Who Was Who in American History

**Biographical Reference Works
Published by Marquis Who's Who, Inc.**

Who's Who in America

Who's Who in America / Index by Professions

Who Was Who in America

   Historical Volume (1607-1896)

   Volume I (1897-1942)

   Volume II (1943-1950)

   Volume III (1951-1960)

   Volume IV (1961-1968)

   Volume V (1969-1973)

Who Was Who in American History — Arts and Letters

Who Was Who in American History — The Military

Who's Who in the World

Who's Who in the East

Who's Who in the South and Southwest

Who's Who in the West

Who's Who in the Midwest

Who's Who of American Women

Who's Who in Religion

Who's Who in Finance and Industry

Who's Who in Government

World Who's Who in Science

Directory of Medical Specialists

Directory of Osteopathic Specialists

International Scholars Directory

Marquis Who's Who Publications / Index to all Books

Who Was Who
in American History–
The Military®

A Component of
Who's Who in American History

MARQUIS
Who's Who

Marquis Who's Who, Inc.
200 East Ohio Street
Chicago, Illinois 60611 U.S.A.

Library of Congress Catalog Card Number 75-29616
ISBN 0-8379-3201-7

Distributed in the United Kingdom by
George Prior Associated Publishers
Rugby Chambers, 2 Rugby Street
London WC1N 3QU

Table of Contents

Preface

"Be there a thousand lives, My great curiosity has stomach for 'em all." In the two hundred years since James Boswell thus expressed his "great curiosity," our interest in biography has remained insatiable.

Today's increased demand among researchers for biographical reference books, in addition to the desire of Marquis Who's Who, Inc. to contribute to the commemoration of our nation's Bicentennial, has made possible both the growth of the Who's Who in American History series and the appearance now of WHO WAS WHO IN AMERICAN HISTORY — ARTS AND LETTERS and WHO WAS WHO IN AMERICAN HISTORY — THE MILITARY, the first two of several projected new volumes in the series.

Who's Who in America, the major component of the Who's Who in American History series, has advanced the highest standards of biographical compilation throughout its more than three-quarters of a century of continuous publication, while the WHO WAS WHO IN AMERICA books have sought to reflect the history and genealogical heritage of America.

Basically, however, the WAS books (to use the shortened form by which they are perhaps better known) inherited those unique characteristics that made *Who's Who in America* an internationally respected reference book and a household word here in the country of its origin.

Sketches in each WAS volume, for example, have not only been prepared from information supplied by the biographees themselves, but have been approved personally — and frequently revised — before being printed in a Marquis publication during the subject's lifetime. As with all WAS volumes, many of these sketches have been scrutinized and revised by relatives or legal representatives of the deceased biographee. Except for the resulting changes, and those occasional variations interjected by the compilers, the WAS biographies are printed precisely as they last appeared during the subject's lifetime. As a result, many contain personal data unavailable elsewhere. The preface to the first volume of *Who's Who in America* selected this fact as one of that volume's outstanding characteristics, and stated: "The book is autobiographical, the data having been obtained from first hand." It follows that WHO WAS WHO IN AMERICAN HISTORY — ARTS AND LETTERS and WHO WAS WHO IN AMERICAN HISTORY — THE MILITARY are autobiographical to a distinctive degree. In that respect, they are unique among American biographical directories. And although condensed to the concise style that Marquis Who's Who, Inc. has made famous, their sketches contain all essential facts.

There results far more than a biographical directory of some 90,000 deceased American notables within the covers of the WAS volumes. WHO WAS WHO IN AMERICA is a vital portion of American history from the early days of the colonies to mid-1973. It is authentic history. It is the autobiography of America.

Table of Abbreviations

The following abbreviations are frequently used in this book:

*Following a sketch signifies that the published biography could not be verified.

††Non-current sketches of WHO'S WHO IN AMERICA biographees who were born 95 or more years ago (see Preface for explanation).

A.A., Associate in Arts.
A.A.A., Agricultural Adjustment Administration; Anti-Aircraft Artillery.
A.A.A.S., American Association for the Advancement of Science.
AAC, Army Air Corps.
a.a.g., asst. adjutant general.
AAF, Army Air Forces.
A. and M., Agricultural and Mechanical.
A.A.H.P.E.R., American Association for Health, Physical Education and Recreation.
A.A.O.N.M.S., Ancient Arabic Order of the Nobles of the Mystic Shrine.
A.A.S.R., Ancient Accepted Scottish Rite (Masonic).
A.B.C.F.M., American Board of Commissioners for Foreign Missions (Congregational).
A.B. (also **B.A.**), Bachelor of Arts.
A.,B.& C. R.R., Atlanta, Birmingham & Coast R.R.
ABC, American Broadcasting Company.
AC, Air Corps.
acad., academy; academic.
A.C.L. R.R., Atlantic Coast Line R.R.
A.C.P., American College of Physicians.
A.C.S., American College of Surgeons.
actg., acting.
a.d.c., aide-de-camp.
add., additional.
adj., adjutant; adjunct.
adj. gen., adjutant general.
adm., admiral.
adminstr., administrator.
adminstrn., administration.
adminstrv., administrative.
adv., advocate; advisory.
advt., advertising.
A.E., Agricultural Engineer.
AEC, Atomic Energy Commission.
A.E. and P., Ambassador Extraordinary and Plenipotentiary.
AEF, American Expeditionary Forces.
aero., aeronautics, aeronautical.
AFB, Air Force Base.
A.F.D., Doctor of Fine Arts.
A.F. and A.M., Ancient Free and Accepted Masons.
AFL (or **A.F. of L.**), American Federation of Labor.
A.F.T.R.A., American Federation TV and Radio Artists.
agr., agriculture.
agrl., agricultural.
agt., agent.
Agy., Agency.
a.i., ad interim.
A.I.A., American Institute of architects.
AID, Agency for International Development.
A.I.M., American Institute of Management.
AK—Alaska
AL—Alabama

Ala., Alabama
A.L.A., American Library Association.
Am., American, America.
A.M. (also **M.A.**), Master of Arts.
A.M.A., American Medical Association.
A.M.E., African Methodist Episcopal.
Am. Inst. E.E., American Institute of Electrical Engineers.
Am. Soc. C.E., American Society of Civil Engineers.
Am. Soc. M.E., American Society of Mechanical Emgineers.
A.N.A., Associate National Academician.
anat., anatomical.
ann., annual.
ANTA, American National theatre and Academy.
anthrop., anthropological.
antiq., antiquarian.
A.O.H., Ancient Order of Hibernians.
A.P., Associated Press.
appmnt., appointment.
apptd., appointed.
apt., apartment.
a.q.m., assistant quartermaster.
AR—Arkansas
A.R.C., American Red Cross.
archeol., archeological.
archtl., architectural.
Ark., Arkansas
Ariz.—Arizona.
Arts D., Doctor of Arts.
arty., artillery.
AS, Air Service.
A.S.C.A.P., American Society of Composers, Authors and Publishers.
ASF, Air Service Force.
assn., association.
asso., associate; associated.
asst., assistant.
astron., astronomical.
astrophys., astrophysical.
A.T.S.C., Air Technical Service Command.
A.,T.& S.F. Ry., Atchison, Topeka & Santa Fe Ry.
Atty., attorney.
AUS, Army of the United States.
Aux., Auxiliary.
Av., Avenue.
AZ—Arizona

b., born.
B., Bachelor.
B.A. (ALSO **A.B.**), Bachelor of Arts.
B.A.A.S., British Association for the Advancement of Science.
B.Agr., Bachelor of Agriculture.
Balt., Baltimore.
Bapt., Baptist.
B.Arch., Bachelor of Architecture.
B.& A. R.R., Boston & Albany R. R.
B.A.S. (or **B.S.A.**), Bachelor of Agricultural Science.
batn., batin., batt., battalion.
B.B.A., Bachelor of Business Administration.
BBC, British Broadcasting Company.
B.C., British Columbia.

B.C.E., Bachelor of Civil Engineering.
B.Chir., Bachelor of Surgery.
B.C.L., Bachelor of Civil Law.
B.C.S., Bachelor of Commercial Science.
bd., board.
B.D., Bachelor of Divinity.
B.DI., Bachelor of Didactics.
B.E. (or **Ed.B.**), Bachelor of Education.
B.E.E., Bachelor of Electrical Engineering.
BEF, British Expeditionary Force.
bet., between.
B.F.A., Bachelor of fine Arts.
bibl., bibilcal.
bibliog., bibliographical.
biog., biographical.
biol., biological.
B.J., Bachelor of Journalism.
Bklyn., Brooklyn.
B.L. (or **Litt.B.**), Bachelor of Letters.
Bldg., building.
blk., block.
B.L.S., Bachelor of Library Science.
Blvd., Boulevard.
B.& M. R.R., Boston & Marine R.R.
Bn. (or **Batn.**), Battalion.
B.O. (or **O.B.**), Bachelor of Oratory.
B.& O. R.R., Baltimore & Ohio R.R.
bot., botanical.
B.P., Bachelor of Painting.
B.P.E., Bachelor of Physical Education.
B.P.O.E., Benevolent and Protective Order of Elks.
B.Pd. (or **Pd.B.**, or **Py.B.**), Bachelor of Pedagogy.
Br., branch.
B.R.E., Bachelor of Religious Education.
brig., brigadier, brigade.
brig. gen., brigadier general.
Brit., British; Britannica.
Bro., Brother.
B., R. & P. Ry., Buffalo, Rochester & Pittsburg Ry.
B.S. (also **S.B.** or **ScB.**), Bachelor of Science.
B.S. in Ry. M.E., Bachelor in Railway Mechanical Engineering.
B.S.A., Bachelor of Agricultural Science.
B.S.D., Bachelor of Didactic Science.
B.S.T., Bachelor of Sacred Theology.
B.Th., Bachelor of Theology.
bull., bulletin.
bur., bureau.
bus., business.
B.W.I., British West Indies.

CA—California
C.A., Central America.
CAA, Civil Aeronautics Adminstrn.
CAB, Civil Aeronautics Board.
CAC, Coast Artillery Corps.
Cal., California.
Can., Canada.
Cantab., of or pertaining to Cambridge University, Eng.
capt., captain.
C. & A. R.R., Chicago & Alton R.R., now Alton Ry. Co.
Cath., Catholic.

cav., cavalry.
CBI, China - Burma - India theater of operations.
C.,B.& Q. R.R., Chicago, Burlington & Quincy R.R. Co.
CBS, Columbia Broadcasting System
CCC. Commodity Credit Corporation.
C.,C.,C.& St.L. Ry., Cleveland, Cincinnati. Chicago & St. Louis Ry.
C.E., Civil Engineer (degree), Corps of Engineers.
CEF, Canadian Expeditionary Forces.
C.& E.I. R.R., Chicago & Eastern Illinois R.R.
C.G.W. R.R., Chicago Great Western Railway.
ch., church.
Ch.D., Doctor of Chemistry.
chem., chemical.
Chem.E., Chemical Engineer.
Chgo., Chicago.
Chirurg., Chirurgical.
chmn., chairman.
chpt., chapter.
Cia, (Spanish), Company.
CIA, Central Intelligence Agency.
CIC, Counter Intelligence Corps.
C., I.&L. Ry., Chicago, indianapolis & Louis-ville Railway.
Cin., Cincinnati.
CIO, Congress of Industrial Organizations.
civ., civil.
Cleve., Cleveland.
climatol., climatological.
clin., clinical.
clk., clerk.
C.L.S.C., Chautauqua Literary and Scientific Circle.
C.L.U., Certified Life Underwriter.
C.M., Master in Surgery.
C. M., St.P.&P.R.R., Chicago, Milwaukee, St. Paul & Pacific R.R. Co.
C. N. Ry., Canadian Northern Ry.
C.& N.-W. Ry., Chicago & Northwestern Railway.
CO—Colorado
Co., Company;
C. of C.. Chamber of Commerce.
C.O.F., Catholic Order of Foresters.
C. of Ga. Ry., Central of Georgia Ry.
col., colonel.
coll., college
Colo., Colorado
com., committee.
comd., commanded.
comdg., commanding.
comdr., commander.
comdt., commandant.
commd., commissioned.
comml., commercial.
commn., commission.
commr., commissioner.
Com. Sub., Commissary of Subsistence.
condr., conductor.
conf., conference.
confed., confederate.
Congl., Congregational; Congressional.
Conglist., Congregationalist.
CONN—Connecticut.
cons., consulting, consultant.

consol., consolidated.
constl., constitutional.
constn., constitution.
constrn., construction.
contbd., contributed.
contbg., contributing.
contbn., contribution.
contbr., contributor.
conv., convention.
coop. (or co-op.), cooperative.
corp., corporation.
corr., correspondent; corresponding, cor-respondence.
C & O. Ry., Chesapeake & Ohio Ry. Co.
C.P.A., Certified Public Accountant.
C.P.C.U., Chartered Property and Casualty Underwriter.
C.P.H., Certificate of Public Health.
cpl. (or corpl.), corporal.
C.P. Ry., Canadian Pacific Ry. Co.
C. R.I.& P. Ry., Chicago, Rock Island & Pacific Ry. Co.
C.R.R. of N.J., Central Railroad Co. of New Jersey.
C.S., Christian Science.
C.S. Army, Confederate State Army.
C.S.B., Bachelor of Christian Science.
C.S.D., Doctor of Christian Science.
C.S.N., Confederate States Navy.
C.& S. Ry. Co., Colorado & Southern Ry. Co.
C.,St.P.,M.&O. Ry., Chicago, St. Paul, Min-neapolis & Omaha Ry. Co.
Ct., Court.
C.T., Candidate in Theology.
CT—Connecticut.
c.Vt. Ry., Central Vermont Ry.
C.& W.I. R.R., Chicago & Western Indiana R.R. Co.
CWS, Chemical Warfare Service.
cycle., cyclopedia.
C.Z., Canal Zone.

d. (also dau.), daughter.
D., Doctor.
D. Agr., Doctor of Agriculture.
D.A.R., Daughters of the American Revolu-tion.
D.A.V., Disabled American Veterans.
D.C., District of Columbia.-D.C.
D.C.L., Doctor of Civil Law.
D.C.S., Doctor of Commercial Science
D.D., Doctor of Divinity.
D.D.S., Doctor of Dental Surgery.
DE—Delaware.
dec., deceased.
Def., Defense.
deg., degree.
Del., Delaware.
del., delegate.
Dem., Democratic.
D.Eng. (also Dr. Engring., or e.d. Doctor of Engineering.
denom., denominational.
dep., deputy.
dept., department.
dermatol., determatological.
desc., descendant.
devel., development.

D.F.C., Distinguished Flying Cross.
D.H.L., Doctor of Hebrew Literature.
D.& H. R.R., Delaware & Hudson R.R. Co.
dir., director.
disch., discharged.
dist., district.
distbg., distributing.
distbn., distribution.
distbr., distributor.
div., division; divinity; divorce proceedings.
D.Litt., Doctor of Literature.
D.,L.& W.R.R., Delaware Lackawanna & Wes-tern R.R. co.
D.M.D., Doctor of Medical Dentistry.
D.M.S., Doctor of Medical Science.
D.O., Doctor of Osteopathy.
DPA. Defense Production Administration.
D.P.H. (also Dr.P.H.), Diploma in Public Health or Doctor of Public Health or Doctor of Public Hygiene.
Dr., Doctor, Drive.
D.R., Daughters of the Revolution.
D.R.E., Doctor of Religious Education.
D.& R.G.W. R.R. Co., Denver & Rio Grande Western R.R. Co.
D.Sc. (or Sc. D.). Doctor of Science.
D.S.C., Distinguished Service Cross.
D.S.M., Distinguished Service Medal.
D.S.T., Doctor of Sacred Theology.
D.T.M., Doctor of Tropical Medicine.
D.V.M., Doctor of Veterinary Medicine.
D.V.S., Doctor of Veterinary Surgery.

E., East.
E. AND P., Extraordinary and Plenipotentiary.
ECA, Economic Cooperation Administration.
eccles., ecclesiastical.
ecol., ecological.
econ., economic.
ECOSOC, Economic and Social Council of UN.
ed., educated.
E.D. (also D.Eng., or Dr.Engring.), Doctor of Engineering.
Ed.B., Bachelor of Education.
Ed.D., Doctor of Education.
edit., edition.
Ed.M. (or M.Ed.), Master of Education.
edn., education.
ednl., educational.
E.E., Electrical Engineer.
E.E. and M. P., Envoy Extraordinary and Minister Plenipotentiary.
Egyptol., Egyptological.
elec., electrical.
electrochem., electrochemical.
electrophys., electrophysical.
E. M., Engineer of Mines.
ency., encyclopedia.
Eng., England.
engr., engineer.
engring., engineering.
entomol., entomological.
e.s., eldest son.
E.S.M.W.T.P., Engring. Science and Manage-ment War Training Program.
ethnol., ethnological.
ETO, European Theater of Operations.
Evang., Evangelical.

exam., examination; examining.
exc., executive.
exhbn., exhibition.
expdn., expedition.
expn., exposition.
expt., experiment.
exptl., experimental.

F., Fellow.
F.A., Field Artillery.
FAA, Federal Aviation Agency.
F.A.C.P., Fellow American College of Physicians.
F.A.C.S., Fellow American College of Surgeons.
FAO, Food and Agriculture Organization.
FBI, Federal Bureau of Investigation.
FCA, Farm Credit Administration.
FCC, Federal Communications Commission.
FCDA, Federal Civil Defense Administration.
FDA, Food and Drug Administration.
FDIA, Federal Deposit Insurance Administration.
F.E., Forest Engineer.
Fed., Federal.
Fedn., Federation.
Fgn., Foreign.
FHA, Federal Housing Administration.
FL—Florida.
Fla., Florida.
FOA, Foreign Operations Administration.
Found., Foundation.
frat., fraternity.
F.R.C.P., Fellow Royal College of Physicians (England).
F.R.C.S., Fellow Royal College of Surgeons (England).
frt., Freight.
FSA, Federal Security Agency.
Ft., Fort.
FTC, Federal Trade Commission.

G.-1 (or other number), Division of General Staff.
gastroent., gastroenterological.
GA—Georgia.
Ga., Georgia.
G.A.R., Grand Army of the Republic.
GATT, General Agreement on Tariffs and Trade.
G.,C.& S.F. Ry., Gulf, Colorado & Santa Fe Ry. Co.
G.D., Graduate in Divinity.
g.d., granddaughter.
gen., general.
geneal., genealogical.
geod., geodetic.
geog., geographical; geographic.
geol., geological.
geophys., geophysical.
g.g.d., great granddaughter.
g.g.s., great grandson.
G.H.Q., General Headquarters.
G.,M.& N. R.R., Gulf, Mobile & Northern R.R. Co.
G., M.& O. R.R., Gulf, Mobile & Ohio R.R. Co.
G.N. Ry., Great Northern Ry. Co.
gov., governor.

govt., government.
govtl., governmental.
grad., graduated; graduate.
g.s., grandson.
Gt., Great.
G.T. Ry., Grand Trunk Ry. System.
GU—Guam.
G.W. Ry. of Can., Great Western Ry. of Canada.
gynecol., gynecological.

Hdqrs., Headquarters.
H.G., Home Guard.
H.H.D., Doctor of Humanities.
HHFA, Housing and Home Finance Agency.
H.I., Hawaiian Islands.
HI—Hawaii.
hist., historical.
H.M., Master of Humanics.
HOLC, Home Owners Loan Corporation.
homeo., homeopathic.
hon., honorary; honorable.
Ho. of Reps,, House of Representatives.
hort., horticultural.
hosp., hospital.
Hts., Heights.
H.Ty. (or H.T.), Hawaiian Territory.
Hwy., Highway.
Hydrog., hydrographic.

IA— Iowa.
Ia., Iowa.
IAEA, International Atomic Energy Agency.
IBM, International Business Machines Corporation.
ICA, International Cooperation Administration.
ICC, Interstate Commerce Commission.
I.C.R.R., Illinois Central R.R. System.
ID—Idaho.
Ida., Idaho.
I.E.E.E., Institute of Electrical and Electronics Engineers.
IFC, International Finance Corp.
I.G.N. R.R., International - Great Northern R.R.
IGY, International Geophysical Year.
IL—Illinois.
Ill., Illinois.
ILO, International Labor Organization.
Illus., Illustrated.
IMF, International Monetary Fund.
IN— Indiana.
Inc., Incorporated.
Ind., Indiana, Independent.
Indpls., Indianapolis.
Indsl., Industrial.
inf., infantry.
ins., insurance.
insp., inspector.
inst., institute.
instl., institutional.
instn., institution.
instr., instructor.
instrn., instruction.
internat., international.
intro., introduction.
I.O.B.B., Independent Order of B'nai B'rith.

I.O.G.T., Independent Order of Good Templars.
I.O.O.F., Independent Order of Odd Fellows.
I.R.E., Institute of Radio Engineers.

J.B., Jurum Baccalaureus.
J.C.B., Juris Canonici Bachelor.
J.C.L., Juris Canonici Lector.
J.D., Doctor of Jurisprudence.
j.g., junior grade.
jour., journal.
jr., junior.
J.S.D., Doctor of Juristic Science.
Jud., Judicial.
J.U.D., Juris Utriusque Doctor: Doctor of Both (Canon and Civil) Laws.

Kan.—Kansas.
K.C., Knight of Columbus.
K.C.C.H., Knight Commander of Court of Honor.
K.P., Knight of Pythias.
K.N.S. Ry., Kansas City Southern Ry.
KS—Kansas.
KY—Kentucky.
Ky., Kentucky.

lab., laboratory.
lang., language.
laryngol., laryngological.
lectr., lecturer.
L.H.D., Doctor of Letters of Humanity.
L.I., Long Island.
lieut., lieutenant.
L.I. R.R., Long Island R.R. Co.
lit., literary; literature.
Lit. Hum., Literae Humanores (classics Oxford U., Eng.).
Litt.B. (or B.L.). Bachelor of Letters.
Litt.D., Doctor of Letters.
LL.B., Bachelor of Laws.
LL.D., Doctor of Laws.
LL.M. (or ML.). Master of Laws.
L.& N. R.R., Louisville & Nashville R.R.
L.O.M., Loyal Order of Moose.
L.R.C.P., Licentiate Royal Coll. Physicians.
L.R.C.S., Licentiate Royal Coll. Surgeons.
L.S., Library Science.
L.S.A., Licentiate Society of Apothecaries.
L.S.& M. S. Ry., Lake Shore & Michigan Southern Ry.
lt. or (lieut.), lieutenant.
Ltd., Limited.
Luth., Lutheran.
L.V. R.R., Lehigh Valley R.R. co.

m., marriage ceremony.
M.A. (OR A.M.), Master of Arts.
mag., magazine.
M.Agr., Master of Agriculture.
maj., major.
Man., Manitoba.
M.Arch., Master in Architecture.
Mass., Massachusetts.
Math., mathematical.
M.B., Bachelor of Medicine.
M.B.A., Master of Business Administration.

MBS, Mutual Broadcasting System.
M.C., Medical Corps.
M.C.S., Master of Commercial Science.
mcht., merchant.
M.C. R.R., Michigan Central R.R.
Md., Maryland
MD—Maryland
M.D., Doctor of Medicine.
M.Di., Master of Didactics.
M.Dip., Master in Diplomacy.
mdse., merchandise.
M.D.V., Doctor of Veterinary Medicine.
Me., Maine.
ME—Maine.
M.E., Mechanical Engineer.
mech., mechanical.
M.E. Ch., Methodist Episcopal Church.
M.Ed., Master of Education.
med., medical.
Med. O.R.C., Medical Officers' Reserve Corps.
Med. R.C., Medical Reserve Corps.
M.E.E., Master of Electrical Engineering.
mem., member.
Meml. (or Mem.), Memorial.
merc., mercantile.
met., metropolitan.
metall., metallurgical.
Met.E., Metallurgical Engineer.
meteorol., meteorological.
Meth., Methodist.
metrol., metrological.
M.F., Master of Forestry.
M.F.A., Master of Fine Arts.
mfg., manufacturing.
mfr., manufacturer.
mgmt., management.
mgr., manager.
M.H.A., Master of Hospital Administration.
M.I., Military Intelligence.
MI—Michigan.
Mich., Michigan.
micros., microscopical.
mil., military.
Milw., Milwaukee.
Mineral., mineralogical.
Minn., Minnesota.
Miss., Mississippi.
M.-K.-I. R.R., Missouri - Kansas-Texas R.R. Co.
M.L. (or LL. M.), Master of Laws.
M.Litt., Master of Literature.
Mlle., Mademoiselle (Miss).
M.L.S., Master of Library Science.
Mme., Madame.
M.M.E., Master of Mechanical Engineering.
MN—Minnesota.
mng., managing.
Moblzn., Mobilization.
Mont., Montana.
M.P., Member of Parliament.
Mpls., Minneapolis.
M.P. R.R., Missouri Pacific R.R.
M.Pd., Master of Pedagogy.
M.P.E., Master of Physical Education.
M.P.L., Master of Patent Law.
M.R.C.P., Member Royal College of Physicians.
M.R.C.S., Member Royal College of Surgeons.

M.R.E., Master of Religious Education.
MS—Mississippi.
M.S. (or M.Sc.). Master of Science.
M.S.F., Master of Science of Forestry.
M.S.T., Master of Sacred Theology.
M.& St. L. R.R., Minneapolis & St. Louis R.R. Co.
M.,St.P.& S.S.M. Ry., Minneapolis, St. Paul & Sault Ste. Marie Ry.
M.S.W., Master of Social Work.
MT—Montana.
Mt., Mount.
mtn., mountain.
M.T.O.U.S.A., Mediterranean Theater of Operations, U.S. Army.
mus., museum; musical.
Mus.B., Bachelor of Music.
Mus.D. (or Mus. Doc.), Doctor of Music.
Mus. M., Master of Music.
Mut., Mutual.
M.V.M., Massachusetts Volunteer Militia.
M.W.A., Modern Woodmen of America.
mycol., mycological.

N., North.
N.A., National Academician; North America; National Army.
N.A.A.C.P., National Association for the Advancement of Colored People.
NACA, National Advisory Committee for Aeronautics.
N.A.D., National Academy of Design.
N.A.M., National Association of Manufacturers.
NASA, Nàtional Aeronautics and Space Administration.
nat., national.
NATO, North Atlantic Treaty Organization.
N.A.T.O.U.S.A., North African Theater of Operations, U.S. Army.
nav., navigation.
NB—Nebraska.
N.B., New Brunswick.
NBC, National Broadcasting Co.
NC—North Carolina.
N.,C.& St.L. Ry., Nashville, Chattanooga & St. Louis Ry.
NDCR, National Defense Research Committee.
N.E., Northeast; New England.
N.E.A., National Education Association.
Neb., Nebraska.
neurol., neurological.
Nev., Nevada.
New Eng., New England.
N.G., National Guard.
N.G.S.N.Y., National Guard State of New York.
N.H., New Hanpshire.
NH—New Hampshire.
NIH, National Institutes of Health.
N.J., New Jersey.
NJ—New Jersey
NLRB, National Labor Relations Board.
N.Ph.D., Doctor Natural Philosophy.
N.P. Ry., Northern Pacific Ry.
No., Northern.
NPA, National Production Authority.

nr., near.
NRA, National Recovery Administration.
NRC, National Research Council.
N.S., Nova Scotia.
NSC, National Security Council.
NSF, National Science Foundation.
NSRB, National Security Resources Board.
N.T., New Testament.
numis., numismatic.
N.W., Northwest
N.& W. Ry., Norfolk & Western Ry.
NV—Nevada.
N.Y., New York.
NY—New York.
N.Y.C., New York City.
N.Y. Central R.R. (or **N.Y.C. R.R.**), New York Central Railroad Company.
N.Y.,C.& St.L. R.R., New York, Chicago & St. Louis R.R. Co.
N.Y., N.H.& H. R.R., New York, New Haven & Hartford R.R. Co.
N.Y.,O.& W. Ry., New York, Ontario & Western Ry.

O—Ohio.
OAS, Organization of American States.
O.B., Bachelor of Oratory.
obs., observatory.
obstet., obstetrical.
OCDM, Office of Civil and Defense Mobilization.
ODM, Office of Defense Mobilization.
OECD, organization European Cooperation and Development.
OEEC, Organization European Economic Cooperation.
O.E.S., Order of the Eastern Star.
ofcl., Official.
OH—Ohio.
OK—Oklahoma.
Okla., Oklahoma.
Ont., Ontario.
OPA, Office of Price Administration.
opthal., ophthalmological.
OPM, Office of Production management.
OPS, Office of Price Stabilization.
O.Q.M.G., Office of Quartermaster General.
O.R.C., Officers' Reserve Corps.
orch., orchestra.
OR—Oregon.
Ore., Oregon.
orgn., organization.
ornithol., ornithological.
O.S.B., Order of Saint Benedict.
O.S.L. R.R., Oregon Short Line R.R.
OSRD, Office of Scientific Research and Development.
OSS, Office of Strategic Services.
osteo, osteopathic.
O.T., Old Testament.
O.T.C., Officers' Training Camp.
otol., otological.
O.T.S., Officers' Training School.
O.U.A.M., Order United American Mechanics.
OWI, Office of War Information.
O.-W.R.R.& N. Co., Oregon-Washington R.R. & Navigation Co.
Oxon., Of or pertaining to Oxford University, Eng.

PA—Pennsylvania
Pa., Pennsylvania
Pa. R.R., Pennsylvania R.R.
paleontol., paleontological.
pass., passenger.
path., pathological.
Pd.B. (or B.Pd., or Py.B.), Bachelor of Pedagogy.
Pd.D., Doctor of Pedagogy.
Pd.M., master of Pedagogy.
P.E., Protestant Episcopal.
Pe.B., Bachelor of Pediatrics.
P.E.I., Prince Edward Island.
P.E.M., Poets, Playwrights, Editors, Essayists and Novelists (Internat. Assn.).
penol., penological.
pfc., private first class.
PHA, Public Housing Administration.
pharm., pharmaceutical.
Pharm.D., Doctor of Pharmacy.
Pharm.M., Master of Pharmacy.
Ph.B., Bachelor of Philosophy.
Ph.C., Pharmaceutical Chemist.
Ph.D., Doctor of Philosophy.
Ph.G., Graduate in Pharmacy.
Phila., Philadelphia.
philol., philological.
philes., philosophical.
photog., photographic.
phys., physical.
Phys. and Surg., Physicians and Surgeons (college at Columbia University).
Physiol., physiological.
P.I., Philippine Islands.
Pitts., Pittsburg.
Pkwy., Parkway.
Pl., Place.
P.& L.E. R.R., Pittsburgh & Lake Erie R.R.
P.M., Paymaster.
P.M. R.R., Pere Marquette R.R. Co.
polit., political.
poly., polytechnic.
pomol., pomological.
P.Q., Province of Quebec.
P.R., Puerto Rico.
prep., preparatory.
pres., president.
Presbyn., Presbyterian.
presdl., presidential.
prin., principal.
Proc., Proceedings.
prod., produced (play production).
prodn., production.
prof., professor.
profl., professional.
Prog., Progressive.
propr., proprietor.
pros. atty., prosecuting attorney.
pro tem, pro tempore (for the time being).
psychiat., psychiatrical; psychiatric,
psychol., psychological.
P.T.A., parent-Teacher Association.
PTO, Pacific Theatre of Operations.
pub., public; publisher; publishing; published.
publ., publication.
pvt., private.
PWA, Public Works Administration.
Py. B., Bachelor of Pedagogy.

q.m., quartermaster.
Q.M.C., Quartermaster Corps.
q.m. gen., quartermaster general.
Q.M.O.R.C., Quartermaster Officers' Reserve Corps.
quar., quarterly.
Que., Quebec (province).
q.v., quod vide (which see).

radiol., radiological.
R.A.F., Royal Air Force.
R.A.M., Royal Arch Mason.
R.C., Roman Catholic; Reserve Corps.
RCA, Radio Corporation of America.
RCAF, Royal Canadian Air Force.
R.C.S., Revenue Cutter Service.
Rd., Road.
R.D., Rural Delivery.
R.E., Reformed Episcopal.
rec., recording.
Ref., Reformed.
Regt., Regiment.
regtl., regimental.
rehab., rehabilitation.
Rep., Republican.
rep., representative.
Res., Reserve.
ret., retired.
Rev., Reverend, Review.
rev., revised.
RFC, Reconstruction Finance Corporation.
R.F.D., Rural Free Delivery.
rhinol., rhinological.
RI—Rhode Island
R.I., Rhode Island
R.N., Registered Nurse.
rontgenal., rontgenological.
R.O.S.C., Reserve Officers' Sanitary Corps.
R.O.T.C., Reserve Officers' Training Corps.
R.P., Reformed Presbyterian.
R.P.D., Rerum Politicarum Doctor (Doctor Political Science).
R.R., Railroad.
R.T.C., Reserve Training Corps.
Ry., Railway.

s., son.
S., South.
S.A., South Americe.
S.A. (Spanish) Sociedad Anonima, (French) Société Anonyme.
SAC, Strategic Air Command.
S.A.L. Ry., Seaboard Air Line Ry.
san., sanitary.
S.A.R., Sons of the Am. Revolution.
Sask., Saskatchewan.
S.A.T.C., Students' Army Training Corps.
Sat.Eve.Post, Saturday Evening Post.
Savs., Savings.
S.B. (also B.S. or Sc.B.), Bachelor of Science.
SC—South Carolina.
S.C., South Carolina; San. Corps.
SCAP, Supreme Command Allies Pacific.
Sc.D. (or D.Sc.), Doctor of Science.
S.C.D., Doctor of Commercial Science.
sch., school.
sci., science; scientific.
S.C.V., Sons of Confederate Veterans.
SD— South Dakota.

S.D., South Dakota.
S.E., Southeast.
SEATO, Southeast Asia Treaty Organization.
SEC, Securities and Exchange Commission.
sec., secretary.
sect., section.
seismol., seismological.
Sem., Seminary.
sgt. (or sergt.), sergeant.
SHAEF, Supreme Headquarters, Allied Expeditionary Forces.
SHAPE, Supreme Headquarters Allied Powers in Europe.
S.I., Staten Island.
S.J., Society of Jesus (Jesuit).
S.J.D., Doctor Juristic Science.
S.M., Master of Science.
So., Southern.
soc., society.
social., sociological.
sos, Services of Supply.
S. of V., Sons of Veterans.
S.P. Co., Southern Pacific Co.
spl., special.
splty., specialty.
Sq., Square.
S.R.C., Signal Reserve Corps.
sr., senior.
S.R., Sons of the Revolution.
S.S., Steamship.
SSS, Selective Service System.
St., Saint; Street.
Sta., station.
statis., statistical.
Stblzn., Stabilization.
S.T.B., Bachelor of Sacred Theology.
S.T.D., Doctor of Sacred Theology.
S.T.L., Licentiate in Sacred Theology; Lector of Sacred Theology.
St.L.-S.F. R.R., St. Louis - San Francisco Ry. Co.
supr., supervisor.
supt., superintendent.
surg., surgical.
S.W., Southwest.

T.A.P.P.I., Technical Association Pulp and Paper Industry.
T. and S., Trust and Savings.
Tb (or TB), tuberculosis.
Tchrs., Teachers.
tech., technical; technology.
technol., technological.
Tel.&Tel., Telephone and Telegraph.
temp., temporary.
Tenn., Tennessee.
Tex., Texas.
T.H. (or H.T.), Territory of Hawaii.
Th.D., Doctor of Theology.
ThM., Master of Theology.
theol., theological.
TN—Tennessee.
Tng., Training.
topog., topographical.
T.P.A., Travelers Protective Assn.
T.&P. Ry., Texas & Pacific Ry. Co.
trans., transactions; transferred.
Transl., translation; translations.
transp., transportation.

treas., treasurer.
TV, television.
TX—Texas.
TVA, Tennessee Valley Authority.
Twp., Township.
Ty. (or **Ter.**), Territory.
Typog., typographical.

U. (or **Univ.**), University.
UAR, United Arab Republic.
UAW, United Automobile Workers.
U.B., United Brethren in Christ.
U.C.V., United Confederate Veterans.
U.D.C., United Daughters of the Confederacy.
U.K., United Kingdom.
UN, United Nations.
UNESCO, United Nations Educational Scientific and Cultural Organization.
UNICEF, United Nations International Childrens Emergency Fund.
UNRRA, United Nations Relief and Rehabilitation Administration.
U.P., United Presbyterian.
U.P. R.R., Union Pacific R.R.
urol., urological.
U.S., United States.
U.S.A., United States of America.
USAAF, United States Army Air Force.
USAC, United States Air Corps.
USAF, United States Air Force.
USCG, United States Coast Guard.
U.S.C.T., U.S. Colored Troops.
USES, United States Employment Service.

USIA, United States Information Agency.
USIS, United States Information Service.
USMC, United States Marine Corps.
USMHS, United States Marine Hospital Service.
USN, United States Navy.
USNA, United States National Army.
U.S.N.G., United States National Guard.
U.S.O., United Service Organizations.
USNG, United States National Guard.
USNRF, United States Naval Reserve Force.
USPHS, United States Public Health Service.
U.S.R., U.S. Reserve.
U.S.R.C.S., U.S. Revenue Cutter Service.
U.S.S., United States Ship.
USSR, Union of Soviet Socialist Republics.
U.S.V., United States Volunteers.
UT—Utah.

v., vice.
VA—Virginia.
Va., Virginia.
VA, Veterans Administration.
vet., veteran; veterinary.
V.F.W., Veterans of Foreign Wars.
V.I., Virgin Islands.
VI—Virgin Islands.
vice pres. (or **v.p.,**), vice president.
vis., visiting.
vol., volunteer; volume.
vs., versus (against).
VT—Vermont.
Vt., Vermont.

W., West.
WA—Washington (state).
WAC, Women's Army Corps.
Wash., Washington (state).
WAVES, Womens Reserve. U.S. Naval Reserve.
W.C.T.U., Women's Christian Temperance Union.
WHO, World Health Organization.
W.I., West Indies.
WI—Wisconsin.
Wis., Wisconsin.
W.& L.E. Ry., Wheeling & Lake Erie Ry. Co.
WPA, Works Progress Administration.
WPB, War Production Board.
W.P. R.R. Co., Western Pacific R.R. Co.
WSB, Wage Stabilization Board.
WV—West Virginia.
W. Va., West Virginia.

YMCA, Young Men's Christian Association.
YMHA, Young Men's Hebrew Association.
YM and YWHA, Young Men's and Young Women's Hebrew Association.
Y.& M.V. R.R., Yazoo & Mississippi Valley R.R.
yrs., years.
YWCA, Young Women's Christian Association.

zoöl., zoölogical.

ALPHABETICAL PRACTICES

Names are arranged alphabetically according to the surnames, and under identical surnames according to the first given name. If both surname and first given name are identical, names are arranged alphabetically according to the second given name. Where full names are identical, they are arranged in order of age—those of the elder being put first.

Surnames, beginning with De, Des, Du, etc., however capitalized or spaced, are recorded with the prefix preceding the surname and arranged alphabetically under the letter D.

Surnames beginning with Mac are arranged alphabetically under M. This likewise holds for names beginning with Mc; that is, all names beginning Mc will be found in alphabetical order after those beginning Mac.

Surnames beginning with Saint or St. all appear after names that would begin Sains, and such surnames are arranged according to the second part of the name, e.g., St. Clair would come before Saint Dennis.

Surnames beginning with prefix Van are arranged alphabetically under letter V.

Surnames containing the prefix Von or von are usually arranged alphabetically under letter V; any exceptions are noted by cross references (Von Kleinsmid, Rufus Bernhard; see Kleinsmid, Rufus Bernard von).

Compound hypenated surnames are arranged according to the first member of the compound.

Compound unhyphenated surnames common in Spanish are not rearranged but are treated as hyphenated names.

Since Chinese names have the family name first, they are so arranged, but without comma between family name and given name (as Lin Yutang).

Parentheses used in connection with a name indicate which part of the full name is usually deleted in common usage. Hence Abbott, W(illiam) Lewis indicates that the usual form of the given name is W. Lewis. In alphabetizing this type, the parentheses are not considered. However if the name is recorded Abbott, (William) Lewis, signifying that the entire name William is not commonly used, the alphabetizing would be arranged as though the name were Abbott, Lewis.

Who Was Who in American History-
The Military

ABBOT, CHARLES WHEATON naval officer; b. in R.I., Nov. 18, 1829. Apptd. purser U.S. Navy, Sept. 2, 1856; promoted pay insp., Mar. 3, 1871; pay dir., July 3, 1871; retired, Nov. 18, 1891; advanced to rank of rear adm., June 29, 1906; for services during Civil War. Home: Warren, R.I. Died 1907.

ABBOT, FREDERIC VAUGHN army officer, b. Cambridge, Mass., Mar. 4, 1858; s. Henry Larcom and Mary Susan (Everett) A.; grad. Flushing (L.I.) Inst. 1873; grad. U.S. Mil. Acad., 1879; m. Sara Julie Dehon, Oct. 15, 1885; children - Marion Beatrice, Elinor Russell, Henry Dehon. Second lt. engr. corps, June 13, 1879; advanced through grades to col., June 24, 1909, brig. gen. N.A., Aug. 5, 1917. Survey of boundary line bet. Md. and Va., 1883-84; asst. to chief of engrs. U.S. Army, Aug. 12, 1900-10; charge defensive works southern and eastern entrances to N.Y. Harbor, and of river and harbor works, 2d N.Y. Dist., Apr. 30, 1915-Oct. 15, 1917; prin. asst. of chief of engrs. U.S. Army and comdg. officer, post of Washington Barracks, 1917; acting chief of engrs., U. S. Army, 1918-19; retired May 10, 1920. Home: Washington, D.C. Died Sept. 26, 1928.

ABBOT, HENRY LARCON soldier, engr.; b. Beverly, Mass., Aug. 13, 1821; s. Joseph Hale and Frances Ellingwood (Larcom) A.; grad. West Point, 1854; LL.D., Harvard, 1886; m. Mary Susan Everett, Apr. 2, 1856. Served in Civil War; mustered out as col.; retured from regular army as col., 1895; advanced to brig.-gen., retired 1904. Home: Cambridge, Mass. Died Oct. 1, 1927.

ABBOT, JOEL naval officer; b. Westford, Mass., Jan. 18, 1793; s. Joel and Lydia (Cummings) A.; m. Mary Wood, Jan. 1820; m. 2d, Laura Wheaton, Nov. 29, 1825; 10 children. Apptd. midshipman U.S. Navy, 1812; served under Commodore John Rodgers in frigate President, 1812; captured by English while acting officer of ship, 1813, exchanged; served in Commodore Thomas Macdonough's squadron on Lake Champlain; on spl. mission disguised as Brit. officer destroyed large supply ships' parts; took part in Battle of Lake Champlain, 1814, received sword of honor from Congress for his service there; commd. lt., 1818; discovered frauds against U.S. Govt. while on duty at Charleston (S.C.) Navy Yard, 1822, preferred charges on his commandant Capt. Isaac Hull, offered no proof, court martialed and suspended 2 years; commd. capt., 1850; picked by Commodore M.C. Perry to command frigate Macedonian in fleet in expdn. to Japan, 1852, visited Japanese, Bonin, Philippine, Formosa islands; made comdg. officer of fleet on his return to U.S. Died Hongkong, China, Dec. 14, 1855.

ABBOTT, JO lawyer, congressman; b. near Decatur, Ala., Jan. 15, 1840; s. William and Mary A.; m. Rowena W. Sturgis, Dec. 15, 1868. Served in C.S. army as 1st lt. 12th Tex. cav.; admitted to Tex. bar; mem. Tex. legislature, 1869-71; judge 28th jud. dist. Tex., 1879-84; mem. Congress, 1887-97. Democrat. Home: Hillsboro, Tex. Died 1908.

ABBOTT, JOSEPH FLORENCE sugar refining; b. Clarksville, Tenn., Mar. 3, 1888; s. Florence F. and Elizabeth (Boillin) A.; grad. Saint Mary's Coll., law study Georgetown U., 1907-11; m. Laura C. Griswold, June 5, 1920; children-Charles Griswold, Joseph Alan. Admitted to D.C. bar, 1912, and began practice at Washington; gen. counsel Am. Sugar Refining Co., 1926-29 pres., 1929-53, dir., 1929-, chmn bd., 1953-57; dir. Am. Express Co., Emigrant Industrial Savings Bank. Served as lt. F.A., U.S. Army, World War I. Clubs: Round Hill (Greenwich, Conn.); Blind Brook (Port Chester, N.Y.). Home: Greenwich, Conn. Office: 120 Wall St., N.Y.C. Died Nov. 17, 1961; buried Putnam Cemetery, Greenwich.

ABENDROTH, WILLIAM HENRY, army officer; b. Ft. Mead, S.D., Dec. 24, 1895; s. William Henry and Alice Amelia (Smith) A.; grad. Cav. Sch., 1930, Chem. Warfare Sch., 1940, Command and Gen. Staff Sch., 1946; m. Veda Mae Kirkman, May 5, 1934; children—William Henry, Wesley Wallace. Enlisted Ida. N.G., 1913, fed. service on Mexican Border, 1916-17; served Inf. and C.E., U.S. Army, World War I; commd. 2d lt. Cav., Ida. N.G., 1927, advanced through grades to maj. gen., 1952; insp. gen dept., 1941; provost marshal, hdqrs. comdt. IX Corps, Hawaii, P.I., Japan. U.S., World War II; detailed Office Chief of Staff, U.S. Army, apptd. resident N.G. mem., 1947-49; comdg. gen. D.C. Nat. Guard, 1949-68; chief army div., N.G. Bur., 1951-55; purchasing agt., budget dir., State of Ida., 1932-37; rural electrification mgr. Ida. Power Co., 1938-40; adj. gen., State of Ida., Apr. 1946, state dir. Selective Service Aug. 1946. Recipient Legion of Merit. Mem. exec. council Boy Scouts Am., Washington. Mem. Nat. Rifle Assn., N.G. Assn., Am. Legion, Vets. Fgn. Wars. Elk. Home: Falls Church VA Died Sept. 3, 1970; buried Arlington Nat. Cemetery, Arlington VA

ABERNATHY, ALONZO educator; born Sandusky County, O., Apr. 14, 1836; s. Jebiel Anna Mary (Ettinger) A.; A.B., U. of Chicago, 1866; - Ph.D., Lenox Coll., Ia., 1886; m. Louise E. Eaton, Jan. 21, 1868. Pvt. to col. 9th Ia. Vols., 1861-65; participated in 40 engagements; twice wounded. Mem. Ia. Ho. of Rep., 1866-68; prin. Des Moines Coll., 1870-71, since then on bd. trustees same; supt. pub. instrn., Ia., 1871-76; pres. U. of Chicago, 1876-78; prin. Cedar Valley Sem., 1881-1902; mem. bd. regents, State U. of Ia., 1890-1909. Author: Iowa Under Territorial Government, and the Removal of the Indians, 1906; History of Iowa Baptist Schools, 1907; Glimpses of Abraham Lincoln, 1909. Editor Whitman's Early Life of Jesus, and New Light on Passion Week, 1913. Home: Des Moines, Ia. Died Feb. 1915.

ABERNATHY, CHESS, JR., aerospace co. exec.; b. Gastonia, N.C., Mar. 2, 1912; s. Chess and Myra (Herman) A.; A.B., Emory U., 1934; postgrad. U. Mich., 1939, Pub. Relations Soc. Am. Inst., Cornell U., 1962; m. Martha Virginia McDonald, Sept. 24, 1937; children—Martha Virginia, Margaret Louise. Editor in chief Cobb County Times, Marietta, Ga., 1934-40; alumni sec., editor, then alumni dir. Emory U., Atlanta, 1940-50; pres. Brumby Inc., Times-Jour., Inc., Marietta, Ga., 1950-52; pub. relations coordinator Lockheed-Ga. Co., Marietta, 1953-58, pub. information mgr., 1958-69. Instr. journalism Emory U., 1940-43, Ga. State Coll., 1955-56. Mem. regional expansion council U.S. Dept. Commerce. Dir. Met. Atlanta Community Services, Cobb County Emergency Aid Assn.; bd. dirs. Cobb YMCA; alumni council Emory U. Served to capt. AUS, 1942-45; maj. Res. Decorated Legion of Merit. Recipient honor award Emory U., 1950; Rosenwald fellow, 1939-40. Mem. Pub. Relations Soc. Am. Cobb County C. of C., Assn. U.S. Army, Navy League, Army Aviation Assn. Am., Sigma Alpha Epsilon, Sigma Delta Chi. Methodist. Home: Marietta GA Died May 3, 1969.

ABERNETHY, ROBERT SWEPSTON ret. army officer; b. Gonzales County, Tex., Aug. 5, 1874; s. Benjamin Roberts and Anna Elizabeth (Swepston) A.; grad. U.S. Mil. Acad., 1897; grad. Sch. Submarine Defense, 1905-06, Army War Coll., 1911-12. Commd. 2d lt. arty. U.S. Army 1897, promoted through grades to brig. gen. 1932; temp. major U.S. Vols., 1899-1901; temp. col. Nat. Army, 1917-20. Served in Spanish-Am. War. in Philippines. 1898-1901; comdr. 165th F.A. Brigade, AEF, served in France and Germany, 1917-18; last command, San Francisco Port of Embarkation, Fort Mason, Cal.; retired. 1938. Decorated Silver Star with two clusters, Order of Purple Heart, with one cluster. Nat. pres. Nat. Sojourners, Inc., 1937-40. Mason (33rd degree. hon.) Home: Summerton, S.C. Died June 10, 1952

ABERT, SILVANUS THAYER civil engr.; b. Philadelphia, Pa., July 22, 1828; ed. at Princeton; entered service U.S. Govt. in 1848 and was active in canal construction; on staff Gens. Banks and Meade in Civil War; in river surveys for Columbian govt., 1865-66; re-entered U.S. service, and in 1873 took charge of geog. div. from Washington to Wilmington, N.C. Died 1903.

ACHESON, ALEXANDER W. (SANDLE), M.D. born Washington, Pa., Oct. 12, 1842; s. Judge Alexander Wilson and Jane (Wishart) A.; non. A.B., Washington and Jefferson Coll., 1866; M.D., U. of Pa., 1867; m. Sarah M. Cooke, June 20, 1864 (deceased). 1 dau., Mrs. Alice A. Sproule. Pvt. 13th Pa. Regt., 1861; pvt. 140th Pa. Regt., 1862; sergt., 1862; capt., 1863; a.-d.-c. on staff of Gen. Nelson A. Miles, 1863; was the 1st U.S. Army officer on the captured Confederate breastworks at tlhe "bloody angle," in the charge at Spottsylvania, Va.; shot through the face there. Began practice at Phila.; removed to Denison, Tex., 1872. Was mayor of Denison 4 terms; Rep. candidate for gov. of Tex., 1906, for U.S. senator, 1916, for mem. Congress, 1920; city physician, 1923-29. Hon. Life v.p. Red River Flood Control and Navigation Assn.; Tex. dir. Miss. Valley Ass.; del. to rivers convs. at New Orleans, Washington and Chicago. Presbyn. Club: Elks. Home: Denison, Tex. Died Sept. 7, 1934.

ACHESON, WILLIAM MCCARTHY civil engr.; born Cohoes, N.Y., July 16, 1878; s. James Francis and Mary (McCarthy) A.; prep. edn., Troy (N.Y.) Acad.; student Rensselaer Poly. Inst., 1895-98, also Union U., Royal Engrs. Sch., Chatham, Eng., 1917; hon. E.D., Syracuse U., 1927; m. Inger Thira Miller, Apr. 25, 1908; children-Margaret Miller, Thomas Temple. Began in water works dept., Troy, N.Y.; in Isthmian Canal Service, Panama, 1904-10; supervising engr. with contractor, later div. engr. N.Y. State Highway Dept., Buffalo, same, Syracuse Div., 1915-16; chief engr. Crescent Portland Cement Co., 1916-17 div. engr. N.Y. State Dept. Highways, Syracuse, 1917, 1919-23; div. engr., Bur. of Highways and Bur. of Canals, N.Y. State Dept. Pub. Works, 1923-27, in charge div. engring., later chief engr., 1927-; lecturer on engring., Syracuse U., 1922-. Served as capt., later maj. engrs. U.S. Army, assigned to staff of chief of roads and railroads, 1917, chief of road service, 1918; maj. Engr. R.R., 1919, lt. col., 1920. Mem. Nat. Research Council. Citation from Gen. Pershing and Maj. Gen. Langfitt, chief of engrs., World War. Republican. Catholic. Consultant on pub. works to Republic of Cuba. Home: Syracuse, N.Y. Died Jan. 25, 1930.

ACKERSON, JAMES LEE naval officer; b. Lowell, Mich., Aug. 8, 1881; s. John Elbert and Katherine (Labadie) A.; grad. U.S. Naval Acad., 1901; M.S., Mass. Inst. Tech., 1906; m. Martha Alleston Buist, Apr. 21, 1906. Promoted ensign, June 7, 1903; master, Dec. 1, 1903; lt. comdr., Aug. 21, 1916; comdr., Oct. 1, 1917. Naval constr., 1903-; v.p. and trustee U.S. Shipping Bd. Emergency Fleet Corp., 1918. Episcopalian. Died Sept. 13, 1931.

ACKLEY, CHARLES BRECK clergyman; b. Oconomowoc, Wis., Apr. 13, 1878; s. Henry Meyers and Josephine McKenzie (Breck) A., B.L. Hobart ll., Geneva, N.Y., 1899, S.T.D. 1926; postgrad. Theol. Sem., 1900-03. Deacon, 1903, priest, 1904, P.E. Ch.; vicar St. Bartholomew's Ch., N.Y., 1905-08; missionary archdeacon in Cuba, 1908-12; pastor St. Bartholomew's Chapel, 1912-18; rector St. Mary's Ch, N.Y.C., 1919-. Chaplain Fire Dept., N.Y.C., 1903-05; civilian chaplain 9th Regt. U.S. Marines, 1918; commd. chaplain capt., U.S. Army, 1918 chief chaplain Camp Grant, Rockford, Ill. Rec. sec. Episcopal Actors' Guild; also trustee St. Lukes Home, N.Y.C. Mem. N.Y. Soc. Order of Founders and Patriots Am., Sigma Chi. Mason Order of St. Galahad. Lectr. on travel and church history. Home: 521 W. 162th St., N.Y.C. 10027. Died 1964.

ACRET, GEORGE EDWARD (A'KRET), lawyer; b. Brooklyn, NY., Dec. 23, 1886; s. George W. and Katherine (Franklin) A.: student Brooklyn Manual Training High Sch., 1902-05, Worcester Poly. Inst., 1905-06, U. of Wis., 1906-09; legal edn. in law office; m. 3d, Marian McMillan, July 1, 1943: children by previous marriage-Mary, John, James. Admitted to Wash. bar, 1919, to Calif. bar, 1923, and since practiced at Los Angeles; admitted to bar of Wash., D.C., 1938; formerly asso. with firm of Hanna & Morton; formerly asso. with late Sen. William G. McAdoo; dist. atty. Grays Harbor Co., Wash., 1921-22; city atty. Venice, Calif., 1923-25; apptd. mem. Nat. Bituminous Coal Commn., 1935-37; acting dir. div. of trials and hearings, 1937-38. In air service, A.E.F., World War, 1917-19, and with Wash. Nat. Guard, 1920-22, retiring as capt. Mem. State Bar of Calif., Los Angeles Bar Assn., Lawyers Club, Am. Legion. Democrat. Episcopalian. Home: El Rancho Paraiso, 10428 Penrose St., Sun Valley, Calif. Office: 650 S. Grand Av., Los Angeles. Deceased

ACUFF, HERBERT (A'KUF), surgeon; b. Washburn, Tenn., Aug. 22, 1886; s. Joel and Sarah A.: Pharm. G.,Ky. Sch., 1911; Honoris Causa, U. of Argentina; m. Lola Pruden, Oct. 20, 1915; 1 dau., Betty Rose (Mrs. Lawrence Barker). In practice at Knoxville, Tenn.; chief of staff, St. Mary's Memorial Hospital; vis. surg. East Tenn. Bapt. Hosp., Knoxville General Hospital, Fort Sanders Hospital, cons. surgeon and chmn. operating com., Beverly Hills Sanitorium; chief cons. surgeon of Pruden Coal & Coke Co., surgeon, Southern Ry. System; pres. and surg. dir. surgery, Acuff Clinic. Served as maj., Med. Corps, U.S. Army, World War I. Mem. Tenn. Hosp. Licensing Bd.; sec. Internat Bd. Cancerology. Life fellow Am. Coll. Surgeons, Southeastern Surg. Congredd (pres., 1947-48), Internat. Coll. Surgeons (treas., 1946-48; pres. U.S. Chapt., 1946-48; founder fellow Qualification Bd. since 1947; pres. since 1950); hon. fellow Mcd. and Surg. Society of Sao Paulo, Brazil, Surg. Soc. of Rome, Italy, Piemontese Soc. of Torino, Italy; mem. Am. Goiter Assn., American

Coll. Chest Physicians (asso.), Am. Cancer Soc. (bd. dirs., 1945-46; bd. dirs. & service dir., Tenn. div. since 1945), World Med. Assn. (mem. bd. dirs., U.S. Com., Inc.), Knoxville Acad. Medicine (pres. 1945-46), Am. Assno. Ry. Surgeons. Clubs: Civitan (internat. pres. 1926-27), Cherokee Country. Contrb. papers to med. lit. on surg. subjects. Home: 632 Cherokee Blvd. Office: 514 Church Av., Knoxville, Tenn. Died Nov. 2, 1951.

ADAIR, WILLIAM army officer; b. Macomb Co., Mich., Dec. 15, 1848; s. Edmund Phelps and Adelia (Ferris) A.; M.D., Univ. of lfich., 1870; m. Cincinnati, O., Jan. 23, 1877, Margaret Fitzpatrick. Apptd. first lt. asst. surgeon U.S.A., Nov. 10, 1874; capt. asst. surgeon Nov. 10, 1879; maj. surgeon, Sept. 11, 1891; lt. col. deputy surgeon-gen., Jan. 1, 1902; col. asst. surgeon-gen. and chief surgeon, Dept. of Dak., since apr. 6, 1905. Mem. Assn. Mil. Surgeons, Mil. Service Assn. Address: Army Bldg., St. Paul, Minn.

ADAMS, ANDREW Continental congressman, jurist; b. Stratford, Conn., Dec. 11, 1736; s. Samuel and Mary (Fairchild) A.; B.A., Yale Coll., 1760, LL.D. (hon.), 1796; m. Eunice Canfield. Admitted to Conn. bar, 1763; mem. upper house Conn. Gen. Assembly, 1776-77, 82-89; mem. Conn. Council of Safety; commd. maj., later col. Conn. Militia; apptd. del. to Continental Congress, 1777; signer Articles of Confederation; asso. judge Conn. Superior Ct., 1789, chief justice, 1793-97. Died Litchfield, Conn., Nov. 26, 1797.

ADAMS, CHARLES surgeon; b. Northamptonshire, Eng., May 29, 1847; s. John and Elizabeth (Clarke) A.; brought to America at 10 yrs. of age; M.D., Hahnemann Med. Coll., Chicago, 1872; M.D., Rush Med. Coll., 1898; m. Mary Curtis, of Wellingborough, Eng., 1875 (died 1888); 2d, Mrs. Elizabeth Mitchell Gaylord, 1889. In gen. practice, Chicago, 1873-95, exclusivly in surgery, 1892-; prof. surg. pathology, Hahnemann Med. Coll., 1873-75; prof. principles and practice of surgery, Chicago Homoe. Coll., 1875-84; cons. surgeon, Chicago Nursery. Evanston, Passavant, and St. Joseph's hosps. Surg. maj. 1st Inf., Ill. National Guard, 15 yrs.; maj. and brigade surg., U.S. Volunteers, 1898; surg. gen. I.N.G., 1908-13; apptd. 1st lt. M.R.C., U.S. Army, 1911. Home: Chicago, Ill. Died May 6, 1924.

ADAMS, CHARLES FELLEN author; b. Dorchester, Mass., Apr. 21, 1842; s. Ira and Mary Elizabeth (Senter) A.; ed. common sch. Was in 13th Mass. Inf. in Civil War, wounded and taken prisoner at Gettysburg; m. Harriet Louise Mills, Oct. 11, 1870. In 1872 began contributing to periodicals humorous poems in German dialect. Author: Leedle Yawcob lets-Dot Long-Handled Dipper, Vas Marriage a Failure? and Der Oak nd and Der Vine: Yawcob Strauss and Other Poems (complete poems), 1910. Home: Boston, Mass. Died Mar. 15, 1918.

ADAMS, CHARLES FRANCIS, publicist; b. Boston, Mass., May 27, 1835; s. Charles Francis and Abigail Brown (Brooks) A.; A.B., Harvard, 1856 (LL.D.) 1895, Princeton, 1909); admitted to bar, 1858; served in Union Army through Civil War; hon. mustered out, Sept. 1, 1864; lt.-col. 5th Mass. Cav., Sept. 8, 1864; col., Mar. 14, 1865; bvtd. brig.-gen. vols., Mar. 13, 1865; resigned Aug. 1, 1865; m. Mary Hone Ogden, Nov. 8, 1865. Identified with ry. interests; mem. Bd. R.R. Commrs. of Mass., 1869-79 (chmn. 7 yrs.); mem. b.d. Arbitration, Trunk Line R.R. Orgn., 1879-84; govt. dir. U.P. R.R., 1877-90, pres., 1884-90; overseer Harvard, 1882-94 and 1895-1907. Pres. Mass. Hist. Soc., 1895; fellow Am. Acad. Arts and Sciences; mem. Am. Acad. Arts and Letters. Author: Chapters on Erie and Other Essays; Railroads, Their Origin and Problems; Notes on Railway Accidents: Massachusetts, Its Historians and Its History; Three Episodes of Massachusetts History; Life of Charles Francis Adams; Richard Henry Dana, a Biography, and others. Home: South Lincoln, Mass. Died Mar. 20, 1915.

ADAMS, CHARLES FRANCIS lawyer ex-secretary of navy; b. Quincy, Massachusetts, August 2, 1866; s. John Quincy and Fanny (Crowninshield) A.; great-great-grandson of John Adams; A.B., cum laude, Harvard, 1888; LL.B., 1892; read law in office of Sigourney Butler, of Boston; admitted to Suffolk bar, 1893; m. Frances Lovering, April 3, 1899. Began practice with his law preceptor, but later with Judge Everett C. Bumpus until death of father, 1894; became interested in many business enterprises in Boston, Mass., and elsewhere; secretary of navy, by appointment President Hoover, Mar. 4, 1929-Mar. 4, 1933; now chmn. bd. State Street Trust Co., Boston; dir. many corps. Mem. Quincy City Council, 1893-95, mayor, 1896, 97. Treasurer of Harvard Coll., 1898-1929; elected pres. Harvard Alumni Assn. 1933. Amateur skipper on yacht "Resolute" which won Internat. Yacht Races, 1920. Clubs: Eastern Yacht, Quincy Yacht, etc. Home: 177 Commonwealth Av., Boston: summer address: The Glades, Minot, Mass. Office: 15 State St., Boston. Died June 11, 1954: buried Quincy Mass.

ADAMS, CLAUDE MITCHELL govt. ofcl.; b. Humboldt, Tenn., Oct.2, 1895; s. Jeremiah John Robert and Annie (Senter) A.; ed. Fitzgerald-Clarke Sch., U. of Tenn., grad. Inf. Sch. Command and Gen. Staff Sch.; m. Ruth Cornelia Graves, Sept. 14, 1921. Enlisted N.G. of Tenn., June 1916; served as 1st lt. in 119th Inf., 30th Div., World War I, and advanced through the grades to brig. gen., 1943; served as adjutant, executive officer and aide-de-camp to Gen. G.C. Marshall, Chief of Staff, U.S. Army; served as military attache to Brazil, 1942-44; state dir. Civil Def., 1951-52; exec. asst. Gov. Browning, 1952. Awarded Order of Military Merit (Brazil); Legion of Merit (U.S.); Legion of Honor (France); Medalha de Guerre (Brazil). Mem. Sigma Alpha Epsilon. Clubs: Cumberland (Nashville); Arlington (Portland, Ore.): Army and Navy (Washington); Humboldt Country. Home: Humboldt, Tenn. Died Mar. 26, 1958; buried Rose Hill Cemetery, Humboldt

ADAMS, DANIEL WEISSIGER lawyer, army officer; b. Lynchburg, Va., 1820; s. George and Anna (Weissiger) A.; ed. U. Va. Began practice law in La., 1842; apptd. mem. mil. bd. to organize La. for war, 1861; apptd. lt. col. inf. Confederate Army, advanced through grades to brig. gen., 1862; comdr. cavalry brigade; comdr. Dist. of Central Ala., 1864; comdr. State of Ala., North of Gulf Dept., 1865; participated in defense of Selma, 1865, in battle at Columbus (Ga.), 1865; resumed law practice, New Orleans, 1865-72. Died New Orleans, June 13, 1872.

ADAMS, EDWARD FRANCIS editorial writer; b. Augusta, Me., Dec. 30, 1839; s. Thomas (D.D.) and Catherine (Lyman) A.; Western Reserve Coll., 1860; m. Roah Elmira Shattuck, Jan. 30, 1860 (died 1866), 1 son, Edward Thomas; m. 2d, Delia Ray Cooper, Dec. 25, 1868 (died 1918); children-Evangeline (widow of Dr. A. Spozio), Mrs. Katherine Hicks (dec.), Marion, William, Frank. Pvt. 41st Ohio Inf., Civil War. Active for many yrs. in promoting cooperation in econ. and civic lines; editorial writer San Francisco Chronicle on econ., financial and agrl. topics. Pres. or v.p. Commonwealth Club of Calif. for its first 10 yrs. Presbyn. Author: the Modern Farmer, 1899; Critique of Socialism, 1905; Inhumanity of Socialism, 1913. Home: San Franciso, Calif. Died Nov. 19, 1929.

ADAMS, ERNEST GERMAIN, investment banking; b. Honolulu, T.H., Sept. 15, 1874; s. Edward Payson and Ellen Germain (Fisher) A.; student Harvard, 1896-97; m. Mary Edith Russell, of Weston, Mass., Oct. 14, 1902; children—Margaret Germain (dec.), Elizabeth Fisher, Edward Payson, Mary Rogers. Began with E. Rollins Morse and Bro., Boston, 1897; mgr. Providence office Kidder Peabody & Co. since 1922; pres. Union Mills Co.; dir. Boston Consolidated Gas Co. Pvt. and 2d lt. 1st Corps Cadets, Mass. Vol. Militia, 10 yrs.; in U.S. Navy, World War, advancing to lt. comdr. Trustee and chmn. bd. Unitarian Foundation; head of campaign, 1920, which raised 2,400,000 for the denomination; trustee Lincoln Sch. Mem. Unitarian Laymen's League. Republican. Clubs: Turks Head (Providence); Harvard (Boston); Army and Navy (Washington). Home: 57 Barnes St. Office: 100 Grosvenor Bldg., Providence RI

ADAMS, FRANK DURWARD clergyman, author; b. Tama Co., Ia., Apr. 18, 1876; s. Newell H. and Lenora (McKinney) A.; A.B., Dixon Coll. (now defunct), 1900; M.A. in letters, IA. Christian Coll., 1904; B.D. Ryder Divinity Sch. (Lombard Coll.), 1905, D.D., 1919; m. Helen Follett, July 26, 1897; children- Evelyn (Mrs. Russell T. Costello), Lillian (Mrs. Jack Robinson). Ordained Universalist ministry, 1905; pastor Avon, Ill. 1904-08, Urbana, Ill., 1908-09, Indpls., 1909-14, Spokane, Wash., 1914-15, Urbana, Ill., 1916-20, Elgin, Ill., 1920-23, Ch. of Our Father, Detroit, 1923-32, Unity Ch. Oak Park, Ill., 1933-44, Lansing, Mich., 1945-49, Universalist Church, Farmington, Mich., 1950-53, emeritus, 1953-62; interim minister Waterloo, IA., 1956-57. Served as 1st lt. inf., U.S. Army, 1917-18; instr. O.T.C., Camp Grant, Ill., and Camp Lee, 1st state Chaplain Am. Legion, - Dept. of Ill., 1919-20. Pres. Universalist Ch. of Am., 1927-31; pres. Ill. Universalist Ch. of Am., 1927-31; Lombard Coll., Meadville Theol. Sch. at U. Chgo.; pres. Mich. Universalist Conv., 1945-49; mem. Unitarian-Universalist Joint Commn. organizing and incorporating Free Ch. of America; Universalist mem. Council Free Ch. Am. Chmn. Mayor's Unemployment Com., Detroit, 1931-33. Mem. Chgo. Soc. of Bibl. Research, Pi Gamma Mu. Mason, Odd Fellow. Clubs: Lowell, Rotary, Torch, Detroit Wranglers. Author: Did Jesus Mean It?, 1923; Re-discovered Countries, 1924; God and Company, Unlimited, 1927; Glimpses of Grandeur, 1930; Are You Mentally Healthy?, 1934; Divine Purpose in a World of Chaos, 1941; The Ladder of Excellence, 1943; contbr. Best Sermons of 1925; contbr. to ch. periodicals and various mags. Address: R.F.D. 2, Orchard Lake, Mich. Died Jan. 26, 1962

ADAMS, GEORGE BETHUNE jurist; b. Phila., Pa., Apr. 3, 1845; s. Andrew W. and Mary A. A.; ed. public schools, Philadelphia and by private tuition; m. Helen Jean Balfour, July 12, 1904. Served with 3 months vols., May to Aug. 1861; also went to the front at the time of Lee's invasion of Pa.; on receiving discharge entered q.m.'s dept. remaining until 1871, when he engaged in mercantile pursuits. Studied law in office of Frederick S. Dickson. Admitted to practice in lower courts, 1878, in Supreme Court of Pa., 1880; mem. Wilcox, Adams & Green; became judge U.S. Dist. Court, Southern dist. New York, Aug. 30, 1901. Republican. Home: New York, N.Y. Died 1911.

ADAMS, GRANGER army officer; b. Williamson, N.Y., Sept. 28, 1852; s. Orlando and Emily (Granger) A.; grad. U.S. Mil. . 1876, Arty. Sch. 1882; m. Mary Ingham Williams, Sept. 14, 1881 (died 1902). Commd. 2d lt. 5th Arty., June 15, 1879; advanced through grades to brig. gen., July 1, 1916; retired after 44 yrs. service, Sept. 28, 1916. Prof. mil. science and tactics, St. John's Coll., Fordham, N.Y., 1893-95; sr. instr. arty. tactics, U.S. Mil. Acad., 1895-1900; comdg. Morro Castle, Santiago, Cuba, 1903-04; apptd. pres. Field Arty. Bd., 1910. Home: Front Royal, Va. Died Mar. 27, 1928.

ADAMS, HENRY HEBERLING army officer; b. Short Creek Harrison County, O., Sept. 4, 1845; s. Joshua and Jane (Brown) A.; ed. pub. schs. of Ohio; m. Mary Stiles, Oct. 31, 1878. Began mil. career as pvt. Co. F, 78th battalion Ohio Nat. Guard, 1863, in pursuit of command of Gen. John Morgan in his raid through Ohio; joined Co. C, 98th Ohio Vol. Inf., at Rossville, Ga., Mar. 1864; and served in Sherman's army until Mar. 1865; took part in engagements at Tunnel Hill, Rocky Face Ridge, Ga., battles of Resaca, Rome, Dallas, Peach Tree Creek, Kenesaw Mountain, Atlanta and Jonesboro; then with 3d div., 14th A. C., in pursuit of Gen. Forrest in N. Ga. and Ala.; later to Rome, Ga., and Atlanta, and on the March to the Sea, then on campaign in Carolinas, battle of Avensboro and Bentonville, N.C., where received gun-shot wound in face which caused his discharge, June 26, 1865. Apptd. 2d lt. U.S. Army, Feb. 23, 1866; served in South until 1879, when went to Mont.; took part in campaigns against Sitting Bull and Gall, and other duties until 1884; in 1885 with co. at Ft. Reno, Ind. Ty.; later on recruiting duty at Pittsburgh and after that in Ind. Ty., Texas, etc. Promoted 1st lt., 1885, capt., Oct. 1886, maj., Mar. 1899, col., Feb. 10, 1903; served with regt. at Iloilo, P.I., 1899; afterward comd. various posts; commandant at Plattsburgh Barracks, N.Y., Feb. 1903-. Died 1907.

ADAMS, HENRY MARTYN army officer; b. in Mass., May 28, 1844. Grad. U.S. Mil. Acad., 1866. Apptd. 2d lt. U.S. Engrs., June 18, 1866; 1st lt., July 10, 1866; capt., Sept. 2, 1874; maj., Jan. 10, 1887; lt. col., May 2, 1901; col. asst. chief engrs., U.S. Army, June 26, 1905. Died 1909.

ADAMS, JAMES DEXTER rear adm. U.S. Navy; b. Catskill, N.Y., May 4, 1848; s. Frederick Chollet and Mary Dexter (Reynolds) A.; grad. U.S. Naval Acad., 868; m. Margaret J. Phelps, May 6, 1873. Ensign Apr. 17, 1869; advanced through grades to rear admiral, Oct. 25, 1908. Comdt. Navy Yard, Charleston, S.C., Jan. 2, 1909-June 1, 1910; retired, May 4, 1910. Clubs: Army and Navy, Chevy Chase (Washington); New York Yacht. Home: Washington, D.C. Died Feb. 19, 1922.

ADAMS, JAMES FORSTER ALLEYNE physician; b. Boston, March 20, 1844; s. William Joseph and Deborah Forster (Chickering) A.; ed. Dedham, Mass., High School and Lawrence Scientific School, Harvard; grad. Harvard Med. School, 1866; med. cadet U.S.A., 1862-63; acting asst. surgeon U.S.N., 1864-65; served in Washington (Judiciary Square Hosp.), and in East Gulf Blockading Squadron; m. Washington, Oct. 20, 1870, Annah E. N. Bailey. Practicing since 1866. Mem. Am. Med. Assn., Mass. Med. Soc., Loyal Legion, S.A.R., G.A.R. Wrote: Health of the Farmers of Mass., Report of Mass. State Bd. of Health, 1874; Cremation and Burial, same, 1875; Intermittent Fever in Mass., same 1881; Sanitary Forest Culture, Proc. Mass. Med. Soc., 1884; The Prevention of Diseases in Mass., Shattuck Lecture, 1892, Mass. Med. Soc. Address: 114 Wendell Av., Pittsfield, Mass.

ADAMS, JAMES HOPKINS gov. S.C.; b. S.C., Mar. 15, 1812; s. Henry Walker and Mary (Goodwyn) A.; grad. Yale, 1831; m. Jane Margaret Scott, Apr. 1832. Joined S.C. States Rights Party, 1832; mem. S.C. Ho. of Reps., 1834-37, 40-41, 48-49, S.C. Senate, 1850-53; served as brig. gen. S.C. Militia; gov. S.C., 1854-56; elected one of commrs. to U.S. Govt. to negotiate transfer of U.S. property in S.C. to the state govt., Washington, D.C. Died Columbia, S.C. July 13, 1861.

ADAMS, JAMES TRUSLOW writer; b. Brokln., N.Y., Oct. 18, 1878; s. William Newton and Elizabeth Harber (Truslow) A.; A.B., Poly. Inst. Brooklyn, 1898; A.M., Yale U., 1900; LL.D., R.I. State Coll., 1923; Litt.D., Columbia U., 1924; L.H.D. from Wesleyan U., Conn., 1931, Lehigh U., 1933, U. of Pittsburgh, 1939; Litt.D. Princeton U., 1933, and New York U., 1937; m. Kathryn M. Seely, Jan. 18, 1927. Mem. N.Y. Stock Exchange frim until 1912; with Col. House Commn. to prepare data for Peace Conf., early in World War; later capt. Mil. Intelligence Div., Gen. Staff U.S. Army; detailed spl. duty at Peace Conf., Paris, 1919. Trustee of Bridgeport-People'sSavings Bank. Mem. Am. Acad. Arts and Letters, Mass. Hist. Soc., Am. Antiquarian Soc., Am. Hist. Assn. (exec. council 1927-28), Am. Philos. Soc.; fellow Royal Soc. of Lit. (Eng.); hon. fellow N.Y. State Hist. Soc.; hon. mem. New Eng. Hist. Geneal. Soc., N.Y. Hist. Soc. Clubs: Century (N.Y. City); Pequot Yacht (Conn.); Authors' (London, Eng.) Author: Memorials of Old Bridgehampton, 1916; History of Town of Southampton, 1918; Founding of New England, 1921 (winner Pulitzer prize of $2,000 for best book on history of U.S., 1922); Revolutionary New England, 1691-1776, 1923; New England in the

Republic (1776-1850), 1926; Provincial Society (1690-1763), 1927; Hamiltonian Principles, 1928; Jeffersonian Principles, 1928; Our Business Civilization, 1929, republished in England as A Searchlight on America, 1930; The Adams Family, 1930; The Epic of America, 1931, trans. into French, German, Danish, Hungarian, Italian, Portuguese, Rumanian, Spanish and Swedish; The Tempo of Modern Life, 1931; The March of Democracy (2 vols.), 1932-33; Henry Adams, 1933; America's Tragedy, 1935; The Record of America (with C. G. Vannest), 1935; The Living Jefferson, 1936; Building the British Empire, 1938; Empire on the Seven Seas, 1940; The American, 1943; Frontiers of American Culture, 1944; Big Business in a Democracy, 1945. Contributing editor of New Frontier Social Science Series, three volumes, 1936-37; editor in chief of Dictionary of Am. History, Six volumes, 1940; revised and enlarged J. M. Beck's Constitution of the United States, 1941; Album of American History, (vol. 1, 1944, vol. II, 1945, vol. III, 1946, vol. IV, 1948). Editor in chief, The Atlas of American History, 1943. Member advisory council, Yale Review, 1926-27. By request of senators appeared before Senate Judiciary Com. in opposition to President's Supreme Court Plan, 1937. Contributor to revised Ency. Brit., Dictionary Am. Biography and leading periodicals in U.S. and England. Mem. Pulitzer prize jury in history, 1924-32, chmn., 1930-32. Awarded prize ($1,000) by Yale Rev. for article on pub. affairs of 1932. Incorporator Sons of the Middle Border and Museum, Mitchell, S.D. Inspected 30,000 miles of Am. railways, and helped open Meadows Valley, Ida., to settlement, 1908. Home: Sheffield House, Southport, Conn. Address: care Charles Scribner's Sons, 597 Fifth Av., New York, N.Y. Died May 18, 1949.

ADAMS, JED COBB laywer; b. Kaufman, Tex., Jan. 14, 1876; s. Z. T. and Elizabeth (Ratliff) A.; student Southwestern U., Georgetown, Tex., 1889-91, Bingham Sch., Asheville, N.C., 1892-93; hon. LL.D., Jefferson Sch. of Law, 1931; m. Allie Nash, Dec. 1, 1897; children - Nash Ratliff, Elizabeth Michaux. Admitted to Tex. bar, 1895; state's atty. Kaufman County, Tex., 189O-1902; del. Dem. Nat. Conv., St. Louis, 1904; Dem. presdl. elector at large, 1908; moved to Dallas, Tex., 1909; U.S. atty. Northern Dist. of Tex., Oct. 1919-Jan 1920 (resigned); mem. U.S. Board of Tax Appeals, May 1933-; mem. Dem. Nat. Exec. Com. from Tex., 1924-34. Maj. J.A.G.'s Dept., U.S. Army hdqrs. Governor's Island, N.Y., Oct. 1918-Apr. 1919, World War; lt. col. R.C., U.S. Army Methodist. Home: Dallas, Tex. Died Jan. 29, 1935.

ADAMS, JOHN 2d Pres. U.S.; b. Braintree (now Quincy), Mass., Oct. 30, 1735; s. John and Susanna (Boylston) A.; grad. Harvard, 1755; m. Abigail Smith, Oct. 25, 1764; children—John Quincy (6th Pres. U.S.), Thomas, Charles, Abby. Admitted to Boston bar, 1758; rep. from Boston to Mass. Gen Ct., 1770; joined Sons of Liberty; one of Mass. dels. to 1st Continental Congress, 1774; apptd. chief justice Superior Ct. of Mass., 1775; signer Declaration of Independence, 1776, proposed Washington for gen. Continental Army; resigned office of chief justice Superior Ct. to become mem. newly-created Board of War, 1777; elected commr. to France, 1777; minister to United Provinces, 1780; with Jay and Jefferson negotiated treaty of Paris with Gt. Britain, 1785; elected 1st vice pres. U.S., 1788, reelected, 1792; elected 2d Pres. U.S., 1796, signed Alien and Sedition Acts, resisted pressure to declare war on France, 1797, one of last acts was to appoint John Marshall as chief justice U.S. Supreme Ct., defeated for 2d term by Thomas Jefferson, 1800. Author numerous published works, including: Thoughts on Government, 1776; Defense of the Constitutions of the United States of America Against the Attacks of Mr. Turgot, 1787; Novanglus and Massachusetensis, 1819. Died Quincy, July 4, 1826; buried under old 1st Congregational Ch., Boston.

ADAMS, JOHN army officer; b. Nashville, Tenn., July 1, 1825; grad. U.S. Mil. Acad., 1846; m. Georgia McDougas, 1852. Commd. 2d lt., 1st Dragoons, J.S. Army, Mexican War, served at Rayado, Las Vegas, N.M., 1850-51, promoted lst lt; lt. col., aide-de-camp to gov. Minn., 1853; capt. Dragoons, 1856; resigned commn., 1861; commd. col. Confederate Army, 1862. Killed at Battle of Franklin (Tenn.), Nov. 30, 1864.

ADAMS, JOHN GREGORY BISHOP; b. Groveland, Mass., Oct. 6, 1841; enlisted, April 19, 1861, in Maj. Ben Perley Poore's Rifle Battalion (afterward merged in 19th Mass. vols.); served private to capt., 1861-65, in Army of Potomac except during nine months when he was a prisoner of war and when he was in hospital from wounds received at Gettysburg; has held several local offices; was three times post comdr. G.A.R., Lynn, Mass.; comdr.-in-chief, G.A.R., 1893-94. Home: Lynn, Mass. Died 1900.

ADAMS, JOHN QUINCY 6th Pres. U.S.; b. Braintree (name now Quincy), Massachusetts, July 11, 1767; son of John (2d Pres. U.S.) and Abilgail (Smith) A.; graduate of Harvard, 1787; m. Louisa Johnson, July 26, 1797, 4 children including Charles Francis. Admitted to Mass. bar, 1790; apptd. U.S. minister to Netherlands by Pres. Washington, 1794; elected to Mass. Senate, 1802; mem. U.S. Senate from Mass., 1803-08, resigned, 1808; U.S. minister to Ct. of St. Petersburg (Russia), 1809-11; nominated to U.S. Supreme Ct., 1811; declined; one of negotiators of peace after War of 1812; U.S. minister to Gt. Britain, 1815; U.S. sec. of state, 1817-25, considered prin. author of Monroe Doctrine drawn up during his term; 6th Pres. U.S., 1825-29, defeated for 2d term by Andrew Jackson, 1828; mem. U.S. Ho. of Reps. from Mass., 22d-30th congresses, 1831-48, leading opponent of slavery, gag rule efforts of So. reps., also instrumental in getting favorable vote for establishment of Smithsonian Instn., 1846. Author: Memoirs (edited by Charles Francis Adams), 12 vols., 1874-77; Writings (edited by W. C. Ford), 7 vols., 1913. Died Washington, D.C., Feb. 23, 1848; buried Quincy.

ADAMS, MELVIN OHIO lawyer; b. Ashburnham, Mass., Nov. 7, 1850; s. Joseph and Dolly W. (Whitney) A.; A.B., Dartmouth, 1871 (LL.D., 1912): LL.B., Boston U., 1874; m. Mary Colony, Jan. 20, 1874. Practiced, Boston, 1876-; asst. dist. atty., 1876-86; U.S. atty., 1895-1906; pres. Boston, Revere Beach & Lynn R.R. from 1891; v.p. Liberty Trust Co. from 1907; trustee Dartmouth Coll.; pres. Trustees, Cushing Acad.; asst. adj. gen. on staff Gov. Brackett, 1890-91, with rank of col. Republican. Home: 36 Beacon St., Boston, Mass. Died Aug. 9, 1920.

ADAMS, MILTON BUTLER army officer; b. Beaver Falls, Pa., Apr. 11, 1845; s. Samuel Plummer and Ellen (Barker) A.; ed. Calvin Moore's Sem. (Quaker), Salem, O., 1853-61; grad. U.S. Mil. Acad. 1865; m. Cleveland, O., 1878, Anna Lewis. Commd. 1st lt. engrs., June 23, 1865; capt., 5, 1898; col, Apr. 23, 1904. Episcopalian. Home: Salem, O. Address: War Dept., Washington.

ADAMS, MYRON EUGENE social worker; b. Palmyra, N.Y., Feb. 19, 1876; s. Myron II. and Lydia (Brewster) A.; A.B., Syracuse U., 1898; Rochester Theol. Sem., 1901; D.D., Syracuse U., 1920; m. Roma M. Howell, July 7, 1914; children - Brewster Howell, Grant Howell. Dir. 1st playground, Rochester, N.Y., 1899; Cleveland, 1901; resident worker and probation officer, Welcome Hall Settlement, Buffalo. 1901-04; head worker, West Side Neighborhood House, New York, 1904-06; ordained Baptist ministry, 1905; pastor Midland, Mich., 1906-09, Warren Av. Ch., Detroit, 1909-12, 1st Baptist Ch., Chicago, 1912-16. Organized and became 1st dir. dept. of morale (afterwards a dept. under Chief of Staff U.S. Army) R.O.T.C., Ft. Sheridan; capt. administrative staff Adj. Gen. Ill., exec. sec. Nat. Rehabilitation Com., 1922; associated with Marshall Field and Albert A. Sprague in the Public Service Associates, inc., for pub. service purposes, 1922-26; consultant Reorganizarion Hosp. Service, downtown, N.Y. City, 1924-25; made plans for Chicago Centennial Celebration, 1925; sec. Pub. Health Inst. Mason (32o). Home: Hubbard Woods, Ill. Died Jan. 17, 1930.

ADAMS, OSCAR SHERMAN mathematician; b. nr. Mt. Vernon, O., Jan. 9, 1874; s. David W. and Louisa (McElroy) A.; B.S., 1st honors, Kenyon Coll., 1896 (valedictorian), A.M., 1915, Sc.D., 1922; m. Mary Edna Fuller, June 20, 1900 (dec.); children-Catherine Fuller, Jane Elizabeth, George David; m. 2d, Mrs. Pauline Gleeson Pealer; 1 dau., Carola Ann. Supt. Schs., Ohio, 1899-1903; Dover, Ohio, 1903-05, Rock Creek, 1905-06; prin. Madison Twp. High School, North Madison, O., 1906-10; geodectic computer and mathematician, U.S. Coast and Geodetic Survey, 1910-44. Served in Co. L 4th O. Vol. Inf., Spanish-Am. War, Puerto Rico Campaign; 1st lt. Engr. O.R.C., 1917. Mem. Math. Assn. Am. (pres. lfd.-Va.-D.C. sect. 1921-22). Washington Philos Soc. (rec. sec. 1929-30, v.p. 1931-32, pres. 1933), Washington Acad. Scis. (sec. 1938-39), Grange, Am. Geophys. Union, Phi Beta Kappa, Sigma Xi (sec. of D.C. Chapter, 1937-39). Methodist. Author: Application of Least Squares to Adjustment of Triangulation, 1915; General Theory of Lambert Projection, 1918; General Theory of Polyconic Projections, 1919; Latitude Developments, 1921; Elements of Map Projection (with Chas. H. Deetz), 1921; Radio-Compass Bearings, 1921; Elliptic Functions Applied to Conformal World Maps, 1925; Tables for Albers Projection, 1927; The Bowie Method of Triangulation Adjustment, 1930. Co-Author: Manual of Plane Coordinate Computation, 1935; Manual of Traverse Computation on the Lambert Grid, 1935; Manual of Traverse Computation on the Tranverse Mercator Grid, 1935. Compiler: Triangulation in Colorado, 1930; Triangulation in North Carolina, 1935. Home: Route 3, Mt. Vernon, O. 43050. Died Mar. 5, 1962, Buried Arlington Nat. Cemetery, Va.

ADAMS, PARMENLO congressman; b. Hartford, Conn., Sept. 9, 1776; attended common schs. Moved to Phelps Corners, Batavia, Genesee County (now Attica, Wyoming County), N.Y., 1806; served with N.Y. Militia, 1806-16, as lt. light inf., capt. Grenadiers, 2d and 1st maj., div. insp. Inf.; served as maj. and commandant N.Y. Volunteers, in War of 1812; sheriff of Genesee County, 1815-16, 18-21; engaged in agrl. pursuits, also as constrn. contractor on Erie Canal; mem. U.S. Ho. of Reps. from N.Y. (contested election), 18th, 19th congresses, Jan. 7, 1824-27. Died Alexander, N.Y., Feb. 19, 1832.

ADAMS, PORTER (HARTWELL) educator; b. at Andover, Mass., Aug. 10, 1894; s. Charles Albert and Jeannie Hortense (Porter) A.; prep. edn. Stone Sch. and Chauncy Hall Sch., Boston; student U. of Redlands, Calif., Mass. Inst. Tech.; hon. M.Sc., Norwich U., 1933, Sc.D., 1935; m. 2d, Due Shorter, July 27, 1931. With Cooper Aircraft Co., Bridgeport, Conn., 1915; associated with Donald Douglas on first proposed world flight, 1916; development work, 1920-22. Intelligence and communications officer, U.S. Navy, Rockland, Me., and Boston, 1917-18; aide to comdg. officer, Naval Air Sta., Chatham, Mass., 1918-19; lt. comdr. U.S.N.R., retired. Executor and trustee of various estates; pres. of Norwich U., Dec. 1933-June, 1939, now pres. emeritus. Pres. Village Soc. of Thetford, Vt., since 1929; mem. Thetford Water Bd.; mem. Thetford Bd. of Selectmen, 1933-36; mem. Vt. Ho. of Reps. 1933-34; mem. Vt. Chamber of Commerce, Chmn. exec. com. Nat. Aeronautic Assn., 1922-26 and since 1928, pres. 1926-28; chmn. Municipal Air Bd., Boston, since 1922; Vt. airport supervisor for aeronautics branch, Dept. of Commerce and Civil Works Adminstrn.; dir. Miniature Aircraft Tournament under Playground Recreation Assn. America, Nat. Glider Assn.; v.p. Internat. Air Congress, Rome, Italy, 1927; tech. adviser for Am. delegation, Internat. Civil Aeronautics Conf., Washington, 1928; mem. Fed. Bd. of Maps and Surveys; mem. Am. Olympic Com., 1928; chmn. First Intercollegiate Aeronautical Conf., Yale U., 1928; chmn. aviation med. sect., First Nat. Aeronautical Safety Conf., 1928; chmn. first aviation com., Am. Legion, Dept. of Mass.; mem. advisory council on student flying activities, Mass. Inst. Tech.; mem. special com. on Aeronautical Research in Ednl. Instns. of Nat. Advisory Com. for Aeronautics; mem. New Eng. Planning Com. of Nat. Resources Bd., also chmn. aviation com.; chmn. Aeor Com. of A.L. Dept., Vt., 1935; Vt. chmn. for Navy Day, 1933-40; apptd. by gov. chmn. Vt. Aviation Commn. for term, 1936-40. Mem. Vt. advisory bd. for N.Y. World's Fair. Trustee Norwich U.; elected chmn. spl. com. of trustees to administer James Jackson Cabot professorship of air traffic regulation and air transportation, and also appointed first James Jackson Cabot prof. of air traffic regulation and air transportation at Norwich Univ., Aug, 1935; trustee Thetford Acad.; v.p. Vt. Boy Scouts. Fellow A.A.A.S.; mem. Inst. of Aeronautical Sciences, Am. Soc. M.E. (exec. com., aeronautics sect.), Navy League of U.S., Soc. Automotive Engrs., Am. Acad. Air Law, Vt. Histo. Soc., Vt. Soc. Engrs., U.S. Naval Inst., Naval Order of U.S., Mil. Order of World War, Nat. Grange (7th degree), Newcomen Soc., New Eng. Railroad Club, Pi Gamma Mu, Epsilon Tau Sigma; also hon. mem. foreign aeronautical socs. Conglist. Clubs: Metropolitan, Aero (trustee), Army and Navy (Washington); St. Botolph, Wardroom, Engineers, Aero Club of Mass. (dir., ex-vice pres.), Aero Club of New England (dir., ex-pres.), Woodland Country (Boston); University (Boston and Northfield, Vt.); Newcomen Soc. (England). Contbr. to periodicals on subject of aviation. Inventor of aeroplane brakes, 1916, Adams type of wind tunnel balance for aerodynamical research, 1933, Adams system of combustion for steam submarines, aircraft, tanks, etc. Home: "Aero Acres," Thetford, Vt. Address: Norwich University, Northfield, Vt. Died Dec. 5, 1945.

ADAMS, ROBERT NEWTON Presbyterian clergyman; b. Fayette Co., O., Sept. 15, 1835; s. Albert and Nancy A.; grad. Miami Univ., 1861 (D.D., 1890); m. Athens, O., Dec. 27, 1867, Nellie W. Whipple (died Oct. 10, 1900). Entered army April, 1861 in a co. of students as private and served 3 months; reenlisted for 3 yrs. Aug. 30, 1861 in Co. C, 81st Ohio Vol. inf.; elected capt.; afterward became lt. col. and col. same regt.; at close of war in command 2d brigade and 4th div., 15th army corps, and in March, 1865, was apptd. bvt. brig.-gen.; ordained Presbyn. minister 1870. Address: 6201/2 Nicollet Av., Minneapolis

ADAMS, WILLIAM HENRY jurist; b. Lyons, N.Y., Mar. 27, 1841; s. John and Rebecca B. A.; ed. pub. schs., and in prep school at Geneva, N.Y. (LL.D., Coll., 1899); m. Charlotte L., d. U.S. Senator Elbridge G. Lapham. Sept. 27, 1865. Served in Union army in Civil War as lt. and capt. 98th N.Y. vols. and asst. adj. gen. on staff of Gen. J. J. DeForrest; admitted to bar; elected, 1887, and re-elected 1901, justice Supreme Court, N.Y., renominated on both Republican and Democratic tickets, 1901, and vote practically unanimous (term to expire 1915); now presiding justice Appellate div. Supreme Court, 4th dept. Republican. Home: Canadaigua. N.Y. Died 1903.

ADAMS, WILLIAM MILTON plastic surgeon; b. Ripley, Miss., Apr. 26, 1905; s. Dr. R. M. and Patty Etter (Murray) A.; B.S., U. Miss., 1928; M.D., Tulane, 1930; m. Catherine Taylor, May 22, 1934; children-William Milton, Robert Franklin, Ann Taylor, Catherine Sue. Intern N.Y. Post Grad. Hosp., N.Y. City, 1931-32; asso. prof. surgeru U. Tenn. 1951—, chief plastic surgery dept. U. Tenn., John Gaston Hosp., 1935—; chief surgery Meth. Hosp., 1947, chief staff, 1948; senior attending plastic surgery Bapt. Meml., John Gaston, Meth., St. Joseph's hosps.; chief cons. plastic surgery Kennedy V.A., U.S. Marine hosps. Mem. Examining Bd. Plastic Surgery, 1947—. Diplomate Am. Bd. Plastic Surgery. Fellow Internat. Coll. Surgeons, A.C.S.; mem. Am. Soc. Plastic and Reconstructive Surgery (pres. 1954; asso. editor Jour.), Am., Brit. assns. plastic American Association Surgery Trauma, Am. Med. Assn., Southern, Tenn., Shelby Co., Memphis med. assns., Southeastern Surg. Congress, Southwestern

Surg. Assn., Memphis Surg. Soc., La.-Miss. Ophthal. and Otolarygnol. Soc. (hon. mem.), Clubs: Rotary, Memphis Country (Memphis). Contributor articles medical journals. Home: 689 East Drive., Memphis 2. Office: 1073 Madison St., Memphis 3. Died Apr. 4, 1957; buried Memorial Park, Memphis.

ADAMS, WILLIAM WIRT army officer; b. Frankfort, Ky., Mar. 22, 1819; s. Judge George and Anna (Weissiger) A.; grad. Bardstown (Ky.) Coll., 1839; m. Sallie Mayrant, 1850. Served as pvt. under Col. Burleson's command Republic of Tex. Army, 1839; mem. Miss Legislature, 1858, 60; assisted in securing withdrawal of La. from the Union, 1861; commd. brig. gen. Confederate States Army, 1863; surrendered Ala., 1865; revenue agt. Miss., 1880-85; apptd. postmaster of Jackson (Miss.) by Pres. Cleveland, 1885. Died in street duel with John Martin, Vicksburg, Miss., May 1, 1888.

ADAMSON, ALFRED rear adm.; b. Brownsville, N.Y., Sept. 19, 1836. Apptd. 3d asst. engr. U.S. Navy, May 13, 1861; promoted 2d asst. engr., Dec. 17, 1862; 1st asst. engr., Jan. 1, 1865; chief engr., May 19, 1879; retired on account of age, Sept. 19, 1898; advanced to rank of rear adm. retired, June 29, 1906, in recognition of service during Civil War. Home: Boston, Mass. Died Feb. 22, 1915.

ADCOCK, CLARENCE LIONEL army officer; b. Waltham, Mass., Oct. 23, 1895; s. Charles John and Jennie Abbie (Leonard) A.; B.S., U.S. Mil. Acad., 1918; grad. The Engr. Sch., 1921, Command and Gen. Staff Sch., 1935, The Army War Coll., 1939; m. Inez Elise Genrich, Mar. 5, 1947; children by previous marriage-Charles Warren, Robert L. Commd. 2d lt. C.E., U.S. Army, 1918, advanced through grades to maj. gen., 1945; asst. chief of staff II Corps, for invasion of N. Africa, 1942-43, and under Gen. Mark W. Clark, Fifth Army, 1943, for G-4 (supply) with Gen. Eisenhower's hdqrs. in N. Africa and Italy, 1943-44, G-4 with 6th Army group in France and Germany, 1944-45; dep. to Gen. Clay in Berlin with Mil. Govt., 1946, ret. 1947; recalled active duty, 1948; U.S. chmn. Bipartite Control office, Frankfurt, Germany, supervising German Economic Govt. of Brit. and Am. zones of Occupation, 1947-49; ret., 1949. Asst. to the pres. Continental Can Co., N.Y.C., 1950-67. Decorated D.S.M. with 2 oak leaf clusters, Legion of Merit with one oak leaf cluster: hon. Comdr. Most Excellent Order of Brit. Empire; officer Legion of Honor, Croix de Guerre with Palm. Home: 450 E. 63rd St., N.Y.C. 21. Office: 100 E. 42d St., N.Y.C. 17. Died Jan. 9 1967.

ADDEMAN, JOSHUA MELANCTHON banker, lawyer; b. New Zealand, Nov. 15, 1840; s. Thomas and Mary (Fligg) A.; brought to U.S., 1843; A.B., Brown U., 1862, A.M., 1865; m. Louise W. Winsor, Oct. 25, 1872. Served in U.S. Vols., 1862-65; mustered out as capt.; admitted to bar, 1866; clk. Common Council, Providence, R.I., 1867-81; sec. of State R.I., 1872-87; commr. to revise the R.I. Public Statutes, 1880 v.p. Industrial Trust Co., 1895 - . Mason. Republican. Episcopalian. Home: Providence, R.I. Died Oct. 13, 1930.

ADDICKS, WALTER ROBARTS pub. utility exec.; b. Philadelphia, Pa., Apr. 14, 1861; s. John Edward Charles O'Sullivan and Margaretta Turner (McLeon) A.; prep. edn., Episcopal Acad., Phila.; grad. U.S. Naval Acad., 1882; m. Margaret Jardine, Jan. 22, 1890. Resigned from U.S. Navy, 1883; draftsman, Pa. R.R., Altoona, Pa., 1883-84, in charge surveys of shops and shop yards east of Pittsburgh and Erie, 1885-86; chief engr., Brookline Gas Light Co. and cons. engr. Mass. Pipe Line Gas Co. and N.E. Gas and Coke Co., 1887-1903; 1st v.p. and trustee Consol. Gas Co. of N.Y., 1903-25, v.p., 1925 - , acting pres., 1904-09; pres. United Electric Light & Power Co., 1904-12; pres. Municipal Lighting Co., 1906-13. Served as lt., sr. grade, U.S. Navy comdg. U.S.S. Eileen and U.S.S. Huntress, Spanish Am. War. Mem. nat. com. on gas and electric service, Council Nat. Defense, and in charge Govt. plants producing tuluol, carbon soda lime. World War, Republican Baptist. Home: Mt. Kisco, N.Y. and New York City. Died Apr. 14, 1931.

ADDISON, JAMES THAYER clergyman; b. Fitchburg, Mass., Mar. 21, 1887; s. Charles Morris and Ada (Thayer) A.; student Groton Sch., 1900-05; A.B., Harvard, 1909; B.D., Episcopal Theol. Sch., Cambridge, Mass., 1913; S.T.M., Harvard Div. Sch., 1917; D.D., Theol. Sem. of Va., 1931; m. Margaret B. Crocker, Dec. 18, 1917; children-Helen Crocker, Martha Lothrop. Ordained to ministry P.E. Ch., 1913; minister in charge St. Mark's Ch., Nowata, and St. Paul's Ch., Claremore, Okla., 1913-15; lecturer Episcopal Theol. Sch., 1915-17, asst. prof. history of religion and missions, 1919-26, prof., 1926-40; acting master Kirkland House, Harvard, 1932-33; vice president National Council of the Protestant Episcopal Church, 1940-46. Chaplain 1st Gas Regt., A.E.F., France, 1918-19. Trustee Am. Univ., Cairo, Egypt. Author: Story of the First Gas Regiment, 1919; Chinese Ancestor Worship, 1925; Our Father's Business.

ADKINS, HOMER MARTIN gov. Ark.; b. Jacksonville Ark., Oct. 15, 1890; s. Ulysses and Lorena (Wood) A.; student Draughons Bus. Coll., 1907-08, Pharmacy Coll., 1910-11; m. Estelle Elise Smith, Dec. 18, 1921. Registered pharmacist, Little Rock, 1911-16; salesman Darragh Co., Little Rock, 1916-17, 1919-22; sheriff and collector Pulaski firm of Adkins & Williams, 1926-33; Fed. Internal Revenue collector, 1933-40; gov., State of Ark., 1941-45. Served as capt., Med. Adminstrn., U.S. Army, in U.S. and France, 1917-19. Mem. Am. Legion, Woodmen of World. Democrat. Methodist. Mason. Elk. Club: Little Rock. Home: 1601 Dennison, Little Rock. Died Feb. 28, 1964.

ADLER, DANKMAR architect; b. Langsfeld, Saxe Weimar, July 3, 1844; ed. public schools; studied architecture, Detroit and Chicago, 1857-62; m. Dila, d. Abraham Kohn, of Chicago, June 25, 1872. Served, 1862-65, Bat. M, 1st Ill. Artillery. Began practice of architecture in Chicago, 1869; with A. J. Kinney, 1869-71; with Edward Burling, 1871-78; with Louis H. Sullivan, 1881-95; architect of Unity Ch., Grace M.E., and 1st M.E. Chs., Sinai, Zion, Anshe Maariv and Isaiah synagogues, Central Music Hall, McVicker's Theatre, The Auditorium, Stock Exchange bldg., and Schiller bldg., Chicago; Pueblo (Colo.) Opera House; Union Trust, Wainwright and St. Nicholas Hotel bldgs., St. Louis; Guaranty bldg., Buffalo, N.Y.; I.C. R.R. passenger station, New Orleans; asso. architect Carnegie Music Hall, New York, etc. Home: Chicago, Ill. Died 1900.

ADSON, ALFRED WASHINGTON surgeon; b. Terril, , Mar. 13, 1887; s. Martin and Anna (Bergeson) A.; B.Sc., U. of Neb., 1912, A.M., 1918; M.D., U. of Pa., 1914; M.S. in surgery, U. of Minn., 1918; hon. D.Sc., U of Neb., 1948, St. Olaf Coll.; m. Lora G. Smith, Aug. 3, 1911; children-William Walter, Mary Louise, Martin Alfred. Successively fellow in surgery, Mayo Clinic, 1st asst., jr. surgeon, neurol. surgeon, chief neurol. surgeon; now senior neuro-surgeon professor neuro-surgery Mayo Foundation Grad. Sch. of U. of Minn. Colonel Med. R.C., United States Army. Mem. Minn. State Board of Med. Examiners since 1929, pres., 2 years. Mem. Medical Council of the Veterans Administration, Council on Medical Service and Public Relations of A.M.A., adv. com. Med. Unit of Div. of Social Welfare of Minn. Dept. of Social Security; mem. Commn. on Associated Med. Care Plans; chmn. Minn. State Med. Service Com.;pres. Northwest National Conference. Fellow American College of Surgeons; member A.M.A., American Surg. Assn., American Neurol. Assn., American Neurosurgical Assn. (pres. 1932), Internat. Neurol Assn. Internat. Congress of Surgeons, Western Surg. Assn. (v.p. 1936), Minn. State Med. Assn. (pres. 1937; del. to A.M.A.), Am. Bd. Neurol. Surgery (chmn.), Minn. Soc. of Neurology & Psychiatry (pres. 1943), also numerous local, state and district medical societies, Phi Rho Sigma, Sigma Xi, Alpha Omega Alpha. Republican (chmn. co. com.). Mason (32 degrees, K.T., Shriner). Clubs: University, Golf. Contbr. more than 242 articles to med. jours. in development and improvement of surg. technique in removal of brain and spinal cord tumors; development of operations for treatment of glossopharyngeal neuralgia, cervical ribs, Reynaurd's disease, Hirschsprung's disease and essential hypertension. Home: 831 9th Av. S.W., Rochester, Minn. Died Nov. 12, 1951

AGETON, ARTHUR ret. naval officer, author, corp. exec.; b. Fromberg, Mont., Oct. 25, 1900; s. Peter Benjamin and Minnie Anna (Drummond) A.; student State Coll. Wash., 1918-19; B.S., U.S. Naval Acad., 1923; certificate, Naval Postgrad. Sch., 1931; M.A., Johns Hopkins, 1953; m. Jo Lucille Gallion, Nov. 24, 1933; children—Mary Jo, Arthur Ainslie. Commd. ensign USN, 1923, advanced through grades to rear adm., 1947, ret., 1947; ambassador to Paraguay, 1954-57; business rep. 1957-63. Decorated Legion of Merit, Bronze Star Medal (U.S.); Gran Cruz Orden Nacional del Merito (Paraguay). Mem. U.S. Naval Inst. Republican. Episcopalian. Clubs: Army and Navy, Army and Navy Country (Washington). Author: Dead Reckoning Altitude and Azimuth Table, 1932; Naval Officer's Guide, 1942; Naval Leadership and the American Bluejacket, 1944; Manual of Celestial Navigation, 1942; Mary Jo and Little Liu, 1945; The Jungle Seas, 1954; Admiral Ambassador to Russia (with Adm. William H. Standley), 1955; The Marine Officers Guide (with Gen. G. C. Thomas and Col. R. D. Heinl), 1955; Hit the Beach, 1961. Home: Annapolis MD Died May 1971.

AGG, THOMAS RADFORD (AG), highway engring.; b. Fairfield, Ia., May 17, 1878; s. Henry and Sarah Jane (Tansey) A.; B.S. in E.E., Ia. State Coll., Ames, Ia., 1905, C.E., 1914; m. Lois Woodman, Dec. 27, 1906; children—Muriel Lois, Alice Jane. Instr. in theoretical mechanics, U. of Ill., 1905-08; road engr. Ill. Highway Dept., summers, 1906, 1907, and full time, 1908-13; prof. highway engring., Ia. State Coll., 1913-30, asst. dean of engring., 1930-32, dean of engring. and dir. Engring. Expt. Sta., 1930-46; resident prof. highway engring. since July 1946, also cons. practice. Developed outstanding instrn. and research in highway engring. at Ia. State Coll. Entered Engineering Officers Training Camp, May 1917; commissioned captain, later major; served with 109th and 98th Engineers. Received George S. Bartlett award for outstanding contribution to highway progress, 1936. Member American Society Civil Engrs. (dir. Dist. 16, 1938-40); (v.p. Zone 3, 1943-44), Am. Soc. for Testing Materials, Soc. for Promotion Engring. Edn., Iowa Engring. Soc., Newcomen Soc., Tau Beta Pi, Sigma Xi, Phi Kappa Phi, Acacia. Republican. Episcopalian. Mason (32 degree). Me. Rotary Internat. Author: Construction of Roads and Pavements, 1916, 5th edit., 1939; American Rural Highways, 1920; (with Dr. John E. Brindley) Highway Administration and Finance, 1927; (with W. L. Foster) Preparation of Engineering Reports, 1935; (with Anson Marston) Engineering Valuation, 1936. Home 325 Pearson Av., Ames, Ia. Died May 7, 1947.

AGNEW, WILLIAM JOHN CLARKE med. officer; b. High Falls, N.Y., Dec. 6, 1891; s. William J. C. and Mary Martha (Stephens) A.; student L.I. Coll. Hosp., Bklyn., 1910-11; M.D., U. Vt., 1914; m. Drika Fisher, Apr. 29, 1937. Interne, St. Johns Riverside Hosp., Yonkers, N.Y., 1914-16; resident N.Y., Nursery and Childs Hosp., N.Y.C., 1916 N.Y. Orthopedic Hosp., N.Y.C., 1916-17; entered M.C., U.S. 1917; promoted through grades to rear adm., Sept. 1942; now dist. med. officer. 11th Naval Dist. Fellow A.C.S.; mem. Alpha Kappa Kappa, Theta Nu Epsilon. Clubs: Army and Navy (Washington); Chevy Chase, Columbia Country (Chevy Chase, Md.). Editor: Handbook of the Hospital Corps, U.S. Navy, 1939. Home: 1041 Encino Row, Coronado, Cal. Address: District Medical Officer, 9th Naval District, Great Lakes, Ill. Died Jan. 26, 1955

AGNUS, FELIX editor; b. Lyons, France, July 4, 1839; ed. Coll. Jolie Clair, near Paris; traveled around the world 4 yrs.; vol. under Napoleon III during Franco-Austrian War; also served under Garibaldi; came to U.S., 1860; m. a d. of Charles C. Fulton, of Baltimore, Dec. 13, 1864. Enlisted as sergt. in Duryea's 5th N.Y. Zouaves, May 9, 1861; 2d lt., Sept. 6, 1861, for saving life of Gen. Judson Kilpatrick at Big Bethel; 1st lt., July 8, 1862; capt. 165th N.Y. Inf., Nov. 6, 1862; maj., Sept. 2, 1863; resigned, July 26, 1865. Bvtd.; lt.-col., Mar. 13, 1865, "for gallant and meritorious services at battle of Gaines' Mill," June 13, 1862 (wounded); col., Mar. 13, 1865, for same at battle of Port Hudson, La. (wounded); brig-gen. vols., Mar. 13, 1865, for same during the war. Apptd. asst. assessor internal revenue, Baltimore, 1865; business mgr., later editor and publisher Baltimore American and Baltimore Star; retired. Home: Stevenson. Md. Died Oct. 31, 1925.

AGUINALDO, EMILIO, Filipino leader; b. Cavite Province, P.I., Mar. 22, 1869; s. Carlos Aguinaldo; m. Hilaria del Rosario, 1896 (dec. 1930), 6 children; m. 2d, Maria Agoncillo, 1930 (dec. 1963). Became leader Filipino revolt against Spain, 1896, was exiled to Hong Kong by peace treaty that ended hostilities; fought with U.S. forces during Spanish-Am. War; organized and assumed presidency of Philippine Republic with capital at Malolos, 1898 (Republic not recognized by U.S. peace treaty); fought against U.S. occupying forces until captured by Brig. Gen. Frederick Funston, 1901, then swore allegiance to U.S.; defeated by Manuel Quezon in presdl. election, 1935; wore black bow tie as symbol of mourning for Philippine Republic until Philippines was granted independence from U.S., 1946; accused of cooperating with Japanese in Philippines during World War II, taken into custody, 1945, but never tried. Died Veterans Meml. Hosp., Manila, P.I., Feb. 6, 1964.

AIKEN, WILLIAM APPLETON mfr.; b. Manchester, Vt., Apr. 18, 1833; s. John and Mary Means (Appleton) A.; ed. pub. and pvt. schs., Lowell, Mass., Dummer Acad., Byfield, Mass., Phillips Acad., Andover, Mass., to 1851; m. Eliza Coit, d. Gov. William A. Buckingham of Norwich, Conn., Aug. 28, 1861. Acting asst. paymaster U.S. Navy, 1861-62; q.-m.- gen. of Conn., 1862-65. Was pres. Norwich Nickel & Brass Co. Republican. Home: Norwich, Conn. Died Nov. 7, 1929.

AIKEN, WYATT ex-congressman; b. Abbeville Co., S.C., Dec. 14, 1863; s. D. Wyatt (M.C.) and Virginia Carolina A.; ed. Cokesbury, S.C., and Washington, D.C.; m. Mary Barnwell, Apr. 27, 1892. Farmer since boyhood; served in 1st S.C. Vols. in Spanish-Am. War; battalion adj. and regimental q.-m. Official court stenographer, Abbeville, S.C., 1884-1903; mem. 58th to 64th Congresses (1903-17), 3d S.C. Dist.; Democrat. Address: Abbeville, S.C. Died Feb. 6, 1923.

AINSWORTH, FRED CRAYTON major-general U.S.A.; b. Woodstock, Vt., Sept. 11, 1852. M.D., Univ. Med. Coll. (New York U.), 1874. Apptd. from Vt. asst. surgeon, Nov. 10, 1874; capt. asst. surgeon, Nov. 10, 1879; maj. surgeon, Feb. 27, 1891; col. and chief of Record and Pension Office, May 27, 1892; brig. gen., Mar. 2, 1899; maj. gen. and mil. sec. U.S.A., Apr. 23, 1904; maj. gen. and the adj. gen. U.S.A., Mar. 5, 1907, with rank from Apr. 23, 1904; retired at own request, Feb. 16, 1912. Home: Washington, D.C. Died June 5, 1934.

AINSWORTH, WALDEN L. naval officer; b. Mpls., Nov. 10, 1886; S. William Green and Mary Lee (Walden) A.; student U. Minn., 1905, B.S., U.S. Naval Acad., 1910; m. Katharine Gardner, June 10, 1916; children-H. Gardner, Katharine Walden (Mrs. Benedict Joseph Semmes). Served on various ships and stations including Asiatic Sta., Panama, advanced through grades to rear adm. Dec. 1941; ret. as vice adm., 1948. Decorated Navy Cross for Battle of Kula Gulf; D.S.M. for Solomons Campaign; Legion of Merit as comdr. destroyers-cruisers, Pacific Fleet. Mem. Soc. of

Cincinnati. Clubs: Army-Navy (Washington), N.Y. Yacht. Home: Wonalancet, N.H. Died Aug. 7, 1960. Buried Arlington (Va.) Nat. Cemetery.

ALBERT, ALLEN DIEHL, JR., sociologist, historian; b. Washington, D.C., Apr. 27, 1902; s. Allen Diehl and Janet Clark (Jones) A.; student DePauw U., 1920-21; Ph.B., U. of Chicago, 1924, M.A., 1932, Ph.D., 1936; student Harvard Grad. Sch. Bus. Adminstrn., 1926-27; m. Emily Bartlett Davis, Sept. 6, 1934; 1 stepdaughter, Emily Carson (Mrs. Albert Hanahan). Employee, Jacksonville (Fla.) Gas Co., 1925, Evanston (Ill.) News-Index, 1927-28, Century of Progress Expdn., Chgo. 1928-29; prof. Old Testament and Semitic Langs., Seabury-Western Theol. Sem., Evanston, 1932-41; ordained deacon, Episcopalian Ch., 1938, priest, 1939; prof. sociology, Emory U., since 1946, chairman of division of social science, 1947-48, on leave as pub. relations mgr. Lockheed Aircraft Corp., Ga. div., since 1951. Hon. canon, Cathedral of St. Philips', Atlanta since 1948. Consultant to advisory committee of State Board of Health on Hospital Locations since 1950; chairman Local Govt. Commn., Atlanta and Fulton County. Captain to lt. col., Inf., U.S. Army, 1941-46; aide-de-camp to Gen. Omar N. Bradley, Maj. Gen. Leven C. Allen, 1941-42; asst. exec. officer to Maj. Gen. Fred L. Walker and Maj. Gen. John W. O'Daniel, all at Fort Benning Inf. Sch., Office Strategic Services, 1944; lt. col. Inf., U.S. Army Reserve. Mem. bd. Ga. Citizens Council, 1946-49, Atlanta Housing Authority (vice-chairman), Met. Planning Commission of Atlanta 1946-50, Community Planning Council, 1946-49, Commn. on Crime and Delinquency, Y.M.C.A. Commission on Boys' work. Greater Atlanta Area Greater Atlanta Chamber of Commerce, 1948-49, 52-53, Jr. League Sch. Speech Correction, 1946-52, Nat. Conference of Christians and Jews (Atlanta chpt.), Ga. Cooperative Services for the Blind. Mem. Army Adv. Com. of Greater Atlanta, Travelers' Aid Soc. Mem. Soc. of Planning Officials, Nat. Assn. of Housing ofcls., Pub. Relations Soc. Am. (pres. Atlanta chapt. 1952), Ga. Rose Soc., Am., So. social socs., Ga. Acad. Social Sciences, Ga. Ednl. Assn. Beta Theta Pi, Kappa Phi Kappa, Alpha Phi Omega. Democrat. Episcopalian. Clubs: Capital City, Rotary (award for contbn. to city, 1951). Author articles and papers on ancient Oriental cities; population studies of southeastern cities; delinquency and the family. Specializes in city studies. Author of law, Plan of Improvement, 1952. Elected life mem. for civic leadership, Atlanta Jr. C. of C., 1951. Home: Atlanta GA Deceased.

ALBRIGHT, FRANK HERMAN army officer; b. Putnam County, O., Aug. 2, 1865; s. William L. and Mary (Shierlow) A.; grad. U.S. Mil. Acad., 1887, Army War Coll., 1915; m. Minnie Louise, d. Chaplain Winfield Scott, U.S. Army, Mar. 4, 1891. Commd. 2d lt. 12th Inf., June 12, 1887, and advanced through grades to brig. gen. N.A., Aug. 15, 1917. Service in Cuba and P.R., 1898, in Philippines, 1899-1902, 1907-09; prof. mil. science and tactics, U. of N.D., 1898, Purdue U., 1903-05; comdg. 151st Inf. Brigade, Camp Devens, Ayer, Mass., Aug. 25, 1917, later with A.E.F. in France; hon. disch as brig. gen., Nov. 27, 1918; retired. Republican. Home: San Diego, Calif. Died Apr. 10, 1940.

ALCORN, DOUGLAS EARLE, neuropsychiatrist; b. Victoria, B.C., Can., Nov. 1, 1906; s. Duncan Rudolph and Addie L.B. (Olmstead) A.; student Victoria Coll., 1923-25; M.D., C.M., McGill U., 1931; postgrad. Harvard, U. Ia.; m. Doreen Evelyn Lougheed, Jan. 30, 1942. Intern, Royal Victoria Hosp., Montreal, Que., Can., 1931-32, Lenox Hill Hosp., 1935, Maudesley Hosp., London, 1937-38; practice medicine, specializing in neuropsychiatry, Victoria, 1938-41, 46-68; mem. staff Royal Jubilee, Veterans, Queen Alexandra Solarium hospitals (all Victoria), Hollywood Hosp., New Westminster, B.C. Served to maj., Royal Canadian Army Med. Corps, 1941-46. Fellow Am. Psychiat. Assn. (past pres. N. Pacific br.), A.A.A.S., Am. Geriatrics Soc., Am. Acad. Forensic Scis., N. Pacific Soc. Neurology and Psychiatry (past pres.). Home: Victoria BC Canada. Died Nov. 9, 1968; cremated.

ALCORN, JAMES LUSK senator, gov. Miss.; b. Golconda, Ill., Nov. 4, 1816; s. James and Louisa (Lusk) A.; ed. Cumberland Coll.; m. Mary C. Stewart, 1839; m. 2d, Amelia Walton Glover, 1850. Dep. sheriff, Livingston, Ky., 1839; mem. Ky. Legislature, 1843; admitted to Ky. bar, 1843; mem. Miss. Ho. of Reps., 1846, 56, 65, Miss. Senate, 1848-56; served as brig. gen. Miss. Militia during Civil War; pres. Miss. Levee Bd.; elected to U.S. Senate, 1865, not permitted to take seat; gov. Miss., 1869-71; mem. U.S. Senate from Miss., 1871-77; defeated as Independent candidate for gov. Miss., 1873. Died "Eagle Nest," Coahoma County, Miss., Dec. 20, 1894; buried "Eagle Nest."

ALDEN, BERTRAM F. surgeon; b. Vallejo, Calif., Jan. 5, 1873; s. Eugene Beaubarnois and Lydia (Webster) A.; M.D., Cooper Med. Coll., 1894; m. Leonie E. Gless, May 11, 1903; 1 dau., Victoria. House surgeon Lane Hosp., 1895; surgeon French Hosp., 1903-20; mem. attending staff S.P.R.R. Gen. Hosp. Served as capt. Med. R.C., Fort Riley, Kan., 1917; maj. later lt. col. Med. Corps. U.S. Army, chief of surg. service, Base Hosp., Fort Riley, Ft. McArthur, Tex., and Toul, France, World War. Democrat. Mason (Shriner). Home: San Francisco, Calif. Died May 14, 1939.

ALDEN, CHARLES HENRY architect; b. Hingham, Mass., Sept. 27, 1867; s. Charles Henry and Katherine Russell (Lincoln) A.; student U. Minn., 1884-87; B.S. in Architecture, Mass. Inst. Tech,. 1890 Began practice in Boston, 1897; with Howard and Galloway, supervising architects Alaska Yukon Pacific Expn. and U. Wash., 1906-09; in charge specifications and archtl. dept., div. of works Panama-Pacific Expn., 1913-15; practiced at Seattle, 1909—; lectr. on architecture U. Wash. Mem. Mass. N.G., 1891-1900; commd. capt., O.R.C., U.S. Army, 1917; apptd. supply officer, 311th Sanitary Train, 86th Div., later asst. depot q.m., Boston, 1917; asst. q.m. 6th A.C., 1918; adj. 122d Engrs. supply officer and asst. to engr. officer in charge constrn., Am. Embarkation Center, Le Mans, France, 1918-19; maj. to col. Q.M. Res. Corps, 1919-31. Mem. Seattle Zoning Commn. Building Code Revision Commn., Seattle City Planning Commn. (chmn. zoning commn.), King County Planning Commn., 1939; state chmn. Pub. Works of Art Project, 1933-34; mem. Com. on City & Local Planning of Wash. Planning Council, 1934; chmn. planning com. Assn. of Wash. Cities, 1940; trustee Seattle Traffic & Safety Council, 1937. Engr. Seattle Municipal Def. Commn. Fellow A.I.A. (pres. Wash. Chpt.); mem. Fine Arts Soc. of Seattle (pres.), Pacific N.W. Acad. Arts, Mil. Order Loyal Legion, Municipal League of Seattle (dir.). Chi Psi. Episcopalian. Clubs: University, Cosmos. Home: University Club. 1004 Boren Av. Office: Arcade Bldg., Seattle. Died 1951

ALDEN, CHARLES HENRY brig. gen. U.S. Army; retired; late asst. surgeon gen. U.S. Army; b. Phila., April 28, 1836; grad. Brown, 1856; Pa. Med. Coll., 1858; (hon. M.D., U. of Pa., 1901); m. Katherine Russell, Oct. 25, 1864. Pres. Army Med. School. Deceased.

ALDEN, ICHABOD army officer; b. Duxbury, Mass., Aug. 11, 1739. Commd. lt. col. Continental Army, 1775; in command of 25th Continental Inf., then col. 7th Mass. Regt., 1776. Killed in attack by raiding party of Indians, Tories and British, Cherry Valley, N.Y., Nov. 11, 1778; buried Ft. Schuyler, N.Y.

ALDEN, JAMES naval officer; b. Portland, Me., Mar. 31, 1810; s. James and Elizabeth (Tate) A. Commd. midshipman U.S. Nary, served on ship Concord, 1828; served as lt. in Wilkes' South Sea exploring Expdn., 1838-42; served at battles of Veracruz and Tabasco in Mexican War; commd. comdr., 1855; commanded ship Richmond in battles of New Orleans and Vicksburg; promoted capt., 1863; commanded ship Brooklyn at Battle of Mobile Bay; commd. commodore, 1866; ret. as rear adm. Died San Francisco, Feb. 6, 1877.

ALDIS, GRAHM real estate exec.; b. Chgo., Nov. 12, 1895; s. Arthur Taylor and Mary (Reynolds) A.; A.B., A.M., Harvard, 1917; m. Dorothy Keeley, June 15, 1922; children-Mary Cornelia (Mrs. Roy Porter), Owen, Ruth (Mrs. E. L. Timberman, Jr.), Peggy (Mrs. Allen Westphal). Partner, Aldis & Co., Chgo., since 1922; dir. First Fed. Savs. & Loan Assn. Chgo.; trustee, dir. various real estate enterprises. Pres. Civic Fedn. Chgo., 1939-41; Chgo. Council on Fgn. Relations, 1931-33, Chicago Real Estate Bd., 1949-50; mem. Ill. Housing Bd., 1949-53. Trustee U. Chgo. since 1946. Served as 1st lt., inf. U.S. Army, World War I; Army real estate dir. for Ill., Mich., Wis., 1941-42; later served in Iceland, U.K., OSS, War Dept.; maj., Gen. Staff Corps, U.S. Army, 1945. Received War Dept. citation. Mem. Am. Inst. Real Estate Appraisers, Bldg. Mgrs. Assn. Chgo. (pres. 1934-39). Republican. Episcopalian. Clubs: Tavern (pres. 1947-49), University, Commercial (Chicago); Onwentsia (Lake Forest, Ill.). Contbr. numerous articles to real estate publs. Office: 53 W. Jackson Blvd., Chgo. Died Apr. 21, 1966.

ALDRICH, DONALD BRADSHAW clergyman; b. Fall River, Mass., Aug. 14, 1892; s. Earl Hulbert and Grace (Bradshaw) A.; A.B., Darmouth, 1917, D.D., 1927; B.D., Episcopal Theol. Sch., 1921; L.H.D., Kenyon Coll., 1935; D.D., Rutgers U., 1950; m. Frances Learned, May 18, 1918; children-Suzanne, William. Deacon, 1920, priest, 1921, P.E. Ch.; mem. staff Cathedral Ch. of St. Paul, Boston, 1920-25; also chaplain Mass. Ho. of Rep., 1923-2 Ascension, N.Y.C., 1925-45, ret.; dean Princeton U. Chapel. Trustee Pomfret Sch., Wooster Sch., 1946. Served to ensign USN, 1917-18, champlain, lt. comdr., 1942-45. Dean, Princeton U. chapel, 1947. Elected Bishop-Coadiutor of Mich., 1945. Life trustee Princeton U., 1928; trustee Barnard Coll., 1940; chmn. Ch. Congress. Mem. Psi Upsilon. Club: Century. Died Jan. 19, 1961

ALDRICH, WILLIAM SLEEPER educator; b. Phila., Mar. 3, 1863; s. George Wells and Sallie Edith (Sleeper) A.; grad. U.S. Naval Acad., 1883; M.E., Stevens Inst. Tech., 1884; m. Mary Lavinia Purdy, of Phila., July 1, 1886. Asst. Boys' High Sch., Reading, Pa., 1885-87, Central Manual Training Sch., Phila., 1887-89; instr. drawing, 1889-91, asso. in mech. engring., 1891-92, Johns Hopkins; prof mech. engring, and dir. mechanic arts, W. Va. U., 1893-99; prof. and head dept. elec. engring., U. of Ill., 1899-1901; dir. Thomas S. Clarkson Memorial School of Technology, 1901-11; U.S. Reclamation Service, Shoshone Project, Powell, Wyo., 1911-13; acting prof. elec. and mech. engring., U. of Ariz., 1913-14. Passed asst. engr. (with relative rank of lt. USN), attached to the U.S.S. Vulcan, with Admiral Sampson's fleet in Cuban waters, May 12-Oct. 18, 1898. Fellow A.A.A.S.; mem. Am. Inst. Elec. Engrs., Am. Soc. Mech. Engrs., Soc. Promotion Engring. Edn. Contbr. papers to engring. and scientific societies and tech. press. Author: Notes on Building Construction and Architecture (with William H. Browne, Jr.): Manual for Electrical Engineering Laboratory. Address: Tucson, Arizona.

ALESHIRE, JAMES BUCHANAN army officer; b. at Gallipolis, O., Oct. 31, 1856; s. Reuben and Margaret (Shepard) A.; ed. Galia Acad., Gallipolis, O.; grad. U.S. Mil. Acad., 1880; m. Harriet A. Dana, Nov. 3, 1886. Commd. 2d lt. U.S. Cav., June 12, 1880; advanced through the ranks to q.m. gen., U.S.A., Apr. 27, 1914. Served in operations against hostile Apache Indians, Oct., 1881-Apr., 1882; Sioux campaign, S.D., Nov., 1890-Feb., 1891; in Cuba, Jan.-July, 1899, and Nov., 1899-Aug., 1900; China Relief Expdn., Sept. 1, 1900-Feb., 1901; Philippines, Feb., 1901-Sept. 1, 1903. Retired for disability in line of duty, Sept. 12, 1916. Home: Sheridan, Wyo. Died June 1, 1925.

ALESSANDRONI, WALTER EDWIN state ofcl.; b. Phila., Dec. 27, 1914; s. Joseph and Sally (Asrpino) A.; B.S., Villanova U., 1935, LL.D., 1958; LL.B., U. Pa., 1938 Litt.D. (hon.), Del. Valley Coll., 1964; m. Ethel Decius; children-Eugene Victor II, Eric Gregory. Admitted to Pa. bar, 1938; gen. practice of law, 1938-; faculty Villanova U., 1938-43; exec. sec. to mayor Phila., 1940-47; exec. dir. Phila. Housing Authority, 1947-59; U.S. atty. Eastern Dist. Pa., 1959-61; atty. gen. Pa., 1963-66. Mem. Phila. County Bd. Law Examiners chmn. citizens adv. com. on Traffic Ct.; dir. World Affairs Council, Health and Welfare Council, United fund. Served from 2d lt. to maj. USI)CR, World War II. Mem. Am. (house of dels.), Pa. (Distinguished Service award 1959), Phila. (chmn bd. govs., chancellor) bar assns., Am. Judicature Soc., Medico-Legal Inst., Inst. Jud. Adminstrn; Am. Soc. Pub. Adminstrn., Am. Legion (nat. exec. committeeman, past state comdr., past nat. vice comdr). Clubs: Lawyers, Socialegal (Phila.); Ocean City (N.J.) Yacht. Died May 9, 1966.

ALEXANDER, BARTON STONE army officer; b. Nicholas County, Ky., Sept. 4, 1819; s. John and Margaret (Davidson) A.; grad. U.S. Mil. Acad., 1842. Joined Corps Engrs., U.S. Army, 1842, advanced through grades to lt. col., brevetted brig. gen., 1865; took part in 1st Battle of Bull Run, Peninsular campaign, during Civil War; designed Ft. McPherson. Died San Francisco, Dec. 15, 1878.

ALEXANDER,BEN pres. Masonite Corp.; b. Wausau, Wis., Oct. 6, 1804; s. Walter and Sarah (Strobridge) A.; B. Forestry, Biltmore (N.C.) Forest Sch., 1914; student U. of Wis., 1914-15; B.S., U. of Calif., 1917; m. Josephine Foster, Oct. 9, 1926; children— Foster, Sarah, Thomas, William. With Silver Falls Timber Co., Silverton, Ore., 1919-21; laborer Wausau Paper Mills Co., 1922-24; became woods supt. Walter Alexander Co., Wausau, 1922; with Masonite Corp., Chicago, since 1925, pres. since 1926; pres. Lake Superior Lumber Co., Yawkey-Alexander Lumber Co., Wausau Paper Mills Co., Northern Logging Co.; v.p. and dir. Silver Falls Timber Co., Alexander Yawkey Timber Co., Stewart and Alexander Timber Co.; asst. sec. and treas. Alexander Stewart Lumber Co.; treas. and dir. Yawkey-Bissell Lumber Co. (Wis.); sec. and dir. Walter Alexander Co. (Wis.); dir. Employers Mutual Liability Ins. Co., Marathon Paper Mills, Naval Stores Investment Co., Mont. Dakota Power Co., Mont. Dakota Utilities Co., Ontanagon Fibre Co., Tomahawk Kraft Paper Co., McCloud River Lumber Co. Served as capt. of inf., U.S. Army, during World War. Trustee Lawrence Coll., Appleton, Wis. Mem. Zeta Psi. Republican. Methodist. Mason. Clubs: Chicago, Chicago Athletic, Onwentsia Tavern (Chicago). Home: Lake Forest, Ill. Office: 111 W. Washington St., Chicago, Ill. Died July 6, 1944.

ALEXANDER, CHARLES TRIPLER brig.-gen. U.S.A.; b. Indian Ty., May 3, 1833. Apptd. from Ark., asst. surgeon U.S.A., Oct. 1, 1856; capt. asst. surgeon, Oct. 1, 1861; maj. surgeon, Feb. 9, 1863; lt.-col. surgeon, July 26, 1886; col. chief med. purveyor, Sept. 11, 1891; retired by operation of law, May 3, 1897; advanced to rank of brig. gen. retired, by act of Apr. 23, 1904. Bvtd.: lt. col., Mar. 13, 1865, "for faithful and meritorious services during the war"; col. Feb. 27, 1890, "for gallant services in action at Clearwater, Ida., July 11 and 12, 1877." Died Feb. 28, 1918.

ALEXANDER, CLYDE C. army officer; b. Cal., July 1, 1892; grad. F.A. Sch., 1926, Command and Gen. Staff Sch., 1934, Army Indsl. Coll., 1936. Served as 2d lt. later 1st lt. F.A., Cal. N.G., 1916-17; comd. 2d it. F.A., U. Army, Aug. 1917, and advanced through the grades to brig. Gen., 1943. Address: A.P.O. 501, care Postmaster, San Francisco. Died Jan. 4 1965.

ALEXANDER, EDWARD PORTER engr.; b. Washington, Ga., May 26, 1835; s. Adam Leopold and Sarah Gilbert A.; grad. U.S. Mil. Acad., 1857; m. Bettie Mason, 1860; 2d, Mary L., d. Augustine S. Mason, of Hagerstown, Md., Oct. 1, 1901. Apptd. 2d lt. U.S. engr.

corps.; resigned, 1861; entered C.S.A. and served through war; was brig.-gen. and chief of arty., Longstreet's Corps, at Appomattox, 1865; prof. of mathematics and engring., U. of S.C., 1866-70; gen. mgr. and pres. of various railroads (including L. N., Central of Ga., Ga. R.R. Bank Co.), 1871-92; capitol commr., State of Ga., 1883-88; mem. bds. on navigation of Columbia River, Ore., and on ship canal between Chesapeake and Delaware bays, 1892-94; govt. dir. U. R. R.R. Co., 1895-97; arbitrator boundary survey between Costa Rica and Nicaragua. Rice planter on South Island, Georgetown, S.C. Author: Railway Practice; Military Memoirs of a Confederate. Home: Savannah, Ga. Died 1910.

ALEXANDER, HOOPER lawyer; b. Rome, Ga., Oct. 6, 1858; s. Thomas Williamson and Sarah Joyce (Hooper) A.; A.B., U. of Ga., 1879; m. May H. Field, Jan. 28, 1889 (died 1890); m. 2d, Amelia Hutchins, Oct. 17, 1894; children—Mrs. Amelia Greenawalt, Hooper, Mrs. Hallie Turner, Miller. Thomas W., Mrs. Joyce Rhine. President S. Georgia Agr. and Mech. Coll., Thomasville, 1880-84; admitted to Georgia bar, 1884, and since practiced in Atlanta; mem. Ga. Ho. of reps., 1904-12, and 1928-30; U.S. atty. Northern Dist. of Ga., 1913-21; resumed pvt. practice. 1st lt. Gate City Guards, Atlanta, 1888; trustee Decatur Pub. Schs., 1908-17. Democrat. Presbyn. Home: Decatur, Ga. Deceased.

ALEXANDER, JAMES F. M.D.; b. Greenville Dist., S.C., May 28, 1824; ed. Oglethorpe Univ. and at Lawrenceville, Ga.; grad. Med. Coll. of Ga., Augusta, 1849; located at Atlanta; delegate to secession conv., 1861; surgeon 7th Ga. regt., C. S. A.; m. Georgia Orme, 1855 (died 1876); m. 2d, Ada Reynolds; chmn. Fulton County Dem. Com. during reconstruction times; several yrs. pres. Atlanta Bd. of Health; has been pres. Ga. State Med. Assn. Home: Atlanta, Ga. Died 1901.

ALEXANDER, JAMES WADDELL, II, mathematician; b. Sea Bright, N.J., Sept. 19, 1888; s. John White and Elizabeth A. Alexander; B.S., Princeton, 1910, M.A. (Gordon Macdonald fellow), 1911, Ph.D., 1915, D.Sc., 1947; student U. Faris, U. Bologna; m. Natalie Levitzkaja, Jan. 11, 1918; children—Irina, John. Instr., Princeton U., 1911-12, 15-16, asst. prof., 1920-26, asso. prof., 1926-28, prof., 1928-33, prof. Inst. for Advanced Study, 1933-51; Rouse Ball lectr. Cambridge (Eng.) U., 1936; a founder of modern topology. Served with tech. staff, ordnance dept. U.S. Army, overseas, 1917-18; ret. as capt.; mem. N.J. Nat. Guard. Recipient Bocher prize Am. Math Soc., 1928. Mem. Nat. Acad. Sciences, Am. Philos. Soc., Am. Math. Soc., Math. Assn. Am., A.A.A.S., Phi Beta Kappa. Clubs: American Alpine; Quadrangle; Nassau. Contbr. articles math. publs. Home: Princeton NJ Died Sept. 23, 1971.

ALEXANDER, JOHN surgeon; b. Phila., Pa., Feb. 24, 1891; s. Lucien Hugh and Mazie (Just) A.; student Episcopal Acad., Phila., 1903-04, Chestnut Hill Acad., 1904-08; B.S., U. of Pa., 1912, M.A., 1913, M.D., 1916 (hon. Sc.D., 1940); m. Emma Ward Woolfolk, July 11, 1936. Formerly mem. surg. & teaching staff U. of Pa.; now prof. surgery, U. of Mich.; surg. in charge sect. thoracic surg., U. of Mich. Hosp.; chief surg., Mich. State Sanatorium; cons. thoracic surg. various sanatoria and hops. Surg. with French Army; lt. U.S.M.C., World War I. Awarded Samuel D. Gross prize of Phila. Acad. Surgery 1925; Henry Russel award, U. of Mich., 1930; Trudeau medal, Nat. Tuberculosis Assn., 1941. Henry Russel lectureship, U. of Mich., 1944. Fellow Am. Coll. Surgeons; mem. Am. Surg. Assn., Soc. of Thoracic Surgery of Great Britain and Ire. Sociedad de Argentina de Cirujanos (hon.); Societe' Belge de Chirurgie (hon.); Sociedad Parguaya de Tisiologia (hon.); Sociedad de Tisiologia de Cordoba, Argentina (corr.); Tuberculosis Assn. of India (corr.); Detroit Heart Club; Am. Trudeau Soc. (pres. elect 1946), Am. Bd. Surg. (founders' group), Soc. of Clin. Surg., Internat. Soc. of Surgery, Am. Assn. for Thoracic Surg. (p. 1935), Detroit Acad. of Surgery (hon.), Central Surg. Assn. (founders' group), A.M.A., Mich. State Med. Soc. (chmn. sect. on surgery, 1932). Mich. Tuberculosis Assn. (trustee 1936-42, pres. 1938-39), Nat. Tuberculosis Assn. (dir. 1941-44, v.p. 1945), Mich. Trudeau Soc., Alpha Omega Alpha, Alpha Mu Pi Omega, Nu Sigma Nu (hon.), Sigma Xi, Phi Kappa Phi, Delta Tau Delta. Republican. Presbyterian. Author: The Surgery of Pulmonary Tuberculosis, 1925; The Collapse Therapy of Pulmonary Tuberculosis, 1937; also articles on thoracic surgery. Mem. adv. editorial bd. Journal of Thoracic Surgery. Home: 788 Arlington Blvd. Office: U. of Mich. Hospital, Ann Arbor. Died July 16, 1954; buried Forest Hills Cemetery

ALEXANDER, JOHN MACMILLAN clergyman; b. Jackson, Miss., Oct. 31, 1891; s. Charlton Henry and Matilda (Macmillian) A.; student Southwestern Coll. (now in Memphis, Tenn.), 1906-09; A.B., Princeton, 1914; B.D., Union Theol. Seminary of Va., 1921, D.D., 1926; m. Victoria M. Holladay, June 19, 1923; children-Victoria Holladay (Mrs. Henry Sharp), Matilda Caroline (lMrs. George W. Bryan) John Macmillan. With A.E.F., France, World War, 1917-19; 1st lt. Med. Dept. Sanitary Corps, 1918-19; ordained ministry Presbyn. Ch. in U.S., 1921; pastor First Ch., Columbia, Mo., 1924-32, First Church, Birmingham, Ala., 1932-39, First Church, Fayetteville, N.C., 1939-46; dir. radio com., Presbyn. Church U.S. 1946—. Moderator of Synod of Mo., 1930; Synod of Ala., 1936; commr. Gen. Assembly Presbyn. Ch. in U.S., 1927, 30, 32, 34, 43, 46; mem. Assembly's Com. on Union of Presbyn. and Reformed Chs., 1930-33, and mem. Assembly's Ad-Interim Com. on Salaries and Retirement Allowances, 1933-34; chmn. Assembly's Ad-Interim Com. on Minimum Income for Ministers, 1934-35; chmn. Assembly's Ad-Interim Com. on Pastoral Changes, 1935-36; mem. Assembly's Com. on Stewardship and Finance, 1935-39; chmn. Assembly's special com. on radio, 1943—; pres. Birmingham Protestant Pastors' Union, 1934-35; del. from Presbyn. Ch. of U.S. to World's Conf. on Life & Work, Oxford, 1937, and World's Conf. on Faith & Order, Edinburgh, 1937; interchange preacher representing American Committee in France and Great Britian, 1937; chairman Defense Service Council, Synod of N.C., 1941-46; member Assembly's Defense Service Council, 1944-46; mem. executive com. Federal Council of Chs. of America, 1941-51, N.C. Council of Chs. 1941-46; fraternal del. Assembly of Presbyn. Ch. U.S.A., 1943; sec. div. Radio and TV, Presbyn. Ch., U.S.A.; mem. exec. com. broadcasting & film commn. Nat. Council Chs.; pres. Protestant Radio & TV Center, Incorporated; Rep. Presbyn. Bd. World Missions in Radio Survey Brazil, 1952. Recieved citation Nat. Council Chs. for work in religious radio. Mem. Kappa Sigma. Democrat. Clubs: Kiwanis, Athletic (Atlanta). Asso. editor Presbyterian Outlook. Home: 16691 Dyson Dr., N.E., Atlanta 7. Office: 1717 Clifton Rd. N.E., Atlanta. Died Aug. 7, 1957; buried Jackson, Miss.

ALEXANDER, ROBERT army officer; b. Md., Oct. 17, 1863; s. Judge William Alexander, of Baltimore; distinguished grad. Army Sch. of the Line, 1909; grad. Army Staff Coll., 1910; LL.D., St. John's Coll., Annapolis, Md., 1920; LL.D., Coll. of Puget Sound, Tacoma, Wash., 1931; m. Mollie Augur, d. Brig. Gen. Earl D. Thomas, 1892; children—William Denison, Robert. Pvt., sergt. and 1st sergt. Co. G, 4th U.S. Inf., 1886-90; 2d lt. 7th Inf., Dec. 17, 1889; promoted through grades to brig. gen. N.A., Feb. 9, 1918; maj. gen. (temp.), Aug. 26, 1918-Aug. 1, 1919; brig. gen., N.A., Apr. 30, 1921, maj. gen., Aug. 26, 1927; retired Oct. 17, 1927. In Indian campaign 1890-91, Spanish-Am. War, 1898, also in Philippines, Cuba, and Mexico; insp. gen. Line of Communications, A.E.F., in France, Nov. 1917-Feb. 1918. Decorated D.S.C. (U.S.); Croix de Guerre (2 citations), and Comdr. Legion of Honor (France). Apptd. comdr. 3d F.A. Brigade, Aug. 4, 1921. Elected to Wash. State Conv., 1933. Mason (33 degree). Home: La Jolla, Calif. Died Aug. 26, 1941.

ALEXANDER, SUYDENHAM B. congressman; b. Mecklenburg Co., N.C., Dec. 2, 1840; A.B., Univ. of N.C., 1860; enlisted pvt. 1st N.C. Vol. Inf., C.S.A., 1861; capt. Co. K, 42d N.C. Inf., June, 1862; insp.-gen. on staff Maj. Gen. R.F. Hoke, 1864; engaged in farming after war. Master State Grange and ex-officio mem. State Bd. Agr., N.C., 1877; mem. N.C. State senate, 1878-90; mem. Congress, 8th N.C. dist., 1891-95; Democrat. Trustee N.C. Agrl. and Mech. Coll. Address: Charlotte, N.C.

ALEXANDER, WILFORD S. ex-govt. ofcl.; b. Eastport, Me., Sept. 25, 1878; s. Wilford F. and Nellie M. (Swett) A.; grad. Boynton high sch., Eastport, m. Mary P. White, July 19, 1905 (died Apr. 1, 1948); children-Katherine Marcia (Mrs. Cyril Coleman), Sheila (Mrs. Richard Joyce Smith), Agnes, Alison (Mrs. Edward C. Tredennick), Wilford S., Jr. (1st lt. USMC, killed in action, Okinawa, May 5 1945). Clerk Eastport Savings Bank, 1896; was asst. cashier Frontier Nat. Bank, Eastport; then cashier Oxford Paper Co., Rumford, Me.; securities salesman Paine, Webber & Co., Boston until 1920; treas. Puritan Bank & Trust Co., Meriden, Conn., 1920-27, pres., 1927-36; adminstr. Fed. Alcohol Adminstrn. 1936-40 (dept. merged with alcohol tax unit under President's reorgn. plan); dist. supr. and dist. co-ordinator Dist. No. 1 Alcohol Tax Unit, Bur. of Internal Revenue, Me., Vt., N.H., Mass., R.I. and Conn., 1940-49; city mgr. City of Eastport, Mem. 1950-53. Served as capt. inf., U.S. Army, 5 mos. on Mexican Border and 20 mos. in France, World War. Express. Meriden Pub. Health & Visiting Nurse Assn. Meriden C. of C.; past dept. comdr. Conn. Am. Legion. Home: 139 Main St., Southport, Conn. Died Apr. 24, 1959.

ALEXANDER, WILL WINTON ret. authority on race relations; b. Marrisville, Mo., 1884; s. William Baxter and Arabella A. (Winton) A.; A.B. Scarritt-Morrisville (Mo.) Coll., 1908; B.D., Vanderbilt U., 1912; hon. degs. Berea Coll., So. Coll., Boston U., La State U.; m. Mabelle A. Kinkead, Oct. 1914; children-Edgar Kinkead, John Winton, William McLees. Ordained to ministry Meth. Ch. South, 1901; pastorates at Nashville and Murfresboro, Tenn., 1911-17; withdrew from ministry, 1917; exec. dir. Commn. on Interracial Coop. 1919-30; acting pres. Dillard U., New Orleans, 1931-35; asst. adminstr. U.S. Resettlement Adminstrn., 1935-36; adminstr. Farm Security Adminstrn., U.S. Dept. Agr., 1937. V.p. Julius Rosenwald Fund. Served as exec. sec. Army Y.M.C.A. Southeastern Mil. Dept., 1917-19. Chmn. adv. com. on race studies of problems & policies com. Social Sci. Research Council, 1927-28; Am. del. to Internat. Conf., Jerusalem, 1928; Weil lectr. U. N.C., 1929; mem. Com. on Minority Groups in Econ. Recovery, 1934-35; mem. on care and edn. of Am. youth, Am. Council Edn. Vice Pres., treas. Am. Council Race Relations and Staff War Manpower Commn., World War II. Recipient Harmon Nat. Award for service in Am. peace relations, 1928. Trustee Antioch Coll., Cookman Coll., Atlanta U., Morehouse Coll., Spelman Coll. Mem. Alpha Tau Omega. Democrat. Club: Cosmos (Washington). Co-author: Collapse of Cotton Tenancy, 1935. Home: R.R. 3, Chapel Hill, N.C. Deceased

ALEXANDER, WILLIAM (known as Lord Stirling), army officer; b. N.Y.C., 1726; s. James Alexander; m. sister of Gov. Livingston of N.J. Surveyor Gen. Stirling, 1756, claim rejected by English Ho. of Lords, 1762; mem. N.J. Common Council, asst. to gov. N.J.; fought in French and Indian War; commd. col. 1st N.J. Regt., 1775, brig. gen. Continental Army, 1776; comdr.-in-chief N.Y.C., 1776, built fts. Lee and Washington for defense of city, also Ft. Sterling (named for him), Brooklyn Heights, N.Y., 1777; head right wing Continental Army at Battle of L.I., 1776; fought at Battle of Trenton, promoted maj. gen., 1777; led div. Battle of Brandywine, commanded reserves Battle of Germantown, left wing Battle of Monmouth; served on ct. inquiry at trial of Benedict Arnold, 1780; an early gov. King's coll. (now Columbia). Died Albany, N.Y., Jan 15, 1783.

ALEXANDER, WILLIAM LEIDY brig. gen.; b. in Iowa, Sept. 9, 1842. Apptd. 1st lt. 30th Ia. Vol. Inf., Sept. 23, 1862; capt., Oct. 1, 1863; hon. mustered out, July 27, 1865; apptd. capt. commissary of subsistence U.S.A., Oct. 4, 1889; advanced through grades to col. asst. commissary-gen., July 27, 1903; brig. gen. and retired at own request, Jan. 19, 1905. Died Dec. 1, 1915.

ALGER, FREDERICK M(OULTON) JR. ex-ambassador; b. Detroit, Aug. 3, 1907; s. Frederick M. and Mary (Swift) A.; student Milton Acad., Philips Acad.; Harvard, 1926; m. Suzette de Marigny Dewey, 1929; children-Suzette (Mrs. Reese E. Howard), Frederick Moulton, David Dewey. Asst. to Am. financial adv. to Polish Govt., Warsaw, 1928-29; successively sec.-treas., v.p., pres. Allen Corp., 1930-46; dir. First of Mich. Corp., 1936-46; sec. state State of Mich., 1946-52; U.S. ambassador to Belgium, 1953-56. Republican nominee for rep. U.S. Congress 14th Mich. Congl. Dist., 1936; 1st pres. Wayne Co. Rep. Precinct Orgn., 1935; Rep. nominee for gov. of Mich., 1952. Asst. treas., trustee Jennings Meml. Hosp., Detroit, 1934, trustee Alma (Mich.) Coll. from 1951. Commd. lt. U.S.N.R., 1939; active duty advancing to comdr., 1941-45, in Honolulu, 1942 with 11th Naval Dist., 1943-45. Mem. S.A.R., Mil. Order World Wars, Am. Legion, Vets. Fgn. Wars, Det. Bd. Commerce. Elk, Mason. Clubs: Country, Yondotega, Detroit Racquet, Scarab. Metamora (Det.); Grosse Pointe, Hunt (Grosse Pointe, Mich.); Bloomfield Open Hunt; St. Clair Flats Shooting; Country, Press, City (Lansing, Mich.); United Hunts Racing Assn., Racquet and Tennis, Turf and Field (N.Y.C.); Chevy Chase (Md.); Everglades, Seminole Golf (Fla). Home: 294 Lincoln Rd., Grosse Pointe, Mich. Office: Free Press Bldg., Detroit. Died Jan. 5, 1967.

ALGER, RUSSELL ALEXANDER senator; b. Lafayette Township, Medina County, O., Feb. 27, 1836; orphaned at 12 yrs. of age and for 7 yrs. worked on farm, earning money to defray expenses at Richfield (O.) Acad. during winters. Taught school 2 winters; admitted to bar, 1859; began practice in Cleveland; removed to Mich., Jan. 1, 1860; began lumbering in a small way; enlisted, Sept. 2, 1861, and served as capt. and maj. 2d Mich., lt. col. 6th Mich., col. 5th Mich. cav.; bvtd. brig. gen. and maj. gen. vols. In lumber business after war; head of Alger, Smith & Co., and Manistique Lumbering Co. Was gov. Mich., 1885 and 1886; a leading candidate for pres. in Rep. Nat. Conv., 1888; 1 term comdr.-in-chief G.A.R.; Sec. of War of U.S., 1897-99, resigned; apptd. U.S. senator Sept. 27, 1902, to succeed James McMillan deceased, and elected Feb. 1903, for term expiring 1907. Author: The Spanish-American War, 1901. Home: Detroit, Mich. Died 1907.

ALKIN, WILFORD MERTON personnel cons.; b. New Concord, O., Sept. 22, 1882; s. James Henderson and Mary Jane (Dew) A.; B.S., Muskingum Coll.; 1907, LL.D., 1933; M.A., U. Mich., 1913; student Columbia U., 1917-18; m. Lena Graham, Feb. 21, 1907 (div. 1940); 1 son, Norman Edward; m. 2d Marjorie Jackson, 1940; children-Marjorie Lois, Jane. Teacher, 1907; teacher Bowling Green (O.) High Sch., 1907-08, Jackson (Mich.) High Sch., 1908-10, Ann Arbor (Mich.) High Sch., 1910-13, prin., latter, 1913-16 dir. Scarborough Sch., Scarborough-on-Hudson, N.Y., 1918-22, John Burroughs Sch., St. Louis, 1922-35; asst. prof. edn., Ohio State U., 1916-18, became prof. of edn. 1935; cons. on personnel management and tng. Standard Oil Co. of Cal. Expert cons. civilian tng. Office Q.M. Gen. U.S. Army, Dec. 1, 1942; chief civilian tng., office Sec. of War, 1942-46. Chmn. commn. on Relation of Schs. and Colleges since 1930; field rep. U.S. Office Edn. Mem. Am. Ednl. Research Assn., Nat. Assn. Secondary Schs., Prins. Assn. Presbyn. Author: English Literature, 1914; (with Thomas E. Rankin) American Literature, 1916; The Story of the Eight-Year Study; also author articles. Editor: Report of Commission on the Relation of School and College. Address: 1350 Chaning Av., Palo Alto, Cal. 84301. Died Feb. 16, 1965; buried Skylawn Meml. Gardens, San Mateo, Cal.

ALLAIRE, WILLIAM HERBERT army officer; b. Pocahontas, Ark., Jan. 1, 1858; s. William Herbert and Nancy Green (James) A.; grad. U.S. Mil. Acad., 1882; m. Florence Benton Whitehead, May 14, 1902. Served as 2d lt., 1st lt., then capt., 23rd Inf., 1898; advanced through grades (in various inf. cos.) to brig. gen., Aug. 15, 1917. Served in the Southwest until 1893; instr. U.S. Mil. Acad., 1893-97; in Philippines during insurrection, 1899-1901; under Gen. Wood in P.I., expdns. against Moros, 1903-05; mil. attache at Vienna, 1907-11; served under Gen. Pershing in Mexico, 1916-17; with first expdn. to France, June, 1917; apptd. provost marshal gen. A.E.F. in France, Aug. 30, 1917. Died May 1, 1933.

ALLAN, JOHN J. Salvation Army exec.; b. Hazelton, Pa., March 24, 1887; s. James and Phoebe (Strong) A.; ed. Salvation Army Training Coll., 1906; m. Maud Eva Parsons, Nov. 25, 1909; children-Maud (Mrs. George McChain), Jean (Mrs. Bert Willenbrock), John, Vera (Mrs. Harry Sheffer), Elizabeth. Professional musician, 1901; served in various positions with Salvation Army, 1906-18, officer Young Peoples Soc. N.Y., N.J., 1923-42, dir. pub. relations, comdr, Central Territory (11 north central states), 1942, chief of staff Internat. Salvation Army, 1946-53, special international delegate for the General camp, since 1953. Organized pioneer youth summer music camp, 1920, helped organize U.S.O. trustee Salvation Army, Senior chaplain 77th Division in World War I; staff Gen. Hdqrs., chaplain, 1940-42, staff chief of chaplains, U.S. Army; grade of lt. col. Decorated Croix de Guerre: Officer Order of Orange-Nassau. Mem. Nat. Assn. Social Workers, Mil. Order Fgn. Wars, Am. Legion (life). Rotarian. Died Nov. 1, 1960.

ALLEN, ALFRED REGINALD neurologist; b. East Greenwich, R.I., May 26, 1876; s. Rev. George Pomeroy (D.D.) and Elizabeth Marshall (Howe) A.; ed. Lehigh U., 1893-94; M.D., U. of Pa., 1898; m. Helen, d. E. Burgess and Emma (Bolton) Warren, Jan. 21, 1904. Practiced in Phila., 1898—; lecturer in neurol. electrotherapeutics, U. of Pa., 1908-11; pathologist, Eastern Pa. State Instn. for Feeble Minded and Epileptic, 1909; asso. in neurology, and in neuropathology, U. of Pa., 1912—. Grad. Inf. Sch. of Arms, Ft. Sill; commd. maj., 314th U.S. Inf.; dir. Sch. of Automatic Arms, in Inf. Sch. of Arms, of 79th Div. and was some time actg. comdt. same. Mem. Am. Psychopathol. Assn. (pres. 1914, 15), Am. Neurol. Assn. (sec. and treas. 1909-17),Phila. Neurol. Soc. (pres. 1910); sec. of U.S. delegation to 16th Internat. Med. Congress, Budapest, 1909; U.S. Govt. del., also sec. of delegation to 17th Internat. Med. Congress, London, 1913. Republican. Author of various clin. and exptl. works in neurology. Home: Philadelphia, Pa. Died 1918.

ALLEN, CHARLES JULIUS brig. gen. U.S.A.; b. Buffalo, N.Y., Jan. 31, 1840; s. Charles H. and Melissa M. (Kissam) A.; grad. U.S. Mil. Acad., 1864; m. Elizabeth Wallbridge, Jan. 20, 1869. Commd. 1st lt. engrs., June 13, 1864, and advanced through grades to lt. col., Feb. 5, 1897; brig.-gen., Jan. 22, 1904; retired at own request after 40 years service, Jan. 23, 1904. Served in Div. of West Miss. and Dept. of La. during Civil War; in charge of defenses of Natchez; acting chief engr. 16th Army Corps at siege of Spanish Ft., Ala., etc.; chief engr. Army of Observation on Rio Grande, Tex., June-Aug., 1865; in charge defenses of Washington during Spanish-Am. War, 1898. Died June 15, 1915.

ALLEN, CLINTON L. insurance exec.; born Brooklyn, October 3, 1893; s. Frank J. and Nellie Lorraine (Fowler) A.; ed. pub. schs., Hartford, Conn.; m. Anna Mizelle Perkins, Oct. 5, 1917 (died 1944); 1 son, Clinton L.; m. 2d, Beatrice M. Goodrich, Apr. 27, 1945; 1 daughter, Gail Goodrich. Special agent Aetna Ins. Co., Mich., 1922, asst. sec. home office, Hartford, Conn., 1939, sec. 1943, vice pres. and mgr. Western dept., 1945; exec. vice pres. Aetna Ins. Co., 1949-50, pres., 1950-59, chmn. bd., 1959-; dir. Reinsurance Corp. of N.Y. Served Conn. Cavalry, Troop B, Mexican Border, 1916; 2dlt., 26th Div., 101st Machine Gun Bn., U.S. Army, 1917-19; overseas. Director Chamber of Commerce of United States. Republican. Clubs: Dauntless (Essex, Conn.); Hartford, Hartford Golf; Off Soundings (Springfield, Mass.). Home: 49 Fernwood Rd., West Hartford. Conn. Office: 55 Elm St., Hartford 15, Conn. Died Sept. 29, 1960; buried Riverside Cemetery, Farmington, Conn.

ALLEN, EDGAR VAN NUYS physician; b. Cozad, Neb., June 22, 1900; s. Charles Edgar and Sue (Morrow) A.; B.Sc., U. of Neb., 1923, M.A., 1923, M.D., 1925, Doctor of Science (honorary), 1952; M.Sc., Univ. of Minnesota, 1933; student of medicine, Germany and England, 1929-30; m. Margaret Wise, Nov. 23, 1929; children-Katherine Lee, Charles van Nuys, David Wise. Fellow and first asst. in medicine, Mayo Foundation, U. of Minn., Rochester, Minn., 1925-29; fellow Nat. Research Council, studying in Germany and Eng., 1929-30; consultant in medicine, Mayo Clinic since 1930, also chief of sect. div. medicine, 1935-47 (on mil. leave of absence from both positions, 1942-46); sr. cons. med. since 1948; instr., U. of Minn., Rochester, Minn., 1931-34, asst. prof. 1934-37, asso prof., 1937, prof. med. since 1947. Served in S.A.T.C., 1918; commissioned lieut. col. Med. Corps, Army of U.S., Aug. 1942, promoted col., Feb. 1944; med. consultant 7th Service Command, 1942-46. Awarded Legion of Merit, 1946; Gold Heart award, Am. Heart Assn., 1959, Albert Lasker award, 1960, Distinguished Service medal, 1957. Diplomate of the American Board of Internal Medicine; Am. Bd. Cardiovascular Diseases. Member American College of Physicians, A.M.A. (member Ho. Dels. 1942-60); member American Soc. Clin. Investigation, Central Soc. Clin. Research, (pres. 1948). Am. Heart Assn. (dir., pres. 1956-57), Med., Minn. Med. Assn., Soc. Med. Cons. for World War II, Alpha Omega Alpha, Sigma Xi, Phi Chi. Republican. Presbyterian. Author: Thromboangitis Obliterans (with George E. Brown), 1928; Peripheral Vascular Diseases (with N.W. Barker and E.A. Hines, Jr.), 1946; also numerous sci. articles. Home: 1121 Plummer Circle. Office: Mayo Clinic, Rochester, Minn. Died June 14, 1961; buried Mankato, Minn.

ALLEN, ETHAN army born in Litchfield, Conn., Jan. 21, . 1738; s. Joseph and Mary (Baker) A.; m. Mary Bronson, 1762; m. 2d, Mrs. Frances (Montresor) Buchanan, 1784; 8 children including Fanny, Hannibal, Ethan. Served in French and Indian War, 1757; lived in N.H. Grants (area over which control was disputed by N.Y. and N.H.), 1769; became col. comdt. Green Mountain Boys (group formed for purpose of making N.H. Grants into the separate province of Vt.), 1770; his activities caused gov. of N.Y. to offer reward of 20 pounds for his capture, 1771 (increased to 100 pounds, 1774); apptd. (with others) at Westminster meeting to prepare petition to King, 1775; his efforts to make Vt. a separate state were interupted by Battle of Lexington; captured Ft. Ticonderoga (on instructions from Conn.), 1775; captured while serving in expdn. against Canada, 1775, exchanged for Col. Archibald Campbell, 1778; brevetted col. Continental Army by Gen. George Washington; presented Vt. claims to Continental Congress (with no success), 1778; promoted maj. gen. Vt. Militia; corresponded with comdr. of Brit. forces in Canada (not known whether Allen actually wanted Vt. to become Brit. province, or used correspondence to pressure Congress into making Vt. a separate state) 1780; moved to Burlington Vt., 1787. Author: An Animadversory Address to the Inhabitants of the State of Vermont, 1778; A Narrative of Col. Ethan Allen's Captivity (does not mention Benedict Arnold's aid in capturing Ft. Ticonderoga), 1779; Reason the Only Oracle of Man; or, A Compendious System of Natural Religion, Bennington, 1784. Died Burlington, Feb. 2, 1789; buried with mil. honors in a valley nr. Winooski, Vt.

ALLEN, EZRA GRIFFEN naval officer; b. Scranton, Pa., Mar. 11, 1885; s. Thomas H. and Maria (Smith) A.; B.S., U.S. Naval Acad., 1907; m. Elizabeth F. Travers, June 11, 1931. Commd. ensign U.S. Navy, 1907, and advanced through the grades to rear adm. Decorated Navy Cross (U.S.); Chevalier Legion of Honor (France). Mason. Clubs: Army and Navy, Army and Navy Country, Chevy Chase (Washington); New York Yacht (N.Y.C.). Home: 2419 California St., Washington. Died Jan. 4, 1952

ALLEN, FREDERICK HENRY housing planning cons.; b. N.Y.C., Dec. 2, 1909; s. William Harvey and Isabel (Dangaix) A.; student Ecole des Roches, France, 1921-24; B.Arch., U. Va., 1929; postgrad. Columbia, 1920-31; m. Helen Minnigerode, Oct. 9, 1936 (div. 1949); children-Dangaix, Anthonie Galt; m. 2d, Katherine Price, Dec. 26, 1951; step-sons, Hugh E. Price, Thomas A. Price. With Starrett Bros. & Eken, 1929-30, R.H. Macy, 1931, Liberty Mut. Ins. Co., 1932; with Bowery Savs. Bank, 1932-46, dep. mortgage officer, 1941-46; partner Harrison, Ballard & Allen, from 1946, serving as pres., dir.; v.p. Albert B. Ashforth, Inc., N.Y.C. ; housing planning cons., N.Y.C., Norfolk, Va., other, 1946-; pres. Urban Motor Hotels, Inc. Co-author N.Y. Urban Redevel. Law, 1939; head mortgage portfolio survey N.Y.C. and suburbs, 1939-42; chmn. com. on redevel. Manhattan, 1942. Pres., trustee Five Points House. Served as capt. USMCR, 1942-46. Mem. Nat. Assn. Housing Ofcls., Citizens Union, N.Y.C. Welfare and Health Council, Am. Inst. Planners (affiliate), Lambda Alpha, Sigma Chi, Arista, Scarab. Club: University. Author: Your Mortgage, 1950 N.Y. City in Relation to Real Estate Investment, 1951. Contbr. articles profl., popular publs. Home: 49 E. 86 St., N.Y.C. 28. Died Dec. 1965.

ALLEN, FREDERICK HOBBES lawyer, economist; b. Honolulu, T.H.; s. Elisha H. (mem. Congress, later chief justice of Hawaiian Kingdom, E.E. and M.P. to U.S.) and Mary Harrod (Hobbes) A.; studied in . Switzerland and under tutors; A.M., LL.B., Harvard, 1883; m. Adele Livingston Stevens, 1892, children—Frederic Stevens, Mary Dorothy Adele (dec.), Barbara Frances (Madame Andre Vagliano), Joan Livingston (Mrs. Goodhue Livingston, Jr.), Julian Broome Livingston, Priscilla Alden Sampson. Became sec. of Hawaiian Legation, Washington, D.C., 1882; charge d'affaires same, 1883; mem. Adams & Allen, New York, 1894-1900, then Allen & Cammann; served as corp. counsel and pres. Pelham Manor, and chmn. Dem. County Com., Westchester Co.; mem. Dem. Nat. Finance Com., 1912, 20, 24, 28, 32; mem. com. sent to Europe to study agrl. production, distribution and rural credits (report of com. was basis for Fed. Farm Loan Act). Rep. of Pan-European Am. Coop. Com. at Pan-European Congress, Vienna, 1926; observer for Pan-European Council of Economic Conf., Geneva, 1927. Mem. com. of 4 which secured formation of Lafayette Escadrille, 1916; commd. lt. comdr. U.S.N.R. Flying Corps, Aug. 20, 1917, and served as aide to comdr. of U.S. aviation forces in Europe, hdqrs. in Paris. Lt. comdr. U.S.N.R.F. Res. Decorated Officer Legion of Honor (French); Officer Order of Leopold II (Belgian); Star of Order of Polonia Restituta (Polish); Comdr. Order of the White Lion (Czechoslovakia). Home: Newport, R.I. Died Dec. 12, 1937.

ALLEN, HARRIS CAMPBELL, architect; b. Rutland, Vt., Nov. 22, 1876; s. Charles Linnacus and Gertrude Margaret (Lyon) A.; B.A., Stanford U., 1897; student U. of Calif., 1897-98. Draftsman, 1898-1908; architect, 1908-17 and since 1919; editor Pacific Coast Architect, 1919-29, Calif. Arts and Architecture, 1929-34, Bulletin of State Assn. of Calif. Architects, 1934-42; zone architect Zone 5, Federal Housing Adminstrn., 1938-41; architectural examiner Federal Housing Adminstrn., War and Veterans Housing, 1941-45. Served as capt. U.S. Air Service, 1917-19. Fellow Am. Inst. Architects (v.p. No. Calif. Chapter 1925-27, pres. 1927-29, dir. 1922-25 and 1929-32); mem. State Assn. of Calif. Architects (pres. 1933, dir. 1930-32 and 1934-36), San Francisco Soc. Architects (pres. 1933-38), Am. Legion of Calif. (chmn. aviation com. 1921-25), Sons of the American Revolution, Nat. Aeronautic Assn., Phi Kappa Psi. Republican. Episcopalian. Mason (Shriner). Club: Bohemian (San Francisco). Contbr. to professional jours. Address: Bohemian Club San Francisco

ALLEN, HENRY BUTLER inst. exec.; b. Greenfield, Mass. July 20, 1887; s. Franklin and Nettie (Butler) A.; student Amherst Coll., 1905-09, D.Sc., 1949; Metall. Engr., Sch. of Mines, Columbia, 1911; D.Sc., Temple U., 1937; D.Eng., Drexel Inst., 1949; m. Ione A. Ralli, May 29, 1915; children-Ione (Mrs. Frank Itgen), Julia (Mrs. M. L. L. Short), Margaret (Mrs. H. Spencer Potter), Lois Elizabeth (Mrs. Runyon Colie). U.S. examiner iron and steel Port of N.Y., 1912-13; metall. engr. Henry Disston & Sons, Inc., 1913-17, 22-26, chief metallurgist, 1926-35; v.p. Dodge Steel Co., 1920-22; adminstrv. sec., dir. Franklin Inst., Phila., 1935-47, exec. v.p., sec. since 1947; editor Jour. Franklin Inst. Served as capt. Ordnance Dept., U.S. Army, A.E.F., 1917-20. Asso. trustee Bd. Grad. Edn. and Research, U. Pa.; bd. dirs. Atwater-Kent Mus.; chairman Phila. Adv. Council for Vocational Edn. Fellow A.A.A.S.; mem. Am. Inst. Mining and Metall. Engrs., Am. Soc. for Metals, Am. Assn. Mus. (v.p.); Am. Soc. for Testing Materials, Newcomen Soc., S.R., Sigma Delta Kappa — Epsilon. Decorated Chevalier of Legion of Honor (Fr.); Presdl. Medal for Merit, 1948. Republican. Unitarian. Clubs: Rittenhouse, Engineers, Cricket, Rotary, Poor Richard, Physics. Died Mar. 21, 1962; buried Green River Cemetery, Greenfield, Mass.

ALLEN, HENRY TUREMAN army officer; b. Sharpsburg, Ky., Apr. 13, 1859; s. Sanford and Susan (Shumate) A.; prep. edn. in Ky., and at Peekskill Mil. Acad., and Georgetown Coll., A.M., 1898; grad. U.S. Mil. Acad., 1882; LL.D., Lincoln Memorial U., 1915, Georgetown, 1922; m. Dora Johnston, July 12, 1887. Commd. 2d lt. 2d Cav., June 13, 1882; promoted through grades to lt. col., vols., 1901, and to brig. gen. regular army, 1917; maj. gen. N.A., Aug. 5, 1917; maj.gen., Mar. 6, 1921; retired Apr. 13, 1923. Instr. U.S. Mil. Acad., 1888-90; mil. attache Russia, 1890-95, Germany, 1897-98; served in Santiago campaign as maj. and adj. gen., in Philippines at lt. col. 43d Regt.; gov. Island of Leyte, Apr.-July, 1901; started orgn. of Philippine constabulary, July, 1901, as its chief; brig. gen and chief of constabulary by act of Congress, Jan. 1903; later lt. col. Gen. Staff in charge of cav. sect.; with Mexican Punitive Expdn., 1916; assigned comdr. 90th Div., Camp Travis, Tex., Sept. 1917; apptd. comdr. 90th Div., A.E.F., Sept. 1917, participating in Toul sector, St. Mihiel and Meuse-Argonne offensives; assigned as comdr. 8th Army Corps, Nov. 24, 1918; 9th A.C., Apr. 20, 1919, 7th A.C., May 5, 1919; apptd. comdr. Am. Forces in Germany, July 2, 1919. Decorated D.S.M.; Croix de Guerre with palm and Comdr. Legion of Honor (France); Comdr. Order of Leopold (Belgium); plaque Order of Prince Danilo; medal de la Solidaridad (Panama); Grand Cordon of Order of the Crown (Italian); Croix de Guerre with palm (Belgian). Author: Reconnaissance of Copper, Tannana and Kuyukuk Rivers, 1886; Military System of Sweden, 1895; My Rhineland Journal, 1923; The Rhineland Occupation, 1926. Home: Washington, D.C. Died Aug. 30, 1930.

ALLEN, HUBERT A. army officer; b. Buchanan Co., Ia., Apr. 4, 1872; s. Joel M. and Mary Jane (McGary) A.; ed. Ia. State Coll.; m. Jessie M. Mainus, Oct. 2, 1805. Dist. comml. mgr., Ia. Telephone Co. Actively identified with Ia. N.G. about 25 yrs.; served as capt., Spanish-Am. War, 1898; apptd. brig. gen. N.A., Aug. 5, 1917; assigned Camp Cody, Deming, N.M. Mem. United Spanish War Vets. Republican. Mason, K.P. Home: 3127 3d Av., Cedar Rapids, Ia. Died May 31, 1942.

ALLEN, IRA pioneer, army officer; b. Cornwall, Conn., May 1, 1751; s. Joseph and Mary (Baker) A.; m. Jerusha Enos, circa 1789, 3 children including Ira H. Lived in N.H. Grants (now Vt.) with brothers Ethan, Herman, Heber and Levi, 1772, mem. Green Mountain Boys; represented Colchester in Dorset Conv. (Vt.), 1776; mem. Constl. Com. of Windsor Conv. (Vt.), 1777, wrote preamble to constn. sec. Council of Safety; mem. V.t Gov.'s Council, 1777 1st treas. Vt., 1778; involved in plot with Gt. Britian to make Vt. a province of England, 1780-81, apparently hoped to force Continental Congress to recognize independence of Vt.; negotiated comml. treaties with Quebec; gave land valued at 4,000 pounds to build U. Vt.; in England to secure arms for Vt. Militia (of which he was maj. gen.), obtained them in France instead, captured by British while sailing -.. home in ship Olive Branch, 1796, Brit. courts decided in his favor; returned to U.S., 1801, found that his land had been seized, thrown into prison released by Vt. Legislature, granted immunity from arrest for 1 year; fled to Phila. Author: Natural and Political History of the State of Vermont, 1798; Particulars of the Capture of the Ship Olive Branch, 1798; also pamphlets listed in M.D. Gilman's Bibliography of Vermont, 1897. Died Phila., Jan. 15, 1814.

ALLEN, JAMES brig. gen. U.S. Army; b. Laporte, Ind., Feb. 13, 1849; s. Mark and Matilda A.; grad. U.S. Mil. Acad., 1872. Commd. 2d lt. 3d U.S. Cav., June 14, 1872; advanced through the grades to brig. gen. chief signal officer U.S. Army, Feb. 10, 1906; retired Feb. 13, 1913. Served in Cuba, Puerto Rico, Philippine Islands and Alaska. Died Feb. 19, 1933.

ALLEN, JOHN BEARD U.S. senator, lawyer; b. Crawfordsville, Ind., May 18, 1845; ed. Wabash Coll.; served private 135th Ind. vols., Civil War; after war in Rochester, Minn., until 1870; admitted to bar; removed to Washington Ty., 1870; U.S. atty. for Washington Ty., 1878-85; was reporter for Territorial and U.S. courts for years; author 1st volume of Washington Territory Reports; elected to Congress for term 1889-91, but resigned on being elected U.S. senator on admission of Washington as State; took seat, Dec. 2, 1889. Mem. firm Struve, Allen, Hughes & McMicken. Home: Seattle, Wash. Died 1903.

ALLEN, JULIAN banker; b. Pelham Manor, N.Y., Apr. 8, 1900; s. Frederick Hobbes and Adele (Stevens) A.; grad. St. Paul's Sch., 1915; m. Alice Harding, Oct. 1, 1936; children-Mary Elizabeth, Fredrick Harding. With Bankers Trust Co., N.Y.C., 1919-33; mgr. Morgan & Cie, Paris, 1933-45; v.p., 1949-55, pres., 1955-59; v.p. in charge European Offices, v.p., gen. mgr. Paris office Morgan Guaranty Trust Co., 1959-. Served with Am. Field Service, 1915-17, as lt. Coldstream Guards, British Army, 1917-19, as colonel USAAF, 1942-46. Decorated Legion of Merit with one cluster, Bronze Star lfedal; Order of British Empire; Legion of Honour, Croix de Guerre (twice) (France). Clubs: Brook (N.Y.C.); Guards, White's (London); Travellers, Jockey (Paris). Home: Bolton Priory Pelham Manor, N.Y. Office: 14 Place Vendome, Paris, France. Died Oct. 1967.

ALLEN, RILEY HARRIS editor; b. Colorado City, Tex., April 30, 1884; s. Riley Harris and Anna (Beck) A.; Ph.B. in Litt., U. Chgo., 1904; Alumnus Summa Lauda Dignatus, U. Wash., 1958; m. Suzanne McArdie, Sept. 6, 1910 (dec. July, 1950). Began as reporter for Honolulu Evening Bull. Feb.-Sept. 1905, Seattle Post-Intelligencer, 1906; editor Wash. Mag., Seattle, 1907; reporter, sports writer Seattle Post-Intelligencer, 1907-10; city editor Honolulu Evening Bull. 1910-12; editor Honolulu Star-Bull. (consolidation Hawaiian Star and Evening Bull.), since 1912, except when in mil. service; v.p., sec. Honolulu Star-Bull., Ltd.; v.p. sec., Hilo Tribune-Herald; v.p. Hawaiian Broadcasting System; v.p., sec. Honolulu Lithograph Co. In Siberia with A.R.C., Nov. 1918-July 1920; 1st lt., maj., lt. col. and acting commr. for Siberia; hon. discharged, Apr. 1921. Comd. S.S. Yomei Maru (children's relief ship) on voyage from Vladivostok to Finland July-Oct. 1920, returning to homes in Petrograd 775 Russian children rescued by A.R.C. in Siberia, completing repatriation of children and war prisoners in Jan. 1921. Decorated White Russian Govt. Pres. Honolulu C. of C. 1920, Honolulu Advt. Club, 1930; v.p. Pacific Fgn. Trade Council; chmn. Hawaii Group, Inst. Pacific Relations, 1940-42; chmn. Honolulu chpt. Nat. Found. for Infantile Paralysis, 1943-48. Recipient Nat. V.F.W. Citzenship Medal, 1952; degree distinguished service in journalism U. Mo. Sch. Journalism, 1956. Mem. Beta Theta Pi. Republican. Presbyn. Contbr. short stories and articles to mags. Home: 3275 Pacific Heights Rd. Office: 125 Merchant St., Honolulu. Died Oct. 2, 1966.

ALLEN, ROBERT congressman; b. Augusta County, Va., June 19, 1778; attended Coll. William and Mary; studied law. Practiced law; moved to Carthage, Tenn., 1804, became a mcht.; became clk of Smith County; served as co., commanded regt. Tenn. Volunteers under Gen. Andrew Jackson, War of 1812; mem. U.S. Ho. of Reps. (Democrat) from Tenn., 16th-19th congresses, 1819-27; del. Tenn. Conv., 1834. Died Carthage, Aug. 19, 1844; buried Greenwood Cemetery Lebanon, Tenn.

ALLEN, ROBERT army officer; b. Ohio, July, 1812; grad. U.S. Mil. Acad., 1836. Commd. 2d lt. 2d Arty., U.S. Army, served in Seminole War; commd. capt., 1846; served as q.m. under Gen. Zachary Taylor during Mexican War; treas., chief q.m. Mil. Govt. of Cal.; promoted maj., became q.m. Dept. of Mo., U.S. Army (under Gen. John Fremont), 1861; held temporary rank col. U.S. Army, 1862; commd. brig. gen. U.S. Volunteers, 1836; chief q.m. various Union campaigns in West against Confederacy; commd. col., 1866; ret., 1878. Died Geneva, Switzerland, Aug. 5, 1886.

ALLEN, ROBERT GRAY mfg. exec.; b. Winchester, Mass., Aug. 24, 1902; s. Arthur Harrison and Sally (Gray) A.; grad. Philips Acad., 1922; student Harvard, 1926, spl exec. course Sch. Bus. Adminstrn., 1928; m. Katharine Hancock Williamson, Jan. 17, 1925; children-Katharine Hancock (Mrs. Warren A. Morton), Robert Gray, Mary Williamson. Trainee to sales mgr. Walworth Co., 1925-37; mem. U.S. Congress 28th Dist. Pa., 1937-41; pres. Duff-Norton Mfg. Co., 1940-45; sales mgr. Baldwin Locomotive Co., 1945-46 v.p. Gt. Lakes Carbon Corp., 1947-54; pres. Pesco Products div. Borg-Warner Corp., 1954-57; v.p., then exec. v.p. Bucyrus-Erie Co., South Milwaukee, Wis., 1957-58, pres., 1958-; chmn. bd. Bucyrus-Erie, Ltd., Gulph, Ont., Ruston-Bucyrus Ltd., Lincoln, Eng.; dirs. First Wis. Nat. Bank. Served as lt. col. AUS, 1942-45; exec. officer Phila. Ordnance Dist., sector comdr. Central Pacific Command, Honolulu. Home: Quiet Entry Farm, Keene, Va. Died: Aug. 1963.

ALLEN, ROBERT H. army officer; b. Buchanan, Va., July 19, 1870; s. Judge John J. and Elizabeth M. A.; ed. Washington and Lee U., Lesington, Va.; hon. grad. Sch. of the Line, 1920; grad. Gen. Staff Sch., 1921; m. Stella McIntyre, June 3, 1907; 1 dau., Elizabeth A. (Mrs. John Neff). Enlisted in U.S. Army, June 8, 1893; commd. 2d lt. infantry, Oct. 31, 1895; promoted through grades to col., July 1, 1920; served as col. N.A., Aug. 5, 1917-Aug. 31, 1919; promoted chief of inf., rank of maj. gen., period of 4 yrs., beginning Mar. 28, 1925; retired with rank of maj. gen., 1929. In command of 356th Inf., 89th Division, during Meuse-Argonne offensive, 1918; with Army of Occupation in Germany until May 10, 1919. Awarded D.S.M. "for exceptionally meritorious and distinguished services" in the performance of duties of great responsibility as commanding officer, 356th Inf., 89th Div., during the Meuse-Argonne offensive, during the march into Germany, and during the occupation of enemy territory. Protestant. Home: 1048 Granada Av., San Marion 9, Calif. Died. Oct. 10, 1949.

ALLEN, RODERICK RANDOM, army officer; b. Marshall, Tex., Jan. 29, 1894; s. Jefferson Buffington and Emma (Albers) A.; B.S., Tex. A. and M. Coll., 1915, LL.B., 1946; Univ. of Toulouse, France, 1919; grad. Cav. Sch., 1923, Comd. and Gen. Staff Sch., 1929, Army War Coll., 1935, Naval War Coll., 1936; m. Maydelle Campbell, Apr. 25, 1917; children—Nancy Campbell, Gail Random. Commd. 2d lt., 16th U.S. Cav., Nov. 29, 1916, and advanced through the grades to major general, October 29, 1944; Captain 3d Cavalry A.E.F., France, October 1917-July 1919; comdr. combat Comd. A., 4th Armored Div., April 1942-Oct. 1943; comdg. gen. 20th Armored Div., Oct. 1943-Sept. 1944; comdg. gen. 12th Armored Div., Sept. 1944-Aug. 1945; comdg. gen. 1st Armored Div. (Germany), Aug. 1945-Feb. 1946; Dir. Operations, Plans and Training for U.S. Forces, European Command 1945-47; dir. Intelligence, Army Ground Forces, 1947-48; comdg. gen., 3d Armored Div., Ft. Knox, 1948-50; dep. chief of staff Gen. Hdqrs., Far Eastern Command and U.N. Command, Japan, and chief of staff Korean operations, Japan, 1950-51; comdg. gen. XVI Corps, Japan, 1951-52, 9th Inf. Div., Feb-July 1952, New Eng. Subarea and Boston Army Base and Ft. Devens, Massachusetts, July, 1952, till retirement, 1954. Honorary Kentucky Colonel. Decorations: Distinguished Service Medal, Silver Star Medal, Legion of Merit, Bronze Star Medal, Army Commd. Ribbon, Distinguished Marksman; Officer Legion of Honor, Croix de Guerre with Palm (French); Order of the White Lion and Victory, War Cross (Czechoslovakia). Clubs: Army-Navy, Army-Navy Country (Washington). Home: Washington DC Died Mar. 1970.

ALLEN, SAMUEL EDWARD army officer; b. New Lebanon, Ind., Aug. 12, 1858; s. Arthur P. and Rachel Josephine (Dodds) A.; grad. U.S. Mil. Acad., 1881. Coast Arty. Sch., Ft. Monroe, Va., 1892; m. Conchita Alvarez de la Mess, Dec. 9, 1885. Commd. 2d lt. 5th Arty., June 11, 1881; advanced through the grades to col. Coast Arty. Corps, Feb. 2, 1911. Instr. philosophy, U.S. Mil. Acad., 1892-96; retired at own request, after 42 yrs. service, July 1, 1919. Died Dec. 11, 1926.

ALLEN, TIMOTHY FIELD M.D.; b. Westminster, Vt., Apr. 24, 1837; grad. Amherst Coll., 1858 (LL.D., Amherst, 1885); M.D., Univ. City of New York, 1861; M.D., Univ. of State of New York and Hahnemann Med. Coll., Phila., 1865; m. Julia Bissell, 1862. Acting asst. surgeon, U.S. Army, 1862-64. Prof. materia medica and dean N.Y. Home. Med. Coll.; pres. bd. trustees N.Y. Home. Med. Coll.; pres. N.Y. Ophthalmic Hosp. Author of numerous works on med. topics, etc. Home: New York, N.Y. Died 1902.

ALLEN, WALTER CLEVELAND mfr., b. Farmington, Conn., Aug. 9, 1877; s. George Lewis and Albina (Marble) A.; ed. high sch., Stamford, Conn.; m. Susie C. Travis, Apr. 22, 1897; children—Mildred Louise (Mrs. Frederick L. Reid), Mary Frances (Mrs. Arthur W. Rossiter, Jr.). With Yale & Towne Mfg. Co., Stamford, until retirement Jan. 1, 1939, pres., 1915-32, chmn. bd., 1932-39; dir. First-Stamford Nat. Bank, Stamford Savings Bank. Served as maj., later lt. col., Air Service, U.S. Army, Oct. 1917-Mar. 1919. Citation for Conspicuous Service (U.S.), French Legion of Honor. Pres. Fergusom Library (Stamford). Republican. Methodist. Home: 655 Shippan Av., Stamford, Conn. Died Nov. 13, 1945.

ALLEN, WILLIAM HENRY naval officer; b. Providence R.I., Oct. 21, 1784; s. Gen. William and Sarah (Jones) A. Became midshipman U.S. Navy, 1800, served aboard frigate George Washington under Capt. William Brainbridge; promoted 3d lt. aboard frigate Chesapeake, commanded gun div. when Chesapeake attacked by Brit. ship Leopard, 1807; successfully petitioned (with 6 officers) to have Commodore James Barron removed from command of Chesapeake (after Barron Surrendered without engaging Leopard in action); 1st lt. in frigate United States under commodore Decatur, 1809; took part in capture of Brit frigate Macedonian, 1812, took command of Macedonian with rank of master-comdt., 1812, then given command of ship Argus; sailed (with Crawford, Am. minister to France, aboard) for France, 1813, after landing Crawford at l'Orient, harried Brit. commerce in Irish Channel. Mortally wounded when Argus was captured by British brig Pelican, Aug. 14, 1813, died Mills Prison hosp., Aug. 18, 1813.

ALLEN, (WILLIAM) HERVEY author; b. Pittsburgh, Pa., Dec. 8, 1899; s. William Hervey and Helen Ebey (Myers) A.; U.S. Naval Acad., 1910-11; B.Sc., U. of Pittsburgh, 1915, Litt.D., 1934; studied Harvard, 1920-22; hon. Litt.D., Washington and Jefferson Coll. 1947; m. Ann Hyde Andrews, June 30, 1927; children—Marcia Andrews, Mary Ann, Richard Francis. Instr. English, Porter Mil. Acad., Charleston, S.C., 1920-21; instr. English, high sch., Charleston, 1922-24; with dept. of English, Columbia University, 1924-25; lecturer on Am. Lit., Vassar College, 1926-27; lecturer on modern poetry. Bread Loaf (Vt.) Sch. of English and Writers Conf., 1930, 31. Midshipman U.S. Navy, 1909-10; 2d lt. 18th Pa. Inf., on Mexican border, 1916; 1st lt. 111th Inf., 28th Div., A.E.F., 1917-19, World War; wounded in action, Aug. 1918; instr. English, French Mil. Mission. Regional information rep., War Manpower Commn., consultant, 1944. Mem. bd. govs. St. Johns College, Annapolis, Md.; trustee, U. of Miami. Fellow Royal Soc. of Arts; mem. Nat. Inst. Arts and Letters, Miami Hist. Soc., Poetry Soc. America, MacDowell Colony, Poetry Soc. of South Carolina (founder), Hist. Cos. Southern Florida, Hist. Soc. of Pennsylvania; Hist. Soc. of Maryland, Phi Beta Kappa, Sigma Chi, Omicron Delta Kappa. Clubs: Surf (Miami Beach); Hamilton Street (Baltimore); Biscayne Bay Yacht. Author: Wampum and Old Gold, 1921; The Bride of Huitzil, 1922; Carolina Chansons (with Du Bose Heyward), 1922; The Blindman, 1923; Earth Moods, 1925; Towards the Flame, 1926; Israfel (Biography of E.A. Poe), 1926; Poe's Brother (with Thomas Ollive Mabbott), 1926; New Legends, 1929; Sarah Simon, 1929; Songs for Annette, 1929; Anthony Adverse, 1933; Action at Aquila, 1937; It Was Like This, 1939; The Forest and the Fort, 1943; Bedford Village, 1944; Toward the Morning, 1948. Editor, Rivers of America series, since 1943. Home: The Glades Estate, Box 99, Rt. 2, Miami, Fla. Address: care Rinehart & Co., Inc., 232 Madison Av., New York, N.Y. Died Dec. 28, 1949.

ALLEN, WILLIAM VINCENT senator; b. at Midway, O., Jan. 28, 1847; s. Rev. Samuel and Phoebe (Pugh) A.; g.g.s. Capt. Ananias A., 2d Sussex, N.J., Regt. in Revolutionary War; removed with family to Ia., 1857; ed. Upper Ia. U.; pvt. 32nd Ia. Inf., Civil War; admitted to bar, May 31, 1869; m. Blanche Mott, May 2, 1870. Practiced law in Ia. until 1884, after that in Neb. until 1891; judge 9th Jud. Dist. of Neb., 1891-93; U.S. senator from Neb., 1893-99 and by appmt., Dec. 18, 1899-Mar. 27,1901; dist. judge by appmt., Mar. 9-Dec. 13, 1899; reelected dist. judge Nov., 1899, but did not take seat because of appmt. to Senate; again judge 9th Jud. Dist. of Neb., 1917-21. Permanent pres. Populist State Conv., 1892, 1894, 1900 and of Populist Nat. Conv., 1896. Home: Madison, Neb. Died Jan. 12, 1924.

ALLEN, WILLIS BOYD author; b. Kittery Point, Me., July 9, 1855; s. Stillman Boyd and Harriet (Seaward) A.; A.B., Harvard, 1878; LL.B., Boston U., 1881; unmarried. Practiced law several years in firm Allen, Long & Savage, Boston. On staff Gov. John D. Long, with rank of lt. col., 1881-82. Republican. Author: Pine Cones, 1885; Silver Rags, 1886; Christmas at Surf Point, 1886; Northern Cross, 1887; Mountaineer Series (5 vols.), 1887; Kelp, 1888; Cloud and Cliff, 1889; The Red Mountain of Alaska, 1889; Forest Home Series (5 vols.), 1889; The Lion City of Africa, 1890; In the Morning (verse), 1890; John Brownlow's Folks, 1891; The Boyhood of John Kent, 1891; Gulf and Glacier, 1892; Lost on Umbagog, 1894; Snowed In, 1894; The Mammoth Hunters, 1895; Son of Liberty, 1896; Called to the Front, 1897; Great Island, 1897; Around the Yule Log, 1898; Cleared for Action, 1898; Navy Blue, 1898;

Pineboro Quartette, 1898; The Head of Pasht, 1900; Play Away, 1902; Under the Pine Tree Flag, 1902; Sword and Ploughshare, 1904; The North Pacific, 1905; Gold Hunter of Alaska (2d edit.), 1906; The Violet Book, 1909. Home: Boston, Mass. Died Sept. 9, 1938.

ALLISON, JAMES NICHOLLS brig. gen. U.S.A.; b. Catlettsburg, Ky., Sept. 4, 1848; s. James Willetta and Mary McClellan (Boal) A.; ed. pub. schs., Ironton, O., to 1863, and from close of Civ. War to 1867; grad. U.S. Mil. Acad., 1871; m. Susan Whalley, May 12, 1887. Served as pvt. 39th Ky. Inf., Aug. 10, 1863-June 3, 1865; advanced through the grades to col., asst. commissary gen., Oct. 13, 1907; brig. gen., retired after 46 years service, June 7, 1912. Sec. Mil. Service Instn. of U.S., and editor Journal same; sr. v. comdr. N.Y. Commandery Loyal Legion; sr. v. comdr. George Washington Post, G.A.R. (New York). Died May 2, 1918.

ALLISON, NOAH DWIGHT, editor; b. Spencer Ind., Feb. 9, 1899; son of Clayton Benbridge and Pearl (Coble) A.; A.B., DePauw U., 1921; grad. Command and Gen. Staff Sch.; grad. Brit. Sr. Staff Coll.; m. Tomi Charpentier, July 3, 1923 (dec.). Reporter, 1921; news editor Post-Enquirer, Oakland, Calif., 1922-24; Sunday editor The Record, Fort Worth, Tex., 1925; mng. editor The Light, San Antonio, 1928-67; Lozano prof. journalism Trinity University, 1968-71. Served as 2d lt. Royal Air Force, Gt. Britain, World War I; lt. col., Mil. Intelligence Res., U.S. Army, World War II; 36th Div. V Corps, Hdqrs. ETO, 12th Army Group; chief liaison officer, 12th to 21st Army Group (Brit.) in Continental operations; campaigns: Normandy, Northern France, Ardennes, Rhineland, Central Europe. brig. gen. AUS (ret.). Decorated Bronze Star, Bronze Service Arrowhead, Order of British Empire. Mem. Tex. Cavaliers, Beta Theta Pi, Sigma Delta Chi. Democrat. Mason. Club: Argyle. Home: San Antonio TX Died Mar. 22, 1971.

ALLISON, RICHARD army med. officer; b. nr. Goshen, Orange County, N.Y., 1757. Surgeon's mate 5th Pa. Regiment, Continental Army, 1778-83; transferred to 1st Pa. Regiment, 1783; surgeon's mate 1st Inf. Regt., U.S. Army, 1784-88, promoted regtl. surgeon, 1788; stationed at Ft. Bibiography; went to Europe, 1888; works include: campaigns under Gen. Josiah Harmar and Gen. Arthur St. Clair; apptd. surgeon to Legion of U.S., 1792, honorably discharged when Legion dissolved, 1796; practiced medicine, Cincinnati, 1796-1816. Died Cincinnati, Mar. 22, 1816; buried Wesleyan Cemetery, Cumminsville, O.

ALLSOPP, CLINTON BONFIELD telegraph-cable co. exec.; b. Austin, Nev., Aug. 8, 1887; s. George Fulford and Jennie Edith (Dyer) A.; student U. Cal.; m. Carola Hess Apr. 3, 1918; children-Jane Ellen, Peter Bonfield. Ckl. in plant dept. Pacific Tel. & Tel. Co., San Francisco, 1909, traffic mgr. at Oakland Main Exchange, eight months later, then traffic mrg. entire San Francisco suburban dist. and pay stations, div. traffic agt., 1913-19, acting supt. traffic in charge Ore., Wash., part Ida., 1919-20; div. supt. traffic for same ty., 1920-23; div. supt. traffic N.E. Tel. & Tel. Co., 1923-26, div mgr. in charge all comml. activity in met. div., 1926-29, gen. comml. mgr., 1929; v.p. in charge sales and publicity Postal Telegraph-Cable Co., N.Y.C., 1929, v.p. in charge of comml. operations since 1929; pres. Postal Telegraph Sales Corp., 1931; v.p., dir. Postal Telegraph-Cable Corp., 1941; v.p. Internat. Tel& Tel. Corp. Apptd. mem. adv. com. Chief Signal Officer, U.S. Army, mem. tel. & tel. coms. Def. Communication Bd., Jan. 1941. Commd. maj. Signal Corps Res., Feb. 1941; lt. col. AUS Feb. 1942, col., Dec. 23, 1942; comdg. officer Communications Security Br., Army Communications Div., Signal Corps. Clubs Army and Navy (Washington, D.C.); Army and Navy Country (Arlington). Address: Ranhita La Jota, Angwin, Cal. Died Oct. 12, 1962.

ALMAND, CLAUDE MARION univ. dean, composer; b. Winsboro, La., May 31, 1915; s. Claude F. and Pearl (Harrsion) A.; A.B., La. Coll., 1934, Mus. B., 1934; student Sherwood Sch. Music, Chgo., 1934-35; Mus. M., La. State U., 1938; Ph.D., U. Rochester 1940; m. Lenoir Patton, July 27, 1950. Asso. prof. music George Peabody Coll. for Tchrs., 1940-43, prof. 1943-44; prof. music, sch. ch. music So. Bapt. Theol. Sem., 1944-48, lectr. theory, composition, musicology,1948-53; prof. composition, condr. chorus U. Louisville, 1944-48, asst. to dean, prof. music, head theory dept. 1948-53, dir. grad. dept., 1952-53; dean sch. music Stetson U., 1953—. Recipient state, nat. honors Nat. Fedn. Music Clubs Composition Contest, 1940; one of six contemporary composers awarded commns. Louisville Orchestra, 1948, 49. Mem. Chamber Music Soc. Louisville (dir.), Louisville Community Concerts Assn., Daytona Beach Symphony Soc. (dir.), Fla. Music Tchrs. Assn. (v.p.), Phi Kappa Phi, Phi Mu Alpha (province gov.), Delta Omicron (nat. patron), Lambda Chi Alpha, Kappa Phi Kappa, Phi Delta Kappa. Clubs: Arts, (Louisville); Athenian (DeLand). Composer: Pondy Woods, 1938; The Legend of Last Isle, 1939; The Waste Land. 1940; String Quartet, 1941; Chorale, 1943; Toccata, 1944; John Gilbert-A Steamboat Overture, 1949; Concerto, 1949; Roustabout, 1952; also piano sonatas, chamber music, songs schoral works, piano & organ pieces. Works performed by Eastman-Rochester Orchestra, New Orleans Orchestra, Peabody Chamber Orchester, Little Symphony Nat. Gallery Art, Louisville & Cin. orchestras. Home: 210 W. Washington Av., Deland Fla. Died Sept. 12, 1957

ALMY, JOHN JAY naval officer; b. Newport, R.I., Apr. 24, 1815; s. Samuel Almy. Became midshipman U.S. Navy, 1829; served on brig Concord in Mediterranean Sea, 1830-32; served in Mexican War; promoted Lt., 1846; served on blockading duty off Confederate coast during Civil War; captured or destroyed over $1,000,000 in Confederate blockade runners in 1864 alone; commd. rear adm. (ret.), 1877, had served longest period of active duty of any officer up to that time. Died May 16, 1895.

ALTER, DINSMORE, astronomer; b. Colfax, Wash., Mar. 28, 1888;2s. Joseph and Jeannette (Copley) A.; B.S., Westminster Coll., New Wilmington, Pa., 1909; M.S., U. of Pittsburgh, 1910; Ph.D., U. of Calf., 1916; D.Sc., Monmouth Coll., 1941; m. Ada McClelland, Dec. 26, 1910; children—Helen Jeannette, Dinsmore (dec.). Instr. and adj. prof. physics and astronomy, U. of Ala., 1911-14; instr. astronomy, U. of Calif., 1914-17; asst. prof. of astronomy, U. of Kan., 1917-19, asso. prof., 1919-24, prof., 1924-36; dir. Griffith Observatory, Los Angeles, 1935-58, dir. emeritus, 1958. Served to maj. C.A., U.S. Army, World War I; col. T.C. Reserve; on active service, col. T.C., A.U.S., 1942-1947, World War II. Fellow, Royal Astron. Soc., Am. Meteorol. Soc. (v.p. 1926-27), American Geophysical Union, Institute of Math. Statistics, British Astron. Assn., Astron. Soc. of Pacific, A.A.A.S., American Astronomical Society American Legion, Forty and Eight, Sigma Xi. Democrat. United Presbyn. Contbr. to Lick Obs. bulls., Astron. Jour., numerous others. Known for original research in meteorol. periodicities and math. methods pertaining to same. John Simon Guggenheim memorial fellow in England for statistical research on rainfall, 1929-30. Home: Berkeley CA Died Sept. 1968.

ALTER, NICHOLAS M(ARK), pathologist, lab. dir.; b. Csanytclek, Hungary, Oct. 12,21892; s. Joseph M. and Katherine (Csany) A.; M.D., U. Hungary, 1913, U. Vienna, 1914; grad. study U. Lelpzig, 1913, U. Heidelberg, 1914; m. Eleanor Cochran Reed, Apr. 11, 1931; children—Eleanor, Katherine, Nicholas Albert, Ernest Henry. Came to U.S., 1914, naturalized, 1923. Pathologist, lab. dir. H. A. Kelly Hosp., Baltimore, 1915-19, also asst. dept. pathology Johns Hopkins Hosp.; resident pathologist, instr. med. sch. Yale, 1919-20; pathologist W. Penn Hosp., Pittsburgh, 1920-22; asst. prof. internal medicine U. Mich., 1922-23; prof. pathology U. Colo., 1923-25, N.Y. Post Grad. Med. Sch., N.Y. City, 1925-30; later pathologist, lab. dir. Margaret Hague Hosp., Jersey City. Mem. bd. Mus. Assn. Jersey City, Internat. Inst., Jersey City Philharmonic Symphony. Served as lt. comdr., U.S. Navy, 1933-41. Diplomate Am. Bd. Pathology (anat. and clin. pathology). Fellow A.M.A.; mem. A.A.A.S., Am. Assn. Pathologists and Bacteriologists, N.Y. Path. Soc., N.J. Soc. Pathologists, China Inst. Study Oriental Art. Club: Hajji Baba. Home: Slatersville RI Died Mar. 1970.

ALTMAN, OSCAR LOUIS, govt. ofcl.; b. N.Y.C., Jan. 17, 1909; s. Benjamin and Rose (Sokoloff) A.; A.B., Cornell U., 1929, A.M., 1930; Ph.D., U. Chgo., 1936; m. Alberta Smith Neblett, 1942 (div. 1951);children—Peter A., Leslie V.; m. 2d, Adeline Furness Roberts, 1952 (div. 1965); 1 son, William H.F. Instr. econs. Ohio State U., 1936-38; sr. economist SEC, 1938-40; prin. economist Nat. Resources Planning Bd., 1940-42; with French Supply Council, 1945-46; with Internat. Monetary Fund, 1946-68, dep. dir. research, 1954-66, treas., 1966-68. Bd. dirs. D.C. Inst. Mental Hygiene, 1967-68, Washington Drama Soc., 1964-68. Served to lt. col. USAAF, 1942-45. Decorated Legion of Merit. Mem. Am. Econ. Assn., Phi Beta Kappa, Phi Kappa Phi Fraternity. Democrat. Jewish religion. Clubs: Army/ Navy Country, also Cosmos (Washington); Army Navy Country (Arlington, Virginia). Author: Saving, Investment and National Income, 1942; also articles. Home: Washington DC Died Dec. 22, 1968.

ALVORD, BENJAMIN army officer; b. Rutland, Vt., Aug. 18, 1813; s. William and Lucy (Claghorn) A.; grad U.S. Mil. Acad., 1833; m. Emily Louise Mussey, 1846, 6 children. Commd. in 4th Inf., U.S. Army, 1833; served in Seminole War, 1835-37, cheif paymaster in Mexican War. 1846-48, and in Ore. 1854-62; commd. brig. gen. U.S. Volunteers, 1862; paymaster gen. U.S. Army, 1872-80. Author numerous articles on mathematics and geography. Died Oct. 16, 1884

ALVORD, BENJAMIN army officer; b. Wash., May 15, 1860; s. Brig. Gen. Benjamin A. (U.S. Army); grad. U.S. Mil. Acad., 1882. Inf. and Cav. Sch., Ft. Leavenworth, Kan., 1887. Commd. 2d lt. 20th Inf., June 13, 1882; advanced through the ranks to brig. gen. and adj. gen. A.E.F., France, 1917. Died Apr. 13, 1927.

ALVORD, ELLSWORTH CHAPMAN lawyer; b. Washburn, Wis., Oct. 21, 1895; s. Elias Chapman and Miriam Lucy (Moore) A.; A.B., U. of Wis., 1917; LL.B., Columbia, 1921; LL.D. (honorary), Northland College, 1956; m. Kathryn McLean Watson, Dec. 31, 1921; children-Ellsworth Chapman, Betty Pierpont (Mrs. William R. Loweth), Katharyn Joanne (Mrs. Henry Remsen), Robert Watson. Admitted to N.Y. bar 1921, Supreme Court of U.S., 1926, U.S. Dist. Court for D.C., 1931; asst. legislative counsel U.S. Senate, 1921-24, Ho. of Rep., 1924-26; spl. asst. to Sec. of Treasury, 1926-30; private practice since 1930; member Alvord & Alvord, Washington, D.C., 1934-; dir. Gen. Dynamics Corp., SC, Corp., Crown Drug Co., Metro-Goldwyn-Mayer Inc., State Loan & Finance Corp., Jonnell Gas. Formerly treas., mem. com. on federal finance U.S. C. of C.; chmn. com. on taxation and trustee U.S. Council of Internat. C. of C., vice chmn., com. on taxation; chmn. bd. trustees Northland Coll.; pres. bd. trustees Alvord Found.; dir. Found. for Research of N.Y. Acad. Osteopathy; trustee Lovelace Found. for Med. Research; dir. Wis. Eastern Alumni Scholarship Fund; bd. visitors Columbia U. Sch. Law; mem. Columbia Law Sch. Fund. Served to 1st lt. F.A., U.S. Army, 1917-19. Mem. tax Inst. (adv. council), Mining and Metallurgy Soc. Am. (com. on taxation and depletion), Internat. Fiscal Assn., Newcomen Soc. N.Am., Acad. Polit. Sci., Am. Bar Assn., Am. Judicature Soc., D.C. Bar Assn., Am. Mining Congress (com. on taxation), Phi Delta Phi. Ind. Republican. Conglist. Clubs: Burning Tree, Metropolitan, Columbia Country, National Press (Washington); Duquesne (Pitts.); Chicago (Chgo.); Columbia Univ., Marco Polo, Bankers, Deepdale Garden City, Metropolitan, Pinnacle (N.Y.C.); Everglades, Seminole Golf, Bath & Tennis (Palm Beach); Eldorado (Palm Desert, Cal.); Winged Foot Golf (Marmaroneck, N.Y.); Royal & Ancient Golf of St. Andrews (Fife, Scotland). Contbr. numerous articles on govt. finance and taxation to periodicals. Home: 3521 Lowell St. N.W. Office: World Center Bldg., Washington 6. Died Jan. 16, 1964

AMADAS, PHILLIP naval officer; flourished 1584-85. A comdr. in Walter Raleigh's fleet, sent out by Queen Elizabeth to discover new lands; left Eng., Apr. 1584, went 1st to Canary Islands, then to W.I., reached coast of N.C., July 1584, discovered Wokokon isle nr. Pamlico Sound; visited Ohanoak (Roanoke) Island; took 2 Indians back to Eng. on return trip, Sept. 1584; went with Sir Richard Grenville, to colonize new colony (named Va. by Queen Elizabeth), 1585.

AMEN, JOHN HARLAN lawyer; b. Exeter, N.H., Sept. 15, 1898; s. Harlan Page and Mary (Rawson) A.; grad. Phillips Acad., Exeter, 1915; A.B., Princeton U., 1919; student Harvard Law Sch., 1919-23; m. Marion Cleveland, July 25, 1926; 1 son, Grover Cleveland. Admitted to N.Y. bar, 1923; asso. with Shearman & Sterling, New York, 1923-28; partner Duryee, Zunino & Amen, N.Y., 1928-38; partner Parker & Duryee 1938; mem. Amen, Weisman & Butler, N.Y.C.; special assistant to United States atty. gen. on cases involving violations of federal anti-trust laws, 1928-38, apptd. (Oct. 26, 1938) special prosecutor to supersede dist. atty. of Kings County in connection with investigation of official corruption in Brooklyn; apptd. (Aug. 23, 1940) asst. atty. gen. of the State of N.Y. to conduct city-wide investigation of contracts for constrn. of pub. highways and sewers in Kings, Queens, New York, Bronx and Richmond Counties. Published: Report on Probation Department of Kings County Court, 1941; Report on Department of Correction in Kings County, 1942;Report of Kings County Investigation (1938-42), 1942. Conducted investigation of N.Y. City Police Dept. in connection with gambling racket, 1942. Served as 2d lt. U.S. Marine Corps, Reserve Flying Corps, during World War; commd. lt. col., U.S. Army, Aug. 1942; col., 1944—. Asso. trial counsel, chief interrogations div. office U.S. Chief of Counsel in war criminal trials, at Nuernburg, Germany, 1945-46. Awarded Legion of Merit with Oak Leaf Cluster (U.S.); Royal Order of St. Olaf, rank of commander (Norway); Order of the White Lion (Czechoslovakia). Pres. Phillips Exeter Acad. Alumni Assn., 1940-41. Mem. Loyalty Review Bd., Am. Bar Assn., Assn. of Bar of the City of N.Y. Clubs: Ivy, Princeton, River Club of N.Y. Home: 430 E. 57th St. Office: 17 E. 63d St., N.Y. City 21. Died Mar. 10, 1960.

AMES, NORMAN BRUCE univ. prof.; b. Richmond, Va., July 1, 1896; s. Nathaniel Turner and Mary Farley (Peck) A.; B.S. in Elec. Engring., Miss. State Coll., 1915; B.S., George Washington U., 1916, LL.B., 1925, E.E., 1929; S.B. in Elec. Engring., Mass. Inst. Tech. 1917, S.M., 1935; S.B. in Elec. Engring., Harvard, 1917; Dr. Sci. Tech., Swiss Federal Instn. Tech., Zurich, 1956; m. Mary Olive Jennings, June 9, 1921; children-Ruth Barbara (Mrs. Joseph Vivari), Phyllis (Mrs. Milton D. Willford). With Pa. R.R., Bethlehem Shipbldg. Corp., Stone & Webster, B.F. Goodrich Rubber Co., 1919-20 with George Washington U. since 1920, prof. since 1929. head of elec. engring. dept.; dir. and sec. Murphy & Ames, Inc., Arlington, Va. Fulbright lectr. elect. engring., U. Ceylon, 1956-57. Chmn. Montgomery County (Md.) Charter Bd., 1946, pres. Montgomery County Charter Com., 1947-50. Registered engr., Md. Served as 2d lt., aviation sect., Signal Corps, U.S. Army, 1918-19; in France and Germany, 15 mos.; on active duty, U.S. Army, Sept. 1940-Sept. 1941; recalled to active duty, 1941, asst. exec. and div. executive Hdqrs. of USAF, 1941-45, lt. col. 1942; disch. 1946; following service in Hdqrs. U.S.A.F., was information and education officer for AAF, M.T.O. U.S.A., later for ground forces M.T.O. Fellow Am. Inst. E.E. (chmn. Washington sect. 19 48); mem. Am. Assn. of University Professors, Tau Beta Pi, Sigma Tau, Delta Tau Delta, Omicron Delta Kappa, Phi Kappa Phi. Grand Regent

Theta Tau, 1948-50. Democrat. Mem. Christian Ch. (elder). Mason. Home: 5208 Westwood Dr. Washington, 16. Office: 725 21st St., Washington 6. Died Mar. 5, 1960; buried Arlington Nat. Cemetery, Arlington, Va.

AMES, ROBERT PARKER MARR physician; b. Springfield, Mass., Oct. 20, 1856; ed. pub. schs. and acad.; grad. Jefferson Med. Coll., Phila., 1880; was resident surgeon Jefferson and Phila. hosps.; surgeon U.S. Marine Hospital Service, 1881-90; now practices at Springfield; m. April 20, 1882, Mary, d. Dr. David Benson, Hoboken, N.J.; mem. Am. Med. Assn., Mass. Med. Assn. and Hampden Med. Assn. Mem. House of Delegates, 1904-05. Address: Cooley Blk., Springfield, Mass.

AMES, WILLIAM soldier, mfr.; b. Providence, R.I., May 15, 1842; s. Hon. Samuel and Mary T. (Dorr) A.; A.B., Brown U., 1863, A.M., by spl. vote, 1891; m. Henriette F. Ormsbee, Nov. 8, 1871 (died 1875); m. 2d Mrs. Anne Ives Carrington Dwight, Apr. 27, 1882 (died 1904). Entered army as 2d lt. 2d R.I. Inf., June 5, 1861; advanced through grades to col., Oct. 10, 1864; bvtd. brig. gen vols., Mar. 13, 1865, "for meritorious services during the war"; hon. mustered out, Aug. 27, 1865. Connected with Allen's Print Works, 1865-69; collector U.S. internal revenue, 1st R.I. dist., 1870-75; agt. and mgr. Fletcher Mfg. Co., Providence 1875-1904, pres. and treas. same, 1904—; pres. Blackstone Canal Nat. Bank, 1877—. Mem. Providence Common Council, 1872-73; mem. R.I. Ho. of Rep., 1898-99; chmn State House Commn. Republican. Home: Providence, R.I. Died Mar. 8, 1914.

AMMEN, JACOB educator, army officer; b. Fincastle, Va., Jan. 7, 1807; s. David and Sally (Houtz) A.; grad U.S. Mil. Acad., 1831; m. Caroline L. Pierce; m.2d, Martha Beasley, Prof. mathematics Bacon Coll. (now Transylvania U.), 1837, 48-55, Jefferson (mo.) Coll., 1839-40, 43-48, U. Ind., Bloomington, 1840-43; civil engr., Ripley, O., 1855-61; commd. capt. 12th Ohio Volunteers, later lt. col. 1861; commd. brig. gen. U.S. Volunteers, 1862, resigned conmm., 1865. Died Lockland, O., Feb. 6, 1894.

AMMONS, TELLER, ex-gov.; b. Denver, Colo., Dec. 3, 1895; s. Elias M. and Elizabeth (Fleming) A.; student U. of Denver, 1919-21; LL.B., Westminster Law Sch., 1929; m. Esther Davis, Sept. 9, 1933; 1 son, Davis. Admitted to Colo. bar. 1929; mem. State Senate, 1930-35; city atty. for City and Co. of Denver, 1935-36; gov. of Colo., 1936-38. Served with 154th Inf., A.E.F., World War I; commd. lt. col. A.U.S. 1942. On selection and assignment bd. all officers of mil. government under provost marshal gen. to 1944; served in provost court, chief justice, court of appeals, investigator and later trial judge advocate, Guam; separated Dec. 1945. Mem. Am. Legion, Vets. of Fgn. Wars, Sigma Alpha Epsilon, Phi Alpha Delta. Dem. Clubs: Denver Law, Denver Athletic. Address: Denver CO Died Jan. 1972.

AMORY, HARCOURT, bus. exec.; b. Beverly, Mass., July 7, 1894; s. Harcourt and Gertrude Lowndes (Chase) A.; A.B., Harvard, 1916; m. Susannah Stoddard Wood, Feb. 17, 1923; children—Harcourt, Susannah Lowndes. With Smith Barney & Company (previously Edward B. Smith & Co.), 1925-42, partner, 1931-42; dep. vice chmn. War Prodn. Bd., 1942-44; v.p. Hawaiian Pineapple Co., Ltd., 1945-47; v.p. Castle & Cooke, Ltd., 1945-47, Smith, Barney & Co., 1947-69; dir., mem. exec. and finance com. Ranco, Inc., Witco Co., Ranco, Ltd., Am. Motors. Vice pres. Lenox Hill Neighborhood Assn. Capt. U.S. Army, 1917-19. Treas. Mass. Rep. State Com., 1936-42; pres. Rep. Club of Mass., 1940-42. Mason, Clubs: Harvard, Racquet and Tennis, The Links, Recess (N.Y.C.); Southampton; The Detroit. Home: New York City NY Died Dec. 1969.

AMOSS, HAROLD L(INDSAY) (A'MOS), physician; b. Cobb, Ky., Sept. 8, 1886; s. David Alfred and Waters (Lindsay) A.; B.S., State U. Ky., 1905, M.S., 1907; M.D., Harvard, 1911, Dr. P. H., 1912; hon. Sc.D., George Washington U., 1922; m. Marguerite Dupree Moore, May 17, 1917; children-Harold Lindsay, Dudley Moore. Chemist Ky. Agrl. Expt. Sta., 1905; asst. chemist Hygienic Lab., USPHS, 1905-07, Bur. Chemistry U.S. Dept. Agr., 1907-09; physiol. chemist Western Pa. Hosp., 1909; instr. preventive medicine & hygiene, Harvard Med. Sch., 1909-12; asst. in pathology and bacterology, 1912-14, asso., 1914-19, asso. mem., 1919-22, Rockefeller Inst. Med. Research; asso. prof. medicine Johns Hopkins U. and asso. physician Johns Hopkins Hosp., 1922-30; prof. medicine, Duke, 1930-33. Cons. in medicine Greewich, Grasslands, White Plains, United and No. Westchester Hosps. editor "Medicine," 1922-25 Commd. 1st lt. Med. R.C., 1915, capt. M.C. N.A., 1917; maj., 1918; honorably discharged, July 15, 1919. Chmn. Med. Adv. Bd. No. 5, Conn. Med. Adv. Food Panel. Mem. A.M.A., A.C.P., A.A.A.S., Assn. Am. Physicians, Assn. Am. Chest Physicians, Am. Soc. Clin. Investigation, Am. Soc. Exptl. Pathology, Am. Climatol. Soc., Am. Assn. Immunologists Am. Heart Assn., Harvey Soc., Interurban Clin. Club So. Interurban Clin. Club, Sigma Xi, Phi Beta Kappa, Omicron Delta Kappa, Pi Kappa Alpha, Phi Chi. Independent. Episcopalian. Mason. Contbr. various articles on physiol, chemistry, infectious diseases, immunology, epidemiology and clin. medicine. Home: 68 Deerfield Dr., Greewich, Conn. Died Nov. 2, 1956; buried Maplewood Cemetery, Princeton, N.Y.

ANAST, JAMES LOUIS engineering executive; born Columbus, O., May 27, 1918; s. Louis D. and Kally (Drosos) A.; B.E.E., Ohio State U., 1940; m. Marie Ellen Pirpiris, Apr. 25, 1946; 1 son, Louis J. Research engr. U.S. Air Force, 1946-49, chief engr. All Weather Flying Center, 1949-52; dir. missile intelligence Hdqrs. USAFE, 1952-53; chief systems engr. Air Navigation Development Bd., 1954-55; tech. asst. to spl. asst. to Pres. for aviation planning, 1955-56; tech. dir. Airways Modernization Bd., 1957-58 v.p. tech. planning Lear, Inc., 1958, pres. 1959; dir. Bur. Research and Devel., Fed. Aviation Agy., 1959-61; director of European operations for Ling Temco Vought Corporation, 1961-. Served from pvt. to lt. col., AUS, 1940-46, 1952-53. Decorated Air Medal. Mem. Sigma Epsilon Phi. Mem. Greek Orthodox Ch. Developed 1st translantic automatic flight system, 1947. Home: 15 Rue Vineuse, Paris, France. Died Aug. 1964, buried Cabourg, Calvados, France.

ANDERSON, CHARLES HARDIN, air force officer; b. Cape Girardeau, Mo., Nov. 3, 1907; s. Daniel Hardin and Marie (Boysen) A.; B.S., U.S. Mil. Acad., 1932; grad. Advanced Flying Sch., 1933, Air Command and Staff Sch., 1947, Air War Coll., 1948, Nat. War Coll., 1950; m. Mary Kathryn Glass, Feb. 20, 1936 (dec.); children—Kathryn Marie (Mrs. Waterbury), Patricia, Mary Sheridan. Commd. 2d lt., U.S. Army, 1932, advanced through grades to maj. gen. USAF, 1956; assigned 1st Pursuit Group, 1933-37; spl. duty Philippine A.C., 1938-39; comdg. officer Advanced Flying Sch., 1942-43; overseas duty, 1944-45; faculty Air War Coll., 1947-49; dir., office manpower requirements Office Sec. Def., Washington, 1953-55; asst. chief staff, Air and Spl. Operation, SHAPE 1955-58; asst. atomic energy, Hq. USAF, 1958-60; comdr. Lowry Tech. Tng. Center, 1960-67. Decorated Legion of Merit with oak-leaf cluster, D.F.C., D.S.M., Air Medal, Bronze Star Medal, Commendation Medal with 2 oak-leaf clusters (U.S.); Distinguished Service Star of Philippines. Address: Denver CO Died May 27, 1971; buried Arlington Nat. Cemetery, Arlington VA

ANDERSON, CHARLES LOFTUS GRANT, surgeon; b. near Hagerstown, Md., Mar. 8, 1863; s. George Washington and Anna Maria (Winter) A.; student Claverack (N.Y.) Coll., 1877-79; U. of Pa., 1881; M.D., Coll. Physicians and Surgeons (Columbia), 1884; m. Ruby Scruggs, July 7, 1910. House physician and surgeon, Jersey City Hosp., 1885; commd. 1st lt. and asst. surgeon, U.S. Army, 1886; resigned, 1888; acting asst. surgeon, U.S. Army, with 5th Army Corps, Santiago Campaign, Spanish-Am. War, 1898, then on duty at gen. hosps., Ft. Myer, Va., and Savannah, Ga.; maj. and surgeon, U.S. Vols. in Philippines, 1899-1901; asso. in surgery Emergency Hosp., Washington, D.C., 1905; physician, Isthmian Canal Commn., Canal Zone, Panama, 1905-07. Amateur swimmer of note. Major Med. R.C., active service with A.E.F., in France, with 2d Div. and in comd. of hosps.; promoted to lt. col. Med. Corps.; lt. col. Med. Res. Corps, retired, 1928. Med. specialist, U.S. Vets. Bur. Founder and v.p. Spanish-Am. Athenaeum. Fellow A.M.A., Am. Geog. Soc.; mem. Assn. Mil. Surgs. of U.S., Med. Soc. of D.C., Anthropol. Soc. Washington (pres.), Washington Acad. Sciences, United Spanish War Vets, Am. Legion, Institute de las Espanas. K.T. Clubs: University (Washington, D.C.); Army and Navy (New York). Author: Old Panama and Castilla del Oro, 1914; Life and Letters of Vasco Nunez de Balboa, 1941; also various articles on lit., med. and scientific topics. Home: 2407 15th St. N.W., Washington DC

ANDERSON, CLIFFORD LE CONTE lawyer; b. Macon, Ga., July 7, 1862; s. Clifford and Anna (Le Conte) A.; A.B., Mercer U., 1880, LL.B., 1883; m. Kitty Van Dyke, Sept. 10, 1884; children—Mrs. John Geizer, Jr., Clifford V.; m. 2d, Mary Alice Van der Grifft, April 30, 1910; 1 son, Jackson V. Practiced at Macon, Ga., 1883-86, at Atlanta, 1886—; sr. mem. Anderson, Rountree, Crenshaw & Hansell. Commr. roads and revenue, Fulton County, Ga., 1899-1914, inclusive. Brig.-gen. comdg. Ga. N.G. (retired). Home: Atlanta, Ga. Died Sept. 17, 1933.

ANDERSON, EDWARD clergyman; b. Boston, Mass., Nov. 19, 1833; s. Rufus (D.D., LL.D.) and Eliza (Hill) A.; ed. in Boston schs.; pvt. instrn.; studied theology with father and pastor; m. Harriet Flora Shumway, July 29, 1857. Ordained Congl. ministry, 1858; pastor, St. Joseph, Mich., 1858-60, Qunicy, Ill., 1874-80, Toledo, O., 1880-84, Norwalk, Conn., 1884-89, Danielson, Conn., 1890-95. Served with John Brown in Kansas; chaplain 37th Ill. Vols. till after the Mo. campaign, 1862; col. 12th Ind. Vol. Cav. until close of war. Mason. Home: Qunicy, Mass. Died May 21, 1916.

ANDERSON, EDWARD LOWELL lawyer; b. at Cincinnati, O., Oct. 4, 1842; s. Larz and Catharine (Longworth) A.; ed. pub. schools and tutors to 1861; left school to enter army; LL.B., U. of Cincinnati, 1866; m. Mary Fore, Dec. 5, 1865. Served 1st lt. and capt. 52d Ohio Inf., 1862-65; capt. on staff Gen. William T. Sherman; was in battles of Perryville, Murfreesboro, Chickamauga, Mission Ridge, Kenesaw Mountain, Jonesboro (wounded), and other engagements; mustered out at close of war; admitted to bar, 1866. Author: Northern Ballads, 1874, Soldier and Pioneer, 1879; Six Weeks in Norway, 1877; Modern Horsemanship, 1884; Curb, Snaffle and Spur, 1894; Riding and Driving (with Price Collier), 1905; Horses and Riding, 1909. Home: Cincinnati, O. Died Mar. 29, 1916.

ANDERSON, EDWARD WHARTON army officer; b. Manhattan, Kan., Sept. 23, 1903; A.B., Stanford U., 1928; grad. Air Corps Primary Flying Sch., 1934, Tactical Sch., 1940, Apptd. 2d lt., Air Res., 1929; commd. 2d lt., Air Corps, U.S. Army, 1930, and advanced through the grades to brig. gen., 1944; comd. 41st Pursuit Squadron, 31st Pursuit Group, Jan.-Apr. 1941; group operations officer, 31st Pursuit Group, Apr.-May 1941, group exec. officer, May 1941-Mar. 1942; comdg. officer 20th Fighter Group, Mar.-Aug 1942; became comdr. 4th Fighter Group, Sept. 1942, later becoming Fighter Wing comdr. European Theater Operations. Decorated Silver Star, Air Medal with two oak leaf clusters. Address: care the Adjutant General's Office, War Dept., Washington 25, D.C. Deceased.

ANDERSON, EDWIN ALEXANDER naval officer; b. Wilmington, N.C., July 16, 1860; grad. U.S. Naval Acad., 1882. Ensign, July 1, 1884; promoted through the grades to rear adm., Nov. 28, 1918. In service on Marblehead and as comdr. Sandoval, Spanish-Am. War, 1898; advanced 5 numbers in rank "for extraordinary heroism" during Spanish-Am. War; comdr. 2d Regt. of Bluejackets at capture of Vera Cruz, Mexico, 1915; awarded Congressional Medal of Honor "for extraordinary heroism in battle on that occasion"; rear adm. Nov. 28, 1918. D.S.M. for services during World War; vice adm. comdg. European Forces, 1922; comdr. in chief Asiatic Fleet, 1922-23; retired, 1923. Home Wilmington, N.C. Died Sept. 23, 1933.

ANDERSON, FREDERICK L., ret. Army officer; b. Kingston, N.Y., October 4, 1905; s. Frederick L. and Anna Elizabeth (Haulenbeck) A.; grad. U.S. Military Acad., 1928; m. Elizabeth Ann Travis, Aug. 30, 1928; children—Mary Winn, Travis. Commd. 2d lt., 1928, advanced through grades to major gen., 1943; graduate Kelly Field and Brooks Field, receiving his wings, 1929; served in Philippines, Hamilton Field, Lowry Field, and Washington; transferred to bombardment aviation in 1931; operations officer 7th Group; selected to start the first Bombardier's Instructor Sch., 1940; head of bombardment tactics bd. sent to England in 1941; deputy dir. bombardment, Washington, 1942; rep. of General Arnold on bombardment matters in Northern Africa and England, 1942; comdr. Fortress Wing in United Kingdom, 1943; comdg. gen., VIII Bomber Comd., Eng., 1943; dep. comdr. operations, Hdqrs. U.S. Strategic Air Forces in Europe, England, France, 1944-45; asst. chief, air Staff for Personnel, 1945-47, retired 1947; U.S. ambassador to NATO, 1952-53; dir. Lear Siegler, Inc., Am. Bakeries Co., Fed. Petroleum, Inc., Royal Industries, Inc., U.S. Leasing Corp.; trustee the Rand Corp. Trustee Menlo Sch. and Coll. Decorated Silver Star, D.F.C., D.S.M. with Oak Leaf Cluster, Air Medal, Legion of Merit, Order of Suvorov 3d Degree (Russian), Commander of the Bath (British), Legion of Honor, (French), Croix de Guerre with Palm (French). Mem. Nat. Aeronautical Soc. Club: Army-Navy (Washington, D.C.); The Links (N.Y.C.); Cypress Point (Pebble Beach, Cal.); Menlo Country (Woodside, Cal.), San Francisco Golf. Home: Woodside CA Died Mar. 2, 1969; buried Arlington Nat. Cemetery, Washington DC

ANDERSON, GEORGE LUCIUS army officer; b. Delafield, Wis., Apr. 9, 1849; s. Archibald A. and Clarissa E. (Clarke) A.; A.B., Lawrence U., 1870, A.M., 1873; grad. West Point, 1874, U.S. Arty. Sch., 1876, Naval War Coll., 1897; unmarried. Apptd. 2d lt., June 17, 1874; promoted through grades to col. and insp. gen., Oct. 1, 1908; retired Apr. 9, 1913. Elec. engr. Calif. Power & Light Transmission Lines, Palo Alto, 1913-17; on duty in office of Board of Ordnance and Fortification, Washington, 1917-18. Asst. prof. mathematics, West Point, 1885-89; instr. electricity and submarine mines, U.S. Arty. Sch., Ft. Monroe, 1889-95; mil. attache to U.S. Embassy at St. Petersburg, 1897; mem. U.S. Ordnance Bd., New York, 1903-06; insp. gen. Dept. of Calif., 1906-09. Author: Handbook for U.S. Electricians in the Management and Care of the Machinery of Sea Coast Fortifications, 1902; Instructions in Electricity for Non-Commissioned Officer, 1894. Home: Washington, D.C. Died 1934.

ANDERSON, GEORGE MINOR physician, state health officer; b. Santa Rosa, Cal., July 12, 1873; s. Rev. John (D.D.) and Virginia (Drace) A.; A.B. amd A.M., Central Coll., Fayette, Mo., 1898; student U. Mo., 1900; M.D., U. Chgo., 1903; postgrad. Sch. Pub. Health, U. Cal., 1938; m. Nancy Esther Holden, Jan. 5, 1903; children-Stephen M., Virginia Lewis (Mrs. James H. Carlisle), Dorothy (Mrs. Morrie Dowd). Intern Chgo. Lying-In Hosp., 1903; practiced medicine, Casper, Wyo., 1917-23; state health officer and sec. Wyo. State Bd. of Health, 1923—. Mem. bd. regents U. Denver, 1912-14. Mem. exec. com. Assn. State & Territorial Health Officers, 1937-38. Served as capt. M.C., U.S. Army World War I. Mem. A.M.A., Wyo. State Med. Soc., Cheyenne Forum, Am. Legion, Sigma Nu.

Democrat. Presbyterian. Home: 220 East 3d Av. Office: State Board of Health, Capitol Bldg., Cheyenne, Wyo. Died May 20, 1958

ANDERSON, GEORGE SMITH army officer; b. Bernardsville, N.J., Sept. 30, 1849; s. John Hill and Susan Ogden (Lewis) A.; unmarried. Grad. U.S. Mil. Acad., 1871; commd. 2d lt. 6th Cav., June 12, 1871; advanced through the grades to brig. gen., U.S.A., Mar. 20, 1911. retired Oct. 16, 1912. Home: Bernardsville, N.J. Died Mar 7, 1915.

ANDERSON, GEORGE THOMAS army officer; b. Ga., Mar. 3, 1824; s. Joseph Stewart and Lucy (Cunningham) A. Served as 2d lt. Ga. Mounted Volunteers, 1847-48; capt. 1st Cavalry, 1855-58; commd. col. 11th Ga. Regt., 1861; commanded brigade during Seven Days' conflicts in Peninsular Campaign, 1862, wounded 2d Battle Manassas, 1862; commd. brig. gen., 1862; served in battle for Round Top Hill, wounded at Devil's Den during Battle of Gettysburg. 1863; joined Gen. Longstreet in siege of Knoxville; served under Gen. Robert E. Lee until surrender at Appomattox; chief of police Atlanta (Ga.). Died Anniston, Ala., April 4, 1901.

ANDERSON, HARRY REUBEN army officer; b. Chillicothe, O., Jan. 20, 1844; s. Col. William Marshall and Eliza (McArthur) A.; captain's clerk in U.S. Navy, May 2, 1863-June 30, 1864; cadet U.S. Mil. Acad., July 1, 1864-Jan. 18, 1865; grad. Arty. Sch., 1875; m. Florence Allison, Aug. 26, 1869. Capt. 6th U.S. Vol. Inf., Apr. 28, 1865-June 12, 1866; 2d lt. 6th U.S. Inf., Mar. 7, 1867; advanced through the grades to col., Mar. 26, 1906; brig. gen., retired Apr. 5, 1907. Participated in campaign against Sioux Indians on Powder River, Neb., 1865; apptd. a.-d.-c. to Gen E. R. S. Camby, 1868; in campaign against Modocs, 1873 (hon. mention); against Sioux Indians, under Gen. Crook, 1876; against Bannocks, in Ore., 1877-78; served in Cuba and P.R. during Spanish-Am. War. Home: Circleville, O. Died Nov. 22, 1918.

ANDERSON, HENRY WATKINS lawyer; b. Dinwiddie County, Va., Dec. 20, 1870; s. Dr William W. and Laura (marks) A.; LL.B., Washington and Lee U., 1898, LL.D., 1916. Practiced at Richmond, 1898—, mem. Hunton, Williams, Anderson, Gay & Moore, 1901—. Rep. nominee for gov. of Va., 1921; apptd. trustee by U.S. Govt. for Armour & Swift interests in stock yards, 1921; special asst. to atty. gen. U.S., 1922-23; U.S. agent Mexican Claims Commn. 1924-26; counsel for recievers of Seaboard Air Line Ry., 1931-32, co-reciever, 1933-46; now chmn. bd. dirs. Seaboard Air Line R.R. Co. Mem. Nat. Comn. Law Observance & Enforcement, 1929. Pres. War Relief Assn. Va., 1915-17; chmn. Richmond chpt., dir. for Va., A.R.C., 1917; chmn. Roumanian Commn. Am. Nat. Red Cross, rank lt. col. in Roumania, fall of 1917-18; commr. of A.R.C. to Balkan States with rank lt. col., charge relief - there, Oct. 1918-Nov. 1919. Grand Comdr. Order of St. Sava, 1st Class, also 2d class, and Red Cross (all of Serbia); Comdr. Order of Regina Maria, 1st Cross Order of Regina Maria, 2d Class, Grand Officer Order of the Star, Comdr. of Crown, with swords (all of Roumania); Comdr. Royal Order of Saviour (Greece); Comdr. Order of St. Anne, with swords (Russia); Comdr. Order of Prince Danilo I (Montenegro); War Cross of Czechoslovakia; War Medal (Italy). Clubs: Commonwealth, Country of Va. (Richmond); Metropolitan (Washington). Home: Whippernock Manor, Sutherland P.O., Dinwiddie Va. Office: Electric Bldg., Richmond 19, Va. Died Jan. 7, 1954; buried Hollywood Cemetery, Richmond, Va.

ANDERSON, JAMES PATTON army officer; b. Franklin County, Tenn., Feb. 12, 1822. Raised Battalion of Miss Militia in Mexican War; elected to Miss Legislature, 1850, apptd. U.S. marshall for Territory of Wash., 1853; del. from Territory of Wash. to U.S. Congress, 1855; commd. col. in Fla. Militia, 1861; commd. brig. gen., 1862, fought at battles of Shiloh, Perryville, Murfreesboro, Chickamauga; commd. maj. gen. Confederate Army, 1864; comdr. Dist. of Fla.; surrendered at Greensboro, N.C., editor of agrl. paper, Memphis, Tenn., after Civil War. Died Memphis, Sept. 1, 1873

ANDERSON, JAMES ROY army officer; b. Racine, Wis., May 10, 1904; s. Niels and Inger Kerstine (Klausen) A.; B.S., U.S. Mil. Acad., 1926; M.S., Ordnance Tech. Sch. (U.S. Army), 1934; grad. Army Air Force Primary and Basic Flying Sch., 1936, Advanced Flying Sch., 1937, Tactical Sch., 1940; student special course, Columbia, 1940; m. Ester Katherine Hsu, June 1, 1927; children—Nancy Jo, James Roy. Commd. 2d lt., U.S. Army, 1926, promoted through grades to brig. gen., 1945; served with ordnance dept., 1931, with air corps, 1931-45; rated air observed, air pilot, sr. air pilot. Decorated Am. Defense Medal, European Theater Medal, Asiatic-Pacific Theater Medal. Home: 100 S. Hickory St., Fond du Lac, Wis. Address: care The Adjutant General's Office, War Dept., Washington 25, D.C. Died Feb. 27, 1945.

ANDERSON, JOHN EDWARD psychology; b. Laramie, Wyo., June 13, 1893; s. John August and Julia (Wilhelmson) A.; A.B., U. Wyo., 1914, LL.D., 1942; A.M., Harvard, 1915, Ph.D., 1917; m. Dorothea Lynde, Dec. 3, 1918; children-Frances Julia (Mrs. Louis J. Moran), John Lynde, Richard Davis, Theordore Robert, Dorothea Jean (Mrs. Martin A. Antman). Instr. psychology, Yale, 1917, 1919-21, asst. prof., 1921-25; prof. psychology Inst. Child Devel., U. Minn., 1925-61, dir. Inst., 1925-54, emeritus 1961-; vis. prof. U. Chgo., U. Cal. at Los Angeles, summers 1939, 49. Chmn. sect. child welfare Minn. Def. Council 1941-45. Served as 1st lt. U.S. Army, chief psychol. examiner, sr. instr. Sch. Mil. Psychology Camp Greenleaf, 1917-19. Chmn. com. on edn. and tng. infant and presch. child, White House Conf. on Child Health and Protection, 1929-31; mem. White House Conf. on Children and Youth, 1940, 1950; NRC (chmn. com. on child devel. 1928-32; mem. div. anthropology and psychology, 1931-34, 1943-46); mem. Social Sci. Research Council, 1929-32; chmn. Com. on Exceptional Child, Nat. Congress Parents and Tchrs., 1937-43, Nat. Conf. on Aging, 1950, Minn. Commn. on Aging 1951-53 (chmn. com. on Living Arrangements); mem. nat. adv. com. for 1960 White House Conf. on research in psychol. and social scis. Fellow A.A.A.S. (sec. psychol. sect. 1929-33, v.p. 1934); mem. Soc. for Exptl. Biology and Medicine, Am. Psychol. Assn. (sec., 1923-25; mem. council, 1926-28, 1934-37; pres. 1942-43; pres. div. on Childhood and Adolescence, 19 Assn., Sr. Neighbors Chattanooga (mem. bd.), Soc. Research in Child Devel. pres. (1942), Minn. Acad. Sci. (v.p. 1944-45), Gerontol. Soc., Phi Beta Kappa, Sigma Xi, Phi Delta Kappa, Delta Sigma Rho, Sigma Alpha Epsilon. Club: Campus. Author numerous books, 1927-, also editor Editor: Psychological Aspects of Aging, 1956. Asso. editor Gerontologist, 1961-. Home: Wideview, Route 4, Chattanooga 9. Died May 10, 1966.

ANDERSON, JOSEPH senator, jurist; b. nr. Phila Nov. 5, 1757; s. William and Elizabeth (Inslee) A: m. Only Patience Outlaw, 1797, Capt., 1777, maj., 1783; admitted to bar; apptd. U.S. judge of Territory South of the Ohio River, 1791-96; mem. U.S. Senate from Tenn., 1797-1815; 1st comptroller U.S. Treasury, 1815-36; trustee Blount Coll., Washington Coll. (Tenn.); charter mem. Del. chpt. Soc. of the Cincinnati; Anderson County (Tenn.) named for him. Died Washington, D.C., Apr. 17, 1837; buried Congressional Cemetery, Washington.

ANDERSON, LARZ diplomat; b. Paris, France, Aug. 15, 1866; s. Gen. Nicholas Longworth and Elizabeth Coles (Kilgour) A.; ed. abroad and at Phillips Exeter Acad.; A.B., Harvard, 1888; spent 2 yrs. in travel around the world; m. Isabel, d. Commodore George Perkins, U.S. Navy, June 10, 1897. Second sec. U.S. Legation and Embassy at London, 1891-93; 1st sec. and charge d'affaires, U.S. Embassy, Rome, 1893-97; capt. and asst. adj. gen. U.S.V., during Spanish-Am. War, 1898, acting as adj. gen. 2d Div. 2d Army Corps. E.E. and M.P. to Belgium, Aug., 1911-13; apptd. ambassador extraordinary and plenipotentiary to Japan, Nov., 1912, resigned with change of administration, 1913. Comdr. Order of St. Maurice and St. Lazarus (Italy). Grand Officer of Crown of Italy; Grand Cordon, 1st Class, Order of Rising Sun, Japan; Grand Cordon Order of Crown, Belgium. Republican. Episcopalian. Home: Washington, D.C. Died Apr. 13, 1937.

ANDERSON, RICHARD HERON army officer; b. Statesburg, S.C., Oct. 7, 1821; s. Dr. William Wallace and Mary (MacKenzie) A.; grad. U.S. Mil. Acad., 1842; m. Sarah Gibson, 1850, 2 children; m. 2d, Martha Mellette, 1874. Served with U.S. Army during Mexican War, also on Western Frontier; brevetted 1st lt. for services during Battle of Vera Cruz, 1848 esied commn., 1861; commd. col. 1st S.C. Inf. Regt., 1861l, brig. gen. 1861, Confederate Army, 1861; brigade comdr. Army of No. Va., 1862; commd. maj. gen., 1862, div. comdr.; served in battles of Seven Pines, Seven Days, 2d Bull Run, Manassas, Harper's Ferry, Chancellorsville, Crampton's Gap, Fredericksburg, Gettysburg, Spotsylvania Court House, Cold Harbor; one of 3 famous div. comdrs. of Robert E. Lee; held temporary rank of lt. gen., 1864; employed by S.C. R.R. Co. after Civil War; state insp. Phosphates S.C. Died Beaufort, S.C., June 26, 1879.

ANDERSON, ROBERT EARLE naval architect, writer: b. Trenton, N.J., Feb. 18, 1881; s. Robert Morris and Frances (Baily) A.; C.E., Princeton U., 1903; student naval architecture, U. Glasgow, 1903-04; m. Emily Hays Farr, June 6, 1906; children-Edith (Mrs. Harold E. Smith), Helen (Mrs. James B. Daly), Robert Earle. Began as naval architect, 1904; with U.S. Navy Dept., Bur. Constrn. and Repair, 1904-13; asst. to mng. dir. Lake Torpedo Boat Co., 1913-14; gen. mgr. Augusta-Savannah Nav. Co., 1914-15, successively asst. to gen. supt., indsl. engr., comptroller, treas., and v.p. in charge finance Winchester Repeating Arms Co., 1915-24, also officer or dir. various subsidiaries and pres. Barney & Berry, Inc., sec. and treas. Winchester Co. and v.p. Simmons Hardware Co., comptroller, later gen. supt. and treas. R. Hoe & Co., N.Y.C., 1924-26; comptroller, later treas. and in gen. charge contracts, bus. relations, etc., Elec. Research Products, Inc. and officer various subsidiary cos., 1927-35; pres. Exhibitors Reliance Corp.; financial v.p. Paramount Pictures, Inc., and officer various subsidiary cos., 1935-36; in private cons. practice, 1937; dir. finance U.S. Maritime Commn., 1938-64; mem. adv. bd. Columbus Circle Br., l)frs. Trust Co. N.Y. Fellow Am. Geog. Soc.; mem. Princeton Engring. Assn. (ex-pres.), Soc. Colonial War, Soc. Naval Architects and Marine Engrs., Am. Acad. Polit. and Social Sci., (asso.) U.S. Naval Inst., Propeller Club, Port of N.Y., Phi Beta Kappa. Republican. Presbyn. (elder) Author: General Specifications for Building Ships of the United States Navy, 1908; The Merchant Marine and World Frontiers, 1945; Liberia, America's African Friend, 1952; numerous articles in tech. and bus. periodicals. Inventor of cage mast used on U.S. battleships. Home: 11 Sussex Av., Chatham, N.J. Died Winston-Salem, N.C. Mar. 1967.

ANDERSON, RUDOLPH JOHN biochemist; b. Harna, Sweden, Sept. 13, 1879; s. Anders and Johanna (Johanson) A.; came to U.S., 1893; Ph.G., New Orleans Coll. of Pharmacy, 1903; B.S. Tulane U., 1906, grad. work, 1906-07; grad. work, Upsala U., Sweden, 1909-10, Berlin U., 1910-11, 14, Univ. Coll., London, 1914-15; Ph.D., Cornell University 1919; hon. Ph.D., Lund University, Sweden, 1947; m. Clara Tillinghast, Jan. 3, 1920. Asso. in chemistry, N.Y. Agrl. Expt. Sta., Geneva, N.Y., 1911; biochemist same 1919; chief in research biochemistry, also prof. Cornell U., 1920-27; prof. chemistry, Yale U., 1927-48; fellow Calhoun College. Mem. editorial board Jour. of Biol. Chemistry; mem. board of scientific advisors, The Jane Coffin Childs Memorial Fund for Medical Research. Served as captain San. Corps, U.S.A., 1917-18; sr. instr. Sch. of Nutrition, Camp Greenleaf, Ga., July-Dec. 1918; maj. San Res. Corps since 1921. Awarded Trudeau Medal, 1948. Fellow A.A.A.S.; mem. Am. Chem. Soc., Trudeau Soc. (hon.), Am. Soc. of Biological Chemists (v.p., 1939-40; pres., 194-43), Soc. for Exptl. Biology and Medicine, National Academy of Science, Sigma Xi. Republican. Specializing in chem. problems dealing with plant products having biol. significance and in the chemistry of bacteria. Contbr. to Jour. Biol. Chemistry, Jour. Am. Chem. Soc., etc. Home: 101 Cottage St., New Haven, Conn.; also Nut Plains Rd., Guilford, Conn. Died Apr. 6, 1961; buried Brookside Cemetery, Englewood N.J.

ANDERSON, RUDOLPH MARTIN zoologist, govt. official, writer; b. near Decorah, Ia., June 30, 1876; s. John Emmanuel and Martha Ann (Johnson) A.; Ph.B., U. of Ia., 1903, Ph.D., 1906; m. Mae Belle Allstrand, Jan. 22, 1913 (dec. Mar. 1960); children-Dorothy, Mary, Isabel. Asst. in zoology, asst. curator Mus. Natural History, U. Ia., 1902-06; instr. and asst. comdt. Blees Mil. Acad., Macon, Mo., 1906-08; field agt., asst. in mammalogy and explorer, Am. Mus. Nat. History, New York, 1908-13; zoologist Geol. Survey of Can., Ottawa, Can., 1913-20; chief of div. of biology National Museum of Canada, 1920-46, hon. curator in mammalogy since 1946. Active in biol. and anthropol. exploration, Arctic Alaska. Yukon, Ty., and Northwest Territories, Can., 1908-12; chief of southern party Canadian Arctic Expdn., 1913-16; gen. editor sci. reports of expdn. since 1919; investigated 28 provisional wildlife sanctuaries in Prairie provinces, Nat. Parks Bur., 1918-19; naturalist on Canadian Arctic expdn. to Greenland and Canadian Arctic Archipelago, 1928; Columbia and Kootenay valleys, Southern B.C., and Nat. Parks, 1938-39. Served with Co. I, 52nd Iowa Inf., Spanish-Am. War, 1898; 54th Inf., N.G. of Ia., 1900-06; staff capt., N.G. of Mo., 1906-08. Awarded Spanish-Am. War medal, expert rifleman medal with bars; King George VI Coronation medal. Knight Officer International Order, St. Hubert, 1951. Mem. adv. bd. on wild life protection. Can., 1917-46; mem. library com. of Geol. Survey and Nat. Mus. of Can., also Northern adv. bd. and interdeptl. reindeer com. Fellow Royal Soc. of Can.; mem. Wildlife Soc., Biol. Soc. of Washington, D.C., (hon.) Ornithologische Verein zu Dresden, (corr.) Zool. Soc. (London), La Societe Provancher d'histoire naturelle du Can., Am. Soc. Mammalogists (charter mem. 1919; bd. dirs. 26 yrs.; vice pres. 1946), Am. Ornithol. Union (asso. 1906, mem. since 1914), Am. Soc. Ichthyologists and Herpetologists (bd. govs, since 1946), Pacific Northwest Bird and Mammal Soc., Ottawa Field-Nat. Club. Wilson Ornithol. Club, Cooper Ornithol. Club of Calif., Sigma Xi, Sigma Alpha Epsilon. Mason. Author: Birds of Iowa, 1907; Methods of Collecting and Preserving Vertebrae Animals, (bull.), 1932, revised edit., 1948; Catalogue of Can. Recent Mammals (bull.), 1947. Asst. editor Can. Naturalist since 1917. Contbr. numerous papers in sci. jours. and govt. reports. Hon. mem. Arctic Inst. N.A., 1956. Home: 58 Driveway. Office: National Museum of Canada, Ottawa, Ont., Can. Died June 21, 1961; buried Beechwood Cemetery, Ottawa, Ont., Can.

ANDERSON, SAMUEL congressman, physician; b. Middletown, Pa., 1773; studied medicine. Began practice medicine, 1796; became asst. surgeon U.S. Navy, 1799, promoted surgeon, 1800-01; began practice medicine, Chester, Pa., 1801; raised a co. volunteers known as Mifflin Guards, War of 1812; commd. capt. Pa. Militia, 1814, promoted lt. col. 100th Regt., 2d Brigade, 3d Div., 1821; mem. Pa. Ho. of Reps., 1815-18, 23-25, 29-35, speaker, 1833; sheriff Delaware County, 1819-23; reentered naval service as spl. physician to Adm. David Porter (comdr. W. Indian Squadron), 1823, resigned because of ill health; mem. U.S. Ho. of Reps. from Pa., 20th Congress, 1827-29; apptd. insp. customs, 1841; justice of peach, 1846-50. Died Chester, Jan. 17, 1850; buried Middletown Presbyn. Cemetery, nr. Media, Pa.

ANDERSON, THOMAS MCARTHUR army officer; b. Chillicothe, O., Jan. 21, 1836; s. William Marshall and Eliza (McArthur) A.; grad. Mt. St. Mary's Coll., Md., 1855 (LL.D.); grad. Cincinnati Law Sch., 1858; admitted to Ohio bar, 1858, Ky. bar, 1859; practiced law, 1858-61; m. Elizabeth Van Winkle, 1869. Pvt. Co. A, 6th Ohio Inf., Apr. 20, 1861; advanced through the grades to brig. gen. U.S. Army, Mar. 31, 1899; retired by operation of law, Jan. 21, 1900. Bvtd.: maj., Aug. 1, 1864, "for gallant services in Battle of Wilderness"; lt. col., Aug. 1, 1864, for same in battle of Spottsylvania. Comd. 1st land forces taking Manila, Aug. 13, 1898; comd. 1st div. 8th Army Corps in battles of Santana, San Pedro, Passe and Guadalupe, Feb. 5-Mar. 17, 1898. Mason. Home: Vancouver, Wash. Died May 8, 1917.

ANDERSON, WILLIAM A. lawyer; b. Boteourt County, Va.; s. Judge Francis T. and Mary Ann (Alexander) A.; ed. Washington Coll. (now Washington and Lee U.); LL.B., U. of Va., 1866; hon. LL.D. from Hampton-Sydney Coll., Virginia; m. Maza Blair, Aug. 9, 1875; children—Ruth Floyd (wife of Dr. Charles McCulloch), Anna Aylette (Mrs. C. S. McNulty), Maj. W. D. A., Judith N., Ellen Graham. Served in 4th Va. Inf., Stonewall Brigade, 1861; wounded, battle Manassas. Admitted to bar, 1866. Mem. Va. Senate, 1869-73; House of Delegates, 3 terms; U.S. commr. Paris Expn., 1878; atty.-gen. of Va., 1902-10. Mem. Va. Constl. Conv., 1901-02. Trustee Washington and Lee U., 1885—, and rector, 1914-23. Home: Lexington, Va. Died June 21, 1930.

ANDRADE, CIPRIANO rear adm. U.S. Navy; b. Tampico, Mex., Sept. 1, 1840; s. Cipriano and Elizabeth (Edwards) A.; ed. pub. and pvt. schs., Phila., to 1857; studied engring. at Franklin Inst., in connection with practical course at Southwark Foundry, Phila., 1858-61; m. Annie A. Berry, June 1, 1870. Apptd. 3d asst. engr., July 1, 1861; advanced through the grades to capt. navy on active list, Mar. 3, 1898; rear adm., retired, July 1, 1901, under naval personnel act. Took part in various engagements in Civil War, and afterward in active service as engr. officer of navy; active service during Spanish War on shore and afloat. Died 1911.

ANDRESS, ROBERT JOSEPH business exec.; b. Cin., May 16, 1910; s. William Thomas and Stella (Frankenstein) A.; student pub. schs.; m. Christine Rimes, Feb. 14, 1937; children-Sharon Christine, William Charles. Exec. sec. tax survey com. Tex. State Legislature, 1931-32; sec. to mgr. Tex. Motor Transp. Assn., 1932-35, acting mgr., 1935-36; admitted to Tex. bar, 1935, Okla., 1947; mgr. Herman Clary Trucking Co., 1936-38; sec., div. mgr. B.F. Walker, Inc., 1938-42; practice law, Ft. Worth, 1946; asst. traffic mgr. Eervice Pipe Line Co., 1946-47, dir. since 1948, v.p., 1952-55, exec. v.p., 1955-. Served as 2d lt. to capt. Transp. Corps, AUS, 1942-45). Decorated Bronze Star, Croix de Guerre, (France) Mem. Am. Okla., Tex. bar assns., I.C.C. Practitioners Assn., Shippers Oilfield Traffic Assn. (chmn), Am. Petroleum Inst., Am. Dialect Soc. Clubs: Tulsa Traffic, Tulsa. Home: 3126 E. 41st St., Tulsa 5. Office: 116 E. Sixth St., Tulsa. Died Oct. 19, 1966.

ANDRETTA, S(ALVADOR) A(NTONIO) govt. ofcl.; b. Hartford Conn., Sept. 2, 1898; s. Antonio Salvador and Felicia (Pallotti) A.; A.B., Tuck Sch. Bus. Adminstrn., Dartmouth, 1920; LL.B., Yale, 1923; m. Patricia Collins, Apr. 10, 19 marriage)-Daniel Bennett, Gage. Admitted to bar 1934, in practice of law, 1923-26, 1932-35; pres. Pallotti, Andretta & Co., Inc., New Haven and Hartford; v.p., dir. Riverside Trust Co., Hartford, 1926-31; spl. asst. to atty. gen. Dept. Justice, 1935-44, exec. asst., 1944-45, adminstrv. asst., 1945-50; apptd. adminstrv. asst. atty. gen., 1950. Served chief q.m. (aviation) USNR, World War I. Mem. Am. Bar Assn., Conn. Bar, Phi Sigma Kappa, Dragon Sr. Soc. Home: 2500 Q St., N.W., Washington. Died Oct. 18, 1965; buried Greenwood Cemetery, West Avon, Conn.

ANDREW, A(BRAM) PIATT congressman; b. La Porte, Ind., Feb. 12, 1873; s. Abram Piatt and Helen (Merrell) A.; B.A., Princeton, 1893, M.A. (hon.), 1923; univs. of Halle, Berlin, Paris, 1897-99; A.M., Ph.D., Harvard, 1900. Instr. and asst. prof., economics, Harvard, 1900-09; expert asst. and editor of publs. of Nat. Monetary Commn., 1908-11; dir. of the mint, Nov. 1909-June 1910; asst. sec. of the Treasury, 1910-12; elected mem. 67th Congress, 6th Mass. Dist. to fill vacancy, Sept. 1921; reelected 68th to 74th Congresses (1927-37). Republican. Commd. maj. U.S.N.A., Sept. 1917; lt. col. Sept. 1918; served in France, first with the French, later with U.S. Army, Dec. 1914-May 1919; organized and directed Am. Field Service with the French Army (consisting of 44 vol. ambulance and transport sections), 1914-17. Awarded Croix de Guerre and named Chevalier de la Legion d'Honneur, 1917; Officier de la Legion d'Honneur, 1927; D.S.M. (U.S.), 1919; Officer Order of Leopold (Belgium). Treas. Am. Red Cross, 1910-12; del. Internat. Conf. of Red Cross, 1912; del. Rep. Nat. Conv., 1924 and 1928; del. of Am. Legion to Fidac Congress, Rome, 1925. Trustee Princeton U. Home: Gloucester, Mass. Died June 3, 1936.

ANDREW, HENRY HERSEY b. Boston, Mass.; Apr. 26, 1858; s. Gov. John A. (was gov. of Mass.) and Eliza Jones (Hersey) A.; student Harvard, 1880-81; U. of Ga.

Law Sch., 1888; 3 yrs. in Europe; married; children—Beatrice, Margaret Forrester; m. 2d, Mary Raymond Garrettson, Jan. 16, 1901; 1 son, John Albion II (dec.). Admitted to W.Va. bar, 1888; Rep. nominee for W.Va. Senate, 1898; founder West Virginia News, Ronceverte, 1898. Commd. capt. W.Va. Militia, Nov. 16, 1887; raised 2d Regt. and commd. col., Mar. 31, 1888; with Am. Red Cross in France and Eng., May 6-Nov. 7, 1918; rank of capt. U.S.A. (assimilated). Republican. Episcopalian. Mason. Home: New York, N.Y. Died Aug. 9, 1934.

ANDREWS, ADOLPHUS retired naval officer, business executive; born in Galveston, Texas, on October 7, 1879; son of Adolphus Rutherford and Louise Caroline (Davis) A.; ed. U. of Tex., 1896-97; grad. U.S. Naval Acad., 1901, U.S. Naval War Coll., 1920; m. Berenice Waples Platter, Sept. 16, 1914; children—Frances Waples, Adolphus. Ensign, 1901; promoted through grades to rear admiral Jan. 1934; attached to U.S.S. Dolphin as jr. naval aide to President Theodore Roosevelt, 1904-06; aide to supt. U.S. Naval Acad., 1911-14; gunnery officer U.S.S. Michigan, took part in landing at Vera Cruz, 1914; exec. officer U.S.S. Mississippi, 1917-18; comdg. U.S.S. Massachusetts, 1918; comdg. U.S.S. Mayflower, sr. naval aide to President Harding, 1922; escorted President Harding to Alaska; comdg. U.S.S. Mayflower, sr. naval aide to President Coolidge, 1923-26; naval rep. Disarmament Conf. Geneva, 1926, 27; comdg. Submarine Base, New London, Conn., 1927-29, U.S.S. Texas, 1929-31; chief of staff Naval War Coll., 1931-33; chief of staff Battle Force, 1933; chief of staff, U.S. Fleet, 1934, 35; chief of Bur. of Navigation, 1935-38; vice admiral commanding Fleet Scouting Force, 1938-41; comdt. Third Naval Dist. and comdr. North Atlantic Naval Frontier, 1941-42; vice adm. comdg. Eastern Sea Frontier, 1942-43; vice admiral retired on special duty, Navy Dept., Washington, D.C.; relieved of active duty, July 1, 1945; commr. Pacific Ocean Areas Nat. Red Cross, Honolulu, T.H., 1945-46; now president Waples-Platter Co., Fort Worth, Texas. Episcopalian. Mason. Home: Dallas, Tex. Office: Andrews Bldg., Dallas, Tex. Died June 19, 1948.

ANDREWS, CHRISTOPHER COLUMBUS soldier, diplomat; b. at Hillsboro, N.H., Oct. 27, 1829; s. Luther and Nabby (Beard) A.; attended Francestown Acad. and Harvard Law Sch.; admitted to Mass. bar, 1850; m. Mary Baxter, Dec. 1868 (died 1893). West to Kan., 1854, later St. Cloud, Minn.; served in Union Army as capt. 3d Minn. Inf., Nov. 4, 1861; lt. col., Dec. 1, 1862; col., Aug. 9, 1863; brig. gen. vols, Jan. 5, 1864; bvtd. maj. gen. vols., Mar. 9, 1865; hon. mustered out, Jan. 15, 1866, U.S. Minister to Sweden and Norway, 1869-77; supervisor U.S. Census, Minn., 1880; counsul gen., Rio de Janeiro, 1882-85; forestry commr. of Minn., 1895-1911; sec. Minn. Forestry Bd., 1899-1923. Author: History of Campaign of Mobile, 1867; Brazil, Its Conditions and Prospects, 1886; Administrative Reform, etc. Furnished report on forestry of Sweden to U.S. Dept. of State, 1872; 16 of his ann. reports on forestry have been published. Home: St. Paul, Minn. Died Sept. 21, 1923.

ANDREWS, CLARENCE EDWARD college prof.; b. N.Y. City, Nov. 25, 1883; s. William Sturgis and Ida Augusta (Clark) A.; B.A., Yale, 1906, M.A., 1908, Ph.D., 1912; unmarried. Instr. English, Yale, 1908-09; Amherst, 1909-11, asst. prof. same coll., 1911-14; asst. prof. English, Ohio State U., 1915—. Commd. 1st lt., Air Service U.S.A., Oct. 8, 1917, duty at Washington, D.C.; with A.E.F. in France, 1918-19; attached to Balkan Div. of Am. Commn. to Negotiate Peace, Paris, Feb.-May 1919; officer Am. relief adminstrn. in Serbian Macedonia, summer 1919. Awarded Madaille de Misericorde (Serbia); Chevalier Order of St. Sava (Seroia). Author: Richard Brome, A Study of His Life and Works, 1913; From the Front, 1918; Writing and Reading of Verse, 1918; Old Morocco and the Forbidden Atlas, 1922; The Innocents of Paris, 1928. Compiler and editor: Romantic Poetry (with M.O. Percival), 1924; Victorian Poetry (with same), 1924; The Poetry of Eighteen Nineties (with same), 1926. Home: Columbus, O. Deceased.

ANDREWS, CLAYTON FARRINGTON surgeon; b. St. Paul, Neb., Jan. 4, 1891; s. Ernest Irving and Pearl Josephine (Waite) A.; Ph.G., Creighton Coll. Pharmacy, Omaha, 1909; postgrad. U. Neb., 1910-12; M.D., U. Pa., 1916; M.S. in Surgery, Mayo Clinic and Post Grad. Sch., U. Minn., 1923; m. Mildred Rae Wells, Aug. 28, 1919; 1 son, David Irving. Began practice surgery, 1923; attending surgeon Lincoln Gen. and Bryan Meml. hosps. Chmn. med. sect. Neb. Civilian Def. Com. Served as 1st lt. M.C., U.S. Army, 1917-19; comdr. M.C. USNR (ret.). Treas. Neb. Med. Found.; mem. Exec. Council, Order of deMolay. Fellow A.C.S., Ex-residents Assn. of Mayo Clinic; Diplomate Am. Bd. Surgery; mem. A.M.A., Neb. State Med. Soc. (past pres.), Lancaster County Med. Soc. (past pres.), S.A.R., Delta Upsilon (past pres.), Phi Rho Sigma, Republican. Ch. of Holy Trinity (sr. warden emeritus). Mason (33 , K.T.), Shriner; Past Protentate Sesstoris Temple; pres. Central States Shrine Assn., 1946; imperial potentate 1959-60). Clubs: Country (pres. 1938), University, Polemic (Lincoln); Newcomen Society (Eng.). Contbr. surg. articles to various. med. jours. Home: 2626 S. 24th St., Lincoln 2, Neb. Died Mar. 27, 1964.

ANDREWS, E(LISHA) BENJAMIN educator; b. at Hinsdale, N.H., Jan. 10, 1844; s. Erastus and Almira (Bartlett) A.; served pvt. to 2d lt. in Union Army in Civil War; wounded at Petersburg, Aug. 24, 1864, losing an eye; A.B., Brown U., 1870, A.M., 1873; Newton Theol. Inst., 1872-74; matriculated universities of Berlin and Munich, 1882-83 (D.D., Colby, 1884; LL.D., U. of Neb., 1884, Brown, 1900, U. of Chicago, 1901; Ph.D., U. of Neb., 1912); m. Ella Anna Allen, Nov. 25, 1870. Principal of the Conn. Lit. Instn., Suffield, 1870-72; ordained Bapt. ministry, 1874; pastor Beverly, Mass., 1874-75; pres. Denison U., Granville, O., 1875-79; prof. homiletics, Newton Theol. Instn., 1879-82; prof. history and polit. economy, Brown U., 1882-88; prof. polit. economy and finance, Cornell, 1888-89; pres. Brown U., 1889-98; supt. schs., Chicago, 1898-1900; chancellor U. of Neb., 1900-08, emeritus. Author: Institutes of Constitutional History, English and American, 1884; Institutes of General History, 1885, 1895; Institutes of Economics, 1889, 1900; Outlines of the Principles of History (transl. from Droysen), 1890; Eternal Words (sermons), 1893; An Honest Dollar, 1894; Wealth and Moral Law, 1894; History of the United States, 1894, 1902; History of the Last Quarter Century in the United States, 1896; Cosmology, 1900; History of the United States in our Own Times, 1904; The Call of the Land, 1913. Died Oct. 30, 1917.

ANDREWS, ELMER FRANK indsl. relations cons. and consulting engr.; b. N.Y.C., Nov. 22, 1890; s. Frank Henry and Lillian Marcella (Baker) A.; C.E., Rensselaer Poly. Inst., 1915; m. Ruth Mivda Reid, Feb. 21, 1913 (dec. Dec. 8, 1944); children-William Reid (USNR), Jean Elinor, Daphne Frank; m. 2d, Mildred Gwin Barnwell, June 2, 1945. Began as civil engr., 1915; engaged in railway constrn., U.S. and Cuba, and in safety engring.; served on compensation Ins. Rating Bd., N.Y.C.; mgr. bridges and highways bur. Queensboro (N.Y.) C. of C., 1927-29; cons. engr., Queens Boro Planning Commn., N.Y.C., 1927-29; dep. indsl. commr. of N.Y. State, 1929-33, indsl. commr., 1933-38; mem. Anthracite Fact Finding Commn., NLRB, 1933; 1st adminstr. wage and hour div., U.S. Dept. of Labor Conf., Geneva, Switzerland, 1934; mem. nat. panel Am. Arbitration Assn. Lt., pilot, U.S. Army, World War I. Mem. Am. Assn. for UN, Soc. Profl. Engrs., Am. Soc. Safety Engrs., Am. Legion, Delta Tau Delta. Conglist. Mason. Contbr. articles engring. and labor to periodicals. Address: Boxley Hill, Box 96, Vienna, Va. Died Jan. 17, 1964; buried Arlington Nat. Cemetery, Arlington, Va.

ANDREWS, FRANK MAXWELL army officer; b. Nashville, Tenn., Feb. 3, 1884; s. James David and Louise (Maxwell) A.; student Montgomery Bell Acad., Nashville, 1897-1901; grad. U.S. Mil. Acad., 1906; student Air Corps Tactical Sch., 1927-28, Command and Gen. Staff Sch., 1928-29; grad. Army War Coll., 1933; m. Jeannette Allen, Mar. 16, 1914; children—Josephine, Allen, Jean. Commd. 2d lt. cav., June 12, 1906; through grades to col., Aug. 1, 1935; rank of lt. gen. (temp.), Sept. 19, 1941. Served in Philippine Islands, 1906-07; in Hawaii, 1911-13; served with Signal Corps (aviation sec.), 1917-20; served with Am. Forces in Germany, 1920-23; returned to U.S. as exec. officer. Kelly Field, 1923-25; mem. War Dept. Gen. Staff, 1934-35; apptd. temp. brig. gen., Air Corps, Mar. 1, 1935; temp. maj. gen., Air Corps, Dec. 27, 1935; commanding G.H.Q. Air Force, Mar. 1, 1935-Feb. 28, 1939. Apptd. brig. gen. U.S. Army, July 14, 1939; mem. War Dept. Gen Staff, 1939-40; comdr. Panama Dept. 1942; apptd. comdr. U.S. forces in European theater, Feb. 1943. Decorated Comdr. Order of the Crown (Italy). Clubs: Army and Navy, Metropolitan (Washington). Killed in airplane accident over Iceland, May 3, 1943.

ANDREWS, GARNETT lawyer; b. Washington, Ga., May 15, 1837; s. Judge Garnett and Annulet (Ball) A.; ed. Washington Male Acad. and Univ. of Ga.; m. Rosalie Champ Beirne of Va., 1867. Lt.-col. C.S.A., comd. 8th battalion Confed. Inf.; fought last action of any troops attached to Army of Northern Va., at Salisbury, N.C., April 12, 1865, three days after Appomattox, where, with 600 men, resisted Gen.Stoneman's whole div. until trains with officials and treasure from Richmond passed South; desperately wounded there in hand-to-hand combat, shot and sabered. Lawyer Yazoo City, Miss., until 1882; took leading part in overthrow of carpet-bag govt.; mem. Miss. legislature 1879-80; removed to Chattanooga 1882; mayor 1891-92. Author: Andrews' Mississippi Digest, 1881. Home: Chattanooga, Tenn. Died 1903.

ANDREWS, GEORGE LEONARD army officer, engr., educator; b. Bridgewater, Mass., Aug. 31, 1828; s. Manasseh and Harriet (Leonard) A.; grad. U.S. Mil. Acad., 1851. Assisted in constrn. of fortifications in Boston Harbor, 1851-54; instr. civil and mil engring. U.S. Mil. Acad., 1854-55; civil engr. in pvt. practice 1855-61; engr. Amoskeag Mfg. Co., Mfg. Co., Youngstown, O.; organizer Imperila Coal Manchester, N.H., 1855-57; commd. lt. col. 2d Mass. Inf., 1861; in command of a regt. at battles of Winchester and Cedar Mountain 1861-62; commd. col., 1862; commd. brig. gen. U.S. Volunteers, 1862; chief-of-staff of Gen. Banks, 1863; brigade comdr. Red River expdn., 1863; comdr. Corps d' Afrique (later known as U.S. Colored Troops), 1864; provost marshal gen. Army of Gulf, 1865; chief-of-staff to Gen. Canby, 1865; U.S. marshall for Mass.,

1867-71; prof. French, U.S. Mil. Acad., 1871-82, prof. modern langs., 1882-92; ret. from active duty, 1892. Died Brookline, Mass., Apr. 4, 1899.

ANDREWS, GEORGE LIPPITT brig. gen. U.S. Army; b. Providence, R.I., Apr. 22, 1828; s. George and Cornelia Augusta (Lippitt) A., ed. in grammar schs., Providence, R.I.; m. Alice Beverly Potter; m. 2d, Emily Kemble (Oliver) Brown, May 13, 1874; father of George A. In business life, June, 1841, at Providence, R.I., afterward New York, and St. Louis, 1858. Entered R.I. Militia, 1844, maj., 1848, col., 1853; resigned 1856; 2d lt. 2d Co., Mo. N.G., 1859; advanced through the grades to col. 25th U.S. Inf., Jan. 1, 1871; retired for age, Apr. 22, 1892; advanced to rank of brig. gen. retired, by act of Apr. 23, 1904. Supt. Indian Affairs for Ariz., July 1869-71. Served at beginning of Civil War through campaign under Gen. Nathan Lyon, 1861; wounded and horse killed under him at battle of Wilson's Creek, Mo., Aug. 10, 1861, while comdg. brigade and regt.; with Army of Potomac and engaged in its operations, 1862-63; organized and recruited 17th and 13th Inf., U.S. Army, 1863-66; in Indian Country west of the Mississippi for 25 yrs. Bvtd.: lt. col., Aug. 30, 1862, "for gallant and meritorious services at 2d Bull Run"; col. May 3, 1863, for same at Chancellorsville. Republican. Episcopalian. Home: Washington, D.C. Died July 19, 1920.

ANDREWS, JOHN NEWMAN brig. gen. U.S. Vols., retired April 1, 1899. b. "Andrusial" Wilmington, Del. Sept. 16, 1838; grad. U.S. Mil. Acad., 1860; m. Lucy McEntee. Served through Civil war; bvtd. capt. for gallantry, Cedar Mountain; maj., for same, Franklin, Tenn.; and lt. col. Served in Indian country and Spanish-Am. war. Home: Wilmington, Del. Died 1903.

ANDREWS, JUSTIN M(EREDITH) pub. health scientist and adminstrn.; b. Providence, Aug. 28, 1902; s. Clark Willett and Annie F. (Bliven) A.; Ph.B. cum laude, Brown U., 1923; ScD., Johns Hopkins 1926, LL.D., 1951; m. Arline S. Anderson, Sept. 24, 1927 (div.); children-Donald C., Theodore H.; m. 2d, Jean Simone Grant, Apr. 6, 1957; 1 stepson, Richard W. Grant. Instr. Johns Hopkins Sch. Hygiene and Pub. Health, 1926-27, asso. protozoology, 1927-30, asso. prof. protozoology, 1931-38; spl. mem. Rockefeller Found., 1929; vis. prof. parasitology U. Philippines, Manila, 1930-31; dir. div. malaria and hookworm service, Ga. Dept. Pub. Health, Atlanta, 1938-42; sr. zoologist U.S.P.H.S., Atlanta, 1941-42, dir., profl. functions, office Malaria control in war areas, 1946, dep. officer in charge, 1946-51, officer in charge communicable disease center, 1952, asst. surgeon gen., Bur. State Services, USPHS, 1953-75; dir. Nat. Inst. of Allergy and Infectious Disease, Nat. Insts. of Health, Bethesda, Md., 1957—. Cons. amebiasis, Fresnillo, Mex., 1931, malaria Venezuela, 1947, Iran, 1948, enteric infections Armed Forces Epidemiol. Bd., Europe and N. Africa, 1956; cons. med. adv. council Iran Found., 1953—; mem. Armed Forces Epidemiol. Bd. Commn. Enteric Infections, 1953—; mem. adv. com. malaria eradication PanAm. San. Bur., 1955—; mem. expert panel on malaria, AID; mem. psittacosis bd. Surgeon Gen. Pub. Health Service; dir. Gorgas Meml. Inst.; lectr. Harvard Med. Sch., Tulane Med. Sch., Emory U., Army and Navy Med. Grad. Schs. Served from maj. to col., AUS, 1942-46. Awarded Legion of Merit, 1944; Le Prince award Am. Soc. Tropical Medicine and Hygiene, 1960. Mem. bd. of editors Pub. Health Reports, 1952-55; editorial com. protozoologic mem. Journal Parasitology, 1949-53, editorial bd. Journal Nat. Malaria Soc., 1942-44, expert adv. panels on malaria and insecticides World Health Assn. (governing council, 1954—), A.A.A.S., Am. Acad. Microbiology, Royal Soc. Tropical Med. and Hygiene; mem. Am. Epdiemiol. Soc., Assn. Mil. Surgeons, Am. Acad. Tropical Med. (council 1947-51, treas. 1952-53), Am. Soc. Tropical Med. and Hygiene (pres. 1957), Am. Soc. Parasitologists (pres. 1961), Helminthological Soc. Washington, D.C. Pub. Health Assn., Belgian Soc. Tropical Med., Mexican Soc. Parsitology, Tropical Med. Assn. Wash. (Pres. 1955-56), Sigma Xi. Author: Problems and Methods of Reserach in Protozoology (with Robert Hegner), 1930. Contbr. to profl. publs. numerous articles on epidemiologic phases of protozoan diseases. Home: 8 North Dr., Bethesda 14. Office: Nat. Inst. of Allergy and Infectious Diseases, Nat. Insts. of Health, Bethesda, Md. Died June 29, 1967.

ANDREWS, LINCOLN CLARK ret. army officer; b. Owatonna, Minn., Nov. 21, 1867; s. Charles T. and Mary (Clark) A.; student Cornell U., 1888-89; grad. U.S. Mil. Acad., 1893; m. Charlotte Graves, Oct. 5, 1899; 1 son, John Graves. Commd. 2d lt., 3d Cav., June 12, 1893; promoted through grades to lt. col., June 28, 1917; served as brig. gen., U.S. Army. Aide to Gen. Sumner, comdg. cav. div., Battle of Santiago, 1898; instr. physics, U.S. Mil. Acad., 1899; in Phillippines, 1899-1903; 1st gov. Island of Leyte; participated in campaign against Lake Lanoa Moros; instr. cav. tactics, U.S. Mil. Acad., 1903-06; in Cuba, 1908-09; insp. instr. cav. N.Y. Nat. Guard, 1911-15; charge cav. instrs. 1st Plattsburg (N.Y.) Tng. Camp. 1915; duty, Phillippines, 1916-17; insp. gen. and charge tng. and instrn. of officers P.I. Div. Nat. Guard; col. inf., Camp Dix, N.J., Organized 3rd O.T.C., Dec. 1917, 304th Cav., U.S. Army, Leon Springs, Tex., Feb. 1918; brig. gen. 172d. inf. Brigade, 86th Div., Camp Grant, Ill.; took brigade to France, Aug. 1918; after armistice served as dep. provost marshal gen. at G.H.Q. til end of orgn.; ret. from active service at own request after 30 yrs. service, Sept. 30, 1919. In charge mil. tng. N.Y. State Universal Tng. Commn., Nov. 1920-May 1921; chief exec. N.Y. Transit Commn., May 1921-Jan. 1923; apptd. to recievership N.Y. and Queens County Ry. Co., 1923; asst. sec. of treasury, Apr. 1, 1925-Aug. 1, 1927; pres. Guardian Investment Trust, Hartford, Conn., Nov. 1, 1927-June 1928; pres. The Rubber Inst., Inc., June 1928-May 15, 1929; became chmn. bd. Internat. Development Corp., 1930. Author: Basic Course for Calvary, 1914; Fundementals of Military Service, 1916; Leadership & Military Training, 1918; Man Power, 1921; Military Man Power, 1921. Address: Grand Isle, Vt. Died Nov. 23, 1950

ANDREWS, LORIN coll. pres.; b. Ashland, O., Apr. l, 1819; s. Alanson and Sally (Needham) A., attended Kenyon Coll, 1838-40; m. Sarah Gates, Oct. 30, 1843; 3 children Supt. Union Sch., Massillon, O.; a founder Ohio State Tchrs. Assn., 1847; pres. Kenyon Coll., Gambier, O., 1853-61; col. 4th Ohio Volunteers, 1861. Died Gambier, Sept. 18, 1861; buried Kenyon Coll. Cemetery.

ANDREWS, MARTIN REGISTER coll. prof.; b. Meigs, O., Apr. 6, 1842; s. Seth and Elvira Thora A.; grad. McConnelsville (O.) High Sch., 1859; pvt. 62d Ohio Inf., 1861; in signal corps U.S. Army, 1863; 2d lt. and adj. 43d Battalion, Ohio Vol. Inf., 1863-64; A.B., Marietta Coll., 1869, A.M., 1872; m. Amanda Laughlin, Aug. 12, 1869; m. 2d, Susan K. Hook, Sept. 1, 1891. Supt. Steubenville (O.) Pub Sch., 1870-79; prin. Marietta Acad., 1879-94; prof. history and polit. science, Marietta Coll., 1895-1910; emeritus prof. on Carnegie Foundation, 1910—. Home: Marietta, O. Died Apr. 20, 1913.

ANDREWS, PAUL SHIPMAN lawyer: b. Syracuse, N.Y., Aug. 2, 1887; s. William Shankland and Mary Raymond (Shipman) A.; A.B., Yale, 1909; LL.B., Columbia, 1912; LL.D., St. Johns U., Bklyn., 1939; m. Hannah Sargent Sessions, Dec. 3, 1917; children-Nigel Lyon, William Shankland. Admitted to N.Y. bar, 1912, and began practice in Syracuse; mem. Andrews & Fox, 1914-17, Andrews & Andrews, 1919-26, Andrews, Andrews & McBride, 1926-36; part time instr., Syracuse U. Coll. Law, 1916-23, dean Coll. Law, 1927-52, dean emeritus since Sept. 1952; spl. cons. to Office of Sec. Defense, 1952-53; resumed legal practice as partner law firm, with Harold Herkimer McBride and Nigel Lyon Andrews, Syracuse, N.Y. On leave of absence, served as lt. col., A.U.S., dir. liaison and member faculty, Sch. of Military Govt., Charlottesville, Va., Apr. 1942-Aug. 1943. County atty. Onondaga Co., 1916-20; spl. asst. to atty. gen. (later Chief Justice) Harlan F. Stone, and dir. War Transactions Sect. of Dept. of Justice, 1924-26; spl. counsel in water power cases for State of Ny., 1930-32; counsel railway consolidation cases for Syracuse C. of C. and Syracuse Mfg. Assn., 1933; counsel Syracuse Charter Com. (draftsman of present charter of Syracuse). 1935. Served as capt. 151st F.A., U.S. Army, with A.E.F., 1917-18; officer Allied Mil. Govt., overseas, 1943-46; assigned as civil affairs officer in charge area in Italy, also commanding officer of group of refugee camps near Ancona; organized Italian committees for relief of devasted areas, Rome and Florence. Sec. finance com. N.Y. finance State Constitution Convention, 1915, co-chairman United World Federalists (N.Y. State Branch) since April 1948 (mem. Nat. and World Councils). Former pres. bd. trustees Court of Appeals Library, Syracuse, Gen. Hosp. of Syracuse. Mem. bd. trustees Manlius Sch., Manlius, N.Y. chmn. minimum wage bd. hotel industry State of N.Y. Mem. Internat., Am., N.Y. State Bar Assns., Onondaga County Bar Assn.; hon. mem. Vt. Bar Assn., Delta Kappa Epsilon. Republican. Episcopalian. Clubs: University, Century (Syracuse). Editor in chief Columbia Law Review, 1911-12. Home: "Wolf Hollow," Onondaga Rd., Onondaga Hill P.O., N.Y. Office: S.A. & K. Bldg., Syracuse, N.Y. Died Apr. 1967.

ANDREWS, PHILIP naval officer; b. N.Y. City, Mar. 31, 1866; grad. U.S. Naval Acad., 1886; m. Clara Fuller. 1 dau., Jean Andrews (Wife of C.C. Champion, Jr., U.S.N.). Ensign, July 1, 1888; promoted through grades to rear adm., July 1, 1918. Served on Bennington during Spanish-Am. War, 1898; on duty with gen. bd., Navy Dept. 1904-06; Bur. of Navigation, 1906-07; served on Kansas, 1907-09; at Naval War Coll., Newport, R.I., 1090; aide to Sec. of Navy, 1909-11; chief Bur. of Navigation, with rank of rear adm., 1911-13; duty gen., bd., 1913; comd. Montana, 1913, Maryland, 1913-14; comdr. Naval Training Sta., San Francisco, 1915-16; Naval War Coll., Newport, R.I., 1916-17; apptd. chief of staff, 5th Naval Dist., Mar. 29, 1917; comdr. Mississippi, Jan. 1918, U.S. Naval base, Cardiff, Wales, Sept. 1918, U.S. Navy Yard, Norfolk, Va., 1921-23; also comdt. 5th Naval Dist., Jan.-June 1923; U.S. naval forces Eastern Mediterranean, 1919-21; comdr. U.S. Naval Forces, Europe, with rank of vice adm., June 1923-Oct. 10, 1925; rear adm. comdg. 1st Naval Dist. and Navy Yard, Boston, 1925-30; retired Apr. 1, 1930. Address. Navy Dept., Washington. Died Dec. 19, 1945.

ANDREWS, ROLAND FRANKLYN editor; b. Hartford, Conn.; s. Charles B. and Alice J. (Andrews) A.; ed. Cayuga Lake Mil. Acad.: student Cornell U., 1896-98; m. Florence Benedict, June 17, 1916. Began as reporter, Syracuse Standard, later with Hartford Telegram; mng. editor Waterbury Republican, 1900-02; asso. editor Waterbury American, 1902-12; mng. editor Hartford Times, 1912-20; editor Worcester (Mass.) Telegram-Gazette, 1920—. Pvt., lt. and capt. Conn. N.G., 1910-17; served on Mexican border, 1916; capt. comdg. motor supply train 429, U.S. Army, 1917-18. Mem. U.S. Naval Inst. Unitarian. Mason. Home: Worcester, Mass. Died Dec. 21, 1930.

ANDREWS, SCHOFIELD, lawyer; b. N.Y.C., Aug. 7, 1889; s. Avery De Lano and Mary Campbell (Schofield) A.; grad. St. Paul's Sch., Concord, N.H., 1906; A.B., Harvard, 1910; LL.B., U. Pa., 1913; m. Lillian Forsyth Brown, Apr. 21,1921 (died May 1972); children—Schofield, Stuart Brown, Stockton Avery; m. 2d, Marie D. Grant, May 9, 1929. Admitted to Pa. bar, 1913, practiced in Phila.; mem. firm Ballard, Spahr. Andrews and Ingersoll, Phila., 1919-73. Served with U.S. Army, 1917-19; lt. col., asst. chief of staff, 90th Div., with A.E.F. Decorated D.S.M. Republican. Episcopalian. Club: Philadelphia. Home: Philadelphia PA Died May 1973.

ANDREWS, TIMOTHY PATRICK army officer; b. Ireland, 1794. Served in U.S. Navy in War of 1812; paymaster in army, 1822-47; commanded regt. of volunteers during Mexican War, 1847; served in Battle of Molino del Rey; brevetted brig. gen. for gallant conduct in Battle of Chapultepec; dep. paymaster gen. 1851; paymaster gen with rank of col. U.S. Army, circa 1861-64. Died Washington, D.C., Mar. 11, 1868.

ANDREWS, WALTER GRESHAM congressman; b. at Evanston, Ill., July 16, 1889; s. William Henry and Kate (Gresham) A.; grad. Lawrenceville (N.J.) Sch., 1908; LL.B., Princeton, 1913; unmarried. Head coach Princeton football team, 1913; dir. and mem. exec. com. Pratt & Lamberg, Inc. Mem 72d to 80th Congresses (1931-49), 42d New York Dist.; chmn. armed services com. With U.S. Army, Mexican Border and France, 1916-19, advancing to rank of major, 107th Inf.; wounded in attack on Hindenburg Line, 1918. Decorated Distinguished Service Cross. Member Am. Legion. Republican. Presbyterian. Clubs: Saturn, Buffalo; Tiger Inn (Princeton); Metropolitan (Washington). Home 172 Summer St. Office: U.S. Court House, Buffalo, N.Y. Died Mar. 5, 1949.

ANDRUS, CLIFT, army officer; b. Fort Leavenworth, Kan., Oct. 12, 1800; s. Edwin Proctor and Marie Josephine (Birdwell) A.; Cornell Univ., 1912; F.A. Sch., 1927-28, Command and Gen. Staff Sch., 1928-30, Army War Coll., 1933-34, Naval War Coll., 1934-35, 1939-40; D.Sc (hon.), Drexel Inst. Technology, 1951; m. Marion Eleanor Lightfoot, Feb. 15, 1918; children—Margaret Josephine (dec.), Marion (Mrs. Seferlis). Commd. 2d lt., 4th F.A., 1912, advanced through grades to major gen., 1945, ret., 1952. Decorated Distinguished Service Cross, Distinguished Service Medal, Silver Star with oak leaf cluster, Legion of Merit with oak leaf cluster, Soldiers Medal, Bronze Star Medal with oak leaf cluster. Mem. Seal and Serpent, Scabbard and Blade, Semaphore (Cornell). Died Sept. 1968; buried Arlington Nat. Cemetery, Arlington VA

ANDRUSS, E(LIAS) VAN ARSDALE brig. gen U.S.A.; b. Newark, N.J., Dec. 18, 1839; s. Isaac Mix and Lydia I. A.; grad. U.S. Mil. Acad., 1864, Arty. Sch., 1876; m. Elizabeth Kinne, 1868. Acting midshipman U.S.N., 1854-56; commd. 2d lt. 1st Arty., June 13, 1864; promoted through grades to col. Arty. Corps. Sept. 23, 1901; retired at own request after 40 yrs. service, Apr. 1, 1902; brig. gen. retired, by act of Apr. 23, 1904. Bvtd.; 1st lt., Apr. 2, 1865, for capture of Petersburg, Va.; capt. Apr. 9, 1865, for campaign ending with surrender of Confederate Army of Northern Va. Comd. defenses of the Delaware during Spanish-Am. War. Home: Brooklyn, N.Y. Died 1910.

ANGAS, W(ILLIAM) MACK civil engr.; b. Great Burdon, Eng., July 5, 1892; s. William Moore and Elizabeth (Mack) A.; came to U.S., 1895, naturalized, 1917; student Chestnut Hill Acad., Phila., 1911-13; B.S., Mass. Inst. Tech., 1917; m. Elizabeth Abbie Gale, Dec. 26, 1917 (dec. 1952); children-Elizabeth Gale, (Mrs. W.T. Hardaker), Mary Mack (Mrs. Arnold Dreyer, Jr.), Jean Moore (Mrs. Willard Starks), Frances Louise (Mrs. Fred Weaver), and Roberta Martin (Mrs. George B. Douglas); m. 2d, Katherine Tracy L'Engle, July 27, 1954. Instr. in nav., tng. officers for merchant service, Shipping Bd., Boston and Baltimore, 1917; commd. lt. (j.g.), Civil Engr. Corps, U.S. Navy, 1918 and advanced through the grades to rear adm., 1948; pub. works officer in charge constrn. work, Naval Air Sta., Pensacola, Fla., 1929-32, Navy Yard, Charleston, S.C., 1938-42, N.Y. Naval Shipyard (Brooklyn Navy Yard), 1942-43; joined staff comdr., 7th Fleet, Southwest Pacific area, 1943; officer in charge 3d Naval Constrn., Brigade and comdr. Constrn. Forces, 7th Fleet, in charge Seabees. Southwest Pacific Area, 1944-45; superintending civil engr. with consulting supervisory responsibility Bureau of Yards and Docks constrn. on East Coast 1945-48; dir., Atlantic Div., Bur. of Yards and Docks, with additional duty on staff of

Comdr. in Chief, U.S. Atlantic Fleet and on staff of Comdr. Eastern Sea Frontier, Mar. 1948-May 1950, ret. from active duty in navy with rank of vice admiral; apptd. chmn. civil engring. Princeton U.; cons. to State N.J. on beach erosion problems. Awarded Wason medal by Am. Concrete Inst., 1944; commended by sec. of navy for duty at N.Y. Naval Shipyard. Decorated Legion of Merit. Mem. Am. Soc. C.E., Am. Concrete Inst., N.J. Soc. Profl. Engrs., Theta Chi. Episcopalian. Clubs: N.Y. Yacht (N.Y.C.); Nassau. Author: Rivalry on the Atlantic, 1939. Contbr. tech. and semi-tech. articles to various tech. and boating publs. Home: 59 Coll. Rd. W., Princeton, N.J. Died Dec. 12, 1960; buried Arlington Nat. Cemetery, Ft. Myer, Va.

ANGELL, ISRAEL army officer; b. Providence, R.I., Aug. 24, 1740; s. Oliver and Naomi (Smith) A.; m. Martha Angell; m. 2d, Susanne Wright; m 3d, Sarah Wood; 17 children. Commd. maj. R.I. Volunteers at beginning of Revolutionary War; commd. maj. 11th Continental Inf., 1776; lt. col., then col. 2d R.I. Regt., 1777; served in siege of Boston, 1776-76, battles of Brandywine, Red Bank, 1777, Monmouth, 1778, Springfield, 1780; ret., 1781 Died Smithfield, R.I., May 14, 1832.

ANGELL, MONTGOMERY B(OYNTON), lawyer; b. Rochester, N.Y., May 18, 1889; s. Edward B. and Florence (Montgomery) A.; Litt.B. cum laude, Princeton, 1911; LL.B. cum laude, Harvard U., 1915; m. Ellen Shipman, Sept. 8, 1917; children-Montgomery B., Ellen Whitney(Mrs. Frank Streeter), Nicholas Biddle. Admitted to N.Y. bar, 1916, D.C. bar, 1921; with ICC, Washington, 1915-17; gen. counsel's office Fed. Res. Bd., Washington, 1919-21; with Stetson, Jennings & Russell and successor firms, now Davis, Polk, Wardwell, Sunderland & Kiendl, 1921—, mem. firm, 1927—. Commr. Taconic State Park Commission of N.Y., 1948-58, served as a major in the infantry of the U.S. Army, 1917-19. Decorated Crois de Guerre with gold star, French Army Corps citation, Mem. Am., N.Y. State bar assns., N.Y. Co. Lawyers' Assn. City N.Y. Clubs: Century Assn. Princeton, Down Town Assn. (N.Y.C.). Author: Valuation Problems, 1945. Contbr. articles law revs. Home: 1 E. 87th St., N.Y.C. 28. Office: 15 Broad St., N.Y.C. 5. Died Nov. 1959

ANGIER, ROSWELL PARKER psychologist; b. St. Paul, Minn., Oct. 21, 1874; s. Albert Edgar and Emma Frances (McNeil) A.; A.B., Harvard, 1897, A.M., 1901, Ph.D., 1903; studied at univs. of Berlin and Freiburg, Germany, 1903-06; A.M., Yale, 1917; m. Genevieve Severy, Sept. 2, 1907; children—Roswell Parker, James Severy, Philip Holt. Asst. Physiol. Lab., U. of Berlin, 1905-06; instr. psychology, Yale, 1906-08, asst. prof. 1908-17, prof., 1917-41, dir. Psychol. Lab., 1917-41, dean of freshmen, 1920—; prof. of psychology and dir. of Lab. of Psychology, emeritus, since 1941. Visiting prof. Harvard, 1917, U. of Chicago, 1925. Capt. sanitary corps, U.S. Army, 1918-19. Mem. Am. Psychol. Assn., Am. Philos. Assn., Am. Physiol. Cos., Delta Upsilon, Sigma Xi. Home: R.F.D. Route 4, Box 686, Tucson, Ariz. Died June 24, 1946.

ANGLE, GEORGE KEYSER oculist, aurist; b. Hainesburg, N.J., Oct. 12, 1865; s. Jacob Jay and Elisa Fulmer (Keyser) A.; A.B., Lafayette Coll., 1885, A.M., 1890; M.D. Bellevue Hosp. Med. Coll., 1891; m. Helen Goldthorpe Williams, Sept. 16, 1896; children—Mary Elisabeth (dec.), Katherine Goldthorpe, Richard Williams. Practiced at Richmond, Ind., Easton, Pa., Silver City, N.M., Albuquerque, N.M., 1916—. Capt. Med. Corps. U.S. Army, 1917; Gen. Hosp., Ft. Des Moines, Ia., June 1918 to close of war; sec. med. sect. N.M. Council Defense. Del. Dem. Nat. Conv., Baltimore, 1912. Wrote 1st state paper on Malta Fever in the Southwest, 1907; and many others on med. subjects. Home: Albuquerque, N.M. Deceased.

ANGLE, WESLEY MOTLEY telephone-tv mfr.; b. Rochester, N.Y., Dec. 17, 1882; s. Charles Edwin and Ida Jane (Motley) A.; grad. Bradstreet Prep. Sch., 1899; A.B., Harvard, 1903, A.M., 1904; m. Ann Van Vranken Warner, Nov. 24, 1909; children-Charles Edwin, Richard Warner, Eleanor (Mrs. Thomas Thacher Richmond), Janet (Mrs. E.A. Mays, dec.), George Motley. With Stromberg-Carlson Co., 1903-49, cable machine operator, stockroom clk., assembler, cost ckl., office mgr., asst. sec., asst. treas., sec., v.p., pres., chmn. bd. (pres. 1934-45, chmn. 1945, hon. chmn. 1949, dir., 1914-55); dir. Gen. Dynamics Corp.; dir. R. W. Angle Corp. (Marion, Mass.), Security Trust of Rochester. Served as capt. Q.M.C., U.S. Army, as chief purchase records br. Office of Dir. of Purchase, Washington, 1918-19. Dir., U.S.-Ind. Telephone Assn., 1940-49; dir. Asso. Inds. N.Y. State, 1935-50, N.A.M., (1941-43). Dir. Genesee Hosp.; hon. dir., Vis. Nurse Assn. Trustee Rochester Bur. Municipal Research; dir. Rochester Civic Music Assn, 1930-45. Trustee Rochester C. of C. Republican. Presbyn. Clubs: Country, Genesee Valley, Harvard (N.Y.C.); Brook-Lea. Home: 43 E. Blvd., Rochester, N.Y. Died Sept. 3, 1960.

ANKCORN, CHARLES M. brig. gen. U.S. Army, ret. Address: care Office of the Adjutant General, Dept. of the Army, Pentagon, Arlington, Va. Died Oct. 1, 1955.*

ANSELL, SAMUEL TILDEN, lawyer; b. Coinjock, N.C., Jan. 1, 1875; s. Henry Beasley and Lydia (Simmons) A.; grad. U.S. Mil. Acad., 1899; LL.B., U. of N.C., 1904; m. Elmeda Tracy, Feb. 16, 1904 (dec. 1944); children—Elmeda (dec.), Burr Tracy, Samuel Tilden, Nancy Lydia; m. 2d, Anne Clay Clay, Nov. 8, 1948. Commd. 2d lt. 11th Inf., Feb. 15, 1899; promoted through grades to brig. gen., Oct. 5, 1917. Instr. law, U.S. Mil. Acad., 1902-04, 1906-09; duty with civil govt. in Philippines as pros. atty., Moro Province, 1909-11; atty. for Porto Rico and Philippine Islands before Federal Courts of U.S., by spl. assignment of War Dept.; acting judge advocate gen. U.S. Army, 1917-18; inaugurated movement resulting in reformation of army courtmartial system and adoption of liberalized articles of war; resigned from army to resume practice of law, July 21, 1919. Awarded D.S.M. "for especially meritorious and conspicuous service" as acting judge advocate gen. Episcopalian. Home: 1957 Biltmore St., Washington, D.C.; (country) Rehoboth Beach, Del. Office: Tower Bldg., Washington DC

APPEL, THEODORE BURTON M.D.; b. Lancaster, Pa., Sept. 8, 1871; s. Rev. Theodore (D.D.) and Susan Burton (Wolff) A.; A.B., Franklin and Marshall, 1889, A.M., 1892; Sc.D., 1915; M.D., U. of Pa. 1894; m. Mary Calder, June 18, 1900; children—Mary Calder, Susan Burton, Ellen Ellery, Theodore Burton, James Ziegler. Interne. Presbyn. Hosp., Phila., 1894-96; in practice at Lancaster; med. dir. Lancaster Gen. Hosp., 1906-20; sec. Health Com., Pa., 1927-35. First lt. and asst. surgeon Battery C, N.G., Pa., 1905; commd. capt., Med. R.C. June 6, 1917; maj., Sept. 18, 1917; lt. col. Med. Corps U.S. Army, Nov. 6, 1918; lt. col. Med. O.R.C., 1919; col., 1924. Home: Lancaster, Pa. Died July 31, 1937.

APPLETON, FRANCIS HENRY agriculturist; b. Boston, June 17, 1847; s. Francis Henry and Georgiana Crowninshield (Silsbee) A.; A.B., Harvard, 1869. A.M., 1872, student Mass. Inst. Tech., m. Fanny Rollins Tappan, June 2, 1874 (died); m. 2d, Mary Spencer Tappan, Nov. 6, 1907 (died). Pvt. to capt. Mass. Vol. Militia; later commissary gen. of Mass.; then maj. gen., retired. Mem. Mass. Ho. ofRep., 1891, 1892, Senate, 1902, 1903; del. Rep. Nat. Conv., 1892. Curator Bussey Inst., 1873-75; mem. Mass. Bd. Agr., 1891-1907 (elected sec., 1887,but declined); reporter on agr. for Mass. commrs., Vienna Expn.,1873; mem. bd. commrs., Jamestown Expn., mem. bd. control Mass. Agrl. Expt. Sta. Pres. Perkins Instn. and Mass. Sch. for Blind, Watertown, Mass., for 33 years, retiring in 1933; trustee Peabody Mus. (Salem), Mass. Gen. Hosp., Mass. Soc. Promoting Agr. (sec. and ex-pres.). Home: Boston, Mass. Died Apr. 5, 1939.

APPLETON, FRANCIS RANDALL lawyer; b. New York, Aug. 5, 1854; s. Daniel F. and Julia (Randall) A.; A.B., Harvard, 1875; LL.B. Columbia, 1877; m. Fanny, d. Charles Lanier, October 7, 1884. Mem. Robins & Appleton, New York; dir. Waltham Watch Co., Mt. Morris Bank, Nat. Park Bank, etc. Overseer, Harvard U., 1903—. Maj. and insp. rifle practice, 2d Brigade, 1st Div., N.G.S.N.Y. Home: New York, N.Y. Died Jan. 2, 1929.

APPLETON, JESSE clergyman, coll. pres.; b. New Ipswich, N.H., Nov. 17, 1772; s. Francis and Elizabeth (Hubbard) A.; grad Dartmouth, 1792; m. Elizabeth Means, 1800, 6 children including Jane Means (wife of Pres. Franklin Pierce). Ordained to ministry Congregational Ch., Hampton, N.H., 1797; minister Congregational Ch., Hampton, 1797-1807; pres. Bowdoin Coll., 1807-19; mem. Acad. Arts and Scis.; trustee Phillips Exeter Acad. Author: The Works of Jesse Appleton, D.D., 1836, 3 editions. Died Brunswick, Me., Nov. 12, 1819.

ARCHER, ALLEN THURMAN ins. broker, counselor; b. Sedalia, Mo., Jan. 4, 1889; s. Richard Pinckney and Belle (Macdonald) A.; student Occidental Acad., Los Angeles, 1904-07; LL.B., U. of Southern Calif., 1910; m. Violet McIlwraith, June 25, 1924; children-David, John, Richard. Pres. Allen T. Archer Co., ins. brokers and counselors, Los Angeles, since 1921. Commd. 2d lt. and served as pilot, A.A.F., World War I; served on war bond coms.; chmn. spl. groups including social, fraternal and service orgns., clubs and professional groups in Los Angeles area, World War II. Mem. Nat. Assn. Ins. Brokers,Inc. (pres. 1946, bd. dirs. 1945-58), Ins. Brokers Soc. of Southern Calif. (pres. 1944), Town Hall of Los Angeles (pres. 1943), U. of Southern Calif. (hon. fellow 1938-49), Friends of the Colls. at Claremont (bd. dirs. 1938-49), Calif. State Bd. Edn. (1928-35), Gen. Alumni Assn. U. of Southern Calif. (pres. 1927-28). Mason (Shriner). Clubs: California, Los Angeles Country (Los Angeles, Cal.). Home: 10401 Wilshire Blvd., Los Angeles 24. Office: 3450 Wilshire Blvd., Los Angeles 5. Died Aug. 15, 1959; buried Forest Lawn Cemetery, Los Angeles.

ARCHER, CLIFFORD PAUL, educator; b. Troy, Ia., Nov. 18, 1893; s. John Franklin and Martha Emiline (Hunt) A.; grad. So. Ia. Normal, 1911; A.B., Ia. State Tchrs. Coll., 1920; M.A., U. Ia. 1923, Ph.D., 1927; m. Myrtle Blair, July 5, 1918; children—Blair, Philip, Helen (wife of Dr. Wilfred Lundblad), Stephen. Rural sch. tchr., Davis Co., Ia., 1912-13; prin. Libertyville (Ia.) Schs., 1913-14; supervisor rural schs., Limecreek, Ia., 1916-17; supt. schs., Hudson, Ia., 1920-22; instr. summer sch. Ia. State Tchrs. Coll., 1921-23; head dept. edn. State Tchrs. Coll., Moorhead, Minn., 1923-26, 27-37; asst. prof. edn., dir. bur. recommendations U. Minn., 1938-42, asso. prof., 1942-50, prof., 1951-68, program coordinator Peace Corps project 1962-63; chief field party Inst. Inter-Am. Affairs, Bolivia, 1950-51; edn. program officer, Washington, 1952-53. Chmn. Minn. Commn. Study and Improvement Instrn., 1955-57. Chief boatswain's mate USNR, 1918-19; lt. col. U.S. army, comdt. Armed Forces Inst., Southwest Pacific, 1943-45. Mem. Nat. Instnl. Tchrs. Placement Assn. (pres. 1946-47), Minn. (pres. 1938-40), Western Minn. (past exec. sec.) edn. assns., N.E.A. (chmn. com. internat. edn. rural dept.; president department of rural edn. 1960-61), Am. Ednl. Research Assn., Nat. Elementary Sch. Prins. Assn., Nat. Dept. Rural Edn. (pres. 1960-68), Am. Assn., Suprs. and Curriculum Dirs., Nat. Council Tchrs. English, Nat. Council Research in English, W. Minn. Schoolmasters (pres., exec. sec. 1924-37), Minn. Soc. Study (pres. 1958-59), Minn. Elementary Prins. Assn. (life), Phi Delta Kappa, Psi Chi, Delta Sigma Rho, Kappa Delta Pi. Mason. Author: Elementary Education in Rural Areas, 1957. Contbr. profl. jours. Home: St Paul MN Died Nov. 18, 1968; buried Sunset Meml. Park, Minneapolis MN

ARCHER, JAMES J. army officer; b. Stafford, Hartford County, Md., Dec. 19, 1817; attended Princeton, also Bacon Coll., Georgetown, Ky. Served in Mexican War; brevetted maj. U.S. Army for gallantry at battle of Chapultepec; discharged 1848; reentered U.S. Army as capt., 1855; entered Confederate Army, 1861; commd. brig. gen., 1862; led Archer's brigade in battles of Seven Days, Cedar Mountain, Second Manassas, Antietam, Fredericksburg, Chancellorsville, and Gettysburg, captured at Battle of Gettysburg, held prisoner for over year; died soon after release. Died Oct. 24, 1864.

ARCHER, JOHN physician, congressman, army officer; b. Hartford County, Md., May 5, 1741; B.A., Princeton, 1760; A.M., 1763, B.M., Phila. Coll. Medicine, 1768; m. Catherine Harris, 10 children (5 became doctors), including Stevenson. Commd. maj. Continental Army, 1776; mem. conv. which framed Md. Constn. and Bill of Rights, 1776; a founder, exec. mem. Med. and Chirurg. Facualty Md., 1799; presdl. elector; mem. U.S. Ho. of Reps. from Md., 7th-9th congresses, 1801-07; introduced Senega in treatment croup; contbd. to Med. Repository N.Y. Died Hartford County, Sept. 28, 1810; buried Presbyn. Cemetery, Churchville, Md.

ARCHIBALD, JAMES FRANCIS JEWELL, war corr.; b. New York, Sept. 22, 1871; s. Dr. F. A. and Martha Washington (Jewell) A.; grad. Ohio Wesleyan University. Served in Chinese-Japanese War; with Gen. Miles through labor riots, in the Sioux campaign, and the last Apache campaign; vol. a.-d.-c. 5th Army Corps through Spanish War; served in Santiago campaign; was on first scouting expdn. that landed in Cuba about a month before the Santiago expdn.; first man wounded in war with Spain; was in Chippewa campaign on Leach Lake; with army of occupation of Cuba with staff of Gen. Ludlow; with British forces in Soudan, 1899; with Boer Army in the South African War; with Castro's army during Barcelona campaign in Venezuela and later followed events of allied forces against Venezuela; with Philippine constabulary against Ladrones; with Russian Army from beginning Russo-Japanese War representing Collier's Weekly; with French Army in Morocco, 1910; with Turkish Army during the revolution in Albania, 1910; in Lisbon during Portuguese revolution, 1911; with Chinese troops during revolution, 1913; with Austrian and German armies for a time in 1915. While on way to Europe, from U.S., Aug., 1915, was detained by authorities of British Govt. and charged with carrying dispatches to representatives of govts. of Germany and Austria, at Berlin and Vienna; released, but dispatches confiscated, Sept., 1915; returned to U.S. Fellow Royal Geog. Soc. and Royal Soc. Arts, London, etc. Author: Blue Shirt and Khaki; Tales from the Trenches. Plays produced: The Outpost; The Field Hospital; The Last Bet; The Nick of Time. Address: 47 W. 34th St., New York NY

ARGALL, SAMUEL maritime explorer, colonial gov.; b. Bristol, Eng., 1572. Discovered shortest Northern route from Eng. to Va., 1609; captured Pocahontas and brought her to Jamestown, 1612; regained French settled coast of Me. and Nova Scotia for Eng., destroyed French settlements St. Croix and Port Royal, 1613 dep. gov. Va., 1617-19; captained expdn. against Algerines, 1620; adm. Brit. Naval Force in Cecil's expdn. against Spain, 1625; knighted by King James I, 1626; mem. New Eng. Royal Council Died 1639.

ARMISTEAD, LEWIS ADDISON, army officer; b. Newbern, N.C., Feb. 18, 1817; s. Gen. Walker Keith and Elizabeth (Stanley) A.; m. Cecelia Lee Love. Commd. 2d lt. 6th Inf., U.S. Army, 1839, 1st lt., 1844; served in Mexican War at battles of Contreras, Churubusco and Molina del Rey, 1846-47; commd. capt., 1855; comdr. detachment which defeated Indians from Ft. Mohave (Colo.), 1859; apptd. col. 57th Va. Regt., Confederate States Army, 1861, brig. gen., 1862;

served at Battle of Antietam, 1862; in charge of brigade in Gen. George Pickett's Div. at Battle of Gettysburg (Pa.), 1863. Killed at Battle of Gettysburg, July 3, 1863.

ARMS, FRANK THORNTON naval officer; b. Dec. 9, 1866; entered U.S. Navy, 1892, and advanced through the grades to rear adm., 1924; retired, 1925. Home 51 Glenwood Av., New London, Conn. Address: care Chief of Naval Personnel Navy Dept., Washington 25, D.C. Died Apr. 18, 1848.

ARMS, THOMAS SEELYE, army officer (ret.); b. Cleveland, O., Mar. 22, 1893; s. Charles Carrol and Sarah Elizabeth (Seelye) A.; B.S. Va. Mil. Inst., 1915; student basic course, Infantry Sch., 1923-24, advanced course, 1928-29; Command and Gen. Staff Sch., 1929-31; m. Gladys Josephine Schauweker, June 21, 1917; children—Thomas Seelye, Robert Joseph, William Henry. Commd. 2d lt., Inf., U.S. Army, Nov. 30, 1916; promoted through grades to brig. gen., April 27, 1942. Served on Mexican border, and during World War I, in U.S. and Siberia, later in P.I. and China; instr. R.O.T.C., Emory U., 1924-28; instr. tactics, Infantry Sch., Fort Benning, Ga., 1931-35; instr. Ohio Nat. Guard, 1935-40; comdg. officer 159th Inf., 1941-42; instr. with Chinese Army, 1942-46, ret., 1946; operator Armsley Farms, Easton, Md., 1946-70. Authors: Notes on Infantry Training for the Chinese Army (with others), 1942. Home: Easton MD Died Nov. 1970.

ARMSTEAD, HENRY HOWELL cons. mining engineer; b. Chicago, Ill., Aug. 4, 1872; s. of the late Henry Howell and Alice Mary (McPherson) A.; ed. pvt. schs. and Columbia Sch. of Mines; unmarried. Maj. of Engrs., U.S.A., World War; retired col., Officers Reserve Corps, Apr. 30, 1928. Mason. Home: New York, N.Y. Deceased.

ARMSTONG, FRANK C. mem. Commn. to treat with the Five Tribes in the Indian Territory; b. Choctaw Agency, Ind. Ter., 1835; s. Frank W. and Anne M. (Millard) A.; ed. Holy Cross Coll., Worcester, Mass.; went to Tex., 1854, and made a trip across State from Corpus Christi to El Paso with his stepfather, Gen. Persifer F. Smith, U.S. Army, for bravery in an encounter with Indians on this trip was apptd., June, 1855, lt. 2d U.S. dragoons, serving in Tex., Kan. and Neb. until 1857, then went to Utah with Gen. Albert Sydney Johnston; resigned commn., 1861, and joined C.S. army; apptd. adj. gen. under Gen. McCulloch in Ark., and after McCulloch's death, apptd. maj. and soon after elected col. 3d La. inf. Under orders from Gen. Bragg organized cav. command and engaged in Miss. and Ala.; attacked and captured Federal camp, Courtland, Ala., and afterward was successful in actions at Bolivar and near Benmark; apptd. brig. gen.; assigned to brigade under Van Dorn, and later under Forrest; commd. brigade during campaign in Tenn., and on retreat to Chattanooga, took important part at Chickamauga, comd. cav. div. Moved with Longstreet to E. Tenn., under Gen. Jos. Wheeler, then moved to Ga. and served until after fall of Atlanta; later in Tenn. and Miss.; surrendered to Gen. Canby. Last battle was at Selma, Ala., under Gen. Forrest. After war engaged in Overland mail service in Tex.; U.S. indian insp. 1885-89; asst. commr. Indian Affairs, 1893-95; became interested in mining, etc., in Mexico. Died 1909.

ARMSTRONG, CLARE HIBBS, army officer; b. Albert Lea, Minn., Jan. 23, 1894; s. DeWitt Clinton and Anna Caroline (Hibbs) A.; ed. Army and Navy Prep. Sch., Washington, D.C., 1913; B.S., U.S. Mil. Acad., 1917; grad. Coast Arty. Sch., 1930; Chem. Warfare Sch., 1930, Command and Gen. Staff Sch., 1936, Air Corps Tactical Sch., 1942, Ordnance Field Officer Motor Course, 1942; m. Mary Denard Coombs, May 1, 1917 (died 1938); children—Clare Hibbs, Elizabeth Anne (Mrs. Richard Louis Hennessy), DeWitt Clinton, Mrs. L. Bughman; 1 stepson, M. Nelson Taylor; m. 2d, Mary Weber Harter, June 5, 1939; m. 3d, Catherine Hays Taylor. Commd. 2d lt., U.S. Army, 1917, advanced through the grades to brig. gen., 1943, ret., 1953. Mason (Scottish Rite, Shriner). Club : Army and Navy Country (Washington, D.C.). Home: Albert Lea MN Died Aug. 1969.

ARMSTRONG, EDWIN H(OWARD) elec. engr.; b. New York, N.Y., Dec. 18, 1890; s. John and Emily Gertrude (Smith) A.; E.E., Columbia, 1913, Sc.D., 1929; Sc.D., Muhlenberg College, 1941; married Marian MacInnis, December 1, 1923. Assistant in dept. elec. engrng., Columbia, 1913-14; asso. with Prof. Michael I. Pupil in research, Marcellus Hartley Research Lab., at Columbia U., 1914-35; prof. of elec. engrng., Columbia, since 1934. Served as capt. and major, Signal Corps, with A.E.F., 1917-19. Chevalier, Legion of d'honneur, 1919. Awards: Medal of Honor, Inst. of Radio Engrs., 1917; Egleston medal, Columbia U., 1939; "Modern Pioneer" plaque, Nat. Assn. Mfrs., 1940; Holley medal, Am. Soc. Mech. Engrs., 1940; Franklin medal, Franklin Inst., 1941; John Scott medal, Bd. of City Trusts, City of Phila., 1941; Edison medal, Am. Inst. of Elec. Engrs., 1943; award to be known as Armstrong Medal, established by Radio Club of America, 1935; Medal for Merit, 1947; Washington award for 1951 Western Soc. Engrs. Mem. Inst. Radio Engrs. Rep. Presbyn. Contributor to tech. jours. Inventions: regenerative circuit, 1912; superheterodyne, 1918; super-regenerative circuit, 1920; method of eliminating static in radio by means of frequency modulation, 1939. Home: 435 E. 52d St., N.Y. City. Died Feb. 1, 1954; buried Locust Grove Cemetery, Merrimack, Mass.

ARMSTRONG, FRANK ALTON, JR., air force officer; b. Hamilton, N.C., May 24, 1902; s. Frank Alton and Annie Elizabeth (Hobbs) A.; LL.B., A.B., Wake Forest Coll., 1925; m. Vernelle Hudson, Mar. 15, 1929; 1 son, Frank Alton III. Began as flying cadet, U.S. Army, 1928; commd. 2d lt. AC, 1929, and advanced through grades to lt. gen., 1956; served at airfields throughout U.S; as combat observer, Eng., 3 mos., 1940; and as asst. chief A-3 sect. AF staff, Washington; comd. 1st U.S. heavy bombing flights over France, Germany; comd. 101st Combat Wing, and 17th Training Wing, U.S., 315th Wing, Guam; leader B-29 bombing mission, Guam to Akita, Japan; comdr. in chief Alaskan Command, 1957-69. Decorated D.S.C., D.S.M., Silver Star, D.F.C. with oak leaf cluster, Air Medal; British Flying Cross (first air medal awarded U.S. airman, World War II). Mem. Kappa Alpha (Southern). Pioneered first polar flight from Alaska to Norway. Home: Nashville NC Died Aug. 20, 1969.

ARMSTRONG, JOHN army officer, Continental congressman; b. County Fermanagh, Ireland, Oct. 13, 1717; s. James Armstrong; m. Rebecca Lyon; children-John, James. Surveyor, laid out Town of Carlisle (Pa.); commd. capt. Pa. Militia, 1756, lt. col., 1756; fought in French and Indian War, led successful night attack on Delaware l ' Indians at Kittanning, 1756 (Called Hero of Kittanning); commd. brig. gen. Continental Army, 1776, maj. gen., 1777; mem. Continental Congress, 1778-80, 87-88. Died Carlisle, Mar. 9, 1795; buried Old Carlisle Cemetery.

ARMSTRONG, JOHN army officer, explorer; b. N.J., Apr. 20, 1755; s. Thomas and Jane (Hamilton) A.; married a dau. of Judge William Goforth; 1 son, William Goforth. Served as officer Pa. Militia, 1777-84, Continental Army, 1784-93; commandant Ft. Pitt, 1875-86, Ft. Hamilton, 1791; explored Wabash River to Lake Erie, 1790; served in Gen. Josiah Harmar's unsuccessful expdn. against Indians in what is now Ind., 1790, Unsuccessful expdn. of Arthur St. Clair against same Indians, 1791; treas. Northwest Territory; founder Armstrong's Station on the Ohio River, 1796. Died Armstrong's Station, Feb. 4, 1816.

ARMSTRONG, JOHN army officer, sec. of war, diplomat; b. Carlisle, Pa., Nov. 25, 1758; s. John and Rebecca (Lyon) A.; attended Princeton, 1775; m. Alida Livingston, 1789. Aide-de-camp under John Frances Mercer and Horatio Gates in Revolutionary War; author Newburgh Letters threatening army action if Congress refused to pay arrears in soldiers' salaries, 1783; after war became sec. of state, adj.-gen. Pa.; del. Continental Congress, 1787; mem. U.S. Senate from N.Y., 1800-02, 03-04; U.S. minister to France, 1804-10; believed to have contbd. to outbreak of French-British War, 1812; commd. brig. gen. in command N.Y.C., 1812; sec. of war U.S., 1813-14; considered responsible for failure of Montreal and Plattsburg campaigns and Brit. capture of Washington, D.C., 1814. Died Red Hook, N.Y., Apr. 1, 1843; buried Rhinebeck (N.Y.) Cemetery.

ARMSTRONG, JOSEPH GILLESPIE 3D clergyman; b. Warren, Pa., Oct. 15, 1901; s. Joseph Gillespie and Minnie (Houston) A; A.B., Johns Hopkins, 1928; S.T.B., Gen. Theol. Seminary, 1931, S.T.D., D.D., Philadephia Divinity School; married Louise McKelvey, Nov.24, 1950 Ordained deacon, P.E. Chl., 1931, priest, 1931; rector Severn Parish, Anne Arundel County, Md., 1931-35, Christ Ch., Georgetown, D.C., 1935-40, St. Mary's Ch., Ardmore, Pa., 1930-49; suffragen bishop of Pa. 1949-60: Bishop Coadjutor of the Diocese, Pa., 1960-63; bishop of Diocese of Pa., 1963-64. Served as ambulance driver, World War I; chaplain, U.S. Navy, 1942- Unit mem. bd. trustees Gen. Theol. Sem. Mem. Mil. Order World Wars, Ch. Hist. Soc. Republican. Clubs: Merion Golf (Ardmore, Pa.), Merion Cricket (Haverford, Pa.); Rittenhouse. Home: 128 N. Roberts Rd., Bryn lfawr. Pa. Office 202 S. 19th St., Philadelphia 3. Died Apr. 1964.

ARMSTRONG, PAUL GALLOWAY state dir. Selective Service; b. Leadville, Colo., Oct. 26, 1890; s. Rev. Arthur Edson and d Luvia Adelma (Russell) A.; student Fairmont Sch. (Denver) and West Denver High Sch.; m. Blanche Astrid Larson, Dec. 4, 1916; children—Don Wellington, Patricia Lorraine, With Parker, Schmidt & Tucker Paper Co., Chgo., 1919—, as clk., salesman and v.p.; dir. 1st lfutual Savings Assn.; state director S.S.S.; for Illinois, 1940—. Served with 8th U.S. Regular Inf. in France, World War I. Awarded Legion of Merit: Medaille' de la France Liber'e for World War II services. Mem. S.A.R., Am. Legion (past state commander). Republican. Presbyterian. Mason. (Shriner, 33 degree). Clubs: Lake Shore, Illinois Athletic. Address: 1831 S. Holmes St., Springfield, Ill. Died Jan. 11, 1958; buried Rosehill Cemetery, Chgo.

ARMSTRONG ROBERT army officer; b. Abingdon, Va., Sept. 28, 1792; s. Trooper Armstrong; m. Margaret Nichol, June 1814. Served to sgt. U.S. Army in War of 1812; served as lt. arty. under Andrew Jackson during Creek Indian campaign; wounded at battle of Enotochapho, 1814; mem. Jackson's staff at Battle of New Orleans; postmaster Nashville (Tenn.), 1829-35; commd. brig. gen. during Second Seminole War, 1836-37; engaged in Battle of Wahoo Swamp; unsuccessful candidate for gov. Tenn., 1837; consul at Liverpool, 1845-49; propr. Washington (D.C.) Union, 1851-54. Died Washington, Feb. 23, 1854.

ARMSTRONG, SAMUEL CHAPMAN army officer, educator; b. Hawaiian Islands, Jan. 30, 1839; s. Rev. Richard and Clarissa A.; grad. Williams Coll., 1862; m. Emma Walker, 1869; m. 2d, Mary Ford, 1890. Commd. capt. 125th N.Y. Volunteer Regt., 1862, commd. 9th Colored Regt., U.S. Colored Troops (in this capacity developed interest in the Negro); brig. gen., 1865; agt. Freedmen's Bur , 1866; founder Hampton (Va.) Normal and Indsl. Inst. for Negroes, 1868. Died Hampton, May 11, 1893.

ARMSTRONG, SAMUEL TREAT physician; b. St. Louis, Nov. 2, 1859; s. David Hartley and Laura Armstrong (Milligan) A.; Ph.B., St. Louis U., 1879, Ph.D., 1886; M.D., St. Louis Med. Coll. (Washington U.), 1879; m. Alice Cobin, Dec. 6, 1882; children—Mrs. Laura Lovejoy, Clairette Papin, Donald, Francis Tuttle, U.S. Marine Hospital Service Feb. 1881; resigned July 1890; maj. and brigade surgeon U.S.V., May 1898; resigned, June 1901. Companion Mil. Order Foreign Wars, Order Spanish-Am. War.; mem. A.A.A.S., N.Y. Acad. Sciences. Clubs: Army and Navy (Washington, D.C.). Contbr. med. monographs to various publs. Home: Hillbourne Farms, Katonah, N.Y. Died Aug. 31, 1944.

ARN, WILLIAM GODFREY, civil engr.; b. Terre Haute, Ind., Feb. 7, 1877; s. Godfrey and Elizabeth (Van Brunt) A.; B.S. in C.E., Rose Poly. Inst., Terre Haute, Ind., 1897; unmarried. With L. & N. R.R. Co., 1897-1906, as rodman, masonry insp., building insp., asst. engr. and roadmaster; engr. and supt. Southern Bitulithic Co., Nashville, Tenn., 1906; with I.C.R.R. Co., 1907-17, and since 1919 as asst. div. engr., asst. engr., roadmaster, asst. engr. maintenance of way and asst. chief engr., Chicago Terminal Improvement. Served in U.S. Army, May 8, 1917-June 1, 1919; capt., maj. and lt. col. 13th Engrs.; with A.E.F., in France; now lt. col. engrs., O.R.C. Mem. Am. Soc. C.E., Am. Ry. Engrng. Assn., Western Soc. Engrs., Soc. Am. Mil. Engrs., A.A.A.S., Am. Legion, Mil. Order World War, Maintenance of Way Club of Chicago. Citation by Gen. Pershing. Republican. Methodist. Mason (32 deg., Shriner). Clubs: University, Engineers', Prairie, Sojourners, Adventurers', Cambridge, Lincolnshire Country. Home: 5202 Cornell Av. Office: I.C.R.R. Station, Chicago IL

ARNEILL, JAMES RAE (AR'NEL), physician; b. DePere, Wis., Mar. 6, 1869; s. John and Elizabeth (Rae) A.; A.B. Lawrence U. (Wis.), LL.D., 1923; M.D., U. Mich., 1894; m. Sarah Hyatt Taylor, Sept. 1900. Instr. clin. medicine U. Mich., 1897-1903; settled in Denver; was prof. medicine U. Colo. Mem. bd. of Regents A,C,P,; mem. A.M.A., Colo. Med. Soc. Served as capt., M.C., U.S. Army, World War. Author: Clinical Diagnosis & Urinalysis, 1905. Contbr. Reference Handbook of Med. Scis. Home: 741 Washington St. Office: 1765 Sherman St., Denver, Died Jan. 27, 1950; buried Fairmont Cemetery, Denver.

ARNESEN, SIGURD J(OHANNESEN) ret. publisher; b. Stava ger, Norway, July 31, 1887; s. Johannes and Lena Elizabeth (Levardsen) A.; grad. Stavanger Cathedral High Sch., 1902, Bay Ridge Evening High Sch., 1911; m. Martha Marie Musaus, May 1, 1920; children-Norma Elizabeth, Paul Musaus, Ruth Marie, Siguard John. Came to U.S., 1904, naturalized, 1909. pub. Nordisk Tidende, 1911-58; trustee Bay Ridge Savs. Bank. Served as 1st lt. inf. AEF, U.S. Army, 1918-19; col. intelligence corps, 1942-45, asst. chief staff G-2, First Army, 1942, mem. gen. staff corps, 1943, asst. mil. attache Am. Legation, Stockholm, Sweden, 1944-45; now col. M.I. Res., ret. Decorated Knight Comdr. Order St. Olav, King Haakon Liberation Cross (Norway); Army Commendation (U.S.). Mem. nat. council Boy Scouts Am., former mem. Greater N.Y. Councils Exec. Bd., chmn. advancement com., chmn. activities com. and vice chmn. camping com., served as scout commr. Bklyn. Council Exec. Bd., mem. Honor Soc. Order of Arrow (recipient Silver Beaver, Silver Antelope awards). Mem. Norwegian-Am. C. of C. (dir.), Norwegian Am. Hist. Soc. (past pres.), Sons of Norway (past pres. Eastern dist.), Luth. World Relief (treas.), N.Y. Soc. lMil. and Naval Officers World War, M.I. Res. Soc., Am. Legion. Republican. Lutheran (nat. council). Clubs: Rotary (Bklyn.); Norwegian. Home: 9801 Shore Rd., Bklyn. Died 1966.

ARNOLD, ABRAHAM KERNS brig. gen. U.S.V.; b. Bedford, Pa., March 24, 1837; grad. U.S. Mil. Acad., 1859; bvt. 2d lt., 2d cav.; commd. 2d lt., June 28, 1860; promoted through grades to brig. gen., U.S. Vols., 1898. Bvtd. capt. June 27, - at Todd's Tavern; Congressional medal of honor for gallantry in action at Davenport Bridge, N. Anna River, Va., May 18, 1864; comd. cav. div. at Chickamauga; comd. 5th cav. in Civil war; served against Indians on frontier; served in war with Spain in the field from April 22, 1898; comdg., 1899, 2d div., 7th Army corps, in Cuba. Died 1901.

ARNOLD, BENEDICT army officer; b. Norwich, Conn., Jan. 14, 1741; s. Benedict and Hannah (Waterman) A.; m. Margaret Mansfield, Feb. 22, 1767; m. 2d, Margaret Shippen, Apr. 1779; 8 children including Benedict, Richard, Henry. Commd. capt. Conn. Militia, then col, 1775; captured Ft. Ticonderoga from British, 1775; defeated in attack on Quebec, 1775; commd. brig. gen., 1776; twice stopped British in their attempted expdn. down Lake Champlain, 1776; promoted maj. gen., 1777, played major role in defeat and surrender of Burgoyne at Battle of Saratoga; mil. comdr. of Phila., 1778; commanded Am. post at West Point (N.Y.), 1780; started correspondence with Sir Henry Cointon, Brit. comdr-in-chief in N.am. (after a court martial, congressional slights and opposition to the French Alliance); correspondence culminated in his arrangement with Maj. John. Andre' of Clinton's staff to betray West Point, 1780; fled to British after discovery of his treason, became brig. gen. Brit. Army, 1780; led raids on Va., 1780, on Conn., 1781; granted land in Canada, 1797. Died London,Eng., June 14, 1801.

ARNOLD, BION JOSEPH electrical engr.; b. Casnovia, near Grand Rapids, Mich., Aug. 14, 1861; s. Joseph and Geraldine (Reynolds) A.; U. of Neb., 1879-80; B.S., Hillsdale (Mich.) Coll., 1884, M.S., 1887; grad. course Cornell, 1888-89; E.E., U. of Neb., 1897; hon. M.Ph., Hillsdale, 1889, hon. diploma, 1903; D.Sc., Armour Inst., 1907; D.Eng., U. of Neb., 1911; m. Carrie Estelle Berry, Jan. 14, 1886 (dec.); m.2d, Mrs. Margaret Latimer Fonda, Dec. 22, 1909. Chief designer, Ia. Iron Works, Dubuque; mech. engr., C.G.W. Ry.; later cons. engr. for Chicago office Gen. Electric Co.; independent cons. engr. since 1893. Designed and built Intramural Ry., Chicago Expn.; cons. elec. engr. Chicago & Milwaukee Elec. Ry., Chicago Bd. of Trade, C.,B. & Q. R.R., Grand Trunk Ry. on electrification of St. Clair tunnel; cons. engr. Wis. State Ry. Commn., 1905-07; devised plan for electrically operating trains of N.Y. Central R.R. in and out of New York, and mem. Electric Traction Commrs. engaged in carrying on the work; mem. electric traction com. Erie R.R., 1900-04; cons. engr. for city of Chicago to revise street ry. systems of city, 1902; chief engr. rebuilding Chicago traction system at cost approx. $140,000,000 and chmn. bd. supervising engrs. same since 1907; cons. engr. Pub. Service Commn., 1st Dist., N.Y., matters connected with subway and st. ry. properties, New York; chief subway engr. city of Chicago and cons. engr. on traction matters for cities of Pittsburgh, 1910, Providence, Los Angeles, San Francisco, 1911, Toronto and Cincinnati, 1912; appraised properties of Seattle Electric Co., Puget Sound Electric Ry. Co., Southern Calif. Co., Los Angeles, 1911; Chicago Telephone Company's System, 1911; Internat. Ry. Co., Buffalo, N.Y., 1911; Met. St. Ry. System of Kansas City, Toronto St. Ry., and Lincoln (Neb.) Tel. & Tel. Co., 1913; Mountain States Tel. & Tel. Co., Denver, 1914; Denver Tramway Co., 1915; Brooklyn R.T. Co. surface lines, 1917-18. Chosen by the Citizens' Terminal Plan Com. of Chicago to review plans submitted by Pa. Ry. Co. and others for terminals and to recommend a comprehensive system of steam ry. terminals for city; mem. of Chicago Ry. Terminal Commn. until 1921; mem. Traction and Subway Commn., 1916-17; retained by Mass. Pub. Service Commn. to report on rys. and by Bay State Ry. Co., Boston, 1916-17; adviser to Des Moines, Omaha, Winnipeg, Sacramento, New Orleans, Detroit, Harrisburg, Rochester, Syracuse, Jersey City, Toronto, etc. Pres. The Arnold Engineering Co. Inventor of combined direct-connected machines, a magnetic clutch, storage battery improvements, and new systems and devices for elec. rys.; pioneer in alternating current, direct current and in single phase electric traction systems. Mem. Naval Consulting Board; chairman com. Am. Inst. Elect. Engrs. on Nat. Reserve Corps Civilian Engrs., 1915. Commd. maj. Engr. R.C., Jan. 23, 1917; transferred to regular army, Dec. 14, 1917, with rank lt. col., Aviation Sect., Signal Corps; assigned to equipment div. production sect. of aircraft, Washington, D.C., and continued to act in advisory capacity to Army and Navy; made 2 surveys of aircraft production and report on aluminum situation; had control for 5 mos. previous to armistice over development and production of aerial torpedoes; hon. discharged Feb. 6, 1919; commd. maj. Aviation Sect., O.R.C., Mar. 28, 1919, col. Aux. Corps, Aug. 14, 1925; col. Inactive Reserve since 1929. Trustee Hillsdale Coll.; mem. bd. mgrs. Lewis Inst.; trustee Illinois Inst. of Technology since 1940. Pres. Am. Inst. E.E., 1903-04, elected hon. mem., 1937, was also del. for Inst. at Internat. Elec. Congress, 1900, pres. Western Soc. Engrs., 1906-07, elected hon. mem., 1927, and received Washington Award, 1929, "for devoted, unselfish and preeminent service in advancing human progress"; member A.A.A.S. (vice pres.), American Soc. Promotion Engring. Edn.; 1st v.p. and chmn. exec. com. Internat. Elec. Congress, St. Louis, 1904; chmn. com. on award Anthony N. Brady medals of N.Y. Mus. Safety; chmn. Am. Committee on Electrolysis; mem. of Inventors Guild, Aero Club of Ill. (past pres.), N.Y. Elec. Soc. Mil. Order World War (comdr. Chicago chapter, 1932-33, state comdr. for Ill. 1937); pres. Air Bd. of Chicago, etc. Clubs: Engineers' (New York); Union League, South Shore, Commercial, Engineers, Army and Navy (pres. 1926-27). Home: 4713 Kimbark Av. Office: 231 S. LaSalle Street, Chicago, Ill. Died. Jan. 29, 1942.

ARNOLD, CONWAY HILLYER rear-admiral U.S.N.; b. New York, Nov. 14, 1848; s. Comdr. Henry Nathan Tewkesbury (U.S.N.) and Cornelia Van Vleck (Sleight) A.; ed. pvt. schs.; grad. U.S. Naval Acad., 1867; m. Fanny, d. William W. W. Wood, engr.-in-chief U.S.N., Nov. 17, 1870. Commd. ensign, 1868; master, 1870; lt., 1874; lt. comdr., 1892; comdr., 1898; capt., Sept. 17, 1902; rear-admiral, Jan. 30, 1908. Pres. Naval Examining and Retiring Bds. Home: New York, N.Y. Died July 16, 1917.

ARNOLD, HAROLD DEFOREST physicist; b. Woodstock, Conn., Sept. 3, 1883; s. Calvin and Audra Elizabeth (Allen) A.; Ph.B., Wesleyan U., 1906, M.S., 1907, D.Sc., 1930; fellow in physics U. of Chicago, 1907-09, Ph.D., 1911; m. Leila Stone Beeman, Sept. 3, 1908; children—Audra Elizabeth, Dorothy Edith. Asst. in physics, Wesleyan U., 1906-07; prof. physics, Mt. Allison U., Sackville, N.B., Can., 1909-10; research engr., Western Electric Co., N.Y. City, 1911-24; dir. research, Bell Telephone Labs., N.Y. City 1925—. Capt. Signal Corps, U.S.R., 1917. Received John Scott medal and award, 1928 for development of 3-electrode high vacuum thermionic tube. Methodist. Home: Summit, N.J. Died July 10, 1933.

ARNOLD, HENRY H. army officer; b. Gladwyne, Pa., June 25, 1886; s. H.A. and Louise (Harley) A.; grad. U.S. Mil. Acad., 1907, Army Indsl. Coll., 1925, Command and Gen. Staff Sch., 1929; D. Aero. Sc., Pa. Mil. Coll., 1941; D.Sc., U. So. Calif., 1941; LL.D., Iowa Wesleyan Coll., 1942; m. Eleanor A. Pool, Sept. 10, 1913; children— Lois E., Henry H., William, David L. Commd. 2d lt. inf., 1907; and advanced through grades to gen., 1943; gen. of the Army (5-star), Dec. 1944. Detailed to Signal Corps Aviation Sect., 1916-17; comdg. officer 7th Aero Squadron, Panama, 1917-18; dept. air service officer, San Francisco, 1919-22; comdg. officer various air fields, 1922-36; flight comdr. U.S. Alaska Flight, 1934; asst. chief Air Corps, 1936-38; became chief of Army Air Corps, 1938; apptd. dep. chief of staff for Air, 1940; became comdg. gen. Army Air Forces, 1942, now gen. of the Air Force. Awarded Distinguished Flying Cross, 1934; Clarence H. Mackay Trophy, 1912 and 1935; Distinguished Service Medal, 1942. Baptist. Mason. Clubs: Army and Navy, Columbia Country. Author: Air Men and Aircraft, 1926; Bill Bruce Series, 1928; This Flying Game (with I.C. Eaker), 1936 (rev. 1944); Winged Warfare (with I.C. Eaker), 1941; Army Flyer (with I.C. Eaker), 1942. Home: Fort Myer, Va. Died Jan. 15, 1950.

ARNOLD, HORACE DAVID physician; b. Boston, Nov. 4, 1862; s. George Jerome and Anna Elizabeth (Bullard) A.; A.B., Harvard, 1885, M.D., 1889; m. Ida P. Lane, June 8, 1892. House officer Boston City Hosp., Boston Lying-in Hosp., 1889-90; asst. supt. Boston Dispensary and Boston City Hosp.; instr., later prof. clin. medicine, Tufts Coll. Med. Sch., 1896-1910; dean Harvard Grad. Sch. of Medicine, 1912-16, dir. same, 1916. Mem. Nat. Bd. Med. Examiners, 1915. Major, Med. R.C., Apr. 11, 1917. Mem. A.M.A. (chmn. council on med. edn., 1917), Mass. Med. Soc., Am. Climatol. Assn., Boston Soc. for Med. Improvement, Boston Soc. Med. Sciences, etc. Mason. Clubs: Union, Harvard (Boston). Home: 427 Beacon St. Office: 520 Commonwealth Av., Boston. Died Apr., 1935.

ARNOLD, JAMES E., naval officer, ret.; b. North Troy, Vt., May 5, 1895; s. Cyrus and Annie (Blenkhorn) A.; student Worcester Poly. Inst., 1915-17, U.S. Naval Acad., 1918, U.S. Navy Submarine Sch., 1918; m. Margaret Lewis, May 22, 1919; children—Barbara (Mrs. Vincent Thorpe), Hope (Mrs. Albert Barre), Margaret (Mrs. Henry Snelling), Ann (Mrs. Paul Driscoll), James E. Entered U.S. Navy, 1917; served with submarines and destroyers, 1918-27; sales engr., Leland-Gifford Co., 1927-40; on active duty with U.S.N., 1940-45; present rank, rear admiral, U.S.N.R.; became comdg. officer, Advanced Amphibious Base, Falmouth, Cornwall, 1943; comdg. officer (U.S. Navy) Normandy Beach during assault, France, June 6, 1944; comdg. officer U.S. Naval Base, Le Havre, France, 1944-45; pres. Gen. Court Martial, 1st Naval Dist., 1945, rear adm. U.S. N.R. (Ret.); pres. Arnold Realty Trust, Wilowood Corp.; mem. bd. Leland-Gifford Co. of Can.; Washington rep. Inland Constrn. Co., Omaha, Neb., 1951-71. Mem. Mass. Gen. Court, Ho. of Reps., 1932-34. Decorated Legion of Merit with one gold star (U.S.), Croix de Guerre (France). Mason. Club: Army and Navy (Washington). Home: Washington DC Died Nov. 1971.

ARNOLD, JOHN JR. congressman; b. Elmira, N.Y., Mar. 11, 1831; attended Yale, did not graduate. After death of father became banker in Elmira; pres. Village of Elmira, 1859-64, pres. bd. village trustees, 1859, 60, 64; served as paymaster with rank of maj., U.S. Army, stationed in Elmira, during Civil War; mayor Elmira (after it was chartered as a city), 1864, 70, 74; mem. U.S. Ho. of Reps. (Democrat) from Y.Y., 48th, 49th congresses, 1883-Nov. 20, 1886. Died Elmira, Nov. 20, 1886; buried Woodlawn Cemetery.

ARNOLD, JOHN ANDERSON lawyer; b. Bloomington, Ill., July 26, 1907; s. John Alexander and Ellen Jane (Anderson) A.; student Ill. Wesleyan U., 1925-27, Okla. U., 1931; LL.B., U. Colo., 1934; m. Mildred Chapin Fox, June 14, 1920; children-John Fox, Robert Chapin, David Fryar. Admitted to Mo. bar, 1934, since practiced in St. Louis; mem. firm. Green, Hennings, Henry, Evans & Arnold. Mem. Mo. Supreme Ct. Grievance Com. for 22d Jud. circuit, 1953-. Served as lt. USNR, World War II; lt. comdr. Res. Mem. Mo. Bar (bd. govs. 1958-, exec. com. 1959-60), Am. Bar Assn., Bar Assn. St. Louis (pres. 1957-58), Phi Delta Phi, Phi Gamma Delta. Republican. Presbyn. Mason. Clubs: Westborough Country (pres. 1951-52), Missouri Athletic. Home: 521 Oakwood, Webster Groves 19, Mo. Office: Boatmen's Bank Bldg., St. Louis 2. Died Nov.21, 1963; buried St. Paul's Ch. Yard.

ARNOLD, LESLIE PHILIP business exec.; born New Haven, Conn., Aug. 28, 1894; s. Frank Leslie and Cora (Fiske) A.; B.A., Norwich Univ., 1924: married. Asst. to pres. Trancontinental and Western Air Lines, 1929-37; vice pres. and dir. Pa. Central Airlines, 1937-40; v.p. Eastern Airlines since 1940. Served as 1st lt., A.A.F., 1917-1928; col., 1942-45. Home: Leonia, N.J. Office: 10 Rockefeller Plaza, N.Y.C. Died Mar. 21, 1961.

ARNOLD, LEWIS GOLDING army officer; b. N.J., Jan. 15, 1817; grad. U.S. Mil. Acad., 1837. Served with 2d Arty., U.S. Army in Seminole War, 1837-38; commd. 1st lt., 1838; served at siege of Veracruz in Mexican War; brevetted capt. and maj., 1847; served with 2d Arty. in Fla. War, 1853-56; commd. maj. 1st Arty., 1861; brevetted lt. col., 1861; served at Santa Rosa Island (Fla.), 1861, Ft. Pickens, 1861-62; brig. gen. U.S. Volunteers, New Orleans, 1862; commanded Dept. of Fla., 1862; lt. col. U.S. Army, 1863; lt. col. 2d Arty., 1863; ret. 1864. Died Boston, Sept. 22, 1871.

ARNOLD, RICHARD army officer; b. Providence, R.I., Apr. 12, 1828; s. Lemuel Hastings and Sally (Lyman) A.; grad. U.S. Mil. Acad., 1850. Commd. in U.S. Arty., 1850, served in Fla. and Cal.; engaged in road building and exploration in Northwest for 2 years; promoted 1st lt., 1854; a.d.c. to Gen. John E. Wool, 1855-61; promoted capt. 5th U.S. Arty., 1861; participated in 1st Battle of Bull Run; chief of arty. in Gen. William Franklin's division, 1862; spent most of Peninsular Campaign on staff 6th Corps, served at battles of Savage Station, Glendale, Malvern Hill (Battle of Seven Days) (all Va.); brevetted maj. U.S. Volunteers for services at Malvern Hill; chief of arty. Dept. of Gulf, 1862; brig. gen. U.S. Volunteers, 1862, went to New Orleans; participated in seige of Port Hudson, La., 1863, commander of cavalry at Red River Expdn., 1864; his field service ended with capture of Ft. Morgan, Ala.; promoted maj. 5th Arty., 1875. Died Governor's Island, N.Y. Harbor, Nov. 8, 1882.

ARNOLD, SAMUEL GREENE senator, historian; b. Providence, R.I., Apr. 12, 1821; s. Samuel Greene and Frances (Rogers) A.; grad Brown U., 1841; LL.B., Harvard, 1845. After graduation visited St. Petersburg, Russia, admitted to R.I. bar, 1845; spent much time travelling in S.Am., Eng., France, Egypt, Syria, elsewhere; lt. gov. R.I., 1852, 61-62; mem. U.S. Senate (Republican) from R.I., Dec. 1, 1862-Mar. 3. 1863; commanded battery of infantry, a.d.c. to Gov. William Sprague of R.I. during Civil War; trustee R.I. Reform Sch., Butler Hosp.; pres., contbr. to Charitable Baptist Soc., pres., speaker R.I. Hist. Soc. Author: History of Rhode Island and Providence Plantation, 1859; Memorial Papers on A. C. Greene, William Staples, and Usher Parsons; Historical Sketches of Middletown, 1880. Died Providence, Feb. 13, 1880; buried Swan Point Cemetery, Providence.

ARNOLD, WILLIAM RICHARD bishop; b. Wooster, O., June 10, 1881; s. Augustine Adam and Catherine Mary (Dalton) A.; A.B., St. Joseph's Coll., Rensselaer, Ind., 1902; student St. Bernard's sem., Rochester, N.Y., 1902-08. Ordained priest Roman Catholic Ch., 1908; chaplain U.S. Army, 1913-45, chief of chaplains 1937-consecrated bishop 1945, mil. del. to Armed Force, with Mil. Ordinate, 1945. Decorated D.S.M. Ecclesiastical honors; Papal Chamberlain, 1940, Domestic Prelate, 1942. Home: 1088 Park Av., N.Y.C. 28. Address: The Military Ordinariate, 30 E. 51st St., N.Y.C. 22 Died Jan. 7, 1965; buried Nat. Cemetery, Arlington, Va.

ARNOTE, WALTER JAMES, lawyer; b. McAlester, Okla., Jan. 19, 1905; s. James Samuel and Stella (Rock) A.; A.B., LL.B., Okla. U., 1928; student Harvard Law Sch., 1929; m. Jean Black, Jan. 30, 1939; 1 dau., Christie (Mrs. Tony Ashmore). Admitted to Okla. bar, 1928, since practiced in McAlester; partner firm Arnote, Bratton & Allford, 1929-65; city atty., McAlester, 1949-65. Dir. atty. First Nat. Bank McAlester, Okla. Automatic Telephone Co.; sec. treas., dir., atty. Great Lake Oil & Gas Co.; dir. Mid-Continent Casualty Co. Mayor of McAlester, 1946-47. Served to lt. col. AUS, 1941-45; ETO. Decorated Legion of Merit; Croix de Guerre with gold star (France); Mil. Cross of Valor (Italy). Fellow Am. Coll. Trial Lawyers, American Bar Foundation; member of the American, Okla. (pres. 1961), Pittsburgh County (pres. 1946) bar assns., U. Okla. Coll. Law Assn. (pres. 1959), Nat. Conf. Bar Presidents, McAlester C. of C., Am. Legion, Vets. Fgn. Wars, Harvard Law Sch. Assn., Okla. U. Alumni Assn., Phi Beta Kappa, Kappa Alpha. Mem. Christian Ch. Mason (33 deg.), Elk, Rotarian. Clubs: Country, Fin and Feather, Knife and Fork (McAlester). Home: McAlester3OK Died Aug. 13, 1965.

ARPS, GEORGE FREDERICK psychologist; b. Cary, Ill., Jan. 23, 1874; s. August H. and Ida (Hansen) A.; A.B., Leland Stanford Jr. U., 1904; A.M., Ind. U., Ph.D., Univ. of Leipzig, 1908; m. Alice Mary Black, Oct. 18, 1905; children—Leslie H., Margaret M. Asso. prof. psychology, Ind. Univ., 1909-10; asst. prof. psychology, U. of Ill., 1910-12; prof. psychology and head of dept., Ohio State U., 1912—, dean Coll. of Edn., 1920-37, dean Grad. School, 1937—. Appointed capt. Sanitary Corps, U.S.A., major, Feb. 9, 1918-Aug. 14, 1919; served as chief psychol. examiner Camp Sherman, O., also as chief camp morale officer; appt. chief ednl. officer U.S.A. Gen. Hosp. 36, Detroit, Dec. 5, 1918, also chief hosp. morale officer; maj. reserve officer, Sanitary Corps, 1920—. Home: Columbus. O. Died Sept. 16, 1939.

ARRICK, CLIFFORD b. St. Clairsville, O.; s. of Clifford and Margaret Josephine Cochran (Templeton) A.; ed. pub. and prep. schs.; m. Florence Gertrude Miller, Feb. 22, 1892. Began as topographer, U.S. Geol. Survey, 1884; pvt. sec. to W. H. H. Miller, atty. gen. U.S., 1892-93; with Union and Marion Trust cons., Indianapolis, 1899-1908; spl. agt. Bell Telephone System, Indianapolis, 1908-12; mgr. publicity Central Group of Bell Telephone cons., Chicago, 1912-20; v.p. Nat. City Bank, 1920—. Maj. and p.-m. U.S. Vols., Spanish-Am. War, 1898; commd. maj. q.-m. O.R.C., Jan 10, 1917. Republican. Home: Chicago, Ill. Died July 13, 1922.

ARTHUR, HAROLD JOHN, gov. Vt.; b. Whitehall, N.Y. Feb. 9, 1904; s. Roma Sholes and Almina Calista (Wells) A.; grad. Albany (N.Y.) Bus. Coll., 1928; LL.B., LaSalle Extension U., 1932; LL.D. (hon.), Norwich U., Northfield, Vt., 1950; m. Mary Catherine Alafat, Nov. 11, 1939; 1 dau., Portia Mary. Bank clk. Brandon (Vt.) Nat. Bank, 1922-26; stenographer for Ambassador Warren R. Austin, Burlington, Vt., 1928-32, after admittance to Vt. State bar, 1932, practiced as asso. to 1940; mem. firm Arthur & Arthur, civil and criminal trial practice, 1940-71; justice of the peace, Chittenden Co., 1947-49. Clk. ho. of reps., State of Vt., 1939-43, 1947-49; lt. gov., 1949-50, gov. 1950-51. Enlisted as private, 172d inf., Vt. N.G., 1928; active service as lt. to maj., A.C., U.S. Army, 1941-46. Served as civic service chmn. Boy Scouts, 1935-39. Mem. Vt., Chittenden County bar assns., United Comml. Travelers (grand counselor N.E.), Am. Legion, Amvets, Farm Bur., S.A.R. Republican. Unitarian (trustee). Elk (pres. Vt. State assn., 1939-49), Vt. State Grange (master, 1946-58), Mason (K.T., 32 deg., Shriner), Eastern Star, Eagle, K.P., Odd Fellow. Compiler, pub., House Precedents, 1939. Home: Burlington VT Died July 19, 1971; interred Arthur Mausoleum, Lakeview Cemetery, Burlington, Vt

ARTHUR, WILLIAM HEMPLE army officer; b. Philadelphia, Pa., Apr. 1, 1856; s. Robert and Mary (Hemple) A.; M.D., U. of Md., 1877; m. Laura Bouvier, Sept. 26, 1881. Apptd. asst. surgeon U. S. Army, Feb. 18, 1881; capt. asst. surgeon, Feb. 18, 1886; promoted through grades to brig. gen., Oct. 2, 1917. Comd. hosp. ship Spanish-Am. War; with China Relief Expdn, 1900; in Philippines, 1900-02; duty at Soldiers' Home and Walter Reed Hosp., D. C., until 1911; duty in Philippines until 1915; apptd. comdt. Army Med. Sch., Washington, Oct. 1, 1915; retired Dec. 3, 1918. Med. dir. Georgetown Univ. Hosp., Mar. 10, 1919 - . Home: Washington, D. C. Died Apr. 19, 1936.

ASBOTH, ALEXANDER SANDOR army officer; b. Keszthely, Hungary, Dec. 18, 1811. Mem. Austrain army; fought under Louis Kossuth in Hungarian revolt, 1848-49, came with Kossuth to U.S.; became Am. citizen and officer in U.S. Army; on staff Gen. John Fremont, 1861; commanded division under Gen. Samuel Curtis in campaign in Ark. and Mo., winter 1861; wounded at Battle of Pea Ridge (Ark.), 1862; commd. brig. gen. U.S. Volunteers, 1862, later in command in Columbus, Ky., and Ft. Pickens, Fla.; wounded in Marianna, Fla., 1864; left army with rank of brevetted maj. gen., 1865; U.S. minister to Uruguay and Argentina, 1866-68. Died Buenos Aires, Argentina, Jan. 21, 1868.

ASCH, MORRIS JOSEPH physician, army officer; b. Phila., July 4, 1833; s. Joseph M. and Clara (Ulman) A.; grad. Jefferson Med. Coll., 1852, M.D., 1855. Clin. asst. to Dr. Samuel Gross, Jefferson Med. Coll.; asst. surgeon U.S. Army in Civil War, worked in surgeon gen.'s office, 1861-62; surgeon-in-chief to arty. reserve of Army of Potomac; med. insp. Army of Potomac, med. dir. 24th Army Corps. med. insp. Army of the James and staff surgeon to Gen. Philip H. Sheridan, 186573, served at battles of Chancellorsville, Mine Run, Gettysburg and Appomatox Ct. House; brevetted maj. for Civil War services 1865; while on Sheridan's staff active in Cholera epidemic of 1866 and yellow fever epidemic of 1867; with Sheridan in Chgo. until 1873; practiced medicine, N.Y.C., specialized in laryngology; a founder Am. Laryngol. Assn.; surgeon to throat dept. N.Y. Eye and Ear Infirmary, Manhattan Eye and Ear Hosp. Author articles including "A New Operation for Deviation of the Nasal Septum," (known as Asch operation). Died Oct. 5, 1902.

ASCHAM, JOHN BAYNE (AS'KAM) clergyman; born Vanlue, O., Feb. 12, 1873; s. Frederick Augustus and Minnie (Ault) A.; A.B., Ohio Wesleyan U., 1900 (Phi Beta Kappa), A.M., 1902; A.M., Harvard, 1906; Ph.D., Boston U., 1907; spent 6 mos. in travel and study, Italy and Germany, 1907; spl. student, Am. Sch. Oriental Research, Jerusalem, 1913, and made extensive tour of Palestine; m. Jessie Biggs, Aug. 15, 1895; 1 dau., Mrs. Margaret Greene, Entered minsitry, M.E. Ch., 1897; served Marysville (Ohio) Circuit, 1897-98, 1900-01, Spencerville Circuit, 1901-01; ordained, 1899; pastor Trinity Ch., Delphos, O., 1902-05, 1907-10, Epworth Church, Toledo, 1910-16, Avaondale Church, Cincinnati, Sept. 1916-Sept. 1925; retired since May 1, 1943. Trustee Ohio Wesleyan University, Ohio Methodist Children's Home, etc. First lt., assimilated rank, , U.S. Army; chaplain Base Hosp. No. 25, Allerey, France, July 1918-Feb. 1919; sr. chaplain of hosp. center at Allerey; capt.-chaplain inactive, O.R.C., U.S. Army. Special visitor from Am. Waldensian Aid Soc. to The Waldensian Ch. of Italy, 1921; del. Fifth Ecumenical M.E. Conf., London, 1921. Traveled in Eurpoe as corr. Christian Advocate, etc., summers 1922, 23, 24. Social service rep. of The A. Nash Co., and ednl. adviser of Turk Ojaq, of Turkey, 1925-28. Exec. v.p., The Children's Home, Cincinnati, 1928-43; chmn. children's div. Ohio Welfare Conf., 1933. Mem. Nat. Council for Social Work, Am. Social Soc., Am. Acad. Polit. Science, Am. Assn. on Mental Deficiency, Am. Psychol. Assn., Nat. Com. for Mental Hygiene, Am. Eugenics Soc., Am. Assn. of Church History, Am. Assn. of Social Workers, Am. Legion. Republican. Mason. (32degree, Shriner). Clubs: Cincinnati, Torch, Clergy, Author: Help from the Hills, 1910; A Syrian Pilgrimage, 1914; The Religion of Israel, 1918; The Religion of Judah, 1919; Apostles, Fathers, & Reformers, 1921; Home: The Cincinnati Club, Cincinnati. Died Nov. 14, 1950; buried Spring Grove Cemetery, Findlay, O.

ASH, NICHAEL WOOLSTON congressman, lawyer; b. Phila., Mar. 5, 1789; studied law. Admitted to Pa. bar, 1811, began practice law in Phila.; served as 1st lt. and lt. col. First Regular Pa. Volunteers, War of 1812; became law partner of James Buchanan (15th Pres. of U.S.), Phila., after War of 1812; mem. U.S. Ho. of Reps. from Pa., 24th Congress, 1835-37. Died Phila., Dec. 14, 1858; buried Christ Ch. Burial Ground, Phila.

ASHBURN, PERCY MOREAU med officer, U.S.A.; b. Batavia, O., July 28, 1872; s. Allen W. (M.D.) and Julia M. (Kennedy) A.; grad. Batavia High Sch., 1890; M. D., Jefferson Med. Coll., 1893; m. Agnes Davis, July 6, 1896; children - Allen D. (dec.), Frank D., Ann Virginia Apptd. contract surgeon U.S.A., May 30, 1898; commd. 1st lt. asst. surgeon, Dec. 12, 1808; promoted through grades to col. M.C., May 15, 1917. Participated in Philippine Campaign, 1899; pres. army bd. for study of tropical diseases in P. I., 1906-07; attached to U. S. Commn. to Republic of Liberia, 1909; again detailed pres. army bd. for study tropical diseases of P. I., and at Ancon, Panama, June 1913; gen. insp. Health Dept., Panama Canal, 1914-15; comdr. Med. Officers' Training Camp, Ft. Benjamin Harrison, Ind., 1917; on duty in A.E.F., July 1918-July 1919; comdt. Med. Field Serv. Sch., Aug. 1, 1920-Aug 1, 1923; prof. mil. hygiene, U.S. Mil. Acad., 1923-27; librarian Army Med. Library, Washington, D.C., 1927-32 (retired); apptd. supt. Columbia Hosp. for Women, Sept. 20, 1934. Author: The Elements of Military Hygiene, 1909; History of the Medical Department of the United States Army, 1929. Home: Washington, D.C. Died Aug. 20, 1940.

ASHBURN, THOMAS QUINN army officer; b. Batavia, O., Nov. 17, 1874; s. Allen Wright and Julia (Kennedy) A.; grad. U.S. Mil. Acad., 1897, B. Sc., 1937; grad. Sch. of Submarine Defense, Ft. Totten, N. Y., 1907; m. Frances Marshall Fee; 1 son, Thomas Quinn. Commd. add. 2d lt. U.S.A., June 11, 1897; promoted through grades to col. C.A.C., July 1, 1920; twice promoted by act of Congress to brig. gen., June 3, 1924. maj. gen., Feb. 28, 1927; suggested Inland Waterways Corp. and chmn. bd. and pres. until 1939; pres. Warrior River Terminal Co. Served in Spanish-Am. War, Philippine Insurrection and World War; mil. and civ. gov. in P.I.; organizer and comdr. Met. Police, Manila; expert mil. witness before Spanish Claims Commn.; served as chmn. Claims Bd. for Transportation and chief of Inland Coastwise Waterway Service; chmn. American Waterways Assn. Silver star citation (U.S.); Purple Heart (U.S.); Croix de Guerre and Legion of Honor (France); Condecoracion de Merito Militar, primer clase (Mexico); Spanish-American, Cuba Occupation, Philippine and World War medals; wounded in action insignia. Author: History of 324th Field Artillery, 1919; Waterways and Inland Seaports (govt. printing office), 1925; Technical Discussion Concerning Waterways (Internat. Congress of Navigation, Brussels, Belgium), 1926; Annual Reports (govt. printing office), 1923-36; Inland Waterway Transportation - A National Problem, 1933. Home: Washington, D.C. Died May 2, 1941.

ASHBY, TURNER army officer; b. Plantation Rose Bank, Fauquier County, Va., Oct. 23, 1828; s. Turner and Dorothy (Green) A. Collected a band of men which merged with 7th Va. Cavalry at outbreak of Civil War; served as scout; commd. lt. col. Va. Militia, 1861, promoted col., 1862; fought with Stonwall Jackson in Shenandoah Valley; commd. brig. gen. Confederate Army, 1862. Killed in battle, Harrisonburg, Va., June 6, 1862.

ASHE, GEORGE B(AMFORD), naval officer (ret.); b. Raleigh, N.C., Jan. 19, 1891; s. Samuel A'Court and Hannah Emerson (Willard) A.; B.S., U.S. Naval Acad., 1911; m. Ellen Lane Jett Williams, June 10, 1916. Commd. ensign U.S. Navy, 1912, advanced through grades to rear adm., 1947; served at occupation of Vera Cruz, Mexico, 1914; with destroyer fiotilla, Queenstown, Ireland, 1917-18; stationed in China, destroyer squadrons, 1926-29; with amphibious forces, South Pacific, 1942-44; ret. from active duty, Jan. 1, 1947. Awarded Legion of Merit (World War II). Mem. Sons of Confed. Vets., Queenstown Assn., Soc. of the Cincinnati. Democrat. Episcopalian. Author: (with John I. Hale) Engineering Materials and Processes, 1926. Home: Berryville VA Died May 1971.

ASHE, JOHN colonial legislator, army officer; b. Grovely, N.C., 1720; s. John Baptista and Elizabeth (Swann) A.; m. Rebecca Moore, Speaker, N.C. Colonial Assembly, 1762-65; mem. Com. of - Com. of Safety, Provincial Congress (all N.C.); commd. col. N.C. Militia 1775, brig. gen., 1778; defeated at Brier Creek by Gen. Prevost, 1779 (gave British control of Ga., and made communication possible between Ga. and the Carolinas and the Indians), censured for cowardice by mil. tribunal, 1779; Asheville and Ashe County (N.C.) named for him. Died Sampson County, N.C., Oct. 24, 1781.

ASHE, JOHN BAPTISTA congressman; b. Rocky Point, N.C., 1848 s. Samuel and Mary (Porter) A.; m. Eliza Montfort, children include Samuel. Command. capt. Continental Army, 1776, later lt. col.; mem. N.C. Ho. of Commons, 1784-86; speaker, 1786; mem. Continental Congress, 1787-88; mem. N.C. Senate, 1789; mem. N.C. Conv. to ratify U.S. Constn.; mem. U.S. Ho. of Reps. (Federalist) from N.C., 1st-2d congresses, 1789-93 elected gov. N.C., 1802, died before inauguration. Died Halifax, N.C., Nov. 27, 1802; buried Churchyard Cemetery, Halifax.

ASHE, SAMUEL A'COURT lawyer; b. near Wilmington, N.C., Sept. 13, 1840; s. William Shepperd and Sarah Ann (Green); ed. Rugby Acad., 1852-54, Oxford (Md.) Mil. Acad., 1854-55, Naval Acad., 1855-58; LL.D., U. of N.C., 1916; m. Hannah Emerson Willard, Aug. 10, 1871 (died 1892). Capt. and asst. adj. gen. Pender's Brigade, 1862; ordnance officer Battery Wagner, 1863; asst. to comdg. officer, Fayetteville Arsenal, 1863-65, C.S.A. Admitted to bar, 1867; practiced, 1867-79; mem. N.C. Assembly, 1870-72; chmn. Dem. State Com., 1877-80; editor Raleigh News and Observer, 1879-94; postmaster Raleigh, 1885-89; pres. Willard Mfg. Co., 1896-1906; v.p. Raleigh Hosiery Co., 1900-07; expert employee, Finance Com. of U.S. Senate, 1912-17; clerk U.S. District Court, Raleigh, N.C., 1918-36. Editor hist. vols. and author articles in mags. Home: Raleigh, N.C. Died Aug. 31, 1938.

ASHE, WILLIAM FRANCIS JR. physician, educator; b. Braddock, Pa., Dec. 14, 1909; s. William Francis and Catherine Nancy (Euwer) A.; A.B., Oberlin Coll., 1932; M.D., Western Res. U., 1936; m. Kathleen Terry Little, Dec. 24, 1945; children-James Allyn, Nancy E., Sarah A., Susan K., Carl Francis, Lynn Terry. Intern U. Hosp., Cleve., 1936-38; resident U. Cin. Coll. Medicine, 1937-40; research in indsl. medicine Kettering Lab. Applied Physiology, Cin., 1940-42; dir. Inst. Indsl. Medicine, U. Cin. Coll. Medicine, 1946-50; chief internal med. dept. Holzer Clinic and Hosp., Gallipolis, O., 1950-54; prof., chmn. dept. preventive medicine Ohio State U. Coll. Medicine, 1954-; cons. on thermal environmental problems in industry to Govt. India; med. cons. VA Hosp., Dayton, O.; vis. staff U. Hosps., Columbus. Dir. nutrition survey Armed Forces, Spain, 1958, Chile, 1960. Served from capt. to lt. col. M.C. AUS, 19 Order al Merito Bernardo O'Higgins (Chile). Diplomate Am. Bd. Preventive lfedicine in occupational medicine, 1955. Fellow, A.C.P., A.A.A.S., Am. Coll. Preventive Medicine, Am. Acad. Occupational Medicine, Aerospace Med. Assn.; mem. A.M.A., Am. Pub. Health Assn. Home: 2006 Collingswood Rd., Columbus 21, O. Died Feb. 27, 1966; buried Union Cemetery, Columbus.

ASHFORD, BAILEY KELLY med. officer; b. Washington, D.C., Sept. 18, 1873; s. Francis Asbury (M.D.) and Isabella Walker (Kelly) A.; grad. Washington High Sch., 1891; Columbian (now George Washington) U., 1yr.; M.D., Georgetown U. Med. Sch., 1896; grad. Army Med. Sch., 1898; Sc.D., Georgetown, 1911, Columbia Univ., 1933, U. of Puerto Rico, 1933; hon. M.D., U. of Egypt, 1932; m. Maria Asuncion Lopez, June 24, 1899; children - Mahlon, Gloria Maria, Margarita. Resident phys. Children's Hosp., Washington, D.C., 1895-96; apptd. 1st lt. U.S. Army, Nov. 6, 1897; promoted through grades to col., May 15, 1917. Served with mil. expdn. to P.R., July 1898, and in Battle of Hormigueros, Aug. 13, 1898; div. surgeon 1st Div., June-Oct. 1917; in charge battle training of med officers, Zone of Armies, A.E.F., Nov. 1917-Nov. 1918; battle clasps for Aisne-Marne and Argonne-Neuse. In 1899 determined cause of the anemia of agrl. class of Puerto Rico, later popularized as "hookworm disease"; founded, 1904, P.R. Anemia Commn., which began first campaign against disease in Western Hemisphere. Del. from U.S. to Internat. Cong. Indsl. and Alimentary Hygiene, Brussels, 1910; mem. med. commn. to Brazil, Rockefeller Foundation, 1916; del. from U.S. to Internat. Cong. of Tropical Medicine and Hygiene, Cairo, 1928. Prof. tropical medicine and mycology Columbia U., collaborating with Sch. of Tropical Medicine (Puerto Rico). Hon. mem. and pres. Am. Soc. Tropical Medicine, Puerto Rico Med. Assn.; fellow Am. Coll. Physicians, Am. Coll. Surgeons. Awarded D.S.M. (U.S.); Companion of St. Michael and St. George (Eng.); Grand Cordon, officer 1st class, Order of the Nile. Author: Anemia in Porto Rico, 1904; Uncinariasis in Porto Rico (with Gutierrez), 1911; also The Organization and Administration of the Medical Department, in the Zone of the Armies (Keen's Surgery, Vol. VII); Sprue (Tice's Loose-leaf Medicine), 1931; A Soldier in Science, 1934. Home: San Juan, P.R. Died Nov. 1, 1934.

ASHFORD, MAHLON surgeon; b. Washington, Mar. 24, 1881; s. Francis Asbury and Isabella Walker (Kelley) A.; M.D. Georgetown U. 1904; grad. U.S. Army Med. Sch. 1908, U.S. Army War Coll., 1925; m. Elizabeth Beale, Dec. 20, 1911; 1 son, Beale. Commd. 1st lt., M.C., U.S. Army, 1908, advanced through the grades to col., 1934; chief surgeon Panama Dept., 1935-36; retired from army, 1936; exec. sec. com. on med. edn., N.Y. Acad. Medicine, editor Bull. of N.Y. Acad. Medicine, ú 1936-51, ret. Fellow A.C.S., A.C.P.; mem. Theta Delta Chi. Presbyn. Club: Army & Navy (Washington). Home: Washington. Deceased.

ASHHURST, RICHARD LEWIS lawyer; b. Naples, Italy, Feb. 5, 1838; s. John and Harriet (Eyre) A.; grad. U. of Pa., 1856 (A.M., 1859), law dept., 1859; m. Sarah Frazier, May 30, 1861. Admitted to bar, June 1859. Mustered into Union army 1st lt. and adj. 150th Pa. Vols., Aug. 11, 1862; hon. disch. for wounds received at Gettysburg, Sept. 5, 1863; bvtd. capt. for services at Chancellorsville; bvtd. maj. U.S. Vols., for distinguished gallantry at Gettysburg. Vice dean Shakespeare Soc.; vice-chancellor Phila. Law Assn. Postmaster, Phila., 1906 - . Republican. Home: Phiadelphia. Died 1911.

ASHMORE, JOHN DURANT congressman; b. Greenville, Dist., S.C., Aug. 18, 1819; attended common schs.; studied law. Admitted to the bar, never practiced law; engaged in agrl. pursuits; mem. S.C. Ho. of Reps., 1848-52; comptroller gen. State of S.C., 1853-57; mem. U.S. Ho. of Reps. (Domocrat) from S.C., 36th Congress, 1859-Dec. 21, 1860, resigned; col. 4th S.C. Regt., resigned before regt. called into service; mcht. in Greenville. Died Sardis, Miss. Dec. 5, 1871; buried Black Jack Cemetery, nr. Sardis.

ASHMUN, GEORGE COATES M.D.; b. Tallmadge, O., Jan. 31, 1841; s. Russell A. and Marcia (Wright) A.; M.D., Western Reserve U., 1873; m. Laura J. Post, May 20, 1880; m. 2d, Alice Ford, Nov. 27, 1888; children - Russell Ford, Louis Henry, George Slaght, Bernice. Served in Civil War, 1861-62 and 1863-65; U.S. examiner for pensions, Cleveland, 1873-86; health officer, Cleveland, 1881-91; lecturer on hygiene, Case Sch. of Applied Science, 1903-07; prof. hygiene and preventive medicine, 1893-1909, registrar and bursar. 1893-1907, then prof. emeritus med. jurisprudence and ethics, Med. Coll., Western Reserve U. Maj. surgeon 5th Regt. Inf., Ohio N.G., 1889-98. Mem. Cleveland City Council, 1898-99 and 1902-03; mem. Bd. of Edn., 1909-1915. Home: Cleveland Heights, O. Died June 25, 1929.

ASHTON, WILLIAM EASTERLY gynecologist; b. Phila., Pa., June 5, 1859; s. Samuel Keen and Caroline M. (Smiley) A.; M.D., U. of Pa., 1881; M.D., Jefferson Med. Coll., 1884; LL.D., Ursinus, 1904; m. Alice Elizabeth Rosengarten, Oct. 5, 1891; 1 dau., Dorothy (dec). Mem. faculty of hosp. and Jefferson Med. Coll., 1884-92; gynecologist to hosp. and prof. gynecology, Medico-Chirurg. Coll., 1892-1916; prof. gynecology, Grad. Sch. of Medicine, U. of Pa., 1916 - . Enlisted U.S. Army, 1917; commd. maj. and assigned as regtl. surgeon 309th F.A., 78th Div.; served in France 11 mos., St. Mihiel and Meuse-Argonne offensives; commd. lt. col., Feb. 1919; hon. disch., Camp Dix, N.J., Apr. 1919; gassed in Argonne and retired from practice on leaving army; awarded D.S.C., "for extraordinary heroism," 1918. Fellow Am. Coll. Surgeons. Rep. Epis. Author: Essentials of Obstetrics, 1888 (trans. into Chinese); The Practice of Gynecology (textbook), 1905. Contbr. on surg. subjects. Inventor surg. instruments and appliances; first who substituted pads of gauze for marine sponges. Cited by Maj. Gen. Mark L. Hersey, for award of Congressional Medal of Honor, for "Action beyond call of duty." Home: Philaelphia, Pa. Died 1933.

ASPER, JOEL FUNK congressman, lawyer; b. Adams County, Pa., Apr. 20, 1822; attended local coll. in Warren, O.; studied law. Admitted to Ohio bar, 1844, began practice law in Warren; justice of the peace. 1846; pros. atty. Geauga County, 1847; del. Free-Soil Conv., Buffalo, N.Y., 1848; editor Western Reserve Chronicle, 1849; moved to Ia., 1850; publisher Chardon (Ia.) Democrat; raised a co., served as capt., 1861, during Civil War; wounded in Battle of Winchester, promoted to lt. col., 1862, mustered out of service because of wounds, 1863; moved to Chillicothe, Mo., 1864, practiced law; founded the Spectator, 1866; del. Republican Nat. Conv., Chgo., 1868; mem. U.S. Ho. of Reps. (Radical Republican) from Mo., 41st Congress, 1869-71. Died Chillicothe, Oct. 1, 1872; buried Edgewood Cemetery.

ASPINWALL, WILLIAM physician; b. Brookline, Mass., June 4, 1743; s. Thomas and Joanna (Gardner) A.; grad. Harvard, 1764; m. Susanna Gardner, 1776, 7 children. Served as volunteer in Battle of Lexington, 1776; brigade surgeon in Continental Army, served as deputy dir. army hosp., Jamaica Plain, Mass., 1776-81; established inoculation hosp. for smallpox, Brookline; practiced medicine, Brookline until 1823; mem. Mass. Gen. Ct., Mass. Senate, Gov.'s Council. Died Apr. 16, 1823.

ASTON, RALPH naval officer; b. Middletown, Conn., Jan. 31, 1841; s. Henry Hungerford and Ann (Sheppard) A.; ed. Chase Sem. and pvt. tutors; m. Jennie R. Preswich, Oct. 1869 (died, 1876); 2d, Salena Hinman, Oct. 26, 1882. Apptd. 3rd asst. engr. U.S.N., 1861, and advanced to capt., Mar. 3, 1899; rear-admiral and retired 1902. First service on steam gunboat Cayuga, West Gulf Sta., which first to pass lower forts at capture of New Orleans. Served in Sampson's fleet during Spanish-Am. War, on cruiser Cincinnati, from which transferred to U.S. cruiser Brooklyn, completing sea service April 23, 1899. Home: Brooklyn, N.Y. Died 1904.

ASTOR, JOHN JACOB capitalist; b. Rhinebeck, N.Y., July 13, 1864; s. William and Caroline Webster (Schermerhorn) A.; g.gs. John Jacob Astor; B.S., Harvard, 1888; traveled abroad, 1888-91; m. Ava. Lowle Willing, 1891; 2d, Madeline Talmage Force, Sept. 9, 1911. Mgr. family estates, 1891-; built, 1897, Astoria Hotel, New York, adjoining Waldorf Hotel, which built by Wm. Waldorf Astor, cousin, two now forming one building under name of Waldorf-Astoria Hotel, one of largest and probably most costly hotels in world. Col. staff of Gov. Levi P. Morton, and May, 1898, commd. lt. col. U.S.V.; presented to govt. mountain battery for use in Spanish war, said to cost over $10,000. After assisting Maj. Gen. Breckinridge, Insp. gen. U.S.A., in inspection of camp and troops at Chickamauga Park, Ga., assigned to duty on staff of Maj. Gen. Shafter and served in Cuba in operations ending in surrender of Santiago. Has invented bicycle brake, pneumatic road improver, improved turbine engine, vibrator disintegrator, for getting power gas from peat, and steamship chair, held in place by suction cups. Author: A Journey in Other Worlds, 1890, etc. Home: New York, New York. Died Apr. 15, 1912.

ASTOR, WILLIAM VINCENT b. New York, Nov. 15, 1891; s. John Jacob and Ava Willing A.; now head of Astor family in U.S.; ed. St. George's Sch. and Harvard, 1911-12; m. Helen Dinsmore Huntington, Apr. 30, 1914 (div.); m. 2d, Mary Benedict Cushing, Sept. 27, 2940 (div. 1953); married 3d, Brooke Russell Marshall. Chmn, bd. Weekly Publs., Inc.; dir. U.S. Lines Co. Gov. New York Hospital; trustee N.Y. Pub. Library. Served as ensign, lt. (e.g.) and lt. U.S. Navy, World War I, active duty in European waters; capt., U.S. Naval Res.; on active duty with U.S. Navy, World War II. Mem. War Soc. of Cruiser & Transport Force, Humane Soc. of N.Y. (life), Am. Museum Natural History (life), Saint Nicholas Soc. (life); Navy of U.S. (life), Society Naval Architects & Marine Engrs. (asso.), U.S. Naval Inst., Naval History Soc., Honor Legion of Police Dept., City of N.Y. (hon. Mem.), Holland Lodge (life), U.S. Naval Reserve Officers Assn., County Soc. of City of N.Y. (life), Nat. Assn. Audubon (life), Mil. Order World War (life); charter mem. Geog. and Hist. Soc. of the Americas. Clubs: City (life), Harvard (life), Nat. Golf Links America, The Brook (life), The Links Golf Raquet & Tennis (life), N.Y. Yacht (life), Cedar Creek, Aero of America (life), India House; River of New York; Newport Reading Room (Newport, R.I.); Ft. Orange (Albany, N.Y.); Clove Valley Rod & Gun. Office: 405 Park Av., N.Y.C. 22. Died Feb. 3, 1959; buried Ferncliff, Rhinebeck, N.Y.

ATCHISON, DAVID RICE senator; b. Frogtown, Ky., Aug. 11, 1807; s. William and Catherine (Allen) A.; grad. Transylvania U., 1828. Admitted to Ky. bar, 1830; mem. Mo. Ho. of Reps., 1834, 38; mem. U.S. 14, 1 Senate from Mo., Oct. 24, 1843-Mar. 3, 1855; elected pres. pro tem., 1846-49. 52-54; maj. gen. Mo. Militia; Atchison County (Mo.), City of Atchison (Kan.) named after him. Died Gower, Clinton County, Mo., Jan 26, 1886; buried Greenlawn Cemetery, Plattsburg, Mo.

ATHERTON, GEORGE W. pres. Pa. State Coll., 1882 - ; b. Boxford, Essex Co., Mass., June 20, 1837; left fatherless at 12; helped support mother and two sisters; worked in cotton mill, then on farm, later as teacher; worked way through Phillips Exeter Acad. and Yale; grad. 1863; LL.D., Franklin and Marshall Coll., 1883; m. Frances D. W. Washburn, Dec. 25, 1863. Served as lt. and capt. 10th Conn. vols., 1861-63; taught in Albany Boys' Acad., 1863-67; prof. St. John's Coll., 1867-68, Univ. of Ill., 1868-69; prof. polit. economy and constl. law. Rutgers, 1869-82; mem. Bd. of Vistors to U.S. Naval Acad., 1873, 1891; on commn. to investigate Red Cloud Indian agency, 1875; chmn. commn. to digest and revise State system of taxation, N.J., 1878; admitted to N.J. bar, 1878; first pres. Am. Assn. of Agrl. Colls. and Expt. Stas. (Reelected for purpose of recognizing his services in drafting and securing passage of act of Congress establishing agrl. expt. stas. in every State and Territory). Author: Magna Charta, a Comparative View of the Barons' Articles and the Great Charter. Home: State College, Pa. Died 1906.

ATKIN, ISAAC CUBITT RAYMOND banker; b. Springfield, Ont., Can., Jan. 2, 1892; s. William Isaac and Martha (Calk) A.; ed. Springfield, Ont., pub. and high schs. m. Alice Winnifred Falnagan, Sept. 27, 1922; children—Donald Raymond, Frances Winnifred (dec.), James Blakesley. Came to U.S., 1925, naturalized, 1940. Asso. with Traders Bank of Can. and Royal Bank of Can., 1909-25; with J.P. Morgan & Co. since 1925, partner, 1939-40, vice-pres. & dir. since incorp., Apr. 1, 1940; dir. Johns-Manville Corp., Can. Life Assurance Co. Internat. Nickel Co. of Can., Ltd., Monsanto Can., Ltd. Served as capt. 102d Can. Inf. Batt., C.E.F., 1915-19. Decorated Mil. Cross & bar. Episcopalian. Clubs: Baltusrol Golf, Short Hills (Short Hills, N.J.). Home: 95 Knollwood Rd., Short Hills, N.J. Office: 23 Wall St., N.Y. City Died Jan. 25, 1957.

ATKINS, SMITH DYKINS newspaperman; b. Horseheads, N.Y., June 9, 1836; s. Adna Stanley and Sarah (Dykins) A.; ed. Rock River Sem., Mt. Morris, Ill.; m. Eleanor Hope Swain, Aug. 27, 1865. Admitted to bar, 1854; pros. atty. 14th Jud. Dist., Ill., 1860. Enlisted as pvt., 11th Ill. Inf., Apr. 17, 1861; capt. Co. A, Apr. 30, 1861; maj., Mar. 21, 1862; resigned, Apr. 17, 1862; col. 92d Ill. Inf., Sept. 4, 1862; bvtd. brig. gen. vols., Jan 12, 1865, "for gallant and meritorious services"; hon. mustered out, June 21, 1865. Editor Freeport Daily Journal, 1878 - ; postmaster of Freeport. Republican. Home: Freeport, Ill. Died Mar. 27, 1913.

ATKINSON, ARCHIBALD congressman, lawyer; b. Isle of Wight County, Va., Sept. 15, 1792; attended law dept. Coll. William and Mary, Williamsburg, Va. Served in War of 1812; Admitted to bar; practiced in Smithfield, Isle of Wight County; mem. Va. Ho. of Dels., 1815-17, 28-31; mem. Va. Senate, 1839-43; mem. U.S. Ho. of Reps. (Democrat) from Va., 28th-30th congresses, 1843-49; pros. atty. Isle of Wight County. Died Smithfield, Jan. 7, 1872; buried graveyard of Old St. Luke's Ch., nr. Smithfield.

ATKINSON, HENRY army officer; b. N.C., 1782; m. Mary Ann Bullitt, Jan. 16, 1826; 1 son, Edward. Commd. capt. 3d Inf., U.S. Army, 1808, col. 45th Inf., 1814, col. 6th Inf., 1815; commanded Yellowstone Expdn. instituted by Sec. of War John C. Calhoun, fought against the Indians and Brit. fur traders; brig. gen. in charge of Western Dept., 1820; reappt. col. 6th Inf. after a revision of army rattings, 1821; commanded expdn. to Upper Mo. River, 1825; appt. commr. to make treaties with Indians; selected site for Jefferson Barracks, Mo., 1826; dispatched mission which resulted in the establishment of Ft. Leavenworth, 1827; served in Black Hawk War, 1832; supr. removal of Winnebago Indians from Wis. to Neutral Ground, Ia. Died Jefferson Barracks, Mo., June 14, 1842.

ATKINSON, JOHN BRADSHAW shoe importer; b. Cambridge, Mass., June 17, 1894; s. Thomas E. and Sarah E. (Flaherty) A.; A.B., Boston Coll., 1916; postgrad. Suffolk Law Sch.; M.Pub. Adminstrn., Harvard, 1949, M.A. (hon.), 1951; m. Louise May O'Shea, June 7, 1922; 1 son, Thomas. Pres., treas. Atkinson Shoe Corp., Boston; treas. LeSol, Inc., dir. Scully Signal Co. (Cambridge), Sporting Shoe Co. of Can.; trustee Cambridge Savs. Bank; city mgr., Cambridge, 1942-52, Regent Boston College; mem. Harvard overseers com. to visit govt. Served with U.S. Army, 28 mos., World War I; with Mass. N.G. retiring with rank of col.; mil. aide to Gov. Joseph B. Ely, 4 yrs. Mem. Internat., Mass. (past pres.) city mgrs. assns., Mass. Soc. Pub. Adminstrn. (past pres.), Cath. Alumni Sodality (past pres), Am. Legion Boston Coll. Alumni Assn. (past pres.). Roman Catholic. Clubs: Harvard, Clover, Gridiron (Boston); Cambridge, Harvard Faculty; Hatherly Country: Royal Canadian Yact. Home: 515 Beacon St., Chestnut Hill 67. Mass. Office: 145 Lincoln St., Boston. Died Apr. 28, 1965.

ATTERBURY, WILLIAM WALLACE ry. official; b. New Albany, Ind., Jan. 31, 1866; Ph.B., Yale, 1886; hon. A.M., 1911; LL.D., U. of Pa., 1919, Yale U., 1926, Villa Nova Coll., 1927, Temple U., 1929; E.D., Pa. Mil. Coll., 1932; m. Mrs. A. R. MacLeod. Began as apprentice in Altoona shops, Pa. R.R., 1886, road foreman on various divs., 1889-92; asst. engr. of motive power Pa. Lines (Northwest System), 1892-93; master mechanic Pa. Co., Ft. Wayne, Inc., 1893-96; gen. supt. motive power, lines east of Pittsburgh and Erie, 1896-1903; gen. mgr. same, 1903-09; 5th v.p. in charge transportation Pa. R.R., Mar. 24, 1909-Mar. 3, 1911, and 4th v.p., Mar. 3, 1911-May 8, 1912, v.p. in charge operations, May 8, 1912. Granted leave of absence, Aug. 6, 1917, to direct constrn. and operation U.S. mil. rys. in France; commd. brig. gen. U.S.A., Oct. 5, 1917-May 31, 1919; v.p. in charge operation Pa. R.R. system, Mar. 1, 1920; v.p. without designation, Nov. 15, 1924; elected pres. Pa. R.R. Co., Oct. 1, 1925; dir. Chicago Union Station Co., N.Y. Connecting R.R. Co., Richmond, Fredericksburg & Potomac R.R. Co., Washington Terminal Co., Pennroad Corp., N.&W. Ry. Co., Phil. Nat. Bank, Guaranty Trust Co. of N.Y.; trustee Penn Mut. Life Insurance Co. D.S.M. (U.S.);

Comdr. Legion of Honor (France); Companion of Most Honorable Order of Bath (Great Britain); Comdr. Order of Crown (Belgium); Royal Order of White Eagle (Serbia); Grand Officer of Order of Crown (Roumania). Republican. Home: Philadelphia, Pa. Died Sept. 20, 1935.

ATTWOOD, FREDERIC, business exec.; b. East Haddam, Conn., Apr. 23, 1883; s. Frederic J. H. and Margaret (MacConnell) A.; grad. Bklyn. Latin Sch., 1900; M.E., E.E., Columbia, 1904; m. Gladys Hollingsworth, Oct. 27, 1917; 1 son, William Hollingsworth. Traffic engr. N.Y. Telephone Co., 1904-07; European rep. Air. Reduction Co., 1915-17; gen. European rep. Ohio Brass Co., elec. mfrs., 1919; v.p., dir. Canadian Ohio Brass Co., Ohio Brass Co. from 1927; dir. Melville Shoe Corp. Commd. maj. C.E., A.E.F., Nov. 1917; attached to Gen. Hdqrs. A.E.F., C.W.S., Gen. Tech. Bd. War Damages Bd. Am. Commn. to Negotiate Peace, U.S. Liquidation Commn.; hon. disch. Oct. 1919; col. O.R.C. Decorated Officer Legion of Honor (France). Pres. U.S. nat. com. Internat. Conferences Large Elec. Systems; World Power Conf., Internat. Electrotech. Commn. Mem. Inst. Elec. and Electronic Engineers, Phi Gamma Delta. Republican. Episcopalian. Clubs: Bankers, Engineers, Columbia University (New York City); St. Cloud Country; University; Interallied (Paris, France). Home: New Canaan CT Died Aug. 26, 1969; buried Lake-View Cemetery, New Canaan CT

ATWATER, JOHN WILBUR ex-congressman; b. Chatham Co., N.C., Dec. 27, 1840; academic edn.; enlisted Co. D., 1st N.C. vols., C.S.A., and served with Gen. Lee to close of war; State senator, 1890, 1892 and 1896, first term as Dem., and last two as Populist; mem. 56th Congress, 4th N.C. dist. Address: Rialto, N.C.

ATWOOD, ARTHUR R. banker; b. Champlain, N.Y., Nov. 21, 1891; s. Levi E. and Ida M. (Waters) A.; m. Florence E. Doane, July 6, 1920; 1 son, John Deane (killed World War II). With U.S. Treasury Dept., 1931-35; dir. and v.p. Colonial Trust Co., Pitts., 1935ú ú 1935—, ú now exec. v.p. sec. dir. McClane Mining Co., P. McGraw Wool, U.S. Concrete Pipe Co., Pa. Industries, Inc., Ft. Pitt Coal & Coke Corp., Harmon Creek Coal Corp., Unity Rys. Co., The Waverly Oil Works Co.; partner A.R.M. Coal & Coke Sales Agy. Capt., 367th F.A. Res. Presbyn. Mason. Clubs: Duquesne, Pittsburgh Field, Home: 78 Woodhaven Dr., Mt. Lebannon, Pa. Office: Colonial Trust Co., 414 Wood St., Pitts. 22. Died June 13, 1954; buried Champlain, N.Y.

ATWOOD, EDWIN BYRON soldier; b. Portage Co., O., Sept. 18, 1842; s. Edwin and Eliza (Byron) A.; ed. Farmington Sem., Trumbull Co., O., and Allegheny Coll., Meadville, Pa.; m. Henrietta M. King, Nov. 23, 1878. In 41st Ohio Inf. as sergt. maj., Sept. 19, 1861, 2d lt., Jan. 1, 1862, 1st lt., Sept. 8, 1862, capt., May 1, 1864; bvt. maj. vols., Mar. 13, 1865, for "valuable and conspicuous service during war"; mustered out Nov. 27, 1865; apptd. 2d lt. 16th U.S. Inf., May 11, 1866, and advanced to col. asst. q. m. gen., Nov. 1, 1900. Bvtd. 1st lt. Mar. 2, 1867, for "gallant and meritorious services" in battle of Murfreesboro, Tenn.; capt., Mar. 2, 1867, for same at Chickamauga, and maj., Mar. 2, 1867, for same at Mission Ridge. Brig.-gen. U.S.A., Aug. 2, 1903, retired Aug. 3, 1903, at own request, being senior col. in q.m. dept. U.S.A., and serving as chief q.m., Div. of Philippines, at Manila. Home: Chicago, Ill. Died 1909.

ATWOOD, HENRY (ELKINS) banker; b. Keeseville, N.Y., Nov. 22, 1892; s. John N. and Harriet (Jocelyn) A.; A.B., Dartmouth, 1913; A.M., Harvard, 1914; m. Marion Woodward, June 19, 1917; children—John A., Roger W., Carol (Mrs. Harvey N. Daniels). Instr. in French, Syracuse (N.Y.) U., 1914, U. Minn., 1915-17; investment business, Mpls., 1919-24; bond officer Mpls. Trust Co., 1924-33; v.p. First Nat. Bank of Mpls., 1933-36, pres. 1945—, also dir.; v.p. B. F. Nelson Mfg. Co., Mpls., 1936-45; v.p., dir. First Bank Stock Corp.; dir. First Service Corp., B. F. Nelson Mfg. Co., 1st Bancredit Corp., N.W. Fire & Marine Ins. Co., N.W. Nat. Life Ins. Co., Soo Line R.R. Co., Mpls. & Eastern Ry. (pres.). Trustee Mpls. Found,; dir., mem. exec. com. Minn. Community Research Council, Inc. Mem. Fed. Adv. Council. Served as capt. Cav., U.S. Army, World War I. Clubs: Minneapolis, Minikahda (Mpls.); Minnesota (St. Paul); Woodhill Country (Wayzata); Chicago. Home: Maplewood, Wayzata, Minn. Doed Aug. 27, 1950.

ATWOOD, ROY FRANKLIN stock broker; b. Plymouth, Mass., Sept. 8, 1899 s. Herbert Franklin and Lucy (Shurtleff) A.; student Bryant-Stratton Sch., 1915-17; m. Whitney Bourme, Feb. 4, 1954 (div. May 1961). Mgr. stock dept. Paine Webber & Co., Springfield, Mass., 1919-27; founder J.R. Timmins & Co., N.Y.C., Montreal and Toronto, 1927, resident partner, N.Y.C., 1927-; pres. Can. Oil Lands, Ltd., Calgary Alta., 1952-; dir. Greyhound Corp., R.F.A., Inc. Served with Air Corps, U.S. Army, World War I; to col. USAAF, World War II. Decorated Legion of Merit, Bronze Star medal; comdr. British Empire; Legion of Honor, Croix de Guerre with palm (France); comdr. Cross St. Olaf (Norway). Republican. Epsicopalian. Clubs: Links, Brook (N.Y.C.); Nat. Golf Links (Southampton, L.I.); Piping Rock (Locust Valley, L.I.); Bucks(London, Eng.); Rolling Rock (Pa.). Home: 767 Fifth Av., N.Y.C. 22. Office: 61 Broadway, N.Y.C. 6. Died July 26, 1963.

AUCHINCLOSS, CHARLES C. broker; b. New York, N.Y., Sept. 24, 1881; s. Edgar Stirling and Maria LaGrange (Sloan) A.; A.B., Yale 1903; LL.B., Harvard, 1906; m. Rosamond Saltonstall, June 19, 1906; children-Rosamond (Mrs. T. Plowden-Wardlow), Josephine (Mrs. Harry I. Nicholas, Junior), and Richard Saltonstall Auchincloss. Admitted to N.Y. bar, 1906 and since practiced in that state; mem. firm Littlefield & Littlefield, N.Y. City, 1908-17; partner F.S. Moseley & Co., N.Y. City 1917-. Director Am. Can Co., Nat. Biscuit Co. Capt. F.A., O.R.C., World War I; chmn. Officers Service Com. World War II. Mem. Prison Assn. of N.Y. (treas). Clubs: Links (past pres.), Racquet and Tennis, Grolier, Yale, University (New York); Nat. Golf Links (Southampton, L.I.); Somerset (Boston). Home: 120 e. 70th St. N.Y.C. 21 Office: 120 Broadway, N.Y.C. 5. Died May 14, 1961.

AUCHMUTY, RICHARD TYLDEN philanthropist; b. N.Y.C., July 15, 1831; s. Richard Tylden and Mary (Allen) A at 1831. 1831; s. Richard Tylden and Mary (Allen) A.; attended Columbia, 1847-49; studied architecture with James Renwick, N.Y.C., circa 1852; m. Ellen Schermerhorn. Became partner (with James Renwick) in archtl. firm, circa 1856; commd. capt. 5th Corps. U.S. Army, 1861; served at Battle of Gettysburg, 1863, brevetted col.; helped prepare defenses of Washington, D.C. against Early's expdn., 1864; returned to practice of architecture, N.Y.C., after Civil War; active in affairs of Lenox, Mass. (where he owned summer home), from circa 1866; founded N.Y. Trade Sch. (for young men to learn trades without spending excessive apprenticeship terms), 1881, maintained sch. until 1892, when endowment received from J.P. Morgan; active in Trinity (Episcopal) Ch., N.Y.C., served as vestryman. Died Lenox, July 18, 1893.

AUD, GUY surgeon; b. Cecilia, KY., Aug. 29, 1887; s. Charles Zachary and Lura (Bayne) A.; A.B., St. Xavier Coll., Louisville, 1904; M.D., U. Louisville, 1909; Fellow in surgery Mayo Clinic, Rochester, Minn., 1911-15. Surg. interne Lying-in Hosp., N.Y.C., 1909, N.Y. Hosp. for Relief of Ruptured and Crippled, 1910, Bellevue Hosp., 1911; pvt practice surgery, Louisville, since 1919; faculty Sch. of Medicine, U. Louisville, since 1915, prof. surgery since 1946; attending surgeon Louisville Gen. Hosp., St. Joseph Infirmary and Kosair Crippled Children's Hosp. Served to maj. M.C., U.S. Army, 1917-19; comdg. officer Base Hosp. 210, Toul, France, 1918, lt. col. Med. Res. Corp., 1919-35; ret. 1935; surg. cons. to Med. Examining Bd., Selective Service Bd., 1942-46. Received Congl. Selective Service medal, 1947; Citation U. Louisville for 34 yrs. outstanding service, 1915; 1949 medal Am. Cancer Soc., Ky. div., for work in cancer control. Diplomate Am. Bd. Surgery, 1937. Fellow A.C.S., So. Surg. Assn. (v.p. 1950); mem. Am. Cancer Soc. (pres. 1951, regional dir. since 1944, chmn. exec. com. Ky. div., 1942-50), So. Med. Assn., Ky. State Med. Assn. (pres. 1948), Ky. Surg. Assn., Med. Research Commn. State of Ky., Phi Chi. Democrat. Catholic. Contbr. chpts. in Ency. Medicine, Book of Health. Contbr. articles on surgery in med. jours. Editor Jour. Ky. State Med. Assn. Died Feb. 27, 1959; buried Calvary Cemetery, Louisville.

AUDRIETH, LUDWIG FREDERICK chemist, educator; b. Vienna, Austira, Feb. 23, 1901; s. Ludwig Anton and Fredericka (Herrmann) A.; brought to U.S., 1902, naturalized, 1912; B.S., Colgate U., 1922; Ph.D., Cornell, 1926; m. Maryon Laurice Trevett, Mar. 27, 1937; children-Kaaren Laurice (Mrs. J.R. Tague, Jr.), Elsa Craven, Anthony Ludwig. Research asst. Cornell, 1926-28; faculty mem. dept. chemistry U. Ill., 1928-67, prof. emeritus, 1961-67; NRC fellow U. Rostock, Germany, 1931-32; chem. cons., 1937-67 sci. attache Am. embassy, Bonn, West Germany, 1959-63; faculty Sch. Fgn. Affairs, Fgn. Service Inst., Washington, 1964-67. Mem. Chem. Corps Adv. Council, 1952-57. Served Res. officer, Chem. Corps, 1930-42; active duty, capt., maj. Ordnance Dept., Picatinny Arsenal, as chief research div., 1942-46. Mem. Am. Chem. Soc., Ges. Deutscher Chemiker, A.A.A.S., Ill. Acad. Scis, Phi Beta Kappa, Sigma Xi, Sigma Nu, Alpha Chi Sigma, Phi Lambda Upsilon (nat. pres. 1950-54, editor Register 1938-42), Phi Mu Alpha, Sigma Gamma Epsilon, Phi Kappa Phi. Clubs: Cosmos (Washington). Author: The Chemistry of Hydrazine (with B. A. Ogg), 1950; Non-Aqueous Solvents (with J. Kleinberg), 1953. Bd. editors Inorganic Syntheses, 1934-67. Editor-in-chief, 1945-50. Contbr. profl. jours. Patentee in field. Home: 1515 Waverly Dr., Champaign, Ill. Died Jan. 28, 1967; buried Mt. Hope Cemetery, Champaign.

AUER, JOSEPH LAWRENCE business exec.; b. N.Y.C., Mar. 18, 1898; s. Jacob S. and Augusta (Hodes) A.; ed. pub. schs.; evening engring. courses Columbia and N.Y. univs.; m. Ernestine Lorch, Apr. 28, 1925; children-Joan Lorelei, Edmund R. Began as apprentice and machinist De La Vergne Machine Co., Bronx, N.Y., 1912, advancing to position as works mgr., 1926-30; supt. Crocker-Wheeler Electric Mfg. Co., Ampere, N.J., 1930-37; works mgr. R. Hoe & Co., Inc., N.Y.C., 1937-42, v.p., gen. works mgr., 1942-46, pres. 1946-53, dir. 1946-54; mem. Bronx adv. com. Chase Manhattan Bank. Dir., v.p. Bronx Bd. Trade. Dir., mem. council Greater N.Y. Fund; dir. Bronx region Nat. Conf. Christians and Jews; mem. N.Y. State Payroll Savs. Adv. Commn. Served as chief spl. mechanic USN, World War I; overseas, Brest, France; chmn. maj. caliber anti-aircraft integrating com., later chmn. moblie carriage recoil mechanism com. Ordnance Dept., War Dept. during World War II. Recipient Ordnance Dept. citation for meritorious service, July 1944; certificate of appreciation from sec. of war, 1945. Mem. Am. Soc. for Metals, Am. Ordnance Assn. (chmn. recoil, recuperator and equilibrator com.), Bronx C. of C., Nat. Printing Equipment Assn. (dir.), Newcomen Soc. N.A. Democrat. Roman Catholic. Clubs; Rotary (Bronx); Cloud, Schnorer, N.Y. Athletic; Winged Foot Golf; Larchmont (N.Y.) Shore. Died May 24, 1963; buried St. Raymond Cemetery, Bronx, N.Y.

AUERBACH, HERBERT S. merchant; b. Salt Lake City, Utah, Oct. 4, 1882; s. Samuel H. and Eveline (Brooks) A.; student Fresenius Labs. and J.J. Meier Sch., Wiesbaden, Germany, 1897-99; Lausanne Tech. Sch., Lausanne, Switzerland, 1901; Mining Engr., Columbia University Sch. of Mines; M.A., Columbia University, Electro Metallurgy; unmarried. Mining engr. in charge properties in Ida. and Colo., 1906-10; engaged in real estate, building and mercantile bus., Salt Lake City, since 1911; pres. and mgr. Auerbach Co. Dept Store; pres. Auerbach Realty Co., Brooks Co.; chmn. bd. dirs. Federal Reserve Bank (Salt Lake City branch, Dist. 12). Major, Ordnance sect. U.S. Army, 1918. Mem. Army Ordnance Assn., Washington (1918-43). Pres. Utah State Hist. Soc. Mem. Am. Soc. of Composers, Authors and Publishers. Clubs: Rotary, Sons of Pioneers, Timpanogos (Salt Lake City). Home: 368 S. State St. Office: Broadway at State St., Salt Lake City, Utah. Died Mar. 19, 1945.

AUGSPURGER, OWEN BEAL, lawyer; b. Buffalo, June 19, 1913; s. Owen Beal and Mabel (Moulter) A.; B.A., Princeton, 1934; LL.B., U. Buffalo, 1937; m. Paula Norris, Mar. 13, 1945; children—John, Susan, Robert. Admitted to N.Y. bar, 1937, since practiced in Buffalo; partner firm Jaeckle, Fleischmann, Kelly, Swart & Augspurger, and predecessors, 1946-69. Sec., dir. Roblin Steel Corp., Jones Rich Milk Co., Backers Realty Corp., Lake Erie Rolling Mill, Inc., Erie Forge & Steel Corp.; secretary, director Rand Capital Corporation. Dir., sec. Greater Buffalo Development Found.; chmn. devel. campaign U. Buffalo, 1952; chmn. Buffalo chpt. A.R.C., 1953-55, vice chmn. nat. conv., Seattle, 1963, chmn. adv. com. Eastern Area, 1960-61; chmn. joint United Fund-A.R.C. com. Buffalo, 1956-59; mem. N.Y. State Commn. on War 1812, 1964-69; mem. council U. Buffalo, 1953-63. City councilman, Buffalo, 1950-51, vice chmn. University of Buffalo, 1950-51. Served to lt. col. AUS, 1941-46; PTO; brig. gen. N.Y. Guard. Fellow Company Mil. Historians; mem.. Am., N.Y., Erie County (bd. dirs. 1954-56) bar assns., N.Y. State Jr. (pres. 1940), Buffalo Jr. (pres. 1938) chambers commerce, Buffalo Hist. Soc. (pres. 1964-69), Phi Delta Phi. Republican. Presbyn. Clubs: Buffalo Country, Buffalo Athletic. Author: World War II History of the 102d AAA Battalion, 1961; also articles. Home: Buffalo NY Died 1969.

AUGUR, CHRISTOPHER COLUMBUS army officer; b. Kendall, N.Y., July 10, 1821; s. Ammon and Annis (Wellman) A.; grad. U.S. Mil. Acad., 1843; m. Jane Arnold, 1844. Served as aide-de-camp to Brig. Gen. Hopping and Gen. Caleb Cushing during Mexican War, 1846-47; commd. capt., 1852; served in campaigns against Indians in Ore. and Wash. territories, 1852-56; promoted maj., 1861; comdt. cadets U.S. Mil. Acad., 1861; commd. brig. gen. U.S. Volunteers at start of Civil War, 1861; brevetted maj. gen. U.S. Volunteers, col. U.S. Army for services in Battle of Cedar Mountain, 1862; commanded action at Port Hudson Plains, 1863, Dept. of Washington, Oct. 1863-Aug. 1866; promoted brig. gen. for service at Port Hudson, 1865, commanded Dept. of the Platte, 1867; commd. brig. gen. U.S. Army, 1869, brig. gen. Dept. of Tex., 1869-75, of the Gulf, 1875-78, of Dept. of the South and Mo., 1878-85; ret., 1885. Died Georgetown, D.C., Jan. 16, 1898.

AUGUR, JACOB ARNOLD soldier; b. Ft. Niagara, N.Y., Aug. 21, 1849; s. Gen. Christopher C. and Jane Elizabeth (Arnold) A.; grad. U.S. Mil. Acad., 1869; m. Katherine J. Dodge, Nov. 14, 1872. Commd. 2d lt., 5th Cav., June 15, 1869; promoted through grades to col., 10th Cav., June 9, 1902; employed chiefly on frontier service until 1880; served with Republican River Expdn., 1869, and engaged in affair on Prairie Dog Creek, and in Ute Expdn. during fall and winter of 1879; was instr. at U.S. Mil. Acad., 1883-87; on frontier duty Ind. Ty. and Tex., 1887-97; instr. Inf. and Cav. Sch., 1897-99, 1901-02; in Philippines, 1899-1901; on duty in Neb., 1902-07, in Philippines, Apr. 2, 1907 - . Died 1909.

AULD, GEORGE P. (AWLD) accountant; b. at Rutland, Vt., Jan. 28, 1881; s. Joseph and Annie C. (Howe) A.; A.B., U. of Vermont, 1902, LL.D., 1937; m. Madeleine G. Swift, Nov. 19, 1910 (died Jan. 1949); 1 dau., Elizabeth (Mrs. Robert H. Perry); married 2d Margaret A. Adair, October 21, 1950. Officer of Supply Corps, U.S. Navy, 1902-20; comdr., 1918; chief accounting officer United States Navy, 1915-18; aide to Adm. Sims, London, 1918, asst. financial adviser U.S. Peace Mission, 1919; accountant-gen. Inter-Allied

Reparation Commn., 1920-24; asst to Owen D. Young, first agent gen. under Dawes plan, Berlin, 1924; joined Haskins & Sells, C.P.A.'s 1924 (partner since 1930); chmn. Accountants Advisory Com. to N.Y. State Regents Inquiry, 1936; served as civilian in Navy Dept., 1941-42, organizing field inspection of contract audits, then chief cost and audit branch (Office Procurement & Material) and mem. Navy Price Adjustment Bd. Trustee U. of Vermont, 1942-44. Mem. Am. Inst. of Accountants (mem. 1933 com. on federal securities act; chmn. 1937 com. on fed. reorganization), Council on Foreign Relations, Am. Econ. Assn., N.Y. State Society C.P.A.'s (hon. life mem.), Sigma Phi, Phi Beta Kappa. Awarded U.S. Navy Cross (World War I); Officer Legion of Honor (France). Clubs: Century (New York); Army and Navy (Washington). Author: The Dawes Plan and the New Economics, 1927; Rebuilding Trade by Tariff Bargaining, 1936. Formerly writer international affairs, N.Y. Herald-Tribune, Foreign Affairs, Atlantic Monthly, and others. Home: New Canaan, Conn. Office: 2 Broadway, N.Y.C. 4. Died Sept. 8, 1962; buried Sleepy Hollow Cemetery, Concord, Mass.

AULTMAN, DWIGHT EDWARD army officer; b. Allegheny, Pa., Feb. 2, 1872; s. Matthias W. and Mary (Beach) A.; grad. U.S. Mil. Acad., 1894; m. Alma Y. Hickok, Jan. 5, 1898; children - Edith H. (Mrs. Mark H. Doty), Dwight E., Anita B. Commd. 2d lt. 4th Cav., June 12, 1894; promoted through grades to col., May 15, 1917; brig. gen. N.A., Apr. 18, 1918; brig. gen. U.S.A., Apr. 27, 1921. Participated in Battle of San Juan Hill, July 1-3, 1898, and siege of Santiago, Cuba; a.d.c. to Gen. Wheaton in Cuba, Dec. 1898-Jan. 1899, later a.d.c. to Gen. Keifer; organized and comd. Cuban Arty., 1901-02, instr. same, 1903-06; on staff comdg. gen. Army of Cuban Pacification, 1906-07; instr. dept. of langs., 1914-15; grad. Army War Coll., 1916; instr. same, 1916-17; comdr. 5th F.A., 1st Div., A.E.F., Oct. 1917-May 1918; comdr. 51st Brigade F.A., 26th Div., 1st A.C., A.E.F., May 8-Aug. 15, 1918; apptd. chief of Arty., 5th Corps, Oct. 1918, and of 2d Army, Dec. 1918; participated in battles, Champagne-Marne, Aisne-Marne, St. Mihiel and Meuse-Argonne. Grad. Gen. Staff Coll., 1920. Decorated D.S.M.; Comdr. Legion of Honor, Croix de Guerre (France). Author: Military Strength and Resources of the United States, 1917. Died Dec. 13, 1929.

AUMAN, WILLIAM brig. gen. U.S.A.; b. Berks Co., Pa., Oct. 17, 1839; s. Henry and Catherine (Breyman) A.; ed. pub. schs., Pottsville, Pa., to 1852; Wyoming Sem., Kingston, Pa., 1865; m. Emma Eliza Rosengarten, Sept. 27, 1866. Served as pvt. Washington Arty., of Pottsville, 25th Pa. Vols. (1st troops to arrive for defense of Nat. Capitol), Apr. 15-July 29,1861; corp. to capt. Co. G, 48th Pa. Vols., Sept. 9, 1861-July 17, 1865; commd. 2d lt. 13th Inf., May 11, 1866; promoted through grades to brig. gen., Apr. 16, 1902. Bvtd. capt. vols., Apr. 2, 1865, "for gallant and meritorious services before Petersburg, Va." (wounded). Participated in 17 general engagements and many minor affairs; assisted in mining and blowing up Confederate fort before Petersburg, Va., July 30, 1864. Was in campaigns against Crow Indians in Mont., 1868 (severely wounded); Ute Indians, Southern Utah, 1872; Sioux Indians, Red Cloud, Neb., 1874; comd. 13th Inf., July 1-24, 1898, in Santiago campaign which regiment captured Spanish block house and flag in the assault on San Juan Hill, July 1, 1898; comd. sta. of Santa Cruz, Laguna, P.I., 1901; obtained surrender of Col. Julie Herrera and his command; pres. exam. bds. and bds. of survey. Northern Luzen, 1901-02; retired at own request, May 10, 1902. Home: Buffalo, N.Y. Died May 21, 1920.

AURELL, GEORGE EMANUEL, fgn. service officer; b. Kobe, Japan, Jan. 8, 1905; s. Karl Emanuel and Hannah Antoinette (Christensen) A.; student Park Coll., 1922-23, Northwestern U., 1923-24; B.S., Okla. State U., 1927; m. Maxine Reagor, June 22, 1934; children—John Karl, Jane A. Croft. Vice consul Dept. of State, Yokohama, Japan, 1927-30; comml. manager Southwestern staff Gen. MacArthur, Dept. of Def., Tokyo, Japan, 1946-53; staff Far Eastern Affairs, Dept. State, Washington, 1953-56; spl. asst. ambassador, Manila, P.I., 1956-60; State Dept., Washington, 1960-62; spl. asst. to sec. gen. SEATO, Bangkok, Thailand, 1962-66, served to lt. col. AUS, 1942-46. Decorated Legion of Merit, Bronze Star with cluster. Mem. Phi Kappa Alpha, Alpha Kappa Psi. Episcopalian. Home: McLean VA Died Feb. 1970.

AUSTIN, FRED THADDEUS army officer; b. at Hancock, Vt., Dec. 28, 1866; s. Julius Tilden and Manora (Keith) A.; B.S., Norwich U., 1888, M.S., 1894, (C.E., 1896; m. Lenore Harrison, Oct. 21, 1909. Practiced architecture Brockton and Boston, Mass., 1889-98; 1st lt. and adj. 5th Mass Inf. Vols., July 1, 1898; hon. mustered out, Mar. 31, 1899; 1st lt. 46th U.S. Inf., Aug. 17, 1899; hon. mustered out, June 30, 1901; 1st lt. Arty. Corps. Aug. 22, 1901; promoted through grades to col., Sept. 27, 1925; maj. gen. chief of field artillery, Dec. 20, 1927. Col. N.A., Aug. 5. 1917; brig. gen. N.A., Apr. 18, 1918; dir. Arty. Sch., Fort Sill, Okla., 1920; later in insp. gens. department. Died Feb. 26, 1938.

AUSTIN, JAMES HAROLD prof. research medicine; b. Phila., Pa., Sept. 22, 1883; s. James Smith and Louisa McKee (Sloan) A.; B.S., University of Pennsylvania, 1905; M.D., 1908; married Thelma Frances Wood, June 21, 1924; children—Thelma Frances Wood (Mrs. W. Warrin Fry), James Harold, John Brander, 3d. Interne Univ. Hosp., Phila., 1908-10; asst. demonstrator in pathology, U. of Pa., 1910-11, asso. in research medicine and medicine, 1911-17; asst. Rockefeller Inst., New York, 1919-20, asso., 1920-21; prof. of research medicine, University of Pennsylvania, 1922-50, emeritus prof. since 1950. Dir. William Pepper Lab. of Clin. Medicine, 1942-50; exec. sec. Coll. Physicians of Philadelphia since 1949. Successively 1st lt., captain, major Medical Corps, U.S. Army, 1917-19. Mem. A.A.A.S., A.M.A., Assn. Am. Physicians, Assn. of Pathol. Bacteriology, Soc. Exptl. Biology Soc. Clin. Investigation, Soc. Biol. Chemistry, Harvey Soc., Coll. of Physicians of Phila., Phi Beta Kappa, Sigma Xi, Alpha Omega Alpha, Delta Upsilon. Episcopalian. Club: University (Phila.). Editor Jour. Clin. Investigation, 1926-35; asso. editor Medicine since 1929. Home: 138 Chamounix Rd., St. Davids, Pa. Office: 19 S. 22d St., Phila. 3. Died lMar. 29, 1952; buried West Laurel Hill Cemetery, Bala Cynwyd, Pa.

AUSTIN, JONATHAN LORING commonwealth ofcl.; b. Boston, Jan. 2, 1748; s. Hon. Benjamin and Elizabeth (Waldo) A.; grad. Harvard, 1766; m. Hannah Ivers, 1781, 1 son, James T. Served as maj. in volunteer N.H. Regt., 1775; sec. Mass. Bd. War, circa 1775-76; sent to Paris (France) to advise Benjamin Franklin of Gen. Burgoyne's surrender at Battle of Saratoga, 1777, pvt. sec. to Franklin in Paris, 1777-79; mem. Mass. Senate from Boston, 1801, Mass. Ho. of Reps. from Cambridge, 1803-06; sec. Commonwealth of Mass., 1806-08, treas., 1811-12. Died Boston, May 10, 1826.

AVERELL, WILLIAM WOODS army officer, inventor; b. Cameron, N.Y., Nov. 5, 1832; s. Hiram and Huldah (Hemenway) A.; grad. U.S. Mil. Acad., 1855; attended Cavalry Sch. for Practice, Carlisle, Pa., 1857; m. Kezia Hayward, Sept. 24, 1885. Drug clk., Bath, N.Y., until circa 1851; commd. brevet 2d lit. of mounted rifles U.S. Army, circa 1855; stationed Jefferson Barracks, Mo., 1855-56, ordered to frontier in N.M., 1857; received leave of absence due to wounds, 1859; became asst. adj. gen. on Gen. Andrew Porter's staff, 1861, served in 1st Battle of Bull Run; apptd. col. 3d Pa. Cavalry, U.S. Volunteers, Aug. 1861; lead charge with his brigade in Battle of 2d Manassas, Mar. 1862; served at Yorktown, Williamsburg, Fair Oaks Malvern Hill, White Oak Swamp (all Va.), 1862; commd. capt. U.S. Army, apptd. brig. gen. U.S. Volunteers, 1862; made raids in Va., Dec. 1862; in command of 2d Cavalry Div. at Battle of Kelly's Ford (Va.), 1863, brevetted maj. U.S. Army for this action; served in Stoneman's Raid, Richmond, Va., May 1863, then transferred to W. Va.; brevetted lt. col. after Battle of Droop Mountain, 1863; took part in raids in Tenn., brevetted col. U.S. Army; commanded 2d Cavalry Div. in several battles under Gen. Philip Henry Sheridan, 1864; brevetted brig. gen. and maj. gen. U.S. Army, 1865, resigned 1865; apptd. U.S. consul gen. for Brit. N. Am. at Montreal, 1865-68; had interests in mfg. and engring.; invented and patented asphalt paving, 1879, insulating conduits for wires and conductors, 1884-85; insp. gen. Soldiers' Home, Bath, N.Y., 1880-98; awarded $700,000 in patent infringement suit against Barbour Asphalt Paving Co., 1898. Died Bath, Feb. 3, 1900.

AVERILL, JOHN THOMAS congressman, mcht.; b. Alna, Lincoln County, Me., Mar. 1, 1825; grad. Me. Wesleyan Sem., Readfield, 1846. Sch. tchr. short time; lumberman for 1 year; moved to Winthrop, Me., merchant 3 years; moved to Northern Pa., 1852, lumberman until 1857; moved to Lake City, Minn. Senate, 1858-60; served in Union Army during Civil War; commd. lt. col. 6th Regiment, Minn. Volunteer Inf., 1862, promoted col., 1864; mustered out, 1865; brevetted brig. gen. Volunteers for meritorious service in recruitment of Army of U.S., 1865; moved to St. Paul, Minn., 1866, in wholesale paper and stationery business; mem. Republican Nat. Com., 1868-80; mem. U.S. Ho. of Reps. (Rep.) from Minn., 42d-43d congresses, 1871-75. Died St. Paul, Oct. 3, 1889; buried Oakland Cemetery.

AVERY, ALPHONSO CALHOUN lawyer; b. at Swan Ponds, Burke Co., N.C., Sept. 11, 1835; A.B., U. of N.C., 1857; studied law under Chief Justice Pearson of N.C.; served in 6th N.C. regt as 1st lt. and capt. and as asst. insp.-gen. with rank of maj. on staffs of Gens. D. H. Hill and J.B. Hood, C.S.A.; was organizing regt. and had appmt. of col. when Lee surrendered. Mem. N.C. Ho. of Rep., 1866; elected to Senate, 1868, but was not allowed to take his seat; mem. Constl. Conv., 1875; Tilden elector, 1876; judge Superior Ct., 1878-88; judge Supreme Ct., N.C., 1888-96; defeated for reelection, 1896. Was recommended for U.S. circuit judge, to fill vacancy caused by death of Judge Bond. Address: Morgantown, N.C.

AVERY, COLEMAN lawyer; b. Cincinnati, O., Feb. 22, 1880; s. William Ledyard and Johanna (Ummethun) A.; A.B., U. of Cincinnati, 1902; LL.B., Cincinnati Law Sch., 1905; m. Elinor Coates Baer, June 7, 1904 (died 1929); children - John Coleman, Ledyard, Elinor Louise, Mary Frances, Elizabeth Coates; m. 2d, Sara L. Loving, May 23, 1934. Began law practice, Cincinnati, 1905; asst. prosecuting atty., Hamilton Co., O., 1909-11; asst. solicitor of Cincinnati, 1911-13; spl. counsel representing the state in cases against George B. Cox, for perjury and Jacob Baschang, for bribery, in Supreme Court of Ohio, 1912-13; Dem. candidate for Court of Common Pleas, Hamilton Co., 1914; prof. law, Cincinnati Law Sch., 1916-18; spl. asst. U.S. atty., Southern Dist. of Ohio, 1918-19; asso. justice Supreme Court of Ohio, June-Dec. 1920; Dem. candidate for asso. justice Supreme Court of Ohio, 1920. Maj. 2d Bn., Cincinnati Home Guard, 1917-19; mem. Legal Advisory Bd., etc., World War. Presbyn. Home: Cincinnati, O. Died Mar. 14, 1938.

AVERY, ISAAC WHEELER lawyer-journalist; b. St. Augustine, Fla., May 2, 1837; grad. Oglethorpe Univ., Ga., 1854; admitted to bar at Savannah, Ga., 1860; in Confederate army 1861-65, private to col. of cav.; practiced law at Dalton, Ga., 1866-69 then at Atlanta. Founded Atlanta Constitution, and was several years its editor; propr. Atlanta Herald, 1875-76 and afterward for one year of Atlanta Evening Capitol; del. to Nat. Dem. Conv., 1872; mem. and sec. State Dem. com. same year; chief Public Dept. Div. U.S. Treas., 1887-89; started in 1892 successful movement for direct trade between southern U.S. and foreign ports; m. Emma Bivings, 1868. Author: History of Georgia; Digest of Ga. Supreme Court Reports. Home: Atlanta, Ga. Died 1897.

AVERY, JOHN congressman, physician; b. Watertown, Jefferson County, N.Y., Feb. 29, 1824; studied medicine Grass Lake Acad., Jackson Mich.; grad. Cleve. Med. Coll., 1850. Practiced medicine, Ionia, Mich., 1850-52, Otsego, Mich., 1852, Greenville, Mich., 1868; asst. surgeon 21st Regt., Mich. volunteer Inf. during Civil War; served in Army of Cumberland in Ky. and Tenn.; with Sherman on his march to the sea; mem. Mich. Ho. of Reps., 1869-70; apptd. mem. Mich. Bd. Health, 1880, 86; mem. U.S. Ho. of Reps. (Republican) from Mich., 53d-54th Congresses, 1893-97. Died Greenville, Jan. 21, 1914; buried Forest Home Cemetery.

AVERY, ROBERT lawyer; b. Tunkhannock, Pa., Sept. 22, 1839; s. Abel Marcy and Euphemia Pell A.; ed. Wyo. Sem., Kingston, Pa.; admitted to bar, 1870; m. Virginia C. Risley, July 4, 1874. Capt. 102d N.Y. Inf., Dec. 17, 1861; promoted through grades to lt. col. and retired, Dec. 31, 1870; advanced to rank of col. retired, by act of Apr. 23, 1904. Bvtd. lt. col. vols., Mar. 13, 1865, "for gallant and meritorious services at Chancellorsville"; col. and brig. gen., Mar. 13, 1865, for same at Lookout Mountain (lost right leg); maj. gen. vols.; Mar. 13, 1865, for same. Pres. Union Loan & Investment Co., Niagara Tin Smelting Co., Argenteau Kennels; v.p. Burlington and S.E. Ry. Co., Della Realty Co. Home: Brooklyn, N.Y. Died Oct. 2, 1912.

AVERY, WILLIAM TECUMSAH congressman, lawyer; b. Hardeman County, Tenn., Nov. 11, 1819; grad. Jackson Coll., nr. Columbia, Maury County, Tenn.; studied law. Admitted to bar; moved to Memphis, Tenn., 1840, practiced law; mem. Tenn. Ho. of Reps., 1843; mem. U.S. Ho. of Reps. (Democrat) from Tenn., 35th-36th congresses, 1857-61; served as lt. col. Confederate Army in Civil War; clk. criminal court, Shelby County 1870-74. Drowned in Ten Mile Bayou, Crittenden County, Ark. (opposite Memphis), May 22, 1880; buried Elmwood Cemetery, Memphis.

AXLINE, GEORGE ANDREW educator; b. Fairfield, Ia., Sept. 22, 1871; s. Andrew and Almira (Stever) A.; A.B., Parsons Coll., Iowa, 1892, A.M., 1895 (LL.D., 1917); student Chicago Normal Sch., 1899 m. Mabel Estella Rea, Oct. 20, 1898. Prin. mgn school, Cawker City, Kan., 1892-95; supervising prin. pub. schs., Kirwin, Kan., 1895-96, supt. pub. schs., Humeston, Ia., 1896-1903, Corning, Ia., 1903-04; pres. State Normal Sch., Albion, Ida., 1904-, also ranching. Pvt. and corporal, Co. M, 50th Ia. Regt., Spanish-Am. War. Republican. Presbyn. Mason. Mem. State Council of Defense, 1917-. Address: Albion, Ida. Died Oct. 11, 1919.

AXTON, JOHN THOMAS chief of chaplains, U.S.A.; b. Salt Lake City, July 28, 1870; s. John and Matilda Loretta (Webb) A.; ed. Salt Lake pub. schs.; D.D., Middlebury Coll., Middlebury, Vt., 1919, Ursinus Coll., Pa., and Elon Coll., N.C., 1923; m. Jane Bean, Aug. 28, 1891; children - John T. (U.S.A.), Matilda, Anna (wife of R. D. Daugherity, U.S.A.), Lily Jane (wife of Frederick R. Pitts, U.S.A.). Was general sec. Y.M.C.A., 1893-1902; apptd. chaplain U.S.A., rank of capt., 1902; maj., 1917; apptd. col. and chief of chaplains, July 15, 1920; retired Apr. 6, 1928, on account of disabilities in line of duty; chaplain Rutgers U., 1928-32. Served in P.I. twice, on Mexican border 5 yrs.; duty at Port of Embarkation, Hoboken, N.J., during World War, in gen. charge philanthropic, social and religious orgns. Officiated at interment of America's unknown soldier, Arlington Nat. Cemetery, Nov. 11, 1921. Awarded D.S.M., 1919; Chevalier Legion of Honor (French), 1922; Croce di Guerra (Italian), 1922, Republican. Conglist. Mason. Home: Washington, D.C. Deceased.

AYER, RICHARD SMALL congressman; b. Montville, Waldo County, Me., Oct. 9, 1829; attended common schs. Agriculturist and mcht. many years; enlisted as pvt. in Co. A., 4th Regiment, Me. Volunteer Inf., Union Army in Civil War, 1861, promoted to 1st lt., mustered out as capt., for disability, 1863; moved to Va., 1865, lived nr. Warsaw; del. Va. Constl. Conv., 1867; mem. U.S. Ho. of Reps. (Republican) from Va., 41st Congress, Jan. 31, 1870-71; moved back to Montville; mem. Me. Ho. of Reps., 1888. Died Liberty, Waldo County, Dec. 14, 1896; buried Mt. Repose Cemetery, Montville.

AYLWIN, JOHN CUSHING naval officer; b. Que., Can., circa 1780; s. Thomas and Lucy (Cushing) A. Worked on Brit. naval vessel, although he disliked practice of impressment, promoted to mate of his ship, 1795; kidnapped by his capt. after a dispute, forced to sail on gun-brig. for 6 years; never jointed Brit. Navy; allowed to rejoin his parents in Boston, after his health failed; later became capt. of several Boston mcht. vessels; served as lt. in frigate Constitution, U.S. Navy, 1812, aided in capture of Brit. frigate Guerriere, and saw capture of ship Java before dying in battle. Died at sea, Jan. 28, 1813.

AYRES, JOSEPH GERRISH, rear adm.; b. Canterbury, N. H., Nov. 3, 1839; s. Charles H. and Almira S. (Gerrish) A.; ed. U. of Vt. and Columbia U.; m. Olinda A. Austin, July 11, 1884. Served in 15th N.H. Vols. as 2d and 1st lt., Oct. 1, 1862-Aug. 13, 1863; apptd. acting asst. surgeon U.S.N., Dec. 17, 1864; advanced through grades to med. dir. U.S.N., Dec. 12, 1898; retired with rank of rear adm., Nov. 3, 1901, for services during Civil War. Home: Montclair, N.J. Died Mar. 21, 1922.

AYRES, QUINCY CLAUDE educator, engr.; b. Columbus, Miss., May 30, 1891; s. Claude Hutchins and Sallie M. (Whitfield) A.; student Sewanee Military Acad., 1906-08, U. of South, 1908-09; B.S., U. of Miss., 1912, B.E., 1912, C.E., 1920; m. Mary H. Herron, Aug. 18, 1917 (dec. Apr. 1946); 1 dau., Sally Ruth (Mrs. L. W. Shroyer III); m. 2d, Anne Pleasants Hopkins, June 17, 1947; children-Quincy, Marsha. Pvt. practice, municipal, drainage and flood control engring., Greenville, Miss., 1912-15; drainage engr. Dept. of Agr., 1916-19 asst. prof. civil engring. U. of Miss., 1919-20; asst. prof. agrl. engring. Ia. State University of Science and Technology, 1920-21, associate, prof., 1921-44, professor since 1945, patent mgr. (part time) since 1935; visiting prof. U. Tenn., summers 1937, 38. Research in field soil and water conservation, 1916-40; cons. engr. (summers) various engring. and indsl. firms, Served as 2d lt., 1st lt., corps engrs. - U.S. Army, with combat divs. overseas. 1917-19; lt. comdr., comdr. C.E.C., U.S.N.R., active duty, 1941-45, capt., 1951. Recipient Iowa Engring. Soc. award for outstanding service, 1944, Faculty citation Ia. State U., 1962. Member Am. Soc. Engring. Edn., Am. Soc. Agrl. Engrs. (chmn. reclamation div., 1929, mem. gov. council, 1929-32), Am. Soc. C.E. (pres. Ia. sect., 1930), Ia. Engring. Soc. (pres., 1936), Ames C. of C. (dir.), Kappa Alpha. Episcopalian. Club: Rotary. Author Ia. Engring. Expt. Sta. bulls.; Land Drainage and Reclamation (with D. Scoates), 1928, rev., 1939; Soil Erosion and Its Control, 1936 (trans. in Spanish); Engineering for Agricultural Drainage (with H. B. Roe) 1954 (transl. in Spanish). Editor 13 books in McGraw-Hill Agrl. Engring. Series, 1945-56. Cons. editor McGraw-Hill Book Co., 1940-. Contbr. Ency. Brit., McGraw Hill Ency. Sci. and Tech., others. Home: 424 N. Franklin Av., Ames, Ia. Died May 1, 1963; buried Ames, Ia.

AYRES, ROMEYN BECK army officer; b. Montgomery County, Dec. 20, 1825; grad. U.S. Mil. Acad., 1847. Served with U.S. Army at various posts throughout U.S., promoted capt., 1861; participated in 1st Battle of Bull Run; served with Army of Potomac throughout Civil War; capt., chief arty. for a div., later a corps; promoted brig. gen. U.S. Volunteers, 1862; commd. lt. col. U.S. Army, 1866; col 2d U.S. Arty., 1879. Died (still on active duty) Port Hamilton, N.Y., Dec. 4, 1888.

AYRES, SAMUEL LORING PERCIVAL rear adm.; b. Stanford, Conn., July 29, 1835; s. Dr. Chauncey and Deborah Ann (Percival) A.; high sch. edn.; m. Almira J. Stonaker, Aug. 17, 1867. Apptd. 3d asst. engr. U.S.N., July 21, 1858; promoted through grades to chief engr., Mar. 21, 1870; retired, July 29, 1897; advanced to rank of rear adm., June 20, 1906, for services during Civil War. Home: Philadelphia, Pa. Died Apr. 29, 1917.

BABBITT, EDWIN BURR army officer; b. N. Y., July 26, 1862; s. Col. Lawrence Sprague (U.S. Army) and Fannie (McDougall) B.; grad. U.S. Mil. Acad., 1884, Arty. Sch., 1889; s. Maud Ainsworth, Feb. 23, 1924. Commd. 2d lt., June 15, 1884; promoted through grades to brig. gen. N.A., Oct. 2, 1917; brig. gen., U.S. Army, Feb. 12, 1918; maj. gen., Apr. 14, 1923; retired Sept. 19, 1924. Commdg. brigade in Marne, St. Mihiel and Argonne offensives; with Army of Occupation. Awarded D.S.M. "for exceptionally meritorious and conspicuous services"; Officer Legion d'Honneur (French); Comendador Order of El Sol del Peru (Peru); Abdon Calderon, first class (Equador). Home: Santa Barbara, Calif. Died Dec. 9, 1939.

BABBITT, LAWRENCE SPRAGUE army officer; b. Boston, Mass., Feb. 18, 1839; s. Col. Edwin Burr (U.S. Army) and Sarah Stedman (Sprague) B.; grad. West Point, 1861; m. Fannie, d. Surgeon McDougall, U.S. Army, Oct. 22, 1861. Has served in U.S. Army since 1861 as officer, becoming col. Apr. 7, 1809, and on duty in ordnance dept., U.S. Powder Depot, Dover, N.J., until retired Feb. 18, 1903. Home: Dover, N.J. Died 1903.

BABCOCK, CHARLES HENRY, stock broker; b. Lafayette, Ind., Sept. 24, 1899; s. Charles Henry and Ella (Park) B.; B.S., U. Pa., 1920; m. Mary Reynolds, Dec. 16, 1929 (dec.); children—Mary Katharine (Mrs. Kenneth Mountcastle, Jr.), Charles Henry, Barbara Frances, (Mrs. Frederic H. Lassiter), Betsy Main; m. second, Winifred Penn Knies, September 8, 1954. With Guaranty Trust Co. of N.Y., N.Y.C., 1920-23; v.p. Mahjongg Corp. of Am., San Francisco, 1923-24; with Guaranty Co. of N.Y., Phila., 1924-31; sr. partner Reynolds & Co., N.Y., 1931-67; director Piedmont Publishing Co., Winston-Salem. Commr. pub. housing, Winston-Salem. Pres., treas. Mary Reynolds Babcock Found; vice pres., treas. Smith Reynolds Found. Served as pvt. U.S. Army, World War I, maj., World War II. Mem. Grolier Soc., Alpha Chi Rho. Clubs: Down Town Assn., University, Bankers (N.Y.C.); Twin City, Forsyth Country, The Old Town (Winston-Salem). Home: Winston-Salem NC Died Dec. 13, 1967; buried Winston-Salem NC

BABCOCK, JOHN BRECKINRIDGE army officer; b. in La., Feb. 7, 1843. Sergt. Co. G, 37th N.G.S.N.Y., May 29, 1862; disch., Sept. 2, 1862; 3d lt. 174th N.Y. Inf., Nov. 13, 1862; advanced through grades to brig. gen. vols., June 3, 1898; col. asst. adj. gen. U.S. Army, Feb. 21, 1901; brig. gen., Aug. 7, 1903; retired at own request, over 30 yrs. service, Aug. 8, 1903. Bvtd. 1st lt., capt. and maj., Mar. 2, 1867, for battles of Sabine Cross Roads, Pleasant Hill and Cane River Crossing, La.; lt. col., Feb. 27, 1890, for action against Indians at Tonta Creek, Ariz., June 16, 1873, and at Four Peaks, Ariz., Jan. 16, 1874; awarded medal of honor, Mar. 2, 1899, for most distinguished gallantry in action at Spring Creek, Neb., May 16, 1869. Died 1909.

BABCOCK, ORVILLE ELIAS engr., army officer; b. Franklin, Vt., Dec. 25, 1835; s. Elias and Clara (Olmstead) B.; grad. U.S. Mil. Acad., 1861; m. Annie Eliza Campbell, Nov. 8, 1866. Assigned to Corps Engrs., U.S. Army as 2d lt., 1861, then ordered to Army of Potomac; mem. staff of Gen. W. B. Franklin, 1862; apptd. acting chief engr. Dept. of Ohio, 1864, in charge of positions, defenses, bridges, etc.; promoted to lt. col, 1864; a.d.c. to Gen. Ulysses S. Grant, 1864-68; served in Battle of Wilderness, subsequent battles of Army of Potomac; breveted brig. gen. U.S. Volunteers, 1865; promoted to col. U.S. Army; served as Pres. Grant's pvt. sec., 1868-71; appt. supt. engr. of pub. bldgs. and grounds, 1871; indicted by grand jury of St. Louis because of connections with John McDonald (one of the known leaders of the Whiskey Ring), 1875, acquitted through Pres. Grant's intercession; returned to duties at White House, ret. shortly afterwards. Drowned in Mosquito Inlet, Fla., June 2, 1884.

BABCOCK, WARREN LA VERNE hosp. dir.; b. Eden, Erie County, N.Y., Mar. 14, 1873; s. David H. and Eliza C. (Belknap) B.; desc. James Babcock, Mass., 1642; M.D., Coll. Physicians and Surgeons, Baltimore, Md., 1893; m. Helen M. Wood, Dec. 30, 1896; children—Warren Wood (M.D.), Lyndon Ross, Kenneth Belknap (M.D.), Mrs. Margaret Carter Lovell. Mem. med. staff, Md. State Hosp., Catonsville, Md., 1893-94; Binghamton State Hosp., 1894-95, St. Lawrence (N.Y.) State Hosp., 1895-1902; chief surg. N.Y. State Soldiers' and Sailors' Home, Bath, N.Y., 1902-04; dir. Grace Hosp., Detroit, 1904-37, treas. and trustee since 1937. Commd. mem. Med. Corps U.S. Army, May 1917; served as comdg. officer Am. Red Cross Hosp. No. 3, Paris, later comdg. officer Base Hosp. No. 6, Bordeaux; hon. disch. as col., Feb. 1919. Officer Legion of Honor (France), 1919. Treas. and trustee Mich. Hosp. Service; mem. A.M.A., Mich. State Med. Assn., Wayne Co. Med. Assn. (ex-pres.), Am. Hosp. Assn. (ex-sec. and ex-pepres.), Detroit Philatelic Soc. (ex-pres.). Baptist. Mason. Home: 245 Willis Av. E., Detroit, Mich.; (winter) 2945 6th Av. N., St. Petersburg, Fla. Died Dec. 27, 1942.

BABCOCK, WILLIAM WAYNE, surgeon; b. E. Worcester, Otsego County, N.Y., June 10,21872; s. William Wayne and Sarah Jane (Butler) B.; grad. Binghamton (N.Y.) High Sch.; M.D., Coll. Physicians and Surgeons, Baltimore, 1893; studied summer sch., Harvard, 1893; M.D., Sch. of Medicine, U. of Pa., 1895; M.D., Medico-Chirurg. Coll., Phila., 1900; hon. A.M., Pa. Coll., Gettysburg, 1904; LL.D., Temple U., 1932; D.Sc., Ursinus Coll. 1944; L.H.D. Villenova, 1947; Med. Alumni Award, D.Sc., U. of Md., 1948; m. Marion C. Watters, May 14, 1918; children—Jane Butler, Catherine, Bonnie, William Wayne 3d (deceased). Resident physician St. Mark's Hosp., Salt Lake City, 1893-94, tng., Phila., 1895-1903; prof. gynecology Temple Coll., 1903, prof. surgery, clin. surgery, 1903-44, now emeritus; prof. oral surgery Phila. Dental Coll., 1907-08; surgeon to Temple U., cons. Phila. Gen. hosps., Phila. Has conducted researches leading to improved methods in surgery and invented a number of surg. instruments. Commd. capt., Med. Res. Corps, May 9, 1917; entered service Camp Greenleaf, Ga.; regtl. surgeon 318th F.A., Camp Jackson, August 1917; surg. chief, General Hospital No. 6, Fort McPherson, Georgia, September 1917-September 1919; commd. major, November 1917; lt. colonel, June 1918. Fellow Am. Coll. Surgeons, A.A.A.S; asso. mem. Academie de Chirurgie of France; hon. mem. Royal Soc. of Medicine (proctology), England; mem. A.M.A., Am. Therapeutic Soc. (pres. 1917-18), Pathol. Soc. Phila., Am. Assn. Obstetricians, Gynecologists and Abdominal Surgeons (pres. 1933-34), Internat. Coll. Surgeons, Am. Bd. Surgery, Societe des chirurgiens de Paris, Nat. Soc. Surgeons of Cuba, Phi Chi. Mason. Episcopalian. Clubs: Union League, Rotary. Home: 11 St. Asaph's Rd., Bala-Cynwyd, Pa. Office: 3401 N. Broad St., Philadelphia

BABIN, HOSEA JOHN naval officer; b. in Can., Dec. 15, 1842. Apptd. acting asst. surgeon U.S.N., from Mass., Feb. 10, 1865; asst. surgeon, Mar. 13, 1865; passed asst. surgeon, June 23, 1869; surgeon, Mar. 17, 1876; med. insp., June 22, 1894; med. dir., May 7, 1898; retired, Dec. 15, 1904; advanced to rank of rear admiral for service during Civil War. Mem. Bd. of Inspection and Survey, Jan. 23-June 22, 1894; pres. Med. Examining Bd., N.Y., Oct. 5, 1897-May 7, 1898; in charge Naval Hosp., New York, 1900-04. Address: Care C. A. Betts, 126 Broadway, Brooklyn.

BACHE, DALLAS asst. to surgeon-gen. U.S. Army, with rank of col.; b. in Pa.; apptd. asst. surgeon U.S. Army, May 28, 1861; bvt. capt. and maj., 1865; capt. and asst. surgeon, May 28, 1866; maj. and surgeon, Aug. 5, 1867; lt. col. surgeon, Feb. 9, 1890; col. and asst. surgeon-gen., Apr. 18, 1895. Died 1902.

BACHE, FRANKLIN physician, educator; b. Phila., Oct. 25, 1797; s. Benjamin Franklin and Margaret (Markoe) B.; grad. U. Pa., 1810, M.D., 1814; m. Aglae Dabadie, 1818. Entered U.S. Army as asst. surgeon, 1813, promoted to full surgeon, 1814, served until 1861; practiced medicine, Phila., 1816-24; physician to Walnut Street Prison, Phila., 1824-36; prof. chemistry Franklin Inst., Phila., 1826-32; an editor N.Am. Med. and Surg. Jour., 1826-31; fellow Coll. Physicians and Surgeons, Phila., 1829; prof. chemistry Phila. Coll. Pharmacy, 1831-41, Jefferson Med. Coll., Phila., 1841-64; pres. Am. Philos. Soc., 1853-55. Author: System of Chemistry for the Use of Students in Medicine, 1819; Dispensatory of the United States of America, 1833. Died Phila., Mar. 19, 1864.

BACHE, HAROLD L., corporation executive; b. N.Y.C., June 17, 1894; s. Leopold S. and Hattie (Stein) B.; student Ethical Culture Sch., N.Y.C., to 1910, Gunnery Sch., Washington, Conn., 1910-12, Cornell U., 1912-14; m. Alice Kay Bache. Asso. with J. S. Bache & Co., N.Y.C., excepting few assignments with affiliated cos., became partner, 1926, firm incorporated, 1945; pres., chmn. bd. Bache & Co., Inc., 1945-68; former officer several produce exchanges, firm mem. nat. and fgn. bds. of trade and produce exchanges. Dir. Far-East Am. Council, Japan Fund, Japan Soc., N.Y.C. Youth Bd., Queens Boys Club: trustee The Gunnery School, Museum of the American Indian, Jewish Federation, Cornell University. Served from pvt. to capt. U.S. Army, 1917-18; lt. col. Res. Mem. Commerce and Industry Assn. of N.Y. Inc. (dir.), N.Y. Bd. Trade, C. of C. N.Y. Clubs: Westchester Country; Cornell, Wall Street, Terrace, Sky (N.Y.C.). Home: New York City NY Died Mar. 15, 1968; buried Salem Fields Cemetery, NY

BACHMAN, JONATHAN WAVERLY clergyman; b. Roseland, Sullivan County, Tenn., Oct. 9, 1837; s. Jonathan and Frances (Rhea) B.; Emory and Henry Coll., Va.; Union Theol. Sem.; (D.D., Central U., Ky., 1880. Washington and Lee U., Va., 1911); m. Eva Dulaney, Oct. 20, 1863. Pvt. C.S.A., May, 1861; became capt. and comd. 60th Regt. Tenn. Vols. at Vicksburg, during siege, 1863; after being exchanged, comd. regt. until ordained Presbyn. ministry, Oct., 1864, then became chaplain same regt. until close of war; pastor First Ch., Chattanooga, 1873-Sept. 30, 1923. Delegate Am. Conf. on Internat. Arbitration, Washington, 1896; moderator Gen. Assembly Presbyn. Ch. in U.S., 1910. Chaplain genl., U.C.V., 1913-. Mason. Home: Chattanooga, Tenn. Died Sept. 26, 1924.

BACHMEYER, ARTHUR CHARLES (BAK'MI-ER), med. adminstr. b. Cincinnati, O., Dec. 6, 1886; s. Henry and Caroline (Weist) B.; IM.D., U. of Cincinnati, 1911, hon. D.Sc., 1935; D. Sc. (honorary), University of Nebraska, 1949; m. Lulu K. Troeger, Nov. 23, 1911 (died May 3, 1933); children—Robert Wesley, William Leonard, Janet Ann; m. 2d Mary L. Hicks, July 5, 1934. Interne and resident surg. Cinn. Gen. Hosp., 1911-13, asst. later acting supt. 1913, supt., 1914-35, also supt. Cincinnati Tuberculosis Sanatorium, 1914-35; prof. hosp. admn. 1920-35; dean College of Medicine, U. of Cincinnati, 1925-34; prof. asso. dean biol. div., dir. of clinics, U. of Chicago, 1935-52; asso. dean biol. scis., prof. emeritus since 1952; vice chairman Commission on Survey of Medical Edn., since 1948. First lt., Med. Corps, O.N.G., 1916; capt. and maj. Med. R.C., U.S. Army, 1917-19; lt. col. Med. O.R.C. since 1919. Recipient of study Award of Merit, Am. Hosp. Assn., 1943. Dir. of study, Commn. on Hosp. Care, 1944-46, mem. exec. com. Commn. on Financing Hosp. Care since 1951. Mem. A.M.A., Ohio State Med. Assn., Chgo. Hosp. Council, Chgo. Hosp. Service Corp. (mem. bd.), Am. Coll. Hospital Administrators (pres. 1940-41; hon. mem. 1952), Assn. Am. Med. Colls. (treas. 1938-49, president 1950-51), National Security Resources Board, (med. Adv. committee 1948-50), Cincinnati Acad. Medical, Inst. Med. of Chicago, American Hospital Assn. (past pres., treasurer since 1946), Am. Pub. Health Assn., A.A.A.S., Am. Acad. Polit. and Social Sciences, Alpha Kappa Kappa, Alpha Omega Alpha. Methodist. Mason. Chmn. editorial bd., Modern Hosp. Author: Hospital in Modern Society (with G. Hartman), 1943; Hospital Care in U.S. (report), 1947; Hospital Trends & Developments, 1948; Medical Schs. of Western Europe, 1952; Address: Box 180, R.D. 2, Loveland, O. Died May 22, 1953 buried Spring Grove Cemetery, Cin.

BACK, GEORGE IRVING, army officer; b. Sioux City, Ia., Feb. 25, 1894; s. Aaron and Carline (Dorum) B.; A.B., Morningside Coll., 1921; grad. work, Yale, 1920-21; m. Rosalie Henry Rives, Nov. 26, 1927. Commd. 2d lt., Signal Corps, U.S. Army, 1917, and advanced through the grades to brig. gen., 1945; student, communications engring., Yale, 1920-21; asst. dept. signal officer, Hawaiian Dept., 1922-24; chief, wire communications engring. section, Office Chief Signal Officer, Washington, 1924-29, Signal Corps Laboratories, 1929-33; student Signal Corps Sch., 1933-34; chief, Army Communications Service, 1934-38; student Command and Gen. Staff Sch., 1938-39; sec. Signal Corps Bd., 1939-41; chief communications div. signal section, G.H.Q., 1941-42; exec. officer, engring. and supply service, Office Chief Signal Officer, 1942-43, dir. distribution div., 1943-44; chief signal officer Mediterranean Theatre of Operations from 1944; chief Army Communications Service 1945-46; Signal Officer G.H.Q., F.E.C. and chief Civil Communications Sect., S.C.A.P. from 1947. Awarded Distinguished Service Medal, Legion of Merit (U.S.), Commander of British Empire (Gt. Britain), Grand Official and Order of Crown (Italy), Brazilian War Medal. Home: St Petersburg FL Died Sept. 1972.

BACKUS, SAMUEL WOOLSEY immigration commr.; b. Pine Plains, Dutchess Co., N.Y., Nov. 6, 1844; s. Gurdon and Julia Ann (Woolsey) B.; ed. grammar and high schs.; m. Nellie Grant Sanborn, of Watsonville, Santa Cruz Co., Cal., June 7, 1883. Enlisted in Co. L, 2d Mass. Cav., Jan. 22, 1863; served in Army of Potomac and Army of Shenandoah until transferred to Co. F, 2d Cal. Cav., as 2d lt., June 30, 1865, and served in Indian campaigns; mustered out with regt., June 30, 1866. Engaged in shipping and commn. business, San Francisco, 1868-78; postmaster San Francisco, 1882-86 and 1890-94; publisher newspapers, 1884-88; pres. West. Expanded Metal Co., 1895-11; pres. Ford & Sanborn Co., mchts., Monterey Co., Cal.; was U.S. commr. of immigration Northern Cal. and Nev. Progressive. Christian Scientist. Past sr. vice comdr. in chief G.A.R., 1886-87; comdr. Cal. Commandery, Loyal Legion, 1892; pres. Veterans' Home, Cal., since 1895; mem. S.A.R. K.T. Clubs: Commercial, Union League and Masonic. Home: 1109 Jones St., San Francisco, Calif.

BACON, ALBERT WILLIAMSON rear adm.; b. Philadelphia, Jan. 5, 1841; s. James Ware and Alice Ann (Riggs) B.; ed. pub. and pvt. schs. at Frankfort, Ky., and Phila.; m. Kate S. Stoughton, Jan. 23, 1873. Apptd. captain's clk., U.S.N., 1861; advanced through grades to pay dir., 1900; retired with rank of rear adm., Jan. 5, 1903. Attached to Admiral Farragut's fleet during Civil War; afterwards on N. Atlantic sts.; in charge U.S.N. depots at Rio de Janeiro, Brazil, and Nice, France; on duty Navy Dept., and Mare Island Navy Yard. Republican. Roman Catholic. Home: Santa Barbara, Calif. Died Sept. 23, 1922.

BACON, ALEXANDER SAMUEL lawyer; b. Jackson, Mich., Nov. 20, 1853; s. John Arthur and Harriet (Smith) B.; grad. U.S. Mil. Acad., 1876; m. Harriet Whittlesey Schroter, Sept. 1, 1886. Was apptd. 2d lt. 1st U.S. Arty., June 15, 1876; resigned, Mar. 15, 1878; admitted to bar, 1879; practice has extended to many states and Eng., France, Japan and Central America. Was capt., maj. and lt. col. 23d regt., N.G.S. N.Y., and col. 2d Provisional regt., N.G.S. N.Y. Baptist. Democrat. Mem. N.Y. Assembly, 1887. Author: The Woolly Horse; The Illegal Trial of Christ; Masonic Nobility; Mohammed and Islam; Ancient Calendars. Home: Brooklyn, N.Y. Died May 30, 1920.

BACON, AUGUSTUS OCTAVIUS senator; b. Bryan Co., Ga., Oct. 20, 1839; s. Rev. Augustus Octavius and Mary Louisa (Jones) B.; A.B., U. of Ga., 1859, LL.B., 1860 (LL.D., 1909); m. Virginia Lamar, Apr. 18, 1864. Adj. 9th Ga. Regt., C.S.A., and capt. on gen. staff; in law practice at Macon, Ga., 1866-; presdl. elector, 1868; mem. Ga. Ho. of Rep., 1870-82, 92, 93 (speaker 1873-82, except 1875-76, when was speaker pro tem); frequently del. to Dem. State convs. (pres. 1880); del.-at-large Dem. Nat. Conv., 1884; several times candidate for Democratic nomination for gov. (within 1 vote of nomination, 1883, when equivalent to election); elected U.S. senator, 1894, 1900, 1907. chmn. com. Engrossed Bills; mem. various coms. Regent Smithsonian Instn.; trustee U. of Ga. Home: Macon, Ga. Died Feb. 14, 1914.

BACON, GASPAR GRISWOLD lawyer; b. Jamaica Plain, Mass., Mar. 7, 1886; s. Robert and Martha (Cowdin) B.; grad. Groton Sch., Mass., 1904; A.B., Harvard, 1908, LL.B., 1912; m. Priscilla Toland, July 16, 1910; children—William Benjamin, Gaspar Griswold, Robert. Admitted to Mass. bar, 1912, since practiced in Boston. Mem. Mass. State Senate, 1925-32 (pres. 1929-32); lieut. gov. of Mass., 1933-34; now prof. govt., Boston U. Served in World War as capt. and maj. F.A., Aug. 1917-Feb. 1919; with 81st Div., School of Fire, Ft. Sill, Okla., and 16th Div.; now col., chief of staff, Mass. State Guard; commd. maj. Air Corps, A.U.S., March, 1942; attached to 8th Air Force, E.T.D., 1942; 3d Army, 1943-44; commd. lt. col., Oct. 1944. Awarded Croix de Guerre with silver star (Fr.); Am. Service Medal; European-African-Middle Eastern Service Medal; Legion of Honor. Vis. prof. of govt. (by invitation), U. of N.C., 1947; completed 20 yrs. Gaspar G. Bacon Lectureship on Constituion of U.S., Boston U., 1947. Pres. Franco-American Review. Mem. Am. Bar Assn., Mass. Hist. Soc., Phi Beta Kappa. Republican. Episcopalian. Mason (K.T., 32 degree), K.P., Elk, Moose. Clubs: Republican, Roosevelt, Somerset, Tennis and Racquet, Harvard, Middlesex (Boston); Norfolk Hunt (Mass.); Harvard, Racquet and Tennis (New York). Author: The Constitutions of the United States, 1928; Government and the Voter, 1931; Individual Rights and the Public Welfare, 1935. Home: 222 Prince St., Jamaica Plain, Mass. Address: Boston U., 688 Boylston St., Boston. Died Dec. 25, 1947.

BACON, JOHN MOSBY colonel U.S.A.; b. in Ky., Apr. 17, 1844. Enlisted 2d lt. 11th Ky. Cav., Sept. 22, 1862; promoted through grades to col. 8th Cav., June 29, 1897; brig. gen. vols., May 4, 1898; hon. disch. from vol. service, Feb. 24, 1899; retired at own request, over 30 yrs. service, May 8, 1899. Bvt. maj. Mar. 2, 1867, for siege of Resaca, Ga.; lt. col., Feb. 27, 1890, for actions against Indians on the Rio Pecos, Tex., June 7, 1867, and nr. headwaters of Salt Fork of Brazos River, Tex., Oct. 28, 29, 1869. Col. and a.-d.-c. to Gen. Sherman, 1871-84. Died Mar. 19, 1913.

BACON, RAYMOND FOSS chem. engr.; b. Muncie, Ind., June 29, 1880; s. Rev. Charles and N. V. (Wiggs) B.; direct desc. of Bacons who settled in Mass., 1640; B.S., DePauw U., 1899, M.A., 1900.Ph.D., U. of Chicago, 1904; D.Sc., U. of Pittsburgh, 1918, DePauw, 1919; m. Edna Hine, Aug. 4, 1905. Chemist in U.S. Bur. of Science, Manila, P.I., 1905-10; asst. chemist Bur. of Chemistry, Washington, D.C., 1910-11; sr. fellow Petroleum Fellowship, Dept. Indsl. Research, U. of Pittsburgh, 1911-12; asso. dir., 1912-14, dir., 1914-21, Mellon Inst. Indsl. Research, U. of Pittsburgh; cons. chem. engr., New York, since Oct., 1921; scientific adviser to Philippine Govt., 1939. Col. Chem. Warfare Service, U.S. Army, Dec. 1, 1917-Dec. 16, 1918, spending 9 months in France as chief Tech. Div., C.W.S., A.E.F. Awarded D.S.M., 1922. Mem. Am. Inst. Chem. Engrs., A.A.A.S., Societe de Chimie Industrielle, Chem. Soc. of London, D.K.E., Alpha Chi Sigma, Phi Lambda Upsilon. Clubs: Chemists', Siwanoy Country, Union League, Hudson River Country. Author: (with W.A. Hamor) American Petroleum Industry (2 vols.), 1916; (with same) American Fuels (2 vols.), 1922; also numerous papers on chemistry, technology of essential oils, reports, etc. Inventor of processes for mfr. of gasoline, recovery of cuprous sulphide from ores, for hydrogenating vegetable oils and for mfr. of sulphur from sulphide ores. Home: 98 Rockledge Rd., Bronxville, N.Y. Office: 500 Fifth Av., New York, N.Y. Died Oct. 14, 1954.

BACON, ROBERT ambassador; b. Boston, July 5, 1860; s. William B. and Emily C. (Low) B.; A.B., Harvard, 1880; m. Martha Waldron Cowdin, Oct. 10, 1883. Entered Banking House of Lee, Higginson & Co., Boston, 1881; became mem. E. Rollins Morse & Bro., 1883, until 1894; mem. J. P. Morgan & Co., New York, 1894-1903. Asst. sec. of state, U.S., 1905-09, except from Jan. 27-Mar. 6, 1909, when was Sec. of State, succeeding Elihu Root, elected to Senate; ambassador extraordinary and plenipotentiary to France, Dec., 1909-Jan. 1912. Mem. Bd. Overseers, Harvard U., 1889-1901 and 1902-08; fellow, Harvard, Jan., 1912. Commd. maj., U.S.P., May, 1917; assigned to staff of Gen. Pershing with A.E.F. in France. Home: New York, N.Y. Died May 29, 1919.

BACON, ROBERT LOW congressman; b. Jamaica Plain, Boston, Mass., July 23, 1884; s. Robert and Martha Waldron (Cowdin) B.; A.B., Harvard, 1907, LL.B., 1910; m. Virginia Murray, Apr. 14, 1913; children - Alexandra Murray, Virginia Murray, Martha. With U.S. Treasury Dept., 1910-11; mem. Kissel, Kinnicutt & Co., Banking, 1911-23. Mem. Rep. State Com., N.Y.; formerly mem. Rept. County Com., Nassau Co., N.Y.; del. Rep. State Conv., N.Y., 1915, 19 and 1920-23 inclusive; del. Rep. Nat. Conv., Chicago, 1920; mem. 68th to 75th Congresses (1923-39), 1st N.Y. Dist.; mem. Rep. Congressional Com. Attended original Plattsburg T.C., 1915; enlisted in N.G.N.Y.; 1st lt N.Y.F.A., Mexican border service, 1916; with Field Arty., U.S.A., Apr. 24, 1917-Jan 2, 1919; served as asst. to chief of F.A., Washington, D.C., and promoted maj.; grad. sch. of Fire for F.A., Ft. Sill, Okla., Nov. 10, 1918; lt. col. and col. O.R.C., U.S.A.; comdg. officer 304th Cav., 61st Div., Jan. 1923-Jan. 1924; now col. F.A., O.R.C. Awarded D.S.M. Mem. bd. visitors U.S. Naval Acad.; mem. 150th Anniversary Commn. Battle of Bunker Hill. Episcopalian. Mason. Home: Westbury, L.I., N.Y. Died Sept. 12, 1938.

BADEAU, ADAM army officer, diplomat; b. N.Y.C., Dec. 29, 1831; s. Nicholas Badeau. Commd. aide-de-camp U.S. Volunteers, 1862; commd. lt. col., served as mil. sec. to Gen Grant, 1864-69; ret. as brevet brig gen U.S. Army, 1869; sec. U.S. legation, London, Eng., 1869-70; U.S. consul gen. at London, 1870-81, Havana, 1882-84; known as "court historian" of Grant administrn. Author: The Vagabond, 1859; Military History of Ulysses S. Grant, 3 vols, 1868, 81, Grant in Peace (a study of Grant's activities), 1887; Conspiracy, a Cuban Romance, 1885. Died Ridgewood, N.J., Mar. 19, 1895

BADGER, CHARLES JOHNSTON naval officer; b. Rockville, Md., Aug. 6, 1853; s. Commodore Oscar Charles (U.S.N.) and Margaret M. (Johnston) B.; apptd. to U.S. Naval Acad., at-large, by Pres. Grant, 1869, grad. 1873; m. Sophia J. Champlin, Oct. 4, 1882. Promoted capt., July 1, 1907; supt. U.S. Naval Acad., 1907-09; comdg. battleship Kansas, 1909-11; promoted rear adm., Mar. 8, 1911. Retired by operation of law, Aug. 6, 1915, but continued on active duty as mem. Gen. Bd. until Feb. 28, 1921. Home: Cleveland Park, D.C. Died Sept. 7, 1932.

BADGER, LUTHER congressman, lawyer; b. Partridgefield (Now Peru), Mass., Apr. 10, 1785; attended Hamilton Coll., 1807; studied law. Admitted to bar, 1812; practiced in Jamesville, Onondaga County, N.Y.; served as judge advocate 27th Brigade, N.v. Militia, 1819-27; mem. U.S. Ho. of Reps. from N.Y., 19th Congress, 1825-27; moved to Broome County, N.Y., 1832; examiner in chancery, 1833-47; apptd. commr. of U.S. loans, 1840-43; dist. atty. Broome County, 1847-49; practiced law, Jordan, Onondaga County. Died Jordan, 1869; buried Jordan Cemetery.

BADGER, OSCAR CHARLES commodore U.S. Navy retired, 1885; b. Windham, Conn., Aug. 12, 1823; entered Navy from Philadelphia as midshipman, 1841; grad. Naval Acad., 1847; m. Margaret M. Johnston, Rockville, Md., 1852; served through Mexican and Civil wars; took part in many engagements; promoted through grades to commodore and comdt. Boston Navy yard. Died 1899.

BADGER, OSCAR CHARLES corporation consultant, naval officer, retired; born in Washington, June 26, 1890; son of Charles Johnston (rear admiral, U.S. Navy), and Sophia Jane (Champlin) B.; student St. John's Coll., Md., 1905-07; B.S., U.S. Naval Academy, 1911; grad. Naval War College, 1932; married Isabelle Edna Austen, October 31, 1917; children—Isabelle Edna (Mrs. John Power Schroeder), Jane Austen (Mrs. Frederick John Leary). Commd. ensign, U.S. Navy, 1911 and advanced through the grades to vice admiral, 1945; served on USS Utah-landings at Vera Cruz, 1914; USS Porter-European waters, 1917; comd. USS Sultana and USS Worden, 1918; gunner officer Squadron 15. destroyers Atlantic Fleet, 1922; aide to CinCAsiaticFLt., 1923; at Bureau of Ordnance, 1923-25, 1928-31; USS Maryland, 1925-28; duty at Naval Acad., 1933-36; sec. of General Board Navy Dept., 1939-40; chief of staff to CinCUSLantFlt. 1940-41; comd. USS North Carolina, 1941-42; comd. destroyers Atlantic Fleet, 1942; asst. chief, Naval Operations for Logistics Plans, 1943-44; comdr. Service Squadrons South Pacific Force, 1944; tactical comdr. Heavy Striking Force of Third Fleet, 1944-45; comdr. Service Force U.S. Pacific Fleet, 1945-47; comdt. 11th Naval Dist., 1947-48; comdr. U.S. Naval Forces Far East, 1948-49; special adv. on Far Eastern matters at Navy Dept., 1949-50; comdr. Eastern Sea Frontier, comdr. Atlantic Reserve Fleet, 1950-52, retired with rank of adm., 1952; consultant Sperry Corp., 1952—; dir. Prudential Ins. Co. Sr. naval representative of Joint Chiefs of Staff on military staff committee of Security Council UN, 1951; commr. Civil Def., 1952-53. Recipient of Congressional Medal of Honor; Navy Cross; Legion of Merit with three gold stars; Mexican Service Medal; Victory Medal with destroyer clasp; American Defense Service Medal with fleet clasp; American Campaign Medal; Asiatic-Pacific Campaign Medal; European-Africa-Middle Eastern Campaign Medal; World War II Victory Medal; China Service Medal; Philippine Liberation Ribbon with two bronze stars, Order of the British Empire (Honorary Commander.). Clubs: N.Y. Yacht; Army-Navy, Army-Navy Country (Wash.); Garden City Golf; Seawanhaka-Corinthian Yacht; Piping Rock. Address: 57 Duck Pond Rd., Glen Cove, N.Y. Died Nov. 30, 1958; buried Arlington Nat. Cemetery.

BADING, GERHARD ADOLPH diplomat; b. Milwaukee, Wis., Aug. 31, 1870; s. of John and Dorothea (Ehlers) B.; student Northwestern U., Watertown, Wis.; M.D., Rush Med. Coll., Chicago, 1896; m. Carol Royal Clemmer, Dec. 15, 1895. House physician, Milwaukee Hosp., 1896-97; instr. sugr. pathology Milwaukee Med. Coll., 1897-1901; asso. in surgery, 1901-05, prof. operative surgery, 1905-07, Wis.

Coll. Phys. & Surg.; surgeon Johnston Emergency Hosp., 7 yrs.; cons. surgeon, Milwaukee County Hosp., 4 yrs. Commr. of health, Milwaukee, 1906-10; mayor of Milwaukee 2 terms, 1912-16; E.E. and M.P. to Ecuador, by appmt. President Harding, 1922; apptd. A.E. on special mission by President Collidge, 1925; A.E. on special mission by President Hoover, 1929; resigned from the diplomatic service, 1930. U.S. examining surgeon for pensions, 1897-1912. Mem. Light Horse Squadron, W.N.G., 1890-93; served as lt. col. N.G., P.I.; 1st lt. M.O.R.C., 1917, capt. 1917, maj. 1919; served at Fort Riley, Kans., 4 months, 34th Div., Camp Cody, N.M., 7 months, P.I., 9 months, China expedition, Tientsin, 3 months; hon. discharge, Camp Grant, Ill., July 1919. Decorated Al Merito primera classe, Ecuador. Regent Marquette Univ., Milwaukee. Lutheran. Mem. A.M.A., Am. Pub. Health Assn., Wis. State, Milwaukee Col. and Milwaukee med. socs., Am. Legion, Phi Rho Sigma. Clubs: Town, City. Home: 2711 N. Hackett Av., Milwaukee. Died Apr. 11, 1946.

BAEHR, CARL ADOLPH army officer; b. Mpls., July 28, 1885; s. Charles and Katherine (Groppre) B.; B.S., U.S. Mil. Acad., 1909; grad. Command and Gen. Staff Sch., 1923, Army War Coll., 1926; m. Emilie A. Bischoff, Sept. 15, 1910; children-Carl (killed in action on Bataan), Katherine (Mrs. St. John) Elizabeth. Commd. 2d lt., 1909, advanced through grades to brig. gen., 1941; served in Alaska and on Mexican Border; instr. Plattsburg, 1915-16; served with 3rd F.A., France, 12th F.A., Meuse-Argonne, World War I; prof. mil. sci. and tactics, U. Okla., 1920; instr. Mo. N.G., 1923; exec. 11th F.A. Brigade, Hawaii, 1926; instr. and dir. F.A. Sch., 1930; later chief of staff Philippine Div. and chief of staff 2d Army Corps, comdg. 71st F.A. Brigade; comdg. VI Corps Arty., Italy, France, Germany, Austria Army of Occupation. Decorated Silver Star, Bronze Star, Air medal, African-European, Mexican border, World War Distinguished Service, Legion of Merit, American Theater, Army of Occ. (U.S.) medals, Legion of Honor, Croix de Guerre (French); Hon. Comdr., Order Brit. Empire (British). Mem. Nat. Army and Navy YMCA Com., Manila, 1938-40. Dir. YMCA A.R.C. Clubs: Racquet (Phila.); Army and Navy Country (Washington). Contbr. to F.A. Jour. and other service publs. Home: 5302 Baltimore Av., Chevy Chase, Md. Died Dec. 22, 1959.

BAER, JOSEPH LOUIS surgeon; b. Chicago, Apr. 29, 1880; B.S., U. of Chicago, 1902, M.S., 1903. M.D., Rush Med. Coll., 1904; post-grad. studies, Berlin and Vienna, 1908; married Gretchen Winslow Shattuck, July 28, 1913 (died Mar. 2, 1926); m. 2d, Janet Bachrach, Jan. 22, 1931. Interne Michael Reese Hosp., Chicago, 1904-07, anaestetist, 1907-13, attending obstetrician and gynecologist, 1913-36, sr. attending gynecologist and obstetrician, 1936—. Instr. dept. gynecology and obstetrics, Rush Med. Coll., 1917-21, asst. prof., 1921-27, asso. prof. 1927-35, prof., 1935-46, prof. emeritus, 1946—; bd. dirs. Blue Cross Plan for Hosp. Care, 1937—. Vice Pres. and dir. Am. Bd. Obstetrics and Gynecology, 1927—. Captain Medical Corps, United States Army, Base Hospital, Camp Custer, Michigan, November 1918-Jan. 20, 1919. Fellow Am. Coll. Surgeons, Am. Gynecol. Soc.; mem. A.M.A., Chicago Gynecol. Soc., Chicago Inst. of Medicine. Mason. Contbr. articles to med. press. Home: 1642 E. 56th St. Office: 104 S. Michigan Av., Chgo. Died Dec. 8, 1954.

BAETJER, FREDERICK HENRY intgenologist; b. Baltimore, Md., Aug. 7, 1874; s. Henry and Fredericka B.; A. B., Johns Hopkins, 1897, M.D., 1901; m. Mary Yarnall Carey, Oct. 14, 1903. Prof. roentgenology and roentgenologist, Johns Hopkins U. and Hosp.; cons. roentgenologist, Union Memorial Hosp., Church Home and Infirmary, Hosp. for the Women of Md., Children's Hosp. Sch. Maj. Med. Corps U.S. Army, May 1917-Feb. 1919. Pres. Am Roentgen Ray Soc., 1911-12. Home: Catonsville, Md. Died July 17, 1933.

BAGGETT, SAMUEL GRAVES lawyer, author: b. Coryell County, Tex., Sept. 1894; s. William Tillman and Sarah Elizabeth (Linder) B.; LL.B., U. Tex., 1917; m. Mrs. Esther Ann Wadsworth, Feb. 18, 1933. Gen. law practice, Austin, San Antonia, 1919-22; atty. Atlantic Refining Co. interests in Mexico, 1922-24; sec. Mexico office Assn. Producers of Petroleum in Mexico, 1924-26; atty. Latin Am. br. law dept., United Fruit Co., 1926-27. atty. for tropical operations, 1927-39, gen. atty., 1939, 47, v.p. and Gen. counsel, 1947-59, also dir. Dir. Keystone Custodian Funds, Inc.; v.p. Framingham Union osp. Served to 1st lt., 345th F.A., 90th Div., A.E.F., 1917. Dir. Nat. Fgn. Trade Council, Inc.; observer Am. delegation 9th Conf. Am. States, Bogota, 1948. Mem. Am. Bar Assn., Internat. Bus. Relations Council, Am. Arbitration Assn., Internat. C. of C. (trustee U.S. council), Tex. Folklore Soc., Delta Sigma Rho. Mason (K.T., Shriner). Clubs: Army and Navy (Washington); Lawyers (N.Y.). Author: Gods on Horseback, 1952. Contbr. articles to law jours. Died Dec. 28, 1964; buried Austin (Tex.) Meml. Park.

BAGLEY, DAVID WORTH navy officer; b. Raleigh, N.C., Jan. 8, 1883; s. William Henry and Adelaide Ann (Worth) B.; student N.C. State Coll., 1898-99; B.S., U.S. Naval Acad., 1904; m. Marie Louise Harrington, Feb. 16, 1918; children-David Harrington, Worth Harrington, Tennent Harrington. Commd. ensign USN, 1906, advanced through the grades to adm. 1947 (ret.). Served as flag lt. to comdr. in chief China Sta., during Chinese Revolution, 1911-12; comdr. destroyer in war zone during WW; naval attache, The Hague, Holland, 1919-20; chief of staff U.S. Naval Forces, Europe, 1926-28; comdt. U.S.S. Pensacola, 1931-33; comd. mine force 1937-38; comdt. Navy Yard, Mare Island, Cal., 1938-41; comdr. Battleship Div. 2, Jan. 1941-Apr. 1942; comdt. 14th Naval Dist. and Hawaiian Sea Frontier Apr. 1942-Mar. 1943; comdt. 11th Naval Dist. and Naval Operations Base, San Diego, Mar. 1943-Feb. 1944; comdr. Western Sea Frontier Feb.-Nov. 1944; comdt. 14th Naval Dist. and Hawaiian Sea Frontier, Nov. 1944-July 1945; naval rep. Inter-Am. Def. Bd., U.S.-Mexican Def. Bd., U.S.-Canadian Def. Bd., July 1945-Dec. 1946. Decorated D.S.M., Legion of Merit, World War Victory Medal, Distinguished Service award (U.S.); Order of the Savior (Greece); Naval Order of Merit (Spain); Order of Aviz (Portugal). Home: 2721 Glenwick Pl., La Jolla, Cal. Died May 24, 1960; buried Arlington Nat. Cemetery.

BAGSTER-COLLINS, ELIJAH WILLIAM, college prof.; b. Pawtucket, R.I., Apr. 16, 1873; s. Henry and Elizabeth (Hollingworth) Collins; A.B., Brown, 1897; A.M., Columbia, 1898; studied Berlin, 1891-93, Leipzig, 1902-03; m. Edith Lilian Bagster, of London, Eng., 1897; children—Ashlyn H., Robert D., Jeremy F. Adj. prof. German, Teachers Coll. (Columbia), 1903, asso. prof., 1904-39; now retired. Mng. editor Modern Lang. Jour., 1916-19; mng. editor German Quarterly, 1927-37. Capt. U.S.A., Mil. Intelligence Div. Gen. Staff, 1918-19. Mem. Nat. Inst. Soc. Sciences, Modern Languages Assn. America, Am. Assn. Teachers of German (acting pres. 1927), Alpha Delta Phi, Phi Beta Kappa, Phi Delta Kappa. Author: Teaching of German in Secondary Schools, 1904; First Book in German, 1912; History of Modern Language Teaching in the United States, 1930. Editor: A First German Reader, 1925. Home: Montrose NY

BAILEY, CLARENCE MITCHELL brig. gen. U.S.A.; b. New York, Nov. 26, 1841; ed. pvt. and pub. schs. in Ind. and Pa.; married. Apptd. from Ind., 2d lt. 6th U.S. Inf., Aug. 5, 1861; promoted through grades to col. 16th Inf., Nov. 1, 1898; retired for disability in line of duty, May 5, 1899; advanced to rank of brig. gen. retired, by act of Apr. 23, 1904. Home: Ft. Wayne, Ind. Died May 21, 1920.

BAILEY, DAVID JACKSON congressman, Lawyer; b. Lexington, Ga., Mar. 11, 1812; studied law. Admitted to bar, 1831, practiced law, Jackson, Butts County, Ga.; served as capt. of co. in Seminole and Creek Wars; mem. Ga. Ho. of Reps., 1835, 47; mem. Ga. Senate, 1838, 49-50, 55-56, se., 1839-41, pres., 1855-56; del. Democratic county convs., 1838, 50; mem. U.S. Ho. of Reps. (State Rights Dem.) from Ga., 32d-33d congresses, 1851-55; mem. Ga. Secession Conv., 1861; served with Confederate Army, became col. 30th Regt., Ga. Inf.; moved to Griffin, Spalding County, Ga., 1861. Died Griffin, June 14, 1897; buried Oak Hill Cemetery.

BAILEY, FRANK HARVEY naval officer; b. Cranesville, Pa., June 1851; s. James and Sarah Ann (Hurd) B.; B.S., Scio (Ohio) Coll., 1873; grad. U.S. Naval Acad., 1875; m. Anna J. Markham, Dec. 28, 1881. Commd. asst. engr., July 1, 1877; advanced through grades to capt., July 1, 1908; rear admiral, Feb. 13, 1913; retired on account of age, June 29, 1913. Instr. in marine engring. dept., Cornell U., 1882-85. Served on Raleigh, in Philippine Islands, during Spanish-Am. War and was advanced 3 numbers "for eminent and conspicuous conduct in battle." On duty at Bur. of Steam Engring., Navy Dept., during war with Germany. Republican. Methodist. Home: Gowanda, N.Y. Died Apr. 9, 1921.

BAILEY, JAMES EDMUND senator, lawyer; b. Montgomery County, Tenn., Aug. 15, 1822; attended Clarksville Acad., U. Nashville; studied law. Admitted to bar, 1843; practiced in Clarksville, Montgomery County; Whig mem. Tenn. Ho. of Reps., 1853; served as col. 49th Tenn. Regiment, Confederate Army in Civil War; apptd. mem. court of arbitration by Tenn. gov., 1874; mem. U.S. Senate (Democrat, filled vacancy) from Tenn., Jan. 19, 1877-81. Died Clarksville, Dec. 29, 1885; buried Greenwood Cemetery.

BAILEY, JOSEPH army officer; b. Pennsville, O., May 6, 1825; studied engring., Ill.; m. Mary Spaulding, 1846. In lumber business and engring. constrn., Kilbourn City, Wis., 1847-61; organized company in 4th Wis. Volunteer Regt., 1861, had rank of capt., became maj., 1863, lt. col., 1863, col., 1864, brig. gen., 1864, brevetted maj. gen., 1865; served in Point Hudson, New Orleans, also on Red River expdn. (built dams for withdrawal of Bank's army); moved to Vernon County, Mo., 1865; sheriff Vernon County, 1866. Murdered by 2 criminals he had placed under arrest, Nevada, Mo., Mar. 21, 1867.

BAILEY, MILUS KENDRICK physician and surgeon; b. Euharlee, Ga., Sept. 4, 1891; s. Edward and Martha Jane (Kendrick) B.; student Daniel Baker Coll., 1908-12, U. Tex., 1915; M.D., Emory U., 1919; m. Martha Williams, Dec. 24, 1920 (dec.); m. 2d Frances Riley Dec. 10, 1950; 2 children. Interne, Emory U. Hosp., 1919-21; practice medicine and surgery, Hamilton, Ga., 1921-25, specializing in genito-urinary surgery since 1925; prof. urology and chmn. dept. urology Emory U. Sch. Medicine Atlanta, since 1934. Served as maj. M.C., AUS, 1942-45. Diplomate Am. Bd. Urology. Mem. A.M.A., Am. Urol. Assn., Phi Chi. Democrat. Presbyn. Clubs: Kiwanis, Druid Hills Golf. Author articles on genito-urinary surgery. Home: 578 Ridgecrest Rd. N.E., Atlanta. Died June 21, 1964.

BAILEY, THEODORUS senator, congressman, lawyer; b. nr. Fishkill, Dutchess County, N.Y., Oct. 12, 1758; attended rural schs.; studied law. Admitted to bar, 1778; practiced in Poughkeepsie, N.Y.; adjutant in Col. Freer's Regt., N.Y. Militia, later in Col. Morris Graham's Regt., in Revolutionary War; maj. N.Y. State Militia, 1786, lt. col., 1797, brig. gen., 1801-05; mem. U.S. Ho. of Reps. (Democrat) from N.Y., 3d-4th, 6th, (filled vacancy) 7th congresses, 1797-97, 99-1801, Oct. 6, 1801-03; mem. N.Y. State Assembly, 1802; mem. U.S. Senate from N.Y., 1803-Jan. 16, 1804; postmaster City of N.Y., 1804-28. Died N.Y.C., Sept. 6, 1828; buried Dutch Burying Ground, reinterred Rural Cemetery, Poughkeepsie, N.Y., Jan. 8, 1864.

BAILEY, THEODORUS naval officer; b. Chateaugay, N.Y., Apr. 12, 1805; s. William and Phoebe (Platt) B.; m. Sarah Ann Platt, June 23, 1830. Apptd. midshipman U.S. Navy, 1818; served on coast of Africa, then transferred to Pacific 1818-20; 1st command was store-ship Lexington, 1846; served in Lower Cal. during Mexican War; promoted to comdr., 1849, capt., 1855; comd. St. Mary's in the Pacific, 1853-56, frigate Colo. in blockade of Fla., 1861; 2d in command under Admiral David Farragut in attack on New Orleans, La., 1862, led Union fleet up Mississippi River and accepted surrender of New Orleans; comd. East Gulf blockading squadron, 1862-64, Portsmouth Navy Yard, 1864-66; promoted to rear adm., 1866. Died Washington, D.C., Feb. 10, 1877.

BAILIE, EARLE investment banking; b. Milwaukee, Wis., Sept. 17, 1800; s. John and Cornelia Purdy (Conklin) B.; A.B., U. of Minn., 1913; LL.B., Harvard, 1915, S.J.D., 1916; m. Margaret Iselin Henderson, June 11, 1923; children - David Henderson, Susanah Conklin, Joanna De Peyster. Admitted to N.Y. bar, 1916; with Cravath & Henderson, 1916-17 and 1919; with J. W. Seligman & Co., 1919-, partner, 1923-; chmn. bd. Tri-Continent Corp., Selected Industries Co., Broad St. Investing Corp., Capital Administrations, General Shareholdings, Union Securities Corp. Spl. fiscal asst. U.S. Treasury Dept., 1933. Served in U.S. Army, 1917-18, retiring as capt. F.A.R.C. Home: Wilton, Conn. Died Nov. 15, 1940.

BAILY, ELISHA INGRAM army officer; b. in Pa., Nov. 14, 1824. Apptd. from Pa., asst. surgeon, Feb. 16, 1847; capt. asst. surgeon, Feb. 16, 1852; maj. surgeon, May 15, 1861; lt. col. surgeon, June 26, 1876; col. surgeon, Jan. 30, 1883; retired, Nov. 14, 1888; advanced to rank of brig. gen. retired, Apr. 23, 1904. Bvtd. lt. col., Mar. 13, 1865, for services during the war. Died 1908.

BAINBRIDGE, WILLIAM naval officer; b. Princeton, N.J., May 7, 1774; s. Dr. Absolom and Miss (Taylor) B.; m. Susan Hyleger, 1798, 5 children. Commd. lt. comdt. U.S. Navy, 1798, given command ship Retaliation; commd. master comdt., given command consort Norfolk; promoted capt. (at that time highest rank in navy), 1800, given command frigate George ashington; comdr. frigate Philadelphia, 1803, ran aground in harbor of Tripoli, taken prisoner, ship later burned by Stephen Decatur (so it would not be used against Am. fleet); received command ship President, 1808; comdt. Charlestown (Mass.) Navy Yard, 1812, obrained command flag ship Constitution; supt. constrn. war ship Independence, 1813; established 1st U.S. naval sch. at Boston Navy Yard, 1815, presided over 1st bd. examiners, 1819; commanded battleship New Columbus, 1820; commanded Phila. Navy Yard, 1821, Charlestown Navy Yard, 1823; U.S. naval commr., 1823. Died Phila., July 27, 1833.

BAINBRIDGE, WILLIAM SEAMAN surgeon; b. Providence, R.I.; s. Rev. William Folwell and Lucy Elizabeth (Seaman) B.; grad. Mohegan Lake School, Peekskill, N.Y., 1888; student Columbia; M.D., Coll. of Physicians and Surgeons (Columbia), 1893; grad. Presbyn. Hosp., 1895, Sloane Maternity Hosp., 1896; post-grad. Coll. Phys. and Surg., 1896; abroad 2 yrs.; hon. A.M., Shurtleff Coll., Ill., 1899; M.S., Washington and Jefferson Coll., 1902; Sc.D., Western U. of Pa., 1907; LL.D., Lincoln Memorial U., and Coe College; Litt.D., Lincoln Memorial U., 1923; Dr. Honoris Causa, U. of San Marcos, Peru, 1941; m. June Ellen Wheeler, Sept. 9, 1911; children—Elizabeth (dec.), William Wheeler, John Seaman, Barbara (Mrs. Angus McIntosh). Professor operative gynecology, New York Post-graduate Medical School, 1900-06; professor surgery, New York, Poly. Med. Sch. and Hosp., 1906-18; surgeon N.Y. Skin and Cancer Hosp., 1903-18; surg. dir. N.Y. City Children's Hosps. and schs., Manhattan State Hosp., Ward's Island; cons. surg. or gynecologist to 16 metropolitan and suburban hosps.; hon. prof. med. faculty, Univ. Santo Domingo, Dominican Republic. Dir. Equitable Life Assur. Soc. of U.S., The Americas Foundation. Member Reserve Corps United States Navy, 1913-17; since Apr. 6, 1917 served as lieut. comdr., comdr. and capt. (med. dir.), M.C., U.S.N.R.; during World War operating surgeon on U.S.S. George

Washington; med. observer for U.S. with allied armies in the field, later attached to surgeon general's office to write report; cons. surgeon and chief, Physiotherapeutic Division, U.S. Naval Hospital, Brooklyn, New York, made consulting surgeon 3rd Naval Dist.; now cons. surgeon 3d Naval Dist. and attending specialist in surgery, U.S. Pub. Health Service, N.Y. City and vicinity. Official rep. of U.S. Govt. since 1921 at internat. congresses mil. medicine, surgery and sanitation; pres. 8th session Internat. office Medico-Military Documentation, Luxemburg, 1938, chmn. 9th session, Washington and New York, 1939. On official mission to all republics of Central and South America for Navy Dept. and State Dept., 1941. Decorated U.S. Naval Reserve Medal; Conspicuous Service Cross (N.Y. State); Officer, later Comdr. Legion of Honor (French); Officer Order of Leopold and Military Cross, 1st Class (Belgian); Commander, later Grand Officer Order of Crown of Italy, Vittorio-Veneto, Commemorative Cross (Italian); Medaille Commemorative, Medaille Reconnaissance (French): Silver Medal of Merit (Italian R.C.); Officer, later Comdr. Order Polonia Restituta; Comdr. Order of White Lion (Czechoslovakia); Grand Officer Order of Crown (Rumania); Officer Orden del Libertador (Venezuela); Order of Gediminas (Lithuania); Cross of Merit (Hungary); Gold Cross of Merit (Poland); Comdr. Order of the Crown (Belgium); Comdr. Order of the Crown, Medal of Red Cross (Jugoslavia); Cruz de la Orden del Merito Naval (Spain); comdr. Order of Saints Mauritius and Lazarus (Italy); Comdr. Order of the Sun (Peru); Comdr. of the Oak Leaved Crown (Luxemburg); Order of Merit, first class, Knight, Order of White Rose (Finland); Gold Medal Order of Distinguished Auxiliary Service, Salvation Army. Hon. mem. Royal Acad. Medicine of Belgium, Royal Acad. Medicine Rome. Soc. of Surgeons of Poland, Soc. of Surgeons of Paris, Assn. Mil. Surgeons of Mexico, Union Medicale Latine, Assn. Mil. Surgeons of Hungary, Acad. of Surgery of Peru, Nat. Acad. Medicine Mexico, Acad. Sciences and Arts, Mexico, Nat. Acad. Med. Venezuela, French Gynecol. Soc., Nat. Acad. of Medicine of Spain; fellow Am. Assn. Obstet., Gynecol. and Abdominal Surgeons, Internat. Coll. Surgeons (internat. treas., 1935-46; surg. regent, New York State; chairman board trustees of U.S. chapter), American Geriatrics Society (hon.), International College Anesthetists, Royal Institute Pub. Health (life), fellow Royal Soc. Medicine (Eng.), A.M.A., N.Y. Acad. Medicine; mem. N.Y. State Med. Soc., Greater N.Y. Med. Assn., Assn. Mil. Surgeons of U.S. (pres. 1935), Internat. Med. Club of New York (pres. 3 terms, 1934-38), Am. Acad. Physical Medicine (pres. since 1941), St. Andrews Soc., Colonial Wars, S.R., S.A.R., Huguenot Soc., Soc. of Cincinnati (hon.), Mil. Order Foreign Wars (comdr. gen. Nat. Comdry., 1926-32), Military order World War, Society Legion of Honor, Am. Soc. French Legion of Honor, St. Nicholas Society, Soc. of Am. Wars, Am. Legion (comdr. Tiger Post 1932-35), Delta Upsilon, The Newcomen Soc., various foreign societies. Clubs: Authors, Columbia University, Pilgrims of United States, Quill (pres. 1938-39), Foreign Students Cosmopolitan, Union League, Nat. Arts, Rotary (pres. N.Y., Rotary 1933), Army and Navy of America (New York); Inter-allied Officers (London and Paris); Union, Interalliee (Paris). Author: A Compend of Operative Gynecology, 1906; Life's Day Guide-Posts and Danger Signals in Health, 1909; The Cancer Problem, 1914 (French, Italian; Spanish, Polish, Arabic edits.); also brochures, med. papers and repts. Address: 34 Gramercy Park, New York, N.Y. Died Sept. 22, 1947.

BAINES, EDWARD RICHARDS, business exec. b. Bklyn., Mar. 20, 1887; s. James Clarence and Lillian Mary (Rea) B.; student Comml. High Sch., Brooklyn, 1904; m. Ada Z. Vermilye, Mary 25, 1907 (dec.); 1 son, Robert Edward (dec.); m. 2d, Alice Horan Haley, Feb. 9, 1933. Asst. treas. Gen. Vehicle Co., Long Island City, N.Y., 1906-17; vice pres. and comptroller Underwood Corp., N.Y. City, 1919-47, v.p. finance and internat. operations, 1947-59. Served as maj., Motor Transport Corps, U.S. Army, 1917-19. Mem. Controllers Inst. America, Nat. Assn. Cost Accountants. Clubs: Wee Burn Country, National Republican. Home: Greenwich CT Died Jan. 24, 1969.

BAIRD, ABSALOM brig. gen. U.S. Army (retired, 1888); b. Washington, Pa., Aug. 20, 1824; grad. Washington Coll., 1841; studied law; grad. West Point, 1849; m. Cornelia W. Smith. Oct. 17, 1850 (dec.). Served in Florida, 1850-53; asst. prof. mathematics West Point 1853-59; served during Civil war in Va., Tenn., and in the march to the sea; became bvt. maj. gen.; after war, insp. general. Died 1905.

BAIRD, GEORGE WASHINGTON rear admiral U.S.N.; b. Washington, Apr. 22, 1843; s. Matthew and Ophelia (Cauthorn) B.; ed. in pub. schs. and acad.; m. Miss L. J. Prather, 1873. Apptd. 3d asst. engr. U.S.N., Sept. 19, 1862; promoted through grades and retired with rank of rear admiral, Apr. 22, 1905. Pres. Bd. of Edn., Washington. Protestant. Mason. Home: Washington, D.C. Died Oct. 4, 1930.

BAIRD, GEORGE WILLIAM army officer; b. Milford, Conn., Dec. 13, 1839; s. Jonah Newton and Minerva (Gunn) B.; grad. Hopkins Grammar School, New Haven, 1859; entered Yale, 1859 (given diploma with class of 1863); m. Julia C. Rogers, July 31, 1866. Served in Civil War as pvt. Aug. 25, 1863 to Mar. 18, 1864; promoted from pvt. to col. 32d U.S. colored troops; served in S.C., Ga. and Fla., battles St. John's Bluff, Honey Hill, Deveaux' Neck, James Island, Siege of Charleston, Morris Island, S.C. Entered regular army May 11, 1866, as 2d lt. 19th inf., transferred Sept.21 to 37th inf.; promoted 1st lt. Apr. 27, 1867; transferred to 5th inf. May 19, 1869; served on Western frontier from Tex. to Mont. and in Indian campaigns, Mar. 1867, to July 1878; left field wounded; adj. 5th inf. and adj. gen. of Gen. N.A. Miles's field commands Jan. 1, 1871, to June 23, 1879; twice recommended for bvts. for gallant services in action; received medal of honor "for most distinguished gallantry in action against hostile Nez Perce Indians at Bear Paw Mountain, Mont., Sept. 30, 1877, where he was twice severely wounded"; promoted maj. and paymaster U.S.A., June 23, 1879; lt. col. and deputy paymaster gen., July 12, 1899; brig. gen, U.S.A., Feb. 19, 1903; on duty as chief disbursing officer, paymaster-gen.'s office, Apr. 1899-Feb. 1903. Wrote "Gen. Miles's Indian Campaigns," The Century, July 1901. Home: Milford, Conn. Died 1906.

BAIRD, HENRY W. army officer; b. Md., Aug. 13, 1881; student Mounted Service Sch., 1st yr. course, 1915; maj. Philippine Scouts, 1917; Cav. Sch. Field Officers Course, 1922; Command and General Staff Sch., 1923; 2d lt. Cav., Feb. 11, 1907; promoted through grades to maj. gen., July 11, 1941; became comdr. 4th Armored Div., U.S. Army. Died Oct. 1963.

BAITER, RICHARD ENGLIS, soap products mfr.; b. Short Hills, N.J., Dec. 11, 1913; s. Charles William Grevel and Madeleine (Englis) B.; A.B., Princeton, 1936; m. Barbara Dumont Baker, Sept. 12, 1936; children—Richard Englis, Peter B., David D., Barbara L. Vice pres. Standard Brands, 1953-56; merchandising mgr. Lever Bros. Co., 1956-60, marketing v.p. charge Pepsodent div., 1961-63, marketing v.p. Household Products division, 1963-66, trade development v.p., 1966-68, chmn., chief exec. officer subsidiary Glamorene Products Corp., 1968. Vice chmn. grad. inter club com. Princeton. Served to lt. col. USAAF, 1941-45. Clubs: Wee Burn Country (gov.) (Darien); Tiger Inn (gov., pres. Princeton, N.J.); Princeton of N.Y. Home: Darien CT Deceased.

BAKENHUS, REUBEN EDWIN cons. engr.; b. Chgo., Sept. 10, 1873; s. Deitrich and Wilhelmnia (Kemper) B.; B.S., Mass. Inst. Tech., 1896; grad. Naval War Coll., 1924; m. Edith Steacy Rogers, 1901 (dec. 1946), 1 dau., Mrs. Dorinda Bakenhus Beck; m. 2d, Ethel Berg von Linde, July 22, 1953. Instructor civil engring., Mass. Inst. of Tech., 1896-97; with U.S. Civil Service Commn., 1898-99; with U.S. Engineer Office, 1899-1901; commd. jr. lt. U.S. Navy, Feb. 27, 1901; advanced through grades to rear adm. C.E. Corps, Nov. 11, 1932, ret. Oct. 1937; sec. Am. Inst. Cons. Engrs., 1948-52, now secretary emeritus. Awarded Navy Cross, World War. Fellow A.A.A.S., mem. Am. Soc. C.E. (ex-pres. Met. Sect.; former mem. bd. dirs.; sec., 1947-51), Society Engring. Edn., Soc. Am. Military Engrs. (ex-pres. nat. soc., ex-pres. N.Y.C. post); Am. sect. Permanent Internat. Assn. of Navigation Congresses; ex-pres. Am. Inst. Cons. Engrs. (mem. council), N.Y. Soc. Military and Naval Officers, World War, Military Order World War (ex-comdr. N.Y. Chapter), Amateur Fencers League of Am. Clubs: Army and Navy (Washington); N.Y. Yacht, Military Naval, Explorers. Author: The Panama Canal (with Capt. H.S. Knapp, and Emory R. Johnson), 1914. Editor of Activities of Bureau of Yards and Docks during World War, Manual of Bur. of Yards and Docks, Navy Dept. Contbr. to tech. mags. Home: 51 5th Av., New York 3. Office: care Am. Inst. of Consulting Engineers, 33 W. 39th St., N.Y.C. Died Oct. 7, 1967.

BAKER, ARTHUR MULFORD clergyman, editor; b. Wanakoneta, O., Oct. 11, 1880; s. John Mulford and Alice Maria (Arthur) B.; A.B., Defiance (O.) Coll., 1906; grad. McCormick Theol. Sem., 1909; studied Columbia U. and Ind. U.; Ph.D., Ind. U., 1928; m. Glenna Maude Helser, June 20, 1907; children - Margaret (Mrs. Arthur M. Adams). Daniel Arthur. Ordained Presbyn. ministry, 1909; pastor various chs., 1908-24; asst. editor Am. S.S. Union Publs., 1924-30. editor, 1930-. Chaplain 120th Inf., U.S. Army, with A.E.F., 1918-19; capt. Co. K. 151st Ind. N.G., 1923-24; chaplain O.R.C. Author: If I Were a Christian. 1930: Hoofbeats in the Wilderness, 1930; The River of God, 1930. Died Sept. 22, 1941.

BAKER, ASHER CARTER naval officer; b. Matawan, N.J., Dec. 18, 1850; s. Elihu and Charlotte (Carter) B.; grad. U.S. Naval Acad., 1871; m. Mary Elizabeth Reese, Feb. 10, 1880. Served on various ships; served 3 yrs. on deep-sea investigations for U.S. Fish Commn.; commr. to Mexico for Chicago Expn. and later supt. marine div., Transportation Dept., same; connected with Transportation Exhibits Dept. of U.S. Commn. to Paris Expn., 1900; decorated Order of Legion of Honor; asst. chief Dept. Transportation, St. Louis Expn., 1904; dir. exhibits and chief, dept. transportation exhibits, Panama-Pacific International Expn., San Francisco, 1915. Capt. U.S.N. and retired, June 30, 1905. Called to active duty, Apr. 3, 1917, and in France to July 1, 1919; dep. dir. gen. of transportation and dir of ports, on staff Gen. Pershing. Died June 5, 1926.

BAKER, BRYANT, sculptor; b. London, England, July 8, 1881; s. John (sculptor) and Susan (Bryant) B.; student City and Guilds Tech. Inst., London; grad. Royal Acad. Arts, London, 1910; unmarried. Executed bust and heroic statue of King Edward VII; bust of King Olav of Norway; also busts of many notable persons of Eng. Came to U.S., 1916; made busts from life of Pres. Coolidge, Col. John Coolidge, Sens. H. C. Lodge, W. A. Clark and J. H. Bankhead. Gens. Pershing, March and Gorgas, Chief Justices White, Taft and Hughes, John Hays Hammond, Herbert Hoover, Newton Baker, Josephus Daniels, Percival Lowell, George Harvey, Cordell Hull; heroic statue of Chief Justice Edward D. White, New Orleans; heroic bronze statues of Grover Cleveland, Millard Fillmore and Young Lincoln, Buffalo, N.Y., Chief Justice John Marshall, Warrenton, Va., Elbert Gary, Gary, Ind.; John F. Kennedy heroic bronze statue, McKeesport, Pa.; 4 marble busts, U.S. Supreme Ct.; marble statues Caesar Rodney, John M. Clayton, patriots of Del., Statuary Hall, Washington, D.C.; Gov. Reuben Fenton statue, Jamestown, N.Y.; Bishop Freeman. Meml. Washington Nat. Cathedral; colossal bronze statue of George Washington, Masonic National Memorial Building, Alexandria, Va.; bronze bust of Sir Winston Churchill, in National Portrait Gallery, Washington, D.C. Works in bronze or marble throughout U.S., Europe. Ideal works in various private collections and in art galleries. Exhibitor at Royal Acad., from 1910, also Paris Salon, Corcoran Art Gallery, Etc. Served as sgt., M.C., U.S. Army, 1918-19. Winner of Marland competition for Pioneer Woman Statue, Ponca City, Okla.; D.A.R. medal for Americanism and achievement, also N.Y. State grand lodge medal for achievement, 1960. Fellow Nat. Sculpture Soc.; mem. N.A.D. Studio: New York City NY Died Mar. 29, 1970; buried Fordcombe England

BAKER, CHAUNCEY BROOKE army officer; b. Lancaster, O., Aug. 26, 1860; s. Emanuel Ruffner Peter and Eliza (Stoneberger) B.; grad. U.S. Mil. Acad., 1886; honor grad. Inf. and Cav. Sch., Ft. Leavenworth, Kan., 1889 (B.S., Ohio State U., 1904); m. Lucy, d. Gen. Alexander McD. McCook, U.S.A., June 19, 1889 (died 1923); m. 2d, Ella Turner, Dec. 1924 (died 1932); m. 3d, Emily Burr, Oct. 3, 1934. Commd. 2d lt. 7th Infantry, July 1, 1886; advanced through grades to col. q.m. dept., U.S.A., May 15, 1917; brig. gen. N.A., Aug. 5, 1917; retired from active service April 21, 1921. Regtl. officer and a.-d.-c. at frontier posts, 1886-98; depot q.m., Havana, 1898-1900; chief, q.m., Havana, Aug. 1900-May 1902; various assignments in q.m. dept. to 1914; duty Office Q.M. Gen., 1914-16; sr. mem. Mil. Commn. to France, May-July 1917. chief embarkation service, Office Chief of Staff, War Dept., Aug. 7, 1917-Feb. 1918. Presbyn. Mason. Author: Notes on Fire Tactics, 1889; Transportation of Troops and Material, 1905; Handbook of Transportation by Rail and Commercial Vessels, 1916; Co-ordination between the Transportation Companies and the Military Service, 1916. Chairman bd. Market Exchange Bank Co., Columbus; chmn. bd. Am. Nat. Fire Ins. Co. Home: Bexley, O. Died Oct. 18, 1936.

BAKER, EDWARD DICKINSON senator; b. London, Eng., Feb. 24, 1811; m. Mary A. Lee, Apr. 27, 1831. Came to U.S., 1825, moved to Springfield, Ill., 1830; admitted to Ill. bar, 1830; mem. Ill. Gen. Assembly from Sangamon County, 1837-40; mem. Ill. Senate, 1840-44; mem. U.S. Ho. of Reps. from Ill. as Whig (defeated Lincoln), 29th Congress, 1845-Dec. 30, 1846, as Republican, 31st Congress, 1849-51; raised a co. of vol raised a co. of volunteers, 1846, col. in Mexican War, participated in siege of Veracruz, commanded brigade at Battle of Cerro Gordo; mem. U.S. Senate from Ore., Oct. 2, 1860-Oct. 21, 1861; col. 71st Regt., Pa. Volunteer Inf., in charge of a brigade, 1861; commd. col., then maj. gen. U.S. Volunteers, 1861. Killed in Battle of Ball's Bluff (Va.), Oct. 22, 1861; buried Lone Mountain Cemetery, San Francisco.

BAKER, GEORGE BARR b. Wyandotte, Mich., Apr. 1, 1870; s. George Payson and Celestia Barr (Hibbard) B.; m. Laura Pike, May 10, 1910. Reporter, Detroit Tribune, 1895-96, Detroit Journal, 1897-99; European corr., Detroit Journal, 1900-01, McClure's Magazine (English office), 1902; art critic "Academy and Literature" (Eng.); 1903; Am. corr., London Daily Express and Paris Matin, 1904-05; journalist sec. to Joseph Pulitzer, 1906; asso. editor Everybody's Mag., 1907-10; lit. editor Delineator, 1911-14. Dir. Am. Relief Administration, exec. com. Commn. for Relief in Belgium Ednl. Foundation; mem. exec. com. Am. Relief Administration Children's Fund; dir. Am. Child Health Assn.; chmn. Internat. Conf. between Authors and Motion Picture Producers, 1923-24; mem. council Authors' League America. Ship's writer U.S.S. Yosemite through Spanish-Am. War; mem. Commn. for Relief in Belgium, 1916; comdr. U.S.N.R.F., exec. officer U.S. Naval Cable Censorship, 3d Naval Dist., 1917; attached to force comdr. in European waters, 1918; attached to dir.-gen. of relief under Supreme Economic Council, Paris, during Peace Conf., 1919. Dir. publicity Coolidge presidential campaign, 1924, head of naturalized citizens organizations for Rep. Nat. Com. in Hoover campaign, 1928; general consultant, White House Conference on Child Health and Protection, 1930-31; now retired. Officer Crown of Belgium; Comdr. Order of Leopold (Belgium); Order of the White Rose of Finland, Order of Restituta (Poland).

Republican. Mem. Soc. Colonial Wars, S.R. Clubs: Players, Dutch Treat, Brook (New York); National Press (Washington); Burlingame (Calif.); Bohemian (San Francisco); West Indian (London, England). Home: Burlingame, Calif. Office: Graybar Bldg., New York, N.Y. Died July 29, 1948.

BAKER, HENRY MOORE lawyer; b. Bow, N.H., Jan. 11, 1841; s. Aaron W. and Nancy (Dustin) B.; A.B., Dartmouth, 1863, A.M., 1866; LL.B., Columbian (now George Washington) U., 1866; (LL.D., Howard U., 1911); unmarried. Pvt. U.S. Treasury Guards, 1864-65; admitted to D.C. bar, 1866, Supreme Ct. of U.S., 1882; began practice in Washington, 1874; judge advocate gen. with rank of brig. gen. N.H. N.G., 1886-87; mem. N.H. Senate, 1891-92; mem. 53d and 54th Congresses (1893-97), 2d N.H. Dist. mem. N.H. Constl. Conv., 1902; mem. N.H. Ho. of Rep., 1905-07, 1907-09. Pres. trustees Pembroke Acad., 1904-; trustee Howard U., 1906-12; pres. trustees of Mary Baker G. Eddy and her executor. Home: Concord, N.H. Died May 30, 1912.

BAKER, HUGH POTTER univ. pres. emeritus; b. St. Croix Falls, Wis., Jan. 20, 1878; s. Maj. J(oseph) Stannard and Alice (Potter) B.; B.S., Mich. State Coll., 1901; M.F., Yale, 1904; Dr. Econs., U. Munich, 1910; LL.D., Syracuse U., 1933; LL.D., R.I. State Coll., 1945, Amherst Coll., U. Mass., 1947; D.Sc. in Edn., Boston U., 1945; m. Fleta Paddock, Dec. 27, 1904 (now dec.); children—Carolyn, Steven Paddock (dec), Clarence Potter; m. 2d, Richarda Sahla, Nov. 27, 1929. For 10 years with the U.S. Forest Service, examining pub. lands for forest reserves in Central Ida., Wyo., Neb., N.M., Wash., and Ore. Prof. forestry, Ia. State Coll., 1904-07, Pa. State Coll., 1907-12; dean and prof. silviculture, N.Y. State Coll. Forestry, Syracuse, 1912-20, dean, 1930-33; exec. sec. Am. Paper and Pulp Assn., 1920-28; mgr. trade assn. dept. C. of C. of U.S., 1928-30; pres. Mass. State Coll., 1933-47. Mem. 2d R.O.T.C., Ft. Sheridan (Ill.), Aug.-Nov. 1917; with 46th Inf., and mem. Gen. Staff; maj. O.R.C. Fellow A.A.A.S., Royal Geog. Soc. (London); mem. Soc. Am. Foresters, S.A.R., Loyal Legion. Mason. Clubs: Cosmos (Washington); University (Boston, N.Y.C.). Address: U. Mass., Amherst, Mass. Died May 24, 1950; buried St. Croix Falls, Wis.

BAKER, JAMES HEATON soldier; b. Monroe, O., May 6, 1829; s. Henry and Hannah Woodruff (Heaton) B.; A.B., Ohio Wesleyan U., 1852, A.M., 1851; m. Rose Lucia Thurston, 1851 (died 1873); 2d, Zula Bartlett, Dec. 23, 1879. Sec. of State of Ohio, 1854-56; elected sec. State of Minn., 1857; re-elected, 1861 (resigned to enter army, 1861); commd. col. 10th Minn. Vol. Inf., Nov. 16, 1862; served with Gen. H. H. Sibley in Indian War, 1862-63; ordered to Mo., 1862; placed in command of post of City of St. Louis under Gen. Schofield; provost marshal, Dept. of Mo., under Gen. G. M. Dodge; bvtd. brig-gen. vols., March 13, 1865. "for faithful and meritorious services"; mustered out of service, Oct. 21, 1865. U.S. commr. of pensions under Pres. Grant, 1871-75; surveyor-gen. of Minn. 1875-79; state railroad commr., 1881-86. Purchased, 1879, The Union and Record, Republican newspapers, Mankato, Minn., combined the two and formed the Mankato Free Press, of which was editor and pub. for several yrs. Methodist. Author: The Lives of the Governors of Minnesota, 1908. Home: Mankato, Minn. Died May 27, 1913.

BAKER, J(AMES) NORMENT surgeon, state health officer; b. Abingdon, Va., Apr. 11, 1876; s. James Biscoe and Sallie Claiborne (Barksdale) B,; A.B., U. of Va., 1895, M.D., 1898; post-grad. courses Johns Hopkins Hosp., Baltimore, and Mass. Gen. Hosp., Boston; m. Marguerite Rice, Apr. 29, 1908; children—Samuel Rice, J. Norment (dec). Interne, St. Vincent's Hospital, Norfolk, Va., 1898-99; surgeon in charge Plant System hosps., Waycross, Ga., 1899, Montgomery, 1900-01; practice of gen. surgery and female urology, Montgomery, Ala., since 1918; surgeon for Atlantic Coast Line and Central of Ga. R.R., U.S. Employees Compensation Commn., Southern Bell Telephone Co.; visiting surgeon Memorial Hosp. and Highland Park Sanitarium; state health officer of Ala. since 1930. Maj. Med. Corps, World War. Sec. State Bd. of Med. Examiners of Ala.; mem. Nat. Bd. Med. Examiners of U.S.; pres. (1940-41) Conf. of State and Provincial Health Authorities of N.A.; ex-pres. Fed. of State Med. Boards of U.S. Fellow Am. Pub. Health Assn. (pres. Southern Branch); Am. Coll. Surgeons; mem. Am. and Southern med. assns. (ex-chmn. pub. health sect.), Southern Surg. Assn. (v.p. 1921), Phi Kappa Psi, Pi Mu. Democrat. Episcopalian. Club: Country (Montgomery). Home: 602 S. Perry St. Office: 519 Dexter Av., Montgomery, Ala. Died Nov. 9, 1941.

BAKER, LAWRENCE SIMONS agt. Seaboard Air Line; b. Gatesville, N.C., May 15, 1830; s. Dr. John and Mary (Wynns) B.; grad West Point, 1851; m. Elizabeth Earl Henderson, March 13, 1855. Apptd. 2d lt. U.S.A., resigned as 1st lt. mounted rifles, U.S.A., 1861. Apptd. col. 1st N.C. cav., May 20, 1861; brig. gen., Aug. 1, 1863; severely wounded - right arm shattered, Aug. 1, 1863, at battle of Brandy Station; in command eastern dept., N.C., from June 1864 until close of Civil War. Home: Suffolk, Va. Died 1907.

BAKER, REMEMBER army officer; b. Woodbury, Conn., June 1737; s. Remember and Tamar (Warner) B.; m. Desire Hurlbut, Apr. 3, 1760, 1 son, Ozi. Served in French and Indian War, 1757—circa 1760; settled in Arlington (in what now is Vt.), 1764; became involved in controversy between N.Y. and N.H. over control of territory that is now State of Vt.; joined Green Mountain Boys under Ethan Allen to enforce claims to grants made by N.H. govt. to settlers in territory, 1770-74. Killed in encounter with Indians while serving in Gen. Schuyler's scouting expdn. up Lake Champlain, at St. John's, N.Y., Aug. 1775.

BAKER, WILLIAM CLYDE JR. army officer; b. Alexander, N.C., May 9, 1904; s. William Clyde and Anna Mae (Clontz) B.; student U. Tenn., 1921-22; B.S., U.S. Mil. Acad., 1926; C.E., Cornell U., 1928; student Command and Gen. Staff Sch., 1937-38; grad. Nat. War Coll., 1950; m. Hazel Marie Keily, July 24, 1934; 1 son, William Clyde III. Commd. 2d lt. U.S. Army, 1926, advanced through grades to maj. gen. C.E.; instr. U.S. Mil. Acad., 1933-37; exec. Engr. Bd., U.S. Army, 1938-42; chief staff 106th Inf. Div., World War II; chief econs. br. Civil Affairs and Mil. Govt. Div., Dept. Army, 1947-49; engr., asst. chief staff G-4, 8th Army, Korean War; asst. chief engrs. U.S. Army, 1953-56; comdg. gen., Ft. Leonard Wood, Mo., 1956-57; asst. chief staff G-4, U.S. Army Pacific, 1957-60; comdg. gen. Theater Army Support Command, Europe, Verdun, France, 1960-61; dep. chief staff, logistics Army, Europe 1961-62, chief of staff, 1962-64, ret.; asst. to Sec. Am. Battle Monuments Commn., 1964-. Decorated Distinguished Service medal, Legion Merit with 2 oak leaf clusters, Bronze Star with Oak leaf cluster and numerous foreign. Member Sons of the Am. Revolution, Soc. Am. Mil. Engrs., Sigma Nu, Sigma Delta Psi, Pi Delta Epsilon, Alpha Phi Epsilon, Kappa Pi, Chi Beta Phi, Sigma Delta Kappa, Theta Alpha Phi, Sigma Upsilon. Clubs: Army and Navy, Army and Navy Country (Washington). Mason (32 , 33 ,). Home: 301 W. Broad St., Clinton, Tenn. Died Oct. 5, 1966; buried Arlington Nat.

BAKER, WILLIAM JESSE urolgist; b. Dallas City, Ill.; May 1, 1894; s. Eugene Hamilton and Elizabeth Edity (Prescott) B.; B.S., Knox Coll., 1917; M.D. Rush Med. Coll., 1923; m. Eloise Parsons, Aug. 30, 1923; children—William, Robert. Intern, resident intern urology Cook County Hosp., Chicago, 1924-26; asso. urologist, 1932-46; chief urol. dept. 1946—; urologist St. Luke's Hosp., 1926—; prof. urology Northwestern U. Med. Sch., 1955—; cons. urologist Municipal Contagious Hosp. Served with med. dept. U.S. Army, 1917-19, as lt. col., M.C., AUS, World War II. Fellow A.C.S.; mem. A.M.A., Am. Urol. Assn., Am. Assn. Genito-Urinary Surgeons, Clin. Soc. Genito-Urinary Surgeons, Internat. Soc. Urologists, Chgo. Urol. Soc., Am. Neissereian Soc., Tau Kappa Epsilon, Delta Sigma Rho, Nu Sigma Nu, Alpha Omega Alpha, Pi Kappa Epsilon. Conglist. Mason. Clubs: University, South Shore Country (Chgo.). Home 5830 Stony Island Av., Chgo. Office: 7 W. Madison Street, Chgo. 2. Died Dec. 3, 1958.

BAKEWELL, CHARLES MONTAGUE ex-congressman, educator; b. Pitts, Apr. 24, 1867; s. Thomas and Josephine Alden (Maitland) B.; A.B., U. Cal., 1889; LL.D., 1943; A.M., Harvard, 1892, Ph.D., 1894; student univs. of Berlin, Strassburg and Paris, 1894-96; hon. A.M., Yale, 1905; m. Madeline Palmer, Dec. 21, 1889 (died May 15, 1947); children—Henry Palmer, Bradley Palmer (dec.), Mildred Palmer (Mrs. Richard Hooker, Jr.). Instr. philosophy Harvard, 1896-97; instr. philosophy U. Cal., 1897-98, asso. prof., 1900-03, prof., 1903-05; asso. prof. philosophy Bryn Mawr Coll., 1898-1900; prof. philosophy Yale, 1905-33, now emeritus; mem. 73d Congress, Conn. at large. Mem. Conn. Senate, 1920-24 (chmn. edn. com.); chmn. Commn. To Revise and Codify Edn. Laws of Conn. Mem. Am. Philos. Assn (pres. 1910), A.A.A.S., Nat. Inst. Social Scis., Brit. Inst. Philosophy, N.H. Hist. Soc. Author: Source Book in Ancient Philosophy, rev. ed,. 1939; Story of the American Red Cross in Italy; George Herbert Palmer (with W.E. Hocking). Also various essays in ethical and philos. criticism; editor and part author, Thomas Davidson's The Education of the Wage Earners; editor Everyman edit. of William James' Selected Papers on Philosophy, and Emerson's Poems, and Plato's Republic in Scribner's philosophy series. Insp. and historian with of maj., and dep. commr. Italian Commn. of A.R.C. in Italy, 1918-19. Decorated Order of The Crown (Italy); Silver Medal of Honor (Italian Red Cross). Mem. Beta Theta Pi, Phi Beta Kappa. Republican. Clubs: Century (N.Y.C.0; Graduate, New Haven Country (New Haven); Metropolitan (Washington); Hammonassett Fishing Assn. Address: 437 Humphrey St., New Haven. Died Sept. 19, 1957.

BAKKEN, CLARENCE JOHN, ednl. adminstr.; b. Pequot, Minn., Sept. 28, 1902; s. John P. and Caroline (Brunes) B.; LL.B., YMCA Coll. of Law, Mpls., 1926; B.S., U. Minn., 1927; M.A., U. Denver, 1957, Ed.D., 1959; m. Cora Opland, June 30, 1931; children—Colette (Mrs. William Kerlin), Clarence Opland. Admitted to Minn. bar, 1926, commd. 2d lt. U.S. Army, Res. 1927, advanced through grades to col., 1956; with civilian conservation corps, 1933-42, inspector gen. Pacific, 1942-45, 5th Army, 1947-50; mil. post Heidelberg, Germany, 1950-53, Ft. Benning, 1953-56; ret., 1956; pvt. practice law, 1926-29; high sch. tchr. Mandan, N.D., 1929-32; counselor Parsons Coll., Fairfield, Ia., 1960-62; mem. student personnel faculty Cal. State Coll., Long Beach, 1962-67, dir. financial aids, 1963-67. Active in Boy Scouts Am., 1914-67, named Silver Beaver, 1952. Decorated Bronze Star. Mem. N.D., (pres. 1938-39), S.D. (v.p., pres. 1941-46), res. officers assns., Am. Acad. Polit. and Social Sci., Am. Personnel and Guidance Assn., Am. Coll. Personnel Assn., Phi Delta Kappa, Kappa Delta Pi. Mason, Lion. Author monograph The Legal Basis for College Student Personnel Work, 1960. Home: Garden Grove CA Died Sept. 19, 1967; buried Ft. Logan Cemetery Denver CO

BALCH, GEORGE BEALL naval officer; b. in Tenn., Jan. 3, 1821. Apptd. from Ala., midshipman U.S.N., 1837; promoted through the grades to rear adm., June 5, 1878. Served in Mexican War, 1846-47, participating in attack on Alvarado and in joint bombardment of Vera Cruz, at surrender of that city; on duty Naval Acad., 1860-61; on board Sabine, 1861-62; comd. Pocahontas, 1862, Pawnee, 1862-65, S. Atlantic Blockading Squadron, 1862; engaged with battery at Stono, S.C., Aug., engagements in Stono River, S.C., July, 1864, bombardment of battery Pringle on James Island, S.C.; on duty Navy Yard, Washington, 1865-68, 1871-72; comd. Albany, flagship, N. Atlantic Squadron, 1868-70; gov. Naval Asylum, 1873-76; mem. Light-House Bd., 1876-77; mem. Exam. Bd., 1878; supt. Naval Acad., 1879-81; comdr.-in-chief Pacific Sta., 1881-82; retired Jan. 3, 1883. Home: Baltimore, Md. Died 1908.

BALDERSTON, JOHN LLOYD writer; b. Phila., Pa., Oct. 22, 1889; s. Lloyd and Mary F. (Alsop) B.; student Columbia U., 1911-14; m. Marion Rebicam, Mar. 6, 1921; 1 son, John Lloyd, Jr. New York corr. Phila Record, 1912-14; went to Europe as free lance war corr., 1915; war corr. McClure Newspapers, 1916-18; dir. information, Gt. Britain and Ireland, for U.S. Govt. Com. on Pub. Information, 1918-19; editor The Outlook, London, 1920-23; chief London corr. New York World, 1923-31; took part through writings, broadcastings, etc., in defense movement, 1940-41; Washington observer for Com. to Defend America by Aiding the Allies, 1940; organized and conducted William Allen White Com. News Service from Washington, 1940; lectr. drama, U. of So. Cal., 1952—. Clubs: Century (New York); Athenaeum; Savile (London). Author: Genius of the Marne, 1919; A Mortality Play for the Leisure Class, 1924; Berkeley Square, 1929; Chicago Blueprint, 1943; A goddess to a God; also author Cleopatra and Cesar (play) (London), 1952. Co-author (plays): Cracula, 1927; Frankenstein, 1931; (motion pictures) Lives of a Bengal Lancer, Berkeley Square, Smilin'Through, Gaslight, Tennessee Johnson, Prisoner of Zenda and others. Home: 615 N. Rodeo Dr., Beverly Hills, Cal. Died Mar. 8, 1954; buried Colora, Md.

BALDWIN, ABRAHAM senator, univ. pres.; b. North Gilford, Conn., Nov. 22, 1754; s. Michael and Lucy (Dudley) B.; grad. Yale, 1772. Licensed minister; tutor Yale, 1775-79; chaplain 2d Conn. Brigade, Continental Army, 1779-83; admitted to Fairfield County (Conn.) bar, 1783, Ga. bar, 1784; mem. Ga. Ho. of Assembly from Wilkes County, 1785; mem. Continental Congress, 1785-88; founder U. Ga., 1785, 1st pres., 1786-1800, pres. bd. trustees, 1800-07; mem. U.S. Constl. Conv., 1787; mem. U.S. Ho. of Reps. (Federalist) from Ga., 1st-5th congresses, 1789-99; mem. U.S. Senate from Ga., 1799-1807, pres. pro tem, 1801; U.S. commr. to treat regarding ceding of Ga. lands to U.S. Govt., 1802; an original mem. Conn. br. Soc. of Cincinnati; Baldwin counties (Ga. and Ala.) named for him, Died Washington, D.C., Mar. 4, 1807; buried Rock Creek Cemetery, Washington.

BALDWIN, ARTHUR DOUGLAS, lawyer; b. Hawaiian Islands, Apr. 8, 1876; s. Henry P. and Emily (Alexander) B.; A.B., Yale, 1898; LL.B., Harvard, 1901; Dr. Humanities, Western Reserve U., 1939; m. Reba Williams, June 18, 1902; children—Henry P., Louise (Mrs. Woods King), Fred C., A. Alexander, Sarah (Mrs. Irwin C. Hanger), Lewis W. Admitted to Ohio bar, 1902; mem. firm Garfield, MacGregor & Baldwin (now Garfield, Baldwin, Jamison, Hope & Ulrich) since 1916; dir. and counsel North Electric Mfg. Co., Galion, O.; dir. and mem. exec. com. Sherwin-Williams Co., Cleve.; dir. Land Title Guarantee & Trust Co. Ex-chmn. bd. Western Reserve U. Chmn. bd. Cleve. Hosp. Service Assn., Legal Aid Society, Spies Com. for Clin. Research (affiliated with Northwestern U.). Awarded Cleveland C. of C. Medal for Distinguished Service to City of Cleveland, 1940; Cleveland Community Fund Distinguished Service Medal, 1941; hon. award, Am. Hosp. Assn., 1948. Served as lt., later capt., F.A., U.S. Army, World War I. Republican. Presbyterian (mem. bd. trustees Ch. of the Covenant). Clubs: Union, Kirtland Country, Tavern, Chagrin Valley Hunt. Author: Memoirs of Henry P. Baldwin, 1904. Home: 9534 Lake Shore Blvd.,Cleveland 8. Office: National City Bank Bldg., Cleveland 14

BALDWIN, BIRD THOMAS college prof.; b. Marshalltown, Pa., 1875; s. Bird L. and Sarah R.B.; B.S., Swarthmore (Pa.) Coll., 1900; studied U. of Pa., 1901-02, Harvard 1902-03, 1904-05, U. of Leipzig, summer, 1906; A.M., 1903, Ph.D., 1905, Harvard; m. Claudia W. Wilbur, Sept. 1904 (died 1925); children - Bird Wilbur,

Alan Wilbur and Jervas Wilbur (twins), Patricia. Supervising prin. Friends' schs., Morristown, Pa., 1900-02; asst. in edn., Harvard Summer Sch., 1903; asst. in psychology and logic, Harvard, 1903-04; prof. psychology, West Chester (Pa.) State Normal Sch., 1905-09; lecturer on psychology and edn., Swarthmore, 1906-10, U. of Chicago, 1909-10; asso. prof. edn. and head Sch. of Art of Teaching, U. of Tex., 1910-12; prof. edn., U. of Tenn., summers, 1912, 1913; prof. psychology and edn., Swarthmore, 1912-16; prof. ednl. psychology, Johns Hopkins, summers, 1915, 16, 17; lecturer in ednl. psychology, Johns Hopkins, 1916-17; research prof. in ednl. psychology and dir. Ia. Child Welfare Research Sta., State U. of Ia., 1917- Chmn. Child Development Com. of Nat. Research Council. Washington, D.C. Mem. Friends Ch. Writer of numerous published articles, bulls, and reviews on ednl. and psychol. topics; collaborating editor psychol. and ednl. jours. Maj. Sanitary Corps U.S.A., Mar. 1, 1918-Aug. 1, 1919; in office of Surgeon Gen. of the Army, and chief psychologist and dir rehabilitation of disabled soldiers, Walter Reed General Hosp., Washington, D.C. Author: Physical Growth and School Progress; Physical Growth of Children from Birth to Maturity; The Mental Growth Curve of Normal and Superior Children; The Psychology of the Preschool Child. Home: Iowa City, Ia. Died May 12, 1928.

BALDWIN, CHARLES JACOBS clergyman; b. Charleston, N.Y., Aug. 10, 1841; s. George Colfax and May Cynthia (Jacobs) B.; A.B., Madison (now Colgate) U., Hamilton, N.Y., 1864; grad. Rochester Theol. Sem., 1868; (D.D., Denison U., 1900); m. Adelaide Fosdick, of Groton, Mass., Aug. 3, 1870. Ordained Bapt. ministry, 1868; pastor Chelsea, Mass., 1868-74, 1st Church, Rochester, N.Y., 1974-86, Granville, O., 1886-. Served as 1st lt. and adj., 157th N.Y. Vols., 1863-65, campaigns of Chancellorsville, Gettysburg and siege of Charleston. Republican. Author: Modern Miracles, 1895; The First American, 1911. Address: Granville, O.

BALDWIN, FRANK DWIGHT army officer; b. Manchester, Mich., June 26, 1842; s. Francis Leonard and Betsy Ann (Richards) B.; ed. pub. schs., Constantine, Mich., and Hillsdale Coll.; m. Alice Blackwood, Jan. 10, 1867. Served in Civil War as 2d lt. Mich. Horse Guards, Sept. 19-Nov. 22, 1861; 1st lt. 19th Mich. Inf., Aug. 12, 1862; capt., Jan. 23, 1864; mustered out of vols., June 10, 1865. In regular army as 2d and 1st lt. 19th Inf., Feb. 23, 1866; promoted through grades to brig. gen. U.S.A., June 9, 1902. Bvtd. Capt. Feb. 27, 1890, "for gallantry in action against Indians in Texas," and maj., "for gallantry and successful attack on Sitting Bull's Camp of Indians on Red Water River, Mont.," Dec. 18, 1876; medal of honor "for distinguished bravery in battle of peach tree creek, Ga., July 20, 1864," while serving as capt. 19th Mich. Inf.; medal of honor "for distinguished gallantry in action against Indians in Texas, Nov. 8, 1874." Comd. first body of civilized troops that ever successfully reached the south shore of Lake Lanao (Island of Mindanao), and after desperate encounter with Moros at battle of Byian, May 2, 1902, completely overcame them, Americans losing 51 killed and wounded out of 471, and the Moros losing over 300, less than 30 escaping; in command S.W. Division, Retired June 26, 1906. Adj. gen. of Colo., Apr. 1, 1917-Apr. 21, 1919. Hon. LL.D. conferred by Hillsdale Coll., Mich. 1904. Died Apr. 22, 1923.

BALDWIN, GEOFFREY P. army officer; b. Madison Barracks, N.Y., May 10, 1892; s. John Arthur and Lucy Frances (Prescott) B.; B.S., U.S. Mil. Acad., 1916; grad. Inf. Sch., 1922; distinguished grad. Command and Gen. Staff Sch., 1926; grad. Army War Coll., 1928; unmarried. Commd. 2d lt., U.S. Army, 1916 and advanced through the grades to brig. gen., 1942; served as capt. and maj. (tem.) with 5th Div., A.E.F., France, 1918; formerly assigned to War Dept. Manpower Bd., Washington; retired from service, 1946; chief of CARE mission in Italy since May 1946. Decorated D.S.C., Silver Star, Victory Medal with three battle clasps (U.S.), Knight Comdr. (Mil. Class) Order St. Gregory the Great (Papal), Knight Comdr. Order of la Concordia (Italy). Hom. mem. Scabbard and Blade. Roman Catholic. Clubs: Army and Navy (Washington); University (Boston). Home: care the Adjutant General, Washington. Office: CARE, Inc. Via Lucullo 6, Rome, Italy. Died Aug. 30, 1951.

BALDWIN, JOHN FINLEY JR. congressman; b. Oakland, Cal., June 28, 1915; s. John Finley and Nellie (Linekin) B.; B.S., U. Cal., 1935, LL.B., 1949; m. Mary Isaacs, Dec. 20, 1944; children-Georgia, Doris, Sylvia. Asst. mgr. South-Western Pub. Co., San Francisco, 1936-41; pvt. practice, Martinez, Cal., 1949-. Mem. 84th to 87th Congresses, 6th Cal. Dist., 88th and 89th Congresses, from 14th Cal. Dist. Served as dir. tng. Army Finance Sch., 1943-44; chief fgn. fiscal affairs Office of Fiscal Dir., War Dept., 1954; exec. officer Office of Fiscal Dir., MTO, 1946. Mem. Contra Costa Pub. Health Assn., East Contra Costa U. Cal. Alumni. Kiwanian. Club: Sierra (life). Home: 1010 Ulfinian Way, Martinez, Cal. Office: House Office Bldg., Washington 25. Died Mar. 9, 1966; buried Oakmont Meml. Park, Lafayette, Cal.

BALDWIN, JOSEPH CLARK ex-congressman; b. N.Y.C., Jan. 11, 1897; s. Joseph Clark and Fanny (Taylor) B.; B.A., Harvard, 1920; m. Marthe Guillon-Verne, Dec. 5, 1923; children—Fanny Taylor, Joseph Clark, Jeanne Neumayer, Stephen Verne. Was reporter N.Y. Tribune; asso. editor North Westchester Times; asso. editor The Independent; contbg. editor The Independent Outlook; salesman Russell Miller & Carey; asst. v.p. Murray Hill Trust Co.; now sr. partner Baldwin, Munson & Mann; v.p., dir. Nitralloy Corp.; v.p. Dunn & Fowler; pres., dir. United Dydwood Corp. Mem. Bd. of Aldermen, N.Y.C., 1928-34, minority leader, 1929-34; mem. N.Y. State Senate, 1934-36, Constnl. Conv., N.Y., 1937, N.Y.C. Council, 1937-41; mem. 77th-79th Congresses, 17th N.Y. Dist. Served in USN, 1917, U.S. Army with AEF, 1918; commd. 2d lt., 1918; now capt. Inf. Res. Decorated Officer French Legion of Honor. Republican. Episcopalian. Mason, Elk. Clubs: Racquet and Tennis, Brook, National Republican (N.Y.C.); Porcellian (Harvard). Home: 222 E. 71st St., N.Y.C. 21. Died Oct. 27, 1957; buried Woodlawn Cemetery, N.Y.C.

BALDWIN, LOAMMI civil engr.; b. North Woburn, Mass., Jan. 21, 1745; s. James and Ruth (Richardson) B.; m. Mary Fowle, 1772; m. 2d, Margery Fowle, 1791; 2 sons, George, Loammi. Apprenticed in cabinet making; engaged in surveying and engring., Woburn, Mass., circa 1765; apptd. lt. col. 38th Infantry Regt. in Continental Army, 1775; served with Washington's army in attack on Trenton, N.J., 1776; discharged due to ill health, 1777; represented Woburn in Mass. Gen. Ct., 1778-79, 1800-04; sheriff Middlesex County (Mass.), 1780-circa 1785; chief engr. Middlesex Canal (connecting Charles and Merrimac rivers), 1793-1803; discovered strain of apple known as Baldwin in later years; mem. Am. Acad. Arts and Scis. Died Woburn, Oct. 20, 1807; buried Woburn.

BALDWIN, NEILSON ABEEL physician; b. Brooklyn, Feb. 28, 1839; s. Rev. John Abeel and Elizabeth Elmendorf (Van Kleeck) B.; grad. Lafayette Coll., 1858, A.M., 1861; Med. Dept. Yale Univ., 1861; Blanche Chandler Ballam, Sept. 1, 1877. Surgeon U.S. vols. in Civil war, 1862-65, then in practice in Brooklyn; surgeon Nat. Guard, S.N.Y., 1866-70; health insp. Brooklyn, 1870-71; police suregon, Brooklyn, 1872-75. Republican. Med. supt. Sanitarium, 1890-1900; fellow Am. Acad. Medicine, 1878-. Home: Brooklyn, N.Y. Deceased.

BALDWIN, NOYES army officer, mcht.; b. Woodbridge, Conn., Sept. 8, 1826; at least 1 son. Went to Cal., 1849; served as capt. 1st Nev. Volunteers at Ft. Churchill, 1861-63, transferred to Ft. Bridger; promoted maj., transferred to Camp Douglas, Utah, then to Post Provo, 1864; commander Ft. Bridger, 1865; engaged in trading and merchandising, Wyo., 1869-89; del. Wyo. Constl. Conv., 1889, did not sign constn. Died lander, Wyo., Jan. 12, 1893.

BALDWIN, ROLAND DENNIS banker, Masonic exec.; b. Yonkers, N.Y., May 29, 1896; s. William Dalavan and Helen Runyal (Sullivan) B.; student The Lawrenceville (N.J.) Sch., 1911-13, Berkley-Irving Sch., N.Y. City, 1913-16; m. Pearl Sheldon Smith, Apr. 4, 1925; children—William Delevan, Sheldon Smith. Pres. Baldwin Lumber Co., Jacksonville, Fla., 1919-22; asst. vice pres., Barnett Nat. Bank, Jacksonville, 1922-29; asst. vice pres., Barnett Nat. Bank, Jacksonville, 1922-29; partner firm of Vanderholf & Robinson, mems. of N.Y. Curb Exchange, N.Y. City, 1929-32; mgr. Jacksonville office of Merrill, Lynch, Pierce, Fenner & Bean, 1932-42, 1944-45; asst. vice pres., Atlantic Nat. Bank since 1945. Enlisted U.S.M.C., 1917; service in France; disch. as sergt., 1920; commd. 1st lt., 1942; returned to inactive service as capt., 1944. County chmn., 6th, 7th, and 8th War Loan Drives; treas. local U.S.O., 1942; treas. Greek Relief, 1942. Recipient Purple Heart, World War I. Mem. Am. Legion (mem. since inception; treas. 1926-27), Am. Cancer Soc. (local treas., 1946-49), Fla. C. of C., Children's Home Soc. of Fla. (state dir., 1935-50), Jacksonville Jr. C. of C. (charter mem., treas., 1925-29), Jacksonville C. of C. (gov., 1941-42, treas. 1942), Gen. Soc. Mayflower Descendants (life mem.). S.A.R. Episcopalian. Mason; mem. since 1921; R.A.M. (life mem., treas. 1928-29) K.T. (life mem., treas., 1928-29); 32 degree (life mem. Knight Comdr. of Court of Honour, 1947); Royal Order Jesters (dir. 1940, 41, 42); Royal Select and Super Excellent Master (1943); Hon. mem. of De Molay (1950); Shrine (treas., 1928-29), potentate, 1938, Imperial rep. to Imperial Council, 1938-42, mem. Imperial Divan of Imperial Council, 1942, deputy Imperial Potentate of Imperial Council, 1950-51; chmn. Shrine Room Com., The George Washington Nat. Masonic Memorial Bldg., 1946; mem. bd. trustees. Shriners' Hosps. for Crippled Children, 1949). Mem. Y.M.C.A. (dir., 1944-45, advisory com., 1945-46). Clubs: Rotary (past dir., Jacksonville), Timuquana Country, Florida Yacht (Jacksonville, Fla.). Home: 1846 Montgomery Pl., Jacksonville 5. Office: 121 Forsyth St., Jacksonville 2, Fla. Died May 20, 1951.

BALDWIN, THEODORE ANDERSON brig. gen.; b. in N.J., Dec. 31, 1839. Served pvt. and q.m. sergt, 19th Inf., May 3, 1862-May 3, 1865; promoted through grades to brig. gen. vols., Oct. 6, 1898; hon. discharged from vol. service, Jan. 31, 1899; col. 7th Cav., May 6, 1899; brig.-gen., Apr. 19, 1903; retired at own request after 40 years.' service. Apr. 20, 1903. Died Sept. 1, 1925.

BALL, NORMAN T(OWER), lawyer; b. Toledo, Ohio, February 14, 1905; son John Stanley and Nina Belle (Frary) B.; student U.S. Naval Acad., 1924-27, Universite de Poitiers, 1927; B.S., U. of Toledo, 1928; B.F.S., Georgetown U., 1929; J.D., George Washington U., 1934; student Harvard, 1943, Mass. Inst. Tech., 1943; m. Margaret Herrmann, Oct. 24, 1936. Aeronautics patent examiner, U.S. Patent office, 1928-37, classification examiner, 1937-47; exec. dir., com. on tech. information, Research and Development Bd., 1947-50; economic commissioner European Recovery Program, American Embassy, London, England, 1950-51; cons. electronics and microwave labs. Stanford U., 1952-53; program dir. Nat. Sci. Found., 1953-54, exec. sec. interdepartmental com. on sci. research and development, 1954-59, U.S. del. to com. cooperation and applied research Orgn. European Econ. Cooperation, Paris, 1956-59; counsel Nat. Council Patent Law Assns., 1960-61. Pres. Seacrest chpt. American Field Service, 1963-64, Fla. Atlantic Arts Inst. of Fla. Atlantic U., 1966-68. Served from lt. to comdr., 1940-46; U.S. Navy, Naval Intelligence, Western European sect., 1940-43; design of electronics aids to air navigation systems, 1944-46. Nat. Inventors' Council, 1940. Mem. A.A.A.S., I.E.E.E., Am. Patent Law Association. Mason. Author: sects. of books, also articles to profl. jours. Home: Delray Beach FL Died Nov. 22, 1971.

BALL, RAYMOND NATHANIEL banker; b. Wellsville, N.Y., June 10, 1891; s. Charles Alley and Clara M. (Pooler) B.; B.S., U. Rochester, 1914; LL.D., Alfred (N.Y.) U., 1954; m. Margaret Quick, May 13, 1918; children-Virginia Eloise (Mrs. George W. Hamlin, II), Margaret Elizabeth (Mrs. Raymond Wessman), Richard Raymond. Alumni exec. sec. U. Rochester 1919, comptroller 1922, v.p. and treas. 1923-30, chmn. finance com. 1932-52, chmn. bd. trustees, 1952-59; pres. Lincoln Rochester Trust Co., 1929-54, chmn. bd. dirs., 1954-61, mem. adv. bd. 1961-66; hon. dir. Pfaudler Permutit Inc., 1961-66; dir. McCurdy & Co., Rochester Telephone Corp., Rochester Gas & Elec. Corp., Eastman Kodak Co.; dir. Fed. Res. Bank of N.Y. (Buffalo br.) 1932-34, 41-43. Chmn. Dist 2, N.Y., State War Finance Com., 1942-46. Hon. trustee U. Rochester; trustee Rochester C.of C. (pres. 1941), George Eastman House, Inc.; mem. adv. council Rochester Community Chest (pres. 1947-48). Pres. N.Y. State Bankers Assn., 1936-37; mem. Banking Bd. State N.Y., 1943-50. Enlisted U.S. Army, 1917, capt. Co. A, 308th Machine Gun Bn., 78th Div.; participated in St. Mihiel and Argonne offensives. Mem. Delta Upslion. Republican. Presbyn. Clubs: Ad, Genesee Valley, Country. Home: 45 Elm Lane. Office: Lincoln Rochester Trust Co., Rochester, N.Y. Died Oct. 8, 1966.

BALL, WILLIAM LEE congressman; b. Lancaster County, Va., Jan. 2, 1781; had liberal edn. Served as paymaster in War of 1812, with 92d Va. Regiment; mem. U.S. Ho. of Reps., (Democrat) from Va., 15th-18th congresses, 1817-Feb. 28, 1824. Died Washington, D.C., Feb. 28, 1824; buried Congressional Cemetery.

BALLARD, BLAND WILLIAMS frontiersman; b. Fredericksburg, Va., Oct. 16, 1759; s. Bland Ballard; no formal edn.; m. Elizabeth Williamson, 1783; m. 2d, Diana Matthews, Aug. 17, 1835; m. 3d, Mrs. Elizabeth Garrett, Oct. 28, 1841. In Ky., 1779-80, cative in war against Indians; with Gen. George Rogers Clark, 1781-82; in war in Pickaway towns in Ohio; with Gen. Clark in expdn. against Indians on Wabash River, 1787; survived Indian attack on homestead in Shelbyville, Ky., 1787; participated in Battle of Fallen Timbers, 1793; became farmer in Shelbyville; mem. Ky. Legislature for 5 terms between 1703-1810; participated in Battle of Tippecanoe, 1811; served with Col. John Allen's Regt. in War of 1812, at Battle of Raisin River, 1813. Died Shelbyville, Sept. 5, 1853; buried State Cemetery, Frankfort, Ky.

BALLARD, ERNEST SCHWEFEL lawyer; b. Philadelphia, Pa., Aug. 29, 1885; s. Ellis Ames and Nina (Schwefel) B.; prep. edn. William Penn Charter Sch., 1894-1903; A.B., Yale, 1907; LL.B., U. of Pa., 1916; m. Elisabeth Sloan Duryee, Aug. 27, 1913; children—Elisabeth Sloan (Mrs. Frank F. Fowle, Jr.), Susan Rankin (Mrs. Stewart Boal), Ellis Ames, Joseph Duryee, Mary (Mrs. John H. Hobart), Ernest Schwefel, Jr., Samuel Sloan. Began practice as asst. to gen. solicitor N.Y. Central Lines, N.Y. City, 1910, commerce counsel at Chicago, 1915-17, asst. gen. solicitor at Chicago, 1917-19; partner Pope & Ballard and predecessor firms since 1919. Commissioned 1st lt. February 5, 1918; with A.E.F. in France, 1918-19; appointed officer General Staff A.E.F., Feb. 17, 1919; promoted captain, Feb. 19, 1919; honorably discharged, May 19, 1919. Knight Order of Black Star (France), 1919. Pres. Winnetka Bd. of Edn., 1923-30. Pres. Chicago Br. English-Speaking Union, 1930-32. Senior Warden Christ Church, Winnetka, Ill.; trustee Glenwood Manual Training Sch. Mem. Ill. and Chicago bar assns., Assn. I.C.C. Practitioners, Psi Upsilon, Order of Coif. Ind. Republican. Episcopalian. Clubs: Chicago, Indian Hill, Commercial, Commonwealth Church

(Chicago); Century (N.Y.). Home: 6 Kent Road, Hubbard Woods, Ill. Office: 33 N. La Salle St., Chgo. Died Mar. 18, 1952.

BALLARD, FREDERIC LYMAN lawyer; b. Phila., Mar. 20, 1888; s. Ellis Ames and Nina (Schwefel) B.; A.B., U. Pa., 1909, LL.B., 1912; m. Frances Stoughton, June 18, 1916; children-Frederic Lyman, Jean Tod, Augustus Stoughton, John Ames, Francis. Admitted to Pa. bar, 1912, practice in Phila.; partner Ballard, Spahr, Andrews & Ingersoll, since 1918; mrg. Western Savs. Fund Soc.; dir. Western Md. Ry. Co., Muskogee Co. Trustee U. Pa., Phila. Mus. of Art, St. Georgis Sch., Newport, R.I., 1940-47. Served as capt. U.S. Army, A.E.F., 1918. Republican. Episcopalian (vestryman). Clubs: Rittenhouse, Philadelphia. Died Dec. 25, 1952.

BALLENTINE, JOHN JENNINGS, naval officer; b. Hillsboro, O., Oct. 4, 1896; s. George McClelland and Ora (Eakins) B.; B.S., U.S. Naval Acad., 1917; naval aviator, Pensacola, Fla., 1920; m. Catherine Howard Sheild, June 10, 1922; 1 son, John Jennings; Commd. ensign, U.S.N., 1917, advancing through the grades to vice adm., 1949; served with battleships during World War I; aviation assignments since, 1920, including command of torpedo and bombing squadrons in Orient and on U.S.S. Saratoga, later on duty in Navy Dept., Washington, D.C., testing and developing bombsights and allied equipment; exec. officer on carrier, Atlantic Command and in Pacific; comdg. officer U.S.S. Long Island, 1942 and U.S.S. Bunker Hill, 1942-44; dep. comdr. Air Force Pacific; comdr. Div. 7, Third Fleet; fleet liaison officer Supreme Commander Allied Powers, Tokyo, 1944; mem. U.N. Military Staff Com., 1946-47. Com. Car. Div. 1, 1947-49; comdr. Sixth Fleet in Mediterranean, 1949-51; comdr. Air Force, Atlantic Fleet, 1951-54, ret., 1954. Decorated Legion of Merit (twice, 2V), Bronze Star Medal, Commendation (V), Presidential Unit (Bunker Hill) Citation, Victory, Yangtse Campaign, Am., European, Pacific Areas (5 stars), World War II; Legion of Honor (comdr.); Grand Cordon Order Phoenix (Greece). Clubs: Chevy Chase (Washington); N.Y. Yacht. Home: Millbank Dogue VA Died May 21, 1970; interred Emmanuel Episcopal Ch., Port Conway VA

BALLOU, CHARLES CLARENDON army officer; b. Orange Tp., N.Y., June 13, 1862; s. William Hosea and Julia A. (Hendrick) B.; U.S. Mil. Acad., grad., 1886; Inf. and Cav. Sch., 1897-98; Field Officers' Sch., 1916; War Coll., 1916-17. Commd. 2d lt. 16th Inf., July 1, 1886; promoted through grades to col., July 19, 1916; brig. gen. N.A., Aug. 5, 1917; maj. gen. N.A., Nov. 28, 1917; retired June 13, 1926. Served as maj. 7th Ill. Inf. Vols., July 8-Oct. 20, 1898; regt. q.m., P.I., 1899; participated in Battle of Zapote River, June 13, 1899, and minor engagements, also assualt on Angeles, Aug. 16, 1899; comdr. 92d Div. (colored), A.E.F., Oct. 27, 1917-Nov. 19, 1981; comdr. 6th Army Corps. Oct. 23-Nov. 11, 1918; comdr. 89th Div., Nov. 19, 1981-Feb. 1, 1919. Participated in Battle of the Argonne, battle of Nov. 10th and 11th, on Moselle River, and various engagements in St. Die sector, Notable achievement was passing safely, with one attendant, through the camp of over 5,000 hostile Sioux Indians, soon after the Battle of Wounded Knee, in 1890. Awarded silver star citation by President Coolidge, Mar. 10, 1927, "for gallantry in action"; decorated Croix de Guerre with Palm and Officer Legion of Honor (French). Home: Spokane, Wash. Died July 23, 1928.

BALTZELL, ROBERT C. judge; b. Lawrence County, Ill., Aug. 15, 1879; s. Henry H. and Margaret C. (Roderick) B.; student Northern Ill. Normal Coll., Dixon, Ill., 1899, Marion (Ind.) Normal Sch., 1903-04; LL.B., Marion Law Sch., 1904; m. Vienna N. Carlton, Mar. 28, 1904 (dec.); 1 son, Robert Carlton (dec.). Teacher public schools in Ill., 1898-1903; admitted to Ind. bar, 1904, and began practice with brother, Charles O., at Princeton; elected judge of Gibson Circuit Court, Princeton, Nov. 1920, served until Jan. 19, 1925; U.S. district judge, by apptmt. of President Collidge, since Jan. 19, 1925. Served as maj. inf., Dec. 26, 1917-May 10, 1919. World War. Mem. Ind. State Bar Assn., Am. Bar Assn., Mem. Christian (Disciples) Ch. Mason. Club: Columbia (Indianapolis). Home: 5637 Central Av. Address: Federal Bldg., Indianapolis. Died Oct. 18, 1950.

BANCROFT, GEORGE historian, sec. of navy, diplomat; b. Worcester, Mass., Oct. 3, 1800; s. Aaron and Lucretia (Chandler) B.; grad Harvard, 1817; Ph.D., M.A., U. Gottingen (Germany), 1820; D.C.L. (hon.), Oxford (Eng.) U., 1849; m. Sarah H. Dwight, Mar. 1, 1827; m. 2d, Mrs. Elizabeth (Davis) Bliss; 3 children. A founder Round Hill Sch., Northampton, Mass., 1823; wrote series on "German Literature," published in Am. Quarterly Review, 1827-28 (1st comprehensive treatment of German literature and philosophy to appear in Am.); collector Port of Boston, 1838; a Mass. del. to Democratic Nat. Conv., 1844; U.S. sec. of navy, 1845-46, established U.S. Naval Acad., Annapolis, Md., 1845; U.S. minister to Gt. Britain, 1846-49, to Prussia, 1867-71, to German Empire, 1871-74; correspondent Inst. of France; pres. Am. Geog. Soc., devoted most of his time and energies to writing of History of the United States in which he expounded his democratic theories. Author: History of the United States, 10 vols., 1834-74; Literary and Historical Miscellanies, 1855; History of the Formulation of the Constitution of the United States, 1886; Martin Van Buren to the End of his Public Career, 1889. Died Washington, D.C., Jan. 17, 1891.

BANCROFT, HUGH publisher; b. Cambridge, Mass., Sept. 13, 1879; s. William Amos and Mary (Shaw) B.; A.B., Harvard, 1897, A.M., 898; LL.B., Harvard Law Sch., 1901; m. Mary A. Cogan (died 1903); 1 dau., Mary (Mrs. Sherwin C. Badger); m. 2d, Jane Wallis Waldron Barron, Jan. 15, 1907; children - Jessie (Mrs. William C. Cox), Hugh, Jr., Jane. Asst. dist. atty., Middlesex Co., 1902-06, dist. atty., 1907; chmn. bd. dirs. Port of Boston, 1911-14; pres. Boston News Bur. Co., Cohasset Nat. Bk.; also pres. Dow, Jones & Co., pubs. Wall St. Journal, pub. Barron's Weekly and Phila. Financial Jour. Mem. Mass. Vol. Militia, pvt. to brig. gen., 1894-1909, retired as maj. gen.; 1st lt. and adj. 5th Mass. Inf., U.S. Vols., Spanish-Am. War. Republican. Episcopalian. Author: Inheritance Taxes (with A. W. Blakemore), for investors, 1911 1912. Home: New York, N.Y. Died Oct. 17, 1933.

BANDHOLDTZ, HARRY HILL brig. gen.; b. Constantine, Mich., Dec. 18, 1864; s. Christopher John and Elizabeth Ann (Hill) B.; grad. U.S. Mil. Acad., 1890; m. May Cleveland, July 15, 1890; m. 2d, Inez C. Gorman, Apr. 19, 1922. Commd. 2d lt., June 12, 1890; advanced through grades to maj. gen., Nov. 3, 1923. Prof. military science and tactics. Michigan Agrl. College, 1896. Served with 7th Inf. during Santiago campaign; with 2d Inf. in Philippine insurrection campaigns; gov. of Tayabas Province, Mar. 4, 1902-Apr. 1903; only regular army officer elected to such a position; apptd. col. and asst. chief of Philippine Constabulary, Apr. 1903, in comd. Dist. of Southern Luzon; conducted campaign against Simeon Ola in Albay, resulting in destruction of Ola's forces; transferred to comd. Dist. of Central Luzon, Oct. 1905; forced surrender of outlaws Montalan, Sakay and others and accomplished destruction of Felizardo; brig. gen. and chief Philippines Constabulary, June 30, 1907-Sept. 1, 1913; maj. 30th Inf., 1915; chief of staff N.Y. Div. on Mexican border, 1916; chief of staff 27th Div. (N.Y.) till Feb. 9, 1918; comd. 58th Inf. Brig., Feb. 9-Sept. 27, 1918; provost marshal gen. A.E.F., Sept. 27, 1918-Aug. 5, 1919; Am. rep. on Interallied Mil. Mission to Hungary, Aug. 5, 1919; comd. 13th Inf. Brig., Sept. 1,-1920-Sept. 1, 1921; in command Dist. of Washington, Sept. 1, 1921-; suppressed Miners' Insurrection in W.Va., Sept. 1-12, 1921. Awarded D.S.M.; Comdr. French Legion of Honor; Comdr. Belgian Order of the Crown; Comdr. Italian Order of the Crown; Grand Cross Crown of Roumania; Montenegrin decoration. Mason. Home: Constantine, Mich. Died May 7, 1925.

BANDLER, CLARENCE G. surgeon, b. Owego, N.Y., Nov. 6, 1880; s. William and Eva (Fox) B.; A.B., Columbia, 1901, M.D., 1904; m. Miriam R. Zack, Aug. 17, 1951. Intern Bellevue Hosp., N.Y.C., 1904, adjunct attending urologist, chief of clinic, dept. urology, 1906-12; inst. asso. in urology, med. dept. Columbia, 1906-25; prof. urology N.Y. Post-Grad. Med. Sch. and Hosp. of Columbia U., 1909—; attending urologist Post-Grad. Hosp., 1934—, dir. dept. urology; cons. surgeon Home for Aged and Infirm, Yonkers, N.Y., 1908—; cons. urologist St. Francis Hosp., Port Jervis, N.Y., St. Vincent's Hosp., S.I., N.Y., U. Hosp., N.Y.U. Bellevue Med. Center, Bd. dirs. Asso. Hosp. Service. Served as capt., Med. Officers Res. Corps, World War I; sec. med. adv. bd. for draft registrants; with procurement and assignment com. Med. Adv. for Selective Service, World War II; with emergency med. service Office Civilian Def. Repicient Certificate, Medal of Merit, World War II. Diplomate Am. Bd. Urology (v.p.). Fellow A.C.S.; mem. Associete 'Internationale d'Urologie, N.Y. State, N.Y. County med. socs. Clubs: Columbia University (N.Y.C.); Fairview Country, (Elmsford, N.Y.). Author numerous med. articles, including Tumors of the Urogenital Tract in the Young, Nephroptosis and Nephropexy, Urinary Obstruction. Home: 440 Park Av., N.Y.C. 22. Office: 77 Park Av., N.Y.C. Died Nov. 15, 1957.

BANGS, ISAAC SPARROW soldier; b. Canaan, Me., March 17, 1831; s. Capt. Isaac Sparrow B.; ed in Me. and New York; m. Oct. 20, 1857, Hadassah J. Milliken. Left position as cashier Waterville Bank to enter Union service, Aug. 9, 1862, as private; mustered in as capt. Co. A, 20th Me. vol. inf., Aug. 29, 1862; served in Army of Potomac in Md. campaign, Sept. and Oct., 1862, including battle of Antietam, Sept. 17, Shepardstown Ford, Sept. 18 and 19, in Va., Oct., 1862, to Feb., 1863; battle of Fredericksburg; expdn. to Ellis and Richard's fords, Burnside's 2d campaign ("Mud March"), etc.; lt. col. U.S. colored troops, Feb. 26, 1863; comd. 4th regt., Ullman's brigade (later named 81st U.S. colored inf.); served in Dept. of Gulf; took part in siege of Port Hudson, La.; pres. of examining bd., Oct. 3, 1863; col. 10th U.S. colored heavy arty., Nov. 10, 1863; comdg. Forts Jackson, St. Phillip, Livingston and Pike, and defenses of New Orleans until hon. disch. July 19, 1864. Bvtd. brig. gen. U.S. vols. Mar. 13, 1865, for gallant and meritorious service during war. Home: Waterville, Me. Died 1903.

BANISTER, JOHN Continental congressman, army officer, b. Bristol Parish, Va., Dec. 26, 1734; s. John and Willmuth (or Wilmet, or Wilmette) Banister; m. Patsy Bland; m. 2d, Anne Blair. Mem. Middle Temple, 1753; mem. Va. Conv., 1776; mem. Va. Ho. of Burgesses, 1777; mem. Continental Congress from Va., 1778-79, a framer and signer Articles of Confederation, lt. col. Va. Cavalry in Revolutionary War, 1778-81. Died Sept. 30, 1788; buried on family estate Hatcher's Run, nr. Petersburg, Va.

BANISTER, WILLIAM BRODNAX colonel in medical corps U.S.A.; b. Huntsville, Ala., Oct. 14, 1861; s. John Monro and Mary Louisa (Brodnax) B.; Trinity (Ala.) High Sch.; M.D., Hosp. Coll. of Medicine, Med. Dept., Central U. of Ky., 1883; m. Mary Caroline Noltenius, of Petersburg, Va., Jan. 12, 1893. Contract surgeon U.S.A., 1883; asst. surgeon, Jan. 26, 1886; capt. asst. surgeon, Jan. 26, 1891; maj. brigade surgeon vols., June 4, 1898; hon. discharged Apr. 30, 1899; maj. surgeon vols., Nov.11, 1899; vacated Apr. 2, 1901; maj. surgeon U.S.A., Apr. 2, 1901; lt.-col., Jan. 1, 1910; col., July 1, 1916. Served in Geronimo Campaign, 1885-86; Pine Ridge Campaign, winter, 1890-91; Santiago Campaign, 1898, and Philippine Insurrection, 1900-02; chief surgeon, China Relief Expdn., 1900, Dept. of Dakota, 1910; sanitary insp. Central Div., 1911-13; apptd. chief surgeon 2d Div. U.S.A., Feb. 15, 1913. Comdg. officer, Hosp. Centre of Limoges, France, July 15, 1918-Mar. 9, 1919; dept. surgeon, Central Dept., Chicago, May6-Sept. 30, 1919, Philippine Dept., Nov. 22, 1919-. Holds 4 campaign medals from Govt. Recommended for brevet lt.-col. vols., San Juan Hill Fight, Cuba, for brezet maj., Tientsin fight, China, July 13, 1900. Democrat. Episcopalian. Mem. Assn. Mil. Surgeons, A.M.A., S.A.R., Legion of Honor, Mil. Order of Dragon, Mil. Order of Carabao, Soc. Army of Santiago. Address: War Dept., Washington, D.C.

BANKHEAD, HENRY MCAULEY, commercial attache; b. Moscow, Ala., Dec. 19, 1876; s. John Hollis and Tallulah (Brockman) B.; student U. of Ala., 1893-96; m. Alice B. Stickney, Nov. 3, 1903; children—John Long, Harriet, Katherine (Mrs. Flamen B. Adae). Capt. U.S. Vols., Spanish-Am. War; commd. 2d lt. U.S. Army, 1899; advanced through grades to lt. col.; retired, 1922; promoted to rank of col. retired by act of Congress. In real estate business, Miami, Fla., 1926-33; mem. City Council of Miami, 1928-30; commercial attache U.S. Legation, Ottawa, Can., since July 1, 1933. Address: 100 Wellington St., Ottawa Canada*

BANKS, LINN congressman; b. Madison (then Culpeper) County, Va., Jan. 23, 1784; studied law. Admitted to Madison County bar, 1809; mem. Va. Ho. of Dels., 1812-38, speaker 20 successive years; mem. U.S. Ho. of Reps. (Democrat, filled vacancy, contested election) from Va., 25th-27th congresses. April 28, 1838-Dec. 6, 1841, practiced law; served as col. in Va. Militia. Drowned while attempting to ford Conway River nr. Wolftown, Va., Jan. 13, 1842; buried family burying ground on his estate nr. Graves Mill, Madison County.

BANKS, NATHANIAL PRENTISS gov. Mass., congressman; b. Waltham, Mass., Jan. 30, 1816; s. Nathanial P. and Rebecca (Greenwood) B.; m. Mary Palmer, Mar. 1847, 3 children, including Maude, Admitted to Mass. Bar, 1839; mem. lower house Mass. Legislature, 1849, speaker, 1851; pres. Mass. Constl. Conv., 1853; mem. U.S. Ho. of Reps. from Mass., 33d-34th, 39th-42d, 44th-45th, 51st congresses, 1853-57, 65-73, 75-79, 89-91, speaker 1856-57; governor of Mass., 1858-60; served with U.S. Volunteers during Civil War, from 1861, comdr. 5th Corps, Dept. of Shenandoah, U.S. Army Upper Potomac, 1861, Shenandoah Valley, 1862, led unsuccessful attack at Cedar Mountain, 1862, captured Port Hudson, 1863; apptd. U.S. marshall for Mass., 1879-88; called the Bobbin Boy. Died Waltham, Sept. 1, 1894; buried Grove Hill Cemetery, Waltham.

BANNING, KENDALL editor, author; b. New York, Sept. 20, 1879; s. William Calvin and Helen Josephine (Mellen) R.; A.B., Dartmouth, 1902; m. Hedwig v. Briesen, May 19, 1906 (died July 7, 1912); 1 daughter, Barbara (Mrs. Harrison Tweed); m. 2d, Dorothy Carter Sanders, November 15, 1915; 1 son, William Calvin. Managing and associate editor, System, 1903-17; managing editor, Hearst's Mag., Cosmopolitan, 1919-21; editor, Popular Radio, 1922-28; editorial dir. New Fiction Pub. Corp., also of Leslie-Judge Co., 1923-27; vice pres. New Fiction Pub. Corp., Leslie-Judge Co., Popular Radio, Inc., 1922-28; editorial dir. Pub. Utilities Fortnightly, 1929-34. Officer N.Y. and Ohio N.G., 1902-09; capt. 1st Aero Squadron (provisional), N.Y., 1913-14; maj. Signal Corps, U.S. Army, 1917; dir. div. of pictures, Com. on Public Information, Washington, 1917. Maj., Gen. Staff, U.S. Army, 1918-19; officer in charge of compilation of pictorial record and history of the war; lt. col. Signal Reserve since 1922; with Office of Chief of Ordnance since 1943; chief historian Army Ordnance Dept., 1943-44. Member Society 1812, Order Founders and Patriots America, Veteran Corps Arty., Phi Delta Theta. Clubs: The Players (New York); Army and Navy Club (Washington, D.C.). Editor: Songs of the Hill Winds, 1902 (Darthmouth anthology); Songs for a Wedding Day, 1907; How to Build Your Own Radio Receiver (with L.M. Cockaday), 1924. Author: Flotsam, 1903; Bookplates, 1906; Songs of the Love Unending, 1912; The Squire's Recipes, 1912; The Sun Dial (song cycle, with Gena Branscombe), 1912; Bypaths in Arcady, 1914; Pirates, 1916; Mon Ami

Pierrot, 1916; Songs of the Unafraid (song cycle, with Gena Branscombe), 1918; Phantom Caravan, 1920; The Great Adventure, 1925; Mother Goose Rhymes, Censored, 1930; Drum Beats (1936 Kaleidograph Book award), 1937; West Point Today, 1937; Annapolis Today, 1938; The Fleet Today, 1940; Submarine, The Story of Undersea Fighters, 1942; Our Army Today, 1943; "Copy," one-act play, prod. by Edmund Breese, 1911-12; The Garden of Puchinello, pantomime, prof. with Mlle, Dazie, 1917; A Garden Fate, pantomime prod. 1919; and miscellaneous songs. Contbr. to mags. Address: Old Lyme, Conn. Died Dec. 27, 1944; buried in Arlington National Cemetery.

BARACH, JOSEPH H. physician, research medicine; b. Calvary, Poland-Russia, 1883; s. Zorach and Deborah (Oppenheim) B.; came to U.S., 1888, citizenship derived from father; student Park Inst., 1895-99; M.D. Univ. of Pittsburgh, 1903; m. Edna S. Levy, Sept. 21, 1915; children—Joseph L., Richard L. Resident pathologist and interne West Pa. Hosp., Pittsburgh, 1904; asso. prof. medicine U. Pitts., also med. dir. U. Clins. Sch. Medicine 1930—; sr. staff med. center hosps, 1910—; cons. dept. health Carnegie Inst. Tech., Pitts., 1910; cons. in medicine, Sewickley (Pa.) Valley Hosp., 1925—. Chmn metabolism and endocrinology sect., research grants div. U.S.P.H.S., 1946-51, nat. council arthritis and metabolism sect., research grants div. since 1952. Served as capt. med. corps., World War I; chief selective service Dist. 1, Western Pa., World War II. Name inscribed on the Wall of Fame of the American Common-World's Fair of 1940, New York, for "having made notable contribution to our living, ever-growing democracy devoted to peace and freedom." Fellow A.A.A.S., A.C.P., Am. Diabetes Assn. mem. council 1941, pres., 1944-46, chmn. sect. on metabolic and endocrine diseases, etc., member A.M.A., Sigma Xi. Republican-Liberal. Mem. Congregation Rodef Shalom, Pitts. Clubs: Cosmos (Washington); Concordia, Deep Creek Yacht. Author: Self Help for the Diabetic, 1934; Diabetes and its Treatment, 1946; Diabetes, The Patients Book, 1948; Diabetes and Its Treatment, 1949; Diabetes, The Foods and Facts on Diabetes, 1949. Contributor many articles to med. lit. in U.S. and abroad. Home: 5745 Beacon St., Pittsburgh 17, (summer) Maneto, N.C., Roanoke Island. Office: 3601 Fifth Av., Univ. Clinic Med. Center, Pitts. 13. Died Mar. 7, 1954.

BARBER CHARLES NEWELL ret. univ. adminstrv. officer; b. Barre, Vt., Sept 8, 1884; son Charles Newell and Ella Laura (Granger) B.; B.S., in civil engineering, Norwich University, Northfield, Vermont, 1908, D.Sc., 1952; married Ida Demis Stickney, May 12, 1917; children—Jane (Mrs. Marc Martin Lainwohl), Caroline. Instructor in physics, Norwich U., 1908-16, asst. mathematics and physics, 1916-24, asso. prof. physics, 1924-34, sec.-treas. of the univ. since 1934, now retired; director Selective Service State of Vt., 1940-47; v.p., dir. Northfield Trust Co. Rep. to General Assembly of Vt., 1953, Chairman of advisory committee for rent control for Washington and Caledonia counties, 1948-49; mem. Governor's adv. council on education, 1956—. Member Vt. Nat. Guard, 1904-19 and 1920-41; retired with rank of major; col. comdg. Vt. State Guard, 1941-42; U.S. Property and Disbursing Officer, Vt., 1921-38; Mexican Border Service,1916; U.S. Army, 1917-19. Awarded President's Certificate of Merit, 1946. Trustee Vt. Soldiers Home since 1924, president bd. since July, 1946. Dem. candidate (Vt.) lt. gov., 1924, 34. Del. Constl. Conv. State of Vt., 1933. State chmn. Infantile Paralysis Fund, 1940-45. Mem. Am. Legion (dept. comdr., 1923-24; mem. nat. com. edn. of orphans of veterans). Mil. Order Fgn. Wars (dept. comdr., 1924-25). Vt. Soc. Profl. Engrs., Vt. Hist. Soc., Newcomen Soc., Theta Chi. Mason, K.P., Granger, Elk. Home: Jefferson Av., Northfield, Vt. Died Apr. 22, 1958.

BARBER, CHARLES WILLIAMS army officer; b. Gloucester Co., N.J., Sept. 21, 1872; s. George W. and Ellen (Taggart) B.; ed. pub. schs. and business coll.; studied law in office of Hon. H. S. Grey, attny. gen. of N.J., 1899; m. Katherine Runge, Mar. 8, 1894; 1 son, Russell George. Commd. 2d lt. 4th N.J. Inf., Spanish-Am. War, July 16, 1898; 1st lt., Sept. 27, 1898; capt., Mar. 3, 1899; hon. mustered out. Apr. 6, 1899; 1st lt. 28th U.S. Inf., July 5, 1899; hon. mustered out vol. service, May 1, 1901; commd. 2d lt. 2d Inf. U.S. Army, Feb. 2, 1901; 1st Lt., Nov. 11, 1901; capt. 4th Inf., Mar. 11, 1911; assigned to 3d Inf., Jan. 1, 1915; retired as maj., Sept. 1, 1916; brig. gen., N.A., July 15, 1917. Served in Philippines, 1899-1901, 1902-03, 1906-08; duty with Isthmian Canal Commn., Panama, 1908-15; Mexican border service, 1916; in charge orgn. state troops for war, registration and selection of drafted men, etc.; comdg. 29th Div., July 28-Aug. 25, 1917; comdg. 57th Infantry Brigade, Camp McClellan, Anniston, Ala., Sept. 11, 1917; in command 57th Inf. Brig. in front line sectors and as chief of staff, Base Sect. No. 2, Bordeaux (Gen. staff officer, A.E.F.), June 1918-July 1919; returned to status of retired officer, Aug. 1919; brig. gen. retired, June 21, 1930. Special representative Atlantic Refining Co. in Mexico, 1920; gen. mgr. Antilles Molasses Co., 1920-21; pres. and dir. Charles W. Barber & Son, Inc., investment bankers, New York; chmn. bd. and dir. Thermoid Co., Trenton, N.J.; dir. Southern Asbestos Co., Charlotte, N.C., Brager-Eisenberg, Inc., Baltimore. Officer Legion of Honor (France); D.S.M. (U.S.); D.S.M. (State of N.J.). Mem. Mil. Order Carabao. Republican. Methodist. Mason. Clubs: Army and Navy (Manila and Washington), Bankers (New York). Home: Short Hills, N.J. Office:111 Broadway, New York, N.Y. Died Jan. 7, 1943.

BARBER, FRANCIS army officer; b. Princeton, N.J., 1751; grad. Princeton, 1767; m. Mary Ogden; m. 2d, Anne Ogden. Rector of academy, Elizabethtown, N.J., circa 1769-76; maj. 3d N.J. Regt., 1776, lt. col., 1776; took part in Prenceton campaign, battles of Brandywine and Germantown; asst. insp. gen. to Gen. von Steuben, Valley Forge; wounded at Battle of Monmouth; transferred to 1st N.J. Regt., 1781; quelled mutiny of underpaid soldiers from Pa. and N.J., therby winning commendation of Gen. Washington; commanded batallion of light infantry under Lafayette at Battle of Green Spring. Killed by falling tree while army was stationed at Newburgh, N.Y., Feb. 11, 1783.

BARBER, GEORGE HOLCOMB naval officer; b. Glastonbury, Conn., Nov. 15, 1864; s. Ralph and Mary Henrietta (Holcomb) B.; S.B., Mass. Agrl. Coll., 1885; S.B., Boston U., 1885; M.D., Coll. Phys. and Surg. (Columbia), 1888; unmarried. Apptd. asst. surgeon U.S.N., May 23, 1889; promoted through grades to med. dir., rank of rear admiral, Oct. 15, 1917. Service at sea, 14 yrs., mostly in foreign waters, comdg. hosp. ship relief as last duty; shore duty 14 yrs., on receiving ships, at U.S. Naval Acad., training sta., at Newport, R.I., and naval hosps., New York, Boston, Phila., Olongapo, P. I., and Ft. Lyon, Colo. Conglist. Has specialized in treatment of tuberculosis. Died Aug. 24, 1926.

BARBER, GERSHOM MORSE lawyer; b. Groton, Cayuga Co., N.Y., Oct. 2, 1823; s. Rev. Phineas B. and Opha (Morse) B.; grad. Univ. of Mich., 1850 (LL.D., Ohio Wesleyan); m. July 2, 1851, at Berlin, O., Huldah L. Seeley of New York. Served in Civil war, 1862-65; capt. sharpshooters; lt.-col. 197th Ohio vol. inf.; bvtd. col. and brig.-gen.; judge Superior Court, Cleveland, O., 1873-75; judge Court of Common Pleas, 1875-85; prof. med. jurisprudence, 1869, Homoe. Hosp. Med. Coll., Cleveland, O. Author: Book of the Law; Notaries' Guide; etc. Residence: 585 Sibley St. Office: 10 Wick Bldg., Cleveland, O.

BARBER, HENRY A. JR. army officer; b. Ft. Reno, Okla., July 31, 1896; s. Henry Anson and Inez (Smith) B.; B.S., U.S. Mil. Acad., 1917; grad. Inf. Sch., Ft. Benning, Ga., 1922. Command and Gen. Staff Sch., Ft. Leavenworth, Kan., 1935, Army War Coll., 1937; m. Margaret Wahl, Aug. 16, 1920; children—Henry Anson, III, Natalie (dec.), Anne. Commd. 2d lt. Inf. U.S. Army, 1917, advanced through grades to brig. gen., 1943; served on War Dept. Gen Staff, 1937-38, 41-43; participated in seizure of Adak, Aleutian Islands, 1942. Decorated D.S.C. (U.S.); Legion of Honor, Croix de Guerre with Palm (France), World War I. Died Apr. 29, 1956.

BARBEY, DANIEL EDWARD, naval officer; b. Portland, Ore., Dec. 23, 1889; s. John and Julia Anna (Chlopeck) B.; B.S., U.S. Naval Acad., 1912; m. Katharine Graham, June 16, 1927. Commd. ensign USN, 1912, and advanced to vice adm., 1944; in charge War Plans sect. Bur. Nav., 1941-42; chief of staff, comdg. Service Force, also Amphibious Force, Atlantic Fleet, 1942; established and in charge Amphibious Warfare sect., staff comdr.-in-chief, Washington; as comdr. 7th Amphibious Force, conducted all amphibious operations S.W. Pacific area (eastern end New Guinea through Bismarck Archipeligo to Philippines); comdr. mopping-up amphibious landings, Philippines, N. Borneo, also landing Balikpapan, Borneo; participated at surrender Japanese comdr. of Korea, 1945; handled repatriation of over two million Japanese from Korea and China; served as comdt. Caribbean Sea Frontier; comd. 13th Naval Dist., 1950; ret., 1951. Dir. Civil Def., State of Wash., 1951-57. Decorated Navy Cross, D.S.M. with gold star, D.S.M. (Army), Legion of Merit (U.S.) Spl. Grand Order of Orange Nassau with Swords by Royal Decree (Netherlands), hon. Comdr. Mil. Div. Order Brit. Empire; Comdr. Order of Liberator (Venezuela); Grand Order of The Cloud and Banner (China); Order of Christopher Columbus, Degree of Great Cross, Silver Plaque; Order of Merit Juan Pablo Duarte, Degree of Great Cross, Silver Plaque (Dominican Rep.). Clubs: Army and Navy (Washington); New York Yacht; Seattle Yacht. Contbr. articles on nat. def. to well known mags. Currently writing a history of amphibious operations in S.W. Pacific in World War II. Home: Olympia WA Died Apr. 11, 1969; buried Portland (Ore.) Meml. Cemetery.

BARBOUR, JAMES senator, sec. of war; b. Barboursville, Va., June 10, 1775; s. Col. Thomas and Mary (Thomas) B.; D.C.L. (hon.), Oxford (Eng.) U., 1829; m. Lucy Johnson, 1792, 5 children. Admitted to Va. bar, 1794; supported Va. resolutions of 1798; mem. Va. Ho. of Dels., 1798-1812, speaker. 1809, drew up bill which established Va. Literary Fund, 1810; gov. Va., 1812-15; mem. U.S. Senate (Democrat) from Va., 1815-25, chmn. coms. mil. affairs, fgn. relations; U.S. sec. of war, 1825-28; apptd. U.S. minister to Gt. Britain, 1828-29; pres. Va. Agrl. Soc. Died Orange County, Va., June 7, 1842.

BARBOUR, JOHN STRODE congressman, lawyer; b. Fleetwood, nr. Brandy Station, Culpeper County, Va., Aug. 8, 1790; grad. Coll. William and Mary, 1808; studied law. Admitted to bar, 1811; practiced in Culpeper, Va.; a.d.c. to Gen Madison in War of 1812; mem. Va. Ho. of Dels., 1813-16, 20-23, 33, 34; mem. U.S. Ho. of Reps. (State Rights Democrat) from Va., 18th-22d congresses, 1823-33; mem. Va. constl. Convs., 1828, 30; chmn. Nat. Dem. Conv., Balt., 1852. Died Fleetwood Jan. 12, 1855; buried family burying ground on his estate.

BARBOUR, JOHN S(TRODE) lawyer; b. nr. Brandy Station, Va., Aug. 10, 1866; s. James and Fanny Thomas (Beckham) B.; student Cables Acad., 1881-82; LL.B., U. Va., 1888; m. Mary Browning Grimsley, Apr. 4, 1894. Admitted to Va. bar, 1887; law clk. Commonwealth's Atty. for Culpeper Co., 1888-1911; established, pub. Piedmont Advance weekly newspaper, Culpeper, 1886-88; candidate for Commonwealth's atty., 1891; mayor, Culpeper, 1897; elected to represent Culpeper, Co., Va. Constl. Conv., 1901-02; mem. Barbour, Garnett, Pickett & Keith, and predecessors, Fairfax, Va. and Washington, 1907-13, since 34; gen. atty. Washington Ry. & Electric Co., Potomac Electric Power Co., Washington Utilities Co., and other affiliates, Washington, 1913-34. Served as pvt. to 1st sgt. Culpeper Minute Men, 3d Regt., inf., Va., N.G.; commd. capt., adj., 3d Regt.; maj., asst. adj. gen., 1st Brigade. Mem. Am., D.C., Va. State (Nat. v.p.), Fairfax Co. bar assns., Clubs: Lawyers, University (Washington); Washington Golf and Country (Arlington, Va.); Fairfax Hunt (Sunset Hills, Va.): Court House Country (Fairfax, Va.). Home: The Oaks, Fairfax, Va. Died May 6, 1952.

BARCLAY, MCCLELLAND artist and illustrator; b. St. Louis, Mo., May 9, 1891; s. Robert and Minnie G. (Hamilton) B.; prep. edn., Central High Sch., St. Louis and Western High Sch., Washington, D.C.; studied art, Cocoran Sch. of Art, Washington, 1909-12, Art Students' League, New York, 1912-14, Art Inst., Chicago, 1919-22; awarded perpetual life scholarship, St. Louis Mus. Fine Arts. Began as advertising illustrator, 1912, also known for sculpture and portrait painting. Awarded 1st prize, World War I for recruiting poster, by Conf. Com. on Nat. Preparedness, 1917; 1st prize for poster "Fill the Breach," for 2d Red Cross drive; 1st prize, "The Human Cross," Marine Corps Recruiting Poster, 1918; 1st prize for "At the Front of the Front," Chicago Assn. Commerce, 1920, etc. Creator of the "Fisher Body Girl," designer of covers for Ladies' Home Jour., Pictorial Rev., Saturday Evening Post, illustrations for Cosmopolitan, etc. Naval camoufleur., 1918, also made posters for Am. Protective League. Appointed lieut. U.S.N.R., June 13, 1938, lieut. comdr., May 21, 1942; called to active duty, Oct. 19, 1940; transferred to Class D, Sept. 1942. Reported missing in action while passenger on ship torpedoed in Solomon Sea, July 18, 1943. Awarded Purple Heart posthumously August 26, 1944. A founder Artists Guild of Chicago; mem. Artists' Guild New York, Art Inst., Chicago; Democrat. Episcopalian. Mason. Clubs: Players, New York Athletic, Lotos (N.Y.) Maidstone (East Hampton, N.Y.). Address: 36 W. 59th St., New York. Died July 19, 1943.

BARCLAY, THOMAS Loyalist, diplomat; b. N.Y.C. Oct. 12, 1753; s. Henry and Mary (Rutgers) B.; ed. Columbia, m. Susanna De Lancey, Oct. 2, 1775. Commd. maj. Loyalist forces in N.Y., 1777, fled to Can. at end of Am. Revolution; held office under Brit. govt. in N.S., circa 1781-circa 1811, also speaker of assembly, adj. gen. N.S. militia, commissary for prisoners; commr. to carry out terms of Jay Treaty, 1795; consul gen. N.Y., 1799-1830; commr. under 4th and 5th articles Treaty of Ghent; consul of Gt. Britain for Northern and Eastern states in U.S., 1802-12. Died N.Y.C., Apr. 21, 1830.

BARD, ROY EMERSON securities and grain broker; b. Cleve., May 20, 1888; s. George Morris and Helen (Norwood) B.; student Lawrenceville Sch., 1906-07; Litt.B., Princeton, 1911; m. Dorothy Channon, Nov. 2, 1921. With bond dept. Harris Trust & Savings Bank, Chg., 1911-20; partner firm of Bard, Esch & Co., 1920-25; v.p. Ralph A. Bard & Co., 1926-28; partner Bard & Co., 1928-30, Sutro Bros. & Co., 1930-41, Clement, Curtis & Co., 1941-45, Shearson, Hammill & Co., ; dir. Chgo. Rivet & Machine Co. Served as capt., F.A., U.S. Army, World War I. Republican. Presby. Clubs: University, Attic (Chicago); Indian Hill (Winnetka). Home: 526 Greenwood, Kenilworth, Ill. Office: 208 S. LaSalle St., Chgo. 4. Died Aug. 1959.

BARING, MAURICE, author; b. London, Eng., Apr. 27, 1874; s. Edward Charles and Emily (Bulteel) B.; student Eton Coll., 1887-91, Trinity Coll., Cambridge, 1903-04; unmarried. In British diplomatic service, 1899-1904; war corr. to Morning Post, 1905; spl. corr. to Morning Post, 1905-07; spl. corr. in Turkey to Times, 1912. Served in Royal Flying Corps and Royal Air Force, 1914-18. Decorated Chevalier Legion d'Honneur, 1915, Officer, 1933; O.B.E., 1918. Roman Catholic. Clubs: Athenaem, White's, Beefsteak (London). Author: Outline of Russian Literature, 1914; Puppet Show of Memory, 1921; Collected Poems, 1921; Cat's Cradle, 1925; C, 1924; Daphne Adeane, 1927. Address: Half-Way House, Rottingean Sussex England

BARKER, ALBERT SMITH rear adm.; b. Hanson, Mass., Mar. 31, 1843; s. Josiah and Eliza (Cushing) B.; Naval Acad. from Mass., 1859-62; m. Ellen Blackmar Maxwell, 1894. Promoted ensign, Nov. 25, 1862; advanced through grades to rear adm., Oct. 10, 1899. Served Mississippi, W. Gulf Blockading Squadron, 1861-63; participated in bombardment and passage of Fts. Jackson and St. Philip, Chalmette batteries and capture of New Orleans, 1862; in attack on Port Hudson, Mar. 14, 1863, where the Mississippi was destroyed; joined the Monongahela; took part in the siege of Port Hudson; torpedo duty, 1873-74; Naval Acad., 1874-76; comd. Palos, 1876-77; lighthouse insp. 8th dist., 1878-81, 2d dist., 1886-89; comd. iron-clad Montauk, 1882; comd. Enterprise, and ran a line of deep-sea soundings around the world, 1882-86; Bur. of Navigation, 1890-91; comd. Philadelphia, 1892-94; Navy Yard, Mare Island, 1895-97; comd. Oregon, 1897; mem. of Bd. of Strategy at beginning of Spanish War, 1898; comd. Newark, May-Aug., 1898; comd. Oregon and also spl. service squadron to the Pacific, Aug., 1898-May, 1899; relieve Admiral Dewey of command of Asiatic Fleet, May, 1899, temporarily; comdt. Navy Yard, Norfolk, 1899-1900, Navy Yard, New York, 1900-03; comdr.-in-chief, N. Atlantic Fleet, 1903-05; retired, Mar. 31, 1905. Was first one in the U.S. to fire high explosives in shells. Home: Washington, D.C. Died Jan. 29, 1916.

BARKER, HAROLD RICHARD army officer; b. R.I., Aug. 4, 1881; commd. 2d lt. R.I.N.G., 1916; capt. U.S. Army, 1917; served in World War I; maj. Res., 1920, advancing to brig. gen., 1937; Fed. service since Feb. 1941; assigned commd. 68th F.A. Brigade, 43rd Div., Camp Blanding, Fla.; arty. comdr. 43rd Inf. Div., June 1942; assigned outside continental limits of the U.S., Oct. 1942. Died May 1965.

BARKER, JEREMIAH physician; b. Scituate, Mass., Mar. 31, 1752; s. Samuel and Patience (Howland) B.; studied medicine under Dr. Bela Lincln; m. 5 times, Ship's surgeon during Revolutionary War, served in privateer, then in Penobscot expdn.; after war practiced medicine in Gorham, Me.; mem. Mass., Me. med. socs. Author: Vade Mecum; A Book of Anatomy. Died Oct. 4, 1835.

BARKER, JOHN, JR., lawyer and insurance company executive; born at Brookline, Massachusetts, Mar. 18, 1906; s. John and Miriam A. (Trowbridge) B.; A.B. cum laude, Williams Coll., 1927; LL.B., Harvard University, 1930; married Mary Cleave, January 15, 1944; one son, John Cleave. Admitted to Mass. bar, 1930; asso. Choate, Hall & Stewart, Boston, 1930-36; atty. New Eng. Mutual Life Ins. Co. Boston, 1936-42, counsel, 1942-48, gen. counsel, 1948-59, vice president, 1950-64, sr. v.p., 1964-66, sr. v.p., gen. counsel, 1966-70, chmn. agy. adminstrn. com., 1960-66, dir., 1960-70; dir. Boston Safe Deposit & Trust Co., Boston Co., Inc. Dir. Massachusetts Hosp. Service, Incorporated, 1953-56, Mass. Higher Edn. Assistance Corp., New Eng. Med. Center Hosps., Medic Alert Found., Internat., World Affairs Council; trustee Dexter School, Brookline. Served as comdr., U.S. Navy, 1942-46, comdr., USNRF. Mem. American Bar Assn. (mem. ho. dels., 1955-58, standing com. unemployment and social security) Nat. Conv. Lawyers and Life Ins. Cos. (co-chmn. 1950-55), Assn. Life Ins. Counsel (exec. com. 1951-59, pres. 1954-55), Life Ins. Assn. Am., Am. Life Conv. (chmn. legislative com. 1956-57), Res. Officers Assn., Phi Beta Kappa, Delta Kappa Epsilon. Epicopalian (sr. warden). Clubs: Country (Brookline); Somerset (Boston); Algonquin. Articles on ins. profl. jours. Contbg. author: Life and Health Insurance Handbook. Home: Chestnut Hill MA Died Dec. 11, 1970.

BARKER, JOSIAH ship builder; b. Marshfield, Mass.; s. Ebenezer and Priscilla (Loring) B.; m. Penelope Hatch, Dec. 9, 1787. Learned ship building trade on North River, Pembroke, Mass.; constructed his 1st ships at St. Andrews and St. Johns, N.B., Can., 1786-87; opened shipyard, Charlestown, Mass., 1795; during War of 1812 built Frolic and was master carpenter for Independence (1st U.S. Navy ship of line); U.S. Naval constructor, 1826-46; built ships Vermont, Virginia and Cumberland; rebuilt Constitution, 1834; designed and built Portsmouth, 1843. Died Charlestown, Sept. 23, 1847.

BARKER, M. HERBERT physician; b. Villisca, Ia., Aug. 20, 1899; s. William Asa and Bessie May (Kimel) B.; student U. of Minn., 1919-21; B.S., U. of S.D., 1923; M.D., Rush Med. Coll. (U. of Chicago), 1925; M.S., Northwestern U., 1931; m. Nancy Maes Henderson, Mar. 3, 1928; 1 dau., Nancy Marion; m. 2d, Marjorie Leigh, Feb. 15, 1945. Interne Wesley Memorial Hospital, Chicago, 1925, and 1926; research in cardio-renal disease at Harvard Medical Sch. and Peter Bent Brigham Hosp., 1927-29; resident in medicine, Passavant Memorial Hosp., Chicago, 1930-31, now asst. prof. medicine, Northwestern U. Med. Sch.; attending physician Memorial Hosp.; expert consultant to U.S. Surgeon Gen.; former cons. in cardio-renal disease, Vets. Diagnostic Center, Edward Hines Hosp. Served with U.S. Marines, 1918-19. Col. U.S. Army, Medical Corps, World War II. Mem. Com. on Hypertension for America and Great Britain; mem. advisory counsel Ill. State Pneumonia Control Commn.; chmn. Com for Nomenclature of Renal-vascular Disease; mem. Central Clin. Research Club. Fellow Central Society Clinical Research (peripheral cardio disease, vascular sect.), American College Physicians; mem. Society Medical History, A.M.A., Sigma Nu, Phi Chi, Sigma Xi, Pi Kappa Epsilon. Received citation, Legion of Merit, 1944. Clubs: Saddle and Cycle, Chicago Yacht, Racquet (Chicago). Contbr. numerous articles to med. jours. and papers to med. meetings. Home: 444 Wrightwood Av. Office: 720 N. Michigan Av., Chicago 11, Ill. Died Aug. 14, 1947.

BARKER, PRELATE DEMICK postmaster; b. North Branford, Conn., Sept. 29, 1835; s. Jonathan Brooks and Frances Jane (Appell) B.; pub. schs., New Haven, Conn., and Stratford (Conn.) Acad.; m. Joan Elizabeth Ferguson, of Selma, Ala., Aug. 1, 1865 (died Mar. 21, 1910); m. 2d, Grace Salome Pettit of Grand Rapids, Mich., Apr. 29, 1914. Served in the Confederate Army as asst. to Maj. C. E. Thames, post q.m., Selma, Ala., 1861 to close of Civil War; sec. and treas. Ala. & Mills. R.R., 1866-71; in lumber, iron and cottonseed oil business, Selma, 1871-79; sec. Empire Refining Co., New York, 1879-83; in cotton compress and storage business, Mobile, 1886-90; dir., press and storage business, Mobile, 1886-90; dir., sec. and treas. Mobile Land Improvement Co. County supt. edn., Dallas Co., Ala., 1870-71; collector U.S. internal revenue, Ala., by appmt. of Pres. U.S. Grant, 1871-78, reapptd. by Pres. Arthur and served until after Pres. Cleveland's inauguration; postmaster of Mobile, 1890-13; except during Cleveland's 2d administration; del. 1st Dist. of Ala., to 8 Rep. nat. convs.; chmn. Ala. delegation to Phila., 1900, and mem. com. that notified McKinley of his nomination; mem. Rep. Nat. Com., Ala., 1908-12, 1912-16. Methodist. 32ff Mason, K.T. Home: 974 Government St., Mobile, Alabama.

BARKER, THEODORE GAILLARD lawyer; b. Charleston, S.C., Aug. 24, 1832; s. Samuel Gaillard and Ellen (Milliken) B.; A.B., S.C. Coll., 1849; m. at Flat Rock, N.C., Louisa Preston, d. Hon. Mitchell King. of Charleston, Oct. 12, 1875. Admitted to bar, 1853, and practiced at Charleston to 1900; also extensive rice planter in S.C., 1874-1904. Served to rank of maj. C.S.A., 1861-65; mem. S.C. Ho. of Rep., 1866; del. Constl. Conv., 1895; del.-at-large Dem. Nat. Conv., 1880. Address: Charleston, S.C.

BARKSDALE, ALFRED DICKINSON, judge; b. Halifax, Va., July 17, 1892; s. William Randolph (judge Sixth Judicial Circuit of Virginia) and Hallie Poindexter (Craddock) B.; ed. Cluster Springs Academy, 1907-08; B.S., Va. Mil. Inst., 1911; LL.B., U. Va., 1915; m. Louisa Estill Winfree, Dec. 15, 1934; children—Louisa Estill Winfree, Mary Owen. Admitted to Va. bar, Aug. 13, 1915, and began practice in Lynchburg; judge Sixth Judicial Circuit of Va., 1938-40; judge U.S. Dist. Court, Western Dist. of Va., 1940-72. Mem. Va. Senate, 1924, 26, 27. Served as capt. 116th Inf., U.S. Army, with A.E.F., World War. Decorated Distinguished Service Cross; Chevalier Legion of Honor, Croix de Guerre. Trustee Hollins Coll.; bd. visitors U. Va. Mem. Am., Va., Lynchburg bar associations, Kappa Alpha, Phi Delta Phi, Phi Beta Kappa. Democrat. Episcopalian. Clubs: Boonsboro Country (Lynchburg); Farmington Country (Charlottesville). Home: Lynchburg VA Died Aug. 16, 1972; buried Spring Hill Cemetery Lynchburg VA

BARKSDALE, JOHN WOODSON, surgeon; b. Vaiden, Miss., Nov. 20, 1876; s. Charles Henry and Emily St. Albans (Woodson) B.; ed. pvt. schs. and under tutors until 1893; M.D. U. of Ala., 1899; m. Emily Meade Hawkins, Apr. 18, 1900; children—Elizabeth Vaiden (Mrs. Wm. D. Lawson, Jr.), Emily Woodson (Mrs. Wm. G. Humphrey), Charlotte Milstead (Mrs. Thomas A. Turner, Jr.), Theresa Hawkins (Mrs. Geo. Vinsonhaler), John Woodson, Henry Edward, Battle Malone. Began practice at Birmingham, Ala., 1899; instr. surgery Memphis (Tenn.) Hosp. Med. Coll., 1905-06; surgeon and pres. Winona (Miss.) Infirmary since 1910; surgeon and chief of staff, Jackson Infirmary, since 1923; visiting surgeon Miss. State Charity Hosp.; div. surgeon I.C. R.R., Miss. Sanatorium for the Tubercular; dir. Miss. Fire Ins. Co., Plaza Investment Co. Served as lt. col., sr. surgeon Hosp. Center, Rimaucourt, France, and comdg. officer Base Hosp. 58, World War; now col. Med. Sect. O.R.C. Fellow Am. Coll. Surgeons (gov.), Southern Surg. Soc.; mem. A.M.A., Southern Med. Assn., Miss. State Med. Soc. (ex-pres.), Tri-State Med. Soc. (ex-pres.), Miss. Reserve Officers' Assn. (ex-pres.); hon. mem. West Tennessee Medical and Surgical Soc., Newcomen Soc. of Engineers (chmn. Mississippi Committee). Mem. Founders Group American Bd. Surgery. Democrat. Episcopalian. Mason, Elk. Clubs: University (ex-pres.), Jackson County (ex-pres.), Rotary, Tennessee (Memphis). Home: 1440 N. State St. Address: Jackson Infirmary, 121 N. President St., Jackson MS*

BARLOW, JOHN WHITNEY brig. gen.; g. Perry, Wyoming Co., N.Y., June 26, 1838; s. Nehemiah and Orinda (Steel) B.; grad. U.S. Mil. Acad., 1861; m. Ilessie McNaughton Birnie, Dec. 26, 1861; m. 2d, Alice Stanton Turner, Sept. 17, 1902. Apptd. 2d.lt., 2d U.S. Arty., May 6, 1861; promoted through grades to col. engrs., May 10, 1895; brig. gen. and chief of engrs., U.S.A., May 2, 1901; retired May 3, 1901, at own request, after 40 yrs.' service. Bvtd.: capt., May 27, 1862, "for gallant and meritorious services in battle of Hanover C.H., Va."; maj., July 22, 1864, for same in Atlanta campaign; lt. col., Mar. 13, 1865, for same in battles before Nashville, Tenn. Was with light battery at first Bull Run; with horse battery M, in Peninsular campaign; at Yorktown, Williamsburg, Hanover C.H. (where recommended for medal of honor for holding in check, with one gun, a div. of the enemy); in 7 days' battles before Richmond, notably Malvern Hill; afterward with engr. battalion, Army of the Potomac, building bridges, making roads, building block houses and erecting defensive works; in Ga. campaign, July 12-Aug. 27, chief of engr. 17th Army Corps; in charge defenses of Nashville, Nov. 1864-Oct. 1865. etc. Senior commr. of U.S. in marking boundary between U.S. and Mexico, 1892-96. Episcopalian. Republican. Home: New London, Conn. Died Mar. 1, 1914.

BARNARD, JOHN GROSS army officer, engr.; b. Sheffield, Mass., May 19, 1815; s. Robert Foster and Augusta (Porter) B.; grad. U.S. Mil. Acad.; m. Jane Brand, circa 1840; m. 2d, Mrs. Anna Boyd, 1860. Commd. lt. in Corps Engrs., U.S. Army, assigned to coastal defenses, 1833; supervising engr. fortifications several prots including N.Y., Portland and Mobile during 1840's supervised fortifications at base of Tampico during Mexican War; brevetted maj. for services; . survey for railroad across isthmus of Panama for Tehuantepec R.R. Co. of New Orleans, 1850; supt. U.S. Mil. Acad., 1855-56; planned defenses of Washington (D.C.) following beginning of Civil War, 1861; commd. brig. gen. of Volunteers, 1861, brevetted maj. gen., 1864; chief engr. for Gen. McClellan during Peninsular campaign, 1862; chief engr. all field armies on Gen. Grant's staff, 1864; chmn. adv. bd. on improvements of mouth Mississippi River, 1871; retired from army, 1881; pres. Permanent Bd. Engs. for Fortifications and River and Harbor Improvements, 1881; author many articles including A Report on the Defenses of Washington, 1871, The Phenomena of the Gyroscope Analytically Examined, 1858. Died May 14, 1882.

BARNES, ALFRED VICTOR chmn. bd. American Book Co.; b. Brooklyn, N.Y., July 25, 1870; s. Alfred Cutler and Josephine (Richardson) B.; student Brooklyn Poly., Brooklyn Latin Sch., Yale, 1891; m. Martha E. Sitt, Sept. 6, 1923. Served as chief of mfg. Am. Book Co., dir. since 1907, later vice-pres. chmn. bd. since 1931. During World War served as lieut. col., U.S.A. Ordnance Dept., and dist. chief Baltimore Dist. Clubs: Society of Colonial Wars, Yale, St. Anthony, New Canaan, Country, Woodway Country. Home: New Canaan, Conn. Office: 88 Lexington Av., New York, N.Y. Deceased.

BARNES, GLADEON MARCUS army officer, engr.; b. Vermontville, Mich., June 15, 1887; s. Frank E. and Selinda (Cross) B.; B.C.E., U. Mich., 1910, M.E., 1941; Eng. D., Ill. Inst. Tech., 1942; grad. Ordnance Sch. Tech., 1914; student Ordnance Sch. Application, 1916-17, Army Indsl. College, 1935-36, Army War Coll., 1937-38; m. Evelyn Mary Kofp, Apr. 3, 1912; 1 dau., Barbara Tufts (Mrs. Roderick Hamilton Sears). Commd. 2d lt., Coast Artillery, U.S. Army, 1910 and advanced through grades to major gen., 1943; charge design and prodn. of ry. and seacoast artillery, 1917-21, inspector fgn. munitions plants and materials, European countries, 1922, charge development anti-aircraft artillery. 1922-27, inspector Govt. Ordnance and Mfg. plants, Europe, 1928; chief engr. charge development and engring., Watertown Aresenal, 1928-32; chief proof of officer, automotive div., Aberdeen (Md.) Proving Ground, 1932-35; charge procurement planning office, asst. sec.-war, 1936-37; chief tech. staff, 1939-40, asst. chief indsl. service in charge research and engring. ordnance dept., 1940-42; asst. chief ordnance, 1942-46, ret. 1946; cons. Porter International, Washington; v.p. charge engring. Budd Co., Phila., 1946-53. Decorated D.S.M.; Comdr. of Order Brit. Empire; Chevalier French Legion of Honor; recipient Elliott Cresson gold medal Franklin Inst., 1946. Mem. Am. Ordnance Assn., Newcomen Soc. Eng. Tau Beta Pi. Episcopalian. Clubs: Racquet (Phila.); Chevy-Chase, Army-Navy (Washington). Author: Weapons of World War II. 1947. Home: Osterville, Cape Cod, Mass.; also 4000 Cathedral Ave., Washington 16. Died Nov. 15, 1961; buried Arlington Nat. Cemetery, Arlington, Va.

BARNES, HAROLD ARTHUR army officer; b. Oneida, N.Y., Aug. 7, 1887; commd. 1st lt. Q.M. Corps, 1917, advanced through the grades to brig. gen. 1943; became officer in charge, Civilian Conservation Corps br., Office Q.M. Gen., Washington, 1940; exec. to Q.M. Gen. for civilian personnel affairs, 1940; named chief, Organized Planning and Control Div., Office Q.M. Gen., Washington, 1942; named dep. Q.M. Gen., 1943. Address: Quartermaster General's Office, War Dept., Washington. Died Aug. 7, 1953.

BARNES, JAMES army officer, engr.; b. Boston, Dec. 28, 1801; s. William Barnes; grad. U.S. Mil. Acad., 1829; Assigned to Arty., U.S. Army, commd. 1st lt., 1836, resigned 1836; became railroad engr. and supt., also engaged in railroad constrn.; col. 18th Mass. Volunteers, 1861; took part in battles of Mechaniesville,

Antietam; commd. brig. gen. U.S. Volunteers, 1862; brevetted maj. gen. 1864; wounded at Battle of Gettysburg, Died Springfield, Mass., Feb. 12, 1869.

BARNES, JOHN BRYSON soldier, author; b. Pennsboro, W.Va., Sept. 18, 1876; s. Henry and Adaline (Hupp) B.; ed. pub. schs.; distinguished grad. Army Sch. of Line, 1906; grad. Army Staff Coll., 1907, Army War Coll., 1920; m. Caroline Rayfield Bitting, Aug. 31, 1904. 1 son, John Bryson. Enlisted in U.S. Army, 1895; served through Spanish-Am. War, Philippine Insurrection and Cuban Pacification: commd. 2d lt. from ranks, Feb. 2, 1901; promoted through grades to col., June 21, 1930; maj., lt. col. and col. N.A., 1917-19; retired on account of physical disability Nov. 15, 1922. With Isthmian Canal Commn., 1908-09; insp. instr. Vt. N.G., 1911-12; asst. chief of staff (operations), 5th Div., 80th Div. and 9th Corps, A.E.F.; mem. Gen. Staff, Washington, 1921-22; prof. Kemper Mil. Sch., Boonville, 1922-34. Awarded D.S.M. (U.S.); officer Etoille Noir, and Croix de Guerre with Palm (French). Republican. Methodist. Mason (32 degree Shriner). Clubs: Army and Navy (Washington and New York); Sojourners, Rotary. Author: Elements of Military Sketching, 1911. A Plattsburg Patriot, 1917. Home: Boonville, Mo. Died Oct. 23, 1956.

BARNES, JOSEPH K. army officer, surgeon; b. Phila., July 21, 1817; s. Judge Joseph Barnes; M.D. U. Pa., 1838; m. Mary Fauntleroy. Apptd. asst. surgeon U.S. Mil. Acad., 1840; served in Seminole War, 1840-43; served under gens. Zachary Taylor and Winfield Scott in Mexican War; attending surgeon, Washington, D.C., 1862; apptd. surgeon-gen., chief Med. Dept., U.S. Army, 1864; attended deathbed of Pres. Lincoln, personal physician to Sec. of State William H. Seward after attempted assassination, attended Pres. James Garfield after he was shot; hon. mem. royal med. socs. of London, Eng., Paris, France and Moscow, Russia. Died Washington, D.C., Apr. 5, 1883; buried Oak Hill Cemetery, Washington.

BARNETT, CHARLES ELDRIDGE surgeon; b. Wapakoneta, O., Sept. 30, 1866; s. Rev. William Clarkson and Frances Mead (Sullivan) B.; B.S., Edgewood (Tenn.) Lit. Coll., 1888; M.D., Ind. U., 1890; univs. of Berlin and Vienna, 1905, 08, 11, 13; m. Mrs. Grace L. Kelley, at Inverness, Fla., Dec. 24, 1936. Practiced in Tenn. 6 mos., Neb. 6 years, Ft. Wayne, Ind., since 1896; specializes in genito-urinary surgery; prof. surg. anatomy, genito-urinary surgery, Fort Wayne Coll. Medicine, 1896-1905; adj. pro. genito-urinary surgery, Purdue U., 1906. Surgeon capt. 157th Ind. Vol. Inf., Spanish-Am. War, 1898; surgeon capt. Med. R.C., as chief of venereal (urologic) sect. Base Hosp., Camp Sherman (83rd Div.), 1917; state committeeman for Nat. Council of Medical Defense, for Council American National Red Cross. Fellow Am. Coll. of Surgeons; mem. A.M.A., Mississippi Valley (pres. 1922), Ind. State, 12th Dist., and Allen Co. (pres. 1910), med. assns., Am. Urol. Assn. Lutheran. Mason (32ff, K.T., Shriner). Clubs: University, Commercial, Country. Author of about 40 published addresses and articles relating mainly to results of original research; mem. staff Internat. Abstract of Surgery, of the Urologic and Cutaneous Review. Address: 220 21st Av. S., St. Petersburg, Fla.

BARNETT, WILLIAM congressman, physician; b. Amherst County, Va., Mar. 4, 1761; studied medicine. Moved to Ga. with his father; returned to Va. at outbreak of Revolutionary War; joined military company from Amherst County under Marquis de Lafayette, present at surrender of Cornwallis at Yorktown; returned to Ga. at end of war, settled on Broad River, Elbert County; practiced medicine, Elbert County; sheriff Elbert County, 1780; mem. Ga. Senate, also pres.; mem. U.S. Ho. of Reps. (State Rights Democrat, filled vacancy) from Ga., 12th-13th congresses, Oct. 5, 1812-15; apptd. commr. to establish boundaries of Creek Indian Reservation, 1815; moved to Montgomery County, Ala. Died Montgomery County, Oct. 25, 1834; buried Smyrna Churchyard, - Washington, Wilkes County, Ga.

BARNETTE, WILLIAM JAY naval officer; b. Morrisville, N.Y., Feb. 2, 1847; s. Dr. Milton and Caroline (Shepherd) B.; grad. U.S. Naval Acad., 1868; m. Evelyn G. Hutchins, Nov. 29, 1877. Served midshipman Asiatic Fleet, 1868; ensign, Apr. 19, 1869, master, July 12, 1870; lt., Dec. 28, 1872; lt.-comdr., Apr. 16, 1894; comdr. Mar. 3, 1899; capt., Oct. 11, 1903; rear-adm., Aug. 1, 1908; Comd. Dorothea, June, 1898; Saratoga, 1898-1901; mem. Gen. Bd. (Navy), 1902-04; mem. Joint Bd. (Army and Navy) July 21, 1903 to June 14, 1904; comdg. U.S. battleship Kentucky, June, 1904-Jan., 1906; mem. Gen. Bd. and Joint Bd., Jan., 1906; retired, Feb. 1, 1909. Republican. Clubs: University (Phila.), Metropolitan (Washington). Address: care Navy Dept., Washington. Deceased.

BARNEY, JOHN congressman; b. Balt., Jan. 18, 1785. Apptd. capt., asst. dist. q.m. gen. U.S. Army, 1814, discharged, 1815; mem. U.S. Ho. of Reps. (Federalist) from Md., 19th-20th congresses, 1825-29; engaged in literary pursuits until 1857. Died Washington, D.C., Jan. 26, 1857; buried Greenmount Cemetery, Balt.

BARNEY, JOSHUA naval officer; b. Balt., July 6, 1759; s. William and Frances (Holland) B.; m. Anne Bedford, Mar. 1780; 1 child. Commd. lt. U.S. Navy, 1776; taken prisoner by British, exchanged, 1777; lt. in ship Virginia, 1777, took several Brit. ships as prizes; commanded several armed mcht. ships, 1778-80, captured by British, 1780, imprisoned in Eng., escaped, 1781; commanded armed merchantman Hyder-Alley, 1782, by brilliant maneuvering captured larger Brit. ship General Monk, received sword from Pa. for services in engagement; declined appointment as 1 of 6 capts. U.S. Navy, 1794; served as commodore French Navy, 1796-1802; commanded privateers during War of 1812; commanded spl. force to defend Washington, D.C., 1814, fought with distinction nr. Bladensburg; served as naval officer at Balt., 1815. Died Pitts., Dec. 1, 1818

BARNHARDT, GEORGE COLUMBUS army officer; b. Gold Hill, N.C., Dec. 28, 1868; a Marshal L. and Sarah Pines (Dunlap) B.; grad. U.S. Mil. Acad., 1892, Army Staff Sch., 1920, Army War Coll., 1921; m. Floy Rice, d. of late Col. John B. Rodman, U.S. Army, Dec. 19, 1895. Commd. 2d lt. 6th Cav., June 11, 1892; promoted through grades to col. N.A., Aug. 5, 1917; brig. gen. (temp.), Oct. 1, 1918; brig. gen. regular army, June 23, 1927. Served at Ft. McKinney, Wyo., 1892-94; comd. troop in Santiago Campaign, 1898; duty Ft. Leavenworth, Kan., 1898-1900; with China Relief Expdn., Aug.-Nov., 1900; in Philippines, 1900-01, 1902-03, participating in Lake Lanao Expdn.; regtl. q.-m. at Santa Clara and Cienfuegos, Cuba, 1907; duty with Provisional Govt. of Cuba, 1907-09; adj. 15th Cav., 1909-12; duty Gen. Staff Corps, 1912; on Mexican border, 1913-16; with Q.-M. Corps, 1916-17; comdr. 329th Inf. at Camp Sherman and in France, 1917-18; comdr. 28th U.S. Inf., 1st Div., July-Oct. 10, 1918, during St. Mihiel and Argonne-Meuse operations; comdr. 2d Brigade, 1st Div., Oct. 10-24, 1981; assigned to 178th Inf. Brig., Nov. 13, and served with it in France and Germany, returning to the U.S. May 31, 1919; gen. staff, 1921-25; comdg. 6th Cav., Aug. 1925-June 1927; comdg. Dist. of Washington, July-Sept., 1927; 22nd Inf. Brig. (Hawaii), Oct. 1927-. Decorated D.S.M. (U.S.); Officer Legion of Honor, Croix de Guerre with palm (France). Address: Schofield Barracks, T.H. Died Dec. 11, 1930.

BARNITZ, ALBERT major U.S.A.; b. Everett, Pa., Mar. 10, 1835; s. Dr. Martin Eichelburger and Martha (McClintie) B.; ed. pub. schs. and Kenyon Coll.; admitted to Ohio bar; m. Jennie Platt, of Cleveland, O., Feb. 11, 1867; father-in-law of Bernard Abert Byrne (q.v.). Sergt. Co. G, 2d Ohio Cav., Aug. 22, 1861; 2d lt., June 1, 1862; 1st lt., Feb. 18, 1863; capt., Feb. 26, 1863; maj., Mar. 20, 1865; hon. mustered out, Sept. 11, 1865; capt. 7th U.S. Cav., July 28, 1866; retired, Dec. 15, 1870; advanced to rank of major retired, by act of Apr. 23, 1904. Bvtd.: maj., Mar. 2, 1867 "for gallant and meritorious services at Ashland Sta., Va.,"; lt. col., Mar. 2, 1867, for same at Sailor' Creek, Va.; col., Nov. 27, 1868, "for distinguished gallantry in battle of Washita, I.T." (severely wounded). Mem. Mil. Order Loyal Legion. Author of vol. of poems, 1857; also poems and prose articles, which appear in various collections. Address: Care Adjutant-General U.S.A., Washington.

BARNUM, HENRY A. army officer; b. Jamesville N.Y., Sept. 24, 1833; s. Alanson Levi and Beersheba (Pixley) B.; grad Syracuse Inst.; m. Lavinia King; m. 2d. Josephine Reynolds; 3 children. Commd. capt. 1st Co., 12th N.Y. Volunteers 1861, served Battle of Bull Run and Battle of Blackburn's Ford; promoted maj., 1861, served in Peninsula Campaign; wounded and captured at Battle of Malvern Hill, July 1, exchanged July 28, 1862; recruiter and col. 149th N.Y. Volunteers, 1862, served at battles of Gettysburg and Lookout Mountain, also in Gen. William Sherman's campaign in Ga., led Union forces which occupied Savannah, Ga.; brevetted brig. gen., then maj. gen., 1865, resigned, 1866; insp. of prisons N.Y., 1865-69; dep. tex. commr. N.Y.C., 1869-72, harbor master, port warden, 1888-92; mem. N.Y. Legislature, 1885; recipient medal of Honor, U.S. War Dept., 1889, Gold medal U.S. Congress, 1889. Died N.Y.C., Jan. 29, 1892.

BARNUM, MALVERN-HILL army officer; b. Syracuse, N.Y., Sept. 3, 1863; s. Gen. Henry A. and Luvina (King) B.; grad. U.S. Mil. Acad., 1886; distinguished grad. Inf. and Cav. Sch., 1893; grad. Army War Coll., 1915; grad. Gen Staff Coll., 1920; m. Martha Maginness, Oct. 24, 1889; children—Frances (Mrs. F. E. Davis), Malvern-Hill (dec.). Commd. 2d lt. 3d Cav., July 1, 1886; promoted through grades to col., July 1, 1916; brig. gen. N.A., Oct. 31, 1917; brig. gen. regular army, Mar. 2, 1923. Duty Rock Island (Ill.) Arsenal, 1893-94; adj. of 10th Cav. during Santiago Campaign, 1898; wounded at San Juan Hill, July 2, 1898 (awarded citation for bravery); duty U.S. Mil. Acad., 1899-1902; a.d.c. to Maj. Gen. J. F. Weston, P.I., 1905-09; insp. small arms practice, Philippine Div., 1908-09; adj. 8th Cav., 1910-11; duty Gen. Staff, 1915-17; apptd. comdr. 183rd Brigade Inf., 92nd Div., Oct. 31, 1917; arrived in France, June 19, 1918; chief of Am. Sect. Inter-Allied Armistice Commn., Dec. 1918-July 1919. Comdr. U.S. Disciplinary Barracks, Ft. Leavenworth, Kan., Sept. 1920-Mar. 1923; brig. gen. U.S. Army, Feb. 9, 1923, comdg. 18th Inf. Brigade, 1923; maj. gen., June 13, 1927; retired, Sept. 3, 1927. Awarded D.S.M., order of the Purple Heart (U.S.). Commander Legion of Honor (French); Comdr. Order of the Bath (British); Comdr. Order of Leopold, and Croix de Guerre (Belgium); Order St. Maurice and St. Lazarus (Italian), Comdr. Mass. Commandery Loyal Legion (also comdr. Nat. orgn.), Naval and Mil. Order Spanish-Am. War; mem. S.R. Phi Gamma Delta. Episcopalian. Clubs: Army and Navy (Washington, D.C., Manila, Boston); Phi Gamma Delta (New York); Algonquin; Santaky Head Golf. Home 194 St. Paul St., Brookline, Mass. Address: care War Dept., Washington, D.C. Died Feb. 18, 1942.

BARNWELL, ROBERT Continental congressman; b. Beaufort, S.C., Dec. 21, 1761; ed. common schs., pvt. tutors; at least 1 son, Robert Woodward. Volunteered in Revolutionary War at age 16; received 17 wounds in Battle on Johns Island, S.C., recovered, served as lt. with his company at siege of Charleston, 1780, when Charleston fell became prisoner aboard ship Pack Horse, released in gen. exchange prisoners, 1781; pres. bd. trustees Beaufort Coll. many years; mem. Continental Congress from S.C., 1788, 89; mem. S.C. Conv. to ratify U.S. Constn., 1788; mem. U.S. Ho. of Reps. (Federalist) from S.C., 2d Congress, 1791-93; mem. S.C. Ho. of Reps., 1795-97, speaker, 1795; mem. S.C. Senate, 1805, 06, pres., 1805. Died Beaufort, Oct. 24, 1814; buried St. Helena's Churchyard.

BARON, STEPHEN EMORY fire underwriter; b. Oxford, Mass., Dec. 24, 1848; s. Capt. David and Julia (Porter) B.; ed. pub. schs., Oxford, Mass., until 1863; m. Hastings, N.S., Joyce Willmot, June 28, 1870 (died Apr. 12, 1871); m. 2d, Lizzie W. Tracy, of Norwich, Conn. Entered army in U.S. mil. telegraph service, Dept. of South and Army of the Potomac, until close of Civil War; served 4 yrs. on Atlantic cables, 1867-71; fire ins. agt., 1872-. One of incorporators Am. Nat. Red Cross and many yrs. 2d v.p. same; chmn. Central Cuban Relief Com. under appmt. of President McKinley, Jan., 1898-July 15, 1899. Mem. Boston Chamber of Commerce. Clubs: Exchange (Boston), Republican (new York). Asso. editor (with George S. Barton, of Worceter, Mass.), of the Barton Genealogy. Contbr. on Red Cross, ins. and other topics. Home: Hotel Buckminster. Office: 60 Congress St., Boston, Mass.

BARON, THOMAS HARRY industrialist; born Marlin, Tex., Sept. 20, 1881; s. Thomas Killebrew and Mary Estelle (Johnson) B.; student Tex. A. and M. Coll., 1897-99, LL.D.; LL.D., U. Ark., Harding Coll. and Coll. of Ozarks; student 3d Army Orientation Course, Ft. Leavenworth, 19 married to Madeline Mary Larimer, July 13, 1925; children-Clark N., T. Killebrew. Pres. El Dorado Natural Gas Co., 1921-24, Nat. Gas & Fuel Corp., El Dorado, 1924-28; pres., dir. Lion Oil Co., El Dorado, 1929-47, chmn. bd., 1947-55; mem. finance com., dir. Monsanto Chem. Co., 1955-59; pres., dir. The Sonbar Corp., The Barton Corp. Ark. Radio and Equipment Co., (operating sta. KARK and KARK-TV, Little Rock); past dir. Southwestern Bell Telephone Co. Mem. exec. com. Boy Scouts Am.; national asso. Boys' Clubs of Am.; mem. bd. trustees Nat. Soc. Cripple Children and Adults. A founder, past pres. Ark. Livestock Show Assn., Little Rock; dir. Bd. Fundamental Edn.; mem. Nat. Monument Commn. Trustee, past mem. exec. com. Cordell Hull Found.; pres., dir. The Barton Found.; mem. bd., finance com. Nat. Freedom Shrine Found.; past bd. trustees George Peabody Coll. for Tchrs. Served as capt. 36th Div., U.S. Army, World War I; later col. U.S. Res. Chosen Arkansan of the Year, 1952; recipient Ark. Jr. C. of C. trophy for distinguished service to state, 1942; Golden Boy award Boys' Clubs Am.; Silver Beaver award DeSoto area Boy Scouts Am.; Distinguished Citizenship award Harding Coll., 1958. lMem. Am. Petroleum Inst. (hon. life mem. bd. dir.), Newcomen Soc. Eng., 25-Year Club Petroleum Industry, Am. Legion, 40 and 8, Mil. Order World War, Beta Gamma Sigma, Lambda Chi. Mason (Shriner, Jester). Clubs: Boston, International House (New Orleans): City, Petroleum (Dallas); Bankers of America (N.Y.C.); National Press, Jefferson Islands (Washington); Pipe Liners, Little Rock (Little Rock); El Dorado (Ark.) Golf and Country. Barton Found. erected Barton Library, El Dorado, T. H. Barton Inst. Med. Research, Hendrix Coll. expansion program, also contbr. Boy's Club, hosps., colls. Home: Country Club Colony. El Dorado. Office: Lion Oil Bldg., El Dorado Ark. Died Dec. 24, 1960; buried Arlington Cemetery, El Dorado, Ark.

BARR, DAVID GOODWIN, army officer; b. Nanfalia, Ala., June 16, 1895; s. William Walter Barr; student Ala. Presbyn. Coll.; grad. Inf. Sch., 1921, Tank Sch., 1924, Army War Coll., 1939; commd. 2d lt., Inf. Reserve, 1917; 1st lt. Inf., U.S. Army, 1920, advanced through grades to maj. gen. (temp.) Feb. 1944; m. Vivian Louise Bell, Nov. 5, 1924; children—Virginia Lane, Patricia Bell. Became asst. G-4, Armoured Corps, 1940, asst. chief of staff G-4, Armored Force, 1941; chief of staff, Armored Force, 1942; dep. chief and chief of staff, European Theater of Operations, 1943; chief of staff North African Theater of Operations, and chief of staff 6th Army Group, 1944-45; G-1 Army Ground Forces, 1945-48; chief, Army Adv. Group, Nanking, 1948-49; comdg. gen. 7th Inf. Div., 1949-51; comdg. gen. Armored Center, 1951. Served with 1st U.S. Inf. Div., World War I. Decorated Silver Star with oak leaf cluster, D.S.C., D.F.C., D.S.M. with 2 oak leaf clusters, Legion of Merit, Air Medal with 3 oak leaf clusters, French Legion of Honor, Commander's Degree, Croix de Guerre with Palm, Brazilian Order of Military Merit; Gold Cross of Merit with Swords (Polish). Home: Arlington VA Died Sept. 26, 1970; buried Arlington Nat. Cemetery, Arlington VA

BARR, RICHARD ALEXANDER surgeon; b. Sumner County, Tenn., Sept. 8, 1871; s. B.B.M.L. and Mary Laura (Alexander) B.; B.A., Vanderbilt U., 1892, M.D., 1894; m. Sarah Elizabeth Kirkpatrick, Nov. 18, 1897; 1 son, Richard A. Practiced in Nashville, 1895—; prof. clinical surgery, Vanderbilt U., 1902—. Maj. surgeon, 1st Tenn. Vol. Inf., Spanish-Am. War and Philippine Insurrection, 1898-99; lt. col M.C., U.S. Army, comdg. officer Hosp. Unit "S" (Vanderbilt), AEF, France, 1918. Fellow A.C.S.; mem. A.M.A., So. Surg. Assn., Phi Delta Theta, Phi Beta Kappa. Presbyn. Address: R. 4, Gallatin, Tenn. Deceased.

BARRETT, CHANNING WHITNEY gynecologist; b. Blissfield, Mich., Dec. 14, 1866; s. David Fowler and Martha C. (Dewey) B.; student Fayette (O.) Normal U., Hillsdale (Mich) Coll.; M.D., Detroit Coll. Medicine, 1895; m. Luella May Alvord, July 22, 1896; children—Russell Alvord, Florence Louise, Helen Elizabeth, Ruth Esther. Intern St. Luke's Hosp., Detroit, 1893-96; asst. surgeon Marion Sims. Hosp., Chgo., 1893—; prof. gynecology Chgo. Clin. Sch., 1900-06; prof. gynecology Chgo. Policlinic Sch.; prof., chief dept. gynecology U. Ill. Med. Sch. to 1930; now prof. gynecology Loyola U. Med. Sch.; chief dept. of gynecology Cook County Hosp. Maj. M.C. World War. Fellow Assn. Obstetricians and Gynecologists, Am. Gynecol. Soc., Chgo. Gynecol. Soc. (ex-pres.); mem. A.M.A., and kindred orgns. Cited for Legion of Honor by French govt. Republican. Methodist. Clubs: City, Press. Contbr. med. jours. Home: 6224 Kenmore Av. Office: 6 N. Michigan Av. Chgo. Died Jan. 29, 1958.

BARRETT, CHARLES D marine officer; b. Henderson, Ky., Aug. 16, 1885; s. Robert South and Kate (Waller) B.; student Episcopal High Sch., Alexandria, Va., 1901-03; attended field officers course, Marine Corps Schs., Quantico, Va., 1932-33; brevetetat Maj. Ecole Superieure de Guerre, Paris, 1929; m. Emily Hawley Beach Johnson, Mar. 2, 1918; children—Charles Dodson, Constance Cardigan. Commd. 2d lt., U.S. Marine Corps, 1909, 1st lt., 1916, capt., 1916, maj., 1918, lt. col., 1934, col., 1937, brig. general, 1942, major general, Oct. 1943. Received Mexican Service medal, 1914; Victory medal (with Meuse-Argonne clasp), 1918; Expeditionary medal, 1922. Mem. U.S. Naval Inst. (former dir.). Home: 213 S. Pitt St., Alexandria, Va. Office: headquarters, U.S. Marine Corps, Washington, D.C. Died Oct. 1943.

BARRETT, CHARLES F., soldier; b. Galion, O., Jan. 1, 1861; s. John E. and Charlotte (Reynolds) B.; student Kan. State Agr. Coll., Manhattan, 1880-81; m. Capitola Millard, of Perry, Okla., Sept. 26, 1900; children-Charles F., Helen and Wanda (twins). Admitted to Okla. bar, 1894, and began practice at Shawnee, Okla.; founder, and pub. 1901-06, Shawnee Herald. Capt. Okla. N.G., 1897; served as pvt. and 1st sergt. Territorial Vol. Inf., Spanish-Am. War; commd. 2d lt., Okla. N.G., 1899; promoted through grades to brig. gen., 1919; apptd. adj. gen. of Okla., 1919, resigned, 1923; commd. col. inf., U.S.A.; retired, 1925; reapptd. adj. gen. of Okla., rank of brig. gen., 1925. Sec. Okla. State Bd. of Agr., 1908-10; mem. Okla. Ho. of Rep., 1911-12, Senate, 1913-16; clk. Okla. constl. conv., 1906-07; mem. publicity bureau Dem. State Com., 1917-18. Mason (K.T., Shriner). Club: Sojourner. Home: 2600 N. Francis St. Office: State Capitol, Oklahoma City, Okla.

BARRETT, CHARLES J(OSEPH) army officer; b. South Orange, N.J., Feb. 15, 1900; s. Charles J. and Jennie (Grimes) B.; student Seton Hall Prep. Sch., 1912-16; B.S., U.S. Mil. Acad., 1922; M. Maxine Fulton, Aug. 16, 1937; 1 dau., Diane Fulton. Commd. 2d lt. C.E., U.S. Army, 1922, advanced through grades to brig. gen.; trans. F.A., 1924; pvt. 29th Div., World War I; with 1st Cav. Div., 1923-26; attached Spanish cav. regt., Madrid, Spain, 1926-27; gen. staff War Dept., 1941-42, spl. staff Civil Affairs Div., 1945-47; chief staff, later arty. comdr. 84th Inf. Div., 1942-45; asso. prof. mil. sci. and tactics Colo. State Coll., 1933-36; instr. Spanish U.S. Mil. Acad., 1927-30, asst. prof., 1930-31, instr. French, Spanish, 1937-40, asst. prof., 1940-41, prof. fgn. langs. (in grade of col.) since 1947, head dept. since 1948, exec. sec. bd. visitors, 1951-62. Decorated Silver Star, Legion of Merit, Bronze Star medal, Commendation Ribbon with oak leaf cluster, campaign badges (World War I and II); Order of Fatherland (Russia); Comdr. with swords Order of Orange Nassau (Netherlands); Croix de Guerre with palm (France); Cruz de Merito Militar (Mexico); Medalha do Pacificador (Brazil), 1958; D.S.M. (posthumously). Club: Army-Navy Country (Arlington, Va.). Mem. Am. Olympic team, 1928, chmn. Modern Pentathlon com. Olympic Games of 1948. Home: Quarters 102, West Point, New York. Died June 30, 1963; buried West Point, N.Y.

BARRETTE, JOHN DAVENPORT army officer; b. in Louisiana, May 14, 1862; s. John Dunsworth and Margaret Elizabeth (Maybanks) B.; grad. U.S. Mil. Acad., 1885; m. Katherine Biddle, June 13, 1894; children - Margaret (Mrs. John Barber Harper), Katharine Biddle (Mrs. Maurice Place Chadwick), Mary Lydia (Mrs. William Taylor Sinclair), Elizabeth Biddle, Louisa Biddle (Mrs. Norman Henry Blanch). Commd. 2d lt. 3d Arty., June 14, 1885; promoted through grades to brig. gen. National Army, Aug. 5, 1917; brig. gen. U.S.A., Feb. 2, 1818; retired May 14, 1926. Instructor of mathematics, U.S. Mil. Acad., 1892-96; instr. Arty. Sch., 1903-07; dir. dept. arty. and gun defense, Coast Arty. Sch., Ft. Monroe, Va., 1907-09; comd. Ft. McKinley, 1910; comdg. arty. dist. of Charleston, lt. col. 1st Provisional Regt., Coast Arty., and coast defense officer Eastern Dept., 1911; comd. coast defenses of Baltimore, 1912, of L.I. Sound, 1913-14; adj. gen. Western Dept., 1915, Philippine Dept., 1916; comd. 152d Brigade, Field Arty., 1917; actg. chief of Coast Arty., Dec. 1917-May 1918; comdg. A.E.F. Arty. Sch., Saumur, June-Nov. 1918; comdg. Coast Arty. dists., Jan. 1919-May 1926, Southeastern Dept., July-Oct. 1919, Hawaiian Div., Dec. 1921-Feb. 1922, 1st Corps Area, Nov. 1924-Feb. 1925. Died July 16, 1934.

BARRIER, JOSEPH HENRY, ins. exec.; b. Yazoo County, Miss., Sept. 30, 1890; s. Forester and Cady (Wood) B.; B.S., Miss. State Coll., 1910; m. Annie Milton Norman. Instrument man, draftsman Bogue Hasty Drainage Dist., Miss., 1910-12; field engr. drainage projects Capt. West, Greenville, Miss., 1912-14; resident engr. Miss. Levee Bd., 1914-17; mortgage loan insp. Guaranty Bank & Trust Co., Memphis, 1919-20; field engr. oil terminal Doullott & Williams, Tampico, Mexico, 1920-21; mortgage loan insp. Jefferson Standard Life Ins. Co., 1921-25, mgr. mortgage loan dept., 1925-46, v.p., 1945-55 dir., exec. and finance com., 1947-51. Served as capt., F.A., U.S. Army, 1917-19. Mem. S.A.R., George Rifles Club. Methodist Episcopal. Mason (Shriner), Elk. Clubs: Merchants and Manufacturers; Greensboro Country. Address: Greensboro NC Died July 21, 1970; buried Green Hill Cemetery, Greensboro NC

BARRIGER, JOHN WALKER brig. gen.; retired; b. nr. Shelbyville, Ky., July 9, 1832; s. Josiah and Paulina (Elliott) B.; grad. West Point, 1856; m. Sarah A.F. Wright, Mar. 4, 1863. Promoted 2d lt., July 1, 1856; 1st lt., May 2, 1861 (bvtd. capt., for gallantry, at Bull Run, July 21, 1861); apptd. capt. on staff, com. of subsistence, Aug. 3, 1861; lt. col. staff, U.S. vols., Nov. 17, 1863, to Aug. 1, 1865; bvt. maj., lt. col., col. and brig. gen., Mar. 13, 1865, for faithful and meritorious services during war; apptd. maj. staff, commissary subsistence, Nov. 21, 1875; lt. col., later col. staff, asst. commissary apptd. brig. gen., U.S.A. Apr. 23, 1904. Author: Legislative History of Subsistence Department of the United States Army, 1775-1876. Home: New York, N.Y. Died 1906.

BARRINGER, PAUL BRANDON, JR., lawyer; b. Davidson, N.C., Aug. 28, 1887; s. Paul Brandon and Nannie (Hannah) B.; B.A., U. Va., 1907; LL.B. U. Mich., 1914; m. Lucy Landon Minor, Nov. 28, 1917; children—Charles Minor, Rufus. Engaged in bus., N.C., 1907-10, Tex., 1912-13; admitted to N.Y. bar, 1915, also U.S. Supreme Ct.; asst. counsel Nat. Biscuit Co., 1914-15, Am. Sugar Refining Co., 1916-17; asso., then partner firm Jackson, Nash, Brophy, Barringer & Brooks, and predecessors, N.Y.C., 1919-73. Trustee, mayor Village of Matinecock, L.I., N.Y., 1928-38. Trustee Soc. St. Johnland, 1940-63, Locust Valley Pub. Library, 1937-73. Served to capt. U.S. Army, 1917-19; AEF in France. Mem. Am., N.Y. State bar assns., Assn. Bar City N.Y., Am. Law Inst., Phi Beta Kappa, Order of Coif, Zeta Psi, Phi Delta Phi. Democrat. Episcopalian (vestry). Clubs: Century Assn., Pilgrims, Down Town Assn. (N.Y.C.); Piping Rock (Locust Valley). Home: Locust Valley NY Died Jan. 27, 1973.

BARRINGER, RUFUS army officer; b. Cabarrus County, N.C., Dec. 2, 1821; s. Paul Barringer; grad. U. N.C., 1842; m. 1st, Eugenia Morrison, 1854; m. 2d, Rosalie Chunn; m. 3d, Margaret Long. Admitted to N.C. bar, practiced in Concord, 1845; mem. N.C. Assembly (Whig), 1848, apptd. capt. 1st N.C. Cavalry, 1861, served in Confederate Army of No. Va.; participated in battles of Peninsular campaign, 2d Bull Run, Antietam, Fredericksburg and Chancellorsvillep promoted maj., 1863, also lt. col.; promoted col., brig. gen., 1864; led brigade in Gen. W.H.F. Lee's cavalry div. 1864-65; assisted in Lee's retreat from Richmond, 1865; practiced in Charlotte, N.C., 1865-84; joined Republican Party in N.C., active in politics; del. N.C. Constl. Conv., 1875; unsuccessful candidate for lt. gov. N.C., 1880. Died Charlotte, Feb. 3, 1895; buried Charlotte.

BARRON, ELBERT MACBY, lawyer, business exec.; b. Van Alstyne, Tex., Feb. 13, 1903; s. John Macby and Rilla (McWilliams) B.; LL.M., Cath. U. Am., 1940; Sapientiae Mundane Dr., Boswell-Johnson Inst. Great Britain, 1960. Admitted to bar, 1924; member firm Hay, Finley, Wolfe & Barron, Sherman, Tex.; pres. Southern Gem Mining Co.; engaged in general civil practice and represented oil, r.r. and utility cos. until 1939, except 4 yrs. as counsel govt. agencies; assigned War Dept. Gen. Staff, Jan. 1940; following emergency served as chief legislative officer and chief of War Dept. litigation, later served PTO; ret. with rank of col.; formerly officer Tex. N.G. Mem. Tex. ligislature, 1932-35; exec. head and author report of legislative tax survey commn. which led to reorg. Tex. tax structure. Mem. bd. devel. U. Tex. Western Coll.; mem. devel. bd., founding mem. chancellor's council U. Tex. Bd. dirs. El Paso Mus. Fine Arts, Witte Meml. Mus. Mem. Tex., Oklahoma, D.C. and U.S. Supreme Ct. bars. British Gemmological Assn., Alumni Assn. Loyola U., Am. Gem. Soc., Heroes of '76, Disabled Officers of World Wars, El Paso Geol. Soc. (chmn.), Del. several Dem. nat. convs. Author: Current Reports on Mexican and Southwestern Minerals; Minerals of Mexio. Home: El Paso TX Died Jan. 5, 1969; buried Van Alstyne (Tex.) Cemetery.

BARRON, JAMES naval officer; b. probably Norfolk, Va., Sept. 15, 1768; s. James and Jane (Cowper) B.; no formal edn. Commd. lt. U.S. Navy, 1798, capt., 1799; commanded ship President in Mediterranean Fleet, 1800-05; surrendered Chesapeake to Brit. warship which demanded alleged deserters, nr. Norfolk, 1807, court martialed, 1808; served in French Navy while under suspension from U.S. Navy, 1808-13; fought duel with Commodore Stephen Decatur (leader of group of officers opposed to his restoration to active duty), 1820, subsequently never restored to active service. Died Norfolk, Apr. 21, 1851; buried Norfolk.

BARRON, WILLIAM ANDROS JR. business exec.; b. Newburyport, Mass., Dec. 16, 1892; s. William Andros and Mary Lawrence (Todd) B.; grad. Middlesex Sch., Concord, Mass., 1910; A.B., Harvard, 1914; m. Emily Wesselhoeft, July 10, 1920 (died Aug. 24, 1945); children-William Andros III, Richards Bradley; married 2d Josephine T. Dyer, June 28, 1946. Partner, investment firm White, Weld & Co., New York, Boston, 1914-45; chmn. The Gillette Co., 1945-56; dir. Incorporated Investors, Boston Safe Deposit & Trust Co., Greenville Electric Light Co., St. Croix Paper Co. Trustee Suffolk Savings Bank for Seamen and others. Served with U.S. Army, 1942, and advanced through the grades to brig. gen., 1944; chief of staff 1st Service Command, 1943-45. Awarded Legion of Merit. Trustee Mass. Memorial Hospitals, Boston; pres. sec. bd. trustees Middlesex Sch., Concord, Mass.; mem. bd. overseers Boys Club of Boston, Inc. Clubs: Manchester Yacht, Country (Brookline, Mass.); Madison Square Garden (gov.), Somerset, Tennis and Racquet, Harvard, Downtown (Boston); Essex Country, Harvard, The Brook (N.Y.). Home: 351 Bath Club Blvd. N., North Redington Beach, Fla. 33708. Office: 15 W. First St., Boston. Died Sept. 29, 1964; buried Oak Hill Cemetery, Newburyport, Mass.

BARROW, DAVID surgeon; b. Bayou Sara, La., Aug. 31, 1858; s. David and Susan (Woolfolk) B.; M.D., Tulane U., 1880; m. Mary Parham, of New Orleans, La., Apr. 15, 1881; children-Woolfolk (dec.), Mrs. Artemisia Briggs, Mrs. Sue Hunt, Mrs. Betty Woolfolk, John Parham, David (dec.). Practiced in Lexington, Ky., since 1887; visiting consulting surgeon Good Samaritan and St. Joseph's hosps. Fellow Am. Surg. Assn., Am. Coll. Surgeons; mem. A.M.A., Ky. State Med. Assn. Lt. col. Med. Corps U.S.A. and was comdg. officer Base Hosp. No. 40. Home: 203 E. 4th St. Office: 190 N. Upper St., Lexington, Ky.

BARROWS, ARTHUR STANHOPE former under sec. USAF; b. Chgo., Aug. 22, 1884; s. John Henry and Sarah Eleanor (Mole) B.; student Oberlin Coll.; grad. Yale, 1906; m. Bessie Gordon, Mar. 29, 1909; children-Eleanor (Mrs. Waterbury), Frederick G., John M. Began with Hibbard, Spencer, Bartlett & Co., Chgo., 1906-10; in retail hardware bus., Washington, Ind., 1910-16; with McKinney Co., Binghamton, N.Y., 1916-17, Montgomery Ward & Co., 1917-25, A.S. Barrows Co., San Francisco, 1925-26; joined Sears, Roebuck & Co., 1926, bd. dirs. 1935, v.p. in charge Pacific Coast terr., Jan. 1941, pres. 1942-46, vice chmn. bd. dirs., 1946-47; dep. dir. econ. div. Ofcl. Mil. Govt. U.S. in Germany, 1947; under sec. Air Force, Dept. Def., 1947-50. Conglist. Home: Edgar Manor, Greenwich, Conn. Died Sept. 20, 1963; buried Oberlin (O.) Cemetery.

BARROWS, DAVID PRESCOTT, univ. prof.; b. Chicago, Ill., June 27, 1873; s. Thomas and Ella Amelia (Cole) B.; B.A., Pomona Coll., 1894; M.A., U. of Calif., 1895, Columbia, 1896; Ph.D., in anthropology, U. of Chicago, 1897; LL.D., Pomona, 1914, U. of Calif., 1919, Mills Coll., 1925; Dr. honoris causa, U. of Bolivia, 1928; Litt.D., Columbia U., 1933; m. Anna Spenser (Nichols), July 18, 1895; children—Anna Frances (wife of Brig. Gen. Floyd W. Stewart, Army of United States), Ella Cole (Mrs. Gerald Hagar), Thomas Nichols, Elizabeth Penfield (wife of Lieut. Col. F. G. Adams, United States Army); m. 2d, Mrs. Eva S. White, 1937. City supt. of schools, Manila, P.I., 1900; chief, Bureau Non-Christian Tribes of P.I., 1901; gen. supt. (afterwards styled director) of education for P.I., 1903-09; prof. edn. 1910, dean Grad. Sch., 1910, prof. polit. science, July 1, 1911, dean of faculties, 1913, and pres., 1919-23, prof. polit. science, emeritus, since 1943, Univ. of California. Pres. trustees Mills Coll., Calif., 1910-17; mem. bd. dirs. Calif. State Sch. for Deaf and Blind, 1912-17; mem. Calif. State Commmn. on Rural Credit and Colonization, 1915-17; dir. East Bay Pub. Utility Dist., 1924-27, 1932-34; trustee Carnegie Endowment for Internat. Peace. Mem. Belgian Relief Com., in charge food supply of Brussels, 1916, Commd. maj. of cav., N.A., 1917; lt. col. cav. U.S. Army, 1918; active duty in P.I. and Siberia, 1917-19; on original gen. staff list, U.S. Army 1919; col. 159th Inf., N.G., Calif., 1921; brig. gen. 79th Inf. Brigade, Calif. N.G., 1925; maj. gen. Army U.S., comdg. gen. 40th Div., Calif. N.G., 1926-37. First state comdr. for California, American Legion, 1920. Carnegie visiting prof. of Internat. Relations (Latin-America), 1928; Theodore Roosevelt prof., U. of Berlin, 1933-34; expert consultant to Secretary of War, 1941; representative Office Strategic Services, 1942; radio commentator, 1943-44; columnist International News Service, 1943-49. Decorated Chevalier Legion of Honor (French), promoted to officer, 1932; Order of the Crown (Belgian), Croix de Guerre (Czecho-Slovak); Order of the Sacred Treasure (Japanese); Order of the Crown (Italian); Comdr. Order of Polonia Restituta (Polish). Corr. mem. Royal Acad. of Polit. and Moral Science (Madrid), 1923. Republican. Conglist. Mem. Phi Beta Kappa. Clubs: Faculty (Berkeley); Bohemian (hon.), University (hon.), Commonwealth (San Francisco); Army and Navy (Los Angeles). Author: The Ethno-Botany of the Coahuilla Indians, 1900; A History of the Philippines, 1903, rev. 1924; A Decade of American Government in the Philippines, 1915; British Politics in Transition (with E. M. Sait), 1925; (with Thomas Barrows) Government in California, 1926; Berbers and Blacks (also transl. into French), 1927. Traveled in Asia, Malaysia, Central and South America and in Africa (Timbuktu, the French Sudan and British Nigeria). Home: 85 Parkside Dr., Berkeley 5 CA

BARRY, EDWARD BUTTEVANT rear adm.; b. New Oct. 20, 1849; s. Garrett Robert and Sarah Agnes (Glover) B.; grad. U.S. Naval Acad., 1869; m. Mary Wycliff Clitz, Apr. 7, 1875 (died 1906). Promoted ensign, July 12, 1870; advanced through grades to rear adm., Feb. 1, 1909. Served on various vessels to 1875; mem. bd. to organize training service, 1875; on Alaska, 1878-80; admiral's sec., Richmond and Monocacy, 1880-83; at Naval Acad., 1883-86, made 2 practice cruises on sailing frigate Constellation; on Alliance and Lancaster, S. Atlantic sta., 1886-89; with Bur. of Navigation, 1889-91; Asiatic sta., 1891-94; office naval intelligence, 1894-97; S. Atlantic and Cuban blockade, 1897-99, present at attack on Matanzas, Cuba, and Ponce, P.R.; comd. collier Marcellus, 1900; at gun factory, Washington, War Coll. and comdg. Vicksburg, Asiatic sta., 1900-02; comd. Kentucky, 1905-07; recruiting duty, New York, 1907; supervisor naval auxiliary service, 1908-09; comdr. 2d div. Pacific Fleet, 1909. Asso. Soc. Naval Architects. Home: New York, N.Y. Died Nov. 27, 1938.

BARRY, HENRY W. congressman, lawyer; b. Schoharie County, N.Y., Apr. 1840; grad. law dept. Columbian Coll. (now George Washington U.), 1867. Prin., Locust Grove Acad., Ky.; enlisted in Union Army in Civil War; organized regt. Colored troops in Ky.; commd. 1st lt. 10th Regt. Ky. Volunteer Inf., 1861; col. 8th U.S. Colored Artillery, 1864; brevetted brig. gen. Volunteers for faithful and meritorious services, 1865; admitted to bar, 1867; practiced in Columbus, Lowndes County, Miss.; del. Miss. Constl. Conv., 1867; mem. Miss. Senate 1868; mem. U.S. Ho. of Reps. (Republican) from Miss., 41st-43d congresses, Feb. 23, 1870-75. Died Washington D.C., June 7, 1875; buried Oak Hill Cemetery.

BARRY, HERBERT lawyer; b. Wilmington, N.C., Feb. 25, 1867; s. Maj. (U.S. Army) Robert Peabody and Julia Kean (Neilson) B.; prep. edn. various private schs.; B.L., U. of Va., 1888; m. Ethel M. Dawson, Feb. 16, 1898; children—Herbert, Eleanor, Stuyvesant. Admitted to Va. bar in 1888, N.Y. bar, 1890; mem. firm Davies, Auerbach, Cornell & Barry, 1897-1913; sr. partner, Barry, Wainwright, Thacher & Symmers since 1913. Mem. Troop A, later Squadron A., N.G.N.Y., 1891-1908; capt., 1900-08, and mem. Gov. Hughes staff; maj. Squadron A. Cav., N.Y.G. Dec. 1917; commd. maj. inf. U.S. Army, May 1918; served overseas, May 1918-June 1919; hon. discharged, July 1919; subsequently commd. lt. col. 302d Regiment Cav., O.R.C., 1923. retired, 1931, with rank of col. Pres. Bd. of Edn., West Orange, for many yrs. Mem. Am. Bar Assn., Assn. Bar City of New York, New York County Bar Assn., N.Y. State Bar Assn., S.R., Soc. Colonial Wars, and other patriotic and civic bodies; former gov. The Virginians of N.Y. City; former pres. Ex-members Assn. of Squadron A. Republican. Episcopalian. Clubs: University, Downtown, Rock Spring Club. Contributed to Virginia Law Review, papers on many subjects published in each year, 1923-37, later compiled under title Viewed History of First Fifty Years of Squadron A. (pub. by Assn. of Ex-Mems. of Squadron A). Home: Llewellyn Park, West Orange, N.J. Office: 72 Wall St., New York, N.Y. Died June 19, 1947.

BARRY, JOHN navy officer; b. County Wexford, Ireland, 1745; s. John and Catherine B.; no formal edn.; m. Mary Burns; m. 2d, Sarah Austin, July 7, 1777. Commanded ship Lexington in U.S. Navy, 1776; promoted capt., given command of Effingham, 1777; comdr. Raleigh, captured many Brit. ships, 1778-81; in command of Alliance, captured Brit. ships Atalanta and Trepassy, 1781; ret. from Navy, 1783; appt. sr. capt. in command of the ship United States during Algerine conflict, 1794, in command of U.S. naval forces in West Indies, 1798; commanded U.S. naval sta. at Guadaloupe, 1800-01. Died Sept. 13, 1803.

BARRY, THOMAS HENRY major gen.; b. New York, Oct. 13, 1855; s. David and Margaret (Dimond) B.; ed. pub. schs. and Coll. City of New York; grad. U.S. Mil. Acad., 1877; m. Ellen Bestor, Jan. 23, 1884. Second lt. 7th Cav., June 15, 1877; promoted through grades to lt. col., asst. adj. gen. U.S.A., Jan. 10, 1900; brig-gen. U.S.V., June 18, 1900, to June 30, 1901, serving with China relief expdn. and in Philippines till July 18, 1901; col. asst. adj.-gen. U.S.A., July 15, 1902; brig-gen., Aug. 18, 1903; maj-gen., Apr. 29, 1908. Adj. gen. 8th Army Corps and dept. of Pacific in P.I., Aug. 1898-Feb. 1900; chief of staff, Div. of the Philippines, Nov. 14, 1900-July 18, 1901; comdg. army of Cuban pacification, 1907-Apr. 1, 1909; comdg. dept. of Cal. to Aug. 1910; apptd. supt. U.S. Mil. Acad., Aug. 31, 1910; comdg. Eastern Department, Governor's Island, New York, 1913, Philippine Dept., until 1915, Central Dept., Chicago until Aug. 1917; comdr. Camp Grant, Rockford, Ill., and 86th Div., N.A., Aug. 1917-Feb. 1918; again comdg. Central Dept., Chicago, Mar. 1918 - . Died Dec. 30, 1919.

BARRY, WILLIAM FARQUHAR army officer; b. N.Y.C., Aug. 18, 1818; grad. N.Y.C. High Sch., 1831, U.S. Mil. Acad., 1838; m. Kate McNight, 1840. Began service with 2d Arty. Corps. U.S. Army, 1838; participated in Mexican War as adjutant gen. at Veracruz; served in Seminole Indian War in Fla., 1857-58; in charge of arty. under Gen. McDowell at Battle of Bull Run, 1861; promoted capt., 1852, maj., 1861; commd. brig. gen. U.S. Volunteers, 1862; brevetted col. U.S. Army and maj. gen. volunteers, 1864, brig. gen. and maj. gen. U.S. Army, 1865; commd. col. U.S. Army, 1865; served as head of arty. Army of Potomac, 1862; insp. arty. Armies of the U.S., Washington, D.C., 1862-64; chief of arty. for Gen. Grant, 1864, for W. T. Sherman, 1864-65; commanded 2d Arty. U.S. Army in service on No. border during Fenian conflicts, 1866; organized, headed U.S. Army Arty. Sch., Ft. Monroe, Va., 1867-77. Died . McHenry, Balt., July 18, 1879; buried Ft. McHenry.

BARRY, WILLIAM TAYLOR senator, postmaster gen.; b. Lunenburg, Va., Feb. 5, 1785; s. John and Susannah (Dozier) B.; grad. Coll. William and Mary, 1803; m. Lucy Overton; m. 2d, Catherine Mason. Admitted to bar, 1805; mem. U.S. Ho. of Reps. (Democrat) from Ky., 11th Congress, Aug. 1810-11; sec. and aide-de-camp to Gen. Isaac Shelby during War of 1812, served in Battle of the Thames, 1813; mem. U.S. Senate (Democrat) from Ky., 1814-16; judge 11th Circuit Ct. of Ky., 1816-17; mem. Ky. Senate, 1817-21; lt. gov. Ky., 1820; tried to establish an effective system of pub. edn.; prof. law, politics Transylvania U., 1822-24; sec. of state Ky., 1824; chief justice Ky. Ct. of Appeals, 1825; postmaster-gen. U.S., 1829-35; apptd. U.S. minister to Spain, 1835, died before serving. Died Liverpool, Eng., Aug. 30, 1835; buried Frankfort (Ky.) Cemetery.

BARRY, WILLIAM TAYLOR SULLIVAN congressman, army officer; b. Columbus, Miss., Dec. 10, 1821; s. Richard and Mary (Sullivan) B.; grad. Yale, 1841; m. Sally Fearn, Dec. 20, 1851. Admitted to Miss. bar, practiced in Columbus, circa 1844; mem. Miss. Legislature, 1849, 50; mem. U.S. Ho. of Reps. from Miss., 33d Congress, 1853-55; mem., speaker Miss. Lower House, 1855-61; became leader of states' rights secessionist branch of Democratic Party during 1850's; pres. Miss. Conv. which passed secession ordinance, 1861; del. to Montgomery (Ala.) Conv. which organized Confederate Covt., 1861; mem. Confederate Provisional Congress from Miss., 1861-62; organizer, col. 35th Miss. Inf. Regt., Confederate Army, 1862; participated in Corinth and Vicksburg campaigns; captured at Mobile, Ala., 1865; practiced law in Columbus, 1866-68. Died Columbus, Jan. 29, 1868; buried Columbus.

BARSANTI, OLINTO MARK, army officer; b. Tonopah, Nev., Nov. 11, 1917; s. Silvio and Agatha (Vangeliste) B.; B.A., U. Nev., 1940; M.A. in Internat. Affairs, George Washington U., 1962; grad. Nat. War Coll., 1958, Command and Gen. Staff Coll., 1946; m. Aletha Imogene Howell, Oct. 22, 1942; 1 dau., Bette (Mrs. Harvey Daniels). Commd. 2d lt. U.S. Army, 1940, advanced through grades to maj. gen., 1967; assigned Europe, 1943-45. Korea, 1950-52; chief staff, Berlin, Germany, 1955-57; assigned Army Staff, 1958-60, Joint Chiefs Staff, 1961-62; comptroller U.S. Army, Europe, 1963-65, Army Material Command, 1966; comdg. gen. 101st Airborne Div., Vietnam, 1967-68; chief staff 5th U.S. Army, 1968-71; mem. faculty Command Gen. Staff Coll., 1946-49; ret., 1971. Decorated D.S.C., D.S.M., Silver Star (5), Purple Heart (7), Legion of Merit (2), Bronze Star (8), D.F.C. Mem. Assn. U.S. Army, Sigma Nu. Lion. Kiwanian. Home: Northbrook IL Died May 3, 1973; buried Arlington Nat. Cemetery, Washington DC

BARSTOW, JOHN LESTER governor; b. Shelburne, Vt., Feb. 21, 1832; s. Heman and Laura (Lyon) B.; ed. Shelburne; (LL.D., Norwich U., 1909); m. Laura Maeck, Oct. 28, 1856 (died in 1885). Served in Union Army, 1861-64, to rank of maj.; was made brig. gen. state troops at time of St. Albans raid. Mem. Vt. Ho. of Rep., 1864-65, Senate, 1866-68; U.S. pension agt., Burlington, Vt., 1870-78; lt. gov., 1880-82; gov., 1882-85. Dir. Burlington (Vt.) Savings Bank, 1887 - . Home: Shelburne, Vt. Died June 28, 1913.

BARSTOW, WILLIAM AUGUSTUS gov. Wis.; b. Plainfield, Conn., Sept. 13, 1813; s. William Barstow; m. Maria Quarles, Apr. 1844. Sec. of state Wis., 1850; pres. St. Croix & Lake Superior R.R. Co., 1855; elected gov. Wis. (Democrat) 1854, reelected, 1856 (election contested by Republicans, and Wis. Supreme Ct., for 1st time in history of any Am. state, removed gov. from office after installation); commd. col. U.S. Army, 1861; provost-marshal gen. Kan., 1862; brevetted brig. gen. U.S. Volunteers, 1865. Died Leavenworth, Kan., Dec. 14, 1865.

BARTELL, FLOYD EARL educator; b. Concord, Mich., June 16, 1883; s. William and Margaret (Allman) B.; A.B., Albion (Mich.) Coll., 1905; A.M., U. Mich., 1908, Ph.D., 1910; m. Lawrence Bunting Sims of Newport News, Va., Aug. 30, 1921; children-Margaret W. (dec.), Lawrence Sims. Instr. chemistry, Simpson Coll., 1905-07, same, U. Mich., 1910-16, asst. prof. chemistry, 1916-18, asso. prof., 1918-24, prof. 1924-53, emeritus, 1953-. Served as capt. nitrate div. Ordnance Dept. U.S. Army, 1917-18; cons. War Dept., 1938-43; gen. cons. OSRD, 1943-45. Fellow A.A.A.S.; mem. Am. Chem. Soc., Delta Tau Delta, Phi Beta Kappa, Sigma Xi, Phi Kappa Phi, Phi Lambda Upsilon, Gamma Alpha, Alpha Chi Sigma. Conglist. Contbr. to sci. jours. Home: 1919 Scottwood Av., Ann Arbor, Mich. Died Mar. 5, 1961; buried Concord, Mich.

BARTH, CHARLES H., JR. Army officer; born Kan., Oct. 1, 1903; B.S., U.S. Mil. Acad., 1925; grad. Civil Enginring. Cornell U., 1927; commd. 2d lt. Corps of Engrs., 1925, and advanced to brig. gen., 1943; served as chief of staff to comdg. gen. U.S. Forces in Iceland, 1943; killed in airplane crash, Iceland, May 3, 1943.

BARTH, GEORGE BITTMAN, army officer; b. Leavenworth, Kan., Dec. 19, 1897; s. Charles H. and Harriet (Bittmann) B.; B.S., U.S. Mil. Acad., 1918; grad. F.A. Sch., Ft. Sill, Okla., 1926, Command and Gen. Staff Sch., 1936; m. Mary S., June 21, 1935. Commd. 2d lt. U.S. Army, 1918, advanced through grades to maj. gen., Mar. 16, 1953; served with inf., also F.A., assigned R.O.T.C. duty, Auburn, Ala.; instr. arty. N.Y.N.G., 27th Div.; chief staff 9th Inf. Div., North Africa, Sicily, Normandy landing; regtl. comdr. 357th Inf., 90th Inf. Div., Normandy; with Gen. Patton's Third Army in breakthrough across France, 1944; prof. mil. sci. N.Y. Mil. Acad., 1946; dir. operations, tng. dept. Command and Gen. Staff Coll., Ft. Leavenworth, Kan., 1948, chief staff, 1949; arty. comdr. 25th. Inf. Div., Japan, 1949-50; assigned 24th Inf. Div., Korea, 1950, 25th Inf. Div., 1950-51; asst. div. comdr. 5th Inf. Div., Indiantown Gap, 1951; comdg. 5th Inf. Div., 1952-53; chief C.I.C., Sept.-Oct. 1953; chief Joint U.S. Mil. Aid Group, Greece, 1953-55; dep. comdg. gen. 1st Army, 1955-57. Decorated D.S.C., Silver star with 2 oak leaf clusters, Legion of Merit with 2 clusters, Bronze Star with cluster, Air Medal, Purple Heart. Mem. Alpha Tau Omega. Club: Rotary. Home: Leavenworth KS Died Aug. 1969.

BARTH, THEODORE H. inventor; b. New York, N.Y., Nov. 13, 1891; s. Ignatius and Johanna (Wollner) B.; unmarried. Co-inventor U.S. Norden bombsight, 1923; co-inventor U.S. Navy catapult and arresting gear for launching and landing aircraft on the U.S.S. Saratoga and U.S.S. Lexington, 1928. Address: Carl L. Norden Inc., 141 Broadway, N.Y.C. Died June 19, 1967.

BARTHOLF, JOHN CHARLES PALMER, army officer; b. Plattsburg, N.Y., Oct. 26, 1891; s. John Henry and Isabella (Palmer) B.; student Phillips Exeter Acad., 1908-09, A.B., Harvard, 1913; m. Madeline Edith Tomlinson, Jan. 15, 1918; children—Edith Isabelle (Mrs. Charles Robert Clark), Anne Palmer Rawlings, John Copeland (brig. gen. USAF). Commd. 2d lt. inf., 1913, and advanced through grades to brig. gen., 1943; Aviation Section Signal Corps, 1916; junior military aviator, 1916; engaged primarily in training and test pilot duties during World War I. Club: Army-Navy (Washington, D.C.). Home: Great Barrington MA Died Sept. 22, 1969; buried Arlington Nat. Cemetery, Arlington VA

BARTHOLOMEW, TRACY research engr.; b. Austin, Tex., Nov. 14, 1884; s. George Wells and Hettie Julia (Cole) B.; student Ohio State U., 1902-03; E.M., Colo. Sch. of Mines, 1906; m. Sarah Jane Anderson, Oct. 6, 1921; children—George Anderson, Jane Anderson. Construction engr. Federal Lead Co., Flat River, Mo., 1906-07; designing and test engr. Nev. Consol. Copper Co., McGill, Nev., 1907-09; gen. mgr. Alkali-Proof Cement Div. of Colo. Portland (now Ideal) Cement So., Denver, Colo., 1909-11; mgr. Rico Tropical Fruit Co., Garrochales, P.R., 1911-21, pres. since 1921; sr. fellow Mellon Inst. of Industrial Research, Pittsburgh, 1921-39; mgr. of research Duquesne Siag Products Co., 1929-40; cons. engr. since 1940. Served as captain 374th Inf., United States Army, 1918-19. Mem. A.A.A.S., American Institute Mining and Metallurgical Engineers, American Society Civil Engineers. Am. Chem. Soc., Am. Ceramic Soc., Am. Soc. Municipal Engrs., Am. Sox. Testing Materials, Am. Concrete Inst., Engrs. Soc. of Western Pa., Beta Theta Pi, Phi Lambda Upsilon. Republican. Presbyterian. Mason (K.T., Shriner). Clubs: Faculty (U. Pittsburgh); Longue Vue. Home: 1545 Beechwood Blvd., Pitts. 17. Died Dec. 7, 1951.

BARTLETT, BOYD WHEELER educator, army officer; b. Castine, Me., June 20, 1897; s. Boyd and Louise (Wheeler) B.; A.B., Bowdoin Coll., 1917, Sc. D. (hon.), 1949; B.S., U.S. Mil. Acad., 1919, Mass. Inst. Tech., 1921; A.M., Columbia, 1926, Ph.D., 1932; grad. study U. Munich, 1934-35; m. Helen A. Allen, July 3, 1920. Served at 1st lt. C.E., U.S. Army, 1919-22; physicist Bell Telephone Labs., N.Y.C., 1922-27; asst. prof. physics Bowdoin Coll., 1927-29, asso. prof., 1929-31, prof., 1931-42, coordinator civilian pilot tng., 1940-42; maj. advancing to col. AUS, 1942-44, asst. prof., acting prof. physics U.S. Mil. Acad., now brig. gen. U.S. Army ret.; prof., head dept. electricity, mem. acad. bd., 1945-61. Bid overseers Bowdoin Coll., 1952-61, trustee, 1961-. Trustee Assn. Grads., U.S., Mil. Acad., chmn. athletic bd. U.S. Mil. Acad. Decorated Legion of Merit with oak leaf cluster. Fellow A.A.A.S.; mem. Am. Soc. Engring. Edn. Am. Phys. Soc., Am. Assn. Physics Tchrs., Phi Beta Kappa, Delta Kappa Epsilon. Unitarian. Contbr. sci. jours. Address: Castine, Me. Died June 24, 1965; buried Castine.

BARTLETT, CHARLES WARD commodore U.S.N.; b. Worcester, Mass., Aug. 11, 1850; s. Theodore H. and Elizabeth W. B.; grad. U.S. Naval Acad., 1871; m. Henrietta F. Williams, Nov. 25, 1879. Promoted ensign, June 14, 1872; master, Mar. 17, 1875; lt., Nov. 4, 1882; lt. comdr., Mar. 3, 1899; comdr., Oct. 9, 1901; capt., June 29, 1906; commodore and retired, June 30, 1908. Astron, work for latitude and longitude in the W.I.; surveying coast of Lower Cal., comd. Piscataqua in cruise to China, U.S.S. Isle de Cuba and Petrel on Asiatic sta., U.S.S. Florida in U.S. Coast Squadron; asst. to chief Bur. of Ordnance; comd. U.S.S. Ohio in cruise of Atlantic Fleet to San Francisco. Home: Worcester, Mass. Died 1910.

BARTLETT, FRANK W. author, naval officer; b. Boston, Aug. 15, 1856; s. James W. and Achsah (Ballou) B.; grad. U.S. Naval Acad., 1878; m. Hattie Owen, of Detroit, Jan. 3, 1883; children—Owen, Marjorie, Bradford. Apptd. asst. engr., June 20, 1880; passed asst. engr., June 19, 1890; chief engr., Sept. 19, 1898; rank changed to lt., Mar. 3, 1899; promoted lt.-comd., Apr. 14, 1901; comdr., May 6, 1906; capt., Mar. 17, 1910; served on Indiana, 1901-02, Maine, 1902-03, Chicago, as fleet engr., 1904-06; retired Aug. 15, 1920. Author : Mechanical Drawing, 1901; Engineering Descriptive Geometry, 1910; Engineering Descriptive Geometry and Drawing, 1917, prize article, Jour. Am. Soc. of Naval Engrs., for 1902, subject, "Repair Ships." Home: Annapolis. Md. Address: Navy Dept., Washington, D.C.

BARTLETT, FREDERIC HUNTINGTON physician; b. Fayetteville, N.Y., July 3, 1872; s. Delancey and Almeria (Farnham) B.; A.B., Harvard, 1895; A.M., Columbia, 1899, M.D., 1905; m. Eleanor Pearson, June 1902; children—Phyllis Brooks (Mrs. John Pollard), Frederic Pearson; m. 2d, Isabelle Reid Woolley, Sept. 11, 1923. Teacher of English, Pomfret (Conn.) Sch., 1985-97, Belmont Sch., 1899-1900, Stanford U., 1900-01; engaged in practice of medicine since 1907; associated with Dr. L. Emmett Holt, 1907-11; attending physician, Babies Hosp., New York, N.Y., 1909-23; chief of pediatrics, Fifth Av. Hosp., 1923-34, attending physician Babies Hosp., since 1934. Served as major, Med. Corps, U.S. Army, 1917-19; medical chief, base hospital, Camp Jackson, S.C. Mem. Am. Pediatric Soc., N.Y. Acad. of Medicine, Am. Med. Assn., N.Y. State and County med. socs. Clubs: Harvard, Century Association (New York). Author: Treatment of Internal Diseases (translation of Nicholas Ortner), 1908; Infants and Children: Their Care and Feeding, 1933. Home: 26 Jones St. Office: 115 E. 82d St., New York, N.Y. Died Oct. 19, 1948.

BARTLETT, GEORGE TRUE army officer; b. N.H., Apr. 29, 1856; s. Thomas and Elizabeth W. (Titcomb) B.; student U. of Kans.; B.S., U.S. Mil. Acad., 1881; grad. Arty. Sch., 1890; m. Cornelia Terrell, Sept. 18, 1884 (died Feb. 14, 1888); children—Charles Terrell, Geoffrey; m. 2d. Helen Walton, Nov. 28, 1893 (died Dec. 26, 1940). Commd. 2d. lt. 3d Arty., June 11, 1881, advanced through grades to maj. gen., 1917; 1st lt., Dec. 10, 1889; maj. commissary of subsistence, vols., June 3, 1898; hon. discharged vols., June 13, 1899; capt. arty., Mar. 2, 1899; maj. Arty. Corps, Mar. 26, 1906; lt. col. Coast Arty. Corps. Dec. 4, 1909; col., Dec. 5, 1911; brig. gen., May 15, 1917; maj. gen. N.A., Aug. 5, 1917; Prof. mil. science and tactics, Pa. Mil. Coll., 1885-88, and Agrl. and Mech. Coll., Tex., 1894-98; chief commissary, Dept. of Santiago, Cuba, 1898; adj. Arty. Sch., Ft. Monroe, Va., 1903-06; mem. bd. to revise drill regulations for Coast Arty., 1902-06; mem. Gen. Staff Corps, Dec. 10, 1909-Dec. 20, 1911, and July 10, 1916-June 22, 1917; hon. discharged from N.A. Mar. 26, 1918; retired at his own request after more than 40 years service, Sept. 25, 1918. Served in World War as comdr. brigade Railroad Arty., A.E.F., July 12-Sept. 8, 1917; comdr. Base Sect., No. 3, A.E.F., in France, Oct. 7, 1917- Mar. 22, 1918. Mem. Interallied Mil. Commn., in Greece, Apr. 21, 1917-Nov. 8, 1918; mil attache at Athens, Mar. 22-Oct. 21, 1918; retired 1918. Republican. Episcopalian. Home: Terrell Road, San Antonio, Tex. Died March 11, 1949.

BARTLETT, JOHN HENRY; b. Sunapee, N.H., March 15, 1869; s. John Z. and Sophronia A. (Sargent) B.; A.B., Dartmouth, 1894, A.M., 1920; LL.D., U. N.H., 1920; m. Agnes Page, June 1, 1900; 1 son, Calvin Page. Teacher in grammar schs. and high sch., Portsmouth, 4 yrs.; admitted to N.H. bar, 1898; practiced at Portsmouth since 1898; now mem. law firm Bartlett and Mitchell; postmaster, Portsmouth, 1899-1908; mem. staff of Gov. John McLane, 1905-06, rank of col.; elected gov. of N.H., 1918, term 1919-21; pres. Civil Service Commn., Washington, D.C., 1921-22; 1st asst. p.m. gen., Mar. 1922-May 1929; chmn. U.S. Sect. Internat. Joint Commission, U.S. and Can., 1929-39; pres. Portsmouth Trust & Guarantee Co., 1920-40. Pres. N.H. Soc. for Prevention of Cruelty to Children and Animals. Club: National Press. Author: Spice for Speeches, 1926; Folks is Folks, 1927; Legend of Ann Smith, 1931; The Bonus March and the New Deal, 1937: A Synoptic History of the Granite State. Home: Portsmouth, N.H. Died Mar. 19, 1952.

BARTLETT, JOHN RUSSELL state ofcl., bibliographer; b. Providence, R.I., Oct. 23, 1805; s. Smith and Nancy (Russell) B.; m. Eliza Ann Rhodes, May 15, 1831; m. 2d, Ellen Eddy, Nov. 12, 1863; children. Mem. Franklin Soc.; mem. R.I. Hist. Soc., 1831; corr. sec. N.Y. Hist. Soc.; apptd. by Pres. Taylor U.S. commr. to establish boundary between U.S. and Mexico, 1850; explored extensively in Tex., N.M., Cal., also Chihuaha and Sonora (Mexico); sec. of state R.I., 1855-72; founder (with Albert Gallatin) Am. Ethnol. Soc. Author: Records of the Colony of Rhode Island, 1636-1792, 10 vols.; The Process of Ethnology, 1847; Dictionary of Americanisms, 1848; Naval History of Rhode Island, 1880; John Carter Brown Catalogue (bibliography of early Americana), 1882. Died Providence, May 28, 1886.

BARTLETT, JOHN RUSSELL rear adm. (retired, 1897); b. New York, Sept. 26, 1843; s. John R. and Eliza A. (Rhodes) B.; ed. Cambridge, Mass., and U.S. Naval Acad. (Sc.D., Brown, 1898); m. Jeanie R. Jenckes, Feb. 6, 1872. Ordered into service May, 1861; served during Civil war at passage of Fts. Jackson and St. Philip and capture of New Orleans; on Admiral Dahlgren's staff off Charleston, 1863-64; comd. co. in naval attack on Ft. Fisher; investigated Gulf Stream, 1877-82, in commd U.S. Coast Survey Str. Blake; in charge hydrographic office, 1882-88; last command Monitor Puritan. During war with Spain, 1898, in charge of naval intelligence office, and was supt. U.S. Coast Signal Service and chief U.S. Auxilliary Naval Force. Home: Lonsdale, R.I. Died 1904.

BARTLETT, JOSIAH gov. N.H.; b. Amesbury, Mass., Nov. 21, 1729; s. Stephen and Hannah (Webster) B.; studied medicine privately, 1745-50; M.D. (hon.), Dartmouth, 1790; m. Mary Bartlett, Jan. 15, 1754, 12 children. Began practice medicine, Kingston, N.H., 1750; mem. N.H. Provincial Assembly from Kingston, 1765-75; justice of peace, Kingston, 1767; col., regt. N.H. Militia, 1767; del. to Continental Congress, 1775, 76, 70; signer Declaration of Independence, 1776, Articles of Confedn., 1779; chief justice N.H. Ct. Common Pleas, 1779-82; asso. justice N. H. Superior Ct., 1784-88, chief justice, 1788-89; mem. Constl. Conv., Phila., 1787; res. State of N.H., 1790-93; secured charter for N.H. Med. Soc., 1791, 1st pres.; 1st gov. N.H., 1793-94. Died Kingston, May 19, 1795; buried Kingston.

BARTLETT, ROBERT ABRAM explorer; b. Brigus, Newfoundland, Aug. 15, 1875; s. William James and Mary J. (Leamon) B.; ed. Brigus High Sch., and Meth. Coll., St. Johns, Newfoundland. passed exam. for Master of British Ships, Halifax, N.S., 1905; hon. A.M., Bowdoin Coll., 1920; unmarried. Began explorations wintering with R.E. Peary, at Cape D'Urville, Kane Basin, 1897-98; on a hunting expdn., Hudson Strait and Bay, 1901; capt. of a sealer off Newfoundland coast, 1901-05; comd. the Roosevelt, 1905-09, taking active part in Peary's expdn. to the pole, reaching 88th parallel; comd. ship on pvt. hunting expdn. to Kane Basin, 1910; with Can. Govt., Arctic Expedition, 1913-14, as captain of the C.G.S. Karluk, which was crushed by ice, Jan. 1914; with 17 persons reached Wrangel Island; leaving 15 persons on island; with one Eskimo crossed ice to Siberia and returned with rescuing party, reaching Wrangel Island in Sept. 1914, and Sept. 12, 1915, reached Nome, Alaska, with 13 survivors. Comdr. 3d Crocker Land Relief Expdn. to N. Greenland, returning with party, 1917; marine supt. Army Transport Service, New York, since Oct. 1917. Was sent 1925, by Nat. Geog. Soc. to locate bases for aircraft, N.W. Alaska, and shores Arctic Ocean, also recording times and currents and dredging for flora and fauna. Expdn. to North Greenland and Ellesmere Lane, 1926, to Fox Basin and West Shores Baffin Land, 1927, to Siberia, 1928, to Labrador, summer 1929, head of expdn. to N.E. coast of Greenland for Mus. of Am. Indian and Mus. of Natural History of Phila., 1930, expdn. to Greenland for Am. Mus. Natural History, Bot. Gardens of N.Y. City and Smithsonian Instn. (Washington), 1931, to N.W. Greenland (erecting monument in memory of miral R. E. Peary), 1932, to Baffin Land, 1933, to N.W. Greenland, Ellesmere and Baffin Lands, under auspices of Acad. of Natural Sciences of Phila., 1934, to N.W. Greenland under auspices of Field Scientific research in Eastern Arctic, 1936-41; in government service, Hudson Bay, Baffin Land and Greenland (on own schooner Morrissey), 1942-44. Awarded Hubbard gold medal, National Geographic Society, 1909; Hudson-Fulton silver medal, 1909; silver medal, English Geog. Soc., 1910; Kane medal, Phila. Geog. Soc., 1910; silver medal, Italian Geog. Soc., 1910; gold medal, Harvard Travelers Club, 1915; awarded the Back Grant, Royal Geog. Soc., 1918, "in recognition of splendid leadership after the Karluk was lost"; gold medal Am. Geog. Soc. Hon. mem. "Society of Dorset Men in London," England, Boy Scouts of America; life mem. Am. Mus. Natural History; mem. Marine Soc. (New York), Am. Geophys. Union, Am. Legion, Vets. Fgn. Wars, New York Garrison 194, Army and Navy Union of U.S.A.; corr. mem. N.R.F., 1920. Mason. Clubs: City, Travelers' (Boston); Ends of the Earth, Explorers', Travel, Aero of America, Cruising of America, Coffee House (New York); Wilderness, Boone and Crockett. Author: Last Voyage of the Karluk, 1916; The Log of Bob Bartlett, 1928; Sails over Ice, 1934. Home: Brigus, Newfoundland. Address: Explorers' Club, 10 W. 72d St., New York, N.Y. Died Apr. 28, 1946.

BARTLEY, MORDECIA gov. Ohio, congressman; b. Fayette County, Pa., Dec. 16, 1783; s. Elijah and Rachel (Pearshall) B.; m. Miss Welles, 1804. Adj. with rank of capt. under Gen. Harrison in Northwest during War of 1812; mem. Ohio Senate, 1817; register Ohio Land Office, 1818-23; mem. U.S. Ho. of Reps. from Ohio, 18th-21st congresses, 1823-31; gov. Ohio, 1844-46. Died Mansfield, O., Oct. 10, 1870; buried Mansfield Cemetery.

BARTOL, JOHN WASHBURN, physician; b. Lancaster, Mass., Jan. 10, 1864; s. George Murillo and Elizabeth (Washburn) B.; grad. Phillips Exeter Acad., Exeter, N.Y., 1883; A.B., Harvard, 1887, M.D., 1891; m. Charlotte H. Cabot, Oct. 2, 1900; children—Janet, Dorothy, Ann, Priscilla, George M., Louis C. Began practice at Boston, 1893; asst. in clin. medicine, Harvard Med. Sch., 1905-10. Mem. Mass. State Bd. of Health, 1902-07. Served as lt., advancing to maj., Med. Corps, U.S. Army, 1917-19. Pres. Boston Med. Library, 1927-33; mem. corp. Simmons Coll., Boston, 1906-39. Mem. Am. Med. Assn., Mass. Med. Soc. (pres. 1921-23). Unitarian. Home: 1 Chestnut St., Boston MA

BARTON, JOHN KENNEDY rear adm.; b. Phila., Pa., Apr. 7, 1853; s. Joseph and Margaret B.; grad. U.S. Naval Acad., 1873; m. Mildred S. Scott, 1898. Apptd. cadet engr., Oct. 1, 1871; promoted through grades to capt., July 8, 1907; engr. in chief, rank of rear adm., and retired by reason of physical disability incurred in line of duty, Dec. 22, 1908. Served on Richmond, Spanish-Am. War, 1898; at U.S. Naval Acad., 1902-07; head Dept. Steam Engring., Navy Yard, League Island, Pa., 1907-08; engr. in chief and chief Bur. Steam Engring., Navy Dept., Washington, D.C., 1908; mem. Navy Examining Bd., Washington, 1909-10. Episcopalian. Home: Philadelphia, Pa. Died Dec. 23, 1921.

BARTON, WILLIAM army officer; b. Warren, R.I., May 26, 1748; s. Benjamin and Lydia B.; m. Rhoda Carver, 1770. Hatter in R.I., 1770; became R.I. Militia capt., 1775, maj., 1776, lt. col., 1777; conceived and executed capture of Brig. Gen. Prescott by R. I. Militia, 1777, during occupation of R.I. by Brit., received sword from Congress in recognition of exploit; mem. R.I. Conv. to ratify U.S. Constn., 1790. Died Providence, R.I., Oct. 22, 1831; buried Providence.

BARTON, WILLIAM PAUL CRILLON naval surgeon, botanist; b. Phila., Nov. 17, 1786; s. William and Elizabeth (Rhea) B.; grad. Princeton, 1805; studied medicine under uncle B.S. Barton, 1805-08; m. Esther Sergeant, Sept. 1814. Apptd. surgeon USN, 1809, served in hosps. in Phila., Norfolk, Pensacola; prof. botany U. Pa. (though still on Navy active list), 1815-18; charges brought by fellow Navy surgeons that he had criticized marine hosps. unjustifiably were dismissed, 1818; prof. medicine Jefferson Med. Sch., circa 1825; 1st chief Bur. Medicine and Surgery, USN, 1842-44; as mem. inactive Navy list served as pres. Bd. Med. Examiners 1852. Author: Vegetable Materia Medica of United States, 1817-19 (description medicinal plants). Died Phila., Feb. 29, 1856; buried Phila.

BARTOW, EDWARD chemist; b. Glenham, New York, January 12, 1870; s. Charles Edward and Sarah Jane (Scofield) B.; B.A., Williams Coll, 1892; Ph.D., U. Gottingen, 1895, Golden diploma, 1956; D.Sc., Williams Coll., 1923; m. Alice Abbott, Sept. 3, 1895 (dec. May 15, 1951); 1 dau., Virginia. Assistant in chemistry, 1892-94, instructor, 1895-97, Williams Coll.; instr. in chemistry, 1897-99, asso. prof., 1899-1905; U. of Kan.; asso. prof., 1905-06, prof. sanitary chemistry, 1906-20, U. of Ill. Dir. State Water Survey, 1905-17; chief Water Survey Div., Dept. Registration and Education, Illinois 1917-20; prof. and head dept. of chemistry and chem. engring., State Univ. of Ia., 1920-40, prof. emeritus, since 1940; research consultant, Johns-Manville Corp., 1940-41. Del. 9th Internat. Congress Chemistry, Madrid, 1934, 10th, Rome, 1938; mem. council Internat. chem. Union, 1922-25, 27-30, 33-38, v.p. for U.S.A., 1934-38. Sec. Lake Mich. Water Commn., 1908; Commn. on Standards of Water for Interstate Carriers, 1913, 22; sec.-treas. Ill. Water Supply Association, 1909-17. Served from maj. to lt. col., san. corps, U.S. Army, A.E.F., 1917-19. Awarded

Medaille d'Honneur, des Epidemies, d'Argent (France). Mem. of American Chemical Society (dir. 1933, pres. 1936), A.A.A.S., Societe Chim. Industrielle (France), Soc. Chem. Industry (Great Britain), Am. Water Works Assn. (trustee, 1913, v.p., 1921, pres., 1922), Am. Inst. Chem. Engrs. (dir. 1923-25, 1936-39), Am. Soc. Civil Engrs. (life mem. 1946), Am. Assn. U. Profs., Franklin Inst., Am. Pub. Health Assn., Kan. Acad. Sci. (pres. 1904), Am. Soc. Testing Materials, American Soc. for Engineering Education, Am. Public Works Assn., Nat. Security League, Mil. Order World War, Nat. Inst. Social Science, Acad. Polit Science, Am. Veterans Assn., Am. Legion, Illinois Acad. Science, Iowa Engrig. Society, Ia. Acad. Science (vice-president, 1933, president, 1934), Am. Inst. Chemists, American Philatelic Society, Society Philatelic Americans, Spanish Academy Science (corresponding mem.), Trans-Miss. Stamp Soc., Phi Beta Kappa, Sigma Xi, Alpha Chi Sigma, Tau Beta Pi, Theta Delta Chi, Phi Lambda Upsilon. Conglist. Clubs: University, Chaos (Chgo.); Chemists (NYC, Chg.). Author 14 vols. report on Ill. waters; also papers relating to field. Asst. editor Chem. Abstracts, 1911—. Home: 304 Brown St. Office: Chemical Bldg., Iowa City, Ia. Died Apr. 12, 1958; buried Fishkill, N.Y.

BARZYNSKI, JOSEPH E., army officer; b. St. Paul, Neb., Mar. 13, 1884; s. John and Virginia (Wilkosheski) B.; B.S., U.S. Mil. Acad., 1905; student Ecole de l'Intendence, Paris, 1924-26, Command and Gen. Staff Sch., 1931-33; m. Theresa M. New. Sept. 23, 1908; children—Joseph E. (col. A.C., U.S. Army), Eunice (2d lt. W.A.C., U.S. Army). Commissioned 2d lieutenant Inf., U.S. Army, 1905, and advanced through the grades to brig. gen., 1940; with Inf., Wyo., 1905-12, Philippine Islands, 1912-15; Mexican Punitive Expdn., 1916-17; Q.M., 86th Div., Camp Grant, and sailed with the 86th Div. to France; Q.M., 32d Div., France and Germany, 1918-19; duty with U.S. Liquidation Commn., Paris, 1919; Am. Legation, Warsaw, Poland, 1920; mem. War Dept. Gen. Staff. Washington, D.C., 1927-31; chief of motor transportation, 1940-41; comdg. gen. Chicago Q.M. Depot Oct. 1941-72. Received Mexican Punitive and World War I service decorations. Mem. Soc. Automotive Engrs. Clubs: Army and Navy, Army and Navy Country (Washington, D.C.); South Shore Country, Union League, Tavern (Chicago). Address: Chicago IL Died Aug. 1972; buried Arlington Nat. Cemetery.

BASDEVANT, PIERRE JULES French diplomat; b. Grenoble, Isère, France, Mar. 22, 1914; s. Jules and Renee (Mallarmé) B.; student Faculté de Droit de Paris, Ecole Libre des Sciences Politiques; diplomas in pub. law, economics, polit. sci.; m. Huguette Mallet, Oct. 20, 1949; children-Patrick, Francois, Isabelle, Valerie. Consul, Bratislava, 1945-46; attache, then sec. French embassy, Washington, 1946, 53; service in French Fgn. Ministry (defense problems), 1953-56; sr. polit. adviser NATO Internat. Staff, 1957-61; consul gen., San Francisco, 1961—. Served to capt. French Army, 1935-37, 39-42, 45. Decorated Knight Legion of Honor. Home: 2010 Broadway. Office: 740 Taylor St., San Francisco. Died Jan. 6, 1968.

BASH, LOUIS HERMANN army officer; b. Chicago, Ill., Mar. 7, 1872; s. Daniel N. and Virginia (Ballance) B.; prep. edn., Lake Forest (Ill.) Acad.; grad. U.S. Mil. Acad., 1895, Army Sch. of Line, Ft. Leavenworth, Kan., 1920; m. Bertha Runkie, October 26, 1940 (deceased January 4, 1958). Commissioned 2d lieutenant inf., U.S. Army, June 12, 1895, and advanced through grades to col., July 1, 1920; brig. gen., Sept. 19, 1929. Served in Cuba, Spanish-Am. War, participating in assault on San Juan Hill and siege of Santiago; served in P.I., Filipino Insurrection; aide de camp to Gen. Loyd Wheaton, 1900-02; service in field, Cavite Province, Jan.-July 1905; chief commissary, Dept. Mindanao, Apr. 1906-Sept. 1907; chief commissary, Dept. Tex., 1907-09; maj., inf., Mexican border and Mexican punitive expdn., 1916-17; served as adj. gen., Service of Supply, France, Feb. 1918-July 1919; transferred to Q.M.C., 1920; asst. to q.m., 4th Corps Area, 1920-21; gen. supt. army transport service, San Francisco, 1924-28; asst. to q.m. gen., chief of constrn. service, 1929-34; apptd. q.m. gen., with rank of maj. gen., 1934; retired from active service account of disability, Mar. 31, 1936. D.S.M.; silver star citation "for gallantry in action" at Battle of Santiago de Cuba; decorated Officer Legion of Honor (France). Home: Palo Alto, Cal. Died May 24, 1952; buried Presidio of San Francisco.

BASS, EDGAR WALES col. U.S.A.; b. Prairie du Chien, Wis., Oct. 30, 1843; s. Jacob Wales and Martha Darrah (Brunson) B.; pvt. and q.m. sergt. 8th Minn. Inf., Aug. 13, 1862-June 30, 1864; grad. West Point, 1868; studied Post-Grad. Sch. for Mil. Engrs., Willets Point, N.Y.; m. Adele Smith, June 26, 1879. Bvt. 2d lt. U.S. Engrs., June 15, 1868; 2d lt., Feb. 15, 1869; 1st lt., Feb. 14, 1871; prof. mathematics, West Point, Apr. 17, 1878; col. U.S.A.; retired at own request, after 36 yrs. service, Oct. 7, 1898. Asst. astronomer, U.S. Transit of Venus Expdn. to New Zealand, 1874-75; U.S. Expdn. Eclipse of Sun, Colo., 1878. Author: Introduction to the Differential Calculus, 1888; Elements of Trigonometry (Ludlow's). 1888: Elements of Differential Calculus, 1896-1905. Home: Bar Harbor, Me. Died Nov. 6, 1918.

BASS, IVAN ERNEST naval officer; b. Carley, Miss., July 29, 1877; s. Isaac E. and Mary Eliza (Wilkes) B.; grad. U.S. Naval Acad., 1901; m. Florence Victoria Bouche, Nov. 26, 1915. Commd. ensign, 1903, advanced through grades to rear adm., 1934; engr. officer Navy Yard, Boston, 1917-20, Navy Yard, N.Y., 1920-23; asst. to chief Bur. Engring., 1929-31; fleet engr. U.S. Asiatic Fleet, 1931-34; naval insp. machinery Newport News Ship Building & Dry Dock Co. (Va), 1934-39; gen. insp. machinery Bur. Engring., sr. mem. Compensation Bd., U.S. Navy Dept., 1939-41; ret., 1941; mem. compensation bd., Navy Dept., 1942-44; sr. mem. Contract Settlement Rev. Bd., Bur. Ships, Navy Dept., 1944-47; returned to inactive duty 1947. Mem. U.S. Naval Inst. Awarded medals Spanish-Am. War, Philippine Campaign, World War I, Yangtze Patrol, Am. Def., World War II; spl. commendation from Navy Dept. for service during World War I. Mem. Nat., Miss. geneal. socs., Inst. Am. Geneaology. Clubs: Army and Navy Country (Washington); New York Yacht. Author: History of Esau Bass (Rev. Soldier), Hos Brother Jonathan, and Their Descendants, 1955; Thomas Wilkes (circa 1735-1809) and His Descendants, 1965. Address: 3601 Connecticut Av., Washington 20008. Died 1967.

BASSETT, CHARLES A. II astronaut; b. Dayton O., Dec. 30, 1931; s. Charles A. and Belle (James) B.; student Ohio State U., 1950-52; B.S. in Elec. Engring. with high honors, Tex. Tech. Coll., 1960; postgrad. U. So. Cal.; m. Jean Marion Martin; children-Karen Elizabeth, Peter Martin. Commd. 2d lt. USAF, 1952, advanced through grades to capt.; formerly exptl. test pilot, engring. test pilot Fighter Projects Office, Edwards AFB, Cal.; now astronaut with Manned Spacecraft Center, NASA. Mem. Am. Inst. Aeros. and Astronautics, Phi Kappa Tau. Home: 6848 Lindbergh St., Edwards, Cal. Died Feb. 1966.

BASSETT, JOHN publisher; b. Omagh, County Tyrone, Northern Ireland, Feb. 7, 1886; s. Edward and Elizabeth (Tough) B.; student National Sch. and Christian Bros. Sch. of Omagh; Royal U. of Ireland; D.C.L. (hon.), Bishop's U., Lennoxville, Quebec, 1939; LL.D., U. New Brunswick, 1947, McGill University, Montreal, Canada, 1955; married Marion Wright Avery, Sept. 21, 1914; children—Elizabeth (Mrs. Baldwin Smith), John. Parliamentary corr. Montreal Gazette, Ottawa, 1911-26 (pres. Parliamentary Press Gallery, 1925-26), dir. Gazette Printing Co., Ltd., Montreal, 1913-20, v.p. and dir., 1920-37, president and managing director, 1937-56, chairman of the board, 1956—; president and publisher Sherbrooke Daily Record, 1936—; chancellor Bishop's U., Lennoxville, Que., 1950—. Staff ofcr. to Lt. Gen. Hon. Sir Sam Hughes in Can., England, Belgium and France, 1914-16. Decorated by Belgian Govt. with Order de Reconnaissance, 1918. Can. del. to Third Imperial Press Conf., Australia, 1926. Clubs: Mt. Royal, St. Jame's (Montreal); Rideau (Ottawa); St. George's (Sherbrooke, P.Q.). Home: 1227 Sherbrooke St., W., Montreal; also Bondville, P.Q., Can. Office: 1000 St. Antoine St., Montreal, P.Q. Died Feb. 12, 1958; buried Knowlton (Que.) Cemetery.

BASTEDO, PAUL HENRY naval officer (ret.); b. Buffalo, Feb. 25, 1887; s. Walter Stanley and Catherine Ann (Henry) B.; B.S., U.S. Naval Acad., 1908; m. Helen Prindeville Griffin, May 4, 1920; stepchildren—Rosemary (wife of Capt. John F. Greenslade), Thomas Francis Griffin, Richard Bulen. Commd. ensign USN, 1910, advanced through grades to capt., 1936; staff officer to comdr. U.S. Naval Forces, European waters, World War I, acting chief of staff to comdr., Europe, World War II; naval attache, London, Eng., 1943; ret. with rank of rear adm., 1944 and continued on active duty until 1946. Trustee and treas. Naval Hist. Found. Decorated D.S.M., Cuban Pacification, Mexican, World War I, German occupation, Am. Defense, Eruopean Theatre medals; Valore medal silver and Fatiche di Guerra medal (Italy); Order of Leopold II (Belgium); Comdr. Order of the So. Cross (Brazil). Presbyn. Clubs: Alibi, Chevy Chase, Metropolitan (Washington); N.Y. Yacht (N.Y.C.). Home: 73 Catherine St., Newport, R.I. Deceased.

BASTER, LIONEL DAVID MACKENZIE broker; b. Pittsburgh Twp., Ont., Can., Aug. 16, 1889; s. John D. and Nora (Wagner) B.; m. Elsie Middlecott, June 3, 1920; children—Robert MacKenzie, Peter Kionel. Pres. Osler, Hammond & Nanton, Ltd., Winnipeg, Can., Calgary & Edmonton Corp., Osler & Nanton Trust Co., Anglo-Canadian Oil Co., Ltd., Calgary. Home Oil Co., Central Manitoba Mines, Ltd., Manitoba Bridge & Iron Iron Works, Ltd., Manitoba Rolling Mill Co., Ltd., Winnipeg, Dominion Bank, Toronto, Guarantee Co. of N.A., Montreal. Served with 1st Canadian Div., 1914-18; advanced to lt. col. Decorated Order of Brit. Empire. Mem. Canadian Legion (pres. Dominion Command). Home: 137 Westgate St., Manitoba, Can. Deceased.

BATCHELDER, RICHARD N. brig. gen. (retired, July 27, 1896); b. Lake Village, N. H., July 27, 1832; ed. at Manchester, N.H. Entered volunteer service, 1861; rose through successive ranks until bvtd. brig. gen., March 13, 1865; after war in regular service, and became brig. gen. and q.m., U.S. Army, June 26, 1890. Awarded medal of honor for most distinguished gallantry in action during Civil war. Unmarried. Died 1901.

BATCHELLER, GEORGE SHERMAN judge Internat, Tribunal (mixed courts) of Egypt; b. Batchellerville, Saratoga Co., N.Y., July 25, 1837; s. Sherman Batcheller; fitted for coll. Ft. Edward Inst.; grad. law dept., Harvard, 1857; admitted to bar, 1858; practiced at Saratoga Springs; m. Catherine Phillips, d. Gen. James M. Cook, of Saratoga. Elected to N.Y. legislature at 21 yrs. of age, 1858. Entered army as capt. 115th regt., N.Y. vols., 1862; taken prisoner at Harper's Ferry, 1862; exchanged, and was in Va. campaigns; later at Hilton Head, and in siege of Charleston; deputy provost marshal gen., Dept. of South, 1863; lt. col. vols.; Jan. 1, 1865, and insp. gen. vols. and Nat. Guard of State of N.Y. Specially designated by govt. to accompany body of Pres. Lincoln through State of N.Y. Resumed practice at Saratoga; mem. N.Y. legislature, 1873-74 (chmn. ways and means and mem. judiciary com.); apptd. 1875, by Pres. Grant, judge Internat. Tribunal of Egypt; chosen by colleagues of all the powers presiding justice; resigned, 1885; elected N.Y. legislature, 1886, 1888-89; 1st asst. sec. Treasury U.S., 1889-91; U.S. minister to Portugal, Nov., 1891; diplomatic representative in Europe, headquarters, Paris, 1893-95; mgr. of governmental affairs of various Am. cos., 1895-96; apptd. by Pres. McKinley to preside over deliberations (in French language) Universal Postal Congress, Washington, 1897; at request of Egyptian govt. again apptd. to Internat. Tribunal, Nov. 1898; promoted by President Roosevelt to Supreme Court of Appeal, May, 1902; companion Mil. Order Loyal Legion; grand officer (with insignia) Imperial Order of the Medjidieh; grand cordon (with cross and insignia), Order Crown of Italy (King Humbert, 1897). Died 1908.

BATE, WILLIAM BRIMAGE U.S. senator from Tenn., 1887-1905; b. nr. Castilian Spring, Tenn., Oct. 7, 1826; academic edn.; was steamboat clerk on Mississippi; private in Mexican war in La. and Tenn. regts.; on return, mem. Tenn. legislature; grad. Lebanon Law School, 1852; practiced at Gallatin, Tenn.; atty. gen. Nashville dist., 1854-60; presdl. elector, 1860, on Breckinridge-Lane ticket; private to capt., col., brig. gen. and maj. gen. in C.S.A., 1861-65; thrice dangerously wounded. Practiced law at Nashville after war; del. Nat. Dem. Conv., 1868; mem. Nat. Dem. Exec. Com. 12 yrs.; presdl. elector, 1876; gov. Tenn., 1883-86. Home: Nashville, Tenn. Died 1905.

BATES, ALEXANDER BERRY rear admn.; b. Brooklyn, Nov. 25, 1842; s. John A. and Anna M. (Berry) B.; ed. Milton Acad., Md.; m. Fannie J. Everts. Entered naval service as 3d asst. engr., Jan. 16, 1863; served in navy through to end of Civil War on N. Atlantic Squadron; minor engagements in James River. and Albemarle Sound, N.C., with Confederate ram Albemarle; after end of war sent to European sta. and with Admiral Farragut's fleet until end of 1868; afterward served principally on N. Atlantic and Pacific stas.; in Spanish War with Flying Squadron, and Admiral Sampson's fleet before Santiago, and engagement on July 3, 1898, with Spanish fleet, as chief engr. of U.S. battleship Texas; advanced 3 numbers of grade of chief engr. for action at Santiago; transferred from engr. corps. to the line, with rank of comdr. and promoted to capt.; also received advancement of 3 numbers in grade of comdr. for service at Santiago, Cuba; retired at own request, July, 1903, with rank of rear-admiral. Home: Binghamton, N.Y. Died Feb. 19, 1917.

BATES, ALFRED ELLIOTT paymaster gen. U.S.A.; b. Monroe, Mich., July 15, 1840; s. Alfred G. and B. Ann B.; Canandaigua, N.Y., Acad., 1853-54, 1856-57; grad. U.S. Mil. Acad.; m. Caroline McCorkie, Dec. 1, 1875. Served 2d U.S. cav., June 1865, to March 1875; scouting and frontier work, Dept. Mo. and The Platte, ranging through the northern border, Tex. to Mont.; instr. cav., West Point, Sept. 1869, to June 1873; paymaster, Dept. Tex., 5 yrs.; Dak., 2 yrs.; Washington 4 yrs.; Dak., 4 yrs.; New York, 4 yrs.; San Francisco, 4 yrs.; mil. attache Court of St. James, 1897-99; at Washington as acting paymaster gen., May 1899; made paymaster gen., with rank of brig. gen., July 12, 1899; maj. gen. U.S.A., Jan. 12, 1904; retired Jan. 14, 1904. Died 1909.

BATES, JAMES L., naval architect; b. Mt. Vernon, O., Jan. 18,1880; M.E., Cornell U., 1903; m. Mabel Parmele, Apr. 26, 1904; children-Marian Parmele, Janet Louise, James Lawrence, Gilbert Landon. Began as mold loftsman and asst. shipfitter, St. Clair, Mich., 1903; with N.Y. Navy Yard, 1903-06; with Navy Dept., Washington, 1906-38, dir., tech. and inspection div., Maritime Commn., Washington, 1938-. Chmn., Chesapeake Sect., Soc. Naval Architects and Maine Engrs., 1945-46. Mem. Soc. Naval Architects and Marine Engrs., Naval Engrs., Am. Welding Soc. Presbyn. Home: 23 Bryant St. N.W. Office: U.S. Maritime Commn., Washington, Died Oct. 1962.

BATES, JOHN COALTER lt. gen. U.S.A.; b. St. Charles Co., Mo., Aug. 26, 1842; s. Edward and Julia Davenport (Coalter) B.; ed. Washington U., St. Louis (LL.D., 1904); unmarried. Apptd. from Mo., 1st lt. 11th

U.S. Inf., May 14, 1861; promoted through grades to brig. gen. U.S.V., May 4, 1898, maj. gen., July 8, 1898; hon. disch., Apr. 13, 1899; brig. gen. U.S.V., Apr. 13, 1899; maj. gen., Jan 2, 1900; hon. disch., Feb. 28, 1901; brig. gen. U.S.A., Feb. 2, 1901; maj. gen., July 15, 1902; lt. gen. and chief of staff of the army, Feb. 1, 1906; retired at own request, over 40 yrs'. service, Apr. 14, 1906. Bvtd.; maj. Aug. 1, 1864, "for faithful and meritorious services in the field"; lt. col., Apr. 9, 1865, "for operations resulting in fall of Richmond." Served in Civil War 2 yrs. with regt. and 2 yrs. as a.-d.-c. to comdg. gen. Army of the Potomac; in Spanish-Am. War comd. Bates' Independent Brigade and later 3d Div., 5th Army Corps; comd. dists. of Mindanao and Jolo and 1st Div., 8th Corps, and Dept. of Southern Luzon, P.I., 1899-1901. Home: St. Louis. Died Feb. 4, 1919.

BATES, WALTER IRVING editor, pub.; b. Meadville, Pa., June 15, 1873; s. of Samuel P. (LL.D.) and S. Josephine (Bates) B.; A.B., Allegheny Coll., 1896; studied Sorbonne, Paris, 1896-97; m. Marion Sackett, Feb. 7, 1901; children - Elizabeth (Mrs. Merwin G. Shryock), Edward Irving. Sarah Josephine (Mrs. Donald W. Gapp), Robert S. Admitted to Pa. bar, 1895; was Paris corr. Philadelphia Press; pres. and editor Meadville Tribune-Republican, 1899-; v.p. McCroskey Tool Corp. Recruited company for Spanish-Am. War, 1898, and chosen capt.; maj. 21st Regt. N.G. Pa., Aug. 15, 1898. Rep. presdl. elector, 25th Pa. Dist., 1916, del. to Rep. Nat. Convs., 1928, 32. Pres. Meadville Bd. of Edn.; trustee Pa. State Teachers' College, Edinboro. Baptist. Mason. Home: Meadville, Pa. Died May 5, 1934.

BATES, WILLIAM WALLACE, shipbuilder; b. Nova Scotia, Feb. 15, 1827; s. Stephen and Elizabeth (Wallace) B.; ed. common schs., Calais, Me., beyond that self-educated; also self-educated in naval architecture; m. Marie Cole, Sept. 11, 1856. Began in shipwright trade, 1839; built 1st clipper schooner, "Challenge," at Manitowoc, on the Great Lakes, 1851; editor Nautical Magazine and Naval Journal. New York, 1854-58; capt. in Union Army, 1861-63; in shipbuilding and drydock business, Chicago, 1866-81; dry-dock building, Portland, Ore., 1881-83; mgr. Inland Lloyds. Buffalo. 1885-88; U.S. commr. navigation, Washington, 1889-92; retired. Republican. Author: Rules for Shipbuilding, 1876, 1894; American Marine, 1892; American Navigation, 1902. Home: Denver, Colo. Died Nov., 1912.

BATTEY, ROBERT surgeon; b. Augusta, Ga., Nov. 26, 1828; s. Cephas and Mary (Magruder) B.; attended Phila. Coll. Pharmacy, 1856; M.D., Jefferson Med. Coll., 1857; m. Martha Smith, Dec. 20, 1849, 14 children including Dr. Henry H. Performed successful operation for vesico-vaginal fistula, 1858; served as surgeon 19th Ga. Volunteers, Confederate Army, Civil War, established hosp., Macon, Ga., 1864; editor Atlanta Med. and Surg. Jour., 1872-76; founder Martha Battey Hosp., Rome Ga.; performed Battey's Operation (removal of normal human ovaries to establish menopause), 1872; prof. obstetrics Atlanta (Ga.) Med. Coll., 1873-75; pres. Ga. Med. Assn., 1876; introducted iodized phenol in gynecol. work, 1877; mem. Atlanta Acad. Medicine, Am. Gynecol Soc., A.M.A. Died Rome, Ga., Nov. 8, 1895.

BATTLE, CULLEN ANDREWS lawyer, soldier, journalist; b. Powelton, Ga., June 1, 1829; s. Dr. Cullen and Jane A. B.; preparatory edn. Brownwood Inst., nr. La Grange, Ga., 1846-48; grad. Univ. of Ala.; m. Georgia F. Williams, 1851. Admitted to bar, 1852; practiced law in Ala. until 1860; Breckenridge and Lane elector, 1860, and canvassed Ala. with Hon. William L. Yancey. Entered C. S. army as private; elected maj. 3d Ala. regt., April 1861; lt. col., July 1861; col., June 1862; distinguished in battle; promoted brig. gen. on field at Gettysburg, July 1863; maj. gen., Oct. 1864; wounded 7 times; since the war devoted his time chiefly to journalism. Home: New Bern, N.C. Died 1905.

BATTLEY, JOSEPH F., retired army officer; b. Norfolk, Va., Dec. 19, 1896;2s. Joseph Franklin and Effie Ada (Sadler) B.; student Norfolk (Va.) Academy; M.B.A., Harvard University, 1926; graduate Army Indsl. Coll., 1933, Chem. Warfare Sch., 1938, Army War College, 1946; m. Joyce Russell Zannia. In Federal service with Va. Nat. Guard, 1917; commd. 2d lt., Engrs Reserve Corps, U.S. Army, 1918, and advanced through the ranks to brig. gen., 1944; served with Chem. Warfare Service, France, 1918; exec. officer Chem. Warfare Service Arsenal, Edgewood, Md., 1920-23; with Office of Under Sec. of War, 1932-36, on loan to NRA to serve as div. adminstr., chem. div., 1933-36, later asst. to adminstr. W.P.A. in New York, N.Y., to 1936; assigned to Edgewood Arsenal, 1936-39, chief, protective development div., developing and perfecting fully molded gas mask and plastic lenses, also chief, war plans div. to 1939; mem. joint Army and Navy Munitions Bd. for indsl. and manpower phases of plans for emergency, 1939-41; assistant construction, Q.M.C., 1940-41; chief manpower and liaison div., Office of Under Secretary of War, 1941-42, also consultant, labor div., O.P.M. (later W.P.B.), 1942; also nat. occupational adv. Selective Service System, 1940-42; chief, administrative mgt. br., control div., Army Service Forces, 1942; exec. for Service Comds. Office Chief of Administrative Services, Oct. 1942-May 1943; exec. officer dept. chief of staff for Service Comds., 1943-44, dep. chief of staff, 1944-46, asst., Office of Comdg. Gen. Army Service Forces, charge Army Service Forces pub. relations, 1946; spl. around world mission Aug.-Sept. 1945; exec. chief pub. information, Office Gen. Eisenhower, 1946, retired 1947. Exec. asst. pres. Sands, Las Vegas, Nev.; partner Labor-Mgmt. Sales Consultants. Pres. Nat. Clean-up Paint-up Bureau. Member of National Planning Council; sponsor Atlantic Council U.S. Awarded Army Commendation Ribbon with two clusters, D.S.M., Legion of Merit. Mem. Nat. Paint Varnish and Lacquer Assn. (pres. 1947-61). Clubs: Nat. Press; Harvard; Harvard Business School of S.C., SKAL. Internat.; Army Navy. Home: Riverside CA Died Dec. 18, 1970.

BAUER, LOUIS HOPEWELL (BOU'ER) physician; b. Boston, Mass., July 18, 1888; s. Charles Theodore and Ada Marian (Shute) B.; A.B., Harvard, 1909, M.D., cum laude, 1912; honor grad. U.S. Army Med. School, 1914, U.S. Army School of Aviation Medicine, 1920; grad. Army War Coll., 1926; D.Sc., University of Sydney (Australia), 1955; m. Helena Meredith, Dec. 27, 1913; 1 son, Charles Theodore; m. 2d, Margaret Louise Macon, Aug. 9, 1930; 1 step-daughter, Joan Macon (Mrs. William B. Lawrence, Jr.). Intern, Mercy Hosp., Springfield, Mass., 1912-13; entered Med. Corps, U.S. Army, 1913, successively ranked as lt., capt., major, lt. col. (emergency); resigned, 1926; med. dir. aeronautics branch U.S. Dept. of Commerce (now Fed. Aviation Agy.), 1926-30; engaged in pvt. practice, confined to cardiology, Hempstead, N.Y., 1930-53; chmn. bd. dirs. United Med. Service, Inc., 1954-59, now cons. Past mem. N.Y. State Public Health Council. Mem. bd. of visitors Air University, 1957-59. Served as lt. col. and col., Med. Res. Corps, 1927-39; col., U.S. Army, retired. Recipient John Jeffries Award from Inst. Aeronautical Sciences, 1940; Theodore C. Lyster Award, Aero. Med. Assn. 19 French Army, 1947; Carlos Finlay award Cuba, 1954: Bancroft medal, Queensland br. Brit. Med. Assn., in Australia, 1955; hon. gold key, Medical Faculty Univ. of Vienna, 1955; Paracelsus medal, German Medical Association, 1960. Diplomate Am. Bd. Internal Medicine, Am. Bd. Preventive Medicine (Aviation Medicine). Fellow A.C.P., Aero. Med. Assn. (pres. 1929-31); member World (sec. general 1948-61, now consultant), American (trustee 1944-51, chairman 1949-51, president 1952-53) med. assns., Med. Soc. State N.Y. (pres. 1947-48, pres. 2d dist. br. 1939-41), Nassau County Med. Soc. (pres. 1938-39), Am. Heart Assn., Alpha Omega Alpha, Kappa Gamma Chi, Phi Beta Kappa (hon. Harvard); Hon. mem. Cuban, Burma med. assns. Mason. Club: Harvard (N.Y.C., Boston). Editor in chief Journal of Aviation Medicine (bi-monthly), 1930-54, now editor-in-chief emeritus. Author: Aviation Medicine (textbook), 1926; Private Enterprise or Government in Medicine, 1947. Contributor chapter Medicine and Aeronautics in Tice's Practice of Medicine, 1942, Aviation Medicine chpt. in Cyclopedia of Medicine, Surgery and the Specialties, 1942, Aviation Medicine chpt. in Oxford Loose Leaf Medicine, 1943 (also pub. as monograph). Contbr. numerous articles on aviation medicine and cardiology to med. jours; The First Decade Report on the World Medical Association, 1958. Home: 341 Harvard Av., Rockville Centre, N.Y. Office: 10 Columbus Circle, N.Y.C. 10019. Died Feb. 3, 1964; buried Arlington, Va.

BAUER, WALTER physician; b. Crystal Falls, Mich., June 7, 1898; s. John and Caroline (Schmid) B.; B.S., U. of Mich., 1920, M.D., 1922; M.A., honoris causa, Harvard, 1942; m. Margaret Zeller, Sept. 12, 1931; children-Walter Dale, Gretchen, Nancy Wallace. Interne, L.I. Coll. Hosp., Brooklyn, N.Y., 1922-23, asst. resident in medicine, 1923-24; resident physician, Mass. Gen. Hosp., Boston, 1924-27, asst. in medicine 1928-29, asst. physician, 1929-32, asso. physician, 1932-37, physician, 1937-51, chief med. service since 1951; instr. medicine Harvard Med. Sch., 1928-29, faculty instr. and tutor in medicine, 1929-32, asst. prof., 1932-36, asso. prof., 1936-51, Jackson prof. clin. medicine since 1951. Cons. physician Mass. Eye and Ear Infirmary; cons. in med. research, Robert B. Brigham Hosp.; cons. Beth Israel, Lemuel Shattuck hosps. Director Robert W. Lovett Memorial Foundation for Study of Crippling Diseases, 1929-58. Chmn. sci. adv. com., v.p. bd. trustees Helen Hay Whitney Foundation. NRC fellowship in England (with Sir Henry H. Dale), 1927-28. Certified by Am. Bd. of Internal Medicine, 1937. Col., U.S. Army Med. Corps, med. consultant and dir. med. activities, 8th Service Comd., 1942-45. Fellow N.Y. Acad. Med. Royal Society of Medicine. (London, honorary); mem. A.M.A., Assn. of American Physicians (president 1959), Association Profs. Medicine, Royal Society of Medicine, American Coll. Physicians, Am. Soc. Clin. Investigation, Am. Rheumatism Assn., Am. Physiol. Soc., Assn for Study of Internal Secretions, Mass. Med. Soc., Boston Soc. of Biologists, Am. Acad. Arts and Scis., A.A.A.S., Soc. of U.S. Med. Consultants in World War II; bd. dirs. Arthritis and Rheumatism Found.; hon. mem. Swedish Med. Soc., Pan Am. Med. Assn., Danish Soc. Medicine; Liga Argentina contra el reumatismo. Clubs: Harvard of Boston, Interurban, Peripatetic, Boston Orthopedic. Home: 10 Emerson Pl., Boston 02114. Office: Mass. General Hospital, Boston 02114. Died Dec. 2, 1963; buried Still River, Mass.

BAUER, WILLIAM WALDO physician, author; b. Milw., July 23, 1892; s. Robert William and Anna Katherina Lizzette (Bunteschu) B.; B.S., U. Wis., 1915; M.D., U. Pa., 1917; LL.D. George Williams Coll., 1960; m. Florence Ann Marvyne, Feb. 8, 1920; children-William Waldo (dec.), John Robert, Erminie Anne (Mrs. Maurice F. Wetzel), Charles Marvyne. Physician, Milw. Health Dept., 1922-23; commr. of health and supt. of charities, Racine, Wis., 1923-31; lectr. in pub. health, Marquette U., 1923-24 and 1930-31; statis. cons. Wis. Anti-Tb Assn., 1930; with A.M.A. as dir. Dept. Health Edn., 1932-61, emeritus, 1962—, asso. editor Hygeia, 1949-58; now health edn. cons., free lance writer; editor Today's Health, 1945-57. Dir. radio programs, 1932-58, ednl. TV, 1947-58. Mem. President's Conf. on Fitness of Am. Youth, 1956; mem. adv. coms. of Summer Roundup, Nat. Congress Parents and Tchrs., 1932—; on Maternal and Child Welfare, U.S. Childrens Bur., 1935-51, Dept. Health and Welfare, Nat. Com. for Traffic Safety, 1946. Vis. expert pub. heal Am. Sch. Health Assn., 1958. Diplomate Am. Bd. Preventive Medicine, Pub. Health. Fellow Am. Pub. Health Assn.; mem. Chgo. Med. Soc., A.M.A., Ill. State Med. Soc., Milw. Acad. Med. (hon.), Am. Sch. Health Assn., N.E.A., Scabbard and Blade, Am. Acad. Phys. Edn., Nat. Soc. Med. Research, Broadcast Pioneers, Am. Fedn. TV and Radio Actors, Screen Actors Guild, Am. Acad. Preventive Medicine, Soc. Pub. Health Educators, Am. Med. Writers Assn. (Honor award 1953), Phi Beta Kappa, Alpha Omega Alpha, Phi Beta Pi. Presbyn. Author: Stop Annoying Your Children, 1947; Santa Claus, M.D., 1950; (with others) Health and Personal Development (series sch. health textbooks); Your Health Today, 1955; Moving Into Manhood, 1964; (with Florence Marvyne Bauer) Way to Womanhood, 1965. Daily syndicated health column, Health for Today, 1953—. Editor: Today's Health Guide, 1965. Contbr. technical and popular articles on health to jours. Home and office: 400 E. Randolph St., Chgo. 60601. Died Dec. 25, 1967.

BAXTER, HENRY army officer, diplomat; b. Sidney Plains, N.Y., Sept. 8, 1821; s. Levi and Lois (Johnson) B.; m. Elvira E. George, 1854. Commd. capt. U.S. Army, 1861, col., 1862, brig. gen. U.S. Volunteers, 1863; commanded brigade at battles of Fredericksburg and Gettsburg; wounded in battles of Antietam and Fredericksburg; served in Battle of Five Forks; mustered out, 1865; brevetted maj. gen. U.S. Volunteers, 1865; U.S. minister to Honduras, 1866-69, to Holland, 1869-72. Died Jonesville, Mich., Dec. 30, 1873.

BAXTER, JOHN BABINGTON MACAULAY chief justice of New Brunswick; b. Saint John, N.B., Feb. 16, 1868; s. William and Margaret (MacAuley) B.; B.C.L., King's Coll. Law Sch.; hon. D.C.L., King's Coll.; LL.D., St. Josephs Coll.; LL.D., Univ. of N.B.; m. Grace Winnifred Coster, Jan. 14, 1924; children—John Babington MacAulay, Jr., Eleanor Cowden, Frederick Coster Noel, Mary Faith. Began as atty. at law, Oct. 16, 1890; barrister, 1891, King's counsel, 1909; atty. gen. of N.B., 1916-17; premier of N.B., 1925-31. Mem. Parliament (Can.), 1921-25; mem. Provincial Parliament, N.B., 1911-21, 1925-31; judge Supreme Court, N.B., 1931-35, chief justice since 1935. Served as lt. col., 3d N.B. Regt. of Arty., 1907-12. Alderman, St. John, 1892-94, 1899-1902, 1904-09. Mason (33 degree). Clubs: Cliff (St. John); City (Fredericton, N.B.). Author: New Brunswick Regiment of Artillery, 1793-1896, pub. 1896; Simon Baxter, His Ancestry and Descendants, 1944. Home: 34 Dufferin Row. Office: Provincial Bldg., St. John, N.B., Can. Died Dec. 27, 1946.

BAYARD, NICHOLAS colonial ofcl., mayor N.Y.C.; b. Alphen, Holland, 1644; s. Samuel and Anna (Stuyvesant) B.; m. Judith Varlet, May 22, 1666, 1 son, Samuel. Came to Am., 1647; clk. N.Y. Common Council, 1664; sec. Province of N.Y., 1664; pvt. sec. to Gov. Stuyvesant of N.Y., 1665; continued as provincial sec. N.Y. under Dutch occupation, 1672, commd. receiver gen., 1672; lt. Dutch Militia, 1672 given power of atty. to collect debts for Dutch Gov.; commd. mayor N.Y.C., 1685-87; mem. N.Y. Gov.'s Council; comdr.-in-chief N.Y. Militia, 1688. Died N.Y.C., 1707.

BAYLEY, RICHARD physician; b. Fairfield, Conn., 1745; studied medicine under John Charlton, N.Y.C.; studied anatomy under William Hunter, London, Eng., 1769-71; m. Miss Charlton. Went to London, 1769-71; during croup epidemic made study of disease's causes and treatment which cut mortality rate in half, 1774; in England, 1775-76; surgeon Brit. Army under Gen. Howe, Newport, R.I., 1776-77; practiced medicine, N.Y.C., 1777; prof. anatomy and surgery Columbia, 1792; 1st physician in Am. to amputate arm at shoulder-joint; health physician Port of N.Y., 1795. Author: An Account of the Epidemic Fever which Prevailed in the City of New York during Part of the Summer and Fall of 1795, published 1796; Letters from the Health Office Submitted to the New York Common Council. Died Aug. 17, 1801.

BAYLEY, WARNER BALDWIN rear adm.; b. Baldwinsville, N.Y., Sept. 9, 1845; m. Annette Williamson, Oct. 1890; 1 son, Warner W. Apptd. from N.Y., acting 3d asst. engr., Aug. 4, 1864; promoted through grades to capt., July 1, 1905; retired with rank of rear adm., Apr. 18, 1906. Advanced 2 numbers in rank for "eminent and conspicuous conduct in battle" while attached to the Massachusetts during the Spanish-Am. War. Died Apr. 22, 1928.

BAYLY, THOMAS MONTEAGLE congressman, lawyer, planter; b. Hills Farm, nr. Drummondtown, Accomac County, Va., Mar. 26, 1775; attended Washington Acad., Md.; grad. Princeton, 1794; studied law; at least 1 son, Thomas Henry. Admitted to bar, circa 1796; practiced in Accomac County; became planter; mem. Va. Ho. of Dels., 1798-1801, 19, 20, 28-31; mem. Va. Senate, 1801-09; col. of militia during War of 1812; mem. U.S. Ho. of Reps. (Democrat) from Va., 13th Congress, 1813-15; del. Va. constl. convs., 1829, 30. Died on his plantation Mt. Custis, nr. Accomac, Va., Jan. 7, 1834; buried family cemetery at Mt. Custis.

BAYNE, HUGH AIKEN lawyer; b. New Orleans, La., Feb. 15, 1970; s. Thomas Levingston and Anna Maria (Gayle) B.; A.B., Yale, 1892; LL.B., Tulane 1894, LL.D. (hon.) 1946; m. Helen Cheney, Oct. 8, 1895; children—Helen, Elizabeth C.; m. 2d, Emily Ford, 1919 (died 1937); 1 son, Hugh G. (lt. Air Corps). Admitted to bar, 1894, prac. New Orleans, 1894-98; N.Y. City, 1898-1919; mem. firm Stong & Cadwalader, N.Y. City, 1905-14; mem. legal service of Reparations Commn. under treaties of Versailles and St. Germain, 1919-28; served as one of three judges deciding claim of Belgium vs. Austria to Treasure of Order of Golden Fleece and to Tryptich of San Ildenphonse (Rubens), claim of Czechoskovakia as successor to Kingdom of Bohemia to 500 works of art taken from Bohemia by Austria between 1616 and 1914; claim of Standard Oil Co. vs. Reparations Commn. to 21 oil tankers of Standard's German subsidiary, appropriated by Reparations Commn. to pay Germany's reparations. Also sole judge of two questions of interpretation of disarmament clauses of Versailles treaty submitted by ambassadors of France, Italy, Great Britain and Japan. Served as major judge advocate, U.S. Army, 1917, in France, J.A., S.O.S., of A.E.F., counsel Prisoners of War Mission, 1918, lt. col., 1919. Decorated Distinguished Service Medal (U.S.), Legion of Honor, Palmiers Universitaire, grade of officers publ. instrn. (France). Clubs: Yale (New York); Skull and Bones (Yale); Graduates (New Haven); Boston (New Orleans). Home: Graduates Club, 155 Elm St., New Haven. Died Dec. 24, 1954; buried Magnolia Cemetery, New Orleans.

BAYNE, THOMAS MCKEE congressman, lawyer; b. Bellevue, Allegheny County, Pa., June 14, 1836; attended Westminster Coll., New Wilmington, Pa.; studied law. Served as col. 136th Regt., Pa. Volunteer Inf., Union Army, in Civil War, 1862; in battles of Fredericksburg and Chancellorsville; admitted to Allegheny County bar, 1866; elected dist. atty. Allegheny County, 1870-74; mem. U.S. Ho. of Reps. (Republican) from Pa., 45th-51st congresses, 1077-91; retired from public life and business activities. Died Washington, D.C., June 16, 1894; buried Uniondale Cemetery, Pitts.

BAYNE-JONES, STANHOPE, bacteriologist; b. New Orleans, La., Nov. 6, 1888; s. Stanhope and Minna (Bayne) B.; A.B., Yale, 1910; M.D., Johns Hopkins, 1914, M.A., 1917, Sc.D., U. Rochester, 1943, Emory University, 1954; LL.D., Tulane University, 1956; married Nannie Moore Smith, June 25, 1921. Interne, Johns Hopkins Hosp., 1914-15; Rockefeller fellow in pathology, 1915-16, asso. prof. bacteriology, same, 1922-23; prof. bacteriology Sch. of Medicine, U. of Rochester, 1923-32; dir. Rochester Health Bur. Labs., 1926-32; prof. bacteriology, Yale Sch. of Medicine, 1932-47, and dean of the School of Medicine, 1935-40; also master of Trumbull Coll. (Yale), 1932-38. Served as capt. and maj., M.C., with British and Am. armies in France, Italy and Germany, 1917-19; sanitary insp. 3d Army, in Germany, 1919; brigadier gen. medical corps, U.S. Army, dept. chief preventive med. service, Office of the Surgeon Gen., 1942-46; adminstr. Army Epidermiological Board. Director, United States of America Typhus Commn., 1944-46; chmn. div. med. scis. National Research Council, 1932-33. Director Board of Scientific Advisers, Jane Coffin Childs Memorial Fund for Med. Research, 1937-47; scientific dir. Internat. Health Div., Rockefeller Foundation, 1939-41; director Josiah Macy, Jr. Foundation, 1939-41 and from 1948; president Joint Administration Board of New York Hospital-Cornell Medical Center, 1947-53; tech. dir. research Army Med. Research and Development Program, 1952-56; mem. Army Sci. Adv. Com., from 1954; chmn. sec.'s cons. on med. research and edn. U.S. Dept. Health, Edn. and Welfare, 1957-58; mem. Surgeon gen.'s com. on smoking and health USPHS from 1962. Mem. N.Y.C. Bd. Hosps., 1950-52, Nat. Manpower Council, 1951, Commn. on Financing Hosp. Care, 1951, Hosp. Council of Greater N.Y., 1948-51; mem. Yale Corp., 1956-57. Mem. A.A.A.S., A.M.A. (council on pharmacy and chemistry, 1930-34), Society Am. Bacteriologists (president 1929-30), Am. Assn. Immunologists (pres. 1930-31), Soc. Exptl. Biology and Medicine, Assn. Am. Physicians, Am. Assn. Pathologists and Bacteriologists (pres. 1940-41), Am. Pub. Health Assn., Am. Soc. Tropical Medicine, Assn. of Am. Med. Coll. (exec. council 1938-40), Am. Soc. for Control of Cancer (exec. com. 1938-1940), Am. Assn. for Cancer Research, Leonard Wood Memorial (med. advisory board 1937-41), Nat. Bd. Med. Examiner (1936-41), Zeta Psi, Nu Sigma Nu (hon. council), Phi Beta Kappa, Alpha Omega Alpha. Decorated Mil. Cross, Croix de Guerre, Distinguished Service Medal, U.S. of America Typhus Commn. Medal, Army Commendation Ribbon, Silver Star (with 2 oak leaf clusters), Order of British Empire (hon. comdr.). Episcopalian. Clubs: University, Metropolitan, Army and Navy, Cosmos. Contbr. on pathology and bacteriology. Home: Washington DC Died Feb. 20, 1970; buried Arlington Nat. Cemetery, Arlington VA

BEACH, EDWARD LATIMER naval officer; b. Toledo, O., June 30, 1867; s. Joseph Lane and Laura Colton (Osborn) B.; apptd. from Minn., and grad. U.S. Naval Acad., 1888; m. Lucie Adelaide Quin, of Brooklyn, May 11, 1895. Asst. engr. U.S.N., July 1, 1890; lt., Mar. 3, 1899; commander, Mar. 11, 1910; promoted captain, Dec. 12, 1914; retired, 1921, to become lecturer at Stanford U.; served on different ships, in N. Atlantic, S. Atlantic, European, Asiatic and Pacific stas.; was an officer of Admiral Dewey at battle of Manila Bay, May 1, 1898, and at capture of Manila, Aug. 13, 1898, serving aboard U.S.S. Baltimore; engr. officer in charge of machinery, ordnance and elec. repairs to U.S. war vessels, Navy Yard, Boston, May 20, 1910; comdg. U.S.S. Vestal during Am. occupation of Vera Cruz, Mex., and commandant Fortress San Juan de Ulloa; chief of staff of Admiral Caperton and in comd. "Washington" during pacification of Haiti and Santo Domingo, 1915; comd. "Memphis " when the ship was engulfed by tidal wave without warning, Aug. 29, 1916, and destroyed; comdg. Naval Torpedo Sta., Newport, R.I., 1917; comd. U.S.S. New York in North Sea during latter part of World War, and at time of surrender of German fleet, Nov. 21, 1918; late commandant navy yard station, Mare Island, Calif. Now city assessor, Palo Alto, Calif. Decorations: Dewey Medal, Spanish Campaign Medal, Philippine, Mexican, Haitian and Santo Domingan campaign medals, also D.S.C. at close of World War. Clubs: St. Botolph, Authors (Boston); New York Yacht. Author: An Annapolis Plebe, 1907; An Annapolis Youngster, 1908; An Annapolis Second Classman, 1909; An Annapolis First Classman, 1910; Roger Paulding, Apprentice Seaman, 1911; Roger Paulding, Gunner's Mate, 1912; Ralph Osborn, Midshipman at Annapolis, 1909; Midshipman Ralph Osborn at Sea, 1910; Ensign Ralph Osborn, 1911; Lieutenant Ralph Osborn, 1912; Roger Paulding, Gunner, 1912; Roger Paulding, Ensign, 1913; Dan Quin of the Navy. Home: 525 Channing Av., Palo Alto, Calif.

BEACH, GEORGE CORWIN JR. army officer; b. Topeka, Kan., Oct. 28, 1888; s. George Corwin and Laura (Rosseau) B.; M.D., Kansas City U. Med. Coll., 1911; grad. Army Med. Sch., 1917; m. Jessie Spencer, Nov. 16, 1914. Interne University Hosp. of Kansas City, 1911-12; asst. surgeon Soldiers Home, Hampton, Va. 1912-14; commd. 1st lt., Med. Corps, U.S. Army, 1914; promoted through grades to brig. gen., 1943; asst. surg. gen., Army Med. Center, Washington, D.C. Awarded D.S.M., World War I. Second v.p. United Services Automobile Assn. Fellow Am. Coll. Physicians, A.M.A.; diplomate Am. Bd. Internal Medicine; mem. Assn. Mil. Surgeons, Phi Beta Pi; hon. mem. Tex. Internists Soc. Episcopalian. Club: San Antonio Country. Home 204 Artillery Post, Fort Sam Houston, Tex. Address: care War Dept., Washington, D.C. Died Nov. 18, 1948.

BEACH, LANSING HOSKINS army officer; b. Dubuque, Ia., June 18, 1860; s. Myron Hawley and Helen Mary (Hoskins) B.; grad. U.S. Mil. Acad. 1882; m. Anna May Dillon, June 18, 1890; 1 son, Lansing Dillon. Commd. additional 2d lt. engrs., June 13, 1882; promoted through grades to col., Feb. 27, 1913. Commr. on part of U.S. in determining boundary between Tex. and Indian Terr., 1886; engr. commr. of D.C., 1898-1901; while in that position initiated the improvement of Rock Creek Park and obtained first appropriation from Congress for the purpose; secured abolition of railroad grade crossings in Washington and originated the plan for removal of Pa. R.R. from the Mall and establishment of a union station; personally selected names now borne by streets in street extension plan of D.C., Div. engr. Gulf Div. embracing all states touching the Gulf of Mexico, 1908-15; mem. Miss. River Commn., 1913-20; div. engr. Central Div. embracing Ohio River basin, 1915-20; sent by U.S. to Europe, 1911, to study and report upon conditions of navigation there; advanced maj. gen. and chief of engrs. Jan 9, 1920; retired, June 18, 1924. Mem. U.S. Commn. to confer with Mexican Commn. to determine equitable div. of waters of Rio Grande and Colorado rivers. Mem. Am. Soc. C.E., Am. Soc. Mil. Engrs. (ex-pres.). Clubs: Army and Navy (Washington, D.C.); Los Angeles (Calif.) Athletic; Twilight (Pasadena). Address: 690 Bradford St., Pasadena, Calif. Died Apr. 2, 1945.

BEACH, WILLIAM DORRANCE army officer; b. Brooklyn, N.Y., June 18, 1856; s. Joshua M. and Sarah E. (Ford) B.; grad. U.S. Mil. Acad., 1879; m. Miss Bullens, Apr. 27, 1882. Comd. 2d lt. 3d Cav., June 13, 1879; promoted through grades to brig. gen. N.A., Aug. 5, 1971; brig. gen. regular army, Feb. 28, 1927 (retired). Served at Camp Eagle Pass, Tex., 1888-91; instr. in charge dept. engring., Inf. and Cav. Sch., Ft. Leavenworth, 1892-98; comd. cav. troop, Chickamauga Park, Ga., 1898; engr. cav. div. 5th Army Corps, and mem. Gen. Wheeler's staff at battles of Las Cuasimas and San Juan, Cuba, 1898; acting insp. gen. 5th Army Corps, 1898-99; participated in various minor engagements. Philippines, 1899; duty Gen. Staff. 1903-06, 1909-12; gov., Santa Clara Province, Cuba, 1908; chief of staff, Philippine Dept., 1910-12; pres. Bd. on Cav. Drill Regulations, 1916; comdg. 176th Inf. Brigade, Camp Dodge, Des Moines, Ia., Sept. 1917 and 88th Div. there and in France, May-Aug. 1918. Decorated D.S.M. (U.S.); 2 citations "for gallantry in action"; Legion of Honor, Croix de Guerre (France). Republican. Episcopalian. Home: San Diego, Calif. Died June 18, 1932.

BEACHAM, JOSEPH (WILLIAM), JR. ret. army officer; b. Bklyn., Apr. 8, 1874; s. Joseph William and Mary (Dovey) B.; LL.B., Cornell U., 1897; distinguished grad. Army School of Line, 1915; grad. Army Staff Coll., 1916, Army War Coll., 1921; m. Bernadett Herman, June, 1925 (died Apr. 14, 1948). Served with U.S. Army, Spanish-American War, 1898. Philippine Insurrection, 1901, World War I, 1918; commd. 2d lt. U.S. Army, 1899, advanced through grades to brig. gen., 1940; instr. Army War Coll., 1921-25; prof. mil. sci. and tactics Cornell U., 1927-32, U. Pa., 1934-38; retired, 1938. Coach, Army football team, 1908-11; mem. Football Rules Com., 1909-14; chmn. Cornell Football Com., 1927-32. Mem. Psi Upsilon. Decorated D.S.M., Silver Star (U.S.); croix de Guerre and Etoile Noir (France); Order of Redeemer (Greece); Order of Danilo (Montenegro). Presbyn. Clubs: Army and Navy, Chevy Chase (Washington); N.Y. Athletic. Lambs (N.Y.C.). Address: Army and Navy Club, Washington. Died July 1958.

BEALE, GEORGE WILLIAM clergyman; b. Westmoreland County, Va., Aug. 21, 1842; s. Gen. Richard Lee T. and Lucy Maria (Brown) B.; ed. pvt. schs., Fleetwood and Piedmont Acads. and Culpeper Military Inst., So. Bapt. Theol. Sem.; D.D., Wash. and Lee U., 1894; m. Mary A. Bouic, Dec. 3, 1879. Entered C.S.A. Apr. 30, 1861, as pvt. in Co. C, 9th Va. Cav.; advanced to 1st lt.; comd. co. 2 campaigns; was wounded twice, in battles of Reams Station and Hatcher's Run. Ordained Bapt. ministry, Oct. 18, 1868; pastor Machodoc and Pope's Creek, 1868-73, Georgetown, 1874-79, Halifax, Va., 1879-83, Buchanan and Hollins Inst., 1883-94, Heathsville, 1894-05, Richmond and Westmoreland counties, 1905-15. Pres. Gen. Bapt. Assn. Va., 1901, 1902; trustee Richmond Coll., v.p. Va. Bapt. Orphanage, Salen, Va. Democrat. Mem. Soc. of Cincinnati, Va. Bapt. Hist. Soc. (v.p.). Author: History 9th Virginia Cavalry, 1895; A Lieutenant of Cavalry in Lee's Army, 1918. Editor of Semple's History of Virginia Baptists. Home: Hague, Va. Died July 15, 1921.

BEALE, RICHARD LEE TURBERVILLE army officer, congressman; b. Hickory Hill, Va., May 22, 1819; s. Robert and Martha (Turberville) B.; grad. U. Ho. of Reps. (Democrat) from Va., 30th Congress, 1847-49; del. Va. Constl. Conv., 1851; mem. Va. Senate, 1858-60; commd. 1st lt. Lee's Legion, Confederate Army, 1861; maj., 1862; col., comdr. brigade, 1864, brig. gen., 1865; mem. U.S. Ho. of Reps. from Va., 46th Congress, 1879-81. Died Apr. 21, 1893

BEALL, ELLIAS JAMES physician, surgeon; b. Macon, Ga., Feb. 5, 1835; s. Dr. Jeremiah B.; prep. edn. high schs.; M.D., U. of La. (now Tulane); M.D., Mo. Med. Coll. (now med. dept. Washington U.); studied Coll. Phys. and Surg. (Columbia), and in hosps. of London, Paris and Berlin; m. Fannie Van Zandt, whose father was minister from Republic of Tex. to U.S., and negotiated treaty of annexation. Was surgeon 15th Tex. Cav., chief surgeon Walker's div., med. insp. Trans-Miss. Dept., on staff Lt.-Gen. Holmes, C.S.A., in Civil War. Emeritus prof. principles and practice surgery and clin. surgery, and pres. faculty, med. dept. Ft. Worth U. Has written communications on med. and surg. subjects to various med. jours.; letters from Europe to Daniels' Medical Journal. Home: Cor. 5th and Lamar Sts. Office: Hoxie Bldg., Ft. Worth, Tex.

BEALL, JOHN YATES army officer; b. Jefferson County, Va., Jan. 1, 1835; s. George and Miss (Yates) B.; attended U. Va., circa 1855-59; studied law. Served in Stonewall Brigade, Confederate Army, 1861; apptd. acting master Confederate Navy, 1862, sabotaged Union ships in Chesapeake Bay area, 1862-63; captured several Fed. vessels including Alliance; attempted from base in Canada to capture Union warship on Lake Erie and to free some Confederate prisoners, 1864, plan failed because of mutiny; arrested following attempts to derail trains in N.Y., tried, 1864, convected of espionage, executed despite please for clemency by Gov. Andrew of Mass. and Thaddeus Stevens. Executed Ft. Lafayette, N.Y., Feb. 24, 1865.

BEALL, REASIN congressman; b. Montgomery County, Me. Dec. 3, 1769; limited schooling. Served as officer under Gen. Harmer, 1790; apptd. ensign U.S. army, 1792, battalion q.m., 1793; served under Gen. Wayne in campaign against Indians; moved to New Lisbon, O., 1803; commd. brig. gen. Volunteers, 1812; moved to Wooster, O., 1815; mem. U.S. Ho. of Reps. (Whig filled vacancy) from Ohio, 13th Congress, Apr. 20, 1813- June 7, 1814, resigned; register land offices, Canton, Wooster, O., 1814-24; presided over Whig

Conv., Columbus, O., 1840; Whig presdl. elector, 1840. Died Wooster, Feb. 20, 1843; buried Wooster Cemetery.

BEALL, SAMUEL WOOTTON polit. leader; b. Montgomery County, Md., Sept. 26, 1807; s. Lewis and Eliza B.; grad. Union Coll., Schenectady, N.Y., 1827; m. Elizabeth Cooper, 1827. Apptd. receiver of public land sales in N.W., Green Bay, Wis., 1827-34, Cooperstown, N.Y., 1834-40; moved to Wis., settled in Fond du Lac County, 1840, became farmer; advocated statehood for Wis. Territory; del. Wis. Constl. Conv., 1846, 47; drafted constn. for new state, Madison, Wis.; lt. gov. Wis., 1851-53; Indian agt. for Wis. tribes, 1853-59; led expdn. to Pike's Peak, Colo., 1859; a founder Denver (Colo.), helped obtain charter for Denver in Washington, D.C., 1860; returned to Wis., 1861; served as lt. col. 18th Wis. Inf. Regt. during Civil War, 1862-62; participated in campaigns of Shiloh and Vicksburg; moved to Helena, Mont., 1866. Killed in newspaper office in Helena in controversy with editor George Pinney of Montana Post, Sept. 26, 1868; buried Helena.

BEALS, FRANK LEE, retired army officer, educator, author; b. Morganton, Tenn., Sept. 2, 1881; s. Francis (M.D.) and Sadie Louisiana (Dawson) B.; ed. Reidville (S.C.) High Sch., George Washington U., U. Chgo.; B.S., De Paul U., 1930. A.M., 1932; m. Alice Alexandra Barnes, Apr. 17, 1909; children—Elena Louise (dec.), Bettina Byrd (Mrs. Iwersen); m. Ida Catherine Dushek, May 1, 1941 (dec. May 1972). Enlisted in U.S. Army, 1898; commd. 2d lt., Oct. 9, 1903; retired for disability in line of duty, May 1, 1908; 1st lt. retired, Oct. 30, 1916; capt. retired, Jan. 1918; maj. retired, Jan. 6, 1922. Served in Philippines, 1899-1900, 1905-06; San Francisco earthquake and fire; mil. attach., Brazil, 1909-10; comdt. Northwestern Mil. and Naval Acad., 1911-17, examining officer for Wis. state O.T.C., 1917; prof. mil. science and tactics; supr. phys. edn., high schs. Chgo., 1917-32; est. Camp Roosevelt (summer tng. camp for boys), 1919; pres. Racine (Wis.) Mil. Acad., 1930-33; asst. supt. schs., Chgo., 1935-46, supt. compulsory Edn., 1946-48. Wounded at the Battle of Big Bend, P.I., 1899. Awarded Purple Heart, 1932. Author: Topographical Primer, 1914; Squad Leaders' Note Book, 1917; Beal (e,l,s) the Ancient Name, 1929; Look Away Dixieland, 1937; Kit Carson, David Crocket, 1941; Chief Black Hawk, Buffalo Bill, 1943; The Story of Robinson Crusoe; The Story of Lemuel Gulliver in Lilliput Land; Rush for Gold, 1945; The Story of the Three Musketeers, Boswell in Chicago, 1946; The Story of Treasure Island, 1947; The Story of Moby Dick, 1949; The Patriot Silversmith, 1949; The Story of Deerslayer, 1950; Backwoods Baron, The Life Story of Claude Albert Fuller, 1951; The Story of Two Years Before the Mast, 1952; The Story of the Prince and The Pauper, 1953; American Heroes Series, 1954; Spanish Adventure Trails, 1960. Home: Eureka Springs AR Died Aug. 31, 1972.

BEALS, WALTER BURGES judge; b. St. Paul, Minn., July 21, 1876; s. James Burrill and Katharine (McMillan) B.; LL.B., U. Wash. 1901; m. Othilia Gertrude Carroll, July 14, 1904. Admitted to Wash. Bar, 1901, and began practice at Seattle; 1st asst. corp. counsel, Seattle, 1923-26; judge Superior Ct., King County, 1926-28; apptd. judge to fill vacancy, Supreme Ct. Wash., Apr. 15, 1928, elected term 1928-34, reelected for term 1934-40, 40-46, 46-52. Left Olympia for Nurnberg, Germany, Oct. 1, 1946; mil. leave of absence from Supreme Ct. Wash., 1946-48; designated presiding judge of Mil. Tribunal I, by lt. gen. Clay. Tribunal convened Dec. 9, to try 1st case assigned to it, pursuant to an indictment - filed by chief of counsel for War Crimes. Chief justice, 1933-34, 1945-46. Served as maj., lt. col., judge advocate 1917-19; participated in Meuse-Argonne offensive; pvt. advancing to lt. col. Wash. Nat. Guard, 1909-28. Mem. Wash. State Bar Assn., Am. Bar Assn., S.A.R., Mil. Order Loyal Legion, Vets of Foreign Wars, Am. Legion, Legion of Honor, France. Republican. Mason (320). Home: 726 S. Percival St. Office: Temple of Justice, Olympia, Wash. Died Sept. 1960.

BEAMAN, BARTLETT army officer b. Princeton, Mass., July 20, 1891; A.B., Harvard, 1913. Flying cadet, 2d Air Interceptor Command, Tours, France, 1917; commd. 1st lt., 1918, later served with 3d Air Command and with 5th Air Depot; participated in Meuse-Argonne Offensive; with 12th Aero Squadron, Am. Forces in Germany; disch., 1919; commd. 1st lt., aviation section Signal Res., 1919, and advanced through the grades to brig. gen., 1944; on active duty since 1941; assigned with intelligence div. Office Chief of Air Corps, Washington, D.C., Feb.-July 1941, chief, evaluation unit, July 1941-Jan. 1942; become wing exec. officer, Hdqrs. 1st Bombardment Wing, European Theatre of Operations, 1942; chief of staff, 1st Bombardment Div., 1943-45. Decorated Legion of Merit, Bronze Star, Air Medal, Distinguished Service Medal. French Croix de Guerre and Legion of Honor. Home: 3700 Massachusetts Av., N.W., Washington, D.C. Died Nov. 14, 1947.

BEAMAN, GEORGE WILLIAM rear adm.; b. Rutland, Vt., May 7, 1837; s. George Hudson and Eleanor Kettele (Gookin) B.; ed. Rutland High Sch., Troy Conf. Acad.; m. Rebecca Swift Goldsmith, May 2, 1866; 1 son, William Major B. Enlisted as pvt. 3d Regt., Mo. U.S. Reserve Corps, May 1861, and took part in capture of Camp Jackson; was war corr. Missouri Democrat. Aug. 1861-Mar. 1862; was with Fremont in S.W. Mo. campaign, and later with Grant in battles Fts. Henry and Donelson; apptd. acting asst. p.-m. U.S.N., Mar. 1862; asst. p.-m., June 1862; promoted p.-m., 1866; pay insp., 1890; pay dir., Apr. 1899; retired with rank of rear admiral. May 7, 1899. Served in S. Atlantic and Gulf Blockading squadrons, and on Miss. River during Civil War; was in several engagements; subsequently served on various ships and stas. Was general storekeeper at Boston and Mare Island navy yards, 1887-93; made last cruise on flagship New York as fleet-paymaster N. Atlantic Sta. Mem. Loyal Legion (Mass. Commandery). Home: Cambridge, Mass. Died. May 3, 1917.

BEAMAN, ROBERT PRENTIS banker; b. Norfolk, Va., Dec. 13, 1891; s. Nathaniel and Katherine Lewis (Prentis) B.; grad. Norfolk Acad., 1908; A.B., Washington and Lee U., 1911; m. Salome Lydia Slingluff, Feb. 24, 1923; children—Robert Prentis, Nathaniel III. Began as clk. with Nat. Bank of Commerce, 1911, asst. cashier, 1924-17, cashier, 1919-21, v.p. 1921-26, resigned, 1926; pres. Commerce Corp., dir. Chesapeake Ferry Corp.; mem. banking and industrial com., 5th Federal Res. Dist. Served in World War as lt. and later capt., U.S. Army, in St. Mihiel and Meusse-Argonne offensives. Mem. Commn. revision of Charter, City of Norfolk, 1933; pres. Norfolk Community Fund, 1940-41; pres. Norfolk-Portsmouth Clearing House Assn.; mem. exec. com. Industrial Commn., Tax Equalization Assn., Hampton Roads Defense Council; mem. Committee of National Credit Association No. 1, Fifth Federal Reserve Dist.; mem. Va. Com. of Deposit Liquidation Com. of Reconstruction Finance Corp.; mem. Tax Com. of Va. State Chamber of Commerce; mem. bd. of dirs. Norfolk Assn. of Commerce; mem. board of management, Navy Y.M.C.A. Selected First Citizen of Norfolk, 1940. Mem. Virginia Bankers Assn. (legislative committee), New York Southern Soc., Va. Hist. Soc., Soc. of Colonial Wars in State of Va., Am. Legion (comdr. Norfolk post, 1926-27), Sigma Alpha Epsilon. Democrat. Episcopalian. Clubs: Norfolk Yacht (Norfolk, Va.); Bankers, Lotos (New York); Surf Club, Princess Anne Country (Virginia Beach, Va.). Home: 5220 Edgewater Dr., Norfolk, Va. Died May 30, 1953; buried Arlington Natl. Cemetery.

BEARBORN, DONALD CURTIS coll. pres.; b. Oscoola, Neb., Mar. 20, 1910; s. Ralph Eaton and Olive (Curtis) B.; A.B., Hastings Coll., 1931; M.A., U. Neb., 1933; Ph.D., Duke, 1936; m. Mary Katherine Omwake, July 1, 1937; children-Katherine C., Ralph O., Elizabeth H. Grad. asst. U. Neb., 1931-33; math. techr. Catawba Coll., 1935-63; prof., 1942-63, registrar, 1940-47, dean coll., 1947-63, pres., 1963—. Mem. bd. edn., Salisbury, 1947-57. Dir. Air Force Coll. Tng. Detachment, 1942-44. Mem. Math. Assn. Am. N.C. Acad. Sci., Am. Arbitration Assn., Phi Beta Kappa, Sigma Xi. Mem. United Ch. of Christ (exec. council). Club: Civitan (gov. N.C. dist. 1947-48). Address: Catawba Coll., Salisbury, N.C. Died Nov. 11, 1967.

BEARD, OLIVER THOMAS lawyer; b. New York, Nov. 13, 1832; studied in local schools and Nazareth, Pa.; crossed plains to Calif., 1849; mined, built wharves, etc.; later built railroads in S. America, served in Civil war, 1861-65, private 71st N.Y. vols. to lt.-col. 48th N.Y. vols.; practiced law in Ohio and Mich.; was editor The Post and Tribune, Detroit; inherited from father large warehouse property in Brooklyn and moved to New York. Author: Bristling With Thorns: etc. Address: New York.

BEARDALL, JOHN REGINALD naval officer; b. Sanford, Fla., Feb. 7, 1887; s. William and Florence (Bonser) B.; grad. Porter Mil. Acad., 1904; B.S., U.S. Naval Acad., 1908; LL.D., Temple U., 1942; Sc.D., U. So. Cal., 1943; m. Edith Jett McCormick, Feb. 10, 1917; children-Edith A. (Mrs. Y. Fitzhugh Hardcastle), John Reginald (U.S. Navy), Geoffrey Bonser. Commd. ensign U.S. Navy, 1910, promoted through grades to rear adm., 1941; cond. co. of U.S.S. Vermont at seizure of Vera Cruz, Mexico, 1914; attached to U.S.S. Kansas and gunnery officer U.S.S. New Hampshire during World War; aide to comdr. Spl. Service Squadron, 1923-25; comd. U.S.S. Sands, 1925; on duty in Europe, 1926-29, Naval War Coll., 1931-33; exec. officer U.S.S. Minneapolis, 1933-35; staff comdr. Battle Force, 1935-36; aide to sec. of Navy, 1936-39; comdr. U.S.S. Vincennes, 1939-41; aide to Pres. of U.S., 1941-42; supt. U.S. Naval Acad. 1942-45; apptd. comdt. 15th Naval Dist., comdr. S.E. Pacific, 1945; ret. 1946. Awarded Mexican Service, Victory and Navy Expeditionary, Navy and Marine Corps, Legion of Merit with oak leaf cluster; Abdon Calderon (Ecuador), Orden del Sal (gran official), Orden Militar de Ayacucho (Peru). Episcopalian. Club: Army and Navy (Washington). Home: Orlando, Fla. Home: 1403 Green Cove Rd., Winter Park, Fla. 32789. Died Jan. 4, 1967; buried Arlington Nat. Cemetery.

BEARDSLEE, LESTER ANTHONY rear adm.; b. Little Falls, N.Y., Feb. 1, 1836; entered Navy March 5, 1850; grad. Naval Acad., June, 1856; m. Evelyn, d. Isaac Small, Little Falls, N.Y., Jan. 1863 promoted regularly through all grades to rear adm. in 1895; comdr.-in-chief of naval forces on the Pacific sta., 1894-97; apptd. naval mem. U.S. bd. for testing and reporting upon Am. metals; participated in exec. officer monitor Nantucket in attack on Charleston, April, 1863; participated in capture of Confederate steam sloop Florida in Bahia, Brazil, Oct., 1864, and as prize master brought her to U.S.; in 1870 took tug Palos to China, carrying on her the first U.S. flag through the Suez Canal; while comdg. the U.S.S. Jamestown, 1879-80, in Alaskan waters, discovered, surveyed and named Glacier Bay. Retired from active service on reaching 62 yrs. of age, Feb. 1, 1898; Was one of the officers serving under Commodore Mathew C. Perry; participated in the landing of the commodore at Kurihama, Japan, July 14, 1853, and the interview with the two princes representing the Emperor, to whom commodore presented President Fillmore's letter. As one of few survivors of that event visited Japan, 1900-01, to advocate the erection of a monument by the Japanese on the site of the historic interview; the monument was unveiled with imposing ceremonies July 14, 1901. Home: Beaufort, S. C. Died 1903.

BEARDSLEY, FRANK GRENVILLE clergyman; b. Ovid, Mich., Nov. 9, 1870; s. Grenville Sterling and Mary Elizabeth (Clark) B.; A.B., Western (now Coe) Coll., Cedar Rapids, Ia., 1894; A.M., Ill. Wesleyan U., 1896; Ph.D., 1897; student Chgo. Theol. Sem. and U. Chgo.; B.D., Oberlin Theol. Sem., 1900; S.T.D., Kansas City U., 1912; m. Mary E. Riddell, Dec. 22, 1896; children— Frank Grenville, Mary Elizabeth, Martha Lydia, Margaret Theodosia, Theodore Sterling, Edity Allene, Whitmore Everett. Ordained Congl. ministry, 1897; pastor in Ia., at Salem, 1897-99, Rock Rapids, 1900-02, Greenwood Ch., Des Moines, 1902-04, Harlan, 1904-08; prof. Theology, Talladega (Ala.) Theol. Sem., 1908-09; pastor 1st Ch., Kansas City, Kan., 1909-14, 1st Ch., Keokuk, Ia., 1914-17, 1st Ch., Aurora, Ill., 1917-22, Fountain Park Ch., St. Louis, 1922-31, 1st Ch., Minot, N.D., 1931-42; pastor, 1st Church, Zumbrota, Minn., 1942—. Trustee at large Ill. Congl. Conf., 1917-22; sec. exec. com. Mo. Congl. Conf., 1922-27. Del. Nat. Congl. Council several times. Chaplain Mo. Soc. S.A.R., 1925-28, sec. 1928-29, pres. 1929-30; pres. Capm Jackson Union Soldiers' Monument Assn., 1926-31; chaplain Mo. Dept. Sons of Union Vets. of Civil War, 1926-30, dept. comdr., 1930-31, nat. chaplain, 1933-34; chaplain N.D. Dept. United Spanish War Vets, 1936-47; adv. com. Salvation Army, 1935-43. Mem. Am. Soc. Ch. History, Am. Numismatic Assn., S.A.R., Sons of Vets., Internat. Brotherhood Magicians. Republican. Mason, Odd Fellow. Author: History of American Revivals, 1904 (awarded George Wood prize and gold medal by Am. Tract Soc.); Christian Achievement in America, 1907; The Builders of a Nation, 1921; The Miracles of Jesus, 1926; A Mighty Winner of Souls, 1937; The History of Christianity in America, 1938; Heralds of Salvation, 1939; The Christ of the Ages, or Christianity Attested by Its Historical Effects, 1941; Religious Progress Through Religious Revivals, 1943. Home: Commercial St., Wellfleet, Mass. Died July 31, 1954; buried Geneva, Ill.

BEARDSLEY, GRENVILLE state's atty. gen.; b. Salem, Ia., Jan. 12, 1898; s. Frank Grenville and Mary Elizabeth (Riddel) B.; student Kansas City U., 1913-14; A.B., Knox Coll., 1917; student Ill. Wesleyan U. Law Sch., 1917-18, U. Tex. Law Sch., 1918; LL.B., John Marshall Law Sch. Chgo., 1923; m. Leona Marian Murray, Apr. 16, 1927; 1 son, Frank Grenville II. Admitted to Ill. bar, 1923, practiced in Chgo., 1923-53; asst. state's atty. Cook County, Ill., 1929-33; 1st asst. atty gen. Ill., 1953-59, atty. gen., 1959-. Served in U.S. Army, World Wars I and II; col. AUS ret. Decorated Legion of Merit. Home: 1834 W. 107th St., Chgo. Office: Supreme Ct. Bldg., Springfield, Ill. Died June 3, 1960; buried Holy Sepulchre Cemetery, Chgo.

BEARY, DONALD BRADFORD naval officer; b. Helena, Mont., Dec. 4, 1888; s. Lorenzo Dow and Melinda (Ervin) B.; A.B., U.S. Naval Acad., 1910; M.S., Columbia U., 1917; grad. Naval War Coll., 1937; m. Alice Lovett Keene, Jan. 15, 1919 (dec. Mar. 1953); 1 dau., Alice Ervin; m. 2d. Mary Louise Robnett, 1955. Commd. past midshipman, U.S. Navy, 1910; advanced through grades to vice adm., Oct. 16, 1948; comdr. of destroyer, World War I, transport div.; commandant, Naval Operating Base, Iceland; comdr. Fleet Operational Tng. Command, Atlantic Fleet; comdr. Service Squadron Six, Pacific Fleet, World War II; pres. The Naval War Coll., ret. Oct. 1, 1950; comdt. 12th Naval Dist.; comdr. Western Sea Frontier. Awarded Navy Cross, Distinguished Service Medal, Legion of Merit with Gold Star, Bronze Star Medal, campaign badges, Mexico, Nicaragua, China. Mem. U.S. Naval Inst. Episcopalian. Address. 820 Margarite Av., Coronado, Calif. Died Mar. 7, 1966, buried Naval Acad., Annapolis, Md.

BEASLEY, REX WEBB army officer; b. Linden, Tenn., Oct. 16, 1892, s. John Miller and Nannie Eck (Webb) B.; B.S., U.S. Mil. Acad., 1917; m. Elinor Dorothy Leonard, Aug. 2, 1943; children-Rex Webb, Martha Jean. Commd. 2d lt., F.A., US Army, 1917, advanced through grades to major gen; served with 1st Division, France, World War I; comdr. div. arty. 81st Div., World War II. Decorated Purple Heart; Silver

Star. Mem. Delta Kappa Epsilon. Address: 555 Lakeshore Dr., Asheville, N.C. Died Feb. 25, 1961; buried Arlington Nat. Cemetery.

BEATH, ROBERT BURNS fire ins.; b. Phila., Jan. 26, 1839; s. David and Robena (Wilson) B.; pub. sch. edn.; m. Margaret E. Blinkhorn, 1863. Pvt. to lt. col., Pa. Vols. in Civil War; wounded at Chapin's Farm, Va., Sept. 29, 1864, requiring amputation of right foot; Surveyor-gen. of Pa., 1872-75; agt., spl. agt., and sec., 1881-92, pres. 1892-, United Firemen's Ins. Co. of Phila. Sec., 1885-1902, pres., 1902-, Nat. Bd. of Fire Underwriters. Republican. Comdr. Dept. of Pa. G.A.R., 1873-74, comdr.-in-chief, 1883-84. Author: History of the Grand Army of the Republic, 1888; Historical Catalogue St. Andrew's Soc. of Pa., 1907, 1913; Grand Army Blue Book, Its Decisions and Laws (last edit.), 1910. Home: Philadelphia, Pa. Died Nov. 25, 1914.

BEATON, LINDSAY EUGENE physician; b. Chgo., Jan. 25, 1911; s. David and Vera (de Lipkau) B.; A.B. summa cum laude, Darmouth, 1932; M.D., Northwestern U., 1938, M.S., 1939, student Inst. Neurology, 1940-42; m. Eileen Barrows, June 28, 1962; children-Kathleen Fraser, Jeremy de Lipkau. Intern, Passavant Meml. Hosp., 1939-41; inst. anatomy and neurology Northwestern U. Med. Sch., 1936-38; lectr. dept. physiology U. Ariz.; attending physician St. Mary's Hosp., Tucson Med. Center, St. Joseph's Hosp.; cons. VA Hosp., Tucson, U.S. Army Hosp., Ft. Huachuca, Ariz. Mem. Ariz. Hosp. Bd, 1952. Pres., Family Service Agy., 1956-57, Tucson Child Guidance Clinic, 1958-59; chmn. social planning and priorities com. Tucson Community Council. Served from capt. to lt. col. M.C., AUS, 1941-46. Diplomate, asst. examiner Am. Bd. Psychiatry and Neurology. Fellow Am. Psychiat. Assn., Acad. Neurology, Am. Acad. Forensic. Scis.; mem. A.M.A. (del. Ho. Dels.; vice council mental health), Ariz. Med. Assn. (past pres.). Pima County Med. Soc., Am. Assn. Med. Colls. (editorial com. 1962), Phi Beta Kappa, Sigma Xi, Alpha Omega Alpha, Beta Theta Pi, Phi Kappa Epsilon. Contbr. chpt.: The Crisis in American Medicine, 1962; Today's Health Guide, A.M.A., 1964. Asso. editor U.S. Army Med. History of World War II, Neuropsychiatry in the War Against Japan, 1964. Contbr. numerous articles sci. jours. Home: 1615 N. Norton St. Office: 123 S. Stone Av., Tucson. Died Feb. 1967.

BEATTY, CHARLES CLINTON clergyman; b. Antrim County, Ireland, circa 1715; s. John and Christiana (Clinton) B.; attended "Log Coll.," Neshaminy, Pa.; m. Anne Reading, June 24, 1746. Licensed to preach, 1742; assisted in William Tennent's ch., Neshaminy, 1743, pastor, 1743; missionary in Va. and N.C., 1754; chaplain Pa. troops engaged in fighting in Indian wars, 1755; active in organizing relief funds for ministers' widows and in conversion of Indians; moderator Presbyn. Synod of N.B. (Can.), 1764; became trustee Coll. of N.J. (now Princeton), 1763. Author: Journal of a Two Months Tour among the Frontier Inhabitants of Pennsylvania, 1768. Died Barbados, W.I., Aug. 13, 1772; buried Barbados.

BEATTY, FRANK EDMUND, Naval officer; b. Azatlan, Wis., Nov. 26, 1853; s. Edmund and Annette (Brayton) B.; grad. U.S. Naval Acad., 1875; m. Anne Meem, d. William Daingerfield and Lelia Russell (Meem) Peachy, Apr. 29, 1891. Promoted through the various grades to rank of capt., July 1, 1908; rear adm., Apr. 27, 1912. Served on various ships; comd. Battleship Wisconsin on tour of world, 1908; commandant Navy Yard, Washington, and supt. Naval Gun Factory, 1910-13; comdr., 1st div., Atlantic Fleet, on U.S.S. Florida, 1914; apptd. comdr. Navy Yard, Norfolk, Va., Jan. 1915; temporarily detached May 10, 1915, to take command of the "Red," enemy forces in a strategical Navy Dept. problem; was successful and constructively defeated the U.S. Fleet and landed 20,000 men on U.S. shores. Episcopalian. Retired Nov. 26, 1915; ordered to active duty, 1917, and assigned as commandant 6th Naval Dist., Charleston, S.C. Home: Washington, D.C. Died Mar. 16, 1926.

BEATTY, JOHN soldier; b. Sandusky, O., Dec. 16, 1828; pub. sch. edn. Raised a co. of vols., Apr. 1861; lt. col., 3d Ohio Inf., Apr. 27, 1861; col., Feb. 12, 1862; brig. gen. vols., Nov. 29, 1862; was with McClellan in W. Va. campaign; accompanied O. M. Mitchel in dash through Tenn. to Northern Ala.; apptd. provost marshal Huntsville, Ala.; returned with Buell's army to Louisville in pursuit of Bragg; fought his regt. in battle of Perryville, Ky., Oct. 8, 1862; comd. brigade at Stone River; in Tullahoma campaign, 1863; in battle of Chickamauga, and march to Knoxville for the relief of Burnside; resigned Jan. 28, 1864. Presdl. elector, 1860; mem. 40th Congress to fill unexpired term (1868-69); mem. 41st and 42d Congresses (1869-73), 8th Ohio Dist.; presdl. elector-at-large, 1884. Republican. Pres. Ohio, Chickamauga and Chattanooga Nat. Mil. Park Commn. Author: The Citizen Soldier, 1876; Belle o' Becket's Lane, 1882; High Tariff or Low Tariff, Which?, 1894; Answer to "Coin's Financial School," 1896; The Acolhuans, 1902; McLean, A Romance of the War, 1904. Home: Columbus, O. Died 21, 1914.

BEAUMONT, JOHN COLT naval officer; b. Wilkes-Barre, Pa., Aug. 27, 1821; s. Andrew and Julia (Colt) B.; m. Fanny Dorrance, Oct. 27, 1852; m. 2d, Fannie King, 1874. Commd. midshipman U.S. Navy, 1838, lt., 1852; ship comdr. during Civil War; played leading part in capture of Ft. Wagner, July 1863; commanded Miantonomah (1st monitor to cross Atlantic Ocean); commd. capt., 1867; commandant Portsmouth Navy Yard, 1882; ret. as rear adm., 1882. Died Durham, N.H., Aug. 2, 1882; buried Arlington (Va.) Nat. Cemetery.

BEAUMONT, JOHN COLT officer Marine Corps; b. Washington, D.C., Oct. 7, 1878; s. John Colt and Frances Sayer (King) B.; student St. John's Coll., Annapolis, 1895-96, Fordham U., 1897-99; grad. Naval War Coll., 1930, Army War Coll., 1931; m. May Lansing Gates 1906 (died 1916); 1 dau., Natalie; m. 2d, Helen Ferguson Tucker, April 3, 1937. Commd. 2d lt. U.S.M.C., 1900, and promoted through grades to Col., apptd. brig. gen., July 25, 1935; served in the Philippines, 1902-04, Nicaraguan Revolution, 1912, Vera Cruz occupation, 1914, Haitian Revolution, 1915, World War, 1917-18; on staff comdr.-in-chief U.S. Marine Corps Forces in China, 1933-36; comdr. of 2d Brigade Marines, Shanghai, during China-Japan hostilities Sept. 1937-Feb. 18, 1938. Awarded Order de Merite by President of Nicaragua; Navy Cross, World War. Catholic. Clubs: Army and Navy (Washington); University (Phila.); Chevy Chase (Md.). Address: Navy Dept., Washington, D.C. Died Apr. 12, 1942.

BEAUMONT, WILLIAM surgeon; b. Conn., Nov. 21, 1785; s. Samuel and Luctetia (Abel) B.; m. Mrs. Deborah Platt, 1821, 1 son, 2 daus. Apprenticed to physician, St. Albans, Vt., 1810-13; licensed to practice medicine by 3d Med. Soc. of Vt., 1812; surgeon 6th Inf., Plattsburg, N.Y., 1812-15; practiced medicine, Plattsburg, 1815-20; post surgeon Ft. Mackinac, Mich., 1820-25; treated patient with stomach wound and made important discoveries regarding digestive processes, 1822, conducted expts. with patient (Alexis St. Martin) until 1834 while stationed as post surgeon at Ft. Niagara, 1825-26, Ft. Howard, 1826-28, Ft. Crawford, 1828-34, corresponded with leading scientists about gastric fluids in digestion; served in St. Louis, 1834-39; resigned from Army Med. Corps, 1839; practiced medicine, St. Louis, until 1853. Author: Experiments and Observations on the Gastric Juice and the Physiology of Digestion (pioneer studies on digestion including over 200 expts.), 1833, 2d edit., 1847. Died St. Louis, Apr. 25, 1853; buried Bellefontaine Cemetery, St. Louis.

BEAUREGARD, AUGUSTIN TOUTANT naval officer; b. San Antonio, Dec. 1, 1885; s. Richard Toutant and Aglae (Phillips) B.; student U.S. Naval Acad., 1903-06, Naval War Coll., Newport, R.I., 1936-37; m. Elizabeth Henry Munford, Nov. 18, 1915; 1 dau., Elizabeth Toutant (wife of Capt. Porter Fryman Bedell, U.S.N.). Commd. ensign, USN, 1908, advanced through grades to capt., 1932; commd. rear adm., 1941; naval aide to President-elect Brum of Uruguay on visit to U.S., 1918. Prestes of Brazil on visit to U.S., 1930, Herbert Hoover on South Am. tour, 1928-29; mem. naval mission to Brazil, 1922-27; naval attache, Paris and Madrid, 1934-36; chief U.S. Naval Mission to Brazil, 1939-41; staff comdr.-in-chief U.S. Pacific Fleet, 1911-12, 16-17; staff comdr. 4th Div. Atlantic Fleet, 1914-15; staff comdr.-in-shief U.S. Fleet, 1932-33; commd. rear admiral, 1941, apptd. naval attache Am. Embassy, Rio de Janeiro, Brazil, 1941; retired because of physical disability, 1942; relieved of all active duty, 1943 while chief of naval mission to Brazil. Decorated Officer Legion of Honor (France); Commemorative Medal of Founding of Republic, Comdr. Order of Naval Merit, Grand Officer of Order of Southern Cross, Army Medal (Brazil); Order Abdon Calderon, 1st class (Ecuador); Victory medal with patrol clasp, World War I, Mexican Campaign Medal, 1914, U.S. Legion of Merit for service of distinguished character in Brazil, Defense ribbon, service in Am. theatre of operations, 1941-43. Club: Army and Navy (Washington). Died Apr. 8, 1951; buried Arlington Nat. Cemetery.

BEAUREGARD, PIERRE GUSTAVE TOUTANT army officer, state ofcl.; born in St. Bernard Parish, Louisiana, May 28, 1815; the son of Jacques and Helene (de Reggio) B.; grad. U.S. Mil. Acad., 1838; m. Laure Villere, Sept. 1841; m. 2d, Caroline Deslonde, 1860. Served in Corps Engrs., U.S. Army, La., 1838-46; mem. staff Gen. Scott as engr. during Mexican War, 1846-47; received brevets for conduct at battles of Cerro Gordo and Contreras; promoted capt., 1853, served in Corps Engrs.; apptd. supt. U.S. Mil. Acad., 1860, resigned to join Confederate Army, 1861; commd. brig. gen. Confederate Army, 1861, maj. gen., 1861; 2d in command at 1st Battle of Bull Run, 1861; in command Confederate Army at Battle of Shiloh, 1862; retreated from Corinth (Miss.) after fortifying it; in charge of coastal defense of Ga. and S.C., 1863; served in Va. theater, defeated Gen. Butler, fought at Battle of Petersburg, 1864; 2d in command to Gen. J. E. Johnston in Carolinas, circa 1865; pres. New Orleans, Jackson & Miss. R.R., Circa 1866-71; served as adjutant gen. of La. for many years after war. Author: Principles and Maxims of the Art of War, 1863; A Commentary on the Campaign of Manassas, 1891. Died New Orleans, Feb. 20, 1893.

BEAVER, JAMES ADDAMS governor; b. Millerstown, Pa., Oct. 21, 1837; s. Jacob and Ann Eliza (Addams) B.; grad. Jefferson Coll., Cannonsburg, Pa., 1856; (LL.D., Dickinson, Pa., and Hanover, Ind., 1889, and U. of Edinburgh, Scotland); m. Mary A., d. Hon. H. N. McAllister, Dec. 26, 1865. Admitted to bar, 1858; practiced Bellefonte, Pa., 1859-61: Served as 2d lt. 2d Pa. Inf., Apr. 21, 1861; lt. col. 45th Pa. Inf., Oct. 21, 1861; col. 148th Pa. Inf., Sept. 8, 1862; bvtd. brig. gen. vols. "for highly meritorious and distinguished conduct throughout the campaign, particularly for valuable services at Cold Harbor while comdg. a brigade," hon. disch., Dec. 22, 1864; shot through body, Chancellorsville, May 3, 1863; shot in side, Petersburg, Va., June 1864; lost a leg at Ream's Station, Aug. 24, 1864; resumed law practice at Bellefonte; was maj. gen. Pa. N.G., 1870-87; defeated for gov. by Robert E. Pattison, 1882; gov. Pa., 1887-91; judge Superior Ct., Pa., 1896-1906, 1906-16. Pres. bd. trustees pa. State Coll.; del. Rep. Nat. Conv., 1880; vice-moderator Presbyn. Gen. Assembly, 1888, 1895; mem. President's commn. for investigation of War Dept., 1898; del. to Gen. Missionary Conf., Edinburgh, 1910. Died Jan. 31, 1914.

BECK, CLAUDE SCHAEFFER, surgeon; b. Shamokin, Pa., Nov. 8, 1894; s. Simon and Martha (Schaeffer) B.; A.B., Franklin and Marshall Coll., 1916, D.Sc. (hon.), 1937; M.D., Johns Hopkins Univ., 1921; m. Ellen Manning, May 26, 1928; children—Mary Ellen, Kathryn Schaeffer, Martha Ann. House officer, Johns Hopkins Hosp., 1921-22; Meml. Cemetery, Chicago ILCabot fellow in research surgery, Harvard, and asso. surgeon Peter Bent Brigham Hosp., Boston, 1923-24; Crile fellow in surgery, Western Reserve Univ., Cleveland, 1924-25, various positions dept. of surgery since 1925, prof. neurosurgery, 1940-51, professor of cardiovascular surgery since 1951; with University Hospitals since 1924, asso. surgeon specializing in surgery of the heart since 1933; chief consultant neurosurgery, Crile Veterans Hosp., Cleveland, since 1945; visiting neurosurgeon, Cleveland City Hosp.; cardiac consultant Mt. Sinai Hospital, Cleve. Colonel, M.C., U.S. Army as surgeon consultant Fifth and Sixth Service Commands, 1942-45; awarded Legion of Merit, 1945. Spl. consultant Surgery Study Group, Nat. Institutes of Health since 1949. Fellow A.C.S. Mem. Am. Surgical Assn., Assn. for Thoracic Surgeons, Soc. Clinical Surgery, Am. Soc. for Exptl. Pathology, A.M.A., Am. Heart Assn., Am. Bd. of Surgeons, Am. Bd. Thoracic Surgeons (founders group), Eastern and Central surgical socs.; Cleveland Surgical Soc. (pres.), Cleveland Heart Soc. (pres.). Club: Halsted Contbr. about 125 chpts. and articles in med. books and jours. Home: East Cleveland OH Died Nov. 1971.

BECK, D. ELDEN educator; b. Spanish Fork, Utah, Apr. 11, 1906; s. Mitchell R. and Ruth Ellen (Davis) B.; A.B., Brigham Young U., 1929, M.A., 1930; Ph.D., Ia. State Coll., 1933; m. Florence Robinson, May 30, 1933; children-Janet (Mrs. Jon Clark), Brent, Linda (Brent Bullough), Larry. Chmn. biology dept. Dixie Coll., St. George, Utah, 1933-38; mem. faculty Brigham Young U., 1938-, prof. zoology, chmn. dept., 1960-; expdns. to Can., Mexico. Pres., Utah Mosquito Abatement Assn., 1964-. Served to capt. AUS, 1943-45; PTO. Mem. Am. Soc. Parasitologists, Wildlife Disease Assn., Utah Acad. Arts and Letters, Sigma Xi. Mem. Ch. of Jesus Christ of Latter-Day Saints. Author books, articles in field. Editor, Utah mag., 1935-48. Home: 1398 N. 9th East, Provo, Utah 84601. Died Aug. 11, 1967; buried Provo, Utah.

BECK, ROBERT MCCANDLASS, JR., army officer; b. Westminster, Md., May 9, 1879; s. Robert McCandlass and Amelia (Stieg) B.; B.S., U.S. Mil. Acad., 1901, Gen. Staff Sch., France, 1918, Army War Coll., 1926; distinguished grad., Sch. of the Line, 1921; m. Jessie Hamilton, Nov. 18, 1908 (dec. 1956); m. 2d, Mary Kelly Mayer, Nov. 1, 1958. Commd. 2d lt., Cavalry, U.S. Army, 1901 and promoted through grades to brig. gen., 1936, maj. gen., 1938. Served in Philippines, 1903-05, and 1909-11; participated in Aisne-Marne, Oise Aisne and Meuse Argonne offensives, World War; with Army of Occupation, Germany, 1918-19; exec. officer War Plans Div. of Gen. Staff, 1920; instr. in Cav. Sch., 1921-23; instr. Command and Gen. Staff Sch., 1926-30; instr. Army War Coll., 1931-35; comdg. gen. 2d Cav. Brig., 1936-38; asst. chief of staff, Operations and Training Div., War Dept. Gen. Staff, 1938-39, retired 1939. Awarded D.S.M.; Croix de Guerre with Palm, Officer Legion of Honor (French). Lutheran. Mason. Club: Army and Navy (Washington). Home: Washington DC Died July 4, 1970; buried Arlington Nat. Cemetery, Arlington VA

BECK, WILLIAM HENRY brig. gen.; b. Phila., June 29, 1842; s. John Rogers and Jane Owen (Ward) B.; ed. grammar and high schs., Phila.; m. Rachel Wyatt Elizabeth Tongate, Aug. 21, 1863. Corporal Co. B, 10th Ill. Vol. Inf., Apr. 16-July 29, 1861; promoted through grades to col. 49th U.S. Vol. Inf., Sept. 9, 1809; maj. 6th U.S. Cav., Feb. 2, 1901; hon. disch. vol. service, June 30, 1901; transferred to 8th Cav., Feb. 25, 1903; lt. col. 3d Cav., Apr. 15, 1903; brig. gen. U.S.A., Apr. 7, 1905; retired at own request, Apr. 8, 1905. Died 1911.

BECKER, ELERY RONALD zoology, parasitology; b. near Sterling, Ill., Dec. 5, 1896; s. William Edgar and Emma Catherine (Gerdes) B.; A.B., U. of Colo., 1921, D.Sc., Johns Hopkins, 1923; m. Helen Pauline Grill, June 24, 1925; children-Helen Catherine, Ronald Ernest, William Elery. Instr. Zoology, Princeton, 1923-25; asso. prof. zoology, Ia. State Coll., 1925-35, prof., 1935-58; prof. zoology Arizona State Univ., 1958-61. Served as private, Medical Dept., World War I; maj., Sanitary Corps, A.U.S., World War II. Sec.-treas. Ia. Acad. Sci., 1941-43. Member American Society of Zoologists, Am. Society of Parasitologists (pres. 1954), Beta Beta Beta, American Soc. Naturalists, Soc. Protozologists (sec.-treas. 1949-52, pres. 1959), Am. Soc. Tropical Medicine and Hygiene, Sigma Xi, Phi Beta Kappa, Phi Kappa Phi, Gamma Sigma Delta. Conglist. Author of Coccidia and Coccidiosis, 1934; Brief Directions in Histological Technique. Contbr. on sci. subjects. Editor Jour. of Parasitology. 1959-61. Home: 724 E. Granada Dr., Tempe, Ariz. Died Nov. 20, 1962; buried Green Acres Meml. Park, Scottsdale, Ariz.

BECKER, HOWARD (PAUL) sociologist; b. New York, N.Y., Dec. 9, 1899; s. Paul John and Letitia Dickson (Stevenson) B.; B.S., Northwestern U., 1925, A.M., 1926; exchange fellow, U. of Cologne, 1926-27; Ph.D., U. of Chicago, 1930; m. Frances Bennett, Mar. 16, 1927; children-Elizabeth Fairchild, Christopher Bennett, Ann Hemenway. Began work at 14 as unskilled laborer, later became indsl. engr.(Dort Motor Co., Internat. Harvester Co., etc.); admitted to college by examination 1922; began teaching as grad. instr. of sociology, U. of Chicago, 1928; instr. sociology, U. of Pa., 1928-31; asso. prof. sociology, Smith Coll., 1931-37; prof. sociology, U. of Wis., 1937-, chmn. dept. sociology and anthropology, 1951-55; research cons. Internat. Order of DeMolay, 1955-; sociology lectr. Harvard, 1935, Birmingham, England, 1951, Toronto, Canada, 1952, lecturer summer schools Harvard, Columbia and Stanford Universities. Member American Sociologial Soc. (pres.-elect 1958), German Sociol. Soc. (hon.), Midwest Sociol. Soc. (pres. 1946-47), Sociol. Research Assn., Institut Internat, de Sociologie, Phi Beta Kappa. Research fellowship abroad, Social Science Research Council, 1934-35. Mem. O.S.S., World War II; leader of Morale Operations Unit for Germany. with Secret Intelligence; chief higher education with O.M.G., Hesse, Germany, 1947-48. Mason (32ff, Shriner). Clubs: University, Fourth Monday, Professional Men's (all of Madison, Wisconsin). Author: German Youth: Bond or Free, 1946, also German translation, 1948; Family, Marriage and Parenthood (with Reuben Hill, Marguerita Steffenson, editors) 2d ed., 1955; Through Values to Social Interpretation, 1950, also German translation, 1959; Systematic Sociology (with Leopold von Wiese), revised edition, 1950, Social Thought From Lore to Science, second edition (with H. E. Barnes), 1952, also Spanish translation, 1952, Portuguese translation, 1959; Man in Reciprocity, 1956; Societies around the World (with Irwin Sanders, et al.), 1956; Modern Sociological Theory in Continuity and Change (with Alvin Boskoff, et al.), 1957. Contbr. to profl. publs. and jours. Home: 3501 Sunset Dr., Shorewood Hills, Madison 5, Wis. Died June 8, 1960.

BECKWITH, THEODORE DAY bacteriologist; b. Utica, N.Y., Dec. 8, 1879; s. Theodore George and Jane (Day) B.; B.S., Hamilton Coll., 1904, M.S., 1907; Ph.D., U. of Calif., 1920; m. Cornelia Lyon, June 14, 1910; children—Josephine Day, Jane Crosby, Stephen Lyon, Theodore Day. Algologist, U.S. Dept. Agr., 1904-05, scientific asst., 1905-07; asst. prof. bacteriology and plant pathology, N.D. Coll., 1907-10, prof., 1910-11, asst. botanist, N.D. Expt. Sta., 1907-11; head dept. bacteriology, Ore. State Coll., and bacteriologist Expt. Sta., 1911-20; asso. prof. of bacteriology U. of Calif., and mem. Calif. Stomatological Research group, 1920-32; asso. prof. bacteriology, U. of Calif. at Los Angeles, 1932-33, prof. since 1933, head dept. since 1934; research asso. Calif. Expt. Sta., 1934-35; cooperated with Huntington Library in research dealing with foxing of paper, 1933-39; consultant for pulp and paper industry. Capt. Sanitary Corps, U.S. Army, 1918-19. Fellow A.A.A.S., Calif. Acad. Sciences; mem. Soc. Exptl. Biology and Medicine (sec. Pacific Coast sect., 1925-32; chmn. Southern Calif. sect., 1935-36; council mem., 1935-36), Soc. Am. Bacteriologists (chmn Southern Calif. sect.; council mem., 1936-37), Am. Pub. Health Assn., Southern Calif. Pub. Health Assn. (exec. com. 1938-1942); pres., 1941-42 Western Soc. Naturalists, Inst. Food Technology, Southern Calif. Dental Assn. (hon.), Phi Beta Kappa, Sigma Xi, Alpha Zeta, Gamma Alpha, Kappa Psi, Delta Upsilon, Delta Omega. Presbyterian. Mason. Author: Causes and Prevention of Foxing in Books (with T. M. Iiams), 1937. Contbr. many articles on water supply, sewage germicides, metabolism, paper faults, medical and dental bacteriology. Home: 333 19th St., Santa Monica, Calif. Died July 18, 1946.

BEDINGER, GEORGE MICHAEL army officer, congressman; b. Va., Dec. 10, 1756; s. Henry and Magdalene (von Schlegel) B.; m. Nancy Keane; m. 2d, Henrietta Clay; 9 children. Commanded a battalion in St. Clair's expdn., 1791; commd. maj. inf., U.S. Army, 1792-93; mem. Ky. Legislature from Bourbon County, 1792, 94; mem. U.S. Ho. of Reps. from Ky., 8th-9th congresses, 1803-07. Died Blue Licks, Ky., Dec. 8, 1843; buried cemetery at Licking River, Ky.

BEE, BARNARD ELLIOTT army officer; b. Charleston, S.C., Mar. 1824; s. Bernard E. Bee; grad. U.S. Mil. Acad., 1845. Commd. 2d lt. 3d Inf., U.S. Army, 1845; brevetted for meritorious conduct at Battle of Chapultepec; promoted 1st lt., 1851; served as capt. on Utah expdn. against Mormons, 1855, commd. maj. inf. Confederate Army, then Brig. gen., 1861; gave Thomas J. Jackson the nickname "Stonewall." Killed at Battle of Bull Run, July 21, 1861.

BEE, HAMILTON PRIOLEAU army officer; b. Charleston, S.C., July 22, 1822; s. Bernard E. Bee; m. Mildred Taruer, 1854. Sec., U.S.-Tex. Boundary Commn., 1839; sec. Tex. Senate, 1846; served as lt. Tex. Rangers, Mexican War; mem. Tex. Ho. of Reps., speaker for 1 term; commd. brig. gen. Tex. Militia, 1861; brig. gen. Confederate Army, 1862, primarily occupied with administry. work concerning importing munitions from Europe through Mexico; served at Battle of Sabine Cross Roads, 1864; promoted maj. gen. 1865. Died San Antonio, Tex., Oct. 2, 1897.

BEE, THOMAS Continental congressman; b. Charleston, S.C., 1725; educated in Charleston, also Oxford (Eng.) U.; studied law. Admitted to Charleston bar, 1761; practiced in Charleston; became planter; mem. Commons House, Province of S.C. for St. Pauls, 1762-64, for St. Peters, 1765, for St. Andrews, 1772-76; justice of peace, 1775; del. 1st and 2d Provincial Congresses, 1775, 76; mem. S.C. Ho. of Reps., 1776-79, 82, speaker, 1777-79; played active part in Revolutionary War; mem. council of safety, 1775,76; law judge, 1776-78; mem. S.C. Legislative Council, 1776-78; lt. gov. S.C., 1779, 80; mem. Continental Congress from S.C., 1790-82; apptd. judge U.S. Ct. for Dist. of S.C. by Pres. Washington, 1790; published reports of dist. ct. of S.C., 1810. Died Pendleton, S.C., Feb. 18, 1812; buried Woodstock Cemetery, Goose Creek, S.C.

BEEBE, LEWIS C. army officer; b. Ia., Dec. 7, 1891; s. Dr. Addison James and Ida Elizabeth (Hamblin) B.; grad. Inf. Sch., 1923, Command and Gen. Staff Sch., 1932, Army War Coll., 1939; m. Dorothy McRae, Dec. 26, 1923; children—William Wallace, John McRae. Commissioned 2d lt., Regular Army, 1917, and advanced through grades to brig. gen., March, 1942. Served as regimental staff officer in 3d div., World War I; instr. Infantry Sch., 1923-26; 1927-30; asst. chief of staff, later dep. chief of staff for Gen. MacArthur on Corregidor; chief of staff for Gen. Wainwright until surrender of U.S. forces in the Philippines, May 6, 1942; Japanese prisoner of war until Aug. 27, 1945; chief of staff for Gen. Wainwright, 1946-47; served in Europe, 1947-50, now retired. Received Distinguished Service Medal, Distinguished Service Cross, French Croix de Guerre, Purple Heart. Mem. Am. Legion (life), Tau Kappa Alpha. Episcopalian. Mason. Address: Faribault, Minn. Died Feb. 17, 1951; buried Arlington Nat. Cemetery.

BEEBE, ROYDEN EUGENE JR. ret. air force officer; b. Ft. Douglas, Utah, July 26, 1908; s. Royden Eugene and Sara (Reid) B.; B.S., U.S. Mil. Acad., 1931; postgrad. Mass. Inst. Tech., 1935; student Nat. War Coll., 1946-49; m. Janet Benedict. Oct. 29, 1932; 1 son, Hugh Grenville. Commd. 2d lt. U.S. Army, 1931, advanced through grades to maj. gen. USAF, 1951; 19th Pursuit Squadron, 1932-35; base operations, Mitchel Field, 1936-39; 9th Bomb Group, 1939-41; operations 3d Air Force, 1941-42; dir. operations Far East Air Force, then chief staff Allied Air Forces S.W. Pacific area, 1942-45; assigned office Sec. Def., 1949-53; dep. chief of staff operations USAF, Europe, 1953-56; mem. strategic survey com. Joint Chiefs of Staff, Washington, 1956-59, ret. Decorated D.S.M.; Comdr. Order Brit. Empire (Eng.). Home 1676 32d St., Washington 7. Died May 3, 1959; buried Arlington Nat. Cemetery.

BEECHER, PHILEMON congressman, lawyer; b. Kent, Litchfield County, Conn., 1775; classical edn.; studied law. Admitted to bar, practiced law; moved to Lancaster, O., 1801, practiced law; mem. Ohio Ho. of Reps., 1803, 05-07, speaker 1807; maj. gen. Ohio Militia; mem. of U.S. Ho. of Reps. (Federalist) from Ohio, 15th-16th, 18th-20th congresses, 1817-21, 23-29. Died Lancaster, Nov. 30, 1839; buried Elmwood Cemetery.

BEEHLER, WILLIAM HENRY commodore, U.S.N.; b. Baltimore, Apr. 2, 1848; s. Francis and Charlotte Maria (Bowers) B.; Concordia Coll., St. Louis; Baltimore City Coll.; grad. U.S. Naval Acad., 1868; Naval War Coll., Newport, R.I.; m. Lelia Potter, June 3, 1886. Served in Union League Co. for 3 weeks in defense of city of Baltimore, June-July, 1863, before battle of Gettysburg; ensign, 1869; master, 1870; lt., 1874; lt. comdr., 1896; comdr., 1899; capt., 1904; commodore, 1907; retired Nov. 12, 1910. Naval attache, Berlin, Rome, Vienna, 1899-1902. Chmn. World's Congress of Meteorology, Chicago, 1893; v.p. World's Congress of Navigation, Paris, 1900; life mem. U.S. Naval Inst. Awarded 2 medals, Spanish-Am. War service and San Juan. Invented and patented a self recording weighing machine, 1879, but did not market it; patented the solarometer, 1892, and instrument to determine position and compass error at sea (now in use nautical colls. U.S. and Germany). Episcopalian. Author: The Cruise of the Brooklyn, 1884; History of the Italian-Turkish War, 1912, 2d edit., 1913. Home: Annapolis, Md. Died June 23, 1915.

BEEKMAN, FENWICK surgeon; b. N.Y.C., June 1, 1882; s. William Bedlow and Katherine Morris (Parker) B.; student in St. Mark's Sch., Southboro, Mass., 1896-1901, Columbia, 1901-03; M.D., U. of Pa., 1907; m. Sabina Wood Struthers, Oct. 12, 1912; children-Fenwick, Gerardus, Robert Struthers: m. 2d, Vera Byerley Lindo, Dec. 8, 1933. Cons. surgeon Hospital for Special Surgery; cons. surgeon Lincoln and Bellevue Hosps., North County Community Hospital, Glen Cove, N.Y.; consulting pediatric surgeon Fitkin Memorial Hosp. (Neptune, N.J.). Trustee N.Y. Soc. Library, Greenwood Cemetery, Bklyn. Served A.E.F., World War, discharged as maj. Med. Corps. Cited for "meritorious service in Battle of Cambrai." Fellow Am. Coll. Surgeons; mem. A.M.A., N.Y. Co., Med. Soc., N.Y. State Med. Soc., N.Y. Acad. of Medicine, N.Y. Surgical Soc., N.Y. and New Eng. Assn. Ry. Surgeons, N.Y. Hist. Soc. (trustee, past pres.), Am. Assn. for Surgery of Trauma, Am. Assn. Oral and Plastic Surgery. Republican. Episcopalian. Mason. Clubs: Union, St. Anthony, St. Nicholas, Grolier, Pilgrims (exec. com.). Author: Office Surgery, 1932; also surg. papers. Home: 136 E. 64th St., N.Y.C. 10021. Died Nov. 21, 1962; buried Greenwood Cemetery.

BEERS, ALFRED BISHOP lawyer; b. New Rochelle, N.Y., Apr. 23, 1845; s. Alfred and Mary Elizabeth (Bishop) B.; ed. pub. and grammar schs; m. Callie H. House, Feb. 29, 1872. Served as pvt., corporal, orderly sergt., Co. I, 6th Conn. Vol. Inf.; capt. Co. B. same regt., Civil War; enlisted Aug. 25, 1861, discharged Aug. 21, 1865. Prac. law in Bridgeport, 1871; mem. Beers & Foster, 1900-; clk. City Ct., 1873; asst. city atty., 1875; judge of City Court, 1877-93; city atty., 1897-01; pres. Standard Assn., pubs. Bridgeport Standard; v.p. United Illuminating Co. Republican. Episcopalian. Mason. Comdr. in chief n.A.R., 1912-13. Mem. Soldiers' Hosp. Board of Conn., 1886-1906 (chmn, exec. com.). Home: Bridgeport, Conn. Died Mar. 30, 1920.

BEERS, BARNET WILLIAM, army officer, ret.; b. Petosky, Mich., July 18, 1896; s. William and Lucy Ethel (Kennedy) B.; student U. Ill., 1918; m. Marie Caroline Ball, Sept. 11, 1946. Served as officer U.S. Army, 1917-19; bldg. constrn. engr., 1921-31; prodn. engr. Eastman Kodak Co., 1931-39; reentered U.S. Army, 1940, advanced through grades to col., staff officer, dir. security div. 2d Service Command, Governor's Island, N.Y., 1940-44; chief civilian def. survey team U.S. Strategic Bombing Survey, Germany, Eng., Japan, 1944-46; with War Dept. gen. staff, sec. War Dept. Civil Def. Bd., 1946-47; exec. officer civil def. planning Office Sec. Def., 1947-48, asst. for Civil Def. Liaison, 1949-51, Asst. for Civil Def. Office Sec. Def., 1951-53; retired; now adminstr., Capitol Area Br. of FCDA, 1956-62; spl. liaison officer, OCBM, Washington Chmn. bd. trustees Nat. Inst. for Def. Moblzn. Recipient Legion of Merit. Army Commendation Medal with two oak leaf clusters. Mason. Home: Chevy Chase MD Died July 27, 1971.

BEERS, WILLIAM HARMON architect; b. Greensburg, Ind., May 26, 1881; s. William Harmon and Caroline Ryder (Gately) B.; student U. of Gottingen, 1897, U. of Dresden, 1898; B.S., Columbia, 1903; architect diploma of the French Government, Ecole des Beaux Arts, Paris, France, 1910; married Elizabeth Lee Dodge, April 23, 1927; 1 daughter Elizabeth Lee (Mrs. Marvin Stephens). Draftsman, Welles Bosworth, 1909-12; in practice of architecture, New York, N.Y., since 1912; partner firm Beers & Farley; architecture editor New York Herald Tribune, 1928-33. Served as capt. U.S. Army, World War I; overseas 1-1/2 years; commnd. major, U. S. Army, 1942, promoted lieut. col., 1943, col. 1945; served in England, North Africa, Italy and France. Received citation from Gen. Pershing, World War I; decorated Bronze Star (World War II); Croix de Guerre, 1944; 5 battle stars. Fellow Am. Inst. Architects (past chmn. pub. information committee; past vice pres. and past sec. New York chapter); mem. Columbia School of Architects, Soc. of Architects, given diploma by French Govvt. Clubs: Racquet and Tennis, Century Association (N.Y.); Bedford (N.Y.) Country. Home: Bedford Village, N.Y. Office: 238 E. 49th St., New York, N.Y. Died July 1, 1949; buried at Newton, Conn.

BEESON, CHARLES HENRY univ. prof.; b. Columbia City, Ind., Oct. 2, 1870; s. Henry Norris and Magdalena (Wekerie) B.; A.B., Ind. U., 1893, A.M., 1895, studied U. of Chicago, 1896-97, 1901-03; U. of Munich, 1903-05, 1906-07, Ph.D., 1907; LL.D., Indiana U., 1939; m. Mabel Banta, 1897. Tutor and instr. Latin, Indiana U., 1893-96; instr. Latin, U. of Chicago, 1906, Univ. High Sch., 1907-08; instr. Latin, 1908; asst. prof., 1909; asso. prof., 1911, prof. since 1918, U. of Chicago; annual prof. Am. Academy in Rome, 1930-31. Capt. Mil. Intelligence Div. Gen Staff, U.S. Army, 1918-19; capt. O.R.C., 1919. Fellow Mediaeval Acad., America (pres. 1936-39), Am. Acad. Arts and Sciences, Am. Philos. Soc.; mem. American Philological Assn., Classical Assn., Middle West and

South, Phi Beta Kappa, Phi Kappa Psi. Asso. editor Classical Philogy (mng. editor 1936-38); asso. editor Archivum Latinitatis Medii Aevi (Bulletin Du Cange). Club: Quadrangle. Author: Secome Latin Book (with F. J. Miller), 1901; Hegemonius Acta Archelai, herausgegeben im Auftrage der Kirchenvater-Commission der konigl. Preussischen Akademie der Wissenschaften, 1906; Isidor-Studien, Quellen und Untersuchungen zur lateinischen Philologie des Mittelaters, begrundet von Ludwig Traube, 1913; New Second Latin Book (with H. F. Scott), 1916; Third Latin Book (with F. W. Sanford and H. F. Scott), 1923; Primer of Medieval Latin, 1925; Lupus of Ferrieres, as Scribe and Text Critic, 1930. Home: 1228 E. 56th St., Chicago, Ill. Died Dec. 1949.

BEESON, HENRY WHITE congressman, farmer; b. Uniontown, Fayette County, Pa., Sept. 14, 1791; attended public schools. Became farmer; served as col. Fayette County Militia; mem. U.S. Ho. of Reps. (Democrat, filled vacancy) from Pa., 27th Congress, May 31, 1841-43. Died North Union Twp., nr. Uniontown, Oct. 28, 1863; buried Oak Hill Cemetery.

BEHAN, WILLIAM JAMES sugar planter; b. New Orleans, Sept. 25, 1804; s. John Holland and Katherine (Walker) B.; ed. U. of La., Western Mil. Inst., Nashville, Tenn.; m. Katie Walker, June 7, 1866; children - Mrs. Bessie Lewis and Mrs. Andre Dreux. Was extensively engaged in sugar planting (retired). Enlisted in Washington Artillery, New Orleans, and served through Civ. War in Army of Northern Va. (surrendered at Appomattox); a leader in reconstruction period and commanded, 1874, fight in New Orleans which deposed radical carpet-bag govt., mag. gen. La. State Nat. Guard, 1874-82; mayor of New Orleans, 1882-84; mem. State Senate, 1888-92. Left Dem. party during Cleveland administration because of efforts to place sugar on free list; chmn. Rep. State Exec. Com., 1900-12; del. to all Rep. nat. convs., 1896-; Rep. candidate for governor of La., 1904. Maj. gen. U.C.V., 1889-91; comdr. Washington Artillery Veterans' Assn., 1905-. Active in war work during World War; visited the Aisne and Somme sectors of the battle front in France, 1917. Home: New Orleans, La. Died May 4, 1928.

BEHN, SOSTHENES telephone official; St. Thomas, Virgin Is., Jan. 30, 1882; s. William and Louise (Monsanto) B.; ed. St. Thomas, Ajaccio, Corsica. Ste. Barbe, Paris, France; m. Margaret Dunlap; children—Edward John, William Charles, Margaret Cecilia. Chmn. Internat. Tel. Tel. Corp. (ret.), Internat. Std. Electric Corp.; chmn bd., pres., Cuban Telephone Co.; pres., dir., Port of Havana Docks Co., Havana Docks Corp., Radio Corp. Cuba, Standard Products Distby. Co. (Cuba), Internat. Tel. & Tel. Co. (Espana); chmn., dir. Porto Rico Tel. Co., Radio Corp, P.R., dir., chmn. finance com., Fed. Electric Corp.; dir. Am. Cable & Radio Corp., Capehart Farnsworth Co., The Coolerator Co., Fed. Telecommunications Labs., Inc., Fed. Telephone & Radio Co., Internat. Telephone Bldg. Corp., Kellogg Credit Corp., Kellogg Switchboard & Supply Co., Cia Standard Electric Argentina, Cia de Telefonos de Chile, Standard Electric Corp., P.R., Standard Elektrizitats-Gesellschfat A.G., Standard Electrica, S.A.R.L., Lisbon, Standard Electrica, S.A., Madrid, The Nat. City Bank N.Y. (ret.), L. M. Ericsson Telephone Co. Ltd., Sweden. Del. Rep. nat. conv., 1912; mem. Rep. nat. com., 1912-16. Commd. capt., Signal Corps, U.S. Army, June 19, 1917, later maj. and lt. col.; with A.E.F., France, until Feb. 1919; commanded 332 Field Signal Bn., Chateau Thierry, St. Mihiel, Argonne. Awarded D.S.M., Medal of Merit (U.S.); Comdr. Legion d'Honneur (France); Grand Cross Order of Isabela la Catolica of Spain; grand officer Order of St. Gregory. Clubs: Metropolitan (Washington); New York Yacht, Links, Knickerbocker (N.Y.); Union, Country, Yacht, Tennis (Havana). Office: 67 Broad St., N.Y.C. Died June 6, 1957; buried Arlington Nat. Cemetery.

BEHRENS, WILLIAM WOHLSEN naval officer; b. Lancaster, Pa., June 6, 1898; s. Henry Conrad and Anna Dorothy (Wohlsen) B.; ed. U. Pa., Temple U.; LL.D. (hon.), Franklin and Marshall Coll., 1943; m. Nellie V. Vasey, Oct. 22, 1921; children-William W. Jr., Patricia Anne (Mrs. Duryea Cameron). Commissioned ensign, USNR, 1918, advanced through grades to rear adm. USN, 1945; comd. Submarine Chaser No. 26, 1919-20; served in U.S. ships Quincy, Ramapo and Conner, 1920-22; duty at Naval Torpedo Sta., Newport, R.I., 1922; in U.S.S. Bruce, 1923-24, U.S.S. Whitney, 1924-26; in charge Naval Exhibit Afloat, Sesquicentennial Expn., Phila., 1926; service in U.S.S. Wyoming, 1927; duty at Receiving Barracks, Phila., 1927-28; exec. officer in U.S. ships Mahan and Lansdale, 1928-31, Wyoming, 1931, Claxton, 1931-32; comd. U.S.S. Iuka, 1932; aide to comdt. 4th Naval Dist., Phila., 1932-34; asst. 1st lt., U.S.S. Minneapolis, 1934-35; service in U.S.S. Henderson, 1935-36; comd. U.S.S. Southard, 1936-37; aide to comdt., Navy Yard, Phila., 1937-39; comdr. U.S.S. Cimarron, 1939-40; exec. officer U.S.S. Concord, during Pearl Harbor Attack and subsequent duty in Pacific, 1940-42; duty with Bur. Naval Personnel, Navy Dept., Washington, 1942-43; comdr. U.S.S. Houston, 1943-45; comdr. Naval Training Center, Bainbridge, Md., 1945-48; in charge Bur. Engring. and Constrn., Commonwealth Pa.; dep. sec. commerce Pa., sec. commerce. Decorated Navy Cross, Purple Heart, Victory Medal with submarine chaser clasp, World War I, American Nat. Defense Service Medal with fleet clasp, Am. Area Medal, Pacific-Asiatic Campaign Medal with 4 campaign stars, Victory Medal, World War II, Philippine Liberation Medal with star. Mason. Mem. Pa. Soc. Clubs: Army-Navy Country (Washington); Rotary (Harrisburg, Pa.). Home: Riverview Manor. Address: Meadow Lake, 5501 Devonshire Rd., Harrisburg, Pa. Died Jan. 27, 1965; buried Arlington Nat. Cemetery.

BEINECKE, EDWIN JOHN, business exec.; b. N.Y. City, Jan. 6, 1886; s. Bernhard and Johanna Elizabeth (Weigle) B.; ed. Philips Acad., Andover, Mass., 1901-03; grad. Yale Coll., 1907; D.H.L. (hon.), Bowdoin, 1950, Dr. Humane Letters; m. Linda Louise Maurer, Apr. 22, 1909; children—Sylvia L. (wife of Dr. John N. Robinson) Edwin John. Pres. Henry Maurer & Son, 1921-23; pres., chmn. bd. Sperry and Hutchinson Co., 1923-67, also dir.; dir., pres. chmn. U.S. Realty & Improvement Co., 1936-42; chmn. bd. Plaza Hotel Co., 1936-42; chmn. bd. George A. Fuller Co., 1941-56, dir., 1941-65; chmn. bd. Patent Scaffolding Co., 1957-61; dir. Hotel Waldorf Astoria Corp., Mfrs. Hanover Trust Co. N.Y.C. (hon.). Served as capt. construction div., U.S. Army, World War I; dep. commr. Am. Red Cross in Great Brit., World War II. Awarded Medal of Freedom. Past chmn. council fellows Pierpont Morgan Library, Yale Library Assos. Mason. Clubs: Com. of 25 (Palm Springs, Cal.), Bath and Tennis, Everglades (Palm Beach), Yale, Lawyers, Whitehall, Regency Whist, Marco Polo, Fifth Avenue, Grolier (N.Y.C.); Westchester (N.Y.) Country; Blind Brook (Port Chester, N.Y.); Portland, Savile (London). Home: Greenwich CT Died Jan. 21, 1970; buried Kensico Cemetery, Valhalla NY

BEINECKE, FREDERICK WILLIAM, advt. exec.; born N.Y.C., Apr. 12, 1887; s. Berhnard and Johanna Elizabeth (Weigle) B.; student Phillips Andover Acad.; Ph.B., Sheffield Sci. Sch., Yale, 1909; m. Carrie Sperry, Nov. 14, 1912; children—William S., Richard S. Insp. Bethelehm Steel Corp., South Bethlehem, Pa., 1909-10; asst. supr. N.Y.C. R.R., N.Y.C., 1910-11; chief engr. Red Hook (N.Y.) Light & Power Co., 1911-14; partner Washington Engine Works, N.Y.C., 1914; asst. supt. Tex. Corp., N.Y.C., 1914-19; pres. Studebaker Sales Co., Newark, 1919-29; partner Coady, Beinecke & Co., N.Y.C., 1929-32; pres. Houghton & Dutton, Boston, 1933-36; v.p. Sperry & Hutchinson Co., 1938-71, dir., chmn. exec. committee. Served as captain in U.S. Army, World War I. Established Beinecke Rare Book and Manuscript Library, Yale, 1963. Mason. Clubs: Manhattan, Metropolitan, Grolier, Yale (N.Y.C.); Wyantenuck Country (Great Barrington, Mass.). Home: New York City NY Died Aug. 1971.

BELCHER, FRANK GARRETTSON banker; b. Los Angeles, June 30, 1905; s. Frank J., Jr., and Virginia Acheson (Garrettson) B.; B.S., Princeton, 1928; m. Harriet Holbrook, Sept. 20, 1930; children—John Garrettson, Frank Garrettson, David Holbrook, Virginia Carolyn. Dir. J.D. & A. B. Spreckels Cos., San Diego; v.p., dir. First Nat. Trust & Savings Bank, San Diego; maintains Belbrook Stables at Corta Madera Rancho, Cal.; owner Electronic Engineering Assos. Ltd. San Carlos, Cal. Pres. Cal. Pacific Internat. Expn. at San Diego, 1935-36. Dir. Calif. Fish & Game Development Assn., Golden Gate Internat. Expn., San Francisco, Coronado Nat. Horse Show Assn. Chmn. Rep. Nat. Central Com. for No. Cal. USN attache, Venezuela, S.A., 1942; comdr. USN, World War II. Clubs: Bohemian (San Francisco); Cuyamaca (dir.), Coronado Riding (dir.), Marlin of Southern Calif. (founder, dir.); Campus (Princeton); Princeton (New York). Home: 1890 Spindrift Dr., La Jolla, Cal. Died Jan. 12, 1959; buried Fort Rosecrans, San Diego, Cal.

BELKNAP, CHARLES ret. univ. vice chancellor; b. Oakland, Md., Sept. 6, 1880; s. Charles and Fanny (Wheelwright) B.; student St. Pauls Sch., Concord, N.H., 1897-99; grad. U.S. Naval Acad., 1903; m. Helen M. Rockwood, Oct. 5, 1918. Commd. ensign USN, 1903, resigned, 1919, rank of comdr.; pres. Gen. S.S. Corp., San Francisco, 1919-21; v.p., later pres. Merrimac Chem. Co., Boston, 1921-35; v.p., later pres. Monsanto Chemical Co., St. Louis, 1935-46; vice chancellor Washington U. St. Louis, 1946-51; dir. Wabash R.R., Boatmen's Nat. Bank, Dir. St. Luke's Hosp., St. Louis chpt. A.R.C. Republican. Episcopalian. Clubs: Noonday, Country (St. Louis); University (N.Y.C.). Home: 45 Westmoreland St., St. Louis. Died Dec. 29, 1954.

BELKNAP, GEORGE EUGENE rear adm. (retired Jan. 22, 1894); b. Newport, N.H., Jan. 22, 1832; s. Sawyer B. Apptd. midshipman, 1852; promoted through grades to rear admiral, 1889; m. Ellen D. Reed, Dec. 8, 1861; m. 2d, Frances G. Prescott, Calcutta, Ind., Dec. 23, 1866. Fighting service in China, capture of the Barrier Forts, 1856, and through Civil war, participating in bombardment of forts and batteries in Charleston harbor, in both fights at Ft. Fisher, etc. In 1873 ordered to steamer Tuscarora to make deep-sea soundings in North Pacific, with view to submarine cable; discoveries concerning topography of ocean bed recognized by scientists world over; senior officer Honolulu at time of disturbances at election of King Kalakaua; at various times in command navy-yards at Norfolk, Pensacola and Mare Island, and supt. Naval Observatory, Washington; pres. torpedo bd.; pres. Naval Bd. of Inspection and Survey; in command Alaska, South American waters, at time of difficulty between Chile and Peru. Author: Deep Sea Soundings; etc. Honored by leading scientific socs. of Europe and America; LL.D., Dartmouth, 1894. Comd. U.S. fleet in the Asiatic Sta., 1889-92. Chairman Bd. Commrs., Mass. Nautical Training School; mem. Loyal Legion, U.S.; Naval Order of the U.S.; Sons of Am. Revolution, and G.A.R. Home: Brookline, Mass. Died 1903.

BELKNAP, MORRIS BURKE merchant; b. Louisville, Ky., June 7, 1856; s. William Burke and Mary (Richardson) B.; brother of William Richardson B. (q.v.); Ph. B., Sheffield Scientific Sch. (Yale), 1877; m. Lily, d. Gen. S.B. Buckner, C.S.A., June 14, 1883; m. 2d, Marion S. Dumont, July 16, 1900. Served pvt. to lt. col. Ky. N.G., 1879-98; lt. col. and col., 1st Ky. Vol. Inf., Spanish-Am. War, 1898. Rep. candidate for gov. of Ky., 1903. V.p. Belknap Hardware & Mfg. Co. Pres. Louisville Bd. of Trade; U.S. del. Congres Internat. of Chambers of Commerce, Liege, 1905; pres. Yale Alumni Assn. of Ky. Republican. Presbyn. Home: Louisville, Ky. Died 1910.

BELKNAP, REGINALD ROWAN naval officer, ret.; b. Malden, Mass., June 26, 1871; s. Rear Adm. George Eugene and Frances Georgiana (Prescott) B.; grad. U.S. Naval Acad., 1891; m. Julia Pomeroy Averill, March 3, March 31, 1900; children—Averill (Mrs. Andrew R. Mack), Frances G. (Mrs. Malcolm Edgar), Emilia F. (Mrs. Leonard Cresswell), Mary (Mrs. John Howard), Barberie Ann. Commd. ensign, July, 1893; promoted through grades to capt.; rear adm. by special act Congress for war service, Mar. 3, 1927; retired, 1927. Served in Spanish-American War, Chinese Boxer Campaign and Philippine Insurrection; naval attache Berlin, 1907-10, Rome and Vienna, 1908-09; Bureau of Navigation, 1902-04, asst. chief, 1912-13; Office of naval operations, planning section, 1917; in charge Am. orgn., Messina earthquake, building dwellings, etc., for 16,000 homeless; war observer, Germany, Aug.-Oct. 1914; naval aide to Ex-President Theodore Poosevelt, special ambassador at funeral Edward VII, 1910; senior officer Santiago de Cuba Insurrection, 1917; invented and patented collapsible anti-submarine net; organized, equipped, trained and commanded U.S. Mine Squadron, personnel, laying 56,500 mines in North Sea, June-Oct. 1918; dir. strategy dept., Naval War Coll., 1921-23; commanded U. S. S. San Francisco, Delaware, Colorado and Naval Training Station, Hampton Roads, Va. Bursar, treas. Gen. Theol. Sem. N.Y.C., 1929-50. Awarded D.S.M. (U.S.); Officer Order Leopold (Belgium), Officer Legion of Honor (France). Exec. chmn. Mass. Bay Tercentenary, 1928; comdr. New York chpt. Mil. Order World War, 1931-35; nat. v.-comdr. in chief, 1933-36, comdr. in chief, 1936-37; comdr. gen. Naval Order, U.S., 1932-37; pres. Naval Academy Grads. Assn. of N.Y., 1934; mem. Nat. Aero. Assn., Loyal Legion of United States (comdr.-in-chief, 1947), Founders and Patriots of America. Episcopalian; warded of Trinity Ch.; mem. bd. mgrs. Seamen's Ch. Inst., N.Y.C.; mgr. Episcopal Gen. Conv., 1934; pres. Am. Ch. Union, 1937; del. to Episcopal Gen. Conv., 1937-49; chmn. Army Day Com., New York, 1934-46; chmn. exec. com., treas., Bundles for America; chmn. of exec. com., Laymen's National Com., 1945-50. Trustee Cathedral of St. John the Divine, 1941-53. Trustee Laake and Watts Childrens Home. Clubs: Yacht, Military-Naval (Washington); Aero of N.E. (v.p.); Union, Century, Church (New York); Army and Navy (Washington). Writer on naval subjects. Home: Field Elders, Madison, Conn. Died Mar. 30, 1959; buried Arlington Nat. Cemetery.

BELKNAP, WILLIAM WORTH army officer, sec. of war; b. Newburgh, N.Y., Sept. 22, 1829; s. Gen. William G. and Ann (Clark) B.; grad. Princeton, 1852; m. Cora LeRoy; m. 2d, Carrie Thompson; m. 3d, Mrs. John Bower. Admitted to D.C. bar, 1851; mem. Ia. Legislature (Democrat), 1857-58; commd. maj. 15th Ia. Inf., U.S. Army, 1861, served at battles of Shiloh, Corinth and Vicksburg; commd. brig. gen. U.S. Volunteers, 1864, served under Gen. William Sherman in Ga. campaign; commanded 14th div. 17th Army Corps; collector internal revenue in Ia., 1865; U.S. sec. of war under Pres. Grant, 1869-76, impeached for accepting bribes from John Evans in return for appointing Evans post-trader at Ft. Sill, allowed (by Grant) to resign before his trial, found not guilty (but most of senators who voted in his favor did so because they believed him no longer under their jurisdiction). Died Washington, D.C., Oct. 13, 1890.

BELL, GEORGE soldier; b. Hagerstown, Md., 1828; s. William Duffield B.; grad. West Point, 1853; served before Civil War mainly on Tex. Indian frontier and in Seminole Indian disturbances in Fla. During Civil War instructing vol. commissaries and in Army of the Potomac on 1st movement to Richmond, in charge of sub-depots of Washington and Alexandria; chief commissary of various depts. and New York sub-depots. Bvtd. maj., lt. col., col and bvt. brig. gen. Apr. 9, 1865; col. U.S.A. Died 1907.

BELL, HENRY HAYWOOD naval officer; b. N.C., Apr. 13, 1808; Commd. midshipman U.S. Navy, 1823, lt., 1831; served on ship Grampus against pirates in

Cuban waters, 1828-29; commd. comdr., 1854; commanded San Jacinto in East India Squadron, 1856; promoted to commodore, 1862; fleet-capt. West Gulf Squadron, 1862; served in battles of Ft. Jackson, St. Philip in opening Mississippi River; commanded East India Squadron, 1865; commd. rear-adm., 1866, ret., 1867. Died Osaka, Japan, Jan. 11, 1868; buried Hiogo, Japan.

BELL, HIRAM PARKS congressman; b. Jackson Co., Ga., Jan. 19, 1827; academic edn.; admitted to bar, 1894; has since practiced at Cumming, Ga.; State senator, 1861-62; opposed secession originally, but served in C.S.A., becoming col. 43d Ga.; dangerously wounded Chickasaw Bayou, Dec. 29, 1862; mem. 2d Confederate Congress, 1863-64; U.S. Congress, 1873-75, 1877-79; presdl. elector, 1868; Democrat; mem. gen. conf. M.E. Ch., South, St. Louis, 1890. Mem. Ho. Reps., Ga., 1899-1902; State senator, 1901-02; chmn. Com. on Constitutional Amendments, Trustee Wesleyan Female Coll., Macon Ga., and Emory Coll. Home: Cumming, Ga. Died 1907.

BELL, HUGH MCKEE, coll. prof.; b. Frostburg, Pa., July 9, 1902; s. Frank W. and Mary (Smitten) B.; A.B., Willamette U., 1926; A.M., Stanford U., 1928, Ph.D., 1941; m. Eva Tacheron, June 14, 1928. Banker, Monmouth and Corvallis, Oregon, 1919-22; exec. sec. (Monmouth) Ore. Normal Sch., 1926-27, Stanford, 1927-28; teacher of psychology, dean lower dir., Chico (Calif.) State Coll., 1928-42, prof. psychology, 1956-67, dean of students, 1946-56; visiting prof. psychology, U. Maine, summer, 1954; vis. prof. U. Minn., summers 1938, 47, Denver U., summer 1956; vis. prof. ednl. psychology U. Wash., summer 1960, 66; cons. counseling psychology Office Edn., 1962-63; cons. Cal. Dept. Mental Hygiene, 1962-63; cons. Portland pub. schs. in counseling and guidance, 1959; faculty rep. Far Western Conf., 1959-60. Mem. Wesley Found. bd. Chico State Coll. Served as capt. U.S. Army, 1942-45; training specialist, Vets. Adminstrn., Washington, 1945-46, now cons. Mem. Cal. State Psychology Examining Com., 1957-67, chmn., 1958-59. Mem. Cal. Council Ednl. Research, 1948-64; mem. bd. dirs. Jour. Counseling Psychology, 1964-67; president Chico Family Service Assn., 1957. Fulbright lectr. U. Exeter (England), 1967. Recipient distinguished univ. awards. Diplomate Am. Bd. Examiners in Profl. Psychology. Mem. Shakespeare Soc. Am., Cal. Psychol. Assn. (pres. 1954), American Coll. Personnel Assn. (v.p. and mem. exec. council), Am. Psychol. Assn. (pres. div. of counseling and guidance), Nat. Vocational Guidance Assn., Western Psychological Association (pres. 1965-66), California Educational Research Association (pres.), Sigma Xi, Kappa Delta Pi, Pi Gamma Mu. Author: Theory and Practice of Personal Counseling, 1939; Adjustment Inventory (student form), 1934, rev. 1962, (adult form), 1938; School Inventory, 1936; Personal Preference Inventory, 1948. Contbr. numerous articles in ednl. publs. Methodist. Home: Chico CA Died Dec. 25, 1967.

BELL, J(AMES) FRANKLIN maj. gen. U.S.A.; b. Shelbyville, Ky., Jan. 9, 1856; s. John Wilson and Sarah Margaret Venable (Allen) B.; grad. U.S. Mil. Acad., 1878; m. Sarah Buford, Jan. 5, 1881. Additional 2d lt. 9th Cav., June 14, 1878; promoted through grades to brig. gen. U.S.V., Dec. 5, 1899; brig. gen. U.S.A., Feb. 19, 1901; maj. gen., Jan. 3, 1907. Served on plains in 7th U.S. Cav., 1878-94; captured band of half-breed Cree Indians, near Ft. Buford, S.D., 1883; in Sioux campaign, Pine Ridge, S.D., 1891; adj. of regt. and sec. Cav. and Light Arty. Sch., 1891-94; aid to Gen. J. W. Forsyth, Honor, Nov. 27, 1899, "for most distinguished gallantry in action, Sept. 9, 1899, nr. Porac, Luzon, P.I."; comd. 4th Brigade, 2d Div., 8th Army Corps, and 3d dist., Dept. N. Luzon, to July, 1900; provost marshal gen. of Manila, P.I., to Feb., 1901; comd. 1st dist., Dept. N. Luzon to Nov., 1901, and 3d Brigade, Dept. of S. Luzon to Dec., 1902; returned to U.S. 1903; comdt. of Inf. and Cav. Sch., Signal Sch. and Staff Coll. to Apr. 1906; chief of staff, U.S.A., Apr. 1906-Apr. 1910; comdr. Philippines Div., Jan. 1911-Apr. 1914, 2d Div., U.S.A., Texas City, Tex., May 1914-Dec. 1915; comdr. Western Dept., San Francisco, Calif., to May 1917, Eastern Dept. to Sept. 1917, 77th Div. N.A., Camp Upton, Sept. 1917. Died Jan. 8, 1919.

BELL, JAMES MONTGOMERY brig. gen. U.S.A.; b. Williamsburg, Pa., Oct. 1, 1837; s. William B.; grad. Wittenberg Coll., Springfield, O., 1862, A.M.; m. Emily M. Hones, of Pittsburgh, Mar. 2, 1872. Entered Union Army, 1st lt. 86th Ohio Inf., June 10, 1862; promoted through grades to brig. gen. U.S. Vols., 1900-01; brig. gen. U.S.A., Sept. 17, 1901; retired Oct. 1, 1901. Bvtd.; 1st lt. and capt. "for gallant and meritorious services in battle of the Wilderness, Va."; maj. for same at Ream's Station, Va., and lt. col. for same against Indians, Canon Creek, Mont., Sept. 30, 1877. Participated in 16 engagements in Civil War. Served on frontier of Kan., Tex., Indian Ty., Colo., Neb., N. and S. Dak., Mont., and Wyo., 1866-91; Tex., N.M. and Ariz., 1894-96; Okla. and Kan., 1896-98. Served through Civil War, Cuban war, and in the P.I., Oct. 26, 1899-Apr. 1901. Took part in Cheyenne, Arapahoe, and Kiowa war of 1867-69; Sioux wars of 1876-81; Nez Perces war of 1877. Served as guard to engrs. and construction parties on Kan. Pacific, U.P., N.P. and G.N. Trans-Continental railroads, 1867-87; 3 times wounded; Indian agt. of Ogalia Sioux Indians, Pine Ridge Agency, 1886. Comd. Bell's expeditionary brigade to the Camarines provinces, Southern Luzon, Feb., 1900; comdg. 3d dist., Dept. 2. Luzon, Mar. 1900-Mar. 1901; mil. gov. 3d dist., Dept. S. Luzon, Apr. 1900-Mar. 1901, composed of Ambos Camarines, Albay and Sorsogon provinces, and the Island of Catanduanes. Home: Pasadena, Calif. Died Sept. 17, 1919.

BELL, JOHN senator, sec. of war; b. Nashville, Tenn., Feb. 15, 1797; s. Samuel and Margaret (Edmiston) B.; grad. Cumberland Coll., Nashville, 1817; m. Sally Dickinson; m. 2d, Jane Yeatman. Admitted to bar, 1817, began practice law in Franklin, Tenn.; moved to Nashville, practiced law, circa 1819; mem. U.S. Ho. of Reps. from Tenn., 20th-26th congresses, 1827-41, opposed Jackson's bank policy and nomination of Van Buren, 1836; became Whig in late 1830's U.S. sec. of war under Pres. Harrison, 1841; mem. U.S. Senate from Tenn., 1847-59, opposed Kan.-Neb. Act and LeCompton Constn. in Kan.; became mem. Am. Party, late 1850's; advocated moderation on slave issue; Constl. Union Party candidate for Pres. U.S., 1860; favored compromise to save Union, but after Ft. Sumter advised Tenn. to join Confederacy; lived in Confederacy during Civil War. Died Stewart County, Tenn., Sept. 10, 1869; buried Stewart County.

BELL, JOSEPH CLARK radiologist; b. Punxsutawney, Pa., Aug. 10, 1892; s. Franklin Welch and Mary (Smitten) B.; A.B., U. of Ore., 1917; M.D., Harvard, 1923; m. Lorraine Seeley, May 20, 1925; children-Nathaniel S., Edith M., Joseph Clark. Interne med. service, Presbyn. Hosp., N.Y. City, 1923-24, asst. resident in medicine, fall 1924, resident in radiology, 1924-25; pvt. practice medicine specializing in radiology, Louisville, since 1925; head dept. radiology, Norton Meml. Infirmary since 1931; cons. in radiology Kosair Crippled Children's Hosp. 1933-, Ky. State Tuberculosis Sanatorium since 1936; sr. consultant in radiology U.S. V.A. Hosp., Nichols, since 1945; asso. prof. radiology, U. of Louisville Med. Sch., 1949-52, clin. prof. roentgenology, 1952-53, professor of roentgenology, 1953-57, prof. radiology, 1957-; consultant Armed Forces Institute of Pathology 1952-57; bd. dirs. Ky. Physicians Mut. Ins. Co. (Blue Shield). Served with MC Army, 1917-19; staff sergeant, 91st Division, A.E.F., 1918-19; lt. comdr., U.S.N.R., 1934-37; served with Jones Gen. Hosp., Battle Creek, Mich., 1942-45; disch. to inactive service as lt. col. Awarded Army Commendation ribbon; Silver medal by Am. Roentgen Ray Soc. for exhibit, abdominal arteriography (with associates), 1950. Certified Am. Bd. Radiology, 1934. Fellow Am. Coll. Radiology (chmn. commn. on pub. relations, 1947-51, member bd. chancellors, 1953-57); member Am. Roentgen Ray Soc. (mem. pub. com. 1950-54), Radiol. Soc. North America (bd. dirs. 19ú5-50, ú chmn. bd. dirs. 1950; pres. 1951-52), A.M.A., Southern (chairman sect. on radiology 1950-51), Ky. State and Jefferson Co. assns., Ky. Radiol. Soc. (pres. 1945-46), member local med. socs. Epsicopalian. Club: Louisville Country (bd. dirs., 1947-49). Editor: Case discussion sect. Kentucky State Med. Jour., 1954-57. Home: Glenview, Ky. Office: Heyburn Bldg., Louisville 2. Died Apr. 25, 1960.

BELL, PETER HANSBOROUGH army officer, gov. Tex.; b. Fredericksburg, Va.; Mar. 11, 1810; s. James and Elizabeth (Hansborough) B.; m. Ella Eaton, 1857. Moved to Tex., 1836; asst. adj. gen. (apptd. by Sam Houston, pres. Republic of Tex.), 1837-39; asst. adj. gen., insp. gen., 1839-40; commd. capt. Tex. Rangers, 1845; commd. lt. col. U.S. Volunteers, 1846; gov. Tex, 1849-53; mem. U.S. Ho. of Reps. from Tex., 33d-34th congresses, 1853-57. Died Littleton, N.C., Apr. 20, 1898; buried City Cemetery, Littleton

BELL, ULRIC exec., writer; b. Louisville, Ky., Dec. 13, 1891; s. William James and Caroline (Wellington) B.; LL.D., George Washington U., 1935; children—Elizabeth (Peddie), George Ulric, Ulrica; m. Vivian Hall, Jan. 22, 1955. Reporter Louisville Courier-Journal, 1910, city ed., 1919-20. Washington corr., 1921-41; exec. chmn. Fight for Freedom, Inc., 1941; asst. dir. U.S. Office Facts and Figures Jan.-July 1942; dep. dir. overseas br., O.W.I., 1942-44; exec. v.p. Americans United for World Orgn., 1944-46; executive asst. to pres. 20th Century Fox Film Corp., 1947—; press advisor Cordell Hull, U.S. delegate, 7th International Conf. of Am. States, Montevideo, Uruguay, and during Sec. Hull's tour of S. America, 1933-34. Capt. 83d Inf., 17th Div., at close of World War I. Contbr. to mags. Clubs: Gridiron (pres. 1935), Nat. Press (pres. 1926); Salmagundi. Co-author: Why Korea (motion picture academy award documentary), 1951. Home: 44 West 10th St., N.Y.C. 11. Office 444 West 56th St., N.Y.C. 19. Died Jan. 1960.

BELL, WILLIAM HEMPHILL brig. gen. U.S.A.; retired Jan. 28, 1898; b. West Chester, Pa., Jan. 28, 1834; s. Hon. Thomas S. B. (jurist); grad. West Point, 1858; bvt. 2d lt., Dec. 6, 1858; promoted through the grades to brig. gen. and commissary gen. U.S.A., Nov. 14, 1897. Served during Civil War in line of the army, in field, and in subsistence dept.; much of service west of the Missouri, in Alaska, and on the frontier. Home: Arvada, Colo. Died 1906.

BELLINGER, JOHN BELLINGER army officer; b. Charleston, S.C., Apr. 15, 1862; s. Amos Northrop and Maria Louisa (Whaley) B.; ed. pvt. schs. in Charleston; m. Marie Clarisse Coudert, Apr. 19, 1892; children - John Bellinger, Frederic Coudert, Edmund Bellinger and Rene Duchamp. Grad. U.S. Mil. Acad., 1884, commd. 2d lt., 7th Cav., June 15, 1884; transferred to 5th Cav., Oct. 13, 1884; apptd. capt. and asst. quartermaster, Aug. 11, 1894; promoted through grades to brig. gen., asst. to quartermaster gen., Dec. 4, 1922; retired from active service by operation of law, Apr. 15, 1926, having served 45 years, 9 mos. and 15 days. Served as maj. and lt. col. of vols. July 16, 1898-May 17, 1901; with cav. regt. in Wyo., Kan. and Indian Ty. (now Okla.), Oct. 1884-Aug. 1888; instr. at U.S. Mil. Acad., Aug. 1888-Aug., 1892; studied law and admitted to bar, 1894; quartermaster and disbursing officer, U.S. Mil. Acad., Sept. 1894-May 1898, and June 1900-July 1903; moved 5th Corps (Shafter's) from Tampa to Port Tampa for embarkation to Cuba; moved 7th Corps (Fitzhugh Lee's) by Army transports from Savannah, Ga., to ports in Cuba, Dec. 1898-Jan. 1899; planned and executed return of U.S. troops, due to fear of yellow fever, from Cuba and Puerto Rico through quarantine stations, Fla. and Ga., Feb.-May 1899; depot quartermaster and gen. supt. (Pacific) Army Transport Service, San Francisco, Oct. 1906-June 1909; in charge of preparing plans, constructing buildings, water system, sewage, organizing and equipping shops, railroad system and operating them for building of Ft. Mills on top of Corregidor Island, Manila Bay (City of approximately 5,000 people). 1909-11. Awarded D.S.M. "for exceptionally meritorious and distinguished services," as dept. quartermaster P.I., 1921. Originated and executed the supplying of Siberian A.E.F. at Vladivostok (specifically mentioned therefore in report of comdg. gen. of expdn.) and the purchasing of foods in the Orient and shipping them to U.S. on army transports. Also aided Philippine govt. in its problems. Received thanks of the Philippine Senate by resolution adopted Feb. 4, 1920. Died Sept. 22, 1931.

BELLINGER, PATRICK NIEWSEN LYNCH naval officer; b. Cheraw, S.C., Oct. 8, 1885; s. Carnot and Eleanor (Lynch) B.; student U.S. Naval Acad., 1903-07; m. Miriam Benoist, Apr. 16, 1921; children-Frederick, Miriam, Patricia, Marie Eleanor. Commd. ensign, U.S. Navy, and advanced through grades to vice admn., 1943. Catholic. Home: Earlehurst, Va. Died June 1962.

BELLOWS, JOHNSON MCCLURE impresario, musical and dramatic critic; b. New York, N.Y., Mar. 19, 1870; s. George Gates and Mary (McClure) B.; grad. General Theol. Sem., 1893. Ordained ministry Protestant Episcopal Ch., 1893; asst. rector St. James Ch., New York, 1894-95; rector Grace Ch., Norwalk, Conn., 1895-1901; apptd. chaplain U.S. Navy, by Theodore Roosevelt, 1902; served with rank of jr. lt., 1902-08; resigned from Navy and ch., 1908 to take up profession of music. Pupil of Sargent and Bissell. Music critic on Hartford Globe and Times, 1908-11; same, St. Paul Dispatch and Pioneer Press, 1911-15; for several years manager of Chicago Office, Columbia Concerts Corp., of Columbia Broadcasting System; retired. Mem. Soc. Colonial Wars, New York. Address: Care Bankers Trust Co., 529 5th Av., New York, N.Y. Died Apr. 8, 1949.

BELMONT, PERRY b. N.Y. City, Dec. 28, 1850; s. late August and Caroline Slidell (Perry) B.; A.B., Harvard, 1872; studied civil law, U. of Berlin; LL.B., Columbia, 1876; m. Jessie Robbins, 1899. Admitted to bar, 1876; in practice, 1876-81; mem. 47th to 50th Congresses (1881-89), chmn. Com. on Foreign Affairs, 1885-89; E.E. and M.P. to Spain, 1888-89; del. Dem. Nat. Conv., 1890, 96, 1900, 04, 12; maj. insp. gen. 1st U.S. Q.-M. Corps, U.S. Army, May 1917. Mem. advisory bd. Am. Defense Soc. Mem. Soc. of the Cincinnati. Comdr. Legion of Honor of France; Sacred Mirror (Japan). Clubs: Metropolitan (New York and Washington, D.C.); Knickerbocker, Brook, New York Yacht, Army and Navy, Union, Harvard, Jockey, Turf and Field (pres.), United Hunts Assn. (pres.), Coaching. Democratic. Manhattan, Newport Reading Room. Author: National Isolation an Illusion, 1924; Survival of the Democratic Principle, 1926; Return to Secret Party Funds, 1927; Political Equality, Religious Toleration, 1928; An American Democrat, 1940. Home: Newport, R.I. Died May 25, 1947.

BELO, ALFRED HORATIO pres. A.H. Belo & Co., publishers Galveston News and Dallas News; b. Salem, N.C., May 27, 1839; elected capt. Forsyth Rifles, April 1861; served in army of Northern Va. (Confederate); wounded at Gettysburg and at Cold Harbor; went to Texas at close of war; became mgr. Galveston News; established Dallas News, 1885. Home: Dallas, Tex. Died 1901.

BEMIS, HAROLD MEDBERRY, naval officer (ret.); b. Oshkosh, Wis., July 15, 1884; s. Eric Eugene and Sarah Elizabeth (Storr) B.; B.S., U.S. Naval Acad., 1906; grad., Naval War Coll., 1934; m. Hazel Haynes, Nov. 20, 1926. Commd. ensign U.S. Navy, Sept. 12, 1906, advanced through grades to rear adm., Jan. 10, 1941; ret. from active service upon reaching statutory retirement age, Aug. 1, 1946; pres. and chmn. of bd., Compania Anonima Venezolana Lummus, Caracas, Venezuela, 1947-53. Awarded D.S.M., Victory medals

(World Wars I and II), Am. Defense and Am. Campaign medals, Star of Calderon (Ecuador). Clubs: Army Navy (Washington), Chevy Chase (Md.), Caracas Country, Americano (Venezuela). Home: Washington DC Died Feb. 1970; buried Arlington Nat. Cemetery, Arlington VA

BENEDICT, JAY LELAND army officer; b. Hastings, Neb., Apr. 14, 1882; s. Fred Jay and Eliza (Calvert) B.; B.S., U.S. Mil. Acad., 1904; hon. grad. Command and Gen. Staff School, 1925; grad. Army War Coll., 1926; m. Dr. Loretta K. Maher, June 14, 1924; 1 dau.; Margaret Ann (wife of Capt. Wilbur H. Vinson, Jr., U.S. Army). Private and sergt., Neb. Nat. Guard, 1898-99; commd. 2d lt. inf., U.S. Army, 1904, and advanced through the grades to maj. gen., Oct. 2, 1940; instr. U.S. Mil. Acad., 1908-12 and 1916-17; maj. and lt. col. field arty. and col. inf. during World War I; gen. staff War Dept., 1920-24; and 1926-30; insp. gen. Hawaiian Dept., 1930-34; chief of staff 8th Corps Area, 4th Army Corps, Nov. 1940-Sept. 1941; comdg. 9th Corps Area, 1941-42; on duty in War Dept., 1942-46; Retd. May 1, 1946. Awarded D.S.M., Legion of Merit. Episcopalian. Clubs: Army and Navy, Army-Navy Country. Home: 4606 Langdrum Lane, Chevy Chase 15, Md. Died Sept. 16, 1953.

BENET, (JAMES) WALKER army officer; b. at Richmond, Ky., July 16, 1857; s. Brig. Gen. Stephen V. (chief of ordnance U.S.A.) and Laura (Walker) B.; grad. U.S. Mil. Acad., 1880, grad. Arty. School, 1884; m. Frances Neill Rose, of Phila., Pa., June 25, 1883. Commd. 2d lt. 15th inf., June 12, 1880; trans. to 5th Arty., Mar. 18, 1881; 1st lt., July 18, 1886; trans. to ordnance, Oct. 26, 1886; capt., June 12, 1894; maj., Jan. 19, 1904; lt. col., Aug. 9, 1907; col., Aug. 5, 1911. Asst., Frankford Arsenal, Phila., 1890-94; at Bethlehem Iron Works, S. Bethlehem, Pa., 1894-98; insp. ordnance, hdqrs. Buffalo, 1898-99; asst., Watervliet Arsenal, N.Y., 1899-1904, Rock Island (Ill.) Arsenal, 1904-05; comdg. Benicia (Cal.) Arsenal, and armament officer Western Dept., 1905-11; comdg. Augusta (Ga.) Arsenal Aug. 1911-Mar. 1919; comdg. Ordnance Training Corps, Camp Hancock, Augusta, Ga., June 1918-Feb. 1919; comdg. Watervliet Arsenal, N.Y., since Mar. 1919. Mem. Loyal Legion. Agnostic. Club: Union (Troy, N.Y.). Address: Watervliet Arsenal, N.Y.

BENET, LAURENCE VINCENT mech. engr.; b. West Point, N.Y., Jan. 12, 1963; s. Brig. Gen. Stephen V. and Laura (Walker) B.; prep. edn., Emerson Inst., Washington; Ph.B., Yale, 1884; m. Margaret Cox, Dec. 20, 1899 (died July 20, 1941). With La Societe Hotchkiss & Cie., Paris, since 1885; now hon. pres. Ensign U.S. Navy, Spanish-Am. War, 1898; with Am. Ambulance and Hosp. Service, Aug. 1914-1917; rank of comdt.; mem. advisory com. Purchasing Bd., A.E.F., Sept. 1917-Jan. 1918. Past pres. and gold medalist Am. Chamber of Commerce in France, Am. Aid Soc. Decorated Grand Officer Legion of Honor, Medal of Honor, 1st Class (France); Comdr. Mil. Order of Christ (Portugal); Comdr. Order of Crown of Rumania; Officer of Osmania (Turkey); Am. Field Service, First Class, etc. Mem. Am. Soc. Mech. Engrs., Yale Engring. Assn., Nat. Councillor Chamber Commerce of the U.S., Ingenieurs Civiles de France, U.S. Naval Inst., S.R., S.A.R., Loyal Legion, Mil. Order of Foreign Wars of the U.S., U.S. Army, Ordnance Assn., United Vets of Spanish-Am. War; fellow Am. Geog. Soc., St. Augustine's Hist. Soc. Republican. Episcopalian. Clubs: Metropolitan, Army and Navy (Washington); University (New York); Cercle Interallie. American (Paris). Home: 2101 Connecticut Av., Washington, D.C. Died May 21, 1948; buried in Arlington Nat. Cemetery.

BENHAM, ANDREW ELLICOTT KENNEDY rear admiral U.S.N., retired Apr. 1894; b. New York, Apr. 10, 1832; m. 1863, Emma H. Seaman. Apptd. from N.Y., Nov. 24, 1847; served in East India squadron, 1847-51, and asstd, in capture of piratical Chinese junk; slightly wounded; in home squadron, 1851-52; Naval Acad., 1852-53; promoted passed midshipman, June 10, 1853; promoted through grades to rear admiral, Feb. 1890. During Civil war served in S. Atlantic and Western Gulf blockading squadrons; took part in the battle of Port Royal and other engagements; was in command in one of the divs. in the naval display nr. New York, Apr. 1893; in 1894 comd. squadron at Rio de Janeiro, Brazil; forced comdr. of insurgent squadron to raise blockade of city and to discontinue firing upon Am. mcht. vessels; in 1898, prize commr. at Savannah, Ga. Died 1905.

BENHAM, HENRY WASHINGTON army officer, engr.; b. Quebec, Montreal, Can., Apr. 8, 1813; s. Jared and Rebecca (Hill) B.; grad. U.S. Mil. Acad., 1837; m. Elizabeth McNeill, Oct. 3, 1843; 3 children U.S. Army, brevetted 2d lt. engrs., 1837, commd. 1st lt., 1838; served in Mexican War; brevetted captain for services at Battle of Buena Vista, 1847; capt. engrs., 1848; in charge of repairs for defenses of N.Y. Harbor, 1848-53; built Boston Lighthouse; asst. in U.S. Coast Survey Office, 1853-56; Ch Coast Survey Office, 1853-56; chief engr. Dept. of Ohio, U.S. Army, 1861; commd. maj. engrs. U.S. Army, 1861; brevetted col.; commd. brig. gen. U.S. Volunteers; charged with violation of orders during Battle of Secessionville (S.C.), 1862, appointment of brig. gen. revoked, revocation cancelled by Pres. Lincoln, 1836; commanded engr. brigade Army of the Potomac, 1863; commd. lt. col. engrs., Army, 1863; brevetted brig. gen., also maj. gen. U.S. Army, brevetted maj. gen. U.S. Volunteers, 1856; commd. col. engrs. 1867; in charge defense of Boston, N.Y. harbors 1865-82. Died N.Y.C., June 1, 1884.

BENJAMIN, JOHN FORBES congressman, lawyer; b. Cicero, Onondaga County, N.Y., Jan 23, 1817; attended public schs.; studied law. Moved to Tex., 1845, to Mo., 1848; admitted to bar, 1848; practiced in Shelbyville, Shelby County, Mo., 1848; mem. Mo. Ho. of Reps., 1850-52; Democratic presdl. elector, 1856; entered U.S. Army as pvt., 1861, promoted to capt., maj., lt. col., brig. gen.; provost marshal 8th Dist. of Mo., 1863, 64; del. Nat. Republican Conv., Balt., 1864; mem. U.S. Ho. of Reps. (Radical Rep.) from Mo., 39th-41st congresses, 1865-71; moved to Washington, D.C., 1874, became banker. Died Washington, Mar. 8, 1877; buried pvt. cemetery, Shelbina, Shelby County.

BENJAMIN, JUDAH PHILIP senator, Confederate cabinet officer; b. St. Croix, B.W.I., Aug. 5, 1811; s. Philip and Rebecca (de Mendes) B.; attended Yale, 1825-27; m. Natalie St. Martin, 1833. Admitted to La. bar, 1832; became mem. La. Legislature, 1842; del. La. Constl. Conv., 1844-45; Whig presdl. elector, 1848; prin. organizer Jackson R.R. (now I.C. R.R.), 1852; mem. U.S. Senate (Whig) from La., 1853-61; apptd. atty. gen. Provisional Govt. of Confederate States Am., Feb. 1861; acting sec. of war Confederate States Am., Sept.-Nov. 1861, sec. of war (censured severly and unjustly for Confederate losses of Roanoke Island, Forts Henry and Donelson), Nov. 1861-Mar. 1862, resigned during Confederate Congress investigation of Roanoke Island affair; appt. sec. of state by Jefferson Davis, was highly unpopular with Southern People, but possessed Davis' firm confidence; advocated arming of slaves and providing for ultimate emancipation, winter 1864-65 (plan rejected by Confederate Congress); promoted Hampton Roads Conf., Feb. 1865, believed in viability of Confederate regime until the end, but with Davis refused to make essential concessions in negotiations with U.S. Govt. in 1865; escaped to Eng. following collapse of Confederacy, Apr. 1865; admitted to bar at Lincoln's Inn, June 1866; practiced law before English courts, 1866-83, revealed logical capacities of highest order, specialized in appeal and chancery cases; argued important cases involving principles of criminal jurisdiction over foreigners, constl. issues, corporation law; ret. to residence in Paris, France, 1883. Author: Treatise on the Law of Sale of Personal Property, 1868. Died Paris, May 8, 1884.

BENNETT, ALBERT ARNOLD, mathematician, b. Yokohama, Japan, June 2, 1888; s. Albert Arnold and Mela Isabelle (Barrows) B.; came to U.S. in 1902; A.B., A.M., Brown Univ., 1910, Sc.M., 1911; Ph.D., Princeton, 1915; studied univs. of Paris, Gottingen, Bologna and Chicago; m. Velma McAfee Ely, June 17, 1922; one daughter, Betsy Bennett Miller. Instructor Princeton Univ., 1914-16; adj. professor U. of Tex., 1916-21, asso. prof., 1921-25; prof. and head of dept., Lehigh U., 1925-27; prof. mathematics, Brown U., from 1927. Editor in chief, Math. Monthly, 1923; mathematics editor Prentice-Hall, Inc. Student 1st O.T.C., Leon Springs, Tex., and Ft. Monroe, Va.; commd. capt. C.A.R.C., Aug. 15, 1917; trans. to ordnance, June 1918; hon. discharged Jan. 15, 1919; mathematics and dynamics expert, Ordnance Corps, June 1919-Sept. 1921; maj. Ordnance Corps, A.U.S., 1942-46, lt. col., 1946. Member Am. Math. Soc., Math. Assn. America (trustee 1922, v.p. 1925, 33), Am. Academy Arts and Sciences, Progressive Edn. Assn. (adv. council, 1933), A.A.A.S., Am. Assn. Univ. Profs., Am. Soc. Engring. Education, Assn. Computing Machines, Assn. Symbolic Logic (council), 1935, Assn. Teachers Math. New England (president 1941), Nat. Council Teachers of Math., Institute Math. Statistics, Rhode Island Sch. Design (Corp. mem.), Phi Beta Kappa, Sigma Xi, Delta Upsilon. Author: Introduction to Ballistic (Ordnance Dept. U.S.A.), 1921; Tables for Interior Ballistics (same), 1922; (with C.A. Baylis) Formal Logic, 1939. Address: Providence RI Died Feb. 17, 1971.

BENNETT, ANDREW CARL, naval officer; b. Goodland, Kan.; s. Andrew Pierce and Harriet Winefred (Kirkpatrick) B.; grad. U.S. Naval Acad., 1912; past grad. student various service schools; m. Jessie Crawford Biggam, Oct. 16, 1920; children—Betty Duff (wife of Lt. Donald Francis Banker, U.S.N.), Anne Douglas (wife of Lt. Charles Francis Helme, Jr., U.S.N.). Commd. ensign, U.S. Navy, 1912, advancing to rear adm., 1942; comd. submarines and submarine units, 24 yrs. also served in battleships and cruisers; comd. U.S.S. Savannah (light cruiser), 1940-42; unit comdr., Oran, Algeria, area of invasion of North Africa, Nov. 8, 1942; comdt. 8th Naval Dist., hdqrs. in New Orleans, La. since 1943. Decorated Navy Cross, also 6 campaign medals (U.S.); Legion of Honor (France). Mason (32 deg., Scottish Rite, Shriner). Clubs: Army-Navy Country (Washington, D.C.); Boston (New Orleasn, La). Home: Carmel CA Died 1972.

BENNETT, CALEB PREW gov. Del.; b. Chester County, Pa., Nov. 11, 1758; s. Joseph and Elizabeth (Prew) Wiley B.; m. Catherine Britton, Apr. 5, 1792. Joined Continental Army, 1775, sgt., 1777, served at Valley Forge, winter 1777-78; commd. 2d lt., 1778, served at battles of Brandywine and Germantown; commd. 1st lt., 1780; treas. New Castle County (Del.), 1807-33; maj. arty. Del. Militia, 1813; in command Port of New Castle during War of 1812; 1st Democratic gov. Del., 1833-36. Died Wilmington, Del., May 9, 1836; buried Friends Meeting House Cemetery, Wilmington.

BENNETT, EUGENE DUNLAP, lawyer; b. Newton Kan.; s. Dr. George Dunlap and Nellie (Akin) B.; LL.B. Hastings Coll. Law, U. Cal., 1920; m. Gertrude Douglass, Dec. 29, 1926. Practiced law, San Francisco, 1920-68; partner Pillsbury, Madison & Sutro, 1936-68; chief dep. U.S. atty. No. Dist. Cal., 1925-27; counsel Cal. Dept. Fish and Game, 1927-33; civilian aide to sec. of army, 1950-68. Mem. U.S. Commn. on Jud. and Congl. Salaries, 1953-54; chmn. U.S. sect. Inter-Am. Tropical Tuna Commn.; commr. Pacific Marine Fisheries Commn., 1948-59; nat. trustee Ducks Unlimited. Served as 1st lt. Inf. World War I, col. inf., World War II. Fellow Cal. Acad. Scis. (trustee 1950-67), Am. Coll. Trial Lawyers; mem. Am. (chmn. sect. internat. and comparative law 1961-62), Cal., San Francisco bar assns., National Rifle Association (dir.), Am. Bar Foundation, American Judicature Society (director 1959-64), Am. Legion. Clubs: Pacific Union, St. Francis Yacht, Olympic, Press, Union League, Commonwealth, Stock Exchange (San Francisco). Home: San Francisco CA Died Dec. 16, 1968; buried Cypress Lawn Meml. Park, Colma CA

BENNETT, FRANK MARION naval officer; b. Marcellus, Mich., May 7, 1857; s. William I. and Lovisa (Brokaw) B.; grad. U.S. Naval Acad., 1879; m. Mary Henderson Eastman, June, 1893. Ensign, USN, 1879, advanced through grades to capt., 1910, now commandant navy yard, Pensacola, Fla. Clubs: Army and Navy (N.Y.C.); Army and Navy (Washington). Author: The Steam Navy of the United States, 1897; The Monitor and the Navy Under Steam, 1900. Contbr. to naval and engring. jours. Home: Cassopolis, Mich. Deceased.

BENNETT, HENDLEY STONE congressman, lawyer; b. nr. Franklin, Williamson County, Tenn., Apr. 7, 1807; attended public schs., West Point, Miss.; studied law. Admitted to bar, 1830; practiced in Columbus, Miss.; judge circuit ct., 1846-54; mem. U.S. Ho. of Reps. (Democrat) from Miss., 34th Congress, 1855-57; moved to Paris, Tex., 1859, practiced law; served as capt. Co. G., 32d Regt. Tex. Cavalry, Confederate States Army, 1861-62; returned Tenn., 1886, settled in Franklin, practiced law. Died Franklin, Dec. 15, 1891; buried Oakwood Cemetery, Syracuse.

BENNETT, JOHN JAMES lawyer; b. Bklyn., Mar. 2, 1894; s. John James and Kathryn (O'Brien) B.; ed. St. Francis High Sch., Bklyn., 1908-10; LL.B., St. Lawrence U., 1926, LL.D., 1932; LL.D., St. John's U., 1938; LL.D., Manhattan Coll., 1942; m. Evelyn Anne Cogan, Sept. 4, 1923; children-Marie Louise, John James, Joan, Evelyn. Connected with bus. houses, 1910-15; asst. to Edward R. Stettinius of J. P. Morgan & Co., 1915-25; admitted to N.Y. bar, 1927; prof. law Bklyn. Law Sch., 1928-31; atty. gen. of N.Y., 1931-45, 1956-; corp. counsel, City of N.Y., 1946; dep. mayor City of N.Y., 1947-49; chief justice Ct. Spl. Sessions, 1950; chmn. N.Y.C. Planning Commn., 1951-55. Del., N.Y. State Constnl. Conv., 1938; Democratic candidate Gov. N.Y. 1942. Pres., Am. Legion Mountain Camp Corp., N.Y., 1930-55. Served as lt., A.S. U.S. Army, World War I; lt. col. AUS, World War II. Mem. Am. Bar Assn., Bklyn. Bar Assn. Assn Bar City N.Y., N.Y. State Bar Assn., Am. Legion (comdr. N.Y. 1929-30), Phi Delta Phi. Democrat. Club: Army Athletic (N.Y.). Home: 9707 4th Av., Bklyn. 9. Office: 29 Broadway, N.Y.C. 6. Died Oct. 4, 1967.

BENNETT, RAWSON, cons. engr.; b. Chgo., June 16, 1905; s. Rawson and Cora A. (Jones) B.; B.S., U.S. Naval Acad., 1927; M.S. in Elec. Engring., U. Cal., 1937; m. Mary F. Wyman, 1931 (dec.); children—Rawson, Sally Ann; m. 2d, A. Louise Holmes, 1949; children—Holmes, Gregory. Commnd. ensign USN, 1927, advanced through grades to rear adm., 1956; electronics dir. design Bur. Ships, 1943-46; comdg. officer, dir. Navy Electronics Lab., San Diego, Cal., 1946-50; dir. electronics prodn. resources Dept. Def., 1950-51; head minesweeping Bur. Ships, 1951-53, asst. chief electronics, 1954-56; chief of Naval Research, Washington, 1956-61; sr. v.p., dir. engring. Sangamo Electric Co., Springfield, Ill., 1961-63; cons. engr., 1963-69; dir. Washington Assos., Inc. Registered profl. engr., Cal. Fellow A.A.A.S., Am. Inst. Aeros. and Astronautics, I.E.E.E., Acoustical Soc. Am. Home: Arlington VA Died Dec. 8, 1968.

BENNETT, THOMAS GRAY mfr.; b. New Haven, Conn., Mar. 22, 1845; s. Thomas and Mary Ann (Hull) B.; Gen. William H. Russell's Sch. to 1861; Ph.B., Yale, 1870; m. Hannah Jane Winchester, May 9, 1872. Apptd. to drill troops for state of Conn., 1861; commd. 1st lt. and adj., Aug. 28, 1862; 3d lt. 28th Conn. Vols., Nov. 26, 1862; 1st lt. 29th Conn. Vols., Jan. 20, 1864; wounded at Battle of Chapin's Farms, Sept. 27, 1864; promoted to capt. 29th Conn. Vols., Sept. 27, 1864; hon. mustered out Nov. 1865. Entered employ of Winchester Repeating Arm Co., Aug. 1, 1870; sec. same 1871-75; dir., 1875-, treas., 1881-82, v.p., 1882-90, pres., 1890-

1911; resigned presidency, Jan. 20, 1911, and elected consulting dir. Mem. Corp. Yale U., 1884-1902; trustee Sheffield Scientific Sch.; mem. bd. mgrs. Observatory, in Yale Coll. Received decoration of the Medjidi, Turkey. Home: New Haven, Conn. Died Aug. 19, 1930.

BENNETT, THOMAS WARREN congressman; b. Union County, Ind., Feb. 16, 1831; grad. law dept. Ind. Asbury (now DePauw) U., 1854. Admitted to bar, 1855; practiced in Liberty, Union County; elected mem. Ind. Senate, 1858, resigned, 1861, 64-67; commd. capt. 15th Regt., Ind. Volunteer Inf., 1861; became maj. 36th Regiment, 1861, col. 69th Regt., 1862, apptd. brig. gen. 1865; returned to Richmond, Ind.; mayor Richmond, 1869, 70, 77-83, 85-87; gov. Territory of Ida. (apptd. by Pres. Grant), 1871-75; mem. U.S. Congress (Independent, contested election) from Ida. Territory, 1875-June 23, 1876; practiced in Richmond. Died Richmond, Feb. 2, 1893; buried Earlham Cemetery.

BENNETT, VICTOR WILSON marketing consultant and instr.; b. Frostburg, Md., May 19, 1895; s. William Sellman and Frances Susan (Wilson) B.; B.A., Gettysburg Coll., 1917, M.A., 1918; M.A., U. of Pittsburgh, Pa., 1924; Ph.D., U. of Wash., 1937; student U. of Wis., Stanford, and Boston U. Coll. of Bus. Adminstrn.; m. Mary Nell Wright, July 20, 1944 (dec. Sept. 1954); 1 dau., Nellie Susan. Instr. accounting, Boston U., 1919-20; asst. prof. accounting, U. of Pittsburgh, Pa., 1920-23; asso. prof. bus. adminstrn., Emory U., Atlanta, Ga., 1923-24; asst. prof. marketing, U. of Hawaii, 1928-31; asso. prof. and head dept. of marketing, U. of Md., 1939-42; chmn. marketing dept., U. of Miami, Fla., 1946—; accounting and marketing counselor to private firms, 1920—; management counselor Farm Credit Adminstrn., Washington, D.C., 1933-39. Mem. national panel American Arbitration Assn. Served at lt., training Platsburg Barracks, in New York and Troy, N.Y., World War I; maj. U.S. Army, World War II, directing ground training at B-26 Transition Sch., Del Rio, Tex.; personal affairs officer Blackland Army Airfield, Waco, Tex.; dir. counselor training Separation Center, Ellington Field, Houston, Tex. Mem. Advt. Fedn. of Am., Am. Marketing Assn., (past v.p., Washington chpt.; national director), Artus, Am. Legion, Philo Literary Soc. (Gettysburg Coll.), Tau Kappa Alpha, Delta Sigma Phi, Delta Sigma Pi. Dem. Meth. Mason (K.T., Shriner), Elk. Clubs: Rotary, Coral Gables Country, U. Miami Propeller (pres.), Sales Execs. Co-author: Current Economic Policies, 1934; author articles and surveys. Home: 3709 Monserrate St., Coral Gables 34, Fla. Died Mar. 1, 1955; buried Fairview Cemetery, Hubbard City, Tex.

BENNING, HENRY LEWIS laywer, army officer; b. Columbia County, Ga., Apr. 2, 1814; s. Pleasant Moon and Matilda (White) B.; grad. Franklin Coll. (now U. Ga.), 1834; m. Mary Howard Jones, Sept. 12, 1839, 10 children. Admitted to Ga. bar, 1835, practiced law, Columbus, Ga., 1835-75; mem. Ga. Gen. Assembly; secessionist del. to Nashville Conf. of 1850 which met to consider fed. legislation on expansion of slavery; asso. justice Ga. Supreme Ct., 1853-59; del. Nat. Democratic Conv., Charleston, S.C., 1860; v.p. Nat Dem. Conv., Balt., 1860; del. Ga. Secession Conv., 1861; Ga. commr. to Va. conv. to Consider Ordinance of Secession, 1861; served as brig. gen. Confederate Army, participated in battles of Sharpsburg, Antietam, Chickamauga, Gettysburg, The Wilderness. Died Columbus, Ga., July 10, 1875.

BENSON, CHARLES EMILE univ. prof.; b. Clinton, Ia., Sept. 9, 1881; s. Peter Emil and Anna (Peterson) B.; B.Ed., State Teachers Coll., Peru, Neb., 1911; A.B., U. of Neb., 1911, A.M., 1912; Ph.D., Columbia, 1922; m. Luella Linder, Oct. 10, 1906; 1 son, Frederic Rupert. Formerly teacher in rural schs. and prin. village schs.; supt. schs., Chelan, Wash., 1905-06. Nelson, Neb., 1907-09; fellow dept. psychology, U. of Neb., 1910-12; supt. schs., Lexington, Neb., 1912-14; prof. psychology and edn., State Normal Sch., Kearney, Neb., 1914-15; head dept. psychology, Southeast Mo. State Teachers Coll., Cape Girardeau, Mo., 1915-21; acting dean Sch. of Edn., 1922-23, and dir. of summer session, 1923, U. of Okla.; asst. prof. ednl. psychology, New York U., 1923-24, asso. prof., 1924-45, prof., 1925-45, prof. emeritus since 1945, also chmn. dept. of educational psychology; organizer, dir., Psycho-Education Clinic, 1925-45; educational adviser Berkeley Secretarial School, East Orange, N.J., also in New York, N.Y., and White Plains, N.Y.; psychologist Maine experiment in rehabilitation of disabled veterans, World War II, summer 1944; pres. bd. trustees, The Mills School, N.Y., 1938-41. Commissioned first lieutenant, Sanitary Corps (div. psychology), U.S. Army, February 6, 1918; served at Camp Greenleaf, Ga.; clin. psychologist, Camp Grant, Rockford, Ill.; hon. discharged, Dec. 12, 1918; retired U.S. Army, 1928. Mem. N.Y. Acad. of Pub. Edn., N.E.A. (life), Nat. Soc. for Study of Edn., Coll. Teachers of Edn., Am. Psychol. Association, National Committee for Mental Hygiene, Association of Applied Psychologists, also New York Schoolmasters Club (president 1957-58), Phi Delta Kappa, Kappa Delta Pi, Pi Gamma Mu. Horace Mann League, Kiwanis Club (honorary); fellow A.A.A.S.; associate fellow New York Academy of Medicine. Republican. Methodist. Author: The Output of Professional Schools for Teachers, 1922; Psychology for Teachers (with others), 1926, revised, 1933; Psychology for Advertisers (with D. B. Lucas), 1930. Home: 55 N. Mountain Av., Montclair, N.J., (summer) Boothbay, Me. Died Mar. 23, 1963; buried Mt. Hebron Cemetery, Upper Montclair, N.J.

BENSON, HENRY KREITZER, indsl. chemist; b. Lebanon, Pa., Jan. 3, 1877; s. William Frank and Catherine (Kreitzer) B.; A.B., Franklin and Marshall Coll., Lancaster, Pa., 1899, A.M., 1902, D. Sci., same coll., 1926; studied Johns Hopkins Univ., 1903-04; Ph.D., Columbia Univ., 1907; m. Eva A. Ronald, June 15, 1905; children—William Ronald, Margaret Elizabeth, Henry K., Betty. Prof. indsl. chemistry and chemical engineering, U. of Washington, 1905-47, professor emeritus since 1947; dir. research, I. L. Loucks' Laboratories, Inc., Seattle, 1949; former administrative head chem. dept. With U.S. Bureau of Soils, 3 summers; with U.S. Bur. Foreign and Domestic Commerce, as comml. agent, 1914, studying lumber by-products; state dir. with U.S. Naval Advisory Bd., 1916. Served as capt. research sect. of nitrogen div. of Army Ordnance, July 6, 1918-Feb. 20, 1919. Chmn. div. chemistry and chem. technology, Nat. Research Council, Washington, D.C., 1931-32. Del. Internat. Chem. Conf., Rome, Italy, 1938; chmn. Washington State Chemurgic Com. since 1942; Mem. Tech. Assn. of the Pulp Paper Industry, Am. Chem. Soc., Am. Inst. Chem. Engrs., Am. Legion (dist. comdr. 1923), Sigma Xi, Tau Kappa Epsilon, Phi Lambda Upsilon. Republican. Mem. Congl. Ch. Mason. Author: Industrial Chemistry, 1913; By-Products of the Lumber Industry, 1915; Chemical Utilization of Wood, 1932; Potential Chemical Industries of Washington, 2 vols., 1936. Contbr. of some 90 articles to tech. jours. Home: 6027 Princeton Av., Seattle 5 WA

BENSON, STUART editor; b. Detroit, Mich., Jan. 3, 1877; s. George Stewart and Martha (Bennett) B.; student U. of Mich., 1896-98; Detroit School of Art; m. Mary Helen Duggett, 1921. Began as illustrator, 1900. later advt. writer, publicity magr. art editor, Collier's Weekly, 1910-13; prodn. mgr. Erickson Co., 1913-17; syndicate mgr.; mem. New York Stock Exchange firm, Morgan, Livermore & Co., 1919-24; art editor Collier's Weekly, since 1924. Served overseas as capt. and maj. inf., 1917-19. Decorated Legion d'Honneur, Etoile Noire and Croix de Guerre (France). Clubs: Players, Dutch Treat, Westport Country. Author: (play) Find Cynthia (prod. by Kilbourn Gordon, Inc., 1922). Contbr. short stories and spl. articles. Home: Weston, Conn. Office: 250 Park Av., New York. Died Oct. 19, 1949.

BENT, SILAS naval officer; b. St. Louis, Oct. 10, 1820; s. Silas and Martha (Kerr) B.; m. Ann Eliza Tyler, 1857. Apptd. midshipman U.S. Navy, 1836, promoted lt.; flag lt. aboard ship Mississippi in Japan Expdn. led by Commodore Matthew Perry, made extensive hydrographic surveys of seas around Japan, studied Kuro Siwo current (similary to Gulf Stream); assigned to Hydrographic div. of Coast Survey, 1860; resigned because of So. sympathies, 1861. Died Shelter Island, L.I., N.Y. Aug. 26, 1887; buried Louisville, Ky.

BENTLEY, MADISON psychologist; b. Clinton, Ia., June 18, 1870; s. Charles Eugene and Persis Orilla (Freeman) B.; B.S., U. of Neb., 1895 (LL.D., 1935); Ph.D., Cornell U., 1898. Assistant in psychology, instr. asst. prof., Cornell, until 1912; prof. psychology, and dir. psychol. labs., U. of Ill., 1912-28; Sage prof. psychology, Cornell, 1928-38; consultant for psychology, Library of Congress, 1938-40, lecturer in psychology, Cornell Univ., 1942-44; chmn. division anthropology and psychology, Nat. Research Council, 1930-31. Capt. Air Service, 1917-18; major, U.S. Army, 1924-34. Fellow A.A.A.S.; mem. Am. Psychol. Assn. (pres. 1925), Phi Beta Kappa, Sigma Xi, and Phi Kappa Psi. Wrote section on History in A Manual of American Literature, 1909; also articles on psychol. subjects in New Internat. Ency., Internat. Year Book, Ency. Americana, United Editors' Ency.; mag. articles. Editor of American Journal Psychology, 1903-51. Author: Studies in Social and General Psychology, 1916; Critical and Experimental Studies in Psychology, 1921; The Field of Psychology, 1924; Studies in Psychology from the University of Illinois, 1925; The New Field of Psychology, Pt. 1, The Psychological Functions and Their Government, 1934; The Problems of Mental Disability in England, 1938; Cornell Studies in Dynasomatic Psychology, 1938; The Theater of Living in Animal Psychology, 1943; Tools and Terms in Recent Researches since, 1943; Sanity in the Life Course, 1946; Towards a Psychological History of the Hominids, 1947; Primary Factors in the Government of certain Biomechanical Systems, 1952. Address: 733 Oregon Av., Palo Alto, Cal. Died May 29, 1955.

BENTLEY, WILLIAM BURDELLE chemist; b. Maple Valley, N.Y., Aug. 8, 1866; s. William Henry and Elizabeth (Cummings) B.; A.B., Harvard, 1889, A.M., 1890, Ph.D., 1898; m. Susan E. Prescott, Dec. 15, 1891 (died 1923); children—William Prescott, Harold Jackson; m. 2d, Henrietta J. Prescott, July 1925 (died May 19, 1956). Asst. in chem. lab. Harvard, 1889-91. U.S. Torpedo Sta., Newport, R.I., summer 1890; adj. and asso. prof. chemistry Ohio U., 1900-36, now emeritus. Served as capt. Ordnance Dept., U.S. Army, 1918-19, stationed Watertown (Mass.) Arsenal. Mem. Am. Chem. Soc., A.A.A.S. Mason (K.T.). Home: Athens, O. Died July 14, 1945; buried Athens.

BENTON, GUY POTTER univ. pres.; b. Kenton, O., May 26, 1865; s. Daniel Webster and Harriet (Wharton) B.; A.B., Baker U.; A.M., Ohio Wesleyan; also studied U. of Wooster, and in Berlin; D.D., Baker, 1900, Ohio Wesleyan U., 1905; LL.D., Upper Iowa U., 1906, U. of Vt., 1911, Middlebury Coll., 1912, U. of Miss., 1914; Miami U., 1916; L.H.D., Norwich U., 1916; m. Dollar Konantz, Sept. 4, 1889; children - Mrs. Helen Minnich, Pauline. Supt. of schs., Ft. Scott, Kan., 1890-95; asst. state supt. pub. instrn., Kan., 1895-96; prof. history and sociology, Baker U., 1896-99; pres. Upper Iowa U., 1899-1902, Miami U., 1902-11; pres. U. of Vt., 1911-19; chief ednl. consultant, pres. U. of Philippines, 1921-24; retired. With A. E. F., 1917-19; gen. sec. Y.M.C.A. for City of Paris, Sept., Oct. and Nov. 1917; chief organizing sec. for Y.M.C.A. with membership on staff of Brig. Gen. Sample, comdr. in chief of advance sect., A.E.F., Nov. 1917-June 1919; chief sec. 8th Region, A.E.F., 1919; mem. U.S. Army Ednl. Corps and chief ednl. dir. Am. Army of Occupation with hdqrs. at Coblenz, Germany, to June 30, 1919; hon disch. from U.S.A., July 24, 1919. Awarded D.S.M. by President of U.S. for war service, Apr. 19120. Author: The Real College, 1909. Home: Minneapolis, Minn. Died June 28, 1927.

BENTON, JACOB congressman, lawyer; b. Waterford, Caledonia County, Vt., Aug. 19, 1814; grad. Burr and Burton Sem., Manchester, 1839; studied law. Tchr. several years; moved to Lancaster, Coos County, N.H., 1842; admitted to bar, 1843; practiced in Lancaster; mem. N.H. Ho. of Reps., 1854-56; del. Nat. Republican Conv., Chgo., mem. U.S. Ho. of Reps. (rep.) from N.H., 40th-41st congresses, 1867-71. Died Lancaster, Sept. 29, 1892; buried Summer Street Cemetery.

BENTON, JAMES GILCHRIST army officer; b. Lebanon, N. H., Sept. 15, 1820; s. Calvin and Mary (Gilchrist) B.; grad. U.S. Mil. Acad., 1842; m. Catherine Webb, Aug. 17, 1859. Brevetted 2d lt. U.S. Ordnance Corps, 1842, commd. 2d lt., 1847, 1st lt., 1848, capt., 1856; instr. ordnance and gunnery U.S. Mil Acad., 1857-61; prin. asst. to chief of ordan chief of ordnance, 1861-63; commanded Washington Arsenal, 1863-66; maj., 1863, brevetted lt. col. and col., 1865; commanded Nat. Armory, Springfield, Mass., 1866-81; promoted lt. col., 1874, col., 1875; inventor electro-ballistic chronograph for determining velocity of shells, a velocimeter, a spring dynamometer, a cap-filling machine, made improvements on Springfield rifle. Died Springfield, Aug. 23, 1881.

BENTON, LEMUEL congressman, farmer; b. Granville County, N.C., 1754; Moved to Cheraw Dist. (now Darlington County, S.C.), became planter, large landowner; elected maj. Cheraw Regt., 1777, served throughout Revolutionary War; promoted to col., 1781, resigned commn., 1794; mem. S.C. Ho. of Reps., 1781-84, 87; county court justice Darlington County, 1785, 91; escheator Cheraw Dist. (now Chesterfield, Darlington and Marlboro counties), 1787; del. S.C. Conv. to ratify U.S. Constn., 1788; sheriff Cheraw Dist., 1789, 91; del. S.C. Constl. Conv., Columbia, 1790; mem. U.S. Ho. of Reps. (Democrat) from S.C., 3d-5th congresses, 1793-99. Died Darlington, S.C., May 18, 1818; buried on his estate Stony Hill, nr. Darlington.

BENTON, THOMAS HART educator; b. Williamson County, Tenn., Sept. 5, 1816; s. Samuel Benton; attended Marion (Mo.) Coll.; m. Susan Culbertson, 1851. Conducted 1st classical sch. in Ia., 1838-39; mem. 1st Ia. Senate, 1846-48, chmn. com. on schs.; supt. pub. instrn. State of Ia., 1848-54; exec. sec. Ia. Bd. Edn., 1858-62; commd. col. 29th Ia. Inf., U.S. Volunteers, 1862, brevetted brig. gen., 1865; collector U.S. revenue for 6th Dist. of Ia., 1866-69. Died St. Louis, Apr. 10, 1879; buried Marshalltown, Ia.

BENYAURD, WILLIAM H. H. lt. col. corps of engrs. U.S.A., July 2, 1889-; b. Philadelphia, May 17, 1841; grad. West Point, 1863; entered army, 1st lt. corps of engrs., June 11, 1863; bvtd. capt. and maj. for services in Richmond campaign and battle of Five Forks; promoted capt., May 1, 1866; maj., Mar. 4, 1879; received Congressional medal of honor for most distinguished gallantry at battle of Five Forks, Va., Apr. 1, 1864; was in many other battles; after war was asst. prof. engring., West Point, 1866-69; since then largely engaged as supt. of river and harbor improvements in all sections of the country. Died 1900.

BERENS, CONRAD ophthalmologist; b. Phila., Dec. 2, 1889; s. Conrad and Mary E. (Brockett) B.; prep. edn. Protestant Episcopal Acad., Phila.; M.D., U. Pa., 1911; m. Katherine Simpson Storrs, June 15, 1916 (dec. 1917); 1 son, Richard; m. 2d, Katherine Andrea Parker, July 12, 1923; m. 3d, Frances Penington Cookman; children-Lawrence Penington, Rodney Bristal. Adv. attending surgeon-cons. pathologist, cons.-dir. research N.Y. Eye and Ear Infirmary; lectr. ophthalmology N.Y. U. Post-grad. Med. Sch.; prof. clin. ophthalmology Columbia, 1943-46; cons. ophthalmology St. Clare's Hosp., French Hosp., Midtown Hosp., Glen Cove Community Hosp., Nassau Hosp.; mem. med. bd. Doctor's Hosp.; vis. staff Hempstead Gen. Hosp.; cons.

Riverview Hosp.; chmn. Council for Research in Glaucoma and Allied Diseases; staff Southside Hosp.; mng. dir. Ophthal. Found., Inc.; former cons. ophthalmology air surgeon, U.S. Army. Pres. Snyder Ophthalmic Found.; trustee Seeing Eye; dir. N.Y. Assn. for Blind, Nat. Soc. Prevention Blindness; chmn. Am. Com. on Optics and Visual Physiology; v.p. Internat. Assn. Prevention Blindness; v.p. Internat. Council on Ophthalmology chmn. Am. Bd. Ophthalmology, 1938-43, cons., 1948-59, emeritus. Commd. lt., Med. Res. Corps, 1917; France, World War I; lt. col., 1924-. Fellow A.C.S.; mem. A.M.A. (chmn. sect. ophthalmology 1943), Med. Soc. State N.Y. (chmn. eye sect. 1931), Am. Acad. Ophthalmology (chmn. 1945), Assn. Research Nervous and Mental Diseases, A.A.A.S., Illuminating Engring. Soc., Assn. Mil. Surgeons U.S., Optical Soc. Am. Pan-Am. Med. Assn. (exec. sec. 1929-32, treas. and sec. N.Am. Sect. on ophthalmology 1934) Pan-Am. Assn. Ophthalmology (pres. 1948), Air Service Med. Assn. (pres. 1933), Med. Soc. County N.Y. (pres. 1944), Societe Francaise D'Ophtalmologie (Am. rep.). Clubs: Racquet and Tennis, Piping Rock, Seawanhaka Yacht, University. Author: The Eye and Its Diseases, 1936, 49; Diagnostic Examination of the Eye (with Zuckerman), 1946; Ency. of the Eye (with Siegel), 1950; Abstracts on Aviation and Military Ophthalmology, 5 vols. (with Sheppard and Bickerton), 1953-59; Ocular Surgery Manual (with Loutfallah); 1950, rev. (with King), 1956; also articles and sci. papers. Home: Center Island, Oyster Bay L.I. Office: 708 Park Av., N.Y.C.; also 13 Walnut Rd., Glen Cove, N.Y. Died Mar. 1963.

BERGER, ADOLPH oral surgeon; b. Hungary, Dec. 12, 1882; s. Ignatz and Theresa (Goldberger) B.; D.D.S., N.Y. Coll. Dentistry, 1909; Came to U.S., 1903, naturalized, 1911. Practiced gen. dentistry, 1909-16, specializing in oral surgery, 1916-; prof. oral surgery, Columbia, 1923-51, emeritus 1951; attending oral surgeon Hosp. for Joint Diseases, 1918-51, cons. oral Surgeon 1951; attending oral surgeon Beth Israel Hosp., 1917-45, cons. oral surgeon 1945-; attending dental surgeon Presbyn. Hosp., 1928-51, cons. oral surgeon, 1951-; cons. Hosp. for Joint Diseases, all N.Y.C. lt. commr. U.S.N.R. Dental Corps, 1935-38, comdr., 1938-. Diplomate, Bd. Oral Surgery of N.Y. State. Fellow Acad. Internat. Dentistry; asso. fellow N.Y. Acad. Medicine; mem. Am. Med. Editors and Authors Assn., Am. Dental Assn., N.Y. State Dental Soc., 1st Dist. Dental Soc., Omicron Kappa Upsilon, S.E.D. Author: Principles and Technique of Oral Surgery, 1923; Principles and Technique of the Removal of Teeth, 1929. Contbr. articles on oral Surgery and dental edn. to jours. Home: 9 E. 96th St. Office: 654 Madison Av., N.Y.C. Died Apr. 1961.

BERGIN, CHARLES KNIESE naval officer; b. Balt., Jan. 25, 1904; s. Denis Lee and Katherine Irene (Kniese) B.; grad. Balt. Poly. Inst., 1921; B.S., John Hopkins, 1923, U.S. Naval Acad., 1927; postgrad. Naval Postgrad. Sch., 1933-36; grad. advanced mgmt. program Harvard, 1949; grad. Nat. War Coll., 1952; m. Katherine M. Philbrick, Oct. 21, 1936; children-Cecelia Jeannette, Katherine Drake, Patricia Ruth. Commd. ensign, U.S. Navy, 1927, advanced through grades to rear adm., 1955; ship's officer U.S.S. Maryland, U.S.S. Gilmer, U.S.S. Blakeley, U.S.S. Dobbin, U.S.S. Ralph Talbot; staff comdr. destroyers, battle fleet staff com. 5th Amphibious Force; staff com. Operational Dev. Force; comdr. U.S.S. Monssen, 1944, Destroyer Div. 122, 1945, U.S.S. Des Moines, 1952-53, Des Flotilla 3, 1955-56; comdr. destroyers, West Pacific, 1955-56; shore assignments include pt. exptl. officer Naval Proving Ground, Dahlgren, Va., 1940-43, dir. gun systems, ordnance ship bldg. program Navy Bur. Ordnance, 1949-51; asst. chief Navy Bur. Ordnance Research and Devel., 1953-55; staff Office Sec. of Def., 1956-59; comdr. mine force U.S. Pacific Fleet, 1959-60; comdr. operational test and evaluation force U.S. Atlantic and Pacific Fleets, 1960-63; supt. (pres.) U.S. Naval Postgrad. Sch., Monterey, Cal., 1963-. Decorated Navy Cross, Bronze Star. Mem. Newcomen Soc. N.A. Clubs: Harvard Business School, Army-Navy (Washington); New York Yacht. Died Dec. 6, 1964; buried Arlington Nat. Cemetery.

BERGTOLD, WILLIAM HARRY, M.D. b. Buffalo, s. Joseph Edward and Louisa (Hoffer) B.; M.D., U. of Buffalo, 1886; post-grad. student, Columbia, 1888; (hon. M.Sc., Hobart, 1891); m. Adele D. Smith, June 20, 1898; children - Adele (dec.), Mrs. Louise Harriet Woolfenden. Began med. practice at Buffalo, 1886; removed to Denver, Colo., 1894; asst. instr. histology, Coll. Phys. and Surg. (Columbia), 1888; prof. pathology, U. of Buffalo, 1893-94. U. of Denver, 1897-1900. Capt. asst. surgeon 74th Regt., N.G.N.Y., 1890-1904, inclusive; commd. maj. Med. Corps, U.S.A., Sept. 13, 1918; chief of med. service U.S. Gen. Hosp. No. 21, Denver, Sept. 13, 1918-June 17, 1919; was col. O.R.C. Author: A Study of the Incubation Periods of Birds, 1917; A Guide to the Birds of Colorado, 1928. Home: Denver, Colo. Died Mar. 1936.

BERKELEY, NORBORNE steel mfg. exec.; b. Danville, Va., May 13, 1891; s. Landon Carter and Anne Poe (Harrison) B.; LL.B., U. Va., 1916; m. Dorothea Winslow Randolph, May 4, 1918; children-Dorothea (Mrs. David M. Brush), Norborne. Employed with the law firm Cravath & Henderson, N.Y., 1916-17; with legal dept. Bethlehem Steel Co., 1919, asst. sec., 1922, asst. to pres., 1930, vice president, 1945-; dir. Bethlehem Steel Corp. (holding co.), 1935, v.p., 1958-. Mem. bd. visitors U. Va. Served as capt. 313th F.A., U.S. Army, World War I; grad. Army Gen. Staff Coll., Langres, France; maj. F.A., G-3, 80th Div.; participated Saint-Mihiel, Meuse-Argonne. Mem. Am. Iron and Steel Inst. Episcopalian. Clubs: University, Links (N.Y.C.); Saucon Valley Country, (Bethlehem, Pa.); Maidstone (East Hampton, N.Y.); Farmington (Charlottesville, Va.). Home: R.D. 3 Office: Bethlehem Steel Co., Bethlehem, Pa. Died May 26, 1964.

BERKELEY, RANDOLPH CARTER officer U.S. Marine Corps; b. Staunton, Va., Jan. 9, 1875; s. Carter and Lovie Jane (Gilkeson) B.; ed. Potomac Acad., Alexandria, Va.; grad. Marine Corps Field Officers Sch., Quantico, Va., and Army War Coll.; m. Carrie Anna Phillips, Sept. 12, 1906 (died 1907); m. 2d, Bessye Bancroft Russell, Oct. 2, 1911; 1 son, Randolph Carter, Jr. (lt col., aviator U.S. Marine Corps). Stenographer Richmond and Danville R.R. (now Southern Ry. Co.), 1893, city passenger agent, 1896; 2d lt. Marine Corps, Spanish-Am. War, 1898; through grades to maj. gen., 1939; now retired; shore service in Philippine Islands, Panama, Haiti, Nicaragua, Guam, Cuba; sea service on battleships Oregon and Kentucky and in Chinese waters on river gunboat U.S.S. Helena; pres. Naval Examining Bd., Marine Corps., 1936-39; retired Feb. 1, 1939. Holder of Congressional Medal of Honor, Navy Distinguished Service Medal, Navy Cross, Nicaraguan medals and various campaign badges. Mason. Episcopalian. Club: Army and Navy Country. Home: R.F.D. Beaufort, S.C. Died Jan. 31, 1960; buried Arlington Nat. Cemetery.

BERKNER, LLOYD VIEL sci. reserach adminstr.; b. Milw., Feb. 1, 1906; s. Henry Frank and Alma Julia (Viel) B.; B.S. in Elec. Engring., U. Minn., 1927 student physics George Washington U., 1933-35; D.Sc. (hon.), Bklyn. Poly. Inst., 1955, U. Calcutta, 1957, Dartmouth and U. Notre Dame, 1958, Columbia, 1959; D.Sc. (hon.), U. Rochester, 1960, Tulane U., 1961; D.Eng., Wayne State U., 1962; Ph.D. U. Uppsala (Sweden), 1956; LL.D., U. Edinburgh, 1959; m. Lillan Frances Fulks, May 19, 1928; children-Patricia Ann Booth (Mrs. Charles Harrington), Phyllis Jean Ashley (Mrs. James Clay). Began as engr. in charge radio sta. WLB-WGMS, Mpls., 1925-27; elec. engr. airways div. U.S. Bur. Lighthouses, 1927-28; engr. 1st Byrd Antarctic Expdn., 1928-30, Nat. Bur. Standards, 1930-33; physicist, dept. terrestrial magnetism Carnegie Instn. Washington, 1933-41 (Australia 1938-39, Alaska 1941), head sect. of exploratory geophysics of atmosphere, 1947-51; exec. sec. Research and Devel. Bd., Dept. 1946-47; spl. asst. sec. state on fgn. mil. assistance, 1950; pres., bd. trustees, chmn. eexec. com. Asso. Universities, Inc., 1951-60; pres. Grad. Research Center of Southwest, 1960-65, chmn. exec. com., 1965—, dir. Southwest Center for Advanced Studies, 1965—. Cons. several univs., govtl. agys. 1940—. Mem. com. on Rockefeller pub. service awards, 1954—. Chmn. 1957-59, 1962—. Mem. or officer of numerous U.S. delegations internat. sci. confs., 1936—. Naval aviator USNR, 1926—, rank of rear adm., 1955—; on active duty, head radar sect. Bur. Aero., USN, 1941-45. Decorated Legion of Merit (U.S.), Hon. Officer Order Brit. Empire; recipient spl. Congl. gold medal, silver medal Aero. Inst., sci. award Washington Acad. Scis., 1941, Cleve. Abbe award Am. Metrol. Soc., 1962. Fellow Am. Acad. Arts and Scis., I.E.E.E., Am. Phys. Soc., Arctic Inst. N.A., N.Y. Acad. Scis.; mem. Internat. Acad. Astronautics (corr.), Royal Swedish Acad. Sci., Am. Soc. Astronautics, Aerospace Med. Assn. (hon. mem.), Nat. Acad. Scis., (treas. 1960—, chmn. space sci. bd., 1958-62), Am. Philos. Soc., Philos. Soc. Washington, Washington Acad. Scis., Am. Geophysical Union (John A. Fleming award), Acacia (Founders award), Eta Kappa Nu (Eminent Members award), Theta Tau, Scabbard and Blade also several fgn. socs. Democrat. Conglist. Clubs: Cosmos (Washington); Explorers, Century Assn. (N.Y.C.); Bohemian (San Francisco, Cal.). Contbr. to scientific and prof. jour. Home: 3632 N.E. 24th Av., Fort Lauderdale, Fla. Office: Grad. Research Center, Box 8478, Dallas 5. Died June 4, 1967.

BERL, EUGENE ENNALLS, Dem. nat. committeeman, lawyer; b. New Orleans, Mar. 2, 1889; s. William and Marie (Waggaman) B.; A.B., Princeton, 1912; LL.B., Harvard, 1915. Admitted to Del. bar, 1915, and since practiced in Wilmington; mem. firm Ward & Gray, and successor firm Berl Potter and Anderson, attys.-at-law, since 1927. City solicitor, Wilmington, 1933-35; nominee for U.S. Senate, 1942; Dem. nat. committeeman since 1948. Served as 1st lt. U.S. Ambulance Service, 1917-18, capt. Claims Service, 1918-19; lt. col. to col. U.S. Army, 1943-46, with Italian Mil. hdqrs., 1943-44, asst. chief of staff G/5 13th Corps. Engr., France, Belgium, Holland and Germany, 1944-45; col. Gen Staff Corps., 1945-46. Decorated Silver Star medal with two oak leaves, Legion of Merit, Bronze Star medal (U.S.); Croix de Guerre. Mem. Am. and Del. State bar assns. Democrat. Roman Catholic. Clubs: Wilmington, Wilmington Country (Del.); Princeton (N.Y.C.); Army and Navy (Wash.). Home: 1303 Market St., Wilmington. Office: Delaware Trust Bldg., Wilmington 28, Del. Died Apr. 1, 1954; buried Cathedral Cemetery, Wilmington, Del.

BERLINER, HENRY ADLER, engring. exec.; b. Washington, Dec. 13, 1895; s. Emile and Cora (Adler) B.; student Cornell U., Mass. Inst. Tech.; B.S. in Mech. Engring., Harvard, 1918; m. Josephine Mitchell, Sept. 15, 1921; children—Josephine (Mrs. George Vargas), Cora Ann (Mrs. R. Cunningham), Henry Adler. Helicopter research, 1919-26; pres. Berliner Aircraft, Washington, 1926-29; v.p. prodn. Berliner-Joyce Aircraft Co., 1929-30; chmn. Engring & Research Corp., Riverdale, 1930-54; pres., chmn. bd. Tecfab, Inc., Beltsville, Md., 1955-62. Served from private to sergeant A.S. Signal Corps., 1917-19; maj. to col., U.S. Army, 1942-44. Awarded Distinguished Service Medal by USAF, Hon. Comdr. Brit. Empire. Fellow Inst. Aeros. Clubs: Army-Navy, University (Washington); Wings, Nat. Press. Patentee in field, also metal working machinery, home appliances and constrn. Home: Washington DC Died May 1970; buried Rock Creek Parish Cemetery, Washington DC

BERMAN, MORRIS army officer; born N.Y., Aug. 10, 1891; grad. Air Service Pilots School, Bombardment Sch.; commd. 2d lt. Inf., 1917; transferred to Air Service and advanced to brig. gen., Sept. 1942. Died Nov. 11, 1945.

BERNADOU, JOHN BAPTISTE naval officer; b. Phila., Nov. 14, 1858; s. George W. and Helen (Hay) B.; apptd. to U.S. Naval Acad. by the President, at large, 1876, grad. 1882. Promoted to midshipman, June 22, 1882; ensign, jr. grade, Mar. 3, 1883; ensign, June 26, 1884; lt., jr. grade, July 1, 1892; lt., June 1906. Served in Bureau of Navigation, 1882; spl. duty Smithsonian Instn., 1882-83; spl. duty in Korea, under Smithsonian Instn., 1883-84; various assignments to 1897; comd. Winslow during Spanish War, 1898; was advanced ten numbers in rank for eminent and conspicuous conduct in battle during Spanish War; served in Bureau of Ordnance, Navy Dept. 1898-99, Indiana, 1899-1900, Kentucky, 1900, Dixie, 1900-02; office of naval intelligence, 1902-04; exec. officer Kearsarge, 1904-06; Naval War Coll., 1906; naval attache, Am. Embassy, Rome and Vienna, Dec. 1906-. Author: A Trip Through Northern Korea in 1883-84; Pyro-Collodion Smokeless Powder; Smokeless Powder, Nitro-Cellulose, and Theory of the Cellulose Molecule, 1901 W9. Translated (from the Russian, by Vice Admiral Makaroff) Questions in Naval Tactics, 1898. Home: Winslow, N.J. Died 1908.

BERNE, ERIC LENNARD, psychiatrist, author; b. Montreal, Can., May 10, 1910; s. David Hillel and Sara (Gordon) B.; B.A., McGill U., 1931, M.D., C.M., 1935; student N.Y.C. Psychoanalytic Inst., 1941-43, San Francisco Psychoanalytic Inst., 1947-56; children—Ellen, Peter, Ricky, Terry, Robin Way, Janice Way (Mrs. Michael Farlinger). Intern Yale Psychiat. Clinic, 1936-38; clin. asst. psychiatry Mt. Sinai Hosp., N.Y.C., 1941-43; attending psychiatrist, mental hygiene clinic VA Hosp., San Francisco, 1950-56; pvt. practice, N.Y.C. and Norwalk, Conn., 1940-43, San Francisco, Carmel, Cal., 1946-70; cons. to surgeon gen. U.S. Army, 1951-56; adj. psychiatrist Mt. Zion Hosp., San Francisco, 1952-70; lectr. psychiatry U. Cal. Med. Sch., 1960-70; cons. group therapy McAuley Clinic, San Francisco, 1962-70. Served to maj., M.C., AUS, 1943-46. Diplomate Am. Bd. Psychiatry and Neurology. Fellow American Psychiatric Association (life member); member of the International Transactional Analysis Association (chairman board of trustees); corr. member Indian Psychiat. Society. Author: The Mind in Action, 1947; Layman's Guide to Psychiatry and Psychoanalysis, 1957; Transactional Analysis in Psychotherapy, 1961; The Structure and Dynamics of Organizations and Groups, 1963; Games People Play, 1964; Principles of Group Treatment, 1966; The Happy Valley, 1968. Home: Carmel CA Died July 1970.

BERNE-ALLEN, ALLAN, chem. engr., educator; b. S.I., N.Y., Aug. 13, 1902; s. Allan and Harriet Anna (Mallory) Berne-A.; B.S.E., U. Mich., 1924; Chem.E., Columbia, 1933. Ph.D., 1936; m. Helen Louise Kelsey, June 24, 1926. Research development tech. service Standard Oil Co. N.J., 1924-31. Vacuum Oil Co. (now Mobile Oil Co.), 1931-32; research, development, tech. asst. operation E.I. du Pont de Nemours & Co., Inc., 1934-47; prof. mech. engring. U. Cal. at Berkeley, 1947; prof. head dept. chemical engineering Clemson Agricultural College, 1948-55, profl. engr., 1955-69. Charter mem. bd. dirs. Fats and Protein Research Found., 1962-66. Served as maj. C.W.S., AUS, 1942-46; ret. lt. col. Reserves. Registered profl. engr., N.Y., S.C. Fellow Am. Inst. Chemists, A.A.A.S.; member Am. Oil Chemists' Soc., Am. Chem. Soc. (chmn. Va. sect 1941), Am. Inst. Chem.E., Am. Soc. Engring. Edn., Am. Assn. U. Profs., Va. Acad. Sci. Fla. Academy of Sciences, Res. Officers Assn. (pres. Staunton Va. 1936-37, pres. Gulf Coast chpt. 1958-59), Mil. Order World Wars, N.Y. Acad. Scis., Sarasota Power Squadron, Sigma Xi, Phi Lambda Upsilon, Phi Kappa. Phi, Phi Gamma Delta. Mason (past master). Clubs: Chemists (N.Y.C.); Army and Navy (Washington); Sarasota (Florida) Yacht; Michigan Union (Ann Arbor); Fla. N.; Highlands (N.C.) Country. Contbr. tech. mags. Patentee in field. Home: Sarasota FL2Died Apr. 15, 1969; Meml. Army Marker in New Drop Moravian Cemetery.

BERNHARD, ALVA DOUGLAS naval officer; b. Pa., Mar. 9, 1886. Commd. ensign, USN, advanced to capt., 1937, rear admiral, 1941; designated naval aviator. Deceased.

BEROLZHEIMER, EDWIN MICHAEL chmn Eagle Pencil Co.; b. N.Y. City, Jan. 16, 1887; s. Emil and Gella (Goldsmith) B.; student Phillips Exeter Acad.; Harvard; m. Myra Bessie Cohn, Jan. 26, 1911; children—Emile Albert Berol, Margaret Gella (Mrs. Frank B. Craig). Supt. Eagle Pencil Co., New York City, 1919, vice pres., 1921, pres., 1925-46, chmn. bd. since 1946; chmn bd. Hudson Lumber Co.; v.p. and dir. Blaisdell Pencil Co.; mem. adv. bd. Chemical Bank & Trust Co.; owner Cloister Kennels. Served as capt., Ordnance, U.S. Army, World War I. Mem. Nat. Panel of Arbitrators of Am. Abritration Assn.; perpetual mem. N.Y. Soc. Mil. and Naval officers of World Wars. Trustee Mt. Sinai Hosp., N.Y. City, 1928-41. Vice pres. Irish Setter Club of America. Republican. Clubs: Harvard, Anglers, Armor and Arms. Home: The Cloisters, Tarrytown, N.Y.; also Davant Plantation, Ridgeland, S.C. Office: 710 E. 14th St., New York 9, N.Y. Died Mar. 15, 1949.

BERRIEN, FRANK DUNN naval officer; b. Galesburg, Ill., Aug. 17, 1877; s. Leonard Budd and Harriet May (Smith) B.; B.S., U.S. Naval Acad., 1900; grad. U.S. Naval War Coll., 1917; Army War Coll., 1926; m. Mary Elizabeth Whittelsey, Nov. 9, 1907; children—Frank Whittelsey, Mary Elizabeth (Mrs. Harry Hager Lugg). Served on U.S.S. Cincinnati in West Indies in Spanish-Am. War, 1898, Asiatic Station, participating in Philippine Campaign and Boxer War, 1900-04; with Atlantic Fleet on warships Kentucky and Missouri, 1904-07; on staff Rear Adm. C. M. Thomas, on flagships Minnesota and Connecticut, 1907-08; head football coach Naval Acad., 1908-10; comdr. U.S. Destroyer, Trippe, 1910-14; participated in Mexican Campaign, 1914; in charge Naval Magazine, Hingham, Mass., 1914-16; apptd. comdr. U.S. warships Nicholson and Wilkes at Queenstown, Ire., 1917; comdr. U.S. hops. ship, Comfort, 1918; following the armistice became naval post officer at Bordeaux, France, remaining until summer of 1919; chief of staff to comdr. of the Destroyer Force of the Pacific Fleet, 1920; capt. submarine base, New London, Conn., 1921-25; est. and commanded naval unit at Yale Univ., 1926; qualified as naval observer, Naval Air Sta., Pensacola, Fla., 1928; comdr. U.S. airplane carrier, Lexington, 1928-30; capt. Navy Yard, Washington, 1930; rear admiral, 1935—; on active duty as troop convoy comdr. between San Francisco and South Australia, Mar.-Aug. 1942. Decorated Distinguished Service Medal (U.S.), Order of St. Michael and St. George (Gr. Brit.), Comdr. Order of the Savior (Greece). Mem. Queenstown Assn., Mil. Order World War, Mil. Order of the Dragon, Mill. Order of Carabao; Huguenot Soc., Phi Gamma Delta. Republican. Conglist. Clubs: New York Yacht (N.Y.C.); Army and Navy, Army and Navy Country (Washington). Died Jan. 31, 1951; buried Naval Acad. Cemetery, Annapolis.

BERRY, ALBERT GLEAVES rear adm. U.S.N.; b. Nashville, Tenn., Sept. 16, 1848; s. William Tyler and Mary Margaret (Tannehill) B.; grad. U.S. Naval Acad., 1869; m. Lilliam Reed Merriman, Sept. 28, 1881 (died 1931); children - Mary Lillian, Albert Gleaves. Ensign, 1871; master, 1872; lt., 1875; lt. comdr., 1897; comdr., 1900; capt., June 16, 1905; rear adm., June 18, 1909; retired, 1910. Served at sea in European, S. Atlantic Asiatic (twice), Pacific and N. Atlantic squadrons; also spl. duty and in spl. service squadron; exec. officer Amphitrite during Spanish-American War. Awarded medal for action at San Juan, P.R., May, 1898, clasp for action off Cardenas, Cuba; medal for Spanish-Am. War. Home: Coronado, Calif. Died May 12, 1938.

BERRY, CHARLES WHITE soldier, city ofcl.; b. Green County, N.Y., Apr. 11, 1871; s. Frank M. and Almira (Horn) B.; M.D., Columbia, 1896; D.P.H. course N.Y.U.; m. Nina La Plante, Dec. 1922; 3 children. Practiced medicine in Bklyn. many yrs.; chmn. N.Y. Fair Price Coal Commn., 1924-25; mem. Reconstrn. Labor Bd. of N.Y., 1919-21; comptroller City of N.Y., 1926—. Served from pvt. to capt. N.Y., N.G., 1903-17; maj. 14th Inf. later 106th Inf., AEF, 1917-18, participated battles at Somme Defensive, Dickebusch Lake, Vierstraat Ridge, Hindenburg Line (Somme offensive), Canal de la Sambre; brig. gen. N.Y. N.G., 1919-23; adj. gen. State N.Y.; comdr. N.Y. N.G., 1923-25. Decorated N.Y. Conspicuous Service Cross; Croix de Guerre with palms (Belgium); Comdr. Order Polonia Restituta; cited for gallantry in action. Democrat. Presbyn. Home: Romer Rd., Dongan Hills, S.I., N.Y. Office: Municipal Bldg., N.Y.C. Died 1941.

BERRY, HIRAM GREGORY army officer; b. Rockland, Me., Aug. 27, 1824; s. Jeremiah and Frances (Gregory) B.; m. Almira Merriman, Mar. 23, 1845. Mem. Me. Legislature, 1852; mayor Rockland, 1856; commd. col. 4th Me. Regt. during Civil War; commd. brig. gen. then maj. gen. U.S. Volunteers, 1862; distinguished at battles of Williamsburg and Fair Oaks; gen. of div. 3d Corps. Killed at Battle of Chancellorsville (Va.), May 3, 1863.

BERRY, JAMES EDWARD lt. gov. of Okla., banker; b. Oak Grove, Mo., Oct.2, 1881; s. William Edward and Martha (Brown) B.; grad. bus. coll.; student Okla. A. and M. Coll.; m. Edwina Morrison, Oct. 21, 1908 (dec. Aug. 1965); children-William Morrison, Virginia (Mrs. J. D. Harrison), James Edward (dec), George Malcolm, Frank Gilman, Robert Nelson (dec), Sarah Jane (Mrs. James W. Rodgers, Jr.). Pres., Stillwater (Okla.) Nat. Bank, Stillwater Milling Co.; v.p. First Nat. Bank, Cushing, Okla.; lt. gov. of Okla., 1935-55. Candidate, U.S. Senate, 1944. Treas., Payne County (Okla.) Salvation Army Com., Infantile Paralysis Payne County chpt. Served as capt. Rainbow Div., AEF, World War I; ret. Maj., 45th Inf. Div., Okla. N.G. Inducted into Okla. Hall of Fame, 1953. Mem. Am. Legion (past post comdr.), V.F.W., Okla. Bankers Assn. (past dist. chmn.) Okla. C. of C., Pi Kappa Alpha. Democrat. Methodist Episcopalian. Mason. Home: 502 Duck St., Stillwater. Died Nov. 22, 1966; buried Fairlawn Cemetery, Stillwater.

BERRY, KEARIE LEE army officer; b. Denton, Tex., July 6, 1893; s. Thomas Eugene and Viola Eugenia (Riley) B.; student U. Tex., 1912-16, 24-25; m. Alice Celeste Fleming, May 7, 1917; children-Kearie Lee, Viola Celeste (Mrs. William Robison Reilly, IV), Thomas Eugene. Attended First Officers' Tng. Camp, Leon Springs, Tex.; commd. 2d lt., inf. sect., O.R.C., Aug. 15, 1917, and advanced through the grades to brig. gen. (temp.) Jan. 18, 1946; joined 2d Tex. Inf., May 17, 1916, spent 10 months on Mexican Border; joined 21st inf., Balboa Park, San Diego, Aug. 1917; served with 27th inf. at Verknie-Udinsk, Vladivostok, Siberia, 1919-20, then in Manila and Hawaii; service in various U.S. camps as comdr. and athletic officer, 1921-33; machine gun co. comdr., athletic and recreation officer 15th inf., China 1933-36; service instr. and camp comdr. U.S. camps, 1936-41; sr. instr. 1st Philippine Constabulary Regt., acting q.m. and ordnance officer, South Luzon Force, Nov.-Dec. 19 with the enemy, Jan.-Feb. 1942; comd. 1st Philippine div. until surrender of Bataan, Apr. 9, 1942; prisoner of war of Japanese in prison camps, Luzon, Formosa, Kyushu and Manchuria, Apr. 1942-Aug. 20, 1945; attended orientation courses for former prisoners of war at The Inf. Sch., Field Arty. Sch., Coast Arty. Sch., Cavalry Sch., Armored Sch., Mar.-June 1946; exec. officer Tex. Mil. Dist., Austin, Tex., 1946-47; adj. gen. of Tex., 1947-61; maj. gen. Tex. N.G., 1947; ret. from regular Army as brig. gen., 1947; apptd. lt. gen. Tex. N.G., 1961; D.S.M., Silver Star, Purple Heart, Combat Infantryman's badge, Comdr. Philippine Legion of Honor, Bronze Star Medal, D.S.M. (N.G. Assn. U.S.); named to Longhorn Hall of Fame, U. Tex. Mem. Tex. Heritage Found., Delta Kappa Epsilon, Sigma Delta Psi. Mem. Christian Ch. Mason (Shriner, Jester). Clubs: Headliners, Wainwrights Travellers. Address: 3201 Highland Terrace W. Austin, Tex. Died Apr. 27, 1965; buried Ft. Sam Houston Nat. Cemetery, San Antonio.

BERRY, ROBERT MALLORY rear adm. U.S.N.; b. Henry Co., Ky., Jan. 28, 1846; s. Edmond T. and S. F. B.; apptd. from Ky., and grad. U.S. Naval Acad., 1866; m. Mary A. Brady, 1895. Promoted ensign, Mar. 12, 1869; advanced through grades to rear adm., June 29, 1906. On bd. the Macedonian, in summer of 1864, in pursuit of the Confederate steamers Florida and Tallahassee; served in the Sabine and Gettysburg, 1866, Guerriere and Huron, 1867-68, Kansas, 1869, Cyane and Pensacola, 1869-72, Tigress, 1873. Dictator, 1874, Franklin, 1874-77; torpedo duty, 1877; exec. officer Saratoga, 1878-80; Navy Yard, Washington, 1881; comdr. of U.S.S. Rogers in search of the Jeanette, 1881-82; exec. officer St. Mary's, 1882-86, Atlanta, 1886-88; torpedo duty and at Naval War Coll., 1889; light house insp., 16th dist., 1889-92; comd. Michigan, 1893-94; Navy Yard, New York, 1895-96; comd. Castine, 1896-99; Naval Home, Phila., 1899-1901; mem. Naval Examining Bd., Washington, 1901; comd. Dixie, 1901-02; Navy Yard, Norfolk, 1902; comd. Kentucky, 1903-04; comdt., Naval Sta., Charleston and 6th naval dist., 1904-05; comdt., Navy Yard, Pensacola and 8th naval dist., 1905-06; comdt., Navy Yard, Norfolk, and 5th naval dist., 1906-07; retired, Jan. 28, 1908. Comdr. U.S. Naval Unit, U. of Mich., Sept. 23, 1918-Jan. 3, 1919. Home: Detroit, Mich. Died May 19. 1929.

BERRY, ROBERT W. army officer; b. New Jersey, Mar. 20, 1902; B.S., U.S. Mil. Acad., 1924; grad. Coast Arty. Sch., battery officers course, 1933, Command and Gen. Staff Sch., 1940. Commd. 2d lt., Coast Arty. Corps, U.S. Army, 1924, and advanced through grades to maj. gen., 1955; comdg. officer Atlantic sector Panama Canal Zone; comdg. gen., 35th A.A.A. Brigade, Ft. Bliss, Tex., 1948-50; gen. Western Army Antiaircraft Command, 1950-53; dir. J/1 div. Hdqrs. U.S. European Command, 1953; dep. commandant mil. affairs. Nat. War Coll., 1944-48; comdg. gen. 1st region ARADCOM, Fort Totten, N.Y., 1958-. Decorated D.S.M., Legion of Merit Medal. Home: Quarters 131, Weaver Av. Office: 1st Region, ARADCOM, Fort Totton 59, N.Y. Died Apr. 1, 1960; buried Presidio of San Francisco.

BERTRAM, JOHN sea capt., mcht.; b. Jersey Island, Feb. 11, 1796; s. John and Mary (Perchard) B.; m. Mary G. Smith, 1823; m. 2d, Mrs. Clarissa Millett, 1838; m. 3d, Mary Ann Ropes, 1848. Moved with family to Am., 1807; cabin boy in merchantman Hazard, 1812, later served in privateers Monkey and Herald; held prisoner (after Herald was captured by English) until end of War of 1812; became mate, 1821, held 1st command in ship General Brewer; entered mcht. business by gathering hides from Patagonia coast; made last voyage as capt. aboard Black Warrior, 1830-32; began full-scale mcht. business, 1832; sent 1st ship from U.S. to Cal. during gold rush; founded Bertram Home for Aged Men, Salem Fuel Fund. Died Mar. 22, 1882.

BERTRANDIAS, VICTOR EMILE army officer; b. San Francisco, May 14, 1893; ed. St. Mary's Coll., Oakland, Cal.; grad. Air Service Pilots Sch., 1919, Bombardment Sch., 1921. Served with U.S. Army, 1917-19; with 1st Aviation Instrn. Center, France, 1917, with 94th Aero Squadron, 1918; commd. 1st lt., San. Corps, and assigned motor inspector, med. dept., Chief Surgeon's Office, A.E.F.; later, dir. ambulance service, Port of Embarkation, Hoboken, N.J., disch. 1918; commd. 2d lt., and promoted 1st lt., Air Service, U.S. Army, 1920; transpn. officer, Hdqrs. Am. Forces in Germany, 1920-21; resigned and was apptd. major Specialist Res., advanced through the grades to brig. gen., 1944; comdg. officer 4th Air Depot, 5th Air Forces Service Command, 1942; comd. advanced echelon 5th Air Forces Service Command, 1943-44; comdg. officer, Air Force Area Command, Southwest Pacific Area, 1944; assigned chief of maintenance, Hdqrs. Army Transport Service Command, Wright Field, Dayton, Ohio; test pilot, Gen. Aviation Co., 1929-31; with Douglas Aircraft Co., Inc. 1931-42, becoming v.p. Decorated Air Medal. Address: War Department, Washington 25, D.C. Died Mar. 1961.

BESLEY, FREDERIC ATWOOD surgeon; b. Waukegan, Ill., Apr. 19, 1868; s. William and Sylvia (Jocelyn) Besley; M.D., Northwestern University, 1894; married Mrs. Myra E. Busey, October 6, 1910. Began practice Chicago, 1894; prof. surgery, Northwestern U. Med. Sch.; mem. staff Victory Memorial Hosp., Waukegan, Ill. Commd. maj. Med. R.C., 1917, later col. Med. Corps U.S. Army, and on duty in France. Fellow Am. Coll. Surgeons (sec.; pres. 1937); mem. Am. Surg. Assn., A.M.A., Lake County Med. Soc., Chicago Surg. Soc. Clubs: University. Home: 1505 N. Sheridan Rd., Waukegan, Ill. Died Aug. 16, 1944.

BESTIC, JOHN BRERETON, air force officer; b. Fargo, N.D., Aug. 18, 1915; s. Arthur Edward and Anna (Doleshy) B.; student U. Minn., 1933-35; B.S., U.S. Mil. Acad., 1939; m. Frances Leona Powell, Oct. 18, 1939; children—John Brereton, Philip Brereton, Jeffrey Brereton. Commd. 2d 1t. U.S. Army, 1939, advanced through grades to maj. gen. USAF, 1961; assigned New Guinea, Philippines, Okinawa, Japan, World War II; staff Hdqrs. Army Air Forces, Pentagon, 1946-49; dep. dir. communications and electronics Joint Chiefs Staff, 1949-50; chief communications electronics SAC, 1950-57; comdr. Pacific Area Airways and Air Communications Service, 1957-58; dep. dir. communications-electronics Hdqrs. USAF, 1958-61, dir. telecommunications, 1961-62; dep. dir. Nat. Mil. Command System, Hdqrs. Defense Communications Agency, Washington, 1962-67; comdr. electronic systems div. Air Force Systems Command, Bedford, Mass., 1967-68; v.p. corporate operations MACRO Systems Assos., 1968-69. Decorated Legion Merit with 1 oak leaf cluster. Mem. Armed Forces Communications and Electronics Assn. (v.p.), Club: SAC Aero (pres. Offutt AFB, Neb., 1955). Contbr. articles to mags. in field. Home: Corona Del Mar CA Died Dec. 6, 1969; buried Pacific View Meml. Park, Newport Beach CA

BESTON, HENRY, author; b. Quincy, Mass., June 1, 1888; B.A., Harvard 1909, M.A., 1911; studied U. of Lyons, France, 1 year; Litt.D., Bowdoin Coll., U. Me.; m. Elizabeth Coatsworth, June 18, 1929; children—Margaret Coatsworth, Catherine Maurice. Mem. editorial staff Atlantic Monthly Co.; editor The Living Age, 1919-23; with Am. Field Service attached to French Army, 1915-16; with U.S. Navy, 1918. Recipient Thoreau Emerson medal Acad. Arts and Scis., 1954; Outermost House (Cape Cod, Mass.) dedicated as Nat. Lit. Monument, 1964. Mem. Portland (Me.) Soc. Natural History, Josselyn Bot. Soc. Me., Audubon Soc., P.E.N., Vets. U.S. Submarine Service Assn., Am. Legion, Phi Beta Kappa (hon.). Clubs: Authors' (London), The Grange, Maine Guild of Herbalists. Author: Full Speed Ahead, 1919; Firelight Fairy Book, 1919 (school edit. same with preface by Theodore Roosevelt, 1921); Starlight Wonder Book, 1923; The Book of Gallant Vagabonds, 1925; The Sons of Kai, 1926; The Outermost House, 1928, London, 1929; (Armed Services edit., 1945); Herbs and The Earth, 1935; American Memory, 1937; The Runaway Tree, 1941; The St. Lawrence River in the "Rivers of America" series, 1942; (Armed Services edit., 1944); Northern Farm, 1948; White Pine and Blue Water, 1950. Hon. editor Nat. Audubon Mag. Contbr., Human Events, to Brit. edit. The St. Lawrence, 1951. Home: Nobleboro ME Died Apr. 15, 1968; buried Chimney Farm Burying Ground, Nobleboro ME

BETTELHEIM, EDWIN SUMMER, J. mil. orgn. executive; b. N.Y.C., Apr. 11, 1887; (desc. Annetje Jans, 1st white girl born on Manhattan Island); s. Edwin Summer and Emma Ethel (Hutcheson) B.; B.S., Columbia, 1911; LL.B., George Washington U., 1924, LL.M., 1925, A.B., 1926, A.M., 1927; grad. Command and Gen. Staff Sch. (Res.), 1938; m. Dorothy English

Caldwell, Oct. 22, 1928. First engaged in constructural engring., later in newspaper work. Served as 2d lt., F.A., U.S. Army, Mexican Border, 1916; 1st lt., 104th and 17th F.A., France, England, Belgium and Germany during World War I; apptd. capt. F.A. Res., 1919, and advanced through grades to col.; past asst. chief of staff Mil. Dist. Washington, ret., 1948; mil. analyst Dept. State; mil. biographer Inter-Am. Mil. Assn.; became asst. chief field forces, Bureau of War Risk Ins., 1919; nat. legislative dir. Vets. Foreign Wars, 1921-31; adj. gen. and exec. officer (treas. gen.) Mil. Order of World Wars since 1931. Mem. Washington Bd. of Trade, Commd. by U.S. Govt. to head expdn. to northern Russia to search for the return to U.S. bodies of Americans lost in Polar Bear Campaign, 1929. Dir. Goodwill Industries, Presidents Com. for Employment Physically Handicapped; trustee Boys Club A.; mem. council Boy Scouts Am.; mem. Health and Welfare Council Dist. Columbia. Decorated Mexican Border, Victory with bars, German Occupation, Am. Defense and N.Y. State War Service medals, Am. Sector medal, World War II badge and commendation ribbon with palms. Knight Royal Order Scotland, knight chevalier Ordre de la Couronne de Charlemagne I, knight star and ribbon Grand Duke Cyril of Russia, L'Odre St. Anne with crossed swords, Cross and Star Merite Civique (France); Wojsk Poliskiah, Krzyz Walecz Nosci, Polonia Restituta (Poland); Cruz Merite San Juan Bautista (Puerto Rico); Abdon Calderon 1st Cl. (Ecuador). Mem. Vets. Fgn. Wars (past comdr.), Am. Legion (founder mem.), Mil. Order Fgn. Wars (past comdr. gen.), Res. Officers Assn. (past pres.), Disabled Am. Vets., Fgn. Service Order (grand sec.), Nat. Sojourners (past pres.), Heroes of '76 (past nat. comdr.), Am. Coalition (v.p.), D.C. Bar Assn., St. Andrews Soc., Nat. Council for Friendship with Arab World (treas.), Delta Theta Phi. Episcopalian. Mason (past master, 32ff, Shriner, K.T., grand master D.C.; K.C.C.H. (past high priest, past Ill. master), Elk, Odd Fellow. Clubs: Old Guard (N.Y.); Army and Navy, Army-Navy Country (member board govs.), University, National Press, Rotary (Washington). Author: Nooks and Corners of Old New York - Memorabilia, 1917; My Experiences in Northern Russia, 1929; Army Mobilization, 1934. Home: 3927 Massachusetts Av. N.W. Office: 1700 I St., Washington 6. Died July 1959.

BETTERS, PAUL V(ERNON) orgn. exec.; b. Morris, Minn., Apr. 19, 1906; s. Burt Henry and Olivia (Christianson) B.; grad. Pillsbury Acad., Owatonna, Minn., 1921; United States Naval Academy, 1923-24; B.S., Univ. of Minnesota, 1928; M.S., Syracuse University, 1929; graduate study George Washington Univ., 1931; local govt. sch., Selwyn Coll., Cambridge, Eng., summer 1932; m. Myra Graff Keck, June 8, 1929; children; Richard Keck, Judith Keck, Barry Keck, Paula Keck. Fellow and instr. in pub. adminstrn. Sch. of Citizenship and Pub. Affairs, Syracuse Univ., 1929-30; staff New York Commn. on Revision of Pub. Service Laws, State of New York, Albany, New York, 1930; staff The Brookings Instn., Washington, D.C., 1930-32; tech. adv. to Governor of N.C. at Raleigh, 1931; sec. Govtl. Research Assn., Washington, 1931-32; exec. dir., organizer Nat. Inst. Municipal Law Officers, Washington, D.C., 1933-35; exec. dir. the U.S. Conf. of Mayors, Washington, D.C., since 1932; co-founder Nat. Inst. of Governmental Purchasing, Washington, 1945; exec. dir. and founder Nat. Inst. of City and Town Clerks, Washington, 1946. Cons. C.A.A., Office Prodn. Management, Fed. Works Agency, War Assets Adminstrn., U.S. Air Coordinating Com., 1933—; Adv. to administrator Civil Works Adminstrn., Washington, 1934-35; liaison officer Pub. Works Adminstrn., 1934-35. Del. U.S. Govt. to Internat. Congress of Local Authorities, London, 1932, Lyon, France, 1934, Paris, France, 1947, The Hague, 1948, Geneva, 1949, Brighton, Eng., 1951, Vienna, 1953; del. Pan-Am. Congress Municipalities, Havana, 1939; del. U.S. cities Helsinki (Finland) Anniversary, 1950; del. U.S. cities Canadian Ann. Confs. of Mayors since 1937; U.S.A.F. Civilian Seminar, Air Univ., Maxwell Field, 1947; dept. of defense Civilian Orientation Conf., 1951. Served as lt. col. assigned to Gen. Staff Corps, U.S. Army, 1942-44. Recipient Citation and Award for Distinguished Service to Am. Cities, U.S. Conf. of Mayors, 1942, 47, 52; distinguished service award, First Nat. Inst. Governmental Purchasing, 1950. Decorated Order Orange-Nassau, The Netherlands, 1948; Knight's Cross, First Class, Royal Order of St. Olaf (Norway) 1950, Helsinki Anniversary Medal, 1950. Advisor to U.S. dir. Civilian Def., 1941-42, aide to U.S. chmn. Permanent Joint Bd. on Def., U.S. and Can., 1940-47; asst. to spl. U.S. Ambassador to Brazil, 1945. Mem. Nat. Aviation Clin., Pres. Conferences on Highway and Fire Safety. Mem. Am. Acad. Polit. and Social Sci., Am. Polit Sci. Assn., Govtl. Research Assn., Nat. Municipal League, Internat. City Mgrs. Assn., Am. Pub. Welfare Assn., Am. Soc. Planning Ofcls., Nat. Assn. Housing Ofcls., Civil Service Assembly of U.S. and Can., Municipal Finance Officers Assn., Nat. Planning Assn., Urban Land Inst., A.A.A.S., Acad. of Polit. Sci., Internat. Union of Local Author ties (mem. exec. com.), Atty. General's Conf. on Crime, U.S. Fed. Works Agency Constrn. Adv. Council. Am. Society of Public Administration, Nat. Tax Assn., Am. Ordnance Assn., Assn. of U.S. Army, Am. Com. for Internat. Cooperation (vice chmn.), U.S. Bur. Census (adv. com.), Defense Orientation Conf. Assn., Nat. Safety Council. Unitarian. Clubs: Nat. Press, Army and Navy (Wash.); Wings (N.Y.C.). Author: Personnel Classification Board, 1931; U.S. Shipping Bd., 1932; Federal Services to Municipal Governments, 1932; State Centralization in North Carolina, 1932; City Problems, 1933-50 (ed. annual vols.). You and Your City, 1946; America Cannot Afford Slums, 1947; Government of the People, 1948. Editor: The United States Municipal News since 1933. Contbr. articles, reports and bulls. dealing with municipal affairs, including European Unions of Cities, 1932; Municipal Cooperation in Europe, 1934; Civil Airports in Europe, 1938. Home: Windy Hill, Burnt Mills Hills, Silver Spring, Md. Office: 730 Jackson Pl. N.W., Washington 6. Died May 12, 1956; buried Arlington Nat. Cemetery.

BETTS, EDWARD C. army officer; b. Ala., June 9, 1800; LL.B., U. of Alabama, 1911; grad. Inf. Sch., 1925. Commd. capt., inf., U.S. Army, 1917, and advanced through the grades to brig. gen., 1943; prof. of law, U.S. Mil. Acad., 1938-42; theater judge advocate, European Theater of Operations, U.S. Army, since Apr. 1942. Address: care Judge Advocate General's Office, War Dept. Washington 25, D.C. Died May 6, 1946.

BEUKEMA, HERMAN army officer; b. Muskegon, Mich., Jan. 29, 1891; s. Charles J. and Wyke (Banninga) B.; student U. of Chicago, 1909-10; B.S., U.S. Mil. Acad., 1915; grad. Field Arty. Sch., 1922, advanced course, 1927, Command and Gen. Staff Sch., 1928; hon. Dr. Science of Edn., Washington and Jefferson Coll., 1943; LL.D., Rutgers U., 1944, Norwich U. 1944; m. Margaret Whitman Shaw, Mar. 18, 1916; children-Margery Alden (wife of Maj. Gen. C. F. Leonard, Jr.), Alice Wyke (wife of Col. J.G.K. Miller, G.S.C.), Maj. Henry Shaw (dec. 1954). Commd. 2d lt. F.A., U.S. Army, 1915, and advanced through grades to col., 1940; ret. as brig. gen., 1954; dir. Overseas Program, U. Md., 1954-; served as capt. and maj., World War I; assigned dept. econs. U.S. Mil. Acad., 1928, prof., head dept. social scis. since 1930; organized War Dept. Orientation Course, 1941, dir. to Apr. 1942; organized Army Specialized Training Program, 1942, dir. 1942-44, also mem. Gen. Staff; lecturer. Recipient Distinguished Service Medal, Victory Medal with 1 clasp, Purple Heart. Econ. com. U.S.C. of C.; bd. of cons. N.Y. State Bd. of Edn. Mem. Council Fgn. Relations Am. Polit. Science Assn., American Military Institute, American Soc. of Professional Geograph Republican. Episcopalian. Co-author: World Political Geography, 1948; Twentieth Century America, 1949; Economics of National Security, 1950. Author monographs; contbr. to encys., periodicals. Home: 20 Kirschgarten St., Heidelberg, Germany. Office: U. Md., APO 403, N.Y.C. Died Nov. 26, 1960; buried West Point, N.Y.

BEVERIDGE, ANDREW BENNIE, lawyer; b. Jellico, Ky., Sept. 28, 1915; s. Andrew and Annie (Bennie) B.; B.S. in Elec. Engring. U. Md., 1936; J.D., George Washington U., 1941; m. Elizabeth Griffith, Aug. 19, 1939; children—Susan W. (Mrs. Pericles G. Perikles), Lynn A. Admitted to D.C. bar, 1941 also U.S. Supreme Ct.; patent atty. Gen. Elec. Co., 1947-51; partner firm Browne, Beveridge & DeGrandi, and predecessors, Washington, 1951-72. Served to lt. col. USAAF, 1941-46; col. Res. (ret.). Mem. Am. (chmn. sect. patent, trademark and copyright law 1970-71), D.C. (chmn. sect. patent, trademark and copyright law 1963-64), Fed. bar assns., Am. Patent Law Assn., Internat. Assn. for Protection Indsl. Property, Canadian Patent and Trademark Assn., Order of Coif, Tau Beta Pi, Omicron Delta Kappa. Democrat. Presbyn. Rotarian. Clubs: Prince George Country (pres. 1965, 67, dir.) (Landover, Md.); Nat. Lawyers (Washington). Home: Hyattsville MD Died Feb. 10, 1972; buried St. John's Cemetery, Beltsville MD

BEYER, HENRY GUSTAV med. dir. U.S.N., retired, 1912; b. Saxony, Oct. 28, 1850; s. Carl and Wilhelmine (Scheibe) B.; ed. pub. schs., Hohenstein Ernstthal to 1864; pvt. instrn. (classical) till 1866, pharmacy till 1869; M.D., Bellevue Hosp. Med. Coll. (New York U.), 1876; M.R.C.S., London, 1881; Ph.D., Johns Hopkins, 1887; m. Harriet W. Wescott, May 6, 1880 (died Jan. 4, 1891). Apptd. from N.Y., asst. surgeon U.S.N., May 19, 1876; passed asst. surgeon, Apr. 30, 1880; surgeon, May 19, 1893; med. insp., 1905; med. dir., 1910. Naval Hosp., Brooklyn, 1876-77; various assignments to 1897; on U.S.S. Amphitrite, 1897-99, and during Spanish-Am. War; Wabash, Boston, 1899-1901; U.S.S. Prairie, 1901-03; fleet surgeon Pacific Fleet, 1905-07. Mem. bd. on barracks, visiting Eng. and Germany (spl. commn.), 1903-04; prof. hygiene, Naval Med. Sch., Washington, from 1904; lecturer on naval hygiene, War Coll., Newport, R.I. Del. Internat. Congress, Stockholm, Amsterdam, Berlin and Rome, 1907; chmn. exhibition, Congress on Tuberculosis, Washington, 1909; del. Internat. Hygiene Expn., Dresden, 1911; pres. sec. mil., naval and tropical hygiene. Internat. Congress Hygiene, Washington, 1912. Died Dec. 9, 1918.

BICKNELL, GEORGE AUGUSTUS rear adm.; b. Batsto, N.J., May 15, 1846; s. George A. and Elizabeth Haskins (Richards) B.; Scandinavian lineage; early education in private schools; appointed acting midshipman from Indiana, Dec. 2, 1861; served as 1st lt. U.S. Vol. Inf. during Morgan raid in Ind. until regt. was mustered out; grad. U.S. Naval Acad., 1866; Naval Torpedo Sch., 1874 and 1896, U.S. Naval War Coll., 1896 and 1900; m. Annie Sloan, May 22, 1878. Served on Iroquois, Asiatic Fleet, 1867-70; was at opening of ports of Kobe and Osaka, Japan, to trade, 1868; in landing party repelling attack of Prince Hizen and later 2d in command of marines protecting Yokohama until order was restored. Promoted ensign, Apr. 1868; advanced through grades to rear adm., Feb. 8, 1907. Served on numerous vessels and stas.; navigator of Marion, 1880-82, cruised from Montevideo to Heard's Island, about 7,000 miles; rescued 30 survivors of shipwrecked bark Trinity; comd. U.S.S. Niagara in Spanish-Am. War, and in other service in Puerto Rican and Cuban waters until Sept. 1898; comd. Monocacy at Shanghai, China, Dec. 1899, cruised with Hon. E. H. Conger, Am. minister, and suite to Han Kow and river ports, visiting 2 viceroys of river provinces, etc.; comdt. Naval Sta., Key West, Fla., 1902-04; comdg. flagship Texas, flagship U.S. Coast Squadron, 1904-06; comdt. Pensacola Navy Yard, July 1, 1906-Feb. 13, 1907; comdt. Navy Yard, Portsmouth, N.H., 1907-08; retired, May 15, 1908. Life mem. U.S. Naval Inst. Episcopalian; del. Gen. Convs., 1910, 13; sr. warden same ch. in which father and g.f. held same office. Pres. Sinking Fund Commn., City of New Albany. Democrat. Home: New Albany, Ind. Died Jan. 27, 1925.

BICKNELL, LEWIS WILLIAMS judicial executive; b. Minneapolis, Dec. 14, 1885; s. George Simpson and Alice Bertha (White) B.; LL.B., U. of Minn., 1907. Admitted to Minn. bar, 1907, S.D., bar, 1908; states atty. Day Co., S.D., 1933-37; chmn. South Dakota Relief Administration, 1933-35, South Dakota Public Welfare Board, 1935-37; member S.D. Judicial Council, 1933—, pres., 1951—. Dem. nominee for gov. S.D., 1940-42; mem. adv. com. S.D. Code, 1937-39; gen. counsel Farm Credit Adminstrn., Omaha, Neb., 1943-48; mem. Dem. Nat. Com., 1948-52; del. Dem. Nat. Conv., 1916-28, 1936. Served as capt. to maj. U.S. Army, 1917-19. Mem. Am. and S.D. bar assns. Club: Minneapolis. Home: 818 1st St. West. Office: Box 615, Webster, S.D. Died Oct. 20, 1953; buried Lakewood Cemetery, Mpls.

BIDDLE, A. J. DREXEL ambassador to Spain; b. Philadelphia, Dec. 17, 1896; s. A(nthony) J(oseph) Drexel and Cornelia Rundell (Bradley) B.; grad. St. Paul's Sch., N.H., 1915; LL.D., Temple U., 1938. Drexel Institute of Technology, 1955; married Mary Duke; married 2d, Margaret Thompson Schulze, 1901; m. 3d, Margaret Atkinson Loughborough, 1946. Engaged in shipping business; mining bus., South Africa, 1931-34; minister to Norway. 1935-37; ambassador to Poland, 1937. Accompanied Polish govt. in forced move from Warsaw to several capitals in Poland, 1939, and to Angers, France. Interim ambassador, France, 1940, when French govt. moved seat to Tours, then to Bordeaux; A.E. and P. to govts. Poland, Belgium, Netherlands, Norway, Greece, Yugoslavia, Czechoslovakia, also minister to Luxembourg, 1941-44; ret. from diplomatic service, 1944. Chmn. Pa. Aeros. Commn., State Armory Bd., Govtl. Reorgn. Commn.; ex-officio mem. State Vets. Commn.; ex-officio mem. bd. trustees Soldiers and Sailors Home; trustee Temple U. Asst. sec. Dem. nat. conv., Phila., 1936. Served with U.S. Army, 1917-18, advancing to capt.; active duty as lt. col., U.S. Army, 1944, advancing to brig. gen., 1951; dep. chief European allied contact sect. SHAEF; chief allied contact sect. USFET, 19 dep. fgn. liaison officer, Gen. Staff Corps, Dept. Army, Washington, 1948, fgn. liaison officer, 1950-51; exec. Nat. Mil. Reps., SHAPE, 1951-53; spl. asst. to chief of staff Dept. Army, Washington, 1953-55; adj. gen. Pa., with rank maj. gen., until 1961; U.S. ambassador to Spain, 1961-. Pres. Assn. U.S. Army, 1958-60. Recipient Meritorious Service medal State of Pa., for cementing Polish-Am. relations; Pa. Distinguished Service medal, 1958; Legion of Merit (U.S.); Palmes d'Academie. Legion of Honor, Croix de Guerre with palm (France); Grand Cross Order of White Lion, Medal of Merit (1st class) (Czechoslovakia); Medal of Valor, Gold Cross of Merit with crossed swords, Grand Cross Polonia Restituta (Poland); Order Cross of Yugoslavia, Medal of Merit (1st class) (Yugoslavia); Grand Cross Order of St. Olaf (Norway); Officer Order of Leopold I, Mil. Order (1st class) (Belgium); Order Brit. Empire; Commenda dell' Ordine della Corona d' Italia (Italy); Comdr. Order Couronne de la Cheve (Luxembourg); Grand Cross Orange-Nassau (Netherlands); Grand Cross Royal Order of Phoenix (Greece); Medal of Mil. Merit (1st class) (Mexico); Order of Merit (Brazil); Comdr. Order of St. Charles (Monaco). Clubs: Philadelphia, Racquet and Tennis (Phila.); Brook, Knickerbocker, Union, Racquet and Tennis, River (N.Y.C.); Travelers (Paris). Mem. Am. court tennis teams competing for Bathurst Cup, 1932,33, 34; winner court tennis championship, France, 1933. Address: Am. Embassy, Madrid, Spain. Died Nov. 13, 1961; buried Arlington Nat. Cemetery, Va.

BIDDLE, A(NTHONY) J(OSEPH) DREXEL author, explorer, lecturer; b. W. Phila., Pa., Oct. 1, 1874; s. Edward and Emily (Drexel) B.; ed. pvt. sch., Phila., and Heidelberg, Germany; m. Cordelia Rundell Bradley, June 11, 1905. Lived in Maderia Islands, studying conditions there, returning to U.S., 1891; joined staff of Phila. Public Ledger, also contbd. to mags. and humorous jours.; revived Phila. Sunday Graphic, 1895, and became its editor; head pub. house of Drexel Biddle, 1897-1904; founder of movement known as Athletic Christianity; founder, 1907, and pres. Drexel Biddle Bible Classes (200,000 members) in U.S., England, Ireland, Scotland, W.I., W. Africe, S. Australia and Canada. Prof. on faculty of Bureau of Investigation, Training School of Dept. of Justice. Served in France as captain U.S. Marine Corps., 1918; now colonel in U.S. Marine Corps Reserve. Commanded U.S. Marine Corps Combat Team, exhibiting at Phila. Sesqui-Centennial; instr. of individual combat, U.S. Marine Corps. Fellow Royal Geographical Society; corr. mem. Societe Archeologique de France. Amateur boxing champion. Author: A Dual Role, 1894; All Around Athletics, 1894; An Allegory and Three Essays, 1894; The Froggy Fairy Book, 1896; The Second Froggy Fairy Book, 1897; Shantytown Sketches, 1898; Word for Word and Letter for Letter, 1898; The Flowers of Life, 1898; The Madeira Islands (2 vols.), 1900; The Land of the Wine (2 vols.), 1901; Do or Die, Military Manual of Advanced Science in Individual Cambat (pub. by U.S. Marine Corps), 1937. Office: 112 Drexel Bldg., Philadelphia, Pa. Died May 27, 1948.

BIDDLE, CLEMENT army officer, mcht.; b. Phila., May 10, 1740; s. John and Sarah (Owen) B.; m. Mary Richardson; m. 2d, Rebekah Cornell; 13 children, including Clement Cornell. Signed Phila. Nonimportant Agreement, 1765; partner father's shipping house, 1771; apptd. q.m. gen. with rank of col. for militias of Pa. and N.J., by 2d Continental Congress, 1776; participated in battles of Trenton, Princeton, Brandywine and Portsmouth; aide-de-camp to Gen. Green, 1776; commissary gen. of forage, 1777; q.m. gen. (col.) Pa. Militia, 1781; justice Pa. Ct. Common Pleas, 1788; apptd. U.S. marshall Pa. by Pres. Washington, 1789; Gen. Washington's factor (purchasing agt., seller produce of Mt. Vernon), 1780's-1790's. Died Phila., July 14, 1814.

BIDDLE, JAMES naval officer; b. Phila., Feb. 18, 1783; s. Charles and Hannah (Shepard) B.; attended U. Pa., circa 1798-1800. Apptd. midshipman U.S. Navy, 1800, served in Tripolitan War, 1802-03; promoted to lt., 1803, master-commandant, 1813, capt., 1814, commodore, 1822; commanded sloop-of-war Syren, 1810; 1st lt. on Wasp which captured Brit. brig Frolic, 1812; commanded Hornet, 1813-15, captured Brit. Penguin; sailed to Columbia River to take possession of Ore, Territory, 1817; commodore of West India station, 1822; on duty in S.Am. and Mediterranean seas, 1826-32; pres. Naval Asylum, Phila., 1838-42; commodore East Indian Squadron, signed 1st treaty between China and U.S., 1846; commanded Pacific Coast Squadron during Mexican War. Died Phila., Oct. 1, 1848; buried Phila. 62

BIDDLE, JAMES brig. gen.; b. Phila., Dec. 11, 1832; s. Edward R. and Eliza Terry (Davis) B.; ed. U. of New York; m. Ellen F. McGowan, First lt. 10th N.Y. Inf., May 2, 1861; hon. mustered out of vol. service, Aug. 31, 1861; capt. 15th U.S. Inf., Aug. 5, 1861; col. 6th Ind. Cav., Nov. 11, 1862; bvtd. maj. U.S.A., Sept. 1, 1862, "for gallant and meritorious services at battle of Richmond, Ky."; lt. col. U.S.A., Dec. 16, 1864, for same at battle of Nashville; brig. gen. vols., Mar. 13, 1865, for same during the war; hon. mustered out, June 27, 1865; maj. 6th Cav., Feb. 21, 1873; lt. col. 5th Cav., Oct. 19, 1887; col. 9th Cav., July 1, 1891; retired, Dec. 11, 1896; advanced to rank of brig. gen., retired, by act of Apr. 23, 1904. Mem. Loyal Legion, S.A.R. Home: Berkeley Springs, W.Va. Died 1910.

BIDDLE, JOHN army officer; b. Detroit, Mich., Feb. 2, 1859; s. William S. and Susan D. (Ogden) B.; grad. West Point, 1881; unmarried. Commd. 2d lt. engrs., June 11, 1881; promoted through grades to col., Feb. 27, 1911; brig. gen. U.S.A., May 15, 1917; maj. gen. N.A., Aug. 5, 1917. In charge of river and harbor work at Nashville, Tenn., 1891-98; lt. col. and chief engr. U.S. vols. during war with Spain; served in expdn. to P.R.; in Cuba, 1898-99, P.I., 1899-1901; commr. D.C., 1901-07; in charge river and harbor work at San Francisco, June 1907-Aug. 1911; on duty War Dept., Gen. Staff, 1911-14; in charge rivers and harbors, Savannah, July-Sept. 1914; observer with Austro-Hungarian Army in Austria and Poland, Dec. 1914-June 1915; in charge river and harbors. Baltimore, Oct. 1915-July 1916; supt. U.S. Mil. Acad., 1916-17; comdg. 6th U.S. Engrs., June 1917; comdg. U.S. Ry. regts. in France, July-Oct. 1917; asst. chief of staff, Nov. 1917-Mar. 1918; comdg. Am. forces in Eng., Mar. 1918-June 1919; comdg. Camp Travis, Tex., Aug. 1919-20, Camp Custer, Feb.-Sept. 1920; retired Dec. 1, 1920; retired Dec. 1, 1920. Died Jan. 18, 1936.

BIDDLE, NICHOLAS navy officer; b. Phila., Sept. 10, 1750; s. William and Mary (Scull) B. Given command of privateer Franklin with rank of lt. by Continental Congress, 1775; commd. capt., given command of Andrea Doria, 1775; captured numerous ships in N. Atlantic, 1775-76; comdr. ship Randolph, assigned to West Indies, 1776, captured ships including British vessel Triton, 1777. Killed in explosion of Randolph during engagement with Brit. ship Yarmouth nr. Charleston, S.C., Mar. 7, 1778.

BIDDLE, WILLIAM PHILLIPS maj. gen. U.S.M.C.; b. Phila., Dec. 17, 1853; s. John Barclay B. (M.D.) and Caroline (Phillips) B.; ed. pvt. schs. and tutor and U. of Pa.: m. Mrs. Martha Reynolds Adger, Apr. 12, 1908. Commd. 2d lt. U.S.M.C., June, 1875; 1st lt., 1884; capt., 1894; maj., 1899; lt. col., 1903; col., 1905; maj. gen., comdt. Marine Corps, Feb. 3, 1911. Commanded marines, Peking relief expdn., marine barracks, Cavite, P.I., and 1st Regt., 1st Brigade 1900-03; pres. Marine Exam. Bds., Washington, 1903; comd. 1st Regt. marine expeditionary forces, Isthmus of Panama, 1903-04; comd. marine barracks, Phila., 1904-06; comd. 1st Brigade marines, Manila, P.I., 1906-08; comd. marine barracks, New York, 1908-09; Nicaraguan expeditionary marines, Panama, 1909-10; retired, Feb. 26, 1914. Awarded Dewey medal, for Battle of Manila; Spanish War, Philippine and Peking relief campaign medals. Episcopalian. On active duty during World War at San Diego, Calif. Died Feb. 26, 1823.

BIERER, ANDREW GORDON CURTIN, JR. lawyer; b. Guthrie, Okla., Dec. 1, 1899; s. Andrew Gregg Curtin and Nancy (Stamper) B.; student University of Wisconsin, 1920; A.B., University of Oklahoma, 1921; LL.B., Harvard, 1925; m. Vinita McDonald, June 29, 1927; children: Andrew Gordon Curtin, III, Alva McDonald. Admitted to Oklahoma bar, 1925, and since practiced in Guthrie; mem. firm Bierer & Moser, 1952—. Mem. Okla. State Bar Commn., later Com. State Bar Examiners, 1927-39; mem. exec. com. Nat. Conf. of Bar Examiners, 1931-41, chmn. 1938,39. Enlisted Central Machine Gun Officers Training Sch., Camp Hancock, Ga., during World War I; maj., U.S. Army, J.A.G.D.; mem. bd. of review No. 4, Judge Adv. Gen.'s Office, Washington, World War II to Jan. 1946. Pres. State League of Young Democrats of Okla., 1930. Mem. Southwestern Council, U.S. C. of C. Mem. American Bar Assn., Okla. State Bar Assn., Guthrie Bar Assn., Am. Legion (past comdr.), Kappa Sigma. Democrat. Episcopalian. Mason (33ff, Shriner). Clubs: Oklahoma, University (Oklahoma City); Harvard of Oklahoma; Guthrie Country. Author of various bar journal articles. Lecturer before professional socs. Home: 800 East Cleveland Av. Office: Bierer Bldg., Guthrie, Okla. Died Aug. 27, 1956; buried Summit View Cemetery, Guthrie, Okla.

BIERI, BERNHARD HENRY, naval officer; b. Walnut Lake, Minn., June 24, 1889; s. Bernhard and Elsie (Schild) B.; B.S., U.S. Naval Acad., 1911; grad. U.S. Naval War Coll., 1936; m. Elsie Genther, June 27, 1913; children—Bernhard, John Genther, David, Robert, James. Commd. ensign, U.S. Navy, 1911, advancing through the grades to vice adm., 1945; served in U.S. ships, Delaware, 1911-12, Nashville, 1913, Montana, 1914, Virginia, 1914-15, Texas, 1915-19 and 1929-30, Utah, 1928, Altair, 1933-35; comd. U.S.S. Corry, 1921-25; staff comdr. Battleships, 1938, Battle Force, 1939; staff comdr. in chief U.S. Fleet, 1939-40; comd. U.S. Chicago, 1941-42; staff comdr. in chief U.S. Fleet, 1942-45, this period including duty with Allied Comdr. North African Invasion Forces and Supreme Comdr. Allied Forces in Europe; dep. chief Naval Operations, 1945-46; comdr. U.S. Naval Forces in Mediterranean, 1946-48; comdt. 11th Naval Dist., 1948-49; rep. U.S. chief naval operations, on mil. staff Com. of Security Council, U.N., 1949-51. Decorated service bars, Mexican, World War I. Pacific, European-African fronts, World War II. Home: Bethesda MD Died Apr. 10, 1971; buried Arlington Nat. Cemetery.

BIGELOW, JOHN army officer; b. New York, N.Y., May 12, 1854; s. John and Jane Tunis (Poultney) B.; ed. in Paris, Bonn, Berlin, Freiberg and Providence, R.I.; apptd. from N.Y., and grad. U.S. Mil. Acad., 1877; m. Mary Braxton Dallam, Apr. 28, 1883; children - John (dec.), Gladys (dec.), Braxton (dec.), Jan Poultney. Second lt., June 15, 1877; 1st lt., Sept. 24, 1883; capt., Apr. 15, 1893; maj. 9th Cav., Dec. 8, 1902; adj. gen. D.C. militia, 1887-89; prof. mil. sci., Mass. Inst. Tech., 1894-98; wounded in attack on San Juan, July 1, 1898; retired at own request, over 30 yrs. service, Sept. 15, 1904. Prof. French, M.I.T., 1905-10; on duty with organized militia of Mass., Feb. 10, 1906-Aug. 1, 1910; prof. mil. sci., Rutgers Coll., Oct. 15, 1917-May 18, 1918; on duty in hist. branch Gen. Staff, till July 5, 1919. Author: Mars-la-Tour and Gravelotte, 1884; Principles of Strategy, 1894; Reminiscences of the Santiago Campaign, 1899; The Campaign of Chancellorsville, 1910; American Policy, 1914; World Peace, 1915; Breaches of Anglo-American Treaties, 1917. Home: Washington, D.C. Died Feb. 29, 1936.

BILLADO, FRANCIS WILLIAM adj. gen.; b. Rutland, Vt., Mar. 3, 1907; s. Jason A. and Regina (Horan) B.; student Norwich U., 1933; m. Ruth Bourquin, Nov. 26, 1938; children-Francis William, Barrie Lynne, Virginia Helen. Commd. 2d lt. U.S. Army, 1933, advanced through grades to maj. gen., 1955; assigned 172d inf. Regt., 43d Inf. Div., 1941, War Dept. gen. staff, 1942-45 (subcom. on logistic aspects Occupied Europe, Joint Chiefs Staff), C-4 European sect., operations div. War Dept. Gen. Staff, exec. officer new development div. War Dept. Spl. Services, 1945-46; exec. officer 172d Inf. Regt., 43d Inf. Div., 1946-50; adj., insp., q.m. gen. of Vt., 1955-64; chmn. gen. staff com. on Army N.G. policy, 1964-. Mem. Vt. Ho. of Reps., 1947, 53, 55; chmn. Vt. State Vets. Bd.; pres. Rutland Bd. Sch. Commrs., 1953. Trustee U. Vt., 1947-53, Vt. Soldiers' Home. Mem. Vt., Rutland County (pres. 1952) bar assns., Am. Legion, Theta Chi. lMason (Shriner). Home: 864 S. Prospect St., Burlington, Vt. Died Dec. 13, 1966.

BILLINGS, FRANK M.D.; b. Highland, Iowa Co., Wis., Apr. 2, 1854; s. Henry M. and Ann (Bray) B.; M.D., Northwestern U., 1881, M.S., 1890; interne Cook Co. (Ill.) Hosp., 1881-82; studied in Vienna, London and Paris, 1885-86; Sc.D., Harvard, 1915; m. Dane Ford Brawley, May 26, 1887; 1 dau., Margaret (Mrs. Geo. R. Nichols, II). Demonstrator of anatomy, 1882-86, prof. physical diagnosis, 1886-91, prof. medicine, 1891-98, Northwestern U.; prof. medicine, 1898 - , dean of faculty, 1900 - , Rush Med. Coll. (affiliated with U. of Chicago); professional lecturer, 1901-05, prof. medicine, 1905-24, U. of Chicago. First lt., 1908, major, 1917, Med. R.C. Presbyterian Hosp., 1898-1920; cons. phys same; retired. Shattuck lect. (Boston), 1902; Lane and lecturer (Leland Stanford U.), 1915. Chmn. Am. Red Cross Mission to Russia, 1917. Mem. Ill. State Council Defense; mem. advisory bd. of Am. Red Cross War Council; major Med. R.C. U.S.A. as aide to gov. of Ill. in orgn. advisory med. bds. for army draft; col. Med. Corps. U.S.A.; served in A.E.F. and office of provost marshal gen. and office of surgeon gen., Feb. 1, 1918-June 28, 1919. Pres. Ill. State Bd. Charities and of State Charities Commn., 1906-12. Home: Chicago, Ill. Died Sept. 20, 1932.

BILLINGS, JOHN SHAW surgeon, librarian; b. Switzerland Co., Ind., Apr. 12, 1839; s. James and Abbie (Shaw) B.; A.B., Miami U., 1857, A.M., 1860; M.D., Med. Coll. of Ohio, 1860; (LL.D., U. of Edinburgh, 1884, Harvard, 1886, Buda-Pesth, 1896, Yale, 1901, Johns Hopkins, 1902; M.D., Munich, 1889, Dublin, 1892; D.C.L., Oxford, 1889); m. Kate M. Stevens, Sept. 3, 862. Demonstrator anatomy, Med. Coll. of Ohio, 1860-61; served in U.S.A., as asst. surgeon, Apr. 16, 1862; maj. surgeon, Dec. 2, 1876; lt. col. deputy surgeon gen., June 6, 1894; bvtd. capt., maj. and lt. col., Mar. 13, 1865. "for faithful and meritorious services during the war"; in hosp. service during Civil War; later med. insp. Army of the Potomac, in charge of library of Surgeon-general's office until his appmt., Dec. 28, 1883, as curator Med. Mus. and Library; retired Oct. 1, 1895. In charge vital statistics 10th Census, vital and social statistics, 11th Census. Prof. Hygiene, U. of Pa., 1891, and dir., 1893-96; dir. N.Y. Pub. Library, Astor, Lenox and Tilden foundations, 1896-; chn. bd. Carnegie Instn., 1905-. Fellow Am. Acad. Arts and Sciences; pres. A.L.A., 1901-02. Author: Principles of Ventilation and Heating, 1886; Index Catalogue of the Library of the Surgeon-General's Office U.S.A. (16 vols.), 1880-1894; National Medical Dictionary (2 vols.), 1889. Home: New York. Died March. 11, 1913.

BILLINGS, LUTHER GUITEAU naval officer; b. in New York, 1842; s. Hon. Andrew and Abbie (Sheldon) B.; apptd. acting asst. p.-m. U.S.S. Water Witch, Oct. 22, 1862; took active part in engagement June 4, 1864, when Water Witch was boarded by Confederates, several of whom, including their comdg. officer, he killed in hand to hand conflict, but was wounded and captured, taken to hosp. and later to prison; escaped from moving train, but was recaptured by aid of bloodhounds; imprisoned in Charleston and later in Libby Prison; exchanged late in 1864; promoted 15 numbers in his grade for "eminent and conspicuous conduct in battle"; afterward served on various stas.; was on the Wateree when it was carried about one mile inland during earthquake, Aug. 14, 1868; commd. p.-m. U.S.N., May 4, 1866; gen. insp. pay corps, Sept., 1897; pay dir. with rank of rear adm., Jan. 9, 1895; retired, Mar. 14, 1898. After retirement, was ordered to duty during the Spanish War, and organized the Coast Signal Service, from Eastport, Me., to the Rio Grande; again ordered to active duty, Mar. 8, 1917, as purchasing officer for Eastern Dist., Baltimore. Home: Chappaqua, New York. Died Dec. 30, 1920.

BINGHAM, DAVID JUDSON army officer; b. Massena, N.Y., May 16, 1831; s. Alfred Sidney and Mary (Purcell) B.; grad. U.S. Mil. Acad., 1854, Arty. Sch., Ft. Monroe, Va., 1860; m. Marguerite Gonzalez, Nov. 20, 1856. Apptd. 2d lt. 2d Arty., July 1, 1854; advanced through the grades to maj. q.-m. U.S.A., July 29, 1866; lt. col. deputy q.-m. gen., Mar. 3, 1875; col. asst. q.-m. gen., July 2, 1883; retired by operation of law, May 16, 1895; advanced to rank of brig. gen. retired by act of Apr. 23, 1904; bvtd. maj., lt. col. and col., Mar. 13, 1865, for faithful and meritorious services during the war; bvtd. brig. gen., Apr. 9, 1865, for es in the field during the war. Died 1909.

BINGHAM, GONZALEZ SIDNEY army officer; b. Pensacola, Fla., Oct. 10, 1857; s. Judson David and Marguerite (Gonzalez) B.; B.S., Columbian (now George Washington) U., 1877; m. Antoinette Collins Lynch, of Nashville, Tenn., Dec. 13, 1888; children-Sidney Vincent, Dorothy Campbell (Mrs. Walter Steves). Commd. 2d lt. 7th Inf., Oct. 10, 1883; promoted through grades to col., Feb. 6, 1909; retired June 26, 1920. (For details of career see Vol. XI, 1920-21). Home: 831 Grayson St., San Antonio, Tex.

BINGHAM, HENRY HARRISON congressman; b. Phila., Dec. 4, 1841; s. James and Ann (Sheller) B.; A.B., Jefferson Coll., Pa., 1862, A.M., 1866; (LL.D., Washington and Jefferson, 1906). First lt. 140th Pa. Inf., Aug. 22, 1862; capt. Sept. 9, 1862; maj. judge advocate vols., Sept. 20, 1864; bvtd. maj. vols. Aug. 1, 1864, "for good conduct and conspicuous gallantry, especially at the Wilderness, Spottsylvania and Gettysburg"; lt. col.

vols., Apr. 9, 1865, "for highly meritorious services during campaign terminating with surrender of Gen. R.E. Lee"; col. and brig. gen. vols. Apr. 9, 1865, "for conspicuous gallantry and meritorious services the war"; awarded medal of honor, Aug. 26, 1893, for Battle of Wilderness; hon. mustered out, July 2, 1866; thrice wounded. Read law with Atty.-Gen. Benjamin H. Brewster; m. Mary H. Alexander, Feb. 4, 1874. Postmaster of Phila., 1867-72; clerk courts of oyer and terminer and quarter sessions of the peace, Phila., 1872-78; mem. 46th to 62d Congresses (1879-1913), 1st Pa. Dist. (longest continuous service of any mem. now in House). Del. Rep. Nat. convs., 1872 (at-large), 1876, 1884, 1888, 1892, 1896, 1900, 1904. Home: Philadelphia. Died Mar. 23, 1912.

BINGHAM, HIRAM explorer, ex-senator; b. Honolulu, H.I., Nov. 19, 1875; s. Rev. Hiram and Minerva Clarissa (Brewster) B.; A.B., Yale, 1898; M.A., U. of Calif., 1900; M.A., Harvard, 1901, Ph.D., 1905; Litt.D., U. of Cuzeo, 1912; m. Alfreda Mitchell, Nov. 20, 1900; children: Woodbridge, Hiram, Alfred Mitchell, Charles Tiffany, Brewster, Mitchell, Jonathan Brewster; m. 2d, Suzanne Carroll Hill, June 28, 1937. Austin teaching fellow in history, Harvard, 1901-02 and 1904-05; preceptor in history and politics, Princeton U., 1905-06; explored Bolivar's route across Venezuela and Colombia, 1906-07; lecturer on South Am. geography and history, Yale, 1907-09; asst. prof. Latin Am. history, 1909-15, prof., 1915-24; Albert Shaw lecturer on diplomatic history, Johns Hopkins, 1910. Del. U.S. Govt. to 1st Pan.-Am. Scientific Congress, Santiago de Chile, 1908; explored Spanish trade route, Buenos Aires to Lima, 1908-09; dir. Yale Peruvian Expdn., 1911, discovered ruins of Machu Picchu, located Vitcos, last Inca capital, and made the first ascent of Mt. Coropuna, 21,703 ft.; dir. Peruvian expdns., 1912, 14-15, auspices of Yale U. and Nat. Geog. Soc.; adviser on the South Am. collections in the Yale U. Library; lecturer on South Sea Islands, Naval Training Schools, 1942-43. Alternate Rep. Conv., Chicago, 1916; del. at large, Cleveland, 1924, Kansas City, 1928, Chicago, 1932, Cleveland, 1936; presdl. elector, 1916; lt. gov. of Conn., 1923-24, elected gov., 1924, resigning Jan. 8, 1925; elected U.S. Senator, Dec. 16, 1924, re-elected for term, 1927-33; mem. President Coolidge's Aircraft Bd. (Morrow Bd.), 1925; chairman American Samoan Commission, 1930; chairman Loyalty Review Board, Director Washington Loan & Trust Co. Capt. 10th Field Arty., Conn. Nat. Guard, 1916; organized U.S. schools of military aeronautics; commd. lt. col., Air Service, Mil. Aeronautics, U.S. Army, Oct. 23, 1917; chief Air Personnel Div., Washington, Nov. 1917-Mar. 1918, and A.E.F., Tours, 1918; comdg. officer Aviation Instrn. Center, Issodoun, France (Allies' largest flying school), Aug.-Dec. 1918. Officer de l'Ordre de l'Etiole Noire (French): Gran Oficial de la Orden del Libertador (Venezuela); Gran Oficial de la Orden "E Sol del Peru"(Peru); awarded Mitre medal of Hispanic Soc.; H.G. Bryant Gold Medal. Fellow Royal Geog. Society; honorary life member National Geog. Society; member Geographic Soc. of Phila., Hispanic Soc. America (hon. president), American Antiquarian Society; honorary member Nat. Acad. Hist. (Bogota); corr. member Lima Geog. Soc., Nat. Acad. Hist. (Caracas, Venezuela). Mem. Sigma Psi. Clubs: Elizabethan, Grad. (New Haven), Century (N.Y.), Metropolitan, Chevy Chase, Alfafa (Wash). Author: Journal of an Expedition across Venezuela and Colombia, 1909; Across South America, 1911; Vitcos, the Last Inca Capital, 1912; In the Wonderland of Peru, 1913; The Monroe Doctrine, An Obsolete Shibboleth, 1913; The Future of the Monroe Doctrine, 1920; An Explorer in the Air Service, 1920; Inca Land, 1922; Freedom under the Constitution, 1924; Machu Picchu, 1930; Elihu Yale, Governor, Collector and Benefactor, 1938; Elihu Yale - The American Nabob of Queen Square, 1939; Lost City of the Incas, 1948. Home: 1818 R St., Washington 9. Died June 6, 1956; buried Arlington Nat. Cemetery.

BINGHAM, JOHN ARMOR congressman, diplomat; b. Mercer, Pa., Jan. 21, 1815; son of Hugh Bingham; attended Franklin Coll., 2 years; m. Amanda Bingham (cousin), 3 children. Admitted to Ohio bar, 1840; dist. atty. Tuscarawas County, O., 1846-49; mem. U.S. Ho. of Reps. (Republican) from Ohio, 33d-37th, 39th-42d congresses, 1855-63, 65-73; served as maj., judge advocate U.S. Army, 1864; helped frame 14th Amendment to U.S. Constn.; U.S. minister to Japan, 1873-85. Died Cadiz., O., Mar. 19, 1900; buried Cadiz Cemetery.

BINGHAM, THEODORE ALFRED brig. gen. U.S.A.; b. Andover, Tolland Co., Conn., May 14, 1858; s. Joel Foote and Susan (Grew) B.; grad. West Point, 1879; hon. A.M., Yale, 1896; m. Lucile Rutherfurd, Dec. 15, 1881 (died 1920); m. 3d, Addison Mitchell, Oct. 2, 1926. Commissioned 2d lt., June 13, 1879; promoted through grades to brig. gen., July 11, 1904; retired July 12, 1904. Served in various duties as engineer officer, 1879-90; military attache, U.S. Legation, Berlin, 1890-92, Rome, 1892-94; in charge Pub. Bldgs. and Grounds, Washington, with rank of col., Mar. 9, 1897-May 17, 1903; in charge of engring. dist., Lake Ontario and Lake Erie, light engr. 10th light house dist., 1903-04. Police commr., New York, Jan. 1, 1906-July 1, 1909; chief engr. highways, New York, May 10th-July 10, 1911; consulting engr., dept. of bridges N.Y. City, 1911-15 (resigned); recalled to active service in U.S.A., Oct. 11, 1917; in command of 2d engring. dist., N.Y. City; chief engr. on staff of comdg. gen. Dept. of the East, Governor's Island, N.Y. City; discharged from active service and returned to retired list, June 10, 1919. Died Sept. 6, 1934.

BINGHAM, WALTER VAN DYKE psychologist; born Swan Lake, Ia., Oct. 20, 1880; s. Lemuel Rothwell and Martha Evarts (Tracy) B.; U. of Kan., 1897-98; B.A., Beloit (Wis.) Coll., 1901, U. of Chicago, 1905-06, U. of Berlin, 1907; M.A., Harvard, 1907; Ph.D., University of Chicago, 1908; Sc.D., Beloit College, 1929, Illinois Wesleyan University, 1950; married Millicent Todd, Dec. 4, 1920. Asso. in psychology, U. of Chicago, 1906-07; instr. ednl. psychology, Teachers Coll. (Columbia), 1908-10; asst. prof. psychology, Dartmouth, 1910-15, also dir. summer session, 1912-15; prof. psychology and head div. of applied psychology, Carnegie Inst. Tech., Pittsburgh, 1915-24; dir. Cooperative Reserach, same, 1921-24; dir. Personnel Research Fedn., Inc., 1924-34; mem. bd. Psychol. Corp. since 1920 (pres. 1926-28); professional lecturer in psychology, Stevens Inst. Tech., 1930-40; consultant, Occupational Information Service, U.S. Office of Edn., 1938-39; chief psychologist Adj. Gen.'s Office, War Dept., 1940-47. Exec. sec. com. on classification of personnel in the army, 1917-18; lt. col., Personnel Br. Gen. Staff, U.S. Army, 1918-19. First chmn. Div. of Anthropology and Psychology, Nat. Research Council, 1919-20. Chmn. com. on classification of military personnel, 1939-46; chmn. bd. on clin. psychol. advisory to the Surgeon Gen., U.S. Army, 1944-47; chmn. council, adv. to dir. personnel and adminstrn. Army Gen. Staff, 1946-48; consultant on personnel policies to Sec. of Defense since 1949. Awarded sec. of war's Emblem for Exceptional Civilian Service, 1944. Hon. corr. British Nat. Inst. Indsl. Psychol.; fellow A.A.A.S. (sec. council, 1917); mem. Am. Psychol. Assn. (sec. 1911-14). Am. Assn. Applied Psychol. (pres. 1941), Am. Assn. for Applied Psychology (pres. 1939), Psychometric Soc., Internat. Musical Soc., Sigma Xi, Phi Beta Kappa. Repn. Episcopalian. Clubs: Cosmos (Washington); Century (New York). Author: Studies in Melody, 1910; Aptitudes and Aptitude Testing, 1937, revised 1951. Joint author: Procedures in Employment Psychology, 1926; How to Interview, 1931; Psychology Today, 1932. Cons. editor Jour. of Applied Psychology, Personnel Psychology. Address: 1661 Cresdent Pl., Washington 9. Summer home: Medomak, Me. Died July 7, 1972; buried Arlington Nat. Cemetery.

BINGHAM, WILLIAM J., ednl. adminstr.; b. Norristown, Pa., Aug. 8, 1889; s. Robert and Martha (Clyde) B.; grad. Phillips Exeter Acad., 1912; A.B., Harvard, 1916; m. Florence Patee, May 29, 1917; children—William J., Richard I. Banking, Houston, 1919-20; head track coach and asst. grad. treas. Athletiç Assn., Harvard, 1920-22, dir. athletics and chmn. com. on regulation athletic sports, 1926-51, chmn. faculty athletic com. 1951; with Department of Defense, Washington, 1951-52; president and treas. Ernest Monnier, Inc., importers, Boston, 1922-37; dir. Cambridge Trust Co. Dir. Boston Garden, Harvard Coop. Soc. Nat. Football Hall of Fame. Chmn. Am. Olympic Track Com. and Olympiad (1936-Berlin); sec. Nat. Collegiate Football Rules Com., 1932-43, chmn., 1943-50; also pres. various sports coms., 1927-51). Served as pvt. to capt. U.S. Army, 1917-19; maj. to col., 1942-45, dir. security and intelligence First Service Command. Decorated Croix de Guerre, Legion of Merit. Clubs: Harvard (Boston and N.Y. City), Faculty (Harvard). Home: Marlboro NH Died Sept. 7, 1971.

BIRCHARD, GLEN ROBBINS air force officer; b. Grand Rapids, Mich., Feb. 5, 1914; s. Glen R. and Lula Mae (Garrison) B.; A.B., Bay City (Mich.) Jr. Coll., 1934, U.S. Army Air Corps Flying Sch., 1939, Air War Coll., 1953; m. Virginia Leigh Brooks, Jan. 11, 1941; children-Geoffrey Robbins, Christopher. Commd. 2d lt. USAAF, 1939, advanced through grades to maj. gen. USAF, 1960; comdr. 307th Bombardment Group, Solomon Islands, 1942-44; operations officer Berlin Airlift, 1948-49; dep. comdr. Airlift Force, Korea, 1950-51; comdr. 1707th Transp. Tng. Wing, 1951-52; staff officer Hdqrs. USAF, 1953-56 dep. chief staff, operations, Mil. Air Transp. Service, 1958-61; comdr. Western Transp. Air Force, 1961-63; vice comdr. Mil. Air Transport Service, 1963-. Decorated Legion of Merit with oak leaf cluster, D.F.C., Air medal with 9 oak leaf clusters; Order Brit. Empire. Home: 1314 McKinley Av., Bay City, Mich. Office: Hdqrs., Mil. Air Transport Service, Scott AFB, Ill. 62226. Died June 3, 1967; buried Arlington.

BIRD, CHARLES brig. gen.; b. Wilmington, Del., June 17, 1838; s. James T. and Elizabeth (Kettle) B.; grad. Lawrenceville (N.J.) Sch.; m. Mary C. Bowman, Nov. 15, 1866. First lt. 1st Del. Inf., May 20, 1861; hon. mustered out, Aug. 16, 1861; 2d lt. 2d Del. Inf., Apr. 11, 1862; advanced through the grades to col., May 30, 1865; bvtd. 1st lt. and capt., Mar. 2, 1867, "for gallant and meritorious services in battle of Fredericksburg, Va."; maj., Mar. 2, 1867, for same in battle of Spottsylvania, Va.; various assignments to 1882; capt. asst. q.m., Mar. 14, 1882; maj. q.m., Jan. 14, 1895; lt. col. chief q.m. vols., May 9, 1898; col. q.m. vols., July 10, 1898; brig. gen. vols., Jan. 3, 1901; hon. disch. from vol. service, June 20, 1901; lt. col. deputy q.m. gen., Feb. 2, 1901; brig. gen., Apr. 16, 1902; retired by operation of law, June 17, 1902. Home: Wilmington, Del. Died Mar. 22, 1920.

BIRDSALL, SAMUEL congressman, lawyer; b. Hillsdale, Columbia County, N.Y., May 14, 1791; attended common schs.; studied law in office Martin Van Buren. Admitted to bar, 1812; practiced in Cooperstown, N.Y.; master in chancery, 1815; moved to Waterloo, Seneca County, N.Y., 1817; division judge adv. with rank of col., 1819; counselor in Supreme Ct. and solicitor in chancery, 1823; surrogate Seneca County, 1827-37; bank commr., 1832; mem. U.S. Ho. of Reps. (Democrat) from N.Y., 25th Congress, 1837-39; admitted to U.S. Supreme Ct. bar, 1838; dist. atty. Seneca County, 1846; postmaster, Waterloo, 1853-63. Died Waterloo, Feb. 8, 1872; buried Maple Grove Cemetery.

BIRDSEYE, CLAUDE HALE topographic engr.; b. Syracuse, N.Y., Feb. 13, 1878; s. George Frederick Hurd and Katharine Lamb (Hale) B.; A.B., Oberlin, 1901, Sc.D., 1931; post-grad. work, U. of Cincinnati and Ohio State U.; m. Grace Gardner Whitney, Nov. 23, 1904; children - Charles W., Frederick H., Florence W. Instr. in physics, U. of Cincinnati, 1901; field asst., later topographer U.S. Geol. Survey, 1901-06; surveyor Gen. Land Office, 1907-08; with U.S. Geol. Survey, 1909-29 (except when in war service), as topographer, geographer and from Oct. 1919 to Sept. 1929, as chief topographic engr.; pres. Aerotopograph Corp. of America, 1929-32; asst. to dir. U.S. Geol. Survey, 1932; chief, division of engraving and printing, U.S. Geol. Survey, 1932-. Captain Corps of Engineers, U.S.A., Mar.-July 1917; maj. July 1917-Aug. 1918; lt. col. C.A.C., Aug. 1918-June 1919; served in France, on staff of chief of army arty., Aug. 1917-Jan. 1919. Then col. engr., O.R.C. Decorated Officier de l'Instruction Publique (French), 1919; Daly medal (American Geog. Soc.), 1924. Author of engring. and tech. repts. Home: Chevy Chase, Md. Died May 30, 1941.

BIRGE, HENRY WARNER army officer; b. Hartford, Conn., Aug. 25, 1825. Mcht., Norwich, Conn., before Civil War; commd. maj. 4th Inf. Conn. Volunteers, 1861, col. 13th Inf., 1862, promoted brig. gen., 1863; participated in expdn. to take New Orleans, 1862; mem. picked force to storm Port Hudson before its surrender, 1863; commanded brigade under Gen. Banks in Red River campaign, 1864; served with Schofield's army in N.C., 1865, commanded dist. of Savannah; resigned from army, 1865; engaged in cotton and lumber enterprises in Ga. after Civil War. Died N.Y.C., June 1, 1888; buried N.Y.C.

BIRKHEAD, CLAUDE VIVIAN lawyer; b. Phoenix, Oregon, May 27, 1880; son of Joseph Chenoweth and Mary Jane (Jennings) B.; student Fort Worth U., 1898-99; hon. LL.D., 1941; m. Lillian Alice Guessaz, Dec. 6, 1905; children—Betty Jane, Mary Ann. Admitted to Tex. bar, 1899, practiced at San Antonio since 1904; sr. mem. Birkhead, Beckmann, Standard, Vance & Wood; apptd. judge 73d Dist. Fed. Loan Agency; pres. and gen. counsel, Commercial Cattle Loan Co.; gen. counsel Grayburg Oil Co., San Antonio Ins. Exchange, San Antonio Real Estate Bd.; coastal land claims before Congress, 1939. Chairman San Antonio U.S.-Tex. Centennial Com., 1936-37; chmn. Dem. Nat. Campaign Com., Bexar County, Tex., 1936-37; chmn. Fire and Police Civil Ser Service Bd., 1931-36. Col. 131st F.A., U.S. Army, A.E.F., 1917-19; chief of staff, 36th Div., Tex. Nat. Guard, 1919-23; brig. gen., 1923-36; maj. gen. (N.G.U.S.) Army of U.S., comdg. 36th Div., Tex. Nat. Guard, 1936; command gen. Camp Bowie, Tex., and 36th Div. Army of U.S., 1940-41; comdg. gen. Internal Security Forces, 3d Service Comd., 1942; retired from active service, June 30, 1942; lt. gen. Tex. State Gurad Reserve Corps, comdg. Awarded meritorious service medal (Texas), 1933. Mem. Am., Tex. State and San Antonio bar assns. Fraternal Soc. Law Assn., Internat. Assn. of Ins. Counsel; Founders, Am. Legion; Am. Legion (1st comdr., Dept. of Tex., chmn. bd. trustees of Permanent Fund, 1930-36); Nat. Guard Assn. of U.S. (pres. 1932-33); Military Order of the World War. Democrat. Presbyterian. Mason (K.T.). Club: Ft. Sam Houston Officers'. Home: 4001 N. New Braunfels Av. Address: Majestic Bldg., San Antonio, Tex. Died Nov. 19, 1950; buried Ft. Sam Houston Nat. Cemetery, San Antonio.

BIRKHIMER, WILLIAM EDWARD brig. gen.; b. Somerset, O., Mar. 1, 1848; s. Nathan and Temperance (Hood) B.; ed. Denmark (Ia.) Acad.; grad. U.S. Mil. Acad., 1870 (LL.D., Univ. of Oregon, 1889); m. Geraldine, d. late R.V.W. Howard, U.S. Army, Sept. 22, 1876. Served as pvt., Co. M, 4th Ia. Vol. Cav., Mar. 21, 1864-Aug. 8, 1865; commd. 2d lt. 3d U.S. Arty., June 15, 1870; hon. grad. Arty. Sch., 1873; 1st lt., Apr. 10, 1879; promoted through grades to maj. arty corps, U.S.A., Aug. 1, 1901; lt. col., May 20, 1905; brig. gen., Feb. 15, 1906; retired at own request, over 40 yrs.' service, Feb. 16, 1906. Asst. prof. natural and experimental philosophy, U.S. Mil. Acad., 1874-76; judge advocate Dept. of the Columbia, 1886-90; ú asso. justice Supreme Ct. (the Audiencia), Manila, 1899. Awarded medal of honor "for most distinguished gallantry at San Miguel de Mayumo, Luzon, May 13, 1899." Author: Law of Appointment and Promotion in the Army of the United States, 1880; Historical Sketch of the Organization, Administration, Material and Tactics of the Artillery, United States Army, 1884; Military Government and Martial Law, 2d edit., 1904. Home: Washington, D.C. Died June 10, 1914.

BIRMINGHAM, HENRY PATRICK surgeon U.S.A.; b. in N.Y., Mar. 15, 1854; M.D., U. of Mich., 1876 Apptd. asst. surgeon U.S.A., Feb. 18, 1881; capt. asst. surgeon, Feb. 18, 1886; maj. brigade surgeon vols., June 4, 1898; hon. discharged vols., Feb. 20, 1899; maj. surgeon U.S. Army, Dec. 15, 1989; maj. Med. Corps. Dec. 15, 1898; lt. col., Apr. 23, 1908; col., June 7, 1911; brig. gen., Oct. 2, 1917. Died May 4, 1932.

BIRNEY, DAVID BELL army officer; b. Huntsville, Ala., May 29, 1825; s. James Gillespie and Agatha (McDowell) B.; 6 children. Family moved to Cincinnati, 1833; admitted to Mich. bar, 1848; moved to Phila., 1848; commd. lt. col. Pa. Militia, 1860; commd. lt. col. 23d Pa. Volunteers, 1861; col., then brig. gen. U.S. Volunteers, 1862; div. comdr. Army of the Potomac, 1862-63; brevetted maj. gen. volunteers for service at Battle of Chancellorsville, 1863; took part in Battle of Gettysburg, Died from fever contracted during army service, Phila., Oct. 18, 1864.

BIRNEY, WILLIAM lawyer; b. Madison Co., Ala., May 28, 1819; s. James Gillespie B.; m. Catherine Hoffman, 1845. While pursuing studies in Paris took part in the revolution of 1848; was apptd., on public competition, prof. English literature in the coll. at Bourges, France; enlisted in U.S. vols. as private, 1861; rose through all the grades to bvt. maj. gen.; comd. div., 1863-65; practiced law in Washington, 1874-1900, counsel for D.C., 1874-77. Author: Life and Times of James G. Birney; Plea for Civil and Religious Liberty; etc. Died 1907.

BIRNIE, ROGERS army officer; b. Glen Burn farm, Carroll Co., Md., Apr. 5, 1851; s. Rogers and Amelia Knode (Harry) B.; grad. U.S. Mil. Acad. No. 1 in class, 1872; m. Helen Gunn, Dec. 30, 1879. Second lt. 13th Inf., June 14, 1872; advanced through grades to col., Oct. 10, 1907. Regimental q.m., Feb. 1874; served at Camp Douglas, Utah, 1872-74; in engr. service with U.S. Geog. Survey, W. of 100th meridian, 1874-79; attended maneuvers of the 9th Corps d'Armee in France, 1880; served in the 7th Army Corps and in Havana during Spanish-Am. War; formerly inspector West Point Foundry, Cold Spring, N.Y.; acting chief of ordnance U.S.A., Oct. 1912-July 1913; pres. Ordnance Bd., July 3, 1913-15; retired Apr. 5, 1915. Chevalier Legion d'Honneur, France. Home: 530 Fifth Av., New York. Died Spet. 25, 1939.

BIRNIE, UPTON, JR. army officer; b. Carlisle, Pa., July 7, 1877; s. Upton and Susan Alice (Galt) B.; B.S., U.S. Mil. Acad., 1900; distinguished grad. Inf. and Cv. Sch., 1907; grad. Army Staff Coll., 1908; Army War Coll., 1912, 21; m. Susan Turner Schenck, Apr. 15, 1903; children—Elizabeth Schenck (dec.), Sue Schenck (Mrs. Francis I. Brady), Mrs. Margaret Birnie Capron. Apptd. 2d lt. arty., 1900; advanced through grades to col. F.A., 1929; apptd. maj. gen., chief of field arty., 1934; relieved, 1938; retired with rank of maj. gen., 1938. Decorated D.S.M. (U.S.), Officer Legion of Honor (France); Officer Order of Leopold (Belgium); Officer Order of St. Maurice and St. Lazare (Italy). Presbyn. Home: 1702 Surrey Lane, N.W., Washington 7. Died Oct. 15, 1957; buried Arlington Nat. Cemetery.

BISBEE, SPAULDING business exec.; b. Buckfield, Me., 1890; student Hebron Acad., Colby Coll., Boston U. Law Sch. Vice Pres., dir., asst. sec., asst. treas. Keyes Fibre Co., Portland, Me. Dir. civil def. Me., 1949-53; mem. Me. bar. Served as maj. World War I; as col., World War II; ret. as brig. gen., 1950. Episcopalian. Mason. Club: Cumberland (Portland). Home: Falmouth Foreside. Portland 99. Office: 465 Congress St., Portland, Me. Died Aug. 29, 1958; buried Evergreen Cemetery, Portland, Me.

BISBEE, WILLIAM HENRY brigadier-gen. U.S. Army, retired; b. in R.I., Jan. 28, 1840. Pvt. and 1st sergt. Co. A., and sergt.-maj. 2d Battalion 18th Inf., Sept. 2, 1861-July 11, 1862; 2d lt. 18th Inf., June 9, 1862; 1st lt., Dec. 31, 1862; bvtd. capt., Dec. 31, 1862, "for gallant and meritorious services in battle of Murfreesboro, Tenn."; and capt., Sept. 1, 1864, for same during Atlanta campaign and in battle of Jonesboro, Ga.; promoted through grades to rank of brig.-gen., Oct. 2, 1901. Served in campaigns and many battles under Gens. Thomas, Buell, Halleck, Rosecrans, Sherman; wounded at Hoover's Gap, Tenn., June 26, 1863, at siege of Atlanta, Aug. 1864; long service on western frontier; built Ft. Phil Kearny, Dak., 1866, participating in frequent engagements with Sioux Indians; adj.-gen. U.S. Troops in Chicago riots, 1877; engaged in suppressing Coeur d'Alene miners outbreaks, 1892; comd. U.S. troops Ogden, Utah, and Pocatello, Ida., in Debs riots and Commonwealers outbreaks, 1893-94; comd. battalion at Jackson's Hole in Bannock Indian disturbances, 1895; comd. regt. through Santiago campaign; with Capron's battery at battles of El Caney and San Juan, Cuba; had charge of payment of $3,000,-000 appropriation to Cuban army; served in Philippines, 1899-1902; comd. sub-dist. embracing 19 native towns in provinces of Pangasinan and Nueva Ecija, Luzon; comdg. all troops north of Manila on Island of Luzon; retired Oct. 1, 1902. Mem. Loyal Legion (hon. comdr. in chief), S.A.R., Army of the Cumberland, Soc. Santiago de Cuba. Home: 30 Babcock, S. Brookline, Mass. Address: Care Adj.-Gen. U.S. Army, Washington, D.C. Died June 11, 1942.

BISHOP, BRUCE CLAY, lawyer; b. Chattanooga, Jan. 31, 1919; s. Jacob Walter and Ola (McGaughey) B.; B.B.A., U. Chattanooga, 1940; postgrad. George Washington U. Law Sch., 1940-41; LL.B., Stetson U., 1946; m. Dorothy Pepiot, Apr. 26, 1944; children—Bruce Clay, Beverly, Leslie. Admitted to Tenn. bar, 1947, practiced in Chattanooga, 1947-68; mem. firms Thomas, Folts & Brammer, 1947-48, Folts, Bishop & Thomas, 1949-62, Bishop, Thomas, Leitner, Mann & Milburn, 1962-68. Corporate dir. Indsl. Water Chems., Inc., Chamberlain-Realtors, Inc., Smith Elevator Co., Inc. (all Chattanooga). Mem. adv. council U. Chattanooga, 1964-68; active United Fund campaigns. Commr. Town of Signal Mountain, 1959-63. Served to comdr. USNR, 1941-46. Decorated D.F.C. with three oak leaf clusters, Air medal with twelve oak leaf clusters. Mem. Fedn. Ins. Counsel, Internat. Soc. Barristers, Internat. Acad. Law and Sci., Fla. Bar, Bar Assn. Tenn., Phi Alpha Delta, Pi Kappa Alpha. Democrat. Baptist (deacon, Sunday sch. supt. 1960-68). Rotarian (v.p. 1960). Clubs: Mountain City, Signal Mountain Golf and Country (Signal Mountain, Tenn.). Contbr. articles to profl. publs. Home: Signal Mountain TN Died Dec. 1, 1968.

BISHOP, JOHN PEALE author; b. Charles Town, W.Va., May 21, 1892; s. Jonathan Peale and Margaret Miller (Cochran) B.; Litt.B., Princeton, 1917; m. Margaret Grosvenor Hutchins, June 17, 1922; children—Jonathan Peale, Robert Grosvenor, Christopher. Mng. editor Vanity Fair, 1920-22. Director of Publications Program, 1941-31, later spl. consultant, Officer of Coordinator of Inter-Am. Affairs. Served as 1st lt. Inf., U.S. Army, 1917-19, with Hdqrs. Troop, 84th Div., A.E.F. Mem. Phi Beta Kappa. Club: Princeton Quadrangle, Editor (with Allen Tate); American Harvest; Twenty Years of Creative Writing in the United States, 1942. Author: Green Fruit (poems), 1917; Undertaker's Garland (poems, with Edmund Wilson), 1922; Many Thousands Gone (stories), 1931; Now with His Love (poems), 1933; Act of Darkness (novel), 1935; Minute Particulars (poems), 1936; Selected Poems, 1941. Contbr. articles, verse fiction to mags. Home: Sea Change, South Chatham, Mass. Died Apr. 4, 1944.

BISHOP, JUDSON WADE capitalist; b. Evansville, N.Y., June 24, 1831; s. Rev. John F. and Elena (Brown) B.; ed. Fredonia and Union Acad., Belleville, N.Y.; studied civil engring. Asst. engr. Grand Trunk Ry., 1853; later engr. in Minn.; then surveyor, Chatfield, Minn.; publisher Chatfield Democrat, 1859-61; capt. 2d Minn. Inf., June 26, 1861; maj., May 15, 1862; lt.-col., Oct. 15, 1862; col., Mar. 26, 1865; bvtd. brig.-gen. vols., June 7, 1865, "for meritorious services"; hon. mustered out, July 11, 1865. After war built and operated railroads in Minn.; now retired. Comdr. Minn. Commandery Loyal Legion. Address: 193 Mackubin St., St. Paul, Minn.

BISHOP, PERCY POE army officer; b. Powell, Tenn., May 27, 1877; s. John McElroy and Margaret (Wood) B.; B.S., U. Tenn., 1898; honor grad. Arty. Sch., 1902; grad. Army War Coll., 1926; m. Grace Waldron Calvert, Apr. 17, 1911. Commd. 2d lt. 4th Arty., July 9, 1898; promoted through grades to col., Feb. 6, 1918; brig. gen. (temp.), U.S. Army, Oct. 1, 1918-Nov. 1, 1919; brig. gen. (permanent), 193 Instr. U.S. Arty. Sch., 1902-03; asst. to chief of Coast Arty., 1907-11 and 1914-17; detailed mem. Gen. Staff Corps, Oct. 16, 1917-Mar. 21, 1918; sec. of Gen. Staff, Mar.-Sept. 1918; chief of Personnel Br. of Gen. Staff, Sept. 10, 1918-Oct. 1921; duty in Philippines, Honolulu, both coasts U.S., asst. comt. Coast Arty. School, command 4th Coast Arty. Dist., harbor defenses Manila and Subic bays, Philippine Div., and 7th Corps Area since 1921. Awarded D.S.M. "for especially meritorious and conspicuous service as sec. of Gen. Staff, and in the organization and coordination of matters relating to the commissioned personnel of the Army during the World War." Clubs: Army and Navy (Washington, D.C.); Fort Monroe Club (Fort Monroe, Va.); Omaha (Omaha, Neb.). Home: 98 Park St., Portland, Me. Address: War Dept., Washington, D.C. Died Apr. 8, 1967.

BISSELL, CLAYTON LAWRENCE, army officer; b. Kane, Pa., July 29, 1896; s. Thomas Francis and Isabelle (Collins) B.; LL.B., Valparaiso U. Law Sch., 1917; student Air Corps Tactical Sch.; Command and Gen. Staff Sch.; Chem. Warfare Sch.; Army War Coll.; Navy War Coll.; m. LeClair Gaillard, June 3, 1925; 1 dau., LeClair. Began as pvt. 1st class, Aviation Sec. Signal Corps, 1917, and advanced through the grades to maj. gen., 1943. Served with 148th Fighter Squadron, comd. 638th Fighter Squadron in France and in Coblentz with U.S. Army of Occupation. Awarded D.S.C., D.S.M. and Silver Star (U.S.), Distinguished Flying Cross (United States), Air Medal, Order of British Empire, British Distinguished Flying Cross, Order of Crown of Italy, Italian War Cross, Polonia Restituta, Order of Merit (Chile), Abdon Calderon (Equador). Inspected fgn. aviation in Eng., France, Germany, Italy, Holland, 1921; asst., General Billy Mitchell, 1921-24; advance officer first round the world flight, U.S. to Japan and Greenland to U.S. with Stilwell in China, 1941-42; commanded 10th Army Air Force, 1942-43. Chief Army Air Force Intelligence 1943, Asst. Chief of Staff, G-2 in charge of Intelligence U.S. Army, 1944 to end of war; Mil., Mil. Air Attache, Am. Embassy, London, 1946-48. Author: History U.S. Army Air Corps, 1923. Home: Sewanee TN Died Dec. 23, 1972; buried Arlington Nat. Cemetery.

BISSELL, HERBERT PORTER judge; b. New London, Oneida Co., N.Y., Aug. 30, 1856; s. Amos Alanson and Amelia Susan (Wilsey) B.; ed. De Veaux Coll., Suspension Bridge, N.Y., 1869-73; Gymnasium, Braunschweig, Germany, 1873-75; A.B., Harvard, 1880; m. Lucy Agnes Coffey, Oct. 30, 1883. Admitted to N.Y. bar, 1883, and practiced in Buffalo; apptd. justice Supreme Court of N.Y. to fill vacancy, 1912; elected to same office, 1913, for term of 14 yrs. Mem. State Hosp. Commn., N.Y., 1911, 1912; pres. Bd. of Edn., East Aurora, N.Y., 1905-12; formerly judge-advocate and maj. 4th Brigade, N.G.N.Y. Trustee DeVeaux Coll., 1887-99. Democrat. Episcopalian. Mason. Home: East Aurora, N.Y. Died Apr. 30, 1919.

BISSELL, PELHAM ST. GEORGE jurist; b. N.Y. City, Apr. 11, 1887; s. Rev. Pelham St. George and Helen Alsop (French) B.; student at Cutler School, N.Y. City; A.B., Columbia, 1909, A.M., 1910, LL.B., 1912; LL.D., Hobart and William Smith Colls., 1943; m. Mary Valentine Yale Bissell, Nov. 10, 1910; children—Helen Alsop (Mrs. Charles Hecker Stout), Pelham St. George III, Mary Sackett (Mrs. James J. Christie), Nancy Wemple (Mrs.) David Lawrence), Ruth Mason (Mrs. Joseph M. Schwartz), Ophelia Louise (Mrs. William W. Molla), George Henry, Elizabeth Goodwin (dec.). Began the practice of law in N.Y. City, 1912; special attorney U.S. Dept. of Justice, Customs Div., 1921-24; counsel to U.S. appraiser Port of N.Y., 1922-24; dep. asst. atty. gen. State of N.Y., 1929; justice Municipal Court, New York, since Jan. 1, 1931 (re-elected 1940), designated acting pres. justice, 1934, pres. justice since June 7, 1934, (redesignated, 1939, 41). Chmn. Mayor's Board of Survey, settling N.Y. City Building Service Employees strike, 1936; instituted small claims parts of Municipal Court in each of five boroughs of City, 1934; centralized jury cases in Brooklyn, Bronx, and Queens and non-jury cases over $100 in Manhattan with centralized motion calendar. Sponsored and instituted Government Project whereby lawyers in needy circumstances are assigned by Municipal Court as trial counsel for indigent litigants, 1935. Rep.-Fusion-Independent Progressive candidate for justice Supreme Court, First Dist., New York, 1938. Awarded Columbia U. medal for service at bar and on bench, 1940. Commd. 2d lt., Inf. R.C., U.S. Army, May 11, 1917; 1st lt. Inf., N.A., Dec. 31, 1917; capt. inf., U.S. Army, Mar. 26, 1919; maj. Inf. Reserve, June 9, 1922, lt. col. Inf. Res., Dec. 10, 1930; overseas with 77th Div., participated in Baccarat and Vesle sectors, Oise-Aisne and Meuse-Argonne offensives; commended in Argonne by comdg. gen. 77th Div.; awarded Conspicuous Service Cross by State of N.Y. Mem. City Advancement Com. Boy Scouts of America. Mem. Am. Bar Assn., Assn. Bar City New York, N.Y. County Lawyers Assn., St. Nicholas Soc., The Pilgrims, Soc. Colonial Wars (council), S.R. (past pres.), Soc. War of 1812, Mil. Order World War (past N.Y. State comdr.), Mil. Order Foreign Wars (past national commander general), Soc. Am. Wars (past comdr. gen.), La Societe des 40 Hommes et 8 Chevaux (past nat. pres.), Am. Legion (past comdr.), N.Y. Soc. Mil. and Naval Officers of World War, Res. Officers Assn. (state exec. com.), Vets. Foreign Wars (past judge advocate), N.Y. Hist. Soc., Columbia Alumni Fed. (dir.), Grant Monument Assn. (trustee), Grand Street Boys Assn., Ends of Earth Club, Junior O.U.A.M., Phi Delta Phi, Free Sons of Israel, Foresters of America, Phi Sigma Omega; fellow inst. Am. Genealogy. Republican. Episcopalian. Mason (32 degree), Elk, Sojourners (past pres.Manhattan chapter). Clubs: Union League, Military and Naval (v.p.), Church, Columbia Univ., Nat. Republican (New York), Army and Navy (Washington, D.C.). Home: 270 Park Av. Chambers: 8 Reade St., New York, N.Y. Died Sept. 8, 1943.

BISSELL, WILLIAM HENRY gov. Ill., congressman; b. Hartwick, N.Y., Apr. 25, 1811; s. Luther and Hannah Bissell; grad. Jefferson Med. Coll., 1835; attended Lexington (Ky.) Law Sch.; m. Emily James Oct. 1840; m. 2d, Elizabeth Kane, 1852; 2 children. M. Ill. Legislature, 1840; admitted to Ill. bar, 1843; pros. atty. St. Claire County Mexican War, served in Battle of Buena Vista, 1847; mem. U.S. Ho. of Reps. (Democrat) from Ill., 30th-33th congresses, 1849-54; gov. Ill., 1857-60. Died Springfield, Ill., Mar. 18, 1860; buried Oak Ridge Cemetery, Springfield.

BITTINGER, JOHN LAWRENCE retired; b. nr. Chambersburg, Pa., Nov. 28, 1833; common sch. edn. in Ashland Co., O.; m. Annie M. Smith, June 10, 1862. Moved to Green Co., Wis.; worked on farm 3 yrs.; office of Freeport (Ill.) Journal, 1852-55; foreman on several papers in St. Louis, 1855-60; represented St. Louis Typographical Union in nat. conv., 1858, Chicago, and 1859. Boston; removed to St. Joseph, 1860; postmaster, 1861-65; maj. and a.-d.-c. on staff Gen. Willard P. Hall, 1861-62; mem. Mo. Gen. Assembly 7 terms; del. Rep. Nat. convs., 1872, 1896; mng. editor St. Joseph Herald,

27 yrs., Kansas City Journal, 5 yrs.; Am. consul-gen. at Montreal, 1897-1903; retired. Home: St. Joseph, Mo. Died 1911.

BIXBY, WILLIAM HERBERT army officer; b. Charlestown, Mass., Dec. 27, 1849; s. Clark Smith and Elizabeth (Clark) B.; brother of James Thompson B.; student Mass. Inst. Tech., 1866-67; apptd. from Mass., and grad. U.S. lMil. Acad., 1873; grad. French H. Rogers Jones, Dec. 27, 1893. Second lt. engrs., June 13, 1873; promoted through grades to brig. gen., June 12, 1910; retired Aug. 11, 1913. Asst. prof. engring., West Point, 1875-79; sent by U.S. Govt. to attend French Army manoeuvers, 1880, to examine and report upon iron fortifications in Europe, 1881-82, to inspect buildings Charleston, S.C., earthquake, 1887; lecturer on coast defenses, U.S. Naval War Coll., 1887; with Nat. Waterways Commn. to inspect rivers and harbors in Europe, 1909; in charge removal wreck of the Maine from Havana Harbor, 1912; in charge, at different times, of U.S. river and harbor improvements in N.C., S.C., Va., 1884-91, in Conn., R.I., Mass., 1891-95, in the Ohio River basin, 1897-1901, on ship channel of Great Lakes, 1902-04, in Ill. and Ind., 1905-07; also of lighthouse constrn. in N.J., Pa., Del., Md., Va. and of the Ohio and tributaries, 1884-1905; div. engr. of Northwestern and Western U.S., 1905-08; pres. Miss. River Commn., 1908-10; chief of engrs. U.S.A., June 10, 1910-Aug. 11, 1913; returned to active service May 1917-Apr. 1919; again pres. Miss. River Commn., and div. engr. Western Div. River and Harbor Improvements, and insp. 15th Lighthouse Dist. Home: Washington, D.C. Died Sept. 29, 1928.

BJORNSTAD, ALTREA WILLIAM army officer; b. St. Paul, Minn., Oct. 13, 1874; s. Julius B.; preliminary edn. Luther Col.; student U. of Minn., 1893-96; honor grad. Army Sch. of the Line, 1909; grad. Army Staff Coll., 1910; m. Pearl Ladd Sabin, Oct. 3, 1905. Commd. 1st lt. 13th Minn. Inf., May 7, 1898; capt., May 16, 1898; hon. mustered out, Oct. 3, 1899; capt. 42d U.S. Inf., Aug. 17, 1899; hon. mustered out vols., June 24, 1901; 1st lt. 29th Inf., U.S.A., Feb. 2, 1901; promoted through grades to rank of brig. gen., Jan. 17, 1925. Engaged in 34 battles and actions in Philippines, 1898-1904; duty Gen. Staff, 1911-12; mil. attache to Germany, 1912-13; instr. mil. art, Army Staff Coll., 1915-16; duty Gen. Staff, 1917; organized, and directed, 1917, the 16 training camps for officers which produced the original 25,341 officers of the N.A. in the World War; first chief of staff, 30th Div., 1917; organized and directed Army Gen. Staff Coll. in France, 1917-18; brig. gen. N.A., July 12, 1918-July 31, 1919; chief of staff 3d Army Corps, A.E.F., 1918; comdr. 13th Brigade, 1918-19; participated in all major engagements in France; duty Gen. Staff Coll., 1919; comdg. Inf. Sch., Ft. Benning, Ga., 1923-25; retired Aug. 31, 1928. Decorated D.S.C., D.S.M., Purple Heart (Oak Leaf Cluster); Companion St. Michael and St. George (British); Legion of Honor, Croix de Guerre (French). Mason. Home: San Francisco, Calif. Died Nov. 4, 1934.

BLACK, BENJAMIN WARREN physician and medical administrator; b. Fillmore, Utah; s. George Warren and Birdie Susannah (Robison) B.; student University of Utah, 1909-10, Brigham Young U., 1911, U. of Chicago, 1911-12; M.D., Medico-Chirurgical Coll., U. of Pa., 1916; m. Jean Blackburn, Sept. 15, 1909; children—Dr. Benjamin Marden, Margaret Susannah. Teacher and prin., pub. schs., Utah, 1904-09; interne, Dr. W. H. Groves, L.D.S. Hosp., Salt Lake City, Southern Pacific R.R. Hosp., 1916-17; acting asst. surgeon to senior surgeon, U.S.P.H.S.; 1920-24; exec. officer U.S. Vets. Bur., 1924-26, med. dir., 1926-28; med. dir. Alameda County (Calif), Oakland, since 1928. Served in M.R., U.S. Army, 1917-19, advancing from 1st lt. to lt. col.; now lt. col., Med. Res. Pres. Oakland Forum, 1940-42; member exec. com. Oakland Community Chest. Charter fellow Am. Coll. of Hosp. of Mil. Surgeons, Am. Psychiat. Assn., A.A.A.S., A.M.A.; mem. Am. Hosp. Assn. (pres. 1940-41; mem. council on edn.), Kiwanis Internat. (past dist. gov., Calif.-Nev. District; now internat. trustee), Western Inst. for Hospitals, (dir. 1938-40), Western Hosp. Assn. (pres. 1931-33). Calif. Med. Assn., Alameda County Med. Assn., Phi Rho Sigma. Mason (32 degree; K.C.C.H. past master Lodge of Perfection). Author: Medical Policies and Procedures, 1936; also author articles in Hospitals, Modern Hosp., Hosp. Management, etc. Home: 250 Tunnel Rd., Berkeley, Calif. Office: 2701 Fourteenth Av., Oakland, Calif. Died Dec. 1, 1945; buried in Mountain View Cemetery, Oakland.

BLACK, GARLAND C. army officer; b. Dayton, O., Nov. 14, 1894; s. Hiram Criag and Lulu B. (Cone) B.; B.S. in Elec. Engring., U. Mo., 1917; grad. Chem. Warfare Sch., officer course, 1931, Signal Sch., co. officers course, 1933, command and Gen. Staff Sch., 1937; m. Florence M. Biegler, Aug. 7, 1919; children—Garland C., Marrilyn Jean (wife of Robert C. Bagby, USN). Elec. engr. Kansas City Light and Power Co., Kansas City, Mo., 1917; commd. 2d lt., U.S. Army, 1917, advanced through the grades to brig. gen. Decorated Legion of Merit, Bronze Star (U.S); Chevalier Legion of Honor, Croix de Guerre with palm (France). Mem. Phi Kappa Psi. Address: care the Adjutant General's Office, War Dept., Washington 25. Deceased.

BLACK, GEORGE ROBISON congressman; b. nr. Jacksonboro, Screven County, Ga., Mar. 24, 1835; s. Edward Junius Black; attended U. Ga. at Athens, U. S.C. at Columbia; studied law. Admitted to bar, 1857; practiced in Savannah, Ga.; served as 1st lt. Phoenix Rifleman, Confederate Army; promoted lt. col. 63d Ga. Regt.; del. Ga. Constl. Conv., 1865; del. Nat. Democratic Conv., Balt., 1872; mem. Ga. Senate, 1874-77; v.p. Ga. Agrl. Soc.; mem. U.S. Ho. of Reps. (Democrat) from Ga., 47th Congress, 1881-83. Died Sylvania, Screven County , Nov. 3, 1886; buried Sylvania

BLACK, HUGO LA FAYETTE, jurist, b. Harlan, Clay County, Ala., Feb. 27, 1886; s. William La Fayette and Martha Ardella (Toland) B.; ed. pub. schs., Ashland, Ala., LL.B., University of Alabama, 1906; married Josephine Foster, February 1921 (deceased December 1951); children—Hugo La Fayette, Sterling Foster, Martha Josephine; married second Elizabeth Seay DeMeritte, Sept. 11, 1957. Began practice Ashland, Alabama, 1906-07, Birmingham, Alabama, from 1907; served as police judge 18 months, 1910-11; solicitor (prosecuting attorney) Jefferson County, Ala., 1915-17; in gen. practice, Birmingham, 1919-27; U.S. Senator from Ala. 2 terms, 1927-37; apptd. asso. justice U.S. Supreme Court, 1937-71. Entered 2d O.T.C., Ft. Oglethorpe, Ga., Aug. 3, 1917; commd. capt. F.A.; served in 81st F.A. and as adj. 19th Arty. Brigade. Home: Alexandria VA Died Sept. 25, 1971; buried Arlington Nat. Cemetery, Arlington VAArty. Brigade. Home: Alexandria VA Died Sept. 25, 1971; buried Arlington Nat. Cemetery, Arlington, VA

BLACK, JOHN CHARLES lawyer; b. Lexington, Miss., Jan. 27, 1839, 1839; s. Rev. John and Josephine (Culbertson) B.; ed. Wabash Coll.; (A.M., LL.D., Knox Coll.); m. Adaline L. Griggs, Sept. 28, 1867. Pvt. and sergt. maj. 11th Ind. Inf., Apr. 25-Aug. 4, 1861; maj. 37th Ill. Inf., Sept. 5, 1861; lt. col., July 12, 1862; col., Dec. 31, 1862; bvtd. brig. gen. vols., Apr. 9, 1865, "for gallant services in assault on Ft. Blakely, Ala."; awarded medal of honor, Oct. 31, 1893, for Battle of Prairie Grove, Ark., Dec. 7, 1862 (severly wounded); resigned, Aug. 15, 1865. Admitted to bar, 1867; practiced at Danville, Ill., 1867-; candidate for Congress, 1866, 1880, 1884, for lt. gov., 1872; del.-at-large Dem. Nat. Conv., 1884; Dem. Nominee for U.S. senator, 1879; U.S. commr. of pensions, 1885-89; mem. 53d Congress (1893-95), Ill. at-large; U.S. Atty. for Northern Dist. of Ill., 1895-99; mem. U.S. Civil Service Commn., Dec. 1903-13, and pres., Jan. 1904-June 10, 1913. Comdr.-in-chief G.A.R., 1903-04 (comdr. Ill. dept., 1903-04). Home: Chicago, Ill. Died Aug. 17, 1915.

BLACK, ROBERT LOUNSBURY lawyer; b. Norwood, O., Sept. 15, 1881; s. Lewis Cass and Abigail (Lounsbury) B.; grad. Phillips Andover Acad., 1899; B.A., Yale, 1903; LL.B., Harvard, 1906; m. Anna McNaughten Smith, Oct. 14, 1916; children—Robert L., Jr., Harrison, Anne McNaughten (dec.), David de Laine, Frances Harrison. Admitted to Ohio bar, 1906; formerly mem. Black & Black, later Black, Swing & Black; has practiced independently since 1919 retired 1953; president Little Miami R.R. Co.; sec. L. B. Harrison Estate, Inc.; counsel and dir. Security Storage Co.; v.p. and trustee L. B. Harrison Hotel. Served at lt., later capt., U.S. Army, 37th Div., Mil. Intelligence, World War. member American Peace Commn. Mission to Germany. Trustee Y. M. Mercantile Library; trustee Veterans Memorial Fund. Ex-trustee, Cincinnati Orphan Asylum; ex-dir. U. of Cincinnati; formerly member rehabilitation Committee Am. Legion. Mem. Am., Ohio State and Cincinnati bar assns., Bar Assn. City of N.Y. Republican. Episcopalian. Clubs: Queen City, margo (Cincinnati); Yale, Grolier (New York). Author: The Little Miami Railroad, 1940; The Cincinnati Orphan Asylum, 1952. Home: Willow Hills Lane, Cin. Office: Blymer Bldg., Cin. Died Jan. 24, 1954; buried Spring Grove Cemetery, Cin.

BLACK, SAMUEL CHARLES clergyman; b. Monticello, Ia., Sept. 6, 1869; s. William Irvin and Flora A. (Johnson) B.; A.B., Parsons Coll., Ia., 1892, A.M., 1898; grad. McCormick Theol. Sem., Chicago, 1898; (D.D., Blackburn University, 1907, LL.D., Univ. of Pittsburgh, 1919); m. Grace Westcott, Dec. 6, 1892. Telegraph operator, 1884-88; in banking business at Fairfield and Des Moines, Ia., 1892-95; ordained Presbyn. ministry, 1897; pastor, Kewanee, Ill., 1895-97, South Chicago, Ill., 1897-1900, Clinton, Ill., 1900-08, Boulder, Colo., 1908-10; Collingwood Av. Ch., Toledo, O., 1910-19; pres. Washington and Jefferson Coll., June 1, 1919. Instr. Hebrew, U. of Colo., 1908-10; lecturer. Maj. and morale officer, Camp Gordon, Ga., 1918-19. Author: Plain Answers to Religious Questions Modern Men Are Asking, 1907, 1910; Building a Working Church, 1911; Progress in Christian Culture, 1912. Home: Washington, Pa. Died July 25, 1921.

BLACK, WILLIAM MURRAY army officer; b. Lancaster, Pa., Dec. 8, 1855; s. James and Eliza (Murray) B.; ed. Franklin and Marshall Coll., Pa., 1870-73; grad. U.S. Mil. Acad., 1877; Sc.D., Franklin and Marshall Coll., 1912; Dr. Engring., Pa. Mil. Coll., 1920; m. Daisy Peyton, d. Capt. George H. Derby, U.S.A. "John Phoenix"), 1877; m. 2d, Gertrude Totten, d. Comdr. William M. Gamble, U.S.N. Commd. through all grades to col. corps. engrs., U.S.A., apptd. lt. col. and chief engr. U.S.V., May 25, 1898; hon. dis. from vol. service June 13, 1899. Long engaged on works of river and harbor improvement; also asst. instr. practical mil. engring., U.S. N.Y.; asst. in charge works of fortification, office of chief engrs., Washington, 1895-97; commr. of D.C., 1897-98; chief of engr. in campaign in P.R., 1898; chief engr. Dept. of Havana, staff Gen. Ludlow, Jan. 2, 1899-Apr. 30, 1900; chief engr. Div. of Cuba, Jan. 1900-Apr. 1901, staff of Gen. Leonard Wood; charge of engr. work, Havana, and supervision of work in Cuba; comdg. Engr. Sch. Application and 3d batn. engrs., 1901-03, and post of Washington Barracks, D.C., 1901-03; observing work of new Panama Canal Co. under orders of Isthmian Canal Commn., Apr. 1930-July 1904; in charge river and harbor improvements and fortifications, Me., 1904-06; adviser, dept. pub. works, Provisional Gvt. of Cuba, 1906-09; in charge river and harbor improvements, Dist. No. 1, New York, Feb. 1909-Mar. 1916; brig. gen. chief of engrs. U.S.A., Mar. 7, 1916; promoted to maj. gen., Oct. 8, 1917, Sr. mem. of bd. charged with raising wreck of U.S.S. Maine from Havana Harbor, 1910-13; chief engr. officer Eastern Dept. U.S.A.; div. engr. Eastern Division River and Harbor Improvements, 1909-16; sr. officer bd. of engrs. for Rivers and Harbors, 1912-16, chmn. Inland Waterway Transportation Com. of Council Nat. Defense, 1917; member Nat. Research Council; chmn. port and harbors facilities commn. of U.S. Shipping Bd., Feb. 1919; retired from active Service Oct. 31, 1919. Awarded D.S.M., Dec. 1918, for especially meritorious and conspicuous service in planning administering the engring. and mil. ry. services during the war. Episcopalian Author: Improvement of Harbors; South Atlantic Coast; Waterway and Railway Equivalents (prize essays, Trans. Am. Society C.E., 1893-1925); Public Works of United States. Collaborated with Prof. E. B. Phelps in Report on Discharge of Sewage into New York Harbor. Inventor method of purfying sewage G by aeration. Died Sept. 24, 1933.

BLACKBURN, JOHN HENRY surgeon; b. Woodburn, Ky., Aug. 7, 1876; s. Henry M. and Amanda (Deupree) B.; prep. ed. Franklin High Sch.; M.D., Vanderbilt U., 1899; m. Bess Trousdale Hatcher May 25, 1904; children—Henry Hatcher, John Deupree. Began practice at Bowling Green 1900; dir. course post-grad study for county med. socs., 1907-11, dir. Am. Nat. Bank. Commd. capt. M.C., U.S. Army, 1917, advanced through grades to lt. col., 1918; chief of surg. service, Base Hosp. No. 86, Mesves Hosp. Center, France; returned to U.S. as regtl. surgeon, 139th F.A.; hon. discharged 1919. Mem. Ky. Bd. Health, 1934—. Fellow A.C.A.; mem. Am. So. med. assns., Ky. (past pres.), Warren County med. socs., S.E. Med. Congress. Democrat. Methodist. Odd Fellow. Clubs: Country, Gun, Kiwanis. Home 627 E. Main St. Office: 535 10th St., Bowling Green, Ky. Died Feb. 17, 1951.

BLACKFORD, STAIGE D(AVIS) physician; b. Alexandria, Va., Dec. 28, 1898; s. Launcelot Minor and Eliza Chew (Ambler) B.; student Episcopal High Sch., Alexandria, 1908-17; B.S., U. of Va., 1923, M.D., 1925; m. Lydia H. Fishburne, Aug. 20, 1927; children—Staige D., Linda H. Interne, Mass. Gen. Hosp., Boston, 1925-27, student physician and instr. in medicine, 1927-28; asst. prof. of practice of medicine, U. of Va., 1938-40, asso. prof., 1940-46, prof. since 1946; pvt. practice of medicine, specialist in internal medicine, Charlottesville, Va., since 1927 connected with U. of Va. Hosp. Served as pvt., 1st class, U.S.A.A.C., U.S. Army, 1917-19; overseas, France; lt. col., M.C., U.S. Army, 1942-45; overseas, Italy; mem. selective service bd. of appeal No. 4, Va., 1940-42. Certified Am. Bd. Internal Medicine, 1937. Diplomate Nat. Bd. Med. Examiners, 1927. Awarded Croix de Guerre (France, 1917); Legion of Merit (U.S. 1945); Croce di Guerra (Italy 1945). Mem. bd. trustees Episcopal High Sch. Fellow A.C.P.; mem. Am. Clin. and Clomatologic Assn., A.M.A., Delta Kappa Epsilon, Phi Rho Sigma. Alpha Omega Alpha, Sigma Xi. Democrat. Episcopalian. Home: 1403 Hilton Road Office: Univ. Hosp., Charlottesville, Va. Died July 17, 1949.

BLACKSTONE, RICHARD engineer; b. Connellsville, Pa., Oct. 16, 1843; s. James and Nancy Campbell (Johnston) B.; studied Pa. Mil. Acad., Rensselaer Poly. Inst., Troy, N.Y.; m. Mabel R. Noble, Dec. 28, 1871. Enlisted as pvt. in Co. C, 32d Ohio Vols., July 30, 1861; served in W.Va.; taken prisoner at Harper's Ferry Sept. 12, 1862; exchanged, and assigned to Army of Tenn., under Gen. Grant; participated in many battles, siege of Vicksburg, March to the Sea, Grand Review at Washington; mustered out as capt., July 27, 1865. Placer miner, 2 seasons Breckenridge, Colo., 1868 and 1869; draftsman in office U.S. surveyor gen., Denver, 1869-70, Cheyenne, Wyo., 1870-78; went to Black Hills, 1878, and engaged in mining and mine surveying; asst. supt., chief engr., 1883-1914, gen. mgr. and supt., Sept. 1914-18. Homestake Mining Co., Lead, S.D. Built Black Hills & Ft. Pierre R.R.; water system for Homestake; hydro-electric sta. at Englewood; electric light and power plant, and hydro-electric power plant, Spearfish, including 5-mile concrete-lined, diverting dam tunnel; complete elec. equipment of Homestead Mine; etc. Mem. Am. Inst. Mining Engrs., Ohio Commandery Loyal Legion. Republican. Home: Lead, S.D. Died Dec. 21, 1922.

BLACKWOOD, NORMAN JEROME rear adm.; b. Philadelphia, Pa., Jan. 3, 1866; s. William and Emma Jerome (Smith) B.; student Franklin and Marshall Coll., 1882-83, U.S. Naval Acad., Annapolis, Md., 1883-86; M.D., Jefferson Med. Coll., Phila., 1888; m. Rebecca Barnes Wilkinson, Nov. 29, 1892. Commd. ensign, U.S.N., July 17, 1890, and advanced through grades to rear adm., Oct. 10, 1929, retired. Comdr. U.S. naval hosps. at Canacao, P.I., 1911-13, Boston, Mass., 1918-23, New York, N.Y., 1923-27, Puget Sound, Wash., 1927-29; comdr. U.S.S. Solace, 1916-17, U.S.S. Mercy, Mar.-Sept. 1918; retired from active service, Jan. 3, 1930; then med. dir. Provident Hosp., Chicago. Served in Spanish-American War, Cuban Insurrection, World War. Fellow Am. Coll. Surgeons. Awarded Navy Cross. Republican. Episcopalian. Mason. Home: Syracuse, N.Y. Died Apr. 1, 1938.

BLAIR, HENRY WILLIAM senator; b. Campton, N.H., Dec. 6, 1834; s. William Henry and Lois (Baker) B.; acad. edn. in N.H.; (hon. A.M., Dartmouth, 1873); admitted to N.H. bar, 1859; m. Eliza Ann Nelson, Dec. 20, 1859 (died 1907); father of Henry P. B. Served capt. and lt. col. 15th N.H. Vols., Civil War; twice wounded. Solicitor Grafton Co., 1860, for term of 5 yrs.; mem. N.H. Ho. of Rep., 1866 Senate, 1867-68; mem. 44th, 45th and 53d Congresses (1875-79, 1903-05); U.S. senator, 1879-91; declined office judge U.S. Dist. Ct.; apptd. and confirmed U.S. minister to China, 1891, but resigned when Chinese Govt. objected to him because of his opposition to Chinese immigration. Republican. Author Blair bill to extend federal aid to edn. in the states, which 3 times passed Senate; also bills establishing U.S. Labor Dept., the Sunday Rest bill, temperance, financial and other legislation; originator of bills under which about half of the soldiers' pensions are paid; practicing law, 1895 - . Author: The Temperance Movement - or the Conflict of Man with Alcohol. Home: Manchester, N.H. Died Mar. 14, 1920.

BLAIR, JAMES A(LONZO), JR. corp. official; b. Ohio, July 19, 1880; s. James A. and Isabelle B. (Meyers) B.; A.B., Princeton, 1903; unmarried. Chairman of exec. com. Kingsport Press, Inc., pres. Kingsport Sales Agency; dir. The Securities Co., Clinchfield Securities Co., Macon, Dublin & Savannah R.R., Securities Investment Fund, Kingsport Improvement Co., Continental Trust Co. (Baltimore). Served as 2d lt., capt. and maj. N.Y.N.B.; commd. maj. N.A., U.S.A., 1917, and assigned to hdqrs. Eastern Dept.; lt. col., Mar. 10, 1918, duty with Emergency Fleet Corp., later Gen Staff; commd. col. G.S., overseas; twice apptd. Army mem. Am. Aviation Mission, Apr. 1919, to study future aviation policy of Eng., France and Italy; hon. disch., Dec. 20, 1910; col. on G.S. eligible list Jan. 10, 1920. Mem. Met. Mus. Art, Mus. Natural History. Decorated by France, Italy, Belgium and Servia. Republican. Home: New York, N.Y. Died Aug. 15, 1934.

BLAIR, JAMES T(HOMAS), JR. ex-gov. Mo.; b. Maysville, Mo., Mar. 15, 1902; s. James T. and Grace (Ray) B.; student Staunton (Va.) Mil. Acad., S.W. State Coll., Springfield, Mo., U. Mo.; LL.B., Cumberland U., 1924, LL.D.; LL.D., Westminster College, Fulton, Missouri, Missouri College Osteopathy and Surgery, Missouri University; married Emilie C. Chorn, 1926; children-James Thomas, III, Mary Margaret. Admitted to Mo. bar 1924, since practiced in Jefferson City; v.p. Jackson Life Ins. Co., Ozark Fisheries, Inc.; city atty., 1925-29; lt. gov. Mo., 1949-56, gov., 1956-60. Mem. Mo. Ho. of Reps., 1928-32, majority leader, 1931; mayor Jefferson, 1936-42). Chmn. judicial circuit bar com., 1946-. Served as lt. col., AUS, 1942-45. Decorated Air Medal, Bronze Star, Legion Merit, Presdl. Unit Citation, Arrow Head. Mem. Mil. Order World Wars, Am. Legion, Vets. Fgn. Wars, Am. Vets., Civic Music Assn., Mo., Cole Co. hist. assns., S.A.R., Internat. Ins. Counsel Assn., Am., Mo. (pres. 1930), Cole Co. (past pres.) bar assns., Mo. Golf Assn. (dir.), Sigma Chi, Phi Delta Phi, Sigma Nu Phi. Democrat (chmn. city com. 1932-42, co. com. 1932-42; del. nat. conv. 1936). Presbyn. Mason (Shriner), Elk, Moose, Eagle. Clubs: High Twelve, Jefferson City Country, Mo. Athletic. Home: 4 Hobbs Lane. Office: Monroe Bldg., Jefferson City, Mo. Died July 12, 1962; buried Riverview Cemetery, Jefferson City, Mo.

BLAIR, VILRAY PAPIN surgeon; b. St. Louis, June 15, 1871; s. Edmund Harrison and Minnie (Papin) B.; A.B., Christian Brothers Coll., 1890, A.M., 1894; M.D., Washington U., 1893; m. Kathryn Lyman Johnson, 1907; children—Kathryn Lyman, Nancy Lucas, Mary Papin (dec.), Vilray Papin, John Bates Johnson. Practiced in St. Louis, 1893-48; prof. emeritus clinical surgery Washington U. Sch. Medicine, oral surgery, School Dentistry; vis. surgeon, Maternity and De Paul hosps.; asso. surgeon Barnes and St. Louis Children's hosps.; in charge plastic and oral surgery section of the head, U.S. Army, 1917-18, chief cons. maxillo-facial surgery, AEF, 1918-19. Fellow A.C.S., Am. Laryngol. Assn., Am. Surg. Assn.; mem. Internat. Surg. Soc., Nat. Inst. Social Sciences, A.M.A., Assn. Am. Anatomists, So., Western surg. assns. Catholic. Clubs: University, St. Louis Country. Home: R.F.D. 1, Florissant, Mo. Office: Metropolitan Bldg., St. Louis. Died Nov. 24, 1955.

BLAIR, W(ILLIAM) REID zoologist; b. Phila., Pa., Jan. 27, 1875; s. William Reid and Jeannette (Houston) B.; D.V.S., McGill U., Montreal, Can., 1902, LL.D. from same univ. in 1928; m. Mildred Myrtle Kelly, Oct. 29, 1896. Veterinarian and pathologist, N.Y. Zool. Park, 1902-22; prof. comparative pathology, Vet. Dept. New York U., 1905-17; cons. veterinarian, N.Y. State Dept. Agr., Asst. dir. N.Y. Zool. Park, 1922-26, dir., 1926-40; exec. sec. Am. Com. Internat. Wild Life Protecttion since 1938. Pres. Vet. Med. Soc., 1922-23; v.p. and trustee Bronx Soc. of Arts and Sciences; life mem., fellow N.Y. Zool. Soc.; fellow A.A.A.S., Am. Geog. Soc.; life mem. Quebec Zool. Soc.; mem. council N.Y. Acad. Sciences; corr. mem. Royal Zool. Soc. of Ireland, Zool. Soc. of London, Internat. Soc. for Preservation of European Bison; life mem. Soc. for Preservation of Fauna of the Empire; trustee Am. Soc. of Mammalogists; sr. fellow Am. Inst. of Park Execs.; mem. Nat. Inst. of Social Sciences, Am. Vet. Med. Assn., N.Y. Graduates Soc. of McGill U., Phi Beta Zeta. Commd. maj., Veterinary Corps, U.S. Army, 1917; served in France and Germany as chief vet., 4th Army Crops, 1918-19; hon. discharged, June 1919; col. Res. Corps, U.S. Army, 1923. Received Citattion of Merit, Park Assn. of N.Y. City, 1940. Active in wild life conservation of birds and mammals. Clubs: Century. Authors, Boone and Crockett. Author: Diseases of Wild Animals in Confinement (pub. N.Y. Zool. Soc.), 1911; In the Zoo, 1929. Also contbr. scientific publs. on comparative medicine. Home: 271 College Road, Riverdale, New York, N.Y. Died Mar. 1, 1949.

BLAKE, A. HAROLD univ. prof., engr.; b. Salt Lake City, Utah, April 3, 1896; s. John Joseph and Bridget (Ryan) B.; B.S. in M.E., U. of Utah, 1920; M.M.E., Cornell U., 1926; m. Lucile Farnsworth, June 8, 1922; children—Robert Harold, William Farnsworth, John Joseph. Instr. mech. engring., U. of Utah, 1920-26, asst. prof., 1926-33, asso. prof., 1933-39, prof. since 1946. Chmn. cubbing commn., Salt Lake Council, Boy Scouts of Am., 1940-42. Served as 2d lt., U.S. Army Inf., 91st Div., 1917-18; maj., U.S. Army Inf., acting adj. gen., with 3d Mil. Area, 1940-41; lt. col., asst. chief of staff G-1, with Hqrs. 9th Corps Area, 1941-42; lt. col., comdg. officer, with W. Va. Ordnance Works, 1942-43; lt. col., dir. engr. maintenance and supply sch., with Corps of Engrs., 1943-45; col. inf. res., 1946-47; col. Ordnance Dept. Res., since 1948. Mem. Am. Soc. M.E., Utah Soc. of Professional Engr., Phi Delta Theta. Tau Beta Pi, Pi Tau Sigma, Theta Tau. Roman Catholic. Co-Author: Automotive Manual, 1923. Home: 1618 Yale Av., Salt Lake City 5. Died Oct. 29, 1951; buried Mt. Olive Cemetery, Salt Lake City.

BLAKE, CLINTON HAMLIN lawyer and author; b. Englewood, N.J., July 26, 1883; s. Clinton Hamlin and Mary Gibson (Parsons) B.; A.B., Columbia U., 1904 (class sec.), A.M. in Polit. Science, 1905. LL.B., 1906; m. Margaret Duryee Coe, June 10, 1908; children—Margaret Coe (Mrs. Theodore W. Oppel), Marion Stanley (Mrs. William G. Cullimore), Dorothy Dexter (Mrs. George H. Macy), Clinton Hamlin, Jr. Admitted to N.Y. bar, 1906, later to bars of United States Circuit and Dist. courts, Ct. of Appeals, D.C., United States Patent Office and Supreme Ct. of U.S.; member Blake, Voorhees & Stewart, N.Y. City; specializes in laws relating to corporations, architecture and building, and unfair competition; president and director Harper-Gow Corp.; dir. and vice pres. Citizens Nat. Bank & Trust Co., Englewood, 1925-36; chmn of Bd., 1936-41; dir. Pond's Extract Co., Penn Sugar Co.; dir. mem. exec. com., v.p. and gen. counsel Nat. Sugar Refining Col Special lecturer on law of architecture and bldg., Mass. Inst. Tech., 1921-22, 25. Columbia U., 1928, New York U., 1933, and on same subject before various archtl. societies; instr. in architecture New York U., 1928. Councilman at large, pres. Common Council, Englewood, 1914-16; mayor of Englewood 2 terms, 1916-18; resigned to enter Army. Mem. N.J. State Council of Defense, 1917-18; chmn. War Draft Bd., No. 5 Bergen County, N.J., 1917-18; capt. Signal Corps, U.S. Army, 1918-19. Former mem. exec. com. N.J. div. Am. Liberty League; former dir. and mem. exec. com. N.J. div. Assn. Against Prohibition Amendment; charter member com. on Food, Drug and Cosmetic Law. Trustee The Barrington School. Mem. Am. Bar Assn., New York State Bar Assn., Assn. of the Bar of the City of New York, Beta Theta Pi. Republican. Clubs: University, Down Town Assn., Beta Theta Pi (New York), Wyantenuck Gold (Great Barrington). Author: The Law of Architecture and Building, 1916-25; The Architect's Law Manual, 1924; Acquiring The Home, 1925; special report to 14th Internat. Congress of Architects, Paris, 1937; also many serial and special articles in mags. since 1915. Editor legal dept. Am. Architect, 1921-27 and 1934-36. Runnerup New Jersey golf champ., 1904. Home: Seekonk Road, Great Barrington, Mass.; (summer) Sugar Hill, N.H. Office: 20 Exchange Place, New York, N.Y. Died Jan. 25, 1947.

BLAKE, FRANCIS GILMAN M.D., educator; b. Mansfield Valley, Pa., Feb. 22, 1887; s. Francis Clark and Winifred Pamelia (Ballard) B.; A.B., Dartmouth Coll., 1908; M.D., Harvard, 1913; hon. M.A., Yale, 1921; Sc.D., Dartmouth College, 1936; m. Dorothy Dewey, June 1, 1916; children—Francis Gilman, William Dewey, John Ballard. Successively med. interne, asst. resident physician and resident physician Peter Bent Brigham Hosp., Boston, 1913-16; asst. at Hosp. of Rockefeller Inst., New York, 1916-17; asst. prof. medicine, U. of Minn., 1917-19; asso. in medicine, Rockefeller Hosp., New York, 1919-1920; asso. mem. Rockefeller Inst., 1920-21; John Slade Ely prof. medicine, Yale School of Medicine, 1921-27, Sterling professor of medicine since 1927. Physician-in-chief, New Haven Hosp., 1921—; sci. dir., med. research and development bd., surg. gen.'s office, Dept. of Army, 1952; member board of scientific dirs. Rockefeller Inst., 1924-35; mem. Nat. Research Council, Div. Med. Sciences, 1925-36, chmn. of Div. for term 1933-36. Served as 1st lt., capt. and maj. Med. R.C., U.S. Army, from Jan. 1, 1918; active duty, Feb. 1918-Sept. 1919; consultant to secretary of war and mem. Bd. for Investigation of Epidemic Diseases in U.S. Army since 1941 (pres., 1941-46); mem. Nat. Adv. Health Council, U.S.P.H.S., since 1948; chmn. adv. council, Life Ins. Med. Research Fund, 1946-50; chmn. com. on med. scis., Research and Development Bd., Dept. of Defense, since 1948; mem. exec. council Assn. of Am. Med. Colls., 1932-33; mem. bd. sci. dirs. Yerkes Lab. for Primate Biology 1940-52. Fellow A.C.P. (regent 1939-47, v.p., 1948-, mem. Assn. American Physicians (pres., 1949), National Academy Science, American Philos. Society, Am. Acad. Arts and Sciences, American Society for Clinical Investigation (pres. 1931), American Society for Experimental Biology and Medicine, Am. Soc. for Exptl. Pathology, Soc. Am. Bacteriologists, Am. Assn. Immunologists (pres. 1935), Am. Assn. Pathologists and Bacteriologists, Conn. Acad. Arts and Sciences, Harvey Soc., Chi Phi, Phi Rho Sigma, Alpha Omega Alpha, Sigma Xi; A.A.A.S. (v.p. 1946), A.M.A. (chmn. sect. on medicine, 1938). Episcopalian. Clubs: Graduate, New Haven Lawn; Harvard (Boston); Interurban Clinical. Author: (with others) Epidemic Respiratory Disease, 1921; Studies on Exptl. Pneumonia, 1920; Studies on Measles, 1921; Treatment of Scarlet Fever with Anti-Toxin, 1924; Artificial Pneumothorax in Lobar Pneumonia, 1935; Chemo Therapy of Pneumonia, 1939; Penicillin Therapy, 1943; Tsutsugamushi Disease in New Guinea, 1945. Received the Charles V. Chapin Memorial Award, Providence, R.I., 1945; U.S. Typhus Medal, 1945; Medal for Merit, 1945. Home: 1619 19th St., Washington 9. Office: care Surgeon General's Office, Dept. of Army, Washington 25. Died Feb. 1, 1952.

BLAKE, HARRISON GRAY OTIS congressman, lawyer; b. Newfane, Windham County, Vt., May 17, 1818; attended public schs.; studied medicine, Seville for 1 year; studied law. Moved to Medina, O., 1836, became mcht.; admitted to bar; practiced in Medina; mem. Ohio Ho. of Reps., 1846, 47; mem. Ohio Senate, 1848, 49, pres.; mem. U.S. Ho. of Reps. (Republican, filled vacancy) from Ohio, 36th-37th congresses, Oct. 11, 1859-63; col. 166th Regt., Union Army, 1864; declined appointment gov. Ida. Territory; in banking and merc. activities; del. Loyalist Conv., Phila., 1866. Died Medina, Apr. 16, 1876; buried Spring Grove Cemetery.

BLAKE, HOMER CRANE naval officer; b. Dutchess County, N.Y., Feb. 1, 1822; s. Elisha and Marilla (Crane) B.; m. Mary Flanagan, 2 children. Apptd. midshipman U.S. Navy, 1842, commd. lt., 1855, lt. comdr., 1862, comdr., 1866, capt., 1871, commodore, 1879; commanded Hatteras, 1862, destroyed by Confederate raider Alabama; later commanded Eutaw in North Atlantic Squadron. Died Jan. 21, 1880.

BLAKELY, GEORGE, army officer; b. in Pa., July 5, 1870; grad. U.S. Mil. Acad., 1892, Arty. Sch., 1896. Commd. 2d lt. 2d Arty., June 11, 1892; 1st lt., Feb. 13, 1899; capt. Arty. Corps, May 8, 1901; maj. Coast Arty. Corps, Mar. 8, 1909; lt. col., Aug. 25, 1915; insp. gen., Nov. 1, 1915; col., 1917; brig. gen. N.A., Aug. 5, 1917. Apptd. comdr. 61st Field Arty. Brigade, Camp Bowie, Ft. Worth, Tex., Sept. 1917; comdr. S. Atlantic Coast Arty. Dist., July-Oct. 1918; comdr. 38th Arty. Brigade, A.E.F., France, Oct. 1918-Feb. 1919; comdr. N. Pacific Coast Arty. Dist., Mar.-June 1919. Address: War Dept., Washington DC

BLAKELY, JOHN RUSSELL YOUNG naval officer; b. Phila., Pa., July 17, 1872; grad. U.S. Naval Acad., 1892. Commd. ensign, 1894 promoted through grades to rear adm. U.S. Navy, June 4, 1926. Served on Yankee, Merrimac and New Orleans, Spanish-Am. War; on Paducah, 1906-07; exec. officer Wolverine, 1907; navigator, Maine, 1909, Washington, 1909-11; duty Bur. of Navigation, Washington, D.C., 1911-14; comdr. Des Moines, 1914-17, and later comdr. Seattle, World War; comdr. Arizona, 1922-24; comdr. light cruiser div., Asiatic Fleet, 1927-29; comdt. 15th Naval Dist., 1929-30; mem. Gen. Bd., 1930-32; retired, June 1, 1932. Address: Navy Dept., Washington. Died Mar. 28, 1942; buried in Arlington National Cemetery.

BLAKELY, JOHNSTON naval officer; b. Seaford, Ireland, Oct. 1781; s. John Blakely; attended U. N.C., 1797; m. Jane Hoope, Dec. 1813, 1 child. Apptd. midshipman U.S. Navy, 1800, promoted lt., 1807, master comdt., 1813, capt., 1814; participated in Tripolitan War; commanded in Enterprise, 1811-13, Wasp, 1813-14; destroyed Brit. ship Reindeer, 1814, captured Atalanta, 1814; received gold medal and thanks of Congress for triumph over Reindeer, 1814. Died at sea, Oct. 1814.

BLAKESLEE, ERASTUS soldier, minister, author, editor; b. Plymouth, Litchfield Co., Conn., Sept. 2, 1838; s. Joel and Sarah Maria (Mansfield) B.; grad. Williston Sem., 1859, Yale, 1863, B.A., 1864, M.A., 1860, Andover Theol. Sem., 1879; m. Mary Goodrich North, Mar. 30, 1865. Enlisted Co. A, 1st Conn. Cav., Oct. 9, 1861, commd. 2d lt., Oct. 18, 1861; promoted 1st lt. and adj., Nov. 26, 1861, capt., Co. A, Feb. 28, 1862, maj., July 14, 1863 (for gallantry near Harper's Ferry, Va.), lt. col., May 23, 1864, col., May 27, 1864; mustered out, Oct. 26, 1864; commd. bvt. brig. gen. U.S.V. (for gallant conduct at Ashland, Va., June 1, 1864), Mar. 13, 1865. Engaged in business 1865-75. Student at Andover Theol. Sem., 1876-79; pastor 2d Congl. Ch., Greenfield, Mass., 1880-83, 2d Congl. Ch., Fair Haven, Conn., 1883-87; elected pres. Atlanta Univ., Ga., 1887, but declined; pastor 1st Congl. Ch., Spencer, Mass., 1887-92; organized in Conn. 1st State Christion Endeavor Union, and was its pres. until left state. Began, preparation of graded Sunday Sch. Lessons, 1888; removed to Boston, 1892, and then devoted whole time to writing, editing and publishing Bible Study Union Lessons, in 7 grades. Pres. Bible Study Pub. Co. Asso. Victoria Inst., London; mem. Soc. Bibl. Literature and Exegesis, Mass. Commandery and commander in chief, Loyal Legion. Conglist. Republican Author: Brief History 1st Connecticut Cavalry Vols., 1889; also author or editor of over 100 vols. of the Bible Study Union Lessons. Home: Brookline, Mass. Died 1908.

BLALOCK, MYRON GEER ex-Dem. Nat. committman; b. Harrison County, Tex., Jan. 3, 1891; s. William Meredith and Willie Henry (Boothe) B.; A.B., U. Tex., 1914, LL.B., 1916; m. Bertha Mary Storey, Aug. 22, 1917; children—Mary Dorothy, Myron Geer, Jo Ann. Admitted to Tex. bar, 1916, since practiced at Marshall; mem. own firm, 1919—; now mem. Blalock, Blalock, Lohman & Blalock; at Marshall and Houston; chief justice (by appointment) Tex. Court Civil Appeals, 6th Dist., Texarkana, 1932. Served from capt. to maj. U.S. Army, 1917-19; major Tex. N.G. 1923-38; lt. col. (finance officer) 36th Div. (Tex., N.G.) U.S. Army, 1938-41; col., Hdqrs. A.E.F., Washington, 1941-43; on inactive duty. Mem. Tex. Ho. of Reps., 1913-18. Comn. Tex. State Dem. Exec. Com., 1934-38; chmn. Dem.Nat. Campaign Com. for Tex., 1936, 40, 44; Dem. Nat. committeeman for Tex. Mem. State Bar of Tex., Am., Harrison County bar assns., Am. Legion. Methodist. Mason (32ff, Shriner.). Clubs: Marshall Country, Rotary, Dallas Athletic. Home: 205 E. Merritt St., Marshall, Tex. Died Dec. 28, 1950.

BLAMER, DEWITT, naval officer; b. Independence, Ia., Jan. 20, 1872; grad. U.S. Naval Acad., 1891. Ensign, July 1, 1893; lt. jr. grade, Mar. 3, 1899; lt., July 6, 1899; lt. comdr., July 18, 1905; comdr., Mar. 4, 1911; capt., Aug. 29, 1916. Served on Alliance and Apache, Spanish-Am. War, 1898; in charge navy recruiting sta., Chicago, 1905-6; navigator St. Louis, 1906-8; exec. officer Milwaukee, 1908-9; with Bur. of Equipment, Navy Dept., 1909-10; in charge 9th Light House Dist., Chicago, 1910-11; comd. Paducah, 1911; exec. officer Wisconsin, 1911-12; comd. Buffalo, 1912-13; capt. of yard, Navy Yard, Puget Sound, Wash., 1913-15; at Naval War Coll., Newport, R.I., 1915-16; comd. Birmingham, 1916; chief of staff, destroyer force, Atlantic Fleet, 1916-17; comdg. U.S.S. Seattle, 1917-18; chief of staff, cruiser and transport force, Atlantic Fleet, 1917-19; chief of staff, Asiatic Fleet, 1919-20. Address: Navy Dept., Washington DC

BLANCHARD, MURRAY, engineer; b. Peru, Ill., July 25, 1874; s. Murray and Helen A. (Dolliver) B.; B.S. in C.E., Univ. of Mich., 1898, C.E., 1903; m. Alice H. Fish, Feb. 6, 1902; 1 dau., Helen (dec.). Has operated extensively in the U.S. and Can. as engr. water power development, also as hydraulic engr.; with engring. dept. Pa. R.R. as asst. engr. on tunnel in N.Y. City, 1905-09; hydraulic engr. State of Ill., Div. of Waterways, 1920-30; prin. engr. U.S. Engring. Dept., 1930-31; cons. engr., Chicago, 1930-33; engr. U.S. Pub. Works Adminstrn., 1933-37; engr. U.S. Engring. Dept since Feb. 1, 1938. Served in World War as major engrs. U.S. Army, 1917-19. Mem. Am. Soc. C.E. (life), Western Soc. Engrs., Soc., Am. Mil. Engrs., Am. Legion. Republican. Conglist. Clubs: Univ. of Mich., Chicago Engineers'. Home: 132 Peck St. Office: U.S. Engineer Office, Sault Ste Marie MI

BLANCHARD, WILLIAM H. air force officer; b. Feb. 6, 1916; grad. Phillips Exeter Acad.; ed. U.S. Mil. Acad.; m. Anne H.; children-William H., Dale (both from previous marriage), Donald H. Commd. permanent rank maj. gen., 1955, temporary rank lt. gen. USAF, 1961; now vice chief of staff, Bolling AFB. Address: 62 Westover Av., Bolling AFB, Washington 20025. Died June 1966.

BLAND, THEODORICK army officer, congressman; b. Prince George County, Va., Mar. 21, 1742; s. Theodorick and Frances (Bolling) B.; M.D., U. Edinburgh (Scotland), 1763; m. Martha Dangerfield. Commd. capt. 1st troop Va. Cavalry 1776; commd. col. 1st Continental Dragoons, 1779; del. to Continental Congress from Va. 1780-83; mem. Va. Ho. of Dels., 1786-88; unsuccessful candidate for gov. Va., 1786; mem. Va. Conv. to ratify U.S. Constn., 1788, voted against ratification; mem. U.S. Ho. of Reps. from Va., 1st Congress, 1789-90. Died N.Y.C., June 1, 1790; buried Trinity Churchyard, N.Y.C.

BLANDING, ALBERT HAZEN, ret. Nat. Guard officer; b. Lyons, Iowa, Nov. 9, 1876; Abram Ormsby and Sarah Ann (Nattinger) B.; grad. East Florida Seminary (now part of U. of Fla.), 1894; LL.D., University of Florida, 1942; m. Mildred M. Hale, June 1, 1908; children—Sarah Elizabeth, Mildred Louise (Mrs. J. H. Yarborough), William Norris. Mine supt. and asst. mgr. with Dutton Phosphate Co., 1896-1910; est. and operated lumber and naval stores business, 1910-16; with Consol. Lumber Co., 1919-22, Fla. Citrus Exchange, 1922-33; chief U.S. Nat. Guard Bureau, Feb. 1, 1936 to Jan. 31, 1940; lt gen. Fla. Nat. Guard; retired, Nov. 9, 1940. Coordinating dir., Action Divisions and chmn. Division of Civil Protection, State Defense Council of Florida. Mem. bd. of Control of State Instns. of Higher Learning (Fla.), 1922-36; Fla. State Plant Bd., 1922-36, Capt., maj., 1t. col. and col. Fla. Nat. Guard, 1899-1917; duty on Mexican border, 1916-17; mustered into U.S. Army, 1917, as brig. gen. and served in France, World War, 1918-19; apptd. maj. gen. of the line, N.G., U.S., 1924. Awarded D.S.M.; active State Service medal, Florida Cross. Incorporator of the Am. Legion and 1st dept. comdr. of Fla. Democrat. Mason, Elk. Clubs: Army and Navy (Washington, D.C.), Kiwanis. Address: Tallahassee FL Died Dec. 1970.

BLANDY, WILLIAM HENRY PURNELL naval officer ret., business exec.; b. N.Y.C., June 28, 1890; s. Charles Graham and Elizabeth Harwood (Purnell) B.; student U. Del. (then Delaware Coll.), 1906-09, D.S., 1941; B.S., U.S. Naval Acad., 1913; m. Roberta Hope Amies, May 27, 1914; children—Hope Gilmour (wife of Comdr. John M. Lee, U.S. Navy), William Purnell (lt. J.g.)). Commd. ensign, U.S. Navy, 1913, advanced through grades to adm. 1947; chief Bureau Ordnance, Navy Dept., Feb. 1941-Dec. 1943; comdr. Amphibious Group One, Jan. 1944-July 1945; participated in capture Kwajalein, Saipan, Palau, IwoJima and Okinawa; comdr. cruisers and destroyers Pacific Fleet, July-Nov. 1945; dep. Chief of Naval Operations, Special Weapons, Nov. 1945-Dec. 1946, during which period, as comdr. Joint Army-Navy Task Force One, planned and comd. atomic bomb tests at Bikini; comdr. Eighth Fleet, Dec. 1946-Feb. 1947; comdr. in chief Atlantic Fleet, 1947-50; comdr. in chief Atlantic (Unified) Command, 1947-50, ret. from active duty, 1950; now dir. gray Mfg. Co., Perkin-Elmer Corp.; pres. Health Information Found. Sponsor James Forrestal Research Center, Princeton, N.J.; com. pub. policy Inst. War and Peace Studies, Columbia; Adv. council N.Y.C. Civil Def. Decorated D.S.M. with 3 gold stars; Grand Officer Order of the So. Cross (Brazil); Comdr. Order of British Empire. Mem. Am. Ordnance Assn. (dir, v.p.), Council on Fgn. Relations, Mil. Order World Wars (hon. life), Naval Order of U.S. (hon. life), Nat. Security Indsl. Assn. (hon.). Clubs: Yacht, University, Dutch Treat, Economic (N.Y.C.); Army and Navy, Army and Navy Country, Chevy Chase (Washington). Home: 277 Park Av., N.Y.C. 17. Office: 420 Lexington Av., N.Y.C. 17. Died Jan. 12, 1954; buried Arlington Nat. Cemetery.

BLANTON, WYNDHAM BOLLING, M.D. b. Richmond, Va., June 3, 1890; s. Charles Armistead (M.D.) and Elizabeth Brown (Wallace) B.; B.A., Hampden-Sydney Coll., 1910; M.A., U. of Va., 1912; M.D., Coll. Physicians and Surgeons (Columbia), 1916; grad. work, Columbia, Berlin and Edinburgh; Litt.D., Hampden-Sydney Coll., 1933; m. Natalie Friend McFaden, Jan.1, 1918; children-Wyndham Bolling, Frank McFaden, Charles Armistead, Mary Friend Easterly. Began practice at Richmond, Va., 1920; specializes in internal med.; asso. prof. of med., Med. Coll. of Va., 1930-33, prof. history of med., 1933-36, prof. of clin. medicine, 1939-59, prof. emeritus; chief div. of medicine Richmond Meml. Hosp., 1957. Senior surgeon U.S. P.H.S. Reserve. Served as vol. with Dr. Joseph Blake, at Am. Ambulance Hosp., Neuilly-sur-Seine, France, 1915; capt. Med. Corps, U.S. Army, Ft. Benjamin Harrison and Ft. Snelling; chief of lab. service, Cantonment Hosp., Camp Cluster, Mich., 1918-19. Chmn. bd. trustees Union Theol. Sem., Va. Fellow A.C.P., Am. Acad. Allergy (v.p. 1953); mem. Med. Soc. of Va., Richmond Society of Internal Medicine (v.p. 1956), Richmond Acad. Medicine (pres. 1929), Va. Acad. Science, American Association History of Med., Tristate Med. Soc., Southern Med. Soc. (v.p. 1943), Va. Hist. Soc. (pres.), Historic Richmond Found. (pres.), First Families of Virginia, American Clinical and Climatological Assn., Soc. Colonial Wars, Soc. Cin. Va. (pres.), Pi Kappa Alpha, Phi Chi, Omicron Delta Kappa, Sigma Delta Chi, Phi Beta Kappa. Democrat. Presbyn. Author: The Making of a Downtown Church, 1945. Emeritus editor Va. Med. Monthly; contbr. med. lit.; cons. editor Jour. of The History of Medicine and Allied Scis., Bull History Medicine; past asso. editor, Annals Med. History. Home: 3015 Seminary Av. Office: 828 W. Franklin St., Richmond, Va. Died Jan. 6, 1960; buried Hollywood Cemetery, Richmond, Va.

BLATCHFORD, RICHARD MILFORD army officer; b. N.Y., Aug. 17, 1859; m. Elinor Hall, Jan. 1921. Apptd. from civil life, 2d lt. 11th Inf., Oct. 10, 1883; advanced through grades to rank of brig. gen., May 15, 1917; maj. gen. N.A., Aug. 5, 1917, and assigned as comdr. at Panama, C.Z.; disch. from commn. in N.A., Mar. 1918, and continued in command at Panama, as brig. gen. U.S.A., retired Dec. 1, 1922; maj. gen. retired, June 21, 1930. Home: San Francisco, Calif. Died Aug. 31, 1934.

BLAYNEY, T(HOMAS) LINDSEY, educator; b. Lebanon, Ky., Dec. 3, 1874; s. Rev. John McClusky and Lucy Weisiger (Lindsey) B.; A.B., Centre Coll., Ky., 1894, A.M., 1897; univs. Gottingen, Geneva, Grenoble and Faculty of Lit., Florence; Ph.D., U. Heidelberg, 1904; LL.D., Southwestern U., Loyola University, New Orleans, University of Notre Dame, 1923, Austin (Texas) College, 1926, Centre Coll., Ky., 1947; m. Gertrude South, Sept. 9; 1896 (dec. 1945);children—Lucy L. (dec.), John McC., Lindsey; m. 2d, Dr. Ida Walz Kubitz, Mar. 24, 1948. Expdn. interior Morocco, 1899; vice consul, Mannheim, Germany, 1901-04; prof. modern langs., and history European art Central U. Ky., 1904-12; prof. German, William M. Rice Inst., Houston, 1912-24; pres. Tex. State Woman's Coll., 1924-26; dean Carleton Coll., 1926-45, chmn. dept. German, 1926-46. Chmn. first Houston City Planning Commn.; as pres. Houston Art League, planned, negotiated for present site Houston Mus. Art, and self-perpetuating bd. trustees. Am. Albert Kahn fellow to Orient, 1914-15. Served from maj. to 1t. col. AEF, 1917-19. Decorated Croix de Guerre with palm (2), Officer Legion of Honor (France); Hon. Officer Chasseurs Alpins; Order White War Eagle, Serbia; Chevalier Order St. Sauveur (Greece); Comdr. Order Crown of Italy; 6 citations for D.S.M., Order Purple Heart (United States), American Legion del. 17th Congress FIDAC, Warsaw; del. Internat. Ednl. Congress, Heidelberg. Mem., fellow nat. and internat. orgns., Rice U. Alumni Assn. (hon.). Vice pres. Am. Fed. Arts, 1910. Presbyn. Mason, Rotarian (hon.), Author: Thomas Moore, Ein irisch-galischer Dichter, 1906 Ideals of Orient, 1916; To Our Country (verse series); Am. Ideals and Traditions. Contbr. Am., fgn. and lit. press. Pioneered history of art Am. Colls. and univs. Article on Philippine independence credit with slowing down Congressional action. Home: Marine on St Croix MN Died Mar. 13, 1971; buried Frankfort Cemetery, Frankfort KY

BLECKWENN, WILLIAM JEFFERSON neuropsychiatrist; b. Astoria, L.I., N.Y., July 23, 1895; s. Alfred Paul and Julia A. (Lorenz) B.; student N.Y.U., 1913-15; B.S., U. Wis., 1917; M.D., Columbia, 1920; m. Marion J. Dougan, Jan. 28, 1919; children-Marion J. (Mrs. Birkenmeier), William Jefferson (dec.), Alfred T. Intern Bellevue Hosp., N.Y.C., 1920-22; grad. tng. Wis. Psychiat. Inst., 1922-24, asst. dir., 1926; instr. neuropsychiatry U. Wis., 1922-26, asst. prof., 1926-30, asso. prof., 1930-35, prof., 1935-, chmn. dept., 1948-; practice medicine, 1920-, specializing neuropsychiatry, 1922-; cons. neuropsychiatry Surg. Gen. U.S. Army, 1944-; chmn. med. adv. bd. Dept. Vets. Affairs, 1952. Chmn. boxing rules com. Nat. Collegiate Athletic Assn., 1948-. Served with U.S. Army, World War I, col. M.C., World War II. Decorated Legion Merit with oak leaf cluster, Presdl. Citation. Mem. A.M.A., Am. Psychiatry Assn., Central, Milw. neuropsychiat. assns., Wis Mental Health Soc., Sigma Xi, Sigma Sigma, Phi Gamma Delta, Phi Rho Sigma. Presbyn. Clubs: Madison, University. Contbr. articles on neurosyphilis, narcoanalysis, picrotoxin, epilepsy, shock therapy. Discoverer sodium amytal (truth serum). Home: 3441 Crestwood Dr., Madison 5, Wis. Died Jan. 4, 1965; buried Forrest Hills Cemetery, Madison.

BLEECKER, JOHN VAN BENTHUYSEN rear adm.; b. Glen Cove, N.Y., Aug. 16, 1847; s. John V.B. (paymaster U.S.N.) and S. Rosalie (Lynch) B.; grad. U.S. Naval Acad., 1867; promoted ensign, 1868; master, 1870; lt., 1871; lt. comdr., June 30, 1891; comdr., Dec. 8, 1897; capt., June 3, 1902; rear adm. and retired, June 27, 1905. Served 19 yrs. on sea duty at various stas.; shore service at torpedo sta., 1873-74, Navy Yard, Washington, 1877-78; Naval Acad., 1878-81; insp. of steel, new cruisers, 1887-88; torpedo sta., 1889-90; Navy Yard, Boston, 1893-96; Naval War Coll., 1894; comd. U.S.S. Bancroft, 1898, Isla de Luzon, 1899, Marietta, 1901; Naval War Coll., Navy Yard, Puget Sound; comdg. U.S.S. Columbia, until retired. Home: Jamestown, R.I. Died Feb. 20, 1922.

BLESH, ABRAHAM LINCOLN surgeon; b. Lock Haven, Pa., Jan. 6, 1866; s. Rudolph and Sarah Frances (Bartholomew) B.; Campbell Normal Sch., Holton, Kan.; M.D., Northwestern U. Med. Sch., 1889; U. of Vienna, 1910-11; m. 2d, Beatrice Rogers, Jan. 22, 1921. Practiced at Rio, Wis., 1889-90, Hope, Kan., 1890-91, Lost Springs, Kan., 1891-93, Guthrie, Okla., 1893-1908, Oklahoma City, Okla., 1908 - . Practiced surgery exclusively, 1902 - ; prof. clin. surgery, Univ. Med. Sch., Oklahoma City; chief of staff, chief surgeon, Wesley Hosp.; pres. and chief of staff, Oklahoma City Clinic, 1919 - . Fellow and gov. Am. Coll. Surgeons. Mason. Commd. 1st lt. M.R.C., and chief surgeon Base Hosp. No. 1, Ft. Sam Houston, Tex., May 27, 1917; promoted maj., Aug. 23, 1917; detached duty Phila.; chief surgeon, Base Hosp., Camp Sheridan, Montgomery, Ala., June 19-Dec. 29, 1918. Home: Oklahoma City, Okla. Died Feb. 20, 1934.

BLESSE, FREDERICK ARTHUR army officer; b. Ill., Nov. 22, 1888; M.D., Hahnemann Coll., 1913; honor grad. Med. Field Service Sch., 1925, Command and

Gen. Staff Sch., 1932, Army War Coll., 1936. Commd. 1st lt. Med. Sect., O.R.C., Feb. 1918; on active duty from Apr. 1918; advanced through grades to brig. gen., 1942; served as chief surgeon North Africa Theater of Operations; later surgeon gen. of the Army, ret. 1949; dir. Henrico County Health Dept., Richmond, Va., 1950—. Died June 4, 1954.

BLETHEN, CLARENCE BRETTUN newspaper man; b. Portland, Me., Feb. 1, 1879; s. Alden J. and Rose A. (Hunter) B.; m. Rae Kingsley, Aug. 10, 1909; five sons. Connected with Seattle Times in various capacities since 1900, succeeding father who died July 12, 1915, as editor and pub.; pres. Seattle Times Co. since 1921; also pres. Blethen Corp. Mustered into federal service as col. coast arty., U.S. Army, July 25, 1917; at close of war commanded 24th Arty.; brig. gen. U.S. Army, Res., 1924. Inventor and pantentee of various newspaper printing processes. Home: Olympic Hotel. Seattle; and Sunnyview Farm, Medina, Wash. Died Oct. 30, 1941.

BLISS, AARON THOMAS gov. of Mich. for 1900-04; b. Smithfield, Madison Co., N.Y., May 22, 1837; s. Lymand and Anna (Chaffee) B.; ed. country schs.; employed in store, 1854-61; enlisted pvt. Co. D., 10th N.Y. cav., Oct. 1, 1861; elected 1st lt.; promoted capt., 1862; in service 3 yrs. 5 months; captured on field, Ream's Sta., Va.; 6 months in prisons at Salisbury, N.C., Andersonville, and Macon, Ga., Charleston and Columbia, S.C.; excaped from Columbia prison Nov. 29, 1864, and reached Union lines Dec. 16, nearly starved; m. Allaseba M., March 31, 1868, d. Ambrose Phelps of Solsville, Madison Co., N.Y. Lumberman in Saginaw, 1865 - , large mfr. of lumber and salt, and interested in banking, mercantile and farm enterprises. Has been alderman, supervisor and mem. bd. edn., Saginaw; State senator, 1882; mem. bd. to locate Mich. Soldiers' Home; mem. Congress from 8th Mich. dist., 1889-91; aide on staff Gov. Alger, 1885; dept. comdr. n.A.R., 1897; lay del. Gen. Conf. M.E. Ch., 1900; elected gov. Mich., 1900; re-elected, 1902. Republican. Home: Saginaw, Mich. Died 1906.

BLISS, GEORGE LAURENCE, business exec.; b. Rogers Park, Ill., Mar. 5, 1896; s. George Harvey and Robina Margaret (Mount) B.; grad. high sch., Northampton, Mass., 1914; B.S. in econs., U. Pa., 1919 (as of 1918); m. Corinne Constance Sawyer, June 1, 1921; children—George Donald, Arthur Sawyer (dec.), Janet. With Fisk Rubber Company, Chicopee Falls, Mass., and N.Y. City, 1919-22; assistant to president Franklin Soc. for Home-Building and Savings, N.Y. City, 1922-23, v.p., 1923-32; exec. v.p. Fed. Home Loan Bank of N.Y., 1932-34, pres., 1934-41, (on leave as dep. gov. Fed. Home Loan Bank System, Washington, D.C., 1936-37, director 1954-57, vice chairman, 1955-57; president Century Fed. Savings and Loan Assn., N.Y.C., 1941-65, chmn. bd., dir., 1946-65; pres., mng. dir. Council Mut. Savs. Instns., from 1966; Mem. Pres. Eisenhower's Advisory Com. on Housing, 1953; mem. task force on lending agencies Commn. on Orgn. Exec. Branch of Government, 1954-55. Officer candidate, 1st O.T.C., Ft. Niagara, New York, 1917; 2d lt., 1st lt., and captain, 316th Inf., 79th Div., U.S. Army, 1917-19; with A.E.F., July 1918-May 1919; cited for gallantry in action, 1918; 1st lt., captain and maj., 71st Inf., N.Y. Nat. Guard, 1921-28; maj. lt. col., col., 17th Inf., N.Y. Guard, 1940-46; col. 71st Inf., N.Y.N.G., 1946-47; brig. general N.Y. Guard Reserve. President Metropolitan League Savings Assn., 1928-29, N.Y. State League of Savings and Loan Assns., 1931-32; chmn. accounting div. U.S. Savs. and Loan League, 1934-40, chmn. legislative com., 1950-54, director, 1956-58, mem. exec. com., 1958-61; vice chmn. Nat. Thrift Com., 1943-63; mem. council of Internation Union Bldg. Sec., 1956-58. Fellow Royal Society of Arts (London, Eng.); mem. American Savings and Loan Inst., (pres. 1930-31), Am. Finance Assn., Nat. Association Business Economists, American Legion, 316th Inf. Assn. (pres. 1941-42), Internat. Benjamin Franklin Soc. (pres. from 1948). Republican Conglist. Clubs: Army-Navy (N.Y.C., also Washington); University of Pennsylvania (N.Y.C.); Rotary. Home: Mount Vernon NY Deceased.

BLISS, PAUL SOUTHWORTH govt. service; b. Rice Lake, Wis., Apr. 12, 1889; s. Alden Southworth and Olive Irene (Hills) B.; student Hamline Coll., 1907-10; A.B., Harvard, 1913, post-grad. work in drama, 1913-14; unmarried. Wrote for various newspapers, including theatrical and musical criticism, 1913-23; on staff Minneapolis Community Fund, 1923-26; publicity dir. St. Louis Community Fund, 1926-32; exec. sec. St. Louis Chapter Am. Red Cross, 1932-33; field rep. Federal Emergency Relief Adminstrn. of N.D., 1933-35; dir. dept. of intake and certification, Works Progress Adminstrn. of N.Dak., 1935-37; with Social Security Board, 1937-. Served as captain and later maj., U.S. Army, with A.E.F. in France, World War; now col. O.R.C. commanding 406th Inf. Regt., St. Louis. Author: (poetry) Songs for Seven Moods, 1926; After Supper Poems, 1927; Rough Edges and All, 1928; How Pan Shaped the Leaves and Other Poems, 1930; Arch of Spring, 1932; Spin Dance, 1934; Cirrus from the West, 1935; The Rye is the Sea, 1936; Poems of Places, 1937; The Lord Made Kansas for Wheat. Home: Hettinger, North Dakota. Died Dec. 31, 1940.

BLISS, RAYMOND WHITCOMB army officer; b. Chelsea, Mass., May 17, 1888; s. Eli Cooley Weston and Hannah Page (Ham) B.; M.D., Tufts Med. Coll., 1910; postgrad. Army Med. Sch., Washington, D.C., 1912-13; C.S., Harvard Med. Sch., 1921, D.Sc. 1943; D.Laws, U. Louisville, 1948; m. Martha Stuchul, Sept. 15, 1914; children-Raymond Whitcomb, Martha Jane. Commd. 1st lt. Med. Res. Corps., U.S. Army, 1911, advanced through grades to brig. gen., 1943; apptd. dep. surgeon gen. U.S. Army, 1946, surgeon gen., 1947. Fellow A.C.S.; mem. Theta Delta Chi. Mason. Home: 1 Main Dr., Army Med. Center, Washington. Died Dec. 1965.

BLISS, TASKER HOWARD army officer; b. Lewisburg, Pa., Dec. 31, 1853; s. George Ripley (D.D., LL.D.) and Mary Ann (Raymond) B.; ed. Lewisburg Acad., 1867-69, entered Univ. at Lewisburg (now U.), Bucknell 1869 and finished sophomore yr.; grad. U.S. Mil. A 1989-May 20, 1902. Apptd. mem. Army War Coll. Bd., July 21, 1902; apptd. spl. envoy to Cuba to negotiate treaty of reciprocity bet. Cuba and the U.S., Nov. 13, 1902; comdt. Army War Coll., 1903; mem. Joint Army and Navy Bd. and Gen. Staff U.S.A., 1903-05; comdg. Dept. of Luzon, P.I., 1905-06, Dept. of Mindanao, 1906-09, Div. of the Philippines, Dec. 1908-Apr. 1909; mem. Army Gen. Staff and pres. Army War Coll., June-Dec. 1909; asst. chief of staff, Dec. 1909; mem. Joint Army and Navy Bd., 1909-10; acting chief of staff, lMay-Aug. 1910; comdg. Dept. of Calif., Aug. 1910-June 30, 1911; comdg. provisional brigade on Mexican border, Southern Calif., during lMexican insurrection, Mar.-June 15, 1911; comdg. Western div., July 1-July 30, 1911; comdg. Dept. of the East, Aug. 12, 1911-Feb. 14, 1913; comdg. Eastern Div., Jan. 29-Aug. 31, 1912; comdg. Southern Dept. and the Cav. Div., Feb. 15, 1913-Feb. 15, 1915; apptd. mem. Gen. Staff, U.S. Army, and asst. chief of staff, Feb. 15, 1915; mem. Joint Army and Navy Bd., Sept. 23, 1915, maj. gen. U.S.A., Nov. 20, 1915; chief of staff, Sept. 23, 1917; chief of staff with rank of general, U.S.A., Oct. 6, 1917; retired by operation of law, Dec. 31, 1917; continued on active duty by order of the President. Mem. of the Allied Conf., 1917; mem. Supreme War Council in France; mem. Am. Commn. to Negotiate Peace, Paris, 1918-19; detailed by President as Gov. of U.S. Soldiers' Home, May 1, 1920-May 1, 1927. Apptd. brevet gen. by Act of Congress, lfay 20, 1918. Awarded D.S.M. (U.S.). Home: Washington, D.C. Died Nov. 9, 1930.

BLOCH, CLAUDE CHARLES navy officer; b. Woodbury, Ky., July 12, 1878; B.S., U.S. Naval Acad., 1899, hon. D.Sc., 1938; student, Ogden Coll., Ky., Naval War Coll.; m. Augusta Kent, Mar. 3, 1903; 1 dau., Ethel Kent (wife of Col. T.A. Broom, U.S.A.). Commd. ensign U.S. Navy, 1901, advanced through grades to rear admiral, 1923; admiral (temp.) 1937, (Permanent) 1942. Served on the USS Ia., Spanish Am. War, Arizona, Plattsburg, and Mass., World War I; asst. chief bureau ordnance, 1918-21, chief 1923-27; commander battle force, comdr. in chief, U.S. fleet, 1937-40; comdt. Hawaiian Sea frontier, 1941-42; mem. General Bd., 1942-45; chmn. Navy Bd. Products awards, 1942-45. Decorated: Legion of Merit, Navy Cross, Medal for Meritorious conduct, Spanish-Am. War. Clubs: Army and Navy, Chevy Chase, (Wash., D.C.). Home: 2607 36th Pl. Washington 7. Died Oct. 1967.

BLOCH, HERBERT AARON (DAVID) sociologist; born New York, N.Y., Sept. 8, 1904; s. Leon and Johanna (Weisenberg) B.; B.S., Coll. City of N.Y., 1926; A.M., Columbia, 1929, Ph.D., 1934; m. Adeline H. Supove, July 3, 1929; children-Herbert Spencer, Susan Del. Supervisor and teacher, N.Y. City Schs. System, 1926-33; dir. Community Orgn., N.Y. Social Settlements, 1931-34, dir. adult edn. 1931-34; dir. and organizer, Social Settlement Camps, 1931-34; supervisor, Central Registration Bureau for the Homeless. N.Y. City, 1933-34; chmn. dir. social studies St. Lawrence University, 1935-46, became prof. sociology, 1938, chmn. dept. sociology, 1935, chmn. dept. of sociology and anthropology, 1950; visiting professor Bklyn. Coll., 1954-55, prof. sociology, anthropology 1955-, coordinator police sci., 1956-, dir. juvenile delinquency workshops, summers 1957-59, 61-, dir. div. graduate studies, 1963-; adjunct professor N.Y.U., 1958-; associate dean University of City of N.Y., 1963-; chief Pub. Safety Mission, Govt. of Ceylon. Cons. Kings County Narcotics project, also START project, exec. dept. N.Y. State Youth Commn.; chmn. N.Y. conf. pre-profl social work, 1949-; mem. N.Y. Police & Public Safety Adv. Board; cons. editor social problems Random House, Inc.; cons. N.Y. State Division for Youth, 1963-; research cons. Robert Bruce House. Served as exec. officer and chief mil. govt. officer, G-5 Sect. 80th Inf. Div., World War II; supervised repatration and settlement 250,000 war refugees and displaced persons, World War II. Awarded Bronze Star, Croix de Guerre. Fellow Am. Sociol. Soc. (chmn. social problems sect.); mem. A.A.A.S. (chmn. criminology sect.), Assn. Psychiat. Treatment Offenders (dir. research), Am. Criminological Soc., Am. Assn. Univ. Profs., Soc. Study of Social Problems (pres. elect 1958), St. Lawrence County Historical Society, International Criminological Society, Sigma Xi, Alpha Kappa Delta. Universalist. Clubs: Brooklyn College Faculty, N.Y. University Faculty. Author: Concept of Changing Loyalties, 1934; Individual and Social Pathology, 1950; Syllabus in Introductory Sociology, 1949; Disorganization. Personal and Social, published in the year 1952; Delinquency: The Juvenile Offender in America Today (with Frank T. Flynn), 1956; (with Arthur Niederhoffer) The Gang: Study in Adolescent Behavior, 1958; Crime and Insanity, 1959; Crime in America, 1961; Culture and Homicide: A Study of Ceylonese Murder, 1961: (with Gilbert Geis), Man, Crime and Society; also research articles in sociol. jours. Editorial bd. A.P.T.O. Jour.; adv. editor Sociol. Abstracts. Home: 1624 Wales Av., Baldwin, L.I., N.Y. Office: Bklyn. Coll., Bklyn. 11210. Died May 25, 1965; buried L.I. Nat. Cemetery, Pinelawn, L.I., N.Y.

BLOCK, MELVIN A. pharmaceutical exec.; born N.Y. City, May 28, 1908; s. Alexander and Tillie (Goetz) B.; student Polytech. Prep. Sch., 1923-27; B.S., U. Pa., 1931; m. Anita Wangrow, May 8, 1934; children-James, Susan. President Block Drug Co., Jersey City, since 1945; dir. Reed & Carnrick. Chairman Joint Defense Appeal, N.Y., 1954-55; mem. nat. council Anti-Defamation League, 1953-55; trustee Mount Sinai Hospital, N.Y.C., New York Federation of Jewish Charities. Dir. Asso. YM-YWHA's Greater N.Y., pres., 1960-61. Capt. C.E., AUS, 1943-45. Home: 778 Park Av., N.Y.C. 21. Office: 257 Cornelison Av., Jersey City 2. Died Mar. 11, 1963.

BLOCKLINGER, GOTTFRIED rear adm. U.S.N.; b. Dubuque, Ia., Oct. 23, 1847. Apptd. from Ia., and grad. U.S. Naval Acad., 1868; promoted ensign, Apr. 19, 1868; master, July 12, 1870; lt., Apr. 2, 1874; lt. comdr., May 21, 1895; comdr., Mar. 3, 1899; capt., June 1, 1904; rear adm., Oct. 30, 1908; retired, 1909. Was in active service during Civil War; in summer of 1864 on bd. the Marion, in pursuit of the Confederate cruisers Florida and Tallahassee; served successively in the Pacific squadron, Kearsarge, Enterprise, and Adams, 1868-82; various assignments to 1895; exec. officer, Boston, 1895-96, Navy Yard, Mare Island, Calif., 1897; exec. officer, Charleston, 1898-99; in charge recruiting sta., Chicago, 1899-1901; comd. Alert and Concord, 1901, Wheeling, 1902, Vicksburg, 1902, New Orleans, 1903; Navy Yard, Norfolk, Va., 1904; Navy Yard, New York, 1904-06; comdg. Illinois, 1906-08; mem. Naval Examining and Retiring Bds., 1908-09. Died May 18, 1930.

BLOCKSOM, AUGUSTUS PERRY army officer; b. Ohio, Nov. 7, 1854; grad. U.S. Mil. Acad., 1877. Commd. 2d lt. cav., June 15, 1877; maj. insp. gen., Apr. 20, 1905; col. of cav., Jan. 1, 1913; brig. gen., 1917; maj. gen., Aug. 5, 1917. Served on frontier in Ariz. in many campaigns against Apache Indians; operations against Sioux in S.D., 1890, 91; campaign against Santiago de Cuba, 1898; wounded in assault on San Juan Hill, July 1, 1898 (cited by War Dept. in gen. orders for "gallantry in action" and awarded silver citation star); participated in China Expdn. (Boxer campaign), comdg. charge of 6th Cav. Squadron against Boxers (cited by War Dept. in gen. orders for "gallantry in action" and awarded silver citation star); Philippine Insurrection, 1900-02; comdr. Camp Cody, Deming, N.l:., Sept. 1917-Apr. 18, 1918; hon. discharged as maj. gen. N.A., Apr. 18, 1918; brig. gen., comdr. Hawaiian Dept., Apr. 18-Nov. 7, 1918; retired Nov. 7, 1918. Bvtd. 1st lt., July 27, 1890, "for gallant services against Indians at Ash Creek, Ariz., May 7, 1880." Home: Miami, Fla. Died July 26, 1931.

BLODGETT, WELLS HOWARD lawyer; b. Downer's Grove, Ill., Jan. 29, 1839; s. Israel P. and Avis (Dodge) B.; ed. Ill. Inst. (now Wheaton Coll.); admitted to bar, 1861. First lt. 37th Ill. Inf., Aug. 1, 1861; capt., Jan. 1, 1863; judge-advocate Army Frontier, with rank maj. of cav., Mar. 10, 1863; lt. col. 48th Mo. Inf., Sept. 14, 1864; col., Nov. 22, 1864; awarded Congressional Medal of Honor, "for most distinguished gallantry at Newtonia, Mo., Sept. 30, 1862"; hon. mustered out June 20, 1865. Mem. lMo. Ho. of Rep., 1866-68, Senate, 1868-72; asst. atty., 1873-74; gen. atty., 1874-79, St. Louis, Kansas City & Northern R.R.; gen. solicitor, Wabash, St. Louis & Pacific Ry., 1879-84; gen. counsel for receiver, Wabash lines, 1884-89; gen. solicitor, Wabash R.R., 1889-1900, and v.p. and gen. counsel, 1900-09, and counsel for receivers, same corp., Dec. 1911-Nov. 1915. Home: St. Louis, Mo. Died May 8, 1929.

BLOODGOOD, DELAVAN med. dir. U.S.N., retired 1893; b. Springville, N.Y., 1831; grad. Colgate Univ., Hamilton, N.Y., 1852 (A.M.); M.D., Jefferson Med. Coll., Phila.; entered U.S.N.; asst. surgeon, 1857; med. dir., 1884. Served throughout Civil war; on active duty throughout Spanish war; mem. Loyal Legion; Holland Soc.; Order Colonial Wars; Order Foreign Wars. Home: Brooklyn, N.Y. Died 1902.

BLOOMBERG, MAXWELL HILLEL, orthopedic surgeon; b. Rovna, Russia, Feb. 24, 1899; s. Benjamin and Bessie (Kuperman) B.; student Tufts U., 1918-20, M.D., 1924; m. Leah Plutzik, June 30, 1930; 1 dau., Reva. Intern, Beth Israel Hosp., Boston, 1924-25; resident Jewish Hosp., Bklyn., 1925-27, U. Ia. Steindler Clinic, 1927-28; practice orthopedic surgery, Boston, 1928-38, 68; chief orthopedics VA, Pitts., 1938, 42, orthopedic surgeon, East Orange, N.J., 1964-68. Served to lt. col. AUS, 1942-46; ETO. Diplomate Am. Bd. Orthodic Surgeons; Fellow Internat. Coll. Surgeons; mem. Mass. Med. Soc., A.M.A., So. Med. Soc., Am. Med. Writers Assn., Am. Geriatric Soc., Assn. Mil. Surgeons U.S., Pan Am. Med. Soc., New Eng. Med.

Soc., Am. Physicians Fellowship Com. of Israeli Med. Assn. Author; Orthopedic Bracing, 1964; also orthopedic articles. Patentee in field. Home: East Orange NJ Died Oct. 9, 1968

BLUE, VICTOR naval officer; b. Richmond Co., N.C., Dec. 6, 1865; s. John G. and Annie M. (Evans) B.; grad. U.S. Naval Acad., 1887; m. Eleanor Foote Stuart, Oct. 17, 1899. Promoted asst. engr., July 1, 1889; advanced through grades to rear adm., Apr. 1, 1919; retired July 11, 1919. Served in Quinnebaug, 1887-89. Pensacola, 1889-91; duty Union Iron Works, San Francisco, 1891-92; served in Charleston, 1892; Navy Yard, Norfolk, 1892-93, Alliance, 1893-94, Charleston, 1894, Thetis, 1894-95, Bennington, 189S-96, Naval Acad., 1896-98, Suwanee during Spanish War, 1898, was advanced 5 numbers in rank "for extraordinary heroism" during war, and awarded medal for specially meritorious service; various assignments to 1909; comd. Yorktown, Pacific Sta., 1910; chief of staff, Pacific Fleet, 1910-11; duty, Gen. Bd., Navy Dept., May 25, 1911; chief Bur. of Navigation, Navy Dept., with rank of rear adm., Mar. 26, 1913-Aug. 10, 1916; comd. Battleship Texas, operating with British Grand Fleet under Admiral Beatty in the North Sea, 1917-18; took part in receiving the surrender of German Fleet, Nov. 21, 1918; reappointed chief of Bur. of Navigation, Dec. 16, 1918, with rank of rear adm. Awarded D.S.M. "for exceptionally meritorious service" in North Sea; decorated Comdr. Order of Leopold, by King of Belgium. Home: Ft. George, Fla. Died Jan. 22, 1928.

BLUNT, JAMES GILLPATRICK physician, army officer; b. Trenton, Me., July 21, 1862; M.D., Starling Med. Coll., Columbus, O., 1849; m. Nancy Carson Putnam. Served in various mcht. ships, 1841-46; practiced medicine, New Madison, O., 1849-56; moved to Kan., 1856, practiced medicine, also became involved in anti-slavery movement; a friend of John Brown, helped slaves escape to Canada; mem. anti-slavery conv. which drew up Kan. Constn., 1859, chmn. militia com.; lt. col. 3d Kan. Volunteers, U.S. Army, 1861; promoted brig. gen. U.S. Volunteers with command of Dept. of Kan., 1862; took command Army of Frontier after defeating Confederates with their Indian allies at Battle of Old Ft. Wayne (Mo.); promoted maj. gen. 1862; fought on Ark.-Kan.-Mo. Frontier throughout war, helped to keep Kan. and Mo. from being captured by Confederate forces; left U.S. Army, 1865, practiced medicine, Leavenworth, Kan.; solicitor of claims, Washington, D.C., 1869-71; indicted by U.S. Govt. as member of a conspiracy to defraud govt. and band of Cherokee Indians, 1873, charges dismissed by U.S. Dist. Ct., 1875. Died July 25, 1881.

BLUNT, MATTHEW M. soldier; b. New York, Aug. 13, 1830; entered, 1849, grad., 1853, from U.S. Mil. Acad. (A.M., Columbia Coll., 1856). Bvtd. 2d lt., 2d Arty., July 1, and commd. Sept. 30, 1853; promoted 1st lt., 2d Arty., Mar. 31, 1855; capt. 12th Inf., May 14, 1864; maj. 7th Inf., July 30, 1865; transferred to 14th Inf., lfar. 15, 1869; lt. col. 25th Inf., Oct. 7, 1874; col. 16th Inf., July 3, 1883; retired for age, Aug. 13, 1894; advanced in grade to brig. gen., U.S.A., retired, Apr. 23, 1904. In active service during Civ. War in Army of the Potomac and thrice bvtd. for gallant and meritorious services - maj., July 1, 1862 (Malvern Hill), lt. col., Dec. 13, 1862 (Fredericksburg), col., June 19, 1864 (Petersburg). Much of service after war was on frontier in Wyo., Utah and Texas. Died 1907.

BLUNT, STANHOPE ENGLISH army officer; b. Boston, Sept. 29, 1850; s. Charles E. and Penelope Bethune (English) B.; grad Oswego (N.Y.) High Sch., 1868, U.S. Mil. Acad., 1872; m. Fanny Smith, Nov. 18, 1873; children - Katharine, Evelyn B., Frances S. Apptd. 2d lt. 13th Inf., June 14, 1872; promoted through grades to col., June 25, 1906; retired from active service at own request, Sept. 1, 1912; recalled to active duty, Apr. 7, 1917; in Ordnance Office, Washington, D.C., till Aug. 4, 1918. Served in Utah, Wyo. and Colo. with 13th Inf., 1872-74; lt. col. and col. a.d.c. to Gen. P.H. Sheridan, 1885-88; insp. small arms practice, 1885-89; instr. mathematics and in science of ordnance and gunnery, U.S. Mil. Acad., 1876-80; comdg. Rock Island (Ill.) Arsenal, 1897-1907, Springfield (Mass.) Armory, 1907-12. Chmn. Transportation Commn., Springfield, 1912-15; pres. Park Commn., Springfield Planning Commn. Springfield Hosp., 1913-17. Author: Rifle and Carbine Firing, 1885; Firing Regulations for Small Arms, 1889. Home: Springfield, Mass. Died Mar. 22, 1926.

BLYTHIN, ROBERT lawyer; b. Cleve., Jan. 10, 1914; s. Edward and Jane (Rankin) B.; student Oberlin Coll., 1931-32; A.B., Western Res. U., 1935, LL.B., 1937; m. Lois M. Baynes, Feb. 16, 1946. Admitted to Ohio bar, 1937, Ill. bar, 1948, Mich. bar, 1953; pvt. practice law, Cleve., 1937-40; with law dept. Gen. Electric Co., 1940-42, 46-47; counsel Hotpoint, Inc., 1947-52; gen. counsel, sec. Packard Motor Car Co., 1952-54; gen. counsel Studebaker-Packard Corp., 1954-56, counsel Div. of Gen. Electric Co., 1956-. Served as capt. OSS, U.S. Army, 1942-46. Mem. Am. Bar Assn., Phi Delta Phi, Order of Coif. Home: 117 Adrienne Lane, Wynnewood, Pa. Office: 6901 Elmwood av., Phila. Died Mar. 21, 1966; buried Zachary Taylor Nat. Cemetery.

BOAL, PIERRE DE LAGARDE diplomat; b. Thononles-Bains, France, Sept. 29, 1895 (parents Am. citizens); s. Theodore Davis and Mathilde (de Lagarde) B.; ed. Concord, N.H.; m. Jeanne de Menthon, June 10, 1919; children-Mathilde (Mrs. Blair Lee III), Mary Elizabeth (Mrs. Gaston d'Harcourt). Apptd. sec. Embassy, 1919, and assigned to Mexico City; with Dept. State, sec. Internat. Conf. on elec. Communication, Washington, 1920; assigned to Belgrade, Dec. 1920, Warsaw, 1922; 2d sec. Legation, Berne, 1924, Lima, Sept. 1925, 1st sec., Dec. 1925; returned to Dept. State, 1928; sec. Internat. Conf. Am. States on Conciliation and Arbitration, Washington, 1928-29; acting sec. gen. Commn. of Inquiry and Conciliation of Bolivia and Paraguay, Washington, 1929; apptd. asst. chief, div. Western European affairs Dept. State, 1930, chief, 1931; charge d'affaires Am. Legation, Ottawa, Can., 1932-33, consul gen., 1935; assigned to Toronto, 1935 (cancelled) as counselor Legation of Ottawa, 1935; counselor Am. Embassy, Mexico City, 1936; adviser Prep. Commn. for Disarmament Conf., Geneva, 1930; E.E. and M.P. to Nicaragua, 1941-42; A.E. and P. to Bolivia, 1942-44; assigned to Dept. State, 1944; ret., 1947. Designated mem., apptd. by U.S. to Emergency Adv. Com. for Polit. Defense in Montevideo, with rank of ambassador, 1945; special rep. of exec. sec. Internat. Refugee Orgn., Geneva, Switzerland, 1947-48. Served with French army cav., also Lafayette Flying Corps, 1914-15; capt. U.S. AS, 1917-18, comdr. 400th Air Squadron. Decorated Purple Heart, Lafayette Flying Corps ribbon, Legion of Honor, Croix de Guerre (France). Roman Catholic. Clubs: Metropolitan (Washington); Officers Club of 28th Division, Pa. Home: 2911 33d Pl. N.W., Washington. Died May 1966.

BOARDMAN, HARRY CLOW civil engr.; b. Plainfield, Ill., Apr. 29, 1887; s. George Bates and Mary (Clow) B.; B.S., U. Ill., 1910, C.E., 1926; D.Eng. (hon.), S.D. Sch. Mines, 1943; m. Bessie McCumber, May 27, 1923. Draftsman Chgo. Bridge & Iron Co., 1910-16, research engr., 1926—, dir. research, 1945—; engaged automobile tire and accessory bus., Kansas City, Mo., 1919-22; engr., supt. constrn. Internat. Filter Co., Chgo., 1922-24; instr. civil engring. U. Ill., 1924-26. Vice chmn. welding research council Engring. Found., 1949, chmn., 1949-52. Served from pvt. to corpl. N.G., lt. to maj. F.A., U.S. Army, 1917-19. Mem. Am. Welding Soc. (past pres.). Western Soc. Engrs., Am. Soc. C.E., Am. Soc. Metals, A.S.M.E. (chmn. boiler and pressure vessel com.), Am. Soc. Testing Materials, A.A.A.S., Am. Petroleum Inst., Sigma Xi, Tau Beta Pi. Home: 5050 East End Av. Office: 1305 W. 105th St., Chgo. Died Aug. 6, 1956.

BOCOCK, JOHN HOLMES lawyer; b. Hampden-Sidney, Va., Sept. 3, 1890; s. Willis Henry and Bessie (Friend) B.; A.B., U. Ga., 1910; LL.B., U. Va., 1915; m. Elisabeth Strother Scott, May 3, 1928; children—Bessie (Mrs. Robert Carter), Frederic Scott, Mary Buford. Admitted to Va. bar, 1915, since practiced in Richmond; sr. partner McGuire, Eggleston, Bocock & Woods 1947—; spl lectr. law U. Va., 1952-55; dir. First & Mchts. Nat. Bank of Richmond, others. Served as 1st lieutenant, United States Army, 1917-19, maj., 1942-45. Decorated Croix de Guerre with palm (France). Mem. Am., Va. State, Richmond bar assns., Phi Beta Kappa. Clubs: Commonwelath (Richmond); Union (N.Y.C.). Home: 909 W. Franklin St., Richmond 20. Office: Mutual Bldg., Richmond 19, Va. Died Aug. 14, 1958.

BODER, BARTLETT, banker; b. Troy, Kan., Jan. 5, 1885; s. Louis and Fannie (Quimby) B.; student Saint Joseph (Missouri) Schools, 1903; student, London, Paris, and Berlin, 1911-14; m. Vira Price, Apr. 26, 1930 (dec. Sept. 1959); m. 2d, Mary Louise Wallace, Dec. 24, 1960, Bank clk., 1903-05, 1907-08; reporter St. Joseph News-Press, 1905-07; reporter St. Joseph Gazette, 1915-17, editorial writer, 1919; pres. Missouri Valley Trust Co. 1931-—, also dir.; trustee of Harris Trust & Savings Bank, Chicago, St. Joseph Light & Power Co., from 1946; v.p. Tootle-Lacy Nat. Bank, 1949. Pres. St. Joseph Mus. Student Ft. Riley (Kan.) Training Camp, 1917; commd. 2d 1t., 1917; with 127th and 104th F.A., A.E.F.; organized 35th Div. Tank Co., 1923; retired 1935, as lt. col. on 35th Division Staff. Handled Missouri financing for building river bridge at Rulo, Neb., 1938. Originated name, Missourissippi, for world's longest river, July 7, 1942. Chmn. 1st Dist. Missouri State Council of Defense, 1941-45. Mem. President's Washington Conf. on Fire Prevention, 1947. City assessor, 1920-23; city comptroller, 1930-32; police commr., 1932-33. Decorated Knight of Red Cross of Constantine. Mem. Missouri Archeological Soc. (trustee, 1957), American Legion (state vice-comdr. 1927), Forty and Eight (director Nat. Voiture Activities, 1946), Soc. Mayflower Descs., State Hist. Soc. Mo. (v.p.). Sons Revolution, Central Overland Pony Express Assn. (pres. 1959-61). Episcopalian. Mason (Shriner), Nat. Sojourner, Royal Order Jesters. Clubs: St. Joseph Auto (president 1939-40), Benton and St. Joseph Country. Author articles in France-Amerique on history of the early French west of the Mississippi River, 1947; also historical and geographical articles in English. Home: St. Joseph MO Died Jan. 8, 1967.

BOGERT, EDWARD STRONG rear adm.; b. Geneva, N.Y., May 7, 1836; s. Stephen Van Rensselaer and Amanda (Strong) B.; ed. Dwight's High Sch., Brooklyn; m. Helen Hart, June 6, 1866. Apptd. asst. surgeon U.S.N., June 10, 1861; promoted passed asst. surgeon, June 22, 1864; surgeon, Apr. 6, 1866; med. insp., Sept. 10, 1882; med. dir., Nov. 28, 1889; retired, May 7, 1898; advanced to rank of rear adm., June 29, 1906, for services during Civil war. Served on various vessels and at various stas. during Civil War; fleet surgeon, Aug. 1, 1884-Sept. 9, 1886; pres. Naval Examining Bd., New York, Oct. 1-Nov. 28, 1889; in York, charge Naval Hosp., New 1892-95. Died 1911.

BOGERT, MARSTON TAYLOR chemist; b. Flushing, N.Y., Apr. 18, 1868; s. Henry A. and Mary B. (Lawrence) B.; A.B., Columbia, 1890, Ph.B., 1894, Sc.D., 1929; LL.D., Clark U., 1909; R.N.D., Charles U. (Prague); m. Charlotte E. Hoogland, Sept. 12, 1893; children—Annette B. (Mrs. Frank B. Tallman), Elise B. (Mrs. F. K. Huber). Asst. organic chemistry 1894-97, tutor, 1897, instr., 1897-1901, adj. prof., 1901-04, prof., 1904-39, emeritus prof. in residence since 1939; mem. Univ. Council, 1909-11, 1916-17, and 1922-29, Columbia; also rep. Columbia U. on bd. trustees N.Y. Coll. of Pharmacy, 1930-36. Lecturer organic chemistry, New York U., 1919-20. Mem. Am. Advisory Com. of Honor 7th Internat. Congress of Applied Chemistry, London, 1909; pres. Organic Sect., 8th Internat. Congress Applied Chemistry, Washington, D.C. and New York, 1912, chmn. com. of presidents of sections of same and v. chmn exec. com. of same; by invitation of President Roosevelt, mem. of White House Conf. on Conservation of Natural Resources, May 1908; also of the following Conf. with Governors of States and Tys., Washington, D.C., Dec., 1908; mem. Internat. Com. in Honor of Amedeo Avogadro, under patronage of King Victor Emmanual III of Italy; del. of U.S. Govt. and Nat. Research Council and pres. sect. on chemistry and nat. defense, X. Internat. Congress Chemistry, Rome, 1938; pres. Internat. Union Chemistry, 1938-47. Fellow A.A.A.S., London Chemical Soc., Royal Soc. of Edinburgh (hon.). Member Assn. chimica Italiana, Societe Chimique de Paris, Nederland Chem. Ver., Swiss Chemists' Society American Institute Chemists (medalist for 1935-36), Am. Chem. Society (ex-pres.; Nichols medal, 1905; Priestley medal, 1938); hon. mem. Soc. Chem. Industry Eng. (ex-pres.), Chemists Club (ex-pres.), Nat. Acad. Sciences (chmn. chem. sect., 1926-29), Washington Acad. Scis., N.Y. Acad. Scis., Am. Philos. Soc., Am. Acad. Arts and Sciences, Am. Assn. Univ. Profs. (pres. Columbia U. chapter 1932-37), Phi Beta Kappa, Delta Phi, Sigma Xi (councilor 1904; pres. Columbia Chapter, 1906, 1933-37), Phi Lambda Upsilon, Alpha Chi Sigma, Alumni Assn. Graduate Schs., Columbia Unv. (pres. 1935-37; recipient of its Large Scroll 1936); hon. mem. Chemists' Soc. of Poland, Royal Soc. Sciences and Letters (Bohemia), Societe de Chimie Industrielle de France (pres. Am. sect. 1920-21); corr. mem. Am. Inst. in Prague. Medalist of Charles U. (Prague) and of the Comensky U. (Bratislava); Comdr. Order of White Lion of Czechoslovakia. Awarded Egleston Medal of Columbia Engineering School Alumni Assn., 1939. First recipient Medal Award, Society of Cosmetic Chemists; Charles Frederick Chandler medalist and lecturer (selection by Columbia U.), 1948. An incorporator of Museums of Peaceful Arts, now New York Museum of Science and Industry, New York, 1915, member board directors since its organization; member national advisory board, Masaryk Institute. In World War I - member executive bd. Nat. Research Council (organizer and 1st chmn. div. of chemistry and chem. technology, with 32 subcoms.); mem. raw materials div. War Industries Bd.; mem. bd. on Gas Warfare; cons. chemist, Bur. Mines; mem. scientific staff, Bur. Standards; advisory com. War Trade Bd., advisory bd. materials prodn. div., Signal Corps, War Dept.; consultant Fed. Trade Commn., mil. intelligence div. of Gen. Staff, War Dept., bur. investigation Dept. Justice, postal censorship Post Office Dept., etc. Commd. lt. col. and apptd. chief, Chem. Service Sect., U.S. Army, and asst. dir. Gas Service, Mar. 9, 1918; promoted col., July 13, 1918; served as chief of relations sect., intelligence sect., mem. bd. of review, claims bd. and exec. com. hdqrs. staff of Chem. Warfare Service; mem. standardization sect., purchase branch. Gen. Staff U.S. Army, etc.; hon. disch. May 1, 1919. Apptd. U.S. tariff commr. by President Wilson but declined; consultant in research and development work, Chem. Warfare Service, councillor of Internat. Union Pure and Applied Chemistry, 1926-33 and since 1937; 1st visiting Carnegie prof. of internat. relations to Czechoslovakia, 1927-28; v.p. Nat. Inst. Social Science, 1923-25; collaborator U.S. Dept. Agr., 1926-32 (chmn. advisory bd. to Color Lab. 1926-31); mem. board mgrs. N.Y. Bot. Gardens since 1927; mem. council of advisors, Fed. Union, Inc.; pres. supervisory bd., Am. Year Book Corp. Mem. Referee Bd., Chem. Industries Br., Office of Production, Research and Development, War Production Bd., 1942-45. Mem. Mil. Order Foreign Wars, Mil. Order World War. Asso. editor Jour. Am. Chem. Soc., 1924-30; mem. bd. of editors and editor trustee, Jour. Organic Chemistry since 1937; contbr. Jour. Indsl. Engring. Chemistry, Science, Jour. Am. Chem. Soc., Jour. Organic Chemistry, etc. Clubs: Megantic Fish and Game, Columbia Men's Faculty, Chemists' (hon.), Century Assn., Holland Soc. of N.Y.,

St. Nicholas Soc. of N.Y. Home: 1158 5th Av., N.Y.C. 29. Died Mar. 21, 1954; buried Flushing Cemetery, Flushing, L.I., N.Y.

BOGGS, CHARLES STUART naval officer; b. New Brunswick, N.J., Jan. 28, 1811; s. Robert Morris and Mary (Lawrence) B.; m. Sophia Dore, Dec., 4, 1832; m. 2d, Henrietta (Molt) Bull, Apr. 8, 1875. Apptd. midshipman U.S. Navy, 1826; served against North African Pirates passed midshipman, 1832; master ship-of-line North Carolina; 1836; became acting lt., 1836, lt., 1837; served on sloop Saratoga against African slave trade; participated in Mexican War; promoted comdr., 1855; participated in capture of New Orleans under David Farragut, 1862; promoted capt. for bravery; commanded steamer Connecticut, 1866; promoted rear adm., 1870; commanded steamer Connecticut, 1866; promoted rear adm. 1870 commanded European fleet, 1871-72; ret. 1 Died Apr. 22, 1888.

BOGGS, FRANK CRANSTOUN, army officer; b. Swedesboro, N.J., Mar. 16, 1874; s. George Brenton and Hannah Garrison (Thompson) B.; grad. Pub. High Sch., Norristown, Pa., 1890; grad. U.S. Mil. Acad., 1898; m. Marianne Thomson, of Norristown, Pa., June 23, 1900. Commd. 2d lt. engrs., U.S.A., Apr. 26, 1898; 1st lt., Feb. 7, 1900; capt. Apr. 23, 1904; major., Feb. 27, 1911; lt. col., Corps of Engineers U.S.A., May 15, 1917; colonel N.A., Aug. 5, 1917. Quartermaster battalion engineers and Post Willets Point, N.Y., 1898-9; local charge fortification work near Tampa, Fla., 1899-1900; with battalion engrs. and at Engr. Sch., Willets Point and Washington, D.C., 1900-2; adj. engr. battalion, Washington, D.C., and P.I., 1902-4; local charge fortification works, P.I., 1904-5; local charge constrn. dam Monongahela River, Pa., 1906-7; charge Wheeling District, engr. dept., 1907-8; gen. purchasing officer and chief Washington office, Isthmian Canal Commn. 1908-16; in charge U.S. Engring. Dist., Montgomery, Ala., 1916; in charge Engr. Depot and engr. purchasing officer at San Antonio, Tex., 1916-17; comdg. 315th Engrs., at San Antonio and in France, 1917-18; in charge engr. depots and engr. purchasing officer in France for A.E.F., 1918; duty with Gen. Staff, Washington, 1919—. Episcopalian. Mem. Am. Soc. C.E., Engrs. Club (Washington), Nat. Geog. Soc. Club: Army and Navy. Address: War Dept., Washington DC

BOGGS, ROBERT cons. med. edn.; b. Portland, Ore., Sept. 22, 1903; s. Robert William and Martha (Horton) B.; A.B., U. Ore., 1928; M.D., C.M., McGill U., 1933; m. Barbara Field, Feb. 14, 1942 (div. Feb. 1961); children-Robert, Sarah Lenox, Evelyn Marshall; m. 2d, Jane Will Teagle. Research fellow in surgery Harvard also fellow surgery Peter Bent Brigham Hosp., Boston, 1933-34; intern, asst. resident surgery N.Y. Hosp., 1934-36; pvt. practice surgery N.Y.C., 1936-39; instr. N.Y. Med. Coll., 1939-40; asst. prof. anatomy N.Y. U. Coll. Med., 1945-47, asst. dean, 1947-48; acting dean N.Y. Post-Grad. Med. Sch. (formed by consolidation of N.Y. Post-Grad. Med. Sch. and postgrad. div. N.Y. U. Coll. Medicine), 1948, dean, 1949-55; cons. med. edn., 1955-. Chmn., Nat. Com. Resettlement of Fgn. Physicians; chmn. deans com. N.Y. Vets. Hosps., 1953-55; mem. adv. com. Unitarian Service Com. Bd. dirs. Field Found. Commd. lt. (j.g.), M.C., U.S. Navy, 1936; on active duty, 1940-45; promoted comdr., 1942; served in U.S.S. Wichita, P.T.O., 1942-44; capt., 1945. Mem. N.Y. Acad. Medicine, Harvey Soc., Royal Soc. Health, Chi Psi, Alpha Kappa Kappa. Clubs: University, Piping Rock, Links, Golf, Racquet and Tennis, River, Creek, Turf and Field, Seawanhako-Corinthian Yacht; Bath and Tennis, Everglades (Palm Beach, Fla.). Home: Cleft Rd., Millneck, N.Y. Office: 203 E. 62nd St., N.Y.C. Died Oct. 1967.

BOGGS, WILLIAM ROBERTSON soldier; b. Augusta, Ga., Mar. 18, 1829; s. Archibald and Mary Ann (Robertson) B.; grad. U.S. Mil. Acad., 1853; m. Mary Sophia, d. Col. John Symington, U.S.A., Dec. 19, 1855. Mentioned in general orders by Lt. Gen. Scott during winter of 1859-60; resigned from U.S.A., 1861; served in C.S.A. from organization until disbanded in 1865; attained the rank of brig. gen.; served as chief of staff Trans.-Mississippi dept., Jan., 1863, until close of war; has followed occupations of architect, civ. engr., 1865-, and was for 5 yrs. prof. mechanics, Va. Mech. Coll. Home: Winston, N.C. Died 1911.

BOISSEVAIN, CHARLES HERCULES physician; b. Amsterdam, Holland, Oct. 18, 1893; s. Charles Ernest Henri and Maria Barbera (Pijnappel) B.; grad. Gymnasium Amsterdam, 1911; M.D., U. of Amsterdam, 1919; m. Countess Marie Theresa Zwetana von Hartenan, 1925; m. 2d Ruth Davis Dangler, 1928; children—Menso, Maria Barbera. Came to U.S. 1923; naturalized, 1930. Research asso. Institut Pasteur de Brabant, Brussels, 1921-23; visiting research prof., Colo. Coll., Colorado Springs, since 1924; lab. dir. Colo. Foundation for Research in Tuberculosis since 1924; capt. Sanitary Corps, U.S. Army. Serving as maj., U.S. Army Med. Corps; overseas since 1944. Mem. A.M.A., Soc. for exptl. Biol. and Medicine. Clubs: Cheyenne Mountain Country (Colorado Springs); University (Chicago). Home: 16 Fifth St., Broadmoor. Colorado Springs, Colo. Died Oct. 18, 1946.

BOK, CURTIS judge; b. Wyncote, Pa., Sept. 7, 1897; s. Edward and Mary Louise (Curtis) B.; student Hill Sch., Pottstown, Pa., 1910-15; student Williams Coll., 1915-17, Univ. of Va. Law Sch., 1919-21; L.H.D. (honorary), Swarthmore (Pa.) College; m. Margaret Adams Plummer, May 24, 1924; children-Margaret Welmoet, Benjamin Plummer, Derek Curtis; m. 2d, Nellie Lee Holt, Nov. 25, 1934; children-Rachel, Enid. Admitted to Pa. bar, 1921; gen. law practice, Phila., 1921-36; mem. bd. dirs. Eastern State Penitentiary, 1925-27; asst. dist. atty. Philadelphia County. 1928-32; judge Orphans Ct., Phila., 1936-37; president judge Ct. of Common Pleas No. 6, Phila. County 1937-58, associate justice Supreme Court of Pa., 1958-; dep. chief hearing commr. Nat. Prodn. Authority, 1951-53; spl. hearing officer Dept. Justice, 1951-53. Served as lt. (s.g.) U.S. Navy, 1918-19; panel mem. Nat. and 3d Regional War Labor Bds., World War II; compliance commr. and deputy chief compliance commr. War Prodn. Bd., and hearing Officer, SSS (under U.S. Atty.-Gen.), 1942-46, 1950-52. Vice-president and dir. The Curtis Inst. of Music, Phila. since 1924. Sec. of Am. delegation to Coronation of George VI, 1937. Dir. and treas. The American Foundation, Inc. Mem. Phila., Pa., and Am. Bar associations, Am. Law Institute; Delta Kappa Epsilon. Democrat. Member Society of Friends. Clubs: Ocean Cruising (England); Philadelphia, Order of the Coif, Legal. Author: Star Wormwood, The Backbone of the Herring; I, Too, Nicodemus, Maria, 1962. Home: Radnor, Pa. Office: City Hall, Phila. 19107. Died May 22, 1962; buried Radnor Meeting House, Ithan, Pa.

BOLAND, FRANK KELLS surgeon; b. Indianapolis, Ind., May 3, 1875; s. Kells Hewitt and Louise (Bright) B.; A.B., U. of Ga., 1897, Sc.D., 1926; M.D., Emory U., 1900; studied Johns Hopkins; m. Molly Horsley, Apr. 25, 1905; children—Grank Kells, Joseph Horsley. Resident Surgeon St. Joseph's Hosp., Baltimore, 1900-03; practiced at Atlanta since 1903; with Emory U. since 1903, prof. surgery, 1921-30, professor clin. surgery since 1930, prof. surgery, 1942-45; mem. board of trustees, 1937-46; prof. anatomy, Emory U. Sch. of Dentistry, 1907-19, prof. psysiology, 1919-49; visiting surgeon Grady Municipal Hosp., Emory U. Hosp. Served as lt. col. Med. O.R.C., World War; chief of surg. service, Base Hosp. No. 43 (Emory Unit), Flois, France, 1918-19; apptd. col. Med. Officers Reserve Corps. President Crawford W. Long Memorial Assn.; pres. Atlanta Hist. Soc., 1938-42; chmn. Atlanta Chapter Am. Red Cross, 1938-42; pres. Atlanta Chapter, English Speaking Union since 1942. Fellow American College Surgeons, American Surgical Association; mem. A.M.A. (vice chmn. surg. sect. 1930), Southern Surgical Assn. (v.p. 1926, pres. 1934), Am. Assn. for Thoracic Surgery, Amer. Assn. for Traumatic Surgery, Med. Assn. of Ga. (pres. 1925-26), Fulton County Med. Soc. (pres. 1921). U. of Ga. Alumni Soc. (pres. 1941-42), Southeastern Surg. Congress (pres. 1932-33). Societe Internationale de Chirurgie, Chi Phi, Phi Beta Kappa, Phi Beta Kappa Assos., Phi Chi, Omicron Delta Kappa, Alpha Omega Alpha. Citation for "distinguished service" from U. of Ga. Alumni Soc., 1940. Dem. Methodist. Clubs: Rotary, Piedmont Driving. Author: The First Anesthetic, Story of Crawford Long, 1950. Home: 252 Peachtree Circle. Office: 478 Peachtree St., Atlanta, Ga. Died Nov. 11, 1953.

BOLLES, FRANK CRANDALL, army officer (ret.); b. Elgin, Ill., Sept. 25, 1872; s. Elisha and Harriett (Crandall) B.; student Mo. Sch. of Mines, 1890, C.E., 1922; grad. U.S. Mil. Acad., 1896; distinguished grad., Army Sch. of Line, 1915; grad. General Staff Sch., 1920; also grad. Army War Coll., 1921; m. Irene H. Pettit, Jan. 14, 1909; children—Frank Crandall, Seaman P., Elizabeth L., Henrietta, Jonathan. Commd. 2d lt., U.S. Army, 1896; promoted through grades to maj. gen., 1935. Served in Spanish-Am. War, Filipino Insurrection; wounded in action, Battle of Jaro, P.I., Jan. 13, 1899, battle of Tangalan, P.I., Feb. 1900; comdr. 39th U.S. Inf., France, World War; gassed during the 2d Battle of the Marne, 1918, and wounded at Bois de Septarges, Sept. 28, 1918; comdr. 30th Inf., Presidio, San Francisco, 1925-28; comdg. gen. at Ft. D.A. Russell, Wyo., 1928-29; comdg. gen. at Ft. Stotsenburg, P.I., 1929-31; comdg. gen. at Fort Sheridan, Ill., 1931-35; comdg. gen. of Fort Sam Houston, 1935; comdg. gen. of 7th Corps Area, Omaha, Neb., 1935-36; retired; pres. Union State Bank South San Antonio, Tex., since July 19, 1937. Awarded D.S.C. for gallantry in action in battle of Jaro, P.I., 1899; citations for gallantry in action at assault of Moro position in crater at Bud Dajo; awarded D.S.C. and Oak Leaf Cluster for service in France; D.S.M. (U.S.); Croix de Guerre with Palm, and Chevalier of Legion of Honor (France); D.S.M. (State of Mo.), 1936. Mem. Am. Legion. Baptist. Mason. Elk. Clubs: Rotary, Kiwanis, Army and Navy. Sojourners. Author: Economy in Military Administration, 1928; Back to the Land, 1933. Address: 117 Geneseo Rd., San Antonio TX

BOLLING, ALEXANDER RUSSELL army officer; b. Phila., Aug. 28, 1895; s. Robert Hagedorn and Julia Campbell (Russell) B.; student U.S. Naval Acad., 1915-16; grad. Inf. Sch., 1933, Command and Gen. Staff Sch., 1935, Army War Coll., 1938; LL.D., (hon.), Westminister Coll., Dr. Sci. (hon.), University Tampa, 1954; m. Mary J. Hoyer, Nov. 27, 1917; children-Margaret Josephine (Mrs. Roderick Wetherill), Alexander Russell, Barbara Ann (Mrs. Clarence L. Thomas). Commd. 2d lt., U.S. Army, 1917, advanced through grades to lt. gen., 1952, comdr. 3d Army, Ft. McPherson, Atlanta; ret., 1955. Decorated D.S.C, D.S.M. with cluster, Silver Star, Bronze Star, Legion of Merit, Purple Heart (U.S.); Legion of Honor, Croix de Guerre with palm and silver star (France); Croix de Guerre (Belgium); Order of Orange-Nassau (Netherlands), Order of Red Banner, Order of Fatherland (Russia); War Cross (Czechoslovakia). Clubs: Army and Navy, Army and Navy Country (Washington). Home: 405 Glenwood Av., Satellite Beach, Fla. Died June 4, 1964; buried Arlington Nat. Cemetery.

BOLLING, RAYNAL CAWTHORNE lawyer; b. in Ark., 1877; A.B., Harvard, 1900, LL.B., 1902; m. Anna T. Phillips, 1907. Admitted to bar, 1902; then gen. solicitor U.S. Steel Corp.; dir. Tenn. Coal, Iron & R.R. Co.; pres. Ark. Farms Co. Apptd. head of the Aeroplane Bd., 1917; commd. maj., Aviation in France. Home: N.Y. City. Died May 1918.

BOLTON, CHESTER CASTLE congressman; b. Cleveland, O., Sept. 5, 1882; s. Charles C. and Julia (Castle) B.; A.B., Harvard, 1905; m. Frances Payne Bingham, Sept. 14, 1907; children - Charles B., Kenvon C., Oliver P. Identified with steel industry, 1905-17; mem. Ohio Senate, 1923-28; del. Rep. Nat. Conv., 1928; mem. 71st to 74th Congresses (1929-37), 22d Ohio Dist. Mem. Ohio onN.G., 1905-15; at Plattsburg Mil. Training Camp, 1916; capt. O.R.C., U.S.A., ordered to active service, Mar. 1917; with first War Industries Bd., later aide to asst. sec. of war; trans. to Gen. Staff, 1917, and took course of instrn. in officers' field training, 1918; promoted to lt. col. and apptd. asst. chief of staff, 101st Div.; hon. disch. Dec. 1918. Republican. Episcopalian. Home: Cleveland. O. Died Oct. 29, 1939.

BOLTON, WILLIAM JORDAN U.S. storekeeper, Nov. 16, 1882-; b. Norristown, Pa., Oct. 1833; s. James and Mary Ann B.; ed. Norristown public schools and Tremont Sem.; became machinist and engr.; m. Emma Rupert, Frankford, Pa., Feb. 28, 1868, now deceased. Was burgess and councilman of Norristown, Pa.; sheriff Montgomery Co.; in uniformed militia of Pa., 1855-61; pvt. to maj., capt., maj. and col. Pa. vol. inf., 1861-65; bvt. brig. gen. U.S.V., 1865; capt., col., maj. gen. Nat. Guard of Pa., 1868-78. In Civil War served in depts. of Annapolis, Md., Northeastern Va., N.C., Army of Va., Army of Potomac, 1862; dept. of Va., Army of Ohio, Mil. div. of the Mississippi, Sherman's Expeditionary Army, Mil. divs. of the Tenn. and of the Cumberland, Army of Potomac, 1864-65; Middle Mil. div., dist. of Alexandria, Va.; was mil. gov. of Alexandria, Va. In 23 battles ending at Appomattox C.H., and 25 skirmishes. Republican. Home: Philadelphia. Died 1906.

BOMAR, EDWARD EARLE newspaper corr.; b. Aiken, S.C., Nov. 4, 1897; s. Edward Earle and Nancy (Landrum) B.; A.B., Georgetown Coll., Ky., 1919; M.A., Columbia, 1923; m. Mary Rowland Carter, May 26, 1933; children—Mary Rowland, Edward Earle III. Reporter Lexington (Ky.) Herald, 1919-22, Detroit News, 1923-28; on staff Associated Press, Louisville and Baltimore (chief of bur.), 1928-31, chief at Manila, P.I., 1931-35; mem. Washington staff, 1936-42, and since 1946; major to colonel, Army of U.S., 1942-46. Served in U.S. Navy, World War I. Mem. Kappa Alpha. Baptist. Club: National Press (Washington, D.C.). Address: 3055 Foxhall Road N.W., Washington. Died Oct. 27, 1953; buried Arlington Nat. Cemetery.

BOMFORD, GEORGE army officer; b. N.Y.C., 1782; m. Miss Barlow. Apptd. cadet U.S. Army, 1804; commd. 2d lt. engrs., 1805; worked on fortifications in N.Y. Harbor and Chesapeake Bay, 1805-12; promoted 1st lt., 1806, capt., 1808, maj., 1812; assigned to ordnance dept., 1813; invented howitzer; lt. col. ordnance, 1815, col., 1832; chief ordnance U.S. Army, 1832-48; owned large estate "Kalorama" (famous meeting place of diplomats and govt. Washington, D.C.; lost - fortune when cotton mill he owned failed. Died Boston, Mar. 25, 1848.

BOND, EDWIN E. U.S.O. exec.; b. Dover, Mass., Mar. 3, 1904; s. Richard H. and Lillian (Wilson) B.; B.S., Springfield (Mass.) Coll., 1926, Dr. Humanics, 1962; m. Ruth B. Wadman, 1925; children-Barbara (Mrs. Robert Wasserman), Edwin E. Dir. religious edn. Meth. Episcopal Ch., Mamoroneck, N.Y., 1926-27; sec. Westchester and Putnam counties (N.Y.) YMCA, 1928-33, city boys' work sec., White Plains, N.Y., 1933-37, asso. state sec., Me., 1938-42; YMCA-U.S.O. supr. Southwestern, Rocky Mountain areas, 1942-43; dir. operations Mid-Pacific area U.S.O., 1943-46; exec. sec. Armed Services dept., nat. bd. YMCA, 1946-50; exec. dir. Asso. Services for Armed Forces, Inc., 1950-51; bd. govs., mem. exec. com., exec. dir. U.S.O., Inc., N.Y.C., 1951-. Mem. city council, Waterville, lMe., 1941-42. Pres. corp., trustee Springfield Coll. Mem. Nat. Conf. Social Welfare, Assn. YMCA Secs. Presbyn. Club: University (N.Y.C.). Home: Blind Brook Lodge, Rye, N.Y. Office: U.S.O., Inc., 237 E. 42nd St., N.Y.C. 10022. Died Nov. 2, 1966; buried Dover, Mass.

BONDURANT, EUGENE DUBOSE, physician; b. near Greensboro, Ala., Jan. 26, 1862; s. James William and Evelyn (DuBose) B.; student Avery Sch. and Southern U., Greensboro; M.D., U. of Va., 1883; grad. study Heidelberg and Vienna, 1890-91, Edinburgh and London, 1911; m. Annie Laurie Prince, Apr. 19, 1899. Asst. physician, Manhattan Hosp., N.Y. City, 1884-85; asst. phys., Bryce Hosp., Tucaloosa, Ala., 1886-90, asst. supt., 1892-97; prof. nervous and mental diseases, U. of Ala. Sch. of Medicine, 1897-1915, dean, 1911-15; one of condrs. of Inge-Bondurant Sanatorium, Mobile, Ala. Served as maj., later lt. col., Med. Corps., U.S. Army, comdg. officer Gen. Hosp., Dansville, N.Y., 1917-19; col. Med. Res. Corps, U.S. Army, since 1925. Trustee Ala. Insane Hosp. 20 yrs. Fellow A.A.A.S.; mem. A.M.A., Am. Psychiatric Assn., Am. Neurol. Assn., Med. Assn. State of Ala., Kappa Alpha (Southern). Democrat. Episcopalian. Clubs: Athelstan, Mobile Country, Alba Hunting and Fishing. Assn. editor and contbr. to Sajous' Analytic Cyclopedia of Practical Medicine; also contbr. to medical journals. Home: 1600 Government St., Mobile AL

BONESTEEL, CHARLES HARTWELL army officer; b. Ft. Sidney, Neb., Apr. 9, 1885; s. Charles Hartwell and Mary (Greene) B.; B.S., U.S. Mil. Acad., 1908; postgrad. Inf. Sch., 1924-25, Command and Gen. Staff Sch., 1925-26, Army War Coll., 1931-32: m. Caroline Standish Hudson, Dec. 29, 1908; children-Charles Hartwell III, Eleanor Mead (Mrs. N. O. Ohman). Cadet U.S. Mil. Acad., 1904; commd. 2d lt. col., 1932, col., 1937, brig. gen. U.S. Army, 1940, maj. gen., 1946; comdr. U.S. troops in Iceland, 1941-43; ret., 1947. Decorated D.S.M., Bronze Star, Legion of Merit, companion Bath, Legion of Honor. Address: 3133 Connecticut Av. N.W., Washington. Died June 5, 1964; buried Arlington Nat. Cemetery.

BONHAM, MILLEDGE LUKE gov. S.C., congressman, b. Red Bank, Mass., Dec. 25, 1813; s. James and Sophie (Smith) B.; grad. S.C. Coll., 1834; m. Ann Griffin, Nov. 13, 1845. Mem. S.C. Legislature, 1840-44; commd. col. 12th Inf., U.S. Army, 1846; elected solicitor So. dist. S.C., 1848-57; mem. U.S. Ho. of Reps. from S.C. (states rights Democrat), 35th-36th congresses, 1857-60; commd. brig. gen. Confederate Army, reapptd. brig. gen. cavalry, 1865; confederate gov. S.C., 1862; apptd. S.C. railroad commr. to reorganize wrecked railroad system, 1878. Died White Sulphur Springs, Va., Aug. 27, 1890.

BONNER, JOHN WOODROW, gov. Mont.; b. Butte, Mont., July 16, 1902; s. Patrick and Kathleen (Kelly) B.; A.B., LL.B., U. Mont., 1928; m. Josephine Martin, Feb. 3, 1929; children—Jacqueline, Josephine, Patricia, Wilma Jean, Thomas John. Teacher athletic dir. Mont. pub. schs., 1921-23; admitted to Mont. bar, 1928, practicing in Butte, 1928-29; atty. State Highway Commn., 1929-36; atty. and sec. State Bd. Railroad Commn., Pub. Service Commn.; Mont. Trade Commn., 1936-40; elected atty. gen. of Mont., Jan. 5, 1941; elected gov. Mont. 1949-53; asso. justice Mont. Supreme Ct., 1968-70. Commd. major, Judge Advocate General's Dept. U.S. Army Reserve; lt. colonel; assigned as Staff Judge Advocate 104th Inf. Div.; maj. J.A.G.D. Res., May, 1942; served as exec. officer, asst. staff judge adv., acting staff judge dv. 1st U.S. Army. Apptd. chief of War Crimes 1st Army, Apr. 1945; discharged with rank of col., Dec. 10, 1945. Former mem. Bd. of Edn., Mont.; former sec.-treas. State Democratic Central Com.; former chmn. Lewis and Clark County Democratic Central Com.; past pres. Mont. Law Sch. Alumni Assn., State Reserve Officers Assn., Lewis and Clark County Chapter Reserve Officers Assn. Past State Comdr. Vets. Fgn. Wars of U.S. (1947-48). Mem. Lewis and Clark Bar Assn., Mont. Bar Assn. (past pres.), Phi Delta Phi, Sigma Phi, Epsilon; former ex-officio mem. Am. Law Inst. Democrat. Roman Catholic. Elk, Eagle. Author: Handbook on Eminent Domain, 1933. Home: Helena MT Died Mar. 28, 1970; buried Arlington Nat. Cemetery, Arlington VA

BONNER, JOSEPH CLAYBAUGH banker; b. at Chillicothe, O., July 13, 1855; s. James Taylor and Anna McCord (Carson) B.; ed. Chillicothe Acad. and High Sch.; m. Nelly Turney Bell, of Chillicothe, Nov. 4, 1878. Established and pres., Ames-Bonner & Co., mfrs. brushes and mirrors, 1880; pres. Renick Bonner Farm Co.; member firm of Bonner & Co., bankers. Mem. O.N.G. 9 yrs.; col. on staff under Gov. William McKinley, 1891-95; col. provisional regt., Ohio, Spanish-Am. War. U.S. collector of customs, Toledo, 1900-10; chmn. Rep. State Central Com., Ohio, 1892-95; mem. Rep. Nat. Finance Com., 1908. Chmn. Toledo Civic Federation, 1910-16; pres. Toledo Stock Exchange, 1903-16. Inventor the Bonner Rail Wagon. Presbyn. Mem. S.R., Ohio Soc. (New York). Clubs: Toledo, Toledo Commerce. Home: Miltimore Apts. Office: 8 Spitzer Arcade, Toledo, O.

BONNER, PAUL HYDE, author; b. Bklyn., Feb. 14, 1893; s. Paul Edward and Theodora Wilson (Hall) B.; student Adelphi Acad., Bklyn., Poly. Prep. Sch., Bklyn., Phillips Exeter Acad.; student Harvard, 1915; m. Lilly M. Stehli, Apr. 30, 1917 (dec. Jan. 1962);children—Paul Hyde, John Tyler, Henry Stehli, Anthony Edmonde; m. 2d, Elizabeth McGowan, Jan. 10, 1963. Vice pres., gen. mgr., dir. Stehli & Co., Inc., textile mchts., 1919-31; central field commr. Office Fgn. Liquidation, State Dept., 1946; spl. adviser U.S. ambassador to Rome on economics of peace treaty, 1947-51. Served as 2d lt. U.S. Army, 1917-19; from maj. to col., USAAF, 1941-46. Episcopalian. Clubs: Union, The Brook (N.Y.C.); The Travellers (Paris); Rotary (Sommerville, S.C.). Author: S.P.Q.R., 1954; Hotel Talleyrand; Excelsior; The Glorious Morning; With Both Eyes Open; Aged in the Woods; Amanda; The Art of Llewellyn Jones, 1959; Ambassador Extraordinary, 1962. Home: Charleston SC Died Dec. 15, 1968.

BONSAL, STEPHEN newspaper corr., writer; b. Baltimore, Mar. 29, 1865; s. Stephen and Frances (Leigh) B.; ed. at St. Paul's Sch. Concord, N.H., also studied Heidelberg, Bonn and Vienna; m. Henrietta Fairfax Morris, Mar. 1900. Was spl. corr. of the New York Herald in the Bulgarian-Servian War, 1885; In Morocco, 1889. Macedonian uprising, 1890. Chino-Japanese War, 1895; traveled through Siberia, 1896; Cuban insurrection, 1897, Spanish-Am. War; China relief expdn., 1900; Samar, Batangas and Mindanao (P.I.) campaigns, 1901; in Venezuela during Matos revolution and blockade by the powers, 1903; upon outbreak of Russo-Japanese War, 1904, traveled for New York Herald 6 months in the Balkans, Albania, Macedonia, Montenegro, etc.; in Russia during the Revolutionary troubles of 1907; visited all the West Indies and parts of S.A., 1908; in Mexico during the Madero revolution, 1910-11, for New York Times. In U.S. diplomatic service as sec. of legation and charge d'affaires in Peking, Madrid, Tokio and Korea, 1893-97. Apptd. sec. to the governor-gen., P.I., Sept. 1913; commr. Public Utilities, P.I., 1914; spl. mission in Mexico, 1915; with Hindenburg's army on east front, 1915; adviser Am.-Mexican Joint Commn., 1916-17; maj. Nat. Army, 1917 and on duty War Coll., Washington; with A.E.F. in France, 1918; Am. rep. Congress Oppressed Nationalties, Paris, Sept. 1918; lt. col. inf., attached Am. mission to Peace Conf. after armistice; Am. mem. inter-allied mission to Austro-Hungary and Balkan States under General Smuts and spl. mission to Germany and Bohemia, 1919. Traveled 10,000 miles in Soviet Russia, 1931, and in 1934, across North China and Manchukuo. Clubs: Century, Knickerbocker (New York); Metropolitan (Washington). Frequent contbr. sketches and short stories to mags. Author: Morocco as It is., 1892; The Real Condition of Cuba, 1897; The Fight for Santiago, 1899; The Golden Horse Shoe, 1900; The American Mediterranean, 1912; Heyday in a Vanished World, 1927; Unfinished Business, Paris-Versailes, 1919 (awarded Pulitzer Prize), 1944; When The French Were Here, 1915; Suitors and Suppliants; The Lesser Nations at Versailles, 1946. Address: 3142 P St. N.W. Washington. Died June 8, 1951.

BOOK, GEORGE MILTON rear adm. U.S.N.; b. New Castle, Pa., May 25, 1845; s. Col. William and Ann (Emery) B.; apptd. from Pa., and grad. U.S. Naval Acad., 1865; m. Mary Sippy, May 7, 1867. Promoted ensign, Dec. 1, 1866; master, Mar. 12, 1868; lt. Mar. 26, 1869; lt. comdr., May 28, 1881; comdr., Dec. 16, 1891; capt., Mar. 29, 1899; retired for incapacity resulting from an incident of service, with rank of rear adm., Mar. 8, 1900. In summer of 1864, on board the Marblehead, in pursuit of the Confederate steamers Florida and Tallahassee; served Dakotah, 1865, Rhode Island, 1866, Mackinaw, 1866-67; Portsmouth, 1867-68, receiving-ship at Norfolk, 1868-69, Seminole and Benicia, 1869, Swatara, 1870; retired, 1871, but restored to active list, 1875; various assignments to 1896; comd. Marion, 1897; Navy Yard, Mare Island, 1897; comd. Mohican, 1898; Adams, 1898-99. Died Jan. 22, 1921.

BOOTH, EWING E. army officer; b. Bower Mills, Mo., Feb. 28, 1870; s. Nathaniel and Martha B.; honor graduate Infantry and Cavalry Schools, 1903; graduate Army Staff College, 1905; married (wife died Jan. 1943); 1 dau. Gladys (Mrs. P. L. Thomas). Captain 1st Colorado Volunteer Infantry, May 1, 1898; hon. discharge, July 14, 1899; capt. 36th U.S. Inf., July 5, 1899; hon. mustered out, Mar. 16, 1901; 1st lt. 7th Cav., U.S. Army, Feb. 2, 1901; capt. 10th Cav., Aug. 22, 1904; trans. to 7th Cav., May 11, 1905; a.d.c. to Maj. Gen. J. F. Bell, 1912-15; assigned to 1st Cav. Oct. 4, 1915; maj., May 15, 1917; brig. gen. N.A., June 26, 1918; col. cav. U.S. Army, July 1, 1920; brig. gen., July 21, 1924; major gen., Dec. 23, 1929. Served as chief of staff Eastern Dept., June-Aug., 1917; Chief of staff 77th N.A. Div., Aug 5, 1917-June 25, 1918; commanded 8th Brigade, 4th Div. of regular army, June 25, 1918-January 10, 1919. Participated in French sector activities, May, June and July, 1918; 2d Marne offensive, July and Aug. 1918; St. Mihiel salient offensive, Sept. 1918; Meuse-Argonne offensive, Sept. and Oct. 1918; with Army of Occupation, Germany, Nov. 18, 1918-Jan. 10, 1919; asst. chief of staff, G.I. Service of Supply, Jan. 15-June 20, 1919; chief of staff S.O.S., and chief of staff Am. Forces in France, June 21, 1919-Jan 8, 1920; dep. Allied high commr. to Armenia, Jan. 5-June 30, 1920; asst. comdt. Gen Service Sch., Aug. 1, 1920-June 30, 1921; dir. Gen. Service Schs., 1921-23; instr. War Coll., 1923-24; comd. 4th Cav. and 1st Cav. Brigade on Mexican border, 1924-25; comdt. Cav. Sch., Ft. Riley, Kan., 1925-27; asst. chief of staff, G-4, War Dept., 1927-30; deputy chief of staff, Oct. 12-Dec. 21, 1930; comdg. 1st Cavalry Div., Apr. 27, 1931-Jan. 31, 1932; comdg. Philippines Dept., R.I., Apr. 9, 1932-Sept. 7, 1933; retired, Feb. 28, 1934. Commended for action on the Vesle; cited with 7th and 8th brigades for service in the Bois de Fays; decorated D.S.M. (U.S.); Croix de Guerre and Legion of Honor (French); Philippine Congressional medal; Spanish-Am. War medal; Philippine Insurrection medal; Cuban Occupation medal; Mexican border medal; World War with 4 stars; also by Panama. Address: 4707 Harrison St., Chevy Chase, Md. Died Feb. 19, 1949; buried Arlington National Cemetery, Washington.

BOOTH, ROBERT HIGHMAN, army officer; b. Washington, Feb. 20, 1905; B.S., U.S. Mil. Acad., 1930; m. Constance May Ralston; children—Constance R., Barbara L., Robert Highman. Commd. lt. U.S. Army, 1930, and advanced through grades to maj. gen., 1956; chief Def. Atomic Support Agy., Washington. Home: Ft George G Meade MD Died 1972.

BOOTH, WALTER congressman, mfr.; b. Woodbridge, Conn., Dec. 8, 1791; attended public schs. Settled in Meriden, New Haven County, Conn., became mfr.; col. 10th Regt., 2d Battalion of Militia, 1825-27, brig. gen., 1827, 28, maj. gen. 1st Div., 1831-34; judge county court, 1834; mem. Conn. Ho. of Reps., 1838; mem. U.S. Ho. of Reps. (Free-Soiler) from Conn., 31st Congress, 1849-51. Died Meriden, Apr. 30, 1870; buried East Cemetery.

BOOTHBY, WALTER MEREDITH medical research; b. Boston, Mass., July 28, 1880; s. Alonzo and Marie Adelaide (Stodder) B.; student Boston U. Sch. of Medicine, 1901-05; A.B., Harvard Coll., 1902; M.D. Harvard U. Med. Sch., 1906; M.A., Harvard Grad. Sch., 1907; m. Catharine Burns, Nov. 15, 1930; children (by previous marriage) - Gertrude (Mrs. Louis Schulze), Nancy (Mrs. Robert Reinhardt). Interne and house surgeon Boston City Hosp., 1908-09; practiced surgery in Boston, 1909-16; in charge metabolism and respiration labs., Peter Bent Brigham Hosp., 1913-26; instr. in anatomy, Harvard Med. Sch., 1910-16; also lecturer on anesthesia, 1914-16; head of sect. of metabolic research, Mayo Clinic, 1916—; asst. in medicine, Mayo Foundation, 1917-23, asso. prof. in medicine, 1923-26; prof. exptl. metabolism, 1936-48, emeritus professor, 1948—; chmn. Mayo Aero Med. Unit for Research in Aviation Med., 1942-48; guest prof. aviation medicine, Institute of Physiology, Air U., Randolph Field, U.S. Air Force, Texas, 1950-51; Lovelace Found. for Med. research, 1951—. head of dept. of respiratory physiology. Served with A.R.C. Ambulance Hospital, Paris, summer 1915; capt., later major, Med. Corps, U.S. Army, with A.E.F. in France, 22 months; assigned as dir. 1st Corps Gas Sch., Chem. Warfare Service; later instr. Army Med. Sch. Lange, France; at front as chief of surgical team in battles of St. Mihiel and Argonne. President Roosevelt made personal award of Collier Trophy for 1938 to Dr. Walter M. Boothby and Dr. William Randolph Lace II (both of Mayo Foundation) for med. end., and research and to Capt. Harry L. Armstrong, M.C., U.S. Army, for mutual contribution to aviation medicine in general and pilot fatigue in particular; certificate of merit, U. Minn., 1949; awarded order Comdr. of North Star by King of Sweden, 1952. Fellow A.C.S., A.C.P.; mem. A.M.A., Am. Physiol. Soc., Am. Soc. Biol. Chemists, American Soc. for Clin. Investigation, Soc. for Exptl. Biology and Medicine, Assn. Am. Physicians, Am. Inst. Nutrition, Am. Soc. for Exptl. Pathology, Am. Soc. for Pharmacology and Exptl. Therapy, Am. Soc. Anesthetists, Aero Med. Assn. of U.S., Inst. Aeronautical Sciences, Nat. Aeronautic Assn., Mass. Med. Soc., Alumni Assn. of Mayo Foundation, Minn. State Med. Assn., U.S. Inf. Assn., Sigma Xi. Democrat (liberal). Protestant. Author of 300 sci. papers on respiration, metabolism, thyriod diseases, aviation medicine. Home: 2819 Ridgecrest Dr. Office: Lovelace Found., Albuquerque, N.M. Died July 4, 1953.

BOOZ, EDWIN GEORGE management consultant, engr.; b. Reading, Pa., Sept. 2, 1887; s. Thomas H. and Sarah (Spencer) B.; A.B., Northwestern U., 1912, A.M., 1914; m. Helen M. Hootman, Aug. 9, 1918; children—Donald Robert, Marion Elizabeth McGee. Founder, 1914, and now sr. partner Booz, Allen & Hamilton, management cons., Chicago, N.Y.City, San Francisco, Washington, Minneapolis, Los Angeles; clients include U.S. Gypsum Co., Montgomery Ward & Co., Electric Bond & Share, Western Union Telegraph, University of Chicago, R.C.A., Republic Aviation Corp., General Foods, S.C. Johnson & Son, Inc., Kinberly-Clark, General Mills, Schenley Distillers Corp., Columbia Pictures Corp., Sperry Corp., Standard Oil (Indiana), Inc., Bigelow-Sanford Island Creek Coal, Weyerhaeuser Timber Company; firm conducts surveys for bus. and instnl. managements. Enlisted as pvt. 333d F.A., U.S. Army, 1917; and commd. lt. after 4 months; 18 months service as major Inspector General's Dept.; assigned to special staff on bus. orgn., sec. of war. Mem. Assn. Cons. Management engrs. (past pres.), Alpha Delta Phi, Presbyn. Mason (32ff). Clubs: Chicago, Union League, Attic, Executives (Chicago); Glen View Gold (Golf, Ill); Metropolitan (Washington); University (N.Y.C.); Calif. Institute Associates, California (Los Angeles); Tennis, Committee of 25, Thunderbird Country (Palm Springs). Home: 931 Pontiac Rd., Wilmette, Ill. Office: 135 S. LaSalle St., Chgo. Died Oct. 14, 1951.

BORAH, WAYNE G. judge; b. Baldwin, La., Apr. 28, 1891; s. Charles Frank and Fannie (Thomas) B.; student Phillips Exeter Acad., 1908-10, Washington and Lee U., also U. Va., 1910-13; LL.B., La. State U., 1915; m. Elizabeth Pipes, Apr. 25, 1936. Admitted to La. bar, 1915, began practice, New Orleans; mem. firm Borah, Himel, Block & Borah, 1915-23; asst. Asst. U.S. atty. Eastern dist. Ct., Eastern Dist. La., 1928-49; judge U.S. Ct. Appeals 5th Circuit, 1949-. Served as student officer, later capt., inf. U.S. Army, 1917-18. Mem. Sigma Alpha Epsilon; hon. mem. Phi Delta Phi, Phi Kappa Phi. Republican. Episcopalian. Clubs: Boston, New Orleans Country. Home: 1238 Philip St. Chambers: Post Office Bldg., New Orleans, La. Died Feb. 6, 1966.

BORDEN, GEORGE PENNINGTON brig. gen.; b. Ft. Wayne, Ind., Apr. 24, 1844; s. James W. and Emeline (Griswold) B.; ed. pub. schs. and Fairfield Acad., N.Y., to 1862; m. Elizabeth Reynold, May 25, 1869. Enlisted as pvt. Co. C, 121st N.Y. Vol. Inf., July 23, 1862; disch. Oct. 12, 1863; cadet U. S. Mil. Acad., Sept. 16, 1863-Jan. 23, 1864; apptd. from Ind., 2d lt., 5th U.S. Inf., Oct. 1, 1866; 1st lt., Sept. 4, 1878; capt., Feb. 20, 1891; maj. 3d Inf., Sept. 8, 1899; transferred to 5th Inf., Nov. 3, 1899; lt. col. 2d Inf., Nov. 28, 1902; transferred to 5th Inf., Dec. 24, 1902; col. 24th Inf., Apr. 14, 1905; brig. gen. and retired, Jan. 1, 1907. Home: New York, N.Y. Died Apr. 26, 1925.

BORDEN, JOHN explorer, lawyer; b. N.Y.C., May 21, 1884; s. William and Mary (Whiting) B.; B.A., Yale, 1906; student Yale and Northwestern law schs.; m. 3d, Frances Yeaton, July 20, 1933. Admitted to Ill. bar, 1908; founder Yellow Cab Co.; organizer Old Dutch Refinery, nr. Muskegon. Served as lt. comdr. U.S.N.R.F., 1917-19. Decorated Navy Cross. Expdns. to Alaska and Arctic in 1913, 16, 27. Mem. Arctic Brotherhood, Phi Beta Kappa, D.K.E. Home: West Spring Lake, Mich. Office: 105 W. Monroe St., Chgo. Died July 1961; buried West Spring Lake.

BORDEN, WILLIAM CLINE surgeon; b. Watertown, N.Y., May 19, 1858; s. Daniel J. and Mary L. (Cline) B.; ed. Adams (N.Y.) Collegiate Inst.; M.D., Columbian (Now George Washington) U., 1883, Sc.D., 1931; m. Jennie E. Adams, Oct. 27, 1883; children—Daniel Le Ray, William Ayres. Apptd. 1st lt. asst. surgeon U.S.A., Dec. 3, 1883; capt., Dec. 3, 1888; maj. brigade surgeon vols., June 4, 1898-Mar. 31, 1899; maj. surgeon, Feb. 2, 1901; lt. col. and retired, 1909. Comd. Gen. Hosp., Key West, Fla., during Spanish-Am. War; Gen. Hosp., Washington, 1898-1907; also prof. mil. surgery, Army Med. Sch., and prof. surg. pathology and mil. surgery, Georgetown U., 1898-1907; comd. div. hosp. Manila, 1908; prof. surgery, and dean med. dept., George Washington U. and surgeon in chief George Washington U. Hosp., 1909-June 1931. Returned to active service for war as chief of surg. service Walter Reed Army Gen. Hosp., 1917-19. Mem. Med. Soc., Surg. Soc., Med. Hist. Soc. D.C., A.M.A., S.A.R. (N.Y. chap.); a founder and fellow American Coll. Surgeons. Clubs: Chevy Chase, Army and Navy (Washington); Crescent Yacht (Watertown, N.Y.). Author: Use of the Rontgen Ray by the Medical Department of the United States in the War with Spain, 1898 (published by joint resolution of Congress). 1900. Also several secs. in standard surg. works and many med. monographs and articles. Home: 2306 Tracy Pl., Washington. Died Sept. 29, 1934.

BORIE, ADOLPH EDWARD sec. of navy; b. Phila., Nov. 25, 1809; s. John Joseph and Sophia (Beauveau) B.; grad. U. Pa., 1825; m. Elizabeth Dundas McKean, 1839. Became partner in father's mercantile business, 1828, engaged primarily in silk and tea trade with Far East; consul to Belgium, apptd. U.S. sec. of navy by Pres. Grant, 1869; apptd. U.S. sec. of navy by Pres. Grant, 1869; accompanied Grant on his world tour, 1878-79. Died Phila., Feb. 5, 1880.

BORLAND, SOLON diplomat, senator, army officer; b. Suffolk, Va., Sept. 21, 1808; studied medicine, N.C.; m. Mrs. Huldah Wright; m. 2d, Mrs. Hunt; m. 3d, Mary Melbourne; 3 sons, 2 daus. Practiced medicine, Little Rock, Ark., circa 1832-46, 54-61; served as volunteer in Mexican War, 1846-47; mem. U.S. Senate (Democrat) from Ark., Mar. 30, 1848-Apr. 3, 1853; U.S. minister to Nicaragua and C. Am., including Honduras, 1853-54, involved in controversy in Greytown (Nicaragua) over right of Nicaragua to arrest Am. citizen, resulted in U.S. bombardment of Greytown because of insults to him as U.S. rep.; organized, col. 3d Ark. Calvary, Confederate Army, 1861; served in campaigns in Miss. and in Battle of Port Hudson; promoted brig. gen. Confederate Army. Died nr. Houston, Tex., Jan 1, 1864; buried City Cemetery, Houston.

BOSCH, HERBERT MICHAEL engineer; b. Jefferson City, Mo., Mar. 31, 1907; s. Herman and Katherine (Buehrle) B.; B.S., U. Mo., 1929; Master Pub. Health Sch. Pub. Health Johns Hopkins U., 1940; m. Jeanette E. Heinrich, Aug. 17, 1931. Tech. and administrative staff Mo. State Bd. Health, 1929-35, Minn. Dept. Health, 1935-41, 46-50; chief environmental sanitation sect. WHO, U.N., Geneva, Switzerland, 1950-52, mem. panel experts on environmental sanitation, 1952-; prof. environmental health School of Public Health, U. Minn. Mem. Minnesota Bd. Health, 1952-, v.p., 1954-. Mem. Mo. State Planning Bd., 1933-35; mem. com. on san. engring. and environment Nat. Research Council. Cons. san. engring. Surgeon Gen. Dept. Army, 1947-, WHO (govts. Jugoslavia, Finland) 1952, ECA (Brazil), 1954, ICA (Brazil), 1955-56, WHO (Eastern Mediterranean Region), 1956; cons. USPHS, ICA, WHO (Japan) 1957, Pan Am. Health Orgn., 1959; mem. Commn. Environmental Health Study Team to USSR, 1962. Served as 1st lt. to col. San. and Gen. Staff Corps, U.S. Army, 1941-46. Decorated Bronze Star Medal with oak leaf cluster, Legion of Merit (U.S.); Legion of Honor, Croix de Guerre with Palm (France); Commander Order Orange-Nassau (Holland); Croix de Guerre with Palm (Belgium); recipient medal for distinguished service in engring. U. Mo. Fellow Royal Sanitary Institute, London (hon.), Am. Pub. Health Association (governing council 1949, 57-); mem. Am. Soc. C.E., National, Minn. soc. profl. engrs., A.A.A.S., Am. Water Works Assn., Am. Assn. U. Profs., Central States Sewage and Indsl. Waste Assn., Minn. Acad. Sci., Nat. Research Council (exec. com. Div. Med. Scis. 1960-61), New York Academy of Sciences, also Sigma Xi, Tau Beta Pi, Delta Omega. Club: Campus (Mpls.). Home: 315 11th Av. S.E., Mpls. 55414. Office: care Sch. Pub. Health, U. Minn., Mpls. 55414. Died Sept. 16, 1962; buried Nat. Cemetery, Jefferson City, Mo.

BOSTWICK, FRANK MATTESON naval officer; b. Janesville, Wisc., Apr. 13, 1857; s. Joseph Morton and Harriet Maria (Allen) B.; grad. U.S. Naval Acad., 1877; m. Elvira (Gregg) Hartwell, Aug. 14, 1879. Promoted through the various grades to capt., 1909; retired at own request, with rank of commodore, June 30, 1910. Served on Pacific sta. and Navy Yard, Mare Island, Cal., 1877-86; Asiatic sta., 1886-89; on bd. U.S.S. Charleston during Spanish-Am. war 1898; on Charleston, Bennington and Marietta, Philippine sta., 1898-1901; navigator and later 1st lt., Oregon Mar.-Oct., 1901; comdg. Nipsic, Oct., 1901-May 1904, Philadelphia, May-Aug., 1904; Eagle, Sept. 1904-Sept. 1906; lighthouse insp., 10th dist., Sept. 1906-June 1908; comd. Buffalo, June 1908-Apr., 1909; capt. of yard, Navy Yard, Portsmouth, N.H., June 1909-July 1910. Received Spanish and Philippine campaign medals. Episcopalian. Club: University (Buffalo). Address: Care Franklin Nat. Bank, Philadelphia, Pa. Died Dec. 20, 1945.

BOSTWICK, LUCIUS ALLYN naval officer; b. Providence, R.I., Feb. 21, 1869; s. David S. and J. Anna (Tripp) B.; grad. U.S. Naval Acad., 1890; m. Mary S. Wolfer, Sept. 27, 1897. Promoted ensign, July 1, 1892, and advanced through grades to comdr., Mar. 4, 1911; capt., Aug. 28, 1916; rear admiral, June 8, 1923; vice admiral, May 21, 1929; returned to rank of rear admiral, May 21, 1930. Served on Oregon, Spanish-American War, 1898; various assignments to 1914; mem. Gen. Bd., Navy Dept., 1914-17; comdg. South Dakota, Apr. 5, 1917-Sept. 17, 1918, New Mexico, Sept. 27, 1918-May 10, 1919; sr. mem. Naval Overseas Transportation Service Demobilization Bd., New York, May 10-Sept. 19, 1919; duty with office chief of naval operations, Navy Dept., 1919; comdr. U.S.S. California, 1922-23; chief of staff, Battle Fleet, 1923-25; chief of staff, U.S. Fleet, 1925-26; pres. Bd. of Inspection and Survey, Navy Dept., 1926-28; comdr. battleship divs., Battle Fleet, 1929-30; comdt. U.S. Navy Yard, Phila., and 4th Naval Dist., 1930 - . Episcopalian. Died Jan. 14, 1940.

BOTTOM, RAYMOND BLANTON newspaper pub.; b. Richmond, Va., Sept. 8, 1893; s. Davis and Ella Virginia (Alley) B.; ed. pvt. and pub. schs., Richmond, Va., and various service schs. of U.S. Army; m. Dorothy E. Rouse, July 2, 1925; children—Barbara Agens (Mrs. Miles D. Forst), Dorothy Evelyn (Mrs. Langdon B. Gilkey), Raymond Blanton. Rodman, instrumentman and chief of surveying party in railroad location and construction, 1911-17; newspaper publisher, 1931—; pres. and business mgr. Daily Press Inc.; president, Southern Colorprint Corporation; pres. Hampton Roads Broadcasting Corp., 1931—; pres. Peninsula Industrial Finance Corporation; director Citizens Marine Jefferson Bank. Member bd. trustees Virginia War Memorial Museum. Commd. 2d lt., promoted 1st lt., later capt., C.A.C., U.S. Army, 1917-31; aerial observer, U.S. Army Air Corps, France and Germany, 1918-19, with 24th and 50th Aero Squadrons; lt. comdr. (D-VS), U.S.N.R., 1942-44. Chmn. Hampton Roads Regional Defense Council, 1940-42. Decorated Victory and Army of Occupation (Germany) medals. Member Military Staff, Governor of Virginia. Member Va. State Chamber of Commerce (director), American Newspaper Publishers Association, Sigma Delta Chi frat. Clubs: James River Country (Newport News); Yacht (Hampton, Va.); Commonwealth (Richmond); National Press (Washington). Home: 103 Powhatan Parkway, Indian River Park, Hampton, Va. Office: 215 25th St., Newport News, Va. Died Oct. 29, 1953; buried Greenlawn Cemetery, Newport News.

BOUDE, THOMAS congressman, lumber exec., b. Lancaster, Pa., May 17, 1752; attended pvt. schs. Served as lt. under Gen. Anthony Wayne with 2d, 4th, 5th Pa. battalions in Revolutionary War, 1776-83; promoted capt., brevetted maj.; lumber dealer, Columbia, Pa.; mem., an organizer Soc. of Cincinnati; mem. Pa. Ho. of Reps., 1794-96; mem. U.S. Ho. of Reps. (Federalist) from Pa., 7th Congress, 1801-03. Died Columbia, Oct. 24, 1822; buried Brick Graveyard of Mt. Bethel Cemetery.

BOUDINOT, ELIAS Continental congressman; b. Phila., May 2, 1740; s. Elias III and Catherine (Williams) B.; LL.D., Yale, 1790; m. Hannah Stockton, Apr. 21, 1762. Licensed counselor and atty. at law, 1760; sgt. at law, 1770; trustee Coll. of N.J. (now Princeton), 1772-1821; mem. N.J. Com. of Safety, 1775; commissary gen. of prisoners Continental Army, 1776-79; mem. N.J. Provincial Congress; del. from N.J. to Continental Congress, 1777-84, pres., 1782-83, signed peace treaty with Gt. Britain, alliance treaty with France, sec. fgn. affairs com., 1783-84; dir. U.S. Mint, 1795-1805; mem. N.J. Conv. which ratified U.S. Constn.; mem. U.S. Ho. of Reps. from N.J., 1st-3d congresses, 1789-95; 1st pres. Am. Bible Assn., 1816-21. Died Burlington, N.J., Oct. 24, 1821.

BOUDINOT, TRUMAN EVERETT army officer; b. Hamilton, Ia., Sept. 2, 1895; s. George Arthur and Eva Margaret (Tower) B.; grad. Cav. Sch. troop officers course, 1920, Inf. Sch. advanced course, 1928, Command and Gen. Staff Sch., 1937; m. Lolita Margaret Sargent, June 1, 1922; children—Truman Everett (cadet U.S. Mil. Acad.), Burton Sargent. Commd. 2d lt., U.S. Army, 1917, advancing through the grades to brig. gen., 1944; serving in European Theater of Operation since 1943; comdg. C.C.B., 3d Armored Div., in Normandy, France, Belgium and Germany, since July 1944. Decorated Mexican Service Medal (1918), World War I and Defense Service medals, European Theater Service Medal with 3 bronze stars, Legion of Merit, Silver Star with 2 oak leaf clusters, Distinguished Service Medal (posthumously) (U.S.), Chevalier Legion of Honor, Croix de Guerre with palms (France). Mem. Heroes of '76, Theta Xi, Mason, Sojourner. Home: 308 South Doheny Dr., Beverly Hills, Calif. Address: care The Adjutant General's Office, War Dept., Washington 25. Died Dec. 21, 1945; buried in Arlington National Cemetery.

BOUQUET, HENRY army officer; b. Rolle, Switzerland, 1719. Lt. col. 1st battalion Royal Am. Regt., 1755; came to Am., 1756; center of Phila. quartering dispute, 1756; served as col. on Ft. Duquesne expdn., 1758; naturalized by Md., also by Supreme Ct. of Pa., 1762; served in French and Indian Wars, 1756-63; leader Bouquet's Expdn., 1763-65, ordered to relief of Ft. Pitt, defeated Indian attack, 1763, returned to Muskingum River, 1765, negotiated peace treaty with Shawnee and Delaware Indians, thus ending Indian rebellion. on Pa. border; commd. brig. Brit. Army, 1765 contbd. to crushing of Pontiac Indian rebellion. Died Pensacola, Fla., Sept. 2, 1765.

BOURNE, NEHEMIAH ship builder, naval officer; b. London, Eng., circa 1611; s. Robert and Mary Bourne. Came to Am., 1638, settled in Charlestown, Mass., later engaged in shipbuilding, merc. pursuits, Boston; constructed ship Trial for Gov. Winthrop (1st ship built in Boston), 1641; returned to Eng., circa 1645, became rear adm. in Parliamentary Navy, supervised fitting out and supplying of ships of Parliamentary fleet. Died Eng., Feb. 1691; buried Bunhill Fields, Enbg.

BOUSH, CLIFFORD JOSEPH naval officer; b. Portsmouth, Va., Aug. 13, 1854; grad. U.S. Naval Acad., 1876. Promoted ensign, Dec. 1, 1877; lt., jr. grade, Nov. 3, 1884; lt., July 31, 1890; lt. comdr., Mar. 25, 1899; comdr., Jan. 12, 1905; capt., July 20, 1908; rear adm., Mar. 26, 1913. Served in Annapolis during Spanish-Am. War; at Naval War Coll., 1904-05; in Concord, 1905-07; insp. 2d Lighthouse Dist., 1907-08; at Navy Yard, Portsmouth, N.H., 1908-09; comd. Ohio, 1909, North Carolina, 1909-11; mem. Examining and Retiring bds., Washington, D.C., 1911-13; comd. 3d Div., Atlantic Fleet, 1913-15; comdt. Naval Sta., Hawaii, July 17, 1915-Aug. 13 1917; retired, Aug. 13, 1917. Died July 24, 1936.

BOW, WARREN E supt. of schools, univ. pres.; b. Detroit, Mich., June 2, 1891; s. Sandy and Anna (Cushing) B.; B.S., U. of Ill., 1914; A.M., U. of Mich., 1923; LL.D., Battle Creek Coll., 1931; m. Marian Flaherty, Nov. 7, 1920; children—Nancy Ann (dec.), Warren James. Teacher and prin., grade and high schs., 1915-22; asst. dean Detroit Teachers Coll., 1922-25; acting dean, 1925-26, dean, 1926-30; asst. supt. Detroit Schs., 1930-39, first asst. supt., 1939-41, dep. supt., 1941-42, supt. since 1942; pres. Wayne U., Detroit since 1942. Served as capt., maj., Field Arty., 32d Div., A.E.F. Mem. The Citizens Housing and Planning Council of Detroit (v.p. 1941-43), Detroit Bd. of Commerce. Mem. N.E.A., Mich. Edn. Assn., Detroit Teachers Assn., Am. Vocational Assn., Mich. Indsl. Edn. Soc., Engring. Soc. of Detroit, Am. Legion, Phi Delta Kappa, Kappa Delta Pi, Mu Sigma Pi, Sigma Pi. Mason (K.T. Consistory, Shriner). Clubs: Detroit Athletic, Economic, Northwest Kiwanis (pres. 1927), Ridgevale Rod and Gun, St. Andrews Soc., Noontide, University of Michigan (Detroit, Mich.). Home: 18318 Birchcrest Drive. Office: 1354 Broadway, Detroit, Mich. Died May 12, 1945; buried in Evergreen Cemetery, Detroit.

BOWDITCH, CHARLES PICKERING trustee, archeol. student; b. Boston, Sept. 30, 1842; s. Jonathan Ingersoll and Lucy O. (Nichols) B.; A.B., Harvard, 1863, A.M., 1866; m. Cornelia L. Rockwell, June 7, 1866. President Pepperell Mfg. Co. and Mass. Hosp. Life Ins., Co.; dir. Boston & Providence R.R. Corp. Served as 2d lt., 1st lt., and capt., 5th Mass. Vol. Inf., May 1863-Feb. 1864; capt. 5th Mass. Vol. Cav., Feb-Aug. 1864. Fellow Am. Acad. Arts and Sciences, A.A.A.S., Archaeol. Inst. of America. Republican. Author: Maya Numeration, Calendar and Astronomy; Bacon's Connection with the First Folio of Shakespeare; Pickering Genealogy; also 10 pamphlets on Central Am. archeology, and of History of the Trustees of the Charity of Edward Hopkins. Home: Jamica Plain, Mass. Died June 1, 1921.

BOWDITCH, HENRY PICKERING physiologist; b. Boston, Apr. 4, 1840; s. Jonathan Ingersoll and Lucy Orne (Nichols) B.; brother of Charles Pickering B.; A.B., Harvard, 1861, A.M., 1866, M.D., 1868; (D.Sc., Cambridge, Eng., 1898; LL.D., Edinburgh, 1898, Toronto, 1903, U. of Pa., 1904); lt., capt. and maj. U.S. Vol. Cav., 1861-65; studied physiology in France and Germany, 1868-71; m. Selma Knauth, of Leipzig, Sept. 9, 1871. Asst. prof., 1871-76, prof. physiology, 1876-1903, George Higginson prof. physiology, 1903-06, dean Med. Sch., 1883-93, Harvard. Trustee Boston Pub. Library, 1895-1902. Fellow Am. Acad. Arts and Sciences, A.A.A.S. (v.p., 1886, 1900); mem. Nat. Acad. Sciences. Author: Growth of Children, 1877; Hints for Teachers of Physiology, 1889; Is Harvard a University?, 1890; Are Composite Photographs Typical Pictures?, 1894; Advancement of Medicine by Research, 1896. Home: Jamaica Plain, Mass. Died 1911.

BOWDOIN, GEORGE E. corp. exec.; b. Balt., Jan. 23, 1898; s. Henry J. and Julia Morris (Murray) B.; student Gilman Sch., Balt., 1910-16; student Princeton, 1920; m. Harriet Sinton, Nov. 20, 1950. Formerly exec. v.p., dir. U.S. Hoffman Machinery Corp., N.Y.C., now pres. Served with 1st div. USMC, PTO; disch. lt. col. Res. Decorated Bronze Star, Silver Star, Gold Star in lieu of 2d Silver Star. Home: 440 Park Av., N.Y.C. 22. Office: 105 4th Av., N.Y.C. Died Mar. 3, 1959.

BOWEN, HAROLD GARDINER naval officer, ring traveler mfg. exec.; b. Providence, Nov. 6, 1883; B.S., U.S. Naval Acad., 1905; M.A., Columbia, 1914; Sc.D., Brown U. 1947; m. Margaret Edith Brownlie, Sept. 27, 1911; 1 son, Harold Gardiner. Commd. ensign USN, 1907, advanced through grades to capt., 1927, rear adm., 1935, vice adm., 1946; apptd. asst. chief Bur. Engring., 1931, engr. in chief of navy, 1935, dir. Naval Research Lab., also tech. aide to sec. navy, 1939-42, spl. asst. to under-sec. navy and sec. navy, 1942-47, dir. Office Patents and Inventions, 1945, chief Office Research and Inventions, May 1946, chief of Naval Research, Aug. 1946, ret. 1947; exec. dir. Thomas Alva Edison Found., Inc., 1948-55; pres. U.S. Ring Traveler Co., 1944-. Mem. research adv. bd. Franklin Inst., 1946. Decorated D.S.M., nine letters of commendation from sec. navy; recipient Newcomen medal Franklin Inst., 1944. Hon. mem. Am. Soc. M.E. Author: The Edison Effect; (with Charles F. Kettering) Short History of Technology. Home: 65 Arlington Av., Providence 6. Office: U.S. Ring Traveler Co., 159 Aborn St., Providence 3. Died Aug. 1, 1965; buried Arlington Nat. Cemetery.

BOWEN, IVAN lawyer; b. Sleepy Eye, Minn., Jan. 28, 1886; s. John Richard and Florence Maria (Gradner) B.; LL.B., Georgetown U., 1911; m. Mildred Muriel Morehart, Apr. 29, 1912; children—Robert M., William M., Mildred E. (Mrs. Lester H. Bolstead), Ivan. Admitted to Minn. bar, 1911; law practiced Mankato, 1913-17, 19-21; mem. Minn. R.R. and Warehouse Commn., 1921-28; partner Bowen & Bowen, Mpls., 1928—; counsel Greyhound Lines; v.p., dir. (ret.) Greyhound Corp.; gen. counsel (ret.) Nat. Assn. Motor Bus Operators, Adv. to employers delegation 24th Conf. Internat. Labor Orgn., Geneva, Switzerland, 1938. Served as capt., F.A., O.R.C., 89th Div., U.S. Army, 1917-19; with Minn., N.G., 1921-40; ret. as col. Recipient Medal of Merit, State of Minn., Mil. Dept., 1940, Mem. Am. (mem. House of Dels., representing sect. pub. utility law), Minn. State Bar assns., Am. Legion, Vets. Fgn. Wars. Republican. Presbyn. Mason. Home: Route 4, Excelsior, Minn. Office: 1630 Rand Tower, Mpls. 2. Died Sept. 24, 1959.

BOWEN, THOMAS M. lawyer; b. near Burlington, Ia., Oct. 26, 1835; ed. public schools; admitted to the bar at age of 18; mem. Ia. legislature, 1856; removed to Kan., 1858; enlisted as capt. Union army; raised 13th Kan., 1858; enlisted as capt. Union army; raised 13th Kan. Inf. and commanded it until end of war; bvt. brig. gen.; comd. brigade, 1863-65, on frontier and with 7th Army Corps; delegate from Kan. to Nat. Rep. conv., 1864. After war settled in Ark.; pres. constl. convs. of 1866 and 1868; justice Supreme Court, Ark., 1867-71; apptd. gov. Idaho, 1871; resigned and returned to Ark.; was defeated as candidate for U.S. senator; removed to Colo.; was 4 yrs. judge Dist. Court; mem. State legislature, 1882; U.S. senator from Colo., 1883-89. Republican. Has been identified with large mining interests since living in Colo. Home: Pueblo, Colo. Died 1906.

BOWERS, HENRY FRANCIS founder of the "A.P.A."; b. Baltimore, Aug. 12, 1837; ed. at home; removed to Iowa; m. Eliza H., d. Judge Thomas H. Wilson, of Ia. Deputy clerk of cts., 1863; deputy recorder, 1869; co. recorder, 1870-74; admitted to bar, Oct. 1870; practiced in U.S. cts. Spl a.-d.-c., with rank of lt. col., staff of Gov. John H. Gear, 1878-82. Founded, 1887. the Am. Protective Assn.; was its to Gen. Conv. P.E. Ch., 1904. Republican. Home: Galveston, Tex. Died 1910.

BOWERS, THEODORE SHELTON army officer; b. Hummelstown, Pa.; s. George and Ann Maria. Editor, Register, Mt. Carmel, Ill.; served as pvt. 48th Ill. Inf., 1861, commd. 1st lt., 1862, capt., capt., 1862, maj. 1863, promoted lt. col. after Battle of Vicksburg, 1863; clk. in hdqrs. of Gen. U.S. Grant, 1862, also aide; served in Va. campaigns of 1863-65; capt. Q.M. Dept., U.S. Army, 1864. Died after falling under train wheels while trying to board train, Garrison, N.Y., Mar. 6, 1866; buried West Point, N.Y.

BOWES, THEODORE F. lawyer; b. Moshannon, Pa., Dec. 12, 1904; s. Maines J. and Nancy (Fleming) B.; Ph.B., Dickinson Coll., 1927; LL.B., Syracuse U., 1936; asst. to pres. Bankers Investment Trust, 1928-31; prof. law Syracuse U., 1936-41, 46-53; v.p., gen. counsel Onondaga Aviation Corp., 1940-41; gen. counsel Inst. Indsl. Reseach, Syracuse U., 1952-53; U.S. Atty., No. Dist. N.Y., 1953-61; commr. N.Y. State Public Service Commn., 1961-. Trustee N.Y. Ct. of Appeals Library, 1948-. Served as col., USAAF, 1942-46. Decorated Legion of Merit. Mem. Am., N.Y. bar assns., Order of the Coif, Phi Delta Theta, Phi Delta Phi. Methodist. Mason. Club: Syracuse University. Contbr. articles profl. jours. Home: 709 Scott Av., Syracuse, N.Y. Office: 55 Elk St., Albany, N.Y. Died Jan. 8, 1967; buried Oakwood Cemetery, Syracuse.

BOWIE, EDWARD HALL meteroligist; b. Annapolis Junction, Md., Mar. 29, 1874; s. Thomas John and Susanna Hall (Anderson) B.; M.S., St. Johns Coll., Annapolis, Md., 1920; m. Florence C. Hatch, Dec. 12, 1895; children—Mrs. Helen McKinstry Prentiss, Mrs. Margaret Lowndes Wallace, Mrs. Susanna Anderson Lindquist. Entered service U.S. Weather Bur., Dec. 1891; asst. observer at Memphis, 1891-95, Montgomery, Ala., 1896-98; observer, Dubuque, Ia., 1898-1901; section dir., Galveston, Tex., 1901-03; local forecaster, St. Louis, 1903-09; chief forecast div. U.S. Weather Bur., 1910-12, nat. forecaster, 1909-24, prin. meteorologist and dist. forecaster, Pacific States, since 1924. Commd. maj. Signal Corps, July 9, 1917, and ordered to France for meteorol. forecasts for A.E.F.; resigned and returned to Weather Bur., Dec. 1918. Mem. coms. meteorology and scientific hydrology, Am. Geophys. Union. Fellow Am. Meteorol. Soc., Calif. Acad. Sciences; mem. Philos. Soc. Washington, Washington Acad. Sciences. Mason. Clubs: Faculty (Berkeley, Calif.); Family (San Francisco, Calif.). Home 844 Contra Costa Av., Berkeley, Calif. Office: U.S. Weather Bur., San Francisco, Calif. Died July 29, 1943.

BOWIE, JAMES soldier, pioneer; b. Burke County, Ga., 1796; s. Rezin and Alvina (Jones) B.; m. Maria Ursula, Apr. 25, 1831, 2 children. Moved to Texas, 1828; became Mexican citizen, 1830; developed "Bowie knife" as an effective weapon in close-in fighting; fought in Battle of Nacogdoches, 1832; favored Texas resistance to Mexico early after arrival in Tex.; served as col. Tex. Army, 1835-36; killed at The Alamo, San Antonio, Tex., Mar. 6, 1836.

BOWLBY, JOEL MORGAN, corp. exec.; b. Litchfield, Ill., Apr. 26, 1887; s. Joel and Amelia (Smith) B.; grad. So. Ill. U., 1904; LL.D., Xavier U., 1947; m. Alice Fairbairn, Aug. 29, 1928 (dec. Dec. 1951); children—Joel Morgan, III, Dudley Churchill; m. 2d, Dorothy S. Horner, December 23, 1953. With Railway Steel-Spring Co., 1904-09; asso. comml. investment banking bus., 1910-12; pub. accounting, 1913-16; with U.S. Liquidation Commn., also chief machine tool sect., office of dir. sales U.S. War Dept., 1920; asso. Barrow, Wade, Guthrie & Co., C.P.A.'s, 1921-41, gen. partner, 1928-41; pres. Eagle-Picher Co., 1941-49, dir., 1941—, chmn. bd., 1949-55. Served as maj. inf., A.E.F., 1917-19. Mem. Am. Inst. Accountants (past mem. council), Ill. Soc. C.P.A.'s (past pres.), Am. Inst. Mining and Metall. Engrs. Episcopalian. Clubs: Queen City (Cin.); Mid Day (Chgo.); Pacific Union (San Francisco); Links (N.Y.C.). Office American Bldg., Cin. 1. Deceased.

BOWLES, FRANCIS TIFFANY shipbuilder; b. Springfield, Mass., Oct. 7, 1858; s. Benjamin F. and Mary E. (Bailey) B.; grad. U.S. Naval Acad., 1879; (post-grad. degree of Naval Architect from Royal Naval Coll., Greenwich, Eng.); m. Adelaide Hay Savage, Nov. 17, 1886; children-Thomas Savage (dec.), Mrs. Catherine Lowell. In U.S.N. until 1903, serving as constructor at navy yards, etc.; chief constructor U.S.N., with rank of rear adm., 1901-03; pres. Fore River Shipbuilding Corp., Quincy, Mass.; mgr. div. of constrn., afterwards asst. gen. mgr., U.S. Shipping Bd. of Emergency Fleet Corp., Washington, D.C., 1917-19. Mem. Inst. Naval Architects, London; past pres. Soc. Naval Architects and Marine Engrs.; fellow Am. Acad. Arts and Sciences. Home: Boston, Mass. Died Aug. 3, 1927.

BOWLES, PICKNEY DOWNIE lawyer; b. Edgefield, S.C., July 7, 1835; s. Isaac and Emily Holloway B.; ed. in acad. and law depts. U. of Va.; studied in law offices of Judge Samuel McGowan, Abbeville C.H., S.C.; m. Alice Irene Stearns, Feb. 24, 1863. Located in Sparta (then C.H.), Conecuh Co., Ala., Apr. 15, 1859; elected lt. Conecuh Guard, part of Ala. vol. corps, July 4, 1860; elected capt., Apr. 1, 1861; reelected capt. at York Town, Va., May 1, 1862; maj., Aug. 23, 1862; lt. col., Sept. 30, 1862; col., Oct. 3, 1862; brig. gen., Apr. 2, 1865. Opened law office, Evergreen, Ala., 1866; State's pros. atty., 10 yrs.; apptd. postmaster, Evergreen, Ala., spring of 1887; was probate judge, July 1, 1887-Nov. 3, 1898. Democrat. Home: Evergreen, Conecuh Co., Ala. Died 1910.

BOWLEY, ALBERT JESSE army officer; b. Westminster, Calif., Nov. 24, 1875; s. Freeman S. and Flora E. (Pepper) B.; grad. U.S. Mil. Acad., 1897; m. Elsie Ball Wright, Sept. 12, 1931. Commd. 2d lt. 4th Arty., June 11, 1897; promoted through grades to col. May 15, 1917; brig. gen. N.A., June 26, 1918; brig. gen. regular army, Apr. 20, 1921; major gen. Feb. 20, 1931; lieut. gen., Aug. 5, 1939. Participated in Siege of Santiago, Cuba, July 1890; in Philippines, 1899-1901; participated in General Lawton's campaign in Northern Luzon; instr. in chemistry, mineralogy, geology and electricity, and senior inst. arty. tactics, U.S. Mil. Acad., 1901-05; a.d.c. to Maj. Gen. F. D. Grant, at Governor's Island, N.Y., 1906-08, at Chicago, 1908-10; in Philippines, 1910-11; mil. attache to China, 1911-14; duty Fort Sill and Mexican border, 1915-17; organized 17th F.A., 1917, and went to France as its head, Dec. 1917, service Troyon sector, Chateau-Thierry, Belleau Woods, Soissons offensive, Marbache sector, St. Mihiel offensive. Blanc Mont offensive, Meuse-Argonne offensive, Moselle sector; apptd. comdr. 2d F.A. Brigade, 2d Div., A.E.F., June 26, 1918; apptd. chief of arty. 6th Corps, Nov. 6, 1918; at Gen. Staff Coll., 1919-20; mem. Gen. Staff Corps, 1920-21; apptd. comdr. Ft. Bragg, N.C., July 1921; in command 8th Corps Area, June-Dec. 1928, 2d Div., 1928-29; asst. Chief of Staff (G1), Washington, D.C., 1929-31; in command Hawaiian Div., Schofield Barracks, T.H., 1931-34, 5th Corps Area, 1934-35, 3d Corps Area (headquarters at Baltimore), 1935-38, 9th Corps Area, and 4th Army, 1938-39; retired from active service, Nov. 30, 1939. Medals Spanish-Am. War, Cuban Occupation, Philippine Insurrection, Mexican Border, Victory, also Distinguished Service Medal; Officer Legion of Honor, and Croix de Guerre, 4 palms and 1 silver star (France); Order of Chi Hua (Plentiful Rice), by Chinese Govt.; Order of Solididad (Republic of Panama); Order of White Elephant (Siam); Royal Order of St. Olav (Norway); Gen. Staff Medal, War Dept., (U.S.). Club: Army and Navy (Washington, D.C.). Home: 2819 McGill Terrace, Washington 8, D.C. Died May 22, 1945.

BOWMAN, ALPHEUS HENRY brig. gen. U.S.A.; b. Loudon Co., Va., Feb. 28, 1842; s. Henry A. and Martha K. (Polk) B.; ed. Newark (Del.) Acad., Del. Coll., and Chester (Pa.) Mil. Acad., 1855-61; m. Lillie J. Bartlett, Jan. 12, 1898. Entered mil. service in Pa. vols., Dec. 3, 1861; apptd. capt. 9th Inf., 1866; maj. 2d Inf., lt. col. 5th Inf., col. 25th Inf., and brig. gen. U.S.A., retiring Aug. 13, 1903, after more than 40 yrs.' service. Served in command of Co. of Pa. Vols. in Army of the Potomac in Civil War, and from 1866 in regular army, serving in Indian wars, Spanish War, and in the Philippine Islands. Mem. Loyal Legion, S.A.R., Soc. Colonial Wars. Mil. Service Instrn. of U.S., Nat. Geog. Soc. Episcopalian. Home: Washington, D.C. Died Nov. 10, 1926.

BOWMAN, CHARLES GRIMES commodore U.S.N.; b. Delphi, Ind., Oct. 15, 1848; s. John Milton and Elizabeth (Barnett) B.; apptd. from Ind., and grad. U.S. Naval Acad., 1869; m. Josephine McFarlane, Feb. 24, 1876. Promoted ensign, July 12, 1870; master, July 12, 1871; lt., Aug. 9, 1874; lt. comdr., May 4, 1896; comdr., July 8, 1899; capt., Nov. 8, 1904; retired at own request as commodore, June 30, 1907. Served successively on the Sabine, Richmond, Constellation, Yantic and Hartford, 1869-76; Naval Acad., 1876-79; Adams, 1879-82; Naval Obs., 1882-86; Atlanta, 1886-87; Boston, 1887-89; Naval Acad., 1889-93, head dept. astronomy navigation and surveying, 1890-93; exec. officer Marblehead, 1894-97; equipment officer Navy Yard, Mare Island, 1897-1900; comd. Castine, 1900-01, Don Juan de Austria, 1901-02; insp. 6th light house dist., 1902-03, Navy Yard, League Island, Pa., 1903-04; equipment officer Navy Yard, New York, 1904-05; capt. of yard, Navy Yard, Pensacola, Fla., 1905-06; comd. Rhode Island, 1906-07. Ordered to active duty, Apr. 7, 1917. Home: Delphi, Ind. Died Oct. 1918.

BOWMAN, FRANK OTTO army officer, retired; Mesilla Park, N.M., July 27, 1896; s. Henry D. and Carrie (Otto) B.; B.S., U.S. Military Academy, 1918; grad. Engrs. Sch., basic course and civil engr. course, 1921; m. Lucy Reed Curtis, June 17, 1920; children—Frank Otto, Henry D. II. Commd. 2d lt., Corps of Engrs., U.S.A., 1918, and advanced through grades to maj. gen., 1954; chief engr., II Corps, Jacosonville, Fla., and Eng., 1942; later became engr. European Theater of Operations; engr. Allied Force Hdqrs., England and North African Theater of Operations; engr., 5th Army, 1943, Hdqrs. Service of Supply, North Africa, Apr.-July, 1943; engr. 5th Army, Aug. 1943-45; engr.

Yokohma Base, Japan, Oct. 1945; comdg. Ground Forces, Okinawa, May, 1946; asst. chief of staff, G-4, Army Ground Forces, Aug. 1946; comdr. Columbus Gen., Depot, Columbus, O., 1947-49; chief of staff, dep. comdr. Engr. Center, Ft. Belvoir, Va., 1940-53; chief engr. U.S. Army Forces Far East, 1953-55; comdg. gen. Ft. Leonard Wood, Mo., and 6th Armored Div., 1955-56, ret. June 30, 1956. Decorated D.S.M., Legion of Merit with two oak leaf clusters, Purple Heart (U.S.), Comdr. British Empire, Croix de Guerre (French), Comdr. Crown of Italy, Silver Star of Valor (Italy), Military Medal (Brazil), Ulchi Distinguished Mil Service Medal with Gold Star (Korea). Address: P.O. Box 52, Carmel, Cal.

BOWMAN, GEORGE T. officer, U.S. Army (ret.); b. Buffalo, June 12, 1869; s. Dennis and Alice (Mills) B.; student Inst., Politics, Williamstown, Mass., 1923; grad. Army War Coll., Washington, 1922; grad. Naval War Coll., Newport, R.I., 1923; m. Lillian Elizabeth Burrows, June 24, 1896 (died Mar. 6, 1945); 1 son, John William (dec.). Cadet, enlisted man, officer 74th regt. N.G., N.Y., 1885-97; capt. 65th N.Y. vol. inf., 1898; lt. 36th U.S. vol. inf., 1899-01; lt. to col. U.S. Cav., 1901-33, brig. gen., (ret.), 1940—; active service, Spanish-Am. War, 1898; P.I., 1899-04; Cuba, Army of Cuban Pacification, 1906-09; Mexican border, Mexico, Punitive Expedition, 1915-16; France, Belgium, Luxemburg, Germany, 1918-19; mem. gen. staff corps, U.S. Army, 1917-21, War Dept. gen. staff, gen. hdqrs., AEF; faculty Army War Coll., 1923-25; chief of staff 62d cav. div., 1927-33. Decorated D.S.M., medals, distinguished marksman, U.S. Army, Spanish-Am. War, Philippine Insurrection, Army of Cuban Pacification, Mexican Punitive Expedition, World War I (battle stars), occupation of Germany; Legion of Honor (France). Mem. Vets. Assn. (74th regt. N.G. N.Y.), Cav. Assn. (Phila.). Clubs: Army and Navy Country (Washington), Fort Monmouth Officers'. Author: Our Military Rifle, 1909; How to Shoot the U.S. Rifle, 1914. Home: Sycamore Av., Shrewsbury, N.J. Died Feb. 14, 1951; buried Arlington Nat. Cemetery.

BOWMAN, JOSEPH MERRELL, JR., govt. ofcl.; b. Valdosta, Ga., June 23, 1931; s. Joseph Merrell and Martha (Stanley) B.; LL.B., Emory U., 1957; m. Mary Isabella Nichols, Dec. 19, 1953; children—Joseph N., Mary B., Henry H. Admitted to Ga. bar, 1958; legislative asst. to Congressman Flynt, Jr., 1958-59; partner Kennedy, Kennedy, Seay &Bowman, Barnesville, Ga., 1959-62; Congl. liaison officer Dept. Labor, 1962-63; dep. asst. to sec. treasury Congl. liaison, 1963-64; asst. to sec. treasury Congl. relations, 1964-68; asst. sec. treas., 1968-72; mem. firm Corcoran, Foley, Youngman & Rowe. Mem. bd. visitors Emory U. Served to capt. USAF, 1952-56. Mem. Am., Ga., D.C. bar assns., Phi Delta Theta, Phi Delta Phi. Democrat. Methodist. Home: Alexandria VA Died May 16, 1972; buried Culpepper Nat. Cemetery, Culpepper VA

BOWMAN, KARL MURDOCK, physician; b. Topeka, Nov. 4, 1888; s. Homer Caleb and Isabelle Susanna (Murdock) B.; A.B., Washburn Coll., 1909, D.Sc., 1953; M.D., U. Cal. at Berkeley, 1913, LL.D., also Dr. J. Elliott Royer award, 1964; m. Eliza Abbott Stearns, Aug. 18, 1916 (dec. 1957); children—Richard Stearns, Thomas Elliot, Murdock Stearns, Walter Murdock; m. 2d, Anna Lowrey, July 18, 1959. Intern Children's Hosp., Los Angeles, 1913, Seton Hosp., N.Y.C., 1914, Roosevelt Hosp., N.Y.C., 1915, Bloomingdale Hosp., White Plains, N.Y., 1915-17, 19-21; chief med. officer Boston Psychopathic Hosp., 1921-36; asst. prof. psychiatry Harvard Med. Sch., 1921-36; dir. div. psychiatry Bellevue Hosp., N.Y.C., 1936-41; prof. psychiatry N.Y.U. Coll. Medicine, 1936-41; prof. psychiatry U. Cal. Sch. Medicine, San Francisco, 1941-56, prof. emeritus, 1956-73, med. supt. Langley Porter Clinic, San Francisco, 1941-56; vis. prof. U. Philippines Coll. Medicine, 1954-55; dir. div. mental health for Alaska, also supt. Alaska Psychiat. Inst., Anchorage, 1964-67. Sent to China by WHO to assist govt. China in setting up Nat. Psychiat. Inst., Nanking, 1947; cons. USPHS, Office Surgeon Gen., U.S. Army, U.S. Navy, USAF, VA; mem. com. neuropsychiatry NRC, 1944-47; dir. Cal. Sexual Deviation Research, 1950-54; mem. nat. health adv. com. USPHS, 1948-50; mem. profl. adv. com. Office Vocational Rehab., 1944-50; trustee Nat. Com. Mental Hygiene, 1944-47; mem. adv. bd. psychiatry A.R.C., 1938-50. Served as capt., M.C., U.S. Army, World War I; lt. comdr. USNR, 1935-52; ret., 1952. Diplomate in psychiatry Am. Bd. Psychiatry and Neurology (dir. 1943-46, 50-51). Fellow Am. Psychiat. Assn. (life fellow, pres. 1944-46), Physician Philippines (hon.), Am. Coll. Psychiatrists; hon. life mem. Philippine Mental Health Assn.; mem. Cal., San Francisco med. socs., N.Y., Mass. psychiat. socs., A.A.A.S., Boston Soc. Psychiatry and Neurology (sec.-treas. 1933-36), New Eng. Soc. Psychiatry, Assn. Research Nervous and Mental Disease (1st v.p. 1938, 41), Sigma Xi, Phi Delta Theta, Alpha Omega Alpha. Author: Personal Problems for Men and Women, 1931; also numerous articles. Asso. editor Geriatrics, Quar. Jour. Studies on Alcohol, 1942-73. Address: San Francisco CA Died Mar. 2, 1973.

BOWRON, ARTHUR JOHN, JR. banker; b. Birmingham, Ala., Jan. 1, 1907; s. Arthur John and Lillian (Roden) B.; B.S. cum laude, Princeton, 1928; LL.B., Harvard, 1934; m. Virginia Pero, June 25, 1936. Admitted to Ala. bar, 1934; asso. law firm White, Bradley, All & Arant, Birmingham, 1934-42; with First Nat. Bank, Birmingham, 1945-, trust officer, 1945-51, v.p., trust officer 1951-52, v.p. 1953-55, exec. vice pres., 1955-; dir. Elmwood Corporation (Birmingham, Alabama), Bessemer Coal Iron & Land Co., Hayes Aircraft Corp., Chmn. com. met. found. Greater Birmingham Found. Served as maj. ordnance AUS, 1942-45. Mem. Birmingham C. of C. (treas.), Ala., Birmingham bar assns. Presbyn. Home: 4333 Altamont Rd., Birmingham 35213. Office: care First National Bank, P.O. Box 2534, Birmingham, Ala. 35202. Died July 13, 1961.

BOWYER, JOHN MARSHALL naval officer; b. Cass Co., Ind., June 19, 1853; s. Lewis Franklin and Naomi Emeline (Pugh) B.; apptd. from Ia., and grad. U.S. Naval Acad., 1874; m. Cora McCarter, Oct. 29, 1879. Promoted ensign, July 17, 1875; master, May 28, 1881; lt. jr. grade, Mar. 3, 1883; lt., May 26, 1887; lt. comdr., Mar. 3, 1899; comdr., Mar. 21, 1903; capt., Nov. 8, 1907. Served at various stas. and on various vessels until beginning of war with Spain; apptd. exec. officer, Princeton, May 2, 898, patrol duty about west end of Cuba; to Philippines, Jan 11, 1899; detached to Yorktown, Jan. 1, 1900; participated in suppression of Philippine insurrection and the Boxer troubles in N. China; exec. officer, flagship Brooklyn, Sept. 3, 1900; asst. supt. gun factory, Navy Yard, Washington, and head dept. yards and docks, 1901-05; comd. U.S.S. Columbia, July 10, 1905; sr. officer in comd. Columbia at Colon, Marblehead at Panama and 600 marines ashore Isthmus of Panama, during elections, June 1906; aid to asst. sec. navy, Mar. 1907; comd. battleship Illinois, Nov. 25, 1907, and made cruise to Pacific and around the world with Atlantic Fleet; supt. Naval Acad., 1909-11; retired on account of Illness contracted in line of duty, Sept. 14, 1911, and commd. - retired. Medals: West India campaign; Spanish-Am. War; Philippines campaign; China campaign, Home: Washington, D.C. Died Mar. 15, 1919.

BOYCE, CHARLES MEREDITH, investment bankers; b. Balt., Feb. 8, 1920; s. Fred Grayson and Sophie (Meredith) B.; A.B., Yale, 1942; grad. sch. banking Rutgers U., 1952; m. Lila Jones, Oct. 3, 1942; children—Charles Meredith, Lila Capen, Elizabeth Barker. With Merc.-Safe Deposit and Trust Co., Balt., 1946-61, v.p., 1954-60, exec. v.p., 1960-61; partner Robert Garrett & Sons, Balt., 1961-64; exec. v.p. Robert Garrett & Sons, Inc., Balt., 1964-67, pres., 1967-69; dir. Can. Dry-Frostie Corp., F. Bowie Smith & Son, Inc., Baltimore & Annapolis R.R., All. American Engring Co. city council, Balt., 1951-55, city treas., 1959-63. Treas., trustee Peabody Inst.; trustee Union Meml. Hosp., Samuel Ready Sch.; overseer Goucher Coll. Served from pvt. to maj., inf., AUS, 1942-46. Mem. Investment Bankers Association. Clubs: Maryland, Elkridge, Merchants. Home: Baltimore MD Died Mar. 31, 1969; buried Druid Ridge Cemetery.

BOYD, BELLE Confederate spy, actress; b. Martinsburg, Va., May 9, 1843; attended Mt. Washington Coll., 1855-59; m. Lt. Sam W. Hardinge, Aug. 1864; m. 2d, John Hammond, 1869; m. 3d, Nathaniel High, 1885. During Civil War obtained valuable information for Gen. Stonewall Jackson when Federals under Gen. James Shields held war councils at her aunt's house, Martinsburg; twice arrested, released due to lack of evidence; sailed to Eng. with letters from Jefferson Davis, 1864; made debut on English stage in Lady of Lyons at Theatre Royal, Manchester; after successful career in Eng., made Am. debut at Ben De Bar's Theatre, St. Louis; joined Miles and Bates stock co. of Cincinnati, 1868. Died Kilbourne, Wis., June 11, 1900.

BOYD, DAVID FRENCH army officer, coll. pres.; b. Wytheville, Va., Oct. 5, 1834; s. Thomas Jefferson and Minerva Anne (French) B.; grad. U. Va., 1856; m. Esther Gertrude Wright, Oct. 5, 1865, 8 children. Sch. Tchr., Homer and Rocky Mount, La., 1857-60; prof. ancient langs. and English, La. State Sem. of Learning, Pineville, 1860-61; enlisted as pvt. Co. B., 9th La. Volunteers, 1861, sent to Va., rose to maj. in Stonewall Jackson's corps by 1862, transferred to Trans-Miss. Dept. constructed Fort DeRussy on Red River, 1863, captured nr. Black River, La., 1864, imprisoned in New Orleans, 1864; an instigator of law stating that every parish in La. should have 1 or more public schs., one for Negroes, 1 for whites, 1869; supt. La. State Sem., 1865-70, became pres. when sem. was renamed La. State U., 1870, instrumental in merger of La. State U. and La. Agrl. and Mech. Coll., 1874; removed from presidency by La. Legislature, 1880, reinstated, 1884, attempted to expand univ. without operating through bd. of suprs., resigned as a result, 1885, prof. mathematics 1886-88, prof. philosophy, civics, 1897-99; supt. Ky. Mil. Inst., Farmingdale, Ky., 1888-93; tchr. Ohio Mil. Acad., Germantown, 1893-94; prof. Mich. Mil. Acad., Orchard Lake 1894-97. Died Baton Rouge, La. May 27, 1899.

BOYD, HARRY BURTON clergyman; b. Chgo., Ill., Mar. 10, 1882; s. Joseph Warren and Minnie (Brock) B.; B.A., cum laude, Centre Coll., Ky., 1908, D.D., 1928; B.D., McCormick Theol. Sem., 1911; D.D., Hastings (Neb.) Coll., 1922; LL.D., U. of Dubuque, 1928; m. Margaret Elizabeth Denham, Oct. 10, 1911; 1 son, Leslie Randolph. Ordained Presbyn. ministry, 1911; pastor successively Denton, Tex., Olean, N.Y., Iowa City, Ia., until 1918, Park Ch., Erie, Pa., 1919-28, Arch. Street Presbyn. Ch., Phila., 1928-37, First Ch., Indiana, Pa., 1937-55, Garden Crest Ch., St. Petersburg, Fla., 1955. Served as chaplain 313th Engrs., 88th Div., U.S. Army, 1917-18; sr. chaplain 88th Div., U.S. Army, 1917-18; sr. chaplain 88th Div., A.E.F., 1918-19; organized first sch. of chaplains held in U.S. Army, Camp Dodge, Ia., Oct. 1917; organized ednl. work of 88th Div., A.E.F., Jan. 1, 1919, enrolling 3,000 students; hon. discharged June 19, 1919. Mem. bd. dirs. U. of Dubuque, Ia., 1926-50, pres. bd., 1927-36; mem. bd. overseers Centre College, 1949—; v.p. Pa. Lord's Day Alliance; trustee and v.p. U.S.S. Niagara Assn.; trustee Western Theol. Sem. 1940-55; del. Pan-Presbyn. Alliance, 1928; commr. Gen. Assembly, 1921, 1932, 1942; moderator Erie Presbytery, 1921, Kitanning Presbytery 1942; del. to Fed. Coucil of Chs., 1932-34; chmn. Phila. Prohibition Emergency Com., 1933; trustee Pa. Anti-Saloon League, 1935, v.p. 1938-46. Mem. Am. Acad. Polit. and Social Science, Am. Legion, Mem. bd. dirs. Ind. Chapter, Am. Red Cross, 1940, chmn. 1943-45. Mem. Phi Delta Theta. Republican. Mason (33ff). Clubs: Ingleside, Kiwanis. Preacher before shcools and colls.; contbr. religious press. Home: 305-15th Av. N.E., St. Petersburg, Fla. Died July 11, 1959.

BOYD, RALPH GATES, lawyer; b. Chelmsford, Mass., Oct. 30, 1901; s. Richard Turnbull and Jennie (Gates) B.; A.B. cum laude, Harvard, 1922, LL.B., 1925; m. Dorothy Louise Koch, Apr. 2, 1932; 1 son, Douglas. Admitted to Mass. bar, 1926, since practiced in Boston; asso. firm Dunbar, Nutter & McClennen (now Nutter, McClennen & Fish), 1925-34, partner, 1934-54, own practice, and partner firm Boyd & MacCrelish, 1954-61; partner firm Boyd, MacCrellish & Weeks, 1962-72; pres. West Point Mfg. Co., 1950-51, also chmn. bd. dirs. subsidiary and affiliated textile cos.; gen. counsel United-Carr Inc., 1929-65, also dir.; chmn. bd. dirs. Davis-Furber Machine Co.; dir. Roger Boyd, Inc., W. J. Connell Co.; dir., clk. Bankers Service Co. Mem. Beacon Hill Archtl. Com., 1964-71. Mem. nat. bd. dirs. Arthritis and Rheumatism Found., also mem. nat. exec. com., trustee gen. counsel Mass. chpt.; trustee, treas. France G. Lee Found. Served as pvt. Jr. Co., S.A.T.C., 1918; maj. to col., U.S. Army, 1941-46, col., brig. gen. JAGC, U.S. Army Res. 1947-61; ret., 1961. Decorated Legion of Merit, Commendation ribbon, Am., Asiatic, E.T.O. ribbons, Battle star for No. France. Mem. Am. Bar Assn. (chmn. sect. corp., banking and bus. law 1950-51, mem. Ho. of Dels. 1948-52, chmn. com. lawyers in Armed Forces, 1952-53, chmn. com. Mil. Justice, 1953-56; mem. adv. com. to U.S. Mil. Appeals, 1952-72; mem. Judge Advs. Assn. (pres. 1947, dir. 1946-57), Mass. State, Boston bar assns., Assn. U.S. Army (pres., dir. Mass. Bay chpt.). Republican. Conglist. Clubs: Union Algonquin, Harvard, Fort Hill, Downtown (Boston); Harvard (N.Y.C.). Author wartime legislation and Army regulations and manuals; also articles. Home: Boston MA Died Mar. 31, 1972; buried Mt. Auburn Cemetery, Cambridge MA

BOYD, WILLIAM YOUNG lawyer, publicist; b. Auburn, N.Y., Feb. 18, 1884; s. David and Mary (Young) B.; B.S., Syracuse U., 1906; m. Katharine Endsley, Oct. 6, 1910; traveled in West Indies and Central and S. America, 1907-16, representing Am. corps. and studying trade and polit. conditions, Commd. lt. U.S.N., 1917; lt. comdr., 1918; assigned to Dept. Naval Communications, Washington, D.C., selected to coordinate and establish censorship between U.S. and its European allies in Brazil; attache Am. Embassy, Rio de Janeiro, 1917-19; organized system of Brazilian censorship; served as U.S. del. Internat. Cable Censorship Commn., Brazil; U.S. rep. Com. on Pub. Information in Brazil, 1918; invited by French Govt. to reorganize at Brest, France, the S. Am. cable censorship; apptd. mem. commn. to accompany President Passoa of Brazil on trip to U.S. and Can., 1919. Hon. discharged from Navy, 1919, and with Gen. George W. Goethals and others organized firm of Goethals, Wilford & Boyd, Inc., to develop port of Colon and Republic of Panama, also exploring various dists. of Panama; rep. various Am. bondholders in Mexico, 1922-23; negotiated $4,-500,000 loan for Republic of Panama in New York, 1923; by apptmt. of President Chiari of Panama, went to Germany, Holland and Denmark, 1924, to make survey and investigation of the Free Ports of those countries; administr. for govt. of Panama in orgn. and operation of Govt. bonded warehouses; spl. envoy to Germany from Panama, 1925. to adjust questions arising from German emigration to Panama; adviser to government of Panama in negotiating treaty with U.S., 1926. Mem. Council of the "Living Age," 1928-; mem. first Nat. Aviation Commn. of Panama, 1928-29; del. of Republic Panama to Internat. Civil Aeronautic Conf. called by President Coolidge in Washington, D.C., Dec. 1928; established first pvt. commercial air service between Canal Zone and S. America, 1929; organized Panama Chapter of Nat. Aeronautic Assn. of U.S.A., 1929; mem. Free Port Commn. of Panama, 1929-30. Decorated Cross Legion of Honor (French); Cross of Saints Maurizio and Lazzaro (Italian). Compiled survey of compensation insurance and casualty laws of Brazil, Argentina, Venezuela and Colombia for Am. casualty insurance companies. Died Aug. 8, 1932.

BOYKIN, GARLAND LESTER govt. ofcl.; b. Russell, Tex., June 25, 1900; s. James A. and Lyda (Garland) B.; B.S. in Animal Husbandry, Tex. A. and M. Coll., 1922; postgrad. Colo. State U., summers 1924-26, Northwestern U., 1943-44; m. Lucy E. Mathews, Sept. 2, 1924; children-James L., Benjamin M., William E., Martha E. (Mrs. Jordan Wolle). With Palma Soriano Sugar Co. (Cuba), 1922-23; high sch. tchr. and coach, 1923-27, mgr. Clarendon (Tex.) C. of C., 1927-34; county agrl. agt., Tex., 1934-37; state agrl. agt., N.M., 1937-42, dir., then asso. dir. agrl. extension, 1946-52; gen. mgr. Mimbres Valley Farmers Assn., Deming, N.M., 1952-58; agrl. extension adviser U.S. Operations Mission, Manila, P.I., 1958, acting chief, agrl. div., to 1963; ret. Member ICAFAO Agrl. Econ. Survey Team, Nigeria, 1960; cons. in agrl. extension and agrl. prodn. to Ceylon Govt., 1962 (author report for Ceylon and U.S. AID). Dir. Tri-State Asso. Wholesale Grocers, El Paso, Tex., 1952-58. Served from 1st lt. to maj. USAAF, 1942-46; maj. Res. Mason, Rotarian. Home and office: Box 117, Mesilla Park, N.M. 88047. Died Sept. 18, 1966; buried Masonic Cemetery, Las Cruces, N.M.

BOYLE, JEREMIAH TILFORD railroad exec.; s. John and Elizabeth (Tilford) B.; studied law under Gov. William Owsley, Transylvania, Ky.; m. Elizabeth Owsley Anderson, 1842, 12 children. Practiced law, Danville, Ky., until 1861; a slave owner, but supported Union at outbreak of Civil War; commd. brig. gen. of co. of volunteers, 1861; apptd. by Edwin Stanton as mil. comdr. of Ky. after Battle of Shiloh, removed from post because of mil. ineptitude, 1864; organizer, pres. Louisville City R.R. Co.; pres. Evansville, Henderson & Nashville R.R., 1866. Died July 28, 1871.

BOYLE, LEO MARTIN, adj. gen. of Illinois; b. Chicago, Ill., July 20, 1899; s. Frank E. and Margaret (Callahan) B.; grad. Cath. schs., Chgo.; m. Anna Marie Boyle, July 4, 1931 (dec.); one son, George Anthony. Served with U.S. Army, 1917-19; 2d lt., inf., 1924, advancing through the grades to maj. gen., 1945; the adjutant general, chief of staff, Mil. and Naval Dept., State of Ill., 1940-69. Decorated Silver Star for gallantry during World War I. Roman Catholic. Home: Springfield IL Died May 3, 1969.

BOYLE, THOMAS NEWTON clergyman; b. Blairville, Pa., Apr. 26, 1839; s. Thomas and Maria (Adair) B.; ed. Bellefonte (Pa.) Acad., 1856-57; (D.D., Mt. Union Coll., 1884; LL.D., Western U. of Pa., 1894); m. Sarah E. Weatherwax, Mar. 11, 1863. Ordained M.E. ministry, 1859; capt. Co. H, 140th Pa. Vols., Civil War; del. to Gen. Conf. M.E. Ch 5 times; presiding elder 20 yrs. Chaplain-in-chief, G.A.R., 1901; grand prelate, Grand Commandery K.T. of Pa., 1895-. Trustee Mt. Union Coll., Allegheny Coll., Am. U., Beaver Coll., mem. bd. of mgrs., Dixmont and West Pa. hosps., Pittsburgh, Home: Crafton, Pa. Died 1911.

BOYNTON, EDWARD CARLISLE army officer, educator; b. Windsor, Vt., Feb. 1, 1824; s. Thomas and Sophia (Cabot) B.; grad. U.S. Mil. Acad., 1846; m. Mary J. Hubbard. Commd. in Arty., served under Gen. Zachery Taylor in Mexican War; later served in battles of Vera Cruz, cerro Gordo and Contreras under Gen. Winfield Scott; taught at U.S. Mil. Acad., 1849-56; prof. chemistry, mineralogy and geology U. Miss., 1856-61; allowed to leave Miss. at outbreak of Civil War after he took pledge not to take field against Confederacy; as result of pledge declined colonelcy of Vt. regt.; capt. 11th Inf., assigned as adjutant and q.m. of U.S. Mil. Acad., 1861-71; retired to Newburgh, N.Y., 1871; supt. water works for 8 years. Author: History of West Point, and Its Military Importance during the American Revolution; and the Origin

BOYNTON, HENRY VAN NESS soldier; journalist; b. West Stockbridge, Mass., July 22, 1835; s. Rev. Charles B. and Maria (Van Buskirk) B.; removed to Ohio in boyhood; grad. Woodward Coll., Cincinnati, 1854; Ky. Mil. Inst., 1858 (A.M., 1859; C.E., 1860); m. Helen Augusta Mason, 1871. Maj. and lt. col. 35th Ohio vol. inf., 1861-65; comd. regt. in battles of Chickamauga and storming of Missionary Ridge; bvtd. brig. gen. for gallantry at Chickamauga and Chattanooga; awarded Congressional medal of honor for Missionary Ridge. Newspaper corr. in Washington from 1865. Chmn. Chickamauga and Chattanooga Nat. Mil. Park; brig. gen. vols., war with Spain, June 17, 1898. Pres. Bd. of Edn., D.C. Mem. Soc. Army of the Cumberland. Author: Sherman's Historical Raid, 1875; The Chickamauga National Military Park. Died 1905.

BOYNTON, NATHAN SMITH founder Order of Knights of the Maccabees; b. Port Huron, Mich., June 23, 1837; s. Granville F. and Frances B.; ed. dist. schs. and Waukegan (Ill.) High Sch.; m. Annie Fields, June 20, 1859. In mercantile business, Port Huron, Mich., 1856; later in Cincinnati, New Orleans, St. Louis. Served pvt. to maj. 8th Mich. Cav., 1862-65; when lt., cut off retreat of Gen. John Morgan, whom he finally captured. Elected to Mich. Legislature, 1868; mayor Port Huron, 1874-75, again, 2 terms, 1894-98. Was mem. Mich. Constl. Conv., 1907. Was owner and editor Port Huron Press. From 1881 devoted his attention to Order of Knights of the Maccabees, of which he was Supreme and Great Record Keeper, Past Supreme Comdr., Supreme Advisor and was then Great Comdr. of Modern Maccabees. Author: Boynton's Parliamentary Rules: The History of the Maccabees; The Dependency Place; Fraternal Co-operation. Home: Port Huron, Mich. Deceased.

BRADBURY, HOWARD WILLIAM naval officer (ret.); b. Wheeling, West Va., July 5, 1892; s. George Washington and Jessie (Porter) B.; student Hiram Coll., 1910-13; Carnegie Inst. Tech., 1915; m. Alice Farrell Craig, Dec. 5, 1922; children-John Craig, Howard William, George Craig, Harriet Craig, Patricia Craig. Enlisted USN, 1917; commd. ensign U.S.N.R.F., 1918, USN, 1923, advanced through grades to rear adm., 1947; served in S.W. Pacific, 1942-44; comdr. U.S.S. Alhena, cargo attack transport and Naval Insp. Ordnance Norden, 1944-47; ret. from active duty, Jan. 1, 1947. Awarded Presdl. commendation, Bronze Star. Home: 51 Lockwood Rd., Riverside, Conn. 06878. Died Nov. 2, 1964; buried Arlington (Va.) Nat. Cemetery.

BRADDOCK, EDWARD army officer; b. Perthshire, Scotland, 1695; s. Edward Braddock. Commd. maj. gen. Brit. Army, 1754; noted for his continental European mil. experience and stern mil. discipline; came to Hampton (Va.) as comdr.-in-chief of all his Majesty's forces in Am., 1755; built 1st road across Alleghanies in preparation for attack on Ft. Duquesne; victim of primitive Indian "guerrila style" warfare (as opposed to continental column formation) at Battle of Ft. Duquesne; had horse shot from under him before he himself was killed; only the Indians' propensity for scalping dead and familiarity of colonial troops (under Washington) with Indian fighting, allowed fair number of defeated troops to escape safely to rear guard, thence to Ft. Cumberland. Died Great Meadows, Pa., July 13, 1755; buried Great Meadows.

BRADFORD, GERARD engr., ret.; b. N.Y.C., Sept 13, 1887; s. William and Mary (Chittenden) B.; student U. Vt., 1904-05; B.S., U.S. Naval Acad., 1909, post grad., 1914-15; m. Helen Gartley, July 5, 1917; 1 son, Gerard. Commd. ensign USN, 1909, advancing through grades to lt. comdr., 1917; in submarine service, 1911-14; sea duty in SU.S.S. Arizona, San Diego, Louisiana, 1916-18; comdg. officer, naval mine depot, Yorktown, Pa., 1919-22; gunnery officer U.S.S. Pittsburgh, 1922-23; resigned and entered civil life in ins. mgmt., 1924, real estate engring. mgmt., N.Y.C., 1933-40; pres., dir. Witherbee Sherman Corp., 1940, ret. On active duty as comdr. USNR, Washington, 1941-45; placed on retired list, USN, 1943. Decorated Silver Star, World War I. Mem. Am. Inst. Mining and Metall. Engrs., N.Y. Hist. Soc., Sigma Phi. Clubs: University (N.Y.C.); Army and Navy (Washington); University (Hartford). Home: Bill Hill Rd., Old Lyme, Conn. Died Nov. 5, 1955; buried Arlington Nat. Cemetery.

BRADFORD, KARL SLAUGHTER, army officer; b. Washington, D.C., June 28, 1889; s. Ben Boyland and Nellie Irene (Harvey) B.; student U. of Va., 1906-07; B.S., U.S. Mil. Acad., 1911; grad. Machine Gun Officers Sch., Ecole Speciale Militaire, St. Cyr, France, Cavalry Sch., Command and Gen. Staff Sch. and Army War Coll.; m. Loraine Allen Sickel, Dec. 27, 1917; 1 daughter, Sally Harvey (Mrs. Richard Peck, Jr.). Commissioned 2d lt., U.S. Army, 1911; promoted through grades to brig. gen., 1941; served at various times in 2d, 3d, 4th, 15th and 26th Cavalry Regts.; comdr. 1st Cavalry Brigade, Fort Bliss, Tex., 1941-43; instr. U.S. Mil. Acad., 1914-18, and Cavalry School, 1934-36. Member Cavalry Board, 1921-25. Dep. pres. War Dept. Manpower Bd., 1943-46. Retired since Dec. 1946. Awarded Legion of Merit. Mem. Soc. of the Cincinnati, Beta Theta Pi. Clubs: Army and Navy, Army and Navy Country (Washington). Editor of Cavalry Jour., 1926-27. Home: Washington DC Died Aug. 1972.

BRADFORD, TAUL congressman, lawyer; b. Talladega, Ala., Jan. 20, 1835; grad. U. Ala. at Tuscaloosa, 1854; studied law. Admitted to bar, 1855, began practice of law, Talladega; served as maj. 10th Regt. Ala. Inf., then as lt. col. 13th Regt., Confederate Army during Civil War; mem. Ala. Ho. of Reps., 1871-72; mem. U.S. Ho. of Reps. (Democrat) from Ala., 44th Congress, 1875-77. Died Talladega, Oct. 28, 1883; buried Oak Hill Cemetery, Talladega.

BRADFORD, THOMAS publisher; b. May 4, 1745; s. William and Rachel (Budd) B.; attended U. Pa.; m. Mary Fisher, 1768, 6 children including Samuel, William, Thomas. Began working under his father on Pa. Journal and Weekly Advertiser, 1762, became full partner, 1766; took active part in resisting Stamp Act; his press temporarily suspended during Brit. occupation of Phila., 1777; served as capt. Pa. Militia, also lt. col. Continental Army, during Revolutionary War; started paper Mchts.' Daily Advertiser (specialized in news of business world), 1797, changed name to True American 1798, added literary supplement; charter mem. Am. Philos. Soc. Died May 7, 1838.

BRADFORD, WILLIAM BROOKS ret. army officer; b. Tallahassee, Mar. 15, 1896; s. John Taylor and Ida Henley (Brooks) B.; B.S., Va. Mil. Inst., 1916, Ecole de Cavalerie, Saumur, France, 1922-23, U.S. Cav. Sch., 1920-21, Command and Gen. Staff Sch., 1932-34; m. Stella Mae Batsell, 1920 (div.); 1 dau., Anne Batsell (Mrs. Robert N. Denniston); m. 2d Lois M. Blatt; 1 adopted son, Frederick. Commd. 2d lt., 1917, advanced through grades to maj. gen. (temporary), 1951, perm. 1952; civil engr. Everglades Drainage Project, 1916; mem. U.S. Olympic Equestrian Team, 1928, 32, 36 (capt.); dir. Dept. Tactics, U.S. Cav. Sch., 1939-41; chief of staff 2d Cav. Div., 83rd Inf. Div., 33d Inf. Div., 1941-43; asst. div. comdr., 99th Inf. Div., 1943-44, 25th Inf. Div., Pacific Area, Feb.-Sept. 1944; 27th Div. initial occupation of Japan comdg. gen. 1st Cav. Brigade 1945-49; dep. and G-3, Army Field Forces, Ft. Monroe, Va., 1949-52; comdg. gen. Trieste U.S. Troops, 1952-53; ret. 1953. Home: 145 Midland Dr., Asheville, N.C. Died Jan. 1965.

BRADLEY, ALFRED EUGENE army officer; b. Jamestown, N.Y., Nov. 25, 1864; s. Arthur A. and Jane (Parsons) B.; M.D., Jefferson Med. Coll., Phila., 1887; m. Letitia M. Follett, Oct. 4, 1887. Apptd. asst. surgeon, Oct. 29, 1888; capt. asst. surgeon, Oct. 29, 1893; maj. brigade surgeon vols., June 4, 1898; hon. discharged vol. service, Nov. 10, 1899; maj. surgeon U.S.A., Jan. 1, 1902; maj. Med. Corps, Jan. 1, 1902; lt. col., Jan. 28, 1910; col., July 1, 1916; brig. gen. N.A., Aug. 5, 1917; hon. discharged, as brig. gen. N.A., June 20, 1918; retired with rank of col. Mil observer with British, on duty at Am. Embassy, London, May 20, 1916, June 1917; apptd. chief surgeon A.E.F. in France, June 8, 1917, organizing med services of Am. forces abroad. Home: Highland Park, Ill. Died Dec. 17. 1922.

BRADLEY, FOLLETT army officer; b. Omaha, Feb. 12, 1890; s. Brig. Gen. Alfred E. and Letitia (Follett) B.; B.S., U.S. Naval Acad., 1910; grad. Ordnance Sch. of Application, 1915, Air Service Engring. Sch., 1922, Air Corps Tactical Sch., 1927, Command and Gen. Staff Sch., 1928, Army War Coll., Washington, 1932, Naval War Coll., Newport, 1933; m. Katharine Rising, Aug. 11, 1913 (dec. Dec. 1926); children-Carol (Mrs. Frederick Savage Jr.), Elizabeth Foster (Mrs. M.E. Sorte), Follett (1st lt. Air Corps, killed in Eng., June 22, 1941); m. 2d, Hester Henderson Foster, June 21, 1927. Commd. ensign USN, 1910 commd. 2d lt. F.A., U.S. Army, 1912; maj. AS, 1920, and advanced through grades to maj. Gen., Feb. 1942; learned to fly, 1916; served under air comdr. A.E.F., 1917, becoming jr. mil. aviator; instr. Arty. Sch. of Fire, Ft. Sill, Okla. 1919; asst. comdt. AS Tech. Sch., Chanute Field, Ill., 1922-23; comdg. officer France Field and 6th Composite Group, Panama Canal Dept., 1923-26; instr., dir. instrn. AC Tactical Schl. Langley Field, 1928-31; comdg. officer 9th Observation Group, Mitchel Field, N.Y., 1933-34; chief insp., air mail, 1934; War Dept. Gen. Staff, 1934-35; asst. chief of staff, G-2, G.H.Q., Air Force Langley Field, 1935-38; command Moffett Field, Calif., 1938-39; air officer, Puerto Rican Dept., 1939-40; command 13th Composite Wing, P.R., 1940-41; command 3d Bomber Command, MacDill Field, Tampa, Fla., 1941; comd. 1st Air Force, Mitchel Field and spl. mission to Russia for Pres. with personal rank of minister, 1942; insp. for U.S. Army Air Forces and overseas on spl. mission, 1943. Ret. as maj. gen., phys. disability, April 1944; aviation coordinator, asst. to pres. Sperry Gyroscope Co., since Apr. 1944. Decorated Croix de Guerre with palm and bronze star (France); Silver Star (U.S.); D.F.C., D.S.M. Mem. Daedalians, Mil. Order World Wars, Inst. Aero. Scis., Am. Legion. Clubs: Army and Navy Country (founder), Columbia Country (Washington); Garden City Golf; Meadowbrook; Wings (hon. mem. N.Y.). Home: 66 Poplar St., Garden City, N.Y. Died Aug. 4, 1952.

BRADLEY, JAMES L. army officer (ret.); b. Doniphan, Mo., May 18, 1891; B.S., U.S. Mil. Acad., 1914; grad. Inf. Sch. of Arms, Ft. Sill, 1917, Advanced Course Inf. Sch., Ft. Benning, 1924, Command and Gen. Staff Sch. (honor grad.), 1926, Army War College, 1931. Commd. 2d lt., U.S. Army, 1914, advanced through grades to maj. gen. (temp.), June 20, 1942; with 19th Inf., Vera Cruz, Mex., 1914, 22d Inf., Galveston, Tex., 1915; camp and dist. adjutant, Del Rio, Tex., 1916; with 57th Inf., Camp Travis, Tex., to June 1917, Camp Stanley, Tex., to Oct. 1917; inst. Sch. of Arms, Ft. Sill, 1918; sec. Inf. Sch. of Arms, Camp Benning, 1918-20; with 44th Inf., later 21st Inf., Schofield Barracks, Hawaii, 1920-23; with 4th Inf., Fort Missoula, 1923-24; inst. Inf. Sch., Ft. Benning, 1926-31. Command and Gen. Staff Sch., Ft. Leavenworth, 1932-36; exec. officer 16th Inf., Ft. Jay, 1936-38; with 2d Provisional Brig., Puerto Rico, 1938; comdg. officer 16th Inf., Ft. Jay, 1938; at Hdqrs. 9th Area, San Francisco, 1938-40; asst. chief of staff in charge plans and operations, 4th Army, San Francisco, 1940-41; chief, 1941-42; comdg. gen. 96th Inf. Div., 1942-46; participated in campaigns of Leyte and Okinawa. Awarded D.S.M., Legion of Merit, Bronze Star. Retired as maj. gen., 1947. Home: 608 West 11th St., Rolla, Mo. Died July 30, 1957; buried Presidio Nat. Cemetery, San Francisco.

BRADLEY, JOHN JEWSBURY army officer, lawyer; b. Chicago, Ill., Apr. 20, 1869; s. Timothy M. and Emma (Cookson) B.; B.S., U.S. Mil. Acad., 1891; grad. Army Sch. of Line, 1912, Army Staff Coll., 1913; m. Caroline Staden, Sept. 14, 1893; children—Frances Sladen (Mrs. William Elbridge Chickering), John Jewsbury, Jr., Joseph Sladen. Commd. 2d lt., 14th Inf., U.S. Army, 1891, advancing through the grades to brig. gen., 1926; admitted to New York bar, 1928. Washington (state) bar, 1908; now engaged in practice of law, N.Y. City. Served overseas in Philippines, China, France.

Decorated Distringuished Service Medal, Silver Star, Purple Heart (U.S.), Officer Legion d'Honneur (France). Comdr. Order of Crown (Italy). Companion of St. Michael and St. George (England). Trustee Disabled Am. Vets. Service Foundation. Mem. Mil. Order of World Wars, S.R., N.Y. state, West Point Soc. Hon. mem. Guards Club (London), 1918. Clubs: Military and Naval, University (New York); Army and Navy (Washington, D.C.). Home 57 W. 58th St., New York 19. Office: 475 Fifth Av., New York 17, N.Y. Died May 21, 1948; buried at U.S. Military Academy, West Point, N.Y.

BRADLEY, JOSEPH SLADEN army officer; b. Vancouver, Wash., June 9, 1900; s. John Tewsbury and Caroline Louise (Sladen) B.; B.S., U.S. Mil. Acad., 1919; student Mass. Inst. Tech., 1925-26; grad. Inf. Sch. basic course, 1920, Command and Gen. Staff Sch., 1937; m. Susan Lane Shattuck, Oct. 25, 1924; children-Susan Caroline, Joseph Sladen. Commnd. 2d lt. U.S. Army 1919, advanced through grades to maj. gen., 1944; now dep. dir. strategic plans joint staff; served with Am. forces in German Occupation, 1918; with inf. regts. in U.S.A., China and Philippines; on gen. staff, 32d Div., S.W. Pacific Area, 1942; comd. 126th Inf., 32d Div., during Buna Campaign and Saidor Landing, New Guinea; chief tng. group War Dept. Gen. Staff, G-3, 1953-56, ret.; city mgr. Winter Park, Fla., 1957-60. Decorated D.S.C., D.S.M., Siver Star, Bronze Star, Air medal. Mem. S.R. Mason. Club: Army and Navy (Washington). Address: 1850 Summerland Av., Winter Park, Fla. Died Jan. 17, 1961; buried U.S. Mil. Acad., West Point, N.Y.

BRADLEY, LUTHER PRENTICE army officer; b. New Haven, Conn., Dec. 8, 1822; ed. common schs. Lt. col. 51st Ill. Inf., Nov. 6, 1861; col., Oct. 5, 1862; brig. gen., July 20, 1864; resigned, June 30, 1865; apptd. from Ill., lt. col. 27th Inf., July 28, 1866; transferred to 9th Inf., Mar. 15, 1869; col. 3d Inf., Mar. 20, 1879; transferred to 13th Inf., June 14, 1879; retired, Dec. 8, 1886; advanced to rank of brig. gen. retired, by act of Apr. 23, 1904. Bvtd. col., Mar. 2, 1867, for battle of Chickamauga; brig. gen., Mar. 2, 1867, for battle of Resaca, Ga. Home: Tacoma, Wash. Died 1910.

BRADLEY, OTIS T(REAT) lawyer; b. New Haven, Conn., June 21, 1895; s. Otis Belden and Nellie Lucy (Treat) B.; A.B., Yale, 1915; LL.B., Harvard, 1919; m. Marian B. Alling, Nov. 18, 1926; children —Margaret Osborne, Otis T., Marian A., Edward Michael. Admitted to N.Y., State bar, 1920, and since practiced in N.Y. City, mem firm of Davis Polk Wardwell Sunderland & Kiendl and predecessor firms since 1930. Dir. F. Kelly Co., Union Fabric Co., Steel & Busks, Ltd. Admitted to U.S. Supreme Court, 1939. Served with Coast Artillery, U.S. Army, 1917-19; commd. 2d lt., 1917, disch. capt., 1919; served in 56th Artillery, C.A.C. in second battle of Marne, Meuse-Argonne campaigns, 1918; Govt. appeal agt., Selective Service. Trustee Union Coll., Bennington Coll., Union Theol. Sem., Southampton Hosp., Budkley Foundation, Chapin-Brearley Exchange, The Chapin Sch., Ltd. Mem. Am. Bar Assn., N.Y. State Bar Assn., N.Y. County Lawyers Assn., Assn. Bar City N.Y., N.Y. Hist. Soc. (trustee), Phi Beta Kappa, Zeta Psi. Presby. (mem. bd. nat. missions, elder, trustee). Clubs: Nat. Golf Links (Southampton, N.Y.); Grolier, Century, Links, Yale (N.Y. City). Home: 1160 Park Av., N.Y. City 28. Office 15 Broad St., N.Y. C. 5. Died Nov. 22, 1950.

BRADLEY, STEPHEN ROW senator; b. Wallingford (later Cheshire), Conn., Feb. 20, 1754; s. Moses and Mary (Row) B.; grad Yale, 1775; studied law under Tapping Reeve, Litchfield, Conn.; m. Merab Atwater, at least 1 son, William Czar; m. 2d, Thankful Taylor; m. 3d, Belinda Willard. Commd. capt. volunteers Continental Army, 1776, resigned as col. at end of Revolutionary War; admitted to Vt. bar, 1779; state's atty. for Cumberland County, Vt., 1780; register probate for Westminister, Vt., 1782; judge Windham County, Vt., 1783; speaker Vt. Ho. of Reps., 1785; asso. justice Vt. Superior Vt., 1788 mem. Westminster City Council, 1798; mem. U.S. Senate from Vt., Oct. 17, 1791-95, Oct. 15, 1801-13, pres. pro tem, 1802-03, 08, introduced bill to establish nat. flag of 15 stripes and 15 stars, used from 1795-1814 (sometimes called Bradley flag). Died Walpole, N.H., Dec. 9, 1830; buried Old Cemetery, Westminster, Vt.

BRADLEY, THOMAS W. congressman; b. Apr. 6, 1844. Pvt. to capt. 124th N.Y. Vols.; a.-d.-c. to Maj. Gen. Mott, 3d Div., 2d Army Corps; wounded at Gettysburg, Wilderness and Petersburg; awarded Congressional Medal of Honor; bvtd. maj. vols. Mem. del. Rep. nat. convs., 1892, 1896, 1900, 1908; mem. 58th to 62d Congresses (1903-13), 20th N.Y. Dist. Home: Walden, N.Y. Died May 30, 1920.

BRADLEY, WILLIS W. state legislator; b. Ransomville, N.Y., June 28, 1884; s. Willis W. And Sarah Anne (Johnson) B.; B.Sc., U.S. Naval Acad., 1907; M.Sc., George Washington Univ., 1914; post grad. Ordnance and Gunnery, United States Navy, 1913-35; graduate of the Naval War College, 1938; m. Sue Worthington Cox, Oct. 16, 1907; children—Elizabeth (Mrs. John J. Earle), Sue (Mrs. Bruce McCandless), Anne (Mrs. Wallace H. Brucker), Josephine (Mrs. Guy O. DeYoung). Commd. ensign U.S. Navy, 1907, and advanced through grades to capt., 1933; gov. of Guam, 1929-31; retired; 1946. Mem. of the Congress, 18th District of Calif., 1947-49; mem. assembly, Cal. Legislature, 1952. Mem. board visitors U.S. Naval Academy, 1948. Awarded Congressional Medal of Honor, World War I; Silver Medal from Pope Pius XI; Silver Medal from Italian Red Cross for Messina Earthquake. Mem. Am. Legion, Vets. Fgn. Wars, Am. Vets., Disabled Am. Vets. Army and Navy Union, U.S.A., Mil. Order of Carabao, Naval Order of U.S., American Academy Political and Social Science. Republican. Protestant. Mason (32ff, K.T., Shriner). Elk. Moose, National Sojourners (past nat. pres.). Clubs: Army and Navy, Army-Navy Country, Cosmos (Washington, DC); University (Long Beach); Propeller of U.S. Home: 284 Argonne Av., Long Beach 3, Cal. Office: State Capitol, Sacramento. Died Aug. 27, 1954; buried Fort Rosecrans Nat. Cemetery, Point-Loma, San Diego, Cal.

BRADSHAW, FREDERICK JOSEPH, JR., hosp. adminstr.; b. Kiating Sze, China, Aug. 24, 1904 (parents Am. citizens); s. Frederick Joseph and Martha (Philp) B.; B.A., U. Redlands, 1927; B.M., Northwestern U. Med. Sch., 1931, M.D., 1932; m. Edna Margaret Biersdorfer, Dec. 14, 1931;children—Edna Joan (Mrs. Lyle Edward Miller), Frederick Joseph III. Intern, Cal. Hosp., Los Angeles, 1931, Cedars of Lebanon Hosp., Los Angeles, 1932; resident Community Hosp., Long Beach, Cal., 1932-33; med. officer VA, Palo Alto, Cal., 1938-39, St. Cloud, Minn., 1939-41; chief neuropsychiat. service Barnes Gen. Hosp., Vancouver, Wash., 1941-44; asst. clin. dir., instr. neuropsychiatry VA Hosp., Coatesville, Pa., 1946-47; chief profl. services VA Hosp., Gulfport, Miss., 1947-51; mgr. VA Hosp., Ft. Meade, S.D., 1951-57; chief of staff VA Hosp., Tomah, Wis., 1958-63; med. dir. Brentwood Hosp. VA Center, Los Angeles, 1964-71; asst. clin. prof. psychiatry U. Cal., Los Angeles. Served to col. M.C., AUS, 1941-46. Fellow Am. Coll. Physicians, Am. Psychiatric Assn.; mem. A.M.A. Home: Canoga Park CA Died Jan. 6, 1971; inurned Columbarium, Veterans Administration Cemetery, Los Angeles CA

BRADSTREET, JOHN army officer; b. Horbling, Eng., 1711. Sent as young Brit. officer to Am., 1745; served as lt. col. Pepperell's Regt. in expdn. against Louisburg, Me.; made capt., 1745; lt. gov. St. John's, Newfoundland, 1746-55; adjutant gen. to Gov. Shirley, Boston, 1755-57; lt. col. 60th Regt. Royal Americans, 1757-58; participated in attack on Ft. Ticonderoga; served under Lord Jeffery Amherst, 1759; served in Pontiac's War, negotiated Peace Treaty in Detroit, 1764. Died N.Y.C., Sept. 25, 1774.

BRADY, FRANCIS M., army officer; b. Yonkers, N.Y., July 7, 1896; grad. Air Service Pilots Sch., and Observation Sch., 1921, Tactical Sch., 1923, Command and Gen. Staff Sch., 1931, Army War Coll., 1936; rated command pilot, combat observer. Commd. 2d lt., Inf., U.S. Army, Oct. 1917; transfered to Air Corps as capt., 1925; advanced through the grades to brig. gen., Feb. 1942; Gen. Staff Corps, 1938-39; served as 2d and 1st lt., Inf., World War I; decorated Distinguished Service Cross, Silver Star, Purple Heart. Address: Miami Beach FL Died Oct. 1969.*

BRADY, THOMAS JEFFERSON soldier; b. Muncie, Ind., Feb. 12, 1839; s. John and Mary (Wright) B.; ed. Asbury Coll. (De Pauw U.); studied law, but did not practice; m. Emmeline Wolfe, 1864. Supt. Muncie schools, 1860-61; capt. and maj. 8th Ind. inf., 1861-63; col. 117th Ind. inf., 1863-64; col. 140th Ind. inf., 1864-65; bvt. brig. gen. Mar. 13, 1865; U.S. consul, St. Thomas, West Indies, 1870-75; supervisor Internal Revenue, 1875-76; 2d asst. postmaster-gen., 1876-81. Home: Colonial Beach, Va. Died 1904.

BRAGDON, JOHN STEWART govt. ofcl.; b. Pittsburgh, Pa., May 21, 1893; s. Frank Hamilton and Annie (Gaines) B.; B.S., U.S. Mil. Acad., 1915, M.S., Carnegie Tech., 1923; U.S. Engr. Sch., 1919, Command and Gen. Staff Sch., 1928; m. Ruth Josephine Hughes, Apr. 20, 1917; children-Ruth (Mrs. Charles Donovan), Dorothy Mary (Mrs. Robert L. L. McCormick) and John Stewart. Commissioned 2d lieutenant, 1915, and advanced through grades to major gen., Oct. 1950; instr. U.S. Mil. Acad., 1923-24, U.S. Engr. Sch., 1924-27; on Gen. Staff with troops, P.I., 1929-31; contract officer, Engr. Dept., War Dept., 1931-35; asst. div. engr. North Atlantic Div., Engr. Dept., 1935-37, U.S. dist. engr., Providence, R.I., 1937-41, div. engr. South Atlantic Div., 1941-44. Dir. Mil. Constuction, Office Chief of Engrs., U.S.A., 1944-49, asst. chief of engrs. 1948-51, dep., 1949-51; cons. engr., N.Y.C., 1951-53; v.p. Vermilya-Brown Co., 1954; staff Council of Econ. Advisers to President, 1954-55; asst. to President of the U.S. for pub. works planning, 1955-60; mem. Civil Aeronautics Bd., 1960-61; consultant House Com. Public Works, 1961-62. Decorated Purple Heart, D.S.M. with oak leaf cluster. Mem. A.I.A. (honorary), Am. Soc. Mil. Engrs. Conglist. Club: Army and Navy (Washington). Home: 2737 Devonshire Pl., Washington 20008. Died Jan. 7, 1964; buried U.S. Mil. Acad., West Point, N.Y.

BRAGG, BRAXTON army officer; b. Warren County, N.C., Mar. 22, 1817; s. Thomas and Margaret (Crossland) B.; grad. U.S. Mil. Acad., N.Y., 1837; m. Elisa Ellis, 1849. Brevetted capt. U.S. Army, 1846; served with distinction under Zachary Taylor during Mexican War; served as lt. col., maj. gen. La. Militia, 1861; commd. brig. gen. Confederate States Army, 1861, maj. gen., 1862, gen, 1862; fought against Gen. Don Carlos Buell at Battle of Perryville (Ky.), Oct. 8, 1862, forced to retreat into Tenn., battle marked end of Confederate invasion of Ky.; most famous for victory at Battle of Chickamauga, 1863; later defeated by U.S. Grant at Battle of Chattanooga, forced to retreat into Ga., comdr.-in-chief Confederate Army, also mil. adviser to Pres. Davis, 1864; supt. New Orleans Water Works, 1869; chief engr. Gulf, Colorado and Santa Fe. R.R., 1874. Died Galveston, Tex., Sept. 27, 1876.

BRAGG, EDWARD STUYVESANT congressman; b. Unadilla, N.Y., Feb. 20, 1827; s. Joel and Margaretha (Kohl) B.; student Geneva and Hobart colls.; LL.D., Hobart, 1898, Appleton, 1902; m. Cornelia Colman, Jan. 2, 1854. Dist. atty., Fond du Lac County, 1854-56; mem. Charleston Conv., 1860. Capt. 6th Wis. Inf., July 16, 1861; maj., Sept. 17, 1861; lt. col., June 21, 1862; col., Mar. 24, 1863; brig. gen. vols., June 25, 1864; hon. mustered out, Oct. 9, 1865. Del. Dem. Nat. convs., 1861, 1872, 1884, 1892, 1896, Union Conv., Phila, 1866; mem. 45th, 46th, 47 Congresses (1877-83), 49th Congress (1885-87); E.E. and M.P. to Mexico, 1888-89; prominent gold Democrat, 1896; supported McKinley, 1900; consul-gen. at Havana, May 19-Sept. 15, 1902, at Hongkong, China, 1902-06. Home: Fond du Lac, Wis. Died June 20, 1912.

BRAINARD, DAVID LEGGE army officer; b. Norway, N.Y., Dec. 21, 1856; s. Alanson and Maria C. (Legge) B.; ed. State Normal Sch., Cortland, N.Y., m. Sara H. Guthrie, June 1917. Pvt., corporal and sergt. Troop L, 2d Cav., Sept. 18, 1876-July 31, 1884; sergt. Signal Corps, Aug. 1, 1884-Oct. 21, 1886; commd. 2d lt. 2d Cav., Oct. 22, 1886; brig. gen., N.A., Oct. 2, 1917; brig. gen. U.S. Army, July 25, 1918; retired July 27, 1918. Participated in Sioux, Nez Perce and Bannock campaigns, 1877-78; wounded in face and right hand; detailed for duty with Howgate Arctic exploring expdn., 1880; with Lady Franklin Bay Arctic Expdn., under Lt. Greely, 1881-84; associated with Lt. Lockwood in exploring interior of Grinnell Land and the northwest coast of Greenland; on May 13, 1882, reached the then highest point North ever attained, was one of 7 survivors rescued by Comdr. W. S. Schley, June 1884; commd. 2d lt. 2d Cav. "for distinguished and meritorious services in connection with the Arctic Expdn., 1881-84." Awarded the Back Grant of Royal Geog. Soc., 1885, for spl. services in connection with his work of exploration in Arctic regions; Charles P. Daly gold medal, 1926, by Am. Geog. Soc. for Arctic explorations; explorer's medal, Explorers Club, N.Y. City, 1929; Purple Heart, 1933. Fellow Am. Geog. Soc.; mem. Nat. Geog. Soc. Clubs: Explorers, Military-Naval (New York); Army and Navy (Washington). Author: Outpost of the Lost (Arctic Journal), 1929; Six Came Back, Aug. 1940. The only survivor of the Greely Arctic Expedition. Address: Army and Navy Club. Washington. Died Mar. 22, 1946; buried in Arlington National Cemetery.

BRAINE, CLINTON ELGIN, JR. naval officer, ret.; b. N.Y. City, Dec. 9, 1894; s. Clinton Elgin and Ella Bird (Warburton) B.; B.S., U.S. Naval Acad., 1916; m. Miriam Maude Ellis, Feb. 22, 1919; 1 son, Clinton Ellis. Commd. ensign, U.S. Navy, 1916, and advanced through grades to rear admiral, 1945; duty on battleship, 1916-20; on submarine, 1920-30, staff and cruiser, 1930-38; with Bureau of Ordnance, 1938-41; mem. mission to U.S.S.R., 1941; comd. U.S.S. Memphis, 1941-42, chief of staff 4th Fleet, 1942-45; comdg. Naval Operating Base and Training Station, Newport, R.I.; office of Sec. of Navy, 1946-49, ret. 1949; now asst. to pres. Crucible Steel Co. of Am. Decorated Legion of Merit (3 times), Commendation Medal, World War II, China Defense, Atlantic and European service medals of Merit for Air (Brazil). Clubs: New York Yacht, St. Nicholas, Yale (N.Y. City); Duquesne (Pittsburgh). Home: 108 E. 38th St. Office: 405 Lexington Av., N.Y. City. Now deceased.

BRAISTED, WILLIAM CLARENCE navy surgeon; b. Toledo, O., Oct. 9, 1864; s. Frank and Helen Maria (Fiske) B.; Ph.B., U. of Mich., 1883; M.D., with honors, Med. Dept., Columbia U., 1886; LL.D., U. of Mich., 1917, Jefferson Med. Coll., Phila., 1918; D.Sc., Northwestern U., 1918; m. Lillian Mulford Phipps, Apr. 2, 1886. Served Bellevue Hosp., New York, 1/2 yrs.; practiced, Detroit, 1888-90; entered Navy as asst. surgeon, Sept. 26, 1893; surgeon, Mar. 3, med. insp., Oct. 20, 1913; twice instr. in surgery Naval Medical Sch.; fitted out and equipped the hosp. ship Relief, 1904. Represented Med. Dept. in Japan during Russo-Japanese War; asst. chief Bur. of Medicine and Surgery, 6 yrs., 1906-12, and assisted in reorganization of same and of med. service of the Navy; served with Dr. Rixey as attending phys. at White House, President Theodore Roosevelt's administration, 1906-07; fleet surgeon, Atlantic fleet, July 1, 1912-14; surgeon-gen. and chief Bur. of Medicine and Surgery, Feb. 1914-21, rank of rear admiral. Pres. Coll. of Pharmacy and Science, Phila., 1921 - ; dir. Union Trust Co., Washington, D.C. Mem. bd. dirs. Columbia Hosp. for Women; pres. bd. visitors Govt. Hosp. for Insane, Washington, D.C. Mem. exec. com. central com. and war relief bd., Am.

Red Cross, 1914-20. Retired from Navy after 30 yrs.' service, Nov. 1920, with rank of rear admiral. Awarded D.S.M.; decorated by Emperor of Japan, and with Order of Bolivar by pres. of Venezuela. Home: West Chester, Pa. Died Jan. 17, 1941.

BRAMLETTE, THOMAS E. gov. Ky.; b. Cumberland County, Ky., Jan. 3, 1817; m. Sallie Travis, 1837, m. 2d, Mrs. Mary E. Adams, 1874. Admitted to Ky. bar, 1837; states atty. Ky., 1848; judge 6th Jud. Dist, Ky., 1856; U.S. dist. atty., 1862; commd. maj. gen. U.S. Army, 1863; gov. Ky. (Union Democrat), 1863-67; declined Dem. vice presdl. nomination, 1864. Died Louisville, Ky., Jan. 12, 1875.

BRANCH, IRVING LEWIS air force officer; b. Keokuk, Ia., Aug. 1, 1912; s. George Irving and Helen Louise (Lewis) B.; B.S. in Civil Engring., Norwich U., 1934; grad. Air Corps Primary and Advanced Flying Sch., 1935, Armed Forces Staff Coll., 1947, Air War Coll., 1953; m. Margaret Dulaney Rogers, June 19, 1937; children-Christopher Irving, Richard Dulaney. Commd. 2d lt. Air Corps, 1936, advanced through grades to maj. gen. USAF, 1964; pilot pursuit group, comdr. reconnaissance squadron to 1954; liaison officer Anti-submarine Command to sec. war, Washington, 1943; comdr. 1st Bombardment Group, Chinese Air Force, 1943-44; comdr. 72d Fighter Wing, Colorado Springs, 1945-46; chief staff, mem. Air Force delegation Mil. Staff Com. UN, 1947-49; chief air intelligence div. U.S. Air Forces Europe, 1949-53; chief weapons devel. div., chief staff Armed Forces Spl. Weapons Project, Washington, 1953-57; dep. comdr. Air Force Spl. Weapons Center, Alburquerque, 1957-59; asst. dir. div. reactor devel. AEC, chief Aircraft Nuclear Propulsion Office, asst. for nuclear systems Dep. Chief Staff Hdqrs. USAF, Washington, 1959-61; comdr. Air Force Flight Test Center, Edwards AFB, Cal., 1961-. Decorated Legion of Merit, D.F.C., Air medal (U.S.); Yun Hui Order of Cloud Banner, Pilot Wings (China). Mem. Am. Ordnance Soc., Nat. Rifle Assn., Nat. Aero. Assn. (mem. contest bd.), Order Daedalians. Club: Tuesday Musical. Home: 5308 Palo Verde Dr., Edwards, Cal. Office: Hdqrs. Air Force Flight Test Center, Edwards AFB, Cal. Died Jan. 1966.

BRANCH, JAMES RANSOM coal operator; b. Petersburg, Va., Dec. 14, 1863; s. James R. and Martha Louise (Patteson) B.; removed to Richmond, 1864; ed. in schs. of Gen. Robert Ransom, John P. McGuire, Pampatike Acad., Col. Gordon McCabe, Richmond Coll.; m. Mary Lillian Hubball, of Richmond, Va., Oct. 28, 1885. With Merchants' Nat. Bank, Richmond, 1881-85; in stock raising and other business until 1890, when returned to Merchants' Nat. Bank, becoming its spl. corr. and chief of collection dept.; mem. Richmond City Council, 1895; apptd., 1895, national bank examiner for Va., W.Va., N.C. and Tenn.; sec. Am. Bankers' Assn., 1895-1908; trust co. sect., 1900-08, Currency Commn., 1906-07. Pres. Branchland Coal Co., since 1906; pres. Guyandotte Coal co., Guyan River Coal Co., Served pvt. to lt.-col. in Va. Vols.; maj. 7th U.S. Vol. Inf. in Spanish War (7th Immunes). Episcopalian. Democrat. Mem. Southern Soc., Virginians. Clubs: Guyandotte (Huntington, W.Va.), Army and Navy (Washington), Commonwealth (Richmond, Va.), New York Athletic, Home: New York Athletic Club. Offices: Hanover Bank Bldg., New York, and Branchfield, W.Va.

BRANCH, JOHN senator, gov. N.C.; b. Halifax County, N.C., Nov. 4, 1782; s. Col. John and Mary (Bradford) B.; grad. U. N.C., 1801, m. Elizabeth Fort, m. 2d, Eliza Jordan, 9 children. Mem. N.C. Senate, 1811, 13-17, 22, 34, speaker, 1815-17; gov. N.C., 1817-20; mem. N.C. br. Am. Colonization Soc., 1819; mem. U.S. Senate from N.C., 1823-29; U.S. sec. of navy, 1829-31; mem. U.S. Ho. of Reps. from N.C., 22d Congress, 1831-33; mem. N.C. Constl. Conv., 1835; gov. Territory of Fla., 1843-45. Died Enfield, N.C., Jan. 4, 1863.

BRANCH, LAWRENCE O'BRYAN army officer; congressman, b. Enfield, N.C., July 7, 1820; s. John and Susan (O'Bryan) B.; grad. Princeton, 1838; m. Nancy Blount, 1844. Pres., Raleigh & Gaston R.R. Co., (N.C.) 1852-55; mem. U.S. Ho. of Reps. from N.C., 34th-36th congresses, Dec. 3, 1855-61; commd. brig. gen. Confederate Army, 1862. Died Battle of Antietam, Sept. 17, 1862.

BRAND, CHARLES L. naval officer; b. Worcester, Mass., Nov. 11, 1887; s. John L. and Annie E. (Butt) B.; B.S., U.S. Naval Acad., 1910; M.S., Mass. Inst. Tech., 1915; m. Helen May Levin, June 17, 1914; 1 dau., Nancy R. Commd. lt. (j.g.), U.S. Navy, 1912, and advanced through the grades to rear admiral, 1942; served as midshipman, U.S.S. Georgia, 1910-12; at U.S. Navy Yards, Phila., 1915-20, Puget Sound, Wash., 1920-23, Charleston, S.C., 1923-25, Mare Island, Calif., 1927-31, Puget Sound, 1931-32, Phila., 1936-38; staff of comdr. in chief, Battle Force, 1925-27; head constrn. div., Bureau of Ships, Navy Dept., Washington,D.C., 1932-36; mgr. Navy Yard, Boston, 1938-42; became asst. chief for design and shpbldg., Bur. Ships, Navy Dept., Washington, 1942; retired, 1949. Now representative American President Lines. Awarded Victory Medal (World War I), Emergency Medal, 1941; Distinguished Service Medal, Am. Theatre Victory medal, World War II. Mem. Grad. Bd., Mass. Inst. Tech. Mem. U.S. Soc. Naval Architects (past pres.), Am. Soc. Naval Engrs. Address: 32 Riverbank, Beverly, N.J. Died April 18, 1953.

BRAND, HARRISON, JR., association exec.; b. Ilion, N.Y., Aug. 24, 1891; s. Harrison and Marion S. (Eaton) B.; B.S., U.S. Mil. Acad., 1914; m. Helen McCumber, Apr. 21, 1917; 1 son, Harrison; married 2d, Emily Hambrock, June 21, 1960. Commissioned 2d lieut. and advanced through grades to lt. col., Engrs. Corps, U.S. Army, 1914-19; lt. col. Engineers reserve, 1920-32, col., 1932-42, colonel, Army of United States, retired, 1951; federal tax practice, 1920-25; admitted to D.C. bar, 1925; mem. firm McCumber and Brand, Washington, 1925-33; mem. D.C. Pub. Utilities Comm., 1927-29; pvt. practice of law, 1933-37; in charge of supply for W.P.A. of New York, N.Y., 1937-38, purchase of construction equipment, federal W.P.A., 1938; exec. sec. Washington (D.C.) Board of Trade, 1938-41; with the Aerospace Industries Association of America, Inc., and predecessors, Washington, D.C., since 1941, secretary-treasurer, since 1944. Member Washington Board of Trade. National Aeronautic Association, Soc. American Military Engineers (honorary life member; director or officer 1923-37). Mason. Clubs: Army and Navy (Washington); Chevy Chase (Md.). Home: Washington DC Deceased.

BRANDON, WILLIAM WOODWARD gov.; b. Talladega, Ala., June 5, 1868; s. Rev. Franklin Thomas Jefferson and Caroline (Woodward) B.; ed. Cedar Bluff Inst., and high sch., Tuscaloosa; studied law, U. of Ala.; m. Mrs. Lizzie Andrews Nabors, June 27, 1900 (died 1933). Admitted to Ala. bar, 1892, and began practice at Tuscaloosa; city clk., 1891-94; mem. Ala. Ho. of Rep. 3 terms, 1894-98; clk. Ala. Constl. Conv., 1901; state auditor of Ala., 1897-1911; probate judge, Tuscaloosa County, 1911-23; gov. of Ala., term 1923-27; again probate judge, Tuscaloosa County. Capt. Co. F, 2d Ala. N.G., 1895-98; capt. and maj. same regt., Spanish-Am. War; brig. gen. and adj. gen. Ala. N.G., 1898-1907. Democrat. Methodist. Mason. Home: Tuscaloosa, Ala. Died Dec. 7, 1934.

BRANDT, ERDMANN NEUMIESTER editor; b. Savannah, Ga., July 18, 1893; s. Carl Nelson and Clara (Ellis) B.; student Bear Island Acad., Taylorsville, Va., 1903-06; Washington Irving High Sch., Tarrytown, N.Y., 1907-10; m. Jessamine Patteson, Sept. 10, 1927; children-Erdmann Ellis, C. Patteson, Jessamine. With Maxwell-Briscoe Motor Co., Tarrytown, 1910-11; Walker Bin Co., Penn Yan, N.Y., 1911-13; asst. western sales mgr., hdqrs. San Francisco, for Hupp Motor Car Co., Detroit 1913-16; partner Brandt & Brandt, lit. agts., N.Y.C., 1919-34; asso. editor Sat. Eve. Post, 1934-61, ret., 1961. Served with 7th Regt., N.Y.N.G., on Mexican Border, 1916; capt., 106th Inf., 27th Div., 1917-19; lt. col., 107th Inf., N.G., 1926-29. Awarded Silver Star with cluster, Purple Heart. Dir. Merion Civic Assn., Merion Bot. Soc. Mem. N.Y. Soc. Mil. and Naval Officers, 7th Regt. Vet. Assn. Republican. Presbyn. Clubs: Philadelphia Country; Cactus (N.Y.C.). Home: 76 Rayham Rd., Merion Sta., Pa. 19066. Died June 11, 1966; buried Sleepy Hollow Cemetery, North Tarrytown, N.Y.

BRANN, DONALD W. army officer; b. Rushville, Ind., Sept. 26, 1895; s. Oliver Canby and Dorothy B.; student Purdue U., 1913-14, U. of Mich., 1914-15; grad. company officers training course, Inf. Sch., 1931, Command and Gen. Staff Sch., 1935; Army War Coll., 1938; m. Dorothy Teel, Dec. 27, 1922; 1 dau., Dorothy Ballard (wife of Lt. Col. Dorsey E. McCrory). Entered U.S. Army as 2d lt., inf., 1917, advancing through the grades to maj. gen., 1944. Decorated Distinguished Service Medal with oak leaf cluster, Legion of Merit (U.S.); chevalier Legion of Honor, Croix de Guerre with palm, (France) Italian Order of the Crown, Silver Star (Italy); Hon. Comdr. Order British Empire; Polish Gold Cross of Merit with Swords; Czechoslovakian War Cross, War Medal, Order of Military Merit, National Order of Southern Cross (Brazil). Mem. Phi Delta Theta. Office: care The Adjutant General, U.S. Army, Washington. Died Dec. 29, 1945; buried in U.S. Military Cemetery, Castel Florentino, near Florence, Italy.

BRANNAN, JOHN MILTON army officer; b. D.C., July 1, 1819; grad. U.S. Mil. Acad., 1841. Brevetted 2d lt. arty. U.S. Army, 1841, stationed at Plattsburg, N.Y. until 1842; commd. 2d lt., 1842; promoted 1st lt. arty. at outbreak Mexican War, 1846, adjutant 1st Arty., 1847; served in battles of Vera Cruz, Contreras and Churubusco; brevetted capt. for bravery, 1847; wounded in assult on Chapultepc, served in occupation of city; promoted capt., 1854; engaged in battle with Seminole Indians in Fla., 1856-58; apptd. brig. gen. U.S. Volunteers in charge of Key West, Fla., also operations on St. John's River, at beginning of Civil War; brevetted lt. col. U.S. Army for bravery at Jacksonville, 1862; promoted maj., 1863; brevetted col. for bravery at Chickamauga, 1863; served at Battle of Missionary Ridge, 1863; commanded arty. at siege of Atlanta; brevetted brig. gen. U.S. Army for bravery at Atlanta, 1865; commanded garrison at Ogdensburg, N.Y.; promoted lt. col. 4th Arty., 1877, col., 1881; ret., 1882. Died Dec. 16, 1892.

BRANSHAW, CHARLES E. army officer; born Vt., Aug. 6, 1895; grad. Air Corps Tactical Sch., 1935; rated pilot, combat observer, tech. observer, aircraft observer. Began as private, F.A., Colo. Nat. Guard, 1916; commd. 1st lt. Aviation Sect., 1917, and advanced through the grades to maj. gen., June 1943; retired as maj. general for disability incident to the service on Dec. 31, 1944. Served as 1st lt. Aviation Sect., World War I. Awarded Distringuished Service Medal. Legion of Merit. Address: Concan, Texas. Died May 8, 1949. Buried Concan, Tex.

BRASTED, ALVA JENNINGS, army chaplain, ret.; b. Findley Lake, N.Y., July 5, 1876; s. Nathan Russell and Adaline (More) B.; B.S., Des Moines College, 1902; B.D., Chicago U., 1905; LL.D., Sioux Falls Coll., 1946; m. Ada Crocker, June 15, 1910; children—Mary Frances, Robert Crocker, Donald More. Student pastor Wauconda (Ill.) Bapt. Ch., 1902-05; ordained to ministry Bapt. Ch., 1905; pastor Lisbon, N.D., 1905-10, Montevideo, Minn., 1910-12, Ft. Dodge, Ia., 1912-13; 1st lt. chaplain U.S. Army, 1913; capt., 1920, maj., 1927; lt. col., 1933, apptd. chief of chaplains, U.S. Army, with rank of col. term Dec. 23, 1933-Dec. 22, 1937. Member of John More Association, Sons of Am. Revolution, Am. Legion. Republican. Mason (32 deg.); Soujourner. Author of articles and pamphlets on the work of chaplains in the regular army and Civilian Conservation Corps.; (books) Service to Service Men; For Victorious Living; AZ You Were. Home: 204 MacArthur Rd., Alexandria VA

BRATTON, JOHN physician, state legislator; b. Winnsboro, S.C., Mar. 7, 1831; s. Dr. William, Jr. and Isabella (Means) B.; grad. S.C. Coll., 1850; M.D., S.C. Med. Coll., 1853; m. Elizabeth DuBose, 1859. Practiced medicine, Fairfield County, S.C., until Civil War; served with 6th Regt., S.C. Volunteers during Civil War, promoted capt., 1861, col., 1862, brig. gen., 1864, known as "Old Reliable"; mem. S.C. Constl. Conv., 1865, S.C. Senate, 1865-66, S.C. Ho. of Reps., 1884-85. Died Winnsboro, Jan. 12, 1898.

BRATTON, LESLIE EMMETT naval officer; b. Hastings, Neb., Dec. 8, 1885; s. Aleinas Thomas and Harriet (Stevens) B.; B.S., U.S. Naval Acad., 1907; LL.B., George Washington U., 1915; grad. Naval War Coll., 1928; m. Emeline Kooser Wolf, Mar. 31, 1909; children—Elizabeth (Mrs. Lee C. Ashley), Alice Virginia (Mrs. George S. Writer). Commd. ensign U.S. Navy, 1907, and advanced through the grades to comdr.; retired for physical disability 1930; mgr. of safety for Denver, Col., 1930-31; v.p. Daly Gen. Ins. Co., Denver, 1931-40; recalled to active duty 1940; promoted to capt., then rear adm; asst. judge advocate gen. of Navy. Retired. physical disability, 1944. Decorated 1st and 2d World War, and Nicaraguan Campaign medals. Mem. D.C., Colo. bar assns., Phi Delta Phi. Am. Legion, Vets. Foreign Wars. Clubs: Army and Navy, Chevy Cahse (Washington); Denver Club, Denver Country Club. Home: 228 Race St., Denver. Died Aug. 2, 1959; buried Arlington Nat. Cemetery.

BRAUER, JOHN CHARLES, educator; born Sterling, Neb., Sept. 6, 1905; s. John Thomas and Mary Ann (Ross) B.; D.D.S., U. Neb., 1928, A.B., 1934, M.Sc., 1936; student U. Mich., summer 1932; m. Dora Lee Stewart, June 20, 1932; 1 son, James Stewart. Practiced as dentist, Orleans, Neb., 1928-30; instr. operative dentistry, pedodontics, preventive dentistry U. Neb., 1930-36; dir De Los L. Hill, Jr., Meml. Children's Dental Clinic, prof. pedodontics, orthodontics and preventive dentistry, Atlanta Southern Dental Coll., 1936-38; head dept., prof. preventive dentistry and pedodontics, dir. bur. dental hygiene State U. Ia., 1938-42; dir. postgrad. dental edn., exec. officer dept. pedodontics U. Wash. Sch. Dentistry, 1947-50; dean, U. N.C. Sch. Dentistry, 1950-66; sec. Dental Found of N.C., Inc., from 1950; lectr. numerous dental socs., U.S. and Can. Cons. to asst. sec. def. for manpower Dept. Def., from 1958, USPHS, from 1960, W.K. Kellogg Found., Council on Dental Edn., from 1961; studies dir. Com. on Instnl. Cooperation, Big 10 Univs. Commd. 1st lt., Dental Corps, U.S. Army Res., 1928; lt. col., asst. to Maj. Gen. Robert H. Mills, dental div. and chief dental standards br., Surg. Gen. Office, 1942-46. Decorated Legion of Merit. Recipient O. Max Gardner award U. N.C., 1963 Fellow Am. Coll. Dentists; mem. Am. Dental Assn., Am. Soc. Dentistry for Children, Internat. Research Assn., Am. Acad Pedodontics (pres. 1949, chmn. 1946), Sigma Xi, Tau Kappa Epsilon, Omicron Kappa Upsilon, Delta Sigma Delta. Author: Dentistry for Children, 1939. Co-author, co-editor: Dentistry for Children, rev. edit., 1964; The Dental Assistant, rev. edit., 1964. Editor (with Sturdevant, Barton, Harrison) The Art and Science of Operative Dentistry, 1968. Contbr. articles to jours. Address: Carmel CA Died Apr. 9, 1971.

BRAUSE, EDWARD pub. relations exec.; b. Glen Cove, N.Y., May 26, 1908; s. Adolph L. and Marcella (Cassell) B.; B.A., Columbia, 1929; m. Hilda R. Adams, Mar. 27, 1942; children-Peter A., Andrew H. Reporter, N.Y. World, 1930-31, N.Y. Herald Tribune, 1931-36; rewrite editor Havas News Agy., 1936-40, PM and N.Y. Star, 1940-41, 45-49; pub. relations account exec. Barber & Baar, N.Y.C., 1949-50; pub. relations dir. Merritt-Chapman & Scott Corp., N.Y.C., 1950-, v.p.

pub. relations, 1958-. Served to capt. inf. AUS, 1941-45. Mem. Soc. Silurians, Indsl. Publicity Assn., Zeta Beta Tau. Club: Overseas Press (N.Y.C.). Home: 4 Knollwood Rd., Flower Hill, Roslyn, N.Y. Office: 277 Park Av., N.Y.C. 10017. Died Sept. 2, 1967.

BRAXTON, ELLIOTT MUSE congressman, lawyer; b. Matthews, Va., Oct. 8, 1823; attended common schs.; studied law. Admitted to bar, 1849, began practice of law, Richmond, Va.; moved to Richmond County; mem. Va. Senate, 1851-55; moved to Fredericksburg, Va., 1860, continued practice of law; raised company for Confederate Army, elected its capt., during Civil War; commd. maj., served on staff of Gen. J. R. Cooke; mem. Fredericksburg Common Council, 1866; mem. U.S. Ho. of Reps. (Democrat) from Va., 42d Congress, 1871-73. Died Fredericksburg, Oct. 2, 1891; buried Confederate Cemetery.

BRAY, JOHN LEIGHTON metallurgist; b. Millbridge, Me., Aug. 11, 1890; s. Charles Ambergh and Vinetta (Cook) B.; B.S. Mass. Inst. of Tech., 1912, Ph.D., 1930; m. Jean Shaw, Aug. 23, 1925; children—Barbara Vilora, John Leighton. Metallurgist, Braden Cooper Co., Rancagua, Chile, 1912-15, Consolidated Mining & Smelting Co., Trail, B.C., 1915-16, Blackbutte (Ore.) Quicksilver Co., 1916-17, N.Y. & Honduras Mining Co., Honduras, C.A., 1918-20; prof. metallurgy, N.S. Tech. Coll., 1920-21; metallurgist for U.S. Tariff Commn., 1921-23; prof. metallurgy, Purdue U., W. Lafayette, Ind., since 1947, head Sch. Chem. and metallurgical Engring. 1935-47, prof. metall. engring. since 1947. Served as maj., Ordnance Dept., U.S. Army, World War I. Mem. Am. Inst. Mining and Metall. Engrs., Soc. of Metals, Am. Chem. Soc., Am. Inst. Chem. Engrs., Electrochem. Soc., Inst. of Metals (Eng.), Soc. for Promotion Engring. Edn., Scabbard and Blade, Sigma Psi, Tau Beta Pi, Phi Lambda Upsilon, Lambda Chi Alpha, Omega Chi Epsilon. Republican. Presbyn. Author: Textbook of Ore Dressing (with R. H. Richards and C. E. Locke), 1925; Principles of Metallurgy, 1930; German Grammar for Chemists, 1937; Introductory Readings in Technical German, 1940; Non Ferrous Production Metallurgy, 1941; Ferrous Production Metallurgy, 1942; Patent Law and Procedure, 1948. Home: 701 N. Chauncey Av., W.Lafayette, Ind. Died Dec. 6, 1952.

BREARLEY, DAVID jurist; b. Spring Grove, N.J., June 11, 1745; s. David and Mary (Clark) B.; m. Elizabeth Mullen, Circa 1767; m. 2d, Elizabeth Higbee, Apr. 17, 1783. Commd. lt. col. 4th N.J. Regt., Continental Army, 1776, 1st N.J. Regt., 1777; mem. N.J. Constl. Conv., 1779; chief justice Supreme Ct. of N.J., 1779; N.J. del. to U.S. Constl. Conv., 1787; chmn. N.J. Conv. to ratify U.S. Constn., 1788; U.S. dist. judge, 1789-90; v.p. N.J. Soc. of Cincinnati; del to Episcopal Gen. Conv., 1786. Died Trenton, N.J., Aug. 16, 1790.

BRECK, EDWARD author, lecturer; b. San Francisco, July 31, 1861; s. Lt. Comdr. Joseph Berry and Ellen Frances (Newell) B.; ed. Oberlin Coll., Amherst, univs. of Cambridge, Munich, and Leipsic; M.A. and Ph.D., U. of Leipsic, 1887; diploma U.S. Naval War Coll. (corr. course); m. Miss A. Wagner von Kleeblatt, 1889; children - Ellen Frances (Mrs. F. F. Macnee), Margaret Adele (Mrs. H. F. Miller), Josephine Leslie; m. 2d, Mary Louise Stanley, 1923, Was editor and lit. adviser Estes & Lauriat, pubs., Boston; editor in chief of Life, London, 1890-92; Berlin corr. New York Herald and New York, Times; vice consul gen., Berlin, 1895-96; asst. to U.S. naval attache Berlin, during war with Spain; volunteered to go to Spain as secret agent, and operated there till close of war, status of U.S. officer. Lecturer on naval subjects, 1914-16. Lt. comdr. U.S.N.R.F., Feb. 13, 1917; in secret service until Mar. 1918; then apptd. U.S. naval attache to Portugal; executive of hist. sect. Navy Dept., 1919-22; officially retired from U.S.N.R.F., on account of age, as hon. lt. comdr., July 21, 1925. Temporary editor Living Age, 1923. Awarded Navy Cross for distinguished and dangerous service; Chevalier Legion of Honor (French); Comdr. Order of Aviz, Order of Christ and D.S.M. (Portuguese); Italian War Cross. Deist. Author: De Consuetudine Monachorum, 1887; Art of Fencing, 1894; Way of the Woods, 1908; Wilderness Pets, 1910; Sporting Guide, 1909; The American Naval Railway Batteries in France, 1920; Armed Guards on American Merchant Ships, 1921; The Steel-Trap, 1925; The Lady and the Trapper, 1927. Naval contbr. Dictionary of American Biography, 1926-. Address: Washington, D.C. Died May 14, 1929.

BRECK, SAMUEL army officer; b. Middleborough, Mass., Feb. 25, 1834; s. Samuel and Sarah Amelia (Eddy) B.; grad. U.S. Mil. Acad., 1855; m. Caroline J. Barrett, Sept. 23, 1857 (died 1900). Commd. 2d lt. 1st Arty., July 1, 1855; promoted through grades to brig. gen., Sept. 11, 1897; retired Feb. 25, 1898. Author: Genealogy of the Breck Family, 1887; Magoun Memorial, 1891. Home: Brookline, Mass. Died Feb. 23, 1918.

BRECKINRIDGE, HENRY lawyer; b. Chicago, Ill., May 25, 1886; s. Maj. Gen. Joseph Cabell (U.S. Army) and Louise Ludlow (Dudley) B.; A.B., Princeton, 1907; LL.B., Harvard, 1910; LL.D., U. of Ky., 1915; LL.D., Tusculum Coll., Greeneville, Tenn., 1935; hon. Master Phys. Edn., Internat. Y.M.C.A. Coll.; D.C.L. (hon.) Bishops' Univ., Lennoxville, Quebec, 1940; m. Ruth Bradley Woodman, July 7, 1910; children-Elizabeth Foster, Louise Dudley; m. 2d, Aida de Acosta Root, Aug. 5, 1927; married 3rd, Margaret Lucy Smith, March 27, 1947; one daughter, Madeline Houston Breckinridge. In private practice of law at Lexington, Ky., 1910-13; asst. sec. of War, Washington, D.C., 1913-16 (resigned); 1st v.p. Pacific Hardware & Steel Co., San Francisco, 1916-17; law practice, N.Y. City, since 1922; sec.-treas. William Holland Willmer Found. Mem. Citizens Com. on Control Crime in N.Y.; organized first Navy Day; pres. Navy League of U.S., 1919-21; numerous civic, polit. activities. Served from maj. to lt. col., inf., A.E.F., U.S. Army, 1917-19. Mem. Nat. Amateur Athletic Fedn. Am. (pres.), Am., N.Y. State, N.Y. County bar assns., S.A.R., Mil. Order World War, Am. Legion, Loyal Legion, Amateur Fencers League Am. (hon. pres.). Democrat. Presbyn. Clubs: Army and Navy (Washington); Princeton, Fencers (hon. pres.) (N.Y.C.). Author: "...shall not perish ...," 1941. Home: 67-38 B. 190th Lane. Fresh Meadows, L.I.,N.Y. 11365. Office: 24 W. 40th St., N.Y.C.; also 1824 23d St. N.W., Washington. Died May 2, 1960; buried Lexington, Ky.

BRECKENRIDGE, JAMES army officer, congressman; b. Fincastle, Va., Mar. 7, 1763; s. Robert and Letitia (Preston) B.; grad. Coll. William and Mary, 1785; m. Anne Selden, Jan. 1, 1791. Mem. Va. Ho. of Dels. from Botetourt County, 13 sessions between 1780-1824; admitted to the bar, circa 1787, practiced law, 1787-89; commd. maj. gen. Va. Militia during War of 1812; unsuccessful candidate for gov. Va.; mem. U.S. Ho. of Reps. from Va., 11th-14th congresses, 1809-17; leader Federal party in Va.; a founder, mem. bd. vistors U. Va.; promoter Chesapeake & Ohio Canal. Died Fincastle, May 13, 1833.

BRECKINRIDGE, JAMES CARSON maj. gen. U.S. Marine Corps; b. in Tenn., Sept. 13, 1877; advanced through grades to maj. gen., Feb. 1, 1935; now comdr. Marine Barracks, Quantico, Va. Address: Navy Dept. Washington, D.C. Died Mar. 2, 1942.

BRECKINRIDGE, JOHN CABELL vice pres. U.S., senator; b. Lexington, Ky., Jan. 21, 1821; s. Joseph and Mary (Smith) B.; grad. Centre Coll., 1839; attended Transylvania U., Lexington, 1840; m. Mary Burch, Dec. 1843. Mem. Ky. Legislature, 1849; mem. U.S. Ho. of Reps. from Ky., 32d-33d congresses, 1851-55; vice pres. U.S. (Democrat), 1857-61; presdl. candidate of pro-slavery branch Democratic Party, 1860, ran 3d in election after Lincoln and Douglas; mem. U.S. Senate from Ky., Mar 4-Dec. 2, 1861; commd. brig. gen. Confederate Army, 1861, maj. gen., 1862; sec. of state Confederate States Am., 1865; v.p. Elizabethtown, Lexington & Big Sandy R.R., circa 1870. Died Lexington, May 17, 1875; buried Lexington.

BRECKINRIDGE, JOSEPH CABELL, army officer; b. Baltimore, Jan. 14, 1842; s. Rev. Robert Jefferson B.; attended Centre Coll., Ky., and U. of Va.; m. Louise Ludlow Dudley, July 20, 1868. Entered army, 1861, Gen. Nelson's and Gen. Thomas' staffs; commanded light battery F, 2d Arty., at Atlanta; apptd. 2d lt. 2d Arty., Apr. 14, 1862, "for gallantry at Mill Springs, Ky."; promoted through grades to maj. gen., U.S. Army, Apr. 11, 1903. Bvtd.; Capt., July 22, 1864, "for gallant and meritorious services in battle before Atlanta, Ga."; maj., Mar. 13, 1865, for same during the war. Maj. gen. vols., 1898, in Santiago campaign; horse shot under him July 2, 1898; comd. separate army of 44,000 men at Chickamauga, Ga., Aug., 1898; insp. gen. U.S.A., 1889-1940; retired at own request after 40 yrs.' service, Apr. 12, 1903. Traveled throughout Europe and southeastern and western Asia and all over U.S. Del. of Gen. Assembly Presbyn. Ch. in America to Pan Presbyn. Alliance Conf., Liverpool, 1904. Pres. Gen. Nat. Soc. S.A.R., 1900-01; v.p. Soc. Army of the Cumberland, and Soc. of Army of the Tennessee. Home: Washington, D.C. Died Aug. 18, 1920.

BRECKINRIDGE, WILLIAM CAMPBELL PRESTON congressman; b. Baltimore, Aug. 28, 1837; s. Rev. Robert Jefferson B.; grad. Centre Coll., Danville, Ky., April 26, 1855; A.M., LL.D.; also LL.B., U. of Louisville, 1857; LL.D., Central U. Richmond, Ky., and Cumberland U., Tenn. Entered C.S.A., as capt.; became col. of 9th Ky cav. and commd. Ky. cav. brigade when it surrendered; afterward prof. of equity jurisprudence in Ky. U. Mem. Congress, 7th Ky. dist., 1884-95. Nat (gold) Democrat. Home: Lexington, Ky. Died 1904.

BREED, R(ICHARD) E(DWARDS) pub. utilities; b. Pittsburgh, Pa., Mar. 17, 1866; s. Richard E. and Martha Olivia (Lyon) B.; ed. U. of Ky.; m. Julia Porter, Mar. 7, 1904; children - (by 1st marriage) Mrs. Lucy Tucker, (by 2d marriage) Richard Edwards, Jane Porter, George, Organizer, pres., chmn. bd. Am. Gas & Electric Co.; dir., exec. com. Am. Power & Light Co., Electric Power and Light Corp., Carolina Power & Light Co., dir. many corps. Served as mem. mil staffs of Govs. Durbin, Hanly and Goodrich, of Ind., advancing to brig. gen. Republican. Presbyn. Mason. Home: New York, N. Y. Died Oct. 14, 1926.

BREES, HERBERT JAY, army officer, bank president; b. Laramie, Wyoming, June 12,21877; s. Daniel Hickey and Cora (Andrews) B.; B.S., University of Wyoming, 1897, LL.D., 1939; honor graduate U.S. Inf. and Cav. School, 1903, Staff College, 1905, Army War College, 1907; m. Elizabeth Porter Nicholson, July 28, 1926. Commissioned 2d lieutenant, U.S. Army, May 23, 1898; advanced through grades to colonel, July 1, 1920; brig. gen., Nov. 1, 1930; maj. gen., May 2, 1936; lt. gen., Oct. 1, 1940; retired June 30, 1941; pres. Nat. Bank of Fort Sam Houston, San Antonio, Texas, since July 1, 1941. Participated in Spanish-American War, Philippine Insurrection, Mexican Border, World War in Vosges Sector, St. Mihiel, Meuse-Argonne and Ypres-Lys campaigns; chief of staff, 91st div., Sept. 1917-Oct. 1918, 7th Army Corps, 1918-June 1919. Awarded D.S.M., Silver Star (U.S.); Officier Legion of Honor (France). Clubs: Army and Navy, Army Navy Country; San Antonio (Tex.) Country. Address: 310 Arcadia Place, San Antonio 9 TX

BREESE, RANDOLPH KIDDER naval officer; Apr. 14, 1831. Apptd. midshipman U.S. Navy, 1846, assigned to ship Saratoga for duty in Mexican War, 1847; served in ship St. Mary's, 1848, Brandywine, until 1850; sailed in ship St. Lawrence to Eng., 1851; prepared for midshipman's exam., 1851-52; reported to ship Mississippi, commanded by M.C. Perry for voyage to Japan, 1852; ordered to Preble for S. Am. trip, 1858-59; assigned to duty in Portsmouth on African coast, 1860, then stationed in ship San Jacinto until 1861; assigned to command mortar flotilla to help open Mississippi River, 1861; promoted lt. comdr., 1862, joined Adm. Porter's Mississippi Fleet; commanded flagship Black Hawk; fleet-capt. to Adm. Porter's N. Atlantic Squadron, 1864-65; promoted comdr., 1866; asst. supt. U.S. Naval Acad., insp. of ordnance Washington Naval Yard; in command of Plymouth on European Station, 1870; stationed Bur. of Ordnance, Navy Dept., 1872; commandant of midshipman U.S. Naval Acad., 1873; commd. capt., 1874; commanded ship Pensacola, 1878; ordered home on sick leave, 1880. Died Sept. 13, 1881.

BREIDENTHAL, JOHN W., banker; b. Kansas City, Kan., Nov. 4, 1911; s. Willard J. and Mary (Gray) B.; student U. Kan., Kansas City Law Sch.; m. Mary Ruth Pyle, Feb. 11, 1939; children—Julie (Mrs. Henry C. Gold), Nancy, Mary Ann (Mrs. Scott A. Nordheimer), Susan Jane. With Riverview State Bank, 1933-38, 40-42, chmn. bd., 1957-62; asst. cashier Victory State Bank, 1938-40, now dir.; vice chmn. bd., chmn. exec. com. Security Nat. Bank, Kansas City, Kan., 1962-66, chmn. bd., pres., 1966-72; adv. dir. Turner State Bank; dir. Victory State Bank, Fort Riley Nat. Bank, ERC Corp., Employers Reins. Corp., Gas Service Co., Kan. Bankers Surety Co., Kan. & Mo. Ry. & Terminal Co., Ortmeyer Lumber Co., Wyandotte Hotel Co. Chmn. Greater Kansas City Flood Protection Planning Commn.; chmn. dist. 5, Water Resources Assn. Mem. Pres.'s Adv. Com. on Mo.-Ark. Basins Flood Control and Conservation; mem. adv. council Kansas City FAA. Trustee Midwest Research Inst., Ottawa U.; bd. dirs. Central Indsl. Dist. Assn., Civic Council Greater Kansas City, 1st v.p., exec. bd. Agrl. Hall Fame. Served to maj., cav., AUS, 1941-46, PTO; brig. gen. Kan. N.G. Mem. Am. Royal Assn. (exec. com.), Assn. U.S. Army, N.G. Assn. U.S., Newcomen Soc., Mil. Order World Wars, 35th Div. Assn. (exec. com.), Am. Legion. Rotarian. Clubs: Kansas City (Kan.); Ft Leavenworth (Kan.) Officer's Open Mess; Richards-Gebaur Officers; Terrace; Victory Hills Golf and Country; Garden of the Gods (Colorado Springs). Home: Kansas City KS Died Jan. 4, 1972.

BRENNAN, JOHN FRANCIS steamship co., exec.; b. Wallingford, Conn., Nov. 29, 1893; s. Martin J. and Margaret (Brennan) B.; A.B., Yale, 1915. With U.S. Lines Co. (formerly) Internat. Mercantile Marine Co., N.Y.C., 1919—, passenger traffic mgr., 1936-49, v.p. passenger traffic, 1949—, dir., 1951—; dir. One Broadway Corp. Served from ensign to lt. (j.g.), USNRF, 1917-19; from lt. col. to col., Transportation Corps, AUS, 1942-45. Decorated Legion of Merit. Mem. Propeller Club U.S., Am. Legion. Clubs: Rotary (past dir.), Yale, N.Y. Athletic, Downtown Athletic, Skal(N.Y.C.). Home: 320 Park Av., N.Y.C. 22. Office: 1 Broadway, N.Y.C. 4. Died Feb. 9, 1958; buried St. John's Cemetery. Wallingford, Conn.

BRENT, JOSEPH LANCASTER lawyer, sugar planter, soldier; b. Charles County, Md., Nov. 20, 1826; s. William Leigh B. and Maria (Fenwick) B.; ed. Georgetown Coll., Served D.C.; m. Rosella Kenner, Apr. 23, 1870. in arty. and cav., C.S.A.; chief of ordnance under Gen. John B. Magruder in Va., chief of Arty. and ordnance under Gen. Richard Taylor in La., 1862-64; col. arty., Apr. 17, 1864; brig. gen. C.S.A., Oct. 1864; comd. "Brent's Cav. Brigade" (2d, 5th, 7th and 8th La.) cav.; comd. front lines extending from Arkansas line to Gulf (including forts on Red River) at time of Gen. E. Kirby Smith's surrender; comd. wooden gunboats which captured U.S. ironclad Indianola on Mississippi river in Feb. 1863. After war practiced law in Baltimore until 1870, then engaged in farming and sugar planting until 1889, retired. Mem. Calif. legislature, 2 terms; first pres. La. State Agrl. Soc. until 1889; mem. La. legislature 2 terms. Author: Mobilizable Batteries (advocating arming of railways). Home: Baltimore, Md. Died 1905.

BRERETON, LEWIS HYDE air force officer; b. Pitts., June 21, 1890; s. William Denny and Helen (Hyde) B.; student St. Johns's Coll., 1905-07; B.S., U.S. Naval Acad., 1911; grad. Command and Gen. Staff Sch., 1928; m. Icy V. Larkin, Feb. 20, 1931; children-Lewis Hyde, Elizabeth Denny (wife of Col. W. K. Pottinger, USMC); m. Zena A. Groves, Jan. 24, 1946. Served as ensign, U.S. Navy, June 3-5, 1911; commd. 2d lt., U.S. Army, Aug. 1911; commenced flying training, 1912; became mil. aviator, Mar. 1913; instr. Signal Corps Aviation Sch., Jan.-May 1913; pilot 2d Aviation Squadron, Philippine Islands, Oct. 1915-Jan. 1917; served as 1st lt., advancing to lt. col., Air Service, with A.E.F., World War, variously as squardon and group commander, chief of Air Service 1st Army Corps, wing comdr., Chief of staff Air Service Group of Armies, and U.S. Army of Occupation in Germany; air attaché Am. Embassy, Paris, 1919-23; instr. Air Corps Tactical Sch., 1923-27; instr. F.A. Sch., 1928-31; instr. Command and Gen. Staff Sch., 1935-39; brig. gen. and wing comdr. 17th Bombardment Wing, 1940-41; maj. gen., 1941; comdg. gen. Far East Air Force, Manila, P.I., 1941, Darwin, Australia, 1942; Lembang, Java, 1942, 10th Air Force, India, 1942, U.S. Middle East Air Force, and later 9th USAAF, Egypt, 1942, U.S. Army Forces in Middle East and United Kingdom, Egypt, Feb. 1, 1943; comd. lt. gen. (temp.) 1944, apptd. to commd. First Allied Air Borne Army, 1944. Chmn. Mil. Com. to U.S. AEC rep. Inter-Allied Armistice Commn for Aviation; 1946-48; mem. Inter-Allied Control Commission for Aviation, 1919-21. Decorated Legion of Merit, Bronze Star Air Medal, Distinguished Service Cross, Distinguished Service Medal, Silver Star, Purple Heart, Distinguished Flying Cross, Knight of the Bath, Comdr. France Legion of Honor, Croix de Guerre (3 palms), Grand Comdr. Order of Albert of Belgium. Comdr. Order of Danilo (Montenegro now Jugoslavia), Grand Officer Order of Orange Nassau(Netherlands). Mem. Society Automotive Engineers. Club: Army and Navy (Washington, D.C.). Author: The Brereton Diaries, 1946. Home: Winter Park, Fla. Died July 1967.

BRES, EDWARD SEDLEY, cons. civil engr.; b. New Orleans, Sept. 15, 1888; s. Joseph Ray and Sara Ella (Hughes) B.; B.E. in Civil Engring., Tulane U., 1910, C.E., 1931; m. Ann Elizabeth Todd, Sept. 7, 1917; children—Edward Sedley (officer U.S. Army), Elizabeth (Mrs. Samuel D. G. Robbins). In engring. work, harbors, flood control, dredging, docks, highway constrn., New Orleans and State of La.; mem. Eustis & Bres, 1910-17; cons. engr. and contractor, 1919-26; mem. Scott & Bres, cons. and contracting engr., 1926-41. Served from lt. to maj. C.E., AEF, U.S. Army, 1917-19; col. C.E. Res., 1927, reentered Army, 1941, brig. gen., 1945, maj. gen., 1946; ret., 1950; cons. and regional engr. U.S. Army constrn. projects, 1941; dep. chief engr. U.S. Army Forces in Australia, 1942-43; regulating officer Office of G.H.Q., S.W. Pacific Forces, 1942-44; duty Gen. Staff Corps, Washington, 1945-50; mem. N.G. Res. policies com., 1945; exec. for Res. and R.O.T.C. affairs, 1945-47; mem. sec. of army personnel bd., 1947-50. Chmn. La. Com. for Trade Recovery, 1933; La. del. Nat. Rivers and Harbors Conf., 1935; mem. adv. bd. Soil and Foundation Survey, New Orleans and vicinity, 1935; mem. La. State Bd. Engring. Examiners, 1941; mem. housing code rev. com. D.C., 1954-55. Mem., chmn. Battle of New Orleans Sesquicentennial Celebration Commn., 1963 (apptd. by pres.). Mem. Tulane Athletic Council, 1937-40. Decorated Legion of Merit with oak leaf cluster, World War I Victory medal with 3 stars, World War II Victory medal, Asiatic-Pacific medal with 4 stars, and other medals. Recipient Freedom Found. award, 1965. Nat. dir. Soc. Am. Mil. Engrs. 1941; nat. pres. Res. Officers Assn. of U.S., 1939-40, pres. New Orleans chpt., 1930, La. dept. 1932, IV Corps area council, 1934-35; dir. Navy League of U.S., 1953. Mem. Am. Soc. C.E. (life mem., past pres. La. sect., past nat. dir.), La. Engring. Soc. (hon. mem., past pres.), Am. Legion, Tulane Alumni Assn. (sec. 1915, pres. 1941), Soc. War of 1812, Mil. Order World Wars, Delta Kappa Epsilon (nat. hon. pres. 1951), Theta Nu Epsilon, Kappa Delta Phi, Delta Tau Omega, Omicron Delta Kappa, Scabbard and Blade. Clubs: Boston (New Orleans); Army and Navy, Cosmos, Post Mortem (Washington). Home: New Orleans LA Died Sept. 24, 1967; buried Arlington Nat. Cemetery, Arlington VA

BRESNAHAN, THOMAS F., army officer; born Mass., July 4, 1892; B.S., Middlebury Coll., Vt., 1917; grad. Inf. Sch., 1924, Command and Gen. Staff Sch., 1938; commd. 2d lt. Inf., Aug. 1917; advanced through the grades to brig. gen., Sept. 1943; acting comdt. Army War Coll., 1943. Decorated D.S.C., Purple Heart with oak leaf cluster. Home: Fitchburg MA Died 1971.

BRETT, LLOYD M. army officer; b. Dead River, Me., Feb. 22, 1856; s. John and Elizabeth (Brown) B.; grad. U.S. Mil. Acad., 1879; m. Elma Wallace, Feb. 7, 1887. Commd. 2d lt. 2d Cav., June 13, 1879; promoted through grades to brig. gen., Nat. Army, Aug. 5, 1917, Adj. gen. D.C. Militia, 1903-08; supt. Yellowstone Nat. Park, 1910-16; comdg. 160th Inf. Brigade, Camp Lee, Petersburg, Va., Sept. 1917, and overseas, May 1918-June 1919; col. 3d U.S. Cav., Aug. 1, 1919-. Awarded Medal of Honor" for most distinguished gallantry," in action against hostile Sioux Indians, while 2d lt. 2d Cav., Apr. 1, 1880; D.S.M.; Officer of the Legion of Honor; Croix de Guerre. Died Sept. 23, 1927.

BRETT, SERENO E. army officer; b. Portland, Ore., Oct. 31, 1891; s. James and Clara Marie de Lille (Harvey) B.; B.S., Ore. State Coll., 1916; grad. Inf. Sch., 1922, Tank Sch., 1926, Command and Gen. Staff Sch., 1927, Army War Coll., 1934; m. Elizabeth Anderson March, Nov. 5, 1923; children—Elizabeth Ann, James Sereno. Commd. 2d lt. Inf., AUS, 1916, advanced through grades to brig. gen. (temp.) 1942; overseas with 1st Div., AEF, 1917; organized and directed 37 mm. Sch., Army Inf. Specialists Sch., 1917-18; trans. Tank Corps, 1918; instr. in chief Am. TAnk Center, Bourg, France, 1918; organized and comd. 327th bn. Tank Corps, 1918; as maj. led first Am. tank attack, 326th bn. St. Mihiel, 1918; comd. 1st Am. Tank Brigade throughout Meuse-Argonne, 1918; returned to U.S., 1919; mem. first transcontinental truck convoy, Washington to San Francisco, 1919; comd. exptl. tank force, Panama Canal Zone, 1923-24; inst. Inf. Sch., 1927-30; exec. officer Mechanized Force, 1930-31; mem. Inf. Bd., 1931-33, 1935-38; fgn. service, Hawaii, 1934-35; instr. Command and Gen. Staff Sch., 1938-40; chief of staff Armored Force, 1940-41; comdg. officer 31st Armored Regiment, 1941, 5th Armored Div., 1942-43; retired, physical disability. Decorated D.S.C., D.S.M. Silver Star with oak leaf cluster (U.S.); Legion of Honor, Croix de Guerre with Palm (France). Mem. Delta Upsilon. Mason. Address: 201 Calle Palo Colorado, Santa Barbara, Cal. Died Sept. 9, 1952

BREWER, JAMES ARTHUR advt. exec.; b. Los Angeles, Oct. 23, 1886; s. James Biays and Florence Carlton (Keller) B.; ed. Los Angeles Poly. H.S.; m. Ada Troutman Winslow, July 23, 1921; children—Dyke G., Beverly W. (Mrs. Jewel Emmet Colvin, Jr.), Ada W. (Mrs. Henry Parker Grimshaw), Florence Cathryn (Mrs. George L. Skip Allen). With Guaranty Trust & Savings Bank, Los Angeles, California, 1910-17, Seaman Paper Company, N.Y.C., 1920-28; became pres. Brewer-Cantelmo Co., Inc., 1928, now chmn. bd. Served as maj., U.S. Army, 1917-19. Mem. Am. Legion. Mason. Club: Advertising (treas.) (N.Y. City). Contbr. articles on book binding and big game fishing to mags. and newspapers. Home: 49 Highland Av., Montclair, N.J.; also 3819 Cactus Blvd., Tucson. Office: 116 E. 27th St., N.Y.C. Died Mar. 5, 1957. 1

BREWER, LEO lawyer; b. Mayfield, Ky., July 9, 1889; s. Lafayette and Celia (Cross) B.; A.B., U. Ky., 1908; LL.B., Harvard, 1914; m. Dorothy Swearingen, Aug. 16, 1917; 1 dau., Dorothy. Admitted to Ill. bar, 1915, practiced Chgo., 1915-17, Tex. bar, 1919, practiced San Antonio, 1919-26, since 1928, with Brewer, Matthews, Nowlin & Macfarlane since 1943; prof. law U. Tex., 1926-28. Trustee St. Mary's U. Law Sch. Mem. Tex. Economy Commn. Served as 1st lt. to capt. U.S. Army, 1917-19. Decorated Croix de Guerre, Silver Star citations. Mem. Am. (house dels. 1942-50), Am. Legion (comdr. bus. profl. mens post 1937), Order of Coif. Episcopalian. Clubs: San Antonio Country, San Antonio, Petroleum (San Antonio). Contbr. articles, book revs. Mem. bd. editors Tex. Law Rev. Home: 107 E. Gramercy Pl., San Antonio 12. Office: Alamo Nat. Bldg., San Antonio 5. Died Nov. 3, 1965; buried Mission Burial Park, San Antonio.

BREWSTER, ANDRE WALKER army officer; b. in N.J., Dec. 9, 1862; grad. Army War Coll., 1907. Commd. 2d lt. 10th Inf., Jan. 19, 1885; 1st lt. 22d Inf., Dec. 17, 1891; trans. to 9th Inf., Feb. 9, 1892; capt. a.q.m. vols., Oct. 15, 1898; hon. discharge vols., May 12, 1899; capt. U. S. Army, Mar. 2, 1899; trans. to 25th Inf., Jan 29, 1908; maj. 19th Inf., Mar. 15, 1908; insp. gen., 1909-13; lt. col. inf., Dec. 2, 1913; col., July 1, 1916; brig. gen. N.A., 1917; maj. gen. N.A., Nov. 28, 1917; maj. gen. U.S. Army, Dec. 1, 1922; retired Dec. 9, 1925. Address: War Dept., Washington, D.C. Died Mar. 27, 1942.

BREWSTER, DAVID LUKENS marine corps officer; b. Washington, D.C., Dec. 31, 1887; s. Robert John Walker and Leila (Shoemaker) B.; grad. Tech. High Sch., Washington, D.C., 1904-08. Service Staff and Command Schs., 1923 and 1938; m. Mercer B. Taliaferro, Feb. 26, 1919; children—David Andre, Austin (Mrs. Charles D. Barrett, Jr.). Commd. 2d lt., U.S. Marine Corps, 1910, and advanced through the grades to brig. gen.; naval aviator, 1917-22; chief of staff, 1st Marine Amphibious Corps, 1943-44. Decorated Legion of Merit, Distinguished Marksman (U.S.); Portuguese Grand Order of Aviation; Nicaraguan Order of Merit. Home: 1437 44th St. N.W., (7). Address: care The Advocate General's Office, Navy Dept., Washington 25, D.C. Died July 10, 1945.

BRICKER, EDWIN DYSON army officer; b. Chambersburg, Pa., Nov. 24, 1875; s. William H. and Laura (Dyson) B.; grad. U.S. Mil. Acad., 1898, Army War Coll., 1923; m. Emma Lena Braunersreuther, Jan. 23, 1901. Second lt. inf., U.S. Army, Apr. 26, 1898; transferred to Ordnance Dept., Jan. 3, 1901; was promoted through grades to col. Served in Santiago Campaign in Cuba, 1898; in Philippine Insurrection, 1899-1901; chief purchasing officer, Ordnance Dept., A.E.F., ordnance rep. on the Gen. Purchasing Bd., World War I; apptd. asst. to chief of ordnance, rank of brig. gen., Sept. 1, 1930. Commanded Frankford Arsenal, Phila., 1934-39; retired from active service Nov. 30, 1939; recalled to active duty, Nov. 1, 1940; chief, Requisitioning Div., Bd. of Economic Warfare until June 14, 1943. Awarded 2 silver stars and cited for gallantry in action in Santiago Campaign, 1898, Philippine Insurrection, 1899; D.S.M. for service in A.E.F.; Officier de la Legion d' Honneur (France). Clubs: University (N.Y.); Army and Navy (Washington); Chevy Chase (Md.); Racquet, Philadelphia Country (Phila.). Address: 5084 Lowell St. N.W., Washington 16, D.C. Died Apr. 7, 1967; buried Arlington Nat. Cemetery.

BRIDGES, CHARLES HIGBEE army officer; b. Whitehall, Ill., Mar. 1, 1873; s. Jehoshaphat and Annette (Cheney) B.; grad. U.S. Mil. Acad., 1897, Army Sch. of the Line, 1908, Army Signal Sch., 1909, Army War Coll., 1920; m. Mrs. Sadie Awl, 1914. Commissioned 2d lt., U.S. Army, June 11, 1897; promoted through grades to colonel, July 1, 1920; colonel (temp.) World War. Served in Santiago Campaign, War with Spain, 1898; in Philippine Insurrection, 1899-1902; custodial of Aguinaldo, Sept. 1901-Jan. 1902; insp. gen. 2d Div., A.E.F., France, Nov. 1917-Feb. 1918; asst. 2d Div., A.E.F., France, Nov. 1917-Feb. 1918; asst. chief of staff 2d Div., to July 25, 1918; asst. chief of staff 6th Army Corps, France, Mar. 9-Nov. 11, 1918; insp. gen. 5th Div., June-Sept. 1920; insp. 5th Corps Area to July 1921; chief of staff 5th Corps Area to Oct. 28, 1922; brig. gen., asst. adj. gen., July 2, 1927-Feb. 1, 1929; become maj. gen., The Adj. Gen., Feb. 1, 1929; now retired. Clubs: Army and Navy, Chevy Chase. Home: 1870 Wyoming Av., N.W., Washington, D.C. Died Sept. 11, 1948.

BRIDGES, GEORGE WASHINGTON, congressman, lawyer; b. Charleston, Tenn., Oct. 9, 1825; attended E. Tenn. U. at Knoxville; studied law. Admitted to bar, 1848, began practice of law, Athens, Tenn.; also engaged in agriculture; atty. gen. Tenn., 1849-60; raised 10th Regt., Tenn. Cavalry for U.S. Army, during Civil War, served from capt. to col; elected mem. U.S. Ho. of Reps. (Unionist) from Tenn., 37th Congress, arrested enroute to Washington, D.C., held prisoner in Tenn. for more than a year, escaped and served in U.S. Congress, Feb. 25-Mar. 3, 1863; circuit judge 4th Jud. Dist. of Tenn., 1866. Died Athens, Mar. 16, 1873; buried Cedar Grove Cemetery.

BRIGGS, WALTER OWEN, JR., business exec.; b. Detroit, Mich., Jan. 20, 1912; s. Walter Owen and Jane (Cameron) B.; student Canterbury Prep Sch., New Milford, Conn.; B.S., Georgetown Univ., 1934; m. Laura Manly, June 28, 1934; children—Walter Owen, III, Basil Manly, James Rodney. Pres., Briggs Sales Corp. (now Meridian Industries, Inc.), Lake Wales, Fla.; v.p., dir. Detroit Football Co., Fife Electric Supply Co.; pres., dir. Erie Lands, Inc.; dir. Briggs Mfg. Co.; formerly pres. Detroit Baseball Co.; formerly v.p., dir. Detroit Football Co.; exec. v.p., asst. gen. mgr. Briggs Mfg. Co. Former mayor City of Bloomfield Hills, Mich. Dir. Boys Clubs of Detroit; overseer William Beaumont Hosp.; alumni senate Georgetown U. Served from 2d lt. to lt. col. USAAF, 1941-45. Mem. Detroit Urban League, Detroit Indsl. Safety Council, Boy Scouts Am., Detroit Bd. of Commerce, United Found., Old Newsboys, Vets. Fgn. Wars, Mil. Order World Wars, Newcomen Soc., Am. Legion. Elk. Clubs: Touchdown (Washington); Economic, Adcraft, Detroit Athletic (Detroit); Aero of Mich., Bloomfield Open Hunt, The Hundred, Lambs, Variety, Bloomfield Hills Country. Home: Bloomfield Hills MI Died July 3, 1970.

BRIGHAM, JOSEPH HENRY asst. sec. of Agr.; b. Lodi, O., Dec. 12, 1838; ed. common schools and 1 term each at Berea U., Nr. Cleveland, and Normal School, Lebanon, O.; m. Edna Allman, Dec. 1, 1863. Served through Civil War, private to col. in 12th and 69th Ohio regts.; war farmer in Ohio; has held several county offices; served in State senate; master Nat. Grange 5 successive terms; mem. 6 yrs. and pres. 1 yr. Ohio State bd. of agr.; asst. sec. U.S. Dept. Agr., 1897-. Address: Washington, D.C. Died 1904.

BRIND, SIR (ERIC) (JAMES) PATRICK, naval officer; b. Paignton, Devon, Eng., May 12, 1892; s. Col. Edward and Florence (Lund) B.; student Royal Naval Coll., Osborne, 1905, Royal Naval Coll., Dartmouth, 1907; m. Eileen Apperly, Jan. 23, 1918 (dec. 1940); 1 dau., Lady Charles John Hanson; m. 2d Edith Blagrove, Jan. 21, 1948. Apptd. midshipman Royal Brit. Navy, 1909, advanced through ranks to adm., 1949; served various ships including H.M.S. Malaya at Dattle, Jutland, World War I; with naval staff Admiralty, 1934-36; capt. H.M.S. Orion (cruiser) in Home Fleet, 1936, 37, H.M.S. Birmingham, China, 1938-40, H.M.S. Excellent, 1940; chief staff Home Fleet, 1940-42, asst. chief naval staff admiralty, 1942-44; comdg. cruisers Brit. Pacific Fleet, 1944-46; pres. Royal Naval Coll., Greenwich, 1946-48; comdr. in chief Brit. Far East Sta., 1949-51, Allied Forces No. Europe, Mar. 1951-Apr. 1953. Decorated Comdr. Brit. Empire, Knight Grand Cross Order Brit. Empire, Companion Bath, Knight Comdr. Bath Am. Legion Merit. Mem. United Service Instn. Clubs: United Service, Jr. Army and Navy (London, Eng.). Home: Lye Green Forge, Crowborough, Sussex, Eng. Died Oct. 4, 1963.

BRINK, FRANCIS G. army officer; b. Marathon, N.Y., Aug. 22, 1893; s. Lawrence J. and Martha S. (Sheldon) B.; A.B., Cornell U., 1916; grad. Inf. Sch., basic course, 1921, Command and Gen. Staff Sch.,

1936; m. Florence Roos, Aug. 18, 1917; children—Esther Roos, Robert Sheldon, Leilani Tryon. Instr. in physical training, Cornell U., 1916; commd. 2d lt., U.S. Army, 1917, and advanced through grades to brig. gen.; served through World War I; with 2d Inf. Div., 1919-20; inst. Inf. Sch., 1921-23; with 27th Inf., Hawaii, 1923-28; asst. prof. mil. science and tactics Louisiana State U., 1928-34; with 16th Inf., Governor's Island, N.Y., 1937-38; 31st Inf., Philippines, and as force comdr., 1938-41; U.S. Military observer and liaison for War Dept., Singapore, Java and Burma, on Gen Wavell's staff, 1941-42; in first Java Campaign, 1942; in Hawaii, Aleutians, Alaska, China and Burma operations, 1942-44; chief of operations div. Southeast Asia Command, 1944-45, 1945-end of war, G-3 Tactical Hdqrs.; U.S. Army Forces, China, 1945-46; China liaison officer to AFPAC. Manila and Tokyo; duty with USAFC, Shanghai and Japan; chief joint adv. staff, A.A.G., Nanking, China, 1946-49; comdg. general O.M.D. 2d Army 1949-50; chief M.A.A.G. Mission, Saigon, Indo China since 1950. Decorated Distinguished Service Medal, Legion of Merit with Oak Leaf Cluster, Commendation Ribbon, Purple Heart. Comdr. Brit. Empire, Order Yun Hui, Order Pao Ting. Author: Divisional Tactics and Adminstrn., Gen Staff, 1938; Corps, Army Operations, 1938; also several mil. publs. outlining tactics and strategy for operations in Pacific and Asia theaters of operation during World War II. Home: Marathon, N.Y. Address: M.A.A.G., care U.S. Legation, Saigon, Indo China. Died June 24, 1952.

BRINKERHOFF, ROELIFF banker; b. Owasco, N.Y., June 28, 1828; ed. common schs. and Auburn and Homer acads.; taught in common schs. at 16 and 17, went South at 18 and was for 3 yrs. tutor in Hermitage, home of Gen. Jackson; returned North at 21; studied law with Judge Jacob Brinkerhoff, Mansfield, O.; began practice, 1852; editor and propr. Mansfield Herald, 1855-59; m. Mary Bentley. Entered army 1st lt. and q.m. 64th Ohio Vol. Inf.; served 5 yrs. and attained rank of col. in q.m.'s dept. and was bvtd. brig. gen. "for meritorious service." Resumed law practice until 1873, when became cashier Mansfield Savings Bank, later becoming pres. Mem. Ohio State Bd. of Charities, 1878-(chmn. several yrs. past); pres. Nat. Conf. of Charities and Correction, 1880; v.p. Internat. Preson Congress, Paris, Prison 1895, and pres. Am. delegation; v.p. Am. Nat. Prison Congress, 1884-94, with Gen. R. B. Hayes as pres., becoming pres. at latter's death. Organized, 1875, and 1st pres. and pres., 1893-, succeeding Gen. Hayes, Ohio Archaeol. and Hist. Soc. Author: The Volunteer Quartermaster; Recollections of Lifetime, 1900. Address: Mansfield, O. Died 1911.

BRINSER, HARRY LERCH naval officer; b. Middletown, Pa., Nov. 11, 1876; s. Christian and Mary (Lerch) B.; student Harrisburg Acad., 1893-95; grad. U.S. Naval Acad., 1899; m. Natalie Meylert Bulkley,Nov. 1, 1919; 1 son, Harry Meylert. Became ensign U.S. Navy, June 1899; advanced through grades to rear adm., Oct. 1, 1932. Served in Battle of Santiago, Philippine Insurrection, Boxer Rebellion; comdg. U.S.S. Columbia, World War; became dir. of Navy Yars, 1932; later comdr. Cruiser Div. 4; mem. Gen Board, Navy Dept.; retired, Dec. 1, 1940. Awarded Navy Cross, 1924. Died Dec. 9, 1945.

BRINSMADE, WILLIAM BARRETT surgeon; b. Brooklyn, Dec. 24, 1865; s. James Beebee and Jennie (Newman) B.; B.A., Yale, 1888; M.D., Coll. Phys. and Surg. (Columbia), 1892; m. Elizabeth T. Holister Fish, Feb. 19, 1929. Became prof. surgery, Long Island Coll. Hosp., 1914, also surgeon same; sr. surgeon, Brooklyn Hosp.; consulting surgeon, St. Christopher's Hosp. for Children, St. John's Hosp.; retired. Surgeon with rank of comdr. U.S. N.R.F.; dir. Naval Base Hosp. No. 1; cited by General Pershing. Decorated Order of Purple Heart (United States). Fellow Am. Coll. Surgeons; mem. Am. Surg. Assn., Am. Acad. Medicine, A.M.A., Med. Soc. State of N.Y., Kings Co. Med. Soc., N.Y. Surg. Soc., Brooklyn Surg. Soc., Pathol. Soc., etc. Decorated Legion of Honor (French), 1925. Home: Bedford Hills, N.Y.

BRINTON, PAUL HENRY MALLET-PREVOST chemist; b. Richmond, Va., May 8, 1882; s. Col. Joseph P. and Kate (Mallet-Prevost) B.; student, Trinity Coll., Hartford, Conn., and Stevens Inst. Tech., Hoboken, N.J., 1900-02; Chemisches Laboratorium Fresenius, Wiesbaden, Germany, 1907-09; B.S., U. Minn., 1912, M.S., 1913, PhD., 1916; m. Mary Adams Rice, 1906. With various elec. mfg. and mining cos. until 1907; instr. chemistry U. Minn., 1909-12; asst. prof. and prof., U. Ariz., 1912-20; prof. and head of div. of analytical chemistry, U. Minn., 1921-27; resigned to devote time to private research; cons. chemist; vis. prof. chemistry, U. So. Cal., 1932-42. Capt. Chem. Warfare Service, U.S. Army; chief of analyt. research unit, chem. research sect., 1918. Fellow A.A.A.S., Am. Inst. Chemists; mem. Am Chem. Soc., Am. Assn. Univ. Profs., Phi Kappa Phi, Sigma Xi, Phi Lambda Upsilon, Phi Gamma Chi, Psi Upsilon. Christian Scientist. Contbr. numerous papers on analyt. chemistry and chemistry of rare elements. Address: Madre del Oro Mine, Oracle, Ariz. Died Nov. 16, 1966.

BRISBIN, JAMES S. army officer; b. Boalsburg, Pa., May 23, 1837; studied law, Bellefonte, Pa. Editor, Centre Democrat, Bellefonte; admitted to Pa. bar; entered U.S. Army as pvt., 1861, commd. 2d lt. soon after; wounded at 1st Battle of Bull Run, 1861; later promoted capt. 6th U.S. Cavalry; served with Army of Potomac in Peninsular Campaign, 1862; brevetted maj. U.S. Army for services at Battle of Malvern Hill, 1863; commanded Pa. regt. at Battle of Gettysburg, 1863; commd. col. 5th U.S. Colored Cavalry, 1864; brevetted brig. gen., maj. gen. U.S. Volunteers, 1865; brevetted col. U.S. Army, 1865; capt. 6th U.S. Cavalry, 1866-68; commd. maj. 2d Cavalry, 1868, lt. col. 9th Cavalry, 1885, col. 1st Cavalry, 1889; stationed mostly on the frontier, 1868-89, took part in most of Indian battles in Northwest.

BRISCOE, BIRDSALL PARMENAS, architect; b. Harrisburg, Tex., June 10, 1876; s. Andrew Birdsall and Annie Frances (Payne) B.; student San Antonio Acad., Tex. A. and M. Coll., U. Tex.; m. Ruth Dillman, 1927. Pres., Birdsall P. Briscoe, Houston, 1906-71; specializing in residences. Served to maj., inf. U.S. Army, World War I. Fellow A.I.A. Author: (fiction) In the Face of the Sun, 1935, Spurs from San Isidro, 1951. Contbr. tech. articles, short stories to nat. mags. Home: Houston TX Died Sept. 18, 1971; buried Oakhill Cemetery, Goliad TX

BRISCOE, ROBERT PEARCE, naval officer; b. Centreville, Miss., Feb. 19, 1897; s. Pearce Tonstil and Alice Letitia (Ware) B.; B.S., U.S. Naval Acad., 1918; student Marion Inst., 1914-15; m. Katherine Norwood Lewis, Aug. 22, 1923. Commd. ensign U.S. Navy, 1918, advanced through grades to admiral, 1956; served in destroyer convoy escort duty, Europe, World War I; served Near East, 1919-21; asst. engring. officer, U.S.S. West Va., 1926-29; instr., U.S. Naval Acad., 1929-31, 1934-37; China duty, 1931-33; navigation officer, U.S.S. Miss., 1937-39; asst. dir. Naval Research Lab., 1939-41; comdr. U.S.S. Prometheus, Destroyer Squadron 5, U.S.S. Denver, Amphibious Group 14, 1942-44; staff comdr. in chief, U.S. Fleet, 1944; comdr. Operational Development Force, 1945-48; comdr. amphibious force Atlantic Fleet 1950; comdr. 7th Fleet, Korea, 1972; comdr. naval forces, Far East, 1952-54, dep. chief naval operations, 1954-56; comdr. in chief Allied Forces So. Europe, 1956-59, rank adm. Decorated Navy Cross, D.S.M., Legion of Merit with gold star, commendation ribbon, citation from sec. of navy. Mem. Newcomen Soc. Presbyn. Home: Liberty MS Died Oct. 14, 1968; buried Arlington Nat. Cemetery, Arlington VA

BRISKIN, SAMUEL JACOB, motion picture exec.; b. Russia, Feb. 8, 1897; s. Benjamin and Rose (Buchman) B.; brought to U.S., 1898, derivative citizen; student Coll. City N.Y., 1916-17; m. Sara Myers, July 27, 1918; children—Gerald, Bernard. With Brisken, Sohn & Feiman, C.P.A.'s, 1918-20, C.B.C. Film Sales Corp., 1920-26; with Columbia Pictures Corp., 1926-36, 38-42, 58-68 v.p., dir. until 1968. with RKO Radio Pictures, 1936-38, Liberty Films, Inc., 1945-50, Paramount Pictures Corp., 1950-57; chmn. bd. TelAutograph Corp.; bd. dirs. Screen Gems, Inc. Spl. advanced gifts div. Community Chest. Trustee bd. dirs., pres. Cedars of Lebanon Hosp., Mt. Sinai Hosp. (both Los Angeles). Served from major to lt. col. Signal Corps, AUS, 1942-45. Decorated Legion of Merit. Mem. Screen Producers Guild. Western Harness Racing Association. Jewish religion. Mason. Club: Hillcrest Country (Los Angeles). Home: Los Angeles CA Died Nov. 14, 1968; buried Hillcrest Meml. Park and Mausoleum.

BRISTOL, ARTHUR LEROY naval officer; b. Charleston, S.C., July 15, 1886; s. Arthur LeRoy and Alice Marion (Blodgett) B.; student Coll. of Charleston, 1901-02; grad. U.S. Naval Acad., 1906; advanced through grades; commd. rear adm., July 1939. Decorated Navy Cross; Distinguished Service Medal; World War medal; Mexican Campaign medal; Russian Order of Stanislaus. Clubs: Army and Navy (Washington); Chevy Chase (Md.); New York Yacht. Home: Charleston, S.C. Address: care Navy Dept., Washington, D.C. Died Apr. 20, 1942.

BRISTOL, HENRY P. corp. exec.; b. Clinton, N.Y., 1889; s. William McLaren and Mary Seymour (Lee) B.; A.M., Hamilton Coll., Clinton, N.Y., 1930; m. Gertrude Flesh, June 14, 1928. Chmn. board Bristol-Myers Co. (Del.); dir. Irving Trust Co., Lehigh Valley R.R.; trustee East River Savs. Bank. Trustee Com Econ. Development, Hamilton Coll. Served as lt., F.A., Mexican Border Service, 1916; maj., F.A., U.S. Army, World War I. Mem. U.S. Council Internat. C. of C. (trustee), Proprietary Assn. (dir.), Sigma Phi. Clubs: Army and Navy, Bay Head Yacht, Bankers, University, Fort Schuyler. Home: 1 Beckman Pl., N.Y.C. 22. Office: 630 Fifth Av., N.Y.C. 20, N.Y. Died Apr. 14, 1959.

BRISTOL, MARK LAMBERT naval officer; b. Glassboro, N.J., Apr. 17, 1868; s. Mark Lambert and Rachel Elizabeth (Bush) B.; grad. U.S. Naval Acad., 1887; m. Helen Beverly Moore, June 1, 1908. Ensign U.S.N., May 19, 1889; advanced through grades to capt., July 1, 1913; commd. temporary rear admiral, July 1918; commd. rear admiral, July 1921. Served on board battleship Texas at Battle of Santiago and throughout Spanish-Am. War; closely connected with the development of modern gunnery in the Navy, and of torpedoes and aircraft. In charge aeronautical development of Navy, 1913-16; comdg. North Carolina, Apr. 16, 1917, convoying troops to Europe; comdg. Oklahoma Battleship Div. 6, in European waters, July 1918; comd. U.S. Naval Base, Plymouth, Eng., Oct. 1918-Jan. 1919; mem. Internat. Armistice Commn. in Belgium, Nov. 1918; comd. U.S. Naval Detachment Eastern Mediterranean, 1919; apptd. U.S. high commr. to Turkey, Aug. 12, 1919; mem. internat. com. of inquiry into Greek occupation of Smyrna, Sept.-Oct. 1919; U.S. high commr. to Turkey, 1919-27; comdr. in chief Asiatic Fleet, rank of admiral, 1927-29; became chmn. Gen. Bd., Mar. 1930; retired, May 1, 1932. One of Am. delegates to Lausanne Conf., Nov. 23, 1922-Feb. 5, 1923. Address: Washington, D.C. Died May 13, 1939.

BRITTAIN, CARLO BONAPARTE naval officer; b. Pineville, Ky., Jan. 16, 1867; s. Carlo Bonaparte and Lydia Susan (Burch) B.; student Cumberland Coll., Barbourville, Ky.; grad. U.S. Naval Acad., 1888; m. Mary Elizabeth Baldwin, June 29, 1897. Commd. ensign, July 1, 1890; promoted through grades to rear adm. (temp.), Sept. 21, 1918. Comd. forces afloat, 5th Naval Dist., June-Oct. 1918; comd. Battleship Div. One, U.S. Fleet, Nov. 1918-June 1919; chief of staff U.S. Atlantic Fleet, attached to fleet flagship U.S.S. Pennsylvania, June 30, 1919. Mem. U.S. Naval Inst. Awarded Sampson medal for engagement at Santiago, Cuba, U.S.S. Newark, July 2, 1898; also West Indian campaign badge, Philippine campaign badge. Mem. Christian (Campbellite) Ch. Author: Elements of Naval Warfare, 1909. Home: Richmond, Ky. Died Apr. 22, 1920.

BRITTIN, LEWIS HOTCHKISS, engineer; b. Derby, Conn., Feb. 8, 1877; s. Edwin and Mary (Hotchkiss) B.; prep. edn., Gunnery and Ridge schs., Washington, Conn.; student Harvard, 1897-99; m. Arna Torkelson, 1919 (died July 25, 1935). Engineer Newhall Engineering Co., Sierra Madre Land & Lumber Co.; mgr. Nat. Lamp Div. of Gen. Electric Co.; v.p. and gen. mgr. Northwestern Terminal, Minneapolis; founder, vice pres. and gen. mgr. Northwest Airways, Inc.; consultant, Bureau Foreign and Domestic Commerce, U.S. Dept. of Commerce; cons. and collaborator, U.S. Dept. Agr.; cons. Bur. Fgn. and Domestic Commerce, N.Y. Bd. Trade, dir. Edward S. Evans Transportation Research, Washington, D.C. Pres. Chicago Air Traffic Assn.; v.p. St. Paul Assn.; mem. bd. govs. and cons. Aeronautical Chamber Commerce; pres. Nat. Assn. of State Aviation Officials; chmn. Minn. Aeronautics Commn.; dir. Airport Program, Dept. Commerce, State of Minn.; dir. Independent Air-Freight Assn. Cons. aeronautical engr. Cpl. Batt. A, 1st Mass. Vols., Spanish-Am, War; lt. col., assigned duty Gen. Staff, U.S. Army, World War; chmn. Minn. State Defense Com. Mem. Sons of Am. Revolution, Soc. of War of 1812, Sigma Alpha Epsilon, Pi Eta Soc. (Harvard). Clubs: Harvard (New York); Minnesota (St. Paul); Minneapolis (Minn.). Home: 1445 Ogden St., N.W. 813 Arlington Bldg., 1025 Vermont Av., N.W., Washington 5

BRITTON, FREDERICK O. advt. exec.; b. Reading, O., Aug. 28, 1910; s. Frederick and Jane (Shoemaker) B.; student Miami U., Oxford, O., 1929-31, U. Cin., 1932-35; m. Erna M. Schriever, Nov. 29, 1930. Store ckl., meat cutter Kroger Co., Cin., 1932-37, dir. sales and tng., 1934-37; dir. tng. Macy's N.Y.C., 1939-41; v.p. D.G. Terrie, Ltd., 1944-46; asst. to pres. Heyden Chem. Corp., 1946-48; cons. in Arabia, Griffenhagen & Associates, 1949; mem. Facilities Rev. Bd. Def. Prodn. Bd., 1951-52; v.p. McCann Erickson, Inc., Chgo., 1953-59, Rutledge Advt. Co., St. Louis, 1960-. Spl. cons. sec. of war, 1940-41; mem. Army Exchange Adv. Com., 1941. Served from maj. to col. AUS, 1941-44, 48; col. USAF, 1952. Decorated Legion of Merit. Home: 908 Jefferson Av., Reading, Cin. 45215. Office: 1000 Market St., St. Louis. Died May 5, 1960; buried Reading Cemetery.

BROADHURST, EDWIN BORDEN air force officer; b. Smithfield, N.C., Aug. 16, 1915; s. Jack Johnson and Mabel (Borden) B.; student Citadel, 1933; B.S., U.S. Mil. Acad., 1937; grad. Kelly Field Flying Tng. Sch., 1939; m. Viola Seubert, Mar. 11, 1944; children-Edwin Borden, MaryAnn, Barbara Ellen. Commd. 2d lt. U.S. Army, 1937, advanced through grades to lt. gen. USAF, 196 rated command pilot, bombardier and navigator; 20 combat missions in B-17 bombers, World War II; plans officer Allied Hdqrs. S.W. Pacific, 1943; assigned air office War Operations Staff, 1944, Office Asst. Sec. War, 1945-46; chief U.S. Mil. Mission to Chile, 1947-50; chief plans Strategic Air Force, 1950-53; comdr. 5th Reconnaissance Wing, 1953-55, 57th Air Divs., Spokane, 1955-56; insp. gen. Hdqrs. Strategic Air Command, 1956-57, chief staff, Omaha, 1957-61; comdr. 7th Air Div., High Wycombe Air Sta., London, Eng., 1961-62; dep. chief staff operations headquarters Air Force, 1962-64; chief of staff UN Command, Korea, 1964-. Decorated Silver Star, Legion of Merit D.F.C., Air medal, Purple Heart. Mem. Soc. Mayflower Descendents. Home: 622 Hancock St., Smithfield, N.C. Office: Hdqrs. UN Command, APO 301, Seoul, Korea. Died Apr. 4, 1965; buried Riverside Cemetery, Smithfield, N.C.

BROCK, HENRY IRVING, writer; b. Amherst, Va., Aug. 4, 1876; s. Henry Clay and Mary Carter (Irving) B.; A.B., Hampden-Sidney (Va.) Coll., 1895, A.M.,

1896. hon. Litt.D., 1925; m. Nelly Grattan Morton, Oct. 1, 1908; 1 dau., Georgiana Mary. Teacher, prep. schs. Va. and Tenn., 1896-99; reporter Chattanooga (Tenn.) Times, 1899-1900; reporter and writer, New York Times, 1900-06, exchange and foreign editor, 1906-11; editor Saturday Magazine, New York Evening Post, 1912-17; asst. editor New York Sunday Times, 1919-24; polit. editor Unpartizan Review, 1919; writer for N.Y. Times since 1924. Capt. Air Service, U.S. Army, 1918-19. Clubs: Century, Players. Author: A Little Book of Limericks, 1947. Home: 776 Lexington Av., New York; and Bleak Hill, Comorn, Va. Address: New York Times, Times Square, NYC

BRODHEAD, DANIEL army officer; b. Albany, N.Y., Sept. 17, 1736; s. Daniel II and Hester (Wyngart) B.; m. Elizabeth Dupui; m. 2d, Rebecca Mifflin. Brought up on large family holdings in Bucks County, Pa.) dep. surveyor-gen., Reading, Pa., 1773; raised co. of riflemen to join Washington; promoted lt. col. after Battle of L.I., 1776, col., 1777; given command of regt. at Pitts., 1779; raided and terrorized Delaware Indians, 1779-81; acquitted in court martial resulting from complaints from officers and civilians; brevetted brig. gen. by Gen. Washington; strong mil. disciplinarian; served as surveyor gen. Pa. Died Nov. 15, 1809.

BRODIE, ALEXANDER OSWALD army officer; b. Edwards, N.Y., Nov. 13, 1849; s. Joseph and Margaret (Brown) B.; grad. U.S. Mil. Acad., 1865; m. Louise Hanlon, Dec. 15, 1892. Apptd. 2d lt. 1st Cav., June 15, 1870; 1st lt., May 25, 1875; resigned Sept. 30, 1877; pvt. 6th Cav., Aug. 6, 1883-Feb. 4, 1884; served against Apaches in Ariz. and Nez Perce campaign in Idaho. In cattle trade, Kan., 1878-82; mining in Dak. and Ariz., 1882-87; chief engr. Walter Storage Commn., Walnut Grove, Ariz., 1887-90; civ. and mining engr., Prescott, Ariz., 1893-94; county recorder, Yavapal County, Ariz., 1893-94. Maj. 1st U.S. Cav. ("Rough Riders"), May 17, 1898; lt. col., Aug. 11, 1898; served in Tampa and Cuba; in command left flank action at Las Guasimas, June 24, 1898, wounded. Rep. candidate for del. in Congress from Ariz., 1898; apptd. gov. of Ariz., July 1, 1902. Maj. asst. chief Record and Pension Office, Feb. 15, 1905; lt. col. mil. sec., June 10, 1905; lt. col. adj. gen., Mar. 5, 1907; col., Aug. 24, 1912, retired by operation of law, Mar. 13, 1913. Address: Haddonfield, N.J. Died May 10, 1918.

BROKMEYER, HENRY C. politician, philosopher; b. nr. Minden, Prussia, Aug. 12, 1828; s. Frederick William Brockmeyer; m. Elizabeth Robertson (dec. 1864); m. 2d, Julia Keinlen, Jan. 1867; several children. Emigrated to N.Y. at age 16, worked as bootblack, learned trades of currier, tanner, shoemaker; traveled, mostly on foot, to Ohio and Ind., then settled and worked in Memphis for 2 years; entered prep. dept. Georgetown Coll., was dismissed as result of theol. dispute with coll. pres. then studied philosophy with Wayland at Brown U., Providence; returned West, settled and studied philosophy in abandoned cabin, Warren County, Mo., 1854-56; moved to St. Louis, 1856, worked as iron-molder, studied and instructed William Torrey Harris and others in German philosophy; resumed solitary life until illness forced his return to St. Louis; served with Mo. Militia in Civil War, imprisoned for organizing a regt.; elected as War Democrat to Mo. Legislature, 1862-64, opposed disenfranchisement of So. sympathizers; elected alderman of St. Louis, 1866, Mo. senator, 1870; mem. Mo. Constl. Conv., 1887; became lt. gov. Mo., 1876; organized St. Louis Philos. Soc., 1866, gained large following as leader of St. Louis Movement in philosophy; propagated German Idealism with emphasis on Hegel, envisaged St. Louis as future Athens of Am.; later became lawyer for Gould railroads; received largest popular vote in Mo. to that time as elector-at-large, 1884; took several western trips. Contbr. articles to Jour. Speculative Philosophy; wrote some poetry; translated Hegel's Larger Logic (never published). Died July 26, 1906.

BROMER, RALPH SHEPHERD physician; b. Schwenksville, Pa., Mar. 21, 1886; s. Albert and Catherine (Schappert) B.; A.B., Yale, 1908; M.D., U. Pa., 1912; m. Alice Rupp, July 6, 1921; children—Ralph Shepherd, Catherine Brandes (Mrs. John Haughton Wrenn). Interne Pa. Hosp., Phila., 1912-14; house officer in orthopedic surgery Children's Hosp., Boston, 1915, roentgenologist, 1921-51; pvt. practice, specialist in radiology, 1915—; radiologist Episcopal Hosp., 1917-32, Bryn Mawr Hosp., Phila., 1932—; cons. roentgenologist, 1951—; prof. clin. radiology grad. sch. medicine U. of Pa., 1935—. Served with M.C., U.S. Army, World War I; roentgenologist and adj. Base Hosp. 34, comdg. officer Evacuation Hosp. 36, Nantes, France, 1918-19; disch. as lt. col. Fellow Am. Coll. Radiology; mem. Am. Roentgen Ray Soc. (past pres.), Radiol. Sco. N.A., A.M.A. Home: 318 Millbank Rd. Office: Bryn Mawr Hosp., Bryn Mawr, Pa. Died Sept. 25, 1957.

BROMLEY, CHARLES DUNHAM, lawyer; b. Boulder, Colo., Nov. 19, 1899; s. Charles Clark and Theresa (Dunham) B.; LL.B., U. Colo., 1924; m. Priscilla Price, Aug. 19, 1924 (div. 1929); 1 son, Charles P.; m. 2d, Sarah W. Wendelken, June 30, 1932; children—James F., John C. Admitted to Colo. bar, 1924; practice in Denver, 1930-68; mem. firm Bromley & Myers, 1946-68. Mem. Colo. Supreme Ct. Bd. Law Examiners, 1959-62. Del. Republican. Nat. Conv., 1924, alternate del., 1952; sec. Rep. Congl. Com. 2d Congl. Dist., 1924-30. Bd. regents U. Colo., 1928-34, 50-68. Served with U.S. Army, World War I; served to col USAAF, World War II; PTO. Decorated Legion of Merit, Bronze Star medal, commendation ribbon. Mem. Vets Fgn. Wars (judge adv. Colo. 1958-63), Chi Psi, Phi Alpha Delta. Mason. Home: Denver CO Died Jan. 8, 1968.

BROOKE, FRANCIS TALIAFERRO jurist; b. Smithfield, Va., Aug. 27, 1763; s. Richard and Elizabeth (Taliaferro) B.; studied medicine with brother Lawrence; read law with brother Robert; m. Mary Randolph Spotswood, Oct. 1791; m. 2d, Mary Champe Carter, 1804; children include Francis Jr. Commd. lt. Continental Army, 1780; served under Lafayette, 1781, later under Gen. Green; admitted to Va. bar, 1788, practiced law, Monongahela and Harrison counties; apptd. atty. Va. Dist. Ct.; mem. Va. Ho. of Dels, 1794-95; commd. Va., 1796; commd. brig. gen. Va. Militia, 1802; elected mem. Va. Senate, 1800, speaker, 1804; judge Va. Gen. Ct., 1804-11; judge Va. Supreme Ct. of Appeals, 1811-51, pres., 1824-30; v.p. Soc. of Cincinnati. Died Mar. 3, 1851.

BROOKE, JOHN RUTTER army officer; b. Montgomery County, Pa., July 21, 1838; s. William and Martha (Rutter) B.; ed. Freeland Sem. (now Ursinus Coll.), Pa., and Bolmars Sch., W. Chester, Pa.; m. Louisa Roberts, Dec. 24, 1863 (died 1867); m. 2d, Mary L. Stearns, Sept. 19, 1877. Capt. 4th Pa. Inf., Apr. 20, 1861; hon. mustered out, July 26, 1861; col. 53d Pa. Inf., Nov. 7, 1861; brig. gen. vols., May 12, 1864, "for distinguished services during battles of the Old Wilderness and Spottsylvania C.H., Va.;" resigned from vol. service, Feb. 1, 1866; lt. col. 37th U.S. Inf., July 28, 1866; transferred to 3d Inf., Mar. 15, 1869; col. 13th Inf., Mar. 20, 1879; transferred to 3d Inf., June 14, 1879; brig. gen., Apr. 6, 1888; maj. gen., May 22, 1897. Was head of mil. commn. and gov. gen. P.R.; gov. gen. of Cuba and comdg. Div. of Cuba; later comdg. Dept. of the East; retired by operation of law, July 21, 1902. Address: Washington, D.C. Died Sept. 5, 1926.

BROOKE-RAWLE, WILLIAM lawyer; b. Phila., Aug. 29, 1843; s. C. Wallace and Elizabeth Tilghman (Rawle) B.; A.B., U. of Pa., 1863; m. Elizabeth Norris Pepper, Feb. 7, 1872. Served in Civil War, lt. and capt. 3d Pa. Cav.; bvtd. maj. and lt. col. Agt. Penn. estates in Pa. Author: The Right Flank at Gettysburg; With Gregg in the Gettysburg Campaign; Gregg's Cavalry Fight at Gettysburg; The General Title of the Penn Family to Pennsylvania. Home: Philadelphia, Pa. Died Dec. 1, 1915.

BROOKINGS, WALTER DUBOIS lumberman; b. Keokuk, Ia., Feb. 28, 1873; s. John Emory and Emma m. Marian Kinney, Nov. 19, 1909 (died June 3, 1926); children—Robert Somers, Walter DuBois, Henry Nason K., Mary McIntosh; m. 2d, Martha Nutting Brooks, Aug. 27, 1929. Sec. and treas. Brookings Lumber & Box Co., Highland, Calif., 1899-1912, Brookings (Ore.) Timber & Lumber Co., 1912-17; Brookings (Ore.) Land & Town Site Co., 1912-17; v.p. Brookings Commercial Co., 1915-17; investigated pulpwood and forest resources and paper bag industry in France, Great Britain, Germany and Can., for Union Bag & Paper Corp. of New York City, 1919-20; sec., Miss. Flood Control Com., Nat. Water Power Development Com. Captain, Co. E. 2d Batt., 20th Engrs., A.E.F., Oct. 1917-July 1918; in charge securing timber-lands in the Vosges to supply Am. armies in Eastern France with lumber and timber; maj. 1st Batt., 20th Engrs., July 1918-Feb. 1919; in charge six lumbering operations near Pyrenees. As rep. of Herbert Hoover, took first shipload relief food to Baltic region, landing at Libau, Latvia, Mar. 1919, and remained there until Aug. 1919. Citation A.E.F. "for exceptionally meritorious service"; silver medal (Polish). Mem. Pi Eta. Gamma Delta Psi. Clubs: Cosmos, Harvard, Army and Navy Country (Washington). Author: Briefs for Debate (Brookings and Ringwalt), 1896; also numerous articles on problems of natural resources industries. Home: Seminary Hill, Alexandria, Va. Died July 23, 1950.

BROOKS, DAVID congressman; b. Phila., 1756; attended public schs.; studied law. Commd. lt. Pa. Battalion of Flying Camp. Continental Army, during Revolutionary War, 1776; captured at Ft. Washington, 1776, exchanged, 1780; apptd. asst. clothier gen; admitted to bar, practiced law; settled in New York County, N.Y.; mem. N.Y. State Assembly, 1787-88, 94-96, 1810; judge Dutchess County (N.Y.), 1795-1807; mem. U.S. Ho. of Reps. from N.Y., 5th Congress, 1797-99; apptd. commr. to negotiate treaty with Seneca Indians; clk. Dutchess County, 1807-09, 10-11, 13-15; apptd. an officer U.S. Customs Service; an original mem. Soc. of Cincinnati, Died Poughkeepsie, N.Y., Aug. 30, 1838; probably buried Old Rural Cemetery.

BROOKS, (HENRY) HARLOW physician; b. Medo, Minn., Mar. 31, 1871; s. Daniel Walker and Katherine (Riley) B.; High Sch. Minn.; U. of Mich., 1895; post-grad. work, U. of Freiburg, Polyclinic, Munich, Bavaria; hon. M.S., U. of Mich., 1929; m. Louise Dudley Davis, June 14, 1899. Asst. demonstrator anatomy, U. of Mich., 1894; instr. histology and embryology, Bellevue Hosp. Med. Coll., 1895-98; instr. and asst. prof. pathology and spl. pathology, 1898-1900, New York U., asst. prof. clin. medicine, 1904-11, prof. clin. medicine, 1912 - ; visiting phys. Bellevue Hosp.; cons. phys. City Hosp., Montefiore Hosp., Ossining Hosp., Union Hosp., Beth Israel Hospital, Greenwich Hospital; consulting pathologist, Hackensack Hospital. Civilian physician, U.S. Army, 1898-99; mem. 7th Regt. N.G. N.Y., 1896-1915; capt. Med. Corps, 1899, retired; returned to active list as lt. col., chief surgeon 2d Div., July 1916; placed on nat. guard reserve, Jan. 1917; commd. maj., Med. R.C., Aug. 21, 1917; active service, Sept. 7, 1917, med. chief Base Hosp., Camp Upton, Yaphank, L.I.; promoted lt. col., Med. Corps, U.S.A., Aug. 1918; chief consultant in medicine, 1st Army A.E.F., later transferred to 2d Army A.E.F., Nov. 1, 1918; transferred to staff, chief surgeon, 2d Army, A.E.F., Jan. 1, 1919; discharged, Apr. 22, 1919; commissioned col, U.S.R.C., Oct. 14, 1919. Trustee N.Y. Pathol. Soc. Awarded D.S.M. (U.S.). Address: New York, N.Y. Died Apr. 13, 1936.

BROOKS, JOHN army officer; gov. Mass.; b. Medford, Mass., May, 1752; s. Caleb and Ruth (Albree) B.; grad. Dr. Tufts' med. sch., 1773; A.M. (hon.), Harvard, 1787, M.D., 1810, LL.D., 1817; m. Lucy Smith, 1774, 2 children. Served as capt. Reading Co. of Minute Men, fought at Concord; commd. capt. Continental Army, 1776; served as lt. col. 8th Mass. Regt.; mem. lMass. Gen. Ct., 1785-86; commd. maj. gen. Middlesex (Mass.) Militia, 1786; mem. Mass. Conv. to ratify U.S. Constn., 1788; U.S. marshal for Mass. dist., 1791; mem. Mass Senate from Middlesex County, 1719; served as brig. gen. U.S. Army, 1792-96; adj. gen. Mass., 1812-16; gov., 1816-22; pres. Mass. Med. Soc. Mass. Soc. of Cincinnati, Washington Monument Soc.; bd. overseers Harvard, 1815. Died Medford, Mar. 1, 1825.

BROOKS, JOHN G(AUNT), mfg. exec.; b. Chgo., Jan. 9, 1913; s. Overton and Emmilgene (Wortsman) B.; student Northwestern U., 1930-36; m. Ann. Malcolm, Oct. 30, 1941; children—William Blair, Robert Malcolm. With Commonwealth Edison, 1930-36, Zenith Radio Corp., 1936-42, Majestic Radio Corp., 1946-47; with Ekco Products Co., 1947-54, v.p., 1950-54; pres., dir. Siegler Corp., Los Angeles, 1954-62; chmn. of the board and chief executive officer of Lear Siegler, Inc., Santa Monica, 1962-71, pres., 1964-71; dir. Royal Industries, Mattel, Inc., Aircraft Builders Counsel, Inc. Campaign chmn. Los Angeles County Heart Assn.; vice chmn. Nat. UN Day, 1960. Gov. Henrotin Hosp., Chgo.; regent St. John's Hosp., Santa Monica; asso. Cal. Inst. Tech.; founding mem. Claremont Coll.; trustee City of Hope, U. So. Cal., Cal. Council Econ. Edn. Served to capt. USAAF, 1942-46. Mem. Aerospace Industries Assn. (gov.), N.A.M. Air Force Assn., Navy League, U. So. Cal. Assos., U.S. C. of C. (dir., marine resource adv. panel). Clubs: Bel Air Country (Los Angeles); The California, Los Angeles Country. Home: Los Angeles CA Died Jan. 15, 1971; buried Holy Cross Cemetery, Los Angeles CA

BROOKS, MICAH congressman; b. Brooksvale, nr. Cheshire, Conn., May 14, 1775. One of earliest surveyors of Western N.Y.; justice of peace, 1806, mem. N.Y. State Assembly, 1808-09; served as col. on frontier, also at Ft. Erie, 1812-14; served as maj. gen. N.Y. State Inf., 1828-30; mem. U.S. Ho. of Reps. from N.Y., 14th Congress, 1815-17; engaged in agriculture; del. from Ontario County to N.Y. State Constl. Conv., 1821; presdl. elector on Adams ticket, 1824. Died Fillmore, N.Y., July 7, 1857; buried Nunda (N.Y.) Cemetery.

BROOKS, PHILLIPS MOORE, astronautics co., exec.; b. Independence, Cal., Feb. 18,21908; s. Willis Moore and Wilhelmina (Singlaub) B.; student U. Cal., Los Angeles, 1931-34; A.B., U. Cal., Berkeley, 1935; Ph.D., Leland Stanford U., 1943; m. Jean Woodworth Smith, Aug. 21, 1941; 1 son, Phillips Robertson. Scientist Bikini Sci. Resurvey Group, USAF, 1947; head dept. bacteriology, botany, physiology, Riverside (Cal.) Coll., 1947-49; asst. prof. aviation physiology U. So. Cal., Los Angeles, 1949-51; chief nuclear safety analysis group Nuclear Div., Martin Co., Balt., 1960-62; staff physiologist McDonnell Douglas Corp., St. Louis, 1962-—. Lectr. physiology dept. Ohio State U., Columbus, 1958-59; lectr. Washington U., St. Louis, 1963-65, cons. dept. radiation physics, 1965-—; vice chmn. space simulator safety operations subcom. Aerospace Industries Assn. Am., St. Louis, 1962. Served to lt. col., USAF, 1943-47, 52-60. Recipient Huntington Meml. Library scholarship U. Cal., 1933-34; Am. Smelting and Refining Corp., fellowship, Stanford U., 1935-38. Mem. A.A.A.S., Am. Inst. Aeronautics and Astronautics, Health Physics Assn., Aerospace Indsl. Life Scis. Assn., Aerospace Physiologist Assn., Aerospace Bioenvironmental Engrng. and Scis. Assn., Aerospace Med. Assn., Air Force Assn., Nat. Sojourners, Inc., Am. Inst. Biol. Scis., Sigma Xi, Chi Phi. Contbr. articles to profl. jours. Home: Creve Coeur MO Died Dec. 17, 1967.

BROOKS, THOMAS BENTON engr.; b. Monroe, N.Y., June 15, 1836; grad. Union Coll., C.E., 1857 (A.M.); m. Hannah Hulse, 1868 (died 1883); m. 2d, Martha Giesler, 1887. Practiced as civil and mining engr.; in Civil war, lt. 1st N.Y. vol. engrs., serving as engr. officer on staff Gen. Gilmore; bvtd. lt. col. and col.; later State geologist, Mich. and Wis.; published reports on Lake Superior iron regions, 1872-76; later farming; owned live-stock and tobacco plantations in S.W. Ga., spending winters at Bainbridge, Decatur County, Ga. Home: Newburgh, N.Y. Died 1900.

BROOKS, WILLIAM BENTHALL naval officer; b. Portsmouth, Va., Nov. 27, 1832; s. William and Mary Elizabeth (Benthall) B.; ed. pvt. schs. and by pvt. tutor; m. Amelia Wright, Sept. 23, 1858. Apptd. from Va., 3d asst. engr. U.S.N., Feb. 1852; promoted 2d asst. engr., U.S.N., Feb. 1852; promoted 2d asst. engr., Sept., 1855; 1st asst. engr., 1858; lt. chief engr., 1861; retired with rank of capt., Mar., 1892; promoted to chief engr. with rank of rear adm. retired, by act of Congress, June 1896. Episcopalian. Home: Erie, Pa. Died 1910.

BROSMAN, PAUL WILLIAM judge, b; Albion, Illinois, Nov. 9, 1899; s. William Henry and Lida (Leavitt) B.; LL.B., from University of Ill., 1924; A.B., Indiana University, 1926; J.S.D., Yale University, 1929; m. Katherine Elizabeth Lewis, Aug. 21, 1925; 1 son, Paul William. Mem. of Ill. and La. bars, Instr. business law, Ind. U. Sch. of Commerce and Finance, 1924-25, asst. prof., 1925-26; prof. law, Mercer U., Macon, Ga., 1926-28; Sterling fellow in law, Yale, 1928-29; prof. law, Tulane U., New Orleans, since 1929. W. R. Irby prof. of law 1938-51, asst. dean, 1932-37, dean, 1937-52, prof. of law (on leave of absence) since 1951; mem. summer faculty, various law schs.; now judge U.S. Ct. of Mil. Appeals, Washington. Mem. La. Supreme Ct. Adv. Com. on Integration of Bar, 1940-41; mem. La. Civil Service Commn., 1947-48; mem. Nat. Conf. of Commrs. on Uniform State Laws from La. Served as pvt., S.A.T.C., in United States Army, 1918; served with U.S. Army Air Corps, 1942-45; discharged with rank of lt. col.; now col., Judge Adv. Gen.'s Dept., U.S.A.F. Reserve, Awarded Legion of Merit. Mem. Am. (mem. council sect. legal edn. and admission to bar), La. State (ex.-mem. bd. govs.), and New Orleans bar assns., Association American Law Schools, Judge Advocates Assn., American Judicature Society American Law Inst., La. State Law Inst., Am. Acad. Political and Social Science, Order of Coif, Phi Kappa Tau, Phi Alpha Delta, Beta Gamma Sigma, Delta Sigma Rho, Alpha Alpha Alpha, Omicron Delta Kappa. Democrat. Episcopalian. Mason. Clubs: Round Table, Recess, Boston, New Orleans Country (New Orleans); Army and Navy (Washington). Home: 5609 McLean Dr., Bethesda, Md.; also 1776 State St., New Orleans. Office: U.S. Court of Military Appeals Bldg., Washington 25. Died Dec. 21, 1955.

BROUILLETTE, T. GILBERT, art dealer, cons.; b. Warrensburg, Mo., Aug. 2, 1906; s. T. William and Bessie M. (Trumbull) B.; B.A., Westminster Coll., 1928; postgrad. architecture, mus. direction Harvard, 1929-30, 1933-34. Asso., Ehrich-Newhouse Galleries, N.Y.C., 1935-36; asso. Acquavella Galleries, N.Y.C., 1945-50; dealer, art cons., N.Y.C., 1950-60, Falmouth, Mass., 1961-70; organizer old masters exhbns. Denver Art Mus., 1955, Brooks Meml. Art Gallery, Memphis, Tenn., 1952, Wichita (Kan.) Art Assn. Galleries, 1946, 48, 54, Staten Island Mus., 1955, 58, Moravian Coll., Bethlehem, Pa., 1948, Mus. Fine Arts, Little Rock, 1955, Mint Mus. Art, Charlotte, N.C., 1957, Okla. Art Center, Oklahoma City, 1946, 54, 65. Served to capt. USAAF, 1942-45. Mem. Coll. Art Assn. Am., Am. Fedn. Arts, Am. Assn. Museums, Soc. Archtl. Historians, Alumni Assn. Harvard Grad. Sch. Design, Falmouth Hist. Soc., Beta Theta Pi. Presbyn. Club: N.Y. Athletic (N.Y.C.). Address: Falmouth MA Died Jan. 24, 1970.

BROUN, WILLIAM LE ROY educator; b. Loudoun County, Va., 1827; A.M., U. of Va., 1850; LL.D., St. John's Coll., Md., 1874, U. of Ga., 1892; m. Sallie J. Fleming, Nov. 1, 1859. Prof. in a coll. in Miss., 1852-54; prof. mathematics, U. of Ga., 1854-56; in C.S.A. as lt. of arty., 1861, and later as commandant of the Richmond arsenal, with rank of lt. col. in ordnance dept.; at close of war became prof. natural philosophy, U. of Ga.; pres. Ga. Agrl. and Mech. Coll., 1872-75; prof. mathematics, Vanderbilt U., 1875-82; pres. Agrl. and Mech. Coll., Ala., 1882-83; prof. mathematics, U. of Texas, 1883-84; pres. Ala. Poly. Inst., 1884-. Home: Auburn, Ala. Died 1902.

BROUSSARD, EDWIN SIDNEY senator; b. Iberia Parish, La., Dec. 4, 1874; s. John D. and Anastazie (Gousoulin) B.; B.S., La. State U., 1896; studied law Tulane U.; m. Marie Patout, 1905. Teacher pub. schs., 1897-98; capt. 2d U.S. Vol. Inf., Spanish Am. War, 1898; served in Santiago Province, and in Cuba 1 yr.; asst. sec. Taft Commn. to Philippines, 1900; admitted to La. bar; apptd. dist. atty., 1903, and twice elected to the office, once as a Democrat and once as a Progressive; candidate of Progressive Party for lt. gov. of La., 1916; mem. U.S. Senate, 2 terms, 1921-33. Democrat. Home: New Ibernia, La. Died Nov. 19, 1934.

BROWER, WALTER SCOTT lawyer; b. Kewanee, Miss., Nov. 17, 1888; s. Joshua Randolph and Elizabeth Judith (Ingram) B.; awarded scholarship to U. of Texas as 1st honor grad. of Wall Sch., Honey Grove, Tex., 1907; LL.B., U. of Alabama, 1911; m. Elizabeth Jordan, 1920; children-Walter Jordan and William. Began law practice Birmingham, 1911; pros. atty., 1915-16; partner, London, Fitts, Yancey & Brower, 1916-17, London, Yancey & Brower, 1917-34; spl. corp. counsel, City of Birmingham, 1920-23; senator, Alabama State Senate, 1923-27; trade advisor Royal Netherlands Govt., 1921-28; spl. asst. to U.S. Atty. Gen., 1934-40, in charge of mail fraud investigation and prosecution; admitted to N.Y. bar, 1937; mem. firm, counsel, Brower, Brill & Tompkins, New York, N.Y., 1937-46; Brower, Brill, & Gaugel, since January 1, 1948. Impartial chmn. New York Shoe Industry since 1939, N.Y. Clothing Industry since 1937, N.Y. Cleaning & Dyeing Industry since 1939, N.Y. Poultry Industry 1941-43, Phelps-Dodge Copper Products Corp. since 1944, Commercial Finishing & Dyeing Hosiery Industry (N.Y. and Philadelphia) 1940-42; chmn. bd. trustees N.Y. Clothing Unemployment Fund since 1937; pub. mem. and panel chmn. W.L.B., 2d Region, since 1943; mem. Needlecraft Ednl. Commn. since 1937; mem. Nat. Panel of Arbitration, Am. Arbitration Assn. Chmn. Board of Registrars, Birmingham, Alabama. Served with 1st R.O.T.C., commd. capt., inf., U.S. Army, 1917; mem. advance party, 82nd Div. sent to France 1918; promoted maj., J.A.G.D., assigned to Gen. Pershing's Hdqrs., 1918; demobilized 1919. Chairman of board of trustees of New York Clothing Industry Vacation Fund; chmn. board trustees, Sidney Hillman Health Center, since 1948. lMem. N.Y. Southern Society, Southern Social Register, Soc. Am. Legion Founders. Am. Legion (del. 29th div. Paris Conv. 1919), Sons Confederate Vets. Mason (Shriner). Democrat (del. to nat. conv., Chgo. 1932). Clubs: The Club, Mountain Brook (Birmingham). Address: 3648 Clairmont Av., Birmingham, Ala. Office: 165 Broadway. also 45 E. 17th St., N.Y.C. Died Feb. 9, 1962; buried Birmingham, Ala.

BROWN, ALBERT GALLATIN senator; gov. Miss.; b. Chester Dist., S.C., May 31, 1813; s. Joseph Brown; attended Miss. Coll., 1829-32; m. Elizabeth Taliaferro, Oct. 1835; m. 2d, Roberta Young, Jan. 12, 1841; children-Robert Y., Joseph A. Elected col. Copiah County (Miss.) Militia, 1832, commd. brig. gen., 1834; admitted to Miss. bar, 1834; mem. Miss. Ho. of Reps., 1835-39; mem. U.S. Ho. of Reps. from Miss., 26th, 30th-32d congresses, 1839-41, Jan 1848-53; circuit judge, 1841-43; gov. Miss. 1844-48; mem. U.S. Senate from Miss., 1854-60 mem. Confederate Senate from Miss., 1862-65; capt. Brown's Rebels. Died nr. Terry, Hinds County, Miss., June 12, 1880; buried Greenwood Cemetery, Jackson, Miss.

BROWN, AMES THORNDIKE army officer; b. Boston, Nov. 3, 1890. Commd. 1st lt., inf. U.S. Army, 1917, advanced to maj., 1919; with 106th Inf., France, 1918; participated in Ypres-Lys engagement and Somme Offensive; disch. 1919; maj., inf., O.R.C., 1921-24; commd. major, inf., N.Y. N.G., 1924, and advanced through grades to brig. gen., 1940; became adj. gen. State of N.Y., Feb. 1940; on active duty as dir. N.Y. State SSS, since 1940. Decorated D.S.M., Silver Star, Army Commendation Ribbon, Purple Heart, Conspicuous Service Cross. Past Pres. 27th Div. Asso.; mem. Am. Legion, N.Y. Soc. Mil. and Naval Officers World Wars, Mil. Order World War, hon. mem. Vets. Corps Arty.-N.Y. Old Guard of City N.Y. Chmn. Vets.' Affairs Com., Div. Vets. Affairs. State N.Y. Address: 112 State Street, Albany, N.Y. Died May 1961.

BROWN, ARLO AYRES univ. pres.; b. Sunbeam, Ill., Apr. 15, 1883; s. Robert Ayres and Lucy Emma (Sanders) B.; A.B., Northwestern U., 1903; B.D., Drew Theol. Sem., 1907; postgrad. Union Theol. Sem., Northwestern U.; D.D., Cornell Coll., Ia., 1921; LL.D., Syracuse U., 1927; Litt.D., U. Chattanooga, 1929; LL.D., Northwestern, 1938; L.H.D., Boston U., 1939; m. Grace Hurst Lindale, Feb. 14, 1914; children-Arlo Ayres, Robert Lindale. Charges M.E. Ch., 1903-12, deacon, 1907. elder, 1909; asso. pastor Madison Av. Ch., N.Y.C., 1907-09; pastor Mount Hope Church, N.Y., 1909-12; agt. Bd. Fgn. lMissions, M.E. Ch., in Jerusalem. 1912-13; exec. sec. Newark Dist. Ch. Soc., 1913-14; supt. tchr. tng. Bd. of Sunday Schs., M.E. Ch., 1914-21; pres. U. Chattanooga, 1921-29; pres. Drew U., 1929-48. Enlisted in Tng. Sch. for Army Chaplains, June 1, 1918; commd. 1st lt., chaplain 318th Engrs., 6th Div., A.E.F., Aug. 29, 1918, sr. chaplain, Dec. 21, 1918; capt., Mar. 26, 1919; hon. discharged June 12, 1919; capt. chaplain O.R.C. 1921-24, maj. chaplain, 1924-34. Vice pres. Assn. of Am. Colls., 1928-29; chmn. Internat. Council Religious Edn.; pres. Am. Assn. Theol. Schs., 1936-38; pres. Meth. Ednl. Assn., 1939-40; mem. Commn. on Conf. Courses of Study of Meth. Ch.; mem. Bd. Edn., Meth. Ch.; mem. Meth. Commn. on Chaplains; mem. Appraisal Commn. of Laymen's Fgn. Missions Inquiry, 1931-32. Mem. Internat. Com. Internat. Bd. Army and Navy Com., Pub. Relations Com. YMCA. Mem. Phi Beta Kappa. Republican. Mason. Clubs: Rotary (Madison); Aldine, University (New York); University (Evanston, Ill.). Author: Studies in Christian Living, 1914; Primer of Teacher Training, 1916; Life in the Making (co-author), 1917; A History of Religious Education in Recent Times, 1923; Youth and Christian Living, 1929. Address: Drew University, Madison, N.J. Died Dec. 19, 1961; buried Old St. Paul's, Chestertown, Md.

BROWN, ARTHUR WINSTON army officer; b. Davenport, Ia., Nov. 9, 1873; s. Samuel Edward and Mary Louise (Davis) B.; ed. pub. schs. Davenport and Hempstead, N.Y.; LL.B., Cornell U., 1897; m. Jessie M. Emery, June 23, 1908; 1 son, Winston. Private, corpl., sergt. Battery A. Utah Arty., May 1898-Aug. 1899; apptd. 2d lt. U.S. Army, Dec. 1899; advanced through grades to col., Dec. 25, 1927; lt. col. judge advocate, N.A., Aug. 5, 1917, col., May 31, 1919, hon. disch., Mar. 21, 1920; apptd. judge advocate gen. with rank of maj. gen., Nov. 30, 1933; retired, Nov. 30, 1937. On legal staff of Tacna-Arica Plebiscitary Commission (Peru-Chile), 1926-27, and of Nat. Board of Elections of Nicaragua (1928-29), American mem. League of Nations Commn. for Adminstration of the Territory of Leticia (Peru-Chile), 1933-34. Mem. Delta Chi. Episcopalian. Mason. Address: 2221 Bay St. N., St. Petersburg, Fla. Died Jan. 3, 1958; buried Arlington Nat. Cemetery.

BROWN, BENJAMIN GRATZ senator, gov. Mo.; b. Lexington, Ky., May 28, 1826; s. Mason and Judith (Bledsoe) B.; attended Transylvania U.; grad Yale, 1847. Admitted to Ky. bar, 1849; mem. Ky. Legislature, 1852-59; significant figure in formation of Nat. and Mo. Republican parties; commd. col. 4th regt. Mo. Volunteers; mem. U.S. Senate from Mo., Dec. 14, 1863-67; gov. Mo., 1871-73; nominated from vice pres. U.S. on Liberal Republican ticket, 1872. Died St. Louis, Dec. 13, 1885; buried Oak Hill Cemetery, Kirkwood, Mo.

BROWN, ENOCH newspaper exec.; b. Franklin, Tenn., May 19, 1892; s. Enoch and Lulie (Allen) B.; student Vanderbilt U., 1910-14, Georgetown U., 1916-17; L.H.D., Southwestern U., 1951; m. Elizabeth Eggleston, Sept. 8, 1917. Pres. Memphis Pub. Co. since 1948. Mem. Game and Fish Commn., State of Tenn.; state com. officer Ducks Unltd.; State of Tenn. Bd. dirs. Meth. Hosp., Memphis; trustee Vanderbilt U. Battle Ground Acad. Served as capt. E Battery, 114th F.A., 55th F.A. Brigade, France, World War I; lt., col., mil. govt. sect., 5th Army, North Africa and Italy, World War II. Mem. U.S. Field Trials Assn. (pres.), Phi Delta Phi, Delta Tau Delta. Methodist. Mason (32ff, Shriner). Clubs: Country, Tennessee (Memphis). Home: 2391 Germantown Rd., Germantown, Tenn. Died Apr. 20, 1962; buried Mt. Hope Cemetery, Franklin, Tenn.

BROWN, FRANK XAVIER, lawyer; b. N.Y.C., Oct. 18, 1914; s. Frank X. and Emma (Knorr) B.; A.B., Fordham U., 1935; LL.B., Georgetown U., 1940; m. Catherine A. Toomey, Jan. 4, 1947. Admitted to D.C. bar, 1940; spl. asst. Office Undersec. War, 1939-41; asst. gen. counsel War Assets Adminstrn., 1947-49, Gen. Services Adminstrn., 1949-50; asst. gen. counsel Dept. Def., 1950-54, dir. procurement supply and distbn., 1954-56; partner Cox, Langford & Brown, Washington, 1956-68. Served from lt. to col. AUS, 1942-46. Mem. Am. Bar Assn., Bar Assn. D.C. Republican. Roman Catholic. Clubs: Army-Navy, Lawyers, Nat. Aviation. Home: Washington DC Died May 1, 1968.

BROWN, GEORGE naval officer; b. Rushville, Ind., June 19, 1835; s. William J. and Susan (Tompkins) B.; apptd. to U.S. Naval Acad. from Ind., 1849; m. Kate Morris, Oct. 4, 1871. Promoted passed midshipman, June 12, 1855; master, Sept. 16, 1855; lt., June 2, 1856; lt. comdr., July 16, 1862; comdr., July 25, 1866; capt., Apr. 25, 1877; commodore, Sept. 4, 1887; rear adm., Sept. 27, 1893; retired, June 19, 1897; performed spl. duty on western coast during Spanish-Am. War. Home: Indianapolis, Ind. Died June 29, 1913.

BROWN, HARRY JOE, motion picture dir.-producer; b. Pitts., Sept. 22, 1893; s. Nathan and Anna Brown; student U. Mich., 1909-10; LL.B., U. Syracuse, 1915; m. Dorothy Gray, Sept. 1, 1953; 1 son, Harry Joe. Stage and screen actor, dir., producer Warner Bros., Paramount Pictures, Pathe, R.K.O.; pres. Federal TV Prodns., Producers Actors Corp., 1944-72, Murphy Brown Prodns., Sage Prodns. Served as capt., inf., U.S. Army, World War I. Mem. Am. Legion, Screen Producers Guild, Motion Picture Alliance, Motion Picture Arts and Scis. Elk. Clubs: Masquers (pres. 1954-58), Friars (dir.) (Hollywood); Pioneers, Lambs (N.Y.C.); Tamarisk Country; Hillcrest Country; Variety. Home: Beverly Hills CA Died Apr. 28, 1972.

BROWN, HENRY HARRISON lecturer; b. Uxbridge, Mass., June 26, 1840; s. Pemberton and Paulina (Whitmore) B.; ed. Nichols Acad., Dudley, Mass., and 1885-86. at Unitarian Div. Sch., Meadville, Pa.; m. Fannie M. Hancox, Sept. 1873 (divorced). Teacher, 1857-70, except 3 yrs. in war as pvt. 18th Conn. Vols., 1st lt. 29th Conn. Vols. (colored), Jan. 1, 1863; capt. 1st U.S.C.T., Mar. 1864; mustered out Sept. 29, 1865. Preached for Unitarian Soc., Petersham, Mass., 1887-88, Salem, Ore., 1890-92; lecturer on spiritualistic, reformatory and econ. topics, 1870-85; lecturer and soul-culture teacher, 1893-1900; editor, lecturer, etc., 1900-. Pres. "Now" Folk, publishers, San Francisco, and editor "Now" (new-Thought mag.); also author of various pamphlets on Suggestion and the New Thought. Pres. World New Thought Federation, 1905. Established a cooperating community at Glenwood, Calif., 1906. Author: Self-Healing Through Suggestion; How to Control Fate Through Suggestion; Man's Greatest Discovery; Dollars Want Me: Concentration, or, the Road to Success; Success; How Won Through Affirmation. Home: Glenwood, Calif. Died May 8, 1918.

BROWN, HIRAM STAUNTON ret. corp. exec.; b. nr. Chestertown, Md., Oct. 3, 1882; s. Hiram and Mary (Hazzard) B.; A.B., magna cum laude, Washington Coll., Chestertown, Md., 1900; m. Mae Roslyn Maltz, Oct. 21, 1908; 1 son, Hiram Staunton. Began as office boy, N.Y. Herald; later with Washington Times; then in Mexico with Mex. Nat. R.R.; for 15 yrs. in pub. utility business with Hodenpyl, Walbridge & Co. and H.D. Walbridge & Co; pres. U. S. Leather Co.; 1924-29; pres. Radio-Keith-Orpheum Corp., 1929-33; officer or dir. various other corps; asst. coordinator of Nat. Def. Purchases, 1940-41; asst. dir. purchases OPH, 1941-42. Lt. col., chief of finance div. of Air Service, World War I; asst. to U.S. Liquidation Commn. in France. Chmn. bd. Washington Coll. Republican. Methodist. Clubs: Westchester Country, Bankers (N.Y.C.). Home: Rye, N.Y.; and Godlington Manor, Chestertown, Md. Died May 4, 1950; buried Chestertown, Md.

BROWN, HOMER CAFFEE army officer; b. Carthage, Mo., Sept. 25, 1893; s. William Henry Samuel and Edna (Caffee) B.; B.S., U.S. Mil. Acad., 1917; grad. Inf. Sch., company officers course, 1924, advanced course, 1930, Command and Gen. Staff Sch., 1934, Army War Coll., 1935, C.W.S., 1935; m. Helen Lahm, Aug. 8, 1917; 1 dau., Elizabeth Caffee (wife Calvin McVeigh Jenkins, USAAC). Commd. 2d lt. U.S. Army, 1917, advanced through grades to brig. gen.; served with 3d Inf., Eagle Pass, Tex., 1917-20; with 21st Inf., Schofield Barracks, Hawaii, 1920-23, with 16th Inf., Governors Island, N.Y., 1930-32; with 9th Inf., Fort Sam Houston, Tex., 1939-40; asst. G-3, Third Army, San Antonio, 1940-41; comdg. officer, 9th Inf., Fort Sam Houston, 1941-45; in S.W. Pacific area 1942-46; G-3, 4th Army, San Antonio, 1946-48, ret. for phys. disability. Mem. Nat. Security League (N.Y.), Press Club (Manlius School), Phi Mu, Scabbard and Blade. Home: 339 Ridgemont Av., San Antonio 2. Address: care The Adjutant General's Office, War Dept., Washington 25. Died Feb. 18, 1950; buried Ft. Sam Houston Nat. Cemetery, San Antonio.

BROWN, JAMES BARRETT, plastic surgeon; b. Hannibal, Mo., Sept. 20, 1899; s. Albert Sydney and Evelyn (Segsworth) B.; M.D., Washington U., 1923, D.Sc., 1970; m. Bertha Phillips Phillips, Sept. 30, 1946; children—Jane Hamilton, Frances Reith; (by previous marriage)—James Barrett, Charles Sydney. Interne and assistant resident surgical service, Barnes and Childrens' Hospital, 1923-25; engaged in private practice of plastic surgery, Saint Louis, Missouri, since 1925; professor clin. surgery, School of Medicine, Washington U., 1948-68, prof. emeritus plastic surgery, 1968-71; prof. maxillo-facial surgery, Sch. of Dentistry from 1936; mem. surg. staff, Barnes, St. Louis Children's, St. Luke's, Jewish, Deaconess and DePaul hosps., St. Louis Mo. consultant surgeon, Shriners. Barnard Free Skin & Cancer, Ellis Fischel State Cancer Hosps., and others; cons. surgeon M.P. & Frisco R.R.; cons. plastic surg. USAF; consultant Los Alamos Medical Center. Served as colonel, M.C., U.S. Army, 1942-1946; chief consultant plastic surgery, E.T.O., 1942-43; chief plastic surgeon, Valley Forge Gen. Hosp., 1943-45; senior consultant plastic surgery U.S. Army, 1945-46; sr. civilian cons. plastic surg., U.S. Army, Office Surgeon Gen.; chief cons. plastic surg., U.S. Vets. Adminstrn. Decorated Legion of Merit; Am. Design Award, Lord & Taylor, 1944; Alumni Citation, Washington U., 1955; award Am. Assn. Plastic Surgeons, 1967, Modern Medicine, 1968; Certificate Merit, St. Louis Med. Soc., 1969; James Barrett Brown vis. professorship established in his honor Washington U., 1969. Diplomate Am. Bd. Surgery (founders group), Am. Bd. Plastic Surgery (founders group), Fellow A.C.S. (v.p. 1959-60), Am. Assn. Plastic Surgeons (hon.; pres. 1954); mem. Am., Southern, Western (vice president 1955, president 1958), Central surg. assns., Am. Assn. Surg. Trauma. Assn. Mil. Surgs., Am. Society of Plastic and Reconstructive Surgery, International Society of Surgeons (Brussels), Assn. of Medical Consultants, World War II, Surgeons' and Halsted clubs, Am. Soc. Surgery Hands, Society Head and Neck Surgeons, Phi Delta Theta, Nu Sigma Nu, Alpha Omega Alpha. Presbyterian. Clubs: Grolier (New York City); University (St. Louis). Co-author: Skin Grafting, 1958; Plastic Surgery of the Nose, 1951; Neck Dissections, 1957; Surgery of Face, Mouth and Jaws, 1954; Post-Mortem Homografts, 1960; (with Dr. Thomas Zaydon) Early Treatment Facial Injuries, 1964; other books on plastic surgery. Editorial bd. Excerpta Medica, Amsterdam; and others. Contbr. chpts. textbooks and articles in surg. jours. and other sci. publs. Home: St. Louis MO Died Mar. 18, 1971; interred Oak Grove Mausoleum, St. Louis MO

BROWN, JOHN army officer; b. Haverhill, Mass., Oct. 19, 1744; s. Daniel and Mehitabel (Sanford) B.; grad. Yale, 1771; read law with brother-in-law Oliver Arnold, Providence, R.I.; m. Huldah Kilbourne. Admitted to Tryon County (R.I.) bar; began practice law, Johnstown, N.Y.; moved to Pittsfield, Mass., 1773; mem. Pittsfield Com. of Correspondence, 1774; mem. Provincial Congress from Pittsfield 1774-75; went to Montreal (Can.), to discover strength and nature of revolutionary sentiment there, 1775; commd. maj. Continental Army, 1775, served in battles at Lake Champlain, Montreal, Ft. Chambly; served under Gen. Montgomery in unsuccessful attempt to take Que. (Can.), 1776, was clearly insubordinate in this action; resigned commn., 1777; published handbill attacking Benedict Arnold; elected col. Berkshire Militia, 1777, captured Ft. George; returned to law practice; mem. Mass. Gen. Ct., 1778; judge county ct. of common pleas, 1779. Ambushed and killed while leading group of Mass. Militia, Oct. 19, 1780.

BROWN, JOHN senator, Continental congressman; b. Staunton, Va., Sept. 12, 1757; s. John and Margaret (Preston) B.; ed. Princeton, Coll. William and Mary; studied law under Thomas Jefferson; m. Margaretta Mason, 1799. Fought in Am. Revolution; admitted to Va. bar, 1782; represented Ky. in Va. Legislature, 1784-88; del. Continental Congress, 1787-88; mem. Ky. Constl. Conv., 1788; mem. Va. Conv. to ratify U.S. Constn., 1789, voted against ratification; mem. U.S. Ho. of Reps. from Va., 1st-2d congresses, 1789-92; mem. U.S. Senate from Ky., 1792-1805, pres. pro tem, 1803-04; his home "Liberty Hall," Frankfort, Ky., designed by Thomas Jefferson. Died Frankfort, Aug. 29, 1837; buried Frankfort Cemetery.

BROWN, JOHN abolitionist; b. Torrington, Conn., May 9, 1800; s. Owen and Ruth (Mills) B.; m. Dianthe Lusk, 1820; m. 2d, Mary Anne Day, 1832; 20 children. Ardent abolitionist, favored use of violence; kept sta. of Underground Ry. for escaping slaves, located at Richmond, Virginia, led free soil forces of Pennsylvania at the Potawatomie River massacre in Mo., 1856; claimed to be an instrument of God, also influenced by sack of Ft. Lawrence, Kan., by pro-slavery forces; conceived plan of slave refuge base in Md. or Va., polit. basis of which would be a constl. state govt. set up to beat off all attacks (state or fed.), also to promote slave insurrection; captured Harper's Ferry, Va., also U.S. Armory, 1859; captured by Robert E. Lee at Harper's Ferry, Oct. 16, 1859; convicted of treason by State of Va. (although not citizen of that state), hanged Dec. 2, 1859; regarded by abolitionists as martyr; other portions of No. population looked favorably on his sincerity, calm conduct during trial; subject of song John Brown's Body; called "Old Brown of Osawatomie." Executed Charles Town, Va., Dec. 2, 1859.

BROWN, JOHN HERBERT, JR. naval officer; b. Canton, Pa., Oct. 12, 1891; s. John Herbert and Belle (Dartt) Brown; B.S., U.S. Naval Acad., 1914; grad. Submarine Sch., Naval War Coll.; m. Nellie Janvier, Apr. 20, 1916; children-Mariana, John Herbert 3d. Commd. ensign USN, 1914, advanced through grades to rear adm., 1943; served in submarines 17 yrs., in cruisers 3 yrs.; became dep. comdr. submarine force Pacific Fleet; comdr. Cruiser Div. One; comdt. U.S. Naval Base, Portsmouth, N.H. comdr. submarine force Pacific Fleet; comdt. 4th Naval Dist. since 1951. Decorated D.S.M.; Legion of Merit and Gold Star with Combat "V"; Submarine Combat Insignia. Clubs: New York Yacht; Racquet (Phila.); University (Washington). Home: 212 Cass St., Middletown, Del. 19709. Died June 10, 1963.

BROWN, JOHN MARSHALL trustee of estates, army officer; b. Portland, Me., Dec. 14, 1838; s. John Bundy and Ann Matilda (Greely) B.; ed. Portland, Gould's, Bethel and Phillips Andover Acads.; grad. Bowdoin Coll., 1860; A.M., 1863. Commd. 1st lt., 20th Me. Vols., Aug. 29, 1862; apptd. by Pres. Lincoln, June 1863, capt. and asst. adj. gen. vols.; later served in S.C. and Fla.; promoted to lt. col. 32d Me. vols., Mar. 26, 1864; comd. regt. at Totopotomy and Cold Harbor and preliminary movements at Petersburg, where was severely wounded; discharged for physical disability from sounds, Sept. 23, 1864; bvtd. col. and brig. gen.; m. Alida Catherine Carroll, Dec. 18, 1866. Became mem. firm J. B. Brown & Son, owners Portland Sugar Co. Mem. common council, Portland, 1865, commr. to Paris Expn., 1867. Served in Me. Militia as a.-d.-c., col. and brig. gen. Bem. Me. legislature, 1899. Republican. Pres. Me. Agrl. Soc., 1878; was 25 yrs. mem. and 6 yrs. pres. bd. of overseers, and later mem. bd. of trustees Bowdoin Coll. Mem. bd. of mgrs. Nat. Home for Disabled Vol. Soldiers, and local mgr. Eastern branch, 1898-. Home: Falmouth Fireside, Me. Died 1907.

BROWN, JUSTUS MORRIS army officer; b. in Ohio, Dec. 8, 1840; M.D., U. of Pa., 1862. Apptd. from Ohio, asst. surgeon U.S. Army, July 11, 1862; capt. asst. surgeon, col. asst. surgeon gen., Feb. 2, 1901; retired at own request after 40 yrs.' service, Feb. 13, 1903; advanced to rank of brig. gen.; retired, by act of Apr. 23, 1904. Home: Hackensack, N.J. Died Dec. 21, 1912.

BROWN, LEWIS H. corp. official; b. Creston, Ia., Feb. 13, 1894; s. Lewis Henry and Arminta (Cole) B.; A.B., State University of Iowa, 1915; hon. LL.D., Temple Univ., 1942, Brown Univ., 1943; Lake Forest College, 1945; D.C.S., hon., N.Y.U., 1950; m. Mary A. Allen, June 24, 1918; children—Rosalind Louise (Mrs. Philip Inglehart), Beatrice Marie (Mrs. William H. Sweney, Jr.), and Mary Barbara (Mrs. C. E. Bayliss Griggs). With Fort Wayne (Ind.) Corrugated Paper Co., 1915-17, Montgomery Ward & Co., 1919-27; asst. to pres. Johns-Manville Corp., 1927-29, pres., 1929-46, chmn. bd. and chief exec. officer, 1946-51; chairman bd. Canadian-Johns-Manville Co., Ltd., Johns-Manville Internat. Corp., Johns-Manville Sales Corp., Johns-Manville Products Corp.; dir. Johns-Manville Corp., American Telephone & Telegraph Co., Federal Reserve Bank of New York; chmn. exec. committee Tax Foundation, Inc.; chairman American Enterprise Assn.; vice chmn. Freedoms Found.; mem. Com. on the Present Danger; dir. Citizens Nat. Com. Attended 1st Officers Training Camp, May 1917; capt. infantry, U.S. Army, Aug. 1917-May 1919, A.E.F., France. Chmn. Noise Abatement Commn., N.Y. City, 1929; mem. Pres'. Emergency Com. for Employment, 1930-31; pres. Asbestos Inst., 1933; mem. Durable Goods Indus. Com., Mar. 1934-Sept. 1935; dir. New York World's Fair, 1939 and 1940; dir. National Industrial Conference Board; member lay council New York Academy Medicine. General chmn. 23rd and 24th Annual Roll Call, and 1940 Citizens War Relief Com., N.Y. Chapter, Am. Red Cross. Received Vermilye medal, 1939, from Franklin Inst. of Pa. for "outstanding contribution in field of industrial management," Medal for Merit, 1946. Member New York Chamber Commerce, Nat. Assn. Manufactors, National Inst. Social Sciences, Phi Alpha Delta, Beta Gamma Sigma. Republican. Clubs: The Links (New York); Round Hill Country (Greenwich, Conn.); Gulf Stream (Del Ray Beach, Florida); Burning Tree Country (Washington); Union League (New York); Chicago; Minnesota (St. Paul); Pacific Union (San Francisco); Rolling Rock (Pittsburgh); pine Valley Golf (Clementon, N.J.); National Golf Links (Southampton, N.Y.); Everglades (Palm Beach, Fla.). Author: A Report on Germany, 1947. Home: Deer Park, Greenwich, Conn. Office: 22 E. 40th St., N.Y. City. Died Feb. 26, 1951; buried Putnam Cemetery, Greenwich, Conn.

BROWN, LLOYD DAVIDSON ret. army officer; b. Sharon Ga., July 28, 1892; s. Dr. Lawrence Ruffin and Mary A. (Davidson) B.; A.B., U. Ga., 1912; m. Benita Allen, Sept. 10, 1919 (died Dec. 12, 1925); 1 son, Allen Davidson; m. 2d, Katherine Green, July 28, 1928. Commd. 2d lt. U.S. Army, 1917, advanced through grades to maj. gen., 1943. comdt. 28th Div., later stationed Fort Benning, Ga.; retired 1948. Mem. Phi Delta Theta, Phi Beta Kappa. Methodist. Home: S. Alexander Av., Washington, Ga. Died Feb. 17, 1950; buried Washington, Ga.

BROWN, LYTLE army officer; b. Nashville, Nov. 22, 1872; s. James Trimble and Jane (Nichol) B.; grad. U.S. Mil. Acad., 1898; B.E., Vanderbilt U., 1893, C.E., 1894; m. Louise Lewis, Dec. 23, 1902; children—Lytle, Eugene Lewis (dec.), Pauline Lewis, Neill Smith, James Trimble, Lewis Castner. Commd. 2d lt. engrs., 1898; promoted through grades to col. N.A., 1917; brig. gen. Nat. Army, 1918; brig. gen. U.S. Army, 1928. Participated in Santiago Campaign; engaged in Battle of San Juan, July 13, 1898; and siege of Santiago, in Philippines, as city engr. Manila, engr. officer Dept. of Northern Luzon, 1900-02; instr., asst. prof. civil and mil. engring, U.S. Mil. Acad., 1903-07; comdr. Co. E, 2d Bn. Engrs., 1907-08; in charge U.S. Engr. Dist., Louisville, 1908-12; comdr. 2d Batn. Engrs., 1912-16, engr. officer Punitive Expdn., Mexico, 1916; in charge U.S. Engr. Dist., Nashville, 1917-18; comdr. 106th Regt. Engrs., engr. officer 31st Div.; apptd. dir. War Plans Div. and pres. Army War Coll., 1918; in charge U.S. Engr. Dist., Florence, Ala., and Chattanooga, Tenn., 1919; in charge constrn. Wilson Dam, Muscle Shoals, Ala., 1919-20; regtl. comdr. 2d Engrs., 1920-21; sr. instr. engring., Gen Service Sch., Ft. Leavenworth, Kan., 1921-23; dir. Gen. Staff Corr. Sch., 1923-24; dir. and asst. comdt., comdt. General Staff Sch. U.S. Army, 1924-25; comdg. 2d Regt. Engrs., 1925; asst. comdt. Army War Coll., 1926-28; comdg. 19th Brigade, Panama Canal Dept., 1928-29; chief of army engrs., with rank of maj. gen., 1929-33; brig. gen. comdg. Atlantic sector Panama Canal Dept., 1934; maj. gen. comdg. Panama Canal Dept., 1935-36; retired from active service, 1936. Decorated D.S.M. (U.S.); Companion of Bath (Britain); Officer Legion d'Honneur (France). Mem. Nat. Capital Park and Planning Commn., 1932-33; mem. engrs. adv. bd. RFC; mem. Tenn. Conservative Commn., 1939-40; chmn. Gov.'s Adv. Com. on Preparedness; chmn. State Def. Council, 1941; chmn. State Bd. on prevention of stream pollution, state rationing dir., 1942. Home: R.F.D. 5, Franklin, Tenn. Died May 1951.

BROWN, PRESTON army officer; b. Lexington, Ky., Jan. 2, 1872; s. Col. John Mason B.; A.B., Yale, 1892, M.A., 1920; honor grad. Army Sch., of the Line, 1913; grad. Army Staff College, 1914. Army War College, 1920; LL.D., Trinity Coll., Hartford, 1926; m. Susan Ford Dorrance, of Wilkes-Barre, Pa., Feb. 8, 1905; 1 son, Dorrance (died June 1936). Served as private and corpl. Battery A. 5th Arty., Sept. 1894-Mar. 26, 1897; commd. 2d lt. 2d Inf., Mar. 2, 1897; promoted through grades to maj. gen., Dec. 10, 1925; chief of staff, 4th Army Corps in front of Metz, Sept., 1918; comdg. gen. 3d Div., Battle of the Meuse-Argonne, Oct. 1918; asst. chief of staff, A.E.F., at advanced Gen. Hdqrs. in occupied German territory, Nov. 1918; instr., dir. and acting comdt. Army War Coll., Washington, 1919-21. Awarded D.S.M. for exceptionally meritorious and distinguished services. As chief of staff 2d Div. directed the details of the battles near Chateau-Thierry, Soissons and at the St. Mihiel salient; also, in comd. of 3d Div. in the Meuse-Argonne offensive, at a critical time, through his judgment and energetic action, div. was able to carry to a successful conclusion the operations at

Claire-Chenes and Hill 294. Comdg. gen. 3d Inf. Brigade, 1921, 2d Div., 1924, 1st Div., 1925, 1st Corps Area, 1926-30; comdg. gen. Panama Canal Dept., Nov. 24, 1930-Nov. 14, 1933; comdg. gen. 2d Army and 6th Corps Area, 1933-34, retired Nov. 30, 1934. Comdr. Legion of Honor (France); Comdr. Order of the Crown (Belgium). Mem. Soc. of the Cincinnati. Clubs: University (New York); Graduate (New Haven, Conn.); University (Denver). Home: Vineyard Haven, Mass. Died June 30, 1948.

BROWN, ROBERT ALEXANDER army officer; b. Delaware County, Pa., Nov. 7, 1859; s. James and Ann (Stewart) B.; grad. U.S. Mil. Acad., 1885, Inf. and Cav. Sch., 1889, Army War Coll., 1910; m. Virginia Long, Nov. 8, 1893. Commd. 2d lt. 4th Cav., June 14, 1885; promoted through grades to brig. gen. N.A., Aug. 5, 1917. Comd. Indian scouts in Capt. Lawton's command which secured surrender of Geronimo, 1886; participated in Cuban Occupation, 1898-99, in subduing Philippine Insurrection, 1899-1901; instr. Army War Coll., 1910-11, 1912-13; officer of Gen. Staff, and chief of staff, Southern Dept., 1913-14; apptd. comdr. 84th Inf. Brigade, Camp A. L. Mills, L.I., N.Y., Sept. 1, 1917; joined A.E.F. in France, Nov. 14, 1917. Address: Washington, D.C. Died Sept. 30, 1937.

BROWN, SAMUEL ALBURTUS physician; b. Newark, Jan. 7, 1874; s. Isaac Payne and Marie (Aldridge) B.; M.D., N.Y.U., 1894, Dr.P.H., 1926; m. Charlotte Cowdrey, June 15, 1898; children—Charlotte Cowdrey, Alberta Hartley. Mem. faculty med. dept. N.Y.U. (formerly U. and Bellevue Hosp. Med. Coll.), 1896-1932, dean, 1915-32, now dean emeritus; cons. physician, Bellevue, New Rochelle Hosp., Meml. Hosp., Long Branch, French Hosp., North Hudson Hosp., Rockaway Hosp., Fitkin Meml. Host. Acting chmn. bd. trustees Bellevue Medical Center and N.Y. U. Served as asst. surgeon and surgeon, 12th Regt. Nat. Guard N.Y., 1900-10. lt. col. U.S. Res. Fellow A.C.P.; mem. A.M.A. Med. Soc. State of N.Y., (pres. 1924-26), N.Y. Acad. Sciences, S.A.R., Harvey Soc., New York Soc. Mil. and Naval Officers of World War. Am. Legion. Alpha Omega. Phi Gamma Delta, Nu Sigma Nu. Democrat. Episcopalian. Clubs: New York Yacht, Links Golf, Woodmont Rod and Gun, Century. Home: 277 Park Av., N.Y.C.; also Sands Point, L.I., N.Y. Office: 75 55th St., N.Y.C. Died Mar. 16, 1952.

BROWN, SETH W. ex-congressman, lawyer; b. nr. Waynesville, Warren Co., O., Jan. 4, 1843; ed. public schools; served in Civil war in Co. H, 79th Ohio Vol. inf.; admitted to bar, 1873; pros. atty. Warren Co., 1880-83; mem. Ohio Gen. Assembly, 1883-87; presidential elector, 1888; mem. Congress, 1897-1901, 6th Ohio dist.; Republican. Home: Lebanon, O.

BROWN, SYLVANUS millwright, inventor; by. Valley Falls, R.I., June 4, 1747; s. Philip and Priscilla (Carpenter) B.; m. Ruth Salisbury, 1 son, James Salisbury. Learned millwright trade; served aboard Continental Navy vessel Alfred, at beginning of Am. Revolution; worked for State of R.I. arsenal; supervised constr. several grist and saw mills, New Brunswick; made short trip to Europe, returned to Pawtucket, R.I., reestablished machine shop; assisted Samuel Slater in construction Am.'s 1st practical power spinning wheel, 1790, credited with crucial part in turning Slater's memories of English spinning machines into working model; developed many machines essential to profitable constn. of textile machinery; possibly 1st to use slide-crest lathe; superintended furnaces in cannon factory, Scituate, R.I., 1796-1801. Died Pawtucket, July 30, 1824.

BROWN, THADDEUS HAROLD lawyer; b. Lincoln Tp., O., Jan. 10, 1887; s. William Henry and Ella Dell (Monroe) B.; ed. Ohio Wesleyan U. and Ohio State U.; LL.D., Lincoln Memorial U.; m. Marie Thrailkill, Nov. 10, 1915; 1 son, Thaddeus. Journal clk., Ohio Ho. of Rep., 1909-11; asst. sec. 4th Ohio Constl. Conv., Jan.-June 1912; in practice of law at Columbus, O., 1912-17, 1919-20, 1927-29; mem. Civil Service Commn., O., 1920-22; sec. of state, Ohio, 1923-27; chief counsel Federal Power Commn., Sept.-Dec. 1929; gen. counsel Federal Radio Commn., Dec. 1929-Mar. 1932, mem. same, Mar. 1932-July 1934, vice chmn., Apr. 1933-July 1934; mem. Federal Communications Commn., July 1934-. Del. Rep. Nat. Conv., 1928; Ohio Presidental elector, 1928. Captain inf., U.S. Army, July 1917-Feb. 1919; maj. J.A.G. Reserve Corps, 1919-23; lt. col. Inf. R.C., 1923-24; lt. col. J.A.G. R.C., 1924-. Vice chmn. bd. of trustees Lincoln Memorial U. Republican. Presbyn. Mason (32 degree, Shriner). Home: Columbus, O. Deceased.

BROWN, THOMAS F(RANCIS), business exec.; b. Cambridge, Mass., May 19, 1883; s. John and Helen (Melville) B.; student pub. and pvt. schs. of Mass. and Eng. Chemist U.S. Govt., 1905-09; metall. engr., 1910-15; works mgr. Framingham Machine Co., 1915-17; pres. Indsl. Engring. Corp., 1919-22; v.p. U.S. Food Products Corp., 1922-29. Nat. Distillers Products Corp., 1929-53, retired 1953; director and chmn. exec. com. Certainteed Products Corporation; director of the Bestwall Gypsum Company. Served as col. A.U.S., 1942-43. Recipient Legion of Merit. Mem. A.S.M.E., Am. Inst. Chem. Engrs., Am. Inst. Mining and Metall. Engrs., Profl. Engrs. State N.Y., Am. Legion, Mil. Order World Wars, Sons of Vets., Philippine-Pacific War Veterans, Am. Ordnance Assn., Mil. Order of the Carabao. Office: 99 Park Av., N.Y.C. 10016. Died Sept. 11, 1962.

BROWN, WARWICK THOMAS naval officer; b. Kan., Mar. 15, 1890; s. Jackson and Alice Janet (Planck) B.; M.D., Kan. Med. Coll., 1913; postgrad. student Tulane U., 1917-18, U. Cal., 1935; m. Mildred Marie Mills, June 2, 1915; children-Mills, Thomas McGiffin. Commd. lt. (j.g.) M.C., U.S.N., 1917, advanced through grades to vice adm., 1952; asst. surgeon, 1917; asst. surgeon 4th Marine Brigade, France, 1918-19; brigade surgeon, Nicaragua, 1930-32; comdg. officer First Med. Bn., 1941-42; div. surgeon First Marine Div., Guadal Canal, 1942; force surgeon Fleet Marine Force, Pacific, 1944-46; comdg. officer Naval Hosp., Quantico, Va., 1946-49, St. Albans, N.Y., 1949-51; dist. med. officer Fifth Naval Dist., 1951-52; adminstr. Central Dispensary and Emergency Hosp., Washington, 1952-; adminstr. Washington Hospital Center, 1956-. Diplomate Am. Bd. Internal Medicine. Decorated Legion of Merit, Gold Star, Bronze Star, Presdl. Unit Citation, Presdl. Medal of Merit (Nicaragua), 1931. Mem. Kappa Sigma. Club: Army-Navy (Washington). Home: 2800 Woodley Rd. Office: 1711 New York Av. N.W., Washington. Died May 17, 1960.

BROWN, WILLIAM CAREY army officer; b. Traverse des. Sioux, Minn., Dec. 19, 1854; s. Garretson Addison and Sue (Carey) B.; grad. U.S. Mil. Acad., 1877, Infantry and Cavalry Sch., 1883; Army War Coll., 1910. Commd. add. 2d lt. 2d. Cav., June 15, 1877; promoted through grades to col. cav., Apr. 26, 1914. Participated in Bannock Indian Campaign, 1878, Sheepeater Indian campaign, 1879, Sioux Indian campaign, 1890-91; adj. U.S. Mil. Acad., 1885-90; in Santiago campaign and Battle of San Juan, July 1-2, 1898; Philippine Insurrection, 1900-01; an actg. insp. gen., 1900 and 1912-14; comdg. 10th U.S. Cav. at Siege of Naco, Ariz., Oct.-Dec. 1914, and on Mexican Punitive Expdn., Mar. 16-May 3, 1916. Prepared War Dept. report on mobilization nat. guard, 1916; pres. Cantonment Site Bd., Eastern Dept., 1917; in France with 42d Div., insp. Q.M.C., A.E.F., 1917-18, when retired for age after over 41 years of active commissioned service. Bvtd. 1st lt., Feb. 27, 1890, for gallant service in action against Indians at Big Creek, Ida., Aug. 19, 1879, and reconnaissances, Aug. 17 and Sept. 25, 1879. In action at Santa Cruz, P.I., Oct. 13, 1900, and at Malimba River, P.I., Jan. 25, 1901. Devised automatic correction for "drift" of bullet Springfield rifle; invented asbestos stovepipe shield for tents; performing voluntary service in O.M.G.O., Oct. 1919-July 1923, in matters pertaining to Emergency Rations, and in development of New Reserve Rations for U.S. Army. Awarded D.S.M. for services in World War and Silver Star Citation "for gallantry in action" at Santiago, Cuba, 1898. Apptd. brig. gen. U.S. Army, retired Feb. 28, 1927. Engaged in historical research pertaining to Indian Wars. Home: Denver, Colo. Died May 8, 1939.

BROWN, WILSON naval officer; b. Phila., Pa., 1882; s. Wilson and Sarah Ann (Cochran) B.; student Penn Charter Sch., Phila., 1890; grad. U.S. Naval Acad., 1902; m. Lydia Ballou Chappell, Aug. 4, 1924. Commd. ensign, U.S. Navy, 1902, and advanced through the grades to rear adm., 1936; comdg. training squadron, Scouting Force, U.S.S. New York, 1936-37; supt. U.S. Naval Acad., Annapolis, Md., 1938-41; became vice adm. comdg. Scouting Force, Pacific Fleet, 1941; apptd. aide to President Roosevelt. Feb. 1943; retired Dec. 1944. Episcopalian. Clubs: Army and Navy, Chevy Chase, N.Y. Yacht. Home: Waterford, Conn. Died Jan. 2, 1957.

BROWN, WRISLEY lawyer; b. Washington, July 22, 1883; s. Charles Albert and Mary Louise (Wrisley) B.; student; Columbian now George Washington) U., 1901-02; studied under private teachers, 1903-04; LL.B., Nat. U., Washington, D.C., 1907. LL.M., with honors, 1908; m. Mrs. Mozelle Price Whitford, 1920. Apptd. to classified civil service from Me., Feb. 13, 1905, and assigned to Treas. Dept.; law clerk to comptroller of the treas., 1907-09; examiner, Dept. of Justice, Mar. 15-Oct. 8, 1909; spl. asst. to the atty. gen. U.S., 1909-18; also consulting atty., Bureau of Investigation, 1910-Jan. 7, 1918. Conducted the investigation that resulted in impeachment, on July 11, 1912, of Robert W. Archbald, U.S. circuit judge; was counsel for the mgrs. on the part of Ho. of Rep. in the trial before the Senate, culminating in conviction. Represented U.S. before an English commn., at London, June and July 1914, in litigation under the Nat. Banking Laws, Republican. English Lutheran. Commd. 2d lt. D.C.N.G., July 2, 1902; commd. maj. Signal Res. Corps, Dec. 17, 1917; transferred to Air Service, Oct. 18, 1918; commd. lt. col. U.S. Army, July 3, 1919; resigned Sept. 28, 1920. Pres. Potomac Freight Terminals Co.; pres. and gen. counsel, Terminal Refrigerating & Warehousing Corp., Consol. Terminal Corp.; dir. Nat. Bank of Washington, Norfolk & Washington Steamboat Co. Mem. Am. Bar Assn., Am. Acad. Polit. and Social Science, Archeol. Inst. America (pres.), Am. Inst. of Refrigeration, Chamber of Commerce of U.S. (nat. concillor), Washington Board of Trade, English-Speaking Union (dir.), Am. Legion, Mil. Service Legion. Clubs: Bankers of America (New York); University Club, Army and Navy Club, Nat. Press Club, Rotary Internat., Seigniory of Canada. Author of "The Impeachment of the Federal Judiciary," pub. as a public document pursuant to a resolution of the U.S. Senate, Jan. 13, 1914. Address: 2319 Wyoming Av., N.W. Washington, D.C.: (country) "Hollowtree" Sandy Spring, Md. Died Mar. 19, 1943.

BROWNE, CHARLES physician; b. Phila., Pa., Sept. 28, 1875; s. William Hardcastle and Alice (Beaver) B.; A.B., Coll. of N.J. (now Princeton U.), 1896, A.M., 1899; M.D., U. of Pa., 1900; U. of Berlin, 1902-03; m. Georgeanna Gibbs, April 30, 1913; children—Colston Hardcastle, Anthony DeHoojes, Archibald Ayres, Charles Brown. Began practice at Princeton, N.J., 1906; overseer of poor, Princeton, 1913-16; mayor of Princeton, 4 terms, 1916-23; pres. bd. trustees Princeton Hosp., 1919-28; mem. 68th Congress (1923-25), 4th N.J. Dist.; mem. bd. Pub. Utility Commrs., N.J., since Mar., 1925. Dir. 1st Nat. Bank (Princeton), Del & Bound Brook R.R. Co. Mem. Borough Council, Princeton, N.J., 1933-35; mem. N.J. House of Assembly, 1936-39, 1941-42. Assistant to surgeon Old Point Comfort Army Hospital, Spanish-Am. War, 1898; student Plattsburg Camps, 1915-16; commd. 1st lt. Med. Corps, U.S. Army, 1917; capt., Sept. 1918; comdt. U.S. Army Convalescent Hosp. No. 1 at Lawrenceville, N.J. Mem. bd. mgrs. N.J. State Home for Women; mem. Grad. Council Princeton U. Mem. Am. Inst. of Polit. and Social Science. Democrat. Presbyterian. Author: Gun Club Cook Book, 1930; Gun Club Drink Book, 1939. Clubs: University, Princeton, Racquet and Tennis (New York); University, Racquet, Princeton (Phila.). Home: Princeton, N.J. Died Aug. 16, 1947.

BROWNE, FREDERICK WILLIAM army officer; b. St. Charles, Ia., Oct. 25, 1875; s. William Lytle and Mary Pollock (McClure) B.; student U. Ia., 1894-96, Corcoran Sci. Sch., 1896-98; LL.B., George Washington U., 1901; LL.M., Nat. U., 1902; grad. Command and Gen. Staff Sch., 1925; m. Mary Postell Lockwood, June 14, 1906; children-Frederick Lee, William Lytle. Began as stenographer, 1896; commd. maj. C.E., U.S. Army, Sept. 20, 1918; promoted through grades to lt. col. Finance Dept., Oct. 1, 1934; mem. War Dept. Gen. Staff, 1925-33; ret. with rank of col. Nov. 30, 1938; recalled to active duty, Jan. 1, 1939; promoted to brig. gen., Feb. 23, 1942; asst. budget officer, War Dept., 1936-44; inactive status since Jan. 1944. Presbyn. Club: Army and Navy (Washington). Home: 4608 Langdrum Lane, Chevy Chase, Md. Died Dec. 16, 1960; buried Arlington (Va.) Cemtery.

BROWNE, LOUIS EDGAR foreign trade expert; b. Lynn, Mass., Oct. 20, 1891; s. Edgar William and Hattie Westerfield (Adams) B.; ed. U.S. Naval Acad., 1910-12; m. Ouida Risner, May 4, 1920; m. 2d, Eleanor Bode, July 14, 1934; children—Marylou Adams, Virginia Westerfield, Hendrik Adams, Christopher Carter. Began as journalist, 1912; Washington corr. New York Herald, 1913; war corr. Chicago Daily News, New York Globe and Philadelphia Bulletin with Allied Forces in Dardanelles, Suvla Bay, Egypt, India, Mesopotamia, Macedonia; with Servian Army in retreat; with Brit. Forces in France; Holland; Russia, 1917, through Revolution to July 1918; served in U.S.N.R.F., July-Dec. 1918; special corr. Chicago Daily News in Near East, 1919; exec. sec. Am.-Russian Chamber of Commerce 1929-42, 1944—. Lt. col. on active service with U.S. Army, 1942-43, chief U.S.S.R. Sect., Mil. Intelligence Div.; War Dept., Washington. Episcopalian. Mason. Clubs: National Press (Washington); Lotos (New York). Author: Economic Handbook of the Soviet Union, 1932; Handbook of the Soviet Union, 1935. Contbr. articles on fgn. trade to jours. Home: Briarcliff Dr., Gainesville, Fla. Office: 245 Fifth Av., N.Y.C. Died Feb. 10, 1951; buried Gainesville, Fla.

BROWNE, ROBERT H., physician, author; b. New York, Aug., 1835; s. Nimmo and Agnes (Steven) B.; ed. schs. and acad. to 1852; grad. Rush Med. Coll., Chicago, 1868; also read law with Davis, Gridley & Lincoln, Bloomington, Ill.; m. Isabel Graham, Champaign, Ill. Asst. surgeon 25th Ill. vols., 1861; acting asst. surgeon U.S.A. and surgeon 2d Tenn. to close of war; after war practiced medicine at Kirksville, Mo., until 1894; since then at Wichita, Kan.; State senator, Mo., 1870-74; in public life in Mo. to 1892; was abolitionist with Lovejoy; afterward liberal Republican and Independent. Active in G.A.R.; post comdr. Kirksville, Mo.; dept. insp. Mo., 1887-89. Author: Abraham Lincoln and the Men of His Time, 1901 M25. Address: Wichita, Kan.

BROWNING, MILES (RUTHERFORD) ret. naval officer; b. Perth Amboy, N.J., Apr. 10, 1897; s. Oren Fogle and Sarah Louise (Smith) B.; B.S., U.S. Naval Acad., 1917; grad. Naval War Coll., 1936-37; m. Katherine Jame Ejnon, Mar. 30, 1943. Commd. ensign USN, 1917, advanced through grades to rear adm., 1947; served in Atlantic Grand Fleet, World War I; naval aviation, 1924-46; chief of staff, South Pacific Area and Force, 1942-43; comdr. U.S.S. Hornet, 1943-44; air and naval inst. and dir. of naval instrn. Command and Gen. Staff Coll., 1944-46, ret. from active duty, 1947; dir. Md. Civil Def., 1950-52. Decorated D.S.M., Silver Star, Navy Spl. Commendation Ribbon, Army Commendation Ribbon, Presdl. Unit Citation (twice). Contbr. articles on prof. subjects and allied matters to Mil. Rev., Marine Corps Gazette, Sea Power, Jour. of

Ednl. Sociology. Home: 3 Elms Farm, Pumpkin Hill Rd., Warner, N.H. Address: care Navy Dept., Washington. Died Sept. 29, 1954.

BROWNSON, NATHAN gov. Ga., Continental congressman; b. Woodbury, Conn., May 14, 1742; grad. Yale, 1761; studied medicine. Practiced medicine, Woodbury; moved to Liberty County, Ga., circa 1764; mem. Provincial Congress, 1775; served as surgeon in Revolutionary Army; mem. Continental Congress from Ga., 1776-78; mem., speaker Ga. Ho. of Reps., 1781, 88; gov. Ga., 1782; del. Ga. Conv. to ratify U.S. Constn., 1788, Ga. Constl. Conv., 1789; mem. Ga. Senate, 1789-91, served as pres. Died on his plantation nr. Riceboro, Ga., Nov. 6, 1796; buried Old Midway Burial Ground.

BROWNSON, WILLARD HERBERT naval officer; b. Lyons, N.Y., July 8, 1845; s. Morton and Harriet (Taft) B.; grad. U.S. Naval Acad., 1865; m. Isabella King Roberts, July 10, 1872; children - Roswell Roberts, Mrs. Harriet Hussey, r,rs. Caroline Hart. Served in flagship N. Atlantic squadron, 1865-68, Pacific sta., 1868-71, Naval Acad., 1872-75; coast survey, Str. Blake, deep sea investigation. 1882-84; insp. hydrography, 1885-89; comdg. Petrel, 1889-91, Dolphin, 1892, Detroit, at Rio de Janeiro, Brazil, during revolution, 1893-94; comdt. cadets Naval Acad., 1894; bd. of inspection and survey, 1896-98; comdg. Yankee during war with Spain; capt., Mar. 3, 1899; comdg. Alabama, 1900-02; supt. U.S. Naval Acad., Nov. 6, 1902-June 1, 1906; rear admiral, May 6, 1905; comd. 4th div. Atlantic Fleet, July 8-Aug. 15, 1906; comd. spl. service squadron, Aug. 15-Oct. 15, 1906; comdr. in chief Asiatic Fleet, Oct. 15, 1906-Apr. 1, 1907; apptd. chief, Bur. of Navigation, May 20, 1907; retired July 8, 1907, but kept on active duty by order of President. Home: Washington, D.C. Died Mar. 16, 1935.

BRUCE, ANDREW DAVIS, univ. adminstr.; b. St.L., Mo., Sept. 14, 1894; s. John Logan and Martha Washington (Smith) B.; B.S., Agr. and Mech. Coll. of Texas, 1916; LL.D., 1946; graduate Infantry School, Fort Benning, Georgia, 1924, Field Arty. School, Fort Sill, Okla., 1925, Command and Gen. Staff Sch., Ft. Leavenworth, 1933, Army War Coll., Washington, 1936, Naval War Coll., Newport, R.I., 1937; m. Roberta Kennedy, Jan. 28, 1920;children—Andrew Davis Jr., Roberta Linnell, Logan Lithgow. Commd. 2d lt., U.S. Army, June 16, 1917; advanced to lieut. gen., 1951; served as lt. col. (temp.) 2d Div., U.S. Army, in all actions of 2d Div. (Verdun defensive and Aisne-Marne, San Mihiel, Champagne, Meuse-Argonne offensives), World War I; comdg. gen. Tank Destroyer Center, Camp Hood, Tex., 1942-43; comdg. gen. 77th Inf. Div. 1943-46; in Guam, Leyte, P.I.; Kerama Rhetto Ie Shima, and Okinawa operations, occupation of Japan. Comdg. gen. 7th Infantry Div., 1946-47, occupation of Korea, dep. army comdr. 4th Army, 1947-51; comdt. Armed Forces Staff Coll., Norfolk, Va., 1951-54, ret. from Army, 1954; pres. U. Houston, 1954-56, chancellor, 1956-61, chancellor emeritus, 1961-69. Decorated Distinguished Service Cross, the Distinguished Service Medal with Oak Leaf, Navy Distinguished Service Medal, Leg. of Merit, Bronze Star, Air Medal, Commendation, Purple Heart, Victory medal (with 5 stars), Leg. of Honor, 3 Croix de Guerres (2 palms and 1 gold star), 1 Fourragere and numerous campaign ribbons. Mem. First Families of Va., S.A.R. Mason (Shriner). Home: Southern Pines NC Died July 27, 1969; buried Arlington Nat. Cemetery, Arlington VA

BRUCE, JAMES DEACON physician; b. Blackstock, Ont. Can., Oct. 4, 1872; s. John and Mary (Deacon) B.; M.D., Detroit Coll. Medicine and Surgery, 1896; m. Grace A. Campbell, May 25, 1904. Came to U.S., 1892, naturalized, 1896. In gen. practice, Michigan, 1896-1904, 1906-16, and 1919-25; asst. in internal medicine, U. of Mich., 1904-05, dir. internal medicine, Univ. of Mich., and chief med. service of Univ. Hosp., 1925-28, dir. post-grad. medicine, 1925-42, consultant to Univ. med. service, 1925-42; mem. exec. com., Univ. Med. Sch., 1930-42, vice pres. in charge univ. relations, 1931-42, chmn. div. health sciences, 1935-42; vice-pres. emeritus, 1942. Univ. of Mich. Mem. Med. Advisory com., Nat. Com. on Econ. Security, 1934; mem. Nat. Research Council, Div. Med. Sciences, (com. on medicine, 1940-42); mem. Nat. Com. on Grad. Med. Edn., 1937-40; chmn., Asso. States Postgrad. Com., 1937-41; mem. Mich. Tuberculosis Sanatorium Commn., 1932-46; pres. Mich Council on Adult Education, 1941-46; pres. Mich. Com. on Juvenile Delinquency, 1943-46; mem. Mich. Adult Edn. Advisory Com., 1944-46. Served as capt., M.C., Canadian Army, later maj., M.C., U.S. Army, overseas, 1916-19, World War I. Fellow Am. Coll. Surgeons, Am. Coll. Physicians (gov. for Mich.), 1930-36; regent since 1936, pres. 1940-41, regent 1941-46; member Mich. State Med. Soc. (councillor, 1923-34), Washtenaw County Med. Soc., A.M.A., Alpha Omega Alpha, Phi Kappa Phi, Delta Omega, Phi Rho Sigma. Conglist. Mason. Clubs: Crystal Downs Country, University, Barton Hills Country, University of Michigan. Home: 631 Oxford Rd. Address: University Hospital, Ann Arbor, Mich. Died Sept. 5, 1946.

BRUCE, SAUNDERS DEWEES editor Turf, Field and Farm (which he founded, 1865); b. Lexington, Ky., Aug. 16, 1825; Grad. Transylvania U., 1846. Engaged in business, 1848, to Civil War; apptd. Union army, 1861; recruited and was insp. gen. Union Home nuard of Ky., elected col. 20th Ky. vols.; built fortifications mouth of Cumberland river; in command 22d brigade, and in battle of Shiloh; injured by falling horse; in command provisional brigade, opened Cumberland river below Ft. Donelson; recommended for promotion to brig. gen. by Gen. Sherman and Gen. Grant; resigned, 1864, on account of heart trouble, and went to New York. Authority on pedigree of horses. Author: American Stud Book (6 vols.); Horse Breeders' Guide and Handbook; The Thoroughbred Horse. Address: New York, N.Y. Died 1902.

BRUCKER, WILBER M(ARION), lawyer, ex-Sec. Army; b. Saginaw, Mich., June 23, 1894 s. Ferdinand and Roberta (Hawn) B.; LL.B., U. Mich., 1916; J.D. (hon.), U. Detroit, 1931; Ph.D., Hillsdale Coll., Alma Coll., 1932; LL.D., Hope Coll., George Washington U., U. Mich., Norwich U., Defiance (O.) Coll., Dickerson Coll.; married Clara Hantel, Aug. 18, 1923; 1 son, Wilber M. Admitted to Mich. bar, 1919; pvt. practice law, Saginaw, 1919-26; pros. atty. Saginaw County (Mich.), 1922-26; atty. gen. Mich., 1928-30, gov., 1930-32; mem. Clark, Klein, Brucker & Waples, 1937-54; gen. counsel 1st Fed. Savings & Loan Assn., Detroit, 1952-54; gen. counsel Dept. of Def., Washington, 1954-55, Secretary of the Army, Washington, 1955-61; mem. firm Brucker & Brucker, Detroit, 1961-68; dir. Fruehauf Corp., 1st Fed. Savs. & Loan Assn. of Detroit, United States Truck Company, Inc., Detroit. Bd. dirs. Freedom's Found., Valley Forge, Pa. Served with 33d Inf., Mich. N.G., Mexican Border, 1916, 1st lt. Rainbow Div., U.S. Army, 1918-19. Mem. Am. Bar Assn. (chmn. ethics com.), Nat. Assn. Rainbow Div. Vets. (pres. 1933-34), Am. Legion (co-founder Paris br.). Republican. Presbyn. Mason (K.T., most eminent grand master, 33 deg.). Home: Grosse Pointe Farms MI Died Oct. 28, 1968; buried Arlington Nat. Cemetery.

BRUFF, LAWRENCE LAURENSON army officer; b. in Md., Oct. 14, 1851; grad. West Point, 1876. Commd. 2d lt. 3d arty., June 15, 1876; promoted through grades to lt. col., June 25, 1906. Instr. ordnance and gunnery, West Point, 1891-1900; later asst. Watervliet Arsenal, N.Y. Author: Exterior Ballistics, Niven's Method, 1885; Notes on Machine and Rapid Fire Guns, Small-Arms and Ballistic Machines, 1892; Gunpowder and Interior Ballistics, 1892; Exterior Ballistics, Gun Construction, U.S. Sea Coast Guns, 1892; Ordnance and Gunnery, 1906 (all text boosk, used at West Point). Died 1911.

BRUMBY, FRANK HARDEMAN, naval officer; b. Athens, Ga., Sept. 11, 1874; s. John Wallis and Arabella (Hardeman) B.; grad. U.S. Naval Acad., 1895; m. Isabelle Truxtun, June 4, 1907; children—Isabelle Truxtun, Frank Hardeman. Commd. ensign U.S. Navy, July 1, 1897; promoted through grades to rear admiral Sept. 8, 1927, vice admiral in command of Scouting Force, May 1933-June 1934; admiral in command of Battle force June 15, 1934 to April 1, 1935; retired Oct. 1, 1938. Served as capt. (temp.), World War; comdr. U.S.S. Kansas, 1920-21, U.S.S. New Mexico, 1924-26. Episcopalian. Club: New York Yacht. Home: Athens GA*

BRUMBY, THOMAS MASON lt. U.S.N.; b. Marietta, Ga., 1855; grad. U.S. Naval Acad., June 18, 1879; served on various vessels; promoted ensign; was one of survivors of the hurricane off Samoa, March 1889; promoted lt. (jr. grade), April 21, 1887; lt., Aug. 24, 1892; served on New York and Vermont; at Naval Observatory and War Coll., Sept., 1897 to Jan. 1898; flag lt. on Olympia, Asiatic squadron, Jan. 1898, took part in battle of Manila Bay and at surrender of Manila, Aug. 13, 1898, he raised the American flag over Manila. Died 1899.

BRUNS, HENRY FREDERICK naval officer; b. Nov. 24, 1889; entered U.S. Navy, 1914; advanced in Civil Engr. Corps to rear admiral, June 1943. Died Jan. 20, 1947.

BRUNS, THOMAS NELSON CARTER bridge builder; b. Richmond, Va., June 4, 1902; s. Henry Dickson and Kate Virginia (Logan) B.; grad. Prep. Sch., Woodberry Forest, Orange, Va.; student U. Va., 1920-23; B.S. in Civil Engring., Tulane U., 1927, E.C., 1932; m. Bernard Peyton Llewellyn Early, Oct. 27, 1928; children-Thomas Nelson Carter, Peyton Llewellyn Early. Foreman, then supt. Doullut & Ewin, Inc., New Orleans, 1924-37; project mgr. Raymond Concrete Pile Co., N.Y.C., 1937-41; owner, mgr. Bruns Bridge Co., New Orleans, 1946-57; chief engr. Keller Constrn. Corp., 1957-; pres. Brunspile Corp., New Orleans, 1957-. Served as comdr. Civil Engr. Corps, USNR, 1942-46. Fellow Am. Soc. C.E.; mem. La. Engring. Soc., Chi Phi, Tau Beta Pi. Patentee prestressed concrete piling. Contbr. articles to engring. lit. Home: 526 St. Peter St., New Orleans 70116. Office: 7900 Palm St., New Orleans 70125. Died Oct. 1, 1966; buried Christ Ch., Glendower, Va.

BRUSH, DANIEL HARMON army officer; b. in Ill., May 9, 1848; s. Daniel Harmon and Julia F. B.; was pvt. Co. F, 145th Ill. Inf., May 22-Sept. 23, 1864; grad. U.S. Mil. Acad., 1871; m. Harriet Rapp, Feb. 18, 1874. Commd. 2d lt. 17th Inf., June 12, 1871; promoted through grades to brig.-gen. U.S. Army, Feb. 17, 1908; retired May 9, 1912. Home: Baltimore, Md. Died Mar. 8, 1920.

BRYAN, BENJAMIN CHAMBERS naval officer; b. Throggs Neck, N.Y., Aug. 16, 1858; s. Timothy Matlack and Mary Duncan (Chambers) B.; grad. U.S. Naval Acad., 1879; married; 1 dau.,Anne (wife of R. E. S. Williamson, U.S. Army). Asst. engr. U.S.N., June 10, 1881; passed asst. engr., Oct. 3, 1891; chief engr., Jan. 20, 1899; transferred to line as lt., Mar. 3, 1899; promoted through grades to rear adm.; retired Aug. 16, 1922. Served on Delphin, Spanish-Am. War, 1898; with Bur. Steam Engring., Navy Dept., 1903-08; head of Dept. Steam Engring., Navy Yard, Phila., 1908-12; dir. navy yards, Navy Dept., 1912-15; apptd. Commandant Naval Sta., Charleston, S.C., July 8, 1915. Mem. Naval and Retiring Bd. Died July 21, 1930.

BRYAN, HENRY FRANCIS naval officer; b. Cin., May 3, 1865; grad. U.S.N. Acad., 1887. Ensign, July 1, 1889; lt. jr. grade, June 19, 1897; lt., Mar. 3, 1899; lt. comdr., June 16, 1905; comdr., July 1, 1909; capt., July 1, 1913; promoted temporary rank rear adm. Aug. 1918. Served on Newark, Spanish-Am. War., 1989; on Alabama, 1903-06; Office of Naval Intelligence, Navy Dept., 1906-07; at Naval Acad., 1907-10; exec. officer Vermont, 1910-11; comdr. Prairie, 1911-12; duty Office of Naval Intelligence, 1912-14; comd. Kansas, 1914-16; apptd. chief of staff 2d Naval Dist., Mar. 23, 1917. Address: Navy Dept., Washington. Died Mar. 19, 1944.

BRYAN, JOSEPH HAMMOND physician; b. Washington, D.C., July 4, 1856; s. Joseph Brooke and Louisa Steans (Hammond) B.; M.D., U. of Va., 1877, Univ. Med. Coll. (New York U.), 1878; unmarried. Asst. surgeon U.S.N., 1880-85; in practice at Washington since 1887. Maj., M.C. U.S.A., June 19, 1917-Dec. 4, 1918; lt. col. O.R.C., Feb. 4, 1919. Mem. Acad. Sciences, Philos. Soc. Washington, Am. Laryngol. Assn. Clubs: Metropolitan, Cosmos, Chevy Chase. Address: 302 Stoneleigh Court, Washington, D.C.

BRYAN, L. R., JR. vice chmn. bd.; chmn. exec. com.; b. Qunitana, Tex., Aug. 17, 1892; m. Katherine McGown; children—L. R. III, Hoyd, Stephen Austin. dir. Bank of the Southwest, Houston; dir. Fort Worth & Denver Ry. (Fort Worth). Houston Br. Fed. Res. Bank of Dallas, Pres. area found., Boy Scouts Am. Trustee Houston Symphony Soc. Endowment Fund. Trustee San Jacinto Mus. of History Assn. (pres.). Served as maj., U.S. Army, World War I. Mem. Tex. Philos. Soc., Newcomen Soc., Sons Republic of Tex., Tex., Gulf Hist. Assns. Episcopalian. Knight San Jacinto. Home: 3315 Ella Lee Lane. Off:ce: Bank of the Southwest, Houston. Died Jan. 30, 1959; buried Houston.

BRYAN, LOUIS ALLEN naval officer; b. Louisville, Oct. 17, 1908; s. Massie Womack and Nellie (Christmas) B.; student Coll. Engring., U. Ky., 1924-28; B.S., U.S. Naval Acad., 1932; grad. Naval Postgrad. Sch., 1939, Naval War Coll., 1951; m. Virginia Bean, 1932 (dec. 1959); m. 2d, Margaret Hilton, Sept. 9, 1960; children-Nancy (Mrs. M.J. Weller), Margaret, Robert. Commd. ensign USN, 1932, advanced through grades to rear adm., 1960; various on ships and at naval stations, 1932-42; exec. officer U.S.S. Duncan, 1942; comdg. officer U.S.S. Shubrick, 1943; staff comdr. destroyers Atlanitc, 1944-45; comdg. officer U.S.S. Blue, 1945-46; exec. officer phys. tng. dept., football coach U.S. Naval Acad., 1946-47; comdg. officer Naval Acad. Prep. Sch., 1949-50; comdr. Escort Destroyer Div. 62, 1951-52; staff comdr.-in-chief Atlantic Fleet, 1952-54; comdg. officer U.S.S. Sanborn, 1954-55; staff comdr. amphibious force Atlantic Fleet, 1955-57; comdg. officer U.S.S. Northampton, 1957-58; head navy plans br. Office Chief Naval Operations, Navy Dept., 1958-59, dir. ship material readiness div., 1959-61; comdr. Destroyer Flotilla 2, 1961-62; dep. dir. logistics Joint Chiefs of Staff, 1962-64; comdr. naval forces So. Command, also comdt. 15th Naval Dist., 1964-66. Decorated Silver Star, Bronze Star with gold star, Letter of Commendation, Legion of Merit, Purple Heart, numerous other area and service ribbons. Home: 4300 Chesterbrook Rd., McLean, Va. Office: Joint Staff (J-4), The Pentagon, Washington 25. Died Feb. 27, 1966; buried Arlington (Va.) Nat. Cemetery.

BRYANT, ELIOT H. naval officer ret.; b. Rusheville, Ill., Aug. 21, 1896; s. James Reeves and Jennie Elizabeth (Moriarity) B.; B.S., U.S. Naval Acad., 1918; M.S. Columbia, 1927; m. Miriam H. Hawkins, Oct. 30, 1937. Commd. ensign, USN Acad., 1918; and advanced through grades to v. adm.; student Submarine Sch., New London, 1918; duty in various submarines, 1918-30; asst. naval attache, Berlin and other princ. embassies of Europe, 1930-33; staff comdr. Submarines U.S. Fleet, 1933-35; gunnery officer U.S.S. Northampton, 1935-37; on duty Bu. Engring. Submarine Design, Navy Dept., 1937-39; student Sr. War Coll., Newport, R.I., 1939-40, comd. gun boat U.S.S. Asheville in S. China Patrol, 1940; comd. div. of submarines in the Asiatic Fleet, 1940-42; duty Bur. Ships, submarine design, Navy Dept., 1943; comd. squadron submarines, 1943; chief of staff to Comdr. Submarines 7th Fleet, 1944-45; comd. U.S.S. Chicago, 1945; pres. Bd. Review, Discharges and Dismissals, Navy Dept., Washington,D.C., to April

1946; comdr. Cruiser Div. Two, May 1947; now vice adm., retired. Decorated: D.S.M., Legion of Merit, Navy Unit commdenation, Letter of Commendation ribbon, Army Distinguished Unit badge, Victory medal, American Defense Service medal, Fleet clasp, Asiatic-Pacific Area campaign medal with 2 stars, World War II Victory medal, Philippine Defense with 1 star, Philippine Liberation, and Submarine Combat Insignia pin. Presbyn. Club: Annapolis Yacht. Home: Cider Jug Farm, Annapolis, Md. Died Oct. 16, 1955; buried U.S. Naval Acad. Cemetery, Annapolis.

BRYANT, SAMUEL WOOD naval officer; b. Washington, Pa., May 24, 1877; s. William Curry and Sarah (McLean) B.; grad. U.S. Naval Acad., 1900; m. Carolina F. Merry, Dec. 18, 1905; children - Gordon McLean, Samuel Wood. Ensign, May 20, 1902; promoted through grades to rear adm., July 1, 1933; retired because of physical disability incurred in line of duty, March 1, 1937. Commander torpedo boat destroyer off coasts of Ireland and France, and on staff commander United States destroyer flotillas, in European waters, during World War; tech. adviser on elec. communications to Am. del., Limitation of Armament Conf., Washington, 1921-22; asst. naval adviser to Am. delegation at Internat. Conf. on Rules of Warfare, The Hauge, 1922-23; mem. staff U.S. Naval War. Coll., 1925-26 and 1928-30; in comd. U.S.S. Detroit, attached to cruiser divs., U.S. Fleet, 1926-27, and as flagship U.S. Naval Forces to Europe, 1927-28; chief of staff Scouting Fleet, 1930-32; dir. War Plans Div., Navy Dept., 1932-34; comdr. battleship div. U.S. Fleet, 1934-35; chief of staff to comdr. in chief U.S. Fleet, 1935. Presbyn. Home: Asheville, N.C. Died Nov. 4, 1938.

BRYANT, W(ILLIAM) SOHIER physician; b. Boston, May 15, 1861; s. Henry and Elizabeth Brimmer (Sohier) B.; ed. pvt. schs. at home and abroad, St. Paul s Sch., pvt. tutors; A.B., cum laude, Harvard, 1884, A.M., M.D., 1888; m. Martha Lyman Cox, 1887 (dec.); children—Mrs. Mary Cleveland Blanchard, Elizabeth Sohier, Mrs. Alice de Vermandois Frank (dec.), Julia Cox, Gladys de Brion, William Sohier (dec.). Began practice in Boston; was aural surgeon Boston Dispensary; asst. in anatomy and otology, Harvard; sr. asst. surgeon, Mass. Charitable Eye and Ear Infirmary; in N.Y., 1903; was adj. prof. dept. diseases of car. New York Post-Grad. Med. Sch. and Hosp.; cons. otolaryngologist Manhattan State Hosp.; sr. asst. surgeon aural dept., N.Y. Eye and Ear Infirmary; instr. otology Coll. Phys. and Surg. (Columbia); clin. asst. dept. otology Vanderbilt Clinic; asst. surgeon St. Bartholomew's Clinic; clinical instr. and attending surgeon, otol. dept., Cornell U. Med. Sch.; physician in class of nose, throat and ear diseases, Presbyn. Hosp. Dispensary. Mem. Mass. N.G., 1881-98; asst. surgeon 1st Mass. Regt., Heavy Arty., Spanish-Am. War; maj. and brigade surgeon U.S.V. Served with Maj. Gen. Fitzhugh Lee in 7th Army Corps and occupation of Cuba until May 1899, then surgeon, 2 yrs. Battery A., Mass. N.G.; became member of Medical Reserve Corps, 1911; served in World War, 1917, major Medical R.C., with British Army, contract surgeon in charge Royal Victoria Hosp., otolaryngologist British Red Cross Hosp., at Netley, Hants, England; later with French Army, voluntere et benevol, Hospital Auxiliere 49, Orleans, France, at Am. Red Cross Mil. Hosp. 3, Paris, 1918; lt. col. Med. Corps U.S.; dir. med. affairs and del. Emelia Dist., Am. Red Cross in Italy; col. Med. O.R.C., later col. Inactive Res. Awarded Grand Cross Order of St. John of Jerusalem. Fellow Am. Coll. Surgeons, Boylston Med. Soc.; mem. Boston Med. Library Assn., Mass. Med. Soc., Mass. Benevolent Medical Soc., A.M.A. (chairman sect. laryngology and otology), Am. Otol. Siciety, Med. Soc. State of N.Y., Med. Soc. County N.Y., Am. Board Otolaryngology, Am. Laryngol., Rhinol. and Otol. Soc., Assn. Mil. Surgeons of U.S., Naval and Mil. Order of Spanish-Am. War, N.E. Historic Geneal. Soc., Am. Legion, Nat. Rifle Assn., St. Nichols Soc., British Legion, British Great War Vets. of Am., Vets. of Fgn. Wars of U.S. Fedn. of French Veterans, Mass. Soc. of the Cincinnati, N.Y. Soc. Mil. and Naval Officers of World War, S.A.R., Boston Soc. Natural Hist., Soc. Mayflower Descendents, Res. Officers Assn. of U.S., Loyal Legion, United Spanish War Vets., N.Y. Genealogical and Biog. Soc., Military Order World War, Mil. Order Foreign Wars, American Soc. French Legion of Honor, Military Intelligence Res. Soc., Mass. Bay in New England (gov.), Am. Vets. 1812. Delta Kappa Epsilon, Zeta Psi. Decorated Chevalier Legion of Honor (French); Officer Crown of Italy; Grand Cross of the Order of St. Johns the Baptist. Episcopalian. Mason (K.T. 32ff, Shriner). Clubs: Harvard (New York City), Century (New York); Porcellian (Cambridge,Mass.). Author: Anatomy and Physiology of the Ear, and Tests of Hearing (in Burnetts's System of Diseases of the Ear, Nose and Throat), 1893; Ear Section, Knight and Bryant's med. publs. Rowed as No. 7 and stroke, Varsity, 1884. Address: 30 E. 40th St., N.Y.C. Deceased.

BRYDEN, WILLIAM, retired army officer; b. Hartford, Conn., Feb. 3, 1880; s. George and Florence Andrews (Bliss) B.; B.S., U.S. Mil. Acad., 1904; m. Ellen Barry, Oct. 26, 1912; children—Ellen (wife Lt. Col. Alexander D. Surles). Marion (wife Lt. Col. F. W. Moorman). Commd. 2d lt. U.S. Army, 1904, served as officer all grades until promoted to maj. gen., 1940. Decorated D.S.M. with two oak leaf clusters. Mem. Am. Legion, The Newcomen Soc. Clubs: Army and Navy, Army and Navy Country. Address: Washington DC Died 1972.

BUBB, JOHN WILSON brig. gen.; b. Danville, Pa., Apr. 26, 1843; s. Frederick and Sarah J. (Wilson) B.; ed. pub. schs., Danville, Pa.; m. Frances Helena Steele, Nov. 19, 1867. Served pvt., sergt. and 1st sergt. Co. E, 1st Battalion, 12th Inf., Sept. 13, 1861-Apr. 24, 1866; promoted through grades to brig. gen., U.S.A., Apr. 3, 1906. Participated in many battles and campaigns in Civil War, 1862-64; prisoner in Libby, Bell's Island and Salisbury, Aug. 19, 1864-Apr., 1865; chief commissary, Gen. Crook's campaign against Sioux Indians, May-Oct., 1876; served in P.I., 1899-1902, 1904-06, participating in various engagements; recommended for bvtd. of col. in regular service for action nr. Dasmarinas, 1899; comd. Dept. of Visayas, Oct. 29-Dec. 23, 1905, Dept. of Dak., May 21, 1906-Apr. 26, 1907; retired. Home: Wilmington, Del. Died Feb. 23, 1922.

BUCHANAN, DAVID H., army officer; b. Marion, Va., May 8, 1907; s. B.F. and Eleanor Fairman (Sheffey) B.; student Greenbrier Mil. Sch., Lewisburg, W.Va., 1920-24; B.S., U.S. Mil. Acad., 1929; grad. Inf. Sch., 1936;, Nat. War Coll., 1951; m. Katherine Pritchett, Nov. 29, 1929; 1 dau., Cynthia Dee. Commd. 2d lt. U.S. Army, 1929, advanced through grades to maj. gen., 1956; company officer 16th Inf., Governor's Island, N.Y., 45th Inf., P.I., 31st Inf., Manila, 20th Inf., Ft. Francis E. Warren, Wyo.; instr. equitation Inf. Sch., 1936-39; comdr. Hawaiian Div. Pack Train, Schofield Barracks, T. H., 1939; successively div. asst. chief staff G-4, bn. and regtl. comdr. 161st Inf., regt. comdr. 27th Inf. Regt., 25th Inf. Dv., Pacific, World War II; Army instr. Air U., Maxwell Field, Ala., 1946-49; sec. Gen. Staff, Army Ground Forces, Ft. Monroe, Va., 1949-51; chief Joint War Plans G-3, Dept. Army 1951, asst. chief Plans Div. G-3, Dept. Army Gen. Staff, 1952; mem. standing group, North Atlantic Treaty Mil. Com., Washington, 1952; dep. standing group liaison officer North Atlantic Council, 1953-56; chief staff Fifth Army Hdqrs., Chgo., 1956-57; comdg. gen. 1st Inf. Div., Ft. Riley, Kan., 1957-58; chief M. I. Assistance & Adv. Group, Korea, 1958-59; dep. insp. gen. U.S. Army, 1959-61; chief staff U.S. Continental Army Command, 1962, ret., 1962; cons. Research Analysis Corp., 1963-70. Decorated D.S.M., Silver Star, Legion of Merit, Bronze Star Medal, Purple Heart, Combat Inf. Badge, Liberation Philippines. Presbyn. Clubs: Circle Interalliee (Paris, France); Army and Navy (Washington). Home: Washington DC Died Jan. 1, 1972; buried Arlington Nat. Cemetery, Arlington VA

BUCHANAN, JAMES ANDERSON brig. gen.; b. Washington Co., Md., Dec. 11, 1843; s. Dr. James A. and Eleanora Elder (Miller) B.; m. Helen Warren Myers, 1885. Apptd. from Md. 2d lt. 14th U.S. Inf., Mar. 7, 1867; promoted through grades to col. 24th U.S. Inf., Aug. 14, 1903; brig. gen., Apr. 14, 1905; retired, at own request, over 30 yrs.' service, May 31, 1906. Served at principal western posts for more than 30 yrs., in P.R., 1898-1903, and later in P.I. Home: Upperville, Va. Died May 18, 1926.

BUCHANAN, KENNETH army officer; b. Chgo., Aug. 30, 1892; B.S., U. of Ill., 1917; commd. 2d lt., Coast Arty., 1917; 1st lt., Oct. 1918; capt. Nat. Guard, Sept. 1924, and advanced to lt. col. May 1935; active Fed. duty, Supply div., G-4, War Dept. Gen. Staff. Apr. 1936; aide to Gen. George C. Marshall, Chief of Staff, Aug. 1939; promoted to col. Feb. 1940, brig. gen., May 1942; assigned to 28th Inf. Div., Camp Livingston, La. Address: Camp Livingston, La. Died Apr. 1967.

BUCHANAN, ROBERT CHRISTIE army officer; b. Balt., Mar. 1, 1811; s. Andrew and Carolina (Johnson) B.; grad. U.S. Mil. Acad., 1829; m. Miss Windsor, circa 1847. Commd. 2d lt. 4th Inf., U.S. Army, 1830; served in Black Hawk War, 1832; adj. of his regt., 1835-38; commd. 1st lt., 1836; served in Seminole War; commd. capt., 1838; brevetted maj. during Mexican War, 1846, lt. col., 1847; commd. maj. U.S. Army, 1855, lt. col., 1864; brevetted col. for action at Battle of Gaine's Mill; commd. brig. gen. U.S. Volunteers, 1862, col., 1863; brevetted brig. gen., 1865; fought at battles of Antietam, 2d Bull Run, Fredericksburg during Civil War; mem. Ia. Claims Commn., 1867; asst. commr. Freedman's Bur., 1868; comdr. Dept. of La., 1868. Died Washington, D.C., Nov. 29, 1878.

BUCHER, JOHN CONRAD soldier, clergyman; b. Neunkirch, Switzerland, June 10, 1730; s. Hans Jacob and Anna Dorothea (Burgauer) B.; attended U. Marburg (German), 1752-55; m. Mary Magdalena Hoke, Feb. 26, 1760, 6 children. Arrived in U.S., 1755; commd. ensign 1st Battalion, Pa. Militia, 1758, commanded garrison at Carlisle, Pa., 1759-60, promoted to lt. 2d Pa. Battalion, 1760, then to adj. and capt., 1760; began preaching, 1763; ordained to ministry German Reformed Ch., 1767, made occasional missionary trips West; 1st minister to preach in German lang beyond Allegheny Mountains; chaplain "German Regt." under Baron Von Arnt, 1775-77. Died Annville, Pa., Aug. 15, 1780; buried Lebanon, Pa.

BUCK, BEAUMONT BONAPARTE ret. army officer; b. Mayhew, Miss.; Jan. 16, 1860; s. J. G. H. and Martha S. (Garner) B.; grad. U.S. Mil. Acad., 1885, Army War Coll., 1909; m. Susanne Long of Memphis, Tenn., Dec. 30, 1908. Commd. 2d lt. 16th Inf., June 14, 1885; 1st lt. 19th Inf., May 4, 1892; trans. to 16th Inf., Aug. 12, 1892; maj. 2d Tex. Inf., May 13, 1898; hon. mustered out vols., Nov. 9, 1898; capt. U.S.A., Mar. 1, 1899; maj. 13th Inf., July 1, 1912; lt. col. inf., Apr. 28, 1914; col., July 1, 1916; brig. gen. N.A., Aug. 5, 1917; maj. gen., Aug. 8, 1918. Comdt. cadets. U. of Mo., 1889-92, Baylor U., Waco, Tex., 1893-94; distinguished marksman, 1893; at Austin and Dallas, Tex., and Miami and Jacksonville, Fla., 1898; duty in Philippines, 1899-1902, 1906, 1911-14; on Mexican border, 1914; duty MASS. Mass. N.G., 1915-17.Comd. 28th Inf., 1st Div., A.E.F., June 12, 1917, 2d Inf. Brig., 1st Div., Aug. 5, 1917, 3d Div. (regulars), Aug. 8, 1918, 34th Div., Oct. 17, 1918. Participated in the first all-Am. (Catigny) offensive, May 28-29, 1918, and Aisne-Marne, St. Mihiel and Meuse-Argonne offensives; returned to U.S., Nov. 15, 1918; comdr. Camp McArthur, Dec. 20, 1918, Camp Meade, Md., Mar. 1919, Laredo dist., Mexican border, May 1919-Mar. 1920; assigned to 20th Inf., Ft. Cook, Neb., Apr. 13, 1920; at Camp Travis, Tex., Aug. 15, 1921; assigned acting chief of staff, 90th Div. Organized Reserves, at San Antonio, Tex., Aug. 15, 1921. Awarded D.S.C. (U.S.); chevalier and Comdr. Legion of Honor, and Croix de Guerre with two palms (French); Italian War Cross. Address: San Antonio. Died Feb. 10, 1950.

BUCK, PHILO MELVIN, JR. college prof., writer; b. Morristown, N.J., Feb. 18, 1877; A.M., Harvard, 1900; Litt.D., Ohio Wesleyan Univ., 1935; m. Alethia Hall, Aug. 27, 1902; children—Edward MacMillan, Carolyn Laura (Mrs. William Harvey Reeves). Instr. English, Ohio Wesleyan U., 1898-99, high schs., St. Louis, 1900-10; head. dept. English, William McKinley High Sch., St. Louis, 1904-10; asso. prof. rhetoric, 1910-12, prof. rhetoric, 1912-19, dean Coll. of Arts and Sciences, 1919-24, chmn. dept. of comparative lit., 1924-26, U. of Neb.; chmn. dept. comparative lit., U. of Wis., emeritus prof. comparative lit., U. Wis., since 1947; spl. services prof. comparative lit., 1947-49. Lecturer on comparative lit., Utah State Coll., summer 1948. Exchange prof. Baroda Coll., U. of Bombay, India; lecturer on American lit. in other Indian universities, 1922-23; lecturer U. of Utah, summer, 1931, U. of Southern Calif., summer, 1935; Syracuse U., 1947, Utah State Coll., 1948; traveled in the Orient, especially India, 1931, 1938-39. Capt.; adj. gen.'s dept., 34th Div., U.S. Army, 1917-18; in charge publ. section Military Intelligence Division, Gen. Staff, 1918-19. Asso. editor Midwest Quarterly to 1917. Mem. Modern Lang. Assn. America, Inst. Litt. et Artistique, Paris, France, Alpha Tau Omega, Phi Beta Kappa, Phi Kappa Phi, Sigma Delta Chi. Clubs: University, Blackhawk Country. Author: The Art of Composition (with William Schuyler), 1907; Social Forces in Modern Literature, 1913; An Anthology of World Literature, 1934, rev. edit., 1940. Contbr. to Goethe Centenary, Univ. of Wis., 1933; The World's Great Age, 1936; Directions in Contemporary Literature, 1941. Editor various texts; contbr. to mags. and publs. Home: 1852 Summit Av., Madison, Wis. Died Dec. 9, 1950.

BUCK, RAYMOND ELLIOTT, lawyer, ins. exec.; b. Ft. Worth, July 13, 1894; s. Raymond H. and Eula E. (Blackmore) B.; student Tex. Christian U., 1911-13; LL.B., U. Tex., 1917; m. Katherine Camp, Dec. 8, 1921; children—Raymond Elliott Buck (deceased), Katherine Camp Buck (Mrs. McDermott). Admitted to Tex. bar, 1919, since in general practice as member Buck & Buck; city atty., Ft. Worth, 1920-22; gen. counsel, dir. So. Air Transport, 1928-30; president Midway Airport Corp., 1948-52; associate gen. counsel Am. Airlines, Inc., from 1929; dir., gen. counsel Trinity Life Ins. Co., 1934-35; dir., gen. counsel Comml. Standard Ins. Co., 1935-43, chmn., gen. counsel, from 1943, pres., from 1952; chmn., past pres., gen. counsel, chmn. exec. com. Comml. Standard Fire & Marine Co., from 1952, Comml. Standard Life Ins. Co., from 1955, Comml. Standard Title Ins. Co., from 1958; owner, operator Raymond E. Buck Ranch & Cattle Co., from 1938; asso. gen. counsel Convair, div. Gen. Dynamics Corp., from 1941; pres. Bucco Homes, Inc., from 1950, Tarrant Land Co., from 1954; v.p., dir. Geyser Corp., from 1964; dir., sec., mem. exec. com. Ft. Worth Air Terminal, Inc., from 1948; dir. Continental Nat. Bank, Forth Worth, vice chairman of bd., mem. exec. com., from 1967. Active mem. internat. bd. electors Ins. Hall of Fame, 1962-65; co-chmn. U. Tex. Internat. Ins. Seminar, bd. govs. Internat. Invitational Ins. Seminar, 1965-66; mem. ins. adv. council and planning commn. U. Tex., U. Tex. Council Bus. Adminstrn. Foundation. Mem. the Governor's Post War Planning Committee on Taxes and Aviation, 1944-47; member of Texas War Bonds Com., 1942-45; director of Ft. Worth Better Bus. Bur., Tex. Technological College Found. Chmn. Young Democrats Tex., 1931-35; finance chmn. Tex. Democratic Party, 1942; Tex. chmn. Jefferson Day Dinner, 1941-42; chmn. Tex. Dem. Conv., 1956; mem. Dem. Adv. Council, 1955. Lay council St. Joseph's Hosp.; citizens council Scott and White Meml. Hosp.; sponsoring com. Nat. Jewish Hosp. at Denver. Served as capt., inf., U.S. Army, 1917-19; AEF in France. Mem. Am., Tex. bar assns., First Officers Tng. Camp Assn. (pres. 1952-53), Texas Univ. Alumni Assn. of Ft.

Worth (president 1925), Ft. Worth C. of C. (dir. from 1957, pres. 1962-63), Texas Christian University Ex-Student Assn. (pres. 1949-50), Am. Assn. UN (pres. Ft. Worth from 1964). Clubs: Forth Worth (gov. 1946-57, dir., exec. com.), Town, River Crest Country, Ridglea Country, Admirals (Ft. Worth). Home: Ft Worth TX Died Mar. 27, 1971; interred Greenwood Masoleum, Ft Worth TX

BUCK, RICHARD SUTTON civil engr.; b. Georgetown, Ky., Nov. 21, 1864; s. Richard Sutton and Juliana Scott (Randolph) B.; student U. of Miss., 1883; C.E., Rensselaer Poly. Inst., 1887; m. Laura Beverly Miller, June 30, 1890 (died Mar. 1, 1934); children—Richard Sutton, Horace Miller; m. 2d Judith Marshall Fishburn, Jan. 25, 1936 (died July 16, 1942). Served with engineer and quartermaster corps, U.S. Army, 1887-90; manager Carney Phosphate Co., Florida, 1890-92; bridge design, New York City, 1893-95; in charge construction Niagara Falls and Clifton Arch Bridge and Niagara Ry. Arch Bridge, across Niagara River, 1895-98; chief engr. Lewiston and Queenstown Bridge, 1898-99, Manhattan and Queensboro bridges, 1899-1902, Dominion Bridge of Canada, 1902-04; cons. engr. in charge constrn. Manhattan and Queensboro bridges, 1904-07; mem. Sanderson & Porter, N.Y. City, 1907-12; again chief engr. Dominion Bridge Co., 1912-14; maj. 11th Engrs. U.S. Army, with A.E.F. in France, 1917-18; valuation engr. and cons. practice since 1919; served as adviser to legal counsel Brooklyn City R.R., in suit involving $13,000,000; with others reported on projected bridge 9 miles long across San Francisco Bay. Awarded D.S.O. (British) for services on Somme and Arras fronts. Mem. Am. Soc. E.C., Soc. Mil. Engrs., Engring. Inst. of Can. Awarded Rowland prize, Am. Soc. E.C., 1899. Democrat. Clubs: Brooklyn Engineers (past pres.); Cosmos (Washington, D.C.). Home: 2123 R St., N.W., Washington. Died Aug. 1, 1951.

BUCK, WALTER ALBERT naval officer; b. Oskaloosa, Kan., June 4, 1895; s. Walter and Anna (Gramse) B.; B.S., Kansas State Coll., 1913, M.S., 1916; M.B.A., Grad. Sch. Bus. Adminstrn., Harvard, 1924; m. Mildred Ann Reed, Sept. 4, 1920; children—Walter James, John Addison. Commd. ensign, U.S. Navy, 1917, and advanced through the grades to rear adm.; retired March, 1948. Chief Bur. Supplies and Accounts, and Paymaster Gen. of the Navy, 1946-48; pres. Radiomarine Corp. of Am., Mar.-Dec. 1948; operating v.p. RCA Victor Div., 1949-50, v.p. and gen. mgr. since 1950; dir. RCA, Radiomarine Corp. of Am. Decorated World War I medal with Mine-Laying Clasp, Nat. Defense Medal with A, Am. Theater Medal, Legion of Merit (2 times). Mem. Sigma Tau, Scabbard and Blade. Clubs: New York Yacht (N.Y.); Army and Navy, Army-Navy Country (Washington). Home: 514 E. Lancaster Av., Wynnewood, Pa. Office: RCA Victor, Camden, N.J. Died June 12, 1955.

BUCKENDALE, L. RAY business exec; b. Detroit, Mich., Apr. 19, 1892; s. Adolph and Margaret Esther (Ryan) B.; B.Engring., U. of Mich., 1916; unmarried. Employed by The Timken-Detroit Axle Co., Detroit, Mich., 1911-16, engr. at plant No. 3, 1916-17, engr., 1919-36, vice pres. in charge engring., 1936—. Served as capt. Ordnance, U.S. Army, 1917-19. Mem. Soc. Automotive Engrs. (pres.). Engring. Soc. Detroit. Army Ordnance Assn. Club: Detroit Yacht. Home: 14530 Harbor Av., Detroit 15. Office 100-400 Clark Av., Detroit 32. Died Apr. 1952.

BUCKINGHAM, GEORGE TRACY lawyer; b. Delphi, Ind., Apr. 21, 1864; s. Tracy Wilson and Helen (Clark) B.; desc. Thomas Buckingham, Puritan settler of New Haven and Milford, Conn., 1637-38; removed to Ill., 1870; ed. common sch. to 1880 employed on farm, brickyard and store, 1880-90; student at night, law office, Danville, Ill., 1886-90; m. Victoria Donlon, 1894 (died 1922); 1 son, Tracy Wilson; m. 2d, Carol Allen, Jan. 30, 1926. Admitted to Ill. bar, 1890; spl. agt. U.S. Treasury (New York, Boston, Can. and Europe), 1890-94; practiced at Danville, 1894-1908; asst. state's atty., 1894-98; del. to many convs., including Nat. Rep. Conv., 1904,08; settled in Chicago, 1908; mem. Defrees, Buckingham, Jones & Hoffman (firm consisting of 10 partners and 20 associate lawyers). Trustee Illinois State Hosp., Kankakee, 1897-1901; pres. bd. trustees Joliet Prison, 1901-05; dir. or trustee numerous civic instns. Mem. Ill. N.G., 1886-1904; lt. col., Spanish-Am. War; pres. Nat. Security League, World War. Republican. Methodist. Mason. Home: Lake Forest, Ill. Died Sept. 9, 1940.

BUCKLAND, EDWARD GRANT ry. official; b. Buffalo, Dec. 31, 1866; s. Andrew J. And Julia A. (Turner) B.; B.A., Washburn Coll., Topeka, Kan., 1887, LL.D., 1921, Yale, 1889, M.A., 1895, LL.D., 1937; m. Sally Tyler Clark, June 21, 1898; children—Charles Clark, Julia Turner (Mrs. Harrison Fuller), Susan Lord (Mrs. Arthur Milliken), Chester Parsons. In general practice of law New Haven, Connecticut, 1889-98; inst. and asst. prof. of law, Yale, 1889-98; atty., 1898-1906, v.p., 1907-14, v.p. and gen. counsel, 1914-18, pres., 1918-20, v.p. and gen. counsel, 1920-24, v.p. in charge of law, finance and corporate relations, 1914-28, dir., 1918-41, chmn. bd., 1929-47, N.Y., N.H. & H. R.R. Co. and affiliated cos.; officer or dir. various other corps. Seaman, ensign lt. (j.g.), lt.-comdr. and comdr. Naval Batt., C.N.G., 1893-98; lt. col. Home Guard, Conn., 1917-20. Rep. Episcopalian. Mem. Conn. Acad. Science, Phi Delta Phi, Phi Beta Kappa. Mason. Clubs: Yale (New York); Graduate, Lawn, Country, Quinnipiack (New Haven). Home: 254 Prospect St. Office: 71 Meadow St., New Haven. Died Mar. 30, 1953; buried Grove St. Cemetery, New Haven.

BUCKLE, JOHN FRANKLIN, fgn. service officer; b. Salt Lake City, Sept. 22, 1920; s. John Vivian and Gladys Elizabeth (Frink) B.; A.B., U. Utah, 1941; postgrad. Harvard Law Sch., 1941, Fletcher Sch. Internat. Law and Diplomacy, 1942, U. Cal., 1946; M.A., Sch. Advanced Internat. Studies, 1948; m. Eva Roberta Kratzer, Aug. 30, 1942 (div. 1956); children—Eve Roberta, Michele L.; m. 2d, Mary Jane Vinson, Jan. 1957; children—John Franklin, Guy Jerome. With Bur. Economic Affairs, United States Dept. of State, Washington, 1948-50, Bur. European Affairs, 1952-56; 1st. sec. of embassy, counsul American Embassy, Madrid, Spain, 1956-57; officer in charge of economic affairs, Northern Africa, Bur. African Affairs, 1957-62; 1st sec., chief econ. sect. Am. embassy, Lisbon, Portugal, until 1966; assigned Nat. War Coll., 1966-67; sr. regional adviser Office Regional Affairs, Bur. Nr. East and S. Asian Affairs, 1967-68; dir. Office Maritime Affairs, Bureau Economic Affairs, 1968-69. Served as capt. USMC, 1942-46, PTO, as maj., 1950-52. Korea. Mem. Sigma Nu. Mason. Home: Washington DC Died Sept. 18, 1969.

BUCKLEY, OLIVER ELLSWORTH research engr.; b. Sloan, Ia., Aug. 8, 1887; s. William Doubleday and Sarah Elizabeth (Jeffrey) B.; B.S., Grinnell Coll., 1909, D.Sc., 1936; Ph.D., Cornell, 1914; D.Sc., Columbia U., 1948; D. Eng., Case Inst. Tech., 1948; m. Clara Lane, Oct. 14, 1914; children—Katherine Lane (Mrs. R. G. Nuckolls), William Douglas, Barbara (Mrs. Frederick B. Wolf), Juliet Georgiana (Mrs. Patrick Alsup). Instr. Grinnell (Ia.) Coll., 1909, Cornell, 1910-14; with the research department Western Electric Co., 1914-25; with Bell Telephone Labs., 1925-52, asst. dir. research, 1927-33, dir. of research, 1933-36, exec. v.p., 1936-40; pres. 1940-51, chmn. bd., 1951-52, dir., 1940-55; dir. Summit Trust Company,. Mem. bd. of Edn. of South Orange-Maplewood, N.J., 1938-50, pres. 1948-50. Trustee Jackson Memorial Lab., Thomas A. Edison Foundation. Served as major, Signal Corps, A.E.F., World War I, in charge research section Div. Research and Inspection, Signal Corps, Paris; mem. communications and guided missiles divisions Nat. Defense Research Com., World War II. Medal for Merit. Chmn. sci. adv. com. O.D.M. 1951-52, Bd. Multiple Sclerosis Soc. Mem. gen. adv. com. AEC, 1948-54; mem. Army Ordnance sci. adv. com., 1951-55. Fellow Am. Phys. Society, Am. Acad. Scis., Am. Philosophical Society (v.p. 1954-57), Franklin Institute, Engineering Foundation Board (chmn. 1939-42), National Inventors Council, Sigma Xi, Phi Beta Kappa, Phi Kappa Phi. Clubs: Century (N.Y.C.), Cosmos (Washington). Home: 13 Fairview Terrace, Maplewood, N.J. Died Dec. 1959.

BUCKNER, SIMON BOLIVAR soldier; b. on farm, Hart Co., Ky., Apr. 1, 1823; s. Hon. Aylett Hartswell and Elizabeth Ann (Morehead) B.; grad. U.S. Mil. Acad., 1844; m. Delia Claiborne, 1886. Bvt. 2d lt. 2d U.S. Inf., July 1, 1844; ed lt. 6th Inf., May 9, 1846; regimental q.m., Aug. 8-Dec. 17, 1847; bvtd. 1st lt., Aug. 20, 1847, for gallant and meritorious conduct at battle of Churubusco, Mex., and capt., Sept. 8, 1847, for same at battle of Moline del Rey, Mex.; asst. instr. ethics, West Point, 1845-46, asst. instr. inf. tactics, 1848-50; 1st lt., Dec. 31, 1851; capt. commissary of subsistance, Nov. 3, 1852; resigned from U.S.A., Mar. 26, 1855. Insp.-Gen., Ky., 1860-61; brig. gen. C.S.A., Sept. 1861; prisoner of war, Feb.-Aug. 1862; maj. gen., 1863; lt. gen., Sept. 1864, Gov. Ky., 1887-91; mem. Ky. Constl. Conv., 1891; candidate for V.P. of U.S. on Gold Democrat ticket, 1896. Home: Munfordville, Ky. Died Jan. 8, 1914.

BUCKNER, SIMON BOLIVAR JR. army officer; b. Munfordville, Ky., July 18, 1886; s. Simon Bolivar (lt. gen. C.S.A.) and Delia Hayes (Claiborne) B.; student Va. Mil. Inst., 1902-04; B.S., U.S. Mil. Acad., 1908; grad. advanced course, Inf. Sch., Fort Benning, Ga., 1924. Command and Gen. Staff Sch., Fort Leavenworth, Kan., 1925, Army War Coll., Washington, D.C., 1929; m. Adele Blanc, Dec. 30, 1916; children—Simon Bolivar III, Mary Blanc, William Claiborne. Commd. 2d lt. inf., U.S. Army, 1908, advanced through grades to lieut. gen. (temp.), 1943; served as maj. aviation sect., Signal Corps., comdr. training brigs., World War; instr. inf. tactics, U.S. Mil. Acad., 1919-23; inst. Command and Gen. Staff Sch., 1925-28; exec. officer, Army War Coll., 1929-32; asst. comdt. cadets U.S. Mil. Acad., 1932, comdt., 1933-36; comdr. 66th Inf. (light tanks), 1937-38, 22nd Inf., 1938-39; chief of staff, 6th Div., 1939-40; comdg. gen Alaska Defense Force, July 1940; comdg. gen., Okinawa, 1945. Mem. S.A.R., Aztec Club of 1847, Ends of the Earth Club. Democrat. Protestant. Clubs: Army and Navy, Army, Navy and Marine Corps Country (Washington, D.C.). Address: Hdqrs. A.D.C., care Postmaster Seattle, Wash. Killed in action, Okinawa, June 18, 1945.

BUDD, NATHAN P., coll. dean; b. Reading, Kan., Apr. 29, 1911; s. Charles Albert and Ethel (McKeehen) B.; B.S. in Edn., Kan. State Teachers Coll., Emporia, 1946; M.A., U. Colo., 1949, Ed.D., 1956; m. Helen Raikes, Dec. 28, 1941; children—Michael Nathan, Pamela Sue, Joan Elizabeth. Tchr. country schs., Kan., 1930-35, elementary schs., Kan., 1935-37; tchr. math., coach Osage City (Kan.) Jr. High Sch., 1937-40; jr. high sch. prin., Stafford, Kan., 1946-48; mem. faculty Kan. State Tchrs. Coll., 1949-71; dean instrn., 1957-71; visiting prof. Univ. Minn., summers 1964-67. Served to capt. AUS, 1942-46. Mem. Am. Personnel and Guidance Assn. (pres. U. Colo. 1956), N.E.A., Kan. Tchrs. Assn., Emporia C. of C., N. Central Assn. Acad. Deans, (pres. 1966-67), Phi Delta Kappa, Kappa Delta Pi, Blue Key. Methodist (ofcl. bd.). Rotarian. Editor: The Faculty Role in Working with Students as Persons, 1965; Assessment of Teacher Competencies, 1964; The Teacher Education Program as a Total Institutional Responsibility, 1966; Improving Instruction, 1967. Home: Emporia KS Died Nov. 28, 1971; buried Meml. Lawn Cemetery, Emporia KS

BUDGE, WALTER LYTTLETON atty. gen. Utah; b. Paris, Ida., Mar. 3, 1906; s. Alfred and Ella (Hoge) B.; LL.B., U. Ida., 1938; m. Doris Penwell, June 4, 1926; children-Doris Patricia (Mrs. Jack Mallery), Bruce Pensell; m. 2d, Phyllis Edna Simmonds, Feb. 17, 1946. Admitted to Ida. bar, 1939, Utah bar, 1947, also U.S. Supreme and dist. cts.; asso. firm Hanson, Baldwin & Allen, Salt Lake City, 1957-; asst. atty. gen. Utah, 1953-57, dep. atty. gen., 1957-59, atty. gen., 1959-. Served to capt. USAAF, World War II. Mem. Phi Gamma Delta, Phi Alpha Delta. Republican. Mem. Ch. of Jesus Christ of Latter Day Saints. Home: 153 2d Av., Salt Lake City 3. Office: State Capitol, Salt Lake City 14. Died Dec. 10, 1961.

BUEHLER, WILLIAM GEORGE rear adm. U.S.N.; b. Phila., Mar. 25, 1837; s. William Olds and Henrietta Ruhamah B.; removed to Harrisburg, Pa., 1844, and was ed. in pvt. schs. there. Entered U.S.N. as 3d asst. engr., in May 1857; 2d asst. engr., Oct. 8, 1861; 1st asst. engr., Oct. 6, 1862; chief engr., Nov. 10, 1863; capt., June 4, 1894; rear adm. and retired, Mar. 25, 1899; officer U.S.S. frigate Niagara when 1st Atlantic telegraph was laid (received gold medal N.Y. Chamber of Commerce); served during Civ. War, chief engr. U.S.S. Aroostook, 1861-62; U.S.S. Galena, 1863-65; participated in attacks on James River and Ft. Darling, at passage of forts at entrance of Mobile Bay under Farragut, etc.; engr. on various ships until 1888; mem. U.S. Naval Bd. Inspection 4 yrs.; twice mem. Examining Bd. Naval Engrs.; in charge dept. steam engring. Navy Yard, Portsmouth, N.H., 1894-99. Home: Philadelphia. Died Aug. 10, 1919.

BUELL, DON CARLOS army officer; b. nr. Marietta, O., Mar. 23, 1818; s. Salmon D. and Eliza (Buell) B.; grad. U.S. Mil. Acad., 1841; m. Margaret Hunter. Commd. 2d lt. 3d Inf., U.S. Army, 1841; fought in Seminole War; served as 1st lt. at battles of Monterey, Churubusco during Mexican War; brevetted capt., 1846; adj. gen. of his regt., 1847; commd. lt. col. Adj. Gen.'s Dept., 1860; commd. brig. gen. U.S. Volunteers, 1861; an organizer Army of Potomac; commdr. Army of Ohio, 1861; commd. maj. gen. U.S. Volunteers, 1862; fought at battles of Shiloh, Perryville; relieved of command for failure to pursue Confederate Army after Battle of Perryville; resigned commn., 1864; pres. Green River Iron Works, 1865. Died Rockport, Ky., Nov. 19, 1898.

BUESSER, FREDERICK G. physician, educator; b. Troy, N.Y., Apr. 27, 1881; s. Gustavus D. and Nellie (Conners) B.; student U. Vt., 1901-04; M.D., Wayne U., 1905; postgrad. N.Y.C., Chgo., Rochester, Minn., Paris, Lyon and Dijon, France; m. Lela Carpenter, Mar. 1, 1915; children—Frederick G., William Carpenter (dec.), Elizabeth L. (Mrs. John F. Pfender), Anthony Carpenter. With Harper Hosp., Detroit, 1905—, Vol. asst., out-patient dept. of internal medicine, 1905-07, asst. physician, 1908-10, attending physician, 1910-19, physician dept. internal medicine, 1919-22, sr. physician, 1923-45, cons. physician, 1945—; vis. physician Detroit Tb. Sanatorium; cons. physician City of Detroit Receiving Hosp., Charles Godwin Jennings Hosp.; with Wayne U. Coll. Medicine, 1905—, inst. clin. medicine, 1905-07, asst. prof., 1908-19, asso. prof. gastro-enterology, 1919-35, now prof. clin. medicine; former chmn. faculty adv. council; lecturer, Postgrad. Sch. Medicine, U. Mich. Mem. Continuation Sch. of Medicine, Wayne County; mem. State Com. on Med. Procurement and Assignment; mem. med. adv. bd. 1, Mich. Served from lt. to maj. M.C., AEF and BEF, 1917-19. Diplomate Am. Bd. Internal Medicine. Fellow A.C.P., Detroit Acad. Medicine (ex-pres.); mem. A.M.A., Mich., Wayne County med. socs., Assn. Mil Surgeons, Delta Mu, Nu Sigma Nu, Alpha Omega Alpha (hon.) Republican. Episcopalian. Clubs: Detroit Gold, Detroit Athletic. Home: 921 Taylor Av. Office: 1553 Woodward Av., Detroit. Died July 1, 1950.

BUFFINGTON, ADELBERT RINALDO army officer; b. Wheeling, Va., Nov. 22, 1837; grad. U.S. Mil. Acad., 1861; m. Eliza Allston White, May 14, 1873. Commd. add. 2d lt. ordnance, May 6, 1861; 2d lt., May 14, 1861; capt., Mar. 3, 1863; maj., June 23, 1874; lt. col., June 1, 1881; col., Feb. 28, 1889; brig. gen. and chief of ordnance U.S.A., Apr. 5, 1899; retired, Nov. 22, 1901. Was bvtd. maj., Mar. 13, 1865, "for faithful and meritorious services" in Ordnance Dept. In Command Nat. Armory, 1881-82, Rock Island Arsenal, 1892-97. Originator various improvements in ordnance, also methods of mfg. small arms. Home: Madison, N.J. Died July 10, 1922.

BUFORD, ABRAHAM army officer; b. Culpeper County, Va., July 31, 1749; s. John and Judith Beauford; m. Martha McDowell, Oct. 1788. Raised company of minutemen who helped in explusion of Gov. Dunmore of Va., 1774; commd. maj. 14th Va. Regt., 1776; promoted to lt. col. 5th Va. Regt., 1777, col. in command 11th Va. Regt., 1778-81; comdr. 3d Va. Regt., Continental Army, 1781; became large landowner after Am. Revolution; moved to Ky. Died Georgetown, Ky., June 30, 1833.

BUFORD, ABRAHAM army officer, stock raiser; b. Woodford County, Ky., Jan. 18, 1820; s. William B. and Frances (Kirtley) B.; grad. U.S. Mil. Acad., 1841; m. Amanda Harris, 1845, 1 son, William. Commd. 1st lt. U.S. Army during Mexican War, 1846, capt., 1853; stock raiser, specializing in horses and short horn cattle, Ky., 1854-61; commd. brig. gen. Confederate Army, 1862; returned to stock raising after war, also bred race horses. Died Danville, Ind., June 9, 1884.

BUFORD, JOHN army officer; b. Woodford County, Ky., Mar. 4, 1826; s. John and Anne (Bannister) Watson B.; grad. U.S. Mil. Acad., 1848; m. Martha McDonald Duke, May 9, 1854. Brevetted to 2d lt. U.S. Army, 1848, commd. 2d lt., 1849, 1st lt., 1853, regimental g.m., 1855; frontier duty, Tex., N.M., Kan.; took part in Sioux Expdn., 1855; commd. brig. gen. U.S. Volunteers, 1862, assigned to cavalry; wounded at Battle of Centerville, 1862; chief cavalry Army of Potomac, 1862; served in battles of Antietam, Fredericksburg, Gettysburg; promoted maj. gen. volunteers shortly before death. Died on sick leave, Washington, D.C., Dec. 16, 1863; buried U.S. Mil. Acad., West Point, N.Y.

BUFORD, NAPOLEON BONAPARTE army officer; b. Woodford County, Ky., Jan. 13, 1807; s. John and Mary (Hickman) B.; grad. U.S. Mil. Acad., 1827; m. Sarah Childs; m. 2d, Nancy Anne Greenwood. Commd. lt. arty. U.S. Army 1827; asst. prof. natural and exptl. philosophy U.S. Mil. Acad., 1834-35, sec. bd. visitors, 1850; commd. col. 27th Ill. Volunteers, 1861, participating in operations in Ky., Tenn. and Miss., 1861; commd. brig. gen. U.S. Volunteer, 1862, maj. gen., 1865; supt. Fed. Union Mining Co., Colo., 1866; U.S. commr. Indian affairs, 1867; a founder Chgo. Soc. Sons of Va. Died Chgo., Mar. 28, 1883; buried Rock Island, Ill.

BUGG, BENJAMIN LAMAR, ry. executive; b. Palo Alto, Miss., Aug. 8, 1869; s. Thomas Elliott and Emma (Shotwell) B.; edn. high sch. and under private instrn.; m. Mabel Dodd, Mar. 15, 1892; 1 dau., Mildred (dec.). Terminal agt. Central of Ga. Ry., at Savannah, 1901-07; gen. agt. Old Dominion S.S. Co., Norfolk, Va., 1907-10; traffic mgr. Norfolk Southern Ry., 1910-12; apptd. asst. gen. mgr., A.B.&A. Ry., 1912, gen. mgr., 1916, v.p. and gen. mgr. 1917, pres., 1920, receiver, 1921-26; pres. Atlanta, Birmingham & Coast R.R., 1927-45; retired July 1, 1945. Commissioned lieutenant colonel, engineers, United States Army, May 22, 1918; sailed for France in command 66th Regt. Engineers, June 30, 1918; comd. camps Gron. Raymond, St. Pierre des Corps and 20th Grand Div. Transportation Corps; discharged May 29, 1919. Chevalier Legion of Honor (French). Mem. Am. Ry. Engring. Assn., Soc. Am. Mil. Engrs. Baptist. Scottish Rite Mason, Shriner. Home: 34 Inman Circle, N.E., Atlanta GA

BULL, ALFRED CASTLEMAN, banker; b. Austin, Tex., Dec. 20, 1893; s. Richard Platt and Margaret (Castleman) B.; grad. Austin Acad., 1912; B.S., Tex. A. and M. Coll., 1916; m. Edna Hazlewood, July 2, 1924 (dec. 1943); 1 son, Richard Hazlewood; m. 2d, Alice Archer, Oct. 20, 1951. Partner, Bull & DeViney, gen. ins. agy., 1919-25; v.p., dir. Tex. Bank & Trust Co., Austin, 1926-33; v.p., dir. Am. Nat. Bank, Austin, 1936-61, chmn. bd., 1961-67. Mem. Tex. Library and Hist. Com., 1940-44; chmn. Travis chpt. A.R.C., 1945-46. Mem. sch. bd., Austin, 1938-43. Served as capt., inf., U.S. Army, 1917-19. Mem. Austin C. of C. (pres. 1934), Am. Bankers Assn. Episcopalian. Mason (33 deg.). Clubs: Austin, Austin Country. Home: Austin TX Died Dec. 27, 1967; buried Oakwood Cemetery, Austin TX

BULL, JAMES HENRY commodore U.S.N.; b. West Chester, Pa., June 13, 1852; s. James Hunter and Mary Augusta (Sheaff) B.; grad. U.S. Naval Acad., 1870; Naval War Coll., 1892, 1896, 1906; m. Katherine Whittelsey Tillman, Mar. 5, 1878. Ensign, 1871; promoted through grades to commodore, and retired June 30, 1907. For service record see Vol. 12 (1922-23) Home: San Francisco, Calif. Died July 20, 1932.

BULLARD, ROBERT LEE army officer; b. Youngsboro, Ala., Jan 15, 1861; s. Daniel and Susan (Mizell) B.; ed. Agrl. and Mech. Coll. of Ala.; B.S., U.S. Mil. Acad., 1885; LL.D., Columbia U. and Ala. Poly. Inst.; D.M.S., Pa. Military Coll.; m. Rose D. Brabson; children—Robert Lee, Peter C., Rose, Keith; m. 2d, Mrs. Ella R. Wall, Aug. 1927. Commd. 2d lt., U.S. Army, June 14, 1885; advanced through grades to col., Mar. 11, 1911; brig. gen., June 16, 1917; maj. gen., Nov. 27, 1918; retired Jan. 15, 1925. Served in United States with regiment during Spanish-Am. War, and in P.I. during period of insurrection; built Iligan-Lanao mil. rd. and gov., of Lanao Moros, Mindanao, 1902-04; spl. aid and investigator for the U.S. provisional gov. of Cuba, 1907; supervisor (sec.) of pub. instrn. and fine arts, Cuba, 1908. Comdg. regt., dist. and nat. guard brigade in Mexican Border bandit raids, and nat. guard mobilization on border, 1915-16; comdr. O.T.C., Ark., May, 1917; brig. gen. U.S. Army, June 14, 1917; comdg. 2d Brigade, 1st Div., A.E.F. in France, June, July, Aug. 1917; maj. gen. N.A., Aug. 5, 1917; establishing and comg. various inf. officers schs. in France to Dec. 14, 1918; condg. 1st Div. A.E.F. in training maneuvers, trenches and open field in all its engagements and operations against Germans, Dec. 14, 1917-July 14, 1918, 3d Corps, July 14-Oct. 11, 1918; lt. gen., Oct. 16, 1918; maj. gen. (regular army), Nov. 1918; comdg. 2d Army A.E.F. in all its operations and engagements, training, occupation of enemy territory in France and in Luxembourg, Oct. 11, 1918-Apr. 15, 1919; retired, Jan. 15, 1925, with rank of lieutenant general; president of the National Security League since 1925. Wrote the famous message at the opening of the 2d Battle of the Marne, July 1918, which marked the turning point of the war, concluding with the words, "We are going to counter-attack," Awarded D.S.M., 1918; decorations from France, Belgium and Italy. Author of numerous articles in magazines, newspapers and military journals. Home: 2 E. 86th St., New York, N.Y. Died Sept. 11, 1947; buried U.S. Military Academy Cemetery, West Point, N.Y.

BULLARD, WILLIAM HANNUM GRUBB naval officer; b. Media, Del. Co., Pa., Dec. 6, 1866; s. Orson Flagg and Rebecca Ann (Huston) B.; grad. U.S. Naval Acad., 1886; m. Beirne Saunders, Oct. 30, 1889; 1 son, Beirne Saunders. Ensign, July 1, 1888; lt. jr. grade, Sept. 5, 1896; lt., Mar. 3, 1899; lt. comdr., Jan. 1, 1905; comdr., Feb. 1, 1909; capt., July 1, 1912; rear admiral, temporary, July 1, 1918, permanent rank, Oct. 20, 1919. Served on Columbia, Spanish-Am. War, 1898; naviagtor, Maine, 1905-06; exec. officer same, 1906-07; at U.S. Naval Acad., 1907-11 (organized dept. elec. engring. there); comd. San Francisco, 1911-12; supt. naval radio service, 1912-16; comdg. Arkansas, 1916-18. Served in Atlantic Fleet and in Am. div. of battleships in British Grand Fleet; mem. Inter-Allied Commn. at Malta; comd. U.S. naval forces in Eastern Mediterranean; mem. Inter-Allied Commn. to put into effect the naval terms of the armistice with Austria-Hungary, and received surrender of Austro-Hungarian fleet; mem. Inter-Allied Conf. on Radio, Paris, Jan. and Aug., 1919; dir. naval communications, Mar. 1919-21; comdr. Yangtze Patrol Force, U.S. Asiatic Fleet, 1921-22; retired, Sept. 30, 1922. Del. Internat. Safety at Sea Conf., London, 1913. Medals and decorations: West Indian and Philippine campaigns; Victory Medal; D.S.M. (Navy Dept.); Comdr. Legion of Honor (French); Order of the Knights of Polonia Restituta (Poland). Home: Media, Pa. Died Nov. 24, 1927.

BULLENE, EGBERG FRANK ret. army officer; b. Salinas, Cal., Jan. 25, 1895; s. Alfred Frank and Lida (Hatch) B.; Columbia Prep. Sch., 1913-14, B.S., U.S. Naval Acad., 1917, Army Indspl. Coll. 1928, Chem. Warfare Corps, line and staff course, 1926, field officers course, 1933, Command and Gen. Staff Sch., 1937, Army War Coll., 1940; m. Lois Esther Salsman, Sept. 29, 1919; 1 son, Roger. Commd. 2d lt. 1917, advanced through grades to maj. gen., 1951; bn. comdr., 4th Div., World War I; spl. detail in North China when Japanese came over the Great Wall for first time in 1933; served in F.A., Cav., and Corps; instr. at Command and Gen. Staff Sch., 1937-39; comd. joint Am. British secret Army-Navy project overseas, 1944; in European and Pacific Theatres, 1945; mem. mil. commn. which tried and convicted Gen. Yamashita; comd. Army Chem. Center, Md., 1946-50; chief chem. officer of the Army, ret. 1954. Decorated Legion of Merit, Bronze Star, Purple Heart, Commendation Ribbon, Victory Medal with four clasps. Mason. Address: P.O. Box 1968 Carmel, Cal. Died Feb. 21, 1958; buried Nat. Cemetery of the Presidio of San Francisco.

BULLIS, JOHN LAPHAM brig. gen., b. in N.Y., Apr. 17, 1841; s. Abrah R. and Lydia P. B.; ed. at Macedon Center and Lima, N.Y.; m. Alice Rodriguez; 2d, Josephine Withers. Enlisted as corporal Co. H, 126th N.Y. Vol. Inf., Aug. 8, 1862; disch. Aug. 17, 1864; capt. 118th U.S.C.T., Aug. 18, 1864; hon. mustered out, Feb. 6, 1866; apptd. from Ark., 2d lt. 41st U.S. Inf., Sept. 3, 1867; transferred to 24th Inf., Nov. 11, 1869; 1st lt., June 20, 1873; capt., Apr. 29, 1886; maj. Jan. 29, 1897; brig. gen. U.S.A., Apr. 13, 1905; retired at own request after 40 yrs.' service, Apr. 14, 1905. Bvtd. capt., 1890 "for gallant services in action against Indians at Remolina, Mex., 1873," and on Pecos River, Tex., 1875; maj., 1890, for same in action against Indians nr. Saragossa, Mex., 1876, and action against Indians in the Burro Mountains, Mex., 1881. Home: San Antonio, Texas. Died 1911.

BULLITT, WILLIAM CHRISTIAN former ambassador; b. Phila., Pa., Jan. 25, 1891; s. William Christian and Louisa Gross (Howritz) B.; A.B., Yale, 1912; student Harvard Law Sch., 1913-14; LL.D., Temple U., 1935, Dartmouth, 1938, U. of Nancy (France), 1937, U. Montreal, 1941, Georgetown U., 1947; m. Anne Moen Louise Bryant Reed, 1923; 1 dau., Anne Moen (Mrs. Nicholas Benjamin Duke Biddle). Asso. editor, fgn. corr. and Washington corr. Phila. Public Ledger, 1915-17; asst. in Dept. of State, 1917-18; attaché to Am. Commn. to Negotiate Peace, 1918-19; spl. mission to Russia, 1919; spl. asst. to Sec. of State, 1933; mem. Am. Delegation to World Monetary and Econ. Conf., 1933; U.S. ambassador to Union of Soviet Socialist Republics, 1933-36, France, 1936-41; ambassador at large, Nov. 1941-Apr. 1942; spl. asst. to sec. of Navy, June 1942-July 1943. Fgn. corr. for Life Magazine, 1944. Mng. editor, Famous Players-Lasky Corp., 1921. Enlisted in French Army, Aug., 1944; served as major in inf. Decorated Croix de Guerre with palm, comdr. Legion of Honor (France); Officer, Legion of Merit (U.S.). Mem. Phi Beta Kappa. Author: It's Not Done (novel), 1926; Report to the American People, 1940; The Great Glove Itself, 1946. Home: 3440 34th Pl. N.W., Washington. Died Feb. 1967; buried Woodlands Cemetery, Phila.

BULWINKLE, ALFRED LEE ex-congressman; b. Charleston, S.C., Apr. 21, 1883; s. Herman and Frances (McKean) B.; student Law dept., U. N.C., 1903-04; D.C.L., Lenoir-Rhyne Coll., 1941; m. Bessie Lewis, 1911; children—Frances (Mrs. E. Grainger Williams), Alfred Lewis (U.S. Army). Admitted to N.C. bar, 1904, pros. atty., Gastonia, 1913-36. Mem. 67th to 70th and 72d to 81st Congresses, 11th N.C. Dist. Mem. Joint Congl. Policy Bd.,; del. Internat. Aviation Conf., 1944; U.S. adviser Internat. Civil Aviation Organ. Conf., Montreal, Can., and Geneva, Switzerland, 1947. Capt. Inf., N.C.N.G., 1909-17; maj. comdg. 2d bn., 113th F.A., 30th Div., AEF, 1917-19. Mem. exec. bd. United Lutheran Ch. in America. Mem. N.C. State Bar Assn. Democrat. Lutheran. Mason, Elk. Home: Gastonia, N.C. Died Aug. 31, 1950

BUMSTEAD, HORACE educator; b. at Boston, Sept. 29, 1841; s. Josiah Freeman and Lucy Douglas (Willis) B.; A.B., Yale, 1863. A.M., 1866; maj. 43 U.S.C.T., 1864-65, serving in siege of Richmond and Petersburg, later in Tex.; grad. Andover Theol. Sem., 1870; studied in Europe, 1870, 1871 (D.D., New York U., 1881); m. Anna M., d. Albert G. Hoit, portrait painter, Jan. 9, 1872. Ordained Congl. ministry, 1872; pastor Second Ch., Minneapolis, 1872-75; prof. natural science, 1875-80, prof. Latin, 1880-97, pres., 1888-1907, Atlanta U. (for colored students); retired on Carnegie Foundation, 1907; then engaged in religious and philanthropic work. Home: Brookline, Mass. Died Oct. 14, 1919.

BUNCE, ALLEN HAMILTON physician; b. Bulloch County, Ga., Sept. 5, 1889; s. James Allen and Georgia Anne (McElveen) B.; A.B., U. Ga., 1908; Emory U. Sch. Medicine, 1908-09, M.D., 1911; postgrad. U. Chgo., 1909-10; m. Angelina La Riviere, Aug. 28, 1916 (dec. 1939) m. 2d, Isabella Arnold, June 12, 1940. Formerly asso. in medicine Emory U. Sch. Medicine; physician Ga. Bapt. Hosp. (pres. 1928-29), Crawford W. Long Meml. Hosp. (pres. 1924-25, now cons.), Wesley Meml. Hosp., Grady Hosp. (pres. 1927-28), Piedmont Hosp.; cons. St. Joseph's Infirmary. Served as 1st lt. and capt. M.C., U.S. Army, in World War, Nov. 1, 1917-Apr. 7, 1919; with A.E.F. as chief of lab. service Base Hosp. 43. Officer Acad. Francaise for service in France. Pres. Atlanta Tb Assn., 1917-19. Phi Beta Kappa Assn. fellow, 1953. Recipient Lamartine Griffin Hardman award, 1947; 1st D.S.M. Med. Assn. Ga., 1958. Diplomate Am. Bd. Internal Medicine; fellow A.C.P., A.M.A. (vice speaker Ho. of Del.; trustee 1929-39; del. 1916, 1924-39, 1942-50); mem. Med. Assn. Ga. (sec.-treas. 1920-35, pres. 1941-42), Fulton County Med. Soc. (hon. pres. 1951), World Med. Assn. (charter mem.), Internat. Soc. Internal Medicine, Phi Chi, Phi Beta Kappa, Omicron Delta Kappa, Pi Mu Gamma. Democrat. Mason (32ff, Shriner). Club: Lotos (N.Y.). Author: Campus Verse, 1908; Outlines of Physiology (with E.G. Jones), 1912; also numerous articles on internal medicine and allied subjects. Editor Jour. Med. Assn. Ga., 1920-35. Elected chmn. com. on revision of Constn. and By-laws, U.S. Pharmacopeal Conv., 1940-50; revision adopted, 1942, pres. conv., trustee, 1950-60. Club: Capital City (Atlanta). Home: 368 Ponce de Leon Av., N.E. Atlanta 30308. Office: 98 Currier St., N.E., Atlanta 3. Died July 30, 1965; buried Oakland Cemetery, Atlanta.

BUNCE, FRANCIS MARVIN rear adm. U.S.N., retired Dec. 25, 1898; b. Hartford, Conn., Dec. 25, 1836; s. James Marvin B.; grad. U.S. Naval Acad., 1857; lt., 1861; lt. comdr., 1863; comdr., 1871; capt., 1883; commodore, 1895; rear adm., 1898. During Civil war was exec. officer Penobscot, 1862, in blockading service off Wilmington, N.C.; took part in various boat expdns. and skirmishes; served on Pawnee and had charge of naval part in attack and capture of Morris' Island, S.C.; served on monitor Patapsco in siege of Charleston, until wounded by explosion of cartridges, Nov., 1863; afterward on several vessels; in 1865-66 took monitor Monadnock from Phila. to San Francisco - 1st extended seavoyage every made by monitor; comd. Naval Training Sta., Newport, R.I., 1891-94; North Atlantic Sta., 1895-97; navy yard, New York, 1897-99; m. Mary E. Bull, 1864. Home: Hartford, Conn. Died 1901.

BUNDEL, CHARLES MICHAEL army officer; b. Sharon, Pa., June 2, 1875; s. Charles Edward and Sarah Elizabeth (Murphy) B.; grad. U.S. Mil. Acad., 1899, Army Sch. of the Line, 1916, Army Gen. Staff Sch., 1921, Army War Coll., 1925; m. Enid Cal Valentine, June 2, 1913. Commd. 2d lt. U.S.A., Feb. 15, 1899; promoted through grades to col. F.A., Nov. 5, 1921; brig. gen., Mar. 1934. Served in Philippine Insurrection, 1899-1903, Mexican Punitive Expdn., 1916, World War. Episcopalian. Contbr. articles on mil. subjects to mil. jours. and mags. Died Sept. 15, 1941.

BUNDY, OMAR, army officer; b. New Castle, Ind., June 17, 1861; s. Martin L. and Amanda (Elliott) B.; grad. U.S. Mil. Acad., 1883, Inf. and Cav. Sch., 1887, Army War Coll., 1913; LL.D., DePauw U., 1919; m. Miss Harden, Nov. 27, 1889. Commd. 2d lt. 2d Inf., June 13, 1883; promoted through grades to col. 16th Inf., July 20, 1914; adj. gen., Oct. 2, 1915; brig. gen., May 15, 1917; maj. gen. N.A., Aug. 5, 1917. Served in campaign against Sioux Indians, S.D., 1890-91; participated in Battle of El Caney, Cuba, July 1, 1898. and at siege of Santiago; went to Philippines, 1899; operated against insurgents and ladrones until July, 1900; insp. gen. Dept. of Visayas, 1900-01; provost marshal Iloilo, 1901-02; duty Gen. Service and Staff Coll., 1902-05; in Philippines, 1905-07; comd. one of columns in the assault on Moro stronghold at Mount Dajo, Jolo, Mar. 1906; comdg. 2d Div. A.E.F. in France, Oct. 1917-July 1918, 6th and 7th Army Corps, July-Oct. 1918; major gen. regular army, in comd. Philippine Div., 1922; comdr. 5th Corps Area, 1924-25; retired June 17, 1925. Died Jan. 21, 1940.

BUNIM, JOSEPH J(AY) physician, educator; b. Volozin, Russia, Nov. 5, 1906; s. Moses and Minnie (Joselowsky) B.; brought to U.S., 1910, naturalized, 1914; B.Sc., Coll. City N.Y., 1926; M.D., N.Y. U., 1930, Sc.D. in Medicine, 1938; m. Miriam Schild, Dec. 30, 1934; children-Lesley, Elizabeth, Michael. Intern Medicine N.Y.U. div., Bellevue Hosp., 1930-32, resident medicine, 1933-35, successively adjunct vis. physician, asst. vis. physician, asso. vis. and vis. physician, 1936-52, founder, chief prenatal cardiac clinic, 1939-49, chief arthritis clinic, 1949-52; asst. physiology N.Y.U. Coll. Medicine, 1935-36, asst., 1936-39, instr., 1939-42, asst. prof. clin. medicine, 1942-49, asso. prof. medicine, 1949-52; fellow infectious diseases Yale Coll. Medicine, 1932, intern pediatric service New Haven Hosp., 1932-33; cons. Surg. Gen., U.S. Army, Hosp., 1949-52, VA Hosp., 1951-52; asso. prof. medicine Johns Hopkins, 1953-; clin. prof. medicine Georgetown U., 1959-; clin. dir., chief arthritis and rheumatism br. Nat. Inst. Arthritis and Metabolic Diseases, Nat. Insts. Health, USPHS, 1953-; attending physician Walter Reed Army Hosp., 1955-. Sci. adv. com., bd. dirs. Arthritis and Rheumatism Found.; mem. expert adv.-panel on chronic degenerative diseases WHO, 1963-. Recipient Heberden medal for research rheumatic diseases, 1960, Presidential citation N.Y.U., 1965. Diplomate Am. Bd. Internal Medicine. Fellow A.C.P.; mem. Assn. Am. Physicians, N.Y. Acad. Medicine, N.Y., Washington acads. sci., Harvey Soc., A.M.A., Am. Rheumatism Assn. (pres. 1959), Nat. Rheumatism Soc. Argentina, Can., Mexico, NRC, Sigma Xi, Alpha Omega Alpha. Founder, editor Bull. on Rheumatic Diseases. Editorial bd. Jour. Chronic Diseases, Jour. Arthritis and Rheumatism. Contbr. sci. articles med. publs. Home: 7506 Maple Av., Chevy Chase, Md. Office: Nat. Inst. of Health. Bethesda, Md. Died July 8, 1964; buried Montefiore Cemetery, St. Albins, N.Y.

BUNKER, CHARLES WAITE ORVILLE naval officer; b. Viroqua, Ia., Feb. 23, 1882; s. Charles Fremont and Isola B. (Bassore) B.; B.sc., U. Neb., 1901; M.D., Cornell U., 1950; m. Eleanor G. Caldwell, Nov. 12, 1910; children—Garrett, Eleanor L. Asst. Cornell U. Med. Coll., 1901-05; intern Bellevue Hosp., N.Y.C., 1905-07; commd. lt. (j.g.) USN, 1907, advanced through grades to rear adm., 1938; med. officer, 1907-44; retired with rank of rear adm. M.C., 1944. Fellow A.C.S.; mem. A.M.A., Omega Upsilon Phi. Clubs: Garden City (L.I.) Golf, New York Yacht, University (N.Y.C.); Burning Tree (gov.), Army-Navy, Army and Navy Country (Washington). Home: 5312 Moorland Lane, Bethesda 14, Md. Died Sept. 1958.

BUNKLEY, JOEL WILLIAM naval officer, (ret.); b. Macon, Ga., July 3, 1887; s. Thomas Pitt and Anne Martha (Brown) B.; B.S., U.S. Naval Acad., 1909; Navy Post Grad. Sch., 1912-14; grad. Naval War Coll., 1933; m. Sally Shelby Williams, Oct. 6, 1915 (dec. May 19, 1945); children-Joel William, Allison Williams; m. 2d, Jeanne Barbaresi Frese, June 6, 1951. Commd. ensign USN, 1909, and advanced through grades; ret. as rear adm., 1942; served on U.S.S. Conn., 1909-12, U.S.S. Wyo., 1914-15, on Pres.'s Yachts Mayflower and Sylph, 1915-17; exec. officer Naval Ry. Battery at the front in France, World War I, 1917-18; on staff of comdr., Destroyer Forces, 1919-20; staff of comdr. in chief Asiatic Fleet, 1923-24; exec. officer U.S.S. Marblehead, 1933-34; naval mission to the Argentine, 1934-37; comd. Destroyer Squadron 10, 1938-39; commanded U.S.S. Cal., 1940-42 (at Pearl Harbor Dec. 7, 1941); supr. of N.Y. Harbor. Decorated Navy Cross, Legion of Merit, Victory Medal with three bronze stars, Am. Def. Medal with bronze star, Asiatic Pacific Campaign Medal with bronze star, Expert Rifleman Medal, Distinguished Marksman Medal, Ma. Area Campaign Medal, W.W.II Victory Medal (U.S.); Legion Honor (France); Order of the Avis (Portugal). Mem. Inst. of the Aeronautical Scis.; mem. bd. trustees World Wide Broadcasting Found. Presbyn. Clubs: N.Y. Yacht: Ends of the Earth, University, Leash (N.Y.). Author: Military and Naval Recognition Book, 1917, 18, 41, 42, 43; articles Ency. Americana. Home: 846 Palmer Rd., Bronxville, N.Y. Died Dec. 10, 1967.

BUNN, HENRY GASTON chief justice Ark., 1893-1904; b. Nash Co., N.C., June 12, 1838; m. Louisa E. Holmes, Sept. 6, 1865; m. 2d, Arralee Connolly, June 3, 1869. Was student Davidson Coll., N.C., but before graduating joined C.S.A.; served 1861-65; 3d lt., adj., lt. col. and col. under Gens. Ben McCulloch, Van Dorn in Ark. and Mo., and Beauregard, Bragg, E. Kirby Smith and J. E. Johnston; after war practiced law in Camden, Ark.; State senator from Ouachita and Nevada counties, 1873-74; mem. Constl. Conv., 1874. Home: Eldorado, Ark. Died 1908.

BUNN, WILLIAM HALL physician; b. Salineville, O., Dec. 24, 1889; s. William Eliphalet and Alice Ophelia (Hall) B.; student U. Wooster, 1911-12; M.D., Jefferson Med. Coll., 1915; m. Helen L. Rownd, Jan. 17, 1925; children-Nancy, William Hall, Robert. Postgrad. study Sir James MacKenzie, St. Andrews, Scotland, 1921; intern Presbyn. Hosp., Phila., 1915-16; student Nat. Heart Hosp., London, 1924; inst. cardiology Youngstown Hosp. Nurses Tng. Sch., 1924-47; chief cardiac clinic Youngstown Hosps., 1924-56; chief med. services Youngstown Hosp. Assn., 1935-55; lectr. biology Youngstown U. Cons. in cardiology area VA, 1946; cons. FSA Pub. Health Service, 1951, Surgeon Gen. U.S. Army. Bd. govs., exec. com. Youngstown U.; trustee Youngstown YMCA. Chmn. Ohio Nat. Found. Scholarship Com., 1959-60. Served as capt. U.S. Army, 1917-19. Decorated Medaille D'Honneur des Epidemie (France). Diplomate Am. Bd. Internal Medicine, Cardiovascular Disease. Fellow A.C.P. mem. hosp. standards survey group 1956-57; mem. A.M.A., Am. Heart Assn. (dir. 1947-56, v.p. 1954-56), Central Soc. Clin. Research (pres. 1937), Youngstown Area Heart Assn. (past pres.), Mahoning Med. Assn. (pres. 1945), Alpha Omega Alpha. Clubs: Youngstown Country, Youngstown; Union (Cleve). Contbr. articles med. jours. Home: 410 Tod Lane. Office: 275 W. Federal St., Youngstown, O. Died Aug. 15, 1961; buried Youngstown, O.

BURBA, EDWIN HESS, army officer; b. Crowder, Okla., Feb. 18, 1912; s. Joseph L. and Estella B. (Hess) B.; B.S. in Bus. Adminstrn., U. Okla., 1933; grad. Army War Coll., 1954; m. Margaret Elizabeth Monk, Jan. 1, 1934; children—Lallie C. (Mrs. John A. Sheard), Edwin Hess, Margaret E. (Mrs. Clarence T. Babbitt), Alonzo R., Joseph C. Commd. 2d lt. F.A. Res., 1933; sec.-treas. Burba Auto Supply Co., McAlester, Okla., 1933-34; commd. 2d lt. U.S. Army Res., 1935, transferred to Regular Army, 1946, advanced through grades to maj. gen., 1963; co. comdr., dist. staff officer Civilian Conservation Corps, 1935-40; battery and battalion comdr., arty. 1st Armored Div., 1940-43; operations officer, comdr. Combat Command B, 8th Armored Div., 1944-45; various troop staff assignments, 1945-50; mil. asst. to undersec. army, 1950-52; chief staff 3d Inf. Div., Korea, 1953; exec. officer Office Asst. Sec. Army, 1955-58; combat command comdr. 4th Armored Div. and 7th Army Tng. Center in Germany, 1958-60; dep. operations officer Joint Chiefs Staff, 1960-62; comdg. gen. 2d Armored Div., 1963-64; chief joint MAAG, Korea, 1965-66; project mgr. US/FRG Main Battle Tank-70, 1966-68; deputy CG 1st Army, 1968-70. Decorated Silver Star, Legion of Merit with 2 oak leaf clusters, Bronze Star with oak leaf cluster, Purple Heart, Combat Inf. badge, Army Commendation ribbon; Cezch War Cross of 1939; Croix de Guerre with palm (France and Belgium), Mem. Alpha Tau Omega. Democrat. Presbyn. Mason. Home: Ft. Geo. G. Meade MD Died Oct. 1970; buried Arlington Nat. Cemetery, Washington DC

BURBANK, JAMES BRATTLE brig. gen. U.S.A.; b. Hartford, Conn., Sept. 11, 1838; s. David and Julia (Brattle) B.; ed. Hartford Pub. High Sch.; grad. Arty. Sch., U.S.A., Ft. Monroe, Va.; m. Alice Goodrich White, July 17, 1876. Was asst. q.m. gen., State of Conn., 1861; adj. 20th Conn. Inf., 1862; joined 3d U.S. Arty., May 1864; 2d lt. 3d U.S. Arty., Mar. 12, 1865; 1st lt., July 28, 1866; prof. mil. science, Cornell U., 1877-83; capt., Nov. 3, 1882; maj. 5th U.S. Arty., May 8, 1898; lt. col., Feb. 2, 1901; col., Apr. 1, 1902; retired Sept. 11, 1902, advanced to rank of brig. gen.; retired by act. of Apr. 23, 1904. Bvtd. 1st lt., Mar. 13, 1865; bvtd. maj. for gallant conduct at battle of Gettysburg. Home: New York, N.Y. Died Dec. 30, 1928.

BURBRIDGE, STEPHEN GANO army officer; b. Scott County, Ky., Aug, 1831; s. Capt. Robert and Eliza Ann (Barnes) B.; attended Georgetown (Ky.) Coll., Ky. Mil. Inst.; m. Lizzie Goff, 1, dau., Sara R. Studied law; farmed in Logan County, Ky.; commd. col. 26th Ky. Inf. in U.S. Army, 1861; served with Army of Ohio at battle of Shiloh; promoted brig. gen. U.S. Volunteers, 1862; active at Vicksburg campaign; given temporary command of Dist. of Ky., 1864, successful in his mil. operation, his civilian responsibilities; but antagonized moderate Union faction with his civilian policies; accused of using extra legal methods in Ky. in order to assure Lincoln's reelection, 1864; suppressed Ky. Home Guards, disbanded state troops raised to resist guerillas; called for his brutal suppression of guerrilla . forces; relieved of command, 1865; his methods earned such general hatred from populace that he did not feel safe to live in Ky. Died Bklyn., Dec. 2, 1894.

BURCH, CHARLES BELL ins. exec.; b. Auburn, Me., Mar. 8, 1891; s. William Mark and Lizzie (Decker) B.; B.S. in Civil Engring., Norwich U., 1913; grad. student U. Mich., 1921; m. Jane M. Bell, June 1, 1916 (dec.); children—William Mark, Donald C., Walter T. Engr. City of Greenfield, Mass., 1913, U.S. Engrs. Ohio River, 1914-15, H. Koppers Co., Pitts., 1916-17, Pitman-Brown Co., Salem, Mass., 1917; with Mich Mutual Liability Co., Detroit, 1921—; v.p., 1956—. Served as capt. constrn. div. U.S. Army, 1918-20. Mem. Sigma Nu. Clubs: Detroit Athletic, Detroit Yacht. Home: 35 Sylvan Av., Pleasent Ridge, Mich. Office: 26 W. Adams Av., Detroit 26. Died Sept. 20, 1959; buried Roseland Park Cemetery, Detroit.

BURD, GEORGE ELI naval officer; b. Belfast, Me., Apr. 27, 1857; s. Samuel F. and Rebecca (Brown) B.; grad. U.S. Naval Acad., 1878; m. Frances A. Goodwin, Aug. 3, 1882. Promoted asst. engr., 1880; passed asst. engr., 1889; chief engr., 1898; trans. to line as lt., 1899; lt. comdr., 1901; comdr., 1906; capt., 1910; rear adm., 1916. Served as chief engr. U.S.S. Badger, West India Campaign, Spanish-Am. War, 1898; engr. officer at sea, and navy yards, San Francisco, Bremerton, Boston, Phila. and New York; in charge industrial activities, construction and engr. work at Navy Yard, New York 1914 - ; in charge, 1917, of all alternation, reconstruction, engring. and repair work on 723 vessels assigned to 3d Naval Dist., including all troop transports based on New York (these latter vessels carrying over 40 per cent of U.S. Army forces sent to Europe). Home: Brooklyn, N.Y. Died Feb. 18, 1924.

BURDETT, SAMUEL SWINFIN lawyer; b. Leicestershire, Eng., Feb. 21, 1836; s. Rev. Cheney and Elizabeth (Swinfin) B.; student Oberlin Coll., 1853-56; studied law under Hon. Edward Graham, DeWitt, Ia.; m. Nancy Eliza Graham, 1864. Admitted to Ia. Bar, 1859; apptd. supt. schs., Clinton, Co., Ia., 1860; lt. and capt. Co. B, 1st la. Cav., 1861-63; Lincoln presdl. elector, 2d Ia. Dist., 1864; circuit atty., Mo., 1866-67; mem. 41st and 42d Congresses (1869-73), 6th Mo. Dist.; commr. Gen. Land Office, 1874-75; in practice at Washington, 1875 - . Comdr.-in-chief G.A.R., 1885-86. Home: Glencarlyn, Va. Died Sept. 24, 1914.

BURDETT, WILLIAM CARTER foreign service officer; b. Nashville, Tenn., Feb. 3, 1884; s. William Potter and Serafina (Carter) B.; educated at University of Tennessee; m. Elizabeth Hardwick Burke, Jan. 18, 1918; children—William Carter, Edward Burke, Agnes Elizabeth, Mary Elizabeth. Mining engineer and mine operator, South America, 1903-06; Greenville, Tennessee, 1906-17; U.S. Consul, Ensenada, Mexico, 1919-22; Seville, Spain, 1922-25, Brussels, Belgium, 1925-30; consul. gen., Lima, Peru, 1930-32; sec. of Embassy, Lima, 1932; sec. of Legation, Panama, 1933-35; consul gen. Buenos Aires, Argentina, 1935-37; consul gen. Rio de Janeiro, Brazil, 1937-39; counselor of Embassy, Rio de Janeiro, 1939-41; dir. Foreign Service Officers Training Sch., 1941-42; mem. Foreign Service Sch. Bd. since 1941. Served in U.S. Army, Philippine Insurrection, 1900-03; capt. inf., U.S. Army, World War; wounded at battle of Blanc Mount; maj. O.R.C. Awarded D.S.C. (U.S.); Croix de Guerre (France); Purple Heart (U.S.). Mem. S.A.R. Office: (U.S.) care Hermitage Cement Co., Knoxville, Tenn. Address: State Dept., Washington, D.C. Died Jan. 14, 1944

BURDICK, EUGENE L. author, educator; b. Sheldon, Ia., Dec. 12, 1918; s. Jack D. and Marie (Ellerbrook) B.; A.B., Stanford, 1942; Ph.D., Oxford (Eng.) U., 1950; m. Carol Warran, July 3, 1943; children-Katherine, Maggie, Michael. Asso. prof. polit. theory and behavior U. Cal. at Berkeley. Pres. Thomas Dooley Found., 1961-; chmn. Alameda (Cal.) Heart Assn., 1960-; cons. Fund for Republic, 1957-. Bd. dirs. Hope Ship project. Served to comdr. USNR, 1942-46, 50-52. Decorated Navy and Marine Corps medal; recipient 2d prize O'Henry Best Short Story Anthology, 1947; Houghton Mifflin Lit. fellow, 1947. Mem. Rhodes Scholar Assn., Am. Polit. Sci. Assn. Author: The Ninth Wave, 1946; The Blue of Capricorn, 1961; The 480, 1964; Nina's Book, 1965; also numerous articles and stories. Co-author: The Ugly American, 1958; American Voting Behavior, 1959; Fail Safe, 1962. Address: 791 Santa Barbara Rd., Berkeley 7, Died July 26, 1965.

BURGES, DEMPSEY congressman; b. Shiloh, Camden County, N.C., 1751. Mem. provincial Congress, 1775-76; served as maj. Pasquotank Minutemen, later as lt. col. Gregory's Continental Regt. during Revolutionary War; mem. U.S. Ho. of Reps. from N.C., 4th-5th congresses, 1795-99. Died Camden County, Jan. 13, 1800; buried Shiloh Baptist Churchyard.

BURGES, RICHARD FENNER lawyer; b. Seguin, Tex., Jan. 7, 1873; s. William H. and Bettie (Rust) B.; ed. in pub. schs.; m. Ethel Petrie Shelton, Dec. 7, 1898

(died 1912); 1 dau., Jane Rust (Mrs. Preston R. Perrenot). Admitted to Tex. bar, 1894; city atty., El Paso, 1905-07; mem. Tex. Ho. of Rep., 2 terms, 1913, 17; asso. counsel for U.S. in Chamizal Arbitration with Mexico, 1910-11; pres. Internat. Irrigation Congress, 1915-16; counsel for Tex. interests in negotiations between Tex. and New Mexico on division of waters of Pecos River, 1923; special counsel for Tex., Rio Grande Compact Commn., Colo., N.M. and Tex., apptd. commr. for Tex. on same commn. to execute 1929 compact; gen. counsel, El Paso County Water Improvement Dist.; special atty. Dept. of Justice in regard rectification of channel of the Rio Grande, 1935-40. Served as capt. and major 141st Inf., U.S. Army, during active operations in France, World War. Cited by Marshal Petain; awarded Croix de Guerre with gilt star (French). Mem. Am. Bar Assn., Tex. Bar Assn., Am Forestry Assn., Tex. Forestry Assn. (pres. 1921-23). Tex. Hist. and Library, Commn., Tex. Hist. Assn., Va. Hist. Soc. Democrat. Author of El Paso Commission Charter, and of Texas Irrigation Code, and Forestry Act. Partially explored and published first account of Carlsbad (N.M.) Cavern which has since been made a nat. park. Special counsel for Tex. in case of Tex. vs. N.M. in U.S. Supreme Court. Home: 603 W. Yandell Blvd. Office: First Nat. Bank Bldg., El Paso, Tex. Died Jan. 13, 1945.

BURGESS, HARRY army officer; b. Starkville, Miss., Feb. 22, 1872; s. James and Susan Elizabeth (Foster) B.; student Miss. Agrl. and Mech. Coll., 1888-91; grad. U.S. Mil. Acad., 1895; grad. study U.S. Engr. Sch. of Application, 1896-98; m. Mary Lillington McKoy, Feb. 27, 1912. Commd. adj. 2d lt., June 12, 1895, and advanced through grades to col., Corps of Engrs., July 1, 1920. Instr. in engring., U.S. Mil. Acad., 1898-1900; in charge surveys and design, Muscle Shoals power development; mem. Miss. River Commn., 1920-22; engr. of maintenance, Panama Canal, 1924-28, gov. of canal, Oct. 16, 1928 - ; pres. Panama R.R. Co. Served in France, comdr. 16th and 30th Engrs., A.E.F., 1917-19. Home: Balboa Heights, C.Z. Died Mar. 18, 1933.

BURGESS, ROBERT WILBUR, statistician; b. Newport, R.I., July 25, 1887; s. Isaac Bronson and Ellen (Wilbur) B.; grad. Morgan Pk. Acad., 1905; A.B., Brown U., 1908, hon. Sc.D., 1948; Rhodes scholar, 1908-11; B.A., Oxford U., 1910; Ph.D., Cornell 1914; m. Dorothy Cross, Jan. 1, 1925; children—Mary Ellen, Dorothy (Mrs. H. M. Baird Voorhis), Margaret (Mrs. Charles W. Cammack, 3d). Instr. mathematics Purdue, 1911-12; asst. mathematics Cornell, 1912-14, instructor, 1914-16; instr. mathematics, Brown University, 1916-17, assistant professor, 1919-25; statistician and economist, Western Electric Co., 1924-52; cons. statistics from 1952; dir. Bur. of Census, Dept. Commerce, 1953-61. Served as first lieutenant, O.R.C., duty at Washington, D.C., Oct. 1917-May 1918; 1st lt., capt., maj. N.A., duty with statistics br. Gen. Staff, Washington, May 1918-Sept. 1919; maj. O.R.C., 1919-29. Fellow Am. Statis. Association (v.p. 1939); member Conference of Business Economists, Population Assn. Am., Am Econ. Assn., Econometric Soc., Brown Engring. Association (pres. 1942), Economic Principles Commission N.A.M. Delta Upsilon, Phi Beta Kappa and Sigma Xi. Baptist. Clubs: Brown University (N.Y.C.); Cosmos (Washington); Huguenot Yacht. Author: Introduction to Mathematics of Statistics; chapter on research for gen. administration in Scientific Management in Am. Industry. Contbr. math. or statis. articles in Am. Jour. Mathematics, Physical Rev., Am. Oxonian, Encyclopedia Britannica, etc. Home: Pelham NY Died May 27, 1969.

BURGEVINE, HENRY ANDREA fgn. mercenary officer, b. probably Chapel Hill, N.C., 1836; s. Gen. Andrea and Julia (Gillette) B. Fought in Crimean War; next heard of in China; became mercenary officer for Fred Townsend Ward who was attempting to capture Sungkiang (China) from Taiping rebels, 1860, left 3d in command of army (about 4000 men) after Ward's death, 1862, soon came to command entire force; enlisted his army on side of imperial rulers (directly subordinated to Gov. Li Hung Chang); dismissed by gov. for uncontrollable, insubordinate and mutinous conduct; formed small army of 100 and eventually joined remains of Ward's old army and was captured; following his release was delivered to U.S. consul at Shanghai; set free upon his parole to leave China; returned to Fukien on route to join last of Taiping rebels, captured by imperialist forces. Drowned (while being conveyed with other prisoners in small boat which capsized), June 26, 1865.

BURGIN, HENRY T. army officer; b. North Middletown, Ky., Oct. 9, 1882; s. Perry and Sithey Hedges (Gaitskill) B.; grad. U.S. Mil. Acad., 1905; distinguished grad. Coast Arty. Sch., Ft. Monroe, Va., 1908; honor grad. Sch. of the Line, Command and Gen. Staff Sch., 1921; grad. staff class, Command and Gen. Staff, 1922; grad. Army War Coll., 1923; m. Winona Elizabeth Derby, Nov. 7, 1911. Commd. 2d lt. Arty. Corps, U.S. Army, 1905, and advanced through the grades to maj. gen. Oct. 1904 and served as major and lt. colonel, div. ordnance officer, 41st Div., with A.E.F. in France, Dec. 1917-Mar. 1918, and then acting chief of staff of Am. troops on Italian Front; has served at harbor defenses of Puget Sound, San Francisco and San Diego and field arty. at Ft. Sam Houston and duty at Ft. Monroe; foreign service at harbor defenses of Manila and Subic Bays, P.I., and on Gen. Staff, Hawaiian Div.; 3 tours of duty at Washington, D.C. including acting chief of C.A.; comdg. 9th C.A. Dist. June 1937-Aug. 1941; promoted maj. gen., Oct. 1, 1940; in command seacoast and anti-aircraft artillery troops, Hawaiian Dept. August 1941 to June 1944; command Central Pacific Base Command, July 1944-Oct. 1945; retired as major gen., Aug. 1946. Decorated Legion of Merit, Distinguished Service Medal; Fatigue de guerre, Chevalier de St. Maurice et Lazarus (Italy); Victory Medal, Purple Heart, Am. Defense Service Medal, Asiatic Pacific Campaign Medal (U.S.). Home: 537 Hassayampa Dr. Address: 537 N. Hassayampa Dr., Prescott, Ariz. Died July 31, 1958; buried U.S. Mil. Acad., West Point, N.Y.

BURKE, AEDANUS congressman, jurist; b. Galway, Ireland, June 16, 1743; studied theology St. Omer, France; studied law, Stafford County, Va., 1769; never married. Visited West Indies; came to Am., settled in S.C.; resigned commn. as lt. 2d S.C. Continental Regt., 1778; judge S.C. Supreme Ct., 1778-80, 85-1802; served as capt. Continental Army, 1780-82; mem. S.C. Ho. of Reps., 1781, 82, 84-89, favored leniency toward Loyalists; a commr. to prepare digest of S.C. laws, 1785; mem. S.C. Conv. to ratify U.S. Constn., 1788, opposed ratification unless amendment added restricting Pres. to 1 term; mem. U.S. Ho. of Reps. from S.C., 1st tax, favored U.S. assumption of state debts and slavery; chancellor S.C. Ct. of Equity, 1799-1802. Author: (pamphlets including) An Address to the Freemen of South Carolina, 1783; Considerations on the Order of Cincinnati translated into French, German), 1783. Died Charleston, S.C., Mar. 30, 1802; buried "Burnt Church," nr. Jacksonboro. S.C.

BURKE, DANIEL WEBSTER brig. gen. U.S.A.; b. in Conn., Apr. 22, 1841. Served pvt., corporal and 1st sergt. cos. E and B, 2d Inf., June 10, 1858-Nov. 8, 1862; advanced through grades to brig. gen., Oct. 20, 1899; retired at own request after 40 yrs.' service, Oct. 21, 1899. Bvtd.; capt., July 2, 1863, and maj., Jan. 22, 1867, "for gallant and meritorious services in battle of Gettysburg, Pa.;" lt. col. for same during the war; awarded Congl. Medal of Honor, Apr. 21, 1892, "for distinguished gallantry in action at Shepherdstownford, W.Va. Home: Portland, Ore. Died 1911.

BURKHARDT, SAMUEL, JR. army officer; b. Palos, Cook Co., Ill., Sept. 10, 1865; s. Samuel and Margaret Burkhardt; grad. U.S. Military Acad., 1889. Commd. 2d lt. 25th Inf., June 12, 1889; 1st lt. 10th Inf., Jan. 1, 1897; capt., 19th Inf., Sept. 16, 1899; maj., Mar. 11, 1911; lt. col., July 1, 1916; col., July 29, 1917. Participated in Sioux Indian campaign, 1890-91, Santiago campaign, 1898; at Havana and Matanzas, Cuba, Dec. 1898-Nov. 1899; duty Philippines, 1900-02, 1905-07, 1910-12; at Vera Cruz, Mex., Apr.-Nov. 1914. Died Dec. 29, 1929.

BURLESON, EDWARD army officer, legislator; b. Buncombe County, N.C., Dec. 15, 1798; s. James and Elizabeth (Shipman) B.; m. Sarah Owen, 1815. Commd. capt. Mo. Militia, 1816, later col.; commd. col. Tenn. Militia, 1823; moved to Tex., 1831, settled on Colorado River at extreme edge of what was then the frontier; local leader against Indian raids; commd. lt. col. Tex. Army, 1832; participated in Tex. Revolution against Mexico, commanded Tex. Army besieging Mexican Gen. Cos, San Antonio, 1835, participated in Battle of San Jacinto; mem. 1st Senate of Republic of Tex., 1836; commd. col. Tex. Army, 1838, served in Cherokee War, 1839, Comanche War, 1840; v.p. Republic of Tex., 1841, defeated for presidency, 1844; mem. Tex. State Senate, 1849-51. Died Austin, Tex., Dec. 26, 1851.

BURLINGAME, C. CHARLES psychiatrist, univ. prof.; b. Rockford, Ill., Oct. 27, 1885; s. Charles Henry Camlin and Ella S. F. (Dagwell) B.; ed. in public schs., Rockford, Ill., and private tutors; M.D., Ill. Gen. Med. Coll., Chicago, 1908; m. Ruth Beardsley Parsons, Dec. 31, 1912. Asst. phys. Westboro (Mass.) State Hosp., 1908-12; med. dir., asst. supt. and actg. supt. Fergus Falls (Minn.) State Hosp., 1912-15; industrial psychiatrist, Cheney Bros., Manchester, Conn., 1915-17 and 1919-21; exec. officer joint adminstrv. bd. Columbia U.-Presbyn. Hosp. Med. Center, N.Y. City, 1921-28; exec. v.p. Presbyn. Hosp., N.Y. City, 1923-25; in private psychiatric practice, N.Y. City, 1925-31; hosp. cons. govt. of Uruguay and other S. Am. and European countries since 1925; psychiatrist in chief Inst. of Living, 1931-50; asso. in psychiatry Columbia since 1932; cons. in psychiatry U.S. Vets. Hosp., Newington, Conn., since 1931, Neurol Inst., N.Y. City, 1932-39 (now mem. courtesy staff); attending psychiatrist Vanderbilt Clinic, N.Y. City, 1932-34; attending neuro-psychiatrist Vet. Home & Hosp. Commn., Conn.; cons. in psychiatry St. Francis Hosp., Hartord, Conn., since 1933; cons. in psychiatry Charlotte Hungerford Hosp., Torrington, Conn., since 1934; clin. prof. psychiatry and mental hygiene, Yale, 1936-38; cons. Hosp. St. Raphael, New Haven, since 1943; cons. psychiatry Hartford Hosp., 1945; Cons. psychiatry and neurology, Meriden Hosp.; sr. psychiatry U.S. Vets Hosp., Northampton; cons. psychiatry to sec. war (Insp. Gen. Office, Gen. Staff, U.S. Army), 1944-45. Chmn. Adv. Bd. in Am. of The Am. Hosp. in Paris. Served as 1st lt., capt., maj. and lt. col., in U.S. Army Med. Corps, A.E.F.; dir. Med. and Surg. Sec. Dept. Mil. Affairs, Bureau Hosp. Adminstrn., Med. and Surg. Dept. Am. Red Cross in France. Diplomate Am. Bd. Psychiatry and Neurology. Mem. Am. Coll. Physicians, Am. Psychiatric Assn. (former v.p. bd. dirs. Research Council on Problems of Alcohol, Mem. sci. bd., mem. com. pub. edn.), N.Y. Acad. Medicine (chmn. Salmon com. for psychiatry and mental hygiene, mem. sect. neurology and psychiatry), Am. Soc. of Research Psychosomatic Problems (former chmn. com. indsl. medicine), Am. Psychiatric Found. (chmn. sci. com; dir.), Southern Psychiatric Assn., A.M.A., Am. Med. Editors and Authors Assn., Study Internal Secretions, N.Y. Psychiatric Assn., N.Y. Neruol Soc., N.Y. Soc. Clin Psychiatry, N.E. Soc. Psychiatry, Conn. Soc. Psychiatry, N.Y. State Med. Soc., N.Y. Co. Med. Soc., Conn. Soc. Mental Hygiene (v.p. 1938-40), Hartford County Medical Society, Hartford Med. Soc. (pres. 1947), Conn. State Med. Soc. (pres. elect 1950-51, adv. com. Vets. Adminstrn., com. National legislation, trustee bldg. fund, chairman com. pub. relations), Central Neuro-Psychiatric Hosp. Assn., Pan-Am. Med. Assn., Nat. Conf. Bd. Psys. and Surgs., State Bd., Edn., Sociedad Cubana de Neurologia and Psiquiatria, Am. Soc. French Legion of Honor, Am. Legion, Council Fgn. Relations, Psi Upsilon Pho. Awarded Gold Medal of Honor, Officer Legion of Honor (France), Order University of Palms (French Academy), Officer Order St. George and Notre Dame de Mont Carmel (France), National Eagle (Poland), Revolution Medal (Czechoslovakia), Citation for conspicuous and meritorious service with A.E.F. (U.S.), Mem. Commn. to Study Conn. Laws and Facilities pertaining to the Prevention, Treatment and Care of Mental Diseases and defects and Allied Problems. Commn. to Survey the Human Resources of Conn. Chmn. Com. for Formulating Standards for School Psychologists, Conn. State Bd. of Edn. Clubs: Union, Yale, Columbia University, Columbia University Faculty, Vidonian (New York); Sleepy Hollow Country (Scarborough-on-Hudson); Hartford, Hartford Golf, Twentiety Century (Hartford); Bohemian (San Francisco); 100,000 Mile; Grad. (Yale). Editor; Digest of Neurology and Psychiatry; asso. editor; Am. Jour. Psychiatry. Home: 11 Fernwood Rd., West Hartford, Conn.; and 610 Park Av., N.Y., N.Y. Office: 610 Park Av., New York 21, N.Y.; and 459 Marlborough St., Boston. Died July 22, 1950; buried Fairview Cemetery, West Hartford, Conn.

BURNETT, CHARLES army officer; b. Knoxville, Tenn., Oct. 28, 1877; s. Jackson G. and Nancy (Smith) B.; student Blackburn Coll., Ill., 1894-95; B.S., U.S. Mil. Acad., 1901; m. Frances Hawks Cameron, Mar. 15, 1905. Commd. 2d lt. U.S. Army, 1901, and advanced through grades to brig. gen., 1937; chief Bur. Insular Affairs, War Dept., Washington, D.C. 1937 - . Awarded D.S.M., Victory, and Philippine, Spanish-Am., Mexican Campaign medals (all U.S.); decorated by Japanese, French, Italian, Mexican, Swedish and Ecuador gvts. Episcopalian. Died Nov. 28, 1939.

BURNETT, CHARLES HOYT, physician, educator; b. Boulder, Colo., Mar. 7, 1913; s. Clough Turrill and Lucille (Hoyt) B.; A.B., U. Colo., 1934, M.D., 1937; M. Eda Waugh, Apr. 27, 1940; children—Grosvenor Turrill, Mark Hoyt, Margaret Jamie. Asst. resident pathology, asst. pathology Presbyn. hosp., N.Y.C., Columbia U. Coll. Phys. and Surg., 1937-38; intern Harvard med. service Boston City Hosp., 1939-40; asst. resident medicine Mass. Gen. Hosp., Boston, 1940-42, chief resident medicine, 1945-46; asst. medicine, med. sch. Harvard, 1940-42, 45-46; asst. prof. medicine Boston U. Sch. Medicine, 1947-50, asso. prof., 1950; asst. mem. Robert Dawson Evans Meml. Hosp., 1947-50, asso. mem., 1950; prof. medicine, chmn. dept. Southwestern Med. Sch., U. Tex., Dallas, 1950-51; prof. medicine University N.C., Chapel Hill, 1951-67, head dept. medicine, 1951-65; consultant Surgeon Gen.'s Office, 1946-56, 63-67; chief med. service N.C. Memorial Hospital, 1952-65; chief cons. for research Richardson Merrell, Inc., 1965-67. Mem. Nat. Board Medical Examiners medicine test committee, 1955-56, chmn. 1956. Member of sub-com. on shock Nat. Research Council, 1951-54; sci. adv. bd. Armed Forces Inst. Pathology, 1952-56; mem. adv. com. for biology and medicine AEC, 1953-58; council Nat. Inst. for Arthritis and Metabolic Diseases, 1958-62. Served as maj. M.C., AUS, 1942-46. Decorated Bronze Star Medal Fellow A.C.P.: mem. Soc. for Clin. Investigation (emeritus), Assn. Am. Physicians. A.A.A.S., Endocrine Soc., A.M.A., Am. Acad. Arts and Scis., So. Soc. Clin. Research, Assn. Am. Profs. Medicine (v.p. 1963), Alpha Omega Alpha. Author sci. articles. Home: Chapel Hill NC Died Oct. 23, 1967.

BURNETT, HENRY LAWRENCE lawyer; b. Youngstown, O., Dec. 26, 1838; attended Chester Acad.; LL.B., Ohio State Nat. Law Sch., 1859; admitted to bar; married. Capt. 2d Ohio Cav., Aug. 23, 1861; maj. judge adj. vols., Aug. 10, 1863; bvtd. col. vosl., Mar. 8, 1865, vols., "for diligent and efficient services," and brig. gen. vols., Mar. 13, 1865, "for meritorious services" in Bur. of Justice; hon. mustered out, Dec. 1, 1865; with General Holt and John A. Bingham was engaged in prosecution of the assassins of Lincoln. In practice, Cincinnati, 1865-72, New York, 1872 - ; U.S. dist., atty., Southern Dist. of N.Y. Republican. Home: New York, N.Y. Died Jan. 4, 1916.

BURNHAM, FREDERICK RUSSELL explorer; b. Tivoli, Minn., May 11, 1861; s. Rev. Edwin O. and Rebecca (Russell) B.; family removed to Los Angeles, 1870; ed. Clinton High Sch.; was cowboy, scout, guide, miner, dep. sheriff, etc. in West; m. Blanche Blick, 1884 (died Dec. 22, 1939); m. 2d, Ilo K. Willits, Oct. 28, 1943. Went to Africa, 1893; scout in Matabele War in Rhodesia, and for services there the govt. presented him with the campaign medal, and jointly with his two companions was given 300 square miles of land in Rhodesia in recognition of exceptional service. Discovered in the granite ruins of an ancient civilication of Rhodesia a buried treasure of gold and gold ornaments dating before Christian era; led expdn. to explore Barotzeland preparatory to the bldg. of the Cape to Cairo Ry.; took active part in 2d Matabele War on staff of Sir Frederick Carrington; was commd. to capture or kill the Matabele God M'Limo and succeeded in entering his cave in the Matopa Mts. and killing him; operated gold mines in Klondike and Alaska, 1898-1900; was sent for by Lord Roberts, Jan. 1900 to go to S. Africa for service in the Boer War, and was made chief of scouts of the British Army in the field; wounded, June 2, 1901, while on scouting duty (destroying the enemy's ry. base) and invalided home; for services there was commd. maj. in British Army, presented with large sum of money and received personal letter of thanks from Lord Roberts; on arrival in England was comd. to dine with Queen Victoria, spending the night at Osborne House, and was created mem. Distinguished Service Order by Kind Edward, who also presented him with S. African medal with 5 bars and the cross of the D.S.O.; made surveys of the Volta River, W. Africa, 1902, exploring parts of French Nigeria Hinterland of Gold Coast Colony, and took active part in native troubles of that time; comd. an exploration of magnitude from Lake Rudolph to German E. Africa, covering a vast region along Congo basin and head of the Nile, 1903-04; discovered a lake of 49 sq. miles composed almost entirely of pure carbonate of soda of unknown depth; made archaeol. discovery of Maya civilization extending into the Yaqui country, as shown by stone carvings and writings, 1908. Engaged with John Hays Hammond in diverting the Yaqui River through a system of canals into the delta containing 700 sq. miles of land. Vice pres. Dominguez Oilfields Co. Mem. Calif. State Park Commn.; mem. Save the Redwoods League; mem. Exec. council, Boy Scouts of Am. Clubs: Boone and Crockett (New York); Sunset (Los Angeles). Author: Scouting on Two Continents; Taking Chances. Home: P.O. Box 518 Santa Barbara, Calif. Office; Union Oil Bldg. Los Angeles, Calif. Died Sept. 1, 1947; buried at Three Rivers, Tulare County, Calif.

BURNHAM, WALTER HENRY, advt., pub. relations exec.; b. Providence, Aug. 31, 1886; s. Walter Willcutt and Grace Edith (Warner) B.; A.B., Brown U., 1908; m. Anne H. Edwards, Apr. 21, 1917; children—Margrette Louise (Mrs R. Manning Brown, Jr.), Anne Warner (Mrs. William B. Moore), Phoebe Barber (Mrs. E. J. White, Jr.). With Carlisle, Mellick Co., N.Y.C., 1908-11, Richmond Dorrance & Co., Providence, 1911-12; salesman Potter, Choate & Prentice, N.Y.C., 1912-14; dept. Mgr. Crompton Richmond Co., N.Y.C., 1914-17; sec. Doremus & Co., N.Y.C., 1919, v.p., 1932-46, hon. vice chmn., dir. until 1962. Dir., Elizabeth Gen. Hosp., 1925-35, also Social Welfare Soc. Elizabeth. Served as capt., U.S. Army, World War I. Mem. Delta Kappa Epsilon. Clubs: Yacht (Bay Head, N.J.); Tiger Inn (Princeton, N.J.). Home: Bay Head NJ Died June 1, 1968.

BURNHAM, WILLIAM POWER army officer; b. Scranton, Pa., Jan. 10, 1860; s. Maj. David Roe (U.S. Army) and Olive E. (Power) B.; ed. Kan. State Agrl. Coll.; at West Point, 1877-80; grad. U.S. Inf. and Cav. Sch., 1889; m. Grace F. Meacham, Feb. 18, 1890; 1 son, Edward Meacham. Was enlisted man 14th U.S. Inf., 1881-83; promoted from ranks July 1883; served lt. col. 4th Mo. Vols., Spanish-Am. War, and in Philippine Insurrection, 1900-02; maj. U.S. Army, Aug. 20, 1906; mem. gen. staff, 1907-11; lt. col. and comdt. Army Service Sch., Ft. Leavenworth, 1912-14; col. inf., May 1, 1916; comdr. Puerto Rico Regt. of Inf. and Dist. of P.R., 1914-17; served in Canal Zone, May-July 1917; comd. 56th Inf., July-Aug. 1917; brig. gen. N.A., Aug. 5, 1917; assigned to command 164th Inf. Brigade, 82d Div., Camp Gordon, Atlanta, Ga.; maj. gen., Apr. 12, 1918; comd. 82d Div., Dec. 1917-Oct. 5, 1918; in front line sectors (Toul and Moselle River), June-Sept. 1918, St. Mihiel offensive, Sept. 12-16, and Battle of Meuse-Argonne, Sept. 26-Oct. 5, 1918; mil. attache and Am. del. Inter-Allied Mil. Commn., Athens, Greece, Oct. 20, 1918-June 9, 1919; hon. disch. as temp. maj. gen., July 1919, and reverted to rank of col., regular army; comdr. Ft. McDowell, Angel Island, and Presidio, San Francisco, Aug. 1919-Jan. 1924; brig. gen. Jan. 1, 1924, retired Jan. 10, 1924. Companion of the Bath (English); Croix de Guerre and Officer Legion of Honor (French); Medal of Military Merit, 1st class (Greek). Author: Three Roads to a Commission in the States Army, 1892; Duties of Outposts, Advance Guards, etc., 1893. Died Sept. 27, 1930.

BURNS, DANIEL M. mine operator; b. 1845; parents emigrated overland to Ore., 1847, and from thence to Cal.; served on plains against Indians, 2 yrs., during Civil War; read law but never practiced; engaged in mining operations in Mex. and elsewhere; pres. Mexican Candearia Co., S.A., San Dimas Co. Twice co. clerk, Yolo Co., Cal.; sec. of state of Cal., 1879-83; was mem. police commn. of San Francisco and on staff Gov. Markham with rank of col., 1891-95; candidate for U.S. Senate, 1899. Republican. Address: Call Bldg., San Francisco, Calif.

BURNS, JAMES AUSTIN educator, lawyer; b. Oxford, Me., Jan. 25, 1840; grad. Bowdoin, 1862 (Ph.D., 1885); admitted to bar, New Haven, Conn., 1861; m. 1864, Mary J. Granniss; m. 2d, Mrs. Lucie E. McClurkan. Served through war as lt. and capt., 7th Conn. inf.; later on staff duty; after war settled at Atlanta, Ga.; prof. chemistry, Southern Med. Coll., 1882-92. Has published a series of Juxtalinear Translations of Greek and Latin classics. Engaged in practice of law. Home: Atlanta, Ga. Died 1902.

BURNS, OWEN MCINTOSH judge; b. Danville, Ill., Sept. 6, 1892; s. William Charles and Jennie (McIntosh) B.; A.B., U. Ill, 1916, LL.B., 1921; m. Marion Foster, 1930; children—William, Franklin, Jeanne. In general practice of law in fed. and state cts. of Ill. and Pa., 1921-49; U.S. Atty., May 1947-Oct. 1949; judge U.S. Dist. Ct. for Western Dist. of Pa. since 1949. Served as capt., inf., U.S. Army, World War I. Mem. Alpha Epsilon, Phi Delta Phi. Home: 1815 Plymouth St. Office: U.S. Court House Bldg., Erie, Pa. Died Oct. 16, 1952.

BURNS, ROBERT WHITNEY air force officer; b. Wis., Sept. 15, 1908; grad. Air Corps Primary Flying Sch., 1929, Advanced Flying Sch., pursuit course, 1930; m. Caroline Miller; children-Robert Whitney, Marsha. Commd. 2d lt., Air Corps, U.S. Army, 1930 and advanced through the grades to lit. gen., 1958; comdg. gen., Air Force Air Training Comd., 1948; mem. Air Corps Mil. Mission to Chile, 1940-43; asst. dep. chief of staff, operations Hdqrs. USAF, 1951-52; asst. vice chief of staff USAF, 1953-54; comdr. Air Proving Ground Command, Elgin AFB, Fla., 1955-58; comdr. 5th Air Force and U.S. Forces, Japan, 1958-61; chairman Inter-American Defense Bd., 1961; comdr. Air Tng. Command, Randolph AFB, Tex. Served in World War II, 8th Air Force Eto, Okinawa. Awarded Legion Merit (Oak Leaf Cluster), D.F.C., Air Medal (with Oak-Leaf Cluster), Bronze Star; Commander Order British Empire; Croix de Guerre with palm (Belgium); Croix de Guerre (France); Order of Merit, First Class (Chile); Cross of Grand Comdr. of Royal Order of Phoenix (Greece); Order of Rising Sun 1st class (Japan); D.S.M. with oak leaf cluster, Legion of Merit with two oak leaf clusters. Office: Hdqrs. Air Tng. Command, Randolph AFB, Tex. Died Sept. 5, 1964; buried Arlington Nat. Cemetery, Arlington, Va.

BURPEE, CHARLES WINSLOW writer; b. Rockville, Conn., Nov. 13, 1859; s. Colonel Thomas F. and Adeline M. (Harwood) B.; A.B., Yale, 1883; m. Bertha Stiles, of Bridgeport, Conn., Nov. 5, 1885; 1 son, Stiles. Chairman of Yale News, 1882-83; city editor of the Waterbury (Connecticut) American 1883-91; asso. editor Bridgeport (Conn.) Standard, 1891-95; staff Hartford Courant, 1895-1904, mng. editor, 1900-04; with Phoenix Mutual Life Ins. Co., 1904-35. Lit. editor Hartford Times, 1930-35; council Nat. Citizens' League for Sound Banking, pres. Yale Alumni of Hartford County, sec. Hartford Yale Fund. Capt. in Conn. N.G., retiring in 1897; vol. a.d.c. staff of 1st Conn. Vol. Inf., Spanish-Am. War, col. 1st Regt. Conn. S.G., 1917-21. Mem. S.A.R., Conn. Historical Society, Friends of Hartford. Club: Twilight (Hartford). Contbr. to hist. publs., including History of Connecticut, History of Waterbury (Conn.). Wrote: Military History of Waterbury; History of Hartford County, 1928; A Century in Hartford, 1931; Connecticut in Colonial Wars, 1933. Story of Connecticut, "Constitution State" 1939. Home: 19 Forest St., Harford, Conn.

BURR, AARON senator, vice pres. U.S.; b. Newark. N.J., Feb. 6, 1756; s. Aaron and Esther (Edwards) B.; grad. Coll. N.J. (now Princeton), 1772; m. Mrs. Theodosia Prevost, July 1782, 1 dau., Theodosia; m. 2d, Mrs. Stephen Jumel, 1833; Served in Revolutionary War, 1777-79, commd. lt. col. Continental Army, 1777; served in battles of L.I., Monmouth; admitted to N.Y. bar, 1782; practiced law, N.Y.C., 1783; atty. gen. N.Y. State, 1789-91; mem. U.S. Senate from N.Y., 1791-97; mem. N.Y. State Assembly, 1797; tied with Jefferson for U.S. presidency in election of 1800, Jefferson became Pres. on 36th ballot in U.S. Ho. of Reps., (Burr became vice pres. U.S. (Republican), 1801-05 (this situation produced 12th amendment); mortally wounded Alexander Hamilton, a polit. enemy, in duel, Weehawken, N.J., 1804; formulated conspiracy to seize S.W. Territory from Spanish America in order to set up a new republic; arrested 1807, tried for treason before Chief Justice Marshall of U.S. Circuit Ct. in Va., May 22, 1807, acquitted, Sept. 1, 1807; journeyed abroad, attempted to interest France and Eng. in his schemes, 1807, failed, returned home, 1812, resumed law practice, N.Y.C. Died S.I., N.Y., Sept. 14, 1836; buried Princeton, N.J.

BURR, EDWARD army officer; b. Boonville, Mo., May 19, 1859; s. William E. and Harriett Holly (Brand) B.; student Washington U., 1874-8; grad. U.S. Mil. Acad., 1882; m. Katherine Green, June 24, 1886. Commd. 2d lt. U.S. Engrs., 1882 advanced through grades to lt. col. 1898; hon. mustered out of vol. service, 1899; maj., 1903, lt.-col., 1908, col., 1912, brig. gen. N.A., 1917. Apptd. comdr. 166th F.A. Brig., 91st Div., 1918. Mem. Am. Soc. C.E. Clubs: Army and Navy, Chevy Chase. Address: War Dept., Washington. Died Apr. 15, 1952.

BURR, GEORGE WASHINGTON army officer; b. Tolono, Ill., Dec. 3, 1865; s. George W. and Nancy (Scott) B.; grad. U.S. Mil. Acad., 1888; m. Lydia Kent. Commd. 2d lt. 1st Arty., June 11, 1888; promoted through grades to col., July 1, 1916; brig. gen. (temp.), Aug. 6, 1918; maj. gen. (temp.), Mar. 5, 1919; brig. gen., ordnance dept., July 2, 1920. At Presidio. San Francisco, 1890; duty Ft. Hamilton, N.Y., 1891-93; prof. mil. science and tactics, A. and M. Coll. of Miss., 1893-94; various duties to 1907; in Philippines, 1907-10; chief ordnance officer Philippines Div., mem. Fortification Bd., etc.; comdr. Augusta Arsenal, Ga., 1910-11, Rock Island Arsenal, chief ordnance officer, Central Dept., 1911-18; chief ordnance officer, Am. Forces in Eng., and representing U.S. Ordnance Dept. in Eng., 1918; apptd. chief of engring. div. Ordnance Dept., Oct. 1918; apptd. asst. dir. purchase, storage and traffic, Gen. Staff, Washington, D.C., Nov. 29, 1918; apptd. asst. chief of staff and dir. of purchase, storage and traffic, Gen. Staff, Mar. 1, 1919. Mem. War Dept. Claims Bd., settling Govt. war business, 1919; spl. rep. Sec. of War in Europe settling war business with English and other govts., Sept.-Dec. 1920; asst. to chief of ordnance, Washington, D.C., Jan. 1921 - . Awarded D.S.M.; Companion Order of the Bath (British). Died Mar. 4, 1923.

BURR, NELSON BEARDSLEY ry. official; b. Auburn, N.Y., Feb. 3, 1871; s. Charles Porter and Frances (Powers) B.; B.S., Yale, 1893; LL.B., Harvard, 1895; m. Helen Van Courtland Morris, June 29, 1904. Practiced law at N.Y. City, 1895-1910; v.p. St. L. & S.W. Ry. Co., 1910 - ; dir. Am. Writing Paper Co. Trustee Post-Grad. Hosp., Kingsland Av. Children's Home (N.Y.). First lt. Co. B, 12th N.Y. Inf., Spanish-Am. War; lt. col. and col. 12th N.Y. Inf.; col. 212th Arty. (antiaircraft), World War. Republican. Episcopalian. Home: Oyster Bay, L.I., and New York. Died Feb. 11, 1928.

BURRAGE, GUY HAMILTON naval officer; b. Lowell, Mass., June 14, 1867; s. Hamilton and Mary How (Davis) B.; grad. U.S. Naval Acad., 1887; m. Mary Rickets Graham, Sept. 4, 1894. Commd. ensign USN, 1880, advanced through grades to vice adm., 1942; served in U.S.S. Wheeling during Spanish-Am. War; exec. officer U.S.S. Chattanooga, 1905-07, U.S.S. Connecticut, 1910; comd. U.S.S. Albatross, 1910-12; comdt. midshipman, U.S. Naval Acad., 1912-15; comdt. U.S.S. Nebraska, 1915-19; comdt. Navy Yard, Norfolk, Va., 1919; comdt. naval forces in Europe, 1926-28; comdt. 5th Naval Dist. and Naval Operating Base, Norfolk, Va., 1928-31; retired 1931. Home 719 Yarmouth St., Norfolk, Va. Died June 16, 1954; buried Congressional Cemetery, Washington.

BURRAGE, HENRY SWEETSER clergyman; b. Fitchburg, Mass., Jan. 7, 1837; s. Jonathan and Mary Thurston (Upton) B.; A.M., Brown U., 1861; grad. Newton Theol. Instn., 1867; U. of Halle, Germany, 1868-69; D.D., Brown, 1883; LL.D., U. of Me., 1922; m. Caroline Champlin, May 19, 1873 (died 1875); children - Champlin, Thomas Jayne; m. 2d, Ernestine Mai Giddings, Nov. 8, 1881; children -Margaret Ernestine (dec.), Mildred Giddings, Madeleine. Served in 36th Mass. Vol., 1862-65, as sergt. maj., 2d lt., 1st lt., capt. and bvt. maj.; also acting asst. adj. gen. on staff 1st Brigade, 2d Div., 9th Army Corps. Ordained Bapt. ministry, 1869; pastor Waterville, Me., 1870-73; editor Zion's Advocate, 1873-1905; chaplain Nat. Home for Disabled Vol. Soldiers, 1905-12; state historian of Me., 1907 - . Recording sec. Me. Bapt. Missionary Conv., 1875-1905, Am. Bapt. Missionary Union, 1876-1904; pres. Me. Bapt. Edn. Soc., 1893-98. Trustee Colby Coll., 1881-1905, Newton Theol. Instn., 1889-1906, Brown U., 1889-1901 (bd. fellows). Author: The Act of Baptism in the History of the Christian Church, 1879; History of the Baptists in New England, 1894; Gettysburg and Lincoln, 1906; Early English and French Voyages, 1906; Gorges and the Grant of the Province of Maine, 1622, 1923; Thomas Hamlin Hubbard, Bvt. Brig. Gen. U.S. Vols., 1923. Editor: History of the Thirty-sixth Massachusetts Volunteers, 1884; Rosier's Relation of Waymouth's Voyage to the Coast of Maine, 1605, 1887; etc. Home: Kennebunkport, Me. Died Mar. 19, 1926.

BURRELL, GEORGE ARTHUR chem. engr.; b. Cleve., Jan. 23, 1882; s. Alexander A. and Jane (Penny) B.; student Ohio State U., 1902-04, Chem. E., 1918; Sc.D., Wesleyan U., 1919; m. Mary L. Schafer, 1906; 1 dau., Dorothy May; m. 2d, Naomi L. Schafer, June 16, 1914. Chemist U.S. Geol. Survey, 1904-08; in charge research work, gas mine gas, and natural gas and gasoline investigations, U.S. Bureau mines, Pitts., 1908-16; cons. engr. petroleum and natural gas work, 1916-43; asst. to dir. Bureau of Mines, 1917; col. U.S. Army, in charge all research work, C.W.S., 1917-18; located supply of helium gas in Tex. and initiated the govt. helium program. Decorated D.S.M. (U.S. Army). During 1919-20 had charge constrn. of refineries for the Island and Raritan Refining Cos. (N.Y.C.), was pres.

Island Refining Co. and v.p., gen. mgr. Raritan Refining Co.; pres. Burrell Corp., 1923-52, became chmn. bd.; pres. Atlantic States Gas Co., 1936-54; v.p. Commonwealth Gas Corp., 1942-54; retained by Russian govt. to modernize natural gas industry, 1930-31. Inventor Burrell gas detector, Burrell gas analysis appartus; coinventor Burrell-Oberfell process of extracting gasoline from natural gas by charcoal methods; designed and built many natural gasoline refineries. Recipient Lamme medal for achievements in engring. Ohio State U., 1935; Hanlon award, Nat. Gasoline Assn. Am., 1948. Mem. Am. Petroleum Inst., Am. Chem. Soc., Am. Inst. Chem. Engrs., Am. Inst. Chemists, Tau Beta Pi, Sigma Xi. Clubs: Uptown, Westchester Country (N.Y.C.). Author: Handbook of Gasoline, 1917; Recovery of Gasoline from Natural Gas, 1925; An American Engineer Looks at Russia, 1932; and also many papers and govt. publs. on gas, gasoline, petroleum and allied subjects. Home: 101 W. 57th St., N.Y.C. Died Aug. 16, 1957.

BURROUGH, EDMUND WELDMANN naval officer; b. Camden, N.J., Oct. 28, 1890; s. Edmund Y. and Alice (Todt) B.; B.S., U.S. Naval Acad., 1914; M.S., Columbia, 1921; m. Carol Johnson, Mar. 8, 1918; 1 son, Edmund Johnson. Commd. ensign USN, 1914, advanced through grades to rear adm., 1943; sea duty in submarines and battleships, 1914-39; on staff Naval War Coll., 1936-38; comd. U.S.S. Cleveland, 1942-43; Joint War Plans Com. of Joint Chiefs of Staff, Washington, 1943-45, chief Post-War Planning, 1945; comdr. cruiser div. 12, comdr. cruises Mediterranean, sr. naval officer Adriatic, 1946-48; mem. Gen. Bd., Navy Dept., Washington, 1948-50; dep. comdr. Eastern Sea Frontier, comdr. Res. Fleet, 1950-52; ret. vice adm., 1952. Awarded Legion of Merit with combat citation and gold star. Episcopalian. Office: Gen. Bd. Navy Dept., Washington 25. Died May 8, 1962; buried Arlington Nat. Cemetery.

BURROUGHS, SILAS MAINVILLE congressman, lawyer; b. Ovid, N.Y., July 16, 1810; studied saw. Village clk. Medina, Orleans County, N.Y., 1835, village trustee, 1836, 39-43, 45-47; admitted to N.Y. State bar in Orleans County, 1840, began practice law in Medina; village atty., 1845-47; brig. gen. N.Y. State Militia, 1848-58; mem. N.Y. Assembly, 1837, 50-51, 53; mem. U.S. Ho. of Reps. (Republican) from N.Y., 35th-36th congresses, 1857-60. Died Medina, June 3, 1860; buried Boxwood Cemetery.

BURROWS, WILLIAM naval officer; b. Kinderton, Pa., Oct. 6, 1785; s. W. W. Burrows; never married. Appt. midshipman U.S. Navy, 1799, served on ship Portsmouth 1799-1803; acting 1803; served on ship . Constitution in Tripolitan War, 1803-08; promoted to 1st lt., 1809; during furlough went on mcht. voyage to China, 1810-11; given command of Enterprise, 1813; mortally wounded in victory over Brit. brig. Boxer. Died at sea nr. Portland, Me., Sept. 5, 1813.

BURSLEY, JOSEPH ALDRICH educator, corp. exec.; b. Fort Wayne, Ind., June 14, 1877; s. Gilbert Everett and Ellen Rebecca (Aldrich) B.; student U. Mich., 1895-97, 98-99, Cornell U., 1897-98; B.S. in Mech. Engring., U. Mich., 1899; m. Marguerite Knowleton, Apr. 8, 1908 (dec.), children—Anne Knowlton (dec.), Joseph Aldrich (dec.), Jerome Knowlton (dec.), Anne Bursley Steed, Rebecca Bursley Winder, Margery Bursley Angst. Apprentice Pa. Co., Ft. Wayne, 1899-1902; merc. bus., 1902-04; instr. mech. engring., 1904-09; asst. prof. U. Mich., 1909-11, jr. and asso. prof., 1911-47, prof. 1917-47, also dean students 1921-47, emeritus prof. and dean, 1947—; pres. Double A Products Co., Manchester, Mich., 1936—. Mem. common Council. Ann Arbor, Mich., 1925-29. Ednl. adviser Nat. Interfraternity Conf., 1939-46. Served as maj. and lt. col. Ordnance Dept., U.S. Army, World War I; organizer and C. O. Army Stores Course, U. Mich., 1917; chief of instrn. sect., Ordnance Dept., Washington, 1918; chief of plant sect. Detroit Dist. Ordnance Office 1918-19; chief Detroit Dist. Salvage Bd., 1919-20. Col. O.R.C., U.S. Army. Mem. Am. Soc. M.E., Engring. Soc. Detroit, Soc. for Promotion Engring. Edn., Am. Ordnance Assn., S.A.R., Mass. Soc. Mayflower Descs., Tau Beta Pi, Pi Delta Epsilon, Phi Kappa Phi, Phi Eta Sigma. Republican. Episcopalian. Mason (32ff). Clubs: University, Ann Arbor Gold. Author: (with John R. Allen) Heat Engines, 1910, 14, 25, 31, 41. Home: 2107 Hill St., Ann Arbor, Mich. Died Sept. 4, 1950.

BURT, ANDREW SHERIDAN brig. gen.; b. Cincinnati, Nov. 21, 1839; s. Andrew Gano and Anna (Thompson) B.; m. Elizabeth Johnstone Reynolds, Sept. 13, 1862. Enlisted as pvt. Co. A, 6th Ohio Inf., Apr. 20, 1861; disch., July 15, 1861; apptd. from Ohio, 1st lt. 18th U.S. Inf., May. 14, 1861; promoted through grades to brig. gen. vols., May 4, 1898; hon. disch. from vol. service, Dec. 31, 1898; brig. gen. U.S.A., Apr. 1, 1902; retired at his own request, Apr. 15, 1902. Bvtd. capt., June 19, 1862, "for conspicuous gallantry in battle of Mill Spring, Ky." (wounded); maj., Sept. 1, 1864, for Atlanta campaign and battle of Jonesboro, Ga. Author: May Cody, or Lost and Won (W. F. Cody's most successful play). Died Jan. 12, 1915.

BURTIS, ARTHUR naval officer; b. New York, June 29, 1841; s. Rev. Arthur (D.D.) and Grace Ewing (Phillips) B.; ed. pvt. schs. in Buffalo, Union Coll., and Hobart Coll. (A.M.); m. Ida Thomas, 1884. Entered U.S.N., asst. paymaster, July 14, 1862; promoted through all grades to pay dir. with rank of captain, 1899; served on U.S.S. Connecticut, 1862-64, Muscoota, 1865-66, N. Atlantic Squadron; various duties to 1897; on flagship, New York, 1897-99, as fleet paymaster under Rear Admiral W. T. Sampson, off Santiago, Cuba, at destruction of Spanish fleet, July 3, 1898; afterward in navy pay offices in Boston and New York until 1903; retired with rank of rear adm., Nov. 21, 1902. Home: Buffalo, N.Y. Died 1908.

BURTON, GEORGE HALL brig. gen.; b. Millsboro, Del., Jan. 12, 1843; s. Benjamin and Catherine R. (Green) B.; grad. U.S. Mil. Acad., 1865; m. Minnie Larrabee, Nov. 24, 1870. Promoted 2d lt. and 1st lt. 12th Inf., June 23, 1865; promoted through grades to brig. gen. insp. gen. U.S.A., Apr. 12, 1903; retired at own request, over 40 yrs,' service, Dept. 30, 1906. Bvtd. maj., Feb. 27, 1890, "for gallant services" in action against Indians in the Lava Beds, Calif., Jan. 27, 1873, and at the Clearwater, Ida., July 11 and 12, 1877. Served in Modoc Indian War, in northern Calif. and Ore.; Nez Perce War in Idaho, and across the Continent to the Mo. River; Bannock War in Ore.; served on frontier and in the Indian country, 1869-78 and 1880-84. Home: Los Angeles, Calif. Died Oct. 20, 1917.

BURTON, HAROLD HITZ asso. justice; b. Jamaica Plain, Mass., June 22, 1888; s. Alfred Edgar and Gertrude (Hitz) B.; A.B., Bowdoin Coll., 1909, LL.D., 1937; LL.B., Harvard, 1912; LL.D., Oberlin, 1941, Ohio Wesleyan, 1942, Kenyon Coll., Boston U., 1944, Wooster Coll., Heidelberg Coll., 1945, Western Res., Wesleyan (Conn.), 1946; L.H.D., Mt. Union 1943; m. Selma Florence Smith, June 15, 1912; children-Barbara (Mrs. H. C. Weidner, Jr.), William, Deborah (Mrs. R. W. Adler), Robert. Practiced with Gage, Wilbur & Wachner, Cleve., 1912-14; asst. atty. Utah Power & Light Co. and Utah Light & Traction Co., Salt Lake City, 1914-16; atty. Ida. Power Co. and Boise Valley Traction Co. (Ida.), 1916-17; asso. with Day, Day & Wilkin, later Day & Day, Cleve., 1919-25; mem. Cull, Burton & Laughlin, 1925-29, Andrews, Hadden & Burton, 1932-35. Inst. in pvt. corps. Western Res. U., 1923-25. Mem. Bd. Edn., East Cleveland, 1928-29; mem. Ohio Ho. of Rep., 1929; dir. of law, City of Cleve., 1929-32, acting mayor, Nov. 9, 1931-Feb. 20, 1932, mayor, 1935-40; U.S. senator from Ohio, 1941-45; asso. justice U.S. Supreme Ct., 1945-58. Chmn. research, Citizens' Com. on Regional Govt. for Cleve., 1928; chmn. Cleve. Bd. Edn. Com. on Citizenship Tng., 1934-35; chmn. County Charter Commn. of Cuyahoga County, O., 1935. Served as 1st lt., later capt. 361st Inf., 91st Div., U.S. Army, 1917-19; in France and Belgium, 1918-19; maj. Cleve. Grays, 1921-22. Citation and Order of Purple Heart (U.S.); Croix de Guerre (Belgium). Mem., Am., Ohio, Cleve. bar assns., Am. Legion, V.F.W., Army and Navy Union, Phi Beta Kappa, Delta Kappa Epsilon and Phi Alpha Delta. Republican. Unitarian (moderator Am. Unitarian Assn. 1944-45), Mason (33ff), K.P., Rotarian, Kiwanian. Clubs: Grange (hon.), Moose, Eagle, Exchange. Editor: 600 Days' Service-A History of the 361st Infantry Regiment, U.S. Army, 1919. Home: Hotel Cleveland, Cleve. Office: U.S. Supreme Ct., Washington 13. Died Oct. 28, 1964; buried Highland Park Cemetery, Cleve.

BURTON, ROBERT Continental congressman; b. nr. Chase City, Mecklenburg County, Va., Oct. 20, 1747; attended pvt. schs. Became a planter in Granville County, N.C., 1775; served to col. as a q.m. gen. in Revolutionary Army; mem. gov.'s council, 1783, 84; mem. Continental Congress from N.C., 1787-88; mem. commn. to establish boundary line between N.C., S.C., Ga., 1801. Died Granville (now Vance) County, N.C., May 31, 1825; buried on his estate "Montpelier," Williamsboro (now Henderson), N.C.

BURTT, WILSON BRYANT army officer; b. Hinsdale, Ill., Jan. 1, 1875; s. George H. and Ellen M. (Keyes) B.; grad. U.S. Mil. Acad., 1899; honor grad. Army Sch. of the Line, 1911; grad. Army Staff Coll., 1912. Commd. 2d lt. Inf., 1899, advanced through grades to brig. gen. Nat. Army, 1918; with regt. at Havana, Cuba, Mar.-Sept., 1899, in Philippines, 1900-03, 07-10; instr. Ky. State U., 1904-07; inst. N.G. Cal., 1913-15; observer, German armies in the field, 1914-15; in Mexico, 1916; with AEF in France as asst. chief Air Service and chief of staff, 5th Army Corps, 1917-19, served in Vosges sector, St. Mihiel offensive, Meuse-Argonne offensive; appt. instr. Gen. Staff Coll., 1919. Decorated D.S.M. (U.S.); Croix de Guerre with Palm, and Legion of Honor (French); Order of St. Michael and St. George (British); Order of the Crown (Italian). Mason (Shriner). Elk. Address: Care War Dept., Washington. Died Mar. 21, 1957.

BURWELL, ARMISTEAD judge; b. Hillsboro, N.C., Oct. 22, 1839; s. Rev. Robert and Margaret Anna (Robertson) B.; A.B., Davidson Coll., 1859; m. Ella M. Jenkins, Dec. 14, 1869. Capt. C.S.A. during Civil War; admitted to bar, 1869; mem. N.C. Senate, 1881; justice Supreme Ct. of N.C., 1892-95; sr. mem. Burwell & Cansler, 1895 - . Home: Charlotte, N.C. Died May 1913.

BURWELL, WILLIAM TURNBULL naval officer; b. Vicksburg, Miss., July 19, 1846; s. Armistead B. and Priscilla Withers (Manlove) B.; grad. U.S. Naval Acad., 1866; m. Miss Bradford. Promoted ensign, Apr. 1868, master, Mar. 26, 1869, lt., Mar. 21, 1870, lt. comdr., Sept. 1885, comdr., July 3, 1894, capt., Nov. 29, 1900, rear admiral, June 6, 1906; served in various stas and commands; commd. Wheeling, May 31, 1898, to May 1900, Puget Sound Naval Sta., 1900-02; comdg. Oregon, 1902-04, Independence, Nov. 1904; comdr. Navy Yard, Puget Sound, 1905. Died 1910.

BUSBEE, CHARLES MANLY, army officer; b. Raleigh, N.C., July 3, 1893; s. Charles Manly and Elinor (Cooper) B.; B.S., U.S. Mil. Acad., 1915; grad. Command and Gen. Staff Sch., 1926, Army War Coll., 1930; m. Elizabeth C. White, July 9, 1917; 1 son, Charles Manly, Jr.; m. 2d, Lou Taylor Uline, Dec. 26, 1926; children—John Taylor, Willis Uline; m. 3d, Elizabeth Divers, July 3, 1957. Commd. 2d lt., F.A., U.S. Army, June 12, 1915, and advanced through grades to brig. gen., July 25, 1942, ret., 1954. Served in Mexican Campaign, 1916-17, World War I, and with Occupation Forces in Germany after World War II. Decorated Bronze Star, Silver Star, campaign medals. Club; Army and Navy Country (Washington, D.C.). Home: Rocky Mount VA Died Jan. 19, 1970; buried Arlington Nat. Cemetery, Arlington VA

BUSEY, SAMUEL THOMPSON ex-army officer, ex-congressman; b. Greencastle, Ind., Nov. 16, 1835; s. Matthew Wales and Elizabeth (Bush) B.; student Urbana pub. schs.; m. Mary E. Bowen, Dec. 25, 1877. Was sgt. and 1st lt. Urbana Zouaves, 1861-62; town collector, Urbana, Ill., 1862, commd. 2d lt. in recruiting service Union Army, 1862, advanced through col., 1863; led regt. in assault on Ft. Blakeley, Ala., Apr. 9, 1865, was bvtd. brig.-gen. on request of Maj.-Gen. C. C. Andrews and Gen. U.S. Grant, and called by his comrades "The Hero of Fort Blakeley." Mayor and pres. bd. edn., Urbana, 1889-99; organized and conducted Busey's Bank, 1867-88; mem. 52d Congress. Gold Democrat. Address: Urbana, Ill. Died Apr., 1910; buried Woodlawn Cemetery, Urbana.

BUSH, PRESCOTT SHELDON, former U.S. senator; bus. exec.; b. Columbus, O., May 15,21895; s. Samuel Prescott and Flora (Sheldon) B.; M.A., Yale, 1917; m. Dorothy Walker, Aug. 1921; children—Prescott Sheldon, George Herbert Walker, Nancy (Mrs. Alexander Ellis, Jr.), Jonathan James, William Henry Trotter. Partner Brown Bors., Harriman & Co., 1930-72; formerly dir. C.B.S., Prudential Ins. Co. Am.; resigned all corporate directorships. Nat. campaign chmn. U.S.O., 1942; chmn. National War Fund Campaign, 1943-44; chairman Conn. Rep. Finance Com., 1948, del-at-large Rep. Nat. Conv. Served as capt. F.A., AEF, 1917-19. U.S. senator Conn., 1952-63. Trustee Westminster Choir Coll. Mem. U.S. Golf Assn. (pres. 1935). Republican. Episcopalian. Home: Greenwich CT Died 1972.

BUSHNELL, DAVID inventor; b. Saybrook, Conn., 1742; grad. Yale, 1775. Completed man-propelled submarine boat, 1775; originator modern submarine warfare; capt.-lt. Continental Army, 1779, capt., 1781. Died Warrenton, Ga., 1824.

BUSHNELL, GEORGE ENSIGN surgeon U.S.A.; b. Worcester, Mlass., Sept. 10, 1853; s. George and Mary Elizabeth (Blake) B.; A.B., Yale, 1876, M.D., 1880; m. Adra Holmes, 1881 (died 1896); 2d, Ethel M. Barnard, Dec. 24, 1902. Apptd. asst. surgeon, Feb. 18, 1881; capt. asst. surgeon, Feb. 18, 1886; maj. chief surgeon vols., June 4, 1898; maj. surgeon U.S.A., Dec. 10, 1898; maj. Med. Corps, Dec. 10, 1898; hon. disch. from vol. service, Jan. 23, 1899; lt. col. U.S.A., Apr. 23, 1908; col. May 1, 1911. Comd. U.S.A. Gen. Hosp., Ft. Bayard, N.M., about 14 yrs. Retired by operation of law, Sept. 10, 1917. Republican. Author: A Study in the Epidemiology of Tuberculosis, 1920. Deceased.

BUSSEY, CYRUS asst. sec. interior; b. Hubbard, O., Oct. 5, 1833; s. Rev. Amos and Hannah (Tylee) B.; m. Ellen Kiser, May 15, 1855. Engaged in mercantile pursuits; mem. Ia. Senate, as Democrat; del. Baltimore conv., 1860, that nominated Stephen A. Douglas for president; raised 3d Ia. Vol. Cav., Aug., 1861, becoming its col., later brig. gen. and bvt. maj. gen.; comd. a brigade in battle of Pea Ridge, Mar. 7, 1862; comd. 2d Cav. Div., Army of the Tenn.; chief of cav. Grant's army, siege of Vicksburg; led advance Sherman's army against Gen. Johnston's army to Jackson, Miss.; defeated Jackson at Canton, July 18, 1863; comd. 1st Div. 7th Army Corps, at Little Rock, and the last yr. of war comd. 3d Div. 7th Army Corps, Western Ark. and Indian Ty. After war commn. mcht. in St. Louis and New Orleans; pres. New Orleans Chamber of Commerce 6 yrs.; moved to New York, 1881; del. Rep. Nat. Conv., 1868, 1880; del. Meth. Ecumenical Conf., London, 1881. Asst. sec. of the interior, 1889-93; then in law practice. Home: Washington, D.C. Died Mar. 2, 1915.

BUTLER, BENJAMIN FRANKLIN army officer, gov. Mass., congressman; b. Deerfield, N.H. Nov. 5, 1818; s. John and Charlotte (Ellison) B.; grad. Waterbury Coll. (now Colby U.), 1838; m. Sarah Hildreth May 16, 1844, 1 dau., Blanche. Admitted to

Mass. bar, 1840; mem. Mass. Ho. of Reps., 1853, Mass. Senate, 1859; commd. brig. gen. Mass. Militia at beginning of Civil War; occupied Balt., 1861; comdr. in capture of New Orleans, 1862, mil. gov. New Orleans, 1862; controversial politics and regulatory tactics led to charges of corruption and graft; in command Eastern Va. and N.C. dists., 1863; sent to N.Y. to preserve order during election, 1864; mem. U.S. Ho. of Reps. from Mass. 40th-43d, 45th congresses, 1867-75, 77-79; gov. Mass., 1882; U.S. presidential nominee of Anti-Monopoly Party 1884, Greenback Party, 1884. Author: Butler's Book (autobiography), 1892. Died Washington, D.C., Jan. 11, 1893.

BUTLER, CHARLES ST. JOHN M.D.; b. Bristol, Tenn., Mar. 1, 1875; s. Matthew Moore and Mary Taylor (Dulaney) B.; student King Coll.; A.B., Emory and Henry College, 1895; LL.D., 1932; M.D., University of Virginia, 1897; m. Ingeborg Maria Nordqvist, July 4, 1899; children—Maria Nordqvist (wife of Harry L. Brockmann, M.D.), Martha Amanda (Mrs. Erik W. Ehn), Ruth Elizabeth. Began practice at Bristol, 1899; entered Med. Corps, U.S. Navy, as lt., j.g., 1900; and advanced through grades to rear admiral, 1935; retired Apr. 1, 1939. Instr. in bacteriology and tropical medicine, various times, U.S. Naval Med. Sch., 1907-21; occasional lecturer at George Washington U., Jefferson Med. College, 1923-24; commanding officer Naval Med. Sch., Washington, D.C., 1921-24 and 1927-32; comdg. officer U.S. Naval Hosp., Brooklyn, 1932-35; dir. gen. of pub. health of Republic of Haiti, 1924-27; comdg. officer, U.S. Naval Med. Supply Depot, Brooklyn, N.Y., 1935-36; U.S. Navy Med. Center, Washington, D.C. 1936-38. Mem. med. bd. Nat. Research Council, 1924-26. Fellow Am. Med. Assn., Am. Coll. Surgeons, Am. Coll. Physicians, N.Y. Acad. Medicine; diplomate Am. Bd. of Internal Medicine; mem. A.A.A.S., Am. Acad. Tropical Medicine (pres. 1940). N.Y. Soc. Tropical Medicine (pres. 1935), Washington Acad. Sciences, Am. Soc. Tropical Medicine (pres. 1927), Am. Soc. Clin. Pathologists, Mil. Surgeons of U.S., Sigma Alpha Epsilon, Alpha Omega Alpha; hom. mem. Soc. of Medicine of Haiti. Docorated Medal of Honor and Merit (Haiti); letter of commendation from U.S. Navy Dept. for service in World War I. Democrat. Club: Army and Navy (Washington). Author: Syphilis Sive Morbus Humanus, 1936. coll. edit. (2d), 1939; also author of numerous papers dealing with tropical medicine, seasickness, etc. Home: 848 Anderson St., Bristol, Tenn. Died Oct. 7, 1944.

BUTLER, GLENTWORTH REEVE M.D.; b. Phila., Dec. 31, 1855; s. J(ames) Olentworth and Evelyn E. (Reeve) B.; A.B. Hamilton Coll., 1877, A.M., 1880; M.D., L.I. Coll. Hosp., Brooklyn, 1880; Sc.D., Hamilton, 1904; LL.D., Wesleyan, 1908; m. Antoinette Willson, Jan. 1884; 1 dau., Antoinette Reeve (Mrs. Brower Hewitt). In practice of medicine in Brooklyn; asst. phys., St. Mary's Gen. Hosp., 1882-91, M.E. Hosp., 1885-91; chief 2d med. div., M.E. Hosp., 1891-1906, phys.-in-chief, attending phys., Brooklyn Hosp., 1902 - , sr. — phys., 1913. U.S. pension examining surgeon, 1889-93; contract surgeon, U.S.A., Aug.-Nov. 917; maj., later lt. col., M.C., U.S.A., Sept. 1918-May 1919; mem. advisory med. bd. Dept. of Health, New York, Fellow Am. Climatol. Assn., Am. Coll. Physicians. V.p. Packer Inst., 1905 - . Presbyn. Republican. Author: Emergency Notes, 1889; Diagnostics of Internal Medicine, 1901. Home: Brooklyn, N.Y. Died Dec. 6, 1926.

BUTLER, HENRY VARNUM naval officer; b. Peterson, N.J., Mar. 9, 1874; grad. U.S. Naval Acad., 1895. Promoted through grades to vice adm., 1935; former comdr. Aircraft Squadrons, U.S. Battle Fleet; former comdt. and supt. Naval Gun Factory, Navy Yard, Washington; former comdt. Navy Yard, Charleston, S.C., and 6th, 7th and 8th Naval Dists. Retired Apr. 1, 1938. Died Aug. 6, 1957.

BUTLER, JAMES GAY capitalist; b. Saugatuck, Mich., Jan. 23, 1840; s. William N. and Eliza (McKennan) B.; student U. of Mich., 1858-61, leaving coll. to enlist in Union Army; B.S., same univ., 1904; m. Maggie Leggat, Oct. 15, 1868. Mem. 3d Mich. Cav. 4 1/2 yrs., advancing to maj., and comdg. regt. during last 8 mos. of service; entered manufacture of tobacco in St. Louis, 1866, and became dir. Am. Tobacco Co. (retired). Rep. candidate for mayor of St. Louis, 1880; mem. bd. dirs. La. Purchase Expn., 1903-04. Presbyn. Home: St. Louis, Mo. Died Aug. 22, 1916.

BUTLER, JOHN GAZZAM brig. gen. U.S.A.; b. Pittsburgh, Pa., Jan. 23, 1842; s. John Bartlet and Catherine Selina (Gazzam) B.; ed. Western U. of Pa., and grad. U.S. Mil. Acad., 1863; m. Eliza Miller Warnick, Jan. 26, 1866. Second lt. 4th Arty., June 11, 1863; advanced through grades to col., Aug. 16, 1903; brig. gen. Jan. 21, 1904. Served with Battery M, 4th U.S. Arty. in Army of the Cumberland, Tenn., campaign; bvtd. 1st lt., Sept. 20, 1863, "for gallant and meritorious services in battle of Chickamauga;" transferred to ordnance corps, Jan. 1864; served on various spl. duties during 40 yrs.; retired Jan. 22, 1904. Episcopalian. Died Aug. 17, 1914.

BUTLER, MATTHEW CALBRAITH lawyer, U.S. senator; b. nr. Greenville, S.C., Mar. 8, 1836; s. Dr. Williams and Jane T. (Perry) B.; ed. S.C. coll., 1853-56, leaving in jr. yr.; m. Feb. 21, 1858, Maria Simkins Pickens. Admitted to S.C. bar, 1856; practiced at Edgefield Court House; elected to legislature, 1859; served in C.S.A., capt. to maj. gen., losing right leg at battle of Brandy Sta., June 9, 1863; elected to S.C. legislature, 1866; U.S. senator from S.C., 1877-89; Democrat; apptd. maj. gen. U.S. vols. for service in Spanish-Am. war, lMay 28, 1898; after war sent on com. with Admiral Sampson and General Wade, U.S.A., to assist Spanish gov. in evacuating Island of Cuba to be turned over to Cuban govt.; resigned commn. Pres. Mexican Mining and Exploration Co. Died 1909.

BUTLER, SMEDLEY DARLINGTON officer U.S.M.C.; b. West Chester, Pa., July 30, 1881; s. Thomas Stalker and Maud (Darlington) B.; Haverford Sch., 1898; m. Ethel C. Peters, June 30, 1905; children - Ethel Peters (wife of Capt. John Wehle, U.S. Marine Corps), Smedley Darlington, Thomas Richard. Appointed to U.S.M.C., Apr. 8, 1898; promoted through grades to col., Mar. 9, 1919; brig. gen. (temp.), 1918-21; brig. gen., March 5, 1921; maj. gen., July 5, 1929; retired, Oct. 1, 1931. Leave of absence to act as dir. Dept. of Safety, Phila., 1924-25. Served as comdr. Camp Pontanezen, Brest, France, Oct. 15, 1918-July 31, 1919. Awarded 2 congressional medals of honor, for capture of Vera Cruz, Mexico, 1914, and for capture of Ft. Riviere, Haiti, 1917; D.S.M. (U.S.), 1919. Quaker. Candidate for Republican nomination, U.S. Senate, Pa., 1932. Lecturer. Home: Newton Square, Pa. June 21, 1940.

BUTLER, WALTER N. Loyalist; b. Johnstown, N.Y., s. Lt.-Col. John and Catherine Butler; studied law, Albany, N.Y. Fled to Can. with father and other Loyalist leaders from Western N.Y., 1776; mem. Gen. Barry S. Leger's expdn. down Mohawk Valley, 1777; captured by Continental soldiers, 1777, escaped; leader Loyalists and Indians in Cherry Valley Massacre in which over 40 people were murdered, Nov. 11, 1778; killed in Loyalist raid on Mohawk Valley, 1781. Died Oct. 30, 1781.

BUTLER, WILLIAM army officer, congressman; b. Prince William County, Va., Dec. 17, 1759; s. James and Mary (Simpson) B.; M.D., S.C. Coll., 1778; m. Behethland Moore, June 3, 1784; children James, Andrew, George William Frank, Pierce, Emmala, Leontine. Commd. S.C. Militia, 1781; mem. S.C. Ho. of Reps., 1876; del. S.C. Conv. to ratify U.S. Constn., 1787, voted against Constn.; sheriff 96th Dist., 1791; commd. brig. gen. S.C. Militia, 1794, then maj. gen.; mem. U.S. Ho. of Reps. from S.C., 7th-12th congresses, 1801-13. Died Columbia, S.C., Sept. 23, 1821.

BUTLER, WILLIAM congressman, physici[ian; b. Edgefield Dist., S.C., Feb. 1, 1790; s. of William Butler; grad. S.C. Coll. (now U. S.C.), 1810; studied medicine; at least 1 son, Matthew Calbraith. Licensed to practice medicine; served as surgeon Battle of New Orleans, War of 1812, served with U. S. Navy until 1820; mem. U.S. Ho. of Reps. (Whig) from S.C., 27th Congress, 1841-43; agt. of Cherokee Indians, 1849-50. Died Fort Gibson, Indian Territory (now Okla.), Sept. 25, 1850; buried nr. Van Buren, Ark.

BUTLER, WILLIAM ORLANDO army officer, congressman; b. Jessamine County, Ky., Apr. 19, 1791; s. ercival and Mildred (Hawkins) grad. Transylvania U., 1812. Commd. capt. U.S. Army, served under Andrew Jackson, 1813, brevetted a maj., 1816; mem. Ky. Legislature from Gallatin County, 1817-18; mem. U.S. Ho. of Reps. from Ky., 26th-27th congresses, 1839-43; served as maj. gen. during Mexican War, 1846, present at capture of Mexico City, succeeeded Gen. Scott in command of Army in Mexico, voted a sword by U.S. Congress, also by Ky. for bravery in Battle of Monterey; Democratic nominee for vice pres. U.S. 1848; declined appointment by Pres. Pierce as gov. Neb., 1855. Author: The Boatman's Horn and other Poems. Died Carrollton, Ky., Aug. 6, 1880.

BUTLER, ZEBULON naval, army officer; b. Lyme, Conn., Jan. 23, 1731; s. John and Hannah (Perkins) B.; m. Anna Lord, Dec. 23, 1760; m. 2d, Lydia Johnston, Aug. 1775; m. 3d, Phebe Haight, Nov. 1781. Served as Ensign during French and Indian Wars, 1757, lt. and q.m., 1759, capt., 1760; led band of conn. settlers to Wyoming Valley (now luzerne County, Pa.), 1769; dir. Susquehanna Co.; mem. Conn. Assembly from Wyoming, 1774-76; commd. lt. col. Continental Army, 1776, col., 1778. Died Wilkes-Barre, Pa., July 28, 1795.

BUTNER, HENRY W. army officer; b. Pinnacle, N.C., Apr. 6, 1875; s. Frank A. and Sarah E. B.; grad. U.S. Mil. Acad., 1898, Staff College, 1906, Army War Coll., 1920; unmarried. Commissioned 2d lt. arty., Apr. 26, 1898; promoted through grades to col., May 15, 1917; brig. gen., temporary, Oct. 1, 1918; brig. gen., permanent, lMar. 7, 1930; maj. gen., Feb. 1, 1936. Died Mar. 13, 1937.

BUTT, ARCHIBALD WILLINGHAM, army officer; b. Augusta, Ga., Sept. 26, 1866; s. Joshua Willingham and Pamela Robertson (Boggs) B.; grad. U. of the South; unmarried. Apptd. capt. a.q.m. vols., Jan. 2, 1900; hon. disch. from vol. service, June 30, 1901; apptd. capt. q.m. U.S.A., Feb. 2, 1901; maj., Dec. 1911. Served as q.m. in P.I., Mar. 1900-June 1903; depot q.m., Washington, July 1903-Sept. 1906, Havana, Sept. 1906-Apr. 1908; personal aide to President Roosevelt, Apr. 1908-Mar. 4, 1909; personal aide to President Taft, Mar. 4, 1909 - . Home: Washington, Died Apr. 15, 1912.

BUTT, JOHN D. banker. Formerly pres., chmn., trustee Seamen's Bank for Savs., N.Y.C., now trustee, mem. exec. com.; chmn. Am. Trust Co., San Francisco, 1960-; pres., dir. Towers Hotel Corp., Hotel Volney, Chatham Towers, Buttonwood Corp., Beaux Art Properties, Inc.; chmn., dir. Beaux Arts Apts., Inc.; dir. Madison Owners, Inc., Gen. Realty & Utilities Corp. Central and South West Corp., Concord Freeholders, Inc., Parkway Village, Inc.; adv. com. to bd. dirs. Mfrs. Trust Co. Trustee Gen. Theol. Sem., Pace Coll.; bd. mgrs. Bedford br. YlMCA, Ch. Charity Found. L.I.; adv. com. to bd. dirs. The Lighthouse. Served as capt. F.A., U.S. Army, Mexican Border and World War I. Mem. Downtown Manhattan Assn. (pres., dir.). Office: 54 Wall St., N.Y.C. 10005. Died Sept. 1967.

BUTTERFIELD, DANIEL army officer; b. Utica, N.Y., Oct. 31, 1831; s. John and Melinda (Baker) B.; B.A., Union Coll., 1849; m. 1st wife, Feb. 12, 1857; m. 2d, Mrs. Julia L. James, Sept. 21, 1886. Commd. Capt. 71st Regt., N.Y. Militia; commd. col. 12th Regt. (1st Union forces to enter Va., crossing Long Bridge May 24, 1861), 1861; promoted brig. gen. U.S. Volunteers, 1861; decorated Congressional Medal of Honor (1892) for service at Gaines's Mill during Gen. George McClellan's Peninsular Campaign of 1862; commd. maj. gen., in command 5th Army Corps, served at Battle of Fredericksburg, 1862; became chief of staff under Gen. Thomas Hooker, 1863, also at Battle of Lookout Mountain, 1863; served at Battle of Chancellorsville, under Gen. George Meade at Battle of Gettysburg; commanded 3d Div. 20th Army Corps in Gen. William Sherman's march through Ga.; commd. col. U.S. Army, 1863; brevetted maj. gen., 1865, resigned, 1870; apptd. asst. U.S. treas., N.Y.C., 1870; constructed railroad in Guatemala; pres. Albany and Troy Steamboat Co.; owner Bklyn. Annex Steamships; dir. Mechanics & Tracers Bank N.Y.C., grand marshall of parade during Washington Centennial. Celebration, N.Y.C., 1899; pres. Soc. of Army of Potomac; mem. Grand Army of Republic. Died Cold Spring, N.Y., July 17, 1901.

BUTTRICK, JAMES TYLER Marine Corps officer; b. Newsport, R.I., Sept. 8, 1875; s. James Tyler and Mary Eliza (Sheffield) B.; student U.S. Naval Acad., 1893-96, U. Va., 1897-1900, Field Officers Sch., 1926-27, Naval War Coll., 1921-22 and 1935-36; m. Myna Staley Duncan, Apr. 16, 1904; children-Elizabeth (dec.), James Tyler (dec.), Duncan. Commd. 2d lt. USMC, 1900, advanced through grades to brig. gen., 1935; served in Philippines, San Domingo, Vera Cruz, Cuba, Nicaragua, Haiti, World War; service on board various ships USN; became comdt. USMC Schs., May 1937; ret. Oct. 1939. Decorated Navy Cross, Philippine, Cuban Pacification, Vera Cruz, World War, Nicaraguan and Expeditionary campaign medals. Mem. Zeta Psi. Episcopalian. Address: Beach Rd., Jamestown, R.I. Died May 9, 1963; buried Newport, R.I.

BUTTS, ALFRED BENJAMIN educator; b. Durham, N.C., May 3, 1890; s. Alfred Norman and Ada Virginia (Eakes) B.; B.S., Miss. State U. 1911, M.S., 1913; A.M., in govt., Columbia, 1915, Richard Watson Gilder fellow in public law, 1917-18, Ph.D., in pub. law, 1920; LL.B., Yale, 1930; m. Mary Evans Lampkin, Sept. 6, 1916; children-Barbara (Mrs. Read Patten Dunn, Jr.), Lampkin Herbert, Betty (Mrs. John Albert Latimer), Dorothy. Mem. faculty Miss. State U., 1911-35, v.p., head dept. govt., 1930-35; chancellor, prof. law U. Miss., 1935-46; tchr. govt. Yale, 1929-30; summer session tchr. pub. law various univs.; dir. edn. U.S. Department of Army, directing postgrad. edn., regular army officers in civilian universities, 1946-61; consultant Office U.S. Def. Dep. Asst. Secretary for Edn. and Manpower, 1961-. Admitted to Miss. bar, 1928, U.S. Ct. Mil. Appeals, 1952. Chmn. Miss. com. to select Rhodes Scholars, 1935-39, Colonel Judge Advocate General's Corps, United States Army Reserve; on active duty July 1, 1942-January 15, 1944. Member National Association State Universities (spl. mem.), Am., Miss. bar associations, Am. Political Science Assn., Southern Polit. Science Assn. (pres. 1938), Southern Association Colleges and Secondary Schools (v.p., 1933; mem. council on higher instns.), Southern University Conf. (pres. 1944, 1945), Sigma Alpha Epsilon, Phi Alpha Delta, Omicron Delta Kappa, Scabbard and Blade. Democrat. Methodist. Rotarian (past pres., Starkville and Oxford, Miss.). Author: Public Administration in Mississippi, 1919. Contbg. editor to Encyclopedia Britannica. Contbr. to law publs. Home: 5410 Connecticut Av. N.W., Washington 20015. Office: Pentagon Bldg., Washington. Died Sept. 26, 1962; buried Starkville, Miss.

BUTTS, EDMUND LUTHER ret. army officer; b. Stillwater, Minn., Aug. 15, 1868; s. Edmund Gregory and Amelia Augusta (White) B.; B.S., U.S. Mil. Acad., 1890; m. Lilian Stafford Hatie, Jan. 9, 1900. Commd. 2d lt., inf., U.S. Army, 1890. advanced through grades to brig. gen., 1940; retired, 1932; spl. instr. phys. tng. throughout army, 1893-96; comd. 30th inf., 3d Div.,

AEF France, to Aug. 1, 1918, 7th Inf., 3d Div., Aug.-Oct. 1918; participated in 6 major campaigns, including St. Mihiel, Meuse-Argonne and 2d Battle of Marne. Decorated D.S.C. (U.S.); Croix de Guerre with palm (France); 30th Inf. cited by Gen Petain as sustaining principal shock of German attack, July 15, 1918, and regtl. flag received decoration of Croix de Guerre with palm; flag also awarded legend Rock of the Marn, July 14-18, 1918, authorized by Pres. Truman, 1948. Illustrated phys. tng. of soldiers, mus. drill, etc., at 1st mil. tournament, Madison Sq. Garden, N.Y. City. Became sr. instr. Minn. N.G. St. Paul, 1921. Author: Manual of Physical Training for the United States Army, 1897; The Key Point of the Marne, 1930. Home: 1800 Broadway, San Francisco 9. Died June 6, 1950; buried Presidio Nat. Cemetery, Presidio of San Francisco.

BUXTON G. EDWARD b. Kansas City, Mo., May 13, 1880; s. G. Edward and Sarah Amelia (Harrington) B.; prep. edn., Highland Mil. Acad., Worcester, Mass.; 1895-98; Ph.B., Brown U., 1902, LL.D., 1948; LL.B., Harvard, 1906; m. Aline H. Armstrong, Jan. 19, 1910; 1 son, Coburn Allen. Reporter Providence (R.I.) Journal, 1902-03; mgr. Title Guarantee Co. of R.I., 1906-11; admitted to R.I. bar, 1907; asst. to trustee John Carter Brown estate, 1911; treas. Providence Journal Co., 1912-20, war corr., France, Germany and Gelgium, Aug. 1914-Feb. 1915; vice pres. B.B.& R. Knight, Inc., 1920-26; pres. B.B. & R. Knight Corp., 1926-35; pres. Androscoggin Mills, Bates Mfg. Co., Edward Mfg. Co., Hill Mfg. Co., York Mfg Co. (all 5 cos., 1932-40); chairman of bd. Panhandie Production and Refining Co., Inc., since 1946; dir. Fruit of the Loom, Inc. Served as asst. dir. Office of Strategic Services, Washington, resigned June 30, 1945. Member Cotton Textile Industry Commission of NRA; v.p. Cotton Textile Inst., Inc., 1933-34. Mem. R.I.N.G., 1900-03. 1906-16, advanced from 2d lt. to major; served as maj. and lt. col., infantry, U.S. Army, 1917-19; participated engagements St. Mihiel and Meuse-Argonne; 3 citations; col., U.S. Res. Decorated Medal for Merit, Purple Heart (U.S.), Hon. Comdr. Mil. Div. Order Brit. Empire, Polonia Restituta (Poland). Del. to Rep. Nat. Conv., Kansas City, Mo., 1928, and to Rep. Nat. Conv., Cleveland, O., 1936. Republican Nat. Committeeman for Rhode Island. 1940-41; chmn. Brown Univ. Housing and Development Campaign. One of founders R.I. Boy Scouts. Mem. 82d Div. Nat. Assn. (pres. 1929-30). Am. Legion (one of founders in France), Soc. of the Cincinnati, S.A.R., Phi Delta Theta, Republican. Mason. Elk. Clubs: Hope, Art (Providence); Army and Navy (Washington); Knickerbocker, Merchants (New York). Author: Official History 82nd Division A.E.F., 1920. Home: 85 Power St., Providence, R.I. Died Mar. 15, 1949.

BUZZNELL, REGINALD W. army officer; apptd. brig. gen. Inf., Aug. 1942. Address: Camp Blanding, Fla. Died Jan. 23, 1959.

BYERS, WALTER LOUIS, surgeon; b. Cedar Rapids, Ia., June 30, 1910; s. Edward Jacob and Mary Ellen (Fenton) B.; M.D., U. Ia., 1938; m. Barbara Jean Hood, July 21, 1952; children—Kathleen (Mrs. Richard A. Larson), David, Laura, Robert. Intern St. Mark's Hosp., Salt Lake City, 1938-39; resident Highland-Alameda County (Cal.) Hosp., 1945-47, later coordinator vascular surgery; resident Samuel Merritt Hosp., 1947-49; chief surgeon emergency surg. service Alameda County Med. Instns. Bd. dirs., mem. exec. com. Oakland Boys Club; bd. dirs. Alameda County chpt. A.R.C., 1968-69. Served to maj., M.C., AUS, 1940-46. Decorated Bronze Star; recipient Good Govt. award Alameda County, 1965. Diplomate Am. Bd. Surgery. Fellow A.C.S., Am. Coll. Chest Physicians; mem. A.M.A. Republican. Methodist. Mason. Club: Commonwealth of Cal. Address: Oakland CA Died Sept. 14, 1970; buried Chapel of Chimes, Oakland CA

BYLLESBY, HENRY MARISON elec. engr.; b. Pittsburgh, Pa., Feb. 16, 1859; s. Rev. DeWitt Clinton and Sarah (Mathews) B.; ed. Lehigh U., Pa.; m. Margaret Stearns Baldwin, June 15, 1882. Was associated with Thomas A. Edison in the early days of electric lighting in N.J., and has been identified with many movements and advances in elec. enterprises. Pres. H. M. Byllesby & Co., engrs., Chicago; also officer and dir. pub. service cos. in Ala., Ark., Okla., Ia., Colo., etc. Commd. lt. col. U.S.A., and assigned to hdqrs. of Chief Signal Officer, Washington. Purchasing agt. in Great Britain and Scandinavian countries for A.E.F., hdqrs. London, June-Dec. 1918, when hon. disch. Awarded D.S.O. (British). Died May 1, 1924.

BYNUM, CURTIS business exec.; b. Lincolnton, N.C., July 6, 1892; s. Rev. William Shipp and Mary Louisa (Curtis) B.; prep. edn., Horner Mil. Sch., Oxford, N.C.; A.B., U. N.C., 1903; J.D. cum laude, U. Chgo., 1907; grad. study Ecole de Droit, Sorbonne U., 1919; m. Florence Helen Boyd, July 10, 1907; children-Katharine Fullerton (Mrs. Charles Frederic Shepard), William. Dir. Charles S. Boyd Paper Co. and Appleton Coated Paper Co., Appleton, 1907-08; pres. Carolina Creamery Co., Asheville, N.C., and Forsyth Dairy Co., Winston-Salem, 1912-27. Admitted to practice N.C. bar, 1914; served as capt. and adj. 321st Inf., U.S. Army, World War; grad. Army Gen. Staff Coll., Langres, France, 1918. Decorated with German Red Cross, 1933. Mem. Council Meml. Mission Hosp., Asheville, N.C. Ex-pres. Rotary Club of Asheville. Mem. Mass. Soc. Cin., Phi Beta Kappa, Sigma Alpha Epsilon. Republican. Episcopalian. Mason (33ff). Club: Pen and Plate (ex-pres.). Compiler of Marriage Bonds of Tryon and Lincoln Counties. Sec. Sinking Fund Commn. for Buncombe County, 1937-64. Home: Macon Avenue. Office: County Bldg., Asheville, N.C. Died Oct. 13, 1964; buried Calvary Episcopal Ch., Fletcher, N.C.

BYRAM, GEORGE LOGAN army officer; b. Noxubee Co., Miss., Jan. 19, 1862; s. George and Sallie I. (Moseley) B.; student U. of Ala., 1878-81; grad. U.S. Mil. Acad., 1885; m. Jane Lockhart Skiles, Jan. 23, 1889; 1 dau., Cornelia (wife of John E. Lewis, U.S.A.). Commd. 2d lt. 1st Cav., June 14, 1885; promoted through grades to col., and retired July 1916. Participated in Sioux campaign, 1890-91; in operations against Apache Kid, 1893; duty with Colo. N.G., 1893-97; wounded in battle at Las Guasimas, Cuba, June 24, 1898; recommended for Medal of Honor by Maj. James M. Bell, 1st Cav.; acting judge advocate Dept. of the Colo., 1898-99; in Philippines, 1899-1903; acting insp. gen., Jan.-July 1901; q.m. 6th Cav., 1901-05; participated in expedition against renegade Utes, from Utah, in S.D. and Mont., 1906; again in Philippines, 1907-10; comd. expdn. which annihilated Jikiri's band of Moro pirates, July 4, 1909. On Mexican border different periods, 1914-15; recalled to active duty Sept. 1, 1917, as comdt. War Prison Barracks No. 3, Ft. Douglas, Utah. Awarded D.S.C. "for extraordinary heroism in action," at Las Guasimas, Cuba. Mem. Mil. Order of Caraboa. Democrat. Presbyn. Home: Hollywood, Calif. Died June 16, 1929.

BYRD, RICHARD EVELYN explorer, naval officer (ret.); b. Winchester, Va., Oct. 25, 1888; s. Richard Evelyn and Eleanor Bolling (Flood) B.; ed. Shenandoah Valley Mil. Acad., Va., Mil. Inst. and U. of Va.; grad. U.S. Naval Acad., 1912; m. Marie D. Ames, of Boston, Mass., Jan. 20, 1915. Ensign U.S. Navy, 1912; advanced through grades to lt. comdr.; ret. Mar. 15, 1916; promoted to grade of comdr. after north polar flight, 1926; promoted to rank of rear adm., 1930. Entered Aviation Service Aug. 1917; comdr. U.S. Air Forces of Can., July 1918, until Armistice; comdr. aviation unit of Navy-MacMillan Polar Expdn., June-Oct. 1925; made flight in aeroplane with Floyd Bennett over North Pole and back to base at Kings Bay, Spitzbergen, May 9, 1926, covering distance of 1,360 miles in 15-1/2 hours; made trans-Atlantic flight with 3 companions, from New York to France, distance of 4,100 miles, flight lasting 42 hours, June 29-July 1, 1927; flew over South Pole, Nov. 29, 1929; made 1st expdn. to Antarctic, 1928-30, 2d expdn., 1933-May 10, 1935; on both expdns. made important discoveries, among them being Edsel Ford Mountains and Marie Byrd Land; spent 5 mos. of winter night alone at scientific work in shadow of South Pole. In 1939 was made commander of United States Antarctic Service, an expedition sent to the Antarctic by Government; made four noteworthy flights resulting in discovery of five new mountain ranges, five islands, more than 100,000 square miles of area, a large peninsula, and 700 miles of hitherto unknown stretches of antarctic coast. During World War II served with Fleet Admiral King in Washington and Fleet Admiral Nimitz in Pacific; overseas 4 times (3 times in Pacific, once, Western front in Europe); cited 4 times; apptd. commanding officer U.S. Navy Antarctic Expdn., 1946. Advisor Dept. Defense, Polar defense and strategy. Holds 18 honorary degrees from colleges and universities. Presented by President Collidge with Hubbard gold medal, June 23, 1926, "for valor in exploration"; awarded Congressional Medal of Honor, 1926, Special Congressional Medals (1930, 37, and 46), Congressional Life Saving Medal of Honor, Navy D.S.M., Navy Cross, Navy Flying Cross. Patron's medal of Royal Geog. Soc. (British, 1931), and gold medal Reale Societa Geografica (Italy, 1931); Elisha Kent Kane medal of Phila. Geog. Soc.; Langley medal of aerodromics of Smithsonian Instn., David Livingstone Centenary medal of Am. Geog. Soc., D.S.M. of State of N.Y. presented by Gov. Franklin D. Roosevelt; also 65 other medals; received gold star in recognition of services as commander of U.S. Antarctic Service Expedition, 1939-41; 22 citations from Navy Dept.; twice awarded Legion of Merit medal and special citation for service in Pacific, World War II; decorations by Portuguese and Rumanian govts.; also Officer Legion of Honor and Comdr. Legion of Honor (France) Medal, Order of Christopher Columbus, Santo Domingo; Grand Lodge Medal for Distinguished Achievement; Loczy Medal, Hungarian Geog. Society; Vega Medal, Swedish Geog. Society Mem. Phi Beta Kappa, Kappa Alpha, and about 200 other orgns. Episcopalian. Clubs: Century, Explorers (New York); Chevy Chase (Washington); Tavern, University, Somerset, Union Boat, Engineers', Country (Boston); Dedham Polo and Country. Author: Skyward, 1928; Little America, 1930; Discovery, 1935; Exploring with Byrd; Alone, 1938. Address: 9 Brimmer St., Boston. Died Mar. 11, 1957.

BYRD, WILLIAM planter, mcht., colonial legislator; b. London, Eng., 1652; s. John and Grace (Stegg) B.; m. Mary Horsmanden, 1673; 1 son, William Engaged in tobacco trade with Eng. and West Indies; fur trader, land speculator; owner plantation nr. what is now Richmond, Va. imported, used, sold numerous slaves; comdr. Henrico County (Va.) Militia; mem. Va. Ho. of Burgesses, 1677-82, mem. Va. Council of State, 1683-1704, pres., 1703-04; mem. Albany Conv. to treat with Indians, 1685; auditor gen. Va., 1688. Author: A History of the Dividing Line; A Progress to the Mines; also recently published diaries. Died Westover, Va., Dec. 4, 1704.

BYRNE, BERNARD ALBERT soldier; b. Newport Barracks, Ky., Oct. 19, 1853; s. Maj. Bernard Myles and Louisa (Albert) B.; ed. Columbian (now George Washington) U.; m. Bertha, d. Albert Barnitz, Feb. 11, 1892. Apptd. from D.C., 2d lt. 6th Inf., Oct. 15, 1875; promoted through grades to lt. col. 28th Inf., June 15, 1906; retired at own request, over 30 yrs.' service, July 13, 1906. Awarded Congressional Medal of Honor, July 1, 1902, "for gallantry at Bobong Negros, P.I., July 19, 1899." Home: Los Altos, Calif. Died 1910.

BYRNE, CHARLES CHRISTOPHER brig. gen.; b. Pikesville, Baltimore Co., Md., May 7, 1837; s. Charles (M.D.) and Emeline (Cole) B.; ed. Mt. St. Mary's Coll. Emmitsburg, Md.; M.D., U. of Md., 1895; m. Henrietta P. Colt, Oct. 4, 1876. Entered U.S.A. as asst. surgeon, June 23, 1860; attained rank of asst. surgeon-gen.; retired by operation of law, May 7, 1901, with rank of col.; advanced to rank of brig. gen.; retired by act of Apr. 23, 1904. Died Nov. 8, 1921.

BYRNE, RICHARD army officer; b. Cavan County, Ireland, 1832. Came to U.S., 1844; joined U.S. Army, 1849; served with 2d Cavalry against Indians in Fla. and Ore.; commd. lt. at beginning of Civil War, commd. col. 28th Mass. Volunteers, 1862; served with Army of Potomac at Fredericksburg, Chancellorsville and Gettysburg; recruited replacements, given command of Irish Brigade, 1864; mortally wounded at Cold Harbor, Va., Died Washington, D.C., June 10, 1864.

BYRNES, RALPH LEONIDAS physician; b. Walcott, Ia., Mar. 30, 1878; s. Thomas (M.D.) and Jennie (Allen) B.; B.Sc.; State U. Ia., 1902, M.Sc. and M.D., 1906; studied Harvard, 1911; spl. work in bacteriology, New Haven, 1918, in pulmonary tb. Yale Army Med. Sch.; m. Edith Whitney Merritt, Oct. 6, 1908. Hosp. service, 1906-08; practice at Avoca, Ia., 1908-10; at Pottenger's Sanatorium, Monrovia, Cal., 1910; prof. bacteriology and pathology U. Utah, dir. State Bd. Health and Lab., 1911-15; prof. pathology, bacteriology and clin. microscopy U. So. Ca., 1915-16; prof. diseases of the chest Coll. Med. Evangelists, Los Angeles, 1919-23; estab. first endocrine and mental hygiene clinic, Belevedere Health Center, Los Angeles County Health Dept., 1930. Commd. 2d lt. Med. R.C., 1912; 1st lt. Utah N.G., 1912-15; capt. and maj. various mil. camps in U.S., 1917-19; camp surgeon and pres. Bd. Tb Examiners, 1917-19; returned to pvt. practice, 1919. Diplomate Am. Bd. Internal Medicine. Mem. A.M.A., Cal., Los Angeles County med. socs., Am. Pub. Health Assn., A.C.P., Los Angeles Acad. Criminology (dir. and chmn. com., 1924), S.A.R., Am. Legion (chmn and dir. Service Bur., 1928—, Pi Kappa Alpha, Phi Beta Pi. Republican. Episcopalian. Mason (K.T., Shriner). Clubs: Los Angeles Athletic, Am. Legion Luncheon. Optimist (bd. govs.). Home: 3706 W. 4th St. Address: Box 5846 Metropolitan Station, Los Angeles. Died Feb. 16, 1943; buried Family Plot, Walcott, Ia.

BYRON, JOSEPH WILSON army officer; b. Fort Meade, S.D., June 3, 1892; s. Joseph Charles and Jane Frances (Wilson) B.; student Phillips Exeter Acad., 1909-10; B.S., U.S. Mil. Acad., 1914; m. Susanne Rice, Apr. 14, 1917; children—Jane Wilson (Mrs. Vernon N. Simmons, Jr.), Susanne (Mrs. Frank Kent Bradford), Joseph Rice, Edmund Rice (deceased), Sedgwick Rice. Commd. 2d lt., U.S. Army, and served, 1914-19; with W. D. Byron & Sons, tanners, Williamsport, Md., 1919-42, as asst. treas., 1922-24, v.p. and gen. mgr., 1924-28, pres., 1928-42; v.p., chmn. exec. com. Hagerstown Shoe & Legging Co.; resigned to re-enter the Army; was chief Army Exchange Service; maj. gen. dir., Special Services Division; inactive duty, June 23, 1946; recommd. maj. gen. O.R.C., Feb. 27, 1947; pres. First Fed. Savings & Loan Assn., Industry advisor, NRA, 1933; sect. chief (dollar-a-year man), Office Production Management and WPB, 1941-42; v.p. Boy Scout Council (Silver Beaver award); past president Hagerstown Rotary Club. Republican. Presbyterian. Clubs: Army and Navy, Chevy Chase (Washington). Home: 760 Preston Rd., Hagerstown, Md. Died Apr. 12, 1951; buried Rose Hill Cemetery.

BYRON, ROBERT BURNS, JR., game mfg. exec.; b. Chgo., Sept. 13, 1916; s. Robert Burns and Helen (Manchester) B.; grad. high sch.; m. Doris Bloom, Feb. 28, 1963; children—Laura, Barbara. Copy writer, retail sales supr. Montgomery Ward & Co., Chgo., 1938-41; copy writer, media dir. C. Wendel Muench & Co., advt. agy., 1946-47; outdoor advt. buyer, account exec., media dir., v.p., account supr. Young & Rubicam, Inc., 1947-63; v.p. Pacific Outdoor Advt. Co., Los Angeles, 1963-64; v.p., media dir. Wolf, Krautter, Inc., Chgo., 1964-66; v.p., sec. The Fyanes Corp., Chgo., 1966-69. Devel. director of Lawrence Hall, Inc., Chgo., past pres. Served to capt. Signal Corps, AUS, 1941-46. Decorated Bronze Star medal. Mem. Western Advt. Golf Assn., Lawrence Hall Alumni Assn. (past pres.). Home: Des Plaines IL Died Nov. 13, 1969; interred Memory Gardens, Arlington Heights IL

CABEL, GEORGE CRAGHEAD lawyer; b. Danville, Va., Jan. 25, 1837; ed. Danville Acad.; grad. law dept., Univ. of Va., 1857; commonwealth atty., 1858-61; in C.S.A., 1861-65, private to col., 18th Va. inf. - 3 times wounded. Mem. Congress, 1875-87; then city atty. Democrat. Home: Danville, Va. Died 1906.

CABELL, DE ROSEY CARROLL, army officer; b. in Ark., July 7, 1861; grad. U.S. Mil. Acad., 1884, Army War Coll., 1913. Commd. 2d lt. 8th Cav., June 15, 1884; advanced through grades to brig. gen. N.A., Dec. 17, 1917; maj. gen., Oct. 1, 1918; remanded to regular rank of col. after the war. Participated in Geronimo Indian campaign, 1885-86; Sioux Indian campaign, 1890-91; China Relief Expdn., 1900; Philip pines campaigns, 1900-02; chief of staff Punitive Expdn. into Mexico, 1915-16; D.S.M., 1919. Then retired. Home: San Diego, Calif. Died Mar. 15, 1924.

CABELL, EDWARD CARRINGTON congressman; b. Richmond, Va., Feb. 5, 1816; attended Washington Coll. (now Washington and Lee U.), 1832-33, Reynold's Classical Acad., 1833-34; grad. U. Va., 1836. Moved to Fla., 1837, became a farmer, nr. Tallahassee; del. Fla. Constl. Conv., 1838; returned to Va. to study law, admitted to Va. Bar, 1840; returned to Tallahassee; mem. U.S. Ho. of Reps. from Fla., 29th Congress (election contested), Oct. 6, 1845-Jan.

CABELL, SAMUEL JORDAN congressman; b. Amherst County, Va., Dec. 15, 1756; s. Col. William and Margaret (Jordan) C.; m. Sally Syme, 1781. Commd. maj. 6th Va. Regt., 1775, served at Valley Forge and in Washington's campaigns of 1778; commd. lt. col., 1779; lt. Amherst County (Va.) Militia, 1784; mem. Va. Legislature, 1785-86; mem. U.S. Ho. of Reps. from Va., 4th-7th congresses, 1795-1803; an original mem. Va. Soc. of Cincinnati. Died Nelson County, Va., Aug. 4, 1818; buried family burial grounds "Soldiers' Joy" farm, Norwood, Va.

CABELL, WILLIAM LEWIS lawyer; b. Danville, Va., Jan. 1, 1827; grad. U.S. Mil. Acad., 1850; lt. 7th U.S. Inf., 1850-58; capt. q.m.'s dept., 1858; served on Gen. Harney's staff on Utah expdn., 1858; ordered to rebuild old Ft. Kearney on the Platte River, Neb., Jan. 1859; stationed at Ft. Kearney on the Platte River, Neb., Jan. 1859; stationed at Ft. Arbuckle, in Indian Ty., 1860; 1860-61 engaged in building Fort Cobb, in Indian country occupied by the Comanches, Kiowas, and other wild tribes; resigned Mar. 1861; in C.S.A., Apr. 1861-Oct. 1864, becoming brig. gen.; captured on a raid into Kansas; prisoner of war until Apr. 28, 1865. After war practiced law at Ft. Smith, Ark., 1865-72; in Dallas, Tex., 1872 - ; 4 times mayor of city; U.S. marshal Northern Dist. Tex., 1885-89. Home: Dallas, Tex. Died 1911.

CADWALADER, CHARLES EVERT physician; b. Phila., Nov. 5, 1839; s. John and Henrietta Maria (Bancker) C.; grad. Univ. of Pa., 1858; A.M., M.D., 1861; m. Mary B. Ryan, July 15, 1897. During Civil war served pvt. 1st City troop; capt. 6th Pa. cav., and on gen. staff Army of the Potomac as aid to Gens. Hooker and Meade with bvt. rank of lt. col. In med. practice, 1861 - ; and lived in same house in which he was born. Active from 1872 in polit., med. and social reform. Home: Philadelphia. Died 1907.

CADWALADER, THOMAS FRANCIS, lawyer, b. nr. Jenkintown, Pa., Sept. 22, 1880; s. John and Mary Helen (Fisher) C.; student Episcopal Acad., Phila., Pa., 1889-96, St. Paul's Sch., Concord, N.H., 1896-97; A.B., U. of Pa., 1901; LL.B., University of Maryland, 1903; married Elizabeth Middleton Read, November 23, 1911 (died June 27, 1952); children—Thomas Francis, Mary Helen, Anne Cleland, Benjamin Read. Admitted to Md. bar, 1903; practiced as partner in Cadwalader & Whitman, later Cadwalader, Whitman & Mason, Baltimore, 1903-16; practiced alone since 1919; trustee or agt. of various estates, individuals and charitable funds administered in Phila.; dir. Baltimore & Phila. Steamboat Co., 1904-35, pres., 1930-35; trust officer, First Nat. Bank of Baltimore, 1943-45. Served Mexican border with Troop A, First Md. Cav. and in 5th Md. Inf.; mem. First R.O.T.C., Ft. Myer, Va., 1917; 2d lieutenant cavalry, 1st lieutenant and captain field artillery, Camp Lee and Camp Zachary Taylor. Trustee University of Pennsylvania (1928-43), Hannah More Academy (Reisterstown, Md.), St. Paul's Sch. for Boys (Brooklandwood, Md.). Church Home and Hospital of City of Baltimore, St. Andrew's School, Middletown, Del. Mem. Md. State, Harford County and Baltimore City bar assns., Delta Phi, Phi Beta Kappa. Episcopalian (del. to Gen. Conv. P.E. Ch., 1943, 46, 49, 52). Club: University (Phila.) Home: Joppa MD Died Feb. 24, 1970.

CAFFEY, EUGENE MEAD army officer; b. Decatur, Ga., Dec. 21, 1895; s. Lochlin Washington and Helen Eugenia (Mead) C.; B.S., U.S. Mil. Acad., 1918; Engr. Sch., U.S. Army, 1919-20; L. U. Va., 1933; Nat. War Coll., 1948; m. Catherine Frances Howell, June 12, 1918; children-Eugene Mead, Catherine Howell (Mrs. James P. Sturrock), Lochlin Willis, Hester Washburn (Mrs. Richard C. Mallonee), Benjamin Franklin, Francis Gordon, Helen Mead, Mary Winn (Mrs. Paul H. Reistrup), Thurlow Washburn Howell. Commd. 2nd lt., U.S. Army, 1918, advanced through grades to Judge Adv. Gen. of Army, 1954; served in C.E., 1918-30, surveys Republic of Panama, 1922-26, Tacna Africa, Piebiscitary Commn., 1926, Am. Electoral Mission to Nicaragua, 1928-29, Nicaragua Canal Survey, 1929-30; with Judge Adv. Gen.'s Dept., 1930-41, counsel for Philippine Govt., also sec. war, 1935-40; with C.E., 1941-47, comd. 20th Engr. Combat Regt., Morocco and Tunisia, 1st Engr. Spl. Brigade, Sicily, Italy and Normandy; Judge Adv. Gen.'s Dept., 1947-56, Judge Adv. Gen. of Army, 1954-56; ret., 1956; mem. law firm Darden & Caffey, 1957-59, Darden, Caffey & Mechem, 1959-60, Darden & Caffey, 1961. Decorated D.S.C., Silver Star, Legion of Merit (3 awards), Bronze Star, Purple Heart; Order of Brit. Empire, other fgn. decorations. Mem. Phi Beta Kappa, Phi Delta Phi. Democrat. Roman Catholic. K.C. Address: Route 2, Box 216, Las Cruces, N.M. Died May 30, 1961; buried Masonic Cemetery, Las Cruces.

CAHILL, EDWARD lawyer; b. Kalamazoo, Mich., Aug. 3, 1843; s. Abraham and Frances Maria (marsh) C.; ed. Kalamazoo Coll.; m. Lucy Crawford, June 11, 1867. Enlisted as pvt. Co. A, 89th Ill. Inf., Aug. 1862; disch. for disability, Dec. 1862; apptd. by President Lincoln, 1st lt. 102d U.S.C.T., Dec. 1863; promoted capt., Jan. 1864; mustered out, Sept. 30, 1965. Admitted to bar, 1866; practiced in Clinton and Ionia cos., Mich., 1866-71, at Chicago, 1871-73, Lansing, Mich., 1873 - ; counsel for State of Mich. on important cases. Pros. atty., Ingham County, Mich., 1877-81; apptd. justice Supreme Ct., Mich., for unexpired term (1890-91) of James V. Campbell, deceased. Pres., trustee Edward W. Sparrow Hosp. Assn. Mem. Nat. Conf. Commrs. on Uniform State Laws. Address: Lansing, Mich. Died July 26, 1922.

CAHOON, WILLIAM congressman; b. Providence, R.I., Jan. 12, 1774; attended common schs. Moved to Lyndon, Vt., 1791, engaged in milling, agrl. pursuits; mem. Vt. Ho. of Reps., 1802-10; succeeded father as town clk., 1808; Democratic presdl. elector, 1808, messenger to deliver electoral vote of Vt.; county judge, 1811-19; apptd. maj. gen. Vt. Militia, 1808, served during War of 1812; del. Vt. constl. convs., 1814, 28; mem. exec. council, 1815-20; lt. gov. of Vt. 1820-21; mem. U.S. Ho. of Reps. (Anti-Masonic Party) from Vt. 21st-22d congress, 1829-33. Died Lyndon, May 30, 1833; buried Lyndon Town Cemetery, Lyndon Center, Vt.

CALDWELL, CHARLES HENRY BROMEDGE naval officer; b. Hingham, Mass., June 11, 1823; s. Charles H. and Susan (Blagge) C. Commd. midshipman U.S. Navy, 1838, promoted lt., 1852, comdr., 1862, capt., 1866; chief of staff N. Atlantic fleet, 1870; promoted commodore, 1847; acting rear adm. in command S. Pacific fleet, 1876, S. Atlantic fleet 1877. Died Waltham, Mass., Nov. 30, 1877; buried Waltham.

CALDWELL, CHARLES POPE lawyer; b. Bastrop County, Tex., June 18, 1875; s. Charles G. C.; LL.B., U. of Tex., 1898, Yale, 1899; m. Frances Morrison, July 20, 1907: 1 son, Charles Morrison. Admitted to N.Y. bar, 1900. Del. Dem. Nat. Conv., 1912; mem. 64th to 66th Congresses (1915-21), 2d N.Y. Dist.; apptd. asso. justice Ct. of Special Sessions, N.Y. City, 1926. Maj., Ordnance Corps, World War, 1918; founder Veterans' Mountain Camp. Tupper Lake, N.Y. Mason. Home: Kew Kardens, L.I. Died July 31, 1940.

CALDWELL, FRANK MERRILL army officer; b. Rochester, N.Y., Nov. 8, 1866; s. Walter Lester and Jane (Carter) C.; grad. U.S. Mil. Acad., 1890; distinguished grad. Army Sch. of the Line, 1909; grad. Army Staff coll., 1910; m. Mary Hay, June 6, 1894; children - Dorothy (Mrs. C. F. Beach), Jane Carter (Mrs. Harrison Lobdell), Mary Hay (Mrs. David Bath). Commissioned 2d lieut. 3d Cav., June 12, 1890; promoted through grades to brig. gen., Jan. 18, 1925. Served as lt. col. 4th Wis. Inf., Spanish-Am. War; detailed in Insp. Gen.'s Dept., 1916-18; brig. gen. N.A., Apr. 12, 1918-Oct. 31, 1919, World War; comdr. 75th Inf. Brig., 38th Div., May 15-Oct. 14, 1918; comdr. 83rd Inf. Brig., 42 Div., 1918-19; insp. gen., 1920-21; chief of staff, Gen. Staff Corps, 6th Corps Area, 1921-24; comdg. harbor defenses of P.I., 1925-27, harbor defenses of Pacific Coast, 1928-31; retired Nov. 30, 1931. Died Mar. 8, 1937.

CALDWELL, GEORGE ALFRED congressman, lawyer; b. Columbia, Ky., Oct. 18, 1814; studied law. Admitted to Ky. bar, 1837, began practice law in Adair County; mem. Ky. Ho. of Reps., 1839-40; mem. U.S. Ho. of Reps. (Democrat) from Ky., 28th Congress, 1843-45, 31st Congress, 1849-51; commd. maj. and q.m. Volunteers, Mexican War, 1846, maj. inf., 1847, maj. of volunteers, 1847, brevetted lt. col., 1847 for gallant service in Battle of Chapultepec; del. Union Nat. Conv., Phila., 1866. Died Louisville, Ky., Sept. 17, 1866; buried Cave Hill Cemetery.

CALDWELL, GREENE WASHINGTON congressman, lawyer, physician; b. Belmont, Gaston County, N.C., Apr. 13, 1806; grad. med. dept. U. Pa., 1831; studied law. Practiced medicine; asst. surgeon U.S. Army, 1832; admitted to N.C. bar, began practice law in Charlotte; mem. N.C. House of Commons, 1836-41; mem. U.S. Ho. of Reps. (Democrat) from N.C., 27th Congress, 1841-43; apptd. supt. U.S. Mint at Charlotte, 1844; served as capt. of inf., Mexican War, 1846; commd. capt. Third Dragoons, 1847; mem. N.C. Senate, 1849; resumed practice of medicine. Died Charlotte, N.C., July 10, 1864; buried Old Cemetery.

CALDWELL, HENRY CLAY judge; b. Marshall County, W.Va., Sept. 4, 1832; moved with family to Iowa, 1837; ed. in common schs.; admitted to bar, 1852. Pros. atty., Van Buren County, Ia., 1856-58; mem. Iowa legislature, 1859-61; maj., lt. col. and col. 3d Ia. Cav., 1861-64; U.S. dist. judge, Eastern Dist. of Ark., 1864-90; U.S. circuit judge, 8th Jud. Circuit, 1890-1903; resigned. Died Feb. 15, 1915.

CALDWELL, JOHN CURTIS soldier; b. Lowell, Vt., Apr. 17, 1833; s. George M. and Betsey (Curtis) C.; A.B., Amherst, 1855; m. Martha Helen Foster, May 15, 1857. Prin. Washington Acad., E. Machias, 1855-61; col. 11th Me. Inf., Nov. 12, 1861; brig. gen. vols., Apr. 28, 1862; bvtd. maj. gen. vols., Aug. 19, 1865, for faithful and meritorious services; hon. mustered out, Jan. 15, 1866; pres. Mil. Commn., Washington, 1864-65. Admitted to Me. bar, 1866; mem. Me. Senate and adj. gen., 1867-69. Removed to Kan., 1883, chmn. State Bd. Pardons, 1885-92; Am. consul at Valparaiso, Chile, 1869-70; charge d'affaires ad interim to Chile, Aug.-Dec. 1870; minister resident, 1874-76, charge d'affaires, 1876-81, Uruguay and Paraguay; consul at San Jose, Costa Rica, 1897-1909. Died Aug. 30, 1912.

CALHOUN, JOHN CALDWELL vice pres. U.S., senator; b. Abbeville Dist., S.C., Mar. 18, 1782; s. Patrick and Martha (Caldwell) C.; grad. Yale, 1804, Litchfield (Conn.) Law Sch., 1806; m. Floride Bouneau, Jan. 1811, 9 children. Admitted to S.C. bar, 1807; mem. S.C. Legislature, 1808; mem. U.S. Ho. of Reps. from S.C. 12th-15th congress, 1811-17, acting chmn. house com. on fgn. affairs, 1811, one of group called War Hawks, presented resolution recommending declaration of war on Eng., 1812; resigned U.S. Ho. of Reps. to become U.S. sec. of war, 1817-25; vice pres. U.S. under John Q. Adams, 1825-29, under Andrew Jackson, 1829-32 (resigned because of dispute with Jackson over states rights and nullification); leader and polit. theoretician of states rights point of view; formulated S.C.'s policy during nullification crisis, declaring that a state can nullify laws it considers unconstl., 1832-33; mem. U.S. Senate from S.C., 1832-43, 45-50, leading senatorial champion of slavery and the So. cause of states rights under his philosophy of "concurrent majorities" or mutual checks whereby each sect. of the country was to share equally in fed. power; U.S. sec. of state under Tyler, 1843-45. R.K. Crallé published compilation of Calhoun's works, 6 vols., 1851-55. Died Washington, D.C., Mar. 31, 1850; buried St. Philip's Churchyard, Charleston, S.C.

CALHOUN, JOHN CALWELL financier; b. nr. Demopolis, Ala., July 9, 1843; s. Andrew Pickens and Margaret Maria (Green) C.; g.s. John Caldwell Calhoun, v.p. of U.S., 1825-29; brother of Patrick C.; ed. Thalian Acad., nr. Pendleton, S.C.; entered S.C. Coll., class of 1863, but left to enter C.S.A. at battle of Ft. Sumter; served in cav. through war, becoming capt.; m. Linnie Adams (1870), grandniece Richard M. Johnson (v.p. U.S., 1837-41). Planter after war in Ala., Miss. and Ark.; del.-at-large from Ark. to Cotton Expn., Louisville, 1883, New Orleans, 1884; v.p. conv. in Washington, 1884, which memorialized Congress with reference to improvement of Miss. River; spl. ambassador to France of S.A.R., 1897. Pres. Baltimore Coal Mining & Railraod Co., Albertite Oilite & Cannel Coal Co., Ltd. Home: New York, N.Y. Died Dec. 18, 1918.

CALIFF, JOSEPH MARK brig. gen.; b. E. Smithfield, Pa., Aug. 31, 1843; s. Hosea and Mary (Pierce) C.; ed. pub. schs. and acads.; m. Katharine Wendell Hardy, June 4, 1902. Commd. 2d lt., U.S.C.T., Oct. 8, 1863; 1st lt., Mar. 5, 1865; bvt. capt., Mar. 13, 1865; hon. mustered out, Oct. 13, 1866; apptd. 2d lt., 3d U.S. Arty., Aug. 17, 1867; honor grad. Arty. Sch., 1871; 1st lt., capt., maj., arty. corps, 1875-1901; lt. col., May 20, 1904; brig. gen., Mar. 24, 1906; retired, Mar. 28, 1906. Served during Civil War in Va., and Dept. of the South; comd. battery of field arty. in Cuba and P.R. during Spanish-Am. War. Author: History of the 7th Regiment, United States Colored Troops, 1878; Notes on Military Science, 1889, 1906. Home: Towanda, Pa. Died Dec. 9, 1914.

CALLAN, ROBERT EMMET army officer; b. Baltimore, Md., Mar. 24, 1874; s. Frank J. and Sarah (Riley) C.; grad. U.S. Mil. Acad., 1896; m. Margaret Valentine Kelly, Oct. 10, 1912. Commd. add. 2d lt. 5th Arty., June 12, 1896; promoted through grades to lt. col., July 19, 1916; col. (temp.), Aug. 5, 1917; brig. gen. N.A., Aug. 8, 1918; brig. gen. regular army, June 9, 1921, maj. gen., Apr. 1, 1931. In campaign, Western Puerto Rico, 1898; instr. mathematics, U.S. Mil. Acad., 1899-1903; mem. Torpedo Bd., Ft. Totten, 1904-07; asst. to chief of Coast Arty., 1907-12; comdr. Fort Andrews, Mass., 1912-14; pres. Coast Arty. Bd., Ft. Monroe, Va., 1914-15; duty Gen. Staff Corps, Philippine Dept., 1915-17; organized 65th Regt. Heavy Arty., and arrived in France in command of regt., Apr. 8, 1918; chief of staff of Army Arty., 1st Army, June-Aug. 1918; comdr. 33d Heavy Arty. Brig. Aug.-Dec. 1918; mem. Arty. Mission in France, Italy, Eng. and

U.S. Jan.-May 1919; assigned duty with technical staff, Ordnance Dept., June 1, 1919. Grad. Army War Coll., June 1, 1921; comdg. 2d Coast Arty. Dist. Hdqrs., Ft. Totten, N.Y., July-Nov. 1921; comdg. Panama Coast Arty. Dist. Hdqrs., Ft. Amador, C.Z., 1921-24; comdg. Third Coast Arty. Dist., and Coast Arty. Sch., Ft. Monroe, Va., 1924-29; comdg. Hawaiian Separate Coast Arty. Brigade, hdqrs., Ft. De Russy, July 1929-Jan. 1931; asst. chief of staff, War Dept., Washington, Jan. 1931-Jan. 1935; comdg. 3d Corps Area Hdqrs. Baltimore, Md., Feb. 18, 1935-Jan. 31, 1936; retired. Awarded D.S.M.; Commander Order of the Crown (Italy); Officer Legion of Honor (France). Catholic. Died Nov. 20, 1936.

CALLENDER, GEORGE RUSSELL, pathologist, army officer; b. Everett, Mass., May 13, 1884; s. Thomas Russell and Martha Ellen (Bemis) C.; grad. Mt. Hermon (Massachusetts) Sch., 1903; M.D., Tufts College Medical School, 1908, Sc.D. (honorary), 1954; graduate Army Medical School, 1913; married Gladys Foster Moore, August 28, 1913 (dec. 1969); children—Janet (Mrs. Merrill Buffington), George Russell, Gladys Catherine (Mrs. R. L. Gellein). Instr. pathology and bacteriol., Tufts Med. Sch., 1909-12; commd. 1st lt. M.R.C., U.S. Army, 1912, 1st lt. M.C., 1913, advanced through grades to brig. gen., 1945; chief of lab. Army Gen. Hosp., Ft. Bayard, N.M., 1913-15, Hawaiian Dept., 1916-18; asst. Div. of Lab. and Infectious Diseases, Surgeon Gen's. Office, 1918, chief, 1919; asst. curator Army Med. Mus., 1919-20, curator, 1920-22, 1924-28; mem. Med. Dept., Research Bd., Manila, 1922-24, pres., 1922-23; pres. Philippine Leprosy Research Bd., 1923-24; adviser in pathology, Philippine U. Med. Sch., 1923-24; instr. pathology Army Med. Sch., 1924-32; prof. gross pathology Georgetown U. Med. Sch., 1925-28; chief lab. 8th Corps Area, 1932-35; pres. Army Med. Research Bd., Canal Zone, 1935-38; pathologist, Army Med. Center, 1939; asst. comdt. Med. Dept., Professional Service Schs., 1940-45, comdt., 1946, retired, 1946; dir. pathology VA, 1947-59; advisor Gorgas Meml. Inst. Organizer, 1930, American Registry Pathology; mem. adv. bd. Armed Forces Inst. Pathology, until 1967. Served in Mass. N.G., 1907-12; 1st lt., M.C., 1911-12. Awarded Sternberg Medal, 1913; The Strong Medal, 1946; D.S.M., 1945; U.S.A. Typhus Com. Medal, 1946; Medale de la Reconnaissance Francaise, 1947. Diplomate Am. Bd. Pathology, Am. Bd. Preventive Med. Pub. Health Fellow A.C.P.; member A.M.A., Am. Assn. Pathologists and Bacteriologists (pres. 1930), Am. Soc. Tropical Med. (pres. 1933), Internat. Assn. Med. Mus. (pres. Am. and Canadian sect. 1932), Am. Acad. Tropical Medicine (pres. 1954) Armed Forces Inst. Pathology (sci. advisory bd.), Walter Reed Memorial Association, Am. Urol. Assn., Association of Mil. Surgeons of U.S., International College of Surgeons, com. on pathology Nat. Research Council, Nat. Adv. Cancer Council, Am. Found. Trop. Med., A.P.H.A., Acad. of Medicine of Washington, Massachusetts Society of Cincinnati, Alpha Kappa Kappa. Mason. Club: Army and Navy (Washington, D.C.). Wrote Pathology of the Acute Respiratory Diseases (Vol. XII, The Med. Dept., U.S. Army in World War), 1929—Co-author of "Malaria in Panama." Contributor technical articles to jours. Home: Washington DC Died Feb. 26, 1973.

CALVER, GEORGE WEHNES, physician; b. Washington, D.C., Nov. 24, 1887; s. Dr. Thomas and Elizabeth (Wehnes) C.; M.D., George Washington U., 1912; m. Jessie Willits, Mar. 15, 1916; children—Jessie Carleton (wife of Captain Paul F. Dickens, U.S.N.), Georgianna Elizabeth (wife of Capt. Eldon C. Swanson, U.S.N.). On active duty as naval med. officer, from 1913; commd. rear adm. M.C., USN, 1945, later vice adm.; with Naval Hosp., Washington, D.C., 1913, naval med. sch., Naval Sta., Guam, 1914-15, Naval Sta., Cavite, P.I., 1915-16, Yangtze River Patrol, 1916, Naval Hosp., Yokohoma, Japan, 1916-17, Charleston, S.C., 1917-19, U.S.S. Bridgeport, 1919-22; Naval Hosp. and Hosp. Corps Training Sch., 1922-25, U.S.S. Henderson, 1925-27; visiting surgeon U.S. Naval Dispensary, Washington, D.C., 1927-28; attending physician Congress of the U.S., 1928-66; dir. research lab. Naval Med. Research Institute, Bethesda Naval Medical Center, from 1966; consultant internal medicine and med. research Nat. Naval Med. Center; trustee Worcester Found. Research, Southwest Foundation for Research (San Antonio). Honorary consultant for Army Medical Library. Diplomate Bd. Internal Medicine. Fellow A.C.S., A.C.P., Am. Coll. Cardiology (trustee, pres. 1958-59), Am. Geriatrics Soc., A.A.A.S.; member A.M.A., D.C., George Washington U., Pam Am. (past president), Southern med. socs., Am. Heart Assn., Assn. Mil., Surgeons U.S., Medical Library Assn., Endocrine Soc., Pan Am. Med. Soc. (pres.), Laurentian Hormone Conf., Phi Chi. Mason. Clubs: International Medical, Carabao, Washington Clinical, Army-Navy Country, Chevy Chase (Washington): New York Yacht. Home: Washington DC Died Feb. 27, 1972; buried Arlington Nat. Cemetery, Arlington VA

CALVER, HOMER NORTHUP, health edn., pub. relations; b. N.Y.C., Nov. 22, 1892; s. William Louis and Mary Ella (Northup) C.; B.S. in Sanitary Engring., Mass. Inst. Tech., 1914; m. Hulings Elizabeth Lappe, Apr. 17, 1922; children—Cornelia and Judith Margaret. Hydrographic asst. Metropolitan Sewage Commission, New York City, 1913; asst. prof. hygiene, N.Y. U. Med. Sch., 1928-32; sec. pub. health com. of the Paper Cup and Container Inst., 1934-58, sec. pub. relations com., 1942-58; editor Health Officers News Digest, 1936-57; vis. prof. pub. health Am. U., Beirut, 1957, 59. Secretary Am. Mus. of Health, Inc., 1938-54; director Health exhibits N.Y. World's Fair, 1939 and 1940; consultant in health edn.; coordinator of Inter-Am. Affairs, 1943-46; mem. nat. adv. com. on emergency feeding FCDA; vice president nat. citizens com. WHO. Secretary-treasurer of Empire State Health Council. With American Ambulance in France, 1915; 1st lieutenant and captain Sanitary Corps, U.S. Army, 1917-19; asst. san. insp. 89th Div., Camp Funston, Kan.; comdr. 89th Div. Mobile Field Lab.; lecturer A.E.F. Univ., Beaune, France; captain Sanitary Officer Reserve, 1919-20. Recipient of the Ling Medal, 1930. Fellow of American Public Health Assn. (governing council, 1931-37; vice-chmn. Pub. Health Edn. Sect., 1934-36, chmn., 1936-37; chmn. com. on scientific exhibits 1932-42); fellow Royal Soc. Promotion Health (hon.), Am. Med. Writers Assn.; mem. S.R., Soc. Am. Bacteriologist, Pub. Relations Soc. Am., Soc. Pub. Health Educators, Kappa Sigma, Delta Omega. Club: University (N.Y.). Home: Clinton Corners NY Died Sept. 15, 1970.

CALVERT, LEONARD colonial gov.; b. Eng., 1606; s. George (1st lord Baltimore) and Anne (Mynne) C.; m. Anne Brent; children-William, Anne, Came to Md., 1634, took possession for King of Eng.; established seat of govt., St. Mary's, Md.; commd. 1st gov. Md., also comdr.-in-chief armed forces, chief magistrate, chancellor and chief justice 1637; lost Md. due to an insurrection, 1644, recovered possession, 1646; monument erected in his memory by State of Md., 1890. Died Md., June 9, 1647.

CAMAC, CHARLES NICOLL BANCKER M.D.; b. Phila., Pa., Aug. 6, 1868; s. William and Ellen (lMcIlvaine) C.; A.B., U. of Pa., 1892, M.D., 1895; student, Guy's Hosp. Med. Sch., London, 1893; Johns Hopkins U. Med. Sch., grad. studies, 1895-97; m. Julia Augusta Metcalfe, Nov. 17, 1897; m. 2d, Christie M. Fraser, May 25, 1935. Instr. physiology, U. of Pa., 1895; asst. resident phys., Johns Hopkins Hosp., 1896-97; organizer and dir. lab. of clin. pathology, 1899-1905, instr. physical diagnosis, chief of med. clinic, lecturer in medicine, 1905-09, prof. clin. medicine, 1909-10, Cornell U. Med. Coll., New York; asst. prof. clin. medicine, College Physicians and Surgeons (Columbia), 1910-38; visiting phys., 1899-1916, cons. physician, 1916-35, N.Y. City Hospital; cons. physician, N.Y. Polyclinic Hosp. and Med. Sch., 1934-36 (emeritus prof. medicine). During World War served as physician in American War Hospital, England, and Ocean Ambulance Hospital, Belgium; chmn. Physicians, Surgeons and Dentists Fund for purchase of hosp. instruments and equipment for French mil. hosps., 1916; med. dir. Gouverneur Hosp. of the Bellevue and Allied hosps., N.Y. City, 1916-23; cons. phys., 1923 - . Commissioned 1st lt. Med. R.C., Apr. 1917; student officer, Camp Greenleaf, Ft. Oglethorpe, Ga., and Sch. of Gas Defense, Ft. Sill, Okla.; apptd. instr. in gas defense, Inf. Sch. of Arms, U.S. Army, Ft. Sill, Okla., Sept. 1917; promoted maj., Med. R. C., Oct. 1917; apptd. med. chief U.S. Army Gen. Hosp. No. 6, Ft. McPherson, Ga., Oct. 1917; apptd. dir. Officers' Training Sch., Ft. McPherson, Apr. 1918; promoted lt. col. M.C., Nov. 1918; apptd. med. chief Gen. Hosp. No. 38, Eastview, N.Y., Jan. 1919; hon. disch., July 1919. Author: Imhotep to Harvey - The Backgrounds of the History of Medicine, 1931. Home: Altadens, Calif. Died Sept. 27, 1940.

CAMERON, CHARLES RAYMOND, consular service; b. York, N.Y., June 25, 1875; s. John and Catherine (McDougall) C.; A.B., Cornell, 1898 (Phi Beta Kappa); unmarried. Mercantile business, 1898-1901; entered Philippine Civil Service, 1901; supt. schs., Moro Province and Province Mindanao and Sulu; asst. to dept. gov., dept. sec. and treas.; census asst. Capt. Aviation Sect. Signal Corps U.S.A., World War, 1917-18; maj. Air Service, 1918-19. Consul at Tacna, Chile, 1919-20, Pernambuco, Brazil, 1920-23, Tokyo, 1923-25; assigned to the Department of State, 1925; consul at Sao Paulo, Brazil, 1930-33, at Habana, Cuba, 1934-36, at Osaka, Japan, 1936-37, at Tokyo, Japan, since 1937. Chairman U.S. delegation to Second International Coffee Congress, Sao Paulo, May-June 1931. Author: Sulu Writing—an Explanation of the Sulu Arabic Script as Employed in Writing the Sulu Language of the Southern Philippines; also numerous magazine articles. Address: Dept. of State, Washington DC

CAMERON, GEORGE HAMILTON army officer; b. Ottawa, Ill., Jan. 8, 1861; s. Dwight Foster and Fanny Elizabeth (Norris) C.; student Northwestern U., 1878-79: grad. U.S. Mil. Acad., 1883: m. Nina Dean, d. Lt. Col. J. G. Tilford, U.S. Army, May 22, 1888; children-Douglas Tilford, lt. U.S. Army, killed in action in France, Nov. 3, 1918, Nina Tilford (wife Brig. Gen. John B. Thompson), Margaret Hughes (wife Lt. Col. Buckner M. Creel). Commd. 2d lt. 7th Cav., June 13, 1883; promoted through grades to col., July 1, 1916; brig. gen. N.A., Aug. 5, 1917; maj. gen. U.S. Army, Nov. 28, 1917. Served in Dak. and Kan., 1883-88; duty as instr. and asst. prof., dept. of drawing, U.S. Mil. Acad., 1888-95; duty in Wash. and Calif., 1895-98; equipped first U.S. horse transport Tacoma, and sailed for Manila. P.I., Aug. 5, 1898; participated in Lawton's northern campaign and Schwan's southern campaign in Luzon; sec. Sch. of Application for Cav. and Field Arty., Ft. Riley, Kan., 1901-06; at Camp Overton, Mindanao; P.I., 1906; sec. and asst. comdt., Mounted Service Sch.; 1907-10; at Camp Stotsenburg, P.I., 1910-12; comdg. Big Bend Dist., Tex., to Aug. 1913; at Army War Coll., 1913-14: Gen. Staff, to Dec. 10, 1916; comdg. 5th and 25th Cav., to Aug. 25th, 1917; comdg. 80th Inf. Brigade, N.G., Camp Kearny, Cal., to Dec. 4, 1917; comdg. 4th Div. Regular Army at Camp Greene, Charlotte, N.C., and in France to Aug. 16, 1918, participating in offensive from Marne to Vesle; comdg. 5th Corps A.E.F., to Oct. 12, 1918, in St. Mihiel and Argonne-Meuse offensives; comdr. Camp Gordon, Ga., to May 1, 1919; comdt. Cavalry Sch., Fort Riley, Kan., to Sept. 1, 1921; chief of staff, 76th Div. Org. Res., Hartford, Conn., to July 31, 1924; retired after 45 yrs. service. Home: Fishers Island, N.Y. Died Jan. 28, 1944.

CAMERON, JAMES DONALD sec. of war; b. Middletown, Pa., May 14, 1833; s. Simon C. (U.S. senator and sec. of war in President Lincoln's cabinet); A.B., Princeton, 1852, A.M., 1855; m. Mary McCormick, (died 1874); m. 2d, 1878. Elizabeth, d. Judge Sherman, of Ohio and niece of Gen. W. T. Sherman. Clerk, cashier, and then pres. Nat. Bank of Middletown; pres. Northern Central R.R. Co., of Pa., 1863-74; had large coal, iron and mfg. interests. Sec. of War in cabinet of President Grant, May 22, 1876-Mar. 3, 1877; elected U.S. senator, 1877, for unexpired term of his father, resigned, and reelected, serving until 1897; del. Rep. Nat. Convs., 1868, 1880; chmn. Rep. Nat. Com., 1880. Home: Harrisburg, Pa. Died Aug. 30, 1918.

CAMERON, ROBERT ALEXANDER colonist, army officer; b. Bklyn., Feb. 22, 1828; s. Robert A. C.; grad. Ind. Med. Coll., 1849; m. Miss Flower. Owner Valparaiso (Ind.) Republican, 1857; served in Ind. Legislature, 1860; commd. capt. 9th Ind. Volunteers 1861, lt. col. 19th volunteers, 1861, col. 34th volunteers, 1862; brig. gen. 3 divs. 13th Corps, U.S. Army, 1863; comd. Lafourche dist. Dept. of Gulf, 1864; brevetted Maj. gen., 1865; v.p. Union Colony which settled in Colo., 1869, pres., 1871; supt. Fountain Colony, founded Colorado Springs, 1871; founded Ft. Collins, 1873; warden of penitentiary, Canon City, Colo., 1865-87; immigration agt. Ft. Worth & Denver City R.R. Died Mar. 15, 1894.

CAMERON, SIMON senator, sec. of war, b. Lancaster County, Pa., Mar. 8, 1799; s. Charles and Martha (Pfoutz) C.; m. Margaret Brua; 5 children. Editor Bucks County (Pa.) Messenger, 1821; owner Harrisburg Republican, 1824; state printer Pa., circa 1825-27; adj. gen. Pa., 1826; constructed network of railroads in Pa. united into No. Central R.R.; founder Bank of Middleton, 1832; commr. for setting Winnebago Indian claims, 1838; mem. U.S. Senate from Pa., 1845-49, 57-61, 67-77 (radical Republican, 1867-77); leader Rep. Party in Pa., 1857-77, one of most successful machine politicians of his time, had strong support as Rep. presdl. nominee in conv., 1860; U.S. sec. of war, 1861-62; appt. U.S. minister to Russia, 1862. Died Lancaster County, Pa., June 26, 1889; buried Harrisburg, Pa.

CAMERON, WILLIAM EVELYN governor; b. at Pettersburg, Va., Nov. 29, 1842; s. Walker Anderson and Elizabeth Byrd (Walker) C.; ed. Petersburg Classical Acad., N.C. Mil. St. Acad., Washington U., Louis; graduation prevented by Civil War; m. Louisa Clara Egerton, Oct. 1, 1868. In C.S.A. from May, 1861; served pvt. to asst. adj. gen. in all battles of Lee's army from Seven Pines to fall of the Confederacy; wounded at 2d Manassas; surrendered at Appomattox. Edited leading newspapers in Va., 1866-76; admitted to bar, 1876. Mayor of Petersburg, 1876-82; governor of Va., 1882-86; mem. Constl. Conv., 1891-92. emocrat. Author: Life and Character of Robert E. Lee, 1902; History of the Chicago Exposition, 1903: The World's Fair, 1904. Now editor-in-chief The Virginian-Pilot, Norfolk, Va. Home: Norfolk, Va. Died Jan. 26, 1927.

CAMP, JOHN LAFAYETTE army officer, territorial ofcl.; b. nr. Birmingham, Ala., Feb. 20, 1828; s. John L. and Elizabeth (Brown) C.; grad. U. Tenn., 1848; m. Mary Ward. Practicied Practiced law, Gilman, Tex., 1848-91; elected col. 14th Tex. Calvary, 1865; elected to U.S. congress from Tex. dist., 1866, not permitted to take seat; del. Tex. Constl. Conv., 1866; de. Nat. Democratic Conv., 1872; mem. Tex. Senate 1874; judge Tex. Dist. Ct., 1878; registrar Ariz. Land Office, 1884-86: Camp County (Tex.) named after him. Died San Antonio, Tex., July 16, 1891.

CAMPBELL, ARTHUR GRIFFITH army officer; b. Lexington, Va., Nov. 15, 1884; s. John Hammond and Mattie (Steele) C.; B.S., Va. Mil. Inst., 1906; grad. Coast Arty. Sch., 1915 (advanced course 1923), Command and Gen. Staff Sch., 1924, Army War Coll., 1928; m. Virginia Roberts, Feb. 19, 1921. Comdt. Hoge Meml. Mil. Acad., 1906; asst. prof. Va. Mil. Inst., 1907; commd. 2d lt. CAC, 1908, promoted through grades to brig. gen., 1940; command and staff duties with arty. of AEF, 1917-18; mem. War Dept. Gen. Staff, 1918-21; asst. chief of staff, 6th Corps Area, 1928-32, 8th Corps Area, 1939-40; retired as brig. gen., 1944. Decorated Chevalier Legion of Honor, France, 1920. Mem. Kappa

Alpha. Presbyn. Mason. Club: Army and Navy (Washington). Home: Fort Adams Newport, R.I. Address: care Adjutant General, U.S. Army. Washington 25. Died Jan. 25, 1957.

CAMPBELL, BRUCE JONES, retail merchandising exec.; b. in Flagstaff, Ariz., Aug. 20, 1912; s. William Alexander and Mina B. (Jones) C.; B.S. in Bus. Adminstrn., U. So. Cal., 1934, M.B.A., 1939; m. Susanne Margaret Jones, Aug. 10, 1940; children—Barbara Jones, Robert William. Partner Campbell & Guill, pub. accountants, 1946-50; supervising auditor Cal. Bur. Milk Control, 1946-50, chief, 1950-52; controller Golden State Co., Ltd., 1952-54; controller Foremost Dairies, San Francisco, 1954-56, v.p., comptroller, 1956-59, financial v.p., 1959-61; financial v.p., treas. Food Giant Markets, Inc.; v.p. dir. Meyenberg Old Fashion Products Co., Giant Realty Co. Served as maj. AUS, 1941-46. Mem. Financial Execs. Inst., Cal. Soc. C.P.A.'s. Methodist. Mason. Home: Whittier CA Died May 26, 1968.

CAMPBELL, CHANDLER marine corps officer; b. Wheeling, W.Va., Feb. 10, 1880. Apptd. 2d lt. USMC, 1900, and advanced through grades to col., 1932; ret. from active duty, 1936; brevetted with rank of brig. gen., 1942; participated Philippine campaign, 1902, Nicaraguan campaign, 1912, Haitian campaign, 1915, Dominican campaign, 1916; comd. 10th Marine Regt., 1918. Died Oct. 28, 1956; buried Nat. Cemetery, Arlington, Va.

CAMPBELL, DELWIN MORTON veterinary editor and publisher; b. Topeka, Kan., Jan. 19, 1880; s. Newton Josephus and Mary Jean (Mitchell) C.; student Kansas State Normal Coll., 1897-98; Kan. State Agrl. Coll., 1903-05; D.V.M., Kansas City Vet. Coll., 1907; m. Gertrude Elma Hole, lfay 1, 1907; children-Eloise Belle (Mrs. Harner Selvidge), Dorothea Gertrude (Mrs. Joseph Calvin Sides), Delwin Morton, Jr. Editor, Vet. Medicine, 1908-49, consulting editor since 1949. Col. Veterinary Corps, U.S. Army, 1941-44. Mem. Am. Vet. Med. Assn., Am. Pub Health Assn., A.A.A.S., Assn. Mil. Surgs. U.S. Democrat. Author: Colics of the Horse, 1945; Veterinary Account Book, 1917; Veterinary Service in Wartime, 1942; Army Veterinary Service, 1944. Co-author: Veterinary Military History of the United States (2 vols.), 1935; vet. sect. The Americana Annual since 1946. Address: 7632 S. Crandon Av., Chicago 49. Died Mar. 27, 1952; buried Arlington Nat. Cemetery.

CAMPBELL, EDWARD HALE, naval officer; b. South Bend, Ind., Oct. 4, 1872; s. Myron and Abbie Johnson (Fifield) C.; grad. U.S. Naval Acad., 1893; m. Lilian, d. George Henry Strong, Aug. 30, 1899; children—Edward S., Georgiana. Ensign, July 1895; promoted through grades to judge advocate gen. of navy with rank of capt., 1907; capt. 1918; service at Pacific, Asiatic, S. Am. and Atlantic stations; chief of staff, comdr. Battle Force, Pacific Fleet, 1921; comdg. U.S.S. Pennsylvania, 1922, Navy Yard, Mare Island, Calif., 1923-24; with Bureau of Navigation, Navy Dept., Washington, D.C., 1924-25; judge advocate gen. with the rank of rear adm., 1925-29; comdr. Special Service Squadron, 1929-30; comdt. 13th Naval District and Puget Sound Navy Yard, Bremerton, Wash., 1931-34; comdr. Scouting Force, with rank of vice-admiral, 1934-35; comdt. 12th Naval Dist., San Francisco, 1935-36; retired, Nov. 1, 1936. Club: Rainier (Seattle). Address: Overlake Drive, Medina WA

CAMPBELL, ELDRIDGE surgeon; b. Alderson, W.Va., Dec. 21, 1901; s. Eldridge H. and Bessie (Spessard) C.; B.S., U. Va., 1923; B.A. (Rhodes Scholar), Balliol Coll., Oxford U., 1925; M.D., Johns Hopkins, 1927; m. Eleanor Brown, July 2, 1930; children-Elizabeth Spessard, Jean McComb, Thomas Richardson Brown. Intern, asst. resident, resident surgery and neurological surgery Johns Hopkins Hospital, 1927-34; faculty Albany Med. Coll., 1934-, prof. surgery, 1946-; practice neurological surgery, Albany, 1934-; surgeon-in-chief Albany Hosp., 1946-. Served as col. M.C., U.S. Army, 1942-46, unit dir., surgeon in chief 33rd Gen. Hosp., acting neurosurg. cons. M.T.O.; neurosurg. cons. Surgeon Gen., Japan, Korea, 1952. Decorated Legion of Merit. Diplomate Am. Bd. Surgery, Am. Bd. Neurol. Surgery. Fellow A.C.S., mem. Am. Surg. Assn., Am. Neurological Assn., Harvey Cushing Soc., Halsted Surg. Soc., So. Surg. Soc., Excelsior Surg. Soc., Soc. U. Med. Cons. in World War II, Soc. Neurological Surgeons, Soc. Univ. Surgeons, Internat. Soc. Surgeons. Clubs: Schuyler Meadows (Loundonville); Ft. Orange (Albany). Home: Old Niskayuna Rd., Loudonville. Office: Albany Hospital, Albany, N.Y. Died Feb. 15, 1956; buried Albany Rural Cemetery.

CAMPBELL, HAROLD DENNY, marine corps officer; b. Middlesex, Vt., Mar. 30, 1895; s. Eugene Ellsworth and Bertha (Denny) C.; C.E., Norwich University, 1917; graduate Air Corps Tactical Sch., 1929, Marine Corps Schools, 1935; student Senior Officers Course (British), England, 1942; married Mildred Fairbanks Shattuck, Mar. 10, 1898; children-Marilyn Denise, Harold Denny, Nancy Jean (dec.). Commd. 2d lt., U.S. Marine Corps, 1917. and advanced through the grades to maj. gen., 1946; served overseas 27 months during World War I; became marine aviator, 1921; chief aviation section Marine Corps Sch., 1931-35; air officer Fleet Marine Force. 1935-39; Am. adviser to Lord Louis Mountbatten. 1942-43; served in Central, South and Western Pacific areas, 1943-45, comdg. 4th Marine Air Wing, later 2d Marine Air Wing and as island comdr., Peleliu; comdg. gen. Marine Corps Air Bases and 9th Wing; 1st island comdr., Peleliu, Western Carolines. Western Pacific. Decorated Purple Heart, Legion of Merit, Navy-Marine Corps Medal, 11 campaign ribbons. Awarded Schiff Trophy for world's record of greatest number of hours in air as pilot without accident, 1926. Member Quiet Birdmen, Am. Legion, Marine Corps League, Phi Kappa Delta, Sigma Nu (life). Author: Employment of Marine Corps Aviation in Small Wars, and Flying over Nicaragua (syndicated mga. article). Home: 90 S. Main St., Waterbury, Vt. Address: care Marine Corps Headquarters, Washington 25. Died Dec. 29, 1955; buried Arlington Nat. Cemetery.

CAMPBELL, JACOB MILLER, congressman, businessman; b. "White Horse." nr. Somerset, Pa., Nov. 20, 1821; attended public schs. Learned printing trade in the office of the Somerset Whig; later connected with mag. publishing co., Pitts., newspapers in New Orleans; engaged in steamboating on lower Mississippi River, 1814-47, gold mining in Cal., 1851; aided in bldg. Cambria Iron Works. Johnstown, Pa., 1853, with co., 1853-61; del. 1st Republican Nat. Conv., Phila., 1856; served in Union Army as 1st lt. and q.m. Co. G, 3d Regt., Pa. Volunteer Inf., recruited the 54th Regt. of Inf., commd. as its col., 1862. brevetted brig. gen. for gallant service in Battle of Piedmont (Va.), 1865; surveyor gen. (later sec. internal affairs) of Pa., 1865-71; mech., indis. pursuits; mem. U.S. Ho. of Reps. (Rep.0 from Pa., 45th, 47th-49th congresses, 1877-79, 81-87; financial interests in banking and steel mfg.; chmn. Pa. Rep. Conv., 1887. Died Johnstown, Sept. 27, 1888; buried Grand View Cemetery.

CAMPBELL, JAMES HEPBURN congressman, diplomat; b. Williamsport, Pa., Feb. 8, 1820; s. Francis and Jane (Hepburn) C.; grad. Dickinson Coll., 1841; LL.D., Carlisle (Pa.) Law Sch., 1841; m. Juliet Lewis, 1843. Admitted to Pa. bar. 1841; mem. U.S. Ho. of Reps. from Pa., 34th, 36th-37th congress, 1855-57, 59-63, chmn. spl. com. on Pacific R.R.; served as lt. col. in command 39th Pa. Volunteers, 1863; apptd. U.S. minister to Sweden by Pres. Lincoln, 1864-67; declined appointment as U.S. minister to Bogota, Columbia, 1866. Died Wayne, Pa., Apr. 12, 1895, buried Woodlands Cemetry, Phila.

CAMPBELL, JAMES HOBART, public utility exec.; b. Jackson, Mich., Oct. 18, 1910; s. Birum Gould and Helen May (Chapel) C.; B.S.M.E., Purdue U., 1933; student Mass. Inst. Tech. (Alfred P. Sloan fellow), 1939-40; D. Engring. (honorary), Purdue U., 1964; m. Jane Hewett, June 11, 1936; children—Bruce Hobart, James Birum, Scott Richard. Power engr., Consumers Power Co., Lansing, Mich., 1933-39; power engr., Ohio Edison Co., Youngstown, 1940-42; asst. to division mgr. Consumers Power Co., Grand Rapids, Mich., 1946-47, division mgr., 1947-49, asst. to pres., 1949-50, v.p., Jackson, Mich., 1950-56, sr. v.p. Consumers Power Co., 1956-60, president, chief operating officer, 1960-72, also dir.; dir., v.p. mem. exec. com. Power Reactor Devel. Co.; dir. Nat. Bank of Jackson, Tecumseh Products Co. (Mich.), Hayes-Albion Corporation. Vice pres., dir. Atomic Indsl. Forum. Chmn. Nat. Assn. Electric Cos., 1962-63. Served from 1st lt. to lt. col., Fifth Army, AUS, 1942-46; ETO. Mem. Am. Gas Assn. (director), Newcomen Society, Beta Theta Pi. Clubs: Town, Country, Rotary (Jackson); Metropolitan (Washington). Student history of Am. Revolution. Home: Jackson MI Died Jan. 24, 1972; buried Campbell Cemetery, Parma MI

CAMPBELL, JAMES ROMULUS congressman; b. Crook Tp., Hamilton Co., Ill., May 4, 1853; s. John and Mary (Coker) C.; ed. U. of Notre Dame, Ind.; admitted to bar, 1877; m. Kittie B. Benson, Dec. 18, 1879. Pub. McLeansboro Times, 1879-99; pres. First Nat. Bank (McLeansboro), Campbell Milling Co. (Carmi, Ill.). Mem. Ill. Ho. of Rep., 1884-88, Senate, 1888-96; mem. 55th Congress (1897-99), as Democrat; resigned seat in Congress, 1898. Col. 9th Ill. Vols., June 28, 1898; hon. mustered out, May 20, 1899; lt. col. 30th U.S.V. Inf., July 5, 1899; brig. gen. vols., Jan. 3, 1901; hon. disch., Mar. 25, 1901; served in Cuba and P.I. Home: McLeansboro, Ill. Died Aug. 12, 1924.

CAMPBELL, JOHN (4th earl Loudoun), army officer; b. Scotland, May 5, 1705; s. Hugh (3d earl Loudoun) and Margaret (Dairymple) C.; never married. Entered Scots Greys as cornet, 1727, rose to capt. with rank of lt. col. 3d Foot Guards, Brit. Army, by 1739; Scottish rep. in English Ho. of Lords (one of few Scottish peers allowed to sit), 1734; became gov. Stirling Castle, 1741; elected fellow Royal Soc., 1738; a.d.c. to King George II; adj. gen. to Sir John Cope during Jacobite rebellion, 1745; col. 30th Regt., Brit. Army, 1749, commd. maj. gen., 1755; comdr. in chief all forces in N.Am., col. in chief Royal Am. Regt., gov. gen. of Va., 1756-57; made improvements in tng. and transp. of troops in Am.; unsuccessful in attempt to take Louisbourg, recalled, 1757; commd. lt. gen., 1758; became gov. Edinburgh Castle, 1763; promoted gen., 1770, col. Scots Guards. Died Loudoun Castle, Scotland, Apr. 27, 1782.

CAMPBELL, JOHN soldier; b. New York, Sept. 16, 1831; s. Archibald and Mary C.; apptd. asst. surgeon, U.S.A., Dec. 1847; served in war with Mexico and afterward at several posts; promoted surgeon, May 1861, serving throughout Civil war; bvtd. col.; promoted lt. col., 1877, and col., and retired Sept. 16, 1885; commd. brig. gen., U.S.A., retired Apr. 23, 1904. Home: Cold Spring, N.Y. Died 1905.

CAMPBELL, JOHN ALLEN diplomat, gov. Wyo. Territory; b. Salem, Columbiana County, O., Oct. 8, 1835. Served as adj. gen. on Maj. Gen. Schofield's staff during Civil War; brevetted brig. gen., 1864; apptd. asst. sec. of state, 1875-77; U.S. consul at Basel, Switzerland, 1877-80. Died Washington, D.C., July 14, 1880.

CAMPBELL, JOSIAH A. PATTERSON judge; b. Waxaw Settlement, S.C., Mar. 2, 1830; s. Rev. R. B. and Mary (Patterson) C.; ed. Camden Acad. and Davidson Coll., N.C.; (LL.D., U. of Miss.); admitted to bar, 1847; m. Eugenia E. Nash, May 23, 1850. In practice Kosciusko, Miss., 1848-65, except war period; at Jackson, Miss., 1876 - . Mem. Ho. of Rep., 1851-59 (speaker, 1859); one of 7 Miss. dels. to conv. which organized Confed. States; capt. lt. col. of inf. and col. of cav., C.S.A., 1862-65; judge Circuit Ct., 1865-70; judge of Supreme Ct., 1876-94 (chief justice 6 yrs.). Mem. Miss. Code Commn., 1870; prepared Miss. code, 1880, still almost wholly in force. Democrat. One of the 49 who signed the constitution of the Confed. States of America. Home: Jackson, Miss. Died Jan. 10, 1917.

CAMPBELL, LEWIS DAVIS editor, congressman, diplomat; b. Franklin, Warren County, O., Aug. 9, 1811; s. Samuel and Mary (Small) G.; m. Jane Reily, 3 children. Admitted to Ohio bar, 1835; mem. U.S. Ho. of Reps. (Whig, later Democrat) from Ohio, 31st-35th, 42d congresses, 1849-59, 71-73, chmn. com. ways and means, 34th Congress; commd. col. 69th Regt., Ohio Volunteers, during Civil War; U.S. minister to Mexico, 1866-67. Died Hamilton, O., Nov. 26, 1882; buried Greenwood Cemetery, Hamilton.

CAMPBELL, SAMUEL congressman; b. Mansfield, Conn., July 11, 1773; attended common schs. Became farmer in Columbus, N.Y.; supr. Town of Columbus, 1807-08, 21, 40; mem. N.Y. State Assembly, 1808-09, 12, 20; served on staff Maj. Gen. Nathaniel King as div. q.m., War of 1812; asso. judge Chenango County (N.Y.) Ct., 1814; justice of the peace, Columbus, 25 years; sheriff Chenango County, 1815-19; mem. U.S. Ho. of Reps. from N.Y., 17th Congress, 1821-23; became a Whig. Died Columbus, June 2, 1853; buried Lambs Corners Cemetery.

CAMPBELL, THOMAS DONALD mech. and agrl. engr.; b. Grand Forks, N.D., Feb. 19, 1882; s. Thomas and Almira Cathrine (Richards) C.; A.B., U. N.D., 1903, M.E., 1904, LL.D., 1929; postgrad. Cornell U., 1904-05; D. Eng., U. So. Cal., 1929; m. Bess McBride Bull, Oct. 3, 1906; children-Thomas D. (dec.), Elizabeth Ann, Jean, Cathrine. Engaged in farming since 1898; operated 95,000 acres of land in Mont. and raised wheat and flax; spl. investigator available farm lands on Indian reservations for U.S. Dept. Interior, World War I; pres. and chief engr. Campbell Farming Corp. since 1922; spl. adviser, cons. engr. for Russian Govt. to assist in forming plans covering operation 10 million acres in Russia, 1929; spl. adviser to Brit. Govt. on increased wheat prodn. and agro. mechanization, 1941; made report for French Govt. on increased wheat prodn. in N. Africa, 1948. Serving as col. AC, U.S. Army, since 1942, overseas, 1943, 45; brig. gen., Apr. 1946; now gen. Army Res. Awarded Commandeur Degree, French Legion of Honor. Mem. Am. Soc. M.E., Am. Soc. Agrl. Engrs., Am. Assn. Engrs., Soc. Am. Mil. Engrs., Am. Inst. Cons. Engrs. Delta Tau Delta. Republican. Presbyn. Mason (Shriner). Clubs: University (Los Angeles); Twilight, Valley Hunt (Pasadena); Union League (Chgo.); University (Washington); Cornell (N.Y.C.). Author: Russia, Market or Menace. Inventor, Campbell Grain Dryer; developer Campbell windrow method of harvesting and threshing grain and furrow dammers on grain drills for conserving moisture. Home: Harden, Mont.; and Albuquerque. Office: Korber Bldg., Albuquerque. Died Mar. 1966.

CAMPBELL, WILLIAM army officer; b. Augusta County, Va., 1745; s. Charles and Miss (Buchanan) C.; m. Elizabeth Henry. Served as capt. Va. Militia; Indian fighter; justice Fincastle County (Va.), 1773; campaigned in Lord Dunmore's War, 1774; signed address from Fincastle County to Continental Congress delcaring loyalty to Crown and willingness to fight for "constitutional rights," 1775; led his company to Williamsburg to help expel Gov. Dunmore 1776; became boundary commr. between Va and Cherokees, 1778; became lt. col. and justice Washington County (Va.), 1777; del. to Va. Legislature; commd. col., 1780; led 400 men from Washington County to join Evan Shelby and John Sevier, fought Gen. Ferguson in Carolinas, 1780; led Va. Militia at Battle of Guilford, 1781, voted thanks, horse and sword by Continental Congress elected to Va. Legislature, 1781; apptd. brig. gen. Va. Militia, 1781; fought under Lafayette in Battle of Jamestown. Died Rocky Mills, Va., Aug. 22, 1781.

CAMPBELL, WILLIAM BOWEN gov. Tenn., congressman; b. Sumner County, Tenn., Feb. 6, 1807; s. David and Catherine (Bowen) C.; m. Frances Owen, 1835. Admitted to Tenn. bar, 1829, mem. lower house Tenn. Legislature, 1855; served as capt. of co. in Seminole War, 1836; mem. U.S. Ho. of Reps. from Tenn., 25th-27th, 39th congresses, 1837-43, 66-67; elected to command 1st Regt. Tenn. Volunteers during Mexican War; last Whig gov. Tenn., 1851-53; circuit judge, 1857; commd. brig. gen. U.S. Volunteers, 1862. Died Lebanon, Tenn., Aug. 19, 1867; buried Cedar Grove Cemetery, Lebanon.

CAMPNEY, RALPH OSBORNE lawyer, Canadian govt. ofcl.; b. Picton, Ont., June 6, 1894; s. Frank Bowerman and Mary Emily (Cronk) C.; A.B., Queen's U., 1921; m. Vera Wilhelmina Farnsworth, Nov. 25, 1925; 1 son, Alan. Called to the bar, Ont., 1924, B.C., 1929, created Dominion King's Counsel, 1940; asso. pvt. sec. to Prime Minister W.L. Mackenzie King, 1924-26; pvt. sec. to Hon. James Malcom, 1926-29; mem. firm Campney, Owen, Murphy & Owen, Vancouver, 1936—. Chmn. Nat. Harbours Bd., 1936-40; mem. Canadian House of Commons for Van Centre, 1949—; Parliamentary asst. to Minister of Nat. Def., 1951, solicitor gen. of Can., 1952, asso. minister of Nat. def., 1953-54, minister of nat. def., 1954—. Canadian rep. council meetings NATO, 1954-56. Past dir. Air Cadet League Can.; trustee, mem. univ. council Queen's U. Served in CEF, 1915-17, Royal Flying Corps, 1917-18. Home: 4629 W. 2d Av., Vancouver, B.C. Office: Dept. Nat. Defence, Ottawa, Ont., Can. Died Oct. 6, 1967.

CANADA, JOHN WALTER lawyer; b. Memphis, Tenn., Dec. 27, 1876; s. W. W. and Sallie T. (Brewster) C.; grad. Memphis Inst., 1895; student Millsaps Coll., Jackson, Miss., 1895-97; m. 2d, Virginia Broaddus, Mar. 16, 1934. Admitted to Tenn. bar, 1897; gen. atty M.P.R.R.; v.p. and gen. counsel Union Railway Co. since 1905; gen. counsel and mem. exec. com. and bd. of dirs. Union Planters Nat. Bank & Trust Co., Plough, Inc., gen counsel Ark. & Memphis Ry., Bridge & Terminal Co., Memphis Union Station Co.; counsel for Tenn. and Miss. for St.L.&S.L. R.R.; gen. atty. for Tenn. M.P.R.R.; atty. St. Louis Southwestern Ry. Co. Served in Cuba as capt. 4th Tenn. Vols., Spanish-Am. War; retired at Col. Tenn. Nat Guards. Mem. Kappa Alpha. Democrat. Episcopalian. Clubs: University, Tennessee, Memphis Country (Memphis). Home: Adanac Lodge, Memphis. Office: 2910 Sterick Bldg., Memphis, Tenn. Died June 11, 1944.

CANADA, ROBERT OWEN, JR., retired naval med. officer; b. Grottoes, Va., July 16, 1913; s. Robert Owen and Mary Patterson (Crawford) C.; grad. Augusta Mil. Acad., Ft. Defiance, Va., 1931, M.D., U. Va., 1937; m. Julia Dent Salter, July 16, 1938; 1 son, Robert Owen III. Intern U. Va. Hosp., 1937-38; commd. lt. (j.g.) U.S. Navy, 1938, advanced through grades to rear adm., 1964; med. officer oiler U.S.S. Salinas, 1940-41; sr. med. officer U.S.S. Pasadena, 1944-45; then shore assignments naval hosps. Charleston, S.C., Oakland, Cal., Portsmouth, Va., Sampson, N.Y., Fitzsimons Gen. Hosp., Denver; comdg. officer U.S. Naval Hosp., Jacksonville, Fla., 1961-62, Bethesda, Md., 1962-65; dep. surg. gen., asst. chief Bur. Medicine and Surgery, Navy Dept., 1965-68; comdg. officer Nat. Naval Medical Center, Bethesda, 1968-69; ret., 1969; mem. staff Greenbrier Clinic, White Sulphur Springs, W. Va., 1969—. Decorated Legion of Merit. Diplomate Am. Bd. Internal Medicine. Fellow A.C.P. (gov. for Navy), Am. Coll. Chest Physicians; mem. Am. Clin. and Climatol. Assn., Am. Thoracic Soc., A.M.A. Home: Lewisburg WV Died Dec. 6, 1972; buried Arlington Cemetery, Washington DC

CANBY, EDWARD RICHARD SPRIGG army officer; b. Ky., Aug. 1817; s. Israel T. Canby; grad. U.S. Mil. Acad., 1839. Served as 2d lt. 2d Inf., U.S. Army, 1st lt., 1846; asst. adj. gen. with rank col., 1847-48; served in Mexican War, 1847; commd. maj. 10th Inf., 1855, col. 19th Inf., 1861; commanded Dept. of N.M., 1861-62; brig. gen. U.S. in N.M.; maj. gen. U.S. Volunteers, 1864; comdr. La. Army and Mil. Div. of West Mississippi, 1864; captured Mobile Ala., 1865; commd. brig. gen. U.S. Army, 1866; assigned a command on Pacific Coast, 1870. Died Siskiyou County, Cal., Apr. 11, 1873.

CANDLER, ALLEN DANIEL governor; b. Lumpkin Co., Ga., Nov. 4, 1834; s. Daniel G. and Nancy C. (Matthews) C.; A.B., Mercer U., Ga., 1859, A.M., 1866 (LL.D., 1908); m. Eugenia Williams, Jan. 12, 1864. Served pvt. to col., C.S.A., 1861-65; founded Clayton High Sch., and was prin. same, 1859-61 and 1867-69; v.p. Monroe Female Coll., 1865-66; pres. Bailey Inst., 1870-71; mem. Ga. Ho. of Rep., 1872-78, Senate, 1879-80; was pres. of a ry., 1879-92; mem. 48th to 51st Congresses (1883-91); sec. of state of Ga., 1894-98; gov. Ga., 1898-1902; state historian. 1903 - . Democrat. Home: Atlanta, Ga. Died 1910.

CANDLER, JOHN SLAUGHTER lawyer; b. Villa Rica, Ga., Oct. 22, 1861; s. Samuel Charles and Martha (Beall) C.; A.B., Emory Coll., 1880, A.M., 1883, LL.D., 1924; m. Lula Garnier, January 16, 1884 (now deceased); children-Asa Warren (dec.), Allie Garnier (Mrs. J. Sam), Guy; m. 2d, Florida George Anderson, August 1, 1906 (died Oct. 7, 1935); m. 3d, Martha Erwin, Dec. 31, 1936. Admitted Ga. bar, 1882; solicitor gen. 1887-96; judge Stone Mountain Jud. Circuit of Ga. Superior Courts, 1896-1902: asso. justice Supreme Court, Georgia, 1902-06, resigned to resume law practice. Alderman, City of Atlanta, 1909-14; mayor pro tem. and pres. Gen. Council, 1911, 12, 14. A.-d.-c. on staff Gov. Alexander H. Stephens, with rank of lt.-col.; mil. judge advocate gen. Ga., 1886-93; col. 5th Inf. Ga. N.G., 1893-1901; col. 3d Ga. Vol. Inf., in Spanish-Am. War, 1898. Mem. Gen. Conf. M.E. Ch., S., 5 times between 1890 and 1934; mem. Commn. on Unification of the two branches of the denomination; pres. Bd. of Edn., North Ga. Conf.; mem. S.R., Kappa Alpha, Phi Beta Kappa, Phi Delta Phi, Omicron Delta Kappa. Democrat. Mason (32ff, Shriner). Home: 199 Tuxedo Road. Office: 410 Palmer Bldg., Atlanta, Ga.* Died Dec. 9, 1941.

CANDLER, SAMUEL CHARLES, merchant; born Oxford, Ga., Dec. 9, 1895; s. Warren Akin and Sarah Antoinette (Curtright) C.; A.B., Emory U., 1916; m. Mary Frances Godfrey, Nov. 29, 1917; children—Caroline (Mrs. Lowry W. Hunt), Frances (Mrs. Frances C. Shumway). Pres., Godfrey's Warehouse, Madison, Ga., 1937-70, ret. chmn. bd. Mem. Southeastern Jurisdictional Conf., 1948, 52, member comm. on chaplains, 1948-64. Trustee emeritus Emory University, Atlanta, Georgia; ret. trustee Wesleyan Christian Advocate, Salem Camp Ground. Served as capt., inf., U.S. Army, World War I. Mem. Am. Legion, Kappa Alpha. Mason. Clubs: Atlanta Athletic. Home: Madison3GA Died Feb. 10, 1973.

CANHAM, CHARLES DRAPER WILLIAM army officer; b. Kola, Miss., Jan. 26, 1901; s. Thomas and Helen (Moll) C.; B.S., U.S. Mil . Acad., 1926; grad. Inf. Sch., 1931, Command and Gen. Staff Sch., 1939; m. Alma Brayton, Mar. 31, 1921; children-Robert C., Charles Draper William, Jr. Thomas R. Entered U.S. Army, as pvt., F.A., 1919, advancing through the the grades to maj. gen.; served overseas during World War I and World War II. Director of the Army Council of Review Boards. Decorated Distinguished Service Order (British), Distinguished Service Cross, Silver Star, Bronze Star, Purple Heart, Presidential Unit Citation, Combat Infantryman Badge (U.S.). Address: care Adjutant General, War Dept., Washington, D.C. Died Aug. 1963.

CANN, JAMES FERRIS lawyer; b. Savannah, Ga., Dec. 11, 1868; s. James Ferris and Anna Sophia (Turner) C.; ed. pub. schs. Savannah and Ga. Mil. Acad.; studied law summers, U. of Va.; m. Eliza Chisholm, Oct. 10, 1916; 1 son, James Ferris. Admitted of Ga. bar, 1889, and since practiced in Savannah; partner G. T. and J. F. Cann and successors, now Anderson, Cann & Dunn; state senator, 1900-02; mem. Ga. Ho. of Rep., 1902-05; pres., dir. Industrial Savings & Loan Co., Tybee Beach Co., Savannah Warehouse & Compress Co., Chatham Fertilizer Co., Blum Corp.; v.p., dir. Cann Estate; former chmn. council Savannah Beach Tybee Island since 1920; judge adv. gen. of Ga., 1910-16. Pres. Savannah Benevolent Assn. Member Savannah Cotton Exchange. Served as capt. Co. C, Savannah Vol. Guards, 1896-1903; capt. Co. K, 2d Ga. Inf. Vols. Spanish-Am. War, 1898; maj., div. judge adv. Nat. Army, World War, 1917. Mem. Am., Ga. State and Savannah bar assns., Ga. Hist. Soc., Telfair Acad. Arts and Sciences, Am. Legion, Spanish Am. War Veterans, Naval Mil. Order Spanish Arm. Am. War, Sons of Revolution, Sigma Alpha Epsilon. Democrat. Episcopalian (vestryman St. John's Church in Savannah). Clubs: Oglethorpe (ex-pres.), Savannah Golf (ex-pres.), Savannah Yacht (ex-commodore). Home: 111 E. 54th St. Office: Blun Bldg., Savannah, Ga. Died Feb. 14, 1944.

CANNAN, ROBERT KEITH, organization exec.; b. Fowler, Cal., April 18, 1894; son of David and Mary (Cunningham) C.; B.Sc., University of London (England), 1914, M.Sc., 1923, D.Sc., 1929; married Catherine Ann Smith, Aug. 4, 1920; 1 dau., Cecily (Mrs. Henry M. Selby); m. 2d, Hildegard Wilson, Aug. 21, 1953. Asst. biochemistry U. London, 1919-23; Rockefeller traveling fellow in United States, 1924-25; lecturer, U. of London, 1925-30; prof. chemistry N.Y.U., 1930-52; vice chmn., div. med. scis. Nat. Research Council, 1952-53, chairman 1953-67; spl. asst. to pres. Nat. Acad. Sciences, 1967-70. With B.E.F., France, 1914-19; lt. 2d East Lancashire Regt., 1914-15; capt. 66th Div. Trench Mortar, 1916-19. Mem. Nat. Acad. Scis. Clubs: Cosmos (Washington); Century Assn., (N.Y.). Home: Washington DC Died May 24, 1971.

CANNON, JOHN KENNETH U.S.A.F. officer; b. Salt Lake City, Mar. 9, 1892; s. John M. and Margaret (Peart) C.; student Utah State Coll., 1910-14, Air Corps Tactical Sch., 1935-36, Command and Gen. Staff Sch., 1936-37; m. LaVon Bennion, June 16, 1922; children-Joan, Marion, Margaret. Commd. 2d lt., U.S. Army, 1917; promoted through grades to general. October 29, 1951; rated command pilot, command observer; chief U.S. Mil. Mission to Argentina, June 1938-Oct., 1941; with American Army abroad; chief of staff, 1st Air Force, Mitchel Field; comdg. gen. 1st Intercepter Command, Feb.-Sept., 1942; comd. 12th Air Support Comd. in support of Western Task Force during invasion French Morocco, North Africa; organized Air Training Command Mediterranean Theatre of Operations; dep. comdr. Mediterranean Allied Tactical Air Force for Sicilian Campaign and Invasion of Southern Italy; assumed comd. U.S. 12th Air Force and Mediterranean Allied Tactical Air Force, 1943; air comdr.-in-chief, All Allied Air Forces in Mediterranean and European Theatre, 1945. Comd. Air Training Command, 1946-48; comdr.-in-chief U.S. Air Forces in Europe, 1948-51; now in command Tactical Air Command. Sigma Chi. Address: U.S.A.F., Air Adjutant General's Office, Washington. Died Jan. 12, 1955.

CANNON, NEWTON gov. Tenn. congressman; b. Guilford County, N.C., May 22, 1781; s. Minos and Lettia (Thompson) C.; m. Leah Perkins, Aug. 26, 1813; m. 2d, Rachel Wellborn, Aug. 27, 1818; 11 children. Mem. Tenn. Senate, 1811; served as col. Tenn. Mounted Rifles during War of 1812; served briefly as col. of a regt. mounted volunteers during Creek War, 1813; mem. U.S. Ho. of Reps. (Democrat) from Tenn., 13th-14th, 16th-17th congresses, 1814-17, 19-23; commr. to Chickasaw Indians, 1819; 1st Whig gov. Tenn., 1835-39. Died Harpeth, Tenn., Sept. 16, 1841; buried pvt. estate, Williamson County, Tenn.

CAPERS, ELLISON P.E. bishop of S.C., 1893 - ; b. Charleston, S.C., Oct. 14, 1837; s. William and Susan C.; grad. S.C. Mil. Acad., Nov. 18, 1857; asst. prof. same, 1858-60; m. Charlotte Rebecca Palmer, Feb. 24, 1859. Served maj., lt. col., col. and brig. gen. in C.S.A., 1861-65; severely wounded at Jackson, Miss., May 14, 1863; at Chickamauga, Sept. 20, 1863, and at Franklin, Tenn., Nov. 30, 1864; sec. state S.C., 1867-68. Entered P.E. ministry, 1867; rector Christ Ch., Greenville, S.C., for 20 yrs.; St. Paul's Selma, Ala., 1 yr.; Trinity, Columbia, S.C., 6 yrs. Home:Columbia, S.C. Died 1908. S. America during World War; rep. with rank of A.E. and P. at inauguration of President Alves, of Brazil, also spl. naval del. at inauguration of Dr. Brum, as president of Uruguay, 1919; relieved of command of fleet, Apr. 30, 1919; retired June 30, 1919. Decorations: Spanish Campaign; Cuban Pacification; Mexican Service medal; Haitian Campaign; Dominican Campaign; Victory Medal - patrol clasp; D.S.M. with citation; Bust of Bolivar (Venezuela); Grand Officer Southern Cross (Republic Brazil). Founder and hon. mem. Mil. Order Foreign Wars of U.S. (European comdry., Paris, 1927); hon. life mem. Mil. Order Foreign Wars of U.S. (comdg. gen. 1914-17), Mil. Order World War, etc. Died Dec. 21, 1941.

CAPERTON, WILLIAM BANKS admiral U.S.N.; b. Spring Hill, Tenn., June 30, 1855; s. Samuel B. and Mary Jane (Childress) C.; desc. John Caperton, from Scotland to Va. abt. 1753; Spring Hill Academy; B.Sc., U.S. Naval Acad., 1875; grad. Naval War Coll., 1896; m. Georgie Washington Blacklock; 1 daughter, Marguerite. Ensign, U.S. Navy, Aug. 3, 1877; promoted through grades to rear adm., Feb. 13, 1913; advanced to rank of adm., retired, June 30, 1919. Served on various ships and stas., 1875-96; Naval Intelligence, Washington, D.C., 1896; U.S.S. Brooklyn, 1897; exec. officer U.S.S. Marietta, 1899; insp. ordnance Naval Gun Factory, 1901; exec. officer U.S.S. Prairie, 1904; Naval War Coll., 1904; lighthouse inspector 15th Dist., 1907; comdr. U.S.S. Denver, 1908, U.S.S. Maine, 1909; naval sec. Lighthouse Bd., 1910; Naval War Coll., 1910; mem. Naval Examining and Retiring Bd., 1912; comdt. Naval Sta., Newport, R.I., and 2d Naval Dist., 1913; apptd. comdr. in chief Atlantic Reserve Fleet, Nov. 25, 1914; comdr. Cruiser Squadron of Atlantic Fleet, 1916; in command naval forces that intervened in Haiti, 1915-16; comdr. Naval Forces, Vera Cruz, 1915; comdr. naval forces intervening and suppressing Santo Domingo Revolution, 1916; designated comdr. in chief U.S. Pacific Fleet, July 28, 1916, with rank of admiral. In charge patrol of east coast of east coast of S. America during World War; rep. with rank of A.E. and P. at inauguration of President Alves, of Brazil, also spl. naval del. at inauguration of Dr. Brum, as president of Uruguay, 1919; relieved of command of fleet, Apr. 30, 1919; retired June 30, 1919. Decorations: Spanish Campaign; Cuban Pacification; Mexican Service medal; Haitian Campaign; Dominican Campaign; Victory Medal — patrol clasp; D.S.M. with citation; Bust of Bolivar (Venezuela); Grand Officer Southern (Republic Brazil). Founder and hon. mem. Mil. Order Foreign Wars of U.S. (European comdry., Paris, 1927); hon. life mem. Mil. Order Foreign Wars of U.S. (comdg. gen. 1914-17). Mil. Order World War, etc. Died Dec. 21, 1941.

CAPPS, WASHINGTON LEE naval officer; b. Portsmouth, Va., Jan. 31, 1864; s. Washington Tazewell and Frances (Bernard) C.; grad. U.S. Naval Acad., 1884; B.S., U. of Glasgow, 1888, D.Sc., 1912; m. Edna Ward, d. of Rear Admiral and Mrs. Aaron Ward, of Roslyn, L.I., 1911. Promoted ensign, July 1, 1886; apptd. asst. naval constructor, June 6, 1888; promoted naval constructor, Jan. 28, 1895. Served on the U.S.S. Tennessee, and on the staffs of Rear Admirals Luce and Jouett, 1884-86; spl. duty Glasgow, Scotland, and abroad, 1886-89; Navy Dept. and Cramp's Shipyard, 1889; Navy Yard, New York, 1889-92; Bur. of Constrn. and Repair, Navy Dept., 1892-95; superintending constrn. for the Navy at Union Iron Works, San Francisco, 1896-98; spl. duty on staff of Admiral Dewey, comdr.-in-chief Asiatic sta., 1898-99; superintended raising of several sunken Spanish ships;

mem. Bd. Inspection and Survey, Washington, 1899-1901; then head of the construction dept. of Navy Yard,New York, 1901-03; chief constr. of the Navy and chief of Bur. Constrn. and Repair, with rank of rear admiral, 1903-07, re-apptd., 1907; resigned as chief of bur., Oct. 1910, and given permanent commn., as chief constr., with rank of rear admiral, from Oct. 1, 1910. Spl. duty abroad, 1909 and 1910-11; spl. duty as mem. Navy Yd. Commn., 1916-35, as pres. Navy Compensation Bd., 1917-35; pres. Naval War Claims Bd., 1925-35; pres. bds. on hull changes for U.S. naval vessels bldg. on Atlantic Coast, 1912-29. Gen. mgr. Emergency Fleet Corp., July-Dec. 1917. U.S. commr. Internat. Maritime Conf., London, 1913, and chmn. Conf. Com. on Safety of Constrn.; transferred to retired list, 1928, but continued on active duty by request of sec. of navy. Awarded Navy D.S.M. "for exceptionally meritorious services in a position of great responsibility" during the World War; specially commended, 1924, for services on Naval Compensation Board during preceding seven years. Remained on duty as mem. Navy Yard Commn., pres. Navy Compensation Bd., and pres. Naval War Claims Bd. until day of death, at his home, May 31, 1935.

CAPRON, HORACE agriculturist; b. Attleboro, Mass., Aug. 31, 1804; s. Dr. Seth and Eunice (Mann) C.; m. Louisa V. Snowden, June 5, 1834; m. 2d, Margaret Baker, 1854. Owner, supt. cotton factory, Laurel, Md., 1836-51; nationally known for his progressive farming techniques; commd. lt. col. 14th Ill. Cavalry during Civil War, 1863, commd. brig. gen. U.S. Volunteers, 1865, U.S. Army, 1866; U.S. commr. of agriculture, 1867-71; agrl. commr., chief adviser Japanese Govr., 1871-75; his farming methods revolutionized Japanese system of agriculture. Died Washington, D.C., Feb. 22, 1885.

CAPT, JAMES CLYDE govt. official: b. Tex., June 12, 1888; s. Felix W. and Carrie (Bell) C.; ed. pub. schools, San Antonio. Tex., and Baylor U., Waco, Tex.; divorced; children-Thelma (Mrs. Milton L. Conner), Berlette (Mrs. Robert S. Swain); m. 2d. Katherine Gordon Parker, Dec. 14, 1946. Has been engaged in business successively as railroad employee, small businessman, owner and operator system of dairy products plants, field rep. for Tex. Relief Commn., exec. officer Work Projects Adminstrn.; asst. to director of Bureau of the Census, 1939-41, dir. since Mar. 25, 1941. Served as capt. U.S. Army, with A.E.F., 1917-18. Home: The Westchester, Cathedral Av. N.W., Washington 16; 510 E. Quincy St., San Antonio, Tex. Office: Bureau of the Census, Dept. of Commerce, Washington 25. Died Aug. 30, 1949; buried Arlington (Va.) Nat. Cemetery.

CARD, BENJAMIN COZZENS soldier; b. in R.I., Feb. 15, 1825. Apptd. from Kan., 1st lt. 12th U.S. Inf. and capt. asst. q.m., Sept. 27, 1861; col. q.m. vols., Aug. 2, 1864-Jan. 1, 1867; maj. q.m., June 6, 1872; lt. col. deputy q.m. gen., Aug. 31, 1883; retired by operation of law, Feb. 15, 1889; advanced to rank of col. retired, by act of Apr. 23, 1904. Bvtd.; maj., lt. col. and col., Mar. 13, 1865, "for faithful and meritorious services during the war," brig. gen., Mar. 13, 1865, for same in q.m. dept. during the war. Died Feb. 14, 1916.

CAREY, ASA BACON brig. gen.; b. Windham Co., Conn., July 12, 1835; s. James B. C.; apptd. from Conn., and grad. U.S. Mil. Acad., 1858; m. Laura lf., D. Hon. S. B. Colby, of Vt., July 29, 1867. Commd. 2d lt. 7th Inf., Oct. 1858; advanced through grades to col. asst. p.m. gen., June 10, 1898; brig. gen. p.m. gen., U.S.A., Jan. 30, 1899; retired operation of law, July 12, 1899. Bvtd.: maj., Mar. 28, 1862, "for gallant and meritorious services in battle of Apache Canon, N.M."; lt. col., Mar. 13, 1865, for same in war against Navajo Indians. Author: Legislative History of Pay Department U.S. Army. Home: Vineyard Haven, Mass. Died Apr. 4, 1912.

CARLETON, GUY army officer; b. Austin, Tex., Sept. 9, 1857; s. William and Elizabeth Carleton; grad. U.S. Mil. Acad., 1881, Army War Coll., 1909; m. Cora B. Arthur, June 20, 1883. Commd 2d lt. 2d Cav., June 11, 1881; 1st lt., 1888; capt. 10th Cav., 1898; q.-m., 1901; assigned to 13th cav., 1905; maj. 4th Cav., 1906; lt. col. cav., 1912; assigned to 3d Cav., 1912; col. of cav., 1915; brig. gen., N.A., 1917; maj. gen., 1918. Was at Forts McGinnis and Custer, Mont., and Sherman, Ida., 1881-90; at Fts. Walla Walla, Wash., Ft. Lowell, Ariz., and Ft. Wingate, N.M., 1890-95; on recruiting duty and at Ft. Riley, Kan., 1895-98; comd. troop Montauk Pt., N.Y., Huntsville, Ala., and San Antonio, 1898-99; comd. Dist. of Campechuela, Cuba, 1899, Manzanillo, and Bayamo, Cuba, 1899-1900; in Philippines, 1901-03, 07; duty Gen. Staff and dir. Army War Coll., 1909-12; insp. gen. Philippine Dept., 1916-17; comdr. 159th Depot Brigade, Camp Taylor, Louisville, Ky., 1917; apptd. comdr. Provisional Depot for Corps and Army Troops, Camp Wadsworth, Spartanburg, S.C., 1917. Retired as col. regular army, 1921. Mem. Order of Carabao. Democrat. Episcopalian. Odd Fellow. Clubs: Army and Navy (Washington and Manila). Home: San Antonio. Died Jan. 8, 1946.

CARLETON, HENRY (original name Henry Carleton Cox), jurist, author; b. Va., circa 1785; grad. Yale, 1806; m. Aglae D'Avezac de Castera, May 29, 1815, a dau., Aglae Marie, m. 2d, Mrs. Maria (Vanderburgh) Wiltbank. Served as lt. inf. U.S. Army under Jackson defending New Orleans against British, 1814-15; U.S. dist. atty., 1832; asso. justice Supreme Ct. La., 1837-39; Author: Liberty and Necessity, 1857; Essay on the Will, 1863; translator (with Louis Moreau Lislet) Las Slete Partidas (the Spanish legal code in La.). Died Phila., Mar. 28, 1863.

CARLIN, WALTER JEFFREYS lawyer; b. Brooklyn, N.Y.; s. Joseph and Margaret (Driscoll) C.; LL.B., N.Y. Law Sch., 1904; LL.D., St. John's U., St. Mary's Coll., 1936, Fordham U., 1939, St. Lawrence U., 1940; m. Jeannette King, Nov. 8, 1911 (dec.); 1 dau., Marjorie Jean. Admitted N.Y. bar, 1904; chmn. bd. Lafayette Nat. Bank of Brooklyn; president Lafayette Safe Deposit Co.; director Namm's, Inc., 35 Park West Corporation. Served as pvt. N.Y.N.G. and promoted through grades to colonel, 1899-1901, 1903-21; lt. colonel, Judge Advocate Gen.'s dept., United States Army Reserves, 1922-37. Decorated Chevalier of the Legion of Honor; Cavaliere Order of the Crown of Italy; Officer of the Acad. (France); Officer Order of Crown of Belgium; Caballero, Orden del Merito Juan Pablo Duarte (Dominican Republic); Caballero, Orden de Cristobal Colon (Dominican Republic), Shell of the Holy Land, Master Knight, Sovereign Military Order of Malta; Knight, Grand Cross, Equestrian Order of Holy Sepulchre, Knight of St. Gregory the Great. Member of New York City Milk Commission, 1913, N.Y.C. Commn. on Plan and Survey, 1926, N.Y.C. Board of Education, 1933-39; chmn. Appeal Bd. No. 11, Selective Service, pres. National Catholic Community Service of Brooklyn and L.I., 1941-; mem. exec. com., War Com., Bar of City of N.Y., 1942-46. Member American, N.Y. State, City bar assns., Brooklyn Bar Assn. (ex-trustee), Soc. Med. Jurisprudence (past pres.), N.P. Soc. Mil. and Naval Officers World Wars, C. of C. (dir.), Phi Kappa Psi. Democrat. Catholic. K.C. Clubs: Montauk, Cathedral (Bklyn.); Lawyers (N.Y.C.). Home: 11 Fifth Av. Office: 37 Wall St., N.Y.C. Died Apr. 24, 1958; buried Holy Cross Cemetery, Bklyn.

CARLIN, WILLIAM PASSMORE brig. gen., retired, Nov. 24, 1893; b. Greene Co., Ill., Nov. 24, 1829; grad. U.S. Mil. Acad., 1850. Bvtd. 2d lt., 6th regt., U.S. inf., and served with regt. until 1861, participating in Sioux war, 1855-56; Cheyenne, 1857; Mormon rebellion, 1858. Apptd. col. 38th Ill. vol. inf., 1861; comd. 4,500 men, battle of Fredericktown, Mo., Oct. 21, 1861; promoted brig. gen. vols., Nov. 29, 1862, and bvt. maj. gen., U.S.A. After being mustered out of vol. army, was returned to rank maj., regular army; promoted brig. gen., U.S.A., May 17, 1893, and assumed command dept. of the Columbia; retired by age limit. Home: Carrollton, Ill. Died 1903.

CARLISLE, HAROLD WALTER editor; b. Columbua, O., Mar. 7, 1910; s. Walter Ewing and Blanche (Sniff) C.; student Ohio State U., 1927-31; m. Louise F. Eyerman, Jan. 7, 1932; 1 dau., Eugenia Louise. Polit. writer Ohio State Jour., 1931-40, exec. editor since 1950; city editor Columbus (O.) Dispatch, 1946 50, assistant to the publisher, 1959-; member bd. dirs. Dispatch Printing Co., Columbus Automobile Club. Trustee, Center of Sci. and Industry. Served as lt. col. USAAF, World War II. Mem. Ohio Legislative Corr. Assn., Franklin County Historical Society (trustee), also mem. Air Force Assn., Columbus Zool. Soc., Sigma Delta Chi. Pi Kappa Alpha. Mason (Shriner). Clubs: Nat. Press; Athletic, Young Business Men's (Columbus); Army-Navy (Washington). Home: 1298 Lakewood Rd., Columbus 9, Office: 34 S. 3d St., Columbus 16, O. Died Nov. 7, 1966; buried Arlington (Va.) Nat. Cemetery.

CARLSON, ANTON JULIUS physiologist; b. Bohusian, Sweden, Jan. 29, 1875 s. Carl and Hedwig (Anderson) C.; A.B., Augustana Coll., 1889, A.M., 1899; Ph.D., Stanford U., 1903; honorary degrees of M.D., LL.D., Sc.D. from 8 univs. and colls.; m. Esther Shegren, Sept. 26, 1905; children—Robert Bernard, Alice Esther, Alvin Julius. Came to U.S., 1891. Research asso. Carnegie Instn., 1903-04; asso., asst. prof., prof. and chmn dept. of physiology, U. of Chicago, 1904-40, now Frank P. Hixon Distinguished Service prof., emeritus. Consultant U.S. Food and Drug Administrn., U.S.P.H.S.; lecturer in China under auspices of Rockefeller Found., 1935; with Am. relief expedition in Europe, 1918-19; mem. Internat. Congresses of Physiology in Vienna, 1909, Groningen, 1913, Edinburgh, 1923, Stockholm, 1927, Boston, 1930, Leningrad and Moscow, 1935, Copenhagen, 1950, Montreal, 1953; member medical and research committees of the National Foundation of Infantile Paralysis. Served O.S.R.D. Lt. Colonel, Md. Corps, U.S. Army, 1917-19. Awarded Distinguished Service Gold Medal (A.M.A.), Distinguished Service Citation (Minn. Med. Assn); voted Humanist of Year, 1953. Fellow A.A.A.S. (past pres.); pres. Nat. Soc. for Med. Research, Research Council on Problems of Alcohol, Chicago Com. on Alcoholism; past pres. Am. Biol. Soc., Am. Physiol. Soc., Fedn. of Am. Socs. for Exptl. Biology, Inst. of Medicine, Am. Assn. Univ. Profs.; mem. American Gerontological Society (president), Nat. Acad. Sci., National Research Council, A.M.A. Am. Inst. Nutrition, Am. Inst. Chemists, etc.; mem. biological and med. socs. of France, Germany, Sweden, China and Argentina. Author (books): Control of Hunger in Health and Disease; The Machinery of the Body; also some 200 research reports. Contbr. to Am. and German jours. on physiological subjects. Home: 5228 Greenwood Av., Chgo. 15. Died Sept. 2, 1956.

CARLSON, EVANS FORDYCE Marine Corps officer; b. Sidney, N.Y., Feb. 26, 1896; s. Thomas Alpine and Joetta (Evans) C.; student George Washington Univ.; spl. student internat. law and politics, 1935-36, 37; m. Peggy Tatum; children-Evans Charles (officer U.S.M.C.), Anthony John. Entered U.S. Army, 1912: served in Philippine Islands, Hawaii, Mexican Border; commd. capt., F.A., 1917; in France and Germany 1917-19; asst. adj. gen. 87th Div., mem. staff of Gen. John Pershing, and with Army of Occupation; returned to civilian life, 1920-21; entered U.S. Marine Corps, 1922; served in West Indies, with Battle Fleet and in Nicaragua; observer with Chinese armies, 1937-38; joined Chinese guerrilla forces in penetrations behind Japanese lines; resigned U.S.M.C. to lecture and write, 1939; reentered Marine Corps, 1941, becoming comdr. 2d Marine Raider Bn. (Carlson's Raiders) with rank of lt. col., and advanced through the grades to brig. gen.; retired, 1946, as result of wounds in action. Decorated Navy Cross (3), Legion of Merit, Purple Heart (2), Presidential Unit Citation (3), Mexican Border Medal (World War I), German Occupation, Marine Corps Expeditionary, Yangtze Service, Nicaraguan Campaign, Asiatic-Pacific Theater (with 6 stars) and Am. Theater medals (U.S.); Italian War Cross; Presidential Medal of Merit, Medal of Distinction (Nicaragua). Mem. Inst. Pacific Relations, Inst. Ethnic Relations; consultant Nat. Inst. Social Relations. Mason (Scottish Rite). Club: Army and Navy (Washington, D.C.). Author: Twin Stars of China, 1940; The Chinese Army, 1940. Home: Brightwood, Ore. Died May 27, 1947.

CARLTON, CALEB HENRY brig. gen.; b. Cleveland, Sept. 1, 1836; s. C. C. and Jane (Stow) C.; grad. U.S. Mil. Acad., 1859; m. Sara Pollock, Mar. 3, 1863. Bvt. 2d lt. 7th Inf. July 1, 1859; commd. 2d lt. 4th Inf., Oct. 12, 1859; 1st lt., May 14, 1861; capt. June 30, 1862; col. 89th Ohio Inf., July 7, 1863; hon. mustered out of vol. service, June 23, 1865; assigned to 10th Cav., Dec. 15, 1870; maj. 3d Cav., May 17- 1876; lt. col. 7th Cav., Apr. 11, 1889; col. 8th Cav., Jan. 30, 1892; brig. gen., June 28, 1897; retired at own request after 40 yrs.' service, June 30, 1897. Bvt. maj., July campaign; lt. col., Sept. 20, 1863, for battle of Chickamauga, Ga. Died Mar. 21, 1923.

CARMAN, EZRA AYERS b. Metuchen, N.J., Feb. 27, 1834; s. M. F. and Ann Maria (Ayers) C.; early edn. in Middlesex Co., N.J.; grad. Western Mil. Inst., Ky., 1855; asst. prof. mathematics Univ. of Nashville, Tenn., 1855-56 (A.M., U. of Nashville, 1858); m. Ada Salmon, Nov. 22, 1859. Civil pursuits, 1859-60; lt. col. 7th N.J. inf., Sept. 5, 1861; col. 13th N.J. inf., July 8, 1862, and bvt. brig. gen., U.S.V., Mar. 13, 1865; served in Army of the Potomac, Sept. 1861-Sept. 1863; in Army of the Cumberland, Sept. 1863, to end of war, June 8, 1865. Comptroller Jersey City, 1871-75; chief clerk U.S. Dept. of Agr., July 1877-Apr. 1885; mem. Antietam Battlefield Bd., Oct. 1894-July 1898; chmn. Chickamauga and Chattanooga Park Commn., June 1905-. Republican. Died 1909.

CARMODY, THOMAS EDWARD surgeon; b. Shiawassee County, Mich., May 22, 1875; s. Thomas and Mary Ann (Gorman) C.; D.D.S., Dental Sch., U. of Mich., 1897, D.D.Sc., 1898; grad. Sch. of Medicine, U. of Colo., 1903; m. Mary Jane McBride, Nov. 7, 1899; children-David, Ruth P. (Mrs. William G. Summers), Mary Alice (Mrs. Howard D. Cobb). In practice as physician and surgeon since 1903, specializing in otorhinolaryngology, bronchoesophagology, oral and plastic surgery; prof. bacteriology and histology, Dental Coll., U. of Denver, 1898-1905, prof. oral surgery and rhinology, 1905-32. asst. in laryngology and otology, Med. Sch., U. of Colo., 1905-33: chief of otolaryngology, child research council research dept., U. of Colo., 1928-36. Surgeon general of Colo., 1909-11. Served as 1st lt., Med. Res. Corps, U.S. Army, 1917; major, Med. Corps, U.S. Army, 1918-19. Fellow Am. Coll. Surgeons, Am. Coll. Dentists, Internat. Coll. Surgeons. Mem. Denver County Med. Soc. (sec., 1904, pres., 1923), Denver Dental Soc. (pres., 1907), Colorado Otolaryngol. Soc. (1st pres.), Col. Soc. for Crippled Children (1st pres.), Am. Acad. of Opthal. and Otolaryn. (pres., 1923), Am. Bronchoesophagological Soc., Am. Laryn., Rhenol. and Otol. Soc. (pres. 1936), Am. Laryn. Assn. (pres., 1941), Am. Otol. Assn., Am. Soc. of Oral and Plastic Surgs., Am. Soc. of Plastic and Reconstructive Surgery, Am. Med. Assn. (chmn. otolaryn. sec., 1931); mem. 1st Internat. Otolaryn. Congress, Copenhagen, Denmark, 1929; mem. bd. dirs. Nat. Soc. for Crippled Children. Home: 1901 Hudson St. Office: 227 16th St., Denver, Colo. Died Aug. 30, 1946.

CARPENDER, ARTHUR S. naval officer (retired); b. New Brunswick, N.J., Oct. 24, 1884; s. John N. and Annie S. (Kemp) C.; student St. Paul's Sch., Concord; Rutgers Prep. Sch.; grad. U.S. Naval Acad., 1908; grad. sr. course, Naval War Coll.; completed course in submarine instrn., 1922; m. Helena B. Neilson, Apr. 30, 1912. Commd. ensign, U.S. Navy, 1910, advanced through grades to rear adm., 1941, temporary vice adm., 1942, retired as adm., 1946; comd. U.S.S. Fanning; staff commander U.S. Naval Forces, Europe, World War I;

comdr. destroyers, U.S. Atlantic Fleet, later comdr. S.W. Pacific Force; comdt. 9th Naval Dist., World War II; U.S. Navy dir. pub. relations. Supt. Admiral Farragut Academies, Pine Beach, N.J., and St. Petersburg, Fla., since 1948. Decorated D.S.M., Legion of Merit with gold star, Army D.S.M., Distinguished Service Order; Comdr. Mil. Div., Order British Empire, Order Orange-Nassau with Swords (Netherlands). Mem. Navy League of U.S. (v.p.), Clubs: Army and Navy (Washington); Chevy Chase (Md.); New York Yacht. Home: Riverside Dr., Pine Beach, N.J. Address: Admiral Farragut Academy, Pine Beach, N.J. Died Jan. 10, 1960.

CARPENTER, AARON EVERLY, mfg. exec.; b. Woodbury, N.J., Aug. 1, 1883; s. Charles Everly and Florence Rebecca (Browne) C.; A.B., U. Pa., 1906; m. Elizabeth Ryder Williams, 1904 (div.); children—Florence (Mrs. Carpenter Murray), Aaron Everly (dec.); m. 2d, Edythe Aramantha Anderson, July 6, 1914 (dec.). With E. F. Houghton & Co., Phila., mfr. oils, leathers, 1905-69, being successively fgn. rep., treas., 1st v.p., pres. and gen. mgr., chmn. bd., 1950-69; editor The Houghton Line; mem. conseil d'administration Societe des Produits Houghton; dir. E. F. Houghton & Co. of Can., Ltd., E. F. Houghton & Co. of Eng., Ltd., Edgar Vaughan & Co., Ltd., Birmingham, Eng. Bd. mgrs. Germantown Dispensary and Hosp.; trustee Phila. Mus. Art. Served as capt. inf. A.E.F., World War I; maj. USAAF, World War II. Fellow Royal Geog. Soc., St. Andrews Soc., Newcomen Society England; mem. Sigma Alpha Epsilon. Mason (K.T.), National Sojourner. Clubs: Bay Head (New Jersey) Yacht; Racquet, Army and Navy (Washington, D.C.); Manasquan River Marlin and Tuna (Brielle, N.J.); Philadelphia Country; Germantown (Pa.) Cricket. Home: Philadelphia PA Died May 15, 1969.

CARPENTER, BENJAMIN merchant; b. Chicago, Sept. 16, 1865; s. George B. (Greene) and Elizabeth Curtis Carpenter; S.B., Harvard Univ., 1888; m. Helen Graham Fairbank, Sept. 18, 1893; children - Benjamin, Jr., Cordelia Fairbank (wife of Dr. N. S. Davis, III), Elizabeth Webster (Mrs. Thos. L. Marshall), Fairbank. In business, 1888 - ; pres. Geo. B. Carpenter & Co.; v.p. Anniston (Ala.) Cordage Co. Lt. col., Q.M.R.C., on active duty July 1917-Feb. 1919. Mem. Art. Inst., Chicago (life), Chicago Hist. Soc. (life), Field Mus. (life). Home: Chicago, Ill. Died. Feb. 23, 1927.

CARPENTER, CYRUS CLAY gov. Ia.; b. Susquehanna County, Pa., Nov. 24, 1829; s. Asahel and Amanda (Thayer) C.; m. Susan Burkholder, 1864. Tchr. 1st sch. opened, Ft. Dodge, Ia., 1854; mem. Ia. Gen. Assembly, 1857, 1884; commissary of subsistance in U.S. Army under Gen. Sherman; brevetted col., 1865; register Land Office Ia., 1866; gov. Ia., 1871-75; comptroller of treasury U.S., 1875; mem. U.S. Ho. of Reps. from Ia., 46th-47th congresses, 1879-83; postmaster Ft. Dodge. Died Ft. Dodge, May 29, 1898; buried Oakland Cemetery, Ft. Dodge.

CARPENTER, FORD ASHMAN meteorologist, aeronaut; b. Chicago, Ill., Mar. 25, 1868; s. Lebbaeus Ross and Charlotte (Eaton) C.; ed Dilworth Acad.; Carson Astronomical Obs.; U.S. Balloon and Airship Schs., etc.; LL.D., Whittier (Calif.) Coll., 1913; Sc.D., Occidental Coll., Los Angeles, Calif., 1921. With U.S. Weather Service various stations, 1888-1919; special observer, 1940-41; mgr. dept. meteorology and aeronautics, Los Angeles Chamber of Commerce, 1919-41. Hon. lecturer, summer sessions U. of Calif. 1914-16, 1939-41; lecturer, U.S. Army Aviation School, San Diego, 1915, Monterey Mil. Encampment, 1916-17; mem. faculty (lecturer meteorology) Southern br. U. of Calif., 1919-30; lecturer on meteorology, Air Service, War Dept., 1915-44, Babson Inst., 1921-35, Columbia, Cornell, and Northwestern, 1923-38, New York U., West Point Mil. Acad., Annapolis Naval Acad., Poly. Inst. Brooklyn, Carnegie Inst. Pittsburgh, Field Mus., 1925-38, Goodyear-Zeppelin Co., 1926-29, War Coll. (Washington), etc., Meteorological adviser Palos Verdes Estates, 1914-20, Pauba Rancho, 1921-31, TWA, 1927-30, Santa Fe Ry. Co., 1922-35, American Airways, TWA, United Airlines, 1927-38, Los Angeles Municipal Airport, 1927, Hollywood Bowl, 1928, Amer-Hawaiian Steamship Co., 1934-40. Climatol. adviser to Frank A. Vanderlip, 1927-37. Selected and surveyed L.A. Municipal Airport, 1927. Served as pvt., Signal Corps, U.S. Army, 1888; lt. U.S.N.R., class 5, 1920-21; lt. col. Inactive Res., U.S. Army aide, 9th Civilian Defense Area. Meteorol. in defense, World War I: in Intelligence, World War II, lecturing to pre-aviation cadets, 1943-44. Meteorol. observer of aerial bombing of former German battleships, 1921. Radio broadcaster over Stations KFI, KFAC, and KMTR, 1923-41. International balloon pilot No. 913, Fédération Aeronautique Internationale since 1921. Meteorological and aeronautic adviser to naval affairs com. of 72d Congress, 1930; nat. councilor U.S. Chamber of Commerce, Washington, 1933-38. Mem. 8th Internat. Geog. Congress, Washington, D.C., 1904, Internat. Congress Tuberculosis, Washington, D.C., 1908; mem. photographic com. standards, U.S. Dept. Agr., 1908. Climatol. commr. Seattle Expn. (gold medal for meteorol. exhibit), 1909; first photographed red snow in natural colors, 1911; asst. in U.S. Weather Bur. meteorograph ascents into stratosphere, alt. 108,000 ft., 1913; mem. Pan Am. Med. Congress, 1915, 1st International Aero Congress (v.p.), Omaha, 1921. Past fellow A.A.A.S., Royal Meteorol. and Geog. Socs. (London), Am. Seismol. Soc., Am. Assn. Univ. Profs., S.A.R.; fellow San Diego Soc. Nat. History, Southern Calif. Acad. Science (pres. 1929-31, v.p. 1932-39), Nat. 'Assn., Assn. Mil. Engrs., Sigma Xi, Phi Beta Kappa. Republican. Episcopalian. Mason (32ff, Shriner). Clubs: University, Sunset, Scribes (Los Angeles, Calif.); Sojourners, Army and Navy (Washington, D.C.). Author of monographs, pamphlets, articles, etc., including the following: Climate and Weather of San Diego; Influence of the College Spirit; Aviator and Weather Bureau; Meteorological Methods; Aerial Pathways; Roadbeds of the Air; Weather and Flight; Aids to Air Pilots; Climatic Comparisons; Old Probabilities mate; Commercial Climatology; Gen. "Billy" Mitchell As I Knew Him; Sailing Around America's Shores of Two Oceans; Climatology of a Block of Ice, 1945. Contbr. Atlantic Monthly, Scientific Am., Nation's Business, etc. Editor, Meteorology and Aeronautics, 1919-41. Inventor of anemometric scale, hythergraph, televentscope and ventograph. Home: University Club; Office: 108 W. 6th St., Los Angeles 14. Died Nov. 1947.

CARPENTER, GILBERT SALTONSTALL brig. gen. U.S. Army, retired, Jan. 1900; b. Medina, O., Apr. 17, 1836; s. Judge James G. C.; grad. Western Reserve Coll., 1859; admitted to Ohio bar, 1861; m. Elizabeth Thacher Balch, Mar. 1863. Entered army as lt., 19th Ohio vol. inf., 1861; 18th U.S. inf., 1861-66; bvtd. capt. for gallantry, battle Stone River; served in Indian campaigns; maj. 4th U.S. inf.; lt. col. 7th inf.; promoted brig. gen. vols. for gallantry at El Caney, from Sept. 21, 1898, to May 12, 1899; as col. 18th inf. comd. at the battles of Jaro and Pavia, Island of Panay, P.I. Was made brig. gen. U.S.A. and retired Jan. 1900. Home: Montclair, N.J. Died 1904.

CARPENTER, JOHN SLAUGHTER rear admiral; b. Louisville, Ky., May 18, 1860; s. John Slaughter and Ellen Blake (Cosby) C.; ed. pub. and pvt. schs. and under pvt. tutor; studied law Columbian (now George Washington) U.; m. Charlotte Freeman Clark, Oct. 8, 1889; 1 dau., Evelyn Fessenden (Mrs. Everard Stowell Pratt). Apptd. fleet pay clk, European Sta., 1877, and by President Arthur as asst. p.m. with rank of ensign, Oct. 29, 1881; promoted through grades to rear adm., 1921 (the first officer of Supply Corps to reach permanent flag rank in U.S. Navy, upon recommendation of Selection B.); retired May 18, 1924. Attached to Battleship Texas, Spanish-Am War, and participated in Battle of Santiago and minor engagements; served twice as asst. p.m. gen.; fleet p.m. Pacific Sta., 1903-05; then in charge Supply Corps Sch. of Application, Washington, D.C., and of gen. edn. activities in Supply Corps. Awarded Sampson medal with 6 bars, Spanish-Am. War medal, Victory medal, also letter of commendation Navy Dept. for services in World War. Home: Washington, D.C. Died June 24, 1929.

CARPENTER, LOUIS HENRY brig. gen.; b. Glassboro, N.J., Feb. 11, 1839; s. Edward and Anna Maria (Howey) C.; A.B., Central High Sch., Phila., 1856; student Univ. of Pa., class 1859; unmarried, Pvt., corporal and sergt. cos. C. and L, 6th U.S. Cav., Nov. 1, 1861-Sept. 20, 1862; 2d lt. 6th Cav., July 17, 1862; advanced through grades to brig. gen. U.S.V., May 4, 1898; hon. disch., June 12, 1899; brig. gen. U.S.A., Oct. 18, 1899; retired at own request, over 30 yrs.' service, Oct. 19, 1899. Bvtd.: 1st lt., July 3, 1863, for Gettysburg; capt., Sept. 19, 1864, for Winchester, Va.; maj. and lt. col., Mar. 13, 1865, for gallant and meritorious services during the war; col., Oct. 18, 1868, for Beaver Creek, Kan.; col. volunteers, Sept. 28, 1865, for meritorious services during the war; awarded Congressional Medal of Honor, Mar. 26, 1898, for distinguished conduct during Indian campaign in Kan. and Colo., Sept. and Oct., 1868, and in forced march, Sept. 23-25, 1868, to the relief of Forsyth's scouts. Served in Army of Potomac in Civil War, participating in many battles, and as a.d.c. to Gen. Sheridan; served on Indian frontier, 1866-79; comd. Ft. Robinson, Neb., 1883-85, Ft. Myer, Washington, 1887-91; dir. Cav. Sch. of Application, Ft. Riley, Kan., 1892; pres. bd. to revise cav. tactics, 1896; comd. Ft. Sam Houston, Tex., 1897-98; comd. 1st Div., 3d Corps, and 3d Div., 4th Corps, in Spanish-Am. War; mil. gov. Province of Puerto Principle, 1898-99. Home: Philadelphia. Died Jan. 21, 1916.

CARPENTER, WILLIAM H. wholesale coal; b. Nyack, N.Y., Oct. 26, 1878; s. George W. and Sarah Elizabeth (Waldron) C.: ed. high sch.; m. Elizabeth Epperson, Jan. 15, 1920; 1 dau., Betty. Pres. Dexter-Carpenter Coal Co. since 1922, Black Oak-Leland Coal Co., Black Oak Coal Mining Co., Dexcar Queen Coal Co., Carpenter Coal Mining Co., Cammos Coal Mining Co. Served as capt. A.E.F., World War I. Republican. Mason. Clubs: Whitehall, Bankers, Metropolitan (N.Y.C.); Lake Placid (N.Y.); Sleepy Hollow Country (Scarboro-on-Hudson, N.Y.): Blind Brook (Port Chester, N.Y.). Home: 25 East End Av. Office: 30 E. 42d St., N.Y.C. 10017. Died 1965.

CARR, CAMILLE CASATTI CADMUS brig. gen.; b. Harrisonburg, Va., Mar. 3, 1842; s. Dr. Wattson and Maria (Graham) C.; prep. edn. Wheeling, Va., and Chicago; entered University of Chicago, 1859, left in senior yr. before graduation to enter army (hon. A.M., 1873); m. Mrs. Marie C. Camp, Nov. 1878 (dec.). Served pvt. to regimental sergt. maj. 1st U.S. cav., Aug. 15, 1862; advanced through grades to brig. gen., Aug. 17, 1903. Bvtd. 1st lt. (Todd's Tavern), May 6, 1864: capt. (Winchester, Va.), Sept. 19, 1864; maj. (Nez Perce campaign, Idaho), Aug. 20, 1877. Wounded Todd's Tavern, Va., and in battle of Cedar Creek, Va., Oct. 19, 1864. Engaged in Apache campaigns, Ariz., 1866-69, 1871-73, and 1881-82; Nez Perce campaign, 1877; Bannock campaign, 1878, etc.; over 20 yrs. campaigning in Indian country; asst. instr. and instr. cav. in U.S. Inf. and Cav. Sch., Ft. Leavenworth, Kan., 1885-94; insp. gen. Dept. Columbia, 1894-95; command in western part of P.R., 1898-99; comd. regt. in P.I., 1900-01; comdg. post and comdt. Sch. of Application for Cav. and Field Arty. at Ft. Riley, Kan., 1901; comd. Dept. of Mo., Jan. 15-Feb. 24, 1904, Dept. of Dak., 1904-06; retired by operation of law, Mar. 3, 1906. Died July 24, 1914.

CARR, CLARENCE ALFRED rear admiral; b. Crawford County, Pa., July 26, 1856; s. Alfred B. and Chloe R. (Stebbins) C.; grad. U.S. Naval Acad., 1879; M.E., Stevens Inst. Tech., 1884; m. Blanche Lanman, Oct. 19, 1898. Asst. Engr. U.S. Navy, June 10, 1881; chief engr., Apr. 24, 1898; transferred to line as lt., Mar. 3, 1899; lt. comdr., Sept. 28, 1901; comdr., July 22, 1906; capt., July 1, 1910; rear adm., Sept. 26, 1919. Insp. machinery, Seattle, 1902-04; fleet engr. Coast Squadron, and in charge steam engring. on Texas, 1904-06; head dept. steam engring., Navy Yard, Mare Island, Calif., 1906-10; insp. machinery, Bayonne, N.J., 1911-17; engr. officer, Navy Yard, Phila., July 1917-Sept. 1919; insp. machinery, 3d Naval Dist., N.Y. City, Sept. 1919. Catholic. Retired July 22, 1921. Home: New London, Conn. Died Mar. 9, 1930.

CARR, EUGENE ASA brig. gen.; b. Concord, N.Y., Mar. 20, 1830; s. Clark Murwin and Delia Ann (Torrey) C.; brother of Clark Ezra C.; apptd. from N.Y., and grad. U.S. Mil. Acad., 1850; m. Mary P. Magwire, 1865. Bvt. 2d lt. mounted riflemen, July 1, 1850; 2d lt., June 30, 1851; advanced through grades to col. 3d Ill. Cav., Aug. 16, 1861; commd. brig. gen. vols., Mar. 7, 1862, "for distinguished services in battl OF pEA rIDGE, aRK.;" NON. MUSTERED service, Jan. 15, 1866; maj. 5th Cav., July 17, 1862; lt. col. 4th Cav., Jan. 7, 1873; transferred to 5th Cav., Apr. 10, 1873; col. 6th Cav., Apr. 29, 1879; brig. gen., July 19, 1892. Bvtd.: lt. col., Aug. 10, 1861, "for gallant and meritorius services in battle of Wilson's Creek, Mo.;" col., May 7, 1863, for same in action of Black River Bridge, Miss.; brig. gen., Mar. 13, 1865, for same in capture of Little Rock, Ark.; maj. gen., Mar. 13, 1865, for same in the field during the war; also maj. gen. vols., Mar. 11, 1865; awarded Congressional Medal of Honor, Jan. 16, 1894, "for distinguished gallantry in battle of Pea Ridge, Ark." Served on frontier from Missouri River to Pacific and from Mont. to Tex.; was wounded in Texas, 1854, and was in 13 Indian fights; served through Civil War, and was at the battles of Wilson Creek, Mo., Pea Ridge, Ark. (wounded there 3 times), battles of Clarendon, Poison Spring and Jenkins Ferry, Ark., Port Gibson, Champion Hills, Black River Bridge, siege and capture of Vicksburg, siege and capture of Mobile. Received resolutions of thanks from legislatures of Neb., Colo. and N.M.; retired, Feb. 15, 1893. Died 1910.

CARR, IRVING J., army officer; b. Chippewa Falls, Wis., May 29, 1875; s. Joseph Shannon and Ella (Wentworth) C.; C., Pa. Mil. Coll., Chester, 1897; grad. Inf. and Cav. Sch., 1907, Army Signal Sch., 1909, Army Staff Sch., 1920, Army War Coll., 1921, Army Industrial Coll., 1926; m. Margaret Lisle Halley, Apr. 25, 1912 (deceased 1932); m. 2d, Betty Guinn, Mar. 17, 1942. Commd. 2d lieut. inf., U.S. Army, July 9, 1898, advanced through grades to maj. gen., July 1, 1931; chief of staff, Hawaiian Div., 1921-25; dir. Army Industrial Coll., 1926-30; exec. to asst. sec. of war, 1931; chief signal officer, July 1, 1931-Dec. 31, 1934; retired Dec. 31, 1934. Served in the Philippine Islands, 1899-1902, 1903-05, 1909-11; with Punitive Expdn. to Vera Cruz, Mexico, 1914; signal officer 2d Div., 4th Army Corps and 3d Army, France, World War. Awarded silver star citation for gallantry in action against insurgents, Magalang, Luzon, P.I., 1899; meritorious service citation certificate by comdg. gen. A.E.F., for service as chief signal officer; Officer Order of Black Star (France); Purple Heart. Club: Chevy Chase (Md.). Home: Army and Navy Club, Washington DC

CARR, JOHN congressman; b. Uniontown, Ind., Apr. 9, 1793; attended public schs. Fought in Battle of Tippecanoe; apptd. lt. in a co. of U.S. Rangers (authorized by Act of Congress for defense of western frontiers), 1812; brig. gen. and maj. gen. Ind. Militia until death; clk. Clark County (Ind.), 1824-30; Democratic presdl. elector, 1824; mem. U.S. Ho. of Reps. (Dem.) from Ind., 22d-24th, 26th congresses, 1831-37, 39-41. Died Charlestown, Ind., Jan. 20, 1845; buried Old Cemetery.

CARR, JOSEPH BRADFORD army officer; b. Albany, N.Y., Aug. 16, 1828; s. William and Ann C. Commd. Col. N.Y. State Militia, 1849, col. of a militia regt., 1859, col. 2d N.Y. Inf., 1861, commanded a brigade in Peninsula Campaign and 2d Battle of Bull Run; commd. brig. gen. U.S. Volunteers, 1862, led troops at center of Union line at Battle of Gettysburg, 1863; apptd. maj. gen. N.Y. Militia, 1865; sec. of state N.Y. State, 1879, 81, 83; unsuccessful Republican nominee for lt. gov. N.Y., 1885; maj. gen. in command 3d Div. N.Y. Militia, 1893. Died Troy, N.Y., Feb. 24, 1895.

CARR, ROBERT FRANKLIN pres. Dearborn Chemical Co.; b. Argenta, Ill., Nov. 1871; s. Robert F. (M.D.) and Emily A. (Smick) C.; B.S., Univ. of Ill., 1893, LL.D., 1929; m. Louise B. Smiley, 1906 (died Sept. 7, 1925); children-Louise (Mrs. W. P. Hodgkins, Florence (Mrs. Edgar L. Marston, II), Robert Franklin. With Dearborn Chemical Co., Chicago, since 1894, pres. since 1907; director Wilson & Co., Continental Illinois Bank and Trust Co., Peoples Gas Light & Coke Co. (all of Chicago); director Chicago & Eastern Illinois Railroad. Served as major General Staff, U.S. Army, Purchase, Storage and Traffic Division under General Goethals, July 1918-Jan. 1, 1919. Pres. Home for Destitute Crippled Children (Chicago) 1921-33; trustee U. of Ill., term 1915-21, pres. of bd., 1920, 21 (donor of fellowship in chemistry); trustee Northwestern Mut. Life Ins. Co., Milwaukee; chmn. U. of Illinois Memorial Stadium Com. ($1,850,000 stadium completed Oct. 1924, funds all raised among alumni, faculty and students; dedicated to 180 U. of Ill. men who lost lives in World War); chmn. com. to finance and build Illinois Students Union, Mem. Bd. of Edn., Chicago, 1931-33; director general Analine and Film Corporation; trustee Century of Progress Expn., Chicago; trustee Passavant Hospital. Member American Chemical Society, Art Inst. Chicago (life), Chicago Historical Soc., Field Mus. of Chicago (life), Kappa Sigma. Democrat. Episcopalian. Clubs: University (ex-president), Chicago, Commercial, Old Elm, Onwentsia, Shoreacres, Casino, Saddle & Clyde (Chicago); Seigniory (Quebec); Everglades (Palm Beach, Fla.). Home: 545 Deerpath Av., Lake Forest, Ill. Office: 310 S. Michigan Av., Chicago, Ill.* Died Jan. 22, 1945.

CARRINGTON, EDWARD Continental congressman; b. Goochland County, Va., Feb. 11, 1748. Mem. county com., 1755-76; served in Continental Army, commd. lt. col. Arty., 1776, served as q.m. gen. on staff Gen. Greene, commanded Arty. at battle of Hobkirks Hill, 1781, also at Yorktown; mem. Continental Congress from Va., 1785-86; apptd. by Pres. Washington as marshal of Va., 1789; foreman of jury in Aaron Burr treason trial, 1807. Died Richmond, Va., Oct. 28, 1810; buried St. John's Cemetery.

CARRINGTON, GORDON DE L. army officer; b. Evansville, Ind., Nov. 15, 1894; s. Dr. Paul (U.S.P.H.S.) and Belle (Gordon) C.; student San Diego Jr. Coll., 1914-15, U. of Calif., 1915-16; grad. Coast Arty. Sch., 1922, Command and Gen. Staff Sch., 1932, Army War Coll., 1936; m. Jeannie Garnham, June 10, 1917; children-George Baker, William Miles, Virginia Fairholm. Commd. 2 lt., Coast Arty., U.S. Army, 1916, and advanced through the grades to brig. gen. (temp.), 1942. Mem. Theta Xi.† Died Aug. 21, 1944.

CARRINGTON, HENRY BEEBEE brig. gen.; b. Wallingford, Conn., Mar. 2, 1824; A.B., Yale, 1845, A.M., 1848; Yale Law Sch., 1847; (LL.D., Wabash Coll., 1878); m. Margaret Irvin McDowell (author "Absaraka, Home of the Crows"); m. 2d, Frances Courtney, 1871 (widow of Lt. G. W. Grummond); father of James Beebee C. Practiced law, Columbus, O., 1848-61 (Dennison & Carrington); chmn. com. to organize new party, July 13, 1854; adj. gen., 1857-61; escort of legislatures of Ky. and Tenn. to Columbus; of Prince of Wales from Cincinnati to Columbus; of Pres.-elect Lincoln from Springfield to Columbus; at beginning of war moved 9 militia regts. into Western Va.; apptd. col. 18th U.S. Inf., May 14, 1861, and brig. gen. vols., Nov. 29, 1862; served in important commands; also comd. Dist. of Ind.; organized and sent to front 120,000 Ind. vols.; exposed disloyal "Sons of Liberty;" rejoined Army of Cumberland, 1865; opened wagon route to Mont., through Wyo., 1866; comd. Rocky Mountain Dist.; planned and built Ft. Phil Kearney; in active war with the opposing Sioux; wounded in skirmish with the Sioux Indians; comd. Ft. McPherson, Neb., and Ft. Sedgwick, Colo.; detailed as mil. prof. Wabash Coll.; on increased disability retired from active service, 1870; in 1875 was granted access by Great Britain and France to all revolutionary archives; surveyed and mapped the battlefields; made treaty with Flathead Indians of Mont., 1889; in 1891 moved to the Indians through Missoula, across Mission Ridge Range to the Rocky Mountains, to Jocko Reservation, Western Mont.; took detailed census of Six Nations, N.Y., and Cherokees, N.C., 1890. Author: Washington, the Soldier, 1899. Home: Hyde Park, Mass. Died Oct. 26, 1912.

CARROLL, HENRY soldier; b. in N.Y., May 20, 1838. Served pvt., sergt. and 1st sergt., Co. E, 3d Arty., Jan. 13, 1859-Jan. 13, 1864; pvt. and sergt., Co. G. 3d Arty., Feb. 3- June 4, 1864; promoted through grades to lt. col., 6th Cav., May 23, 1896; apptd. brig. gen., vols., June 8, 1898; hon. disch., Nov. 30, 1898; col. 7th Cav., Mar. 29, 1899; retired at own request after 40 yrs.' service, May 6, 1899; advanced to rank of brig. gen. retired, by act of Apr. 23, 1904. Bvtd. maj., Feb. 27, 1890, for action against Indians on main fork of Brozos River, Tex., Sept. 16, 1869, and against Indians in San Andreas Mts., N.M., Apr. 7, 1880 (severely wounded). Died 1908.

CARROLL, PAUL THOMAS army officer; b. Woonsocket, R.I., Apr. 6, 1910; s. Peter Christopher and Cora (McLaughlin) C.; student R.I. State Coll., 1928-29; B.S., U.S. Mil. Acad., 1933; student Inf. Sch., 1939, Armed Forces Staff Coll., 1948, Nat. War Coll., 1952-53; m. Ruth Cooper; children—Paul Thomas, Robert Cooper, David Warringer. Commd 2d lt. U.S. Army, 1933, advanced to brig. gen., 1953; unit comdr. 5th Inf. div., 1941-44; mem. War Dept. Gen. Staff, 1944-48; instr. Command and Gen. Staff Coll., 1949, Army War Coll., 1950; mil. asst. Supreme Allied Comdr. Europe, 1951-52; mil. liaison officer The White House, 1953—, staff sec., 1954—. Home: 7405 Alaska Av., N.W., Washington. Died Sept. 17, 1954; buried Arlington Nat. Cemetery.

CARROLL, SAMUEL SPRIGG army officer; b. Washington, D.C., Sept. 21, 1832; s. William Thomas Carroll; grad. U.S. Mil. Acad., 1856. Quartermaster, U.S. Mil Acad., 1860-1861; commd. 1st lt. 10th Inf., U.S. Army, 1861, capt. 1861; commd. col. 8th Ohio Inf., 1861; commanded brigade in operations in central Va., 1862; participated in No. Va. Campaign and Battle Cedar Mountain; commanded brigade at battles of Fredericksburg, Chancellorsville and Gettysburg; commd. brig. gen. U.S. Volunteers, 1864; commd. lt. col. 21st Inf., 1867, maj. gen. (ret), 1869. Died Washington, D.C., Jan. 28, 1893; buried Oa, Hill Oak Hill Cemetery, Washington.

CARROLL, WILLIAM gov. Tenn.; b. Pitts., Mar. 3, 1788; s. Thomas and Mary (Montgomery) C.; m. Cecelia Bradford, circa 1813. Moved to Nashville, Tenn., 1810; commd. capt. Tenn. Militia, 1812, served as col. during Creek War, 1813, commd. maj. gen., 1814; gov. Tenn., 1821-27, 29-35, noted for reform policies. Died Nashville, Mar. 22, 1844.

CARROLL, WILLIAM HENRY lawyer; b. Panola County, Miss., Feb. 18, 1843; s. Gen. William H. and Elizabeth (Breathitt) C.; student U. of Tenn. through sr. yr.; m. Mattie McKay, June 15, 1888. Enlisted in C.S. Army at outbreak of Civil War, drilling a regt. raised by father; became mem. staff of Gen. Thomas H. Bradley, as vol. and aide; was made adj. 37th Tenn. Regt.; in comd. of Gen. James R. Chalmer's escort; resigned shortly before close of war on account of ill health. Engaged in cotton business in Memphis; admitted to bar, 1875; asso. in practice with Julius H. Taylor, later with Gen. Chalmers; then mem. Carroll & Scott. For many yrs. a leading figure in Tenn. politics; chmn. Dem. State Central Com.; del. Dem. Nat. Conv., 1876, 1880; Dem. presdl. elector from Tenn., 1900. Home: Memphis, Tenn. Died 1916.

CARSON, CHRISTOPHER (Kit Carson), Indian agt., army officer; b. Madison County, Ky., Dec. 24, 1809; s. Lindsay and Rebecca (Robinson) C.; m. Alice (an Indian girl), 1836, 1 dau., Adaline; m. 2d, Maria Josepha Jaramillo, Feb. 6, 1843. Fur trapper in Far West, 1829-41; guide to Fremont's expdns., 1843-44, 45; apptd. lt. Mounted Riflemen by Pres. Polk, appointment rejected by U.S. Senate, 1847; Indian agt., 1853-61; an organizer 1st New Mexican Volunteer Inf., commd. lt. col., 1861, col., 1861; brevetted brig. gen. U.S. Volunteers for gallantry in Battle of Valverde and for distinguished services in N.M., 1865; led campaigns against S.W. Indians during Civil War; took command Ft. Garland in Colo., 1866; dictated account of his life to Lt. Col. DeWitt C. Peters, 1857-58, published as The Life and Adventures of Kit Carson, The Nestor of the Rocky Mountains, 1858. Died Ft. Lyon, Colo., May 23, 1868.

CARSON, CLIFFORD, army officer; b. N. Greenfield, Ohio, Apr. 4, 1876; s. Leonard W. and Laura B. (Conn) C.; B.S., U.S. Mil. Acad., 1900; graduate, Gen. Staff Sch., 1922, Sch. of the Line, 1921, Cav. and F.A. Sch., 1904, Coast Arty. Sch., 1916; unmarried. Commd. 2nd lt., U.S. Army, 1900, and advanced through grades to col. (temp. arty.), 1918; prof. mil. sci. and tactics, Va. Poly. Inst., 1916-17, 1919-20; service in France as maj., lt. col., and col., 6th Art'y, as commander, Tractor Arty. Schs., AEF and with Inspector Gens. Dept., 1917-1919; ret. (own request), 1922; active duty, recruiting service, Knoxville and Chattanooga, Tenn., 1926-28. Recipient D.S.M., in France, 1919. Hon. Alumnus, Va. Poly Inst., 1920. Home: Mount Dora FL

CARSON, JOHN MILLER army officer; b. Phila., June 26, 1864; s. Capt. John Miller and Annie L. (Miller) C.; B.Sc., U.S. Mil. Acad., 1885; m. Margaret Forster Sumner, Dec. 14, 1887; 1 dau., Margaret Sumner (Mrs. Henry C. Holt). Commd. 2d lt. 5th Cav., 1885, promoted through grades to brig. gen. (temp.), 1918; brig. gen. Q.M. Corps, 1920; retired after 40 yrs. service, 1922; adj. U.S. Mil. Acad., 1890-95; adj. 5th Cav., 1895-97; q.m. at hdqrs. U.S. troops in P.R. 1898; asst. to chief q.m. Dept. of P.R. 1898-99, in Philippines, 1899; duty Officer Q.M. Gen., 1900-03; q.m. and disbursing officer and officer in charge of constrn., U.S. Mil. Acad., 1903-11; constrn. q.m., Corregidor Island, P.I., 1911-14; asst. to depot q.m., N.Y.C., 1914-16, depot q.m., 1916-17, gen. supt., Army Trans. Service, N.Y.C., 1917, chief q.m., Line Communications, AEF, France, 1917-18; dep. chief q.m., 1918-19, acting chief q.m., 1919; spl. duty Officer Q.M. Gen., Washington, 1919; zone supply officer, N.Y.C., 1919-20; asst. q.m. gen., 1920-22. Decorated D.S.M.; Spanish-Am. War; Occupation of Puerto Rico; Philippine Insurrection; World War medals; Comdr. Legion of Honor, France; Polonia Restituta, Class IV, Poland. Mem. Loyal Legion, Soc. Foreign Wars, Mil. Order of World Wars. Address: Chandler Farms, Pomfret, Conn. Died Jan. 18, 1956; buried U.S. Mil. Acad. Cemetery, West Point, N.Y.

CARSON, JOSEPH KIRTLEY, JR. lawyer, state senator; born McKinney, Kentucky; December 19, 1891; son of Joseph Kelly and Sallie Elizabeth Adeline (Johnson) C.; Bachelor of Laws, University of Ore., 1917; hon. LL.D., Univ. of Portland (Ore.), 1942; m. Hazel Irene Jenkins, March 26, 1926 (died 1928); m. 2d, Myrtle Cradick, June 19, 1937; children—Joan Cradick, Lucian Joseph. Admitted to Ore. bar, 1917, U.S. Supreme Ct., 1936; gen. practice of law, Portland; commr. U.S. Maritime Commn., 1947-50. Mayor of City of Portland, Ore., 1933-41; now Oregon state senator. Served in the United States Army, 1917-19; colonel O.R.C.; served in World War II, 1942-46. Decorations: Bronze Star Medal; St. Olav's Medal (Norway); Order Orange-Nassau (Netherlands); Order Leopold II (Belgium); Military Medal (Czechoslovakia). Democrat. Episcopalian. Mem. Ore. Bar Assn., Delta Theta Pi. Mason. Maccabees, Woodmen. Clubs: University, Multinomah, Aero, Arlington (Portland); Army and Navy, Nat. Press (Washington); Columbia Edgewater Country (Portland). Home: 7119 N. Fowler Av. Office: Yeon Bldg., Portland, Ore. Died Dec. 20, 1956.

CARSON, MATTHEW VAUGHAN, JR., corp. exec.; b. Cleburne, Tex., Nov. 12, 1910; s. Matthew Vaughan and Mary (Brady) C.; LL.B., U. Tex., 1934; m. Gwendolyn Strieber, Nov. 30, 1933; 1 son, Matthew Vaughan III. Admitted to Tex. bar, 1934, U.S. Supreme Ct. bar, 1949; practiced law, 1934-40; adminstrn. Oil Import Adminstrn., Washington, 1957-60; dir. Office Oil and Gas, Dept. of Interior, 1958-61; vice president of Sinclair Refining Co., Washington, 1961-65; corporate sec. Sinclair Oil Corp., N.Y.C., 1965-69; v.p. Sinclair Oil & Gas Co., Tulsa, 1966-69. Served with USNR, World War II; captain USN (ret.). Decorated Legion of Merit (U.S.); Medal Naval Merit (Spain). Recipient Distinguished Service medal from United States Department of Interior, 1961. Member Texas State Bar, Internat. Petroleum Assn. Home: Sea Island GA Died Oct. 26, 1971; buried Arlington Nat. Cemetery, Arlington VA

CARSTARPHEN, WILLIAM TURNER (KÄR-STÄR), physician; b. Garysburg, N.C., Aug. 25, 1875; s. John R. and Willie E. (Turner) C.; A.B. Wake Forest (N.C.) Coll., 1897; M.D., Jefferson Med. Coll., Phila., 1904; grad. work, same coll., 1910. Began practice Garysburg, N.C., 1904, removed to Kittrell, 1908; prof. physiology, later prof. pharmacology, biochemistry and prof. ednl. hygiene, Wake Forest Coll., 1910-17, splty. gastroenterology; chief med. sect., Works Progress Administration, N.Y. City. Apptd. by War Relocation Authority chief med. officer, Rohwer, Ark., 1942, Granada, Col., 1943. Commissioned capt. Med. R.C., May 1917; major Med. Corps, U.S. Army, Feb. 1918; lieut. col., March 4, 1919; hon. discharged, Aug. 26, 1919. Served as special insp. and instr. at Camp Pike, Ark., sanitary insp. 87th Div. in England, area insp. in France, in comd. 5th Sanitary Train, 5th Div., Luxembourg, and post surgeon, Foreign Office, Paris. Fellow A.M.A.; mem. N.Y. County, N.Y. State med. socs., Union County Med. Soc., Southern Sociol. Congress, Sigma Phi Epsilon, etc. Democrat. Baptist. Mason. Home: Westport, Conn. Died Nov. 2, 1947.

CARTER, A(NDREW) F(RANCIS) naval officer; b. Little Rock, S.C., Jan. 17, 1883; s. William Joseph and Mary (Cottingham) C.; commd. ensign U.S. Naval Acad., 1905; children (by previous marriage)-Mary Cottingham (Mrs. Robert C. Savage), Anne; m. 2d, Chellis Baker, Apr. 14, 1938. Dir., v.p. Russell Co., Boston (Wm. A. Russell Trust), 1920-28, during part of this period, and in connection with activities Russell Co., served as dir., mem. exec. com. Merrimac Chem. Co.; mgr. New Eng. Oil Refining Co., 1928-29; pres., Shell Eastern Petroleum Products, Inc., 1929-33: ind. investigations and bus. in oil industry, 1934-42; organizer Commonwealth Oil Refining Co., 1953. Active duty USN, 1905-20, incl. command of U.S.S. Monocacy in Yangtze River, China, 1914-16; aide to chief naval operations 1916-19; resigned commn., 1920; reentered mil. service, 1942-45 (rear adm. USNR) with petroleum liaison work, dir. petroleum and tanker div. Office Chief Naval Operations, Army-Navy petroleum bd. (exec. officer). Clubs: University (N.Y.C.); Houston Country, Army and Navy (Washington, D.C.), Country (Brookline, Mass.). Awarded: Navy Cross; World War medal, one bronze star; French Fgn. Legion, Chevalier, (all during World War I), D.S.M. (Navy), World War II. Home: Route 3, Dillon S.C. 29536. Died Aug. 2, 1966; buried Arlington Nat. Cemetery.

CARTER, ARTHUR HAZELTON b. Hillsboro, Marion County, Kan., Jan. 6, 1884; s. Thomas Allen and Ada (Jetmore) C.; grad. U.S. Mil. Acad., 1905; C.P.A.; m. Marjorie Sells, July 6, 1910. Served as maj. lt. col. and col. ordnance, World War; lt. col. and col. F.A.;

organized and commanded Field Arty. Central O.T.S., Camp Zachary Taylor, Ky.; hon. discharged Mar. 31, 1919; temp. brigadier gen., 1941; major gen., Apr. 1943. Awarded D.S.M. "for exceptionally meritorious and conspicuous service" in orgn. and administrn. Field Artillery Central O.T.S., World War I. Awarded Oak Leaf Cluster to D.S.M., in lieu of 2d D.S.M., for service in World War II. Partner Haskins & Sells, certified pub. accountants. Pres. bd. govs. Good Samaritan Hosp., Palm Beach, Fla. Mem. Am. Inst. Accountants. Republican. Episcopalian. Clubs: Union League, University, Racquet and Tennis, The Recess, Accountants Club of America (New York); Round Hill (Greenwich); Army and Navy (Washington); Philippine; Blind Brook; Everglades; Gulf Stream. Home: Doubling Rd., Greenwich, Conn. Office: 2 Broadway, N.Y.C. 10004. Died Jan. 3, 1965.

CARTER, CLIFTON CARROLL ret. army officer, educator; b. Lexington, Ky., July 12, 1876; s. John Hubbell and Judith Ann (Coons) C.; grad. U.S. Mil. Acad., 1899, Coast Arty. Sch., 1903, Sch. of Submarine Defense, 1907; B.S. in E.E. Mass. Inst. Tech., 1909; m. Mai Angevine Coleman, Oct. 1, 1902; children—Clifton Coleman, Marshall Sylvester. Commd. 2d lt. arty., 1899, advanced through grades to col. Arty. Corps, 1921; chief ordnance officer and chief signal officer, Dept. of Havana, Cuba, 1899-1901; various stations in U.S., 1902-11; mem. Gen. Staff Corps, chief of staff, Dept. of Hawaii, at Honolulu, 1911-12; pres. Coast Arty. Bd., 1913; adj. U.S. Mil. Acad., 1914-17; prof. natural and experimental philosophy, 1917-40; ret.; promoted to brig. gen. ret. 1948. Spl observer in France, 1918. Mem. Society for Promotion of Engring. Edn., Institute of Aeronautical Sciences. Medals: Spanish-Am. War, Army of Cuban Occupation, Victory Medal (service in France). Author: Simple Aerodynamics and the Airplane. Home: 3133 Connecticut Av., Washington 8. Died Sept. 20, 1950; buried Arlington Nat. Cemetery.

CARTER, GEORGE MILTON adj. gen., Me.; b. Washburn, Me., June 11, 1894; s. Calvin D. and Faustina A. (Dickinson) C.; A.B., in Edn., Univ. of Me., 1918; A.M., Columbia, 1939; Honorary LL.D., University of Maine, 1948; married Myrtle Ruby Stairs, Aug. 16, 1917; children—G. Milton, W. Berkeley. Teacher Secondary Washburn High Sch., 1920-21; supt. schs. Union No. 122, Washburn, 1921-23, No. 124, Caribou, Me., 1923-41. Served in R.O.T.C., 1917; commd. 2d lt. inf., transferred to arty., Sept. 1917; left for fgn. service, Sept. 1917; served as officer 102d F.A., 16th Div. and as instr. Saumur arty. sch., France, 6 mos.; returned to U.S.A. with 102d F.A., Apr. 1919; commd. capt. F.A., Me. Nat. Guard, 1931; comdg. officer Battery B, 152d F.A., Me. Nat. Guard, 1931-40; apptd. adj. gen. State of Me., 1941; became maj. gen., 1954, also state dir. selective service, 1948. Recipient Distinguished medal, N.G. Assn. U.S., 1955. Member Mathematics Teachers Assn., 1920-47; N.E.A. (life); Me. Teachers Assn. (treas. pres. 1938-39), Kappa Phi Kappa. Republican. Methodist. Home: 41 School St. Office: State House, Augusta, Me. Died Sept. 11, 1958.

CARTER, JAMES FRANCIS, naval officer; b. St. Clair, Pa., Mar. 25, 1869; grad. U.S. Naval Acad., 1891. Ensign, July 1, 1893; lt. jr. grade, Mar. 3, 1899; lt., May 26, 1900; lt. comdr., June 3, 1906; comdr., July 1, 1911; capt., July 1, 1917. Served on Mayflower, Spanish-Am. War, 1898; in charge 12th Lighthouse Dist., 1906-8; navigator Georgia, 1908-11; supervisor New York Harbor, 1912; duty at Navy Yard, N.Y., 1912-14; comd. Castine, 1914-16; Navy Yard, Phila., 1916; apptd. comdr. Alabama June 9, 1916. Home: Pottsville PA

CARTER, JESSE MCILVAINE army officer; b. in Mo., Apr. 12, 1863; grad. U.S. Mil. Acad., 1886; married; children - Clara McIlvaine (dec.), Betty Landon, Mary Allen. Commd. 2d lt. 3d Cav., July 1, 1886; promoted through grades to brig. gen., Nov. 16, 1917; maj. gen. N.A., Aug. 8, 1918; brig. gen. U.S.A., retired, Oct. 1, 1921. Duty Gen. Staff, 1909-13; assigned to Militia Bur., War Dept., 1916, chief of bur., 1917; organized and comd. 11th (Regular) Div., Aug. 1918-Feb. 1919. Awarded D.S.M., Feb. 13, 1919, "for exceptionally meritorious and conspicuous service to U.S. Govt." Mgr. Tex. properties Missouri-Lincoln Trust Co. Home: Magnet, Tex. Died June 23, 1930.

CARTER, LANDON pioneer, public ofcl.; b. Va., Jan. 29, 1760; s. John and Elizabeth (Taylor) C. m. Elizabeth Maclin, 1784. Served in Revolutionary War, 1780-83, as capt. in John Sevier's expdn. against the Cherokee Indians, 1780; apptd. maj. N.C. Militia, by N.C. legislature, 1788; lt. col., comdr. S.W. Territory) Militia, Washington Dist. 1790; served as col. during Indian campaign, 1792-93; from Washington County mem. N.C. Ho. of Commons, 1784, 89; sec. State of Franklin, 1784-89, Jonesborough Conv. of 1784, also speaker 1st Senate of Franklin, advocate of entry Franklin as state; treas. Washington dist. Govt. of S.W. Territory; elected by 1st Tenn. Legislature as treas. for dists. of Washington and Hamilton (Tenn.), 1796; trustee, incorporator Marin Acad.; trustee Greenville Coll.; Carter County (Tenn.) named after him; Elizabethton (Tenn.) named for his wife. Died June 5, 1800.

CARTER, OBERLIN MONTGOMERY capt. corps in engrs., U.S.A.; b. in Ohio, 1856; entered Mil. Acad. from Ohio apptd. by Pres. Grant, June 14, 1876; 2d lt. engs., 1880; 1st lt., June 15, 1882; capt., Dec. 14, 1891. Mem. Am. Soc. C.E.'s. Address: War Dept., Washington. Died July 1944.

CARTER, ROBERT colonial ofcl.; b. Lancaster County, Va., 1663; s. John and Sarah (Ludlow) C.; to m. Judith Armistead; m. 2d, Elizabeth Landon sev eral children. Mem. Va. Ho. of Burgesses, 1691-92, 95-99, speakers, 1696, 99; mem. Gov.'s Council, 1699-1732, pres. of council, 1726-32; treas. of Va., 1699-1705; col. and comdr.-in-chief Lancaster County; agt. for proprietors of Northern Neck of Va., 1702-11, 22-32; one of wealthiest men in Va.; rector, trustee Coll. William and Mary: built Christ Ch., Lancaster County. Died Aug. 4, 1732.

CARTER, SAMUEL POWHATAN naval and army officer; b. Elizabethtown, Tenn., Aug. 6, 1819; s. Alfred Moore and Evaline (Parry) C.; attended Washington Coll., Princeton; grad. U.S. Naval Acad., 1846; m. Carrie Potts. Commd. Midshipman U.S. Navy, 1846; asst. prof. mathematics U.S. Naval Acad., 1850-53 asst. to exec. officer, 1857-60; detailed from U.S. Navy to spl. duty at War Dept., 1861; brig. gen. Tenn. Volunteers, defeated Morgan, 1862; commanded 1st important cavalry raid by U.S. Army at battles of Holsten, Carter's Station and Jonesville; commd. lt. comdr. U.S. Navy, 1863, comdr., 1865; comdr. steamer Monacacy, 1866; commd. capt. 1870; commandant U.S. Naval Acad, 1870-73; mem. Lighthouse Bd., 1877-80; commodore, 1878, rear adm. (ret.), 1882; only Am. officer to be both rear adm. U.S. Navy and maj. gen. U.S. Army. Died Washington, D.C., May 26, 1891; buried Oak Hill Cemetery, Washington.

CARTER, WILLIAM clergyman; b. Pittington, England, May 22, 1868; s. Joseph and Thomasina (Whitford) C.; came to U.S., 1883; B.A., Parsons Coll., Ia., 1891, M.A., 1894; grad. McCormick Theol. Sem., 1894; D.D., Knox College, 1907; LL.D., Parsons College, 1925; m. Alice Kellogg, May 17, 1893; children-Mrs. Florence Carter Snow, Mrs. Louis A. Cerf. Jr., William K., Whitford van Dyke. Ordained to ministry of Presby. Ch., 1893; pastor 1st Ch., Sterling, Ill., 1894-99, 1st Ch., Kansas City, Mo., 1899-1906, Madison Av. Ref. Ch., N.Y. City, 1906-12; sec. Internat. Peace Forum, 1912-14; pres. Ch. and Sch. Social Service Bur., New York, 1914-16; pastor Throop Av. Presbyn. Ch., Brooklyn, 1915-33. Chmn. of Interdenominational Fellowship of the Spirit since 1933. Am. corr. for Christian Herald, Messina Earthquake, 1908; special corr. for Brooklyn Eagle in Far East, 1922. Chaplain Junior Plattsburg (N.Y.) Camp, 1917; Y.M.C.A. traveling chaplain through southern camps, 1918; lieut. col. chaplain U.S. Res. (past nat. and N.Y. state chaplain); sr. chaplain 77th Div., 2d Corps Area, Reserve. Lecturer N.Y. City Board of Edn., 1909-19. Special tariff speaker for Rep. Nat. Com., following Woodrow Wilson through New England, 1912; speaker for Rep. Nat. Com., 9th Congl. Dist., Va., 1912, 14, Republican, Presbyterian. Clubs: Chi Alpha, Sigma Chi, Union League (New York); Authors' (London); Army and Navy (Washington, D.C.). Mem. Institut Litteraire et Artistique de France. Author: The Gates of Janus (epic story of the World War), 1919; The Other Side of the Door, 1927; A Nation's Sire, 1931; World Poetry, Its Origins and Developments, 1943; (brochures) Milton and His Masterpiece; Studies in the Pentateuch. Extensive traveler, and lecturer on history, literature and current events. Home: 25 E. 99th St., New York, N.Y. Died July 26, 1949.

CARTER, WILLIAM HARDING major gen. U.S. Army; b. Nashville, Tenn., Nov. 19, 1851; s. Samuel Jefferson and Anne (Vaulx) C.; ed. pvt. and pub. schs., Nashville and Ky. Mil. Inst., Frankfort; mounted messenger in Civil War, 1864-65; grad. U.S. Mil. Acad., 1873; m. Ida Dawley, Oct. 27, 1880. Apptd. 2d lt. 8th Inf., June 13, 1873; promoted through grades to maj. gen., Nov. 13, 1909. Awarded Congressional Medal of Honor "for distinguished bravery in action against Apache Indians at Cibicu Creek, Ariz., Aug. 30, 1881;" D.S.M., World War. Student of army orgn. and adminstrn.; chiefly responsible for tech. details of army orgn., 1901-03. Comdg. 2d Div. U.S. Army, 1913, Hawaiian Dept., Jan. 1914-15; retired by operation of law, Nov. 19, 1915; recalled for active service, Aug. 26, 1917; comd. Central Dept., Chicago, Aug. 1917-Feb. 1918. Author: Horses, Saddles and Bridles, 4th edit., 1918; From Yorktown to Santiago with the Sixth Cavalry, 1900; Old Army Sketches, 1906; Giles Carter of Virginia, 1909; The American Army, 1915; Life and Services of Lieutenant General Chaffee, 1917. Died May 24, 1925.

CARTER, WILLIAM V., army officer; b. Fort Lowell, Ariz., Jan. 30, 1883; s. Maj. Gen. William Giles Harding and Ida (Dawley) C.; B.S., U.S. Mil. Acad., 1904; m. Helen C. Hunter, Aug. 14, 1907 (now dec.); 1 son, William H. (dec.); m. 2d, Margaret B. Woodbury, Jan. 5, 1921; children—Woodbury, Leigh, David Giles. Commd. 2d lt., U.S. Army, 1904, and advanced through the grades to brig. gen., 1940; began service in the cavalry; transferred to Adj. Gen. Dept., 1922; later in charge personnel bureau; retired, Aug. 31, 1942. Awarded Victory medal, World War. Club: Army and Navy Country (Washington, D.C.). Home: Westerly RI Died Jan. 1971.

CARTY, JOHN J. elec. engr.; b. Cambridge, Mass., Apr. 14, 1861; ed. Cambridge Latin Sch.; D. Engring., Stevens Inst. Tech., 1915, New York U., 1922; D.Sc., U. of Chicago, Bowdoin, 1916, Tufts, 1919, Yale 1922, Princeton, 1923; LL.D., McGill, 1917, U. of Pa., 1924; m. Marion Mount Russell, Aug. 8, 1891; 1 son, John Russell. Began with Bell System in Boston, 1879, served in various positions, including chief engr. New York Telephone Co., 1889-1907, chief engr. Am. Telephone & Telegraph Co., 1907-19, v.p. same, 1919-30. A pioneer in development of telephone, for which invented many improvements. Trustee of Carnegie Instn., Washington, Carnegie Corp. (New York). Fellow Am. Academy of Arts and Sciences, American Institute E.E. (pres. 1915-16); hon. mem. Franklin Inst., etc. Longstreth medal, 1903, and Franklin medal, 1916. Franklin Inst.; Edison medal, 1918, Am. Inst. E.E.; John Fritz medal, 1928, engring. societies. Commd. maj. Signal Officers' R.C. Jan. 1917; col. (temp.) U.S. Army, 1917; served on staff chief signal officer U.S. Army, and in France on staff chief signal officer A.E.F.; signal officer during armistice, in charge of communications, Am. Commn. to Negotiate Peace; brig. gen. U.S. Army Res. Decorated D.S.M. (U.S.); Officer Legion of Honor (French), Order Rising Sun and Order Sacred Treasure (Japanese). Home: Winter Park, Fla. Died Dec. 27, 1932.

CARVER, JOHN Pilgrim father, colonial gov.; b. Nottinghamshire or Derbyshire, Eng., circa 1576. Went to Holland, 1609; joined Leyden Pilgrims, circa 1610-11; agt. to Eng. to secure charter from Virginia Co.; responsible for Common Stock agreement under which Mayflower Pilgrims sailed for New World, hired Mayflower to go to New Eng.; 1st gov. Plymouth Colony 1620-21; obtained treaty with Indian chief Massasoit, 1621. Died Plymouth, Mass., Apr. 5, 1621.

CARY, ROBERT WEBSTER naval officer (ret.), business exec.; b. Kansas City, Mo., Aug. 18, 1890; s. Robert Webster and Lalla (Marmaduke) C.; student William Jewell Coll., 1907, U. Mo., 1907-09; B.S., U.S. Naval Acad., 1914; student Naval War Coll., 1936-37; m. Jane McCollum Watt, July 6, 1915 (dec. Jan. 10, 1931); children-Lalla Jane (wife of Comdr. William McCormick), Barbara Frances (Mrs.Louis Pembroke Brown), Robert Webster; m. 2d Helen Jane Christian, Sept. 7, 1932; stepchildren-Elizabeth Craven Harris, Jane VanRennselear Harris (wife of Comdr. Walter L. Small). Commd. ensign US Navy, 1914, and advanced through grades to commodore, 1944; ret. with rank of rear adm., Dec. 1, 1946; mem. staff 3d naval dist. N.Y., and destroyer, Queenstown, Ireland, 1917-19; comdr. U.S.S. Jacob Joses, 1931-32; exec. officer U.S.S. Chicago, 1939-40; dir. of base maintenance div., Office of Chief of Naval Operations, 1942-43; comdr. U.S.S. Savannah, Sicily and Italy, 1943, U.S.S. Brooklyn, Anzio, Italy, 1943-44, Naval Training and Distribution Center, Treasure Island, San Francisco, 1944-46; dir. planning group, office of pres., Willys-Overland Motors, Inc., 1946-47, personnel and indsl. relations, 1947-48, asst. to exec. v.p., since 1947. Awarded Congressional Medal of Honor, Navy Cross, Legion of Merit with 4 gold stars, Commendation ribbon, various service medals; decorated comdr. Order of Orange Nassau with swords (Netherlands), Distinguished Service Order (Gt. Britain). Mem. Acad. of Polit. Sci., Am. Acad. of Polit. and Social Sci., U.S. Naval Ints., Am. Legion, Legion of Valor, Am. Vets., Phi Delta Theta, Protestant Episcopal. Clubs: Army Navy, Army Navy Country (Washington), Toledo (O.), Bohemian (San Francisco). Home: 2043 Mt. Vernon Rd., Toledo 7. Office: Willys-Overland Motors, Inc., Wolcott Boulevard, Toledo, 1. Died July 16, 1967.

CASE, JAMES THOMAS surgeon, roentgenologist; b. San Antonio, Tex., Jan. 5, 1882; s. of James Henry and Fannie Elizabeth (Robertson) C.; M.D., Am. Med. Missionary Coll. U. of Ill. Med. Sch., 1905; D.M.R.E., U. of Cambridge, 1920; m. Helena Margaret Kellogg, Sept. 1908; children-Herbert Roland, Margaret Frances. House surgeon, Battle Creek Sanitarium, 1908-10, asst. surgeon, 1910-19, chief surgeon, 1919-29, consultant, 1929-51, dir. of sanitarium's Roentgen department; also president of board of trustees, 1944-51: formerly director of X-ray dept. St. Luke's Hosp., Chicago and Evanston (Ill.) Hospital professor roentgenology, Northwestern University Medical School, 1912-47, professor emeritus since 1947; mem. exec. com. Chicago Tumor Inst., 1947-52, pres., 1949-52; radiologist U.S. Marine and Highland Park hosps., 1929-52; dir. Meml. Cancer Found., Santa Barbara, 1951-. Pres. Race Betterment Found. 1942-51. Served as lt. col. Med. R.C., 1917; in general charge of X-ray work, A.E.F., in France, 1917-18; col., 1920-32; exec. officer 108th Med. Regt., 33d Div., 1932-37. Decorated with Order of the Purple Heart (U.S.); with Order of Merito Militar (Mexico), 1948; Cuban Order of Merit, Carlos Finlay, 1955; Colombian Orden de Boyaca, 1955; recipient gold medal, Interamerican Congress of Radiology, 1955; honorary professor radiol. U. of San Marcos, Lima (Peru), 1949. Editor Annals of Roentgenology, 1920-38. Pres. Am. Roentgen. Ray Soc., 1919-20. Caldwell lectr., gold medalist, 1939; pres. Am. Radium Society, 1923-24 (Janeway lecturer and medalist 1959), American Coll. Radiology, 1929-30; treas. Internat. Coll. Surgeons, 1949-56; fellow A.C.S., Royal Soc. Medicine (Eng.), Radiol . Soc. of N.A. (Carman lectr., 1937; gold medalist, 1950); mem. Interam. Congress Radiology (pres. 1955): hon. mem. roentgen and radiology profl. socs. Am., France Spain, Brazil, Peru and other countries; mem. fgn. and domestic scientific socs. Del. to and sometimes officer of several internat. profl. congresses. Republican. Author X-ray Examination of the Alimentary Tract (4 vols.), 1914, Spanish Edition, 1918; also chapters in various med. books. Translator German books in field. Home: 416 Samarkand Dr. Office: 2315 Bath St., Santa Barbara, Cal. Died May 25, 1960.

CASE, NORMAN STANLEY lawyer, former gov. of R.I.; b. Providence, Oct. 11, 1888; s. John Warren and Louise Marea (White) C.; A.B., Brown U., 1908; studied law, Harvard U., 1909-11; LL.B., Boston U., 1912; LL.D., Manhattan Coll., 1930, R.I. State Coll., 1931; m. Emma Louise Arnold, June 28, 1916; children-Norman Stanley, John Warren (dec. France, 1944), Elizabeth Richmond. Admitted to bar, R.I., 1911, Mass., 1912, Supreme Ct. of U.S., 1923, Mem. City Council, Providence, 1914-18; mem. Soldiers' Bonus (Bd. R.I.), 1920-22; U.S. atty., Dist. R.I., 1921-26; lt. gov. R.I., 1927-Feb. 4, 1928, succeeding as gov. R.I. upon death of Gov. Pothier, serving 3 terms, 1928-33; chmn. exec. com. Governors Conf., 1930-32; mem. F.C.C., 1934-43. Alumni trustee Brown U., First lt. Troop A, R.I. Nat. Guard, Mexican border, 1916, World War service, July 25, 1917-July 19, 1919, as capt. Co. A, 103d Machine Gun Batt., 26th (Yankee) Div., later with Gen. Staff, A.E.F.; colonel Cav. Res. Chevalier de L'Etoile Noire (France), 1918. Mem. Delta Upsilon. Republican. Baptist. Mason. Clubs: University, Dunes, Squantum Assn. (R.I.). Home: 70 Main St., Wakefield, R.I. Died Oct. 9, 1967.

CASE, ROLLAND WEBSTER ret. army officer; b. Manchester, Mich., May 26, 1882; s. Clarence Webster and Dora (Robinson) C.; B.S., U.S. Mil Acad., 1905; attended Ordnance Sch. of Tech., 1912-13. Command and Gen. Staff Sch., 1922-23, Army War Coll., 1928-29; m. Jessie Tucker, July 17 (dec.); 1 dau., Lucy Imogene (Mrs. Clyde Wendelken, Jr.); m. 2d, Mary Gertrude King, Aug. 18, 1933. Commd. 2d lt., Inf., U.S. Army, 1905, 1st lt., Ordnance, 1909, 1st lt., Inf., 1911; was capt., Ordnance, 1911-13; commd. capt. Inf., 1916; served as maj. (temp), 1917-18; commd., maj., Inf., 1920; transferred to Ordnance Dept., 1920; commd. lt. col., Ordnance, 1929, col., 1935, brig. gen. (temp.) 1940; retired 1944; dir. research, Coll. of Engring., N.Y.U., 1944-48, ret. Mem. Army Ordnance Assn. Republican. Episcopalian. Mason. Clubs: Army and Navy, Army and Navy Country (Washington); Engineers (N.Y.C.). Home: Washington. Died Dec. 16, 1957.

CASEY, SILAS army officer; b. East Greenwich, R.I., July 12, 1807; grad U.S. Mil Acad., 1826. Commd. 2d lt. inf., U.S. Army, 1826; fought in Seminole War in Fla., 1837-42; commd. capt., 1839; fought at battles of City of Mexico, Churubuseo, Chapultepec, during Mexican War, 1847; prepared tactics manual adopted by Army, 1862; commd. lt. col. 9th Inf., 1855, col., 1861, brig. gen. U.S. Volunteers, 1861, maj. gen., 1862; ret. 1868. Died Bklyn., Jan. 22, 1882.

CASEY, SILAS rear adm.; b. E. Greenwich, R.I., Sept. 11, 1841; s. Gen. Silas and Abbie (Pearce) C.; apptd. to U.S. Naval Acad. from N.Y., 1856, grad. 1860; m. Sophie Gray Heberton, Oct. 1865. Midshipman, June 15, 1860; promoted through grades to rear admiral, Mar. 3, 1899. Served on the Niagara, 1860-62; engagements with batteries at Pensacola, Fla., Oct. 1861; served on Wissahicken, S. Atlantic Blockading Squadron, 1862-63; engagements with Ft. McAllister, 1862; Quaker City, N. Atlantic Blockading Squadron, 1863-65; first attack on Charleston under Admiral Dupont; attack on Ft. Fisher, Dec. 1864; Winooski, Atlantic Squadron, 1865-67; Naval Acad., 1867-69; various duties to 1897; comdt. Navy Yard, League Island, 1897-1901; comdr.-in-chief, Pacific Fleet, 1901-03; retired, Sept. 11, 1903. Died Aug. 14, 1913.

CASEY, THOMAS LINCOLN army officer; b. at West Point, N.Y., Feb. 19, 1857; s. Gen. Thomas Lincoln and Emma (Weir) C.; brother of Edward Pearce C.; ed. pvt. schs., Washington and Sheffield Scientific Sch., Yale, class of 1877; grad. U.S. Mil. Acad., 1879; m. Laura Welsh. June 1, 1898. Second lt. corps of engrs., June 13, 1879; 1st lt., June 17, 1881; capt., July 23, 1888; maj., July 5, 1898; lt. col., Sept. 26, 1906; col., Sept. 21, 1909. In charge of defense of Hampton Roads, Va., during Spanish-Am. War, and at many stations in charge of works of river and harbor improvement; asst. astronomer, under Prof. Newcomb, Transit of Venus expedition, Cape of Good Hope, 1882; Greer County Commn., Tex., 1886; Miss. River Commn., 1902-06, and numerous other spl. bds; in charge of U.S. engring. exhibit, St. Louis Expn., 1904; mem. and engr. sec. Light House Board, 1906-10; retired from active service, Mar. 1, 1912. Home: Washington, D.C. Died Feb. 3, 1925.

CASS, LEWIS senator, territorial gov.; b. Exeter, N.H., Oct. 9, 1782; s. Jonathan and Mary (Gilman) G.; m. Elizabeth Spencer, 1806. Admitted to Ohio bar, 1802; mem. Ohio legislature, 1806; U.S. marshall for Ohio, 1807-12; apptd. col. 3d Ohio Regt. War of 1812; commd. col. brig. gen. U.S. Army, 1813; gov. Mich. territory, 1813-31; U.S. sec. of war under Pres. Jackson, 1831-36; apptd. U.S. minister to France, 1836; mem. U.S. Senate (Democrat) from Mich., 1845-48, 49-57; Democratic nominee for U.S. Pres., 1848, supported "squatter sovereignty", defeated by Zachary Taylor; U.S. sec. of state under Pres. Buchanan, 1857-60. Author: France, Its King, Court and Government, 1840; also articles on mil., western, Indian subjects. Died Detroit, June 17, 1866.

CASSADY, JOHN HOWARD, naval officer; b. Spencer, Ind., Apr. 3, 1896; s. William Franklin and Samantha (Haxton) C.; ed. Spencer (Ind.) High Sch., and Army and Navy Prep. Sch., Annapolis, Md.; grad. U.S. Naval Acad., 1918; m. Sallie Dold, Feb. 3, 1925; children—John Howard, William Francis. Commd. ensign, U.S. Navy, 1918, and advanced through the grades to rear adm., 1943; served in U.S. ships Cassin, Olympia, Wilkes, Truxton, McCormack, Colorado, Aroostook, Saratoga, Ranger, Virginia, Yorktown and Wasp; designated naval aviator, 1927; asst. naval attache and naval attache for air, Am. Embassy, Rome, Italy, 1937-39; operations officer on staff of commander aircraft, Atlantic Fleet, 1940-41; chief of staff of to commander of operational training command, Jacksonville, Fla., 1941-42; dir. aviation training div. Bureau of Aeronautics, Navy Dept., Mar.-Aug. 1943; comdg. officer, U.S.S. Saratoga, 1943-44; asst. dep. chief of naval operations (air) Navy Dept., Washington, D.C., 1944-45; comdr. carrier div. Atlantic Fleet, 1945-47; assistant chief of naval operations for air, 1947-49; comdr., air fleet, Jacksonville, Fla., from 1949. Decorated Legion of Merit with gold star, Victory Medal World War I with destroyer clasp, Am. Defense Service Medal with fleet clasp, Am. Area Campaign Medal, Asiatic-Pacific Area Campaign Medal with 4 stars, Victory Medal World War II (U.S.), Order British Empire, Comdr. of Bath (Gt. Britain), Order of the Phoenix (Greece). Home: Boca Raton FL Died Jan. 30, 1969.*

CASSIDY, GEORGE LIVINGSTON association exc.; b. Brooklyn, N.Y., July 24, 1902; s. George and Dr. Caroline (Macdermott) C.; A.B., Brown Univ., 1926; student, N.Y. Univ., 1942-43; m. Dr. Mary-Light Schaefer, Oct. 8, 1926; children-Martin Macdermott, Patrick Livingston. Reporter. Providence (R.I.) Journal, 1922-23; reporter, Brooklyn (N.Y.) Times, 1927-34; legislative correspondent, asso. ed., N.Y. Post, 1934-40; mem. N.Y. State Labor Relations Bd., 1941-43; chief roving European corr., also war corr., N.Y. Post, 1946-47, editorial page editor, 1947; asst. to gen. mgr., N.Y. Post Home News, mng. editor, 1948; pub. relations counsel, 1948-; exec. director America-Israel Society, 1954-; mem. mgr. Am.-Israel Soc.-Princeton Theol. Sem.-Link Marine Archaeological Expdn. to Israel, 1960. Member labor relations panel American Arbitration Association. Served U.S. Army, advancing from maj. to lt. col., 1943-46; chief manpower, S.H.A.E.F. mission to Belgium, 1944; chief, manpower sect., U.S. Zone, Germany, 1945. Awarded Bronze Star, Army commendation ribbon, European-North African theatre ribbon with battle star; decorated officer, Order of the Crown (Belgium). Mem. Soc. of Silurians, Delta Upsilon. Democrat. President Episcopal. Club: Brown Univ. (New York City). Home: 405 Bedford Rd., Pleasantville, N.Y. Office: Willard Hotel, Washington 20004. Died Oct. 14, 1962.

CASTLEMAN, JOHN BRECKINRIDGE retired; b. Fayette County, Ky., June 30, 1841; s. David and Virginia (Harrison) C.; ed. Transylvania U., from which at 19, entered C.S.A. at outbreak of war; trooper Morgan's cav., 1861-Oct. 1864, and maj. of Morgan's old regt.; comd. expdn. to release Confederate prisoners confined in Ill. and Ind., when he was captured and placed in solitary confinement 9 months, being released on parole, July, 1865, to leave the U.S. never to return; parole revoked by President Johnson; studied in Europe; LL.B., U. of Louisville, 1868; m. Alice Barbee, Nov. 24, 1868. Mgr. Royal Ins. Co. of Liverpool, 1869-1902. Adj. gen. Ky. under Gov. Knott; chmn. Dem. State Central Com., 1890-92; comdg. officer Louisville Legion, 1878 - ; pres. Louisville bd. park commrs., 1891 - ; enlisted the 1st regt. Ky. Vol. Inf., 1898, for service Spanish-Am. War, which participated in P.R. campaign; apptd. brig. gen. U.S.V.; declined comn. commn. of brig. gen. U.S. Army tendered by President McKinley; comd. Ky. troops during troubles following assassination of Gov. Goebel. His fellow citizens in Ky. have erected in his honor an equestrian statue in recognition of distinguished pub. service. Author: Active Service. Home: Louisville, Ky. Died May 23, 1918.

CASTNER, JOSEPH COMPTON army officer; b. N.J., Nov. 18, 1869; B.Sc., Rutgers Coll., 1891, M.S., 1916; grad. Inf. and Cav. Sch., 1895. Army War Coll., 1915 and 1921, Gen. Staff Sch., 1920. Commd. 2d lt. 4th Inf., Aug. 1, 1891; 1st lt., Apr. 26, 1898; capt. squadron Philippine cav., Apr. 3, 1900; hon. mustered out service, June 30, 1901; capt. U.S. Army, Feb. 2, 1901; q.m. Feb. 26, 1908; promoted through grades to brig. gen., Nov. 14, 1921; served as brig. gen. N.A., with A.E.F., World War; retired, Nov. 30, 1933; later advanced to rank of major gen. Received 3 silver star citations, two for gallantry against insurgent forces, Philippine Islands, 1809, one for gallantry in action during World War, and Distinguished Service Medal during World War I. Mem. Phi Beta Kappa. Home 360 Euclid Av., Oakland, Calif. Died July 8, 1946.

CASWELL, RICHARD army officer, gov. N.C., Continental congressman; b. Cecil County, Md., Aug. 3, 1729. Surveyor, Raleigh, N.C., dep. surveyor N.C. clk. Orange County (N.C.) mem. N.C. Assembly, 1754-71, speaker, 1770-71; presided over N.C. Provincial Congress during Am. Revolution; presided over N.C. Constl. Conv., 1776; N.C. del. to Continental Congress 1774-76; commd. col. N.C. Partisan Rangers, Continental Army, 1776-77; maj. gen. N.C. Militia, 1780-83; 1st gov. N.C., 1776-80, 5th gov., 1785-87; comptroller gen. N.C., 1782; pres. N.C. Senate, 1782-84, 89; presided over N.C. Conv. to ratify U.S. Constn., 1789. Died Fayetteville, N.C., Nov. 10, 1789; buried in family cemetery, Lenoir County, N.C.

CASWELL, THOMAS THOMPSON rear adm.; b. Providence, R.I., Jan. 4, 1840; s. Alexis and Esther Lois (Thompson) C.; A.M., Brown U., 1861; widower. Apptd. from R.I. asst. p.m. U.S. Navy, Sept. 9, 1861; p.m., 1863; pay insp., 1881; pay dir., 1892; retired with rank of rear admiral, June 1899. Home: Annapolis, Md. Died July 18, 1913.

CATES, CLIFTON BLEDSOE, Marine Corps officer; b. Tiptonville, Tenn., Aug. 31, 1893; s. Willis Jones and Martha (Bledsoe) C.; LL.B., U. of Tenn., 1916; grad. Field Officers' Course, Marine Corps Schs., Army Indsl. Coll., Army War Coll.; m. Jane Virginia McIlhenny, Oct. 7, 1920; children—Clifton Bledsoe (lt. comdr. U.S.N.), Ann Willis. Commd. 2d lt., Marine Corps, 1917, advancing through the grades to major general 1944; promoted to rank of general, 1948; served with 96th Company, 2d Battalion, 6th Marines, 2d Div., Jan. 1918-Sept. 1919; participated at Verdun sector, Aisue defensive, Bouresches and Belleau woods, Aisne Marne offensive, Marbach sector, St. Mihiel offensive, Blanc Mont sector, Meuse-Argonne offensive; with Army of Occupation in Germany; twice wounded during World War I; commander, 1st Marine Regiment, 1st Marine Division, Guadalcanal, Solomon Islands, August-December, 1942; comdt. Marine Corps Schools, Quantico, Va., 1943-44; participated Saipan and Tinian offensives, July 1944-August 1944, Iwo Jima Operation, February-March, 1945; comdg. gen. 4th Marine Div., July 1944-Nov. 1945; comdg. gen. Marine Barracks and Marine Corps Schools, Quantico, Va., June 1946-Dec. 1947. Appointed commandant of the Marine Corps, 1948; comdt. Marine Corps Schools, Quantico, since 1952. Decorated Navy Cross, Distinguished Service Cross (Army) with oak leaf, Distinguished Service Medal with gold star, Legion of Merit, Silver Star with oak leaf, Purple Heart with oak leaf, Presidential citation with 3 stars, Victory Medal with 5 bronze stars, World War II Victory Medal, Army of Occupation of Germany, Marine Corps Expeditionary, Yangtze, China and Am. services, Asiatic-Pacific Area Medal with 5 bronze stars (U.S.), Legion of Honor, Croix de Guerre (3) with 2 palms and 1 gold star, Fourragere (France). Comdr. Order Orange of Nassau with Crossed Swords (Netherlands). Mem. Phi Gamma Delta, Phi Alpha Delta. Clubs: Army and Navy, Army-Navy Country, Alfalfa (Washington); Chevy Chase. Address: Quantico VA Died June 6, 1970.

CATHCART, ROBERT SPANN surgeon; b. Columbia, S.C., Sept. 25, 1871; s. William Richard and Mary Eliza (Kelly) C.; Ph.G., U. of S.C., 1890; M.D., Med. Coll. State of S.C., 1893; m. Katherine Julia Morrow, Jan. 5, 1898; children-Mary Frances (Mrs. William Smith Stevens), Katherine Morrow (Mrs. William G. Hamm), Robert S., Hugh. Began practice at Charleston, South Carolina, 1893; professor of surgery Emeritus, Medical College of State of S.C.; surgeon A.C.L. R.R., S.A.L. Ry., South Carolina Power Co., The Citadel (mil. coll.). Commd. 1st lt., Med. R.C., 1917; maj. chief of surg. service, Camp Wadsworth, Spartanburg, S.C., later Camp Sevier, Greenville, S.C., and Gen. Army Hosp., Parkview, Pa., 1917-18; commd. lt. col. Med. Reserve Corps, June 4, 1924 (inactive); col. on Citadel staff, 1934. Diplomate Am. Bd. of Surgery (founder's group). Fellow Am. Coll. Surg.; mem. Am., Southern Tri-State (past pres.) S.C. State med. assns., Southern Surg. Assn., (past pres.), Medical Society of South Carolina (past president), St. George's Society, S.C. Society. Democrat. Episcopalian. Mason (K.T., Shriner). Home: 2 Water St. Office: 75 Hasell St., Charleston 8, S.C. Died Apr. 29, 1949.

CATHCART, THOMAS EDWARD (TOM CATHCART), editor; b. Chgo., Aug. 12, 1894; s. Alexander and Mary (Elliot) C.; ed. pub. schs., Chgo. and Phila., and Wharton Sch. of Finance and Commerce (U. Pa.); m. Elizabeth Swanson, Jan. 15, 1920; 1 son, Tom. Began as apprentice mechanic, 1912, later sales engr. Standard Roller Bearing Co., advt. mgr. Vim Motor Truck Co., Packard Motor Car Co.; promotion mgr. Crowell Pub. Co., 1922-29; spl. editorial work, 1929; editor Country Home, 1930-34, editorial dir., 1935; dir. promotion This Week mag., 1935-44, mgr. newspaper relations, 1946-48, vice president and director from 1949, exec. vice president, 1957-60; pres. Newspaper and Magazine Special Services. Served as 1st lt. inf., Motor Transport Corps, U.S. Army, 1917; capt., attached to hdqrs. 1918-19. Republican Episcopalian. Clubs: Nat. Press (Washington); Old

Lyme Country and Beach (Lyme, Conn.). Home: Lyme CT Died Dec. 31, 1968; buried Hamburg Cemetery, Lyme CT

CATHER, DAVID CLARK naval med. officer; b. Clearbrook, Va., Dec. 19, 1879; s. Clark and Cornelia (Shaull) C.; ed. Shenandoah Valley Acad., Winchester,Va., 1893-97; M.D., U. of Pa., 1903; m. May Haynes Sumpter, Aug. 20, 1915 (died Feb. 16, 1940). Commd. lt., j.g., Med. Corps, U.S. Navy, July 28, 1904, and advanced through the grades to rear adm., Nov. 1, 1939; retired Dec. 1, 1942. Fellow Am. Coll. Surgeons; mem. A.M.A. Mason. Clubs: Army and Navy (Washington, D.C.); Jonathan (Los Angeles, Calif.). Home: Jonathan Club, 545 S. Figueroa St., Los Angeles, Calif. Died June 25, 1944.

CATLIN, ALBERTUS WRIGHT officer U.S.M.C.; b. Cowanda, N.Y., Dec. 1, 1868; s. Buckley Dary and Adeline (Cook) C.; grad. U.S. Naval Acad., 1890; grad. Army War Coll., May 1917; m. Carrie Abbott, Aug. 29, 1902 (died 1915); m. 2d, Martha Ellen Gallant, Aug. 22, 1917; 1 dau., Martha Ellen. Commd. 2d lt. U.S.M.C., July 1, 1892; promoted through grades to brig. gen., and retired Dec. 10, 1919. Comd. marine guard, U.S.S. Marine when destroyed in Havana Harbor, 1898; comd. marines on S.S. St. Louis during Spanish-Am. War; in Philippines, 1902-04; comd. first marines landed in Cuba, 1906, and served there until 1909; comd. marines from fleet, landed at Vera Cruz, Mexico, Apr. 21-22, 1914; comd. 6th Regt. Marines, 4th Brigade, 2d Div., 1st A.C., A.E.F., 1917-18; wounded in action at Belleau Wood, June 6, 1918; assigned as comdr. 1st Brigade Marines, Hayti, Nov. 1918. Awarded Congressional Medal of Honor "for distinguished conduct," at Vera Cruz, Apr. 22, 1914; Croix de Guerre with Palm and Legion of Honor (French) for service at Chateau Theirry, June 1918. Republican. Methodist. Home; Washington D.C. Died May 31, 1933.

CATLIN, ISAAC SWARTWOOD brig. gen.; b. Owego, N.Y., July 8, 1835; s. Nathaniel and Jane (Brodhead) C.; ed. Owego; m. Virginia H. S. Bacon, Oct. 1862. Raised 1st co. of vols. for the Civil War on the day of Mr. Lincoln's call for 75,000 troops; capt. 3d N.Y. Inf., May 14, 1861; resigned Mar. 14, 1862; 1st lt., adj. 109th N.Y. Inf., Aug. 2, 1862; lt. col., Aug. 28, 1862; col., July 29, 1864; hon. mustered out, June 4, 1865; capt. 45th U.S. Inf., May 6, 1867; retired with rank of col., May 6, 1870; brig. gen. U.S.A. retired by act of Apr. 23, 1904. Bvtd.; brig. gen. vols., Mar. 13, 1865, "for gallant and meritorious services during the war"; maj. gen., Mar. 13, 1865, for same in battles before Petersburg, Va. (lost right leg); maj. May 6, 1867, for same in Battle of Wilderness; lt. col., May 6, 1867, for same at Petersburg; awarded Congressional Medal of Honor "for most distinguished gallantry in action at the explosion of the mine at Petersburg." Asst. U.S. dist. atty., 1871; elected dist. atty., Kings Co., 1877; re-elected, 1880; nominated for mayor of Brooklyn, 1885; nominated for Congress, but declined nomination, 1893; offered, but declined, nomination for lt. gov., 1896; originally Republican, then Cleveland Democrat; supported war policy of Presidents McKinley and Roosevelt. Then retired from business. Writing "Memoirs of Civil and Military Career." Home: Brooklyn, N.Y. Died Jan. 19, 1916.

CATTELL, HENRY WARE medical editor; b. Harrisburg, Pa., Oct. 7, 1862; s. Rev. William C. (pres. Lafayette Coll.) and Elizabeth (McKeen) C.; A.B., Lafayette, 1883, A.M., 1886; U. of Leipzig, 1883-84; M.D., U. of Pa., 1887; unmarried Demonstrator of morbid anatomy, U. of Pa., 1892-97; dir. Ayer Clin. Lab., Pa. Hosp., 1899-1901; pathologist at different times to Blockley, Presbyn., and other Phila. hosps.; expert in many murder trials. Served in France as a major, 1918-19, and had charge of the post mortem records of the A.E.F., and was pathologist to Base Hosp. No. 17 and to the Central Med. Dept. Laboratory; grad. Oct. 13, 1925. Med. Field Service Sch., U.S.A., Carlislie, Pa.; lt. col. Med. Res., U.S.A. (Ret.). Editor Internat. Med. Magazine, 1894-97, Internat. Clinics, 1900-03, 1910-16, 1922-32 (edited 78 vols. before retiring). Del. of U.S. to 5th Internat. Congress of Military Medicine and Pharmacy, London, 1929. Republican. Presbyn. Author: Post-Mortem Pathology, 1903, 05, 06. Editor: Lippincott's Medical Dictionary, 1910, 3d edition, 1913. Translator: Ziegler's Special Pathological Anatomy, 1896-97. Home: Brown Mills, N.J. Died Mar. 8, 1936.

CAULDWELL, OSCAR RAY marine corps officer (ret.); b. Rockville, Ind., Aug. 14, 1892; s. John Monroe and Christina (Ward) C.; student Wabash Coll., 1910-12; B.S., U.S. Naval Acad., 1916; student Purdue U., 1947-48; m. Margaret MacFarland Brown, July 19, 1924; children—Nancy (Mrs. D. C. Fisher), Sara (Mrs. Marco Ambrosini) (deceased). Commissioned 2d lt. USMC, 1916, advanced through grades to maj. gen., 1946; served in France, World War I (wounded in action); comdr. 3d regt., World War II; asst. div. comdr. Bougainville campaign, 1943; ret. from active duty, 1946. Mem. Alpha Gamma Rho. Presbyn. Home: Avon Old Farms, Avon, Conn. Died Sept. 1959.

CAUSEY, WILLIAM BOWDOIN civil engr.; b. Suffolk, Va., June 24, 1865; s. Charles Henry and Martha Josephine (Prentis) C.; ed. pvt. schs.; unmarried. Began as chairman Atlantic & Danville R.R., Va., 1883; with engring. depts. various rys., including U.P. Ry., N.Y., N.H. & H. R.R., C. & N.W., C. & A. R.R., C.G.W. R.R., also was chief engr. E. J. & E. Ry., supt. Ill. lines C. & A. R.R., supt. C. G. W. Ry.; v.p. and gen. mgr. Norwood-White Coal Co., Des Moines, Ia., 1914-17; city mgr. Norfolk, Va., 1923-25; then v.p. White Construction Co. and M.E. White Co., gen. contractors, Chicago. Commd. capt. engrs., June 13, 1917, and assigned to 17th Engrs., U.S.A.; landed in France Aug. 1917; maj., Mar. 1918; lt. col., Sept. 1918; mem. Am. sect. Inter-Allied Mission sent to Vienna from Paris by Supreme War Council to investigate financial, economic and fuel transportation conditions in former Austro-Hungarian Empire, Dec. 1918-July 1919; was coal and transp. expert of the Mission, pres. Allied Ry. Mission, Austro-Hungary, Jan.-Oct. 1919; tech. adviser to Austrian Govt., Sept. 1919-July 1923; then lt. col. O.R.C., U.S.A. Asst. U.S. commr. to Century of Progress Expn., Chicago, July 1932-Apr. 15, 1935. Decorated Officer Legion of Honor (France); Order of Saint Sava 2d class (Kingdom of the Serbs, Croats and Slovenes - Jugo-Slavia); The Great Silver Cross of Honor (Republica of Austria); citation from Gen. Pershing "for distinguished services" in France. Republican. Episcopalian. Mason. Home: Chicago, Ill. Died Aug. 10, 1936.

CAZIARC, LOUIS VASMER brig. gen.; b. Boston, July 4, 1844; s. Etienne and Maria Louisa Susetta (de Rochemont) C.; ed. pub. schs., Boston; (M.A., Bowdoin Coll., 1879); m. Esther Alexander Ritchie, 1873. Served as sergt. and 1st sergt., Co. I, 38th Mass. Vol. Inf., Aug. 16, 1862-Apr. 19, 1864; 1st lt. 89th U.S.C.T., Apr. 24, 1864; promoted through grades to col. Arty. Corps. Jan. 23, 1904; brig. gen. and retired at own request, after over 40 yrs.' service, 1906. Bvtd. capt. vols., Mar. 26, 1865, for campaign against city of Mobile, Ala. Was a.d.c. to Gen. George L. Andrews, 1864-65, to Gen. Canby, U.S.A., and adj. gen. 1st, 2d and 5th mil. districts and Dept. of Columbia, 1866-73; was mil. prof. and acting prof. internat. and constl. law, Bowdoin Coll.; exec. officer signal and weather bureau, 1881-84; adj. Arty. Sch., Ft. Monroe, 1887-91; served in Cuba on staffs of Gens. Bates, Wilson, Ludlow and Wood, 1898-1901. Home: Charleston, S.C. Died June 19, 1935.

CECIL, CHARLES PURCELL naval officer; b. Sept. 4, 1893; entered U.S. Navy, 1912; and advanced through grades to rear adm., 1943. Decorated Navy Cross (twice). Address: Navy Dept., Washington 25. Deceased.

CESNOLA, LOUIS PALMA DI trustee and dir. Metropolitan Museum of Art, 1878 - ; b. Rivarolo, Piedmont, Italy,Jn June 29, 1832; ed. in Turin (LL.D., Columbia; also Princeton). At 17 took part in war against Austria for independence of Italy and was promoted lt. on battlefield at Novara, 1849, for merit; came to New York, 1860; apptd., 1861, maj., then lt. col., 11th N.Y. cav; promoted col., 4th N.Y. cav., 1862; at the battle of Aldie, Va., was severely wounded, taken prisoner and 9 months in Libby Prison; promoted brig. gen.; U.S. consul at Cyprus, 1865-77; made extensive archaeol. explorations, unearthed statues, inscriptions, sarcophagi, architectural remains, vases, terracottas, bronzes, gold and sliver jewels at Curium, etc.; all are now exhibited in the Metropolitan Museum of Art; awarded, Dec. 1897, Congressional medal of honor; gold medal and several knightly orders from King of Italy. Author: Cyprus: Its Cities, Tombs and Temples. Died 1904.

CHADBOURNE, WILLIAM MERRIAM lawyer; b. San Francisco, Feb. 11, 1879; s. Forrest Simeon and Caroline Augusta (Merriam) C.: A.B., Harvard, 1900, A.M., 1901, LL.B., 1903. Admitted to N.Y. bar, 1904, and began practice with Hornblower, Byrne, Miller & Potter; now mem. Chadbourne, O'Neill & Thomson. Chmn. Felmont Petroleum Corp.; dir. Drilling & Exploration Co., Pittston Co., Park Sheraton Corp., Fgn. Indsl. Equipment Corp.; counsel U.S. Liquidation Commn. in Paris, 1919. Pvt. Squadron A, N.Y.N.G., 1908-14: 2d and 1st lt. 12th N.Y. Inf., 1914-17, including 9 mons. on Mexican border; 1st lt. and maj. N.A., 1917-18; adj. gen.'s dept. and Chem. W.S.; rep. of latter at Gen. Hdqrs., A.E.F., for 6 mos.; participated in St. Mihiel and Meuse-Argonne campaigns; colonel C.W.S.O.R.C. Decorated Officer Legion of Honor (France), Jugoslovenska Kruna II (Yugoslavia), Order of Jade (China), Order of Brit. Empire. Mem. bd. mgrs. State Charities Aid; pres. Honest Ballot Assn.; an organizer Progressive Party in N.Y.; del. Prog. Nat. Conv., 1916; del. Rep. Nat. Conv., 1936, 40, mem. Fusion com., 1913, 17, 21, N.Y.C. municipal campaigns; mgr. N.Y.C. Fusion Campaigns, 1933, 37, 41; mem. Adv. Com. of Salvation Army; dir. N.Y. World's Fair, Inc., 1939 and 1940. Mem. exec. com. Serbian Child Welfare Assn., Am. Jugoslav Soc.; pres. Am. Friends Jugoslavia; chmn. United Yugoslav Relief Fund of Am.; dir. CARE; v.p. Bundles for Britain; dir. N.Y.C. Def. Recreation Com.; mem. Am., N.Y. State bar assns., Bar Assn. City of N.Y., S.R. (past pres. N.Y. State), Am. Legion, N.Y. Soc. Mil. and Naval Officers World Wars, Soc. Colonial Wars, Civil Service Reform Assn., Nat. Econ. League, Council on Fgn. Relations, China Soc. (hon. v.p.), Phi Beta Kappa. Episcopalian. Republican. Mason. Clubs: University, Harvard Republican, City, Downtown, Explorers, Adirondack Mountain, Appalachian Mountain (N.Y.C.); Union Interaliée (Paris). Home: 550 Park Av., N.Y.C. 21. Office: 70 Pine St., N.Y.C. 5 Died May 2, 1964; buried Arlington Nat. Cemetery.

CHADWICK, FRENCH ENSOR rear adm.; b. Morgantown, W.Va., Feb. 29, 1844; s. Daniel Clark and Margaret Eliza (Evans) C.; apptd. to U.S. Naval Acad. from W.Va., 1861, grad 1864; m. Cornelia J. Miller, Nov. 20, 1878. Ensign, Nov. 1, 1866; promoted through grades to rear adm., Oct. 11, 1903. Summer of 1864, was attached to the Marblehead in pursuit of the Confederate steamers Florida and Tallahassee; various assignments to 1882; naval attache, Am. Embassy, London, 1882-89; comd. Yorktown, 1889-91; chief, intelligence office, 1892-93; chief Bur. of Equipment, 1893-97; comd. New York, and chief of staff of Admiral Sampson, during war with Spain, participated in the most important engagements in the Atlantic during the war, and was advanced 5 numbers in rank for eminent and conspicuous conduct in battle; pres. Naval War Coll., Newport, 1900-03; duty in connection with Naval War Coll., 1903-04; comdr.-in-chief S. Atlantic Squadron, 1904; retired, Feb. 28, 1906. Mem. Nat. Inst. Arts and Letters. Interested in municipal government, on which he often wrote and spoke. Mem. Newport Representative Council 2 terms, and mem. Newport Park Commn. Author: Causes of the Civil War (Am. Nation Series, Vol. XIX), 1906; Relations of the United States and Spain, 1776-1898. Home: Newport, R.I. Died Jan. 27, 1919.

CHAFEE, ADNA ROMANZA army officer; b. Junction City, Kan., Sept. 23, 1884; s. Adna Romanza and Anna Frances (Rockwell) C.; B.S., U.S. Mil. Acad., 1906; grad. Mounted Service Sch., Ft. Riley, Kan., 1908, advanced course, same, 1912. Gen. Staff Coll., Langres, France, 1917, Sch. of the Line, Ft. Leavenworth, Kan., 1921, Army War Coll., Washington, D.C., 1925; m. Ethel Warren Huff, Dec. 15, 1908; 1 son, Adna Romanza. Commd. 1st lt., 1912, advanced through grades to brig. gen., Nov. 1, 1938; maj. Inf., Nat. Army, and assigned as adj., 81st Div., Cap Jackson, S.C., 1917; served in St. Mihiel and Meuse-Argonne offensives and with Army of Occupation, World War; comdg. gen. 7th Cavalry Brigade (mechanized), 1938-. Awarded D.S.M. Episcopalian. Died Aug. 22, 1941.

CHAFFEE, ADNA ROMANZA lt. gen. U.S.A.; b. Orwell, O., Apr. 14, 1842; s. Truman B. and Grace (Hyde) C.; ed. pub. schs. of Ohio; (LL.D., Tufts Coll., 1905); m. Annie Frances Rockwell, Mar. 31, 1875. Pvt., sergt. and 1st sergt., Troop K, 6th Cav., July 22, 1861-May 12, 1863; 2d lt. 6th Cav., Mar. 13, 1863; advanced through grades to maj. gen. U.S.V., July 8, 1898; hon. disch., Apr. 13, 1899; brig. gen. U.S.V., Apr. 13, 1899; maj. gen., July 19, 1900; col. 8th U.S. Cav., May 8, 1899; maj. gen., Feb. 4, 1901; lt. gen., Jan. 9, 1904. Bvtd.: 1st lt., July 3, 1863, for Gettysburg; capt., Mar. 31, 1865, for Dinwiddie C.H., Va.; maj., Mar. 7, 1868, for engagement with Indians, Paint Creek, Tex., Mar. 7, 1868; lt. col., Feb. 27, 1890, for Red River, Tex., Aug. 30, 1874, and against Indians at Big Dry Wash, Ariz., July 17, 1882. Served in Army of Potomac during Civil War; mostly on the plains, 1865-98; in Spanish-Am. War comd. 3d Brigade, 2d Div., 5th Army Corps, June-Aug. 1898; comd. 2d Div., 5th Corps, Aug.-Sept., 1st Div., 4th Corps, Nov.-Dec. 1898; chief of staff, Div. of Cuba, Dec. 25, 1898-May 1900; comd. China relief expdn., June 24, 1900-May 21, 1901; comd. Div. of the Philippines, July 4, 1901-Oct. 1, 1902; comd. Dept. of the East, 1902-03; asst. to chief of staff, 1903-04; chief of staff, U.S.A., Jan. 9, 1904-Feb. 1, 1906; retired at own request, over 40 yrs.' service, Feb. 1, 1906. Died Nov. 1, 1914.

CHAFFEE, ROGER B. astronaut; b. Grand Rapids, Mich., Feb. 15, 1935; s. Donald L. Chaffee; B.S. in Aero. Engring., Purdue U., 1957; postgrad. Air Force Inst. Tech., Wright-Patterson AFB. O.; m. Martha Louise Horn; children-Sherly Lyn, Stephen Bruce. Joined USN, 1957, advanced through grades to lt. comdr.; former safety officer, quality control officer Navy Photog. Squadron 62, Jacksonville (Fla.) Naval Air Sta.; now astronaut with Manned Spacecraft Center, NASA. Mem. Tau Beta Pi, Sigma Gamma Tau, Phi Kappa Sigma. Office: care Manned Spacecraft Center, NASA, Houston 1. Died Jan. 27, 1967.

CHAISSON, JOHN ROBERT, marine corps officer; b. Swampscott, Mass., Sept. 27, 1916; s. Joseph and Annie Josephine (Donovan) C.; A.B. cum laude, Harvard, 1939; m. Marguerite Martin, Feb. 22, 1946; children—Joseph M., Dorothy (Mrs. Robert Jones), Jane, Thomas M. Commd. 2d lt. USMC, 1941, advanced through grades to lt. gen., 1971; assigned 1st Marine Div., 1942-45, 53-54; chief staff USMC, 1971-72; ret., 1972; dep. dir. regulations AEC, 1972. Decorated D.S.M., Silver Star, Legion of Merit, Bronze Star, Navy Commendation medal. Home: Washington DC Died Sept. 20, 1972; buried Arlington Nat. Cemetery, Arlington VA

CHALLE-LONG, CHARLES soldier, diplomat; b. Princes Anne, Somerset Co., Md., July 2, 1842; s. Littleton Long of Chaille and Anne Mitchell (Costen) Long; ed. Washington Acad., Md., 1860; LL.B., Columbia, 1880; m. Marie Amelie Hammond, July 16, 1890. Served all ranks to capt., 11th Md. Vols., 1862-65;

apptd. lt. col. Egyptian army, 1869; chief 1st, 2d and 3d sects. gen. staff, Egyptian army, 1869-73; chief staff to Gen. Gordon, gov. gen. Egyptian Soudan, 1874-77; executed treaty with King M'Tesa, annexing Uganda to Egypt, 1874; discovered Lake Ibrahim, solving problem of Nile source, Aug., 1874; wounded at M'Rossi, Aug. 17, 1874; cited in general orders No. 18, decorated Cross Medjidieh, for expdns. Niam-Niam and East Coast Africa; promoted col. and bey. Nov. 16, 1874; retired Aug. 31, 1877. Acting consul of U.S. at Alexandria, when titular agents had abondoned consulate, June-Aug., 1882, making consulate refuge for all nationalities after bombardment; decorated Cross Osmanieh; sec. legation and consul gen. U.S. to Corea, 1887-89; sec. Universal Postal Congress, Washington, 1897; sec., Aug. 1897, and charge d' affaires, Oct. 1897-Sept. 1898, U.S. Spl. Commn. to Paris Expn., 1900. Chevalier Legion d' Honneur of France; hon. mem. Institut Egyptien. Gen assembly of Md. conferred by unanimous vote resolutions of thanks and gold medal for services to science and valiant conduct in Centrial Africa and Egypt, Mar. 3, 1904; awarded gold medal by Am. Geog. Soc. for final solution of Nile source problem, Feb. 15, 1910. Died Mar. 24, 1917.

CHALMERS, JAMES RONALD army officer, congressman: b. Halifax County, Va., Jan. 11, 1831; s. Joseph Williams and Fannie (Henderson) C., grad. S.C. Coll., 1851; m. Rebecca Arthur, circa 1865, 1 daughter. Admitted to Miss. bar, 1853; dist. atty. Miss., 1858; chmn. com. on mil. affairs Miss. Secession Conv., 1861; commd. capt. Confederate Army, 1861, col., 1861, brig. gen., 1862; comdr. 1st div. Forrest's Cavalry Army Corps, 1865; mem. Miss. Senate, 1875, 76; mem. U.S. Ho. of Reps. from Miss., as Democrat, 45th-47th congresses, 1877-83, as Independent, 48th Congress, 1884-85; spl. asst. to U.S. dist. atty. 1883-84. Died Memphis, Tenn., Apr. 9, 1898; buried Elmwood Cemetery, Memphis.

CHAMBERLAIN, DANIEL HENRY governor, S. Carolina; b. W. Brookfield, Mass., June 23, 1835; s. Eli C.; prep. edn. Phillips Acad., Andover, Mass., and high school, Worcester; grad. Yale Univ., 1862, A.M., 1867 (LL.D., Univ. of S.C.); grad. Harvard Law School, 1863; m. Alice C. Ingersoll, Dec., 1869. Served in Union army; capt. 5th Mass. colored inf., 1864-65; cotton planter, S.C., 1866 del. S.C. Constl. Conv., 1868; atty gen. S.C., 1868-72; gov. S.C., 1874-77. Home: Columbia, S.C. Died 1907.

CHAMBERLAIN, JOHN LOOMIS army officer; b. New York, Jan. 20, 1858; s. Jabez Lewis and Charity (Hart) C.; prep. edn. Geneseo State Normal Sch., 1872-76: apptd. from N.Y., and grad. U.S. Mil Acad., 1880; m. Carolyn Marrow, Sept. 9, 1896 (died Feb. 9, 1947); children-John Loomis, Mary Carolyn. Commissioned second lieutenant First Artillery, June 12, 1880) promoted through grades to major general, March 28, 1921. Instructor U.S. Mil. Acad., 1884-88; grad. Arty. Sch., 1890; spl. field officer's course, Army Service Sch., 1912; army War Coll., 1912-13; in campaign against Sioux Indians, 1890-91; chief ordnance officer dept. of Mo., 1891-93; instr. mil. science and tactics, Peekskill Mil. Acad., 1895-96; mil. attaché, Vienna, 1897-98; with U.S. siege train and 7th Army Corps, U.S. Volunteers, 1898-99; insp. gen. Calif. and P.I., 1901-05, and in campaign against Moros, Apr. 1903; insp. gen. Pacific Div., Dec. 1906-June 30, 1907, Dept. of the East, Aug. 13, 1907-June 30, 1909, Philippine Div., Sept. 1, 1909-Sept. 15, 1911, Western Div., Nov. 11, 1911-Aug. 15, 1912, Western Dept., Aug. 1, 1913-Sept. 1914; dept. insp., Eastern Dept., 1914; insp.-gen. U.S. Army, with rank of brig. gen., Feb. 21, 1917; promoted to maj. gen., I.G., Oct. 6, 1917. Tour of inspection A.E.F. in France, July 10-Sept. 20, 1918; retired Nov. 6, 1921; tour of inspection of all activities under the War Dept. in Great Britain and Europe July, Aug., and Sept. 1920; four months tour of Europe, the Near East and Africa July, Aug., Sept. and Nov. 1921. Awarded D.S.M., 1919, "for exceptionally meritorious service to U.S. Govt." Club: Army and Navy. Home: 1319-30th St. N.W., Washington. Died Nov. 14, 1948; buried in Arlington Nat. Cemetery.

CHAMBERLAIN, JOSHUA LAWRENCE soldier, governor; b. Brewer, Me., Sept. 8, 1828; s. Joshua and Sarah Dupee (Brastow) C.; A.B., Bowdoin, 1852, A.M., 1855; grad. Bangor Theol. Sem., 1855; (LL.d., Pa. Coll., 1866, Bowdoin, 1869); m. Frances Caroline Adams, Dec. 7, 1855. Lt. col. 20th Me. Inf., Aug. 8, 1862; col., May 20, 1863. Congressional Medal of Honor for "daring heroism, holding position Little Round Top and carrying Great Round Top, in battle of Gettysburg, July 2, 1863"; comdg. brigade 5th Corps, Aug. 15; promoted brig. gen. U.S.V. on field of battle, June 18, 1864, by General Grant for "meritorious and efficient services in battle and specially gallant conduct in leading his brigade against the enemy in the assault on Petersburg"; bvtd. maj. gen. U.S.V., Mar. 29, 1865, for "conspicuous gallantry in action"; apptd. to command parade at formal surrender of Lee's army, Appomattox, Apr. 1865; comdg. 1st Div. 5th Corps thence to dissolution of Army of the Potomac; assigned to spl. command from that date; declined colonelcy regular army, and hon. disch. Jan. 15, 1866; thrice wounded. Gov. of Me., 1866-71; maj. gen., Me., charged with protection of peace and institutions of the state in absence of civil govt. and contest thereover, 1879-80. Prof. rhetoric and oratory, 1856-62, modern langs., 1861-65, rhetroic and oratory, 1865-66, trustee, 1867 - , pres., 1871-83, prof. mental and moral philosophy, 1874-79, lecturer polit. science and pub. law, 1883-85, Bowdoin Coll. U.S. commr. Paris Expn., 1878; medal from French Govt. for his services there. Pres. Soc. Army of Potomac, 1884; comdr. Loyal Legion U.S., 1866, G.A.R. of Me., 1903; pres. Me. branch Am. Nat. Red Cross; sr. v.p. Am. Bible Soc.; life mem. A.B.C.F.M. U.S. surveyor of customs, port of Portland, 1900 - ; leave of absence to visit Egypt to observe methods of English rule, 1901. Home: Brunswick, Me. Died Feb. 24, 1914.

CHAMBERLAIN, ORVILLE TRYON soldier, lawyer; b. Leesburg, Kosclusko Co., Ind., Sept. 1, 1841; s. Joseph Wright (M.D.) and Caroline (Tyron) C.; U. of Notre Dame, Ind., 1860-62 (hon. A.B., 1868); m. Helen M. Mead, of Elkhart, Ind., Sept. 1, 1869 (died May 31, 1911); 1 dau., Edith C. (Mrs. Louis M. Simpson). Enlisted as pvt. Co. G. 74th Ind. Vol. Inf., Aug. 6, 1862; hon. discharged as capt., June 9, 1865; awarded Congressional Medal of Honor "for most distinguished gallantry" in Battle of Chickamauga, Sept. 20, 1863. Admitted to Ind. bar, 1866, and practiced at Elkhart until 1901; was town atty. Elkhart, and its first city atty.; served as dist. atty., 34th Jud. Dist. Elected comdr. Army and Naval Medal of Honor Legion of U.S.A., 1916, reelected 1917; div. comdr. 10th Dist. of Ind., G.A.R., under original orgn.; comdr. Elmer Post No. 37, Elkhart, 3 terms; was judge advocate, G.A.R., Dept. of Ind.; mem. Loyal Legion. Republican. Author of act of Congress, approved Apr. 27, 1916, granting spl. pensions to soldiers and sailors of the Union Army and Navy who were awarded the Congressional Medal of Honor "for conspicuous gallantry, at risk of life, above and beyond the call of duty." Address: 417 W. Franklin St., Elkhart, Ind.†

CHAMBERLAIN, WILLIAM congressman, lt. gov. of Vt.; b. Hopkinton, Mass., Apr. 27, 1755; attended common schs. Moved to Loudon, N.H., 1774; served as sgt., Revolutionary War; became land surveyor and farmer; moved to Peacham, Vt., 1780, clk, of the proprietors Town of Peacham, 1780, town clk., 1785-87, town rep., 12 years; mem. Vt. Ho. of Reps., 1785, 87-96, 1805, 08; justice of the peace, 1786-96; del. Vt. constl. convs., 1791, 1814; brig. gen. Vt. Militia, 1794, maj. gen., 1799; asst. judge Orange County, 1795; chief judge Caledonia County, 1796-1803; sec. bd. trustees Caledonia County Grammar Sch., 1795-1812, pres. 1813-28; state councilor State of Vt., 1796-1803; Federalist presdl. elector, 1800; mem. U.S. Ho. of Reps. (Federalist) from Vt., 8th, 11th congresses, 1803-05, 09-11; lt. gov. of Vt., 1813-15. Died Peacham, Spet. 27, 1828; buried Peacham Cemetery.

CHAMBERLAINE, WILLIAM army officer; b. in Va., Mar. 1, 1871; grad. U.S. Mil. Acad., 1892; honor grad. Arty. Sch., 1896. Commd. add. 2d lt. 2d Arty., June 11, 1892; advanced through grades to brig. gen., Dec. 18, 1918. Duty U.S. Mil. Acad., 1899-1901; asst. to chief of arty., War Dept., May 1901-Oct. 1903; mem. Coast Arty. Bd., 1903-06; mem. Gen Staff, 1906-10; asst. chief of staff. Philippines, Div.; dir. Coast Arty. Sch., 1911-13; adj. gen. Fort Totton, 1917; organized and took to France 6th Prov. Regt. Coast Arty., Aug. 1917; chief of arty. 2nd Div., May and June 1918, during capture by marines of Belleau Woods; comd. gen. ry. arty. A.E.F.; comd. ry. arty. St. Mihiel and Meuse-Argonne operations; comd. gen. coast arty. training center; detailed Gen. Staff Corps, 1919, chief staff Hawaiian Dept. Officer de l'Legion l'Honneur; Croix de Guerre with Palm. Died June 9, 1925.

CHAMBERLIN, HARRY DWIGHT army officer; b. Elgin, Ill., May 20, 1887; s. Dwight Allen and Corinne Leona (Orth) C.; student Elgin Acad., 1905-06; B.A., U.S.M.A., 1910; distinguished grad. French Cavalry Sch., Saumur, France, 1923, Italian Cavalry Sch., Tor di Quinto, Italy, 1924; grad. Command and Gen. Staff Sch., Ft. Leavenworth, 1928, Army War Coll., 1933: m. Sally Garlington, June 24, 1912; m. 2d, Helen Bradman, Aug. 13, 1933; children-Lydia, Frederica Dwight. Commd. 2d lt., U.S. Cavalry, June 15, 1910; advanced through grades to brig. gen., Apr. 1941; chief of Staff 1st Cavalry Div., 1938-39; comd. 2d U.S. Cavalry (oldest cav. regt. in U.S.), Fort Riley, Kan., 1939-41; comd. task force of Army, Navy, Marines and Air Corps which occupied New Hebrides Islands, Apr. 1942; returned to U.S. for major operation, June 1942; comd. Southwestern Security Dist., La Jolla Calif., March 1943; comd. Fort Ord, Calif., Sept. 1943. Decorated Mexican Campaign medal, World War Campaign medal (2 stars), Belgian Mil. Cross. Episcopalian. Club: Army and Navy (Washington). Mem. Equitation Team in Inter-Allied Games, Paris, 1919; 2d individual place, 1920; mem. Olympic Team, Antwerp, Belgium, 1922; capt. Army polo team, 1926; won Nat. 12-Goal and Nat. 20-Goal championships, 1926-27; mem. U.S. Olympic Equestrian Team, Amsterdam, 1929; capt. Army Equestrian Team, Germany, Ireland and Poland, 1928; captain United States Olympic Equestrian Team, Los Angeles, Calif., 1932, won first Individual place in 3-day event, won second place in Prix des Nations. Author: Riding and Schooling Horses, 1934; Training Hunters, Jumpers and Hacks, 1937; also many articles. Home: Presidio of Monterey, Calif. Died Sept. 29, 1944, buried in Nat. Cemetery, Presidio of Monterey, Calif.

CHAMBERLIN, STEPHEN J., army officer; b. Spring Hill, Kan., Dec. 23, 1889; s. Clark and Minnie (Hare) C.; B.S., U.S. Mil. Acad., 1912; grad. Inf. Sch., 1924, Command and Gen. Staff Sch. (hon. grad.), 1925, Army War Coll., 1933; m. Sarah Chapman Shanks, Mar. 2, 1918; children—Sarah Shanks, Stephen Jones. Commd. 2d lt., U.S. Army, 1912, and advanced through the grades to lieut. general, 1943; served with regt. at San Francisco, El Paso, Philippines, 1912-17; chief troop movement sect., Port of Embarkation, Hoboken, N.J., 1917-18; with 16th Div., General Staff, Camp Kearney, Calif., then chief passenger traffic sect., Office of chief Embarkation Service; asst. chief of staff, Port of Embarkation, Hoboken, N.J., and at Gen. Staff Coll., Washington, D.C., 1918-20; transportation officer, Panama Canal Dept., and with regiment and brigade, 1920-23; with regt., Fort McPherson, Ga., 1923; instr. Nat. Guard, Staunton, Va., 1925; Office, Chief of Inf., Washington, D.C., 1926-30; with regt., Fort McPherson, Ga., 1930-32; asst. chief of staff, G-3, Hawaii Dept., 1933-36; R.O.T.C. duty, Los Angeles high schools, 1936-38; chief Constrn. Div., G-4, War Dept. Gen. Staff, 1938-41; G-4 and chief of staff, U.S. Army Forces, Australia, 1942; G-3, Southwest Pacific Area, U.S. Army Forces Pacific, 1942-45; dep. chief of staff and acting chief of staff, U.S. Army Forces, Pacific and for Supreme Comdr. for Allied Powers, 1945-46; dir. Intelligence, Dept. of the Army, 1946-48; comdg. gen. 5th Army, Chicago. Awarded D.S.M. with 3 Oak Leaf Clusters, Navy Distinguished Service Cross, Silver Star, Phillipine Distinguished Service Star; Order British Empire, Al Merito Militarde, Chile; Odu Nile Grand O, Egypt; Order de la Couronne arec Palme, Croix de Guerre, Belgium; Order of Orange of Nassau with Swords, Netherlands; Egyptian O'Ordre d'Ismail de 28eme classe; French Officer Legion of Honor. Home: Laguna Hills CA Died Oct. 23, 1971; buried Arlington Nat. Cemetery.

CHAMBERS, CHARLES CARROLL foundry exec.; b. Galena, Ill., July 2, 1888; s. Mathew Robert and Mary Josephine (Smith) C.; grad. Culver Mil Academy, 1908, U. Wis., 1912; m. Marjorie Graham, Dec. 25, 1917; children—Marjorie Ann (Mrs. Joe W. Beckham), Charles Carroll. Instr., English, mil., athletics, Culver (Ind.) Mil. Acad., 1912-13; salesman E.F. Houserman Co., Cleveland, 1915-20, sales mgr., 1920-22; treas., v.p. Wrought Iron Range Co., St. Louis, 1932-36; vice-pres., general mgr. So. Malleable Iron Co., East St. Louis, Ill., 1935-38; pres., gen. mgr. Tex. Foundries, Inc., Lufkin, Tex., 1939—, Sec. dir. Culver Ednl. Found. 1930-53, v.p. 1953. Served as lt. col., U.S. Army, 1916-19; col. Gen Staff, War Dept., Washington, 1922; col., chief staff 37th Div., Ohio N.G., 1920-23; now col., inf., retired. Decorated D.S.C., Silver Star, Purple Heart (U.S.); Belgian War Cross; French Cross of War. Mem. Vets. Fgn. Wars, Am. Legion, S.A.R., Am. Foundrymans Assn., Nat. Assn. Mfrs., Malleable Founders Soc. (dir., pres. 1951-52), Texas Bur. for Econ. Understanding (dir. 1953-55), Phi Gamma Delta (field sec., 1913-15), Sigma Delta Chi. Mason (Scottish Rite Shriner), Episcopalian. Clubs: Houston, Ramada, Petroleum, Coromado (Houston); Army & Navy (Washington); Lufkin, Lufkin Country. Home: 1017 Grove St. Office: Texas Foundries, Inc., Box 180, Lufkin, Tex. Died Mar. 15, 1958; buried Garden of Memories, Lufkin.

CHAMBERS, FRANK TAYLOR rear admiral; b. Louisville, Ky., July 1, 1870; s. Henry and Annie Cowan (Weisiger) C.; A.B., Male High Sch., Louisville, 1888; C.E., Rensselaer Poly. Inst., 1892; m. Mrs. Florence Newell Pease, Feb. 14, 1920. Apptd. jr. lt. C.E. Corps U.S.N., July 19, 1897; promoted through grades to rear adm., Apr. 6, 1927. Mem. Chesapeake & Delaware Canal Commn., 1905, 06, Nat. Advisory Bd. on Fuels and Structural Materials, 1906-07, Army and Navy Bd., 1908, studying and reporting upon Deep Draft Ship Canal between Chesapeake and Delaware bays, also upon deep draft ship channel from Golden Gate, San Francisco, to Mare Island Navy Yard; apptd. mem. Navy Yard Commn., 1917; chief engr. and mem. port facilities com. U.S. Shipping Bd.; visited Eng. and France, 1918, and reported on port and harbor facilities, information to be applied to improvement of home ports; cons. engr. on port facilities to Bd. of Engrs. for Rivers and Harbors, War Dept.; rep. of Navy Dept. on Assn. of Port Authorities; then dir. Naval Petroleum Reserves and Naval Oil Shale Reserves. Mem. Permanent Internat. Commn., Permanent Internat. Assn. of Navigation Congresses. Died Nov. 10, 1932.

CHAMBERS, W(ASHINGTON) IRVING naval officer; b. Kingston, N.Y., Apr. 4, 1856; s. Jacob and Margaret Ann (Ayers) C.; grad. U.S. Naval Acad., 1876; m. Isabella Reynods, of Kingston, Dec. 3, 1892. Commd. midshipman, June, 1876; ensign, Nov. 30, 1878; lt. jr. grade, Jan. 1, 1886; lt., May 29, 1891; lt.-comdr., July 1, 1899; comdr., Apr. 22, 1905; capt., Dec. 23, 1908. Served on bd. U.S.S. Pensacola, Portsmouth, Marion, 1876-83; Office Naval Intelligence, 1883-84; Greely relief expdn., Apr.-Oct., 1884; spl. survey Nicaragua Canal, Oct.-Dec. 1884; Office Naval Intelligence, 1885-88; Navy Yard. New York, 1888-89; U.S.S. Petrel, 1889-91, Atlanta, 1891-92; Naval War Coll., 1892-94; insp. ordnance, 1894-95; U.S.S. Minneapolis, 1895-97; Puritan, 1897; recorder, armor factory bd., 1897-98; naval torpedo sta., 1898-99; U.S.S. Texas, 1899-1900; Annapolis, 1900-02; comd. Frolic,

Mar.-Oct., 1902; Naval Torpedo Sta., 1902-04; Gen. Bd., Navy Dept., 1904-05; comd. Nashville, 1905-06; Florida, July-Sept., 1906; Newark, Sept.-Nov., 1906; Florida, 1906-07; asst. chief, Bur. Ordnance, 1907-09; comd. Louisiana, May-Dec., 1909; asst. to aid for material, 1909-11; mem. Gen. Bd., Mar.-Apr., 1911; Bur. Navigation in charge development of aviation, 1911-13; retired June 1, 1913; continued duty at Navy Dept. under Div. of Operations. Bronze medal, Philippine wars. Mem. U.S. Naval Inst. (gold medal 1884), Soc. Naval Architects, and Marine Engrs., N.Y. Aeronautical Soc. (dir., gold medal 1913), Soc. Automotive Engrs. Clubs: Army and Navy, Aero Club of America, Arts Club of Washington, Home: Kingston, N.Y. Address: 1834 I St. N.W., Washington, D.C.

CHAMBERS, WILLIAM naval officer; b. Phila., Aug. 25, 1884; M.D., Jefferson Med. Coll., 1907; grad. Naval War Coll. Senior Course; post-grad course in aviation medicine (flight surgeon); grad. Naval Med. Sch., Gen Course; rear admiral Med. Dept., Sept. 1942; med. officer in command; later vice adm., comdr. Naval Med. Center, Bethesda. Address: Naval Medical School, Navy Dept., Washington. Deceased.

CHAMBERS, WILLIAM EARL army officer; b. Chicago, Ill., Feb. 9, 1882; s. William Henry and Charlotte (Stilson) C.; B.S., U.S. Mil. Acad., 1916; graduate Infantry Sch., 1922; distinguished grad. Command and Gen. Staff Sch., 1926; grad. Army War Coll., 1934; Air Corps Tactical Sch., 1937; m. Aline Ingram, Dec. 11, 1920; children—William E., Margaret Aline (wife of Hiram W. Rainey, Jr.); married 2d Thekla Glenn Harshberger, Sept. 14, 1950. Commd. 2d lt., U.S. Army, June 12, 1912. Promoted through grades to brig. gen., June 20, 1942. Decorated Distinguished Service Medal, Legion of Merit, Philippine Distinguished Service Star. Mem. Mass. Soc. of Cincinnati, S.A.R., Tau Kappa Epsilon. Address: P.O. Box 563, Ithaca. Died Feb. 11, 1952; buried West Point, N.Y.

CHAMBLISS, HARDEE educator; b. Selma. Ala., Dec. 4, 1872; s. Nathaniel Rives and Anna Dummett (Hardee) C.; grad. Va. Mil. Inst., 1894; M.S. Vanderbilt U., 1899; Ph.D., Johns Hopkins, 1900; m. Julita McLane Sturdy, 1903 (died 1916); children-Joseph Hardee, John Lockwood, Hardee C., Allan McLane Francis, m. 2d, Emma Marie Henne, June 27, 1918. Instr., Columbia U., 1900-01; research chemist Moore Electric Co., Newark, N.J., 1901-03; Gen. Chem. Co., New York, 1903-09; prof. in charge chemistry, Oklahoma Coll., Stillwater, 1909-15; asst. commr. of health, Okla., 1915-16; chem. dir. Commercial Acid Co., St. Louis, Mo., 1916-17. Commd. maj. O.R.C., Aug. 1917; called to active duty, Dec. 7, 1917, and assigned to Gun Div., Ordnance Dept.; trans. to Nitrate Div. of Ordnance, Feb. 3, 1918, and directed researches, N.Y. City, conducted by War Dept. in cooperation with Gen. Chem. Co.; later put in charge all research work of Ordnance Dept., Nitrate Div., in New York and vicinity; detailed as comdg. officer U.S. Nitrate Plant No. 1, Sheffield, Ala., Feb. 1919; promoted lt. col., July 1919; hon. discharged, Nov. 29, 1920, and apptd. plant mgr, U.S. Nitrate Plant 1, resigned Sept. 1, 1921; prof. chemistry, Catholic U. of Am., 1921, dean Sch. of Science, 1925-30, dean Sch. of Engring., 1930-34; retired; now cons. chemist. Promoted col. O.R.C., 1929. Fellow A.A.A.S.; mem. Am. Chem. Soc., Sigma Alpha Epsilon, K.C. (4ff). Democrat. Home: 1715 Varnum St. N.W., Washington. Died June 1, 1947.

CHAMPION, EPAPHRODITUS congressman, businessman b. Westchester parish, Colchester, Conn., Apr. 6, 1756; attended common schs. Served in commissary and purchasing depts. Continental Army, Revolutionary War; moved to East Haddam, Conn., 1782; served as capt. 24th Regt., Conn. Militia, 1784-92, maj., 1793-94, lt. col., 1795-98, brig. gen. 7th Brigade, 1800-03; was a mcht., shipowner, exporter, importer, mem. Conn. Assembly, 1791-1806; mem. U.S. Ho. of Reps. (Federalist) from Conn., 10th-14th congresses, 1807-17. Died East Haddam, Dec. 22, 1834; buried Riverview Cemetery.

CHAMPLIN, STEPHEN naval officer: b. South Kingston, R.I., Nov. 17, 1789; s. Stephen and Elizabeth (Perry) C.; m. Minerva Pomeroy, Jan. 5, 1817, 5 children. Became sailing master U.S. Navy, 1812; participated in expdns. against York and Ft. George; fired 1st shot in Battle of Lake Erie; served in Battle of Mackinac; promoted lt., 1814; in command of Porcupine on survey of Canadian boundary, 1816-18; involved in little active service, 1818-45; in command of lake station ship Michigan, 1845-48 promoted capt., 1850; commd. commodore (ret.) 1867. Died Buffalo, N.Y., Feb. 20, 1870.

CHANCE, EDWIN MICKLEY pres. United Engineers and Constructors, Inc.; b. Phila., Pa., Jan. 13, 1885; s. Henry Martyn and Lillie E. (Mickley) C.; grad. DeLancey Sch., 1903; B.S. in Chemistry, U. of Pa., 1907; m. Eleanor Kent, Jan. 11, 1909 (died Nov. 21, 1940); children—Henry Martyn II, Britton. Assaying and mining in Nev., 1907-09; chemist and engr. Phila. & Reading Coal & Iron Co., Pottsville, Pa., 1909-13; cons. practice, Wilkes-Barre, 1913-17; engring. mgr. Day & Zimmerman, Inc., Phila., 1919-25; v.p. Day & Zimmerman, Inc., Phila., 1925-28; pres. Day & Zimmerman Engring. & Constrn. Co., Inc., 1928; v.p. United Engrs. & Constructors, Inc., 1928-31, pres., 1931—; pres. Dwight P. Robinson & Co., Inc., U.G.I. Contracting Co. Served as capt. to lt. col. Ordnance Dept., Chem. Warfare Service, U.S. Army, in charge design, construction and operation of poison gas, shell filling plant, Edgewood Arsenal, 1917-18; with A.E.F., 1918. Trustee and mem. ex. bd. U. of Pa., chmn. bd. grad. edn. and research member bd. (U. of Pa.), trustee Henry Phipps Inst. (U. of Pa.). Mem. Acad. Natural Science (Phila), Franklin Inst., Army Ordnance Assn Awarded Edward Longstreth medal of merit, Franklin Institute. Clubs: Midday, Racquet (Philadelphia); New York Yacht, Mantoloking Yacht, Cruising Club of America, Sportsmen's Club of America. Contbr. tech. publs.; chem. and metall. inventions. Home: Ocean Av., Mantoloking, N.J. Office: 1401 Arch St., Phila. 5. Died Nov. 26, 1954.

CHANCE, JESSE CLIFTON brig. gen.; b. Alliance, O., Jan. 26, 1843; s. Henry and Charlotte Temple (Trego) C.; ed. pub. schs., Alliance, O., m. Elizabeth Hafford Roberts, April 8, 1867; m. 2d, Jean Sleeth McWatty, September 1, 1887. Enlisted private Company E, 25th Ohio Infantry. August 9, 1862; mustered out of vol. service as 2d lt., Apr. 16, 1866; apptd. 2d lt. 13th U.S. Inf., Jan. 22, 1867, and after serving through every grade was retired from active service, Aug. 15, 1903, with rank of brig. gen. U.S.A., after more than 40 yrs.' service. Methodist. Republican. Home: Petersburg, Fla. Died May 16, 1914.

CHANDLER, CHARLES DEFOREST aeronautics; b. Cleveland, O., Dec. 24, 1878; s. Francis Marion and Effie May (Barney) C.; student Case Sch. of Applied Science, 1899-1901; grad. Army Signal Sch., Fort Leavenworth, Kan., 1911; unmarried. Served as 1st lt. U.S. Vol. Signal Corps, June 1898-May 1899; apptd. 1st lt. U.S.A., Feb. 2, 1901, and advanced through grades to col., Aug. 5, 1917; trans. to Air Service, July 1, 1920; retired, Oct. 18, 1920; aeronautic editor Ronald Press Co., 1925 - . Served in Spanish-Am. War, Philippine Insurrection, punitive Expdn. in Mexico; chief of balloon sect., Air Service, U.S.A., in France, World War. Comdr. U.S. Cableship Burnside, laying of 1st submarine cables to Alaska, 1903-04; 1st winner of Lahm trophy for balloon racing, 1907; comdr. 1st Army aviation sch., College Park, Md., 1911-13. Awarded D.S.M. (U.S.); Officer Legion of Honor (France). Republican. Author: Free and Captive Balloons (with R. H. Upson), 1926; Balloon and Airship Gases (with W. S. Diehl), 1926. Home: Washington, D.C. Died May 18, 1939.

CHANDLER, JOHN army officer, senator; b. Epping, New Hampshire, February 1, 1762; s. Capt. Joseph and Lydia (Eastman) C.; m. Mary Whittier (also spelled Whitcher), Aug. 28, 1783. Served with Continental Army, 1777, 80, Participated in Battle of Saratoga, mem. Mass. Senate, 1803, 04, 19; mem. U.S. Ho. of Reps. from Mass., 9th-10th congresses, 1805-09; sheriff Kennebec County, Mass. (now Me.), 1809-12; commd. brig. gen. U.S. Army during War of 1812; del. Me. Constl. Conv., 1819; pres. Me. Senate, 1820; mem. U.S. Senate from Me., dir. U.S. Br. Bank, Portland, Me., 1829-30; founder Monmouth Acad.; trustee Bowdoin Coll., 1821-38; U.S. collector of customs Dist. of Portland and Falmouth, 1829-37. Died Augusta, Me., Sept. 25, 1841.

CHANDLER, JOHN GORHAM brig. gen.; b. Lexington, Mass., Dec. 31, 1830; s. Daniel and Susannah C.; grad. U.S. Mil. Acad., 1853; m. Mrs. Louise Carnegie Maurice, Oct. 9, 1890. Bvt. 2d lt., 3d Arty., July 1, 1853; commd. 2d lt., Dec. 24, 1853; 1st lt., May 31, 1856; regtl. adj., Dec. 27, 1857-May 17, 1861; capt. asst. q.m., May 17, 1861; lt. col. q.m. vols., Jan. 1, 1863-Aug. 1, 1865; maj. q.m., Jan. 18, 1867; lt. col. deputy q.m. gen., Mar. 4, 1879; col. asst. q.m. gen., Dec. 11, 1892; retired by operation of law, Dec. 31, 1894; advanced to rank of brig. gen. retired, by act of Apr. 23, 1904. Bvtd. maj. lt. col. and col., Mar. 13, 1865, "for faithful and meritorious services during the war." Home: Los Angeles. Died June 31, 1915.

CHANDLER, JOSEPH RIPLEY journalist, congressman; b. Kingston, Mass., Aug. 25, 1792; s. Joseph and Saba (Ripley) C.; ed. U. Pa. Editorial writer U.S. Gazette, 1822, became part owner, 1826, editor until 1847; editor Graham's Am. Monthly Mag. of Lit., Art and Fashion; pres. bd. dirs. Girard Coll., 1848; mem. U.S. Ho. of Reps. from Pa., 31st-33d congresses, Dec. 3, 1849-55; U.S. minister to the Two Sicilies, 1858-60; sent by Phila. Soc. for Alleviating Miseries of Public Prisons to Internat. Congress, London, Eng., 1872. Author: Outlines of Penology, Grammar of the English Language, 1848; The Beverly Family or Home Influence of Religion, 1875. Died Phila., July 10, 1880.

CHANDLER, LLOYD HORWITZ naval officer; b. Washington, D.C., Aug. 17, 1869; grad. U.S. Naval Acad., 1888. Commd. ensign, U.S. Navy, 1890, and advanced through the grades to rear adm., 1930; retired, 1921; served on U.S.S. San Francisco, Spanish-Am. War, 1898, U.S.S. Connecticut, 1906-07; comd. U.S.S. Salem, 1911-12, Illinois, 1912, Nebraska, 1912, Illinois 1912-13, New Hampshire, 1916-18; chief of staff, Battleship Force One, Atlantic Fleet, 1918-19. Decorated Navy Cross. Address: Navy Department, Washington 25. Died Jan. 17, 1947; buried in Glenwood Cemetery, Washington.

CHANDLER, THEODORE EDSON naval officer; b. Annapolis, Md., Dec. 26, 1894; s. Lloyd Horwitz and Agatha Buford (Edson) C.; B.S., U.S. Naval Acad., 1915, post-grad. work in explosives, 1921, M.S. in Chem. Engring., Univ. of Mich., 1922, Army Indsl. Coll., 1931; m. Beatrice Bowen Fairfax, Apr. 28, 1919; children-Theodora Edson (Mrs. John James Green). Commd. ensign 1915, and advanced through the grades to rear admiral (temp.) 1942; during World War I served on U.S.S. Conner, a destroyer basing at Brest, France; commanded U.S.S. Pope on the Asiatic Station, 1929-30, U.S.S. Buchanan in the Battle Force, 1934-35 and U.S.S. Omaha, 1941-43; asst. naval attaché at Paris, Madrid, Lisbon, 1935-38; comdr. of All Forces, Aruba-Curacao, 1943-44; comdr. Assault Group Allied Invasion Southern France, 1944; comdr. Battleship Div. 2, Philippine Invasion and Battle of Leyte Gulf, 1944; comdr. Cruiser Div. 4, Invasion of Lingayen Gulf, Philippines, 1945. Decorated: Navy Cross, Distinguished Service Medal (Army), Silver Star Medal. Legion of Merit, Gold Star in lieu 2d Legion of Merit (Combat V), Purple Heart Medal, Victory Medal with Destroyer Clasp, World War I, Yangtze Service Medal, Am. Defense Medal with bronze A, Am. Campaign Medal, European-African-Middle Eastern Campaign Medal with bronze star, Asiatic-Pacific Medal with 3 bronze stars, World War II Victory Medal, Philippine Liberation Medal with 2 bronze stars; Officer Legion of Honor (France): Nat. Order of Cruzeviodo Sul (officer), War Service Medal with Diploma and Citation (Brazil); Hon. Companion of Distinguished Service Order (Great Britain); Order of Orange Nassau (Netherlands). Recipient letter of commendation from Sec. of Navy. Clubs: New York Yacht, Chevy Chase, Army-Navy Country, Army-Navy, (Washington). Home: 2811 Albemarie St., Washington. Killed in action, Jan. 6, 1945.

CHANDLER, WALTER (CLIFT) lawyer; b. Jackson, Tenn., Oct. 5, 1887; s. William Henry and Knoxie (Clift) C.; LL.B., U. Tenn., 1909; hon. LL.D., Southwestern Coll., Memphis, 1947; m. Dorothy Wyeth, October 10, 1925 (dec. Nov. 16, 1949); children-John Wyeth, Lucia Mary (Mrs. W. F. Outlan). Practiced law, Memphis, 1909-; mem. firm of Chandler, Manire, Johnson & Chandler: mem. Tenn. Ho. of Rep., 1917, Senate, 1921-23; city atty. Memphis, 1928-34; mem. 74th to 76th Congresses (1935-41), 9th Tenn. Dist. (resigned 1940); mayor of Memphis, 1940-46, 55; v.p. U.S. Conf. of Mayors, 1946; mem. Tenn. Constl. Conv. Served in 114th F.A., 30th Div., U.S. Army, 1917-19; participated in battles of San Mihiel, Meuse-Argonne, Woevre Offensive; hon. disch. as capt. Decorated Officer of Orange of Nassau, 1946. Recipient certificate Am. Bar Found., 1964. Mem. Am. (gen. council, 1931-35), Tenn. State (pres. 1928). Memphis (pres.) bar assns., Phi Kappa Phi, Sigma Alpha Epsilon, Omicron Delta Kappa and Order of the Coif, Democrat. Episcopalian. Mason. Home: 1530 Peabody Av. Office: Home Fed. Bldg., Memphis. Died Oct. 1967.

CHANDLER, WILLIAM EATON secretary of the Navy; b. Concord, N.H., Dec. 28, 1835; s. Nathan S. and Mary Ann (Tucker) C.; LL.B., Harvard, 1854; admitted to bar, 1855; (A.M., 1866, LL.D., 1901, Dartmouth). In law practice Concord, N.H., from 1855; reporter decisions Supreme Ct. of N.H., 1859; mem. N.H. Ho. of Rep., 1862, 1863, 1864, 1881 (speaker 1863-64); solicitor and judge adv. gen., Navy Dept., Mar 9-June 17, 1865; 1st asst. sec. of the treasury, June 17, 1865-Nov. 30, 1867; apptd. solicitor gen. of U.S., Mar. 31, 1881, but rejected by Senate; sec. of the Navy, in cabinet of President Arthur, 1882-85; organized Greeley relief expdn., 1884; U.S. senator, for unexpired term (1887-89) of Austin F. Pike, deceased; reelected for terms 1889-95, 1895-1901; pres. Spanish Treaty Claims Commn., 1901-07. Del.-at-large Rep. nat. convs., 1868, 1880; sec. Pep. Nat. Com. during Grant's administration; mem. N.H. Constl. convs., 1876, 1902. Home: Concord, N.H. Died Nov. 30, 1917.

CHANEY, JAMES EUGENE army officer; b. Chaney, Md., Mar. 16, 1885; s. Dr.Thomas Morris and Emma (Chaney) C.; student Baltimore City Coll., 1900-04; grad. U.S. Mil. Acad., 1908, Air Corps Tactical Sch., 1925, Command and Gen. Staff Sch., 1926, Army War Coll., 1931; m. Miriam Clerk, 1910. Served as 2d lt., with 9th Inf. at Ft. Sam Houston, Tex., and in P.I., 1908-12; apptd. maj. A.S., 1917; with A.E.F. in France, 1918-19; air attaché Am. Embassy, Rome, 1919-24; comdt. Air Corps flying schs., Brooks Field and Kelly Field, Tex., 1924-28; lt. col. Air Corps, 1932; chief War Plans Div., Air Corps, Washington, 1932-34; brig. gen., asst. chief of Air Corps, 1934-38, and comdg. Air Corps Tng. Center, San Antonio, Tex., 1935-38; comd. Mitchel Field, L.I., N.Y., 1938-40; apptd. brig. gen., to comd. first Air Defense, 1940; apptd. major gen. commanding 1st Air Force, 1940-41; in office of chief of staff, Washington, 1941-42; commanding U.S. Forces in British Isles, 1942; comdg. gen., First Air Force, 1942-43, Air Forces Western Tech. Training Command, 1944; comdg. Army Forces in seizure, occupation and development, Iwo Jima, 1945; Western Pacific Base Command, 1945; Pres. Sec. of War's Personnel Bd., 1946-47, retired from active service, 1947. U.S. delegate to International Aviation Congresses, Monte Carlo, 1921, Prague, 1921 and Rome, 1924; tech. advisor U.S. Delegation, Geneva Disarmament Conf., 1932. Mem. Gen. Marshall's military mission to Brazil, 1939. Awarded Victory Medal, D.S.M., Legion of Merit with Oak Leaf Cluster (U.S.); Am. Defense; Am. Campaign; European and Asiatic-Pacific Campaigns; War Cross, Officer of the Crown (Italy); comdr. Order of Prince Danilo I (Montenegro); comdr. Order Southern cross (Brazil); Mil. Command Pilot. Address: 3410 Reservoir Rd., N.W., Washington. Died Sept. 1967.

CHAPIN, WILLIS MCDONALD army officer; b. St. Johns, Mich., June 27, 1893; B.S., U.S. Mil. Acad., 1916; grad. Coast Arty. Sch., battery officers course, 1923, advanced course, 1930, Command n and Gen. Staff Sch., 1934. Commd. 2d lt. CAC, U.S. Army, 1916, and advanced through grades to brig. gen., 1944; antiaircraft def. comdr., Fourth Coast Arty., Fort Amador, Panama, C.Z., Mar.-Nov. 1939; became comdg. officer, 73d Coast Arty., Nov. 1939; comd. Antiaircraft Arty. Tng. Center, Fort Bliss, Tex., July-Sept. 1942; assigned to hdqrs. at overseas sta. Sept. 1944. Address: War Dept., Washington 25. Died Oct. 1960.

CHAPLINE, VANCE DUNCAN, naval officer; born Red Cloud, Neb., Sept. 19, 1887; s. William Ridgely and Henrietta (Duncan) C.; student U. of Neb., 1904-05; B.S., U.S. Naval Acad., 1909; m. Marion Pilsbury, Aug. 9, 1938; children by previous marriage—Dorothy Drake (Mrs. Richmond D. Fitzgerald), Frances Drake; step-daughters, Cynthia Billings Morgan (Mrs. William C. Wilcox), Frances Pilsbury Morgan (Mrs. Charles C. Hartigan). Commd. ensign, U.S. Navy, 1911, and advanced through the grades to rear admiral; comd. destroyers operating out of Brest, France on Troop Convoy, World War I; dir. Fleet Maintenance Div., Office of Operations, Navy Dept., Washington, World War II; retired Nov. 1, 1946; asst. to the pres. Marine Transport Lines Inc., 1946-54. Decorated Navy Cross, Legion of Merit (U.S.), officer Legion of Honor (France), Hon. Comdr. Mil. Div. Order of British Empire. Mem. U.S. Naval Acad. Alumni Assn. Clubs: Army and Navy, Army-Navy Country (Washington); N.Y. Yacht; Chevy Chase Country; Propeller Club of Amrica. Home: Washington DC Died Aug 1970.

CHAPMAN, ANDREW GRANT congressman, lawyer; b. La. Plata, Md., Jan. 17, 1839; s. John Grant; attended Charlotte Hall Acad., St. Mary's County, Md.; grad. St. John's Coll., Annapolis, Md., 1858; grad. law dept. U. Va., Charlottesville, 1860. Moved to Balt., 1860; admitted to Md. bar, 1860, began practice of law, Balt.; moved to Port Tobacco, Md., 1864, continued law practice, also involved in famring; mem. Md. Ho. of Dels., 1867-68, 70, 72, 79, 85; apptd. aide and insp. with rank ofbrig. gen., 1874. Gov. Groome's staff, reapptd. by Gov. from Md., 47th Congress, 1881-83; apptd. dep. collector internal revenue, 1885, collector, 1888; del. Democratic Nat. Conv., St. Louis, 1888. Died at home Normandy, nr. La Plata, Md., Sept. 26, 1892; buried Mt. Rest Cemetery, La Plata.

CHAPMAN, AUGUSTUS ALEXANDRIA congressman, lawyer; b. Union, Va. (now W. Va.), Mar. 9, 1803; studied law. Admitted to bar, 1825, began practice of law, Union; mem. Va. Assembly, 1841-43; mem. U.S. Ho. of Reps. (Van Buren Democrat) from Va., 28th-29th congresses, 1843-47; brig. gen. state militia at outbreak of Civil War, took field with his command 1861, served Confederate Army in Kanawha Valley; resumed practice of law, Union, also involved in farming. Died Hinton, Summers County, W. Va., June 7, 1876, while on way to attend W. Va. Democratic Conv., Charleston; buried Green Hill Cemetery, Union.

CHAPMAN, ELBRIDGE GERRY army officer; b. Denver, Nov. 20, 1895; s. Elbridge Gerry and Florence Fairfield (Lake) C.; A.B., U. Colo., 1917, LL.B., 1920; student New Coll., Oxford U., Eng., 1919, Law Sch., Northwestern U., 1923-24; m. Margaret Elene, June 8, 1927; 1 child, Craig. Commd. 2d lt. Inf., U.S. Army, 1917, advanced through grades to maj. gen. (temp.), 1943; legal staff Gov. Gen., P.I., 1932-35; Command and Gen. Staff Sch., 1938; comdg. gen. Airborne Command, 1942—. Decorated D.S.C., Silver Star with oak leaf cluster, Purple Heart. Mem. Phi Gamma Delta. Mason. Home: Denver. Address: Hdqrs. 13th Airborne Div., Camp Mackall, N.C. Died July 6, 1954.

CHAPMAN, JOHN WAYNE govt. ofcl.; b. Ansley, Neb., Dec. 19, 1889; s. James Harve and Cora Adel (Slater) C.; grad. Neb. Tchrs. Coll., 1907; LL.B., U. Mich., 1911; m. Mary Margaret Riordan, June 12, 1921; children-Julia Adel (Mrs. Frank J. Southerland), Mary Margaret (Mrs. Charles L. Pennington), John Wayne. Admitted to N.M. bar, 1917; asst. counsel N.M., State Tax Commn., 1927-31, chief counsel, 1940-41; dir. N.M. Vets. Service Commn., 1935-39; chief legal adv. to mil. govt. in Free Ty. of Trieste, 1948-49; N.M. state dir. Civilian Def., 1951-55, N.M. state dir. Drought Relief Agy., 1955-58; asso. counsel N.M. Bur. Revenue, 1958-, chief legal counsel, 1961-63. Served as lt. col. to col. AUS, 1941-49; chief legal officer Naples Region, assisted in preparation mil. govt. plans for Sicily and Italy, prepared 1st order for elimination of fascism from Italian instns., 1943; regional commr. (mil. gov.) Naples Region, dir. pub. safety sub-commn. Allied Commn. in Italy, 1944-46. Decorated Order of St. Mauritius and St. Lazarus, Order of Crown of Italy (Italy); Bronze Star medal, Victory medal (World War I and II), Am. Def., Am. Theatre, European-African-Middle East, Occupation Medal campaign ribbons. Mem. Am. Legion (dept. comdr. 1920-21, nat. exec. com. 1921-22). S.A.R., V.F.W. Episcopalian. Mason, Rotarian (dist. gov. 1937-38). Author: Conversations on Communism, 1953. Home: 1316 Morelia St. Office: State Capitol Bldg., Santa Fe. Died Jan. 5, 1963; buried Nat. Cemetery, Santa Fe.

CHARBONNEAU, LOUIS HENRY, lawyer; b. Detroit, Jan. 21, 1897; s. Louis Israel and Mary Ellen (Cadieux) C.; LL.B., U. Detroit, 1920; m. May Ellen Young, Feb. 6, 1922; children—Frank L., Louis H., Mary Helen (Mrs. Bruce Mellett), Ann Elizabeth (Mrs. Stephen Pobutski), Michael J. Admitted to Mich. bar, 1920; asst. v.p. Union Trust Co., 1920-30; v.p. Detroit Life Ins. Co., 1931-35; practice of law, Detroit, 1936-60, 66-71; dean and professor University Detroit (Michigan) School of Law, 1960-66. Served as 1st lt. U.S. Army, World War I; from lt. col. to brig. gen., AUS, World War II. Decorated Bronze Star Medal (U.S.); Croix de Guerre (France); Fourragerre (Belgium). Mem. State Bar of Mich. (commr.), Am., Detroit (past pres., director) bar assns., Am. Legion. Mil. Order World Wars, Mil. Order Fgn. Wars. Delta Theta Phi. Roman Catholic. K.C. Home: Grosse Pointe Park MI Died Aug. 13, 1971; buried Mt. Olivet Cemetery, Detroit MI

CHARLTON, CHARLES MAGNUS, clergyman; b. Maynard, Mass., Oct. 12, 1877; s. Emmanuel Carlson and Bellona Maria (Fisk) C.; student Wesleyan Acad., Wilbraham, Mass., and Boston Univ.; S.T.B., Boston U., 1898; m. Lucia Sarah Chamberlain, June 17, 1904 (deceased); children—Frances Lincoln, Newell Chamberlain, Lucia Woodruff; m. 2d, Jessie M. Caddoo. Ordained M.E. ministry, 1898; minister in Vt. conf., 1898-1901; appointed by Pres. Theodore Roosevelt, chaplain U.S. Navy, Oct. 17, 1901; served in P.I. and on Asiatic Sta., 1901-04; Naval Training Sta., Newport, R.I., 1904-06; U.S.S. Georgia, 1906-09; Navy Yard, Norfolk, Va., 1909-10; Navy Yard, Boston, 1910-13; U.S.S. Nebraska, 1913-15; training sta., Newport, R.I., 1915-17; U.S.S. Pennsylvania, 1917; with U.S. Marines, A.E.F., 1917-19; participated in Belleau Woods, Chateau Thierry, Soissons and St. Miheil operations; Navy Yard and Prison, Portsmouth, N.H., June 1, 1919-Nov. 21, 1921 (resigned); former rector Christ Ch. Parish (Protestant Episcopal), Providence, R.I.; later asso. rector St. Stephens Parish, Lynn, Mass., St. Mark's Ch., Boston; and Gloucester, Mass.; now chaplain and dir., Seamen's Club of Boston. Trustee National Sailor's Home, Duxbury, Mass. Mem. North Sea Mine Force Assn., Mil. Order World Wars, Appalachian Mountain Club. Nat. chaplain-in-chief, Commandery N. and M.; order of Spanish-Am. War and comdr. Mass. Commandery; Mass. Dept. chaplain of V.S.W.V. Mason (32 deg.). Home: 176 Marlborough St. (B 16) Boston, Mass.; and Gloucester MA

CHASE, GEORGE FRANCIS army officer; b. Macomb, Ill., July 29, 1848; s. Rev. James M. and Salina (Venable) C.; grad. U.S. Mil. Acad., 1871; m. Nannie, d. of Col. Ely McClellan, U.S.A., Oct. 30, 1888. Commd. 2d lt. 9th Inf., June 12, 1871; promoted through grades to col. 12th Cav., Oct. 2, 1906; brig. gen., May 16, 1912; retired on account of age, July 29, 1912. Served in Dept. of Platte, 1871-80, participating in many campaigns against Indians and in Tongue River, Rosebud, Slim Buttes, Fort Robinson and Hat Creek battles; at U.S. Arty. Sch., 1880-82; duty against Apaches, 1882-85; comd. squadron of cav. on Texas frontier, 1892; at Chickamauga Park, 1898; provost marshal gen. 2d Army Corps, 1898-99; in P.I., 1899-1900 and 1903-05; comd. 15th Cav. in Cuba, 1906-07; duty, Washington, D.C., 1912. Mem. Mil. Order Carabao, Order of Indian Wars of U.S., Vet. Army of Philippines, Died Dec. 13, 1925.

CHASE, HAROLD STUART, realty developer; b. Boston, July 23, 1890; s. Hezekiah Griggs and Nina Wheeler (Dempsey) C.; B.S., U. Cal. at Berkeley, 1912; m. Gertrude Boyer, July 28, 1917; 1 dau., Barbara (Marchioness of Landsdowne) (dec.); stepchildren—Gertrude (Mrs. Raoul Schumacher). Business career with H. G. Chase Real Estate, Santa Barbara, Cal., 1912-70; pres., dir. La Cumbre Mut. Water Co., Laguna Blanca Water Co., Castro Valley Ranch, Inc., Dune Lakes, Ltd.; chmn. adv. bd. Security-First Nat. Bank, Los Angeles, Santa Barbara br., dir., 1924-70; dir. Burroughts Corp., 1929-70. Mem. Santa Barbara Earthquake Relief Com. of 15, 1925; chmn. Pres.'s Unemployment Relief Com., Santa Barbara, 1931-32, v.p., dir. Community Chest, 1931-39, 45-46, War Chest, 1942-44; mem. U.S. Treasury Def. Savs. Com. for So. Cal., 1941; asso. adminstr. War Savs. Staff for So. Cal., 1942; So. Cal. War Finance Com., 1942-46; chmn. Santa Barbara Co. Def., War and U.S. Savs. Bonds Coms., 1941-49; mem. adv. com. U.S. Treasury Savs. Bonds Dir., So. Cal., 1946-49. Pres. 1952-66 (dir. 1946-70) Santa Barbara Mus. Natural History; dir. Santa Barbara Cottage Hosp., 1927-70, pres., 1958-66, chmn. of bd., 1966-70; pres. Knapp Coll. Nursing, 1958-66, chmn. bd., 1966-70, Santa Barbara Found., 1947-49, trustee, 1941-70; trustee Meml. Cancer Found. Santa Barbara, 1950-62, Jefferson Endowment Fund, 1953-70. Served as capt. inf., U.S. Army, WW I. Mem. Duck Hunters Assn. of Cal. (honorary life member of board of directors), Santa Barbara C. of C. (dir. 1925-27, hon. life pres., 1946-70), Cal. Alumni Assn., Beta Theta Pi. Republican. Episcopalian. Clubs: Detroit; Bohemian (San Francisco); Bankers' of America (New York City); Valley Montecito, Montecito Country, University (honorary life member), also mem. Santa Barbara, Coral Casino Beach, Cabana, Kennel (pres. Santa Barbara); La Cumbre Golf and Country (mem. bd. dirs. 1957-70). Home: Santa Barbara CA Died Apr. 26, 1970.

CHASE, JEHU VALENTINE naval officer; b. Pattersonville, La., Jan. 10, 1869; grad. U.S. Naval Acad., 1890. Ensign, July 14, 1892; lt. Mar. 3, 1899; promoted through grades to rear admiral, Jan. 1, 1922. Served on Newport, Spanish-Am. War, 1898; comd. Whipple, 1902-05, Hull, 1905; comdr. Naval Torpedo Sta., Newport, R.I., 1905-07; navigator Kearsarge, 1907-08; flag sec. to comdr. 3d squadron Pacific Fleet, 1908-10; aide on staff comdr. in chief Pacific Fleet, 1910; comd. Tallahassee, 1910-11; insp. ordnance, whitehead Torpedo Works, Weymouth, Eng., 1911-12; comd. Monterey, 1912-13. Cincinnati, 1913-14; mem. spl. bd. on ordnance, Navy Dept., 1914-17; apptd. comdr. Minnesota, 1917; comdr. fleet base force, 1923. later mem. Gen. Board of U.S. Navy; retired, Feb. 1, 1933. Died May 24, 1937.

CHASE, JOHN F lecturer; b. Hallowell, Me., Apr. 23, 1843; ed. common schools; was cannoneer of 5th Me. battery in war, received medal and thanks from Congress for heroic services at battle of Chancellorsville, May 3, 1863; received 48 wounds at battle of Gettysburg; on staff comdr.-in-chief. G. A. R.: now lecturer and gen. mgr. Cyclorama of the Battle of Gettysburg, St. Petersburg, Fla.; m. Sept. 10, 1866, Maria C. Merrill, Freeport, Me. Address: St. Petersburg, Fla.

CHASE, PAUL ADDISON justice; b. Whitingham, Vt., Nov. 13, 1895; s. Charles Sumner and Carrie Emily (Brigham) C.; student Amherst Coll., M.A. (hon.), 1953; m. Doris Eleanor Dexter, Nov. 27, 1926; 1 son, Charles Dexter. Asst. sec. Vt. Senate, 1921-25; admitted to Vt. bar, 1922, Feb.-July 1925; spl. asst. to atty-gen. U.S., 1925-30; mem. Stickney, Sargent & Chase 1930-48; pres. Ludlow Savs. Bank & Trust Co. 1939-41; apptd. superior judge Vt., Oct. 1948; asso. justice Supreme Ct. Vt., since 1953. Served with Hdqrs., Co., 148th Inf., 37th Div., U.S. Army, A.E.F.; commd. capt. inf., Vt. N.G., Dec. 11, 1934 to July 2, 1937; commd. capt. J.A.G. Dept. U.S. Army, Jan. 12, 1938 to Feb. 13, 1941. Apptd. lt. col. J.A.G. Dept. N.G. U.S. Feb. 1941, assigned to 43d Div. as div. judge adv., promoted to col. June 12, 1943, overseas with 43d Div. as div. judge adv., promoted to col. June 12, 1943, overseas with 43d Inf. Div. and First Island Comd., Oct. 1942-Jan. 1944; hospitalized to U.S., Jan. 1944. With First Service Comd. April 1944-46. P.M.S. and T., Norwich U., Northfield, Vt., Apr. 1944-Jan. 1946; returned to N.G. Status, Aug. 1946. Chmn. Vt. Pub. Service Commn., 1947-48; mem. from Ludlow, Vt. Legislature, 1947. Mem. Am. Legion, Chi Phi. Republican. Universalist. Mason. Odd Fellow. Home: South Newfane, Vt. Died July 31, 1963; buried Morningside Cemetery, Brattleborl, Brattleboro, Vt.

CHASTAIN, ELIJAH WEBB congressman; b. nr. Pickens, S.C., Sept. 25, 1813; studied law. Served as capt., then col. in Seminole Indian War; farmer, Union County, Ga.; mem. Ga. Senate, 1840-50; admitted to Ga. bar, 1849, practiced in Blairsville, Ga.; mem. U.S. Ho. of Reps. (Union Democrat) from Ga., 32d-33d congresses, 1851-55; del. Secession Conv., Milledgeville, Ga., 1860; served as lt. col. 1st Ga. Regt., Confederate Army during Civil War; state's atty. for Western & Atlantic R.R., 1860-61. Died nr. Dalton, Ga., Apr. 9, 1874; buried family cemetery nr. Morganton, Ga.

CHATFIELD, WALTER HENRY army officer; b. New Haven, Conn., Mar. 11, 1852; s. John L. and Mary A. (Riggs) C.; ed. high sch., Waterbury. Conn.; Episcopal Acad., Cheshire, Conn.; m. Frances May Rains, Dec. 21, 1880. Pvt. and corpl. Co. G, and q.-m. sergt. 7th Cav., 1878-80; commd. 2d lt. 5th Inf., Oct. 4, 1880; promoted through grades to col. Inf., May 30, 1914; assigned to 2d Inf., Sept. 1, 1915; retired, Mar. 11, 1916. Served in the Indian country 10 yrs., Cuba 2 yrs., Philippines 2 1/2 yrs., Hawaii 6 mos. On active duty, Feb. 1917-Aug. 1919, recruiting and at Port Embarkation, Hoboken, N.J. Episcopalian. Home: New York, N.Y. Died June 30, 1922.

CHATFIELD, WILLIAM HAYDEN, merchant and mfr.; b. Cincinnati, O., Jan. 26, 1893; s. Albert Hayden and Helen (Huntington) C.; student St. Mark's Sch., Southboro, Mass., 1907-10; A.B., Harvard, 1914; m. Elizabeth Wolcott Henry, Oct. 14, 1916; children—Henry Houston, Frederick Huntington, Helen Huntington, Charles Wolcott, John Snowden. Pres. Chatfield and Woods Co. from 1929; also president Chatfield Paper Corporation, Clements Paper Company, The Scioto Paper Co.; chmn. Chaftield & Woods Co. Pa., Union Paper & Twine C. of O., Union Paper & Twine Co. of Mich.; dir. Cin. Equitable Fire Ins. Co., Emery Industries, Incorporated. Served as capt. 309th Inf., A.E.F., World War I. Dir. Cincinnati

Community Chest, Children's Home. Trustee, Cincinnati Inst. of Fine Arts. Clubs: Camargo, Queen City (Cincinnati). Home: Madeira OH Died Sept. 11, 1970; buried Spring Grove Cemetery, Cincinnati OH

CHAUNCEY, ISAAC naval officer; b. Black Rock, Conn., Feb. 20, 1772; s. Wolcott and Ann (Brown) C.; m. Catharine Sickles; children-Charles W., John S. Served in war with Tripoli, 1802-05; comdr. ships New York, John Adams; commd. capt. U.S. Navy, 1806; comdr. naval forces on lakes Ontario and Erie during War of 1812: transported Gen. Dearborn's Army to York (now Toronto), Ont., Can., 1813; established navy-yard, naval hosp., naval sch.; took command ship Washington, 1815; pres. Bd. Navy Commns., 1821-24, 32-40. Died Washington, D.C., Jan. 27, 1840; buried Congressional Cemetery, Washington.

CHEATHAM, BENJAMIN FRANKLIN army officer: b. Nashville, Tenn., Oct. 20, 1820; s. Leonard Pope and Elizabeth (Robertson) C.; m. Anna Bell Robertson, 1866. Served as capt. Tenn Volunteers during Mexican War, 1847; commd. brig. gen. Tenn. Militia, upon ordinance of secession, 1861; commanded div. in Polk's and Hardee's Corps; commd. maj. gen. Confederate Army, 1862: commanded one of Hood's Corps in Tenn. campaign, 1864; served in battles of Belmont, Shiloh, Chickamauga, Chattanooga, 1861-65; supt. Tenn. prisons, 4 years; apptd. postmaster Nashville by Pres. Cleveland, 1885. Died Sept. 4, 1886.

CHEATNAM, B. FRANK army officer; b. Beech Grove, Tenn., May 20, 1867; s. Gen. Benjamin Franklin and Anna Bell (Robertson) C.; student U. of the South, Sewanee, Tenn.: grad. Gen. Staff Sch., 1920, Army War Coll., 1921: m. Mary Warren Denman, Dec. 7, 1901; children-B. F. III, William D., Virginia. Served as maj., Tenn. Vol. Inf., Spanish-Am. War; commd. capt. Q.M. Corps, U.S.A., Feb. 2, 1901, and advanced through grades to col., July 1, 1920; q.m. gen. rank of maj. gen., 1926-30, retired. Served in P.I., Spanish-Am. War, in France, World War. Mem. Sigma Alpha Epsilon. Awarded D.S.M. (U.S.); decorated Comdr. Legion of Honor (France). Clubs: Army and Navy, Chevy Chase. Home: 2101 Connecticut Ave., N.W. Address: War Dept., Washington. Died Dec. 2, 1944.

CHEATNAN, JOSEPH J. naval officer: b. Tenn. Feb. 11, 1872. Entered Supply Corps, U.S. Navy, Sept. 6, 1894; promoted through grades to capt., July 1, 1917; apptd. paymaster gen., Apr. 1929, with rank of rear adm.; retired Mar. 1, 1936. Address Navy Dept., Washington, D.C. Died Sep. 8, 1942.

CHEEVER, DAVID surgeon, educator; b. Boston, June 25, 1876; s. David Williams and Anne Caroline (Nichols) C.; A.B., Harvard, 1897; M.D., 1901; m. Jane Welles Sargent, June 8, 1907; children—David, Francis Sargent, Charles Ezekiel, Daniel Sargent, Jane Hunnewell. Began practice at Boston, 1901; asst. surgeon, Boston City Hosp., 1905-12; surgeon Peter Bent Brigham Hosp., 1913-39, emeritus, 1939—; asst. and demonstrator in anatomy, Harvard Med. Sch., 1903-13; asst. prof. surg. anatomy, 1913-22, asso. prof. surgery, 1922-39, emeritus, 1939—. Lieut. col. BEF, chief surgeon Base Hosp. 22, in charge Harvard Surg. Unit, 1915-16, Recalled to duty as acting surgeon in chief of Peter Bent Bingham Hosp., 1942. Overseer Harvard U., 1939—; pres. Boston Medical Library, 1941—. Began lectr. Chgo Surg. Soc., 1939; Balfour lectr. U. Toronto, Canada, 1941. Fellow Am. Acad. Arts and Sciences, Societe Internationale de Chirurgie; (hon.) Royal Soc. Medicine (London, Eng.); mem. Am. Surg. Assn. (pres. 1940), Soc. Clin. Surgery, A.M.A., New Eng. Surg. Soc. (pres.). Inter-Urban Surg. Soc., Mass. Med. Soc., Mass. Hist. Cos., Sigma Xi, Alpha Omega Alpha. Republican. Unitarian. Contbr. articles and monographs on surg. subjects. Address: 193 Marlboro St., Boston. Died Aug. 13, 1955; buried Mount Auburn Cemetery, Cambridge, Mass.

CHEFFEY, JOHN HOWARD, physician, naval officer; b. Smithfield, O., Oct. 17, 1916; s. Windsor H. and Zana M. (Galbraith) C.; B.S., U. Pitts., 1938; M.D., Jefferson Med. Coll., 1942; m. Ruby E. Marshall. Commd. lt. (j.g.) U.S. Navy, 1942, advanced through grades to rear adm., 1968; intern U.S. Naval Hosp., Portsmouth, Va., 1942-43; jr. med. officer in U.S.S. Gen. H.W. Butner, 1944-45; resident in surgery U.S. Naval Hosp, Bainbridge, Md., 1945-46; mem. staff U.S. Naval Hosp, Chelsea, Mass., 1946; resident in orthopedic surgery U.S. Naval Hosp., Chelsea, Mass., 1946-48; tng. in children's orthopedics Alfred I. DuPont Inst., Wilmington, Del., 1948; staff U.S. Naval Hosp., Bethesda, Md., 1949-50, chief orthopedics, 1953-56, 58-64; officer in charge E Co., 1st Med. Detachment, 1st Marine Div., Fleet Marine Force, 1950-51; chief orthopedic surgery U.S. Naval Hosp., Key West, Fla., 1951-53; chief orthopedic service U.S. Naval Hosp., Yokosuka, Japan, 1956-58; asst. chief Bur. Medicine and Surgery for Personnel Control and Planning, Navy Dept., Washington, 1964-66; asst. for personnel to dep. asst. sec. def. Dept. Def., Washington, 1966-57; comdr. U.S. Naval Hosp., Newport, R.I., 1967-69, U.S. Naval Hosp. and Hosp. Corps Sch., Great Lakes, Ill., 1969-70, also dist. med. officer 9th Naval Dist., 1969-70. Decorated Legion of Merit. Diplomate Am. Bd. Orthopedic Surgery. Fellow Am. Acad. Orthopedic Surgeons; mem. A.M.A. Home: Barnesville OH Died May 17, 1970; buried Arlington Nat. Cemetery, Arlington VA

CHENERY, CHRISTOPHER TOMPKINS, corp. exec.; b. Richmond, Va., Sept. 16, 1886; s. James Hollis and Ida Burnley (Taylor) C.; student Randolph-Macon Coll.; B.S. in Engring., Washington and Lee University, 1909; LL.D., Randolph Macon College, 1964; m. Helen Clementina Bates; children—Hollis Burnley, Margaret Emily, Helen Bates. Chmn. bd. So. Natural Gas Co., now chmn. emeritus; dir. Offshore Company. Trustee Washington and Lee Univ. Served as capt., later maj., engrs., U.S. Army, World War I. Mem. Am. Soc. C.E., New England Geneal. Sco., Acad. Polit. Sci., Am. Waterworks Assn., Inc., Newcomen Soc., N.Y. So. Soc., Va. Hist. Soc., Va. Thoroughbred Assn., Phi Beta Kappa, Phi Delta Theta, Phi Beta Kappa Assos., Omicron Delta Kappa. Clubs: City Midday, Jockey, Madison Sq. Garden, Turf and Field, Recess, Pinnacle (N.Y.C.); American Yacht, Shenorock Shore (Rye, New York); Pelham Country, Boulder Brook, Union Leaggue, Deep Run Hunt, Country of Virginia, Commonwealth. (Richmond); Metropolitan (Washington); Mt. Brook (Birmingham, Ala.); Blind Brook (Purchase, N.Y.); Everglades. Home: Pelham Manor NY Died Jan. 1973.

CHENEY, SHERWOOD ALFRED army officer (ret.) b. S. Manchester, Conn., Aug. 24, 1873; s. John S. Cheney; grad. U.S. Mil. Acad., 1897, Army War Coll., 1907, Gen. Staff Coll., 1921; m. Louise Delano, Sept. 10, 1921 (died 1923); m. 2d, Charlotte S. Hopkins, Nov. 23, 1925. Comd. additional 2d lieut. engrs., June 11, 1897; 2d lieut., July 5, 1898; advanced through the grades to brig. gen., (temp.), Oct. 1, 1918; brig. gen. U.S. Army, Apr. 1, 1933. In field in Cuba, May-Sept., 1888; in Philippines, 1899-1901; participated in operations about San Fabian, later in Cavite Province and in expdn. to Nueva Caceres, and chief engr. officer Dept. of Southern Luzon; a.-d.-c. to Maj. Gen. J. C. Bates, at Chicago and St. Louis, 1903-05; duty with Gen. Staff, 1907-11; dir. Army Field Engr. Sch., 1914-15; on Mexican border, 1915-17; went to France on special commn., June 1917; comdr. 110th Regt. Engrs., 1918; rep. of chief of engrs. at Gen. Hdqrs., A.E.F., 1918; dir. Army Transport Service later dir. gen. transportation, 1919; Am. mem. Inter-Allied Mil. Mission to Baltic Provinces, Nov. 1919-Jan. 1920, in Baltic States and Germany; mem. Gen. Staff Corps, 1921-24; military attaché to China, 1921-24 retired Aug. 24, 1937. Awarded D.S.M. "for services in organization of engineer units and repatriation of A.E.F. from France." Clubs: Hartford (Hartford, Conn.); Army and Navy (Washington). Home: 34 Park St., Manchester, Conn. Died March 13, 1949.

CHENNAULT, CLAIRE LEE airline exec., ret. army officer; b. Commerce, Tex., Sept. 6, 1893; s. John S. and Jessie (Lee) C.; grad. La. State Normal Coll., La State U.; m. Nell Thompson, Dec. 25, 1911 (div. 1946); children—John S., Max T., Jessie Nell (Mrs. A. R. Lee), Charles L., Pat T., David W., Robert K., Rosemary L. (Mrs. Norman H. Marten); m. 2d Anna Chan, Dec. 2, 1947; 2 daus. Claire, Cynthia. Pub. sch. teacher, La., 1908-13; commd. 1st lt. Inf., U.S. Army, trans. to Aviation Sect., Signal Corps, 1917; flight training, 1918; Mexican Border Patrol, 1919-23, Hawaiian Pursuit Squadron, 1923-26, instr. Brooks Field, 1926-30; spl. aviation training, 1930-31. mem. U.S. Army Pursuit Development Bd. 1931-36, leader Air Corps Exhbn. Group, 1932-36, retired 1937; adv. to Chaing Kai-shek, 1937-41; leader Flying Tigers; recalled to active duty and promoted to brig. gen., 1942. Organized and comd. China Air Task Force, 1942, activated 14th Air Force and comd. 1943-45; maj. gen., 1943, retired 1945; organized CNRRA Air Transport, pres., dir., 1946-48; pres., dir., Civil Air Transport, Inc., 1948-50, chmn., dir., 1950-55; chmn., dir. Asiatic Aviation Co., Ltd., CAT, Inc., 1955—; dir. Chinese Air Transport, Ltd. Decorated D.S.M. Army and Navy, Air Medal, D.F.C., D.F.C. Cluster, Air Medal Cluster, D.S.M. Cluster, Chinese Long Sword, Chinese Cloud and Banner Fifty Class, Blue Sky and White Sun, Chinese Cloud and Banner Second Class, Chinese Army, Navy and Air Force Medal; Comdr. British Empire; Croix de Guerre with Palm, Legion of Honor; Chevalier Polonia Restituta. Mem. Am. Legion, V.F.W. Mason. Protestant. Clubs: American, Columbia Country, Shanghai Amateur Baseball (pres. 1948) (all China). Author: Role of Defensive Pursuit, 1933; Way of a Fighter, 1948; also numerous mil. texts and articles. Home: 12 Uri Chang, Taipeh, Formosa. Office: 801-918 16th St., Washington. Died July 1958.

CHESTER, COLBY MITCHELL rear adm.; b. New London, Conn., Feb. 29, 1844; s. Melville and Frances E. (Harris) C.; apptd. to U.S. Naval Acad. from Conn., 1859, grad. 1863; m. Melancia Antoinette Tremaine, Nov. 25, 1873. Ensign, Oct. 1, 1863; promoted through grades to rear adm., Aug. 10, 1903; retired. Served on Richmond, W. Gulf Blockading Squadron, 1863-65; participated battle of Mobile Bay, and capture of Ft. Morgan, Aug. 1864; capture of Mobile, Apr. 1865; various assignments to 1888; mem. commn. to select site for navy yard on Pacific Coast, 1888-90. Bur. of Navigation, 1890-91; comdt. cadets U.S. Naval Acad., 1891-94; Navy Yard, New York, 1894-95; comd. Richmond, 1896, Newark, 1896-97, Minneapolis, May-July 1897; comdr.-in-chief S. Atlantic Squadron, 1897-98; Cincinnati, 1898-99; gen. insp. Kentucky, 1899-1900; comd. Kentucky, 1900-01; Naval War Coll., 1901-02; supt. Naval Obs., 1902-06; comd. spl. service squadron to witness total eclipse of sun, 1905, retired, Feb. 28, 1906; spl. duty in Bur. of Equipment and in Europe until July 1908. prof. naval science, Yale U., 1917; supt. naval units of Yale and Brown univs., and comdt. U.S. Naval Unit, Yale U., until Apr. 1919. Engaged for 15 yrs. under apptmt. from President Roosevelt in establishing open door for Am. trade in Western Asia. Pres. Inter-ocean Engring. Co.; negotiating concessions for construction of railroads and development of mines and oil wells in Ottoman empire. Wrote Diplomacy of the Quarter-Deck; The Monroe Doctrine. A pioneer of the "A.B.C. policy." Died May 4, 1932.

CHESTNUT, JAMES JR. senator; b. Kershaw County, S.C., Jan. 18, 1815; s. James and Mary (Cox) C.; grad. Princeton, 1835; m. Mary Miller, Apr. 23, 1840. Admitted to S.C. bar, 1837; mem. lower house S.C. Gen. Assembly from Kershaw County, 1840-46, 47-48, 49-52; mem. S.C. Senate, 1852-58, pres., 56-58; mem. U.S. Senate from S.C., 1858-60; mem. drafting com. S.C. Ordinance of Secession, 1860; expelled from U.S. Senate upon his appointment to Confederate Provisional Congress, July 11, 1861; mem. Exec. Council S.C., 1861-62; col. cavalry Confederate Army on Pres. Davis' staff; commd. brig. gen. in command S.C. Res. Forces, 1864; del. Democratic Nat. Conv., 1868; chmn. exec. com. taxpayer's convs., S.C. 1871, 74; chmn. Kershaw County Dem. Conv., 1876. Died Saarsfield, nr. Camden, S.C., Feb. 1, 1885; buried Knights Hill Cemetery, nr. Camden.

CHETLAIN, AUGUSTUS LOUIS soldier; b. St. Louis, Dec. 26, 1824; s. Louis and Julia (Droz) C.; ed. com. schs.; m. Emily Tenney, Oct. 1847; m. 2d, Mrs. Melancthon Smith, Apr. 6, 1865; father of Arthur Henry C. Assisted in raising a co. of Galena (Ill.) vols., and elected capt., Apr. 18, 1861; lt. col., 12th Ill. Inf., May 2, 1861; col., Apr. 2, 1861; brig. gen. vols., Dec. 18, 1863; bvtd. maj. gen. vols., June 18, 1865, for gallant and meritorious services during the war; mustered out, Jan. 15, 1866. Asst. U.S. collector internal revenue, Utah, 1867-69; U.S. consul gen., Brussels, 1869-72; mem. bd. of edn., Chicago, 1876-77; organized Home Nat. Bank, Chicago, 1872, and was its pres., organized Industrial Bank of Chicago, 1891, and elected its pres.; retired. Author: Recollections of Seventy Years, 1898. Home: Chicago, Ill. Died Mar. 15, 1914.

CHEVALIER, WILLARD TOWNSHEND publisher; b. Brooklyn, N.Y., Jan. 29, 1886; s. William H. and Elizabeth J. (Kellett) C.; grad. high sch., Brooklyn; student Cooper Union and Pratt Inst., N.Y. City; C.E., Poly. Inst., Brooklyn, 1910; Dr. Engring, Colo. Sch. of Mines, 1936, S. Dak. Sch. of Mines, 1938; m. Josephine Blackmore, June 12, 1911. Civil engr. with Arbuckle Bros., Brooklyn, 1903-05; with Consol. Telegraph & Elec. Subway Co., N.Y. City, 1905-10; N.Y. City Rapid Transit Subway constn., 1910-12; with Atlantic Gulf & Pacific Co., 1912-16; sales mgr. Am. Bitumastic Enamel Co., New York, 1916-17; gen. mgr., 1919-21; cons. tech. advt. and promotion work, 1921-22; asso. editor Engring. News-Record, 1922-23, business mgr., 1923-27; publishing dir. civil engring. and constrn. publs., McGraw-Hill Pub. Co. 1927-38, vice-pres. and dir. since March 1934; publisher Business Week, 1938-45; exec. asst. to pres., 1945-50, exec. v.p. 1950-55, v.p., executive assistant to the president, 1955-57; dir. all McGraw-Hill Cos.; cons. Nat. Indsl. Conf. Bd. Angio-Am. Council on Productivity, Mut. Security Agy., 1948-51, mem., 1951-52. Capt., maj. and lt. col., 11th U.S. Engrs., France, World War I; col. C.E. Res., 1937-48, Hon. Res., 1948-50 ret., 1952. Mem. corp. Poly. Inst. Mem. Am. Soc. C.E. (former dir., pres. N.Y. sect. 1928-29), N.A.M., Internat. C. of C. (trustee 1952), Am. Standards Assn., Am. Water Works Assn. (Honorary Member 1945) Am. Roadbuilders Assn. (pres. 1936-37), Highway Industries Assn. (pres. 1931-35), Water Works Mfrs. Assn. (pres. 1932), Polytechnic Alumni Assn. (past pres.), Soc. Am. Mil. Engrs. (past dir., 2d v.p., 1937), Tau Beta Pi. Clubs: Brooklyn Engineers (past pres.), New York University. Recipient John M. Goodell prize of American Water Works Assn., 1934. Home: 145 Brewster Rd., Scarsdale, N.Y. Office: 330 W. 42d St., N.Y.C. 10036. Died June 29, 1961; buried Greenwood Cemetery, Bklyn.

CHEVER, JAMES W. sea capt.; b. Salem, Mass., Apr. 20, 1791; s. James and Sarah (Browne) C. Went to sea as cabin boy, 1804; 2d in command of ship Fame, 1810; in command of ship Belisarius, 1811; served as prizemaster during War of 1812; capt. of privateer America (owned by Crowninshields), 1813, took 25 ships as prizes, 1813-15; skipper Salem mcht. vessels for many years, retired, circa 1840; owned wharf, Salem. Died May 2, 1857.

CHICKERING, WILLIAM ELBRIDGE ret. army officer; b. Smithville, N.J., Jan. 8, 1895; s. Charles Holland and Margaret Turner (Reick) C.; B.S., U. Pa., 1916; m. Frances Sladen Bradley, Apr. 2, 1921; children—William Elbridge, Jr., Elizabeth Sladen (Mrs. John Swinton King), John Bradley. Commd. 2d lt. Inf., 1917, advanced through the grades to brig. gen., 1944; retired, 1946; v.p. Internat. Group Am. Machine &

Foundry Co. Awarded Legion of Merit (with Oak Leaf Cluster), Silver Star, Purple Heart; Order of the British Empire; Czechoslovak War Cross, 1939. Mem. Sigma Alpha Epsilon. Clubs: University (N.Y.C.); Army and Navy (Washington). Home: Island Heights, N.J.; also 314 E. 41 St., N.Y.C. 17. Died Mar. 2, 1959; buried Arlington Nat. Cemetery.

CHILDERS, JAMES SAXON writer, pub.; b. Birmingham, Ala., Apr. 19, 1899; s. Hayden Prior and Pattie Undine (Goldwire) C.; B.A., Oberlin Coll., 1920; Rhodes Scholar from Ala., Oxford U., B.A., 1923, M.A., 1927; Litt.D., Oglethorpe University, 1954; Litt.D., Birmingham Southern College, 1955; married Maurine White. Prof. lit. Birmingham So. Coll., 1925-42; columnist, feature writer Birmingham News, 1925-42; asso. editor Atlanta Journal, 1951-53, editor, 1953-57; lectr. U.S. State Dept. in Far East and Middle East, 1958-59; pres. Tupper and Love, Inc., book pubs., 1959-. Served in the Naval Air Force as pilot, World War I; served as col., USAF, 1942-45; ETO. Member of the Alpha Tau Omega, Phi Beta Kappa, Omicron Delta Kappa. Episopalian. Author many books latest being: The Nation on the Flying Trapeze, 1960. Home: 8200 Jett Ferry Rd., Dunwoody, Ga. 30043. Office: 3030 Peachtree Rd. N.W., Atlanta. Died July 17, 1965; buried Elmwood Cemetery, Birmingham, Ala.

CHILDS, CEPHAS GRIER engraver, editor, publisher; b., Bucks, County, Pa., Sept. 8, 1793; s. Cephas and Agnes (Grier) C. Enlisted in Washington Guards, 1813; commd. col. 128th regt. Pa. Militia, 1834; comml. litography pioneer in U.S.; engraved, published periodical Childs Views in Phila., 1827-30; a founder lithographic firm Pendleton, Kearny & Childs, Phila., 1829, publishers of Phila. Comml. Herald (merged with North Am. mag. 1840); propr., editor mag. Comml. List and Phila. Price Current, 1835-52; pres. New Creek Coal Co., 1855-64; sec. bd. dirs. Phila. Bd. Trade, 1839-51; dir. Bank of Northern Liberties, Pa. Acad. Fine Arts. Died July 7, 1871.

CHILDS, THOMAS army officer; b. Pittsfield, Mass., 1796; s. Dr. Timothy and Rachael (Easton) C.; grad. U.S. Mil. Acad., 1814; m. Ann Eliza Coryton, Jan. 5, 1819, 9 children. Served in Niagara campaign, 1814; commd. 1st lt. U.S. Army, 1818, capt., 1826; planned attack on Ft. Drane during Seminole War, 1836, for which he was brevetted maj. 1st Arty.; promoted lt. col., 1841; mil. gov. stationed at Jaiapa in Mexican War, 1847; made brig. gen. for his defense of Puebla, 1847; in command of mil. operations East Fla., 1852-53. Died Ft. Brooke, Fla., Oct. 8, 1853.

CHIPERFIELD, BURNETT MITCHELL congressman; b. Dover, Ill., June 14, 1870; s. Rev. Thomas and Hannah M. (Reynolds) C.; ed. Hamline Univ., 1888-89 (non-grad.); m. Clara Louise Ross, Nov. 12, 1895; children - Margaret Ross (dec.), Robert Bruce, Claude Burnett. Began law practice, Canton, Ill., 1891; identified with much important litigation in Ill.; mem. Chiperfield & Chiperfield. City atty., Canton, 1894-96; state's atty., Fulton Co., Ill., 1896-1900; sec., trustee W. Ill. State Normal Sch., 1901-05; mem. Ill Ho. of Rep., 8 yrs., 1903-13 (chmn. judiciary com., 1909-11); chmn. com. of House and Senate which made extensive investigations and submitted exhaustive report concerning submerged and shore lands owned by the State; mem. 64th Congress (1915-17), Ill. at large, also 71st and 72d Congresses (1929-33), 15th Ill. Dist.; del. to Rep. Nat. Conv., 1920, 36. Adjutant and lt. col. 1st Cav. Ill. N.G., also judge advocate gen.; organized regt. Spanish-Am. War; mem. mil. staff several Ill. govs.; assisted, 1917, in writing draft law and regulations for World War; asst. to provost marshal gen. of U.S.A., in charge 1st draft in Ill. until Aug. 1917; commd. major, judge advocate general's dept. O.R.C., 1917; judge advocate 33d Div., U.S.A., Camp Logan, Houston, Tex., and in France; div. liaison officer; judge advocate gen. 3d Army Corps, Army of Occupation, in Germany, in charge civil affairs area across Rhine; judge advocate gen. State of Ill., for 10 years, rank of col., retired, 1934, with rank of brig. gen., after 30 years' service with Ill. N.G. Cited for "exceptionally meritorious and conspicuous service," by Gen. Pershing, and for "gallantry in action against the enemy," by comdr. 33d Div., A.E.F.; recommended on 4 distinct occasions for D.S.M. Pres. First Nat. Bank, Canton. Mem. Bd. Cons. Biologists and Conservationists, Emergency Conservation Com.; mem. Nat. Council Jews and Christians. Methodist. Home: Canton, Ill. Died June 24, 1940.

CHIPMAN, NORTON PARKER judge; b. Milford, O., Mar. 7, 1838; s. Norman and Sarah Wilson (Parker) C.; prep. edn., Washington Coll. and Mt. Pleasant Acad., Ia.; LL.B., Cincinnati Law Sch., 1859; m. Mary Isabel Holmes, Jan. 30, 1865. Began practice at Washington, Ia., 1859; lt. Co. H. and adj. 2d Ia. Inf., 1861; commd. maj., Sept. 23, 1861; col. and a.a.d.c., Apr. 17, 1862, staff of Maj. Gen. Samuel R. Curtis; brig. gen. vols., Mar. 13, 1865, "for meritorious service in Bureau of Military Justice"; hon. mustered out, Nov. 30, 1865, and resumed practice of law. Apptd. sec. District of Columbia, 1871 (resigned and elected); del. to Congress from D.C., 1871-75; removed to California, 1875, and engaged in law practice; commr. Supreme Ct. of Calif., 1897-1905; apptd. presdg. justice Dist. Ct. of Appeals, 3d Dist., San Francisco, 1905, and elected to same office, Nov. 1906. Pres. Calif. State Bd. of Trade; dir. Calif. Development Bd. Republican. Episcopalian. Died Feb. 1, 1924.

CHISOLM, ALEXANDER ROBERT army officer, financier; b. Beaufort, S.C., Nov. 19, 1834; s. Edward N. and Mary (Hazzard) C.; attended Columbia, 1851, m. Helen (Schieffelin) Graham, Apr. 7, 1875. Commd. lt. col. S.C. Militia, 1861; served on Gen. Beauregard's staff during Civil War; fought at battles of Bull Run, Shiloh, Charleston; moved to N.Y.C., 1869; founded A. R. Chisolm & Co., stockbrokerage; founded Mining Record, 1877 (named changed to Financial and Mining Record), co-editor, 1882-90. Died N.Y.C., Mar. 10, 1910.

CHISOLM, JOHN JULIAN surgeon, oculist; b. Charleston, S.C., Aor. 16, 1830; s. Robert Trail and Harriet Chisolm; M.D., Med. Coll. S.C., 1850; m. Mary Edings Chisolm, Feb. 3, 1852; m. 2d, Elizabeth Steel, Jan. 14, 1854. Practiced medicine, Charleston, 1852-61; conducted free hosp. for slaves, also 1 of 1st Am. summer schs. of medicine 1853-58; prof. surgery Med. Coll. of S.C., 1856-61, dean, 1865-69; 1st commd. med. officer in Confederate Army, 1861; served as chief surgeon mil. hosp., Richmond, Va., later dir. plant for manufacture of medicines, Charleston: prof. eye and ear surgery U. Md., 1869, dean, 1869-95, prof. emeritus, 1895-1903; founder Balt. Eye and Ear Inst., 1870; founder Presbyn. Eye and Ear Charity Hosp., Balt., 1877, chief surgeon, 1877-98; limited his practice to ophthalmology, after 1873; 1 of 1st to use cocaine in eye surgery and to use chloroform anesthesia. Died Petersburg, Va., Nov. 2, 1903; buried Greenmount Cemetery, Balt.

CHITTENDEN, HIRAM MARTIN brig. gen.; b. Western N.Y., Oct. 25, 1858; s. William F. and Mary Jane (Wheeler) C.; apptd. from N.Y., and grad. U.S. Mil. Acad., 1884; grad. Engr. Sch. of Application, 1887; m. Nettie M. Parker, Dec. 30, 1884. Second lt. engrs., June 15, 1884; 1st lt., Dec. 31, 1886; capt., Oct. 2, 1895; lt. col. chief engr. vols., May 9, 1898-Feb. 25, 1899; maj. engrs., Jan. 23, 1904; lt. col., July 28, 1908; brig. gen., Jan. 25, 1910. Had charge govt. works in Yellowstone Nat. Park and on Missouri, Ohio and other Western rivers; also of reservoir surveys in arid regions; chief engr. 4th Army Corps in Spanish-Am. War, 1898; retired for disability incident to the service, Feb. 10, 1910. Mem. Fed. commn. on Yosemite Nat. Park, 1904, commn. of engrs. on Sacramento flood control; port commr., Port of Seattle, Sept. 5, 1911-Oct. 15, 1915; cons. engr. Spring Valley Water Co., San Francisco, 1912, and on Dayton, O., flood problem, 1914-15. Author: Yellowstone National Park (12 edits.). Died Oct. 9, 1917.

CHIVINGTON, JOHN MILTON clergyman, army officer; b. Warren County, O., Jan. 27, 1821; s. Isaac and Jane (Runyon) C.; m. Martha Rollason, 1840; m. 2d, Mrs. Isabella Arnzen, 1873; children-Thomas, Elizabeth Jane, Sarah. Worked with his brothers in family's small timber business, later because carpenter's apprentice; converted to Methodism, 1842; ordained to ministry Methodist Ch., 1844; became mem. Order of Masons, 1864; itinerant preacher in Ohio, 1844-48; itinerant preacher to both Whites and Indians on frontier, 1848-54; founded 1st Masonic order in Kan., 1854; anti-slavery advocate, supported Free-Soil group during Kan. Border Wars, 1854-56; became known as the Fighting Parson; apptd. maj. 1st Colo. Volunteers, 1861, promoted col., 1862, served in Colo. and N.M. campaigns against Confederacy; apptd. comdr. of mil. dist. of Colo., 1863; wanted policy of unconditional surrender from various Plains Indian tribes; led controversial attack on Indians at Sand Creek, Colo., Nov. 1864 (variously referred to as a battle or a massacre); 3 separate hearings were held on matter, but no ofcl. action of any type was instituted against him; he was personally castigated both at hearings and for years afterward; engaged in freighting bus., Neb., 1865-67; returned to Colo., 1883, engaged in newspaper work, held various public offices. Died of cancer, Denver, Colo., Oct. 4, 1894; buried Denver.

CHRISMAN, EDWARD ROBERT army officer; b. Connersville, Ind., Aug. 13, 1866; s. Jesse Swisher and Catharine Verlinda (Price) C.; grad. U.S. Mil. Acad., 1888, Sch. of Submarine Mining, Willetts Point, N.Y., 1892; m. Florence Isabella Ryan, Mar. 28, 1892; children - Catharine Verlinda, Ord Gariche. Commd. 2d lt. inf., U.S.A., 1888, and advanced through grades to col., May 15, 1917; retired Jan. 31, 1921; brig. gen. on retired list, June 21, 1930; prof. mil. science and tactics, S.D. State College, 1909-11; on active duty as prof. mil. science and tactics, U. of Idaho, 1919-36, comdt. of cadets, 1932-35, prof. military science and tactics, emeritus for life, by act of Congress, approved Apr. 15, 1936, comdt. of cadets, emeritus, by board of regents, University of Idaho, 1935. Participated in Sioux Indian Campaign, 1890-91; Spanish-American War, Cuba, 1898 (cited for gallantry in action); Philippine Insurrection, 1899-1902; Leyte Campaign, Pulujan (P.I.) Outbreak, 1906-07; served in Panama Canal Zone, and brig. gen. comdg. U.S. forces in Puerto Rico, World War. Mason. Home: Moscow, Ida. Died Jan. 15, 1939.

CHRISTENBERRY, CHARLES W(ILKES) assn. exec., ret. army officer; b. Anson, Tex., Jan. 28, 1895; s. Charles McLeod and Georgia (Jones) C.; student Tex. Christian U., 1914-17; grad. Inf. Sch., Ft. Benning, Ga., 1926; B.S., Columbia, 1927; m. Vestal Diane Tompkins; children-Charles Wilkes, Helen Agnes (Mrs. Jacob R. Moon, Jr.). Commd. 2d lt. Inf., 1917, advanced through grades to maj. gen., 1953; prof. mil. sci. and tactics N.Y. U., 1928-35; with Office Adj. Gen., 1935-36; officer in charge publs. br. Adj. Gen. Dept., Washington, 1936-39; dept. adj. gen. Philippine Dept., 1939-41; adj. gen. V Corps., 1941-43, adj. gen. SOS, North Africa, 1943; chief staff Replacement Tng. Command, North Africa, Italy, 1944; theater adj. gen. Am. and Brit. Forces, Italy, also adj. gen. M.T.O.U.S.A., 1944-46; adj. gen. 1st Army, 1946-48, comdr. Recruiting Publicity Bur., Governors Island, N.Y., 1948-51; chief spl. services div. Office Adj. Gen., Dept. Army, Washington, 1951-52; dep. chief staff Gen. Van Fleet, Korea, 1952-53; asst. chief staff Hdqrs. Far East and UN Commands, Japan, 1953-54; pres. Am.-Korean Found., 1954-, C.S. Com. on Publ. for N.Y. State, 1956-. Decorated D.S.M. (twice) Legion of Merit, B.S.M. (U.S.); Order Brit. Empire; Decoration Fgn. Legion (France); Medale La Guerre (Brazil); Crown of Italy; received silver replica Paul Revere Bowl for outstanding service for peace Citizens of Mass., 1954. Home: 160 Riverside Dr., N.Y.C. Office: 345 E. 46th St., N.Y.C. 17; also 551 Fifth Av., N.Y.C. 17. Died Dec. 24, 1963; buried Arlington Nat. Cemetery.

CHRISTIAN, WILLIAM army officer; b. Berkeley County, Va., 1732; s. Israel and Elizabeth (Stark) C.; m. Anne Henry. Commd. capt. Col. William Byrd's Regt., 1763; represented Fincastle County in lower house Va. Legislature, 1773-75, Fincastle and Botetourt counties in Va. Senate, 1776, 80-83; mem. Va. Com. of Safety, 1775; commd. col. Va. Militia by Va. Council Defense, 1776; one of 3 commrs. of Va. to negotiate Cherokee treaty signed at L.I., July 20, 1777. Killed nr. Jeffersonville, Ind. while leading pursuit party against marauding Wabash Indians, Apr. 9, 1782.

CHRISTIANS, WILLIAM F(LORIAN) educator; b. Victor, Colo., Oct. 2, 1903; s. Ward and Flora (Peak) C.; Ph.B., U. Chgo., 1925, M.S., 1932, Ph.D., 1938; Am. Field fellow, U. Grenoble, France, 1926-27; m. Magdalene Schaffer, June 23, 1927; 1 dau., Dagny Schaffer (Mrs. Anthony J. Tarrell, Jr.). With accident acturial dept. Travelers Ins. Co., Hartford, Conn., 1927-28; asst. traveling auditor Internat. Harvester Co., Chgo., 1929-31; instr. geography Syracuse U., 1932-33; fellow dept. geography U. Chgo., 1933-34; instr. U. Pa., 1934-39; asst. prof., 1939-44, asso. prof., 1944-54, prof., 1954—. Wage analyst Wage Adminstrn. Agy., 1942-45; geographer OSS, China, 1945-46. Served as lt. col. AUS, 1949, now lt. col. Res. Mem. Assn. Am. Geographers, Sigma Xi, Lambda Chi Alpha. Author: Economic Geography of South America (with R. H. Whitbeck and F. E. Williams), 1940. Contbr. Global Geograph., 1944, India, Pakistan and Ceylon, 1951; World Political Geography, 1956; Ency., Americana, Ency. Brit. Home: 311 Overhill Rd., Wayne, Pa., Office: U. Pa., Phila. 4. Died Mar. 13, 1956; buried Valley Forge Gardens, King of Prussia, Pa.

CHRISTIE, ARTHUR CARLISLE physician, radiologist; b. W. Sunbury, Butler County, Pa., Dec. 29, 1879; s. Milton Hughes and Harriet Josephine (Rhodes) C.; grad. high sch., Corry, Pa., 1898; M.D., Cleveland Coll. Physicians and Surgeons (medical department Ohio Wesleyan University), 1904; M.S., Ohio Wesleyan, 1919; D.Sc., The American University, 1942; grad. Army Med. Sch., Washington, D.C., 1907; m. Maude Irene Hopkins, June 1, 1904; children—Mrs. Geneva Irene Morris, Carlisle Van Dyke, Milton Arthur, Harriet Inez Beck. Practiced Clymer, N.Y., 1904-06; joined Med. Corps, U.S. Army, 1906; served in Philippines, 1907-10, Columbus Barracks, 1910-12; prof. operative surgery and Roentgenology, Army Med. Sch., Washington, D.C., 1912-16; resigned as capt.; in World War as maj., lt. col. and col. M.C.; gen. charge X-ray work for Army, 1917-Aug. 1918; apptd. sr. consultant in Roentgenology, A.E.F. in France, Sept. 1918; hon. discharged, Feb. 1919; col. M.R.C. Formerly prof. of radiology George Washington U. Med. Coll. Mem. firm Drs. Groover, Christie & Merritt, specializing in Roentgenology; formerly prof. clinical radiology Georgetown Univ. Med. School; consultant U.S. Public Health Service. Mem. special advisory group Veterans Administration; consultant in radiology Walter Reed General Hosp. Pres. Fifth Internat. Congress of Radiology, Chicago, 1937; chmn com. on Radiology, Natl. Research Council; hon. consultant U.S. Army Medical Library. Hon. fellow British Faculty of Radiologists, 1950. Mem. editorial bd. Am. Jour. Roentgenology and Radium Therapy. Fellow Am. Med. Assn., Am. Coll. of Physicians, International College Surgeons; member Am. Roentgen Ray Soc. (pres.). Radiol. Soc. N. Am., Am. Coll. Radiology (pres.), Med. Society of D.C. (president). Republican. Methodist. Mason (32ff). Club: Army and Navy, Rotary. Author: Manual of X-ray Technique, 1913, 17; Roentgen Diagnosis and Therapy, 1924; Economic Problems of Medicine, 1935. Home: Crescent City, Fla. Office: 1835 I St. N.W., Washington 6. Died June 22, 1956.

CHRISTY, WILLIAM C. army officer; b. Ariz., Nov. 25, 1885; B.S., U.S. Mil. Acad., 1907; grad. Cav. Sch., 1924; honor grad. Command and Gen. Staff Sch., 1925; grad. Army War Coll., 1928; commd. 2d lt. Cav., 1907, advanced through grades to brig. gen., 1943; served on Gen. Staff Corps, 1928-32, 35-39, 42—. Address: A.P.O. 830. care Postmaster, New Orleans. Died Jan. 31, 1957.

CHURCH, BENJAMIN carpenter, army officer; b. Plymouth, Mass., 1639; s. Richard and Elizabeth (Warren) C.; m. Alice Southworth, Dec. 26, 1671. Engaged in carpenter's trade, Plymouth Colony, circa 1658; moved to Little Compton. R.I., by 1674; played prominent role in King Philip's War, 1675, organized English settlers' forces against Indian attacks, urged necessity for pursuing Indians after encounters; wounded in Great Swamp Fight, 1675, nr. South Kingston, R.I., took Indian leader Philip prisoner, 1676; lived in Plymouth Colony, 1676-88, served as selectman and magistrate; served as maj. Plymouth forces during King William's War, 1689-97, also Queen Anne's War, 1791-14; led expdn. against French town of Les Mines, 1704; resumed carpenter's trade, Little Compton, circa 1690. Died Little Compton, Jan. 17, 1718.

CHURCH, EARL D. commr. of pensions; b. Rockville, Conn.; s. Philo H. and Jennie T. (Ide) C.; grad. high sch., Rockville, 1890; student Yale, 1891-92; m. Elysabeth Remington, Sept. 26, 1905. With Travelers Ins. Co., 1896-1929, pvt. sec. to pres., 1896-1901. supt. life policy loan div., 1905-18, in casualty agency dept., 1920-29, asst. supt. of agencies, 1929; U.S. commr. of pensions, May 24, 1929-. Served as maj., later lt. col., Ordnance Dept., U.S. Army 1917-20; took part in Battle of Cambral, on the Somme, at Verdun, in battles of St. Mihiel and the Argonne. Awarded D.S.M. (U.S.); Croix de Guerre with bronze star (France); Gen. H.Q. citation certificate for "exceptionally meritorious and conspicuous service": French citation at St. Mihiel; cited in 80th Div. gen. orders in battle of Argonne. Pres. Bd. of Councilmen, Hartford, 1905-06. Bd. of Aldermen, 1907-08. Republican. Home: Washington, D.C. Died May 9, 1930.

CHURCH, JOHN HUSTON army officer; b. Pa., June 28, 1892; s. William and Elizabeth (Kime) C.; grad. Bucknell Acad., Lewisburg, Pa., 1910; student N.Y.U., 1915-17; grad. Inf. Sch., 1921, Command and Gen. Staff Sch., 1937; m. Jean Haller, Sept. 1, 1922; 1 dau., Martha J. Commd. 2d lt., inf. U.S. Army, 1917, advancing through grades to maj. gen.; comdr. 24th Div., Korea, 1950; comdr. Inf. Center, Ft. Benning, Ga., 1951-52. Decorated D.S.C., Silver Star, Legion of Merit, Purple Heart with 2 clusters. Office: care Dept. of the Army, Washington 25, D.C. Died Nov. 3, 1953.

CHURCH, WILLIAM E. lawyer; b. Brooklyn, N.Y., Dec. 7, 1841; s. John R. and Anstiss (Howard) C.; A.B., Williams Coll., 1861; studied law at Morristown, N.J., 1861-62, and New York, 1865-66; enlisted in 11th N.Y., av., Aug. 1862; served in Md., Va., and La.; apptd. asst. adj. gen. vols. with rank of capt., Mar. 29, 1865, and assigned to 1st Brigade, 1st Div., 13th Army Corps; went with his command, in May, 1865, to occupy Shreveport, La., and to receive the surrender of Kirby Smith's army; was post adj. of Shreveport until Aug. and afterward on staff of Gen. Sheridan until mustered out, Oct. 23, 1865; m. Mary Jones, Nov. 2, 1870. Admitted to N.Y. bar, 1866; practiced there until 1872; at Morristown, N.J., 1872-83; asso. justice Supreme Ct. of Dak. Ty., 1883-87; located in Chicago, 1890; sr. mem. Church & McMurdy. Republican. Apptd. judge-advocate, Dept. Ill., G.A.R., July 1913. Home: Evanston, Ill. Died Apr. 20, 1917.

CHURCHILL, EDWARD DELOS, surgeon; b. Chenoa, Ill., Dec. 25, 1895; s. Ebenezer Delos and Maria A. (Farnsworth) C.; B.S., Northwestern U., 1916, A.M., 1917; M.D. cum laude, Harvard, 1920; Dr. Honoris Causa, of Algiers, 1944; D.Sc., Princeton, 1947, U. Ala., 1959, Harvard, 1961; LL.D., Queen's U., 1954; m. Mary Lowell Barton, July 7, 1927; children—Mary Lowell, Frederick Barton, Edward Delos, A. Coolidge. Student intern Faulkner Hosp., Boston, 1919-20; surg. intern Mass. Gen. Hosp., 1920-22, resident, 1922-23, chief West Surg. Service, 1931-48, chief Gen. Surg. Services, 1948-72; asso. surgeon and dir. Surg. Research Lab., Boston City Hosp., 1928-30; asst. in surgery Harvard, 1922-23, Alumni asst. in surgery, 1923-24, instr. surgery, 1924-28, Moseley traveling fellow, 1926-27, asso. prof. surgery, 1928-31, John Homans prof. surgery, 1931-62, emeritus, 1962-72. Adv. med. bd. Am. Hosp., Paris, 1957-72; mem. adv. council Shiraz Med. Center, Nemazee Hosp., Iran, 1957-72; charter mem. sci. adv. bd. Walter Reed Inst. Research, Washington, 1958. Served in Med. Res., U.S. Army, 1918, 1st lt., 1924-29; col. M.C., cons. surgeon N. African and Mediterranean theatres, 1943-46. Decorated Legion of Merit, 1944; European Theater Service medal with 4 bronze battle stars; Cross of Knight Legion of Honor, 1953; War medal of Brazil; comdr. Order Crown of Italy; hon. officer Mil. Div. Order Brit. Empire, 1945; D.S.M., 1946; officer de l'Ordre National du Cedre (Lebanon). Chmn. med. adv. com. to sec. of war, 1946-48; vice chmn. task force, Fed. Med. Services, Commn. on Orgn. Exec. Br. Govt., 1948-49, 1953-55; mem. Armed Forces Med. Adv. Com. to Sec. Def., 1948-51; chmn. com. on surgery NRC, 1946-49; sr. civilian cons. in thoracic surgery to Surgeon Gen., 1953-72; cons. to Surgeon Gen., 1954-55; mem. edit. bd. Annals of Surgery. Fellow Royal Coll. Surgeons Eng. (hon.), Royal Coll. Univ. Surgeons Denmark (hon.), Am. Acad. Arts and Sci.; lectr. Royal Coll. Physicians and Surgeons (Can.); mem. Am. Assn. for Thoracic Surgery (pres. 1948-49), Am. Bd. Surgery Founders' Group (mem. bd. 1937-49), A.C.S., A.M.A., Am. Soc. for Clin. Investigation (emeritus 1941-72), Am. Surg. Assn. (pres. 1946-47), Assn. Mil. Surgeons U.S., Internat., New Eng. Boston, Excelsior (hon.) surg. socs., Halsted Club, Mass. Med. Soc., No. Pacific Surg. Assn. (hon.), Soc. Clin. Surgery (pres. 1949-50), Soc. U.S. Med. Cons. in World War II, Trudeau Soc., Korean Communications Zone Med. and Dental (hon.), 38th Parallel Med. Soc. of Korea (hon.), So. Honshu Med. Soc., Alpha Omega Alpha, Sigma Xi, Delta Tau Delta; hon. mem. U.S. and fgn. surg. socs. Presbyn. Clubs: Tavern, Century Assn., Harvard (Boston and N.Y.C.), Aesculapian. Home: Belmont MA Died Aug. 28, 1973.

CHURCHILL, FRANK SPOONER M.D.; b. Milton, Mass., Aug. 28, 1864; s. Charles Marshall Spring and Susan Elizabeth (Spooner) C.; A.B., Harvard, 1886, M.D., 1890; grad. Mass. Gen. Hosp., Boston, 1891; m. West Medford, Mass., Lucretia Mott Hallowwell, Dec. 31, 1894; children-Richard Hallowell (dec.), Lucretia Mott, Winthrop Hallowell. Surgeon Calumet & Hecla Mining Co., 1891-92; removed to Chicago, 1892; specialist in diseases of children; former med. insp. Bd. of Health, Chicago; asso. prof. pediatrics, Rush Med. Coll.; until 1906 visiting phys. Cook Co. Hosp.) attdg. phys. Children's Memorial Hosp. 10 yrs. Commd. maj. Med. R.C., 1917; hon. discharged, Jan. 1919, and removed to Milton, Mass. Med. dir. pub. schs. of Milton since Sept. 1919. One of editors Am. Jour. Diseases of Children. Unitarian. Mem. Am. Pediatric Soc. (pres. 1916-17), Chicago Pediatric Soc., A.M.A. (pres. sect., Diseases of Children, 1913-14), Chicago Med. Soc. Home: Milton, Mass.

CHURCHILL, MARLBOROUGH army officer; b. Andover, Mass., Aug. 11, 1878; s. John Wesley and Mary (Donald) C.; A. B., Harvard, 1900; m. Mary Smith, Oct. 7, 1904. Comd. 2d lt. Arty. Corps, July 16, 1901; 1st lt., Jan. 25, 1907; assigned to 3d Field Arty., June 6, 1907; trans, to 1st Field Arty., Aug. 2, 1910; capt., Apr. 13, 1911; trans. to 5th Field Arty, Jan. 8, 1912; maj., May 15, 1917; lt. N. A., Aug. 5, 1917; col. N. A., June 12, 1918; brig. gen. N. A., Aug. 8, 1918. Instr., Sch. of Fire for Field Arty., 1912-14; insp.-instr., Field Arty. of Organized Militia of Va., Pa. and D. C., 1914-16; editor Field Artillery Jour., July 1914-Jan. 1916; mil. observer with French, Armies in the field, Jan. 1916-Apr. 1917; exec. officer Am. Mil. Mission, Paris, Apr.-June 1917; gen. staff, A. E. F., Aug. 1917-Jan. 1918; acting chief of staff, Army Arty., 1st Army, A. E. F., Jan.-May 1918; returned to U. S., June 1918; gen. staff, U. S. Army, since June 6, 1918, as chief, mil. intelligence br., June-Aug. 1918, asst. chief of staff and dir. of mil. intelligence, since Aug. 1918; spl. duty, Am. Commn. to Negotiate Peace, Dec. 1918-Apr. 1919; hon. discharged from temporary commn. as brig gen., June 30, 1920. Decorated D. S. M.; Officer Legion of Honor (France); Companion of the Bath (Eng.); Comdr. Order of the Crown (Italy); Comdr. Order of Leopold (Belgium). Clubs: Army and Navy (Manila and Washington); Harvard (N. Y. City), Metropolitan, Racquet (Washington). Home: 2301 Connecticut Av. Address: Care War Dept., Washington. Died July 9, 1942.

CHURCHILL, THOMAS J. planter; b. Louisville, Ky., Mar. 10, 1824; s. Col. Samuel C.; grad. St. Mary's Coll., Ky.; studied law Transylvania Univ., Lexington, Ky.; m. Annie Maria, d. Senator A.H. Sevier, July 31, 1849; First col., Humphrey Marshall's regt. cav., in war with Mexico; postmaster ittle Rock, Ark., during Buchanan's administration; col. 1st regt. mounted riflemen in Civil war; promoted to brig. gen. for gallant conduct and afterwards to maj. gen.; State treas. Ark. for 3 terms; gov. Ark., 1881-83. Home: Little Rock, Ark. Died 1905.

CILLEY BRADBURY congressman; b. Nottingham, N.H., Feb. 1, 1860; attended common schs. Involved in farming; U.S. marshal for dist. of N.H. (appt. by Pres. John Adams), 1798-1802; mem. U.S. Ho. of Reps. (Federalist) from N.H., 13th-14th congresses, 1813-17; col., aide Gov. Gillman's staff, 1814-16; retired from pub. life. Died Nottingham, Dec. 17, 1831; buried Gen. Joseph Cilley Buring Ground in Nottingham Square.

CILLEY, GREENLEAF retired naval officer; b. Thomaston, Me., Oct. 27, 1829; apptd. midshipman, U.S.N., Feb. 26, 1841; in Mediterranean squadron, 1843-45; ordered to Naval School, 1846; a month later went to seat of war in Gulf of Mexico for active service in Mexican war; returned to Naval School, Jan., 1848: grad. passed midshipman July, 1848; master and lt., 1855; lt.-commander, 1862; commanded Unadilla and afterward monitor Catskill during Civil war. On retired list March 18, 1865; promoted to commander, May 12, 1867. Has large interests in Argentina. Address: San Isidoro, Buenos Ayres, Argentina.

CILLEY, JONATHAN PRINCE soldier; b. Thomaston, Me., Dec. 29, 1835; s. Jonathan and Deborah (Prince) C.; A.B., Bowdoin, 1858; admitted to bar, 1860; m. Caroline A. Lazell, Oct. 10, 1866; m. 2d, Abby (Butler) Burpee, Dec. 25, 1897. Capt. 1st Me. Cav., Oct. 19, 1861; maj., May 15, 1862; lt. col., July 1, 1864; hon. mustered out, Aug. 1, 1865. Bvtd.: col. vols., Mar. 13, 1865, "for gallant and meritorious services during the war"; brig. gen. vols., June 12, 1865, for same. In practice, Rockland, Me., 1865-; mem. Ho. of Rep., 1867; U.S. ct. commr., 1867-80; adj. gen. of Me., 1876-78; editor Maine Bugle, 1894. Author: Cilley Genealogy, 1879; The Mount Desert Widow, 1896. Died Apr. 7, 1920.

CILLEY, JOSEPH army officer, legislator; b. Nottingham, N.H., 1735; s. Capt. Joseph and Alice (Rollins) C.; m. Sarah Longfellow, Nov. 4, 1756, 10 children. Mem. N.H. Provincial Congress; coast guard duty; took part in Siege of Boston, battles of L.I., Trenton, Princeton; commd. maj. 2d N.H. Inf., 1775, 8th Continental Inf., 1776; participated in Battle of Ticonderoga, 1777; commd. col. 1st N.H. Inf., 1777; promoted maj. gen. N.H. Militia, 1786; mem. N.H. Senate, 1790-91, N.H. Ho. of Reps., 1792; mem. N.H. Council, 1797-98. Died Nottingham, Aug. 25, 1799.

CIST, HENRY MARTYN soldier, lawyer; b. Cincinnati, Feb. 20, 1839; s. Charles and Janet (White) C.; grad. Farmer's (now Belmont) Coll., 1858, A.M.; studied law; m. Mary E. Morris, g.d. U.S. Senator Thomas A. Morris of Ohio, Sept. 22, 1868; m. 2d, Jennie E., d. Martin Bare, Cincinnati, April 12, 1882. Enlisted April 21, 1861, pvt. 6th Ohio vols.; became 2d lt. 52d Ohio vol. inf.; adj. 74th Ohio vols.; post adj. Camp Chase during confinement of prisoners of war captured at Ft. Donelson; served in middle Tenn., 1862; adj. Miller's brigade, Sept. 1862; later asst. adj. gen. Dept. of the Cumberland, on staff Gens. Rosecrans and Thomas; resigned Jan. 4, 1866; attained rank of maj. and asst. adj. gen., with bvts. of lt. col., and col. and brig. gen. After war practiced law, Cincinnati; mayor of College Hill, O., 2 terms; corr. sec. Army of the Cumberland, 1869-92 (edited 20 ann. reports of soc.). Author: The Army of the Cumberland 1882; Life of Maj. Gen. George H. Thomas (with late Col. Donn Piatt). Died 1902.

CLAGETT, JOHN ROZIER maj. U.S. Army; b. Washington, D.C., Apr. 1852; of family settled in Md. under Lord Baltimore; ed. under private tutors. Second lt. 23d inf., 1875; promoted 1st lt., 1884; capt., 1892; maj. 2d inf., Mar. 2, 1901; m. Cornelia M., d. Col. H. M. Black, U.S. Army, Jan. 1884. Served on Crook's campaign against Northern Cheyenne Indians, 1876-77; on duty at St. Louis during riots, 1877; on campaign against Northern Cheyenne Indians when they broke from reservation in Indian Ty., 1878; campaigns against Ute Indians, Colo., 1880; Apache Indians, Ariz., 1882. Served on 2d Philippine expdn., May 1898; engaged in assault and capture Manila, Aug. 1898; defense of Manila during Tagalog insurrection, Feb. 1899; on expdn. to Sulu Islands, May 1899, and took possession of same; returned to U.S. in command Home Battalion 25th inf. after 2 yrs.' service in Philippines. Died 1902.

CLAGHORN, GEORGE army officer, shipbuilder; b. July 6, 1748; s. Shubael and Experience (Hawes) C.; m. Deborah Brownell, 4 sons, 4 daus. Served as 1st lt., then capt. 2d Bristol Regt., wounded in Battle of Bunker Hill, later commd. maj., then col.; shipbuilder, New Bedford, N.H., launched ship Rebecca, 1785; naval constructor of ship Constitution, 1794 (launched 1797). Died Seekonk, R.I., Feb. 3, 1824.

CLAPP, WILLIAM WARLAND editor; b. Boston, Apr. 11, 1826; s. William Warland and Hannah (Lane) C.; m. Caroline Dennie, 1850, 3 children. Owner and editor Saturday Evening Gazette, Boston, 1847-65; editor Boston Jour., 1865-91; Republican, polit. views reflected in his papers. Author: A Record of the Boston Stage, 1853; also several plays including La Flaminna, John Gilbert and His Daughters, My Husband's Minor. Died Boston, Sept. 13, 1891.

CLARK, ALFRED EDWARD lawyer; b. Ont., Can., Aug. 17, 1873; s. John and Mary Jane (Caldwell) C.; ed. pub. schs. Minn.; m. Dehlia E. Wagner, Mar. 1918. Practiced law, Mankato, Minn., 1897-1905; located in Portland, Ore., 1906; chmn. Charter Commn. City of Portland, 1911 to revise judicial system of Oregon and modes of pleading and procedures; mem. Portland Civil Service Commn., 1913-15. Mem. Am. and Ore. State bar assns. Commd. maj. asst. judge adv. gen., U.S. Army, Sept. 1917; hon. disch., Aug. 1919, with rank of col. Apptd. rep. War Dept., Sept. 1919, to sit with Imperial Munitions Bd. in adjusting war claims and contracts between U.S. and Can. Clubs: University, Aero (Portland); Nat. Republican (New York). Author articles and monographs on Internat. and constl. law. Home: Portland, Ore. Office: Yeon Bldg., Portland, Ore. Died Jan. 30, 1951; buried Riverview Cemetery, Portland, Ore.

CLARK, BENNETT CHAMP judge; born Bowling Green, Mo., Jan. 8, 1890; s. Champ and Genevieve (Bennett) C.; A.B., U. of Mo., 1913; LL.B., George Washington U., 1914; LL.D., Marshall Coll., Bethany Coll., Washington and Lee U., U. of Missouri; m. Miriam Marsh, Oct. 2, 1922; (dec. 1943); children—Champ, Wilbur Marsh, Kimball; married 2d Violet Heming, Oct. 6, 1945. Parliamentarian U.S. House of

Rep., 1913-17; admitted to Mo. bar, 1914; in practice in St. Louis since 1919. Commissioned capt. U.S. Res., Aug. 1917; lt. col. 6th Mo. Inf., Aug.-Sept. 1917; lt. col. 140th U.S. Inf., Sept. 1917-Sept. 1918; col. Gen. Staff, 1919. Elected U.S. senator from Mo. for term ending Jan. 3, 1939; apptd. senator to fill unexpired term of Harry B. Hawes, Feb. 3, 1933; re-elected senator for term ending January 3, 1945; associate justice of the United States Court of Appeals, District of Columbia, since 1945. Past nat. comdr. Am. Legion; past comdr. 35th Div. Vets. Assn.; ex-pres. Nat. Guard Assn. of U.S.; mem. Order of the Coif, Phi Beta Kappa, Delta Tau Delta, Phi Delta Phi, Delta Sigma Rho. Democrat. Presbyterian. Mason, Odd Fellow. Club: Chevy Chase (Washington). Author: John Quincy Adams, "Old Man Eloquent." 1932. Compiler: Constitution Manual and Digest of Practice, U.S. House of Representatives, 1913, 14, 15, 16. Joint author: Social Studies, 1934. Home: St. Louis County, Mo. Address: U.S. Court of Appeals, Washington. Died July 13, 1954; buried Arlington Nat. Cemetery.

CLARK, CHARLES gov. Miss.; b. Cincinnati, 1810; m. Ann Darden. Went to Miss., 1831; mem. Miss. Legislature (Whig), 1838-44, 56-61; served as col. in Mexican War; mem. state conv. to consider Miss. relations to Union, 1851; rep. Miss. Legislature, 1856-61; del. Nat. Democratic convs., Charleston and Balt., 1860; commd. brig. gen. Miss Militia, 1860, advanced to maj. gen.; commd. brig. gen. Confederate Army; gov. Miss., 1863-65; arrested and imprisoned by U.S. Army for governorship of unrecognized state; chancellor 4th dist. Miss., 1876. Died Dec. 18, 1877.

CLARK, CHARLES EDGAR rear adm.; b. Bradford, Vt., Aug. 10, 1843; s. James Dayton and Mary (Sexton) C.; apptd. from Vt., and grad. U.S. Naval Acad., 1863; (LL.D., U. of Pa., 1905); m. Marie L. Davis. Promoted ensign, Oct. 1, 1863; advanced through grades to rear adm., June 16, 1902. Served on board Ossipee, W. Gulf Bloc Kading Squadron, 1863-65; battle of Mobile Bay, and capture of Ft. Morgan, Aug., 1864; Vanderbilt, Pacific Squadron, 1865-67; comd. Ranger, 1883-86, Mohican, 1893-94, Monterey, 1896-98; comd. battleship Oregon during the cruise from San Francisco to Key West, and in the battle of Santiago, July 3, 1898; for eminent and conspicuous conduct in this battle was advanced 6 numbers in rank; was again advanced 7 additional numbers in rank, and promoted rear-adm., June 16, 1902; gov. Naval Home, Phila., 1901-04; pres. Naval Examining and Retiring Bd., 1904-05; retired, Aug. 10, 1905. Home: Washington, D.C. Died Oct. 1, 1922.

CLARK, CYRUS J. med. officer; b. Carmel, Ind., Nov. 16, 1900; s. Cyrus J. and Ella L. (Hershey) C.; m. Edith Lakey, Sept. 29, 1929; children—Cyrus J., III, Kenton Eric, Patricia Ellen. Began career as physician; chief med. staff, Indianapolis City Hosp., clinical prof. cardiology, Ind. U. Sch. Med. (chmn. dept. post grad. edn.). Col. M.C., A.U.S.; comdg. officer, 32nd Gen. Hosp., World War II. Home: 1501 E. 38th St. Office: 6325 Guilford Av., Indpls. Died Jan. 22, 1953; buried Summit Lawn, Westfield, Ind.

CLARK, EDWARD BRAYTON, newspaper man; b. Utica, N.Y.; s. Erastus and Frances (Beardsley) Clark; grad. Free Academy, Utica; cadet U.S. Mil. Acad., 1879-81; m. Eliza Frances Obee, of Highland Park, Ill.; one daughter, Frances Clark Devereux (deceased). Enlisted in United States Army, 1887, and served as non-commissioned officer and instr. of recruits, and later with 6th U.S. Inf.; assisted in raising an Ill. regt. for Spanish-Am. War and commd. capt. by Ill. legislature (services of regt. not required). Began newspaper work as reporter, Boston Herald, 1882; reporter and spl. article and editorial writer in Chicago, 1890-1903; Washington corr. Chicago Evening Post, 1903-31; was corr. in field in Sioux Indian war, 1890-91, in Garza uprising, Tex., 1892, in France, 1915. An organizer, 1897, and v.p. Ill. Audubon Soc. for Protection of Birds; life mem. Franklin Inst.; mem. permanent orgn. West Point Class of 1884. Republican. Episcopalian. Clubs: Gridiron, Nat. Press, Army and Navy, Overseas Writers; The Tavern (Chicago). Contbr. newspapers and mags. on polit. and natural history topics; wrote interview with Theodore Roosevelt, on "The Nature Fakers," for Everybody's Mag. Commd. capt., N.A., Dec. 18, 1917; major, July 1918; lt. col., R.C., Aug. 18, 1919; col., O.R.C., 1923; with A.E.F. in France 5 months; participated in two major mil. operations. Decorated Chevalier Legion of Honor (France), wife awarded same decoration. Home: 2100 Massachusetts Av., Washington DC

CLARK, EMMONS soldier; b. Huron, N.Y., Oct. 14, 1827; s. William and Sophronia (Tillotson) C.; grad. Hamilton Coll., 1847; m. Adella Augusta Hallett, Nov. 15, 1859. In commercial pursuits in New York, 1850-66; apptd. fire commr., Metropolitan dist., 1868, and consul to Havre by Pres. Harrison, 1889, but declined both positions. Enlisted private Co. B, 7th regt., N.G.S.N.Y., 1857; promoted 1st sergt., 1859; 2d lt., 1859; 1st lt., 1859; capt., 1860; mustered into U.S. service as capt., 1861; served as such in campaigns, 1861-62-63; promoted to col. 7th regt., 1864, and after serving in that capacity 25 yrs. was, by spl. act of legislature of N.Y., promoted to bvt. brig. gen. Sec. Bd. of Health, New York, 1866-1901. Mem. 7th Regt. Vet. Assn., 7th Regt. Active and Vet. League. Author: History of the Seventh Regiment of New York. Died 1905.

CLARK, FRANK HODGES ret. naval officer; b. in Mass., Dec. 18, 1871; grad. U.S. Naval Acad., 1893. Commd. ensign USN, 1893, advanced through grades to rear adm., 1927; apptd. comdr. Destroyer Squadrons, Scouting Fleet, 1927; then head of Fleet Tng. Div.; became mem. Gen. Bd. USN, 1933. chmn., 1934; retired, 1936. Address: 45-2126 Connecticut Av., Washington 8. Deceased.

CLARK, FRED GEORGE, found. exec.; b. Cleve., Nov. 2, 1890; s. Frederick George and Mary Angeline (Winter) C.; student Kenyon Coll., Gambier, O., 1909-13; LL.D., Morningside Coll., Sioux City, Ia.; m. Margaret L. Moore, June 26, 1915 (div. Dec. 1931); m. 2d, Sibyl Young Hine, Jan. 16, 1932 (div. Sept. 1948); m. 3d, Diana M. Brodie, Dec. 18, 1948. Oil tester Fred G. Clark Co., oil refining, Cleve., 1913, office mgr., 1914-16, salesman, 1916-17, v.p., 1920-24, pres., 1924-32; pres. Conewango Refining Co., Warren, Pa., 1926-32; pres. Clark, Curtin & Norton, Inc., ins., N.Y., 1932-65; organizer, nat. comdr. Crusaders against Nat. Prohibition, 1929-33; nat. radio broadcaster for econ. enlightenment, 1933-36; established, chmn. bd. Am. Factfinders, 1936; founder, chmn. bd. Am. Econ. Found., ednl. research, 1939-72; moderator radio program, Wake Up Am., 1939-46. Served as capt. U. S. Army, in charge all lubricating oil purchases for U.S. Army, 1917-18. Mem. Soc. Colonial Wars, Huguenot Soc., Colonial Lords of Manors in Am., Nat. Inst. Social Scis., Psi Upsilon. Clubs: Racquet and Tennis, Sky, River (N.Y.C.); Atlantic Beach (L.I.). Author: Magnificent Delusion, 1940: (with Richard S. Rimanoczy) How We Live, 1944; Money, 1946; How To Be Popular Though Conservative, 1948; How to Think About Economics, 1952; What Every Supervisor Should Know About the Principles of Economics, 1960; Where the Money Comes From 1961; editorials. Composer, Wake Up America, 1932. Lectr. Home: New York City NY Died Jan. 7, 1973; buried Lake View Cemetery, Cleveland OH

CLARK, FREDERICK TIMOTHY surgeon; b. Granville, Mass., Mar. 27, 1874; s. William Calvin and Mary Newberry (Ripley) C.; M.D., Albany Med. Coll. (Union U.), 1896; m. Emily Fletcher Rogers, June 18, 1902. Interne Albany City Hosp., 1896-97; asst. phys. Hudson River State Hosp., Poughkeepsie, N.Y., 1897-1900; settled in Westfield, Mass., 1901; surgeon in charge Eye, Ear, Nose and Throat Dept., Noble Hosp.; surgeon Sarah Gillet Home and Shurtleff Mission. Fellow Am. Coll. Surgeons, 1913. Conglist. Mason. Capt. M.C., U.S.A., Oct. 2, 1918; maj., Dec. 1918; chief eye, ear, nose and throat dept. Gen. Hosp. 1, New York; hon. disch., Oct. 25, 1919. Home: Westfield, Mass. Died Aug. 16, 1927.

CLARK, GEORGE jurist; b. Eutaw, Ala., July 18, 1841; s. James B. and Mary (Erwin) C.; ed. Univ. of Ala.; served pvt. to capt., 11th Ala. regt. in C. S. A., 1861-65; wounded at Gaines' Mill, 1862, Gettysburg, 163, and Ream's Station, 1864; m. Austin, Tex., Nov. 4, 1874, Mary Pauline Johns. Studied law with his father after war; admitted to bar, 1866; removed to Tex., Jan. 1867; practiced at Weatherford until Dec., 1868; after that at Waco. Sec. of State, Tex., 1874; atty.-gen., 1874-76; commr. on revision of statutes to 1878; judge Court of Appeals, 1879-80. Address: Waco, Tex.

CLARK, GEORGE RAMSEY naval officer; b. Monroe O., Mar. 20, 1857; s. Peter Williamson and Louisa Jane (Boyd) C.; grad. U.S. Naval Acad., 1878; m. Mary Winchell Brown, Oct. 29, 1889. Commd. ensign, U.S. Navy, 1884, and advanced through the grades to rear admiral, 1918; retired, 1921; served in Spanish-Am. War, Philippine Insurrection, Boxer Rebellion; apptd. judge advocate general, 1918. Decorated Navy Cross, Distinguished Service Medal. Author: (with others) The Navy, 1775-1909, 2 vols., 1910; Short History of U.S. Navy, 1911. Address: Navy Dept., Washington 25, D.C. Died Dec. 14, 1945.

CLARK, GEORGE ROGERS army officer; b. nr. Charlottesville, Va., Nov. 19, 1752; s. John and Ann (Rogers) C. Minor exploring attempts on Ohio River, 1772; served as capt. Va. Militia in Dunmore's War, 1774; surveyor in Ky., organizer, leader frontier defense against British-supported Indian raids, 1776-77; set out to conquer Ill., largely under auspices of Gov. Patrick Henry of Va., captured key points, Kaskaskia, Cahokia and Vincennes, thus assuring Colonial control Ky. and Ill. countries (Northwest); commd. brig. gen. Va. Militia, engaged in several battles and expdns. to protect Northwest region, 1779-83; mem. bd. commrs. which supervised allotment of lands in Ill. grant; served on commn. making a treaty with Indians of Northwest; set out on retaliatory expdn. against Wabash tribe, not wholly successful, 1786: polit. and econ. fortunes declined toward end of life. Author: Memoir, 1791. Meml. to him erected by U.S. Govt., Vincennes, Ind., 1928. Died Louisville, Ky., Feb. 13, 1818; buried Cave Hill Cemetery, Louisville.

CLARK, GRENVILLE, laywer; b. N.Y.C., Nov. 5, 1882; s. Louis Crawford and Marian de Forest (Cannon) C.; A.B., Harvard, 1903, LL.B., 1906, LL.D., 1951; LL.D., Princeton, 1951, Dartmouth, 1953; m. Fanny Pickman Dwight, Nov. 27, 1909; children—Mary Dwight, Grenville, Louisa Hunnewell; m. 2d, Mary Brush, January 1, 1965. Admitted New York State bar, 1906, began practice with Carter, Ledyard & Milburn, N.Y.C.; mem. Root, Clark & Bird, and successor firms, 1909-46; counsel to Cleary, Gottlieb, Steen and Hamilton, 1954. Afounder Mil. Tng. Camps Assn., 1915-16; chmn. Nat. Emergency Com. for Selective Service, 1940-41; chmn. Citizens Com. for Nat. War Service, 1944-45. Served from maj. to lt. col. Adj. Gen.'s Dept., U.S. Army, 1917-18. Decorated D.S.M.; awarded Theodore Roosevelt Meml. Medal, 1940; gold medal Am. Bar Assn., 1959; 2d Ann. Publius award N.Y. Met. Com. of United World Federalists, 1965. Member of Pres. and Fellows Harvard College, 1931-50; member American Bar Association (chairman committee bill of rights 1938-40), Assn. Bar City of N.Y., N.Y. Law Inst., United World Federalists (v.p.), Phi Beta Kappa. Clubs: Century, Downtown Assn., Somerset Author: A Plan for Peace, 1950; (with L. B. Sohn): World Peace through World Law, 1958, rev. edit., 1960; also articles on civil govt., world orgn. and legal subjects. Home: Dublin NH Died Jan. 12, 1967.

CLARK, HARVEY CYRUS lawyer; b. in Morgan Co., Mo., Sept. 17, 1869; s. James C. and Melissa (Myers) C.; Wentworth Mil. Acad., Lexington, Mo., 1887-88; A.B., Scarrett Coll., Neosho, Mo., 1891; m. Sudye C. Berry, Dec. 7, 1909. Admitted to Mo. bar, 1893; mem. Graves & Clark until partner was elected chief justice of Mo., 1908; pros. atty. Bates Co., 1896-1901; apptd. dist. atty. Mo.P. Ry., 1910; atty for K.C. Southern Ry. Co., Western Coal Mining Co., etc. Commd. capt. 2d Mo. Inf., Oct. 8, 1888; maj., July 1, 1897; lt. col. 6th Mo. Ind., July 20, 1898. and served during Spanish-Am. War; brig. gen. Mo. N. G., Feb. 2, 1899; comd. Mo. troops on Mexican border, June 19-Dec. 31, 1916; brig. gen. N.A., Aug. 5, 1917; apptd. comdr. 60th Depot Brigade, Camp Doniphan, Okla., Aug. 5, 1917; hon. disch. account Physical disability, Dec. 26, 1917; apptd. adj. gen. of Mo., Jan. 1, 1918. Democrat. Presbyn. Mason. Home: Nevada, Mo. Died Apr. 1921.

CLARK, HENRY BENJAMIN, business exec.; b. near Walworth, Wis., Apr. 15, 1874; s. James Dallas and Adelia Violet (Church) C.; Ph.B., Beloit (Wis.) Coll., 1895; B.S., U.S. Mil. Acad., 1899; grad. Army Staff Coll., 1905, Army War Coll., 1920; m. Lena Sefton Wakefield, Nov. 20, 1912; children—James Dallas, Henry B., Jr. Commd. 2d lt., U.S. Army, 1899, and advanced through grades to col., 1921; served with China Relief Expdn. (Boxer Rebellion), 1900, Philippine Insurrection, 1900-02, Moro Expedition, Mindanao, 1902, A.E.F., France, 1918; on War Department General Staff, 1921-22; ret., 1922; vice pres. Sefton Mfg. Corp., Chicago, 1922-25, pres., 1925-28; dir. Container Corp. of Am. since 1931; retired. Mem. Beta Theta Pi. Republican. Presbyn. Mason. Clubs: Union League (Chicago); Army-Navy (Washington); Cuyamaca (San Diego). Home: 3810 Narragansett Av., San Diego 7 CA

CLARK, JOHN gov. Ga.; b. Edgecombe County, N.C., Feb. 28, 1766; s. Gen. Elijah Clarke; m. Nancy Williamson 1787. Commd. capt. Continental Army, 1782; commd. maj. Ga. Militia, 1787, maj. gen., 1811; received generous grant of bounty lands after Revolution; presdl. elector, 1816; gov. Ga., 1819-23; apptd. Indian agt., Fla., 1827. Died of yellow fever at St. Andrew's Bay, Fla., Oct. 12, 1832.

CLARK, JOHN BULLOCK lawyer; b. Fayette, Mo., Jan. 14, 1831; grad. Harvard Law School, 1854; served in C.S.A., lt. to brig. gen.; resumed law practice at Fayette, Mo.; mem. Congress, 1873-83; then clerk of House of Reps. several yrs. Died 1903.

CLARK, JOHN EMORY mathematician; b. Northampton, N.Y., Aug. 8, 1832; s. Rev. John and Sarah Miller (Foote) C.; A.B., U. of Mich., 1856, A.M., 1859; (hon. A.M., Yale, 1873); m. Caroline C. Doty, Aug. 20, 1856 (dec.). Professor of mathematics, Mich. State Normal Sch., 1856-57; asst. prof. mathematics, U. of Mich., 1857-59; studied at univs. of Heidelberg, Munich and Berlin, 1859-60; U.S. deputy surveyor in Dak., 1861-62, in Colo., 1869; capt. and maj. 5th Mich. Cav., 1862-65; bvtd. lt. col. U.S. Vols., Mar., 1865; prof. mathematics and astronomy, Antioch Coll., 1866-72; asst. astronomer, Northern Boundary Commn., 1872; prof. mathematics, 1873-1901, emeritus, Sheffield Scientific Sch. (Yale). Home: Springfield, Mass. Died Jan. 3, 1921.

CLARK, JOHN HOWE rear adm.; b. Greenland, N.H., Apr. 16, 1837; s. Samuel Wallace and Rebecca E. (Howe) C.; A.B., Dartmouth Coll., 1857; M.D., Harvard, 1862; unmarried. Entered U.S.N. as asst. surgeon, Oct. 19, 1861; promoted surgeon, May 14, 1867; med. insp., Jan. 8, 1885; med. dir., Mar. 4, 1893; retired with rank of rear adm., Apr. 16, 1899. Home: Amherst, N.H. Died Nov. 30, 1913.

CLARK, JOSEPH JAMES, retired naval officer; born in Pryor, Okla., November 12,21893; s. William Andrew and Lillie Belle (Berry) C.; student Okla. A. and M. Coll., 3 1/2 yrs.; grad. U.S. Naval Acad., 1917; children—Mary Louise, Catherine Carol; m. 4th, Olga Choubaroff. Commissioned ensign, USN, 1917, advancing through grades to admiral; comdr. of 7th Fleet, USN, retired, 1953; chmn. bd. Hegeman Harris, Inc., New York City. Decorated two D.S.M.'s (Navy), D.S.M. (Army), Navy Cross, Silver Star, Commendation Ribbon. Clubs: N.Y. Yacht, Larchmont Yacht, N.Y. Athletic; Chevy Chase; Long Island. Home: New York City NY Died July 1971.

CLARK, J(OSHUA) REUBEN JR. ch. official, atty.; b. Grantsville, Tooele County, Utah, Sept. 1, 1871; s. Joshua Reuben and Mary Louisa (Woolley) C.; student Latter-day Saints College, 1890-91; B.S. Univ. of Utah, 1898; L.L.B., Columbia Univ., 1906; LL.D., U. of Utah, 1934, Brigham Young U., 1952; m. Luacine A. Savage, Sept. 14, 1898 (dec.); children-Mrs. Louise Bennion, Mrs. Marianne Sharp, J. Reuben, III, Mrs. Luacine Fox, Prin. high sch., Heber City, Utah, 1898-99; admitted to N.Y. bar, 1905; apptd. spl. ambassador to attend the inauguration of President Rubio, Mexico, Feb. 1930; A.E. and P. to Mexico, 1930-33. Apptd. mem. gen. bd. Y.M.M.I.A., 1925. Sustained as 2d Counselor in 1st Presidency of Ch. of Jesus Christ of Latter-day Saints, 1933, since 1951; sustained as first counselor same, 1934; ordained Apostle, Ch. of Jesus Christ of Latter-day Saints, 1934, first counselor, 1959-; mem. Gen. Ch. Bd. Edn., 2d v.p. bd. trustees, Brigham Young U. Commd. maj. Judge Advocate Gen.'s R.C., Feb. 3, 1917, assigned to active duty June 13, 1917; under order of Atty. Gen., Dept. of Justice, June 18, 1917; relieved from duty in office of Judge Advocate Gen. and apptd. adj. of provost marshal gen., Sept. 13, 1918; hon. discharged, Dec. 18, 1918; undersec. of state, Aug. 31, 1928-June 20, 1929. Awarded D.S.M., 1922. Mem. U.S. delegation to VII Pan-Am. Conf., Montevideo, Nov. 1933; pres. Foreign Bondholders Protective Council, Inc., 1934-38, chmn. exec. com., 1938-45, dir., 1934-53; vice chmn., dir. U.-I Sugar, Z.C.M.I., Beneficial Life Ins. Co., Hotel Utah, KSL Radio & TV; vice president and director Zion's Securities Corporation; dir. cos. U.S. rep. Com. for Study Internat. Loan Contracts, Geneva, Switzerland, since 1936; mem. exec. com. Foreign Bondholder Council, 1945-50. Member Com. of Experts on Codification of Internat. Law established under Resolution of 7th Pan-Am. Conf. Trustee Herbert Hoover Found., Theodore Roosevelt Assn. Republican. Mem. Am. Soc. Internat. Law, Phi Delta Phi. Clubs: Cosmos (Washington); India House (N.Y.C.). Home: 80 D St. Office: 47 E. South Temple St., Salt Lake City. Died Oct. 6, 1961; buried Salt Lake City.

CLARK, ROLAND EUGENE banker; b. Houlton, Me., July 3, 1879; s. Michael McGuirk and Henrietta (Braden) C.; A.B., Bowdoin College, 1901, M.A. (hon.), 1952; LL.B., Georgetown U., 1904; m. Gladys Goodin Tingle, Feb. 14, 1941. Admitted to Me. bar, 1905; pvt. sec. to Congressman Llewellyn Powers, 1901-05; practiced law Houlton, 1905-17; v.p. charge trust dept. Fidelity Trust Co., Portland, Me., 1919-33, Nat. Bank Commerce, Portland since 1933. Trustee Portland Pub. Library; mem. bd. trustees, treas. Bowdoin Coll., since 1949; mem. bd. overseers, 1939-49. Served as 2d lt. to maj. 1st Inf. Div., U.S. Army, 1917-19, asst. div. adj. 1st Inf. Div., asst. adj. gen. 1st army, A.E.F. Pres. trust div. Am. Bankers Assn., 1939. Mem. Psi Upsilon. Republican. Conglist. Club: Cumberland (Portland). Home 15 Clifford St., Portland 4. Office: National Bank of Commerce, Portland, Me. Died Nov. 1, 1958.

CLARK, STEPHEN CARLTON corp. officer; b. Cooperstown, N.Y., Aug. 29, 1882; s. Alfred Corning and Elizabeth (Scriven) C.; A.B., Yale, 1903, Dr. of Humane Letters (hon.), 1959; LL.B., Columbia, 1907; m. Susan Vanderpoel Hun, Feb. 20, 1909; children-Elizabeth Scriven, Stephen Carlton, Alfred Corning, Robert Vanderpoel, Mem. N.Y. Assembly, 1910; v.p. Safe Deposit Co. N.Y.; dir. Singer Mfg. Co., N.Y. Trust Co. Served as adj. 80th Div., with rank of maj., later adj. gen. 2d Army Corps, rank of lt. col.; in France from May 1918 to close of World War. Awarded D. S.M. Chmn. bd. N.Y. State Hist. Assn., Met. Mus. Art; pres. Clark Found.; dir. Scriven Found.; pres. Farmers' Mus., Inc., Nat. Baseball Hall of Fame and Museum, Inc. Republican. Episcopalian. Mason. Clubs: Union, University, Yale, Century, Racquet and Tennis, National Golf, St. Anthony. Home: 46 E. 70th St., N.Y.C. 21. Office: 149 Broadway, N.Y.C. 6. Died Sept. 17, 1960.

CLARK, WALTER judge; b. Halifax Co., N.C., Aug. 19, 1846; s. David and Anna M. (Thorne) C.; A.B., Susan W., d. Gov. and U.S. Senator and Sec. of Navy W. A. Graham of N.C., Jan. 28, 1874. Lt. col. C.S.A., 1864, at 17 yrs. of age; admitted to bar, 1868; judge Superior Ct. of N.C., 1885-89; judge Supreme Ct., 1889-1902, chief justice, Jan. 1, 1903-. Author: Annotated Code of Civil Procedure, 3d edition. Translated from original French, Constant's Memoirs of Napoleon, 3 vols., 1895. Home: Raleigh, N.C. Died May 19, 1924.

CLARK, WILLIAM explorer, territorial gov.; b. Caroline County, Va., Aug. 1, 1770; s. John and Ann (Rogers) C.: m. Julia Hancock, Jan. 1808; m. 2d, Harriet Kennerly, 1821; 5 children, including Meriwether Lewis, George Rogers Hancock, Jefferson Kennerly. Commd. lt. inf. U.S. Army, 1792, in charge of rifle corps, 1793, served under Gen. Anthony Wayne in Battle of Fallen Timbers, 1794, resigned commn., 1796; Meriwether Lewis proposed Clark should accompany him as joint leader expdn. which Pres. Jefferson was sending to explore continent, find route to Pacific Ocean, 1803, expdn. recruited in Ill., 1803-04, embarked to Missouri River, May 14, 1804, descended Columbia River, reached Pacific, returned to St. Louis, Sept. 23, 1806; apptd. brig. gen. La. Territorial Militia, 1807; gov. Mo. Territory, 1813-21, protected frontiers from Indian Territory, 1813-21, protected frontiers from Indian invasions during War of 1812, at war's end reconciled Western Indians by series of treaties; U.S. supt. Indian affairs, St. Louis, 1813-38; surveyor gen. for Ill., 1824-25; attempted to effect permanent peace with Indians in Treaty of Prairie du Chien, 1825; laid out Town of Paducah (Ky.), 1828: mapmaker, wildlife artist; diary of Lewis and Clark published as Expeditions Under the Commands of Captains Lewis and Clark, 1814. Died St. Louis, Sept. 1, 1838.

CLARK, WILLIAM judge; b. Newark, N.J., Feb. 1, 1891; s. J. William and Margaretta (Cameron) C.; grad. Newark Acad., 1904; grad. St. Mark's Sch., 1908; B.A., Harvard, 1911, M.A., 1912, LL.B., 1915; m. Marjorie Blair, Sept. 20, 1913 (div. 1947); children—Anne, John William, Blair; married 2d Sonia Tomara, Oct. 4, 1947. Admitted to N.J. bar, 1916, counsellor at law, 1920; mem. Lindabury Depue & Faulks, 1920-23; apptd. judge N.J. Court of Errors and Appeals, 1923; judge U.S. Dist Court, N.J., 1925-38; judge U.S. Circuit Court of Appeals for the Third Circuit, July 5, 1938—. Apptd. legal cons. to Gen Lucius Clay, U.S. Military Government in Germany, Jan. 1948; apptd. chief judge, Mil. Govt. Courts of Germany, Sept. 1948; chief justice high commn. courts, Germany, 1949-54. Entered First R.O.T.C., Ft. Meyer, Va., May 1917; commd. 2d lt., Aug. 1917, and assigned to 314th F.A.; 1st lt., Jan. 1918; capt. Sept. 1918; oversea service 1 yr.; silver star citation "for for gallantry in action"; maj., F.A., O.R.C.; received Certificate of Graduation from Business and Professional Men's Company at Plattsburgh Barracks, New York, Aug. 3, 1940; entered U. S. Army, March 24, 1942, with rank of lt. col.; served overseas, Pacific and European theatres, North Africa, Sicily, Italy, Normandy and Belgium; promoted to col. Wounded. Decorated Comdr. British Empire, Trustee of New Jersey Historical Society, and New Jersey Museum Assn., Member Am., N.J. and Essex County bar assns., Assn. Bar City of New York, Am. Law Inst., Am. Soc. Internat. Law, Am. Acad. Polit. Science. Republican. Presbyterian. Home: 12 Battle Rd., Princeton, N.J. Died Oct. 10, 1957; buried Arlington Nat. Cemetery.

CLARK, WILLIAM ANDREWS senator; b. nr. Connellsville, Pa., Jan. 18, 1839; s. John and Mary (Andrews) C.; ed. Laurel Hill Acad., and other acads; studied law Mt. Pleasant (Ia.) U.; m. Kate L. Stauffer, Mar. 1869 (died 1893); 2d, Anna E. La Chapelle, May 25, 1901. Did not enter legal profession; taught sch., Mo., 1859-60; went to Colo., 1862, to Mont., 1863; then banker, mine-owner, having large interests; pres. or dir. United Verde Copper Co., Mayflower, Moulton, Ophir Hill Consolidated mining cos., L.A. & S.L. R.R., Butte Elec. Ry. Co., Clark-Mont. Realty Co., Colusa-Parrot Mining & Smelting Co., Los Alamitos Sugar Co., Mont. Land Co., Natural Mineral Water Co., W.A. Clark & Bro., bankers, Butte, Mont., Waclark Realty Co., Waclark Wire Co. State orator, representing Mont. at Centennial Expn., 1876. Major Butte battalion, leading it in Nez Perce campaign, 1878; pres. Constl. convs., 1884, 1889; commr. from Mont. to New Orleans Expn., 1884; Dem. candidate for del. to Congress, 1888; nominated by Democrats for U.S. senator, 1890, and claimed election, but was denied seat; candidate for U.S. senate, 1898, and elected; a contest ensued at Washington, but before investigation concluded he resigned; elected U.S. senator by legislature for term, 1901-07. Mason. Home: Butte, Mont. Died Mar. 2, 1925.

CLARK, WILLIAM HENRY, banker; b. St. Louis, Nov. 9, 1909; s. Arthur P. and Elizabeth (Haigh) C.; B.A., De Pauw U., 1932; M.B.A., Northwestern U., 1952; m. Alice M. Hein, Aug. 27, 1938; 1 dau., Carolyn E. With First Nat. Bank & Trust Co., Evanston, Ill., 1933-69, successively messenger, teller, asst. cashier and v.p., exec. v.p., pres., 1960-68, vice chmn., 1968-69, dir., 1960-69. Pres. United Community Services, Evanston, Ill., 1963-65. Dir. St. Francis Hosp., Evanston, 1959-69. Served to capt. AUS, 1943-45. Mem. Evanston C. of C. (pres. 1960-62), Chgo. Bankers Club, Chgo. Economic Club, Northwestern U. Assos., Delta Kappa Epsilon. Republican. Episcopalian. Clubs: University, Rotary (officer), Westmoreland Country, John Evans (Northwestern U.). Home: Evanston IL Died Dec. 18, 1969.

CLARK, WILLIAM SMITH army officer, scientist, coll. pres.; b. Ashfield, Mass., July 31, 1826; s. Dr. Atherton and Harriet (Smith) C.; grad. Amherst Coll., 1848; Ph.D., Gottingen U., 1852; m. Harrietta Richards, May 25, 1853, 11 children, Tchr. natural scis. Williston Sem., 1848-50; prof. chemistry Amherst (Mass.) Coll., 1852, prof. Zoology, 1853, prof. botany, 1854; mem.-at-large Mass. State Bd. Agr., 1859-61; commd. maj. 21st Mass. Volunteers, 1861, lt. col., 1862, col., 1862; returned to Amherst; presdl. elector, sec. Electoral Coll., 1864; mem. Mass. Gen. Ct., 1864, 65, 67; pres., also prof. botany and horticulture Mass. Agrl. Coll., 1867-79; organizer, pres. Imperial Coll. of Agr. in Japan, 1867-77. Author: The Phenomena of Plant Life, 1875. Died Amherst, Mar. 9, 1886.

CLARK, WILLIAM THOMAS soldier; b. Norwalk, Conn., June 29, 1831; s. Levi and Fanny C.; served pvt. to bvt. maj.-gen. Union army in Civil war; chief of staff and adj.-gen. Army of Tenn., until battle of Atlanta, July 22, 1864, when he received two bvts.; took command of brigade and div.; left army, 1866, as div. comdr.: engaged in business, Galveston, Tex.; m. Nov. 13, 1856, Laura Clark of Hartford, Conn. Mem. Congress, 1869-73, from Galveston dist.; Republican; secured first appropriation of $100,000 for harbor, which resulted in the completion of the jetties, making Galveston one of the most important ports of U.S. Is last surviving adj. and chief of staff of Grant's old Army of the Tenn. Address: 1528 U St. N.W., Washington.

CLARKE, ELIJAH army officer; b. Edgecombe County, S.C., 1733; m. Hannah Arrington, at least 1 son, John Clar,. Commd. capt. Ga. Militia, 1776, later col., brig. gen., 1781; served at battles of Kettle Creek, Musgrove's Mill, Beattie's Mill and both sieges of Augusta (Ga.) in Revolutionary War; given estate in Wilkes County by State of Ga. for his mil. services; participated in battle with Indians at Jack's Creek, 1787; involved in French minister Edmond Genet's scheme to seize Spanish lands in Am., commd. maj. gen. French Army, 1793, plans failed when Genet was recalled; attempted to set up state in Creek Indian territory, 1794, established several forts but forced to give up venture by Ga. Militia. Died Wilkes County, Ga., Jan. 15, 1799.

CLARKE, JAMES FREDERIC surgeon; b. Fairfield, Ia., Feb. 23, 1864; s. Charles Shipman and Sarah Louisa (Wadsworth) C.; student Parsons College, Fairfield, Ia., 1881, 82, Sc.D., 1933; B.S., State Univ. of Ia., 1886, A.M., 1889; M.D., Univ. of Pa., 1889; studied Johns Hopkins Univ. and Univ. of Göttingen, Germany; m. Melinda Eliza Clapp, Oct. 13, 1891. Interne Phila. Gen. Hosp. 2 yrs.; practiced at Fairfield since 1889; lecturer on hygiene, U. of Ia., 3 yrs.; lecturer on fungi and bacteria, Parsons Coll., Fairfield. Maj., surgeon 49th Ia. Inf., U.S. Army, Spanish-Am. War, in Cuba, and introduced trained nurses to U.S. Army; lt. col. M.C., World War, in France; organizer and comdr. Hosp. Unit R; built second county hosp. in Ia. at Fairfield; developed cretin children by thyroid feeding. Served as mayor of Fairfield; mem. Ia. Ho. of Rep., 1906-07 . Fellow Am. Coll. Surgeons; mem. Am. and Ia. State med. socs., etc., Delta Tau Delta. Democrat. Conglist. Mason (K.T., Shriner). Club: Fairfield Rotary (organizer and pres. 1st 3 years). Home: Fairfield, Ia. Died Apr. 12, 1942.

CLARKSON, MATTHEW army officer, philanthropist; b. N.Y.C., Oct. 17, 1758; s. David and Elizabeth (French) C.; m. Mary Rutherford, May 24, 1785; m. 2d, Sarah Cornell, Feb. 14, 1792. Participated in Battle of L.I. as a volunteer and aide-de-camp to Benedict Arnold, 1778-79; attached to staff of Gen. Benjamin Lincoln, served with him until end of Revolutionary War, 1779-83, participated in siege of Savannah Ga., defense of Charleston, S.C., present at surrender of Yorktown, 1781; asst. to U.S. Sec. of War Benjamin Lincoln; commd. brig. gen., then maj. gen. N.Y. State Militia; regent State U. N.Y.; mem. N.Y. State Assembly, 1789-90; U.S. marshal, 1791-92; mem. N.Y. State Senate, 1794-96; one of commrs. apptd. by N.Y. State Legislature to build new prison, 1796; pres. N.Y. Hosp., 1799; pres. Bank of N.Y., 1804-25; Federalist candidate for U.S. Senate, 1802, defeated by DeWitt Clinton; supported numerous socs. and movements for pub. improvement. Died N.Y.C., Apr. 25, 1825.

CLARKSON, PERCY WILLIAM army officer; b. San Antonio, Dec. 9, 1893; s. William Banton and Alice Ann (Peples) C.; B.S. in Elec. Engring., Tex. A. and M. coll., 1915, LL.D., 1946; Army Schs.; grad. Signal Sch., Co. Officers Course, 1922, Advanced Course, 1924; Inf. Sch., Advanced Course, 1927; Command and Gen. Staff Sch., 1934; m. Lucy Kent Chappell, Nov. 23, 1920; 1 son, William Kent. Commd. 2d lt., 1916, advanced to maj. gen. 1942; served in 26th Inf. 1st Div., during World War I; asst. prof. chemistry and electricity U.S. Mil. Acad., 1928-33; on War Dept. Gen. Staff, 1940-41; chief staff, 36th Inf Div. (Tex. N.G.), asst. div. comdr., 91st Inf. Div., Camp White, Ore., 1940-41; comdg. gen. 87th Inf. Div. 1942-43; comdg. gen. 33rd Inf. Div. (Ill. N.G.) 1943-45, in Hawaiian Islands, S.W. Pacific, Japan; comdg. gen., X Corps, dep. chief of staff, Army Forces in Pacific, Tokyo, Japan. Awards: D.S.M. with oak leaf cluster, Legion of Merit, Silver Star and Bronze Stars, Air medal, Order of Silver Palms (French); Purple Heart. Address: 304 Primera Dr., San Antonio. Died Sept. 14, 1962; buried Fort Sam Houston Nat. Cemetery.

CLARKSON, THADDEUS STEVENS gen. mgr. Trans-Miss. and Internat. Expdn. Omaha, 1898; b. Gettysburg, Pa., April 26, 1840; grad.. St. James Coll., Washington Co., Md., 1857; m. 1862, Mary B. Matteson, Chicago. Went to Chicago, 1857; read law, 1858; clerk in Chicago, 1859-61; served in army, 1861-65, private 1st Ill. to maj. 3rd Ark. cav., U.S. vols.; in all battles in S.W. Mo. and Ark.; moved to Omaha, 1866; dept. comdr. of Neb., 1890; junior vice comdr.-in-chief, 1891; comdr.-in-chief, 1896 to 1897. G. A. R.; postmaster Omaha, 1890-95. Address: 3706 Olive St., St. Louis.

CLARY, ALBERT G. commodore U.S. Navy, retired 1874; b. Mass., 1812; apptd. to navy, May 8, 1832; served in Pacific squadron, 1834-36; naval sch., New York, 1837; passed midshipman, July 8, 1839; lt., Apr. 11, 1845; served in Mexican war; comd. U.S.S. Anacostia, Potomac flotilla, 1861; engagement Aquia Creek, May 31, and battle Port Royal, Nov. 7, 1861; comdr., July 16, 1862, in blockade service to end of Civil War; capt., Nov. 21, 1866; commodore, 1873. Died 1902.

CLAY, CECIL veteran soldier, U.S. civ. service official; b. Phila., Pa., Feb. 13, 1842; s. Joseph Ashmead and Cornelia (Fletcher) C.; grad. Univ. of Pa., 1859, A.M.; m. Anna Wood Kester, June 8, 1865. Capt. 58th Pa. vols. Feb. 1862; maj. Sept. 30, 1864; lt. col. Nov. 19, 1864; col. Nov. 20, 1864; bvtd. col. and brig. gen. U.S.V.; mustered out Jan. 24, 1866; congressional medal of honor for distinguished bravery at storming of Ft. Harrison, Va., Sept. 29, 1864 (lost right arm and was badly wounded in left hand). Pres. St. Lawrence Boom & Mfg. Co., 1870-79; 1883 to 1903, chief clerk, now gen. agt. U.S. Dept. of Justice, Col. 2d D.C. Nat. Guard, 1887-97. Pres. Bd. Reform Sch., D.C. Home: Washington, D.C. Died 1907.

CLAY, GREEN army officer, legislator; b. Powhatan County, Va., Aug. 14, 1757; s. Charles Clay; m. Sally Lewis, 7 children including Cassius Marcellus, Brutus J. Came to Ky. circa 1777; dep. surveyor Lincoln County (Ky.), 1781; amassed a fortune by locating lands; settled in Madison County, Ky.; became trustee Town of Boonesborough (Ky.), 1787; mem. Va. Legislature, 1788, 89; mem. lower house Ky. Legislature, from Madison County, 1793-94; mem. Ky. Senate, 1795-98, 1807; represented Madison County at conv. to draft 2d constn. for Ky., 1799; commd. maj. gen. Ky. Militia, marched with 3000 state troops to relieve Gen. Harrison at Ft. Meigs; Clay County (Ky.) named in his honor. Died Madison County, Oct. 31, 1826.

CLAY, JOSEPH mcht., Continental congressman; b. Yorkshire, Eng., Oct. 16, 1741; s. Ralph and Elizabeth (habersham) C.; m. Ann Legardere, Jan. 2, 1763; children include Joseph. Rice planter, mcht., asso. at various times with Joseph Clay Co., Seth John Cuthbert & Co., Clay, Talfair & Co.; partner William Fox & Co.; mem. Ga. Revolutionary Com., 1774; participated in seizure 600 pounds of powder from King's magazine, Savannah, Ga., May 11, 1775; mem. Ga. Council of Safety, 1775; mem. Provisional Congress, 1775; paymaster gen. So. dept. Continental Army, 1777; mem. Continental Congress, 1778-80; one of 25 rebel leaders indicted for treason by Royalist Assmbly, 1780; state treas. Ga., 1782; mem. bd. created by Ga. Gen. Assembly to establish instn. higher edn., thus became a founder U. Ga. (1st state univ. chartered in Am.). Died Savannah, Nov. 15, 1804; buried Colonial Park Cemetery, Savannah.

CLAY, MATTHEW congressman; b. Halifax, County, Va., Mar. 25, 1754; s. Charles and Martha (Green) C.; m. Polly Williams; m. 2d, Miss Saunders. Commd. Ensign 9th Va. Regt. 1776, 2d lt., 1777, 1s5 lt., 1778; q.m. 1st Va. Regt., 1778-81; mem. Va. Ho. of Dels., 1790-94; mem. U.S. Ho. of Reps. from Va., 4th-12th, 14th congresses 1795-1813, Mar. 4-May 27, 1815. Died Halifax Court House. Va., May 27, 1815; buried family burying ground Pittsylvania County, Va.

CLAYTON, BERTRAM TRACY army officer; b. Clayton, Ala., Oct. 19, 1862; s. Gen. Henry De Lamar and Victoria Virginia (Hunter) C.; bro. of Henry De Lamar C.; student of U. of Ala., 1880-82; grad. U.S. Mil. Acad., 1886; m. Louise M. Brasher, June 12, 1887; m. 2d, Mary D. Watson, Dept. 2, 1907. Second lt. 11th Inf., July 1, 1886; resigned, May 31, 1888, to enter civil engring. practice at Brooklyn. Adj. 13th Regt. N.G.S.N.Y., 1890; maj. and engr. 2d Brigade, 1894; organized troop C and elected capt., 1896, comdg. same during Spanish-Am. War; in action at Coama, P.R., Aibonito Pass; col. 14th Regt., N.G.S.N.Y., 1899-1901. Mem. 56th Congress (1899-1901), 4th N.Y. Dist. Democrat. Apptd. capt. and q.-m. U.S. Army, Feb. 2, 1901; maj. and q.-m., Mar. 3, 1911. As constructing q.-m. had charge of completing the new riding hall and the erection of the new academic bldg. of the U.S. Mil. Acad., 1911-13; was q.-m. of U.S. troops in Canal Zone to 1917; chief q.-m. 1st Div., 1st Army Corps, A.E.F. in France, 1917 - . Died May 30, 1918.

CLAYTON, JOSHUA physician, gov. Del.; b. Dover, Del., Dec. 20, 1774; s. John and Grace Clayton; attended U. Pa., 1756-62; m. Rachael McCleary, 1776. Commd. maj., 2d in command Bohemia Bn. of Md., 1776; commd. col., apptd. mem. staff of Gen. Washington; elected mem. Del. Ho. of Assembly, 1785, 87; state treas. Del., 1786; pres. Del., 1789-92; 1st gov. Del., 1792-96; mem. U.S. Senate from Del., Jan. 19-Aug. 11, 1798. Died Bohemia Manor, Del., Aug. 11, 1798.

CLEARY, DANIEL FRANCIS govt. ofcl.; b. Chicago, June 4, 1910; s. Daniel Francis and Anna Margaret (Early) C.; A.B., Loyola, 1934; J.D., 1937; m. Gertrude Scanlan, Apr. 10, 1937; children—Mary Denise, Ann Deirdre, Daniel F. Admitted to Ill State bar, Dec., 1937, practice of law, Chicago, 1937-42; mem. firm Garvey, Cleary & Doyle; retraining splist. Dept. of Labor, Washington, 1945-46; sr. atty. Vets Adminstrn., Washington, 1946-49; chmn. War Claims Commn., since 1949. Served as 1st lt., capt. and maj., U.S.A.A.F., 1942-45; disch. to A.A.F. Res. as maj. Mem. Chicago bar assn., Am. Legion, Disabled Am. Vets., Internat. Brotherhood Elec. Workers (A.F.of L.). Democrat. Roman Catholic. Club: National Press (Washington). Home: 3735 Oliver St., Washington 15. Office: Tariff Bldg., Washington 25. Died Dec. 5, 1953; buried Arlington Nat. Cemetery.

CLEARY, PETER JOSEPH AUGUSTINE brig. gen.; b. Malta, N.Y., Nov. 7, 1839; s. Patrick and Laura (Celli) C.; gen. edn. at Queen's U., Ireland; M.D., Royal Coll. Surgeons, London, 1860; m. Sarah M., d. Judge Charles Fleming Keigh, of Athens, Tenn., ept. 28, 1865. Apptd. from N.Y., asst. surgeon U.S.V., Oct. 4, 1862; surgeon U.S.V., Apr. 13, 1863; hon. mustered out, Aug. 10, 1865; asst. surgeon U.S. Army, Oct. 9, 1867; capt. asst. surgeon, Dec. 26, 1867; maj. surgeon, Jan. 30, 1883; lt. col. deputy surgeon gen., Nov. 15, 1897; col. asst. surgeon gen., Feb. 4, 1901; brig. gen., Aug. 6, 1903. Bvtd. lt. col. vols., Aug. 9, 1865, "for faithful and meritorious services." Served during Civil War chiefly with Army of the Cumberland, participating in Chickamauga campaign and siege of Chattanooga; in regular service on Western frontier, Western Tex., Ind. Ty., Colo., Ariz., N.M., etc.; chief surgeon Dept. of Tex., 1896-98, 1900-03, Dept. of the Gulf, 1898-1900; retired at own request, Aug. 7, 1903. Died Nov. 5, 1914.

CLEAVELAND, PARKER educator, scientist; b. Byfield, Mass., Jan. 15, 1780; s. Parker and Elizabeth (Jackman) C.; grad. Harvard, 1799. Taught sch., York, Me., 1799-1802; tutor mathematics and natural philosophy Harvard, 1803-05; prof. mathematics and natural philosophy Bowdoin Coll., Brunswick, Me., 1805-58; prof. materia medica Med. Sch. of Me., Brunswick, 1820-58; mineral Cleavelandite named for him. Author: Elementary Treatise on Mineralogy and Geology (1st Am. work on subject), 1816: Agricultural Queries, 1827. Died Oct. 15, 1858.

CLEAVES, WILLIS EVERETT naval officer (ret.); b. Chebeague Island, Me., Sept. 30, 1902; s. George Lewis and Annie Marie (Strout) C.; B.S., U.S. Naval Acad., 1924; Harvard, 1931; m. Barbara Goss Jacobs, Nov. 28, 1925; children-Jane, Joan, Barbara. Commd. ensign USN, 1924, advanced through grades to rear adm., 1946; entered naval aviation, 1926; comd. patrol squadron, 1942, U.S.S. Casco (seaplane tender), 1942; comdr. U.S. Naval Air Sta., Daytona Beach, Fla., 1943; asst. chief naval communications for aeros., 1944; comdr. U.S.S. Palau (aircraft carrier), 1945; ret. from active duty, 1946; mgr. aviation sales Collins Radio Co., since 1946. Awarded Silver Star, Purple Heart, Republican. Clubs: Rotary (Cedar Rapids, Ia.), Army Navy Country (Arlington, Va.), Yacht (N.Y.C.). Home: Chebeague Island, Me. Office: 11 West 42d St., N.Y.C. 18. Died May 1966.

CLEBORNE, CHRISTOPHER JAMES naval officer; b. Edinburgh, Scotland, Dec. 16, 1838; grad. Univ. of Pa., 1860. Apptd. from Pa., asst. surgeon U.S. Navy, May 9, 1861; promoted past asst. surgeon, Oct. 26, 1863; surgeon, Nov. 24, 1863; med. insp., Jan. 7, 1878; med. dir., Sept. 18, 1887; retired with rank of rear admiral, Nov. 10, 1899. During Civil War attached to various ships and participated in destruction of the Alvarado, Aug. 5, 1861, expdn. to Stono River; operations off Mobile, both attacks on Ft. Fisher, etc. Judge advocate Naval Retiring Bd., 1865, 1867; served in European Squadron, 1872-74; Naval Sta., Portsmouth, N.H., 1875-78, 1881-84; fleet surgeon N. Atlantic Squadron, 1879-81; mem. Med. Examining Bd., 1884-87; dir. naval hosps., Norfolk, Va., 1888-91, Chelsea, Mass., 1891-94, Norfolk, Va., 1894-99, Phila., Jan.-Nov. 1899. Home: Washington, D.C. Died 1909.

CLEBURN, PATRICK RONAYNE army officer; b. County Cork, Ireland, Mar. 17, 1828; s. Joseph and Mary Ann (Ronayne) C. Came to New Orleans, 1849; admitted to Ark. bar, 1856; served with Confederate Army in Tenn., also in battles of Shiloh, Richmond, Chattanooga, Atlanta, 1861-64; organized Confederate mil. co. called Yell Rifles, which seized Fed. Arsenal, Little Rock, Ark., promoted to brig. gen. in command 3d brigade Army of Miss., 1862; commd. maj. gen., 1862; known as Stonewall Jackson of the West for his stand at Battle of Missionary Ridge; composed letter recommending liberation of slaves and their enlistment into Confederate cause (considered inexpedient by Jefferson Davis). Died Battle of Franklin (Tenn.), Nov. 30, 1864; buried Helena, Ark.

CLEM, JOHN LINCOLN army officer; b. Newark, O., Aug. 13, 1851; s. of Roman and Mary (Weber) C.; grad. Arty. School, Ft. Monroe, Va., 1875; m. Anita Rossetta, d. General W. H. French, U.S. Army, May 24, 1875 (died 1899); m. 2d, Bessie, d. Daniel Sullivan, of San Antonio, Tex., Sept. 23, 1903; children-John L., Anne E. Attempted to enlist as drummer in 3d Ohio and 22d Mich. vols., May 1861, but was rejected on account of youth; enlisted as drummer, 22d Michigan Inf., May 1, 1862; promoted sergt. at battle of Chickamauga, Sept. 20, 1863; apptd. 2d lt. 24th U.S. Inf., Dec. 18, 1871; promoted through grades to brig. gen., Aug. 13, 1915, retired as maj. gen., Aug. 29, 1916. Chmn. Fredericksburg-Spottsylvania Battle Grounds Commn. With Army of Cumberland, Civil War, and participated in battles of Shiloh, Chickamauga, Perryville, Stone River, Resaca, Kenesaw, Atlanta, Nashville, etc. Chief q.-m. Philippine Div., 1903-06, Dept. of Tex., 1906-11, Dept. of the Lakes, Chicago, 1911-15. Republican. Catholic. Home: San Antonio, Tex. Died May 13, 1937.

CLEMENS, JEREMIAH senator, novelist; b. Huntsville, Ala., Dec. 28, 1814; s. James and Miss (Mills) C.; attended La. Grange Coll.; grad. U. Ala., 1833; studied law Transylvania U., Lexington, Ky.; m. Mary Read, Dec. 4, 1834, Admitted to Ala. bar, 1834; U.S. dist. atty. for No. Ala., 1838-39; mem. Ala. Ho. of Reps. 1838-41, 43-44; served as lt. col. Army of Tex. in Tex. War for independence, 1842; apptd. maj. 13th Inf. U.S. Army, 1847, lt. col., 1847; chief dept. civil and mil. purhcases in Mexico, 1848; mem. U.S. Senate (Democrat) from Ala., Nov. 30, 1849-53; spent several years writing hist. novels; editor Memphis (Tenn.) Eagle and Enquirer, 1859; mem. Ala. Secession Conv., 1861; apptd. maj. gen. Ala. Militia, 1861, never saw active service; Unionist; lived in Phila., 1862-65. Author: Bernard Lile: An Historical Romance of the Texan Revolution and the Mexican War, 1856; Mustang Gray, 1858; The Rivals, 1860; Tobias Wilson: A Tale of the Great Rebellion, 1865. Died Huntsville, May 21, 1865; buried Maple Hill Cemetery, Huntsville.

CLEMENT, CHARLES MAXWELL army officer; b. Sunbury, Pa., Oct. 28, 1855; s. John Kay and Mary S. (Zeigler) C.; ed. Sunbury and Klinesgrove acads. and at mil. acad., Burlington, N.J.; m. Alice Virginia Withington, Nov. 19, 1879. Began practice in Sunbury, 1878; deputy sec. Commonwealth of Pennsylvania, 1890-91; sec., later chmn. Rep. County Com., Northumberland County, 1879-88. Enlisted as pvt. Co. E. 8th Inf., N.G. Pa., Sept. 3, 1877; 1st lt., May 6, 1878; advanced through grades to maj. gen., Pa. Div., Dec. 22, 1915; retired, Apr. 1, 1919; maj. gen. N.A., Aug. 5, 1917. Served as lt. col. 12th Inf., Spanish-Am. War, 1898; maj. gen. 7th Pa. Div., Mexican border, 1916-17; comdg. 28th Div., Camp Hancock, Ga., Aug. 1917; hon. disch. Dec. 11, 1917. Republican. Episcopalian. Mason. Home: Sanbury, Pa. Died Sept. 9, 1934.

CLEMENT, WILLIAM TARDY marine officer; b. Lynchburg, Va., Sept. 27, 1894; s. William Joseph and Mary Elizabeth (Frees) C.; B.S., Va. Mil. Inst., 1914; widower; children—John Cristy, David Alexander, Nancy Carrington; married 2d, Mrs. Ethel G. Mathiesen; 1 son, Robert Andrew Mathiesen. Commissioned 2d lieutenant, United States Marine Corps, 1917 and advanced through grades to lt. gen., 1944; expeditionary duty Republic of Haiti, 1917-19; duty at Quantico, Va., 1919-23; with Am. Legation Guard, Peking, China, 1923-25; duty at San Diego, Calif., 1925-27 and 1929-30; expeditionary duty, Shanghai, China, 1927-29; comdr. marine detachment, U.S.S. West Virginia, 1930-32; Naval Ammunition Depot Guard, Bremerton, Wash., 1932-34; student and instr., Marine Corps Sch., Quantico, Va., 1934-38; comdr. 1st bn., 5th Marines, 1938-40; fleet marine officer for U.S. Asiatic Fleet aboard U.S.S. Augusta and U.S.S. Houston, 1940-41; at outbreak of war, joined 4th Marines and served throughout Bataan; escaped from Bataan, 1942, and returned to U.S.; mem. staff of comdr. U.S. Naval Forces in Europe, 1942-43; asst. comdr. and comdr. Marine Corp. Schs., Quantico, Va., 1943-44; asst. div. comdr., 6th Marine div., during seizure of Okinawa Shima, Ryukyu Islands and later during occupation of Tsingtao, China, 1944-45; comdr. 3d Fleet Landing Force in initial landings and occupation at Yokusuka Naval and Air Base, Japan, 1945; comdg. gen. 3d Marine Brigade (formerly 6th Div.) Tsingtao area, June 1946; returned to U.S., Sept. 1946; pres. Naval Retiring Bd., 1947-49; dir. Marine Corps Reserve, April 1947, Hdqrs. M.C.; comdg. gen. Marine Corps Recruit Depot, San Diego, Cal., 1949-52. Awarded Navy Cross for service in Bataan, Legion of Merit for Okinawa, 2d Legion of Merit, occupation of Japan, 3d Legion of Merit services in China, U.S. Army Presdl. Citation for Bataan, Bronze Star Medal, U.S. Navy Presdl. Citation, World War I Medal with star, Haitian Campaign Medal, Marine Corps Expeditionary Medal with two stars, Yangtze Campaign Medal, China Service Medal, Asiatic-Pacific Theatre Ribbon with three stars, European Theatre Ribbon, U.S. Theatre Ribbon, Philippine Defense Medal (U.S.), Medal and Diploma of Special Collar Order of Yun Hui, Pao Ting Medal (China); Commander Order of Orange (Nassau). Home: 6120 Avenida Cresta, La Jolla, Cal. Died Oct. 17, 1955; buried Arlington Nat. Cemetery.

CLENDENIN, DAVID congressman. Moved from Harford County, Md. to nr. Stuthers, Mahoning Valley, O., circa 1806; pioneer iron and steel industry, built 2d stack constructed in Ohio; lived in Trumbull County, O.; served as 1st lt. Capt. James Hazlep's co. of arty. attached to regt. of Ohio Militia in War of 1812; lt. paymasted 2d Regt., Ohio Militia, 1812-13; asst. dist. paymaster U.S. Army, 1814; mem. U.S. Ho. of Reps. (filled vacancy) from Ohio, 13th-14th congresses, Oct. 11, 1814-17.

CLEPHANE, WALTER COLLINS lawyer; b. West Haven, Conn., July 17, 1867; s. Lewis and Annie M. (Collins) C.; LL.B., George Washington U., 1889, LL.M., 1890, LL.D., 1932; m. Nellie Mathilda Walker,

Jan. 20, 1896; children—Beatrice A. (dec.), Douglas W., John W. Clerk wholesale store, N.Y., 1884; court stenog. Washington 1889—; mem. Clephane Latimer & Hall; became prof. law George Washington U., 1897, now emeritus; dir., mem. exec. com. Nat. Savings & Trust Co.; mem. Nat. Ry. Labor Panel and many ry. arbitration and presdl. emergency boards. Judge adv. U.S. Army, 1918-20; later col. judge adv., O.R.C. Ex-pres. bd. trustees Indsl. Home Sch., D.C. Mem. Am., D.C. bar assns., Columbia Hist. Soc., Order of Coif, Phi Delta Phi, Kappa Alpha. Republican. Presbyn. Clubs: Cosmos (Washington); Chevy Chase (Md.). Author: Clephane on Organization and Management of Business Corps., 1905; Clephane on Equity Pleading and Practice, 1926. Home: 6000 Connecticut Av., Chevy Chase 15, Md. Office: Investment Bldg., Washington 5. Died Aug. 15, 1951; buried Arlington Nat. Cemetery.

CLEVELAND, BENJAMIN army officer, legislator; b. Prince William County, Va., Mar. 26, 1738; s. John and Martha (Coffee) C.; m. Mary Graves. Justice Wilkes County Ct., N.C.; elected mem. N.C. Ho. of Commons, 1778; mem. N.C. Senate, 1780; commd. capt. 2d regt. N.C. Militia; hero Battle of King's Mountain (defeated the English in the South), 1780. Died Tugalo Valley, S.C., Oct. 1806.

CLEVELAND, GROVER (STEPHEN GROVER CLEVELAND), President of the United States; b. Caldwell, N.J., Mar. 18, 1837; s. Rev. Richard Falley and Ann (Neal) C.; family removed to Onondaga County, N.Y., 1841; attended village sch. and clerked in store; teacher in Inst. for Blind, New York, 1 yr.; (LL.D., Princeton, 1897); m. Frances Folsom, June 2, 1886. Went to Buffalo, 1855, became clerk in law offices of Rogers, Bowen & Rogers, 1855, and was admitted to bar, 1859; asst. dist. atty. Erie County, 1863-66; sheriff Erie County, 1870-73; established law practice; in 1881 was elected mayor of Buffalo. His veto of extravagant appropriations directed outside attention to him and led to his nomination and election as gov. the following year; in 1884 elected Pres. of U.S. as Democrat, over James G. Blaine, Republican, by majority of 37 electoral votes; in 1888 again Democratic nominee, but defeated by Benjamin Harrison; returned to law practice, locating in New York; in 1892 again elected President as Democrat, defeating Pres. Harrison; in 1896 the Democratic party having declared for the free coinage of silver in the platform of its Nat. Conv., Mr. Cleveland withheld his support from the ticket and platform. He took up his residence, after his second retirement from the White House, at Princeton, N.J. Elected trustee, holding a majority of the stock of the Equitable Life Assurance Soc. of U.S., June 10, 1905. Chmn. Assn. of Life Ins. Presidents, Jan. 1907 - . Mem. exec. com. Nat. Civic Federation. Trustee Princeton Univ. Home: Princeton, N.J. Died 1908.

CLEXTON, EDWARD WILLIAM ret. naval officer, corp. exec.; b. S.I., N.Y., Aug. 15, 1900; s. Andrew Ritter and Ann Veronica (Finnerty) C.; student Columbia, 1918; B.S., U.S. Naval Acad., 1924; M.S., Mass. Inst. Tech., 1929; m. Zita Mary Langhorne, June 14, 1930 (dec. Apr. 1948); children-Nancy Anne, Zita Langhorne, Julia Anna, Mary Spencer, Edward William Catherine Cary. Commd. ensign USN, 1924, advanced through grades to vice adm., 1956; designated naval aviator, 1934; gunnery and foretop gunnery spotter U.S.S. Mississippi, 1924-26; shop supt. Naval Aircraft Factory, Phila., 1929-33; asst. to air officer U.S.S. Lexington, 1934-35; asst. chief engr. catapult and arresting gear design Naval Aircraft Factory, Phila., 1935-37; airplane design Bur. Aeros.;, Navy Dept., 1937-41, dir. maintenance, 1944-47; comdr. Air Force Atlantic Fleet staff, 1941-44; asst. dir. Office Budget and Reports, Navy Dept., 1947-50, dir., 1950; asst. comptroller, dir. Budget and Reports, Office of Comptroller, 1951-56, dep. comptroller, 1956; chief Navy Material, 1956-60, ret.; vice pres. Grumman Aircraft Engring. Corp., Bethpage, L.I. Awarded Legion Merit. Sec. Navy Commendation ribbon, World War I and II victory medals, Am. Def. medal, Am., Asiatic and European area medals, D.S.M. Mem. Inst. Aerospace Scis., Delta Kappa Epsilon, Roman Catholic. K.C. Club: Army and Navy Country (Arlington, Va.). Home: 291 Country Club Dr., Jupiter, Fla. Office Grumman Aircraft Engring. Corp., Bethpage, L.I., N.Y. Died Aug. 18, 1966.

CLIFFORD, EDWARD lawyer b. Virginia, Cass County, Ill., Dec. 21, 1873; s. James H. and Eliza Jane (Kikendall) C.; Ph.B., Ill. Coll., 1896, A.M., 1920; LL.B., Washington U., 1900, LL.D., 1936; m. Anne W. Lambert, Jan. 1, 1901. Admitted to Ill. bar, 1900, and practiced in Virginia, Ill., Chgo.; now practicing in Washington; del. Republican Nat. Conv., 1916; asst. sec. treasury (U.S.) May 3, 1921-July 9, 1923. Served as lt. col. U.S. Army in World War; staff duty in Washington, France. Awarded D.S.M. Mem. Phi Delta Phi, Republican. Episcopalian. Clubs: University (Chgo.); Metropolitan, Army and Navy, Chevy Chase (Washington). Home: 1804 45th St. N.W., Washington 7. Died June 13, 1963; buried Oak Hill Cemetery, Washington.

CLIFTON, JOSEPH CLINTON naval officer; b. Paducah, Ky., Oct. 31, 1908; s. Thomas C. and Pearl (Cook) C.; student U.Ky., 1926; B.S., U.S. Naval Acad., 1930; grad. Naval War Coll., 1954; m. Virginia Cobb, Oct. 26, 1950. Commd. engisn U.S.Navy, 1930, advanced through grades to rear adm., 1958; designated naval aviator, 1932; various assignments in ships and with flying squadrons, 1930-42; comdg. officer Fighter Squadron 12, 1942, 44; comdr. Air Group 12, 1944, Combined Air Groups from H.M.S. Illustrious and U.S.S. Saratoga, 1944; flight tng. officer Naval Air Sta., Green Cove Springs, Fla., 1944-45; exec. officer carrier U.S.S. Wasp, 1945-46, also comdg. officer, 1946; assigned air warfare div. Office Dep. Chief Naval Operations, 1946-49; mem. staff comdr. fleet logistics support wings, Pacific Area, 1949; comdr. Transport Squardon 8, 1949-51; comdg. officer seaplane tender U.S.S. Corson, 1951-52; dep. chief staff tng. staff comdr. air forces U.S. Pacific Fleet, 1952-53; comdg. officer Naval Air Sta., Memphis, 1954-56; comdr. Barrier Atlantic, also Airborne Early Warning Wing Atlantic and Fleet Air Detachment, Argentina, 1956-58, Naval Air Advanced tng. Command, 1958-60, Carrier Div. 7, Seventh Fleet, 1960-61; chief Naval Air Tech. Tng., Command, 1961—. Decorated Legion of Merit with gold star, D.F.C. with gold star, Air medal (2); Distinguished Service Order (Great Britain). Address: Care Litton Systems, Inc., Woodland Hills, Cal. Died Dec. 1967.

CLINCH, DUNCAN LAMONT congressman, army officer: b. Ard-Lamont, Edgecombe County, N.C.. Apr. 6, 1787. First lt. 3d Infantry, U.S. Army, 1808, promoted capt., 1810; apptd. lt. col. 43d Regt. U.S. Infantry, 1813, apptd. col. 8th Regt., 1819; brig. gen., 1829; in command at Battle of Ouithlacoohee against Seminole Indians, 1835; resigned, 1836; settled on plantation nr. St. Marys, Ga.: mem. U.S. Ho. of Reps. (Whig, filled vacancy) from Ga., 28th Congress, Feb. 15, 184 Bonaventure Cemetery, Savannah, Ga.

CLINGMAN, THOMAS LANIER senator, army officer b. Huntsville, N.C., July 27, 1812; s. Jacob and Jane (Poindexter) C.; grad. U. N.C., 1832. Admitted to N.C. bar, 1834; mem. N.C. Legislature, 1835, N.C. Senate, 1840; mem. U.S. Ho. of Reps (Whig) from N.C., 28th Congress, 1843-45, 30th-35th congresses, 1847-58; determined highest peak in Smoky Mountains (Clingman's Peak), 1858; mem. U.S. Senate (Democrat) from N.C., Dec. 6, 1858-1861; del. Confederate States Conv., Montgomery, Ala., 1861: commd. col. 25th N.C. Volunteers, 1861; brig. gen. Confederate Army, 1862; del. Nat. Dem. Conv., N.Y.C., 1868; mem. N.C. Constl. Conv., 1875; made many contbns. to geology and mineralogy. Author: Follies of the Positive Philosophers, 1878. Died Morganton, N.C., Nov. 3, 1897: buried Riverside Cemetery, Asheville, N.C.

CLINNIN, JOHN V. lawyer; b. Huntley, Ill., Apr. 5, 1876; s. James Gregory and Jane (Dougherty); children—Muriel, John V. Chief dep. recorder Cook County, 1903-13; asst. corp. counsel City of Chgo., 1915-16; 1st asst. U.S. Dist. Atty., 1921-22; chmn. Ill. Athletic Commn., 1929-31; mem. Ill. Civil Service Commn., 1932—. Enlisted 1st Ill. Inf., 1894; served in Santiago de Cuba campaign during Spanish-American War; col. comdg. 130th Inf., AEF, 1918, retired with rank brig. gen., 1922; major gen. comdg. Ill. Res. Militia, 1940, retired 1943. Decorated D.S.M., Silver Star, Purple Heart; recipient citations Gen. Barry, Gen. Pershing. Gen. George Bell, Jr. Comdr. Columbia Camp U.S. War Vets., Ill. branch Soc. of Army of Santiago de Cuba, North Shore Post Am. Legion, 1920-21; sr. vice comdr. Am. Legion Dept. Ill., 1923-24; nat. comdr. Disabled Am. Veterans, 1926-27; comdr. Chipilly Post, Am. Legion, 1928-29. Republican. Home: 332 Washington Av., Wilmette, Ill. Office: 11 S. LaSalle St., Chgo. Died Sept. 16, 1955.

CLINTON, GEORGE naval officer, colonial gov.; b. Eng., 1686; s. Francis and Susan (Penniston) C.: m. Anne Carle, 2 children including Henry. Joined Brit. Navy, 1708, commd. capt., 1716, commodore, comdr.-in-chief Mediterranean squadron, 1737, rear adm., 1743; gov. Newfoundland, 1732-41; gov. N.Y., 1743-53, allowed colonial assembly to take excessive control over civil affairs, contrary to his instructions; mem. Brit. Ho. of Commons from Saltash, 1754-60; returned to Eng., 1754, became adm. White Fleet, Brit. Navy. Died July 10, 1761.

CLINTON, GEORGE vice pres. U.S., gov. N.Y.; b. Little Britain, Ulster (Now Orange County), N.Y., July 26, 1739; s. Charles and Elizabeth (Denniston) C.; m. Cornelia Tappan, Feb. 7, 1770, 6 children. Del. N.Y. Provincial Assembly, 1768; del. Continental Congress, 1775-76; commd. brig. gen. Continental Army, 1777; 1st gov. N.Y., 1777-95; 1801-04; pres. N.Y. State Conv. to ratify U.S. Constn., 1788, opposed ratification; his opposition resulted in writing of the Federalist (by Madison, Hamilton and Jay) to destroy his influence; vice pres. U.S. under Jefferson and Madison, 1805-13. Died Washington, D.C., Apr. 20, 1812; buried Congressional Cemetery, Washington.

CLINTON, JAMES army officer; b. Orange County, N.Y., Aug. 9, 1733; s. Col. Charles and Elizabeth (Denniston); m. Mary DeWitt, 1764, 1 son, Dewitt: m. 2d, Mrs. Mary Gray. Commd. capt. N.Y. Militia, 1756; lt. col., 1775; elected dep. Provincial Congress N.Y., May 1775; commd. col. N.Y. State Militia, 1775; commd. brig. gen. Continental Army, 1776, in command of No. Dept., Albany, N.Y., 1780; N.Y. State commr. to adjust boundary line between Pa. and N.Y., 1785; mem. N.Y. State Conv. ratified U.S. Constn. Died Orange County, Dec. 22, 1812; buried Little Britain, Orange County.

CLINTON, MARSHALL surgeon; b. Buffalo, N.Y., July 22, 1873; s. Spencer and Sarah (Riley) C.; M.D., U. of Buffalo, 1895; m. Alethe Evans, Dec. 12, 1900 (divorced): children-DeWitt II, Karl, Geoffrey (dec), Marcia, Marshall; m. 2d, Virginia Shepherd, M.D. Practiced, Buffalo, 1895-Dec. 1940; prof. surgery U. of Buffalo, later emeritus attending surgeon Buffalo Gen. Hosp.; retired 1938. Asst. surgeon 202d N.Y. Regt., Spanish-Am. War, 1898; chief surgeon consultant, 2d Army, A.E.F., World War I, commd. maj. Med. R.C., June 12, 1917; lt. col., June 6, 1918; dir. Buffalo Base Hosp. No. 23, 1917-19. Fellow Am. Coll. Surgeons, Am. Surg. Assn.; mem. Buffalo Acad. Medicine, etc. Republican. Episcopalian. Home: Bluff City, Tenn. Died Sept. 3, 1943; buried Morning View Cemetery, Bluff City.

CLOPTON MALVERN BRYAN surgeon; b. St. Louis, Mo., Oct. 8, 1875; s. William H. and Belle (Bryan) C.; prep. edn., St. Louis High Sch.; student U. of Va., classical course, 1893-95, M.D., 1897; m. Mrs. James T. Walker, 1909 (died 1911); m. 2d, Mrs. Rachel Lowe Lambert, 1934. Began practice at St. Louis, 1897; interne Johns Hopkins Hosp., 1898-1900; clin. prof. surgery, Washington U. Sch. of Medicine; asst. surgeon Barnes Hosp.; asso. surgeon St. Louis Children's Hosp.; chief of staff St. Luke's Hosp., 1933-37; consulting surgeon Jewish Hosp. Lt. col. Med. Corps, U.S. Army, 1917-19; with Base Hosp. No. 21 and C.O. Mobile Hosp. No. 4, A.E.F. Fellow Am. Coll. Surgeons; mem. A.M.A., Am. Southern and Western surg. assns., St. Louis Surg, Soc., Soc. Clin. Surgery. Member board directors Washington Univ. Democrat, Episcopalian. Clubs: University, Racquet, St. Louis Country, Log Cabin Club, Round Table. Contbr. to med. jours. Home: Clarksville, Mo. Office: Beaumont Medical Bldg., St. Louis, Mo. Died Apr. 21, 1947; buried in Bellefontaine Cemetery, St. Louis.

CLOSSON, HENRY WHITNEY brig. gen.; b. Whitingham, Vt., June 6, 1832; s. Henry and Emily (Whitney) C. Grad. U.S. Mil. Acad., 1854; m. Olivia A. Burke, Oct. 26, 1857; m. 2d, Julia W. Terry, June 2, 1868. Commd. 2d lt. 1st Arty., July 1, 1854; advanced through grades to col. 4th Arty., Apr. 25, 1888; retired by operation of law, June 6, 1896; advanced to rank of brig. gen. retired, by act of Apr. 23, 1904. Bvtd. maj., July 8, 1863, for services at capture of Port Hudson, La.; lt. col., Aug. 23, 1864, for services at capture of Ft. Morgan, Ala. Served on frontier against Indians in Tex. and Fla., until 1861; in defense of Ft. Pickens, 1861-62; chief arty. dist. of Pensacola, May-Dec. 1862; comdg. Baton Rouge, La., to Mar. 1863; on Teche campaign comdg. arty. of Gen. Grover's div., 19th Army Corps, Oct. 1863-July 1864; chief arty. Mobile expdn., engaged in sieges of Forts Gaines and Morgan; chief arty. and ordnance cav. corps, Middle Mil. Div., Nov.-Dec. 1864. Home: Washington, D.C. Died July 16, 1917.

CLOTHIER, ROBERT CLARKSON, educator; b. Phila., Jan. 8, 1885; s. Clarkson and Agnes (Evans) C.; ed. Haverford Sch., 1894-1903; Litt.B., Princeton, 1908, LL.D., 1932; LL.D., U. of Pittsburgh and Tusculum Coll., 1932, Dickinson Coll., 1933, New York Univ., 1935; Lafayette Coll., 1938; Litt.D., Temple U., 1934; LL.D. U. Del., 1950, U. State of N.Y., 1951, Rutgers U., 1952, University of Rhode Island, 1952; m. Natalie Wilson, June 24, 1916; children—Agnes Evans, (Mrs. Charles P. Whitlock), Arthur Wilson (deceased), Robert C. With Curtis Publishing Co. Phila., 1910-17; v.p. The Scott Co., Philadelphia, 1918-23; asst. headmaster Haverford Sch., 1923-29; dean of men, U. Pitts., 1929-32; pres. Rutgers U., 1932-51, pres. emeritus, 1951-70. Dir. Mut. Benefit Life Ins. Co., Pub. Serv. Gas & Electric Co., Newark, Delaware and Bound Brook R.R. Company. Member Committee on Classification of Personnel, Washington, and A.E.F., World War I; commissioned lt. colonel. President of the New Jersey State Constitutional Conv. 1947. Mem. Dutch Reform Church. Clubs: Century Assn., University (N.Y. City and Phila.). Author: Personnel Management (with Walter Dill Scott), 1923. Home: Haverford PA Died Mar. 1970.

CLOUD, MARSHALL MORGAN surgeon; b. Carroll Co., Va., Oct. 9, 1868; s. Columbus Henry and Mary Emily (Parker) C.; M.D., honor medalist, U. of Kan., 1892; grad. U.S.A. Med. Sch., 1897; B.S., U. of Southern Calif., 1904, A.M., 1906; grad. study Stanford, 1905. U. of Chicago, 1906; m. Mary Frances Moore, June 19, 1894; children - Dorothy (Mrs. Frederick B. Pinkus), Marguerite (Mrs. Allison J. Wallace, Jr.), Mary Frances. Asst. supt. Kan. State Hosp., Topeka, 1893-95; commd. 1st lt., Med. Corps, U.S.A., 1896, and advanced through grades to maj., 1919; retired for disability in line of duty, 1921; clin. prof. ophthalmaology, U. of Southern Calif., 1910-13, prof. mil. medicine, 1920-23; ophthalmologist, Nat. Soldiers Home, Sawtelle, Calif., 1910-13; same, Santa Fe Ry., 1910-21; examining surgeon, U.S. Pension Bur.; on staff Hollywood Hosp. and Gen. Hosp., Los Angeles; partner Angeles Mesa Land Co.; owner Cloud Heights Subdivision, La Crescenta, Calif. Comdr. div. hosp., Mobile, Ala., Miami, Fla., and Anniston, Ala., Spanish-Am. War;

served on operations div., commd. personnel br., Gen. Staff, World War. Fellow Am. Coll. Surgeons. Democrat. Episcopalian. Author: Sanitary Analysis of Water, 1905; Curing Our Nerves, 1934; Facts About Alcoholic Drinks, 1934. Inventor, with M. F. Volkman, of horizontal-base range finder for artillery fire, 1904. Home: Los Angeles, Calif. Died: 1937.

CLOUS, JOHN WALTER army officer; b. Wurttemberg, Germany, June 9, 1837; s. John and Fredericka (Dieterle) C.; ed. in the higher schs. of Germany; began the study of civil law; came to the U.S., 1855; m. Caroline M. Strickle, Nov. 24, 1874. Served as pvt. 9th Inf., Feb. 2, 1857-Nov. 5, 1860; pvt. and corp. and q.m. sergt. 6th Inf., Feb. 9, 1860-Nov. 29, 1862; 2d lt. to capt. 38th Inf., Jan. 22, 1867; transferred to 24th Inf., Nov. 11, 1869; maj. and judge advocate, Apr. 1, 1886; lt. col. and deputy judge adv. gen., Feb. 12, 1892; brig. gen. U.S.V., Sept. 21, 1898; hon. disch. from vols., Mar. 24, 1899; col. and judge adv., Feb. 2, 1901; brig. gen. and judge adv. gen. U.S.A., May 22, 1901; retired at own request after over 40 yrs.' service, May 24, 1901. Twice bvtd. for gallant conduct at Gettysburg, Pa.; adj. gen. 2d Mil. Dist. during reconstruction, 1866-67; acting a.d.c. to Maj. Gen. Sheridan during Indian campaign, 1868-69; finished law studies and admitted to bar U.S. Supreme Court; served on frontier and Indian campaigns, 1868-86; commended in War Dept., orders for gallant conduct in Indian engagement, 1872; asst. to judge adv. gen., 1886-90; prof. law, U.S. Mil. Acad., 1890-95; on staff Maj. Gen. Merritt to 1898; on staff Maj. Gen. Miles while in the field during Spanish-Am. War; sec. and counsel of commn. for evacuation of Cuba, Aug. 20, 1898-Jan. 10, 1899; on staff Maj. Gen. Brooke as judge advocate to May 21, 1901. Home: New York, N.Y. Died 1908.

CLOVER, RICHARDSON rear adm.; b. St. James' Coll., Hagerstown, Md., July 11, 1846; s. Rev. Lewis P. and Sarah Ann (Ackerman) C.; grad. U.S. Naval Acad., 1867; m. Mary Eudora, d. late Senator John F. Miller, May 19, 1886. Ensign, Dec. 18, 1868; master, Mar. 21, 1870; lt., Mar. 21, 1871; lt. comdr., May 19, 1891; comdr., Sept. 14, 1897; capt., Apr. 11, 1902; rear adm., Oct. 9, 1907. Served in various stas. and depts., with 22 yrs. of sea service; in charge survey of S.E. Alaska, 1885-86; hydrographer Bur. of Navigation, 1889-93; chief Office Naval Intelligence, 1897-98; mem. bd. on constrn. of vessels, Navy Dept., 1897-99; mem. war and strategy bd., Mar. 15 to Apr. 25, 1898; comd. U.S.S. Bancroft, May 1, 1898, to end of Spanish War; returned to Naval Intelligence Office; naval attache, London, 1900-03; comdg. U.S.S. Wisconsin, Asiatic Sta., 1904-05; pres. Bd. of Inspection and Survey, 1906-08; retired, 1908. Home: Washington, D.C. Died Oct. 14, 1919.

CLOWRY, ROBERT CHARLES capitalist; b. Will Co., Ill., Sept. 8, 1838; pub. sch. edn.; m. Caroline A. Estabrook, Aug. 29, 1865 (died 1896). Capt. asst. q.m. vols., Oct. 27, 1863; bvtd. maj. and lt. col. vols., Mar. 13, 1865, "for meritorious services and devoted application to duty"; hon. mustered out, May 31, 1866. In charge mil. telegraph lines, 1863-66; after the war served in various capacities with Western Union Telegraph Co., of which was pres. and gen. mgr., Apr., 1902-Nov. 23, 1910; was also pres. and gen. mgr. of its subsidiary cos. Home: Tarrytown, N.Y. Died Feb. 26, 1925.

CLUETT, SANFORD LOCKWOOD, civil and mechanical engr.; b. Troy, N.Y., June 6, 1874; s. Edmund and Mary Alice (Stone) C.; student Albany (N.Y.) Acad., 1889; grad. Troy Acad., 1894; C.E., Rensselaer Poly. Inst., 1898, D.Eng., 1952; D.Sc., Russell Sage Coll., 1958; m. Camilla E. Rising, Feb. 1916; children—Gregory Stone, Sanford Lockwood, Camilla Trent, Marvin Vaughan. With Walter A. Wood Mowing & Reaping Machine Co., Hoosick Falls, N.Y., successively as chief engr., asst. supt., v.p., and v.p. and gen. supt., 1901-19; with Cluett, Peabody & Co., Inc., Troy, N.Y., 1919-68, in charge engring. and research until 1944; dir. from 1921, vice pres. from 1927; trustee Troy Savings Bank; director Albany & Vermont R.R. Co., Saratoga & Schenectady Railroad Company. Member board directors Troy Orphan Asylum. Enlisted as private, Nat. Guard N.Y., 1897, later N.Y. Vol. Inf., Spanish Am. War; trans. to 1st U.S. Vol. Engrs., June 1898; promoted lt. and capt.; served in Porto Rican campaign; again with N.G.N.Y., 1904-17, advancing to maj. Signal Corps.; Reserve list, May 11, 1917. Designed one-horse and two-horse vertical lift mowing machines; steel work for Govt. locks on Big Sandy River, Kentucky, 1900; valves for St. Andrews Rapids locks, Manitoba; etc. Trustee, v.p. Rensselaer Poly. Inst. Received Modern Pioneer award N.A.M.; Longstreth medal Franklin Inst., Holley medal Am. Soc. M.E., 1952. Fellow Am. Numis. Soc., Am. Soc. M.E.; hon. mem. Rensselaer Soc., Soc. Engrs.; mem. N.Y. State Hist. Assn., Franklin Institute, Mil. Order of Foreign Wars, Society Colonial Wars, Founders and Patriots America, Sons of the Revolution, Army Ordnance Association, U.S. Naval Institute, Soc. Am. Mil. Engrs., U.S. Inst. for Textile Research, Sigma Xi, Chi Epsilon. Republican. Episcopalian. Clubs: Troy, Troy Country; Univ., New York Yacht (N.Y.C.); Bath and Tennis, Everglades (Palm Beach, Fla.). Inventor of Sanforized process, Clupak (extensible paper). Home: Palm Beach FL Died May 17, 1968; buried Troy NY

CLUETT, W. SCOTT, b. Williamstown, Mass., June 16, 1912; grad. Hotchkiss Sch., Williams Coll., 1935. Sr. v.p., dir. Drexel Harriman Ripley, Inc., N.Y.C.; v.p., dir. Middlebrook Farm, Inc. Served to maj. USAAC, 1942-46. Decorated Bronze Star. Mem. Investment Bankers Assn. Am., Nat. Assn. Securities Dealers (gov.). Clubs: Bond (gov.), University (N.Y.C.). Address: Wilton CT Died Oct. 25, 1971.

CLUVERIUS, WAT TYLER naval officer, coll. pres.; b. New Orleans, La., Dec. 25, 1874; s. Wat Tyler and Martha Lewis (Manning) C.; grad. U.S. Naval Acad., 1896; m. Hannah Walker Sampson, Apr. 5, 1900 (died Jan. 20, 1938); children—Elisabeth Sampson, Martha, Wat Tyler. Commd. ensign U.S. Navy, 1898; promoted through grades to rear adm., May 30, 1928. Participated in West Indian, Philippine and Mexican campaigns and with Mining Squadron in North Sea, World War; later apptd. comdt. Navy Yard, Norfolk, Va.; commanded second div. of battleships, U.S. Fleet; chief of staff U.S. Fleet; comdr. fourth cruiser div., U.S. Fleet; comdt. 9th Naval Dist.; comdr. base force, U.S. Fleet; comdt. 4th Naval Dist., Phila.; retired Jan. 2, 1939; now president Worcester (Mass.) Poly Institute, Worcester Chapter American Red Cross. Mem. Worcester Council of Boy Scouts; trustee Worcester Academy; dir. Worcester Community Chest. Naval Bd. Prodn. awards. World War II. Member United States Naval Inst., Am. Soc. Naval Engrs., American Society for Engineering Education, Am. Assn. for Advancement of Science, Hampton Roads Chemist Club, American Society of Mechanical Engineers, American Antiquarian Society, Worcester Engring. Society, Newcomen Society of England (American Branch). National Aeronautical Society, Engring. Society of Western Mass., Navy League of U.S., Naval Order of the U.S., Military Order of World War, United Spanish War Vets., Mil. Order Fgn. Wars, Phi Delta Theta (past president), Sigma Xi. Episcopalian. Clubs: Army and Navy (New Orleans); Worcester; Engineers (Phila.); Rotary, Lions. Home: 1 Drury Lane, Worcester 5, Mass. Died. Oct. 28, 1952; buried Arlington Nat. Cemetery.

COATES, EDWIN MORTON brig. gen.; b. New York, Jan. 29, 1836; s. Charles and Catherine (Staley) C.; ed. Albany (N.Y.) Acad.; m. Isaelta Stewart, Oct. 1882. Mem. Chicago Zouaves, Col. E.E. Ellsworth commdg., 1859-60; entered Union Army, Apr. 1861, as 1st lt. N.Y. Fire Zouaves; 2d lt. 2d N.Y. Dragoons, June 1861; 2d lt. 2d U.S. Cav., Aug. 5, 1861; transferred to 12th Inf., Sept. 20, 1861; 1st lt., Oct. 24, 1861; advanced through grades to col. 7th Inf., July 23, 1898; retired, Jan. 29, 1900; advanced to rank of brig. gen. retired, by act of Apr. 23, 1904. Bvtd. capt., Aug. 1, 1864, "for gallant services in battle of the Wilderness and during the campaign before Richmond." Died Sept. 13, 1913.

COBB, AMASA lawyer; b. Crawford Co., Ill., Sept. 27, 1823; s. John and Nancy (Briggs) C.; ed. Crawford Co., Ill., public schools; m. Dec. 26, 1849, Mrs. Sudduth (died 1896). Served in Mexican war, 6th regt., Ill. vols., 1 yr. as private soldier; served in both houses Wis. legislature, 2 yrs. each; was speaker lower house; col. 5th Wis. vol. inf., June 4, 1861-Dec. 27, 1862; comd. regt. in battle of Williamsburg, May 5, 1862; comd. Hancock's brigade at battle of Antietam, Sept. 17, 1862; raised and comd. 43rd regt. Wis. vols., Sept. 10, 1864 to July 7, 1865; received bvt. rank of brig. gen. for gallant and meritorious service at Williamsburg, Golden's farm, Malvern Hill and Antietam. Was elected to Congress 4 times, twice while in actual mil. service; mem. Congress, 1863-71; mayor of Lincoln, Neb., 1873; judge Supreme Court, Neb., 1878-92 (4 yrs. chief justice). Republican. Home: Los Angeles, Calif. Died 1905.

COBB, CHANDLER lawyer; b. Chicago, Apr. 18, 1887; s. Henry Ives and Emma Martin (Smith) C.; A.B., Harvard, 1907; reading, Oxford (Eng.) Univ., 1907-08; LL.B., New York Law Sch., 1910; m. Beatrice Carpenter, Dec. 20, 1910; children—Beatrice (Mrs. Alexander Loudon), Florence C. (Mrs. Thomas B. Husband). Admitted to New York, Federal bars, 1911; in practice, N.Y. City, 1911—; asst. U.S. Atty. for Southern Dist. of N.Y., 1917-19; comml. attache Am. Embassy, London, 1921-23, liaison attache on Settlement Brit. War Debt. 1922; gen. practice of law in Europe, 1932-40; mem. local draft bd., Selective Service System, N.Y. City, 1940-42, N.Y. City dir., Selective Service System, 1946—; mem. N.Y. State War Finance Com. and down-State chmn., Seventh War Loan, 1943-45; dir. Holland-Am. Mchts. Corp., Kreutoll Relization Corp., Nat. Varnished Products Corp. Served as maj., U.S.A., 1942-43. adminstr., N.Y. City Selective Service Hdqurs. Awarded Army Commendation Ribbon, NY State Conspicuous Service Cross, Congl. Selective Service Medal; officer Order of the Orange-Nassau (Netherlands). President and trustee, Protestant Epis. chs., Rome and Florence, Italy, Nice and Paris, France; mem. vestry. Am. Pro-Cathedral, Paris, 1937-46; mem. bd. and finance com., Fresh Air Assn. of St. John; chmn. exec. com., dir., Fedn. of Protestant Welfare Agencies. Mem. Am. C. of C. of France (sec., 1st v.p., 1936-38), Mil. Order of World Wars, N.Y. Soc. of Mil. and Naval Officers. Clubs: India House, Union, Harvard (N.Y.C.); Marlborough (London); Harvard of France (pres. 1938-40). Home: 49 E. 86th St. Office: 20 Exchange Pl., N.Y.C. 5. Died May 24, 1955.

COBB, DAVID army officer, congressman, jurist: b. Attleborough, Mass., Sept. 14, 1748; s. Thomas and Lydia (Leonard) C.; grad. Harvard, 1766. del. to Mass. Provincial Congress, 1775; commd. lt. col. Mass. Militia, 1777, brevetted brig. gen., 1783, commd. maj. gen., 1786; judge Bristol County (Mass.) Ct. of Common Pleas, 1784-96; speaker Mass. Ho. of Reps., 1789-93; mem. U.S. Ho. of Reps. (Federalist), from Mass. 3d Congress, 1793-95; pres. Mass. Senate, 1802-05; lt. gov. Mass., 1809; chief justice Hancock County, (Mass.), 1812; mem. Mass. Bd. of Mil. Defense, 1812. Died Taunton, Mass., Apr. 17, 1830; buried Plain Cemetery, Taunton.

COBB, ROBERT lawyer; b. Eddyville, Ky., May 21, 1836; academic edn.; studied law, Univ. of Va., 1855-56; m. Aug. 3, 1865, Monroe Co., Miss., Virginia, d. John A. and Mary Boone (Grimes) Walker. Practiced law in native town, 1858-61; volunteered, June, 1861, in Co. F, 3d Ky. Inf., C.S.A.; was elected first lieutenant, transferred to light arty. service, became capt. and for nearly 3 yrs. comd. Cobb's battery; commissioned maj. of art., Feb. 22, 1864, and comd. Cobb's battalion of art, until end of war; participated in 41 engagements during war; after war planted cotton in Miss., and engaged in business pursuits at Paducah, Ky., until 1885; removed to Tex. and established as lawyer. In 1892 apptd. maj.-gen. to command dept. of Northwest Tex., of United Confederate Veterans, and served as such 5 yrs. Address: Wichita Falls, Tex.

COBB, STEPHEN ALONZO congressman: b. Madison, Somerset County, Me., June 17, 1833; attended Beloit Coll. 2 years; grad. Brown U., 1858. Settled in Wyandotte, Kan., 1859, practiced law; entered Union Army, 1862; became capt. and commissary sgt. of Volunteers, 1864; brevetted maj., 1865; mayor Wyandotte, 1862, 68: mem. Kan. Senate, 1862, 69, 70; mem. Kan. Ho. of Reps., 1872, speaker; mem. U.S. Ho. of Reps. (Republican) from Kan., 43d Congress, 1873-75. Died Wyandotte (now part of Kansas City), Aug. 24, 1878: buried Oak Grove Cemetery, Kansas City, Kan.

COBB, THOMAS REED congressman, lawyer; b. Springville, Lawrence County, Ind., July 2, 1828; attended Ind. U.: studied law. Admitted to bar, 1851, practiced in Bedfort, Ind.: commd. maj. Ind. Militia, 1852; moved to Vincennes, Ind., 1867; mem. Ind. Senate, 1858-66; Democratic presdl. elector, 1868; pres. Ind. Dem. Conv., 1876; del. Nat. Dem. Conv., St. Louis, 1876; mem. U.S. Ho. of Reps. (Democrat) from Ind., 45th-49th congresses, 1877-87; became farmer; retired from public life. Died Vincennes, June 23, 1892; buried Old Vincennes Cemetery.

COBB, THOMAS REED ROOTES army officer, Confederate Legislator; b. Jefferson County, Ga., Apr. 10, 1823; s. John H. and Sarah (Rootes) C.; grad. U. Ga., 1841; m. Marion Lumpkin, at least 3 children, Callendar, Belle, Marion. Admitted to Ga. bar, 1842; advocated Ga.'s immediate secession upon Lincoln's election to Presidency; mem. Ga. Secession Conv.; Ga. del. to Montgomery Conv. of Seceding states, 1861; prin. contributor to the Confederate Constn., mem. Confederate Provisional Congress, 1861; commd. brig. gen. Confederate Army, participated in Battle of Fredericksburg (Va.). Author: Digest of the Laws of Georgia, 1851; Inquiry into the Law of Negro Slavery in the U.S., 1858; Historial Sketch of Slavery, 1859. Killed in Battle of Fredericksburg, Dec. 13, 1862.

COBURN, JOHN lawyer; b. Indianapolis, Ind., Oct. 27, 1825; s. Henry P. C.; grad. Wabash Coll., 1846, A.M., 1852; LL.D., 1898; studied law at Indianapolis; m. Caroline A. Test, Mar. 9, 1852. Mem. Ind. legislature, 1850-51; judge Court of Common Pleas, 1859-61; col. 33d regt., Ind. vols., Sept. 16, 1861-Sept. 20, 1864; bvt. brig. gen. for gallant and meritorious services; served in Army of the Cumberland; judge of circuit court, 1865-66; mem. Congress, 1867-75; mem. U.S. Hot Springs (Ark.) Commn., 1877-79; judge Supreme Court of Mont., 1884-86; Whig and Republican. Home: Indianapolis, Ind. Died 1908.

COCHEU, FRANK SHERWOOD army officer; b. Brooklyn, N.Y., Nov. 22, 1871; s. Theodore and Catharine Elizabeth (Benson) C.; grad. U.S. Mil. Acad., 1894; Army War Coll., 1908, 21, Gen. Staff Coll., 1919, Gen. Staff Sch., 1920; m. Kathleen Lacey, Aug. 4, 1897. Commd. 2d lt. inf., U.S.A., June 12, 1894; advanced through grades to maj. gen. of the line, Mar. 1934; col. N.A., brig. gen. U.S.A., World War. Participated in Santiago Campaign, 1898, Philippine Insurrection, 1899-1902; in France, 1918-19, battles Artois Sector, St. Mihiel and Meuse-Argonne offensives. Mem. Gen. Staff Corps, 1907-11, 1914-17, 1921-25; asst. dir. Army War Coll., 1908-11: asst. comdt. Int. Sch., 1925-27; retired, Nov. 30, 1935. Awarded D.S.M. (U.S.); Conspicuous Service Medal (N.Y. State). Mason (K.T.). Home: The Highlands, Washington. Address: War Dept., Washington. Died July 11, 1940.

COCHRAN, CLAUDE A. lawyer; b. Star, N.C., Jan. 27, 1884; s. D.C. and (Leach) C.; ed. U. N.C., class 1906; m. Margaret Reese, 1929. Admitted to N.C. bar, 1909, since practiced in Charlotte; mem. Cochran, McCleneghan & Miller; city atty. Charlotte, 1920-26, 1928-30. Capt., inf., U.S. Army, France, World War I.

Served as sec.-treas. Co-op. Nursing Assn.; chmn. Salvation Army Fund Drive, 1920; chmn. Ann. Red Cross Roll Call, 1943, chmn. local chpt. A.R.C. Mem. Am., N.C. bar assns., Mecklenburg County Tb and Health Assn. (1st pres.). Mason (32ff, Shriner, potentate 1935, life mem. Temple). Clubs: Charlotte Country (past pres.), Good Fellows, Manufacturers (past pres.). Home: 320 Feuton Pl., Charlotte. Office: Low Bldg., Charlotte, N.C. Died Jan. 26, 1958.

COCHRAN, JOHN surgeon; b. Sudsbury, Pa., Sept. 1, 1730; s. James and Isabella; m. Mrs. Gertrude Schuyler, Dec. 4, 1760. A founder N.J. Med. Soc., pres., 1769; apptd. physician surgeon gen. Middle Dept. Continental Army, by George Washington, 1777, later chief physician and loans for N.Y., 1785. Died Palatine, N.Y., Apr. 6, 1807.

COCHRAN, ROBERT LEROY ex-gov.; b. Avoca, Neb., Jan. 28, 1886; s. Charles A. and Jane (Wilkinson) C.; B.S. in C.E., U. Neb., 1910; LL.D., Midland Coll., 1938; m. Aileen Gantt, Mar. 18, 1919; children-Mary Aileen (Mrs. Lee Grimes), Robert LeRoy (lt. U.S. Armored Forces). Practiced with county surveyor, North Platte, Neb., July-Dec. 1910; with A.T.&S.F. R.R., 1911; county surveyor North Platte, 1912-16; state bridge insp., Neb., 1915-16; dept. state engr., 1917; dist. engr. State Dept. Pub. Works, Neb., 1919-22; state engr., 1923-34; elected gov. Neb. 1934, served 3 terms to 1941; chmn. govs. conf. and council state govts., 1937, 39; asst. commr. Fed. Pub. Housing Authority, 1942-43, commr., 1943-44; rep. Dir. gen. UNRRA, Mediterranean Theater, 1944-45; chief, civil works br. Bur. Budget U.S. Govt. 1945-47, 48-56; expert witness for Colo. River Bd. of Cal., 1956-57; receiver N. Loop River Pub. Power and Irrigation Dist., 1956-62; dep. chief Am. Mission to Greece, 1947. Enlisted U.S. Army, 1917; 1st lt., capt. A.E.F., Dec. 1917-Feb. 1919; hon. disch. as capt. C.A.C. Col., U.S. Army, 1941-42. Mem. Am. Soc. C.E., Am. Legion, Alpha Tau Omega (life). Democrat. Episcopalian. Elk (life), Mason (32ff, Shriner, K.T.). Clubs: University (Lincoln). Home: 3128 Cedar Av., Lincoln 2, Neb. Died Feb. 23, 1963; buried Lincoln Meml. Park Cemetery.

COCHRANE, EDWARD LULL ret. naval officer; b. Mare Island, Cal., Mar. 18, 1892; s. Brig. Gen. Henry Clay (U.S. Marine Corps) and Elizabeth (Lull) C.; student U. Pa., 1909-10; S.B. (with distinction), U.S. Naval Acad., 1914; post grad., 1916; M.S., Mass. Inst. Tech., 1920; at U.S. Naval War Coll., 1939; LL.D., Hahnemann Med. Coll., 1943; E.D. (hon), Poly. Inst. Bklyn., 1946; Stevens Inst. Tech., 1954; Sc.D. (hon.), Tufts Coll., 1950; m. Charlotte Osgood Wilson, June 3, 1916; children—Richard Lull (Comdr. United States Navy), Edward Lull, Jr. (lt., U.S.N.). Commissioned ensign U.S. Navy, 1914, and advanced through the grades to vice admiral, 1942; on U.S.S. Rhode Island, 1914-16; selected for post-grad. in naval constrn., 1915; assigned Phila. Navy Yards, 1917; in charge of constrn. of 2 battle cruisers, 1920-24; Bur. Constrn. and Repair, Navy Dept., 1924-29; submarine and general design; tech. adviser Internat. Conf. Safety of Life at Sea, London, 1929; in charge of design and constrn. submarines, Navy Yard, Portsmouth, N.H., 1929-33; Force constrn. staff, comdr. Scouting Force, U.S. Fleet, 1933-35; New Design Bur. Constrn. and Repair, Navy Dept., 1935-39; Bur. of Ships, Navy Dept., as hull asst. to head design div., 1939-40, also head preliminary design branch, 1941-42; asst. naval attache, Am. Embassy, 1940; chief of Bur. of Ships, Nov., 1942-Nov., 1946; chief Material Div., Navy Dept., 1946-47; ret.; professor of naval construction head dept. of naval architecture and marine engring., Mass. Inst. Tech., 1947-50; chmn. Fed. Maritime Board and Maritime Adminstr. Dept. of Commerce, 1950-52; dean engring. Mass. Inst. Tech., 1952-54, v.p. indsl. and governmental relations, 1954—. Awarded Mexican campaign medal, 1915; Victory medal World War I; Nat. Def. medal, 1944; Am. Def. medal, Asiatic-Pacific campaign medal, Am. Theatre medal, Victory medal, World War II; David W. Taylor medal for notable achievement in naval architecture and marine engring., 1945; Knight Comdr. Mil. Div., Order British Empire, Navy Distinguished Service Medal. Mem. Soc. Naval Architects and Marine Engrs., Am. Soc. Naval Engrs., British Inst. Marine Engrs., British Instn. Naval Architect. U. S. Naval Inst., Nat. Acad. Scis., Am. Acad. Arts and Scis., United Seaman's Service (pres. 1954), Am. br. Newcomen Soc. Eng. Clubs: Army and Navy, Chevy Chase (Washington); Country (Brookline, Mass.); Army and Navy Country (Arlington, Va.); University (N.Y.C.). Home 2 Larchwood Dr., Cambridge 38, Mass. Died Nov. 14, 1959; buried Arlington Nat. Cemetery.

COCHRANE, HENRY CLAY brig. gen.; b. Chester, Pa., Nov. 7, 1842; s. James L. and Sarah Jane (Gillespie) C.; ed. Upland Normal Sch. and Friends' Central High Sch., Phila.; m. Elizabeth F., d. Capt. E. P. Lull, U.S.N., June 30, 1887. Apptd. in naval service, Sept. 7, 1861; served in Civil War, in railroad strikes of 1877, Spanish-Am. War, Boxer compaign, China, 1900, and in P.I.; retired with rank of brig. gen., Mar. 10, 1905. Was present at bombardment of Alexandria, Egypt, by the British, 1882, and at coronation of Czar, Alexander III, Moscow, 1883; maj. of marine battalion that held the heights at Guantanamo, Cuba, June, 1898; detailed as gov. of Manzanillo; comd. 1st brigade of marines in P.I. and acted as gov. Peninsula of Cavite, 1900-01; comd. regt. marines in Boxer war in China. Decorated with Cross of Legion of Honor by Pres. Carnot of France for services at Universal Expn., 1889; has Civil War, Spanish War, China and Philippine medals. Republican. Episcopalian. Home: Chester, Pa. Died. Apr. 27, 1913.

COCHRANE, JOHN congressman; b. Palatine, N.Y., Aug. 27, 1813; s. Walter Livingson and Cornelia (Smith) C.; grad. Hamilton Coll., 1831. Admitted to N.Y. bar, 1834; surveyor Port of N.Y., 1852; mem. U.S. Ho. of Reps. from N.Y., 35th-36th congresses, 1857-61; commd. brig. gen. U.S. Volunteers, 1862, participated in battles of Fair Oaks, Malvern Hill, Antietam, Williamsport, Fredericksburg, under Gen. Couch; atty. gen. N.Y., 1863-65; nominated vice pres. U.S. on ticket with John C. Fremont for Pres., 1864; U.S. collector Internal Revenue, 1869; Mem. Soc. of Cincinnati, pres. until 1898; pres. Common Council, N.Y.C., 1872; chmn. N.Y. Delegation to Liberal Republican Nat. Conv., 1872. Died N.Y.C., Feb. 7, 1898; buried Rural Cemetery, Albany, N.Y.

COCKE, JOHN congressman; b. Brunswick, Nottoway County, Va., 1772; s. William Cocke; attended public schs. in Tenn.; studied law. Admitted to bar, 1793; practiced in Hawkins County; mem. Tenn. Ho. of Reps. 1796-96, 1807, 09, 12, 37, speaker, 1812, 37; mem. Tenn. Senate, 1799-1801, 43; served as maj. gen. Tenn. Volunteers in Creek War, 1813; served as col. regt. Tenn. riflemen under Gen. Andrew Jackson at New Orleans; mem. U.S. Ho. of Reps. from Tenn., 16th-19th congresses, 1819-27; became farmer; founded school for deaf-mutes, Knoxville, Tenn. Died Rutledge, Tenn., Feb. 16, 1854; buried Methodist Ch. Cemetery.

COCKE, JOHN HARTWELL planter, army officer; b. Surry County, Va., Sept. 19, 1780; s. John Hartwell and Elizabeth (Kennon) C.; grad. Coll. William and Mary, 1798; m. Ann Barraud, Dec. 25, 1802, several children including Philip St. George. Promoted new agrl. methods, founded agrl. socs., promoted steam navigation, various other pub. improvements; commd. brig. gen., commander Va. Militia guarding Richmond in War of 1812, 1814-15; served on Am. Bd. Commrs. for Fgn. Missions; sr. v.p. Am. Colonization Soc. from its orgn. to his death, 1819-66; elected pres. U.S. Temperance Soc., 1836; a founder U. Va., mem. bd. visitors, 1819-52. Died Fluvanna County, Va., July 1, 1866.

COCKE, PHILIP ST. GEORGE planter, army officer; b. Fluvanna County, Va., Apr. 17, 1809; s. John Hartwell and Ann (Barraud) C.; grad. U.S. Mil. Acad., 1832; m. Sally Bowdoin, June 4, 1834: 11 children. Owner 7 plantations in Va. and Miss.; served as 2d lt., adj., 2d U.S. Arty., 1832-33; pres. Va. Agrl. Soc., 1853-56; served 9 years on bd. Va. Mil. Inst., founded there 1st sch. of sci. agr. in Va.; commd. brig. gen. Confederate Army, 1861, assigned command of mil. dist. along Potomac. Author: Plantation and Farm Instruction, 1852; Address to the Virginia Farmer's Assembly, 1856. Died Powhatan County, Va., Dec. 26, 1861.

COCKE, WILLIAM army officer, senator; b. Amelia County, Va., 1748; s. Abraham Cocke; m. Sarah Maclin; m. 2d, Mrs. Kissiah Sims. Fought in Revolutionary War; mem. Va. Assembly, 1777, N.C. Legislature, 1778; leader attempt to establish separate state of Franklin, 1784-88, brig. gen. Militia of State of Franklin, 1784-88; mem. Tenn. Constl. Conv., 1796; mem. U.S. Senate from Tenn., 1796-97, 1799-1805; judge 1st Tenn. Circuit Ct., 1809-12, impeached, removed from judgeship, 1812; fought in wars against Seminole and Creek Indians, 1812-15; Indian agt. Chickasaw Nation, 1814-15; mem. Miss. Legislature, 1822; a founder U. Tenn. Died Columbus, Miss., Aug. 22, 1828; buried Columbus.

COCKE, WILLIAM HORNER educator; b. City Point, Va., Sept. 12, 1874; s. Henry Teller and Elizabeth Welsh (Horner) C.; C.E., Va. Mil. Inst., 1894; B.L., Washington U., 1898; Army Gen. Staff College, Langres, France, 1918; LL.D., Washington and Lee U., 1929; m. Anne Jeannette Owen, Dec. 20, 1905. Comdt. cadets and prof. mathematics, Kemper Mil. Acad., Booneville, Mo., 1894-97; practiced law. St. Louis, Mo., 1899-1907; founder, 1907, pres. until 1936, Southern Acid & Sulphyr Co. (formerly Commercial Acid Co.), St. Louis, Mo.; supt. Va. Mil. Inst., Oct. 1, 1924-July 1, 1929; apptd. mem. board visitors of same instn., 1930. Served as 1st lt. 4th Mo. Inf. (U.S. Vols.), Spanish-Am. War; maj. Inf., U.S.A., 1917-19, World War; brig. gen. Va. Volunteers, 1924; aide on staff gov. of Va., 1930. Chmn. Va. Assn. Against the Prohibition Amendment. Democrat. Episcopalian. Home: Claremont, Va. Died June 9, 1938.

COCKERILL, JOSEPH RANDOLPH congressman, lawyer, b. Loudoun County, Va., Jan. 2, 1818; attended public schs.; studied law. Moved to Scott Twp., Adams County, O., 1837, settled in Youngstown; taught sch.; county surveyor, 1840; admitted to bar, 1851, practiced in West Union, O.; clk. Ct. Common Pleas; mem. Ohio Ho. of Reps., 1853, 54, 68-71; mem. U.S. Ho. of Reps. (Democrat) from Ohio, 35th Congress, 1857-59; served as col. 70th Ohio Volunteer Inf. in Union Army during Civil War; brevetted brig. gen. of Volunteers, 1865. Died West Union, Oct. 23, 1875; buried West Union Cemetery.

CODD, LEO A., editor; b. Balt., Apr. 20, 1895; s. John and Amelia (Dittmar) C.; A.B., Loyola, 1916; A.M. Georgetown U., 1923, LL.B., 1922, LL.M., 1923, L.H.D., 1964; m. Gertrude Jane Callahan, Dec. 27, 1919. Asst. sec. Am. Ordnance Assn., 1923, sec., 1928, exec. v.p., 1940-64; editor Ordnance mag., 1928-65, contbg. editor, 1945-71, instr., Georgetown Coll., 1917, Cyrus Fogg Brackett lectr., Princeton, 1937. Served as chemist, Ordnance Dept., U.S. Army, World War 1; exec. asst. to chief of ordnance, AUS, World War II; capt., Ordnance Res., 1920, col. 1943-71. Decorated Legion of Merit. Mem. D.C., Md. bar assns. Roman Catholic. Clubs: Army and Navy (Washington); University (N.Y.). Author: American Industry and the National Defense, 1937. Lectr. in U.S., Can. and Eng. Home: Washington DCDied Sept. 4, 1971; buried Oak Hill Cemetery, Washington DC

CODE, JAMES A., JR., telephone co. exec., ret. army officer; b. San Francisco, Jan. 17, 1893; s. James Arthur and Katherine (Shaw) C.; B.S., U.S. Mil. Acad., 1917; M.S., Yale, 1920, E.E., 1933; postgrad. Ohio State U., 1920-23, U. Cal., 1934-38; m. Isabelle Elizabeth Black, Jan. 17, 1929. Commd. 2d lt., C.A.C., U.S. Army, 1917, and advanced to capt., 1930; maj. S.C., 1932, lt. col., 1940, col., 1941; brig. gen., dep. chief signal officer, 1942, maj. gen., asst. chief signal officer, 1942-45; chief signal officer, ETO (France), 1945; ret. 1945. Chmn. bd. Telephone Services, Inc.; dir., v.p. Asso. Tel. & Tel. Co. (Wilmington, Del.); chief exec. Gary Group; v.p., dir. Anglo-Canadian Telephone Co., Automatic Elec. Co. (1946), Internat. Automatic Elec. Corp., Pan-Am. Tel. & Tel. Co., Continental Telephone Co., Dominican Dir. Co., Can., Tex., Home and Citizens Telephone Cos., Allied Syndicate, Inc., Gen. and Telephone Investments, Inc., Ohio Consol., Ill. Telephone Co.; v.p., dir. Gary Services and Investment Co., Tel. Bond & Share Co., Linwood Investment Co., Antel Services, Ltd., Asso. Telephone Services Ltd.; dir. various other telephone cos.; v.p., trustee Pt. Roberts & Gulf Telephone Co.; cons. Automatic Electric Co., Diablo Labs., 1963, Lenkurt Electric Co., 1959. Decorated Bronze Star medal, D.S.M.; Croix de Guerre, L'Ordre de la Legion d'Honneur (France), Commandeur de l'Ordre de la Couroune (Belgium). Asso. mem. Am. Inst. E.E.; sr. mem. Inst. Radio Engrs.; mem. Armed Forces Commn., Am. Soc. Legion of Honor, West Point Soc., Yale Alumni Assn., Army Athletic Assn., Assn. Grads. U.S.M.C., Am. Signal Corps Assn., Am. Legion, Mil. Order of World Wars, S.A.R., Scabboard and Blade, Pi Tau, Pi Sigma. Republican. Episcopalian. Clubs: Olympic; Army and Navy; Lake Shore: South Shore Country; Chicago; University. Address: Palo Alto CA Died Oct. 29, 1971.

CODMAN, JULIAN lawyer; b. Cotuit, Mass., Sept. 21, 1870; s. Charles Russell and Lucy L. P. (Sturgis) C.; A.B., Harvard, 1892, LL.B., 1895; m. Norah Chadwick, Apr. 27, 1897; children - Lucy Sturgis, Hester Schuyler. Admitted to Mass. bar, 1895, and then practiced at Boston; with C. P. Greenough, 1897-1902; mem. Warren, Perry & Codman, 1902-10, Wheelwright & Codman, 1910-26; then asso. with David F. Sibley; pres. Fabreeka Belting Co. Commd. Q.M. Dept., U.S.A., 1916; capt. Q.M. Dept., World War, 1917-19; with A.E.F. 9 mos.; lt. col. J. A. Gen's. Dept., O.R.C., 1924-26. Gen. counsel for A.F. of L. and all assns. opposed to prohibition in hearings before House and Senate coms. on bills for the modification of the Volstead Act. Home: Boston, Mass. Died Dec. 29, 1932.

CODY, WILLIAM FREDERICK scout, showman; b. Scott Co., Ia., Feb. 26, 1846; father killed in the "Border war". In Kan.; pony express rider, 1860-61; Govt. scout and guide and mem. 7th Kan. Cav., 1861-65; m. Louisa Frederici, Mar. 6, 1866. Contracted to furnish Kan. Pacific Ry. with the buffalo meat required to feed the laborers engaged in construction, and in 18 months (1867-68) killed 4,280 buffaloes, earning name of "Buffalo Bill," by which he is best known; govt. scout and guide, 1868-72, serving in operations against Sioux and Cheyenne; mem. Neb. Legislature, 1872; joined 5th Cav. as scout, 1876. In battle of Indian Creek killed Yellow Hand, Cheyenne chief, in hand-to-hand fight; 1890-91, gen. Neb. N.G., Sioux outbreak; headquarters Pine Ridge Agency; Battle of Wounded Knee. At head of "Wild West Show," 1883 - . Judge-advocate-gen. Wyo. N.G.; pres. Shoshone Irrigation Co. Co-author: The Great Salt Lake Trail. Home: Cody, Wyo. Died Jan. 10, 1917.

COE, FRANK WINSTON army officer; b. Kan., Nov. 27, 1870; grad. U.S. Mil. Acad., 1892, Arty. Sch., 1896; m. 1895, Anne Chamberlaine; 1 son, William Chamberlaine; m. 2d, 1923, Martha Pratt Donnellan, Commissioned add. 2d lt. 1st Artillery, June 11, 1892; promoted through grades to colonel, May 15, 1917; brig. gen., U.S. Army, Aug. 5, 1917; maj. gen. and chief of Coast Arty., May 24, 1918; retired, Mar. 1926. Instr. mathematics, U.S. Mil. Acad., 1898-1902; adjutant U.S. Mil. Acad., 1903-07: asst. to Chief Coast Arty., Washington, 1908-09; apptd. dir. Coast Arty. Sch., Monroe, Va., 1909; chief of staff, Western Dept., San Francisco, 1916; chief of staff, First Div., A.E.F., June-

Aug. 1917; comdr. 30th Brigade, Heavy Arty., A.E.F., Sept. 1917-May 1918. D.S.M., 1919. Address: War Dept., Washington, D.C.* Died May 25, 1947.

COE, HENRY CLARKE gynecologist; b. Cincinnati, Feb. 21, 1856; s. Erastus Pease and Mary (Ross) C.; A.B., Yale, 1878, A.M., 1881; M.D., Harvard, 1881, Columbia, 1882; M.R.C.S., Eng., 1884; m. Sara Livingston Werden; children - Fordyce B., Henry C., Arthur P. Practiced at N.Y. City from 1884; prof. gynecology, Univ. and Bellevue Hosp. Med. Coll. (New York U.), 1896-1915 (emeritus); consulting surgeon to Bellevue, Woman's Memorial, Polyclinic, and Beth Israel hosps. Col. M.C.U.S.A., 2 yrs. foreign service in war; then col. U.S.A., Ret. Fellow Am. Coll. Surgeons. Republican. Episcopalian. Home: New York, N.Y. Died Apr. 21, 1940.

COFER, JOHN DALY, lawyer; b. Gainesville, Tex., Mar. 11, 1898; s. Robert Emmet and Corinne (Able) C.; A.B., U. Tex., 1919, LL.B., 1921; M. George Hume, Sept. 28, 1922; children—George Hume, Patricia (Mrs. Frances A. Brogan, dec.). Admitted to Tex. bar, 1921, practiced in Austin, 1921-71; spl. justice, Supreme Ct., Tex., 1928; spl. counsel Anti-Trust Litigation, Tex., 1931-38. Mem. Nat. Democratic Advisory Committee Tex., 1952-56; chief counsel United States Senate Preparedness Investing Sub-Committee, 1956. Entered the U.S. Army, 1942; mil. gov., Fuerth-Rothenburg, Bavaria, 1945-46; member Gen. Mil. Govt. Ct., Bavaria, 1945-46. Charter mem. World Peace through Law Center. Awarded Ribbon, World War I; 2 Theatre. Occupation ribbons; 4 Battle Stars, Bronze Star medal, World War II. Mem. Am., Tex., Travis Co. bar assns., Delta Sigma Rho, Sigma Nu. Democrat. Meth. Club: Austin. Home: Austin TX Died Feb. 28, 1971; buried Oakwood Cemetery, Austin TX

COFER, MARTIN HARDIN army officer, jurist; b. Elizabethtown, Ky., Apr. 1, 1832; s. Thomas and Mary (Hardin) C.: m. Mary E. Bush, 1853; s. Thomas and Mary (Hardin) C.; m. Mary E. Bush, 1853. Admitted to Ill. bar. 1856; editor Elizabethtown Democrat; lt. col. 6th Ky. Inf., Confederate Army, 1861-64; made provost marshal Confederate Army of Tenn., 1864; judge Circuit Ct., Ky., 1870-74; asso. justice Ky. Ct. Appeals, 1874-81, chief justice, 1881. Author: A Supplemental Digest of Decisions of the Court of Appeals of Kentucky, 1853-67, published 1867 (standard authority on judicial procedure in Ky.). Died Frankfort, Mar. 22, 1881.

COFFEY, JOHN WILL army officer; b. N.Y.C., Jan. 12, 1897; B.S., U.S. Mil. Acad., 1917. grad. Ordnance Sch., 1923; Command and Gen. Staff Sch., 1933; AC Tactical Sch., 1939; Army War Coll., 1940. Commd. 2d lt. CAC, 1917; transferred to Ordnance and advanced through the grades to brig. gen., 1943; prof. ordnance U.S. Mil. Acad. Address: Ordnance Dept., Indianatown Gap, Pa. Deceased; buried Mil. Cemetery, West Point, N.Y.

COFFEY, ROBERT LEWIS, JR. ex-congressman; b. Chattanooga, Tenn., Oct. 21, 1918; s. Robert Lewis and Curry Ethel (Brindley) C.; student U.Pitts., 1935-38, Pa. State Coll., 1938-39, AC Advanced Flying Sch., 1939-40, Command and Gen. Staff Coll., 1943; m. E. Eileen Mercado-Parra, Oct. 15, 1942; children—Robert Lewis, Eileen Maria, David Mario. Coal miner, track worker, shot firer, motorman, in coal mines, 3 yrs.; mining engr., coal inspector, 1 yr. mil. air attache, U.S. Embassy, Chile, 1946-48; mem. 81st Congress, 26th Dist., Pa. Served from 2d lt. to col. USAF, 9 yrs.; active as col. in USAF Res. Decorated Distinguished Flying Cross, (3 times), Chilean Order of Merit. Mem. Am. Legion, Am. Vets., Vets Foreign Wars, Officers Reserve Assn.. Clubs: Army and Navy; North Fork Country. Home: Creek Pkwy., Silver Spring, Md. Office: House Office Bldg., Washington. Died April 21, 1949; buried Arlington Nat. Cemetery.

COFFIN, SIR ISAAC naval officer; b. Boston, May 16, 1759; s. Nathaniel and Elizabeth (Barnes) C.; m. Elizabeth Greenly, Mar. 1811. Entered Royal Navy, 1773, lt., 1778, capt. ship Shrewsbury, 1782; served under Lord Rodney in victory over Count de Grase, 1782; apptd. rear adm., 1804; created baronet, 1804; commd. vice adm., 1808, full adm., 1814; mem. Brit. Parliament, 1818; philanthropic efforts include founding Coffin Sch., Nantucket, Mass., 1827. Died Cheltenham, Eng., July 23, 1839.

COFFIN, JOHN Loyalist; b. Boston, 1756; s. Nathaniel and Elizabeth (Barnes) C.; m. Ann Mathews, 1 dau., Judity. Apptd. ensing Brit. Army by Gen. Gage for gallantry at Battle of Bunker Hill, 1775; organized and commanded Orange Grangers in battles of L.I. and Germantown; with N.Y. Volunteers (Loyalist) at battles of San Lucie, Bryars Creek, 1778, 79, Camden, 1780, Hampton, Hobkerks Hill, Eutaw Springs, 1781; commd. col., 1797, maj. gen., 1803, gen., 1819; mem. Canadian Assembly; chief magistrate Kings County (N.B., Can.); mem. Kings County Council. Died Kings County, June 12, 1838.

COFFIN, LEWIS AUGUSTUS JR., architect; b. N.Y.C., July 21, 1892; s. Lewis A. and Grace (Geer) C.; grad. Choate Sch., 1908; B.A., Columbia, 1912, grad. Archt. Sch., 1914; m. Lois G. Smith, Oct. 6, 1925; children-Joan Emory (Mrs. Gordon Buchaman Leib), Lewis A. III. Founding partner firm Polhemus & Coffin, N.Y.C., 1919-. Served to capt. F.A., U.S. Army, World War I; AEF in France, Recipient medals of Merit, Soc. Beaux Arts Architects, 1913, 14. Mem. Delta Phi. Club: Union (N.Y.C.). Prin. works include: office bldg., 232 E. 33d St., Doctors office bldg., 150 E. 54th St. (both N.Y.C.), various bldgs. Choate Sch., Wallingford, Conn., Mil. Park Bldg., Newark, N.J., Helen Hartley Geer Meml. Gateway, Barnard Coll., N.Y.C.; residences for Harry F. Guggenheim (Charleston, S.C.), Mrs. Daniel Guggenheim (Sands Point Port Washington, L.I.), Roger Straus residence, Kenneth Taylor residence (both N.Y.C.), Mrs. Drexel Dahlgren residence (Newport, R.I.), L. Gordon Hamersley residence (N.Y.C.) George Vanderhoef residence (Sea Island, Ga.), numerous others. Author: Small French Buildings, 1921; Colonial Houses, 1919; The Fog Boat, 1957. Home: 163 E. 81st St., N.Y.C. 10028. Deceased.

COFFMAN, DE WITT naval officer; b. Shenandoah Co., Va., Nov. 28, 1854; grad. U.S. Naval Acad., 1876; married; 1 son, Richard Boush. Ensign, July 10, 1879; promoted through grades to vice adm., June 19, 1916. Served on Terror during Spanish-Am. War; comd. Boston, 1905-07; insp. charge naval magazine, Fort Mifflin, Pa., 1907-08; in charge naval magazine, St. Jullen's Creek, 1908-09; comd. New Jersey, 1909-11; comdt., Navy Yard, Boston, Mar. 18-Nov. 6, 1914, Naval War College, Newport, Nov. 7-Dec. 3, 1914; comdr. 3d Div. Atlantic Fleet to Apr. 15, 1916, 6th Div. Atlantic Fleet to June 19, 1916; promoted vice admiral, June 19, 1916, and battleship squadron comdr. Atlantic Fleet (comdr. Atlantic Fleet, Aug.-Oct. 22, 1917); comd. Battleship Force Two until Aug. 30, 1918; comd. 5th Naval Dist. and Naval Operating Base, Hampton Roads, Va.; retired by opeation of law, Nov. 28, 1918; commd. vice adm., retired, June 21, 1930. Mem. Bd. of Awards, Medals and Honors. Navy Dept., until Oct. 30, 1919. Died June 27, 1932.

COFFMAN, RAY HAROLD govt. ofcl.; b. Spearville, Kan., Sept. 27, 1918; s. Harold Coe and Aletha (Morrow) C.; B.A. with honors, Swarthmore Coll., 1940; student Nat. Inst. Pub. Affairs, Washington 1940-41, Am. U., 1947-50; m. Beverly Ann Gorman, Mar. 4, 1946; children-Terrianne Marie (foster dau.), Harold Stephen. Economist, Dept. Agr., 1940-41; tng. analyst VA 1946-49; chief staff development br. Dept. Health, Edn. and Welfare, 1949-54, dep. exec. sec., 1954-55, mgmt. adviser Office of Se., 1955-56; dep. chief pub. administrn. division U.S. Operations Mission to Iran, 1956-60, also Mission to Pakistan, 1960-62, chief pub. administrn. div., 1958-. Chmn. citizens adv. council Arlington County Sch. Bd. Served from pvt. to capt., AUS, 1941-46. Decorated Bronze Star medal; Rockefller fellow, 1940-41. Mem. Am. Soc. Pub. Administrn., Soc. Personnel Administrn., Soc. Advancement Mgmt., Internat. Inst. Administrv. Scis., Adult Edn. Assn. Unitarian (chmn. bd. trustees 1954-55). Author monographs, articles on supervision and mgmt. Home: care Dr. H. C. Coffman, 2380 Alta Vista Dr., Vista, Cal. 92083. Office: International Cooperation Administrn., Washington 25. Died Apr. 7, 1962; buried Arlington Nat. Cemetery, Arlington, Va.

COGGESHALL, CHESTER, physician; b. Champaign, Ill., Apr. 27, 1909; s. Trovalo Chester and Jessie (McCann) C.; student Knox Coll., 1926-27, U. Chgo., 1927-29, Cambridge (Eng.) U., 1930-31; B.S., U. Ill., 1933, M.D., 1936; m. Marion Frances Campbell, June 7, 1938; children—John Campbell, Susan Campbell (Mrs. George P. Adinamis), Sarah Campbell (Mrs. Gene P. Stute), Marion Campbell (Mrs. Don P. Schmidt). Intern, Presbyn.-St. Luke's Hosp., Chgo., 1936-37, resident in medicine, 1937, sr. attending staff medicine, until 1970; Joslin fellow diabetes New Eng. Deaconess Hosp., Boston, 1938-39; sr. attending staff medicine Cook County Hosp., Chgo., 1946-51; asso. medicine Northwestern U., 1946-70; asst. clin. prof. medicine U. Ill. Med. Sch., 1970; med. dir. Arthur Andersen & Co. Med. cons. various indsl. corps. Served to lt. col., M.C., USAAF, 1942-46. Diplomate Am. Bd. Internal Medicine. Mem. Am., Chgo. (founder, dir.) diabetes assns., Chgo. Med. Soc., Am. Heart Assn., Chgo. Inst. Medicine, A.A.A.S., A.M.A., Am. Legion, Sigma Xi, Beta Theta Pi. Home: Chicago IL Died June 2, 1970; buried Glen Oaks Cemetery, Westchester IL

COGGESHALL, GEORGE sea captain; b. Milford, Conn., Nov. 2, 1784; s. William and Eunice (Mallett) C.; m. Sarah; m. 2d, Elizabeth. Received 1st command, 1809, sea capt., nearly 26 years; capt. privateers David Porter and Lev, during War of 1812. Author: Voyages to Various Parts of the World, 1851; History of the American Privateers and Letters-of-Marque, 1856. Died Milford, Aug. 6, 1861.

COGHLAN, JOSEPH BULLOCK naval officer; b. Frankfort, Ky., Dec. 9, 1844; s. Cornelius and Lavinia (Fouke) C.; apptd. to U.S. Naval Acad. from Ill., 1860, graduated 1863. Promoted ensign, May 28, 1863; advanced through grades to rear adm., Apr. 11, 1902. Served Sacramento spl. service, 1863-65; Brooklyn, Brazilian Squadron, 1865-67; training-ship Portsmouth, 1868; Hydrographic Office, 1871-73; sick leave, 1873-74; comd. Saugus, 1875-76, Colorado, 1877, Monongahela, 1877-79, receiving-ship Independence, 1879-82, Adams, 1883-84; Navy Yard, Mare Island, 1886-88; comd. Mohican, 1888-90; insp. ordnance, Navy Yard, League Island, 1891-94; light-house insp. 8th dist., 1894-97; comd. Richmond, Feb., Mar., 1897; comd. Raleigh, Asiatic Fleet, during war with Spain, 1898; participated in battle of Manila Bay, May 1, 1898; advanced 6 numbers in rank for eminent and conspicuous conduct in battle of Manila Bay; comdt., Naval Sta., Puget Sound, 1899-1900; Naval War Coll., 1901; capt. of yard, Navy Yard, New York, 1901-02; 2d in command of N. Atlantic Fleet, 1902-04; comdt., Navy Yard, New York 1904-07; retired, Dec. 9, 1906. Died 1908.

COGSWELL, JAMES KELSEY naval officer; b. Milwaukee, Sept. 27, 1847; s. George and Celestia Anne Jeannette (Stone) C.; ed. Milwaukee Univ., St. Aloysius Acad. and pub. schs., 1855-60, Racine Coll. Grammar Sch., 1860-62, U.S. Naval Acad. at Newport, R.I., and Annapolis, lfd., grad. 1868; m. Annie Miller Hatch, July 16, 1884. Midshipman, S. Pacific Sta., U.S.S. Powhatan, 1869; ensign U.S.S. Saginaw, 1870-71, wrecked on Ocean Island, Pacific Ocean; master on Saranae and flagship Pensacola, Pacific Sta.; promoted in turn to lt., lt. comdr.; served on Ticonderoga, Essex, Kearsarge, Tallapoosa, Marion on N. and S. Atlantic Stas; shore duty at Torpedo Sta., Newport, R.I., and at Hydrographic Office, Washington; Portsmouth (N.H.) Navy Yard, ins. ordnance S. Boston Iron Works, Navy Yard, Washington; U.S. Battleship Oregon, 1897-98; promoted comdr., 1899; lighthouse insp., 1st dist.; comdr. Marietta and Isla de Luzon, Asiatic Sta., Philippine Islands; promoted capt., 1904; comd. U.S.S. Cleveland, N. Atlantic Sta., 1903-04; retired with rank of rear-admiral, 1904. Advanced 5 numbers for service as exec. officer on U.S.S. Oregon in Spanish War and battle of Santiago. Episcopalian. Democrat. Home: Portsmouth, N.H. Died 1908.

COGSWELL, WILLIAM congressman, lawyer; b. Bradford, Mass., Aug. 23, 1838; attended Phillips Acad., Andover, Mass., also Dartmouth; grad. Dane Law Sch., Harvard, 1860. Admitted to bar, practiced in Salem, Mass.; served in Union Army in Civil War; commd. capt. 2d Regt. Mass. Volunteer Inf., 1861, lt. col., 1862, col., 1863, brevetted brig. gen. of Volunteers, 1864; mayor Salem, 1867-69, 73, 74; mem. Mass. Ho. of Reps., 1870, 71, 81-83; mem. Mass. Senate, 1885, 86; del. Nat. Republican Conv., Mpls., 1892; mem. U.S. Ho. of Reps. (Rep.) from Mass., 50th-54th congresses, 1887-95. Died Washington, D.C., May 22, 1895: buried Harmony Grove Cemetery, Salem.

COGSWELL, WILLIAM STERLING lawyer; b. Jamaica, N.Y., Dec. 29, 1840; s. William Johnson and Alma Canfield (Sterling) C.; A.B., Trinity Coll., Conn., 1861, A.M., 1867; m. Henrietta Spader, Apr. 18, 1872. First lt. Co. I, 5th Conn. Inf., July 22, 1861; detailed to signal service, Aug. 1861; capt. Nov. 1861; major, Aug. 1863; lt. colonel, Nov. 1864; not mustered as lt. col. because regt. then had less than requisite number of men; bvtd. lt. col. U.S.V.; mustered out, Aug. 1865; served under Banks until Antietam, then in Army of Potomac until after Gettysburg; transferred to Army of Cumberland, 1863; with Thomas until after capture of Atlanta; went with Sherman to the Sea and through the Carolinas to Raleigh. Engaged in law practice, in Brooklyn, N.Y., — until 1899; then in New York (Manhattan). Pres. Maple Grove Cemetery Assn.; commr. of taxes of City of New York, 1902-04. Episcopalian. Republican. Trustee Trinity Coll., Brooklyn Law Library; mem. chapter of the Cathedral, Diocese of L.I. Home: Jamaica, L.I., N.Y. Died July 18, 1935.

COHEN, IRVIN JOSEPH, hosp. adminstr.; b. Bklyn., June 5, 1908; s. Louis J. and Anna S. (Cohen) C.; Ph.G., U. Md., 1926, M.D., 1930; m. Elsa Bondy Kaufman, Sept. 2, 1928; children—Barbara Louise (Mrs. Thomas Noel Casselman), Abby Ruth (Mrs. Marius Clarke Smith). Intern, Mass. Gen. Hosp., 1930-31; asst. resident pediatrics Children's Hosp., Phila., 1931-32; resident pediatrics Beth-El Hosp., Bklyn., 1932-33; exec. physician Bklyn. Hebrew Orphanage, 1933-35; practice medicine, specializing in pediatrics, Bklyn., 1935-42; asst. chief, chief profl. services VA Hosp., Bronx, N.Y., 1946-52; dir. VA Hosp., Balt., 1952-54; dir. hosps. VA., Washington, 1954-56, dir. hosps., clinics, 1956-59, asst. chief med. dir. profl. services, 1959-62; exec. v.p. Maimonides Med. Center, Bklyn., 1962-70; prof., chmn. health care and hosp. adminstrn. program Coll. Health Related Professions, State U. N.Y. Downstate Med. Center, 1967-70; VA rep. Intrgovtl. Working Group on Aging, 1956-59; VA rep. Fed. Council Aging, 1959-60; cons. Welfare Fedn. Cleve., 1961-66, Social Security Administrn., Washington, 1965-70; adv. council for extended care services VA, 1966-70; adv. com. on comprehensive ambulatory care N.Y. City Department of Health, 1967-70. Mem. joint com. Am. Hosp. Assn. and Nat. Assn. Social Workers. Served to maj., M.C., AUS, 1942-46. Recipient Meritorious Service award VA, 1959, Exceptional Service award, 1961. Diplomate Am. Bd. Pediatrics. Fellow A.C.P.; mem. A.M.A., Am., Greater N.Y. (bd. govs. 1965-68) hosp. assns., Nat. Assn. Social Workers (chmn. joint com. 1963-69), Am. Pub. Health Assn. Home: Rockville MD Died Oct. 29, 1970; cremated.

COHEN, JOHN SANFORD editor; b. Augusta, Ga., Feb. 26, 1870; s. Philip Lawrence and Ellen Gobert (Wright) C.; prep. edn., Richmond Acad. (Augusta, Ga.), Shenandoah Valley Acad.; U.S. Naval Acad., 1885-68; LL.D., Washington and Lee U., 1924; m. Julia Lowry Clarke, Nov. 11, 1897; children - John Sanford, Mary Clarke, Began newspaper work on Augusta Chronicle, later on staff New York World; war corr. Spanish-Am. War, sailing with fleet under Admiral Bob Evans; identified with Atlanta Journal most of time, 1890, editor, 1917-, also pres. Atlanta Journal Co.; served as Washington corr. and spl. writer on politics. Commd. 1st lt. Co. A, 3d Ga. U.S. Vol. Inf., 1898, Spanish-Am. War; promoted capt. and maj.; was with Army of Occupation in Cuba. Originator Nat. Highway, built under joint supervision of Atlanta Journal and New York Herald, from N.Y. City to Jacksonville, Fla.; aided building of "Greater Emory University," Atlanta, and refounding Oglethorpe U., Atlanta; patron of art and music; dir. Atlanta Music Festival Assn.; trustee Georgia School of Technology. Mem. Dem. Nat. Com. from Ga., Apr. 1924 - . Apptd. U.S. senator to fill vacancy caused by death of William J. Harris, Apr. 25, 1932, term ending Jan. 10, 1933; vice chmn. Dem. Nat. Com., 1932 - . Episcopalian. Mason. Home: Atlanta, Ga. Died May 13, 1935.

COHN, ALFRED EINSTEIN physician; b. N.Y. City, Apr. 16, 1879; s. Abraham and Maimie (Einstein) C.; A.B., Columbia, 1900; M.D., Coll. Physicians and Surgeons (Columbia), 1904, D.Sc. (hon.), 1940; studied U. of Freiburg, U. of Vienna and Univ. Coll., London; m. Ruth Walker Price, Apr. 24, 1911. In practice in N.Y. City, 1909-11; with Rockefeller Inst. for Med. Research since 1911, mem. since 1920, mem. emeritus since 1944. Lt. Col. M.C., U.S. Army, cons. in cardio vascular diseases, 1918; served in France. Mem. bd. of govs. N.Y. Tuberculosis and Health Assn., 1925-45; chmn. of com. on research N.Y. Heart Assn., 1921-48 (mem. advisory commn. on research 1946-48); councillor to VA, Washington, 1921-46; member executive committee group on adult edn. Carnegie Corp., 1924-26; member Lasker Found., 1928-40; mem. China Med. Board, 1934-45; mem. Com. on Library, 1934-41; member bd. of editors Bulletin of N.Y. Acad. of Medicine; mem. Am. Com. on Refugee Scholars, Writers and Artists (treas. from 1945); mem. med. bd. Irvington House, Irvington-on-Hudson, 1930-45; chairman subcom. on heart diseases and rheumatic fever, N.Y. World's Fair, 1937-40. Mem. exec. committee Internat. Student Service, 1934-42; mem. bd. directors, sec.-treas., Student Service of America, Incorporated, 1943-47; member Club for Research on Ageing, from 1939; vice pres. Com. for Nat. Morale, 1940-42; chmn. exec. com., 1942-49; chmn. science com. Research Council of Dept. of Hosps., New York, 1935-51, treas., 1943-51. Spl adviser Board of Economic Warfare, 1942-44; mem. Health Com. Office of Foreign Relief and Rehabilitation Operations, 1943-44; bd. dirs., Iranian Inst. and Sch. Asiatic Studies, 1944-49, pres., 1947-49; bd. dirs. Sydenham Ins., 1947-48; member health committee American Jewish Joint Distribution Committee since 1944; Council on Foreign Relations since 1946. Visiting prof. medicine, Union Med. Coll., Peking, China spring of 1925. Fellow N.Y. Academy of Medicine; mem. Am. Soc. Pharmacology and Experimental Therapeutics, Am. Assn. Hist. Medicine, Assn. Am. Phys., Am. Assn. Anatomists, Am. Physiol. Soc., Am. Assn. Pathol. and Bacteriol., Am. Soc. Clin. Investigation, Am. Med. Assn., Botanical Soc. of Am. (physiol. sect.), Hist. of Science Soc., Harvey Soc. (pres. 1930), Internat. Assn. Geographical Pathology, New York Academy of Sciences, So. for Experimental Biology and Medicine (councillor 1929-33). A.A.A.S., Am. Assn. Adult Edn., Am. Soc. for Research in Psychomatic Medicine, N.Y. Scientists Assn., since 1945. Am. Assn. on Indian Affairs, 1945-47. Author: Medicine, Science and Art, 1931; Minerva's Progress, 1946; No Retreat from Reason, 1948; The Burden of Diseases in the United States (with Claire Lingg), 1950; also about 180 med. investigations. Home: 200 E. 66th St., N.Y. C. 21. Died July 20, 1957.

COLBERN, WILLIAM H. army officer; b. Mo., June 26, 1895; grad. F.A. Sch., 1924, Cav. Sch., 1925. Polish Cav. Sch., 1932, Command and Gen. Staff Sch., 1937; commd. 2d lt. Inf., 1917; transferred to F.A. as capt., 1923, advanced through grades to brig. gen, 1942; served on Gen. Staff Corps, 1939-40. Address: Field Artillery, Fort McClellan, Ala. Died Apr. 30, 1959.

COLBURN, ALBERT E. army officer; brig. gen., May, 1942. Address: Camp Hulen, Tex. Deceased.

COLBY, HARRISON GRAY OTIS rear adm.; b. New Bedford, Mass., Jan. 28, 1846; s. Harrison Gray Otis and Jane Standish (Parker) C.; grad. U.S. Naval Acad., 1867; m. Mary Catherine Thompson, Apr. 20, 1881 (dec.); 1 son, Francis Thompson. Promoted through grades to capt., June 18, 1902; rear adm. and retired, Jan. 28, 1908. Served on U.S.S. Dakotah during Civil War; comdr. U.S.S. Hannibal and 2d Dist. coast defense, also selecting proper vessels for the govt. to purchase during Spanish-Am. War; capt. of Olympia; comdr. European Squadron, 1904-05; in command cruiser div. N. Atlantic Fleet, winter, 1904-05; comdr. spl. squadron to Havana, Mar. 1905. Was exec. officer yacht "America" in race for the Queen's Cup with the "Cambrial" and other yachts; afterwards in command of "America"; comdr. U.S. Coast and Geod. Survey schooner "Eagre" (late "Mohawk" and steamer "Blake"; then hydrographic insp. of U.S. Coast and Geod. Survey; insp. 2d Light House Dist. With Mrs. Colby worked in Paris for Am. Fund for French Wounded and Am. Red Cross, 1916-18; ordered to active duty U.S.N., Sept. 1918. Home: Boston, Mass. Died Nov. 3, 1926.

COLBY, LEONARD WRIGHT soldier, lawyer; b. Ashtabula Co., O., Aug. 5, 1864; s. Rowell and Abigail (Livingston) C.; A.B. and C.E., U. of Wis., 1871, LL.B., 1872, A.M., 1874; m. 2d, Marie C. Miller; 1 son, Paul Livingston. Judge of 18th Jud. Dist. of Neb.; asst. atty. gen. of U.S., 1890-93; mem. Neb. Senate, 2 terms. Republican. Pvt. Co. B, 8th Ill. Inf., June 12, 1864-Oct. 16, 1865; served in Sioux Indian campaign, 1890-91, comdg. brigade of Neb. troops; lt. to brig. gen. Neb. N.G.; brig. gen. U.S. Vols., June 3, 1898-Feb. 24, 1899, in Spanish-Am. War; adj. gen., Neb., 1901-03. Organized Cuban-Am. Vol. Legion, 1897. Chairman Gage County Defense Council, U.S. Govt. Draft Agt. Mason. Mem. Christian Ch. Home: Beatrice, Neb. Died Nov. 15, 1925.

COLE, CHARLES H., corpn. exec.; b. Boston, Mass., Oct. 30, 1871; s. Charles H. and Mary Lyon (Ball) C.; grad. English High Sch., Boston, 1888; m. Grace F. Blanchard, of Brookline, Mass., July 1910. Clk., later cashier, office of several mining cos., Boston, 1888-98; treas. U.S. Smelting Co., Centennial Eureka Mining Co., Am. Zinc, Lead & Smelting Co., 1898-1900; mgr. and dir. Coeur d'Alene mines, Murray, Ida., 1900-06; police commr., Boston, 1905-07; in mining business, 1907-12; fire commr., Boston, 1912-14; adj. gen., Mass., 1914-16; in mining business, 1917; became treas. Bay State Film Co., 1919; president Colbres Chemical Co., United States Chemical Co. Enlisted as pvt. and advanced through grades to 1st lt., Mass. N.G., 1890-1905, col. and insp. gen. rifle practice for Mass., 1905, resigned, 1906, and reenlisted as pvt., 1906, advancing through grades to brig. gen., 1914, resigned 1916; reenlisted as pvt., World War, 1917, later capt.; apptd. brig. gen. U.S.A., Aug. 1917; overseas, 1917-19; in battles of Apremont, Zivray-Marvoisin, Chateau-Thierry, St. Mihiel, Meuse-Argonne. Del. at large to Dem. Nat. Conv., 1924, 28 and 32; was adjutant gen., chief of staff, Commonwealth of Mass., Jan. 7, 1937. Dem. candidate for gov. of Mass., 1928. Chmn. State Racing Commn., 1934-35; now chmn. Mass. State Bd. of Conciliation and Arbitration. Unitarian. Clubs: Algonquin (Boston); Manhattan (New York). Home: 34 Gloucester St. Office: 329 Newbury St., Boston MA*

COLE, CYRUS W(ILLARD), naval officer (ret.); b. Marshall, Mich., June 21, 1876; s. Willard Churchill and Mary Underhill (Weeks) C.; B.S., U.S. Naval Acad., 1899; student U.S. War Coll., 1923-24; m. Julia Anna Busby, June 8, 1908; 1 s., Cyrus Churchill. Commd. ensign, U.S. Navy, Jan. 28, 1901, and advanced through grades to rear admiral, 1932; commanded U.S. Naval Transports, 1918, Squalus Salvage Unit, May-Sept. 1939; Command Submarine Force, U.S. Fleet 1934-36; ret. July 1, 1940. Pres. Calif. State bd. of pilot commrs. for San Diego since June 1942. Awarded Navy Cross, World War I; Navy D.S.M. (Squalus rescue and salvage), 1939. Republican. Clubs: San Diego (Calif.). Carabao. Hobby: sculpture. Home: 2878 Rosecrans Blvd., San Diego 6 CA

COLE, ELI KELLEY officer U.S.M.C.; b. Carmel, N.Y., Sept. 1, 1867; s. Oncken Willard and Cornelia (Walker) C.; grad. U.S. Naval Acad., 1888; Army War Coll.. 1908; m. Emilie de R. Maxwell, May 10, 1893 1 son, Maxwell. Apptd. 2d lt. U.S.M.C., July 1, 1890; promoted through grades to maj. gen. June 3, 1924. Comd. Marine Barracks, Puget Sound, 1899-1901; duty Philippines, 1902-03; comd. marine battalion, Panama, 1903-04; duty Marine Barracks, Washington, 1904-05; with 2d Regt. and post, Olongapo, P.I., 1905-06; comd. battalion fortifying Grande Island, P.I., 1907; comd. marine regt., spl. duty, Panama, 1908, 10; duty Marine Barracks and Sch. of Application, Port Royal, S.C., 1909-11; duty Office of Maj. Gen. Comdt., Marine Corps, Navy Dept., 1911-14; comd. Marine Barracks, Annapolis, Md., 1915; comd. 2d Regt., 1st Provisional Brigade of Marines, Haiti, 1915-16; apptd. comdr. 1st Provisional Brigade of Marines, Haiti, Nov. 10, 1916; comd. Marine Barracks and Recruit Depot, Parris Island, S.C., Jan.-Aug. 1918; comd. 5th Brigade, U.S. Marines, A.E.F., Sept. 1918-Apr. 1919; comd. 1st Depot Div. (41st), A.E.F., Oct. 1918-Jan. 1919; comd. Am Embarkation Center A.E.F., Jan.-Feb. 1919; spl. duty hdqrs. U.S. Marine Corps, May 1919; comdg. Marine Barracks, avy Yard, Phila., June-July 1919, Marine Barracks, Parris Island, S.C., 1919-24, Marine Barracks, Quantico, Va., 1925-27; comdg. gen. Dept. of Pacific hdqrs. San Francisco, July 2, 1927 - . Home: Carmel, N.Y. Died July 4, 1929.

COLE, HOWARD I(RVING) chemist; b. New Rochelle, N.Y., Apr. 12, 1892; s. Abram Henry and Anna Marie (Kammermeyer) C.; B. Chem., Cornell U., 1914, Ph.D., 1917: m. Nancy Ruth Fields, May 27, 1927. Expert chem. microscopist A. D. Little & Co., Cambridge, Mass., 1919-20; prof. chem. U. Ore., 1920-22; organic research chemist Bur. Sci., Manila, P.I., 1922-24; head dept. chemistry Robert Coll., Istanbul, Turkey, 1924-26; chief chemist Philippine Health Service Culion Leper Colony, 1926-34; expert League of Nations, stationed Rio de Janeiro, 1935-39; exec. dir. com. on biol. warfare. Research and Devel. Bd., Sec. Def., Washington, 1947-54; mem. staff Nat. Acad. Scis., Washington. 1955-57. Served as lt. Gas Def., Service, U.S. Army, 1917-18; capt. 42d and 1st Inf. divs. Chem. Warfare Service, 1918-19; maj., lt. col. Chem. Warfare Service, 1942-47. Awarded Legion of Merit. Fellow A.A.A.S.; mem. Am. Chem. Soc., Internat. Leprosy Assn., Washington Acad. Scis., Sigma Xi. Clubs: Army and Navy (Manila): Army-Navy (Washington), Pan-Am. Doctors (Huasca, Mexico); Cosmopolitan (Santa Barbara). Home: 2279 Alston Rd., Santa Barbara, Cal. Died Nov. 28, 1966; buried Santa Barbara (Cal.) Cemetery.

COLE, NELSON brig. gen. U.S. vols.; veteran officer of vols. in Civil war; after war engaged in business in St. Louis; has been prominent in G.A.R.; apptd., May 28, 1898, from civil life, brig. gen. U.S.V., and placed in command 3d brigade, 2d div., 2d corps. Home: St. Louis, Mo. Died 1899.

COLE, WILLIAM CAREY naval officer; b. Chicago, Ill., Aug. 23, 1868; s. Jirah Delano and Julia Elizabeth (Tucker) C.; grad. U.S. Naval Acad., 1889; grad. Naval War College, 1916; m. Minnie Wetmore, Aug. 13, 1895; 1 dau., Mrs. Louise Chapin, Ensign, July 1, 1891; lt. jr. grade, Jan. 13, 1899; promoted through grades to rear admiral, Dec. 31, 1921. Served on Dolphin, Spanish-Am. War, 1898; various assignments to 1917; apptd. comdr. Frederick, Apr. 10, 1917, comdr. Nevada to Oct. 10, 1918; U.S. Dutch ship mission, May 17, 1919; operations, Navy Dept., Nov. 1919; comdg. Spl. Service Squadron, Apr. 22, 1922; chief of staff U.S. Fleet, Aug. 6, 1923; comdt. Navy Yard, Norfolk, Va., Nov. 16, 1925; comdg. Battleship Div. Four, Battle Fleet, 928-29, Scouting Fleet, June 21, 1929-July 1930; comdr. 12th Naval Dist., San Francisco, 1930-32; retired, Sept. 1, 1932. Baptist. Died May 28, 1935.

COLEMAN, FREDERICK WILLIAM army officer; b. Baltimore, Md., July 16, 1878; s. Frederick William and Clara Pauline (Adams) C.; B.A., Rock Hill (Md.) Coll., 1897; grad. Command and Gen. Staff Sch., 1904, Army War Coll., 1922; m. Blanche Lippincott Forbes, Dec. 8, 1902; children-Emile Tyler (dec.), Frederick William III. Apptd. 2d lt. inf., U.S. Army, Sept. 9, 1898; and advanced through grades to col., Apr. 27, 1921; maj. gen. chief of finance, U.S. Army, 1932-36; retired from active service, Sept. 30, 1936. Gov. U.S. Soldiers' Home Washington, D.C., since May 1, 1936. Served in Spanish-Am. War, Philippine Insurrection, on Mexican border: lt. col. and col. asst. chief of staff. 91st Div., World War. Awarded D.S.M.; Silver Star with Oak Leaf Cluster (U.S.). Mason. Clubs: Army and Navy Country, Chevy Chase, Alfalfa. Address: U.S. Soldiers' Home, Washington. Died Jan. 5, 1945; buried in Arlington National Cemetery.

COLEMAN, THOMAS DAVIES M.D.; b. Augusta, Ga., Jan. 13, 1865; s. Dr. John S. and Carolina Wyatt (Starke) C.; A.B., Ky. U., 1885, A.M., 1902; U. of Ga. (M.D., ad eunendem); post-grad. Johns Hopkins, 1886-87; M.D., Univ. Med. Coll. (New York U.), 1890; m. Annie Lee Adams, June 18, 1890. Asst. physiology, Johns Hopkins, 1887-88; asst. physiology, medical dept. U. City of New York, 1889-90; prof. physiology, 1893-95, physiology and pathology, 1895-1901, medicine, 1901 - , principles and practice of medicine, 1903 - , med. dept. U. of Ga.; pres. Bd. of Health, Augusta, Ga., Jan. 1903-May 1904; cons. physician Univ. Hospitals; U.S. Pub. Health Hosp. for psychiatric cases. Maj. Med. R.C., 1917. hon. disch., Feb. 1, 1919; lt. col. O.R.C. Fellow Am College Physicians. Home: Augusta, Ga. Died Aug. 2, 1927.

COLES, WALTER congressman, farmer; b. Coles Ferry, Halifax County, Va., Dec. 8, 1790; s. Isaac Coles; attended Hampden-Sydney Coll., Washington Coll. (now Washington and Lee U.), Lexington, Va. Served as 2d lt. 2d Regt. of Light Dragons in War of 1812; promoted to capt. of riflemen on Northern frontier, discharged, 1815; became farmer in Va.; justice of peace; mem. Va. Ho. of Dels., 1817-18, 33-34; mem. U.S. Ho. of Reps. (Democrat) from Va., 24th-28th congresses, 1835-45. Died Coles Hill, nr. Chatham, Va., Nov. 9, 1857; buried family burying ground at Coles Hill.

COLEY, BRADLEY LANCASTER surgeon; b. N.Y.C., Dec. 23, 1892; s. William Bradley and Alice (Lancaster) C.; A.B., Yale, 1915; M.D., Columbia, 1919; m. Phyllis Greenfield Macdonell, Sept. 5, 1922; children-William Bradley, Geoffrey Macdonell, Bradley Lancaster. Intern surgery St. Luke's Hosp., 1919-21; attending surgeon bone tumor dept. Meml. Hosp., 1936, Hosp. Spl. Surgery, 1938; chief surgeon N.Y.C. R.R. since 1932; asso. prof. clin. surgery Cornell, 1948; attending surgeon James Ewing, Univ., Bellevue, Flower and Fifth Av. hosps.; prof. clin. surgery N.Y. Med. Coll., clin. prof. surgery Post Grad. Med. Sch. Served as col. U.S. Army, World War II. Decorated Legion of Merit. Diplomate Am. Bd. Surgery. Mem. A.M.A., A.C.S., Internat., Am., So., Eastern, N.Y. surg. socs., Am. Cancer Soc., Am. Radium Soc. Republican. Club: Century Association (N.Y.C.). Author: Neoplasms of Bone. Co-author: Tumors of Bone, Asso.

editor Am. Jour. Surgery. Home: Sharon, Conn. Office: 140 E. 54th St., N.Y.C. 22. Died June 1, 1961; buried Hillside Cemetery, Sharon.

COLLINGS, KENNETH BROWN writer; b. Lincoln, Neb., Sept. 22, 1898; s. Franklin Wallace and Mary Deborah (Brown) C.; student of law George Washington U., 1916-19; student Army and Navy Acad., washington, D.C., 1917; m. Luceille Hendley Smoot, Oct. 20, 1917 (divorced); 1 son, Kenneth Hendley; m. 2d, Mary Katherine Dovel, Nov. 12, 1927; 1 son, Kirby Brown Dovel. Served as private, later corpl., 3d D.C. Inf. (Nat. Guard), on Mexican Border, 1916; 2d lt., later 1st lt. and capt. (naval aviator), U.S. Marine Corps, 1917-22, with A.E.F., 1918, and service in Haiti, 1920-21; officer in Marine Corps Reserve, 1922 - ; naval aviator, 1917 - . Broker, 1922-23, ins. underwriter in aviation hazards, 1923 - ; licensed civil pilot, 1927 - ; chief pilot and chief instr. Newark Air Service, 1928-29; pilot Pan Am. Airways, 1929; free lance writer and foreign corr., 1935 - , covering Italo-Ethiopian War for Liberty Mag., 1935, German occupation of Sudetenland, 1938, and 2 World War on German-Russian front, 1939; lecturer, 1937 - . Nat. trustee Marine Corps League (also one of incorporators). Author: With Allenby in the Holy Land (with L. J. Thomas), 1938; Just for the Hell of It, 1938; These Things I Saw, 1939. Home: Rockville Centre, L.I., N.Y. Died May 6, 1941.

COLLINS, ALFRED MORRIS, retired mfr.; b. Phila., Pa., May 3, 1876; s. Henry Hill and Edith Earl (Conrad) C.; A.B., Haverford (Pa.) Coll., 1897; m. Mrs. Helen Wilson Glenn, Sept. 6, 1928; stepchildren—Helen, Thomas F., Harry W., Shirley. With A. M. Collins Mfg. Co., cardboard and photographic mounts, 1897-1929, v.p. and gen. mgr., 1899-1929. Mem. 1st Troop Phila. City Cav., 1905-12; commd. maj. Ordnance U.S.A., Jan. 1918. Fellow Royal Geographical Society; patron Field Museum Natural History (Chicago); hon. life mem. Acad. Natural Sciences, Zoological Society (Philadelphia), Am. Museum Natural History (New York); mem. Alumni Assn. Haverford Coll. (pres. 1917-18), Phila. Geog. Soc. (pres. 1922, 25, 26, 27, 29, 31), Main Line Citizen's Assn. (pres. 1916-21). Polo player and big game hunter; in charge hunting and scientific expdn. to Brit. E. Africa, in interest of Acad. Natural Sciences, Phila., 1911-12; made hunting trip through Alaska, N.E. Siberia and as far north as Wrangel Island, 1914; a dir. of Collins-Day S. Am. expdn., traveling 4,-000 miles across S. Am., in interest of Am. Mus. Natural History, N.Y., and the Field Museum, Chicago, 1916; sent expdn. to W. Africa, in interest of Smithsonian Instn. of Washington, 1917; led Central African expdn. in interest of Field Mus. Chicago, 1923-24; expdn. to Tanganyika and S. Africa, 1928; now pres. San Luis Valley Land & Cattle Co. Republican. Episcopalian. Clubs: Wilderness (pres.), Explorers, Penn Athletic, Boone and Crockett, Racquet, Phila. Barge, Phila. Country, Merion Cricket, Bryn Mawr Polo. Home: Crestone CO

COLLINS, CONRAD GREEN, physician; b. New Orleans, Apr. 23, 1907; s. Charles and Amelie Marie (Haydel) C.; B.S., Tulane, 1926, M.D., 1928, M.S., 1931; m. Louise Carroll, Oct. 9, 1935; children—Louise Carroll, Conrad G., Claudia Elizabeth. Intern Touro Hosp., New Orleans, 1928-29; asst. resident obstetrics and gynecol. Touro Infirmary, 1929-30, and 1930-31; pvt. practice splty., New Orleans, from 1931; sr. vis. surgeon Charity Hosp. of La. from 1938; sr. consultant Hotel Dieu, Vets. Hosp., U.S. Marine Hosp., Flint Goodridge and Sara Mayo hosps. Instr. gynecol. and lab., Sch. Med., Tulane, 1931-32, asst. prof. gynecol., 1932-38, asst. prof. clin., obstet. and gynecol., 1938-45, prof., chmn., 1945-50, chmn. dept. gynecol., 1949-50, prof., chmn. dept. obstet. and gynecol., from 1950; nat. cons. obstet. and gynecol. Surgeon Gen., USAF, 1952-62. Served as maj., U.S.A., 1942-46; Asiatic-Pac. Theatre, 1942-43, European Theatre, 1944-45. Diplomate Am. Bd. Obstetrics and Gynecol.; fellow A.C.S., mem. A.M.A., Am. Assn. Obstetrics and Gynecology, Am. Coll. Obstetricians and Gynecol., Am. Gynecol. Soc., Sigma Psi. Club: American Gynecological; Boston (New Orleans). Home: New Orleans LA Died Dec. 15, 1971.

COLLINS, JAMES LAWTON army officer; b. New Orleans, Dec. 10, 1882; s. Jeremiah Bernard and Catherine (Lawton) C.; student Tulane U., 1901-03; B.S., U.S. Mil. Acad., 1907; Army War Coll., 1919-20, Command and Gen. Staff Sch., 1925-26; m. Virginia Caroline Stewart, Dec. 1, 1915; children-James Lawton (U.S. Army), Agnes Beattle, Virginia Stewart, Michael, Commd. 2d lt. U.S. Cav., 1907, promoted through the grades to brig. gen., 1939; 2d lt., 8th cav., Ft. Robinson, Tex., 1907-10; with 8th cav., also a.d.c. to Gen. Pershing, Philippines, 1911-13; with 11th cav. also a.d.c. to Gen. Pershing, Mexican Punitive Expdn., 1916-17; sailed for France with Hdqrs. A.E.F., as a.d.c. to Gen. Pershing, May 1917; transferred to F.A., June 1917; mem. Gen. Staff, A.E.F., May-Sept. 1918; comdg. 1st Bn., 7th F.A. in Meuse-Argonne and march into Germany, Oct.-Dec. 1918; War Dept. Gen. Staff, 1920-24; rep. War Dept. in India with Brit. Army, Jan.-May 1922; mil. attaché, Rome, Italy, 1928-32; comdr. 1st F.A., Sch. Troops, Fort Sill, Okla., May-Oct. 1932; asst. chief of staff 2d Corps Area, Governors Island, N.Y., 1934-37 attended coronation King George VI, London, as a.d.c. to Gen. Pershing, 1937; comdg. 6th F.A., Ft. Hoyle, Md., 1937-38, 2d F.A. Brigade, Ft. Sam Houston, Tex., 1939-40; apptd. maj. gen. (temp.) Oct. 1, 1940. Comdg. 2d Div., Ft. Sam Houston, Tex., Oct. 1940-Apr. 1941; comdr. P.R. Dept., Apr. 17, 1941-44; now comdg. VII Corps Western Front. Decorated D.S.M., Silver Star Citation (U.S.); Officer Legion of Honor, Croix de Guerre (France); Officer of Crown (Italy); Officer of Crown (Belgium); Grand Croix de l'Orde Honneur et Merite (Haiti). Address: Hdqrs. Puerto Rican Dept., San Juan, P.R. Died July 1963.

COLLINS, JOHN BARTHOLOMEW commodore, U.S. Navy; b. New Orleans, Jan. 20, 1850; s. Bartholomew and Ann (Douglas) C.; grad. U.S. Naval Acad., 1870; widower. Midshipman, July 26, 1866; promoted through grades to capt., Feb. 28, 1906; commodore and retired, June 30, 1909. Served in Behring Sea, Atlantic, Pacific and Indian oceans, on the prin. rivers - Mississippi, Rio Grande, Orinoco, Amazon, Rio de la Plata, Guayaquil, Columbia, etc.; on the Wilmington during war with Spain; comd. Princeton, Rainbow, Brooklyn. Indiana, and at navy yards, Pensacola, Fla., Mare Island, Calif., and Phila. Mason. Home: Annapolis, Md. Died Apr. 12, 1917.

COLLINS, NAPOLEON naval officer; b. Pa., Mar. 4, 1814, Commd. lt. U.S. Navy 1846; participated sieges of Tuspan and Tabasco on sloop Decatur during Mexican War, 1846-48; commanded ship Anacosta, Potomac fleet, 1861, gunboat Unadilla, So. Atlantic squadron, 1861-62; Union comdr. Octorara, West Indian squadron, 1862; caputred ship Florida in harbor of Bahia, Brazil, 1864, towed her to U.S. authorities at Hampton Roads, Va.; when Brazil demanded her return or rendition, Sec. Seward disavowed the act of Comdr. Collins, who was tried by Navy ct.; commd. capt. 1866; comdr. ship Sacramento, 1867; commd. commodore, 1871; lighthouse insp. until 1874; rear adm. in command S. Pacific squadron, 1874. Died Callao, Peru, Aug. 9, 1875.

COLLINS, STEWART G. army officer; b. Minn., Oct. 29, 1880; B.S., U. of Minn., 1904; commd. capt. Inf., Minn. Nat. Guard, Nov. 1918; maj. F.A., June 1919, advanced to brig. gen., Dec. 1940; Fed. Service. Feb. 1941; command of 68th Inf. Brigade, 34th div., in training, Camp Claiborne, La., since 1941. Address: Camp Claiborne, La.* Deceased.

COLLINS, VIVIAN army officer; brig. gen., 1942. Address: Selective Service, St. Augustine, Fla. Died Aug. 22, 1955.

COLLIS, CHARLES H. T. lawyer; b. Cork, Ireland, Feb. 4, 1838; s. William and Mary Anne (Lloyd) C.; academic edn. in Eng.; m. Septima M. Levy, Dec. 13, 1861. Enlisted Union army, April, 1861; served until surrender of Gen. Lee as pvt., sergt., maj., capt., col., brig. gen., maj. gen. Participated in all battles of Army of Potomac, excepting Gettysburg; after war twice elected city solicitor, Phila.; 15 yr. dir. of city trusts; commr. public works, New York, during the Strong adminstrn. Republican. Home: New York, N.Y. Died 1902.

COLMAN, NORMAN JAY sec. of agr.; b. nr. Richfield Springs, Otsego Co., N.Y., May 16, 1827; s. Hamilton and Nancy (Sprague) C.; ed. dist. sch. and sem.; removed to Ky., 1847; taught sch.; LL.B., Louisville Law Sch., 1851; (LL.D., U. of Mo., 1905; D.Agr., U. of Ill., 1905); m. Clara Porter, 1851 (died 1863); m. 2d, Catherine Wright, 1866 (died 1897). Practiced law, New Albany, Ind., 1850-52; elected dist. atty., 1852; removed to St. Louis, 1852; established Colman's Rural World, and became its editor; dean of agrl. editors in U.S. Alderman St. Lunouis, 1855-56; lt. col. 85th Enrolled Mo. Militia, in Civil War; mem. Mo. Ho. of Rep., 1865-66; defeated for lt. gov., 1868, elected for term 1875-77; U.S. commr. of agr., 1855-89, and when dept. was elevated to an exec. branch of the govt., became first sec. of agr., U.S., Feb. 11-Mar. 4, 1889. Democrat. Issued call, and presided over conv. of dels. from agrl. colls. in U.S., 1885, and urged adoption of laws upon Congress creating the present system expt. stas. in connection with agrl. colls. in U.S.; selected by a commn. to head the govt. horse-breeding farm at Ft. Collins, Colo., for the establishment of a breed of Am. trotting-bred carriage-horses. Officier du Merite Aqricole, France, 1889. Home: St. Louis, Mo. Died 1911.

COLQUITT, ALFRED HOLT senator, gov. Ga.; b. Walton County, Ga., Apr. 20, 1824; s. Walter T. and Nancy (Lane) C.; grad. Princeton, 1844; m. Dorothy Tarver, May 1848; m. 2d, Sarah Tarver. Admitted to Ga. bar, 1845; served as maj. U.S. Army during Mexican War, 1846-48; mem. U.S. Ho. of Reps. from Ga., 33d Congress, 1853-55; mem. Ga. Legislature, 1859; presdl. elector-at-large, 1860; del. to Ga. Secession Conv., 1861; commd. brig. gen., then maj. gen. Confederate Army during Civil War; pres. Ga. Democratic Conv., 1870; gov. Ga., 1876-82; mem. U.S. Senate from Ga., 1883-94. Died Washington, D.C., Mar. 26, 1894; buried Rose Hill Cemetery, Macon, Ga.

COLSTON, RALEIGH EDWARD army officer; b. Paris, France, Oct. 31, 1825; s. Dr. Raleigh Edward and Elizabeth (Marshall) C.; grad. Va. Mil. Inst., 1846; m. Louise Gardnier, 1846. Came to U.S., 1842; asst. prof. French, Va. Mil. Inst., 1846-54, prof., 1854-61; commd. brig. gen. Confederate Army, 1861; commanded div. at battles of Chancellorsville, Lynchburg; reinforced Gen. Magruder, Seven Pines, 1862; after Thomas (Stonewall) Jackson's death (1863) in command defenses St. Augustine River in Gen. Beauregard's dept.; established mil. sch., Wilmington, N.C.; served on mil. staff Khedive of Egypt, in Egypt, 1873-79, went on 2 expdns. exploring South country between Egypt and the equator, 1873-74, 74-76; recipient firman, also decorated knight comdr. Turkish Imperial Order Osmanish by Sultan. Died Richmond, Va., June 29, 1896.

COLSTON, WILLIAM AINSLIE lawyer; b. Louisville, Ky., Nov. 3, 1873; s. John William and Belle (Ainslie) C.; LL.B., Jefferson Sch. of Law, Louisville, 1907; m. Cora Virginia Brown, 1923; children - Margaret Virginia, Ann Ainslie. Began as messenger in mail dept., L. & N. P.R., and continued with the rd. in various positions in accounting dept. and in law dept. up to gen. solicitor; dir. finance, Interstate Commerce Commn., Washington, D.C., 1920-22; v.p. and gen. counsel N.Y.,C. & St. L. R.R., at Cleveland, O., 1922-32, v.p. in charge corporate relations, Jan. 1932 - ; dir. Railroad Credit Corp. Served as capt. 1st Ky. Inf., Spanish-Am. War; col. 138th F.A. and comdg. 63d F.A. Brigade, A.E.F., World War. Democrat. Episcopalian. Home: Shaker Heights, Cleveland, O. Died Nov. 6, 1934.

COLTON, GEORGE RADCLIFFE governor; b. Galesburg, Ill., Apr. 10, 1866; s. Francis C.; ed. Knox Coll., Ill. Ranchman in N.M., 1881-86; mem. Neb. Ho. of Rep., 1889-90; nat. bank examiner Dist. of Neb., 1897; went to P.I. as lt. col. 1st Neb. Vol. Inf.; organized customs service at Manila upon Am. occupation, and served with lt. until 1905, then went to Santo Domingo and organized Dominican customs receivership under the modus vivendi between U.S. and Santo Domingo; insular collector of customs for P.I., 1907-09; drafted and presented to Congress the tariff for Philippines, enacted by spl. session of Congress, 1909; also took part in drafting provisions of the Payne Bill relating to free trade between the U.S. and Philippines; gov. P.R. Nov. 7, 1909-Nov. 15, 1913. Mason. Home: New Canaan, Conn. Died Apr. 7, 1916.

COLVOCORESSES, GEORGE MUSALAS naval officer; b. Chios, Greece, Oct. 22, 1816; s. Constantine and Franka (Grimaldi) C.; m. Eliza Halsey, May 17, 1846: m. 2d, Adeline Swasey, July 19, 1863; had four children including George Partridge. Came to U.S., 1822; apptd. midshipman U.S. Navy, 1832, passed midshipman, 1838; sailed with Wilkes Exploring Expdn. in Antarctic and South Pacific, 1838-42: commd. lt., 1843; served in Pacific Squadron during Mexican War, in Mediterranean, 1847-49, in East India Squadron, 1854-56; commd. comdr., 1861; commanded storeship Supply, 1861-63, Saratoga off Ga. coast, 1864, St. Mary's on Pacific coast off S.Am., 1865-66; ret. as capt., 1867. Author: Four Years in a Government Exploring Expedition, 1852. Killed by thieves in the street, Bridgeport, Conn., June 3, 1872.

COLVOCORESSES, GEORGE PARTRIDGE rear adm.; b. Norwich, Vt., Apr. 3, 1847; s. George M. and Eliza Freelon (Halsey) C.; grad. U.S. Naval Acad., 1869; hon. A.M., Norwich U., Vt., 1898; m. Mary D. Baldwin, Oct. 7, 1875; children - Edith Baldwin (dec.), George Musalas, Harold. Captain's clk. on board ships Supply and Saratoga, 2 yrs., in Civil War; commd. ensign, 1870; master, 1872; lt., 1875; lt. comdr., 1897; comdr., 1900; capt., 1905; retired as rear admiral June 1907. Advanced 5 numbers in grade "for eminent and conspicuous conduct at Battle of Manila Bay." Served in nearly all parts of the world; instr. Naval Acad., 1886-90 and 1893-96; comdt. of midshipmen, 1905-07; served at Torpedo Sta., War Coll., and in comd. Naval Sta., Key West; comd. U.S. Ships Lancaster, Yankee and Newark. Episcopalian. Home: Litchfield, Conn. Died Sept. 11, 1932.

COMBA, RICHARD soldier; b. in Ireland, July 11, 1837; m. Frances Mary Logan, Nov. 23, 1874. Enlisted in U.S.A. as pvt., Jan. 30, 1855; served as such and as non-commissioned officer, 7th inf., to March 26, 1863; apptd. 2d lt. 7th inf. Feb. 19, 1863; advanced through grades to col. 5th Inf. June 30, 1898. Brevets: 1st lt., July 2, 1863 (in the field); capt. and maj., U.S.A., March 13, 1865, for gallantry in battle of Gettysburg, Pa.; lt. col., Feb. 27, 1890; for gallant services in action against Indians at Big Hole, Mont., Aug. 9, 1877. Comd. 12th inf. in Santiago campaign and battle of El Caney, Cuba; bri. gen. vols. Sept. 7, 1898, for distinguished service in Cuba; comd. 2d brigade, 1st div., 4th corps; hon. disch. vol. service, Apr. 15, 1899; comd. 5th inf. in Philippines; comd. province of Abra, Northern Luzon, P.I., 1900-01; brig. gen. U.S.A., retired. Died 1907.

COMBS, THOMAS SELBY vice admiral, U.S. Navy; b. Lamar, Mo., Mar. 25, 1898; s. Orin Preston and Grace (Davis) C.; student Marion Mil. Inst., 1915-16; B.S., U.S. Naval Academy, 1919; M.S., Mass. Inst. Tech., 1932; m. Agnes M. Williamson, Feb. 17, 1923. Commd. ensign, U.S.N., 1919, and advanced through the grades to vice admiral, 1953; chief of staff aircraft, S.W. Pacific, 1942-43; commodore comdg. Aircraft

S.W. Pacific, 1943-44; also Fleet Air Wing Ten and Fleet Air Wing 17, 1943-44; comdg. officer, U.S.S. Yorktown, 1944-45, operating against Japanese in Philippines, South China Sea, Formosa, and in attacks on Tokyo, Iwo Jima and Okinawa; chief of staff to comdr. Seventh Fleet, 1945-46; deputy chief, Bureau of Aeronautics, Navy 1946-48; comd. Carrier Div. 2, 1949-50; chief of staff and aide to comdr. in chief Atlantic Fleet, 1950-51; chief Bur. Aeronautics, Dept. of Navy, 1951-53; commander 2d Fleet, Atlantic, 1953-54, 6th Fleet Mediterranean, 1954-55; mem. NACA, 1955-56; dep. chief of naval operations (FO and R), Navy Department, 1956-58; commander Eastern Sea Frontier, New York, 1958-60; ret., 1960; vice chmn., dir. Fla. Jud. Council, 1962-. Decorated D.S.M., Silver Star, Legion of Merit with Oak Leaf Cluster, Commdn. Ribbon, American Defense Medal, Pacific Medal (seven battle stars), Victory Medal (World Wars 1 and 2) Philippine liberation medal, Grand Cordon of Yun Hui, Cloud Banner 2nd Grade, (Chinese); Order of Naval Merit (Spain). Clubs: Army-Navy, Army-Navy Country (Washington); Metropolitan, New York Yacht, India House (New York City). Home: 303 DeSoto St., Tallahassee. Died Dec. 9, 1964; buried Arlington Nat. Cemetery, Arlington, Va.

COMLY, SAMUEL PANCOAST rear adm.; b. Woodbury, N.J., July 13, 1849; s. Nathan Folwell and Mary (Wood) C.; grad. U.S. Naval Acad., 1869; m. Laura L. Carpenter, Dec. 17, 1884; m. 2d, Mrs. Hannah L. Hamill, Aug. 14, 1895. Promoted ensign, 1870; advanced through grades to rear adm., 1909. Practice cruise to Europe in Sabine, 1869-70; on Junita in Polaris search expdn. to Greenland, 1874; on Adams, in S. Atlantic and S. Pacific, 1876-79; on various ships until apptd. insp. ordnance and steel, Midvale Steel Works, and mem. Spl. Torpedo Bd., 1886-89; on Alliance, China, Japan, and various Pacific ports, 1890-93; navigator Indiana, 1895-98 and during Spanish-Am. War; in action San Juan, P.R., Bombardments of Santiago and destruction of Cervera's fleet; comd. training ship Alliance, 1901-02; insp. 4th lighthouse dist.; Phila., 1904-05; comd. Battleship Alabama, 1905-07; mem.Light House Bd., 1907-09; in comd. 4th div. U.S. Atlantic Fleet, June 10, 1909-Jan. 1910, 3d div. until Oct. 1910; court martial duty, Oct. 1910, until retired, July 13, 1911. Home: Woodbury, N.J. Died April 10, 1918.

COMPTON, CHARLES ELMER army officer; b. Mauricetown, N.J., Jan. 28, 1836. Served as 1st sergt. Co. A, and sergt. maj. 1st Ia. Inf., May 7-Aug. 21, 1861; comd. capt. 11th Ia. Inf., Oct. 19, 1861; hon. mustered out of vol. service, May 4, 1863; maj. 47th U.S.C.T., May 5, 1863; lt. col. 53d U.S.C.T., Dec. 9, 1864; hon. mustered out, Mar. 8, 1866; maj. 40th Inf., July 28, 1866; assigned to 6th Cav., Dec. 15, 1870; lt. col. 5th Cav., Apr. 29, 1879; col. 4th Cav., Oct. 19, 1887; brig. gen. vols., May 4, 1898; hon. discharged from vol. service, Dec. 6, 1898; retired for age, June 9, 1899; advanced to rank of brig. gen. retired, by act of Apr. 23, 1904. Bvtd. lt. col., Mar. 2, 1867, for campaign against Mobile, Ala.; col., Feb. 27, 1890, for action against Indians on Red River, Tex., Aug. 30, 1874. Home: Washington, D.C. Died 1909.

COMPTON, GEORGE BROKAW lawyer; b. Ovid, N.Y., Dec. 21, 1883; s. Charles Covert and Catherine (Little) C.; A.B., Columbia, 1909; LL.B., 1913, valedictorian; unmarried. Farm manager, 1899-1900; began as railway postal clerk in 1901; U.S. customs insp., 1905-13; editor Columbia Alumni News, 1911-14; organizer Columbia Alumni Fed. and exec. sec., 1913-14; admitted to N.Y. bar, 1914; state transfer tax appraiser (N.Y. County), 1915-20; mem. Peaslee and Compton, 1920-23, Compton and Delaney, 1923-31, Compton, Dillon and Clark, 1931 - ; dir. Nat. Bondholders Corp., United Air Lines Transport Corp. (chmn. stockholders protective com. 1934), Alma Egan Hyatt Foundation; mem. N.Y. City Charter Revision Commn., 1934; spl. master Federal Court to determine fairness and feasibility of plan of reorganization of Hotel Waldorf-Astoria Corp., 1934-36; trustee in bankruptcy Greyling Realty Corp. and 10 affiliated mortgage and subsidiary corps. in reorganization of Nat. Surety Co., 1934-36. Capt. F.A., 2d Army, U.S.A. in Marbache sector and Metz offensive, comdr. of a battalion and recommended for promotion, World War; now maj. O.R.C.; one of organizers of Am. Legion, organizer and first comdr. in N.Y. County; resigned as county comdr., Mar. 1920, in personal protest of nat. exec. com. for bonuses for ablebodied, was first Legion official to make public stand in opposition; presided at reception to King Albert of Belgians, Madison Sq. Garden, 1919; presented Legion standard of colors to Prince of Wales, 1920. Chairman Fusion Speakers Bureau, Mayoralty Campaign, New York, 1933; chmn. Mayor's Committee to Welcome Columbia Univ. Football team, Rose Bowl champions, 1933-34. Vol. organizer for Rep. Nat. Com. and campaign mgr. Hughes Nat. Coll. Men's League, 1916; mgr. campaign for new city charter, New York, 1936. Awarded conspicuous Columbia Alumni service medal, 1933. Presbyn.; trustee Fourth Presbyn. Ch., New York. Home: New York, N.Y. Died Mar. 24, 1938.

COMSTOCK, CYRUS BALLOU brig. gen.; b. West Wrentham, Mass., Feb. 3, 1831; s. Nathan and Betsey (Cook) C.; grad. West Point, 1855, in engrs.; m. Elizabeth Blair, Feb. 3, 1869. Bvt. 2d lt. engrs., July 1, 1855; advanced through grades to col., Apr. 7, 1888; bvtd. maj., July 4, 1863, for gallant and meritorious services in siege of Vicksburg; lt. col., May 6, 1864, for same in battle of the Wilderness; col., Jan. 15, 1865, for same in capture of Ft. Fisher; brig. gen., Mar. 13, 1865, for same in campaign ending with capture of Mobile; col. and brig. gen. vols., Jan. 15, 1865, for same in capture of Ft. Fisher; maj. gen. vols., Mar. 26, 1865, for same during campaign against Mobile. Chief engr. Army of the Potomac, 1862-63; sr. engr. at siege of Vicksburg; chief engr. in assault and capture of Fort Fisher, N.C.; sr. a.-d.-c. to Lt. Gen. U. S. Grant, 1864-66; col. a.-d.-c. to Generals Grant and Sherman, 1866-70. Mem. and pres. Miss. River Commn.; mem. permanent Bd. Engrs. for Fortifications; retired, Feb. 3, 1895; advanced to rank of brig. gen. retired, by act of Apr. 23, 1904. Author: Primary Triangulation of the U.S. Lake Survey. Edited Some Descendants of Samuel Comstock of Providence, R.I., 1905. Died 1910.

CONDIT, JOHN surgeon, congressman; b. West Orange, N.J., July 8, 1755; s. Samuel and Mary (Smith) C.; m. Abigail Halsey, 1776; m. 2d, Rhoda Halsey, 1785; 8 children-including John S., Abigail Smith, Jacob A. Silas. Served as surgeon in Col. Van Cortland's battalion, Heard's brigade, during Revolutionary War, 1776; a founder Orange (N.U.) Acad., 1785; mem. N.J. Legislature, 1788-89; mem. N.J. Council; mem. U.S. Ho. of Reps. from N.J., 6th-7th, 16th congresses, 1799-1803, 19-20; mem. U.S. Senate from N.J., 1803-17; asst. collector customs Port of N.Y.; hon. mem. N.J. Med. Cos., 1830. Died Orange Twp., N.J., May 4, 1834; buried Old Graveyard, Orange, N.J.

CONE, HUTCHINSON INGHAM naval officer; b. Brooklyn, Apr. 26, 1871; s. Daniel Newman and Annette (Ingham) C.; removed with parents in infancy to Fla.; grad. Fla. Agrl. Coll., 1889; grad. U.S. Naval Acad., 1894; m. Patty Selden, Oct. 16, 1900; children - Elizabeth, Hutchinson I.; m. 2d, Julia Mattes, Dec. 17, 1930. Commissioned asst. engr., May 23, 1896; jr. lt., July 1, 1899; lt., Feb. 9, 1902; lt. comdr., Jan. 1, 1908. Served on U.S.S. Baltimore during war with Spain; was in Manila Bay, May 1, 1898, and during war; comdr. torpedo boat Dale on trip from Mapton Roads to Manila, 1903; comdr. flotilla of torpedo boats on voyage from Hampton Roads to San Francisco, 1908; fleet engr. Atlantic Fleet, on trip around the world, June 1908-Mar. 1909; head Bur. Steam Engring. with rank of rear admiral and engr.-in-chief, May 21, 1909; then exec. officer Utah; comdg. U.S.S. Dixie; marine supt. Panama Canal; in command U.S. Naval Aviation Forces, foreign service, Aug. 1917-Oct. 1918; wounded on bd. S.S. Leinster when she was sunk in the Irish Sea by a German submarine, Oct. 10, 1981; retired, July 11, 1922; served as v.p. and gen. mgr. U.S. Shipping Bd. Emergency Fleet Corpn. (resigned 1925); apptd. commr. U.S. Shipping Bd., 1928; now chmn. board Moore and McCormack Co., Inc. Distinguished Service Medal (U.S. Navy), Comú Distinguished Service Order (British), Officer Legion of Honor (French), Order of St. Maurice and St. Lazarus (Italian). Episcopalian. Home: Washington, D.C. Died Feb. 12, 1941.

CONGDON, EDWARD CHESTER mining; b. St. Paul, Minn., Mar. 1, 1885; s. Chester Adgate and Clara Hesperia (Bannister) C.; grad. Hill Sch., Pottstown, Pa., 1904; A.B., Yale, 1908; m. Dorothy House, May 5, 1920; children - Mary Mecracken, Stephen House, Thomas Edward. Began in father's office, Duluth, 1908, continuing in business there after the death of father, 1916; principally exploration and mine development; dir. First and Am. Nat. Bank of Duluth. Served as 2d lt., O.R.C., 1916-17; capt., inf., U.S.A., Camp Dodge, 1917. Dir. St. Luke's Hosp. Assn. of Duluth, Duluth Community Fund. Republican. Conglist. Home: Duluth, Minn. Died Nov. 27, 1940.

CONGDON, JOSEPH WILLIAM judge; b. New York, Nov. 26, 1844; s. George and Sarah A. (Wentz) C.; acad. edn. Binghamton, N.Y.; m. Kate De Forest Burlock, Jan. 3, 1867. From Feb. 1, 1886, engaged as mfr. silk products; formerly pres. Phoenix Silk Mfg. Co. (Paterson, N.J.), Adelaide Silk Mills (Allentown, Pa.), Tilt Silk Mills (Pottsville, Pa.), was alderman, Paterson, N.H., 1879-83; pres. Railroad Commn. of N.J., 1907-08; asso. judge Ct. of Errors and Appeals of N.J., Mar. 1909 - . Republican. Served in N.G. S.N.Y., lt. and capt. 22d Regt., and col. 22d Regt. Veteran Corps, New York; formerly maj. comdg. Paterson (N.J.) Light Guard, lt. col. comdg. 1st Battalion N.G.N.J.; commd. brig. gen. and insp. gen. N.G.N.J. Mason. Home: Paterson, N.J. Died May 1, 1914.

CONKLIN, ARTHUR STEWART army officer (ret.); b. nr. Rochester, N.Y., Nov. 27, 1872; s. Melvin Mott and Jeanette (Hutchins) C.; student mech. engring. Cornell U., 1891-93; grad. U.S. Mil. Acad., 1897, Sch. Submarine Def., Ft. Totten, N.Y., 1906, Army War Coll., 1925, Command and Gen. Staff Sch., Ft. Leavenworth, 1926; m. Beatrice O'Meara, July 25, 1926. Served as 2d lt., inf., June 11, 1897; trans. to arty., Apr. 2, 1898; promoted through grades to brig. gen., July 1, 1935. Served in P.R. campaign, Spanish-Am. War, 1898-99, in Philippine Insurrection, 1900-03; comd. battery coast arty., 1903-05; mine comdr. and arty. engr., Ft Wadsworth, N.Y., 1906-07; mine comdr. Ft. Monroe, Va., 1911-12; also instr. dept. engring., Coast Arty. Sch., Ft. Monroe; mem. Coast Arty. Bd., 1911-12; chief of staff Hawaiian Dept., Gen. Staff Corps, 1912-16; served on Mexican border, 1916; in charge instrn. 3 brigades N.G., Camp Wilson, San Antonio, 1916-17; material officer N. Atlantic Coast Arty. Dist., 1916-17; organized and comd. 303d F.A. and 161st F.A. Brigade. Camp Devens, Mass., fall of 1917; comd. 303d F.A. in France, later half of 1918; participated in St. Mihiel and Meuse-Argonne engagements; comd. regt. in Woevre sector; comd. Torpedo Depot, Ft. Totten, 1919-21, Gen. Intermediate Depot, Washington, 1921-24; comd. harbor defs. Chesapeake Bay, Ft. Monroe, Va., 1926-28; chief of staff Gen. Staff Crps, 3d Corps Area, Balt., 1928-36; comdr. 1st Coast Arty. Dist., Boston; now ret. Recommended for promotion to brig. gen. 3 times during World War. Dep. N.Y. State Dir. Civilian Def., July 1941 to Apr. 1944. Mem. N.Y. Soc. Mil. and Naval Officers of World War, Mil. Order of World War. Conglist. Club: Army and Navy (Washington). Home: 1870 Wyoming Av., Washington. Died May 1960.

CONKLIN, JOHN F., army officer; b. Kansas, Apr. 20, 1891; B.S., U.S. Mil, Acad., 1915; grad. Engr. Sch., 1921, Command and Gen. Staff Sch., 1927, Army War Coll., 1934. Commd. 2d lt., U.S. Army, 1915, and advanced through the grades to brig. gen., 1945. Decorated Distinguished Service Medal, Legion of Merit, Bronze Star. Home: Westmoreland Hills MD Died Jan. 25, 1973.

CONLEY, EDGAR THOMAS army officer; "Green Ridge," Fairland, Md., Apr. 12, 1874; s. Charles William and Martha Ellen (Larrick) C.; student Lehigh U., 1892-93; grad. U.S. Mil. Acad., 1897; m. Clare Madeline Geary, Dec. 7, 1904; children—Edgar Thomas, Mary (wife of Capt. Thomas Morgan Wathington, Jr.), Reginald Geary. Commd. 2d lt. inf., June 11, 1897; promoted through grades to brig. gen., 1933. Served in Santiago Campaign in Cuba, 1898; in Philippine Insurrection, 1899-1901; in charge prisoners of war div. Office of Provost Marshall Gen., A.E.F., 1919; maj. gen., The Adjutant Gen., 1935-38, retired, Apr. 30, 1938. Awarded Silver Star medal "for gallantry in action against Spanish forces at Santiago"; D.S.M. "for exceptionally meritorious and distinguished services A.E.F." Episcopalian. Author: Riflemen's Score Book for Krag and Springfield, 1906; Field Equipment Manual for Officers and Men of 30th Infantry, 1916; Training in Bayonet Fighting, 1916. Home: R.F.D. 2, Silver Spring, Md. Died Aug. 20, 1956.

CONNELL, CARL W. army officer; born Ala., Mar. 16, 1899; grad. Air Service Engring. Sch., 1921, Air Corps Tactical Sch., 1929, Command and Gen. Staff Sch., 1931, Army War Coll., 1937; rated command pilot, combat observer, tech. observer. Began as sergt. Signal Corps June 1917; commd. 1st lt. Aviation Sect., Signal Corps, June 1917, and advanced through the grades to brig. gen., June 1942: served as capt. Signal Corps, World War I. Address: Air Corps, A.P.O. 501, care Postmaster, San Francisco, Calif.* Died Jan. 7, 1946.

CONNELL, KARL surgeon; b. Omaha, Neb.; s. William J. and Mattie (Chadwick) C.; M.D., Coll. Physicians and Suregons, Columbia, 1900; m. Frank Hovey-Roof, Sept. 28, 1922; children - Barbara, Karl, Francis Chadwick. Aso. in surgery, Columbia, 1910-14; asst. attending surgeon Roosevelt Hosp., New York, 1908-19; prof. of surgery, Creighton U., 1919-24; pres. Connell Apparatus, 1930 - . Served as maj. Med. Corps, N.G., 1907-17; mil. surgery, France, 1914; observer in Germany and Austria, 1915; mem. Med. Council of Nat. Defense, 1916-17; Mexican Border Service, 1917; maj. Chem. Warfare Service, U.S. Army, with A.E.F., 1917-19; cited for meritorius service; decorated D.S.M. (U.S.). Pres. Presbyn. Hosp., Omaha, 1920-24. Fellow Am. Coll. Surgeons. Author: Surgical Therapeusis. Holds 10 patents on anesthetic apparatus, etc. Died Oct. 18, 1941.

CONNELY, EMMETT FRANCIS investment banker; b. Adrian, Mich., June 13, 1891; s. Michael Joseph and Kathryn Louise (Hurley) C.; A.B., U. Mich., 1915; m. Harriet Louise Cullom, Oct. 29, 1919; children—Richard Day, Cullom, Molly. Clerk Montgomery Ward Co., Chgo., 1915; prodn. dept., Hudson Motor Car Co., 1916-17, 1919-20; salesman and sales mgr. Detroit Trust Co., 1920-27; v.p., 1927-30; v.p. First Detroit Co., 1930-31; pres., 1931-33; pres. First of Michigan Corp., 1933-43, chmn. bd., 1943-49; dir. Am. Seal-Kap Corp., Chicago Ry. Equipment Supply Corp., Briggs Mfg. Co., Nat. Rubber Machinery Co., Abingdon Potteries. Chairman Detroit A.R.C. 1946-47; dir. Jr. Achievement, Inc. (mem. exec. com.). Served as capt. 10th F.A., 3d Division, U.S. Army, 1918-19; with A.E.F., 9 months; major, 182d F.A., Michigan Nat. Guard, 1920-24; colonel, U.S. Army, 1942-45; Trustee Village of Grosse Pointe Farms, 1932-39. Mem. Advisory bd. U. Detroit; trustee United Found., Greater Detroit Hosp. Fund, 1948-49; trustee Turtle Bay Music School New York; mem. exec. com. Committee for United Europe Mem. of the Investment Bankers Assn. Am. (gov. 1936-39, pres. 1939-41), Sigms Phi. Roman Catholic. Clubs: Detroit, Country of Detroit, Yondotega; The Links, Bond, University of Michigan (N.Y.C.); Eastward-Ho Country (Chatham, Mass.).

Author: Let Business Roll Its Own, 1940. Home: 133 E. 80th St., N.Y.C. 21. Office: 25 Broad St., N.Y.C. 4. Died Feb. 2, 1960.

CONNER, DAVID navy officer; b. Harrisburg, Pa., 1792; s. David and Abigail (Rhodes) C.; m. Miss Physick, June 25, 1828, 2 sons. Commd. midshipman U.S. Navy, 1809; served as lt. on ship Hornet, 1812-15; commd. capt., 1835; mem. bd. commrs. U.S. Navy, 1841-42; commodore West India and home squadron, 1843; head Bur. Constrn., Equipment and Repair, until 1843; commanded Am. naval forces in Gulf and Caribbean, 1843-47, in charge of navy side of Scott's army's landing nr. Vera Cruz, Mexico, during Mexican War, put 10,000 men on beaches in 5 hours; comdt. Phila. Navy Yard, 1849-50. Died Phila., Mar. 20, 1856.

CONNER, FOX, army officer (ret.); born Slate Springs, Miss., Nov. 2,21874; s. Robert H. and Nannie (Fox) C.; grad. U.S. Mil. Acad., 1898, Staff Coll., 1906, Army War Coll., 1908; m. Virginia Brandreth, June 4, 1902; children—Betty Virginia, Fox Brandreth, Florence Slocum. Commd. 2d lt. 2d Arty., Apr. 26, 1898; advanced through grades to lt. col. May 15, 1917; col. (temp.) Aug. 5-Dec. 5, 1917; brig.-gen. (temp.), Aug. 23, 1918; brig.-gen. regular army, April 27, 1921; maj. gen. U.S. Army, Oct. 20, 1925. At Ft. Adams, R.I., 1898, Havana, Cuba, 1900; comd. 123d Co., Coast Arty., at Ft. Hamilton, N.Y., 1901-05; detailed to Gen. Staff, 1907; arrived in France, June 1917; with Insp. Gen.'s Dept. A.E.F., served as mem. Operations Sect. Gen. Staff G.H.Q., A.E.F., and asst. C. of S. for Operations; comdr. Hawaiian Dept., 1928-30, First Corps Area, 1930-38. Address: Brandreth NY

CONNER, JAMES army officer, state ofcl.: b. Charleston, S.C., Sept. 1, 1829; s. Henry and Juliana (Courtney) C.; grad. S.C. Coll., 1849; m. Sallie Enders, 1866. Admitted to S.C. bar, 1851; U.S. atty. for dist. S.C., 1856-60; commd. brig. gen. Confederate Army, 1846; solicitor S.C. R.R.; receiver Greenville & Columbia R.R. Co.; chmn. S.C. Democratic Exec. Com., 1876; atty. gen. S.C., 1861, 1876-77. Died Richmond, Va., June 26, 1883.

CONNER, JOHN COGGSWELL congressman; b. Noblesville, Hamilton County, Ind., Oct. 14, 1842; attended Wabash Coll., Crawfordsville, Ind., U. S. Naval Acad., 1861-62. Commd. 2d lt. 63d Regt., Ind. Volunteer Inf. during Civil War, 1862, 1st lt., 1862-64; served as capt. 41st Regt., U.S. Inf., 1866-69; mem. U.S. Ho. of Reps. (Democrat) from Tex., 41st-42d congresses, Mar. 31, 1870-73. Died Washington, D.C., Dec. 10, 1873; buried Old Cemetery, Noblesville.

CONNER, LEWIS ATTERBURY physician; b. New Albany, Ind., Jan. 17, 1867; s. Charles Horace and Katharine Boudinot (Atterbury) C.; Ph.B., Sheffield Sci. Sch., Yale, 1887; M.D., Coll. Phys. and Surg., Columbia, 1890; m. Emma Witt Harris, Nov. 27, 1900 (died Sept. 14, 1921); children—Katharine Atterbury, William Harris, Edith Harris, Sylvia Colt; m. 2d, Laila Ann Coston, Sept. 27, 1923; 1 dau., Ann Atterbury. Attending physician N.Y. Hosp., 1905-32; cons. physician, 1932—; prof. medicine Cornell U. Med. Coll., 1916-32; prof. clin. medicine 1932 until ret. Col. U.S. Army M.C., 1918-19; brig. gen. Med. R.C., 1920. Fellow N.Y. Acad. Medicine; mem. Assn. Am. Physicians, A.M.A. Editor Am. Heart Journal, 1925-38. Club: University (N.Y.C.). Address: Niantic, Conn. Died Dec. 5, 1950.

CONNOLLY, JOHN army officer; b. Wright's ferry, Pa., 1743; s. John and Susanna (Howard) C.; m. Susanna Semple, before 1767; m. 2d, Margaret Wellington; 2 children. Med. officer Pa. Militia in Indian campaigns, 1762-64; studied Indian langs., Kashaskia, 1767-70; practiced medicine, Pitts., 1770-72; received grant of land in Ky. from Lord Dunmore (gov. Va.), 1773; acted as Dummore's agt. in land speculation; commd. capt. Va. Militia and apptd. magistrate for dist. of West Augusta, 1773; attempted to organize settlers in Western Pa. in Va. Militia, 1774, almost started civil war between Pa. and Va. traders when he stopped Pa. trade with Indians and imposed Va. fur tax on Pitts. traders; made treaty with Iroquois and Delaware Indians wherein they agreed to support British, 1775; commd. lt. col. Brit. Army, 1775; while en route West to lead Brit. and Indian forces captured by colonial forces, 1776, imprisoned, 1776-80; joined Lordr Cornwallis at Yorktown, 1781, again captured and imprisoned, 1781-82; went to England, 1782; sent to Detroit as lt. gov., 1788; attempted to persuade leaders in Ky. to shift allegiance to British, unsuccessful; dep. supt. of Indian affairs, 1799-1800. Died Jan. 30, 1813.

CONNOLLY, MAURICE congressman; b. Dubuque, Ia., 1877; s. Thomas and Ellen (Brown) C.; A.B., Cornell U., 1897; LL.B., cum laude, New York U., 1898; post-grad. work Balliol Coll., Oxford, Eng., and U. of Heidelberg, Germany; unmarried. Pres. Connolly Mfg. Co., Dubuque, 1904 - ; v.p. Dubuque Fire & Marine Ins. Co., etc; mem. 63d Congress (1913-15), 3d Ia., Dist.; Dem. primary nominee for U.S. senator, June, 1914; chmn. Ia. State Dem. Convention, 1914. Regent and mem. exec. com. Smithsonian Instn. Commd. capt. Aviation Sect. Signal Corps, July 5, 1917. Adj. Aviation Sch., Rantoul, Ill.; promoted to maj., Aviation Sect. Signal Corps U.S.A., Oct. 23, 1917; exec. officer temporarily in command Wilbur Wright Aviation Sch., Fairfield, O.; reserve mil aviator, 1918; flew for Liberty Loans; chief corr. br., Dept. Mil. Aeronautics, Washington; recruiting officer, Hazelhurst Aviation Field, L.I., 1919. Internat. Pilot's License. Home: Dubuque, Ia. Died May 29, 1921.

CONNOR, WILLIAM DURWARD army officer; b. nr. Beloit, Wis., Feb. 22, 1874; s. Edward D. and Adeline (Powers) C.; grad. U.S. Mil. Acad., 1897. Army Staff Coll., 1905, Army War Coll., 1909; m. Elsa Van Vleet, Nov. 6, 1907. Commd. add. 2d lt., engrs., June 11, 1897; promoted through grades to lt. col., May 15, 1971; col. N.A., Aug. 5, 1917; brig. gen. N.A., June 26, 1918; brig. gen. U.S. Army, Apr. 27, 1921; maj. gen., Sept. 1, 1925. Served in Philippine Campaign and during Filipino Insurrection, 1898; city engr., Manila, 1899-1900; fortification work, New London, Conn., 1903; in charge 1st and 2d dists., Miss. River improvement, 1905-08; dir. civ. engring., U.S. Engr. Sch., 1910-12; duty Gen. Staff, 1912-16; asst. chief of staff Southern Dept., July-Nov. 1916; dept. engr., Philippine Div., Dec. 1, 1916-May 1917: duty Gen. Staff, A.E.F., July 28, 1917, as asst. chief of staff, A.E.F., Nov. 4 to May 1, 1918; chief of staff, 32d Div., to June 26, 1918; comdr. 63d Inf. Brigade, 32d Div., to Aug. 5, 1918; comdr. Base Sect. No. 2, Bordeaux, to Nov. 12, 1918; chief of staff, Services of Supply, to May 26, 1919; comdg. gen. same, to Sept. 1, 1919, comdg. gen. Am. Forces in France, to Jan. 7, 1920; chief of transportation service, Aug. 15, 1920-July 14, 1921; asst. chief of staff, U.S. Army, Aug. 4, 1921-Nov. 10, 1922; comdr. U.S. Army Forces in China, Apr. 12, 1923-May 13, 1926; comdg. 2d Div., June 15, 1926-Dec. 18, 1927; comdt. Army War Coll., Dec. 22, 1927-Apr. 30, 1932; supt. and comdt. U.S. Mil. Acad., May 1932-Jan. 1938; retired, Feb. 28, 1938; recalled to active duty, May 7, 1941; chmn. Construction Advisory Committee, U.S. War Dept., 1941-42, returned to inactive status, Mar. 21, 1942. Awarded D.S.M. and Silver Star (with Oak Leaf cluster) by U.S.; commander Legion of Honor, Black Star of Morocco, Croix de Guerre (French); Companion Order of the Bath (British). Clubs: Army and Navy, Chevy Chase (Washington); Bass Rocks Beach, Eastern Point Yacht (Gloucester, Mass.). Address: 2412 Tracy Pl. N.W., Washington 20008. Died June 16, 1960; buried U.S. Mil. Acad. Cemetery, West Point, N.Y.

CONOLLY, RICHARD L. naval officer, ret.; univ. adminstr.; b. Waukegan, Ill., Apr. 26, 1892; s. Robert Ballentine and Cora Belle (Carhart) C.; student, Lake Forest Acad., 1906-09, B.S., U.S. Naval Acad., 1914, M.S., Columbia U., 1922; U.S. Naval War Coll., 1930-31; LL.D., Muhlenberg College, Villa Nova Coll.; married Helen Blanche Jacobs, June 25, 1921; children-Ann, Richard Lansing, Robert Carhart. Advanced through grades to admiral, 1946; sea duty on destroyers in World War I and II; successively navigating officer Battleship Tennessee, div. and squadron comdr. destroyers; comdr. of task force which took Guam back from Japanese, July, 1944; attended Paris Peace Conf., 1946; comdr. in chief U.S.N. Forces, E. Atlantic, Mediterranean to 1950; pres. Naval War Coll., 1950-53; president Long Island Univ., 1953-. Awarded Navy Cross, Legion of Merit, with one star and combat V. D.S.M. with two stars, Medal of World War I, Grand Officer Belgian Order of the Crown with Palm; Grand Cross Order of King George I (Greece), 1948; Companion of Bath (Britain); Croix de Guerre with Palm (Belgium); Commander Legion of Honor (France); Grand Cross of Order of St. Olav (Norway); Grand Cross of Dannebrog (Denmark); Grand Cross of Order of Christ (Portugal); Grand Cross Order of Orange Nassau (Netherlands). Splty.: amphibious landings. Address: Long Island University, Box 247, Greenvale, L.I., N.Y. Died Mar. 1, 1962.

CONOOR, SELDEN soldier, pension agent; b. Fairfield, lMe., Jan. 25, 1839; s. William and Mary C.; A.B., Tufts Coll., 1859 (LL.D., 1876); m. Henrietta W. Bailey, Oct. 20, 1869. Pvt. 1st Vt. Inf., May 2-Aug. 15, 1861; lt. col. 7th Me. Inf., Aug. 22, 1861; col. 19th Me. Inf., Jan. 11, 1864; brig. gen. vols. June 11, 1864; wounded in battle of the Wilderness, 1864; hon. mustered out Apr. 7, 1866. Assessor of Internal Revenue, 1869; gov. of Me., 3 terms, 1876-78; U.S. pension agt., 1882-86, and again, 1897-1914. Republican. Home: Augusta, Me. Died July 9, 1917.

CONOVER, (JAMES) MILTON, educator; b. South Harrison Twp., N.J., Aug. 16, 1890; s. Samuel S. and Atlantic Dean (Moore) C.; Ph.B., Dickinson Coll., 1913, Sc.D., 1933; M.A. in Polit. Sci., U. Minn., 1916; M.A., Harvard, 1934; postgrad in politics univs. of Oxford, Munich and Paris (Inst. of Urbanism); LL.B., Vanderbilt U., 1955, J.D., 1969. Corr., Boston Herald, 1908-09; tchr. pub. schs., Swedesboro, N.J., 1909-10, St. Matthew's Episcopal Sch., Burlingame, Cal., 1913-15; admitted to Ind. bar, 1916; bill draftsman Ind. Legislature, 1917; fellow polit. sci. Ind. U., 1916-17; instr. govt. U. Pa. and Camden YMCA, 1919-20, N.Y. U., 1922-24, 46-47; mem. faculty govt. Yale, 1924-35, asso. prof., 1930-35; seminarian Princeton U. and Dropsie Coll. for Hebrew and Cognate Learning, Phila., 1938-39; investigated Indian and French communities in Can., 1941-42; resident researcher Cath. U. Am., Washington, 1942-43; research Middle Am. Research Inst., New Orleans, 1943-44; legal practice, Chgo., 1944-45; law adjudicator U.S. VA, Newark, 1946-48; seminarian in law Columbia, 1948-53; lectr. finance Rutgers U., 1949; mem. faculties of social sci. and law Seton Hall U., 1947-68, asso. prof. law, 1955, prof. law, 1960-68, prof. emeritus law, 1968-72; exec. sec. N.J. Assn. Pvt. Colls. and Univs., 1958-60. Served as pvt. 3d N.J. Inf., 1917, later cpl. 104th Engrs., 29th Div.; commd. 2d lt. inf., Camp Lee, Va.; with 42d (Rainbow) Div. in Argonne drive; convoy officer Army of Occupation, Germany; diplomatic courier to Am. Commn. to Negotiate Peace, Paris, operating in Finland, Lithuania, Poland, Czechoslovakia, Italy and Greece; del. Founders' Conv. of Am. Legion, Paris, 1919; mem. staff Inst. for Govt. Research, Brookings Instn., Washington, 1921-22, asso., 1922-32; visited numerous countries and fgn. univs.; mil.-polit. observations in Europe, mid-Asia and Africa, journeying mainly by land from France to Mongolia and Korea via Siberia, 1929-30, Germany to India and Arabia via Khyber Pass, 1935-37, Latin-Am., finishing journey mainly by land from Alaska to Strait of Magellan, 1939-40; studied Negro self-govt. in Haiti, 1940-41; explored wildlife conditions North of Arctic Circle, 1971; pres. Am. Immigrant Inst. Conn., affillie Nat. Inst. of Immigrant Welfare, 1934-35. Recipient Bernard J. McQuald Distinguished Service Medal Seton Hall U., 1969. Mem. Royal Soc. Tchrs. (London), Holland Soc. of N.Y., Huguenot Soc. of N.J., Swedish Colonial Soc., Van Kouwenhoven-Conover Family Assn., Soc. Colonial Wars, Am., Fed., Inter-Am. bar assns., Order of Founders and Patriots of Am., Assn. Princeton Grad. Alumni, S.A.R., Delta Theta Phi, Phi Kappa Psi, Grange (7), Oxford Soc. Pi Gamma Mu. Club: Harvard. Author: The General Land Office, 1923; The Federal Power Commission, 1923; The Office of Experiment Stations. 1924; Working Manual of Original Sources in American Government, 1924; Working Manual of Civics, 1925; co-author Political Theory, 1959. Contbr. to legal and social sci. publs. Home: Mullica Hill NJ Died May 6, 1972; buried Swedesboro NJ

CONRAD, CASPER HAUZER, JR. army officer (ret.); b. Columbus, O., Sept. 26, 1872; s. Casper H. and Ella (Coton) C.; B.S., U.S. Mil. Acad., 1895; grad. Mtd. Service Sch., 1st yr. course, 1916; hon. grad. Sch. of the Line, 1920; B.S., U. of Ill., 1922; grad. Army War Coll., 1923; m. Eva M. Shacklette, Nov. 28, 1923. Commd. 2d lt. Cav., 1895; advanced through grades to col., 1920; served as col. inf., N.A., 1917-19; brig. gen. regular army, 1928. Served in Cuba, 1898-1901; Philippines, 1901-02; St. Louis Expn., 1904-05; Philippines, 1905-08; Tex., Mexican border, 1908-09; organized, comd. 360th Inf., 90th Div., 1917-18; mem. War Dept. Gen. Staff, 1918-19; Germany comdg. Advance Embarkation Sect., comdg. Base Sect. 1, St. Nazaire, France, 1919; Philippines, 1924-25, Washington, 1926-28; comdr. Ft. Sheridan, Ill., and 12th Inf. Brig., 1929-30; comdr. 23d Inf. Brig. (Philippine Scouts), 1930-31; comdr. Fort William McKinley and Philippine Div., 1931-33, 4th Inf. Brigade, Ft. Francis E. Warren, Wyo., 1933-35, 3d Div., Ft. Lewis, Wash., 1935-36; ret., 1936. Decorated D.S.M., 1920, Mem. Soc. Indian Wars. Episcopalian. Home: 477 Burr Road, San Antonio 9. Deceased.

CONRAD, CHARLES naval officer; b. Washington, Mar. 3, 1875; s. William and Adelaide (Zimmerman) C.; grad. Rockville (Md.) Acad., 1892; M.E., Cornell, 1896; m. Dora E. Allen, May 3, 1898 (dec. 1949); children—Adelaide Zimmerman (Mrs. Kenneth Gordon), Dorothy Allen (Mrs. Theodore G. Haff), Charlotte Allen (Mrs. Maurice K. Brady), Mary Waters Allen (Mrs. Elmer M. Jackson), Barbara Allen (lieut. WAVES), Charles Allen (lieut. comdr. USN); m. 2d, Mrs. Margaret F. Eaton, Jan. 18, 1952. Began as ensign Supply Corps U.S. Navy, May 26, 1898, advanced through grades to rear adm., 1936; served 9 years on various battleships, 8 years as disbursing or supply officer at various navy yards, 5 years in Bur. of Supplies and Accounts, Washington, Philippines, 1901-14, fiscal officer at Vera Cruz, Mexico, 1914; adminstr. of customs and financial ad adviser, Republic of Haiti, 1915-16; under instruction at Naval War Coll., Newport, R.I., 1917; U.S. Shipping Bd., 1919-20; spl. asst. Dir. Budget, 1922-25; gen. insp. Supply Corps, East Coast, 1928-32, Paymaster Gen., chief Bur. Supplies and Accounts, Navy Dept., 1935-39; ret., 1939. Apptd. by exec. order chmn. Interdepartmental War Savs. Bond Com., Apr. 16, 1941. Dir. Nat. Savs. & Trust Co., Washington. Awarded campaign badges for Spanish-Am. War, Mexican, Haitian and San Dominican services, and World War I, World War II, Legion of Merit. Clubs: Army and Navy, Chevy Chase. Home: 2311 Connecticut Av. Address: Navy Dept., Washington. Died June 19, 1954.

CONRAD, CHARLES MAGILL congressman, sec. of war; b. Winchester, Va., Dec. 24, 1804; s. Frederick and Frances (Thruston) C.; m. M.W. Angela Lewis. Admitted to La. bar, 1828; mem. La. Legislature, 1840; mem. U.S. Senate from La., Apr. 1842-Mar. 1843; mem. La. Constl. Conv. 1844; mem. U.S. Ho. of Reps. from La., 31st Congress, 1849-51; U.S. sec. of war under Pres. Fillmore, 1850-53; mem. Confederate Provisional Congress, 1861; represented La. in 1st, 2d Confederate congresses, 1862-64; commd. brig. gen. Confederate Army. Died New Orleans, Feb. 11, 1878; buried Girod St. Cemetery.

CONRAD, VICTOR ALLEN corp. exec.; b. Hammond, Wis., Oct. 21, 1900; s. Henry and Kate (Dennis) C.; B.S., U.S. Mil. Acad., 1924; M.S., Yale, 1927; m. Martha Catherine O'Leary, Sept. 8, 1928; children-Martha C. (Mrs. John R. Rogers), Michael J., Mary E. (Mrsa.Richard V. McGarey), Donald H. Commd. 2d lt. U.S. Army, 1924, advanced through grades to maj. gen. 1954; chief war plans div. Office Chief Signal Officer, Dept. Army, 1942-43; wire officer Allied Forces Hdqrs., N. Africa, 1943-44; comdg. officer Signal Corps Engrng. Labs., 1944-46; signal officer Army Forces, Philippine Ryukyus Command, 1946-48; chief Army Communications Service Div., Office Chief Signal Officer, Dept. Army, 1950-51, asst. chief signal officer for procurement and distbn., 1951-54; comdg. gen., Ft. Monmouth, N.J., 1954-57; chief signal officer SHAPE, 1957-60; tech. adv. to pres. Varian Assos., Palo Alto, Cal., 1960-. Decorated D.S.M., Legion of Merit with cluster. Home: 1034 St. Joseph Rd., Los Altos, Cal. Office: 611 Hansen Way, Palo Alto, Cal. Died Dec. 7, 1964; buried Arlington Nat. Cemetery.

CONVERSE FREDERICK SHEPHERD composer; b. Newton, Mass., Jan. 5, 1871; s. Edmund Winchester and Charlotte Augusta (Shepherd) C.; A.B., Harvard Univ., 1893; studied music at Kgl. Akademie der Tonkunst, Munich; hon. Mus.D., Boston U., 1933; m. Emma Cecil Turdor, June 6, 1894; children - Louise (Mrs. J. S. lforgan, Jr.), Augusta C. (Mrs. D. M. McElwain), Marie T. (Mrs. G. A. McCook), Virginia (Mrs. P. C. Cabot), Frederick (dec.), Elizabeth Edmund W. (dec.). Instr. harmony, N.E. Conservatory of Music, 1899-1901; instr. music, 1901-04, asst. prof., 1904-07, Harvard; prof. theory and composition, N.E. Conservatory of Music, also dean faculty, 1931-38; v.p. Boston Opera Co., 1911-14. Capt. 13th Regt. Mass. N.G., 1918-19; mem. Nat. Com. in Charge Music in Training Camps, 1918-19. Mem. American Acad. of Arts and Letters. Composer: Op. 1, Sonata in A; Op. 2, Suite for Piano; Op. 9, Festival of Pan; Op. 11, Night and Day; Op. 12, La Belle Dame Sans Merci; Op. 14, Three Love Songs; Op. 17, Two Songs for Soprano Voice; Op. 18, Quarter in A minor; Op. 20, Two Songs for Low Voice; Op. 20, No. 2, Silent Noon; Op. 22, Laudate Dominum; The Mystic Trumpeter (a fantasy for orchestra); opera, The Pipe of Desire; oratorio, Job; opera, "The Sacrifice"; symphonic poem, "Ormazd"; opera, "The Immigrants"; cantata, "The Peace Pipe"; tone poem, "Ave atque Vale"; symphony, C minor; symphony, E major; photo music drama, "The Scarecrow"; "Fantasie" (for piano and orchestra); tone poem, "Song of the Sea"; "From the Hills" (piano); Elegy (orchestra); "Fantasy" (for orchestra); "Flivver Ten Million"; tone poem "California"; Trio for violin, violoncello and pianoforte; "The Pirate" (for male chorus); Concertino for Piano and Orchestra; Symphonic Suite for Orchestra - American Sketches; Two Songs for Soprano Voice, Harp and Flute; Tone Poem for Soprano Voice and Orchestra - Prophecy; String Quartet in E inor; Symphony in F major; Symphony No. VI in F minor; Rhapsody for Clarinet and Orchestra; Theme and Variations for Chamber Orchestra. Home: Westwood, Mass. Died June 8, 1940.

CONVERSE, GEORGE ALBERT naval officer; b. Norwich, Vt., May 13, 1844; s. Shubael and Luvia (Morrill) C.; ed. Norwich pub. schs., 1852-58, Norwich U., 1858-61; grad. U.S. Naval Acad., 1865 (B.S., Norwich U.); m. Laura Shelby Blood, Dec. 1871. Served on steam sloop Canadaigua, European squadron, 1865-67; promoted ensign, Dec. 1, 1866; promoted through grades to rear adm., Nov. 8, 1904. In torpedo service, 1869-72; on Asiatic Sta., 1872-74; instr. Torpedo Sta., 1874-77; served in U.S.S. Marion, 1877-79, Lancaster, 1883-84; instr. Torpedo Sta., 1885-89; comdg. Enterprise, 1890-91; in Bureau of Ordnance, 1891-92; in charge Torpedo Sta., 1893-97; comd. U.S.S. Montgomery, cruiser, N. Atlantic squadron, 1897-99; in Bur. of Navigation, 1899-1901; comdg. battleship Illinois, 1901-03; chief Bur. of Equipment, 1903-04; chief Bur. of Ordnance, Mar. 15, to Aug. 1, 1904; chief Bur. of Navigation, Aug. 1, 1904 - . Home: Norwich, Vt. Died 1909.

CONVERSE, GEORGE PEABODY patent mgr.; born N.Y. City, Nov. 18, 1902; s. Walter C. Morrill and Antoinette (Converse); student Germany, Switzerland, France, Sanford Sch., 1914-18, Fryburg Acad., 1919. Bowdoin Coll., 1921; m. Anita Stewart, July 24, 1929 (div.); m. 2d, Dorothy Knight, January 11, 1957. Vice pres., treas. Exhibitors Mut. Producing Corp., Hollywood, Calif., 1926: pres., treas. Aero Radio Corp., 1928; U.S. distbr. Filmax Corp., 1937; pres. Gasparcolor, Inc., 1939 (all Hollywood, Calif.); pres., dir. Sperti Products, Inc., N.Y. City, 1951; v.p. treas., director, Cooper-Hewitt Electric Co., Hoboken, N.J., 1951; dir. pub. relations Tracy Kent & Co., Inc., N.Y.C.; now pres. George P. Converse & Co., Inc., patent management. Served as lt. col. M.I., Gen. Staff, War Dept., World War II. Decorated Legion of Merit (Army), N.Y. State Conspicuous Service Cross. Mem. Beta Theta Pi. Episcopalian. Republican. Clubs; Army-Navy (Washington); Yacht, River (N.Y. City); Silver Spring Country (Ridgefield, Conn.); Weston Gun, Pequot Yacht, Essex Yacht Conn.); Tuna (Catalina, Cal.); Country of Fairfield (Conn.), Fairfield Hunt; Sea Island Ga. Golf. Home: 96 Willow St., Southport. Conn. Office: 18 E. 60th St., N.Y.C. 10022. Died June 11, 1963.

CONWAY, HERBERT, plastic surgeon; b. Ft. Wayne, Ind., June 25, 1904; s. James Francis and Irene (McCarthy) C.; student Miami U., 1921-24; B.S., U. Cin., 1929, M.S., 1932, M.B., 1928, M.D. (Taft fellow in surgery 1928-29), 1929, D. Sc. (hon.), 1969; m. Frances Gallagher, Nov. 7, 1936; children—Karen, Richard William, Catherine Lanning. Asst. resident surgeon Cin. Gen. Hosp., 1929-32; asst. resident surgeon New York Hosp., 1932-33, asst. attending surgeon, 1935-42, attending surgeon, attending surgeon in charge plastic surgery, 1945-69; instr. surgery Cornell U. Med. Coll., 1932-35, asst. prof. surgery, 1935-45, asso. prof. clin. surgery, 1945-55, prof. clin. surgery, 1955-69; cons. plastic surgeon VA Hosp., Bronx, N.Y., 1945-69; cons. plastic surgery White Plains (N.Y.) Hosp., Bellevue Hosp., Hosp. Spl. Surgery; cons. plastic and reconstructive surgery Health Center, Inc., N.Y.C., 1950-69; cons., lectr. plastic surgery St. Albans (N.Y.) Naval Hosp., 1957-69; 1st vis. prof. Found. Am. Soc. Plastic and Reconstructive Surgery to Latin Am. (Brazil), 1965; guest prof. U. Cal. at Los Angeles, 1965; guest prof. N.Y.U. Med. Center, 1966, V.H. Kazanjian lecturer, 1966. Board of directors of Goodwill Industries, New York Society Crippled Children Adults; rep. Acad. Surgery of Peru to American College of Surgeon, 1950-69; pres., trustee Found. Am. Soc. Plastic and Reconstructive Surgery, 1960-61; spl. State Dept. lectr. India, Saudi Arabia, Pakistan, Lebanon, 1962-63. Served as 1t. col. M.C., AUS, 1942-45; chief plastic surgery Lovell Gen. Hosp.; chief surg. service 116th Sta. Hosp., Port Moresby, New Guinea, 54th Gen. Hosp., Hollandia, New Guinea, Batanges, P.I.; plastic surg. cons. S.W. Pacific area. Decorated Bronze Star; hon. surgeon Police Dept. City N.Y.; Colles medal Royal Coll. Surgeons Ireland. Diplomate Am. Bd. Plastic Surgery (chmn.), Am. Bd. Surgery, Mem. New York State, N.Y. County med. socs., New York Regional Soc. of Plastic Surgeons (pres.), A.M.A., N.Y. Acad. Medicine, N.Y. Surg. Soc., N.Y. Soc. Electromicroscopists, N.Y. Cancer Soc., Am. Surg. Assn., Soc. Univ. Surgeons, Internat. Soc. Surgery, Soc. Med. Cons. World War II, Mont Reid Surg. Soc., Am. Soc. Surgery of the Hand, Society Head and Neck Surgery, British Association Plastic Surgeons, A.C.S., American Academy Compensation Medicine (chairman plastic surgery sect. 1949-69), Pan Am. Med. Assn. (chmn. plastic surgery sect. 1952-59), Am. Assn. Plastic Surgeons (trustee 1954-57, president 1960-61), American Soc. Plastic and Reconstructive Surgery (chmn. pub. relations com. 1954-57), Sigma Delta Chi, Delta Upsilon, Alpha Kappa Kappa; hon. mem. Faculty Medicine U. Chile, Acad. Surgery of Chile, Chilean Soc. Plastic and Reconstructive Surgery, Acad. Surgery of Peru, Hollywood Med. Assn., Argentine Med. Assn., French Society of Plastic Surgery, also hon. mem. Argentine Assn. Plastic Surgery. Knights of Malta. Clubs: University (N.Y.C.); Larchmont Yacht; Westchester Country; Everglades, Bathing and Tennis and Seminole Golf (Palm Beach, Fla.). Editor Transplantation Bull.; U.S. editor Revista Latino Americana de Cirurgia Plastica; asso. editor Jour. of Surgery, N.Y. State Jour. of Medicine, Plastic and Reconstructive Surgery, 1956-66. Home: Larchmont NY Died Aug. 25, 1969; buried Gate of Heaven, Valhala NY

CONWAY, THOMAS army officer; b. Ireland, Feb. 27, 1735. Commd. brig. gen. Continental Army, May 13, 1777; recommended for promotion to maj. gen., promotion opposed by Washington, as result, Conway resigned; resignation not accepted, became maj. gen. and insp. gen., Dec. 14, 1777; served in battles of Germantown, Brandywine, 1777; organizer conspiracy Conway Cabal to replace Washington with Gen. Horatio Gates,1778, badly wounded in duel with Gen. Cadwallader, July 4, 1778: gov. gen. French possessions in India, 1787; resigned from Continental Army, 1778; named comdr. Order St. Louis, 1787; called Count de Conway. Died 1800.

CONYINGHAM, GUSTAVUS naval officer; b. County Donegal, Ireland, 1744: s. Gastavus Conyngham; m. Ann Hockley, 1773. Came to Am., 1763; commd. capt. ship Surprise, Continental Navy, 1777, captured ships Joseph, Prince of Orange, 1777; took command ship Revenge; arrived at Phila. with 60 prizes, 1779; captured by British, shipped to Eng., escaped, 1779, re-captured, 1780, exchanged, 1781; became mcht., Phila.; mem. Phila. Common Council during War of 1812. Died Nov. 27, 1819; buried St. Peter's Churchyard, Phila.

COOK, FRANCIS AUGUSTUS rear adm.; b. Northampton, Mass., May 10, 1843; s. Gen. Benjamin E. and Elizabeth Christine (Griffin) C.; apptd. from Mass. and grad. U.S. Naval Acad., 1863; m. Carrie Earle, Sept. 3, 1868. Promoted ensign, Oct. 1, 1863; advanced through grades to rear adm., Mar. 21, 1903. Served Seminole, W. Gulf Blockading Squadron, 1863-65; Vanderbilt, N. Pacific Squadron, 1865-67; N. Atlantic Squadron, 1867-68; Naval Acad., 1868-70; receiving ship Independence, 1870-71; Saranac, 1871-72; Richmond, 1872-74; receiving ship Sabine, 1874-76 Plymouth, 1876-79; Naval Acad., 1879-83; light house insp. 11th dist., 1883-86; comd. Ranger, 1886-89; insp. of ordnance, Boston, 1890-92; equipment officer, Navy Yard, Boston, 1892-93 asst. Bur. of Navigation, 1893-96; comd. Brooklyn, 1896-99; advanced 5 numbers in rank "for eminent and conspicuous conduct in battle," while in command of Brooklyn, at battle of Santiago de Cuba with Admiral Cevera's Squadron, July 3, 1898; mem. Naval Examining and Retiring Bd., 1899-1903; retired, Sept. 5, 1903. Home: Northampton, Mass. Died Oct. 8, 1916.

COOK, GILBERT RICHARD army officer; B. Texarkana, Ark., Dec. 30, 1889; s. Joseph Edward and Mary Agnes (Young) C.; student U. Ark., 1905-06, Ark. Mil. Acad., 1906-07; B.S., U.S. Mil. Acad., 1912; distinguished grad. Command and Gen. Staff Sch., 1925; grad. Inf. Sch., Sch., Advanced Course, 1930, Tank Sch., 1931, Army War Coll., 1932; m. Doris Adair Frederick, Sept. 2, 1914 (dec. 1936); children-Gilbert Richard, CeCe Adair, Martha Hardin (adopted). Commd. 2d lt., U.S. Army, June 12, 1912, advanced through the grades to maj. gen. (temp.), Aug. 10, 1942; served as capt., maj. and lt. col., 58th Inf., 1918-19; comdg. officer of Inf. regt. and asst. div. comdr. in H.I., 1941-42; comdg. gen. of inf. div., 1942-43; comdg. gen. 12th Corps, 1943-44; dep. comdg. gen. 3d Army, 1944; Hq. Army Ground Force, 1945; adv. group, O.C. of S., W.I., 1946-48; ret. 1948. Army adviser Hoover Commn., 1948. Decorated 2 Croix de Guerre with gilt star, Legion of Honor, 2 Silver Stars with oak leaf cluster; 2 Distinguished Service Medals. Address: 8638 Washington St., La Mesa, Cal. Died Sept. 1963.

COOK, HENRY CLAY brig. gen.; b. Fall River, Mass., Sept. 29, 1837; s. Joseph S. and Minerva (Warren) C.; ed. pub. schs. and Pierce Acad., Middleboro, Mass.; m. Teresa Valdes Thom, July 12, 1877. Second lt. 2d R.I. Inf., June 5, 1861; mustered out, Aug. 7, 1861; apptd. 1st lt. 16th U.S. Inf., Aug. 5, 1861; advanced through grades to col. 5th Inf., Apr. 17, 1897; retired for disability in line of duty, 1898; advanced to rank of brig. gen. retired, by act of Apr. 23, 1904. Bvtd. capt., Sept. 1, 1864, for Atlanta campaign and battle of Jonesboro, Ga. Served in Army of Potomac and participated in various battles and campaigns in middle Tenn., and later in Ga.; after war served at various points in south and on reconstruction duty until 1877; served in campaign against Nez Perce and Bannock Indians in Ida. and Mont., 1877-79; later on different frontier posts. Home: Fall River, Mass. Died Feb. 22, 1916.

COOK, JOHN soldier; b. Belleville, Ill., June 12, 1825; s. Daniel P. (for whom Cook Co., Ill., was named) and Julia (Edwards) C.; mother d. of Gov. Ninian Edwards of Ill., ed. Ill. Coll.; m. Susan A. Lamb, October 20, 1847; 2d, Mary E. Baker, Sept. 16, 1889. Was in dry goods and later in real estate business. Springfield, Ill.; mayor, 1855; sheriff Sangamon Co., 1856; q.m. gen. of Ill., prior to Civil War; comd. first regt. raised in Ill.; served through war, comd. 3d brigade, Gen. Charles F. Smith's Div., at Ft. Donelson; received the messenger bearing surrender of Ft. Donelson and transmitted it, through Gen. Smith, to Gen. Grant; promoted brig. gen., Mar. 21, 1862; later bvtd. maj. gen. Gov. Yates (war gov.) on behalf of people of the state presented him with beautiful sword in token of appreciation of services and conduct at Ft. Donelson. Mem. Ill. legislature, 1868; agt. for Brule Sioux Indians, 1879. Home: Ransom, Mich. Died 1910.

COOK, JOSEPH PLATT Continental congressman; b. Stratford (now Bridgeport), Conn., Jan. 4, 1730; grad. Yale, 1750. Represented town in about 30 sessions of Conn. Gen. Assembly, 1763-83; justice of peace, 1764; apptd. col. 16th Regt. of Militia, 1771; accompanied Gen. Wolcott's forces to N.Y. in Revolutionary War, 1776; in command Continental forces when British burned Danbury, Conn., 1777; resigned as col., 1778; mem. Council of Safety, 1778; mem. Conn. Ho. of Reps., 1776, 78, 80-82, 84; mem. Continental Congress from Conn., 1784-88; judge Danbury dist. Probate Ct., 1776-1813; mem. gov.'s council, 1803. Died Danbury, Feb. 3, 1816; buried Wooster Cemetery.

COOK, PHILIP congressman, army officer; b. Twiggs County, Ga., July 30, 1817; s. Philip and Martha (Wooten) C.; grad. Ogelthorpe U., Milledgeville, Ga.; grad. U. Va. Law Sch., 1841; m. Sara Lumpkin, 1842, 1 son, Philip. Admitted to Ga. bar, practiced in Ga. at various times until 1880; mem. Ga. Senate, 1859-60, 63-44; volunteered as pvt. in Confederate Army in Macon County Volunteers, assigned to 4th Ga. Regt., 1861, adjutant, 1862; commd. lt. col. after Battle of Seven Days; promoted col. after battles of Second Manassas and Sharpsburg (Antietam); promoted brig. gen. 1864; wounded and captured at Battle of Petersburg, in hosp. there until 1865; mem. Ga. Constl. Conv., 1865; mem. U.S. Ho. of Reps. (Democrat) from Ga., 43d-47th congresses, 1873-83; mem. Ga. capital commrs. to select new site for capital, 1883-89: sec. state Ga., 1890-94. Died Atlanta, May 20, 1894; buried Rose Hill Cemetery, Macon, Ga.

COOK, VIRGIL Y. soldier, mcht., planter; b. Boydville, Ky., Nov. 14, 1848; s. William D. and Pernecia (Dodds) C.; business edn.; entered C.S.A. at age of 14; 8 months in 12th Ky. Cav., transferred to 7th Ky. Mounted Inf., Forrest's cav. corps, participating in battles and campaigns of that command and paroled at Columbus, Miss., May 16, 1865; m. Mildred, d. Capt. Enos Lamb,

1871. From 1866 has lived in Ark.; conducted mercantile business at Grand Glaize, Olyphant and Elmo; also a plantation of 4,000 acres in the Oil Trough Valley, Upper White River; retired. Officer Ark. N.G. many yrs., retiring with rank of maj. gen.; col. 2d Ark. Inf. during Spanish-Am. War; served in 2d Brigade, 2d Div., 3d and 4th Corps and 1st Separate Brigade, 2d Corps, comdg. at frequent intervals as sr. col. each these brigades and was for ten days in command of all the U.S. troops stationed at Camp Shipp, Anniston, Ala.; mustered out with regt., Feb. 25, 1899. Comdr. Tom Hindman Camp 318, U.C.V., Newport, Ark., many yrs.; also adj. gen. and chief of staff Ark. Div. U.C.V.; maj. gen. 2 yrs; was maj. gen. comdg. Trans-Miss. Dept. U.C.V. Trustee U. of Ark 6 yrs.; was mem. State Bd. Confed. Pensions; mem. bd. mgrs. endowment fund Hendrix Coll., Conway, Ark.; pres. Ark. Hist. Soc.; pres. trustees Conf Vet. Pub. Co., Nashville, Tenn., official organ U.C.V. Home: Batesville, Ark. Died Dec. 3, 1922.

COOKE, CHARLES MAYNARD, JR., naval officer; b. Ft. Smith, Ark., Dec. 19, 1886; s. Charles Maynard and Sarah Bleeker (Luce) C.; B.S., U. of Ark., 1905; B.S., U.S. Naval Acad., 1910; m. Lesley Temple, April 30, 1913 (died 1917); children—Lesley (dec.), Anne Bleeker; m. 2d, Mary Louise Cooper, Oct. 5, 1921; children—Mary Maynard, Carol Ridgely, Charles Maynard, III. Commd. ensign, U.S. Navy, 1912 and advanced through the grades to admiral, 1946; commanded Submarines E-2, R-2. S-5, Submarine Division 11, Battleship Pennsylvania; commandant, Naval Station, Guantanamo; Fleet war plans officer, U.S. Fleet, 1936-38; asst. chief of staff, comdr. in chief, U.S. Fleet, 1942-45. Chief of Staff to Comdr. in chief U.S. Fleet, Sept. 1944-Oct. 1945; deputy chief Naval Operations, 1945; comdr. 7th Fleet, 1946-48, retired May 1, 1948. Awarded D.S.M., Victory Medal (World Wars I and II); Hon. Knight Comdr. Mil. Order of Most Excellent Order of British Empire. Officer dans l'Ordre de la Legion d'Honneur, French Republic. Mem. U.S. Naval Inst. Club: Army and Navy (Washington, D.C.). Home: Sonoma CA Died Dec. 24, 1970.

COOKE, GEORGE HENRY rear adm.; b. Phila., Pa., Dec. 12, 1836; s. Christopher and Dorothea C.; ed. Phila. pub. schs.; M.D., Phila. Med. Coll.; m. Mrs. Sarah Lyon Atkinson, Oct. 16, 1873. Apptd. from N.J., asst. surgeon U.S.N., Sept. 22, 1862; passed asst. surgeon, Jan. 20, 1866; surgeon, Feb. 20, 1870; med. insp., Sept. 15, 1888; med. dir., Sept. 29, 1895; retired Dec. 12, 1898; advanced to rank of rear admiral, June 29, 1906, for services during Civil War. Home: Waverly Ala. Died Feb. 15, 1924.

COOKE, HARRISON RICE, banker; b. Honolulu, Oct. 11, 1908; s. Clarence Hyde and Lily (Love) C.; student Yale, 1928-30; m. Dorothea Sloggett, Apr. 7, 1931. With Bank of Hawaii, 1930-34; v.p., sec. Cooke Trust Co., Honolulu, 1934-41; pres. Honolulu Sporting Goods Co., 1946-73; chmn. Bank of Hawaii, 1963-73; pres. Molokai Ranch Ltd., 1958-73, Molokai Electric Co., 1961-73. Trustee, v.p. Honolulu Acad. Arts. Served to comdr. USNR, 1941-45. Decorated Bronze Star. Home: Honolulu HI Died Feb. 9, 1973.

COOKE, HENRY D. naval officer; ret.; b. Washington, Sept. 21, 1879 s. Henry David and Anna Howell (Dodge) C.; grad. U.S. Naval Acad., 1903; m. Elinor Talbot, Jan. 4, 1921. Midshipman U.S. Naval Acad., 1899; became dir. physical tng. U.S. Naval Acad., 1930, became comdt., 1931, ret.; commd. rear ad. USN, 1939, ret.; resumed active duty 1941. Recipient Bronze Star medal. Mem. S.A.R. Clubs: Army and Navy (Washington); New York Yacht (N.Y.C.). Address: 41 Round Hill Rd., Roslyn, L. I., N.Y. Died July 6, 1958.

COOKE, JAY business exec.; b. Phila., Apr. 2, 1897: s. Jay and Nina L. (Benson) C.; student St. Paul's Sch., 1910-15; A.B., Princeton, 1919; m. Mary F. Glendinning, Apr. 24, 1924; children-Nina (Mrs. A. L. Emlen), Mary Ellen (Mrs. Hallet Johnson, Jr.); m. 2d, Hannah M. Durham, July 25, 1956. Began as clk. with Chas. D. Barney & Co. (now Smith Barney & Co.), Phila., 1921, gen. partner, 1924-35; ltd. partner, 1935-40; chmn. bd. Cooke and Bieler, Inc.; dir. Phila. Nat. Bank, Madison Fund, Inc., Hewitt-Robins, Inc. Trustee Phila. Mus. Art. Commr. Fairmount Park. Served from 1st lt. to capt. inf. U.S. Army, 1917-19, capt. to lt. col., inf., 1941-45. Republican. Episcopalian. Clubs: Phiadelphia, Racquet, Union League, Sunnybrook Golf (Phila.); Brook (N.Y.C.). Home: Box 160, Blue Bell, Pa. Office: Phila. Nat. Bank Bldg., Phila. 7. Died July 10, 1963.

COOKE, LORENZO WESLEY brig. gen.; b. Round Top, N.Y., June 8, 1847; s. Amos B. and Lucy A. (Smith) C.; ed. pub. schs.; m. S. Emma Beatty, Nov. 4, 1869. Served pvt. to brig. gen. U.S.A., 1862-1906; retired, Mar. 24, 1906, at own request, over 40 years' service. Home: Santa Barbara, Cal. Died Feb. 15, 1915.

COOKE, PHILIP ST. GEORGE army officer; b. Leesburg, Va., June 13, 1809; s. Dr. Stephen and Catherine (Esten) C.: grad. U.S. Mil. Adad., 1827; m. Rachel Hertzog; children-John Rogers, Flora. Served as adj., 1st lt., capt. U.S. Army in Blackhawk War. 1831; served as 1st lt. in Tex., Ark., N.M., 1833; commd. capt. 1835; accompanied Col. Kearney through St. Pass, Rocky Mountains, thence to Ft. Leavenworth via the headwaters of Ark. River, 1845; commd. lt. col. 1846, ordered to make exploring expdn. to Cal., making a practical wagon road en route, 1846; reached San Diego Mission, 1847, here acquired for govt. 250,000 sq. miles of territory; commanded battalion Mo. Volunteers in Cal. during Mexican War, 1846-48; maj. 2d Dragoons, 1847; supt. cavalry barracks, Carlisle, Pa., 1848-52; commd. col., 1858; brig. gen. U.S. 1861; in command cavalry Army of Potomac at Siege of Yorktown, also battles of Gaines Mill, Frayser's Farm, Williamsburg, Glendale; gen. supt. recruiting for U.S. Army; ret., 1873. Died Detroit, Mar. 20, 1895.

COOLEY, THOMAS ROSS naval officer; b. Grass Valley, Calif., June 16, 1893; s. Thomas Ross and Mary Adelaide (Cota) C.; B.S., U.S. Naval Acad., 1917; m. Adelaide Prescott Morris, Apr. 21, 1919; children—Adelaide Morris (Mrs. Hal W. Smith), Mary Lawrence. Commd. ensign U.S. Navy, 1917, advanced through grades to rear adm., Mar. 20, 1943; served at sea and shore stations, Europe, Orient, Central and South Am., U.S.; mem. faculty U.S. Naval Acad., 1922-24, 27-29, 37-40; comdg. officer U.S.S. Aimaak, Washington and battleship div., 1941-42, 44-47; dir., officer personnel, U.S. Navy Dept., 1942-44; comdr. U.S. Naval Base, Newport, R.I., since 1947. Served World Wars I and II. Awarded Legion of Merit, Victory medals (both world wars), various campaign and service medals and ribbons, Medal of Merit (Nicaragua). Mem. U.S. Naval Inst., U.S. Naval Acad. Alumni Assn. Roman Catholic. Clubs: Army-Navy (Washington), Acme Gun, Pacific Fleet. Home: Grass Valley, Calif. Office: Quarters A., U.S. Naval Base, Newport, R.I. Died Nov. 1959.

COOLIDGE, CALVIN thirtieth President of the U.S.; b. Plymouth, Vt., July 4, 1872; s. John C. and Victoria J. (Moor) C.; A.B., Amherst, 1895; LL.D., Amherst, 1919, also from Tufts, Williams, Bates, Wesleyan, U. of Vt.; studied law with Hammond & Field, Northampton, Mass.; m. Grace Anna Goodhue, Oct. 4, 1905; children - John, Calvin (dec.). Began practice, Northampton, 1897; councilman, Northampton, 1899; city solicitor, 1900-01; clk. of courts, 1904; mem. Gen. Court of Mass., 1907-08; mayor of Northampton, 1910-11; mem. State Senate, 1912-15 (pres. Senate, 1914-15); lt. gov. of Mass., 1916, 17, 18; gov. of Mass., 2 terms, 1919, 20; elected v.p. of U.S. for term 1921-25; became President after death of Warren G. Harding, the oath of office being administered by his father, a notary public, at the paternal home in the village of Plymouth, Vt., at 2:47 morning of Aug. 3, 1923; elected President, term Mar. 4, 1925-Mar. 3, 1929. Dir. N.Y. Life Ins. Co. Visited Havana, Cuba, Jan. 15-17, 1928, and delivered address before Pan-Am. Conf. Conglist.; hon. moderator, Nat. Council Congl. Chs., 1923 - . Home: Northampton, Mass. Died Jan. 5, 1933.

COOLIDGE, CHARLES AUSTIN brig. gen.; b. Boston, July 19, 1844; s. Charles Austin and Anna Maria (Rice) C.; B.S., Norwich (Vt.) U., 1863; M.D., Wooster Med. Coll., Cleveland, O., 1873; m. Sophie Wager Lowry, Nov. 19, 1867. Pvt. Co. H, 16th U.S. Inf., Oh ; promoted through grades to col. 7th Inf., Mar. 2, 1901; brig. gen. and retired, Aug. 9, 1903. Bvtd. maj., Feb. 27, 1890, for gallant services in action against Indians at the Big Hole, Mont., Aug. 9, 1877 (thrice wounded); served in Cuba, P.I., and China during Boxer troubles 1900. Episcopalian. Home: Detroit, Mich. Died June 1, 1926.

COOLIDGE, LAWRENCE lawyer and trustee; b. Boston, Jan. 17, 1905; s. Harold Jefferson and Edith (Lawrence) C.; student Longwood Day Sch., Brookline, Mass., 1912-17, Groton (Mass.) Sch., 1917-22, U. of Ariz., 1922-23; A.B. cum laude, Harvard, 1927, LL.B., 1931; m. Victoria S. Tytus, Jan. 16, 1932; children—Robert Tytus, Lawrence, Nathaniel Silsbee. Asst. dean, Harvard Coll., 1928-29; admitted to Mass. bar, 1931; asso. firm Loring, Collidge, Nobel & Boyd, 1931-33; partner, 1934-37; partner Gaston, Snow, Rice & Boyd, 1937 and since Dec. 1945, dir. Nat. Shawmut Bank, Boston. Trustee Western Real Estate Trust. University Associates, Suffolk Savings Bank for Seamen, and others. Served with U.S.N.R. (active duty), 1942-45; separated with rank of comdr. Dec. 1945; Awarded 7 campaign stars, commendation ribbon. Trustee Peabody Museum of Salem (Mass.), Boston Floating Hosp., Church Home Soc. (pres.). Overseer Harvard U. Trustee of Donations of Protestant Episcopal Ch. Republican. Presbyterian. Clubs: Somerset, Myopia, Tavern, Union Boat, Harvard (Boston); Harvard (New York). Editor: Thoughts on Thomas Jefferson by Thomas Jefferson Collidge, 1936. Home: Main St., Hamilton, Mass. Office: 82 Devonshire St., Boston. Died Jan. 3, 1950; buried Hamilton Cemetery.

COOMBS, HARRISON S., pediatrician; b. Cornwall, Pa., Apr. 15, 1921; s. Robert Duncan and Harriet (Lord) C.; M.D., Tufts U., 1945; m. Elizabeth Gaskill, July 1, 1944; children—Lee (Mrs. William Earl Benjamin), Harrison S., Christine, Stephen Gaskill. Intern Salem (Mass.) Hosp., 1945-46; pediatric asst. resident Boston Floating Hosp., 1948-50; dist. physician, also pediatric teaching fellow Boston Dispensary, 1950; courtesy staff Stamford (Conn.) Hosp., St. Joseph Hosp., Stamford; attending staff Norwalk Hosp., 1952; chief sch. physician New Canaan sch. system, 1951-71. Trustee Natural Sci. for Youth Found., 1970-71; bd. dirs., also co-founder Genesis, Inc., bd. dirs. New Canaan Nature Center, 1960-71, pres., 1960-62, also co-founder. Served to capt. M.C., AUS, 1946-47. Diplomate Am. Bd. Pediatrics. Mem. A.M.A., Am. Acad. Pediatrics (chmn. by-law com. Conn. chpt. 1971), Northeast Pediatric Soc., New Canaan Field Club (charter), Nat., New Canaan (dir. 1951-71, pres., 1957-59) Audubon socs., Am. Mus. Nat. History, New Canaan Hist. Soc. Episcopalian. Home: New Canaan CT Died May 22, 1971; buried Lakeview Cemetery, New Canaan CT

COONEY, MICHAEL brig. gen.; b. Muroe, Co. Limerick, Ireland, May 1, 1837; s. Maurice and Anne (Ryan) C.; ed. pvt. and Nat. schs. in Ireland; m. Catherine Connolly, July 23, 1868. Pvt. Troop A, 1st Cav., Dec. 4, 1856; corp., May 1, 1859; sergt., Mar. 10, 1856; disch. at end of enlistment, Dec. 4, 1861; reenlisted Dec. 18, 1861; served 1st sergt. and q.-m. sergt. to Dec. 30, 1864; capt. 5th U.S.C. Cav., Jan. 1, 1865; mustered out of service Mar. 16, 1866; 1st lt. U.S. Cav., July 28, 1866; capt., Jan. 1, 1868; maj., Dec. 10, 1888; lt. col., June 2, 1897; col., June 9, 1899; retired Sept. 12, 1899; advanced rank of brig. gen. retired by act of Apr. 23, 1904. Catholic. Home: Washington, D.C. Died Sept. 10, 1928.

COONLEY, PRENTISS LOOMIS, manufacturer of machinery; b. Chicago, July 10, 1880; s. John Clark and Lydia Arms (Avery) C.; student University School, Chicago, 1898; graduate Chicago Latin Sch., 1899; A.B., Harvard, 1903; m. Mary Lord, Nov. 15, 1905 (died July 3, 1944); children—Alice Lord (Mrs. Milton P. Higgins, Eleanor Kavanaugh; m. 2d, Katharine Rogers Sullivan, December 21, 1945 (dec. 1961). Salesman Link-Belt Co., Chicago, 1905-11, v.p., 1911-25; pres. H. W. Caldwell & Son Co., later Caldwell-Moore, 1921-25; pres. C. B. Live Stock Co. and subsidiaries of Chicago, 1907-17; founder and treas., Electric Steel Co., Chicago, 1916-25; dir. Chicago Trust Co., 1906-25; v.p. Walworth Co., New York, 1925-32; became connected with NRA, June 1934 and served successively as dep. adminstr., div. adminstr., code adminstrn. dir., and as dir. Div. of Business Cooperation until Sept. 30, 1935; asst. to chairman of the business advisory council for the U.S. Dept. Commerce, 1938-39; consultant to mgt., 1940-71. With C.W.S. as assistant mgr. army gas defense plant, Long Island City, N.Y., rank of lt. col., World War. Trustee and v.p. Austen Riggs Foundation, Stockbridge, Mass. (pres. 1939, chmn. 1943-46). Republican. Clubs: Metropolitan, Burning Tree (Washington). Home: Washington DC Died Aug. 15, 1970; buried Worcester MA

COONTZ, ROBERT EDWARD naval officer; b. Hannibal, Mo., June 11, 1864; s. Benton and Mary Bacon (Brewington) C.; prep. edn. Ingleside Coll., Palmyra, Mo., 1878-79, Hannibal (Mo.) Coll., 1879-80; grad. U.S. Naval Acad., 1885; LL.D. from University of Missouri in 1926; Dr. Naval Science, Pennsylvania Mil. Acad., 1930; m. Augusta Cohen, Oct. 31, 1890; children - Lt. Kenneth Lee, U.S.N. (dec.), Bertha. Commissioned ensign U.S.N., July 1, 1887; promoted through grades to rear adm., Dec. 24, 1917; adm., Oct. 24, 1919. Was in Alaskan service six years, becoming proficient as pilot in those waters; exec. officer Nebraska, on voyage of fleet around the world, 1908; comdt. of midshipmen, U.S. Naval Acad., 1910-11; gov. of Guam, 1912-13; comdg. officer Georgia, 1913-15, winning fleet gunnery trophy; apptd. comdt. Navy Yard, Puget Sound, July 20, 1915; ordered to command 7th Div., U.S. Atlantic Fleet, Aug. 31, 1918; asst. for Naval Operations, 1918; made trip to pacific with U.S. Fleet, U.S.S. Wyoming, flagship; confirmed by the Senate as Chief of Naval Operations, Oct. 24, 1919; comdr. in chief U.S. Fleet, Aug. 4, 1923-Oct. 3, 1925; comdg. fleet on Hawaiian-Australian-New Zealand Cruise; comdt. 5th Naval Dist. Nov. 30, 1925; retired, 1928; recalled, 1930, to assist in investigation of Alaska railroads. Medals Spanish-Am. War, Philippine Insurrection, Vera Cruz, World War; D.S.M.; awarded Am. Legion D.S.M., Oct. 15, 1923; War Mothers' Medal, 1930. Comdr. Gen. Mil. Order Foreign Wars, 1920-23. Democrat, Mem. M.E. Ch., S. Mason. Home: Bremerton, Wash. Died Jan. 26, 1935.

COOPER, CHARLES LAWRENCE brig. gen.; b. New York, Mar. 6, 1845; s. James G. and Mary E. (Bradford) C.; ed. pub and pvt. schs. of New York; m. Flora Green, Dec. 20, 1865. Enlisted May 27, 1862, in 17st N.Y. State Militia, and, with exception of brief period after Civ. War, has been continuously in service, taking part in many campaigns against Indians on the plains, and participating in Porto Rico campaign in war with Spain. Served, enlisted man and officer, in U.S.V., during Civ. War, apptd. 2d lt. in regular service, July 28, 1866; promoted successively, reaching rank of col. 5th U.S. Cav.; apptd. brig. gen. U.S.A., Aug. 16, 1903; retired, Aug, 17, 1903. On duty with Nat. Guard of Colo., June 30, 1904-. Episcopalian. Republican. Deceased.

COOPER, GEORGE FRANKLIN naval officer; b. Americus, Ga., Sept. 26, 1864; s. George Franklin and Cornelia Irene (Staley) C.; grad. U.S. Naval Acad., 1886; m. Louise Lowell, June 5, 1894. Commd. ensign, June 1888; jr. lt., 1897; lt., 1899; lt.-comdr., 1905; comdr., 1909; capt., 1913. On board Vandalia, in the Pacific, 1886-88; on Boston, in Atlantic, 1888-89, Kearsarge, 1889-91; asst. in electricity at Navy Yard,

N.Y.C., 1891-92; insp. electricity, Bath (Me.) Iron Works, 1892-94; on Raleigh, in Atlantic, 1894-99; served U.S. Naval Acad., 1897-99; on Baltimore in Philippines, 1899; on duty Nautical Sch., Manila, 1899-1900; on Mondanock in Philippines and China, 1900-02; U.S. Naval Acad., 1902-04; naviagtor Denver, N.A. Sta., 1904-05; exec. officer Des Moines, N. Atlantic Sta., 1905-06; exec. officer Indiana, 1906-07; at hydrographic office, Washington, 1907-09; on board Rhode Island, Atlantic Fleet, as exec. officer, June-Dec., 1909; comd. Celtic, Atlantic Fleet, 1900-10; comd. Marietta, Central Am. waters, 1910-11; in charge elec. class Navy Yard, N.Y.C., 1911-12; hydrographer Bur. of Navigation, Washington, 1912-14; comd. Louisiana, Atlantic Fleet, 1914-16, U.S. commr. to Internat. Conf. on Safety of Life at Sea, London, 1913-14; Naval War Coll., 1916-17; 4th Naval Dist., Phila., 1917-19; comdg. U.S.S. Kaiserin Auguste Victoria, 1919; comdt. 8th Naval Dist. and Naval Sta., New Orleans, 1919—. Baptist. Mem. Mil. Order Carabao. Clubs: Chevy Chase, Army and Navy (Washington). Home: Americus, Ga. Died May 6, 1953.

COOPER, JAMES senator; b. Frederick County, Md., May 8, 1810; grad. Washington Coll., 1832. Admitted to Pa. bar, 1834; mem. U.S. Ho. of Reps. from Pa., 26th-27th congresses, 1839-43; mem. Pa. Legislature, 1844-48, speaker Pa. Assembly, 1847; atty. gen. Pa., 1849-49; mem. U.S. Senate from Pa., 1849-55; commd. brig. gen. Md. Volunteers, 1861; in command of Camp Wallace, Columbus, O.; comdr. Camp Chase, nr. Columbus. Died Camp Chase, nr. Columbus. Died Camp Chase, Mar. 28, 1863.

COOPER, MERIAN C., motion picture dir., producer, author; b. Jacksonville, Fla., Oct. 24, 1894; s. John C. and Mary (Coldwell) C.; ed. Lawrenceville Sch., U.S. Naval Acad., 1911-14; m. Dorothy Jordan; children—Mary Caroline, Elizabeth T., Richard. Advanced to capt. U.S. Army, World War I, pilot aviation France, later lt. col. Kosciusko Squadron, Poland, traveled widely in Orient, Africa making moving pictures, as newspaper, mag. corr.; exploration in Arabia, Iran; co-dir., co-author, co-producer motion pictures, Grass, Chang, Four Feathers; sole creator, co-producer, co-author King Kong; producer Flying Down to Rio, Last Days Pompeii, Little Women, Lost Patrol, and others; producer (with John Ford); Three Godfathers, Fort Apache, She Wore a Yellow Ribbon, Wagonmaster, Rio Grande, Quiet Man; co-dir., co-producer (with Lowell Thomas) This Is Cinerama; exec. producer The Searchers; dir., co-producer The Best of Cinerama, 1962. Exec. producer with RKO Studios, Hollywood, 2 yrs.; pres. Argosy Pictures Corp., 1946-56, Merian C. Cooper Enterprises, Inc., 1958-73; v.p. Cinerama Prodn. Corp. Was early supporter civilian aviation, former dir. Pan Am. World Airways, Western Airlines, Gen. Aviation, others. Served as col. USAAF, 1942-45, staff China Air Task Force, 1942, 5th Air Force, New Guinea, 1943-45; to brig. genl. Air Force, 1950. Clubs: Explorers, Brook, Boone and Crockett (N.Y.C.), Daedalians (San Antonio). Recipient Acad. Motion Picture Arts and Scis. spl. award motion picture innovator, 1952, Author: (with Edward A. Salisbury) The Sea Gypsy, 1924; Grass, 1925; Things Men Die For, 1927; (with Edgar Wallace) King kong, 1932. Home: Coronado CA Died Apr. 1973.

COOPER, PHILIP HENRY rear adm.; b. Camden, N.Y., Aug. 5, 1844; s. Hiram H. and Delia A. (Murdock) C.; grad. U.S. Naval Acad., 1863; m. Katharine Jordena Foote, June 24, 1884. Ensign, May 28, 1863; promoted through grades to rear adm., Feb. 9, 1902. Served on Constellation, 1863, Richmond, 1863-65; participated in battle of Mobile Bay, siege of Ft. Morgan; exec. officer of Richmond at surrender of ram Webb in Miss. River; served Powhatan, 1865-67; Naval Acad., 1868-69; Sabine, 1869-79; Tehuantepec surveying expdn., 1870-71; Plymouth, 1871-73; Naval Acad., 1873-74; exptl. battery, 1876; comdg. Alliance, 1881, Swatara, 1882-84; Navy Yard, Norfolk, Va., 1886-88; Bd. Inspection, 1889; comdg. Swatara, 1890-91, San Francisco, 1894; supt. Naval Acad., 1894-98; comd. U.S.S. Chicago, Dec. 1898-Oct. 1899; comd. Iowa, June 1900-Apr. 1901; supt. 2d naval dist., July 1902-Jan. 1903; sr. squadron comdr., Asiatic Sta., Mar. 1903; comdr.-in-chief Asiatic Fleet, 1904; retired Aug. 5, 1904. Home: Morristown, N.J. Died Dec. 29, 1912.

COOPER, SAMUEL army officer; b. Hackensack, N.J., June 12, 1798; s. Samuel and Mary (Horton) C.; grad. U.S. Mil. Acad., 1815. Aide to Gen. Alexander Macomb, 1828-36; chief-of-staff to Col. W. J. Worth during Seminole War, 1836-37; asst. adj. gen. with rank of maj., 1838; commd. lt., 1847; adj. gen. with rank of col. U.S. Army, 1852-61; adj. and insp. gen. Confederate Army during Civil War. Author: A Concise System of Instruction and Regulations for the Militia and Volunteers of the United States, 1836. Died Cameron, Va., Dec. 3, 1876.

COOPER, WILLIAM GOODWIN, naval officer; b. Savannah, Ga., July 22, 1903; s. Albert Sidney and Katherine (Falli) C.; student Ga. Inst. Tech., 1921-22; B.S., U.S. Naval Acad., 1926; student Nat. War Coll., 1950-51; m. Lois Luther, Oct. 19, 1929; children—William Goodwin, Ann, John L. Commd. ensign USN, 1926, designated naval aviator, 1929, vice adm.; comdr. U.S.S. McCalla, U.S.S. Charles J. Badger, Destroyer Div. 98, World War II; successively comdr. Destroyer Squadron 9, U.S.S. Newport News, Destroyer Flotilla 6; Naval Base, Guantanamo; deputy controller USN; commander Anti-Submarine Defense Force, United States Atlantic Fleet, Norfolk, 1958-71. Awarded Navy Cross, Bronze Star Medal. Mem. Naval Inst. (sec. 1948-50, editor proc. 1948-50, dir. 1950-51), Phi Gamma Delta. Clubs: New York Yacht (N.Y.C.); Army-Navy Country (Arlington, Va.). Died Mar. 1971.

COOTE, RICHARD (1st earl Bellomont), colonial gov.; b. 1636; s. Richard and Mary (St. George) C.; m. Catherine Nanfan. Mem. Parliament for Droitwich, 1688-95; treas., receiver-gen. to Queen, 1687; gov. N.Y., Mass. and N.H., 1697-1701; in command Militia for R.I., Conn. and the Jerseys during Queen Anne's War; commd. to deal with colonial problem of illegal trade and piracy; brought about arrest of Captain Kidd, 1699. Died N.Y.C., Mar. 5, 1701; buried N.Y.C.

COPELAN, ROBERT W state ofcl.; b. Cin., Dec. 22, 1894; s. William and Hannah (Sullivan) C.; student U. Cin., 1914-16, Ohio State U., 1916-17: m. Orene Martha Ebert, Feb. 12, 1925; children-Robert W., Orene Louise (Mrs. Harry J. Bothwell). Reporter, Cin. Enquirer, 1914-20; advt. and ins. bus., 1920-24; successively reporter, rewrite-man, make-up editor, asst. city editor, news editor, asso. mng. editor Cin. Times-Star, 1925-52, mng. editor 1952-58; chief information and edn. sect. Ohio Dept. Natural Resources, 1958-64. Served from 2d lt. to 1st lt. U.S. Army, 1917-19; capt. to maj. O.R.C., 1919-42; maj. to col. AUS, 1942-46. Recipient Italian War Cross, World War I, U.S., Legion of Merit, World War II. Episcopalian. Mason (K.T., comdr.). Home: 6404 Beechmont Av., Cin. 45230. Office: 1500 Dublin Rd., Columbus 12, O. Died Apr. 2, 1967; buried Springrove Cemetery, Cin.

COPPEE, HENRY army officer, coll. pres.; b. Savannah, Ga., Oct. 13, 1821: s. Edward and Carolina (De Lavillate) C., attended Yale; grad. U.S. Mil. Acad., 1845; A.M. (hon.), U. Ga., 1848; LL.D. (Hon.), U. Pas., 1866, Union Coll., 1866; m. Julia de Witt, 1848. Engaged in most of battles on Gen. Scott's march from Vera Cruz to Mexico City during Mexican War, 1846-48; brevetted capt. for distinguished service at battles of Contreras and Churubusco, 1847; asst. prof. French, U.S. Mil. Acad., 1848-49; held chair English lit. and history U. Pa., 1855-66; editor U.S. Service Mag., 1864-66; 1st pres. Lehigh U., 1866-75, also prof. history and lit., until 1874, acting pres., 1893-95; regent Smithsonian Instn., 1874-75, also prof. history and lit., until 1874, acting pres., 1893-95; regent Smithsonian Instn., 1874-95. Author: Elements of Rhetoric, 1859; The Field Manual for Battalion Drill, 1862; The Field Manual of Evolution of the Line, 1862: Grant and His Campaigns, 1866; Songs of Praise in the Christian Centuries, 1866; English Literature Considered as an Interpreter to English History, 1873; History of the Conquest of Spain by the Arab Moors, 2 vols., 1881; The Classic and the Beautiful, 1888-92; General Thomas, 1893. Died Bethlehem, Pa., Mar. 21, 1895.

COPPINGER, JOHN JOSEPH army officer; b. Co. of Cork, Ireland, Oct. 11, 1834; s. William J. and lM. (O'Brien) C.; ed. pvt. schs.; m. Alice, d. late James G. Blaine, 1870. Was lt. and capt. in Roman Army; chevalier for gallantry at La Roca, 1860; came to U.S., 1861; commd. capt. 14th Inf., Sept. 30, 1861; col. 15th N.Y. Cav., Jan. 27, 1865; hon. mustered out vol. service, June 17, 1865; transferred to 23d Inf., Sept. 21, 1866; maj. 10th Inf., Mar. 20, 1879; lt. col. 18th Inf., Oct. 31, 1883; col. 23d Inf., Jan. 15, 1891; brig. gen., Apr. 25, 1895; maj. gen. vols., May 4, 1898; retired from U.S.A., by operation of law. Oct. 11, 1898; hon. disch. from vol. service, Oct. 31, 1898. Bvtd. maj., June 12, 1864, for battle of Trevillian Sta., Va.; lt. col., Oct. 19, 1864, for battle of Cedar Creek, Va.; col., Dec. 1, 1868, for operations against Indians, 1866-68. Home: Washington, D.C. Died 1909.

CORBIN, HENRY CLARK army officer; b. Clermont Co., O., Sept. 15, 1842; s. Shadrach and Mary Anne C.; reared on farm; ed. common schools and 2 yrs. in private acad.; studied law, 1860-61; m. Edith Agnes Patten, Nov. 6, 1901. Entered U.S.V., 2d lt. 83d Ohio Inf., July 28, 1862; advanced through ranks to col. U.S.C.T., Sept. 23, 1865; bvtd. brig. gen. U.S.V., Mar. 13, 1865, for meritorious services; hon. mustered out, Mar. 26, 1866; bvtd. maj., Mar. 2, 1867, for gallant and meritorious services in action at Decatur, Ala., and lt. col., Mar. 2, 1867 for same at Nashville. Entered regular army as 2d lt. 17th U.S. Inf., May 11, 1866; promoted through grades to lt. gen. U.S.A., Apr. 15, 1906; retired, Sept. 15, 1906. Served 10 yrs. on plains in Kan., N. Mex., Ariz. and Tex.; in Mar. 1877, detailed for duty at Executive Mansion; sec. Sitting Bull Commn. With Pres. Garfield at the time he was shot and at his bedside at Elberon, where he died. In recognition of his services, and the part he took in war with Spain, Congress conferred upon him rank of maj. gen. Comd. Atlantic Div., 1904; conducted army maneuvers, Manassas, Va., Sept., 1904; comd. Philippine Div., 1904, Northern Div., 1906. Home: Washington, D.C. Died 1909.

CORBIN, MARGARET heroine; b. in what is now Franklin County, Pa., Nov. 12, 1751; d. Robert Cochran; m. John Corbin, 1772. Accompanied husband when he marched to war with 1st Co., Pa. Arty., Continental Army, 1776; took her husband's place when he was killed h while defending a cannon against Hessians in Battle of Ft. Washington 1776; fought until severely wounded, captured, but not held prisoner: went to Phila., granted lifetime pension by Continental Congress for her bravery. Died Westchester County, N.Y., Jan. 16, 1800.

CORBY, WILLIAM clergyman, coll. pres.; b. Detroit, Oct. 2, 1833; ed. U. Notre Dame, 1853-60. Apptd. perfect discipline U. Notre Dame, 1858, prof., dir. Manual Labor Sch., 1860, v.p., 1865, pres., 1866-72, 1877-81, rebuilt univ. during 2d term as pres., added new depts., raised standards; ordained priest Roman Catholic Ch., 1860; chaplain (commd. by gov. N.Y.) to N.Y. "Irish Brigade serving with Army of Potomac, 1861-64; pres. Sacred Heart Coll., Watertown, Wis., 1872-77 founder, comdr. Notre Dame Post 569, Grand Army Republic. Author: Chaplain Life: Three Years in the Army of the Potomac, 1894. Died Notre Dame, Ind., Dec. 28, 1897.

CORCORAN, MICHAEL army officer; b. Carrowkeel, Sligo, Ireland, Sept. 21, 1827. Served in Royal Irish Constabulary, 1846-49; came to N.Y., circa 1849; rose through ranks to col. 69th Regt., N.Y. Militia, 1859; up for trial for refusing to permit his men to parade in honor of Prince of Wales, 1860 court-martial dropped when Civil War began); captured at Battle of Bull Run, imprisoned for 13 months; raised 4 regts. (called Irish Legion) in N.Y., served as brig. gen. of Legion in engagements in Va., 1 year. Died when thrown from his horse, Fairfax Court House, Va., Dec. 22, 1863.

CORKER, STEPHEN ALFESTUS congressman, lawyer; b. nr. Waynesboro, Burke County, Ga., May 7, 1830; attended common schs.; studied law. Admitted to bar, practiced in Waynesboro; became farmer; entered Confederate Army, 1861, served as capt. Co. A, 3d Ga. Regt.; mem. Ga. Ho. of Reps.; mem. U.S. Ho. of Reps. (Democrat, filled vacancy) from Ga., 41st Congress, Dec. 22, 1870-71. Died Waynesboro, Oct. 18, 1879; buried Old Cemetery, Waynesboro.

CORLETT, WILLIAM WELLINGTON congressman; b. Concord, O., Apr. 10, 1842; grad. Willoughby (O.) Collegiate Inst., 1861; attended U. Mich. Law Sch.; grad. Union Law Coll., Cleve., 1866. Enlisted in Union Army, 1862; served in 28th Regt., Ohio Volunteer Inf. short time, transferred to 87th Regt.; captured with command at Harpers Ferry, 1862, paroled; returned to Ohio; sch. tchr., Kirkland, Painesville, O.; reentered Army with 25th Ohio Battery, later placed on detached service with 3d Ia. Battery, served until end of Civil War; returned to Ohio, 1865; admitted to bar, 1866; prof. elementary law State U. and Law Coll.; lectr. several comml. colls., Cleve.; settled in Cheyenne, Wyo., 1867; practiced law; postmaster Cheyenne, 1870; mem. Wyo. Territorial Senate, 1871; pros. atty. Laramie County, 1872-76; mem. U.S. Congress (Republican) from Wyo. Territory, 45th Congress, 1877-79; declined appointment as chief justice Wyo. Territory, 1879; mem. Wyo. Legislative Council, 1880-82. Died Cheyenne, July 22, 1890; buried Lakeview Cemetery.

CORLISS, AUGUSTUS WHITTEMORE soldier; b. N. Yarmouth, Me., Mar. 25, 1837; s. Robert Elwell and Asenath (Field) C.; grad. N. Yarmouth (Me.) Acad., 1851; widower. Served in Civil War from 1862 as lt. col. 2d R.I. Cav.; after war was 2d lt. and later 1st lt., 15th U.S. Inf.; capt. 8th U.S. Inf.; maj. 7th U.S. Inf., 1897; lt. col. 2d U.S. Inf., 1899; col. 2d U.S. Inf., 1901; brig. gen. U.S.A. retired, Apr. 23, 1904. Republican. Home: Denver, Colo. Died 1908.

CORLISS, LELAND MARCHANT, physician; b. Gloucester, Mass., July 5, 1905; s. William Dale and Leonette (Burnham) C.; M.D., Tufts Coll., 1932; postgrad. surgery, U. Edinburgh (Scotland), 1934-35; m. Eleanor Nelson, June 6, 1934; children—Leland Marchant (dec.), Gardner Burnham. Intern Meml. Hosp., Worcester, Mass., 1932-34 resident New Eng. Med. Center, Boston, 1935-36, Community Hosp., Rumford, Me., 1936-37; sch. physician, also engaged in gen. practice, Paris, Me., 1937-42; med. examiner Oxford County, Me., 1939-42; med. dir. Denver pub. schs., 1949-70; Mem. Paris Sch. Bd., 1939-42; initiated pure tone hearing test for pre-schoolers, 1955; a developer pre-sch. vision test, 1955; mem. sci. and research com. Colo. Heart Assn., 1952-70; charter mem., bd. dirs. Colo. Soc. Prevention Blindness, 1956-70; mem. Colo. Adv. Com. Polio, 1955-70; speaker Internat. Conf. Health and Health Edn., 1962; cons. Forsyth Conf. Dental Health Edn., 1963; lectr. seminar Sch. Pub. Health Harvard; cons., group leader USPHS; charter member Joint Com. on School and College Health. Bd. dirs. Colo. div. Am. Cancer Soc. Dir. Meridian (Mut.) Fund, Inc. Recipient Distinguished Service awards Colo. Health Fair, 1961, Am. Sch. Health Assn., 1963, Howe award Am. Sch. Health Association, 1967. Served to lt. comdr. USNR, 1942-47; ETO, Mem. Internat. Union Health Edn., Am. Nat. Council Health. Edn. Pub. (research com), Am. Sch. Health Assn. (life, pres. 1960-61), World, Am. (group chmn. nat. conf. physicians and schs. 1949-70) med. assns., Me., Mass., Colo., Denver med. socs., Colo. Pub. Health Assn., Colo. Health Careers Council, Nat. Colo.

edn. assns., Colo. Schoolmasters Assn., Ret. Officers Assn., U.S. Naval Acad. Found., Phi Chi. Republican. Member of the Universalist Church. Mason (32 deg.), Shriner). Author: The School Physician in the Athletic Program (lecture with audio-visual aids), 1962. Co-author of high school health textbook. Producer: About Your Life, sex education filmstrip, 1958. Contbr. articles profl. jours. Home: Denver CO Died Sept. 18, 1970; buried Gloucester MA

CORNELL, EZEKIEL army officer, Continental congressman; b. Situate, R.I., Mar. 27, 1733; s. Richard and Content (Brownell) C.; m. Rachel Wood, 1790. Dep. adj. gen. 11th Continental Inf., 1776; commd. comdr. with rank brig. gen. R.I. Brigade, 1777; mem. Continental Congress, 1780-83; insp. Continental Army under Washington 1782. Died Milford, Mass., Apr. 25, 1800.

CORNELL, WALTER STEWART, physician; b. Phila., Pa., Jan. 3, 1877; s. Watson and Mary Ella (Hurtt) C.; B.S., U. of Pa., 1897, M.D., 1901, D.P.H., 1922; m. Mabel Bremer Kuhn, 1922. Engaged in private practice of medicine, 1902-12; dir. of med. inspection of public schs., Phila., 1912-43; lecturer in anatomy, U. of Pa. Med. Sch., 1902-26; lecturer in hygiene, Univ. of Pennsylvania, 1919-56; formerly asst. professor of public health and preventive medicine, Temple University Med. Sch.; chmn. exec. com. and dir. Pub. School Health Fund, Phila. Maj. in Med. Corps, U.S. Army, 1917-19; lt. col., then col., Med. Reserve Corps, and surgeon 79th Div., 1919-35. Member American Public Health Association, A.M.A., Am. Sch. Health Assn., Phila. Coll. of Physicians, Phi Beta Kappa, Delta Tau Delta, Alpha Mu Pi Omega, Sigma Xi. Republican. Presbyterian. Mason. Club: Union League (Phila.). Author: Handbook of Osteology, 1909; Health and Medical Inspection of School Children, 1912. Former editor: Diabetic Digest. Home: Philadelphia PA Died Mar. 21, 1969; buried West Laurel Hill Cemetery, Philadelphia PA

CORNISH, LORENZO DANA civil engr.; b. Lee Centre, N.Y., Mar. 30, 1877; s. James Bennett and Frances Emeline (Ward) C.; C.E., Syracuse U., 1902; m. Mary Elizabeth Brodhead, Jan. 15, 1901 (died 1911); 1 son, Eugene Brodhead; m. 2d, Jeanette Welsh, May 18, 1916. Jr. U.S. civ. engr. and supt. constn., at Pittsburgh, 1902-06; asst. engr. Internat. Consulting Bd. Panama Canal, 1906; designing engr. Isthamian Canal Commn., 1907-13; prin. asst. engr. Am. Red Cross Bd. Engrs., China, 1914; prin. U.S. engr., U.S. Engr. Dept., Cincinnati, O., 1915-17; asst. chief engr., 1919, became chief engr., 1928, Div. of Waterways, State of Ill., building Waterways, Lockport to LaSalle. Served as pvt. Co. C, 3d N.Y. Vols., June-Oct. 1898; capt. 15th Engrs., U.S.A., June 11, 1917-Feb. 13, 1919; maj., Feb. 13-Oct. 30, 1919; hon. disch. Oct. 30, 1919. Republican. Baptist, Home: Chicago, Ill. Died May 12, 1934.

CORNMAN, DANIEL army officer; b. Carlisle, Pa., Feb. 8, 1852: s. Ephraim and Barbara (Shrom) C.; grad. high sch., Carlisle, 1869, U.S. Mil. Acad., 1873; m. Julia E. Leighton, Oct. 8, 1877. Second lt. 21st Inf., 1873, 1st lt., 1877, capt., 1888, maj., 1899, lt.-col. 24th Inf., 1901, col. 7th Inf., 1903. Retired 1915. Served in Nez Percé Shoshone and Sioux Indian campaigns, and Spanish-Am. War and Philippine insurrection. Democrat. Episcopalian. Mason. Address: care Adjutant General U.S.A., Washington. Died Feb. 5, 1924.

CORNSTALK (INDIAN NAME KEIGH-TUGH-GUA), Indian chief; b. Pa., 1720. Shawnee Indian chief; ally of French made 1st attack of English settlers, Rockbridge County, Va., 1759; ally of Pontiac, 1863 1763; taken hostage (with brother Silver Heels) and released on parole; remained at peace with settlers during border skirmishes, 1764-74; objected to authorities after his brother was maliciously shot and wounded; Lord Dunmore (gov. Va.) decided to settle matter by force (Lord Dunmore's War, 1764, ended by treaty of Camp Charlotte, 1764); taken hostage at Ft. Pitt (now Ohio) while on mission to warn settlers of impending Shawnee uprising, 1777. Murdered with other hostages after Indians killed a white soldier, Ft. Pitt, 1777.

CORNWALLIS, CHARLES (1ST MARQUIE AND 2D EARL OF CORNALLIS) army officer, gov.-gen. of India; b. Grosvenor Sq., London, Eng., Dec. 31, 1738: s. Charles Cornwallis (1st earl of Cornwallis); attended Eton, also Turin (Italy) Mil. Acad.; m. Jemima Tullikens, 1768, 1 son, Charles. Commd. ensign Grenadier Guards, 1756; promoted capt. 85th Regt., 1759; lt. col. 12th Regt. 1761; col. 33d Regt., 1766; joint vice treas. of Ireland, 1769-70; constable of Tower of London, 1770; promoted maj. gen. Brit. Army, 1775; sent to duty in Am., 1776; served in battles of S.I., L.I., Bklyn., also capture of N.Y.C.; won Battle of Brandywine and occupied Phila., 1777; made 2d in command in N.Am. to Sir Henry Clinton, 1778; drew up plans for invasion of Southern colonies took charge of these operations, 1779, captured Charleston, S.C., 1780; forced to surrender at Yorktown, Va. (after Gen. Washington cut him off from aid by Clinton), 1781, blamed Clinton's inactivity for the failure; gov.-gen. of India (rendered services considered invaluable to the Crown), 1785-93. Died Ghazipore, India (while gen.-in-chief in India), Oct. 5, 1805; buried Ghazipore.

CORWIN, RICHARD WARREN M.D., surgeon; b. Binghamton, N.Y., May 24, 1852; s. Walter Scott and Rhoda (Little) C.; student scientific course, Cornell, 1871-74; M.D., U. of Mich., 1878; interne St. Luke's Hosp., Chicago, 1879-81; studied in European hosps., 1893. 1900; LL.D., U. of Colo., 1905; hon. A.M., U. of Denver, 1906; unmarried. Instr. comparative anatomy and microscopy, U. of Mich., 1874-78; chief surgeon from 1881, supt. sociol. dept. from 1900, Colo. Fuel & Iron Co.; chief surgeon Colo. & Wyo. Ry., Crystal River Ry.; div. surgeon Mo.P. Ry.; local surgeon D. & R.G. Ry., C. & S. Ry.; prof. surgery U. of Colo. Lecturer on med., sociol. and other themes; asst. editor "Physicians and Suregons," 1878-84. Pres. Colo. State Conf. Charities and Corrections, 1906; mem. bd., Colo. State Prison Assn., 1906; Colo. State Normal Sch., 8 yrs., Colo. State Bd. Health, 5 yrs., Colo. State Agrl. Coll., 1905 - , Pueblo Sch. Bd., 1892 - . First lt. C.N.G., 1883-84; capt. and 1st asst. surgeon, 1884-87; maj. and surgeon, 1887-98; col. and surgeon-gen.; 1898; col. and a.-d.-c., 1903, 1904, 1907, 1908. Fellow Am. Coll. Surgeons. Republican. Protestant. Mason. Home: Pueblo, Colo. Died June 1928.

COSBY, FRANK CARVILL naval officer; b. Louisville, Ky., Apr. 10, 1840; s. Fortunatus and Ellen (Blake) C.; ed. in Ky. and Washington, to 1854; receiving teller, U.S. Treasury, 1854-57; m. Charlotte M. Spencer, Dec. 6, 1864. Capt.'s clerk, U.S.N., 1857-61; paymaster Potomac flotilla, 1861-63; depot paymaster S. Atlantic squadron, 1863-64, participating in engagements on Potomac and Rappahannock rivers, off Charleston, etc.; paymaster Baltimore and Annapolis stas., 1865-68; Honolulu, H.I., 1868-69, and various other stas. until became fleet paymaster, European sta., 1877-81; various duties to 1897; mem. Bd. Inspection and Survey of Naval Vessels, 1897-98; pres. Naval Examining Bd., 1897-1901; gen. insp. pay corps U.S.N. with rank of capt., 1898-1902; pay dir. with rank of rear admiral, retired. Home: Washington, D.C. Died 1905.

COSBY, GEORGE BLAKE receiver public moneys of Calif.; b. Louisville, Ky., Jan. 19, 1830; s. Fortunatus and Ellen (Blake) C.; ed. private schools; clerk in commn. house; entered West Point, Sept. 1, 1848; bvt. lt. mounted rifles, July 1, 1852; 2d lt., Sept. 16, 1856; capt., May 9, 1861. Entered C.S.A. as capt. cav.; was chief of staff to Gens. Magruder and Buckner; promoted brig. gen., Jan. 20, 1863; comd. cav. brigade under Gen. Earl Van Dorn. After war went to Calif., where was adj. gen. 5 yrs., and held various other govt. and state offices. Home: Sacramento, Calif. Died 1909.

COSBY, SPENCER army officer; b. Baltimore, Oct. 2, 1867; s. Frank C. and Charlotte M. (Spencer) C.; prep. edn. high sch., Washington, and 3 yrs. in France; grad. U.S. Mil. Acad., 1st in class, 1891; grad. U.S. Engr. Sch. of Application, 1894; m. Yvonne Shepard, of Washington, Sept. 15, 1909. Apptd. additional 2d lt. engrs., June 12, 1891; 2d lt., Apr. 12, 1894; 1st lt., Oct. 13, 1895; maj. engrs. U.S.V., June 13-Dec. 31, 1898; capt., Feb. 2, 1901; maj., June 9, 1907; lt. col., Feb. 28, 1915; col., Aug. 5, 1917. In charge of river and harbor and fortification works, Phila., Mobile and Washington; engr. officer on staff Maj.-Gen. Brooke in P.R. during Spanish-Am. War; in charge lighthouse constrn. in P.I., 1903-05; in charge water supply system, Washington, 1905-09; in charge pub. bldgs. and grounds, Washington, with rank of col., Mar. 15, 1909-13; mil. attaché, U.S. Embassy, Paris, 1913-17; comdg. 5th Regt. Engrs., 1917-18; chief engr. 9th Div., 1918; in charge Galveston engr. dist., 1919-. Officer of Legion of Honor, France, 1917. Mem. Am. Soc. C.E., Internat. Congress Navigation. Clubs: Rittenhouse, University (Phila.), Metropolitan, Chevy Chase, Army and Navy (Washington), Home: 2027 Massachusetts Av. N.W., Washington, D.C.

COSGROVE, JAMES J. lawyer; b. North Braddock, Pa., July 10, 1887; s. Thomas and Mary (Flanagan) C.; A.B., Cornell U., 1909; LL.B., U. Pitts., 1912; m. Louise Callan, Apr. 17, 1922; 1 dau., Mary Lousie Yount. Admitted to Pa. bar, 1912; practiced law, Pitts., 1912-17; spl. atty. to commr. internal revenue, Washington, 1921-22; atty., Tex. Co., N.Y.C., 1922-29; gen. counsel Continental Oil Co., 1929-43, gen. counsel, v.p., 1943-47, chmn. bd. dirs., 1945-. Served with U.S. Army, 1917-20; capt. inf., 1917-18, promoted maj., 1918; assigned bd. of appraisers, War Dept., 1919-20. Mem. Am., Okla., Pa. bar assns., Am. Petroleum Inst. (dir.), Knight of Malta, Phi Kappa Sigma, Phi Delta Phi. Clubs: Metropolitan, Whitehall, Cornell, Siwanoy Country (N.Y.); Blind Brook Country. Home: 277 Park Av. Office: 30 Rockefeller Plaza, N.Y.C. Died Aug. 22, 1960; buried Calvary Cemetery, Pitts.

COTHRAN, JAMES SPROULL congressman, lawyer; b. nr. Abbeville, S.C., Aug. 8, 1830; grad. U. Ga., 1852; studied law. Admitted to bar, 1853, practiced in Abbeville: served from pvt. to capt. Confederate Army, during Civil War; with his Company at surrender Army of Northern Va. at Appomattox; elected solicitor 8th Jud. Circuit, 1876, 80, apptd. judge 8th Jud. Circuit, 1881, elected by S.C. Legislature to same office, 1882, 85; mem. U.S. Ho. of Reps. (Democrat) from S.C., 50th-51st congresses, 1887-91; practiced in Abbeville and Greenville, S.C. Died in sanitarium, N.Y.C., Dec. 5, 1897; buried Upper Long Cane Cemetery, Abbeville.

COTHRAN, PERRIN CHILES insurance exc.; b. Chiles Crossroads (Millway), S.C., Feb. 22, 1886; s. Capt. (CSA) Wade Elephare and Sara (Chiles) C.; B.S., C.E. Clemson Coll., S.C., 1904; m. Annie Wilson Howe, Dec. 31, 1910 (divorced 1916); 1 dau., Josephine (Mrs. Samuel Wilson); m. 2d, Ruth Galbraith, Sept. 18, 1941; children-Perrin Galbraith. Robert Chiles, Asst. resident engr., Carolina, Clinchfield & Ohio R.R., Clinchport, Va., 1904-06; resident engr. Va. Pocahontas Coal Co., Coalwood, W.Va., 1906-08; resident engr. N.&S. Ry., Raleigh, N.C., 1908-10; spl. agt. N.C. Home Ins. Co., Raleigh, N.C., 1910-12, Conn. Fire Ins. Co., Richmond, Va., 1912-17; mgr. Am. Fgn. Ins. Assn. of east coast, S.A., Rio de Janeiro. Brazil. 1919-27; spl. agt. Phoenix Ins. Co., Phila., 1927-28; sec. Phoenix Ins. Co., Hartford, Conn., 1928-35; vice pres. and sec. Phoenix-Conn. group of ins. cos.; dir. Phoenix Ins. Co., Conn. Fire Ins. Co.; pres. and dir. Stock Co. Assn., Washington, D.C.; vice pres. and dir. Reliance Ins. Co., Montreal, Can., dir. First Nat. Bank of Hartford, since 1941. Mem. governing com. New York Fire Ins.: Rating Orgn., New York City, governing com. Md. Rating Bur., Baltimore, Md., bd. of govs. Middle Dept. Assn. of Fire Underwriters, Phila., Pa. Served as capt., major and lt. col. of engrs., 195th engrs., 30th Am. div., III corps, U.S. Army, IV British Army, A.E.F.; col. res. corps engrs., comdg. officer 301st engrs., 76th div., U.S. Army; trans. inactive res., 1949. Mem. bd. of finance, City of Hartford, 1937-44. Democrat. Mason. Clubs: Bankers (New York City); Dauntless (Essex, Conn.); Hartford, Hartford Golf (Hartford, Conn.). Home: 11 Woodside Circle, Office: 30 Trinity St., Hartford, Conn. Died Dec. 23, 1959.*

COTTAM, GILBERT (GEOFFREY) (KOT'TAM) public health official; b. Manchester, England, August 2, 1873; s. Rev. Henry (M.A.) and Eliza Mary (Warburton) C.; came to the United States at the age of 16 years; M.D., St. Louis University, 1893; m. F. May Isham Ruddick, June 16, 1896; 1 son, Dr. Geoffrey Isham Warburton; m. 2d, Grace Elizabeth Pulley, June 21, 1930 (she died on September 24, 1945). Interne, St. Louis (Missouri) Female Hospital, 1893-94; engaged in practice, Rock Rapids, Ia., 1894-1910; Sioux Falls, South Dakota, 1910-30 and 1940-43; Minneapolis, Minnesota, 1930-40; mem. staff Sioux Valley Hosp.; chief of staff, McKennan Hosp., 1943; supt. S.D., State Bd. of Health since 1943. Commissioned captain medical section Officers Reserve Corps, U.S. Army, May 28, 1918, and began active service at Camp Dodge, Iowa; went overseas with Base Hosp. 88, Sept. 1918, and was made chief of surg. service of same, in France; maj., May 19, 1919; chief of surg. service, Ft. Riley, Kan., until discharged, Oct. 9, 1919; col. (inactive) Medical Reserve, U.S. Army. Chief of Emergency Medical Service, Office of Civilian Defense, Sioux Falls, S.D., 1943. Licentiate (founders' group) American Board of Surgery, 1937. Fellow American College Surgeons (bd. govs. 1925), A.M.A.; mem. Western Surg. Assn. (life), State Med. Assn. S. Dak. (pres. 1922-23), Minn. Path. Soc., Minneapolis Surg. Soc., Sioux Valley Med. Assn. (pres. 1927-28), Am. Public Health Assn., and various other medical societies. Mem. Alpha Omega Alpha. Republican. Episcopalian. Mason. Clubs: Minneapolis Professional Men's (pres. 1940; life member). Contbr. to surg. publs. (Mem. editorial bd. Journal Lancet, 1931-37 and since 1940; asso. editor Minnesota Medicine, 1937-40. Home: St. Charles Hotel. Office: State Capitol, Pierre, S.D. Died Mar 4, 1949.

COTTER, CARL HENRY ret. naval officer; b. Bay City, Mich., July 11, 1892; s. William H. and Mary (Nickert) C.; B.S. (C.E.), U. Mich., 1916; m. Elizabeth Howard, June 16, 1914 (dec.): m. 2d, Katherine Elizabeth Murphy, Dec. 20, 1938; children-Mary Katherine, Patricia Lyster. Structural draftsman, 1916; asst. to city engr., Flint, Mich., 1917; entered Navy as asst. civil engr., 1918; promoted through grades to rear-adm. (C.E.C.), 1943; dir. Pacific div. Bur. Yards and Docks, 1943-45; rear adm., ret. 1947; v.p. Blythe Bros. Co., Charlotte, N.C., 1947-48; pres., dir. Merritt-Chapman & Scott Corp., and subsidiaries; v.p. Merritt-Chapman-Lindsay, Ltd., Jamaica, B.W.I., 1949-50; v.p. Blythe Bros. Co.; pres., dir. Blythe Co. of P.R., Capitol Constrn. Co. P.R.; v.p., dir. P.R. Asphalt Co., 1951-59, v.p., dir. Carolina Products Co., Ready Mix Concrete Co., 1951-59, Decorated D.S.M., World Wars I and II medals, Haitian Campaign, Navy Expeditionary and Pacific Area medals (U.S.), Medal Honneur et Merite (Haiti). Mem. Am. Soc. C.E., Am. Concrete Inst., Soc. Am. Mil. Engrs. Clubs: University, U. Mich.; Meyers Park Country (Charlotte). Home: 1615 Queens Rd., Charlotte, N.C. 28207. Died Oct. 9, 1965; buried Arlington Nat. Cemetery.

COTTMAN, VINCENDON LAZARUS rear adm.; b. Donaldsville, La., Feb. 13, 1852; s. Thomas Edmond Huff and Marie Louise (de Tournillon) C.; grad. U.S. Naval Acad., 1872. Ensign, July 15, 1873; master, May 9, 1878; lt., Jan. 8, 1885; lt. comdr., July 1, 1898; comdr., May 15, 1902; capt., Jan. 15, 1907; rear adm., Nov. 7, 1910. Sec. Internat. Marine Conf., Washington, 1889-90; served at Guam and Manila, 1899; comdt. Navy Yard, Puget Sound, Wash., and 13th naval defense dist., 1910-14; retired, Feb. 13, 1914. Home: Seattle, Wash. Died Mar. 15, 1917.

COTTON, CHARLES STANHOPE naval officer; b. Milwaukee, Feb. 15, 1843; s. Lester Holt and Mary Ann C.; apptd. to U.S. Naval Acad. from Wis., 1858; ordered into active service, May, 1861; m. Aug. 30, 1865, Miss R. C. Robertson. Promoted ensign, Nov. 1, 1862; advanced through grades to rear adm., Feb. 27, 1900. Served on St. Lawrence, 1861; on Minnesota, N. Atlantic Blockading Squadron, 1861-63; participated in action between Merrimac and Monitor and the fleet in Hampton Roads, Mar. 1862; on Iroquois, 1863; Oneida, W. Gulf Blockading Squadron, 1864-65; in battle of Mobile Bay, and at surrender of Ft. Morgan, 1864; Shenandoah, Asiatic Sta., 1865-69; duty at Naval Acad., 1869-70; various duties to 1898; comd. Harvard during Spanish War, 1898; Navy Yard, Mare Island, 1898-99; comd. receiving-ship Independence, 1899-1900; mem. Naval Retiring Bd., 1900; commandant Navy Yard, Norfolk, 1900-03; comdr.-in-chief European Squadron, 1903-04; retired, Feb. 16, 1904. Died 1909.

COTTON, FREDERIC JAY surgeon; b. Prescott, Wis., Sept. 24, 1869; s. Joseph Potter and Isabella (Cole) C.; A.B., Harvard, 1890, A.M., 1894; M.D., Harvard Med. Sch., 1894; surg. house officer, Mass. Gen. Hosp.; post-grad. work, Coll. Phys. and Surg., New York, U. of Vienna; m. Jane Baldwin, Feb. 8, 1902. Practiced, Boston, 1897 - ; asst. surgeon, Children's Hosp., 1897-1902; surgeon Boston City Hospital, 1902-1931; surgeon Beth Israel Hospital, 1923-27; asst. in surgery, Harvard Med. Sch., 2 yrs., 1903-04; asst. prof. surgery, Tufts Coll. Med. Sch., 1906-10; lecturer in surgery, Harvard Med. Grad. School. Acting asst. surgeon at Montauk Pt., U.S.A., for 2 mos. during Spanish-Am. War; maj. M.C.U.S.A., 1918-19; consultant in surgery, U.S. Pub. Health Service, 1919 - . Fellow Am. Surg. Assn., Am. Coll. Surgeons (a founder). Presbyn. Author: Dislocations and Joint Fractures, 1910. Home: Boston, Mass. Died Apr. 14, 1938.

COTTON, HENRY ANDREWS medical dir.; b. Norfolk, Va., May 19, 1869; s. George Adolphus and Mary Della (Biggs) C.; grad. Baltimore Poly. Inst., 1894; spl. student Johns Hopkins, 1895; M.D., U. of Md., 1899; studied Royal U., Munich, under Prof. Kraepelin, 1905-06; spl. research student, in Pathol. Lab., same, under Prof. Alzheimer, 1906-07; hon. A.lM., Saint John's Coll., 1914; m. A. Delha Keys, Oct. 15, 1903; children - Henry Andrews, Adolph G. Asst. phys., City Asylum, Bay View, Baltimore, 1899-1900, Worcester (Mass.) State Hosp., 1900-03, Danvers (Mass.) State Hosp., 1903-07; med. dir. N.J. State Hosp., Nov. 15, 1904 - . Served U.S.A., 6 mos., Hosp. Corps, Chickamauga, Spanish-Am. War, 1898; maj. Medical Corps, U.S. Army, World War. Democrat. Presbyn. Author: Defective Delinquent and Insane (Vanuxem lectures, Princeton, 1921). Engaged in investigation of relation of physical factors to causation of mental disorders. Died May 8, 1933.

COUCH, DARIUS NASH army officer; b. Southeast, N.Y., July 23, 1822; s. Jonathan Couch; grad. U.S. Mil. Acad., 1846; m. Mary Caroline Crocker, Aug. 31, 1854. Served as 2d lt. 4th Arty., U.S. Army at Battle of Buena Vista during Mexican War: commd. 1st lt., 1847; stationed on Atlantic coast, 1847-53, 55: on leave of absence to make zool. expdn. to Northern Mexico, 1853-54; resigned comm., 1855. commd. col. 7th Mass. Inf., U.S. Volunteers, 1861, promoted birg. gen., 1861, maj. gen., 1862; served in Peninsular campaign; participated in battles of Fair Oaks, Antietam, Fredericksburg, Chancellorsville, Gettysburg, and Nashville; in charge of ceremones consecrating nat. cemetery at Gettysburg (Pa.) 1863: resigned comm. 1865; collector Port of Boston; pres. of a mining and mfg. company; q.m. and adjutant gen. of Comm. Died Norwalk, Conn., Feb. 12, 1897; buried Tauntaon, Mass.

COUDEN, ALBERT REYNOLDS rear adm.; b. Michigan City, Ind., Oct. 30, 1846; s. Reynolds and Margaret S. (Marshall) C.; apptd. to U.S. Naval Acad. from Utah, 1863, grad. 1867. Promoted ensign, Dec. 18, 1868; advanced through grades to rear-adm., July 12, 1907. Summer of 1864 was in active service on board Marion in pursuit of Confederate steamer Florida; various duties to 1896; charge naval proving ground, Indian Head, 1896-1900; comd. Wheeling, 1900-01, Mohican, 1901-02; commandant Naval Sta., Cavite, 1902-04; gen. insp. of ordnance for navy, 1904-06; comd. Louisiana, 1906-07; mem. bd. on Crozier and Brown systems wire wound guns, 1907; later pres. Bd. Naval Ordnance; retired, Oct. 30, 1908. Recalled to active duty, Sept. 1917, with Bur. Navy Ordnance, War Industries and U.S. Shipping bds.; released from active duty, Nov. 1919. Died Apr. 7, 1923.

COUES, SAMUEL FRANKLIN rear adm.; b. in N.H., Sept. 17, 1825. Apptd. asst. surgeon U.S.N., Feb. 25, 1851; surgeon, Apr. 26, 1861; med. dir., Aug. 15, 1876; retired, June 29, 1906, with rank of rear admiral for services during Civil War. Pres. Naval Examining Bd., Phila., 1884-87; in charge Naval Hospital, Chelsea, Mass., Mar.-Sept. 1887. Home: Cambridge, Mass. Died May 1, 1916.

COULTER, JOHN STANLEY physician: b. Phila., Pa., Sept. 27, 1885; s. Levi and Clara (Kinnier) C.; grad Central High Sch., Phila., 1905; M.D., Univ. of Pa. Med. Sch.; 1909; grad. Army Med. Sch., Washington, D.C., 1911; grad. Univ. of Philippines Med. Sch., 1916; m. Margaret Noyes; 1 son (by previous marriage), John Alfred. Settled in Chicago, 1920; prof. in charge physical therapy depts. of Northwestern Univ. Med. Sch., Ill. Central, St. Luke's, Alexian Brothers, Passavant and Wesley hospitals. Chairman council on physical medicine of American Medical Association. Served with Medical Corps, U.S. Army, as 1st lt., capt., maj. and lt. col., 1910-20. Fellow Am. Coll. Surgeons; mem. Am. Med. Assn., Ill. State and Chicago med. socs., Am. Rheumatism Assn., Am. Congress Physical Medicine, Soc. Phys. Medicine, Inst. of Medicine, Chicago. Democrat, Presbyterian. Asso. editor; Principles and Practice Phys. Therapy, 1934 Medical Cyclopedia Service, Vols. 1935, 36, 37, 38, 39, 40, 41, 42, 43, 44, 45, also 2d edition, 1940. Asst. editor: Archives of Physical Therapy and Acta Americana. Contbr. to Reimann's Treatment in General Medicine, 1939, and Barr's Modern Medical Therapy in General Practice, 1940. Glasser's Medical Physics, 1943. Author: History Physical Therapy, 1933. Home: Westville, Ind. Office: 122 S. Michigan Av., Chicago, Ill. Died Dec. 16, 1949.

COUNTS, GERALD ALFORD army officer, educator; b. Ranger, Tex., Sept. 24, 1895; s. John Ellis and Willa Bailey (Shelton) C.; student U. Cal. at Berkeley, 1913-14; B.S., U.S. Mil. Acad., 1917; B.S. in Civil Engring., Mass. Inst. Tech., 1921; postgrad. Cal. Inst. Tech., 1930-31; m. Anne Earle Harris, Nov. 21, 1921; 1 dau., Anne Harris (Mrs. John M. Minor). Commd. 2d lt. C.E., U.S. Army, 1917, advanced through grades to brig. gen., 1957; assigned 109th Engrs., 604th Engrs., 6th Engrs., World War I; river and harbor engring. Los Angeles, Galveston engr. dists., also field charge constrn. Houston Ship Channel, 1921-25; faculty U.S. Mil. Acad., 1925-30, 31-, acting prof. physics, 1931-34, prof. physics, 1934-46, head dept. physics and chemistry, 1946-57, dean acad. bd., 1957-; dep. chief engr. MTO, 1943-44; dep. G-4, 12th Army Group, Normandy to Germany, German occupation, World War II; ret., 1959. Decorated Legion of Merit with cluster, Bronze Star; Legion of Honor, Croix de Guerre with palm (France); Order of Leopold, Croix de Guerre with palm (Belgium); Courone de Chene (Luxembourg); Order Brit. Empire. Mem. Am. Soc. Engring. Edn., Am. Soc. Mil. Engrs., Kappa Alpha. Episcopalian. Home: Quarters 107. Office: Office of the Dean, West Point, N.Y. Died July 30, 1964; buried West Point, N.Y.

COUPAL, JAMES FRANCIS surgeon U.S.A.; b. Quincy, Mass., Jan. 26, 1884; s. Moses Edward and Mary Ann (Hayes) C.; B.S., Tufts Coll., 1906, M.D., 1909, M.S., 1928; m. Martha L. Wilfert, June 23, 1916. Began practice at Boston, 1910; commd. lt. M.R.C., June 18, 1915; capt. med. dept. Mass. N.G., June 19, 1916; maj. M.C., U.S.A., Feb. 17, 1919; maj. M.C. (regular army), July 1, 1920; apptd. White House physician, July 1, 1924; apptd. col. U.S.A., by act of Congress, Mar. 1928; resigned July 12, 1929. Republican. Author of Gas Gangrene Chapter, U.S. Medical History of World War. Home: Washington, D.C. Died Jan. 3, 1935.

COURTIS, FRANK naval officer; b. Cincinnati, O., June 18, 1844; s. James F. and Jane (Cook) C.; ed. schs. of Cincinnati, 1850-59, acad., Oakland, Calif., 1859-62; grad. U.S. Naval Acad., 1866, as midshipman; m. Maude Carleton, Apr. 17, 1883. Promoted ensign Mar. 13, 1868, master Mar. 12, 1869, lt. Mar. 21, 1870, lt. commdr. Mar. 2, 1885, commdr. July 10, 1894, capt. July 23, 1900; rear admiral, and retired for physical disability, Sept. 27, 1901. Served on various duties and stas.; commd. U.S.S. Essex, 1898-1900; at War Coll., 1900, until placed on sick leave. Died 1908.

COUSINS, RALPH P. ret. army officer, ins. exec.; b. Mexia, Tex., Dec. 1, 1891; s. Robert Bartow and Dora (Kelly) C.; B.S., U.S. Mil. Acad., 1915; M.S., Yale 1922; grad. AC Flying Sch., San Diego, 1916, AC Tactical Sch., Langley Field, 1931; m. Diana Wilson Fitzmaurice, May 10, 1945; stepchildren-Sheila Fitzmaurice (Mrs. William Shay), Patricia Fitzmaurice (Mrs. Les Baxter). Command and Gen. Staff Sch., 1933, Army War Coll., 1937, Commd. 2d, lt., U.S. Army, 1915; advanced through grades to maj. gen., 1942; developed radio beam, built communication systems of model airways, 1926-28; comd. Clark Field, Fort Stotsenburg, P.I., 1928-30; charge aviation units N.G., Washington, 1933-36; asst. chief staff (personnel), Air Force, Langley Field, Va., 1937-41, Air Staff, Washington, 1941-42; Comdg. gen. Army Air Forces Western Flying Tng. Command, Santa Ana, Cal., 1942-46; ret. as maj. gen., 1946. Co-founder Founders' Fire & Marine Ins. Co. Los Angeles, v.p., sec., mem. bd. since 1946, past pres. Los Angeles Airport Commn. Decorations: War Dept. Commendation medal; Air medal; D.S.M.; Cloud Banner of Chinese Govt. Clubs: Army and Navy (Washington); California, Los Angeles. Home: 1125 Angelo Drive, Beverly Hills, Cal. Office: 523 W. 6th St., Los Angeles 4. Died Mar. 15, 1964.

COUZENS FRANK ex-mayor Detroit; b. Detroit, Feb. 28, 1902; s. James (U.S. senator) and Margaret Ann (Manning) C.; student Newman Sch., Hackensack, N.J.; m. Margaret Lang, Oct.19, 1922; children—Frank, Margaret, James, Mary, Barbara, Homer, George. Started as builder, 1922; commr. City Plan Commn., 1927-28. Dept. of Street Rys., Detroit, 1929, 30, 31; elected pres. Detroit Common Council, 1932, acting mayor, 1933; resigned, and elected mayor, Nov. 1933, for term 1934-36, reelected 1936, term, 1936-38. Chmn. bd. Wabeck State Bank of Detroit; pres. Wabeek Corp. Served from maj. to lt. col. U.S. Army, 1942-43. Home: 610 Longfellow Av., Detroit. Died Oct. 31, 1950.

COVELL, LOUIS CHAPIN, army officer; b. at Grand Rapids, Mich., June 22, 1875; s. Elliott Franklin and Laura (Chapin) C.; grad. Grand Rapids High Sch., 1893; m. Florence Davidson, of Grand Rapids, June 12, 1906. Began as salesman, Macy Co., Grand Rapids, 1900, and became sales mgr.; organizer, 1915, and pres. The Covell-Hensen Co., advertising and printing. Enlisted as pvt. Mich. N.G., Apr. 6, 1892; served as capt. Co. H, Mich. Vol. Inf., Spanish-Am. War; advanced to brig. gen. Mich. N.G., Feb. 7, 1917; brig. gen. N.A., Aug. 5, 1917; assigned as comdr. 63d Inf. Brigade, 32d Div.; hon. discharged, Feb. 17, 1919. Now mgr. Reynolds-Chrysler Co., Flint, Mich. Mem. Am. Legion, S.A.R., Mil. Order Foreign Wars. Republican. Conglist. Mason (K.T.). Home: 408 E. First St., Flint MI

COVINGTON, LEONARD congressman, army officer; b. Aquasco, Md., Oct. 30, 1768; had liberal schooling. Entered U.S. Army as cornet of Cavalry, 1792: commd. lt. of Dragoons by Gen. Washington, 1793, joined Army under Gen. Wayne; distinguished himself at Ft. Recovery and Battle of Miami; promoted cap., resigned, 1795; became farmer; mem. Md. Ho. of Dels. many years: mem. U.S. Ho. of Reps. (Democrat) from Md., 9th Congress, 1805-07; apptd. by Pres. Jefferson lt. col. of Light Dragoons, 1809, col., 1809; in command at Ft. Adams on Mississippi River, 1810; took possession of Baton Rouge and portion of West Fla.; ordered to Northern fronter, 1813; apptd. brig. gen. by Pres. Madison, 1813; mortally wounded at Battle of Chryslers Field, 1813. Died Frenchs Mills, N.Y., Nov. 14, 1813; remains removed to Sackets Harbor, Jefferson County, N.Y., Aug. 13, 1820; buried at Mt. Covington.

COWAN, ANDREW merchant, mfr.; b. Ayrshire, Scotland, Sept. 29, 1841; s. William Strong and lMargaret Isabella (Campbell) C.; ed. pub. schs., Auburn, N.Y., and Madison (now Colgate) U.; m. Mary E. Adsit, Feb. 23, 1864; 2d, Anna L. Gilbert, Utica, Jan. 13, 1876. Enlisted as pvt. Co. B, 19th N.Y. Inf., Apr. 16, 1861; assisted in raising 1st N.Y. Independent Battery which was mustered into service Nov. 23d, 1861, and served as capt. same, from Jan., 1862; bvtd. maj. and lt. col., and comd. Arty. Brigade, 6th Corps Army of Potomac in campaign ending at Appomattox; hon. mustered out June 23, 1865. Head of Andrew Cowan & Co., established 1866, wholesale hardware, leather and mill supplies, Louisville; pres. Nat. Oak Leather Co.; v.p. Louisville Leather Co. Mem. 1st and 2d bds. of Park Commrs. which established Louisville Park System, 1891-95, and pres. bd., 1907-08; trustee Am. Printing House for the Blind, from 1897, pres., 1906-18; pres. Ky. Inst. for Edn. of the Blind, 1896-1900, 1908-12; charter mem. and councilor Asso. Charities. Republican. Baptist. Home: Louisville, Ky. Died Aug. 23, 1919.

COWAN, FRANK AUGUSTUS communications engr.; b. Escatawpa, Ala., Aug. 30, 1898; s. James T. and Annie Ellen (Adamson) C.; B.S. in Elec. Engring., Ga. Inst. Tech., 1919; m. Dorothy L. Bush., July 3, 1942. With Am. Tel. & Tel. Co., 1920—, successively spl. services engr., div. transmission engr., asst. dir. operations, asst. dir. operations long lines, 1950—. Served as lt. comdr. USNR, 1942-49. Recipient Lamme Gold Medal, Am. Inst. E.E., 1953. Fellow Am. Inst. E.E. (chmn. communications group N.Y. sect. 1944-45), Inst. Radio Engrs. Hon. 44 E. 67th St., N.Y.C. 21. Office: 32 Av. of Americas, N.Y.C. 13. Died June 21, 1957.

COWDIN, J(OHN) CHEEVER industrialist, internat. sportsman; b. N.Y. City, Mar. 17, 1889; s. John Elliott and Gertrude (Cheever) C.: student St. Paul's Sch. to 1907; m. 2d, Andrea Parker, 1942; 1 son, John Cheever (by previous marriage) (dec.). Began as clk. in firm Morgan & Co.; partner in Bond & Goodwin, San Francisco, until 1919; organized Blair & Co. and Blair & Co., Inc., 1920; v.p. Bancamerica Blair Corp., 1930-34; organized Standard Capital Co. and president same from 1935 to dissolution, 1944; chmn. bd. Universal Pictures Co., Inc., 1936-49; chmn. bd. Ideal Chemical Products, Inc., Jan. 1951-; asso. Cady, Roberts & Co.; occupies leading position in financing Am. Aviation cos.; dir. Curtiss-Wright Corp., Vickers Inc.; mem. adv. bd. Sperry Div., of Sperry-Rand Corp., Studebaker-Packard Corp. Served as major Mil. Aeronautics Div. U.S. Army, World War. Mem. U.S. polo and sports teams Episcopalian. Clubs: The Brook (New York); Buck's (London). Home: 301 Stone Canyon Rd., Los Angeles 24, also, 19 E. 72d St., N.Y.C. Office: 3813 Hoke Av., Culver City, Cal. Died Sept. 16, 1960.

COWEN, BENJAMIN RUSH clerk U.S. Courts, Southern dist. Ohio, 1884 - ; b. Moorfield, O., Aug. 15, 1831; s. Benjamin Sprague and Anne Wood C.; ed. St. Clairsville, O.; studied medicine; m. Ellen Thoburn, Sept. 19, 1854. Engaged in journalism, 1848; chief clerk Ho. of Reps., Ohio 1860-61; private, 1st lt., maj., bvt. lt. col., col. and brig. gen. vols., U.S.A.; sec. of State, Ohio, 1862; adjt. gen., Ohio, 1864-68; asst. sec. of Interior, U.S., 1871-77; Republican; mem. M.E. Ch.

Del. Nat. Rep. Conv., 1868, 1876. Ecumenical Meth. Conf., London, 1881. Mason. Mem. Ohio Centennial Commn., 1903; Hamilton Co. Memorial Bd., Nat. Geographic Soc. Author: Our Beacon Light, 1884; Our Civilization the Product of Christianity, 1889; Do Missions Pay?, 1891. Home: Cincinnati. Died 1908.

COWIE, THOMAS JEFFERSON naval officer; b. Montezuma, Ia., Feb. 15, 1857; s. George and Margaret (Duffus) C.; ed. pub. and pvt. schs., Washington, D.C.; M. Susie A. Gedney, Feb. 15, 1881; 1 dau., Mrs. Clyde R. Robinson, Apptd. asst. p.m. U.S.N., June 16, 1880; promoted through various grades to p.m. gen. with rank of rear admiral, July 1, 1910; was also chief Bur. of Supplies and Accounts. Originator and promotor of navy pay bill whereby the pay of all officers and enlisted men of the army, navy and marine corps was increased; intelligence officer on bd. U.S.S. Monocacy during Japanese-Chinese War, Navy liberty loan officer during World War; presented by sec. of Treas. with first Liberty Loan medal made of German cannon, and highly praised by the Sec. of the Navy for service rendered. Sr. vice comdr. in chief Mil. Order World War, 1922-29, comdr. in chief, 1929-30. Sec. and treas. Navy Mutual Aid Assn., 1921 - . Mason. Died July 16, 1936.

COWLES, CHENEY editor: b. Spokane, Wash., Sept. 7, 1908; s. William Hutchinson and Harriet Bowen (Cheney) C.; student Thacher School, Ojai, California, 1922-26; B.A., Yale University, 1930; married to Sarah E. Ferris, June 14, 1939; children-Phoebe, Frank Cheney. Began as circulation solicitor, 1930; had various positions in newspaper work, business and news, 1930-36; financial editor Spokane Daily Chronicle, 1936; city editor Spokane Spokesman-Review, 1937, exec. editor, 1938; mng. editor Spokane Daily Chronicle, 1939-41. First lt., F.A. Res. since 1938, 2d lt., 1930; ordered to active duty on staff of Maj. Gen. John F. Curry, comdr. Second Air Force, May 1, 1941, at Fort George Wright, Spokane, Wash., promoted capt., maj., 1942; asst. chief of staff, A-2 (Intelligence), on staff of comdg. gen., Second Air Support Command. Colorado Springs, Colo., entire command transferred to Shreveport, La., 1943. Received Spokane Jr. C. of C. distinguished service award, 1937. Republican. Clubs: Spokane City, Spokane Ski, Cheyenne Mountain Country. Home: 2602 W. Second Av. Office: Spokane Daily Chronicle, Spokane, Wash. Died May 1943; buried in Greenwood Cemetery, Spokane.

COWLES, WALTER CLEVELAND rear adm.; b. Conn., July 11, 1853; grad. U.S. Naval Acad., 1873. Advanced through various grades and promoted rear admiral U.S.N., Jan. 14, 1911; comd. Naval Sta., Havana, Cuba, Dec., 1910-Mar., 1913; comd. Pacific Fleet, Apr. 1913-Mar. 1914, Asiatic Fleet, May, 1914-July 1915; retired July 11, 1915. Died Nov. 25, 1917.

COWLES, WILLIAM SHEFFIELD rear adm.; b. Farmington, Conn., Aug. 1, 1846; s. Thomas and Elizabeth (Sheffield) C.; grad. U.S. Naval Acad., 1867. Promoted ensign, U.S.N., 1869; master, 1870; lt., 1871; lt. comdr., 1892; comdr., June 5, 1899; capt., Nov. 2, 1902; rear admiral, Apr. 23, 1908. Served on Mediterranean, Pacific, North Atlantic and Asiatic stas.; served on Isthmus of Panama, guarding property of Am. citizens, 1884; naval aide to Sec. of the Navy, in charge naval militia, 1891-92; naval attacheé, U.S. Embassy, London, 1893-97; comd. the Fern, 1897-98, Topeka, 1898-99; asst. to Bur. of Navigation, Sept. 30, 1899, and naval aide to the President; comdg. Missouri, 1903-05; chief Bur. of Equipment, and mem. Bd. Constn., Feb. 1906; retired, Aug. 1, 1908. Naval rep. to Tercentenary Celebration, Quebec, July, 1908; chief Bur. Equipment until 1910. Mem. Borough Council, Farmington, 3 yrs.; naval aide to Gov. Holcomb, of Conn., 1914; mem. Conn. Ho. of Rep., 1916; enlisted in Farmington Home Guard, 1917; detailed Conn. River Patrol, later to staff Maj. Gen. Lucien Burpee, comdg. Conn. Home Guard; chmn. naval and mil. com. Conn. Council Defense. Home: Farmington, Conn. Died May 1, 1923.

COX, ATTILLA lawyer; b. Owenton, Ky., Feb. 21, 1875; s. Attilla and Kate (Martin) C.; student law dept. U. of Louisville, New York Law Sch., 1898; m. Carrie Rogers Gaulbert, Nov. 22, 1898; 1 dau., Harriet Rogers (Mrs. John V. Collis). Admitted to Ky.bar, 1898, and began practice at Louisville, Ky.; mem. Trabue, Doolan & Cox, 1903-11, Cox & Wells, 1920-30. Dir. of Louisville & Nashville R.R. Co., Fidelity & Columbia Trust Co., etc. Served as maj. judge advocate U.S.A., with A.E.F. in France, 1918-19; served as mem. Franco-American Transportation Commn. Decorated Officerd'Academie, with Palms (France); pilsudski Medal (Poland). Democrat. Episcopalian. Home: Louisville, Ky. Deceased.

COX, CREED FULTON army officer; b. Bridle Creek, Va., June 12, 1877; s. Melville B., and Martha (Fulton) C.; grad. U.S. Mil. Acad., 1901; m. Mrs. Margaret Kennedy Ross, Aug. 12, 1925 (died July 15, 1934). Commissioned 2d lt. cavalry, U.S. Army, Feb. 2, 1901; transferred to arty. Promoted through successive grades to col. Served in Philippines, 1902-04; Cuba, 1906-07; assigned to Army Staff Coll., 1908-09; prof. mil. science and tactics, Shattuck Sch., Minn., 1909-12; instr. cav. various state nta. guards, 1914-17; instr. Sch. of Fire, Ft. Sill, Okla., 1917-18; with A.E.F. in France, May 1918-Jan. 1919; comdg. 13th F.A., Aisne-Marne, 77th F.A., St. Mihiel and Meuse-Argonne, barrage grouping 26th Div. and 4th Div.; gen. staff A.E.F., to war's close; War Dept. exec. staff, 1919; mil. observer S. Russia, Turkey, Bulgaria, 1920-21; mil. attaché Germany, Holland, Denmark, Norway, Sweden, 1921-24; pres. F.A. Bd., 1926-28; assigned to Army War Coll., 1929; asst. to chief Bur. Insular Affairs, 1929-32; comdg. 8th F.A., Regt., T.H., 1932-33; chief Bureau of Insular Affairs, with rank of brig. gen., May 1933-May 1937; retired, Sept. 30, 1937; adviser to President of P.I., 1938-39. Awarded D.S.M. (U.S.). Address: Independence, Va. Died Jan. 15, 1950.

COX, JACOB DOLSON lawyer, governor; b. Montreal, Canada (parents natives of U.S.), Oct. 27, 1828; spent boyhood in New York; removed to Ohio, 1846; grad. Oberlin, 1851; m. Helen C., 1849, dau. Rev. Chas. G. Finney, pres. Oberlin Coll. Studied law and settled in practice at Warren, O.; mem. State senate, 1859-61. Was brig. gen. Ohio militia, at breaking out of Civil war; served from Va. to Sherman's march, first as brig. gen. U.S. vols., then as maj. gen., promoted for services at Antietam. Since war in law practice in Cincinnati. Gov. Ohio, 1866-67; U.S. sec. of the interior, 1869-70; congressman, 1877-79; pres. Cincinnati Univ., 1885; dean Cincinnati Law School, 1881-97. Author: Atlanta; The March to the Sea; etc. Home: Oberlin, O. Died 1900.

COX, JAMES congressman; b. Monmouth, N.J., June 14, 1753; attended public schs. In command company of militia at battles of Germantown and Monmouth; attained rank brig. gen.: mem. N.J. Gen. Assembly, 1801-07, speaker, 1804-07; mem. U.S. Ho. of Reps. (Democrat) from N.J., 11th Congress, 1809-10. Died Monmouth, Sept. 12, 1810; buried Yellow Meeting House Cemetery, Upper Freehold Twp., N.J.

COX, LEANDER MARTIN congressman, lawyer; b. Cumberland County, Va., May 7, 1812; completed academic studies; studied law. Admitted to bar, practiced law; moved to Flemingsburg, Ky.; mem. Ky. Ho. of Reps., 1843-45; capt. 3d Ky. Volunteers in Mexican War, 1847; Whig presdl. elector, 1852; mem. U.S. Ho. of Reps. from Ky., (as Whig) 33d, (as Am. Party candidate) 34th congresses, 1853-57. Died Flemingsburg, Mar. 19, 1865; buried Fleming County (Ky.) Cemetery.

COX, LEONARD MARTIN naval officer; b. New Liberty, Ky., Mar. 21, 1870; s. Attilla and Kate Ware (Martin) C.; C. E., Rensselaer Poly. Inst., 1892; m. Jane Torbitt Castleman, Oct. 16, 1895; 1 dau., Katharine Castleman. Engring. work, Louisville & Nashville Railroad, until 1899; commd. lt. jr. grade, Corps of Civ. Engrs., U.S. Navy, Feb. 23, 1899; lt., Apr. 16, 1907; lt. comdr., Oct. 9, 1909; comdr., Aug. 29, 1916, capt., 1921. Made first American survey of Island of Guam together with report on island conditions, 1901-03; in charge constrn. floating dry dock Dewey, 1903-06; chief engr. Louisville, Henderson & St. Louis R. R., 1906-07; mem. Alaskan R.R. Commn. by presdl. appointment, 1912-13 (commn. made first report on which appropriation for Alaskan railroads was based). During World War pub. works officer, Navy Yard, New York, until Sept. 1917; in charge of all pub. works 12th Naval Dist., South of San Francisco Bay, including constrn. air station and marine expeditionary base, San Diego, until Nov. 1918; asst. mgr. Div. of Shipyard Plants, Emergency Fleet Corp., U.S., Shipping Bd., 1918-19; transferred to Mare Island Navy Yard as public works officer of 12th Naval Dist., June 1919; retired for physical disability, May 31, 1923. Mem. Am. Soc. Civil Engrs. (Norman medal, 1907), Naval Inst., A.A.A.S., Engring. Inst. of Canada, Theta Delta Chi. Republican. Episcopalian. Clubs: Army and Navy (Washington, D.C.); Commercial, Engineers', Commonwealth (San Francisco). Home: Malvern Woods, St. Helena, Calif. Died Dec. 12, 1943.

COX, THEODORE SULLIVAN educator; b. "Emery Place," D.C., Aug. 17, 1804; s. William Van Zandt and Juliet Hazeltine (Emery) C.; A.B., U. of Mich., 1917; LL.B., U. of Va., 1922; m. Christiana Osborne Jones, June 20, 1931. Admitted to Va. bar, 1921; instr. law, U. of Va., 1922-24; engaged in research in history, politics and pub. law, Stanford U., 1925-26, Johns Hopkins U., 1926-27, and in Washington, D.C., 1927-30; prof. jurisprudence since 1930, dean Sch. of Jurisprudence since 1932, Coll. of William and Mary. Served as 1st lt., 314th F.A., U.S. Army; capt., 125th F.A., A.E.F., World War I; capt. Provost Marshall Gen.'s Dept., 1942; maj., later lt. col., Gen. Staff Corps., 1944-46; with 15th Army Group, 7th Army, 8th (British) Army, 6th Army Group, 1st (French) Army, and S.H.A.E.F. and U.S. Forces European Theater: participated in engagements in Sicily, Naples-Foggia, Rome-Arno, Northern France, The Rhine, Ardennes, Central Europe. Decorated Bronze Star Medal. Del. Internat. Congress Comparative Law, The Hague, 1932, 37; dir. Tidewater Automobile Assn. of Va. since 1935; member Williamsburg Planning and Zoning Commn., 1933-43; pres. Williamsburg Chamber of Commerce, 1940-42. Member of American and Virginia bar associations, American Historical Assn., Am. Law Inst., American Judicature Soc., Mil. Order of World War, Soc. Colonial Wars, S.R., Order of Coif, Phi Beta Kappa, Phi Alpha Delta, Omicron Delta Kappa, Phi Kappa Phi. Independent Democrat. Episcopalian. Clubs: Army and Navy, Corinthian Yacht (Washington): Farmington Country (Charlottesville, Va.); Colonnade (University, Va.). Contbr. to Dictionary of Am. Biography and to legal and other periodicals. Home: Jamestown Road at Chandler Court. Williamsburg, Va. Died May 10, 1947; buried in Arlington Cemetery.

COX, WILLIAM RUFFIN cotton planter; b. in Halifax Co., N.C., Mar. 11, 1832; s. Hon. Thomas and Olivia (Norfleet) C.; A.B., Franklin Coll., Tenn., 1851, A.M., 1853; LL.B., Lebanon (Tenn.) Law Sch., 1853; admitted to bar, 1853; practiced, Nashville, 1853-57; m. a.d. James S. Battle, 1857 (died 1880); 2d, Fannie A., d. Rt. Rev. T.B. Lyman, of Raleigh, N.C.; 3d, Mrs. Kate C. Claiborne, June 1905. Commd. maj. 2d N.C. Inf., C.S.A., 1861; lt. col., col. and brig. gen.; wounded 11 times. Pres. Chatham Coal Field R.R., 1866; solicitor, 4th Jud. Dist., 1868-74; chmn. Dem. State Exec. Com., 5 yrs.; del.-at-large Dem. Nat. Conv., 1876; judge 6th Jud. Dist., N.C., 1877-80; mem. 47th to 49th Congresses (1881-87); sec. U.S. Senate, 1893-99. Grand Master Grand Lodge of Masonry in N.C., 4 yrs.; has been pres. N.C. Agrl. Soc. Chmn. Dem. State Exec. Com.; trustee U. of the South, 1883. Home: Penelo, N.C. Died Dec. 26, 1919.

COXE, FRANK MORRELL brig. gen.; b. Phila., Mar. 4, 1844; s. Charles W. and Sarah H. C.; ed. pub. schs., Phila. Served pvt. to capt. and bvt. col., U.S.V., during Civil War; transferred to regular army as capt. 40th Inf., July 28, 1866; transferred to 25th Inf., Apr. 20, 1869; maj. p.m., Mar. 3, 1875; lt. col. deputy p.m. gen., Feb. 24, 1896; col. asst. p.m. gen., Feb. 1, 1899; brig. gen. Jan. 23, 1904; retired at own request over 39 yrs.' service Jan. 24, 1904. Principally on line and staff duty on plains and frontier for past 30 yrs. Died Sept. 15, 1916.

COYNE, JOHN NICHOLAS soldier; b. New York, Nov. 14, 1839; s. John Nicholas and Hannah Anne (Park) C.; ed. schs. and acads. New York and Can.; m. Pauline M. Hemingway, June 6, 1894. Served in 7th regt. N.G.S.N.Y., Apr.-June 1861, in response to Lincoln's first call for troops; then pvt. to capt. 70th N.Y. vols. until July 1, 1864, then as capt., Hancock's Vet. Corps to end of war. Bvtd. maj. and lt. col. for gallantry at Williamsburg, Fair Oaks and Bristoe Sta., Va., and Gettysburg, Pa.; Congressional Medal of Honor for bravery and capture of Confederate flag at Williamsburg, Va.; wounded at Fair Oaks and Gettysburg. Now chief clerk disbursing dept. New York Custom House. Author: History of the Third Army Corps; History of the Excelsior Brigade. Home: East Orange, N.J. Died Mar. 4, 1907.

CRABB, JEREMIAH congressman; b. Montgomery County, Md., 1760. Served as 2d lt., 1st Md. Regt. in Revolutionary War; promoted 1st lt., 1777-78, resigned because of ill health from winter at Valley Forge; extensive landowner, Montgomery County; served as gen. with Gen. Harry Lee in Pa. during Whisky Rebellion: mem. U.S. Ho. of Reps. (Democrat) from Md., 4th Congress, 1795-96 (resigned). Died nr. Rockville, Montgomery County, 1800; buried family burying ground nr. Derwood, Montgomery County.

CRADLEBAUGH, JOHN congressman; b. Circleville, Pickaway County, O., Feb. 22, 1819: attended Kenyon Coll., Gambier, O., Oxford (O.) U.; studied law. Admitted to bar, 1840; apptd. U.S. asso. justice for Dist. of Utah, 1858; moved to Carson City, Nev.; mem. U.S. Congress from Nev. Territory, 37th Congress, Dec. 2, 1861-63; served as col. 114th Regt., Ohio Volunteer Inf., Union Army during Civil War, 1862-63; wounded at Vicksburg; in mining business, Eureka, Nev. Died Eureka, Feb. 22, 1872; buried Forest Cemetery, Circleville.

CRAFT, EDWARD BEECH electrical engr.; b. Cortland, Trumbull Co., O., Sept. 12, 1881; s. Charles C. and Nora A. (Trowbridge) C.; prep. edn., high sch., Warren, O.; D. Engring., Worcester Poly. Inst., 1926; m. Mary Ann Richards, Oct. 21, 1902; 1 dau., Clara Virginia. With Warren (O.) Electric and Specialty Co., 1898-1902 (last 2 yrs. as supt. lamp dept.); with dept. design of communication equipment, Western Electric Co., Chicago, 1902-07; development egnr., in charge telephone apparatus design, Western Electric Co., New York, 1907-17; asst. chief engr. same, in charge development and design, 1917-22; chief engr. same and Internat. Western Electric Co., 1922-25; exec. v.p. Bell Telephone Labs., Inc., New York, 1925 - . Capt. Signal Corps, U.S.A., Mar. 1917; maj., Dec. 1917; tech. adviser U.S. Navy, London, June-Oct. 1918. Vice chmn. div. of engring. and industrial research Nat. Research Council; chmn. bd. Engring. Socs. Library; mem. of council Am. Inst. Weights and Measures. Republican. Home: Hackensack, N.J. Died Aug. 20, 1929.

CRAFTS, LELAND WHITNEY, educator; b. Boston, July 10, 1892; s. Albert E. and Mary H. (Wilkinson) C.; B.S., U. N.H., 1915; M.A., Clark U., 1920; Ph.D., Columbia, 1927; m. Edith L. Honigman, Aug. 16, 1927; 1 dau., Valery. Instr. English and German U. N.H., 1916-17; instr. psychology U. Colo., 1921-24; instr. psychology Washington Sq. Coll. of N.Y.U., 1925-27, asst. prof., 1928-31; asso. prof., 1932-45, prof. 1946-57, head dept., 1949-57. Served as capt. F.A., U.S. Army, 1917-19. Fellow Am. Psychol. Assn.; mem. N.Y. State

Psychol. Assn., Sigma Xi. Author: Recent Experiments in Psychology (with T. C. Schneirla, E. E. Robinson, R. W. Gilbert; rev. edit.), 1950. Contbr. articles profl. jours. Home: Red Bank NJ Died Jan. 23, 1968; buried Fairview Cemetery, Red Bank NJ

CRAGO, THOMAS SPENCER congressman; b. Carmichaels, Pa., Aug. 8, 1866; s. John N. and Permelia (Spencer) C.; A.B., Waynesburg Coll., 1892, Princeton U., 1893; m. Margaret Leah Hoge, Oct. 27, 1897; children - Leah A., John Hughes, Ruth Constance. Admitted to Pa. bar, 1894, and practiced in Waynesburg; mem. 62d Congress (1911-13), 23d Pa. Dist. and 64th to 67th Congresses (1915-23), Pa. at large; spl. asst. to atty. gen. of U.S., 1923-24. V.p. Union Deposit & Trust Co.; dir. South Pa. T. & T. Co., River Coal & Coke Co. Trustee Waynesburg Coll., Southwestern State Normal Sch., California, Pa. Served in Spanish-Am. War, capt. Co. K, 10th Regt. Pa. Vols., later in Philippines, lt. col. 10th Regt., N.G. Pa. Republican. Presbyn. Mason (33ff). Home: Waynesburg, Pa. Died Sept. 12, 1925.

CRAIG, CHARLES FRANKLIN army officer, author; b. Danbury, Conn., July 4, 1872; s. William Edward and Maria Hamlin (Payne) C.; M.D., Yale, 1941, hon. M.A., 1914; D.Sc., Tulane U., 1945; m. Lillian Osmun, July 7, 1893; children-Marjorie Lillian, Edward, Arthur. Acting asst. Surgeon U.S. Army, 1808-1903; advanced through grades from 1st lt. to col. M.C., 1918; pathologist and bacteriologist Sternberg U.S. Army Gen. Hosp., Chickamauga Park, Ga., 1808, Simpson Gen. Hosp., Fortress Monroe, Va., 1898-99, Camp Columbia Hosp., Havana, 1899, U.S. Army Gen. Hosp., Presidio, Cal., 1899-1905, Div. Hosp., Manila,1906; mem. U.S. Army Bd. for Study of Tropical Diseases. Manila, 1906-07; lab. Ft. Leavenworth, Kan., 1907-1909; attending surgeon, N.Y.C., 1909; asst. curator Army Med. Museum, 1909-13, curator, 1919-20; asst. prof. bacteriology and clin. diagnosis Army Med. Sch., Washington, 1909-13, prof. bacteriology, parasitology and preventive medicine, also dir. labs., 1920-22, comdt. and dir. clin. pathology and preventive medicine, 1926-30; asso. prof. bacteriology, med. dept. George Washington U., 1910-11; comdg. officer Central Dept. Lab. U.S. Army, Ft. Leavenworth, 1913-16, Dept. Lab. No. 2, So. Dept., El Paso, Tex., 1916-17, Ft. Leavenworth, 1917-18; organized and comd. Yale Army Lab. Sch., 1918-19; med. insp. Hawaiian Dept., 1922-26; asst. comdt. Army Med. Center, Washington, 1930-31; prof. tropical medicine and dir. dept., sch. medicine Tulane U., 1931-38, emeritus prof. tropical medicine Tulane U., 1931-38, emeritus prof. tropical medicine, 1939—. Asso. editor Am. Jour. Parasitology; editor Am. Jour. Tropical Medicine, etc. Fellow A.C.S., A.C.P., Assn. Mil. Surgeons U.S. (life), A.M.A., Am. Pub. Health Assn.; mem. Am. Soc. Tropical Medicine (pres. 1914-15), Royal Soc. Tropical Medicine and Hygiene, Conn. Med. Soc., Wash. Acad. Sciences, Internat. Leprosy Assn., Soc. Tropical Medicine and Hygiene of Egypt, Internat. Soc. Tropical Medicine (sec. div. research), Am. Soc. Parasitologists (pres. 1934-35), Am. Acad. Tropical Medicine (pres. 1935), Bexas County (Tex.) Med. Soc. (hon.), Am. Soc. Clin. Pathologists. Recipient gold medal Am. Acad. Tropical Med., 19-3, Founder's medal Assn. Mil. Surg., 1948. Mem. Alpha Omega Alpha, Sigma Xi, Nu Sigma Nu; pres. Yale Med. Alumni Assn., 1910-11. Decorated D.S.M., 1922. Club: Army and Navy Country (Washington). Author: The AEstivo-Autumnal Malarial Fevers, 1901; The Malarial Fevers, Haemoglobinuric Fever and the Blood Protozoa of Man, 1909; The Parasitic Amoebae of Man, 1911; The Wassermann Test, 1918, 21; A Manual of the Parasitic Protozoa of Man, 1925; Amebiasis and Amebic Dysentery, 1935; Clinical Parasitology (with Faust), 1937; The Laboratory Diagnosis of Protozoan Diseases, 1941; The Etiology, Diagnosis and Treatment of Amebiasis, 1944. Also wrote chapters in Oster's Modern Medicine, 1907, 14, in Hare's Mod. Treatment 1911; Oxford medicine and Oxford Tropical Medicines, 1919; Musser's Internal Medicine, 1932; Brennemann's Pediatrics, 1935; Riemann's Treatment in General Medicine, 1939; Barr's Modern Medical Therapy in General Practice, 1940; Blumr's Therapeutics of Internal Diseases, 1941. Clinical Tropical Medicine, Bercovitz. Home: 225 Henderson St., San Antonio. Died Dec. 9. 1950; buried Ft. Sam Houston Cemetery.

CRAIG, DANIEL FRANK army officer; b. Mahaska Co., Ia., Oct. 3, 1875; s. Samuel C.; grad. Mounted Service Sch., 1910; distinguished grad. Army Sch. of the Line, 1942; graduate Army Staff College, 1916; graduate General Staff Coll., 1921; m. Florence Elizabeth Burt, May 19, 1906. Commd. 1st lt. 20th Kan. Inf., May 10, 1898; capt., May 9, 1899; hon. disch., July 12, 1899; capt. 36th U.S. Inf., July 5, 1899; hon. mustered out, Mar. 16, 1901; commd. 2d lt. Arty. Corps, May 8, 1901; 1st lt., July 28, 1903; capt., Jan. 25, 1907; assigned to 4th Field Arty., June 6, 1907; maj., May 15, 1917; col. N.A., Aug. 5, 1917; brig. gen. (temp.), Oct. 1, 1918. Served in Philippines, 1898-1901, and 1904-07; at Vera Cruz, Apr. 26-Nov. 26, 1914: with Punitive Expdn., Mexico, May 21-Dec. 1, 1916; detailed as mem. Gen. Staff Corps, Nov. 15, 1916; chief of staff, 12th Div., Dec. 4, 1916-Mar. 24, 1917; asst.chief of staff Southern Dept., Mar. 25-Apr. 6, 1917; with War Coll. Div. Gen. Staff, Washington, D.C., Apr.-Aug., 1917; arrived in France Aug. 5, 1918; comdr. 302d Regt. Field Arty., 151st Brigade, F.A., 76th Div., until Oct. 15, 1918; assigned as comdr. 157th F.A. Brigade, Oct. 21, 1918, 158th F.A. Brigade, Mar. 11, 1919, 5th F.A. Brigade, Apr. 15, 1919, 2d F.A. Brigade, Jan. 24, 1919. Presented with Silver plaque by Republic of France while a brigade comdr.; awarded D.S.M., "for exceptionally meritorious and distinguished services." Mason (K.T., Shriner). Episcopalian. Home: Garnett, Kan. Address: Care the Adjutant General, U.S. Army, Washington, D.C. Died Apr. 17, 1929.

CRAIG, JAMES congressman; b. Washington County, Pa., Feb. 28, 1818; attended public schls.; studied law. Admitted to New Philadelphia (O.) bar, 1839; moved to St. Joseph, Mo., 1844, practiced law; capt. volunteer company in Mexican War, served until 1848; state's atty. for 12th Jud. Circuit, 1852-56; mem. Mo. Ho. of Reps. 1856, 57; mem. U.S. Ho. of Reps. (Democrat) from Mo., 35th-36th congresses, 1857-61; commd. brig. gen. Volunteers by Pres. Lincoln during Civil War, 1862; 1st pres. Hannibal St. Joseph R.R.; 1st comptroller City of St. Joseph; negotiated Platt purchase comprising all N.W. Mo. Died St. Joseph, Oct. 22, 1888; buried Mt. Mora Cemetery.

CRAIG, JOSEPH EDGAR naval officer; b. Medina, N.Y., Feb. 24, 1845; s. Joseph and Elizabeth Warren (Herring) C.; m. Alethe Lowber, July 29, 1868, grad. U.S. Naval Acad., 1865; ensign, Dec. 1, 1866; advanced through grades to rear admiral, Dec. 28, 1904. Comdr.-in-chief European Squadron, Feb. 10-May 18, 1902; capt. of the yard, U.S. Navy Yard, Norfolk, Va., Feb. 2, 1903-Dec. 30, 1904; spl. duty Bur. of Navigation, Jan.-Mar. 1905; commandant Navy Yard, League Island, Pa., 1905-07; retired, Feb. 24, 1907. Author: Azimuth, 1887; Negative-Reciprocal Equations, 1893. Home: Washington, D.C. Died June 21, 1925.

CRAIG, MALIN army officer. b. St. Joseph, Mo., Aug. 5, 1875; s. Maj. Louis Aleck and Georgie (Malin) C.; grad. U.S. Mil. Acad., Apr. 26, 1898; honor grad. Inf. and Cav. Sch., 1904; grad. Army Staff Coll. 1905; Army War Coll., 1910; m. Genevieve Woodruff, Apr. 29, 1901; 1 son, Malin. Commd. 2d lt., 4th Inf., Apr. 26, 1898; trans. to 4th Cav., June 23, 1898; promoted through grades to brig. gen., Apr. 28, 1921; maj. gen., July 24, 1924; general, Oct. 2, 1935; served as lieut. colonel, colonel and brig. gen., World War. In Santiago Champaign from June 12, 1898, China Relief Expdn., June-Oct. 1900; a.d.c. to Brig. Gen. 1900; a.d.c. to Brig. Gen. Barry, in Phillipines, 1900-01, to Gen. Bell, 1902-04; again in Philippines, 1907-09; duty Gen. Staff Corps. 1910-12, 1917-19; arrived in France, Oct. 5, 1917; apptd. comdr. 166th Brigade Inf., 83d Div., 4th Army Corps, A.E.F., July 20, 1918; chief of staff 41st Div., Aug. 25, 1917-Jan. 19, 1918, chief of staff 1st Corps, Jan. 20, 1918-Nov. 12, 1918; chief of staff 3d Army. Nov. 13, 1918-July 2, 1919; apptd. dir. Gen. Staff Coll., Washington, D.C., 1919; comdg. Dist. of Ariz., 1920-21, comdt. Cav. Sch., Ft. Riley, Kan., Sept. 1, 1921-July 1, 1923; comdg. Coast Defenses, Manila and Subig Bay, Sept. 17, 1923-July 10, 1924; maj.-gen. chief of cav., July 24, 1925; asst. chief of staff U.S. Army, Mar. 21, 1926; comdg. 4th Corps Area, Apr. 2-Oct. 5, 1927; comdg. Panama Canal Div., Oct. 13, 1927-Mar. 31, 1928; comdg. Panama Canal Dept., Apr. 1, 1928-Aug. 10, 1930; comdg. 9th Corps Area, Oct. 13, 1930-Jan. 24, 1935, 4th Army, Oct. 3, 1933-Jan. 24, 1935; comdg. Army War Coll., Feb. 3, 1935-Oct. 1, 1935; chief of staff, U.S. Army, Oct. 2, 1935-Aug. 31, 1939, retiring with rank of general. Decorated with D.S.M.; with oak leaf cluster (United States); Commander of Legion of Honor. Croix de Guerre with 2 Palms (French); Companion of Bath (British); Comdr. La Couronne (Belgian); Crown of Italy; Estrelia de Abdon Calderon, 1st Class (Ecuador). Home: 2126 Connecticut Av. Address: care of Adj. General, War Dept., Washington, D.C. Died July 25, 1945.

CRAIG, ROBERT S(PENCER), assn. exec.; b. Savannah, Ill., Mar. 16, 1905; s. Harry C. and Grace (Thompson) C.; student U. Dubuque, 1923-25; m. Thelma Coile, June 14, 1947; children—John, Nessly, Robert, Christaine. Pres. Greenleaf, Inc., Detroit, 1930-41; v.p., gen. mgr. Territorial Motors, Honolulu, 1947-49; partner Hawaiian Economic Service, Honolulu, 1950-57; mng. dir. Robert S. Craig Asso., Honolulu, 1957-62; exec. dir. Downtown Improvement Assn.; pres. Pacific Research Corp. Mem. edn. committee of Traffic Safety Council; mem. Mayor's Citizen's Adv. Com. Community Renewal Program; mem. Mayor's Advisory Council on Urban Renewal; advisory council International Training Agency Center for Cultural and Technical Interchange between East and West. President Volunteer Service bur. Mental Health Assn., 1955-56, pres. assn., 1958-59; chmn. Govs. Conf. on Edn., Hawaiian dels. White House Conf. on Edn., 1955-56. Trustee Joint Council on Econ. Edn., Hawaii Council on Economic Education. Served from 1st lt. to lt. col., AUS, 1942-47. Mem. C. of C. Honolulu, Am. Marketing Assn., Internat. Downtown Exec. Assn., Urban Land Inst. Hawaiian Acad. Scis. Republican. Conglist. Home: Honolulu HI

CRAIGHILL, WILLIAM PRICE chief of engrs. U.S.A.; b. Charlestown, Va., July 1, 1833; grad. West Point, 1853; (LL.D., Washington and Lee, 1897); m. Mary A. Morsell, Oct. 14, 1856; m. 2d, Rebecca Churchill Jones, Sept. 22, 1874. Assigned to engr. corps and superintended work on Ft. Sumter, 1854-55, and Ft. Delaware, 1858; several yrs. instr. West Point; built defenses of Pittsburgh, 1863; bvtd. lt. col., Mar. 1865, for services at Cumberland Gap; afterward engaged on defenses of New York and Baltimore, and many public works. Mem. Light House Bd. several yrs., also of Bd. Consulting Engrs: to Dept. of Docks of City of New York; after centennial of Surrender of Cornwallis, 1881, built the monument at Yorktown, Va., which, though ordered to be built by Continental Congress, did not have funds provided until over a century later; colonel engineers, Jan. 10, 1887; brig. gen., chief of engrs., U.S.A., May 10, 1895, until retired. Feb. 1, 1897. Dir., 1892-93, pres., 1894-95, hon. mem., Mar. 23, 1896 - , Am. Soc. Civ. Engrs.; 7 times deputy from W. Va. to Gen. Conv. P.E. Ch. Author: Army Officers' Pocket Companion, 1862. Address: Charles Town, W. Va. Died 1909.

CRAIGIE, ANDREW financier, apothecary; b. Boston, June 18, 1743; s. Andrew and Elizabeth C.; m. Elizabeth Shaw. Continental apothecary gen., 1775-83; commd. lt. col. Continental Army, 1779; mem. Soc. of Cincinnati, 1783: speculation in govt. certificates and supplies earned him large fortune; dir. 1st U.S. Bank; owned much real estate in Boston and Cambridge (Mass.); owned mansion in Cambridge which became one of most important social centers in New Eng. Died Cambridge, Sept. 19, 1819.

CRAIGIE, DAVID JOHNSTON army officer; b. Broomieside, Scotland, Dec. 6, 1840; s. George and Helen (Young) C.; ed. at various schs. and pvt. teachers; m. Florence Mortimer, Apr. 1869. Served as 1st lt., 8th Ia. Inf., Sept. 12, 1861-July 25, 1864; capt. asst. adj. gen. vols., July 2, 1864; hon. mustered out, Sept. 19, 1865; 2d lt., May 11, 1866; advanced through grades to brig. gen., Aug. 12, 1903; retired, Aug. 13, 1903. Bvtd. 1st lt., Mar. 2, 1867, for battle of Shiloh, Tenn.; capt., Mar. 2, 1867, for battle of Iuka, Miss. Served in P.I., 1901-03. Home: Oskaloosa, Ia. Died Dec. 14, 1913.

CRAIK, JAMES physician; b. Arbigland, Scotland, 1730; studied medicine, U. Edinburgh (Scotland): m. Marianne Ewell, Nov. 13, 1760, at least 1 son, George W. Commd. surgeon Va. Militia, 1754, chief med. officer under Col. George Washington, 1775-63; asst. dir. gen. hosps. of middle dist., Continental Army, 1777-80; chief hosp. physician Continental Army, 1780-81, chief physician and surgeon, 1781-83; dir. gen. hosp. dept. U.S. Army, 1798, physician gen., 1798-1800; attended Pres. Washington during his final illness (with Dr. Elisha Cullen Dick), 1799; owned large plantation and practiced medicine, Port Tobacco, Charles County, Md. Died Alexandria, Va., Feb. 6, 1814.

CRAMER, KENNETH FRANK army officer; b. Gloversville, N.Y., Oct. 3, 1894; s. Frank Henry and Stella Sophia (Brown) C.; Litt.B., Princeton U., 1916, M.A., 1917 (Boudinot fellow in Am. history, 1916-17); grad. Command and Gen. Staff Sch., 1938, Inf. Sch. (Spl. Div. Officers' Class), 1942: m. Ruth Rose Fuller, Jan. 3, 1920; children-Margaret Fuller Van Pelt, Dorothy Ruth Van Pelt. Teacher, Newark and Woodbridge (N.J.) High Sch., 1919-20; wholesale coal business, 1920—; v.p. Harnden-Cramer Coal Co., Inc., 1923-27; pres. K. F. Cramer Coal Co., Inc., 1927-52. Acting adj. gen., State of Conn., Jan.-Mar. 1939; asst. adj. gen., State of Conn., 1939-50. Commd. 2d lt. Inf. O.R.C., Aug. 1917, promoted 1st lt., Oct. 1918; hon. discharged June 4, 1919; commd. 1st lt. Inf. Res., Feb. 1922, maj., May 1931, capt. 43d Tank Co., Conn. Nat. Guard, May 1931, col. 169th Inf., Nov. 1940, inducted into U.S. Army, Feb. 24, 1941, promoted to brig. gen., Aug. 17, 1942; major gen., comdg. 43d Inf. Div., July 12, 1946; recalled to active duty as comdg. gen. 43d Div., 1950; comdg. gen. So. Area Command, 1952—. Member War Department General Staff Committee on National Guard and Reserve Policy. Chief N.G. Bur., 1947-50. Member Connecticut House of Reps., 1929-33, Conn. Senate, 1933-37; sec. Conn. delegation, Rep. Nat. Conv., 1936. Awarded Silver Star with 3 Oak Leaf Clusters, Legion of Merit, Bronze Star, Air Medal, Army Commendation Ribbon, Purple Heart, Victory medal (3 bars), Army Occupation (Germany, Japan), Asiatic-Pacific Theatre with bronze arrowhead and 3 stars Am. Theatre, Victory Medal, World War II, Inter-Allied Victory Medal (French), Philippine Liberation Medals with 3 stars, American Defense Medal. Member Wethersfield Board of Education, 1927-37, Met. District Commission for Hartford County, 1929—, Veterans Home Building Commission, 1931-37; secretary Commn. to reorganized the State Govt., 1935-37, State Library Com., 1937—; mem. Charter Oak Council, Boy Scouts of America, 1927-36. Mem. Phi Beta Kappa Assos., Conn. Hist. Soc., Wethersfield Hist. Soc., Am. Legion (dept. comdr. 1927; nat. exec. com. 1932-33; nat. coms. on constitution and by-laws, legislation and nat. defense), Mil. Order of Purple Heart (dept. comdr.), 78th Div. Vets. Assn., 24th Div. Veterans Assn., (pres.) U.S. Infantry Assn., Conn. National Guard Assn., Reserve Officers Assn. (president Hartford Chapter and dept. v.p.), Soc. Mayflower Descendants, S.A.R., Gen. Soc. War of 1812, Sons Union Vets, of Civil War (camp comdr., chmn. council-in-chief), Wethersfield Business Men's and Civic Assn., Princeton Alumni Assn. of Conn. Valley (v.p.), Phi Beta Kappa. Republican. Conglist. Mason (32ff Shriner). Clubs: Nat. Sojourners, Princeton

Gateway, Hartford Rotary. Recalled to active duty U.S. Army, Sept. 5, 1950. Address: 75 Center St., Wethersfield, Conn. Died Feb. 20, 1954: buried Arlington Nat. Cemetery.

CRAMER, MYRON CADY army officer; b. Portland, Conn., Nov. 6, 1881; s. Norman Landon and Mary Josephine (Cady) C.; student Cazenovia (N.Y.) Sem., 1899-1900; A.B., Wesleyan U., Conn., 1904, LL.B., Harvard, 1907; LL.D., 1943; student Army War Coll., Langres, France, 1918, Command and Gen. Staff Sch., 1928-30; m. Esther Durham; children-Emily Durham (Mrs. Charles Earle Van Sickle), Mary (Mrs. Tom Watson O'Bryon). Practiced law, N.Y.C., 1907-10, Tacoma, 1910-20; dep. pros. atty. Pierce County, Wash., 1915-19; served from pvt. to capt.Troop B., Cav., Wash. N.G., 1911-17; 1st lt., Troop B., Wash. Cav. on Mexican 17; 1st lt., Troop B., Wash. Cav. on Mexican Border, June 1916-Feb. 1917; asst. chief of staff and acting chief of staff, 41st Div., France, June 1917-Aug. 1919; promoted to maj. Judge Adv. Gen.'s Dept., regular army, July 1, 1920; promoted to lt. col. 1935, col., 1939; asst. prof. law U.S. Mil. Acad., 1922-24; judge adv. Philippine Dept., 1935-37; apptd. judge adv. gen. U.S. Army, with rank of maj. gen., Dec. 1, 1941; ret., Nov. 30, 1945; recalled to active duty, July, 1946; apptd. U.S. mem. Internat. Mil. Tribunal for Far East, Tokyo, for trial of maj. Japanese war criminals. Relieved from active duty U.S. Army, Mar., 1949. Decorations: D.S.M., Legion of Merit, Companion Order of the Bath, Officer Order of Black Star. Mem. Am., Fed., Wash. (hon. life) bar assns., Alpha Delta Phi, Phi Delta Phi (hon.). Methodist, Clubs: Army and Navy, Army-Navy Country (Washington); Harvard, University (Tacoma). Home: 3717 Fordham Rd. N.W., Washington 20016. Died Mar. 25, 1966; buried Arlington (Va.) Nat. Cemetery.

CRAMER, STUART WARREN JR. ret. army officer, business exec.; b. Charlotte, N.C., Jan. 28, 1892; s. Stuart Warren and Bertha Hobart (Berry) C.: student, Univ. of N.C., 1907-08, Phila. Textile Sch., 1921-22; B.S., U.S. Mil. Acad., 1913; m. Julia Baxter Scott, Nov. 3, 1923; children-Stuart Warren, John Scott. Commd. 2d lt. U.S. Army, 1913, and advanced through grades to maj., June 7, 1918; mil. career as cav. officer in Mexican campaign, 1915, and World War I: instr., U.S. Mil. Acad., 1917; a.d.c. to aide to pres. elect of Brazil, 1919; general staff corps librarian, Army War Coll., 1919-21; ret. from regular Army, Nov. 20, 1922: with Cramerton Mills, Inc. and Cramerton Mills Co., 1922-46, pres., 1939-46; spl. asst. to chmn., Munitions Bd., Washington, 1947, dep. chmn., 1948—; president John M. Scott & Co., Charlotte, N.C., Linville Resorts, Inc., Linville, North Carolina; director Wachovia Bank & Trust Co., Charlotte News Publishing Company. Chairman Gaston County Republican Exec. Com. 1928, N.C. finance chmn., 1940; mem. N.C. Park Commn., 1929-33; N.C. state chmn., Nat. Indsl. Information Com.; mem. Cotton rill Industry Com. and Combed Cotton Fabrics Industry Adv. Com., W.P.B., 1943-45, Cotton Weavers' Industry Com. and Combed Cotton Fabrics Industry Adv. Com., W.P.B., 1943-45, Cotton Weavers' Industry Adv. Com., O.P.A., 1943-45. Mem. exec. com., Nat. Assn. Mfrs., 1942-44, nat. v.p. in charge of Washington contacts and dir., 1944, also chmn. Govt. War Orgn. sub-com., Dir. Cotton Textile Inst. (also mem. exec. com.), Am. Cotton Mfrs. Assn. (st v.p., 1944; rep. on tour of inspection of French textile industries, 1925), N.C. Textile Found. Awarded citation by adj. gen. for service at Santa Anita during Mexican campaign, 1915, campaign medal for service in France, War Cross (Czechoslovakia). Mem. So. Combed Yarn Spinners Assn. (pres. 1940-41). Republican (del. nat. conv. 1944). Episcopalian. Clubs: Charlotte (N.C.) Country, Augusta (Ga.) Nat. Golf (N.J.), Univ., Chevy Chase, Army Navy (Washington), Racquet and Tennis (New York). Home: (winter) 200 Hermitage Rd., Myers Park, Charlotte; also Palm Shadows, Mountain Lake Club, Lake Wale, Fla.: (summer) Cloudcroft, Linville, N.C. Office: 1618 Johnston Bldg., Charlotte, N.C. Died Jan. 6, 1937.

CRAMPTON, GEORGE S., ophthalmologist; b. Rock Island, Ill., Mar. 10, 1874; s. Richard and Martha (Betty) C.; M.D., U. of Pa., 1898; m. Hazel Smedes, May 16, 1907. Practiced at Phila., Pa., since 1898; prof. emeritus ophthalmology, Grad. Sch. U. of Pa.; adjunct opthalmologist to Pa. Hosp. Served as dir., Field Hosps., 28th Div., U.S. Army, rank of lt. col., 1918-19. Fellow A.M.A., Coll., Phys. of Phila.; mem. Am. Ophthal. Soc., Illuminating Engring. Soc. (ex-nat. pres.), Franklin Inst. Republican. Episcopalian. Home-office 2031 Locust St., Philadelphia 3 PA

CRANE, AARON MARTIN author; b. Glover, Orleans Co., Vt., Feb. 13, 1839; s. John and Nancy (Martin) C.; ed. pub. schs., acad. and 1 term Newbury (Vt.) Sem.; m. Lida D. Flint, Jan. 16, 1867. Pvt. Co. I, 1st Vt. Cav., Aug. 11, 1862; promoted 1st lt. Co. E. 18th Regt., U.S.C.T., Aug. 2, 1864, and afterwards to capt., serving until May 1865; pub. Rep. paper, Winchester, Va., 1865-69; assessor internal revenue, 1869, until office abolished by law, 1873, then continued as spl. agt. in charge at various cities until 1884. Republican. Author: Right and Wrong Thinking and Their Results, 1906, 12th edt., 1911; A Search After Ultimate Truth, 1910. Home: Boston, Mass., and Norfolk, Va. Died 1914.

CRANE, JOHN army officer; b. Braintree, Mass., Dec. 18, 1744; s. Abijah and Sarah (Beverly) C.; m. Mehitable Wheeler, 1767. Served with Mass. Militia during French and Indian War; mem. Sons of Liberty; participated in Boston Tea Party, 1773; commd. capt., later maj. R.I. Arty., 1775; col. 3d Arty., Continental Army, 1777; brevetted brig. gen., 1783; served in siege of Boston and at battles of Saratoga and Red Bank; granted estate in Me. by Mass. Legislature for mil. services; judge Mass. Ct. of Common Please, 1790-1805. Died Whiting, Me., Aug. 21, 1805.

CRANE, JOHN ALDEN army officer; b. St. George, Md., Dec. 2, 1885; s. Charles Thomas and Annie Louis (Levering) C.; A.B., Johns Hopkins, 1907; grad. Army War Coll., 1928; m. Mary McKim, Oct. 21, 1908; children-Alden McKim, Mary McKim, Lizetta Violet. Commd. 2d lt., U.S. Army, 1908, and advanced through grades to major gen., 1943; served in P.I., 1908-10, 19-21; with 1st div. in France, 1917-18; mil. attaché to Turkey and Bulgaria, 1932-36; stationed at Ft. Bragg, N.C., 1940—. Decorated Distinguished Service Cross, Silver Star, Purple Heart, French Croix de Guerre with palm. Officer Legion of Honor, Comdr. Order of the Sword (Sweden). Comdr. Order of St. Alexander (Bulgaria). Mem. Alpha Delta Phi. Mason. Clubs: Army Navy Country (Washington); Army and Navy (Manila). Home: Garrison, Md. Died Nov. 3, 1951.

CRANE, ROBERT CLARK pub. relations cons.; b. Pitts., Sept. 25, 1920; s. Frederick Lea and Gwendolyn (Kershner) C.; ed. Pingry Sch., 1931-38, Dartmouth, 1938-41; m. Frances Hyde Adams, Nov. 22, 1942; children-Geoffrey A., Jonathan C., Deborah Lea. Dir., Elizabeth (N.J.) Daily Jour., 1946-60 asst. to gen. mgr., May 1946, asst. gen. mgr., asst. editor, Oct. 1946, v.p. and gen. mgr., 1947, pres., treas., editor and pub., Jan. 16, 1948-60; pres. Robert C. Crane & Sons, Elizabeth, 1960-; dir. Central Home Trust Co., 1948-. Mem. N.J. Senate from Union County, 1956-62. Rep. elector for N.J., Nat. Election, 1948, chmn. N.J. delegation U.S. Electoral Coll., 1949: state del.-at-large Rep. Nat. Conv., 1952; chmn. N.J. Govs. gasoline price study com., 1950-51; mem. N.J. Price Study Commn., 1952; v.p. Union Co. Park Commn., 1952; mem. Elizabeth Juvenile Conf. Com., 1952-54. Mem. bd. dirs. Union Co. Jr. Achievement, Inc.; mem. bd. mgrs. St. Elizabeth Hosp.; trustee Community Chest Eastern Union Co.; dir. Elizabeth YMCA (pres. 1952-56), hon. life mem. N.J. P.B.A. Hon. chmn. United Jewish Appeal, 1959. Served from pvt. to capt. Q.M.C., AUS, 1942-46. Awarded Bronze Star medal; award N.J. dept. Res. Officers Assn. U.S. for contbns. to civil def., 1956; N.J. Distinguished Service award, 1949; Americanism award B'nai B'rith, 1956; nat. achievement award Jr. Achievement of Union County, 1957; 2d Ann. Community Service award Union County Cath. Youth Orgn. for services as Pub., 1959. Mem. Young Pres. Orgn., Holland Soc. N.Y., Artists and Writers Assn. N.Y. (past pres.), Met. Rod and Gun Assn., U.S. N.J. State (p.p.), Eastern Union Co. (past pres.) (past pres., bd. dirs.) C. of C., N.J. Press Assn. (past pres.), Am. Pub. Relations Assn., Pingry Sch. and Dartmouth alumni assns., Res. Officers Assn. U.S., Mil. Order Fgn. Wars U.S., U.S. Power Squadron, Q.M. Assn., Am. Legion, S.A.R., Sigma Phi Epsilon, Republican. Presbyterian. Mason (Shriner). Elk. Clubs: Plainfield Country; Manasquan River Marlin and Tuna (Brielle, N.J.); Marco Polo, Dartmouth (N.Y.C.); Downtown (Newark), Rotary (pres. 1952-53 Elizabeth). Home: 329 Hillside Av., Westfield, N.J. Died Apr. 24, 1962; buried Evergreen Cemetery, Westfield.

CRANE, WILLIAM MONTGOMERY naval officer; b. Elizabeth, N.J., Feb. 1, 1784; s. Gen. William and Abigail (Miller) C.; m. Eliza King. Commd. midshipman U.S. Navy, 1799, lt., 1803; distinguished in 2d attack on Tripoli, 1804; commanded brig. Nautilus during War of 1812; commanded ship General Pike, Lake Ontario, 1814; commanded Mediterranean Squadron, 1827-29; commandant Portsmouth (N.Y.), Navy Yard, 1832-40; navy commr., 1841-42; chief Bur. of Ordnance and Hydrography, 1842-46. Died Washington, D.C., Mar. 18, 1846; buried Congressional Cemetery, Washington.

CRANE, WINTHROP MURRAY, JR., paper mfr.; b. Dalton, Mass., Sept. 12, 1881; s. W. Murray and Mary (Benner) C.; student Hill Sch., Pottstown, Pa.; A.B., Yale, 1904; m. Ethel G. Eaton, Feb. 9, 1905; children—Barbara (Mrs. George Monaghan), Winthrop Murray, III, Arthur Eaton. Entered family paper mills, 1904; pres. and gen. mgr., Crane & Co., 1923-52, chmn. board. Served as lt. colonel, U.S. Army, World War I. Trustee Mem. Skull and Bones (Yale). Republican. Conglist. Clubs: Yale (New York); Yale (Boston). Home: Dalton MA Died Mar. 28, 1968; buried Dalton MA

CRANMER, WILLIAM H(ENRY) H(ARRISON) mining exec.; b. Denver, Oct. 11, 1881; s. William H. H. and Martin Jane (Hittson) C.; student Andover Acad.; Ph.B., Yale, 1906; m. Margaret Wood, May 27, 1907 (dec.); children-William Henry Harrison (dec.), Robert Loring; m. 2d, Helen Worden Erskine, Jan. 31, 1959. Mgr., Ernest & Cranmer Bldg., Denver, 1907-17; pres. Jones Wheeler Cranmer Engring. Co., 1914-17, Navajo Petroleum Corp., 1926-29; pres., chmn. bd. New Park Mining Co., 1934-; chmn. Oil, Inc., Salt Lake City; pres. Yale Gold Mining Co., East Utah Mining Corp.; dir. Silver Buckle Mining Co., Lead Industries Assn., Cardiff Mining Co. Mem. bd. Pub. Works, Denver, 1912-14. Served as capt. F.A., U.S. Army, World War I. Recipient Distinguished Citizens medal Denver Centenary, 1958. Mem. Am. Inst. Mining Engrs., Utah Mining Assn. (pres.). Mason (K.T., 32ff Shriner). Clubs: Kiwanis, Alta; Yale (N.Y.). Address: 45 E. 62d St., N.Y.C. 10021. Died May 2, 1967; buried Fairmount Cemetery, Denver.

CRANSTON, JOHN physician, colonial gov.; b. Eng., 1625; s. Rev. James Cranston; m. Mary Clarke, June 3, 1658, 1 son, Samuel. Atty. gen. R.I., 1654-56; commr. R.I. Gen. Assembly from Newport, 1655-66; dep. gov. R.I., 1672-78; commd. maj. Mass. Militia during King Phillip's War, 1676: gov. R.I., 1678-80. Died R.I., Mar. 12, 1680; buried Cemetery on Farewell St. Newport.

CRAVEN, THOMAS TINGEY naval officer; b. Washington, D.C., Dec. 20, 1808; s. Tunis and Hannah (Tingey) C.; m. Virginia Wingate; m. 2d, Emily Truxtun; 8 children. Commd. midshipman U.S. Navy, 1828, lt., 1830; comdt. of midshipmen U.S. Naval Acad., Annapolis, Md., 1850-55, 58-60, initiated practice of cruises (still feature of the course at Acad.); promoted comdr., 1852; commd. capt. while in command of Potomac flotilla, 1861, commodore, 1863, rear-adm., 1866; comdt. Mare Island Navy-yard; comdr. Pacific Squadron; ret., 1869; port adm., San Francisco, 1870. Died Boston, Aug. 23, 1887.

CRAVEN, THOMAS TINGEY naval officer ret.; b. Vallejo, Cal., July 8, 1873; s. Henry S. and Eugenie (Von Klinkofstrom) C.; B.S., U.S. Naval Acad., 1897; student (later mem. of staff), U.S. Naval War Coll., 1915; m. Antoinette Merritt, July 25, 1901; children-Thomas Tingey, Ann Craven de Kay, Olga Craven Thurber. Commd. ensign USN, 1896, advanced through grades to vice adm., 1935; with Gen. Bd. of Navy, 1911; dir. target practice and engring. competitions, Washington, 1912: comdr. U.S.S. Sacramento, 1916-17; head U.S. Naval Aviation, France, 1917-18; dir. Naval Aviation, USN Dept., 1919, laid ground work for establishment of Bur. of Aeronautics; dir. naval communications U.S. Navy Dept., 1927-28; promoted rear adm., 1928; chief coordinator Fed. govt. under Pres. Hoover, 1931-33; comdr. battleships, 1935; retired from active duty, 1937; supt. N.Y. State Maritime Acad., 1938-39. U.S. del. to internat. congress for regulation of communications, Washington, 1927. Decorated campaign medals for service in West Indies, P.I., Mexico China; Sampson medal, Navy D.S.M. (U.S.); Double Dragon (China); Legion of Honor (France); War Cross and Victory medal (Italy), Polish Cross.Home; 87 Newton St., Weston, Mass. Died Apr. 5, 1950; buried Greenwood Cemetery, Bklyn.

CRAVEN, TUNUS AUGUSTUS MACDONOUGH naval officer; b. Portsmouth, N.H., Jan. 11, 1813; s. Tunus and Hannah (Tingey) C.; m. Mary Carter, 1838; m. 2d, Marie Stevenson. Served as lt. on ships Falmouth, 1841-43, North Carolina, 1843-46; chief editor U.S. Nautical Mag. (one of 1st periodicals devoted to interests of navy), 1845-46; comdr. ship Dale, in Pacific squadron, assisted in conquest of Cal., 1848; comdr. Atrato expdn. in survey for ship canal across Isthmus of Darien, 1857; comdr., Apr. 1861; comdr. monitor Tecumseh with Adm. Farragut's squadron in Mobile, Ala.; Tecumseh was destroyed by the Confederate ram Tennessee in Battle of Mobile Bay, Aug. 5, 1864, and Craven went down with his ship. Died Aug. 5, 1864.

CRAWFORD, CHARLES army officer; b. Coshocton, O.; s. Thomas and Margaret (Parkhill) C.; grad. U.S. Mil. Acad., 1889; Army War Coll., 1912; m. Miss E. M. Miller (dec. 1919). Commd. 2d lt. 10th Inf., 1889; promoted through grades to col. inf., 1917; brig. gen. N.A., 1918; retired, 1919. Mil. police duty, Oklahoma City, 1889-90; assisted U.S. Commn. dealing with Indian tribes, 1890. Iowas. Sac and Foxes, Shawnees, Kickapoos, Cheyenne and Arapahoes; organized Apache Indian Co., 10th Inf., 1891-92; participated in battle of San Juan Hill, Cuba, 1898, in which his captain in official report commented on his fearlessness under fire; in various fights and skirmishes in P.I., 1890-1902; instr. Inf. and Cav. Sch. and Staff Coll., Ft. Leavenworth, 1903-07; in P.I., 1909-11; on Gen. Staff, 1913-16; in Canal Zone, 1916-17; commd. 6th Brig., 3d Div., AEF in 2d Battle of Marne, July 15, 1918, and in advance north and on Vesle River. Aug. 1918. Author: Six Months with Sixth Brigade; Re-Starting Economic Theory. Presbyn. Home: Paola, Kan. Died Dec. 28, 1945; buried Paola.

CRAWFORD, DAVID MCLEAN army officer; b. Flanders, N.J., Oct. 10, 1889; s. Darwin McLean and Grace May (Graybill) C.; S.B., U.S. Mil. Acad., 1912; S.M., Yale, 1922; Command and General Staff Sch., 1932-34; Army War College, 1940; m. Mrs. Annye Wilson Schleiter, October 21, 1952; children (by previous marriage)- David McLean, Leslie McLean (Mrs. John Jamieson Frost), James Tracy. Commd. 2d lt., U.S. Army, 1912, and advanced through the grades to brigadier general, 1942; instr. and asst. prof. chemistry and electricity, U.S. Mil. Acad., West Point, N.Y., 1916-21; dir. Communications Engring. Dept., U.S. Army Signal Sch., Ft. Monmouth, N.J., 1922-24; signal officer, Panama Canal Div., 1924-27; asst. prof. chem. and electricity, U.S. Mil. Adad., 1927-28; chief, war plans and training div., office chief signal ofcr., War Dept., 1928-32; instr. Pa. N.G., 1934-35; chief communications liaison div. Office Chief Signal Officer, 1936-39; U.S. member International Radio Consulting Com., Bucarest, Romania, 1937; tech. advisor, U.S. del. to Inter-Am. Radio Conf., Havana, Cuba, 1937, to U.S. del. to Internat. Radio Conv., Cairo, Egypt, 1938; U.S. del. to Central Am. Regional Radio Conf., Guatemala City, 1939; signal ofcr. Hq. II Corps Area, Gov.'s Isl., N.Y., 1940; signal ofcr. VII Army Corps, 1941; air defense ofcr. GHQ Air Force Hdqrs., Bolling Field, D.C., 1941-42; chmn. Army Communications Board, War Department, 1942-43; communications chief coordinator, U.S. Joint Army-Navy Communications Bd., and Inter-Allied Combined Communications Bd., 1942-46. Retired, 1946. Awarded Comdr. of the Most Illustrious Order of the British Empire. Mason. Home: Wilson Farm. Mifflin. Juniata Co., Pa. Died May 1, 1963; buried Mifflintown Cemetery, Mifflintown, Pa.

CRAWFORD, GEORGE WASHINGTON gov. Ga., congressman b. Columbia County, Ga., Dec. 22, 1798; grad. Princeton, 1820; studied law. Admitted to bar, 1822, began practice of law, Augusta, Ga.; atty. gen. Ga., 1827-31; mem. Ga. Ho. of Reps., 1837-42 mem. U.S. Ho. of Reps. from Ga. (elected as Whig to fill vacancy), Jan. 7-Mar. 3, 1843; gov. Ga., 1843-47; U.S. sec. of war under Pres. Taylor, 1849-50; presided over Ga. Secession Conv., 1861. Died "Bel Air," nr. Augusta, July 22, 1872; buried Summerville Cemetery.

CRAWFORD, JAMES PYLE WICKERSHAM coll. prof.; b. Lancaster, Pa., Feb. 19, 1882; s. James and Corinne (Wickersham) C.; A.B., U. of Pa., 1902, grad. work, 1902-04, Ph.D., 1906; univs. of Grenoble, Madrid and Freiburg, 1904-06; Litt.D., Franklin and Marshall, 1925; m. Florence May Wickersham, June 3, 1909; 1 dau., Harriet de B. Instr. Romance langs., U. of Pa., 1906, prof., 1914 - . Commd. capt. U.S.A., June 1918 and assigned duty at Washington, D.C.; mil. attacheé to Colombia, S.A., Jan.-July, 1919; hon. discharged Aug. 1919; commd. maj. O.R.C., Nov. 1919. Author: Life and Works of Suarez de Figueroa, 1907; Spanish Composition, 1910; Temas Espana, 1931; Spanish Pastoral Drama, 1915; First Book in Spanish, 1919. Editor: Tragedia de Narciso, 1909. Editor of Modern Language Journal, 1920-24, Hispanic Review, 1933 - . Home: Philadelphia, Pa. Died Sept. 22, 1939.

CRAWFORD, MEDOREM army officer; m. Yamhill Co., Ore., Jan. 27, 1844; s. Modorem (Capt. U.S.V.) and Adaline (Brown) B.; grad. U.S. Mil. Acad., 1867, Arty. Sch., 1875; (hon. A.M., Bowdoin Coll., 1881); m. Rita Shreve Carter, Jan. 15, 1874; 2d, Lola Goodall, Jan. 14, 1885. Commd. 2d lt. 2d Arty., June 17, 1867; promoted through grades to brig. gen., Jan. 3, 1908; retired Jan. 27, 1908. On duty, Ft. Vancouver, Wash., 1867-68; with 1st expdn. to Alaska, where was shipwrecked, 1868-70; Tex., Mexican border and in Old Mexico, 1878-79; prof. mil. science, Bowdoin Coll., 1879-18; served in Cuba, and chief ordnance officer, div. and dept. of cuba, 1898-01; comd. Ft. Kenay, Alaska, 1869-70; Pirotecnia militar, Habana, Cuba, 1899-01; comd. Ft. Schuyler, 1901-03, Ft. McHenry, 1903-05. Ft. Wadsworth, 1905-08. Republican. Home: Washington, D.C. Died Aug. 11, 1921.

CRAWFORD, SAMUEL JOHNSON governor; b. Lawrence Co., Ind., Apr. 15, 1835; s. William and Jane (Morrow) C.; prep. edn. graded schs., Bedford, Ind.; read law, Bedford, and admitted to bar, 1856; LL.B., Cincinnati Law Sch., 1858; removed to Garnett, Kan., 1859; m. Isabel M. Chase, Nov. 27, 1866. Capt. 2d Kan. Cav., May 14, 1861; col. 83d U.S.C.T., Nov. 1, 1863; resigned, Nov. 7, 1864; bvtd. brig. gen. vols., Mar. 13, 1865 "for meritorious services"; col. 19th Kan. Cav., 1868. Farming in Kan., 1869 -. Mfem. Kan. Ho. of Rep., 1861; gov. of Kan., 1865-69. Author: Kansas in the Sixties. Home: Topeka, Kan. Died Oct. 21, 1913.

CRAWFORD, WILLIAM army officer; b. Berkeley County, Va., 1732. Served in French and Indian War; capt., leader of scouts with Gen. Braddock in expdn. against Ft. Duquesne, 1755; served as capt. during Pontiac War, 1763-64; justice Pa. Ct. Quarter Sessions; commd. lt. col. 5th Regt., Va. Militia, 1776, col. 7th Regt., 1776; participated in battles of L.I., Trenton, Princeton, Brandywine, Germantown; in charge of Va. Frontier Militia, 1778; comdr. expdn. against Wyandote and Delaware Indians in Ohio. Captured and killed at "Battle Island," Wyandot County, O., June 11, 1782.

CRAWFORD, WILLIAM HARRIS senator, cabinet officer; b. Nelson County, Va., Feb. 24, 1772; s. Joel and Fannie (Harris) C.; ed. privately in classical studies; student Richmond Acad., Augusta, Ga.; m. Susanna Girardin, 1804. Moved to Edgefield, S.C., 1779, to Columbia County, Ga., 1783; admitted to Ga. bar, 1799; mem. Ga. Senate, 1803-07; mem. U.S. Senate from Ga., 1807-13, pres. pro tem, 1812; minister to France, 1812-13; agt. for sale of land donated to U.S. govt. by Lafayette, 1815; U.S. sec. of war, 1815-16; U.S. sec. of treasury, 1816-25; Democratic candidate for Pres. U.S., 1824, paralytic stroke ruined chance in 1824. Died Oglethorpe County, Ga., Sept. 15, 1834; buried "Woodlawn," nr. Crawford, Oglethorpe County.

CRAWFORD, WILLIAM L. lawyer; b. Estell, Clay Co., Ky., Jan. 23, 1839; s. J. D. and Catharine C.; ed. McKinzie Inst., Clarksville, Tex.; studied law in office of D. B. Culberson, Jefferson, Tex.; admitted to bar, 1866, and began practice at Jefferson, Tex., same year; m. Kate Lester Lamar, Oct. 1, 1896. Lt. col. 19th Tex. Inf., C.S.A., 1861-65; mem. Constl. Conv., Tex., 1875; mem. law firm Crawford & Lamar (L. Q. C. Lamar), Dallas, 1903 - . Home: Dallas, Tex. Died Feb. 17, 1920.

CRAZY HORSE (Indian name: Tashunca-vitco), Indian chief; b. circa 1849; married a mem. of Cheyenne tribe. Chief of Sioux Confederacy; moved North with his bank of 1200 Oglalas and Cheyennes, joined large body under Sitting Bull, Valley of Little Big Horn, Wyo., 1876; led a force of Cheyennes in battle of Little Big Horn, June 25, 1876, surrounded Gen. Custer in flanking movements from the North and West, destroyed Custer's entire command; later surrendered. Killed while resisting imprisonment, Sept. 5, 1877.

CREBS, JOHN MONTGOMERY congressman; b. Middleburg, Loudoun County, Va., Apr. 9, 1830; ed. public schs.; studied law. Moved with family to White County, Ill., 1837 admitted to bar, 1852, began practice of law, White County; commd. lt. col. 87th Regt., Ill. Inf., 1862; served in Miss., Vicksburg and ark. campaigns in Civil War; commanded cavalry brigade in Dept. of Gulf; mem. U.S. Ho. of Reps. (Democrat) from Ill., 41st-42d congresses, 1869-73; practiced law, 1873-90. Died Carmi, White County, June 26, 1890 buried Maple Ridge Cemetery.

CREECH, OSCAR, JR., physician, univ. dean; b., Nashville, N.C., Nov. 14, 1916 s. Oscar and Martha (Gulley) C., student Wake Forest Coll., 1933-37; M.D., Jefferson Med. Coll., 1941; m. Dorothy B. Creech. Intern Charity Hosp., New Orleans, 1941-42; resident Tulane Surg. Service, 1945-49; asst. instr. dept. surgery Tulane Med. Sch., 1946-49, now William Henderson prof. surgery, chmn. dept.; instr. to asso. prof. dept. surgery, Baylor U. Coll. Medicine, 1949-55; now dean Sch. Medicine, Tulane U. Served maj., 9th Inf. Div., AUS, 1942-46. Diplomate Am. Bd. Thoracic Surgery, Am. Bd. Surgery, Mem. A.M.A., Am. Surg. Soc., Soc. U. Surgeons, Soc. Vascular Surgery, Am. Assn. Thoracic Surgery, Soc. Soc. Clin. Research, Soc. Exptl. Biology and Medicine, Sigma Xi, Alpha Omega Alpha. Home: New Orleans LA Died Dec. 22, 1967; buried Ahoskie NC

CREEL, ROBERT CALHOUN, fgn. service officer; b. Kansas City, Mo., Sept. 25, 1913; s. James Randall and Margaret Emerson (Davis) C.; A.B. summa cum laude, Harvard, 1934; LL.B. cum laude, 1938; married to Mariana Mears Evans, January 21, 1956; children—Elizabeth Calhoun and Margaret Evans. Admitted to N.Y. bar, 1939; Richard Sheldon prize fellowship for travel, Europe, 1934-35; atty. Root, Clark, Buckner & Ballantine, N.Y.C., 1938-41; chief counsel, dir. legal div. European hdqrs., area dir. for Europe, Washington hdqrs. Office Fgn. Liquidation Commr., Dept. of State, 1946-47; commd. fgn. service officer, consul career, sec. Diplomatic Service, July 1947; 2d sec., consul, Bucharest, Rumania, 1947-50, 1st sec. embassy New Delhi, India, 1950-51, also Katmandhu, Nepal; chief polit. affairs div. Berlin Element, Office U.S. High Commr. for Germany, 1952-54; detailed Nat. War Coll., 1954-55; officer-in-charge, German Polit. Affairs, Dept. State, 1955-58; counselor embassy, dep. chief mission, Beirut, Lebanon, 1958-61; counselor Am. embassy, dep. chief mission, Vientiane, Laos, 1961-62; dir. Office German Affairs, Dept. State, 1962-64; dep. asst. sec. of state for European affairs, 1964-65; U.S. consul general, Munich, Germany, 1965-70. Served as pvt. to lt. col. U.S. Army, 1941-46; with 101st Cav., 212th C.A.C., N.Y.N.G. 1938-41. Mem. Assn. Ex-Mems. Squadron A. Phi Beta Kappa. Clubs: Metropolitan, Chevy Chase (Washington); Harvard (N.Y.C.). Home: Washington DC Died Oct. 1970.

CREESY, JOSIAH PERKINS sea capt.; b. Marblehead, Mass., Mar. 23, 1814; s. Josiah P. and Mary (Woolridge) C.: m. Eleanor Horton Prentiss, 1841. Commanded clipper ships in trade with China, 1837-65; set sailing record of 89 days from N.Y.C. to San Francisco in ship Flying Cloud; volunteer acting lt. in command of U.S.S. Ino, 1861-62. Died Salem, Mass., June 5, 1871; buried Marblehead.

CRESAP, MICHAEL army officer; b. Alleghany County, Md., July 10, 1742; s. Thomas Cresap; M. Mary Whitehead. Precipitated Dunmore's War by leading Whites in Yellow Creek Massacre (in which several families of peaceful Indians were slaughtered), 1774; capt. Va. Militia which defeated Indians at Point Pleasant, 1774; commd. by Md. Assembly to recruit troops for Continental Army, 1775. Died N.Y.C., Oct. 18, 1775.

CRESAP, THOMAS pioneer; b. Skipton, Eng., circa 1702; m. Hannah Johnson, circa 1717, 1 son, Michael. Came to Md., 1717; one of most prominent men of the Appalachian border; served as capt. Md. Militia, 1734; Indian trader, translator; an organizer Ohio Co., 1749; fought in Am. Revolution. Died circa 1790.

CRESON, LARRY BARKLEY, justice; b. Memphis, Jan. 17, 1906; s. Robert Franklin and Etta (Thomas) C.; student Memphis U. Sch., grad. Vanderbilt U., 1928. LL.B., 1929; m. Gertrude Jean Hooper, Aug. 29, 1934; children—Jean Edrington (Mrs. Allen Cooper Dell), Larry Barkley. Admitted to Tenn. bar, 1929; practiced in Memphis, 1930-65; past mem. firm Laughlin, Watson, Creson, Garthbright & Halle; associate justice Supreme Court of Tennessee, chancellor Chancery Court of Shelby County, Tenn., 1947-54. Past member board trust Vanderbilt U. Served as lt. comdr., air combat intelligence, USNR, World War II. Mem. Vanderbilt Alumni Assn. (dir., past pres., Memphis), Am., Tenn., Memphis and Shelby County, (pres. 1960-61) bar assns., Sigma Alpha Epsilon, Phi Delta Phi. Home: Memphis TN 38103 Died June 19, 1972; buried Calvary Cemetery, Memphis TN

CRESS, GEORGE OSCAR army officer; b. Warsaw, Ill., Sept. 18, 1862; s. George and Mary E. C.; grad. U.S. Mil. Acad., 1884, Army War Coll., 1911; m. Dona Scott Dean, May 26, 1886. Commd. 2d lt. Cav., U.S. Army, 1884, advanced through grades to brig. gen. (temp.), 1918; prof. mil. sci. and tactics Knox Coll., Galesburg, Ill., 1889-93; duty Yellowstone Nat. Park, 1897-98; in Philippines, with Gen. Lawton, 1899-1900; constructing q.m. at Ft. Riley, Kan., 1900-04; prof. mil. sci. and tactics Mich. Mil. Acad., Orchard Lake, Mich., 1904-08; duty Insp. General's Dept., 1916-18; organized 49th F.A., 1918; in charge militia affairs So. Dept., 1919; apptd. comdr. Columbus Barracks, Oct. 6, 1919. Address: War Dept., Washington. Died May 8, 1954.

CRESSWELL, ROBERT newspaper pub.; b. Phila., Pa., May 29, 1897; s. Charles Thomson and Bell C. (Catherwood) C.; grad. St. Paul's Sch., Concord, N.H., 1915; A.B., Princeton U., 1919; m. Catharine R. Henriques, May 28, 1921 (divorced); children-Robert, Henry. With N.Y. Herald Trib., 1922-40, successively as reporter, copy reader, circulation mgr., treas. and dir.; pres., dir. and pub. Phila. Evening Public Ledger Jan. 1, 1941-Jan. 5, 1942; with Office of Strategic Services, Washington. D.C., to Mar. 9, 1942. Commd. lt. col. Army of U.S., Mar 20, 1943. Trustee St. John's Guild. Republican, Episcopalian. Clubs: Century Assn. University (N.Y. City); Philadelphia, Sunnybrook Golf, Franklin Inn (Phila.); Ivy (Princeton). Home 15 W. Bell's Mills Road, Philadelphia, Pa. Died Sept. 1943.

CRESWELL, HARRY I. T., mil. attache; b. Mar. 11, 1891; B.S., Va. Mil. Inst., 1913; grad. advance course, Inf. Sch., 1930, Command and Gen. Staff Sch., 1933. Commd. 2d lt., Inf., 1916; promoted through grades to lt. col., Sept. 22, 1938; now mil. attache, Tokyo, Japan. Address: care Am. Embassy, Tokyo Japan

CREWS, RALPH lawyer; b. Mt. Vernon, Ill., Mar. 29, 1876; s. Seth Floyd and Helena Ridgway (Slocum) C.; Hyde Park High Sch., Chicago; LL.B., Chicago Coll. of Law, 1897; m. Elizabeth Stuart Sherman, June 17, 1901; children - Mary Arthur, Elizabeth Ridgway, Ralph. Admitted to Ill. bar, 1897, and practiced at Chicago until 1917; mem. law firm Shearman & Sterling, New York, 1919 - . Dir. National City Co. Old Ben Coal Corp., Austin Machinery Corp., Brokaw & Co. Maj., lt. col. and col. Ordnance Dept., U.S.A., 1917-18; in charge contract sect., later spl. asst. to chief of ordnance, Washington, D.C. Republican. Episcopalian. Home: New York, N.Y. Died Sept. 6, 1926.

CRILE, GEORGE (WASHINGTON) surgeon; b. Chili, O., Nov. 11, 1864; s. Michael and Margaret (Dietz) C.: B.S., Ohio Northern U., 1885, A.M., 1888; M.D., Wooster U. (now Western Reserve U.), 1887, A.M., 1894; student Vienna, 1893, London, 1895, Paris, 1897; hon. Ph.D., Hiram Coll., 1901; LL.D., Wooster U., 1916; M.Ch., U. of Dublin, 1925; LL.D., U. of Glasgow, 1928; Doctor honoris causa, U. of Guatemala, 1939; m. Grace McBride, Feb. 7, 1900; children-Margaret (Mrs. Hiram Garretson), Elisabeth (Mrs. J. A. Crisler, Jr.), George Jr., Robert, Lecturer and demonstrator histology, 1889-90, prof. physiology, 1890-93, prof. principles and practice of surgery, 1893-1900, Wooster U.; prof. clin. surgery, 1900-11, surgery, 1911-24, Western Reserve U.; visiting surgeon Lakeside Hosp., 1911-24; one of founders Cleveland Clinic Foundation, now dir. research. Brigade surgeon vols., maj., Cuba and Porto Rico, 1898; maj. Med. O.R.C. and professional dir. of U.S. Army Base Hosp. No. 4, Lakeside Unit (B.E.F., No. 9), in service in France, May 1917-May 1918; sr. consultant in surg. research, May 1918-Jan. 1919; lt. col., June 1918, col., Nov. 1918, brig. gen. Med. O.R.C., 1921; brig. general Auxiliary R.C., since 1929. Awarded D.S.M. (U.S.), 1919; hon. mem. Military Div., 3rd Class, Companion of Bath (British), 1919; Chevalier Legion of Honor (French), 1922. Alvarenga prize, Coll. Phys., Phila., 1901; Cartwright prize, Columbia, 1897 and 1903; Senn prize, A.M.A., 1898; Am. med. medal for service to humanity, 1914; Nat. Inst. Soc. Sciences medal, 1917; Trimble Lecture medal, 1921; 3d laureate of Lannelongue Foundation (Lannelongue Internat. medal of surgery presented by Société Internationale de Chirurgie de Paris), 1925; Cleveland medal for public service, 1931; Distinguished Service Gold Key, American Congress of Physical Therapy, 1940. Fellow American Assn. Anatomists, A.A.A.S., American Surgical Association (president 1923), Am. Coll. Surgeons (pres. 1916; mem. bd.

regents since 1913; chmn. bd. regents 1917-39). A.M.A., Am. Physiol. Soc., Am. Assn. Obstetricians, Gynecologists and Abdominal Surgeons, Southern Surg. Assn., Southern Med. Assn., Am. Philos. Soc.; mem. Assn. Am. Pathologists and Bacteriologists, Am. Soc. Clin. Surgery, Soc. Exptl. Biology and Medicine, Nat. Inst. Social Sciences, National Research Council, Assn. Study Internal Secretions, Am. Heart Assn., Am. Med. Editors' Assn., Ohio State Medical Assn., Cleveland Acad. Medicine, Cleveland Med. Library Assn.; Interstate Post Grad. Med. Assn. of N. America (chmn. program com.) ; hon. or corr. fellow or mem. many Am. and European societies. Clubs: Union (Cleveland); 100,000 Mile Club. Author: Surgical Shock, 1897; Surgery of Respiratory System 1899; Certain Problems Relating to Surgical Operations, 1901; On the Blood Pressure in Surgery, 1903; Hemorrhage and Transfusion, 1909; Anemia and Resuscitation, 1914; Anoci-Association (with Lower), 1914. 2d edit., title, Surgical Shock and the Shockless Operation through Anoci-Association, 1920; Origin and Nature of the Emotions, 1915; A Mechanistic View of War and Peace, 1915; Man, An Adaptive Mechanism 1916; The Kinetic Drive, 1916; The Fallacy of the German State Philosophy, 1918; A Physical Interpretation of Shock Exhaustion and Restoration, 1921; The Thyroid Gland (with others), 1922: Notes on Military Surgery, 1924; A Bipolar Theory of Living Processes, 1926; Problems in Surgery, 1928; Diagnosis and Treatment of Diseases of the Thyroid Gland (with others), 1932; Diseases Peculiar to Civilized Man, 1934; The Phenomena of Life, 1936; The Surgical Treatment of Hypertension, 1938; Intelligence Power and Personality, 1941. Home: 2620 Derbyshire Rd. Office: Cleveland Clinic, Euclid Av. at E. 93d St., Cleveland, O. Died Jan. 7, 1943.

CRISP, CHARLES FREDERICK congressman; b. Sheffield, Eng., Jan. 29, 1845; s. William and Elizabeth C.; m. Clara Belle Burton, 1867; 1 son, Charles R. Served as lt. Confederate Army during Civil War; admitted to Ga. bar, 1866; Ga. solicitor gen. Southwestern Jud. Dist., 1872-77, judge Ga. Superior Ct., 1877-82: mem. U.S. Ho. of Reps. from Ga., 48th-54th congresses, 1883-96, speaker, 1891-95. Died Atlanta, Ga., Oct. 23, 1896; buried Oak Grove Cemetery Atlanta.

CRITTENDEN, GEORGE BIBB army officer; b. Russellville, Ky., Mar. 20, 1812; s. John Jordan and Sally (Lee) C.; grad. U.S. Mil. Acad., 1832. Commd. capt. co. of mounted rifles during Mexican War; brevetted maj. for gallantry at battles of Contreras and Churubusco; commd. lt. col., 1856, brig. gen., 1857; commd. maj. gen. Confederate Army, 1861, comdr. S.E. Ky. and part of E. Tenn., 1861; state librarian Ky., 1867-74. Died Danville, Ky., Nov. 27, 1880; buried Frankfort (Ky.) Cemetery.

CRITTENDEN, THOMAS LEONIDAS army officer, state ofcl.; b. Russellville, Ky., May 15, 1819; s. John Jordan and Sally (Lee) C.; m. Kittie Todd. Admitted to Ky. bar, 1840; commonwealth's atty. in Ky., 1842; U.S. consul, Liverpool, 1848-53; commd. maj. gen. Ky. Militia, 1860; commd. brig. gen. U.S. Army, 1861, promoted to maj. gen. (for distinguished service at Battle of Shiloh, 1862-, 1862; commanded corps at battles of Stone River, 1862-63; investigated after his corps retreated at Battle of Chickamauga, 1863, acquitted; trans. to Army of Potomac, comdr. portion of 9th Corps throughout operations during 1864; apptd. state treas. Ky. 1866; brevetted brig. gen., 1867. Died Staten Island, N.Y., Oct. 23, 1893; buried Frankfort (Ky.) Cemetery.

CRITTENDEN, THOMAS THEODORE lawyer; b. Shelby Co., Ky., Jan. 2, 1832; s. Henry and Anna Maria C.; ed. Cloverport, Ky., and Centre Coll., Danville, Ky., grad. 1855; m. Carrie W. Jackson, Nov. 13, 1856, Lt. col. 7th Mo. cav., from May, 1862, to close Civil war; after war practiced law; filled an unexpired term as atty. gen. of Mo.; mem. Congress, 1877-81, 7th dist., Mo.; gov. Mo., 1881-85; U.S. consul gen. at city of Mexico, 1893-97; resumed practice of law. Home: Kansas City, Mo. Died 1909.

CROFT, EDWARD army officer; b. Greenville, S.C., July 11, 1875; s. Edward and Mary Eliza (Pearson) C.; student S.C. Mil. Acad., 1892 to 1896; grad. Inf. Cavalry School, 1904, School of Line, 1920. General Staff School, 1921, Army War College, 1924; m. Maribel Williams, February 8, 1905; 1 son, Edward. Second lieutenant, Infantry, U.S.A., July 9, 1898; advanced through grades to major, May 15, 1917; lt. col., Inf., N.A., Aug. 5, 1917, col., June 17, 1918; lt. col., U.S.A., July 1, 1920; advanced through grades to maj. gen., May 6, 1933; chief of Inf., U.S.A., May 6, 1933 - . Decorated Silver Star, Purple Heart (M.S.A.). Episcopalian. Mason. Died Jan. 28, 1938.

CROGHAN, GEORGE army officer; b. Locust Grove, Ky., Nov. 15, 1791; s. William and Lucy (Clark) c.; grad. Coll. William and Mary, 1810; m. Serena Livingston, May 1816. Aide to Col. Boyd at Battle of Tippecanoe, War of 1812, 1811; aide-de-camp Gen. Harrison, 1813; commanded defense of Ft. Stephenson in No. Ohio, for which he was brevetted lt. col., 1813; postmaster New Orleans, 1824; insp. gen. with rank of col. U.S. Army, 1824; served under Gen. Teylor in Battle of Monterey during Mexican War. Died New Orleans, Jan. 8, 1849.

CROMMELIN, HENRY, naval officer; b. Montgomery, Ala., Aug. 11, 1904; s. John Geraerdt and Katherine Vasser (Gunter) C.; student U. Ala., 1920-21; B.S., U.S. Naval Acad., 1925; m. Sally Huntress Clendening, July 14, 1934; children—Diane, Henry, Sally, Harriet, Commd. ensign U.S.N., 1925, advanced through ranks to rear adm., 1952; assigned battleships, destroyers, 1925-33, 1936-40; staff U.S., Naval Acad., 1933-36; bur. personnel Navy Dept., 1940-42, 1945-46; comdr. destroyer division, destroy-Atlantic, 1947-48; attached Naval Base, Guantanamo Bay, Cuba 1950-51; comdr. cruiser U.S.S. Des Moines 1950-51; staff, comdr. in chief Pacific, 1951-52; asst. chief naval operations personnel, 1952-56; comdr. Battleship Div. 2, 1956-57; comdr. naval base, Newport, R.I., from 1957. Decorated Silver Star, Bronze Star with combat V. Club: Army-Navy Country (Washington). Home: Montgomery AL Died Mar. 1971.

CROMWELL, BARTLETT JEFFERSON rear admiral U.S. Navy; b. nr. Springplace, Ga., Feb. 9, 1840; s. Andrew Forgison and Sarah (Ragon) C.; apptd. to U.S. Naval Acad. from Neb., 1857, grad. 1861; m. Lizzie S. Huber. Dec. 31, 1866. Midshipman, June 3, 1861; promoted through grades to rank of rear admiral, Mar. 3, 1899. Participated in attacks on Morris Island and Battery Gregg; comdg. captured Confed. Ram Atlanta, on passage from Port Royal to Phila., Sept. 14, 1863; insp. ordnance, Navy Yard, Phila., 1874-78; Navy insp. ordnance, Navy Yard, Phila., 1874-78; Navy Yard, Portsmouth, 1882-84; comd. naval rendezvous, Phila., 1884-85; Navy Yard, League Island, 1886-89; ordnance duty, 1889-90; comd. Omaha, 1890-91; capt. of yard, Navy Yard, Norfolk, 1891-94; comd. Atlanta, 1894-95; mem. Naval Examining Bd., 1895-98; commandant, Naval Sta., Havana, Cuba, 1899; pres. Naval Retiring Bd., 1899-1900; commandant, Navy Yard, Portsmouth, 1900-01; comdr.-in-chief, S. Atlantic Station, May-July, 1901, European Station, 1901-02; retired, Feb. 9, 1902. Home: Washington, D.C. Died June 24, 1917.

CRONIN, DAVID EDWARD artist, illustrator; b. Greenwich, N.Y., July 12, 1839; s. Eugene A. and Ellen Dora C.; ed. Washington Acad., Salem, N.Y.; studied and practiced law in New York City several yrs.; studied art in London, Paris, Brussels, Dusselforf and Antwerp, 1857-60. Served pvt., capt. and bvt. maj. 1s5 1st N.Y. mounted rifles in Civil war; was judge advocate Kautz div., Army of the James; after war practiced law in New York; later established, edited and published Binghamton (N.Y.) Daily Times; afterward organized ry. cos. in Texas; was on editorial staff of Phila. Daily Record, 1892-95. Specialty is the hand-illustration of books. Author: (under pen name of Seth Eyland), The Evolution of a Life, 1884-1901; a copy of this work, amplified into 5 large vols. and profusely illustrated by the author, is now in archives of N.Y. Hist. Soc. This copy cost $12,000. Address: 2161 Newkirk St. Philadelphia.

CRONIN, MARCUS DANIEL army officer; b. Worcester, Mass., Jan. 9, 1865; grad. U.S. Mil. Acad., 1887. Army War Coll., 1911; m. Helen Hannay, Aug. 2, 1893. Commd. 2d lt., June 12, 1887; promoted through grades to col., May 15, 1917; brig. gen. N.A., Aug. 5, 1917. Instr. U.S. Mil. Acad., 1893-97; regimental adj. 25th Inf., 1898-99, 1903-07; in Santiago Campaign, Cuba, 1898; col. and asst. chief Philippine Constabulary, 1915-17 (acting chief part of time); officer Gen. Staff, 1908-10; apptd. comdr. 163d Inf. Brigade, Camp Gordon, Ga., 1917. Died Aug. 12, 1936.

CRONKHITE, ADELBERT army officer; b. N.Y., Jan. 5, 1861; grad. U.S. Mil. Acad., 1882, Arty. Sch., 1886. Commd. 2d lt. 4th Arty., June 13, 1882; promoted through grades to brig. gen., 1917; maj. gen. N.A., Aug. 5, 1917; maj. gen. U.S.A., Mar. 7, 1921. Operations against Sioux Indians, 1891; prof. mil. science and tactics. Mich. Mil. Acad., Orchard Lake, 1891-92; q.m. and commissary, F.A. Brig., Cuba and P.R., 1898; q.m., 1904-07; insp. gen.'s dept. and arty. officer, 1907-11; comdg. coast defenses, Eastern N.Y., 1911-14, coast defenses Panama and Panama Canal Dept., 1914-17; at Camp Lee and in A.E.F. comdg. 80th Div., 9th and 6th A.C., Sept. 1917-May 28, 1918; service on British front, St. Mihiel and Meuse-Argonne; retired. Feb. 1, 1923. Died June 15, 1937.

CROOK, GEORGE army officer; b. nr. Dayton, O., Sept. 23, 1829; s. Thomas and Elizabeth (Mathers) C.; grad. U.S. Mil. Acad., 1852; m. Mary Dailey. Commd. 2d lt. U.S. Army, 1852, 1st lt. on frontier duty in N.W., 1852-61; col. 36th Ohio Inf., 1861, in command 3d brigade Army of W. Va., served in battles of Lewisburg, South Mountain, Antietam, 1861; brevetted maj. U.S. Army, 1862; commd. brig. gen. U.S. Volunteers, in command of calvalry div. Army of Cumberland, 1863; brevetted col., 1863, brig. gen., 1864; in command W. Va., also in personal command one of corps in Sheridan's Army of the Shenandoah; commd. maj. gen. U.S. Volunteers: commd. maj. gen. U.S. Army, served in battles of Winchester, Fisher's Hill, Cedar Creek, 1864, battles of Dinwiddie Court House, Sailor's Creek, Farmville, 1865; commd. lt. col. 23d Inf., U.S. Army, 1865, commanded Boise (Ida.) dist., 1865; commd. brig. gen. 1873; commanded Dept. of Platte, 1875, 86-88; participated in Gt. Sioux War, 1876; fought against Apache Indians, 1882-86; maj. gen. in command of Div. of Mo., 1888. Died Chgo., Mar. 21, 1890.

CROOKE, PHILIP SCHUYLER congressman; b. Poughkeepsie, N.Y., Mar. 2, 1810; grad. Dutchess Acad., Poughkeepsie; studied law. Admitted to bar, 1831, began practice of law, Bklyn.; moved to Flatbush, N.Y., 1838; mem. bd. suprs. Kings County. (N.Y.) 1844-52, 58-70, chmn., 1861-62, 64-65; presdl. elector on Democratic ticket, 1852; mem. N.Y. State Gen. Assembly (Republican), 1863; mem. N.Y. State N.G., 40 years, served from pvt. to brig. gen., commanded 5th Brigade in Pa., 1863, during Civil War; mem. U.S. Ho. of Reps. (Rep.) from N.Y., 43d Congress, 1873-75. Died Flatbush, Mar. 17, 1881; buried Greenwood Cemetery, Bklyn.

CROSBY, H(AROLD) E(LLSWORTH) business exec.; b. Maryville, Mo., Jan. 22, 1809; s. Ullyses Grant and Jenny Lind (Pike) C.; B.S. in Archtl. Engring., Ia. State Coll., 1922; m. Lydia Clara Ferber. Dec. 27, 1924. Vice pres. constrn. div. and dir. G.C. Murphy Co.; v.p. and dir. Mack Realty Co. Served as 2d lt., F.A., U.S. Army, World War I, lt. col., Corps of Engrs., and Gen. Staff, World War II. Mem. bd. trustees, chmn. bldg. com. McKeesport Hosp.; dir., chmn. bldg. com. McKeesport YMCA. Mem. Am. Inst. Architects, Alpha Tau Omega, McKeesport, C. of C., Am. Legion. Mason (Shriner). Club: Youghiogheny Country (McKeesport). Home: 1512 Manor Av. Office: 531 Fifth Av., McKeesport, Pa. Died Jan. 12, 1958.

CROSBY, HERBERT BALL army officer; b. Fairmount, Kan., Dec. 24, 1871; s. George Heman and Jane (Ball) C.; grad. U.S. Military Acad., 1893; m. Catherine Adelaide Dakin, Feb. 11, 1902; children - George Dakin, Richard Lansing (dec.), Jane, Gordon Willard, Commd. 2d lt., 1893; promoted through grades to lt. col., 1917; commd. col. 351st Inf., N.A., Aug. 5, 1917; col. Cav., regular army, July 1, 1920. Served in Cuba, 1898-1901; in Mindanao, P.I., campaigns against Moros, 1903-05; in France, 1918-19; was instr. service schs. and asst. comdr. War Coll.; apptd. chief of cav., rank of maj. gen., Mar. 21, 1926, term of 4 yrs.; retired from active service, 1930; commr. of D.C. for term 1930-33; moved to San Antonio, Tex., to enter banking, Nov. 1933. Home: San Antonio, Tex. Died Jan. 11, 1936.

CROSBY, PIERCE naval officer; b. Delaware County, Pa., Jan. 16, 1824; s. John P. and Catharine (Beale) C.; m. Matilda Boyer, Oct. 16, 1850; m. 2d Julia Wells, Mar. 1861; m. 3d, Miriam Gratz, Feb. 15, 1870; m. 4th, Louise Audenried, June 24, 1880. commd. lt. U.S. Navy, 1853; served in Brazilian Squadron, 1857; in command tugs protecting trade in Chesapeake Bay, 1861; served spl. duty under Gen. Butler as harbor master at Hampton Roads, 1861; commanded tug Fanny in capture of Hatterus Inlet, 1861; took command steamer Pinola at Balt., joined Farragut below New Orleans, 1861, attempted to break barrier across river below New Orleans, 1862; fleet capt. N. Atlantic Blockading Squadron, 1862-63; commanded ships Florida, 1864, Keystone State (in same squadron), captured 9 blockade runners; served on ship Metacomet in Gulf Squadron, 1864-65; participated in later operations leading to capture of Mobile, Ala.; promoted capt., 1868; commd. commodore, 1874; became rear adm. comdg. S. Atlantic Squadron, 1882, Pacific Squadron, 1883; ret., 1883. Died June 15, 1889.

CROSBY, WILLIAM DORR surgeon U.S.A.; b. in Mass., July 18, 1857; Ph.B., Beloit (Wis.) Coll., 1879; M.D., Coll. Phys. and Surg. (Columbia), 1882. Apptd. asst. surgeon, Dec. 3, 1883; capt. asst. surgeon, Dec. 3, 1888; maj. brigade surgeon vols., June 4, 1898; hon. discharged vols., June 30, 1900; maj. surgeon U.S.A., Feb. 1, 1901; maj. Med. Corps, Feb. 2, 1901; lt. col., Jan. 1, 1909; col., Dec. 7, 1912. Duty in Philippine Islands, 1917. Address: War Department, Washington

CROSE, WILLIAM MICHAEL naval officer; b. Greencastle, Ind., Feb. 8, 1867; s. John A. and Mary E. (Johnson) C.; DePauw U., 1882-84; grad. U.S. Naval Acad., 1888; m. Edith Wilson, of Cincinnati, O., Mar. 6, 1895. Ensign, July 1, 1890; lt. jr. grade, Mar. 10, 1898; lt., Mar. 3, 1899; lt. comdr., July 1, 1905; comdr., Oct. 15, 1909; capt., July 1, 1914. Served on Wheeling, Spanish-Am. War, 1898, Maryland, 1905-08; on receiving ship Franklin, 1908-09, Delaware, 1909-10; gov. of Tutuila, Samoa, and comdr. naval sta. there, 1910-13; duty at Navy Dept., Washington, 1913; capt. of yard, Navy Yard, Mare Island, 1913-15; comdr. Rhode Island, 1915-16; apptd. comdr. North Dakota, Oct. 11, 1916; comdr. Naval Tr. Sta., Hampton Roads, Va., 1918-20; comdg. Naval Base, Cavite, P.I., Dec. 20, 1920-22; retired, Feb. 8, 1923. Mem. Delta Tau Delta, Philippine Campaign medal; Spanish and World War medals, Navy Cross. Club: Army and Navy (Washington). Home: Coronado, Calif.

CROSLEY, WALTER SELWYN rear adm., b. East Jaffrey, N.H., Oct. 30, 1871; s. Rev. William Jacob and Charlotta (Davis) C.; grad. U.S. Naval Acad., 1893; m. Pauline de Launay Stewart, July 3, 1895; children - Floyd Stewart (lt. U.S.N., retired), Paul Cunningham (lt. U.S.N.). Commd. ensign July 1, 1895; promoted through grades to rank of rear admiral, Feb. 17, 1927. Participated in Brazilian Revolution, 1893, railroad riots, Calif., 1894, Spanish-Am. War, 1898, Philippine Insurrection, 1900, West Indian Campaign, Haitian Occupation, 1915. Santo Dominican Occupation, 1916, World War, 1917-18; naval attacheé at Constantinople, 1910-12, Petrograd, Russia, 1917-18, at Madrid, Spain, 1918; commandant of 7th Naval Dist., Key West, Fla., 9th Naval District at Chicago, Ill., Fifteenth Naval District at Balboa, C.Z.; commanded Squadron One, Fleet Base Force and Battleship Division 3. Elected dir. of Internat. Hydrographic Bur., Monte Carlo, Monaco, Apr. 1937. Decorated Navy Cross, Sampson medal, Spanish campaign medal, Philippine campaign medal, Haitian campaign medal, Dominican campaign medal, Victory medal with star, Chinese Order of Wen Hu, Haitian Medal of Honor. Died Jan. 6, 1939.

CROSS, JUDSON NEWELL lawyer; b. Philadelphia, Jefferson Co., N.Y., Jan. 16, 1838; s. Rev. Gorham and Sophia (Murdock) C.; studied and taught in Oberlin Coll., 1855-61; when he enlisted with the 100 Oberlin students who formed Co. C, 7th Ohio inf., becoming 1st lt.; served through Western Va. campaign under Gens. McClellan, Rosecrans and Cox and was editor of The Ohio Seventh, 1st Union paper pub. by Union soldiers, from a press captured from the enemy. Severely wounded and captured at battle of Cross Lanes, but recaptured by Maj. Rutherford B. Hayes; promoted capt., Nov. 1816, but because of wounds given spl. duty to close of war. Later commandant post at Madison, Ind.; adj. gen. mil. dist. Ind.; asst. provost marshal and on staff mil. gov. of dept. at Washington, D.C. Grad. Albany Law Sch., 1866. Practiced law, Lyons, Ia., 1866-75; mayor Lyons, 1871; practiced at Minneapolis, 1875 - ; city atty., 1883-87; mem. Minneapolis bd. park commrs., 1883; mem. U.S. bd. immigration commrs. sent to Europe by U.S. Govt., 1891. Republican. Home: Minneapolis, Minn. Died 1901.

CROSS, THOMAS JOSEPH army officer; b. Amsterdam, N.Y., July 29, 1894; s. Thomas and Mary Ellen (Kelly) C.; student pub. and parochial schs.; grad. advance course Ft. Benning, 1933-34, Air Force Tactical Sch., 1939; grad. Command and Gen. Staff Sch., 1938; m. Florence Edna Sawyer, Aug. 7. 1971; children-Thomas R., Richard E. Entered N.Y. N.G., 1912, advanced through grades to maj. gen., U.S. Army, 1952; with 3d Div., World War I; chief staff 8th Div., regtl. comdr. 121st Inf. Regt., 8th Div., 1942-45; dep. comdr. IX Corps, Korea, organized Field Tng. Command to retrain all Korean combat troops, comdr. 3d U.S. Inf. Div., 1951-52; on loan from army to Gen. Omar Bradley, adminstr. vet's. affairs, as adviser, 1946-48, dep. administr. in charge all VA activities Cal., Nev., Ariz., Hawaii, Guam and Samoa, 1946-48. Decorated D.S.M., Legion of Merit with oak leaf cluster, Silver Star, Bronze Star with 2 oak leaf clusters, Combat Inf. badge, Army Commendation ribbon, Air medal, Presdl. Unit Citation (U.S.); Legion of Honor, Croix de Guerre with palm (France); Order of Leopold, Croix de Guerre with palm (Belgium); Croix de Guerre (Luxembourg); Order of Mil. Merit, Taiguk (Rep. of Korea), Legion of Honor, Republic of Philippines, grade of comdr. Club: Army and Navy (Washington). Home: 6101 Dorchester St., Springfield, Va. Died July 12, 1963; buried Arlington Nat. Cemetery.

CROSSE, CHARLES WASHBURN naval officer; b. Sun Prairie, Wis., Apr. 1, 1885; ed. high school, Stoughton, Wis.; grad. U.S. Naval Acad., 1907. Commd. ensign, U.S. Navy, 1909, and advanced through the grades to rear adm., 1942; served in U.S. Ships Virginia, Ohio, Maryland, Denver, Missouri, Milwaukee, Charleston, Selfridge. Rigel, Seattle, Gold Star, Marblehead, Argonne. assigned to sea duty, 1941. Decorated Victory Medal with escort clasp, Am. Defense Service Medal with fleet clasp, Nicaraguan Campaign and Asiatic-Pacific Campaign medals. Home: 513 N. Page St., Stoughton, Wis. Address: Navy Dept., Washington 25, D.C. Died Apr. 20, 1949.

CROSSLAND, EDWARD congressman; b. Hickman County, Ky., June 30, 1827; studied law. Admitted to bar, 1852, began practice of law, Clinton, Ky.; sheriff Hickman County, 1851-52; mem. Ky. Ho. of Reps., 1857-58; commd. capt. 1st Ky. Regt., Confederate Army in Civil War, then commd. col. 7th Ky. Regt., served until end of war; judge Ct. of Common Pleas, 1st Jud. Dist. Ky., 1867-70; mem. U.S. Ho. of Reps. (Democrat) from Ky., 41d-43d congresses, 1871-75; judge circuit ct. 1st Jud. Dist. Ky., 1880-81. Died Mayfield, Ky., Sept. 11, 1881; buried Maplewood Cemetery.

CROSSLAND, PAUL MARION, physician; b. Wayne, Neb., June 8, 1904; s. George Washington and Mary Katrina (Schonlau) C.; student Wayne State Tchrs. Coll., 1922-25; A.B., U. Minn., 1926, M.B., 1930, M.D., 1931; postgrad. (fellow) Stanford Sch. Medicine, 1951-52; m. Harriet Kent Dueringer, Sept. 20, 1959; 1 son by previous marriage, William. Commd. lt. (j.g.), M.C., USN, 1930, advanced through grades to capt., 1948; intern U.S. Naval Hosp., San Diego, 1930-31; resident in surgery U.S. Naval Hosp., Newport, R.I., 1939; sr. med. officer U.S. Lend Lease Base, Argentia, Nfld., 1941, USS Montpelier, 1942-43; base med. officer Russell Island, 1943-44; exec. officer U.S. Naval Hosp., Sampson, N.Y., 1944-45; 1st med. officer in command U.S. Naval Hosp., Guantanamo Bay, Cuba, 1946-48; resident in dermatology N.Y. Poly. Med. Sch. and Hosp., 1949-51; practice medicine specializing in dermatology, Santa Rosa, Cal., 1952-69; lectr. dir. dermatology Stanford, Palo Alto, Cal., 1951-53, clin. instr., 1953-55, asst. clin. prof., 1955-59, associate clinical professor, 1959-65, clinical professor dermatology, 1965-69; courtesy staff Meml. Hosp., Santa Rosa; active staff Community Hosp., Santa Rosa, 1952-69, chief dept. dermatology and syphilology, 1955, 58, 60, 62, 65, 67, skin clinic and tumor bd. cons., 1952-68, chmn. pharmacy com., 1957-68, exec. com., 1957-59; courtesy staff Warrack Hosp., Santa Rosa, 1960-69, Stanford Hosp., Palo Alto, 1952-68; staff Presbyn. Hosp., San Francisco, 1961-69. Crossland Lab. at Stanford U. dedicated in his honor, 1970. Diplomate Am. Bd. Dermatology, dermatology sect. Pan Am. Med. Assn. Fellow Am. Acad. Dermatology (dir. 1960-63, chmn. com. nominations 1957, 59, membership com. 1958-63, dir. spl. grad. course 1958-65, mil. affairs com., 1963-64, chmn. com. ionizing radiations 1960-69; mem. Am., Cal (chmn. sect. dermatology 1965-66) med. assns., Internat. Soc. Tropical Dermatology, Am. Dermatol. Assn., Sonoma County Med. Soc., Pacific, San Francisco dermatol. socs., Soc. Investigative Dermatology, Am. Cancer Soc. (dir. Sonoma County br. 1956-68), Acacia, Phi Beta Pi. Republican. Methodist. Mason (32 degree). Author: (with A.C. Cipollaro) X-rays and Radium in the Treatment of Diseases of the Skin, 1967. Contributor articles to med. jours., pamphlets. Home: Santa Rosa CA Died Sept. 30, 1968; buried Memorial Park, Santa Rosa CA

CROSSLEY, ARTHUR WEBSTER, engr., bus. exec.; b. Somerset, Colo., Dec. 16, 1908; s. George Lewis and Sarah Elizabeth (Jowett) C.; B.S., Franklin Inst., 1928; LL.B., Southeastern U., 1939; LL.M., M. P.L., 1940, B.C.S., 1941; m. Margaret M. Neu, Oct. 15, 1932;children—Anne Jowett, Jane Elizabeth, Susan Margaret. Engr. Dennison Mfg. Co., 1928-30, Washington Gas Light Co., 1930-33, H.J. Saunders (cons. engr.), Washington, 1933-34, Pub. Utilities Commn., D.C., 1935-38; asst. dir., chief engr. Pub. Works, D.C., 1938-40, dir., 1940-41; asst. gen. mgr. Potomac Electric Co., 1941-48; treas. Diamond Alkali Co., 1948-55; dir. finance Theo. Hamm Brewing Co., St. Paul, Minn., 1956-60, v.p. finance, 1960-68, sec., dir., 1965-68; chmn. bd. Marquette Corp., from 1969. Served as col. chemical corps AUS, 1942-45. Decorated Legion of Merit with oak leaf cluster, Commendation medal with 2 clusters. Mem. A.I.M. Club: Army-Navy (Washington). Home: Burnsville MN Died Apr. 2, 1971; buried Fort Snelling Nat. Cemetery, Minneapolis MN

CROSSLEY, JAMES JUDSON, lawyer; b. Crawford Township, Madison County, Ia., Aug. 31,21869; s. John Wesley and Cynthia Jane (Hardy) C.; Des Moines Coll., Ia; A.B., State U. of Ia., 1891, A.M., 1897; post-grad. study, Yale, 1897-99; LL.B., U. of Ia. Law Sch., 1900; m. Cherry L. Hyde, Aug. 10, 1910 (dec. July 3, 1932); children—Helen, Jane Hannah, Alice Cherry; m. 2d, Minerva K. Brouillette Brown, May 1, 1934 (dec. Nov. 20, 1944); step-children—Helen, Edwin. Supt. public schools, Madison County, Iowa, 1894-98; began practice at Winterset, Ia., June 6, 1900; mem. Ia. State Senate, sessions, 1900, 02, 04, 06, 07; U.S. atty. 4th Div. of Alaska, 1908-14; resumed practice at Portland, Ore., 1914. Republican. Capt. Co. G, 55th Regt. Iowa Nat. Guard, 1901-04; capt. Co. C, 162d Inf., with A.E.F. 18 mos. in France, Belgium and Germany; was in Champagne, Oise-Aisne and Argonne offensives; promoted to lt. col.; served with 41st ("Sunset"), 42d ("Rainbow"), and 6th (regular) divs. Comdr. Portland Post No. 1, Am. Legion, 1922. Mem. Am. Bar Assn., Ore. State Bar (vice-pres., 1941-42, Vets. of Foreign Wars, Mil. Order World War, Am. Legion, Phi Delta Phi. Conglist. Mason (32 deg.), O.E.S. (past patron), Alaskan Sourdoughs. Home: 3916 N Concord Av. Office: American Bank Bldg., Portland OR*

CROSSMAN, EDGAR GIBSON lawyer; b. Lisbon, N.H., Apr. 26, 1895; s. Edgar Orrin and Florence Alice Lavinia (Gibson) C.; student Phillips Andover Acad., 1912-13; B.A., Yale, 1917; LL.B., Harvard, 1922; m. Helen Greatsinger Farrell, Jan. 21, 1929; children-Edgar Orrin II, Patrick Farrell, John Gibson. Admitted to N.Y. bar, 1923; with firm Winthrop & Stimson, N.Y.C., 1922-25, Davis, Polk, Wardwell, Gardiner & Reed, 1925-28, 29-34, mem. firm, 1934-; legal advisor to Henry L. Stimson, Gov.-Gen. Philippines, 1928-29. Served as 1st lt. F.A., U.S. Army, 1917-19, battery comdr. 1918-19, lt. col. to col., civil affairs work, Gen. MacArthur's Staff, during World War II; Am. co-chmn., Joint Am.-Philippine Finance Commn., acting as personal rep. of Pres. of U.S. with rank of minister, 1947. Awarded Legion of Merit, Philippine Distinguished Service Star. Mem. Assn. Bar City N.Y. (chmn. admissions com. and mem. exec. com.). Conglist. Republican. Home: 1088 Park Av., N.Y.C. 10028. Office: 1 Chase Manhattan Plaza, N.Y.C. 5. Died Jan. 28, 1967; buried Arlington Nat. Cemetery, Washington.

CROUNSE, LORENZO farmer; b. Sharon, Schoharie Co., N.Y., 1834; worked in his father's tannery when young; common school edn. and 2 terms in N.Y. Conf. Sem., Schoharie Co.; taught school; studied law; admitted to practice, 1857; entered army, 1861, as capt., Battery K, 1st regt., N.Y. light art.; wounded while holding Beverly Ford on Rappahannock in 2d Bull Run under Pope; disabled for long time and resigned; m. Mary E. Griffiths, 1860 (died 1882). Removed to Neb., 1864; mem. Territorial legislature, 1866; justice Supreme Court, Neb., 1867-72; mem. Congress, 1873-77; internal revenue collector, dist. of Neb., 1879-83; Asst. Sec. U.S. Treasury, 1891-92; gov., Neb., 1893-95; elected Nov. 1900, State senator, 10th dist. Neb. Republican. Home: Omaha, Neb. Died 1909.

CROW, ORIN FAISON educator; b. West Springs, Spartanburg County, S.C., Mar. 9, 1896; s. Henry and Mary (West) C.; A.B., U. of S.C. 1917; A.M., George Peabody Coll. for Teachers, 1925, Ph.D., 1931; m. Innis Cuttino, Sept. 2, 1919; children-Dorothy, Mary (Mrs. J. R. Anderson). Principal high school, Hartsville, South Carolina, 1919-24; prof. edn., University of S.C., since 1925, acting dir. extension, 1925-26, dean of Sch. of Edn., 1920-53, dean faculty, 1953—, dir. summer sch. 1946-53; instr. summers Winthrop College, Rock Hill, S.C., 1924, George Peabody Coll. for Teachers, 1928. Editor South Carolina Education, 1925-26. Served as 2d lt. F.A., U.S. Army, with A.E.F., World War I; col. F.A., World War II. Vice-pres. National Association Colleges and Depts. of Education, 1935-36; pres. Assn. of Deans of Edn. in Univs. and Land Grant Colleges of South, 1947; chmn. S.C. State Com. on Secondary Schs. of Southern Assn., 1946-52; mem. exec. com., 1951-53. Mem. English-Speaking Union (president Columbia branch 1952-53), A.A.A.S., N.E.A., National Society College Teachers of Edn., Phi Beta Kappa, Phi Delta Kappa, Kappa Phi Kappa (Mem. nat. council 1934-36), Kappa Delta Pi, Sigma Phi Epsilon. Democrat. Baptist. Mason. Clubs: Kosmos, Wardlaw, Forum, Kiwanis (gov. Carolinas dist. 1950; mem. internat. bd. trustees 1951-53). Author: The Selection of Teachers in South Carolina; The Control of the University of South Carolina, 1801-1926. Co-author history of Columbia (S.C.). Founder 1935 and editor, 1935-40, S.C. High School Literary Yearbook. Editor: (also wrote introduction) Loyalty to Facts: The Educational Writings of Patterson Wardlaw, 1949. Rep. of Masonic Grand Lodge of S.C. to Grand Lodge of Italy. Home: 810 Sumter St., Columbia, S.C. Died Sept. 20, 1955; buried Greenlawn Meml. Park, Columbia, S.C.

CROWDER, ENOCH HERBERT army officer; b. in Mo., Apr. 11, 1859; s. John Herbert and Mary C. (Weller) C.; grad. U.S. Mil. Acad., 1881; LL.B., U. of Mo., 1886; LL.D., Harvard, Columbia, Brown, Princeton, U. of Mich., U. of Mo., Havana; unmarried. Commd. 2d lt. 8th Cav., June 11, 1881; 1st lt., July 5, 1886; maj. judge advocate, Jan. 11, 1895; lt. col. judge advocate vols., June 22, 1898, apptd. lt. col. 39th Vol. Inf., Aug. 17, 1899; hon. discharged from vol. service, May 6, 1901; lt. col. judge advocate U.S.A., May 21, 1901; brig. gen. vols., June 20, 1901; hon. discharged from vol. service, June 30, 1901; col. judge advocate U.S.A., Apr. 16, 1903; brig. gen. and judge advocate gen. U.S.A., Feb. 14, 1911; maj. gen. and judge advocate gen. U.S.A., Oct. 6, 1917; retired Feb. 14, 1923. Comdr. of troop in Geronimo and Sitting Bull campaigns; mem. commn. to stave off hostilities between Americans and Flipinos, 1899; served on Supreme Ct. Bench Philippine Islands. Served in Philippine Islands, 1898-1901; in Manchuria, with Japanese Army, Apr. 1904-lfay 1905; in Cuba, Sec. of State and Justice, 1906-08; provost marshal gen. U.S.A., May 1917-July 1919; reapptd. judge advocate gen. U.S.A., Feb. 15, 1919. Del. 4th Pan-Am. Conf., Argentina, July-Aug. 1910; E.E. and M.P. on spl. mission to Chile, Sept. 1910. A.E. and P. to Cuba, 1923-27 (retired). Awarded D.S.M. "for especially meritorious and conspicuous service" as provost marshal gen. during the war, Dec. 1918; Comdr. Legion of Honor (French); Knight Comdr. Order of St. Michael and St. George (British); comdr. Mil. Order of the Crown (Italian); 3d Order of Rising Sun (Japanese); Order of Cespedes (Cuban). Died May 7, 1932.

CROWNINSHIELD, ARENT SCHUYLER naval officer; b. Seneca Falls, N.Y., Mar. 14, 1843; s. Jacob and Mary Miller (Schuyler) C.; grad. U.S. Naval Acad., 1863; m. Mary Bradford, July 27, 1870. Ensign, May 28, 1863; promoted through grades to rear adm., Mar. 16, 1902. Served in both attacks on Ft. Fisher, Civil War; lighthouse insp. 1st dist., 1882-85; comd. nautical sch.-ship St. Mary's, 1887-91; Navy Yard, New York, 1891-92; comd. Kearsarge, 1892-93; senior mem. bd. of inspectors, Navy Yard, New York, 1893-94; comd. receiving-ship Richmond, 1894-95, Maine, 1895-97; chief of Bureau of Navigation with the rank of rear adm., 1897-1920; comdr.-in-chief European Sta., 1902-03; was mem. Bd. of Naval Strategy during war with Spain; retired, Mar. 20, 1903. Home: lft. Desert. Me. Died 1908.

CROWNINSHIELD, BENJAMIN WILLIAMS banker, U.S. sec. of navy; b. Salem, Mass., Dec. 27, 1772; s. George and Mary (Derby) C.; m. Mary Boardman, Jan. 1, 1804. Pres., Mchts. Bank of Salem; mem. Mass Ho. of Reps., 1811, 21, 33; Mass. Senate, 1812; U.S. sec. of navy, 1814-18; mem. U.S. Ho. of Reps. from Mass., 18th-21st congresses 1823-31. Died Boston, Feb. 3, 1851; buried Mt. Auburn Cemetery, Mass.

CROWNINSHIELD, JACOB mcht., sea capt., congressman; b. Salem, Mass., May 31, 1770; S. George and Mary (Derby) C.; m. Sarah Gardner, June 5, 1796. Brought to N.Y. 1st live elephant ever seen in U.S., 1796; mem. Mass. Senate, 1801; mem. U.S. Ho. of Reps. from Mass., 8th-10th congresses, 1803-08; declined appointment as U.S. sec. of navy under Pres. Jefferson, 1805. Died Washington, D.C., Apr. 15, 1808.

CROWSON, BENJAMIN FRANKLIN educator; b. Parksley, Va., Apr. 11, 1889; s. Levin Thomas and Sarah Ayres (Rew) C.; B.S., Va. Mil. Inst., 1910, M.A., 1926; student U. of Pa., summers 1914, 21, U. of Va., summer 1924; m. Gladys Anita Wright, June 26, 1915; children - Benjamin Franklin, Levin Thomas III (dec.), Gladys Wright. Comdt. cadets, Millersburgh (Ky.) Mil. Inst., 1910-11; asst. prof. Va. Mil. Inst., 1911-15, co-dir. summer sessions, 1913, 15, 16, asso. prof. English, 1920-27; supervising prin. Roanoke (Va.) Jr. High Sch., 1915-16; prin. Charlotte Hall Sch., 1916-20, and 1927 - . Dir. County Trust Co. of Md. Capt. field arty., Va. Vols., 1911-15, lt. col. engrs., same, 1920-28. Democrat. Episcopalian. Mason. Home: Charlotte Hall, Md. Died July 12, 1938.

CROZET, CLAUDE mil. engr., educator; b. Villefrauche, France, Jan. 1, 1790; ed. Polytechnic Sch. in Paris, France. Came to U.S., 1816; served as engr. U.S. Army; asst. prof. U.S. Mil. Acad., 1816, prof., head dept., 1817-23; state engr. Va., 1823; mem. original bd. visitors Va. Mil. Inst., pres. until 1845; prin. Richmond Acad., 1858-64; introduced study of descriptive geometry to Am. Author: A Treatise of Descriptive Geometry for the use of the cadets of the United States Academy (1st Am. textbook on the subject), 1821. Died Jan. 29, 1864.

CRUGER, DANIEL congressman; b. Sunbury, Pa., Dec. 22, 1780; attended public schs.; studied law. Learned printer's trade; publisher Owego (N.Y.) Democrat; admitted to bar, 1805, started practice of law, Bath, N.Y.; served as maj. in War of 1812; mem. N.Y. State Assembly, 1814-16, 26, speaker, 1816; mem. U.S. Ho. of Reps. (Democrat) from N.Y., 15th Congress, 1817-19; dist. atty. 7th Dist. N.Y., 1815-18, Steuben County, 1818-21; moved to Wheeling, Va. (now W.Va.). Died Wheeling, July 12, 1843; buried Stone Ch. Cemetery.

CRUIKSHANK, WILLIAM MACKEY (KROOK'SHANK), army officer; b. Washington, D.C., Nov. 7, 1870; s. John C. and Euphrasia (Antisell) C.; grad., U.S. Mil. Acad., 1893, Sch. of Submarine Defense, 1903, Army War Coll., 1920; m. Cornelia B. Holabird, Apr. 30, 1904; 1 dau., Mary Holabird. Commd. 2d lt. Arty., June 12, 1893; promoted through grades to col. May 15, 1917; brig. gen. N.A., July 12, 1918; hon. discharged as brig. gen., temp., Aug. 31, 1919; brigadier general regular army, Sept. 1, 1925; retired November 30, 1934. Instr. mathematics, U.S. Mil. Acad., 1895-98 and 1898-99: in Santiago Campaign, July 22-Aug. 30, 1898; dist. and post arty. engr. at Ft. Howard, Md., 1904-07; adj. 5th F.A. in Philippines, 1907-09; arrived in France with 1st Div., June 26, 1917; apptd. comdr. 3d Brigade Field Arty., 3d Div., 3d Army Corps. A.E.F., May 22, 1918, chief of arty., 4th Corps, Oct. 30, 1918-Jan. 1, 1919; with Army of Occupation in Germany, Nov. 17, 1918-Jan. 1, 1919, and Apr. 22, 1919-Aug. 5, 1919; General Staff Corps. Aug. 1920-24; comdt. F.A. Sch., Fort Sill, Okla., 1930-34; retired, Nov. 30, 1934. D.S.M. (U.S.); Officer Legion of Honor (French). Episcopalian. Mem. Mil. Order Loyal Legion. Clubs: Army and Navy. Home: 2126 Connecticut Av., Washington, D.C. Died Feb. 23, 1943.

CRUMB, FREDERICK WAITE coll. pres.; b. Watervilet, N.Y., Apr. 20, 1909; s. Frederick Waite and Marie (Birdsall) C.; A.B., N.Y. State Tchrs. Coll., Albany, 1930, A.M., 1935: Ed.D., Columbia, 1942; D.Hum. (honorary), Saint Lawrence Univ., 1950, H.H.D.., 1950; L.H.D., Clarkson Coll. Tech., 1951; m. Doris Esther Arnold, June 24, 1931; children-Frederick Waite, III, Walter John Arnold, Peter Benjamin. Supervising prin. central rural schs., E. Nassau, N.Y., 1930-32, Narrowsburg, N.Y., 1932-36, Burnt Hills, N.Y., 1936-38, Whitesboro, N.Y., 1938-42; research asst. Met. Sch. Study Council, Columbia, 1941; pres. State University Coll., Potsdam, N.Y., 1946-. Served with A.U.S., November 1942-April 1946, lt. col.; in Edn. Br., Information and Edn. Div. War Dept. Spl. Staff in Washington, D.C., Pacific Ocean area, West Indies, Europe, England, China-Burma-India theatre; now lt. col. O.R.C. Mem. Nat. Soc. for Study Edn., Nat. Ednl. Assn., N.Y. State Council of Sch. Supts., N.Y. State Teachers Assn., Phi Delta Kappa, Kappa Phi Delta, Kappa Delta Pi. Mem. Kappa Delta Rho. Episcopalian (vestryman, lay del. Diocese of Albany to Anglican Congress, Toronto, 1963). Clubs: University (Albany); Torch; National Republican Club (New York City). Author: Tom Quick, Early American, 1934. Contbr. to various prof. periodicals. Appeared in frequent radio broadcasts on American Foklore, 1934-38. Lay dep. of Diocese of Albany to Triennial Conv. Episcopal Ch., 49, 52, 55; mem. joint commn. on approaches to unity Gen. Conv. Episcopal Ch. Home: 69 Pierrepont Av., Potsdam, N.Y. Died Jan. 8, 1967.

CRUSE, THOMAS army officer; b. Owensboro, Ky., Dec. 29, 1857; s. James Barnhill and Mildred Davis (King) C.; Center Coll., Ky., 1874-75; grad. Mil. Acad., 1879; honor grad. Inf. and Cav. Sch., Ft. Leavenworth, Kan., 1891; grad. Army War Coll., 1916; m. Beatrice Cottrell, Feb. 14, 1882; children-Fred Taylor, James Thomas (dec.). Commd. 2d lt. 6th Cav., in Ariz., June 13, 1879; N lt., Sept. 28, 1887; captain, a.-q.-m., December 1, 1896; major q.-m. U.S. Vols. May 12, 1898; hon. discharged from vol. service, May 1, 1901; maj. q.-m., July 5, 1902; lt. col., dept. q.-m. gen., Feb. 17, 1910; col. Q.-M. Corps, Feb. 1, 1913; brig. gen., Jan. 9, 1917; retired Jan. 1918. Awarded Medal of Honor. "for distinguished gallantry in action with hostile Indians." Aug. 1882; also Indian Campaign Medal, Philippine Campaign Medal. Democrat. Baptist. Mason. Clubs: Army and Navy (Washington and Manila); University (St. Louis). Home: Longport, N.J. Address: War Dept., Washington. Died June 8, 1943.

CRUTCHFIELD, WILLIAM congressman; b. Greeneville, Tenn., Nov. 16, 1824; attended common schs. Became farmer, Jacksonville, Ala., 1844; moved to Chattanooga, Tenn., 1850; served as hon. capt. Union Army during Chickanauga campaign in Civil War, with Gen. Thomas during siege of Chattanooga; served as asst. to Gen. Steedman, other comdrs. until close of war; mem. U.S. Ho. of Reps. (Republican) from Tenn., 43d Congress, 1873-75. Died Chattanooga, Jan. 24, 1890; buried Old Citizens Cemetery.

CRYER, MATTHEW HENRY oral surgeon; b. Manchester, Eng., July 21, 1840; s. Henry and Elizabeth (Cookson) C.; grad. Phila. Dental Coll., 1876; M.D., U. of Pa., 1877; m. Martha Gates Phillips, June 17, 1889. Came to America, 1851; enlisted in 6th Ohio Cav., 1861, and advanced to maj., Apr. 8, 1856; participated in Shenandoah Valley campaign, 1862, battles of the Wilderness, Trevilian Station, Mallory's Cross Roads, St. lMary's Ch. (two horses shot under him); wounded at Deep Harbor, Va., July 28, 1864; in command of regt. at Battle of Boydton Plank Road, Oct. 27, 1864, and at Battle of Appomattox; opened the last fight between Grant and Lee, Apr. 9, 1865. Practiced in Phila., 1877 - ; prof. oral surgery, U. of Pa., 1898 - ; visiting surgeon, Phila. Gen. Hosp.; consulting dental surgeon, Univ. Hosp. Republican. Author: Regional Anatomy, 1886; Studied of Internal Anatomy of the Face, 1901; Imperial Stereoscopic Anatomy of Head (with D. J. Cunningham and David Waterston), 1909. Wrote chapter on Extraction of Teeth, in American Textbook of Operative Denistry, and one on General Hygiene of Mouth, in Musser and Keller's Handbook of Practical Treatment. Home: Lansdowne, Pa. Died Aug. 12. 1921.

CUDAHY, MICHAEL FRANCIS, meat packer; b. Milwaukee, Wis., May 27, 1886; s. Patrick and Anna (Madden) C.; A.B., U. of Wis., 1909; m. Mrs. Alice Dickson Pinto, July 15, 1921 (died 1942); 1 son, Richard Dickson. Actively identified with packing business, 1910-70; chmn. Cudahy Bros. Co., 1960-69, name changed to Patrick Cudahy, Inc. Captain Qm. Corps, U.S. Army, World War I. Founder Patrick and Anna M. Cudahy Fund (for charitable purposes). Catholic. Clubs: Milwaukee, University. Home: Milwaukee WI Died May 20, 1970.

CULBERSON, DAVID BROWNING congressman; b. Troup County, Ga., Sept. 29, 1830; s. David B. and Lucy (Wilkinson) C.; studied law in office William P. Chilton, Tuskegee, Ala.; m. Eugenia Kimbal, Dec. 2, 1852, at least 1 son, Charles A. Admitted to Ala. bar, 1851; practiced in Dadeville, Ala., 1851-56, Upshur County, Tex., 1856-60, Jefferson, Tex., 1865-1900; mem. Tex. Ho. of Reps., 1859-60, 64; commd. lt. col., later col. 18th Tex. Inf., Confederate States Am., 1862, resigned, 1863; adjutant and insp. gen. of Tex., 1863-64; mem. Tex. Senate, 1873-75; mem. U.S. Ho. of Reps. (Democrat) from Tex., 44th-54th congresses, 1875-97; mem. commn. to codify laws of U.S., 1897-1900. Died Jefferson, May 7, 1900; buried Jefferson.

CULBERTSON, ALBERT L. ret. army officer; b. Ill., 1884; commd. 2d lt., Inf., Ill. Nat. Guard, Oct. 1904; advanced to capt. 1913; commd. capt. Fed. Service, 1917, maj. Reserve and Nat. Guard, 1919; col. and lt. col., 1922; brig. gen. of the line, 1940: Fed. service 1941, in command 66th Inf. Brigade, 33d div., Camp Forrest, Tenn., ret. 1945. Decorated Purple Heart, World War I. Address: Delavan, Ill. Died 1956.*

CULBERTSON, WILLIAM SMITH lawyer; b. Greensburg, Pa., Aug. 5, 1884; s. George and Jennie (Smith) C.; A.B., Coll. of Emporia, Kan., 1907, LL.D.; A.B., Yale, 1908; Ph.D., 1911; spl. studies univs. Leipzig and Berlin: LL.D., Georgetown U., 1931; m. Mary J. Hunter, Dec. 28, 1911; children-Junia Wilhelmina (Mrs. T.D. Luckenbill) (dec.), Margaret Jane (Mrs. Kendall A. L. Foster), Mary Josephine (Mrs. Edmund E. Pendleton, Jr.). Examiner U.S. Tariff Bd., 1910-12; practice law, Washington, 1912-15; mem. firm McLanahan, Burton & Culbertson, 1914-15; rep. FTC, 1915-16, spl. counsel, mem. bd. rev., 1916-17; mem. U.S. Tariff Commn., 1917-25, vice chmn., 1922-25; E.E. and M.P. to Rumania, 1925-28; A.E. and P. to Chile, 1928-33; col. Gen. Staff Corps, U.S. Army, 1942-45; chmn., with rank ambassador, spl. mission to French N. Africa, Middle East, Italy, France, 1944; ambassador of U.S. on spl. mission to coronation Majesty King Faisal II of Iraq, 1953; now mem. firm Culbertson, Pendleton & Pendleton; prof., mem. exec. faculty Sch. Fgn. Service, Georgetown U., 1919-56. Mem. Council on Fgn. Relations, Am., Fed., Pa. Franklin County, D.C. bar assns., Am. Soc. Internat. Law (mem. council), Internat. Law Assn. (pres. Am. br. 1943-49), Am. Econ. Assn., Phi Beta Kappa, Phi Alpha Delta (nat. supreme justice, 1934-36), Delta Phi Epsilon (nat. pres. 1922). Republican. Presbyn. (pres. Nat. Presbyn. Corp.). Clubs: Chevy Chase, Metropolitan (Washington); Monterey (Pa.) Country. Author books, 1911-latest being: Liberation, 1953. Recipient several fgn. decorations. Home: 2101 Connecticut Av. N. W., Washington 20008. Office: 1155 15th St. N. W., Washington 20005. Died Aug. 12, 1966; buried Arlington Nat. Cemetery.

CULIN, FRANK LEWIS army officer (ret.); b. Seattle, Mar. 31, 1892; s. Frank Lewis and Elizabeth Irene (Harding) C.; B.S., U. of Ariz., 1915, M.S. in M.E., 1916; grad. Infantry Sch., 1928, Command and Gen Staff Sch., 1930, Army War Coll., 1940; m. Ella Greene Sneed, Dec. 27, 1918; children-Virginia Elizabeth (Mrs. James Boyce Scott), Frank Lewis, III, John Edward. Commd. 2d lt., Inf., Nov. 30, 1916; promoted through grades to lt. col., Oct. 1, 1938; apptd. col. (temp.), Oct. 14, 1941, brig. gen. (temp.), June 24, 1943, major gen. (temp.), Mar. 1945, ret. Nov. 1946. Awarded Silver Star, 1918; Oak Leaf Cluster, 1943; second Oak Leaf Cluster, 1945; Bronze Star, 1945; Air Medal, 1945, D.S.M., 1945; Chevalier Legion of Honor, Croix de Guerre with Palm (France), Croix de Guerre with Palm (Belgium). Mem. Kappa Sigma, U. of Ariz. Alumni Assn.; hon. mem. 1st Co. Gov.'s Foot Guard, Hartford, Conn. Address: Monterey Peninsular Country Club, Del Monte, Cal. Died Dec. 31, 1967.

CULLEN, FREDERICK JOHN, physician, med. cons.; born Kokomo, Indiana; son of John and Mildred (Ristley) C.; Ph.G., Winona Coll. Pharmacy, Indianapolis, 1907; M.D., U. Colo., 1913; m. Marie Eloise Stone, Aug. 1, 1936. Gen. practice medicine, State of Washington, 1914-16 and 1919-29; chief, drug control div., Food and Drug Adminstrn., Washington, 1929-34; exec. v.p. and med. dir. Proprietary Assn., Washington, 1934-56; cons. to Proprietary Drug & Pharm. Industries, 1956-68; former professorial lectr. Sch. Pharmacy George Washington U. Served M.C., U.S. Army, 1916-19; retired with rank of maj. Recipient Purple Heart, Silver Star with palms. Registered pharmacist and physician, Wash. state. Past pres. Nat. Drug Trade Conf.; hon. mem. Can. Proprietary Assn., Am. Found. for Pharm. Edn.; sec. Therapeutic Research Found. Mem. George Washington U. Med. Soc., Med. Alumni Assn. U. Colo., Am. Pharm. Assn., Association of Military Surgeons of U.S., Am., National Capitol orchid socs., Disabled Am. Vets., Disabled Officers Assn., Am. Med. Writers Assn. Am. Legion. Clubs: Army and Navy, Congressional Country (Washington); Farmington Country (Charlottesville, Va.). Author: Your Medicine Chest; also articles on Fed. and state laws in field drugs. Home: Washington3DC Died June 10, 1968; buried Arlington Nat. Cemetery, Arlington VA

CULLEN, VINCENT, corp. exec.; b. Balt., Sept. 1, 1884; s. Simon V. and Caroline (Knowles) C.; ed. St. Vincent's Sch., Balt., Balt. Poly. Inst.; m. Bernadine M. Thumel, Aug. 1, 1917. Spl. agt. Am. Bonding Co., 1903-10; gen. agt.Fidelity and Deposit Co., 1903-10; gen. agt. Fidelity and Deposit Co., 1920-28; v.p. in charge Greater N.Y. Dept. of Nat. Surety Co. and Corp., 1928-May 24, 1933; became pres. Nat. Surety Corp., Third Av. Transit Corp.; trustee E. Bklyn. Savs. Bank. Pres. Ins. Soc. N.Y. Served as capt. 136th F.A., 37th div., France, 1917-19, Clubs: Metropolitan, The Recess, Larchmont Yacht (N.Y.). Home: 11 Woodbine, Larchmont, N.Y. Office : 90 John St., N.Y.C. Died Jan. 1962.

CULLUM, GEORGE WASHINGTON army officer; b. N.Y.C., Feb. 25, 1809; s. Arthur and Harriet (Sturges) C.; grad. U.S. Mil. Acad., 1833; m. Elizabeth Hamilton Halleck, Sept. 23, 1875. Commd. , Corps Engrs., U.S. Army, 1833; asst. to chief engr., Washington, D.C., 1834-36; superintending engr. govt. works, notably those at Fts. Trumball, Warren, Independence, Winthrop, Sumter, and at Battery Griswold; staff aide-de-camp to Gen. Winfield Scott, comdr.-in-chief U.S. Army; capt., 1838, maj., 1861; brig. gen. U.S. Volunteers, 1861, lt. col. engrs., 1863; engaged in a number of engring. operations during Civil War, including fortification of Nashville, 1864; supt. U.S. Mil. Acad., 1864-66; commd. col., 1867; an organizer Assn. Grads. U.S. Mil. Acad., 1870; ret., 1874; v.p. Am. Geog. Soc. of N.Y., 1877-92; left bequests of $250,000 for bldg. at U.S. Mil. Acad., $100,000 to Am. Geog. Soc. Author: Biographical Register of the Officers and Graduates of the United States Military Academy. Died N.Y.C., Feb. 28, 1892.

CULP, CHARLES CANTRELL food packer; b. Louisville, June 20, 1891; s. William Newton and Nelab (Allen) C.; student pub. schs.; m. Carolyn M. O'Bannon, Jan. 15, 1920; children-Carolyn O'Bannon, Charles William. Commll. agt. L.&N. R.R., Louisville, 1910-17; partner Lewis & Culp, Louisville, also Lexington, Ky., 1919-28; v.p., dir. Stokely-Van Camp, Inc., Indpls.,

1928-56; ret., 1956. Served as capt. 334th F.A., A.E.F., 1917-19. Mem. S.A.R. Presbyn. Clubs: Univ., Woodstock, Athletic (Indpls.) Home: 4950 N. Meridian St. Office: 941 N. Meridian St., Indpls. Died May 19, 1963; buried Cave Hill Cemetery, Louisville.

CULVER, HARRY H(AZEL) banker, realtor; b. Milford, Neb.; s. Jacob H. and Ada I. (Davidson) C.: ed. Doane Coll., Crete, Neb., and U. of Neb.; LL.D., Loyola U., Los Angeles, Calif., 1930; m. Lillian Roberts, June 11, 1916; 1 dau., Patricia. Founder and builder of Culver City, Calif., 1914, University City Calif., 1927. Pres. Harry H. Culver & Co., Culver City Co., Arizona Development Co. (Phoenix, Ariz.), Pacific Military Acad.; formerly dir. Security-1st National Bank of Los Angeles. Served as sergt. maj., cav., U.S. Vols., Spanish-American War; lt. col., U.S. Army Specialists Res.; now asst. real estate officer, war Dept. Engrs., Pacific Div. Ex-pres. National Assn. Real Estate Boards, Calif. Real Estate Assn., Los Angeles Real Estate Bd.; chmn. finance com. Los Angeles Chamber of Commerce; executive vice-pres. Royce-Linnard Hotels; mgr. Fairmont Hotel, San Francisco. Mem. bd. regents Loyola U., Los Angeles. Republican. Conglist. Mason (32ff, Shriner). Clubs: California, California Country, Los Angeles Country. Address: 1705 E. Central Av., Balboa, Calif. Died Aug. 17, 1946; buried at Inglewood, Calif.

CUMMINS, HENRY JOHNSON BRODHEAD congressman; b. Newton, Sussex County, N.J., May 21, 1831; attended public schs., Muncy, Pa.; studied law. Editor newspaper, Schuylkill County, Pa., 1850; admitted to bar, Williamsport, Pa., 1855; moved to Winterset, Ia., 1856; pros. atty. Madison County (Ia.). 1856-58; served as capt. Co. F., 4th Regt., Ia. Volunteer Inf., 1861— 1861-62, as col. 39th Regt., 1862-64; became propr., editor Winterset Madisopian, 1869; mem. U.S. Ho. of Reps. (Republican) from Ia., 45th Congress, 1877-79. Died Winterset, Apr. 16, 1909; buried Winterset Cemetery.

CUNNINGHAM, ANDREW CHASE officer U.S. Navy, civ. engr.; b. Mohawk, Herkimer Co., N.Y., Feb. 15, 1858; s. Thomas and Cleste (Chase) C.; grad. U.S. Naval Acad., 1879, C.E., Rensselaer Poly. Inst., 1885; m. Jessie E. Thomas, 1879. Line officer U.S.N. until 1883, when resignation was accepted; took up study of civ. engring.; followed profession until Spanish-Am. War, in which served as vol. ensign; at end of war apptd. to corps of civ. engrs. U.S.N. Inventions cover floating dry docks, coaling ships at sea, and burning of liquid fuel. Republican. Died Jan. 13, 1917.

CUNNINGHAM, JOHN LOVELL underwriter; b. Hudson, N.Y., Apr. 5, 1840; s. Jeremiah and Bethiah (White) C.; ed. pub. and pvt. schs.; LL.B., Albany Law Sch. (Union U.), 1861; m. Elizabeth Fowler (now deceased). Admitted to bar, 1861; 1st lt., capt. and maj. 118th N.Y. Vols., 1862-65; bvtd. lt.-col. vols.; collector internal revenue, 16th dist., N.Y., 1866-67. Republican. Gen. agt. 1868-91, sec. 1891-92, pres. 1892-1914, now dir. and mem. exec. com. Glens Falls Ins. Co. Mem. Soc. Army Potomac. Considerable contbr. to fire insurance literature; publisher "Now and Then," insurance paper. Address: Glens Falls, N.Y.

CUNNINGHAM, JULIAN W., army officer; b. Blairsville, Pa., May 1, 1893; s. Samuel Howard and Julia (Zimmers) C.; A.B., George Washington Univ., 1915, law sch., 1916-17; m. Margaret L. McGarry, June 27, 1925; children—Julian W. Jr. (deceased), Gary Craig. Commd. 2d lt. Cav., July 1917, and advanced through the grades to brig. gen., Sept. 1943. Mem. Phi Gamma Delta, Theta Delta Chi, Phi Delta Phi. Mason. Home: Alexandria VA Died Aug. 1972.

CURLEE, FRANCIS M. lawyer; b. Corinth, Miss., Feb. 1, 1877; s. William Peyton and Mary Elizabeth (Boone) C.; LL.B., U. Miss., 1902; children-Francis M. Curlee (dec.), Shelby Hammond III. Admitted to Miss. bar, 1902, and began practice at Corinth; moved to St. Louis and began practice there, 1905. Pres. Curlee Clothing Co. Served from capt. to lt. col., F.A., U.S. Army, 1917-19. Mem. Am., Mo. (pres. 1920-21), St. Louis bar assns., Delta Psi. Democrat. Mason. Club: Glen Echo Country. Home: Defiance, Mo.; also 5724 Chamberlain Av., St. Louis. Office: 1001 Washington Av., St. Louis 1. Died Mar. 1958.

CURRAN, HENRY HASTINGS b. N.Y.C., Nov. 8, 1877; s. John Elliott and Eliza Phillips (Mulford) C.; A.B., Yale, 1898; LL.B., N.Y. Law Sch., 1890; m. Frances Ford Hardy, Oct. 12, 1905. Reporter and editor N.Y. Tribune, 1898-1903; law practice and newspaper corr., 1903-11. Alderman, 1911-17, magistrate, 1917, pres. Borough of Manhattan, 1920-21; Rep. nominee for mayor N.Y.C., 1921; U.S. commr. immigration at Port of N.Y., 1923-26; counsel to City Club N.Y., 1926-28; pres. Assn. Against Prohibition Amendment, 1928-32; dir. Nat. Economy League, 1932-36; magistrate, 1936-38; dep. mayor N.Y.C., 1938-39, chief magistrate, 1939-45; justice of ct. spl. sessions 1945-47, ret. Maj. U.S. Army, 77th Div., 1917-19. Episcopalian. Clubs: Century, University. Author: Van Tassel and Big Bill, 1923; John Citizen's Job, 1924; Magistrate's Court, 1940; Pillar to Post (autobiography), 1941. Home: 40 5th Av., N.Y.C. Died Apr. 8, 1966.

CURRIER, JOHN C. treas. Veteran's Home Assn. and dir. and sec. Columbian Banking Co., San Francisco; b. Auburn, N.H., Sept. 19, 1842; s. David C.; grad. Pinkerton Acad., Derry, N.H.; studied medicine nearly 2 yrs., Georgetown Coll., Washington, 1867-68; m. Manchester, N.H., 1869, Nataline B. Smith. Entered vol. army, June, 1862, for Civil War as pvt.; apptd. 2d lt., 11th N.H. vols., 1862; engaged in battles of Fredericksburg, Vicksburg, Knoxville, Jackson, The Wilderness, South Side Road, Poplar Spring Church, etc.; severely wounded in face (jaw shattered) at Wilderness and Poplar Spring Church; promoted to capt. (bvtd. for gallantry in action); apptd. to U.S.A., 1869; resigned, 1871; U.S. Pension Agt., San Francisco, 1889-93; past pres. Calif. Soc. Sons Am. Revolution; past comdr. Calif. Commandery, Mil. Order Loyal Legion; Republican. Residence: 1804 Broadway. Office: 320 Sansome St., San Francisco.

CURRY, JEBEZ LAMAR MONROE educator; b. Lincoln Co., Ga., June 5, 1825; grad. Univ. of Ga., 1843; Dane Law School, Harvard, 1845 (LL.D., Mercer U., Ga., and U. of Ga.). lMem. Ala. legislature, 1847-48, 1853-54, 1855-56; mem. Congress, 1857-61; mem. Confederate Congress, 1861-65; aid on staff Gens. Jos. E. Johnson and Jos. Wheeler, and lt. col. of cav., C.S.A., 1864-65; pres. Howard Coll., Ala., 1866-68; prof. English philosophy and constitutl. and internat. law, Richmond Coll., Va., 1868-81; U.S. minister to Spain, 1885-88; pres. Bd. of Foreign Missions of Southern Bapt. Conv. and of Bd. Trustees Richmond Coll.; pres. Southern History Assn., etc. Is gen. agt. Peabody Edn. Fund and of John F. Slater Edn. Fund Author: Protestantism, How Far a Failure, 1870; Struggles and Triumphs of Virginia Baptist, 1873; Establishment and Disestablishment, of Progress of Soul Liberty in the United States; Francis Strother Lyon as Commissioner and Trustee of Alabama, 1889; Constitutional Government in Spain, 1889; William Ewart Gladstone, 1891; The Southern States of the American Union in Their Relation to the Constitution and the Resulting Union, 1895; History of the Peabody Edn. Fund, 1898; Civil History of the Confederate Government, 1901. Died 1903.

CURTIN, AUSTIN supt. Soldiers' Orphan School since May, 1896; b. Curtin's Eagle Iron Works, nr. Bellefonte, Pa., March 19, 1835; ed. common schools, and at Lewisburg (Pa.) Acad., and Milnwood Acad.; clerked and managed iron works, 1852-55; in business at Polo, Ill., 1856-58, and in Pa., at iron works, 1858-61; raised a co., 1861, and served, 1861-65, in 45th Pa. regt., 9th corps, in Army of Potomac; comd. co. and was on staffs of Gens. Welch, Ferrero and Burnside; apptd. lt.-col.; dept. comdr., G. A. R., 1885; staff officer, Pa. Nat. Guard, since 1884; now on staff Gen. Snowden, comdg. div., N. G. P.; m. June 1, 1858, at Polo, Ill., Rachel C. Fraser, New York. Address: Roland, Centre Co., Pa.

CURTIS, CARLTON BRANDAGA congressman; b. Madison County, N.Y., Dec. 17, 1811; studied law. Admitted to bar, Erie, Pa., 1834, began practice of law, Warren, Pa., 1834; mem. Pa. Ho. of Reps., 1836-38; mem. U.S. Ho. of Reps. (Democrat), 43d Congress, 1873-75; became a Republican, from Pa., 32d-33d congresses, 1851-55, (Republican), 1855; served from lt. col. to col. 58th Regt. Pa. Volunteer Inf., U.S. Army, 1862-63; moved to Erie, 1868, continued practice of law, also engaged in banking and oil prodn.; an originator and builder Dunkiri & Venango R.R. Died Erie, Mar. 17, 1883; buried Oakland Cemetery, Warren.

CURTIS, CHARLES ALBERT army officer; b. Hallowell, Me., Oct. 4, 1835; s. Charles Stubbs and A. F. (Ham) C.; B.A., Bowdoin Coll., 1861; m. Harriet L. Hughes, May 17, 1866. Second lt. U.S.A., Apr. 14, 1862; 1st lt., Mar. 30, 1864; retired, Dec. 15, 1870, on account of wounds received in line of duty; advanced to rank of capt. of inf. retired, by act of Apr. 23, 1904. Bvtd. capt., Sept. 27, 1865, for meritorious services during the war. Prof. mil. science and tactics in various instns., 1870 - ; col. Wis. N.G. Episcopalian. Author: Captured by the Navajos, 1904. Home: Madison, Wis. Died 1907.

CURTIS, CHARLES BOYD lawyer; b. Penn Yan, N.Y., Sept. 24, 1827; s. Samuel F. and Amelia (Boyd) C.; grad. Hamilton Coll., N.Y. (A.M.); admitted to N.Y. bar, 1849; served in Civil war, capt. 57th regt. N.Y. vols., 1861; m. Isabel Douglass, Aug. 23, 1876. Author: Catalogue of the Works of Velasquez and Murillo, London, 1883; Rembrandt's Etchings, 1888. Died 1905.

CURTIS, CHARLES CLARENCE army officer; b. Wiconisco, Pa., Oct. 29, 1893; s. Harry D. and Mary (Knitey) C.; student pub. schs.; m. Clara Horn, Nov. 21, 1921; 1 son, Charles H. Tehr. pub. schs., 1910-16; newspaper advt. mgr., 1919, later becoming advt. dir. Allentown (Pa.) Call-Chronicle. Promoted from pvt., 1916, to lt., 1917; served in France with 109th Machine Gun Bn., 28th Div., participating in 6 maj. operations: later with 213th Coast Arty.; promoted to brig. gen., 1941; now in command 33d Antiaircraft C.A. Brigade, Camp Huler, Tex. Mem. Pa. Newspaper Pub. Assn. (exec. com.), Alpha Delta Sigma. Republican. Lutheran. Clubs: Lehigh Delta Sigma. Republican. Lutheran. Clubs: Lehigh Valley Motor (dir.), Lexington; Brookside Country (Allentown), Lehigh Valley Country. Home: 2625 Allen St., Allentown, Pa. Died June 24, 1960: buried Greenwood Cemetery, Allentown.

CURTIS, HARRY ALFRED chemist; b. Sedalia, Colo., Feb. 16, 1884; s. Frederick A. and Lydia A. (Cramer) C.; B.S., U. Colo., 1908, M.A., 1910; Sc.D., 1930; Ph.D., U. Wis., 1914, Sc.D., 1937; D. Eng. (hon.), U. Louisville, 1948; m. Irene Hall, May 14, 1911 (dec.); children-Jeanne Carol, Patricia. Instr. later prof. chemistry, U. Colo., 1908-17; prof. chemistry Northwestern U., 1919-20; chief chemist, later plant supt. Internat. Coal Products Corp., Irvington, N.J., 1920-21; gen. mgr. Clinchfield Carbocoal Corp., South Clinchfield, Va., 1921-23; chief nitrogen survey U.S. Dept. Commerce, 1923-24; prof. chem. engring. Yale, 1923-30, chmn. dept. chem. engring., 1929-30; chmn. div. chemistry and chem. tech. NRC, 1930-34; dir. research Vacuum Oil Co., 1931-33; chief chem. engr. TVA, 1933-38; dean Coll. Engring., U. Mo., 1938-48, dir. TVA 1948-57. Mem. Pres. Coolidge's Muscle Shoals Commn. Mem. Colo. N.G., 1915-17; Mexican border service 3 mos., 1916; capt. ordnance, U.S. Army, World War I; assigned to nitrate div. ordnance and engaged in chem. engring. Mem. Am. Chem. Soc., A.A.A.S., Sigma Nu, Alpha Chi Sigma. Club: Cosmos (Washington). Home: 3730 Dellwood Dr., Knoxville, Tenn. Died July 1, 1963.

CURTIS, JOHN TALBOT lawyer; b. Stratford, Conn., Aug. 15, 1900; s. Howard Junior and Ellen Virginia (Talbot) C.; student Army and Navy Prep. Sch., 1917-18; B.S., U.S. Mil. Acad., 1920; LL.B., Yale, 1926; m. Isobel Ramsay Buckley, Nov. 5, 1928; children-Charles Buckley. Clare Howard (Mrs. Charles P. Rimmer, Jr.), Mary Talbot. Admitted to Conn. bar, 1926, N.Y. bar, 1928; practicing lawyer, Bridgeport, Conn., 1926-27, and since 1933, N.Y. City, 1928-32; legal staff R.F.C., Washington, 1932-33; mem. Curtis & Gerety; dir. Southport Savs. Bank, Pepperidge Farm, Inc., Southport Area Association, J. Pedersen Manufacturing Company. Past president Pequot Library Assn. Southport; trustee Bridgeport Protestant Orphan Asylum. Served as 1st lt. Inf., U. S. Army, 1920-22; col., dir. procurement, Boston Q.M. Depot, 1942-45; base q.m. Base K. Leyte, P.I., 1945. Mem. Am., Conn. State and Bridgeport bar assns. Clubs: Army and Navy (Washington); University (Bridgeport); Country (Fairfield, Conn.); Pequot Yacht (Southport); Fairfield County Hunt (Westport, Conn.). Home: 174 Old South Rd., Southport. Office: 955 Main St., Bridgeport 3, Conn. Died May 21, 1958.

CURTIS, NEWTON MARTIN soldier; b. De Peyster, N.Y., May 21, 1835; s. Jonathan and Phebe (Rising) C.; attended Gouverneur Wesleyan Sem., 1854-55; (LL.D., St. Lawrence U., 1906). Postmaster, De Peyster, 1857, 1861; capt. 16th N.Y. Inf., May 15, 1861; lt. col. 142d N.Y. Inf., Oct. 22, 1862; col., Jan. 21, 1863; bvtd. brig. gen. vols., Oct. 28, 1864, for distinguished services nr. New Market, Va.; maj. gen. vols., Mar. 13, 1865, for gallant and meritorious services at capture of Ft. Fisher; awarded medal of honor, May 28, 1891, for being the 1st man at Ft. Fisher, Jan. 15, 1865, to pass through stockade; hon. mustered out, Jan. 15, 1866. Mem. N.Y. legislature, 1884-90; pres. N.Y. State Agrl. Soc., 1880; sec. N.Y. Agrl. Expt. Sta., 1879-85, pres., 1885-80; mem. Congress St. Lawrence-Jefferson dist., 1891-93, St. Lawrence-Saratoga dist., 1893-97. Asst. insp. gen. Nat. Home for Disabled Vol. Soldiers, 1898 - . Pres. Soc. Army of the Potomac, 1907-08. Author: From Bull Run to Chancellorsville, 1906 P2. Home: Ogdensburg, N.Y. Died 1910.

CURTIS, SAMUEL RYAN army officer, engr., congressman; b. Champlain, N.Y., Feb. 3, 1805; s. Zarah and Phalley (Yale) C.; grad. U.S. Mil. Acad., 1831; m. Belinda Buckingham, Nov. 3, 1831. Served as col. 3d Ohio Inf. during Mexican War; chief engr. of improvement Des Moines River; city engr. St. Louis, 1850; mayor Keokuk *Ia.), 1856; mem. U.S. Ho. of Reps. from Ia., 35th-38th congresses, 1856-62; commd. brig. gen. U.S. Army, 1861; commanded U.S. Army which defeated Confederates at Pea Ridge (Ark.); commd. maj. gen., in command Dept. of Mo., 1862, Dept. of Kan., 1864, Dept. of N.W., 1865; peace commr. to Indians, 1865; commr. to insp. Union Pacific R.R., 1865-66. Died Council Bluffs, Ia., Dec. 26, 1866; buried Oakland Cemetery, Keokuk, Ia.

CURTISS, WILLIAM HANFORD glass mfg. exec.; b. Olean, N.Y., Jan. 15, 1884; s. William O. and Ella (Hanford) C.; A.B., Williams Coll., 1906; m. Emily Frost, Sept. 11, 1915; children-William Hanford, Jr., Ruth (Mrs. John Elliot Leggat). Employed in sales, shipping and spare parts depts. Walter A. Wood Mowing & Reaping Machine Co., 1907-20; asst. to pres. Corning Glass Works, 1920-29, v.p., 1929-53, sec., 1936-53, dir. 1937—, exec. com., 1946—, hon. v.p., 1954—; pres. The Corning Museum of Glass 1952—; dir. Corning Fibre Box Corp., Corhart Refractories Co. Served from capt. to lt. col. U.S. Army, 1916-19. Awarded Croix de Guerre. Dir. and mem. Steuben Area Council, Boy Scouts of Am. and mem. Region 2 exec. com. Pres. bd. trustees Corning Pub. Library, 1929-35. Clubs: Corning Country. University, Williams, St. Anthony (New York). Home: 148 E. 5th St. Office: Corning Glass Works, Corning, N.Y. Died Jan. 1960.

CUSHING, CALEB atty. gen. U.S., diplomat; b. Salisbury, Mass., Jan. 17, 1800; s. John and Lydia (Dow) C.; grad. Harvard, 1817; m. Caroline Wilde, Nov. 23, 1824. Admitted to Mass. bar, 1821; mem. U.S. Ho. of Reps. from Mass., 24th-27th congresses, 1835-43; spl. U.S. envoy to China, 1843-45, negotiated Treaty of Wang Huja, July 3, 1844, which opened for trade 5 Chinese ports and limited Am. citizens to jurisdiction of Am. laws and ofcls.; served as col., brig. gen. in Mexican War, 1847; atty. gen. U.S., 1852-57; chmn. commn. to revise and codify statutes of U.S., 1865-67; U.S. diplomat to Bogota, Colombia, 1868; sr. counsel for U.S. before tribunal of arbitration Treaty of Washington, 1871-72, negotiated settlement Ala. claims; U.S. minister to Spain, 1874-77. Author: History of the Town of Newburyport, 1826; The Practical Principles of Political Economy, 1826; Historical and Political Review of the Late Revolution in France, 2 vols., 1833; Reminiscences of Spain, 2 vols., 1833; Growth and Territorial Progress of the United States, 1839; Life of William H. Harrison, 1840; The Treaty of Washington, 1873. Died Newburyport, Mass., Jan. 2, 1879; buried New Burial Ground, Newburyport.

CUSHING, HARRY COOKE investment banker, financial advisor to corps.; born in Boston, Mass., June 10, 1895; son of Harry Cooke and Adelaide C.; student Columbia, Class 1917; son, Harry Cooke, 4th; m. 2d, Frances Sarah Peters, June 30, 1937. Partner, Herrick, Berg & Co., 1920-32; exec. Ladenburg, Thalmann & Co., 1932-37; v.p. E. H. Rollins & Sons, Inc., New York City, 1937-47; director American-Moroccan Corporation, Tower Petroleum Corporation; president and director Security Management Corporation; financial adviser Northfield Mines, Inc., Westfield Mines, Inc. Served as pvt. Troop B, Squadron A. New York Cav. on Mexican Border, 1916; served during World War I as capt. of Field Arty., U.S. Army, and asst. to chief of staff, 2d Army Corps, A.E.F., during Ypres-Lys and Somme offensives, 1918. Fellow Am. Geog. Soc.; mem. Sons of Revolution, Mil. Order of Foreign Wars, Mil. Order of Loyal Legion, Am. Legion, Delta Phi. Republican. Episcopalian. Clubs: Union, Racquet and Tennis, Piping Rock, Creek, The Leash, Westminster Kennel, Church, Town-Town Assn., Knickerbocker (gov.), Brook (gov.), Pilgrims (N.Y.C.); Brook's, White's (London); Travelers (Paris). Author: Liaison in Foreign Financial Relations, 1931; Winning the Peace, 1942. Home: Oxon Hill, Oyster Bay, N.Y.C. Office: 44 Wall St., N.Y.C. 5. Died Nov. 25, 1960.

CUSHING, HARVEY surgeon; b. Cleveland, O., Apr. 8, 1869; s. Henry Kirke and Betsey M. (Williams) C.; A.B., Yale, 1891, hon. A.M., 1912, Sc.D., 1919; A.M. and M.D., Harvard, 1895, Sc.D., 1931; hon. fellow Royal Coll. Surgeons, Eng., 1913, Ireland, 1918. Edinburgh, 1927; M.D., hon. causa, Belfast, 1918, Strasbourg and Brussels, 1930, Budapest and Bern, 1931, Paris, 1933; Sc.D., Washington U., 1915; LL.D., Western Reserve U., 1919, Cambridge, 1920. Edinburgh and Glasgow Univs., 1927; Litt.D., Dartmouth Coll., 1929; m. Katharine Stone Crowell, June 10, 1902; children - Mary Benedict, Betsey, Henry Kirke, Barbara. Engaged in practice surgery, 1895-1933; asso. prof. surgery, etc., Johns Hopkins, 1902-12; prof. surgery, Harvard, and surgeon-in-chief, Peter Bent Brigham Hosp., 1912-32; Sterling prof. neurology, Yale, 1933 - . Dir. U.S.A. Base Hosp., No. 5, attached to B.E.F., in France, May 1917-Mar. 1919; sr. consultant in neurol. surgery, A.E.F., 1918; col. M.C. D.S.M. (U.S.); Companion of the Bath; Officer Leégion d'Honneur. Mem. Nat. Acad. Sciences; pres. Am. Neurol. Assn., 1923, Am. Coll. Surgeons, 1923. Charles Mickle fellowship, U. of Toronto, 1922; Cameron prize, U. of Edinburgh, 1924; Lister medal (London), 1930. Author: The Pituitary Body and Its Disorders, 1912; Tumors of the Nervus Acusticus, 1917; The Life of Sir William Osler, 1925 (Pultizer prize); A Classification of the Gliomata (with P. Bailey), 1925; Consecratio Medici and other Essays, 1928; Intracranial Tumours, 1932; Pituitary Body and Hypothalamus, 1932. Died Oct. 8, 1939.

CUSHING, SAMUEL TOBEY army officer; b. Providence, R.I., Sept. 14, 1839; s. George W. and Sarah (Cooke) C.; early edn. common schools, Providence; grad. West Point Mil. Acad., July 1, 1860; m. Kate Dewey, May 27, 1869. Bvtd. 2d lt., Jan. 1861; 1st lt., Feb. 1862; capt., Feb. 1863; capt. subsistence dept., May 1863; maj. by bvt., Aug. 1888; maj. subsistence dept., Jan. 1897; brig. gen. and commissary gen. U.S. Army. in New Mex. during Navajo war, 1860-61; signal officer, and during Civil War, 1862-63, chief signal officer Army of the Potomac; chief commissary of subsistence in field during Bannock War, 1878. Died 1901.

CUSHING, WILLIAM BARKER naval officer; b. Delafield, Wis., Nov. 4, 1842; s. Milton and Mary (Smith) C.; ed. U.S. Mil. Acad., 1857-61; m. Katherine Forbes, Feb. 19, 1870, 2 children. Master's mate U.S. Navy, captured 1st Civil War prize, a tobacco schooner, 1861; lt. in command gunboat Ellis, 1862; exec. officer ship Commodore Perry; commanded ship Commodore Barney; commanded ships Strokokon and Monticello, 1863; noted for torpedoing Confederate ram Albemarle, 1864; lt. comdr., 1853; commanded ships Lancaster, 1865-67, Maumee, 1868-69; promoted comdr., 1872. Died Washington, D.C., Dec. 17, 1874.

CUSHMAN, ALLERTON SEWARD chemist; b. (U.S. Consulate) Rome, June 2, 1867; s. Edwin and Emma (Crow) C.; B.S., Worcester Poly. Inst., 1888; Freiberg, and Heidelberg, 1889-90; A.M., Harvard, 1896, John Harvard fellow, Ph.D., 1897; pvt. to capt., 6th Mass. Vol. Inf., 1898; m. Sarah Dunn Hoppin, June 20, 1901 (died 1921); children - Charles Van Brunt, Agnes Hoppin (dec.). Asso. prof. chemistry, Bryn Mawr Coll., 1900-01; asst. dir. Office of Pub. Roads, U.S. Dept. Agr., and chemist in charge of investigations, 1902-10; founder and dir. Inst. of Industrial Research, Washington, 1910-24. Commd. maj. Ordnance R.C., June 4, 1917; stationed at Frankford Arsenal, Pa.; promoted lt. col. Ordnance, U.S.A., Jan. 1918; discharged Dec. 1918. Prin. researches: extraction of potash from feldspathic rocks; use of ground rock as fertilizer; properties of road materials; cause and prevention of the rusting of iron and steel. Franklin medal, 1906. Author: The Corrosion and Preservation of Iron and Steel, 1910; Chemistry and Civilization, 1920. 2d. edit., 1925. Died May 1, 1930.

CUSHMAN, AUSTIN SPRAGUE lawyer; b. Duxbury, Mass., Sept. 9, 1827; s. late Robert Woodward C., D.D. (Bapt. clergyman) and Lucy (Sprague) C.; grad. Brown, 1848; admitted to Mass. bar, 1853; of N.Y., 1879; m. Carrie L. Hathaway, Nov. 17, 1861. Clerk in U.S. War Dept., 1894; collaborated with Dr. Stone in reporting (by Isaac Pitman's phonography) trial of Dr. Webster for murder of Dr. Parkman (Published 1850); private sec. to Pres. Fillmore, 1852; 3d lt. U.S. Revenue Marine Service, 1853; U.S. Commr., Mass. dist., May 24, 1855; lt. in 3d Mass. inf., 1858-61; promoted adj. 3d regt. Apr. 19, 1861; on duty at burning of Gosport Navy Yard - among first troops in Va.; raised co.; capt. and maj., 47th Mass. inf., 1862-63; U.S. register bankruptcy, 1867; practiced admiralty and patent law; sec. Am. Patent Protective Assn.; editor Republic Mag., 1890. Prominent in G.A.R.; was 1st of Mass. 32ff Mason. Died 1907.

CUSHMAN, HORACE O., army officer; b. Ill., Jan. 4, 1893; grad. Inf. Sch., Officers Course, 1928, Command and Gen. Staff Sch., 1936, Army War Coll., 1938; m. Kathleen O'Neill; 2 sons, 2 daus. Commd. 2d lt. Inf., Apr. 1917, and advanced through the grades to brig. gen., Oct. 1942; served as 2d lt. to capt., Inf., World War I; Gen. Staff Corps, 1939-40; ret. 1953. Address: Fort Devens MA Died Nov. 1972.

CUSHMAN, PAULINE Union spy, actress; b. New Orleans, June 10, 1833; m. Charles Dickinson; m. 2d, August Fichtner, 1872; m. 3d, Jerry Fryer, 1875. Appeared in The Seven Sisters, Wood's Theater, Louisville, Ky., 1863, during one performance publicly toasted Southern cause, fired from cast; took oath of allegiance to U.S. Govt., commd. Union secret agt.; expelled from Nashville (Tenn.) under guise as ardent Southern sympathizer; her mission was to penetrate as far South as possible and collect mil. information; apprehended near Gen. Bragg's hdqrs. (Tullahoma, Tenn.) with mil. documents, tried and sentenced to be hanged, left behind as Bragg retreated under Gen. Rosecrans advance from North, 1863, supplied Rosecran's forces with valuable information, became too well known to continue spying; returned to stage as lectr. after Civil War; Committed suicide San Francisco, Dec. 2, 1893; buried plot of Grand Army of Republic.

CUSTER, GEORGE ARMSTRONG army officer; b. New Rumley, O., Dec. 5, 1839; s. Emmanuel and Maria (Ward) C.; grad. U.S. Mil. Acad., 1861; m. Elizabeth Bacon, Feb. 9, 1864. Commd. 2d lt. 2d U.S. Cav., 1861, 1st lt. U.S. Army, 1862; served in 1st Battle of Bull Run and Peninsular campaign; promoted brig. gen. U.S. Volunteers for conduct at Battle of Aldie, 1863; promoted capt. U.S. Army, 1864, later brevetted lt. col., then col.; brevetted maj. gen. U.S. Volunteers, 1864; had distinguished Civil War record; brevetted brig. gen., maj. gen. U.S. Army, 1865; promoted maj. gen. U.S. Volunteers, 1865; reverted to rank of capt. U.S. Army, 1865; became lt. col. in command of 7th U.S. Cavalry upon its orgn., 1866, served in various Indian campaigns in Kan., N.D.; sent to take part in Sioux campaign, 1876, in course of fighting his regt. became divided; met (with 5 troops of cavalry) an overwhelmingly large Indian force under Sitting Bull. Killed with all his command in Battle of Little Bighorn, nr. present day Little Bighorn, Mont., June 25, 1876.

CUTCHEON, BYRON M. lawyer, soldier, congressman; b. Pembroke, N.H., May 11, 1836; s. James M. and Hannah (Tripp) C.; grad. U. of Mich., 1861; A.M., (LL.B., 1866; m. Marie Amnie Warner, June 22, 1863. Served in Civil war, capt. and maj. 20th Mich., 1862; lt. col. and col., 1863; bvt. brig. gen., 1865. Admitted to bar, 1866; regent Univ. of Mich., 1875-83; mem. Congress, 1883-91; mem. U.S. Bd. of Ordnance and Fortification, 1891-95. Editorial writer, 1895-98; practicing law, 1898 - . Republican. Home: Grand Rapids, Mich. Died 1908.

CUTCHEON, FRANKLIN W(ARNER) M. b. Dexter, Mich., Mar. 6, 1864; s. Byron M. and Marie A. (Warner) C.; Ph.B., U. of Mich., 1885; studied law, same univ., 1885; m. Sarah Gibson Flandrau, Feb. 5, 1891. Began practice of law at St. Paul, Minn., 1885; moved to New York, 1899; retired, 1924. Sec.-gen. Am. Red Cross (war council), 1917. Commd. capt. Q.M.R.C., Dec. 17, 1917; lt. col. U.S.A., May 8, 1918; chmn. Bd. of Contracts and Adjustments A.E.F., Jan. 30, 1918, to Nov. 13, 1918; thereafter adviser to spl. rep. of sec. of war in Europe; dir. U.S. War Finance Corp., 1920; U.S. citizen mem. Reparation Commn., 1927-29. Decorated D.S.M.; Grand Officer Legion of Honor (French); Grand Officer Order of Leopold (Belgian); Companion St. Michael and St. George (British); Officer Order of Crown of Italy. Chmn. bd. trustees Santa Barbara (Boys) Sch. Died Nov. 12, 1936.

CUTLER, CONDICT WALKER JR. surgeon; b. Morristown, N.J., Aug. 9, 1888; s. Condict Walker and Cora (Carpenter) C.; B.S., Columbia, 1910, M.D., 1912; unmarried. Interne Roosevelt Hosp. 1913-15, asst. surg., 1927-32, asso. surg., 1932-38, attending surgeon, 1948-53, cons. surgeon 1953—, sec. med. bd., 1948-53; cons. resident gynecologist Sloane Hosp. for Women, 1915-16; attending surg. Lincoln Hosp., 1929-31; dir. surgery Goldwater Meml. Hosp., 1939-63; pres. med. bd. 1949-51, cons. surgeon, 1953—; dir. surgery Morristown (N.J.) Meml. Hosp., 1952-54, consulting surgeon, 1954—; consulting surgeon and trustee N.Y. Dispensary, 1932-48; Rock- and State Hosp., since 1943; instr. surgery, Columbia, 1920-28, asso. prof. clin. surgery 1947, prof. clin. surgery, 1947-54; chief Emergency Med.Service, Manhattan Nat. Office of Civilian Defense, 1941-43; surg., mem. cons. bd. and chmn. procurement and assignment service, New York, War Manpower Commn., 1940-43; pvt. practice, N.Y.C. since 1916. Served as 1st Lt. M.C., U.S. Army, A.E.F., 1918-19; Lt. Col. M.C., U.S. Army, 1943-44, Col., 1945-46; surg. consultant, 1st Service Command. Received Legion of Merit, 1946. President citation, 1943. Congressional Medal for Meritorious Service, 1946, Columbia Medal for Excellence 1944, Alumni medal, 1946. Trustee Columbia, 1940-43, 1949-51, N.Y. Acad. Medicine, 1941— (chairman committee on medical education, 1945-47, chairman section of surgery, 1935-36); member joint administrator board Columbia-Presbyn. Med. Center, 1949-51. Fellow A.C.S.; mem. Am. Surg. Assn., Internat. Surg. Assn., N.Y. Acad. Medicine, Society Consultants to Armed Forces, American Assn. Surg. of the Hand (president, 1950), A.M.A., Med. Soc. of County of New York (treas., 1947-52), Am. Legion (past comdr. Columbia U. post), Mil. Order Fgn. Wars, Asso. Alumni Columbia College (pres., 1938-40); asso. Alumni Coll. Physicians and Surgeons (pres. 1950). Republican. Methodist, Club: University of New York City. Author: The Hand: Its Diseases and Disabilities, 1941. Co-author: History of Roosevelt Hospital, 1956. Contbr. numerous monographs and articles to med. publs. Home: 225 Central Park West, N.Y.C. 24. Office: 630 Park Ave., N.Y.C. 21. Died July 6, 1958.

CUTLER, ELLIOTT CARR prof. surgery; b. Bangor, Me., July 30, 1888; s. George Chalmers and Mary Franklin (Wilson) C.; A.B., Harvard, 1909, M.D., 1913: hon. doctorate U. of Strasbourg, 1938; D.Sc., U. of Vermont, 1941, University of Rochester, 1946; m. Caroline Parker, May 24, 1919; children-Elliott Carr, Thomas Pollard, David, Marjorie Parker (dec.), Tarrant, Surgical house officer, Peter Bent Brigham Hosp., 1913-15; resident surgeon, Harvard Unit, Am. Ambulance Hosp., Paris, 1915; resident surgeon, Mass. Gen. Hosp., 1915-16; alumni asst. in surgery, Harvard, 1915-16; voluntary asst., Rockefeller Inst., N.Y. City, 1916-17; resident surgeon, Peter Bent Brigham Hospital, 1919-21, associate in surgery, 1921-24; instructor in surgery, Harvard, 1921-24; professor of surgery, Western Reserve Univ., School of Medicine, 1924-32; dir. of Surgical Service, Lakeside Hosp., Cleveland, 1924-32; consulting surgeon, New England Peabody Home for Crippled Children, since 1932, Children's Hosp., Boston, since 1945; Moseley Prof. of surgery, Harvard, since 1932; surgeon in chief, Peter Bent Brigham Hosp., since 1932; chief consultant to professional services division, Vet. Administrn., 1945; civilian consultant to Sec. of War since May, 1946; acting asst. med. dir. Vets. Adminstrn., since 1947. Trustee, Dexter Sch., 1938-43 (chmn. med. com., 1938-43), Noble and Greenough School, Boston Sch. Occupational Therapy, Mass. State Infirmary; mem. exec. com., High Cabot Memorial Fund; mem. Mass. Med. Benevolent Soc., trustee, 1934-37; sponsor Walter Cannon Memorial Fund, 1946. Served as lt. Med. Reserve Corps, 1916-17; capt., M.O.R.C., 1917-18, major, 1918-24, lt. col., 1924-42, col., 1942-45, brig. gen., A.U.S., 1945, retired April, 1946; chief surgical consultant, E.T.O., U.S. Army, 1942-45; chief, professional services div., E.T.O., U.S. Army, 1945. Awarded Distinguished Service Medal with Battle Clasps for Champagne-Marne, Aise-Marne, St. Mihiel, (Meuse-Argonne Defensive Sector), Victory Medal World War I; Campaign Medal, E.T.O., World War II, Legion of Merit, Croix de Guerre with Palm, Order of British Empire; Oak Leaf Clusters & D.S.M., World War II. Fellow, Am. Coll. Surgeons, Boston Med. Library, Internat. Society of Surgery (chmn. Am. Com., 1929-47, del., chmn., U.S. Exec. Com., 1932). Mem. A.A.A.S., Am. Assn. Advancement of Sci., Am. Geog. Soc., Mass. Foundation, Am. Acad. Surgery, Am. Assn. for Thoracic Surgery, Am. Bd. of Surgery, Founders Group, 1937, Am. Bur. for Med. Aid to China, Inc., Am. Soc. for Clinical Investigation (emeritus, 1931), Am. Heart Assn., Inc., A.M.A., Am. Soc. for Exptl. Pathology Am. Surgical Assn. (pres. 1947), Am.-Soviet Medical Soc. (regional v.p. 1945-47; American

Committee for the Protection of Medical Research, (chmn., 1926-42), Assn. Mil. Surgeons of the U.S.; Boston Surgical Soc.; Boylston Med. Soc. of Harvard U. L'Europe Medicale (hon. scientific mem. patronage com.), Friends of Med. Progress; Federation of Am. Socs. for Exptl. Biology (chmn. of com. for defense of Biological Research), Gerontological Soc., Inc., Harvard Med. Alumni Assn., Mass. Med. Soc.; Med. Exchange Club; New England Heart Assn.; New England Surgical Soc.; Norfolk Med. Soc., Omaha Med. Soc., Soc. for Exptl. Biology and Medicine, Soc. of Clinical Surgery, (senior mem. 1943, pres., 1941-46); Soc. of Univ. Surgeons, (hon. mem. 1938); Suffolk Dist. Med. Soc., Soc. U.S. Med. Consultants of World War II (pres. 1946). Mem. Town of Brookline Unemployment Com., U.N. (official, Mass. Com), Mass. Foundation, exec. com., Mass. com. on Public Safety, (dir. Med. Div.), Mass. Com. for retaining wild life, Parker River Wild Life Refuge, Mem. Alpha Omega Alpha, Sigma XI, American Legion Inc. (Also corresponding member of many foreign medical societies). Unitarian. Clubs: Harvard, Somerset, Thursday Evening, Friday Evening, (all Boston), Aesculapian, Asso. Harvard Clubs (pres. 1936), Porcellian, Hasty Pudding (all affiliated Harvard U.), Harvard (New York), Mayfield Country (Cleveland), Country (Brookline), N. American Yacht Racing Union, Vineyard Haven Yacht Club (Commodore, 1938-42; 1946), Bonaventure Assos., Rotary (distinguished service award, 1946); Henry Jacob Bigelow medal from Boston Surg. Soc., 1947. Editor: America Clinica (adv. bd.), American Heart Journal, (adv. bd.), Macmillan Co. Surgical Monograph Series, (editor), Journal of Clinical Investigation (editorial com.), Surgery (adv. council), Am. Jour. of Surgery, (asso. editor), Brit. Jour. Surgery, (editorial bd. and exec. com.), Washington Inst. of Medicine, (editorial and consulting bd. in surgery). Author: Atlas of Surgical Operations (with R. Zollinger), 1939. Home: 61 Heath St., Brookline, Mass. Office: Peter Bent Brigham Hospital, 721 Huntington Av., Boston 15, Mass. Died Aug. 16, 1947.

CUTLER, MANASSEH clergyman, congressman; b. Windham County, Conn., May 13, 1742; s. Hezekiah and Susanna (Clark) C.; grad. Yale, 1765, A.M., 1768, LL.D. (hon.), 1789; m. Mary Balch, Sept. 7, 1766. Admitted to Mass. bar, 1767; licensed to preach, 1770; ordained, Congregational Ch., 1771, pastor, Ipswich Hamlet (now Hamilton), Mass., 1771-1823; served as chaplain in Revolutionary War: an organizer Ohio Co., colonizers Ohio River Valley, 1786; a founder Marietta (O.), 1787; instrumental in drafting Ordinance of 1787 for adminstrn. N.W. Territory; declined position as judge Supreme Ct. of Ohio Territory, 1795; rep. from Ipswich to Mass. Gen. Ct., 1800; mem. U.S. Ho. of Reps. (Federalist) from Mass., 7th-8th congresses, 1801-05; botanist, systematized and catalogued flora of New Eng. by Linnean system; mem. Am. Philos. Soc. (1784), Am. Acad. Arts and Scis. (1791), Phila. Linnaean Soc. (1809), Am. Antiquariran Soc. (1813), New Eng. Linnaean Soc. (1815). Died Hamilton, Mass., July 28, 1823.

CUTTER, GEORGE WASHINGTON army officer, poet; b. Quebec, Can., 1801; m. Mrs. Frances Ann Drake; married a 2d time. Mem. Ind. Legislature, 1838-39; helped raise a co. of volunteers, 1847; commd. capt. 2d Ky. Regt., 1847; served in Battle of Buena Vista during Mexican War; works include: Buena Vista and Other Poems, 1848; The Song of Stream and Other Poems, 1857; Poems, National and Patriotic, 1857. Died Washington, D.C., Dec. 25, 1865; buried St. John's Masonic Lodge's plot, Congressional Cemetery, Washington.

CUTTING, BRONSON senator; b. Oakdale, L.I., N.Y., June 23, 1888; s. William Bayard and Olivia Peyton (Murray) C.; Harvard, 1910; unmarried. Moved to Santa Fe, N.M., 1910; pres. N.M. Printing Co., 1912-18, Santa Fe New Mexican Pub. Corp., 1920 - ; pub. Santa Fe New Mexican, El Nuevo Mexicano; dir. Sunmount Sanatorium Co.; apptd. senator, Dec. 1927, to fill unexpired term of Andrieus A. Jones, dec., and elected Nov. 1928, for full term ending Mar. 3, 1935. Commd. capt. U.S.A., Aug. 5, 1917; asst. mil. attacheé, Am. Embassy, London, 1917-18. Regent N.M. Mil. Inst., 1920; chmn. bd. commrs. N.M. State Penitentiary, 1925. Treas. Prog. State Central Com., 1912-14, chmn., 1914-16; mem. exec. com. N.M. Taxpayers' Assn., 1915-17. Decorated British Mil. Cross. Episcopalian. Home: Santa Fe, N.M. Died May 6, 1935.

CUTTING, CHARLES SUYDAM, naturalist; b. New York, N.Y., Jan. 17,21889; s. Robert Fulton and Helen (Suydam) C.; prep. edn. Groton Sch., 1903-09; A.B., Harvard, 1912; m. Helen McMahon, 1932 (dec. 1961); m. 2d, Mary Pyne Filley, Apr. 8, 1964. Trustee Robert F. Cutting Estate from 1913; field work on expdns. to Central Asia for Am. Museum Natural History, Field Museum of Natural History, Chicago, Pitt River Museum of Oxford, Eng. Trustee Am. Museum Natural History, New York Zool. Soc. Hon. fellow Field Museum of Natural History, Chicago. Served as 1st lt., U.S. Army during World War; with A.E.F. in France 15 months. Performed active duty abroad as lt. col., U.S. Army. Decorated Croix Noire (French), Croix de Guerre with Gold Star, Honorary Comdr. Most Excellent Order of British Empire. Member of Bombay Natural History Society, Royal Geog. Soc., Royal Central Asia Soc. (all Brit.); Himmalyan Club. Republican. Episcopalian. Clubs: Knickerbocker, Brook, Racquet (New York). Author: The Fire Ox and Other Years, 1940; also series of articles pub. by Am. Museum Natural History. Home: Bernardsville NJ Died Aug. 24, 1972.

DABNEY, ROBERT LEWIS clergyman, educator; b. Louisa County, Va., Mar. 5, 1820; s. Charles and Elizabeth R. (Price) D.; attended Hampden-Sydney Coll., 1836-37, U. Va., 1840-42, Union Theol. Sem., 1844-46; m. Lavinia Morrison, Mar. 28, 1848. Ordained minister Presbyn. Ch., 1846; tchr. Union Theol. Sem., Richmond, Va., also preacher chapel, occaionally tchr. at Hampden-Sydney Coll., 1853-83; became prof. Princeton, also minister Fifth Avenue Presbyn. Ch., N.Y.C., 1860; opposed South with religious fervor when war began; served as chaplain Confederate Army, 1862, commd. maj. Thomas J. (Stonewall) Jackson's staff; proposed saving "spiritual" South by mass migrations from conquered "geographical" South to Australia or Brazil; became prof. philosophy U. Tex., 1883, a founder Austin Sch. of Theology; infirm and totally blind, 1890 until death, but continued to lecture until 1897. Author: Life and Campaigns of Lt.-Gen. Thomas J. Jackson, 1866; A Defense of Virginia and the South, 1867; (theologically Calvinist, politically reactionary) Practical Philosophy, 1897; also many other philos. books andessays. Died Victoria, Tex., Jan. 3, 1898.

DABNEY, VIRGINIUS educator; b. "Elmington," Gloucester County, Va., Feb. 15, 1835; s. Thomas Smith Gregory and Sophia (Hill) D.; attended U. Va., 1853-55, 57-58; m. Ellen Maria Heath; m. 2d, Anna Wilson Noland. Served in Confederate Army during Civil War, discharged as capt.; established Loudoun Sch., Middleburg, Va., 1867; in charge of prep. sch., Princeton, N.J., 1873-74; N.Y. Latin Sch., N.Y.C.; mem. editorial staff N.Y. Comml. Advertiser. Author: The Story of Don Miff, 1886; Gold that did not Glitter, 1889. Died N.Y.C., June 2, 1894.

DABO, LEON artist; b. Detroit, July 9, 1868; s. Ignace Scott and Madelene (Oberle) D.; studied at Ècole des Arts Dècoratifs, Acadèmie Julian, and with Daniel Urabietta Vierge, Paris, and with Galliardi in Rome and Florence. Represented in the Luxembourg Mus., Paris; Met. Mus. Art, N.Y., Imperial Mus. Art, Tokyo, Japan; Nat. Gallery, Ottawa, Can.; Mus. Arts and Scis., Bklyn., Nat. Gallery, Washington; Mus. of Art, Detroit, Art Inst. Chgo., John Herron Inst. Indpls., Mus. of Art, Toledo; Muncie (Ind.) Art Assn.: Saginaw (Mich.) Art Assn.; Poland Springs (Me.) Mus., City Mus. St. Louis; Mus. of Art, Montclair, N.J., Milw. Art Assn.; Mus. of Art, Boston, Hackley Art Gallery, Muskegon, Mich., Nat. Arts Club, N.Y., Arbuckle Inst., Bklyn., Montreal Art Assn.; Tuskegee (Ala.) Inst., Mus. of Art, Lyons, France; Balt. Mus. of Art, Delgado New Orleans Art Mus., Montrela Art Mus., Newark Mus. Art; Ft. Worth Mus. Art, Beloit (Wis.) Coll. Art Gallery, Rochester (N.Y.) Meml. Art Gallery; Reading (Pa.) Art Gallery; Mpls. Mus of Art, others. Executed mural paintings of Ascension and Stas. of Cross, and designed cartoons for opal glass windows, Ch. of St. John the Bapt., also murals Holy Cross Ch. of St. John the Bapt., Flower Meml. Library, Watertown, N.Y. Chevalier Legion of Honor. Served as 1st lt., later capt. A.E.F., 1918-19; with Corps of Interpreters attached 27th Div., later with Army of Occupation, and a.d.c. to Maj. Gen. Mark L. Hersey; hon. mustered out 1919. Mem. Nat. Acad. Design, Soc. Nationale des Beaux Arts (Paris), Soc. des Amis des Arts (Versailles), N.Y. Hist. Soc., Four Arts Soc. (N.Y.). Clubs: University (Paris); National Arts (N.Y.). Lectr. Author numerous monographs; also illustrations for History of Fourth Division, U.S. Address: 140 E. 72St., N.Y.C. Died Nov. 1960.

DADE, ALEXANDER LUCIEN army officer; b. in Ky., July 18, 1863; grad. U.S. Mil. Acad., 1887, Inf. and Cav. Sch., 1893; Army War Coll., 1910. Comd. 2d lt. 13th Inf., June 12, 1887; trans. to 10th Cav., Feb. 27, 1888; 1st lt. 2d Cav., June 13, 1895; trans. to 3d Cav., Nov. 7, 1895; maj. 47th Vol. Inf., Sept. 9, 1899; hon. disch. vols., June 30, 1901; capt. 13th U.S. Cav., Feb. 2, 1901; promoted maj., 1911, col., 1917. Cav.; brig. gen. N.A., Oct. 29, 1917. Assigned as dir. aviation training, Central Dept., hdqrs., Chicago, Mar. 1918; hon. disch. as brig. gen., Signal Corps Aviation Sect., May 3, 1918; col. (cav.), Insp. Gen.'s Dept., May 24, 1918; duty in office Insp. Gen., Feb. 12, 1919; dept. insp., Central Dept., Chicago, Feb. 13, 1919-Sept. 30, 1920 (retired). Died Jan. 8, 1927.

DAGGETT, AARON SIMON army officer; b. Greene Corner, Me., June 14, 1837; s. Aaron and Dorcas C. (Dearborn) D.; ed. Greene, Me., Monmouth Acad., Me., and Wesleyan Sem., Bates Coll.; m. Rose Bradford, June 14, 1865. Enlisted in Co. E, 5th Me. Inf., Apr. 27, 1861; 2d lt., 1st lt., capt., maj., same, 1861-63; lt. col. 5th U.S. Vet. Vol. Inf., Jan. 23, 1865; hon. mustered out, May 10, 1866; capt. 16th U.S. Inf., July 28, 1866; maj. 13th Inf., Jan. 2, 1892; lt. col. 25th Inf., Oct. 1, 1895; brig. gen. vols., Sept. 21-Nov. 30, 1898; col. 14th Inf., Mar. 31, 1899; brig. gen., Feb. 21, 1901. Bvts.: col. and brig. gen. vols., Mar. 13, 1865, "for gallant and meritorious services during the war"; maj., Mar. 2, 1867, for same in battle of Rappahannock Sta., Va., Nov. 7, 1863; lt. col., Mar. 2, 1867, for same in battle of the Wilderness. Participated in battles of First Bull Run, West Point, Gaines Mill, Savage Sta., White Oak Swamp, Malvern Hill, Va., Crampton's Gap, Antietam, Fredericksburg, Marie's Heights, Salem Church, Va., Gettysburg, Rappahannock Station, Mine Run, Wilderness, Spottsylvania C.H., North Anna, Coal Harbor, Petersburg, Va.; in Spanish-Am. War, served in Santiago campaign, taking part in battle of El Caney; in Philippines engaged at Imus river and Bacoor; in China at Yangtsun, Peking and Imperial City; retired, Mar. 2, 1901. Author: America in the China Relief Expedition, 1903. Home: Washington, D.C. Died May 14, 1938.

DAHLGREN, JOHN ADOLPHUS BERNARD naval officer; b. Phila., Nov. 13, 1809; s. Bernard Ulric and Martha (Rowan) D.; m. Mary C. Bunker, Jan. 8, 1839; m. 2d, Sarah Madeleine Vinton Goddard, Aug. 2, 1865; 10 children, including Capt. Charles Bunker, Lt. Paul, John Vinton, Ulric, Eric. Apptd. acting midshipman U.S. Navy, 1826, passed midshipman, 1832, lt., 1837; assigned to make observations of solar eclipse, 1836; on leave to undergo treatment for on coming blindness, 1837-43; patented percussion lock, 1847; chief Bur. of Ordnance, Washington, D.C., 1847-63, 68-69, established ordnance system used by U.S. Navy during Civil War; formulated and equipped Navy Ordnance Yard, Washington inventor 11 inch Dahlgren gun; introduced to navy, 1850; commd. comdr., 1855, capt., 1862, rear adm., 1863; commanded S. Atlantic blockading squadron, 1868; prof. gunnery U.S. Naval Acad.; mem. A.A.A.S.: commdr. Washington Navy Yard, 1869-70. Author: 32 Pounder Practice for Ranges, 1850; The System of Boat Armament in the United States Navy, 1852; Naval Percussion Locks and Primers, 1853; Shells and Shell Guns, 1856. Died Washington Navy Yard, July 12, 1870 *

DALBEY, JOSIAH T. army officer; b. Eufaula, Ala., Jan. 10, 1898; s. Charles Richard and Lila (Hart) D.; B.S., U.S. Mil. Acad., 1919; grad. Inf. Sch., 1920, Command and Gen. Staff Sch., 1940; m. Jimmie Derrington, Dec. 20, 1924. Commd. 2d lt., U.S. Army, 1918, advanced through grades to brig. gen., 1944; in Fed. service with La. N.G., Mexican Border, 1916-17; served in France and Germany, 1919, P.I., 1925-27, China, 1931-33, ETO (Eng.), 1943, France-Germany, 1945; comdg. gen., airborne center, Camp Mackail, N.C., since 1944, qualified parachutist since 1945; dep. comdr. Am. Sector, Berlin, 1945-46; post comdr., Munich, 1946-47; supr. Organized R.C., N.Y., since 1948. Decorated Bronze Star. Home: 5603 West End Blvd., New Orleans 19. Died May 1964.

DALE, RICHARD naval officer; b. Norfolk County, Va., Nov. 6, 1756; s. Winfield and Ann (Sutherland); m. Dorothea Grathorne, Sept. 15, 1791; children—Richard, John M. served with Brit. Navy, 1776-77; joined colonial cause, 1777; served as 1st lt. on Bon Homme Richard under John Paul Jones in battle with Serapis, 1779; commd. lt., 1781; served with Mcht. Marine, 1783-94; commd. capt. U.S. Navy, 1794; commanded squadron in Mediterranean during hostilities with Tripoli, 1801-02. Died Phila., Feb. 26, 1826.

DALE, SAMUEL pioneer, soldier; b. Rockbridge County, Va., 1772. Govt. scout on Southern Frontier, 1798-96; became guide for immigrants going to Miss.; took part in Creek War, 1812-14; mem. Gen. Assembly Ala., 1817-29; one of those charged with transporting Choctaw to West of the Mississippi River, 1832; Dale County (Ala.) named after him. Died Lauderdale County, Miss., May 24, 1841.

DALE, THOMAS army officer, colonial gov.; b. England; m. Elizabeth Throckmorton, 1611. Created knight, 1606; apptd. marshal of Va., 1609; acting gov. Colony of Va. 1611, 14-16; placed colonists under marshall law for insubordination, noted for his discipline, his legislative code (known as "Dales Code") precipitated the phrase "five years of slavery," 1611-16; gained disfavor with the colonists but favor from the Linden Co.; returned to Eng. with Thomas Rolfe and his wife, Pocahontas, 1616; comdr. East India Co. Fleet, 1617. Died Masulipatam, India, Aug. 9, 1619.

DALEY, JOHN PHILLIPS army officer; b. Washington Barracks, D.C., July 17, 1910; s. Edmund Leo (U.S. Army), and Beatrix Otelie (Koehler) D.; student George Washington U., 1926-27; B.S., U.S. Mil. Acad., 1931; student F.A. Sch., 1934-35, Command and Gen. Staff Sch., 1947, Nat. War Coll., 1947-48, Army War Coll., 1950-51; m. Katherine Hadley White, Aug. 6, 1932; children-Katherine Anne (Mrs. David D. Cramer), John Michael (U.S. Army). Commd. 2d lt. U.S. Army, 1931, advanced through grades to lt. gen., 1961; instructor physics U.S. Mil. Acad., 1937-42; instr. gunnery and survey F.A. Sch., 1943; arty. sect. 12th Army Group, Europe, 1944-45; asso. prof. physics U.S. Mil. Acad., 1946-47; internat. group G-3, Dept. Army, 1948-50; faculty Army War Coll., 1950-52; assigned I Corps Arty., Korea, 1952; comdg. officer 2d Div. Arty., Korea, 1952-53; chief staff, mem. mil. armistice commn., Korea, 1953-54; comdg. officer III Corps Arty., 1954-55; dir. spl. weapons research and development Dept. Army, 1955-58; commanding gen. USA SETAF, 1958-60; dep. chief staff operations USAREUR, 1960-61; dep. comdg. gen. for developments U.S. Continental Army Command, 1961-

62; comdg. gen. Combat. Devels. Command, 1962—. Mil. adviser Geneva Conf., 1954. Decorated Legion of Merit with clusters, D.S.M. Address: U.S. Army Combat Developments Command, Fort Belvoir, Va. Died July 21, 1963; buried U.S. Mil. Acad., West Point, N.Y.

DALLAS, TREVANION BARLOW cotton mfr.; b. Washington, Sept. 11, 1843; s. Alexander and Mary Byrd (Willis) D.; ed. in Va.: m. 1st, May 11, 1869, Ella Douglas (died 1870); 2d, Jan. 18, 1876, Ida Bonner, Nashville. Served in C.S.A., 1861-65, pvt. to capt. arty. under Gen. Braxton Bragg. Was voluntary aide in Prussian army during war between Prussia and Austria, 1866; engaged in banking, 1866-69; in dry goods business, Nashville, from 1869, and later cotton mfr., operating large mills at Nashville, and Huntsville, Ala. Address: Nashville, Tenn.

DALLENBACH, KARL M., psychologist; b. Champaign, Ill., Oct. 20, 1887; s. John J. and Anna Caroline (Mittendorf) D.; B.A., U. of Ill., 1910; M.A., U. of Pittsburgh, 1911; Ph.D., Cornell U., 1913; m. Ethel Leila Douglas, Aug. 22, 1914; children—John Wallace, Elizabeth Ann, Frederick Douglas. Asst. in psychology, U. of Ill., 1909-10; fellow in psychology, U. of Pittsburgh, 1910-11, Sage fellow, Cornell U., 1911-12; instr. in psychology, U. of Ore., 1913-15, Ohio State U., 1915-16, Cornell, 1916-18, 1919-21; asst. prof. Cornell U., 1921-30, prof., 1932-45. Sage prof. psychology, 1945-48; distinguished professor of psychology, University of Texas, from 1948, chmn. dept., from 1950; visiting prof. Columbia, 1930-32. Capt., U.S. Army, 1918-19, O.R.C., 1919-42, 1946-48, lt. col., Adj. Gen.'s Dept., Army of U.S., 1942-46, ret., 1948. Asso. and business editor Am. Jour. Psychology, 1921-25, editor from 1926. Chmn. emergency com. in psychology, The National Research Council, 1940-46. Fellow A.A.A.S. (v.p., chmn. Sec. I, 1940); mem. Am. Psychol. Assn. (dir. 1928-30, 1951-54, pres. div. I, 1951), Soc. of Exptl. Psychologists, Am. Assn. Univ. Profs., Southern Soc. Philosophy and Psychology (council member 1952-55, president 1954), Texas Psychological Assn., Eastern Psychol. Assn. (dir. 1937-38; pres. 1939), Psychometric Soc., Am. Legion, Sigma Xi, Phi Kappa Phi, Phi Delta Kappa, Delta Upsilon, Nu Sigma Nu, Psi Chi, Acacia. Republican. Mason. Club: Rotary. Author articles and monographs on psychology. Editor: Washburn Commemorative Volume, 1927; General Index, Am. Jour. Psychology, vols. 1-30, 1926; vols. 31-50, 1942; Golden Jubilee Volume, Am. Jour. Psychology, 1937. Home: Austin TX Died Dec. 23, 1971; buried Champaign IL

DALLSTREAM, ANDREW JOHN lawyer; b. Hoopeston, Ill., Apr. 29, 1893; s. Andrew John and Lida (Loveless) D.; B.S., James Millikin U., 1915, LL.D., 1953; Ph.B., U. Chgo., 1917, J.D., 1917; m. Dorothy Ricketts, Aug. 18, 1917; children-Andrew John, Dorothy Ann (Mrs. Michael Meyer). Admitted to Illinois bar, 1917; practice of law, Centralia, 1919-27, member Noleman, Smith & Dallstream (formerly Noleman & Smith), 1920-27; member Dallstream, Schiff, Hardin, Waite & Dorschel (formerly Pam, Hurd & Reichman), Chgo., 1927-; member exec. committee and director Celotex Corp., Jessop Steel Co.; dir. UARCO, Inc., Tube Turns Plastic, Inc., Binks Mfg. Co., Jessop Steel, Ltd., Jackson & Church Co., Green River Steel Corporation. First National Bank of Barrington (Illinois). Member of board examiners C.P.A.'s. Ill. Member zoning commn. Cook Co., 1937-40, mem. zoning bd. appeals, acting chmn. since 1940; mem. mayor's com. on policemen, firemen awards, com. on selection nominees for membership bd. edn., 1953; mem. exec. com. Citizens Com., for jud. amendment Ill. constn., 1953; pres. Village of Barrington Hills, Ill. Mem. vis. bd. U. Chgo. Law Sch.; dir., member exec. committee Chgo. Lighthouse for Blind, Alumni Fund Found James Milliken U.; trustee, cmmn. planning bd. Miliken University; advisory mem. bd. dirs. Am. Bar Foundation. Served as capt. U.. Found.; Bar of City of New York, National Alumni Assn. James Millikin U. (pres., dir.), Am. (member house dels., 1953), Ill., Chgl. (bd. mgrs., 1948-50, v.p. 1950-52, pres. 1952-53) bar assns., Am. Judicature Soc., U. Chgo. Law Sch. Alumni Assn. (pres.), Sigma Alpha Epsilon, Clubs: Law, Legal, University, Casino (Chgo.); Lawyers (N.Y.C.); Barrington Hills Country (past pres.); Executive, Economics, Fox River Valley Hunt. Home: Andora Hill, 134 Brinker Rd., Barrington Hills, Ill. Office: 231 S. La Salle St., Chgo. 60604. Died June 10, 1962; buried Evergreen Cemetery, Barrington, Ill.

DALTON, ALBERT CLAYTON, army officer (ret.); b. Lafayette, Ind., Oct. 2, 1867; grad. Inf. and Cav. Sch., Ft. Leavenworth, Kan., 1895, Gen. Staff Sch., 1920, War Coll., 1921; m. Caro Gordon, 1907. Pvt., corpl. and sergt. Co. A, 22d Inf., Jan. 18, 1889-Aug. 1, 1891; 2d lt. 22d Inf., July 31, 1891; promoted through grades to brigadier-gen. Q.M.C., Dec. 8, 1922. Participated in Cheyenne Indian Campaign, 1890, Sioux Campaign, 1891, Santiago Campaign, 1898, Philippine Campaign, 1899-1902; with Army of Cuban Occupation, 1907-09, Vera Cruz Expdn., 1914; on Mexican border, 1916-17; organized Expeditionary Depot, Phila., Sept.-Oct. 1917; gen. supt. Army Transport Service, New York, Nov. 1, 1917-Nov. 5, 1918; comdr. 18th Inf. Brig., 9th Div., Nov. 6, 1918-Feb. 5, 1919; duty in France, May-Aug. 1919; apptd. asst. q.m. gen., Washington, D.C., Dec. 8, 1922; retired, July 7, 1926; apptd. pres. U.S. Shipping Bd. Merchant Fleet Corp., July 8, 1926, later v.p. and gen. mgr. same. Awarded Silver Star for gallantry in action, 1899; D.S.M. for World War service; decorated with Grand Officer Crown of Rumania. Home: 4000 Cathedral Av. Address: 318 Metropolitan Bank Bldg., Washington DC

DALTON, JAMES L. army officer; b. New Britain, Conn., Jan. 20, 1910; s. Charles and Gladys D.; B.S., U.S. Mil. Acad., 1933; m. Kaye Starbird, Oct. 16, 1937; children-Catherine Starbird, Elizabeth Hodgman. Commd. 2d lt., U.S. Army, 1933, and advanced through the grades to brig. gen., 1945; stationed at Schofield Barracks, Hawaii, at time Japanese attack, 1941; served in Guadacanal, New Georgia and Solomon Islands campaigns; landed Lingayen Gulf, P.I., Jan. 1945, fought up to Balete Pass; killed by sniper fire, May 1945. Decorated Silver Star with oak leaf cluster, Bronze Star, Combat Infantryman's Badge, Purple Heart. Died May 1945.*

DALTON, JOHN CALL physiologist, coll. pres. b. Chelmsford, Mass., Feb. 2, 1825; s. Dr. John Call and Julia (Spalding) D.; grad. Harvard, 1844; M.D., Harvard, 1847; studied physiology under Claude Bernard, Paris, France; never married. Never practiced medicine; became 1st U.S. physician to devote life to exptl. physiology and related scis.; recipient annual prize from A.M.A. for essay on Corpus Luteum, 1851; prof. physiology U. Buffalo (N.Y.), 1851-54, U. Vt., 1854-56; prof. physiology Coll. Physicians and Surgeons, N.Y.C., 1855-83, pres., 1884-89; with L.I. Coll. Hosp., 1859-61; served as surgeon with rank of brig. gen. med. corps. 7th N.Y. Regt., in Civil War, 1861-64; became mem. Nat. Acad. Scis., 1864. Author: Treatise on Human Physiology, 1859; A treastise on Physiology and Hygiene, 1868; Doctrines of the Circulation, 1884; other med. works. Died N.Y.C., Feb. 12, 1889.

DALTON, JOSEPH N. army officer; b. Winston-Salem, N.C., June 27, 1892; s. David Nicholas and Louisa Wilson (Bitting) D.; B.S., Va. Mil. Inst., 1912; student U. of South, 1912-13, grad. Command and Gen. Staff Sch., 1934, D.C.L. (hon.), 1946. Instr. Culver Summer Sch., 1912; asst. comdt. and comdt. of cadets Sewanee Mil. Acad., 1912-16; commd. 2d lt. U.S. Army, 1916, advanced through grades to brig. gen., 1942; maj. gen., 1943; served as co. and bn. comdr. 55th Inf., A.E.F., World War I; Am. mem. food com. Interallied Rhineland High Commn., 1919-20; with Am. Relief Administrn., Moscow, 1922; aide to Maj. Gen. Hanson Ely, 2d Corps Area, 1935-38; adj. gen. IV Corps, Ft. Benning, Ga., 1940; adj. gen., I Corps, Columbia, S.C., 1940-41; adj. gen. P.R. Dept., 1941-42; dir. personnel Army Service Forces, 1942-46; ret. as maj. gen., 1946. Club: Army-Navy (Washington). Address: Army-Navy Club, Washington. Died Nov. 1961.

DALY, JOHN FIDLAR, physician, educator; b. Overton, Neb. Oct. 12, 1905; s. William H. and Jessie Huff (Fidlar) D.; B.S., Knox Coll., 1926, student Northwestern U. Sch. Medicine, 1926-28; M.D., U. Pa., 1930; m. Catharine Gardette Maury, Mar. 15, 1930. Intern Hosp. of U. Pa., 1930-32; gen. practice of medicine, 1932-40; grad. tng. in dermatology Columbia-Presbyn. Med. Center, N.Y.C., 1946-49; prof. dermatology, chmn. div. U. Vt., from 1949; pvt. practice specializing dermatology, Burlington, Vt., from 1949. Served as maj. M.C., AUS, 1940-46. Decorated Silver Star. Diplomate Am. Bd. Dermatology and Syphilology. Fellow Am. Acad. Dermatology and Syphilology; mem. A.M.A. Canadian Dermatol. Assn., New Eng., Montreal dermatol. socs. Home: Hivesburg VT Died Jan. 16, 1969; buried Village Cemetery, Hivesburg VT

DANA, CHARLES ANDERSON editor; b. Hinsdale, N.H., Aug. 8,1819; s. Anderson and Ann (Denison) D.; ed. Harvard; A.B. (hon. as of Class of 1843), 1861; m. Eunice Macdaniel, 1846, 4 children. Tchr., mng. trustee Brook Farm, 1841-46; asst. editor Boston Daily Chronotype, 1846-47; city, then mng. editor N.Y. Tribune, 1847-62, covered European revoltuions, 1848; editor (with George Ripley) New American Cyclopedia, 16 vols., 1858-63; asst. sec. of war U.S., 1863-64; editor Chgo. Republican, 1865; owner, editor N.Y. Sun, 1868-97, fought against Tweed Gang, also Grant's administrn.; pioneer modern news editing, noted for new style of journalism, stressing "human interest". Author: The Art of Newspaper Making, 1895; Recollections of Civil War, 1898; Eastern Journeys, 1898. Died West Island, L.I., N.Y., Oct. 17, 1897.

DANA, NAPOLEON JACKSON TECUMSEH soldier; b. Ft. Sullivan, Eastport, Me., Apr. 15, 1822; s. Capt. Nathaniel G. D., 1st U.S. arty.; ed. Portsmouth Acad., N.H., 1833-38; grad. U.S. Mil. Acad., West Point, 1842; m. Sue Lewis Martin Sandford, 1844. Engaged in Mexican war, 1st with Gen. Taylor from beginning through siege of Fort Brown and campaign of Monterey, and next with Gen. Scott in siege of Vera Cruz and battle of Cerro Gordo; was banker in St. Paul, 1855-61; was col. 1st Minn. vols. at Ball's Bluff in Civil war, then brig. gen. in all battles of Army of the Potomac up to and including Battle of Antietam; then maj. gen. and comdg. div. and corps and dept. to end of war. Was wounded at Cerro Gordo and again at Antietam. After war engaged in mining in west; gen. agt. Am. Russian Commercial Co. in Alaska and Washington, 1866-71; afterward connected with several railroads; retired. Died 1905.

DANDY, GEORGE BROWN colonel U.S.A.; b. Macon, Ga., Feb. 11, 1830; s. Rev. James Hervey and Charlotte (Temple) D.; who moved to N.J. same year; ed. private schools, N.J.; m. Anne Eliza Slaughter, Feb. 11, 1873. Enlisted April, 1847, in 10th Inf., raised for service in Mexican War, and served until its close; began study of medicine, Salem, N.J.; cadet U.S. lMil. Acad., 1849-52; pvt., sergt., and 1st sergt. Co. A, 1st Arty., 1854-57; promoted through grades to col. 100th N.Y. Inf., Aug. 29, 1862; hon. mustered out of vol. service, Aug. 28, 1865; maj. q.m., Mar. 3, 1875; lt. col. deputy q.m. gen., Nov. 11, 1887; retired, Feb. 11, 1894; advanced to rank of col. retired, by act of Apr. 23, 1904. Bvts.: maj., Sept. 6, 1863, "for distinguished and gallant conduct in siege of Ft. Wagner, S.C."; lt. col., Aug. 14, 1864, "for gallant services in action in Deep Bottom, Va."; col., Mar. 13, 1865, "for gallant and meritorious services at Fort Gregg, Va."; brig. gen., Mar. 13, 1865, for same in the field during the war. Served in Spokane Indian expdn. and Snake expdn.; assigned to duty Gen. McDlellan's headquarters; captured Folly Island, S.C.; took part in assault and capture Morris' Island and Ft. Wagner, S.C.; battles at Port Walthall junction, Drury's Bluff, Deep Bottom, Deep Run, Fussell's Mills and siege of Petersburg, Va.; placed in command 3d Brigade, 1st Div., 24th Army Corps; 1865 took prominent part in assault and capture of Ft. Gregg, south of Petersburg, Va., and comd. his brigade at Appomattox C.H., last battle of war. Since war in q.m. dept.; built Fort Phil Kearney at base of Big Horn Mountains, 1866, and Ft. Abraham Lincoln, N.D., 1873-75; in charge gen. depot q.m. and subsistence depts., Yuma, Ariz., 1868; later at various cities. Hon. mem. Buffalo Hist. Soc. Home: Omaha, Neb. Died 1911.

DANENHOWER, JOHN WILSON naval officer; b. Chgo., Sept. 30, 1849; s. William W. Danenhower; grad. U.S. Naval Acad., 1870; 2 children. Served in ships Plymouth and Juniata in European Squadron, 1870; served in vessel Portsmouth in survey of North Pacific, 1873-74; rank of master, 1873; spent 2 months in insane asylum, 1878; after release served in ship Vandalia, in Mediterranean; while in Smyrna (Turkey) heard of proposed Arctic expdn. in ship Jeannette, offered services and was accepted; exec. officer in Jeannette from Havre (France) to San Francisco; began trip via Bering Strait to Arctic; 1879; commd. lt., 1879; incapacitated by inflammed left eye, 1879; when Jeannette was crushed in ice (latitude 77 degree 15 feet north, longitude 155 degree east), 1881, escaped (with others) over ice to Asia mainland, arrived in U.S., 1882; asst. comdr. of cadets U.S. Naval Acad., Annapolis, Md.; assigned command in Constellation, 1887, grounded vessel going out of harbor, Norfolk, Va.; returned to Annapolis, committed suicide (probably because of this incident). Author: Lieutenant Danenhower's Narrative of the Jeannette, 1882. Died Annapolis, Apr. 20, 1887.

DANFORD, LORENZO congressman, lawyer; b. Belmont Co., O., Oct. 18, 1829; reared on farm; ed. common schools and 2 years at coll. at Waynesburg, Pa. Admitted to bar, 1854; pros. atty., Belmont Co., 1857-61; in Union army from April, 1861, as private, and 1892; member Congress, 16th Ohio dist., 1873-79, and 1895 - . Republican. Chmn. Com. Immigration and Naturalization, 55th Congress. Home: St. Clairsville, O. Died 1899.

DANFORTH, CHARLES H., army officer; b. District of Columbia, Feb. 5, 1876; grad. Infantry and Cavalry Sch., 1903, Air Service Pilots Sch. and Air Service Bombardment Sch., 1921. Began as pvt. U.S.A., June 16, 1898; commd. 2d lt. inf., Feb. 2, 1901; advanced through grades to col.; chief of Air Corps, rank of brig. gen., for term 1930-34; reverted to rank of col., 1934; now retired. Address: War Dept., Washington DC

DANFORTH, GEORGE WASHINGTON naval officer, retired; b. Charleston, Mo., Feb. 22, 1868; s. Lewis William and Mary Jane (Yates) D.; State Normal Sch., Cape Girardeau, Mo., 1883-84; Manual Training Sch., Washington Univ., St. Louis, 1884-85; grad. U.S. Naval Academy, 1889; post-grad. course and practical engring. and engine bldg., Navy Yard, New York, 1891-92; m. Aileen R. Hennicke, of Brooklyn, Dec. 15, 1896. Commd. in engr. corps, U.S.N., July, 1891; engineering duties of various kinds at sea and on shore, July 1, 1891-June 1, 1899, retired. Insp. machinery for Navy Dept., at Union Iron Wks., San Francisco, 1902-03 and 1906-07; Navy Dept. detail at St. Louis Expn., 1904; instr. engring. dept., Naval Acad., 1908-11; in charge summer naval sch., Culver (Ind.) Mil. Acad., 1912; chief Machinery Exhibits Dept., Panama-Pacific Internat. Expn., 1912-15; insp. engring. material for U.S.N. in central dist. of Pa., 1917-19. Mem. Soc. Naval Engrs. Mason. Club: Army and Navy (Washington). Author: Mechanical Processes, 1917. Home: Charleston, Mo. Address: Navy Dept., Washington.

DANIEL, FERDINAND EUGENE editor; b. Greenville (now Emporia) Co., Va., July 18, 1839; s. R. W. T. and Hester Jordan (Adams) D.; ed. pub. schs., Vicksburg, Miss., 1850-56, Jackson, Mfiss., 1856-60;

M.D., New Orleans Sch. of Medicine, 1862; m. Minerva Patrick, July 4, 1863; m. 2d, Fanny Ragsdale Smith, Oct. 10, 1872; m. 3d, Josephine Draper, June 3, 1903. Pvt. 18th Miss. Inf., C.S.A., May-Sept., 1861; surgeon (maj.), C.S.A., upon exam. before Army Bd. Med. Examiners, Army of Tennessee, Tupelo, Miss.; commd. July 8, 1862; registrar Army Bd. Med. Examiners, July-Nov., 1862; judge advocate, gen. court martial. Army of Tenn., Nov., 1862-Feb., 1863, at Chattanooga; in charge Confederate hosps. at Chattanooga, Tenn., Marietta, Kingston, and Covington, Ga., and Lauderdale, Miss., until close of war. Practiced medicine and surgery, Galveston, Tex., 1866-75, Jackson, Miss., 1875-80, in Texas, 1880-85; retired and founded Texas Med. Jour., July, 1885, editing and publishing it. Sec. Texas Quarantine Dept., 1890-98; had charge at Lake Miss. of epidemic of yellow fever, 1878; U.S. quarantine officer, Vicksburg, Miss., 1879. Prof. anatomy and later of surgery, Tex. Med. Coll., Galveston, 1867-68. Pres. Am. Internat. Congress on Tuberculosis, 1905-06. Democrat. Author: Recollections of a Rebel Surgeon, 1899; The Strange Case of Dr. Bruno, 1906. Home: Austin, Tex. Died May 14, 1914.

DANIEL, HENRY congressman; b. Louisa County, Va., Mar. 15, 1786; attended public schs.; studied law. Admitted to bar, started practice of law, Mt. Sterling, Montgomery County, Ky.; mem. Ky. Ho. of Reps., 1812, 19, 26; served as capt. 8th Regt., U.S. Inf. in War of 1812, 1813-15; mem. U.S. Ho. of Reps. (Jackson Democrat) from Ky., 20th-22d congresses, 1827-33. Died Mt. Sterling, Oct. 5, 1873; buried Macphelah Cemetery.

DANIELS, ARTHUR SIMPSON univ. dean; b. N.Y.C., Dec. 21, 1905; s. Anthony Joseph and Anna (Komarek) D.; B.S., Springfield (Mass.) Coll., 1931; M.A., Columbia, 1935, Ed.D., 1943; m. Alice Abge Miller, June 3, 1931; 1 dau., Carolyn Frances (Mrs. Stanley G. Lyons). Asst. prof. phys. edn., dir. intramural sports, coach football, swimming, track, Allegheny Coll., 1931-37; asso. prof. phys. edn., asst. varsity football coach U. Ill., 1937-45; instr. summer sessions Columbia Tchrs. Coll., 1936-42; prof. phys. edn., Ph.D. adviser univ. grad. council Ohio State U., 1945-57; dean Sch. Health, Phys. Edn. and Recreation, Ind. U., 1957-. Spl. adviser Pres. Kennedy's Council on Youth Fitness; adv. com. ednl. policies commn. N.E.A.; adv. bd. Athletic Inst.; mem. bd. trustees Am. Coll. of Sports Medicine. Served to lt. col. USAAF, 1941-45. 1941-45. Recipient citation for outstanding service phys. edn. USAAF, 1945. Fellow Am. Acad. Phys. Edn. (citation for outstanding work adapted phys. edn. coll. level 1948), Am. Coll. Sports Medicine; mem. Am. Assn. Health, Phys. Edn. and Recreation (Nat. Honor award 1957; dir., president 1961-62; past chmn. numerous coms.), Midwest Dist. Ind. assns. health, phys. edn. and welfare, Coll. Phys. Edn. Assn. (pres. 1957). Presbyn. (ruling elder). Kiwanian (dir.). Author: Adapted Physical Education, 1965; also chpts. in books, reports and articles. Home: 2431 Barbara St., Bloomington, Ind. Died June 18, 1966; buried Rosehill Mausoleum, Bloomington, Ind.

DANIELS, JOSEPH J., lawyer; b. Indpls. Apr. 13, 1890; s. Edward and Virginia (Johnston) D.; A.B., Wabash Coll., 1911; LL.B. cum laude, Harvard, 1914; m. Katharine A. Holliday, June 20, 1918 (dec. Apr. 1935); 1 dau., Katharine (Mrs. L.I. Kane); m. 2d, Robertine B. Fairbanks Apr. 2, 1945; 1 stepson, Michael B. Fairbanks (dec.). Practiced in Indpls., 1914-67, ret., 1967; counsel firm Banker & Daniels; dir. Electric Steel Castings Co.; hon. dir. Nat. Starch & Chem. Corp. Hon. gov. Riley Hosp.; bd. corps. Crown Hill Cemetery, Indpls. Served from 1st lt. to capt. U.S. Army, 1917-1919. Mem. Phi Beta Kappa, Phi Beta Kappa Assos., Beta Theta Pi. Clubs: Indianapolis Literary, University (Indpls.). Home: Indianapolis IN Deceased.

DANIELS, JOSEPHUS ex-ambassador, ex-sec. Navy; b. Washington, N.C., May 18, 1862; s. Josephus and Mary (Cleves) D.; ed. Wilson (N.C.) Collegiate Inst., law, U. of N.C.; Litt.D., Washington and Lee U.; LL.D., University of North Carolina, Wesleyan University and other universities and colleges; m. Addie W., d. Maj. W. H. Bagley, May 2, 1888; children-Josephus, Worth Bagley, Jonathan Worth. Frank A. Became editor of Wilson (North Carolina) Advance at age of 18; admitted to the bar. 1885; but did not practice; state printer for North Carolina, 1887-93; chief clerk Dept. of Interior, 1893-95; became editor Raleigh (N.C.) State Chronicle, 1885; consolidated the State Chronicle and the North Carolinian with the News and Observer, 1894, and since editor News and Observer; secretary of the navy in cabinet of President Wilson, March 5, 1913-March 6, 1921; Am. ambassador to Mexico, 1933-42. Member of Democratic National Com. from N.C., 1896-1916; dir. publicity Bryan and Wilson campaigns. Trustee and mem. exec. com. U. of N.C.; trustee Wilson Foundation, Jefferson Memorial Commn.; mem. Woodrow Wilson and Franklin D. Roosevelt Foundations. Author: The Navy and the Nation (addresses), 1919; Our Navy at War, 1922; Life of Worth Bagley, 1898; Life of Woodrow Wilson, 1924; Tar Heel Editor, 1939. Editor: In Politics, 1940; The Wilson Era (Peace 1913-17), 1944; The Wilson Era (War 1917-23), 1945; Shirt Sleeve Diplomat, 1947. Methodist (mem. gen. Conf.). Home: Raleigh, N.C. Died Jan. 15, 1948.

DANIELS, MILTON J. ex-congressman; b. Cobleskill, N.Y., Apr. 18, 1838; s. Hon. John V. and Hester Ann (Wheeler) D.; ed. lMiddlebury (N.Y.). Acad.; m. Jennie E. Booth, May 27, 1869. Enlisted 9th Minn. Inf., Apr., 1861; 2d lt., Aug. 28, 1862; 1st lt., Apr. 24, 1864; capt., May 20, 1864; bvtd. maj. vols., Dec. 9, 1865, hon. mustered out, Dec. 13, 1865. Engaged in banking in Minn., 1868; mem. Minn. Legislature, 1882-9; mem. 58th Congress, (1903-5), 8th Calif. Dist.; Republican. Mem. G. A. R., Loyal Legion. Address: Riverside, Calif. Died Dec. 1, 1914.

DANIELSON, CLARENCE HAGBART army officer; b. Lead, S.D., Aug. 7, 1889; s. Ole and Hannah (Berg) D.; R.S., U/S. Military Acad., 1913, Command and General Staff School, 1930-32, Army War College, 1937-38; National War College, 1946; married Edith May Baird, December 2, 1914; children-Ole, Willis. Commissioned 2d lieut., Infantry, 1913, and advanced through the grades to maj. gen., 1944; Mexican border service, 1913-17; Mexican Punitive Expdn., 1916; Hawaiian Dept., Honolulu, T.H., 1917-18; Insp. Gen. Dept., Camp Custer, Mich., Camp Grant, Ill., Washington, D.C., 1918-19; Adj. Gen. Dept-, 1923; Adj. Gen. Office (both Washington, D.C.), 1920-23, 1926-30, 1933-36; adj. gen. Harbor Defenses, Manila, Subic Bay, Ft. Mills, Corregidor, P.I., 1923-25; asst. adj. gen. 2d Army Corps Areas, 1925-26; Adj. Gen. Office, Washington, 1926-30; asst. adj. gen., Hawaiian Div., Schofield Barracks, T.H., 1932-33; Adj. Gen. Office, Washington, D.C., 1933-36; Gen. Staff Corps, War Dept. Gen. Staff, 1936-37; adj. gen., U.S. Military Acad., 1938-41; adj. gen., 1st Army, Governors Island, N.Y., 1941-42; appt. dir. Office Procurement Service, 1942; comdg. gen. Seventh Service Comd., Jan. 1944; retired, Oct. 1946. Decorations: Legion of Merit with Oak Leaf Cluster: Army Commendation Ribbon: D.S.M.; Estrella Abdon de Calderon, 1st Class (Ecuador). Mason. Clubs: Army-Navy, Columbia Country (Washington); Army-Navy (Arlington, Va.). Home: 3202 Riverview Blvd. W., Bradenton, Fla. Office: c/o Adjutant Gen. Army, Washington. Died May 22, 1952; buried U.S.M.A., West Point, N.Y.

DANIELSON, WILMOT ALFRED army officer; b. Des. Moines, July 25, 1884; s. Alfred and Emma Charlotte (Gustafson) D.; B.S. in E.E., Ia. State Coll., 1907; M.S., Mass. Inst. Tech., 1926; m. Sybil Lenter, 1911; 1 dau., Emma Louise (Mrs. Lynn Paulson); m. 2d, Gertrude Bechtel, 1938; 1 son, William Karth. Served in Ia. N.G., 1905-08; apprentice Gen. Electric Co., 1907-08; lt. CAC, 1908-13; elec. engr. and asst. gen. mgr. Olympic Power Co., 1914-15; recommd., 1916; served in Coast Arty., F.A., Insp. Gen's. Dept. and Q.M.C. as capt., maj., lt. col., col. and brig. gen.; was in charge $100,000,000 def. program, Panama, C.Z.; specialized in air field devel. for more than 20 yrs.; comdg. gen., Memphis Army Service Forces Depot during World War II; ret., 1946; now engring. and mgmt. cons. Awarded Liberty medal for service in France; Legion of Merit, World War II. Mem. Am. Soc. Heating and Ventilating Engrs. (chmn. research com. 1936-37, mem. gov. council since 1945), Am. Inst. E.E., Soc. Am. Mil. Engrs., Am. Legion, Mil. Order World War (past comdr.) council Boy Scouts Am. Clubs: Army and Navy Country (Washington): Army and Navy (Manila); Rotary, Engineers (Memphis); Tennessee. Writer tech. articles. Radio broadcaster and speaker. Home: Tru-Dan Acres, 4559 Stage Rd., Memphis, Tenn. Died Mar. 3, 1966.

DARGUE, HERBERT ARTHUR army officer; b. Brooklyn, N.Y., Nov. 17, 1886; s. Arthur Percy and Madeline (Newins) D., B.S., U.S. .fil. Acad., 1911; grad. Air Corps Engring. Sch., 1920, Command and Gen. Staff Sch., 1924, Army War Coll., 1929, Navy War Coll., 1930; m. Marie Virginia Salmon, Nov. 17, 1915, 1 son, Donald Salmon. Commd. 2d lt. C.A.C., U.S. Army, 1911, and advanced through the grades to maj. gen. U.S. Army, 1941; formerly command of Observers School, Air Corp, Post Field, Okla., comdg. gen. 19th Wing, 1938; comdg. 1st Air Force, Mitchell Field, New York since 1941. Decorated Distinguished Flying Cross, 1927. Mem. Daedalian, Early Bird Presbyterian. Mason (Shriner). Club: Army and Navy (Arlington, Va.). Home: 3215 Rowland Place N.W. Address: War Dept., Washington, D.C. Died Dec. 8, 1942.

DARKE, WILLIAM army officer; b. Philadelphia County, Pa., May 6, 1736; s. Joseph Darke; m. Sarah Delayea, 3 sons including Capt. Joseph, 1 dau. Served as cpl. in Rutherford Rangers during French and Indian Wars, 1758-59; capt. Va. Volunteers at beginning of Revolutionary War; captured at Battle of Germantown, 1777; aboard prison ship, N.Y. until 1780; recruited Berkeley and Hampshire (Va.) regts., 1781; served at siege of Yorktown; retired as lt. col.; mem. Va. Conv. to ratify U.S. Constn., 1788; elected mem. Va. Legislature, 1791, served only 3 days; resigned to accept commn., under Gen. Arthur St. Clair to fight Indians; wounded in defeat by Miami Indians, 1791; promoted brig. gen., given 8,000 acres of public lands for his mil. service. Died Jefferson County, Va., Nov. 26, 1801.

DARLING, CHARLES HIAL lawyer; b. Woodstock, Vt., May 9, 1859; s. Jason L. and Ellen L. (Paul) D.; A.B., Tufts, 1884, LL.D., 1903; m. Agnes Christmas Norton, Nov. 6. 1889 (died Jan. 27, 1941); children-Margaret Norton (Mrs. John Randall Roberts) (dec.), Alice Godfrey (Mrs. Hamilton Armstrong), Elizabeth Paul (Mrs. Donald Armstrong). Admitted to bar, 1886; municipal judge, 15 yrs.; pres. village of Bennington, 1895; mem. Gen. Assembly, Vt., 1896-97; asst. sec. of the navy, 1901-05; collector of customs, dist. of Vt., 1905-14; now pres. Am. Fidelity Co. Trustee Tufts Coll. State dir. Am. Red Cross Christmas membership drive, 1917, and for 3d Liberty Loan. Mem. Vt. Bar Assn. (pres. 1900). Zeta Psi (nat. pres. 1904), S.A.R. (pres. Vt. Soc.). Mason (33ff), Grand Master of Masons of Vt., 1914-16. Address: 184 S. Winooski Av., Burlington, Vt. Died Oct. 31, 1944.

DARLING, CHARLES KIMBALL lawyer; b. Corinth, Vt., June 28, 1864; s. Joseph and Mary Alice (Knight) D.; grad. Barre (Vt.) Acad., 1881; A.B., 1885, A.M., 1893, Dartmouth; cadet for 2 yrs. at U.S. Mil. Acad., West Point; LL.B., 1896, Boston U. Law Sch.; m. Elizabeth R. Holmes, 1903. Admitted to bar, 1896, and began practice in Boston; instr. criminal law, Boston Univ. Law Sch., 1896-99; U.S. marshal for Dist. of Mass., 1899-1908; clk. U.S. Circuit Court of Appeals, 1st Circuit, U.S. Circuit Court and U.S. Dist. Court, Dist. of Mass. 1908-14; also U.S. commr.; referee in bankruptcy, Suffolk Co. Dist., 1914 - . Has been prominent in mil. affairs, 1887 - , when he was apptd. sergt. maj. 6th Regt. Mass. Vol. Militia, adjt., 1889, maj., 1893; served in Spanish-Am. War as sr. field officer of regt.; elected and commd. col. of regt. after it again became part of M.V.M.; retired brig. gen., M.N.G., 1904. Comdr. in chief Sons of Veterans, 1897-98. Died Dec. 29, 1926.

DARLING, CHARLES WILLIAM soldier, historical writer; b. New Haven, Conn., Oct. 11, 1830; s. Rev. Charles Chauncey D.; ed. N.Y. Univ.; became mem. mil. cabinet of Gov. E. D. Morgan, N.Y.; aide on staff Gen. B. F. Butler, Army of the James; mil. engr.-in-chief, N.Y., on staff of Gov. R. E. Fenton, with rank of brig. gen.; m. Angeline E. Robertson. Was several yrs. pres. Y.M.C.A., Utica, N.Y.; corr. sec. Onedia Hist. Soc.; writer on hist. subjects; received decoration for gratuitous service rendered in connection with hist. literature from Soc. of Science, Letters and Art of London. Home: Utica, N.Y. Died 1905.

DARLING, JOHN AUGUSTUS ("AUGUST MIGNON"), soldier; b. Bucksport, lMe., June 7, 1835; s. Amos Buck and Caroline (Hooper) D.; grad. Pa. Mil. Acad., 1849; m. Encarnacion Yniguez, Jan. 28, 1866; 2d, Clara L. Hastings, Oct. 22, 1895. Commd. 2d lt. U.S. Arty., Aug. 5, 1861; 1st lt., May 31, 1862; hon. mustered out, Jan. 1, 1871; apptd. capt. arty., Apr. 24, 1878, with former rank and date of commn. from Dec. 9, 1867; assigned to 1st Arty., Mar. 20, 1879; maj. 5th Arty., July 1, 1892; transferred to 3d Arty., Oct. 7, 1896; retired at his own request, being 62 yrs. of age, June 7, 1897; advanced to rank of lt. col. retired, by act of Apr. 23, 1904. Bvtd. capt. and maj., Mar. 13, 1865, "for gallant and meritorious services during the war." Has published many well-known vocal and instrumental compositions in U.S. and Europe, under pen-name August Mignon. Home: Bucksport, Me. Deceased.

DARLING, SID L(OUIS), trade assn. exec.; born West New York, N.J., Aug. 9, 1894; s. John Sidney and Abigail Bates (Crossley) D.; student N.Y.U. Law Sch., 1914-16; m. Mabel Elizabeth Burridge, Sept. 22, 1920; children—Bruce Burridge, Laird Burridge (dec.). Began as law student, clk. Marshall VanWinkle, Jersey City; then credit mgr. Republic Rubber Co., credit dept. B.F. Goodrich Rubber Co.; asst. treas. George Borgfeldt & Co., N.Y. City; then exec. vice president Nat.-Am. Wholesale Lumber Assn. Mem. Nat. Distbn. Council, U.S. Dept. Commerce. Served from private to capt. U.S. Army, 1917-19, Mem. Am. Soc. Assn. Execs., Nat. Assn. of Wholesalers (Washington trustee), N.Y. Lumber Salesmen's Assn. (hon.), Hoo-Hoo, Delta Chi. Republican. Presbyn. Mason (32 deg., K.T., Shriner). Club: Nylta (N.Y. City). Author articles in lumber trade jours. Home: Leonia NJ Died Aug. 6, 1971; buried Fairview Cemetery, Fairview NJ

DARLINGTON, CHARLES GOODLIFFE, pathologist: b. Bklyn., Jan. 28, 1892; s. Gustavus Cornelius and Kate Annabel (Bearns) D.; student Haverford Coll., 1909-10; M.D., Medico Chirurgical Coll. of Phila., 1915; m. Mabel Heinz, June 16, 1915; 1 dau., Annabel (Mrs. Ricker). Intern Flushing (L.I.) Hosp., 1915, Met. Hosp., N.Y.C., 1916; pathologist, serologist Bellevue Hosp., N.Y.C., 1917-19; asst. pathology N.Y.U. Coll. Medicine, 1919, instr., 1920, asst. prof., 1923, asst. prof. pathology Coll. Dentistry, 1925, asso. prof., 1932, prof. pathology, 1934-, dir. Undergraduate Cancer Teaching, Coll. Dentistry; asst. pathologist N.Y. Founding Hosp., 1920, asso. pathologist, 1926, pathologist, 1935-39; pathologist St. Vincent's Hosp., N.Y.C., 1922-24; pathologist, dir. Pathology Lab., Muhlenberg Hosp., Plainfield, N.J., 1924-53, now cons. tissue pathology; pathologist Beekman-Downtown Hosp., N.Y.C., 1926-47, Somerset Hosp., Somerville, N.J., 1928-48; cons. pathologist Seton Hosp., N.Y.C., 1940-43; cons. oral pathologist VA Hosp., N.Y.C., 1954-. Served from 1st lt. to capt., U.S. Army, 1917-19, as col. AUS, 1943-45. Diplomate Am. Bd. Pathology. Fellow Coll. Am. Pathologists; mem. A.M.A., N.Y. Acad. Medicine, Acad. Medicine No. N.J., Am., N.J. socs. clin. pathologists, N.Y. State Soc. Pathologists, N.Y. Acad. Sci., N.Y. Path. Soc., Harvey Soc., Internat. Assn. Dental Research, Sci. Research Soc. Am., Am. Legion, Mil. Order World Wars, Res. Officers Assn., N.Y. Soc. Mil. and Naval Officers World Wars, S.R., Sigma Xi. Home: 802 Belvidere Av., Plainfield, N.J. Office: 421 First Av., N.Y.C. 10010. Died Nov. 5, 1960.

DARLINGTON, HENRY (VANE BEARNS) ret. clergyman; advt. exec.; b. Brlyn., June 9, 1889; s. Bishop James Henry and Ella L. (Bearns) D.; student Dickinson Coll., 1907, D.D., 1927; A.B., Columbia U., 1910; grad. Gen. Theol. Sem., 1913; grad. student Columbia; D.D., Greek Sem. of St. Athanasius, 1923; married Dorothy Stone-Smith, Nov. 24, 1920; children-Peter (USAFR), Henry (USNR). Deacon, 1913, priest, 1914. P.E. Church; curate St. Thomas' Church, New York, 1913-14; missionary in charge three chs. and founded Mission Serepta, 1914-15; rector St. Barnabas Ch., Newark, 1915-22, Ch. of the Heavenly Rest, N.Y., 1922-25, Ch. of the Heavenly Rest and Chapel of Beloved Disciple, 1925-50. Headmaster, Day School, Church of the Heavenly Rest, 1929-50; acct. exec. Necrgaard, Miller & Co., N.Y.C., 1951-54, limited partner Hill, Darlington & Co., N.Y.C., 1955—. Pioneer Ministry Spiritual Healing, and held regular services in the Parish, 1935-50. Organized, built and operated Turnpike Bridge Co., Delaware, N.J., 1914-26. Commd. 1st lt. chaplain N.A., Feb. 18, 1918; chaplain Coast Defense, East N.Y.; chaplain 50th C.A.C., 1st Army, A.E.F., France; hon. discharged, Feb. 1919; commd. capt. chaplain, N.Y. Nat. Guard. Feb. 28, 1924; assigned junior chaplain 44th Inf. Div. N.J. Nat. Guard, 1924; promoted chaplain major, June 12, 1933, advanced to senior; transferred to chaplain major 27th Div. N.Y. Nat. Guard; resigned, Sept. 1940; recommd. sr. chplain lt. col., Hdqrs. N.Y. Guard, Nov. 1940; promoted col., Jan. 1945; permanent chaplain, association ex-members of Squadron A.; transferred back to N.Y. Nat. Guard, promoted brig. gen., Oct. 1949; now on state reserve list. Chmn. Protestant Council's Commission in Ministry to Veterans and Service Personnel. Chaplain general S.A.R., 1938-41, also various posts Am. Legion. Dir. N.Y. Co. Red Cross, 1949—; mem. N.Y. Co. Red Cross blood bank, 1950—; mem. veterans com., N.Y. Welfare Council. Decorated Officer Order of George I of Greece; received 10 and 15 Year medal New York National Guard, 10 and 15 yr. medal Squadron A, 10 yr. medal N.J. Nat. Guard. Formerly trustee Bard College, 1925-40; trustee The Protestant-Episcopal School. Member Society Colonial Wars, Sons Revolution, Society of Cincinnati (chaplain Rhode Island Soc.), Huguenot Soc., Pilgrims, Mil. Order Foreign Wars (chaplain gen., 1951), Mil. Order World Wars (chaplain, 1947). Mil . Chaplains Assn. U.S.A. (pres. 1952), S.A.R., N.Y. Chpater Mil. and Naval Officers World War, St. Nicholas Soc., Sojourners, St. Andrews Soc., Phi Delta Theta, Mason (32ff, K.T., Shriner grand chaplain, N.Y.). Clubs: Union, Columbia U. Author of many pamphlets, sermons and the like. Address: 2 E. 93rd St., N.Y.C. 28. Died Dec. 20, 1955; buried Woodlawn Cemetery.

DARLINGTON, THOMAS physician; b. Brooklyn, Sept. 24, 1858; s. Thomas and Hannah Anne (Goodlife) D.; C.E., and Ph.B., New York Univ.; Litt.D. from Juniata (Pa.) Coll. 1924; M.D.; Coll., Physicians and Surgeons (Columbia), 1880; m. Josephine A. Sargeant, June 9, 1886 (died 1890); children-Clinton Pelbam, Dorothea. Practiced Newark, N.J., 1880-82, New York, 1882-88, Bisbee, Ariz., 1888-90, New York, since 1891. Commr. and pres. New York Bd. of Health, 1904-10; mem. New York State Workmen's Compensation Commn., 1914-15; cons. physician N.Y. Foundling Hosp. Formerly lecturer indsl. hygiene, Stevens Inst., Tech., and Fordham U. Sanitary engr. N.Y. City Dept. of Health until January 1, 1934. Trustee, 1st v.p. Met. Savings Bank (New York); dir. Morris Plan Bank. Chmn. Mayer's Com. on Sanitation and Harbor Pollution, 1927-28. Trustee N.Y. City Mission Society, also trustee of Grant Monument Association. Maj. Med. Corps, U.S. Army, 1917-18. Asst. to pres. Am. Iron and Steel Institute. Fellow A.A.A.S., N.Y. Acad. of Science; mem. Soc Med. Jurisprudence, A.M.A., Am. Institute, Am. Climatol, and Clin. Asso., Am. Assn. for Promoting Hygiene and Pub. Baths (v.p.), Nat. Inst. of Social Science (v.p.), Harvey Soc., Internat. Sunshine Soc. (care of blind children), Med. Soc. of County of N.Y., N.Y. Acad. Medicine, Greater N.Y. Med. Assn. (v.p.), Physicians Mut. Aid Assn., Sachen Tammany Soc. (Grand Sachem), Thomas Hunter Assn. (pres. 1923-24, 1929-37), Alumni N.Y. Univ., N.Y. Chamber of Commerce (hon. physician), N.Y. Soc. Mil. and Naval Officers World War. Huguenet Soc., St., Nicholas Soc., Soc. Colonial Wars, S.R., Alpha Mu Pi Omega; hon. mem. Kings County Med. Soc. Deacon 1st Presbyterian Ch., trustee Archdeaconry of New York, 1905-11. Club: Iroquois (New York). One of 14 exec. members Congress of Physicians and Surgeons, 1907-39. Writer on med. and climatol. subjects and sanitation. Home: R.D. No. 1, Monticello, N. Y. Died Aug. 23, 1945: buried in Woodlawn Cemetery, New York.

DARNALL, CARL ROGERS army officer; b. Weston, Tex., Dec. 25, 1867; s. Joseph Rogers and Mary Ellen (Thomas) D.; student Carlton Coll., Bonham, Tex., and Transylvania U., Lexington, Ky.; M.D., Jefferson Med. Coll., Phila., 1890; grad. Army Med. Sch., Washington, D.C., 1897; m. Annie Estella Major, Apr. 27, 1892; children - Joseph Rogers, William Major, Carl Robert. Commd. 1st lt. and asst. surgeon, U.S.A., Oct. 26, 1896, and advanced through grades to col., May 15, 1917; brig. gen., Dec. 5, 1929; comdr. Army Med. Center, Washington, D.C., 1929-31, retired Dec. 31, 1931. Served in Spanish-Am. War, Philippine Insurrection, Boxer Rebellion, World War. Fellow Am. Coll. Surgeons. Awarded: D.S.M. (U.S.). Died Jan. 18, 1941.

DARNALL, MARCY BRADSHAW editor; b. nr. Edgar, Ill., Jan. 27, 1872; s. Aaron and Arietta (Bradshaw) D.; ed. Northwestern Normal Sch., Stanberry, Mo., and under pvt. tutorage; m. Lutie Milliken, Jan. 23, 1899; children-Dorothy (dec.), Louise (Mrs. Albert L. Martin) (dec.), Marcy B. Jr. (dec.). Contbr. to music publs., 1897-1905; editor Daily Citizen, Key West, Fla., 1906-13, 1920-21; mem. Fla. Ho. of Rep., 1912-13; postmaster Key West, 1913-21; editor and pub. Herald, Florence, Ala., since Jan. 1, 1922; editor Darnall's Newspaper Service; won first honors in contest for "best weekly newspaper." Chgo., 1923; 2d honors, 1926, 27 and 28 in Nat. Editorial Assn. contests for "greatest community service"; 1st honors, 1926, 27 and 28 in Nat. Editorial Assn. contests for "greatest community service"; 1st honors and silver trophy, same assn., 1929; Hanson trophy for best weekly newspaper in Ala., 1930. Served as pvt. 20th U.S. Inf., Santiago Campaign Spanish-Am. War 1898; bandmaster 9th U.S. Arty. Band, 1901-06; lt. (s.g.) USNRF, World War I; was comdg. officer Key West Naval Tng. Camp, exec. officer and navigator U.S.S. Tallapoosa and sr. watch and div. officer Battleship Louisiana. Mem. Nat. Editorial Assn. (v.p. Ala., 1927-32), nat. council Nat. Econ. League, Ala. Press Assn. (pres., 1930-31), Am. Legion (past post comdr.), United Spanish War Vets. (Past camp comdr.), Civil Legion (life-founder mem.), Pi Gamma Mu. Democrat. Episcopalian. Mason (K.T. 32ff, Shriner), Elk. Clubs: Civitan (pres. 1924), Elks, Florence Golf and Country. Home: Florence, Ala. Died Jan. 18, 1960; buried Greenview Meml. Gardens, Florence.

DARRACH, WILLIAM (DAR'RA), surgeon; b. Germantown, Phila., Pa., Mar. 12, 1876; s. William and Edity Romeyn (Aertsen) D.: grad. The Hill Sch., 1893; A.B., Yale, 1897, hon. A.M., 1920; A.M., M.D., Columbia, 1901 (1st Harsen prize), D.Sc., 1929; LL.D., St. Andrews U., 1928; D.Sc., Jefferson, 1930; m. Florence Borden, May 22, 1907; children-Edith, William Effie Brooks (dec.), Judith (dec.). Interne, 1901-03, asso. attending surgeon, 1913-16, Presbyn. Hosp.; demonstrator anatomy, 1903-09, instr. surgery, 1903-16, prof. of clinical surgery since 1916, and dean of the med. faculty, 1919-30, dean emeritus since 1930, Coll. Phys. and Surg. (Columbia); attending surgeon Vanderbilt Clinic, 1903-06; 2d asst. attending surgeon, 1906-08, 1st asst. 1908-10, jr. surgeon, 1910-13, Roosevelt Hosp.; dir. 1st surg. div., Bellevue Hosp., 1916-19; attending surgeon, Presbyn. Hosp., to 1946, now cons. surg.; cons. surg. Neurol. Inst., N.Y. Orthopedic Dispensary and Hosp., Greenwich, Beckman St. Babies', Sloane, Willard Parker, Morristown Memorial, N. Westchester hosps., Neuro-Psychiatric Inst. of Hartford (Conn.) Retreat. Captain Med., May 10, 1917, later major and lt. col. N.A., col. M.C., U.S. Army; sailed for France, May 14, 1917; comdg. officer, Base Hospital 2, U.S.A. (No. 1 General Hospital, B.E.F.), February 20-July 30, 1918; consultant surgeon 42d Division, A.E.F., later asst. consultant 1st Corps then 1st Army, then sr. consultant 3d Army; participated in Passchendael Campaign, B.E.F., and Château-Thierry, St. Mihiel, Meuse-Argonne campaigns, A.E.F.; hon. discharged, Apr. 12, 1918; col. M.C., U.S. Civilian cons. to Surg. Gen., and Vets. Administrn. Trustee, Fay Sch. Fellow Am. Coll. Surgeons (mem. bd. govs.), Chicago Surg. Soc. (hon.), Am. Assn. Surgery of Trauma (hon.); mem. Am. Acad. Orthopedic Surg.; mem. A.M.A., Assn. Am. Anatomists, Am. Surg. Assn. (pres. 1944), N.Y. Surg. Soc., Soc. Clin. Surgery (pres. 1929-31), N.Y. State Med. Soc., N.Y. County Med. Soc., Société de Chirurgiens de Paris, N.Y. Acad. of Medicine, Société Internationale de Chirurgie, Nat. Research Council (sub-com. on orthopedics), A.A.A.S., Am. Philos. Soc., Soc. Colonial Wars, Psi Upsilon, Phi Beta Kappa, Sigma Xi, Alpha Omega Alpha, etc. Republican. Episcopalian. Clubs: Century, Manursing Island. Contbr. articles on surgery, anatomy and med. edn. Home: Greenwich, Conn. Office: 180 Fort Washington Av., New York, N.Y. Died May 24, 1948.

DARRAH, THOMAS W(ALTER) army officer; b. Marquette, Kan., July 11, 1873; s. Samuel Jones and Mary (Temperly) D.: grad. U.S. Mil. Acad., 1895, Army Sch. of the Line, 1920, Gen. Staff Sch., 1921, Army War Coll., 1923; m. Rose Wood, Apr. 19, 1899; children-Marion Maxwell (Mrs. Warren D. Brewster), Jean West (Mrs. Woodlief Thomas). Commd. 2d lt. inf., U.S. Army, 1S95, advanced through grades to brig. gen., 1931; with subsistence dept. U.S. Army, 1901-05; instr. dept. chemistry U.S. Mil. Acad., 1907-11; sr. regtl. instr. O.T.C., Fort Benjamin Harrison, Ind., 1917; participated in Champagne-Marne Defensive, Aisne-Marne, Oise-Aisne and Meuse-Argonne offensives, World War; chief of staff, 4th Corps Area, 1924-26; comd. 34th Inf., U.S. Army, 1926-28; chief to staff, 3d Corps Area, 1928-31; comdg. Pacific sector Panama Canal Dept., 1932-34; retired, 1937. Decorated two Silver Star Medals for gallantry in action. Santiago, Cuba. Legaspi, Luzon, P.I. Home: 122 E. 82d St., N.Y.C. Died Jan. 21, 1955; buried Arlington Nat. Cemetery.

DASHER, CHARLES LANIER, JR., army officer; born Savannah, Ga., July 11, 1900; s. Charles Lanier and Eloise (Wilder) D.; student George Washington U., 1919-20; B.S., U.S. Mil. Acad., 1924; grad. F.A. Sch., 1930, Command and Gen. Staff Coll., 1940; m. Helen Catherine Rowzee, Feb. 10, 1925; children—Beverly Anne, Charlene Catherine. Commd. 2d lt. U.S. Army, 1924, advanced through grades to maj. gen., 1953; successively instr. tactics, instr. gunnery, exec. officer F.A. Sch., Ft. Sill, Okla., 1940-43; arty. officer 3d Armored Corps. Camp Polk, Ia., 1943; asst. arty. officer 19th Corps, 1943-44; comdg. officer 32d F.A. Brigade, 1944-45; arty. comdr. 75th Div. Arty., 1945; corps arty. comdr. 18th Corps (airborne), 1945; comdr. Rome area Allied Commd., 1945-47; mil. attache, Spain; 1947-50; asst. div. comdr. 8th Inf. Div., 1951-52; 3d Inf. Div., 1952; div. comdr. 24th Inf. Div., 1952-53; dep. comdr. 5th Army, 1954-55, U.S. Comdr., Berlin, 1955-57, Caribbean, 1958-60. Decorated D.S.M., Legion of Merit with 2 oak leaf clusters, Bronze Star medal with two oak leaf clusters. (V), Purple Heart (U.S.); Legion of Honor, Croix de Guerre with palm (France); Order of Orange Nassau (Dutch); Croix de Guerre with palm (Belgium); Ulchi Distinguished Service medal with gold star (Korea); Presdl. Unit Citation; grand officer Order of Crown (Italy); UN Service medal. Mem. Delta Tau Delta, Baronial Order Magna Charta. Home: Bethesda MD Died Oct. 31, 1968; buried Arlington Nat. Cemetery.

DASHIELL, WILLIAM ROBERT army officer; b. Mecklenburg Co., Va., Apr. 3, 1863; s. Thomas M.D.; grad. U.S. Mil. Acad., 1888; Army Sch. of the Line, 1909; Army War Coll., 1915; m. Ida L. Pearson, Nov. 6, 1889. Commd. add. 2d lt. 8th Inf., June 11, 1888; promoted through grades to col., May 15, 1917; brig. gen. N.A., Apr. 12, 1918. Served in Sioux Indian campaign, 1890-91; prof. mil. science and tactics, N. Ga. Agrl. Coll., 1892-95; at posts in Ariz. and Utah, 1896-99; in Philippines in comd. Co. C, 24th Inf., 1899; with Lawton's Column on march through San Isidor and San Joseé; again in Philippines, 1906-08; comd. Madison Barracks, N.Y., Feb.-May 1908; comdt. Va. Poly. Inst., 1909-11; at Ft. Sheridan, Ill., 1911-13, Texas City, Tex., 1913-14; Army War Coll., Washington, D.C., 1914-15, Ft. Shafter, H.T., 1915-17. Organized 43d Inf. at Ft. Douglas, Utah, Aug.-Nov. 1917; at Camp Pike Ark., 1917-18, New Orleans, Feb.-May 1918, Camp Forrest, Ga., May-June 1918, Camp Uton, N.Y., June-July 1918; arrived in France, July 26, 1918; apptd. comdr. 11th Brigade Inf., 6th Div., 5th Army Corps, A.E.F., July 1918; in training area to Sept. 3; in Vosges sector, Sept. 3-Oct. 12; comd. div. in support of 1st Army during Meuse-Argonne drive, Oct. 26-Nov. 6; occupied Artoise, Nov. 4-6; marched to Verdun, Nov. 6-12, 1918; left France for U.S., June 5, 1919; assigned sta. Schofield Barracks, H.T., July 12, 1919. Home: Norfolk, Va. Died Mar. 16, 1939.

DAUBIN, FREELAND ALLEN naval officer; b. Lamar, Mo., Feb. 6, 1886; s. Crittenden Clay and Ella Nettie (Bowen) D.; grad. U.S. Naval Acad., 1909; m. Elizabeth Virginia Scott, June 3, 1912; children—Freeland Allen, Elizabeth Bowen, William Scott, Scott Crittenden. Commd. ensign, USN, 1909, advancing through the grades to rear adm., 1941; served in battleships, destroyers and submarines; comdr. submarines Atlantic, 1942-44; commdt. Navy Yard, New York, 1944—, Decorated Distinguished Service Medal. Home: Quarters "B," Navy Yard. Office: Navy Yard, N.Y. Died Oct. 24, 1959; buried Fort Rosecrans Nat. Cemetery, San Diego, Cal.

DAVENPORT, FRANKLIN senator; b. Phila., Sept. 1755; studied law, Burlington, N.J. Admitted to bar, 1776, began practice of law, Gloucester City, N.J.; clk. Gloucester County Ct., 1776; enlisted as pvt. Capt. James Sterling's Co., N.J. Militia, commd. brigade maj., 1776; served in battles of Trenton and Princeton; apptd. brigade q.m., 1778; asst. q.m. Gloucester County, 1778-79; commd. col. N.J. Militia, 1779, then maj. gen.; prosecutor of please, 1777; moved to Woodbury, N.J., 1781; apptd. 1st surrogate Gloucester County, 1785; mem. N.J. Gen. Assembly, 1786-89; presdl. elector, 1792, 1812; served as col. N.J. Militia during Whisky Rebellion, 1794; apptd. brig. gen. Gloucester County Militia, 1796; mem. U.S. Senate from N.J. (filled vacancy), Dec. 5, 1798-99; mem. U.S. Ho. of Reps. from N.J., 6th Congress, 1799-1801; apptd. master in chancery, 1826. Died Woodbury, N.J., July 27, 1832; buried Presbyn. Cemetery, North Woodbury, N.J.

DAVENPORT, GEORGE army officer, trader; b. Lincolnshire, Eng., 1783. Moved to N.Y., 1804; sgt. U.S. Army, circa 1804-05, circa, 1814-15; supply agt. for Col. William Morrison; established trading business, Rock Island, 1825; with Am. Fur Co., 1826; served as col., acting q.m. during Black Hawk War; founder Davenport (Ia.), 1833; accompanied Sauk and Fox

Indian chief delegation to Washington, D.C., assisted in negotiating 2d Black Hawk purchase,1837. Murdered by robbers, July 4, 1845.

DAVENPORT, JOHN congressman; b. Stamford, Conn., Jan. 16, 1752; grad. Yale, 1770; studied law. Taught at Yale, 1773-74; admitted to bar, 1773, began practice of law, Stamford; mem. Conn. Ho. of Reps. 1776-96; served with commissary dept. Continental Army during Revolutionary War, commd. maj., 1777; mem. U.S. Ho. of Reps. (Federalist) from Conn., 6th-14th congresses,1799-1817. Died Stamford, Nov. 28, 1830; buried North Field (now Franklin Street) Cemetery.

DAVENPORT, RICHARD GRAHAM rear adm., U.S.N.; b. Washington, D.C., Jan. 11, 1849; s. Capt. Henry Kollock (U.S.N.) and Jennie Brent (Graham) D.; apptd. from Ga., Sept. 29, 1864, and grad. U.S. Naval Acad., 1869; instrn. in torpedoes and electricity at torpedo station, Newport, R.I., 1875 and 1881; ordnance instrn. duty, Washington, D.C., Navy Yard, in winter 1880-81; attended course of lectures in internat. law and naval science, Naval War Coll., Newport, terms of 1887 and 1902; m. Serena Hall Gilman, Nov. 20, 1884. Commd. ensign U.S.N., July 12— tiring after more than 42 yrs.' active service, June 30, 1907, as commodore, while in command of 1st class battleship Georgia. On shore duty served as aid to rear adm. representing Navy Dept. at Centennial Expn., Phila., 1875-76; on temporary duty at Chicago Expn., 1893; served as mem. Bd. Civ. Service Examiners for Nautical Experts. Pres. permanent Gen. Court Martial, also navigation and equipment officer and sr. mem. bd. of inspection, Labor Bd. and Wages Bd., Navy Yard, Washington, D.C., May 1902-Aug. 1906, also mem. Naval Examining and Retiring bds., 1906; asst. to chief of Bur. of Navigation and in charge of the detail of officers, Bur. of Navigation, 1897-98, and in charge from time to time of various divisions of the Hydrographic Office, Bur. Navigation; afloat served as a midshipman and as watch and division officer, navigating and exec. officer in N. Atlantic, S. Atlantic, Pacific, Asiatic, Training and European squadrons, also as aid on staff of comdr.-in-chief of Asiatic Sta., served as flag lt. to Commodore J. C. Watson, during war with Spain, 1898-99, 2d in command of fleet blockading on coast of Cuba and later comdr.-in-chief Eastern Squadron; was attached to and abroad U.S.S. Oregon, off Santiago, Cuba, when Spanish gen. comdg. capitulated; as a lt. comdr. in command U. S.S. Fishhawk, investigated radius of dispersion of star fish in waters of Narragansett Bay, and in 1898-99, with party of scientists aboard, made biol. survey of waters around island of Puerto Rico and vicinity, and as comdr. in 1900-02 comd. U.S. training ship Essex and as capt. comd. battleship Georgia at opening of Jamestown Expn., 1907. Awarded West India Campaign Medal, War with Spain, 1898-99, and (Admiral) Sampson Medal, with bars for naval engagements. During World War on active duty, Jan. 26, 1918-June 1, 1919, at Navy Yard, Brooklyn, as sr. mem. Permanent Bd. of Investigation. Home: Washington, D.C. Died May 30, 1926.

DAVENPORT, WALTER, journalist; b. Talbot County, Md., Jan. 7, 1889; s. John and Mary Elizabeth (Dillon) D.; ed. in prep. schs.; student U. of Pa., 2 yrs.; m. Barbara Scollard Brown, Oct. 16, 1919; children—Michael, Anthony. Mem. original staff, Liberty Mag., 1923-24; gen. journalistic writer, specializing in politics, Collier's magazine, 1925, asso. editor 1925-46, editor, 1946-48, became asso. editor and columnist 1948. Served as capt., 111th Infantry, 28th Div., A.E.F., during World War I. Clubs: The Players, Dutch Treat (New York); National Press (Washington). Author: Power and Glory: The Story of Boies Penrose, 1931; (with James C. Derieux) Ladies, Gentlemen and Editors, 1960. Home: Southern Pines NC Died Dec. 9, 1971; cremated.

DAVIDSON, JAMES HAMILTON lawyer; b. Burlington, O., Jan. 25, 1839; s. James and Mary Frances (Combs) D.; A.B., Ohio Wesleyan, 1861. A.M., 1864; m. Abigail Ashley Lamb, July 1, 1861. Enlisted pvt. Co. B, 14th Ky. Inf., 1861; promoted 1st lt. and capt.; promoted maj. 49th Ky. Inf., 1863; col. 122d U.S. C.T., 1864; hon. discharged, 1866; lt. U.S.A., 1866; declined. In fall of 1864 was pres. mil. bd. to examine all applicants for commns. in U.S.C.T. at Lexington, Ky., and was asst. supt. of orgn. of colored troops in Ky. Removed to St. Paul, 1866; city editor Daily Press (now Pioneer Press) until 1870; admitted to bar, 1867; gen. counsel N. Western Union Packet Co., 1870. and later Keokuk No. Line Packet Co. and other corps. until 1885; practiced law, Chgo., 1895-1906: returned to St. Paul, 1906. Platform lectr., debater, campfire talker. Chmn. Minn. State Waterways Commn., 1910-11. Republican. Methodist. Mem. G.A.R., Loyal Legion. Address: Pioneer Bldg., St. Paul. Deceased.

DAVIDSON, JAMES WOOD clerk U.S. Treasury Dept., author; b. Newberry Co., S.C., Mar. 9, 1829; s. Alexander and Sarah J. D. D.; grad. S.C. Coll. (now U. of S.C.), 1852 (A.M., 1855). Prof. Greek, Mt. Zion Collegiate Inst., Winnsboro, S.C., 1854-59; then taught the classics in Columbia, S.C.; was adjt., 13th regt., S.C. vols., in Stonewall Jackson's army corps, under Lee in Va., during Civil war; after war engaged in journalism; moved to Washington; 1873-84, lived in New York; m. Mrs. Josephine Allen, 1884, and moved to Lake Worth, Dade Co., Fla.; mem. Fla. State Constl. Conv., 1886; legislature, 1887; is still a citizen there, though from 1887 clerk in Treasury Dept., residing in Washington. Author: The Living Writers of the South, 1869; A School History of South Carolina. Home: West Palm Beach, Fla. Died 1905.

DAVIDSON, JOHN WYNN army officer; b. Fairfax County, Va., Aug. 18. 1823; s. William Benjamin Davidson; grad. U.S. Mil. Acad. 1845; m. Miss McGunnegle. Served in battles which secured possession of So. Cal. during Mexican War, 1846; commd. capt., 1855; refused commn. in Confederate Army, 1861; commd. brig. gen. U.S. Volunteers, 1862; brevetted lt. col. and col. U.S. Army, 1862; commanded brigade Army of Potomac during Peninsular campaign, 1862; commanded St. Louis dist. Army of S.E. Mo., 1862; commanded Army of Ark., 1863-64; chief of cavalry div. W. Miss., 1865; assisted in capture of Little Rock, Ark.; brevetted brig. gen., also maj. gen., 1865; served in Insp. Gen.'s Dept. of Mo., 1866; prof. mil. sci. and tactics Kan. Agrl. Coll., 1868-71; commd. col. 2d Cavalry, 1879. Died St. Paul, Minn., June 26, 1881.

DAVIDSON, LYAL AMENT navy officer; b. Muscatine, Ia., Dec. 2, 1886; s. Joseph Trimble and Judith (Ament) D.; B.S., U.S. Naval Acad., 1910, M.S., Columbia, 1917; m. Carolyn Gwathmey, June 3, 1916; children-William Gwathmey, Judity Ament, Caroline Tayloe. Commd. ensign 1911 and advanced through grades to rear adm. 1941; comdr. 9th Destroyer Div., U.S. Fleet, 1934-36; comdg. officer U.S.S. Relief, 1938-39, U.S.S. Omaha, 1939-40; comdr. Cruiser Div. 8, U.S. Atlantic Fleet; comdr. cruisers Atlantic Fleet; Task Force comdr. assaults on French Morocco, Sicily, Italy and Southern France; retired with rank of vice adm., 1946. Prof. naval science and tactics U. Mich., 1940-41, U.S. Naval War Coll., 1942. Decorated D.S.M. with gold star, Legion of Merit with gold star, Mexican Service Medal, Victor Medal, 2d Nicaraguan Campaign Mil. Order of the Bath (British), mentioned in dispatches (Eng.), Officer Legion of Honor, Croix de Guerre with palm (French). Mem. U.S. Naval Inst., Am. Soc. Naval Engrs., Quarterdeck Soc. (Univ. Mich.). Clubs: Rotary, Army and Navy (Washington), University (Michigan). Home: 2009 34th St., Washington 8. Died Dec. 29, 1950; buried Arlington Nat. Cemetery.

DAVIDSON, ROYAL PAGE educator: b. Somerville, N.J.; s. Harlan Page and Adelaide S. (Ford) D.: grad. Northwestern Mil. Acad., 1889; studied Mass., Agrl. Coll.: U. of Wis.; m. Clara M. Colwell, July 4, 1892. Comdt., 1891-1911, supt. since 1912, Northwestern Mil. & Naval Acad., Lake Geneva, Wis. Col. Res., U.S. Army. Conglist. Mem. S.A.R., Delta Upsilon (Wis. Chapter): pres. North Central Academic Assn., 1914; sec.-treas. Assn. of Mil. Colls. and Schs. of U.S., 1919-21, pres. 1925. Inventor first military automobile in U.S., 1889; later designed field hospital, radio and other military equipment. Contributor to numerous publications on military and pedagogical subjects. Clubs: Union League, University of Wisconsin, Army and Navy (Chicago); Big Foot and Lake Geneva (Wis.). Country. Home: Avon Park, Fla. Address: Northwestern Military and Naval Academy, Lake Geneva, Wis. Died Jan. 16, 1943; buried on grounds of Northwestern Military and Naval Academy, Lake Geneva.

DAVIDSON, WARD FOLLETT elec. and mech. engring.; b. Commonwealth, Wis., Oct. 21, 1890; s. Otto Conrad and Charlotte S. (Dickinson) D.; B.S., U. Mich., 1913; M.S., 1920; m. Elizabeth Thurber Bostwick, Aug. 17, 1917; children-Ward F., Elizabeth Sargent (Mrs. Ralph Smith-Johannsen). Student, jr. engr. Westinghouse Electric & Mfg. Co., 1914-16; instr. in elec. engring. U. Mich., 11 1916-17, 19-20, asst. prof., 1920-22; dir. research Bklyn. Edison Co. and Consol. Edison Co. of N.Y., since 1922. Cons. to chmn. and dep. exec. officer Nat. Def. Research Com., 1941-46; cons. Smaller War Plants, 1943-46. Awarded Presdl. Certificate of Merit. Served as lt., later capt. C.E., U.S. Army, 1917-19; with A.E.F. in Eng., France and Germany; maj., Engr. Res., 1919-42. Sec. conf. on elec. insulation NRC, 1927-39, chmn. 1939-48; mem.-at-large Div. Engring. and Industrial Research, NRC, 1950-54; chmn. com. on electric power cables Am. Standards Assn., 1927-54; chmn. joint com. on plant coordination, Edison Elec. Inst., 1933-37; mem. U.S. delegation Internat. Electro-tech. Commn., Torquay, 1938; cmhn. engring. sub-com. U.S. Nat. Com., Conference international des Grande Reseaux Electriques á Haut Tension (Cigre). Fellow Am. Inst. E.E. (chmn. com. on basic scis. 1936-38; chmn. com. on research, 1938-40, chmn. com. on nucleonics 1950-52), Am. Soc. M.E.; asso. fellow Inst. Aero. Scis.; mem. Instn. Elec. Engrs. (London), I.R.E., Instn. Mech. Engrs. (London), Am. Phys. Soc., Am. Chem. Soc., Am. Meteorol. Soc. Am. Geophys, Union, Sigma Xi, Tau Beta Pi. Clubs: Engrs. (N.Y.); Cosmos (Washington); Manhasset Bay (N.Y.) Yacht. Author numerous tech. papers, including several on nuclear (atomic) power, Home: 12 Summit Rd., Port Washington, L.I., N.Y. Office: 4 Irving Place, New York 3, N.Y. Died July 12, 1960.

DAVIDSON, WILLIAM LEE army officer; b. Lancaster, Pa., 1746; s. George Davidson; m. Mary Brevard. Commd. maj. 4th N.C. Regt., 1776; joined Washington's Army in N.J., 1776, participated in battles of Brandywine, Germantown, and Monmouth; commd. lt. col., 1777; brig. gen. in command Salisbury (N.C.) dist., 1780; detached by Gen. Greene to interrupt passage of Cornwallis across Catawba, 1781. Killed in action at Cowan's Ford Mecklenburg County, N.C., Feb. 1, 1781.

DAVIE, WILLIAM RICHARDSON officer, gov. N.C.; b. Egremont, Cumberlandshire, Eng., June 20, 1756; s. Archibald Davie; grad. with 1st honors Princeton, 1776; m. Sarah Jones,1782, 6 children.. Helped raise cavalry troop, nr. Salisbury, N.C., 1777-78, commd. lt., then capt., maj.; licensed to practice law, 1780; commissary gen. under Gen. Nathanael Greene in Carolina campaign, 1780; apptd. commissary gen. N.C. Bd. of War, 1781; lawyer, riding N.C. circuits, 1782; mem. N.C. Legislature, 1786-98; gov. N.C., 1793-99; a founder U. N.C.; influential in obtaining state laws, in sending reps. to Annapolis and Phila. constl. convs., also in ceding Tenn. to Union and fising of state boundaries; commanded N.C. troops, 1797; chmn. boundary commns., 1798; brig. gen. in undeclared naval war with France, 1798-99; peace commr. to France, 1799; under presdl. appointment negotiated Tuscarora treaty, 1802; 1st pres. S.C. Agrl. Soc. Died nr. Waxhaw Church, S.C., Nov. 29, 1820.

DAVIES, CHARLES educator; b. Washington, Litchfield County, Conn., Jan. 22, 1798; son of Thomas John Davies; grad. U.S. Mil. Acad. 1815; LL.D. (hon.), Geneva (N.Y.) Coll., 1849; m. Mary Ann Mansfield. Brevetted 2d lt. U.S. Army, 1815, assigned to Engr. Corps., 1816, resigned soon after; prof. mathematics, natural and exptl. philosophy U.S. Mil. Acad., 1816-37; toured Europe, 1836-37; prof. mathematics Trinity Coll., 1837-41; paymaster with rank of maj. West Point, 1841-46; prof. mathematics, philosophy U. City N.Y., 1848-49; prof. higher mathematics Columbia, 1857-65, emeritus prof. mathematics, 1856-76. Died Fishkill-on-Hudson, N.Y., Sept. 17, 1876.

DAVIES, HENRY EUGENE army officer; b. N.Y.C., July 2, 1836; s. Henry Ebenezer and Rebecca (Tappan) D.; grad. Columbia Law Sch., 1857; m. Julia Rich, Aug. 10, 1858. Admitted to N.Y. bar, 1858; commd. capt., then maj. 5th N.Y. Inf., U.S. Army, 1861, lt. col., 1862, col., 1863; brig. gen. U.S. Volunteers, 1863, maj. gen., 1865, resigned, 1866; pub. adminstr. N.Y.C., 1866-69; asst. dist. atty. So. dist. N.Y., 1870-72. Author: Ten Days on the Plains, 1871; General Sheridan, published posthumously, 1895. Died Middleboro, Mass., Sept. 6, 1894.

DAVIS, ABEL b. Chicago, Dec. 26, 1874; s. Peter and Keile (Hochsberger) D.; LL.B., Northwestern U., 1901, LL.D., 1930; m. Marjorie Mayer, Dec. 28, 1922; children - Florence, Abel, Jean A. Admitted to Ill. bar, 1901; mem. Gardner, Stern, Anderson & Davis until 1904, Stern, Anderson & Davis, 1910-12. Mem. Ill. Ho. of Rep., 1902-04; Cook County recorder, 1904-12; mem. Ill. State Constl. Conv., 1920; v.p. Chicago itle & Trust Co., 1912-31, chmn. bd., 1931 - . Served as pvt. in Cuba, Spanish-Am. War; maj. on Mexican border; col. 132d Inf. in France, World War; brig. gen. 66th Inf. Brig., Ill. N.G.; retired from Ill. Nat. Cuard, Jan. 1935. Mem. Chicago Plan Commn.; trustee Century of Progress Expn., Chicago, 1933, Chicago Community Trust, John Crerar Library. Awarded .S.M., D.S.C. (U.S.); Officer Legion of Honor (France). Republican. Reformed Jewish religion. Mason. Home: Glencoe, Ill. Died Jan. 7, 1937.

DAVIS, ADDISON D. army officer; b. New Richmond, O., Jan. 23, 1883; s. Robert Allen and Frances Marshall (Dimmitt) D.; student Miami U., 1900-02, U. Cin., 1902-04; M.D., Jefferson Med. Coll., 1906; student Army Med. Sch., 1908-09, Med. Field Service Sch., 1934; hon. ScD., Dickinson Coll., 1943; m. Alma Virginia McAllister, Oct. 16, 1907; children-Addison D., Robert McAllister. Began as physician, 1907; commd. 1st lt. M.C., U.S. Army, June 2, 1909, advanced through grades to brig. gen., Dec. 19, 1940; served as lt. col. during World War I. Awarded medals for Philippine Campaign, Mexican Punitive Expdn., World War I, Yangste Valley Campaign, 1932; Am., European Theatre medals, World War II, Legion of Merit and Legion of Honor of Haiti. Mem. A.M.A., Assn. Mil. Surgeons, Beta Theta Pi, Nu Sigma Nu. Address: 119 Edisto Av., Columbia, S.C. 29205. Died June 8, 1965: buried Florence (S.C.) Nat. Cemetery.

DAVIS, ALEXANDER MACDONALD army officer; b. Ft. Adams, R.I., Sept. 16, 1868; s. Brig. Gen. Edward (U.S.A.) and Margaret J. (Davis) D.; grad. U.S. Mil. Acad., 1892; m. Cecil McCormick, of Baltimore, Sept. 21, 1892. Commd. 2d lt. 8th Cav., June 11, 1892; 1st lt. 4th Cav., Jan. 20, 1899; capt. commissary subsistence, Jan. 3, 1901; maj., Mar. 17, 1904: lt. col. Q.M. Corps, July 1, 1916; col., Oct. 5, 1917. Prof. mil. science and tactics, Vincennes (Ind.) U., 1897-98; aide to Brig. Gen. W. J. McKee, 1898; participated in various actions in P.I., 1900-01; again in P.I., 1902-03, 1912-14. Mem. Mil. Order Loyal Legion. Episcopalian. Clubs:

Army and Navy (Washington); Fort Monroe (Ft. Monroe, Va.); University (Kansas City, Mo.). Home: 38 W. 68th St., N.Y.C.

DAVIS, ALVA RAYMOND educator: b. Cascade, Ia., Feb. 15, 1887; s. John William and Elizabeth (Orr) D.; A.B., Pomona Coll., 1912, D.Sc. (h.c.), 1948; Ph.D., Washington U., 1915; LL.D., U. Cal., 1957; m. Eugenie Scharle, Aug. 31, 1916; children-Alva R., Jr., Margaret Ellen (Mrs. Robert Imrie). Rufus J. Lackland research fellow Washington U., 1912-15; Yale fellow Bishop Mus., Honolulu, 1925-26; instr. Woods Hole Biol. Lab., summers, 1913-14; research asst. Mo. Bot. garden, 1915-16; instr. Pomona Coll., summer 1915: asst. prof. botany and plant pathology U. Neb., 1916-19; instr. soil chemistry and bacteriology U. Cal., 1919, asst. prof. plant nutrition, 1921, asso. prof. plant physiology, 1925-29, prof. since 1929; chmn. dept. botany, 1936-47, dean Coll. Letters and Sci., 1947-55, vice chancellor, 1955-56, ret., 1956: acting chancellor, July-Aug., 1953, Aug.-Sept. 1954. Mem. Dept. State-ICA Mission U. Concepcion, Chile, 1959; chmn. Nat. Acad. Scis. survey Chilean univs., 1960. Adv. com. Regional Park Bd., San Francisco Bay Area; mem. exec. com. Assn. Land Grant Colls. and Univs. Chmn. bd. trustees Willis Lynn Jepson Found. Served in USN, 1903-07; capt. U.S. Army (CAC), 1917-19; lt. col. (CAC, AA), 1942-45; comdt. enlisted specialists schs., Camp Callan; dir. Centralized schs. Anti-aircraft Replacement Tng. Center, Fort Bliss, Tex., 1944-45. Mem. acad. adv. bd. (chmn.) U.S. Maritime Acad., Kings Point, L.L., N.Y., Knight first class Royal Norwegian Order St. Olaf. Fellow A.A.A.S. (mem. exec. com. Pacific Div., 1932-37); mem. Soc. Plant Physiologists (pres. Pacific div. 1946-47), Bot. Soc. Am., Cal. Bot. Soc., (pres. 1940-41), Western Soc. Naturalists (v.p. 1932), Phi Beta Kappa, Sigma Xi (pres. U. Cal. chpt. 1937). Clubs: Sierra, Sierra Ski, Faculty (pres. U. Cal. 1946); Commonwealth, Bohemian (San Francisco). Author numerous tech. pubs. on various phases plant metabolism. Editor Univ. of Cal. Bot. series, 1938-40. Home: 1159 Keeler Av., Berkely 8, Cal. Died July 15, 1965; buried Pacific View Meml. Park, Corona del Mar, Cal.

DAVIS, ARTHUR CAYLEY naval officer; b. Columbia, S.C., Mar. 14, 1893; s. Ellery William and Annie (Wright) D.; student U. Neb., 1909-11; B.S., U.S. Naval Acad., 1915; student Naval Postgrad. Sch., 1920; M.A., U. Chgo., 1922; m. Elizabeth Holden; Sept. 16, 1946; children-Arthur Cayley, John Holden; m. 2d Katherine Shoemaker, Apr. 8, 1928; m. 3d Eunice Tompkins, Jan. 10, 1947. Commd. ensign USN, 1915, advanced through grades to vice adm., 1951; spl. qualifications in math., gunnery and aviation ordnance; naval aviator since 1923; aircraft carrier comdr., 1939, 42 (U.S.S. Enterprise), chief of staff 5th Fleet, 1944-45; comdr. Carrier Task Force, 1945; dep. asst. sec. def. for Internal Security Affairs, 1952-55, ret. as adm., 1955; now exec. v.p. M. ten Bosch, Inc. Awarded Navy Cross, D.S.M. (2), Legion of Merit (3), Presdl. Unit Citation, Victory Medals, World War I and II, Am. Def. Service, Pacific, Atlantic campaign medals. Mem. Sigma Xi, Delta Upsilon. Club: Chevy Chase, Md. Home: 3915 Thornapple St., Chevy Chase, Md. 20015. Died Feb. 10, 1965; buried Arlington Nat. Cemetery.

DAVIS, CHARLES EDWARD LAW BALDWIN brig. gen.; b. New Haven, Conn., Feb. 16, 1844; s. Charles S.A. and Mary Jeannette (Downs) D.; 1 yr. in acad. dept., Yale, 1861-62; grad. U.S. Mil. Acad., 1866; unmarried. Second lt. engrs., U.S.A., June 18, 1866; 1st lt., Mar. 7, 1867; capt. Sept. 12, 1877; maj., Apr. 7, 1888; lt. col., May 3, 1901; col., Oct. 15, 1905; brig. gen., Jan. 29, 1908; retired, Feb. 16, 1908. Served in the depts. of the Atlantic Gulf, and Lakes, Pacific Coast, and P.I. Home: Atlantic City, N.J. Died June 1, 1925.

DAVIS, CHARLES HENRY naval officer; b. Boston, Jan. 16, 1807; s. Daniel and Lois (Freeman) D.; m. Harriet Mills, 1842, 6 children in including Charles Henry, Anna Cabot, Evelyn. Commd. midshipman U.S. Navy, 1824, lt. , 1827, comdr., 1854; served as chief of staff, capt. of fleet in expdn. under Dupont which captured Port Royal, S.C., 1861; exec. head Bur. of Detail for selecting, assigning officers during Civil War; assumed command Upper Mississippi Gunboat Flotilla above Ft. Pillow, 1862: commd. chief Bur. of Navigation, 1862; commd. rear adm., 1863; a founder Nat. Acad. Scis., 1863; supt. Naval Observatory, 1864-66, 70-73; commanded Brazilian Squadron, 1867-69, Norfolk (Va.) Navy Yard, 1870-73. Author: The Coast Survey of the United States, 1849; Narrative of the North Pole Expedition of the U.S.S. Polaris, 1876. Died Washington, D.C., Feb. 18, 1877.

DAVIS, CHARLES HENRY rear adm.; b. Cambridge, Mass., Aug. 28, 1845; s. late Rear Admiral C. H. D.; apptd. from Mass., and grad. U.S. Naval Acad., 1864. Ensign, Nov. 1, 1866; master, Dec. 1, 1866; lt., 1868; lt. comdr., 1869; comdr., 1885; capt. 1898; rear admiral, U.S.N., Aug. 24, 1904. Served on various stas. and duties; connected with the various expdns. for determination of the difference of longitude by means of submarine telegraph cables; supt. Naval Obs., 1897-98; comd. auxiliary cruiser, Dixie, N. Atlantic Squadron, Apr.-Sept., 1898; returned to Naval Obs.; comd. Alabama, 1902; div. comdr. battleship squadron, 1904; U.S. commr. Internat. Commn. of Inquiry on N. Sea incident, Paris, 1904-05; comdr. 2d Squadron Atlantic Fleet, 1905; retired by operation of law, Aug. 28, 1907. Author: Chronometer Rates as Affected by Temperature and Other Causes; Telegraphic Determination of Longitude; Life of Rear Admiral Davis, 1899; etc. Apptd. mem. Perry's Victory Centennial Commn., 1912. Died Dec. 27, 1921.

DAVIS, CHARLES K(RUM) corp. official; b. Lebanon, Pa., Jan. 7, 1889; s. Walter Scott and Mary M. (Krum) B.; student U. of Ill., 1907-08; LL.D. (hon.), Lebanon Valley Coll., 1950; m. Bertha B. Buscher, July 15, 1912; children-Roberta L. (Mrs. Robt. A. Massey), Dorothy (Mrs. Harold A. Mitchell), Charles Krum, and William Roy. Chemist with Aluminum of Am., 1905-06, American Steel Foundries, 1906-07, Am. Smelting & Refining Co., 1908-10; gen. foreman South America, 1911-15; supt. E.I. du Pont de Nemours & Co., Hopewell, Va., 1915-19; dir. of mfr., later asst. gen. mgr., pres. and dir. DuPont Viscoloid Co., 1919-31; pres., gen. mgr. and dir. Roessler & Hasslacher Chem. Co., 1932-33; pres., gen. mgr. and dir. Remington Arms Co. of Bridgeport, 1933-54, chmn. bd., 1954—; chmn. bd. First Nat. Bank & Trust Co. of Bridgeport, Rem-Cru Titanium Inc.; hon. chmn. bd. Rem-Cru, Inc., Dir. Bridgeport Hosp., Winterthur Mus.; dir. Hartford-Springfield Post. Mem. (life) Am. Ordnance Assn. (vice chmn. council, chmn. small arms and small arms ammunition com.). Founder mem. and former trustee Am. Wildlife Found. Mem. adv. bd. Ordnance Dist. (Springfield, Mass.). Awarded Rice Gold Medal by Army Ordnance Assn., 1947; Certificate of Appreciation from U.S. Ordnance Dept., and from U.S. War Dept., Fellow in perpetuity Met. Mus. of Art, N.Y.C. Mem. Am. Inst. of Chem. Engrs., Nat. Rifle Assn. (life), Soc. Preservation New Eng. Antiquities (hon. life mem.), U. of Ill. Alumni Assn., Ill. U. Found., Conn. Hist. Soc. (council of Fairfield), New Haven Colony Hist. Assn. (hon. life), Pewter Collectors Club Am. Rep. Mason. Shriner. Club: Brooklaw Country. Home: Winton Park, Fairfield, Conn. Office: 1241 Main St., Bridgeport 2, Conn. Died Jan. 9, 1968.

DAVIS, CHARLES LUKENS brig. gen.; b. New Brighton, Pa., Feb. 27, 1839; s. Benjamin and Elizabeth (Hamill) D.; ed. Lawrenceville (N.J.) High Sch.; m. Margaretta M. S. Bowers, 1880. Civ. engr. on rys. in Pa. and Del. before Civ. War; pvt. Commonwealth Arty. of Pa. and 2d lt. 31st Pa. Inf., Aug. 20, 1861; promoted through grades to col. 5th U.S. Inf., July 11, 1901; brig. gen., Jan. 26, 1903, Bvtd. maj. vols., Apr. 9, 1865, "for gallant and meritorious services during operations resulting in the fall of Richmond"; capt. U.S.A., Mar. 2, 1867, for same in campaign from the Rapidan to the James; maj. U.S.A., Mar. 2, 1867, for same in siege of Petersburg. Chief signal officer, Dept. of Va. and N.C., 1862; mem. exam. bd. of officers at New Orleans for appmt. in signal corps, 1863; served with Army of Potomac, 1863-65; chief signal officer Army of Potomac, Jan. 1, 1865; served on Mexican and Indian frontiers, 1866-93; coll. duty, N.C., 1893-97; with gov. N.C., organizing and discharging vols., 1898-99; mil. collector customs. customs, P.R., 1899-1900; comd. Governor's Island, N.Y., 1900-01; Philippines, Apr. 1901-Dec. 1902; retired, Feb. 10, 1903. Home: Schenectady, N.Y. Died Nov. 10, 1919.

DAVIS, DWIGHT FILLEY ex.-gov. gen. P.I.; b. St. Louis, July 5, 1879; s. John Tilden and Maria (Filley) D.; A.B., Harvard U., 1900; LL.B., Washington U., 1903; m. Helen Brooks, Nov. 15, 1905 (died Oct. 10, 1932); children-Dwight F., Alice Brooks (Mrs. Roger Makins), Cynthia (Mrs. William McC. Martin). Helen Brooks (Mrs. Allen Hermes); m. 2d, Pauline Sabin, May 8, 1936; President of Davis Estate. Mem. Pub. Baths Commn., 1903-06; PUblic Library Bd., 1904-07; bd. control Mus. Fine Arts, 1904-07 and 1911-12; Public Recreation Commn., 1906-07; mem. St. Louis Ho. of Dels., 1907-09; Bd. Freeholders, 1909-11; City Plan Commn., 1911-14; park commr., 1911-14. Capt., 5th Mo. Inf., May 16, 1917; maj., Nov. 1917; lt. col., Oct. 1918; col., O.R.C., 1923. Director general Army Specialist Corps, 1942. Mem. executive committee Nat. Municipal League, 1908-12. Playground and Recreation Assn. America, 1910-14; dir., Civic League, 1904-07; v.p. St. Louis. Playgrounds Assn., 1905-08; dir. Tenement House Assn., 1907-09, Soc. Prevention Tuberculosis, 1909-12; mem. Bd. of Overseers, Harvard, 1915-21, 1926-32; dir. War Finance Corp., 1921-23; asst. sec. of war, 1923-25, sec., 1925-29; governor gen. of the Philippine Islands, 1929-32. Mem. bd. dirs. Lehman Corporation, 1941-42. Chmn. bd. trustees Brookings Instn. since 1939. Awarded D.S.C., Mar. 1923, "for extraordinary heroism" in operations at Baulny and Chaudron Farm France, Sept. 29-30, 1917; also awarded Legion of Honor (France), 1932. Republican. Baptist. Member Alpha Delta Phi, Phi Delta Theta, Phi Delta Phi. Comdr. St. Louis Post No. 4, Am. Legion, 1919, Clubs: Noonday Club (St. Louis, Mo.); Chevy Chase, Metropolitan, Burning Tree, Alibi (Washington, D.C.); University (New York). Home: Meridian Plantation, Tallahassee, Fla., and Washington, D.C. Died Nov. 28, 1945; buried in Arlington National Cemetery.

DAVIS, EDMUND JACKSON gov. Tex.; b. St. Augustine, Fla., Oct. 2, 1827; m. Ann Britton, 1858. Dep. collector of customs on the Rio Grande under the Filmore administrn., 1850-52: dist. atty. Rio Grande Valley Dist., 1853-55; judge Dist. Ct. of Austin, Tex., 1855-61; commd brig. gen. U.S. Army after Battle of Mansfield, 1861; del. Tex. Constl. Conv., 1866; pres. Tex. Reconstrn. Conv., 1868-69; gov. Tex., 1869-74. Died Austin, Feb. 7, 1883.

DAVIS, EDWARD brig. gen.; b. Louisville, Ky., July 7, 1845; s. Benjamin Outran and Susan Fry (Speed) D.; grad. U.S. Mil. Acad., 1867; m. Margaret J. Davis, Sept. 18, 1867. Commd. 2d lt. 5th Ky. Vol. Cav., Sept. 20, 1862; resigned, Nov. 2, 1863; commd. 2d lt. 3d U.S. Arty., June 17, 1867; 1st lt., Apr. 14, 1873; grad. Arty. Sch., 1876; capt., Sept. 1, 1896; maj. asst. adj. gen. vols., May 12, 1898; hon. disch. from vols., Apr. 15, 1899; maj. arty. corps, U.S.A., July 1, 1901; asst. adj. gen., Dec. 3, 1902; lt. col. Arty. Corps, Jan. 23, 1904; asst. adj. gen., June 22, 1904; brig. gen., Apr. 11, 1905; retired at own request after 40 yrs.' service, Apr. 12, 1905. Bvtd. 1st lt., June 17, 1867, "for gallant and meritorious services in battle of Chickamauga, Ga., Sept. 19 and 20, 1863." Died Aug. 2, 1918.

DAVIS, EDWIN G., lawyer; b. Samaria, Ida., July 9, 1874; s. Thomas J. and Elizabeth (Williams) D.; grad. U.S. Mil. Acad., 1900; m. Elsie Poll, of Salt Lake City, Utah, July 23, 1900. Served in Philippines, 1900-1; instr. law, U.S. Mil. Acad., 1903-7; capt. U.S.A., retired, Feb. 28, 1910; maj., lt. col. and col. J.A. Gen.'s Dept., Washington, D.C., World War. Rep. candidate for gov. of Ida., 1916, for U.S. senator, 1920; U.S. dist. atty. for Ida. since Jan. 1, 1922. Episcopalian. Elk. Kiwanian. Author: A Text Book of Constitutional Law, 1905. Home: Boise ID

DAVIS, GEORGE BURWELL chief asst. office Commissary-Gen. of Subsistence, U.S.A.; b. Buffalo, N.Y., Oct. 9, 1862: grad. West Point, 1886; assigned 23d inf.; promoted 5th inf., 1803; transferred 4th inf.; apptd. capt. commissary of subsistence, 1897; maj. Dec. 13, 1900. Grad. Inf. and Cav. Sch., 1891; during Spanish-Am. war was chief asst. to commissary-gen. with rank of col.; depot commissary, Manila, 1900-01. Address: Office Commissary-Gen., Washington.

DAVIS, GEORGE GILMAN ch. ofcl.; b. Boston, Aug. 13, 1881; s. Charles Griffin and Martha Anne Harrison (Sawtelle) D.; prep. edn., Boston Latin Sch. and Hopkinson Sch. at Boston; A.B., Harvard, 1903; student Harvard Law Sch., 1903-06; m. Helen Palmer Davidson, Feb. 21, 1906 (dec. Mar. 1910); children-Eliot, Gilman, Helen (Mrs. Kenneth L. Grant); m. 2d, Mildred Ann Albee, June 28, 1921. Admitted to Mass. bar, 1905; exec. sec. Am. Unitarian Assn., 1926-28, 30-37, dir. dept. ch. extension and maintenance, 1937-49, treas., 1949-52, now financial cons. Sec. treas., trustee Lombard Coll., Galesburg, Ill., 1928, pres., 1929-40 (coll. now functioning in co-operation with Meadville Theol. Sch., Chgo. Served from pvt. to maj. U.S. Army. 1917-18, in St. Mihiel and MeuseArgonne offensives; asst. chief of staff, 8th Army Corps; asst. to port comdr. Army of Occupation, Coblenz, Germany; lt. col. O.R.C., 1919-29. Dir. Summer Insts. for Religious Edn., Isles of Shoals, N.H., 1923-27. Trustee and treas. Unitarian Found.; dir. Religious Edn. Assn.; dir. Beacon Press, Inc., Religious Arts Guild, Christian Register, Inc. Trustee and vice-chmn. Meadville Theol. Sch., clk. Unitarian Ch. of Larger Fellowship. Life mem. Sigma Alpha Epsilon, Pi Gamma Mu, Phi Kappa Phi. Home: 137 Garden St., Needham 92, Mass. Office: 25 Beacon St.,Boston 8. Died July 23, 1957.

DAVIS, GEORGE ROYAL dir. gen. World's Columbian Expn., 1890-94; b. Palmer, Mass., 1840; prepared for college at Williston Sem., but enlisted as private, 8th Mass., 1861; served through war; rose to col., 3d R.I. cav.; received staff appointment regular army, but resigned, 1871; located in Chicago; mem. Congress, 1879-85; treas. Cook Co., Ill., 1886-90; long a member and officer Nat. Republican Committee; m. Gertrude Schulin, 1867. Home: Chicago, Ill. Died 1899.

DAVIS, GEORGE WHITEFIELD maj. gen.; b. Thompson, Conn., July 26, 1839; s. George and Elizabeth (Grow) D.; ed. Nichols Acad., Dudley, Mass., and State Normal Sch., New Britain, Conn.; m. Carmen Atocha, Apr. 30, 1870. Q.m. sergt., 11th Conn. Inf., Nov. 27, 1861; disch., Apr. 5, 1862; 1st lt. 11th Conn. Inf., Apr. 5, 1862; promoted through grades to brig. gen. U.S.V., May 4, 1898; hon. disch., Apr. 14, 1899; brig. gen. U.S.V., Apr. 14, 1899; col. 23d U.S. Inf., Oct. 19, 1899; brig. gen., Feb. 2, 1901; maj. gen., July 21, 1902. Bvtd.; Maj. vols., Mar. 13, 1865, "for faithful and meritorious services during the war." Asst. engr. in completion of Washington Nat. Monument, 1878-85; instr. in Inf. and Cav. Sch., Ft. Leavenworth, Kan., 1888-89; mgr. of a mfg. enterprise, Chicago, 1889-1900; mil. gov., Puerto Rico, 1899-1900; provost marshal gen. Div. of Philippines, 1901; comdg. Dept. of Mindanao and Luzon, P.I., 1901-02, Div. of Philippines, 1902-03; gen. mgr. and v.p. Nicaragua Canal Constrn. Co., 1900-03; retired by operation of law, July 26, 1903. Spl. duty in office of Sec. of War, 1903-06; pres. Bd. Publ. Official Records of Union and Confederate Armies, 1904-06; mem. Isthmian Canal Commn., 1904-05; gov. Panama Canal Zone, 1904-05; chmn. bd. of cons. engrs. on type of Panama Canal, 1905-06; E.E. and M.P. to Guatemala on spl. mission, 1907; spl. agt. Dept. of State of Govt. of Guatemala, 1913. Mem. Am. Nat. Red Cross (chmn. Central Com., 1907-15). Died July 12, 1918.

DAVIS, HOWLAND SHIPPEN, trustee; b. Seabright, N.J., Sept. 5, 1886; s. Howland and Anna Elizabeth (Shippen) D.; A.B., Harvard, 1908; LL.D. (honorary), Bard College, 1960; married Laura Suffern Livingston, Sept. 26, 1914; children—Howland, Catherine Livingston (Mrs. Oliver Gordon Stonington). Clerk, Blake Brothers and Co., New York, N.Y., 1908-15, partner, 1915-38; officer, New York Stock Exchange, 1938-48; executive vice pres., 1940-48; trustee Bank for Savings (New York), The Grant Foundation; member bd. directors W. T. Grant Company (New York). Past mem. Tivoli Bd. Edn. Trustee Bard Coll. Served as private, advancing to major, Headquarters 77th Division, A.E.F., World War I. Chairman Taconic (New York) State Park Commission; chmn. bd., Leake and Watts Children's Home (N.Y. City); manager New York Institute for Edn. of Blind; v.p. Fedn. Protestant Welfare Agys. N.Y. Mem. St. Paul's Ch. (vestryman). Clubs: Down Town Assn., Union (N.Y.C.). Home: Tivoli NY Died July 15, 1969; buried St. Paul's Ch., Tivoli NY

DAVIS, JEFFERSON pres. Confederate States Am.; b. Christian (now Todd) County, Ky., June 3, 1808; s. Samuel and Jane (Cook) D.; entered Transylvania U., 1821 (did not graduate); grad. U.S. Mil. Acad., 1828; m. Sarah Taylor (dau. Zachary Taylor), July 1835; m. 2d, Varina Howell, Feb. 26, 1845. Commd. 2d lt. U.S. Army, 1828; served on frontier, 1828-35, resigned commn., 1835; Miss. planter, 1835-45; mem. U.S. Ho. of Reps. from Miss., 29th Congress, 1845-46; resigned to participate in Mexican War, 1846, led advance regt. in attack on Monterey, resigned, 1846; mem. U.S. Senate from Miss., 1847-51; U.S. sec. of war under Pres. Franklin Pierce, 1853-57; mem. U.S. Senate, 1857-61, announced to Senate the secession of Miss. and his senatorial resignation, Jan. 21, 1861; commd. maj. gen. Miss. Militia, 1861; inaugurated pres. Confederate States Am. by Provisional Congress, Feb. 18, 1861; elected by popular vote, inaugurated, Richmond, Va., Feb. 22, 1862; policies promoted opposition and conflict between states' rights advocates and himself; suspected of planning emancipation of slaves; determined to demand independence for Confederacy following Battle of Gettysburg: fled from Richmond, Apr. 3, 1865; captured, Irwinville, Ga., May 10, 1865; imprisoned at Fortress Monroe, Va., 1865-67; indicted for treason, released on bond, May 14, 1867; last years of life spent in retirement and relative poverty at home provided by a bequest. Author: The Rise and Fall of Government, 2 vols., 1878-81. Home: "Beauvoir," Biloxi, Miss. Died New Orleans, Dec. 6, 1889; buried Hollywood Cemetery, Richmond.

DAVIS, JEFFERSON COLUMBUS army officer; b. Clark County, Ind., Mar. 2, 1828; s. William and Mary (Drummond) D.; m. Mariette Woodson Achon. Mem. 3d Ind. Regt. during Mexican War: brevetted 2d lt. 1st Arty., U.S. Army for gallantry at Battle of Buena Vista, 1848; commd. 1st lt., 1852; stationed Ft. Sumter at time of bombardment, 1861; commd. capt. 1st Arty., 1861; col. 22d Ind. Infantry Volunteers, 1861; brig. gen., 1861; commanded division at Battle of Pea Ridge and siege of Corinth; murdered Gen. William Nelson after quarrel in hotel lobby, Louisville, Tenn., 1862; returned to duty unpunished (because of his mil. service and polit. influence of Gov. Oliver P. Morton); commanded at Murfreesboro, Chickamauga, Sherman's march to sea and Carolinas' campaign; discharged from volunteer service, 1866; col. 23d Inf., U.S. Army, 1866; fought in Modoc War, Oregon, 1873. Died Chgo., Nov. 30, 1879.

DAVIS, JOHN congressman; b. Bucks County, Pa., Aug. 7, 1788; attended common schs. Lived in Md., 1795-1812; settled in what is now Davisville, Pa., 1812, engaged in farming and business pursuits; served from capt. to maj. gen. of militia in War of 1812; mem. U.S. Ho. of Reps. (Democrat) from Pa. 26th Congress, 1839-41; surveyor Port of Phila. (apptd. by Pres. Polk), 1845-49; del. to several Pa. and nat. Dem. convs. Died Davisville, Apr. 1, 1878; buried Davisville Baptist Ch.

DAVIS, JOHN LEE naval officer; b. Carlisle, Ind., Sept. 3, 1825; s. John Wesley and Ann (Hoover) D.: m. Frances Robinson, Dec. 12, 1855, 1 dau. Commd. midshipman U.S. Navy, 1841, lt. comdr., 1862; commanded gun boat Wissahickon in sining of Confederate ship Georgiana, Charleston Harbor, 1863; lt. comdr. in monitor Montauk, engaged in battles at fts. Sumter, Gregg, Moultrie, Battery Bee, 1863; commd. comdr., 1866, capt., 1873, commodore, 1882, rear adm., 1885; commanded flagship of European Squadron, 1877-78; commanded Asiatic Squadron, 1883-86; ret., 1887. Died Washington, D.C., Mar. 12, 1889; buried Rock Creek Cemetery, Washington.

DAVIS, JOHN MOORE KELSO brig. gen.; b. Washington, Jan. 31, 1844; s. Dr. A. McD. and Martha (Kelso) D.; 1st lt. 3d Md. Cav., July 1863; apptd., Sept. 1863, from Ark. and grad. U.S. Mil. Acad., 1867; honor grad. Arty. Sch., 1869; m. Fanny Sanger, June 7, 1870. Commd. 2d lt. 1st Arty., June 17, 1867; promoted through grades to brig. gen. U.S.A., May 25, 1907. Comd. Dept. of the Gulf, July 1907-Jan. 31, 1908; retired by operation of law, Jan. 31, 1908. Home: Hartford, Conn. Died May 20, 1920.

DAVIS, JOHN STAIGE plastic surgeon; b. Norfolk, Va., Jan. 15, 1872; s. William Blackford and Mary Jane (Kentie) Howland; Ph.B., Yale U., 1895, A.M., 1925; M.D., Johns Hopkins, 1899; m. Kathleen Gordon Bowdoin, Oct. 26, 1907; children-Kathleen Staige (Mrs. Charles E. Scharlett, Jr.), William Bowdoin (capt. Med. Corps, U.S. Army), Howland Staige (Lt. comdr. Naval Aviation). Surgeon, Baltimore, Md., since 1899; asso. prof. surgery, Johns Hopkins U. since 1923; visiting plastic surgeon, Johns Hopkins Hosp., Union Memorial Hosp., Hosp. for Women of Md., Children's Hosp. Sch. Served as capt., M.C., U.S. Army, 1917-19. Fellow Am. Coll. Surgeons; mem. Am. Surg. Assn. (vice pres. 1939), Am. Bd. of Surgery, Southern Surg. Assn. (pres. 1940), Am. Assn. for Surgery of Trauma, Interurban Surg. Soc., Surg. Research Soc., Am. Assn. Plastic Surgeons (pres. 1945). Chmn. Am. Board of Plastic Surgery. Democrat. Episcopalian. Clubs: Maryland, Yale (New York). Home: 215 Wendover Rd., Baltimore 18. Office: 701 Cathedral St., Baltimore 1, Md. Died Dec. 23, 1946.

DAVIS, JOSEPH JONATHAN congressman; b. nr. Louisburg, Franklin County, N.C., Apr. 13, 1828; attended Louisburg Acad., Wake Forest (N.C.) Coll., Coll. William and Mary; grad. law dept. U. N.C. at Chapel Hill 1850. Admitted to bar, 1850, began practice of law, Oxford, N.C., later in Louisburg; served as capt. Co. G., 47th Regt., Confederate Army, during Civil War; mem. N.C. Ho. of Reps., 1868-70; mem. U.S. Ho. of Reps. (Democrat) from N.C., 44th-46th congresses, 1875-81; apptd. justice N.C. Supreme Ct., 1887. Died Louisburg, Aug. 7, 1892; buried Oaklawn Cemetery.

DAVIS, JOSEPH ROBERT army officer; b. Woodville, Miss., Jan. 12, 1825; s. Isaac and Susan (Garthy) D.; grad. Miami U., Oxford O.; m. Miss Peyton, 1848; m. 2d, Margaret Green 1879; 3 children including Jefferson. Mem. Miss. Senate, 1860-61; commd. lt. col. 10th Miss. Regt., Confederate Army, 1861; commanded a brigade of Miss. troops Army of No. Va., 1862; commd. brig. gen. Confederate Army, 1862; served in battles of Cold Harbor, Gettysburg and Wilderness. Died Sept. 15, 1896.

DAVIS, MILTON FENNIMORE army officer, educator; b. Montorville, Minn., Nov. 15, 1864; s. Evan Richard and Julia Ann (Ryder) D.; grad. U.S. Mil. Acad., 1890; hon. M.A., U. of Ore.; m. Bessie Aitken Hall; children - Margaret Hall (wife of Frank A. Pattillo, U.S.A.), Dorothy (dec.), Helen Dorman, Milton F. Commd. 2d lt. cav., June 12, 1890; promoted through grades to maj., June 14, 1909 (retired); lt. col., ret., July 9, 1918; col. ret., May 29, 1921. Mapped Yosemite and Sequoia parks and Sierra Forest Reserve, 1891-96; explored Grand Canyon of the Colorado, 1895; adj. gen. 3d Brigade, Philippine Insurrection, 1900-03; exec. sec. of staff, Inf. and Cav. Sch., U.S.A., 1903-07; with Gen. Staff and aide to chief of staff, 1907-09; made comdt., sec. and treas. New York Mil. Acad., 1909, now supt. Served as chief of training and executive, U.S. Air Service, World War; brig. gen. A.C. Res., 1920. Silver star citation "for gallantry" at Battle of Santiago, 1898; D.S.M., World War. Sec. treas. New York Mil. Acad. Realty Co.; v.p. Cornwall Nat. Bank. Fellow Am. Geog. Soc. Mem. Chamber of Commerce of U.S. (nat. councillor), Hudson Valley Federated Chamber of Commerce (pres.); nat. councillor Boy Scouts America. Republican. Presbyn. Mason. Died May 31, 1938.

DAVIS, REUBEN congressman, army officer; b. Winchester, Tenn., Jan. 18, 1813; s. Rev. John Davis, M. Mary Halbert, Dist. atty. 6th Miss. Jud. Dist., 1835-39; judge Miss. High Ct. Appeals, 1842; served as col. 2d Miss. Volunteers in Mexican War; mem. Miss Legislature, 1855-57; mem. U.S. Ho. of Reps. (Democrat) from Miss., 35th-36th congresses, 1857-61; maj. gen. Miss. Militia, 1861; mem. Confederate Congress, 1861-64. Author: Recollections of Mississippi and Mississippians, 1889. Died Huntsville, Ala., Oct. 14, 1890.

DAVIS, RICHMOND PEARSON army officer; b. Statesville, N.C., June 23, 1866; s. Hayne and Mary Williams (Pearson) D.; grad. U.S. Mil. Acad., 1887; grad. torpedo course, Willets Pt., N.Y., 1889 (1st in class); m. Bertha Marie Bouvier. Commd. 2d lt. 2d Arty., June 12, 1887; promoted through grades to col., Jan. 24, 1914; brig. gen. N.A., Aug. 5, 1917; brig. gen. regular army, Dec. 1, 1922; major general, Oct. 4, 1927. Instructor, asst. prof. and acting prof. chemistry and electricity, U.S. Mil. Acad., 1891-96, 1898-1904, 1906; dir. Sch. Submarine Defense, Fort Totten, N.Y., 1904-06, Coast Arty. Sch., Ft. Monroe, Va., 1907-11; asst. chief C.A., 1911-12, 1915-16; assisted materially in development of coast arty. service, development of system of submarine mines; apptd. comdr. 162d F.A. Brigade, Camp Pike, Ark., Aug. 1917; comdr. 151st F.A. Brigade at St. Mihiel and Camp de Songe, France, 1918-19, also chief of arty., 9th Corps; comdr. coast defenses, Manila Bay, 1919-21; comdr. Coast Arty. Sch., Ft. Monroe, Va., 1921-22, 22d Brigade, Hawaii, 1922-29, retired, Dec. 22, 1929. Episcopalian. Died Sept. 16, 1937.

DAVIS, ROBERT COURTNEY army officer; b. Lancaster, Pa., Oct. 12, 1876; s. Thomas J. and Lydia (Leaman Audenreld) D.; grad. U.S. Military Academy, 1898; Sc.D., Washington and Jefferson College, 1941; m. Ruby Caroline Hale, Nov. 12, 1902.Commissioned 2d lt. 17th Inf., Apr. 26, 1898; promoted through grades to major gen., Sept. 1, 1922; brig. gen. N.A., June 26, 1918; col. U.S. Army, July 1, 1920; brig. gen., July 3,-1920; commission expired Mar. 4, 1921; maj. gen., the adj. gen., 1922, reappointed, 1926: retired July 1, 1927. Participated in campaign against Santiago de Cuba, 1898, taking part in battles of El Caney and San Juan, Philippine Insurrection, 1899-1901; with Rio Grande Expedition, later in numerous engagements with Filipino insurgents; instructor Department of Tactics, U.S. Military Academy, 1901-05; with Army of Cuban Pacification, 1906-09; a.d.c. to Major Gen. Barry, 1900-11; adj. U.S. Mil. Acad., 1911-12; inspector and instr. Philippine Scouts, 1914-16; duty office of the adj. gen., U.S. Army, 1917; arrived in France, July 28, 1917; asst. to adj. gen. A.E.F., Jan. 23-Apr. 30, 1918; apptd. adj. gen., A.E.F., May 1, 1918; returned to U.S. Sept. 8, 1919; designated by Sec. of War to take charge of Dept.'s part in administrn. of World War Adjusted Compensation Act, upon its passge, May 19, 1924. Exec. dir. N.Y. chapter, Am. Red Cross since 1932; pres. Assn. of Grads. U.S. Mil. Acad., 1936-38. Chmn. Commercial Radio Internat. Com. since 1942. Awarded D.S.M. (U.S.); Silver Star, with Oak Leaf Cluster (U.S.); campanion of the Bath (Great Britain); Comdr. Legion of Honor (France); Comdr. Order of the Crown (Italy); Comdr. Order of the Crown (Belgium); Grand Officer, Order of Prince Danilo (Montenegro); Order of La Solidaridad, 2d Class (Panama). Clubs: Knollwood Country (White Plains, N.Y.); Army and Navy, Chevy Chase (Washington, D.C.). Home: 277 Park Av. Office: 315 Lexington Av., New York, N.Y. Died Sep. 2, 1944.

DAVIS, SAM army scout; b. nr. Smyrna, Tenn., 1842. Joined Confederate Army, circa 1861; sent as scout into Union territory by Gen. Bragg to secure mil. information; captured by Union forces while returning, Giles County, Nov. 19, 1863: brought before Maj. Gen. Dodge of U.S. Army to explain how he received the information; sentenced to be hanged; uttered famous last words from scaffold: "If I had a thousand lives I would lose them all before I would betray my friends or the confidence of my informer." Hanged Nov. 27, 1863.

DAVIS, THOMAS FRANCIS army officer; b. N.Y. City, May 8, 1853; s. James and Mary A. (Lennon) D.; grad. U.S. Mil. Acad., 1875; m. Paulina S. Hart, May 12, 1886 (died 1910). Commd. 2d lt., 15th U.S. Inf., June 16, 1875; promoted through grades to brig. gen., May 16, 1913. Collector of customs, Santiago, Cuba, 1899; mil. sec. and adj. gen. by detail, 1905; gov. Lanao Dist., Mindanao Province, P.I., 1909; comd. 5th Brigade, 2d Div., U.S.A., Galveston, Tex., 1913-14, 6th Brigade, Texas City, Tex., and Naco and Douglas, Ariz., Feb. 1, 1914; comdg. Ariz. Dist. and 3d Provisional Inf. Div., Douglas, Ariz., to May 8, 1917, when retired by operation of law. Catholic. Home: El Paso, Tex. Died Dec. 10, 1935.

DAVIS, WILLIAM CHURCH army officer (ret.): b. nr. McGraw, N.Y., May 11, 1866; s. Samuel and Roxana (Brown) D.; ed. State Normal Sch., Cortland, N.Y., 1881-85; B.S., U.S. Mil. Acad., 1890; grad. U.S. Arty. Sch., 1894-96, U.S. Sch. Submarine Defense, 1903-04; m. Margaret Turner Schenck, Sept. 9, 1896; children-Margaret Brown, William Schenck, Samuel. Commd. 2d lt. U.S. Army, 1890, advanced through grades to maj. gen., 1942; ret. 1921. Served in U.S. Army, U.S. Vols. and O.R.C., in P.I., Europe, and U.S.; prof. mil. science Colo. State Agr. Coll., 1896-97; depot Q.M., Baltimore, 1898-99; in charge of Army Transport Service, Manila, 1899-1900; in command, Forts Revere and Strong, Boston Harbor, 1908-09, Fort Rosecrans, San Diego, Calif., 1913-14, Fort Barrancas, Pensacola, Fla., 1915-17; general staff, 1910-11, 20-21; in command artillery brigades 31 and 32 Europe, 1918-19, Decorated; D.S.M.; Spanish War; Filipino Insurrection; Victory (with 3 clasps); cited, in order of comdg. gen. 5th U.S. Army Corps, for service in Meuse-Argonne, France, 918. Hon. mem. bd. of dirs., A.R.C., Berkeley, Cal. Mem. Am. Legion, S.A.R. Republican. Home: 2440 Oregon St., Berkeley 5, Cal. Died Sept. 23, 1958; buried Presidio Cemtery, San Francisco.

DAVIS, WILLIAM THORNWALL ophthalmologist; b. Little Rock, Arkansas; son William Thornwall and Terese (Akin) D.; student Ky. Military Institute, 1890-92; M.D., George Washington, 1901; grad. U.S. Army Med. Sch., 1902-03, Univ. of Vienna, 1906. 12 Royal Ophthalmic Hosp., London, 190y; m. Reneé Tolson, 1912; children-William Joseph Graham, Roger Has Brouck, René Sheldon, Akin Thornwall. Interne Garfield Memorial Hosp., Washington, D.C., 1901-02; 1st lt., later capt. Med. Corps. U.S. Army, 1902-13 (under Gen. Leonard Wood, Moro campaigns, 1904-05; surgeon under Gen. Frank McCoy, Datto Ali Campaign, 1905); maj. Med. Corps, U.S. Army, World War; prof. ophthalmologh, U.S. Army Med. Sch., 1917-18; prof. same, George Washington, since 1920; sr. surgeon Episcopal Eye and Ear Hosp.; cons. ophthalmologist at Garfield, Columbia, Gallinger, Casualty hosps.; ophthalmologist in chief George Washington U. Hosp.; consultant in ophthalmology to the surg. gen. U.S. Army, Feb. 1943. Mem. advisory bd. Selective Service Draft, 1941. Mem. bd. dirs. Washington Loan & Trust Co. Official Orden Nacional de Merito Carlos J. Finley (Cuba). Fellow American College Surgeon; mem. A.M.A., Southern Med. Assn.,

Am. Acad. Ophthalmology and Otolaryngology, Med. Soc. of D.C., S.A.R., Mil. Order of Foreign Wars of U.S., Soc. of the Cinnati of State of Va., The Filson Club of Ky., Pan-Am. Med. Assn., Acad. of Medicine (Washington, D.C.), Mil. Order Carabao, Spanish Am. War Veterans, Am. Legion (A.P. Gardner Post), Phi Sigma Kappa, Sigma Xi. Episcopalian. Mason. Rotarian. Clubs: Army and Navy, Metropolitan (Washington); Chevy Chase (Maryland). Contributed papers read before Am. Acad. Ophthalmology, Ophthal. Sect. A.M.A., etc. Office: 927 Farragut Sq., Washington, D.C. Died June 16, 1944.

DAVIS, WILLIAM WATTS HART journalist; b. Southampton Twp., Pa., July 27, 1820; s. John and Amy (Hart) D.; grad. Norwich Univ., 1842; instr. Mil. Acad. Portsmouth, Va., 1842-44; admitted to bar, 1846; entered Harvard Law Sch., 1846, but left to enlisted in Mass regt. for Mexican War; mustered out at close, July 19, 1848, as capt.; practiced law 5 yrs. in N.M., 1853-57, as U.S. dist. atty., atty. gen., sec. of Ty., acting gov., supt. Indian affairs, and supt. pub. bldgs.; published Santa Fe Gazette (Spanish and English) 2½ yrs.; engaged in journalism, 1858 - ; comd. co., regt., brig., and div. in Civil War, reaching bvt. rank brig. gen.; shot 3 times; twice Dem. nominee for Congress, defeated with party; U.S. commr. Paris Expn., 1878; U.S. pension agt., Phila., 1885-89. Home: Doylestown, Pa. Died 1910.

DAVIS, WIRT brig. gen.; b. Richmond, Va., May 28, 1839; s. John F. and Delight T. D.; ed. Hampton-Sidney Coll. and U. of Va.; m. Anna J. Berry, 1884. Served as pvt. and corp. Co. K, 1st Cav., promoted through grades to col. 3d Cav., Jan. 10, 1900; retired at own request, after 40 yrs.' service, Apr. 29, 1901; advanced to rank of brig. gen. retired, by act. of Apr. 23, 1904. Bvtd.: "for gallant and meritorious services in Civ. War"; 1st lt., Sept. 19, 1863 (for Chickamauga); capt., Feb. 20, 1864 (cav. expdn. in Miss.); maj., Apr. 2, 1865 (capture of Selma, Ala.); also bvtd. lt. col., Feb. 27, 1900, "for gallant services on N. fork of Red River, Texas, Sept. 29, 1872," and in action against Indians in the Big Horn Mountains, Mont., Nov. 25, 1870. Died Feb. 10, 1914.

DAVISON, DONALD ANGUS army officer; b. San Carlos, Ariz., Oct. 26, 1892; s. Lorenzo Paul and Carolyn (Shannon) D.; student, Colgate Univ., 1910-11, B.S., U.S. Military Acad., 1915; m. Marjorie Risk, Dec. 28, 1920; children-Carolyn Maclean (Mrs. Hugh McCormick Hayden), Wilhemina Shannon, Margaret Angeline. Commd. 2d lt., 1915, and advanced through grades to brig. gen., 1942; Corps of Engrs., 1917-42; awarded Legion of Merit, 1943. Chief engr., Northwest African Air Force, 1943. Christian Scientist. Clubs: Army-Navy, Country (Washington, D.C.). Home: 3804 Fulton St. N.W., Washington, D.C. Died May 5, 1944.

DAVISON, EDWARD, poet; b. Glasgow, Scotland, July 28, 1898; s. Robert and Evelyn Mary (Ford) D.; foundation scholar, St. John's Coll., Cambridge Univ., Eng., 1921, B.A., 1921, M.A., 1925; hon. Litt.D., U. of Colorado in 1934; m. Natalie Eva Weiner, April 27, 1926 (dec. 1959); children—Peter Hubert, Lesley (Mrs. Forrest Perrin); married second to Rose Landver, July 26, 1960. Editor Cambridge (England) Review, 1920-22; editor The Challenge, London, 1922-24; general mgr. The Guardian, London, 1924-25; came to U.S., 1925; prof. English literature, Vassar Coll., 1926-27; editor "The Wits' Weekly," Saturday Review of Literature, 1928-30; engaged in lecturing, 1925-70. John Simon Guggenheim Memorial fellow in poetry, Europe, 1930; visiting prof. English lit., U. of Miami, Fla., 1934-35; dir. Writers' Conf. in the Rocky Mtns., Boulder, Colo., 1935-42; prof. English lit., U. of Colo., 1935-46. Served as ordinary seaman, advancing to paymaster sub-lt. Brit. Royal Naval Div., 1914-18; expert cons. to Sec. of War, 1943; commd. major, A.U.S., 1943 (Army Edn. and Information Div.); lt. col., dir. Army's re-edn. program for enemy prisoners of war, Provost Marshal Gen.'s Office, 1944-46. Awarded Army Commendation, Legion of Merit, 1946. Apptd. George M. Laughlin prof. English lit. and chmn. Eng. dept., Washington and Jefferson Coll., Washington, Pa., 1946, dean of college, 1947-49; prof. English, dean Sch. Gen. Studies, Hunter Coll., City U. N.Y., 1953-68, dean and professor emeritus, 1968-70. Member Poetry Society America (pres. 1955-56), Cum Laude Society (honorary). Author: Poems, 1920; Poems by Four Authors (collaborator), 1923; Harvest of Youth, 1925; Some Modern Poets, 1927; The Heart's Unreason, 1931; The Ninth Witch, 1932; Nine Poems, 1937; Collected Poems, 1940. Editor: Cambridge Poets, 1914-20, 1921. Home: New York City NY Died Feb. 8, 1970.

DAVISON, PETER WEIMER army officer; b. Waupun, Wis., May 15, 1869; s. James and Sarah (Weimer) D.; grad. U.S. Mil. Acad., 1892; m. Esther Fleming, Apr. 11, 1913. Commd. 2d lt. 22d Inf., June 11, 1892; 1st lt., Apr. 26, 1898; capt. a. q.-m. vols., lMay 12, 1900; hon. disch. vols., Mar. 21, 1901; capt. 26th Inf., U.S.A., Feb. 2, 1901; advanced through grades to col. N.A., Aug. 5, 1917; brig. gen. (temp.), Aug. 8, 1918-Oct. 31, 1919. Served on Gen. Staff, 1910; a.d.c. to Maj. Gen. J. Franklin Bell, 1911-12; with allied armies, Tientsin, China, fall of 1913; served in Mont., 1892-96, Neb., 1896-98; a.d.c. to Gen. Ludlow during Spanish-Am. War, serving in campaign in Cuba, and in action at El Caney and Santiago; with regt. in Philippines, 1899-1902, 1903-05, 1911-Sept. 1914; on Tex. border, 1914-15; in Alaska, 1908-10 and 1916-Sept. 1917; comd. 166 Depot Brigade, Oct. 1917-June 1918; comd. 8th Inf. to Sept. 1918, and as brig. gen. comd. 16th Div., Oct. 1918-Feb. 1919; comd. Ft. D. A. Russell, Cheyenne, Wyo., to May 1919; duty at Port of Embarkation, New York, May 1919. Recommended twice, 1899, for brevet, "for gallantry in action," in Philippine Campaign; awarded Naval Cross, "for distinguished services," 1919. Mason. Episcopalian. Died Feb. 12, 1920.

DAVISON, THOMAS CALLAHAN surgeon; b. Woodville, Ga., Nov. 13, 1883; s. Charles C. and Elizabeth (Calahan) D.; M.D., Emory U., Atlanta, 1906; m. Lucile Goodwin, Apr. 15, 1931; children-Betty, Margaret. Intern Ga. Bapt. Hosp., 1906-07; practiced Atlanta, 1907—; chief surg. service, Grady Hosp., 1928-40, chief staff, cons., 1940-53; pres., founder, Sheffield Cancer Clinic, 1934, attending, cons. surgeon, 1937—; chief staff, chief surg. service, Ga. Bapt. Hosp., 1940—; asso. prof. clin. surgery Emory U. Med. Sch. Served as col., U.S. Army M.C., World War I. Diplomate Am. Bd. Surgeons (mem. founders group), Am. Bd. Thoracic Surgery, Fellow A.C.S., Internat. Coll. Surgeons; mem. Fulton Co. Med. Soc. (pres. 1931), Med. Assn. Ga., So. Surgeons Assn., Southeastern Surgeons Congress (founder 1929; pres. 1939), A.M.A., Am. Goitre Assn. (pres. 1950), Am. Assn. Thoracic Surgeons, Am. Legion, Phi Chi. Club: Piedmont Driving. Contbr. over 100 articles to med. jours. Home: 25 Valley Rd. N.W. Office: 478 Peachtree St. N.E., Atlanta. Died Sept. 17, 1953; buried Westview Cemetery, Atlanta.

DAVISON, WILBURT CORNELL, pediatrician; b. Grand Rapids, Mich., Apr. 28, 1892; s. William L. (D.D.) and Mattie E. (Cornell) D.; A.B., Princeton, 1913; Sr. Demy (Rhodes scholar 1913-16), Magdalen Coll., Oxford, Eng., 1915-17; B.A., Oxford U., 1915, B.Sc., 1916, M.A., 1919; M.D., Johns Hopkins, 1917; D.Sc., Wake Forest Coll., 1932; LL.D., U. N.C., 1944, Duke, 1961; m. Atala Thayer Scudder, June 2, 1917; children—William Townsend, Atala Jane Scudder Levinthal, Alexander Thayer. Instr., asso. prof., acting head dept. pediatrics, asst. dean, Johns Hopkins Med. Sch., 1919-27; asso. pediatrician, acting pediatrician in charge, editor Bull. Johns Hopkins Hosp., 1919-27; dean, James D. Duke prof. pediatrics Duke Sch. Medicine, 1927-61; cons. Womack Army Hosp; mem. medico adv. bd. CARE; trustee Duke Endowment; v.p. bd. dirs. Doris Duke Found. Mem. div. med. scis. NRC, vice chmn. 1942-43; cons. office Surgeon Gen., U.S. Army; adv. group Armed Forces Med. Library; mem. com. on vets. med. problems; mem. com. atomic casualties NRC; mem. med. adv. com. N.C. Bd. Mental Health; mem. med. adv. panel Oak Ridge Inst. Nuclear Studies; mem. council chief cons. VA; mem. dean's com. Durham VA Hosp.; mem. N.C. gov.'s working com. Research Triangle Devel. Council, N.C. Nuclear Energy Adv. Com; dir. Playtex Park Research Inst.; med. adv. com. Research Found.; nat. adv. com. Chronic Disease and Health of Aged; trustee Ednl. Council Fgn. Med. Grad.; mem. Civilian Health and Med. Adv. Council; chmn. OSD Hosp. Planning Group. Served with AEC, 1914-15. France, Serbia; capt. M.C., U.S. Army AEF, 1917-19; served to col. AUS. Recipient Alvaranga prize, 1917. Master A.C.P.; mem. Am. Acad. Pediatrics, Am. Coll. Clin. Adminstrn. (hon.), Am. Pediatric Soc., Soc. for Pediatric Research, Am. Soc. Clin. Investigation, N.C. Pediatric Soc., Am. Acad. Gen. Practice (hon.), Assn. Pediatricians de Guatemala (hon.), Phi Beta Kappa, Sigma Xi, Omicron Delta Kappa, Alpha Omega Alpha (pres.). Democrat. Methodist. Clubs: Cosmos (Washington). Hope Valley Country, Roaring Gap Yacht. Author: Pediatric Notes, 1925; (with S.A. Waksman) Enzymes; 1926; The Compleat Pediatrician, 1934, 38, 40, 44, 46, 49, 57, 61. Contbr. articles to profl. jours. Home: Roaring Gap NC Died June 26, 1972; cremated.

DAWES, CHARLES GATES former ambassador, ex-vice-pres. of U.S.; b. Marietta, O., Aug. 27, 1865; s. Gen. Rufus R. and Mary Beman (Gates) D.; A.B., Marietta Coll., 1884, A.M., 1887; LL.B., Cincinnati Law Sch., 1886; m. Caro D. Blymyer, Jan. 24, 1889; children—Rufus Fearing (deceased), Mrs. Carolyn Ericson, Dana McCutcheon, and Virginia (Mrs. Richard T. Cragg). Admitted to bar of state of Nebraska, 1886; in practice of law at Lincoln, Neb., 1887-94; interested in gas and electric business at various places. Was executive of McKinley movement in Ill., resulting in McKinley instructions at Springfield Conv., 1896; mem. exec. com. of Rep. Nat. Conv. in campaign of 1896; comptroller of the currency, 1897-1901; organized Central Trust Co. of Ill., Chicago, 1902, of which he was pres., 1902-21, chmn. bd., 1921-25, hon. chmn. bd., 1930-31; hon. chmn. bd. Central Republic Bank & Trust Co., 1931-32; chmn. bd. City Nat. Bank & Trust Co. since Oct. 6, 1932. Commd. maj. engrs., U.S. Army, June 1917; lt. col., July 1917; col., Jan. 1918; brig. gen., Oct. 1918. Arrived in France, July 1917, as lt. col. ry. engrs.; apptd. to administrative staff of comdr. in chief of A.E.F., Sept. 1917, and served as chmn. Gen. Purchasing Bd., and gen. purchasing agt. A.E.F.; later mem. Military Bd. of Allies Supply, mem. Liquidation Commn. of A.E.F. and mem. Liquidation Bd. of War Dept.; resigned from Army, 1919, and returned to U.S., Aug. 1919. Decorated D.S.M. (U.S.); Companion of the Bath (British); Comdr. of SS. Maurice and Lazarus (Italian); Order of Leopold (Belgium), 1919; Comdr. Legion d'Honneur (French), 1919. Apptd. 1st dir. U.S. Bur. of the Budget, 1921; apptd., 1923, by Reparations Commn., as pres. com. to investigate possibilities of German budget, resulting in the "Dewes Plan," which was put into effect Sept. 1, 1924; nominated by Rep. Nat. Conv. for vice-pres. of U.S., and elected Nov. 1924, for term 1925-29; A.E. and M.P. from U.S. to Great Britain, 1929-32; pres Reconstruction Finance Corp. (controlling $2,000,000,000 of credits), 1932. Awarded the Nobel Peace prize for 1925 jointly with Sir Austen Chamberlain, British foreign secretary, and turned over his share of the prize to endowment of Walter Hines Page School of Internat. Relations, Chmn. Econ. Commn. of Am. Experts visiting Santo Domingo, 1929; chmn. finance com. "Chicago World's Fair 1933" since 1929. Clubs: Chicago, Commercial, Union League, University, Onwentsia, Glenview, Evanston Country. Author: The Banking System of the United States, 1892; Essays and Speeches, 1915; A Journal of the Great War, 1921; The First Year of the Budget of the United States, 1923; Notes as Vice-President, 1935; How Long Prosperity, 1937; A Journal of Reparations, 1939; Journal as Ambassador to Great Britain, 1939; A Journal of the McKinley Years, 1950. Home: 225 Greenwood Blvd., Evanston, Ill. Office: 208 South La Salle St., Chicago 4. Died Apr. 23, 1951.

DAWES, WILLIAM revolutionary leader; b. Boston, Apr. 6, 1745; s. William and Lydia (Boone) D.; m. Mehitable May, May 3, 1768; m. 2d, Lydia Gendall, Nov. 18, 1795; 2 children. Rode with Paul Revere from Lexington, Mass. to Concord, Mass., to spread the alarm British troops were attempting raid on countryside, Apr. 18, 1775; started by way of Brighton Bridge and the Cambridge Rd.; slipped through Brit. lines and met Revere at Parson Clark's, Lexington, where John Hancock and Samuel Adams were staying; either Dawes or his accomplice got through and gave the alarm it is not known which one); joined Continental Army as commissary. Died Feb. 25, 1799.

DAWSON, CECIL FORREST business management; b. Hardin, Mo., Feb. 13, 1803; s. Edward Forrest and Lines (Moore) D; student William Jewell Coll., 1911-15; m. Mary Robertson, Mar. 15, 1919; children-William Forest, Frank Robertson. Began as salesman, 1914, later in manufacture paper products, chiefly drinking cups and containers, then in research in connection with development of railway artillery; vice pres. Dixie Cup Co., Easton, Pa., 1926-47, pres., 1948-54, chmn. bd., 1955-57, dir., 1926-57; chmn., dir. Dixie Cup Co. (Can.), Ltd., 1926-57; chmn., dir. Individual Drinking Cup Co., Inc., 1937-57; cons., dir. Am. Can. Co., 1957—. Mem. exec. com. Nat. Interfraternity Conf., 1957—; mem. bd. Keep Am. Beautiful, Inc., 1953—, v.p., 1956-58, pres. 1958—. Served as capt., CAC, U.S. Army, World War I. Mem. industry panel of the Sixth Regional War Labor Bd. Dir. Paper Cup and Container Inst., Inc. (chmn. war and priorities com.). Mem. Am. Mgmt. Assn., Marketing Execs. Soc., Phi Gamma Delta (pres. 1952-54). Mason. Clubs: Phi Gamma Delta (N.Y. City); Country Club of Northampton Country, Pomfret (Easton, Pa.); University (Chgo.). Recipient of citation for achievement from William Jewell Coll., 1944. Home: 373 Shawnee Dr. Office: Dixie Cup Div. Am. Can Co., 24th and Dixie Av., Easton, Pa. Died July 30, 1960; buried Carrollton, Mo.

DAWSON, WILLIAM WARREN prof. law; b. Wooster, O. Mar. 2, 1892; s. Rev. William Chambers and Mary Elizabeth (Nail) D.; A.B., Ohio Wesleyan U., 1914; LL.B., Western Reserve U, 1921; student Harvard U. Law Sch., Jan.-June 1927; hon. LL.D., Washington & Jefferson Univ., 1942; married Marguerite Sague Shafer, Sept. 3, 1929. Admitted to Ohio bar, 1920; practiced with Stanley & Horwitz, Cleveland. 1920-23, Dawson & Meyer, 1923-27; instr. law. Western Reserve U., 1927-30, asso. prof., 1930-33, prof. since 1933 (on leave since 1942); pub. rep. Regional Labor Bd., 1935-42. Mayor Brecksville, O., 1934-36. Enlisted 166th Inf., 42d Div., U.S. Army, 1917, commd. 2d lt., July 1918, 1st lt., Jan. 1919; hon. disch., July 1919; commd. maj. Inf., A.U.S., Oct. 1942; asst. exec. Tank Destroyer Sch., Camp Hood, Texas; promoted lt. col., June 1943; enrolled, Sch. of Mil. Govt., Charlottesville, Va., Sept. 1, 1943; dir. Training Division, European Civil Affairs Div., Aug. 1944; promoted to col., Mar. 1945; dir. office Military Govt. Wuerttemberg-Baden, Germany, July 1945: director regional government, Coordinating Office, August 1946. Awarded Bronze Star, Jan. 1946, Legion of Merit, 1947; Croix de Guerre with palm, Chevalier de la Legion d'Honneur (France). Mem. Cuyahoga County Charter Commission, 1935. Mem. American Ohio and Cleveland bar assns., Phi Beta Kappa, Beta Theta Pi (pres. 1940-47), Phi Delta Phi. Omicron Delta Kappa. Republican. Methodist. Clubs: University, Philosophical (Cleveland). Author: Ohio Appellate Review, 1935; Dawson & Andrews Ohio Forms, 1928. Editor: Am. Bar Assn. Inst. on Federal Rules, 1938. Address: Windover, Brecksville, O. Died Feb. 10, 1947; buried in Arlington National Cemetery.

DAY, BENJAMIN FRANKLIN rear adm.; b. Plymouth, O., Jan. 16, 1841; s. Benjamin Franklin and Prussia Bunnell (King) D.; apptd. to U.S. Naval Acad. from Ohio, 1858; resigned, Nov. 24, 1860; reinstated,

June 29, 1861; m. Flora Inez Baldwin, Sept. 22, 1869; children - Philip Baldwin, Benjamin Clark. Lt., Aug. 1, 1862; promoted through grades to rear admiral, Mar. 29, 1899. Served New London, on Colorado, W. Gulf Blockading Squadron, 1861-64; wounded in a night engagement, July 9, 1863; on Saugus, N. Atlantic Blockading Squadron, 1861-64; wounded in a night engagement, July 9, 1863; on Saugus, N. Atlantic Blockading Squadron, 1864-65; engagements with Howlett House batteries in James River, and attacks on Ft. Fisher; Tuscarora, 1865-68; Contocook, 1868-70; Hydrographic Office, 1870-71; Ticonderoga, 1871; Congress, 1871-74; receiving-ship New Hampshire, 1874-75; comd. Manhattan, 1875-76. Rio Bravo, 1877-78; Navy Yard, Norfolk, 1879-80; Light-house insp. 8th dist., 1881-84; comd. Mohican, 1885-88; Navy Yard, Boston, 1889-92; comd. Boston, 1892-93, Baltimore, 1894-96; pres. Steel Bd., 1896-97; mem. Naval Exam. and Retiring bds., 1897-1900; retired 1900. Home: Buena Vista, Va. Died July 3, 1933.

DAY, EWING WILBER physician; b. Deerfield, O., Nov. 1, 1862; s. Edgar M. And Frances (Reed) D.; A.B., Allegheny Coll., Meadville, Pa., 1884, A.M., 1886; M.D., Georgetown U., 1889; m. Annie A. Mosier, July 23, 1890; children-Edgar Mortimer (dec.), Ewing W., Kenneth Mosier, Percival Eaton, Mrs. Elizabeth Autrey (dec.). Practiced in Pittsburgh, Pa., 1899-1928 (retired); emeritur prof. otology of the U. of Pittsburgh; member of the Collegium Oto-Rhino-Laryngololicum. Mem. A.M.A., Pa. State Med. Soc., Am. Laryngol., Rhinol. and Otol. Soc. (pres.), Am. Otol. Soc. (pres.), Allegheny County Med. Soc. (pres.), Pittsburgh Acad. Medicine (pres.), S.A.R., Patriots and Founders of America, Episcopalian. Lt. col. Med. R.C., 1917. Club: University. Home: 616 Commercial St., Provincetown, Mass. Office: 121 University Pl., Pittsburgh, Pa. Died Nov. 24, 1942.

DAY, FRANK PARKER educator; b. Shubenacadie, N.S., Can., May 9, 1881; s. George Frederick and Keziah (Hardwick) D.; B.A., Mount Allison U., Sackville, N.B., 1903, LL.D., 1927; B.A., Oxford U., 1907, M.A., 1909; grad. study U. Berlin; Litt. D., N.Y.U., 1929; m. Mabel Eliza Killam, 1910; 1 son, Donald Frank. Prof. English, U. N.B., 1909-12; prof. English, Carnegie Inst. Tech., 1912-14, dean of freshmen and dir., 1919-26; prof. English, Swarthmore, 1926-28; pres. Union Coll., Schenectady, 1929-33. Served as maj., later lt. col. Canadian Inf., 1914-19. Clubs: Mohawk (Schenectady); Century (N.Y.C.); Twenty Club (Oxford). Author: River of Strangers (novel), 1926; Autobiography of a Fisherman, 1927; Rockbound, 1928; John Paul's Rock, 1930. Home: Lake Annis, N.S., Can. Died 1950; buried Yarmouth, N.S.

DAY, KARL S., airline exec.; b. Ripley County, Ind., May 30, 1896;2s. Franklin Groves and Edith (Schmolsmire) D.; B.A., Ohio State U., 1917; m. Margaret Raine, Oct. 16, 1925; children—John Franklin, Nancy (Mrs. Howard M. Trowern, Jr.). Served from 2d lt. to lt. gen., USMC and USMC Res., 1917-57; operations mgr. Curtiss-Wright Flying Service, 1929-32; with Am. Airlines, Inc., 1932-62, successively instrument instr., pilot, check pilot, asst. flight supt., flight supt., 1932-46, dir. flight dispatch, 1946-62. Marine Corps mem. Res. Forces Policy Bd., 1954-57; pres. Marine Corps Res. Officers Assn., 1953-56, chmn. bd. dirs., 1961-68, chmn. emeritus, 1968-73. Died Jan. 19, 1973; buried Arlington National Cemetery.

DAY, WILLIAM PLUMMER rear adm.; b. New York, Sept. 30, 1848; s. William Harrison and Mercy Carter (Church) D.; grad. U.S. Naval Acad., 1869; m. Jenetta Maria Eliza Grace Master, of Bath, Eng., Mar. 3, 1873. Promoted ensign, July 12, 1870; master, Oct. 31, 1871; lt., Jan. 23, 1875; lt. comdr., Dec. 12, 1899; capt., Jan. 12, 1905; retired as rear adm., U.S.N., June 11, 1906. Served successively on Juniata, Franklin, Powhatan, Wyoming, Dicator, receiving ships Vermont and Colorado, Despatch, Wyandotte, Passaic, and Hartford, 1869-79; Quinnebaug, 1881-84; Powhattan, 1884; Yantic, 1885; Alliance, 1886-89; Franklin, 1891-93; exec. officer Bancroft and Machias, 1893; Franklin, 1894; Machias, 1894-96; exec. officer Richmond, 1897-98; New Orleans, 1898-99; comd. Vixen, 1899-1900 light house insp. 13th dist., 1900-02; comd. Mohican, 1902-04; lighthouse insp. 12th dist., 1904-05; Navy Yard, Mare Island, Calif., 1905-06. Died Dec. 28, 1919.

DAYTON, ELLAS army officer, Continental congressman: b. Elizabethtown (now Elizabeth), N.J., May 1, 1737; s. Jonathan Dayton; m. Miss Rolfe, 8 children including Jonathan. Commd. lt. N.J. Militia, 1756, capt., 1760; apptd. to enforce measures recommended by Continental Congress, 1774; muster master Essex County (N.J.), 1775; commd. col. 3d Battalion, N.J. Militia, 1776; commd. brig. gen. Continental Army on recommendation of George Washington, 1783: maj. gen. N.J. Militia; mem. Continental Congress from N.J., 1787-88; recorder Elizabeth (N.J.), 1789; mem. N.J. Assembly, 1791-92, 94-96; pres. N.J. Soc. of Cincinnati. Died Elizabethtown, Oct. 22, 1807.

DAYTON, JAMES HENRY rear adm.; b. South Bend, Ind., Oct. 25, 1846; s. Daniel and Anna M.D.; apptd. from Ind. and grad. U.S. Naval Acad., 1866; unmarried. Ensign, Apr. 1868; master, Mar. 6, 1839; lt., Mar. 27, 1870; lt. comdr., Nov. 1884; comdr., Jan. 1894; capt., Mar. 29, 1900; rear adm., Feb. 28, 1906. Served on various duties and stas.; comd. Detroit, 1897-99; comdt. naval sta., San Juan, Oct. 11, 1899; comd. Chicago, 1901-03; pres. Naval Bd. Inspection and Survey, 1904-05; comdg. Philippine Squadron, Asiatic Fleet, 1906-07; comdr.-in-chief Pacific Fleet, 1907-08; retired Oct. 25, 1908. Courtmartial duty, Jan. 1918-May 1919. Home: South Bend, Ind. Died Nov. 15, 1938.

DAYTON, JOHN HAVENS ret. naval officer; b. Rock Island, Ill., Feb. 3, 1869; s. Frederick Lord and Almira (Olds) D.; grad. U.S. Naval Acad., 1890; m. Nancy Maupin Reed, Apr. 14, 1896. Commd. ensign USN, 1892, advanced through grades to vice adm., 1928; served on Mangrove, Spanish-Am. War, 1898. Iowa, 1904-05; duty U.S. Naval Acad., 1905-08; navigator, Charleston, 1908-10; capt. of yard, Naval Sta., Cavite, P.I., 1910-11; duty Gen. Bd., Navy Dept., 1911; aide to Admiral of the Navy, 1911; comd. Naval Tng. Sta., Newport, R.I., 1911-13; comd. Saratoga, 1913-15; asst. to Bur. of Navigation, Navy Dept., 1915-16; apptd. comdr. receiving ship and Naval Training Sta., Norfolk Va., 1916; comdg. Michigan, 1918, Arizona, 1918-20; comdt. Washington Navy Yard, 1920-23; comdr. spl. service squadron, 1923-25; comdt. Navy Yard, Mare Island, 1925-28; comdr. U.S. Naval Forces, Europe, 1928-29; retired, 1930. Clubs: Army and Navy, New York Yacht. Home: Jamestown, R.I. Died Sept. 7, 1953.

DEAKYNE, HERBERT (DE-KIN'), army officer; b. Deakyneville, Del., Dec. 29, 1867; s. Napoleon B. and Mary A. (David) D.; student Delaware Coll. (now U. of Del.), 1884-85; grad. U.S. Mil. Acad., 1890; Engr. Sch. of Application, 1893; Army War Coll., 1917; m. Sadie M. Nickerson, June 15, 1899; children-Ramona (Mrs. John B. Hughes), Rosalind (Mrs. George W. Waldron). Commd. additional 2d lt. engrs., June 12, 1890; promoted through grades to lt. col., Feb. 27, 1914; col. Nat. Army, July 6, 1917; brig. gen. (temp.), Oct. 1, 1918-May 31, 1919; col. engrs., Feb. 6, 1920; brig. gen., June 27, 1926; retired, Dec. 31, 1931. River and harbor improvements, California, 1893-96; fortification works, Calif., 1896-1900; mem. Calif. Debris Commn., 1897-1901; in charge fortification works and river and harbor improvements in Fla., 1901-03; at Fort Leavenworth, Kan., 1903-05; in Philippines, 1905-07; chief engr. officer Philippines Div., Aug.-Nov. 1907; mem. Bd. Engrs. for Rivers and Harbors, 1909-12; at Phila., Pa., in charge of fortification works and river and harbor improvements, 1908-12; at Kansas City, Mo., in charge of river and harbor improvements, 1912-16; duty office of Chief of Engrs., Washington, D.C., 1916; at Army War Coll., 1916-17. Organized 19th Engrs. (Rh.) at Phila., May-Aug. 1917: sailed for France via Halifax and Eng., Aug. 9, 1917; arrived in France Aug. 30, 1917; comd. 19th Engrs. at St. Nazaire, Sept. 1917-Jan. 1918; comd. 11th Engrs. (Ry.) on British Front and with A.E.F., Jan.-May, 1918; at G.H.Q., A.E.F., as dir. of Light Rys. and Roads, May-July 1918; chief engr. Paris Group, Aug.-Sept. 1918; chief engr., 2d Army, Sept. 1918-Apr. 1919; at New Orleans, La., in charge of fortification works and river and harbor improvements, May 1919-Sept.. 1920; mem. Miss. River Commn., Mar.-Sept. 1920; at San Francisco, Calif., as div. engr. Pacific Div., and in charge fortification works and river and harbor improvements, Sept. 1920-Jan. 1925; mem. California Debris Commn., 1920-25; as division engineer Northeast division and in charge river and harbor improvements, Feb. 1925-June 1926; asst. chief of engrs., June 1926-June 1930; acting chief of engrs., Aug. 8-Sept. 30, 129. Mem. Board of Engineers for Rivers and Harbors, Feb. 6, 1925-Dec. 31, 1931; mem. Permanent Internat. Commn. of Internat. Assn. of Navigation Congresses; pres. Soc. Am. Mil. Engineers, 1932; cons. engr. to Chamber of Commerce. Eureka, Calif., Mar.-May, 1934, to Trinity River Canal Assn., Fort Worth, Tex., Jan.-May 1937. Clubs; Army and Navy, Army, Navy, and Marine Corps Country (Washington. D.C.). Home: San Francisco. Calif. Address: 2248 Washington St., San Francisco 15, Calif. Died May 28, 1945.

DEALEY, EDWARD MUSGROVE (TED), journalist; b. Oct. 5, 1892; s. George Bannerman and Olivia (Allen) D.; A.B., U. of Tex., 1913; A.M., Harvard, 1914; student Sch. Bus. Harvard, 1914-15; m. Clara MacDonald, Mar. 1, 1916 (dec.); children—Edward Musgrove (dec.), Joseph MacDonald, Clara Patricia; married 2d, Mrs. Trudie Kelley, June 29, 1951. Reporter on Dallas News, 1915-20, staff corr., 1920-24, Sunday editor and editorial writer, 1924-28; dir. A. H. Belo Corp., pubs. Dallas Morning News and Texas Almanac, 1926-69, asst. to publisher, 1928-32, v.p., 1932-40, pres., 1940-69, chmn., 1960-69, pub., 1964-69; mem. conf. and editorial boards This Week mag. Dir. Southland Paper Mills, Inc. Trustee Texas Research Found. Colonel on staff Gov. Ross Sterling, 1931-33. Major, comdg. 29th Bn., Tex. Defense Guard, 1941-42; maj. Army Specialist Corps, U.S. Army, 1942-43. First vice president Associated Press, 1948; director of the American Newspaper Publishers Association, 1940-45. Member Texas Newspaper Publishers Association (president 1935-36 and 1936-37), Southern Newspaper Publishers' Association (president 1937-38, chairman board, 1938-39), Advertising Fedn. of America (dir. 1936-41), Dallas Hist. Soc., Dallas Citizens Council, English-Speaking Union, Phi Delta Theta, Sigma Delta Chi, Order of the T (football, Texas U.). Independent Democrat. Presbyterian. Mason (33 deg.). Clubs: Athletic, Dallas Country, Skeet and Gun (Dallas), Advertising, Anglers, Leash (N.Y.C.); Koon Kreek Hunting and Fishing (Athens, Texas); Pine Island Hunting and Fishing (Lufkin, Tex.); Carmen Mountain Hunting (Coahuila, Mexico); Welsh Terrier of America (gov.). Contbr. fiction to publs. Home: Dallas TX Died Nov. 1969.

DEAN, ARTHUR DAVIS educator; b. Cambridge, Mass., Sept. 15, 1872; s. Daniel H. and Lizzie (Reed) D.; grad. Rindge Tech. Sch., Cambridge, 1891: B.S., Mass. Inst. Tech., 1895; Sc.D., Alfred U., 1913; m. Amy Joanna Chattle, Dec. 24, 1806; m. 2d, Rose Elizabeth Sherman, September 8, 1941. Asst. prin., Tech. High Sch., Springfield, Mass., 1899-1905; supervising evening schs. of Y.M.C.A. in Mass. and R.I., 1906-07; chief div. vocational schs. N.Y. State Edn. Dept., Sept. 1980-17; prof. of vocational edn., Teachers Coll. (Columbia), 1917-23. Investigated possibilities of industrial and agrl. edn. in P.R. for insular govt.; editor of investigation of conditions in shoe industry, bull. 8, Nat. Soc. Promotion Industrial Edn., 1908; asst. in investigation apprenticeship systems, for bull. U.S. Dept. Interior, 1907; dir. survey of N.Y. Prison Survey Com., 1919; asso. editor, Industrial Edn. Mag. Maj. U.S. Army, in reconstruction work in army hospitals, 1918-19. Filled U.S. Civilian Defense assignment to Connecticut State Forestry Service, 1942-43. President Eastern Art and Manual Training Teachers' Assn., 1911, etc. Club: Nat. Arts (New York). Author: The Worker and the State, 1910; Our Schools in War Time-and After, 1917; Just Between Ourselves, 1923; also newspaper syndicate feature "Your Boy and Your Girl" and "Let's Talk it Over," since 1924. Address: National Arts Club, 15 Gramercy Park, New Yor, N.Y. Died Nov. 19, 1949.

DEAN, BASHFORD zoologist, armor expert; b. New York, Oct. 28, 1867; A.B., Coll. City of New York, 1886; A.M., Columbia, 1889, Ph.D., 1890; m. Mary Alice, d. Isaac Michael Dyckman, of Kingsbridge, New York, 1886-90; instr. biology, 1891-96, adj. prof. zoology, 1896-1904, prof. vertebrate zoology, 1904-27, hon. prof., 1927 - . Columbia. Asst. N.Y. State Fish Commn., 1886-88; asst., 1889-92, biologist, 1900-01, spl. investigator U.S. Fish Commn.; dir. Biol. Lab., Cold Spring Harbor, N.Y., 1890; mem. Advisory Bd., New York Aquarium, 1902 - ; curator of herpetology and ichthyology, 1903-26, hon. curator of ichthyology, 1926 - , Am. Mus. Natural History; curator arms and armor, Met. Mus. Art, 1903 - ; prof. Fine Arts, New York U., 1925; pres. Dyckman Inst., curator Dyckman House Mus. Trustee N.Y. Museum. Chevalier Legion of Honor. Adviser on armor U.S. War Dept.; maj. of Ordnance U.S.A.; mem. Mission to France, Belgium, England, 1917. Author of numerous works on palaeichthyology and embryology of fishes (myxinoid, chimaeroid and ganoid), and of bibliography of fishes (50,000 titles). Many pubs. on armor and arms. Home: Riverdale, New York, N.Y. Died Dec. 6, 1928.

DEAN, BASIL editor; b. Newbury, Eng., Nov. 12, 1915; s. James Arthur and Winifred Elsie (Baverstock) D.; diploma journalism U. Coll., London, Eng., 1936; m. Florence Jean Brown, Dec. 25, 1941; children-Michael Thomas James, Christopher Allen. Editorial staff Daily Herald, London, Eng., 1936-38, Spectator, Hamilton, Ont., 1938-41; London corr. Southam Newspapers of Can., 1945-49; asso. editor, chief editorial writer Calgary Herald since 1949. Served as squadron leader Royal Canadian Air Force, 1941-45. Mem. United Mil. Services Inst. Calgary. Club: Ranchmen's (Calgary). Home: 436 47th Av., S.W., Calgary, Alberta, Can. Died Dec. 18, 1967.

DEAN, JAMES THEODORE army officer; b. Ironton, O., May 12, 1865; s. Ezra Van Ness and Charlotte Anne (Weaver) D.; grad. U.S. Mil. Acad., 1887; grad. Army War Coll., Washington, 1911; unmarried Commd. 2d lt. 3d Inf., June 12, 1887; 1st lt. 14th Inf., Aug. 14, 1894; maj. chief ordnance officer vols., July 18, 1898; hon. mustered out vols., May 12, 1899; capt. 10th Inf. U.S.A., Mar. 2, 1899; promoted through grades to brig. gen. N.A., Aug. 5, 1917; retired, rank brig. gen. U.S.A., June 21, 1930. Maj. and chief ordnance officer in Puerto Rico and Cuba, Spanish-Am. War; in Alaska, 1906-08, P.I., 1912-15; apptd. comdr. 156th Inf. Brigade, Camp Dix, Wrightstown, N.J., Aug. 25, 1917, and in France, 78th Div., May 1918-May 1919; was in St. Mihiel and Meuse-Argonne campaigns; col. 29th U.S. Inf., Aug. 15, 1919-Aug. 23, 1920; apptd. adj. gen. Aug. 23, 1920; adj. Philippine Dept., Manila, P.I., Dec. 2, 1920-Nov. 18, 1922; col. 11th U.S. Inf., Dec. 12, 1922-Feb. 25, 1924; in charge New York Dist. Gen. Recruiting Service assigned Apr. 23, 1924; asst. chief of staff 77th Div. Organized Reserves, N.Y. City, Jan. 28, 1927-Sept. 3, 1928 (retired). Died June 15, 1939.

DEAN, LEE WALLACE otolaryngolgist; b. Muscatine, Ia., Mar. 28, 1873; s. Henry Munson and Emma (Johnson) D.; B.S., State U. of Ia., 1894, M.S., 1896, M.D., 1896; studied in Vienna, 1896-97; m. Ella May Bailey, Dec. 29, 1904; 1 son, Lee Wallace. Prof. and head of otolaryngology and oral surgery, State U. of Ia. until July 1, 1927; also dean Coll. of Medicine, same univ., 1912-27; prof. otolaryngology, Washington U.

Sch. of Medicine, since 1927; mem. staff Barnes, St. Louis Children's and Jewish hosps.; otolaryngologist in chief McMillan Eye, Ear, Nose & Throat Hospital and Oscar Johnson Research Inst., St. Louis (emeritus 1943). Served as lieut. col. Med. O.R.C., comdg. offr. Gen. Hosp. No. 54, World War. Mem. Am. Bd. Otolaryngology; editor Annals of Otology, Rhinology and Laryngology. Fellow Am. Coll. Surg.; mem. Am. Laryngol. Assn. (past pres.), Am. Laryngol., Rhinol. and Otol. Soc. (past pres.), Am. Otol. Soc. (past pres.), Am. Peroroal Endoscopists, Mo. State Med. Soc., Am. Acad. of Ophthalmology and Otolaryngology (pres.), La Societe de Laryngologie des Hopitaux de Paris. Home: Kirkwood, Mo. Recipient of de Roaldes prize award, 1937. Address: Washington University Medical School, St. Louis, Mo. Died Feb. 9, 1944.

DEAN, RICHARD CRAIN rear admiral; b. Harrisburg, Pa., May 27, 1833; s. Alexander Tracy and Mary Adeline (Crain) D.; student Yale; M.D., Jefferson Med. Coll., 1854; (hon. A.M., Yale, 1854); m. Anna Mulford, 1856; m. 2d, Sarah Elizabeth Bingham, 1888. Apptd. asst. surgeon U.S.N., Apr. 7, 1856; promoted past asst. surgeon, Mar. 25, 1861; surgeon, Aug. 1, 1861; med. insp., June 8, 1873; med. dir., June 10, 1880; retired May 27, 1895; advanced to rank of rear admiral, June 29, 1906, for services during Civil War. Served on various vessels and at various stas. during Civil war; fleet surgeon N. Atlantic Fleet, 1876-77; sr. mem. Examining Bd., 1877-79; mem. Bd. of Inspection, 1879-80; mem. Naval Examining and Retiring Bds., 1886-87; mem. Examining Bd., Washington, 1891-93, pres., 1902-03. Died 1910.

DEANE, GARDINER ANDRUS ARMSTRONG land commr., Mo. Pacific R.R., since 1891; b. Franklin, Mass., July 21, 1840; grad. Franklin Acad., 1858; m. 1866, Eliza J. Margeaux, New York. Private 3d Iowa cav., Aug. 23, 1861; capt., 1st Ia. inf., A.D., Oct. 11, 1863; lt.-col., same, May 9, 1864; was insp. arty. on staff Brig. Gen. Buford; asst. insp.-gen., staff Maj. Gen. A. McD. McCook, and Maj.-Gen. J. J. Reynolds; mustered out while asst. insp.-gen., dept. Ark., Oct. 15, 1865; in mercantile business, Milwaukee, 1865-67; chief clerk land dept., C.B.U.P.R.R., 1867; later asst. land commr., asst. supt. and supt. construction up to 1891. Mem. Loyal Legion, Soc. Colonial Wars; 32 degree Mason. Residence: Little Rock, Ark.

DE ANZA, JUAN BAUTISTA explorer, colonial gov.; b. Fronteras, Sonora, Mexico, 1735. Capt., Presidio of Tubac, 1760; commd. lt. col., 1774; leader Anza expdn. to Alta, Cal., 1775-76; founder San Francisco, 1776; gov. N.M., 1777-88; established Colorado River Colonies, 1780 (wiped out by Yuma Indians, 1781).

DEARBORN, HENRY army officer, physician, congressman, sec. of war; b. North Hampton, N.H., Feb. 23, 1751; s. Simon and Sarah (Marston) D.: m. Mary Bartlett, 1771; m. 2d, Dorcas Marble, 1780; m. 3d, Mrs. Sarah Bowdoin, 1813; 1 son, Henry Alexander Scammell D. Organizer, capt. company, N.H. Milita, 1772; commd. maj. 3d Hampshire Regt., 1777; commd. brig. gen., then maj. gen. N.H. Militia; dep. q.m. gen. with rank of col. on Gen. Washington's Staff, 1781; apptd. U.S. marshall for Dist. of Me., 1790; mem. U.S. Ho. of Reps. from Mass., 3d-4th congresses, 1793-97; U.S. sec. of war under Pres. Jefferson, 1801-09; collector Port of Boston (apptd. by Pres. Madison), 1809-12; apptd. sr. maj. gen. U.S. Army by Madison, 1812, served in War of 1812; U.S. minister to Portugal, 1822-24; Dearborn (Mich.) named after him. Died Roxbury, Mass., June 6, 1829; buried Forest Hills Cemetery, Boston.

DEARBORN, HENRY ALEXANDER SCAMMELL congressman; author; b. Exeter, N.H., Mar. 3, 1783; s. Gen. Henry and Doreas (Marble) D.; grad. Coll. 1805; apptd. to superintend erection new fts. in Portland harbor, 1806; officer Boston Custom House, collector, 1812-29; served as brig. gen. Mass. Militia, 1812; mem. Mass. Legislature from Roxbury, 1829-30; mem. Mass. Gov's Council, 1830; del. Mass. Constl. Conv., 1830; mem. Mass. Senate from Norfolk County, 1830; mem. U.S. Ho. of Reps. from Mass., 22d Congress, 1831-33; adj. gen. Mass., 1835-43; mayor Roxbury, 1847-51. Author: Memoir on the Commerce and Navigation of the Black Sea and the Trade and Maritime Geography of Turkey and Egypt, 1819; Defence of General Henry Dearborn Against the Attack of General William Hull, 1824; Letters on Internal Improvements and Commerce of the West, 1839; A Sketch of the Life of the Apostle Eliot, 1850. Translated from French: Monography of the Genius Camelia (Abbe Lorenzo Berlese), 1838. Died Portland, Me., July 29, 1851; buried Forest Hills Cemetery, Roxbury.

DEAS, ZACHARIAH CANTEY mcht., army officer; s. Col. James Sutherland and Margaret (Chunut) D.; m. Helen Gaines, May 16, 1853. Cotton broker, Mobile, Ala.; served as aide-de-camp to Gen. J. E. Johnston, Confederate Army, commd. col., 1861; recruited (with Maj. Robert B. Armistead) 22d Ala. Inf.; commanded brigade, wounded at Battle of Shiloh, 1862; promoted brig. gen., 1862, served in Battle of Murfreesboro; led brigade at Battle of Chickamauga, 1863, Missionary Ridge, 1863; returned to cotton brokerage, N.Y.C., after war. Died N.Y.C., Mar. 6, 1882.

DE BARDELEBEN, HENRY FAIRCHILD industrialist; b. N.Y. State, July 22, 1841; s. Henry and Jennie (Fairchild) De B.; m. Ellen Pratt, Feb. 4, 1863; m. 2d, Miss McCroffin; at least 2 sons, Henry Charles. Became ward of Ala. industrialist Daniel Pratt, 1856; served with Pratville Dragoons, Confederate Army, participated in battles of Pensacola, Shiloh; mgr. Red Mountain Iron & Coal Co., 1872; inherited Daniel Pratt's fortune, 1873; investor Eureka Coal Co., nr. Birmingham, Ala., 1877, became Pratt Coal & Coke Co., 1878; went to Mexico for health reasons, 1881-82; formed De Bardeleben Coal & Iron Co., 1886; organized Pinchard & De Bardeleben Land Co., merged with Tenn. Coal & Iron Co., 1891, v.p., 1891-93, lost entire fortune in attempt to take over control of co., 1893. Died Dec. 6, 1910.

DE BOLT, REZIN A., congressman; b. nr. Basil, Fairfield County, O., Jan. 20, 1828; attended common schs.; studied law. Employed as a tanner; admitted to bar, 1856, began practice of law, Lancaster, O.; moved to Trenton, Mo., 1858; commr. of common schs. Grundy County, 1859-61; commd. capt. 23d Regt., Mo. Volunteers, U.S. Army, 1861, captured at Battle of Shiloh, 1862, resigned commn., 1863; judge circuit ct. 11th Jud. Circuit Mo., 1863-75; served as maj. 44th Regt., Mo. Volunteer Inf., 1864-65; mem. U.S. Ho. of Reps. (Democrat) from Mo., 44th Congress, 1875-77. Died Trenton, Oct. 30, 1891; buried Odd Fellows Cemetery.

DE BONNEVILLE, BENJAMIN LOUIS EULALIE, army officer, explorer; b. Paris, France, Apr. 14, 1796: s. Nicholas and Margaret (Brazier) de B.; grad. U.S. Mil. Acad., 1815; m. Ann Lewis. m. 2d, Susan Neis, 1870. Came to Am., Aug. 1803; aided Lafayette on his tour of U.S., 1825: went on leave of absence from Army to exploit Northwestern country for comml. gain, 1832-35; served as maj., then lt. col. in Mexican War; comdt. Benton Barracks, St. Louis, 1862-65, brig. gen., Civil War, 1865; subject of Washington Irving's Adventures of Captain Bonneville. Died Ft. Smith, Ark., June 12, 1878.

DE BOWER, HERBERT FRANCIS b. Dane, Wis.; s. Gerd and Mary (Buffmire) de B.; LL.B., U. of Wis., 1896. Practiced at Madison, Wis., several yrs.; developed organization for extensive training in business and law; founded Alexander Hamilton Inst., New York, 1909; v.p. and chmn. exec. com.; dir. various other cos. Capt. Signal R.C. attached to Hdqrs. U.S.A., A.E.F., 1917-19. Commr. of Conciliation, Dept. of Labor, 1922. Author: Advistising Principles, 1917. Co-author of Effective Speech, 1927. Home: Long Beach, N.Y. Died Mar. 16, 1940.

DE CAPRILES, JOSE RAFAEL, lawyer, r.r. ofcl.; b. Mexico City, Mexico, Feb. 13, 1912; s. A. M. and Cristina (Treserra) de C.; LL.B., New York University, 1942, LL.M., 1954; M. Adela Casanova, July 4, 1943; children—John Robert, Charles Michael. Came to U.S., 1920, naturalized, 1936. Admitted to N.Y. bar, 1945; atty. Lehigh Valley R.R., 1945-49, claims atty., 1949-55, trial counsel, 1955-58, gen. counsel, 1958, v.p., 1959-69; pres. Ablalan Corp., Communipaw, Inc.; v.p. United Real Estate Co.; dir. Bayshore Connecting R.R., Osuasco River Rwy., Buffalo Creek R.R. Co., Ironton R.R. Member U.S. Olympic Fencing Com., 1936-61, chmn., 1953-57; dir. U.S. Olympic Com., 1965-69. Trustee Robert Packer Hospital, Sayre, Pennsylvania. Served from pvt. to maj., USAAF, World War II. Decorated Bronze Star, Presdl. Citation; Croix de Guerre (France). Mem. Assn. Am. R.R., Am. Bar Assn., N.Y. State Assn. R.R. (exec. com.), Assn. R.R. N.J. (exec com.), Nat. Assn. R.R. Trial Counsel, Assn. ICC Practitioners, N.Y. R.R. Club, Fedn. Internat. d'Escrime (dep. pres. 1961-64), Amateur Fencers League Am. (pres. 1953-57), Fencers Club N.Y., A.I.M. Founder, editor: Am. Fencing mag. 1948-69. Mem. U.S. Olympic Fencing Team, 1936, 40, 48, 52, capt., 1956; nat. fencing champion, 1939, 46, 51; capt. Pan-Am. Sabre Team, 1955; fencing ofcl. Olympic games, Tokyo, 1964, Mexico, 1968. Home: Middletown NJ Died Feb. 21, 1969.

DECATUR, STEPHEN naval officer: b. Newport, R.I., 1752; s. Stephen and Priscilla (Hill) D.; m. Ann Pine, Dec. 20, 1774, 4 children, Ann, James, John, Stephen, Master sloop Peggy, 1774; U.S. privateer during Revolutionary War; comdr., part owner mcht. ships Ariel and Pennsylvania, 1782-98; commd. capt. U.S. Navy, 1798; commanded Delaware as sr. officer of squadron operating off No. Cuba during hostilities with French, 1798-99; commanded Philadelphia as head Guadeloupe Squadron, 1800-01, discharged, 1801; established gunpowder works, Millsdale, Pa. Died Millsdale, Nov. 14, 1808; buried St. Peter's Churchyard, Phila.

DECATUR, STEPHEN naval officer; b. Sinepuxent. Md., Jan. 5, 1779; s. Stephen and Priscilla (Hill) D.; m. Susan Wheeler, Mar. 8, 1806. Apptd. midshipman U.S. Navy, 1798, acting lt., 1799; 1st lt. in ship Exxex in Commodore Dale's squadron to Tripoli, 1801-02; in command of ship Enterprise in Tripolian waters, 1803, noted for daring exploit in recapturing and burning Am. frigate Philadelphia, 1804; capt. in command of gunboat div. in attacks on Tripoli, 1804; served as commander ship United States (defeated Brit. ship Macedonia 1812) and ship President (defeated ship Endymion in War of 1812): served in expdn. to Algeria, 1815, forced a peace on U.S. terms with so-called Barbary Pirates; mem. newly-created naval commn., 1816-20. Killed by naval officer James Barron in duel, nr. Bladensburg, Md., Mar. 22, 1820; buried St. Peters Churchyard, Phila.

DE CELERON DE BLAINVILLE, PIERRE JOSEPH army officer, explorer; b. Montreal, Que., Can., Jan. 9, 1694; s. Jean-Baptiste and Helene (Picote de Belestre) de C. de B.; married 3 times; at least 1 son, Paul Oouis. Joined French Army, 1715, promoted lt., 1731; commandant French post Michilimackinac, Can., 1734, 37-40,41-42; accompanied expdn. against Chickasaw Indians, 1739-40; promoted capt., 1740; in command of posts at Detroit, Niagara and St. Frederic (now Crown Point) until 1748; sent on expdn. to drive English from Ohio River Valley, 1749, during this campaign left lead plates buried along river banks claiming that region for France; commandant of Detroit, 1750-53; promoted maj., 1750; served at Battle of Lake George, 1755. Died Apr. 12, 1759.

DECHERD, H. BEN, newspaper exec.; b. Dallas, Mar. 14, 1915; s. Henry Benjamin and Fannie (Dealey) D.; B.A. in Govt., U. Tex., Austin, 1936; m. Isabelle Thomason, Dec. 17, 1938; children—Dealey (Mrs. H. David Herndon), Robert W. With A.H. Belo Corp., pub. Dallas Morning News, Tex. Suburban Dailies and Tex. Almanac; owner radio-TV stas. WFAA, TV sta. KFDM, Beaumont, Tex., 1936, 38-72, v.p., sec., 1960-64, chmn. exec. com., 1964-68, chmn. bd., 1968-72; with Balt. Sunpapers, 1937. Past pres. Family Guidance Center, Incarnation Bay Sch., S.W. Sch. Printing, St. Marks Sch. Tex.; bd. dirs. Central Bus. Dist. Assn., Dallas Zool. Soc., Dallas Symphony Orch., Southwestern Legal Found., St. Marks Sch. Tex.; trustee Dallas Hist. Soc., Tex. Research Found. Served to lt. col., inf., AUS, 1942-46. Decorated Bronze Star. Mem. Tex. Daily Newspaper Assn. (past pres.), Phi Beta Kappa, Phi Delta Theta. Episcopalian. Clubs: City, Dallas Country, Northwood, Petroleum, Idlewild (Dallas). Home: Dallas TX Died Nov. 18, 1972.

DECHERT, HENRY TAYLOR lawyer; b. Philadelphia, Feb. 2, 1859; s. Henry Martyn and Esther S. (Taylor) D.; A.B., U. of Pa., 1879, LL.B., 1881; desc. of Gen. Andrew Porter; m. V. Louise Howard, Jan. 30, 1896. In practice at Phila., 1881 - . Lt. col. 2d Regt., N.G. of Pa. in U.S. service Spanish Am. War; after close of war elected col. of regt., serving 5 yrs. and then declined reelection. Home: Philadelphia. Died Oct. 14, 1915.

DECKER, BENTON CLARK naval officer; b. Lima, N.Y., Dec. 28, 1867; grad. U.S. Naval Acad., 1887. Ensign, July 1, 1889; promoted through grades to capt., July 1, 1913; rear admiral, temporary, July 1, 1918. Served on Indiana, Spanish-Am. War, 1898; insp. powder, Wilmington, Del., 1899-1901; on Helena, and Philippine service, 1901-04; Naval Acad., 1904-06; navigator and exec. Virginia, 1906-09; War Coll. and Dept., 1909-10; on Chester, 1910-12; War Coll., 1912-14; on Tennessee, 1914-15; Washington, 1915-16; War Coll., 1916-17; naval attaché, Madrid, 1917-18; Naval Sta., New London, 1918-19; 7th Naval Dist. and Naval Sta., Key West, 1919; Naval Operating Base, Hampton Roads, Aug.-Dec. 1920; 1st Naval Dist., Boston, Mass., Dec. 1920 - . Died Mar. 22, 1933.

DECKER, ORLADY PAUL banker; b. Chgo., Mar. 20, 1903; s. O. P. and Mathilda K. (Froehlinger) D.; Ph.B., U. Chgo., 1927; m. Alice C. Thompson, Jan. 6, 1936; 1 dau., Arabella M. With S. W. Straus & Co., 1927-28; treas. Wolff Co., 1928-30; with Am. Nat. Bank & Trust Co., 1930-56, chmn. investment com., 1953-56; pres., dir. Nat. Boulevard Bank Chgo., 1956-; dir. H. L. Green Co., F. M. Hubbell Son & Co. (Des Moines, Ia.), Glencoe Nat. Bank (Ill.), B. G. Foods, Inc., C. & N.-W. Ry., Chgo., Mpls., St. Paul & Omaha Ry., Consol. Foods Corp. (all Chgo.), John Morrell & Co. (Ottumwa, Ia.). Trustee Thompson Trust, Des Moines. Served from maj. to col., AUS, 1942-45. Decorated Legion of Merit. Mem. Phi Beta Kappa, Lambda Chi Alpha. Clubs: Chicago, Attic, Casino Racquet (Chgo.); Exmoor Country (Highland Park, Ill.); Mountain Lake (Lake Wales, Fla.). Home: 999 Lake Shore Dr., Chgo. 60611. Office: 400 N. Michigan Av., Chgo. 60611. Died Aug. 15, 1962; buried Des Moines.

DEES, RANDALL EUESTA, naval officer; b. Oct. 8, 1893; entered U.S. Navy, 1913, and advanced through the grades to commodore, 1943; formerly chief of staff Newport Naval War Coll. Decorated Silver Star. Address: Newport RI Died July 1972.

DEETER, PAXSON lawyer; b. Reading, Pa., Dec. 23, 1880; s. Ammon S. and Lydia K. (Paxson) D.; B.S., U. of Pa., 1903, LL.B., 1906; m. Helen M. Bowen, 1911. Admitted to Pa. bar, 1906, and began practice at Phila.; lecturer in law, Wharton Sch. (U. of Pa.), 1906-11; dir. Atwater Kent Mfg. Co. Served as capt. Ordnance Dept., U.S.A., 1918-19. Sec. and trustee Atwater Kent Fonnundation, Inc. Republican. Presbyn. Home: Bryn Mawr, Pa. Died June 24, 1933.

DE FLOREZ, LUIS consulting engineer, born in New York City, Mar. 4, 1889; s. Rafael and Marie Stephanie (Bernard) deFlorez; B.S., in M.E., Mass Inst. Tech.,

1912; D.Sc., Rollins College, 1939; D.Eng., Stevens Institute of Technology, 1946, Northwestern University, 1948; Doctor of Science, Tufts Coll., 1946; married Marian Elizabeth King, July 2, 1912; 1 son, Peter Rafael. Began as research engr. Burgess Co., Marblehead, Mass., 1912, W. A. Hall, chem. engr., 1913; chief engr. Hall Motor Fuel Co., Ltd., Eng., 1914-16; cons. engr. N.E. and Invincible Oil crops, 1919-21; chief engr. N.E. Oil Refining Co., 1921-23: cons. engr. A. D. Little & Co., Gasoline Products Co. and Pierce Oil Company, 1923-25; cons. engr. Texas Co. and Gulf Refining Co. 1926-56, Standard Oil Co. of N.Y., Vacuum Oil Company and Gasoline Products Co., 1929-46; director The deFlorez Company, Incorporated; director American-Optical Co., Nat. Aviation Corporation, Douglas Aircraft Company, Incorporated; engaged in the design, construction and operation of cracking plants for various oil refineries in U.S. and foreign, 1913-40; now aviation and mechanical engrs. cons. inventions; deFlorex Cracking Process, deFlorex Temperature Control System, deFlorez Vertical Stills, Safety Drilling Systems, Remote Control Devices. Former pres. Flight Safety Found. Served Inspector naval construction in charge of research, design and prodn. instruments and accessories, aviation, U.S. Navy Dept., Washington, 1918-19; served as naval aviator U.S. Navy, 1940; spl. asst. to chmn. Bur. of Aero., Navy Department, 1940-43; director special devices division Bureau Aeronautics, 1943-45; dep. chief of Office Research and Inventions, Navy Dept., 1945-46, dep. chief Naval Research, Navy Dept., Aug. 1946-Oct. 1946, Rear Admiral inactive service since Oct. 1946. Awarded the Collier Trophy 1943, for development Naval Aviation synthetic tng.; decorated D.S.M., Legion Merit, D.F.C., Comdr. Mil. div. Order Brit. Empire. Mem. Am. Soc. M.E.; asso. fellow Royal Aero. Soc.; fellow Inst. Aeronautical Sciences, Professional engr. N.Y. State. Catholic. Clubs: Union, St. Anthony, Century Assn. (N.Y. City); Metropolitan (Washington). Comdr. of tech. articles to mags. Home: Pomfret, Conn. Office: 200 Sylvan Av., Englewood Cliffs, N.J. Died Dec. 6, 1962; buried Arlington Nat. Cemetery.

DE FONTIANE, FELIX GREGORY journalist; b. Boston, 1834; s. Louis Antoine and Miss (Allen) De F.; m. Georgia Moore, 1860. Founder, editor Daily South Carolinian, Columbia, S.C., 1860-65; corr. for N.Y.C. newspapers; sent to N.Y. Herald 1st account bombing of Ft. Sumter to appear in Northern press; mil. corr. with rank of maj. 1st S.C. Regt., Confederate States Army, 1861-65; sec. conv. to consider abuses of carpet bag govt., Columbia, 1867; mag. editor N.Y.C. Telegram, 1867-70; financial editor, later art and drama editor N.Y. Herald, 1870-96. Author: A History of American Abolitionism Together with a History of the Southern Confederacy, 1861; Marginalia, 1864; The Fireside Dickens, 1883; De Fontiane's Long-Hand and Rapid-Writer's Companion, 1886. Died Columbia, Dec. 11, 1896.

DE FOREST, HENRY PELOUZE obstetrician, surgeon; b. Fulton, N.Y., Dec. 29, 1864; s. John Teller and Emeline (Stephens) D.; Ph.B., Cornell, 1884, grad. course, 1886-87, M.S. (with distinction), 1887; med. student Columbian U., 1887-88; M.D., Coll. Phys. and Surg. (Columbia), 1890; m. Anna Catherine Gilmour (A.B., Smith 1889), Dec. 6, 1891. Began practice Brooklyn, 1890; in M.E. Hosp., Brooklyn, 1890-91, Vienna U. and Hosp., 1891-92, U. of Freiburg, 1892, Sloane Maternity Hosp., New York, 1892-93, U. of Paris and hospitals, 1897, Dublin and Edinburgh hospitals, 1902, Dresden and Berlin hospitals, 1907; police depts. of Christiana, Stockholm, Helsingfors, St. Petersburg, Moscow and Copenhagen, studying methods of personal identification, 1912. Inventor Dactyloscope, 1912; est. first finger print file in U.S., 1902. Sanitary inspector Department of Health, New York City, 1894-1902; medical examining departments, fire and police, N.Y. City, 1902-03; policy surg., New York, 1902-12; chief med. exam. municipal civil service commn., 1912-19; pres. med. bd., Teachers' Retirement System, City of N.Y., 1917-28. Lecturer on obstetrics, New York Post-Grad. Med. Sch., 1903-21. Capt., asst. surgeon 13th Inf. Nat. Guard. N.Y., 1893-98; acting asst. surg. 3d Div. Hosp. 7th Corps, Spanish-Am. War, 1898-99; maj. and surg. 13th C.A., Nat. Guard, N.Y., 1899-1912; maj. M.C. (retired). Mem. N.Y. Acad. Medicine, Brooklyn Pathol. Soc. (pres. 1900-02), U.S. Soc. Mil. Surgeons, Brooklyn Gynecol. Soc. (pathologist 1898-1902), N.Y. State Med. Soc.; sec. Am. Soc. Sanitary and Moral Prophylaxis, 1911-15; pres. Cornell Asn. Class Secs., 1912-14; pres. Internat. Soc. of Personal Identification, 1920-35; grand historian Alpha Mu Pi Omega, 1919-25; librarian Cornell Club of N.Y. since 1924; charter mem. University Club of Brooklyn, Asso. Physicians of Long Island; hon. member Assn. of Alumni of the College of Physicians and Surgeons. Contributor and member editorial staff Medico-Surgical Bulletin, 1897-99, Brooklyn Medical Jour., 1890-1903, Annals of Surgery since 1890, The Post Graduate, 1904-21; Diseases of the Blood and Ductless Glands in Butler's "Internal Medicine," 1902. Wrote (at personal request of Clara Barton) Textbook for First Aid Classes of the Am. Red Cross, 1903. Author: One Thousand Miles Afoot, 1895; Class Secretaries and Their Duties, 1913; Infectious Abortion of Cattle-As a Complication of Pregnancy in Women, 1917; The Evolution of Dactyloscopy in the United States, with an Historical Note on the First Fingerprint Bureau in the United States and a Bibliography of Personal Identification, 1931; Peanut Worms and-Pellagra-Is the Indian Meal Moth, Plodia interpunctella, the Cause of Pellagra?, 1933; also about 100 miscellaneous articles on med. subjects. Life sec. Class of 1884 (Cornell), Class of 1890 (Columbia); rep. of Coll. of Physicians and Surgeons in Columbia Fed., 1930-39; medalist Columbia U., 1933. Inventor binaural stethoscope, Vienna, 1892. Home: 419 E. 57th St. Address: The Harbor, 667 Madison Av., New York, N.Y. Died June 13, 1948; buried in Mount Adnah Cemetery, Fulton, N.Y.

DE FOREST, JOHN WILLIAM army officer, author; b. Humphreysville (now Seymour), Conn., May 31, 1826; s. John H. and Dotha (Woodward) DeF.; A.M. (hon.), Amherst Coll., 1859; m. Harriet Silliman Shepard, June 5, 1856. Travelled extensively and related his experience in books; in Europe at outbreak of Civil War, immediately returned to Am. and recruited company (Company 1, 12th Conn. Volunteers), New Haven, Conn.; acted as insp. gen. 1st Div., XIX Corps, U.S. Army, also aide on corps staff; brevetted maj. U.S. Volunteers, 1865; wrote descriptions of battle scenes for Harper's Monthly during Civil War; commd. capt. Vet. Res. Corps of Company 1, 14th Regt., after Civil War; dist. comdr., Freedman's Bur. with hdqrs. at Greenville, S.C.; mustered out of service, 1868; spent most of rest of life at New Haven. Author: History of the Indians of Connecticut, 1851; Oriental Acquaintance, 1856; European Acquaintance, 1858; Miss Ravnel's Conversion from Secession to Loyalty (novel), 1867. Died July 17, 1906.

DEFREES, JOSEPH ROLLIE naval officer, ret.; b. Smithboro, Ill., June 12, 1876; s. Newton Talmage and Anna Marcia (Johnson) D.; grad. U.S. Naval Acad., 1900; m. Bernice Fairbanks, May 29, 1913; children-Helen Fairbanks (wife of Lt. J. J. Tomanichal, USN), Joseph Rollie (killed in action, World War II). Commd. ensign USN, 1902, advanced through grades to rear adm., 1933. During World War Comdr. of U.S. transport; then comdr. Submarine Force, Atlantic Fleet, later Asiatic Fleet; comdr. Torpedo Sta., Newport, R.I., for some time; later chief of Staff Scouting Force; then comdt. Navy Yard, Washington, and comdr., Submarine Force, U.S. Fleet; dir. Shore Establishments div. UN; later comdt. 11th Naval Inspector of naval material, Los Angeles, 1941-45; now retired. Decorated Navy Cross, Spanish Campaign Badge, Victory Medal. Clubs: Army and Navy (Washington); Chevy Chase. Home: 143 S. Orange Grove Av., Pasadena, Cal. Died Aug. 1958.

DE GALVEZ, BERNARDO provincial adminstr.; b. Macharaviaya, Spain, July 23, 1746; s. Matias and Josefa Gallardo (Madrid) de G.; m. Felicitas de St. Maxent. Served with Spanish Army against Portugal, in New Spain against Apaches, in Algiers, 1772-76; apptd. gov. and intendant, Province of La., 1776; captured Baton Rouge, La. and Natchez, Miss. during war with Gt. Britain, 1779, Mobile, Ala., 1780, Pensacola, Fla., 1781, enabled Spain to obtain both Floridas in the peace settlement, 1783, and to control mouth of the Mississippi River and Gulf of Mexico; commd. maj. gen., 1784; capt. gen. La. and the Floridas; capt. gen. Cuba, 1784; viceroy of New Spain, 1785; aided in obtaining comml. cedula of 1782, shaping policy of Spain in regard to Indian affairs, immigration, boundary dispute with U.S., navigation of Mississippi River. Died Mexico, Nov. 30, 1786.

DEGROAT, GEORGE BLEWER, govt. ofcl.; b. Binghamton, N.Y., Sept. 27, 1898; s. George Steven and Frances (Blewer) DeG.; m. Helen Elizabeth Walker, July 31, 1921 (dec. Apr. 1952); children—Shirley (Mrs. Conrad Hovik), Barbara (Mrs. Thomas Watson). Various positions Erie R.R., Hornell, N.Y., Huntington, Ind., also N.Y.C., Jersey City, 1916-42; dir. rys. Japan and Korea, War Dept., 1947-48; gen. mgr. Myers Y. Cooper Co., Cin., 1948-53; transportation adviser UN Command and Econ. Coordinator, ICA, Dept. State, 1955-61; U.S. rep. UN meeting, Bangkok, Thailand, Internat. Transp. meetings, Taipei, Taiwan. Bd. suprs., bd. appointments, chmn. hwy. commn., chmn. equalization commn., chmn. laws commn. Steuben County, N.Y., 1933-42. Served to col AUS, 1942-46; assigned 3d Transportation Ry. Command, U.S. Army, 1953-55. Decorated Legion of Merit, Bronze Star, Presdl. citation (U.S.); Ulchi medals (2) (Korea). Mem. Nat. Def. Transportation Assn. (past chpt. pres.). Mason. Clubs: Cincinnati, Buckeye (Cin.). Home: Ft Lauderdale FL Died Nov. 17, 1969.

DE HAAS, JOHN PHILLIP army officer; b. Holland, 1735; s. John Nicholas De Haas; m. Eleanor Bingham. Brought to Am., 1737; commd., ensign Provincial Battalion of Pa. during French and Indian Wars, 1757; took part in expdn. against Ft. Duquesne, 1758. magistrate Lancaster County (Pa.), 1765-79; apptd. col. 1st Pa. Battalion, Continental Army, 1776; participated in Canadian campaign under Gen. Benedict Arnold, 1776; commd. brig. gen., 1777 resigned, 1777; organized local militia for campaign against Indians in Wyoming Valley, 1778, relieved of his command by Arnold. Died Phila., June 3, 1786.

DE HART, WILLIAM MATTHIAS dentist; b. Mason, O., Apr. 23, 1838; s. Dr. Gideon and Malinda (Patton) D.; pub. sch. edn.: m. Carolyn E. Vassar, of Poughkeepsie, N.Y., Oct. 5, 1880. Elected pros. atty. for Carroll, Cass, Howard, Miami, Wabash and Huntington cos., Ind., 1860. Served in Civil War (claims first enlistment U.S.V.) from Apr. 13, 1861, as pvt., corporal and sergt. Co. D, 9th Ind. Inf.; reenlisted Co. D, 46th Ind. Vols., Oct. 4, 1861: maj. 46th Ind. Vet. Inf., 1864-65; prisoner in Camp Tyler and Gross, Texas, Apr. 8-Dec. 5, 1864; was in 43 battles; wounded nr. Ft. Pillow, 1862; mustered out Sept. 4, 1865. Registering officer-at-large for Russell Co., Va., and pres. bd., 1867-68; studied dentistry; in practice since 1869. Mem. G.A.R. Address: Logansport, Ind.

DE HAVEN, EDWIN JESSE naval officer; b. Phila., Ma6 7, 1816; s. William and Maria (MacKeever) De H.; m. Mary Norris Da Costa, May 7, 1844. Apptd. midshipman U.S. Navy, 1829; served in West Indies, 1829-32, with Brazil Squadron, 1832-35, in Pacific Squadron, 1837; passed midshipman, 1835, acting master, 1839; with Wilkes expdn. to Antarctic and Pacific, 1839-42; commd. lt., 1841; served in Steamer Mississippi during Mexican War; in command expdn. to Arctic region to search for Sir John Franklin (explorer who had disappeared 1845), 1850-51, failed to find Franklin but discovered and named Grinnell Land; with Coast Survey, 1853-57; ret., 1862. Died Phila. May 1, 1865; buried Old Christ Ch. Graveyard, Phila.

DEITZLER, GEORGE WASHINGTON abolitionist, mayor: b. Pine Grove, Pa., Nov. 30, 1826; s. Jacob and Maria Deitzler; m. Anna McNeil, Sept. 1864. Aide-de-camp to comdr. free-state forces in Kan., 1855; mem. free-state Territorial Legislature, Kan., 1857-58; speaker Kan. Ho. of Reps.; mem. Kan. Senate under Topeia Constn.; became mayor Lawrence (Kan.), 1860; active in organizing 1st Regt., Kan. Volunteer Inf., apptd. col., promoted to brig. gen., 1862, became comdr.-in-chief with rank of maj. gen., 1864; dir. Leavenworth, Lawrence Ft. Gibson R.R. Co.; treas. U. Kan., 1866. Died Ariz., Apr. 10, 1884.

DE KAY, GEORGE COLMAN naval officer; b. N.Y.C., Mar. 5, 1802; s. George and Catherine (Colman) De K.; m. Janet Halleck Drake, 1833, 7 children. Became mcht. capt., 1822: commd. capt. Argentine Navy during dispute with Brazil over possession of what is now Uruguay, 1826; promoted lt. col., 1827; engaged in shipbldg. business, 1828-31; in naval service of Sultan of Turkey, 1831-32; returned to shipbldg. business 1832; in charge of Macedonian in transport foodstuffs (paid for mostly by himself) to Ireland during famine of 1847. Died Washington, D.C., Jan. 31, 1849.

DE KRUIF, PAUL, writer; b. Zeeland, Mich., Mar. 2, 1890; s. Hendrik and Hendrika J. (Kremer) de K.; B.S., U. Mich., 1912, Ph.D., 1916; m. Rhea Barbarin, Dec. 11, 1922 (dec. July 1957); m. 2d, Eleanor Lappage, Sept. 1, 1959. Bacteriologist, U. Mich., 1912-17, Rockefeller Inst., 1920-22; reporter for Curtis Pub. Co., 1925-71; cons. Chgo. Bd. Health, Mich. State Health Dept. Labs. Served from lt. to capt. San Corps, U.S. Army, 1917-19. Mem. Mich. Med. Soc. (hon.). Collaborator with Sinclair Lewis, on Arrowsmith, 1925. Author: Our Medicine Men, 1922; Microbe Hunters, 1926; Hunger Fighters, 1928; Seven Iron Men, 1929; Men Against Death, 1932; Why Keep Them Alive?, 1936; The Fight for Life, 1938; Health Is Wealth, 1940; Kaiser Wakes the Doctors, 1943; The Male Hormone, 1945; Life Among the Doctors, 1949; A Man Against Insanity, 1957; The Sweeping Wind, 1962. Contbr. to Readers Digest. Home: Holland MI Died Mar. 1971.

DELACOUR, REGINALD BEARDSLEY adj. gen., Conn.; b. Wichita, Kan., Nov. 8, 1886; s. Joseph Walter and Margaret Starr (Beardsley) D.; grad. Stratford High Sch., 1904; Comd. and Gen. Staff Sch., Leavenworth, Kan., spl. class 1926, Army War Coll., Washington, D.C., spl. G-1 class, 1927. Enlisted 1st Ill., Cav., Ill. Nat. Guard, Nov. 8, 1915; disch. sergt., Dec. 1916; commd. 1st lt., inf. Plattsburg Training Camp Aug. 1917; 1st lt. machine gun co., 165th Inf., 42d Div. (Rainbow), A.E.F., disch. capt. May 9, 1919. Mem. Officers Reserve Corps., capt. inf. advancing to col., inf., commd. brig. gen., A.G.D., Conn. Nat. Guard, Sept. 19, 1939; commd. adj. gen., rank of major gen., Apr. 1947. Mem. Conn. Gen. Assembly, 1925-27. Vice chmn. State Aeronautics commn. Conn.; chief of staff, Governors Staff, Conn., 1947. Awarded Distinguished Service Cross, Silver Star, Purple Heart, Conspicuous Service Cross, (N.Y.). Mem. Sons of American Revolution, Huguenot Society of North Carolina, Society of Colonial Wars, Army-Navy Legion of Valor. Republican. Mason (K.T., 32ff, Shriner), Sojourners, Elk. Clubs: Wings, Army-Navy, Washington, D.C. Hartford Golf, Hartford (Hartford, Conn.). Home: Prayer Spring Farm, Oronoque, P.O., Stratford, Conn. Office: State Armory, 3360 Broad St., Hartford, Conn. Died Mar. 21, 1948.

DELAFIELD, JOHN ROSS lawyer; b. Fieldston, N.Y., May 8, 1874; s. Maturin Livingston and Mary Coleman (Livingston) D.; A.B., Coll. of N.J. (now Princeton U.), 1896; A.M., Princeton, 1899; LL.B., Harvard, 1899; m. Violetta S. E. White, June 14, 1904;

children-John White, Richard, Janet; m. 2d, Elsie Lush Funkhouser, September 6, 1950. Practice of law N.Y.C., 1899—; member Delafield, Hope, Linker & Blane; pres. Pemeta Oil Company; dir. United States Asphalt Corporation; member board trustees The Green-Wood Cemetery. Served as col., 9th C.A.C., N.G.N.Y.; col. Ordnance Dept. U.S. Army, chmn. War-Dept. Bd. Contract Adjustment; brig. gen. Ordnance Res., U.S. Army, 1923. Pres. Reserve Officers' Assn. of U.S., 1923-26; comdr. in chief Mil. Order World War, 1930-33, now hon. comdr. in chief. Awarded D.S.M. (U.S.); Comdr. Legion of Honor (France); Comdr. Order of Crown (Italy); comdr. Cuban Red Cross; Crowell Gold Medal of Army Ordnance Assn. Member Bar Assn. City of New York, Soc. of Cincinnati, St. Nicholas Soc., Constitution Island Assn. (chairman bd.), Delafield Family Assn. (pres.), Hudson River Conservation Soc. Episcopalian. Clubs: Down Town (N.Y.C.); Army and Navy (Washington); Edgewood (Tivoli, N.Y.). Author: Delafield 2 vols., 1945. Home: Montgomery Pl., Annandale, N.Y. Office: 342 Madison Av., N.Y.C. 10017. Died Apr. 8, 1964; buried Woodlawn Cemetery, N.Y.C.

DELAFIELD, RICHARD mil. engr., ednl. adminstr.; b. N.Y.C., Sept. 1, 1798; s. John and Ann (Hallett) D.; grad. U.S. Mil. Acad., 1818; m. Helen Summers: m. 2d, Harriet Covington; 6 children. Commd. 2d lt. U.S. Army, 1818, advanced through grades to maj. gen., 1855; supt. U.S. Mil. Acad., West Point, Ga., 1838-45, 56-61; superintending engr. N.Y. Harbor Defenses, 1845-56; mem. Mil. Commn. to Crimea, 1855; commd. brig. gen., chief of engrs. U.S. Army, 1864, in command Corps Engrs., also in charge of Engr. Bur., Washington, D.C., 1864-66; ret., 1866: mem. Commn. for Improvement Boston Harbor; regent Smithsonian Instn. Author: Report on the Art of War in Europe in 1854-6 (published by order of U.S. Congress), 1860. Died Washington, D.C., Nov. 5, 1873.

DE LA MOTHE, ANTOINE (SIEUR DE CADILLAC), colonial gov.; b. Gascony, France, 1660; s. Jean de la Mothe and Jeanne de Malenfant; m. Marie Therese Guyon, 1687. In command post of Mackinac (most important position in Western country), 1694; capt. colonial troops of the Marine, 1699; obtained grant of Detroit and title of lt. of the King; set out with colonists to found Detroit, 1701; gov. La., 1713-16. Died Castle Sarrazin, France, Oct. 18, 1730.

DE LANCEY, OLIVER colonial legislator, army officer; b. N.Y.C., Sept. 16, 1718; s. Stephen and Anne (van Cortlandt) De L.; m. Phila Franks, 4 children. Alderman for the Outward, 1754-57; raised N.Y.C. Regt. for expdn. against Crown Point, 1758; mem. N.Y.C. delegation to N.Y. Assembly, 1759-60; mem. N.Y. Provincial Council, 1760-76; receiver gen., 1763; col.-in-chief So. Mil. Dist. 1773; Loyalist, commd. brig. gen. Brit. Army (highest ranking American), raised 3 battalions of troops which carried his name, became symbol of Loyalist during Am. Revolution; went to Eng., 1783. Died Beverley, Eng., Oct. 25, 1785.

DELANEY, MATTHEW A. medical officer U.S. Army; b. Waymart, Pa., Mar. 6, 1874; s. Sylvester and Elizabeth (Burns) DeL.; grad. Pa. Normal Inst., 1896; M.D., U. of Pa., 1898; grad. Army Med. Sch., Washington, 1902; studied U. of Vienna, 1913-14; C.P.H., Harvard U. Sch. of Health, 1928; hon. D.Sc. from Dickinson College, 1935; m. Elizabeth Voltz, Apr. 17, 1918. With Med. Dept., U.S.A., Feb. 6, 1901 - ; promoted through grades to brig. gen., Jan. 1, 1932. Served in Philippine Insurrection; White House physician under President Taft, 1909-13; served in Mexican border trouble, 1916; went to France in command Pa. Base Hosp. No. 10, 1917; liaison officer Brit. War Office, London, comdg. all Am. med. officers with Brit. Army, 1918; exec. officer Surgeon General's Office, 1919-21; surgeon Field Arty. Sch., Ft. Sill, Okla., 1924, Camp Devens, Mass., 1927-28; med. adviser in pub. health and sanitation to Gov. Gens. Henry L. Stimson and Dwight Davis, of Philippines, 1921-31; corps area surgeon Fifth Corps Area, 1931; asst. surgeon gen., 1931-36; comdt. Med. Field Service Sch., Carlisle, Pa., 1933-36, retired. Fellow Am. Coll. of Surgeons, Am. Pub. Health Assn., Am. Coll. Physicians, A.M.A. Awarded D.S.M. (U.S.); Order St. Michael and St. George (British); mentioned in dispatches for "gallantry in the field" by Field Marshal Sir Douglas Haig; member Order of St. Lazare of Jerusalem. Died Nov. 1, 1936.

DE LANGLADE, CHARLES MICHEL army officer; b. Mackinac, Can., May 1729; s. Augustin Monet and Domitelle (Ottawa Indian) De L.; m. Charlotte Bourassa, 1754, several children. Commd. cadet French Colonial Army, 1750, ensign, 1755, lt., 1760; led Indian allies in battles at Lake Champlain, Ft. William Henry, Quebec, and Montreal during French and Indian War; became Brit. subject, 1760; as capt. in Brit. army led Indian auxiliaries against Col. George Rogers Clark during Am. Revolution; granted lands in Canada for services to England. Died Green Bay, Wis., 1801.

DELANO, FRANCIS HENRY rear adm., b. Mt. Carmel, O., Apr. 14, 1848; s. Henry Franklin and Maria (Carter) D.; apptd. from Mass., and grad. U.S. Naval Acad., 1867; m. Evelina Frances Paine, Jan. 29, 1874. Ensign, Dec. 1868; promoted through grades to capt., Oct. 1903; rear adm., June 29, 1905, and retired at own request. Served on Susquehanna, Contoocook and Yantic, N. Atlantic Fleet, 1867-69; Mohican, Pacific Fleet, and Ashuelot, Asiatic Fleet, 1870-73; Portsmouth, Pacific Fleet, 1874-75; on various stas. and duties to 1896; flagship Olympia, Asiatic Fleet and Minneapolis, N. Atlantic Fleet, and comd. Fish Hawk, N. Atlantic Fleet, 1896-98; ordnance officer navy yard, Boston, 1898-99; comdg. training ships Alliance and Topeka, and Marietta, N. Atlantic Fleet, 1899-1902; capt. of yard, navy yard, League Island, Pa., Mar.-Dec., 1902; ordnance officer an navy yard, Portsmouth, 1902-03; Naval War Coll. and comdg. Dixie, Jan.-Nov., 1903; assigned to court martial duty and served as comdg. officer of receiving ship Lancaster, 1903-05. Died Jan. 31, 1929.

DELANO, FREDERIC ADRIAN retired; b. at Hong Kong, China, Sept. 10, 1863; s. Warren and Catherine Robbins (Lyman) D. (both natives of Mass.); lived most of boyhood at Newburgh, N.Y.; A.B., Harvard, 1885; married Matilda A. Peasley, November 22, 1888 (deceased, 1943); children-Mrs. Alexander G. Grant (dec.), Mrs. J. L. Houghteling. Began railway service with the C., B.&Q., Railroad Company, with engineering party in Colorado, Aug. 1, 1885; entered Aurora (Ill.) shops, same road, Oct. 1, 1885, as apprentice machinist; apptd. temporarily acting engr. of tests at Aurora, Apr. 1887; placed in charge bur. rail inspn. at Chicago, July 1,1887; asst. to 2d v.p. at Chicago, Apr. 1889; supt. freight terminals at Chicago, July 1890; supt. motive power at Chicago, Feb. 1, 1899; gen. mgr. at Chicago. C., B.&Q. R.R., July 1, 1901-Jan. 10, 1905. Pres. Wheeling & Lake Erie R.R. Co., Wabash-Pittsburgh Terminal Ry. Co., May 1, 1905-08; 1st v.p. Wabash R.R., May 1-Oct. 5, 1905; pres., Oct. 5, 1905-Dec. 1911, and one of receivers, Dec. 1911-Dec. 1913; pres. C., I. & L. (Monon) Ry. Co., Dec. 1913-Aug. 10, 1914. Mem. Federal Reserve Bd., for 6-yr. term, and designated as vice-gov. for 2 years; resigned, June 1918, to enter army. Commd. maj. Engr. Corps, July 17, 1918; assigned to staff of Gen. Atterbury, dir. gen. of transportation at Tours, France; promoted lt. col. Trans. Corps and apptd. deputy dir. transportation at Paris, Oct. 26, 1918; promoted col. Trans. Corps and apptd. deputy dir. transportation at Paris, Oct. 26, 1918; promoted col., Trans. Corps, May 2, 1919; hon. disch., Oct. 25, 1919; commd. col. Engr. R.C., Jan. 1, 1920. Awarded D.S.M. for service in France, Sept. 9, 1921; Legion of Honor (France), 1919; Order of Sheng Li (Victory) from Chinese govt., 1948. Appointed receiver by Supreme Court of U.S. in Red River Boundary Case, Okla. vs. Texas, U.S. Intervenor, Chmn. Internat. Commn. League of Nations on inquiry into the production of opium in Persia and the possible substitution of other crops or industries. Formerly regent Smithsonian Instn. Chmn. Nat. Capital Park and Planning Commn. of Washington; retired Aug. 1942 after 18 years service. Formerly chmn. Nat. Resources Planning Bd., 1934-43; now retired. Chairman emeritus Am. Planning and Civic Assn. Clubs; University (Chicago); Metropolitan, Cosmos (Washington, D.C.). Home: 2400 16th St., Washington. Died Mar. 28, 1953; buried Fairhaven, Mass.

DELANO, JANE ARMINDA nurse; b. Townsend, N.Y., Mar. 12, 1862; d. George and Mary Ann (Wright) Delano; grad. Bellevue Hosp. Sch. Nursing, N.Y.C., 1886. Supt. nurses of a hosp., Jacksonville, Fla., 1887, U. Pa. Hosp. Sch. Nursing, 1891-96; dir. girls' dept. House of Refuge, Randall's Island, N.Y., 1900-02; dir. Bellevue Hosp. Sch. Nursing, 1902-06; chmn. nat. com. A.R.C., 1909; supt. Nurse Corps, U.S. Army, 1909, made Red Cross Nursing Service the reserve of Army Nurse Corps; pres. bd. dirs. Am. Jour. Nursing; pres. Am. Nurses' Assn., 1909-12; in charge of selection and assignment of all mil. nursing units, 1916; dir. Dept. of Nursing (World War I orgn.), 1918; went to France, 1919. Author: American Red Cross Textbook on Elementary Hygiene and Home Care of the Sick, 1913. Died Savenay Hosp. Center, France, Apr. 15, 1919.

DELANY, MARTIN ROBINSON physician, army officer; b. Charles Town, Va. (now Charleston, W. Va.), May 6, 1812; s. Samuel and Pati D.; entered Harvard, 1849, after having been rejected in N.Y., Pa.; m. Kate A. Richards, Mar. 15, 1843, 11 children. Went to Pa., 1822; with Frederick Douglass issued Northern Star, Rochester, N.Y., 1847; originator, pres. Nat. Emigration Conv., 1854, apptd. to lead expdn. to Niger Valley, Africa, to explore possibilities of returning Negroes to the area; commd. maj. U.S. Army (1st Negro maj.), 1865; judge, Charleston S.C.; fought vigorously against polit. corruption, but defeated when he stood for election on Independent Republican ticket as lt. gov. S.C., 1874. Author: Condition, Elevation and Destiny of the Colored People of the United States Politically Considered, 1852. Died Xnia, O., Jan. 24, 1885.

DELEUW, CHARLES EDMUND, cons. engr.; b. Jacksonville, Ill., July 3, 1891; s. Oscar Anthony and Bessie Mary (Tribbey) DeL.; B.S., U. of Ill., 1912, C.E., 1916; married Martha Guthrie, Aug. 21, 1917 (dec.); 1 dau., Martha Guthrie (Mrs. Donald E. Stende); m. 2d, Ethel Buckmaster, July 29, 1927 (divorced 1948); children—Charles E., Sally (Mrs. Jon Peak) m. 3d, Sylvia Ffennell, Feb. 25, 1948 (dec. Oct. 1960); m. 4th, Emilene Brown, November 11, 1961. Chmn. bd. De Leuw, Cather & Co., cons. engrs.; transit and highway reports and plans for Chgo., Det., Los Angeles, Montreal, Toronto, Balt., Washington, Cleveland, Cin., Louisville, Boston, St. Louis, Providence, Buffalo, NY., Portland, San Francisco, Caracas, El Paso, Milwaukee, Norfolk, Oakland, Richmond, Istanbul, Sydney, Australia, Perth, Australia, New Jersey Turnpike; New York Thruway, Ohio Turnpike, Okla. Turnpike; consulting engineer for Department of Subways, City of Chicago, 1936-40, chief engr. 1941-44. Served as capt., 4th U.S. Engrs., 1917-19. Awarded D.S.C. Mem. Engring. Inst. of Can., Am. Institute Cons. Engrs., Am. Soc. C.E., Soc. Am. Mil. Engrs., Western and Ill. socs. engrs., Am. Transit Assn., Inst. Civil Engrs., Inst. Traffic Engrs., Phi Delta Theta. Clubs: University, Tavern; Mid-America. Home: Chicago IL Died Oct. 1970.

DEMAREE, ALBERT LOWTHER educator; b. Bloomsburg, Pa., Apr. 24, 1894; s. William L. and Katharyn S. (Reifsnyder) D.; A.B., Dickinson Coll., 1923; M.A., Columbia, 1929, Ph.D., 1940; m. Helen Jackson, June 25, 1937. Asst. purchasing agt. Certain-Teed Roofing Co., 1928-35; tchr. history Dartmouth, 1927-61, instr., 1927-35, asst. prof., 1935-41, prof., 1941-61, chmn. dept., 1956-60. Served USN, 1917-22; comdr. USNR, 1941-46. Mem. Am. Hist. Assn., U.S. Naval Inst. Author: The American Agricultural Pres, 1819-60, 1941; Naval Orientation, 1943—. Home: 19 E. Wheelock St., Hanover, N.H. 03755. Died Jan. 15, 1964; buried Bloomsburg. Pa.

DE MEZIERES Y CLUGNY, ATHANASE army officer, explorer; b. Paris, France, c. 1715: s. Louis Christophe de Mezieres and Marie Antoinette Clugny; m. Marie Petronelle Felicione de St. Denis, Apr. 18, 1746; m. 2d, Dame Pelagie Fazende. Served from ensign to lt. col.; a commr. to determine Tex.-La. boundary at Gulf of Mexico, 1756; as ruler Red River Valley, supervised Indian trade, won tribes of La., Tex., Ark. and Okla. to Spanish allegiance; promoted lt. col. by King of Spain, 1772; created knight Order of St. Louis; apptd. gov. Tex., 1779. Died before taking office, Nov. 2, 1779. buried Cathedral of San Fernando, San Antonio, Tex.

DE MILHAU, LOUIS JOHN DE GRENON, lawyer; b. N.Y. City, July 27, 1884; s. John Jefferson (surgeon. bvt. brig. gen. U.S. Army) and Katherine Louise (Manning) de M.; A.B., Harvard University, 1906; LL.B., New York Law School, 1911; married Renee Noel Gourd, December 29, 1909; children—John Waddington, Renee D. (Mrs. de Milhau Davis), Louis John. Admitted to New York bar, 1911, and practiced at N.Y. City. Mem. Squadron A, Cadet Corps, N.Y. City, 1889-1901; mem. 9th Training Regt., Plattsburg, N.Y., 1916; capt. Signal Corps U.S. Army, Dec. 1917-Mar. 1919; capt. J.A.G.D., O.R.C., 1921; lt. col. ret. Govt. appeal agt. Local Bd. No. 133, N.Y. County, June-Dec. 1917. Trustee Inc. Village Old Brookville, L.I., N.Y., 1930-34, police justice, 1935-39. Treas. and mem. bd. mgrs. Lincoln Hall; member bd. trustees and president emeritus St. Vincent de Paul Inst., Tarrytown. Past comdr. N.Y. Commandery Mil. Order Loyal Legion; com. visitors Peabody Mus.; Univ. Mus., Harvard, 1908-21. Republican. Clubs: Harvard, Explorers (honorary mem., historian, director), End of the Earth (N.Y.C.); Army and Navy (Washington); Harvard Travelers (fellow; Boston). Mem. Harvard U. expdn. to Iceland, 1905; de Milhau-Harvard expdn. to S. America, 1907-09; explorations in Peru and Bolivia; donor Icelandic birds to Peabody Mus. Wrote introd. to "Indians of Eastern Peru," by Farabee, 1923. Author: "Sprengisandur Holiday" in Explorers Club Tales, 1937. Home: New York City NY Died 1968.

DE MOTTE, MARK L. lawyer, congressman; b. Rockville, Ind., Dec. 28, 1832; s. Rev. Daniel and Mary (Brewer) D.; ed. Ind. log sch. house until 1848; grad. Asbury (now De Pauw) U., A.B., 1853, A.M., 1856; grad. law sch. same, LL.B., 1855 (LL.D., De Pauw, 1903); m. Elizabeth Christy, Dec. 16, 1856 (died 1891); m. 2d, Clara Stephens, Jan. 12, 1893. Admitted to Ind. bar, Feb. 19, 1855; pros. atty. 31st jud. circuit, Ind., Oct. 1856; entered Union service as ranking 1st lt., 4th Ind. battery, Aug. 1861; promoted capt. and a.q.m., May 1862. Mem. 47th Congress, 10th Ind. dist., 1881-83; mem. Ind. senate, 1886-90; dean Northern Ind. Law Sch., Valparaiso, Ind., 1879 - . Methodist. Republican. Address: Valparaiso, Ind. Died 1908.

DENBY, CHARLES lawyer, diplomat; b. Mt. Joy, Va., 1830; educated at Georgetown Univ. (LL.D.); grad. Va. Mil. Inst.; taught school 2 yrs.; located as lawyer in Ind. in Union army as lt. col., 42d Ind. vols., and later col., 80th Ind. vols., in Civil war; U.S. minister to China, 1885-98; apptd. by President, 1898, mem. of commn. to investigate conduct of war against Spain; mem. U.S. Philippines Commn., 1899. Home: Evansville, Ind. Died 1904.

DENBY, EDWIN sec. of the navy; b. Evansville, Ind., Feb. 18, 1870; s. Hon. Charles and Martha (Fitch) D.; bro. of Charles D.; ed. Evansville High Sch. and U. of Mich.; went to China, 1885, with father, then U.S. minister; in Chinese Imperial Maritime Customs Service, 1887-94; returned to U.S., 1894; LL.B., U. of Mich., 1896; m. Marion Bartlett Thurber, Mar. 18, 1911; children - Edwin, Marion. Admitted to bar 1896, and began practice at Detroit. Gunner's mate, U.S.S.

Yosemite, during Spanish-Am. War, 1898; pvt. U.S. Marine Corps, 1917; on reserve as maj., Jan. 1, 1919. Mem. Mich. Ho. of Rep., 1903; mem. 59th to 61st Congresses (1905-11), 1st lMich. Dist.; apptd. chief probation officer Recorder's Court, City of Detroit, and Circuit Court of Wayne Co., Dec. 1920; sec. of Navy, Mar. 4, 1921-Mar. 10, 1924 (resigned). Republican. Episcopalian. Home: Detroit, lfich. Died Feb. 8, 1929.

DENFELD, LOUIS EMIL, retired naval officer; b. Westboro, Mass., Apr. 13, 1891; s. Louis E. and Etta May (Kelley) D.; A.M., Naval Acad., 1912; m. Rachel Metcalf, June 5, 1915. Commd. ensign, June 1912 and advanced through grades to admiral; served in Virginia, Ark., Paducah, and N.J., 1912-17; on Destroyers Ammen and Lamberton on escort duty during World War I; comd. Destroyers Wadsworth and Brooks and Submarine S-24, 1919-29; aide to Chief of Bur. of Navigation, 1929-31; staff of Comdr. Battle Force and Comdr. in Chief, U.S. Fleet, 1931-33; Bur. of Navigation, 1933-35; comd. Destroyer Div. 11, Battle Force, 1935-37; adminstrative aide to Chief of Naval Operations, 1937-39; comd. Destroyer Div. 18 and Destroyer Squadron 1, 1939-41; special naval observer in London, Chief of Staff for Comdr. Support Force, Atlantic Fleet, 1941; asst. chief naval personnel, Bur. of Naval Personnel, Navy Dept., 1942-44; comdr. battleships, Div. 9, Pacific, 1945; chief of Naval Personnel, 1945-47; comdr.-in-chief Pacific and U.S. Pacific, 1947; chief of naval operations, and mem. Joint Chiefs of Staff, 1947-49; ret. as adm., 1950; cons. Sun Oil Co., 1950-71. Decorated D.S.M., Legion of Merit with gold star. Episcopalian. Clubs: Chevy Chase (Md.); Army-Navy, Metropolitan, Carlton, 1925 F Street. Home: Westboro MA Died Mar. 28, 1972.

DENHARDT, HENRY H. lawyer, soldier; b. Bowling Green, Ky., Mar. 8, 1876; s. William and Margaret (Denhardt) D.; student Ogden Coll., Bowling Green; LL.B., Cumberland U., 1899; student Arty. Sch. of Fire, Ft. Sill, Okla.; Army War Coll. Admitted to Ky. bar, 1899, and began practice at Bowling Green; pres. Times Journal Pub. Co. Pros. atty. City of Bowling Green, 1900-10; judge Warren County (Ky.) Court, 1910-18; del. from state at large to Dem. Nat. Conv., 1924; lt. gov. of Ky., 1923-27. Officer Ky. N.G., June 1898; maj. 3rd Ky. Inf., Mexican border service, 1916-17; maj. 3d Ky. Inf., with 139th F.A. and 319th F.A., 1917-18, lt. col. F.A., 1918-19; participated in St. Mlihiel and Argonne-Meuse offensives; cited and promoted; hon. disch., Mar. 22, 1919; now brig. gen. comdg. 75th Brigade, N.G., U.S.A., comprising 149th Ky. Inf. and 150th W.Va. Inf.; comd. troops during riots at Newport, Ky., 1921-22; serving as adjutant gen. of Ky., Dec. 1931-Dec. 1935. Chmn. Ky. Disabled Ex-Service Men's Bd.; v.p. and former mem. legislative com. Nat. Guard Assn. of U.S. Former moderator Ky. Synod Cumberland Presbyn. Church. Mason. Had charge of rescue of Floyd Collins, cave explorer, 1925. Presented saddle horse by citizens of Newport, and silver service, by citizens of Ft. Thomas, for quelling riots. Home: Bowling Green, Ky. Died Sept. 20, 1937.

DENIG, ROBERT GRACEY commodore U.S.N.; b. Columbus, O., May 22, 1851; s. Robert McClintock and Jane (Harry) D.; grad. U.S. Naval Acad., 1873; m. Jeannie Livingston Hubbard, Apr. 11, 1878. Promoted through the various grades to commodore and retired, June 30, 1908. On board Tallapoosa, Saranac, Tuscarora, Benecia, during revolution in Panama, and in Honolulu at the time Kalakaua was elected king; aboard Huron when she was wrecked on coast Nov. 24, 1877, and one of 29 saved; Trenton, flagship European sta.; flagship Brooklyn on tour around the world; flagship Baltimore, cruise around the world; flagship Philadelphia, Atlantic Coast; gunboat Machinas, U.S.S. Petrel, wintering in Manchuria during war between China and Japan; served during war with Spain on Niagara, Topeka, participating in bombardment of San Juan and battle of Nipe Bay; flagship Chicago, as fleet engr., cruise around Africa and S. America; shore duty at Mare Island, Portsmouth, N.H., U.S. Naval Acad., Naval Training Sta., Newport, R.I.; inspection duty state of Pa.; head of dept. steam engring., Phila. Navy Yard; Spl. duty, applied mathematics, Hamilton Coll. Republican. Episcopalian. Medals: Battle of Nipe Bay, Spanish-Am. War, U.S. Campaign Medal. Home: Sandusky, O. Died Apr. 9, 1924.

DENNIE, CHARLES CLAYTON, physician; b. Excelsior Springs, Mo., Oct. 20, 1883; s. Arthur Doggett and Catherine (Heffley) D.; B.S., Baker U., 1908; M.D., U. of Kan., 1912; m. Glynn Bowden, July 29, 1940. Interne, Kan. City Gen. Hosp., 1912-13, Mass. Gen. Hosp., 1913-15; house officer and instr. in syphilis, Harvard Med. Sch., 1914-15; prof. of dermatology, Med. Sch., U. of Kan., from 1938, becoming prof. emeritus; clin. prof. medicine U. Mo.; dermatologist to Kansas City Gen., Mercy, St. Luke's, hosps. Served A.U.S., 1918-19; major, Med. Corps. A.E.F. Mem. Am. Bd. Dermatology and Syphilology, Am. Med. Assn., Am. Dermotol. Assn. (pres., hon. mem.), Am. Acad. Dermatology and Syphilology, Pan-Am. Med. Assn., French Soc. Dermatology and Syphilology, Brazilian (asso.), N.Y. (hon.) dermatol. assns. Author: Congenital Syphilis, 1940; A History of Syphilis, 1962; also monograph, Syphilis, 1928. Translator of Francisco Lopez de Villalobos book relating to syphilis, written 1498 (pub. in Bull. of History of Medicine). Home: Kansas City MO Died Jan. 13, 1971.

DENNIS, ALFRED LEWIS PINNEO writer; b. Beirut, Syria, May 21, 1874 (parents were temporarily residing abroad); s. James Shepard and Mary Elizabeth (Pinneo) D.; A.B., Princeton, 1896; student Columbia, Heidelberg, Harvard, 1896-1901; Ph.D., Columbia, 1901; m. Mary Boardman, d. George W. Cable, June 7, 1899; children - Mary Elizabeth (Mrs. Alexander Standish), Louise Cable. Instr. and prof. history and polit. science, Bowdoin Coll., 1901-04 lecturer history, Harvard, 1905-06; prof. history, U. of Wis., 1906-20; resigned to engage in research work; prof. history and internat. relations, Clark U., Worcester, Mass., 1923 - . Temp. sec. Wis. State Council Defense, 1917. Capt. Mil. Intelligence Div. Gen. Staff, 1918-19; asst. mil. attacheé, Am Embassy, London reporting to Peace Conf., Paris, 1919. Awarded British Mil. Cross. Author: Eastern Problems at the Close of the XVIII Century, 1901; Anglo-Japanese Alliance, 1923; Foreign Policies of Soviet Russia, 1924; John Hay (in Secretaries of State Series); Adventures in American Diplomacy, 1928. Died Nov. 14, 1930.

DENNIS, JOHN HANCOCK journalist; b. Concord, Mass., May 28, 1835; s. Samuel and Cynthia D.; educated pub. schools, Concord, Mass., Boston High Sch., and Goodnow's Prep. Inst., Concord; left for Cal., 1853; unmarried. Reporter San Francisco Herald, 1854; editor Eldora Times, Placerville, Cal., 1862; editor Austin (Nev.) Reveille, 1868-73, Eureka (Nev.) Sentinel, 1873-77, Tuscarora (Nev.) Times Review, 1877-81, Salt Lake City (Utah) Democrat, 1882-83, Virginia City Chronicle, 1893, Nev. State Jour., 1901-04; retired. Served as melter and refiner Carson City Mint, 1886-89. Mem. Cal. Assembly, 1860-61; removed to Nev., 1863; sheriff, co. clerk and co. commr., Lander Co., Nev.; State senator, Elks Co., 1884; Nev. mem. Nat. Dem. Com. since 1896. Was maj. on staff Gov. Bradley, and comd. troops in campaign against White Pine Indians, 1875. Democrat. Address: Reno, Nev.

DENNISTON, HENRY MARTYN rear adm.; b. Washingtonville, N.Y., June 13, 1840; s. Robert and Mary (Scott) D.; ed. at home and at Yale, 1858-61, leaving in beginning of senior yr., A.B., 1862, A.M., 1892; m. Emma J. Dusenbury, Jan. 21, 1869. Entered U.S.N. pay corps, Sept. 9, 1861; promoted paymaster, Apr. 14, 1862, pay insp., Aug. 19, 1876, pay dir., July 31, 1884; retired June 13, 1902, with rank of rear admiral. Presbyn. Republican. Home: Dobbs Ferry, N.Y. Died May 23, 1922.

DENNY, EBENEZER army officer, mayor Pitts.; b. Carlisle, Pa., Mar. 11, 1761; s. William and Agnes (Parker) D.; m. Nancy Wilkins, July 1, 1793, 3 sons-Harmer, William, St. Clair, also 2 daus. Commd. ensign 1st Pa. Regt., 1776, fought nr. Williamsburg, Va.; served with advance units at siege of York, 1776; served under St. Clair in Carolinas, became adjutant to Harmer, aide-de-camp to St. Clair; mem. 1st Pa. Constl. Conv. from Bedford County, 1777; commd. capt., 1794, commanded LeBoeuf expdn.; treas. Allegheny County (Pa.), 1803, 08; 1st mayor Pitts., 1816: dir. br. of Bank of U.S., Bank of Pitts. Died July 21,1822.

DENNY, FRANK LEE officer U.S. Marine Corps; b. Indianapolis, Ind., July 20, 1858; s. James Cook D. (atty. gen. Ind.) and Caroline D., d. John Wesley Davis, speaker U.S. Ho. of Rep.; m. Julia Graham, d. Gen. Innis Nelson Palmer, U.S.A., Oct. 6, 1886. Apptd. 2d lt. U.S. Marine Corps, June, 1880, 1st lt., Dec., 1884; capt. asst. q.m., Feb., 1892; maj. q.m., June, 1897; col. chief q.m., Mar., 1899. Had 6 yrs. sea service; shore service Alexandria, Egypt, 1882, after British bombardment, Isthmus Panama, 1885, Spanish-Am. War; revoluntarily retired, May 1, 1913, after 30 yrs.' service. Now v.p. Real Estate Trust Co., Washington. Home: Washington, D.C. Died July 8, 1914.

DENNY, HARMAR DENNY govt. ofcl.; b. Allegheny, Pa., July 2, 1886; s. Harmar Denny and Elizabeth Bell (Marshall) D.; B.A., Yale, 1908; LL.B., U. Pitts., 1911; m. Mary Blair Burgwin, Apr. 10, 1915; children-Elizabeth Marshall (Mrs. John B. Saxman), James O'Hara, Anne Burgwin (Mrs. Archbald Angus). Admitted to Pa. bar, 1911; asso. Patterson, Sterrett & Acheson, Pitts., 1912-17; Dalzell, Fisher & Dalzell, Pitts., 1920-26; mem. Burgwin, Scully & Burgwin, Pitts., 1926-1933; dir. pub. safety, Pitts., 1933-34; investment counsel Cromwell & Co. Inc., Pitts., 1938-50; asso. Rose, Eichnauer & Rose, Pitts., since 1949. Republican candidate mayor Pitts., 1941; mem. 82d Congress, 29th Dist. Pa. Mem. Civil Aeros. Bd., 1953—, vice chmn., 1954—. Mem. nat. exec. bd. Boy Scouts Am., Carnegie Hero Fund Commn. Served with U.S. Army, A.S., World War I, as bombing pilot, 1st lt.; U.S. Army A.C., World War II, as lt. col., asst. air insp. Eastern Flying Command, Maxwell Field, Ala. Mem. S.A.R., Soc. of Cin., Phi Delta Phi, Zeta Psi. Presbyn. (trustee, session). Clubs: Columbia Country (Washington); Duquesne; Pittsburgh Golf; Fox Chapel Golf; Yale (N.Y.C.). Home: 3062 Porter St., Washington 8. Office: 3601 Connecticut Av., Washington 8. Died Jan. 1966.

DENT, FREDERICK RODGERS, JR., retired air force officer; b. Mercer, Pa., Feb. 12, 1908; son Reverend Fred and Jane Margaret (Hoon) D.; B.S., U.S. Mil. Acad., 1929; A.B., St. Mary's University, San Antonio, 1930; M.S., Mass. Institute Technology, 1938; student Air Corps Engring. Sch., Wright Field, 1936, Harvard Bus. Sch. Advt. Management Program, 1947; m. Corra Lynn Robinson, Jan. 24, 1931; children—Frederick Rodgers III, Corra Lynn, David Haley. Commd. 2d lt., U.S. Army, 1929, ret. maj. gen. Air Force; instr. Kelly Field, Tex., 1931; engr. officer and armament officer, Luke Field, Hawaii, 1931-32; instr. Randolph Field, Tex., 1933; engr. officer and test pilot, Wright Field, 1938-43; chief U.S. Air Tech. Sect., Eng., 1943, comdr. 44th Bomb group, Eng., 1943-44, comdr. 95th Bomb Wing, 1944, wounded and returned to U.S.; chief aircraft div. A.A.F. Bd., Orlando, Fla., 1944-45, chief engring. br., material div. A.A.F. Hdqrs., Washington, 1945; chief, aircraft and physical requirements sub-div., Wright Field, 1945-47, chief equipment lab., 1947, asst. to chief, engring. div., 1947-48, chief operations engring. div., 1948-49, dep. chief, engring. div., 1949-50, chief, 1950-51, comdg. gen. Wright Air Development Center, 1951-52; mil. dir. production and requirements Munitions Board, 1952-53; Commander Mobile Air Materiel Area, Brookley AFB, 1953-57, ret.; program manager of missile The Martin Co., Baltimore. Decorated the Silver Star, Legion of Merit, D.S.M., D.F.C., Air medal with 1 Oak Leaf Cluster, Commendation ribbon, Purple Heart (United States); Croix de Guerre with palm (Belgium); Croix de Guerre with palm (France). Mem. com. on operating problems NACA, 1947-51. First glider pilot in Air Force. Home: Towson MD Died Sept. 11, 1969.

DENT, FREDERICK TRACY army officer; b. St. Louis County, Mo., Dec. 17, 1821; s. Frederick, F. and Ellen (Wienshall) D., grad. U.S. Mil. Acad., 1843. Apptd. brevet 2d lt. 6th Inf., U.S. Army, 1843; served in Indian Territory; served in battles of Veracruz, San Antonio, Contreras, Churubusco, and Molino del Rey during Mexican War; commd. 1st lt., capt., 1848; later served on Pacific R.R. Survey, Yakima and Spokane expdns., various Indian campaigns in N.W.; commanded regt. in Army of Potomac during Civil War; commd. lt. col., 1864; a.d.c. to Gen. Grant, 1864-65, 66; mil. gov. of Richmond (Va.), 1865; promoted brig. gen. U.S. Volunteers, 1865, col. U.S. Army, 1866; mil. sec. to Pres. Grant, 1868-73; resigned commn., 1883. Died Dec. 24, 1892.

DENTON, WINFIELD K., lawyer; born Evansville, Ind., Oct. 28, 1896; s. George K. and Sara Linda (Chick) D.; A.B., DePauw U.; LL.B., Harvard; m. Grace Abernethy, Dec. 27, 1927; children—Beth (Mrs. Jim Bamberger), Mary, Sara (Mrs. D. Ong). Admitted to Ind. bar, and practiced in Evansville; prosecutor Vanderburgh County, Ind.; mem. Ind. State Legislature, caucus chmn., 1939, minority leader, 1941; mem. 81st, 82d, 84th-89th U.S. Congresses, from eighth congressional district Indiana; attorney at law Denton and Gerling. Served as 2d lieutenant, Aviation Corps, U.S. Army, World War I, from maj. to lt. col., USAAF, World War II; judge adv. gen. dept. Mem. Am. Legion, Vets. Fgn. Wars, Phi Kappa Psi. Democrat. Mason (32 deg., K.T., Shriner). Elk. Home: Evansville IN Died Nov. 2, 1971.

DE PEYSTER, JOHN WATTS soldier, author; b. New York, March 9, 1821; s. Frederic de Peyster (of Holland and Huguenot descent); and Mary Justina, d. Hon. John Watts (of Scotch and Huguenot descent); ed. Columbia Univ., but was not graduated because of ill health (A.M., same, 1872; LL.D., Neb. Coll., 1870; Litt.D., 1892; LL.D., 1896; Ph.D., 1899, Franklin & Marshall Coll.); elected col., N.Y. State inf., 1846; assigned to command 22d regimental dist., N.Y., 1849; apptd. brig. gen. N.G.S.N.Y., 1851; mil. agt., State of N.Y., in Europe (endorsed by U.S.A.), 1851-53; assisted in organizing present police system, New York, and made first reports favoring paid fire dept., 1852-53; adj. gen. State of N.Y., 1855; bvtd. maj. gen. State of N.Y., "for meritorious services," by spl. act of legislature, 1866. His hundreds of published works include Life of Leonard Torstenson, Field Marshal Generalissimo of Sweden, 1855; The Dutch at the North Pole and the Dutch in Maine, 1857; Carausius, the Dutch Augustus, 1858; The Ancient, Medieval and Modern Netherlanders, 1859; Life of Lieut. Gen. Menno, Baron Cohorn, 1860; Personal and Military History of Maj. Gen. Philip Kearny, 1869; The Pearl of Pearls (novel), 1865; Bothwell (hist. drama), 1884. Home: Tivoli, N.Y. Died 1907.

DERBY, GEORGE HORATIO humorist; b. Dedham, Mass., Apr. 3, 1823; s. John Barton and Marg (Townsend) D.; grad. U.S. Mil. Acad., 1846; m. Mary Ann Coons. Very early noted for his wit and practical jokes, especially at Mil. Acad.; apptd. to Engr. Corps shortly after graduation; served in Mexican War; brevetted 1st Lt. for gallantry; served in Topographical Bur., 1847-48; mem. various U.S. Army exploring expdns. in Minn. Territory, 1848-49; had duty on Pacific Coast, 1849-56; managed to get some humorous sketches published, 1850, continued writing them therafter; while temporary editor San Diego Herald, 1853, became famous even in East for his humor; transferred to East by army, 1856; promoted capt., 1860; one of foremost and earliest writers of so-called

Western style of humor. Author: (sketches) Phoenixiana; or Sketches and Burlesques, 1856; The Squibob Papers, 1865. Died N.Y.C., May 15, 1861.

DERBY, GEORGE MCCLELLAN colonel U.S. Army; b. at sea, Nov. 1, 1856; s. Capt. George H. Derby, U.S.A. and Mary A. (Coons) D.; ed. pvt. schs. Paris, Dresden and Lausanne, Switzerland, 1865-71; Washington U., St. Louis, 1872-73, Symonds Acad. Sing Sing, N.Y., 1873-74; grad. U.S. Mil. Acad., 1878, U.S. Engrs. Sch. of Application, 1881; m. Clara Matteson McGinnis, Nov. 6, 1878; m. 2d, Bessie Kidder, Apr. 4, 1904; children-George Townsend (U.S.A.), Roger Barton (U.S.A.), Hollis Hasket, Elizabeth Crowinshield. 2d lt. Engr. Corps, 1878; 1st lt., 1881; capt., 1888; maj., 1898; lt. col. chief engr. U.S.V., May 9, 1898; hon. discharged, May 12, 1899; lt. col. engrs., U.S.A., 1906. On duty with battalion of engrs. U.S.A., 1878-81; asst. to Gen. John Newton in local charge of works at Hell Gate, E. River, and other river and harbor work in N.Y. and N.J., 1881-89; instr. practical mil. engring., U.S. Mil. Acad., 1889-93, and was mem. Academic Bd., U.S. Mil. Acad.; asst. to engr. commr., D.C., 1893-94; in charge 4th dist. Miss. River improvement, 1894-1902; chief engr. 5th Army Corps in Cuba during Santiago campaign, and chief engr. 2d Army Corps, 1898; in charge Louisville and Portland canal and other river and harbor work, Louisville, Ky., 1902-03; in charge reservoirs at headwaters of Miss. River, etc., Minn., 1903-06; retired at own request after 33yrs. service, June 7, 1907. On active duty in charge 4th dist. Miss. River improvement, 1917-19; promoted col. U.S.A., 1919. Cited for gallantry try in action. Fellow A.A.A.S.; mem. Am. Soc. of Civil Engrs. Active in civic and social work in New Orleans, 1899-1921, serving on Parking Commn. and other commns.; was pres. La. S.P.CC.; for 10 yrs. pres. of La. S.P.C.A.; dir. New Orleans Charity Orgn. Soc., La. Free Kindergarten Assn., Home for Homeless Men, etc. Club: Round Table (New Orleans). Home: 1015 S. Carrollton Av., New Orleans. Died Oct. 1948.

DERBY, GEORGE STRONG ophthalmologist; b. Boston, May 29, 1875; s. Hasket and Sarah (Mason) D.; A.B., Harvard, 1896; M.D., Harvard Med. Sch., 1900; surg. interne, Mass. Gen. Hosp., 1900-01; student in pathology and ophthalmology, Austria, Germany, Holland, France and England, 1901-02; m. Mary Brewster Brown, Aug. 5, 1901. Ophthalmic chief, Mass. Charitable Eye and Ear Infirmary; prof. ophthalmology, Harvard Med. Sch.; mem. advisory com. Mass. Commn. for the Blind. Served in M.C., U.S.A., May 5, 1917-Feb. 8, 1919; commd. lt. col., Oct. 1919; asst. consultant in ophthalmology, A.E.F., July 1918-Feb. 1919. Episcopalian. Home: Boston, Mass. Died Dec. 12, 1931.

DERN, GEORGE HENRY secretary of war; b. Dodge Co., Neb., Sept. 8, 1872; s. John and Elizabeth (Dern) D.; grad. Fermont (Neb.) Normal Coll., 1888; student U. of Neb., 1893, 94; m. Charlotte Brown, June 7, 1899; children - Mary Joanna (Mrs. Harry Baxter), John, Louise (dec.), William Brown, Margaret (dec.), Elizabeth Ida, James George. Began mining in Utah, 1894; treas. Mercur Gold Mining & Milling Co., 1894-1900; gen. mgr. Consol. Mercur Gold Mines Co., 1900-13; mgr. various other metal mining enterprises; v.p. and gen. mgr. Holt-Christensen Process Co. (owner Holt-Dern patents). Mem. Utah Senate, 1915-23; mem. State Council of Defense, World War; gov. of Utah, 1925-32; chmn. Governor's conf., 1929, 30; secretary of war, Mar. 4, 1933 - . Democrat. Congregationalist. Mason. Joint inventor, with Theodore P. Holt, of Holt-Dern ore roaster. Was author of Workmen's Compensation Law, Corrupt Practices Act. State Mineral Land Leasing Law, etc. Home: Washington, D.C. Died Aug. 27, 1936.

DE ROSSET, WILLIAM LORD bus. exec.; b. Wilmington, N.C., Oct. 27, 1832; s. Armand John and Eliza Jane (Lord) DeR.; ed. St. Timothy's School and St. James Coll., Md.; student U. N.C.; m. E. S. Nash, June 10, 1863. Worked at machinist trade Lawrence, Mass.; in mercantile bus. Wilmington, N.C., 1852-61; col. 3d N.C. inf., C. S. A.; since the war in business pursuits; maj.-gen. comdg. N.C. div., United Confederate Vets., 1895-1900. Address: Wilmington, N.C. Died Aug. 14, 1910.

DERUSSY, ISSAC DENNISTON brig. gen.; b. Ft. Monroe, Va., June 13, 1894; s. René Edward (U.S.A.) and Ann Alida D.; ed. Episcopal High Sch., Alexandria, Va., and Rutgers Coll.; m. Laura Lee Requa, May 19, 1891. Apptd. from N.Y., 2d lt., 1st Inf., U.S.A., Apr. 27, 1861; promoted through grades to col., 11th Inf., May 19, 1891; brig. gen., Apr. 1, 1902; retired Apr. 15, 1902, at own request, after 40 yrs.' service. Served in Puerto Rican campaign and in P.I. Bvtd. maj., Mar. 13, 1865, "for faithful and meritorious services during the war." Home: New York, N.Y. Died Feb. 16, 1923.

DE ST. VRAIN, CERAN DE HAULT DELASSUS fur trader, army officer; b. Spanish Lake, nr. St. Louis, Mo., May 5, 1802; s. Jacques Marcellin Ceran DeHault Delassus and Marie Felicite Chauvet (Dubreuil) de St. V.; m. Luisa Branch, 3 children. Embarked in fur trade, circa 1823; with Francois Guerin conducted expdn. to the Southwest outfitted by Bernard Pratte & Co. of St. Louis, 1824; received passport at Santa Fe to State of Sonora for pvt. trade, 1826; formed partnership with Charles Bent under name Bent, St. Vrain & Co. (became one of leading furtrading cos. of West), 1831; became citizen of Mexico; with Cornelio Vigil received land grant from Mexican govt., 1844, comprising 4 million acres in valleys Huerfano, Apishapa, Purgatoire, other tributaries; organizer, capt. of a volunteer co., 1846-48, lt. col., 1854-55, apptd. col. 1st N.M. Cavalry, 1861. Died Mora, N.M., Oct. 28, 1870.

DESJARDINS, ARTHUR ULDERIC physician; b. Waterville, Me., May 6, 1884; s. Samuel and Sarah Marie (Mercier) D.; student Montreal (Can.) Coll., 1898-99, St. Joseph's Coll., Three Rivers, Can., 1900-01; M.D., U. Pa., 1912; spl. course radiol. physics U. Cambridge, Eng., 1920; M.S. Radiology, U. Minn., 1924; m. Marie Laure d'Argy, Nov. 28, 1942 (dec. Sept. 1924); m. 2d, Helen Beatrice Hardy, Apr. 10, 1926; children-Adrienne Aymard, Paul Arnault, Vincent (dec.). In charge Fairfield (Me.) Tb Sanitorium, 1913-14; asst. surgeon, Am. Ambulance, Am. Hosp., Paris, 1914-15; asst. to Dr. Joseph Blake Hosp. Militaire 76, Ris Orangis, France, 1915-16; fellow surgery, Mayo Found., 1917, fellow roentgenology, 1920, fellow pathologic anatomy, 1917; head sect. therapeutic radiology, Mayo Clinic, 1920; prof. radiology, Mayo Found., since 1936; hon. mem. staff, trustee Miles Meml. Hosp., Damariscotta, Me. Instr. mil. surgery Ft. Riley, Kan., 1917-18; pathologist Central Med. Dept. Lab., Dijon, France, 1918, Evacuation Hosp. No. 2, Baccarat, France, 1918; pathologist and commd. officer,3d Army Lab., Coblenz, Germany, 1919; capt. to lt. col. M.C., U.S. Army, 1917-24; now col. Diplomate Am. Bd. Radiology. Fellow A.C.P., Am. Coll. Radiology; mem. Me. Med. Soc., Radiol. Soc. N.Am., Am. Roentgen Ray Soc., Am. Radium Soc., N.Am., Am. Roentgen Ray Soc., Am. Radium Soc., Roentgen Soc. Eng., A.M.A., Alumni Assn. Mayo Found. Ret. Home: South Bristol Rd., Walpole, Me. Died Jan. 15, 1964; buried Old Harrington Cemetery, Bristol, Me.

DE SOLLAR, TENNEY COOK cons. mining engr.: b. Denver, Mar. 15, 1881; s. Henry Cook and Ellen Josephine (Waggoner) D.; E.M., Colo. Sch. of Mines, 1904; m. Edythe Longnecker Hoffman, June 20, 1906. Engaged in mining projects, Rico, Idaho Springs, Eldora, Col., Hancock, Mich., 1908-24; Bessemer, Ala., 1924-42. Capt., C.E., 1918, lt. col., 1942-43, Distinguished Achievement medal Colo. Sch. of Mines, 1954. Licenses cons. engr. (mining). Mem. Am. Inst. Mining and Metall. Engrs. (Legion of Honor 1954), Colo. Colorado Sci. Sco., Am. Soc. Mil. Engrs., Am. Legion, S.A.R., Betta Theta Pi. Episcopalian. Mason (Shriner). Address: 1160 Lafayette St., Denver 80128. Died Jan. 22, 1966.

DE STEIGUER, LOUIS RODOLPH admiral U.S. Navy, retired; b. Athens, Ohio, Mar. 18, 1867; s. Judge R. and Mary (Carpenter) de S.; student Ohio University, Athens, hon. LL.D.; graduate United States Naval Academy, 1889; m. Katharine Constable. Commd. ensign, 1891; promoted through grades to rear admiral, Dec. 31, 1921. Served on Montgomery, Spanish-Am. War, 1898; Nashville Philippine insurrection, 1900, O.N.I. Washington; U.S. Ill., 1901-04; supervisor New York Harbor; ordnance officer, Ill. and exec. officer U.S. Conn. in cruise around the world, 1907-09; in charge 5th lighthouse dist., Baltimore, 1909-11; comdg. U.S. Panther. 1911-13; capt. yard and acting comdt., Norfolk, Va.: comdg. U.S. Kearsage and receiving ship (Maine) Navy Yard, New York; Naval War. Coll., 1916-17; chief of staff, 3d naval dist., comdg. U.S. Arkansas British Grand Fleet, U.S. fleet comdt. Navy Yard, Portsmouth, N.H., 1920; hydrographer, Washington, D.C., 1921; comdr. U.S. Train, 1922; comdt. Navy Yard, Boston; comdg. 4th div. battle fleet; vice adm., comdr. battleship divs.; adm. comdr.-in-chief Battle Fleet, 1927; comdt. 3d Naval Dist. and Navy Yard, New York, until retired, Apr. 1, 1931. Clubs: Army-Navy Country, Army and Navy (Washington, D.C.); New York Yacht (New York). Address: 1302 18th St. N.W., Washington, D.C. Died April 18, 1947.

DE TOUSARD, ANNE LOUIS army officer, diplomat; b. Paris, France, Mar. 12, 1749; s. gen. Charles Germain and Antoinette de Poitevin (de la Croix) de T.; grad. Arty. Sch., Strasbourg, France, 1769; m. Maria Francisca Joubert, Jan. 1788; m. 2d, Anna Maria Geddes, 1795. Commd. 2d lt. Royal Arty. Corps, French Army, 1769; arrived in Portsmouth, N.H., 1777; took part in battles of Brandywine and Germantown; brevetted lt. col. by Congress and voted a life pension for gallantry, 1778; decorated chevalier of St. Louis (France), 1779; commd. maj. Provincial Regt. of Toul, France, 1780, lt. col. Regt. du Cap, 1784; went to Santo Domingo, 1784, served with distinction against Negro revolt; accused of counter revolutionary principles, resistance to orders, 1792, arrested, sent to prison in France; released, 1793, returned to U.S.; reinstated in U.S. Army, 1795, commd. maj. 2d Arty., col., 1800; promoted to insp. of arty., 1800; returned to Santo Domingo, then France, 1802; sent to Am. in charge of comml. relations at New Orleans, 1805; moved to Phila. as vice consul; ordered to New Orleans as consul ad interim, 1811-16. Died Paris, May 8, 1817.

DE TROBRIAND, REGIS DENIS DE KEREDEN army officer, author; b. nr. Tours, France, June 4, 1816; s. Baron Joseph and Rochine (Haghin de Courbeville) de T.; grad. College de Tours, 1834; grad. in law, Poiters, 1837; m. Mary Mason Jones, 1843, 1 dau. Came to U.S., 1841; lived with wife in Venice, Italy, until 1847; a leading figure in N.Y. society and literary circles; editor Revue de Nouvean Monde, 1849-50; contbr. to Le Courier des Etats-Unis; became Am. citizen, 1861, also col. "Garges Lafayette" of N.Y. State Militia; brevetted maj. gen. U.S. Volunteers, 1865; apptd. col. U.S. Army, 1866; made many trips to France; served on frontier with Army while in Am.; succeeded to title of count on death of his brother, 1874; ret. from Army, 1879, lived in New Orleans. Author: Les Gentilshommes de L'Ouest, 1840; Quatre Ans de Campagnas a L'Armee du Potomoc, 2 vols., 1867-68. Died Bayport, L.I., N.Y., July 15, 1897.

DE VARGAS ZAPATA Y LUJAN PONCE DE LEON, DIEGO Spanish gov. N.M.; b. Madrid, Spain, circa 1650; s. Alonso and Maria Margarita (de Contreras) de Vargas Zapata y Lujan; m. Juana. Chief magistrate Real de Minas de Talpugajua in Mexico; apptd. colonial gov. and capt. gen. of N.M., 1688; controlled much land in Spain and Mexico through his wife; reconquered upper Rio Grande Valley from Pueblo Indians who had defeated Spanish settlers in 1680, 1692; engaged in suppressing Indian uprisings, 1693-97; reapptd. gov. of N.M. by viceroy of New Spain (Mexico), 1696, imprisoned by gov. apptd. by Spanish king on charges brought by town council of Santa Fe; gov. N.M. (reapptd. by king), 1701-03; created marques de La Nava de Brazinas. Died Sandia mountains, N.M., on campaign against Faraon Apaches, Apr. 4, 1704.

DEVENS, CHARLES army officer, jurist, atty. gen.; b. Charlestown, Mass., Apr. 4, 1820; s. Charles and Mary (Lithcow) D.; grad. Harvard, 1838, LL.D., 1877; Admitted to Mass. bar, 1840; mem. Mass. Senate, 1848-49; U.S. marshal for dist. Mass., 1849-53; city solicitor Worcester (Mass.), 1856-58; commd. brig. gen. Mass. Militia; commd. maj. 3d Mass. Battalion, 1861, col. 15th Mass. Regt., 1861; commd. brig. gen. U.S. Volunteers, 1862; brevetted maj. gen., 1865; served in battles of Balls' Bluff, Fredericksburg, Chancellorsville, Cold Harbor during Civil War; apptd. justice Mass. Superior Ct., 1867; judge Mass. Supreme Ct., 1873; U.S. atty. gen., 1877-81; pres. Harvard Alumni Assn., 1886; comdr. Mil. Order, Loyal Legion, Mass.; nat. comdr. Grand Army Republic, 1874; Camp Devens, Ayer, Mass., named for him. Died Boston, Jan. 7, 1891.

DEVER, PAUL ANDREW ex-gov. Mass.; b. Boston, Jan. 15, 1903; s. Joseph Patrick and Anna Amelia (McAlevy) D.; LL.B. cum laude, Boston U., 1926. Admitted to Mass. bar, 1926, since in practice at Boston; rep. to the Gen. Ct. of Mass., 1928-34; atty. gen. Mass., 1935-41; lectr. sch. law Boston U., 1941-42; gov. Mass., 1949-53. Comdr. USNR, 1942—. Mem. Ancient and Honorable Arty. Co. Mem. Am., Boston, Cambridge bar assns., Woolsack Soc., Phi Delta Phi. Democrat. Catholic. K.C. Home: 86 Buckingham St., Cambridge, Mass. Died Apr. 11, 1958.

DEVEREUX, F. RAMSAY mfg. exec.; b. Utica, N.Y., Nov. 14, 1892; s. Nicholas E. and Mary (McMahon) D.; A.B., Harvard, 1916; m. Ruth A. Lindsay, Feb. 25, 1930. Pres. Oneita Knitting Mills, Andrews, South Carolina, 1925-53, chairman of the board directors, 1953—; director Marine Midland Bank of Mohawk Valley, Am. Mutual Liability Ins. Co., Am. Policyholders Ins. Co., Utica Radiator Corp.; trustee Savs. Bank of Utica. Served as capt., inf., U.S. Army, World War I. Home: Hart's Hill, Whitesboro, N.Y. Office: 350 Fifth Av., N.Y.C. 10001. Died Nov. 13, 1963.

DEVIN, THOMAS CASIMER army officer; b. N.Y.C., Dec. 10, 1822. Joined N.Y. Militia, lt. col. at start of Civil War; apptd. capt. 1st N.Y. Cavalry, 1861; col. 6th N.Y. Calvalry, 1861: served in battles of 2d Bull Run and Antietam; after Battle of Fredericksburg (1862) apptd. brigade comdr., 1863; took part in battles of Chancellorsville and Gettysburg; apptd. brig. gen. U.S. Volunteers, 1865; apptd. lt. col. 8th U.S. Cavalry, 1866; col. 3d U.S. Cavalry, 1877; served mostly on frontier duty, after Civil War, ret., 1878. Died N.Y.C., Apr. 4, 17p878.

DEVINE, JAMES GASPER, army officer; born Calif., Apr. 19, 1895; grad. Coast Arty. Sch., 1924, Advanced Course, 1932. Commd. 2d lt. C.A.C., Calif. Nat. Guard, May 1915; 1st lt. and capt., Calif. Nat. Guard, World War I; advanced through the grades, U.S. Army, to brig. gen., C.A., Mar. 1943. Address: Fishers Island NY Died 1972.

DEVINE, JOHN M., ret. army officer; b. Providence, June 18, 1895; s. Patrick and Bridget (Nangle) D.; B.S., U.S. Mil. Acad., 1917; M.S., Yale U., 1922; grad. Field Arty. Sch., 1929, Command and Gen. Staff Sch., 1938; m. Anne C. Whitelegg, May 15, 1918; children—Austin, Ruth Mildred, Dorothy Anne, Donald Whitelegg. Commd. 2d lt., 1917; promoted through grades to maj. gen. (temp.), May 2, 1945, permanent, 1948; asst. prof. English, U.S. Mil. Acad., Aug. 1932-June 1936; asst. prof. mil. science and tactics, Yale U., July 1938-July 1940; with Armored Force since July 1940, overseas (Europe) with 90th Div. Arty., became comdg. gen., 8th Armored Div., Oct. 1944; comdg. gen. Universal Mil. Training Exptl. Unit, Fort Knox, Ky., 1946-47; chief of staff of Army Ground Forces, dep.

chief Army Field Forces, 1948; comdg. gen. 1st Cav. Div., 1949, 9th Div., 1950; chief Information and Edn. Div., Office Sec. of Def., 1950-52, ret.; comdt. of cadets Virginia Poly. Inst., 1952-60. Awarded Bronze Star, Silver Star, Legion of Merit, Distinguished Service Medal; French Legion of Honor, Croix d'Guerre; Knight Comdr. with Swords Netherlands Order of Orange-Nassau; War Cross and Order of White Lion (Czechoslovakia). Home: Leesburg VA Died Mar. 8, 1971; buried West Point Cemetery, West Point NY

DEVOE, RALPH GODWIN army officer; b. Indiana, Pa., June 15, 1883; s. Arthur and Sarah Alice (Coleman) DeV.; student U. Wash., 1903-04; M.D., U. Pa., 1908; grad. Army Med. Sch., 1910, Command and Gen. Staff Sch., 1925; m. Frances Reba Terard, June 15, 1908; 1 son, Arthur Gerard. Commd. lt. M.C., U.S. Army, 1909, advancing through grades to brig. gen., 1944; comdg. officer Base Hosp. No. 34, Nantes, France, 1917-18, Hosp. Center Nantes, 1918, comdg. officer Halloran Gen. Hosp., S.I., N.Y., 1943; now mgr. Bronx Vets. Hosp., N.Y.C.; asst. prof. mil. sci. and tactics, N.Y.U., 1921-24, 1929-33. Decorated Chevalier Legion of Honor (Fr.); Legion of Merit (U.S.); Comdr. Order of Brit. Empire (Eng.). Mem. Nat. Inst. Social Scis., Mil. Order World Wars, A.M.A., Assn. Mil. Surgeons, Kappa Alpha, Nu Sigma Nu. Address: VA Hosp., 130 W. Kingsbridge Rd., Bronx 63, N.Y. Died July 29, 1966.

DEVOL, CARROLL AUGUSTINE army officer; b. Waterford, O., Apr. 17, 1859; s. Hiram Fosdick and Adelaide (Dyar) D.; C.E., pa. Mil. Coll., 1878, Sc.D., 1914; m. Dora Dean Scott, Feb. 17, 1887; children - Lucile Scott (Mrs. A. G. Bates), Mary Adelaide (Mrs. George H. Brett). 2d lt. 25th Inf., Sept. 1, 1879; 1st lt., Oct. 19, 1886; capt. a.q.m., Aug. 21, 1896; maj. q.m. U.S. Vols., Oct. 17, 1898; lt. col., Fe.Feb. 6, 1899; hon. disch. from vol. service, May 1, 1901; maj. q.m., May 5, 1902; lt. col., Oct. 31, 1909; col. a.q.m. gen., Sept. 22, 1911; brig. gen. q.m. corps, Feb. 16, 1913. Served with the line oftn the army in Tex., S.D., Minn., Mont., Yellowstone Park and Wyo., with U. of Wis., 1896; in Philippine Islands, 1898-1900; with quarter master corps in N.Y. City, Phila., San Francisco, Washington, D.C., Tex.; chief q.m. Isthmian Canal Commn., Panama Canal, July, 1908-Apr. 1, 1913; retired with rank of maj. gen., Oct. 31, 1916. Asst. to provost marshal gen. in registration and draft office, June 24, 1917; zone supply officer and zone transportation officer, 13th Supply Zone, San Francisco, Sept. 5, 1917. Awarded D.S.M., June 6, 1919; also awarded Distinguished Service Cross. Acting chmn. and gen. mgr. Am. Nat. Red Cross. Awarded campaign badge Spanish-Am. War and Philippine Insurrection; Panama Canal Medal. Presbyn. Home: Menlo Park, Calif. Died June 3, 1930.

DEVORE, DANIEL BRADFORD army officer; b. Monroe Co., O., May 14, 1860; s. John Wesley and Mary J. (Gray) D.; grad. U.S. Mil. Acad., 1885, Army War Coll., 1908; m. Helen Gray, d. Alexander Stewart, of Washington, D.C. Commd. 2d lt. 23d Inf., June 14, 1885; promoted through grades to col., July 1, 1916; brig. gen. N.A., Aug. 5, 1917. Asst. prof. mathematics, U.S. Mil. Acad., 1892-97; spl. duty with Sec. of War, 1897-98; purchased 538 reindeer in northern Norway, and delivered 537 of them at Seattle, Wash., for use in Alaska, winter of 1897-98; in Philippines, 1899-1901, 1903-06; comd. post. Holguin, Cuba, 1908-09; justice of the peace, at Malabang, 1903-04; expdns. against Moros, Lake Lanao region, Cottabalo Valley and Jolo, 1904-05; civil gov. Lake Lanao Dist., 1904-06; constructing q.m., Madison (N.Y.) Barracks, 1906-07; with regt. at Jamestown Expn., and dedication McKinley Monument, Canton, O., 1907; duty, Gen. Staff 1911-14; in comd. 10th inf., Panama, C.Z., 1916-17; organized 45th and 46th regts. inf. from 10th Inf., June 1917; mustered into federal service the Ill. N.G., July-Aug. 1917; comd. 167th Brig. in France, Sept.-Dec. 1918; comd. Camp Logan, Houston, Tex., Jan.-Apr. 1919; duty Hdqrs. Central Dept., Chicago, Bur. Nat. Guard, 1919-20; comd. 10th Inf., Camp Sherman, O., 1920-21; adj. gen. 2d Corps Area Governor's Island, New York Harbor, Sept. 1921-22; retired Apr. 5, 1922. Clubs: Army and Navy, Chevy Chase (Washington, D.C.); Army and Navy (New York). Home: 2202 Massachusetts Av.,Washington, D.C.

DEWEERD, JAMES A., clergyman; b. Olivet, Ill., May 23, 1916; s. Fred and Lelia Z. (Benedict) DeW.; student Marion Coll., M.A., Ball State U., 1967; A.B. Taylor U., 1937. D.D., 1949; postgrad. Cambridge U. (Eng.), 1958; m. Mildred J. Geyer, June 5, 1963. Pub. speaker evangelist, lectr. 1937-72; pres. Christian Witness Assn., editor monthly publ. The Christian Witness 1947-57; pres. Kletzing Coll. (now Vennard Coll.), 1949-51; daily broadcast and weekly TV over WLW. Cin., 1952-57; chaplain gen. S.A.R., 1969-71. Sec. bd. edn. pub. schs., Fairmount, 1946-49; chmn. Jay County (Ind.) United Fund Drive, 1969-1970, bd. dirs., 1967-72; chmn. Juvenile Delinquency Study Commn., State of Ind., 1952-56. Pres. bd. trustees Bethany (Ky.) Children's Home, 1948-57, bd. dirs., 1946-72. Served as chaplain (capt.) U.S. Army, northern France, 1943-45. Recipient Purple Heart, Oak Leaf Cluster, Silver Star; George Washington Honor award Freedoms Found., 1970. Mem. S.A.R. (Gold Good Citizenship medal 1969, Patriot's medal 1970, Minuteman award, 1971), Nat. Assn. Conf. Evangelists (v.p. 1969-72), Nat. Assn. Evangs. (mem. commn. on evangelism and spiritual life), Assn. for Advancement of Ethical Hypnosis, Internat. Platform Assn., N.E.A., Y.M.C.A., Am. Legion, Military Chaplain's Assn. Mason. Author: The Realities of Christian Experience, 1940; Memory is Bitter-Sweet, 1952; Stories My Mother Told Me, 1955; What is Worthwhile, 1970. Address: Pennville IN Died Mar. 28, 1972.

DEWEY, LLOYD ELLIS educator; b. Tomah, Wis., Jan. 13, 1897; s. Ira Norman and Emma (Grassman) D.; B.C.S., N.Y.U., 1923, Sc.B., 1925, J.D., 1929, A.M., 1932; m. Anne Huise, May 29, 1921; 1 dau, Margaret (adopted). Instr. finance, sch. commerce N.Y.U., 1923-29, asst. prof., 1929-33, asso. prof., 1932-42, prof. since 1942, prof. finance grad. sch. bus. adminstrn. since 1942, vice chmn. dept. banking and finance, 1946-56; cons. Alexander Hamilton Inst. Trustee Scudder Sch., N.Y. City, 1937-51. Served with U.S.N., World War I; lt. col. C.E., U.S. Army, World War II. Mem. Am. Econ. Assn., Am. Finance Assn., Am. Marketing Assn., S.A.R., American Assn. of University Professors, Order Founders and Patriots of America, also member of American Legion, Kappa Sigma, Delta Sigma Pi. Club: Young Republican (N.Y.). Author: Organizing and Financing Bus. (with J. H. Bonneville, rev. edit.), 1959; Financial Handbook (with others), 1947. Home: Red Creek Rd., Hampton Bays, L.I., N.Y. Died March 24, 1960; buried Arlington Nat. Cemetery.

DEWHURST, J(AMES) FREDERIC economist; b. Seattle, Wash., Mar. 23, 1895; s. Clarence Ely and Sara (Robertson) D.; B.S., U. Wash., 1918; A.M., in Economics, U. Pa., 1922, Ph.D., 1928, D.Sc. in Econs. (hon.), 1962; m. Julie T. Gill, July 1, 1949 (dec. 19620; 1 son, John Richard (by previous marriage); m. 2d, Marjory C. Buchanan, June 1, 1964. Research chemist E. I. du Pont de Nemours Co., 1920; instr. in industry, Wharton Sch. of Finance and Commerce, U. of Pa., 1920-24, asst. prof., 1924-29, prof., 1929-32, lectr. in marketing, 1941-42; chief statistical div. Fed. Res. Bank of Phila., 1923-28; research asso., dept. of indsl. research, U. Pa., 1928-30; chief div. of econ. research, U.S. Dept. Commerce, 1930-32; economist Am. Iron and Steel Inst., 1933; economist 20th Century Fund, 1933-35, 1937-53, exec. dir., Aug. 1953-56; econ. adviser, dir. Fund's Survey of Europe's Needs and Resources, 1957-60. Econ. adviser to Code Authority of Hat Mfg. Industry, 1934-35; dir. com. on social security, Social Science Research Council, 1935-37, staff cons., 1937-45; mem. bd. dirs. and exec. com. 1946-52, chmn. investment com., 1950-55; tech. adviser to Am. delegation to Internat. Conf. on Govt. Statistics, League of Nations, Geneva, 1928, same to Preparatory Commn. for World Econ. Conf., Geneva, 1932; mem. Com. on Govt. Statistics and Information Services, Washington, 1934-35; mem. Census Advisory Com., 1936-50. Trustee Twentieth Century Fund. Served as 2d lt., 1st lt., capt., 3d U.S. Cav., 1917-19. Distribution Hall of Fame; recipient Paul D. Converse Award, 1957. Fellow Am. Acad. Arts and Scis., Am. Statis. Assn. (v.p. 1939), A.A.A.S.; mem. Am. Econ. Assn., Am. Com. for Cultural Freedom Clubs: Cosmos (Washington); Army and Navy (N.Y.C.). Author: University Education for Business (with J. H. S. Bossard), 1931; Does Distribution Cost Too Much? (with P. W. Stewart), 1939; America's Needs and Resources: A New Survey (with others), 1955; Europe's Needs and Resources (with others), 1961; also articles and reports. Home: 23 Braeburn Dr., Princeton, N.J. Died May 26, 1967.

DE WITT, CALVIN soldier; b. Harrisburg, Pa., May 26, 1840; s. Rev. William R. (D.D.) and Mary Elizabeth (Wallace) D.; ed. Harrisburg Acad.; A.B., Princeton, 1860; A.M., 1863; M.D., Jefferson Med. Coll., Phila., 1865; m. Josephine Lesesne, 1877. Served in Army of Potomac, capt. 49th Pa. Vol. Inf., Oct. 1861-Jan. 1863. Apptd. 1st lt., asst. surg. U.S.A., May 14, 1867; advanced through grades to col. asst. surg. gen., May 7, 1901; brig. gen., U.S.A., Aug. 9, 1903; retired from active service Aug. 10, 1903. Served as med. officer U.S.A., in many mil. stas. in various parts of U.S., in several campaigns against Indians and in Cuba. Instr. in mil. hygiene, Gen. Staff Coll., Ft. Leavenworth, Kan.; prof. mil. medicine and later pres. Army Med. Sch., Washington, D.C. Died 1908.

DEWITT, JOHN LESESNE army officer; b. Fort Sidney, Neb., Jan. 9, 1880; s. Calvin and Josephine (Lesesne) D.; student Princeton; grad. Army Sch. of Line, 1907, Army War Coll., 1920; A.M. Princeton, 1932; m. Martha Estes, June 3, 1903; 1 son, John Lesesne. Apptd. 2d lt. inf. U.S. Army, Oct. 10, 1898; promoted through grades to col., May 9, 1921; q.m. gen. rank of maj. gen., 1930-34; brig. gen., Mar. 1934, maj. gen., Dec. 1936, lt. gen., Dec. 1939; served in Philippines 4 times to 1937; instr. at O.T.C., Plattsburg, N.Y., May-Aug. 1917; to France with 42d Div., Sept. 1917; duty Gen. Hdqrs., A.E.F., Jan. 1918; asst. chief of staff for supply 1st Corps, A.E.F., Feb.-July 1918; asst. chief of staff for supply 1st Army, Aug. 1918 to Jan. 1919; participated in Aisne-Marne, St. Mihiel, Meuse-Argonne and Champagne-Marne operations; instr. Army War Coll., 1919-20; mem. War Dept. Gen. Staff, 1919-24 and 1926-28; asst. comdt. Army War Coll., 1928-30; comdg. 1st Brig., 1st Div., 1934-35; comdg. 23d Brig., Philippine Div. 1935-36; comdg. latter Div. 1937; comdt. Army War Coll., July 1937-Dec. 1939; lt. gen. comdg. 4th Army and 9th Corps Area, Dec. 5, 1939; comdg. 4th Army, Nov. 9, 1940; comdg. Western Def. Command and 4th Army, Mar. 17, 1941-Sept. 17, 1943; comdt. Army and Navy Staff Coll., Washington, Sept. 1943-Nov. 1945; Office Chief of Staff, U.S. Army, Nov. 1945-Apr. 1947; ret. from active duty June 10, 1947, 4 star gen., 1954. Awarded D.S.M. (2 oak leaf clusters) (U.S.A.), D.S.M. (U.S.N.); Office Legion of Honor (Fr.); Order Aztec Eagle (Mex.), 1943. Clubs: Army and Navy, Army and Navy Country (Washington). Home: 3505 Davis St. N.W. Office: Adjutant General, Dept. of Army, Washington, D.C. Died June 20, 1962; buried Arlington Nat. Cemetery.

DIBRELL, GEORGE GIBBS congressman, industrialist; b. White County, Tenn., Apr. 12, 1822; s. Anthony and Mildred (Carter) D.; m. Mary Leftwich, Jan. 13, 1842; children-Wamcen, Joseph. Clk. of Sparta, br. Bank of Tenn., 1840-46; clk. White County Ct., 1846-60; mem. Tenn. Gen. Assembly, 1860-62; commd. lt. col. of a regt. Confederate Army, 1861; in command Nathan B. Forest's "Old Brigade," 1863; commd. brig. gen., 1864; dir. Southwestern R.R., 1866, became pres., 1869; participated in Tenn. Counstl. Conv., 1870; mem. U.S. Ho. of Reps. from Tenn., 44th-48th congresses, 1875-85. Died Sparta, May 6, 1888.

DICK, GEORGE FREDERICK internist; b. at Fort Wayne, Ind., July 21, 1881; s. Daniel and Elizabeth H. (Binsley) B.; M.D., Rush Med. Coll., 1905; m. Gladys R. Henry, Jan. 28, 1914. In practice of medicine, Chgo., since 1905; interne Cook County Hosp., 1905-07; prof. and chmn. dept. of medicine, U. of Chgo., since 1933. Mem. staff McCormick Memorial Inst. for Infectious Diseases. Served as maj., M.C., U.S. Army, World War. Mem. A.M.A., Ill. State and Chgo. med. socs., Inst. of Medicine of Chgo., Chgo. Pathol. Soc., Chgo. Soc. Internal Medicine, Assn. Am. Physicians, Am. Assn. Pathology and Bacteriology. With wife isolated the germ of and originated serum for scarlet fever. Clubs: University, Glenview Country. Home: 1915 Greenwood Blvd., Evanston, Ill. Office: 950 E. 59th St., Chgo. Died Oct. 11, 1967.

DICK, SAMUEL Continental congressman; b. Nottingham, Prince Georges County, Md., Nov. 14, 1740: studied medicine, Scotland. Began practice of medicine, Salem, N.Y., 1770; mem. N.J. Provincial Congress, 1776; served as col. 1st Battalion, Salem County (N.U.) Militia, 1776, then as asst. surgeon Continental Army in Canadian campaign, mem. 1st N.J. Gen. Assembly; apptd. collector of customs Western Dist. N.J., 1778; mem. Continental Congress from N.J., 1783-84; del. N.J. Conv. to ratify U.S. Constn., 1787; surrogate Salem County, 1785-1804. Died Salem, Nov. 16, 1812; buried St. John's Episcopal Churchyard.

DICK, SAMUEL BERNARD retired R.R. pres.; b. Meadville, Pa., Oct. 26, 1836; ed. Allegheny Coll.; was col. comdg. 9th regt., Pa. vols., serving in Civil War over 2 yrs. until disabled by wounds; mem. Congress, 1879-81; engaged in contracting and operating railroads; built and was pres. of the P.B. & L.E. R.R.; pres. Colo. & N. Western R.R., Phoenix Iron Works, Meadville Malleable Iron Co., Meadville Gas Co. Widower. Address: Meadville, Pa.

DICKERSON, OLIVER MORTON educator; b. Jasper County, Ill., Sept. 8, 1875; s. Stephen Lee and Margaret (Consley) D.; grad. Ill. State Normal U., Normal, Ill., 1899; A.B., U. of Ill., 1903, A.M., 1904, Ph.D., 1906; studied Harvard; research British Mus., London, Eng.; m. Nora Mae Simmons, Nov. 10, 1906 (dec. Nov. 1954); m. 2d, Alma M. Jensen, May 5, 1956. Tchr. schools, Jasper County, Ill., 1894-97; prin. pub. schs., Macon, Ill., 1899-1901; teaching fellow, U. of Ill., 1903-04, 1905-06; teacher history and civics, Ill. State Normal U., summers 1903, 05, 06; prof. history and social science, Western Ill. State Normal Sch., Macomb, Ill., 1906-13, Winona (Minn.) State Normal Sch., 1913-19; pres. Moorhead (Minn.) State Teachers Coll., 1920-23; prof. of history and polit. science, Colo. State Teachers Coll., 1923-35; head div. of social studies, Colo. State Coll. of Edn., 1935-40, prof. emeritus, history and political science since 1940; pres. Greely Civil Service Commn. 1940-46. In U.S. mil. service 1917-19; commd. captain Inf., 1917, maj., 1918; comdr. 35th Machine Gun Bn., 12th Div.; lt. col. Infantry R.C. (inactive) ret. Mem. Am. Hist. Assn., Am. Acad. Polit. and Social Science, Nat. Council for the Social Studies, Miss. Valley Historical Assn., Colo. Edn. Assn., Colorado Social Science Assn., State Hist. Soc. of Colo., Colo.-Wyo. Acad. of Science, Colonial Society of Massachusetts (corr. mem.), Am. Legion, Phi Beta Kappa, Kappa Delta Pi, Phi Alpha Theta. Mason. Congregationalist. Republican. Club: Kiwanis. Author: History of the Illinois State Constitutional Convention of 1962, 1905; American Colonial Government, 1912: Boston Under Military Rule, 1768-1769, 1936; Writs of Assistance as a Cause of the Revolution, 1939; John Hancock, Notorious Smuggler or Near Victim of British Revenue Racketeers?; Navigation Acts as Cause of the Revolution, 1951; British Control of American Newspapers on the Eve of the Revolution, 1951; Commissioners of Customs and the Boston Massacre; Use Made of the Revenue from the Tax on Tea, 1958. Home: 183 Third Av., Chula Vista, Cal. Died Nov. 26, 1966.

DICKERT, DAVID AUGUSTUS planter; b. Lexington, S.C., Aug. 2, 1845; s. Capt. A. G. and M. W. (Dixon) D.; ed. St. John's Primary Sch.; m. 1st, Miss M. C. Cromer; 2d, Monticello, S.C., July 18, 1886; Mrs. M. A. Coleman. Entered C.S.A. Feb. 1861; promoted capt., Dec., 1862, 3d S.C. vols.; comd. regt. in Valley campaign of Gen. Early, 1864; was in all great battles of east (with two exceptions), at Chickamauga and Knoxville: surrendered with Johnson at Greensboro, N.C., Apr., 1865; col. 3d S.C. State troops, 1877-80. Author: History of Kershaw's Brigade, Longstreet's Corps, 1899. Wrote army reminiscences for papers and mags., 1870-1900. Address: Newberry, S.C.

DICKEY, THEOPHILUS LYLE jurist, army officer; b. Paris, Ky., Oct. 2, 1811; s. James Henry and Polly (De Pew) D.; grad. Miami U., Oxford, O., 1831; m. Juliet Evans, Dec. 6, 1831; m. 2d Mrs. Beulah Hirst, summer 1870. Admitted to Ill. bar, 1835; raised co. for 1st Ill. Inf., at outbreak Mexican War, commd. capt.; judge Ill. Circuit Ct., 1848-52; del. 1st Republican Conv., Bloomington, 1854: raised 4th Ill. Cavalry, 1861, commd. capt., fought under Gen. Grant in West, 1861-63; nominated for congressman-at-large Ill., 1866; asst. atty. gen. U.S., 1868-70; corp. counsel, 1874; judge Ill. Supreme Ct., 1857-85. Died Atlantic City, N.J., July 22, 1885.

DICKEY, WILLIAM DONALDSON judge; b. Newburgh, N.Y., Jan. 11, 1845; s. William and Esther (James) D.; ed. Newburgh Acad. and Mt. Retirement Sem., Deckertown, N.J.; law course in Albany Law Sch.; m. Kate of Richmond, June 25, 1868. Served 3 yrs. in army of Potomac before 21 yrs. of age; entered as private and promoted to maj. and bvt. col.; recd. bvts. as maj., lt. col. and col. for "gallant and meritorious services"; awarded Congressional Medal of Honor. Admitted to bar; mem. N.Y. Const. Conv., 1894; justice Supreme Ct. of N.Y., Jan. 1, 1896-Dec. 31, 1909. Republican. Home: Brooklyn, N.Y. Died May 14, 1924.

DICKINS, FRANCIS WILLIAM rear admiral; b. Beckmanville, N.Y., Nov. 2, 1844; s. George and Eunice (Pearce) D.; grad. U.S. Naval Acad., 1864; m. Edith Pratt, Apr. 9, 1902. Promoted ensign, Nov. 1, 1866; advanced through grades to rear adm., June 17, 1904. On various duties to 1873; exec. officer Monocacy, Asiatic Sta., 1873-Jan. 1875, Kearsarge, Jan.-Apr. 1875, Yantic, Apr.-July 1875; Kearsarge, July 1875-Mar. 1876, Yantic, Mar.-Apr. 1876; comd. Yantic, Apr.-July 1876; leave, 1877; Naval Acad., 1878-80; exec. officer Constitution, 1881; Hydrographic Office, 1882; Kearsarge, 1882; comd. Onward, 1883-84; Tallapoosa, 1887-89; Navy Yard, Washington, head of Dept. of Yards and Docks, 1890-92; spl. duty Asiatic Sta., 1892; Navy Yard, Washington, 1892-93; spl. duty, Jan., Apr.-June, 1893; comd. Monogahela, 1893, Essex, 1894, training sta., Newport, R.I., and training-ship Constellation, 1894-96; asst. to Bur. Navigation, 1896-99; comd. Indiana, 1899-1900, Oregon, 1900-01; Brooklyn, 1901; mem. Examining Bd., 1902; comd. receiving-ship Independence, 1902-03; comdt. Navy Yard, Pensacola, 1903-04, Navy Yard, League Island, 1904-05; comd. Coast Squadron, N. Atlantic Fleet, 1905-06; spl. duty, 1906; retired, Nov. 2, 1906. Home: Washington, D.C. Died 1911.

DICKINSON, (CLINTON) ROY editor, writer; b. Newark, N.J., Mar. 14, 1888; s. Philemon Olin and Anna Elizabeth (Van Riper) I; grad. Newark Acad., 1905; Litt.D., Princeton, 1909; m. Marjorie S. Bostick, Feb. 15, 1910; children-Philemon, Katharine (Mrs. James L. Macwithey), Clinton Roy, Jr. With Cosmopolitan Mag., 1910-15, Puck, 1915-16, New York Times, 1916, Frank Presbrey Co., advt. agts., 1916-17; also. editor Printers' Ink Monthly, 1919-33; pres. Printers' Ink and Pub. Co., 1933-42; resigned to enter Army of the U.S. with rank of colonel, 1942. First lt. and later capt. and major, office of chief of staff U.S. Army, World War; lt. col. O.R.C. Mem. President Harding's Unemployment Conf. (with Samuel Gompers signed minority report against cut in wages). Dir. Council for Democracy. Mem. National Publishers Assn. (dir.), Asso. Business Papers, Inc. (dir.). Methodist. Clubs: Princeton, Dutch Treat, Advertising, Players, Essex County Country, National Press. Contbr. short stories to Harper's, Scribner's, Ladies' Home Journal, Am. Legion Monthly, Elks Magazine, Liberty, etc., articles to Printers' Ink, etc.; included in O'Brien's Best Short Stories of the Year, 1918, 26 and 28. Author: Wages and Wealth, 1931; The Cowards Never Started, 1933; The Ultimate Frog, 1939. Office: 21st and C St. N.W., Washington, D.C.* Deceased.

DICKINSON, DWIGHT commodore U.S.N.; b. Jamestown, N.Y., Oct. 31, 1847; s. Edward Alexander and Sarah Mariah (Fletcher) D.; ed. Jamestown Acad.; M.D., U. of Buffalo 1869; m. Syria Elana Browne, of Oakland, Cal., May 12, 1882. Commd. asst. surgeon U.S.N., Apr. 21, 1869; passed asst. surgeon, Nov. 10, 1872; surgeon, Dec. 6, 1879; med. inspr., Sept. 25, 1895; med. dir., Nov. 11, 1899; retired from active service, Oct. 31, 1909, with the rank of commodore. Mem. A.M.A., Spanish-Am. War Veterans, S.R. Clubs: Metropolitan, Army and Navy (Washington), New York Yacht. Home: 1806 R St., N.W., Washington.

DICKINSON, EDWARD FENWICK congressman, lawyer, b. Fremont, O., Jan. 21, 1829; grad. St. Xavier Coll., Cincinnati. Admitted to bar, began practice of law, Fremont; pros. atty. Sandusky County (O.), 1852-54; commd. lt. U.S. Army during Civil War, promoted capt., served as regimental q.m. Co. G., 8th Regt., Ohio Volunteer Inf.; probate judge Sandusky County, 1866-69, 77-79, 85-91; mem. U.S. Ho. of Reps. (Democrat) from Ohio, 41st Congress, 1869-71; elected mayor Fremont, 1871, 73, 75. Died Fremont, Aug. 25, 1891.

DICKINSON, HUNT TILFORD corp. exec.; b. N.Y.C., Nov. 4, 1899; s. Andrew G., Jr., and Katharine Hunt (Earle) D.; grad. St. Paul's Sch., Concord, N.H., 1919; A.B., Princeton, 1922; m. Betty Ward Gilbert Sept. 8, 1923; children-Patricia Earle (Mrs. Chandler Bates, Jr.), Katharine Ward (Mrs. L. Jerome Alexandre), Hunt Tilford, Chmn. bd., treas. William Edwin Ridge, Inc., printing house, N.Y.C., 1924-; chmn. bd. Automatic Nut Co.; dir. Broad St. Investing Corp., Capital Administrn. Co., Ltd., Whitehall Fund, Incorporated; member trust board of First National City Trust Company; director, mem. exec. com. Seatrain Lines, Inc. Fire commr., Locust Valley, 1932-48. Co-chmn. North Shore Community Hosp. fund drive, Glen Cove, N.Y., 1952. Served as maj., USAAF, 1945. Episcopalian. Clubs: Ristigouche Salmon (Can.); Piping Rock (Locust Valley); Seminole Golf (pres. 1950), Everglades (gov.), Bath and Tennis, Palm Beach, Fla.); Racquet and Tennis, Links (N.Y.C.); Connetquot River, Inc. (Oakdale, N.Y.); Waterhen Lodge (Can.). Home: Locust Valley, N.Y. Office: Chrysler Bldg., 405 Lexington Av., N.Y.C. 10017. Died Mar. 10, 1967.

DICKINSON, JACOB MCGAVOCK sec. of war; b. Columbus, Miss., Jan. 30, 1851; s. of Henry and Anna (McGavock) D.; A.B., U. of Nashville, 1871, A.M., 1872; studied law at Columbia Coll., New York, U. of Leipzig, and L'Ecole de Droit, Paris, and attended lectures at Sorbonne; LL.D., Columbia, 1905, U. of Ill., 1905, Yale, 1909, Lincoln U., 1971; m. Martha Overton, Apr. 20, 1876; children - John Overton, Henry, Jacob McGavock. Admitted to bar, 1874; practiced at Nashville, 1874-99, Chicago, 1899-1909; served several times by spl. commn. on supreme bench of Tenn.; asst. atty. gen. of U.S., 1895-97; counsel for U.S. before Alaskan Boundary Tribunal, 1903; gen. solicitor I.C. R.R. Co., 1899-1901, and gen. counsel, 1901-09; sec. of war in Chicago, Ill. Died Dec. 13, 1928.

DICKINSON, JOHN Continental congressman; b. Talbot County, Md., Nov. 8, 1732; s. Samuel and Mary (Cadwalader) D.; LL.D., Coll. of N.J. (now Princeton), 1768; m. Mary Norris, July 19, 1770. Admitted to Middle Temple, London, Eng.; admitted to Phila. bar, 1757; mem. Assembly of Lower Counties (Del.), 1760, later became speaker; mem. Pa. Legislature from Phila., 1762-64, 70-76; printed pamphlet The Late Regulations Respecting the British Colonies on the Continent of America Considered, 1765; del. to Stamp Act Congress from Pa., 1765; chmn. Com. of Correspondence, 1774; mem. Continental Congress, 1774-76, 79-81; cmmn. of a com. of safety and defense, 1775; advocated concilation with Eng.; voted against Declaration of Independence; col. 1st Battalion raised in Phila.; pres. Supreme Council Del., 1781; pres. Supreme Council Pa., 1782-85; del. U.S. Constl. Conv. from Del., 1787; noted for published series of letters urging adoption of Constn., signed Fabius. Author: Letters from a Farmer in Pennsylvania to the Inhabitants of the British Colonies (urged non-importation instead of violence), 1768. Died Wilmington, Del., Feb. 14, 1808.

DICKINSON, PHILEMON army officer, Continental congressman; b. Croisia-dore, Talbot County, Md., Apr. 5, 1739; s. Judge Samuel and Mary (Cadwalader) D.: grad. U. Pa., 1759; m. Mary Cadwalader, July 14, 1767; m. 2d, Rebecca Cadwalader. Commd. col. Hunterdon County (N.J.) Battalion, 1775; commd. brig. gen. N.J. Militia, 1775, maj. gen., comdr.-in-chief, 1776; defeated a Cornwallis raiding expdn. interrupting Brit. retreat to N.Y. before Battle of Monmouth, 1777; apptd. commr. N.J. Loan Office, 1781; mem. Continental Congress from Del., 1782-83; v.p. N.J. Council, 1783-84; apptd. a commr. by Continental Congress to select site for U.S. Capitol, 1785. Died nr. Trenton, N.J., Feb. 4, 1809.

DICKMAN, JOSEPH THEODORE army officer; b. Dayton, O., Oct. 6, 1857; s. Theodore and Mary (Weinmar) D.; grad. U.S. Mil. Acad., 1881; hon. grad. Inf. and Cav. Sch., 1883; grad. Army War Coll., Washington, 1905; (LL.D., U. of Vt.); m. Mary Rector, Sept. 26, 1882. Commd. 2d lt. 3d Cav., June 11, 1881; promoted through grades to brig. gen. U.S.A., 1917; maj. gen. N.A., Aug. 5, 1917; retired as maj. gen., Oct. 6, 1921. Awarded D.S.M. (U.S.); Croix de Guerre, Comdr. Legion of Honor (French); Knight Comdr. of the Bath (Eng.); Order of Leopold (Belgian); Grand Officer Crown of Italy, etc. Died Oct. 23, 1927.

DICKSON, FRANK STODDARD, adj. gen., ex-congressman, tchr.; b. Hillsboro, Ill., Oct. 6, 1876; s. Prof. J. M. and Illinois (Stoddard) D.; grad. pub. schs., 1891, county sch., 1892, Decatur (Ill.) High sch., 1896; m. Theresa Dixon Scott. Jan. 20, 1903; children-Dorothy Lambur, Mrs. Heaton Buckley. Enlisted pvt. Co. I, 4th Ill. Vol. Inf. in Spanish-Am. War; saw service in Cuba; was successively regimental commissary and q. m.; now capt. q. m., 4th Inf., I. N. G. Engaged as tchr., 1903—. Republican; mem. Congress, 23d Ill. dist., 1905-07; adj. gen. Ill., 1910-12. Methodist. Club: Hamilton (Chgo.). Address: Ramsey, Ill. Died Feb. 24, 1953.

DICKSON, JOSEPH planter, congressman; b. Chester County, Pa., Apr. 1745; ed. in Rowan County, N.C. Became cotton and tobacco planter; mem. Rowan County Com. of Safety, 1775; commd. capt. Continental Army, 1775, served under Col. McDowell, 1780, as maj. "Lincoln County Men" at Battle of Kings Mountain; promoted col. for bravery in opposing Lord Cornwallis' invasion of N.C., 1781; commd. brig. gen. before end of Revolutionary War; clk. Lincoln County Ct., 1781; mem. N.C. Senate, 1788-95; a commr. to establish U. N.C. at Chapel Hill; mem. U.S. Ho. of Reps. from N.C., 6th Congress, 1799-1801, helped elect Thomas Jefferson over Aaron Burr; moved to Tenn., 1803, became planter, Dvaidson (now Rutherford) County; mem. Tenn. Ho. of Reps., 1807-11, speaker, 1809-11. Died Rutherford County, Apr. 14, 1825; buried on his plantation N.E. of Murfreesboro, Tenn.

DICKSON, SAMUEL HENRY naval officer; b. Farmington, Conn., July 20, 1849; s. Samuel Henry and Marie Elizabeth Sealbrook (Du Pré) D.; pvt. schs., Phila.; M.D., Jefferson Med. Coll., Phila., 1870; m. Henrietta George, of Baltimore, Md., Jan. 17, 1894. Apptd. asst. surgeon U.S. Navy, Mar. 19, 1875; promoted through various grades; med. dir., Oct. 31, 1909; retired July 20, 1911. Served at sea and on shore in many parts of the world, also in Spanish-Am, War. Called into active service, Mar. 30, 1917; pres. Naval Examining Bds., Navy Yard, Boston. Awarded Spanish-Am. War medals. Mem. A.M.A. Democrat. Episcopalian. Mason. Clubs: Army and Navy (Washington), New York Yacht; Graduates' (New Haven, Conn.). Home: Nantucket, Mass.

DICKSON, TRACY CAMPBELL army officer; b. Independence, Ia., Sept. 17, 1868; s. Capt. Campbell and Lucy Ellen (Tracy) D.; grad. U.S. Mil. Acad., 1892; m. Isabella Kendrick Abbott, Nov. 7, 1894. Commd. 2d lt. 2d Arty., June 11, 1892; promoted through grades to lt. col., Sept. 2, 1912; retired with rank of col., Aug. 16, 1915; recalled to active service, Mar. 7, 1917; col., Jan. 10, 1918; brig. gen., Feb. 18, 1918-May 30, 1919. Asst. to comdr. Springfield Armory, 1894-99; asst. to comdg. officer Rock Island Arsenal, 1899-1902; mem. bd. that tested and recommended magazine rifle model of 1903; recorder Bd. Ordnance and Fortification, 1903-06; asst. to chief of ordnance, 1902-06; at Sandy Hook Proving Ground, 1906-10; insp. of shops under chief engr., Panama Canal, 1910-14; pres. Ordnance Bd. and comdr. Sandy Hook Proving Ground, 1914-15; comdr. Watertown Arsenal, 1917-18; asst. to chief of ordnance, Jan.-June 1918; in charge all army work at Bethlehem Steel Co., June-Oct. 1918; comdr. Watertown Arsenal Oct. 14, 1918 - . Home: Cleburne, Texas. Died May 17, 1936.

DIEHL, CHARLES SANFORD journalist; b. Flintstone, Md., Aug. 8, 1854; s. Carl F. and Amanda F. D.; ed. pub. schs., Ottawa, Ill.; m. Ellen Watson Chandler, Sept. 9, 1879 (died May 21, 1937); children-Chandler (dec.). Grace Chandler (Mrs. S. F. Shaw). Published "Our Boys," 1871-73: on staff Chicago Times, 1873-83; day mgr. Associated Press service Chicago office. 1883, supt. Pacific coast division, San Francisco, 1887-93, assistant general manager at New York and Chicago, 1893-1911; owner and publisher San Antonio (Tex.) Light (with Harrison L. Beach), 1911-24. Reported Sioux Indian campaign of 1876, 1877, and winter campaign against Sioux, 1881; prepared plans to report Spanish-American War for Associated Press, 1898, taking personal charge staff war corrs. in field during war. Organized 1st Regt. Ill. N.G., 1874 (now 131st Inf., 33d Div., U.S. Army), filling all grades from 2nd lt. to lt.-col. Author: The Staff Correspondent, 1931. Club: San Antonio Country. Home: 301 Terrell Rd., San Antonio, Tex. Died Aug. 19, 1946.

DIEHL, SAMUEL WILLAUER BLACK naval officer; b. Reading, Pa., Sept. 20, 1851; s. William W. and Jeriah C. D.; early edn. pub. schs., Reading, Pa.; grad. U.S. Naval Acad., 1873; m. Caroline Wilbank O'Connor, Apr. 4, 1892. Midshipman, U.S.N., 1869; ensign, 1874; promoted through grades to judge advocate gen. with rank of capt. U.S.N., June 4, 1904 - . Served on bd. U.S.S. Alaska, Wabash Congress, Hartford, Plymouth, Marion, Boston, Detroit, Machias, Cincinnati; comd. U.S.S. Eagle, Marietta, Newport, Boston; also in Hydrographic Office; Bur. of Navigation; Bur. of Equipment; Naval Intelligence Office; Supt. of compasses; judge advocate gen. Author: Practical Problems and the Compensation of the Compass, U22. Died 1909.

DIFFENDERFER, GEORGE M. clergyman; b. East Petersburg, Lancaster County, Pa., Jan. 5, 1869: s. Emanuel G. and Frances L. (Knier) D.; A.B., Gettysburg (Pa.) Coll., 1893, A.M., 1896, D.D., 1911; grad. Luth. Theol. Sem., Gettysburg, 1896; attended lectures in philosophy, U. of Berlin, 1910; m. Laura A. Diehl, June 30, 1896; children-Isabel Romayne (Mrs. John Russell Yates), George M. Ordained Luth. ministry, 1896; pastor St. Paul's Ch., Newport, Pa., 1896-1900, First Ch., Carlisle, 1900-14 (built ch., O0,-

000, and hosp., 15,000), Luther Place Memorial Ch., Washington, D.C., 1919-30. Lecturer on Comparative Religions, Dickinson Coll., 1910-11, Washington Sch. of Religious Edn., 1922-24, on Evolution of North American Indian, Oberammergau, God's Garden of Wonders. Chaplain U.S. Industrial Indian Sch., Carlisle, 1900-10; exec. sec. ministerial relief, Luth. Ch., 1914-17; mem. Pa. Relief Bd.; chaplain at Newport News, Va., 1917-18; maj., chaplain O.R.C., U.S. Army. Pres. Washington Fed. of Chs., 1922-23: trustee Tressler Orphanage (v.p. since 1924); trustee Standard Woman's Coll. since 1923; mem. Com. on Army and Navy Chaplains. Washington Com. of Federal Council Churchs of Christ; trustee United Christian Endeavor Soc. Grand Chaplain Pa. A.F. and A.M., 1924-25; K.P. Republican. Editor of Army Chaplain. 1934-36. Home: 2 N. Hanover St., Carlisle, Pa.* Died May 16, 1943.

DIGGS, MARSHALL RAMSEY, lawyer; b. Paris, Tenn., Nov. 7, 1888; s. Robert Albert and Anna (Sauls) D.; A.B., Epworth U. (now Oklahoma City Univ.), 1910; LL.B., Yale, 1913; m. Alice Muse, Nov. 7, 1919; children—Helen (Mrs. Frank Quiggen), Marshall Ramsey, Alice Muse (Mrs. Chas. K. Nulsen, Jr.). Admitted to Ill. bar, 1913, Minn., 1916; practiced in Chicago, 1913-16, Minneapolis, 1916-17; organized Three Captains Co., 1919; sec. and general manager Walraven Advt. Service, 1921-28; exec. asst. comptroller of the currency, 1934-38, 1st dep., Jan. 1938; acting comptroller of currency, 1938. Served as lt., capt., U.S. Army, instr. O.T.C., 1917-19. Mem. Am. Judicature Soc. Am. Bar Assn., Phi Alpha Delta. Meth. Mason (Shriner). Clubs: Yale (N.Y.C.); Burning Tree. Yale, Metropolitan (Washington). Home: Washington DC Died Sept. 26, 1968; buried West Springfield NH

DILKS, WALTER HOWARD JR. lawyer; b. Phila., Oct. 29, 1902; s. Walter Howard and Clara L. (Durfor) D.; A.B., Princeton, 1924; LL.B., Harvard, 1927. Admitted to Pa. bar, 1927, practiced in Phila. 1927-65; partner firm Dilworth, Paxson, Kalish, Kohn & Dilks, 1939-65. Dir. Delaware Fund, Decatur Income Fund, Pecora, Inc., Sutro-Wheatley, Inc. Pres. Magee Meml. Hosp. Convalescents; v.p. Episcopal Hosp.; treas. Musical Fund Soc. Phila. Served to lt. col. AUS, 1942-46. Mem. Am., Pa., Phila. bar assns. Clubs: Union League, Phila. Country, Racquet, Midday (Phila.). Home: 2101 Delancey P.I., Phila. 19103. Office: Fidelity-Phila. Trust Bldg., Phila. 19109. Died July 23, 1965.

DILLER, GEORGE E., educator; b. Pittsburgh, Mar. 7, 1906; s. Theodore and Rebecca Chambers (Craig) D.; A.B., Princeton, 1926, Ph.D., 1933; m. Constance Dorothea Weeks, June 18, 1938 (dec. Oct. 1957); children—George T., John E.; m. 2d, Angele Belval, Dec. 11, 1958. Bank clk. Paris and N.Y., 1926-30; instr. in French, Princeton, 1933-34, Rutgers U., 1934-36; instr. in French, Dartmouth Coll., 1936-38, asst. prof., 1938-47, prof. of French, 1947-69. Mem. sch. bd., Norwich, Vt., 1946-49. Served with Army Air Force, U.S., India and Guam as intelligence officer, 1942-45; disch. rank of major. Mem. Modern Lang. Assn. of Am., Am. Assn. Teachers of French, Am. Assn. Univ. Profs. Socialist. Author: several books, including La France d'autrefois et d'aujourd'hui (with Charles R. Bagley), 1951. Awarded Bronze Star medal, 1945. Home: Norwich VT Died Aug. 1969.

DILLINGHAM, ALBERT CALDWELL naval officer; b. Phila., June 3, 1848; s. Simeon and Mary Elizabeth (Raymond) D.; served in 7th Pa. Inf. in Civil War; grad. U.S. Naval Acad., 1869; m. Grace Gillmor, June 21, 1897. Promoted through various grades to capt., U.S.N., Feb. 19, 1906; rear adm., Dec. 10, 1910. Served on various stas. and in prin. parts of the world; was promoted for "gallant and conspicuous conduct" in battle during war with Spain; in charge of U.S. affairs in Santo Domingo waters, 1904, stopped the revolution in that republic and established a definite govt.; on diplomatic duty to Santo Domingo, 1905, and with the U.S. minister accomplished an agreement with that republic which secured uninterrupted commerce, security to lives and properties of foreign residents and a guarantee that the debt of the republic be paid, the agreement doing away with the means of revolution by placing the customs of the republic under control of the U.S. Retired by operation of law, June 3, 1910. Recalled to active duty, June 7, 1917; in charge of development of Naval Operating Base, Hampton Roads, Va. Awarded Navy Cross with citation: "for exceptionally meritorious service in a duty of great responsibility, for excellent and thorough work in charge of the development of the Naval Operating Base at Hampton Roads, Va." Home: Norfolk, Va. Died Dec. 6, 1925.

DILLINGHAM, CHARLES BANCROFT theatre mgr.; b. Hartford, Conn., May 30, 1868; s. Edmund Bancroft and Josephine (Potter) D.; ed. pub. schs. Produced 200 plays, mostly musical, from 1900, and managed 50 prominent stars; mgr. Globe theatre and partner of A. L. Erlanger in 20 other theatres. Commd. capt. Aviation Corps, U.S.A., 1917. Died Aug. 30, 1934.

DIMITROFF, GEORGE ZAKHARIEFF educator, astronomer; b. Svistove, Bulgaria, Aug. 24, 1901; s. Zakharia and Elenka Hadji (Nikolova) D.; student Robert Coll., Constantinople, 1916-17, 19-20; B.S., Boston U., 1927; M.A., Harvard, 1929; Ph.D., 1937; M.A. (hon.) Dartmouth, 1947; m. Mary Alice Sweeney, June 14, 1928; children-John David, Barbara Ann. Came to U.S., 1921, naturalized, 1930; Asst. prof. physics. Colo. State Coll., 1929-34; instr. astronomy, tutor div. phys. scis. Harvard, also Radcliffe Coll., 1934-37; supt. Oak Ridge sta. Harvard Obs., also research asso. astronomy Harvard, 1937-42; prof. astronomy Dartmouth, 1946—. Mem. Combined Priorities Tech. Missions to Europe and Japan, 1943-46; dir. tng. research res. program Office Naval Reserach, 1951-52. Served as comdr. USNR, 1943-46, and 1951-52, captain reserve, 1960—. Fellow Royal Astronomical Society, A.A.A.S.; mem. International Astron. Union, Am. Astron. Soc., Am. Phys. Soc., Am. Optical Soc. Author: General Physics for the Laboratory, 1930; Telescopes and Accessories 1945; Astronomy in Brief, 1956. Home: R.F.D. 1, Hartland Vt. Office: Shattuck Observatory, Dartmouth Coll., Hanover, N.H. Died Jan. 3, 1968.

DIMMICK, EUGENE DUMONT brig. gen.; b. Athens, N.Y., July 31, 1840; s. Elnathan Ni and Emily Jane D.; ed. Athens and Hudson, N.Y.; m. Mary Caldwell, 1863 (died 1882); 2d, Mrs. Florence Palmer Hazard, 1896. Enlisted pvt. Co. G, 2d N.J. State Militia, Apr. 26, 1861; disch. July 31, 1861; 1st sergt., Co. M, 5th N.Y. Cav., Oct. 7, 1861-May 8, 1862; 2d lt. same, May 9, 1862; 1st lt., Oct. 10, 1862; capt., July 5, 1863; hon. mustered out, Nov. 6, 1863, on account of wounds; 2d lt., Vet. Reserve Corps., Feb. 3, 1864; hon. mustered out, June 30, 1866; apptd. 2d lt., 9th U.S. Cav., Aug. 9, 1867; advanced through grades to col. Cavalry, Feb. 22, 1903; retired at own request, after 40 yrs. service, Mar. 2, 1903; advanced to rank of brig. gen., retired, by act of Apr. 23, 1904. In Civil War was in actions of Harrisonburg, Culpeper; battles of Cedar Mountain (comdg. co.), 2d Bull Run (escort to Gen. Banks), South Mountain, Antietam, Brandy Sta., Chantilly; actions of Warrenton Junction, Thoroughfare Gap, Beverly Ford, Hanover Junction; battle of Gettysburg, and actions of Boonsboro and Hagerstown (severely wounded, taken prisoner and paroled). Comd. squadron D, and H. Troop, 9th Cav., at affair at Crow Agency, Mont., Nov. 5, 1887, when "Sword Bearer" was killed; in campaign against Indians under Victorio and Nan, N. Mex., Ariz. and Mexico. Butd. Capt. for gallantry in action against Indians, Black Range Mts., N.M. Took part in Santiago Campaign, and comd. 2nd Cav. at Matanzas, 1898. Died Nov. 16, 1935.

DINKELSPIEL, LLOYD W. lawyer; b. San Francisco, Nov. 19, 1899; s. Samuel L. and Beatrice (Bachman) D.; A.B., Stanford, 1920; LL.B., Harvard, 1922; m. Florence Hellman. February 26, 1926 (dec. Jan. 1954); children-Frances (Mrs. William H. Green), Lloyd W.; m. 2d, Anna R. Ward, July 26, 1958. Admitted to Cal. bar, 1921, pvt. practice San Francisco since 1922; partner Heller, Ehrman, White & McAuliffe 1927—. Pres. Jewish Welfare Fedns. of San Francisco, Marin Co. and Peninsula, Nat. Research Inst., president Stanford, trustee 1953-58. Served as 2d lt. Inf., United States Army, 1918; maj. to lt. col., U.S.A.A.F., 1943-45. Decorated Legion of Merit. Mem. Am., San Francisco (pres. 1942-43) bar assns. Home: 2800 Broadway. San Francisco 15. Office: 14 Montgomery St., San Francisco 4. Died May 1959.

DINKINS, JAMES banker; b. Madison Co., Miss., Apr, 18, 1845; s. Alexander Hamilton and Cynthia (Springs) D.; ed. country sch., 1853-60, N.C. Mil. Inst., 1860-61; m. Sue Hart, Nov. 15, 1866. Entered C.S.A. at 16; pvt. 18th Miss. Inf.; 1st lt. cav., Apr. 9, 1863; capt. Co. C, 18th Miss. Cav., Dec. 15, 1864; participated in every engagement of his command, including Leesburg, Dam No. 2, Savage Station, Malvern Hills, Harper's Ferry, Sharpsburg, Fredericksburg; served from Apr. 1863, as a.-d.-c. to Gen. J. R. Chalmers; took part in all the daring and desperate raids and campaigns of Forrest, battles of Coldwater, Okalona, West Point, Brice's Cross Roads, Ft. Pillow, Oxford, Memphis, Harrisburg, Columbia, Franklin and Nashville. Entered service I.C. R.R., 1874; served road 28 yrs. in various capacities; Jan. 1, 1903, opened Bank of Jefferson, Gretna, La., opposite New Orleans. Long edited Confederate column. New Orleans Picayune, contributing war reminiscences. Author: 1861 to 1865, by an Old Johnnie, 1897. Home: New Orleans, La. Died July 19, 1939.

DISMUKES, DOUGLAS EUGENE rear admiral (retired); b. Macon, Miss., Oct. 1, 1869; s. George and Agnes Salina (Harrison) D.; grad. U.S. Naval Academy, 1890; married Maude A. Hench, September 16, 1897; children-Ann Ellen (deceased), Judith Lee, Douglas Eugene. Advanced through grades to captain, United States Navy, 1918; promoted by special act of Congress to rear admiral upon retirement from active service, 1925, in recognition of bring U.S.S. Mt. Vernon into port after being torpedoed 200 miles off coast of France. Served in Spanish-Am. War; comd. U.S.S. Petrel, Haiti Resolution, 1911; capt. eastern terminal port, Panama Canal Zone, 1913-14; comdr. U.S. Naval Training Sta., Newport, R.I., 1919-21; comdr. U.S.S. Nevada, special mission to Rio de Janeiro Internat. Expn., 1922; comdt. Navy Yard, Portsmouth, N.H., 1923-25; recalled to active duty, Jan. 1942; comdg. Me. Maritime Acad., Castine, Me. Awarded D.S.M.; citation for "exceptionally meritorious services" (U.S.); decorated Officer Legion of Honor (France). Home: 32 Livermore St., Portsmouth, N.H. Died Dec. 2, 1949.

DISQUE, BRICE P. army officer, exec.; b. California, O., July 19, 1879; s. Henry Jacob and Ella (Pursell) D.; ed. pub. schs., Cincinnati, O., July 19, 1879; s. Henry Jacob and Ella (Pursell) D.; ed. pub. schs., Cincinnati, O., and Walnut Hill Sch.; distinguished grad. Inf. and Cav. Sch., 1906, Army Staff Coll., 1907; m. Mary Florence Coulter, Oct. 22, 1901; children-Brice Pursell, Gordon Coulter. Served from 2d lt. to brig. gen., U.S. Army, 1899-1919; brig. gen. U.S. Army Reserve Corps, 1919-49; served in Philippine Insurrection and World War; captured Aguinaldo's southern comdr., Emeterio Funes, and his troops, Feb. 21, 1901. Served as mgr. of Michigan State Prison (developed system providing gainful employment for all inmates and operated the prison at profit without financial aid from State), 1916-17; organizer and comdr. Spruce Division, U.S. Army, and pres. U.S. Spruce Corp., 1917-19; organizer, 1918, pres. 1918-19. Loyal Legion Loggers and Lumbermen for lumber industry in the Pacific Northwest (cont. after war period as coordinating agency, bringing industrial peace between employer and employes). Pres. G. Amsinck & Co., 1919-21, Johnson Cowdin & Co., 1921-27, United Industrial Bancstocks, 1930; v.p. The Aviation Corp., 1929; pres. U.S. Distributing Corp., Pattison and Bowns, Inc., 1933-36, Jansen Creek Orchards, Inc.; Pres. Anthracite Inst., 1931-33; dir. Murray Hill Trust Co., 1924-28, Peoples Nat. Bank & Trust Co., 1934-55; past pres. of the Coal Consumers Protective Assn., N.Y. City. Active duty War Department, 1941-42. Chmn. Area Advisory Com. on Local Distbn., Solid Fuels Adminstrn. for War, N.Y., 1943-46. Mem. S.R. Awarded D.S.M. (U.S.); Comdr. Order S.S. Maurice and Lazarus (Italy): commendation from govts. of Great Britain and France. Mem. Disciples of Christ Ch. Clubs: Metropolitan, Uptown (New York); Army and Navy (Wash.) Army and Navy (Manila). Home: Spuyten Duyvil, New York, N.Y.; (farm residence) Linlithgo, N.Y. Died March 1960.

DISQUE, ROBERT CONRAD, educator; b. Burlington, Ia., Mar. 14, 1883; s. Frederick Jacob and Marie Louisa (Holstein) D.; B.L., U. of Wis., 1903, B.S. in E.E., 1908; Sc.D., Northwestern, 1942; D.Eng., Stevens Inst., 1946; grad. study, U. of Pa., 1925-31; m. Laura Maud Crafts, June 14, 1921; children—Sarah Marie, Robert Otis, Helen Cushman. Teacher high sch., Burlington, Ia., 1903-05; engr., Milwaukee Electric & Ry. Co., 1908; instr. in elec. engring., U. of Wis., 1908-17; prof. elec. engring., Drexel Inst., Philadelphia, Pa., 1919-24; academic dean, 1924-32, dean of the faculty, 1932; acting president, 1943-44. Educational consultant Walter P. Murphy Foundation. Served as 1st lt. Air Service, United States Army, 1917, capt. 1918; maj. United States Res., 1918-24. Dir. School Dist. of Swarthmore. Fellow Am. Inst. E.E.; mem. Am. Society for Engring. Edn., The Newcomen Soc., Phi Beta Kappa, Sigma Xi, Tau Beta Pi, Alpha Sigma Phi, Eta Kappa Nu, Phi Kappa Phi. Democrat. Mason. Home: Swarthmore PA Died May 7, 1968.

DITTO, ROLLO C. army officer; born Pa., Sept. 27, 1886; grad. Command and Gen. Staff Sch., 1923. Army War Coll., 1927. Served as private, corpl. and sergt., C.A.C., U.S. Army, Mar. 1907-Nov. 1909; commd. 2d lt., Inf., Nov. 1909; transferred to Chem. Warfare Service as major, 1921, and advanced through the grades to brig. gen., Sept. 1941; served as major, Inf., World War I; on Gen. Staff Corps, 1929-31. Awarded Silver Star with oak leaf cluster, Purple Heart. Address: Huntsville Arsenal, Huntsville, Al.* Died Jan. 7, 1947.

DIVEN, ALEXANDER SAMUEL army officer, railroad promoter; b. Tioga County, N.Y., Feb. 10, 1809; s. John and Eleanor (Means) D.; m. Amanda Beers, 1835; m. 2d, Maria Joy, 1876; 8 children. Admitted to N.Y. bar, 1832; an organizer Republican Party in N.Y.; dir. N.Y. & Erie R.R., 1844; chiefly instrumental in orgn. of company which built Binghamton-Corning Line and the Williamsport & Elmira R.R. (pres. latter throughout constrn.), 1849, mem. N.Y. Senate from Chemung County, 1858-59; Free Soil candidate for gov. N.Y., 1859; mem. U.S. Ho. of Reps. from N.Y., 37th Congress, 1861-63, mem. judiciary com., 1861-63; commd. lt. lt. col. U.S. Army, col. 1862, asst. adj. gen., 1863, brig. gen., 1864, distinguished service in Va. campaigns, 1862, 63; v.p. N.Y. & Erie R.R., 1865-68; mayor Elmira, N.Y., 1868. Died Elmira, June 11, 1896.

DIX, JOHN ADAMS army officer, gov. N.Y.; sec. of treasury; b. Boscowen, N.H., July 24, 1798: s. Col. Timothy and Abigail (Wilkins) D.; m. Catharine Morgan, 1826, 1 son, Morgan. Served in War of 1812; admitted to Washington (D.C.) bar, 1824; travelling aide to Maj. Gen. Jacob Brown; spl. U.S. messenger to Copenhagen, (Denmark), 1826; practiced law, active in politics, Cooperstown, N.Y., 1828; adj. gen. sec. of state N.Y., 1833-39; founder lit. and sci. jour. Northern Light, 1840-43; mem. U.S. Senate (Democrat) from N.Y., 1845-49 unsuccessful Free Soil nominee for gov. N.Y., 1848; pres. Chgo. and Rock Island R.R., also Miss. and Mo. R.R., 1854-57; U.S. sec. treasury, served as maj. gen. U.S. Army, comdr. depts. Md. and the East during Civil War; U.S. minister to France, 1866-69; gov. N.Y., 1873-75. Author: A Winter in Madeira; A Summer in Spain and Florence, 1850; Speeches and Occasional Addresses, 2 vols., 1864; Stabat Mater, 1868. Died N.Y.C., Apr. 21, 1879.

DIXON, GEORGE PELEG assn. exec., ret. army officer; b. Worcester, Mass., Jan. 29, 1889; s. Rufus S. and Cora I. (Remis) D.; student Worcester Poly, Inst., 1912; m. Edna M. Spitzer, May 27, 1946; children-Patricia, Peter (by former marriage), Penelope Ann. Student engr. Pacific Tel. & Tel. Co., San Francisco, 1912-17; engr. Western Electric Co., N.Y.C., 1919-20; traffic supervisor, insp. N.Y. Telephone Co., 1920-25; gen. mgr. Worcester Spiral Ramp Garage Co., 1925-27; N.Y. Tleephone Co., 1927-29; communications engr. Nat. City Bank, and asso. cos., N.Y.C., 1929-40; v.p. Internat. Tel. & Tel. Corp., 1945-50, regional v.p., Brazil, 1946-48; exec. v.p., editor Armed Forces Communications Assn., Washington, since 1950. Trustee Worcester Poly. Inst. Mem. Cal. N.G., 1916-17, served Mexican Border, 6 months; lt. to capt. Signal Corps, U.S. Army, 1917-19, overseas with 91st Div. and S.O.S., 1918-19; lt. col. Signal Corps, col. A.C., 1940-45; signal officer II Corps area, 1940-42; signal communications officer 8th Air Force Service Command, chief signal officer 8th Air Force, dir. communications, U.S.S.T.A.F., E.T.O., 1942-45; Signal Res., 1945-49. Decorated Silver Star (2), Legion of Merit, Bronze Star Medal (4), Commendation Medal, Victory Medal (World War I and II), Mexican Border Medal, World War I Occupation Medal, Am. Def. Medal, E.T.O. Medal, Am. Theatre Medal, World War II Occupation Medal; Officer Order Brit. Empire; Chevalier Legion of Honor, French Cross of War (2), Gen. Service Medal, Gold Palms Hon. Officer French Acad. Sci. (France); Belgium Cross of War. Mem. Am. Inst. Radio Engrs., Radio Engrs. Soc. (Gt. Britain), S.A.R., Armed Forces Communications Assn. (a founder), N.Y. Acad. Scis., Am. Legion, N.Y. State Soc. Mil. and Naval Officers, Mil. Order World Wars, Phi Gamma Delta. Episcopalian. Clubs: Army and Navy (Washington); Belle Haven Country (Alexandria, Va.); Governors land Officers (N.Y.C.); Internacional (Rio de Janeiro). Home: 20 Belfield Rd., Belle Haven, Alexandria, Va. Office: 1624 Eye St., Washington 6. Died July 9, 1956; buried Arlington Nat. Cemetery.

DIXON, WILLIAM (BILLY) frontiersman; b. Ohio County, Va. (now W.Va.), Sept. 25, 1850; m. Olive King, Oct. 18, 1894. Driver in govt. mule trains, Colo. and Okla., 1865-69; became buffalo hunter, 1869; took part in Battle of Adobe Walls (28 whites withstood attack of about 700 Comanche Indians), in what is now Hutchinson County, Tex., 1874; scout for U.S. Calvary, 1874-83; received (with 4 companions) Congressional medal of honor for surviving attack of over 125 Indians; homesteaded on claim in Hutchinson County, 1883, later served as postmaster, land commr., justice of peace, in what is now Cimarron County, Okla., 1906. Died Mar. 9, 1913.

DIXON, WILLIAM PALMER, investment banker; N.Y.C., Mar. 19, 1902; s. William H. and Josephine Theodora (Williams) D.; student Eton Coll., Eng.; A.B., Harvard University, 1925; m. Joan Deery, Feb. 21, 1941; children—Palmer, Peter T. With J. Henry Schroder Banking Corp., N.Y., 1926-29; partner Rhoades & Co., N.Y.C., 1929-38, Loeb, Rhoades & Co., mem. N.Y. Stock Exchange, 1938-68; dir. Loeb, Rhoades & Co., Inc., USLIFE Holding Corp. (N.Y.), also dir. U.S. Life Insurance Co. of N.Y., Am. Home Assurance Co. (N.Y.C.), Am. Internat. Life Assurance Co. of N.Y., The Lighthouse (N.Y.), Loeb, Rhoades Internat., Inc. Trustee, member finance com. Midtown Hospital, New York City; dir. American Field Service. Served as colonel USAAF, World War II, assistant chief staff 9th Air Force, 1944. Decorated Legion of Merit with Oak Leaf Cluster; Croix de Guerre with Palm (Belgium). Mem. N.Y. C. of C., Nat. Inst. Social Scis., Newcomen Soc., N.Y. Philharmonic Soc. Clubs: Recess, Racquet and Tennis, River, Harvard, Madison Sq. Garden, Marco Polo, Turf and Field, Links Golf, The Brook (New York City, N.Y.); Philadelphia (Pennsylvania); Racquet (Montreal), Racquet (Detroit); Jesters, White's, Old Etonian Racquets and Tennis (London, Eng.); Harvard Varsity (pres.) (Cambridge, Mass.), Nat. Champion U.S., Squash Racquets, 1925, 26. Home: New York City NY Died July 25, 1968; buried St. James Ch., New York City NY

DOBIE, ARMISTEAD MASON judge; b. at Norfolk, Va., Apr. 15, 1881; s. Richard Augustus and Margaret Kearns (Cooke) D.; B.A., U. of Va., 1901, M.A., 1902, LL.B., 1904; S.J.D., Harvard Law School, 1922; m. Elizabeth McKenny, July 16, 1958. Began career with law practice in St. Louis, 1904-07; adjunct prof. law. U. of Va., 1907, prof. law, 1909-39, dean, 1932-39; lecturer, summer law schs., Cornell, 1924, of Mich., 1929, U. of N.C. and U. of Chicago, 1930, U. of Kansas, 1931; apptd. U.S. Dist. judge, Western Dist. of Virginia, June 2, 1939; U.S. circuit judge, 4th Circuit, Dec. 19, 1939. Exec. dir. Univ. of Va. Centennial Endowment Fund, 1920-21. Legal adviser Conflict of Laws Sect. of Am. Law Inst.; mem. U.S. Supreme Court's Advisory Com. to draft rules of procedure in lower federal courts; spl. asst. to atty. gen. of U.S. since 1935. Commd. capt. U.S.R., inf., sect., and aide to Maj. Gen. Cronkhite, Camp Lee, Va., 1917; maj., Gen. Staff, 1919; chief of intelligence publs. sect., Gen. Hdqrs. A.E.F.; asst. chief of staff, G 2, 80th Division; hon. disch. June 5, 1919. Decorated Officer d' Académic (Palms, French). Mem. Am. Bar Assn., Am. Law Inst., Virginia Bar Assn., La. Bar Assn. (Hon. life mem.), Am. Judicature Soc., Phi Gamma Delta, Phi Delta Phi, Phi Beta Kappa. Democrat. Episcopalian. Clubs: Colonade (University, Va.); Farmington Country (Charlottesville, Va.). Author and co-author several law books. Contbr. to legal periodicals. Home: Preston Pl., Charlottesville, Va. Died Aug. 7, 1962; buried Univ. Cemetery, Charlottesville.

DOBYNS, A(SHBEL) WEBSTER lawyer; b. Austin, Tex., June 6, 1879; s. John Robert and Lilly (Webster) D.; B.A., Millsaps Coll., Jackson, Miss., 1899; M.A., Gallaudet Coll., Washington, D.C., 1900; LL.B., U. of Ark., 1908; m. Nancy McClerkin, Oct. 26, 1927. Teacher in schs. for deaf, Washington, Minnesota and N.Y. City, and later prin. Ark. Sch. for Deaf, 1900-08; admitted to bar, Miss. and Ark., 1908; practiced law as mem. firm Riddick & Dobyns, Little Rock, Ark., 1908-19; asso. with Rose, Hemingway, Cantrell & Loughborough, 1919-23, mem. firm since 1923, firm name now Rose, Dobyns, Meek and House. Assistant adjutant general, 1918; capt. U.S. Army, and asst. adj., 97th Div., 1918; Judge Advocate General, Ark. Nat. Guard, and major, Judge Advocate General, U.S. Army Res., 1919-22. Mem. bd. trustees Southwest Legal Found., Dallas. Mem. and sec. of sub-com. which wrote constn. of Am. Legion at first conv., Minneapolis, Minn., 1919. Mem. Am. (house of dels., 1940-48; board govs., 1944-47), Arkansas (chairman exec. com., 1941-42), Little Rock (president 1925-26) bar assns., Am. Judicature Soc., Am. Law Inst., Newcomen Soc., Kappa Alpha (Southern),Phi Alpha Delta. Democrat. Presbyterian. Home: 1615 Battery St. Office: 314 W. Markham St., Little Rock, Ark. Died Mar. 26, 1950.

DOCHEZ, ALPHONSE RAYMOND physician, teacher; b. San Francisco, Calif., Apr. 21, 1882; s. Louis and Josephine (Dietrich) D.; A.B., Johns Hopkins, 1903, M.D., 1907; Sc.D., N.Y.U., 1925, Yale U., 1926, Western Reserve U., 1931, Columbia U., 1954; unmarried. Formerly member staff Rockefeller Inst. for Med. Research; asso. prof. medicine, Johns Hopkins Med. Sch., 1919-21; asso. prof. medicine, Coll. Phys. and Surg. (Columbia), 1921-25, prof., 1925-37, John E. Borne prof. of med. and surg. research, 1939-49, emeritus professor medical and surgical research since 1949; visiting physician Presbyn. Hospital. Former trustee Rockefeller Institute for Med. Research. Maj. Medical Corps, U.S. Army. World War. Mem. Assn. Am. Physicians, Am. Soc. for Clin. Investigation, Am. Soc. for Exptl. Pathology, Soc. for Exptl. Biology and Medicine, Harvey Soc. Nat. Acad. Science, Alpha Delta Phi. Democrat, Catholic. Clubs: University, Century, Maryland. Developer antitoxin for scarlet fever, also serum for lobar pneumonia; identified viral origins of common cold. Home: 1 W. 54th St., N.Y.C. Office: 620 W. 168th St., N.Y.C. 10032. Died June 30, 1964; buried Balt.

DODD, GEORGE ALLAN army officer; b. Rose's Valley, Pa., July 26, 1852; s. of Allan Grinnell and Emily (Stiger) D.; grad. U.S. Mil. Acad., 1876; m. Agnes Clara Steele, June 1880. Commd. 2d lt. 3d Cav., June 15, 1876; advanced through grades to col. 12th Cav., Apr. 14, 1908; brig. gen., July 1, 1916, and retired by operation of law, July 26, 1916. Participated in numerous campaigns against Indians, 1876-83; introduced improved system of handling and training cavalry, 1888 and 1891-93; duty Chicago during Pullman strike, 1894; visited Eng. in connection with mil. tournaments, 1895; inaugurated U.S. mil. tourments, Madison Sq., New York, 1896-97; duty in Cuba, 1898, in Philippines, 1899-1901; chief umpire of Div., Aug.-Sept. 1906; duty Gen. Staff, 1907-08; comd. 2d Cav. Brigade, Douglas, Ariz., 1915-16; comd. western column Mex. punitive expdn., 1916. Recommended for bvt. "for gallantry in action and returning to firing line while wounded," Battle of San Juan, Cuba, July 1, 1898; for bvts. as maj. and lt. col., by Gens. Lawton and Young, "for gallant service in attacking in the darkness, and dispersing a large force of the enemy in a most dangerous and difficult pass," 1899, later as col. for same affair; for bvts. Gen. Wheaton, "for most gallant conduct in action." Home: Ithaca, N.Y. Died. June 28, 1925.

DODD, WALTER FAIRLEIGH lawyer; b. Hopkinsville, Ky., Apr. 7, 1880; s. J. M. and Laura A. (Imbler) D.; A.B., Fla. State Coll., 1898; B.S., John B. Stetson U., 1901; Ph.D., U. Chgo., 1905; m. Sue Hutchinson, 1919 (dec. 1944); children-Walter H., Laura Alice. In charge sect. fgn. law Library of Congress, 1904-07; held research appointment Johns Hopkins, 1908-10; asso. in polit. sci. U. Ill., 1910-11, asst. prof. 1911-14, asso. prof., 1914-15; asso. prof. polit. sci. U. Chgo., 1915-17; sec. Ill. Legislative Reference Bur., Springfield, 1917-18; maj., Q.M.C., U.S. Army, 1918-19; in charge collection data for Ill. Constl. Conv., 1919-20; practiced law Chgo., 1920-60; also prof. law, Yale, 1927-30, and research asso. with rank of prof., 1930-33. Mem. Am. Polit. Sci. Assn. (pres. 1946), Am. Ill., Chgo. bar assns., Am. Law Inst., Am. Judicature Soc., Assn. Bar City of N.Y. Clubs: Union League (Chicago); Cosmos (Washington, D.C.). Author: Modern Constitutions (2 vols.), 1909; Government of the District of Columbia, 1909; Revision and Amendment of State Constitutions, 1910; State Government, 1922, 28; Government in Illinois (with Sue Hutchison Dodd), 1923; Appellate Jurisdiction and Practice in Illinois (with Palmer D. Edmunds), 1929; Cases and Authorities on Constitutional Law, 1933-54, supplement to 1956; Administration of Workmen's Compensation, 1936; Annotations of Illinois Civil Practice Act, 1936. Office: 141 W. Jackson Blvd., Chgo., Died Apr. 1960.

DODDS, EUGENE MAXWELL corp. official; b. Enon Valley, Pa., Aug. 7, 1892; s. Rowen Thompson F. and Grace (Stebbins) D.; student U. of Idaho Prep. Sch., 1907-09, U. of Idaho, 1910-12; m. Carmilla Betty Johnson, Dec. 14, 1918; 1 dau., Jeanne (Mrs. J. C. Williams, Jr.). With U.S. Cold Storage Corp. since 1919, chmn. bd. consol. co. operating in Chgo., Ft. Worth, Omaha, Dallas, Detroit, Kansas City and Port Lavaca, Tex., 1955—; pres., dir. Continental Investment Company; member of board of directors St. Louis-San Francisco Ry., Fed. Res. Bank of Kansas City; chmn. bd. Tranin Egg Products Co. Pres., dir. Am. Royal Live Stock and Horse Show 1956-57, now chmn. exec. com. and dir.; president Kansas City Crime Commn., Kansas City chpt. Quartermaster Assn.; mem. City (Kansas City) Plan Commn., 1939-44; mem. Bd. Police Commrs., 1944-46; refrigeration consultant War Department, 1941-45. Served as 2d lt. Engr. O.R.C., later capt. U.S. Army, 1917-18. Mem. Am. Soc. Refrigerating Engrs., Sons of Revolution. Republican. Presbyterian. Clubs: Mission Hills Country, Saddle& Sirloin, Kansas City (Missouri); Racquet, Tavern, Union League, (Chicago). Home: 310 W. 49th St., Kansas City 12, Mo. Office: 500 E. 3d St., Kansas City, Mo. Died May 1, 1960; buried Mt. Moriah Cemetery, Kansas City, Mo.

DODDS, OZRO JOHN congressman, lawyer; b. Cincinnati, Mar. 22, 1840; attended Miami U., Oxford, O., 4 years, received degree after Civil War; attended Cincinnati Law Sch. Organized Capt. Dodd's Univ. Co. during Civil War, enlisted as capt. Co. B., 20th Ohio Volunteer Regt., 1861; served as capt. Co. F, 81st Ohio Volunteer Inf., and acting asst. q.m., 1861-63 promoted lt. col. 1st Ala. Union Cavalry, 1863; admitted to bar, 1866, began practice of law, Cincinnati; mem. Ohio Ho. of Reps., 1870-71; mem. U.S. Ho. of Reps. (Democrat, filled vacancy) from Ohio, 42d Congress, Oct. 8, 1872-73. Died Columbus, O., Apr. 18, 1862; buried Spring Grove Cemetery, Cincinnati.

DODGE, FRANCIS SAFFORD army officer; b. Danvers, Mass., Sept. 11, 1842; s. Francis and Rebecca Appleton (Brown) D.; grad. Danvers High Sch., 1860; attended Henniker (N.H.) Acad., 1860-61; m. Mary Hunt Weston, Dec. 3, 1878. Pvt. and corp. Co. F, 23d Mass. Inf., Oct. 9, 1861-Dec. 19, 1863; 1st lt. U.S. colored cav., Dec. 20, 1863; promoted through grades to brig. gen. p.m. gen., Jan. 23, 1904; retired by operation of law, Sept. 11, 1906. Bvtd. maj., Feb. 27, 1890, for action against Indians at Milk Creek, Colo., Sept. 29-Oct. 1, 1879; awarded medal of honor, Mar. 22, 1898, for "most distinguished gallantry" against Indians nr. White River Agency, Colo. Oct. 2, 1879. Served in N.C. and S.C., 1861-63, in Va., 1863-64, Tex., 1864-65; after the war at various posts in the west, etc. Dir. and mem. exec. com. Garfield Memorial Hosp.; dir. Am. Surety & Trust Co. Home: Washington, D.C. Died 1908.

DODGE, GRENVILLE MELLEN civil engr.; b. Danvers, Mass., Apr. 12, 1831; s. Sylvanus and Julia T. (Phillips) D.; grad. Capt. Partridge's Mil. Acad.; C.E., Norwich U., Vt., 1850 (A.M., M.M.S., LL.D., 1892; LL.D., Cornell Coll., Ia., 1904). Was engr. Ill. Central and Rock Island roads; later on U.P. R.R. survey and banker at Council Bluffs, Ia. Entered Civil War as col. 4th Inf., July 6, 1861; brig. gen. vols., Mar. 21, 1862; maj. gen. vols., June 7, 1864; resigned May 30, 1866. Chief engr. U.P. R.R. and supervised its building, 1866-70; chief engr. Tex. & Pacific Ry., 1871-81. Mem. 40th Congress (1867-69), 2d Ia. Dist. Republican. Succeeded Gen. Sherman as pres. Soc. Army of the Tenn.; comdr.-in-chief Mil. Order Loyal Legion, 1907-08. Apptd. maj. gen. U.S.V., 1898, but declined; apptd., 1898, pres. of the President's commn. to inquire into the management of the war with Spain; chmn. bd. dirs. C. & S. Ry. to Feb. 1909; dir. Ft. Worth & Denver City Ry.; v.p. Abilene & Southern Ry. Died Jan. 3, 1916.

DODGE, HENRY army officer, senator, territorial gov.; Vincennes, Ind., Oct. 12, 1782; s. Israel and Mary Ann (Hunter) D. m. Christina McDonald, 1800, 1 son, Augustus Caesar. Succeeded his father as sheriff Ste. Genevieve, Missouri Dist., 1805-21; marshall Territory of Mo., 1813; rose to maj. gen. Mo. Militia; apptd. by Pres. Jackson as maj. of bn. of mounted rangers recruited to patrol the frontier of Upper Mississippi Valley; commd. col., 1833; gov. Territory of Wis., 1836-41, 45-48: del. U.S. Congress from Territory of Wis., 27th-29th congresses, 1841-45; mem. U.S. Senate from Wis., 1848-57. Died Burlington, Ia., June 19, 1867.

DODGE, OMENZO GEORGE naval officer; b. Mendon, Mich., June 1, 1856; s. George E. and Sarah S. D.; ed. pub. schs. of Mich. and Kan.; apptd. from Kan., and grad. U.S. Naval Acad., 1877; postgrad. course 2 yrs., Smithsonian Instn., Washington; m. Ada E. Jacobs, of Wamego, Kan., 1879. Midshipman U.S.N., 1873; ensign, 1880; lt., 1887; prof. mathematics, U.S.N., June 29, 1892; rank of comdr., 1899; capt., 1908, Mem. Am. Inst. Elec. Engrs. Club: Army and Navy (Washington). Address: Navy Dept., Washington.

DODGE, THEODORE AYRAULT army officer; military historian; b. Pittsfield, Mass., May 28, 1842; s. Nathaniel S. D.; military edn. in Berlin; grad. U. of London, Eng., 1861, LL.B., Columbian, 1865; m. Jane Marshall Neil, 1865; m. 2d, Clara Isabel Bowden, 1893. Entered Union Army, 1861, as pvt.; served in vol. forces in every regtl. rank; thrice wounded; lost right leg at Gettysburg; commd. in regular army, July 1866; served in War Dept., Chief of Bureau, 1864-70; on retired list U.S.A., 1870 - . Author: History of the Art of War - Alexander, Hannibal, Caesar, Gustavus Adolphus, Napoleon (12 vols.), 1890-1907; The Campaign of Chancellorsville, 1881; Bird'seye View of Our Civil War, 1883; Patroclus and Penelope, 1885; Great Captains, 1889; Riders of Many Lands, 1894. Home: Paris, France, Died 1909.

DODSON, JOHN MILTON M.D.; b. Berlin, Wis., Feb. 17, 1859; s. Nathan Monroe and Elizabeth Osborn (Abbot) D.; A.B., U. of Wis., 1880, A.M., 1888; Sc.D., 1925; M.D., Rush Med. Coll., Chicago, 1882, Jefferson Med. Coll., Phila., 1883; post-grad. med. study, Berlin, 1896; m. Male Van Slyke, July 1, 1884 (died 1887); 2d, Jessie Palmer Kasson, Nov. 12, 1890 (died 1914); children - Kasson M. (dec.), Elizabeth Palmer (Mrs. Lester J. Michael); m. 3d, Mary Hyde Webb, Jan. 17, 1923. Practiced in Wis. and Chicago, Mar., 1882 - ; lecturer and demonstrator anatomy, 1889-92, prof. physiology and demonstrator anatomy, 1892-98, prof. pediatrics, 1899 - , jr. dean, 1890-1901, dean of students, 1901-24, Rush Med. Coll.; professional lecturer on medicine, and dean med. courses, U. of Chicago, 1901-24; dir. Bur. Health and Pub. Instrn., A.M.A.; prof. pediatrics, Northwestern U. Woman's Med. Coll., 1894-97. Maj. M.C., U.S.A., med. aide to gov. of Ill., 1918-19. Home: Chicago, Ill. Died Aug. 15, 1933.

DOERING, EDMUND JANES physician; b. New York, Nov. 7, 1854; s. Rev. Dr. C. H. and Nancy (McLaughlin) D.; M.D., Northwestern U., 1874; studied univ. of Berlin and Vienna, 1875 (M. Sc., Northwestern U., 1916); m. Julia Whiting, May 24, 1877 (died Oct. 1939); 1 son, Edmund Janes. Practiced in Chicago since 1881; cons. physician, Chicago Lying-In and Michael Reese hosps. Editor Chicago Med. Recorder, 1891. First lt. U.S.A. Med. Res. Corps, 1911; capt., later major, 1917; lt. col. M.C., U.S.A., 1918; col. M.R.C., Sept. 1922; apptd. sr. surgeon U.S. P.H.S., Oct. 1919. Late surgeon U. S. Marine Hosp. Service; pres. U.S. Examining Bd., Med. R.C., 1918; apptd. dist. med. officer for Ill., Mich. and Wis. of Federal Bd. for Vocational Edn., 1919; chief cons. U.S. Vet. Bur. of Chicago. Fellow Am. Coll. Surgeons; mem. A.M.A., Ill. Med. Soc., Chicago Med. Soc. (pres. 1886-87), Chicago Gynecol. Soc. (ex-pres.), Medico-Legal Soc. (pres.), Inst. Medicine of Chicago (gov.). Sr. v. comdr. Hyde Park Post Am. Legion; pres. Ill. Div. Med. R.C., U.S.A.; gov. Nat. Reserve Officers' Assn., 1922-23 (hon. pres. Med. Chapter); gov. Mil. Order World War (elected comdr. Chicago Chapter 1930). Clubs: Chicago Athletic, University, South Shore Country, Physicians, Executives, Chicago Medical (Chicago); Army and Navy (Washington and Chicago). Mem. adv. council The Living Age. Mem. Bd. Pub. Health Advisors in Dept. of Pub. Health, State of Ill., 1936. Home: 215 E. Chestnut St., Chicago. Died March 1, 1943.

D'OLIER, FRANKLIN insurance; b. Burlington, N.J., Apr. 28, 1877; s. William and Annie (Woolman) D.; B.A., Princeton, 1898; LL.D., University of Newark, 1940; married Helen Kitchen, November 11, 1903. President and treasurer, Franklin D'Olider & Co., Inc., founded by father, 1869, until 1926; pres. 1937-45; chmn. bd. Prudential Ins. Co., 1946, 1947; director Howard Savings Institution of Newark, National Biscuit Co., Pennsylvania R.R., General Refractories Company (Philadelphia), Morristown (N.J.) Trust Co. Trustee Princeton U. Commd. capt. U.S. Army, Apr. 1917; arrived in France, July 1917; organized salvage service of A.E.F.; hon. disch. as lt. col. Gen. Staff, Apr. 1919. Awarded D.S.M. (U.S.); Comdr. Legion of Honor (France). Elected first nat. comdr. Am. Legion, Nov. 12, 1919; mem. American Legion mission to England, 1941; N.J. State chmn. U.S.O., 1943-46; National War Fund and Treasury Bond Drives; chairman U.S. Strategic Bombing Survey in Germany and Japan, 1944-46. Received the Medal of Merit from the United States. Episcopalian. Clubs: Princeton (Phila.); University, Princeton (N.Y. City); Morristown, Essex. Mem. Soc. Colonial Wars. Home: R.D. 1, Basking Ridge, N.J. Office; 744 Broad St., Prudential Insurance Company, Newark 1, N.J. Died Dec. 10, 1953; buried St. Mary's Church Graveyard, Burlington, N.J.

DONAHUE, CHARLES, lawyer; b. Portland, Me., Aug. 14, 1912; s. Charles Louis and Helen Katherine (Cunningham) D.; grad. Canterbury Sch., New Mildford, Conn., 1930; A.B., Princeton, 1934; LL.B., Harvard, 1937; m. Bertha Halsted Terry, Nov. 14, 1942 (div.); children—William Halsted, Christopher Cunningham, Charles, Helen Cunningham, Peter Waldron; m. 2d, Jeanne Coleman Small, June 6, 1968. Admitted to Me. bar, 1937, D.C. bar, 1938; atty. Nat. Cath. Welfare Conf., 1938-39, Dept. Labor, 1939-43, 46-49; labor counsel U.S. Senate Majority Policy Com., 1949; asst. solicitor of labor for employment security, 1949-51, asst. solicitor of labor for legislation, 1951-52; research dir. United Assn. Plumbers and Pipefitters, 1953-61; became solicitor of labor Dept. Labor, 1961; now in pvt. practice law. Served to capt. AUS, 1943-46. Mem. Am., Fed. bar assns., U.S. Judge Advocates Assn., Indsl. Relations Research Assn., Internat. Soc. Labor Law and Social Legislation (exec. com.), Princeton Alumni Assn., Harvard Law Sch. Alumni Assn., Nat. Lawyers Club. Club: Nat. Press. Author labor law rev. articles. Home: Fenit County Kerry Ireland Died Oct. 27, 1972; buried Churchill, County Kerry Ireland

DONALDSON, THOMAS QUINT army officer; b. Greenville, S.C., June 26, 1864; s. T. Q. and Susan B. (Hoke) D.; grad. U.S. Mil. Acad., 1887; distinguished grad. Army Sch. of the Line, 1909; grad. Army Staff Coll., 1910; m. Mary Elizabeth Willson, Oct. 26, 1892. Commd. add. 2d lt. 3d Cav., June 12, 1887; brig. gen. (temp), Feb. 18, 1918; brig. gen. (perm), Jan. 16, 1925; promoted to rank of major general, Dec. 11, 1927. Participated in campaign against Sioux Indians in S.D., 1890-91; in action at Wounded Knee and White Clay Creek; prof. mil. science and tactics, Patrick Mil. Inst., Anderson, S.C., 1891-93, Clemson Agrl. Coll., Ft. Hills, S.C., 1893-95; in Cuba, 1898-99; with 8th U.S. Cav. in Philippines, 1905-07, 1910-14; assigned duty Insp. Gen.'s Dept., 1914; arrived in France, Sept. 1, 1918; insp. gen. Service of Supply, Tours, France, Sept. 1918-June 1919; retired, 1931. Decorated D.S.M.; Legion of Honor (French). Competitor div. and army cav. competitions, 1903, 1904, and also mem. Nat. Cav. Rifle Team, 1907. Methodist. Home: Greenville, S.C. Died Oct. 26, 1934. .

DONGES, RALPH WALDO EMERSON, lawyer; b. Donaldson, Pa., May 5, 1875; s. John W. (M.D.) and Rose (Renaud) D.; grad. Rugby Acad., Phila., 1892; LL.D., Rutgers University, (South Jersey br.); married Eleanor M. Deakyne, January 5, 1945. Admitted to N.J. bar, 1897; counsellor at law since 1900; pres. Pub. Utilities Commn. of N.J., 1913-18; judge Circuit Court of N.J., 1920-30; asso. justice Supreme Court of N.J., 1930-48, judge appellate division, Superior Court, 1948-51, ret. Served as lieut. col., U.S. Army, 1918-19. Mem. Am., N.J. State and Camden County bar assns. Democrat. Episcopalian. Mason, Moose, Elk. Home: Park View Apts., Collingswood 6, N.J. Address: 709 Market St., Camden 2 NJ

DONIPHAN, ALEXANDER WILLIAM lawyer, army officer, b. Maysville, Ky., July 9, 1808; s. Joseph and Anne (Smith) D.; grad. Augusta Coll., 1826; m. Elizabeth Thornton, Dec. 21, 1837, 2 children. Began practice of law in Mo., 1830, became leading Mo. lawyer specialized in criminal cases; mem. Mo. Legislature, 1836, 40, 54; commanded a brigade against Mormons, refused to carry out the later revoked ct. martial sentence of death against Joseph Smith; comdg. officer in N.M. during Mexican War, 1846-48; lead regt. of Missourians from Valverde, N.M. to Chihuahua, Mexico (one of most brilliant long marches ever made), 1846-47; Mo. del. to Washington (D.C.) Peace Conf., 1861; maj. gen. in command Mo. Militia, 1861. Died Richmond, Mo., Aug. 8, 1887.

DONNELL, PHILIP STONE b. Minneapolis, Minn., Dec. 16, 1889; s. Edwin Cone and Laura (Shipman) D.; A.B., Clark U., Worcester, Mass., 1910; M.E.E., Harvard, 1915; M.A. (hon.), Cambridge University, Eng.; married Pauline Gardner, June 17, 1917; children-Sylvia (dec.), Barbara, Richard Gardner (dec.), Franklin, Robert. With U.S. Coast and Geodetic Survey in U.S. and P.I., 1910-13, Alaska, 1915; engr. cos. and schs., 1915-29; dean Coll. Engring., Okla. State University, 1929-54, v.p., 1947-54, ret. as v.p. emeritus; supr. Public Utilities, San Antonio; head division special studies City Water Bd. (on leave, writing book), San Antonio, on leave, attending Cambridge U., Eng., 1956-57. Director Public Works Adminstrn., State of Okla., 1933-36; reg. profl. engr., Okla., Tex., Me. Del. 2d World Power Conf., Berlin, 1930, 3d Conf., Washington, 1936. Former mem. nat. council Boy Scouts America. Served as lieutenant Signal Corps, AEF, U.S. Army, 1917-19; lt. col. signal corps, div. signal officer of 45th Div., U.S.N.G., 1926-40; col. 180th Inf., 45th Div. U.S. Army, 1940-42; base section engr., chief of staff, acting base section Comdr., Western Base Sect. and comdg. officer, Training Within Civilian Agencies for U.K., ETO, 1942-45; ret. as col. AUS, 1949. Decorated Bronze Star Medal, Legion of Merit, Order of the British Empire and Army Commendation Ribbon during European Tour. Recipient Engineer of the year award, San Antonio. Former pres. Okla. Bd. of Registration for professional engrs. Fellow Am. Inst. E.E. (life mem.); mem. Nat. Assn. Profl. Engrs., Am. Soc. for Engineering Education, A.A.A.S., Am. Soc. Mil. Engineers, Theta Xi, Phi Kappa Phi, Sigma Tau, Eta Kappa Nu, Pi Tau Sigma, Iota Lambda Sigma, Scabbard and Blade. Democrat: Presbyterian. Mason. Clubs: Rotary. Torch. Address: Sheepscott, Me. Died Dec. 25, 1962.

DONNELLY, ARTHUR BARRETT army officer; b. St. Louis, Mo., May 31, 1875; s. James J. and Elizabeth (Taaffe) D.; m. Anna Pike Renick, May 10, 1898. Dept. mgr., 1901-06, asst. supt. factory, and buyer, 1906-08, Hamilton-Brown Shoe Co., St. Louis; pres. Arthur D. Donnelly & Co. (leather), Interstate Mercantile Co., Inc., Mo. Paint & Varnish Co. Enlisted in Co. F, 1st Inf., N.G. Mo., Dec. 7, 1892; promoted through grades to adj. gen. of Mo., with rank of brig. gen., Jan. 8, 1971, but granted indefinite leave of absence by gov., Mar. 25, 1917, in order to assume command 1st Mo. Inf.; apptd. brig. gen. N.A., Aug. 5, 1917. Served in Spanish-Am. War as capt. Co. F, 1st Mo. Inf., 1898; comd. regt. on Mexican border, June 18-Sept. 25, 1916; comdg. 69th Inf. Brigade, Camp Doniphan, Ft. Sill, Okla., Aug. 25, 1917. Republican. Catholic. Home: St. Louis, Mo. Died July 29, 1919.

DONNELLY, EDWARD TERENCE army officer; b. London, Eng., Aug. 22, 1871; s. Edward C. D., of N.Y. City; ed. Manhattan Coll., Columbia U.; LL.B., New York Law Sch.; grad. Sch. of Application for Cav. and Field Arty., 1905; m. Mrs. Flora Fitten Bewick, Nov. 22, 1909. Commd. capt. 8th N.Y. Inf., May 17, 1898; hon. mustered out, Nov. 3, 1898; 1st lt. 43d U.S. Inf., Aug. 17, 1899; hon. mustered out, July 5, 1901; 1st lt. Arty. Corps, Aug. 1, 1901; capt., Jan. 25, 1907; assigned to 1st Field Arty., June 6, 1907; trans. to 6th Field Arty., June 11, 1912, to 3d Field Arty., Mar. 20, 1913, to 5th Field Arty., Nov. 1, 1915; maj., July 1, 1916. later lt. col.; col. N.A., Aug. 5, 1916; brig. gen. N.A., Apr. 12, 1918. Served in Spanish-Am. War, Philippine Insurrection, and on Mexican border; comdr. 164th Brigade F.A., 89th Division, A.E.F., in France, July 1918-May 1919. Awarded Croix de Guerre (France). Catholic. Died Feb. 8, 1929.

DONOVAN, RICHARD army officer; born at Paducah, Kentucky, Dec. 2, 1885; B.S., U.S. Military Acad., 1908; M.S., Mass. Inst. Tech., 1921; grad. Army War Coll., 1931, Command and Gen. Staff Sch., 1926, Coast Arty. Sch. (advanced course), 1925. Commd. 2d lt., Coast Arty. Corps, 1908; promoted through grades to maj. gen., Apr. 1941; retired with rank of maj. gen., 1947. Home: Melrose Hotel, Dallas, Tex. Died Feb. 7, 1949.

DONOVAN, WILLIAM JOSEPH lawyer, commr.; b. Buffalo, Jan. 1, 1883; s. Timothy P. and Anna (Lennon) D.; A.B., Columbia, 1905, LL.B., 1907; LL.D., Niagara U., 1919, U. of Notre Dame, 1929, Syracuse Univ., 1931; m. Ruth Rumsey, July 14, 1914; children-David Rumsey, Patricia (dec.). Began practice at Buffalo, 1907; counsel for N.Y. State Fuel Administration, 1924; Republican candidate for lieut. gov. of New York, 1922; U.S. dist. atty., Western District of N.Y., 1922-24; mem. U.S. delegation to customs regulations conf. between U.S. and Can., 1923; asst. atty. gen. of U.S., 1924-25; the asst. to the atty. gen., Mar. 1925-29; U.S. commr. and chmn. Rio Grande River Compact Commn., 1928-29; U.S. commr. chmn. Colo. River Commn. since 1929; mem. Donovan, Leisure, Newton and Irvine; counsel for Assn. Bar City New York and New York and Bronx County bar assns. in bankruptcy investigation, 1929; counsel to com. for revision New York state pub. service commn. laws, 1929. Ambassador of U.S. to Thailand, 1953-54. Member Board Arbitration, under Nat. Mediation Bd., controversy between Am. Train Dispatchers Assn., and B. & M. R.R. Rep. candidate for gov. of N.Y., 1932. Served as capt. Troop I, 1st Cav., N. Y. Nat. Guard: asst. chief of staff, 27th Div., A.E.F., World War; maj., brigade, adj., 51st Brigade; maj. 165 Inf. (old 69th N.Y.) advancing to rank of col.; wounded three times; unofficial observer for sec. of navy, Great Britain, July-Aug. 1940, southeastern Europe, Dec. 1940-Mar. 1941; apptd. coordinator of information, July 1941; dir. Office of Strategic Services, June 1942; rank of maj. gen., J.S. Army. Decorated (World War I) Congressional Medal of Honor for conduct in action near Landres and St. Georges, France, Oct. 14-15, 1918; D.S.C. for conduct in crossing River Ourcq, July 28-31, 1918, D.S.M. for services in Bacarat sector, July 28-31, and Meuse-Argonne Offensive, Oct. 1918 (U.S.), Legion of Honor, Croix de Guerre with palm and silver star (France), Croci di Guerra (Italy); (World War II) Oak leaf cluster on D.S.M. for services as dir. of strategic services (U.S.), Order of Crown (Italy), Knight Comdr. Order of British Empire (Gt. Britain), Comdr. Legion of Honor (France), Grand officer Order of Leopold with palm (Belgium), Papal Lateran medal, Order St. Sylvester (Papal), Comdr.'s Cross with star of Polonia Restituta (Poland), 1st Class of Most Exalted Order of White Elephant, Santi Mala medal (Siam), Comdr. Cross with star Royal Order of St. Olay (Norway); Alexander Hamilton medal Assn. Alumni Columbia Coll. Mem. Assn. Bar City New York (exec. com. 1931), Phi Kappa Psi, Phi Delta Phi. Republican. Roman Catholic. Home: Chapel Hill Farm, Berryville, Va. Died Feb. 8, 1959.

DOOLEY, THOMAS ANTHONY III physician, author; b. St. Louis, Jan. 17, 1927; s. Thomas Anthony and Agnes (Wise) D.; student U. Notre Dame; M.D., St. Louis U., 1953; postgrad. U. Paris. Served with USNR, 1944-46, 53-56; served at Naval Hosp., Camp Pendleton, Cal., 1 year, trans. to Naval Hosp., Yokosuka, Japan; volunteered for duty in USS Montague, transporting no. Vietnamese refugees to Saigon, 1954; later French interpreter, med. officer Navy preventive medicine unit, Haiphong, 1954; duty at Naval Hosp., Yokosuka, 1955; made lecture tour of U.S. under auspices U.S. Navy, 1956; an organizer Med. Internat. Corp. (MEDICO). Named 1 of ten outstanding men of 1956, Look mag.; decorated Legion of Merit; officer Ordre National de Legion of Merit; officer Ordre National de Vietnam. Author: Deliver Us from Evil, 1955; The Edge of Tomorrow, 1958; The Night They Burned the Mountain, 1960. Died Mar. 1961.*

DOOLITTLE, CHARLES CAMP cashier Merchants' Nat. Bank of Toledo, O.; b. Burlington, Vt., March 16, 1832; ed. high school, Montreal, Can.; removed to New York, 1847; later moved to Mich.; m. Emily H. Parsons, Feb. 28, 1856. Became, May 16, 1861, 1st lt. 4th Mich. regt.; col. 18th Mich., July 22, 1862; served in Peninsular campaign in Ky., 1862-63; in Tenn., 1863-64; comd. Decatur, Ala., during 1st day's defense against Gen. Hood; led brigade at Nashville; comd. there, 1865; comd. northern dist., La., fall of 1865; brig. gen. vols., Jan. 27, 1865; bvt. maj. gen., June 13, 1865; mustered out Nov. 30, 1865. Home: Toledo, O. Died 1902.

DOREY, HALSTEAD army officer; b. St. Louis Mo., Feb. 7, 1874; s. William A. and Georgiana (Banks) D.; grad. Shattuck Sch., Fairbault, Minn., grad. U.S. Mil. Acad., 1897; m. Theodora Cheney, Sept. 20, 1905; children-Georgiana (wife Col. M. F. Grant, U.S. Army), Ednah Cheney. Additional 2d lt., June 1897; promoted through grades to maj. gen. Nov. 1, 1933; retired, 1936. In santiago Campaign, Spanish-Am. War, 1898; Philippine Insurrection, 1899-1901; various fights with Moros, 1903-05; Vera Cruz Expdn., 1908; comdr. 4th Inf. (emergency col.), in France, May-Oct. 1918; participated in battles, Aisne, Aisne-Marne, Champaigne-Marne, St. Mihiel, Meuse-Argonne. Decorated D.S.C. and D.S.M. (U.S.); Officer Legion of Honor and Croix de Guerre (French); Purple Heart and Silver Star (U.S., each 3 oak leaf clusters). Episcopalian. Clubs: Army and Navy (Washington, and Manila); University (New York). Address: Saisipuedes, Boerne, Tex. Died June 19, 1946; buried at West Point, N.Y.

DORNIN, THOMAS ALOYSIUS naval officer; b. Ireland, May 1, 1800; s. Bernard and Eliza Dornin; ed. St. Mary's Coll., Balt.; m. Mrs. Jane Thorburn Howison, 1837. Entered U.S. Navy, 1815, served in Mediterranean and against W. Indian pirates; promoted lt., 1825; served in Pacific, 1826; served in ship Falmouth in Pacific, 1831-34; in command of receiving ship, Phila., 1834-36; promoted commander, 1841; with Ordnance Dept., Washington, D.C., 1844-51; stationed in Pacific to watch over William Walker's expdn. to Lower Cal., also blocked Brit. and French aggressive naval moves in Hawaii, 1851-55; promoted capt., 1855, commanded Norfolk Navy Yard, 1855-59; on duty in Mediterranean and in suppression of African slave trade, 1859-61; promoted commodore, 1862; commanded Balt. Navy Yard, 1862-65. Died Savannah, Ga., Apr. 22, 1874; buried Norfolk , Va.

DORRANCE, GORDON publicist, writer; b. Camden, N.Y., June 14, 1890; s. Daniel James and Edith Lillian (Turner) D.; prep. edn. Manlius (N.Y.) Sch., Forest Engineer, Biltmore (N.C.) Forest Sch., 1913, supplementary work at Technische Hochschule, Darmstadt, Germany; studied Grad. Sch., U. Pa., 1919-20, m. Emile Berthe de Vanite, Sept. 12, 1922. With State Bd. Forestery, Md., 1913-17; pres., chmn. bd. Dorrance & Co., Inc., 1920-40. Served as lt. Engrs., U.S. Army, in France, 1918-19; capt. to maj. Reserves, 1925-30; maj. to lt. col. U.S. Army, 1942-45, with office of under sec. of war (internal security), later M.I., 1942: with gen. staff corps, 1943, U.S. Joint Chiefs of Staff and duty with War Dept. Gen. Staff, 1943-45; commn. M.I. Res. 1946; recalled to active duty, Feb., promoted to col. Sept. 1947. Decorated Comdr. Order of the Phoenix, 1930. Mem. Pa. Forest Commn., 1936. Mem. Soc. Mayflower Descs. Presbyn. Mason. Author: Broken Shackles, 1920; The Bonapartes in America, 1939 (co-author), Ten Commandments for Success (with others), 1947. Editor: The Pocket Chesterfield, 1920; Contemporary Poets, An Anthology of Fifty, 1927. Contbr. Sci. Am., Popular Sci. Monthly, London Times Imperial Trade Supplement, New York Times Annalist. Magazine of Wall St., etc. Address: 33 Roumfort Rd., Mt. Airy, Phila. 19. Died Mar. 22, 1957.

DORSEY, GEORGE AMOS anthropologist, journalist; b. Hebron, O., Feb. 6, 1868; s. Edwin Jackson and Mary Emma (Grove) D.; A.B., Denison, 1888, LL.D., 1909; A.B., lHarvard, 1890, Ph.D., 1894; m. Ida Chadsey, Dec. 8, 1892; children - Dorothy Ann, George Chadsey; m. 2d, Sue McLellan. Conducted anthrop. investigations in S. America for Chicago Expdn., 1891-92; supt. archaeology, dept. anthropology, same, 1892-93; asst. in anthropology, 1894-95, instr., 1895-96, Harvard; asst. curator anthropology, 1896-98, curator, 1898-1915. Field Mus. of Natural History, Chicago; prof. comparative anatomy, Northwestern U. Dental Sch., 1898-1913; asst. prof. anthropology, 1905-08, asso. prof., 1908-15, U. of Chicago. Editor writer for Dem. Nat. Com., 1916. Lecturer on anthropology, New School for Social Research, New York, 1925 - . Visited Europe, Egypt, India, Ceylon, Java, Australia, Bismarck Arch., New Guinea, P.I., China and Japan, for Field Mus., 1908; mem. edit. staff and fgn. commr. Chicago Tribune, 1909-12, investigating sources of emigration in Italy, Austria, Hungary, Roumania, Servia and Bulgaria, and studying polit. conditions in India, China, Japan, Australia and South Africa. U.S. del. Internat. Congress Anthropology and Prehistoric Archaeology, Paris, 1900; mem. Jury Awards Dept. Anthropology, St. Louis Expn., 1904. Commd. lt. U.S.N.R.F., Mar. 1918; lt. comdr., Sept 1919; asst. naval attaché. Madrid, 1918; naval attaché. Lisbon, 1919-21; adviser on Spanish problems to Am. Commn to Negotiate Peace, Paris. Comdr. mil. orders of Aviz and Santiago. Author: Young Low (novel), 1917, 27; Why We Behave Like Human Beings, 1925; The Nature of Man, 1927; The Evolution of Charles Darwin, 1927; Hows and Whys of Human Behavior, 1929. Home: New York, N.Y. Died Mar. 29, 1931.

DORSEY, STEPHEN W. senator; b. Benson, Vt., Feb. 28, 1842; s. John W. and Marie H. D.; m. Laura, d. Job P. and M. S. Bigelow, of Washington and London. Served pvt. to col. in Union Army, 1861-65. Removed to Ark.; mem. Rep. Nat. Com., 1868, 72, 76, 80; chmn. exec. com., 1876-80; elected U.S. Senator from Ark., by combination of Democrats and Republicans, term, 1873-79. Home: Los Angeles, Calif. Died Mar. 20, 1916.

DORST, JOSEPH HADDOX army officer; b. Louisville, Ky., Apr. 2, 1852; s. John Henry and Catharine (Mershon) D.; grad. U.S. Mil. Acad., 1873; m. Esther J. Archer, Aug. 21, 1890. Commd. 2d lt. 4th Cav., June 13, 1873; 1st lt., Mar. 20, 1879; capt., Mar. 2, 1885; lt. col. asst. adj. gen. vols., May 9, 1898-May 12, 1899; col. 45th U.S. Inf. Vols., Aug. 17, 1899-June 3, 1901; maj. 2d U.S. Cav., Nov. 7, 1898; insp. gen., Feb. 28, 1901; lt. col. 12th Cav., June 26, 1901; col. 3d Cav., Apr. 15, 1903. Participated in campaigns against Kiowa, Comanche and Cheyenne Indians, 1874-75; Powder River expdn. against Sioux and Cheyennes, 1876-77, against Utes, 1879-81, against Apaches in Ariz., 1881, against Geronimo's band, 1885-86, against Santiago de Cuba, 1898, and against insurrectos in Philippines, 1899-1901; retired, Aug. 10, 1911. Home: Warrenton, Va. Died 1915.

DOSTERT, LEON EMILE, educator; b. Longwy, France, May 14, 1904; s. Leon Emile and Marie (Hollet) D.; came to U.S., 1921; naturalized, 1941; student Occidental Coll., 1924-26; B.S., Georgetown U., 1928, Ph.B., 1930, M.A., 1931; graduate student Johns Hopkins, 1935-36; Litt.D. Franklin and Marshall College, 1957; LLD., Georgetown University, 1958; Litt.D. (hon.), Occidental College, 1960; children—Leon Emile (dec.), Anne Marie, Pierre, Francois; m. 2d, Bozena Henisz, May, 1965. Instr. French, Georgetown U., 1926-29, asst. prof., 1929-32, acting chmn. faculty modern languages, 1930-36, chmn. dept., 1936-41, asso. prof., 1932-36, prof., 1936-41; prof. French civilization Scripps Coll., 1941; attache French embassy, Washington, 1939-40; with O.S.S., 1942; dir. simultaneous interpretation div., U.N., 1946-47; administrative counsellor Internat. Telecommunication Union, Geneva, 1948-49; sec. gen. Internat. High Frequency Broadcast Conf., 1948-49; dir. Inst. Languages and Linguistics, Georgetown U., 1949; prof. French, chmn. dept. langs. and linguistics Occidental Coll., Los Angeles, 1963-69, prof. emeritus of langs. and linguistics, 1969-71; lang. cons. internat., U.S., fgn. govts., pvt. corps. Served from maj. to col., 1942-46; served as liaison officer to Gen. Henri Giraud, 1942-44, interpreter to Gen. Eisenhower, 1942-45; chief language div., Nurenberg Trials, 1945-46; U.S. Army Reserve Officer. Decorated U.S. Legion of Merit with cluster, Bronze Star with cluster, France Knight Legion of Honor, Croix de Guerre with Palms, Morocco and Tunisia. Mem. Modern Language Association of America, Linguistic Soc. Am., Phi Beta Kappa Assos., Phi Beta Kappa. Club: Cosmos (Washington). Editor Monograph Series on Langs. and Linguistics, 1952-56. Author: Spoken French, 1956; Francais Premier Cours, 1958; Francais, Cours Moyen; Francais, Styles Litteraires. Contbr. articles on langs. to profl. jours. Home: Pasadena CA Died Sept. 2, 1971; buried Mountain View Cemetery, Pasadena CA

DOTY, PAUL mech. engr.; b. Hoboken, N.J., May 30, 1869; s. William Henry Harrison and Anna (Langevin) D.; M.E., Stevens Inst. Tech., 1888; m. Mary Reddy, Apr. 8, 1913; 1 dau., Diana. Engr. with United Gas Improvement Co., Phila., 1888-95; engr. with Am. Light and Traction Co., New York, 1895-1917; v.p. and gen. mgr. St. Paul Gas Light Co., 1904-17; chmn. Minn. Bd. Registration for Architects, Engrs., and Land Surveyors, 1921 - ; v.p. St. Paul Trust & Savings Bank, 1921-24; regional reconditioning supervisor Home Owners' Loan Corp., Atlanta, Ga., 1934-35. Served as lt. col. Corps of Engrs., U.S.A., 1917-18; gen. staff U.S.A., constrn. adviser to Sec. of War. Washington, 1918-19. Democrat. Catholic Home: St. Paul, Minn. Died Dec. 3, 1938.

DOUBLEDAY, ABNER army officer, originator baseball; b. Ballston Spa, N.Y., June 26, 1819; s. Ulysses Freeman and Hester (Donnelly) D.; grad. U.S. Mil. Acad., 1842; m. Mary Hewitt, 1852. Commd. 2d lt. arty., U.S. Army, 1845, 1st lt., 1847; served in battles of Monterey, Buena Vista during Mexican War, 1846-48; capt., 1855; maj. 17th Inf., 1861; aimed 1st shot fired from Ft. Sumter against Confederate attack; brig. gen. U.S. Volunteers, then maj. gen, 1862; commanded brigade in 2d Battle of Bull Run; led div. at battle of Antietam, Fredericksburg: commanded corps during 1st day Battle of Gettysburg, div. on 2d, 3d days; lt. col. U.S. Army, 1863, col., 1867. Author: Reminiscences of Forts Sumter and Moultrie in 1860-61, published 1876; Chancellorsville and Gettysburg, 1882. Declared orginator of baseball (Cooperstown, N.Y., 1839) by high commn. of baseball experts in formal report, 1907. Died Mendham, N.J., Jan. 26, 1893; buried Arlington (Va.) Nat. Cemetery.

DOUGHERTY, WILLIAM EDGEWORTH brig. gen. U.S.A.; b. Aranmor, Co. Roscommon, Ireland, Sept. 29, 1841; s. Michael Templeton and Barbara (D'Aignon) D.; ed. pvt. schs., Eng. and Germany; m. Maria L. McCarthy, May 9, 1866. Pvt., corporal, sergt. and 1st sergt., cos. K and G, 1st U.S. Inf., Mar. 10, 1860-Mar. 17, 1863; promoted through grades to col. 8th Inf., Mar. 5, 1901; brig. gen., Jan. 24, 1904; retired at own request after over 43 yrs.' service, Jan. 25, 1904. Bvtd. 1st lt., July 4, 1863 for siege of Vicksburg. Served in Army of the Potomac, 1862-63; Vicksburg, Teche and Red River campaigns, 1863-64; provost marshal Jefferson and Orleans parishes, La., 1865-66; served on plains, 1874-82; in Cuba, 1898; in P.I., 1901-02. Home: Fruitvale, Calif. Died July 13, 1915.

DOUGLAS, BEVERLY BROWNE congressman, lawyer; b. Providence Forge, New Kent County, Va., Dec. 21, 1822; attended Rumford Acad., Yale, U. Edinburgh (Scotland); grad. law dept. Coll. William and Mary, 1843. Admitted to bar, 1844, began practice of law, Norfolk, Va., then practiced in King William County, from 1846; del. Va. Constl. Conv., 1850, 51: mem. Va. Senate, 1852-65; Democratic presdl. elector, 1860; commd. 1st lt. Lee's Ranger's, Confederate Army, in Civil War, promoted maj. 5th Va. Cavalry; mem. U.S. Ho. of Reps. from Va. (as Conservative), 44th Congress, 1875-77, (as Democrat), 45th Congress, 1877-78. Died Washington, D.C., Dec. 22, 1878; buried family burying ground at "Zoar," nr. Aylett, Va.

DOUGLAS, FREDERIC HUNTINGTON curator, anthropologist; b. Evergreen, Colo., Oct. 29, 1897; s. Charles Winfred and Mary Josepha (Williams) D.; A.B., U. of Colo., 1921; post-grad. U. of Mich., 1921-22; student Pa. Acad. Fine Arts, 1922-26; Doctor Sci., University of Colorado, 1948; married Freda Bendix Gillespie, May 21, 1926; children-Ann Pauline and Eve (twins), David. Painter and wood-carver, 1926-29; pres. sch. bd. Evergren, Colo., 1929-34; curator, dept. Indian Arts, Denver Art Museum, 1929-47, curator, dept. Native Arts, since 1947; dir. Denver Art. Mus., 1940-42; asst. prof. anthropology U. Denver, from 1934; lecturer in anthropology U. Colo., from 1946; research fellow in ethnology Harvard, 1952; director of edn. Fed. Indian Exhibit, San Francisco Fiar, 1938-39; co-dir. North Am. Indian Art, Museum Modern Art, N.Y.C., 1940-41; member Anglo-Am. group inspecting Swedish and Finnish musuems, 1946; commr. Fed. Indian Arts and Crafts Board, from 1946. Served as private, U.S. Inf., 1918; commd. capt. Med. Adm. Corps, Nov. 1942, major, 1944, lt. col., 1945; registrar 31st Gen. Hosp., 25 mos., on New Hebrides and Luzon; disch., Feb. 1946. Trustee Denver Art Museum, Museum of Northern Arizona, Museum of Man, San Diego; mem. of the editorial board F. W. Hodge Anniversary Fund. Sec. Clearinghouse for Southwestern Museums, 1938-51. Research in design, styles and techniques appearing in work of Indian tribes north of Mexico, in last 150 yrs. with special emphasis on history of each design, style and technique. Fellow A.A.A.S. (v.p. Southwest Div., 1942-47, pres., 1947-48), Royal Anthrop. Soc Soc. for Am. Archeology, Am. Folklore Soc., Societe des Americanistes de Paris; mem. Phi Gamma Delta, Sigma Delta Chi, Mu Alpha Nu. Republican. Episcopalian. Clubs: Denver Country, University, Mile-High, The Westerners (Denver, Colorado). Author and editor, Denver Art Mus. publs. in Indian art; Indian Leaflet Series, since 1930, Indian Design Series since 1938, etc.; author (with Rene d'Harnoncourt), Indian Art of the United States, 1941; The Inner Light (verses, 4 vols.), 1946-53. Contbr. articles to newspapers and jours. Home: 745 S. Jackson St. Office: 1300 Logan St., Denver. Died Apr. 23, 1956; buried Fairmount Cemetery, Denver.

DOUGLAS, HENRY KYRD lawyer; b. Shepherdstown, W.Va., Sept. 29, 1840; s. Rev. Robert and Mary (Robertson) D.; grad. Franklin and Marshall Coll., 1859; grad. of Judge Brockenbrough's Law School, Lexington, Va., 1860; unmarried. Private, sergt., lt., capt., maj. col., brig.-comdr. C.S.A.; a.-d.-c. to Stonewall Jackson, asst. adj.-gen. to Gens. Edward Johnston, J. B. Gordon, Early, Pegram, Johnston, and Walker; comdr. Light Brigade from Petersburg to Appomattox the brigade that fired the last shot at Appomattox and was last to stack arms; capt., lt. col., col., adj. gen. of MD., maj. gen. comdg. Md. troops on strike of 1894; candidate for Congress, 6th Md. dist., 1888; judge 5th judicial circuit, Md. Gold Democrat. Home: Hagerstown, Md. Died 1903.

DOUGLAS, ORLANDO BENAJAH physician; b. Cornwall, Vt., Sept. 12, 1836; s. Amos and Almira (Balcom) C.; acad. edn. Brandon, Vt.; M.D., Univ. Med. Coll. (New York U.), 1877; m. Mary A. Rust, Dec. 27, 1864 (died Aug. 31, 1873); m. 2d, May L., d. Rev. A. C. Manson, Sept. 16, 1875 (died 1913). Pvt., lt. and adj. 18th Mo. Vols. and acting asst. adj. gen. in Civil War; twice wounded. Asst. surgeon, 1877-83, surgeon and dir., 1883-1902, cons. surgeon, 1902 - , Manhattan Eye, Ear and Throat Hosp.; prof. diseases of nose and throat, New York Post-Grad. Med. Sch. and Hosp., 1889-1901.

Pres. N.H. Orphans' Home, 1905 - ; mem. exec. com. Y.M.C.A. of N.H. Cons. surgeon N.H. Soldiers' Home. Mason. Home: Concord, N.H. Died Dec. 1920.

DOUGLAS, WILLIAM army, naval officer: b. Plainfield, Conn., Jan. 16, 1743; s. John and Olive (Spaulding) D.; m. Hannah Manfield, July 5,1767, children-William, John, Olive, Hannah. Commd. maj. Conn. Militia, 1775, maj. in a volunteer regt., 1776; commd. col. under Gen. Washington, 1776; participated in battles of L.I., Philips Manor, Croton River, White Plains, Harlem Heights; apptd. commodore of vessels on Lake Champlain by Continental Congress; elected to Conn. Assembly, 1777. Died Northford, Conn., May 28, 1777.

DOUGLASS, DAVID BATES civil engr., army officer, coll. pres.; b. Pompton, N.J., Mar. 21, 1790; s. Nathaniel and Sarah (Bates) D.; grad. Yale, 1813, LL.D. (hon.); m. Ann Eliza Ellicott, Dec. 1815. Commd. 2d lt. engrs., sent to U.S. Mil. Acad., 1813; commd. 1st lt., brevetted capt., 1814; asst. prof. natural philosophy U.S. Mil. Acad., Jan. 1, 1815; prof. natural philosophy Univ. City N.Y., 1832-33; became civil engr., architect; designed N.Y.U. bldg. in Washington Sq.; as engr. N.Y. commrs. selected Croton water shed, determined essential features of system including crossing Harlem River on a high bridge; system supplied N.Y.C. with water, 65 years; pres. Kenyon Coll., 1840-45; prof. mathematics and natural philosophy Hobart Coll. 1848. Died Geneva, N.Y., Oct. 21, 1849; buried Greenwood Cemetery, N.Y.C.

DOUGLASS, FREDERICK diplomat, journalist; b. Tuckahoe, Md., circa Feb. 1817; unknown White father and Harriet Bailey; m. Anna Murray, Sept. 1838; m. 2d Helen Pitts, 1884. Born a slave to Capt. Aaron Anthony, escaped, 1838; employed as agt. Mass. Anti-Slavery Soc., 1841; became central figure in "One Hundred Conventions" of New Eng. Anti-Salvery Soc.; visited Gt. Britain and Ireland to avoid possible re-enslavement as result of his biography Narrative of the Life of Frederick Douglass, 1845-47; returned to America with money to buy his freedom, established newspaper North Star (for Negro race), 1847; asissted in recruiting 54th and 55th Mass. Colored regts. during Civil War; sec. Santa Domingo Commn., 1871; marshal and recorder of deeds D.C., 1877-86; U.S. minister to Haiti, 1889-91; vigorous supporter of woman suffrage. Died Washington, D.C., Feb. 20, 1895.

DOW, NEAL temperance reformer; b. Portland, Me., Mar. 20, 1804; s. Josiah and Dorcas (Allen) D.; m. Maria Maynard, Jan. 20, 1830, 9 children. Del. from Portland Young Men's Temperance Soc. to Me. Temperance Conv., 1834; organized Me. Temperance Union, 1838; mayor Portland, 1851-58; secured passage of anti-liquor bill ("Maine law") in Me. Legislature, 1851; pres. World's Temperance Conv., N.Y.C., 1853; mem. Me. Legislature, 1858-59; col. 13th Regt., Me. Volunteers, 1861; brig. gen. U.S. Volunteers, 1862; captured, imprisoned, later exchanged for Gen. Fitzhugh Lee, 1864; Prohibition Party candidate for U.S. Pres., 1880; known as "father of the Maine law." Died Portland, Oct. 2, 1897.

DOWD, WALLACE RUTHERFORD naval officer; b. Ft. Smith, Ark., Oct. 22, 1896; s. Andrew Scales and Emala Elise (Rutherford) D.; student U. Ark., 1913-15; B.S. with distinction, U.S. Naval Acad., 1919; M.S., Mass. Inst. Tech., 1923; m. Alpha Hines, Aug. 18, 1920; children-Wallace Rutherford, Andrew S. Commd. ensign, U.S.N., 1919, promoted through grades to rear adm., 1949; design and maintenance naval vessels; supr. shipbldg., Chgo., 1942-43; mat. control Bur. Ships, 1944-46, asst. chief, 1950; comdr. Mare Island Naval Shipyard, 1947-49, Pearl Harbor Naval Shipyard, 1950, ret. Decorated Legion of Merit, Gold Star (Navy). Mem. Am. Soc. Naval Architects, Am. Soc. Naval Engrs., Kappa Alpha. Episcopalian. Clubs: Army-Navy Country, Army-Navy (Washington). Home: 1510 Sobre Vista Dr., Sonoma, Cal. Died Apr. 22, 1962; buried at sea.

DOWDELL, JAMES FERGUSON congressman, lawyer; b. nr. Monticello, Jasper County, Ga., Nov. 26, 1818; grad. Randolph-Macon Coll., Ashland, Va., 1840; studied law. Admitted to bar, 1841, began practice of law, Greenville, Ga.; engaged in agriculture, Chambers County, Ala., 1846; Democratic presdl. elector, 1852; mem. U.S. Ho. of Reps. (States Rights Democrat) from Ala., 33d-35th congresses, 1853-59; served as col. 37th Regt., Ala. Volunteer Inf., under Gen. Price, Confederate Army, 1862-65; pres. E. Ala. Coll., Auburn, 1868-70. Died nr. Auburn, Sept. 6, 1871: buried City Cemetery, Auburn.

DOWELL, BENJAMIN B(UTTERWORTH) govt. ofcl., lawyer; b. Silver Spring, Md., Oct. 18, 1895; s. Julian C. and Cynthia E. (Noyes) D.; LL.B., George Washington U., 1924; m. Edna C. Maedel, Nov. 16, 1927. Admitted to D.C. bar, 1923: mem. patent law firm Dowell & Dowell, Washington, 1923-40; dir. contract termination program, dep. Bur. Aero. Gen. Rep., Central dist., USN, Wright Field, O., 1944-47; indsl. adviser NPA, Def. Prodn. Adminstrn., 1950-53; spl. cons. Bus. and Def. Services Adminstrn., Dept. Commerce, 1955; chmn. Govt. Patents Bd., 1955—. Served as officer (pilot), USN, World War I, as Procurement and Contract adminstrn. officer, World War II; capt. Res. (ret.). Mem. Am., Fed., D.C. bar assns., Am. Patent Law Assn., Am. Judicature Soc., Early Naval Aviators, Naval Res. Officers Assn., Navy League U.S., Vets. Fgn. Wars, Sigma Alpha Epsilon. Republican. Club: Capitol Hill (Washington). Home: 2300 Connecticut Av. Washington 8. Office: Govt. Patents Bd., Dept. of Commerce Bldg., Washington 25. Died Oct. 29, 1958; buried Arlington Nat. Cemetery.

DOWELL, GREENSVILLE physician; b. Albemarle County, Va., Sept. 1, 1822; s. James and Francis (Dawton) D.; attended U. Louisville, 1845-46; M.D., Jefferson Med. Sch., 1847; m. Sarah Zelinda White, June 29, 1849; m. 2d, Mrs. Laura Baker Hutchinson, 1868. Practiced medicine, Como, Miss., Memphis, Tenn., also Tex.; surgeon Cook's Heavy Arty., Confederate Army, later surgeon-in-chief Confederate Hosp. Dept.; prof. anatomy Soulé U. (now Tex. Med. Coll.); in charge of Galveston (Tex.) Hosp.; founded Galveston Med. Jour., 1869. Author: The Radical Cure for Hernia, 1873; Yellow Fever and Malarial Diseases,. . ., 1876. Died June 9, 1881.

DOWLING, NOEL THOMAS, educator, lawyer; b. Ozark, Ala., Aug. 14, 1885; s. Angus and Laura Lavinia (Boswell) D.; A.B., Vanderbilt U., 1909; A.M., Columbia, 1911, LL.B., 1912, LL.D., 1954; m. Elizabeth Brown Molloy, June 19, 1918; children—Janet Cameron Brown, Elizabeth Molloy (dec. June 1972). Asst., Legislative Drafting Research Fund, Columbia, 1912-14, 16-17; prof. law U. Minn., 1919-22; asso. prof. law Columbia, 1922-24, prof. law, 1924-30, Nash prof. law, 1930-46, Harlan Fiske Stone prof. constl. law, 1946-54, emeritus, 1954-69; acting prof. law Stanford, 1925; vis. prof. law U. Va., 1940. Spl. asst. legislative counsel U.S. Senate, 1921, 27; asso. dir. Bur. War Risk Ins. (now VA), commr. mil. and naval ins., 1918-19; mem. sec. navy com. to prepare report on orgn., methods and procedures of naval courts, 1943, mem. bd., 1945. Chmn. N.Y. Mayor's factfinding bd., city bus strike, 1941. Vice pres. Riverside Ch., N.Y.C., 1941-45, pres., 1945-46, hon. trustee 1959-69; trustee, vice chmn. Nat. Child Labor Com. Served as maj., judge adv. general U.S. Army, World War I. Recipient Distinguished Pub. Service award U.S. Navy, 1948. Mem. Acad. Polit. Sci. (trustee, sec. 1936-46), Am. Univ. Union (dir. Brit. div. 1928-29), Am. Bar Assn., Assn. Bar City N.Y., Am. Law Inst., Phi Beta Kappa, Sigma Alpha Epsilon (mem. supreme council, editor The Record 1918-20). Club: Century (N.Y.C.). Author: (with Joseph P. Chamberlain, Paul R. Hays) The Judicial Function in Federal Administrative Agencies, 1942. Editor; Cases on Constitutional Law, 6th edit., 1959, (with Gerald Gunther), 7th edition, 1965. Co-editor: Cases on Public Utilties, 1926, 36; Cases on Conflict of Laws, 1936-41; Materials for Legal Method, 1946, 52; American Constitutional Law, 1954. Contbr. articles to law reviews. Home: New York City NY Died Feb. 11, 1969; buried Grove Hill Cemetery, Shelbyville KY

DOWMAN, CHARLES EDWARD surgeon; b. Quincy, Fla., Apr. 1, 1882; s. Charles Edward and Julia Robena (Monroe) D.; A.B., Emory U., Atlanta, Ga., 1901; M.D., Johns Hopkins, 1905; m. Caroline Westmoreland, Mar. 1908; 1 son, Charles Edward. Asst. pathol. instr., Charlottenburg Krankenhaus, Berlin, 1905-06; asst., Univ. Chirurg. Klinik, Breslau, Germany, 1906-07; clin. clk., Nat. Hosp. for Paralyzed and Epileptic, London, 1907; attending surgeon, Hillman Hosp., Birmingham, Ala., 1909-15; also prof. pathology. Birmingham Med. Coll., 1911-13, and asso. in surgery, U. of Ala., 1913-15; instr., asso. and asst. prof. surgery, Emory U., 1915-24; neurol. surgeon, Scottish Rite Hosp. for Crippled Children, Eggleston Memorial Hosp., Grady Memorial Hosp., Ga. Bapt. Hosp., Piedmont Hosp., 1918 - . Served as capt., later maj., Med. Corps, U.S.A., 1917-19; chief of surg. team, mobile hosps., St. Mihiel and Argonne offensives. Fellow Am. Coll. Surgeons. Democrat. Methodist. Home: Atlanta, Ga. Died Nov. 14, 1931.

DOWNES, JOHN naval officer; b. Canton, Mass., Dec. 23, 1784; s. Jesse and Naomi (Taunt) D.; m. Maria Gertrude Hoffman, Oct. 30, 1821, at least 1 son John. Purser's steward in U.S. frigate Constitution; apptd. acting midshipman, 1800, midshipman, 1802; served in war against Tripoli pirates; promoted lt., 1807; as 1st lt. joined Essex, 1812; served as prize capt. from Essex, capturing ships which he turned into tiny flotilla; promoted master comdr., 1813, capt., 1817; on tour of duty in Mediterranean Sea, 1815-18; served in Pacific, 1818-28; comdr. in Java in Mediterranean 1828-30; commanded Potomac in Pacific, 1830-34; commandant Boston Navy Yard, 1835-42, 49-52; port capt. of Boston, 1843-45. Died Charleston, Mass. Aug. 11, 1854.

DOWNES, JOHN naval officer (ret.); b. Dorchester, Mass., Nov. 16, 1879; s. John and Emma Homer (Nazro) D.; B.S., U.S. Naval Acad., 1901; hon. LL.D., St. Ambrose Coll., 1943; m. Agnes Carlyle Bryant, Oct. 31, 1906; children-John, William Bryant, Sarah Fairfax Carlyle; m. 2d, Edith A. Steinbrecher, Aug. 12, 1952. Serve as midshipman 3d class, Spanish Am. War, 1897; commd. ensign U.S. Navy, 1901, advanced through grades to rear adm., 1935; aide to supt. U.S. Naval Acad., 1916-18; comdr. heavy cruiser div., 1937-38; chief of staff to comdr. scouting forces, 1934-35; comdt. 9th Naval Dist., 1935-36, 40-44; additional duty as comdg. officer Naval Training Center, Great Lakes, Ill., 1935-36, 40-42; ret. from active duty, 1944; with Chgo. chpt. A.R.C., 1944, Ford Motor Co., 1945; dir., Ill. Service Recognition Bd. (vets. bonus), 1947—. Decorated Spanish Am. War and spl. engagement medals, West Indian campaign medal, Victory medal with silver star (World War I), Legion of Merit (World War II). Republican. Clubs: Yacht (N.Y.C.); Army Navy (Washington); Chevy Chase (Md.); Chicago, Old Elm (Lake Forest, Ill.): University, Union League, Tavern (Chgo.). Home: 40 E. Shiller St., Chgo. 10. Office: 160 N. La Salle St., Chgo. Died. Feb. 10, 1954; buried Annapolis, Md.

DOWNEY, GEORGE FABER army officer; b. in Ariz. Ty., July 30, 1866. Comd. maj. add. p.-m. vols., May 17, 1898; maj. p.-m., U.S.A., Feb. 2, 1901; promoted through grades to brig. gen. Apr. 27, 1921; retired. Home: Washington, D.C. Died Apr. 1, 1935.

DOWNIE, ROBERT C cons.; b. New Concord, O., Mar. 3, 1905; s. John and Mary Belle (Collins) D.; A.B., Monmouth Coll., 1917, LL.D., 1947; LL.B., University of Pittsburgh, 1932; LL.D., Duquesne University, 1952; married Kathleen Wahl, May 18, 1935; children-Robert Wahl, David Collins, Richard Kyle. Admitted to Pennsylvania bar, 1932; engaged in gen. practice of law, 1932-35; gen. atty. Dravo Corp., 1935-38; trust officer Peoples-Pittsburgh Trust Co., 1938-40, pres. since 1944; pres., chmn. bd. Peoples First Nat. Bank & Trust Co., 1946-55; gen. partner Arthurs, Lestrange & Co., Pitts., 1956; asst. to pres., asst. gen. mgr. Superior Steel Corp., 1957-58; asst. to pres. Nat. Electric Products Corp., 1958; bus., financial cons., 1958—; chmn., dir. Carman-Pitts. Co., Inc.; dir. Heppenstall Co. Dir. Pitts., Allegheny Conf. on Community Devel. Served as a colonel with U.S. Army from 1940; assigned dept. dist. chief Pitts. Ordnance Dept., 1940-43, dist. chief, 1943, reappointed, 1949. Mem. Am. Ordnance Assn. Pitts (dir.), Mil Order of World Wars. Order of Coif. Clubs: Duquesne (Pitts.). Home: 4716 Ellsworth Av., Pitts. 15213. Died Mar. 12, 1965; buried Mt. Lebanon, Cemetery, Pitts.

DOYLE, MICHAEL FRANCIS lawyer; b. Philadelphia, Pa.; s. John J. and Mary (Hughes) Doyle; LL.B., U. Penn., 1897; LL.D., Villanova Coll., 1935, St. Johns U., 1944, Nat. U., Ireland, 1959; m. Nancy O'Donoghue, 1918. In gen. practice, including internat. law. Mem. Permanent Court Internat. Arbitration (The Hague), 1938-52; mem. Citizen's Relief Com., Comprehensive Plans Com., Phila.; special agent Dept. of State, 1915; actg. counsellor Am. Legation, Switzerland, Am. Embassy, Vienna, 1915; counsel for Sir Roger Casement, on trial for treason, London, 1916. Spl asst. chief of ordnance, War Department, 1917-18; counsel various individuals and units Irish revolutionary movement; adviser Irish Free State Com. in drafting Nat. Constn., 1922; counsel 1st Irish delegation to League of Nations, Hayti-San Domingo before State Dept., 1922; Chmn. Am. Com., Geneva, League of Nations, 1920-39; hon. v.p. U.N. Association. Member delegations representing U.S. internat. confs.; 1937; appointed by Pres. mem. Permanent Court Internat. Arbitration, The Hague, 1938; reappointed 1944; v.p. Cath. Assn. Internat. Peace; adviser Interparlimentary Union, London, 1957. Chairman bd. dirs. George Washington Boyhood Home. Dem. Presdl. elector, 1928, 32, 44, 48; chairman Dem. Presdl. electors, inauguration of Pres. Roosevelt, 1933, 41. Pres. Electoral College, U.S., 1945-49, 53, hon. pres., 1957. Trustee Nat. Fund for Med. Edn., James Monroe Found., 1956, Assumption Coll., 1956; mem. adv. com. Xavier U. (La.). Villanova (Pa.) College, 1957; director Christian Muslim Continuing Committee, 1957. Mem. nat. state and local bar assns. and legal socs.; dir. Am. Czeckoslovakia Independence Com.; founder counsel Cath. Near East Welfare Association; v.p. Mexican Commn. against Religious Persecution; hon. master Philadelphia Navy Yard; dir. Catholic Missionary Soc. President Thomas Jefferson Memorial Association; dir. Patrick Henry Memorial Foundation, Recipient numerous civil and secular honors and decorations, 1929—, latest being Cross of Merit (Naval) Spain, 1952; Emmanuel D'Alzon medal Assumption Coll., 1956; apptd. pvt. chamberlain Pope John XXIII; hon. bencher Kings Inns of Court. Ireland. Mem. Am. Peace Soc. (v.p.). Clubs: Penn, Contemporary, Lawyers, Friendly Sons of St. Patrick, others. Home: 1906 S. Rittenhouse Sq. Office: Girard Trust Bldg., Phila. Died Mar. 27, 1960.

DOYLE, ROBERT MORRIS naval officer; b. Dyersburg, Tenn., May 5, 1853; s. James Henry and Jane (Sampson) D.; grad. U.S. Naval Acad., 1875; m. Kate Amelia, d. Dr. Thomas Snowden, of Peekskill, N.Y., Oct. 19, 1882. Promoted through the various grades to rank of rear adm., June 7, 1913; retired May 5, 1915. Navigating officer U.S.S. Dixie, during Spanish-Am. War, 1898; comd. Culgoa, Chicago; comd. Missouri on cruise of battleships around the world, 1908; comdt. Norfolk Navy Yard, 1911-13; comdr.-in-chief pacific Reserve Fleet, 1913-15; recalled to active duty and comdt. 14th Naval Dist. and U.S. Naval Sta., pearl Harbor, Hawaii, June 13, 1918-May 15, 1919. Episcopalian. Died Dec. 15, 1925.

DRAEMEL, MILO FREDERICK, naval officer; b. Fremont, Neb., May 30, 1884; s. Frederick William and Johanna (Nilson) D.; B.S., U.S. Naval Acad., 1906; degrees from Villanova, Temple U., Univ. of Pa.; m. Marguerite Clise, Oct. 25, 1911; children—Frederick Clise, Eleanor Clise. Commd. ensign, U.S. Navy, 1906, and advanced through the grades to rear adm., 1938; during World War I served as flag lt. on staff comdr. Battleship Force, U.S. Fleet until Sept. 1918, then officer in charge Code and Signal Sect., Navy Dept., until end of war; became comdt. midshipmen, U.S. Naval Acad., 1937-39; comdr. Destroyer Flotilla, 1940; chief of staff and aide to comdr.-in-chief, Pacific Fleet, 1941-42; task force comdr. Eastern Sea Frontier, comdt. Fourth Naval Dist., 1942-46; inactive list Aug. 1946. Vice pres. Temple Univ., Phila.; sec. Dept. Forests and Waters, Commonwealth of Pa. as mem. of Gov. James H. Duff's Cabinet, 1947-52. Decorated: D.S.M. (Navy), Legion of Merit, Am. Defense, Victory Medals, Pacific and Am. Theatre Medals; French Legion of Honor; Venezuelan Order of Bolivar; Grand Officer of Southern Cross (Brazil); Grand Officer Order of Orange-Nassau (Netherlands). Episcopalian. Clubs: Chevy Chase, The Philadelphia, New York Yacht. Gulph Mills. Home: Wynnewood PA Died Mar. 25, 1971; buried Mount Pleasant Cemetery, Seattle WA

DRAIN, JAMES ANDREW past nat. comdr. Am. Legion; b. Warren County, Ill., Sept. 30, 1870; s. Andrew Hazlett and Virginia (Wornem) D.; ed. high sch. and Western Normal Coll., Shenandoah, fa.; m. Ethel Mary Marsland, June 24, 1801. Mem. Supreme Court of U.S., Dist. of Columbia, Wash. State and Am. bar assns.; owner pub. and editor Arms and the Man, New York and Washington. Brig. gen. and adj. gen. Nat. Guard of Washington; chmn. exec. com. Nat. Guard Assn. of U.S.; chmn. Nat. Militia Bd., etc. World War, Apr. 20, 1917-June 9, 1919; original ordnance officer 1st Div., A.E.F., France, June 1917; D.S.M. (U.S.); Legion of Honor (French); Cross of Italy. Nat. comdr. Am. Legion, 1924-25. Lawyer Spokane, Wash., and Washington, D.C. Staff Social Security Board; asst. to Federal Security Administrator, Clubs: University, National Press, Washington Golf and Country. Author: Stories of Some Shoots, 1912; various articles. Home: Stoneleigh Court, Washington, D.C. Died May 30, 1943.

DRAKE, FRANCIS MARION banker, gov.; b. Rushville, Ill., Dec. 30, 1830; s. John Adams and Harriet Jane (O'Neal) D.; removed to Ft. Madison, Ia., 1837; ed. there; family removed, 1846, to Davis Co., Ia., founding there the village of Drakeville; m. Mary Jane Dord, Dec. 24, 1855 (died 1883). In 1852 with company of 16 men rossed the plains with ox-teams, arriving safely after a severe but successful encounter with Pawnee Indians; again crossed, 1854, with a drove of cattle, but returning by water narrowly escaped death in the wreck of the steamer Yankee Blade, lost in the Pacific, engaged in mercantile business at Drakeville and later at Unionville, Ia. Served, 1861-65, all grades, from private to col. and bvt. brig. gen. of vols. in Union army; was severely wounded; after war practiced law and engaged in railroad and banking enterprises; now pres. Albia & Centerville Ry. Co.; pres. Centerville (Ia.) Nat. Bank, and 1st Nat. Bank of Albia; pres. bd. of trustees Drake Univ., Des Moines, which he has liberally endowed; was gov. Iowa, 1896-93. Home: Centerville, Ia. Died 1903.

DRAKE, FRANCIS SAMUEL hist. writer; b. Northwood, N.H., Feb. 22, 1828; s. Gardiner and Louisa (Elmes) D. Lt., Boston Light Guards, 1848; served as adjutant to Union Army during Civil War; became hist. writer after Civil War; works include: Dictionary of American Biography Containing Nearly Ten Thousand Notices, 1872; The Life and Correspondence of Henry Knox; The Town of Roxbury, 1878; Indian History for Young Folks, 1885. Died Washington, D.C., Feb. 22, 1885.

DRAKE, FRANKLIN JEREMIAH rear adm.; b. Yates, N.Y., Mar. 4, 1846; grad. U.S. Naval Acad., 1868. Promoted ensign, Apr. 19, 1869; master, July 12, 1870; lt., Nov. 15, 1872; lt. comdr., Oct. 1, 1893; comdr., Mar. 3, 1899; capt., Sept. 11, 1903; retired as rear admiral, Dec. 10, 1906. In the summer of 1863, on board the Marion, in pursuit of Confederate steamer Tacony; served on the Gettysburg, 1868-69; signal duty at Washington, 1869-70; Colorado, 1870-73; on torpedo duty, 1873-74; Portsmouth, Jamestown and Independence, 1874-75; Navy Yard, Mare Island, 1875-76; coast survey steamer Hassler, 1876-78; Ticonderoga, 1878-81; Navy Yard, New York, 1881-83; spl. duty with Rear Admiral Shufelt, 1883-85; Pensacola, 1885-88; insp. of torpedo boats, 1888; insp. ordnance, 1888-92; spl. duty at Chicago Expn., 1893; Navy Yard, Boston, 1893-94; comd. Fish Commn. steamer Albatross, 1894-96; exec. officer Oregon, 1896-97; Navy Yard, Mare Island, 1897-1900; comd. Culgoa, 1900-01; comdt. naval - Cavite, and comdg. Monterey, 1901-03; Navy Yard, Mare Island, 1903-05; comd. Wisconsin, 1905-06. Tech. expert, Hague Tribunal, 1913-15; operations, revision of regulations, U.S.N., 1918-1920. Died Jan. 30, 1929.

DRAKE, FRED RAYMOND; b. Easton, Pa., June 12, 1865; s. Samuel and Sarah (Arndt) D.; A.B., Lafayette Coll., 1886, A.M., 1889; m. Pearce Kinkead Fox, June 15, 1911; children - Margaret Kinkead, Frederick Raymond. Entered mercantile business, 1886; pres. Drake & Co., Inc., wholesale grocers; v.p. First Nat. Bk. & Trust Co.; pres. Fire Ins. Co. of Northampton County, Jan. 5, 1925 - ; dir. Wahnetah Silk Co., Catasauqua, Pa. Assisted in recruiting Easton City Guard; mustered into service, Pa. N.G., July 12, 1898, for Spanish-Am. War; elected 1st lt. at muster, capt., Sept. 27, 1898; apptd. aide, brigade staff of Gen. J. P. S. Gobin, Dec. 14, 1900; aide, div. staff, rank of maj., Apr. 6, 1906; retired Jan. 5, 1912. V.p. bd. Easton Pub. Library. Mem. Bd. Trade, Easton (hon.). Home: Easton, Pa. Died July 17, 1932.

DRAKE, JAMES MADISON newspaper publisher; b. Somerset Co., N.J., Mar. 25, 1837; s. James S. and Eunice (Martin) D.; ed. pub. schs., Elizabeth, N.J.; m. Margaret B. Taylor, Jan. 7, 1859. Publisher Mercer Standard, Trenton, N.J., 1853-54; started Evening News, 1857; Wide Awake, 1860. Alderman, Trenton, N.J., 1860-61. Served in Union army, 1861-65; unfurled first Union flag on Virginia soil, May 24, 1861; taken prisoner, May 15, 1864, at Drury's Bluff, Va.; escaped from Charleston, S.C., Oct. 6, 1864, reaching Union lines at Knoxville, Tenn., Nov. 22, 1864; awarded Congressional Medal of Honor for distinguished gallantry; capt. 9th N.J. Veteran Vols.; bvtd. brig. gen. by spl. act of N.J. legislature. Publisher Daily Monitor, Elizabeth, N.J., 1868-81, Elizabeth Sunday Leader, 1882-87, and Elizabeth Daily Leader 1887-1900. Historian 9th N.J. Vols., and Medal of Honor Legion. Home: Elizabeth, N.J. Died Nov. 28, 1913.

DRAKE, SAMUEL ADAMS editor and author; b. Boston, Dec. 1833; s. Samuel G. Drake, author and publisher, Boston; ed. in public schools of Boston. Insp. and adjt. gen. Kan. militia, 1861; col. 1st regt. same, 1863; brig. gen. same, Feb. 1864; col. 17th Kan. vol. inf., July 1864; engaged in mil. operations in Kan. and Mo. during Civil war, 1861-65. Author: The Making of New England, 1886; The Making of the Great West, 1887; Burgoyne's Invasion, 1889; The Taking of Louisburg, 1891; The Battle of Gettysburg, 1892; The Making of Virginia, 1893; The Making of the Ohio Valley States, 1894; The Campaign of Trenton, 1895; The Border Wars of New England, 1897; On Plymouth Rock, 1898; The Myths and Fables of To-day, 1900 L 6; The Young Vigilantes, 1904. Died 1905.

DRAPER, FRANK WINTHROP physician; b. Wayland, Mass., Feb. 25, 1843; s. James Sumner and Emmeline Amanda(Reeves) D.; ed. Brown Univ., A.B., 1862, A.M., 1865, Harvard, M.D., 1869; m. Fanny V. (Jones) Draper, Nov. 1, 1870. Served in Civ. War as pvt. 35th Mass. Vol. Inf.; promoted capt. 39th U.S.C.T., Apr. 1864, resigned June 10, 1865. In practice of medicine from 1869; visiting physician, Boston City Hosp.; editor Mass. Registration Reports; asst. editor Boston Med. and Surg. Jour.; med. examiner, Suffolk Co., Mass.; lecturer forensic medicine, asst. prof. and now prof. legal medicine, Harvard. Fellow Am. Assn. Arts and Sciences. Mem. State Bd. of Health, and of Loyal Legion. Unitarian. Republican. Author: Legal Medicine, 1904. Home: Brookline, Mass. Died 1909.

DRAPER, WARREN FALES, executive medical officer; b. Cambridge, Mass., Aug. 9,21883; s. William Burgess and Carrie Maria (Drew) D.; prep. edn. Waban (Mass.) Sch. for Boys, 1900-02; A.B. Amherst Coll., 1906, D.Sc., 1945; M.D., Harvard, 1910; m. Margaret Gansevoort Maxon, Apr. 6, 1910; children—Warren Fales, Anne Gansevoort. Commd. asst. surgeon, U.S. Pub. Health Service, 1910, surgeon, 1920, asst. surgeon gen. in charge div. domestic quarantine, 1922-31; health commr. of Va., 1931-34; in charge extra cantonment sanitation, Camp Lee, Petersburg, Va., 1917-18, Newport News, Va., Aug.-Sept. 1918; asst. surgeon gen. in charge div. personnel and accounts, 1934-39; dep. surgeon gen., 1939-47, ret.; maj. gen. charge pub. health br. Supreme Hdqrs. Allied Expdnry. Force, 1944-45; asst. to v.p. for health services Am., Nat. Red Cross, 1946-48; exec. med. officer United Mine Workers of America Welfare and Retirement Fund, 1948-69. Alternate mem. Civilian Health and Medical Adv. Council, Office Assistant Secretary of Def., 1956-69; cons. Dept. Occupational Health, United Mine Workers Am., 1969-70. Decorations: Distinguished Service Medal (U.S.); Companion of the Bath (Brit.); Officer Legion of Honor, Croix de Guerre with Palm, Officer Order of Public Health (France); Officer Order of Leopold II (Belgium); Grand Officer Order of Orange-Nassau (Netherlands). Former professorial lectr. on pub. health adminstrn. George Washington U., Jefferson Med. Coll., Phila.; lectr. pub. health U. Mich., Johns Hopkins U. Mem. Nat. Bd. of Med. Examiners, 1940-48. Mem. pub. health adv. com. Commonwealth Fund, 1925-46. Diplomate Am. Bd. Preventive Medicine. Member A.M.A. (house of delegates, 1942-46; former chairman sect. on preventive and industrial medicine and public health; charter member and former member Council on Industrial Health, Com. on Coordination of Medical Activities), mem. American Public Health Association (former mem. governing counsel; former chmn. health officer sect.); hon. life mem. Internat. Soc. of Med. Health Officers, Conf. State and Provincial Health Authorities of N.A., Assn. Mil. Surgeons (pres. 1946-47); mem. Smith-Reed-Russell (hon. med. soc. George Washington U.), Sigma Xi, Alpha Omega Aplha. Club: Cosmos (Washington). Episcopalian. Author many published articles on pub. health adminstrn. and preventive medicine. Home: Arlington VA Died Mar. 19, 1970; buried Columbia Gardens Cemetery, Arlington VA

DRAPER, WILLIAM FRANKLIN diplomat; b. Lowell, Mass., Apr. 9, 1842; s. George and Hannah (Thwing) D.; ed. common schs. and 2 yrs. at acad.; m. Lydia W. Joy, 1862; 2d, Susan Preston, 1890. Enlisted, 1861, Co. B, 25th Mass.; served through war, becoming lt. col. and bvt. brig. gen. of vols. After war engaged in fg. cotton machinery; pres. Home Market Club, Boston, 1890; mem. Congress, 1892-97; U.S. Ambassador to Italy, 1897-1900. Home: Hopedale, Mass. Died 1910.

DRAYTON, PERCIVAL naval officer; b. S.C., Aug. 25, 1812; s. William and Ann (Gadsden) D. Apptd. midshipman U.S. Navy, 1827, passed midshipman, 1833, lt., 1838, comdr., 1855; apptd. aide to Commodore William Branford Shubrick, 1858; apptd. to command ship Pocahontas in Samuel Francis DuPont's expdn. against Port Royal, S.C., 1861; served as capt. in command of monitor Passaic, 1862; fleet capt. West Gulf Blockading Squadron, 1863; chief Bur. of Navigation, 1865. Died Washington, D.C., Aug. 4, 1865.

DRAYTON, THOMAS FENWICK plainter, railroad pres., army officer; b. S.C., 1807; s. William and Ann (Gadsden) D.: grad. U.S. Mil. Acad., 1828; m. Catherine Pope, 8 children. Commd. lt. 6th Inf., U.S. Army, 1828; capt. of a company S.C. Militia, 1842-47; mem. S.C. Bd. Ordnance, 1851-52; mem. upper house S.C. Gen. Assembly, 1853-56; pres. Charleston & Savannah R.R. (constructed and successfully operated under his direction), 1853-61; commd. brig. gen. Provisional Confederate Army, 1861; in command Port Royal, S.C. when attacked by Union ships under DuPont, 1861; commanded brigade in Dist. of Ark., later in charge of sub-dist. in Tex.; pres. S.C. Immigrant Soc., 1878. Died Charlotte, S.C., Feb. 18, 1891.

DRAYTON, WILLIAM army officer, congressman; b. St. Augustine, Fla., Dec. 30, 1776; s. William and Mary (Motte) D.; ed. English prep. schs.; m. Ann Gadsden; m. 2d, Maria Miles; 9 children including Thomas Fenwick, Percival. Asst, in elk.'s office S.C. Ct. Gen. Sessions; admitted to S.C. bar. 1797; mem. S.C. Ho. of Reps., 1806-08; commd. lt. col. 10th Inf., U.S. Army, 1812, col. 18th Inf., 1812, insp. gen., 1814; recorder judge City Ct. Charleston, 1819-24; mem. U.S. Ho. of Reps. from s. c. (union democrat Filling Vacancy), 19th-22d congresses, Dec. 15, 1825-Mar. 3, 1833; declined appointments as U.S. sec. war and minister to Eng. under Pres. Jackson opposed nullification, 1830; moved to Phila., 1833; pres. Bank of U.S., 1840-41. died Phila., May 24, 1846; buried Laurel Hill Cemetery, Phila.

DRELLER, LOUIS, naval officer; b. Portsmouth, N.H., Mar. 6, 1897; s. Abram and Eva Celia (Polimer) D.; B.S. in E.E., U. of N.H., 1918; LL.D., 1947; student Post Grad. Sch., U.S. Naval Acad., 1920-21; M.S. Columbia, 1925; m. Edythe Molly Maharam, May 22, 1924; children—Selma Dreller Kerr, Doris M. Commd. ensign (engring. duty), U.S. Navy, 1918, and advanced through the grades to rear adm. (engineering duty), 1946; service included sea duty on battleships, destroyers, aircraft carriers; two tours of duty, Elec. Design Sect., Bureau of Engring. and Bureau of Ships; at outbreak of World War II was engr. officer attached to Scouting Force Staff; design supt., planning officer and prodn. officer, Philadelphia Navy Yard, 1942-46; comdr. Pearl Harbor Naval Shipyard, Hawaii, 1946-48; chief office Indsl. Survey for Secretary Navy, 1948-49; Assistant Chief of Naval Material, 1950-51. Decorated Legion of Merit, Asiatic-Pacific Campaign with 2 stars, American Theater, Defense with 1 star, World War I and World War II ribbons (U.S.) Order of Southern Cross (Brazil), Order of Orange-Nassau (Netherlands). Mem. Soc. Naval Architects and Marine Engrs., Am. Soc. Naval Engrs., Naval Order of U.S. (gen. commandery). Mason. Club: Army-Navy Country (Washington); Rotary (hon.); Propeller. Home: Alexandria VA Died May, 1970.

DRENNAN, MICHAEL C. medical dir. U.S.N.; b. Easton, Pa.; m. Ellen Johnson, June 1864. Apptd. from Pa., acting asst. surgeon U.S.N., Apr. 15, 1863; asst. surgeon, June 30, 1868; passed asst. surgeon, June 13, 1870; surgeon, Apr. 20, 1879; med. insp., May 28, 1895; med. dir., Apr. 16, 1899; retired, with rank of rear adm. for services during Civil War, Oct. 24, 1899. Served on board flagship New York as surgeon of the fleet, N. Atlantic Squadron, 1895-98. Home: Easton, Pa. Died Mar. 23, 1915.

DRESBACH, GLENN WARD, author; b. Lanark, Ill., Sept. 9, 1889; s. William Henry and Belle M. (Weidman) D.; spl. course, U. of Wis., 1908-11; m. Mary Angela Boyle, Jan. 29, 1921 (died 1943); m. 2d, Beverley Githens, April 9, 1944. Agency accountant Panama Canal, 1911-15. In charge med. supply depots Camp Mead, Md., and Med. Supply O.T.S., U.S. Army, rank of capt., 1917-19. Joint recipient with wife of gold medal for Outstanding Lit. Couple from former Pres. of Philippines. Life fellow Internat. Inst. Arts Letters; member United Poets Laureate International, Society of Midland Authors, Bookfellows, also mem. Am. Legion, Authors' Club (London). Episcopalian. Author: The Road to Everywhere, 1916; In the Paths of the

Wind, 1918; Morning, Noon and Night, 1920; In Colors of the West, 1922; Enchanted Mesa, 1924; Cliff Dwellings and Other Poems, 1926; Star-Dust and Stone (winner Poetry Society of Texas award), 1928; This Side of Avalon, 1929; The Wind in the Cedars, 1930; Selected Poems, 1931; Collected Poems (1914-1948), 1949; and also represented in anthologies, textbooks for high schs. and colls. Contbr. verse to Poetry, Sat. Even. Post, Am. Mercury, Atlantic Monthly, Virginia Quarterly Review, McCall's, The Ladies' Home Journal, New York Times, The Yale Review, etc. Winner George Sterling memorial prize, 1929; Grace D. Sperling sonnet prize, 1928, 30; Am. Literary Assn. prize, 1928; Star-Dust prize, 1929; Gypsy sonnet prize, 1930; Poetry World prize, 1930; Talaria prize, 1937; Lily Reed Zortman sonnet prize, 1937. Winner Ruth Baldwin Pierson award, 1939; George Sterling memorial prize, 1939; Hamlin Garland memorial prize, 1940; Beulah May Sea Poem Prize, 1940; recipient Karta of Award and laurel wreath with bronze medallion United Poets Laureate Internat., 1964. Selected to give poetry program at Ill. Host House Auditorium Century of Progress Expn., 1933; selected as one of five internat. speakers at Lions Internat. Conv., 1937. Prin. speaker Nat. Poetry Day, State of Ark., 1950. Has given his poetry programs for The League of Am. Pen Women. Society of Midland Authors, Order of Bookfellows, Junior League, D.A.R., Friends of Am. Writers, etc., and for many schools, colls., and women's clubs. Featured in radio programs; works translated into German and Ukrainian; display Internat. Outdoor Poetry Show, New Orleans, 1954. Works appear in anthologies and compilations. Judge Nat. Fedn. State Poetry Socs., 1960. Hon. chancellor Nat. Fedn. State Poetry Socs., 1963. Home: Eureka Springs AR Died June 27, 1968; buried Fayetteville Nat. Cemetery.

DREW, FRANK GIFFORD pres. Winchester Repeating Arms Co.; b. Phila., Pa., Dec. 1, 1872; s. David Abbott and Elizabeth (Gifford) D.; ed. pub. schs., Phila.; m. Anne Powell Patterson, Dec. 30, 1896; children - Anne (Mrs. William A. Reynolds), Elizabeth, Frances, Ethel. In wholesale hardware business, Phila., 1887-1903; with Winchester Repeating Arms Co., New Haven, Conn., 1903 - , pres., 1924 - ; pres. The Winchester Co.; v.p. Winchester-Simmons Co., Simmons Hardware Co. Served as capt. 1st Inf. and maj. 3d Inf., Spanish-Am. War, 1898; mem. Advisory Bd. Bridgeport Ordnance Dist., War Dept. U.S., 1927. Mem. Chamber Commerce of U.S., Conn. and New Haven, Mason. Republican. Episcopalian. Home: New Haven, Conn. Died Oct. 1928.

DREW, FRANKLIN MELLEN lawyer; b. Turner, Me., July 19, 1837; s. Jesse and Hannah Gorham (Phillips) D.; A.B., Bowdoin Coll., 1858. A.M., 1861; admitted to bar, 1861; m. Araminta Blanche Woodman, Jan. 3, 1862. Began practice at Presque Isle, Me., 1861; served in Civil War, as capt., maj. and bvt. col., 15th Regt. Me. Vols., Oct. 22, 1861-Jan. 26, 1865; clk. Maine House of Reps., 1866-67; sec. of state of Maine, 1868-72; U.S. pension agent, Augusta, Me., 1872-77; removed to Lewiston, Me., in 1878; judge of probate, 1888-1904. Republican. V.p. Lewiston Trust and Safe Deposit Co.; treas. Bates Coll., 1893-1916. Conglist. Mason. Home: Lewiston, Me. Died Feb. 27, 1925.

DRIGGS, LAURENCE LA TOURETTE author, lawyer, aviation specialist; b. Saginaw, Mich.. Dec. 1, 1876; b. LeRoy Channing and Mary (La Tourette) D.; ed. U. of Mich.: LL.B., New York Law Sch., 1900; m. Mary Ogden, June 29, 1904; children-Ogden, Laurence L. Practiced law in N.Y. City. Rep. nominee for Congress 11th N.Y. Dist., 1908; dep. atty. gen. of N.Y. State, 1909-10; apptd. mem. Market Commn. of N.Y., 1913; operated cattle ranch in Tex. Panhandle, 1913-16; mem. Rep. County Com., 1908-20 Mem. Troop C, N.G.N.Y., 1902-05; mem. Veteran's Corps Artillery since 1906; learned to fly, 1913; invited by British Govt. to visit battle front in France, 1914-16, as aviation specialist; attached to Royal Air Force headquarters, 1918; examined German aviation fields after Armistice. Formed Am. Flying Club at the front, 1918, composed of Am. aviators who had flown over lines, and elected first pres. of the club, at New York, 1919, reelected, 1920; organized New York-Toronto aeroplane races, 1919, aviators' armistice dinner, aviators' annual ball. Commd. maj. N.Y.G. Air Service 1921; organized 102 Observation Squadron, N.Y.G., ascomdg. officer; commd. lt. col. by governor and attached to staff, 1921. Lecturer on aviation throughout U.S. since 1919; engaged in commercial air transport in N.Y. and N.E. since 1927; pres. Prudential Airways; v.p. Colonial Air Transport, Colonial Western Airways, Canadian Colonial Airways. Special rep. of sec. of agr. in lending govt. funds to form credit corps. in drought area, 1931. Mem. Early Birds. Club: Cosmos (Washington). Author: Arnold Adair, 1917; Heroes of Aviation, 1918, 26; Fighting the Flying Circus (with Eddie Rickenbacker), 1919; Golden Book of Aviation, 1920; Arnold Adair with the English Aces, 1921; Secret Air Service, 1930: The Secret Squadron, 1931; Flight, 1933. Home: Broadwater, Oxford, Md. Died May 26, 1945.

DRUM, HUGH ALOYSIUS business exec.; b. Fort Brady, Mich., Sept. 19, 1879; s. Capt. John (U.S.A.) and Margaret (Desmond) D.; father killed at Battle of San Juan, Santiago, Cuba; honor grad. Army Sch. of the Line, 1911; grad. Army Staff Coll., 1912; A.B., Boston College, 1921; hon. Sc.D., Manhattan College, 1940; honorary LL.D., Boston Coll., 1923, St. Lawrence Univ., Fordham Univ., 1941, Loyola U., Columbia Univ., 1942, Rutgers Univ., New York Univ., 1943; hon. D.M.S., Pa. Military Coll., 1942, Georgetown Univ., 1943; University of Delaware, 1944; m. Mary Reaume, Oct. 14, 1903; 1 dau., Anna Carroll (Mrs. Thomas H. Johnson). Commd. 2d lt. 12th U.S. Inf., Sept. 9, 1898; promoted through grades to maj., May 1917; lt. col. (temp.), Aug. 5, 1917; col. (temp.), July 30, 1918; brig. gen. (temp.), Oct. 1, 1918; brig. gen. (tem.), Sept. 21, 1920-Mar. 4, 1921; brig. gen., U.S. Army, Dec. 6, 1922; maj. gen., U.S. Army, Dec. 1, 1931; lt. gen., Aug. 5, 1939. In Philippine Islands, 1898-1901, participating in Philippine Islands Insurrection; participated in campaign against Moros, also Lake Lanao Campaign; recommended for brevet as captain; aide de camp to General Baldwin; aide and adjutant general, Southwestern Division until 1906; again in Philippine Islands, 1908-10; instructor, director and assistant commandant Command and General Staff School, 1912-14; duty on the Mexican border, 1914; served as assistant chief of staff under Gen. Funston at Vera Cruz; asst. instr. in mil. art at army schs., later aide to Gen. Funston until latter's death, Feb. 19, 1917; asst. to chief of staff under Gen. Pershing, when latter succeeded Gen. Funston; detailed to Gen. Staff, June, 1917, and accompanied Gen. Pershing to France, as asst. chief of staff; chief of staff 1st Army, A.E.F., July 4, 1918-Apr. 1919; chief of staff Services of Supply, A.E.F., Apr.-July 1919; remainded to regular rank of maj. of inf.; dir. Army Sch. of the Line since 1919; comdt. General Service Schools, 1920-21; assigned to comd. coast and air defenses, 2d Corps Area, 1922; asst. chief of staff, in charge operations and training, Washington, 1923-26; comd. 1st Inf. Brigade, 1st Div., 1926-27; assigned to comd. 1st Div. Oct. 15, 1927; apptd. insp. gen., U.S. Army, rank of maj. gen., Jan. 29, 1930; comdr. 5th Corps Area and First Army, 1931-33 permanent rank of major general, Dec. 1, 1931; apptd. dep. chief of staff, Feb. 23, 1933; comdr. of Hawaiian Department, Honolulu, 1935-37; comd. Second Army and Sixth Corps Area, Chicago, Ill., 1937-38; comdg. First Army and Second Corps Area, Governors Island, New York, since 1938; appointed lt. gen., U.S. Army, Aug. 5, 1939; comdg. gen. Eastern Defense Command and First Army, Nov. 1940-Sept. 1943; apptd. lt. gen. N.Y. State Guard, 1943; apptd. chairman N.Y. State Veterans Commn., 1944; pres. Empire State, Inc. since 1944. Awarded silver star "for gallantry in action" at Battle of Bayan, Philippine Islands. Distinguished Service medal, with cluster; Commdr. Legion of Honor, and Croix de Guerre with 2 palms (French); Commander Order of Crown (Belgian); Commander Order of Crown (Italian), Comd. (with star) Royal Order of St. Olaf (Norway) Spanish War, Philippine Campaign, Mexican Service (Vera Cruz Expdn.), Mexican Border Service medals, Victory Medal with 4 battle clasps, Am. Defense and Am. Theatre ribbons; Medal of Merit, 1943. Roman Catholic. Mem. Am. Legion, Loyal Legion, Knights of Malta, Soc. of Friendly Sons of St. Patrick (N.Y.), Assn. Ex-members Squadron A (hon. 1942), Mil. Intelligence Res. Sec. (2d Service Command), Scabbard and Blade, Council on Foreign Relations, N.Y. Chamber of Commerce, N.Y. Soc., Mil. and Naval Officers of World Wars, 1944, St. Nicholas Soc. of the City of N.Y. Clubs: Union, University, India House, Overseas Press, Downtown Athletic Lotos, Rotary, Officers of Army and Navy, Chevy Chase (Washington). Address: Empire State Bldg., N.Y.C. Died Oct. 3, 1951.

DRUM, RICHARD COULTER army officer; b. in Pa., May 28, 1825; s. Simon and Agnes (Lang) D.; ed. Jefferson Coll., Phila.; m. Lavinia Morgan, 1850. Enlisted as pvt. Co. K, 1st Pa. Inf., Dec. 16, 1846; participated in siege of Vera Cruz; 2d lt. inf., Feb. 18, 1847, promoted through grades to col. Arty., Feb. 22, 1869; brig. gen. adj. gen., June 15, 1880; retired May 28, 1889. Bvtd. 1st lt., Sept. 13, 1847, for battle of Chapultepec, Mex.; col., Sept. 24, 1864, for services during the war; brig. gen., Mar. 13, 1865, for services in adj. gen.'s dept. during the war. Home: Bethesda, Md. Died 1909.

DUANE, JAMES CHATHAM mil. and civil engr.; b. Schenectady, N.Y., June 30, 1824; s. James and Harriet (Constable) D.; grad. Union Coll., 1844, U.S. Mil. Acad., 1848; m. Harriet Brewerton, 1850, 3 children including Alexander. Participated in Utah expdn. under Albert S. Johnston, 1858; instr. engring. U.S. Mil. Acad., 1858; treas., 1859-61; with McClellan's Army of Potomac during Civil War, made notable contbn. with his orgn. of engr. battalion and equipment; chief engr. Army of Potomac, 1862; brevetted lt. col. and col. U.S. Army for distinguished service; commd. brig. gen., chief of engrs. U.S. Army, 1886-88; ret., 1888; mem. Croton Aqueduct Commn. after 1888. Died N.Y.C., Nov. 8, 1897.

DUANE, WILLIAM journalist; b. Lake Champlain, N.Y., May 17, 1760; m. Catharine Corcoran; m. 2d, Margaret Bache, 1800; 5 children. Went to India, 1787, established Indian World, Calcutta, deported because of resistance ot East India Co.; returned to London; Parliamentary reporter Gen. Advertiser, came to Phila.; co-editor Phila. Aurora, editor 1798-1822 (made it a powerful Jeffersonian newspaper); was arrested under Sedition Act, charges dropped under influence of Pres. Jefferson; served as lt. col. Rifles, 1808, adjutant gen. during War of 1812; traveled to S. Am., 1822-23; prothonotary Pa. Supreme Ct., 1823-35. Author: A Visit to Colombia in the Years 1822 and 1823, pub. 1826; Military Dictionary, 1810; Handbook for Riflemen, 1813. Died Phila., Nov. 24, 1835.

DU BARRY, BEEKMAN brig. gen. U.S. Army, retired; b. Pa., Aug. 20, 1824; entered West Point July 1, 1845; bvt. 2d lt., July 1, 1849; commd. 2d lt. 1st art., April 1, 1850; advanced through grades to brig. gen. inspector gen., Sept. 22, 1885; retired, Aug. 20, 1888. In Civil war served as brig. gen. and bvt. maj. gen. vols. from April 1862, until mustered out of vol. service, Sept. 1, 1866; bvtd. lt. col. and col. U.S. Army, 1865, for faithful and meritorious services. Died 1901.

DU BOIS, COERT diplomat; born at Hudson, N.Y., Nov. 10, 1881; s. John C. (M.D.) and Eva (Kimball) du B.; ed. Biltmore Forest Sch.; m. Margaret Mendell, August 1, 1910. With United States Forest Service, 1900-17, dist. forester, Calif. Dist. 1911-17; consul assigned Paris, 1919. Naples, 1920, Port Said, 1922, in charge Visa Office. State Dept., Washington, 1924-27; consul gen., Batavia. Java, 1927-30; fgn. service inspector, India, 1930; consul gen., Genoa, Italy, 1931, Naples, Italy, 1931-37. Havana, Cuba, 1937-41; in charge Caribbean Office, State Dept., Washington, D.C., Oct. 9, 1941; Jan. 1944; apptd. on President's Anglo-Am. Caribbean Commn., March 14, 1942; sec. in diplomatic service, Aug. 1935; now retired. Liaison officer, State Dept. and War Assets Adminstrn., Central and So. Am. and Caribbean, 1946-47; U.S. del., U.N. Security Council's Com. of Good Offices, Java. N.E. Indies, Jan.-July 1948, rank of minister. Commd. maj. engrs. U.S. Army, Aug. 1917; lt. col., Sept. 1918; served with 10th Engrs. in France, Sept. 1917-Sept. 1918; duty Office of Chief of Engrs., Sept.-Dec. 1918; hon. disch., Dec. 4, 1918 Sent to England, Ireland and the Continent of Europe, 1925, as rep. of U.S. Govt. to arrange for the examination of immigrants before leaving home countries. Club: Metropolitan (Washington). Episcopalian. Home: 13 Elm St., Stonington, Conn. Died March 6, 1960.

DUBOIS, EUGENE FLOYD physiologist; b. West New Brighton, N.Y., June 4,1882; s. Eugene and Anna Greenleaf (Brooks) DuB.; A.B., Harvard 1903; M.D., Coll. Phys. and Surg. (Columbia), 1906; Sc.D., U. Rochester (N.Y.), 1948; m. Rebeckah Rutter, June 4, 1910. Interne Presbyn. Hosp., N.Y., 1907-08, asst. pathologist, 1909; instr. applied pharmacology, Cornell U. Med. Coll., N.Y., 1910-17; asso. prof. medicine, 1919-30, prof. medicine, 1930-41, prof. physiology, 1941-50, emeritus prof., 1950—; med. dir. Russell Sage Inst. Pathologh, 1913-50; dir., vis. physician Second Med. Div. of Bellevue Hosp., 1919-32; cons. physician, 1932—; physician-in-chief N.Y. Hosp., 1932-41. Chmn. com. on aviation medicine NRC, 1940-45. Lt., lt. comdr. Med. Corps, USNRF, 1917-18; capt. 1927; during war had charge of investigations dealing with aviation, gas warfare and submarine ventilation. Served as capt. M.C., USNR. 1942-45, Bur. Medicine and Surgery, USN. Decorated Navy Cross. Mem. Assn. Am. Physicians, Am. Assn. Clin. Investigation, Am. Physiol. Soc., Nat. Acad. Scis. Democrat. Episcopalian. Club: Century Assn. Author: Basal Metabolism in Health and Disease, 1924, 27, 36; The Mechanism of Heat Loss and Temperature Regulation. Compiler of Harvard University Songs, 1902. Research in metabolism. Home: 1215 Park Av., N.Y.C. 28. Died Feb. 1959.

DUBOIS, JULES newspaper corr., author; b. N.Y. C., Mar. 31, 1910; s. Paul and Edith (Gordon) D.; student U. Panama, 1939-40; m. Maria Luella de la Guardia, Jan. 22, 1937; children-Lucille Isabel, Jules Edward, Victor Allen, Mary Helen, Reporter, N.Y. Herald Tribune, 1927-29, The Panama Am., 1929-30, 31, The Star and Herald, Panama, 1930-31; sports editor, spl. editions editor, local advt. mgr. The Star and Herald, 1931-40; editor Panama Times, 1931-32; corr. Universal Service, 1930-31; stringer NBC, 1939-40; editor, pub. Panama Free Press-Prensa Libre, 1940; asst. to pres., pub. The Star and Herald, 1946-47; Latin Am. corr. Chgo. Tribune, 1947—. Dept. pres. C.Z. Res. Officers Assn., 1938-39; served to col. AUS, 1940-46. Decorated Medal of Merit; Order Cruzeiro do Sul (Brazil); Mil. Order Ayacucho (Peru); Order Vasco Nunez de Balboa (Panama); Order Sanchez Mellay Duarte (Dominican Republic); medal, Hero of Freedom of Press and Tom Wallace award Inter Am. Press Assn., 1962; citation William Allen White Nat. Found., 1960; Maria Moors Cabot award Columbia, 1952; Medal Journalist Merit, Guayaquil, Ecuador, 1964; diploma of honor Press Circle Uruguay, 1955; Edward Scott Beck award Chgo. Tribune, 1947, 59. Mem. Am. Acad. Polit. Sci., Inter Am. Press Assn. (sec. 1950-51), Com. Freedom of the Press (bd. dirs., exec. com.; chmn. com. freedom press 1950.—). Authors League Am., Sigma Delta Chi. Republican. Roman Catholic. Clubs: Nat. Press (Washington); Overseas Press (N.Y.C.); Country of Coral Gables; Union (Panama). Home: 423 Palermo Av., Coral Gables, Fla. 33134. Office Chgo. Tribune, Chgo. 60611. Died Aug. 16, 1966.

DUBORD, RICHARD JOSEPH, lawyer, Democratic nat. committeeman; b. Waterville, Me., Nov. 17, 1921; s. F. Harold and Blanche (Letourneau) D.; B.S. cum laude, Holy Cross Coll., 1943; LL.B., cum laude, Boston U., 1948; m. Evelyn P. Parnell, Sept. 4, 1943; children—Stephen F., William P., Susan P. Admitted to Me. bar, 1948, practiced in Waterville as partner Marden, Dubord, Bernier & Chandler; atty. gen. State Me. Mayor, City of Waterville, 1952-56; mem. Dem. Nat. Com. Served as capt. USAAF, 1942-46. Mem. Am., Me., Kennebec Co. (pres.) Waterville (pres. 1953) bar assns., Am. Legion, Vets. Fgn. Wars. Club: Kiwanis, Elks. Home: Waterville ME Died Jan. 1970.

DU BOSE, DUDLEY MCIVER congressman, lawyer; b. Shelby County, Tenn., Oct. 38, 1834; attended U. Miss. at Oxford: grad. Lebanon (Tenn.) Law Sch., 1856. Admitted to bar, 1857, began practice of law, Memphis, Tenn. moved to Augusta, Ga., 1860; served as col. 15th Regt., Ga. Volunteer Inf., Confederate Army, during Civil War, promoted brig. gen. Western Army; moved to Washington, Ga.; mem. U.S. Ho. of Reps. (Democrat) from Ga., 42d Congress, 1871-73. Died Washington, Ga., Mar. 2, 1883; buried Rest Haven Cemetery.

DU BOSE, WILLIAM RICHARDS naval officer; b. Sparta, Ga., Sept. 12, 1854; s. Charles Wildes and Catharine Ann (Richards) D.; U. of Ga., class of 1873; M.D., U. of Va., 1875; m. Katie Bibb, of Charlottesville, Va., Oct. 26, 1875. Commd. asst. surgeon, U.S.N., Oct. 16, 1875; passed asst. surgeon, 1878; surgeon, 1891; med. insp., 1903; med. dir., Mar. 5, 1910; retired, 1918, rank of commodore. Surgeon on board U.S.S. Texas, Spanish-Am. War, 1898; asst. Bur. of Medicine and Surgery, Navy Dept., Washington, 1903-06. Mem. A.M.A., Sigma Alpha Epsilon. Presbyn. Clubs: Army and Navy, Chevy Chase. Home: 1850 Kalorama Rd., Washington, D.C.

DU COUDRAY, PHILIPPE CHARLES JEAN TRONSON army officer; b. Rheims, France, Sept. 8, 1738. An army engr., adj. gen. of arty.; volunteered service in Am. Revolution; promised rank of maj. gen. by Benjamin Franklin, but named insp. gen. instead (compromise to allay jealousy of colonial leaders); placed in charge of fortifications along Delaware River. Drowned nr. Phila. after 4 months of service, Sept. 11, 1777.

DUDLEY, EDGAR SWARTWOUT brigadier-general U.S.A.; b. Oppenheim, N.Y., June 14, 1845; s. James Madison and Maria (Swartwout) D.; grad. U.S. Mil. Acad., 1870; LL.B., Albany Law Sch. (Union U.), 1875; (LL.D., U. of Neb., 1904-; m. Mary S. Hillabrandt, Sammonsville, N.Y., June 22, 1870. Lt. 1st N.Y. Light Arty., May May 28-Nov. 28, 1864; 2d lt. 2d U.S. Arty., June 15, 1870; 1st lt., Oct. 29, 1875; capt. asst. q.m., Dec. 20, 1892; maj. judge advocate, Feb. 2, 1901; lt.-col. judge advocate, May 24, 1901; col. judge advocate, Nov. 22, 1903; brig.-gen., retired at age limit, June 14, 1909. Prof. mil. science and tactics, U. of Neb., 1876-79 and 1884-88; maj. and lt.-col. U.S. vols., judge advocate, Div. of Cuba, and legal adviser in civ. and mil. affairs, of mil. govs. of Cuba (Gens. John R. Brook and Leonard Wood), Dec., 1898-May 21, 1901; prof. law, U.S. Mil. Acad., July 31, 1901, until retirement. Pres. Alumni Assn. Albany Law Sch., 1909-10; mem. Am. Soc. Internat. Law, Nat. Geog. Soc., Johnstown (N.Y.) Hist. Soc. (a founder), N.Y. State Hist. Soc., Soc. Colonial Wars, S.A.R., Soc. War 1812, Loyal Legion, Soc. Army of Potomac, Naval and Mil. Order Spanish-Am. War. Mason (33ff); past grand comdr. K.T., Neb.; hon. mem. Supreme Council of Colon, and Masonic Vet. Assn., Cuba; etc. Clubs; Union League, Army and Navy (New York), Army, Ft. Monroe (Va.), Ft. Thomas (Ky.), Ft. Leavenworth (Kan.), West Point (N.Y.), Colonial (Johnstown, N.Y.). Author: Military Law and the Procedure of Courts-Martial, 1907. Address: 101 S. Melcher St., Johnstown, N.Y. Died 1911.

DUDLEY, NATHAN AUGUSTUS MONROE brig. gen.; b. Lexington, Mass., Aug. 20, 1825; s. John and Ester Eliza (Smith) D.; ed. pub. schs. of Roxbury, Mass.; m. Elizabeth Gray Jewett (dec.). Was engaged in commercial pursuits until 1855; served 6 yrs. in Mass. Militia and was mem. Ancient and Hon. Artillery Co. of Boston, 1851-55, and served 3 yrs. as brigade and div. inspr. of Boston Troops. Apptd. from civ. life as 1st lt. 10th U.S. Inf., Mar. 3, 1855; promoted through grades to col. 1st Cav., June 6, 1885; retired by operation of law, Aug. 20, 1889; advanced to rank of brig. gen. retired, by act of April. 23, 1904. In Civ. War served as col. 30th Mass. Inf., Mar. 1, 1862-Feb. 16, 1865, when was hon. mustered out of vol. service. Received bvts. of maj., lt. col. and col. U.S.A. for gallant services in Civ. War, and bvtd. brig. gen. Vols., Jan. 18, 1865. Was insp. gen. Dept. of the Gulf, or chief of staff to Gen. Banks; spent 30 yrs. in campaigning against Indians on frontier, before and after Civ. War, until retired - with Harney on Sioux expdn., 1855, with Albert Sidney Johnston on Utah expdn., 1857-60; with Crook against Apaches, and comd. cav. on Buell expdn. into Mexico (cooperating with Mexican forces in killing of Victorio and capture of his band). Home: Roxbury, Mass. Died 1910.

DUDLEY, WILLIAM WADE lawyer; b. Weathersfield Bow, Vt., Aug. 27, 1842; ed. Phillip's Acad., Danville, Vt., and Russell's Collegiate Inst., 1860; engaged in milling business; became capt. City Grays there; co. enlisted July 4, 1861; mustered into U.S. service, July 29, 1861, in 19th Ind. vols.; served with distinction and became col. and bvt. brig. gen., taking part in 15 battles; wounded at Gettysburg, losing right leg; afterward served as insp. and judge adv.to close of war; m. Theresa, d. Rev. George Fiske, Richmond, Ind., 1864; m. 2d, Nannie R. Finch, 1899. Clerk of courts, Wayne Co., Ind., 1866-74; admitted to bar; cashier Richmond Savings Bank, 1875-79; U.S. marshal, dist. of Ind., 1879-81; U.S. commr. of pensions, 1881-85, in business, 1885-87; mem. law firm, 1887; became treas. Nat. Rep. Com., 1888; from 1889 in law practice at Washington. Home: Washington, D.C. Died 1909.

DUER, WILLIAM Continental congressman: b. Devonshire, Eng., Mar. 18, 1747; s. John and Frances (Frye) D.; ed. Eton Coll.; m. Catherine Alexander, 1779; 2 children-William Alexander, John. Commd. ensign Brit. Army; aide-de-camp to Lord Clive, 1762, accompanied Clive to India, 1764; came to N.Y., 1768; cotton mfr., N.Y. and N.J., prior to Am. Revolution; del. to N.Y. Provincial Congress, 1775; col., dep. adj. gen. N.Y. Militia; del. to N.Y. Constl. Conv., 1776, mem. com. to draft constn.; mem. N.Y. Com. of Public Safety, 1776; del. from N.Y. to Continental Congress, 1777-79, mem. bd. of war; 1st judge common please Charlotte (now Washington) County (N.Y.), 1777-86; signer Articles of Confederation; instrumental in causing failure of Conway Cabal's plan to remove Washington from command; chmn. commn. for conspiracies (established by Congress), 1780; a founder Bank of N.Y., 1784; sec. to Bd. of Treasury under Articles of Confedn., N.Y.C., 1786; mem. N.Y. Assembly, 1786; asst. sec. U.S. Dept. of Treasury (founded 1789), 1789; became involved in land and other specualtions, imprisoned for debt, 1792. Died in prison, N.Y.C., May 7, 1799; buried Jamaica, L.I., N.Y.

DUFF, EDWARD ALOYSIUS clergyman; b. Philadelphia, Pa., Jan. 5, 1885; s. Patrick James and Mary Eleanore (Bergen) D.; student St. Charles Coll., Md., 1901-03, St. Charles Seminary, Overbrook, Pa., 1904-06; A.B., St. Mary's Seminary, Baltimore, also A.M. and S.T.B. Ordained priesthood Catholic Ch., 1911; sec. to bishop, Cathedral St. John the Baptist, Charleston, S.C., 1911-13; chaplain Charleston New Yard, 1911-13; appt. chaplain U.S. Navy 1915 and has served on ships at sea, Navy Headquarters, London, Graves Registration Unit, Paris, Navy Yards at Philadelphia, New York, U.S. Marine Base, Paris Island, Bureau of Navigation; commd. Capt., U.S. Navy; appt. chief of Chaplain Corps; retired Sept. 1, 1938. Served on staff of Admiral Sims, comdr. U.S. Naval forces in European Waters, World War. Decorated Chevalier of the Crown of Italy. Accompanied body of Unknown Soldier from France to U.S. Clubs: Army and Navy, Army and Navy Country. Lecturer. Home: 3200 16th St. N.W., Washington, D.C. Died Feb. 11, 1943.

DUFFIELD, GEORGE clergyman; b. Lancaster County, Pa., Oct. 7, 1732; s. George and Margaret Duffield; grad. Coll. of N.J. (now Princeton), 1752; m. Elizabeth Blair, Mar. 8, 1756; m. 2d, Margaret Armstrong, Mar. 5, 1759; at least 1 son George. Tutor, Coll. of N.J., 1754-56; licensed to preach, 1756; pastor Presbyn. Ch., Carlisle, Pa., 1757-72, 3d Presbyn. Ch., Phila., 1772-90; ordained to ministry Presbyn. Ch., 1759; capt. local militia; strong patriot, commd. chaplain Pa. Militia, co-chaplain Continental Congress trustee Coll. of N.J., 1777-90; clk. Pa. Gen. Assembly. Author: A Sermon Preached in the Third Presbyterian Church in the City of Philadelphia on Thursday, Dec. 11, 1783, published 1784. Died Feb. 2, 1790.

DUFFIELD, HENRY MARTYN lawyer; b. Detroit, May 15, 1842; s. Rev. George and Isabella Graham (Bethune) D.; A.B., Williams Coll., 1861; m. Frances Pitts, Dec. 29, 1863 (died 1906); father of Pitts D. Enlisted as pvt. 9th Mich. Inf., Aug., 1861; 1st lt. and adj., Oct. 12, 1861-Oct. 14, 1864; asst. adj.-gen. 23d Brigade, Army of the Cumberland, 1862; post adj., Chattanooga, 1863; asst. and acting provost marshal gen. Army of the Cumberland. Admitted to bar, 1865; became sr. mem. H. M. & D. B. Duffield; city counsellor, 1881-87. Brig. gen. vols., May 27, 1898; hon. disch., Nov. 30, 1898. Umpire German-Venezuelan Arbitration Commn., 1903. Comdr. in chief Naval and Mil. Order of Spanish-Am. War, 1910-11. Home: Detroit, Mich. Died July 13, 1912.

DUFFY, FRANCIS PATRICK clergyman; b. Cobourg, Ont., Can., May 2, 1871; s. Patrick and Mary (Ready) D.; grad. St. Michael's Coll., Toronto, Can., 1893; M.D., St. Francis Xavier's Coll., N.Y.C., S.T.B., Catholic U., Washington, D.C., 1898. Entered St. Joseph's Sem., Troy, N.Y., 1894; ordained priest Roman Catholic Ch., 1896; became U.S. citizen 1902; prof. philosophy and moral theology St. Joseph's Sem., Dunwoodie, until 1912; pastor Our Savior parish, Bronx, N.Y., 1912; served as chaplain Fighting 69th Regt., N.Y. N.G., accompanied regt. to Mexican border, 1916; became chaplain 165th Regt., AEF, at outbreak World War I, went to Europe with regt., 1917; earned nicknames "Iron lMan" and "Front Line" Duffy during war; decorated D.S.C., D.S.M., Cross of Legion of Honor, Croix de Guerre with palm, badge of Canadian War Vets; returned to N.Y. after war; pres. Cath. Summer Sch., Cliff Haven; pastor Holy Cross parish, N.Y.C., 1920-32. Author: Father Duffy's Story, a Tale of Humor and Heroism, of Life and Death with the Fighting Sixty-Ninth, 1919. Died June 26, 1932.

DUFOUR, WILLIAM CYPRIEN, lawyer; b. New Orleans, Oct. 31, 1871; s. Elmore and Blanche (Generes) D.; ed. Tulane High Sch., New Orleans; m. Helen McLeary, Sept. 1, 1898; children—Helen, Elmore. Admitted to bar, 1892, since in practice, New Orleans; mem. Dufour, St. Paul & Levy. Mem. La. Ho. of Rep., 1896; counsel for Bd. Liquidation, New Orleans since 1905; v. chmn. Spanish-Am. War Claims Commn. of La. since 1908; mem. Inter-Am. High Commn.; counsel Bd. of Assessors, New Orleans; gen. counsel La. Flood Com. Lt. col. 2d La. Vol. Inf. Spanish-Am. War, 1898. V.p., gen. counsel Federal Land Bank of New Orleans, 1917-18. Dir. Marquette U. Democrat. Catholic. Clubs: Boston, Pickwick (New Orleans); Metropolitan, Chevy Chase (Washington, D.C.). Office: Canal Bldg., New Orleans LA

DUGAN, THOMAS BUCHANAN army officer; b. Baltimore, Md., July 27, 1858; s. Cumberland and Hariet (Buchanan) D.; grad. U.S. Mil. Acad., 1882, Army War Coll., 1913; m. Geraldine, d. Gen. Henry W. Wessells, U.S.A., Nov. 24, 1897; children - Cumberland, Thomas B., Eliza Lane. Commd. additional 2d lt. 10th Cav., June 13, 1882; 2d lt., June 26, 1882; promoted through grades to col., Dec. 9, 1915; commanding co. Apache Indian Scouts, 1884-85; brig. gen. N.A., Aug. 5, 1917; retired July 27, 1922; brig. gen. regular army, by spl. act of Congress, Feb. 28, 1927. Served in army posts in Ariz., N.M., Tex., Okla., Mo., to 1898; participated in campaign against Santiago, Cuba, 1898; Battle of San Juan, July 1-3, 1898, and siege of Santiago; in Cuba, 1901, P.I., 1905 and 1916. Comd. brigades in 86th, 85th, 35th and 5th divs., World War; comd. Brigade and Field Officers Sch., Dec. 1917-May 1918; comd. 35th Div., Dec. 1918-Mar. 1919; in Europe, July 1918-July 1919, and was 1st Army in Meuse-Argonne offensive and with 2d Army and Army of Occupation. Campaign badges: Indian wars, Spanish-Am. War, Silver Star Citation, Cuban Occupation, Mexican Border; D.S.M.; Victory Badge with 3 clasps. Catholic. Died Apr. 27, 1940.

DUGANNE, AUGUSTINE JOSEPH HICKEY author; b. Boston, 1823; married. Became newspaper writer; moved to Phila., circa 1845, N.Y.C., 1850; mem. N.Y. Assembly; (Know-Nothing Party) from 6th Dist., 1855-56; helped raise 176th N.Y. Volunteers, commd. lt. col., 1862; imprisoned by Confederates, 1863-64. Author: Home Poems, 1844; Parnassus in Pillory, 1851; Art's True Mission in America, 1853; Poetical Works, 1856; Camps and Prions..., 1865. Died N.Y.C., Oct. 20, 1884; buried Cypress Hills Cemetery, N.Y.

DUGGAN, WALTER TEELING brig. gen.; b. Isle of Man, Apr. 11, 1843. Served as pvt. Co. B, 5th Wis. Inf., June 13, 1861-Aug. 31, 1863; hosp. steward U.S.A., Sept. 7, 1863-Mar. 23, 1867; commd. 2d lt. 10th Inf., Jan. 3, 1867; 1st lt., Nov. 13, 1874; capt., Aug. 1, 1886; maj., Mar. 2, 1899; lt. col., Mar. 2, 1901; col. 24th Inf., Oct. 3, 1902; transferred to 1st Inf., Oct. 18, 1902; brig. gen., June 26, 1906; retired by operation of law, Apr. 11, 1907. Died Jan. 2, 1915.

DUKE, JAMES THOMAS, army officer; b. California, Md., June 10, 1893; s. John and Lilly (Jarboe) D.; B.S., U. of Md., 1916; grad. Cav. Sch. 1923, Equitation Course, 1924, Ecole d'Application de Cavalrie, Saumur, France, 1928, Command and Gen. Staff Sch., 1934, Chem. Warfare Sch., 1934, Army Indsl. Coll., 1940; m. Lupe O'Neill, May 15, 1919; children—James Thomas, Mary Dolores, Ralph Leonard. Commd. 2d lt., Cav., U.S. Army, 1917, and advanced through the grades to brig. gen., 1943; instr. of equitation, U.S. Cav. Sch., Fort Riley, 1924-27, 1928-32; gen. staff, 1st Cav., Ft. Bliss, Tex., 1937-39; exec. officer, Office Chief of Cav., Washington, D.C., 1941-42; gen. staff, Army Ground Forces, Army War Coll., 1942; comdg. gen., Charleston Port of Embarkation, Charleston, S.C., 1942-50; comdg. officer Ft. Myer, 1950-53; ret. 1953. Decorated D.S.M., Victory, Mexican Service, Mexican Border Service, Am. Defense Service medals. Mem. advisory com. Community Development Council, Charleston, S.C. Mem. Am. Legion, Am. Horse Show Assn., Kappa Alpha Southern. Clubs: Propeller; Army and Navy (Washington, D.C.). Author: U.S. Cavalry R.O.T.C. Manual, 1940, 1941. Mem. U.S. Olympic Equestrian Squad, 1932; U.S. Cav. rep. for equestrian events, inter-Am. Fedn. of Sports, and Olympic Games, 1941-42, Capt., Ft. Myer Horse Show Team, 1932; mem. Ft. Riley Horse Show Team, 1924-27, 1928-32. Participated in engagement with Mexicans, Nogales, Ariz., Aug. 1918. Home: Morganza MD Died Dec. 9, 1970; buried Arlington Nat. Cemetery, Washington DC

DUKE, WILLIAM WADDELL physician; b. Lexington, Mo., Oct. 18, 1882; s. Henry Buford and Susie (Waddell) D.; Ph.B., Yale, 1904; M.D., Johns Hopkins, 1908; grad. study, Mass. Gen. Hosp., Boston, 1909-10, U. of Vienna, 1910-12, U. of Berlin, m. Frances Thomas, May 18, 1920; children-Henry Basil, Frances Suzanne. Practicing physician in Kansas City, Mo., since 1912, limiting practice to internal medicine; prof. exptl. medicine U. of Kan. Sch. of Medicine, Rosedale, 1914-18; visiting physician Christian Ch. Hosp., Kansas City, 1918-24. Mem. Council of Nat.

Defense and capt. in Am. Red Cross, World War; lt. col. O.R.C. since World War, Fellow A.M.A.; mem. Am. Coll. Physicians. Awarded silver medal, 1924, by A.M.A. for research in allergy; annual gold medal, 1941, by the Midwest Forum of Allergy for "distinguished and outstanding contributions in the field of allergy." Episcopalian, Mason (K.T., Shriner). Clubs: Kansas City, University, Kansas City Country. Author: Oralsepsis in Relationship to Systemic Disease, 1918: Allergy, Asthma, Hay Fever, Urticaria and Allied Manifestations of Reaction, 1925; also chapters in Practitioners' Library of Medicine and Surgery, Cyclo. of Medicine, Modern Home Med. Adviser. Contbr. tech. articles. Discoverer in field of allergy and physical allergy, oral sepsis, transfusion and anemia, palm color test, bleeding time, relation between platelets and hemorrhagic disease; co-discoverer physiology of heart beat in relationship to the potassium and calcium content of the blood; also made pollen surveys. Home: 1220 W. 62nd St. Office: Professional Bldg., Kansas City, Mo. Died Apr. 10, 1946.

DULING, G(LEN) HAROLD found. exec.; b. Eskridge, Kan., Mar. 27, 1909; s. Edmund M. and Alice (Siddens) D.; A.B., Baker U., 1931; B.D., Garrett Bibl. Inst., 1934; LL.D. Ind. Central Coll., 1958; m. Kathryn Ann Quigg, Aug. 15, 1942. Ordained to ministry Methodist Ch., 1933; pastor Minn. Conf., 1936-41; mem. pub. relations dept. Eli Lilly and Co., Indpls., 1946-50; with Lilly Endowment, Inc. Indpls., 1950—, exec. dir., 1956-61, dir. for religion, 1961—. Bd. dirs. Community Service Council Met. Indpls. 1950-58, chmn. nominating com., 1961-62, reorgn. com., 1961; bd. dirs. Fletcher Pl. Community Center, Indpls.; treas., dir. Concord Center, Indpls.; trustee Found. Library Center. Mem. bus. and finance com. div. Christian edn. Nat. Council Chs.; mem. Ind. Commn. Aging and Aged, 1955-59. Served to maj. Chaplains Corps, AUS, 1941-45; ETO. Decorated Field Citation with 2 oak leaf clusters. Mem. Soc. Sci. Study Religion, Religious Research Assos., Yoke-fellow Assos., Zeta Chi. Mem. Soc. Friends. Clubs: Rotary, Columbia (Indpls.). Contbr. charitable found. jours. Home: 237 E. Westfield Blvd., Indpls. 20. Office: Mchts. Bank Bldg., Indpls. 4. Died Mar. 30, 1964; buried Earlham Cemetery, Richmond Ind.

DULLES, JOHN FOSTER Sec. of State; b. Washington, Feb. 25, 1888; s. Allen Macy and Edity (Foster) D.; B.A., Princeton U., 1908, LL.D., 1946; Sorbonne, Paris, 1908-09; LL.B., George Washington Univ., 1911; LL.D., Tufts, 1939, Wagner College, Northwestern U., 1947, Union Coll., 1948, U. of Pa., 1949, Lafayette, 1949, Amherst, Seoul Nat. U., 1950, U. Ariz., St. Josephs Coll., 1951, St. Lawrence U., Johns Hopkins U., Fordham U., Harvard, 1952. Columbia University, 1954, Georgetown U., 1954, U. S.C., 1955, Ind. U., 1955, Ia. State U., 1956; m. Janet Pomeroy Avery. June 26, 1912; children-John Watson Foster, Lillias Pomeroy (Mrs. Robert Hinshaw), Avery. Began practice, N.Y. City, 1911; mem. Sullivan & Cromwell, 1911-49; past trustee Bank N.Y. Chmn. Rockefeller Found., Carnegie Endowment for Internat. Peace, Gen. Edn. Bd. Past mem. N.Y. State Banking Bd. Past trustee Union Theol. Sem., N.Y. PUb. Library, Secretary of The Hague Peace Conference, 1907; member of the 2d Pan-Am. Scientific Congress, special agent Department of State, in Central America, 1917; captain and major U.S. Army, 1917-18; asst. to Chairman War Trade Bd., 1918; counsel to Am. Commn. to Negotiate Peace, 1918-19; mem. Reparations Commn. and Supreme Econ. Council, 1919; legal adviser. Polish plan of financial stabilization, 1927. American rep. Berlin debt conferences, 1933. Mem. U.S. del. San Francisco Conf. on World Orgn., 1945, United Nations Gen. Assembly, 1946, 47, 50; acting chmn. U.S. delegation U.N. Gen. Assembly, Paris, 1948; adviser to Sec. of State at council of Fgn. Ministers, London, 1945, 1947, Moscow, 1947, Paris, 1949. Apptd. interim United States senator, 1949; consultant to Secretary of State, 1950; spl. rep. of President, with rank of ambassador, negotiated Japanese Peace Treaty, 1951, and Australian, New Zealand, Philippine and Japanese Security Treaties, 1950-51; apptd. Sec. of State, 1952. Member National Aeronautics and Space Administration; U.S. del. 13th UN general assembly. Member Association Bar City of New York, Phi Beta Kappa, Phi Delta Phi. Presybterian. Clubs: University, Down Town Assn., Century (N.Y.): Metropolitan (Washington). Author: War, Peace and Change, 1939; War or Peace, 1950. Writer and speaker on internat. affairs. Home: 610 Park Av., N.Y.C.; also 2740 32d St., N.W., Washington. Office: Secretary of State, Washington. Died May 24, 1959; buried Arlington Nat. Cemetery.

DUMAS, WALTER A(LEXANDER) army officer; born Sherman, Tex., Nov. 25, 1893; s. DeBerry Glenn and Bessie Holland (Leecraft) D.; B.S., Davidson (N.C.) Coll., 1915, M.A., 1916; Ga. Sch. Tech., summer, 1914; Med. Dept., Texas U., 1916-17; grad. Inf. Sch., 1923; Comd. and Gen. Staff Sch., 1933; Chem. Warfare Sch. and Army War Coll., 1936; m. Josephine Lawson. May 12, 1921; children-Joy Lawson (Mrs. John Bispham Walter Arthur. Served with Siberian A.E.F., 1919-20, P.I., 1920-22; instr. Inf. Sch., Ft. Benning, Ga., 1923-27, 1940-41, Tactics Dept., U.S. Mill. Acad., 1927-31; gen. staff 9th Corps Area, Fourth Army and Western Defense Comd., 1936-40, 1941-42; comdr. 317th Inf.; comdr. Tank Destroyer Replacement Training Center, 1942-43; with gen. staff, overseas, 1943; promoted through the grades from 2d lt., 1917, to brigadier general, 1943; plans and operations officer (G-3) U.S.A.F., So. Pacific, 1943-44; 10th Army, 1944-45; G-3 sect. gen. staff Far East Comd. (Gen. lMacArthur), 1945-47. Retired Oct. 1947 for phys. disability. World War II campaigns; No. Solomons, Ryukus (Okinawa) and others. Mem. S.A.R., Pi Kappa Alpha, Sigma Upsilon, Phi Chi. Mason (32ff K.T., Shriner Nat. Sojourners). Decorations; Distinguished Service Medal, Legion of Merit (U.S. Army, U.S. Navy). Home: 3340 Santiago St., S.F. 16. Died Sept. 11, 1952; buried Arlington Nat. Cemetery

DUMONT, EBENEZER, congressman, lawyer; b. Vevay, Ind., Nov. 23, 1814; studied law. Admitted to bar, began practice of law, Vevay; mem. Ind. Ho. of Reps., 1838; Democratic presdl. elector, 1852; served as col. 7th Regt., Ind. Volunteer Inf., during Civil War, promoted brig. gen. U.S. Ho. of Reps. (Unionist) from Ind., 38th-39th congresses, 1863-67; apptd. gov. Ida. Territory by Pres. Grant, died before taking office. Died Indpls., Ind., Apr. 16, 1871; buried Crown Hill Cemetery.

DUNBAR, ARTHUR WHITE, naval officer; b. Sept. 7, 1869. Entered U.S. Navy, Oct. 25, 1894; promoted through grades to rear adm., Dec. 7, 1926; retired Dec. 1, 1934. Address: 3229 Klingle Rd. N.W., Washington, D.C. Home: Westchester Apartments, 4000 Cathedral Av. N.W., Washington 16 DC*

DUNCAN JAMES HENRY congressman, lawyer; b. Haverhill, Mass., Dec. 5, 1793; attended Phillips Exeter Acad.; grad. Harvard, 1812; studied law. Admitted to bar, 1815, began practice of law, Haverhill; served to rank of col. in militia; pres. Essex Agrl. Soc.; mem. Mass. Ho. of Reps., 1827, 37, 38, 57, Mass. Senate, 1828-31; del. Whig Nat. Conv., Harrisburg, Pa., 1839; apptd. commr. in bankruptcy, 1841; mem. U.S. Ho. of Reps. (Whig) from Mass., 31st-32d congresses, 1849-53; engaged in real estate bus. Died Haverhill, Feb. 8, 1869; buried Linwood Cemetery.

DUNCAN JOSEPH gov. Ill.; b. Paris, Ky., Feb. 22, 1794; s. Maj. Joseph and Ann Maria (McLaughlin) D.; m. Elizabeth Caldwell Smith, May 13, 1828. Commd. ensign 17th U.S. Infantry, 1812, promoted 2d lt., 1813; moved to Ill., 1818, farmed, expanded his land holdings; served as maj. gen. Ill. Militia, 1821-23, commanded militia troops in Black Hawk War, 1831; mem. Ill. Senate (Democrat) from Jackson County, 1824-26; mem. U.S. Ho. of Reps. from Ill., 20th-23d congresses, 1827-34; gov. Ill., 1834-38. Died Jacksonville, Ill., Jan. 15, 1844; buried Diamond Grove Cemetery, Jacksonville.

DUNCAN, GEORGE BRAND army officer; b. at Lexington, Ky., Oct. 10, 1861; s. late Henry T. and Lily (Brand) D.; grad. U.S. Mil. Acad., 1886; Army War Col., 1912; m. Mary Kercheval, Oct. 23, 1895. Commd. 2d lt. 9th Inf., July 1, 1886; promoted through grades to brig. gen. N.A., 1917; maj. gen., 1918; brigadier gen. U.S. Army, 1920; promoted maj. gen. U.S. Army, Dec. 6, 1922; retired Oct. 10, 1925. Staff Major Gen. John M. Schofield, 1892-94; adjt. 4th Inf., 1894-98; adjt. gen. provisional div., Santiago, Cuba, July 1898, and provisional div. in P.R. and Dist. of Ponce, Aug.-Oct. 1898; in Philippines, 1899-1902, 1903-09 comdg. batn. Philippine scouts, 1905-09; Gen. Staff, 1914-17; with A.E.F. in France, June 1917-May 1919. Comd. 26th Inf., 1st Div., Sept. 1917-May 1918; first Am. gen. officer comdg. a sector on the battle front, north of Toul, Jan. 1918 (brigade in battle north of Montdidier, Apr.-May 1918); comd. 77th Div., May-Aug. 1918, in battle sector at Baccarat and in battle on the Vesle; comd. 82d Div. during Meuse-Argonne offensive, Oct. 1918 and until demobilization, May 1919; comdg. 7th Crops Area, Omaha, 1922-25. Awarded Croix de Guerre, Comdr. Legion of Honor (French) Companion of the Bath (British); D.S.M. (U.S.). Episcopalian. Clubs: Army and Navy (Washington, D.C.). Home: Lexington, Ky. Died Mar. 15, 1950.

DUNCAN, GREER ASSHETON civil engr.; b. Alexandria, La., Mar. 31, 1887; s. Herman Cope and Maria Elizabeth (Cooke) D.; B.C.E., U. of South, 1911; B.S., U.S. Naval Acad., 1908; C.E., Rensselaer Poly. Inst., 1912; m. Marie Louise Chauvin, June 17, 1911; children-Marie Louise (wife of Capt. Robert F. Jones), Greer Asheton, Jr. (lt. comdr., U.S., Navy). Line officer on cruisers, torpedo boats and battleships, U.S. Navy, 1908-10; mem. Civil Engr. Corps, U.S. Navy, 1911—, advancing through the ranks from ensign to captain; pub. works officer Navy Yard, Mare Island, Cal., 1938-41; asst. naval attache, spl. naval observer, mem. staff Comdr. of Naval Forces in Europe, 1941-43; pub- works officer, 13th Naval Dist., Seattle, 1943-46, Owner's rep. Constrn., Seattle, 1948; cons. engr., 1947—. Hon. life trustee Rensselaer Poly. Inst. Recipient Sec. of Navy Commendation with bronze star, Comdr. Order of Honor and Merit Republic of Haiti, 1931, Marine Expeditionary Medal, 1908, 09, 31, Cuban Pacification Medal, 1908, Victory Medal, 1917, Def. Medal with Star, European Theatre medal, 1941-43, Am. Theatre medal, 1946; World War Victory medal, 1941-46, Mem. Rensselaer Soc. Engr., Soc. Am. Mil. Engrs., Soc. Naval Architects and Marine Engrs., Kappa Sigma. Episcopalian. Mason. (R.A.M., R.&S.M., K.T.). Home: Alexandria, La.; also 3218 Esplanade Dr., Seattle 7. Office: care Bureau of Yards and Docks, Navy Dept., Washington 25. Died June 26, 1962.

DUNCAN, JAMES congressman; b. Phila., 1756; attended Princeton. Served as 1st prothonotary Adams County; commd. lt. in Col. Hazen's Regt., Revolutionary War, 1776, promoted capt., 1778; elected mem. U.S. Ho. of Reps. from Pa., 17th Congress, resigned before Congress assembled. Died Mercer County, Pa., June 24, 1844.

DUNCAN, JOSEPH army officer; b. in tent in army camp on . bank Nueces River, Tex., June 29, 1853; s. Gen. Thomas (U.S.A.) and Mary Shields (Wilson) D.; ed. prep. sch., Griswold (Ia.) Coll., pub. schs., Nashville, Tenn., and Columbian Coll. (now George Washington U.); m. Catherine Amelia Keefer, Oct. 10, 1878. With Prof. F. V. Hayden on geol. survey of the Yellowstone, 1871, and latter part of same yr. was on cattle range in W. Neb.; commd. 2d lt. 21st Inf., Oct. 1, 1873; 1st lt., May 10, 1878; capt., Apr. 24, 1888; maj. 18th Inf., Mar. 2, 1899; lt. col., Oct. 16, 1901; col. 6th Inf., Aug. 9, 1903. Promoted brig. gen. U.S. Army, Jan. 4, 1911. Participated in Indian Wars (including Nez Perce, 1877, Bannock, 1878, Sioux, 1890-91) and numerous expdns. on the plains and mountains for 20 yrs.; took part in battle of San Juan Hill, and siege of Santiago de Cuba, to surrender, Spanish-Am. War; in P.I., 1899-1902, 1905-06; organized expdn. and commanded forces engaged in battle of Bud Dajo, Jolo ("battle of the Lava Cone"). with moros, Mar. 5-8, 1906, 25 per cent of his command having been killed or wounded; detailed on gen. staff, Aug. 15, 1907 - . Bvtd. 1st lt. "for gallantry in battle of Clearwater, Ida., July 11-12, 1877, Nez Perce Indian War"; recommended for maj., by bvt., "for gallantry in front of Santiago de Cuba, July 1, 1898"; recommended by comdg. gen. P.I. Div. for promotion to brig. gen. "for conduct of affairs in three days' battle against Moros." Comdg. Dept. of Texas, Jan. 1911 - . Presbyn. Home: Washington, D.C. Died May 14, 1912.

DUNGAN, PAUL BAXTER naval officer; b. Hastings, Neb., July 21, 1877; s. William Witherspoon and Isabella (Woods) D.; grad. U.S. Naval Acad., 1899; m. Mabel Miller, June 3, 1903; 1 dau., Catharine. Commd. ensign U.S. Navy, Feb. 1901; promoted through grades to rear admiral, Nov. 13, 1933; assigned to engring. duty, Aug. 1917; participated in Spanish-Am. War, Battle of Santiago, Philippine Insurrection, Boxer Campaign in China and World War. Mem. Soc. Naval Engrs., Naval Inst. Congregationist. Home: Hastings, Neb. Died Nov. 27, 1941.

DUNHAM, FREDERIC G(IBBONS) lawyer; b. Buffalo, N.Y., Mar. 22, 1878; s. John C. and Abby Louise (Gibbons) D.: A.B., Cornell U., 1902; LL.B., A.M., Columbia, 1905; m. Caroline L. Allen, Apr. 10, 1909; children-Anna Louise, Elizabeth (Mrs. William M. Aurelius). Admitted to N.Y. bar, 1904; law clk., 1904; mem. Finegan & Dunham, 1905-09; chief Liquidation Bur., N.Y. State Ins. Dept., 1909-16; atty. Assn. of Life Ins. Pres., 1916-27; asst. gen. counsel Metropolitan Life Ins. Co., 1927-36; gen. counsel since 1936. Served as capt. and admiralty claims officer U.S. Army with A.E.F., 1918-19; maj. Judge Advocate Gen. Dept. (Res.), 1920-35. Mem. Am. Bar Assn., Assn. of Bar of City of N.Y., N.Y. County Lawyers Assn. Home: 450 Beverly Rd., Ridgewood, N.J. Office: 1 Madison Av., New York, N.Y. Died Dec. 24, 1943.

DUNHAM, HENRY KENNON physician; b. Fairview, O., Mar. 3, 1872; s. Dr. William Henry and Mary (McPherson) D.; student U. of Cincinnati, 1888 to 1891; Miami Med. Coll., 1891-94; M.D. Univ. of Cincinnati Dept. of Medicine, 1894; post-grad. work Johns Hopkins Hosp. and research work there to demonstrate specific Roentgen markings characteristic of pulmonary tuberculosis; Great Ormond St. Hosp. and St. George's Hosp., London; m. Amelia Hickenlooper, Mar. 14, 1905; children-Harry, Amelia. Assistant in medicine, Miami Medical Coll., 1896-99; prof. electro-therapeutics, U. of Cincinnati Med. Dept., 1904-40; dir. tuberculosis, and asso. prof. of medicine, Medical Coll., U. of Cincinnati, and dir. tuberculosis service of Cincinnati Gen. Hosp. until 1940. Special war work without rank or pay, 1917-18; capt., M.C., U.S. Army, May 1918; maj., Apr. 1919. Ex-pres. Cincinnati Anti-Tuberculosis League. Mem. A.M.A., Am. Roentgen Ray Soc., Cincinnati Acad. Medicine, Am. Coll. Chest Phys., Am. Coll. Tuberculosis Phys., Am. Clinical and Climatological Soc., Nat. Tuberculosis Assn., Ohio State Med. Soc., Ohio Pub. Health Assn., Beta Theta Pi, Nu Sigma Nu. Presbyterian. Clubs: Country, Golf, University, Queen City. Author: Stereo-Roentgenography-Pulmonary Tuberculosis, 1915; also many tech. articles. Home: 3011 Vernon Pl. Office: Union Central Bldg., Cincinnati, O. Died Apr. 27, 1944.

DUNLAP, ANDREW rear adm., U.S.N.; b. Ovid, N.Y., Oct. 7, 1844; s. Andrew and Hannah (Kinne) D.; grad. U.S. Naval Acad., 1867; m. Ellen Grace Derby Adams, Oct. 13, 1875. Midshipman European and Pacific stas., 1867-68; promoted through grades to capt., June 8, 1902; rear adm. and retired at own request after over 43 yrs.' service, June 27, 1905. Served on various sea and shore duties; comd. coast and geodetic steamer Blake, 1896-97; comd. ambulance and hosp. ship Solace during Spanish-Am. War, and Solace afterward as naval transport to W.I. and P.I.; light house insp., 10th Dist., Buffalo, 1900-02; comdt., Naval Sta., San Juan, P.R., 1902-06. Died Apr. 11, 1914.

DUNLAP, JOHN printer; b. Strabane, Ireland, 1747; m. Mrs. Elizabeth (Hayss) Ellison, Feb. 4, 1773. Came to Phila., 1757: apprenticed to uncle William Dunlap as printer, took over shop, 1766; founder weekly The Pa. Packet, 1771, became 1st daily in Am., 1784; founder 1st troop Phila. City Cavalry, 1774, promoted 1st lt., 1781, capt., 1794; printed Declaration of Independence; printer to Continental Congress, 1778; published U.S. Constn. (its 1st publication) in Pa. Packet and Daily Advertiser; mem. Phila. Common Council, 1789-92; maj. in charge of all Pa. Cavalry during suppression of Whisky Rebellion, 1794. Died Nov. 27, 1812; buried Christ Ch., Phila.

DUNLAP, JOHN BETTES banker; b. Dallas, Aug. 22, 1903; s. Frank Bonds and Minnie Fairchild (Bettes) D.; B.S., So. Meth. U., 1925; grad. Command and Gen. Staff Sch., 1943, Army and Navy Staff Coll., 1944; m. John Bullard, Jan. 15, 1926; children-John Bettes, George C. With Internat. Revenue Service, 1933-52, collector 2d Tex. dist., Dallas, 1947-50, agt. charge Tex., 1950-51, commr. internal revenue, Washington, 1951-52; sr. v.p. First Nat. Bank, Dallas, 1953—. Served from maj. to col., AUS, 1940-45; brig. gen. Res. Decorated Legion of Merit; Order Mil. Merit (Mexico). Mem. Am. Petroleum Inst., Ind. Petroleum Assn. Am. (dir.) Mil. Order World Wars, Alpha Kappa Psi. Kappa Alpha. Episcopalian. Clubs: Salesmanship, Lakewood Country, Dallas Athletic Texas, Northshore (Dallas). Home: 4432 McFarlin Blvd., Dallas 5. Office: First Nat. Bank, Dallas. Died Dec. 6, 1944.

DUNN, BEVERLY CHARLES, army officer; b. Fort Monroe, Va., July 16, 1888; s. Beverly Wyly and Stella (Kilshaw) D.; B.A., U.S. Military Acad., 1910, Engr. Sch., U.S. Army, 1911-12, Army Indsl. Coll., 1927-28, Army War Coll., 1937-38; m. Helen Ward Fay, Nov. 22, 1916; children—Beverly Charles, William Wyly. Commd. 2d lt., engring. corps, 1910 and advanced through grades to brig. gen.; served with engr. installations doing flood control and river and harbor improvement work at Rock Island, Illinois, Memphis, Tenn., Pittsburgh, Pa., New Orleans, La., 1st N.Y. District, Seattle, Wash., Jacksonville, Fla. (intercoastal canal from Jacksonville to Miami); Isthmian Canal Commn. in Panama, supt. 13th Lighthouse District; military aide to the President; chief of finance div., Office Chief of Engrs.; dir., procurement branch, office of Asst. Sec. War, mem. Budget Adv. Bd.; troop duty with 1st battalion engrs., Washington Barracks, Washington, D.C., 3rd engrs., Philippines, 10th engrs. (forestry), Washington, D.C., 5th engrs. training regiment and 33d engrs., Ft. Hunphreys, Va., 209th engrs. Camp Sheridan, Ala., 28th engr. regiment (aviation), Marsh Field, Calif., commd. 6th engrs., Ft. Lawton, Wash.; chief engr. Supreme Hdqrs., Allied Expeditionary Force. Decorated D.S.M. with oak leaf cluster; comdr. Order Brit. Empire; Croix de Guerre, Legion d'Honneur (France and Belgium. Mem. Soc. Am. Military Engrs., Am. Soc. Civil Engrs. Clubs: Army and Navy, Chevy Chase (Washington, D.C.); University (N.Y.C.), N.Y. Athletic. Home: New York City NY Died Aug. 14, 1970; buried U.S. Mil. Academy, West Point NY

DUNN, GEORGE M. army officer; b. Madison, Ind., Mar. 20, 1856; s. Brig. Gen. William McKee and Elizabeth (Lanier) D.; LL.B., Columbian (now George Washington) U., Washington, 1880; m. Elizabeth, d. Hon. John Dalzell, of Pittsburgh, Pa., Feb. 14, 1894. Practiced law at Denver, Colo.; commd. maj. 1st U.S. Cav. (vols.), May 9, 1898; hon. mustered out, Sept. 15, 1898; maj. judge advocate, Apr. 17, 1899; vacated Apr. 2, 1901; maj. j.a. U.S.A., Feb. 2, 1901; lt. col., Nov. 22, 1903; col., Feb. 20 lt. col., Nov. ww, 1903; col., Feb. 20, 1913. Served in Cuba, 1899-1902, in Philippines, 1907-09; mil. attache, Italy, 1911-16. Episcopalian. Clubs: Knickerbocker (New York), Metropolitan (Washington). Home: 1745 R.I. Av., Washington, D.C.

DUNN, HERBERT OMAR rear admiral; b. Westerly, R.I., May 29, 1857; s. Edward Maxson and Desire Anne (Gavitt) D.; grad. U.S. Naval Acad., 1877; m. Elizabeth Armada Webb, July 30, 1890 (died 1907); 1 son, Donald Omar; m. 2d, Eleanor Cameron Warwick Palmer, June 22, 1919. Ensign. Mar. 12, 1881; lt. jr. grade, July 1, 1887; lt., Feb. 17, 1893; comdr., July 1, 1905; capt., July 1909; rear admiral, Aug. 6, 1915. Served in principal stas., various parts of world; aboard Baltimore when she took Ericsson's body to Sweden; invented the Dunn anchor; aboard Terror during Spanish-Am. War, operating in West Indies, lt. comdr. Buffalo in Boxer troubles in China; exec. officer Columbia when she took body of Mexican minister to Vera Cruz, 1904, and in charge of military escort to Mexico City; spl. duty with Sec. of the Navy, 1912-13; assigned in charge Battleship Div. Five, Oct. 6, 1916; comd. Naval Base, Punta Delgada, Azores, Jan. 1918-Apr. 1919; comd. 1st Naval Dist., Boston, May 1919-21. Medals and badges; West Indies Naval Engagements, Spanish Campaign, China Relief Expdn., Philippine Campaign, Naval and Mil. Order Spanish War, Order of the Dragon, Mil. Order of the Aviz (Portugal), Order of the Rising Sun (Japan), D.S.M. (U.S.), Pres. Marine Hist. Assn. Hon. v.p. Ye Knyttes of Ye Round Table (London). Home: Westerly, R.I. Died Feb. 13, 1930.

DUNN, WILLIAM MCKEE congressman, judge adv., army officer; b. Hanover, Indiana Territory, Dec. 12, 1814; s. Williamson and Miriam (Wilson) D.; grad. State Sem. (later Ind. State U.), 1832; A.M., Yale, 1835; m. Elizabeth Lanier. Prin. prep. dept. Hanover Coll., 1832; admitted to Ind. bar, 1837; mem. lower house Ind. Legislature, 1837; del. Ind. Costl. Conv., 1850: mem. U.S. Ho. of Reps. (Republican), Ind., 36th-37th congresses, 1859-63, mem. com. mil. affairs, 1861-63; enlisted Ind. Inf., 1861, aide-de-camp to Gen. McClellan, 1861; commd. brig. gen. U.S. Volunteers, judge adv. of volunteers for Dept. of Mfo., 1863-64; del. Phila. Loyalists Conv., 1866; judge adv. gen. U.S. Army, 1875-81. Died "Maplewood," Fairfax County, Va., July 24, 1887: buried Oa, Hill Cemetery, Washington, D.C.

DUNWOODY, HENRY HARRISON CHASE army officer; b. Highland County, O., Oct. 23, 1842; s. William and Sarah (Murphy) D.; grad. U.S. Mil. Acad., 1866; LL.B., Columbian (Now George Washington) U., 1876. Commd. 2d lt. 4th Arty., 1866, advanced through grades to maj. Signal Corps, 1890; lt.-col., 1897; col. chief signal officer vols., 1898; col. U.S. Army, 1898; resigned from vol. service 1898; brig.-gen., 1904; ret. at own request after 40 yrs.' service, 1904. Recorder tactics bd., St. Louis, 1869-71; weather forecaster, signal officer, Washington, 1872-91; has been supervising forecast official. Address: War Dept., Washington. Died Jan. 1, 1933.

DUPONCEAU PIERRE ETINNE (known in U.S. as DuPonceau, Peter Stephen), lawyer, author; b. Isle de Rhe, France, June 3, 1760; hon. LL.D., Harvard, 1820; m. Anne Perry, May 21, 1788. Apptd. capt. Continental Army, Feb. 18, 1788; became aide-de-camp to newly apptd. Maj. Gen. Von Steuben at Valley Forge, Feb. 1788: Livingston's under-sec., Oct. 22, 1781-June 4, 1783: admitted as atty. Ct. Common Pleas, Phila., June 24, 1785; atty. Supreme Ct., 1786; translated from Bynkershoek's original Latin, A Treatise on the Law of War . . . Being the First Book of his Quaestiones Juris Publici, with notes, 1810; internationally recognized for his contbns. to philology, including work on N. Am. Indian langs.; founded Law Acad. Phila., 1821; elected pres. Am. Philos. Soc., 1828; mem. Acad. Arts and Scis. Author: A Dissertation on the Nature and Extent of the Jurisdiction of the Courts of the United States, 1824; A Brief View of the Constitution of the United States, 1834; English Phonologh, 1817; A Discourse on the Early History of Pennsylvania, 1817. Died Phila., Apr. 2, 1844.

DU PONT SAMUEL FRANCIS naval officer; b. Bergen Point, N.J., Sept. 27, 1803; s. Victor Marie and Gabrielle de la Fire (de Pelleport) Du P.; m. Sophie Madeleine (du Pont), June 27, 1833. Apptd. midshipman U.S. Navy by Pres. Madison, 1815; commd. lt., 1826, comdr., 1843; mem. Sec. Bancroft's bd. organizers naval sch. at Annapolis, Md.: comdr. ship Congress, sailed from Norfolk, 1845; mem. bd. apptd. to consider appropriate study course and prepare regulations for govt. of naval acad., 1849; apptd. mem. bd. to investigate light-house establishment by U.S. sec. of treasury, 1851; naval officer representing govt. at N.Y. World's Fair, 1853; mem. naval efficiency bd., 1855; commd. capt., 1855; comdt. Phila. Navy Yard, 1860-61; sr. mem. commn. of conf. which prepared naval operations plans, 1860; in command of S. Atlantic Blockading Squadron, 1861, led successful expdn. against Port Royal, Va.; commd. rear adm., 1862, led operations along So. coast; directed unsuccessful attack on defenses of Charleston, S.C., 1863; mem. naval bd., 1865; monument erected by Act of Congress at Du Pont Circle, Washington, D.C., 1884. Died Phila., June 23, 1865.

DU PONT, HENRY mfr.; b. Eleutherian Mills, Wilmington, Del., Aug. 8, 1812; s. Eleuthère Irénée and Sophie Madelaine (Palmas) Du P.; grad. U.S. Mil. Acad., 1833; m. Louisa Bernard, 1837. Served as 2d lt. Del. Militia, 1833-34, maj. gen.; joined father in mfg. gunpowder, became head E. I. Du Pont de Nemours & Co., 1850, expanded co. with Crimean War profits, bought mills in Pa., began using Peruvian nitrate soda instead of saltpetre, set up factory in Cal., 1861, bought out Hazard and Cal. Powder cos., 1876. Died Del., Aug. 8, 1889.

DU PONT, HENRY ALGERNON senator; b. nr. Wilmington, Del., July 30, 1838; s. Henry; g.s. of Elenthère Irénée du Pont de Nemours; g.g.s. Pierre Samuel du Pont de Nemours, French economist and statesman (died in. Del., 1817); grad. U.S. Mil. Acad., 1861; at head of class; married; children - Louise Evelina (Mrs. F. B. Crowninshield), Henry Francis. Commd. 2d lt. engrs.; 1st lt. 5th Arty., 1861; regimental adj. July 6, 1861; acting asst. adj. gen. of troops in New York harbor, 1862-63; capt. 5th Arty., Mar. 24, 1864; comd. battery at battle of Newmarket, W. Va., as chief of arty., that dept.; took part in battles of Piedmont and Lynchburg; later chief of artillery, Crook's Corps; in battles of Winchester, Sept. 19, 1864, Fisher's Hill, Sept. 22, 1864, and Cedar Creek, Oct. 19, 1864; resigned from Army, Mar. 1, 1875. Bvtd. maj. "for gallant services at Winchester and Fisher's Hill"; bvtd. lt. col. Oct. 19, 1864, "for distinguished services at Cedar Creek"; awarded Congressional Medal of Honor "for extraordinary gallantry" at Cedar Creek. Received in Del. legislature May 9, 1895, 15 of the 30 votes cast for U.S. senator; election contested on question of right of ex-speaker of Del. Senate (then acting as gov.) to vote; without his vote Col. du Pont had majority of 1; U.S. Senate Com. reported in his favor, but he was not seated, not receiving unanimous party support, because of opposition to the free and unlimited coinage of silver; elected U.S. Senator for terms 1906-11, 1911-17; chmn. of Senate Mil. Com. May 1, 1911-Mar. 15, 1913. Pres. and gen. mgr., Wilmington & Norfolk R.R. Col, 1877-99. Retired. Home: Winterthur, Del. Died Dec. 31, 1926.

DURBIN, WINFIELD TAYLOR governor; b. Lawrenceburg, Ind., May 4, 1847; ed. pub. schs.; served in Union army as pvt.; taught sch.; m. Bertha McCullough, Oct. 6, 1875. Went to Indianapolis, 1869; worked in office and traveled for wholesale dry goods house until 1879; removed to Anderson, Ind., 1879, and engaged in banking; was connected with first fuel gas co. that installed a distributing system in Anderson and a fuel supply co.; is interested in several large mfg. industries as well as electric traction lines. Col. 161st Ind. Regt. in Spanish-Am. War; several yrs. on Rep. State Com. of Ind., chmn. exec. com.; mem. Rep. Nat. Com. and also exec. com., 1896-1900; gov. of Ind., 1901-05; Rep. nominee for gov., 1912. Mason. Died Dec. 18, 1928.

DURGIN, CALVIN THORNTON naval officer; b. Jan. 7, 1893; s. Frank L. and Sara (Boal) D.; B.S., U.S. Naval Acad., 1916; completed flight tng. Naval Air Sta., Pensacola, Fla., 1920; M.S. in Aeronautical Engring., Mass. Inst. Tech., 1924; m. Myrtle Fest, Oct. 7, 1916; children-Calvin Thornton (USN), Phyllis (Mrs. Wallace A. Sherrill), Jean (Mrs. Edward Clinchard). Commd. ensign, USN, 1916, and advanced through grades to vice adm., 1949; served in U.S.S. Connecticut and U.S.S. Kimberly, European Theater, World War I; comdr. U.S.S. Wright, 1938, Utility Wing, Pacific Fleet, 1939; comdr. U.S.S. Ranger, 1942, participated in invasion Western Morocco; comdr. Fleet Air, Quonset Point, 1943; comdr. joint U.S.-Brit. Task Group, 1944, participated in invasion So. France; comdr. Escort Carrier Force, Pacific, 1944-45, participated in invasions, Mindoro and Luzon, capture Iwo Jima, capture and occupation Okinawa; became comdr. naval air bases 11th and 12th Naval Dists., 1946; comdr. Fleet Air, Jacksonville, 1943; dep. chief naval operations (Air), Navy Dept., Washington, 1949-50; comdr. First Fleet, Pacific, 1950; pres. bd. inspection and survey Navy Dept., 1951; ret. 1951; pres. State U. N.Y. Maritime Coll., Ft. Schuyler, N.Y.C., 1951-60. Decorated D.S.M., Legion of Merit with 2 gold stars, Commendation Ribbon from Comdr. in Chief Atlantic Fleet, Presdl. Unit Citation, Navy Unit Citation, Expeditionary Medal (USN), Victory Medals World Wars I and II, Am. Def. with Fleet Clasp, Am. Area Service medal, European-African-Middle Eastern Area Service medal with 2 stars, Asiatic-Pacific Area Service medal with 4 stars, Navy Occupation, Philippine Liberation medal with star (U.S.), Legion of Honor, Croix de Guerre with Palm (France); Hon. Comdr. Mil. Div. Order Brit. Empire. Home: Calmert,Dogue,Va. Died Mar. 25, 1965; buried Arlington Nat. Cemetery.

DURHAM, HENRY WELLES, civil engr.; b. Chicago, Sept. 15, 1874; s. Caleb Wheeler and Clarissa Safford (Welles) D.; father inventor of Durham system of house drainage now universally employed in large bldgs.; C.E., Sch. of Mines (Columbia), 1895; m. Josephine Belden Trowbridge, Oct. 1, 1903; 1 dau., Elisabeth Trowbridge. Asst. on surveys for N.Y. Rapid Transit Commn. and with U.S. Geol. Survey, 1895-98, Nicaragua Canal Surveys 1898-1900; asst. engr. in charge of constrn., New York Subway, 1900-04; resident engr. in charge of design and constrn. of all municipal improvements in City of Panama for U.S. Isthmian Canal Commn., 1904-07; resident engr. in charge of surveys and constrn. of Cape Cod Canal, 1907-12; chief engr. of highways Manhattan Borough, 1912-15; engineer, Bergeon Co., N.J., 1916. Mem. Co. I, 7th Inf., N.G.N.Y., 1900-17; Mexican border service, 1916; commd. capt., Engr. R.C., 1917; promoted maj., Engrs. U.S. Army, Dec. 10, 1917, assigned command 41st Engrs.; took battn. overseas, Feb. 25, 1918; in charge forestry operations near St. Dizier, France, advance section, A.E.F., till July, then on staff Brig. Gen. Jadwin, Tours, France, in chg. road maintenance in A.E.F. till July 1919; discharged Oct. 17, 1919; in Peru on studies and plans for sanitation of Lima, Cuzco and other cities, 1920-22; designs, etc., N.Y., Mass. and N.C., 1923-24; engaged in sanitation and paving for govt. of Nicaragua, 1925-30; highway studies in Guatemala, 1931-32; municipal improvements in Barranquilla, Colombia, 1933-34; mine valuation in El Salvador, 1935; paving engr., New York World's Fair 1939, 1936-39; building first highway in Paraguay, 1939-42; C.E., research, Mil. Intelligence, Office Chief of Engrs., U.S. Army, 1943-45. Del. to Third Internat. Road Congress, London, 1913; studied European street paving for President McAneny and Mayor Gaynor; mem. Am. Soc. C.E., Boston Soc. C.E., Permanent Internat. Assn. Road Congresses, A.A.A.S., Am. Road Builders Assn., Am. Public Works Assn., Municipal Engrs. of N.Y., Internat. Engring. Congress, San Francisco, 1915, Soc. Am. Mil.

Engrs., Reserve Officers' Assn. of U.S. Mil. Order World Wars, New York Soc. Mil. and Naval Officers of World Wars, Sociedad de Ingenieros del Peru; fellow Am. Geog. Soc. Officier du Merite Agricole, Sept. 1919, for work on restoration of French highways; Conspicuous Service Cross, N.Y. State, also 7th Regt. Cross (15 yrs. service). Col., Army of the U.S. Hon. Res. (ret.). Clubs: Columbia University, Beta Theta Pi. Author: Street Paving and Maintenance in European Cities, 1915; various monographs and articles. Home: Halfway House Sandwich MA

DURHAM, KNOWLTON lawyer; b. Chgo., Aug. 29, 1880; s. Caleb Wheeler and Clarissa Safford (Welles) D.; A.B., Columbia Coll., 1901; A.M., Columbia U., 1902; LL.B., Columbia Law Sch., 1905; m. Pauline Crook, Sept. 26, 1925; 1 son, Robert Crook. Admitted to N.Y. bar, 1905, with Masten and Nichols, 1905-07, 1910-14, with Frank V. Johnson, 1907-10. gen. practice, 1914—. Served in N.Y. Nat. Guard (Squadron A), 1912-24; Mexican border service, 1946; lt. and capt. Co. C., 105 machine gun Bn., 27th Div., A.E.F., 1917-19; maj. Judge Adv. Gen. Dept. Res., 1925-40; recalled to active duty, Oct. 30, 1940; chief, legal div., N.Y.C. Selective Service Hdqrs., 1940-44; promoted lt. col., Feb. 2, 1943, col., Feb. 29, 1944. Awarded Silver Star with Oak Leaf Cluster, World War I; Selective Service Medal, Army Commendation Ribbon, World War II. Awarded Columbia Univ. Medal for Excellence, 1946. Trustee Am. Seamen's Friend Society. Mem. Mil. Order Foreign Wars, Mil. Order World War, N.Y. Soc. Mil. and Naval Order World Wars, Soc. Colonial Wars, Assn. Ex-members Squadron A., The Pilgrims, Beta Theta Pi. Mason.Presbyn. Clubs: Army and Navy (Washington); Down Town, (N.Y.C.). Author: Billions for Veterans 1932. Home: Eatons Neck. Northport N.Y. Office: 62 William St., N.Y.C. Died Dec. 1961.

DURKEE, JOHN b. Windham, Conn., Dec. 11, 1728; s. William and Susannah (Sabin) D.; m. Martha Wood, Jan. 3, 1753. Innkeeper, justice of peace, Norwich, Conn.: mem. Conn. Gen. Assembly; served from 2d lt. to maj. Conn. Militia, French and Indian Wars; apptd. mem. com. to arrange correspondence system between Conn. Sons of Liberty and those of other colonies; chosen mem. com. to recommend Norwich's refraining from importation of some Brit. manufacture; founder Ft. Durkee (Pa.), 1769, renamed it Wilkes-Barre (for John Wilkes and Col. Isaac Barre); served with Continental Army, 1775-81, maj., then lt. col. 3d Conn. Regt., lt. col., then col. 20th Regt., col. 4th, 1st Conn. regts.; served with Sullivan's expdn. against the Six Nations, 1779. Died Norwich, Conn., May 29, 1782.

DURRELL, EDWARD HOVEY naval officer; b. Boston, Mass., Feb. 10, 1866; s. James MacDaniel and Bathsheba Thaxter (Hovey) D.; grad. U.S. Naval Acad., 1887, U.S. Naval War Coll., Newport, R.I., 1914; m. Anne Hartwell Kendall, of Hyde Park, Mass., June 9, 1890 (died 1910); m. 2d, Mary Jones Nicholson, of Washington, D.C., Jan. 23, 1917. Promoted ensign, July 1, 1889; lt. jr. grade, July 21, 1897; lt., Mar. 3, 1899; lt. comdr., June 26, 1905; comdr.,comdr., July 1, 1909; capt., Feb. 13, 1914. Served on Wheeling, Spanish-Am. War, 1898; duty at U.S. Naval Acad., 1904-06; navigator on New Jersey, 1906-08; exec. officer West Virginia, 1908-09; at Naval War Coll., Newport, R.I., 1909; U.S. Naval Acad., 1909-12; comd. Tacoma, 1912-13; at Naval War Coll., 1913-14; comd. Connecticut, 1914-16, Minnesota, 1916-17; apptd. commandant Naval Training Sta., San Francisco, Jan. 31, 1917; naval attaché to Chile, Peru and Ecuador, Oct. 1919—. Republican. Clubs: Racquet (Phila.), Boston City (Boston). Home: 1563 Beacon St., Brookline, Mass.

DURYEE, ABRAM mcht., army officer; b. N.Y.C., Apr. 29, 1815; s. Jacob and Eliza Duryee; m. Caroline Allen, 1838, 4 children. Became sgt. 142d Regt., N.Y. Militia, 1833, sgt. maj., 1835; sgt. 7th Regt., 1838, commd. capt., 1843, maj., 1845, lt. col., 1845, col., 1849, acting brig. gen., 1861; organized voluntary regt. Duryee's Zouaves, 1861, served at Battles of Big Bethel and Fed. Hill in Civil War; police commr. N.Y.C., 1873, dockmaster, 1884. Died N.Y.C., Sept. 27, 1890.

DUTTON, CLARENCE EDWARD major U.S.A.; b. Wallingford, Conn., May 15, 1841; s. Samuel Henry and Emily (Curtis) D.; A.B., Yale, 1860; m. Emeline C. Babcock, Apr. 18, 1864. First lt. 21st Conn. Inf., Sept. 5, 1862; capt., Mar. 1, 1863; hon. mustered out, June 14, 1864; apptd. 2d lt. ordnance, Jan. 29, 1864; 1st lt., Mar 7, 1867; capt., June 23, 1874; maj., May 1, 1890; retired at own request, over 30 yrs.' service, Feb. 7, 1901. Home: Englewood, N.J. Died 1912.

DUTTON, JOSEPH (IRA BARNES DUTTON), lay missionary; b. Stowe, Vt., Apr. 27, 1843; s. Ezra and Abigail (Barnes) D.; removed to Wis. with parents, 1847; educated under mother, Milton (Wis.) Acad. and by pvt. study. Enlisted as pvt. in Co. B, 13th Wis. Vols., summer of 1861; apptd. q.m. sergt. when regt. was being organized and served as such until Feb. 10, 1863; commd. 2d lt., Feb. 10, 1863; 1st lt., Feb. 15, 1865; apptd. regtl. q.m., Mar. 24, 1865; recommended (unknown to himself) for appmt. as capt. and a.q.m. by Maj. Gens. Thomas, Rousseau, Donaldson and Granger; assigned to staff of Gen. Granger, June 1864, later asst. to Col. Holabird, chief q.m. Dept. of Louisiana; in Govt. service for 10 yrs. after Civil War, principally in adjustment of war claims. Catholic. Lay missionary, leper settlement, Molokai, T.H., July 29, 1886 - ; administered estate of Father Damien, 1889; builder and in charge of the Baldwin Home (for orphan boys, helpless cases, blind - all of them lepers), where 1,284 inmates have been cared for; specially honored, July 1908, on account of services as a soldier and humanitarian, when Admiral Charles S. Sperry, in comd. of Atlantic Fleet on its tour of the world, paraded with colors flying, before the leper settlement. Mem. U.S. Catholic Hist. Soc., Am. Fedn. Catholic Socs. Died Mar. 26, 1931.

DUVAL, ISAAC HARDING soldier; b. Wellsburg, W.Va., Sept. 1, 1824; common school edn.; m. Mary D. Kuhn, June 23, 1853. Was private sec. to ex-Gov. Butler of S.C.; commr. apptd. by Pres. Polk to treat with wild Indians on Texas border, 1847; comd. first co. that crossed the plains, Texas to Calif., 1849, making the trail; was in the insurrection in Cuba, 1851; served through Civil War, maj. 1st W.Va. inf. to brig. gen. and bvt. maj. gen. U.S. vols.; in 32 battles; wounded 3 times. Republican. Mem. Congress, 1869-71; served in both branches W.Va. legislature, adj. gen. State of W.Va.; collector internal revenue 14 yrs.; U.S. assessor 2 yrs., etc. Home: Wellsburg, W.Va. Died 1902.

DUVALL, WILLIAM PENN maj. gen.; b. St. Mary's Co., Md., Jan. 13, 1847; s. Robert E. and Julia (Frame) D.; ed. pvt. and pub. schs.; grad. U.S. Mil. Acad., 1869; m. Maria Cumming Lamar, Nov. 5, 1902. Commd. 2d lt. 5th U.S. Arty., June 15, 1869; 1st lt., Apr. 9, 1877; grad. Arty. Sch., 1892; capt. 1st U.S. Arty., Mar. 8, 1898; maj. insp. -gen. vols., May 12, 1898; hon. disch., July 19, 1898; lt. col. chief ordnance officer vols., July 18, 1898; hon. disch. from vol. service, May 12, 1899; lt. col. 26th U.S. Vol. Inf., July 5, 1899; col. 48th U.S. Vol. Inf., Sept. 9, 1899; hon. mustered out of vol. service, June 30, 1901; maj. Arty. Corps U.S.A., Sept. 23, 1901; lt. col., Feb. 24, 1906; brig. gen., Mar. 2, 1906; maj. gen. U.S.A., Oct. 2, 1907; asst. to the chief of staff; comdg. Philippines Div., Apr. 1909, to end of 1910; retired from active service, Jan. 13, 1911. Placed on active duty and assigned to command Southeastern Dept., Aug. 21, 1917. Home: Charleston, S.C. Died Mar. 1, 1920.

DWIGHT, ARTHUR SMITH mining and metall. engr.; b. Taunton, Mass., Mar. 18, 1804; s. Benjamin Pierce and Elizabeth Fiske (Dwight) S.; assumed maternal surname on coming of age-authorized by Kings' County (N.Y.) Court, Dec. 15, 1886; grad. Poly. Inst., Brooklyn, 1882; E.M., Sch. of Mines (Columbia), 1885, hon. M.Sc., 1914, hon. D.Sc., 1929; m. Jane Earl Reed, June 4, 1895 (died Feb. 1929); m. 2d, Mrs. Anne Howard Chapin. Mining and metallurgical work, 1885-1906, in charge smelting operations at Pueblo and Leadville (Colo.), El Paso (Tex.), Argentine (Kan.), San Luis Potosi and Cananea (Mexico): cons. practice, and directing business of Dwight & Lloyd cps., New York, since 1906; pres. Dwight & Lloyd Sintering Co.: pres. Dwight & Lloyd Metall. Co. Commd. major engrs., U.S.R., Jan. 23, 1971 1917; assisted organizing 1st Reserve Engrs., later 11th Engrs., the first A.E.F. unit in action in France (Cambrai); served in Somme sector, Cambral offensive, Lys defensive, N. Picardy sector, Meuse-Argonne offensive; in France 22 mos., on British front 9 mos., comdg. 1st Batt., 11th Engrs.; later on spl. duty as metall. consultant French companies; engr. salvage officer A.E.F.; now colonel engrs., U.S.R. (inactive); vice chmn. mineral advisory com. Army and Navy Munitions Board. Alumni trustee Columbia U., 1915-21. Mem. American Institute Mining and Metallurgical Engineers (Life, ex-pres.; Douglas medalist), Mining and Metallurgical Society America, Society American Mil. Engrs. (ex-pres. N.Y. Post), Mass. Society of Mayflower Descendants, Mil. Order of the World War, Am. Legion, Great Neck Post, American Vets. Assn., Institution Mining and Metallurgy of London (hon.), Mass. Soc. of the Cincinnati, Sigma Xi, Tau Beta Pi; hon. mem. Soc. Engineers of Louvain Univ., Belgium. Citation by Gen. Pershing; Order of Purple Heart (U.S.); Companion D.S.O. (British); Chevalier Legion d'Honneur (French). Republican. Episcopalian (hon. Warden All Saints Church, Great Neck). Clubs: University, Engineers', Mining, Columbia Univ., North Hempstead Country. Hobe Sound Yacht (vice commodore), Jupiter Island; Army and Navy (Washington); Union Interalliee (Paris). Co-inventor with R. L. Lloyd of Dwight and Lloyd system of ore treatment. Home: West Shore Rd., Great Neck, L.I., N.Y., Pine Hill Road, New Fairfield, Conn. and "Beau Rivage," Hobe Sound, Fla. Office: 19 Rector St., New York, N.Y. Died Apr. 1, 1946.

DWIGHT, TIMOTHY coll. pres., author; b. Northampton, Mass., May 14, 1752; s. Maj. Timothy and Mary (Edwards) D.; grad. Yale, 1769, M.A., 1772; LL.D. (non.), Harvard, 1810; m. Mary Woolsey, Mar. 3, 1777. Headmaster, Hopkins Grammar Sch., New Haven, Conn., 1769-71; tutor Yale, 1771-77; licensed to preach, 1777; chaplain Gen. S.H. Parson's Conn. Brigade, Continental Army, 1777-79; mem. Mass. Legislature, 1781-82; ordained to ministry Congregational Ch., 1783; pres. Yale, 1795-1817, prof. theology, founder med. dept.; a projector Andover Theol. Sem.; missionary for Soc. of Coun.; mem. Am. Bd. Commrs. for Fgn. Missions; mem. group called "Hartford Wits." Author: The Conquest of Canaan (1st Am. epic poem), 1785; Greenfield Hill, 1794; Theology, Explained and Defended, 5 vols., 1818-19; Travels in New England and New York, 1821. Died New Haven, Jan. 11, 1817.

DWIGHT, WILLIAM army officer, cotton mfr.; b. Springfield, Mass., July 14, 1831; s. William and Elizabeth (White) D.; attended U.S. Mil. Acad., 1849-53; m. Anna Robeson, Jan. 1, 1856. Cotton mfr., Boston and Phila.; commd. capt. 13th Inf., U.S. Army, 1861; commd. lt. col. 70th N.Y. Volunteers, 1861, col., 1861; brevetted brig. gen. for gallantry at Battle of Williamsburg, 1862; helped arrange surrender of Port Hudson, 1863; chief of staff under N.P. Banks on Red River expdn., 1864; commanded 1st div. XIX Corps, Sheridan's Army; mgr., dir. White Water Valley R.R. after Civil War. Died Boston, Apr. 21, 1888.

DWORKIS, MARTIN B(ERNARD) educator; b. N.Y.C., June 14, 1919; s. Meyer and Tillie (Lapidus) D.; A.B. with distinction and honors, U. Mich., 1940, A.M., 1941; Ph.D., N.Y. U., 1952; m. Ida Levine, Oct. 23, 1955; 1 son, Charles Norman. Engaged in personnel and tng. R. H. Macy and Co., N.Y.C., 1941-42; instr. govt. Washington Sq. Coll., N.Y. U., 1946-49, Hunter Coll., N.Y.C., 1946-47, Bklyn. Coll., 1949-51, John Marshall Coll., Jersey City, 1946-48; exec. officer Grad. Sch. Pub. Administrn. and Social Service, N.Y. U., 1956-57, lectr., prof. pub. adminstrn., 1950-64; founding pres. Borough of Manhattan Community Coll., U. City N.Y., 1964—; dean N.Y. Inst. Criminology, 1950; vis. prof. Fredonia State Tchrs. Coll., summer 1949, Bklyn. Coll., summer 1954, Hunter Coll., summer 1956; Brookings vis. prof. Center Advanced Study, Washington, 1961-62. Charter cons. N.Y. State Commn. Govtl. Operations of City N.Y., 1959-61, to City Norwalk, Conn., 1959, to City Cranston, R.I., 1960; program cons. United Parents Assn., 1954—, LaGuardia Meml. Assn., 1953—, N.Y. Jour. Am., 1959—; personnel cons. dept. personnel N.Y.C., 1955—, civil service dept. N.Y. State, 1953, City East Rutherford, N.J., 1955; cons. pub. personnel mgmt. Govt. Jamaica, 1960—; chmn. community dists. Citizens Union and Citizens Planning Council N.Y.; mem. adv. council Pres. of State U. N.Y.; chmn. Nat. Com. for Human Rights and Genocide Treaties; pres. N.Y. Pub. Personnel Council, Chmn. bd. dirs. Fed.-Coll. Internship Program, 1959—; treas., bd. dirs. Council Mgmt. Guidance, 1959—; bd. dirs. N.Y. Civil Liberties Union, Second U.S. Inter-Agy. Mgmt. Devel. Program, 1955—, Moral Leadership Tng. Program, N.Y. Naval Shipyard, 1960-62. Candidate for U.S. Ho. of Reps., 1961. Served to capt. USAAF, 1942-46. Mem. Am. Soc. Pub. Adminstrn. (pres. N.Y.C., 1956-57), Municipal Personnel Soc. (pres. 1959-60), N.Y. Pub. Personnel Assn. (pres. 1957-59), A.A.A.S., Am. Assn. U. Profs., Am. Polit. Sci. Assn., Am. Soc. Tng. Dirs., Coll.-Fed. Agy. Council (exec. com. 1957-62), Internat. Inst. Adminstry. Scis., Internat. City Mgrs. Assn. (asso.), Nat. Civil Service League, Nat. Municipal League, Soc. Personnel Administrn. (pres. N.Y. State 1961-62), N.Y. U. Grad. Sch. Alumni Assn. (v.p.), Am. Fedn. Tchrs. (v.p. United Fedn. Coll. Tchrs. N.Y.), N.Y. U. Assn. U. Prof. (v.p.) Mason, K.P. Author: (with others) Readings in Government in American Society, 1949; (with others) Annual Review of United Nations Affairs, 1955; also numerous articles, monographs, reports, Editor: The Impact of Puerto Rican Migration on Governmental Services in New York City, 1957; The Port of New York and Management of its Piers, 1958; The Community Planning Boards of New York, 1960. Contbr. Ency. Britannica, Am. Oxford, Home: 410 W. 24th St., N.Y.C. 10011. Died Aug. 20, 1965; buried Beth Israel Cemetry, Woodbridge, N.J.

DYE, EUGENE ALLEN editor; born Mellette, S.D., June 2, 1898; s. Eugene Allen and Hester (Snyder) D.; A.B., Univ. of S.D., 1920; m. Josephine B. Dunn, Oct. 19, 1935; 1 dau., Josephine B. Chmn. Mont. State Bd. of Equalization (tax commn.), Helena, Mont., 1937-43; editor The Independent-Record, Helena, Mont., since 1943; vice pres. Mont. Record Pub. Co. Western corr. Newsweek mag., 1958-60. Mem. Mont. Bd. Edn., 1958-60. Entered U.S. Army May 1917; commd. Co. D., 26th inf., 1st div., France and Germany; disch. capt. of inf., 1919. Presbyn. Home: 1107 Livingston St., Helena 59601. Office: 317 Allen St., Helena, Mont. Died Nov. 11, 1960; buried Great Falls, Mont.

DYER, ALEXANDER BRYDIE soldier, ordnance expert; b. Richmond, Va., Jan. 10, 1815; s. William Hay and Margaret (Brydie) D.; grad. U.S. Mil. Acad., 1837; m. Elizabeth Allen, Feb. 6, 1840, 6 children. 2d lt., 3d Arty., 1837, in Fla. War, 1837-38; chief ordnance Army in N.M., 1846: capt. Ordnance Corps, Mar. 3, 1853; assigned command Nat. Armory, Springfield, Mass., Aug. 21, 1861; maj. Ordnance Corps, Mar. 3, 1863; chief ordnance U.S. Army (brig. gen.), Sept. 1864; invented cannon projectile: brevetted capt. Mexican War, brevetted maj. gen., Mar. 13, 1865. Died Washington, D.C., May 20, 1874.

DYER, ALEXANDER BRYDIE army officer; b. Fayetteville, N.C., Mar. 28, 1852; s. Bvt. Mlaj. Gen. Alexander Brydie (chief of ordnance U.S.A.) and Elizabeth B. (Allen) D.; apptd. from D.C., and grad. U.S. Mil. Acad., 1873; grad. Arty. Sch., 1878; m. Madeleine Minturn, Mar. 29, 1880. Second lt. 4th Arty., June 13, 1873; promoted through grades to col.

arty. corps, Jan. 25, 1907; assigned to 4th Field Arty., June 6, 1907; retired from active service, Mar. 15, 1913. Adj., Ft. Riley, Kan., 1873-92; served in campaign against Bannock Indians, 1878; sr. instr. arty., U.S. Mil. Acad., 1892-97; chief of arty., 1st Div., 8th Army Corps, under Gens. Anderson and Lawton, in P.I.; participated in battles at Manila, Feb. 10, 1899, and San Piedro, Mar. 13, 1899; recommended for bvt. of maj.; chief of arty., 2d Div., U.S.A. under Maj. Gen. Carter, on Mexican border, 1913. Author: Handbook for Light Artillery, 1896. Home: San Francisco, Calif. Died July 9, 1920.

DYER, ELISHA gov. R.I.; b. Providence, R.I., Nov. 28, 1839; s. Gov. Elisha and Anna Jones (Hoppin) D.; ed. Brown Univ. to sophomore yr.; grad. Univ. of Giessen, Ph.D., 1860; m. a. d. of Col. William and Mary Brayton (Anthony) Viall of Providence. Enlisted sergt. 1st R.I. light battery, but was severely injured on his way to Washington; col. on staff Governor Smith, 1863-66; entered Marine Corps of arty., 1860, as asst. commissary; became lt. col., 1869; resigned 1871; placed in comd. combined arty. of R.I., 1875; State senator R.I., 1878, mem. R.I. gen. assembly, 1881; adj. gen. R.I., 1882-95, retired at brig. gen. 1895, gov. R.I., 1897-1900. 3 terms. Republican. Mason. Home: Providence, R.I. Died 1906.

DYER, ELIPHALET Continental congressman, jurist; b. Windham, Conn., Sept. 14, 1721; s. Col. Thomas and Lydia (Backus) D.; gra A.B., A.M., Yale, 1740, LL.D. (hon.), 1787; A.M. (hon.), Harvard, 1744; m. Huldah Bowen. Apptd. capt. Conn. Militia, 1745, lt. col. regt., 1755; admitted to Conn. bar, 1746: dist. rep. (to Conn. Gen. Assembly, 1747-62; organizer Susquehanna Co., 1753, purchased lands from Six Nations, 1754, laid out Conn. Settlement in Wyoming Valley, West of what was then N.Y. Province, 1774, disputed title with Pa., 1763, argued case before congressional com., 1782, lost title for Conn.; mem. Conn. Gov.'s Council, 1762-84; comptroller Port of New London (Conn.), 1764; Conn. del. to Stamp Act Congress, 1765; asso. judge Conn. Superior Ct., 1766; mem. 1st Continental Congress from Conn., 1774; mem. Conn. Com. of Safety, 1775; Conn. commr. at Hartford Conv., 1780; chief justice Conn. Supreme

DYER, GEORGE LELAND commodore U.S.N.; b. Calais, Me., Aug. 26, 1849; s. George W. and Mary (Kelley) D.; apptd. from Me., and grad. with honors, U.S. Naval Acad., 1870; m. Susan Hart, d. Gen. O. H. Palmer, Mar. 31, 1875. Ensign, July, 1871; promoted through grades to capt., Sept. 8, 1905; commodore, June 30, 1908. Served on various duties and stas.; naval attaché at Madrid at outbreak of Spanish War; comd. gunboat Stranger during war with Spain on blockade off Havana; transferred to command of gunboat Yankton, fall of 1898; detailed for patrol duty and surveying on coast of Cuba; at Naval Acad., July 1901, in charge of ships and head dept. modern languages; comd. flagship Rainbow, Asiatic sta., 1902-03, cruiser Albany, 1903-04; gov. Guam, 1904-05; comdt., Navy Yard, Charleston, S.C.; Navy Sta., Port Royal, S.C., and 6th naval dist., 1906; retired, June 30, 1908. Home: Winter Park, Fla. Died Apr. 2, 1914.

DYER, JESSE FARLEY, marine corps officer; b. Dec. 2, 1877; entered U.S. Marine Corps, 1903, and advanced through the grades to brig. gen., 1932; retired, 1937. Decorated Medal of Honor. Address: care Marine Corps Headquarters, Navy Department, Washington 25 DC*

DYER, LEONARD HUNTRESS inventor; b. Washington, D.C., May 13, 1873; s. George Washington and Kate (Huntress) D.; student Corcoran Scientific Sch., Columbian (now George Washington) U., 1893, Georgetown U. Law Sch., 1895. Nat. Law Sch., Washington, D.C., 1896; D.Sc., Rollins College, Winter Park, Fla., 1949; m. Josephine Duncan, July 10, 1905; children-Duncan (dec.), Katherine Huntress (Mrs. Elmer Puddington); m. 2d, Jessica Hofstetter, Oct. 14, 1927. Was admitted to D.C. bar, 1894; practiced patent law with brother, Frank L. Dyer, until 1897; practiced alone, 1897-1903, with others, in N.Y. City, until 1917. Commd. lt. U.S.N.R.F., Mar. 6, 1917, and apptd. comdr. 2d Sec., 3d Naval Dist., hdqrs. Bridgeport, Conn.; also assigned as comdr. Squadron 6, 3d Naval Dist. Invented an automobile with a direct drive, sliding transmission, selective gear shift and unit power plant; more than 100,000,000 automobiles have been made embodying this invention; also invented the flying boat, elec. steering gear, and improvements in steam turbines, etc. Also a landscape painter. Fellow Am. Geog. Soc. Mem. Soc. Colonial Wars, Spanish Inst. of Florida. Clubs: New York Yacht, University of Winter Park (Fla.); Anglers' Yacht. Author: The Evolution of the Motor Vehicle as Shown by Patents, 1955. Home: Winter Park Fla. Died Nov. 16, 1955.

DYER, LEONIDAS CARSTARPHEN ex-congressman; b. Warren Co., Mo., June 11, 1871; s. James Coleman and Martha E. (Camp) D.; Central Wesleyan Coll., Warrenton, Mo., and Washington U., St. Louis; married. Admitted to Mo. bar, 1893, and since in practice a St. Louis. Asst. circuit atty., St. Louis, 1909-10; mem. 62d Congress (1911-13); received certificate of election to 63d Congress but was unseated after a partisan contest; mem. 64th to 72d Congresses (1915-33), 12th Mo. Dist. Republican. Served Spanish-Am. War, in Santiago campaign; on staff of Gov. Hadley, Mo., with rank of col.; comdr. in chief United Spanish War Vets., 1915-16. Mem. Christian Ch. Mason. Office: Chemical Bldg., St. Louis, Mo. Died Dec. 1957.

DYER, NEHEMIAH MAYO naval officer; b. Provincetown, Mass., Feb. 19, 1839; s. Henry and Sally (Mayo) D.; ed. pub. schs.; followed the sea, 1854-59; mercantile employment, 1859-61; unmarried. Enlisted 13th Mass. Vols., 1861; transferred to vol. navy as acting master's mate, Apr. 4, 1862; promoted for gallant services to acting ensign, May 18, 1863; advanced through grades to capt., July 13, 1897; rear admiral, and retired, Feb. 19, 1901. Served at Navy Yard, Boston, 1862-63; Eugenie, 1863-64, Metacomet, 1864, West Gulf Blockading Squadron; participated in battle of Mobile Bay, and surrender of Ft. Morgan; on various duties and stas. to 1887; comd. Marion, 1887-90; Navy Yard, Portsmouth, 1890-93; spl. duty, 1893-94; Navy Yard, Boston, 1895-96; light-house insp. 1st dist., 1896-97; command Philadelphia, 1897, Baltimore, 1897-99; participated in battle of Manila Bay, May 1, 1898; for eminent and conspicuous conduct in this battle was advanced 7 numbers in rank; Navy Yard, Boston, 1900-01. Chmn. bd. commrs. Mass. Nautical Training Sch., 1903-04; Companion Loyal Legion. Home: Melrose, Mass. Died 1910.

DYKEMA, RAYMOND K., lawyer; b. Grand Rapids, Mich., Feb. 17, 1889; s. Kryn and Mary (Openeer) D.; LL.B., U. Mich., 1911; m. Margery Russel, Aug. 1917; children—John Russel, Mary (wife of Dr. Laurie C. Dickson, Jr.), Raymond K., Jere Hutchins. Admitted to Mich. bar, 1911; with Bundy, Travis & Marrick, Grand Rapids, 1911-12, Angell, Boynton, McMillan, Bodman & Turner, 1912-16, Mich. Central R.R., 1917; pvt. practice law, 1919-23; partner Dykema and Wheat, 1923-26, now Dykema, Wheat, Spencer, Goodnow & Trigg. Member of the advisory board United Foundation. Served as capt. AUS, 1917-19. Mem. Am., Mich., Detroit bar assns., Psi Upsilon. Clubs: Detroit, Country (Detroit); Grosse Pointe; Huron Mountain. Home: Grosse Pointe Farms MI Died 1972.

DYRENFORTH, ROBERT ST. GEORGE lawyer; b. Chicago, Oct. 17, 1844; s. Julius and Caroline D.; cadet at Breslau, Neisse and Berlin, Prussia, 1857-61; grad. Breslau, 1861; in U.S. army, 1861-66; M.E. Poly Sch., Carlsruhe, Baden; Ph.D., U. of Heidelberg; M.D., Columbian (now George Washington) U., 1870, LL.B., 1875 (LL.D.); m. Jane de Lacy, 1866. Enlisted April, 1861, Schambeck dragoons, Ill., cav., serving under McClellan and Rosecrans, in W.Va.; later capt. and maj. 13th, 12th and 17th Ill. Cav.; asst. insp. gen. and signal officer in dept. of the Missouri; as acting engr. officer fortified mouth of Mo. River, in advance of Price's raid, 1864; finished service on plains in Indian campaign, 1865; several times wounded; received several brevets. Was 2d asst., 1st asst. and prin. examiner, examiner-in-chief, asst. commr., U.S. Patent Office, 1871-85; in patent practice at Washington, 1885 - . Gen. and comdr.-in-chief Union Veterans' Union (5th term); comdr. Mil. Order of Merit. Home: Washington, D.C. Died 1910.

DYSON, CHARLES WILSON naval officer; b. Ambridge, Md., Dec. 2, 1861; grad. U.S. Naval Acad., 1883. Promoted asst. engr., July 1, 1885; passed asst. engr., June 1, 1895; transferred to the line as lt., lMar. 3, 1899; lt. comdr., Dec. 31, 1903; comdr., May 15, 1908; capt., July 1, 1911; rear admiral, Oct. 15, 1917. Served on San Francisco, Spanish-Am. War. 1898; on Oregon, 1904-05; fleet engr. Asiatic Fleet, 1905-06; duty Bur. Steam Engring., Navy Dept., 1906-13; insp. machinery, Camden, N.J., 1913-14; duty Bur. Steam Engring., in charge design of naval machinery, 1914 - . Fellow Royal Soc. of Arts (British); D.S.C. Republican. Episcopalian. Home: Washington, D.C. Died Oct. 25, 1930.

DYSON, JAMES LINDSAY educator, geologist; b. Lancaster, Pa., May 23, 1912; s. Herbert Pannebecker and Mary Emma (Lindsay) D.; B.S., Lafayette Coll., 1933; M.A., Cornell U., 1935, Ph.D., 1938; m. Lolita Gill Brown, Oct. 10, 1942; children-Dolores Gill, Deborah Anne. Instr. geology Cornell U., 1935-38; instr. geology phys. scis. Colgate U., 1938-41; ranger-naturalist Nat. Park Service, summers 1935-40, 46, 48; asso. prof. geology Hofstra Coll., 1946-47; mem. faculty Lafayette Coll. 1947—, prof., 1948-64, Markle professor, 1964—, head dept. of geology and geography, 1948—; lectr., cons. geologist, 1947—; cooperating geologist Pa. Geol. Survey, 1952—. Chmn. geology selection com. Fulbright Awards, Nat. Acad. Scis.-NRC, 1961-62, Mission 66 com., 1957-65, Served to lt. col. AUS, 1941-46; col. Res. Decorated Legion of Merit; recipient Thomas L. Jones superior teaching award Lafayette Coll., 1956, 57, 64, Distinguished Alumnus citation, 1964. Fellow Geol. Soc. Am., Am. Geog. Soc., A.A.A.S. (council 1958-60); mem. Pa. Acad. Sci. (past pres.; dir.), Nat. Assn. Geology Tchrs., Am. Alpine Club, Am. Geol. Inst. (chmn. mission 66 com 1956—). Glaciological Soc., Artic Inst. N.A. (asso.), Sigma Xi, Phi Kappa Phi. Author: The World of Ice (Phi Beta Kappa Sci. award 1962), 1962; also articles. Home: 32 McCartney St., Easton, Pa. Died Mar. 1967.

EAGAN, CHARLES PATRICK brig. gen.; b. in Ireland, Jan. 16, 1841; ed. at San Francisco; m. Emma Johnson, Nov. 5, 1863. Served as 1st lt. 1st Wash. Ter. Inf., June 21, 1862-Apr. 1, 1865; apptd. from Wash., 2d lt. 9th U.S. Inf., Aug. 30, 1866; 1st lt., Jan. 2, 1869; assigned to 12th Inf., Dec. 31, 1870; capt. commissary subsistence, June 23, 1874; maj., Mar. 12, 1892; lt. col. asst. commissary gen., Jan. 26, 1897; col., Mar. 11, 1898; brig. gen. commissary gen., May 3, 1898. Bvtd. capt., Feb. 27, 1890, for gallant services in action against Indians in the Lava Beds, Cal., Apr. 17, 1873, where was wounded. Retired at own request, after 30 yrs.' service, Dec. 6, 1900. Home: New York, N.Y. Died Feb. 2, 1919.

EAGAN, EDWARD PATRICK FRANCIS, lawyer; b. Denver, Colo., Apr. 26, 1897; s. John William and Clara (Bartholomew) E.; Ph.B., Yale, 1921; student Harvard Law Sch., 1921-22; A.B., Jurisprudence, Oxford U., Rhodes scholarship, 1924, M.A., 1928; m. Margaret Colgate, Oct. 1, 1927; children—Sidney, Caroline. Toured world with Marquis of Clydesdale, 1926-27; admitted to N.Y. bar, 1932, and since practiced in that state; asst. U.S. Atty., 1933-38; private practice with Daily News legal firm, New York City, 1938-42; now mem. firm Fennelly, Douglas, Eagan, Nager & Voorhees; chmn. N.Y. State Athletic Commn., appointment of Gov. Thomas E. Dewey, 1945-51. Chairman U.S. Olympic Fund Raising Com., 1956, Internat. Sports Com., People-to-People Sports Committee, United States Olympic Finance Com. Served as 2d lt., F.A., U.S. Army, 1918-19; capt. to lt. col., Air Transport Command, A.U.S., 1942-45. Pres. Boys' Athletic League of New York, 1937-38. Member board of trustees of People-to-People. Awarded ribbons in World War I, all three theatre ribbons in World War II; Olympic champion, light-heavyweight, Antwerp, Belgium, 1920; Am. Olympic heavyweight 1924. Mem. Bar Assn. City of N.Y., American Legion, Beta Theta Pi. Republican. Clubs: Book and Snake, Yale (mem. council), Circumnavigators (New York); Am. Yacht, Apawamis (Rye, N.Y.); Author: Fighting for Fun, 1933; 10 Days to a Successful Memory (with Dr. Joyce Brothers). Contbr. articles Sat. Eve. Post. Chmn. People-to-People Sports Com., Inc. Home: Rye NY Died June 14, 1967; buried Greenwood Union Cemetery, Rye NY

EAGER, JOHN M. army officer; b. Baltimore, Md., Aug. 20, 1889; s. John M. and Constance (Colclough) E.; student Georgetown Coll., 1908-09; A.B., Harvard Coll., 1912; grad. F. A. Sch., 1924, Command and Gen. Staff Sch., 1925, Chem. Warfare Sch., 1933; m. Kathryn Tydings, June 22, 1935; children-John Macaulay, IV, Mary Tydings. Commd. 2d lt., F.A., Mar. 1913, advanced through grades to brig. gen., Sept. 1942; asst. mil. attaché and mil. attaché chief of Italy 1919-1923; gen. staff 1937-1943; chief of staff and comdg. gen., 5th Service command (Ohio, Ind., Ky. and W. Va.), 1940-43; organized and commanded Italian Service Units 1944-45 with hdqrs. at Ft. Wadsworth, N.Y. and units operating at all ports of embarkation, most Army depots, arsenals and numerous centers, posts, camps and stations in the U.S.; now Washington rep. of Heyden Chem. Corp. Editor U.S. Field Artillery Journal 1928-32; Clubs: Army and Navy, Army-Navy Country, Harvard (Washington, D.C.); Harvard (New York City). Home: 6301 Broad Branch Rd., Chevy Chase. Office: 917-15th St., N.W., Washington. Died Nov. 15, 1956; buried Arlington Nat. Cemetery.

EAGLESON, JAMES BEATY surgeon; s. William and Elizabeth (Hodsden) E.; commercial course, U. of Valparaiso, Ind.; ed. pvt. schs.; M.D., Coll. Phys. and Surg., Chicago, 1885; m. Blanche Mills, July 1, 1889. Practiced, U.S. Marine Hosp., Chicago, 1885-86, Port Townsend, Wash., 1887-99; pvt. practice in gen. surgery, 1899 - ; v.p. and med. dir. Northern Life Ins. Co. Surgeon gen. N.G. Wash., 1891-96; lt., Med. R.C., 1911-17, maj. 1917, lt. col., 1919, col., 1924; organizer, comdg. officer and dir. Base Hosp. No. 50; organizer and comdg. officer U.S. Gen. Hosp. No. 50. A founder and asso. editor Northwest Medicine, 1901-17; a founder and regent Am. Coll. Surgeons. Fellow Am. Acad. Polit. and Social Science. Home: Seattle, Wash. Died Jan. 26, 1928.

EAGLETON, WELLS PHILLIPS surgeon; b. Brooklyn, N.Y., Sept. 18, 1865: s. Thomas Aston Proud and Mary Emma (Phillips) E.; Polytechnic Inst., Brooklyn; M.D., Coll. Phys. and Surg. (Columbia), 1888; D.Sc. (hon.), Univ. of Newark, 1942; D.Sc. (hon.), Rutgers Univ., 1943; m. Florence Pershine Riggs, May 24, 1913; med. director board trustees Newark Eye and Ear Infirmary; chief division of head surgery, Newark City Hosp.; cons. cranial surgeon St. Barnabas, St. Michael's Memorial, Presbyn., and Beth Israel hosps. (Newark), lMountain Side Hosp. (Montclair), Muhlenberg Hosp. (Plainfield). All Souls Hosp. (Morristown, N.J.), Irvington General Hospital, Orange Memorial Hospital, Elizabeth General Hosp., West Hudson Hosp. of Kearny (all N.J.); cons. ophthalmologist and otologist Women's and Children's Hosp., Newark, Hosp. & Home for Crippled Children, Newark, Morristown (N.J.) Memorial Hosp.; mem. cons. staff of Essex County Hospital, Overbrook, N.J., div. cranial surgery, Essex County Isolation Hosp., Soho; former director Federal Trust Co. Vol. U.S. Army, April 10, 1917; served as chief of surgery of the head Base Hosp., Camp Dix, until after signing of Armistice; col. Officers' Reserve Corps, M.D. President Newark Council of Social Agencies; trustee Welfare Fedn. of Newark, Newark Museum. Recipient first Edward J. Ill award, 1939, Award of Merit Medical Soc., of N.J., hon. membership, 1939; Diplome de Membre, Associe du College International de Chirurgiens, 1940; gold medal, by Kings County Medical Society, 1938. Member of the board of governors, American College of surgeons, A.M.A. (house of delegates), N.J. State Med. Soc. (pres. 1923-24 and chmn. welfare com.), Am. Otol. Soc. (pres. 1921), N.Y. Otol. Soc. (pres. 1929), Am. Acad. Ophthalmology and Otolaryngology (pres. 1934-35), Nat. Med. Acad. Rio de Janeiro (hon.); hon. mem. Kansas City Ophthalmology, Otology, Rhinology and Laryngology Soc., Washington (D.C.) Med. and Surg. Sociedad Otorinoloargingologica (Madrilena, Spain); trustee Am. Coll. of Surgeons; former N.J. rep. on the Med. Adv. Bd. of the Veterans' Bur.; formerly mem. N.J. Com. for the Blind. Clubs: Essex, Essex County Country. Author: Brain Abscess — Its Surgical Pathology and Operative Treatment, 1922; Cavernous Sinus, 1925; Thromboses (both translater into French), 1925; also numerous published speeches and monographs. Home: 212 Elwood Av. Office: 15 Lombardy St., Newark 2, N.J. Died Sept. 11, 1946; buried in Mount Pleasant Cemetery Newark, N.J.

EAMES, HAYDEN industrial consultant; b. of Am. parents in Shanghai, China, Dec. 19, 1863; s. Ithama Bellows and Emma (Hayden) E.; ed. in pvt. and pub. sch. in Mfe.; grad. U.S. Naval Acad., 1882; m. Clare Hamilton, June 18, 1890; children-Clare Jenness (Mrs. Sidney Howard, dec.), Emma Hayden (Mrs. R.L. Yates), Julia Hamilton (dec.), Hamilton. U.S. naval officer, 1878-94; gen. mgr. Pope Tube Co., 1893-99; mgr. carriage dept., Pope Motor Co. and successors, 1895-1900; with Westinghouse ú Electric Co., Pittsburgh, Pa., 1900-03; propr. of orgn. distributing automobile parts, 1903-07, then stockholder same orgn. under title Am. Distributing Co.; consultant and dir. Garford Co., 1903-13; mgr. Studebaker Automobile Co., 1907-10; indsl. Consultant, 1910-; mem. arbitration bd. Nat. Regional Labor Relations Bd., parts of 1934, 35. Lt. col. of ordnance in charge production of small arms, machine guns and their ammunition, World War. Home: Cleveland, O. Died Nov. 24, 1938.

EARL, N. CLARK, JR., bus. exec.; b. Boston, Dec. 16, 1900; s. N. Clark and Alice (Drake) E.; ed. Berkley Prep. Sch., Boston; m. Consuelp Vanderbilt Smith; 4 children by previous marriage. N.E. mgr. Owens Bottle Co., Boston, 1920-28; owner Earl & Co., Boston, 1928-39; sales mgr. Howard Johnsons, Inc., N.Y. City, 1945-49; pres. Childs Co., 1950, exec. v.p. and dir. since 1950, pres. and dir. all subsidiary cos. since 1950; pres. and dir. Louis Sherry, Inc., N.Y. City, since 1950. Entered U.S. Army as maj., 1939, operations officer, post exchanges; post exchange officer, E.T.O., 1942-44; ret. as col., 1945. Clubs: Retired Officers (Washington); Silver Springs Country (Ridgefield, Conn.); Leash, Metropolitan (N.Y. City); Skye Terrior of America (v.p. and dir.), American Kennel, Afghan Hound, Am. Boxer, N.Y. Boxer. Breeder of dogs, Iradell Kennels since 1943. Home: Ridgefield CT Died Feb. 1969.

EARLE, EDWARD MEAD univ. prof.; b. N.Y., City, May 20, 1894; s. Stephen King and Helen Martha (Hart) E.; B.S., with highest honors, Columbia, 1947, Ph.D., 1923, LL.D., 1954; L.H.D., Union Coll., 1941, Colgate U., 1947; LL.D., Princeton U., 1947; m. Beatrice Lowndes, Feb. 11, 1919; 1 dau., Rosamond. Served as 2d and 1st lt., Field Arty., and A.S., U.S. Army, 1917-19, World War. With Nat. City Bank, New York, 1919-20; lecturer in history, Columbia, 1920-23, asst. prof., 1923-26, asso. prof. 1926-34; prof. Sch. of Hist. Studies, Inst. for Advanced Study, Princeton, since 1934; asso. mem. All Souls Coll., Oxford, 1950. Stafford Little lecturer, Princeton, 1941; Lamont lecturer. Yale. 1945; Chichele lectr. U. of Oxford, 1950. Fellow Mil. Sciences, Library of Congress since 1943. Mem. bd. analysts, Office Strategic Services, Washington, 1941-42; spl. consultant to the comdg. gen. Army Air Forces, 1942-45, on temporary duty with 8th and 9th Air Forces, U.S. Strategic Air Forces overseas, 1944-45, Nat. War Coll., 1946-51, Joint Services Staff Coll. (Brit.), 1948-50, Imperial Defence Coll. (Brit.), 1948-51, Royal Naval War Coll. (Brit.), 1950; mem. bd. visitors Air U., U.S.A.F., 1952-55. Vice chairman Foreign Policy Association, 1924-27: ednl. dir. N.Y. chapter Am. Inst. Banking, 1921-27. Trustee Foundation for Social Sciences, U. of Denver; mem. bd. academic cons. Nat. War Coll., 1946-49. Awarded Presidential medal for Merit for war service; medal for Distinguished Public Service, Columbia University; Legion of Honor, Rank of Chevalier (French). Mem. Am. Hist. Assn., Am. Polit. Science Assn., Council on Foreign Relations, Phi Beta Kappa, Alpha Delta Phi. Specialist in military affairs and American foreign relations. Clubs: Century (New York); Army and Navy (Washington). Author: An Outline of Modern History, 1921; Turkey, The Great Powers, and Bagdad Railway (winner of George Louis Beer prize for best work of year on European diplomacy), 1923; Against This Torrent, 1941; American Views on Air Power (with Gen. Carl Spaatz), 1947. Editor and co-author: "Makers of Modern Strategy: Military Thought from Machiavelli to Hitler," 1943; Nationalism and Internationalism, 1950; Modern France: Problems of the Third and Fourth Republics, 1951. Contbr. articles in Pol. Sci. Quarterly, Yale Review, Fgn. Affairs, Am. Hist. Review, etc. Edited and wrote introduction to sesquicentennial edition of the Federalist, 1937. Home: 101 Battle Road. Address: Institute for Advanced Study. Princeton, N.J. Died June 24, 1954.

EARLE, RALPH naval officer, educator; b. Worcester, lMass., May 3, 1874; s. Stephen Carpenter and Mary Eaton (Brown) E.; student Worcester Poly. Inst., 1892, hon. D.Sc., 1925; grad. U.S. Naval Acad., 1896; m. Janet Turner, d. of late Pay Dir. Casper Schenck, U.S.N., Sept. 29, 1898; children—Ralph, Mary Janet. Ensign, U.S.N., May 6, 1898; lt. (jr. grade), May 6, 1901; promoted through grades to rear adm., Dec. 23, 1916, continuing during World War; capt. May 5, 1920; promoted to rank of rear adm., Sept. 1930. Served on U.S.S. Massachusetts, 1896-98; navigator and watch officer, Hornet, Apr.-Sept. 1898, participating in battles of Manzanillo, June 30 and July 18, 1898; on San Francisco, Sept. 19-25, 1898; on Essex, 1898-1901; at naval proving ground, Indian Head, 1901-02; on Lancaster, 1902-03, Yankee, May-Oct. 1903, Missouri, 1903-05; insp. of powder for East Coast, 1905-07; gunnery officer U.S.S. Maine, 1907-08, also navigator part of time; exec., navigator and gunnery officer U.S.S. Galveston, July-Oct. 1908; in charge magazine and chem. lab., P.I., 1908-10; in elec. dept., Naval Acad., 1910-11; exec. officer Iowa, May-Sept. 1911; discipline dept. Naval Acad., 1911-13; head of English dept., same, Aug.-Sept. 1912; mem. spl. bd. on naval ordnance, 1912-13; comd. Balch, Sept.-Oct. 1913, Dolphin, 1913-15, during which time (Apr. 9, 1914) occurred the "Tampico incident"; exec. officer Arkansas, June-Sept. 1915; head dept. of ordnance and gunnery, Naval Acad., 1915-16, dept. of English, June-Aug. 1916; comd. naval proving ground, Indian Head, Md., Sept.-Dec. 1916; apptd. chief Bur. of Ordnance, Navy Dept., Dec. 23, 1916; comd. U.S.S. Connecticut, May 5, 1919-Sept. 28, 1921; chief of staff of control force, U.S.S. Flordia, Oct. 10, 1921-May 31, 1922; Naval War Coll., July 1, 1922-May 26, 1923; comdr. Naval Torpedo Sta., Newport, R.I., May 26, 1923-May 25, 1925; retired Aug. 25, 1925. Pres. Worcester Poly. Inst., 1925. Mem. U.S. Naval Inst. Episcopalian. Author: Life at the U.S. Naval Academy, 1917; Makers of Naval Tradition; (brochure) Practical Interior Ballistics, 1917. Accomplished origination of and developed plans for and provided the material for the mine field across the North Sea, known as the Northern Barrage; directed making a type of mine entirely new to naval warfare; originator of the 14-inch naval ry. batteries in France. Originated plans for depth charges, and many other ordnance projects. Home: Worcester, Mass. Died Feb. 13, 1939.

EARLE, SAMUEL congressman; b. Frederick County, Va., Nov. 28, 1760. Moved to S.C., 1774; served from ensign to capt. (of co. of rangers) Continental Army, during Revolutionary War, 1777-82; mem. S.C. Ho. of Reps., 1784-88; del. S.C. Conv. which ratified U.S. Constn., 1788; del. S.C. Constl. Conv., 1790; mem. U.S. Ho. of Reps. from S.C., 4th Congress, 1795-97. Died Pendleton dist., S.C., Nov. 24, 1833; buried Beaverdam Cemetery, Oconee County, S.C.

EARLY, JUBAL ANDERSON lawyer, army officer; b. Franklin County, Va., Nov. 3, 1816; s. Joab and Ruth (Hairston) E.; grad. U.S. Mil. Acad., 1837; studied law, 1838. Commd. 2d lt. 3d Arty., U.S. Army, 1837, served in Seminole war in Fla.; commd. 1st lt., 1838, resigned, 1838; admitted to Va. bar, 1840; mem. Va. Ho. of Dels. (Whig; youngest mem.), 1841-42; served as maj. 1st Va. Regt., Mexican war, 1847; commanded a div., 1862; brig. gen. Army of No. Va., 1863, then maj. gen.; served in battles of Chancellorsville, Gettysburg and Wilderness campaign; lt. gen., 1864, commanded corps ordered to Shenandoah Valley, defeated Lew Wallace at Monacacy; made unsuccessful attempt to take Washington, D.C., 1864; led raids as far North as Pa., 1864; driven back by Sheridan at battles of Winchester and Cedar Creek, 1864; his command nearly wiped out by Custer at Battle of Waynesboro, 1865; relieved of command by Robert E. Lee, set out westward to join Confederate Army in Miss., but upon hearing of Confederate surrender, fled to Mexico, then to Can.; returned to law practice, Lynchburg, Va., 1869; never took oath of allegiance to U.S. after war, although he had originally opposed secession; asso. with P.G.T. Beauregard in La. State Lottery, circa 1870-90. Author: A Memoir of the Last Year of the War for Independence in the Confederate States of America, 1866. Died Lynchburg, Mar. 2, 1894.

EARLY, STEPHEN manufacturing exec.; b. Crozet, Va., Aug. 27, 1889; s. Thomas Joseph and Ida Virginia (Wood) E.: student pvt. schs. in Va., high schs., Washington, D.C.; m. Helen Wrenn, Sept. 17, 1921; children-Stephen T., Helen Virginia, Thomas Augustus. Mem. Washington staff, United Press, 1908-13, Associated Press, 1913-17 and 1920-27; advance rep. for Franklin D. Roosevelt, campagn of 1920; publicity dir. for bd. dirs. Chamber of Commerce of U.S., 1920-21; Washington rep. Paramount-Publix Corp. and Paramount News, 1927-33; asst. sec. to President Roosevelt, Mar. 4, 1933-July 1, 1937, sec., 1937-45; apptd. spl. asst. to President Truman; awarded D.S.M. by the President; vice pres. Pullman, Inc., 1945-48; v.p. Pullman Standard Car Mfg. Co., Jan. 1948-Apr. 1949; apptd. under sec. of defense, Apr. 1949, dep. sec. of defense Aug. 1949, resigned Sept. 1950; reelected v.p. Pullman, Inc., also Pullman-Standard Car Manufacturing Co., Sept. 1950. Served as capt. inf., U.S. Army, World War I. Awarded Silver Star citation. Democrat. Baptist. Clubs: The Chicago (Chicago), Metropolitan, National Press, Burning Tree. Home: 7704 Morningside Dr., Washington. Died Aug. 11, 1951; buried Arlington Nat. Cemetery.

EARNEST, HERBERT LUDWELL, ret. army officer; b. Richmond, Va., Nov. 11, 1895; s. James Alfred and Mary Elizabeth (Talley) E.; student Fork Union Mil. Acad., Va., 1911-14, Med. Coll. of Va., 1915-16; grad. Cav. Sch., 1924, Ecole d'Application de Cavalerie, Saumur, France, 1926. Command and Gen. Staff Sch., 1934, Chem. Warfare Sch., 1936, Army Indsl. Coll., 1939; m. Frances Alexander Campbell, Oct. 20, 1920; children—Clyde Tener, Frances Elizabeth. Commd. 1d 1t. U.S. Army, Oct. 26, 1917, and advanced through the grades to maj. gen.; during World War II, comd. Task Force A, 3d Army Britany Peninsula; comd. combat command A, 4th Armored Div., Dec.-Jan. 1944, Jan. 1945; 90th Inf., Mar.-Dec. 1945, assistant chief staff G-3, Army Ground Forces, Ft. Monroe, Va. 1945-47, retired October 1, 1947. Decorated: Bronze Star Medal with Two Oak Leaf Clusters; Silver Star Medal; D.S.M.; Legion of Merit; Hon. Companion British Distinguished Service Order; Chevalier Legion d'Honneir, Croix de Guerre with Palm (French); Czechoslovakian War Cross. Club: Army-Navy (Washington); Commonwealth (Richmond, Va.); Chesapeake (Irvington, Va.); Indian Creek Yacht and Country (Kilmarnock, Va.). Home: White Stone VA Died June 11, 1970; buried Old Christ Ch., Irvington VA

EASLEY, CLAUDIUS MILLER (É'LE) army officer; b. Thorp Spring, Tex., July 11, 1891; s. Alexander Campbell and Claudia (Miller) E.; B.S., Tex. A. and M. Coll., 1916; student Army Service Schs., 1927-39; grad. army war coll., 1940; m. Inez Wickline, Oct. 13, 1917; 1 son, Claudius Miller. Commd. 2d Maj. U.S. Army, Aug, 7, 1917, and advanced through the grades to brig. gen. Awarded Distinguished Marksman medal. Mason. Home; Lake Waco, Waco, Tex. Address: 3601 Connecticut Av. N.W., Washington. Died June 19, 1945; buried in 96th Inf. Div. Cemetery, Okinawa.

EASTERBROOK, ARTHUR E. army officer; b. Amsterdam, N.Y., Nov. 4, 1893; s. Col. Arthur Edmund and Fannie (Luscombe) E.; student U. of Wash., 1915-17; grad. Army Field Officers Tactical Sch., Langley Field, Va., 1921; m. Gertrude L. Augustine, May 1, 1920; 1 son, Arthur Edward. Commd. 2d lt., inf., 1917, retired for disability in line of duty with rank of lt. col., 1939; returned to active duty, 1940; promoted brig. gen., 1944; comdg. officer Santa Ana Army Air Base, Santa Ana, Calif., since August, 1944. Decorated Distinguished Service Cross with oak leaf cluster, Purple Heart, Victory Medal with 4 stars (major campaigns in World War 1), German Army of Occupation and Pre-Pearl Harbor ribbons, Legion of Merit; Croix de Guerre (France). Mem. Sigma Chi, Scabbard and Blade. Credited with shooting down 5 planes during World War I. Home: 2220 Greenleaf St., Santa Ana. Cal. Died July 24, 1952; buried Arlington Nat. Cemetery.

EASTERBROOK, EDMUND PEPPERELL chief of chaplains, U.S.A.; b. Torquay, Eng., Dec. 22, 1865; s. William and Mary Jane (Pepperell) E.; student Torquay (Eng.) Public Coll., Drew U., 1889-1903; D.D., Coll. Puget Sound, 1921; LL.D., Little Rock Coll., 1929; m. Fannie Luscombe, Sept. 22, 1892; children-Arthur E., U.S.A., Gladys E. (wife of J. L. Collins, U.S.A.), Wilfred G., William, Ernest F. Ordained ministry M. E. Ch., 1889; pastor M.E. Chs., Troy Conf., 1889-98; chaplain U.S.A., Spanish-Am. War, in Cuba with Army of Occupation; commd. chaplain, U.S.A., by President McKinley, Jan. 31, 1900; on duty in Philippines during Insurrection, 1900-05; served as chaplain, U.S. Arty., World War; sr. chaplain, A.F.G., Germany, 1919-23; stationed at Fort Monroe, Va., 1923-27, Fort Sam Houston, Tex., 1927-28; chief of chaplains, U.S.A., 1928-30 (retired). Decorated Legion of Honor (France). Mason. Home: Washington, D.C. Died Jan. 18, 1933.

EASTERWOOD, WILLIAM EDWARD JR capitalist; b. Wills Point, Tex., Nov. 5, 1883; s. William Edward and Mollie (Busby) E.; ed. pub. schs., Wills Point; m. Mae Coker, Nov. 1928. Began as newsboy and became traveling man and factory rep. of large Eastern concerns; now dir. Dallas Nat. Bank, pres. Vanette Hosiery Mills; large property owner of Dallas. Mem. U.S. Marine Corps, World War, advancing to capt.; col. on staff 8 governors; col. Nat. Air Reserves. Especially active in promotion of aviation; has established many airports in Tex. (3 named for him); donor of $25,000 to Coste and Bellonte, French flyers, for first one-stop flight from Paris to New York and Dallas. Recipient of silver loving cups from various Tex. orgns.; decorated Legion of Honor (France), 1933. Nat. vice comdr. Am. Legion, 1933; organized Am. Legion depts. of Great

Britain, Belgium and Greece, 1933. Chmn. Aviation Com. of City of Dallas, 1935-37. Mem. advisory bd. Southern Meth. Univ.; former v.p. U.S. Marine Corps League; trustee Nat. Soc. for Crippled Children of U.S.; dir. Tex. Soc. for Crippled Children. Awarded special diploma Internat. Expn. (San Francisco) as Ambassador of Good Will for State of Texas, 1939. Awarded citations from Nat. Aeorographic Aviation Aca., Nat. Aeronautic Assn. Methodist. Life mem. Elks, exalted ruler, Dallas, 1936-37. Sponsor Christmas dinners to destitute children and food relief to vets. Presented with nat. citation by Am. Legion for work on Americanism, nat. defense and aviation. Home: Adolphus, Tex. Died Aug. 24, 1940.

EASTMAN, JOHN ROBIE astronomer; b. Andover, N.H., July 29, 1836; s. Royal Friend and Sophronia (Mayo) E.; M.S., Dartmouth Coll., 1862; Ph.D., 1877; m. Mary J. Ambrose, Dec. 25, 1866. Asst., U.S. Naval Obs., 1861-65; prof. mathematics U.S.N., 1865-. Retired for age, July 29, 1898, with rank of capt. U.S.N., but retained on active duty till Oct. 12, 1898; promoted to rank of rear-adm. U.S.N., June 29, 1906. Engaged in astron. observations, computations and research, 1862-. Most of published work in the annual volumes of the govt. observatory. Was first pres. Washington Acad. Sciences. Was in charge of the Meridian Circle work at the observatory, 1874-91; observed total solar eclipses Aug. 7, 1869, at Des Moines, Iowa; Dec. 22, 1840, Syracuse, Sicily; July 29, 1878, at West Las Animas, Colo., and May 28, 1900, at Barnesville, Ga. Prepared and edited the Second Washington Star Catalogue, which contains the results of nearly 80,000 observations made at the U.S. Naval Obs., 1866-91. Author: Transit Circle Observations of the Sun, Moon, Planets and Comets, 1903. Home: Andover, N.H. Died Sept. 26, 1913.

EASTMAN, JOSEPH RILUS surgeon; b. Indianapolis, Ind., Apr. 18, 1871; s. Joseph and Mary Katherine (Barker) E.; B.Sc., Wabash Coll., Ind., 1891 (A.M., 1904); M.D., magna cum laude, U. of Berlin, 1897; spl. work, Princeton Univ., 1 yr.; LL.D. from Wabash Coll., 1926; m. - Frieda Grumpelt, Feb. 1, 1910 (Dec.); 1 son, Joseph Rilus; m. 2d, Neva Bonham, 1926. Surgeon, Indianapolis City Hospital since 1900; prof. surgery, Indiana U. School of Medicine since 1909. Major, M.C. U.S. Army; mem. Gen. Med. Bd. of Council Nat. Defense; dir. American Hosp., Vienna, Austria, 1916. Received Austrian Imperial decoration of the Red Cross, officers class, 1917. Letter of appreciation sent by Austrian govt. to American govt. Fellow Am. Coll. Surgeons (founder and ex-gov.); mem. Am. Surg. Assn., Western Surg. Assn. (pres. 1913-14), A.M.A. (diploma of honor awarded for pathology exhibit), Ind. State Med. Assn. (pres. 1919), Indianapolis Med. Assn. (pres. 1925), Société Internationale de Chirurgie, Sigma Chi, Phi Rho Sigma, Sigma Xi, Republican. Episcopalian. Mason. Clubs; University, Indianapolis Literary. Contbr. many articles to Am. and fgn. med. publs. Original worker in surg. pathology; has devised surg. procedures and instruments. Home: 970 North Meridian St., Indianapolis, Ind. Died Nov. 29, 1942.

EATON, D(ANIEL) CADY coll. prof.; b. Johnstown, N.Y., June 16, 1837; s. Daniel Cady and Harriet Eliza (Cady) E.; B.A., Yale, 1860, M.A., 1863; LL.B., Albany (N.Y.) Law Sch., 1861; practiced law at New York, 1861-66; studied history of art under Prof. Friederichs, U. of Berlin, 186768, under Taine, Gerome and Boulanger, Pairs, 1869-70; m. Alice Young, Dec. 17, 1861. Prof. history and criticism of art, 1869-76 and 1902-09, emeritus prof., 1909-, Yale U. Served in 7th N.Y. Militia, 1861-63; col. N.Y.S.M., N.Y. Militia, 1863. Democrat. Episcopalian. Author: Handbook of Greek and Roman Sculpture, 1884; Handbook of Modern French Painting, 1909. Home: New Haven, Conn. Died May 11, 1912.

EATON, JOHN HENRY senator, sec. of war; b. Halifax County, N.C., June 18, 1790; s. John and Elizabeth E.; ed. U. N.C.; m. Myra Lewis: m. 2d, Peggy O'Neill. Went to Franklin, Tenn., 1809; served in War of 1812; early supporter and polit. adviser of Andrew Jackson; mem. U.S. Senate from Tenn., 1818-29; U.S. sec. of war in Jackson's cabinet, 1829-31; his 2d wife became the center of a battle in Washington society between Jackson forces and their opponents, which contributed to reshuffling of cabinet and Eaton's resignation, 1829; apptd. gov. Territory of Fla. by Jackson, 1834-36; U.S. minister of Madrid, Spain, 1836-40. An author The Life of Andrew Jackson, Major General in the Service of the U.S., 1817. Died Nov. 17, 1856, Washington, D.C.; buried Oak Hill Cemetery, Washington.

EATON, JOSEPH GILES rear adm.; b. Greenville, Ala., Jan. 29, 1847; s. William Pitt and Sarah Farwell (Brazer) E.; ed. pvt. schs., Lockport, N.Y., Union Acad., Worcester Mil. Acad. and U.S. Naval Acad.; m. Mary Anne Varnum, Aug. 8, 1871. Midshipman U.S.N., 1863; ensign, 1869; master, 1870; lt., 1871; lt. comdr., 1888; comdr., 1896; capt., 1901; retired with rank of rear admiral, June 30, 1905. Comd. U.S. ships Enterprise, Resolute, Chesapeake, Oregon and Massachusetts. Has medals for battles of Manzanillo and Santiago, war of 1898. Was engaged in interoceanic surveys, Isthmus of Panama, and Darien, 1870-74; mem. Steel Bd., 1893-95; medal of honor, Spanish-Am. War. Episcopalian. Died Mar. 8, 1913.

EATON, PHILIP BENTLEY coast guard officer; b. Elkins, N.H., Jan. 24, 1887; s. James Everett and Sophia Rebecca (Bentley) E.; ed. pub. sch. and high sch., Collinsville, Conn.; student Cooper Union, New York, N.Y., 1903-05, Webb Inst. of Naval Architecture, 1905-08, Coast Guard Acad., 1908; m. Anita Mera Anese McWynne, Feb. 9, 1917. Commd. ensign (engineering), U.S. Coast Guard, 1908, and advanced through the grades to rear adm., 1943; served 18 yrs. at sea, including 5 Arctic cruises on cutter Bear; apptd. naval aviator, 1917; patrol pilot and comdg. officer Naval Air Station, Chatham, Massachusetts, World War I; asst. engr.-in-chief, 1941-46, retired as rear admiral September 1946. Chief inspector ships Coast Guard, at Bath Iron Works (Bath, Maine), and Camden, N.J., 1931. Decorated Navy and Marine Corps Medal, Victory Medal with aviation clasp, Defense Medal, World War II Medal, Expert Rifleman, Mem. Am. Soc. Naval Engrs. Soc. Mil. Engrs. Newcomen Society of England. Clubs: Propeller Army and Navy (Washington). Home: "Comynholm," Ocean View Highway, Westerly, R.I. Died May 18, 1958; buried Arlington Nat. Cemetery.

EATON, WILLIAM diplomat; b. Woodstock, Conn., Feb. 23, 1764; s. Nathan and Sarah (Johnson) E.; grad. Dartmouth, 1790; m. Eliza Sykes, Aug. 22, 1792. Commd. capt. U.S. Army, 1792, served Army of West, later Ga., 1792-95, Phila., 1795-97; U.S. consul in Tunis, 1798-1804; navy agt. to Barbary States, forced to return to U.S. while attempting to guide faction in Tripolitan civil war, 1804; mem. Mass. Legislature, 1 term. Died Brimfield, Mass., June 1, 1811.

EATON, WILLIAM COLGATE commodore U.S.N.; b. Hamilton, N.Y., Feb. 4, 1851; s. George W. (D.D., LL.D.) and Eliza H. (Boardman)E.; A.B., Colgate U., 1869, A.M., 1872, PH.D., 1881; grad. U.S. Naval Acad., 1874; m. Lizzie Blish, Sept. 6, 1890 (died 1929); 1 son, William W. Commd. chief engr. U.S.N., June 1, 1895, capt., Nov. 18, 1904. Served as fleet engineer Pacific Squadron, 1899-1900; detailed as head dept. of engring., Colgate U., 1888-90; apptd. by Viceroy Li Hung Chang, examiner of naval engring. graduates, Imperial U., Tientsin, China, 1892; retired as commodore at own request, June 30, 1908. On war duty as inspr. engring. material, Cincinnati, 1917-19. Home: Hamilton, N.Y. Died June 1, 1936.

EATON, WILLIAM HANMER paper mfr.; b. East Hartford, Conn., June 3, 1879; s. Arthur W. and Frances M. (Hanmer) E.; student Peekskill Military Acad., 1896; B.S., Trinity Coll., 1899; m. Isabel Westcott Nicholson, July 17, 1901; children-Hope (Mrs. Leonard A. Whipple), Isabel Wilmot (Mrs. Kimball Salisbury), Ethel Frances (Mrs. E. E. Colt), Cynthia Edity (Mrs. William Callan). With Eaton Paper Corp., 1899—, dir., 1901—, chairman co., 1935-53, ret., now bd. chmn. Mem. City Council, Pittsfield, 1904-05. Trustee Trinity Coll. Served as lt. col. U.S. Army, exec. asst. to Chief Ordnance Office A.E.F., World War I; col. F.A. Res., 1922-41; col. Intelligence Div., First Service Command, 1941-45. Club: St. Anthony (New York). Home: 76 Eleanor Road. Office: 75 Church Street, Pittsfield, Mass. Died Oct. 8, 1957.

EBAUGH, FRANKLIN GESSFORD, psychiatrist; b. Reistertown, Md., May 14, 1895; s. Zachariah Charles and Elizabeth Bell (Gessford) E.; A.B., Johns Hopkins, 1915, M.D., 1919; m. Dorothy Reese, Apr. 9, 1921; children—Franklin G., David C., Donald R., Nancy Haines. Res. med. officer, Henry Phipps Clinic, 1919-20; asst. physician, New Jersey State Hospital, 1920-21; director neuro-psychiatric dept., Philadelphia Gen. Hosp., 1920-24; instr. in psychiatry, U. of Pa., 1922-24; dir. Colo. Psychopathic Hosp., Denver, since 1924; clin. prof. psychiatry University of Colorado, Denver, 1924-53, prof. emeritus 1953-72; pvt. practice psychiatry, 1953. Served as col. M.C., AUS, neuropsychiat. consultant Eighth Service Command, Dallas, Texas, 1942-45, served in Pacific area. Office of Chief Surgeon, June 1945-46. Director Division of Psychiatric Edn., Nat. Com. for Mental Hygiene, 1933-42; mem. Am. Bd. of Psychiatric Examiners, 1933-41; chmn. sect. nervous and mental diseases, Am. Med. Assn., 1931-32; pres. Colo. Soc. for Mental Hygiene; chmn. Gov's. Com. Mental Health, Colo., 1960-61; mem. Ft. Logan Mental Health Center Adv. Com., 1964-65; mem. Am. Bd. of Psychiatry and Neurology, 1934-42; cons.-at-large U.S.P.H.S.; cons. office of Surgeon Gen.; mem. editorial bd. Am. Jour. of Psychiatry, Current Med. Digest, Post-Grad. Medicine, Am. Practitioner, Diseases of Nervous System; contbg. editor Am. Jour. of Med. Sciences; mem. advisory bd. Med. Specialties, 1934-42, Council on Mental Health, Colorado, from 1957. Recipient Distinguished Service award American Psychiatric Association, 1966. Fellow of the American Psychiatric Association (council 1931-34); mem. A.M.A., Colo. Med. Soc. (past chmn. com. mental health), Am. Neurol. Assn., Canadian Neuropsychiatric Assn. (hon.), Nat. Research Council (com. on neuropsychiatry), Am. Psychiatric Association (Colorado District branch president 1960-61, chmn. com. on psychiatry in med. edn.), Assn. Research Nervous and Mental Disease (pres. 1944). Central Psych. Assn. (pres. 1930), Grad. Med. Edn. (mem. commn. 1936-41), Alpha Kappa Kappa, Sigma Xi, Alpha Omega Alpha; corr. mem. Royal Medico-Psychol. Assn. since 1929. Rep. Episcopalian. Mason. Clubs: Mile High, Cactus, Denver Country. Co-author: Practical Clinical Psychiatry (with E. A. Strecher), 1925, 8th edit., 1946; Psychiatry in Medical Education (with Charles A. Rymer), 1942. Contbr. to Am. Jour. Psychiatry, Am. Jour. Med. Sciences, Archives Neurology and Psychiatry, Am. Practitioner, Jour. Nervous and Mental Diseases, Postgrad. Medicine. Home: Denver CO Died Jan. 4, 1972.

EBERLE, EDWARD WALTER naval officer; b. Denton, Tex., Aug. 17, 1864; s. Joseph and Mary E.; grad. U.S. Naval Acad., 1885; m. Tazie Harrison, Oct. 24, 1889; 1 son, Edward Randolph. Ensign, June 12, 1896; promoted through grades to rear admiral, Feb. 1, 1918. Served on Oregon, Spanish-Am. War, 1898, and in Philippine insurrection, 1899; Asiatic Fleet, 1899, and Atlantic Fleet, 1903-05; Naval War Coll., 1905; Bd. of Inspection and Survey, Navy Dept., 1905-07; exec. officer Louisiana, 1907-08; comd. Naval training Sta., San Francisco, Calif., 1908-10; comd. Milwaukee, 1910, Wheeling, 1910-1911; comd. Atlantic Torpedo Fleet, 1911-13; at Naval War College, Newport, R.I., 1913-14; comd. U.S.S. Washington and Naval force in Santo Domingo, 1914; comdg. Navy Yard and Naval Gun Factory, Washington, 1914-15; supt. U.S. Naval Acad., 1915-19; comd. Battleship Div. Five, Atlantic Fleet, 1919-20; comdr. Battleship Div. 7, Atlantic Fleet, 1920-21; comdr. in chief Pacific Fleet with rank of Admiral, 1921-22; comdr. in chief Battle Fleet, 1922-23; chief of naval operations, Navy Dept., 1923-. Home: Washington, D.C. Died July 6, 1929.

EBERLY, GEORGE AGLER, judge; b. Ft. Wayne, Ind., Feb. 9, 1871; s. John and Mary (Agler) E.; LL.B., U. of Mich., 1892, LL.M., 1893; m. Rose Psotta, Aug. 2, 1899; children—Lloyd A. (dec.), Lola A. (Mrs. John A. Negley), George D. Resident of Neb. since 1873; admitted to bar, 1893; county atty., Stanton County, 1899-1903, 1905-09; apptd. asso. justice Supreme Ct. of Neb. for term, 1925-31, elected for terms, 1931-37 and 1937-43; retired from Supreme Court Bench, January 7, 1943. Sergeant Spanish-Am. War, May 15-Sept. 11, 1898; successively capt., maj. and col. Neb. Nat. Guard, 1902-17; comdr. 4th Neb. Inf., Mexican border service, 1916-17; apptd. col. Inf., U.S.R.C., Feb., 1917; ordered to active duty, O.T.C., May 5, 1917; served as col. inf., O.R.C. and maj. N.A. until Dec. 3, 1918. Recipient Lincoln (Neb.) Kiwanis International Medal, 1948. Mem. Am., Neb., State and 9th Neb. Dist. bar assns., Neb. State Hist. Society, Sons of Union Veterans Civil War (past state comdr.), Naval and mil. order Spanish-Am. War Vets. (comdr.-in-chief, 1949, United Spanish War Veterans (comdr.-in-chief), Am. Legion, 40 and 8, Mil. Order World War. Republican. Conglist. Mason (32 deg., K.T.); mem. Woodmen, Sons of Hermann, Ben Hur. Clubs: Kiwanis, Hiram (internat.), Interprofessional Inst. Sojourners: Apptd. Judge Advocate Gen. United Spanish War Vets. Home: Stanton, NE Address: 900 S. 18th St., Lincoln NE

EBERSTADT, FERDINAND, investment banker; b. New York, N.Y., June 19, 1890; s. Edward F. and Elenita (Lembcke) E.; A.B., Princeton, 1913; LL.B., Columbia, 1917; D.C.S. honoris causa, New York University; married Mary Van Arsdale Tongue, Dec. 31, 1919; children—Frances Stuart, Mary Van Arsdale, Frederick, Ann Van Arsdale. Began as law clerk with McAdoo, Cotton & Franklin, 1919; partner Cotton & Franklin, 1923-25; partner Dillon, Read & Co., 1925-29; asst. to Owen D. Young, Reparations Conf., 1929; partner F. Eberstadt & Co., investment bankers; dir. F. Eberstadt & Co., Managers and Distributors, Inc.; chairman of The Eberstadt Fund, Inc.; chmn. Chem. Fund, Inc. Hon. dir. Beekman Downtown Hosp. Squadron A, New York Cavalry, 1916-17; with 304th F.A., 77th Division, U.S.A., with AEF, 1917-19; with Army of Occupation, 1919. Chairman Army and Navy Munitions Bd., 1942; v. chmn. War Prodn. Bd., 1942-43; prepared "Eberstadt Report" for sec. Navy, 1945; asst. to B.M. Baruch, U.N. Atomic Energy Commn., 1946; prepared report on operations of Nat. Security Resources Bd., 1948; chmn. com. on Nat. Security Orgn. of the Hoover Commn. (Commn. on Orgn. of Exec. Br. of the Govt.). Bd. advisers, Indsl. Coll. of the Armed Forces. Mem. U.S.N. Civilian Adv. Com., A.U.S. Adv. Com.; mem. bd. Presbyn. Hosp. Corp.; mem. bd. visitors U.S. Naval Acad., 1946; mem. Army Ordnance Assn.; mem. (hon.) Navy Indsl. Assn., Navy League of the U.S., U.S. Naval Inst., Naval Hist. Found., Phi Beta Kappa. Presbyn. Clubs: University, Princeton, Squadron A Assn., Downtown Assn., River, Piping Rock (N.Y.C.); Huntington (N.Y.) Country; Seawanhaka-Corinthian Yacht; Lyford Cay (Nassau, Bahamas). Home: Huntington LI NY Died Nov. 11, 1969; buried Huntington.

EBERT, EDMUND FRANCIS, banker; b. N.Y.C., Aug. 11, 1911; s. Samuel Harvey and Emily Grace (Cash) E.; student N.Y.U., 1930-32, 41; m. Lathelia Marie Keesey, Oct. 22, 1938; children—Beth Lynn (dec.), Douglas Edmund, Joan Marie. Began as messenger Bankers Trust Co. of N.Y., 1928, dept. head, 1934-39, field rep., 1939-42, asst. treas., 1942-46, asst. v.p., 1946-48, v.p., 1948-61, sr. v.p., 1961-70, exec. v.p., 1970-72; v.p., dir. Interstate Color Co., Inc., 1936-51.

Councilman Town of New Castle, N.Y., 1959-63, chmn. bd. ethics, 1970-72). Commd. lt. (j.g.) S.C., USN, 1944, apptd. dep. fiscal dir., 1945; disch. as lt., 1946; lt. res., 1945-52. Bd. dirs., treas. Ednl. Found. for Fashion Industries. Mem. Am. Bankers Assn. (chmn. credit policy com.), Acad. Polit. Sci., Downtown Lower Manhattan Assn. (dir.). Conglist. Clubs: Union League (N.Y.C.); Mt. Kisco Country (pres. 1956, 57), Bankers of N.Y. Inc.; Seaview Country; Economic; Board Room. Home: Chappaqua NY Died May 7, 1972; buried Kensico Cemetery, Valhalla NY

EBERT, RUDOLPH GUSTAV surgeon U.S.A.; b. N.Y., City, Aug. 29, 1854; s. Gustav and Augusta (Wacker) E.; student Holy Angels Coll., Vancouver, Wash., and med. dept. U. of Cal.; M.D., Bellevue Hosp. Med. Coll. (New York U.), 1878; m. Tabitha A. Clarke, of Forest Grove, Ore., Nov. 2, 1878. Apptd. asst. surgeon U.S.A., June 16, 1880; capt. asst. surgeon, June 16, 1885; maj. surgeon, Apr. 17, 1898; lt. col. Med. Corps, Apr. 23, 1908; campaign col., Dec. 27, 1910. Served in against the Crow Indians, 1887, Santiago Campaign, 1898; in Alaska, 1900-01, Philippines, 1906-08; assigned to Hawaii, 1914. Mem. A.M.A., United Service Med. Soc. of Hawaii. Mason (32ff, K.T., Shriner). Club: University (Honolulu). Addresss: War Dept., Washington, D.C.

EBY, IVAN DAVID marine engr.; b. Waterloo, Ont., Can., Mar. 24, 1887; s. Cyrus and Maria (Buehler) E.; ed. pub. schs., Waterloo; m. Ruth Mary Burroughs, Apr. 30, 1920; children-Barbara Kathleen (Mrs. Richard Hopkins Aime), Elsie Patricia, Adelaide (Mrs. Richard Edward Barkhonr). Came to U.S., 1909, naturalized, 1914. Practiced marine engring. principally Trans-Pacific and Trans-Atlantic, 1910-19. Charge engring. and repairs all Moore-McCormack Lines vessels, N.Y.C., 1920-49, v.p. 1949-52. Engr. officer on Naval troop transport, East Coast U.S. ports to France, World War I. Mem. Am. Soc. M.E., Am. Soc. Naval Architects and Marine Engrs. Mason. Holder patents. Home: 299 West 12th St., N.Y.C. 14. Office: Pier 32, North River, N.Y.C. 13. Died Sept. 24, 1967.

ECHOLS, CHARLES PATTON army officer; b. Huntsville, Ala., Sept. 6, 1867; s. William Holding and Mary Beirne (Patton) E.; grad. U.S. Mil. Acad., 1891; unmarried. Commd. additional 2d lt. engrs., June 12, 1891; 2d lt., Oct. 4, 1894; 1st lt., Jan. 6, 1896; in command of A Co. U.S. Engrs. in 3d expden. to Philippines in War with Spain, 1898; asso. prof. mathematics, U.S. Mil. Acad., Nov. 1898, prof., 1904-; on detached service visiting foreign schools, July 1905-June 1906; lt. col., 1904; col., 191 in France, July-Sept. 1918; retired from active service Sept. 1931. Home: Englewood, N.J. Died May 21, 1940.

ECHOLS, JOHN lawyer, army officer, railroad ofcl.; b. Lynchburg, Va., Mar. 20, 1823. s. Joseph and Elizabeth (Lambeth) E.; grad. Washington and Lee U., 1842; post-grad. Va. Mil. Inst., 1843, also Harvard Law Sch.; m. Mary Caperton; m. 2d, Mrs. Mary Cochran Reid. Admitted to Va. bar, 1843; mem. Va. Gen. Assembly; commanded 27th Va. Regt. at 1st Battle of Manassas; commd. brig. gen. Confederate Army, resumed command Dept. of Southwestern Va., 1864; his brigade fought with the Army of No. Va. from Hanover Junction to Cold Harbor; pres. Bank of Staunton (Va.); undertook reorgn. Chesapeake & Ohio & Southwestern R.R. (now C. & O. Ry.), directed railroad for 20 years; active mem. bd. visitors Va. Mil. Inst., Washington and Lee U. Died Staunton, May 24, 1896.

ECHOLS, OLIVER P. army officer (ret.); b. Charlottesville, Va., Mar. 4, 1892; s. William H. and Mary (Blakey) E.; student Va. Poly. Inst., 1908-10, U. of Va., 1910-13; grad. Army Industrial Coll., 1926, A.C., Engring. Sch., 1927, Command and Gen. Staff Sch., 1934, Army War Coll., 1939; m. Margaret Bailey, Dec. 28, 1920; 1 dau., Mary Beirne. Commd. 2d lt. U.S. Army, 1916, and advanced through grades to maj. gen., 1942; served A.C. Exptl. Engring. Sect., 1927-30; chief A.C. Procurement Sect., 1930-31; graduate of Air Corps Tactical School, 1932; chief engr. Material Div., 1934-38, asst. chief, 1939-40, chief, 1940-47. President Aircraft Industries Assn., 1947-49; chmn. bd., chief exec. officer Northrop Aircraft, Inc., Hawthorne, California since 1949. Served with U.S. Air Services, A.E.F., Aug. 1917-Apr. 1919; comd. 1st Observation Group, chief aviation, 1st Army Corps. Participated in battles of Champagne-Marne, Aisne Marne, St. Mihiel, Meues-Argonne, Chief Army A.F. Materiel Div., Oct. 1940-Apr. 1945; chief Internal Affairs and Communication Div., U.S. Control Council, Germany, May-July 1945; asst. dep. mil. gov., U.S. Mil. Govt. (Berlin) Germany July 1945-Apr. 1946; chief civil affairs div., War Dept., Washington, D.C., Apr. 1946-47; retired. Decorations: D.S.M. with Oak Leaf Cluster, Legion of Merit, Purple Heart, Victory Medal with five battle clasps, Hon. Comdr. Order of British Empire. Home: 10425 Charing Cross Rd., Los Angeles 24. Office: Northrop Aircraft, Inc., Hawthorne, Cal. Died May 15, 1954.

ECKEL, EDWIN CLARENCE (EKEL), engr., geologist; b. New York, Mar. 6, 1875; s. August and Helena S. K. (Butt) E.; B.S., New York U., 1895, C.E., 1896; m. Julia Egerton Dibblee, July 9, children - Edwin Butt, Julie Egerton Dibblee, Richard Egerton. Asst. geologist of N.Y., 1900-02; asst. geologist, 1902-05, U.S. Geol. Survey, and geologist in charge sect. of iron ores and structural materials, 1906-07; spl. commr. in charge cement exhibits, Jamestown Expn., 1907; cons. engr. and geologist since 1907; pres. Dominion Cement Co., 1910-12. Expert on southern and eastern iron ores for U.S. Steel Corp. during the Stanley investigation and dissolution suit, 1911-13; iron ore investigations in Europe, 1928-30; cement mill valuations for U.S. Dept., 1931-32; chief geologist Tenn. Valley Authority since 1933. Commd. capt., Engr. R.C., Jan. 23, 1917; maj. engrs., U.S. Army, Apr. 1919; service in France, July 1917-July 1919. Fellow Geol. Soc. America; mem. Soc. of Econ. Geologists Am. Inst. mining Engrs., Delta Kappa Epsilon; life mem. Am. Soc. C.E. Author: Cements, Limes and Plasters, 1905; Portland Cement Industry from the Financial Standpoint, 1908; Building Stones and Clays, 1911; Iron Ores, 1914; Coal, Iron and War, 1920; Le Ciment Portland, 1927; Report on Economic Sanctions, 1931. Wrote Ency. Britannica article on Iron Ore Resources of World; Engineering

ECKERT, THOMAS THOMPSON chmn. bd. Western Union Telegraph Co.; b. St. Clairsville, O., Apr. 23, 1825; learned telegraphy; supervised construction, 1852, and became supt. of line, Pittsburgh to Chicago, so remaining, with extended jurisdiction, when line became part of Western Union Telegraph Co.; resigned, 1859, becoming supt. of a gold mining co. in N.C. until Civil War broke out, when he went to Cincinnati. Supt. mil. telegraph, Dept. of Potomac, with rank of capt.; later gen. supt. mil. telegraph, with rank of maj.; bvtd. lt. col., col. and brig. gen. vols., Mar. 13, 1865, "for meritorious and distinguished services." Asst. Sec. of War, July 27, 1866-Feb. 28, 1867. Gen supt. eastern div., Western Union Telegraph Co., 1866-75; pres. Atlantic & Pacific Telegraph Co., 1875-81; pres. Am. Union Telegraph Co., 1880-81; v.p. and gen. mgr. Western Union Telegraph Co., 1881-92, and pres. from 1892, later chmn. bd. Home: New York, N.Y. Died 1910.

ECKERT, WILLIAM D(OLE), retired air force officer, business executive; born Freeport, Illinois, on January 20, 1909; the son of Frank Lloyd and Harriet Julia (Rudy) E.; B.S., U.S. Mil. Acad., 1930; grad. (with pilot's rating), Air Force Flying Sch., 1931; M.B.A., Harvard, 1940, student Army-Navy Staff Sch., 1944; m. Catharine Douglas Givens, June 15, 1940; children—Catharine Julia, William Douglas. Commd. 2d lt. U.S. Army, 1930; advanced through grades to lt. general; transferred to U.S.A.A.F., 1931; served at Albrook Field, Panama Canal Zone, 1935-57, Randolph Field, Tex., 1937-38; budget officer and exec. to comdg. gen., Air Materiel Command, Wright Field, Dayton, O., 1940-44; group comdr., later chief of supply, 9th AFSC, Europe, 1944; executive to Deputy Chief of Staff, Materiel, 1945, chief of readjustment and procurement div., 1946; exec. to Under Sec. of Air Force, 1947-49; comptroller Air Materiel Command, Wright-Patterson Air Force Base, Ohio, 1949-51, asst. dep. comdg. gen., 1951-52; asst. dep. chief of staff Materiel, Hdqrs. USAF, 1952-56; vice comdr. Tactical Air Command, 1956-61; comptroller USAF, Feb.-Mar. 1961, ret. as lt. gen., 1961; major league baseball commr., 1965-69. Chmn. retirement council Air Force. Bd. Advisers Tantallon Community, Air Force Assn. Mem. exec. council of Harvard Bus. Sch., from 1961; trustee Little League Found., Logistic Management Inst.; member board of directors Baseball Hall of Fame, 1966-69. Decorated D.S.M. with oak leaf cluster, Legion of Merit with 2 oak leaf clusters, D.F.C., Bronze Star, Air medal (U.S.); Croix de Guerre with palm (France and Luxembourg). Mem. Air Force Assn., Am. Soc. Mil. Comptrollers (past pres.), Am. Legion, Air Force Assn., Baseball Writers Assn. Am. Episcopalian. Clubs: Army-Navy Country (past pres., Nat. Rocket (dir.), Harvard of Dayton (O.) (past pres.), Air Force Acad. Parents, Lambs, Aviation, Harvard Busines of N.Y., Gate. Home: Clearwater FL Died Apr. 16, 1971.

EDDINS, HENRY A. business exec.; b. Jewett, Tex., Nov. 27, 1908; s. Sidney J. and Ada (Burns) E.; B.S. in Elec. Engring., Tex. A. and M. Coll., 1931; m. Claire Gaskell, July 2, 1938; children - Marsha, Henry A. With Stone & Webster Service Corp. and affiliated firms, 1931 - , beginning as engr. Central Ill. Gas Co., Rockford, Ill., successively engr. Stone & Webster Service Corp., N.Y.C., 1936-39, gen. mgr. Citizens Gas Co., Stroudsburg, Pa., 1939-40, asst. div. mgr. utility operations Stone & Webster Service Corp., New Eng. area, 1945-48, v.p. Laclede Gas Co., St. Louis, 1948-54, exec. v.p. Okla. Natural Gas Co., Tulsa, 1954-55, pres., 1955 - , Chmn. bd., 1964 - ; dir. First Nat. Bank & Trust Co. of Tulsa, Okla. Cement Co., Transcontinental Gas Pipe Line Corp. Served from 1st lt. to col. C.E., AUS, 1941-45. Decorated Legion of Merit. Mem. Am., So. gas assns., Res. Officers Assn. Clubs: Tulsa; Southern Hills Country. Home: 3731 S. Delaware Pl., Tulsa 74105. Office: 624 S. Boston St., Tulsa. Died Apr. 26, 1966.

EDDY, MANTON S. army officer; b. Chgo., May 16, 1892; s. George Manton and Martha Bishop (Sprague) E.; student Shattuck Mil. Sch., 1909-13, Inf. Sch., co. officer's course, 1920-21, advanced course, 1929-30, Command and Gen. Staff Sch., 1932-34; m. Mamie Peabody Buttolph, Nov. 23, 1921; 1 dau., Martha Sprague. Commd. 2d lt., 1916, and advanced through the grades to lt. gen.; served with 4th Div., AEF, 1918-19; became comdr. 114th Inf., 44th Div., Oct. 1941; asst. div. comdr. 9th Inf. Div., 1942; assigned to command 9th Div., 1942; comdr. of this div. throughout Tunisian campaign, 1943; comdr. 9th Inf. Div. throughout Tunisian and Sicilian campaigns, 1943, Cherbourg campaign and liberation of France, 1944; assigned to command the XII U.S. Army Corps, 1944, comdr. operations in France, Germany, Luxembourg, 1944-45; comd. 3d Service Comd., alt.; dep. comdr. 2d Army, 1946; information chief, 1947; Comd. and Gen. Staff Coll. (comdg. gen.) Leavenworth, Kan., 1948; nominated comdg. gen. U.S. Army in Europe, 1950. Decorations; D.S.C., D.S.M. with oak leaf cluster, Silver Star, Legion of Merit with oak leaf cluster, Bronze Star with oak leaf cluster, Air medal, Army Commendation Ribbon, Purple Heart; Hon. Companion, Order of Bath (Brit.); Legion of Honor, Croix de Guerre with Palm (French); Order War for Fatherland, Medal for Valor (Russian); Comdr. Order Leopold with Palm, Croix de Guerre with Palm (Belgian). Home: 3224 Hillside Dr., Columbus, Ga. Died Apr. 10, 1962; buried Arlington Cemetery, Washington.

EDDY, NORMAN congressman; b. Scipio, N.Y., Dec. 10, 1810; grad. med. dept. U. Pa. at Phila., 1835; studied law. Practiced medicine, Mishawaka, Ind., until 1847; admitted to bar, 1847, began practice of law, South Bend, mem. Ind. Senate, 1850; held various local offices; mem. U.S. Ho. of Reps. (Democrat) from Ind., 33d Congress, 1853-55; apptd. atty. gen. Territory of Minn. by Pres. Pierce, 1855; served as col. 48th Ind. Volunteer Inf. during Civil War; collector internat. revenue, 1865-70; sec. of state Ind., 1870-72. Died Indpls., Ind., Jan. 28, 1872; buried City Cemetery, South Bend.

EDDY, WALTER HOLLIS physiol. chemist; b. Brattleboro, Vt., Aug. 26, 1877; B.S., Amherst, 1898; A.M., Columbia, 1908; Ph.D., 1909, Instr. sci., high sch., Amherst, 1898-1900, Passaic, N.J., 1900-03; head dept. biology, N.Y.C. High Sch. Commerce, 1903-17; asso. in biochemistry Coll. Phys. and Surg. (Columbia), 1908-13; research chemist N.Y. Hosp., 1913—; with Tchrs. Coll. (Columbia), 1919-41, prof. physiol. chemistry, 1922-41, now emeritus; dir. Bur. Food, Sanitation and Health, Good Housekeeping Mag., 1927-41; cons. chemist and conductor, Food Forum program WOR, 1941-48; sci. dir. Am. Chlorophyll, Inc., Lake Worth, Fla., 1948-52, Am. Chlorophyll Div., Strong Cobb Co., 1952; research dir. Mangrove Products, Inc., West Palm Beach, Fla., cons. chem. engr., 1953—; research cons. U.S. Vitamin and Pharm. Corp. Served from capt. to maj. Nutrition Div., U.S. Army, 1917-19; an organizer Div. Food and Nutrition, A.E.F., and made chief div. Author: Experimental Physiology and Anatomy, 1906; Vitamin Manual, 1921; Nutrition, 1928; The Avitaminoses, 1937, rev. edit., 1941, 1945. What Are the Vitamins?, 1941; We Need Vitamins, 1941; Vitaminology 1949, also many articles on foods and vitamins. Home: 1227 N. Lakeside Dr., Lake Worth, Fla. Died Oct. 1959.

EDDY, WILLIAM ALFRED consultant; b. Sidon, Syria (parents Am. missionaries), Mar. 9, 1896; s. William King and Elizabeth Mills (Nelson) E.; Litt. B., Princeton, 1917, A.M., 1921, Ph.D., 1922; LL.D., St. Lawrence Univ., 1936, Colgate U., 1936; L.H.D., Wooster (O.) Coll., 1937; Litt.D., Hobart Coll., 1947; m. Mary Emma Garvin, Oct. 5, 1917; children - William Alfred, Mary Garvin. John Condit, Carmen Frances. Chairman department English Am. Univ., Cairo, Egypt, 1923-28; assistant professor, later prof. English, Dartmouth Coll., 1928-36; pres. Hobard Coll. and William Smith Coll., Geneva, N.Y., 1936-42; E.E. and M.P. to Kingdom of Saudi Arabia, 1944-46; chief spl. diplomatic mission to kingdom of The Yemen, 1946; special assistant to secretary of State, in charge research and intelligence, 1946-47; served as the Middle East consultant Arabian Am. Oil Co., 1947-62. Served as reg. intelligence officer Sixth Marines, 2d Division AEF, later brigade intelligence officer and aide-de-camp; wounded at Belleau Woods, June 25, 1918; active duty as major, United States Marine Corps, 1941, now col.; served as Naval attache, Am. legations, Cairo, 1941, Tangier, 1942; on staff Allied Force Hdqrs., Algiers, 1943. Awarded D.S.C., Navy Cross, Order Purple Heart (2), Silver Star (2), Legion of Merit, Army Commendation Ribbon. Democrat. Episcopalian. Honorary member of Phi Beta Kappa. Clubs: Army and Navy. Author: Gulliver's Travels-A critical Study, 1923; FDR Meets Ibn Saud, 1954. Editor: Oxford Standard Edition of Jonathan Swift (2 vols.), 1932-33; Samuel Butler's Erew-hon, 1933. Home: Tapline, Beirut, Lebanon. Died May 3, 1962; buried Sidon, Lebanon.

EDGE, WALTER EVANS ex-gov., N.J., ex-senator, ex-ambassador; b. Phila., Nov. 20, 1873; s. William and Mary (Evans) E.; student pub. schs.; m. Lady Lee Philipps, June 10, 1907 (died 1915); m. 2d, Camilla Loyall Ashe Sewall, Dec. 9, 1922. Began as printer's devil Atlantic Review, Atlantic City: later established a nat. and internat. advt. agency; was propr. Atlantic City Daily Press, Atlantic City Evening Union, also identified with banking and other lines of business, Journal clk., N.J. Senate, 1897-99; sec. of senate, 1901-04; Rep. presdl. elector, 1908; del. at large Rep. Nat.

convs., 1916-48; mem. N.J. Assembly, 1910, Rep. leader Senate, two terms 1911-16. Rep. leader 1912, pres. 1915, was chmn. economy and efficiency commn. and a leader in securing passage of workmen's compensation bill, state budger budget system bill and central purchasing bureau bill; gov. of N.J. for term 1917-20, resigned, 1919, to take seat in U.S. Senate, term 1919-25, re-elected for term, 1925-31, resigned; A.E. and P. from the U.S. to France, 1929-33; gov. of N.J., 1944-47. With Sec. of Treasury Mellon negotiated Franco-Am. Accord of July 6, 1931. Served as lt. Co. F, 4th N.J. Vol. Inf., Spanish-Am. War; later capt. Co. L, 3d Regt. N.J.N.G.: mem. staffs of Govs. Murphy and Stokes; was lt. col. and chief ordnance dept., staff of Maj. Gen. C. Edward Murray, N.J. Nat. Guard. Episcopalian. Clubs: Union League (Phila.): Book. Union League (N.Y.C.). Home: Princeton. Office: Press-Union Bldg. Atlantic City, N.J. Died Oct. 29, 1956.

EDGELL, GEORGE HAROLD historian of art; b. St. Louis, Mar. 4, 1887; s. George Stephen and Isabella Wallace (Corbin) E.; A.B., Harvard, 1909, Ph.D., 1913, Art D. (hon.) 1948; fellow Am. Acad. in Rome, 1910-12; m. Jean Walters Delano, June 13, 1914; children-George Harold, Delano (dec.), Henry Walters. Asst. in fine arts,1909-10, instr., 1912-14, asst. prof., 1914-22, asso. prof., 1922-25, prof., 1925-35, dean faculty architecture, chmn. council Sch. of Architecture, 1922-35, Harvard; curator of paintings Mus. Fine Arts, Boston, 1934-38; dir. museum, 1935—. American commr. Interallied Commission for Propaganda, Italian General Staff, 1918; annual prof. Am. Acad. in Rome, 1919-20; exchange prof. to U. of Paris, 1929; overseer, Harvard U., 1936-42. Decorated Chevalier of Legion of Honor, 1937. Member Boston Art Commn., 1925-50; chmn. Mass. State Art Commn., 1941-51; trustee Boston Museum of Fine Arts, 1927—; pres. Am. Assn. of Mus., 1949-51. Mem. U.S. Commn. for UNESCO, 1947—. Fellow A.A.A.S.; mem. Archaeol. Inst. Am., College Art Association of America, Phi Beta Kappa (president Harvard Chapter, 1940-42). Republican, Episcopalian. Clubs: Harvard, Tavern (Boston); Harvard, Century (New York). The Athenaeum (London). Author: (with Fiske Kimball) A History of Architecture, 1918; The American Architecture of Today, 1928; A History of Sienese Painting, 1932; The Bee Hunter, 1949. Contbr. to American Journal Acracology, l'Arte, Art in America, Gazette des Beaux Arts, etc. Home: Newport, N.H. Address: Museum of Fine Arts, Boston 15. Died June 29, 1954; buried North Newport, N.H.

EDGERTON, ALONZO JAY senator; b. Rome, N.Y., June 7, 1827; grad. Wesleyan U., Middletown, Conn., 1850; studied law. Moved to Mantorville, Minn., 1855; admitted to bar, 1855, began practice of law, Mantorville; pros. atty. Dodge County; mem. Minn. Senate, 1858-59, 77-79; commd. capt. 10th Minn. Volunteer Regt. in Civil War, 1862, promoted col., 1864, brevetted brig. gen., 1865; railroad commr., 1871-75; Republican presdl. elector, 1876; moved to Kasson, Minn., 1878; mem. U.S. Senate (Republican) from Mar.-Oct. 1881 (filled vacancy); apptd. chief justice Territorial Supreme Ct. Dakota; U.S. judge Dist. of S.C.; pres. S.D. Constl. Conv. Died Sioux Falls, S.D., Constl. Conv. Died Sioux Falls, S.D., Aug. 9, 1896; buried Evergreen Cemetery, Mantorville.

EDGERTON, WILLIAM FRANKLIN, Egyptologist; b. Binghamton, N.Y., Sept. 30, 1893; s. Charles Eugene and Annie Benedict (White) E.; A.B., Cornell U., 1915; Ph.D., U. of Chicago, 1922; student U. of Pa., 1919, Columbia, 1923-24, U. of Munich, 1927; m. Jean Daniel Modell, May 22, 1918 (div. 1956); m. 2d. Lenetta Margaret Cooper, Feb. 16, 1957. Archeol. survey in Mesopotamia and Syria for Oriental Inst., U. of Chicago, 1920; asst. Oriental Inst., same, 1922-23; asst. prof. ancient history, U. of Louisville, 1924-25; asso. prof. history, Vassar Coll., 1925-26; epigrapher, Epigraphic and Archtl. Survey of Oriental Inst., U. of Chicago, Luxor, Upper Egypt, 1926-29; asso. prof. Egyptology, U. Chgo., 1929-37, prof., 1937-59, emeritus. 1959-70, chmn. dept. Oriental langs. and lit., 1948-54; Fulbright research scholar King's College and University of Cambridge (England), 1951-52; visiting professor U. Cal. at Berkeley, 1964-66; collected demotic and other graffiti at Medinet Habu (near Luxor, Egypt) for Oriental Institute, U. of Chicago 1931-33. Sergt. Medical Dept., U.S. Army, 1918-19. Served as captain, Signal Corps, United States Army, 1942-43, major, 1943-45. Mem. Am. Assn. U. Profs. (council 1953-55), Am. Hist. Assn., Am. Oriental Soc. (president 1944-45), Linguistic Soc. of America, Egypt Exploration Society, Phi Beta Kappa fraternity (member of senate 1952-58). Clubs: University (Chicago); Cliff Dwellers, Quadrangel. Author: Medinet Habu, Vol. I, Earlier Historical Records of Ramses III (with H. H. Nelson, J. A. Wilson and others), 1930; Notes on Egyptian Marriage, Chiefly in the Ptolemaic Period, 1931; The Thutmosid Succession, 1933; Historical Records of Ramses III. The Texts in Medinet Habu (with J. A. Wilson), Vols. I and II, 1936; Medinet Habu Graffiti Facsimiles, 1937; (with E. M. Husselman and A. E. R. Boak) Michigan Papyri from Tebtunis, Part II, 1944. Consulting editor Journal of Near Eastern Studies. 1942-49. Contbr. to scholarly jours. Home: Chicago IL Died Mar., 1970.

EDGINGTON, THOMAS BENTON lawyer; b. Ontario, O., Apr. 23, 1837; s. Jesse and Hannah (Mitchell) E.; student Baldwin U., Berea, O., until sophomore yr.; A.B., Ohio Wesleyan U., 1859, A.M., 1862, LL.D., 1905; m. Catherine Vose Baxter, Apr. 5, 1865; children-Hugh, Irving H., Jesse, Katherine B. (wife of Dr. R. B. Underwood, dec.), Mary Rose. Admitted to bar, 1861; mustered into Union Army as 1st sergt., Co. A, 12th Ia. Inf., Oct. 17, 1861; participated in siege of Ft. Henry, battles of Ft. Donelson and Shiloh; comd. co. in latter battle, was wounded and taken prisoner; remained prisoner of war about 7 months; 1st lt., Apr. 9, 1862-Apr. 4, 1863, resigned on account of ill health; aided in organizing Union Mil. forces in W. Tenn., and became maj. 4th regt. 1863. Now senior mem. Edington & Edington. Episcopalian. Democrat. Author: The Monroe Doctrine, 1904. One of speeches, The Race Question, in opposition to the Force Bill, was published (1889) and attracted wide attention; The Waves of Kosmos, 1920; Electronomy, 1923, revised and enlarged, 1924. Home: Memphis, Tenn. Died Jan. 4, 1929.

EDIE, GUY LEWIS surgeon U.S.A.; b. in Va., June 18, 1858; M.D., U. of Va., 1879. Apptd. asst. surgeon U.S.A., Dec. 3, 1883; capt. asst. surgeon, Dec. 3, 1888; maj. brigade surgion vols., June 4, 1898; vacated Feb. 2, 1901; maj. surgeon U.S.A., Reb. 2, 1901; maj. Med. Corps, Feb. 2, 1901; lt. col., Jan. 1, 1909; col., Aug. 6, 1912. At Presidio, San Francisco, 1916. Died Apr. 9, 1930.

EDIE, JOHN RUFUS congressman, lawyer; b. Gettysburg, Pa., Jan. 14, 1814; attended Emmitsburg (Md.) Coll., U.S. Mil. Acad.; studied law. Prin. schs., Gettysburg, several years; admitted to bar, 1840, began practice of law, Somerset, Pa.; mem. Pa. Senate, 1845-46; dept. atty. gen., 1847-50; dist. atty., 1850-54; mem. U.S. Ho. of Reps. (Whig) from Pa., 34th-35th congresses, 1855-59; commd. maj. 15th Regt., U.S. Inf., 1861, promoted lt. col., 1863; brevetted col. for services during Atlanta campaign, 1864; served with 15th, 8th regts. U.S. Inf., until 1871. Died Somerset, Pa., Aug. 27, 1888; buried Union Cemetery.

EDLER, BOWMAN railway corp. exec.; b. Indianapolis, Ind., Mar. 4, 1888; s. William Line and Laura (Bowman) E.; grad. Chestnut Hill (Pa.) Acad., 1907: B.S., U. of Pa., 1911: m. Madeline Fortune, Sept. 30, 1914; children-Anne, William Line. Entered real estate bus. at Indianapolis, with father, as Wm. L. Elder & Bowman Elder, 1912-40; promoted Chamber of Commerce Office Bldg. and became sec.-treas. Chamber of Commerce Bldg., Corp.; receiver Ind. R.R. and as such lessee Pub. Service Company of Indiana and Indiana Service Corporation, 1933-41: vice president Circle Agencies, Inc., 1935-39; pres. and dir. of Southern Indiana Railway, Inc. Consular agent for France at Indianapolis, 1934-40. Commd. lt. C.A. Res. Corps, Nov. 27, 1917: capt., Apr. 5, 1918; served in France, July 30, 1918-Feb. 22, 1919; capt. Res., May 1, 1919; lt. col., July 5, 1923; col., July 16, 1926; mem. 5th Corps Area Advisory Bd., term 1931-39. Del. Dem. Nat. Conv., St. Louis, 1916, del. at large Dem. Nat. Conv., Chicago, 1932, del. Dem. Nat. Conv. Chicago, 1940; treas. Dem. State Com., Indiana, 1924-26. Mem. bd. dirs. American Red Cross; trustee Park School for Boys, 1934-40; trustee Crown Hill Cemetery Association (pres. and mem. bd. of mgrs.). Active in nat. affairs of Am. Legion, 1922—, nat. chmn. distinguished guests com., 1922, mem. nat. exec. com., 1923-27, nat. chmn. of France Conv. Com., in charge 2d A.E.F., 1927 (comprising 20,000 legionnaires, largest orgn. peace time movement in history), nat. treas. Am. Legion, 1928-33; also same. Legion Pub. Corp.; mem. Ind. Soc. Chicago. Indianapolis Chamber of Commerce, U. of Pa. Alumni Association, Indianapolis Real Estate Board. Reserve Officers Assns., Mil. Order Foreign Wars, Newcomen Society of England. Forty and Eight, Sons of Am. Revolution, Friars Sr. Soc. of Univ. of Pa., Zeta Psi. Officer Order Polonia Restituta (Poland); Order Legion of Honor (France). Presbyterian. Mason. Elk. Clubs: Army and Navy (Washington, D.C.); University, Dramatic, Indianapolis Athletic (dir. and treas.). Compiler: History of the 71st Artillery (C.A.C.) in the Great War, 1919. Home: New Augusta, Ind. Office: Chamber of Commerce Bldg., Indpls. 4. Died June 10, 1954; buried Crown Hill Cemetery.

EDMISTON, ANDREW congressman; b. Weston, W.Va., Nov. 13, 1892; s. Matthew and Ella Bennett (Jackson) E.; ed. Friends Select Sch., Washington, 1900-08, Ky. Mil. Inst., Lyndon, 1908-12; student U. W.Va., 1912-14; m. Merle Williams, Apr. 21, 1920 (dec. 1950); 1 dau., Ann Bland; married second to Beth Gage, Jan. 31, 1953. Editor of Weston Democrat, 1920 - ; mayor of Weston, 1924-26; state chmn. Dem. Exec. Com., 1928-32; mem. 73d to 77th Congresses (1933-43) from 3d W.Va. Dist.; sec. and treas. C.A. Borchet Glass Co.; dir. Weston Nat. Bank; State dir. War Manpower, W.Va., 1943-46. Served as 2d lt., U.S. Army, with A.E.F. Awarded D.S.C., Order of Purple Heart; recipient Distinguished Service medal W.Va. Mem. Am. Legion, V.F.W. Democrat. Episcopalian. Mason, Moose. Home: Weston, W.Va. Died Aug. 28, 1966; buried Weston.

EDMONDS, JOHN WORTH jurist b. Hudson, N.Y., Mar. 13, 1799; s. Samuel and Lydia (Worth) E.; grad. Union Coll., Schenectady, N.Y., 1816. Commd. lt. N.Y. State Militia, 1814, later col.; admitted to Columbia County (N.Y.) bar, 1819; recorder Columbia County, 1828-30; elected to N.Y. Assembly (Democrat), 1830; mem. N.Y. State Senate, 1831-36; spl. commr. to Indians on borders of lakes Huron and Superior, 1836-37; apptd. insp. state prisons N.Y., 1843; an organizer Prison Discipline Soc., Prison Soc., Women's Prison Assn. of N.Y.C., 1844; apptd. judge 1st N.Y. Circuit, 1845; justice N.Y. State Supreme Ct., 1847-52; judge N.Y. Ct. Appeals, 1852-53; Author: (with George T. Dexter) Spiritualism, 1853-55; Reports of Select Cases Decided in the Courts of State of New York, 1868; editor Revised Statutes of New York, 1869-72. Died N.Y.C., Apr. 5, 1874.

EDMUNDSON, HENRY ALONZO congressman, lawyer; b. Blacksburg, Va., June 14, 1814; grad. Georgetown U., Washington, D.C.; studied law. Admitted to bar, 1838, began practice of law, Salem, Va.; mem. U.S. Ho. of Reps. (Democrat) from Va., 31st-36th congresses, 1849-61; served as lt. col. 54th Va. Regt., Confederate Army, until 1862; assigned to command of 27th Va. Cavalry, 1862; resumed practice of law after Civil War; engaged in agriculture, 1880. Died "Falling Waters," Shawsville, Va., Dec. 16, 1890; buried Fotheringay Cemetery, Montgomery County, Va.

EDROP, PERCY T., clergyman; b. Birmingham, Eng., Oct. 18, 1883; s. George Thomas and Annie (Lane) E.; came to U.S., 1895; studied for the ministry P.E.Ch., later under Ref. Episcopal Ch., New York and Phila. Synod; D.D., Ref. Episcopal Sem., at Phila., Pa., 1918; m. Marion Lothrop Stafford, of Brooklyn, N.Y., Mar. 16, 1912. Reporter and mem. editorial staff, New York American, 1905-16; ordained ministry, R.E.Ch., 1907; pastor Ch. of the Reconciliation, Brooklyn, 1910-15, serving without salary; mem. editorial staff New York Tribune, 1919; rector First Ref. Episcopal Ch., New York, since 1919. Chaplain N.G.N.Y., 1916, later chaplain 47th N.Y. Inf., and of 53rd Pioneer Inf.; relieved of regtl. duties by order of Sec. of War Baker, to direct 39 military camp publs. during latter part of World War. Was sec. Gen. Wartime Commn. R.E.Ch., and chmn. of Synod Commn.; mem. S.S.Bd. of R.E.Ch. and of gen. com. of gen. council; v.p. Bd. of Home Missions R.E.Ch. Clubs: Hamilton, Rotary (Brooklyn); Clergy, Old Guard, Columbia Yacht (New York). Wrote larger part of "Marching into the Dawn" (war editorials), also brochures, distributed among soldiers; edited "Going Over," etc. Home: 194 Clinton St., Brooklyn NY

EDSON, STEPHEN REUBEN, ret. naval officer; b. Mpls., Nov. 12, 1895; s. James Richards and Mary Barbara (Strauss) E.; ed. pub. schs.; various Naval courses of instruction; m. Mary Bridget McWilliams, June 10, 1925; children—Stephen R., James, Peter, Charles, Mary, Alice. Enlisted, U.S. Navy, 1917, commd. ensign, 1919, and advanced through grades to vice admiral; assigned to patrol craft, Pacific, World War I; various assignments ashore and afloat, 1919-43; served on staff of Admiral Hewitt, comdr. of Amphibious Forces, Atlantic Fleet, during invasion of N. Africa, 1943-45; served on staff of Admiral Hewitt, comdr. Eight Fleet during invasions of Sicily, Italy and Southern France, 1945; executive officer Naval Supply Depot, Mechanicsburg, Pa., 1945-47; supply officer, Naval Gun Factory, Washington, 1947-49; clothing supply officer of the Navy and comdg. officer, Naval Clothing Depot, Brooklyn, 1949-51, dir. procurement div., office naval material, 1951-53; vice chief of naval material, 1953-54; commanding Naval Supply Depot, Mechanicsburg, Pa., 1954-57. Decorated Legion of Merit with combat device; Gold star in lieu of 2d Leg. of Merit; Commendation ribbon with combat device; Croix de Guerre with silver star; World War I and II Victory medals; Am. Defense service with star; American Area, European-African-Middle Eastern area with star. Republican. Roman Catholic. Elk (life). Home: Chevy Chase MD Died Aug. 28, 1969; buried Arlington National Cemetery, Arlington VA

EDWARD, HENRY army officer; b. New York, Oct. 1, 1893; grad. Q.M.C. Sch., 1928, Army Indsl. Coll., 1931, Command and Gen. Staff Sch., 1934, Chem. Warfare Sch., field officers course, 1938, Army War Coll., 1938. Commd. 2d lt., U.S. Army, 1917, and advanced through the grades to brig. gen., 1945. Address: care The Adjutant General's Office, War Department, Washington 25. Deceased.

EDWARDS, ALANSON W. journalist, consul; b. in Lorain Co., O., Aug. 27, 1840; s. Milton W. and Esther (Powers) E.; ed. McKendree Coll., 1856-59, scientific course; m. Elizabeth Robertson, June, 1869. Enlisted in 122d Ill. Inf., 1862, as pvt.; served to end of war; was with Sherman from Atlanta to the sea, and from Savannah, Ga., to Washington, at final review; became capt. 1st Ala. Union Cav. with Kilpatrick; mustered out as capt. and a. a. gen. with Corse at end of war, 4th div., 15th corps; bvtd. maj. After war in newspaper work with Carlinville (Ill.) Democrat, and Chicago Evening Post. In 1878 founded Fargo (N. Dak.) Daily Argus, and became editor of the paper and its successor, the present Fargo Forum; pres. Forum Printing Co. Was warden Ill.

Penitentiary, 1870-73; dir. Dak. (territorial) Penitentiary and chmn. bd. Republican. Am. consul gen. at Montreal, Can., 1902-06. Methodist. Home: Fargo, N. Dak. Died 1908.

EDWARDS, CLEMENT STANISLAUS, consular service; b. N.Y. City, Mar. 4, 1869; s. Clement and Anna (Cameron) E.; prep. edn., pvt. sch., St. Michael's Acad., Chatham, N.B., Can., and high sch., Albert Lea, Minn.; student Parker Coll., Winnebago City, Minn., and Hillsdale (Mich.) Coll.; m. Marguerite Auld, of Burlington, Vt., Mar. 2, 1922. Admitted to Minn. bar, 1894, and began practice at Albert Lea; city atty., Albert Lea, 1896-1900; owner and editor Albert Lea Times-Enterprise, 1904-10; Am. consul, Acapulco, Mexico, 1911-16; service with Citizenship bur., U.S. Dept. State, Washington, D.C., 1916-17; consul in charge legation part of time, Santo Domingo, 1917-19; consul-Paris, France, 1919-21; attached to Am. Commn., Berlin, detailed to Frankfurt am Main, later to Hamburg, Paris and Kovno, Lithuania, 1921-24; consul, Valencia, Spain, 1924-30, Bradford, England, since 1930. Served as capt., inf., Minn. Vols., Spanish-Am. War. Mem. Albert Lea Charter Commn., 1896-1904. Mem. Phi Delta Theta. Mason, K.P. Home: "Waylands," Harrogate, Eng. Office: American Consulate, Bradford England

EDWARDS, DAVID FRANK industrial exec.; b. Jackson, O., July 21, 1881; s. David Frank and Cornelia (Rathburn) E.; A.B., O. Wesleyan U., 1903, LL.D., 1950; A.M., Harvard, 1906; Sc.D. (hon.) Tufts Coll., 1948; m. Edna Fay, Aug. 30, 1906. Teacher secondary schs., later asso. prof. Grad. Sch. Business Adminstrn., Harvard; ednl. dir. William Filene Sons Co., 1909-10; indsl. sec. Boston Chamber Commerce, 1910-11; statistician and asst. to pres. Gen. Motors Co., 1911-12; comptroller and v.p. Olds Motor Works, 1912-16; engaged in reorgn. certain indsl. cos., 1916-26; pres. Saco-Lowell Shops, 1926-52, chmn. bd., 1952-58, 60-61, hon. chmn., 1961- ; dir. Arkwright Mut. Fire Ins. Co., Cambridge Trust Co., United-Carr Fastener Corp., Ashworth Bros.; hon. dir. Liberty Mut. Fire Ins. Co., Liberty Mut. Ins. Co. Served as maj. Ordnance Corps, U.S. Army, World War I. Vice chmn. vis. com. dept. econs., past mem. vis. com. sch. pub. health Harvard; trustee, chmn. com. devel. Northeastern U. Fellow Am. Academy Arts and Sciences (past v.p.); mem. Nat. Assn. Textile Machinery Mfrs. (past president), N. A.M. (past director), United States C. of C. (past v.p., past dir.), Boston Chamber of Commerce (past dir.), Harvard Alumni Assn. (past dir.), Phi Beta Kappa, Phi Delta Theta. Republican. Conglist. Clubs: Union (Boston); Harvard Univ. Faculty (Cambridge); The Country (Brookline); St. Botolph (Boston). Home: 987 Memorial Dr., Cambridge 38, Mass. Office: 60 Batterymarch St., Boston. Died Oct. 8, 1964; buried Mt. Auburn Cemetery, Cambridge, Mass.

EDWARDS, HEBER L. N.G. officer; b. Park River N.D., June 16, 1897; s. William James Edwards and Theodora Georgiana (Hunt) E.; LL.B., U. of N.D., 1927; m. Louise Reed, June 22, 1928; children - Nancy Jo, Judith Lee. Admitted to N.D. bar, 1927. Commd. capt. infantry Nat. Guard, 1920, and advanced through grades to maj. gen., 1954; adjutant gen. for N.D., 1937 - ; state dir. for Selective Service, 1948 - . Served on Mexican border, 1916-17, overseas, 1917-19; student infantry sch. Ft. Benning, Ga., 1924, command and gen. staff sch. Ft. Leavenworth, Kan., 1939. Awarded Legion of Merit, Army Commendation Ribbon. Mem. Am., Nat. Livestock Assn., Vets. of Foreign Wars. Am. Legion, 40 Hommes et 8 Chevaux, Phi Delta Phi. Presbyn. Mason. Elk, Nat. Sojourners, Rotarian. Address: Fraine Barracks, Bismarck, N.D. Died Oct. 18, 1962; buried Ft. Snelling.

EDWARDS, JOHN congressman; b. Louisville, Ky., Oct. 24, 1805; studied law. Admitted to bar, moved to Ind.; mem. Ind. Ho. of Reps., 1845-46; moved to Cal., elected an alcalde, 1849; returned to Ind., 1852; mem. Ind. Senate, 1853; moved to Chariton, Ia., 1855; mem. Ia. Constl. Conv.; mem. Ia. Ho. of Reps., 1856-60, speaker, 1858-60; founder newspaper Patriot, 1857; commd. lt. col. on staff of gov. Ia., during Civil War, 1861; commd. col. 18th Regt., Ia. Volunteer Inf., 1862; settled in Ft. Smith, Ark., at close of Civil War; U.S. assessor of internal revenue (apptd. by Pres. Johnson), 1866-69; mem. U.S. Ho. of Reps. (Liberal Republican) from Ark., 42d Congress, 1871-Feb. 9, 1872 (contested election); settled in Washington, D.C. Died Washington, Apr. 8, 1894; buried Arlington (Va.) Nat. Cemetery.

EDWARDS, JOHN RICHARD naval officer; b. Pottsville, Pa., July 9, 1853; grad. U.S. Naval Acad., 1874. Promoted asst. engr., Feb. 26, 1875; passed asst. engr., Sept. 11, 1881; chief engr., Nov. 5, 1895; transferred to the line as lt. comdr., Mar. 3, 1899; promoted comdr., Sept. 23, 1903; capt. Jan. 3, 1908; rear admiral, Sept. 11, 1911. Served on Puritan during Spanish-Am. War; detailed Bur. Steam Engring., 1895-97, 1900-04; chief engr. officer, Navy Yard, Portsmouth, N.H., 1904-08; insp. machinery, works of Wm. Cramp & Sons Co., Phila., 1908-11; gen. insp. machy. for Navy, 1911-12; pres. Bd. Inspection and Survey for shore stations, 1912-14; comdt. Navy Yard, Charleston, S.C., 1914-15; retired on account of age, July 9, 1915. Sr. mem. Naval Liquid Fuel Bd., 1901 -04; chmn. Am. delegation to Internat. Radio-telegraphic Conf., London, 1912; sr. mem. Naval Fuel Oil Bd., 1915; comdt. U.S. Naval Unit. Brown U., 1918; spl. duty Naval Training Sta., Newport, R.I., 1918-19. Home: Bristol, R.I. Died Dec. 2, 1922.

EDWARDS, OGDEN MATTHIAS JR M.D.; b. Pittsburgh, Pa., Dec. 23, 1869; s. Ogden M. and Sara (Herron) E.; B.S., Princeton 1893; M.D., Coll. Phys. and Surg. (Columbia), 1896; m. Lela Harkness, Nov. 28, 1893; children-Martha Harkness (Mrs. John M. Lazear), Lela Harkness (Mrs. Harry Cook), Harkness, Katherine Harkness (Mrs. H. Willis Nichols, Jr.). Began practice in Pittsburgh, 1894; prof. of pediatrics, 1909-17, actg. dean, 1917-19, Sch. of Medicine U. of Pittsburgh; retired from practice, 1917. Trustee Shady Side Academy, U. of Pittsburgh, Presbyn. Hospital. Presbyterian. Home: Pittsburgh, Pa. Died Dec. 28, 1940.

EDWARDS, RICHARD STANISLAUS naval officer; b. Phila., Feb. 18, 1885; s. Richard S. and Lucy Brooke (Neilson) E.; student Episcopal Acad., Phila., 1896-1903; B.S., U.S. Naval Acad., 1907; m. Hallie Ninan Snyder, Aug. 11, 1914. Commd. ensign, U.S. Navy, 1908; advanced through grades to rear adm., 1940, vice adm., 1942, admiral, 1945; dep. comdr. in chief, U.S. Fleet, vice chief Naval Operations, 1945-47, ret. 1947. Decorated Victory medal and Navy Cross. Clubs: Army and Navy, Chevy Chase (Wash.). Address: 25 Josepha Av., San Francisco 27. Died June 4, 1959.

EDWARDS, ROBERT WILKINSON, microbiologist; b. Portland, Ore., Apr. 6, 1914; s. William Dresser and Lucy (Wilkinson) E.; B.S., Memphis State Coll., 1948; M.S., U. Tenn., 1949; m. Ruth Mae Rawlins, Apr. 19, 1941; 1son, Robert Wilkinson. Civilian pilot, 1930-40; pres. Edwards Aircraft Corp., Memphis, 1938-40; asst. traffic mgr. Chgo. & So. Airlines, Houston, 1945-46; asst. prof. Tenn. Poly. Inst., Cookville, 1949-51; chief bacteriologist Cook County Hosp., Chgo., 1951-53; microbiologist U.S. Army, 1956-66; tech. staff scientist Airtronics, Inc., Washington, 1966-69; cons. applied microbiology. Served to maj. USAAF, 1940-45; USAF, 1953-56. Decorated Bronze Star medal, Air medal. Mem. N.Y. Acad. Scis., Am. Soc. Microbiologists, Soc. Indsl. Microbiologists, Nat. Assn. Corrosion Engrs., Marine Tech. Soc., Am. Assn. Contamination Control, Quiet Birdmen. Club: OX-5 of America (Md.). Home: Braddock Heights MD Died Sept. 24, 1969.

EDWARDS, THOMAS OWEN congressman, physician; b. Williamsburg, Ind., Mar. 29, 1810; studied medicine U. Md. Moved to Lancaster, O., 1836, practiced medicine; mem. U.S. Ho. of Reps. (Whig) from Ohio, 30th Congress, 1847-49; attended John Quincy Adams when stricken with apoplexy while making speech in Ho. of Reps. (Adams died in his arms); insp. marine hosps.; moved to Cincinnati, entered drug bus.; mem. pres. city council; prof. Ohio Med. Coll., Cincinnati; moved to Madison, Wis., then to Dubuze, Ia.; served as surgeon 3d Regt., Ia. Volunteer Inf., during Civil War; resumed practice of medicine, Lancaster, circa 1870; moved to Wheeling, W.Va., 1875. Died Wheeling, Feb. 5, 1876; buried Mt. Wood Cemetery.

EDWARDS, VICTOR EVERETT mech. engr.; b. North Chelmsford, Mass., Sept. 4, 1862; s. Nathan Brown and Sibbyl Robbins (Hutchins) E.; B.S., Worcester Poly. Inst., 1883, D.Engring., same, 1927; m. Janet Gage, Oct. 6, 1896. Asst. chief engr., Merrimack burn & Moen, Worcester, Otis Steel Co., Cleveland, and Charles H. Morgan, Worcester, Mass.; v.p. Morgan Constrn. Co., 1891-; maj. ordnance engring., 1918; maj. Ordnance R.C. Home: West Boylston, Mass. Deceased.

EELLS, WALTER CROSBY educator; b. Mason County, Wash., Mar. 6, 1886; s. Myron and Sarah (Crosby) E.; A.B., Whitman Coll., 1908, Sc.D., 1938; A.M., U. of Chicago, 1911; Ph.D., Stanford, 1927; m. Natalie Esther Soules, Jan. 1, 1912 (died 1947); children - Kenneth Walter, Frances Natalie, Donald Cushing; m. 2d, May Worthington, 1947. Teacher in high schools, Wash., 1908-10; professor mathematics, Whitworth Coll., Tacoma, Wash., 1911-13; instr. mathematics and mechanics, United States Naval Acad., 1913-16; instr. surveying, Harvard, summer, 1916; prof. applied mathematics and sec. alumni assn., Whitman Coll., 1916-27; asso. prof. edn., Stanford, 1927-31, prof. edn., 1931-38; prof. summer schools, U. of Calif., 1939, U. of Colo., 1940, Boston Univ., 1941, U. of Tex., 1942, Univ. Study Center, Army U., Florence, Italy, 1945; coordinator of Cooperative Study of Secondary Sch. Standards, Washington, D.C., 1935-39; exec. sec., Am. Assn. of Jr. Colleges, Washington, D.C., 1938-45; chief of Foreign Education Div., Vets. Adminstrn., 1945-47; adviser on higher edn. staff of Supreme Comdr. Allied Powers, Tokyo, Japan, 1947-51, ret.; vis. univs. in Asia, Australia, Africa, Europe, 1951-53; prof. edn. Cath. U. Am., 1953-54; ednl. cons. Am. Council on Edn., So. Regional Education Board and United States Office Education, 1955-63. Mem. History of Education Soc., Phi Delta Kappa, Phi Beta Kappa, Sigma Xi, Delta Sigma Rho. Republican. Conglist. Author: numerous books, monographs and reports 1928-48; Education in the New Japan (2 vols.) 1948; Educational Progress in Japan, 1951; Communism in Education in Asia, Africa and the Far Pacific, 1954; The Literature of Japanese Education, 1945-54, 1956; College Teachers and College Teaching, 1957, Baccalaureate Degrees Conferred by American Colleges in the 17th and 18th Centuries, 1958; American Dissertations on Foreign Education, 1959; Administration of Higher Education, 1960; Student Financial Aid in Higher Education, 1960; Academic Degrees, 1960; College Presidency, 1900-1960, 1961; Degrees in Higher Edn., 1962; Sabbatical Leave in American Higher Education, 1962; and others. Editor Whitman Alumnus, 1917-27, Junior Coll. Jour., 1930-45. Contbr. articles in various fields. Address: 2700 Wisconsin Av. N.W., Washington 7. Died Dec. 15, 1963.

EGBERT, SHERWOOD HARRY, management and investment consultant; born at Seattle, July 24, 1920; the son of Harry and C. and Charlotte (Brown) E.; student Wash. State Coll., 1937-38, 39-40; m. Doris Ruth McKay, Mar. 1, 1940; children—Sherwood James, Nancy Lee; m. 2d, Diana Nell Johnson, June 4, 1958; children—David Gregory, Robert, Warren, Sherana. With Austin Co., Seattle, 1940-41; asst. to supt. gen. constrn. Boeing Airplane Co., Seattle, 1941-42; with McCulloch Corp., Los Angeles, 1946-61, dir., 1951-61, exec. v.p. all divs., mem. exec. com., 1956-61, also v.p., dir. several divs.; pres., chief exec. officer Studebaker Packard Corporation (name now Studebaker Corporation), South Bend, Ind., 1961-64; chmn. bd. U.S. Filter; pres., dir. Sherwood Prodn. Co., Cascade, Inc.; v.p., dir. Valor Prodn. Co.; dir. Emett & Chandler, Aeronca, Inc., Ind. Gen. Corp., Western Air Lines. Served to maj. USMCR, 1942-46; PTO. Decorated Bronze Star medal. Clubs: Bel Air Country, Eldorado Country. Address: Los Angeles CA Died July 31, 1969; buried Holy Cross Cemetery, Los Angeles CA

EGELSON, LOUIS I. rabbi; b. Rochester, N.Y., Aug. 29, 1885; s. Samuel and Anna F. Egelson; A.B., Coll. City of N.Y., 1904; A.M., Columbia University, 1907; rabbi, Jewish Theol. Sem., New York N.Y., 1908; D.D. (hon.), Hebrew Union Coll.-Jewish Inst. Religion, 1954; married Augusta Cronheim, January 27, 1920; 1 son, Louis I. Administrative sec. Union of Am. Hebrew Congregations since 1942; sec. Com. on Chaplain Procurement, 1942-47. Com. on Emergency Placement of Chaplains, 1943-47; mem. exec. bd. Central Conf. American Rabbis, 1946-49. Sec. Commn. on Information about Judaism, Commn. on Mil. Services. Editor. Liberal Judaism. Served as chaplain, 91st Div., A.E.F., World War I; participated St. Mihiel, Meuse-Argonne and Lys-Scheldt campaigns. Mem. Am. Legion. Mason. Author of pamphlets. Home: 240 Central Park South. Office: 838 Fifth Av., N.Y.C. 21. Died Apr. 10. 1957; buried Walnut Hills Cemetery, Cin.

EICHELBERGER, ROBERT LAWRENCE ret. army ofcr. b. Urbana, O., Mar. 9, 1886; s. George Maley and Emma (Ring) E.; student O. State U., 1903-05; B.S., U.S. Mil. Acad., 1909; grad. Command and Gen. Staff School, 1926, Army War Coll., 1930; m. Emma Gudger, Apr. 3, 1913. Commd. 2d lt., U.S. Army, 1909, and advanced through the grades to maj. gen., 1941, lt. gen., October 1942; served on Mexican border, 1911, Panama Canal Zone, 1911-15; served as major of infantry, 1918-19; assistant chief of staff, American Expedn. Forces, Siberia, 1918, Philippine Dept., 1920; duty in China and Japan, 1920-21; liaison officer with Chinese delegation to Limitation of Armaments Conf., 1922; Gen. Staff, 1921-24; adjutant general U.S. Mil. Acad., 1931-35; sec. Gen. Staff, Washington, D.C., 1935-38; comd. Presidio of San Francisco and 30th Inf., 1938-40; supt., U.S. Mil. Acad., West Point, 1940-Jan. 1942; comd. 77th Inf. Div., 1942, I Corps, U.S. Army, 1942-44, participating in New Guinea and New Britain campaigns; participated Philippines reoccupation campaign, 1944-45; commanded Eighth Army, 1944-48; commanded Allied and U.S. ground forces, Japan, 1946-48; ret., 1948; promoted full gen. (ret.), 1954. Mem. North Carolina State Ports Authority, 1957 - . Decorated D.S.C. (with Oak-Leaf Cluster), D.S.M. 3 oak leaf clusters, D.S.M. (Navy), Silver Star two oak leaf clusters, Bronze Star Medal, Air Medal, Legion of Merit (U.S.), Distinguished Service Star (Philippine Govt.), Knight Comdr. Order of British Empire (Great Britain), Grand Officer Order of Orange Nassau with swords (Netherlands), Abdon Calderon (Educador); Grand Officer Legion of Honor (France); Croix de Guerre with Palm, Grand Officer Crown (Belgium); Legion Honor, P.I.; Grand Officer Mil. Order of Italy. Mem. Phi Gamma Delta. Methodist. Mason (33ff). Clubs: Army and Navy (Washington); Metropolitan (N.Y.C.); Chevy Chase (Md.) Country; Biltmore Forest (N.C.). Author: Our Jungle Road to Tokyo; contbr. current periodicals. Address: 8 Fairway Pl., Biltmore Forest, Asheville, N.C. Died Sept. 26, 1961; buried Arlington (Va.) Nat. Cemetery.

EISENHART, CHARLES MARION air force officer; b. Culbertson, Neb., Feb. 19, 1914; s. George Geiger and Marion Isabell (Herman) E.; B.S., Neb. State Coll., 1937; grad. Air Forces Flying Sch., 1938, Army Command and Gen. Staff Sch., 1944, Armed Forces Staff Coll., 1948, Air War Coll., 1953; m. Dorothy Mary Leonard, Apr. 11, 1942; children-Donald Charles, Marion Katherine. Tchr. elementary schs., Neb., 1933-35; commd. 2d lt. USAAF, 1938, advanced through grades to maj. gen. USAF, 1960; comdr. 505th Heavy Bombardment Group, Marianas, World War II; assigned pub. relations Hdqrs. USAF, 1948-52;

command and staff position Strategic Air Command, 1953-; base and wing comdr. Lockbourne AFB, Ohio, 1953-56; chief staff 2d Air Force, Barksdale AFB, La., 1956-57; comdr. 14th Air Div., Travis AFB, Cal., 1957-59; chief operations war plans div., Strategic Air Command, Offutt AFB, Omaha, 1959, now comdr. 7th Air Div., Strategic Air Command. Exec. bd. Transatlantic council Boy Scouts of Am. Decorated Legion of Merit. D.F.C. with oak leaf cluster, Bronze Star, Air medal with oak leaf cluster, Presdl. Unit citation with 3 oak leaf clusters. Mem. Daedalians, Phi Tau Gamma. Presbyn. Home: 510 W. 1st St., McCook, Neb. Office: Hdqrs. 7th Air Div., APO 241, N.Y.C. Died July 17, 1967.

EISENHOWER, DWIGHT DAVID, 34th Pres. of U.S.; b. Denison, Tex., Oct. 14, 1890; s. David J. and Ida E. (Stover) E.; B.S., U.S. Military Acad., 1915; married Mamie Geneva Doud, July 1, 1916; children—Dwight Doud (dec.), John Sheldon Doud. Commissioned 2d lieutenant infantry, United States Army, 1915, and advanced through grades to gen. of the army, Dec. 1944; became Allied Comdr. in Chief, North Africa, Nov. 8, 1942; apptd. comdg. gen. Allied Powers, E.T.O., Dec. 31, 1943; comdr. U.S. occupation forces in Germany, 1945; chief of staff, U.S. Army, Nov. 1945-48; pres. Columbia U., 1948-52; apptd. Supreme Comdr. Allied Powers Europe, Dec. 1950; resigned from U.S. Army, July 1952; inaugurated President of U.S., Jan. 20, 1953, and Jan. 21, 1957. Recipient hon. degrees from instns. in U.S. and abroad; fgn. and U.S. orders, decorations and medals; Gen. Sylvanus Thayer gold medal and scroll West Point, 1961; 1st Am. Patriot's medal Freedom's Found., 1961. Mem. English-Speaking Union U.S. chmn. nat. bd. dirs.;. Author: Mandate for Change, 1963; Waging Peace: The White House Years, 1956-61, 1965. Chmn. editorial adv. bd. Ency. Americana, 1961-69. Address: Gettysburg PA Died Mar. 29, 1969; buried Abilene KS

EISENSCHIML, OTTO chemist, author; b. Vienna, Austria, June 16, 1880; s. Alexander and Eleanor (Koretz) E.; Chem. Engr., Polytech. Sch. of Vienna, 1901; hon. Litt.D., Lincoln Memorial U., Harrogate, Tenn., 1937; Diploma, Lincoln College, Lincoln, Ill., 1960; m. Bertha Eisenschimel, Jan. 14, 1912; children - Rosalie Ruth, Gerald Alexander, Ralph Eugene. Chemist with Carnegie Steel Co., Pittsburgh, Pa., 1901-04; chief chemist Am. Linseed Co., Chicago, 1904-07, mgr. South Chicago plant, 1907-12; cons. chemist, Chicago, 1912; pres., now chmn. of bd. Scientific Oil Compounding Co., Inc., distributors of materials for paints, varnishes, fungicides, since 1912. Chmn, State Commn. on Purity of Paint Materials (Ill.), 1927-42; chmn. com. cons. Chicago Civil Defense, 1951. Recipient Honor Scroll Award of American Institute Chemists. Mem. National Research Council, American Chemical Society (chmn. 1914), Paint, Oil and Varnish Assn. of U.S., Chicago Hist. Soc., West Side Hist. Soc. of Chicago (president 1936-37, chairman 1938-45), American Institute Chemists (hon.), N.Y. Academy Sciences. Founder, 1st pres. Nat. Soybean Oil Mfrs. Assn. Club: Chgo. Chemists (pres. 1922). Editor Chem. Bull., 1914-17. Author: Why Was Lincoln Murdered?, 1937; Reviewers Reviewed, 1940; In the Shadow of Lincoln's Death, 1940; Without Fame, 1942; The Case of A. L - , Aged 56, 1943; Chicago Murders (co-author), 1945; The Story of Shiloh, 1946. Co-author: The American Iliad, 1947; As Luck Would Have It, 1948; The Celebrated Case of Fitz John Porter, 1950; The Civil War, 1956; What The Civil War?, 1958; The Hidden Face of the Civil War, 1961; The Civil War in Miniature, 1962. Author tech. and hist. treatises. Editor: Vt. Gen., 1960. Lectr. Home: 2300 Lincoln Park W. Office: 1637 S. Kilbourn Av., Chgo. Died Dec. 9, 1963; ashes scattered at Shiloh.

EISNER, J. LESTER business exec.; born Rec Bank, N.J., Mar. 18, 1889; s. Sigmund and Bertha (Weis) E.; student Phillips Exeter Acad., 1906-07; A.B., Harvard, 1911; m. Marguerite Davidson, Jan. 13, 1913 (died Feb. 28, 1924); children-Lester, Jacques (killed in action aboard U.S.S. San Francisco, battle of Savo Island, Nov. 12, 1942), Gerald; m. 2d, Virginia Scharf Steiner, Apr. 18, 1932; 1 step-son, Erwin B. Steiner. With Sigmund Eisner Co., mfr. of uniforms, Red Bank, N.J., since 1911; pres., dir. Sego Trading Co. since 1922. Mem. Tri-State Treaty Compact (N.J., N.Y., Conn.), 1931-36; commr. and v. chmn. Interstate San. Commn., 1936-42 (chmn. N.J. Commn.). Organizer Nat. Recovery Adminstrn. for N.J., 1933, chmn., 1933-34; chmn. State Recovery Adminstrn. of N.J., 1933-34. Organizer Monmouth County (N.J.) Welfare Bd., 1928, vice chmn., 1928-39; mem. bd. overseers Graham-Eckes School, Palm Beach. Fla. Maj., Q.M.C., U.S. Army, 1917-18; lt. col., Q.M. Reserve Corps, 1919-35; lt. col., N.J. N.G., 1930-33, served as A.R.C. dir. of transportation for E.T.O., hdqrs. London and Paris, 1944-45. Mem. at large Nat. Council Boy Scouts of Am., Mem. bd. edn., Red Bank, 1917-20. Asso. mem. New Sch. for Social Research, N.Y. City. Mem. Am. Legion, Mil. Order World War, Mil. Order Fgn. Wars, League for Fair Play (dir.), Com. on Nat. Affairs (dir.), N.J. Taxpayers Assn. (dir.), Monmouth Hist. Soc. Republican. Elk, Mason, Nat. Sojourner. Clubs: Monmouth Boat; Shrewsbury River Ice and Yacht (Red Bank, N.J.); Army and Navy (Washington); Harvard, The Whist (N.Y.C.); Harvard (N.J.); Montauk (L.I.) Yacht; American (London). Home: 920 Fifth Av., N.Y.C. Office: 261 Fifth Av., N.Y.C. 16. Died May 27, 1955.

EKINS, H(ERBERT) R(OSLYN) newspaper editor, pub.; born Minneapolis, May 9, 1901; son George Herbert and Grace (Horton) E.; student Blackstone (Va.) Mil. Acad., 1917-18, and Clark U., Worcester, lMass., 1921-23; m. Alma Rosen, Jan. 31, 1924 (divorced 1937); 1 dau., Dennison; m. 2d, Ted Katherine Lawrance, Feb. 2, 1937; 1 son, Harvey Horton. Reporter and editorial writer Conn. and N.Y. City papers, 1923-25; mgr. Honolulu bureau United Press, 1927-28, Manila bureau, 1928-29, Shanghai bureau, 1930-31, Peiping bureau, 1932; reported Sino-Japanese hostilities, 1931-33; travelled extensively in oriental countries, 1933-35; inaugurated Tientsin bur., United Press, 1935, trans. N.Y.C. office, United Press, 1936 night news editor United Press, N.Y.C., 1936, covered Sino-Japanese hostilities, 1937, with stations in Shanghai, Hankow, Tokyo, Tientsin and Pekin; night editor New York headquarters United Press 1938; bur. mgr. United Press, Rome, July 1939; on United Press war desk, New York, Sept. 1939-Sept. 1, 1943; news editor and commentator, radio sta. WSYR, Syracuse, N.Y., 1943-47; dir. The Citizens Found. Inc., Syracuse, N.Y. 1947-50; editor, pub. The Goldthwaite (Texas) Eagle 1950-53; mng. editor, Schenectady (N.Y.) Union-Star, 1953-59, editor, 1959-61, editor and publisher, 1961 - . Accredited war correspondent Supreme Hdqrs., Allied Expeditionary Forces, Europe, 1944. Hon. sec.-treas. Peking Anglo-American Assn., 1932. Mem. Sigma Delta Chi. Conglist. Clubs: Peking, Peking Golf (Peiping); Polo (Manila); Cercle Sportif Francais (Shanghai), Circumnavigators Club (N.Y.); National Press (Washington). Author: Around the World in 18 Days - And How to Do It; China Fights for Her Life (with Theon Wright), 1937. Contbr. to We Cover the World. Contbr. numerous magazines and periodicals. Home: 1416 Union St., Schenectady, 8, N.Y. Office: 211 Clinton St., Schenectady, N.Y. Died Oct. 14, 1963.

EKSERGIAN, RUPEN consulting engr.; b. Somerville, Mass., Mar. 30, 1889; s. Carnig and Zoe Elizabeth (Huntington) E.; S.B., Mass. Inst. Tech., 1914, S.M., 1915; S.M., Harvard, 1915; Fellow in physics, Clark U., 1916-17, Ph.D., 1928; m. Maydell Hagenbuch, Aug. 14, 1920; 1 dau., Gloria (Mrs. Gilbert Shaw). Asst. to vice pres. in charge engring. Baldwin Locomotive Works, 1920-29, developed methods of analysis on locomotive design; cons. engr., E. I. du Pont de Nemours & Co., 1929-34; chief cons. engr. E. G. Budd Mfg. Co., 1934-45; cons. engr. The Budd Co., 1945-51; responsible for tech. phase of stainless steel train developments, starting with Pioneer Zephyr cons. engr. Bethlehem Steel Co.; sometime cons. Am. Car & Foundry, Lukens Steel Co., Day & Zimmerman, Inc., Atomic Power Development Assos., formerly research adviser Am. Locomotive Co. Mem. bd. mgrs. The Franklin Institute, co-founder, sr. staff adviser The Franklin Institute Laboratories for Research & Development, also serves as editor of Franklins Inst. Journal. Served as 1st lt., capt., major, Ordnance Dept., U.S. Army, during World War I; organized ordnance design office Franklin Inst., also served as tech. consultant to Chief of Ordnance Office, and specialist on arty. and heavy ordnance, World War II. Recipient George R. Henderson medal Franklin 1937, Worcester Reed Warner medal Am. Soc. M.E., 1939. Fellow Am. Soc. M.E. Mem. Div. I, Nat. Defense Research Com. Recipient Louis E. Levy medal of Franklin Inst., 1945. Contbr. of articles for Am. Soc. M.E., including Stresses in Locomotive Frames, The Balancing and Dynamic Rail Pressure of Locomotives, The Design of Light Weight Trains and The Design of Axles and Locomotive Crank Pins; also papers for Franklin Inst., including The Dynamical Analysis of Machines, Some Applications of Normal Coordinates to Engring. Vibration System, The Fluid Torque Converter and Coupling, The Efficiency of Power Units and The Reaction of Fluids and Fluid Jets. Author of a book on ordnance engring. for U.S. Army, 1920. Analytical research in applied dynamics and dynamics of machinery. Home: Rose Tree Rd., Media, Pa. Died Dec. 1961.

ELBERT, SAMUEL gov. Ga.; b. Prince William Parish, S.C., 1743; m. Elizabeth Rae, 6 Children. Commd. capt., grenadier co. Ga. Militia, 1774; mem. Ga. Council Safety, 1775; commd. lt. col. Continental Army, 1776, col. 1776; brevetted brig. gen., 1783; gov. Ga., 1785-86; sheriff Chatham County; v.p. Ga. Soc. Cincinnati; grand master Ga. Masonic Order. Died Savannah, Ga., Nov. 1, 1788.

ELDEN, JOHN ATEN lawyer; b. East Liverpool, O., Apr. 3, 1891; s. Enoch and Mary (Aten) E.; prep. edn. Va. Mil. Inst.; A.B., Adelbert Coll. (Western Reserve U.), Cleveland, O., 1912; LL.B., Western Reserve, 1914; post-grad. work, Columbia U., George Washington U., and Cleveland Law Sch., lM.A., from latter, 1928; m. 2d, Ruth Knox; children-Betty Jane (by first marriage), John A. Admitted to Ohio bar, 1914, then practiced at Cleveland; head of John A. Elden; chmn. advisory bd. Lake Erie Trust Co.; pres. Economy Mortgage Co.; v.p. Franklin Savings & Loan Co., D.C. Pierce, Inc., brokers. Mem. Bd. of Bar Examiners for State of Ohio, term 1926-31; asst. atty. gen. State of Ohio, 1927-28. served as capt. Gas Service, U.S.A., World War, now O.R.C. Republican. Presbyn. Mason. Author: Here and There, 1928. Home: Cleveland, O. Died Jan. 1, 1935.

ELDREDGE, CHARLES HENRY rear adm.; b. Dedham, Mass., Sept. 21, 1839; s. Nathaniel T. and Mary H. (Haven) E.; m. Genevieve Redfield, Feb. 2, 1881. Apptd. from N.Y. asst. p.-m. U.S.N., July 10, 1861; promoted p.-m., Feb. 16, 1862; pay insp., July 3. 1871; pay dir., Aug. 31, 1881; retired with rank of rear adm., Sept. 21, 1901, for services during Civil War. Served on various vessels and at various stas. during Civil War. Home: Norfolk, Va. Died July 16 1916.

ELDRIDGE, FRANK HAROLD commodore U.S.N.; b. Columbus, O., July 14, 1852; s. Charles and Catherine Taylor (Nelson) E.; grad. U.S. Naval Acad., 1875; Promoted through the various grades to commodore and retired, June 30, 1909. Instr. and head of dept. steam engring. and naval constrn., U.S. Naval Acad., 1900-02; prof. engring., Ohio State U., 1882-85; served in Spanish-Am. War and in P.I. Returned to active service, Aug. 23, 1917-Sept. 29, 1919. Died Dec. 1921.

ELIOT, GEORGE FIELDING, author, journalist; b. Brooklyn, N.Y., June 22, 1894; s. Philip Park and Rena (King) E.; B.A., Melbourne U., Australia, 1914; m. Sara Elaine Hodges, Dec. 23, 1933 (divorced 1942); m. 2d. June Cawley Hynd. Jan. 1, 1943. Accountant Haskins & Sells, Kansas City, Mo., 1922-27; began writing for fiction mags., 1926; writer, especially on mil. and internat. affairs, national security, 1928-71; asso. Center Strategic Studies, Georgetown U., 1967-71. Served Australian Imperial Force, Dardanelles and Western Front, 1914-18; capt., later maj., Mil. Intelligence Reserve, U.S. Army, 1922-30. Recipient Honor medal for distinguished service in journalism U. of Mo., 1962, Alfred Thayer Mahan award for lit. accomplishment Navy League U.S., 1964. Mem. Council on Foreign Relations, Army Ordnance Assn., U.S. Naval Inst., Fgn. Policy Assn., Acad. Polit. Science, American Political Science Association. President Committee Nat. Morale, 1942-45; pres. Assn. of Radio News Analysts, 1943, re-elected, 1951. Episcopalian. Clubs: Century (New York); National Press (Washington, D.C.). Author: If War Comes (with R. E. Dupuy), 1937; The Ramparts We Watch, 1938; Bombs Bursting in Air, 1939; Hour of Triumph, 1944; The Strength We Need, 1946; Hate, Hope and High Explosive, 1948; If Russia Strikes, 1949; Caleb Pettengill, USN (novel), 1956; Victory Without War, 1958; Sylvanus Thayer of West Point, 1959; Reserve Forces and the Kennedy Strategy, 1962; Franklin Buchanan, 1962; articles and fiction mags., newspapers; lectr. internat. relations, mil. affairs. Mil. and naval corr. N.Y. Herald-Tribune, 1939-46; mil. analyst Columbia Broadcasting System, 1939-47, M.B.S., 1950-53; columnist N.Y. Post Home News, 1947-49; Gen. Features Syndicate, 1950-67. Mil. editor Collier's Ency. Home: Litchfield CT Died Apr. 21, 1971; cremated.

ELIOT, WALTER GRAEME civil engr.; b. New York, Nov. 16, 1857; s. Augustus G. (M.D.) and Elizabeth (Proctor) E.; E.M., Ph.B., Columbia, 1878, C.D., 1879, Ph.K., 1882; LL.D., St. Francis Xavier Coll., 1892; admitted to senior class, Harvard; m. Maud Staoutenburgh, Feb. 4, 1892; children-Marion Elinor Viola (wife of Lt. Carlton James), Amory Vivion (U.S.A.), Van Cortlandt Stoutenburgh, Priscilla Alden. Insp. tenements, N.Y. Health Dept., 1877-78; judge, municipal, competitions, 1878-80; sanitary engr. of health dept., New York, 1880-81; engring. expert on water supply, 10th Census, 1881; gen. mgr. Am. Photo Litho. Co., 1881-82; sec., auditor Westcott Express Co., 1884-87; editor and a propr. University Magazine, 1890-94; asst. chemist, and insp. foods, health dept., 1896-98. Active for 4 yrs. in orgn. of mild interests of New York; on tech. staff. dept. taxes and assessments, New York, 1898-1902; asst. engr. topog. bur., Borough of Queens, New York, 1902-10, engr. in charge, 1910; commr. parks, Borough of Queens, New York, 1911 license professional engrs.; appted. mem. N.Y. State Board of Licensing for Professional Ergrs., term 1921-30 (chmn. 1925). Member Co. K, 7th Regt., N.G. N.Y. and of its victorious rifle teams of 1904, 05, 06; 1st lt. Co. A, 71st Inf., N.G.N.Y., Oct. 1907-09; maj. Coast Arty. Corps, N.G.N.Y., 1911-13; lt. col. Inf., 1918. Trustee New York Coll. Dentistry, 1903-25. Pres. Technical League of Engrs., 1908-11; a founder and mem. Soc. Municipal Engrs., New York. Episcopalian. Author: Sketch of the Eliot Family, 1889; History of the Stoutenburgh Family, 1905. Home: Hyde Park-on-Hudson, N.Y. Deceased.

ELKIN, DANIEL COLLIER surgeon: b. Louisville, Ky., Mar. 26, 1893; s. Robert and Roberta (Collier) E.; A.B., Yale, 1916; M.D., Emory University, Atlanta, Ga., 1920; Sc.D., Northwestern University, 1952; D.Sc. (honorary), Centre Coll., 1956; married Helen McCarty, November 3, 1923; 1 son, Daniel C. Intern and resident surgeon, Peter Bent Brigham Hosp., Boston, Mass., 1920-24; asst. in surgery, Harvard, 1924; Whitehead prof. of surgery, Emory U., 1929-55, now emeritus. Mem. bd. trustees Univ. Kentucky. Served as colonel Medical Corps, Army of U.S., unit dir. 43d Gen. Hosp., 1941, chief of surg. service Ashford (W. Va.) Gen. Hosp., 1942-46. Apptd. brigadier gen., O.R.C., A.U.S., 1949. Awarded Matas medal for vascular surgery Tulane U., 1940; Legion of Merit, 1945, Fellow

A.C.S. (pres.); mem. Soc. Vascular Surgery (president 1948), Soc. Medical Consultants (president 1949). Southern Surgical Assn. (president 1946), American Surgical Assn. (past pres.), American Assn. Thoracic Surgery, Soc. Clinical Surgery (pres. 1947). Presbyn. Clubs: Piedmont Driving, Capital City, (Atlanta); Pendennis (Louisville); Graduates (New Haven). Author: Medical Reports of John Y. Bassett, 1941. Contributor numerous papers relating to surgery of heart and blood vessels to sci. publs. Home: Lancaster, Ky. Office: Emory University, Ga. Died Nov. 3, 1958; buried Lancaster, Ky.

ELKINS, DAVIS ex-senator; b. Washington, Jan. 24, 1876; s. U.S. Senator Stephen B. and Hallie (Davis) E.; student Harvard; m. Mary Reagan; children-Hallie Katherine, Davis, Maureen. Left coll., 1898, to enlist as pvt. 1st W.Va. Vol. Inf., at beginning of Spanish-Am. War; commd. 1st. lt. and later served as capt. on staff of Brig. Gen. Theodore Schwan, in Cuba and P.R.; assumed charge of business interests of father, upon leaving army; apptd. by Gov. Glassock of W.Va. to U.S. Senate to fill vacancy caused by death of father, serving Jan. 9-Jan. 31, 1911. Commd. maj. U.S. Army, Dec. 27, 1917, and served as adj. 13th Inf. Brigade, 7th Div., in Tex. and France; hon. disch., Dec. 27, 1918, after being elected in absence to U.S. Senate for term 1919-25. Republican. Clubs: The Links, Racquet and Tennis (N.Y.); Deepdale Golf. Home: 2029 Connecticut Av., N.W., Washington. Died Jan. 5, 1959.

ELKINS, STEPHEN BENTON senator; b. Perry Co., O., Sept. 26, 1841; s. Col. Philip Duncan and Sarah Pickett (Withers) E.; A.B., U. of Mo., 1860, A.M., 1868; m. Sallie Jacobs, June 10, 1866; 2d, Hallie, d. Senator Henry Gassaway Davis, Apr. 14, 1875. Admitted to bar, 1864; went to N.M., 1864; mem. territorial legislature, 1864-65; later territorial dist. atty., atty. gen., 1868-69, and U.S. dist. atty., 1870-72; del. in 43d and 44th Congresses, from N.M., 1873-77; removed to W.Va. Became largely interested in coal mining and railroads; founded town of Elkins, W.Va. Sec. of War in cabinet of President Harrison, 1891-93; U.S. senator from W.Va., 1895-1901, 1901-07, 1907-13. Home: Elkins, W.Va. Died 1911.

ELLERY, FRANK naval officer; b. Newport, R.I., July 23, 1794; s. Christopher and Clarissa (Bird) E.; m. Elizabeth Martin, Aug. 4, 1835. Became midshipman U.S. Navy, 1812; wounded at 1st sea battle; received sword and reward from Congress, 1814; served against Algerian pirates; promoted lt., 1820; served under Capt. Jesse D. Elliot, 1825-32; lt. in command in Enterprise, short period in 1839; resigned, rescinded, reinstated waiting for orders until 1861 (became oldest lt. in service); farmed in poverty, Vt.; in command Naval rendezvous, Boston, Phila., later converted ships for blockade; ret. as commodore, 1867. Died Castleton, Vt., Mar. 24, 1871. 1871.

ELLET, CHARLES civil engr.; b. Penn's Manor, Pa., Jan. 1, 1810; s. Charles and Mary (Israel) E.; attended Ecole Polytechnique, Paris, France; m. Elvira Daniel, 1837, 1 son, Charles Rivers. Chief engr. James River and Kanawha Canal, 1836; designed, built wire suspension bridge across Schuylkill River nr. Phila., 1842; designed, built suspension bridge across Niagara River below the falls, 1847; completed Wheeling (W.Va.) Bridge for B. & O. R.R., 1849; engr. Hempfield R.R., 1851-55, Va. Central R.R., 1853-57; served as col. engrs. U.S. Army 1861-62; converted fleet of Mississippi steamers into rams, sank or disabled several Confederate vessels off Memphis, 1862; considered one of Am.'s great engrs. Author: Physical Geography of the Mississippi Valley with Suggestions as to the Improvement of Navigation of the Ohio and Other Rivers, 1853; Coast and Harbor Defenses, or the Substitution of Steam Battering-rams for Ships of War, 1855. Died Cairo, Ill., June 21, 1862.

ELLETT, EDWARD COLEMAN (ELLET), physician; b. Memphis, Tenn., Dec. 18, 1869, s. Henry Thomas and Katherine (Coleman) E.; Southwestern Presbyn. U., Clarksville, Tenn., 1884-86; B.A., U. of the South, Sewanee, Tenn., 1888; M.D., U. of Pennsylvania, 1891; LL.D., Southwestern University, 1942; hon. D.Sc., University of the South, 1943; married Nina Polk Martin, Nov. 12, 1896. Practiced medicine at Phila., 1891-93, Memphis, Tenn., since 1893; prof. diseases of eye, U. of Tenn., 1906-22. Lt. col. M.C., U.S. Army, in active service, 1917. Fellow Am. Coll. Surgeons; mem. Memphis and Shelby County and socs., West Tenn. Med. and Surg. Assn., Tenn. State Med. Soc., A.M.A., Am. Acad. of Ophthalmology and Otolarynogolgy, Am. Ophthalmol. Soc., Kappa Sigma, Phi Alpha Sigma. Clubs: Memphis Country; Memphis University. Home: 1545 Central Av. Office: Exchange Bldg., Memphis, Tenn. Died June 8, 1947.

ELLETT, THOMAS HARLAN architect; b. Red Oak, Ia., Sept. 2, 1880; s. Thomas Ely and Caroline Elizabeth (Bake) E.; certificate in Architecture, Armour Inst. Tech., 1903; B.S. in Architecture, U. Pa., 1906; awarded Arthur Spayd Brook, medal and Cresson traveling fellowship; studied abroad and at Am. Acad. in Rome, 1907-09; m. Jane Poultney bigelow; Aug. 15, 1917; 1 dau., Jane Braston (Mrs. William Hoffman Benjamin). Engaged in gen. practice of architecture, N.Y.C., 1915—; designer Am. Mil. Chapel and development of cemetery at Thiaucourt, France; Cosmopolitan Club, N.Y.; country houses in vicinity of N.Y.; Bronx Post Office, N.Y.; cons. architect U.S. Dept. Treasury, 1934-36, 1939-40. Served as capt. 302d Engrs., A.E.F., World War. Decorated Silver Star medal (U.S.). Fellow of the Am. Inst. or Architects. Awarded silver medal for 1928 by Architectural League of N.Y. for design of residence for J. Seward Johnson. New Brunswick, N.J., and gold medal for 1933, for design of Cosmopolitan Club, N.Y., also gold medal, Montevideo, 1940; winner Covington, Ky., Post Office and Court House competition. Academician Nat. Acad. of Design. Mem. Nat. Inst. of Arts and Letters. Club: Century (N.Y.C.); Highland Country. Home: Garrison-on-Hudson, N.Y. Office: 101 Park Ave., N.Y.C. Died 1951.

ELLICOTT, JOHN MORRIS naval officer: b. St. Inigoes, Md., Sept. 4, 1859; s. James Fox and Elvira Ann (Jones) E.; grad. U.S. Naval Acad., 1883; studied U.S. Naval War Coll. and Torpedo Sch.; m. Annie M. Williams, Dec. 29, 1887. Commd. ensign USN, 1885, ret. as capt., 1912, recalled active duty, 1918-22; in flagship Tennessee, N. Atlantic sta., 1883-85; expdn. occupying Isthmus of Panama, 1885; in Ranger, N. Pacific sta., 1885-88; staff intelligence duty Navy Dept., 1888-91, Bennington, 1891-93; on flagship Chicago, European sta., 1894; instr. ordnance U.S. Naval Acad., 1894-96; Marion and flagship Baltimore, Pacific sta., 1896-98; flagship Baltimore, Asiatic sta., 1898-99; staff Naval War Coll., 1900-01; participated in battle of Manila Bay, May 1: navigator Prairie, 1901-04; supt. of compasses Navy Dept., 1905-06; exec. officer Maryland, Asiatic sta., 1906-07; comd. Solace, 1908; insp. 13th Light House Dist., Portland, Ore., 1909; comdg. U.S.S. Maryland, 1911-13; Navy Yard, Mare Island, Cal., 1914, capt., 1917-20. Recipient medal from Congress for services at Manila. Author: Justified (novel), 1891; Life of John Ancrum Winslow, 1900; Ellicott Valuation Contract Bridge, 1930; others. Address: Quarters 177, Mare Island Naval Shipyard, Cal. Died Sept. 16, 1955; buried Mare Island Naval Cemetery.

ELLIOT, JAMES congressman; b. Gloucester Mass., Aug. 18, 1775. s. James and Martha (Day). E.; m. Lucy Dow. Enlisted as 1st non-commd. officer in col of 2d U.S. Sub-Legion, Springfield, Mass., 1793; admitted to Mass. Bar, 1803; mem. U.S. Ho. of Reps. from Mass., 8th-10th congresses, 1803-09; commd. capt. U.S. Army, 1812; edited Freeman's Journal, Phila.; clk. Windham County Ct., 1817-35; mem. Vt. State Ho. of Reps., 1818, 19, 37; register Probate Ct., 1822-34. Author: The Poetical and Miscellaneous Works of James Elliot, 1798. Died Newfane, Vt., Nov. 10, 1839; buried Prospect Hill Cemetery, Battleboro, Vt.

ELLIOTT, BYRON KOSCIUSKO lawyer; b. Hamilton, O., Sept. 4, 1835; s. William J. and Mary L. E.; ed. Hamiltion (O.) Acad., Furman's Acad., Marion Co. Sem.; admitted to bar, Feb. 8, 1858; m. Harriet A. Talbott, Sept. 5, 1855. Elected city atty., Indianapolis, 1859; served as capt. 132d Ind. Vols.; detailed for duty on staff of Maj. Gen. Milroy, 1864; city atty., 1865, 1867, 1869; judge Criminal Circuit Ct., 1870; city solicitor, 1872; city atty., 1873; elected judge Superior Court of Ind., 1876; judge Supreme Court, 1881-93. Republican. Author: Work of the Advocate (subsequently enlarged into 2 vols. and given the title of "General Practice"); Appellate Procedure; The Law of Roads and Streets; The Law of Railroads; Treatise on the Law of Evidence, 4 vols., vol. 2, 1905. Home: Indianapolis, Ind. Died Apr. 19, 1913.

ELLIOTT, GEORGE FRANK major gen. U.S. Marine Corps, Oct. 12, 1870; promoted 1st lt., lMar. 30, 1878; capt., June 15, 1892; Mar. 3, 1899; lt. col., 11, 1899; N col., Mar. 3, 1903; comdt. U.S. Marine Corps with rank of brig. gen., Oct. 3, 1903; maj. May 13, 1908. lMade Arctic cruise of 2 yrs. and 10 months while comdg. marine guard of U.S.S. Alliance; comd. marine guard in protection of Am. Legation, Seoul, Korea, 1894, and served in China, guarding Am. interests during war between China and Japan; comd. Co. C, 1st Battalion of Marines, organized for service in Cuba during Spanish-Am. War, Apr. 22-Sept. 22, 1898; advanced three numbers in his grade for eminent and conspicuous conduct in battle nr. Guantanamo, June 14, 1898; served in P.I., Sept. 21, 1899-Mar. 22, 1900; comd. marines in the engagement at Novaleta, P.I., Oct. 8, 1899; comd. and expeditionary brigade of marines on the Isthmus of Panama, Dec. 1903-Mar. 1904. Retired. Home: Washington, D.C. Died Nov. 4, 1931.

ELLIOTT, JESSE DUNCAN naval officer; b. Hagerstown Md., July 14, 1722; s. Robert and Ann E.; m. Frances Vaughan, Apr. 7, 1812; at least 1 son, Washington Lafayette. Commd. lt. U.S. Navy, 1810; in command naval forces on Lake Erie, 1812; master comdt., 1813; in command ship Niagara, 1813; 2d in command to Commodore Perry at Battle of Lake Erie; mem. Stephen Decatur's squadron against Algiers, 1815; commanded sloop Ontario, 1815-16; commd. capt., 1818; commanded W. Indian Squadron, 1829-32; comdt. Boston Navy Yard, 1833-35; comdr.-in-chief. Mediterranean Squadron, 1835-38; commanded Phila. Navy Yard, 1844. Died Phila., Dec. 10, 1845.

ELLIOTT, JOHN BARNWELL, M.D.; b. at Greensboro, Ga., Oct. 30, 1870; s. John Barnwell and Lucy Pickney (Huger) E.; B.Litt., U. of the South, Sewanee, Tenn., 1891, M.A., 1891; M.D., Tulane, 1894, LL.D., 1937; m. Noel L. Forsyth, of "Nydrie," Albermarle Co., Va., Feb. 8, 1900. Began practice at New Orleans, La., 1894; prof. medicine, Tulane U. of La., 1910-21; consultant medicine Tours Infirmary, 1921-39. Commd. maj. Med. Corps, U.S.A., Apr. 11, 1917; lt. col., June 6, 1918. With A.E.F. in France, Mar. 4, 1918-Feb. 16, 1919; was dir. Base Hosp. 24; group consultant Gen. Med. Bazoilles, Vittel Centre, Aug. 15, 1918-Jan. 20, 1919. Home: 1323 1st St. Office: Audubon Bldg., New Orleans LA*

ELLIOTT, JOHN HENRY mem. U.S. Railroad Labor Bd.; b. Chatham, N.Y., 1866; s. John and Susan Elizabeth (McGary) E.; ed. common schs.; m. Elizabeth McPherson, June 4, 1912. Began in track dept. Lebanon Springs R.R., 1881; became gen. mgr. T. & P. Ry. Co., resigned 1917; mem. U.S. R.R. Labor Bd. since 1920. Enlisted in A.E.F., serving with Transport Corps during World War; commd. maj., Feb. 25, 1918, lt. col., Oct. 10, 1918; col., May 2, 1919; hon. discharged Dec. 1919. Apptd. Am. del. Inter-Allied Ry. Commn., Trier, Germany, Inter-Allied Waterways Commn. Cologne, Germany. Mem. Am. Soc. Mil. Engrs., Am. Legion. Clubs: Traffic, High Noon. Home: 5125 University Av. Office: 608 S. Dearborn St., Chicago, Ill.

ELLIOTT, MIDDLETON STUART ret. naval officer; b. Beaufort, S.C., Oct. 16, 1872; s. Middleton Stuart and Ann (Rhett) E.: M.D., George Washington U., 1894: m. Alice Miller Sherwood, Sept. 14, 1898; children-Caryl Middleton (wife of Phillip R. Osborne, USN), Alice Sherwood (wife of Joel Newsom, USN). Med. officer USN, 1896, advanced through grades to vice adm., 1942. Received Medal of Honor. Served in Spanish-Am. War. Philippine Insurrection, Vera Cruz, World War. Mem. Huguenot Soc. S.C. Episcopalian. Club: New York Yacht. Home: Beaufort, S.C. Died Nov. 29, 1952.

ELLIOTT, RICHARD HAMMOND, newspaper editor; b. Annapolis, Md., Oct. 3, 1893; s. Richard Goodwin and Julia Virginia (Hammond) E.; Class of 1917, St. John's Coll., Annapolis, Md.; student Johns Hopkins, 1923; unmarried. Mem. staff Baltimore (Md.) American, 1922-26, Baltimore (Md.) Evening Sun, 1926-33; editor, Annapolis (Md.) bureau, Associated Press, 1933-38; mem. staff, The Capital-Gazette Press (including The Evening Capital and The Maryland Gazette), Annapolis, Md., 1938-40, editor from 1941, also assistant manager from 1945. Commissioned second lieut., inf., U.S. Army, 1917, promoted 1st lt., and capt., 1918; retired for disability in line of duty, 1920. Past comdr. G. C. Parlett Post, Am. Legion; past pres. Annapolis Civitan Club; disaster chmn., Red Cross, Anne Arundel Co., 1940-47; past mem. bd. U.S.O. Mgt., Annapolis; past mem. dist. com. Anne Arundel Co. Boy Scouts; mem. Annapolis Salvation Army Adv. Bd.; past mem. bd. Annapolis YMCA. Awarded Mexican Border and Victory medals; award of merit U.S. Navy Recruiting Service, certificate recognition patriotic effort, WPB. Mem. Md. Press Assn. (dir.), C. of C., Military Order World Wars Republican. Clubs: Annapolitan (Annapolis). Home: Annapolis MD Died May 3, 1971; buried St. Anne's Cemetery, Annapolis MD

ELLIOTT, SHELDEN DOUGLASS, coll. prof., lawyer; b. Hollywood, Calif., June 2, 1906; s. Edwin Windsor and Therissa Irene (Gilbert) E.; A.B., Yale, 1927, law, 1927-28; J.D., U. So. Calif., 1931, LL.M., 1932; LL.D., Temple Univ., Willamette University, 1954; m. Hilda Elizabeth Johnston, Dec. 29, 1929; children—Shelden Douglass, Mary Therissa. Admitted to California bar, 1931, New York bar, 1957; served as assistant counsel, California State Legislative Counsel Bur., 1932-33; sec. Com. Bar Examiners, Calif., 1933-34; asst. prof., dir. Legal Aid Clinic, U. So. Calif., 1934-37, asst. prof., 1937-38, asso. prof., 1938-39, prof. law 1939-52 dean 1947-52; prof. law N.Y.U., dir. Inst. Judicial Admnstrn. since 1952, vis. prof. law U. Mich., summer 1948, N.Y.U., fall, 1950, Rutgers University, summer 1953, U. of Utah, 1956, Hastings Coll. Law, summer, 1958; cons. Indian Law Inst., New Delhi, 1960. Mem. adv. com. Fed. Civil Rules; mem. Regional Loyal Bd., U.S. Civil Service Commn.; Adv. Bd. Contract Appeals, A.E.C.; Airframe Com. W.S.B. Mem. Calif. State Constl. Revision Com., 1948; Los Angeles Commn. Reorgn. City Govt., 1951. Mem. bd. dirs. National Legal Aid Soc. Served as capt. to lt. col., hdqrs. 7th U.S. Army, 103d Inf. Div., 1943-46; brig. gen. res. Decorated Croix de Guerre. Mem. Am., New York State, Cal. State and Los Angeles bar assns., Am. Arbitration Assn. (mem. labor panel), Nat. Acad. Arbitrators, Assn. Am. Law Schs. (pres. 1954), Order of Coif, Phi Beta Kappa, Phi Kappa Phi, Phi Delta Phi. Episcopalian. Author: California Administrative Law, 1947; Cases and Materials on Legislation (with Nutting), 1950; Improving Our Courts, 1959; Cases and Materials on Pleading and Procedure (with Karlen), 1961; also articles legal jours. Home: New York City NY Died Mar. 1972.

ELLIOTT, WASHINGTON LAFAYETTE army officer; b. Carlisle, Pa., Mar. 31, 1825; s. Jesse Duncan and Frances (Vaughan) E.; ed. Dickinson Coll.;

attended U.S. Mil. Acad., 1841-44. Commd. 2d lt. U.S. Army, 1846, 1st lt. 1847, capt., 1854, col., 1861, maj., 1861; commd. brig. gen. U.S. Volunteers, 1862; chief of cavalry, 1862; in command Dept. of N.W., 1862-63; commanded 3d div. III Corps, Army of Potomac, 1863; commd. lt. col., 1866, coll, 1878; ret. as maj. gen., 1879; received 5 brevets for distinguished conduct during Civil War; v.p. Cal. Safe Deposit and Trust Co. Died San Francisco, June 29, 1888.

ELLIOTT, WILLIAM congressman, lawyer; b. Beaufort, S.C., Sept. 3, 1838; ed. at Beaufort Coll., Harvard and U. of Va.; admitted to bar in Charleston, April, 1861; officer in C.S.A. during Civil war. Elected, 1866, mem. of legislature and intendant of Beaufort; presdl. elector, 1880; mem. Congress, 1887-1903, 1st S.C. dist. Democrat. Home: Columbia, S.C. Died 1907.

ELLIS, EZEKIEL JOHN congressman, lawyer; b. Covington, La., Oct. 15, 1840; attended Centenary Coll., Jackson, La., 1855-58; grad. law dept. La. State U. at Pineville (now at Baton Rouge), 1861. Commd. 1st lt. Confederate Army, Civil War, promoted capt. 16th Regt., La. Inf., served 2 years; captured at Battle of Missionary Ridge (Tenn.), held prisoner on Johnsons Island, Lake Erie, until end of war; admitted to La. bar, 1866, began practice of law, Covington; mem. La. Senate, 1866-70; mem. U.S. Ho. of Reps. (Democrat) from La., 44th-48th congresses, 1875-85. Died Washington, D.C., Apr. 25, 1889; buried Ellis family cemetery, "Ingleside," nr. Amite, La.

ELLIS, HAYNE, naval officer (ret.); b. Macon, Ga., Aug. 26, 1877; s. Hayne and Ida Louise (Lamar) E.; B.S., U.S. Naval Acad., 1900; hon. LL.D., Lake Forest (Ill.) Coll., 1939; m. Sally America Long, Dec. 17, 1904; children—Martha Lamar (Mrs. John D. Leland), Hayne, Robert A. Long, Lucia Long (Mrs. Edgar J. Uihlein), Long. Commissioned ensign U.S. Navy, 1902, and advnaced through grades to rear adm., 1933; comdr. patrol force, Atlantic fleet, 1939-40; mem. Gen. Bd. of Navy, 1941; ret. from active service upon reaching statutory age, Sept. 1, 1941; v.p. and dir., Long Bell Lumber Corp., Kan. City, Mo., since 1941. Decorated Comdr. and Grand Officer, Crown of Italy; Order of Naval Merit (Spain); Grand Officer, and Grand Cross Order of Duarte (Republic of San Domingo); Grand Cross, Order of Merit (Haiti). Episcopalian. Clubs: Chevy Chase (Md.), Army Navy, Army Navy Country (Washington), Kansas City (Mo.) Country. Home: 1905 Lombardy Rd., San Marino 9, Calif. Office: R. A. Long Bldg., Kansas City 6 MO

ELLIS, MILTON ANDREW life ins. co. exec.; b. Manila, P.I., May 23, 1910; s. Frederick Holt and Edith Hills (Powers) Kimball; A.B., U. Rochester, 1931; m. Kathleen Black, Sept. 19, 1932; children - Sandra (Mrs. Werner G. Lomker), Fred Kimball. With Met. Life Ins. Co., 1931 - , 2d v.p., 1960-63, v.p., 1963 - . Mem. Nat. council Boy Scouts Am. Served to lt. comdr. USNR, 1943-45. Decorated Submarine Combat award with 4 stars. Fellow Soc. Actuaries; mem. Health Ins. Assn. Am. (past chmn. legislative com.), Life Ins. Assn. Am., Am. Life Conv., U.S. C. of C., Delta Upsilon, Kappa Phi Kappa. Home: 108 Serpentine Rd., Tenafly, N.J. Office: 1 Madison Ave., N.Y.C. 10. Died Mar. 28, 1966.

ELLIS, RUDOLPH banker; b. Elkton, Md., Nov. 20, 1837; son of Francis A. and Eliza (Howard) E.; Ed. Elkton; m. Helen Struthers, Apr. 26, 1866. Served pvt. 1st troop Phila. City Cav., May 13, 1861; 1st lt. and adj. 6th Pa. Cav., Nov. 20, 1862; capt., Apr. 11, 1864; mustered out, Dec. 27, 1864. Pres. Fidelity Trust Co.; dir. Pa. R.R. Co., Fourth St. Nat. Bank (Phila.), Am. Telegraph & Telephone Co., Commercial Trust Co. of Phila., Manhattan Trust Co. (New York). Commr. Tp. of Raknor, Delaware Co., Pa. Mem. Loyal Legion (Pa. Commandery). Pres. Radnor Hunt Club. Home: Bryn Mawr, Pa. Died Sept. 21, 1915.

ELLSWORTH, ELMER EPHRAIM army officer; b. Malta, N.Y., Apr. 11, 1837; s. Ephraim D. and Phoebe (Denton) E. Held various jobs as clk; became patent-solicitor, Chgo.; became comdr. volunteer mil. co., introduced "Zouave" drill method (which co. popular with public); took U.S. Zouave Cadets on Eastern tour; became maj. Ill. Nat. Guard; became mem. Abraham Lincoln's campaign staff; mem. of Three Years Regt., became 1st well-known Civil War death. Died Washington, D.C., May 24, 1861; buried Mechanicansville, N.Y.

ELMENDORF, JOHN E (DWARD), JR. physician; b. New Brunswick, N.J., May 28, 1893; s. John Edward and Helen Aline (Decker) E.; B.A., Rutgers U., 1914; D.Sc. (hon.), 1954; M.D., Johns Hopkins, 1918. spl. studies, sch. hygiene and pub. health, 1926-29; m. Virginia Knower, May 20, 1922 (div. 1934); children - Virginia DuBarry (Mrs. Francis A. Sokol), Joan Loomis (Mrs. Russell McCandless); m. 2d, Harriet Camac, Oct. 25, 1935. Intern Johns Hopkins Hosp., 1918-19; asst. resident medicine Barnes Hosp., St. Louis, 1919-20; dir. field studies dept. medicine and pub. health Rockefeller Found., 1920-52; engaged in yellow fever and malaria control work 1930-41; dir. civilian sch. to train army and navy officers in malaria control, 1942-43; dir. Carlos Finlay Yellow Fever Inst., Bogota, Colombia, 1947-51; promoted, planned and organized Superior Sch. of Hygiene, Colombia, and served as sci. dir., 1951-52; now engaged in writing. Served from lt. col. to col., AUS, 1943-47. Decorated Legion of Merit; Hon. Officer Most Excellent Order of British Empire; Distinguished Visitor and Citation (Mexico); Medal and Citation Crux de Boyaca (Colombia). Fellow A.A.A.S., Am. Pub. Health Assn., N.Y. Acad. Medicine; mem. Am. Soc. Tropical Hygiene and Medicine, Soc. Colonial Wars. Clubs: Strollers, Military Naval (N.Y.C.). Office: care Rockefeller Found., 49 W. 49th St., N.Y.C. 20. Died May 25, 1960; buried Elmwood Cemetery, New Brunswick, N.J.

ELMER, EBENEZER congressman, physician, coll. pres.; b. Cedarville, N.J., Aug. 23, 1752; s. Daniel and Abigail (Lawrence) E.; m. Hannah Seeley, 1784; 1 son, Lucius Quintus Cincinnatus. Commd. ensign 3d N.J. Regt., 1776, promoted to lt.; served as surgeon's mate, 1777, surgeon 2d N.J. Regt., 1778; a founder Soc. of Cincinnati, pres. N.J. br.; v.p. state council, 1807-17, 22-32; mem. N.J. Assembly, 1789-91, 93-95, 1817, 19, speaker, 1791, 95, 1817; mem. U.S. Ho. of Reps. from N.J. 7th-9th congresses, 1801-07, collection of customs, Bridgeton, N.J., 1808; v.p. Burlington Coll., 1808-17, 22-32; last surviving Revolutionary officer of N.J.; adj. gen. N.J. Militia in War of 1812, brig. gen. Cumberland Brigade. Died Bridgeton, Oct. 18, 1843; buried Presbyn. Cemetery, Bridgeton.

ELROD, RALPH (PERRY) bacteriologist; b. Oakland, Cal., Jan. 17, 1913 s. Ralph Leroy and Rose (Gyson) E.: A.B., Brown U., 1936, M.S., 1938; Ph.D., Ohio State U., 1941; m. Elizabeth Virginia Keefe, Oct. 30, 1942; children-Perry Keefe, Ralph George. Instr. Brown U., Providence, 1940-41; asso. Rockefeller Inst., Princeton, N.J., 1941-47; prof., chmn. dept. microbiology U. S.D., 1947—. Served as maj. San. Corps, U.S. Army, 1942-45, bacteriologist, serologist, and parasitologist. Mem. Am. Assn. Immunologists, Soc. Am. Bacteriol., Sigma Xi, Alpha Tau Omega. Author numerous articles in field of microbiology. Home: 920 E. Clark St. Office: U.S.D., Vermillion, S.D. Deceased.

ELSER, MAXIMILIAN, JR. ret. pub. relations; b. Ft. Worth, Tex., June 10, 1889; s. Maximilian and Elizabeth (Loving) E.; ed. Balt. City Coll.; grad. Tome Sch., Port Deposit, Md., 1906; A.B., Cornell, 1911; as of 1910; m. Helen Ruth Richter, Mar. 30, 1916; children - Elizabeth Loving, Peter Fielding Davis, Henry Richter Christopher. Began as reporter Ft. Worth Star, 1906; with N.Y. Evening Sun, Summer, 1907 and 1910-11; asso. editor Cornell Daily Sun, 1907-10, Cornell Widow, 1908-09, editor in chief, 1909-10; adv., publicity and booking work for Anna Pavlowa Ballet Russe, Diaghileff Ballet, New York Philharmonic Orchestra, etc., until 1917; founded Met. Newspaper Feature Service, 1919, sold to United Features, subsidiary of United Press, 1930, remaining as vice president through 1935; editorial head of public relations-publicity dept. J. Walter Thompson Co., N.Y.C. to 1947; partner Elser & Assos., pub. relations to 1956, ret. Chmn. press com. Nat. Horse Show Assn., 1933-50. Commd. 1st lt., inf., 2d Plattsburg Training Camp, 1917; overseas with A.E.F.; capt., inf., Siberia, and attached to G.H.Q. staff, 1918-19; maj., later lt. col., A.U.S., Jan. 1942-Dec. 1945; in pub. relations, 1st Army; transport comdr. running to North Africa; transportation officer in New Guinea; with G.H.Q., Australia, New Guinea and Philippines, and with 8th Army in Philippines (intelligence sect.). Mem. S.R., Zeta Psi, Quill and Dagger. Republican. Episcopalian. Clubs: Players, Cornell (N.Y.); Nat. Press (Washington). Home: 60 Gramercy Pk., N.Y.C. 10; also Hopeland Farms. Hopeland, Pa. Died Jan. 3, 1961; buried Arlington (Va.) Nat. Cemetery.

ELSTON, ISAAC COMPTON banker; b. Crawfordsville, Ind., Feb. 5, 1836; s. Isaac Compton and Maria E. (Aiken) E.; student Wabash Coll., Crawfordsville, 1849-53; U. of Mich., 1854-55; m. Sarah S. Vills, Aug. 7, 1852. Enlisted in 11th Ind. Regt. Vols., Apr., 1861, and elected lt. Co. I; promoted capt.; major, Jan., 1862; apptd. a.-d.-c. on staff of Maj. Gen. Wool, with rank of lt. col., and chief of staff to Gen. Lew Wallace, with rank of col.; participated in capture of Ft. Henry, siege of Ft. Donelson, Battle of Shiloh, and other important engagements. Established 1st Nat. Bank of Memphis (Tenn.), 1864; in brokerage business, Cincinnati, 1866; with brothers-in-law, Henry S. Lane and Gen. Lew Wallace, founded Elston & Co., bankers, Crawsfordsville, 1868; mgr. same till 1905; then pres. of its successor, the Elston Nat. Bank; dir. Union Trust Co. (Indianapolis). Republican. Presbyn. Home: Crawfordsville, Ind. Died July 2, 1925.

ELSWORTH, EDWARD banker; b. New York, N.Y., Jan. 6, 1840; s. John and Martha (Van Varick) E.; ed. Rutgers Grammar Sch., New York, Dutchess Co. Acad., N.Y. State and Nat. Law Sch.; (A.M., Rutgers, 1892); m. Mary Johnston, Dec. 26, 1867; m. 2d, Mary Louise Armstrong, Aug. 29, 1906. Admitted to bar, 1861; practiced law in New York, 1861-63, in Rochland Co., 1864-65, in Poughkeepsie, 1865-67; engaged in bus., Poughkeepsie, 1868-91; pres. Fallkill Nat. Bank, Poughkeepsie, 1891-1903 (dir.); pres. Poughkeepsie Savings Bank, 1903-. Maj. and judge advocate 8th brigade, N.G.S.N.Y., 1875-82; mem. bd. of edn., City of Poughkeepsie, 1880-87; mayor, 1887-88 and 1891-92. Trustee and treas. Vassar Coll. Democrat. Home: Poughkeepsie, N.Y. Died 1911.

ELTING, ARTHUR WELLS surgeon; b. S. Cairo, N.Y., Oct. 6, 1872; s. Francis and Margaret M. (Snyder) E.; A.B., Yale, 1894; M.D., Johns Hopkins, 1898; on staff, Johns Hopkins Hosp., 1898-99; (LL.D., St. Lawrence Univ., 1916); m. Mary B. Lord, Sept. 5, 1900; m. 2d, Harriet Corning Rawle, October 24, 1917. Practiced, Albany, N.Y., since 1900 Became prof. of surgery. Albany Medical Coll., May 1911. Lt. col. Med. Corps, U.S. Army, active service in France, 1918. Fellow American Surgical Association (president); chmn. of Am. Board of Surgery; mem. A.M.A., Clin. Surg. Soc., Interurban Surg. Soc., Albany County and N.Y. State med. socs., Eclat Soc., Phi Beta Kappa. Republican. Home: 119 Washington Av., Albany, N.Y. Died Jan 2, 1948.

ELTING, WINSTON, architect; b. Winnetka, Ill., Feb. 11, 1907; s. Victor and Marie (Winston) E.; grad. Hotchkiss Sch., 1924; A.B., Princeton, 1929; grad. student Ecoles des Beaux Arts, Paris, 1929-32, Am. Acad., Fontainbleau, 1931; m. Marjorie Horton, May 13, 1933; children—Elizabeth Dudley (Mrs. Bernard Rogers III), Audrey Horton, John Winston; m. 2d, Onnolee Laabs Conway, Feb. 3, 1962; 1 s., Winston Lachlan. With housing div. Pub. Works Adminstrn., Wash., 1935-36; pvt. practice. Chgo., 1937-41, 56-60, 61-68; partner Schweikher & Elting, architects, Roselle, Ill., 1945-53, Elting & Bennett, 1953-56, Elting, Deknatel & Assos., Inc., 1960-61; asst. prof. architecture Univ. Ill., Chgo., 1961-62, asso. prof. 1963-64, prof., 1965-68; works include Fine Arts Center, Chapel and Theatre, dormitory bldgs. Maryville (Tenn.) Coll., 1950-58, Lang. Center, Vassar Coll., 1957, Unitarian Ch., Evanston, Ill., 1958, D. E. Daggitt House, Benton Harbor, Mich., 1958, Earl H. Closser House, Marquette, Mich., 1960, others. Board of directors Adult Edn. Council of Chgo. Served to lt. comdr. USNR, 1942-45. Recipient design award Progressive Architecture, 1954, 56, award Chgo. chpt. A.I.A. and Chgo. Assn. Commerce and Industry, 1955, 59, 60, award Ch. Archtl. Guild Am., 1953, award House and Home mag., 1957; award merit A.I.A., 1965; Archtl. Record award excellence, 1965. Fellow A.I.A. (director Chicago chapter); member Mich. Soc. Architects, Soc. Contemporary Am. Art (past pres.), Art Inst. Chgo. (gov. life mem.), Chgo. Mus. Natural History (life asso.). Clubs: Cap and Gown, Princeton (Princeton); Arts (dir.), (Chgo.); Cliff Dwellers; Rolling Rock (Pa.). Author: (with Talbot Wegg) Ubran Housing, 1936; also articles. Home: Chicago IL Died Jan. 25, 1968; buried Elting Meml. Burying Ground, New Paltz NY

ELTINGE, LEROY army officer; b. South Woodstock, N.Y., Sept. 17, 1872; s. Lamont Eltinge and Arvelia (Lake) E.; grad. U.S. Mil. Acad., 1896, honor grad. Army Sch. of the Line, 1908; grad. Army Staff Coll., 1909; m. Effee B. Trotter, Dec. 3, 1897; 1 dau., Margaret (Mrs. James L. Bolt). Commd. 2d lt. 4th Cav., June 12, 1896; promoted through grades to rank brig. gen., July 19, 1924. In Philippines, 1898-99 and 1901-03; with Army Cuban Pacification, 1906-07; on Mexican border, 1914, again, 1916, crossing into Mexico after .- arrived in France, July 28, 1917; in operations sect. of gen. staff, Gen. till Apr. 30, 1918; dep. chief of staff - at Gen. Hdqrs., May 1, 1918-June 30, 1919; asst. chief of staff Philippine Dept., 1921-23; asst. chief of staff War Plans Div., Washington. Decorated D.S.M., Croix de Guerre with palm and Comdr. Legion of Honor (French); Comdr. Order of the Crown (Belgian); Comdr. Order of the Crown (Italian); Companion Order of the Bath (British); Order of Solidaridad (Panamanian). Baptist. Died May 13, 1931.

ELWELL, JOHN JOHNSON physician, lawyer; b. Warren, O., June 22, 1820; M.D., Cleve. Med. Coll., 1846; studied law, 1852-54; m. Nancy Chittenden. Began practice medicine, Cleve., 1846; admitted to Ohio bar, 1854, began practice law specializing in medico-legal area; mem. Ohio Legislature from Ashtabula County, 1853-54; lectr. on med. jurisprudence Ohio U., also Western Res. Coll., 1850's; founder Western Law Monthly, 1857, editor, 1857-61; served with Q.M.'s Corps, U.S. Army, 1861-65, became chief q.m. 10th Corps; practiced law, Cleve., from 1865; contbr. articles to many legal jours.; an editor Bouvier's Law Dictionary. Author. A Medico-Legal Treatise on Malpractice and Medical Evidence, Comprising the Elements of Medical Jurisprudence, 1860. Died Cleve., Mar. 13, 1900; buried Cleve.

ELY, HANSON EDWARD army officer; b. Independence, Ia., Nov. 23, 1867; s. Eugene Hanson and Julia (Lamb) E.; grad. U.S. Mil. Acad., 1891; distinguished grad. Inf. and Cav. Sch., 1905; grad. Army Staff Coll., 1906; m. Eleanor Boyle, July 6, 1910. Commd. 2d lt. 22d Inf., 1891, advanced through grades to col. (temp.), 1917; brig.-gen. to maj. gen. Nat. Army, 1918, brig. gen. to major gen. U.S. Army, 1923. Served in Mont., N.D. and Neb., 1891-97; prof. mil. sci. and tactics State U. Ia., 1897-98; with regt. at Camp Wikoff, N.Y., 1898; in Philippines, 1899-1901; comd. Gen. Funston's mounted scouts, later regtl. adj. and adj. gen. 3d Dist., Dept. So. Luzon; observer German maneuvers and studying European armies, 1906; in Philippines,

1907-12; arrived in France, 1917; apptd. col. 28th Inf., 1918; apptd. comdr. 3d Brigade Inf., 2d Div., 1st Army Corps, AEF, 1918, comdr. 5th Div. 3d Army Corps, 1918; comd. 28th Inf. when it captured Cantigny, and the 5th Div. when it forced Meuse crossing; ret. 1931. Decorated D.S.C., D.S.M. (U.S.); Comdr. Legion of Honor; also Officer Legion of Honor; 5 Croix de Guerre. Clubs: Army and Navy (Washington and Manila); Chevy Chase (Washington); Golf and County (Des Moines, Ia.). Address: 2540 Massachusetts Av. N.W., Washington. Died Apr. 28, 1958; buried Arlington Nat. Cemetery.

ELZEY, ARNOLD army officer; b. Elmwood, Md., Dec. 18, 1816; s. Arnold Elzey and Anne (Jackson) E.; grad. U.S. Mil. Acad., 1837; m. Ellen Irwin, 1845, 1 son. Served as lt. U.S. Army in Seminole War; fired 1st gun of Mexican War; commd. capt. arty. Confederate Army, 1861; promoted brig. gen., 1862; commanded Dept. of Richmond, 1862-64; chief of arty. Many of Tenn. Died Balt., Feb. 21, 1871.

EMERSON, EDWIN author; b. Dresden, Saxony, Jan. 23, 1869; s. Edwin and Marie Louise (Ingham) E.; A.B., Harvard Univ., 1891; m. Mary Edith Griswold, May 16, 1906. Served for many years as foreign and war correspondent. Author: College Year Book, 1897; Pepy's Ghost, 1899; In War and Peace, 1899; Rough Rider Stories, 1900; History of the 19th Century, 1902; The Monroe Doctrine in Venezuela, 1903; Both Sides of a War, 1910; Comet Lore, 1910; Central American Dictators, 1911; Nicaraguan Notes, 1912; Mexican Notes, 1913; With the German Armies, 1917; A Revolutionary Wedding, 1919; Benedict Arnold, 1923; Adventures of Theodore Roosevelt, 1928; The Gutenberg Bible, 1929; Hoover and His Times, 1932; German Swordplay, 1936; Sidelights of History, 1943; When Bugles Blew, 1947; Who Got There First on San Juan Hill?, 1948. Served in Cuban campaign with 1st U.S. Vol. Cav. on Gen. Joe Wheeler's Staff, 1898; col. Venezuelan Vol. Cav. in Colombian Campaign, 1901; capt. 1st Field Artillery, N.Y.N.G., 1910-12; mil. observer U.S. Gen. Staff in Nicaragua, 1912, and Mexico, 1913-14; European and Middle East theater, 1914-18; captive of Turkey, Germany, 1919-22; lieutentant colonel and acting adj. general on General O'Ryan's staff, hdqrs. div., N.Y. Nat. Guard, 1913-14. Mem. Am. Hist. Assn., Rough Riders Association, Phi Delta Theta, Pi Beta. Military Orders: Bolivar, Merito of Ecuador, Momotombo, Santiago de Cuba, Cal. Commandery of Spanish-Am. War Clubs: Fencers (Washington); Harvard, (San Francisco); Sportsman's. Home: Veterans' Home, Yountville, Cal. Died Oct. 2, 1959; buried Golden Gate Nat. Cemetery, San Bruno, Cal.

EMERSON, EDWIN, JR., war corr.; b. Dresden, Saxony; s. Edwin and Marie Louise (Ingham) E.; A.B., Cornell, 1890; A.B., Harvard, 1891; unmarried. Was foreign corr. Boston Post, later in editorial work New York Evening Post, Sun and Harper's Weekly; then sec. Teachers Coll., (Columbia) until 1898. Went to front in Spanish-Am. War as corr. Leslie's Weekly; engaged in successful exploration of Porto Rico under direction of Lt. H.H. Whitney, secret agt. U.S. Mil. Information Bur.; joined Roosevelt's Rough Riders, serving in engagement at San Juan and in the trenches before Santiago. Warr corr. Collier's Weekly and Illustrirte Zeitung in S. America; took part in Colombian-Venezuelan war, 1901, as Venezuelan col. vols.; decorated by President Castro with order of Bolivar for gallantry in action. War corr. New York World, Chicago News, Westminster Gazette, Black and White, in Russian-Japanese War. Mem. N.Y. Hist. Soc., Franklin Inst., Japanese Congress (1875-7); resigned from 44th Congress, Dec. 12, 1876; major of New York, Jan. 1, 1877, to Dec. 31, 1878; presdl. elector, 1880; Central Park commr., 1897-8. Democrat. Mem. S.R., Soc. Colonial Wars, Soc. War 1812. Clubs: Century, Manhattan, Democratic. Presbyterian. Home: 47 W. 57th St. Office: 103 Gold St., New York

EMERSON, KENDALL, surgeon; b. Northampton, Mass., June 27, 1875; s. Benjamin Kendall and Mary Annette (Hopkins) E.; A.B., Amherst Coll., 1897, M.A. (honorary), 1922, Doctor of Science, 1950; M.D., Harvard University, 1901; married Josephine Devereux Sewall, Oct. 1, 1903; children—Sewall, Kendall. Intern, Mass. Gen. Hosp., Boston, 1901-02; began practice orthopedic and gen. surgery, Worcester, Mass., 1902; asst. surgeon, Memorial Hosp., Worcester, 1903-10, orthopedic surgeon, 1910-28, cons. surgeon since 1928; mng. dir. Nat. Tuberculosis Assn. 1928-48, retired, 1948, consultant since 1948; president of New York Tuberculosis and Health Association, 1948-49; exec. sec., Am. Pub. Health Assn., 1931-35. Maj., Royal Army Med. Corps (Brit.), 1916-18; maj., Med. Corps, U.S.A., 1918-19, instr., surgeon general's office, Washington, D.C., 1918-19, detailed as spl. Red Cross commr. to Siberia; dir. Am. Hosp. in Paris, 1920; consultant U.S. Pub. Health Serv.; counselor Med. Council of Vets. Adminstrn. Mem. permanent bd. hon. consultants to Army Med. Library. Trustee Smith Coll., Potts Memorial Hosp. Mem. exec. com. Internat. Union Against Tuberculosis; mem. U.S. Commn. to Meeting of Pan-Am. Sanitary Union, Buenos Aires, 1934. Awarded Trudeau Medal for tuberculosis work, 1947. Fellow Am. Coll. Surgs.; mem. A.M.A., N.Y. Acad. Medicine, New York County Med. Soc., Mass. Med. Soc., New England Surg. Soc., Phi Beta Kappa, Alpha Delta Phi. Decorated Order St. Sava, 1st Class (Rumania). Republican. Episcopalian. Clubs: Century (New York); Cosmos (Washington). Contbr. articles to med. jours. Home: 1070 Beacon St., Brookline, MA Office: 1790 Broadway NY 19

EMERSON, MERTON LESLIE engineer; b. Brockton, Mass., Aug. 11, 1882; s. Edwin Leslie and Lora Gertrude (Kingman) E.; student Thayer Acad., Braintree, Mass., 1900; S.B., Mass. Inst. Technology, 1904; m. Frances Elizabeth Dike, Oct. 25, 1906; children - Elizabeth Kingman (dec.), Merton Leslie (dec.), Mary Leslie (wife of Major Thos. B. Mechling, U.S.A.). with U.S. Geological Survey, 1903-04; engr. Boston Pneumatic Transit Co., 1904-06; mng. dir. The Housing Corp., 1920-21; operating mgr. Am. Pneumatic Service Co., 1906-16, v.p., 1916-27, pres., 1927-29; treas. The Lamson Co., 1916-18, pres., 1927-29; pres. Boston Pneumatic Transit Co., New York Pneumatic Service Co., Chicago Pneumatic Service Co., St. Louis Pneumatic Tube Co.; cons. engr. with Scovell Wellington & Co. and Unifed Engrs. & Constructors; dir. Arkwright Mut. Fire Ins. Co., Braintree Nat. Bank. Mem. Tech. Board of Rev., U.S. Fed. Adminstrn. Pub. Works; New England dir, NRA, 1935; consultant Nat. Resources Com., asst. dir. U.S. Drainage Basin Studies; tech. adviser Social Security Bd. Served as major, U.S. Army, chief of adminstrn., gas defense div., Chem. Warfare Service, 1918-19; Army Specialist Corps, 1942. Trustee Wentworth Inst., Boston, Thayer Acad., Thayerlands Sch.; term mem. Mass. Inst. Tech. Corp. Mem. Am. Soc. C.E., Am. Soc. Mil. Engrs., Am. Inst. Cons. Engrs., Soc. Advancement of Management, Am. Soc. Public Adminstrn., Am. Legion, Mil Order World War, Tech. Alumni Council, Tau Beta Pi, Soc. Mayflower Descendants, Republican, Unitarian, lfason. Clubs: Engineers, Technology (New York); University (Boston); Cosmos, Army and Navy Country (Washington). Home: Braintree, Mass.; 218 S. Royal St., Alexandria, Va. Office: 75 Federal St., Boston, Mass. Died Feb. 1945.

EMERSON, WILLARD I. ednl. adminstr.; b. Ithaca, N.Y., Sept. 7, 1894; s. Alfred and Alice (Edwards) E.; A.B., Cornell, 1921; student Cambridge U., Eng., 1919, Columbia, 1922-23; m. Ethel Townsend Mole, June 2, 1923; children - Ann (Mrs. Kenneth E. Weeks), Willard I., Jr., Barbara Harwood (Mrs. Paul B. McMahon), Jonathan Edwards. With Hemphill, Noyes & Co., and predecessor cos., 1921-51, gen. partner, 1935-51, mgr., 1954 - ; v.p. for development Cornell U., 1951-53; dir. Therm, Inc., Norfolk So. Ry.; dir. Durham & S.C. Railroad. Mem. Tompkins County (N.Y.) United Fund Com. Mem. Cornell U. Council. capt., inf., World War I; lt. col. A.C., A.U.S., World War II. Decorated D.S.C., Conspicuous Service Cross (N.Y. State). Mem. S.A.R., N.Y.C., Theta Delta Chi. Clubs: Cornell (N.Y.C., Ithaca, N.Y.); Statler. Address: 1399 Slaterville Rd., Ithaca, N.Y. Died Dec. 3, 1966.

EMERY, AMBROSE R. army officer; born Ind., July 26, 1883; B.S. in Elec. Engring., Ga. Sch. Tech., 1904; grad. Ind. Sch., Advanced Course, 1925, Command and Gen. Staff Sch., 1926, Army War Coll., 1932. Commd. 2d lt., Inf., U.S. Army, Apr. 1905, and advanced through the grades to brig. gen., Oct. 1941; retired Feb. 1944. Address: War Dept., Washington 25, D.C. Died Nov. 28, 1945.

EMERY, FRED AZRO editor; b. Washington, D.C., August 13, 1875; s. George S. and Abbie Adelia (Moxley) E.; ed. high sch.; student law dept. Columbian (now George Washington) U., 1892-93, 1897-98; unmarried. Reporter Evening News, Washington, 1892-93; Washington corr. The Journalist, 1893-94; with Washington bur. Asso. Press, 1893-1918, mainly reporting proceedings of Congress; White House rep. and one of Capitol staff, during Spanish-Am. War, 1898; night mgr. Southern div. of Associated Press, 1905-07, 1910-11, Capitol mgr., 1911-12. Washington corr. Collier's Weekly, 1903-04, contbg. the "Behind the Scenes in Washington" dept., political and Russo-Japanese war features; contbr. "Washington Day by Day" column to New York Tribune, 1903; feature writer Internat. Syndicate, 1913-15; writer "People of Note," "On a War Basis" and "Potential Presidential Candidates," Internat. Syndicate Series, 1924; with Washington bureau Baltimore Sun, 1921-22, assisting in covering Internat. Conf. on Limitation of Armament. Chief Div. of Foreign Intelligence, Dept. of State, Dec., 1918-May, 1921; apptd. "officer to aid in important drafting work in connection with foreign relations," July 1, 1919; conducted national and local publicity campaigns, 1921-23; with United States Daily (now The United States News) reporting Congress, 1926-33; mem. bd. editors U.S. News & World Report, 1933 - ; contbr. to Dictionary of Am. History, 1937. Mem. original Citizens' Com. of 100 on Future Development of Washington; mem. exec. com. on civic orgns. for President Wilson's inauguration, 1913; mem. civic orgns. com. of President Wilson's 2d inauguration, 1917; mem. finance com. United Confed. Vets., 27th Annual Reunion, Washington, 1917; v.p. Connecticut Av. Citizens' Assn., 1920; del. and chmn. com. on nat. representation for D.C., mem. exec. com., Fedn. of Citizens' Assn., 1930-39; vice pres. Chevy Chase Citizens Assn., 1920-21; past v.p., Vt. State Assn. of D.C.; pres. Soc. Natives of D.C., 3 terms; life mem. and past v.p. Columbia Hist. Soc. of D.C.; mem. and a founder, Nat. Press Club (1908) of D.C. (former mem. bd. govs.); mem. Vermont Historical Society of Montpelier, Vermont. Member Association of Oldest Inhabitants (v.p. since 1930); ex-mem. Washington Criminal Justice Assn. (former mem. exec. com.), Wash. Bd. of Trade, Thornton Soc. of Washington, Mem. Rep. State Com. of D.C., 1944-45. Presbyterian. Home: 3900 Connecticut Av. Tilden Gardens 6, Washington. Office: U.S. News & World Report, 24th and N Sts., Washington 7. Died Mar. 22, 1962; buried Rock Creek Cemetery, Washington.

EMERY, JAMES AUGUSTAN lawyer; b. Detroit, Mar. 29, 1876; s. Augustan Havens and Mary (Harrington) E.; student St. Ignatius Coll., San Francisco; A.B., Santa Clara (Cal.) U., 1896; attended Hastings Coll. Law (U. Cal.), 1898; m. Emily Aloise Hartrick, Jan. 30, 1902; children-Mary Aloise, Letitia Alexia, Alice Suzanne. Admitted to Cal. bar, 1903, began practice at San Francisco; counsel Health Bd., San Francisco, 1903-04, Citizens' Indsl. Assn. Am., 1905-08; gen. counsel N.A.M., 1910-46 (resigned Dec. 1946), Nat. Founders Assn., 1920; assisted orgn. Nat. Indsl. Conf. Board, 1916: assisted in orgn. War Labor Board, 1917; adviser Employer Group of 1st Internat. Labor Conf., Washington, 1919, actively participated in presentation of indsl. questions in litigation and legislation; factor in transition of Am. industry from system of employers' liability to workmen's compensation. Roman Catholic. Clubs: Chevy Chase (Washington); and Bohemian (San Francisco). Author : Accident Prevention and Relief (with F. C. Schwedtman), 1911; Workmen's Compensation in the States (legal phase), 1917. Office: Investment Bldg. Washington. Died Sept. 28, 1955.

EMERY, MATTHEW GAULT b. Pembroke, N.H., Sept. 28, 1818; s. Jacob E.; ed. Pembroke, N.H.; left home and went to Baltimore at 18 yrs. of age; apprenticed himself to a stone cutter. In 1840 received 1st govt. contract, cutting of stone in the quarry for P.O. dept. bldg., Washington. Removed to Washington, 1842; did much stone work on Capitol; cut and laid cornerstone for its extension; prepared, cut and squared, and on July 4, 1848, laid cornerstone of Washington Monument. Organized and became capt. of militia co., May 16, 1861. Took charge of sick and disabled soldiers from his State in Washington, and gave up his residence at Brightwood for that purpose. Treas. N.H. Soldiers' Aid Assn., Washington; was mem. bd. aldermen, Washington, and its mayor, 1870, holding position until territorial govt. adopted by Congress for dist. abolished office of mayor. Sold his interest in business, 1872. Has been regent Smithsonian Instn.; trustee Dickinson Coll., Pa.; regent and vice chancellor Nat. Univ.; regent and treas. Am. Univ.; pres. bd. of trustees Metropolitan Meth. Ch. Identified, 1945-, as incorporator, dir. or officer in nearly all fire and life ins. cos. organized in Washington, as well as banks, trust cos., market cos., gas and electric light cos., etc.; pres. 2d Nat. Bank. Home: Washington, D. C. Died 1901.

EMMONS, ARTHUR BREWSTER III fgn. service officer; b. Boston, Aug. 30, 1910; s. Arthur Brewster, II, and Louise Anderson (Hickok) E.; grad. St. Paul's Sch., 1929; B.S., Harvard, 1933; grad. Fgn. Service Sch., 1940; m. Evelyn Treat Voorhees, Oct. 8, 1938; children - Julia Voorhees, Louise Hickok. Mem. Sikong Expdn. to Southeastern Tibet, 1931-33, expdn. mapped and made 1st ascent of Mt. Minya Konka, 24,900 feet altitude, 1932; mem. Brit.-Am. Himalayan Expdn. to India, expdn. made 1st ascent of Mt. Nanda Devi, 25,-645 feet altitude, 1936; mem. Burma-China Expdn., 1936; apptd. fgn. service officer, unclassified, v. consul career, sec. Diplomatic Service, Mar. 1938. v. consul, Montreal, Que., Can., 1939, Hankow, China, 1940, Keijo, Korea, 1940-41; assigned Dept. State, 1942; 3d sec., v. consul, Montevideo, Uruguay, 1942, 2d sec., v. consul, 1945; fgn. service officer Office of U.S. Polit. Adv. to Supreme Comdr. Allied Forces, Japan, 1945; at Seoul, Korea, Apr. 1946, consul, May 1946; 2d sec. embassy Madrid, Spain, 1946; officer in charge Korean affairs, Dept. State, July 1950; mem. U.S. delegation to U.N., Paris, France, Jan. 1952, N.Y., Oct.-Dec. 1952; 1st sec. of embassy, Canberra, Australia, 1953; counselor of Embassy, Dublin, Ireland, 1956; Kuala Lumpur, Fedn. Malaya, 1958; dept. dir. Office Southwest Pacific Affairs, Dept. State, 1959, special asst. SEATO Affairs Bur. Far Eastern Affairs, 1959 - . Fellow American Geog. Society; mem. of Arctic Inst. N.A. Clubs: Am. Alpine; Alpine (London, Eng.); Himalayan, Kenwood Golf, University (Washington). Author: Men Against the Clouds, 1935; also articles mountaineering and exploration. Compiler original maps of regions surrounding Minya Konka and Nanda Devi. Office: Dept. of State, Washington. Died Aug. 22, 1962; buried Dover, Mass.

EMMONS, DELOS CARLETON air force officer; b. Huntington, W.Va., Jan. 17, 1888; s. Carleton D. and Mary (Gibson) E.; grad. U.S. Mil. Acad., 1909; U.S. Army, air service course, Harvard, 1920-21; grad. Air Corps Tactical Sch., 1932, Command and Gen. Staff Sch., 1934; D.Sc., Marshall Coll.; m. Elena McKim, Mar. 1, 1919; 1 dau., Deloise Ann. Commd. 2d lt. inf., June 1, 1909; promoted through grades to brig. gen., 1936, maj. gen. AC, 1939; lt. gen., 1940; trans. from inf. to Signal Corps, Aviation Sect., 1916; comd. 1st Wing,

G.H.Q., Air Force to 1939; then comdg. Air Force Combat Command, Bolling Field, D.C.; apptd. to comd. Hawaiian Dept., USAF, Dec. 17, 1941; apptd. comdr. Western Def. Command, Sept. 1943; comdg. Alaskan Dept., 1944-46; became comdt. Armed Forces Staff Coll. 1946, ret., 1948. Awarded D.S.M. with 2 oak leaf clusters, D.S.M. Legion of Merit (Navy), Legion of Merit, D.F.C., Air medal, several fgn. decorations. Episcopalian. Club: Burlingame Country. Address: 816 W. Santa Inez Av., Hillsborough, Cal. Died Oct. 3, 1965; buried Arlington Nat. Cemetery.

EMMONS, GEORGE FOSTER naval officer; b. Clarendon, Vt., Aug. 23, 1811; s. Horatio and Abigail (Foster) E.; m. Frances Thornton, Jan. 10, 1843. With Wilkes surveying expdn., 1838-42; commd. lt. U.S. Navy, 1841, advanced through grades to comdr., 1856, capt., 1863, commodore, 1868; captured Cedar Keys, Fla., 1862; fleet capt. of South Atlantic blockading squadron under Rear Adm. Dahlgren, 1867; duties after Civil War include head Hydrographic Office, Washington, D.C., also comdt. Phila. Navy Yard; promoted rear Adm., 1872, ret., 1873. Author: The Navy of the United States from the Commencement, 1775-1853, with a Brief History of Each Vessel's Service and Fate, 1853. Died Princeton, N.J., July 23, 1884.

EMMONS, GEORGE THORTON lt. U.S. navy; b. Md.; grad. U.S. Naval Acad., Oct. 15, 1874, ensign, July 17, 1875, master, Oct. 15, 1881, lt. (j.g.), March 3, 1883; lt., Nov. 1, 1887; on duty at World's Columbian Expn., 1892-93. Mem. Nat. Geog. Soc. Address: Navy Dept., Washington. Died June 11, 1945.

EMMONS, HAROLD HUNTER lawyer; b. Detroit, Mich., June 30, 1875; s. Marcus A. and Alma M. (Slaven) E.; A.B., U. of Mich., 1897, LL.B., 1899; m. Marion Clark Scotten, Feb. 10, 1910 (died 1914); children - Mary Margaret, Harold Hunter. Admitted to Mich. bar, 1899; asso. Maybury & Lucking, 1899-1903; mem. Maybury, Lucking, Emmons & Helfman, 1903-13; retired from law to enter mfg. as treas. Regal Motor Car Co.; resumed practice of law, 1917, mem. Clark, Emmons, Bryant & Klein; has practiced independently since 1936; president Indialantic, Incorporated; officer various other cos.; organizer and president, Northwest Airways, Incorporated; served as police commr., City of Detroit, 1930. Was in Naval Reserves, 1900-20, upon declaration of war assigned to Aircarft Production Board of Army in charge of aviation engine constrn., retired with rank of lt. comdr. and record of 32,000 engines constructed under his direction; commd. lt. col. in Specialist Reserve Corps, U.S. Army, 1924. Awarded Distinguished Service Medal, 1919; Comdr. Order of Cross of Rumania. Mem. Am., Mich. and Detroit bar assns., S.A.R., Am. Legion, Mil. Order of World War, Soc. of Colonial Wars, Delta Chi. Republican. Presbyn. Clubs: Detroit Athletic, Detroit Boat, Lawyers, Detroit Golf, University, Athletic Managers. Home: 8005 St. Paul Av., Detroit 14. Office: 1st Nat. Bank Bldg., Detroit 26. Died May 20, 1962; buried Roseland Park Cemetery, Berkeley, Mich.

EMORY, WILLIAM HEMSLEY army officer; b. Queen Annes County, Md., Sept. 7, 1811; s. Thomas and Anna Maria (Hemsley) E.; grad. U.S. Mil. Acad., 1831; m. Matilda Bache, May 1838. Commd. 1st lt. Topog. Engrs., 1838; prin. asst. on N.E. boundary survey between U.S. and Can., 1844-46; commr. and chief astronomer for running boundary line between Cal. and Mexico, 1848-54; commd. capt. Army of the West, 1851; commd. maj. 2d Cavalry, 1855, lt. col. Army of West, 1857; commanded Indian Territory from Ft. Leavenworth, 1861; commanded a div. under gen. Banks in La., 1863; commanded 19th Army Corps in Red River Expdn., 1864; distinguished at Fisher's Hill, 1864; commd. maj. gen. U.S. Volunteers, 1865; commanded Dept. of W. Va., 1865-66, Dept. of Washington, Dist. of Republican, 1869-71, Dept. of Gulf, 1871-75; ret. as brig. gen., 1876. Author: Notes of a Military Reconnaissance from Fort Leavenworth in Missouri to San Diego in California, 1848; Report on the U.S. and Mexican Boundary Survey, 1858-59. Died Dec. 1, 1887, Washington, D.C.

EMORY, WILLIAM HEMSLEY rear adm.; b. Washington, Dec. 17, 1846; grad. U.S. Naval Acad., 1866; promoted ensign, U.S.N., Mar. 12, 1868; master, Mar. 26, 1869; lt., Mar. 21, 1870; lt. comdr., May 26, 1887; comdr., Dec. 29, 1895; capt., Apr. 14, 1901; rear adm., Nov. 2, 1906. Summer of 1863 on the Macedonian in pursuit of Confederate cruiser Tacony; served on Iroquois, 1866-70; Naval Obs., 1870-71; Relief and Constellation, 1871; Asiatic sta., 1872-74; European sta., 1874-76; Naval Acad., 1876-79; Trenton, 1880-81; spl. duty with Admiral Porter, 1881-84; comd. Bear. 1884, Despatch, 1885-86, Thetis, 1887-89; naval attaché, Am. Embassy, London, 1889-92; comd. Petrel, 1894-96; mem. Bd. Inspection and Survey, 1897-98, 1898-1900; comd. Yosemite during Spanish War; Navy Yard, New York, and comdt. Naval Sta., Key West, 1900; comd. Monongahela, 1901, Indiana, 1901-02; insp. merchant vessels, New York, 1902; comd. Indiana, 1902-03, Hancock, 1904-06; comdg. Second Squadron, Atlantic Fleet, 1907; retired by operation of law, Dec. 17, 1908. July 15, 1917.

EMPEY, ARTHUR GUY author, soldier; b. Ogden, Utah, Dec. 11, 1883; s. Robert Arthur and Rose (Dana) E.; ed. pub. schs., Bklyn. Manual Tng. Sch. Traveled around world to gain practical knowledge before beginning to write. in 47th N.G.N.Y., 4th N.G.N.J., and 71st N.G. N.Y., - - several yrs.; also in 11th and 12th U.S. Cav. 6 yrs.; pvt. Brit. Army, in France, 18 mos., 1915-16; discharged on account of wounds received in Battle Somme, July 1916; served in U.S. Tank Corps, 1917-18; commd. capt. U.S.A.; made recruiting tour of U.S. Episcopalian. Pres. Guy Empey Pictures Corp., Nat. Motion Picture Instn. Am., Inc. Starred with Rose Stahl and assisted in direction comedy drama, "Pack Up Your Troubles"; starred and supervised direction of 9-reel feature, "Over the Top"; starred, wrote story, and supervised direction 7-reel feature, "The Undercurrent," "A Millionaire for a Day," "The Danger Tide," Just Orphans," others. Author: Over the Top, 1917; First Call, 1918; The Coward, 1918; Tales From a Dugout, 1918; The Enemy Within, 1918; The Madonna of the Hills, 1921; Liquid Gold, 1921; The God from Out the Sky; The Phantom Shot; also short stories in mags. Mem. Am. Legion, V.F.W., Old Guard. Elk. Bergen Beach Gun, Nassau - Clubs: Trapshooting, Lancaster Gun, Robin Hood Gun, Perry Circle Gun, Long Key Fishing. Home: 201 W. 78th St. Office: 220 W. 42d St., N.Y.C. Died Feb. 1963.

ENDICOTT, H(ENRY) WENDELL b. Dedham, Mass., Nov. 1, 1880; s. Henry Bradford and Caroline Williams (Russell) E.; Harvard, 1899-1901; m. Martha Waldron, d. C. W. Barron, Oct. 2, 1911; 1 dau., Martha Endicott; m. 2d, Priscilla Maxwell, Sept. 12, 1925; children-Bradford Maxwell, Priscilla. With Endicott-Johnson Corp., mfrs. leather and shoes, for many years from 1901, v.p., 1919; dir. Sears Roebuck & Co. (Chicago), Geo. E. Keith Co. (Campello, Mass.); trustee New England Conservatory of Music; president Boston Opera Association; director Metropolitan Opera Assn., Inc.; N.Y. City. Member Massachusetts Committee on Public Safety. Overseas commr. War Department in France and England, later chief research and specifications branch of Clothing and Equipage Division under Q.M. Gen., Washington, World War I, attaining to the rank of major; retired with rank of lt. col.; tech. cons. World War II, overseas; acting commr., Pacific Theater; dep. commr. Fgn. Liquidation Commn. Mem. Unitarian Ch. Clubs: Somerset, Harvard, Harvard Travelers (Boston): Dedham Polo and Country; Swan Island Shooting (N.C.); Moisie Salmon (Canada); Boone and Crockett (N.Y. City). Author: Adventures with Rod and Harpoon Along the Florida Keys, 1925; Adventures in Alaska and Along the Trail, 1928; Saga of the Tented Cities, 1952. Home: Dedham. Office: 831 Shawmut Bank Bldg., Boston. Died Apr. 20, 1954; buried Forest Hill Cemetery, Boston.

ENDICOTT, MORDECAL THOMAS rear adm.; b. May's Landing, N.J., Nov. 26, 1844; s. Thomas Doughty and Ann (Pennington) E.; prep. edn. parochial sch. of Presbyn. ch.; C.E., Rensselaer Poly. Inst., 1868; m. Elizabeth Adams, lMay 29, 1872. In practice from July 1868 as civil engr. and in mining until apptd. civil engr., U.S.N., July 14, 1874. Duty at various navy yards and in navy dept. at Washington as consulting engr.; apptd. mem. Nicaragua Canal Commn., 1895; mem. U.S. Naval Armor factory bd., 1897; apptd. chief Bureau Yards and Docks, Navy Dept., Apr. 7, 1898, with rank of commodore; later advanced to rank of rear adm.; reappointed Apr. 7, 1902, and Apr. 7, 1906; apptd. mem. Isthmian Canal Commn., 1905; rear adm. and retired, Nov. 26, 1906, but continued upon active duties until June 30, 1909. Recalled to active duty in Navy Dept., Oct. 12, 1927. Home: Washington, D.C. Died Mar. 1926.

ENDICOTT, WILLIAM CROWNINSHIELD sec. of war, U.S.; b. Salem, Mass., Nov. 19, 1826; prepared for college in Salem Latin School; grad. Harvard, 1847; studied law in office and at Harvard Law School; admitted to bar, 1850; began practice in Salem, 1851; m. Ellen, dau. George Peabody, of Salem, Dec. 13, 1859. Member, 1852, and later pres., Salem common council; city solicitor, 1857-64. Democratic nominee for atty. gen. of Mass., 1871, 72, 73; for Congress, 1870; for gov. of Mass., 1884. Judge supreme court, Mass., 1873-83; resigned. Sec. of war, U.S., 1885-89. Pres. Peabody Acad. of Science, Salem, 1863-. Home: Danvers Centre, Mass. Died 1900.

ENGEL, ALBERT JOSEPH ex-congressman; b. New Washington, O., Jan. 1, 1888; prep. cdn. Central Y.M.C.A., Chicago; LL.B., Northwestern U., 1910; m. Bertha M. Bieby; children-Margaret Ann, Albert Joseph, Helen Louise. Admitted to Mich. bar, 1910, and since practiced in Lake City; pros. atty. Missaukee County, 1917; mem. Mich. State Senate, 1921, 27, 29, 31; mem. 74th to 81st Congresses, 9th Mich. Dist. Served as 1st lt., later capt., Sheridan, Ill., War Dept., Washington, D.C., and in A.E.F. (23 mos.), 1917-19. Elected hon. alumnus Univ. of Mich., 1937. Republican. Home: Lake City, Michigan. Died Dec. 3, 1959.

ENGLAND, WILLIAM HENRY, chief economist, Fed. Trade Commn.; b. Edinburgh, Ind., Dec. 21, 1876; s. Joseph Henry and Laura (Drake) E.; B.S., Neb. Wesleyan Univ., 1902; student Univ. Chicago, 1902; Ph.D., Univ. of Neb., 1906; student Georgetown Univ. Law Sch., 1916; m. Norah D. Collins, June 2, 1917; children—William Henry, Collin Byfield. High school principal, 1902-03; instructor Nebraska Wesleyan Academy, 1900-02, Nebraska Wesleyan University, 1906-08; special agent, Bureau of Corps., 1908-16; research economist Hooker Electro-Chem. Co., 1916-17, 1919-20; asst. chief economist Fed. Trade Commn., 1920-40, chief economist, dir. division of accounts, statistics and economic reports, 1941-47; ret. Paper 7, Organization of Private Electric and Gas Utilities, 3d World Power Conference, Washington, 1936; directed inquiries into petroleum, lumber, fertilizers, export grain, farm implements, automobile industry, electric and gas utilities, etc.; econ. consultant War Dept. com. to survey decartelization and deconcentration accomplishments of mil. govt. in Germany, 1948-49. Served in Philippines, 1898-99; commander captain and advanced to major, 1917-19. colonel in Officers Reserve Corps since June 13, 1932. Awarded Philippine Congressional medal. Member American Rose Society, Potomac Rose Soc., Sigma Xi. Club: Takoma Horticultural. Home: 1344 Iris St., N.W. Office: 6th and Pennsylvania Av., Washington DC

ENGLEHARD, CHARLES WILLIAM, precious metals co. exec.; b. N.Y.C., Feb. 15, 1917; s. Charles William and Emy Marie (Canthal) E.; student St. Paul's Sch.; B.A., Princeton, 1939; m. Jane Reis-Brian, Aug. 18, 1947; children—Annette (Mrs. Samuel Pryor Reed), Mary Susan, Sophie, Alexandra, Charlene. Chmn. Engelhard Minerals & Chems. Corp.; chmn. Engelhard Hanovia, Inc., Am.-S. African Investment Co., Ltd., Johannesburg, S.Africa Forest Investments, Ltd., Johannesburg, dir. Anglo Am. Corp. S. Africa (N. Am.), Ltd., Anglo Am. Corp. So. Africa, Ltd. Charter Consol., Ltd., Hudson Bay Mining & Smelting Co., Ltd., Internat. Silver Co., Nat. Newark & Essex Banking Co., Pub. Service Elec. & Gas Co., Rand Selection Corp., Ltd., Thomas Barlow & Sons (S. Africa) Ltd., Prudential Ins. Co. Mem. Community Relations Service, Easco Corp. mem. Pres.'s Spl. Com. to Study East-West Trade, 1965; mem. Citizens Com. Higher Edn. N.J.; commr. Port of N.Y. Authority; chmn. Newark Mus.; mem. Greater Newark Devel. Council. Mem. N.J. Democratic Com. Trustee, v.p. Am. Mus. Immigration; trustee John F. Kennedy Meml. Library, Am. Heritage Found., Bernards Library Assn., Com. Econ. Devel., Seton Hall U., Foxcroft Sch. mem. Eleanor Roosevelt Meml. Found.; bd. dirs. U.S. Com. for Refugees, Atlantic Council U.S., Inc., N.Y. Zool. Soc., Thomas Alva Edison Found., Atlantic Salmon Assn. (dir.) World Wildlife Soc. (dir.). Served as capt. USAAF, 1941-45. Mem. Fgn. Policy Assn. (dir.), N.J. C. of C. (dir.). Clubs: Racquet and Tennis, The Brook, Jockey; Chemist, Economic; Metropolitan (Washington). (N.Y.C.); Ivy (Princeton, N.J.); Rand (Johannesburg); Travelers (Paris, France); Monmouth (N.J.) Jockey. Home: Cragwood Far Hills NJ Died Mar. 2, 1971.

ENGLEHARDT, FRED university president; b. Naugatuck, Conn. Apr. 15, 1885; s. Georg John and Helena (Deubel) E.; preparatory edn., Phillips Acad., Andover, Mass., and Haverford (Pa.) Sch.; Ph.B., Yale, 1908, grad. study, 1908-09; A.M., Columbia, 1915, Ph.D., 1924; grad. study, Harvard summers 1909-10, U. of Pa., 1916-17; LL.D., U. of Me., 1940; m. Marion E. Haskell, Aug. 29, 1929. Asst. instr., Yale, 1908-09; teacher and prin. pub. schs., N.Y., and pvt. schs., Pa. and Ill., until 1919; insp., elementary edn., N.Y. State Dept. Edn., 191o; dir. Bur of Adminstrn., Pa. State Dept. Edn., 1919-22; asst. dean, in charge Coll. Liberal Arts, U. of Pittsburgh, 1922-24; prof. ednl. administration, Coll. of Edn., U. of Minn., 1924-37; pres. U. of N.H. since 1937. Visiting prof. (summers), Peabody Coll., 1929, Univ. of Winnipeg, 1932, Stanford Univ., 1933, Duke U., 1934, Northwestern and Yale, 1935. Maj. Heavy Arty., U.S. Army, 1917-19. Mem. bd. trustees Austin-Cate Acad., Brewster Acad., Northern New England Sch. of Religious Edn. Chmn. State Planning and Development Commn. Mem. N.E.A., Nat. Soc. Study of Edn., Nat. Acad. of Polit. Science, Pa. State Teachers Assn., N.H. Hist. Soc., New England Council, Newcomen Society, Am. Legion, Scabbard and Blade, Grange, Phi Delta Kappa, Kappa Delta Pi, Alpha Sigma Pi. Mason. Clubs: Rotary (Dover); University (Boston). Author: Forecasting School Population, 1924: Public School Organization and Administration, 1931; Syllabus for Public School Organization and Administration, 1930. Co-author: Gunnery for Heavy Artillery, 1915; Public School Accounting Procedure, 1927; First Course in Algebra, 1927; Public School Business Administration (with N. L. Engelhardt), 1927; Second Course in Algebra, 1929; School Plant Programs (with N. L. Engelhardt), 1930; Mathematics for Junior High Schools (3 vols.), 1931; Minnesota Public Schools, 1934; Survey of Public Schools Business Administration (with N. L. Engelhardt), 1936; The Story of Fulling Mill Brook, 1937; Secondary Education Principles and Practices (with A. V. Overn), 1937. Editor: Appleton-Century Administration Series. School surveys: Robinsdale, Minnesota, 1925; Aurora, Minnesota, 1926; Superior, Wis., 1926; Austin, Minn., 1927; Albert Lea, Minn., 1927; Ortonville, Minn., 1928; specialist in administration, Nat. Secondary Survey Commn., 1930-32; on staff Chicago Pub. Sch. Survey, 1932; mem. advisory com. Nat. Finance Survey, 1931-33; mem. Commn. for Study of N.H. Resources, 1937. Contbr. to ednl. publs. Home: Durham, N.H. Died Feb. 3, 1944.

ENGLISH, HORACE BIDWELL prof. psychology; b. Eagle, Neb., Oct. 1, 1892; s. S(amuel) S. and Lilla Gertrude (Richardson) E.; student U. of Neb., 1909-11; Rhodes scholar from Neb., at Pembroke Coll., Oxford, 1911-14, B.A., 1914, certificate in cultural anthropology, 1913; Ph.D., Yale, 1916; m. Olive M. Jones, June 26, 1917 (divorced spring 1947); children - Richard, Don Wellesley, Philip Horace, Helen Elisabeth, Kathryn Joanne; m. 2d, Ava H. Champney, Mar. 9, 1952. Asst. prof. psychology, Wellesley, 1916-21; asso. prof. Wesleyan, 1925-27; prof. psychology, Antioch Coll., 1921-25, 27-30; prof. psychology, Ohio State U., 1930 - ; visiting professor edn. psychology U. Sao Paulo, Brazil, 1953; Fulbright lectr. Central Tng. Coll., Pakistan, 1952-53; psychologist U.S. Forest Service (temp.) 1944. Collaborator, Child Development Center, Am. Council on Edn., 1940; cons. in child development, W. Va. State Dept. Edn., 1941. Commd. 1st lt., later capt. Sanitary Corps; served as psychol. examiner, and as chief of edn. service, Base Hosp., Camp Lewis, Wash., World War I; consulting A.G.O., War Department, 1943 and 1946-47; analyst, bombing survey, Japan, 1945. Fellow British Psychol. Society, American Psychol. Assn. (past mem. council dirs., pres. ednl. psych. div. 1950-51); mem. Midwestern Psychol. Assn. (sec.-treas. 1929-32; pres. 1933), Am. Assn. Univ. Profs., Soc. for Psychol. Study of Social Issues (member council 1936-43, 44-46), Ohio Assn. for Applied Psychology (pres. 1939-40), Am. Assn. for Applied Psychology (executive secretary, 1937-39, president 1939-40). Author of books including: The Psychology of Learning - A Study Guide; Child Psychology, 1952; A Comprehensive Dictionary of Psychological and psychoanalytical Terms, 1958; The Dynamics of Child Development, 1961; also articles tech. jours. Editor: Psychological Abstracts, 1959-60; Psychology, Collier's Ency., 1960 - . Address: 1345 Highland St., Columbus, O. Died July 20, 1961.

ENGLISH, ROBERT HENRY rear adm., U.S. Navy; b. Warrenton, Ga., Jan. 16, 1888; s. William Columbus and Mary Cornelia (Fitzpatrick) E.; student Ga. Sch. of Tech., 1904-06; B.S., U.S. Naval Acad., 1911; m. Eloise Shuford Walker, April 19, 1919; children - Eloise Walker, Robert Henry, Eleanor Cornelia. Commd. ensign U.S. Navy, 1911, and advanced through the grades to rear adm., 1942; in command of Pacific Submarine Force, 1943. Decorated Navy Cross, World War I Campaign, Mexican Campaign; D.S.M. (posthumously), Club: Army and Navy Country (Washington, D.C.). Home: 4445 Lowell St., Washington, D.C. Killed in airplane crash, Jan. 21, 1943.

ENGLISH, WILLIAM EASTIN congressman; b. at Englishton Park, Ind., Nov. 3, 1854; s. William H. E. (Dem. candidate for v.p. U.S., 1880) and Emma Mardulia (Jackson) E.; ed. Northwestern Christian (now Butler) U.; LL.B., same, 1887; m. Helen Orr, Jan. 5, 1898; 1 dau., Rosalind Orr. Practiced law at Indianapolis until 1882; always active and prominent in politics, and mem. state, co. and city coms. (chmn. two latter, 1878); mem. Ind. Ho. of Rep., 1879-80; mem. 48th Congress (1883-85), re-election; pres. bd. of park commrs., 1898-99, bd. police and fire commrs., 1901-02, Indianapolis; mem. Ind. State Senate, 1916-28; in practice with daughter under firm name English & English, 1925-. Spent several yrs. in foreign travel; apptd., 1898, capt. U.S. Vols., served a.d.c. on staff Gen. Joseph Wheeler during campaign in Cuba; seriously injured during battle before Santiago, July 1, 1898; col. and p.m. gen. on staff gov. of Ind., 1899-1900, col. and insp. gen., 1900-04, and col. and a.d.c., 1904-20. Has large property interests. Owner English's block, English's Opera House, Hotel English, etc. Vice pres. Ind. Hist. Soc., Western Geneal. Soc.; past comdr. in chief Nat. Assn. United Spanish War Veterans. Mason. Author: History of Masonry; letters from Europe, etc. Republican. Home: Indianapolis, Ind. Died Apr. 29, 1926.

ENGSTROM, HOWARD THEODORE scientist, corp. exec.; b. Boston, Apr. 23, 1902; s. Gustav. W. and Anna K. (Ranvik) E.; B. Chem. Engring., Northeastern U., 1922; M.A. in Math., U. Me., 1925; Ph.D. in Math., Yale, 1929; NRC fellow, Cal. Inst. Tech., 1929-30; Internat. Research fellow, Gottingen, Germany, 1930-31; m. Karin Ekblom, Apr. 18, 1935; children - Karin S. (Mrs. William Agosta), Anna K., Morten H. Engr. Western Union Telegraph Co., 1922-23; instr. U. Me., 1923-25; instr. math. Trinity Coll., Hartford, Conn., 1925-26; instr. Yale, 1926-29, asst. prof. math., 1931-35, asso. prof., 1935-41; founder, v.p. Engring. Research Assos., St. Paul, 1945-52; company bought by Remington Rand Co., 1952; v.p. Remington Rand div. Sperry Rand Co., 1952-56, 58 - ; dep. dir. Nat. Security Agy., 1956-58; chmn. bd. Computer Export Corp., Atlanta, 1958 - . Adviser Dept. of Def. Served with USNR, 1941-45; capt. Res. Decorated Distinguished Service medal, Naval Res. medal, Presdl. Unit citation; Officer British Empire; recipient medal of appreciation Dept. of Def., Nat. Security Agy. medal; fellow Davenport Coll., Yale, Fellow Inst. Radio Engrs. mem. Am. Math. Soc., Math. Assn. Am., Assn. Computing Machinery. Club: Cosmos (Washington). Editor: High Speed Printing Devices, 1950. Author numerous articles in field. Home: Ellisville, Buzzard's Bay, R.F.D., Mass. Office: Remington Rand, 315 4th Av., N.Y.C. 10. Died Mar. 8, 1962; buried Arlington Cemetery

ENOCHS, WILLIAM HENRY congressman; b. nr. Middleburg, O., Mar. 29, 1842; attended Ohio U. at Athens; grad. Cincinnati Law Sch., 1866. Served as pvt. Co. B, 2d Regt., Ohio Inf., during Civil War, 1861; commd. 1st lt. 5th Regt., W. Va. Inf., 1861, capt., 1862, lt. col., 1863; promoted col. 1st Regt., W. Va Inf., 1864; brevetted brig. gen. U.S. Volunteers, 1865; admitted to bar, began practice of law, Ironton, O.; mem. Ohio Ho. of Reps., 1870-71; mem. U.S. Ho. of Reps. (Republican) from Ohio, 52d-53d congresses, 1891-93. Died Ironton, July 13, 1893; buried Arlington (Va.) Nat. Cemetery.

ENOS, GEORGE M(AGEE) univ. prof., engr.; b. Dubuque, Ia., July 8, 1896; s. George Alfred and Evelyn (Magee) E.; B.S. in Metall. Engring., S.D. Sch. of Mines, 1921, Metall. E., 1922; M.Sc., Carnegie Inst. Tech., 1922; Ph.D., U. Cincinnati, 1925; m. Edna Jones, Feb. 21, 1924; children-Robert Jones, Ruth Evalyn. Teacher grade sch., S.D., 1914-15; asst., chem. labs., S.D. Sch. of Mines, 1916-21; jr. metallurgist U.S. Bureau of Mines, Pittsburgh, 1922-23; successively instr., asst. prof., asso. prof. metallurgy, U. Cincinnati, 1923-39; cons. metallurgist various Cincinnati firms, 1923-39; prof. metall. engring. Purdue U. since 1947, also chmn. of div.; cons. metallurgist. Served with U.S. Army, 1939-46: commd. capt. and advanced through grades to col.; comdg. officer, 5560th Organized Reserve Research and Dev. Group; dir. engring. Cincinnati ordnance dist. Ordnance Dept. Mem. Am. Inst. Mining and Metall. Engineers, Am. Soc. for Metals, Am. Ordnance Assn., Reserve Officers Association, Sigma Xi, Tau Beta Pi, Phi Lambda Upsilon. Acacia, Scabbard and Blade. Mason (32ff). Author: Visual Examination of Steel, 1938; (with W. E. Fontaine) Elements of Heat Treatment (in press). Contbr. articles to professional jours. Home: 1215 Vine St., West Lafayette, Ind. Died Oct. 27, 1952.

ENRIGHT, EARL F(RANCIS) ret. naval officer, management cons.; b. Holyoke, Colo., Oct. 5, 1891; s. Thomas F. and Mary Jane (Welch) E.; B.S., U.S. Naval Acad., 1913; student U.S. Navy Post Grad. Sch., 1914, Harvard Bus. Sch., 1916-17; M.S. in Naval Architecture, Mass. Inst. Tech., 1917; m. Lillian Wells, July 2, 1913; children - Lillian (wife H. S. Harnly, USN), Robert E. Commd. ensign USN, 1913, advanced through grades to capt., 1940; served various shipyards Navy Dept. design and constrn. naval vessels, ret. 1944; v.p., dir. Overseas Corp., 1945-49; treas., dir. Fielden Instrument Corp., 1950-52; pres., treas., dir. General Arm & Mfg. Co., 1954-55; mgmt. cons., Phila., 1955 - . Mem. Naval Architects Soc., Franklin Inst. Clubs: Army and Navy (Washington); Engineers (Phila.). Home: 4701 Pine St., Phila. 43. Office: 225 S. 15th St., Phila. 2. Died July 17, 1961; buried Naval Acad. Cemetery, Annapolis, Md.

ENRIGHT, WALTER J(OSEPH), cartoonist; b. Chicago, Ill., July 3, 1879; s. John W. and Mary B. (Croghan) E.; ed. Armour Inst. Tech.; art edn., Art Inst. Chicago; married. Illustrator for Life, Judge, Scribner's Collier's, etc.; drew "Once Upon a Time" strip for McClure Newspaper Syndicate; cartoonist, New York World, 1927-30, New York American, 1930-36; later with Miami Herald. Served as 1st lt., A.S., U.S.A., comdg. officer photog. sect., World War. Clubs: Players, New York Athletic. Author: Once Upon a Time Stories (3 vols. fairy tales retold in pictures), 1926. Home: Delray Beach Fl Died Jan. 1969.

ENSEY, LOT, naval officer; b. Panama Canal Zone, Nov. 9, 1908; s. Charles Ridgeley and Nona Alva (Johns) E.; student Marion Inst., Ala.; B.S., U.S. Naval Acad., 1930; grad. Armed Forces Staff Coll., 1948, Naval War Coll., 1951; m. Kathryn Zeiss, July 9, 1938; 1 son, Lot. Commd. ensign USN, 1930, advanced through grades to vice adm., 1964; various assignments battleship and destroyers Pacific Fleet, 1930-38; insp. turrets Naval Gun Factory, 1938-40; gun officer, exec. officer destroyers North Atlantic, 1940-42; comdr. three destroyers, 1942-45; staff Bur. Naval Personnel, 1945-48; comdr. destroyer div. Pacific Fleet, 1948; staff Naval War Coll., 1949-52; operations officer Atlantic Fleet, 1952-54; comdr. amphibious attack transport Atlantic Fleet, 1955; comdr. Destoyer Squadron Two, Atlantic Fleet, 1956; chief staff Sixth Fleet, 1956-58; asst. comptroller, dir. budget and reports, Navy Dept., 1958-60; dep. controller of the Navy, 1960-63; comdr. Cruiser-Destroyer Flotilla 9, 1963-64; dep. chief naval operations (logistics) Navy Dept., Washington, 1964-67; director logistics Directorate for Logistics, Joint Staff, Joint Chiefs of Staff, Washington, 1967-69. Decorated Bronze Star, D.S.M. Club: Army-Navy Country (Washington). Home: Washington DC Died Oct. 26, 1970.

ENT, UZAL GIRARD army officer; b. Northumberland, Pa., Mar. 3, 1900; s. Oscar Wellington and Elizabeth (Girard) E.; ed. Susquehanna U. (Selinsgrove, Pa.), 1917-18; B.S., U.S. Mil. Acad., 1924; m. Eleanor Marwitz, Nov. 24, 1929; 1 son, Girard Wellington. Promoted through grades from pvt., aviation sec. Signal Corps, 1918, to maj. gen., 1944; mil. attaché, Am. Embassy, Lima, Peru, 1939-42; chief of staff, U.S. Army Forces in Middle East, 1942; comdg. maj. gen. 9th Bomber Command since Mar. 1943. Decorated D.S.C., D.S.M. (with oak leaf cluster), D.F.C. (with oak leaf cluster), Air Medal (with oak leaf cluster), Legion of Merit, Presidential Unit Citation, Peruvian Flying Cross 1st class, Peruvian Order of Ayacucho, Comdr. Bolivian Condor of the Andes, Comdr. Order of the British Empire. Mason. Home: Northumberland, Pa. Died Mar. 5, 1948.

ENTWISTLE, JAMES rear adm.; b. Paterson, N.J., 1937; ed. pub. schs.; entered U.S. Navy in engr. service, Oct. 1861; commd. lt., July 26, 1866; lt. comdr., Mar. 21, 1873; comdr. Jan. 31, 1888; capt., Apr. 1899; rear admiral, Apr. 1899, and retired, having reached age limit. First sea service on gunboat Aroostook in the Western Gulf Squadron under Farragut; afterward served on 21 vessels in all parts of the world; wrecked on Ashuelot in China waters, 1883; was inspector of machinery at Bath (Me.) Iron Works. 1890-95, during construction of harbor defense ram Katahdin, and gunboats Machian and Castine; asst. to gen. insp. at Morgan Iron Works, New York, during the completion of the Atlanta, Boston, Chicago and Dolphin; then at Mare Island Navy Yard, 1895; joined Asiatic Squadron at Yokohama, 1895; apptd. fleet engr., 1887 and assigned to Olympia; took part in Battle of Manila. May 1, 1898, and was highly commended by Admiral Dewey; awarded Dewey medal and recommended by Sec. of Navy and bd. of officers for advancement in numbers for meritorious services at Manila. Home: Paterson, N. J. Died 1910.

EPPLEY, EUGENE C. hotel exec.; b. Akron, O., Apr. 8, 1884; s. Owen and Jessie C. (Phillips) E.; grad. Culver (Ind.) Mil. Acad., 1901; student Stanford, 1902-03: unmarried. Began with McKinley Hotel. Canton, O., 1903; pres. Eppley Hotels Co. 1915-56, operating 22 hotels; chairman of board Sheraton Cadillac Hotel, Detroit; hon. chmn. bd. Sheraton Corp. Am.; director Branliff Internat. Airways, Sheraton Corp. Am. Dir. Culver Ednl. Found.: president Eugene C. Eppley Foundation, Inc. Served as National Food Administrator for Hotels, World War I; food consultant to Sec. of War, World War II. Dir. Mt. Rushmore at. Memorial Society of the Black Hills (South Dakota), Greater Omaha Assn., Omaha Chamber Commerce; mem. Hotel Men's Mut. Benefit Assn. of U.S. and Can (pres. 3 terms), Chi Psi (exec. council). Decorated Gold Cross of Social Welfare (French), 1926. Crowned King Ak-Sar-Ben XXXIX, legendary Nebraskan Empire of Quivera, Omaha, 1933. Mason (32ff, Shriner), Elk. Clubs: Omaha, Omaha Athlete, Omaha Field, Omaha Country. Address: Hotel Fontenelle, Omaha, Neb. Died Oct. 14, 1958; buried Culver (Ind.) Masonic Cemetery.

EPSTEIN, MAX chairman Gen. Am. Transportation Corp.; b. Cincinnati, O., Feb. 6, 1875; s. Morris and Cecelia (Wertheimer) E.; ed. Coll. City of N.Y.; m. Leola S. Selig, 1907. Resident of Chicago, 1891—; chmn. exec. com. Gen. Am. Transportation Corp. and dir. in affiliated cos.; dir. Chicago Daily News; chairman advisory com. Federal Reserve Bank; chairman Draft Board during World War; lt. col., U.S. Army Reserves. Actively interested in philanthropy; donor Max Epstein Clinic of the Univ. of Chicago. Trustee U. of Chgo., Art Inst. of Chgo.; dir. Boy Scouts of Am., Am. Red Cross. Republican. Jewish religion. Home: 915 Sheridan Rd., Winnetka, Ill. Office: 135 S. La Salle St., Chgo. Died Aug. 22, 1954.

EPSTEIN, RALPH C(ECIL) economist; b. Chgo., Sept. 25, 1899; s. Hugo and Ellinor (Schwerin) E.; A.B., Columbia, 1921; A.M., Harvard, 1925, Ph.D., 1926; m. Miriam Abrams, Oct. 14, 1922; children-Elizabeth Frances (Mrs. Edwin N. Barker), Joan Ellinor (Mrs. John D. Gill), Asst. economics, Northwestern U., 1921-22, instr., 1922-23; asst. in economics, Harvard, 1924-25, tutor in div. history, govt. and economics, 1925-26; asst. prof. economics and business orgn., U. Buffalo, 1926-29, prof. since 1929, dean Sch. of Bus. Administrn., 1935-47, head dept. econs., 1939—; chmn. bd. Smith, Keynes & Marshall, Inc., book pubs.; engaged in industrial engring, with Gerard, Graham & Co., 1919-20; econ. and editorial work A. W. Shaw Co., 1922-23; on staff of Com. on Govt. Statistics, Washington, D.C., 1934; cons. economist U.S. Dept. Commerce, 1930-32. Special economic adviser and consultant, War Production Board. Washington, D.C., 1942-43. Expert consultant to War Dept. (HQ, ASF), 1943-45; to Office Contract Settlement, Washington, D.C., 1944-45. Vice pres. Family Service Soc.; mem. nat. bd. govs. Atlantic Union Com. Pres. Buffalo chpt. Atlantic Union Com., representative to interview legislators and heads of state, in seventeen different countries, 1955; mem. of the advisory com. Graduate Faculty Polit. and Social Sci. of N.Y.; fellow Royal Econ. Soc.; mem. Am. Econ. Assn., Acad. Polit. Sci., Am. Statis. Assn. (v.p. 1937-38), Joint Com. on Income Tax Statistics, Auto. Industry Committee of Price Research Conference, Phi Beta Kappa, Clubs: Harvard, Buffalo. Author: The Automobile Industry-Its Economic and Commercial Development, 1928; Supplementary Readings in Economics, 1929; Trends in Buffalo Real Estate Assessments (with F. M. Clark), 1929; Source Book of the Study of Industrial Profits (with F. M. Clark), 1932; Industrial Profits in the U.S., 1934; History of General American Transportation Corp., 1948; Concentration and Price Trends in Rubber Manufacturing, 1949; Growth of the American Rubber Industry, 1953; How To Invest Your Money, 1957; Report on Asia, 1956; Report on Europe, 1956. Contbr. fgn. affairs publs., to econ. jours.; cons. indsl. corps. Address: 41 Irving Pl., Buffalo. Died Nov. 21, 1959.

ERDMANN, WILLIAM LAWRENCE ret. naval ofcr.; b. Greensburg, Ind., Nov. 18 1902; s. William Valentine and Lulu Dolphine (Thomas) E.; B.S., U.S. Naval Acad., 1924; m. Lillian O'Brien, Oct. 27, 1927; m. 2d, Mrs. Charles Read Tucker, Dec. 30, 1951; 1 dau., Patricia Ann. Commd. ensign U.S.N., 1924, advanced through grades to rear adm., 1952; designated naval aviator, 1928; served in various battleships, cruisers and carriers; commanded VP 82, 1940-42; U.S.S. Matanikau, 1944-45, N.A.S. Pasco, 1945-46, U.S.S. Leyte, 1949-50, N.A.S., San Diego, 1950-52, Carrier Div. 14, 1952-53; NATO, 1953-56; Carrier Div. I, 1956-57. Decorated Legion of Merit, Bronze Star, Air Medal. Address: 13 Arroyo Dr., Kentfield, Cal. Died Aug. 1, 1961.

ERNST, EDWIN CHARLES, radiologist; b. St. Louis, Mo., June 26, 1885; s. Charles W. and Catherine (Koche) E.; grad. Moravian Coll., Bethlehem, Pa., 1905; student St. Louis U., 1906-09; M.D., Washington U., St. Louis, 1912; m. Mildred V. Vogt, Aug. 2, 1916; children—Edwin C., Roland, Richard. Began practice at St. Louis, 1912. Commd. maj. Med. R.C., Apr. 15, 1917; served in Base Hosp. 21, France, 1917-18; dir. x-ray dept. and radiologist of the De Paul Hosp., St. Louis; radiologist St. Joseph Hospital, Kirkwood, Mo. President board of dirs. of Beaumont Medical Building. Awarded gold medal of Radiol. Soc. of North America for researches in X-ray unit measurement; the highest IX Internat. Congress Radiology Scientific award, 1959; citation German Roentgen Society of Munic, 1959. Mem. A.M.A., A.C.P., Am. Roentgen Ray Soc., Chgo. Roentgen Soc., Radiol. Soc. of N. America (ex-pres.), Am. Coll. of Radiology, (past pres.), Am. Radium Soc. (past pres.), Radiological Research Inst., Inc. (past pres.), Am. College of Radiology (past pres.), Am. Cancer Soc. (past pres. Mo. div.), Southern Medical Association (2d vice president), Phi Beta Pi. Republican. Protestant. Clubs: University, Mo. Athletic (pres. 1956-57), Algonquin Country. Contbr. to Am. Roentgen Ray Jour. Research in cancer, radiology. Home: Kirkwood MO Died Mar. 1969; buried Sunset Burial Park.

ERNST, OSWALD HERBERT major general U.S. Army; b. near Cincinnati, O., June 27, 1842; s. Andrew Henry and Sarah H. (Otis) E.; attended Harvard. 1858-60; grad. U.S. Mil. Acad., 1864; m. Elizabeth Amory, d. W. R. Lee, of Roxbury, Mass., Nov. 3, 1866; children-Helen Amory, Mrs. Elizabeth Lee Grinnell. First lt. engrs., June 13, 1864; promoted through grades to rank of maj. gen., Aug. 19, 1916. Brevetted captain, Mar. 13, 1865, for faithful and meritorious services. Served asst. chief engr. Army of Tenn., to close of Atlanta campaign; asst. engr. on fortifications Pacific Coast, 1864-68; astronomer with U.S. commn. to observe solar eclipse in Spain, 1870; instr. practical mil. engring., mil. signaling and telegraphy, West Point, 1871-78; engr. in charge of Western river improvements, 1878-86; in charge of harbor improvements on Tex. coast, 1886-89, where he inaugurated the great work which resulted in deepening the channel at the entrance to Galveston harbor from 12 to 16 feet; engr. on numerous bds., 1880-1906; in charge pub. bldgs. and grounds, Washington, 1889-93; supt. U.S. Mil. Acad., 1893-98; served in war against Spain, going to P.R., July 1898; had immediate command of the troops in the affair of Coamo, Aug. 9; mem. Isthmian Canal Commn., 1899-1901, and 1905, 1906; pres. Miss. River Commn., 1903-06; mem. Internat. Commn. upon the condition and use of waters adjacent to boundary lines between U. S. and Can., 1903-15; retired, June 27, 1906. Author: Manual of Practical Military Engineering, etc. Home: Washington, D.C. Died Mar. 21, 1926.

ERPF, ARMAND GROVER, investment banker; b. N.Y. City, Dec. 8, 1897; s. Bartholomew and Cornelia (von Greiner) E.; B.S., Columbia, 1917; L.H.D., Cath. U. Am., LL.D., Manhattan Coll.; m. Sue Stuart Mortimore, Apr. 7, 1965; children—Cornelia, Armand. Asst. sec. Suffern Co. of N.Y., and asst. mgr. Suffern Co. of Brazil, 1917-19; officer and part owner C.E. Erpf & Co., brokers, 1919-23; made survey of textile enterprise in Saxony, Germany, 1923-24; statistician, later officer, dir. and part owner Cornell, Linder & Co., Inc., N.Y. City, 1924-33; dir. statis. and research departments and subsequently, investment adv. department Loeb, Rhoades & Co., 1933-36, gen. partner, from 1936; chmn. exec. com., dir. Crowell Collier & Macmillan, Incorporated; chmn. Aneid Equities; member of bd. dirs. Adela Investment Co., S.A., Gen. Instrument Corp., Adela Investment Co., S.A., Macmillan Co., Jefferson Ins. Co., Chris-Craft Industries, Inc., Dorr-Oliver, Inc., Jersey External Trust, Stein, Roe & Farnham Internat. Fund. Chmn. council Grad. Sch. of Bus., Columbia U.; chmn. bd. dirs. Arkville Erpf Fund; bd. govs. N.Y. Cultural Center; trustee Chamber Music Soc. Lincoln Center. Commd. 1t. col., U.S. Army, 1942; promoted col., 1944; apptd. to Gen. Staff Corps, 1944; assigned Office of Comdg. Gen. hdqrs. A.S.F., Washington, 1942-45; duty with hdqrs. U.S. Army Forces, Western Pacific, and with comdg. gen. USAF, China Theater, 1945-46. Awarded Legion of Merit. Mem. Council on Fgn. Relations, Inc., Affiliated Business Fellows of Columbia U., Whitney Mus. Am. Art (board of trustee), Victorian Soc., Athenaeum Phila. Delta Sigma Phi. Clubs: Art Collectors, Economic, Wall St. Home: New York City NY Died Feb. 2, 1971; buried Arkville NY

ERWIN, HENRY PARSONS investment banker; b. Newark, July 16, 1881; s. Orlando Richard and Mary Elizabeth (Parsons) E.; A.B., U. Mich., 1904; grad. Ill. Inst. Tech.; student U. Chicago, 1916-17; D.Sc. (hon.), George Washington University, 1952; married Helen Peck Blodgett, 1921; children-Eileen (Mrs. John Alvin Croghan), Hope (Mrs. Macdonald Goodwin), Henry Parsons. Engr., mfr., mem. Washington Stock Exchange; dir. Riggs Nat. Bank Fed. Storage Co., Washington. Trustee, sec., chmn. finance com. bd. trustees George Washington U.; mem. Community Chest Fedn. Classification Com.; trustee Boys Club of Washington, treas. Boys Club Found., treasurer of the National Capital Area Boy Scouts. Served as capt., comdr. Paterson (N.J.) Ordnance Depot, Feb.-Nov. 1918; served, Office Chief of Ordnance, Washington, 1918-20; lt. col., active duty. Ordnance Corps, U.S. Army, Washington, World War II; lt. col., U.S. Army Res. since 1943 to time of death, June 3, 1953. Member Am. Ordnance Assn. (founder, dir., treas.), A.S.M.E., Nat. Parks Assn. (sec.), S.A.R., Archaeol. Soc. of Washington (v.p.), Com. of One Hundred (Miami Beach, Fla.). Republican. Episcopalian. Clubs: Circumnavigators Around World; Athletic Assn., Quadrangle (Chicago); Metropolitan. Univ., Army and Navy, Army-Navy Country, Nat. Press (Washington); Chevy Chase (Md.); Surf (Miami Beach). Author: Ordnance Supply in Time of War and Peace. 1939; numerous elec. and hydraulic engring. articles. Home: Arbremont, Upton St. and Linnean Av. N.W., Washington: also (summer) Cragmere, Mackinac Island, Mich. Office: 723 15th St., Washington 5. Died June 3, 1953; buried Arlington Nat. Cemetery.

ERWIN, JAMES BRAILSFORD army officer; b. Savannah, Ga., July 11, 1856; s. Robert and Mary Ann (Gallaudet) E.; student Trinity Coll., Hartford, Conn., 1872-75 (B.S., 1917); grad. U.S. Military Academy, 1880; hon. grad. Inf. and Cav. Sch., Fort Leavenworth, Kan., 1883; m. Isabel Doan, June 27, 1883. Commd. 2d lt. 4th Cav., June 12, 1880; promoted through grades to brig. gen., N.A., Aug. 20, 1917. Participated in Indian campaigns, 1885-86; supt. Yellowstone Nat. Park, 1897-98; in P.I., 1898-1903; in charge relief work, Oakland, Calif., after San Francisco earthquake, 1906; adj. gen., Sept. 1915-Aug. 1916; comdg. 9th Cav., Aug. 19-Dec. 27, 1916; comdg. 7th Cav., Dec. 27, 1916-Aug. 1917, and in punitive expdn. in Mexico; comdg. 157th Depot Brigade, Camp Gordon, Ga., Aug. 25-Nov. 16, 1917; comdg. 82d Div., Nov. 17-Dec. 27, 1917; assigned to 12th Brigade, 6th Div., Dec. 27, 1917; comdg. U.S. troops, Ft. Oglethorpe and Chickamauga Park, Ga., and 6th (regular) Div., Dec. 28, 1917; comd. 6th Div., A.E.F., France, until Sept. 1918; comd. 12th Brig., 6th Div., until Dec. 15, 1918, taking part in two major offensives; comd. 92d Div., Dec. 15, 1918, to its demobilization, Feb. 1919; comd. El Paso Dist., Mar. 27-Sept. 1, 1919, and ordered troops across boundary, attacking Villistas to protect lives and property of citizens of El Paso, June 15-16, 1919; remanded to regular rank of col. of cav. and assigned to 6th Cav., Sept. 7, 1919. Episcopalian. Mason. Died July 10, 1924.

ERWIN, MARION CORBETT naval officer (ret.); b. Hartsville, Tenn., Mar. 15, 1893; s. William Jefferson and Jennie Belle (Filson) E.; student, Bus. Coll., Cincinnati, 1909-10, Navy Electric School, 1914-15; grad. Naval War Coll., 1934; m. Beatrice Helen Chacksfield, Jan. 7, 1919; 1 son, Marion Corbett. Enlisted U.S. Navy as apprentice seaman, 1910, commd. ensign, 1917, advanced through grades to rear adm., 1946: service in Turkey, 1911-12, with Armed Guard and Brit. Grand Fleet, 1917-18 with amphibious forces, Africa, Solomons, Guam, Iwo Jima, P.I., Japan landings, 1941-45; ret. from active duty, 1946; now associated with J. W. Malmberg Co., investments. Awarded 2. Bronze Stars, various campaign and area medals, ribbons and battle stars, letter of commdn. from comdr. in chief, Atlantic fleet. Mem. U.S. Naval Inst. Repub. Episcopalian. Mason. Club: San Diego (Calif.). Home: 3230 Trumbull St., San Diego 6, Cal. Died Oct. 6, 1954.

ESCH, JOHN JACOB congressman. Interstate Commerce commr.; b. Norwalk, Wis., Mar. 20, 1861; s. Henry and Matilda E.; A.B., U. of Wis., 1882, LL.B., 1887; m. Anna Herbst, Dec. 24, 1889; children-Irene (Mrs. V. D. Tremblett), Marie (Mrs. Donald Moore), Ruth (Mrs. Paul Gatterdam), Anna (Mrs. Harold R. Hall), John, Mark, Margaret (Mrs. John O. Weaver). Admitted to bar, 1887, and began practice at La Crosse, Wis.; mem. Esch, Kerr, Taylor & Shipe, Washington, until 1938. Was capt. Cos. I and M, 3d Wis. N.G.; judge-advocate-gen., with rank of col., 1894-96. Mem. 56th to 66th Congresses (1899-1921), 7th Wis. Dist.; mem. Interstate Commerce Commn., 1921-28; joint author with Sen. Cummins of Iowa of "Transportation Act, 1920." Pres. Assn. Practitioners Before Interstate Commerce Commn., 1931; pres. Am. Peace Soc., 1930-38. Republican. Home: La Crosse, Wis. Died Apr. 27, 1941.

ESMAY, RHODOLPH LESLIE N.G. officer; b. Sabula, Ia., May 15, 1898; s. John H. And Eva Louisa (Beesley) E.; student U. Wyo., 1926; m. Florence Mae Neis, May 22, 1926; children - John Charles, Rhodolph Leslie. With Wyo. N.G., Mexican Border Campaign, 1916-17, World War I, 1917-19; adj. gen. State of Wyo., 1921-23, 1929 - ; state dir. Selective Service, 1940 - , Wyo. Civil Def., 1950 - ; maj. gen. Wyo. N.G., 1954 - . Active Community Chest, A.R.C. Decorated Legion of Merit, Purple Heart. Mem. Adj. Gen. Assn. U.S. (past pres.), N.G. Assn. U.S. (exec. council), Am. Legion, V.F.W., Mil. Order Purple Heart. Episcopalian (sr. warden). Rotarian. Home: 115 E. 1st Av., Cheyenne 82001. Office: 600 E. 25th St., Cheyenne, Wyo. Died Nov. 13, 1965; buried Beth El Cemetery, Cheyenne.

ESPOSITO, VINCENT JOSEPH army officer, educator; b. New York, Apr. 29, 1900; B.S., U.S. Mil. Acad., 1925; Engrs. Sch., civil engr. course (B.S. in M.E., Mass. Inst. Tech.), 1939, company officer course, 1930, Command and Gen. Staff Sch., 1939, Armed Forces Staff College; Industrial College of the Armed Forces, National War College, 1943-47; m. Eleanor Vinyard; children - Vincent Joseph, Michael, Curtis. Entered U.S. Army, as pvt., 1918, advanced through the grades to brig. gen., 1945; War Dept. Gen. Staff, 1943-46; mem. faculty Nat. War Coll., 1946-47; prof. mil. art and engring., 1956-63. Mem. Sec. Army Hist. Adv. Com., 1956- . Trustee Am. Mil. Inst., 1957 - . Recipient Distinguished Service medal, 1963. Address: 2 Sunset Lane, Milford, Del. Died June 10, 1965; buried U.S. Mil. Acad., West Point, N.Y.

ESSELEN, GUSTAVUS JOHN research chemist; b. Roxbury, Mass., June 30, 1888: s. Gustavus John and Joanna (Blyleven) E.; A.B. magna cum laude, Harvard, 1901, A.M., 1911, Ph.D., 1912; m. Henrietta W. Locke, Sept. 18, 1912: children-Rosamond (Mrs. Bradford K. Bachrach), Josephine (Mrs. George Byron Hanson), Gustavus John, 3d. Mem. research lab. staff Gen. Electric Co., Lynn, 1912-14; asst. mgr., later mgr., Chem. Products Co., 1914-17; research staff Arthur D. Little, Inc., 1917-21; v.p. and dir. research Skinner, Sherman & Esselen, Inc., 1921-30: pres. and treas. Gustavus J. Esselen, Inc. (name changed to Esselen Research Corp. 1946), Boston, 1930-49; v.p. U.S. Testing Co., Inc., mgr. Esselen Research Div., 1950-52. President American Council of Commercial Laboratories, Incorporated, 1951-52. National Academy of Sciences delegate to Internat. Union of Chemistry, Liege, 1930, Lucerne, 1936. Chmn. bd. trustees Swampscott Pub. Library, 1928-38. Mem. Nat. Research Council, 1936-39 and 1940-43; mem. Mass. Bd. Registration Professional Engrs. and Land Surveyors, 1942-49, chmn. 1943, 48; mem. Referee Bd. Office Prodn. Research and Development, 1942-45 (chmn. joint Army-Navy Committee on Tropical Deterioration, 1943-46). Served as a major and lt. colonel, Chemical Warfare Reserve, 1925-40. Received Pioneer Award of Nat. Assn. of Mfrs., 1940, Norris Award, 1948. Fellow A.A.A.S., Am. Inst. Chemists, Am. Acad. Arts and Scis. (council 1944-48); mem. Am. Chem. Soc. (dir. 1934-41; trustee permanent trust fund), Assn. Cons. Chemists and Engrs. (dir. 1936-39, 1946-49), Am. Inst. Chem. Engrs. (dir. 1931-33, 1934-36), Boston C. of C. (dir. 1943-46), Asso. Industries of Mass., Engineering Socs. N.E., N.E. Council, Tech. Assn. Pulp and Paper Industry, Soc. Chem. Industry of Great Britain (chmn. Am. sect. since 1949), Electrochem. Soc., Soc. Plastics Industry, Soc. Plastics Engrs., Alpha Chi Sigma, Sigma Xi, Conglist. Clubs: Harvard, Rotary, Union, Chemists (New York); Cosmos (Washington, D.C.). Author of numerous tech. papers and chapters on chem. products. Lecturer. Address: 99 Gale Rd., Swampscott, Mass. Died Oct. 22, 1952; buried Swampscott (Mass.) Cemetery.

ESSER, SIGURD EMANUEL, ednl. cons.; born Scandinavia, Wis., July 3, 1903; s. Nels N. and Elida B. (Johnson) E.; B.A., Concordia Coll., 1925; M.S., N.D. U., 1933; grad. student, U. Minn., Stanford; m. Keziah L. Evingson, Dec. 22, 1933; 1 dau., Elisabeth K. Prin. Kindred (N.D.) High Sch., 1925-27, supt. schs., 1927-32; emergency agrl. asst. Dept. Agr., 1933; tchr. Balboa (C.Z.) High Sch., 1933-38, counselor, asst. prin., 1938-41, prin., 1941-47; dir. research C.Z. schs., 1947-48, dir. secondary edn., 1948-53, supt. schs., and chief state sch. officer 1953-64; educational consultant, from 1964. Chairman C.Z. Administration Intern Selection Com.; mem. selection bds. West Point, Annapolis, Air Force Acad. Bd. dirs. C.Z. Tb. Assn., C.Z.A.R.C. Served as 1st lt. Minn. N.G., 1927-33; mem. U.S. Army Res., 1927-41. Recipient Cruz de la Fundacion Internacional Elay Alfaro, 1961; Distinguished Service awards Panama Canal, 1963, Spl. Edn. Assn., 1963; named mem. Esteemed Order Bearers of Master Key to Panama Canal in grade of hon. aide to gov., 1963. Mem. N.E.A., American Assn. School Administrs., Council Chief State Sch. Officers, Mondamin Soc., Phi Delta Kappa, Phi Theta Kappa. Lutheran. Home: Ft Lauderdale FL Died Feb. 11, 1972; buried Kindred ND

ESTABROOK, MERRICK GAY, JR. army officer; b. Boston, July 12, 1886; s. Merrick Gay and Flora (Shaw) E.; student Pub. Latin Sch., Boston, 1900-05; A.B., Harvard, 1909; grad. Air Corps Engring. Sch., 1932. Army Indsl. Coll., 1936; m. Marion Ward Hartley, Sept. 5, 1912; 1 dau., Mary Ward (wife of Maj. William J. Headrick, Jr.). Commd. 1st lt., Aviation Sect., Sigma Corps, U.S. Army, 1917, and advanced through the grades to brig. gen., Sept. 17, 1943; ret. Aug. 1944. Began as mine operator, 1909. With U.S. Army Air Corps, Patterson Field, 1943. Address: Patterson Field, Fairfield, O. Died Dec. 19, 1947.*

ESTES, CHARLES THOMPSON labor relations cons.; b. Gainesville, Ga., June 10, 1891; s. George Presley and Tomie (Thompson) E.; B.S., U. Ga., 1912; grad. French Sch. of Trench Warfare, and Hist. Research, 1917; grad. other Post and Staff Schs.; m. Alice Christina Laidlaw, Feb. 7, 1933. Farmer-mcht., Gainesville, since 1910; partner George P. Estes Co., 1939-56, pres., 1956-64; pres. Charles Poster Advt. Co., 1955-63; partner farms, real estate, financial interests, Cal., since 1934; commd. 1st lt. U.S. Army, May 1917, advanced through grades to maj., 1926; mem. staff 82d, 18th, 26th divs.; 57th Inf. in China, Japan, P.I., 1922-24; 12th Inf., Presdl. Guard, Washington, 1925-26; released from U.S. Army, 1926; fgn. rep. Coca-Cola Co. in Europe and Latin Am., 1926-33; exec. v.p., sales mgr., Citrus Products Co. and Kings Internat., dep. Inc., Chgo., 1933-34; sr. asst. adminstr. NRA, 1935-36; commr. U.S. Conciliation Service (Fed. Mediation and Conciliation Service 1947 -), 1938-40, liaison officer and spl. asst. to dir., 1940-54. Mem. Nat. Soc. for Study Communication, Com. on Adult Speech Edn., Cooperative Forum (founder and chmn.). Democrat. Baptist. Mason (32ff, Shriner). Clubs: Cosmos; Rotary (Gainesville). Lectr. preventative mediation and conciliation, labor-mgmt. relations. Author of brochures: Human Relations, 1946; Speech and Human Relations in Industry, 1946; Communication in Labor-Management Relations, 1949; Can We Learn to Live Together?, 1949. Contbr. to jours. personnel and communications. Home: C-8 Wildwood Circle, Gainesville, Ga. 30501. Died Nov. 2, 1964.

ESTES, GEORGE HENSON army officer (retired); b. Eufaula, Ala., Jan. 30, 1873; s. George H. and Anna (Thornton) E.; student U. of Ga.; grad. U.S. Mil. Acad., 1894, Gen. Staff Sch., 1920, Army War Coll., 1921; m. Frances Farrell, January 4, 1899; children—Henson F., Frances (Mrs. Claude D. Collins). Commd. 2d lt., inf., U.S. Army June 12, 1894, advanced through grades to col., July 1, 1920; insp. gen., U.S. Army, 1921-25, brig. gen., Jan. 2, 1929. Mem. Gen. Staff War Dept., 1921-25; comdt. U.S. Inf. Sch., Ft. Benning, Ga., 1933-37; retired from active duty, Jan. 1, 1937. War Dept. citations for conduct in action. Baptist. Club: Army and Navy (Washington). Address: 124 Bay Haven, Clearwater FL

ETZ, ROGER FREDERICK clergyman; b. Akron, O., Apr. 30, 1886; s. George Emmet and Frances Adelaide (Rogers) E.; A.B., Tufts, 1909, S.T.D, 1929; S.T.B, Crane Theol. Sch. (Tufts), 1910; postgrad. Hartford Sch. Religious Pedagogy, 1917-18; D.D., Lombard Coll., Galesburg, Ill., 1927; m. Verta Atkinson Smith, June 11, 1913; children-Dorothy, John Rogers. Field sec. Young People's Christian Union, 1910-13, also editor Onward; Ordained Universalist ministry, 1913; minister Concord, N.H., 1913-17; asst. pastor Hartford, Conn., 1917-18; sec. Universalist Gen. Conv. and Internat. Ch. Extension Bd., 1919-37; pastor Charlestown, Massachusetts, 1922-29; also general supt. Universalist Ch., 1929-38: pastor Newark, 1938-41; pastor First Universalist Ch., Medford, 1941-50. Sec. Joint Commn. Conglists. and Universalists and Comity and Ch. Unity; pres. Mass. Universalist Conv., 1948. Trustee Medford Pub. Library, 1948. With YMCA in France 1 yr., World War I; Chaplain (capt.), 182d Inf., Mass. N.G., 1922-29. Republican. Mason. Home: 21 Rural Av., Medford, Mass. Died Dec. 19, 1950; buried Oak Grove Cemetery, Medford.

EUBANK, VICTOR (G.C.) newspaperman; b. Nodaway County, Mo., Aug. 14, 1883; s. Reuben B. and Mary Elizabeth (Campbell) E.; ed. pvt. and pub. schs. and Univ. Med. Coll., Mo.; unmarried. Began with Kansas City Star, 1903; with Chicago Inter-Ocean 1904, later with Chicago Record-Herald, Chicago Evening Jour., Chicago Examiner and Chicago Tribune; joined Associated Press, 1913, as editor Chicago Bar.; lit. and supervising dir. Essanay Film Co., Chicago, 1914; in World War as lt. and capt. Signal Corps, U.S. Army, later capt. intelligence sect. O.R.C.; rejoined Associated Press, 1921, Far Eastern cable editor, San Francisco, 1922-24, cable editor, New York, 1924-25, chief Associated Press Bur., Tokyo, Japan, 1925-29; London Five-Power Naval Conf., 1930; chief Moscow Bur., 1930-31; Internat. Financial Conf., London, 1931; transferred to hdqrs. Associated Press, New York, 1931; writing leading Wall Street review daily for Associated Press 1931-48, now writing spl. features. Contbr. playlets, short stories and mag. articles. Home: 1 Bank St., N.Y. City 14. Office: Associated Press. 50 Rockefeller Plaza, N.Y.C. Died Dec. 11, 1955.

EUSTIS, HENRY LAWRENCE engr., educator, army officer; b. Boston, Feb. 1, 1819; s. Gen. Abraham and Rebecca (Sprague) E.; grad. Harvard, 1838, A.M., 1850; grad. U.S. Mil. Acad., 1842; m. Sarah Eckley, May 2, 1844; m. 2d, Caroline Hall, July 10, 1856; 6 children. Asst. prof. engring. U.S. Mil. Acad., 1847-49; prof. engring. Harvard, 1849-85, organized dept. engring. Harvard's Lawrence Scientific Sch., dean sci. faculty, 1862-63, 71-85; commd. brig. gen. U.S. Volunteers, 1863, served in many important battles; fellow Am. Acad. Arts and Scis. Died Cambridge, Mass., Jan. 11, 1885.

EUSTIS, JAMES U.S. senator; b. New Orleans, La., Aug. 27, 1834; classical edn.; grad. Harvard Law School, 1854; practiced at New Orleans; served as judge-advocate Confederate army, under Gens.

Magruder and Joseph E. Johnston, 1861-65; served in La. house, 1872, and senate, 1874-78; U.S. senator, 1877-79, and 1885-91; prof. civil law, Univ. of La., 1879-84; U.S. minister to France, 1893-97. Home: New Orleans, La. Died 1899.

EUSTIS, WILLIAM gov. Mass., U.S. sec. of war; b. Cambridge, Mass., June 10, 1753; s. Benjamin and Elizabeth (Hill) E.; grad. Harvard, 1772, A.M. (hon.), 1784, LL.D. (hon.), 1823; m. Caroline Langdon, Sept. 24, 1810. Served as surgeon during Am. revolution; surgeon in expdn. to suppress Shay's Rebellion, 1786-87; mem. Mass. Gen. Ct., 1788-94; mem. U.S. Ho. of Reps. from Mass., 7th-8th congresses, 1801-05, 16th-17th congresses, 1820-23; U.S. sec. of war, 1807-13; U.S. minister to Holland, 1814-18; gov. Mass., 1823-25; v.p. Soc. of Cincinnati, 1786-1810, 20. Died Boston, Feb. 6, 1825; buried Granary Burying Ground, Boston.

EVANS, ANDREW WALLACE army officer; b. Elkton, Md., July 6, 1829; s. Dr. Amos and Mary (Oliver) E.; ed. Elkton Acad.; under-grad. Harvard, 1846-47; grad. West Point, 1852; m. Feb. 25, 1886, Susan A. Tuite. Asst. U.S. Coast Survey, 1853-58; served through Civil War, becoming col. U.S. vols.; in regular army after war until retired, Sept. 22, 1883, as lt. col., U.S.A. Companion Pa. Commandery, Mil. Order Foreign Wars. Club: Army and Navy (New York). Address: Elkton, Md.

EVANS, CHARLES ROUNTREE lawyer; b. Lancaster, Wis., Apr. 4, 1863; s. Jonathan H. and Sarah (Kilbourne) E.; A.B., U. of Wis., 1881 (hon. A.M., 1907); admitted to bar, 1884. Located in Chattanooga, Tenn., 1885; city atty., 1887, 88, 91; Rep. candidate for judge 4th Jud. Circuit of Tenn., 1892; prof. law, 1899-1900, dean, 1901-, Chattanooga Coll. of Law. Commr. registration, 1894-95; county atty., Hamilton County, 1894-98. In Spanish-Am. War in P.R. as capt. 6th U.S. Vol. Inf., June 20, 1898; promoted maj., Jan. 7, 1899; judge-adv. of gen. court-martial P.R. and Vieques; mem. mil. court, province of Arecibo; hon. disch., Mar. 15, 1899. Rep. candidate for presdl. elector-at-large, 1900, for 62d Congress, 3d Tenn. Dist., 1910; judge 6th Jud. Circuit of Tenn., 1911-12. Judge adv. gen. State of Tenn., with rank of brig. gen., 1913-14. Died Oct. 3, 1920.

EVANS, CLEMENT ANSELM lawyer; b. Stewart County, Ga., 1833; s. Anselm L. and Sarah Hinton (Bryan) E.; ed pub. schs., Lumpkin, G.; LL.B., Law Sch., Augusta, — 1853. Admitted to bar, 1853, and practiced at Lumpkin; Judge County Court of Stewart County, 1855; mem. Ga. Senate, 1859-60. Served in C.S.A. as maj., col., brig. gen. and acting maj. gen., Army of Northern Va. and surrendered with Lee. Devoted principally to lit. work. Democrat. State comdr. of Ga. Div. U.C.V. 12 yrs., dept. comdr. 3 yrs.; comdr.-in-chief U.C.V., 1909. Editor: Confederate Military History (12 vols.). Author: Military History of Georgia, 1895. Home: Atlanta, Ga. Died 1911.

EVANS, CURTIS ALBAN surgeon; b. Wales, Wis., Apr. 20, 1879; s. Rowland Hill and Sarah (Alban) E.; student Ripon Acad. and Coll., 1894; A.B., U. of Mich., 1902, M.D., 1904; m. Nellie S. Schwartzburg, June 24, 1908; children - Robert Curtis, John Alban, Edward Sifton, Nancy Jane. Instr. anatomy, 1904-08, prof., 1908-12, Wis. Coll. Phys. and Surg.; asso. prof. surgery, Marquette U., 1912-25; chief of staff, Milwaukee Hosp., 1928-1941; cons. surgeon Johnson Emergency Hosp.; surg. staff Columbia Hosp.; Cons. Surgeon Milwaukee Children's Hosp. Commd. lt. M.R.C., U.S. Army; May 27, 1916; maj. Aug. 23, 1917; lt. col., Aug. 20, 1918; dir. and chief surg. service U.S. Army Base Hosp. 22, A.E.F., 1917-Mar. 15, 1919; U.S. Army citation, 1919; col. Med. O.R.C. Mem. of Founders Group Am. Board of Surgery. Fellow Am. Coll. Surgeons (mem. bd. govs. since 1925), A.M.A.; mem. Milwaukee Surg. Soc. (pres. 1922), Milwaukee Acad. Medicine (pres. 1922), Phi Rho Sigma, Pi Gamma rMu. Awarded Order of Purple Heart, 1932. Conglist. Club: University. Home: 2914 E. Newberry Blvd. Office: 324 E. Wisconsin Av., Milwaukee, Wis. Died May 3, 1947.

EVANS, DUDLEY b. Morgantown, W.Va., Jan. 27, 1838; s. Rawley and Clarissa (Cow) E.; A.B., Washington (now Washington and Jefferson) Coll., 1859; capt. 10th Va. Cav., C.S.A., 1862; lt. col., 1863-65; mem. Va. Ho. of Rep., 1863-65; m. Nellie Seelye, Sept. 17, 1878. Gen. express agt. Wells Fargo & Co., Portland, Ore., 1872-82; supt. Portland office, 1882-88; v.p., 1892-1902, pres., 1902-, Wells Fargo & Co.; pres. Wells Fargo & Co.'s Bank, New York. Home: Englewood, N.J. Died 1910.

EVANS, EDWARD STEPTON manufacturer; b. Thaxtons, Va., May 24, 1879; s. Thomas Davis and Mary Elizabeth (Murrell) E.; law student Columbian (now George Washington) Univ., Washington, D.C., 2' yrs.; spl. course in library science; m. Virginia Epes McCormick, Apr. 5, 1905; Children - Edward Steptoe, Robert Beverly. In Library of Congress, 1900-04; asst. state librarian, Va., 1904-07; founder, 1915, pres. and treas. Evans Products Co., Inc., mfrs. loading material and devices for loading automobiles loading material and devices for loading freight cars, airplanes and trucks, road and rail locomotives and vehicles and other equipment for railroads, battery separators, heating and

ventilating units for motor vehicles and airplanes, molded plywood, airplane engine mounts, etc.; president and treasurer Saven Corporation, investments; farmer, breeder of registered Guernseys. Served as captain in Q.M.C., U.S. Army, 1918-19 inclusive; Lieutenant colonel specialist reserve attached to U.S. Air Corps. Fellow American Geographical Society; member Society Automotive Engrs. Episcopalian. rfason (32ff, K.T., Shriner). Clubs: Explorers (New York); Detroit, Detroit Athletic, Detroit Boat, Country, Players, Adventurers (Chicago); Commonwealth (Richmond, Va.). Held record for circumnavigating the globe in 28 days, 14 hours and 36 minutes, 1926; mgr. Detroit Arctic Expdn., 1925, 26. Founder and 1st pres. Nat. Glider Assn. Donor annual silver trophy U.S. nat. glider champion and bronze trophy U.S. Army Air Corps grand glider champion presented to U.S. War Department, 1941. Author: Encyclopedic Guide to Richmond, Va., 1907; History of Seals for Virginia (monograph), 1908. Compiler: Calendar of Virginia Transcripts, 1906. Contbr. to numerous mags. on freight transport. Pioneer in aircraft mfr. and air transportation. Home: 1005 Three Mile Drive, Grosse Pointe, Mich. Died Sep. 6, 1945.

EVANS, EVERETT IDRIS surgeon; b. Norfolk, Neb., Apr. 15, 1909; s. Rhys and Mary (Jones) E.; Ph.D., U. of Chicago, 1935, M.D., 1937; m. LaVerne Veatch, Sept. 14, 1936; children-Robert Rhys, Melissa Lee, Richard Idris. House surgeon Pa. Hosp., Phila., 1937-39; asst. resident surgery, Med. Coll. of Va. Hosp., Richmond, 1939-40; Rockefeller Foundation Fellow in surgery. Mass. Gen. Hosp., Boston, 1940-41; resident in surg., Med. Coll. of Va. Hosp., 1941-42, asst. prof. surg., Med. Coll. of Va., 1942-43, asso. prof., 1943-48, prof. surg. and dir. surg. research lab. since 1948; responsible investigator, Office Sci. Research and Development, Med. Coll. of Va., 1940-46, prin. investigator Research and Development Bd., Office Surg. Gen., Dept. of Army since 1948; surg. cons., Atomic Bomb Casualties Commn., Far East Command (Japan) since 1948, Office of Surg. Gen., Dept. of Army since 1948; vis. prof. surgery pro tem, Ohio State Univ., 1950; MacArthur lecturer U. of Edinburgh, 1952-53. Member committee on surg., Nat. Research Council since 1946; mem. com. on blood and blood substitutes Am. Red Cross since 1947, com. on atomic casualties, Nat. Research Council since 1947; mem. adv. bd. on Health Services, Am. Nat. Red Cross, since 1947. Mem. adv. com. on annual scientific award, Am. Pharm. Mfrs. Assn. since 1947. Awarded certificate of appreciation by Depts. of Army and Navy for work during World War II. Mem. Internat. Soc. Surgery, Soc. for Vascular Surg., Am. Surg. Assn., Southern Med. Assn., A.M.A., Am. Physiol. Soc., Am. Surg. Assn., Am. Coll. Surgs., Southern Surg. Assn., Richmond Acad. Med., Sigma Xi, Nu Sigma Nu, Alpha Omega Alpha. Democrat. Episcopalian. Club: Commonwealth. Mem. editorial bd. Annals of Surg. since 1947. Home: Llanfair, River Rd., Richmond. Office: 1200 E. Broad St., Richmond 19, Va. Died Jan. 14, 1954; buried St. Mary's Episcopal Church, Goochland County, Va.

EVANS, FRANK EDGAR officer U.S.M.C.; b. Franklin, Pa., Nov. 19, 1876; s. Frederick and Frances (William) E.; student Princeton 3 yrs. (non-grad.); grad. Naval War Coll., 1925, Army War Coll., 1926; m. Esther Caldwell Townsend, Oct. 16, 1909 (divorced); m. 2d Aileen Fisk Lambert, June 19, 1937. Began service as enlisted man, 1st Wis. Regt., Spanish-Am. War; commd. 2d lt. U.S.M.C., Jan. 26, 1900; 1st lt., Feb. 19, 1902; capt., July 26, 1905; maj., May 25, 1917; lt. col., July 1, 1918; col., June 24, 1924; retired with rank of brig. gen., 1940. Served in Philippines, Panama, Porto Rico and at Culebra; on relief expdn. to West Indies following eruption of Mt. Pelce, Apr. 1902; on Isthmus of Panama, 1904; with 4th Brigade, 2d Div., A.E.F., in France, Nov. 1, 1917-Oct. 1, 1918; regt. adj. 6th Marines, at Belleau Wood; on staff American High Commissioner to Haiti, 1922-24; on staff Naval War Coll., 1926-27; comdt. Garde d'Haiti, with rank of maj. gen., Apr. 1927-Apr. 1930. Member Am. Assn. Internat. Rifleman; adjutant Am. Palma Rifle Team, 1907, Am. Olympic Rifle Team, 1908; capt. U.S.M.C. Rifle Team, 1905-07. Mem. Comite de Patronage Les Amis de la Legion Etrangere. Awarded Navy Cross for services with 6th Regt. Marines in France; officer Legion (France). Republican. Clubs: Chevy Chase (Chevy Chase, Md.), Tiger Inn (Princeton), Princeton (New York); Bohemian (San Francisco); Racquet (Philadelphia). Author: Marvel Book of American Ships (with O. P. Jackson), 1916; Daddy Pat of the Marines, 1919; New Book of American Ships (with O. P. Jackson), 1927. Contbr. of fiction to mags. Died Nov. 25, 1941.

EVANS, FREDERIC DAHL army officer; b. Ill., June 29, 1866; grad. U.S. Mil. Acad., 1887, Army War Coll., 1906. Commd. add, 2d lt., 22d Inf., July 1, 1887: 2d lt. 18th Inf., Oct. 6, 1887; 1st lt. 24th Inf., Jan. 21, 1895; trans. to 18th Inf., May 16, 1895; capt., Mar. 2, 1899; maj. 17th Inf., Mar. 3,1911; adj. gen., Mar. 2, 1912; assigned to 4th Inf., Jan. 31, 1915; col. 1917; brig. gen. N.A., Aug. 5, 1917. Comd. Seminole Negro Indian scouts until Apr. 1892; at Fort Bliss, Tex., 1893-8; ordered with regt. to Philippines, 1898; participated in battles of Manila, Aug. 13, 1898, of Jaro, Feb. 12, 1899, of Jaro River Mar. 16, 1899; adj. of Col. Carpenter's expdn. from Iloilo to Capiz, Panay Island, 1899; again in P.I., 1903-5; mem. Inf. Exam. Bd., Ft. Leavenworth, Kan., 1906-07; apptd. comdr. 152d Inf. Brigade, Camp Devens, Ayer, Mass., Sept. 1917; comdr. 156th Inf. Brig., 76th Div., A.E.F. in France, July 1918; hon. discharged as brig. gen., Nov. 27, 1918. Address: War Dept., Washington. Died May 1, 1953.

EVANS, FRED(ERIC) M(AURICE), lawyer; born Sparta, Wis., Jan. 20, 1895; s. John and Edith Ann (Evans) E.; grad. LaCrosse Normal Sch., 1923; A.B., University Wisconsin, 1925, LL.B., 1932; married to Eluned Davies, December 28, 1954; 1 daughter, Beti Sian. Admitted to the Wisconsin bar, 1932; teacher and coach, Williston, N.D., 1919-22; asst. dir. athletics U. Wis., 1925-31; law practice, Madison, Wis., 1932-41 and since 1950; judge Dane Co., 1941-50. Mem. Gov's. Commn. Human Rights, Wis., 1945-50, chmn., 1945-49; local chmn. Rep. Party, 1934-39, sec. Wis. state central com., 1936; dir. Red Cross (Madison), 1942-49; appeal agt. Selective Service U.S., 1942-47; chmn. War Manpower shows, 1944-45. Elected and installed Welsh bard, 1954. Served as supply officer, lt., Inf., U.S. Army, 1916-19. Mem. Madison Humane Soc. (dir. 1946), Family Welfare Assn. (dir. 1935-39), Am. Bar Assn., Am. Judicature Soc., Wis. Hist. Soc., Madison Business Association (bd. directors 1939-45), Disabled Am. Vets., Am. Legion (post comdr. 1937, 1958-61, judge adv., Wis. dept. 1939-41), 40 & 8 (grand adv. Wis., 1941-50), Ancient and Honorable Cymmrodorian Soc. (v.p.), Welsh Assn. of London, Clwb-Y Cymry (London), Wis. Gymanfa Ganu Assn. (dir.), Wisconsin Institute of Nationalities, Alpha Kappa Psi, Phi Alpha Delta, Phi Pi Phi fraternity (national vice president 1928-29). Elk, Mason (Shriner). Author articles on edn., human rights and legal subjects. Home: Madison WI Deceased.

EVANS, GEORGE WATKIN mining engr.; b. Ystrad, Rhonnda Valley, Wales, Mar. 5, 1876; s. Watkin and Catherine (Hughes) E.; student Internat. Corr. Schs., Scranton, Pa., 1892-96; B.S. and E.M., State Coll. of Wash., Pullman, Wash.; m. Olivia Laird, Mar. 12, 1902; children-Watkin L., Blodwyn E., Lloyd George. Practical work in coal mines, 1888-96; later in the Klondyke and placer mines, Yukon; with Wash. Geol. Survey, 1899-1901; cyanide practice in gold mines, Colo., 1902; practiced as engr., 1903-08; geologist in charge coal surveys Wash. Geol. Survey, 1909-12; cons. mining engr. U.S. Bur. of Mines, 1911—, also cons. Mining Engr. U.S. Navy; dist mining engr. during World War I; cons. engr. for large fuel cos., also Canadian Nat. Rys.; now in practice as cons. mining engr. Mem. Am. Inst. Mining and Metall. Engrs., West Coast Engineers. Unitarian. Rotarian. Home: 3134 37tb Pl., Seattle 44. Died Jan. 11, 1951.

EVANS, JOHN GARY ex-governor; b. Cokesbury, S.C., Oct. 15, 1863; s. Nathan George and Ann Victoria (Gary) E.; ed. Union Coll., Schenectady, N.Y., class of 1883, to close jr. yr.; read law under Judge W. T. Gary, of Augusta, Ga.; m. Emily Mansfield Plume, Dec. 17, 1897; 1 dau., Emily Victoria (Mrs. Dag Knutson). Admitted to S.C. bar, 1886; elected to S.C. Ho. of Rep. 1888, 1890, Senate, 1892, gov. of S.C., 1894-97; pres. S.C. Constl. Conv., 1895. Maj. and insp.-gen. 1st Div, 7th Army Corps, Spanish-Am. War, 1898; transferred to staff of Major-Gen. William Ludlow. Havanna, Cuba; assisted in organizing civic govt. for Havana after war. Del.-at-large from S.C. to Dem. Nat. Conv., 1896, del., 1900, del-at-large, 1912, 16; chmn. State Dem. Exec. Com., 1912-16; chmn. City Democracy; mem. Dem. Nat. Com. for S.C., 1918-30; mem. S.C. Ho. of Rep. Mem. S.C. Hist. Soc., Delta Phi. Episcopalian. Home: Spartanburg, S.C. Died June 27, 1942.

EVANS, JOSHUA, JR. congressman; b. Paoli, Pa., Jan. 20, 1777; attended common schs. Hotel keeper, also farmer; mem. Pa. Ho. of Reps., 1820; 1st postmaster Paoli, 1826-30; pres. Tredyffrin Twp. Sch. Bd., 1836-46; served as brig. gen. Pa. Militia; mem. U.S. Ho. of Reps. (Democrat) from Pa., 21st-22d congresses, 1829-33. Died Paoli, Oct. 2, 1846; buried Great Valley Baptist Ch., New Centerville, Pa.

EVANS, ROBERT KENNON brig. gen.; b. Jackson, Miss., Nov. 19, 1852; s. Samuel Wildes and Mary (Dennon) E.; grad. U.S. Mil. Acad., 1875; s. Jane Findlay Shunk, Nov. 11, 1880. Commd. 2d lt. 12th Inf., June 16, 1875; promoted through grades to brig. gen. Jan. 30, 1911. Served in Nez Perce and Bannock Indian campaigns, 1877-78; mil. attache, Am. Embassy, Berlin, 1892-96; in Cuba during Spanish Am. War and later in Philippine insurrection; chief, div. mil. affairs and asst. to the chief of staff U.S. Army. 1911-12; comdg. gen. Dept. of the Gulf, Atlanta, Ga., Oct. 1, 1912-14, and comdr. 2d Brigade, 1st div., Jan. 1913-14, comdr. Dept. of the East, 1914-15, 2d Brigade, Laredo, Tex., 1915-16; retired, Nov. 19, 1916. Was exec. officer Nat. and Internat. matches, Camp Perry, Ohio, Aug. 15-Sept. 10, 1913. Ordered on active duty and comd. Philippine Dept., Manila, June 30, 1917-Sept. 5, 1918. Episcopalian. Died July 31, 1926.

EVANS, ROBLEY DUNGLISON rear adm.; b. Floyd County, Va., Aug. 18, 1846; s. Dr. Samuel Andrew Jackson E.; ed. pub. schs. of Washington; apptd. from Utah, and grad. U.S. Naval Acad., 1863; m. Charlotte, d. Franck Taylor, of Washington, 1871. Ensign, Oct. 1, 1863; lt., July 25, 1866; lt. comdr., Mar. 12, 1868; comdr., July, 1878; capt., June 27, 1893; rear adm., Feb.11, 1901. Participated in both attacks on Ft. Fisher, Jan. 15, 1865, and in land attack received 4 severe rifle-shot wounds; when in command of the Yorktown at Valparaiso, Chile, 1891, during period of strained relations between Chile and U.S., his actions in connection with various incidents earned him name of Fighting "Fighting Bob." In war with Spain comd. Iowa in Sampson's fleet off Santiago, taking active part in battle with Cervera's fleet, July 3, 1898; was pres. Bd. of Inspection and Survey; comdr.-in-chief Asiatic Sta., Oct. 1902-04; comdg. Atlantic Fleet, 1905-07; comdr.-in-chief Atlantic Fleet, on tour of the world, 1907-08; retired Aug. 18, 1908. Author: A Sailor's Log, 1901. Home: Washington, D.C. Died 1912.

EVANS, WILLIAM LLOYD educator; b. Columbus, O., Dec. 22, 1870; s. William Henry and Anne (Lloyd) E.; B.Sc., Ohio State U., 1892, M.Sc., 1896, LL.D., 1948; Ph.D., U. Chgo., 1905; D.Sc. (hon.) Capital U., 1949; m. Cora Ruth Roberts, Mar. 9, 1911; children-Lloyd Roberts (M.D.), Jane Anne (Mrs. Alvin H. Nielsen), William Arthur (lt. j.g., U.S.N.R.; lost in action Mar. 27, 1944). Chemist with Am. Encaustic Tile Co., Zanesville, O., 1892-94; University fellow, Ohio State U., 1895-96; asst. dept. of ceramics, 1896-98; instr. chemistry colorado Springs High Sch., 1898-1902; Univ. fellow and Lowenthal fellow in chemistry U. Chgo., 1903-05; lectr. chemistry, Starling-Ohio Med. Coll., 1911-15; asst. prof. chemistry Ohio State U., 1905-08, asso. prof., 1908-11, prof., 1911-41, chmn. dept. chemistry, 1928-41, prof. emeritus, 1941—; cons. chemist The Lowe Bros. Co. (Dayton), Columbus Coated Fabrics Corp., Div. Carbohydrates Nat. Insts. Health. Mem. Nat. Research Council Com. on Carbohydrate Research, 1926-27, Nat. Research Council Div. of Chemistry and Chem. Tech., 1934-40. Commd. capt. O.R.C., U.S. Army Oct. 11, 1917; maj. C.W.S., Offense Div., July 19, 1918; disch., Dec. 30, 1918; head of lab. insp. div. Edgewood Arsenal, World War I. Del. 10th Congress Internat. Union Chemistry, Liege, Belgium, 1930. Fellow A.A.A.S., Am. Acad. Arts and Sciences; mem. Am. Chem. Soc. (chmn. organic div. 1928; mem. exec. com. organic div. 1929; councilor at large 1934-40; pres-elect 1940; pres., 1941), Ohio Acad. Sci. (pres. 1939-40; fellow: v.p. chemistry sect. 1933-34), Scabbard and Blade, Sigma Xi, Phi Eta Sigma, Phi Beta Kappa (hon.), Phi Lambda Upsilon, Alpha Chi Sigma, Gamma Alpha. Sigma Chi. Conglist. Mason (32ff). Clubs: Ohio State University Faculty (pres. 1928). Torch (pres. 1933): Engineers (Dayton, O.). Author: Study and Quiz Outline in Chemistry, 1923. Co-Author: Laboratory Exercises in General Chemistry (with Wm. McPherson and W. E. Henderson), 1928: An Elementary Course in Qualitative Analysis (with J. E. Day and A. B. Garrett), 1938; Semimicro Qualitative Analysis (with A. B. Garrett and L. L. Quill), 1940. rev. edit. (with A. B. Garrett and H. H. Sisler), 1951. Mem. exec. bd., Ohio Jour. Science; mem. bd. editors Jour. of Higher Edn.; chmn. bd. editors. Songs of Ohio State U. (1st and 2d edits). Contbr. Jour. Am. Chem. Soc. and Jour. Chem. Edn. Awarded William H. Nichols medal, 1929; gold medal Am. Inst. of Chemists, 1942. Home: 1975 Indianola Av., Columbus 1, O. Died Oct. 18, 1954; buried Columbus, O.

EVE, HENRY PRONTAUT, lawyer; b. Augusta, Ga., Oct. 17, 1917; s. William Ralford and Helen (Davies) E.; B.S., Davidson Coll., 1936; LL.B., Emory U., 1939; m. Caroline Hull, Jan. 21, 1942; 1 dau., Mary Hull. Admitted to Ga. bar, 1939; practiced in Augusta, 1939-41, 45-69; partner firm Cumming, Nixon, Eve, Waller & Capers, and predecessor, 1945-69. Dir. 1st R.R. & Banking Co. of Ga., Richmond County Bank, 1st Ga. Devel. Corp. Mem. Ga. Ho. of Reps., 1947-49; mem. Ga. Senate, 1949-50. Served to lt. comdr. USNR, 1941-45. Decorated Bronze Star medal. Mem. Am., Augusta (pres. 1967) bar assns., State Bar Ga. (pres. 1965-66), Com. 100, Augusta C. of C. (past dir.), Phi Delta Phi, Sigma Alpha Epsilon. Elk. Clubs: Augusta Country (pres. 1963), Pinnacle (bd. dirs.) (Augusta). Home: Augusta GA Died June 29, 1969.

EVE, PAUL FITZSIMONS surgeon; b. Augusta, Ga., June 27, 1806; s. Capt. Oswell and Aphra (Pritchard) E.; B.A., Franklin Coll. (now U. Ga.), 1826; M.D., U. Pa., 1828; m. Sarah Twiggs; m. 2d, Sarah Duncan, 1852; 3 children including 2 sons who became doctors. Practiced medicine in clinics, London, Eng., also Paris, France, 1828-30; participated as physician in Revolution of July 1831, Paris; offered services to Polish Govt., served in hosp., Warsaw; an organizer Med. Coll. Ga., 1832, prof. surgery, 1839-50; prof. surgery U. Louisville; (Ky.), 1850, U. Nashville (Tenn.), 1851-61, 70-77, Nashville Med. Coll., 1877; served in Mexican War; served as surgeon gen. Tenn., then chief surgeon Gen. Joseph E. Johnston's Army, also surgeon Gate City Hosp., Atlanta, Ga., in Civil War; pres. A.M.A., 1857-58; leading surgeon and tchr. of surgery in South; perfected operation for vesical calculus; 1st Am. surgeon to perform hysterectomy; co-editor So. Med. and Surg. Jour.; asst. editor Nashville Jour. of Medicine and Surgery. Author (most noted med. works): A Collection of Remarkable Cases in Surgery, 1857; A Contribution to the History of the Hip-join Operations Performed During the Late Civil War, 1867. Died Nasvhille, Nov. 3, 1877.

EVELEIGH, NICHOLAS Continental congressman; b. Charleston, S.C., circa 1748; educated in Eng. Commd. capt. 2d S.C. Regt., Continental Army, 1775, served in battle with British at Ft. Moultrie, 1776; promoted col., dep. adj. gen. for S.C. and Ga., 1778; served in Ga. campaign at Ft. Tonyn, 1778; engaged in agriculture; mem. S.C. Ho. of Reps., 1781; mem. Continental Congress from S.C., 1781-82; mem. S.C. Legislative Council, 1782; 1st comptroller U.S. Treasury, 1789-91. Died Phila., Apr. 16, 1791; probably buried Phila.

EVELETH, TRUE BALLENTINE, assn. exec.; b. Portland, Me., Apr. 28, 1904; s. Samuel True and Annie Louise (Bailey) E.; D. O., Kirksville Coll. Osteopathy and Surgery, 1937, Doctor of Science (honorary), in Osteopathy, 1964; D.Sc. in Osteopathy, Chgo. Coll. Osteopathy, 1965; m. Dorothy M. Leland, Oct. 29, 1929. Treas. F. O. Bailey Co., Portland, Me., 1924-32; med. dir. Osteopathic Hosp., Me., 1946-52; exec. asst. Am. Osteopathic Assn., 1952-56, exec. dir., 1956-68, exec. dir. emeritus, 1968-69. Served as lt. col. AUS, 1940-45. Recipient Distinguished Service certificate Am. Osteo. Assn., 1963. Fellow Acad. Applied Osteopathy, Am. Coll. Osteo. Surgeons (hon.); life mem. Ill., Mich., Me. (dir. 1945-52) osteo. assns.; mem. Am. Osteo. Acad. Orthopedics (hon.), Me. Diabetic Soc. (co-founder, treas.), Am. Soc. Assn. Execs. Address: Cape Elizabeth ME Died Dec. 25, 1969.

EVERETT, WILLIAM HENRY rear adm.; b. New York, N.Y., Mar. 6, 1847; s. William Moore and Charlotte M. E.: apptd. from Conn. and grad. U.S. Naval Acad., June 1868; m. Bessie Bell Hackett, Aug. 6, 1885. Promoted ensign, U.S. Navy, Apr. 19, 1869; master, July 12, 1870; lt., Dec. 12, 1873; lt. comdr., Dec. 6, 1894; comdr., lMar. 3, 1899; capt., Feb. 17, 1904; advanced to rear admiral, Oct. 9, 1906, and retired at own request. Home: Newport, R.I. Died June 10, 1912.

EVERHART, JAMES BOWEN congressman, lawyer; b. nr. West Chester, pa., July 26, 1821; s. William Everhart; grad. Princeton, 1842; studied law Harvard, also in Phila.; attended univs. Berlin (Germany) and Edinburgh (Scotland), 2 years. Admitted to bar, 1845; began practice of law, West Chester, circa 1847; served to maj. Co. B, 10th Regt., Pa. Militia, 1862-63; mem. Pa. Senate, 1876-82; mem. U.S. Ho. of Reps. (Republican) from Pa., 48th-49th congresses, 1883-87. Died West Chester, Aug. 23, 1888; buried Oakland Cemetery, nr. West Chester.

EVERHART, WILLIAM congressman; b. Chester County, Pa., May 17, 1785; attended common schs.; married, at least 1 son, James Bowen. Became a civil engr.; served as capt. co. of riflemen in War of 1812; the only passenger saved from shipwreck of Albion, off coast of Ireland, 1822; plotted large addition to City of West Chester (Pa.), after 1822; mem. U.S. Ho. of Reps. (Whig) from Pa., 33d Congress, 1853-55; engaged in business. Died West Chester, Oct. 30, 1868; buried Oakland Cemetery.

EVERSON, WILLIAM GRAHAM clergyman; b. Wooster, Ohio; the son of Jacob Monroe and Annie Louise (Riddell) Everson; A.B., Franklin (Ind.) Coll., 1903; D.D., 1931; B.D., Newton Theol. Instrn., 1908; spl. work, Baylor U. and Harvard; m. Mary Coon (A.B., Franklin), Aug. 31, 1904; children-John David, Mary Louise. Ordained Bapt. ministry, July 18, 1901; pastor Morgantown and Lewis Creek, Ind., 1901-03, First Ch., Columbus, Ind., 1903-05, Glendale Sq., Boston, 1905-08, College Av. Ch., Indianapolis, 1908-11. First Ch., Newport, Ky., 1911-13, Fourth Av. Ch., Louisville, Ky., 1913-15, Norwood Ch., Cincinnati, 1915-21, First Ch., Muncie, Ind., 1921-29, pastor emeritus, 1929-31; pastor First Bapt. Ch. Denver, 1931-32, First Ch., "The White Temple," Portland, Ore., 1932-39; pres. Linfield College, McMinnville, Ore., 1939-43; chmn. advisory com., Shriners Hospital for Crippled Children, Portland, Ore., 1944-47; exec. sec. Ore. Heart Assn., Inc., Portland, 1947—. In Spanish-American and World Wars, in France, Italy, Austria, Dalmatia, Serbia and Mfontenegro; commander only American sector in Italy and all U.S. troops east of Adriatic Sea; rep., United States in Fiume and supervised investigations and food distribution in Austria and Serbia after armistice; hon. disch. with rank of col. June 1919; promoted brig. gen. res., July 1922, and comd. 76th Inf. Brig.; maj. gen., U.S. Army, chief Nat. Guard Bur., 1929-31. Citations and decorations from Eng., France, Italy, Fiume, Serbia, U.S. and three battle clasps. Grad. Command and Gen. Staff School at Ft. Leavenworth, Kan. and Grad. Army War College, Washington, D.C.; retired January 19, 1945 with rank of major general, Chautauqua and Lyceum lecturer, 1919—; mem. Nat. Speakers' Bur. of Am. Legion; nat. chaplain Mil. Order Foreign Wars, 1923-26; past dept. chaplain United Spanish War Vets.; chaplain Am. Legion, 1923-24; past grand chaplain Ind. Masons; chairman Ore. Alien Enemy Hearing Bd. Life mem. Boston Ministerial Association. Member International Lyceum and Chautauqua Association International Law Enforcement Officials, American Legion, United Spanish War Vets., Mil. Order of World Wars. Mil. Order of Fgn. Wars, Army-Navy Union. Scabbard and Blade, Purple Heart, Sigma Alpha Epsilon, Pi Gamma Mu, Phi Kappa Gamma, Pi Kappa Delta. Republican. Baptist. Mason. (32ff, K.T., Shriner, Red Cross of

Constantine). Rotarian. Author: Twenty Outline Studies of the New Testament, 1921; World War and Peace Potentialties, 1924, The Challenge of the Impossible, 1926; The Great Obstacle to World Peace, 1927; Forever As the Stars, 1932; Some Trails of Challenge, 1933. Contbr. on religious, health, peace and other subjects. Honorary life mem. Ind. State Police. Has traveled over 237,000 miles in 18 countries by airplane. Home: 3715 S.E. Tolman St., Portland 2, Ore. Died Sept. 3, 1954; buried Riverview Abbey, Portland.

EVINS, JOHN HAMILTON congressman; b. Spartanburg Dist., S.C., July 18, 1830; grad. S.C. Coll. at Columbia, 1853; studied law. Admitted to bar, 1856, began practice of law, Spartanburg; served from lt. to lt. col. Confederate Army during Civil War; mem. S.C. Ho. of Reps., 1863-64; del. Democratic Nat. Conv., St. Louis, 1876; mem. U.S. Ho. of Reps. (Democrat) from S.C., 45th-48th congresses, 1877-84. Died Spartanburg, Oct. 20, 1884; buried Magnolia Street Cemetery.

EWELL, ARTHUR WOOLSEY, physicist; b. Bradford, Mass., Oct. 20, 1873; s. John Lewis and Emily Spofford (Hall) E.; A.B., Yale, 1897, Ph.D., 1899; studied Johns Hopkins, 1899-1900, U. of Berlin, 1904, Radium Inst., Paris, 1924; hon. D. Sc., Worcester Polytechnic Inst., 1946; m. Jane Dodge Estabrook, Sept. 6, 1905; children—Milicent, Jane Estabrook, John Woolsey. Asst. in physics, Yale, 1897-99; instr. physics, 1900-04, asst. prof., 1904-10, prof. since 1910, dir. of physics and gen. science depts., 1935 to retirement 1938, Worcester (Mass.) Poly. Inst.; trustee Bancroft School, Worcester, Mass., 1915-18, treasurer, 1918-28, president, 1928-30; lecturer Massachusetts Institute of Technology; member research staff Westinghouse Electric Mfg. Co., Bloomfield, N.J.; cold storage engr. Dir. Worcester Airport, Am. Soc. Refrigeration Engrs. Trustee Worcester County Instn. for Savings; v.p. board of Gov. Dummer Acad. Capt. U.S.R., Dec. 15, 1917; head of bomb unit, Air Service, A.E.F., after armistice, in charge expt. development and tests of bombs, until May 1, 1919; lt. col. O.R.C.; apptd. spl. aerial bomb expert War Dept., Nov. 1919. Fellow Am. Acad. Arts and Sciences, Am. Physical Soc. (hon. life mem.); mem. American Society Refrigeration Engineers (dir.; hon. member 1945), French Physical Soc., Newcomen Soc. of England, Am. Legion (past comdr. Devens Post), Phi Beta Kappa, Sigma Xi. Episcopalian. Democrat. Clubs: Century, Yale (New York); Myopia Hunt, Worcester, Worcester Fire Society, St. Wulstan. Author: Physical Chemistry, 1909; Physical Measurements, 1910, 1913; numerous papers upon artifical rotatory polarization, magnetic double refraction, aerial bombs and bombing, electrolytic electrode potentials, properties of gases and vapors, refrigeration, ozone, ultra-violet light, food preservation, etc. Mem. editorial staff Refrigeration Data Book, 1940, 1945. Home: Rowley, Mass. Address: 55 Jackson St., Worcester 8 MA

EWELL, RICHARD STODDERT army officer; b. Georgetown, D.C., Feb. 8, 1817; s. Dr. Thomas and Elizabeth (Stoddert) E.; grad. U.S. Mil. Acad., 1840; m. Leczinska Campbell, 1865. Served in battles of Verz Cruz, Cerro Gordo, Contreras, Churubusco, Molena del Ray, Chapultepec during Mexican War, 1846-48; commd. capt., 1849; participated in Gila and Pinal Apache expdns., 1857-59; commd. col. Confederate Army, brig. gen., 1861, commanded div. in Battle of Blackburn's Ford, promoted maj. gen., 1861; served under Gen. Thomas (Stonewall) Jackson, 1862, in battles of Ft. Royal, Cross Keys, Cedar Mountain, Bull Run; commd. lt. gen., 1863, led 2d Corps at capture of Winchester, battles of Gettysburg, Wilderness, Spotsville Courthouse, 1864; given command defenses of Richmond; considered one of the great Confederate gens. Died Spring Hill, Tenn., Jan. 25, 1872.

EWEN, EDWARD C. naval officer; b. Portsmouth, N.H., May 26, 1897; s. George Swenson and Jessie (Coots) E.; student Tilton (N.H.) Acad., 1914-15; grad. U.S. Naval Acad., 1921, post-grad. 1929-32; m. Elizabeth R. Livingston, Sept. 5, 1923. Commd. ensign, USN, 1921, advanced through grades to rear adm., 1945; in naval aviation service 1924—; comd. U.S.S. Breton, 1943, U.S.S. Independence, 1944; became chief Naval Air Res. Tng., 1946; apptd. comdr. U.S. 1st Carrier Fleet in Pacific, 1950; ret. Decorated Navy Cross. Legion of Merit with gold star, Bronze Star Medal. Commendation Ribbon. Clubs: Chevy Chase, Army and Navy (Washington); Chicago, University (Chgo.); Glen View (Ill.); Onwentsia (Lake Forest, Ill.); Indian Hill (Winnetka, Ill.). Died Aug. 1959.

EWERS, EZRA PHILETUS brig. gen. U.S. Army; b. Wayneport, N.Y., Apr. 13, 1837. Pvt., sergt. and 1st sergt. Co. E, 1st Battalion, 19th Inf., Jan. 18, 1862-Dec. 4, 1863; commd. 2d lt., 19th Inf., Oct. 31, 1863; 1st lt., Mar. 16, 1864; transferred to 37th Inf., Sept. 21, 1866; capt., Sept. 12, 1866; transferred to 5th Inf., May 19, 1869; maj., 9th Inf., Mar. 7, 1893; lt. col., Apr. 30, 1897; brig. gen. vols., July 12, 1898; hon. disch. from vol. service, Apr. 20, 1899; col. 10th U.S. Inf., May 16, 1899; retired by operation of law, Apr. 13, 1901; advanced to rank of brig. gen. retired, by act of Apr. 23, 1904. Bvtd. 1st lt., June 26, 1863, for action at Hoovers Gap, Tenn.; capt., Nov. 25, 1863, for battle of Chattanooga, Tenn.; maj., Feb. 27, 1890, for action against Indians at Tongue River, Mont., Jan. 8, 1877. Died Jan. 16, 1912.

EWING, CHARLES lawyer, army officer; b. Lancaster, Co., Mar. 6, 1835; s. Thomas and Maria Ewing; attended Dominican and Gonzaga colls. Began practice of law, St. Louis, 1860; served as capt. 13th Inf., U.S. Army at beginning of Civil War, served in Ark. and Miss. campaigns; wounded 3 times at Vicksburg; promoted lt. col.; joined Gen. Sherman (his brother-in-law) on march through Ga.; promoted brig. gen., cited for gallantry at Vicksburg and Atlanta; returned to practice of law, 1867; became Indian commr., 1873. Died Washington, D.C., June 20, 1883.

EWING, FAYETTE CLAY otolaryngologist; b. Ariel Plantation, LaFourche Parish, La., May 28, 1862: s. Fayette Clay (M.D.) and Eliza Josephine (Kitredge) E.; ed. U. of the South and U. of Miss.; M.D., Jefferson Med. Coll., Phila., 1884; certificates of internship from several eye, ear, nose and throat hosps., London and N.Y. City; m. Martha Macdonald, 1885 (dec.); children-Fayette Clay (dec.), Ephraim Macdonald (dec.), Presley K., Donald Macdonald; m. 2d, Rowena Annette Clarke, 1924. Practiced gen. medicine, Washington, D.C., 1885-93; specialist in ear, nose and throat, St. Louis, 1896-1918; retired to enter U.S. Army, 1917; one of founders Am. Acad. Ophthalmology and Otolaryngology, 1896 (gen. sec., 1900); fellow A.C.S. (only living founder), Royal Soc. Medicine (Great Britain); mem. Am. Medical Association Command major, M.R.C., United States Army, January 7, 1918; served as chief of ophthalmology and otolaryngology dept., U.S. Rehabilitation Hosp. U.S.P.H.S., Camp Beauregard, 1919-27; now maj. inactive, M.R.C. Awarded Honor Scroll by Jefferson Med. Coll. Alumni, 1947; Golden medal from U. of the South, 1952. Del. of A.M.A. to Internat. Med. Congress, Rome, 1893; del. from Am. Acad. Ophthalmology and Otolaryngology to Internat. Ear Congress, London, 1899; selected by the Congress as sole speaker to rep. U.S. at internat. banquet, London, 1896. Mem. Sons of Revolution (through Gen. Robt. Ewing, Ky.); charter mem. U. Miss. chpt. Beta Theta Pi, only living founder; past pres. Beta Theta Pi Alumni Soc. of St. Louis; hon. mem. Rapides Parish Med. Soc. (past president); past pres. 8th Dist. Med. Soc. La.; former trustee U. of the South; joint-founder (1900) Scottish Terrier Club of Am. (hon. pres.): oldest Scottish Terrier breeder and promoter that ever lived; est. internationally known Nosegay Kennels, 1897: hon. pres. Scottish Terrier Club of Scotland (est. 1888), only American so honored; author of The Book of the Scottish Terrier (standard book of the breed in Britain and Am.): known as "the Father of Scottish Terriers in America," and "Dean of the Fancy"; hon. mem. various nat. canine clubs. Author: Hamlet, an Analytic and Psychologic Study, 1934; also author Shakespearean papers; lecturer on Shakespearean drama and Brit. and Am. poetry; world traveler. Formerly abstract editor of Laryngoscope and The Eye, Ear, Nose and Throat Monthly; contbr. to scientific jours. Democrat. Episcopalian. Home: "Nosegay." Pineville, La. Died Apr. 15, 1956.

EWING, HUGH BOYLE soldier, lawyer; b. Lancaster, O., Oct. 31, 1826; s. Thomas E.; ed. by private tutor and at U.S. Mil. Acad.; went to Calif., 1849, on expdn. sent by his father (then Sec. of the Interior) to the high Sierras to rescue emigrants from snows; returned, 1852. Practiced law, St. Louis, 1854-56, Leavenworth, Kan., 1856-58; in charge of salt works in Ohio, 1858-61; m. Henrietta Young, 1858. Served through war, 1861-65, maj. to brig. gen., and bvt. maj. Gen.; comd. brigade at Antietam and Vicksburg, and a division at Chickamauga, U.S. minister to The Hague, 1866-70; retired. Home: Lancaster, O. Died 1905.

EWING JAMES army officer, legislator; b. Lancaster County, Pa., Aug. 3, 1736; s. Thomas and Susanna (Howard) E.; m. Patience Wright. Served as lt. Pa. Militia during French and Indian War, 1758; mem. Pa. Gen. Assembly, 1771-75; apptd. brig. gen. Pa. Militia, 1776; v.p. Pa., 1782-84; mem. Pa. Senate, 1795-99; trustee Dickinson Coll., 1783-1806. Died Hellam, Pa., Mar. 1, 1806.

EWING, JOHN congressman; b. Cork, Ireland, May 19, 1789; came (with parents) to U.S.; attended public schs. Engaged in comml. pursuits, Vincennes, Ind., 1813; founded Wabash Telegraph; asso. justice Knox County Circuit Ct., 1816-20; apptd. lt. col. Ind. Militia, 1825; mem. Ind. Senate, 1825-33, 42-44; mem. U.S. Ho. of Reps. (Whig) from Ind., 23d, 25th congresses, 1833-35, 37-39. Died Vincennes, Apr. 6, 1858; buried City Cemetery.

EWING, JOHN DUNBRACK editor, publisher; b. New Orleans, La., Feb. 3, 1892; s. Robert and May (Dunbrack) E.; B.S., Va. Mil. Inst., 1913 (capt. basket ball team); m. Helen Hamilton Gray, Dec. 27, 1919; children-Helen May, John D. Circulation mgr. New Orleans States, 1913-15; asst. gen. mgr. Shreveport Times, 1915-17, asst. pub., 1919-31; pub. New Orleans States, 1931-33; pub. and editor Shreveport Times and News-Star-World, Monroe, La., since 1931; co-founder Monroe World, 1929; pres. radio stations KTBS and KWKH since 1934; trustee and pres. Ewing Estate since 1931. Capt. Inf. 32d Div., 1917-19. Awarded Croix de Guerre with Star, 1918, Purple Heart. Pres. Southern Newspaper Pub. Assn., 1938-39, chmn. bd. 1939; dir. K.C.S. and L.&A. Railroads; mem. American Legion (dept. comdr., 1921; chmn. bd. Am. Legion Monthly), Sigma Nu, Democrat. Episcopalian (vestryman). Mason (K.T., Shriner). Clubs: Boston (New Orleans): Shreveport Golf and Country: Augusta (Ga.) Masters; Deepdale (L.I.). Home: 910 Ockley Drive. Office: 408 Marshall St., Shreveport, La. Died May 17, 1952.

EWING, THOMAS army officer. congressman; b. Lancaster, O., Aug. 7, 1829; s. Thomas and Maria (Boyle) E.; ed. Brown U., A.M. (hon.); LL.D. (hon.), Georgetown (D.C.) Coll., 1870; m. Ellen Cox, Jan. 8, 1856. Pvt. sec. to Pres. U.S., 1848-50; leader of anti-Lecompton Constn. forces in Kan.; rep. from Kan. to Peace Conv., Washington, D.C., 1861; 1st chief justice Kan. Supreme Ct., 1861-62; commd. col. 11th Kan. Volunteers, 1862, served in battles of Ft. Wayne, Cane Hill and Prairie Grove; promoted brig. gen., 1863, served in battles in Mo., 1864, held Ft. Davidson, Pilot Knob, Mo.; commanded Border dist., 1863-64; St. Louis dist., 1864; brevetted maj. gen., 1865; mem. Ohio Constl. Conv., 1873-74; mem. U.S. Ho. of Reps. from Ohio, 45th-46th congresses, 1877-81; unsuccessful candidate for gov. Ohio, 1879 founder, pres. Ohio Soc. N.Y.; trustee Ohio U., 1878-83; acting v.p. Cincinnati Law Coll., 1881. Died N.Y.C., Jan. 21, 1896.

EWING, WILLIAM LEE DAVIDSON senator; b. Paris, Ky., Aug. 31, 1795; studied law. Admitted to bar, began practice of law, Shawneetown, Ill.; apptd. by Pres. Monroe receiver of land office, Vandalia, Ill., 1820; served as brig. gen. Ill. Militia; served as col. "Spy Battalion" during Black Hawk War; clk. Ill. Ho. of Reps., 1826-28, 42, mem., speaker, 1830, 38, 40; mem. Ill. Senate, 1832-34, pres. pro tem, 1832; commd. acting lt. gov., 1833; became gov. Ill. for 15 days, 1834; mem. U.S. Senate (Jackson Democrat, filled vacancy), Dec. 30, 1835-37; apptd. auditor public accounts, 1843. Died Vandalia, Mar. 25, 1846; buried Oak Ridge Cemetery, Springfield, Ill.

EXALL, HENRY agriculturist b. Richmond, Va., Aug. 30, 1848; s. Rev. George G. and Angeline (Pierce) E.; ed. in father's pvt. sch.; twice married; m. 2d, May Dickson, Nov. 1887. Served in 10th Va. Cav., C.S.A., spring 1863, to close of war; went to Ky., 1869, to Tex., 1877; del. New Orleans Cotton Expn., 1884; col. and q.-m. Texas state troops, 1884-85; del. Dem. Nat. Conv., 1884; chmn. Dem. State Exec. Com., Tex., 1886-88; del. New York centennial of inauguration of first president, 1889; pres. Texas State Fair, 1889; commr.-at-large Chicago Expn., 1893; pres. Texas Indsl. Congress. Engaged in breeding fine horses and in farming. Home: Dallas, Tex. Died Dec. 29, 1913.

EYANSON, CHARLES LOUIS industrialist; b. Spokane, Wash., Sept. 15, 1892; s. Charles Joseph and Margaret (Kanaley) E.; B.S. in Engring., U. of Pa. 1916; m. Mary Clugston Harrison, Apr. 6, 1920; 1 dau., Mary Lou Reid. Prof. in English and civics, South Phila. Night Sch., 1915-16; prof. engring. adminstrn., Drexel Inst., 1919-20; chief of field staff industrial survey of U.S. by Technology Clubs Associated, 1920; dir. extension dept. Drexel Inst., 1920-22, also mem. adminstrn. bd. of three; sec. gen. The Council of Management Edn.; dean Engring. Economics Foundation since 1923; sec., exec. dir. and asst. treas. Mfrs. Assn. of Conn., 1922-46; president Naugatuck Valley Indsl. Council, 1946 - ; chmn. Naugatuck Valley River Control Commn., 1955 —. Trustee Waterbury, Conn. Community Work Shop. Mem. New England Traffic League, National Industrial Traffic League, N.E. Shippers' Advisory Bd., Conn. Agrl. Soc. Mem. Ind. State Bar. Served in World War as chief of staff Production Engring. Sect. of Council Nat. Defense, 1916-17; attached to Royal Air Force, 1917-19, serving in Eng., Scotland and France; organized and operated school for aero mechanics; assigned to U.S. Air Service, 1919; hon. disch., Mar. 18, 1919; served as clerk of com. on territories and insular possessions of the U.S. Senate, 1929. Fellow Royal Soc. of Arts; mem. Newcomen Soc. of England, Am. Acad. of Polit. and Social Science, Sons of Am. Revolution, Vets. Fgn. Wars, Am. Legion, Theta Delta Chi. Clubs: Engineers, Waterbury (Waterbury, Conn.); Graduate (New Haven); Hartford, University, (Hartford). Author: Old Age Dependency in Connecticut, Unemployment and Its Problems. Contbr. to trade publs. Home: Old South Rd., Litchfield, Conn. Office: 1 Central Av., Waterbury, Conn. Died Nov. 20, 1959; buried Litchfield.

EYSTER, GEORGE SENSENY army officer; b. Halltown, W.Va., Aug. 8, 1895; B.S., U.S. Mil. Acad., 1917; grad. Signal Sch., 1928. Inf. Sch., 1932. F.A. Sch. 1933, Chem. Warfare Sch., field officers course, 1937. Command and Gen. Staff Sch., 1938. Commd. 2d lt., inf., U.S. Army, 1917, and advanced through the grades to brig. gen., 1944; in charge def. housing sect., Fed. Works Adminstrn. Br., G-4, War Dept. Gen. Staff, Washington, 1940-42; chief, later exec. officer, unit tng. br., tng. div., Services of Supply, Washington, 1940-42; chief, later exec. officer, unit tng. br., tng. div., Services of Supply, Washington, 1942-43; chief staff, 76th Inf. Div., Ft. George G. Meade, Md., Jan.-Aug. 1943; became chief, operations br., G-3 sect., Hdqrs. European Theater Operations, Aug. 1943. Home: 3900 Connecticut Av. N.W. Address: care The Adjutant General's Office, War Dept., Washington 25. Died Mar. 9, 1951.*

FABING, HOWARD DOUGLAS, physician; b. Cin., Feb. 21, 1907; s. Henry Charles and Jessie (Ammann) F.; A.B., U. Cin., 1927, M.D., 1931; m. Esther Clare Marting, Dec. 16, 1939; children—Suzannah Jane, Priscilla Ruth, Howard William. Rotating intern Cin. Gen. Hosp., 1931-32, resident neurology, 1932-33; pvt. practice psychiatry and neurology, 1936-70; faculty physiology and neurology dept. U. Cin., 1936-42. Served from maj. to lt. col. M.C., AUS, 1942-46; neurologist Walter Reed Hosp.; chief neuropsychiatry Finney Gen. Hosp.; dir. sch. and standardized treatment combat fatigue ETO; research cerebral blast concussion; chief neurology div. VA, Washington, 1945-46; cons. Surg. Gen. U.S. Army, Korea, 1950. Decorated Legion of Merit. Mem. Am. League Against Epilepsy (chmn. legislation com.), Nat. Multiple Sclerosis Soc. (med. adv. bd.), Am. Neurological Assn., Am. Psychiat. Assn., Assn. Research Nervous and Mental Disease (member Commission 1957) Electroshock Research Assn., Cin. soc. Neurology and Psychiatry (pres. 1941), Ohio Med. Assn. (chmn. sect. nervous and mental diseases 1942), Am. Acad. Neurology (pres. 1953-55), Soc. Biol. Psychiatry (pres. 1955-56), Cin. Acad. Medicine (pres. 1956-57). Author: Fischerisms (rev. edit.), 1956; Epilepsy and the Law (with Roscoe Barrow), 1956. Author sci. papers. Home: Cincinnati OH Died July 29, 1970.

FADDIS, CHARLES I., ex-congressman; b. Loudenville, O., June 13, 1890; s. Samuel C. and Edna (Moredock) F.; student Waynesburg (Pa.) Coll., 1909-11; B.S., Pa. State Coll., 1915; grad. Gen. Staff and Command Sch., Ft. Leavenworth, Kan., 1930; m. Jane Morris, Dec. 1, 1917; children—William George, James M., Edna G., Laura Lucille. In gen. contracting business, Waynesburg, Pa., 1919-26; broker of oil and gas properties, 1926-72. Served as pvt. Pa. Inf., Mexican border, 1916; capt. and lt. col., inf., U.S. Army, World War; in major offensives and occupation of Germany; with O.R.C. since 1924; commd. col., 1930. Citation by Gen. Pershing; awarded Purple Heart. Mem. 73d to 77th Congresses (1933-43), 25th Pa. Dist. Mem. Am. Legion, Vets. of Foreign Wars, B.P.O.E. Democrat. Home: Waynesburg PA Died Apr. 1972.

FAGAN, JAMES FLEMING army officer; b. Clarke County, Ky., Mar. 1, 1828; s. Steven and Kittie (Stevens) F.; m. Mura Ellisiff Beal, 3 children; m. 2d, Lizzy Rapley, 5 children. Mem. Ark. Legislature (Whig) 1 term; served in Gen. Archibald Yell's regt. during Mexican War, discharged with rank of lt.; receiver Ark. State Bank, 1856-57; raised troops, became col. 1st Ark. Infantry at outbreak of Civil War; after battle of Shiloh promoted brig. gen., 1862; transferred to Trans-Miss. Dept., took part in Battle of Prairie Grove, defense of Ark. and repluse of Frederick Steele's Camden expdn.; promoted maj. gen.; did not surrender until 1865; apptd. U.S. marshall of Western dist. at Ft. Smith by Pres. Ulysses S. Grant, 1875; became receiver for Land Office, Little Rock, Ark., 1877. Died Sept. 1, 1893.

FAGAN, WILLIAM LONG farmer; b. Wetumpka, Ala., Nov. 20, 1838; s. Enoch F.; A.M., Howard Coll.; m. Annie E. Avery, Nov. 30, 1874. Capt., C.S.A., 1861-65; surrendered co. of 65 (Co K, 8th Ala. inf.), probably the largest co. in Lee's army, at Appomattox C. H.; contbr. numerous articles to various jours. Compiler Southern War Songs. Address: Havana, Ala. Died May 27, 1914; buried Havana, Ala.

FAGES, PEDRO Mexican gov. Cal.; flourished 1767-96; m. Eulalia Callis, 2 children. Served as lt. 1st Bn., 2d Regt. Catalonia Volunteers (Mexico), promoted lt. col., later capt., 1771; discovered present location of San Francisco; appt. Mexican gov. of Cal., 1782. Died 1796.

FAGLEY, FREDERICK LOUIS clergyman; b. Bethel, O., May 8, 1879; s. Wallace Clark and Fannie (Brown) F.; student U. of Cincinnati, 1903-04; A.B., Evansville (Ind.) Coll., 1905, D.D., 1916; A.M., Oberlin Coll., 1910, D.D., 1948; B.D., Oberlin Theol. Sem., 1911; student Cambridge, summer, 1937: m. Hortense Martin, June 30, 1909; children-Richard Martin, Frances Joan (Mrs. Wm. A. Coury), Robert Earle. Prof. philosophy of edn., Moores Hill Coll., 1905-08; pastor Plymouth Congl. ch., Cincinnati, O., 1911-14; exec. sec. Cincinnati Federation of Chs., 1914-18; exec. sec. Commn. on Evangelism of the Congl. Chs., 1919-22; asso. sec. Nat. Council Congl. Chs., 1922-31; asso. sec. Gen. Nat. Council Congl. Chs., 1922-31; asso. sec. Gen. Council Congl.-Christian Chs., 1931-48, emeritus: exec. sec. Am. Com. Internat. Congl. Council, 1937; dir. German exchange projects Nat. Council Chs. of Christ; mem. exec. com. Fed. Council of Chs. of Christ in Am. (chmn. advisory com., 1945-47), General Commission Army and Navy Chaplains (vice chmn., 1945-47), Commission for Camp and Defense chmn., (1945-47), Commission for Camp and Defense Communities, Service Men's Christian League (vice chmn., 1945-47); chmn. Nat. Committee on Army and Navy Chaplains. Dudliean lectr. Harvard, 1951-52. Citation meritorious service, U.S. Army and USN, 1952. Sec. Congl. Christian Hist. Soc., 1951, Mem. am. Fern Society (past president). Clubs: New England Botanical, Quill (president 1950-51), National Arts (sec., 1948-51). Author: Parish Evangelism, 1923; The Congressional Churches, 1926: Your Church and You, 1928; Handbook on Teaching Religion, 1933; A Little Handook on Adult Education, 1935; An Outline of Church History, 1935; The Religions of Mankind, 1936: A Guide to the Christian Year, 1937; History of American Congregationalism (wigh G. G. Atkins), 1942; History of Congregational Christian Chs., 1956. Home: 60 Gramercy Park, N.Y.C. 10; also Sunapee, N.H. Office: 289 Fourth Av., N.Y.C. 10. Died Aug. 25, 1958.

FAILLA, GIOACCHINO physicist; b. Italy, July 19, 1891; s. Nicolo and Sara (Spoleti) F.; brought to U.S., 1906, naturalized, 1916; E.E., Columbia, 1915, M.A., 1917; D.Sc., U. Paris, 1923; D.Sc. (hon.), University of Rochester, 1949; m. Marie Muller, June 9, 1925 (dec. 1936); children - Marie Louise (Mrs. J. D. Campbell), Evelyn Sara (Mrs. Robert Kent Rockhill); married second Patricia McClement, Jan. 22, 1949. Physicist, establishing physics and biophysics lab. Memorial Hosp., N.Y. City, 1915-42; prof. Coll. Phys. and Surgeons, Columbia, 1943-60, emeritus prof., 1960 - ; sr. physicist (emeritus) Argonne Nat. Lab., Argonne, Ill., 1960 - ; asst. to sci. attache Am. Embassy, Rome, 1918-19; consultant, metall. lab. U. Chicago, 1943-46, Argonne Nat. Lab. 1946-60, Los Almos Sci. Lab., 1947-48, Brookhaven Nat. Lab., 1947-57, Nuclear Engine Propulsion Aircraft Project, 1948-50; member council physical therapy A.M.A., 1941-48, U.S.P.H.S., U.S. V.S since 1942; chief biophysics br., div. biology and medicine A.E.C., 1948, mem. adv. com. biology and medicine, 1951-57, chmn., 1955-57; mem. Nat. Def. Research Com., 1942-45, radiobiology panel, com. growth. Nat. Research Council, 1945-47, subcom. human applications, chmn. Adv. com. isotope distbn., 1947-50; mem. exec. com., chmn. subcom. external radiation, Nat. Com. Radiation Protection, 1946-57; chmn. radiol. instrument panel Armed Forces Spl. Weapons Project, 1948 - . Ofcl. rev. Am. Phys. Soc. to 1st Congress Radiology London, 1925; Am. P Radium Soc. del. to 4th Internat. Congress Radiology Zurich, Switzerland, 1934; chmn. radiophysics sect., hon. chmn. internat. com. radiol. units 5th Internat. Congress Radiology, Chicago, 1937; v.p. emeritus 6th Internat. Congresses Radiology, London, 1950, Copenhagen, 1953, Mexico City, 1956; chairman of biophysics sect. Internat. Cancer Congress, Atlantic City, 1939; chmn. subcom. external radiation Internat. Commn. Radiol. Protection; hon. mem. Brit. Inst. Radiology, Internat. Joint Com. Radiobiology 1950-56. Awarded Pulitzer Scholarship, 1911-15; Leonard prize Am. Roentgen Ray Soc., 1923, 25, Caldwell medal, 1945; Am. Radium Soc., 1939; Gold medal, Radiol. Soc. N.A., 1947; National award Am. Cancer Society, 1956; Ewing Soc. honorary lecture medal, 1961. Fellow A.A.A.S., Am. Phys. Soc.; mem. Optical Soc. Am., N.Y. Acad. Scis., Am. Radium Soc., Am. Roentgen Ray Soc., Radiol. Soc. N.A., Harvey Soc., Corp. Marine Biological Laboratory (trustee), Radiation Research Soc. (president 1954), Internat. Congress Radiation Research, Burlington, Vt., 1958 (organizing com.), Gerontological Soc., Sigma Xi. Author articles in sci. jours. Home: 575 Warren Terrace, Hinsdale, Ill. Office: Radiological Physics Division, Argonne Nat. Lab., Argonne, Ill. Died Dec. 15, 1961.

FAIRBANK, HERBERT SINCLAIR, highway engrineer; b. Baltimore, Md., Sept. 16, 1888; s. Charles Alexander and Sarah Sherwood (Sinclair) F.; C.E., Cornell U., 1910; unmarried. Civil engr. student U.S. Bureau of Mines, Sept.-Nov. 1910; with U.S. Office Pub. Roads since 1910, as civil engr. student, 1910-11, asst., then speaker on Good Roads Trains operated over rys. of South and West, 1912-13, object lesson road building highway research, etc., 1911-17, editor "Public Roads" mag., 1920-27, chief div. of information, 1927, dir. statewide highway planning surveys, U.S. Bur. Pub. Roads in cooperation with highway depts. of 48 states, 1935-43, dep. commr., 1943-55. Chmn. dept. of econs., finance and adminstrn., Hwy Research Bd., Nat. Research Council, 1944-56, mem. com. econs. of size and weight motor vehicles, 1956 - , exec. com., 1959-62. Aternate mem. Pres.'s Sci. Research Bd., 1946. Aide to sec.-gen. Internat. Road Congress, Washington, 1930, del. U.S. Govt., Munich, 1934; v. chmn. U.S. delegation United Nations Conference on Road and Motor Transport, Geneva, 1949. Served as 1st lieut., later capt., Chem. Warfare Service, U.S. Army, 1918-19. Received George S. Bartlett Award for outstanding contribution to highway progress, 1947; Dept. of Commerce award for Exceptional Service, 1949; Roy W. Crum award in highway research, 1953; Thomas H. MacDonald award, 1957. Member Tau Beta Pi. Presbyn. Home: 2041 E. 32d St., Baltimore 21218. Died Dec. 14, 1962; buried Green Mount Cemetery, Balt.

FAIRBANK, LEIGH COLE army officer; b. Genesee County, Mich., Nov. 14, 1889; s. George Kirtland and Abbie (Covert) F.; student Detroit Coll. Medicine, 1908-09; D.D.S., Georgetown U., 1912 Sc.D. (hon.), 1939; Dewey Sch., Orthodontia, 1921, Washington U., St. Louis, 1928, Army Dental Sch., 1934-35; hon. Sc.D., Washington U., 1941; m. May Romig, May 14, 1913; children - Leigh Cole, Justine Louise, Mary Alice. Private practice dentistry, Muskegon, Mich., 1912-14; entered Dental Corps, U.S. Army, as contract dentist, 1914; commd. 1st lt., 1916, advanced through grades to brig. gen., 1938 (first dental officer of U.S. Army to be raised to grad of gen.); brig. gen. asst., surgeon gen., 1938; ret., in grade in 1942. Decorated Palmes d'Officer d'Académie (France); Comdr. Order del Condor de los Andes (Bolivia); Officer Order of Honor and Merit (Haiti); Abdon Calderon (Ecuador); Mexican Border Medal, World War I, Def. medal. Am. Theatre Medal, Mem. Am. Dental Assn., Am. Assn. Orthodontists, Assn. Mil. Surgeons, N.Y. Acad. Denistry, Delta Sigma Delta, Omicron Kappa Upsilon; hon. mem. Southwestern Soc. Orthondontists, Detroit Dist., Indpls. Dist. dental socs., Phila. Acad. Stomatology. Episcopalian. Clubs: Army and Navy (Washington). Author and contbr. of text on oral surgery; contbr. to jours. Am. Assn. Orthodontists, Am. Dental Assn., The Mil. Surgeon. Home: R. 1, Vienna, Va. Address: 1726 I St. N.W., Washington D.C. Died June 28, 1966.

FAIRBANKS, WARREN CHARLES newspaper pub.; b. Indianapolis, Ind., Apr. 25, 1878; s. Charles Warren and Cornelia (Cole) F.; A.B., Ohio Wesleyan U., 1898; m. Ethel Cassidy, Jan 14, 1904; children-Edith Anne (wife of Count Ruggero Visconti di Modrone), Cornelia Warren (wife of Frederick A. Poole, Jr.). With Standard Mfg. Co., Springfield, O., 1898-1901, sec., 1898-1901; sec. Oliver Typewriter Co., Chicago, Ill., 1901-04; pres. and pub. Indianapolis News Publishing Co., Indianapolis, Ind., 1922-; president Indianapolis Switch & Frog Co.; director Pure Oil Company. State director President Hoover's Unemployment Relief. Capt. U.S. Vols., 1898. Trustee McKinley Nat. Memorial Assn., M.E. Hosp. (Indianapolis). Republican. Methodist. Home: Indianapolis, Ind. Died July 27, 1938.

FAIRCHILD, ARTHUR WILSON lawyer; b. Marinette, Wis., Dec. 11, 1876; s. Hiram Orlando and Emma (Hough) F.; B.L., U. of Wis., 1897, LL.B., 1901; m. Edith Hansen, Apr. 19, 1911; 1 dau., Edith Fairchild (Mrs. Arthur J. Frank). Admitted to Wis. bar, 1901, and began practice at Milwaukee; became asso. with firm Miller, Noyes & Miller, 1901, becoming partner, 1905; partner Miller, Mack & Fairchild, 1906-51. Fairchild, Foley & Sammond since 1951; dir. Nat. Rivet & Mfg. Co., T. A. Chapman Co., Square D Co., Mid-State Mfg. Co., Shaler Co., Graham Transmissions, Inc., Riverside Realty Co., Centric Corporatioon, Milwaukee Sanitarium, Kurth Malting Co., Dartwell Co., Fox Point Corporation. Special attorney Federal Trade Commission, Washington, Aug. 1-Oct. 15, 1917. Commd. maj. Ordnance Dept., U.S. Res., 1917; lt. col. Ordnance Dept., U.S. Army, 1918. Mem. Am., Wisconsin and Milwaukee bar assns., Phi Beta Kappa, Phi Delta Phi, Phi Delta Theta. Republican. Clubs: Milwaukee, Milwaukee Country, University, Milwaukee Athletic (Milwaukee); University (Chicago). Home: 2242 N. Lake Drive, Office: 735 N. Water St., Milw. 2. Died Aug. 2, 1956.

FAIRCHILD, LUCIUS gov. Wis., diplomat; b. Dec. 27, 1831; s. Jarius and Sally (Clair) F.; ed. Carroll Coll.; LL.D. (hon.), U. Wis., 1864; m. Frances Bull, Apr. 27, 1864, 3 children. Clk., Circuit Ct. of Dane County (Wis.), 1858; joined 1st Wis. Volunteer Regt., 1861; lt. col. in command 2d Wis. Volunteer Regt. at 2d Battle of Bull Run; commd. col., 1862; commd. brig. gen. U.S. Vols.; sec. State of Wis., 1863-64; gov. Wis., 1866-72; U.S. consul to Liverpool, Eng., 1872-78; U.S. consul gen. to Paris, France, 1878-80; state comdr. Grand Army Republic, 1886, became nat. comdr.-in-chief, 1886; a fed. commr. to settle Cherokee Indian affairs in Okla.; comdr.-in-chief Mil. Order Loyal Legion. Died Madison, Wis., May 23, 1896.

FAIRCHILD, MUIR STEPHEN air force officer; born in Bellingham, Washington, September 2, 1894; son of Harry Anson and Georgie Ann (Crockett) F.; student University of Washington, Seattle, Washington, 1913-17, Air Corps Engring. Sch., Dayton, O., 1928-29, Air Corps Tactical Sch., Montgomery, Ala., 1934-35, Army Industiral Coll., Washington, 1935-36, Army War Coll., Washington, 1936-37; m. Florence Alice Rossiler, Apr. 26, 1924; 1 dau., Betty Anne (Mrs. Ross Hamilton Calvert, Jr.). Commd. 2d lt., Aviation Sect., Signal Officers' Res. Corps, Jan. 1918; promoted through the grades to general, May 1948; mem. Joint Strategic Survey Com., Joint Chiefs of Staff, 1942-46; mem. U.S. del. Dumbarton Oaks Conf.; mil. advisor to U.S. del. Dumbarton Oaks Conf.; mil. advisor to U.S. del. San Francisco U.N. Conf.; became comdg. gen. The Air University, Maxwell Air Force Base, Alabama, January 1946; vice chief of staff United States Air Force, since May 1948. Awarded D.S.M., Legion of Merit, Distinguished Flying Cross, Purple Heart; Croix de Guerre (French); Italian War Medal; Order of Merit (Chile); Order of Condor of the Andes (Bolivia); Order of the Sun (Peru); Order of the Liberator (Venezuela).Mem. Kappa Sigma. Home: Fort Myer, Va. Address: Hdqrs. U.S. Air Force. Washington 25. Died Mar. 17, 1950.

FAIRFAX, DONALD MCNEILL naval officer; b. Va., Mar. 10, 1831; s. George William and Isabella (McNeill) F.; m. Josephine Foote. Apptd. Midshipman from N.C., U.S. Navy, 1837, promoted passed midshipman, 1843, lt., 1851; exec. officer ship San Jacinto, 1861; commanded ships Cayuga, 1862, Nantucket and Montauk, 1863; comdt. of midshipmen U.S. Naval Acad., 1864-65; in charge of ship Susquehanna, 1867; promoted commodore, 1873, comdt. Naval Sta., New London, Conn.; gov. Naval Asylum, New London; 1878; promoted rear adm., 1880. Died Hagerstown, Md., Jan. 10, 1894.

FAIRFIELD, ARTHUR PHILLIP, naval officer; b. Saco, Me., Oct. 29, 1877; s. Rufus Albert and Frances Mary (Patten) F.; student Thornton Acad., Saco, Me., 1892-1895; Bowdoin Coll., Brunswick, Me., 1895-97, hon. A.M., 1924; B.S., U.S. Naval Acad., 1901; m. Nancy Douglas Duval, June 14, 1906. Began as naval cadet, 1897; served as such in U.S.S. Columbia during Spanish-Am. War; advanced through the grades to rear adm., 1934; during World War comdr. U.S.S. McDougal and U.S.S. Gregory, later on staff Adm. Sims, Queenstown, Ireland; mem. Gen. Bd., Navy Dept., Washington, D.C., 1937-39; later comdr. Battleship Div. 3, U.S.S. Idaho, flagship; retired with rank of vice admiral November 1, 1941; in active service after retirement until Dec. 1946. Decorated Spanish-Am. War campaign badge. Victory medal, Navy Cross, Victory medal World War II (U.S.); Order of Crown of Leopold (Belgium), Order of St. Olaf (Norwegian); hon. comdr. Order Brit. Empire. Mem. Naval Inst., Delta Kappa Epsilon. Unitarian. Clubs: N.Y. Yacht, Ends of the Earth (N.Y. City); Army and Navy (Washington, D.C.); Wardroom (Boston). Home: 2400 16th St., N.W. Address: U.S. Maritime Commission, Commerce Bldg., Washington. Died Dec. 1946.

FAIRHURST, WILLIAM mfg. exec.; b. Paterson, N.J., Nov. 10, 1891; s. Joseph and Ida (Thompson) F.; grad. Peddle Sch., 1911; Ph.B., Yale, 1914; m. Josephine Milson, Oct. 22, 1919; children-William Milson, Thomas Johnston. Apprentice Packard Motor Car Co., Detroit, 1914-17; mgr. Detroit and N.Y. City offices Taft-Peirce Mfg. Co., Woonsocket, R.I., 1919-25: sales mgr. Spicer Mfg. Corp., Toledo, 1925-35: v.p. Dana Corp. (hdqrs. Spicer mfg. div.) since 1935. Mem. bd. corporators Peddle Sch. Served as capt., comdg. machine gun co., inf. U.S. Army, France and Germany, 1917-19. Mem. Soc. Automotive Engrs., Army Ordnance Assn., Sigma Chi. Episcopalian (vestryman 1943-50, sr. warden, 1949). Mason (32ff). Clubs: Yale (N.Y. City); Inverness, Toledo (Toledo); Athletic (Detroit). Home: 3759 Sulphur Spring Rd., Toledo 6, Office: 4100 Bennett Rd., Toledo 1. Died Oct. 2, 1953; buried Woodlawn Cemetery, Toledo.

FAISON, SAMSON LANE army officer; b. in N.C., Nov. 29, 1860; grad. U.S. Mil. Acad., June 13, 1883; Army War Coll., 1911. Commd. 2d lt. 1st Inf., June 13, 1883; promoted through grades to Col. Inf., Oct. 2, 1915; brig. gen. N.A., Aug. 5, 1917. Comd. company in engagement with Filipino insurgents, Guadaloupe Ridge, P.I., June 10, 1899; running engagement of 3 days with insurgents, Cavite to San Francisco de Malabon; served as judge Provost Court and judge adv. of Mil. Commn., Manila; mem. Gen. Court Martial at Manila, Apr.-May 1901; again in P.I., in command Camp Downs, Leyte, 1907-08; at Schofield Barracks, H.T., 1916, Brig. gen. N.A., Aug. 5, 1917, and assigned to comd. 60th Inf. Brig., 30th Div., Sept. 1917; comd. 30th Div., Dec. 22, 1917-July 20, 1918; comd. 60th Inf. Sept. 1917-Apr. 1919, when - it was demobilized. Reverted to reg. rank of col. U.S.A., July 15, 1919, comdg. 43d Inf., Camp Lee, Va. Took part in Canal Sector, Belgium, defensive, July and Aug. 1918; Ypres-Lys offensive, Aug. 31 and Sept. 1, 1918, and Somme offensive, Sept. 24-Oct. 20, 1918. Awarded D.S.M.; French Legion of Honor, with rank of Officer, and Croix de Guerre, with Palm. Died Oct. 17, 1940.

FALK, K. GEORGE chemist; b. N.Y. City, Sept. 8, 1880; s. Arnold and Fannie (Wallach) F.; B.S., Columbia, 1901; Johns Hopkins, 1901-03; Ph.D., Strasburg U., 1905; Berlin U., 1905-06; m. Dora Lichten, May 31, 1909; m. 2d, Carolyn Rosenstein, Oct. 16, 1935. Asst. in phys. chemistry, Columbia, 1906-07, tutor in physics, 1907-09; research asso. in phys. chemistry, Mass. Inst. Tech., 1909-11; chemist Harriman Research Lab., Roosevelt Hosp., New York, 1911-28, Harriman Research Fund, New York U., Med. Coll., 1929-31; biol. chemist, Bureau of Labs., Health Dept., N.Y. City, 1931-39; prof. chemical bacteriology in preventive medicine, New York U. Med. Coll., 1933-36: dir. Lab. of Industrial Hygiene, Inc., since 1936; also consultant for various chem. companies. Capt. Sanitary Corps, U.S. Army, 1918-19. Pres. Hebrew Tech. Inst. Mem. Am. Chem. Soc., Am. Pub. Health Assn. Am. Soc. Biol. Chemists, A.A.A.S., Soc. Exptl. Biology and Medicine, Harvey Soc., N.Y. Acad. Sciences, London Chem. Soc., Am. Assn. for Cancer Research, Am. Inst., Am. Inst. of Chemists, Sigma Xi, Phi Lambda Upsilon. Clubs: Chemists, Columbia, Harmonie. Author: Chemical Reactions, Their Theory and Mechanism, 1920; Chemistry of Enzyme Action, 1921, 2d edit., 1924; Catalytic Action, 1922. Contbr. to scientific jours. Home: 40 E. 66th St., N.Y. City 21. Office: 254 W. 31st St., N.Y.C. 1. Died Nov. 22, 1953; buried Ferncliff Cemetery, Hartsdale, N.Y.

FALK, MYRON SAMUEL cons. engr.; b. New York, N.Y., Sept. 13, 1878; s. Arnold and Fannie (Wallach) F.; C.E., Columbia, 1899. Ph.D., 1903; M.E., Stevens Inst. Tech., 1900; m. Milly Einstein, June 3, 1903 (died Nov. 9, 1915); children - Eleanor Arnold (Mrs. Joseph B. Lenzner), Myron Samuel, Mildred (Mrs. Edgar P. Loew). Successively tutor, instr., lecturer in civil engring., Columbia, 1900-10; mem. N.Y. Bay Pollution Commn., 1903-05; cons. engr. N.Y. State Water Supply Commn., 1905-08; chief engr. Godwin Constrn. Co., New York, 1905-30, H.H. Oddie, Inc., 1909-28; chmn. bd. dirs. Wonham, Bates & Goode Trading Corp., 1920-23; v.p. Am. Bemberg Corp., 1925-27. Served as major, later lt. col., Ordnance Dept. U.S. Army, 1918-19. Chmn. bd. trustees Lavanburg Found.; trustee Mount Sinai Hosp. Mem. Am. Soc. Civil Engrs., Am. Soc. Testing Materials. Clubs: Engineers, Columbia University, Harmonie (New York); Century Country (White Plains, N.Y.); Tamarack Country (Port Chester, N.Y.). Author: Cements, Mortars and Concretes, 1904; Graphic Method by Influence Lines for Bridge and Roof Computation (with Wm. H. Burr), 1908; Design and Construction of Metallic Bridges (with Wm. H. Burr), 1908. Address: King St., Greenwich, Conn. Died Nov. 26, 1945.

FALK, OTTO HERBERT soldier, mfr.; b. Milwaukee, June 18, 1865; s. Franz and Louise (Wahl) F.; ed. German-English Academy, Milwaukee; Northwestern Coll., Watertown, Wis.; grad. as capt., Allen Mil. Acad., Chicago, 1884; m. Elizabeth A. Vogel, Dec. 10, 1901; children—Mrs. Elizabeth Eberbach, Otto Herbert. Identified with financial interests of Falk family since beginning of active career, now v.p. The Falk Co., mfrs. steel castings; apptd. receiver Allis-Chalmers Co., 1912, and pres. Allis-Chalmers-Rumely, Ltd., Canada; director Harnischfeger Corporation, First Wis. Nat. Bank, First Wis. Trust Co., Wis. Telephone Co., etc. Chmn. bd. govs. Marquette U. Commd. adj. 4th Batt., Wis. N.G., Mar. 1886; col. and a.-d.-c. to Gov. Rusk, Aug. 1887; lt. col., comdg. 4th Inf., Oct. 1887; q.-m. gen., Jan. 1891; adj. gen., Dec. 1893; commd. maj. and chief q.-m. U.S. Vols., Spanish-Am. War, June 1898; assigned to 1st Div., 3d Army Corps, Chickamauga Park, Ga., apptd. chief q.m. 3d Army Corps, U.S. Army, Oct. 1898, services Cuba and Puerto Rico; hon. discharged from vol. service, June 20, 1899; col. comdg. 1st Regt. Inf., Wis. N.G., June 1899; transferred to gen. staff as chief engr., 1906; retired with rank of brig. gen., Jan. 1911; was in active duty in riots at Milwaukee, 1886, Ashland, 1893; Merrill, 1893, Spooner, 1894, Kenosha, 1909; in charge of relief expedition sent to give aid to starving miners in northern Wis. and Mich., winter of 1893. Dir. Milwaukee Assn. of Commerce (pres. 1909-12) Wis. Mfrs.' Assn. Presented with loving cup as "Milwaukee's foremost citizen," 1924. Home: Milwaukee, Wis. Died May 21, 1940.

FALL, BERNARD B. educator, author; b. Vienna, Austria, Nov. 19, 1926; s. Leon and Anne (Selignan) F.; French citizen; student U. Paris (France), 1948-49, U. Munich (Germany), 1949-50, U. Md., 1950-51, Johns Hopkins, 1952; M.A., Syracuse U., 1952, Ph.D., 1955; m. Dorothy Winer, Feb. 20, 1954; children - Nicole Francoise, Elisabeth Anne, Patricia Madeleine. War crimes research analyst during the Nurnberg Trials, 1946-48; search officer International Tracing Service, UN, 1949-50; asst. dist. mgr. Stars and Stripes, 1950-51; research asst. Cornell U., 1954-55; asst. prof. Am. U., 1955-56; asso. prof. Howard U., 1956-62, prof. internat. relations, 1962 - . Served with French Underground and Army, 1942-46. Decorated Medal Liberated France, 1955. Recipient Polk Journalism award, 1966; awarded Guggenheim fellowship, 1967. Member of the Association for Asian Studies, Am. Assn. U. Profs., Assn. Internat. de Sci. Politique, Am. Polit. Sci. Assn., Centre d'Etudes de Politique Etrangère, French War Vets. (pres. Washington chpt. 1966). Author: The Viet-Minh Regime, 1954; Le Viet-Minh, 1960; Street Without Joy: Indochina at War, 1961; Indochina 1946-62, 1962; The Two Viet-Nams, 1963; Viet-Nam Witness, 1966; Hell in a Very Small Place, 1966. Home: 4535 31st St. N.W., Washington 20008. Died Feb. 21, 1967; buried Rock Creek Cemetery, Washington.

FALLIGANT, ROBERT judge of Superior Court of Eastern jud. circuit of Ga., 1889—; b. Savannah, Ga., Jan. 12, 1839; g.s. Alexander Raiford (soldier in war of 1812); ed. Cherokee Bapt. Coll., nr. Cassville, Ga., then at Univ. of Va., till war broke out; joined "Southern guard"; was one of party that seized Harper's Ferry. Remained in army of Northern Va. until end of war; promoted lt. after Antietam by special order Gen. R. E. Lee. Studied law in office of William Law. Mem. State Legislature, 1882, State senator, 1884; comd. Oglethorpe Light Inf., 18 yrs. Home: Savannah, Ga. Died 1902.

FALLOWS, SAMUEL bishop; b. Pendleton, Lancashire, Eng., Dec. 13, 1835; s. Thomas and Anne (Ashworth) F.; removed to Wis., 1848; A.B., U. of Wis., 1839, A.M., 1862 (LL.D., 1894; D.D., Lawrence U., 1873, Marietta Coll., 1903); m. Lucy Bethia Huntington, Apr. 9, 1860 (died 1916). V.p. Galesville U., 1859-61; chaplain 32d Wis. Inf., Sept. 25, 1862; resigned June 29, 1863; lt. col., 40th Wis. Inf., May 20, 1864; col. 49th Wisconsin Infantry, Jan. 28, 1865; bvtd. brig. gen. vols., Oct. 24, 1865, "for meritorious services"; hon. mustered out Nov. 1, 1865. In M.E. ministry, 1859-75; rector St. Paul's R.E. Ch., Chicago, 1875—; bishop R.E. Ch., 1876—; elected presiding bishop 8 times; Regent U. of Wis., 1866-74; state supt. public instrn., Wis., 1871-7 75; pres. bd. of mgrs. Ill. State Reformatory, 1891-1912; chmn. gen. ednl. commn. World's Congress Auxilliary, 1893; chancellor Univ. Assn; chap- lain-in-chief G.A.R., 1907-08; nat. patriotic instr. G.A.R., 1908-09; dept. comdr. of Ill., G.A.R., 1913-14; chaplain 2d Regt. Illinois N.G., 1890-1916, comdr. Military Order Loyal Legion, Dept. of Ill., 1907. Author: The Bible Looking Glass, 1898; Story of the American Flag, 1903; Complete Dictionary of Synonyms and Antonyms, 1925. Editor-in-chief the Human Interest Library, Pres. Ill. Commn. to Conduct Half Century Anniversary of Negro Freedom in 1915; chmn. Grant Memorial Commn.; pres. Chicago Sch. for Home Nursing, 1919—, Pres. Soc. Army of the Tennessee, 1917. Died Sept. 5, 1922.

FANNIN, JAMES WALKER army officer; b. circa Jan. 1, 1804; son of Dr. Isham Fannin; adopted by his maternal grandfather, J. W. Walker; attended U.S. Mil. Acad. (under name James F. Walker), 1819-21; m. Minerva Fort, 2 daus. Raised on plantation nr. Marion, Ga.; moved to Tex., 1834; active in organizing revolutionary coms. for revolt against Mexico, 1835-36; participated in 1st skirmish of Tex. War for Independence, Oct. 2, 1835; proposed seizure of Mexican port of Matamoras, against wishes of Sam Houston; apptd. to organize and lead expdn. to Mexico, 1836; established control (with force of 420 volunteers) of Goliad on south bank San Antonio River, Feb. 1836; forced to retreat, Mar. 19, 1836, overtaken by Orrea's advance, forced to surrender, Mar. 20. Shot (with over 300 other prisoners) by order of Santa Anna, Mar. 27, 1836.

FANNING, ALEXANDER CAMPBELL WILDER army officer; b. Boston, 1788; s. Barclay and Caroline Henson (Orne) F.; grad. U.S. Mil. Acad., 1812; m. Miss Fowler. Commd. 1st lt., 3d Arty., U.S. Army, 1812, promoted capt., 1813; severely wounded at capture of York, Upper Canada, Apr. 1813; brevetted maj. for his defense of Ft. Erie, 1814; served with Jackson in Seminole campaign, 1818; occupied Spanish post of St. Mark's with force of 200 men; apptd. by Jackson as mem. of court martial which tried and sentenced Robert Ambrister and Alexander Arbuthnot, provost marshall at execution, Apr. 29, 1819; served at Ft. Gadsen, Detroit, Mackinaw, Columbus, arty. sch. at Fortress Monroe, Va., 1821-24; brevetted lt. col., 1824; commd. maj. 4th Arty., 1832; brevetted col. for service in battle at Withlacoochee, Seminole War, 1835; defended Camp Monroe against surprise Seminole attack, 1837; transferred to Canadian frontier, 1840-41. Died Cincinnati, Aug. 18, 1846.

FANNING, DAVID Loyalist; b. Amelia County, Va., circa 1755; son of David Fanning; married, Apr. 1782. Became Loyalist, 1775, commenced marauding expdns. against Whigs; commd. col. in militia, 1781; captured the ofcl. of a jud. ct. (or court martial) sitting at Pittsboro, N.C., July 1781; captured Gov. Burke, Hillsboro, N.C., Sept. 1781; 1 of 3 persons who were excluded from pardon by gen. amnesty act at end of Revolutionary War; mem. provincial parliament, Brunswick, 1791-1801. Died Mar. 14, 1825.

FANNING, EDMUND colonial ofcl., army officer; b. L.I., N.Y., Apr. 24, 1739; s. James and Hannah (Smith) F.; grad. Yale, 1757, LL.D. (hon.), 1803; A.M. (hon.), Harvard, 1764, Kings Coll. (now Columbia), 1772; D.C.L. (hon.), Oxford (Eng.) U., 1774; LL.D. (hon.), Dartmouth, 1803; m. Phoebe Burns, Nov. 30, 1785, 4 children. Admitted to N.C. bar, 1762; col. N.C. Militia; register of deeds N.C.; mem. N.C. Assembly, 1776, 78; apptd. judge Superior Ct. for Salisbury Dist. (N.C.), 1766; pvt. sec. to Gov. Tryon of N.Y., 1771; surrogate N.Y.C., 1771; surveyor gen. Province of N.Y., 1774; raised and commanded corps known as Associated Refugees or King's Am. Regt. of Foot, 1777; property confiscated by N.C., 1779; moved to Nova Scotia; became councillor and lt. gov. N.S., 1783; lt. gov. Prince Edward Island, 1786; commd. col. Brit. Army, 1782, maj. gen., 1783, lt. gen., 1790, gen., 1808. Died London, Eng., Feb. 28, 1818.

FANNING, JOHN THOMAS civil engr.; b. Norwich, Conn. Dec. 31, 1837; s. John Howard and Elizabeth (Pridde) F.; acad. and normal sch. edn.; m. M. Louise Bensley, June 14, 1865. Studied architecture and civil engring. until 1861; served during Civil War, lt. to lt. col., 3d Conn. S.M. After war became prominent in engring., particularly in planning and constructing pub. water works and water powers in N.E., and later in the West, notably on the power of the Miss. River at Minneapolis, of the Spokane River in Washington, and Missouri River nr. Helena and at Great Falls, Mont., and on the Weenatahee River in Wash. for the electrification of the G.N. Ry.'S cascade tunnel; was cons. engr. St. Paul, Minneapolis & Manitoba RR. and G.N. Ry., and v.p. Minneapolis Union Ry. Home: Minneapolis, Minn. Died 1911.

FANNING, NATHANIEL privateersman, officer; b. Stonington, Conn., May 31, 1755; s. Gilbert and Huldah (Palmer) F.; m. Elizabeth Smith, Nov. 21, 1784, 6 children. Sea-fighting privateersman under Franco-Am. auspices, 1778-83; midshipman, pvt. sec. to John Paul Jones in ship Bonhomme Richard; his action in fight with the Serapis, Sept. 22, 1779, did much to bring about Am. victory; commd. lt. U.S. Navy, 1804. Author: Narrative of the Adventures of an American Naval Officer, 1801. Died Charleston, S.C., Sept. 30, 1805.

FARBER, WILLIAM SIMS naval officer; b. Frankfort, Ind., Mar. 16, 1885; s. John Charles and Ruth Margaret (Sims) F.; B.S., U.S. Naval Acad., 1907; postgrad. Naval War Coll., 1937-38, Army Indsl. Coll., 1932-33; m. Louise Natlie Shafer, Sept. 12, 1914. Commd. ensign U.S. Navy, 1909, lt. (J.G.), 1912, lt.,

1915, lt. comdr., 1919, comdr., 1922, capt., 1933, rear adm., 1941, vice adm., 1945. Decorated World War I medal with star, 1919; Mexican Campaign medal, 1914; Nicaraguan Campaign medal, 1927; Haitian medal, 1914; D.S.M., Legion of Merit, Legionaire; Legion of Honor (officer). Presbyterian. Clubs: Chevy Chase (Md.); N.Y. Yacht (New York); Cazenovia (N.Y.). Home: Cazenovia, N.Y. Died Feb. 5, 1963; buried Arlington (Va.) Cemetery.

FARENHOLT, AMMEN, officer Navy Med. Corps; b. Norfolk, Va., Dec. 9, 1871; s. Rear Adm. Oscar Walter and Ella Mortimer (Ames) E.; M.D., Harvard, 1893; m. Mrs. William H. Whiting, Aug. 11, 1926. Apptd. asst. surgeon, U.S. Navy, July 2, 1894; promoted through grades to rear admiral, Dec. 7, 1926. Served with Dewey at Manila, later in Philippine Insurrection and on China Coast; duty on U.S.S. Baltimore, Oregon, Maryland, Independence, etc.; comdr. hosp. ship Mercy, 1921, later comdr. Naval Hospital, Mare Island, California, Great Lakes, Illinois, and Puget Sound, Washington; inspector Naval Medical Corps activities on East Coast, 1930, also asst. to chief of Bur. of Medicine and Surgery, Washington; apptd. insp. Med. Dept. activities of West Coast, Aug. 24, 1931; retired, Jan. 1, 1936. Fellow Am. Coll. Surgeons; mem. A.M.A. Campaign awards, also citation for services in World War. Presbyterian. Club: New York Yacht. Contbr. to Naval Med. Bulletin and Naval Institute. Address: 3626 Hyacinth Drive, San Diego CA

FARENHOLT, OSCAR WALTER rear-admiral U.S.N.; b. nr. San Antonio, Tex., May 2, 1845; ed. in schs. of San Antonio, New Orleans, La., and Pittsburgh, 1861; served on frigate Wabash; participated in engagements and battles at Ft. Hatteras, N.C., Port Royal, S.C., Ft. Pulaski, Ga., etc.; severely wounded at battle of Pocotaligo, S.C., Oct. 22, 1862; sent to Naval Hosp., New York and discharged from navy. Recovered from wounds; reentered navy Feb. 1863, on monitor Catskill; was in almost daily engagements with defences of Charleston, S.C., Apr. 1863-Apr. 1864; participated in unsuccessful storming party of Ft. Sumter, Sept. 1863; promoted acting ensign Aug. 1864, comd. schooner Henry James attached to squardon in Sounds of N.C., participated in recapture of Ft. Fisher, N.C. After war on various duties; commd. ensign, Mar. 12, 1868; master, Dec. 18, 1868; lt. Mar. 21, 1870; lt. comdr., May 11, 1882; comdr., June 19, 1892; capt., Sept. 1900; rear admiral, Sept. 1, 1901, and voluntarily retired from active service after 40 yrs. service. Served on many stations and in varied duties; during Spanish-Am. War stationed at Shanghai China, as Admiral Dewey's base of supplied and information; at Boston Navy Yard and Naval War Coll., Feb. 1899; comdt. navy yard Cavite, P.I., 1900, comd. monitor Monadnock, Asiatic station, 1901. Died June 30, 1920.

FARLEE, ISAAC GRAY congressman; b. White House, Hunterdon County, N.J., May 18, 1787; attended public schs. Engaged in business, Flemington, N.J.; mem. N.J. Gen. Assembly, 1819, 21, 28, 30; clk. Hunterdon County, 1830-40; served as brig. gen. N.J. Militia; mem. U.S. Ho. of Reps. from N.J., 28th Congress, 1843-45; mem. N.J. Senate, 1847-49; judge Ct. of Common Pleas, 1852-55. Died Flemington, Jan. 12, 1855; buried Presbyn. Cemetery.

FARLEY, HUGH D. church council ofcl.; b. Utica, N.Y., Feb. 12, 1913; s. Hugh D. and Jessie E. (Mowers) F.; B.A., Yale, 1934, M.A., 1940; M.A., Columbia, 1943; m. Mary Louise Eldred, Aug. 19, 1939; children - Melissa Wilcox, Hugh Dexter, Mary Allison. Instr. English, Yale-in-China, Changsha, Hunan, China, 1934-36, field rep., New Haven, 1936-37; instr. English, Phillips Exeter Acad., 1937-39, Carleton Coll., 1940-42; dep. sec.-gen. Far Eastern Commn., Washington, 1945-46; asst. chief div. internat. confs. Dept. of State, 1946-48; asst. exec. sec., spl. staff mem. NSC, 1948-54; dir. U.S. Operations Mission to Lebanon, ICA, Beirut, Lebanon, 1954-56; evaluation officer ICA, Washington, 1956-58; asst. dir. for tech. coop. U.S. Operations Mission to Korea, Seoul, 1959-61; exec. dir. church world service, Nat. Council Chs., 1961-65, asso. sec. div. of overseas ministries, 1965- , member of administrative com. Inter-church Aid Refugee and World Service, 1961 - ; chmn. Am. Council Vol. Agys. Fgn. Service, N.Y.C. Com. sec. UN Conf. on Internat. Orgn., San Francisco, 1945; sec.-gen. U.S. delegation, Council Fgn. Ministers, Moscow, 1947; tech. sec. Japanese Peace Conf., 1951. Chmn. bd. trustees Am. Community Sch., Beirut, Lebanon. Served to lt. comdr. USNR, 1942-45; sec. State-War-Navy Coordinating Com. Far East. Lutheran. Home: 10 Walworth Av., Scarsdale, N.Y. Office: 475 Riverside Dr., N.Y.C. 27, Died Nov. 30, 1966.

FARLEY, JOSEPH PEARSON brig. gen.; b. Washington, Mar. 2, 1839; s. Capt. John (U.S.A.) and Anna Maria (Pearson) F.; grad. U.S. Mil. Acad., 1861; m. Miss F. E. Brinley, Apr. 6, 1864. Bvt. 2d lt. and commd. 2d lt. 2d Arty., June 24, 1861; transferred to ordnance, Oct. 24, 1861; 1st lt., Mar. 3, 1863; capt., Apr. 6, 1866; maj., Mar. 25, 1876; lt. col., Feb. 28, 1889; col., July 7, 1898; brig. gen. U.S.A., Feb. 17, 1903; retired at own request over 40 yrs. service, Feb. 18, 1903. Bvtd. capt., Mar. 13, 1865, "for meritorious services in ordnance dept. during the war," Asst. prof. drawing West Point, 1865-67; mem. various statutory bds. ordnance bds., gun-testing bds.; has comd. various arsenals and in the field during Civil War. Author: West Point in the Early Sixties, 1902; Three Rivers, a Retrospect of War and Peace, 1910. Died Apr. 6, 1912.

FARLOW, ARTHUR CLARK advt. exec.; b. New Rochelle, N.Y., Nov. 29, 1904; s. Edwin Castle and Jessie Buxton (Clark) F.; student Columbia, 1922-26; m. Dorothy May Diemer, Mar. 21, 1953; children - Lesley June, Juliet Clark, Alison Emily Burton. With J. Walter Thomson Co., 1927 - , successively member staff, N.Y.C., mgr. office, Buenos Aires, St. Louis, Pacific Coast manager, San Francisco, vice president, N.Y.C., 1927-50, v.p., Chgo. 1950 - , now sr. v.p., v.p. J. Walter Thompson Co., N.Y.C., 1937 - , dir., 1953 - . Served as col. AUS, 1942-45, chief of Army orientation program, World War II. Mem. Columbia U. Alumni Fedn. (dir. 1951-55), Ch. Fedn. Greater Chgo. (chmn. New Chgo. spiritual goals com.), Am. Assn. Advt. Agys. (Pacific Coast Council), Chicago Association Commerce and Industry, Art Inst. of Chgo. Delta Upsilon. Clubs: Columbia University; St. Francis Yacht, San Francisco Advertising (past pres.) (San Francisco); Larchmont (N.Y.) Yacht; Saddle and Cycle (Chicago). Home: 1242 Lake Shore Dr., Chgo. 10; also Siasconset, Nantucket, Mass. Office: 410 N. Michigan Av., Chgo. Died Feb. 10, 1967; buried Nantucket Island, Mass.

FARMER, ALFRED GIBSON ophthalmologist, b. Elizabethtown, Ky., June 4, 1877; s. Benjamin Dew and Elizabeth (Giles) F.; M.D., Ky. U., 1904; grad. work N.Y. Post Grad. Med. Sch., 1915-16, Ohio U., Athens, 1916; m. Minnie L. Cuckler, Jan. 20, 1910; 1 dau., Margaret Louise. Began practice of medicine, 1904; in med. service Panama Canal, U.S. Govt., 1905-15; phys. Gorgas Hosp., dist. phys. Gatun and Cristobal, chief of med. service. Colon Hosp.; med. officer Army and Navy Gen. Hosp., Hot Springs, Ark., 1916-17; since 1919 in Dayton, O., practice limited to eye, ear, nose and throat; cons. ophthalmologist Miami Valley Hospital, Dayton, since 1919; ex-chief of staff Miami Valley Hospital; medical examiner, Civil Aeronautics Adminstrn. Served as med. officer and post surgeon (maj.) aviation service, U.S. Army, Wilbur Wright Aviation Field, Dayton, 1916-19; lt. col. U.S. Army-Med. Res. since 1919. Licentiate of Am. Bd. of Ophthalmology; fellow Am. Coll. Surgeons, A.M.A., Am. Acad. Ophthalmology and Otolaryngology; mem. Aero lMed. Assn., Montgomery County Med. Soc. (pres. 1935), Phi Chi. Methodist. Mason. Contbr. professional articles. Home: 707 Superior Av. Office: Fidelity Medical Bldg., 209 S. Main St., Dayton, O., Died April 2, 1945; buried at Athens, O.

FARMER, DONALD FRANCIS, surgeon; b. Chgo., Feb. 12, 1914; s. James Francis and Mary (Keenan) F.; B.S., Loyola U., Chgo., 1936, M.D., 1938; m. Shirley Gardner, Dec. 28, 1940; 1 dau., Madonna Jean. Intern Little Company of Mary Hosp., Chgo., 1937-38; gen. practice medicine, Chgo., 1938-41, 46-60; med. dir. Fisher Body div. Gen. Motors Corp., Willow Springs, Ill., 1960-67; pres., med. dir. Beverly Blood Center, Inc., Chgo., 1954-67. Served to maj., M.C., AUS, 1941-46. Fellow Internat. Coll. Surgeons; mem. A.M.A., Indsl. Med. Assn., Am. Bd. Abdominal Surgery (founder's group), Chgo. Med. Soc., Med. Dirs. Club of Chgo. Author med. publs. Home: Chicago IL Died Mar. 19, 1967.

FARMER, EDWARD rear-admiral U.S.N.; b. Weathersfield, Vt., Mar. 1, 1836; s. Edward and Lydia A. F.; ed. pub. schs. and pvt. teachers; m. A. Louise Buttrick, of Concord, Mass., June 1, 1869. Apptd. 3d asst. engr. U.S.N., May 3, 1859; 2d asst. engr., Oct. 16, 1861; 1st asst. engr., May 20, 1863; chief engr., Mar. 4, 1871; retired Mar. 1, 1898; advanced to rank of rear-admiral in recognition of services during Civil War, June 29, 1906. Served on various vessels and at various stations during Civil War. Home: 274 Newbury St., Boston.

FARNHAM, ROSWELL lawyer, gov. Vt.; b. Boston, July 23, 1827; s. Roswell and Nancy (Bixby) F.; family removed to Bradford, Vt., 1849; grad. Univ. of Vt., 1849 (A.M. 1852); m. Mary Elizabeth Johnson, Dec. 25, 1848. Admitted to bar, 1857; State's atty., 1859-62; served in army, lt. 1st Vt. regt. to lt. col. 12th Vt. regt., in Civil war; State senator, 1869-70; Presidential elector, 1876; gov. Vt., 1880-82. Republican. Home: Bradford, Vt. Died 1903.

FARNSWORTH, CHARLES STEWART army officer: b. Lycoming County, Pa., Oct. 29, 1862; s. Isaac Francis and Sarah (Moore) F.; grad. U.S. Mil. Acad., 1887; distinguished grad. Army Sch. of the Line and Staff Coll., Ft. Leavenworth, Kan., 1909, 10; grad. Army War Coll., Washington, 1916; m. Laura J. Galey, July 20, 1887 (died May 20, 1890); 1 son, Robert James; m. 2d, Helen D. Bosard, Nov. 28, 1894 (died July 1951). Commd. 2d lt. 25th Inf., 1887, advanced through grades to maj. gen. Nat. Army, 1918; served in Dakota Ty., Mont. and N.D. until 1893; prof. mil. sci. and tactics U. N.D., 1893-97; with 7th Inf., Denver, 1897-98; at Chickamauga Park (Ga.), Tampa (Fla.), Santiago and Havana (Cuba) and Montauk Pt. (N.Y.) during Spanish-Am. War; in Alaska, 1899-1901; constructing cantonments at the Presidio, San Francisco, 1902-03; served in Philippines, Mont., Mich., and Kan., 1911-13; served in Cal., Tex., and Washington, 1913-16; with Pershing's punitive expdn., in Mexico, 1916; comdg. base of communications Columbus, N.M., later asst. chief of staff, El Paso Dist., until 1917; comdt. Inf. Sch. of Arms, Fort Sill, Okla., 1917; comdg. 159th Inf. Brig., Camp Lee, Va., 1917-18, comdg. 37th Div., AEF, 1918-19, participating in occupation of the Baccarat (Vosges Mountains) and Panne (St. Mihiel) sectors and in the offensives in the Argonne-Meuse and Ypres and Lys; comdg. Camp Bowie, Tex., Inf. Sch. and Camp Benning, Ga., 1919-20; chief of Inf., 1920-25, ret. Decorated Silver Star, D.S.M. (U.S.): Croix de Guerre, comdr. Legion of Honor, Verdun Medal (France); comdr. Order of Leopold II (Belgium). Pres. Altadema Citizens' Assn., 1929. Altadena Beautification League, 1930-31; dir. LaVifia Tubercular Sanitarium; dir., v.p. Los Angeles County Conservation Assn., 1934-38; dir. Foothill Health Sch. for Girls. Clubs: Twilight (Pasadena, Cal.); Los Fiesteros (Los Angeles), Army of Santiago de Cuba, Order of Midnight Sun. Home: 556 E. Las Flores Drive, Altadena, Cal. Died Dec. 19, 1955; buried Nat. Cemetery, Presidio of San Francisco.

FARNSWORTH, ELON JOHN b. Greek Oak, Mich., July 30, 1837; s. James Patten and Achsah (Hudson) F.; ed. U. Mich., 1855-58. Joined Gen. A. S. Johnston's Utah expdn. against Mormons, 1857-58; joined 8th Ill. Cavalry, 1861, Commd. 1st lt., regimental adjutant; promoted capt., 1861; commanded for gallant service, 1863; apptd. aide-de-camp by Gen. Pleasanton; acting chief q.m. IV Corps, U.S. Army; commd. brig. gen. U.S. Volunteers, 1863; led charge of right flank of Confederate lines at Battle of Gettysburg, (Pa.), forced several Confederate inf. regts. to withdraw from front lines. Died in Battle of Gettysburg, July 3, 1863; buried Rockton, Ill.

FARQUHAR, JOHN HANSON congressman; b. Union Bridge, Md., Dec. 20, 1818; attended public schs.; studied law. Moved (with family) to Richmond, Ind., 1833; asst. engr. White River Canal, until 1840; admitted to bar, began practice of law, Brookville, Ind.; sec. Ind. Senate, 1842-43; chief clk. Ind. Ho. of Reps., 1844; Republican presdl. elector, 1860; served as capt. 19th Inf., U.S. Army, during Civil War; mem. U.S. Ho. of Reps. (Rep.) from Ind., 39th Congress, 1865-67; moved to Indpls., 1870, became a banker; apptd. sec. of state by Gov. Baker. Died Indpls., Oct. 1, 1873; buried Crown Hill Cemetery.

FARQUHAR, JOHN MCCREATH congressman; b. Scotland, Apr. 17, 1832; s. John and Marion (McCreath) F.; ed. Ayr Acad., Scotland; m. Jane Wood, Sept. 11, 1862. Pres. Internat. Typographical Union, 1860-62. Served throughout Civil War, Army of the Cumberland, pvt. to maj., acting as judge advocate and insp. on staff duty. Awarded Congressional Medal of Honor for bravery at battle Stone River. Tenn. Mem. 49th to 51st Congresses (1885-91); mem. U.S. Industrial Commn. 1898-1902. Republican. Elder emeritus, Calvary Presbyn. Ch., Buffalo. Home: Buffalo, N.Y. Deceased.

FARQUHAR, NORMAN VON HELDREICH rear admiral U.S.N.; b. Pottsville, Pa., Apr. 11, 1840; s. George W. and Amilie (von Schrader) F.; grad. U.S. Naval Acad., 1859; m. Addie W. Pope, Apr. 26, 1862. With squadron, coast Africa, for suppression slave trade, midshipman and acting master, 1859-61; brought to U.S. captured salver, the Triton, with crew 10 men and no other officer; commd. lt., Aug. 31, 1861; served in N. Atlantic blockading squadron; was present at both attacks on Fort Fisher; lt. comdr. Aug. 5, 1865; comdr., Dec. 12, 1872; commodore, 1897. Served in various stations; comd. the Trenton, Pacific sta., when wrecked in great hurricane at Apia, Samoa, March 16, 1889, but saved from drowning the crew of 450 officers and men. Mem. Light House Bd., Oct. 1889; chief bureau yards and docks, Navy Dept., March 6, 1890, later becoming comdt., Norfolk Navy Yard; comdr.-in-chief N. Atlantic sta., Oct. 1899—; chmn. Light House Bd., 1901-02; retired on account of age, 1902. Hon. mem. and prize essayist U.S. Naval Inst. Died 1907.

FARR, CLIFFORD BAILEY, M.D.; b. Landis Twp., N.J., Apr. 17, 1872; s. Lincoln Dow and Hannah (Bailey) F.; A.B., Haverford, 1894, A.M., 1909; M.D., U. of Pa., 1898; m. Katharine Elliott, of Phila., Pa., Nov. 22, 1904; children—Robert Lincoln, Frank Winslow Elliott, James Bailey, Anne Bailey Foot. Began practice, Phila., 1901; teaching staff of med. dept. U. of Pa., 1901-19, advancing to prof. in Grad. Sch.; phys. or asst. to various hosps.; with med. research dept. B.F. Goodrich Co., Akron, O., 1920-22; dir. labs., dept. mental and nervous diseases, Pa. Hosp., 1922-37; psychiatrist, Inst. of Pa. Hospital since 1937. Served as lieut., capt. and maj. Med. Corps, U.S. Army, June 1917-Jan. 1919; with A.E.F. in France 1 yr. Certified by American Board of Psychiatry. Fellow A.M.A.; mem. Pathol. Soc. of Phila., Am. Psychiatric Assn., Coll. Physicians Phila., Phi Beta Kappa. Republican. Epsicopalian. Author: Outlines of Internal Medicine, 5th edit., 1929. Contbr. to Da Costa's Handbook of Med. Treatment, and Craig's Diseases of Middle Life. Home: Bryn Mawr, Pa. Office: 111 N. 49th St., Philadelphia PA

FARRAGUT, DAVID GLASGOW naval officer, b. Knoxville, Tenn., July 5, 1801; s. George and Elizabeth (Shine) F. (adopted by Commodore David Porter); m. Susan Marchant, Sept. 24, 1823; m. 2d, Virginia Loyall,

Dec. 26, 1843, 1 child, Loyall. Commd. midshipman U.S. Navy 1810 (at age 9); served 1st sea duty off U.S. coast, 1811; prize master ship Alexander Barclay during War of 1812; served on board Independence, then Washington, then Franklin in Mediterranean Sea, 1815-20; aide to commodores Bainbridge and Chauncey, also Capt. Gallagher, accompanied Folsom to Tunis; spoke French, Italian, Spanish and Arabic; served as acting lt. brig. Spark, 1821; 1st orders were to Greyhound; commanded Ferret (1st naval vessel command); commd. lt., 1825; exec. officer sloop Natchez, 1833; commanded sloop Erie in Mexican waters to protect Am. citizens and property, 1838; comdr. ship Decatur, 1841; in command of sloop Saratoga, 1847; ordnance duties in Washington and Norfolk, 1850-52, drew up book of ordnance regulations entitled Experiments to Ascertain the Strength and Endurance of Navy Guns; ordered to establish navy Mare Island Rd (Cal.), 1854; commd. capt., 1855; went North when Va. seceded; mem. naval bd. N.Y. Navy Yard to select officers for retirement, 1861; apptd. to command West Gulf Blockading Squadron, 1862; went up Mississippi River; contrary to orders ran by Confederate forts before they were reduced, but New Orleans was taken, 1862; given thanks of the nation by resolution of U.S. Congress; after unsuccessful attempt to take Vicksburg, captured Galveston, Corpus Christi and Sabine Pass; promoted rear adm., 1862; suffered several reverses, 1863; captured Port Hudson (an achievement ranking next to New Orleans), 1863, honored by C. of C. of N.Y.C., Union League Club; comdr. flagship Hartford, led attack against Confederate defenses in Mobile Bay, 1864 (most memorable event of his life; uttered "Damn the torpedoes! Go ahead!" here); promoted to vice adm., 1864, adm., 1866 (both ranks created for him by Congress); took command European Squadron, 1867, led goodwill tour that ended 1868; honored in Am. Hall of Fame. Died Portsmouth, N.H., Aug. 14, 1870; buried Woodlawn Cemetery, Westchester County, N.Y.

FARRAGUT, GEORGE naval, army officer; b. Ciudadela, Minorca, Sept. 29, 1755; s. Anthony and Juana (Mesquida) Ferragut; m. Elizabeth Shine, 1795, 5 children including David Glasgow, William A.C. With Brit. mcht. marine in Mediterranean Sea, 1765-72; mariner in Am. seas, trading chiefly between Havanna, Cuba and Veracruz, Mexico, 1773-75; came to Am., 1776, joined colonial cause, became lt. on privateer; commd. 1st lt. S.C. Navy, 1778; served in defense of Savannah (Ga.), 1779, seige of Charleston (S.C.), 1780; volunteer for Gen. Marion, Battle of Cowpens, 1780; served in N.C. Volunteer Arty. Co. in Battle of Beaufort Bridge; capt. of cavalry troop that he raised; with Am. mcht. marine, 1783-92; sailing master U.S. Navy, 1807; served as sailing master of expdn. dispatched by Gov. William C.C. Claiborne of La. to take possession from Spain of disputed Gulf Coast of Miss. and La. Territory; accompanied personal friend, Andrew Jackson, on Indian campaigns, 1813-14; resigned from U.S. Navy, 1814. Died Point Plaguet, Miss.,June 4, 1817.

FARRAGUT, LOYALL author; b. at Norfolk, Va., 1844; s. Admiral David G. and Virginia L. F.; ed. U.S. Mil. Acad., West Point; m. Miss Gertrude Metcalfe, of New York, 1869. Second lt. 21st Inf., June 15, 1868; resigned Apr. 25, 1872. Author: Life of David Glasgow Farragut, First Admiral of the United States Navy. Address: 113 E. 36th St., New York.

FARRAR, CLARENCE B., prof. psychiatry; b. Cattaraugus, N.Y., Nov. 27, 1874; s. T. Jefferson and Marie (Hawkins) F.; A.B., Harvard, 1896; M.D., Johns Hopkins, 1900; grad. student, univs. Heidelberg, Paris and London, 1902-04; m. Evelyn Lewis, 1911; children—Aida Evelyn, Clarice Elaine (Mrs. B.E. Middleton); m. 2d, Joan Jordan. Asst. physician, Sheppard-Pratt Hosp., Towson, Md., 1900-02, asst. physician and dir. lab., 1904-12; instr. and associate in psychiatry, Johns Hopkins Med. Sch., 1906-13; lecturer in abnormal psychology, Princeton University, also asst. physician, Trenton (N.J.) State Hosp., 1913-16; chief psychiatrist, Dept. S.C.R., Ottawa, Can., 1916-23; med. dir., Homewood Sanitarium, Guelph, Ontario, 1923-25; director Toronto Psychiatric Hospital, and professor psychiatry, University of Toronto, 1925-47; consultant in psychiatry, Hospital for sick children, Toronto, 1936-70. Served as capt. and major, Canadian Army Med. Corps, 1916-19; med. officer, Queen's Field Ambulance, 1916; seconded Mil. Hosp. Commn., 1916-17; pres. standing med. bd., Cobourg (Ont) Mil. Hosp., 1918; with Dept. Soldiers Civil Reestablishment (Can.), 1919-23. Chmn. bd. examiners Ont. Dept. Health, 1934-47. Diplomate Am. Bd. Psychiatry and Neurology. Fellow Royal Coll. Physicians and Surgeons (Can.); mem. Am. Psychiatric Assn., Acad. Medicine (Toronto), A.A.A.S., History of Science Soc. (mem. council), Royal Canadian Inst., Alpha Omega Alpha. Hon. mem. Verein fur Psychiatric und Neurologie Geseilschatider Aertze (Vienna); corr. member Sociedad Argentina, Sexologia, Biotypologia y Eugenesia (Buenos Aires). Mason (32 deg., Scottish Rite). Clubs: Arts and Letters, Aesculapian, Medical Historical (Toronto). Editor Am. Jour. Psychiatry, 1931-65. Asso. editor: One Hundred Years of American Psychiatry, 1944. Contbr. annual article, "Psychiatry" to Funk and Wagnalls New Internat. Year Book, 1940-70. Home: Toronot ON Canada Died June 3, 1970.

FARRELL, PATRICK JOSEPH HOSHIE, b. Calcutta, India, Mar. 18, 1863; s. Gen. G.T. and Louise Helen (Gormanston) F.; ed. in Calcutta, Calif. and Eng.; M.D., U. of Ky., 1892; m. Edna Clare Greatsinger, Sept. 2, 1896; children—Walter Greatsinger (U.S.M.C.), Helen G. (Mrs. Edgar G. Crossman), Jerome G., Louise G. (dec.). Lt., capt. cav., Egyptian, Soudan, & Afendi Wars 1883-86; col. brig gen., Cav., Chilean War, 1889-90; capt. Spanish-Am. and Philippine Wars; commanded first company of U.S. troops that landed in P.I., June 30, 1898. Citation for meritorious service under fire of the enemy; Silver Star medal and medal of Valor for gallantry in action. Major, 1901, col., Cav., 1908. Comdr.-in-chief, Army of the Philippine Vets., 1908-09; comdr.-in-chief, Vets of Foreign Wars of U.S., 1917-18; past comdr. Am. Legion Post. Organized the Boy Scouts of America, 1909; promoted Boy Scouts thousand mile relay race, Washington-Chicago, 1913. Prof. mil. med. hygiene, 1910-16. Fellow Am. Coll. Surgeons. Comdg. officer Advance Sector Hospitals, A.E.F., France, 1918-19. Decorated World War Victory medal, French Medaille Interalliee De La Victoire and Medaille On Ne Passe Pas, Verdun Defense, Surgeon gen. Mil. Order World War, 1925. Col. Res. U.S. Army; brig. gen. Adj. Gen. Calif. Nat. Guard; dir. military and vets. affairs 1939. Clubs: Army and Navy (life mem. ex-pres.); Chicago Athletic, (life mem.); Authors, White Paper, Army and Navy (Washington, D.C.); St. Geroge's (London, England); Los Angeles Athletic, Jonathan (Los Angeles). Home: 2205 W. 6th St., Los Angeles CA

FARRELL, THOMAS FRANCIS cons. engr.; b. Brunswick, Rensselaer County, N.Y., Dec. 3, 1891; s. John J. and Margaret (Connelly) F.; grad. La Salle Inst., Troy, N.Y., 1907; C.E., Rensselaer Poly Inst., Troy, 1912; grad. Engr. Sch., U.S. Army, Ft. Humphreys, Va., 1923; Dr. Engring. (hon.) Renssalaer Poly Inst., 1945; LL.D., Siena Coll., 1947; m. Ynez White, July 23, 1917; children - Thomas F. (killed in action, Anzio, Italy, Feb. 25, 1944), Barbara, Peter B., Patricia Anne, Stephen Stuart. Engring. work, Panama Canal, 1913-17; chief engr. Dept. Pub. Works, Jan. 1930-June 1947; chmn. N.Y. Housing Authority, July 1947-Dec. 1951; dep. adminstr. D.P.A., 1951; asst. gen. mgr. AEC, 1951-52; mng. dir. ARO, Inc. Tullahoma, Tenn., 1952-57; cons. N.Y. Worlds Fair of 1964-65, Power Authority of N.Y. Commd. 2d lt. Corps of Engrs., U.S. Army, 1916, promoted through grades to maj., 1918; served 2 yrs. overseas. On active duty, with rank col., Engrs. Corps, Army of U.S., Feb. 1941-Jan. 1944, brig. gen., Jan., 1944, maj. gen. Nov. 1945; Served as chief engr. China-Burma-India Theatre, Nov. 1944-Jan. 1945; deputy comdr. Atomic Bomb Project, 1945-46; comdg. gen. 301st Logistical Command, and comdg. gen. Camp Rucker, Ala., 1950-51. In chg. of field operations in Mariannas in atomic bomb operns. against Japan. Headed mission to Japan to check damage and Japanese atomic bomb activities; mem. evaluation bd. for test of atomic bomb against naval vessels; advisor to the U.S. rep. on U.N. Atomic Energy Commn. Com. Mem. Am. Society of Military Engineers. Decorated D.S.C., D.S.M., Legion of Merit (with Oak Leaf Cluster). Silver Star Medal (two oak leaf clusters). Order of the Purple Heart (U.S.); N.Y. State Conspicuous Service Cross; 3 citations; Croix de Guerre with Palm (French); Order of British Empire (degree of comdr.). Democrat. Clubs: Army-Navy (Washington), Contbr. to The Military Engineer, Home: 30 W. 60th St. Office: Care Power Authority, 10 Columbus Circle, N.Y.C. Died Apr. 11, 1967; buried Arlington Nat. Cemetery, Washington.

FARRINGTON, JOHN D. ry. official; b. St. Paul, Minn., Jan. 27, 1891; s. Robert Irving and Caroline (Burger) F.; m. Mary Canby, Apr. 11, 1917; (dec. July 1954); m. 2d, Doris Archer, Nov. 1955; children - John D., Dorothy, James W. Began as timekeeper for track gang C., B. & Q. Ry., 1909, foreman, 1911, roadmaster, 1912-16; supt. C., B. & Q. Ry., various divs., 1922-30, gen. supt., 1930-31; gen. mgr. Ft. Worth and D.C. Ry., 1931-36; chief operating officer, C.,R.I. & P.Ry., 1936-42, chief exec. officer 1942-48, pres., dir. to 1955, chairman board, 1955 - , pres., 1961 - ; dir. Archer-Daniels-Midland Co., First Nat. Bank Chgo., Zonolite Co. Served from lt. to maj., 17th U.S. Engrs., 1917-19. Asso. Northwestern University, Clubs: Chicago, Commercial, White Bear Yacht, Hole-in-Wall Golf and Yacht (Naples, Fla.). Home: 190E. Pearson St. Office: 1007 LaSalle St. Station, Chgo. Died Oct. 1961.

FARROW, EDWARD SAMUEL cons. engr.; b. Snow Hill, Md., Apr. 20, 1855; s. William H. and Catherine A. F.; A.B., Baltimore City Coll., 1872; grad. U.S. Mil. Acad., 1876; m. Elizabeth E. Downing, 1897. Commd. 2d lt., 21st Inf., June 15, 1876; 1st lt., Sept. 17, 1883; instr. tactics, U.S. Mil. Acad., 1880-85; resigned from army, Feb. 24, 1892. Served against Indians in Ore., Mont., Dak. and Wash. Ty.; captured the hostile Sheep-Eater Indians, in Salomon Mountains, Ida., 1879, and was recommended for brevets "for conspicuous bravery, energy and soldierly conduct" in Nez Perce, Bannock, Piute and other Indian campaigns. Engring. operations include exploration of mining dists. in eastern Ore. and northwestern Ida.; ry. constn. and timber operations in Adirondacks; surveys and reports on Appalachian fields of Va.; exams. and reports on gold and copper deposits in Black Hills of S.D., mica deposits of Me., arsenical ore deposits in Putnam Co., N.Y., mineral deposits in Bland Co., Va., also reports on Panama Canal and Canal Zone, etc. Founder of Farrow Pub. Library, Pinewarld, and Pinewald Mil. Camp of Instrn. Episcopalian. Author:American Small Arms, 1904; West Point and the Military Academy, 1900; Camping on the Trail, 1902; Dictionary of Military Terms, 1917; Farrow's Manual of Military Training, 1919; Riots and Riot Duty, 1919; Gas Warfare, 1919. Compiler: Farrow's Military Ency. (3 vols.), 1885; owner and editor Pinewald Bull. (newspaper advocating peace). Inventor of toxic gases and gas grenade; discoverer of gravity control by intensification of Hertsian waves. Home: Pinewald, N.J. Died Sept. 25, 1926.

FARWELL, FREDERICK MARCUS business cons.; b. Chgo., Oct. 27, 1906; s. Frederick Marcus and Ann (Davis) Farwell Alling; grad. The Hill Sch., Pottstown, Pa., 1924; B.S., Yale, 1928; postgrad. Northwestern U. Sch. Commerce, 1929-30; m. Dorothy Marie Charbonnet, Jan. 10, 1942; children - Dorothy Ann (Mrs. Meredith William Myers), Dianne Barbara (Mrs. Mikhail R. Parsonnet), Joan Sandra. Started as salesman IBM, 1928-33, asst. mgr. Chgo., 1933, sales mgr. electric accounting machine div., 1935-41; gen. mgr., IBM Plant No. 2, Poughkeepsie, N.Y., 1942, mgr. Washington, 1946-50, v.p. IBM World Trade Corp., Rio De Janeiro, 1950; v.p. and gen. mgr. Munitions Mfg. Corp., Poughkeepsie, N.Y. 1942; exec. v.p. and dir. S.C. Johnson & Son, Inc., Racine, Wisconsin, 1951-55; pres. Ceras Johnson de Mexico, 1954-55; pres., chief exec. officer, exec. com., dir. Underwood Corp., 1955-57; exec. v.p., dir. Internat. Tel. & Tel. Corp., 1957-59; v.p. charge marketing RCA, 1959-62, exec. cons., Camden, N.J., 1962 - ; bus. cons.; dir. D'Armigene Inc. Mem. adv. bd. Procurement Guide. Bd. dirs. Oak Woods Cemetery Assn. Chgo. Served to maj. AUS, 1941-46; spl. staff asst., Ordnance Br., prodn. div., O.P.M., 1941. Awarded Army Commendation and Am. Def. medals. Mem. Berzelius Soc., Fairhope and Eastern Shore C. of C. (chmn. industry com.), U.S. C. of C. (Dir.-at-large), Clubs: Athestan (Mobile, Ala.); Fairhope (Ala.); New Orleans Country; Economic, Yale, New York Sales Managers N.Y.C.); Chicago Athletic Assn. Address: Montrose, Ala. Died July 9, 1965; buried Montrose, Ala.

FASSETT, WILLIAM M., army officer (ret.); b. Nashau, N.H., Jan. 28, 1876; s. James B. and Elien M. (Morrill) F.; B.S., U.S. Mil. Acad., 1897; unmarried. Commd. 2d lt. U.S. Army, 1897, and advanced through grades to brig. gen. 1918; retired 1924; assigned to inf., Spanish-Am. War; served in Santiago, Cuba; Philippine Insurrection, 1899-1902; various army posts in U.S., World War I; now raises citrus fruit. Decorated, silver star, Spanish-Am. War; D.S.M. (U.S.); Belgian War Cross; Officer the French Legion of Honor. Unitarian. Clubs: Orlando (Fla.), Country; Army and Navy (Washington); Officers' (Orlando Air Base) (hon.). Home: Route 5, Orlando FL

FAULKNER, CHARLES JAMES senator; b. Martinsburg, W.Va.; Sept. 21, 1847; s. Hon. Charles James (minister to France) and Mary Wagner (Boyd) F.; early edn. in France and Switzerland; entered Va. Mil. Instn., Lexington, 1862; served with cadets at battle of New Market, and afterwards as aide to Gens. Breckenridge and Wise in C.S.A., to end of war; grad. U. of Va., 1868; admitted to W.Va. bar, 1868. Judge 13th Jud. Circuit, W.Va., 1880-87; U.S. senator, 1887-99; mem. British-Am. Joint High Commn., 1893. Permanent chmn. Dem. State convs., 1888-92; chmn. Dem. Congressional Com., 1894, 96, 98. Mason. Home: Martinsburg, W. Va. Died Jan. 13, 1929.

FAWCETT, ANGELO VANCE mayor; b. Knox Co., O., Mar. 6, 1846; s. Phillip and Martha Ellen (Vance) F.; left Wesleyan U., Bloomington, Ill., to serve in 7th Ill. Inf., Civil War; m. 4th, Margaret J. Smith, 1896. Wounded in Battle of Altoona Pass, Ga., Oct. 1864 (46 out of 51 men in his co. being killed and only three returning unharmed). Began with Kingman & Co., Peoria, Ill., farm machinery, 1877; moved to Tacoma, Wash., 1883, and engaged in same line of business and made $500,000 in 10 yrs.; fortune nearly all swept away in panic of 1893; was head of Fawcett Bros., farm machinery and seeds, Tacoma, also Fawcett Bros., North Yakima and Bellingham, Wash.; pres. Fawcett Wagon Co., Tacoma. County commr. Pierce Co., Wash., 1 term; state senator, 1917-21; has been mayor of Tacoma many terms; secured Cushman Power Plant for city. Republican. Home: Fort Lewis, Wash. Deceased.

FAWCETT, JACOB judge; b. Benton, Wis., Apr. 9, 1847; s. Joshua and Margaret (Nicholson) F.; common sch. edn.; m. Margaret J. Doxey, of Galena, Ill., Apr. 16, 1868. Enlisted at 14 in Co. I, 16th Wis. Inf., 1861; wounded at Shiloh, Apr. 6, 1862, and again in front of Atlanta, July 21, 1864; admitted to Ill. bar, 1874; mem. city council, Galena, 4 yrs.; co. judge Jo Daviess Co., Ill., 1886-87 (resigned); removed to Omaha, Neb., 1887; judge Dist. Ct., Omaha Dist., 1896-1904; commr. Supreme Ct. of Neb., 14 mos., 1907-08; asso. justice Supreme Ct. of Neb., 1908-15. Lecturer in Coll. of Law, U. of Neb., 9 yrs.; trustee German-English Normal Sch., Galena, Ill. On invitation of Wis. delivered dedicatory oration on battlefield of Shiloh, Apr. 7, 1906, at dedication of monument erected by state of Wis. in memory of her soldiers who fell there. Republican. Club: Commercial. Home: 1309 S. 16th St. Office: State House, Lincoln, Neb.

FAXON, WILLIAM OTIS II, engineer; born Stoughton, Mass., Oct. 19, 1910; s. Nathaniel W. and Marie B. (Conant) F.; A.B., Harvard, 1932, M.S., 1933; m. Frances Parker, Sept. 27, 1941; children—David, Susan, Thomas, Roger. Instr. Harvard, 1933-35; comptroller Dorr Co., 1935-42; v.p. Harrison Abrasive Corp., 1946-52, also dir.; v.p. Metals Disintegrating Co., 1952-54; exec. v.p. Tracer Lab., Inc., Boston, 1954-56, dir., 1954-57, pres., 1956-57; pres. Keleket X-Ray Corp., 1956-57, dir., 1954-57, exec. v.p., dir. Comstock & Wescott, Inc., 1957-67, pres., dir., 1967-68. Selectman, Town of Concord. Dir. Manchester (N.H.) Community Chest, 1946-52, Boys Club. Served as lt. comdr. USNR, 1942-46. Registered profl. engr., N.H., Mass. Mem. Harvard Engring. Soc. (sec. 1940-42), Am. Soc. Metals, Am. Soc. Engring. Scis., Am. Metal Powder Inst. Conglist. Home: Concord MA Died Dec. 31, 1968.

FAY, CHARLES W., investment banker; b. San Jose, Cal., Sept. 1, 1903; s. Charles W. and Estelle (Lion) F.; student U. Cal., 1926; m. Dorothy Mein, July 7, 1932; children—Frances (Mrs. John G. Bowes), Dorothy (Mrs. Hamilton Robinson, Jr.), Victoria. Contractor, Fay Improvement Co., 1926-32; real estate broker Buckbee-Thorne & Co., 1932-37; pres., chmn. bd. Hooker & Fay Inc., San Francisco, 1937-63; sr. v.p., mem. exec. com., dir. William R. Staats & Co. (after merger with Hooker & Fay Inc., 1963), 1963-65; sr. v.p., dir. Glore Forgan, Wm. R. Staats Inc. (after merger), 1965-70; sr. v.p. F.I. duPont, Glore Forgan & Co., 1970-72; vice chmn. bd. L. Lion and Sons Co., San Jose, Cal., 1936-67, Roos/Atkins, San Francisco; dir. Clear Lake Water Co., Woodland, Cal., 1939-67. Chmn. mgmt. com. U. Cal. Centennial Fund, 1967; pres. Nob Hill Improvement Assn., 1969-72. Chmn. Bay Area Council A.R.C., 1959-64, now mem.-at-large bd. dirs. Golden Gate chpt.; bd. dirs. United Bay Area Crusade, Nat. Pollution Control Found.; trustee, exec., com. U. Cal. Alumni Found.; trustee Garrison Forest Sch., Balt. Served to lt. comdr. USNR, 1942-45. Mem. U. Cal. Alumni Assn. (alumni council, exec. com.), Delta Kappa Epsilon. Clubs: Bohemian, Pacific Union, Burlingame Country, Golf, Commonwealth of Cal. (San Francisco); California (Los Angeles); Racquet and Tennis (N.Y.C.) Home: San Francisco CA Died June 18, 1972.

FAY, HENRY chemist; b. Williamsburg, Pa., Jan. 12, 1868; s. John (M.D.) and Sarah C. F.; A.B., Lafayette Coll., 1889, A.M., 1892, hon. D.Sc., 1915; Ph.D., Johns Hopkins, 1895; m. Marie F. Phelps, of Boston, Sept. 19, 1908; 1 dau., Margery. Instr. chemistry, Johns Hopkins, 1893-95; instr. analytical chemistry, 1895-1900, asst. prof., 1900-05, asso. prof. 1905-07, prof., 1907-20, prof. anal. chemistry and Metallography, 1920, Mass. Inst. Tech., retired, 1926. Consulting chemist Gillette Safety Razor Company, 1905-12; consulting metallurgist Winchester Repeating Arms Co., 1916-20, and U.S. Arsenal, Watertown, Mass., Naval Acad., 1919. Republican. Unitarian. Fellow Am. Acad. Arts and Sciences; mem. Am. Chem. Soc., British Iron and Steel Inst., Inst. of Metals, Phi Kappa Psi. Author: Microscopic Examination of Steel; An Advanced Course in Quantitative Analysis, 1917. Contbr. articles on chemistry and metallography to various jours. Home: 11 Worthington Rd., Brookline, Mass.

FAY, TEMPLE neurol. surgeon; b. Seattle, Jan. 9, 1895; s. John Purinton and Alice Isabelle (Ober) F.; B.S., U. Wash., 1917; M.D., U. Pa., 1921; m. Marion Hutchinson Button, June 8, 1923; children - Jane Dundas (Mrs. Quinley R. Schulz), Alice Amelia (Mrs. Robert Hutton), Marion Biddle (Mrs. David C. Henry), Marie-Louise (Mrs. Samuel R. Hazlett). Resident physician, U. Pa. Hosp., 1920-23, neurologist, 1922-29; asst. instr. in neurology, Sch. Medicine, U. Pa., 1923-25, asso. in neurology, 1927-29; prof. neurosurgery, Sch. Medicine, Temple U., 1929-36, prof., head dept. neurology, neurosurgery, 1936-43; prof. neurosurgery Women's Med. Coll. Pa., 1949-54; chief neurosurgeon Temple U. Hosp., 1929-43; neurologist Phila. Gen. Hosp.; hon. neuro-surg. cons. Phila. Gen. Hosp.; neuro-surg. cons. Meml. Hosp., Sarasota, Fla.; med. cons. Pa. Bur. Vocational Rehab.; sr. neuro-surg. cons. U.S. Naval Hosp., Phila. Dir. D. J. McCarthy Found. for Investigation Nervous and Mental Diseases, 1928-42; dir. Temple U. Med. Sch. unit for investigation malignancy, Internat. Cancer Research Found. grant, 1935-37. Served with Med. Enlisted Res. Corps and S.A.T.C. during World War I, med. officer base No. 17, Coastal Patrol, 1942-43; mem. U.S.C.G. Aux., 1942 - . Mem. Bd. Appeals Selective Service, Eastern Jud. Area, Pa.; mem. med. adv. com. Nat. Hdqrs. Civil Air Patrol, rank of lt. col.; wing med. officer, Pa. Civil Air Patrol; owner patrol plane lost in action off N.Y. Harbor, 1942. Recipient Gold Medal award, Class A. Sci. Exhibit, A.M.A., 1929, spl. award of merit, 1935. Dir. Neuro-phys. Pehab. Clinic Mem. med. adv. com. Nat. Soc. for Crippled Children and Adults (also Pa. Soc.). Co-founder Harvey Cushing Soc. (pres. 1937), Am. Acad. Cerebral Palsy, 1947; research council United Cerebral Palsy Assn., Inc.; bd. dirs., vice chmn. brs. S.E. chpt. A.R.C. Vice pres. Internat. League Against Epilepsy (pres. Am. chpt. 1937). Diplomate Nat. Bd. Med. Examiners. Fellow A.C.S., Soc. Neurol. Surgeons; mem. Internat. Coll. Surgeons, Am. Neurol. Assn., Am. Psychiat. Assn., A.M.A., Pan-Am., Phila. County med. assns., Phila. Neurol. Soc., Phila. Psychiat. Soc. Royal Soc. Medicine, Assn. Research in Nervous and Mental Diseases, Am. Bd. Neurol. Surgery, Pa. Soc. S.R., Phi Kappa Psi, Nu Sigma Nu, Alpha Omega Alpha, Sigma Xi. Clubs: Country, University, Art Alliance, Art, Pylon, Union League, Rotary, Phila. Cricket (Phila.); Gibson Island Yacht, Rock Hall Yacht, Sportsman Pilot Assn. Contbr. numerous med. papers and articles to sci. publs.; also author: My First Baby, 1933; serial (Sat. Eve. Post), Ambulance Anecdotes, 1932. Home: 7304 Elbow Lane, Philadelphia 19. Office: 8811 Germantown Av., Chestnut Hill, Pa. Died Mar. 7, 1963; buried Ivy Hill Cemetery, Mount Airy, Pa.

FEAGIN, NOAH BAXTER lawyer, humanitarian; b. Midway, Barbour Co., Ala., July 7, 1843; s. James Madison and Almira (Cole) F.; Nashville (Tenn.) Mil. Inst., 1860-61; B.L., Washington Coll. (now Washington and Lee U.), 1870; m. Annie Martin Phillips, Feb. 9, 1876. Pvt. to capt., 15th Ala. Inf., 1861-65; called "boy captain" of his regt.; wounded 5 times; served under "Stonewall" Jackson in 1st Shenandoah Valley campaign, under Gen. Longstreet at Chickamauga, and under Gen. Lee in Va. campaigns. In law practice, 1870—; editor Union Springs (Ala.) Times, 1870-71; mayor, Union Springs, 1875, Anniston, 1886. Apptd. judge Inferior Criminal Ct., Birmingham, Ala., Apr. 1895; elected to same by legislature 3 times; under recent act elected to same by city council as "recorder," last term expired Nov. 1910. Established, 1898, without legal enactment, a juvenile ct. for city of Birmingham after model instituted in Chicago by Judge Hurd; movement resulted in adoption of juvenile ct. law by legislature of Ala., 1908. Upon invitation of President Roosevelt attended Children's Conf., Washington, Jan. 1909; made argument before com. of Congress, 1909, for establishment of a Children's Bur. by Nat. Govt. Home: Birmingham, Ala. Deceased.

FEBIGER, CHRISTIAN army officer; b. Funen, Denmark, 1746; m. Elizabeth Carson. Toured Am. colonies engaging in lumber, fish and horse trade, 1772; enlisted in Essex and Middlesex regt. Mass. Militia; maj. in Benedict Arnold's brigade Continental Army, taken prisoner, 1775; commd. lt. col. 11th Va. Regt., Jan. 1777; commd. col., 1777; chosen by Washington to command one of 4 light regts. for storming Stony Point, 1779; agt. for obtaining and forwarding stores to So. army under Gen. Nathanael Greene, 1780; aided in suppressing Loyalist insurrection in Hampshire County, Va., 1781; superintending officer Va. Militia, 1781; brevetted brig. gen. by Continental Congress, 1783; treas. of Phila., 1789-96. Died Phila., Sept. 20, 1796.

FECHET, JAMES EDMOND army officer; b. Ft. Ringgold, Tex., Aug. 21, 1877; s. Edmond Gustav and Rachel Morrow (Forsythe) F.; A.B., U. of Neb., 1899; grad. Inf. and Cav. Sch., 1904; hon. Dr. Aeronautical Sch., Pa. Mil. Coll., 1929; m. Catharine Luhn, Apr. 10, 1907; children - Catharine, Mary. Enlisted as non-commd. officer cav., U.S. Army, 1898; commd. lt., July 25, 1900; promoted through grades to brig. gen. A.S., Apr. 26, 1925. Identified with A.S. since 1917; comdg. officer Kelly Field, San Antonio, Tex., 1918-20; chief of Training and War Plans Div., Office Chief of A.S., 1920-24; comdg. officer U.S. Training Fields and 3d Attack Group Kelly Field, 1924-25; asst. chief of Air Service, 1925-27; apptd. chief of Air Corps, with rank of maj. gen., Dec. 14, 1927; retired Dec. 1931. Recalled to active duty Mar. 15, 1942; re-retired, Dec. 31, 1946. Decorations: D.S.M., Legion of Merit, African Medal, Pearl Harbor Medal. President Air Corps Promotion Board, Air Corps Decoration Board, Air Corps Procurement Board, Air Corps Naming Bd. Mem. Sigma Chi. Clubs: Army and Navy, Army and Navy Country (Washington, D.C.). Address: Air Corps., War Dept., Washington, D.C. Died Feb. 10, 1948; buried-in Arlington National Cemetery.

FECHTELER, AUGUSTUS FRANCIS naval officer; b. Paderborn, Prussia, Sept. 1, 1857; s. Joseph and Elizabeth (Lucken) F.; brought to U.S., 1865; grad. De La Salle Inst., New York, 1873; U.S. Naval Acad., 1877; m. Maud, d. U.S. Circuit Judge W.W. Morrow of San Rafael, Calif., Oct. 16, 1893. Ensign, Nov. 23, 1880; promoted through grades to rear adm., U.S.N., July 11, 1915. Made first cruise on flagship Trenton to the Mediterranean, later on Shenandoah to the S. Atlantic; duty on Coast Survey, 1882-85; cruise around the world through Suez Canal, 1886-89; with Office of Naval Intelligence, Washington, 1889-92; in Behring Sea, protection of seal herds, 1892-94; in charge hydrographic office, San Francisco, 1894-96; on the Monterey, participating in taking of Manila, then navigator of the Concord, later the Solace, 1896-99; aide to comdt., Mare Island Island Navy Yard, 1899 to 1901; navigator and later exec. Iowa, cruising in Pacific and the Atlantic, 1901-03; at Union Iron Works, San Francisco, 1903-04; at office of Naval Intelligence, 1904-05; in comd. cruiser Dubuque, 1905-06; mem. Bd. of Inspection and Survey, Washington, 1906-10; comdr. battleship South Carolina, 1910-11, cruising to English Channel and the Baltic; pres. Bd. of Inspection, 1911-13; aid for inspection to Sec. of Navy, 1913-14; comdg. div. of battleships in Atlantic Fleet, July 1915; comdt. Navy Yard, Norfolk, Va., Jan. 1918, 5th Naval Dist., Apr. 1919. Died May 26, 1921.

FECHTELER, WILLIAM MORROW ret. naval officer; b. San Rafael, Cal., Mar. 6, 1896; s. Rear Admiral A. F. and Maud (Morrow) F.; grad. U.S. Naval Acad., 1916; m. Goldye Stevens, May 24, 1928; 1 dau., Joan. Commd. ensign, U.S. Navy, June 1916; promoted through the grades to adm., Feb. 1950; formerly dir., officer personnel, Bur. Naval Personnel; dep. chief bur. naval personnel, 1945; comdr. battleships-cruisers, Atlantic Fleet, 1946; deputy chief of Naval Operations (personnel), 1947-50; became comdr. in chief Atlantic Fleet, 1950; named chief of naval operations, 1951-53, comdr.-in-chief Allied Forces So. Europe, 1953-57, ret.; asso. Gen. Electric Co., 1957 - . Decorated D.S.M. with star (Navy), D.S.M. (Army), Legion of Merit, Bronze Star Medal. Clubs: Army and Navy, Chevy Chase (Washington). Home: 5169 Watson St., Washington 16. Office: 777 14th St. N.W., Washington. Died July 4, 1967.

FEE, JAMES ALGER judge; b. Pendleton, Ore., Sept. 24, 1888; s. James Albert and Rose (Maney) F.; A.B., Whitman Coll., 1910, LL.D., 1933; A.M., LL.B., Columbia, 1914: m. Frances Louise Waldo, Feb. 9, 1916 (died Sept. 20, 1935); children-Frances Louise (Mrs. George Conery Martin), Margery Waldo (Mrs. Ray Martin Steele), Lillian Adele (Mrs. Lauren Moore); m. 2d, Alice Emma Tomkins, Dec. 22, 1943. Began practice of law, 1914; mem. firm of Fee & Fee, 1915-16, 1920-27; city atty. Pendleton, 1916-17; mem. legal staff dir. sales, War Dept., 1919-20; judge Circuit Ct. Ore., 1927-31; judge U.S. Dist. Ct., Ore. dist., 1931-54, chief judge, 1937-54: U.S. Circuit judge, 9th Circuit, 1954—. Mem. Jud. Council State of Ore., 1928-31: U.S. Dist. Judges Ninth Circuit exec. sec., 1945-48, 1950-54, pres., 1948-50. Entered 2d O.T.C., Presidio, San Francisco, 1917; commd. 1st lt. Air Service, U.S. Army, 1917; instr., aerial gunnery. Reserve mil. aviator, 1918; 1st lt. Ore. N.G., 1926, advancing to lt. col. and asst. chief of staff, G-1, 41st Div., 1939. Mem. Bd. of Edn., Pendleton, 1922-31. Mem. bd. of overseers Whitman Coll., Chmn., Multomah County Law Library, until 1949. pres. 1941-49. Fellow Am. Bar Found; mem. Am. (chmn. com. on cooperation with Fed. Juciciary, 1950-54), Ore. State bar assns., Am. Law Inst. (mem. council 1949—), N.G. Assn. of U.S. (life), Am. Judicature Soc., Selden Soc. of London (Am. mem.), Am. Legion, Mil. Order World War (Ore. State comdr. 1942-45), Am. Asso. Newcomen Soc., Beta Theta Pi, Phi Beta Kappa; founding mem. Phi Beta Kappa Assos. (bd. dirs. 1945-52). Republican, Episcopalian. Member of the board of editors Columbia Law Review, 1912-14, Oregon Law Review, 1924-31, Law lecturer. Contbr. to legal publs. Clubs: Pacific Union (San Francisco); University (Portland). Home: 901 California St. Office: U.S. Ct. of Appeals, Post Office Bldg., San Francisco. Died Aug. 25, 1959; buried Arlington Nat. Cemetery.

FEE, JEROME JOHN, b. Oct. 13, 1913. Commd. rear adm., U.S. Navy, June 1, 1964, ret., former dir. Queen Mary project, Long Beach, Cal. Home: Long Beach CA Died Mar. 1971.

FEENEY, JOSEPH GERALD, transp. co. exec.; b. Scranton, Pa., May 28, 1910; s. John Patrick and Mary Cecil (Saul) F.; B.A., U. Scranton, 1933; LL.D. (hon.), St. John's U., 1951; m. Mary Eileen O'Toole, Nov. 23, 1942; children—Richard J., Michael J., Erin Eileen. Vice pres. Railway Express Agency, Inc., 1961-68; adminstrv. asst. to President Truman, 1949-52; legislative cons. econs. and transp., 1952-68. Served to capt. USNR, World War II. Decorated Navy Cross, Purple Heart. Mem. Nat. Def. Transp. Assn., Am. Transp. Assn., Newcomen Soc. N. Am., Legion of Valor. Club: Army-Navy (Washington). Home: Washington DC Died Oct. 20, 1968; buried Arlington National Cemetery, Arlington VA

FEGAN, HUGH J. dean and prof. law; b. Washington, D.C., May 7, 1881; s. Hugh J. and Catherine (Wise) F.; A.B., Georgetown U., 1901, A.M., 1902, LL.B., 1907, Ph.D., 1916, LL.D., 1943; grad. work in history English law, Oxford and Cambridge univs., Eng., 1937-38; LL.D., St. Mary's Coll., 1934, Boston U., 1950; unmarried. Asst. solicitor U.S. Dept. Agriculture, 1907-11; prof. law and sec. law faculty Georgetown U., 1911-18, asst. dean, 1919-43, dean Sch. of Law since 1943. Served as capt. J.A.G. Dept., U.S. Army, 1918-19. Spl. atty. U.S. Treasury Dept., 1919. Mem. (life) Am. Law Inst., Am. Bar Assn., Bar Assn. of D.C., Oxford Soc. (Eng.). Club: Cosmos (Washington). Editor: Vance's Cases on Insurance (4th edit.), 1952. Contbr. artlces to law periodicals. Home: 1801 16th St., Washington 9. Died Dec. 19, 1954; buried Rock Creed Cemetery, Washington.

FELAND, LOGAN officer U.S.M.C.; b. Hopkinsville, Ky., Aug. 18, 1869; s. John and Sarah F.; B.S. in Architecture, Mass. Inst. Tech., 1892; m. Katherine Cordner, Feb. 14, 1907. Capt. comdg. Co. F, 3d Ky. Inf., Spanish-Am. War, May 31, 1898; hon. mustered out,

May 16, 1899; apptd. 1st lt. U.S.M.C., July 1, 1899; capt., Mar. 3, 1903; maj., Aug. 29, 1916; lt. col., Mar. 26, 1917; col. (temp.), July 1, 1918; brig. gen. (temp.), Mar. 9, 1919, apptmt. permanent, July 1, 1920; maj. gen., Nov. 12, 1919—. Served in Cuba, the Philippines, Panama, Santo Domingo and various periods at sea; arrived in France, June 13, 1917. Awarded D.S.C. "for energy, courage and disregard of personal safety" in leading troops into action; D.S.M. "for exceptionally meritorious and distinguished service during the World War"; received six awards of the Croix de Guerre, among them one with bronze star, "for generously contributing" to the success of the 116th French Inf., one with palm "for remarkable ardor and tenacity in driving the enemy back for a distance of 11 kilometers," Croix de Guerre with palm "for coolness and skill in command of troops in the Bois de Belleau," Croix de Guerre with palm "for glorious part taken by his regiment in attack in the Champagne, between Blanc Mont and Medeah Farm"; made Officer Legion of Honor, and awarded Croix de Guerre with gold star, "for services in attack South of Soissons," July 18, 1918; awarded Navy, D.S.M. for "distinguished and gallant services"; cited six times in divisional orders for gallantry. Comdg. 5th Regt. U.S. Marines, July 17-Nov. 11, 1918; comdg. 2d Brig., U.S. Marines, San Domingo, Dec. 4, 1919-Oct. 24, 1920. Comdg. Am. forces on shore in Nicaragua, 1927-29; retired as maj. gen., Sept. 1, 1933. Methodist. Home: Columbus, Ohio. Died July 17, 1936.

FELDER, JOHN MYERS congressman; b. Orangeburg Dist., S.C., July 7, 1782; grad. Yale, 1804; attended Litchfield (Conn.) Law Sch. Admitted to bar, 1808, began practice of law, Orangeburg; served as maj. militia in War of 1812; elected trustee S.C. Coll., 1812; mem. S.C. Ho. of Reps., 1812-16, 22-24, S.C. Senate, 1816-20, 40-51; mem. U.S. Ho. of Reps. (Democrat) from S.C., 22d-23d congresses, 1831-35; engaged in agriculture and lumber bus. Died Union Point, Ga., Sept. 1, 1851; buried family burial ground on plantation "midway," nr. Orangeburg.

FELL, HAROLD BERTELS petroleum producer; b. Wilkes-Barre, Pa., Aug. 18, 1880; s. Daniel Ackley and Frances (Bertels) F.; prep. edn., Hillman Acad.; grad. Mereersburg (Pa.) Acad., 1907: C.E., Princeton, 1912; m. Georgie Simpson, Jan. 8, 1919 (div.); children-Frances Alice, Elizabeth Simpson, Engr. Lehigh Valley Coal Co., 1912-17; v.p., gen. mgr. Peerless Steel Co., Ardmore, Okla., 1919-21; v.p., gen. mgr., later pres. Simpson-Fell Oil Co., 1921-57; ret.; owner H. B. Fed. Oil and Gas; pres., dir. Rickey Royalty Co. Mem. adv. council Geol. Engring. Dept., Princeton. Trustee Okla. Pub. Expenditures Council, So. Okla. Meml. Found. Served from 1st lt. to maj. F.A., U.S. Army, 1917-18; col. F.A. Res. Chmn. Okla. State Soldiers Relief Commn., 1921-22; pres. Okla. Am. Legion Endowment Fund Corp., 1925-28. Dir. Internat. Petroleum Expn., Tulsa. Mem. Am. Assn. Petroleum Geologists (asso.), So. Okla. Oil and Gas Assn. (ex-pres.). Am. Inst. Mining and Metall. Engrs., Am. Petroleum Inst., Princeton Engring. Assn., Mid-Continent Oil & Gas Assn. (dir.), Ind. Petroleum Assn. Am. (dir.). Okla. C. of C. (dir.), Ardmore C. of C. (pres. 1932-33), Am. Legion (dept. comdr. 1920-21). Reserve Officers Assn. of U.S. (pres. Okla. dept. 1927-28). Republican. Presbyn. Clubs: Dornick Hills Country (Ardmore); Tulsa; Beacon (Oklahoma City); Tiger Inn (Princeton). Address: P.O. Box 1146, Springfield, Ill. Died Jan. 12, 1959.

FELL, JOHN R(ANDOLPH) investment banker; b. Port Washington, Pa., 1911; s. John Ruckman and Dorothy Randolph F.; student Aiken Prep. Sch., 1924, St. Pauls Sch., Concord, N.H., 1929; m. Josephine Laimbeer, Dec. 7, 1931; children - John Ruckman, Natalie Lee. Partner Lehman Bros., N.Y.C., since 1940; dir., pres. William Assos., Inc.; vice president and director Colorado-Western Pipeline Co.; director Trans-Canada Pipe Lines, Ltd., Monterey Oil Co., Texas Pacific Coal & Oil Company. Member executive committee, board managers Home for Incurables. Served as lt. (j.g.) to comdr., U.S.N.R., 1941-45, comdr. Naval Aviation. Decorated Commendation medal with gold star, Am., Asiatic-Pacific (4 stars), Philippine (2 stars) campaign medals, Presdl. Unit Citation with 2 stars; two USN commendation ribbons with gold star. Mem. Am. Legion, Aviation Commandery of Naval Order of U.S. Roman Catholic. The Brook, India House, Links Golf, Links, Madison Square Garden, Meadow Brook, Nat. Golf Links of American, Piping Rock, Racquet and Tennis, Southampton (N.Y.C.); Seminole (Palm Beach, Fla.); Ft. Worth, Brook Hollow (Tex.); Chevy Chase (Md.). Home: 475 Park Ave., N.Y.C. Office: 1 William St. N.Y.C. 10004. Died Apr. 26, 1961.

FELLERS, CARL RAYMOND educator; b. Hastings, N.Y., Oct. 4, 1893; s. Frank and Mary (Baratier) F.; ed. Mexico (N.Y.) Acad. High Sch.; A.B. in Chemistry, Cornell U., 1916; M.S., Rutgers U., 1916; Ph.D., 1918; m. Josephine Sanders, Mar. 28, 1921; children-Francis X., Mary J., Martha L., Anne M. John C., Paul J., David A., Stephen G. Bacteriologist (1st lt.) U.S. Pub. Health Service at Camps Greene, Bragg and Benning in lab. and field sanitation work, 1918-19; certificate of merit, from Surgeon Gen.; bacteriologist (food law enforcement) U.S. Bur. Chemistry and Soils, Washington, and San Francisco, 1920; research bacteriologist (food law enforcement) U.S. Bur. Chemistry and Soils, Washington, and San Francisco, 1920; research bacteriologist on seafoods and canned foods. Nat. Canners Assn., Seattle and State of Wash., 1921-23; asso. prof., food preservation (teacher and research in food tech., especially fish and marine products), U. of Wash., Seattle, 1924-25; research prof. food tech., Mass. State Coll. (now U. of Mass.) and Expt. Sta., Amherst, Mass., 1926, head of dept., 1941-57; food and nutrition consultant, 1957—. Food research, human and animal nutrition; dir. Blue Channel Corp., Beaufort, S.C. (packing marine products); abstractor for chem. abstracts, editor bd. Food Research and Quick Frozen Foods; food consultant. Served with U.S. Army, res. officer, Chem. Warfare Service, 1926-42; post chem. officer, Ft. Devens, Mass., 1942; army Command and Staff Sch., 1942; major and lt. col., Q.M.C., S.W. Pacific Theater, Australia and New Guinea, 1943-46 (army subsistence and liaison with Australian Govt.). Awarded Bronze Star; Babcock Award, American Institute of Nutrition 1950; Medal of Merit (Cuba). Fellow A.A.A.S., American Public Health Assn. (governing council 6 yrs. and chmn. food and nutrition sect., 1936); mem. Am. Chem. Soc. (councillor and sec.-treas. agr. and food sect., 1941-42, chmn. 1948), Soc. Am. Bacteriologists, Am. Soc. for Hort. Sci., Am. Fisheries Soc., N.Y. Acad. Sci., Inst. Food Tech. (pres. 1949, secretary 1947-48; founder and councillor), Sigma Xi, Phi Lambda Upsilon, Phi Kappa Phi, Theta Kappa Phi, Phi Tau Sigma (honorary pres.). Roman Catholic. K.C. Inventor of methods for pasturizing dried foods, canning Atlantic crabs, ascorbic acid antioxidants and use of chelating agents in foods. Author, many sci. and tech. articles on chemistry, bacteriology and tech. of foods; contbr. to several books, jours. and encys. Home: 52 Fearing St., Amherst, Mass. Died Feb. 22, 1960.

FELLOWS, JOHN R. congressman, lawyer; b. Troy, N.Y., July 29, 1832 attended country schs.; studied law. Admitted to bar, 1855, began practice of law, Camden, Ark.; presdl. elector on Constl.-Union ticket, 1860; del. Ark. Secession Conv., 1861; served with 1st Ark. Regt., Confederate Army, during Civil War; became adj. and insp. gen., after Battle of Shiloh; assigned to Brig. Gen. W.N.R. Bell's staff, commanded dist. in Gen. Van Dorn's dept.; captured at surrender of Port Hudson, La., 1863, imprisoned, released, 1865; mem. Ark. Senate, 1866-67; moved to N.Y.C., 1868, continued practice of law; del. Democratic Nat. Conv., N.Y.C., 1868; asst. dist. atty., N.Y.C., 1869-72, 85-87, dist. atty., 1888-90, 94-96; mem. U.S. Ho. of Reps. (Democrat) from N.Y., 52d-53d congresses, 1891-Dec. 31, 1893. Died N.Y.C., Dec. 7, 1896; buried Trinity Church Cemetery.

FELSING, WILLIAM AUGUST chemist; b. Denton, Tex., May 19, 1891; s. William and Anna Judith (Kurner) F.; A.B., U. of Texas, A.M., 1916; Ph.D., Mass. Inst. Tech., 1918; m. Stella Elizabeth Scorgie, Sept. 8, 1920; children-Barbara Ann, William August. Asst. prof. chemistry, U. of Texas, asso. prof., now prof., part-time research scientist, defense research lab.; with Underwater Sound Lab., Harvard, Mar.-Nov. 1943. Served as 1st lt., later capt., Chem. Warfare Service, U.S. Army, Mar.-Dec. 1918; engaged in making poison gas Edgewood Arsenal. Mem. Tex. Acad. Sciences, Am. Chem. Soc., Sigma Xi, Phi Lambda Upsilon, Phi Beta Kappa, Acacia. Mem. Tex. Acad. Sciences, Am. Chem. Soc., Sigma Xi, Phi Lambda Upsilon, Phi Beta Kappa, Acacia. Mason. Author: Notes on Descriptive Chemistry, 1928; General Chemistry (with E. P. Schooch and G. W. Watt) 1938; (revised edit. 1946). Contbr. more than 50 research articles to sci. jours. Home: 3007 Washington Square, Austin 21, Tex. Died Oct. 5, 1952; buried Austin Meml. Park, Austin, Tex.

FELTON, SAMUEL MORSE, transportation exec.; b. Cincinnati, Feb. 9, 1893; s. Samuel Morse and Dorathea (Hamilton) F.; B.S., Harvard, 1916; m. Louise Merion Garaghty, Oct. 23, 1920; children—Barbara Louise (Mrs. Albert S. Williams, Jr.), Samuel Morse. Engr. J. G. White Management Corp., N.Y. City, 1916-17; mgr. Oil-Shale div., asst. gen. mgr., Minneapolis, and gen. mgr., N.Y. City, Pure Oil Co., 1920-26; dist. mgr. White Motor Truck Co., Phila., 1926-36; gen. sales mgr. railway div., Edward G. Budd Mfg. Co., 1936-45; pres., dir. American Ry Car Inst., N.Y.C., 1946-50, pres., chief exec. officer Shippers' Car Line Corp., 1950-55, now dir., mem. exec. com.; pres. Am. Car and Foundry div. ACF Industries, Inc., 1955-57; retired. Mem. Transportation Council, Dept. Commerce since 1953. With U.S. Army, 1917-19; executive officer to chief engr., A.E.F.; disch. rank major, C.E. Awarded Purple heart. Meritorious Service citation, Chevalier de l'Etoile Noire. Mem. Mil. Petroleum Adv. Bd. A.S.M.E., Pan Am. Ry. Congress Assn. (chmn. indsl. adv. com.), Am. Petroleum Inst., Nat. Petroleum Assn., Colonial Soc. Pa., S.R., Soc. War 1812. Newcomen Soc. Rep. Episcopalian. Clubs: Chicago (Chicago); Railroad-Machinery, Cloud, Harvard Economic, Traffic (N.Y.C.); Harvard, Racquet, Phila. Country (Phila.); Duquesne, Rolling Rock, Traffic (Pitts.); Metropolitan (Washington). Home: Delray Beach FL Died Dec. 1971.

FENNER, CHARLES ERASMUS judge; b. Jackson, Tenn., Feb. 14, 1834; s. Dr. Erasmus Darwin and Annie America (Callier) F.; ed. New Orleans schs., Western Mil. Inst. of Ky., and U. of Va.; law at U. of Va. and U. of La.; (LL.D., U. of the South); m. Carrie Payne, Oct. 16, 1866. Admitted to La. bar, 1855; capt. Fenner's La. battery, light arty., C.S.A., during Civil War; justice Supreme Ct. of La., 1880-94; Democrat. Episcopalian. Pres. Administrators of Tulane U. of La.; trustee Peabody Edn. Fund. Home: New Orleans, La. Died 1911.

FENNER, EDWARD BLAINE naval officer; b. Rochester, N.Y., Aug. 2, 1876; s. Edward Bela and Margaret Virginia (Taylor) F.; student U. of Rochester 2 yrs.; grad. U.S. Naval Acad., 1899; m. Louise Arnold, Sept. 7, 1904. Commd. ensign U.S. Navy, Jan. 28, 1901; promoted through grades to rear adm., Nov. 1, 1930. Served in Spanish-Am. War (Battle of Santiago), Philippine Insurrection, Boxer Campaign N. China, establishment of Republic of Panama, Mexican Campaign; comd. U.S.S. Denver, World War; chief of staff, U.S. Asiatic Fleet, 1923-25; comd. U.S.S. Mississippi, 1928-30; apptd. comd. 16th Naval Dist. and stas. Cavite and Olongapo, Aug. 1930; comdg. Cruiser Div. 2, 1932-33, Cruisers of Battle Force, 1933-34; comdg. 6th, 7th and 9th Naval Dist., May 1934-Mar. 1936; comdr. Battle Div. Ons, April-June 1936; comdr. Cruisers Scouting Force, 1936-37; comdr. 13th Naval Dist. and Puget Sound Navy Yard, July 1937-Aug. 1940; retired Sept. 1940. Mem. Psi Upsilon. Club: Army and Navy (Washington, D.C.). Home: 6230 Wilson Av., Seattle, Wash. Died Feb. 13, 1943.

FENNER, ERASMUS DARWIN orthopedist; b. New Orleans, La., Dec. 21, 1808; s. Charles Erasmus and Caroline (Payne) F.; A.B., Tulane, 1888; student med. dept. U. of Va., 1888-89; M.D., Tulane Med. Coll., 1892; m. Sadie Cameron McDonald, Apr. 28, 1920. Practiced at New Orleans since 1892; emeritus prof. orthonedics and surgical diseases of children, Tulane Med. College; chief in orthopedics and fractures, Independent Unit, Charity Hospital; consultant in orthopedics, Mercy Hospital-Soniat Memorial. Captain Medical Reserve Corps, U.S. Army, June 15, 1917; assigned to duty with Base Hospital 24, Aug. 31, 1917; liaison officer 12th Region, June 1913-Jan. 1919; major Medical Corps, Nov. 9, 1918; hon. disch. Apr. 24, 1919. Decorated Officer d'Académie by French Govt. Fellow Am. Coll. Surgeons; mem. A.M.A., Southern Med. Assn., La. State and Orleans Parish med. socs., Clin. Orthopedic Soc., Am. Acad. of Orthopedic Surgeons, Sigma Chi. Democrat. Episcopalian. Club: Boston. Home: 6323 St. Charles Av., New Orleans. Died June 7, 1944; buried in Metairie Cemetery, New Orleans.

FENNING, FREDERICK ALEXANDER lawyer; b. Washington, D.C., Oct. 23, 1874; s. James Alexander and Mary (Anderson) F.; LL.B., Nat. U. Law Sch., 1900, LL.M., 1901; m. Blanche Alisan Hine, Oct. 18, 1899; children-Katharine Hine (Mrs. Walter L. Wright, Jr.), James Frederick. Resigned as asst, chief clerk, U.S. Disbursing Pension Agency, 1902; in law practice Washington since 1902; dir., mim. trust. com., Nat. Savings and Trust Co. Active duty as capt, and maj. Q.M.C., June 28, 1917-Mar. 15, 1919, in charge of officers allotments branch; col. E.C. Dir. Washington Bd. Trade, 1917-20; v.p. Am. Bar Assn., 1910-11, mem. gen. council, 1911-13, 1915-17; mem. Bd. of Med. Supervisors, D.C., 1915-25; mem. Board of Commissioners, D.C., 1925-1926; general counsel med. soc. D.C., 1924-38, advisory counsel since 1938, also honorary mem. of same society; hon. mem. Med. Soc. of St. Elizabeth's Hosp., D.C. Mem. bd. of trustees Am. Univ., 1921-27. Pres. The Anson Mills Foundation; pres. Washington Law Reporter Co. Mem. Bar Assn. D.C., S.A.R., Kiwanis (honorary), Republican. Presbyn. Clubs: Chevy Chase, Army and Navy. Wrote chapter on "Legal Measures in Their Remedial Bearings," in work White and Jelliffe on Treatment of Nervous and Mental Diseases, 1913; contbr. papers on legal aspect of insanity and medical jurisprudence to law and medical publs. Home: The Kennedy-Warren, Washington, D.C.; (summer) "Grayledge," Brooklin, Me. Office: 1039 National Press Bldg., Washington, D.C. Died Sept. 17, 1944.

FENTON, JEROME D(ESMOND), mgmt. cons.; b. Springfield, Mass., Jan 13, 1908; s. Joseph and Rose (Daly) F.; B.A., U. Ia., 1932; LL.B., Harvard, 1936; m. Elizabeth Clark, Mar. 19, 1938; children - Jerome S. Douglas M. Admitted to Mich. bar, 1937; with firm Clark, Klein, Brucker & Waples, Detroit, 1937-43; asst. v.p. Pan Am. World Airways, 1943-54; spl. asst. to adminstr. VA, 1954; spl. asst. to gen. counsel Dept. of Def., 1954-55, dir. security, 1955-57; became gen. counsel NLRB, 1957; now mgmt. cons.; partner Case and Co., mgmt. consultants, N.Y.C., 1962 - . Mem. Am., Fed., Mich. bar assns., Phi Beta Kappa, Beta Theta Pi. Conglist. Club: Harvard (N.Y.C.). Author: Security at Work, 1956. Home: Cranbury, Rd., Westport Conn. Office: 600 Fifth Av., N.Y.C. Died Nov. 1967.

FENTON, RALPH ALBERT surgeon; b. Lafayette, Ore., Nov. 5, 1880; s. William David and Katherine (Lucas) Fenton; student University of California, 1899-1901; A.B., University of Oregon, 1903, Sc.D., 1943; M.D., Northwestern University, 1906; married Mabel Copley-Smith, June 24, 1908. Senior house surgeon Ill. Charitable Eye and Ear Infirmary, 1906-07; in practice as eye, ear, nose and throat surgeon, Portland, Ore., since 1907; mem. faculty, U. of Ore. Med. Sch., since 1911, prof. and head. dept. of otolaryngology since

1927; mem. staffs Multnomah County Hosp. since 1911, St. Vincents Hosp. since 1907, Portland Sanitarium, Doernbecher Children's Hosp.; senior partner Fenton, Lupton, Bolton & Titus. Served as 1st lieutenant, captain, maj. Med. Corps, U.S. Army, 1917-19; senior consultant in ophthalmology, 3d Army, A.E.F., 1918-19; now colonel Medical Reserve. Awarded The Casselberry prize by American Laryngological Association (with O. Larsell), 1928; De Roaldes Medal, 1943. Member American Board Otolaryngology since 1927. Fellow Am. Coll. Surgeons; mem. Laryngol. Assn. (pres. 1950), Am. Otol. Soc., Am. Laryngol., - Rhinol. and Otol. Soc., Am. Acad. Ophthalmology and Otolaryngology (vice pres. 1927), A.M.A. (trustee 1935-45, Pacific Coast Oto-ophthal. Soc. (pres. 1931), Portland City and County Med. Soc., Ore. Acad. Ophthalmology and Otolaryngology (pres. 1930), Assn. Mil. Surgeons, Chi. Psi, Nu Sigma Nu, Phi Beta Kappa, Sigma Xi, Alpha Omega Alpha. Republican. Protestant. Clubs: Arlington Club, University Club (Portland, Oregon). Contbr. many articles to professional jours.; mem. editorial bd. Archives of Otolaryngology. Home: 13100 S.W. Pacific Hwy., Oswego, Ore. Office: 1020 S.W. Taylor St., Portland 5, Ore. Died Mar. 1960.

FERGUSON, HARLEY B(ASCOM), army officer; b. Waynesville, N.C., Aug. 14, 1875; s. William Burder and Laura Adelaide (Reeves) F.; grad. U.S. Mil. Acad., 1897, Staff Coll., Fort Leavenworth, Kan., 1904, Army War Coll., 1921; m. Mary Virginia McCormack, of St. Paul, Minn., Jan. 3, 1907; children—Adele, Virginia, Harley B. Commd. add. 2d lt. Corps of Engrs., U.S.A., June 11, 1897, and advanced through grades to col., July 1, 1920. With engr. troops in Cuba, 1898, Philippines, 1899; chief engr. China Relief Expdn., 1900; brig. gen. chief engr. 2d Army Corps, France, World War. Dist. engr., Montgomery, Ala., 1907-09; exec. office in charge raising of Battleship Maine, 1910-11; dist. engr., Milwaukee, Wis., 1913-16, Pittsburgh, Pa., 1920, Cincinnati, O., 1927-29, New Orleans, La., 1927, Norfolk, Va., 1930-31, Vicksburg, Miss., since 1932. In charge orgn. industrial mobilization, office of Asst. Sec. of War (established Army Industrial Coll.), 1921-26. Pres. Miss. River Commn. since 1932; mem. Bd. Rivers and Harbors, 1930; mem. St. Lawrence Waterway Bd. Clubs: Army and Navy, Metropolitan, Columbia Country (Washington). Address: Vicksburg MS

FERGUSON, JOHN LAMBUTH clergyman; b. Columbiana, Ala., May 12, 1892; s. John Lee and Claudia Jane (Cole) F.; grad. Birmingham So. Acad., 1910; student Vanderbilt U., 1910-13; A.B., Emory U., 1914, B.D., 1916; postgrad. U. Chgo., 1920-21, U. Edinburgh, 1919; D.D., Southwestern U., 1947; m. Olive Ann Watkins, 1921 (dec. 1924); 1 son, Oliver Watkins; m. 2d, Christine Franklin Beverly, Feb. 25, 1933; children-Franklin Cole, Alice Christine, John Lambuth. Prof. religious edn. Millsaps Coll., Jackson, Miss., 1919-23; ordained to ministry Meth. Ch., 1918; extension sec. Gen. Sunday Sch. Bd., hdqrs. Nashville, extension sec. Gen. Sunday Sch. Bd. , hdqrs. Nashville, 1928-30: v.p. Scaritt Coll., Nashville, 1930-33; dist. supt. Columbia dist. Tenn. Conf. Nashville, 1936-39; minister Belmont Ch., Nashville, 1939—. Served as chaplain U.S. Army, overseas service, 1918-19. Chmn. commn. on World Service and Finance, Tenn. Conf., 1943—. del. gen. conf. M.E. Ch. South, Nashville, 1944—. Mem. Am. Legion (past dept. chaplain), Sigma Upsilon (hon.), Kappa Sigma, Democrat. Mason (grand chaplain). Club: Pew-Pulpit. Contbr. to church sch. lit. and religious press, M.E. Ch. Home: 4005 Harding Pl., Nashville 5. Office: 2007 Acklen Av., Nashville 4. Died Mar. 30, 1950.

FERGUSON, R(USSELL) J(ENNINGS) educator; b. Gowdy, Ind., Jan. 13, 1890; s. James Edward and Elizabeth Charlotte (Dwiggins) F.; A.B., Ind. U., 1921. A.M., 1924, Ph.D., 1928; m. Hannah May Broyles, May 29, 1922; children-Jeanne Anne, Robert Wayne, Elizabeth Ellen. Athletic dir. and instr. history Hanover Coll., 1921-23; acting instr. history and asst. coach Ind. U., 1923-25, instr. history, 1927-28; instr. history U. Pitts., 1925-27, asst. prof. history, 1928-32, asso. prof., 1932-45, prof., 1945—, acting head dept., 1954-55, head dept., 1955—: research asso. Western Pa. Hist. Survey, 1933-36, Served as fireman U.S.S. Kearsarge, USN, 1918; lt. comdr. and comdg. officer at Officer Tng. Unit, World War II. Mem. Am., Miss. Valley, Pa. hist. assns., Western Pa. Hist. Soc. Democrat. Christian (Disciple). Author: Early Western Pennsylvania Politics, 1938; Allegheny County-Sesqui-Centennial Review (Collaborated) Allegheny County Commrs., (1938); contbr. prof. jours. Home: 139 Edgewood Av., Pitts. 18. Died Aug. 20, 1955; buried Elwood, Ind.

FERGUSSON, FRANK KERBY army officer; b. Riddleton, Tenn., Feb. 18, 1874; s. W.W. and Medora C. (Kerby) F.; grad. U.S. Mil. Acad., 1896, Sch. of Submarine Defense, 1906; Army War Coll., 1912; general staff Coll., Washington, D.C., 1920; m. Ocie Hardesty Sheppard, Apr. 1922; 1 dau., (adopted), Dora Margaret (by wife's first marriage). Add. 2d lt. 3d Arty., June 12, 1896; promoted through grades to brig. gen. (temp.), Aug. 8, 1918; col. C.A.C., June 1920; col. gen. staff, Sept. 1920. At various posts, 1896-98; in Galveston, Tex., and on recruiting service, 1898; comd. U.S. Army mine planter, Colonel George Armistead, 1906, duty in submarine mine instrn., 1906-08; comd. Armistead, to Pacific Coast via Straits of Magellan, Dec. 1908-Apr. 1909; a.-d.-c. to Maj. Gen. Barry, 1909-10; coast defense officer, Dept. of Calif., 1910-11; duty at Army War Coll., 1911-12; mem. Ordnance Bd. of the Army, 1912-14; in Philippines, 1914-17; comdr. 8th Regt. C.A.C. (R.R. Arty.), Newport, R.I., and in France, July-Oct. 1917; comdr. Trench Mortar Sch. and on staff at Hdqrs. A.E.F., Training Center, Ft. Monroe and Camp Eustis, Va., Apr. 1, 1918-Feb. 1919; comdr. S. Pacific Coast Arty. Dist., to June June 1919; at Gen Staff Coll., Washington, D.C., 1919; Chief of Staff, 3d Corps Area, Baltimore, Md., Sept. 1920-Apr. 1922; Chief of Staff Philippine Div., Manila, June 1922-24; comdg. 11th Coast Arty. and Coast Defenses, L.I. Sound, Ft. H.G. Wright, N.Y., 1924-28; comdg. 2d Coast Arty. Dist., Ft. Totten, N.Y., 1929; comdg. harbor defenses of Cristobal, Forts DeLesseps and Sherman, Canal Zone, 1930-31, apptd. exec. officer, 2d Coast Arty. Dist., N.Y. City, 1931-34; comdg. 62d Reg. Coast Arty. (Anti-Aircraft), harbor defenses of Eastern New York and the 5th Dist. Civilian Conservation Corps, Ft. Totten, N.Y., 1934-35. Awarded D.S.M. "for conspicuous and specially meritorious service" while comdg. gen. of Coast Arty. Training Center. Died. July 18, 1937.

FERNALD, FRANK LYSANDER capt. U.S.N.; b. Kittery, Me., Nov. 11, 1835; s. William Salisbury and Sarah A. (Hanscom) F.; pub. sch. edn. to 1853; m. Mary Elizabeth Remick, Jan. 8, 1857; father of Chester Bailey F. Served several years in shipbuilding; entered naval service, 1854; apptd. chief draftsman at Navy Yard, Boston, 1868; asst. naval constr., May 4, 1871; constr., with rank of capt., Mar. 12, 1875. In Eng., France and Germany on spl. duty, 1875-79; mem. naval advisory bd. designing and supervising building of Chicago, Boston, Atlanta and Dolphin, 1887-91; supt. building of first Charleston, San Francisco and Monterey at Union Iron Works, San Francisco, 1891-95; in charge of constrn. dept. at Navy Yard, New York, built (old) Maine and Cincinnati; on spl. duty in Eng., 1895-97, and then in China and Burma and at Baltimore, Wilmington and New York superintending new work; retired, Nov. 11, 1897. Home: South Eliot, Me. Deceased.

FERNLEY, GEORGE ANDERSON, bus. exec. and adviser; b. Phila., June 13, 1891; s. T. James and Harriet (Adamson) F.; B.S., U. Pa., 1912, grad. work, 1912-14; m. Mildred Bougher, Mar. 15, 1916; children—Lois (Mrs. Henry S. McNeil), Robert Clute, Joan Adamson (Mrs. Stewart McCracken). Partner firm Fernley & Fernley, Phila., 1943-72. Served as capt., ordnance dept., U.S. Army, 1917-18. Received Award of Merit of Hardware Mchts. & Mfrs. Assn., 1946. Mem. Welsh Pony Soc. Am., S.R., Kappa Sigma. Republican. Episcopalian. Clubs: Riomar Bay Yacht, Riomar Country (Vero Beach, Fla.); Philadelphia Cricket, Down Town. Home: Plymouth Meeting PA Died Jan. 26, 1972.

FERRERO, EDWARD soldier; b. Granada, Spain, of Italian Parentage; came to U.S. in infancy. Conducted a dancing school, New York and taught dancing at Military Acad., West Point; became lt. col. 11th N.Y. militia; in 1861 raised 51st N.Y. regt. and became its col.; commd. brig. gen., Sept. 1862; bvtd. maj. gen., Dec. 1864; mustered out, Aug. 1865. During Grant's final campaign commanded colored div. of 9th corps. Died 1899.

FERRY, DAVID WILLIAM clergyman; b. Belfast, Ireland, Mar. 25, 1876; s. John and Sarah Ann (Reid) F.; came to U.S., 1905, naturalized, 1915; grad. Presbyn. Theol. Sem., Chgo., 1909; D.D., Whitworth Coll., 1918; m. Edith May Fenno, May 19, 1909; children-David Ernest, Frank W. Volunteer with British Forces, Boer War, S. Africa; chaplain of 158th Infantry, A.E.F., World War. Presbyn. clergyman 1909—: pastor First Ch., Yakima, Wash., 1923-43. Medals with clasps for 3 yrs. service in Boer War; victory medal with clasps for service as chaplain in World War. Trustee Whitworth Coll.; moderator Synod of Wash. of Presbyn. Ch., U.S.A., 1936-37. Mason (32ff). Author: Back to the Home, 1926. Home: 601 S. 7th Av., Yakima, Wash. Died Dec. 9, 1955; buried Terrace Hights, Cemetery, Yakima, Wash.

FERRY, ORRIS SANFORD senator; b. Bethel, Conn., Aug. 15, 1823; s. Starr and Esther (Blackman) F.; grad. Yale, 1844; m. Charlotte Bissell, 1847. Editor, Yale Lit. Mag. admitted to Conn. bar, 1846; judge Conn. Probate Ct., 1849-56; states atty. for Fairfield County (Conn.) 1857-59; mem. Conn. Senate, 1855-56, chmn. judiciary com.; mem. U.S. Ho. of Reps. from Conn. 36th Congress, 1859-61, mem. com. Revolutionary claims, also com. of 33; entered U.S. Army, 1861; commd. col. 5th Conn. Volunteers, brig. gen., 1862; changed from redical to moderate polit. course; mem. U.S. Senate from Conn., 1866-75, supported in election of 1873 by Independent Republicans and Democrats. Died Norwalk, Conn., Nov. 21, 1875.

FESSENDEN, FRANCIS soldier; b. Portland, Me., March 18, 1839; s. William Pitt F., sec. of Treasury; grad. Bowdoin, 1858; studied law, Harvard; m. Ellen Winslow Fox, Aug. 26, 1863 (died 1886). Apptd. capt. 19th U.S. inf., May 14, 1861; severely wounded at Shiloh; col. 25th Me. inf., Sept., 1862; col. 30th Me. vet. inf., 1864; brig. gen., May 1864; and maj. gen. vols., Nov. 1865; bvt. maj. gen. U.S.A., 1865; lost a leg at Monetts Bluff, La., 1864; afterward served until Nov. 1, 1866; retired with rank of brig. gen. U.S.A. was mayor of Portland, 1876. Home: Portland, Me. Died 1906.

FESSENDEN, FRANKLIN GOODRIDGE judge; b. Fitchburg, Mass., June 20, 1849; s. Charles and Martha Elizabeth (Newton) F.; Fitchburg High Sch.; LL.B., Harvard U. Law Sch., 1872; studied in Paris, France, 1872; m. Mary J. Rowley, Oct. 3, 1878. Practiced, Greenfield, Mass., 1874-91; served as dist. atty. temporarily justice Superior Court of Mass. Aug. 19, 1891—. V.p. Franklin Savings Instn., Greenfield. Capt. Co. L. 2d Regt., Mass. Vol. Militia, later col. and asst. insp. gen. Democrat. Unitarian. Home: Greenfield, Mass. Died Mar. 16, 1931.

FESSENDEN, JAMES DEERING lawyer, army officer; b. Portland, Me., Sept. 28, 1833; s. William P.H. and Ellen (Deering) F.; grad. Bowdoin Coll., 1852; m. Frances C. Greeley, Nov. 5, 1856. Admitted to Me. bar, 1856; recruited co. 2d U.S. Sharpshooters, 1861, served as capt.; mem. staff Gen. Hunter, 1862; organized, disciplined 1st regt. of Negro soldiers in nat. service; commd. col., 1862; mustered, disbursed troops, 1863; fought under Gen Hooker at battles of Lookout Mountain, Missionary Ridge; participated in Sherman's campaign against Atlanta (Ga.), 1864; commd. brig. gen., 1864; led brigade in Grand Review, Washington, D.C., 1865; commd. maj. gen. U.S. Volunteers, 1866; U.S. register of bankruptcy, 1868-78; mem. Me. Legislature, 1872-74. Died Portland, Nov. 18, 1882.

FESSENDEN, SAMUEL lawyer; b. Fryeburg, Me., July 16, 1784; s. William and Sarah (Clement) F.; grad. Dartmouth, 1806; studied law under Judge Dana; LL.D., Bowdoin Coll., 1846; m. Deborah Chandler, Dec. 16, 1813, 1 son, William Pitt. Admitted to Me. bar, 1809; practiced in New Gloucester, Me., 1809-22; mem. Mass. Gen. Ct., 1815-16, Mass. Senate, 1818-19, maj. gen. 12th Div., Mass. Militia, 1819-33; moved to Portland, Me., 1822; mem. Me. Legislature, 1825-26; (with Thomas A. Deblois) in law firm, Portland, circa 1822-circa 1852. Died Portland, Mar. 19, 1869.

FEST, FRANCIS T. B. physician; b. Wiesbaden, Germany, Nov. 2, 1860; s. Franz C. H. Buechli and Ottilia (von Just) F.; ed. college, Frankfort, U. of Heidelberg, U. of Berlin; M.D., S.C.D.; m. Emilia M. Hartwig, of Homburg, Hessen, 1888. Began practice in the navy of Holland, 1885; came to America, 1886. Col. and surgeon-gen. Med. Reserve Corps, U.S.A.; pres. N.M. Med. Soc., N.M. Assn. for Study and Prevention of Tuberculosis; v.p. Am. Internat. Congress on Tuberculosis; bacteriologist to the Medico-Legal Soc.; mem. A.M.A., Assn. Mil. Surgeons of U.S., Honduras Med. Soc., Red Cross of Japan. Address: E. La Vegas, N.M.

FETTERMAN, WILLIAM JUDD army officer; b. circa 1833; s. Lt. George and Anna Maria C. (Judd) F. Entered U.S. Army at outbreak Civil War, 1861; brevetted for gallant service at battles of Murfreesboro and Jonesboro; promoted capt. 27th Inf., U.S. Army, 1866; stationed at Ft. Phil Kearny, Wyo. Killed (together with force of 80 men) in ambush by Chief Red Cloud nr. Lodge Trail Ridge, Wyo., Dec. 21, 1866.

FEW, WILLIAM banker, senator; b. Balt., June 8, 1748 s. William and Mary (Wheeler) F.; m. Catherine Nicholson, 3 children. Mem. Ga. Gen. Assembly, 1776, 83 mem. Exec. Council of Ga., 1776; surveyor gen. Ga., 1778; served as lt. col. Continental Army, also commr. to Indians during Revolutionary War; mem. Continental Congress from Ga., 1780-82, 85-88; a rep. from Ga. drafting U.S. Constn., signer, 1787; mem. U.S. Senate from Ga., 1789-93; judge 2d U.S. Jud. Circuit of Ga., 1794-97; moved to N.Y.C., 1799; mem. N.Y. Gen. Assembly, 1802-05; insp. N.Y. prisons; alderman N.Y.C.; dir. Manhattan Bank, 1804-14; pres. City Bank of N.Y. Died Fishkill-on-the-Hudson July 16, 1828.

FIALA, ANTHONY explorer: b. Jersey City Heights, N.J., Sept. 19, 1869; s. Anthony and Annie (Kohout) F.; student Cooper Union and N.A.D., N.Y.C.; m. Mary Clare Puryear, Dec. 6, 1905; children-Anthony, Reid Puryear, Mary Maury, Lenore Fontaine, Began business life as stone artist and designer of lithography: asst. in a physical and chem. lab., 5 yrs.; newspaper artist and cartoonist, 1890; cartoonist Grit, Williamsport, Pa., 1893-94; studied processes of photo-engraving and photogravure; installed photo-engraving plant for Bklyn Daily Eagle, 1894, also in charge art and engraving dept., 1894-99; now pres. Fiala Outfits, Inc. War corr. for Bklyn. Daily Eagle while trooper in Troop C, 1st N.Y. Vol. Cav., Spanish-Am, War, 1898; commd. 1st lt. 14th Regt. Nat. Guard, N.Y., 1900, and was instr. mil. engring. Photographer Baldwin-Ziegler Polar Expdn., 1901-02; comdg. officer Ziegler Polar Expdn., 1903-05, reaching 82ff north, discovered and mapped new islands, also surveyed and mapped accurately greater part of Franz Josef Archipelago, maps and records published by Nat. Geog. Soc., Washington, 1907. Commd. 2d lt., q.-m. Squadron C, N.G., N.Y., 1908, capt. 2d Cav., 1911. Fellow A.A.A.S., Royal Geog. Soc.; mem. Am. Geog. Soc.; hon. mem. Internat. Yukon Polar Inst. Cruising Club of Am. Episcopalian (vestryman). Mason. Clubs: Explorers, Artic, Ends of the Earth, Camp Fire of America, Am. Canoe Assn., Squadron C Cavalry. Author: Troop "C" in Service, 1899; Fighting the Polar Ice, 1906. Accompanied Col. Theodore Roosevelt on his trip through the Brazillian wilderness, 1913-14; explored the Papagaio River and descended the Jurnena and Tapajos rivers of Brazil, Capt., Machine Gun Troop, Mexican border service, 1916-17; capt. 4th Co. 102d Ammunition Train, 1917; transferred to Ordnance R.C., Feb. 11, 1918; maj. N.A., July 31, 1918; officer in charge Small Arms Proving Ground, Springfield, Mass., July 1, 1918-June 4, 1919: hon. discharged, June 4, 1919; maj., Ordnance Sect. O.R.C., July 9, 1919. Home: 148 83d St., Bklyn. Office: 10 Warren St., N.Y.C. Died Apr. 8, 1950; buried Arlington Nat. Cemetery.

FICHTE, HAROLD O., banker; b. Chgo., June 16, 1914; s. Otto F. and Lydia (Hildebrandt) F.; B.A., U. Ill., 1936, LL.B., 1938; m. Veryl Von Almen, Apr. 15, 1939; children—Maxine Marie (Mrs. Leo H. Bondurant), Bruce H., Royce J. Claim supr., examiner Lumbermen's Mut. Casualty Co., 1938-46, procedures coordinator, 1946-50, mgr. procedures dept., 1951-65, asst. v.p., 1958-65; v.p. Bank of Chgo., 1965-71; admitted to Ill. bar, 1938. Served to lt. col. USAAF, 1941-46. Decorated Bronze Star medal. Mem. Ill. C. of C., Ill. Bar Assn., Am. Inst. Banking, Phi Beta Kappa, Beta Sigma Psi, Sigma Delta Kappa. Lutheran. Home: Prospect Heights IL Died Apr. 8, 1971.

FICKEL, JACOB EARL ret. army officer; b. Des Moines, Ia., Jan. 31, 1883; s. Joel and Margaret Maria (Jackson) F.; student Des Moines Coll., 1899-1902, Revenue Cutter Service Cadet Sch., 1902-04, Air Corps Tactical Sch., 1924-25, Command and Gen. Staff Sch., 1925-26, Army War Coll., 1930-31; m. Marion Allison, Feb. 15, 1912; children-Arthur Allison, Stanton Livingston. Enlisted in U.S. Army as pvt. 1904; commd. 2d lt., 1907, advanced through the grades to maj. gen. U.S. Army, 1940; 1 aerial gunner 1910; grained as pilot 1918; comd. flying school, 1918, 35; staff AC, 1919-20, 22-23, 31-34; comptroller-treas. U.S. Spruce Production Corp., 1921; exec. Wright Field, 1926-30: staff 9th Corps Areas, 1936-39; dir. aircraft prodn., 1938; command First Wing G.H.Q., Air Force, 1939; asst. chief AC, 1940, comd. S.W. Air Dist., 1940, 4th Air Force, 1941, 3d Dist. Tech. Tng. Command, 1942, Eastern Tech. Tng. Command, 1943, Western Tech. Tng. Command, 1945, ret. 1946. Rated command pilot and combat observer. Methodist. Club: Army and Navy (Washington). Address: San Antonio. Died Aug. 7, 1956.

FICKLIN, ORLANDO BELL congressman, lawyer; b. Scott County, Ky., Dec. 16, 1808; grad. Transylvania Law Sch., Lexington, Ky., 1830. Admitted to bar, 1830, began practice of law, Mt. Carmel, Ill.; served as q.m. in Black Hawk War, 1882; col. Wabash County Militia, 1833; states atty. for Wabash Circuit, 1835; mem. Ill. Ho. of Reps., 1835, 38, 42, 78; moved to Charleston, Ill., 1837; mem. U.S. Ho. of Reps. (Democrat) from Ill., 28th-30th, 32d congresses, 1843-49, 51-53; Dem. presdl. elector, 1856, 84; del. Dem. Nat. Conv.; Cincinnati, 1856, Charleston, S.C. 1860, Chgo., 1864, del., Ill. Constl. Conv., 1869-70. Died Charleston, Ill., May 5, 1886; buried Mount Cemetery.

FIEBEGER, GUSTAV JOSEPH army officer; b. Akron, O., May 9, 1858; s. Joseph and Rosalie (May) F.; grad. U.S. Mil. Acad., 1879; m. Anna Perkins Upson, June 29, 1887; 1 dau., Julia Ford. Additional 2d lt. engrs., June 13, 1879; 2d lt., Oct. 31, 1897; 1st lt., June 15, 1882; capt., Feb. 22, 1891; prof. with rank of col., May 4, 1896. Officer corps engrs. U.S.A., 1879-96, and engr. in charge of improvement of rivers and harbors of Va. and N.C. and of city of Washington; prof. civ. and mil. engring., U.S. Mil. Acad., 1896-1922; retired. Author: Civil Engineering, 1905; Strategy. Awarded D.S.M. Home: Washington, D.C. Died Oct. 18, 1939.

FIELD, B(ENJAMIN) RUSH physician; b. Easton, Pa., Nov. 3, 1861; s. Dr. C.C. and Susan (Freeman) F.; ed. pub. schs. and Lafayette Coll.; M.D., U. of Pa., 1883; m. Nan Edna Rounsavell, Apr. 9, 1902; 1 son, B. Rush. Official phys. Northampton Co., Pa., prison; 10 yrs. phys. for coronor. Mem. and pres. civic council, 1890-93, mayor Easton, 1893-96, and 1899-1902; commr. of Public Safety, 1914-20; chmn. med. board Easton Hospital; also supt. of Easton Hospital, 1926-29. Co-chmn. Civic Assn. of Northampton County; chmn. taxation com. of Easton Board of Trade. Democrat. Capt. Co. E and maj. 2d battallion 11th Pa. Vols., 1898; after Spanish-Am. War, on consolidation of 11th and 13th regts., maj. 13th regt. Pa. N.G., lt. col., 1904; retired at own request, 1908. Trustee Easton Pub. Library, 1902—; trustee, 1915. hon. v.p., 1919, League of Cities of the Third Class in Pa. Chmn. Northampton Co. mil. sect. of Pa. Com. Pub. Safety, 1917; mem. War History Commn. of Pa.; mem. County Com. Citizens Mil. Training Camp.; mem. Internat. Kiwanis Conv., 1919. Author: Medical Thoughts of Shakespeare, 1884, 3d edit., 1905. Editor: Romeo and Juliet (Vol. 5, Bankside Edit. of Shakespeare), 1889. Home: Easton, Pa. Died May 1, 1935.

FIELD, CHARLES WILLIAM army officer; b. Airy Mount, Woodford County, Ky., Apr. 6, 1828; s. Willis and Isabella (Buck) F.; grad. U.S. Mil. Acad., 1849; m. Monimia Mason, 1857, 2 children. Commd. 2d lt. 2d Dragoons, U.S. Army; served in N.M., Tex., Kan., 1849-55; promoted 1st lt., 1855; instr. cavalry tactics U.S. Mil. Acad., 1856; commd. capt., 1861, resigned to enter Confederate Army; commd. capt. Confederate Army, 1861; col. 6th Va. Cavalry, 1861, brig. gen., 1862; commanded brigade at Fredericksburg and Seven Day's battles; served in battles of Cedar Mountain and 2d Bull Run; maj. gen., 1864; present at Appomattox Court House when Lee surrendered; col. engrs. Egyptian Army, 1875, insp. gen. during Abyssinian War; returned to U.S., 1877; doorkeeper U.S. Ho. of Reps., 46th Congress, 1878; U.S. civil engr., 1881-85; supt. Hot Springs (Ark.) Indian Reservation, 1885-89. Died Washington, D.C., Apr. 9, 1892.

FIELD, CROSBY, inventor, engr., mfr.; b. Jamestown, N.Y., Mar. 12, 1889; B.S., N. Y. U., 1909; M.E., Cornell U., 1912; M.S. in Elec. Engring., Union Coll., Schenectady, N.Y., 1914; m. Ethel Henriksen, Nov. 23, 1916; children—Margaret Roberta, Dorothy Henrietta, Patricia Crosby. With Gen. Electric Co., 1912-14; in private practice as cons. engr., 1914-15; chief engr., Standard Aniline Products, Inc., 1915-17; engring. mgr., Nat. Aniline & Chem. Co., in charge all engring. including constrn., maintenance, power plant operating, appraisal and engring. research, 1919-23; v.p., dir. and sec., Brillo Mfg. Co., 1923-45; also with FlakIce Corp., 1923-72. Chem. Machinery Corp., 1923-37. Reserve officer. Army Ordnance Dept., Jan., 1917-72; served as 1st lt., capt., maj., U.S. Army, 1917-19, acting chief, explosives and loading sect. Inspection Div.; in active service, col., Army Ordnance Dept., AUS, 1942-45, assigned as asst. dir. Safety Office of Chief of Ordnance. Decorated Legion of Merit. Registered profl. engr. Fellow Am. Soc. M.E. (medalist 1953, hon. mem.), I.E.E.E., A.A.A.S., Am. Soc. Heating, Refrigerating and Air Conditioning Engrs. (past pres., hon. mem.); mem. Am. Chem. Soc., Am. Inst. Chem. Engrs. (past mem. council), Am. Inst. Chemists, Nat., N.Y. socs. profl. engrs., Am. Ordnance Assn., Sigma Xi, Phi Beta Kappa Alumni Assn., Phi Beta Kappa Assos., Pi Kappa Alpha, Tau Beta Pi, Pi Tau Sigma. Mason. Republican. Episcopalian. Clubs: Andiron, Engineers, Chemists (N.Y.C.); Union League (Chgo.). Contbr. numerous papers on engring. specialties to sci. orgns. Inventor of the Oxide Film Lightning Arrestor, 1912, and continuous ice ribbon freezing process, 1916, continuous steel wool mfg. process, 1923; over 140 U.S. patents including elec., chem., mech. and refrigeration processes and equipment. Home: Brooklyn NY Died Sept. 20, 1972.

FIELD, EDWARD PEARSALL, JR. soap co. exec.; b. N.Y.C., Feb. 12, 1908; s. Edward P. and Gertrude (Baiter) F.; B.S., Princeton, 1926-30; m. Alice Burt, Oct. 23, 1948; children - Edward Pearsall, III, Wency P.; 1 stepson, Lloyd B. Field. Vice pres. Carr, Inc., 1946-52, Colgate Palmolive Co., N.Y.C., 1952 - ; pres., dir. Sterno, Inc.; v.p., dir. Canaan Products. Served to col. USAAF, 1941-46. Decorated Bronze Star. Home: 71 Western Dr., Short Hills, N.J. Office: 300 Park Ave., N.Y.C. Died Sept. 14, 1965.

FIELD, HARRY ASHBY naval officer; b. Baltimore, Md., July 2, 1862; s. John Albert and Susan R. M. (Easter) E.; grad. U.S. Naval Acad., 1883; m. Julia Sewall Waters, Apr. 25, 1900. Ensign, July 1, 1885; lt. jr. grade, Apr. 23, 1895; lt., May 1, 1898; lt. comdr., Jan. 1, 1904; comdr. July 1, 1908; capt., July 1, 1911; rear adm. (temp.), July 1919. Served on the Alert, Independence and Phila., Spanish-Am. War, 1898; insp. equipment, Gen Electric Co., Schenectady, N.Y., 1904-06; exec. officer Tennessee, 1906-08; comd. Yorktown, 1908-09; in charge 6th Light House Dist., 1910-12; comd. Tennessee, 1912-13, Louisiana, 1913-14; capt. of yard, Navy Yard, Portsmouth, N.H., 1914-15; at Naval War Coll., 1915; comd. North Dakota, 1915-16; comdt. Puget Sound Navy Yard, 1913-21; comdr. train Pacific fleet, Apr.-July 1921; pres. bd. of Inspn. Pacific coast July 1921—. Presbyn. Home: Baltimore, Md. Died July 1, 1936.

FIELD, MARSHALL born Chicago, Ill., Sept. 28, 1893; s. Marshall, Jr., and Albertine (Huck) F.; reared and ed. in England; student Eton Coll. and Cambridge U.; m. 3d, Mrs. Ruth Pruyn Phipps, Jan. 15, 1936. Pres. The Field Found., Inc.; pres., dir. Field Enterprises Inc. (which publishes Chgo. Sun-Times, World Book Ency. and Child-craft; owner, operator Simon & Schuster, Pocket Books, Inc., Parade Publs., Inc., N.Y.C. Functional Music Inc., Chgo.; dir. American Houses, Inc. Trustee Chgo. Natural History Museum, Metropolitan Museum of Art, N.Y. Zoological Soc., New School Social Research, Sarah Lawrence College; hon. trustee U. of Chicago; gov. Menninger Foundation. Pvt. 1st Ill. Cavalry, 1917, afterwards 122d F.A., 33d Div.; promoted through grades to capt.; arrived in France, Mar. 1918; participated in St. Mihiel and Meuse-Argonne operations; honorably discharged, Feb. 20, 1919. Elected pres. Child Welfare League of Am., 1951. Democrat. Clubs: Chicago, University, Casino, (Chicago); Knickerbocker, Racquet and Tennis, Brook, Grolier, Meadow Brook, Turf and Field, N.Y. Yacht (N.Y.C.). Home: 740 Park Av., N.Y.C. 21; (country) Lloyds Neck, Huntington, L.I., N.Y. Offices: 250 Park Avenue, N.Y.C. 17; 211 W. Wacker Dr., Chgo. Died Nov. 8, 1956; buried Chgo.

FIELD, RICHARD STOCKTON naval officer; b. Pocahontas, Miss., June 9, 1890; s. Dr. Robert and Belle (Daniel) F.; grad. U.S. Naval Acad., 1911; grad. U.S. Naval War Coll., 1936; m. Mildred Fearn, Oct. 15, 1913; children-Richard Stockton, Fearn. Commd. ensign USN, 1912, advanced through grades to comdr., 1931, ret., 1937; dir. Bur. of Marine Inspection and Nav., U.S. Dept. of Commerce, Washington, 1937—. With USCG, 1942— for duration of war; promoted capt., USN, 1942. Decorated Victory, Haitian, Mexican, Nicaragua campaign medals (U.S.); Commendatore of Order of Crown of Italy. Episcopalian. Club: Chevy Chase. Home: Chevy Chase Club. Chevy Chase. Md. Deceased.

FIELD, WELLS LAFFIN rear-admiral U.S.N.; b. St. Louis, Jan 31, 1846; s. Matthew D. and Clarissa (Laffin) F.; grad. U.S. Naval Acad., 1867; m. Ruth Dunning Clark, Nov. 8, 1894. Promoted ensign, 1868; master, 1870; lt., 1871; lt. comdr., 1892; comdr., Apr. 1898; capt., June 16, 1902; rear admiral and retired, Nov. 20, 1902, after 40 years service in varied sea and shore duties. Died Nov. 27, 1914.

FIELDING, MICHAEL FARLOW radio news and mil. analyst; b. Darjeeling, India, Aug. 7, 1896; s. Percival David and Mary Patricia (Robinson) F.; ed. in Darjeeling, India, Eastbourne, Egn., and Coburg, Germany; student Stoneyhurst Coll., Eng., 1914-15; m. Petrollnia Juan, Jan. 15, 1931. Served as capt. Indian Army, 1915-20; trained in Quetta, Baluchistan; attached to 54th Sikhs on Afghan border; participated in World War I; in Mesopotamia with 6th Cav. Brigade; in 3d Afghan War, Waziristan and Mahsud campaigns; later engaged in varied activities, including work as cowboy, motion picture producer and actor, banker, newspaperman, advt., sales promotion, pub. relations (in U.S. and abroad), radio news and mil. analyst, 1941 - ; now lecturing coast to coast on internat. affairs; guest of Indian Govt. 1945; guest of Pakistan Govt. on Expdn. to Kyber, Afghanistan, Waziristan, Baluchistan, Swat and Kashmir, 1949; dir. Fielding Seminar to Europe, 1951; leader Fielding Adventure Trail tours through Europe, 1951, 52, 53, 54, 55, 56, 57, Fielding-Hemphill Adventure Trail Tour Around World, 1954, 56, Fielding Africa Safari, 1957; Fielding Let's Get Away From it All, South Seas Tour, 1957; v.p. Drake-Fielding Tours, Inc. Clubs: Explorers (N.Y.C.); Chicago Press, Adventures (Chgo.). Author: Pocket Guide to Europe, 1956, 57. Home: Maria Luisa Santander 0141, Dept. H, Santiago, Chile. Died 1966.

FIKE, CHARLES LAIRD marine corps officer (ret.); b. Des Moines, Ia., Mar. 13, 1902; s. Clement Laird and Mary Jane (Campbell) F.; B.S., U.S. Naval Acad., 1924; M.S. in Engring., U. Mich., 1936; m. Helen Elizabeth Lytle, June 28, 1924; 1 son, Robert G. Commd. 2d lt. USMC, 1924, advanced through grades to brig. gen., 1946; Marine Corps aviation, 1926-46, ret., 1946; exec. engr. ry. car div., E. G. Budd Co., Phila. Distinguished Flying Cross, Bronze Star. Mem. Soc. of Automotive Engrs. Home: 1037 Edge Hill Rd., Roslyn, Pa. Died May 3, 1950.

FILLEBROWN, CHARLES BOWDOIN single-tax propagandist; b. Winthrop, Me., Dec. 26, 1842; s. James Bowdoin and Almira (Butler) F.; ed. Kent's Hill, Me., 1858-61; Phillips Acad., Exeter, N.H., 1862; Mass. Inst. Tech., 1866-67; m. Mary Louise Hall, Oct. 9, 1873 (died 1887). In Union Army, 1862-66; in 24th Me. Inf., 9 months; 29th Me. Inf., 3 years; A.-D.-C., 1st brigade, 1st div., 19th Army Corps; brigade staff Bank's 2d Red River Expdn.; div. staff Sheridan's Shenandoah Valley campaign. Pres. and gen. mgr. Glenark Knitting Co., Woonsocket, R.I., 1881-1903. Treas. Mass Single Tax League, 1892, pres., 1899-1909; active as single tax propagandist from 1895. Died Dec. 1917.

FILLMORE, MILLARD Pres. U.S.; b. Locke, N.Y., Jan. 7, 1800; s. Nathaniel and Phoebe (Millard) F.; m. Abigail Powers, Feb. 5, 1826; m. 2d, Caroline Carmichael McIntosh, Feb. 10, 1858; children - Mary Abigail, Millard Powers. Admitted to N.Y. bar, 1823; mem. Anti-Masonic Party; mem. N.Y. State Legislature, 1828-32; mem. U.S. Ho. of Reps. from N.Y. State, 23d, 25th-27th congresses, 1833-35, 37-41, chmn. ways and means com., 1840-42; comtroller N.Y. State, 1847; became vice pres. U.S., Feb. 1849, became 13th Pres. U.S. at death of Pres. Taylor, July 9, 1850, allied with moderate Whigs who favored compromises; achieved Compromise of 1850 regulating slavery boundaries; approved treaty opening Japan to Western commerce; lost Whig presdl. nomination, 1852, unsuccessful candidate on Know Nothing ticket, 1856; 1st chancellor U. Buffalo (N.Y.); a founder of Buffalo Hist. Soc.; a founder, 1st pres. Buffalo Gen. Hosp.; declined D.C.L. from Oxford (Eng.) U., on grounds that his literary or sci. attainments were not great enough, 1855. Died Buffalo, Mar. 8, 1874; buried Forest Hill Cemetery, Buffalo.

FINCH, FREDERICK L. physician; b. Youngstown, O., June 13, 1905; s. Frederick L. and Genevieve Elizabeth (Dobbins) F.; grad. N.Y. Prep Sch., 1925;

student Coll. Wm. and Mary, 1925-28; M.D., Med. Coll. Va., 1932; m. Melba Mayhew Gravely, June 23, 1932; 1 dau., Carole Virginia. Intern St. Lukes Hosp., Richmond, Va., 1932-33; pvt. practice gen. med., Urbanna, Va., 1933-34; internal medicine, asso. indsl. physician Am. Tobacco Co., Richmond, 1934-42, physician-in-charge Va. div., practice internal medicine 1946—; asst. prof. pub. health Med. Coll. Va. 1946—. Entered M.C., USN, 1942; disch. to Res. as comdr., 1946. Fellow Indsl. Med. Assn.; mem. A.M.A., Tri-State Med. Soc., Med. Soc. Va., Richmond Acad. Med., Lambda Chi Alpha, Alpha Kappa Kappa, Theta Chi Delta, Chi Beta Phi. Home: 105 Seneca Rd., Richmond. Office: 1001 Franklin St., Richmond 20, Va. Died May 21, 1957.

FINCH, ISAAC congressman; b. Stillwater, N.Y., Oct. 13, 1783; attended public schs.; studied law. Engaged in agriculture, nr. Jay, Essex County, N.Y.; served as maj. 26th Inf. Regt. during War of 1812; mem. N.Y. State Assembly, 1822-24; mem. U.S. Ho. of Reps. (Democrat) from N.Y., 21st congress, 1829-31. Died Jay, June 23, 1845; buried Central Cemetery.

FINCH, PEYTON NEWELL, JR., metal and pipe co. exec.; b. Selma, Ala., May 1, 1921; s. Peyton Newell and Lucy (Stounmier) F.; B.S., U. Ala., 1942, LL.B., 1948; m. Betty Stith Rowe, Sept. 10, 1947; children—Elizabeth, Susan, Barbara. Admitted to Ala. bar, 1948; patent atty. Comml. Solvents Corp., 1948-51, Chemstrand Corp., 1952-54; patent counsel, asst. sec. U.S. Pipe & Foundry Co., 1955-64, v.p., sec., 1964-69; dir. Rockwin Prestressed Concrete Corp., Sante Fe Springs, Cal. Mem. Ala. Water Improvement Commn., 1964-69; mem. adv. council Ala. Dept. Indsl. Relations, 1962-69; chmn. water and air resources com. Asso. Industries Ala., 1965-69. Bd. dirs. U. Ala. Law Sch. Found., Gorgas Scholarship Found., Jr. Achievement Jefferson County; adv. bd. Salvation Army City Command; trustee Nat. Trade Relations Council. Served to maj. AUS, 1942-46, 51-52. Mem. Am., Ala., Birmingham bar assns., Birmingham C. of C. (chmn. pub. affairs com.), Phi Alpha Delta, Pi Kappa Alpha. Home: Birmingham AL Died Feb. 29, 1968; buried Elmwood Cemetery, Birmingham AL

FINCHER, EDGAR FRANKLIN, neurosurgeon; b. Stone Mountain, Ga., 1900; s. Edgar Franklin and Grace (Maddox) F.; B.S., Emory U., 1922, M.D., 1925; m. Helen Louise Nichols, Feb. 10, 1934; 1 son, Edgar Franklin. Intern Piedmont Hosp., Atlanta, 1925-26; vol. grad. surgery Peter Bent Brigham Hosp., Boston, 1926; fellow neurol. surgery Washington U., St. Louis, 1926-27; fellow NRC, 1927-28; fellow neurol. surgery Mayo Found., U. Minn., 1928-30; instr. neurosurgery Emory U. Sch. Medicine, 1930-33, asso., 1933-37, asst. prof., 1937-55, asso. prof., 1955-59, prof. neurosurgery, from 1959; sect. head neurosurgery Univ. Clinic; chief neurosurgery service Univ. and Henrietta Egleston hosps.; cons. neurosurgery Grady Meml., VA hosps. Served as maj., M.C., AUS, World War II. Diplomate Am. Bd. Neurol. Surgery (founder mem.; pres. 1957-59). Mem. Harvey Cushing Soc. (founder mem.; pres. 1944), Soc. Neurol. Surgeons (sec.-treas. 1949-53, pres. 1956), So. Neurosurg. Soc. (pres. 1950), So. Surg. Assn., A.M.A., A.C.S., Sigma Xi, Alpha Omega Alpha, Phi Delta Theta, Phi Rho Sigma. Methodist. Clubs: Capital City, Commerce (Atlanta); Highlands (N.C.) Country. Author med. articles. Home: Atlanta GA Died Jan. 12, 1969.

FINDLAY, JAMES congressman; b. Franklin County, Pa., Oct. 12, 1777; s. Samuel and Jane (Smith) F.; m. Jane Irwin. Practiced law, Cincinnati; mem. Ohio Territorial Legilsative Council, 1798; U.S. receiver public moneys, Cincinnati, 1800; 1st U.S. marshal of Ohio, 1802; mem. Ohio Ho. of Reps., 1803; mayor of Cincinnati, 1805-06, 10-11; col. 2d Ohio Volunteer Inf., 1812; promoted brig. gen. Ohio Militia; mem. U.S. Ho. of Reps. from Ohio, 19th-22d congresses, 1825-33; built Ft. Findlay, 1812, later became town of Findlay, Hancock County, O.; partner Cincinnati Bell, Brass, and Iron Foundry, Liberty Hall and Cincinnati Gazette. Died Cincinnati, Dec. 28, 1835; buried Spring Grove Cemetery, Cincinnati.

FINK, GEORGE R(UPERT) steel mfr.; b. Brackenridge, Pa., Nov. 1, 1886; s. Peter George and Margaret Jane (Rupert) F.; ed. grammar sch., Brackenridge; Dr. Engring., U. Mich., 1941; m. Esther Malow, Jan. 25, 1917 (dec.); children - George R. (lt. USNR; died in Pacific, June 1945), Eleanor Martha; m. 2d, Elise Morley, Sept. 17, 1929; children - Peter Rupert, Elise Lammert, John Morley, Margaret Ann. Began as steel mill worker with Allegheny Steel Corp., later steel salesman; organizer, operator Mich. Steel Corp. and Gt. Lakes Steel Corp., Detroit; pres. Nat. Steel Corp. Served as capt. Ordinance Dept., U.S. Army, 1918. Presbyn. Clubs: Detroit, Detroit Athletic, Country of Detroit, Gross Pointe (Detroit); Duquesne (Pitts.); Yondotega Club, Union League (N.Y.); Racquet (Chgo.). Home: 69 Cloverly Rd., Gross Pointe Farms 30, Mich. Office: Gt. Lakes Steel Corp., Ecorse, Detroit. Died July 29, 1962; buried Woodlawn Cemetery, Detroit.

FINLAYSON, JOHN DUNCAN life ins. exec.; b. Thessalon, Ont., Can., May 16, 1886; s. Kenneth and Anna (Dickie) F.; student Alma (Mich.) Coll., 1907-08, LL.D., 1928; A.B., U. Mich., 1911; student Union Theol. Sem., and Columbia, 1911-12; B.D., Auburn Theol. Sem., 1914; studied Berlin and Gottingen; Th.D., Harvard, 1916; m. Virginia Joyce Crafts, Sept. 4, 1912; children-Joyce Louise, Judith Ann, Jeanne Tertia, Ordained to ministry Presbyn. Ch., 1914; pastor Ypsilanti, Mich., 1916-19; prof. psychology and philosophy Dubuque (Ia.) Coll., 1919-20; instr. psychology U. Mich., 1921-22; pres. Fairmount Coll., Wichita, Kan., 1922-26, lead successful movement for municipalization of Fairmount Coll., developing it into Municipal U. of Wichita, pres., 1926-27; chancellor U. Tulsa, 1927-34; pres. Beacon Life Ins. Co., 1934-35; dist. mgr. Mass. Mut. Life Ins. Co., 1935—. YMCA regional ednl. dir. AEF, World War I; in charge work in central and so. France and for Army of Occupation in Germany, until Feb. 1919; ednl. dir. U.S. Army, at camps Dodge and Lewis, 1920-21. Mem. Assn. Coll. Pres., N.E.A. (life), Okla. Acad. Sci., Pi Gamma Mu. Presbyn. Mason. Home: 2735 Bedford Rd. Office: First Nat. Bldg., Ann Arbor, Mich. Died June 4, 1950.

FINNEGAN, JOSEPH FRANCIS gov. ofcl.; b. North Adams, Mass., Sept. 12, 1904; s. Dennis J. and Elizabeth (Flanagan) F.; A.B., Columbia, 1928; L.L.B., Fordham U., 1931; m. Maurine C. Schooler, Nov. 14, 1947. Admitted to N.Y. bar, 1931; asst. U.S. atty., So. Dist. of N.Y., 1931-34; mem. Lauterstein, Spiller, Bergerman & Dannett, 1934-48; pvt. practice law, N.Y.C., 1948-55; dir. Fed. Mediation and Conciliation Service, 1955-61; chmn. N.Y. State Bd. Mediation, 1961 - . Served as maj. Air Transport Command, USAAF, 1942-45, asst. chief mil. personnel. Recipient St. John Francis Regis award, U. San Francisco, Berlin award, Coll., Holy Cross, 1957; Rerum Novarum award St. Peters Coll., 1959. Mem. Assn. Bar City of N.Y., Fed., Am. bar assns., Assn. Bar D.C., Catholic Lawyers Guild, Phi Kappa Sigma. Club: N.Y. Athletic. Home: 2510 N. Nelson St., Arlington, Va. 22207. Office: 270 Broadway, N.Y.C. 7. Died Feb. 12, 1964; buried Arlington (Va.) Nat. Cemetery.

FINNELL, WOOLSEY civil engr.; b. Tuscaloosa, Co., Ala., Oct. 24, 1866; s. Adoniran Judson and Narsissa (Durrett) F.; prep. edn., Pleasant Hill Acad. (Jefferson Co., Ala.) and Tuscaloosa Mil. Acad.; C.E., U. of Ala., 1887; m. Margaret Hagler, of Tuscaloosa Co., Oct. 21, 1890; children - Edward Judson, Lillian Margaret (dec.), Julia Judson (Mrs. Joseph J. Wode), Newbie (Mrs. Charles Livingston), Susie (Mrs. C.W. Gross), Woolsey, Mary-Jessie, Harriett M. Began in Jefferson Co. as axeman on K.C., M. & B.R.R. (now St. Louis-San Francisco Ry.), 1887, continuing as asst. engr., resident engr., locating engr. and division engr. several railroads; served as chief engr. various ry. projects; opened office as cons. engr., at Tuscaloosa, Ala., 1894; served as judge of probate, Tuscaloosa Co.; became dir. State Highway Department, Ala., Feb. 1, 1927; now with United States Department of Justice, Bureau of Prisons. Commd. maj. engrs., U.S.A., June 19, 1917; sailed for France with 501st Engrs. and later made engr. officer of Intermediate in command of 18,000 lt. col. 14, 1918; duty at Paris, 1919, with War Damage Peace Bd. of Conf., later field executive of Army Ednl. Corps; hon. discharged, Sept. 16, 1919; col. Engr. Res. Corps, Jan. 20, 1920. Charter mem. Am. Soc. Mil. Engrs., Am. Soc. C.E. Awarded citation by Gen. Pershing "for extremely meritorious service"; Legion of Honor (French). Democrat. Missionary Baptist. Mason (33ff, Scottish Rite; Shriner); in York Rite has held offices of Eminent Comdr. of Commandery, Grand Comdr. K.T. of Ala., v.p. Order of High Priesthood of Ala.; Most Puissant Sovereign Red Cross of Constantine and many others; organized the first Masonic Club in France, Apr. 1918. Home: Tuscaloosa, Ala.

FINNEY, JOHN MILLER TURPIN surgeon; b. June 20, 1863; s. Ebenezer D. and Annie L. (Parker) F.; A.B., Princeton, 1884; M.D., Harvard, 1889, LL.D., 1937; LL.D., Tulane U., New Orleans, 1935; m. Mary E. Gross, Apr. 20, 1892; children - John Miller Train, Eben Dickey, George Gross, Mary Elizabeth. In practice at Baltimore since 1889; prof. surgery emeritus, Johns Hopkins. Fellow Am. Surg. Assn. (ex-pres.), Am. Coll. Surgeons (ex-pres.), Southern Surg. and Gynecol. Assn. Brig. gen., Med. B.C. U.S. Army; chief consultant in surgery A.E.F. Decorated D.S.M. (U.S.); Comdr. de l'Ordre de la Couronne (Belgina); Officer de la Légion d'Honeur (French). Club: Maryland. Home: 200 Goodwood Gardens, Roland Park. Office: 2947 St. Paul St., Baltimore, Md. Died May 30, 1942.

FIRESTONE, ROGER STANLEY, mfg. exec.; b. Akron, O., June 25, 1912; s. Harvey S. and Idabelle (Smith) F.; A.B., Princeton 1935; postgrad. Cal. Inst. Tech.; H.H.D., Central Coll., Pella, Ia., 1961; LL.D., Lycoming Coll., 1963, LaSalle Coll., 1966, Allegheny Coll., 1967; m. Mary Davis, Aug. 22, 1936 (dec.); children—Gay (Mrs. P. G. Wray), Peter, John Davis; m. 2d Anne Joers, April 15, 1946; children—Cinda, Susan. Dist. Sales mgr. with Firestone Tire & Rubber Co., Houston, Tex., 1937-38, dir. since 1945, dir. new prdts. dept., 1945-57; pres. Firestone Rubber & Latex Prdts. Co. Fall River, Mass., 1938-42; pres. Firestone Aircraft Co., Akron, 1945-47; pres. Firestone Plastics Co., Pottstown, 1947. Vice chmn. United Cerebral Palsy Assns.; pres. United Cerebral Palsy Research & Ednl. Found.; v.p., nat. exec. bd. Boy Scouts Am. Mem. Nixon for Pres. adv. com., 1968; adviser Pa. Republican financial com. Bd. dirs., trustees Freedoms Found. at Valley Forge; trustee Ind. Coll. Funds. Am., Ind., Lincoln U., Oxford, Pa.; Pa. chmn. Found. for Ind. Colls., Inc. Served as lt. to lt. comdr. USNR, 1942-45; prodn. div. Navy Bur. Aero, Washington, 1942, logistics plans div. Office Chief Naval Operations. 1944-45. Recipient Silver Beaver, Silver Antelope, Silver Buffalo awards Boy Souts of Am. Mem. Sigma Xi. Republican. Episcopalian. Clubs: Chevy Chase, Metropolitan (Washington); River, Brook (N.Y.C.); Crown Colony (Bahamas); Gulph Mills Golf, Union League, Corinthian Yacht, Racquet, Philadelphia (Phila.); Augusta Nat. Golf; Laurel Valley Golf; Rotary (hon. mem.) (Pottstown, Pa.). Home: Bryn Mawr PA Died Jan. 26, 1970; buried Columbiana OH

FISCHER, ARTHUR FREDERICK museum adminstr.; b. Chgo., Feb. 6, 1888; s. Joseph and Mary Anna (Ebert) F.; C.E., Ohio No. U., 1909; M.F., Yale, 1911; grad. U.S. War Coll., 1927; hon. M.A., Yale, 1939; m. Helen Wyly Campbell, June 21, 1911; children - Arthur Frederick, Ruth Winifred (dec.), Alan Campbell. Asst. to state forester of Ohio, 1910; forester Bureau of Forestry, P.I., 1911-16, acting dir., 1916-17, dir., 1917-36; asst. prof. forest engring. U. Philippines, 1912-17, dean Sch. Forestry. 1917-35, prof. tropical forestry, 1917-; now dir. Natural History Mus. San Diego, adviser on natural resources, Commonwealth Govt. of P.I., 1937-41, Bataan Corregidor campaign, 1941-42; exec. dir. Am. Cinchona plantations U. S. Com. Co., 1943-46; established U.S. Govt. Quinine Plantation in Costa Rica; col. M.I., S.G.O., AUS, now ret. Awarded Legion of Merit, Distinguished Service Star (Philippines), Merite-Agricol (France), Green Dragon Annam. Fellow Soc. Am. Foresters, San Diego Soc. Natural History (sec.-treas.). Presbyn. Clubs: Rotary (pres. 1934-35), Army and Navy, Manila, Polo, Cosmos, Army and Navy (Washington). Home: 1746 Warrington St., San Diego 92107. Office: Natural History Mus., Balboa Park, San Diego 1. Died Oct. 31, 1962; buried Ft. Rosecrans Nat. Cemetery.

FISCHER, LOUIS ALBERT physicist; b. Washington, D.C., Jan. 4, 1865; s. Frederick C. and Anna (Cox) F.; B.S., Columbian (now George Washington) U., 1884; m. Marion G. Garvey, Aug. 6, 1888. In Office of Weights and Measures, U.S. Coast and Geod. Survey, 1891-1901; chief of weights and measures div., Bur. of Standards, with title asso. physicist, 1901-10, physicist, 1910-17; major. Ordnance U.S.A., Aug. 6, 1917-Jan. 30, 1919. Asst. in physics, George Washington U., 1906. Author: Recomparison of United States Prototype Meter, 1904; History of Weights and Measures, 1905. Compiler: Laws Relating to Weights and Measures in United States, 1904. Home: Washington, D.C. Died July 25, 1921.

FISCHLER, PETER K. naval officer; b. Wellsboro, Pa., Sept. 10, 1895; s. Peter and Lillie (Sticklin) F.; B.S., U.S. Naval Acad., 1947; m. Rachel Elizabeth Moore, Nov. 9, 1918; children-Louise Frances (Mrs. David Robert Dieffenbacher), Betty Jane (wife of 1st Lt. Walter Stanley Mattox), Patricia Ann. Commd. ensign USN, 1917, advanced through grades to rear adm., 1943; comdr. U.S.S. Meredith, Breckenridge, Bell, Robinson, Putnam, Preble, Farragut, Alaska; insp. Naval Reserve, Detroit, 1919-39; asst. chief of staff, Comdr. Service Force, Atlantic Fleet, 1941-42; operations officer, staff of comdr.-in-chief U.S. Fleet, 1942-44: comdr. battleship div., 1945; asst. chief of staff, staff of comdr.-in-chief Pacific Fleet, 1945-46; dep. comdr. 19th fleet, 1946-47; comdr. amphibious training command Pacific Fleet, 1947; comdr., amphibious group 1, Pacific Fleet, 1948—. Decorated Bronze Star, Legion of Merit, 2 commendation ribbons. Victory medals (World Wars I and II). 2d Nicaraguan campaign, Yangtze service medals, Navy Expeditionary medal, Am. Defense medal with fleet clasp, Asiatic-Pacific Theatre ribbon with stars. Philippine Liberation medal. Home: 145 E St., Coronado, Cal. Died July 14, 1950.

FISET, SIR EUGENE (MARIE-JOSEPH), lt. gov. Province of Quebec; b. Rimouski, Que., Mar. 15,21874; s. Hon. Jean-Baptiste Romuald and Aimee (Plamondon) F.; student Rimouski Sem.; B.A., Laval U., 1894, M.B., 1896, M.D., M.S., 1898, LL.D., 1940, D.C.L., 1941; Dr. honoris causa, U. of Montreal, 1943, McGill U., 1943; m. Stella Taschereau, 1902; 4 daughters. Dir. gen. Canadian Med. Services, 1903-06; apptd. hon. surgeon-gen. to Gov. Gen. of Can., 1905; dep. minister of militia and defense, Can., 1906; prin. med. officer Coronation contingent, 1902; dep. minister nat. defense and v.p. Defense Council, 1923-24; elected mem. Canadian House of Commons. 1924. 25, 26, 30, 35; lt. gov. Prov. of Quebec since Dec. 1939. Served in S. Africa with 2d Batt. Royal Can. Regt., First Can. Contingent, 1899-1900, present at battle of Paardeberg (dispatches thrice); apptd. mag. gen. Can. Med. Service, 1914. Awarded Queen's medal with four clasps, D.S.O. Created Knight, July 1917. Decorated Companion St. Michael and St. George, 1913; Knight of Grace St. John of Jerusalem, 1941; comdr. Legion of Honour, France (Mil.) and Crown of Belgium; Order of St. Sava of Yougoslavia (1st class); Czecho Slovakian Mil. Cross. Hon. col. Fusiliers du St. Laurent (Can. Mil.). Fellow Royal Coll. Surgeons (Can.). Home: Spencerwood. Address: Government House, Quebec Canada

FISH, IRVING ANDREWS lawyer, b. Racine, Wis., Aug. 25, 1881; son of John T. and Eliza (Sampson) F.; student U. of Wis., 1899-1904; m. Margaret Carswell Richards, Apr. 25, 1908; 1 son, James Fish. Admitted to Wis. bar, 1903, and began practice at Madison; asso. with law firm Burr W. Jones, (Madison); mem. Fish & Storms (Racine, Wis.), Quaries, Spence & Quaries (Milwaukee); now mem. Fish, Marshutz & Hoffman (Milwaukee). Served as 2d lt., capt. and major, Wis. Nat. Guard, 1903-16; major Infantry and Signal corps and lt. col. Cavalry and Field Arty., U.S. Army, 1916-19; col. O.R.C., 1919-27; brig. gen., later major gen., Wis. Nat. Guard, 1927-40; major gen. U.S. Army, since Oct. 1940. Awarded Mexican Border, World War medals, Legion of Merit. Member Am., Wis. and Milwaukee Co. bar assns., Wis. Hist. Soc., Psi Upsilon, Phi Delta Phi Episcopalian. Clubs: Milwaukee, Milwaukee Country. Home: 9185 N. Range Line Rd., Milwaukee 9. Office: Wells Bldg., Milwaukee, Wis. Died Apr. 22, 1948.

FISH, NICHOLAS army officer; b. N.Y.C., Aug. 28, 1758; s. Jonathan and Elizabeth (Sackett) F.; attended Coll. of N.J.; m. Elizabeth Stuyvesant, Apr. 30, 1803; children including Hamilton. Commd. maj. Gen. Scott's Brigade, 1776; commd. maj. 2d, N.Y. Regt., Continental Army, 1776; 2d in command Yorktown campaign; served in battles of L.I., Bemis Heights and Monmouth, commd. lt. col. at war's end; Federalist leader in early N.Y. politics, close friend of Alexander Hamilton; adj. gen. N.Y. State, 1784; alderman N.Y.C., 1806-17; pres. N.Y. Soc. of Cincinnati; chmn. bd. trustees Columiba. Died N.Y.C., June 20, 1833.

FISHBACK, GEORGE WELTON maj. and paymaster, U.S.V., since 1898; b. Smithland, Ky., Nov. 18, 1860; studied in Paris and Hanover, Europe; grad. Harvard, 1884. Sec. legation, Argentine Republic, 1890-96; consular inspector, 1897; additional paymaster, U. S. vols., May 17, 1898; served in Spanish-American war at Santiago, etc.; named chief paymaster, dept. of Porto Rico, stationed at San Juan, Nov. 1, 1898. Unmarried. Address: Army and Navy Club, Washington.

FISHER, FRANKLIN L. illustrations editor; b. Horseheads, N.Y., Aug. 24, 1885; s. Augustus H. and Emily Jane (Garlick) F.; ed. grammar sch. and high sch., Horseheads; m. Ami Dimond, Oct. 22, 1910. Engaged in supplying news and feature photographs to newspapers and mags., N.Y. City, 1907-10; founder, and mgr., 1910-15, Harris & Ewing News Photograph Service, Washington, D.C.; chief of illustrations div. National Geog. Mag. since 1915. Life trustee Nat. Geog. Soc. since May 1945. Served as lt. comdr. U.S. Navy. Mem. U.S. Naval Inst., Nat. Geog. Soc., Photographic Soc. America White House News Photographers Assn., Res. Officers Assn. of U.S. Clubs: Nat. Press, Overseas Writers, Cosmos, Chevy Chase; Elmira (N.Y.) Golf and Country, Elmira City. Home: 2101 Connecticut Av. N.W. Office: 1146 16th St. N.W., Washington. Died Aug. 12, 1953.

FISHER, FREDERICK CHARLES, judge b. at Plymouth, Eng., July 4, 1875; s. Charles Ponsford and Harriett O. F.; brought to U.S., 1885; ed. grammar sch., Witch Creek, San Diego Co., Cal.; m. Teresa Russell, of Manila, P.I., Sept. 10, 1900. Enlisted in Battery K, 3d U.S. Arty., July 1898, and apptd. sergt.; participated in campaign before Manila and against Philippine Insurrection; recommended by Gen. Merritt for Medal of Honor, and promoted 2d lt.; hon. discharged, July 1899. Sec. to Maj. Gen. MacArthur, mil. gov., of P.I., 1899-1901; clk. Supreme Court of P.I., 1901-04; admitted to Philippine bar, 1903, later to bar Supreme Court of U.S.; practiced in Manila; apptd. asso. justice Supreme Court of P.I., 1917. Mem. bd. dirs. Y.M.C.A. of P.I. Mem. Am. Bar Assn., Cal. Bar Assn. Republican. Unitarian. Mason, Elk. Clubs: Spanish Casino, Manila Gun. Author: Code Pleading and Forms (in Spanish), 1903. Address: Manila PI

FISHER, HAMMOND EDWARD ("HAM") cartoonist; b. Wilkes-Barre, Pa., Sept. 24, 1900; s. Edward John and Sadie (Breakstone) F.; grad. Wilkes-Barre High Sch.; self educated in art; 1 dau., Wendy. Became successively, cartoonist Wilkes-Barre Record, Wilkes-Barre Leader, cartoonist, columnist and contbr. to mags. pub. Wilkes-Barre Pictorial; advt. man with N.Y. Daily News, 1927-28; started cartoon, Joe Palooka, for McNaught Syndicate, 1930 now syndicated to 955 newspapers; v.p. Lancaster & Chester R.R.; dir. Am. Title & Mortgage Co., Miami, Fla. Mem. Writer's War Board. Member Society of Illustrators, Artists, Writers and Board of Cartoonists Soc. Am. Legion, Amvets, YMCA, Christian Athletes Fund. Clubs: Kiwanis, Cowboys Turtle Assn. Served as war corr. World War II; also in special work for Army, Navy and Office of War Information; broadcaster to overseas troops; contbr. to Stars and Stripes and camp papers. Awarded citations by Navy, Air, War Dept. and State of Pa. Mt. Joe Palooka, Pa.; statue to Joe Palooka, Bedford, Ind. Author: Boxing; Joe Palooka of War; (monthly comic books) Joe Palooka, Humphrey Pennyworth; (radio program) Joe Palooka (Columbia network), 1943; Hill-Billy comics and books; Little Max and Humphrey Pennyworth. Joe Palooka pictures featured by United Artists, also shorts by Warner Brothers, 1935-37; TV Joe Palooka Story National Syndicated; writer motion pictures for Monogram Pictures Corp. Lecturer. Awarded hon. doctor degree Hamilton Coll. Home: 20 E. 74 St., N.Y.C. Died Dec. 27, 1955.

FISHER, HENRY C. army officer; b. Montgomery Co., Md., May 20, 1867; s. Milton Lyles and Mary Ann (Jones) F.; M.D., Georgetown U., 1891, hon. A.M., 1925; m. Jessie T. Noerr, June 30, 1892. Apptd. 1st lt. and asst surgeon, U.S.A., Oct. 31, 1891, and advanced through grades to col., May 15, 1917; brig. gen., asst. surgeon gen., Oct. 11, 1929; retired May 31, 1931. Served in Spanish-Am. War, Philippine Insurrection, World War. Comdr. Army and Navy Gen. Hosp., Hot Springs, Ark., 1913, Walter Reed Gen. Hosp., 1913; in charge supply div., Surgeon General's Office, 1913-17; gen. med. insp., A.E.F., 1917-19; chief health officer, Panama Canal, 1919-24; comdt. Army Med. Sch., Washington, 1924-29. Fellow Am. Coll. Surgeons. D.S.M.; silver star citation "for gallantry in action" at Battle of Santiago de Cuba; awarded the Victory Medal for service in France; Officer Legion of Honor (France). Methodist. Mason. Home: Arlington, Va. Died Dec. 18, 1936.

FISHER, HORACE NEWTON consul; b. Boston, Oct. 19, 1836; s. Francis and Lydia (Kittredge) F.; A.B., Harvard, 1857, LL.B., 1859, A.M., 1860; studied in Europe, 1859-61; m. Kiameche C. Mason, of Charlestown, Mass., Nov. 13, 1865. Entered army lt. and vol. a.-d.-c. Army of Ohio, Feb. 14, 1862; capt. and mil. engr., May, 1862; capt. and topog. engr., Oct., 1862, Army of Cumberland; lt.-col. and insp.-gen., May-Nov., 1863; resigned, Nov. 10, 1863, on account of wounds in Chickamauga campaign. In commn. business, Boston, 1867-1876; traveled in S.A., 1879-80, securing polit. and commercial data that assisted in shaping U.S. Govt. policy toward S.A. republics; consul of Chili in Boston, since 1876. Lecturer on consular instns. and common law of Spanish America, Boston U., 1903-04; engaged in research for production of work on the Common Law of Spanish America and P.I., for which he obtained at Madrid, 1905, a complete collection of old Castilian laws from time of Alaric, and rare works given by Royal Academy of History; the completed course of 25 lectures was destroyed in the San Francisco earthquake, 1906, but they are being rewritten and enlarged for publication as a treatise. Mem. Sociedad Nacional de Agriculture de Chile, Sociedad de Fomento Fabril de Chile, Loyal Legion. Am. Acad. Polit. and Social Science, etc. Pres. official delegation of Chile, and delegation of Sociedad de Fomento Fabril, at fifth Internat. Congress of Chambers of Commerce, Boston, 1912. Author: Principles of Colonial Government Applicable to Cuba, Porto Rico and the Philippines, 1898; The Objective at Bunker Hill, 1907; also papers on Latin-Am. questions for U.S. State Dept.; articles on internat. law, etc. Address: 256 Walnut St., Brookline, Mass.

FISHER, ROBERT WELLES M.D.; b. Seaford, Del., Oct. 10, 1863; s. Isaac M. and Sarah J. (Vaughan) F.; grad. Phila. Coll. Pharmacy, 1887; M.D., Jefferson Med. Coll., 1890 (Batholow prize); m. Margaret Van B. Terry, 1892; children—Vaughan Terry, Anna Bathsheba, Margaret Louise, Robert Welles. Practiced in Salt Lake City from 1890; physician to St. Mark's Hosp., 1893-1917; prof. materia medica and pharmacy, med. dept. U. of Utah, 1899-1914; sec. State Bd. Med. Examiners, 1901-09; mem. Bd. of Health, Salt Lake City, 1892-1916. Commd. capt. M.R.C., June 15, 1917; served in Base Hosp. 131, France; commd. maj. M.R.C., May 29, 1919. Republican. Home: Salt Lake City, Utah. Died Jan. 16, 1927.

FISHER, THOMAS RUSSELL research analyst; b. Okeene, Okla., June 2, 1895; s. Charles Calvin and Carrie Bell (Uglow) F.; Ph.B., U. Chgo., 1921; A.M., Columbia U., 1928, Ph.D., 1938; LL.B., Syracuse U., 1937; m. Marguerite Juterbock, June 13, 1929; m. 2d, Carole I. Hendley, June 4, 1956; 1 dau., Alice Anne. Instr. in econs., Coll. City of N.Y., 1925-28; instr. polit. sci., Hunter Coll., 1928-29; prof. social legislation, Syracuse U., since 1930, chmn. dept. sociology, anthropology, 1941-49; profl. lecturer, 1930 - ; chief spl. projects sect., div. Exchange Persons, Dept. State, 1949-52; asst. dir. edn. T.C.A., in Dept. 1952-53; fgn. service for Dept. in Jidda, Saudi Arabia, 1952; v.p. Global Trading Corp., 1953-55; cons. the President's Commn. on Vets' Pensions, 1955-56. Served with USN, 1917-19, lt. col., IV Corps, AUS and British 8th Army, 1943-46. Labor Gov. Prov. of Genoa, until 1946. Mem. Selective Service Bd., 1942-43, N.Y. State Bd. Mediation, 1935-43, Nat. Bd. Arbitration, 1937-43, Prison Industries Reorgn. Adminstrn., Washington, 1937. Mem. A.A.A.S., Am. Acad. Polit. and Social Sci., Phi Delta Phi, Alpha Kappa Delta, Phi Delta Kappa. Club: Cosmos, Mem. Christian Ch. Author: Federal Legislation Regulating Industrial Disputes, 1937. Contbr. articles and book revs. to prof. jours. Researcher in social legislation and public law. Home: Hinton, Okla. Died Dec. 1967.

FISK, CHARLES HENRY lawyer; b. Fiskburg, Ky., Aug. 31, 1843; s. John Flavel and Elizabeth Sarah (Johnson) F.; A.B., Miami U., 1863 (Valedictorian), A.M., 1868, LL.D., 1904; LL.B., Cincinnati Law Sch., 1864; m. Margaret A. Emmal, Oct. 23, 1866. Capt. Co. A, 1st Regt, Squirrel Hunters, Ohio Vol. Inf., during Kirby Smith's raid, 1862; admitted to Ky. bar, 1864; practiced, Lexington, 1865, Covington, 1865—; mem. John F. & Charles H. Fisk, 1868-90, then privately; practiced U.S. mil. courts, Lexington, 1865. Sec. Covington & Cincinnati Bridge Co.; 1st pres. Masonic Temple Assn. of Covington; trustee and treas., K.T. & M.M. Aid Assn., Cincinnati. Republican. Mem. Christian (Disciples) Ch.; supt. S.S. for nearly 35 years. Mason. Home: Covington, Ky. Died Oct. 20, 1930.

FISK, CLINTON BOWEN army officer, founder Fisk U.; b. Western N.Y., Dec. 8, 1828; s. Benjamin Bigford and Lydia (Aldrich) F.; m. Jeanette Crippen, 1850. Col., 33d Mo. Volunteers, 1862; commd. brig. gen. U.S. Volunteers, 1862, promoted maj. gen. before mustered out; asst. commr. of bureau of refugees, freedmen and abandoned lands for Ky. and Tenn., Freedmen's Bur., 1865; opened Fisk U. (sch. for Negroes), Nashville, Tenn., 1866; mem. Bd. Indian Commers., 1874, pres., 1881-90; mem. governing com. of Methodist Book Concern after 1876; Prohibitionist candidate for U.S. Pres., 1888. Died N.Y.C., July 9, 1890.

FISKE, BRADLEY ALLEN naval officer; b. Lyons, N.Y., June 13, 1854; s. Rev. William Allen and Susan (Bradley) F.; grad. U.S. Naval Acad. (2d in class), 1874; m. Josephine, d. Joseph Wesley Harper, 1882; 1 dau., Caroline Harper. Ensign, July 17, 1875; promoted through grades to rear-adm., Aug. 3, 1911; retired June 13, 1916. Served on various duties and stations; was on "Yorktown," under Commander Robley D. Evans, in Valparaiso, during critical times following the "Baltimore" incident; on board Admiral Benham's flagship, "San Francisco," in Rio, in 1894, when the U.S. fleet cleared for action, and enforced neutral rights; navigator of "Petrel" at battle of Manila; reported by capt. of "Petrel" for "eminent and conspicuous conduct in battle," and by Admiral Dewey for "heroic conduct" at battle of Manila; navigator of monitor "Monadnock" during 4 mos. following outbreak of the Filipino insurrection; took part in bombardments of Parañaque and Malabon; as exec. officer of "Yorktown" took part in bombardment of San Fernando, Aug. 1899; comd. the Minneapolis, the Arkansas and the Tennessee; comd. 5th, 3d and 1st divs., Atlantic Fleet, 1912; aid for operations, Navy Dept., 1913, till May 1915, when resigned. Mem. 1st Electrical Conf., Phila., 1884; mem. naval wireless telegraph bd., 1904-05; mem. Gen. Bd. of Navy, also Joint Bd. Army and Navy, 1910-11 and 1913-15. Invented boat detaching apparatus, system of elec. communication for interiors of warships, stadimeter, and electric range finger, an electric ammunition hoist, a range indicator, a battle-order telegraph, an elec. engine telegraph, a helm-indicator, a speed and direction indicator, a system of turning turrets of war ships by electricity, the naval telescope mount, the naval telescope sight, gun director system, wireless control of moving vessels, the torpedo-plane, system for detecting submarines, prism system of target practice, electro-magnetic system for exploding torpedoes under ships, and also the reading machine. The naval telescope sight has been adopted by all the navies of the world, and is the main cause of the recent great improvement in the accuracy of naval gunnery; the torpedoplane has been adopted by all the leading navies. Awarded Elliott Cresson gold medal by Franklin Institute, 1893; gold medal for prize essay by U.S. Naval Institute, 1905; gold medal by Aero Club of America for invention of torpedoplane, 1919. Pres. U.S. Naval Inst., 1911-23. Club: Army and Navy of New York (hon. pres.), Author: Electricity in Theory and Practice, 1884; 10 edits.; War Times in Manila; The Navy as a Fighting lMachine, 1917, 2d edit., 1918; From Midshipman to Rear Admiral, 1919; The Art of Fighting, 1920; Invention, 1921; also numerous articles on elec. and naval subjects. Home: Waldorf Astoria, New York, N.Y. Died Apr. 7, 1942.

FISKE, HAROLD BENJAMIN, army officer (ret.); b. Salem, Oregon, Nov. 6, 1871; s. Rufus Eugene and Charlotte (Grubbe) F.; grad. U.S. Mil. Acad., 1897; honor grad. Army Sch. of the Line, 1910; grad. Army Staff Coll., 1911; m. Lucy Brooks Keyes, April 17, 1898; children—Berenice, Virginia. Commd. 2d lt. 18th Inf., Aug. 7, 1897; promoted through grades to maj. gen., Aug. 1, 1933; retired, Nov. 30, 1935. Asst. chief of staff for training, with hdqrs. A.E.F. in France; brig. gen. N.A., June 26, 1918-July 31, 1919; participated in battle at St. Mihiel, Aisne-Marne, Meuse-Argonne. Awarded D.S.M. (U.S.); Comdr. Legion of Honor, Croix de Guerre, with palm (French); Comdr. Crown of Italy; Comdr. Order of Leopold (Belgian). Address: 240 Quince St., San Diego CA

FISKE, JAMES PORTER surgeon; b. New York, N.Y., Nov. 22, 1866; s. Thomas Scott and Clara (Pittman) F.; ed. pvt. instrn.; M.D. Coll. Phys. and Surg. (Columbia), 1891; m. Amy Treadwell, June 14, 1906. Surgeon Charity Hosp. and New York Maternity Hosp., 1891-92; obstetric surgeon Church Hosp. and attending surgeon St. Elizabeth's Hosp., 1892—; attending phys. North Western Dispensary, 1895-97; orthopedic surgeon New York Post-Grad. Hosp., 1895-99; lecturer on surgery, New York Post-Grad. Med. Sch., 1895-99; orthopedic surgeon Roosevelt Hosp., 1893-1901; asst. surgeon and lecturer on surgery, Cornell, 1901-03; asst. surgeon New York Hosp., 1904—. Specialty, deformities and errors of development; introduced into U.S. at Roosevelt Hosp., 1893, the ambulatory treatment of fractures of the leg. Pres. Guild for

Crippled Children of the Poor of New York City, 1905-07; attending surgeon Free Sch. for Crippled Children, 1901-13; charter mem. W.H. Davis Sch. for Crippled Children; mgr. N.Y. State Hosp. for Crippled and Deformed Children, 1908—. Sec. Am. Posture League, New York, 1922—. Fellow New York Acad. Medicine, Commd. capt. and surgeon, Med. R.C., Aug. 5, 1917; maj., Med. Corps U.S.A., Aug. 15, 1918; lt. col., M.O.R.C., 1924; was cons. orthopedic surgeon at various camps and at Washington,D.C. Comdr. European Commandery. Mil. Order of Foreign Wars, 1927-28; vice comdr. gen. Mil. Order of Foreign Wars of U.S., 1932-35; dean at Geneva, Les Amities Internationales, 1930. Died Oct. 24, 1941.

FISKE, JOHN naval officer, mcht.; b. Salem, Mass., Apr. 11, 1744; s. Rev. Samuel and Anna (Gerrish) F.; m. Lydia Phippen, 1766; m. 2d, Martha Lee Hibbert, 1783; m. 3d, Sarah Gerry, 1786; 3 children. Mem. Salem Com. Safety and Correspondence, 1775; capt. brigantine Tyrannicide, 1776; commanded brigantine Massachusetts, harassed enemy shipping off coasts of Western Europe, 1777; mcht., traded with Mediterranian, East and West Indies, purchased several ships after Am. Revolution; mem. Salem Marine Soc., 1791; commd. maj. gen. Mass. Militia, 1792. Died Sept. 28, 1797.

FITCH, JOHN HALL, govt. ofcl.; b. N.Y.C., Mar. 13, 1909; s. Benjamin Homans and Martha Sofia (Johnson) F.; B.S. in Mech. Engring., Rutgers U., 1930; m. Margaret Ridgely, Oct. 27, 1951; children—Lee C., Margo G., John Hall. Various positions prodn. designing, gen. indsl. engring. field, 1930-41; with Fgn. Econ. Adminstrn., 1945; propr. Cladot Trading Corp., 1945-46; gen. mgr. Federal-Huber Co., 1946-47; account exec. Brigg-Stratton Corp., Milw., 1947-48; dir. procurement and prodn. div., staff of asst. sec. def. Dept. Def., 1952-59; dir. budget Air Force and Mil. Assistance Programs, 1959; dep. controller budget Dept. Def., 1959-61; became dep. asst. sec. army for financial mgmt., 1961, later ret.; v.p. for devel. Maremont Corp., Washington, until 1969. Served to col., War Dept. Gen. Staff, AUS, World War II; logistics planner Gen. Hdqrs., Far East Command, Korean War. Clubs: Touchdown; Army-Navy Country (Arlington Va.). Home: Alexandria VA Died Apr. 28, 1969; buried Arlington Nat. Cemetery, Arlington VA

FITCH, WILLIAM EDWARD physician, author; b. Burlington, N.C., May 29, 1867; s. William James and Mary Elizabeth (King) F.; M.D., Coll. Physicians and Surg., Baltimore, Md., 1891; m. Minnie Crump, Oct. 5, 1892; children - Lucille, Elizabeth, William Edward. Specialist in diseases of metabolism. med. hydrology and dietotherapy; lecturer on principles of surgery, Fordham U. Sch. Medicine, 1907-09; attending physician Vanderbilt Clinic; attending gynecologist outpatient dept. Presbyn. Hosp.; asst. in surg. clinic, St. Luke's Hospital; med. dir. and cons. med. hydrologist at French Lick (Ind.) Springs, 1931; cons. med. hydrologist Crazy Hotel and Spa Mineral Wells, Tex. Served as editor Gaillard's Southern Medicine, 1900-09; editor Pediatrics, 1908-17; co-editor and pub. Am. Jour. Electrotherapeutics and Radiology, 1918-19. Served as acting asst. surg. U.S.P.H. and M.H. Service. Spanish-Am. War, 1898; commd. 1st lt. Med. R.C., U.S. Army, July 3, 1912; capt., July 16, 1917; maj., Sept. 25, 1917; comdg. officer hosp. and Ft. Schuyler, N.Y., and chief nutrition and dir. mess, Base Hosp., Camp Jackson, S.C.; later adviser to camp surgeon's office; hon. disch., Dec. 3, 1918. Mem. Hudson-Fulton Celebration Commn. Pres. Alamance Battle Ground Commn. Mem. med. soc. states of Va., Ind., Am. Med. Editors' and authors' Assn., Med. Assn. Greater N.Y., Nat. Soc. Advancement Gastroenterology, Am. Soc. Balneology, Internat. Soc. Med. Hydrology (London), N.Y. Soc. Founders and Patriots Am. (council, gen. court), Soc. Cincinnati, Soc. Fgn. Wars. Soc. Am. Wars. Soc. Vets. World War, Southern Soc. (New York). Democrat. Episcopalian. Clubs: Lotos (New York); Burlington Country. Author: Fitch's Medical Pocket Formulary, 1914, now in 7th edit.; Dietotherapy (3 vols.), 1918, now in 3d edit.; Mineral Waters of the U.S. and Greater American Spas. 1926; Diseases of Metabolism; The Battle of Alamance; also various writings on early history of N. Carolina. Address: 3707 Segovia St., Coral Gables, Fla. Died Sept. 12, 1949; buried Burlington, N.C.

FITCH, WILLIAM KOUNTZ, mfg. exec.; b. Rockford, Ill., Nov. 2, 1889; s. Dr. William H. and Katherine (Kountz) F.; A.B., Yale, 1910; M.E., U. Wis., 1913; m. Mrs. Natalie Stone Austin, Nov. 1, 1947 (divorced). Sales engr. Dravo Doyle Co., 1913-22, dist. mgr. Cleveland office, 1922-27, v.p., 1926-34, pres., 1934-48, now dir.; v.p. Dravo Corp., 1938-46, dir., chmn. bd., 1946-50, ret.; dir. Dir. Allegheny council Boy Scouts America, 1945-51, member exec. com. 1954; director Allegheny County Community Chest, 1943-45, pres., 1945; dir. Fedn. Social Agencies of Allegheny Co., 1942-48, chmn. interim adjustment com., 1947-51. Pres. Sewickley Valley Hosp, 1954-69; pres. Hosp. Council Western Pa., 1959-62; dir. Hosp. Assn. Pa., 1962-69, Harmarville Rehab. Center, 1962-69; treas. Hosp. project 1962-69. Mem. Am. Soc. M.E., Soc. Naval Architects and Marine Engrs., Am. Ordnance Assn. (dir. local, 1947-69, pres. 1955-57), Pa. Economy League (finance com. Western div.), Arthritis and Rheumatism Found. (past pres., now dir. W. Pa. chpt.), Newcomen Soc. Served at 1st lt. Ordnance Dept., U.S. Army, 1917-19; capt. Coast Arty. Res. Corps, 1919-25; mem. Ohio National Guard, 1925-27. Clubs: University, Duquesne, Harvard-Yale-Princeton, Allegheny Country, Rolling Rock, Pittsburgh Golf, Fox Chapel Golf, Sewickley Hunt Newcomen (Pitts.); Yale (N.Y.C.). Home: Pittsburgh PA Died June 29, 1969.

FITE, WILLIAM CONYERS naval officer; b. Jan. 3, 1893; entered U.S. Navy, 1903, advanced through grades to rear adm., 1933. Address: care Chief of Naval Personnel, Navy Department, Washington 25. Died Apr. 1, 1963.

FITHIAN, EDWARD naval officer; b. N.J., Dec. 13, 1820. Apptd. 3d asst. engr. U.S.N., Oct. 31, 1848; promoted 2d asst. engr., Feb. 26, 1851; chief engr., Oct. 23, 1859; retired, Dec. 13, 1882; advanced to rank of rear admiral retired, June 29, 1906, for services during Civil War. Served on Roanoke and at New York during Civil War. Home: Bridgeton, N.J. Died 1908.

FITZ, HUGH ALEXANDER, wholesale merchant; b. Fredericksburg, Va., July 15, 1876; s. William Henry and Mary Ann (Harrison) F. H.; student Epsicopal High Sch., Alexandria, Va., 1891-94, U. of Va., 1894-95; m. Lena Lea, Oct. 19, 1904; 1 dau., Jeanie L. Dir. Mchts. Nat. Bank, Vicksburg. Served as major Q. M. Corps, U.S. Army, 1917-19; lt. col. Reserve Corps, 1919-33. Mem. Phi Kappa Psi. Home: 1403 Baum St. Office: Levee St., Vicksburg MS

FITZ, REGINALD physician; b. Boston, Mass., Feb. 28, 1885; s. Reginald Heber and Elizabeth Loring (Clarke) F.; A.B., Harvard, 1906, M.D., 1909; hon. D.Sc., Western Reserve University, 1943; LL.D. (hon.), Hahnemann Medical Coll., 1947; m. Phoebe Marion Wright, June 29, 1918; children-Phoebe Marion, Reginald Heber, Elizabeth Jean, William Richard Wright, Edith. House officer Mass. General Hosp., 1909-11; vol. asst. Johns Hopkins Med. Clinic, 1911-13; asst. resident physician Peter Bent Brigham Hosp., 1913-15, Rockefeller Inst. Hospital, N.Y.C., 1915-17; staff Mayo Clinic, 1920-22; associate professor medicine Harvard Med. Sch., 1922-36, lecturer in history of medicine since 1936, also assistant dean since 1947; Wade professor of medicine, Boston U., 1936-40; dir. Evans Memorial, 1936-40; clin. asso. Thorndike Memorial Lab., Boston, since 1940; mem. bd. hon. consultants to Army Med. Library (Washington), 1943-52; mem. Nat. Bd. Med. Examiners, 1932-45 and since 1947; chmn. med. adv. bd. No. 13, Selective Service, Boston, 1940-47; med. advisor Boston met. chapter Am. Red Cross. Served as capt. and maj. Med. Corps, U.S. Army, 1917-19. Trustee Perkins Inst. for Blind, 1943-46, pres. since 1946; trustee Brookline Pub. Library, Wellesley Coll., Boston Medical Library; university marshal, Harvard. Mem. Am. Bd. Internal Medicine, 1936-46, chmn., 1944-46. Mem. bd. regents Am. Coll. Physicians, 1939-47, since 1950, 1st v.p., 1947-48, pres., 1949-50; pres. Boston Tuberculosis Assn., 1946-49. Mem. A.M.A. (mem. council med. edn. and hosps. 1929-49), Mass. Heart Association, Mass. Med. Soc. (chmn. com. on med. edn. and diplomas, 1930-40; pres., 1945-46); Suffolk Dist. Med. Soc. (pres. 1938-40), Am. Assn. Hist. Med., Med. Library Assn., Spl. Library Assn., Am. Acad. Arts and Scis., Colonial Soc. Mass. Clubs: Harvard, Tavern (Boston); Century Assn. (New York); Brookline Country. Mem. editorial bd. Archives of Internal Medicine. Home: 56 Walnut Pl., Brookline, Mass. Office: 319 Longwood Av., Boston. Died May 27, 1953.

FITZGERALD, LOUIS pres. Mercantile Trust Co. of New York; b. New York, May 31, 1838; ed. there and engaged in business; became mem. 7th N.Y. regt., later lt. 11th N.Y. Inf.; served through Civil war, becoming col. 1st Miss. regt. On return to New York re-entered 7th N.Y. regt., becoming lt. col., and, 1882-98, brig. gen., resigning Jan. 1898. Active in important reorganizations and financial operations; retired. Home: Garrison, N.Y. Died 1908.

FITZGERALD, ROY GERALD former congressman; b. Watertown, N.Y., Aug. 25, 1875; s. M. G. and Cornelia M. (Avery) F.; ed. high sch., Dayton, O., and coll. courses in econs. and modern langs.; m. Caroline L. Wetecamp, Sept. 5, 1900 (dec. Sept. 1935); children - Mrs. Ruth Hume, Dorothy L. Skinner, Roy Gerald (lt. Col., U.S.A., killed after surviving Battle of Bulge, 1946); m. 2d, Alverda J. Sinks, June 22, 1943. Began practice of law, 1896; dir. Mchts. Nat. Bank & Trust Co.; joined U.S. Army, Aug. 27, 1917; commd. capt. inf., 1917; went to France, June 11, 1918; comd. Hdqrs. Co., 329th Inf.; hon. discharged, 1919; commd. lt. col. Inf. R.C. Mem. 67th to 71st Congresses from 3d Ohio Dist.; chmn. com. on the Revision of Laws; reported Code of Laws of U.S., 1926; author cumulative codification system for statutory law of U.S. and D.C. Del. to Conf. Interparliamentary Union, Paris, 1927, Berlin, 1928, Geneva, 1929, London, 1930, on methods of codifying internat. law. Trustee (pres. bd.) Dayton Public Library, Dayton Law Library Assn.; mem. U.S. Yorktown Sesquicentennial Commn. Mem. Am., Ohio State, Dayton, Fed. Dist. (pres.), bar assns., Dayton Lawyers (pres.), S.A.R., Hist. Soc. (pres.), Dayton, Montgomery County Hist. Socs. (pres.) Am., Dayton philatelic assns. Republican. Episcopalian. Mason (32ff). Clubs: Dayton Chess, Nomad. Climbed Mt. Rainier, 1925; swam Bosphorous, Asia to Europe, 1929. Home: 65 Stoddard Av., Dayton 5. Office: Knott Bldg., Dayton 2, O. Died Nov. 16, 1962; buried Woodland Cemetery, Dayton.

FITZGERALD, THOMAS ret. street ry. exec.; b. Balt., May 30, 1878; s. Thomas and Fanny (Kettlewell) F.; A.B., Johns Hopkins, 1898; m. Laura Unger, Dec. 5, 1899; children-Elizabeth K. (Mrs. Francis P. Browning, dec.), Thomas, Frances K. (Mrs. Lynford A. Keating). Gen. supt. Norfolk, Portsmouth & Newport News Co., 1902-03; gen. mgr. Lexington Ry. Co., 1903-05; purchasing agt., asst. to v.p. Cin. Traction Co., 1905-07; asst. gen. mgr. same and Ohio Traction Co., 1907-13, gen. mgr. both cos., 1913-17; cons. electric ry. engr., Pitts., 1920-24; gen. mgr. Pitts., Rys. Co., 1924-25, v.p., Pitts. Rys. Co. and Pitts., Motor Coach Co., also dir. 37 subsidiaries, 1925-38; trustee and gen. mgr. Rys. Co. and Pitts., Motor Coach Co., 1938-51, ret.; trustee dir. Transit Research Corp., 1937. Pres., dir. Pitts. Conv. Bureau, Maj. inf., U.S. Res., 1917; maj. inf. U.S. Army, 1918, lt. col., 1918-19. Mem. Am. Transit Assn., Soc. Am. Mil. Engrs., Engring. Soc. Western Pa., C. of C. (dir. 1945—), Vets. Fgn. Wars, Am. Legion, Kappa Alpha. Mason (K.T., Shriner). Clubs: Duquesne, University, Traffic, Railway, Fellows, Rotary. Home: 5820 Elwood St., Pitts. 32. Office: 435 Sixth Av., Pitts. 19. Died Nov. 26, 1956.

FITZPATRICK, EDWARD AUGUSTUS coll. pres.; b. N.Y. City, Aug. 29, 1884; s. Thomas and Ellen (Radley) F.; N.Y. City Training Sch. for Teachers; B.S., Columbia, 1906. M.A., 1907, Ph.D., 1911; LL.D., Loyola University (Chicago, Ill.), 1929, St. Mary's Coll., San Francisco, 1948, St. Norbert's Coll., 1954; Litt.D., St. Louis U., 1933; L.H.D., Loyola U., New Orleans, 1939; Ed.D. (hon.), St. Mary's Coll., 1951; D.Pd. (honorary), LaSalle College, Phila., 1958; L.H.D., Mount Mary College, Milwaukee, 1960; m. Lillian V. Taylor, July 15, 1913; children - Edward Augustus (dec.), Francis, Richard, Marjorie Jean (dec.), Robert. Teacher public schs., N.Y.C., 1903-08. Maj. inf. U.S. Army, charge draft adminstrn. for Wis., 1917-19; lt. col. Spl. Res. U.S. Army, 1934-42; active duty, Office Dir. Selective Service, Apr. 1942-Aug. 1945; Indsl. College Armed Forces, June-Sept. 1946. Advisor U.S. Dir. of Selective Service since 1945; advisor, cons. on Manpower, Indsl. Coll. of the Armed Forces, since 1946; col., Army of U.S., 1942; mem. rev. com. deferment govt. employees; dean, Grad. School of Marquette U., 1924-39, and ednl. Dir. Coll. Hosp. Adminstrn. (first of its kind), ame univ., 1924-26; pres. Mount Mary Coll. for Women, Milwaukee (formerly St. Mary's Coll. of Prairie du Chien), 1929-54, pres. emeritus, 1954; investigator publs. U.S. Office Edn. for house com. on labor and edn., 1954; dir. Inst. Human Edn., 1952 - . Cons., mem. adv. bd., Indsl. Coll. of the Armed Forces, 1946 - ; cons. Applied Physics Lab., Johns Hopkins, 1959 - . Mission to France, U.S. Fgn. Econ. Adminstrn., personal rep. of adminstr., 1945; guest prof. U. Mainz (Dolmetscher Inst.), investigator Am. studies in German univs., 1951; pilot study of books about Am. Democracy for U.S. Information Agy., 1956; ednl. cons. Brazilian Center of Ednl. Research, 1956-57. Chairman State Recovery Board and NRA Conciliation Board, 1933. Winner Modern Hospital Essay Contest, 1925, Sachs prize (Columbia), 1927; Medaille de la Liberee (France), 1944, 52; Selective Service Medal (Illinois), 1945; Legion of Merit, 1945. Drafted first minimum wage law for teachers in Wisconsin, 1913; law authorizing establishment of Training School for public service, at U. of Wis., 1917; Wis. ednl. bonus law, 1919; the half time sch. law for children in industry, 1921. Pres. Assn. of Presidents and Deans of Wis. Colleges, 1937. Investigator, Federal Commn. on Industrial Relations. Fellow A.A.A.S.; life mem. Am. Political Science Assn., Nat. Municipal League, State Hist. Soc. of Wisconsin, Am. Hosp. Assn. (chmn. sub-com. on curricular for training hosp. execs., prepared report 1925, and chmn. com., 1927); mem. library com. of Library and Service Bur. of Am. Hospital Conf., 1924-28; mem. (edn.) Nat. Com. on Grading Schs. of Nursing; mem. commn. on Academic Freedom and Tenure; vice chmn. commn. on Higher Christian edn. American Assn. Colleges; chairman committee on liberal arts. Nat. Cath. Edn. Assn., 1948. Author books including: Exploring a Theology of Education, 1949; The Education of Human Beings, 1949; La Salle, Patron of Teachers, 1951. Editor publs. including: Catholic School Jour. since 1929; Highway to Heaven Series, including textbooks and tchrs. manuals, since 1931; Selective Service in Peacetime, 1942; Selective Service in Wartime, 1943; Selective Service as the Tide of War Turns, 1945. Published: Great Books Panasea or What, 1952; Philosophy of Education, 1953; How to Educate Human Beings (translated into German), 1953; Criminology and Crime Prevention. 1958. Home: 2601 Woodley Pl., Washington 8. Died Sept. 13, 1960; buried Arlington Nat. Cemetery.

FITZ-PATRICK, GILBERT obstetrician; b. Columbiana Co., O., Jan. 19, 1873; s. Thomas C. and Mary J. (Gilbert) F.; ed. Ohio Northern U., Ada; M.D., Chicago Home Med. Coll., 1896; m. Elizabeth Sanford, May 1913. Interne Silver Cross Hosp., Joliet, Ill., 1897; house surgeon, Garfield Park Hosp., Chicago, 1898-99, Rotunda Hosp., Dublin, Ireland, 1902, Sloane Maternity Hosp., New York, 1903; formerly head dept.

of obstetrics, Hahnemann Med. Coll. and Hosp., and attdg. obstetrician Cook Co. Hosp.; cons. obstetrician Ill. Masonic Hosp.; attdg. obstetrician Chicago Polyclinic and Henrotin hosps.; mem. visiting staff Passavant Hosp.; trustee Ill. Masonic Hosp. Mem. Ill. State Med. Exam. Bd. Mem. bd. Gorgas Memorial Inst. of Tropical Medicine; fellow and gov. Am. Coll. Surgeons; chmn. Ill. Cancer Committee. Colonel Med. R.C., U.S.A.; chief of surgery, Base Hosp., Camp Gordon, Atlanta, Ga., World War; now comdg. officer U.S. Gen. Hosp. No. 110; del. from Assn. Mil. Surgeons, U.S.A., to Royal Inst. of Pub. Health, Ghent, Belgium, 1927; U.S. del. to 1st Internat. Congress of Pub. Health and Hygiene, Cairo, Egypt, 1928. Republican. Mason. Home: Chicago, Ill. Died Nov. 15, 1936.

FITZROY, HERBERT WILLIAM KEITH, adminstr.; born Thompson, Conn., Nov. 4, 1903; s. Herbert William and Mary Ogilvie (Keith) F.; A.B., U. Pa., 1925, A.M., 1928, LL.B., 1929, Harrison fellow in history, 1930-32; Regents fellow, Trinity Coll., Cambridge U., 1925-26; faculty fellow, law sch., Columbia, 1933-34; LL.D., Virginia Union University, 1961. Assistant instructor history U. Pa., 1926-28, instr. 1934-36; instr. history Princeton, 1937, asst. dean, 1938-42; dir. St. Helena Extension Coll. of William and Mary (a vets. coll.), 1946-48, Marshall-Wythe lectr., Coll. William and Mary, 1948; president U. Center in Virginia (project Gen. Edn. Bd.), 1948-67. Served from 1st lt. to lt. col., USAAF, 1942-46, col. res. Decorated Army Commendation medal, Bronze star. Mem. Am. Hist. Assn., Va. Hist. Soc., Va. Acad. Sci., Richmond Pub. Forum (pres.), English Speaking Union (pres. Va. br.), Phi Beta Kappa, Omicron Delta Kappa. Democrat. Presbyn. Clubs: Appalachian Mountain, Princeton (N.Y.C.). Home: Richmond VA Died Oct. 12, 1967; cremated.

FITZSIMONS, CHARLES soldier, contractor; b. New York, Dec. 16, 1835; removed with parents to Rochester; ed. common schs., and later studied engring. Entered Union Army, 1861, as capt. 3d N.Y. cav.; promoted maj., May 1862; wounded June 1862, and obliged to resign early in 1863 because of wound; after few months rest re-entered service as lt. col; went to front Oct. 1863, with 21st N.Y. cav.; took part in engagements Shenandoah Valley; wounded Ashley's Gap, July 19, 1864; later comd. "remount" camp of cav., Pleasant Valley, Md.; commd. col., June, 1865; served on Western plains until mustered out, Denver, Colo., July 26, 1866, with bvt. rank brig. gen. Entered contracting business, sr. mem. FitzSimons & Connell Co., contractors; constructed substructure of all modern, wide bridges in Chicago, tunnels, cribs and other important works; col. 1st regt. Ill. Nat. Guard, 1882, and same yr. apptd. by Gov. Cullom brig. gen., 1st brigade; apptd. and confirmed brig. gen., U.S.V., June, 1898; but soon after resigned. Home: Chicago, Ill. Died 1905.

FITZ SIMONS, ELLEN FRENCH; b. New York, N.Y., June 15, 1881; d. Francis Ormond and Ellen (Tuck) French; ed. private tutors in England, France and Germany; Alfred Gwynne Vanderbilt, 1901; 1 son, William H. (gov. of R.I., 1938-40); m. 2d, Paul Fitz Simons, lt. comdr., U.S. Navy, 1919. Rhode Island member Republican National Committee, 1930-44; mem. Republican National Executive Com. 1936-44; elected eastern vice chmn. Rep. Nat. Com., 1940-44. Organized Newport County (R.I.) Chapter Am. Red Cross, 1916, and vice chmn., 1916-19; awarded Victory medal of Soc. of Social Sciences for war work, 1919; pres. Newport County Women's Republican Club, 1926-37. Home: "Harbourview," Newport, R.I. Died Feb. 26, 1948; buried at St. Mary's Church, Portsmouth, R.I.

FLAD, HENRY engr., inventor; b. Rennhoff, Germany, July 30, 1824; s. Jacob and Franziska (Brunn) F.; grad. U. Munich (Germany), 1846; m. Helen Reichard, 1848; m. 2d, Caroline Reichard, Sept. 12, 1855 6; 3 children. Served as capt. co. of army engrs. in Bavaria during German Revolution 1848; fled to U.S., 1849; ry. constrn. engr., 1849-60; served from pvt. to col. U.S. Army during Civil War; asst. to James B. Eads in constrn. Eads Bridge over Mississippi River; mem. bd. water commrs. St. Louis 1868-76 (during which time city water-works were completed); mem. Am. Soc. C.E., pres., 1866; founder Engrs. Club of St. Louis, pres. 1868-80; pres. St. Louis Bd. Pub. Improvements, 1877-90; mem. Mississippi River Commn., 1890-98; patented filters, water meters, methods of preserving timber and sprinkling streets, systems rapid transit and cable rys.; devised hydrostatic and hydraulic elevator, deep-sea sounding apparatus, pressure gauges, pile driver. Died Pitts., June 20, 1898.

FLAGLER, CLEMENT ALEXANDER FINLEY army officer; b. in Ga., Aug. 17, 1867; B.S., Griswold Coll., Ia., 1885; grad. U.S. Mil. Acad., 1889, Engring. Sch. of Application, 1892; Army War Coll., 1914. Apptd. add. 2d lt. engrs., June 12, 1889; promoted through grades to brig. gen., Jan. 4, 1918. Instr. civ. and mil. engring., U.S. Mil. Acad., 1894-95; on staff Maj. Gen. J. H. Wilson, Chickamauga Park, Ga., Charleston, S.C., and in Puerto Rico, 1898; engr. officer, Dept. of the East, 1900-02; apptd. mem. Chesapeake & Del. Canal Commn., 1906; on staff Gen Frederick Funston, Vera Cruz expdn., 1914; instr. Army War Coll., 1914-15; duty at Washington, 1916; comd. arty. of 5th Div., at St. Mihiel; promoted maj. gen. and comd. arty., 3d Corps in the Argonne-Meuse; comd. 42d (Rainbow) Div. in the Army of the Rhine, Nov. 21, 1918-Apr. 6, 1919; comdt. Engr. Sch., Camp Humphreys, Va., 1919; dept. engr., Honolulu, 1920; div. engr., Baltimore, 1921. Died May 7, 1922.

FLANAGAN, HENRY CLINTON naval officer; b. Hunter, La., Sept. 9, 1892; s. Henry Clay and Katie Alice (Griffin) F.; student Eastern Ky. State Normal (now Tchrs.' Coll.), 1912-13; tchr.'s certificate U.S. Naval Acad., 1931-33; B.S. in Communications Engring., U. Cal., 1934; m. Mary Dorothy Lorenzen, Feb. 11, 1923. Tchr. rural sch., Sherburne, Ky., 1913-14; asst. sec. to pres. Eastern Ky. State Normal, 1914-15; enlisted in U.S. Navy, 1915; commd. temp. ensign, 1918; permanent commn. as lt. (j.g.), 1921, advanced through grades to rear adm., 1946; served in battleships, submarines, aux. vessels and aircraft carrier, 1919-37; at Navy Yard, Mare Island, Cal., 1926-28; dist. communication officer, 12th Naval Dist., 1937-40; exec. officer, transport, participating in troop landings in Iceland and Ireland, 1940-42; comdr. boat flotilla which landed 1st marine regt. on Guadalcanal, 1942; comd. attack cargo ship and various units of ships, Pacific, 1942-43, attack transport, 1943, transport div., 1943-44, transport squadron, 1944-45; ret., 1946. Awarded Silver Star, Legion of Merit, Bronze Star with 2 gold stars, letter of commendation. Republican. Baptist. Mason. Home: 4464 Hortensia St., San Diego 92103. Died Sept. 26, 1964; buried Ft. Rosecrans Nat. Cemetery, Cal.

FLANAGAN, THOMAS EDMUND govt. ofcl.; b. Fall River, Mass., Aug. 7, 1907; s. Thomas Edmund and Lillian (Butler) F.; student Boston Latin Sch., Harvard, 1925-29; m. Lilian Hasbrouk, Apr. 13, 1934 (dec. Feb. 11, 1941); 1 dau., Catherine; m. 2d, Lois Cooper Holzworth, July 4, 1941; children - Josephine, Mary, Ellen. With N.Y. Sun, 1932-35, Asso. Press, N.Y., 1935-38, Washington, 1938-40, 48-49, London, 1945-57; information officer ECA, Paris, 1949-50, Turkey, 1950-52; country pub. affairs officer U.S. Information Agy., Turkey, 1952-53, India, 1953-56, Indonesia, 1958 - , dep. chief planning div., Washington, 1957-58. Served from lt. (j.g.) to lt. comdr., USNR, 1942-45. Mem. Fgn. Service Assn., Delta Upsilon. Roman Catholic. Home: 631 G St. S.E. Office: 1776 Pennsylvania Av., Washington Died June 8, 1963.

FLANAGAN, WEBSTER lawyer, stockman; b. Cloverport, Ky., Jan. 9, 1832; s. James W. F.; moved to Tex., 1843. Held several local offices before joining C.S.A. as brig. gen.; after war an active Republican; apptd. judge 5th Jud. Dist., Tex., 1865; mem. Tex. Constl. convs., 1869, 1875; lt. gov., 1971-43; mem. Tex. Senate, 1875; pres. Henderson & Overton R.R., 1876-82; collector internal revenue 4th Tex. Dist., 1884-85; collector of customs at El Paso, Tex., 1891-93; apptd. collector of internal revenue, 3d Tex. Dist.; candidate for gov., 1890. Home: Henderson, Tex. Died May 5, 1924.

FLANDRAU, CHARLES EUGENE lawyer; b. New York, July 15, 1828; s. Thomas H. and Elizabeth (Macomb) F.; ed. Georgetown, D.C.; sailor before the mast, 1841-44; worked as sawyer of mahogany veneers, 1845-47; studied law in his father's office, Whitesboro, N.Y.; admitted to N.Y. bar, 1851; settled in practice, St. Paul, Minn., 1853; m. Isabella R. Dinsmore of Ky., Aug. 10, 1859 (died 1867); m. 2d, Mrs. Rebecca B. (McClure) Riddle, Feb. 28, 1871. Served as mem. Territorial Council; Indian agt., Sioux Nation, 1856; mem. constl. conv., 1857; asso. justice, Minn. Ty. and State, 1857-64. Was comdr.-in-chief of vol. forces resisting uprising of Sioux, whom he defeated at defense of New Ulm, Aug. 18, 1862, after desperate battle for 40 hours. Resigned from Supreme Court, 1864; practiced at Carson City, Nev., and later in St. Louis, but returned to Minn.; practiced Minneapolis, and was city atty., 1867, 1st pres. Minneapolis Bd. of Trade; again practicing at St. Paul, 1870—. Chmn. State Dem. Exec. Com., 1868-69; once nominated for gov., another time for chief justice Supreme Court; opposed Bryan on stump in 1896. Home: St. Paul, Minn. Died 1903.

FLANIGAN, HOWARD ADAMS ret. naval officer; b. N.Y.C., Jan. 23, 1889; s. John and Elizabeth (Adams) F.; student Horace Mann Sch., 1899-1905, Seftner Sch., 1905-06, U.S. Naval Acad., 1906-10; m. Lucie Cherbonnier, May 14, 1913; children - Elizabeth Adams, Lucie Cherbonnier; m. 2d, Martha Ruddy Johnson, July 1, 1933; m. 3d Margaret Stewart Dives, June 25, 1949. Ensign U.S. Navy, 1912, advancing through grades to comdr., Oct. 1, 1930; served in Mexican Campaign, 1914; commanded U.S.S. Rowan, World War; ret. Aug. 1, 1936; adminstrv. asst. to pres. N.Y. World's Fair, Inc., 1936-38, exec. v.p., 1938-41; chmn. bd. N.Y. Dock Co. (dir.), N.Y. Ry. (dir.). Recalled to active duty U.S. Navy, June 4, 1941; promoted capt., 1942. Promoted rear adm., Apr. 3, 1945; served as dir. Naval Transp. Service (Washington) to Nov. 1945; ret. Now chmn. bd. Inter-Am. Shipping Services, Inc.; chmn. bd. Flanigan, Loveland, Inc.; pres. Philadelphia Marine Corp. Awarded Navy Cross, World War I; Legion of Merit, D.S.M.; Comdr. Order of British Empire, Officer Legion of Honor, Croix de Gueire with Palm, in World War II. Clubs: New York Yacht, Army-Navy, Recess, Sleepy Hollow Country, India House, Propeller (New York). Home: 145 E. 54th St., New York 22. Address: 44 Whitehall St., N.Y.C. Died Mar. 30, 1967.

FLANNERY, JOHN ROGERS mfr.; b. Pittsburgh, Pa., Nov. 3, 1879; s. James Joseph and Harriet (Rogers) F.; A.B., Mt. St. Mary's Coll., Emmitsburg, Md., 1899, A.M., 1902, LL.D., 1916; LL.B., U. of Pittsburgh, 1902; m. Adelaide Naomi Friday, Oct. 24, 1907; children - John Rogers, Adelaide Elizabeth, Hilda Adelaide. Admitted to Pa. bar, 1902; investigating rubber and mineral concessions, Nicaragua, 1903; began in bolt manufacturing, 1904, vanadium metals manufacturing, 1909; president Flannery Bolt Company, American Vanadium Company, Collier Land Company. In 1914 was scht. by Herbert Hoover into Belgium to assist in organizing Belgian Relief Commission operations and was first American to return from war torn Belgium to United States; active throughout country in securing funds and was decorated by Belgium. Director of service and supplies, American National Red Cross in Washington, May-October 1917; assistant to chairman U.S. Shipping Board, dir. housing, October 1917-May 1918; dir. ry. equipment and supplies, War Industries Bd., May-Nov. 1918; lt. col. ordnance, U.S. Army, 1918. Pres. Mercy Hosp.; trustee Duquesne U., De Paul Inst., St. Barnabas Free Home, St. Paul's Orphan Asylum. Republican. Catholic. Club: Pittsburgh Athletic Assn. Home: 1544 Beechwood Blvd. Office: Flannery Bldg., Pittsburgh, Pa. Died Dec. 26. 1947.

FLEEGER, GEORGE WASHINGTON congressman, lawyer; b. Butler County, Pa., Mar. 13, 1839; attended West Sunbury Acad.; studied law. Entered Union U.S. Army was pvt. Co. C, 11th Regt., Pa. Reserves, 1861, commd. 1st lt., 1862, later brevetted capt., served until 1865; admitted to bar, 1866, began practice of law, Butler, Pa.; mem. Pa. Ho. of Reps., 1871-72; chmn. Pa. Republican Central Com.; del. Rep. state convs., 1882, 90; mem. U.S. Ho. of Reps. (Rep.) from Pa., 49th Congress, 1885-87. Died Butler, June 25, 1894; buried North Cemetery.

FLEISCHMANN, MAX C. mfr.; b. Riverside, O., Feb. 26, 1887; s. Charles and Henriette (Robertson) F.; educated public schools and Ohio Military Institute: LL.D. (hon.), Univ. of Nevada; m. Sarah Hamilton Sherlock, Dec. 20, 1905. Entered mfg. dept. of the Fleischmann Co., Cincinnati, at 18, became chmn. bd.; on acquisition of co. by Standard Brands, Inc. became dir. of latter; dir. Security Nat. Bank. Dir. gen. Nev. State Museum; v.p., trustee Santa Barbara Museum of Natural History; trustee Save-the-Redwoods League. Served in O. Nat. Guard 6 yrs. 2d lt.; 1st lt. Ohio Vol. Cav. Spanish-Am. War; maj. comdg. Balloon Corps, A.E.F., 1917-18. Fellow Roya. Geog. Soc. Republican. Mason (32ff). Clubs: New York Yacht. Explorers (life); Santa Barbara, Valley Club of Montecito. Author: After Big Game in Arctic and Tropic (pvt. circulation), 1909. Home: Glenbrook, Douglas Co., Nev. Office: 595 Madison Av., New York, N.Y.; and 1st Nat. Bank Bldg., Reno. Died Oct. 16, 1951; buried Mountain View Cemetery, Reno.

FLEMING, ADRIAN SEBASTIAN army officer; b. Midway, Ky., Dec. 6, 1872; s. William B. F.; grad. U.S. Mil. Acad., 1895, Sch. of Submarine Defense, 1905; Field Officers' Course, Army Sch. of the Line, 1912; General Staff Coll., 1920; m. Mabel V. Gassen, June 17, 1902. Commd. add. 2d lt. 5th Arty., June 12, 1895; promoted through grades to col., May 15, 1917; brig. gen. N.A., Apr. 12, 1918; brig. gen. O.R.C., July 12, 1921; brig. gen. retired, June 21, 1930. Accompanied Light Battery D, 6th Arty., to Philippines, 1898; in Philippine Rebellion from outbreak, Feb.-July 1898, in numerous engagements on Island of Luzon; cited for gallantry in action against insurgent forces nr. Manila, Feb. 5, 1898, and for gallantry in action at Calumpit River, Luzon, Apr. 25, 1899; comdt. School of Fire for Field Arty., Sept. 1917-May 1918; apptd. comdr. 158th Brigade, F.A., 83d Div., 4th Army Corps, A.E.F., May 1918; with A.E.F., June 1918-May 1919, serving in action during Meuse-Argonne Offensive, with 17th French Corps and 29th, 32d and 91st U.S. divs.; Gen. Staff Corps, Aug. 25, 1920; retired at own request after 30 yrs. service, June 17, 1921. Vice pres. Columbia River Paper Co., Columbia River Paper Mills, Oregon Pulp & Paper Co., Calif.-Oregon Paper Mills. D.S.M.; awarded two oak leaves; officer Legion d'Honneur (France). Presbyterian. Home: Portland, Ore. Died Dec. 1, 1940.

FLEMING, BURTON PERCIVAL civil and mech. engr.; b. Valley, Neb., Aug. 7, 1881; s. Allan Maris and Edith (Clark) F.; B.S. in C.E., Utah Agrl. Coll., 1900; Lawrence Scientific Sch. (Harvard), 1900-01; M.E., Cornell, 1906; m. Florence Foster, June 29, 1909; children—Allaire, Allan, Foster; m. 2d, Ethel Arnold, 1934. Dep. co. surveyor, Cache Co., Utah, 1899-1900, irrigation engr. Wyo. Expt. Sta., 1901-04; with U. S. Dept. Agr., 1906-07; hydraulic engr., Calif. Development Co., 1907; irrigation engr., N.M. Expt. Sta., 1907-09; prof. steam engring. and head of dept. mech. engr., U. of Ia., 1909-29; gen. mgr. Elephant Butte Irrig. Dist., N.M., 1929-32; dean of engring. N.M. State College, 1932-35; cons. engr. Iowa State Bd. Edn., 1923-32; chief engr. U.S. Soil Conservation Service,

1933-35. Capt. Co. M, 34th Engineers, A.E.F., in France, 1918-19; major Engr. R.C., 1919. Episcopalian. Mason. Author: Irrigation and Pumping, 1915. Home: Las Cruces, N.M. Died May 26, 1936.

FLEMING, FRED W. life ins.; b. New Brunswick, Can., Aug. 9, 1866; s. Robert and Lucy S. (Hovey) F.; grad. Ricker Classical Inst., Houlton, Me., 1885; m. Alice Ogden Fleming, Dec. 22, 1896; children—Mrs. Wingate Bixby, Mrs. Marion Goodwin, Kathleen. Bookkeeper and accountant, Kansas City; real estate and loan business on own account. 1887-94; job printing and pub., 1894-1900; sec. and mgr., 1904-11, v.p., 1911-15, chmn. bd., 1915-17, Kansas City Life Ins. Co. Receiver of Kansas City Rys. Co.; pres. Central Surety & Ins. Corp. Vice chmn. Federal Reserve Bank of Kansas City. Col. 3d Regt. N.G. Mo., 1898-1901; served as maj. 3d Mo. Inf. U.S.V., Spanish-Am. War and filled every position in the Nat. Guard from enlisted man to colonel. State oil insp., 1894-97; pres. Dem. Club, 1888-90; del. Dem. Nat. Conv., 1904, 08, 12. Pres. Trans-Miss. Commercial Congress, 1911-13; 1st v.p. Nat. Irrigation Congress, 1911-13. Campaign chmn. Red Cross war fund; pres. Navy League of Kansas City; mem. Mo. Council Defense; federal dir. Nat. War Savings Campaign, 1917. Trustee Y.M.C.A., Christian Coll., Columbia, Mo., Christian Ch. Hosp., Kansas City; treas. Internat. Conv. Disciples of Christ; trustee Horner Inst. Conservatory of Music. Home: Kansas City, Mo. Did Nov. 14, 1929.

FLEMING, PHILIP BRACKEN engr., ex-ambassador; b. Burlington, Ia., Oct. 15, 1887; s. John Joseph and Mary (Bracken) F.; student U. of Wis., 1905-07; B.S., U.S. Mil. Acad., 1911; student Army Eng. School, 1912-13; LL.D., St. Francis Coll.; J.C.D., George Washington U.; m. Dorothy Carson, Dec. 5, 1914; children-Carson, Jocelyn. Commd. 2d lt. C.E., U.S. Army, 1911, and advanced through grades to maj. gen., 1942 (temp. col. during World War); grad. mgr. of athletics West Point, 1926-33; exec. officer and dep. adminstr. Pub. Works Adminstrn., 1933-35; in charge Passamaquoddy Project, 1935-36; co-ordinator Resettlement Adminstrn., 1936-37; dist. engr. St. Paul, 1937-39; adminstr. Wage and Hour Div., Dept. of Labor, 1939-41; Fed. works adminstr., 1941-49; chmn. U.S. Maritime Commn., 1949-50; under sec. of commerce for transportation, 1950-51; ambassador to Costa Rica, 1951-53, ret. Chmn. Pres. Hwy. Safety Conf., 1946-49, Pres. Conf. on Fire Prevention, 1947-49. Mem. Ia., N.H., Minn. hist. socs., Am. Soc. C.E., Soc. Am. Mil. Engrs., Permanent Internat. Assn. Nav. Congresses (chmn. Am. sect., mem. permanent council), Delta Upsilon, Roman Catholic. Clubs: Minnesota, University, Somerset (St. Paul); Army and Navy, Army and Navy Country (Washington); Chevy Chase; Engineers (N.Y.C.). Home: 1554 34th St. N.W. Office: Am. Embassy, San Jose, Costa Rica. Died Oct. 6, 1955; buried Arlington Nat. Cemetary.

FLEMING, ROBERT VEDDER banker; b. Washington, D.C., Nov. 3, 1890; s. Robert Isaac and Bell (Vedder) F.; ed. George Washington U., hon. LL.D., 1939; m. Alice Listen Wright, Nov. 27, 1912; children - Alice Marie (Mrs. William S. Renchard), Robert Wright. Began with Riggs Nat. Bank, Washington, 1907, asst. cashier, 1916-20, cashier and sec. of bd., 1920-21, v.p. and cashier, 1921-24, 1st v.p., 1924-25, pres., 1925-35, pres., chmn. bd., 1935-55, chmn. bd., chief exec. officer, 1955-63, adv. chmn. bd., chmn. exec. and trust and investment coms., 1963 - ; dir. Julius Garfinckel & Co., So. Ry. Co., Chesapeake & Potomac Tel. Co. Hotel Waldorf Astoria Corp., Pan American Airways, Inc., Met. Life Ins. Co. of N.Y., Potomac Elec. Power Co., Cin., New Orleans & Tex. Pacific Ry. Mem. federal advisory council to Bd. Govs. Fed. Reserve System, 5th Fed. Reserve Dist., 1942-45, 47-57, 2d v.p. council, 1948-49, v.p., 1950-55, pres., 1956-57; hon. mem. Bus. Council. Mem. com. econ. devel. D.C. Treas. Nat. Republican Congl. Com., 1926 - . Life trustee, chmn. finance com., Corcoran Gallery Art; chmn. bd. George Washington U., 1937-59, now chmn. bd. George Washington U., 1937-59, now chmn. emeritus, mem. bd. regents, chmn. exec. com., Smithsonian Instn.; chmn. bd. trustees Endowment Fund, A.R.C.; bd. trustees, mem. finance com. Retirement System, Am. Nat. Red Cross; trustee Automotive Safety Found.; trustee, treas. Robert A. Taft Meml. Fund, Inc. Chmn. Pres.'s Adv. Commn. on presdl. Office Space, chmn. D.C. Inaugural Com., 1957. Com. White House Conf. on edn.; chmn., dir. D.C. Com. for Eisenhower Presdl. Library; mem. Nat. Capital Sesquicentennial Commn.; mem Auditorium Com. (apptd. Pres.). Recipient several awards for service to Washington, latest being: Certificate of Merit. Commrs. of D.C., 1953; Washington Bd. of Trade Man of Yr., 1956; Central Bus. Assn. citation, 1960. Commander USNR, retired. Mem. American Bankers Assn. (pres. 1928-29, past chmn., now mem. com. govt. borrowing), Assn. Res. City Bankers (past pres.), Nat. Geog. Soc. (life trustee, v.p., treas.), Navy League of U.S. (nat. dir., mem. adv. council), Air Force Aid Soc. (chmn. finance com.), Am. Road Builders Assn. (dir. at large), Friendly Sons of St. Patrick of City of Washington, Omicron Delta Kappa, Kappa Alpha. Episcopalian. Mason. Clubs: Metropolitan, National Press, Alfalfa (pres. 1949); Burning Tree (pres. 1937-45), Chevy Chase, Rotary (hon.); The Brook (N.Y.C.). Home: 2200 Wyoming Av., Washington 20008. Office: Riggs National Bank, Washington 20013. Died Nov. 28, 1967.

FLEMING, WILLIAM army officer, colonial ofcl.; b. Jedburgh, Scotland, Feb. 18, 1729; s. Leonard and Dorothea Fleming; attended U. Edinburgh (Scotland); m. Anne Christian, Apr. 9, 1763. Came to Norfolk, Va., 1755; served as ensign in regt. under Col. George Washington, 1755-63; col. Botetourt Regt. at Battle of Point Pleasant, 1774; county lt. Botetourt County (Va.), 1776; mem. Va. Legislature, 1777-79, Va. Council, 1780; mem. Danville Conv. (for separate statehood for Ky.), 1784; acting gov. Va., June 1-12, 1781. Died Aug. 5, 1795.

FLETCHER, ANGUS SOMERVILLE (SIR ANGUS FLETCHER) govt. official; b. Queenstown, S. Africa, May 13, 1883; s. Patrick and Agnes (Eaglesim) F.; student South African Coll., Cape Town, South Africa, 1900-03; Law Diploma, Univ. Cape of Good Hope, 1930; D.Litt. (hon.) Muhlenberg Coll. (Pa.), 1942; m. Helen Stewart, Jan. 6, 1926; children - Donald Stewart, peter Stewart, Angus John Stewart. Attached to British War Mission to U.S., 1918; mem. staff Nat. Indsl. Conf. Bd., New York, 1919-22; dir. British Library of Information, New York, N.Y., 1928-41; consultant World Wide Broadcasting Foundation, New York, 1942; British Consul at Buffalo, N.Y., 1943-49. Chairman H.Q. Commn., U.N. 1946. Served with 1st Rhodesia Regt. in German Southwest Africa 1914-15, and Royal Horse Arty., France, 1915-19. Decorated Comdr. Order of British Empire, 1931, Knight Comdr. Order of St. Michael and St. George, 1941. Mem. Scottish History Soc. (Edinburgh). Protestant Episcopalian. Home: Fireplace Landing, East Hampton, N.Y. Died Aug. 6, 1960; buried Scotland.

FLETCHER, BENJAMIN army officer, colonial gov.; b. London, Eng.; s. William and Abigail (Vincent) F.; m. Elizabeth Hodson, at least 3 children including Benjamin. Served from cornet to capt. Brit. Army under Duke of Ormonde, 1663-85; arrived N.Y.C., 1692; gov. N.Y. and Pa., 1692-97; commanded Conn. Militia; brought William Bradford from Phila. prison, set him up as royal printer; liberal benefactor Trinity Ch. (for which he signed charter 1697); deposed and superseded in 1697 (colonists complained of rule), sent to Eng. under arrest, investigated for fraudulent land grants, protection given to piracy. Died Boyle, Ireland, May 28, 1703.

FLETCHER, FRANK FRIDAY admiral U.S.N.; b. at Oskaloosa, Ia., Nov. 23, 1855; s. James Duncan and Nancy Powers (Jack) F.; grad. U.S. Naval Acad., 1875; m. Susan Hunt Stetson, Feb. 1895; children—Sybil Avery, Alice Stetson. Commd. ensign, July 1876; promoted through the various grades to rank of rear admiral, Oct. 1911. Has comd. torpedo boat Cushing, gunboats Kanawha and Eagle, cruiser Raleigh and battleship Vermont; aid to Sec. Navy for div. of material, 1910; comdg. 3d div. Atlantic Fleet, 1913, then 2d Div. and later 1st Div.; comd. naval force on West Coast of Mex., Feb. 1913-Apr. 1914, and Apr. 1921, seized and occupied City of Vera Cruz; comdr.-in-chief Atlantic Fleet, Sept. 1914, and promoted to rank of admiral, Mar. 1915. Mem. War Industries Bd. of Council of Nat. Defense, 1917, and mem. Gen. Bd. of the Navy and Joint Army and Navy Bd.; mem. President's Air Craft Bd., 1925. Inventor of the Fletcher breech mechanism and gun mounts. Awarded medal of honor for distinguished conduct in battle, D.S.M. (Army and Navy). Died Nov. 28, 1928.

FLETCHER, FRANK JACK, naval officer; b. Marshalltown, Ia., Apr. 29, 1885; s. Thomas Jack and Alice (Glick) F.; B.S., U.S. Naval Acad., 1906; grad. U.S. Naval War Coll., 1930, U.S. Army War Coll., 1931; m. Martha Richards, Feb. 10, 1917. Commd. ensign U.S. Navy, 1908, and advanced through the grades to vice adm., 1942; flag lt. and fleet signal officer, U.S. Atlantic Fleet, 1914-15; comd. U.S.S. Dale, Chauncey, Margaret, Benham, Gridley, Whipple, Sacramento, New Mexico, Cruisers Pacific Fleet; in comd. North Pacific Forces; chmn. Gen. Bd. U.S. Navy; retired as adm., May 1947. Decorated Medal of Honor for distinguished service at Vera Cruz, 1914; Navy Cross for distinguished service in command of U.S.S. Benham in war zone, 1918; D.S.M. for distinguished service in command of Task Forces at battles of Coral Sea and Midway; Army D.S.M. for duty in comd. N. Pacific Forces, U.S. Pacific Fleet, 1943-45; Purple Heart; Companion Order of the Bath (British); Order of the Green Dragon of Amxam (French). Clubs: New York Yacht; Chevy Chase, Army and Navy (Washington, D.C.) Home: La Plata MD Died Apr. 1973.

FLETCHER, MONTGOMERY naval officer; b. in Va., Feb. 15, 1830; s. Charles and Sarah (Marshall) F.; unmarried. Apptd. from Pa., 3d asst. engr. U.S.N., June 24, 1850; 2d asst. engr., Feb. 26, 1851; 1st asst. engr., June 20, 1856; chief engr. with rank of capt., Oct. 25, 1859; retired with rank of commodore, Feb. 15, 1892; advanced to rank of rear-admiral, 1906. On Steamer Walker, coast survey, 1850-51; Alleghany, 1851-53; Saranac, 1853-56; Bur. of Steam Engineering, 1856-57; Wabash, 1857-59, Saranac, 1861-65; spl. duty, New York, 1855-56; Navy Dept., Mare Island, 1866-71; fleet engr., Pacific Squadron, 1861-63; insp. of machinery afloat at Mare Island, 1873-76; Navy Yard, Mare Island, 1877-83; mem. Bd. of Inspection, Calif., 1884-90; Bur. of Steam Engineering, 1890-92. Home: Washington, D.C. Died 1908.

FLETCHER, PAUL FRANKLIN gynecologist; b. Sheridan, Wyo., Dec. 24, 1903; s. Thomas Isaac and Margaret (Collins) F.; B.S., U. Santa Clara, 1926; M.D., St. Louis U., 1932, M.S., 1936; m. Margaret Elizabeth Mudd, Feb. 10, 1938; children - Paul Dayton, Margaret Ann, Elizabeth Gay, Nancy Joan, Thomas Gerard, Robert Joseph. Intern St. Luke's Hosp., San Francisco, 1932-33; practice of gynecology, St. Louis, 1936 - ; asst. gynecologist and obstetrician St. Mary's Group Hosps., 1940-45, asso., 1945; attending gynecologist Barnard Free Skin & Cancer Hosp., 1945 - , charge cancer cytology lab., 1951-54; cons. obstetrician and gynecologist Incarnate Word Hosp., Fairfield Meml. Hosp., Fairfield, Ill.; vis. staff St. Louis City Hosp., sr. instr. obstetrics and gynecology St. Louis U. Sch. Medicine, 1946 - , asso. dir. Cancer Cytology Center, dept. pathology, 1951 - . Served as lt. col., M.C., AUS; flight surgeon USAAF. Diplomate Am. Bd. Obstetrics and Gynecology, also Internat. Bd. Surgery. Fellow A.C.S., American Geriatrics Society, International College Surgeons (founder American chapter), American College Obstetrics and Gynecology (founder); mem. A.M.A., St. Louis Gynecol. Soc. (pres. 1951-52), St. Louis Surg. Soc., Central Assn. Obstetricians and Gynecologists (exec. com. 1952-55, v.p. 1955-56), Pan-Pacific Surg. Assn., N.Y. Acad. Scis., Inter-Soc. Cytology Council (mem. founders exec. com.; sec.-treas. 1952-58; clin. representative on exec. committee 1958-60, president, 1961-62), American Academy of Obstetricians and Gynecologists (mem. pub. relations com. 1953-54), St. Louis Medical Soc., Am. Radium Soc., Mo. Med. Assn., Endocrine Soc., Mo. Hist. Soc., St. Louis Zool. Soc., St. Louis Acad. Scis. Clubs: Missouri Athletic, University, Old Warson Country, Harbor Point Yacht, St. Louis Sailing, St. Louis Revolver, Green Head Duck, Missouri Duck Hunters Assn., Ducks Unlimited (St. Louis). Editor St. Louis Med. Soc. Bull., 1946-48. Contbr. sci. articles med. publs. Home: 7345 Westmoreland Dr., University City, Mo. Office: 634 N. Grand Blvd., St. Louis 3. Deceased.

FLETCHER, ROBERT HOWE author; b. Cincinnati, July 21, 1850; s. Robert and Anna (Howe) F.; entered the U.S. Naval Acad. as cadet midshipman at age of 17; after graduation transferred to army; served on Indian frontier and in Calif., until Oct. 1886, when he was retired for disabilities contracted in line of duty; was 1st lt. and bvt. capt. for services in Nez Percès Indian war; m. at San Francisco, Octavia Shreve Miller, of Louisville, Ky., Aug. 1, 1878; 1 son, Robert Howe. Dir. Mark Hopkins Inst. of Art, 1899-1915, and San Francisco Institute of Art, 1907 to 1915. Author: A Blind Bargain; The Johnstown Stage; Marjorie and Her Papa; Annals of the Bohemian Club. Address: Bohemian Club, San Francisco, Calif.

FLETCHER, THOMAS congressman; b. Westmoreland County, Pa., Oct. 21, 1779. Settled in Montgomery County, Ky.; mem. Ky. Ho. of Reps., 1803, 05-06, 17, 20-21, 23, 25; served as maj. Ky. Volunteers under Gen. Harrison in War of 1812, distinguished himself at Ft. Meigs, 1813; mem. U.S. Ho. of Reps. (filled vacancy) from Ky., 14th Congress, Dec. 2, 1816-17. Died nr. Sharpsburg, Ky.; buried pvt. burial ground nr. Sharpsburg.

FLETCHER, THOMAS CLEMENT gov. Mo.; b. Herculaneum, Mo., Jan. 22, 1827; s. Clement B. and Margaret (Byrd) F.; m. Mary Clara Honey, 1851. Admitted to Mo. bar, 1856; land agt. S.W. Br. of Pacific R.R. (now St. Louis & San Francisco R.R.), St. Louis, 1856; asst. provost-marshal gen., St. Louis, circa 1861; served as col. 31st Mo. Regt., 1862, in battles of Vicksburg and Chattanooga; organized 47th and 50th Mo. regts., 1864; gov. Mo., 1865-69; practiced law, Washington, D.C., circa 1870-99. Died Washington, Mar. 25, 1899.

FLETCHER, WILLIAM BARTLETT naval officer; b. St. Albans, Vt., Jan. 7, 1862; s. John Bartlett and Louisa Ballard (Williams) F.; grad. U.S. Naval Acad., 1882, Naval War Coll., 1915; m. Malene R. Asserson, Apr. 4, 1888. Comd. ensign USN, 1884, advanced through grades to rear adm.; served in the battleship Massachusetts, Spanish-Am. War, 1898; at Naval War Coll., Newport, R.I., 1902-04, 1907-09, 11-12, comdr. Birmingham, 1909-11, Montana, 1912-13, Kansas, 1913-14, mem. Gen. Bd. Navy Dept., 1916-17; comdr. Squadron Three, Patrol Force, Atlantic Fleet, 1917, 7th Naval Dist., 1918-19; comdr. 14th Naval Dist., 1919, Naval Sta., Hawaii, 1919. Decorated Medals for West India and Santiago Campaign, Philippine Campaign, Spanish-Am. War. Conglist. Club: Army and Navy (Washington). Home: Orrs Island, Me. Office: care Navy Dept., Washington. Died June 29, 1957; buried U.S. Naval Acad., Annapolis, Md.

FLEWELLING, RALPH CARLIN architect; b. St. Louis, Mich., May 4, 1894; s. Ralph Tyler and Jennie (Carlin) F.; B.S., Wesleyan U., Middletown, Conn., 1916, grad. stdy. Mass. Inst. Tech., 1916-17; m. Carol Hunter, Nov. 19, 1925; 1 son, Ralph Hunter. Practiced architecture in Los Angeles, 1924-; received honor awards from Southern Calif. Cahpter A.I.A., and medals and prizes from art associations and national publications for outstanding structures including pub. bldgs., schools and residences. Served in U.S. Army, 1917-19, resigned as capt., 1919. Awarded U.S. Navy Commendation in 1945, for outstanding services rendered in War Construction Program. Fellow Am. Inst. of Architects (past pres. Southern Calif. cahp.). Mem. Planning and architectural bds., Alpha Delta Phi. Tau Sigma Delta. Author: Town in Transition, 1945. Home: 5147 Oakwood Av., La Canada, Calif. Office: 3112 Los Feliz Blvd., Los Angels 26, Calif. Died Apr. 1960.

FLINT, JAMES MILTON medical dir. U.S.N.; b. Hillsborough, N.H., Feb. 7, 1838; s. Amos and Mary (Stickney) F.; ed. common schs. and Pembroke Acad.; M.D., Harvard, 1860; m. Carolina H. Conant, June 27, 1871; (died 1901). Asst. surgeon, U.S.N., Apr. 14, 1862; surgeon, 1874; med. insp., 1893; med. dir., 1897; retired with rank of rear admiral, Feb. 7, 1900. Connected with U.S. Fish Commn., 1884-87, and at 3 different periods in all about 20 years with Smithsonian Instn. as curator, div. of medicine, U.S. Nat. Mus. Has written reps. and bulls. U.S. Nat. Museum. Died Nov. 21, 1919.

FLINT, JOSEPH MARSHALL, surgeon; b. Chicago, July 8, 1872; s. Francis and Sarah Elizabeth (Dancy) F.; student Princeton U., 1891-93, A.M., 1900; B.S., U. of Chicago, 1895; Johns Hopkins U., 1896-1900, M.D., 1900; U. of Leipzig,1900; Vienna, Bonn, Munich, 1905-07; A.M., Yale, 1907; m. Anne Drusilla Apperson, of Hacienda del Pozo de Verona, Calif., Sept. 15, 1903. Asst. in anatomy, 1897, asso. 1900-01, U. of Chicago; asst. Johns Hopkins Med. Commn. to the Philippines; on spl. plague duty, U.S. Marine Hosp. Service, San Francisco, 1901; prof. anatomy U. of Calif., 1901-07; prof. of surgery, Yale, 1907-21. Chief surgeon New Haven Hosp.; ex-chief surgeon New Haven Disp.; surgeon to Arsakeion Mil. Hosp. during the Graeco-Bulgarian War, summer of 1913; medecin chef. Hopital 32 bis Chateau de Passy, France, July-Dec., 1915; maj. Med. O.R.C., 1917; comdg. officer Base Hosp. No. 39, A.E.F., later Mobile Hosp. No. 39. Mem. med. bd. Council Nat. Defense; liaison officer, chief surgeon's office, A.E.F., to French War Office for mobile sanitary formations; organized first mobile hosp. of A.E.F.; lt.-col. M.C., July 1918; col. Med. R.C. Awarded D.S.M., Mar. 1, 1919; citation for meritorious and conspicuous services, Apr. 19, 1919; Officier de l'Instruction Publique (French), Feb. 17, 1919. Editor Am. Jour. of Anatomy, 1903-07; contbr. on surg. and anat. subjects in med. jours. Fellow Am. Coll. Surgeons, A.A.A.S.; mem. Sigma Xi, Alpha Delta Phi. Clubs: Princeton, University (New York); Graduate (New Haven). Office: 185 Church St., New Haven CT

FLOURNOY, THOMAS STANHOPE congressman; b. Prince Edward County, Va., Dec. 15, 1811; attended Hampden-Sydney (Va.) Coll.; studied law. Became a pvt. tchr.; admitted to bar, began practice of law, Halifax, Va., 1834; mem. U.S. Ho. of Reps. (Whig) from Va., 30th Congress, 1847-49; unsuccessful Am. Party candidate for gov. Va., 1855; mem. Va. Secession Conv., Richmond, 1861; raised cavalry co., Confederate Army, served as capt.; promoted col. 6th Va. Cavalry, wounded, 1864; unsuccessful candidate for gov. Va., 1863; settled in Danville, Va., after Civil War, resumed practice of law; del. Democratic Nat. Conv., St. Louis, 1876. Died Halifax County, Va., Mar. 12, 1883; buried family plot on his estate.

FLOURNOY, WILLIAM WALTON, lawyer; b. Walton Co., Fla., Dec. 5, 1874; s. John and Mary Elizabeth F.; A.B., Florida Agricultural and Mechanical College, 1896; LL.B., Cumberland Univ., Lebanon, Tenn., 1900; m. Marie Alice King, of De Funiak Springs, Fla., June 28, 1900; children—Marie Alice (Mrs. H. L. Pearce), Louise Elizabeth (dec.), Gracie Claude (Mrs. J. P. Ashmore), William W., John Thomas, Willie Louise (Mrs. T. Clyde Beatty), Mary Elizabeth (Mrs. W. Paul Bissett), Eleanor Beatrice. Comdt. cadets and prof. mil. science and tactics, Fla. Agr. and Mech. Coll., 1896-99, inclusive; col. staff, Gov. W. D. Bloxham, 1898. Practiced at De Funiak Springs since 1900; mayor, 1908-11, 1915-21 and 1934-35; mem. Fla. Senate, 1909-11; leading counsel for Gov. S. J. Catts, in Knott-Catts governorship election, 1916. Mem. Bd. of Control of Fla., 1920. Capt. Co. K, 1st Inf. Fla. N.G., at Pensacola, Fla., 1900, at De Funiak Springs, 1904-09. Democrat. Presbyn. Home: De Funiak Springs Fl

FLOWERS, ALAN ESTIS engineer; b. St. Louis, Mo., Oct. 4, 1876; s. William Pitts and Mary Emma (Cummins) F.; M.E., Cornell U., 1902, M.M.E., 1914, Ph.D., 1915; m. Ida Vandergrift Burns, June 29, 1907; children - George Schlaederberg, Nancy Holmes, Priscilla (dec.). Engr. apprentice with Westinghouse Electric & Mfg. Co., 1902-04; instr. and asso. prof. elec. engring., U. of Mo., 1904-12; with Gen. Electric Co., 1912-13; prof. elec. engring., Ohio State U., 1913-18; appraisal engr., Columbus Electric Power & Light Co., 1917-18; capt. Signal Corps, U.S. Army, on duty in radio development sect., Washington, D.C., Mar. 31, 1918-lMar. 8, 1919; test engr. engring. dept., Nat. Aniline & Chem. Co., New York, 1919-20; research engr. in charge of Research Engring. Sect., 1921-22; mgr. and cons. engr. Chem. Machinery Construction co., 1922-23; engr., in charge development, De Laval Separator Co., 1923-43, research engr. since 1943; dir. Flakice Corp. since 1943. Mem. Am. Inst. Elec. Engrs., Am. Soc. Mech. Engrs. (mem. spl. research com. on lubrication), Am. Soc. for Testing Materials (chmn. subm-com. on sampling and gaging), Am. Phys. Soc., Metals, Am. Assu. Univ. Profs., Phi Mu Alpha, Lambria Phi Rho, Sigma Xi, Tau Beta Pi. Conglist. Developed apparatus for measuring cylinder friction and lubrication in steam engines, also invented a viscosimeter; developed processes for oil reclamation, improvements in centrifugal separators and ultra high speed test tube centrifuge. Contbr. on tech. topics.; chapter on "Centrifuges" in Chemical Engineers' Handbook. Home: 148 College Av., Poughkeepsie, N.Y. Died Dec. 4, 1945.

FLOWERS, ROBERT LEE univ. pres.; b. York Collegiate Inst., North Carolina, Nov. 6, 1870; s. George Washington and Sarah (Haynes) F.; grad. U.S. Naval Acad., 1891; hon. A.M., Trinity College (now Duke Univ., Durham, N.C., 1900; LL.D., Davidson College, 1927; LL.D., University of North Carolina, 19 Parrish, June 22, 1905 (died May 22, 1948); children-Virginia, Sybil Parrish. Prof. mathematics, Duke U., 1891-1934; v.p. in charge of business div., 1925-41, pres. 1941-48, trustee of the univ., sec. since 1910, treas. 1928-48, chancellor since 1948. Mem. bd. trustees of the Duke Endowment since 1926. Dir. Durham & Southern Ry. Co., Fidelity Bank. Mem. bd. visitors, U.S. Naval Acad., 1946, Trustee Greensboro Coll., Methodist Orphanage, Oxford Orphanage, N.C. Coll. for Negroes, Lincoln Hosp. for Negroes. Mem. Bd. Edn. of N.C. Conf. M.E. Ch., S., since 1916. Mem. N.C. Acad. Science, Alpha Tau Omega, Omicron Delta Kappa, Phi Beta Kappa. Mason. Rotarian. Home: Durham, N.C. Died Aug. 24, 1951; buried Maplewood Cemetery, Durham.

FLOYD, DAVID BITTLE clergyman, educator; b. Middletown, Md., Mar. 15, 1846; s. Hezekiah and Lydia (Bittle) F.; A.B., Roanoke Coll., Salem, Va., 1872 (2d honor), M.A., 1879; med. dept. U. of Mich., 1866-67; student Bellevue Med. Coll. and Hosp., New York, 1872-73; grad. Luth. Theol. Sem., Gettysburg, Pa., 1876; (D.D., Roanoke Coll. and Susquehanna U., 1906); studied Bible history in Greece, Palestine and Egypt, 1910; m. Mary Elizabeth Cutting, Feb. 15, 1877. Ordained Evang. Luth. ministry, 1876; pastor Uniontown, Md., 1876-82, Boonsboro, 1882-85, Newville, Pa., 1885-99, Funkstown, Md., 1900-1904, Washington, D.C., 1905; prof. Hebrew and Greek langs., Bibl. criticism, Christian ethics and ch. polity. Susquehanna U., 1905—. Served as corpl., sergt. and lt., Co. I, 75th Ind. Regt. Vols., Civil War, 1862-65; fought under Gen Thomas at Chickamauga, and Gen. Grant at Chattanooga, and participated under Gen Sherman in the March to the Sea. Mem. Com. on 100th Anniversary Luth. Gen. Synod; mem. Exam. Com. Md. Synod. Home: Selinsgrove, Pa. Died Jan. 23, 1922.

FLOYD, IVY KNOX clergyman; b. Whitesville, Ky., Sept. 15, 1885; s. Harden Lawrence and Sallie (Douthitt) F.; student Bethel Coll., McKenzie, Tenn., 1911-13; B.S.L., Oskaloosa (Ia.) Coll., 1914; m. Clyde Godbold, May 3, 1908; children-Vernon Lamar, Walter Ray, Floyd Godbold, Melba Laurence, Tchr. pub. schs. 7 yrs.; ordained ministry Cumberland Presbyn. Ch., 1909; pastor Trenton, Tenn., 1912-14, First Ch., Austin, Tex., 1916-17, First Ch., Dallas, 1923—. Moderator Gen. Assembly Cumberland Presbyn. Ch., 1926. Served as chaplain 7th Tex. Inf., 131st M.G. Batt., Development Batt., World War; now chaplain 132d F.A., Tex. N.G. Ch. reporter on Dallas Dispatch, 1926-29; now reporter, religious editorial writer Dallas Jour., in addition to pastoral work. Home: 810 S. Beacon St., Dallas. Deceased

FLOYD, JOHN congressman; b. Beaufort, S.C., Oct. 3, 1769; learned carpenter's trade. Moved (with father) to Camden County Ga., 1791, engaged in boat building; served as brig. gen. 1st (Floyd's) Brigade, Ga. Militia, in War of 1812, also served in expdns. against Creek Indians; mem. Ga. Ho. of Reps., 1820-27; mem. U.S. Ho. of Reps. from Ga., 20th Congress, 1827-29. Died nr. Jefferson, Ga., June 24, 1829.

FLOYD, JOHN surgeon, gov. Va., congressman; b. Floyds Station, Ky., Apr. 24, 1783; s. John and Jane (Buchanan) F.; attended Dickinson Coll., Carlisle, Pa.; M.D., U. Pa., 1806; m. Letita Preston, May, 1804, 9 children. Justice of peace, 1807; surgeon with rank of maj. in War of 1812, became brig. gen. Va. Militia; mem. Va. Ho. of Dels., 1814-15; mem. U.S. Ho. of Reps. from Va., 15th-20th congresses, 1817-29, was 1st to propose occupation and territorial orgn. of Ore. County, 1821; gov. Va., 1830-34; received electoral vote of S.C. for U.S. Pres., 1832. Died Sweetsprings, Va. (now W. Va.), Aug. 1837; buried Sweetsprings.

FLOYD, JOHN BUCHANAN gov. Va., sec. of war, army officer; b. Blacksburg, Va., June 1, 1806; s. Gov. John and Letitia (Preston) F.; grad. S.C. Coll., 1829; m. Sally Preston, 1830; 1 adopted dau. Del. to Va. Gen. Assembly from Montgomery County, 1847-49, 55; gov. Va., 1849-52; ex officio chmn. Va. Bd. Pub. Works; presdl. elector Democratic Party, 1852; apptd. sec. of war by Pres. Buchanan, 1857, served until Dec. 29, 1860 (when S.C. seceded); joined Confederate Cause, 1860; raised a brigade of volunteers, entered Confederate Army; promoted to maj. gen. by Gen. Assembly of Va., 1863. Died Abingdon, Va., Aug. 26, 1863.

FLOYD, RICHARD C(LARK) b. Brookline, Mass., Oct. 28, 1886; s. Eugene Benton and Mary Cleaveland (Taylor) F.; A.B., Harvard, 1911, grad. study, grad. sch. bus. administrn., 1910-11; m. Nancy Ogden, Dec. 7, 1919; children-Mary Cleveland, Nancy Ogden, Richard Clark. Formerly v.p., dir. Bird & Son, Inc.; later asso. dir. Mass. div. Am. Cancer Soc.; dir., mem. exec. com. Norfolk Co. Trust Co.; mem. corp. Brookline Savs. Bank; dir. Coolidge Coop. Bank. Has served Town of Brookline, as park commr., chmn. playground commn., mem. Limited Town Meeting Assembly, mem. sch. com., mem. finance com., chmn. gymnasium and baths commn., dir. citizens com. Dir. Boys Club Camp Wing; mem. boys work com. Boston Y.M.C.A.; trustee Dexter Sch., Longwood, Park Sch., Brookline. Served as capt. C.W.S., U.S. Army, World War I. Mem. bd. dirs. Intercollegiate Assn. Amateur Athletes of Am.; rep. Intercollegiate Assn. to convs. of Amateur Athletic Union and of Am. Olympic Assn.: twice elected mgr. Am. Olympic Team; chmn. com. on rules of athletic competition of Intercollegiate Athletic Assn., mem. games com., Harvard rep. Mem., v. chmn. overseers' com. on athletic sports Harvard; v.p., dir. Harvard Alumni Assn., mem. permament class com., chmn. class 25th reunion; Harvard commencement marshal, dir. Harvard Alumni Bull.; mem. standing com. Harvard Ch. Mem. Boston C. of C., S.R., Delta Kappa Epsilon. Republican. (mem. state com. and exec. com. of Mass.; del., v.p. Mass. state conv.). Episcopalian. Clubs: Harvard (N.Y.C.); Harvard (bd. govs.); Madison Square Garden, University (Boston); Phoenix S-K, Hasty Pudding and Institute of 1770 (Harvard); Country and Polo (Dedham); Longwood Cricket (Chestnut Hill); The Country (sec., mem. bd. govs.), Commercial (Brookline); Lipton League; Middlesex; Republican of Mass., Norfolk County Republican. Address: 207 Fisher Av., Brookline, Mass. Died Sept. 15, 1953.

FLOYD, WILLIAM congressman; b. Brookhaven, N.Y., Dec. 17, 1734; s. Nicoll and Tabetha (Smith) F.; m. Isabella Jones; m. 2d, Joanna Strong. Served as maj. gen. Suffolk County Regt., N.Y. Militia; mem. Continental Congress from N.Y., 1774-77, 78-83; dep. N.Y. Provincial Conv., 1775; 1st N.Y. del. to sign Declaration of Independence; mem. N.Y. State Senate, 1777-78, 83-88, 1808; mem. N.Y. Council, 1787, 89; mem. U.S. Ho. of Reps. from N.Y., 1st Congress, 1789-91; del. N.Y. Constl. Conv., 1801. Died Westerville, N.Y., Aug. 4, 1821; buried Presbyn. Ch. Cemetery, Westerville.

FLOYD-JONES, DE LANCEY soldier; b. Queens Co., N.Y., Jan. 20, 1826; s. Hon. Henry and Helen Watts (De Lancey) F.-J.; grad. U.S. Mil. Acad. and commd. 2d lt., 7th Inf., July 1, 1846; m. Laura Jane Whitney, 1852. Served during Mexican war; took part in seige of Vera Cruz, battles of Cerro Gordo and Molina del Rey, and capture of City of Mexico; bvt. 1st lt. for gallant and meritorious conduct in battle of Molino del Rey; capt. 4th inf., July 31, 1854; served during Civil war, 1861-65, as maj. 11th U.S. inf.; engaged in battles of Yorktown, Gaines' Mill and Malvern Hill; bvt. lt.-col., July 4, 1862, for gallant and meritorious service during peninsular campaign; engaged in battles of Manassas, Antietam, Sharpsburg, Chancellorsville and Gettysburg; bvt. col., July 2, 1863; lt. col. 19th inf., 1863; served on the plains, 1868-79; col., 3d inf., Jan 2, 1873; retired from active service, March 1879. Died 1902.

FLYE, EDWIN congressman, businessman; b. Newcastle, Me., Mar. 4, 1817; attended Lincoln Acad., Newcastle. Engaged in merc. pursuits, also shipbuilding; mem. Me. Ho. of Reps., 1858 pres. 1st Nat. Bank of Damariscotta (Me.), many years; served as paymaster with rank of maj. U.S. Army, during Civil War; del. Republican Nat. Conv., Cincinnati, 1876; mem. U.S. Ho. of Reps. (Rep., filled vacancy) from Me., 44th Congress, Dec. 4, 1876-77. Died while visiting his dau., Ashland, Ky., July 12, 1886; buried Congregational Cemetery, Newcastle.

FLYNN, JOHN E(DWARD) biologist; b. Friendsville, Pa., Aug. 19, 1897; s. William M. and Mary (Murphy) F.; B.S., Pa. State, 1922; M.S., U. Md., 1924; Ph.D., Cornell, 1929; m. Elizabeth Helen Schunk, Nov. 12, 1933; children - Barbara, Patricia. Asst. in botany U. Md., 1922-24; instr. in mycology and plant pathology Cornell, 1924-28; asst. editor Biol. Abstracts, Phila., 1929-37, editor-in-chief, 1938-53; biologist Office Naval Research, N.Y.C., 1954-62, chief scientist, 1962 - , spl. cons. biophysics, 1958 - . Editor: The New Microbiology. Fellow N.Y. Acad. Sci.; mem. Biophys. Soc., Sigma Xi. Roman Catholic. Home: 22 Rockland Pl., New Rochelle, N.Y. Office: 207 W. 24th St., N.Y.C. 11. Died Sept. 22, 1965.

FOERDERER, PERCIVAL EDWARD, b. Phila., Oct. 25, 1884; s. Robert Hermann and Caroline (Fischer) F.; student William Penn Charter Sch., U. Pa.; LL.D., Jefferson Medical Coll.; m. Ethel Tillyer Brown, June 1, 1910; children—Mignon Estabrook (Mrs. John M. Kelso Davis), Florence Rapelye, Shirley Avril (Mrs. Charles Oakes Ames). Pres. Robert H. Foerderer, Inc., mfrs. of Vici Kid, 1908-46; pres. Robert H. Foerderer Estate, Inc.; Mem. storage com. Council Nat. Def.

requirements div., vice chmn. employment mgmt. div. and chief of divisional priorities sect. War Industries Bd., World War I; chmn. Met. Phila. Civilian Aid Com. for AAC, lieutenant col. Army Specialist Corps, World War II. Chmn. Phila. Com. for Econ. Development, 1943-46. Chmn. Tanners Council of America, 1934-36; dir. Found. Tanners Research Lab.; trustee Com. for Econ. Development, Drexel Inst. Tech.; chmn. bd. Jefferson Med. Coll. and Med. Center, 1950-62, trustee 1928-69; vice chmn., dir. Asso. Hosp. Service of Phila. Mem. Numismatic and Antiquarian Soc. of Phila., Newcomen Society, Military Order Foreign Wars of United States, Pannsylvania Commandery, Delta Kappa Epsilon. Clubs: Union League, Gulph Mills Golf, Phila. Country, Poor Richard, Penn, Merion Cricket, Radnor Hunt, Racquet, Rittenhouse (Phila.); Gulf Stream Golf, Everglades, Bath and Tennis (Fla.); Bucks (London, Eng.). Home: Bryn Mawr PA Died Jan. 22, 1969; buried West Laurel Hill Cemetery, Bala-Cynwyd PA

FOLEY, JAMES BRADFORD congressman; b. nr. Dover, Mason County, Ky., Oct. 18, 1807. Worked on flatboat on Mississippi River, 1823; moved to Greensburg, Ind., 1834; engaged in merc. pursuits, 1834-37, later in farming; treas. Decatur County, 1841-43; mem. Ind. Constl. Conv., 1850; apptd. comdr. 4th Brigade, Ind. Militia, 1852; mem. U.S. Ho. of Reps. (Democrat) from Ind., 35th Congress, 1857-59. Died Greensburg, Dec. 5, 1886; buried South Park Cemetery.

FOLGER, WILLIAM MAYHEW rear-admiral U.S.N.; b. Massillon, O., May 19, 1844; s. Robert and Amelia (Hayden) F.; apptd. from Ohio, and grad. U.S. Naval Acad., 1864. Ensign, Nov. 1, 1866; promoted through grades to rear admiral, June 1, 1904. Served receiving ship North Carolina, 1864-65; sch. ship Sabine, New London, to July, 1865; Hartford, Asiatic Squadron, 1865-68; Franklin, 1868-72; ordnance duty, 1872-75; leave in Europe, 1875; Marion, 1876, 1876-77; ordnance duty, Navy Yard, Washington, 1878; Naval Acad., 1878-79; Swartara, 1879-82; Bur. of Ordnance, 1882; ordnance duty, Naval Acad., 1882-85; insp. ordnance, Navy Yard, Washington, 1886-87; comd. Quinnebaug, 1887-88; insp. ordnance, Navy Yard, Washington, 1888-90; chief Bur. of Ordnance with rank of commodore, 1890-93; comdr. Yorktown, 1894-95; light house insp., 11th dist., 1896-98, 3d dist., Jan.-Apr. 1898; comd. New Orleans, 1898-99; gen. insp. Kearsarge, 1899-1900; comd. Kearsarge, 1900-01; light house insp., 3d dist., 1901-04; comd. Philippine Squadron, Asiatic Fleet, to Mar. 1905; comd. Asiatic Fleet, until Mar. 30, 1905; retired, June 30, 1905. Home: Windson, Vt. Died July 22, 1928.

FOLSOM, NATHANIEL Continentalcongressman, army officer; b. Exeter, N.H., Sept. 18, 1726; s. Jonathan and Anna (Foster) F.; m. Dorothy Smith; m. 2d, Mary Sprague. Served in Crown Point expdn. in French and Indian War, 1755; mem. Continental Congress, 1774-75, 77-78, 79-80; signed the Association; mem. N.H. Provincial Congress, 1775; maj. gen. in command of entire N.H. Militia, 1775; served repeatedly in N.H. Legislature; mem. N.H. Com. of Safety; judge Ct. Common Pleas. Died Exeter, May 26, 1790.

FOLTZ, FREDERICK STEINMAN army officer; born Lancaster, Pa., Dec. 15, 1857; s. Surgeon Gen. Jonathan M. (U.S.N.) and Rebecca (Steinman) F.; grad. U.S. Mil. Acad., 1879; m. Mary F., d. Maj. T. B. Keefer, U.S.A., July 11, 1883. Commd. 2d lt. 1st Cav., June 13, 1879; 1st lt., Mar. 26, 1888; capt. 2d Cav., June 23, 1898; maj. 15th Cav., Sept. 13, 1906; lt. col. cav., Feb. 29, 1912; col. of cav., Sept. 27, 1914; assigned to comd. of 1st Cav., Dec. 14, 1914; orig. gen. N.A., Aug. 5, 1917. Duty with Maj. Gen. Miles in Cuba and P.R., July-Aug. 1898; collector of customs, Batavano, Cuba, 1898-99; served successively as supervisor of police, Havana, chief of secret service of Cuba, provost marshal and capt. of Port of Havana; in P.I., 1906; gov. Province of Havana, 1908. Apptd. comdr. 182d Inf. Brigade, A.E.F., Sept. 1917, 91st Div., July 1918; hon. discharged as brig. gen. N.A., Nov. 11, 1918. Mem. Soc. Santiago, Loyal Legion, Aztec Club. Club: Army and Navy. Address: 2022 Columbia Rd., N.W., Washington. Died Aug. 28, 1952; buried Arlington Nat. Cemetery.

FOLWELL, WILLIAM WATTS univ. prof.; b. Romulus, N.Y., Feb. 14, 1833; s. Thomas J. and Joan (Bainbridge) F.; A.B., Hobart Coll., 1857, A.M., 1860, LL.D., 1878; LL.D., Racine, 1870, U. of Minn., 1925; m. Sarah Hubbard Heywood, Mar. 13, 1863. Teacher langs., Ovid Acad., N.Y., 1857-58; adj. prof. mathematics, Hobart, 1858-60; student in Berlin, 1860-61; 1st lt. to maj. and bvt. lt. col., 50th N.Y. Engrs., 1862-65; in business in Ohio, 1865-69; pres., 1869-84, prof. polit. science, 1875-1907, pres. emeritus, 1907—, U. of Minn. Mem. Minn. Centennial Commn., 1876; mem. Bd. Park Commrs., Minneapolis, 1889-1907 (pres. 1894-1900). Author: Minnesota, the North Star State; Economic Addresses; University Addresses; History of Minnesota, 4 vols. Home: Minneapolis, Minn. Died Sept. 18, 1929.

FONTAINE, LAMAR civil engineer; b. Laberde Prairie, Austin's Colony, Tex., Oct. 10, 1829; s. Edward F.; captured by Comanche Indians; prisoner over 4 yrs.; later escaped from camp, head of Zuni River, and returned 750 miles, alone and afoot, to Austin, Tex.; later 6 yrs.; in U.S.N. under instruction of Lt. Matthew Fontaine Maury (his kinsman) and Lt. Louis Herndon; afterward traveled over Europe, Africa, Asia (from Kamtchatka to Chinese Wall and south to Ceylon), South and Central America; was with Russian army at siege of Sebastapol, winning iron cross of Peter the Great for marksmanship; was civ. eng'r. in Central America, 1860; at Pensacola, Fla., Jan., 1861, in capture of navy yard, redoubt, Fts. Barrancas and McRee; pvt. 10th Miss. inf., March, 1861; transferred to his father's co., "K," 18th Miss., June 1861; wounded at 1st Manassas; transferred to Troop I, 2d Va. cav.; scout for Gen. T. J. "Stonewall" Jackson, Nov., 1861, to May, 1853; then courier between Gens. Joseph E. Johnston and Pemberton. During siege of Vicksburg, though suffering from 3 severe wounds and a partially paralyzed right arm, made way through Federal lines on crutches into Vicksburg with 40,000 gun caps and dispatches for Gen. Pemberton, and, 10 days later, with dispatches to Johnston and many soldiers' letters to Jackson, Miss.; famous as marksman; 5 times captured by Federals, but each time made successful daring escape. Was in 27 battles, 57 skirmishes and 100 individual skirmishes and was wounded 67 times. Wrote war songs; All Quiet Along the Potomac; Oenone; Only a Soldier; Good Old Rebel; Dying Prisoner at Camp Chase; etc. m. June 20, 1866, Lemuella S. Brickell. Address: Lyon, Miss. Died Oct. 1, 1921.

FONVILLE, WILLIAM DRAKEFORD superintendent mil. acad.; b. Darlington, S.C., Oct. 14, 1849; s. John Averett and Rachel (Sloan) F.; A.B., Howard Coll., Ala., 1873, A.M., 1875; m. Mary Winn Yancey, of Richmond, Va., Sept. 18, 1883. Commandant of cadets and prof. mathematics, Howard Coll., 1876-78; supt. and propr. Ala. Mil. Inst., 1883-1900; supt. and propr. Mo. Mil. Acad. since 1900. Baptist. Mem. Sigma Alpha Epsilon. Address: Mexico, Missouri.

FOOTE, ANDREW HULL naval officer; b. New Haven, Conn., Sept. 12, 1806; s. Senator Samuel A. and Eudocia (Hull) F.; m. Caroline Flagg, June 22, 1828; m. 2d, Caroline Street, Jan. 27, 1842; 3 children. Became acting midshipman U.S. Navy, 1822; 1st lt. in ship Cumberland in Mediterranean, 1843, formed temperance soc. on board, making Cumberland 1st temperance ship in Navy, chiefly responsible for abolishing liquor ration in U.S. Navy (finally accomplished 1862); in command ship Perry to help destroy slave ships and trade on African Coast, 1849-51; mem. naval efficiency bd., 1855; captured Canton (China) forts in punishment for attacks on Am. flag, 1856; in charge Bklyn. Navy Yard, Civil War, 1861, then in command naval operations on upper Mississippi; in charge naval side of operations in Grant's capture of Ft. Henry, 1862, then in command of naval force at Ft. Donelson (broke Confederate line of defense in No. Tenn.); commd. rear adm., 1862; chief of bureau of equipment and recruiting, 1863; apptd. to succeed DuPont in command of Charleston Squadron, died enroute to South. Author: Africa and the American Flag, 1854. Died N.Y.C., June 26, 1863, buried New Haven.

FOOTE, CHARLES AUGUSTUS congressman; b. Newburgh, N.Y., Apr. 15, 1785; grad. Union Coll., Schenectady, N.Y., 1805; studied law. Admitted to bar, 1808, began practice of law, N.Y.C.; later practiced in Delhi, N.Y.; served as col. 6th div. N.Y. State Militia; trustee Delaware Acad.; pres. Village of Delhi; mem. U.S. Ho. of Reps. (Democrat) from N.Y., 18th Congress, 1823-25. Died Delhi, Aug. 1, 1828; buried pvt. burying ground on father's estate "Arbor Hill."

FOOTE, MORRIS COOPER brig. gen. U.S. Army, retired; b. Madison Barracks, Sackett's Harbor, N.Y., Sept. 16, 1843; s. Lyman (surgeon U.S.A.) and Mary Morris (Cooper) F.; ed. pub. schs., Cooperstown, N.Y. and acad. at Plattsburg, N.Y.; grad. Commercial Coll., Syracuse, N.Y.; m. Annie, d. D.F. Murphy, official reporter to U.S. Senate, Apr. 29, 1891. Entered vol. service as pvt. 44th N.Y. vols., Sept. 1861; served through Civil war as 2d lt., 1st lt. and bvt. capt. N.Y. vols. Entered regular army May 1866, as 2d lt., 9th U.S. Inf.; served as 2d lt., 1st lt., capt., maj. and lt. col. 9th inf.; col. 28th Inf., Apr. 15, 1902; brig. gen. Feb. 18, 1903; retired Feb. 19, 1903. After Civil War served through various Indian campaigns, through the Santiago campaign and battle of San Juan Hill, Cuba, 1898; through the entire campaign for the relief of Peking, China, 1900. Mem. Provisional govt. of Tien-tsin, China, winter of 1900-01; served in the Philippines, summer of 1901 and winter of 1902-03. Home: Cooperstown, N.Y. Died 1905.

FOOTE, PERCY WRIGHT naval officer (ret.); b. Roaring River, N.C., Aug. 13, 1879; s. James Henry and Susan (Hunt) F.; grad. U.S. Naval Acad., 1901, U.S. Naval War Coll., 1929; m. Genevieve Clary, Oct. 1, 1910; children - Lt. Col. Thomas Clary, U.S.A., Diana (wife, Maj. James F. Lawrence). Commd. ensign USN, 1901; advanced through grades to rear adm., 1936 in recognition of distinguished service in combat with the enemy, World War; ret. 1936; recalled to active duty, 1942, and assigned to duty as insp. Naval Material, Houston; ret., 1945. Commanded U.S.S. Pres. Lincoln, sunk in engagement with German submarine U-90, 1918; served as aide to sec. of Navy, 1918-21; comd. forces from U.S.S. Baltimore during Chinese uprising, Shanghai, 1905; commr. Pa. Motor Police, 1937-39. Awarded Meritorious Medal of Pa., by Gov. George H. Earl for services in "leading a great program for highway safety." Decorated with the Order of the Crown of Belgium by King Albert, 1919; also D.S.M. for performance of duty. Democrat. Episcopalian. Mason. Author: Electric Propulsion of Battleships. Clubs: Army and Navy (Washington); New York Yacht. Home: 523 Clement Av., Charlotte, N.C. Died June 23, 1961; buried Arlington (Va.) Cemetery.

FOOTE, STEPHEN MILLER army officer; b. La Salle, Monroe Co., Mich., Feb. 19, 1859; s. of Henry William and Rebecca (Dunlap) F.; apptd. to U.S. Mil. Acad. from Vt., 1880, grad. 1884; grad. Arty. Sch., Ft. Monroe, Va., 1888, Army War Coll., Washington, 1913; m. Sara Brooke, of Radnor, Pa., Apr. 24, 1889. Commd. 2d lt. 4th Arty., 1884; 1st lt. 6th Arty. June 17, 1889; maj. 3d U.S. Vol. Engrs., Nov. 3, 1898; hon. mustered out vol. service, May 17, 1899; capt. 6th Arty., Mar. 2, 1899; maj. Arty. Corps, Feb. 24, 1906; lt. col. Coast Arty. Corps, Mar. 10, 1909; col., Oct. 5, 1911; brig. gen., Aug. 5, 1917. Instr. arty. Sch., 1888-91; with Intercontinental Ry. Commn., Central America, 1892; mil. instr., Vt. Acad., 1895-97, New York Mil. Acad., 1897; a.d.c. Santiago campaign, 1898; in Philippine campaign, comdr. battery of arty. acting as inf., 1899-1901; marched with batln. field arty. from Salt Lake City, Utah, to Cheyenne, Wyo., 500 miles, Apr. 1906; comd. coast defenses on Pacific, Gulf and Atlantic coasts, 1907-11; instr. Army War Coll., 1913-14; comd. South Atlantic Coast Arty. Dist., 1915-16; comd. Coast Arty. Sch., coast defenses of Chesapeake Bay and Training Camp for Reserve Officers, 1916-17; brig. gen., Aug. 5, 1917; comd. 163d Field Arty. Brigade in U.S. and France from its orgn., Aug. 1917, to demobilization, Feb. 1919; comd. training center for 155-millimeter guns at Clermont-Ferrand, France, Sept.-Dec. 1918; with the first Army A.E.F. in the Meuse-Argonne offensive, Oct. 12-22, 1918. Mem. Soc. Army of Santiago de Cuba, Mil. Order of Carabao, S.A.R., Chi Psi. Episcopalian. Clubs: Army and Navy, Chevy Chase. Address: War Dept. Washington, D.C.

FORAKER, JOSEPH BENSON senator; b. on farm nr. Rainsboro, O., July 5, 1846; enlisted July 14, 1862, as pvt. 89th Ohio Inf., and served to end of war, becoming 1st lt. and bvt. capt.; grad. Cornell, 1869; m. Uulia, d. Hon. H.S. Bundy, Oct. 4, 1870. Admitted to bar and began practice at Cincinnati, 1869; judge Superior Ct., Cincinnati, 1879-82; resigned on account of ill health; Rep. candidate for gov. Ohio, 1883; defeated, but elected gov. in 1885 and 1887; again defeated, 1889, for same office; U.S. senator, 1897-1903, 1903-1909. Chmn. Rep. State convs., Ohio, 1886, 1890, 1896, 1900, 04; presented name of William McKinley to the convs. of 1896 and 1900 for nomination to the presidency. Author; Notes of a Busy Life, 1916. Home: Cincinnati, O. Died May 10, 1917.

FORBES, JOHN army officer; b. Dunfermline, Scotland, 1710; s. Col. John Forbes. Joined Scots Greys Regt. of 2d Royal North Brit. Dragoons, 1735, served in War of Austrian Succession; maj., dep. q.m. gen. in Europe, circa 1743, commd. lt. col. Brit. Army, 1745; col. 17th Foot, Eng., 1757; adj. gen. until 1758; brig. gen. Brit. Army in Am. 1757, commanded expdn. against Ft. Duquesne, built forts along the way to preserve eastern communication lines, finally took fort with no resistance from French; raised Brit. flag over Ft. Duquesne (renamed Ft. Pitt), Nov. 25, 1758. Died shortly after successful expdn., Mar. 11, 1759; buried Christ Ch., Phila.

FORBES, STEPHEN ALFRED naturalist; b. Silver Creek, Ill., May 19, 1844; s. Isaac Sawyer and Agnes (Van Hoesen) F.; ed. at Beloit Acad. and Rush Med. Coll.; Ph.D., on exam and thesis, Ind. U., 1884 (LL.D., U. of Ill., 1905); m. Clara Shaw Gaston, Dec. 25, 1873; children—Bertha Van Hoesen, Ernest Browning, Winifred, Ethel Clara, Richard Edwin (dec.). Capt. 7th Ill. Vol. Cav. in Civil War; prisoner 4 months; curator Mus. of Ill. State Natural History Soc., 1872-77; taught zoology, Ill. State Normal U., 1875-78; founded, 1877, and dir. Ill. State Lab. of Natural History to 1917; since chief of natural history survey of Ill.; state entomologist, 1882-1917; prof. zoology, 1884-1909, prof. of entomology, Sept. 1, 1909-21, dean Coll. of Science, 1888-1905, Univ. of Ill. Awarded first class medal of Societe d'Acclimatation de France for scientific publs., 1886; organized Internat. Congress Zoologists, Chicago Expn., 1893; dir. aquarium of U.S. Fish Commn. and prepared natural history exhibit of Ill. at same. Was founder of and has been editor Natural History, 1877—(now Bulletin Ill. State Nat. Hist. Survey). Author: Biennial Reports as State Entomologist, 1883-1916; Studies of the Food of Birds, Fishes and Insects; Contagious Diseases of Insects. Final Report on the Fishes of Illinois and Studies on the Biology of the Illinois River with R.E. Richardson. Home: Urbana, Ill. Died Mar. 13, 1930.

FORBES, THEODORE FRELINGHUYSEN soldier; b. in Hawaii, July 13, 1840; s. Cochran and Rebecca Denman (Smith) F.; acad. edn.; m. Mrs. Henrietta A. Woodward, June 19, 1900. Enlisted pvt. 102d N.Y. Vols., Nov. 9, 1861; apptd. corporal same month;

severely wounded in battle of Cedar Mountain, Va., Aug. 9, 1862, and in hosp. on account of wounds until Feb. 1863; apptd. 2d lt. 102d N.Y. Vols., Aug. 9, 1863; mustered out on account of disability, Mar. 7, 1863; apptd. 2d lt. Vet. Reserve Corps. Aug. 19, 1963, 2d lt. 42d Inf. (Vet. Reserve Corps), July 18, 1866; transferred to 5th Inf., Nov. 15, 1869; promoted 1st lt., Aug. 31, 1875; capt., Oct. 8, 1885; maj. 5th Inf., Feb. 27, 1899; lt. col. 29th Inf., Feb. 28, 1901; col. 27th Inf., July 14, 1902; brig. gen., Aug. 14, 1903, and retired from active service, Aug. 15, 1903. Died Mar. 9, 1917.

FORCE, MANNING FERGUSON comdt. Ohio Soldiers' and Sailors' Home, 1889—; b. Washington, Dec. 17, 1824; grad. Harvard, 1845 (LL.B., Harvard; LL.D., Marietta Coll.). Admitted to bar, Cincinnati, 1850; apptd. maj. 20th O. vol. Inf., Aug. 1861; served through Civil War; mustered out as brig. gen. and bvt. maj. gen., Jackson, Miss., Jan. 1866. Judge of common pleas, Hamilton Co., O., 1867-77; judge superior court, Cincinnati, 1877-87; prof. equity and criminal law, Cincinnati Law School, 1878-88. Author: From Fort Henry to Corinth; General Sherman (Great Comdrs. Series), 1899. Died 1899.

FORCE, PETER mayor Washington, D.C., archivist; b. nr. Passaic Falls, N.J., Nov. 26, 1790; s. William and Sarah (Ferguson) F. Pres., N.Y. Typo. Soc., 1812; served from pvt. to lt., U.S. Army, War of 1812; elected to City Council, Washington, D.C., 1822, later to Bd. Aldermen; mayor Washington (Whig), 1836, 37; established semi-weekly paper Nat. Jour., Washington, 1823, editor, 1823-30; pres. Nat. Inst. for Promotion Science; mem. bd. mgrs. Washington Nat. Monument Soc.; collected and published tracts and other papers, relating principally to origin, settlement and progress of N.Am. colonies (known as Force's Tracts), 1836-46; greatest work: American Archives (considered finest source collection on Am. Revolution and one of best sources of Am. history), 9 vols., 1837-53. Died Washington, Jan. 23, 1868.

FORD, COREY, author; b. New York City, Apr. 29, 1902; s. James Hitchcock and Adelaide C. (Ricketts) F.; educated Columbia, 1919-23; unmarried. Colonel U.S. Air Force. Humorist, magazine writer, playwright, literary parodist under name "John Riddell." Special consultant Dartmouth College. Member of Delta Kappa Epsilon. Clubs: Players, Coffee House, Dutch Treat. Author: numerous books including Cloak and Dagger, 1946; The Last Time I Saw Them, 1946; The Horse of Another Color, 1946; A Man of His Own, 1949; How to Guess Your Age, 1950; The Office Party, 1951; Every Dog Should Have A Man, 1952; Never Say Diet, 1954; Daughter of the Gold Rush, 1958; You Can Always Tell a Fisherman, 1958; Has Anybody Seen Me Lately?, 1958; The Day Nothing Happened, 1959; Corey Ford's Guide To Thinking, 1961; What Every Bachelor Knows, 1961; Minutes of the Lower Forty, 1962; And How Do We Feel This Morning? 1964; Uncle Perk's Jug, 1964; A Peculiar Service, 1965; Where the Sea Breaks its Back, 1966; The Time of Laughter, 1967. Address: Hanover NH Died July 27, 1969; buried Pine Knolls Cemetery, Hanover NH

FORD, GEORGE MICHAEL state supt. schs.; b. Kasson, W.Va., Jan. 7, 1871; s. Frederic G.W. and Jemima Elizabeth (Hebb) F.; student Fairmont (W.Va.) State Normal Sch., 1887; A.B., W.Va. U., 1892, LL.B., 1896; m. Annie L. Linn, Keyser, W.Va., Dec. 22, 1897; children—Margaret Buchanan (Mrs. Harry W. Hall), Jemima Elizabeth (Mrs. Silas E. Richmond), Annie Laurie Linn, Frederick Wayne. Began as teacher pub. schs., 1892; traveling rep. Ginn & Co., pubs., 1900-03; served as prin. schs., Terra Alta, high schs., Grafton and Benwood; pres. Concord State Normal Sch.; head dept. economics and Am. history, Marshall Coll.; supt. schs. Bluefield, Brown's Creek Sch. Dist. pub. schs., Dunbar; state supt. schs., W. Va., Mar. 1922—, 2d term ending 1929. Commd. capt. 2d Inf., W.Va., N.G., May 12, 1911; maj. 1914; served as capt. on Mexican border, 1916-17, and overseas 6 mos. with 150th U.S. Inf., 38th Div., 358th Inf., 90th Div., and 145th Inf., 37th Div.; hon. disch. Apr. 25, 1919; lt. col. 398th Inf. (Res.). Life mem. N.E.A. Methodist. Mason. Home: Dunbar, W.Va. Died Aug. 21, 1941.

FORD, JACOB army officer, powder maker; b. Feb. 10, 1738; s. Jacob and Hannah (Baldwin) F.; m. Theodosia Johnes, Jan. 27, 1767, 6 children. Owner, Middle Forge, Morristown, N.J., 1764, cast shot and shell for Washington's army; built powder-mill., 1776; commd. col. Morris County (N.J.) Militia, 1775; successfully defended Morristown against Brit. raids. Died Jan. 11, 1777; buried 1st Presbyn. Churchyard, Morristown.

FORD, JOHN DONALDSON rear adm.; b. Baltimore, May 19, 1840; s. Thomas C. and Isabella (Logie) F.; grad. Md. Inst. Sch. of Design, 1861, receiving Peabody prize; grad. Potts Sch. of Mech. Engring., 1862; m. Laura Jane Darling, Apr. 30, 1866. Entered U.S.N. as 3d asst. engr., July 30, 1862; promoted 2d asst. engr., Feb. 13, 1864; chief engr., Dec. 27, 1890. During Civil War took part in recapture of Baton Rouge, La., Mar., 1863, battles of Mobile Bay, 1864; was on Arizona, destroyed by fire off Poverty Point, Mississippi River, Feb. 27, 1865, etc.; was wrecked, in the Sacramento, on Coramandel coast of India, June, 1867; served on many expdns. and stas.; detached and ordered to start Baltimore Manual Training Sch., Mar. 13, 1884; at Md. Agrl. and Mech. Coll., 1894-96; on U.S.S. Brooklyn, 1896-98 (relative rank of comdr., 1897); U.S.S. Baltimore (flagship), Jan. 25, 1898; and fleet engr., Pacific Sta.; joined Asiatic fleet; took part in the actions of May 1 and Aug. 13, 1898; the destruction of the Spanish fleet off Cavite; the destruction of the batteries at Cavite and at Sangley Point, and the capture of the forts as Corregidor and the capture of Manila; commd. comdr. Mar. 3, 1899, and later advanced in that grade for "eminent and conspicuous conduct in battle"; promoted capt.; Mar. 5, 1902, rear adm. and retired, May 19, 1902, but continued on duty as insp. machinery and ordnance at Baltimore and Sparrow's Point, Md., until Dec. 25, 1908. Home: Baltimore, Md. Died Apr. 8, 1918.

FORD, RICHARD, physician, educator; b. Cambridge, Mass., Jan. 31, 1915;2s. Jeremiah D.M. and Anna (Fearns) F.; A.B., Harvard, 1936, M.D., 1940; m. Hope Cullinan, Jan. 23, 1942; children—Hope, Faith, Cathleen Charity, Lucy Ann. Intern pathology Peter Bent Brigham Hosp., 1940-41, cons. in pathology, 1953-—; intern surgery Boston City Hosp., 1941-42; research fellow legal medicine and pathology, med. sch. Harvard, 1945-49, acting head dept. legal medicine, asst. prof. legal medicine, 1949-61, asst. clin. prof. legal medicine, chmn. dept., 1961-65; lectr. legal medicine Harvard, Yale, Tufts, and Boston univs. med. schs.; hon. lectr. forensic medicine U. Southern Cal. School of Medicine, 1953; Rockefeller traveling fellow, 1953. Pathologist to State Police, Commonwealth of Mass., 1949-65; asso. med. examiner Suffolk Co. (Boston), 1946-50, med. examiner, 1950-70; cons. in pathology Peter Bent Brigham Hosp., 1953-70; cons. in forensic pathology Mass. Gen. Hosp., 1959-70, Armed Forces Inst. Path., 1959-70, Fed. Aviation Agy., 1960. Served from 1st lt. to maj. AUS, 1942-45. Certified in Forensic Pathology by Am. Bd. Pathology. Decorated Legion of Merit. Fellow Coll. Am. Pathologists; mem. A.M.A., Am. Assn. Pathologists and Bacteriologists, Am. Acad. Forensic Scis., Am. Assn. Neuropathologists (asso.). Home: Peterborough NH Died Aug. 3, 1970; buried Peterborough NH

FORD, WILLIAM MILLER surgeon; b. Brooklyn, N.Y., Nov. 30, 1878; s. A. William and Evelyn M. (Miller) F.; M.D., U. of Va., 1899; grad. St. Vincent's Hosp., 1901, Woman's Hosp., N.Y. City, 1902; m. Theresa E. Dunne, Aug. 30, 1910; children—William Miller, Anne Evelyn, Laurence Maunsell. Junior attending surgeon, Woman's Hosp., 1907-17; attending surgeon, St. Vincent's Hosp., 1905-26; dir. gynecology, 1927-31; attending surgeon, Manhattan Maternity Hosp., 1908—; cons. gynecologist, N.Y. Hosp. for Ruptured and Crippled, 1921—; chief surgeon and dir., Manhattan Maternity Hosp., 1928—; cons. gynecologist, St. Clare's Hosp., N.Y. City, 1935—; pres. med. board, St. Vincent's Hosp., N.Y. City, 1935—; clin. prof. obstetrics, New York U., 1920-33, Capt. N.Y.N.G., 1903-16, on Mexican border, 1916; maj. Medical Corps U.S.A., World War. Fellow Am. Coll. Surgeons. Democrat. Catholic. Home: New York, N.Y. Died Nov. 26, 1938.

FORDYCE, SAMUEL WESLEY capitalist; b. Guernsey Co., O., Feb. 7, 1840; s. John and Mary A.F.; bro. of John Addison F.; ed. Madison Coll., Pa., and North Ill. U., Ill.; m. Susan E. Chadwick, 1866. Enlisted in Co. B, 1st Ohio Cav., 1861, serving throughout Civil War; became capt. of cav. and insp. gen. of cav., Army of the Cumberland; at close of war located in Huntsville, Ala.; mem. Dem. State Central Com., Ala., 1874; removed to Arkansas, 1876; became v.p., and treas., 1881, of Tex. & St. Louis R.R., of which was apptd. receiver, 1885, and when road was reorganized as the St. Louis, Ark. & Tex. Ry. Co. was made its pres.; again apptd. receiver, 1889, and in 1891 road was reorganized as the St. Louis Southwestern Ry., of which was pres., 1891-99; pres. Houston Oil Co., of Tex.; v.p. Jefferson Hotel Co., St. Louis, Eastman and Arlington Hotel cos., Hot Springs, and other corps. Democrat; mem. Dem. Nat. Com. (Ark.), 1884-88. Home: St. Louis, Mo. Died Aug. 3, 1919.

FOREMAN, ALBERT WATSON army officer; b. Wilmington, Del., Aug. 11, 1874; s. Thomas Nicholson and Mary Louise (Watson) F.; grad. Army Sch. of the Line, 1915, Army War Coll., 1921; m. Rebecca Marchand Conner Milligan, Sept. 17, 1901 (died 1930); 1 daughter, Estelle Josephine. Commander 2d lt., Delaware Volunteer infantry, 1898; appointed 1st lt. Regular Army, February 1901, advancing through the grades to col., 1927; retired from active duty, 1938; recalled to active duty, 1942, again retired from active service December 1946; dir. internal security, Hdqrs. 2d Service Command, Governor's Island, N.Y., Sept. 1942; retired from active duty, Oct. 1943; apptd. acting state dir. Selective Service System, Del., Nov. 1943, state dir. since Apr. 1944. Participated in Spanish-Am. War, Philippine Insurrection, Pulajan Campaign (Samar, P.I.), Mex. Border Service and in Mexico, World War I (A.E.F.), World War II (Atlantic Sector). Prof. mil. science and tactics, Miss. Agrol. and Mech. Coll., Starkville, Miss., Nov. 1, 1916-July 1, 1917. Organized and comd. 3d Civilian Conservation Corps Dist., 1st Corps Area, 1933-34. Decorated Distinguished Service Medal, Legion of Merit with oak leaf cluster (U.S.), Cross of Order l'Etoile Noir (France); awarded gov.'s med. by governor of Delaware, 1946, apptd. a.d.c. to gov., 1947; recipient citation for Army Service ribbon from sec. of war. Mem. Order Founders and Patriots Am., Huguenot Soc. N.E., S.A.R., Mayflower Descendants, Mil. Order of Carabao, 80th Div. Vets. Assn., Mil. Order World War, Inf. Assn. (Washington), Soc. Am. Wars, Commandery Commonwealth of Mass., Soc. Colonial Wars, S.R., Magna Charta Soc. (papers finally completed and accepted just prior to death), Ancient and Hon. Arty. Co. of Mass., Soc. War 1812, Am. Legion. A "freeman" of Gov. and Co. of Mass. Bay in N.E. Mason (Lafayette Lodge No. 14, A.F. and A.M. of Wilmington, Del.), Sojourner, Heroes of '76. Clubs: Army Athletic Assn. (West Point); Army and Navy (Washington); Algonquin (Boston); Bedford, Kiwanis, Wilmington Country, Wilmington, Social Service (Wilmington). Home: 803 N. Franklin St., Wilmington 6, Del. Died Aug. 12, 1950; buried Arlington Nat. Cemetery.

FOREMAN, MILTON J. lawyer; b. Chicago, Ill., Jan. 26, 1863; s. Joseph and Mary (Hoffman) F.; ed. pub. schs. and Chicago Coll of Law (night); LL.D., Knox Coll., Ill., 1930; unmarried. Began in employ of Keith Bros.& Co., wholesale hats, Chicago, at 12 and continued 23 yrs.; admitted to Ill. bar, 1899, now mem. Foreman, Bluford, Krinsley & Schultz. Mem. City Council, Chicago, 1899-1911; chmn. Street Ry. Commn., 1900-02; chmn. on Local Transportation, 1907-11, chmn. Chicago Charter Conv., 1905-06; mem. Ill. Liquor Control Commn., 1934—. Enlisted in Ill. N.G., 1895; capt. 1st Ill. Cav., Spanish-Am. War, 1898; col. 1st Cav., Ill. N.G., 1906-17; col. 122d F.A., A.E.F., 1917-19; brig. gen. 33d Div., 1920; apptd. maj. gen. comgd. 33d Div., 1921; retired with rank of lt. gen., 1931. Awarded D.S.C., D.S.M. and Silver Star Decoration with two clusters (U.S.); Crown (Belgian); hon. citizen City of Tarbes, France, Village of Bourseche, France; hon. life mem. Nat. Guard Assn. of U.S.; past nat. comdr. Am. Legion; past comdr. in chief Mil. and Naval Order Spanish-Am. War. Republican. Home: Chicago, Ill. Died. Oct. 16, 1935.

FORMAN, DAVID army officer, jurist; b. Monmouth County, N.J., Nov. 3, 1745; s. Joseph and Elizabeth (Lee) F.; ed. Coll. of N.J.; m. Ann Marsh, Feb. 28, 1767, 11 children. Suppressed Loyalist uprising in Monmouth County, 1776; commd. brig. gen. N.J. Militia, 1777; commanded Jersey Militia at Battle of Germantown, 1777; attached to Maj. Gen. Charles Lee's staff by Gen. Washington's order; judge Monmouth County Ct. of Common Pleas. Died Sept. 12, 1797.

FORNEY, JAMES brig. gen. U.S. Marine Corps; b. Lancaster, Pa., Jan. 17, 1844; s. John W. (journalist) and Matilda (Reitzel) F.; ed. Georgetown U., D.C.; m. Jane R. Richardson, Dec. 1, 1886. Entered U.S. Marine Corps as 2d lt., Mar. 1, 1861; promoted through grades to brig. gen., June 5, 1904; retired, July 1904. Began service on frigate Roanoke, Sept. 1, 1861; was on Brooklyn, Mex. Gulf Squadron, in battles of Ft. St. Philip, Fts. Jackson and Chalmette, and capture of New Orleans, in two attacks at Vicksburg, Baton Rouge, Galveston; landed brigade at Havre de Grace, Md., 1864; comd. marines, Formosa, 1867, and in labor riots, 1877; in Europe on spl. duty, 1873, afterward on various duties, fleet marine office, N. Pacific Squadron, 1876; grad. Torpedo Sch., Newport, R.I., 1879; comd. recruiting rendezvous, Phila., 1879-81; and comd. marines on various stas. and duties; during Spanish-American War commanded the Spanish Camp, consisting of 1,700 prisoners from Admiral Cervera's fleet; comd. 1st brigade, U.S. marines, P.I., 1901-12. Home: Philadephia, Pa. Died Feb. 2, 1921.

FORNEY, PETER congressman; b. nr. Lincolnton, N.C., Apr. 21, 1756; attended public schs.; married, at least 1 son, Daniel Munroe. Served as capt. during Revolutionary War. Engaged in iron mfg.; mem. N.C. Ho. of Commons, 1794-96, N.C. Senate, 1801-02; Democratic presdl. elector, 1804, 08, 16, 24, 28; mem. U.S. Ho. of Reps. (Democrat) from N.C., 13th Congress, 1813-15. Died "Mt. Welcome," Lincoln County, N.C., Feb. 1, 1834; buried pvt. burying ground "Mt. Welcome."

FORNEY, WILLIAM congressman, army officer; b. Lincolnton, N.C., Nov. 9, 1823; s. Peter and Sabina Swope (Hoke) F.; grad. U. Ala., 1844; m. Mary Eliza Woodward, Oct. 4, 1854. Commd. 1st lt. 1st Ala. Volunteers at Siege of Vera Cruz, Mexican War; admitted to Ala. bar, 1848; trustee U. Ala., 1851-60; mem. Ala. Ho. of Reps., 1859; entered Confederate Army as capt. 10th Ala. Regt., 1861, promoted to col. after Battle of Gettysburg (where he was crippled for life), promoted to brig. gen. shortly after Appomattox; mem. Ala. Senate, 1865-66; mem. U.S. Ho. of Reps. from Ala., 44th-52d congresses, 1875-93. Died Jacksonville, Ala., Jan. 16, 1894; buried City Cemetery, Jacksonville.

FORREST, FRENCH naval officer; b. St. Mary's County, Md., Oct. 4, 1796; s. Maj. Joseph and Elizabeth (Dulany) F.; m. Emily Douglas Simms, 1830. Apptd. midshipman U.S. Navy, 1811; served in battles on Lake Erie under Commodore Perry, including battle of Hornet and Peacock during War of 1812 distinguished in operations against Mexican ports in Mexican War;

head Washington (D.C.) Navy Yard, 1855-56; commd. capt. Va. Navy in Civil War, 1861, capt. Confederate Navy, 1861, head bur. orders and detail, 1862; commanded James River Squadron, 1863-64. Died Georgetown, D.C., Nov. 22, 1866.

FORREST, NATHAN BEDFORD army officer; b. Chapel Hill, Tenn., July 13, 1821; s. William and Mariam (Beck) F.; m. Mary Ann Montgomery, 1845. Traded in land, livestock, cotton and slaves, alderman, Memphis, Tenn., after 1849; commd. lt. col. Confederate Army, 1861; led a regt. out of Ft. Donelson, refused to be included in the surrender of that garrison, 1862; commanded a regt. at Battle of Shiloh, 1862; promoted brig. gen., 1862; maj. gen., 1863; commanded a brigade at Battle of Chickamauga, 1863; commanded brigade of Hood's Cavalry in Tenn. Campaign of 1864; considered in some degree responsible for slaughter of Negro soldiers following his capture of Ft. Pillow (Tenn), Apr. 12, 1864; his fame rests upon his record in independent command on long cavalry raids behind Union lines in Tenn., Ky., Miss. and in such engagements as Okolona, Miss., Brice's Cross Bds.; promoted lt. gen., Feb. 1865; surrendered last Confederate command in arms east of Miss., at Gainesville, Ala., May 9, 1865; briefly involved in early activities of Ku Klux Klan; pres. Selma, Marion and Memphis R.R.; considered 1 of greatest Confederate gens. Died Memphis, Tenn., Oct. 29, 1877.

FORREST, NATHAN BEDFORD army officer; b. Memphis, Tenn., Apr. 7, 1905; s. Nathan Bedford and Mattie Patterson (Patton) F.; student Ga. Tech., 1923-24; A.B., U.S. Mil. Acad., 1928; m. Frances Bassler, Nov. 22, 1930. Commd. 2d lt., U.S. Army, 1928, and advanced through the grades to brig. gen., Nov., 1942; became chief of staff, Second Air Force. Reported missing in action while on plane bombing Kiel, Germany, June 1943. Home: 115 W. 9th St., Spokane, Wash. Died June 4, 1944.

FORREST, THOMAS congressman; b. Phila., 1747; attended common schs. Commd. capt. Col. Thomas Proctor's Pa. Arty. during Revolutionary War, 1776, promoted maj., 1777, lt. col., 1778, resigned, 1781; mem. U.S. Ho. of Reps. from Pa., 16th, 17th congresses, 1819-21, Oct. 8, 1822-23. Died Germantown (now part of Phila.), Mar. 20, 1825.

FORREST, URIAH congressman; b. nr. Leonardtown, St. Marys County, Md., 1756. Served as 1st lt., capt., maj. Md. Militia in Revolutionary War; wounded at Battle of Germantown, lost leg at Battle of Brandywine; mem. Continental Congress from Md., 1786-87; mem. U.S. Ho. of Reps. (Federalist) from Md., 3d Congress, 1793-Nov. 8, 1794 (resigned); commd. maj. gen. Md. Militia, 1795; clk. D.C. Circuit Ct., 1800-05. Died "Rosedale," nr. Georgetown, D.C., July 6, 1805; buried Oak Hill Cemetery, Washington, D.C.

FORRESTAL, JAMES sec. of defense; b. Beacon, N.Y., Feb. 15, 1892; s. James and Mary A. (Toohey) F.; student Dartmouth Coll., 1911-12, Princeton U., 1912-15; LL.D. (hon.). Princeton, 1944, Williams Coll., 1946; m. Josephine Ogden, Oct. 12, 1926; Coll., 1946; m. Josephine Ogden, Oct. 12, 1926; children - Michael, Peter. With New Jersey Zinc Co., Tobacco Products Corp., N.Y. City, 1915-16; with Dillon, Read & Co., 1916-40, pres., 1937-40; adminstrv. asst. to President of U.S., June-Aug. 1940; under secretary of navy, 1944-47; sec. of defense, Sept. 17, 1947-Mar. 28, 1949. Served as lt., U.S. Naval Reserve Force, 1917-19. Democrat. Home: 3508 Prospect Av. N.W. Office: The Pentagon, Washington. Died May 22, 1949; buried in Arlington National Cemetery, Washington.

FORSE, CHARLES THOMAS rear adm.; b. Pittsburgh, Dec. 29, 1846; s. William and Marianne (Boyer) F.; apptd. to U.S. Naval Acad. from Ky., Sept. 24, 1863; grad. June 2, 1868; unmarried. Promoted ensign, 1869, master, 1870, commd. lt., 1873, lt. comdr., June 1894, comdr., Mar. 3, 1899; light house insp., 4th dist., Mar. 13, 1900; comdg. Celtic, 1900; promoted capt., Oct. 11, 1903, rear adm., U.S.N., Dec. 26, 1903 and retired. Home: Pittsburgh, Pa. Died Apr. 14, 1925.

FORSYTH, GEORGE ALEXANDER colonel; b. Muncy, Pa., Nov. 7, 1837; s. Orrin and Elizabeth (Frederick) F.; ed. Canandaigua, N.Y., Acad.; m. Natalie S., d. Col. E.B. Beaumont, U.S.A., 1885. Pvt. Chicago Dragoons, Apr. 19-Aug. 18, 1861; 1st lt. 8th Ill. Cav., Sept. 18, 1861; capt., Feb. 12, 1862; maj., Sept. 1, 1863; hon. mustered out of vol. service, Feb. 1, 1866; maj. 9th U.S. Cav., July 28, 1866; lt. col. 4th Cav., June 26, 1881; retired, Mar. 25, 1890; advanced to rank of col. retired, by act of Apr. 23, 1904. Bvtd.: col. vols., Oct. 19, 1864, for gallant and meritorious services at Opequan and Winchester; brig. gen. vols., Mar. 13, 1865, for distinguished services and conspicuous gallantry; lt. col. U.S.A., Mar. 2, 1867, for gallantry at Dinwiddle C.H.; col. U.S.A., for services at battle of Five Forks, Va.; brig. gen. U.S.A., Sept. 17, 1868, for gallant conduct in engagement with hostile Indians, in which he was 3 times wounded. Served through Civil War with Army of W.Va., Army of Potomac, Army of the Shenandoah; took part in 16 pitched battles, 2 sieges and over 60 minor engagements; wounded 4 times in service in Civil War; mil. sec. to Lt. Gen. Sheridan, 1869-73; a.d.c. to same, 1878-81; mem. bd. of officers to inspect the armies of Europe and Asia, 1875-76; on staff and frontier service, 1866-90. Author: Thrilling Days in Army Life, 1900; The Story of the Soldier, 1900. Home: Rockport, Mass. Died Sept. 12, 1915.

FORSYTH, JAMES MCQUEEN rear adm. U.S.N.; b. Long Island, Bahamas, British W.I., Jan. 1, 1842; s. James and Catherine Ann (Taylor) F.; came to U.S., Sept. 1853; grad. Central High Sch., Phila., Feb. 1858 (hon. M.A., 1886); m. Mary J. M. Perkins, Aug. 1, 1871 (dec.); m. 2d, Caroline A. Helfenstein, Oct. 7, 1903. Went to sea as sailor before mast, 1858-61, when he entered vol. navy; apptd., Sept. 25, 1861, acting master's mate, serving through Civil War; took part in capture Fts. Clarke and Hatteras, Aug. 27, 1861; engagements under Farragut on the Miss.; engagement with the rebal ram, Arkansas; engagement with Sumter, Moultrie and other fortifications in Charleston harbor. Promoted acting ensign, Sept. 5, 1862; acting master, Aug. 1, 1864; entered competitive exam. for regular navy; passed No. 23 of 65 admitted out of 900 competing; commd. master Mar. 12, 1868; promoted through grades to capt., Mar. 3, 1899; placed on retired list, Sept. 25, 1901, at his own request, on 40 years service, with rank of rear adm. Comd. at various times. U.S.S. Tallapoosa, U.S. protected cruiser Baltimore, U.S. armored cruiser Brooklyn and U.S. battleship Indiana; comd. naval sta., Key West, Fla., during Spanish-Am. War; commended for efficient service; chief of staff to Rear Admiral J.C. Watson, comdg. Philippine fleet, 1899-1900. Mason. Home: Shanokin, Pa. Died. Aug. 3, 1915.

FORSYTH, JAMES W. maj. gen. U.S.A., retired; b. in Ohio, Aug. 26, 1836; grad. West Point, 1856; assigned to inf.; promoted to 1st lt., Mar. 15, 1861; capt., Oct. 24, 1861. On Gen. McClellan's staff during Peninsular and Md. campaigns; bvtd. maj., Sept. 30, 1863, for gallantry at Chickamauga; in 1864-65, asst. adj. gen. of vols. and chief of staff to Gen. Sheridan; reached rank of brig. gen. vols. and bvtd. brig. gen. regular army; asst. insp. gen. Dept. of the Gulf, 1866-67; aide to Gen Sheridan, 1869-73; later on frontier and garrison service; became col. 7th cav., 1886; brig. gen., 1894, until retirement, 1897, with rank of maj. gen. Home: Columbus, O. Died 1906.

FORT, GREENBURY LAFAYETTE congressman, lawyer; b. French Grant, Scioto County, O., Oct. 17, 1825; attended Rock River Sem.; studied law. Admitted to bar, 1847, began practice of law, Lacon, Ill.; sheriff, 1850; clk. Marshall County (Ill.), 1852; county judge, 1857; apptd. 2d lt. 11th Regt., Ill. Volunteer Inf. during Civil War, 1861, promoted 1st lt. with rank of q.m., 1861, capt., 1861, lt. col. and q.m., 1864; brevetted maj., lt. col. U.S. Volunteers, 1865; mem. Ill. Senate, 1866; mem. U.S. Ho. of Reps. (Republican) from Ill., 43d-46th congresses, 1873-81. Died Lacon, Jan. 13, 1883; buried Lacon Cemetery.

FORTESCUE, GRANVILLE (ROLAND) writer; b. New York, N.Y., Oct. 12, 1875; s. Robert Francis and Marion Theresa (O'Shea) F.; U. of Pa. (left coll. at outbreak of Spanish-Am. War); m. Grace Hubbard Bell, June 4, 1910; children-Thalia, Marion, Helene. Pvt. and corp. 1st U.S. Cav. (Rough Riders), 1898, wounded at San Juan Hill; 1st lt. 26th U.S. Vol. Inf., campaign P.I., 1899-1901; apptd. 2d, lt., 4th U.S. Cav., 1902; grad. staff coll., 1904; 1st lieut., 10th U.S. Cavalry, comdg. Troop A.; military attaché with Japanese Army before Port Arthur. Served as mil. aide to President Roosevelt at White House resigned from U.S. Army, 1906; capt. and spl. agent Cuban rural guard, 1906. Spl. corr. London Standard with Spanish army in Riff War, 1909; exploration interior of Venezuela, headwaters of Orinoco River to mouth; corr. London Daily Telegraph, with Belgian, French, English, Russian and Turkish armies in the field. Commd. maj., O.R.C., N.A., 1917, and in active service with 314th F.A., A.E.V. ret. maj. F.A., 1928. Republican. Awarded certificate of merit and Distinguished Service Cross, Victory Medal, 3 bars; Spanish War medal; Philippine Insurrection War medal; Order of Purple Heart (United States). Order of the Rising Sun (Japan), Japanese War Medal. Clubs: Army and Navy (Washington, D.C.); Metropolitan, Turf and Field (New York). Author: At the Front with Three Armies, 1914; Russia, the Balkans and the Dardanelles, 1915; What of the Dardanelles?, 1915; Fore-Armed, 1916; France Bears the Burden, 1917; (plays) Dolores, 1915; Love and Live, 1921; The Unbeliever, 1925; Front Line and Dead Line, 1937. Fiction editor of Liberty Mag., 1930. Home: Bayport, N.Y. Office: Lantana, Fla. Died Apr. 21, 1952; buried Arlington Cemetery.

FORWOOD, WILLIAM HENRY brig. gen. U.S.A.; b. Brandywine Hundred, Del., Sept. 7, 1838; s. Robert and Rachel Way (Larkin) F.; grad. Crozier Acad., Chester, Pa., 1856; M.D., U. of Pa., 1861; (LL.D., Georgetown U., 1897)); m. Mary A. Y. Osborne, Sept. 28, 1870. Apptd. from Pa. asst. surgeon U.S.A., Aug. 5, 1861; capt. asst. surgeon, July 28, 1866; maj. surgeon, June 26, 1876; lt. col. dep. surgeon gen., June 15, 1891; col. asst. surgeon gen., May 3, 1897; brig. gen. surgeon gen., June 8, 1902. Bvtd. capt. and maj., Mar. 13, 1865, for faithful and meritorious services during the war. Severely wounded in battle, Oct. 1863; in comd. Whitehall Gen. Hosp.; 2,000 beds, 1864-65; served in Indian campaigns; surgeon and naturalist Sheridan's exploring expdns., 1880-82; pres. army exam. bds.; pres. Army Med. Sch.; built Montauk Hosp., 1898; retired, Sept. 7, 1902. Prof. surg. pathology, Georgetown Med. Coll.; prof. mil. surgery, Army Med. Sch., etc. Died May 11, 1915.

FOSKETT, JAMES HICKS naval officer ret.; b. Wollaston, Mass., Aug. 19, 1898; s. Charles Jay and Edith Prudence (Hicks) F.; student U. Mich., 1917-18, 19, Post-Grad. Sch., U.S. Naval Acad., 1927-28; certificate, U.S. Naval War Coll., Newport, R.I., 1928-29; m. Florence Paul Kane, June 9, 1928; children - Margaret Kane, Mary Paul. Enlisted in Navy 1917; commd. ensign, USNRF, 1919; transferred to U.S. Navy and advanced through grades to rear adm., 1946; Naval Intelligence and Joint Intelligence Com., 1941-42; U.S. Naval liaison officer staff of Comdr. in Chief, Brit. Eastern Mediterranean Fleet, 1943-44; comd. U.S.S. Savannah, 1944-45; U.S.S. Augusta, 1945; chief of staff to comdr. 19th Fleet, 1945-46; naval aide to Pres. Harry Truman, 1946-48; comdr. Cruiser div. 12, 1948-49; dir. standing group, mil. com. NATO, 1949-52; chief Mil. Assistance Adv. Group to Norway 1952-54, vice adm. USN, ret. 1954; now v.p. RCA Victor, Argentina, S.A.I.C., Buenos Aires. Awarded Legion of Merit, Commendation ribbon; Comdr. Order British Empire; Grand Officer Order of Phoenix, Greece; Grand Officer Order of Naval Merit. Brazil. Mem. Delta Upsilon. Clubs: Racquet (Phila.); Bohemian (San Francisco); Columbia Country, Army-Navy Country, Army-Navy (Washington). Home: 292 Juan Passo, Martinez, Buenos Aires. Argentina. Died May 1961.

FOSS, WILSON (PERKINS), JR. chmn. bd. New York Trap Rock Corp.; b. Haverstraw, N.Y., Dec. 17, 1890; s. Wilson P. and Anna (De Baun) F.; student Hill Sch., Pottstown, Pa., 1906-10; Ph.B., Sheffield Scientific Sch. (Yale), 1913; m. Mary Burns, Dec. 7, 1923; children-Wilson III, Hugh H., Mrs. Mary Foss Howard, With New York Trap Rock Co., 1914-16, 30—, salesman, 1916-17, now chmn. bd.; pres. Haverstraw Crushed Stone Co., 1916-17; with Tex. Oil Co. in Spain, 1919-26; v.p. Parish-Watson & Co. (works of art), 1920-43. Served as capt. inf., overseas 17 months on special duty with M.I. Div., U.S. Army, World War I. Republican. Presbyn. Mason (32ff). Clubs: Union, Yale, Rockland Country; Creek Country; Triton Fish and Game Club (Quebec, Can.). Home: 155 E. 72d St., N.Y.C. Office: 230 Park Av., N.Y.C. 17. Died Nov. 17, 1957.

FOSTER, BERNARD AUGUSTUS, JR., lawyer; b. Spartanburg, S.C., Aug. 30, 1909; s. Bernard A. and Lillie Harris (Veazey) F.; A.B. with distinction, Wofford Coll., 1931; J.D. cum laude, George Washington U., 1937; m. Cecile Bernice Harrington, Sept. 25, 1937; children—Carolyn Cecile (Mrs. Michael A. Meredith), and Bernard Augustus III. Instr. in English, Kershaw (S.C.) Sch.; law clk Petroleum Adminstrn. Bd., 1933-35; admitted S.C. bar, 1936, D.C. bar, 1937, U.S. Supreme Ct. bar 1941, Md. bar, 1954; chief mediation div. Pub. Works Adminstrn., 1936-41; sr. atty. FTC, 1941-42; spl. counsel Fed. Power Commn., 1946-50, asst. gen. counsel, chief natural gas div., 1951-53; gen counsel President's Water Resources Policy Commn., 1950-51; mem. firm Ross, Marsh & Foster, Washington, 1953-68. Lecturer Southwestern Legal Foundation, 1965; public mem. Adminstrv. Conf. U.S., also chmn. com. on personnel, 1968. Trustee Rocky Mountain Mineral Law Found. Served from 2d lt. to lt. col., AUS, 1942-46; chmn. Joint Army-Navy-Air Force Industrial Review Board, 1945-46. Decorated Legion of Merit, Army Commendation medal with oak leaf cluster; recipient Alumni Achievement award George Washington U., 1946. Fellow Am. Bar Found.; mem. Am. (chmn. natural gas com. 1954-55; council 1955-59; chmn. mineral and natural resources law sect. 1961-62; ho. dels. 1962-66, chmn. spl. com. on cts. of spl. jurisdiction, 1963-64, member of the special committee on legal service, 1963-64, mem. spl. com. on code fed. adminstrv. procedure 1968), D.C., Federal Power (executive committee 1955-59, 66-68), Federal bar assns., Am. Judicature Soc., Internat. Relations Club, Res. Officers Assn. U.S. (pres. Va. 1948-49), Mil. Order World Wars, S.A.R., Scabbard and Blade, Blue Key, Phi Delta Phi, Pi Kappa Phi, Pi Kappa Delta, Sigma Upsilon. Democrat. Episcopalian. Clubs: Army-Navy, Lawyers (Washington); Chevy Chase, Edgemoor Tennis, Sherwood Forest, Jefferson Islands (Md.). Editor George Washington Law Rev., 1936-37. Author: (with others) Water Resources Law, 1950. Home: Chevy Chase MD Died June 7, 1968; buried Parkwood Cemetery, Rockville MD

FOSTER, EDWARD K(INGSBURY) aviation, electronics exec.; b. Tampa, Fla., Sept. 4, 1907; s. Eleazar K. and Eugenia Louise (Noyes) F.; student Waugh Coll. Prep. Sch., Duval High Sch., 1922-25, U. Fla., 1925-28; m. Patricia IM. Goler, Mar. 20, 1937. Stock foreman, later management trainee DeForest Radio Co., Jersey City and Passaic, N.J., 1928-30, purchasing agt., 1930-31, prodn. mgr., 1931-32; prodn. mgr., electronics div. Sylvania Electric Co., Clifton, N.J., 1932-36; works mgr. fan and motor plant F.A. Smith Mfg. Co., Rochester, N.Y., 1938-40; dir. indsl. relations Pioneer Instrument div. Bendix Aviation Corp., Bklyn., 1936-38, gen. factory mgr. Bendix Radio div., Balt., 1940-46, asst. general mgr., 1946-49, gen. mgr. since 1949. also gen. mgr. York and Cin. divs., v.p., mem. adminstrn. com. Bendix Corp., 1951 - , group exec., 1954 - , dir., 1959 - ; cons. mgmt. prof. U. Balt.; dir., mem. bd. incorporators Savings Bank of Balt.; dir. First Nat. Bank of Balt. Mem. President's Com. on Employment Physically Handicapped; dir. Balt. chpt. A.R.C. Recipient Certificate of Appreciation (War Dept.); Certificate of Commendation (Navy) for contbns. World War II; named Man of Year, Towson, Md., 1955. Mem. Soc. Advancement Mgmt. (outstanding mgmt. award Balt. 1955), Balt. Assn. Commerce (v.p., dir.), Armed Forces Communications Assn. (dir.), Am. Ordnance Assn., Air Force 123 Assn., Am. Mgmt. Assn., Radio-Electronics-Television Mfrs. Assn. (dir.), Towson Town Assn. Mason (32ff, K.T., Shriner). Clubs: Detroit Athletic, Traffic, Advertising Wings (N.Y.C.); Nat. Aviation (Washington); Baltimore Country, Merchants (Balt.). Home: Falls Rd., R.D. 1, Box 97, Lutherville, Md. Office: Bendix Radio, Balt. 4, Md. Died Nov. 1967.

FOSTER, GEORGE BURGESS, JR. ret. army officer, physician; b. Salem, Mass., July 27, 1884; s. George Burgess and Maria Christine (Hanson) F.; M.D., Jefferson Med. Coll., Phila., 1907; hon. grad., Army Med. Sch., Washington, 1910; Dr. Ph., Harvard Med. Sch., Boston, 1917; grad. Med. Field Service Sch. (Army), Carlisle, Pa., 1921, advanced course, 1929; m. Sara Ellis Thomas, Sept. 4, 1912; children-Ellis Ane Anne (Mrs. William R. Lonsdale), George Burgess III, Katherine Christine (Mrs. Charles Stuart O'Malley, Jr.). Intern Phila. Gen. Hosp., 1907-09; commd. 1st lt., Med. Corps, U.S. Army, 1909, advancing through the grades to brig. gen., 1944; served overseas in Philippine Islands, Hawaii and France. Comdg. officer, O'Reilly Gen. Hosp., 1941-44; comdg. gen. O'Reilly Gen. Hosp., 1944-46; retired with rank of brig. gen., 1946; med. dir. Cambridge (Mass.) City Hosp. 1946—. Decorated Legion of Merit (U.S.), Legion of Honor (France); Philippine Campaign, Victory (World War II) medals. Fellow Am. Coll. Physicians, Am. Med. Assn.; mem. Mil. Surgeons U.S., Am. Pub. Health Assn., Am., Mass. hosp. assns., Pathol. Soc. Phila., Mass. Med. Soc., New England Hosp. Assembly. Club: Harvard (Boston). Contbr. to med. literature. Address: Oxford Courts, 5 Arlington St., Cambridge 40, Mass. Died Dec. 31, 1949.

FOSTER, GEORGE NIMMONS lawyer; b. Sterling, Neb., Dec. 29, 1885; s. Frank B. and Mary E. (Nimmons) F.; LL.B., U. Neb., 1911; Ph.B., U. Chgo., 1912, J.D., 1914; m. Esther Mosher Burritt, Sept. 2, 1914; children-Georgette, Frank Burritt. Prof. Law, U. Neb., 1912-23, also gen. practice, 1915-22; counsel for Union Auto Ins. Co. and Union Fire Ins. Co., Lincoln, Neb., 1923; moved to Los Angeles, 1925; consul, 1925, v.p., 1926-29, Union Auto Ins. Co., Los Angeles; now gen. practice law at Los Angeles. Served on staff Adj. Gen.'s Dept., World War; maj. Judge Adv. Gen.'s Dept., Am. Legion. Mem. Order of Coif, Acacia, Phi Delta Phi. Republican. Methodist. Mason (33ff). Club: Nebraska. Writer on legal and Masonic subjects. Home: 814 Glenmount Av., Los Angeles. Died Nov. 7, 1952; buried Sterling, Neb.

FOSTER, GEORGE SANFORD surgeon; b. at Barrington, N.H., Apr. 20, 1882; s. George Sanford and Etta Frances (Moulton) F.; student Harvard Summer Sch. of Physical Edn., 1900, Harvard Summer Sch. of Obstetrics, 1905; M.D., cum laude, Tufts Coll. Med. Sch., 1906 (pres. of class); post grad. study in Europe; m. Elizabeth Russell Danforth, Dec. 27, 1905; children - Clayton Reginald, Virginia Frances, George Sanford, Jr., Russell Danforth. Athletic dir. various high schs. and Y.M.C.A.'s for several years; interne Children's Hosp., Boston, Boston City Hosp., Sacred Heart Hosp., Manchester, N.H., 1905-07; began practice at Manchester, Feb. 1, 1907; surgeon and pathologist to Notre Dame Hosp., Manchester, N.H., 1907-25; surgeon Lucy Hastings Hosp., Manchester, 1925-38; cons. surgeon Peterboro (N.H.) Hosp. Trustee Manchester Boys' Club (pres. 12 yrs.). Founded clin. lab. and training school for nurses, Notre Dame Hosp., Manchester; founded Lucy Hastings Hosp., also training schools for nurses and technicians and cancer research lab. at same, Manchester. Served as capt. Med. Corps, U.S. Army, during World War I. Now serving as lt. comdr., Med. Corps, U.S.N.R. Fellow Internat. Coll. Suregons (Geneva). Mem. N.H. Surg. Club, Manchester Med. Soc. (past pres.), Hillsboro County Med. Soc., N.H. Med. Soc., Am. Med. Assn., Am. Assn. for Study of Neoplastic Diseases (founder Northern New England Assn.), Am. Med. Editors and Authors Assn., Wild Life Soc., Am. Forestry Assn., Nat. Assn. Audubon Socs., Mass. Audubon Soc., Northern New England Bird Banding Assn. (treas.), Fed. Boys' Clubs of Am. (exec. com. New Eng. div.), Clin. Congress Surgeons of N. America (rep. from N.H., 1908-11; sen. from N.H., 1911-14), Manchester Hist. Assn., N.H. Hist. Soc., N.H. S.A.R., Manchester Inst. Arts and Sciences, Phi Chi (ex-pres. Delta Chapter), Mil. Order of the World War, Mil. Order of Foreign Wars, Assn. Mil. Surgeons of U.S., Army, Eugene Field Soc. (hon.). Mason. Odd Fellow. Clubs: Manchester County, Y.M.C.A. (Manchester); University (Boston); Army and Navy (Washington). Author: Post Operative Treatment; Qualifications of a Model Nurse; Health Day by Day; Health; Art of Living; Birds and Bird Clubs; They Know Not; Why I Believe in God and Immortaility; Trapping the Common Cold; Our Youth (Helping Them to Help Themselves); also numerous monographs, brochures and articles on med. subjects, etc. Home: Manchester, N.H. Died Aug. 13, 1945.

FOSTER, HENRY BACON judge; b. May 9, 1863; s. Joshua Hill and Frances Cornelia (Bacon) F.; A.B., U. Ala., 1882, A.M., LL.B., 1884; m. Jennie Hester. Tchr. Gadsden, Ala., 1882-83; admitted to Ala. bar, 1884, and began practice at Tuscaloosa; mayor of Tuscaloosa, 1890-94; mem. Ala. Ho. of Rep., 1898-1902; served as Judge Ct. Appeals, Ala. Served as maj. 2d. Regt., Ala. Vols., Spanish-Am. War, 1898. Democrat. Home: Tuscaloosa, Ala. Deceased.

FOSTER, JOHN GRAY army officer; b. Whitefield, N.H., May 27, 1823; s. Perley and Mary (Gray) F.; grad. U.S. Mil. Acad., 1846; m. Mary Moale, Jan. 21, 1851; m. 2d, Nannie Davis, Jan. 9, 1872. Commd. 2d lt. C.E., served in Mexican War; asst. prof. engring. U.S. Mil. Acad., 1855-57; capt. Engrs., July 1, 1860; at Ft. Sumter when bombarded by Confederates, Apr. 1861; brig. gen. Vols., Oct. 23, 1861; col. U.S. Army in command brigade under Gen. Burnside at Roanoke Island, Feb. 1862, at Newbern, Mar., 1862; in command Dept. N.C., July 1, 1862; maj. gen. Vols., July 18, 1862; in command Dept. of South, 1864; brevetted maj. gen. U.S. Army, Mar. 13, 1865; in command Dept. Fla., 1865-67; lt. col. C.E., Mar. 7, 1867; asst. to chief Engrs., 1871-74. Died Nashua, N.H., Sept. 2, 1874.

FOSTER, JOHN WATSON secretary of state; b. Pike Co., Ind., Mar. 2, 1836; s. Judge Matthew Watson and Eleanor (Johnson) F.; A.B., Ind. U., 1855, A.M., 1858; student 1 yr. Harvard Law Sch.; (LL.D., Princeton, 1895, Wabash Coll., 1895, Yale, 1896, U. of Pa., 1907); admitted to Ind. bar and practiced at Evansville, 1857-61; m. Mary Parke McFerson, 1859. Entered Union Army, 1861, as maj. 25th Ind. Vols.; promoted lt. col. at Ft. Donelson, col. at Shiloh; editor Evansville Daily Journal, 1865-69; postmaster, Evansville, 1869-73; chmn. Rep. State Central Co., 1872; minister to Mexico, 1873-80, to Russia, 1880-81; established, 1881, in practice in internat. cases in Washington, representing foreign legations before commns., arbitration bds., etc. Minister to Spain, 1883-85; spl plenipotentiary to negotiate reciprocity treaties with Brazil, Spain, Germany, British W.I., etc., 1891; sec. of state, in cabinet of President Harrison, 1892-93; agt. U.S. in Bering Sea Arbitration, at Paris, 1893; invited by Emperor of China and participated in peace negotiations with Japan; ambassador on spl. mission to Great Britian and Russia, 1897; mem. Anglo-Canadian Commn., 1898; agt. U.S. Alaskan Boundary Tribunal, London, 1903; rep. of China to 2d Hague Conf., 1907. Author: A Century of American Diplomacy in the Orient, 1903; Arbitration and The Hague Court, 1904; The Practice of Diplomacy, 1906. Died Nov. 15, 1917.

FOSTER, JOSEPH rear adm. (retired); b. Gloucester, Mass., June 17, 1841; s. Joseph and Adelaide Coues (Spalding) F.; ed. pub. and pvt. Schs., Portsmouth, N.H.; m. Helen Dickey, Oct. 7, 1875 (died 1904); children—Joseph, Beatrice (dec.), Dorothy (Mrs. L. S. Stewart), Isabel; m. 2d, Josephine Hunt, of Broxbourne, Hertfordshire, Eng., Mar. 17, 1906. Entered U.S.N., Oct. 3, 1862; apptd. actg. asst. p.-m., Oct. 19, 1863; transferred to regular nav., Aug. 10, 1866; advanced through various grades and commd. pay dir., with rank of capt., Aug. 27, 1901; advanced to rank of rear admiral and retired at own request after 40 years service, Dec. 9, 1902. Served during Civil War in S. Atlantic Blockading Squadron, most of the time off Charleston. Mem. bd. of instrn. pub. schs., Portsmouth, N.H., 1909-13. Republican. Theist. Author: The Graves We Decorate, Storer Post G.A.R., Portsmouth, N.H., edits., 1893, 1907, 15, 17, 21, 23; Soldiers' Memorial, Portsmouth, N.H., 1893-1921, tercentenary edit., 1893-1923. Died May 17, 1930.

FOSTER, MILTON HUGH, surgeon; b. Huntingdon, Pa., Mar. 3, 1873; s. Milton Kirk and Martha (Rodgers) F.; Juniata Normal Sch., 1886-90; B.S., Dickinson Coll., 1894, M.A., 1898; M.D., U. of Pa., 1897; m. Louise Griffiths, Jan. 20, 1901 (died Jan. 19, 1906); children—Houston Griffiths, Robert Foster (dec.); m. 2d, Marion Brown, Dec. 15, 1914. Apptd. asst. surgeon Marine Hosp. Service, Mar. 7, 1898; surgeon U.S.P.H.S., Nov. 12, 1912, med. dir., July 1, 1930. Served as chief quarantine officer at Puget Sound and Porto Rico; later in charge marine hosps., Port Townsend, Baltimore, Chicago and Stapleton; was in charge U.S.P.H.S. hosps. at Biltmore, N.C., and Ft. McHenry, Md.; also chief medical officer U.S. Immigration Station, Ellis Island, N.Y.; now retired. Mem. A.M.A., Am. Hosp. Assn., Phi Beta Kappa. Mason. Club: Richmond County Country. Author: Prevention of Diseases and Care of the Sick (with Dr. W. G. Stimpson), 1919; Manual of Hospital Management for Marine Hospitals, 1930. Contbr. to med. jours. Home: 57 Silver Lake Rd., Brighton Heights, Staten Island NY

FOSTER, NELLIS BARNES M.D.; b. Durhamville, N.Y., July 18, 1875; s. Theodore and Loretta (Barnes) F.; A.B., Amherst, 1898; M.D., Johns Hopkins, 1902; post-grad. work European univs.; hon. Sc.D., Amherst College, 1926; m. Julia Catharine Morris, Oct. 26, 1904. Instr. and asso. in biol. chemistry, Columbia U., 1906-12; asso. phys. to New York Hosp., 1907-16; instr. medicine, 1913-14, asst. prof., 1914-17, Cornell Med. Coll. of New York; prof. medicine, U. of Mich. and dir. med. clinic Univ. Hosp., 1917-18. Maj., Med. R.C., 1917, and chief of med. service, Base Hosp., Camp Meade, Md.; lt. col. M.C., 1919; dir. School of Mil. Medicine, Ft. Oglethorpe, Ga.; asso. prof. medicine, Cornell Med. Coll., New York, and asso phys. to New York Hosp., 1919—. Democrat. Home: New York, N.Y. Died Aug. 20, 1933.

FOSTER, PAUL F., consultant; b. Wichita, Kan., Mar. 25, 1889; s. Rev. Festus and Lillian (Howe) F.; B.S., U.S. Naval Acad., 1911; m. Isabelle de la V. Lowe, Sept. 8, 1916; 1 son, Paul Lowe (U.S. Navy). Commd. engign, U.S. Navy, 1911, and advanced in regular Navy until resignation as lieut. comdr., 1929; engaged in bus. and engring., New York City, 1929-39; surveyed resources of Galapagos Islands, 1940-41; organizer and pres., Pacific Development Co., 1941; recalled to active naval duty, 1941; conducted naval and mil. inspections for President Roosevelt, 1942-43, asst. naval inspector gen., 1943-46; retired as vice-admiral, U.S.N.R., Oct. 1946. Vice president Mandel Brothers, Inc., Chicago, 1946-50; with Internat. Bank for Reconstrn. and Development, Washington, until 1954; with AEC, 1954-59, asst. gen. mgr. internat. activities, 1954-58, gen. mgr., 1958, dep. gen. mgr., 1959, U.S. rep. to Internat. Atomic Energy Agy., Vienna, 1959-61. Decorated Congl. Medal of Honor, Navy Cross, D.S.M., Legion of Merit. Commendation Ribbon; recipient Distinguished Service medal AEC. Club: Army and Navy, Metropolitan (Washington). Home: Arlington VA Died Jan. 1971; buried Arlington Nat. Cemetery.

FOSTER, RICHARD CLARKE univ. pres.; b. Demopolis, Ala., July 12, 1895; s. John Manly and Kathleen Mary (Clarke) F.; A.B., U. of Ala., 1914, LL.D., 1936; LL.B., Harvard, 1917; D.C.L., U. of the South, 1937; m. Lida Scarborough, Feb. 27, 1923 (died Sept. 1936); 1 dau., Lida Scarborough. Admitted to the bar, 1919; mem. Foster, Verner & Rice, 1920, Foster, Rice & Foster, 1923-37; pres. U. of Ala. since Jan. 1, 1937; dir. Merchants Bank & Trust Co. of Tuscalosa. Served as lt. and capt. F.A., U.S. Army, 1917-18. Mem. State Dem. Exec. Com., 1924-36; mem. Tuscaloosa County Dep. Exec. Com., 1933-36, Trustee Ala. Insane Hosps. Mem. Am. and Ala State bar assns., Am. Legion, Phi Betta Kappa, Alpha Tau Omega, Omicron Delta Kappa, Phi Delta Phi Democrat. Episcopalian. Mason. Old Fellow, K.P. Clubs: Rotary, Tuscaloosa Country. Died November 19, 1941.

FOSTER, ROBERT SANFORD mcht., soldier; b. Vernon, Ind., Jan. 27, 1834; s. Riley S. and Sarah J. F.; ed. in common school there. Fought through the Civil war with Ind. troops, becoming brig. gen. of vols., 1863, and bvt. maj. gen., 1865. Has resided in Indianapolis since the war; city treas., 1867-72; U.S. marshal for dist. of Ind., 1881-85; now a broker and commission mcht.; unmarried. Home: Indianapolis, Ind. Died 1903.

FOSTER, RUFUS EDWARD judge; b. Mathews County, Va., May 22, 1871; s. Gustavus and Catherine (Moore) F.; student Soule Coll., 1885-88; LL.B., Tulane Univ. Law School, 1895 (hon. LL.D., 1935); m. Blanche Ahrons, Sept. 7, 1899; children - Alice Catherine, Blanche Marian. Second lt. 2d La. Vol. Inf., Spanish-Am. War, May 2, 1898-Apr., 1899; adj.-gen. staff of Brig.-gen. W. W. Gordon, 2d Brigade, 1st Div., 7th Army Corps, Asst. U.S. atty., Eastern Dist., La., 1905-08, U.S. atty., 1908, 1909; apptd. U.S. dist. judge, Eastern Dist. of La. Feb. 2, 1909; U.S. circuit judge, 5th circuit, Jan. 2, 1925. Prof. law, Tulane U., since 1912; dean Coll. of Law, Tulane U., 1920-27 (emeritus); reemployment dir. for La., under NRA. V.p. Am. Olympic Com.; dir. Am. Athletic Union of U.S. Mem. La. Bar Assn., Am. Bar Assn., Am. Law Inst., S.A.R., Phi Delta Phi, Order of Coif. Comdr. in chief United Spanish War Veterans, 1940-41. Republican. Episcopalian. Clubs: Boston, New Orleans Country (both of New Orleans). Home: 21 Richmond Pl. Address: Post Office Bldg., New Orleans Died Aug. 23, 1941; buried in Metairie Cemetery, New Orleans.

FOSTER, THOMAS ARNOLD, pharmacist; b. Camp Hill, Ala., Jan. 26, 1895; s. William Thomas and Eugenia (McLendon) F.; student Howard Coll., Birmingham, Ala., 1911-12; Ph.G., Wilson Sch. Pharmacy, 1916; m. Mary Reeves, Sept. 30, 1919 (dec. Jan. 2, 1942); children—Mary Virginia (Mrs. J. Richard Roberts), Thomas Arnold; m. 2d, Katherine Verschoor, Dec. 8, 1945. Practice pharmacy, Birmingham, Ala., 1917; retail pharmacist, co-owner drug stores, Birmingham, 1919-32; commd. pharmacist USPHS, 1933, advanced through grades to pharmacist dir., 1960; adminstrv. officer, 1933-42, chief supply service hdqrs. Hosp. div., Washington, 1942-44, chief supply officer Office Surgeon Gen., 1944-50, assigned div. civilian requirements, health supplies liaison officer ODM, 1958-60; medical supply cons., Washington, 1960-70; cons. to Office Emergency Planning, Exec. Office Pres., 1964-73. Gen. chmn. convention Assn. Mil. Surgeons, Washington, 1955; Am. Pharm. Assn. del. Conv. Internat. Pharm. Fedn., London, Eng., 1955. Served with U.S. Army, 1917-19. Recipient Founders medal Assn. Mil. Surgeons U.S., 1955, Andrew Craigie award, 1960; medal Swedish Ministry Health, 1959; H.A.K. Whitney award Am. Soc. Hosp. Pharmacists, 1960. Fellow Royal Soc. Health Eng. (life); mem. Am. Pharm.

Assn. (chmn. spl. com. Project Hope 1961-62, hon. pres. 1963, chmn. standing com. on disaster preparedness and nat. security 1963, chmn. standing com. govtl. pharm. service 1964, rep. to surgeon gen.'s profl. adv. com. emergency health preparedness, 1963-64), Am. Soc. Hosp. Pharmacists (chmn. com. laws, legislation and regulations 1967-70), assn. Mil. Surgeons U.S., Am. Legion, Commd. Officers Assn. Pub. Health Service, Am. Surg. Trade Assn. Chgo. (hon. life), Med-Surg. Mfrs. Assn. (hon. life). Home: Washington DC Died Jan. 4, 1973; buried Ft. Lincoln Cemetery, Washington DC

FOUKE, PHILIP BOND congressman, lawyer; b. Kaskaskia, Ill., Jan. 23, 1818; attended public schs.; studied law. Became civil engr.; founder, publisher Belleville Advocate, 1841; admitted to bar, 1845, began practice of law, Belleville; pros. atty. Kaskaskia Dist., 1846-50; mem. Ill. Ho. of Reps., 1851; mem. U.S. Ho. of Reps. (Democrat) from Ill., 36th-37th congresses, 1859-63; served as col. 30th Regt., Ill. Volunteer Inf., during Civil War, wounded at Battle of Belmont; practiced law, Washington, D.C. Died Washington, Oct. 3, 1876; buried Congressional Cemetery.

FOULDS, HENRY W(ILLIAM) mfg. exec.; b. Edinburgh, Scotland, Jan. 10, 1891 (parents U.S. citizens); s. Henry T. and Marie Anne Elizabeth (Pillans) F.; Chem.E., U. Pa., 1914; m. Rose Huntington, 1922; children-Henry William, Ralph H., Robert S., Mrs. John D. Plant, Jr. With Electric Storage Battery Co., Phila., 1914-16, Fairbanks-Morse, Buenos Aires, 1919-25. Servel, Inc., 1926-30. Goulds Pumps, Seneca Falls, N.Y., 1930-34; with Permuitit Co., N.Y.C., 1935, pres., dir., 1944, chmn., 1957; pres., dir. Permutit Co. of Can., Ltd., Montreal, 1936; pres., dir. Simplex Valve & Meter Co., Phila., 1946-57, chmn. bd., 1957. Officer, World War I. Mem. Pan-Am. Soc. U.S., Am. Soc. M.E., Am. Water Works Assn., The Camp Fire Club of Am. Clubs: Union League. Died Apr. 4, 1959.‡

FOULK, GEORGE CLAYTON naval officer, diplomat; b. Marietta, Pa., Oct. 30, 1856; s. Clayton and Caroline (Rudisill) F.; grad. U.S. Naval Acad., 1876; m. Kane Murase, 1887. Served on 2 cruises, Asiatic duty, U.S. Navy, circa 1876; crossed Siberia into Russia (with 2 other naval officers), reported on area to U.S. govt.; commd. ensign upon return to U.S., assigned to Naval Library, 1877; naval attache to Am. legation, Korea, 1883-85, in charge of legation, 1885-87; declined personal offer to become adviser to Korean king; recalled to Washington, D.C., commd. lt. (j.g.), 1884; with Am. Trading Co., Yokahama, Japan, 1888-90; prof. mathematics Doshisha Coll., Kyoto, Japan, 1890-93. Died Aug. 6, 1893; buried Kyoto.

FOULOIS, BENJAMIN army officer, ret.; b. Conn., Dec. 9, 1879; grad. Inf. and Cav. Sch., 1906, Army Signal Sch., 1908, Army Comd. and Gen. Staff Sch., 1925; m. Elisabeth Shepperd Grant, Apr. 1923. Corpl. to Sergt. Co. G, 1st U.S. Engrs., 1898-99; pvt. to 1st sergt., Co. G, 19th Inf., 1899-1901; commd. 2d lt. 17th Inf., Feb. 2, 1901; 1st lt. 24th Inf., Oct. 16, 1906; trans. to 17th Inf., Oct. 30, 1907; 1st lt. Signal Corps, Apr. 30, 1908; assigned to 7th Inf., Apr. 30, 1912; capt., aviation sect., Signal Corps, July 23, 1914; maj., June 27, 1917; brig. gen. Signal Corps (temp.), July 24, 1917. On aviation duty from July 1908 to Dec. 31, 1935; comd. air service troops on Mexican border and in Mexican Punitive Expedition, 1916-17. Drafted the $640,000,000 aviation bill of July 24, 1917; chief of air service, A.E.F., 1917-18; Am. mem. aviation com. of Supreme War Council, 1917-19; Am. mem. mil. com. of Conv. on Rules and Regulations for Internat. Air Navigation, 1919; chief of Am. Sect. of proposed Aeronautical Inter-Allied Commn. of Control, charged with the execution of the air terms of the Treaty of Peace with Germany; asst. mil. observer, Am. Commn., Berlin, Germany, May 1920-Nov. 1921; asst. mil. attaché, Am. Embassy, Berlin, Germany, Nov. 1921-Apr. 1924; apptd. commdg. officer, Mitchel Field, L.I., N.Y., 1925; asst. chief Air Corps, 1927-31; chief of Air Corps, with rank of maj. gen., 1931-35; retired, Dec. 31, 1935. Awarded D.S.M.; Comdr. Legion of Honor (French); Grand Officer Crown of Italy. Episcopalian. Club: Aero (Washington). Home: 3 N. Somerset Av., Ventnor City, N.J. Died Apr. 25, 1967.

FOUNTAIN, SAMUEL WARREN brig. gen.; b. Parkersburg, W.Va., Dec. 13, 1846; s. Chauncy and Ruhama (Ogle) F.; grad. U.S. Mil. Acad., 1870; m. Emily M. Kaufmann, 1879 (died 1885); m. 2d, Katherine G. McGrath, Jan. 11, 1888. Enlisted as pvt. Co. K, 140th Ohio Vol. Inf., May 2, 1864; disch., Sept. 3, 1864; commd. 2d lt. 8th U.S. Cav., June 15, 1870; 1st lt., Oct. 22, 1878; capt., Apr. 11, 1889; maj. 9th Cav., Feb. 2, 1901; asst. adj. gen., Feb. 28, 1901; lt. col. 13th Cav., Aug. 26, 1903; transferred to 4th Cav., Aug. 28, 1903; brig. gen., Apr. 10, 1905; retired, at own request, over 30 years service, Apr. 11, 1905. Served in campaigns against Geronimo, 1885-86; against the Sioux Indians, 1890-91; in Cuba during Spanish-Am. War and as adj. gen. dept. of Mindanao and Jolo, P.I.; comd. Jefferson Gurads at St. Louis Expdn., 1904. Catholic. Home: Devon, Pa. Died Nov. 15, 1920.

FOWLER, CHARLES WESLEY educator; b. Beverly, O., May 22, 1858; s. Royal A. and Emily Jane (Craig) F.; C.E., Ky. Mil. Inst., 1878, M.A., 1879; m. Annie E. Reynolds, of Shelbyville, Ky., July, 1881. Prof. mathematics and natural sciences, Ky. Mil. Inst., 1878-83; pres. Salem Coll., 1883; prin. Brandenburg Acad., 1884-87; practiced engring., 1887-88; prin. Cloverport High Sch., 1888-90; established Ky. Training Sch. at Mt. Sterling, 1890, combined it with Ky. Mil. Inst. and moved sch. to present location nr. Lyndon, Ky., 1896. Originated plan of transporting a mil. boarding sch. to Fla. for winter mos. and returning in spring-trip made in spl. train to Eau Gallie, Fla., and return; holds title of col. by virtue of position as supt. mil. inst.; pres. emeritus, 1919. Red Cross of Constantine. Clubs: Filson, Louisville Rotary; Eau Gallie Yacht (commodore). Author: Inductive Geometry, 1894, 1899, 1905. Address: Lyndon, Ky.

FOWLER, EDMUND P(RINCE), JR. physician; b. N.Y. City, Feb. 16, 1905; s. Edmund Prince and Mabel (Denman) F.; B.S. cum Laude, Storm King Sch., Dartmouth Coll., 1926; M.D., Columbia, 1930, Med. Sc.D., 1934; m. Olivia Jarrett, May 21, 1938; children - Heather, Edmund Prince. Med. interne Presbyterian Hosp., 1931-33; resident, ear, nose and throat Presbyn. Hosp., 1934-35; research fellow in ear, nose and throat, 1933-34; asst. surgeon Manhattan Eye and Ear Hosp., 1931-45; attending otolaryngologist Presbyn. Hosp. since 1937; prof. otolaryngology and dir. of Ear, Nose and Throat Service, Columbia-Presbyn. Med. Center, 1947 - . Past pres. Audiology Found.; president Mirncrocirculatory Conference, 1959. Served as captain, 2d Gen. Hosp. Unit, U.S. Army, 1942; consultant to 8th Air Force, 1944; consultant to air surgeon, 1945; disch. with rank of lt. col., Oct. 1945. Awarded Legion of Merit. Fellow Royal Soc. of Medicine; hon. fellow Royal Coll. of Surgeons (Ireland); mem. Am. Otol. Soc., Trilogical Soc., Am. Acad. of Ophthalmology and Otolaryngology, N.Y. Acad. of Medicine, Collegium Otolaryngolicum, Nat. Research Council Com. on Hearing and Bio-Acoustics, Zeta Psi, Nu Sigma Nu, Sigma Xi, Alpha Omega Alpha. Clubs: University, Omega, Riverdale Yacht, Garison Highlands. Editor: Medicine of the Ear, 1947. Mem. editorial board of Annals of Otology, also of Rhinology and Laryngology, Excerpta Medica, Practica Oto-Laryngologica. Contbr. articles on diseases of ear to med. jours.; research in disease of ear, nose and throat, psychosomatic medicine and micro-circulation. Died Jan. 13, 1964.

FOWLER, FREDERICK CURTIS, II, clergyman; b. Denver, Dec. 2, 1901; s. Frederick Curtis and Mary Mulvina (McConnell) F.; A.B., Princeton, 1924, M.A., 1927; B.D., Princeton Sem., 1927; Litt.D., Colorado College, 1937; D.D. (honorary), Burton Coll., 1949; married Anna Williams Bucher, March 14, 1928; children—Mary Mulvina (Mrs. James Zitzman), Reverend Frederick Curtis III, Rosalie Ann (Mrs. Gordon Arnold), and Paul Bucher. Ordained to ministry Presbyterian Ch. U.S.A., 1927; stated supply Woodside Ch., Buck Co., Pa., 1925-27, Hopewell (N.J.) Ch., 1927; minister English Ch., Marietta, Pa., 1927-30, First Ch., Mt. Union, Pa., 1930-36, Knoxville Ch., Pittsburgh, 1936-54, First Church, Duluth, Minn., 1954, 68; vis. prof. Ref. Theol. Sem., Jackson, Miss., 1969. Moderator Pitts. Presbytery, 1947, chmn. ministerial relations, Duluth Presbytery, 1956-59, moderator Presbytery of Duluth, 1967; member of the council, chmn., com. social edn. and action Pa. Synod, 1949-52; del. to Holland, to form World's Evang. Fellowship, 1951, 53, 56, mem. internat. relations commn., 1951-62; member World Relief Commission. Vice chmn. All Am. Conf. Combat Communism, 1950-53; chmn. March of Freedom, 1953-54; chmn. of the Billy Graham Crusade for Pitts. Dir. Christian Freedom Found., Incorporated, also director Christian Research, Inc., 1962-63, Christian Children's Fund, Inc., 1962-69; chmn. bd. dirs. Nat. Right-to-Work Com., 1965-69; dir. Inst. Applied Citizenship, Protestants and Other Ams. United for Separation Ch. and State. Served as chaplain USNR, Okinawa and Pacific, 1944-46, now ret. Recipient spl. award UN Chaplains' Assn., 1954; Christian Crusade award, 1966; named Distinguished Son of Denver, Colorado, 1959. Member of National Assn. Evangs. (exec. pres. 1950-51, pres. 1950-52, chmn. nat. commn. evang. action 1948-60, member board of directors), Protestants Other Americans United (pres. Pitts. chpt., 1950-53). Am. Legion, Regular Vets. Club: Princeton (N.Y.C.). Author articles religious jours. Frequent broadcaster nat. networks, TV. Home: Elk Park NC Died May 24, 1969; buried Knoxville TN

FOWLER, GEORGE RYERSON M.D., surgeon; b. New York, Dec. 25, 1848; s. Thomas W. and Sarah James F.; ed. public schools, Jamaica, L.I., grad. Bellevue Hosp. Med. Coll., 1871; m. Louise R. Wells, 1873. Surgeon M.E. Hosp.; surgeon-in-chief Brooklyn Hosp.; sr. surgeon German, cons. surgeon, St. Mary's Hosps.; cons. surgeon Relief (E. dist.) Norwegian, and Nassau hosps.; late prof. surgery N.Y. Polyclinic. Fellow Acad. of Medicine; examiner in surgery N.Y. State Bd. of Med. Examiners. Served in war, 1898, as chief surgeon, 3d div., 7th army corps, with Gen. Fitzhugh Lee; later cons. surgeon and chief of operating staff, 7th army corps, accompanying Gen. Lee to Havana, where he organized hosps.; disch., Jan. 31, 1899. Author: Appendicitis, 1894 (enlarged edit., 1900). Home: Brooklyn, N.Y. Died 1906.

FOWLER, (HARRY) ALFRED editor, pub.; b. Paola, Kan., Dec. 1, 1889; s. Harry Turton and m. Eleanor Morrison, Nov. 12, 1918; 1 dau., Gloria Eleanor; m. 2d, Wilma Hall, Nov. 14, 1940. Owner Alfred Fowler, Publisher; formerly editor Print Survey, The Quarterly Notebook, The Golden Galleon, The Bookplate Ann., The Romance of Fine Prints, The Print Collectors' Chronicle, The Print Collectors' Quarterly. Served from lt. to capt. Signal Corps, U.S. Army, World War I; capt. to lt. col. USAAF, 1942-45. Mem. Soc. Print Collectors (dir.), Bibliog. Soc., Am. Inst. Graphic Arts, Am. Soc. Aesthetics. Episcopalian. Clubs: Grolier (New York); Print Collector (London). Author of books on bookplates, radio and fine prints. Address: 311 N. Thomas St., Alexandria 3, Va. Deceased.

FOWLER, RAYMOND FOSTER army officer; b. Alexandria, Neb., Oct. 14, 1884; s. Charles Addison and Abbie V. (Church) F.; student U. of Neb., 1904-06; B.S., U.S. Mil. Acad., 1910; grad. Engr. Sch., 1912; honor grad., Command and Gen. Staff Sch., 1925; grad. Army War Coll., 1935; m. Katharine Van Dorn Wagner, Nov. 24, 1924; children - Helen Frederica (Mrs. Bradford G. Woolley), Gordon (lt. comdr. U.S. Navy). Commd. 2d lt., Corps of Engineers, U.S. Army, June 15, 1910. and advanced through the grades to brig. gen.; served as sect. engr. on constrn. in base sects., A.E.F., and ry. constrn., B.E.F., 1917-18; asst. brigade comdr., 1st Tank Brigade, 1918; chief of supply div., Office of Chief of Engrs., since 1941; div. engrs., South Atlantic Div.; engr. staff 4th Service Command; retired Dec. 1945; exec. Ga. State Ports Authority. Mem. Soc. Am. Mil. Engrs. Clubs: Army and Navy (Washington); Engineers (Phila.); Capital City, Atlanta Athletic. Home: 999 Mt. Paran Rd. N.W., Atlanta, Ga. Died Jan. 19, 1949.

FOWLER, RICHARD LABBITT, naval officer; b. May 13, 1913. Commd. ensign U.S. Navy, 1936, advanced through grades to rear adm., 1964. Deceased.*

FOX, CHARLES EBEN naval officer; b. Chelsea, Mass., Sept. 20, 1851; s. John Lawrence (surgeon U.S.N.) and Elizabeth Amory (Morris) F.; apptd. at-large, and grad. U.S. Naval Acad., 1872; m. Nelly Beckwith, June 10, 1884; lt. comdr., Mar. 1899; comdr., Apr. 1902; capt., Aug. 5, 1906; rear-admiral, Sept. 16, 1910; retired on own application, Aug. 1911. Homes: Washington, D.C., and Cazenovia, N.Y. Died Feb. 12, 1916.

FOX, GUSTAVUS VASA govt. ofcl.; g. Saugus, Mass., June 13, 1821; s. Dr. Jesse and Olivia (Flint) F.; m. Virginia Woodbury, 1856. Apptd. midshipman U.S. Navy, 1841, lt., 1852, resigned, 1856; in charge of evacuation of Ft. Sumter, transported Anderson and his 70 men to N.Y., 1861; chief clk. Navy Dept., 1861, asst. U.S. sec. of navy, 1861, selected Farragut to command expdn. resulting in capture New Orleans and opening of the Mississippi; agt. for U.S. Congress sent to Russia to congratulate Czar Alexander II, 1867; aft. Middlesex Co., Lowell, Mass., 1867; ofcl. papers published posthumously as: Confidential Correspondence of Gustavus Vasa Fox, Assistant Secretary of the Navy, 1861-65 (edited by Robert Thompson) 2 vols., 1918-19. Died N.Y.C., Oct. 29, 1883.

FOX, HERBERT pathologist; b. Atlantic City, N.J., June 3, 1880; s. Samuel Tucker and Hannah Ray (Freas) F.; A.B., Central High Sch., Phila., 1897; M.D., lfed. Dept., U. of Pa., 1901; studied U. of Vienna; m. Louise Carr Gaskill, Nov. 9, 1904 (died Nov. 16, 1933); children - Margaret, John Freas (dec.), Samuel Tucker; m. 2d, Mary Harlan Rhoads, Dec. 3, 1938. Volunteer asso. in William Pepper Clin. Lab. 1903-06; pathologist to Rush Hosp., since 1904; pathologist to Phila. Zool. Soc., since 1906; chief of Labs., Pa. Dept. of Health, 1906-11; dir. William Pepper Lab. of Clinical Medicine, Hosp. U. of Pa., since 1911; pathologist to the Children's Hosp., 1915-26; prof. comparative pathology, U. of Pa., since 1927. Mem. Coll. of Physicians, Am. Philos. Society, Acad. of Natural Sciences, County Med. Soc., Pathol. Society (all of Phila), A.M.A., Am. Assn. Pathologists and Bacteriologists; fellow A.A.A.S. Served as chief contonment lab., Camp Zachary Taylor, Ky., 1917-19; maj. M.C. U.S. Army, Republican. Author: Elementary Bacteriology and Protozoology, 1912, 5th edit., 1931; Text Book of Pathology (with Alfred Stengel), 8th edit., 1927; Disease in Captive Wild Mammals and Birds, 1923. Home: Hamilton Court, 39th and Chestnut Sts., Philadelphia, Pa. Died Feb. 27, 1942.

FOX, HOWARD dermatologist; b. London, Eng., July 4, 1873; s. George Henry and Harriet Lovisa (Gibbs) F.; brought to America in infancy; A.B., Yale, 1894: M.D., Coll. Physicians and Surgeons, Columbia, 1898; post-grad. work univs. of Berlin and Vienna; Sc.D., Rollins Coll., Winter Park, Fla., 1931; unmarried. Practiced, New York, since 1903; prof. dermatology, Dartmouth Med. Coll., Jan. 1913; dermatol. asst., Vanderbilt Clinic, 1903-13; attending dermatologist U.S.P.H.S., Dist. 2; prof. dermatology, N.Y. Polyclinic Med. Sch., 1923-24; emeritus prof. dermatology and syphilology, New York U.: Hon. cons. dermatologist and syphilologist, Bellevue Hosp.; cons. dermatologist various hosps. Lt. Col., M.C. U.S. Army, comdg. officer Base Hosp. No. 136, Vannes, France, 1918-19; active service in war, 1917-19; consultant to Sec. of War in tropical medicine during World War II; now col. Med. R.C. Pres. Am. Bd. of Dermatology and Syphilology, 1932-45; pres. Med. Soc. County of New York, 1938; 1st pres. Am. Acad. Dermatology and Syphilology, 1938; pres. N.Y. Soc. of Tropical Medicine, 1939: 1st pres. Assn. of Dermato-Syphilologists of Greater New York. Mem. Am. Dermatol. Assn. (hon.), (pres. 1924-25), N.Y. Acad. Medicine, Am. Med. Assn., N.Y. State Med. Soc., Psi Upsilon; corr. mem. Swedish Dermatol. Soc., Brit. Assn. of Dermatology and Syphilology, Danish Dermatol. Soc., Med. and Surg. Soc. of Sao Paulo (Brazil); hon. mem. Society of Investigative Dermatology, New York Dermatol, Society, Manhattan Dermatol. Society, N.E. Dermatol. Society, Pittsburgh Dermatol. Soc., Royal Society of Medicine (Sect. of Dermatology), Cuban Dermatol. Soc., Société Francaise de Prophylaxie Sanitaire et Morale, Sociátć Francaise de Dermatologie et de Syphilographia, Hungarian Dermatol. Soc., Spanish Acad. of Dermatol. and Syphilology. Austrian Dermatol. Soc., Polish Assn. of Dermatology and Syphilology, Sociedad de dermatol. y syphilografia of Argentina, Italian Soc. Dermatology and Syphilology (hon.), N.H. State Med. Soc., Plainfield Mod. Soc.; Med. Assn. of Peru; v.p. 8th Internat. Congress Dermatology, Copenhagen, 1930; hon. pres. 9th Internat. Cong. of Dermatology, Budapest, 1935.

FOX, OSCAR CHAPMAN prin. examiner class of Tillage, U.S. Patent Office, July 1, 1873—; b. Pitcher, N.Y., Aug. 23, 1830; s. Daniel and Harriet Amanda (Chapman) F.; grad. Nat. Univ., law dept., 1876; m. Abbie Galt, Sept. 11, 1866. Capt. (bvt. maj.) 76th N.Y. vols.; disch. for wounds, Dec. 1862. Prin. Nelson Acad., Ohio, 3 years. Admitted to bar, 1876. Home: Washington, Ill. Died 1902.

FOX, WILLIAM FREEMAN supt. state forests, N.Y.; b. Ballston Spa, N.Y., Jan. 11, 1840; s. Rev. Norman and Jane (Freeman) F.; ed. Union Classical School, Schenectady, and Union Coll., class of 1860; served in Civil War as capt., maj. and lt. col. 107th N.Y. vols.; wounded at Antietam, Chancellorsville and Resaca; m. Mary Ann Shattuck, Sept. 28, 1865. For past 22 yrs. with State Forestry Dept. Mem. Soc. Am. Foresters; companion Mil. Order Loyal Legion; Mem. N.Y. Hist. Soc.; pres. Chi Psi Alumni Assn., N.Y.; corr. sec., Soc. Army of the Potomac; pres. Soc. Twelfth Army Corps. Author: Forest Tree Nurseries and Nursery Methods in Europe, 1905. Home: Albany, N.Y. Died 1909.

FOY, BYRON CECIL, corporation official; born at Dallas, Tex., June 20, 1893; s. Walter F. and Frances (Smith) F.; student U. of Tex., 1912-16; m. Thelma Chrysler, December 3, 1924 (dec. Aug. 1957); children—Joan Chrysler (Mrs. Raymond French), Cynthia (Mrs. Albert Rupp, Jr.); m. 2d, Virginia Peine Reynolds, Apr. 11, 1961, With Ford Motor Co., Dallas, Balt., Boston, 1916-19; pres. Reo Motor Car Co. of Cal., Los Angeles, 1921-25; v.p. J.H. Thompson Co., Chrysler distbrs., Detroit, 1925-27; v.p. Simons, Stewart & Foy, Chrysler distbrs., N.Y. 1927-29; v.p. Chrysler Corp., Detroit, 1929-46; pres. DeSoto Motor Corp., 1931-42; chmn. bd., pres. Jack & Heintz Precision Inds., Inc., Cleve., 1946-47; dir. Dome Mines, Ltd., Mission Development Co., Exec. officer, jr. lt. Naval Aviation, World War I; lt. col. USAAF, 1943-—. Mem. Phi Gamma Delta. Clubs: Turf and Field, Racquet and Tennis, The Creek, Piping Rock (N.Y.C.); Country, Detroit, Detroit Athletic, University (Detroit); Bath and Tennis, Everglades, Seminole Golf (Palm Beach). Home: New York City NY Died Aug. 1970.

FOY, ROBERT CHERRY army officer; b. Eufaula, Ala., Aug. 20, 1876; s. William Humphrey and Mary Louise (Wilson) F.; B.S., Ala. Poly. Inst., 1894; grad. U.S. Mil. Acad., 1899, Mounted Service Sch., Ft. Riley, Kan., 1915; distinguished grad. Army Sch. of the Line, Ft. Leavenworth, Kan., 1916; grad. Gen. Staff Sch., 1922, Army War Coll., 1923; m. Helene Hummel, Aug. 7, 1923. Commd. 2d lt. U.S. Army, Feb. 15, 1899; promoted through grades to brig. gen., Mar. 1, 1935. Served in Cuba, 1899-1900, in Philippines, 1902-03, Texas, 1903-04; asst. q.m., West Point, N.Y., 1904-08; again in Philippines, 1908-11; on Mexican border with 3d Cav., 1911-14 and 1916-17; in Hawaii with 1st F.A., 1917; organized 332d F.A., Camp Grant, Ill., and comd. the regt. in France, Sept.-Dec. 1918; returned to U.S., Aug. 1919. Comd. 15th F.A. at Fort Sam Houston, Tex., 1920; with 17th F.A., Ft. Bragg, N.C., 1921; mil. attaché, Bucharest, Roumania and Constantinople, Turkey, 1923-26; comd. 4th F.A. at Ft. McIntosh, Tex., 1926-28; served on War Dept. Gen. Staff, Washington, D.C., 1928-32; comdg. officer sch. troops, F.A. Sch., Ft. Sill, Okla., 1932-35; comdr. 2d F.A. Brig., Ft. Sam Houston, Tex., March 1, 1935-March 1937; comdr. 11th F.A. Brigade, Schofield Barracks, Hawaii, 1937-39; retired Dec. 31, 1939. Awarded Polish Commanders' Cross, Order of Polonia Restituta; Czechoslovakia Nat. Order of White Lion. Mem. Sigma Nu. Methodist. Clubs: Army and Navy, Chevy Chase Country (Washington, D.C.). Address: Boerne, Tex. Died Feb. 6, 1944.

FRACHTENBERG, LEE JOACHIM anthropologist; b. Czernautz, Austria, Feb. 24, 1883; s. Abraham and Jeanette (Rottenstreich) F.; grad. Imperial Royal Gymnasium, Przemysl, Austria, 1904; studied Cornell U., 1904-05; M.A., Columbia, 1906, Ph.D., 1910; m. Claudia E. McDonald, May 22, 1913; children—Margaret Janet, Maurice James, Richard (dec.). Asst. supt. Ednl. Alliance, N.Y. City, 1907-09; expert to Commn. on Crime and Dependency, N.J., 1909; asst. U.S. Immigration Commn., 1909-10; chief of fgn. population, U.S. Census for N.Y. City, 1910; lecturer on anthropology, Columbia, 1910-12; ethnologist, Bur. of Am. Ethnology, 1913-17; translator, Dept. of Justice (war work), Com. on Pub. Information, 1917-18; head worker Jewish Welfare Bd., at Camp Humphreys, Va., and Camp Funston, Kan., 1918-19; dir. service clubs, rank of capt., and supervisor service clubs, rank of lt. col., for Central Dept., U.S.A., 1919-20; hon. disch. from army, Nov. 7, 1920; gen. sec. Y.M. Hebrew Assn., Troy, N.Y., June 1921; regional dir. Palestine Foundation Fund, 1922-23, nat. field dir., 1923—, exec. dir. region 4, 1922-17, region 10, 1927—. Researches among Indians of N. America, especially those living on Pacific Coast, seeking establishment of genetic relationships between several langs. spoken by Indians of Northwest Coast. Fellow Am. Ethnological Soc., Am. Geog. Society. Democrat. Author: Coos Texts, 1913; Coos, an Illustrative Sketch, 1914; Lower Umpqua Texts, 1914; Siuslawan, an Illustrative Sketch, 1917; Alsea Texts and Myths, 1919. Home: Chicago, Ill. Died Nov. 26, 1930.

FRAILEY, CARSON PETER pharmacist, assn. exec.; b. Emmitsburg, Md., Aug. 12, 1887; s. Oscar D. and Clara M. (Hoke) F.; Pharm.D., Univ. of Md., 1908, D.Sch., (hon.), 1946; LL.D. (hon.) Southeastern Univ., Washington 1949; m. Rebecca Gray Houck, 1912: 1 son, Carson Gray. With retail drug stores Blue Ridge Summit, Pa., Baltimore, Md., Washington, D.C., 1908-12; Armour & Co. (now The Armour Labs.), Chicago, 1912-14; H. K. Mulford Co., mfg. chemists, Phila., 1914-23; exec. vice pres. and sec. Am. Drug Mfrs. Assn., Washington, D.C. since 1923; professorial lecturer on indsl. pharmacy, George Washington Univ. Commd. major, R.C., U.S. Army; Asst., in studies of med. supply program against a nat. emergency; served as chmn. drugs resources adv. com., Army and Navy Munitions Bd. 1940-44, chmn. com. attached to Office The Surgeon Gen. of the Army since 1944. Mem. Com. on Revision of Constn. and By-Laws of U.S. Pharmacopoeial Conv.; mem. Nominating Com. and bd. trustees U.S. Pharm. Convention, 1950-60. Mem. bd. trustees Southeastern Univ. Mem. Am. Pharm. Assn. (awarded 1 yr. mem. by Md. Bd. of Pharmacy for highest gen. average, 1908, mem. lab. com.), Am. Foundation for Pharm. Edn. (hon. mem.), Nat. Drug Trade Conf. (pres., since 1930), Kappa Psi, Y.M.C.A. (pres. since 1944, chmn. executive com.), S.A.R. Gold Key Award for Service to Youth, Y.M.C.A. Registered pharmacist Md., D.C. Mem. Rho Chi, Mem. Luther Pl. Meml. Ch. (past pres. ch. council). Home: 3704 Livingston St. N.W., Washington 15; and Emmitsburg, Maryland. Office: Albee Bldg., Washington 5. Died Mar. 13, 1954; buried Emmitsburg, Md.

FRAILEY, LEONARD AUGUST rear adm.; b. Washington, Aug. 8, 1843; s. Charles S. and Caroline M. B. F.; ed. Union Acad., Gonzaga Coll. and Young Commercial Coll.; m. Helen Watson Freeman, Sept. 28, 1869. Apptd. acting asst. p.-m. U.S.N., Aug. 20, 1864; passed asst. p.-m. July 23, 1866; p.-m., Jan. 29, 1869; pay insp., May 24, 1894; pay dir., Aug. 29, 1899; retired at own request after 40 years service, Feb. 17, 1905, with rank of rear admiral, for services during Civil War. Home: Washington, D.C. Died Dec. 31, 1913.

FRANCE, CHARLES E. lawyer; b. nr. Cleo Springs, Okla. Terr., Nov. 8, 1900; s. Morris Elmer and Ada (Ginder) F.; student U. Mo., 1919-21; LL.B., U. Okla., 1923; m. Gudrun Engell of Copenhagen, Denmark, July 26, 1945; 1 son, Charles Engell. Admitted to Okla. bar, 1923, since practiced Oklahoma City; mem. firm Burford, Miley, Hoffman & Burford since 1923, now sr. partner successor firm; sec., dir. Suburban Water Company; vice president, general counsel Standard Food Markets, Humpty Dumpty Super Markets, Folding Carrier Corp. and affiliated cos. Volunteered for mil. service in Feb. 1942 as legal officer in Air Force; transferred to Judge Advocate General's Dept. staff Judge Advocate for XII Air Force Service Command and Army Air Force Service Command, Mediterranean Theater Operations; disch. as lt. col. Mem. Okla. City Library Bd. Trustees; sec. and a founder Okla. Art Center; mem. A.R.C. (past county dir., past chmn.). Mem. Am., Okla. (pres. 1945) and Okla. Co. (past dir. and pres.) bar assns., Phi Alpha Delta, Beta Theta Pi. Club: Beacon. An author of law providing public support for Crippled Children's Hosp. and Soc. of Okla. Interested in art and modest collector Am. art and etchings. Home: 321 N.W. 14th St. Office: 16 S. Pennsylvania Av., Oklahoma City. Died Nov. 10, 1952.

FRANCE, ROYAL WILBUR lawyer, assn. exec.; b. Lowville, N.Y., July 27, 1883; s. Joseph and Hannah F. (James) F.; A.B., George Wash. U., 1904, A.M., Hamilton Coll., 1908; student Albany Law School; L.L.D. Centro de Estudios de Mexico; L.H.D. Rollins Coll.; m. Ethel C. Camp, June 13, 1912 (dec. December 1956); children - Marguerite (dec.), Boyd, Hannah (Mrs. Stuart James); married 2d, Ruth E. Crawford, Dec. 27, 1957. Admitted to N.Y. bar, 1906, U.S. Bar 1912, the United States Supreme Court Bar; member law firms Knapp & France, 1906-08, Duell, Warfield & Duell, 1908-16, Konta, Kirchwey, France & Michael, 1918-21, Barber & France, 1928-29; v.p. and gen. mgr. triangle Film Co., 1916-17; vice pres. Salt's Textile Co., 1921-24, pres. 1925-28; vocational advisor Columbia U., 1928-29; prof. economics Rollins Coll., 1929-52; guest prof. Centro de Estudio de Mexico, 1937, Hamilton Coll., 1947, U. of Mass., 1948, 1949; exec. sec. Nat. Lawyers Guild, 1956-61; counsel for civil liberties cases, 1952 - . Member of public panel Nat. War Labor Board, 1943-45, arbitrator labor disputes for Nat. Wage Stabilization Bd., Nat. Conciliation Service. Served as capt. U.S. Army, 1917-18. Mem. National Lawyers Guild, Fellowship of American Civil Liberties Union, New York Bar Association, - Am. Econ. Assn., Am. Assn. U. Profs., Theta Delta Chi., Pi Gamma Mu. Clubs: Winter Park (Fla.) UniYersity, Dubdread Golf. Author: Compromise (novel), 1936; My Native Grounds 1957; contbr. articles to various periodicals. Lecturer on econ. and internat. subjects. Home: 501 W. 213d St., N.Y.C., 10027. Died July 10, 1962.

FRANCHOT, CHARLES PASCAL lawyer; b. Olcan, N.Y., Oct. 8, 1886; s. Nicholas Van Vranken and Annie Conyne (Wood) F.; student Olean (N.Y.) High Sch., 1901-04, Phillips Acad., Andover, Mass., 1905-06; A.B., Yale, 1910; LL.B., Harvard, 1914; m. Lillian Winston, Apr. 8, 1920; 1 dau., Fendall Winston (Mrs. Arthur Burtis Lawrence, Jr.). Admitted to N.Y. Bar 1914, and since in practice at Buffalo and New York; admitted to District of Columbia bar, 1946; member Kenefick, Cooke, Mitchell & Bass, 1920-26; mem. Franchot & Warren, 1928-37, Franchot & Schachtel, 1937-42; practiced alone, Jan. 1943-May 1944, mem. Franchot & Dessner, 1944-46; Franchot, Corwin & Dessner, May 1946-53; with offices in N.Y. and Washington, D.C.; v.p. and gen. counsel Rand Kardex Bureau, Inc., 1926-27; director and general counsel Remington Rand Inc., 1927-45; pres. and gen. counsel Buffalo Electric Furnace Corp.; chmn. bd. dirs. and gen. counsel Sonotone Corp.; Royal Crown Beverage Co., DeLisser Machine & Tool Corporation: pres. and dir. Cheekmaster Systems, Incorporated; spl. legal adviser to dir. Naval Petroleum Reserves, 1946-50, James Petroleum Corp. Served as 1st lt., later capt. and maj. cav. A.E.F., World War I; lt. col., cav. O.R.C. Capt. U.S.N.R.; served as spl. asst. to judge advocate gen. of U.S. Navy, May 1944-May 1946. Received citation by Gen. Pershing, with award of Purple Heart, "for meritorious service" on staff, A.E.F. Awarded Commendation Ribbon by secretary of Navy. Mem. Am., District of Columbia and N.Y. State bar associations, Assn. Bar City of New York, Phi Beta Kappa, Psi Upsilon, Skull and Bones (Yale), Am. Soc. of French Legion of Honor. Republican Episcopalian. Clubs: Yale, Midday (New York), Metropolitan (Washington). Home: 1067 Fifth Av. Office: 1636 Lincoln Bldg., N.Y.C. 17; also 1741 K St. N.W., Washington 6. Died Sept. 8, 1953; buried Olean, N.Y.

FRANCHOT, RICHARD congressman; b. Morris, N.Y., June 2, 1816; attended Hartwick and Cherry Valley acads.; studied civil engring. Polytechnic Inst., Troy, N.Y. Became engaged in agriculture, then in railroad constrn.; pres. Albany & Susquehanna R.R. Co.; mem. U.S. Ho. of Reps. (Republican) from N.Y., 37th Congress, 1861-63; moved to Schenectady, N.Y.; raised 121st Regt., N.Y. Volunteer Inf., during Civil War, commd. col., 1862; brevetted brig. gen. U.S. Volunteers, 1865; asso. with Central Pacific R.R. Co. Died Schenectady, Nov. 23, 1875; buried Vale Cemetery.

FRANCIS, WILLIAM HOWARD JR. lawyer, govt. ofcl.; b. Ft. Worth, Nov. 11, 1914; s. William Howard and Frances (Lysaght) F.; A.B., Rice Inst., 1935; LL.B., Tex. U., 1938; m. Caroline Keith Wiess, May 25, 1946. Admitted to Tex. bar, 1938; with Vinson, Elkins, Weems & Francis, 1938-41, 1945-49; pvt. practice of law, Houston, 1949—; oil operator, 1949—; pres. Texas Fund, Inc., Houston, 1955-57; apptd. asst. sec. defense, 1957—. Served as capt. M.I., AUS, 1941-45. Mem. Am., Tex., Harris County bar assns. Episcopalian. Clubs: Houston Country. River Oaks County, Ramada, Tejas, Bayou, Allegro. Home: 2923 Inwood Dr., Houston. Office: San Jacinto Bldg., Houston 2. Died May 24, 1958.

FRANK, PAT HARRY HART author, journalist; b. Chicago, Ill., May 5, 1907; s. Harry Hart and Doris Aileen (Cohen) F.; student Peddle Sch., Highstown, N.J., 1920-25; U. of Fla., 1925-26; m. 2d, Josephine de Zeng, Mar. 1954 (div.); adopted dau. Anina de Zeng; children by previous marriage - Perry, Patrick Gene. Reporter Jacksonville (Fla.) Journal, 1926-28; New York World, 1928; New York Journal, 1929-32; feature writer Washington, (D.C.) Herald, 1932-38; covered War and State Depts., White House, 1934-40; associated with OWI, 1941; special asst. to Am. Minister and rep. U.S. on Allied Polit. Warfare Council in Australia, 1942-44; conductor polit. warfare against Germans in Turkey, 1944; war corr. on Italian front covering 5th Army and 15th Air Force, 1944-45; resigned to resume fiction writing, 1945; chief of staff, emeritus, Atlantic Beach Navy; cons. Dept. Def.; dir. information Civil Defense Dept., 1964. Awarded distinguished service citation of Reserve Officers Association, 1957; American Heritage award for outstanding citizenship, 1961. Clubs: National Press, Overseas Press. Author: Mr. Adam, 1946, An Affair of State, 1948; Hold Back the Night, 1951; The Long Way Round, 1953; Forbidden Area, 1956; Alas, Babylon, 1959; How To Survive the H-Bomb - and Why, 1962. Contbr. short fiction to nat. mags. Home: Atlantic Beach, Fla. Died Oct. 12, 1964.

FRANK, ROYAL THAXTER army officer; b. Gray, Me., May 6, 1836; s. Alpheus and Nioma (Stimson) F.; grad. U.S. Mil. Acad., 1858. Bvt. 2d lt., 5th Inf., July 1, 1858; 2d lt. 8th Inf., Oct. 19, 1858; 1st lt., May 14, 1861; capt., Feb. 27, 1862; transferred to 1st Arty., Dec. 15, 1870; maj. Jan. 2, 1881; lt. col. 2d Arty., Jan. 25, 1889; col. 1st Arty., Oct. 25, 1894; brig. gen. vols., May 4, 1898; hon. disch. from vol. service, May 12, 1899; brig. gen. U.S.A., Oct. 17, 1899. Bvtd maj., July 3, 1862 for gallant and meritorious services in peninsular campaign; lt. col., Dec. 13, 1862 for same in battle of Fredericksburg, Va. Home: Washington, D.C. Died 1908.

FRANKE, GUSTAV HENRY army officer; b. Manning, Ia., Sept. 7, 1888; s. Gustav Henry with silver star, Mexican Border Service Ribbon, Army Commendation Ribbon. Mem. Scabbard and Blade, Omicron Delta Kappa. Clubs: Army and Navy (Washington). Address: Myrtle Beach, S.C. Died Mar. 19, 1953; buried West Point, N.Y.

FRANKE, LOUIS govt. ofcl.; b. El Campo, Tex., Aug. 7, 1905; s. Paul Conrad and Lydia (Shudde) F.; B.S.A., Tex. A. and M. Coll., 1928; m. Frances Hanna, Oct. 12, 1950; children - Frances, Metche, William, Johanna, Louis, David. Entomologist, Sonora, Mexico, 1928-29; farmer, 1930-33; co. extension agt., Brooks County, Tex., 1934-36; editor Tex. Extension Service, Dept. Agr., 1937-50; on leave as information specialist Nat. Def. Adv. Council, Washington, 1940-41; extension cons. High Commr. Germany, 1950; extension service adviser, then asst. chief party, chief party, dir. agrl. service ICA, Paraguay, 1951-55; food and agr. officer ICA Mission to Guatemala, 1955-60; chief agr. officer ICA Mission to Buenos Aires, Argentina, 1960-62; area devel. officer Agy. Internat. Devel. Mission to Argentina, 1963 - . U.S. del. UN FAO Regional Conf. on Agr., Buenos Aires, 1954, Latin Am. Conf. on Indian Affairs, Guatemala City, 1959. Served to capt. USAAF, 1942-45. Decorated Bronze Star. Home: Av. España 789, Corrientes, Pcia. Corrientes, Misiones, Argentina. Died Aug. 15, 1965.

FRANKFURTER, FELIX ex-asso. justice U.S. Supreme Court; b. Vienna, Austria, Nov. 15, 1882; s. Leopold and Emma (Winter) F.; brought to U.S., 1894; A.B., College City of N.Y., 1902; LL.B., Harvard, 1906, D.C.L., U. of Oxford, 1939; LL.D., Amherst, 1940; Coll. City N.Y., 1947, U. Chgo., 1953; Brandeis Univ., 1956, Harvard, 1956, Yale, 1961; married Marion A. Denman, Dec. 20, 1919. Assistant U.S. atty., Southern District of N.Y., 1906-10; law officer, Bureau of Insular Affairs, War Dept., 1911-14; prof. Harvard Law Sch., 1914-39; George Eastman visiting prof., Oxford U., 1933-34. Maj. and judge adv. O.R.C. U.S. Army; asst. to the Sec. of War, sec. and counsel to the President's Mediation Commn., asst. to the Sec. of Labor, 1917-18; chmn. War Labor Policies Board, 1918; declined Governor Ely's nomination to Mass. Supreme Judicial Court, June 1932. Nominated asso. justice of Supreme Court of U.S. by Pres. Roosevelt Jan. 5, 1939; confirmed by Senate, Jan. 17, took office Jan. 30, 1939; ret. 1962. Hon. Master of Bench, Gray's Inn, London, 1952. Author: The Case of Sacco and Vanzetti, 1927; The Bus. of the Supreme Court (with James M. Landis), 1928; The Labor Injunction (with Nathan Greene), 1930; The Public and its Government, 1930; The Commerce Clause Under Marshall, Taney and Waite, 1937; Mr. Justice Holmes and the Supreme Court, 1939. Editor: Cases under the Interstate Commerce Act, 1915, 2d edit. 1922; Criminal Justice in Cleveland (with Roscoe Pound), 1922; Mr. Justice Holmes, 1931; Cases on Federal Jurisdiction (with Wilbur G. Katz), 1931; Cases on Administrative Law (with J. Forrester Davison), 1931; Mr. Justice Brandeis, 1932; Cases on Federal Jurisdiction (with Harry Shulman), 1937; Of Law and Men, 1956; Felix Frankfurter Reminisces, 1960. Address: Supreme Court of the United States, Washington. Died Feb. 22, 1965.

FRANKLIN, BENJAMIN A. b. Northumberland County, Va., Oct. 15, 1869; s. Benjamin A. and Placidia (Cralle) F.; student Johns Hopkins, 1887-1889; hon. Master Humanics, Internat. Y.M.C.A. Coll., 1924; m. Jeanette Haslett, of England, Apr. 25, 1896; children—Benjamin Allan, Paul Lawrence. With Midvale Steel Col, Phila., 1889-1902; organizer, 1902, Miller, Franklin & Co., efficiency engrs., N.Y. City (of which was treas.), now Miller & Franklin Co.; with Strathmore Paper Co., Springfield, Mass., 1909-32, v.p., 1911-32. Industrial eng. and bus. counsel; sec.-treas. Specialty Paper and Board Affiliates; chmn. bd. Perkins Machine and Gear Co.; trustee Internat. Y.M.C.A. Coll., Springfield branch Northeastern University; chmn. board Am. Youth Council, Inc. Maj., lt. col. and col. Ordnance Dept., U.S.A.; chief Hartford Ordnance District. Distinguished Service Medal, 1919. Republican. Episcopalian. Author: Cost Reports for

Executives, 1913; Experiences in Efficiency, 1915; The Industrial Executive, 1925; Banners in the Wind (a personal philosophy), 1940. Home: Springfield, Mass. Died June 17, 1940.

FRANKLIN, SAMUEL RHOADS rear admiral, U.S.N., retired Aug., 1887; b. York, Pa., Aug. 25, 1825; apptd. midshipman, Feb. 18, 1841; passed midshipman, Aug. 10, 1847; promoted through grades to rear admiral, Jan. 24, 1885; m. dau. of Rear Admiral B. F. Sands, Jan. 10, 1883. A large share of his 46 years of service was passed at sea and included naval operations and actions in the Mexican and Civil Wars. Supt. U.S. Naval Observatory, 1884-85; comdr.-in-chief European sta., 1885-87. Author: Memories of a Rear Admiral. Died 1901.

FRANKLIN, WALTER SIMONDS civil engr.; b. York, Pa., Mar. 1, 1836; s. Walter Simonds and Sarah (Buel) F.; B.S., summa cum laude, Lawrence Scientific Sch. (Harvard), 1857; m. Mary Campbell Small, Dec. 13, 1866. Began work in wholesale store in New York, 1850; chainman and rodman in engring. party of Pa. R.R., 1852; studied, 1854; entered engring. sch., Harvard; on Fernandina & Cedar Keys R.R., Fla., 1857-88; in Europe, 1859; apptd. 1st lt. 12th U.S. Inf., May 1861; served in Army of the Potomac in McClellan's campaign; afterward under Sheridan in Shenandoah Valley, and with Grant until surrender of Lee; on staff of Gen. Sedgwick until he was killed, then with Wright, as insp.-gen. 6th Army Corps, with rank of lt. col.; bvtd. maj. and lt. col. U.S.A., and col. U.S.V.; returned to regt. as capt., 1865, and resigned, 1870. Gen. mgr. Ashland Iron Co., Md., till 1887, then with Md. Steel Co. till 1894 (dir.); pres. Baltimore City Passenger R.R., till consolidation of all the roads; v.p. of the consolidated roads till 1903; retired. Mem. U.S. Lighthouse Bd., 1884—. Presbyn. Democrat. Home: Baltimore, Md. Died 1911.

FRANKLIN, WALTER SIMONDS, ry. official; b. Ashland, Md., May 24, 1884; s. Walter Simonds and Mary Campbell (Small) F.; A.B., Harvard, 1906; LL.D., University of Pennsylvania, 1950; married Cassandra Morris Small, Dec. 6, 1919; children—William Buel II, Cassandra Small (Mrs. Caspar W. Morris, Jr.). Joined Pa. R.R., 1906, advanced to asst. gen. freight agent; became v.p. Am. Trading Co., N.Y., 1919, later pres.; reentered service of Pa. R.R., 1928, apptd. gen. agt. at Det., 1928, gen. supt. Northwestern div., 1929, asst. to v.p. in charge operation, 1931; pres. Det., Toledo & Ironton R.R. Co., 1929-31; became pres. Wabash Ry. Co. and Ann Arbor R.R. Co., 1931, receiver of both Wabash Ry. and Ann Arbor R.R., 1931-33; v.p. traffic, Pa. R.R. Co., 1933-48, exec. v.p., 1948-49, pres., 1949-54; pres. L.I. R.R. Co., 1950-56, resigned Jan. 1, 1956; dir. Curtis Publishing Co., N. & W. Ry. Co., Detroit, Toledo & Ironton R.R. Co., Wabash R.R. Co., Bell Telephone Co. of Pa., Girard Trust Corn Exchange Bank; trustee Western Savs. Fund Soc. Mem. distrbn. com. The Phila. Found. Trustee Presbyterian Hosp. (Phila.) Capt. to lt. col., Transportation Corps, U.S.A. during World War I. Awarded D.S.M. (U.S.); Chevalier Legion of Honor (France); Distinguished Service Order (Gt. Britain). Mem. Pa. Soc. Cin. Presbyn. Clubs: Harvard (N.Y.C.); Gulph Mills Golf, Merion Cricket, Philadelphia, Harvard (Phila.). Home: Ardmore PA Died Aug. 17, 1972; buried St. David's Ch., Devon PA

FRANKLIN, WILLIAM colonial gov.; b. Phila., 1731; illegitimate son of Benjamin Franklin and Deborah Read; M.A. (hon.), Oxford, (Eng.) U., 1762; married twice; m. Elizabeth Downes (1st wife), Sept. 4, 1762; 1 illegitimate son, William Temple Franklin. Often accompanied his father to Europe, also helped in father's scientific experiments; served in King George's War, 1748; comptroller Gen. Post Office, clk. Pa. Provincial Assembly, 1754-56; admitted to Middle Temple, London, Eng., later elected to bar; last royal gov. N.J., 1762-76; began controversy with patriot party in N.J., 1765; at outbreak of Revolutionary War, captured and imprisoned as Loyalist; pres. Bd. Asso. Loyalists, N.Y.C., 1778; Loyalist leanings led to break with father; went permanently to Eng., 1782; reconciled with father, 1784. Died Eng., Nov. 16, 1813.

FRANKLIN, WILLIAM BUEL engr., soldier; b. York, Pa., Feb. 27, 1823; s. Walter Simonds and Sarah (Buel) F.; grad. West Point, 1843; m. Anna L. Clarke, July 7, 1852 (died 1900). Assigned to topog. engrs.; served through Mexican war and engaged in engring. service, becoming col. 12th inf., May 14, 1861; brig. gen. vols., May 17, 1861; maj. gen. vols., July 4, 1862, and afterwards received bvt. rank of brig. gen. and maj. gen. U.S. Army; resigned March 15, 1866; became v.p. Colts Patent Fire Arms Mfg. Co., Hartford; widower. Was pres. of commn. for laying out Long Island City, 1871-72; pres. of commn. for building new State house at Hartford, Conn., 1872-73; cons. engr. of same, 1874; U.S. commr. gen. for Paris Expn., 1889; grand officer French Legion of Honor, Oct. 1889; pres. Bd. Mgrs. Nat. Soldiers' Home until 1899. Hartford, Conn. Died 1903.

FRANKS, JOHN B. army officer; b. Kansas, Mar. 10, 1890; B.S. in Civil Engring., U. of Michigan, 1917; M.S., Mass. Inst. Tech., 1925; grad. Army Indsl. Coll., 1936, Q.M. Sch., 1937. Commd. 2d lt., F.A., U.S. Army, 1918, promoted 1st lt., 1918; commd. 1st lt., Q.M.C., 1920,

and advanced through the grades to brig. gen., 1945. Decorated Legion of Merit, Oak Leaf Cluster; Bronze Star; Croix de Guerre with Palm. Home: 2700 Connecticut Av., Washington, D.C. Died Nov. 13, 1946; buried in Arlington National Cemetery.

FRANTZ, FRANK governor; b. Roanoke, Ill., May 7, 1872; s. Henry J. and Maria (Gish) F.; ed. 2 yrs. Eureka (Ill.) Coll.; m. Matilda Evans, Apr. 9, 1900; children—Frank, Louise, Matie, Virginia. First lt. 1st U.S. Vol. Cavalry "Roosevelt's Rough Riders"), May 1, 1898; capt. July 1, 1898; participated in Cuban campaign and Battle of San Juan Hill, July 3, 4, 1898; mustered out, Sept. 15, 1898. Postmaster Enid, Okla., 1901-03; U.S. Indian agt. for Osage Indians, 1903-04; gov. of Okla., 1905-07. Republican. Real estate broker, 1908-13; petroleum producer, 1913—; became chmn. bd. and gen. mgr. Franko Co.; pres. Roanoke Oil Co. Presby. Mason. Home: Wichita, Kan. Died Mar. 9, 1941.

FRANTZ, ROBERT BENJAMIN, architect; b. Waynesboro, Pa., Mar. 30, 1894; s. Samuel Ryder and Mary Elizabeth (Benson) F.; B.S., U. Mich., 1917, M.S., 1920; married Sarah L'Estrange Stanley, Mar. 1, 1918; children—Peter Benson, Joan Stanley (Mrs. Frederick Meyer). Practice of architecture in Saginaw, Michigan, 1925-71, specializing in schs., hosps., indsl. and comml. bldgs. Mem. Saginaw Planning Commn., 1926-49, pres., 1942-49; pres. Saginaw Mus. Bd. Dirs.; chmn. Commn. Code of Bldg. Ordinances, 1939. Served as 2d lt. 16th F.A., 4th Div. AEF, 1917-19. Mem. Mich. Bd. Registration for Architects, Profl. Engrs., and Land Surveyors, pres., 1951, 57, 64. Registered by National Council Archtl. Registration Bds. Fellow A.I.A. (pres. Saginaw Valley chpt.); mem. Society of Architectural Historians, Architectural League of N.Y., S.A.R. Conglist. Mason (32 deg.). Clubs: Saginaw (past president); Rotary (past pres.); Torch. Home: Saginaw MI Died June 14, 1971; buried Green Hill Cemetery, Waynesboro PA

FRASER, ARTHUR MCNUTT, educator; b. Hamiota, Man., Can., Dec. 29, 1915; s. James Moss and Marie (McNutt) F.; B.A., U. Man., 1945; M.A., Columbia, 1947, Ed.D., 1951; m. Ruth Irvine Gordon, Sept. 12, 1942; children—Loran, Bruce, Susan. Came to U.S., 1949, naturalized, 1966. Asst. prof. Whitworth Coll., Spokane, 1951-54; asso. prof. Howard Coll., Birmingham, Ala., 1954-55; prof., dir. Sch. Music, Montevallo (Ala.) State Coll. Liberal Arts, 1955-63; prof. music, head dept. U. S.C., 1963-72; conductor Huntsville (Ala.) Orch., 1955-59, Columbia Philharmonic Orch., 1964-72. Maj. Canadian Armored Corps, 1942-46. Mem. Music Tchrs. Assn., Am. Symphony Orch. League, Southeastern Choral Conductors Conf. (pres.), Columbia Art Museum, S.C. Arts Commn. (exec. com.). Home: Columbia SC Died Apr. 23, 1972; buried Columbia SC

FRASER, CECIL EATON, educator; born at Champaign, Ill., October 7, 1895; s. of Wilber John and Alice May (Eaton) F.; student U. of Ill., 1914-15, Harvard, 1915-17, B.S. (war degree as of 1918), M.B.A., 1921; M. Clara Foster; children - Diana, Constance. Field agt., Harvard Business Sch., 1921-22, research supervisor, 1922-26, also instr. in finance, 1923-26, asst. prof. finance, 1926-29, asso. prof., 1929-31; treas. and dir. Incorporated Investors, 1930-36; pres. and dir. Boston Fund, Inc. and Boston Management and Research Corp., 1936-39; returned to Harvard. Business School. mem. of staff on industrial mobilization, 1940-47, asso. prof. since 1941 and assistant dean, 1942-47. Pres. and dir. The Buckingham School, 1934-47. Served as 2d lt., later 1st lt. F.A., U.S. Army, A.E.F., Aug. 1917-May 1919; 1st lt. F.A. Res., 1919, capt., 1924, major, 1930-34; instr. Army Air Force since 1942; dir. Army Air Force War Adjustment Commission, 1945. Mem. Harvard Bus. Schl. Alumni Assn. (pres. 1928-29, mem. exec. council 1922-28, 1929-38). Pres. Cambridge Republican Council, 1934, 35; del. Mass. Republican Pre-Primary Convention, 1934; Mass. del. to Rep. Nat. Conv., 1936; mem. Cambridge Sinking Fund Commn., 1935-45; corporator Cambridge Savings Bank, 1934-47, trustee, 1939-47; trustee Avon Home; dir. East End Union; mem. Commn. on Inter-Governmental Relationship, 1942-46. Conglist. Clubs: Harvard (Boston); Harvard (New York); Faculty (Cambridge). Author: Finance (vol. X) of Manuals of Business Management, 1927; Problems in Finance, 1927 (also repub. in 3 vols., Investments, Banking, Corporation Finance, 1928), revised edit. 1930; Analyzing Our Industries (with Georges F. Doriot), 1932. Editor: The Case Method of Instruction, 1931; Industry Goes to War (with Stanley F. Teele), 1942. Home: 20 Gray Gardens W., Cambridge, Mass. Office: Morgan Hall, Harvard Business School, Soldiers Field, Boston, Died Feb. 23, 1947; buried at Fairhaven, Mass.

FRASER, FRANK EDWIN, N.G. officer; b. Tacoma, Mar. 2, 1895; s. Daniel Joseph and Bertha Orienna (Baker) F.; student LaSalle Extension U., 1922, Royal Inst. Fgn. Affairs, London, Eng., 1943; m. Helen Gladys Mitchell, July 5, 1922; children—Frank Edwin (USAF), Mary Elizabeth (wife of Elmer J. Messer, U.S. Army), William H.M. With tax and accounting div. Kennecott Copper Co., 1929-33; revenue adviser Ariz. Legislature in establishment excise revenue div. Ariz. Tax Commn., 1933-40, dir. excise revenue div., comptroller Ariz. Tax Commn., 1933-40; exec. officer Mil. Dept. of Ariz.,

1947-52; adj. gen. Ariz., 1952-58; lt. gen. (ret.); director SSS for Ariz., from 1958; mil. adviser to gov. and state legislature; hon. consul of Luxembourg for Ariz. and N.M. Served as sgt., cav., U.S. Army, 1917-19; served from lt. col. to col., AUS, 1940-46; gen. staff officer Allied Forces, 1942, gen. staff Chief Staff Supreme Allied Command, 1943, mil. govt. officer, liaison to Brit. Army, 1944, chief SHAEF Mission to Luxembourg, dep. chief Mission to Belgium, 1944. Decorated Grand Officer Adolphe of Nassau, Order Couronne du Chene, Croix de Guerre with palm and fourragere (Luxembourg); Legion of Honor, Croix de Guerre with palms, Medal of Verdun, Bronze Liberation Plaque of Metz (France); Comdr. Order of Leopold, Croix de Guerre with palm (Belgium); Order Brit. Empire; Legion of Merit with cluster, Bronze Star Medal, Soldier's Medal (U.S.). Mem. Adjutant's Gen. Assn., Nat. Guard Assn. U.S., Assn. U.S. Army, Am. Legion, Vets. Fgn. Wars, Disabled Am. Vets. Roman Catholic. Elk. Clubs: Phoenix Rotary, Arizona. Address: Sun City AZ Died Mar. 24, 1972.

FRAZER, JOHN chemist; b. Paris, France, Feb. 5, 1882 (parents Am. citizens); s. Persifor and Isabella Nevins (Whelen) F.; B.S. in chemistry, U. Pa., 1903, A.M., 1904, Ph.D., 1907; m. Mary Foxley Tilghman, June 9, 1915; children - Tilghman (dec.), Isabel, John Tench. Instr. chemistry, 1904-06, 07-09, assistant professor 1909-18, 19-21, professor, 1921-33, dean Towne Science School, 1912-18, 19-28, secretary board of deans, 1921-22, chmn. faculty policy com., 1920-21, U. Pa.; Am. exchange prof. applied sci. to French univs., 1922-23; rep. U. Pa. on Coll. Entrance Exam. Bd., 1912-18, 19-21; sec. com. on sci. and arts Franklin Inst., Phila., 1936-56. Active mem. 1st Troop, City Cav., 1903-16, hon. roll, 1921; commd. capt. Chem. Warfare Service, U.S. Army, Aug. 9, 1918; trained in France and detailed as asst. gas officer 1st A.C., and later with 78th and 6th divs. in Argonne, A.E.F., and at Hdqrs. C.W.S., at Tours, France; hon. discharged Jan. 10, 1919; lt. col. O.R.C., C.W.S., U.S. Army, 1921-29. Fellow, life mem. A.A.A.S.; life member Pennsylvania Prison Society; member American Chem. Soc., Franklin Inst. (asst. sec. 1941-56), Franklin Inst. (asst. editor Jour. 1941-48), Hist. Soc. Pa., Soc. War of 1812, Loyal Legion (sr. vice comdr. Pa. 1945), Delta Psi, Sigma Xi, Phi Beta Kappa. Republican. Clubs: St. Anthony, Phila., Mask and Wig (Philadelphia); St. Anthony (N.Y.). Home: 8015 Navajo St., Chestnut Hill, Phila. 18. Office: Franklin Inst., Phila. 3, Pa. Died June 7, 1964; buried Laurel Hill Cemetery, Phila.

FRAZER, PERSIFOR army officer; b. Newton Twp., Pa., Aug. 9, 1736; s. John and Mary (Smith) F.; m. Mary Taylor, Oct. 2, 1766. Took over Sarum Iron Works, 1766; del. to Pa. Provincial Council, 1775; mem. Pa. Com. of Safety; apptd. capt. Pa. Militia, 1776, maj., 1776; lt. col. 5th Pa. Militia, 1776; treas. Chester County (Pa.), 1781; mem. Pa. Gen. Assembly, 1781-82; commd. brig. gen. Pa. Militia, 1782; commr. to Wyoming Valley, 1785; justice Pa. Ct. of Common Pleas, 1786-92; register of wills, Pa., 1786. Died Apr. 24, 1792.

FRAZIER, ARTHUR HUGH diplomatic service; b. Heidelberg, Germany, Aug. 12, 1868; s. Benjamin West and Alice (Clark) F.; A.B., Lehigh U., 1889; studied in Germany, 1889-91; m. Freda Lloyd Davies, 1918; children - Alice Cecile, Joan. Vineyard owner in Calif., 1892-98; mem. Signal Corps, U.S. Vols., Spanish-Am. War, 1898; asst. mgr. Central Aguirre, Porto Rico, 1901-03; pvt. sec. to 2 govs. of Porto Rico, 1903-06; sec. Legation and consul gen., San Salvador, 1908-10; sec. Legation, Bogota, 1910-12; 2d sec. Embassy, Vienna, 1911-14; trans. to Rome, Oct. 1913; 2d sec. Embassy, Paris, 1914-16, 1st sec., 1916-18, counselor, 1918; attached to Supreme War Council, Paris, 1918; chargé d'affaires, Athens, 1920; Am. commr. to Austria, 1920, 21; resigned from diplomatic service, 1922. Fellow Am. Geog. Soc.; mem. Acad. Political Science. Club: University (New York). Address: Dial House, Westport, Conn.

FRAZIER, CHESTER NORTH, prof. dermatology; b. Portland, Ind., Jan. 27, 1892; s. Luther Melanchthon and Etta (North) F.; student Wooster Coll., 1911-13; B.S., Ind. U., 1915, M.D., 1917; Dr. P.H., John Hopkins, 1947; grad. study U. of Paris, 1927, U. of Munich, 1931; A.M. (honorary) Harvard University, 1948; married Sally Harmon, Aug. 3, 1918; 1 son, Philip North. Asst. in dermatology and syphilology, Ind. U., 1919-22, asso. in dermatology, Peiping (China) Union Med. Coll., 1922-26, asso. prof. dermatology and syphilology, 1927-31, professor, 1932-42, librarian, 1937-11, acting dir., 1939-40; head dermatol. service Hosp. of Peiping Union Med. Coll., 1922-42; asst. vis. physician Johns Hopkins Hosp., 1942; prof. dermatology and syphilol., U. of Tex., 1943-48; Edward Wigglesworth prof. dermatol., Harvard U., since 1948; dermatologist-in-chief John Sealy Hospital, 1942-48; consultant in dermatology, M.D. Anderson Hosp. for Cancer Research, 1944-48; cons. Children's Hospital, Boston, 1948; chief dermatol. service Mass. Gen. Hosp. since 1948; cons. Mass. Eye and Ear Infirmary, Army Med. Library (hon.). Served as 1st lt. med. corps, U.S. Army, 1918-19. Chmn. bd. dirs. Peking (China) Am. Sch., 1927-31; vice pres. Internat. Congress Dermatology and Syphilology, Copenhagen, Denmark, 1930; chmn. United China Relief, Galveston, Tex., 1945-46; nat. consultant in dermatology Wartime Post-grad. Meetings, 1945-46; consultant to surgeon gen., U.S. Army, 1945-46. Diplomate, Am. Board of Dermatology and Syphilology. Fellow A.A.A.S., American College of Physicians; member Soc. Exptl. Biology and Medicine, N.Y. Acad. Sci., Hungarian Dermatol. Soc. (corr. mem.), Soc. Investigative Dermatology (dir.), Mass. Soc. for Social Hygiene (president), Swedish Dermatological Society (corr. mem.). Dallas Acad. Ophthalmology (hon.), Human Genetics Soc., Am. Dermatol. Assn. (corr. mem.). Tex. Acad. of Science, Soc. Investigative Dermatology, Assn. Am. Physicians, Am. Assn. History of Med., Am. Acad. Dermatology and Syphilology, N.E. Dermatol. Society, Am. Venereal Disease Assn., Alpha Omega Alpha. Episcopalian. Clubs: Johns Hopkins (Baltimore, Md.); Harvard (Boston); Peking (China). Mem. bd. editors, Jour. Investigative Dermatology; contbr. articles in Am. and Chinese jours. concerning nutritional dermatoses, cutaneous aspects of vitamin deficiency, sex and immunity to syphilis and mode of action of penicillin. Co-author (with H. C. Li): Racial Variation in Immunity to Syphilis; A Formulary for External Therapy of the Skin (with I. H. Blank). Home: Cambridge MA Died Feb. 14, 1973.

FREDERICK, DANIEL ALFRED army officer; b. in Ga., June 10, 1855; grad. U.S. Mil. Acad., 1877. Commd. add. 2d lt. 10th Inf., June 15, 1877; 2d lt. 7th Inf., Aug. 9, 1877; 1st lt., Nov. 14, 1885; capt., Jan. 28, 1897; maj. 45th Vol. Inf., Aug. 17, 1899; hon. discharged vols., June 3, 1901; maj. 21st U.S. Inf., Jan. 31, 1902; a.-a.-g., July 15, 1902; assigned to 22d Inf., Jan. 25, 1906; lt. col. 19th Inf., Oct. 28, 1908; assigned to 17th Inf., Sept. 12, 1911; col. of inf., Sept. 27, 1911; assigned to 22d Inf., Mar. 5, 1912. Comd. Co. A, 7th Inf., during Spanish-Am. War, 1898; participated in Santiago campaign; served in campaigns in provinces of Cavetė and Camarnes, P.I., 1900; mustering officer, P.I., 1901; again in P.I., 1903-05, serving as adj. gen., also as mil. sec. Dept. of Visayas; duty Gen. Staff, 1909-11, Central Dept., Chicago, 1917. Address: War Dept., Washington, D.C.

FREDERICK, ROBERT TRYON, army officer; b. San Francisco, Calif., Mar. 14, 1907; s. Marcus White and Pauline Adelaide (McCurdy) F.; student Staunton (Va.) Mil. Acad., 1923-24; B.S., U.S. Mil. Acad., 1928; grad. Coast Arty. Sch., 1938, Command and Gen. Staff Sch., 1939; m. Ruth Adelaide Harloe, June 9, 1928; children—Jane Adelaide, Anne Tryon. Commd. 2d lt., U.S. Army, 1928; served through the grades to col. in Panama, Canal Zone, Hawaii and U.S.; major gen. since 1944; comdr. 45th Inf. Div. Decorated Distinguished Service Cross with Oak Leaf Cluster, Distinguished Service Medal with Oak Leaf Cluster, Silver Star, Legion of Merit with Oak Leaf Cluster, Bronze Star, Air Medal, Purple Heart with 7 Oak Leaf Clusters, Officer of the Legion of Honor, Croix de Guerre with Palm (France), Distinguished Service Order (Great Britain), Grand Officer Order of St. Charles (Monaco), Liberation Cross of Haakon VII (Norway). Home: Palo Alto CA Died Jan. 1971; buried Presidio Cemetery, San Francisco CA

FREE, EDWARD ELWAY chemist; b. Dagus Mines, Pa., May 3, 1883; s. Spencer Michael (M.D.) and May Irene (Elway) F.; grad. Bellefonte (Pa.) Acad., 1902; A.B., Cornell U., 1906; Ph.D., Johns Hopkins, 1917; m. Marion Allen, Apr. 28, 1922. Asst. chemist Agrl. Expt. Sta., U. of Ariz., 1906-07; physicist and scientist U.S. Dept. Agr., Washington, D.C., 1907-12; cons. chemist, and physicist, 1912—, head E.E. Free Laboratories, New York. Editor Scientific American, 1924-25; owner and editor "The Week's Science" (a news service). Lecturer on Outlines of Science, New York U., 1926-34. Served as capt. Ordnance Dept., U.S.A., 1917-18; maj. C.W.S., 1918-19. Fellow A.A.A.S., Wash. Acad. of Science, Acoustical Soc. America (treas. 1930-34). Died Nov. 24, 1939.

FREEMAN, ALLEN WEIR sanitarian; b. Lynchburg, Va., Jan. 7, 1881: s. Walker Burford and Bettie Allen (Hammer) F.; student Richmond (Va.) Coll., 1895-1900, B.S., 1899; M.D., Johns Hopkins, 1905, LL.D., 1952; Sc.D., U. Richmond (Va.), 1950; married Julia Griffin Brown, June 30, 1906; children-Bettie Charter (Mrs. Cuthbert Rogerson), Margaret Brown (Mrs. L. A. Poole, Jr.). Interne Newark (N.J.) City Hosp., 1905-06; demonstrator in physiology, Med. Coll. of Va., 1906-07; med. insp. Richmond Health Dept., 1907-08; asst. commr. of health, Va., 1908-15; state dir. Rockefeller Hookworm Commission for Va., 1910-14; epidemiologist U.S. P.H.S., 1915-17; state commr. of health, Ohio, 1917-21; with Johns Hopkins U. since 1921, as res. lecturer pub. health administrn., School of Hygiene and Pub. Health, 1921-23, prof., 1923-46, dean, 1934-37, prof. emeritus since 1946; cons. Md. State Health Dept. Commd. major Med. Corps, U.S. Army, 1918; was epidemiologist to bd. for investigation of pneumonia in Army camps, Camp Funston, Kan., and Camp Pike, Ark.; special member Rockefeller Foundation, 1926; lecturer, University of Rio de Janeiro, Brazil, 1926. Fellow American Public Health Assn. (pres. 1942). Mem. A.M.A., Medical Soc. of Va., Phi Gamma Delta, Sigma Xi, Phi Beta Kappa, Delta Omega (nat. pres. 1932). Democrat. Episcopalian. Club: Johns Hopkins (Baltimore). Author: Five Million Patients. Contbr. numerous articles pertaining to epidemiology and public health administrn. Home: Wyman Park Apts., Baltimore 11. Office: 2411 N. Charles St., Balt. 18. Died July 3, 1954; buried Hollywood Cemetery. Richmond, Va.

FREEMAN, CHARLES SEYMOUR, naval officer, retired; b. Nov. 19, 1878; s. Henry Anthony and Margaret Anne (Liston) F.; grad. U.S. Naval Academy, 1900; married Alice Nancy Kimball, Aug. 7, 1909 (deceased August 16, 1943); children—Mildred (wife of Col. K. W. Treacy, U.S. Army), Phyllis (wife of Comdr. R. B. Miller, Med. Corps, U.S. Navy), Kenneth Kimball; married 2d Mrs. Fleet Murdaugh Carney, April 19, 1951. Commissioned ensign United States Navy, and advanced through the grades to vice admiral, June 1942; commander U.S.S. Manchuria, U.S.S. Maui, U.S.S. Orizaba, World War I; supt. Naval Observatory, 1927-30; comd. U.S. Forces in Cuban waters, 1933-34; comdt. Norfolk Navy Yard, Portsmouth, Va., 1935-37; Submarine Force, U.S. Fleet, 1937-39; mem. Gen. Bd. of Navy, 1939-40; successively comdt. Puget Sound Navy Yard, comdt. 13th Naval Dist., comdr. Northwest Sea Frontier, World War II; ret., 1942; vice president National Economic Council, Inc. Decorated Navy Cross, Legion of Merit. Editor: Review of Pre-War Merchant Shipping in Eastern Waters. Clubs: New York Yacht; Army and Navy (Washington); Army-Navy Country (Arlington); The University. Address: Portsmouth VA Died Feb. 22, 1969; buried Arlington National Cemetery, Arlington VA

FREEMAN, CHARLES WEST dentist; b. Sharon, Vt., Jan. 18, 1892; s. Frederick D. and Lucy S. (West) F.; D.D.S., Northwestern U., 1912, M.S., 1925; m. Ruth A. Sprague, Sept. 30, 1916; children - Arthur Gilwer, Robert Sprague. Began practice dentistry, Chgo., 1912; mem. faculty Northwestern U., Dental Sch., since 1912; asst. prof., 1920-25, asso. prof., 1925-33, prof. oral surgery since 1933, asst. dean, 1933-38, dean 1938-53. Served as maj. Dental Corps, U.S. Army, Base Hosp., France, 2 yrs. Editor Bull. Chgo. Dental Soc., 1929-34. Fellow Am. Coll. Dentists; fellow in dental surgery Royal Coll. Surgeons; mem. Am. Dental Assn., Ill., Chgo. dental socs., Inst. Medicine Chgo., Internat. Assn. for Dental Research, Am. Assn. Dental Schs., Sigma Xi, Omicron Kappa Upsilon, Delta Sigma Delta. Republican. Methodist. Mason. Home: 2501 Prospect Av., Evanston, Ill. Office: 311 E. Chicago Av., Chicago 60611. Died June 26, 1960.

FREEMAN, HENRY BLANCHARD brig. gen.; b. Mt. Vernon, O., Jan. 17, 1837; s. Luther and Charlotte (Blanchard) F.; Puritan ancestry; ed. pub. schs., Sloans Acad., Mt. Vernon, O.; m. Sarah E. Darlington, Apr. 26, 1866. Pvt. Co. G, 10th Inf., July 16, 1855-Feb. 5, 1856; promoted through the various grades to col. 24th Inf., Oct. 4, 1898; brig. gen. U.S.A., Jan. 16, 1901; retired by operation of law, Jan. 17, 1901. Bvtd.: capt., Dec. 31, 1862, "for gallant and meritorious services in battle of Murfreesboro, Tenn."; maj., Sept. 20, 1863, for same in battle of Chickamauga, Ga. Awarded Congressional Medal of Honor, Feb. 17, 1894, "for distinguished gallantry in battle of Stone River." Was taken prisoner of war, Chickamauga; escaped from Libby; was recaptured and again escaped; acting asst. adj. gen. 17th Corps; served on frontier in Sioux war, 1867-68, Powder River and Fort Phil. Kearney, in Cheyenne war; in Kan., 1868-69; in Sioux war, 1876, Yellowstone and Custer; in Ute war in Colo., 1879; served in Cuba and P.I. Home: Washington, D.C. Died Oct. 16, 1915.

FREEMAN, HENRY VARNUM judge; b. Bridgeton, N.J., Dec. 10, 1842; of Pilgrim ancestry; s. Henry and Mary (Bangs) F.; A.B., Yale, 1869, A.M., 1874; studied law, New Haven, Conn., and Chicago; admitted to bar, 1872; m. Mary L. Curtis, Oct. 16, 1873. Enlisted Company K, 74th Ill. Inf., Aug. 6, 1862, and made 1st sergt.; capt. 12th U.S. Colored Inf., Aug. 24, 1863; hon. disch., July, 1865; practiced law in Chicago, 1873-93; elected judge Superior Ct., Nov., 1893; reelected, 1898; presiding justice June, 1898. Republican. Professorial lecturer legal ethics and med. jurisprudence, U. of Chicago, and lecturer on legal ethics, law dept. same. Home: Chicago, Ill. Died Sept. 16, 1916.

FREEMAN, JAMES EDWARD bishop; b. New York, N.Y., July 24, 1866; ed. pub. schs., and 15 yrs. in legal and accounting depts. L.I. and N.Y.C. & H.R. rys.; theol. course under Bishop Henry C. Potter and diocesan chaplains; D.D., Seabury Div. Sch., 1913; LL.D., Kenyon College, 1925, Brown U., 1926, Dickinson College, 1931; S.T.D., Bowdoin Coll., 1932; D.C.L., George Washington U., 1933; LL.D., U. of California, 1937; m. Ella Vigelius, April 19, 1890. Deacon, 1894, priest, 1895, P.E. Church; asst. St. John's Ch., Yonkers, N.Y., 1894-95; rector St. Andrew's Memorial Ch., Yonkers, 1894-1910, St. Mark's Ch., Minneapolis, 1910-21, Epiphany Ch., Washington, D.C., 1921; consecrated bishop of Washington, 1923. Layman Beecher lecturer, Yale, 1928. Chaplain, rank of maj., O.R.C. Founder of Hollywood Inn (workingmen's club), Yonkers; also developed similar clubs in Minneapolis. Elected bishop coadjutor of Western Texas, 1911 (declined). Clubs: Cosmos, Chevy Chase (Washington, D.C.); Yale (New York); Elks, Traffic, Dunwoody Country (Yonkers, N.Y.). Author: If Not the Saloon - What? 1902; The Man and the

Master, 1905; Themes in Verse, 1904; The Ambassador, 1928; also Everyday Religion, Little Sermons. Home: Bishop's House, Washington, D.C. Died June 6, 1943.

FREEMAN, JOHN CHARLES univ. prof.; b. Lisle, N.Y., Feb. 14, 1842; s. Charles Waldo and Charlotte (Brockway) F.; A.B., U. of Mich., 1868, A.M., 1871; B.D., Union Theol. Sem., 1872; (LL.D., U. of Chicago, 1880); m. Emma Belden, 1870. Served in Civil War, 27th and 168th N.Y. Vol. Inf., 1862-63; capt., 1st N.Y. Vet. Cav., 1864; asst. insp. gen. cab. corps.; comd. expdn. to Lewisburg and the Greenbrier, Apr. 1865. Asst. prof. Greek, U. of Chicago, 1868-74; prof. Latin, 1874-78, English lit., 1879—, U. of Wis. Republican. U.S. consul at Copenhagen, 1900; U.S. chargé d'affaires to Denmark, 1901. Editor of Xenophon's Memorabilia and of Dialogues of Lucian; History of American Literature. Home: Madison, Wis. Died 1911.

FREEMAN, MILLER publisher; b. Ogden, Utah, July 20, 1875; s. Legh Richmond and Ada Virginia (Miller) F.; ed. pub. sch. Ahtanum, Wash.; hon. A.M., Whitman Coll., Walla Walla, Wash.; m. Bessie Lea Bogle, Oct. 15, 1906: children-William Bogle, Frederick Kemper, Miller. Founder and became pub. The Ranch, 1897 (merged with Wash. Farmer), Idaho Farmer, Oregon Farmer (operated as N.W. Farm Trio) 1912-15, Pacific Fisherman, 1903, Pacific Motor Boat, 1908, Motorship, 1916, Canning Age, 1919, Pulp & Paper, 1926, Mining World, San Francisco, 1939, The Lumberman; pres. Miller Freeman Publs. (Seattle), Western Trade Jours. (San Francisco); dir. Pacific Nat. Bank. Founder Naval Militia, Wash., 1910, rank of comdr., 1910-19; capt. naval res., 1919-37; comdt. U.S. Naval Training Camp, Seattle, 1917-19. Chairman Pacific Fisheries Conf. Cons. N. Pacific Fisheries Treaty. Mem. Rep. National Committee, 1937-40. Mem. Wash. Ho. of Rep., 1913, Wash. State Veterans Commn., 1919-22, International Fisheries Commn., 1925-33, Wash. State Planning Council, 1934-41. Republican. Clubs: Rainier, Seattle Yacht; Overlake Golf and Country (Bellevue). Home: Bellevue, Wash. Office: 71 Columbia St., Seattle. Died Sept. 18, 1955.

FREEMAN, MONROE EDWARD, army officer; b. Washington, Apr. 1, 1906; s. Edward M. and Grace D. (Studeman) F.; B.S., U. Minn., 1928, M.S., 1929, Ph.D., 1931; m. Christina Gray Clinch, Aug. 30, 1929; children—Mary Gray (Mrs. John B. Kelly), Monroe Edward. Instr. chemistry U. Ariz., 1929-30; asst. prof. bio-chemistry U. Me., 1930-36; research prof. chemistry U. Mass., 1936-45; resident prof. research chemistry, 1945-47; chief chem. Walter Reed Army Inst. Research, 1947-53; asst. chief Med. Service Corps, Office Surgeon Gen., 1950-54; research coordinator Army Gen. Staff, 1953-56; comdg. officer European Research Office, U.S. Army, 1956-60; Advanced Project Research Agy. Office Sec. Def., 1960-61; ret., 1961; dir. Sci. Information Exchange, Smithsonian Instn., 1961-71. Served to maj. AUS, 1942-45, to col. U.S. Army, 1947-61. Decorated Army Commendation medal, Legion of Merit. Fellow Am. Assn. Clin. Chemists (pres. 1954), Am. Bd. Clin. Chemists (bd. dirs. 1958-64); mem. A.A.A.S., Soc. Exptl. Biology and Medicine, Internat. Union Pure and Applied Chemistry, Internat. Commn. Clin. Chemistry (sec. 1958-60, pres. 1960-64), Washington Acad. Medicine, Washington Acad. Sci., Internat. Fedn. Clin. Chemists (pres. 1960-64), Sigma Xi, Delta Upsilon. Episcopalian. Club: Cosmos (Washington). Contbr. profl. jours. Home: Washington DC Died Sept. 16, 1972; buried Arlington Nat. Cemetery.

FREEMAN, NATHANIEL jurist, physician; b. Dennis, Mass., Mar. 28, 1741; s. Edmund and Martha (Otis) F.; studied medicine under Dr. Cobb, Thompson, Conn.; studied law under James Otis, Sr. (his great-uncle), Sandwich, Mass., 1765; m. Tryphosa Colton, May 5, 1763; m. 2d, Elizabeth Gifford, Apr. 7, 1799; 20 children including Frederick, Nathaniel. Practiced medicine, Sandwich, 1765-1804; also practiced law; favored colonial cause during Am. Revolution; mem. Sandwich Com. of Correspondence; del. from Sandwich to Watertown Provincial Congress, 1775; apptd. lt. col., then col. 1st Barnstable (Mass.) Regt.; negotiated with Penobscot Indians, served in expdn. against British in R.I.; mem. Mass. Legislature, 1778-80; employed by Gen. George Washington on mission to West Point, 1779; resigned as brig. gen. from Mass. Militia, 1793; chief justice Mass. Ct. of Common Pleas; a founder Sandwich Acad. Author: Charge to the Grand Jury...at Barnstable, 1802. Died Sandwich, Sept. 20, 1827.

FREEMAN, NATHANIEL, JR. congressman; b. Sandwich, Mass., May 1, 1766; grad. Harvard, 1787; studied law. Admitted to bar, circa 1791, began practice of law, Sandwich and Cape Cod dist.; served as brigade maj. Mass. Militia, 16 years; justice of peace, 1793; mem. U.S. Ho. of Reps. from Mass., 4th-5th congresses, 1795-99. Died Sandwich, Aug. 22, 1800; buried Old Burial Ground.

FREEMAN, TALBOT OTIS pub. relations cons.; b. Boston, Sept. 11, 1890; s. Daniel Allen and Lucy Talbot (Swanton) F.; S.B., Harvard, 1914; m. Ellen Roy Goldsborough, July 27, 1934; children-Talbot Otis, Elizabeth Carroll. Mgr. Hartford (Conn.) Home Co., ins., 1921-23; dir. Community Bond & Mortgage Co., Waterbury, Conn., 1925-26; treas., dir., mem. exec. com. Colonial Air Transport, Hartford and N.Y.C., 1926-29; v.p., dir., mem. exec. com. Fairchild Aviation Corp., N.Y.C., 1928-30; dir. Aero Supply Mfg. Co., College Point, N.Y., 1928-30; dir. Aero Supply Mfg. Co., College Point, N.Y., 1928-30; asst. to pres. Aviation Corp., N.Y.C., 1929-30; mem. exec. com. Waco Aircraft Corp., Troy, O., 1929-30; v.p., dir., mem. exec. com. Air Investors, Inc., N.Y.C., 1929-34; v.p., sec., dir., mem. exec. com. Fed. Broadcasting Corp., N.Y.C., 1933-34; regional group supr. Travelers Ins. Co., Hartford, 1934-39; v.p. Pepsi-Cola Co., L.I. City, N.Y., 1940-50; v.p., dir. Compagnia Ingenos Azuoarreros Matanzas, Cuba, 1944-50. Dir., sec., chmn. pub. relations adv. com. Grocery Mfrs. Am., 1946-50; trustee Nutrition Found., Inc., 1947-50; dir., exec. com. Food Industry War Com., and successor Food Industry Council, 1944-47, Mem. soft drink industry adv. com. W.P.B. Mem. gov.'s staff Conn., 1925-31, first aviation insp., 1923-25; pilot inaugural flight, air mail, New York-Boston, July 2, 1926. Served as 1st lt. 140th Air Squadron, overseas, 1917-18; maj., comdg. 43d Div. A.S., Conn. N.G., 1923-25. Mem. Nat. Aero. Assn. (chmn. legislative com. 1926-32), Pub. Relations Soc. Am., Mass. Soc. Mayflower Descs., Am. Arbitration Assn. Republican. Episcopalian. Club: Harvard (N.Y.C.). Co-Author: World Situation on Sugar, 1946. Contbr. to mags. Home: 103 E. 86th St., N.Y.C. Died Dec. 6, 1955.

FREER, ROMEO HOYT ex-congressman; b. Bazetta, O., Nov. 9, 1845; s. Josiah D. and Caroline P. (Brown) F.; ed. Grand River Inst., Austinburg, O.; m. Mary Iams, July 8, 1884. Served in Union Army, 1862-5; subsequently capt., maj., col. 1st reg., W. Va. N.G.; admitted to bar, 1868; asst. pros. atty. Kanawha County, W.Va., 1868-70, pros. atty., 1870-73; U.S. consul Nicaragua, 1873-7; mem. legislature, 1891; pros. atty. Ritchie Co., 1892-97; judge 4th Jud. Dist., 1896-99; mem. 56th Congress; atty.-gen., W.Va., several yrs. from 1901; postmaster of Harrisville, W.Va., 1907—. Republican. Grand Master, I.O.O.F.; dept. comdr. G.A.R. Address: Harrisville, W.Va. Deceased.

FREIBERG, ALBERT HENRY orthopedic surgeon; b. Cincinnati, Aug. 17, 1868; s. Joseph and Amalia F.; U. of Cincinnati; M.D., Med. Coll. of O. (U. of Cincinnati), 1890; univs. Würzburg, Strassburg, Berlin and Vienna; LL.D., Cedarville Coll., 1915; m. Jeannette Frieberg, Dec. 1, 1897; children—Joseph A., Albert M. Practiced at Cincinnati, 1893; prof. orthopedic surgery, med. dept. U. of Cincinnati, 1902-38, emeritus. Cons. orthopedic surgeon, Cincinnati and Children's hosps.; dir. orthopedic service, Jewish Hospital. Was mem. advisory bd. on orthopedics, and maj., M.C., U.S.A. Fellow Am. Coll. Surgeons, Am. Acad. Orthopedic Surgery; mem. Advisory Com. on Crippled Children, to Children's Bureau, U.S. Dept. of Labor. Mem. bd. of govs. Hebrew Union Coll.; mem. bd. of trustees, Cincinnati, O. Died July 14, 1940.

FREIMAN, HENRY DAVID, physician; b. Phila., Nov. 5,21913; s. Philip and Gussie Freiman; M.D., U. Pa., 1937; m. Rose Specter, Apr. 18, 1943; children—David, Marc, Harriet. Intern, Mercy Hosp., Altoona, Pa., 1937-38; resident in pathology Grad. Hosp., U. Pa., Phila., 1946-47, student basic course in internal medicine Grad. Sch. Med., 1947-48; resident in medicine Albert Einstein Med. Center No. Div., Phila., 1948-49, adj. dept. gastroenterology, until 1970. Served to maj., M.D., AUS, 1943-46. Diplomate Am. Bd. Internal Medicine. Fellow A.C.P.; mem. A.M.A. Home: Philadelphia PA Died Aug. 17, 1970; buried Roosevelt Meml. Park, Philadelphia PA

FRELINGHUYSEN, FREDERICK army officer, senator; b. Somerville, N.J., Apr. 13, 1753; s. Rev. John and Dinah (Van Berg) F.; grad. Princeton (formerly Coll. of N.J.), 1770; m. Gertrude Schenck, children include Theodore; m. 2d., Ann Yard. Admitted to N.J. bar, 1774; rep. to N.J. Provincial Congress from Somerset County, 1775-76; Minute Men.; served as maj. Minute Men; capt. arty. N.J. Militia, then maj., col., aide-de-camp to Gen. Philemon Dickinson; commanded arty. corps at battles of Trenton, Springfield, Elizabethtown; participated in Battle of Monmouth Ct. House, 1778; mem. Continental Congress, 1778-83; mem. N.J. Legislative Council until 1782; mem. N.J. Gen. Assembly, 1784, 1800, 1804; mem. N.J. Conv. which ratified U.S. Constn., 1787; brig. gen. in campaign against Western Indians; 1790; served as maj. gen. N.J. Militia during Whiskey Rebellion, 1794; mem. U.S. Senate from N.J., 1793-96; trustee Princeton, 1802-04. Died Millstone, N.J., Apr. 13, 1804; buried Old Cemetery, Weston, N.J.

FRELINGHUYSEN, FREDERICK lawyer; b. Ocean Twp., N.J., Aug. 12, 1903; s. Frederick and Estelle Burnet (Kinney) F.; grad. Newark Acad., 1920; A. B., Princeton, 1924; LL.B., Harvard, 1927; m. Elizabeth Van Cortlandt Lyman, Mar. 3, 1937. Admitted to N.J. bar, 1928, asso. Pitney, Hardin & Skinner (now Pitney, Hardin & Kipp), 1927-31, member firm, 1931 - ; dir. Firemen's Insurance Company, Commercial Insurance Company; mem. board managers Howard Savs. Instn. Trustee Fitkin Meml. Hospital, Neptune, N.J. Served as lt. comdr. USNR, 1942-45. Decorated Bronze Star. Mem. N.J. Hist. Society (trustee), Am., N.J., Essex County bar assns. Home: P.O. Box Holmdel, Pleasant Valley Rd., Marlboro Twp., N.J. Office: 570 Broad St. Newark 2. Died May 26, 1966; buried Mt. Pleasant Cemetery, Newark.

FREMMING, MORRIS A. govt. ofcl.; b. Ft. Dodge, Ia., July 27, 1902; s. Andrew A. and Mathilda (Soder) F.; student Tobin College, 1922-23: married to Patricia Dorothy Morgan, on June 9, 1928; children-Richard Arthur, Michael Douglas, Patrick David. Agent Bureau Internal Revenue, Dallas, 1935-41, group chief field and office group, 1945-51, asst. internal revenue agt. in charge, 1951-52, dist. commr., Birmingham, Ala., 1952-53, regional commnr., San Francisco, since 1953. Served as lt. comdr., U.S. Navy, PTO, 1943-45. Decorated: Am. Def., Am. Area, Pacific Area with 3 battle stars, World War II medals (Navy). Lutheran. Address: 7011 Shook Rd., Dallas. Died Nov. 17, 1953; buried Field of Honor, Restland Meml. Park, Dallas.

FREMONT, JOHN CHARLES army officer, explorer; senator, territorial gov.; b. Savannah, Ga., Jan. 21, 1813; s. Jean Charles and Ann Whiting (Pryor) F.; attended Charleston Coll., 1829-31 (expelled); m. Jessie Benton, Oct. 19, 1851; 1 dau., Elizabeth. Commd. 2d lt. Topog. Corps, U.S. Army explored Des Moines River; helped make surveys in Carolina mountains, also in Ga.; accompanied expdn. of J.N. Nicollet to plateau between Upper Mississippi and Missouri rivers; mapped parts of Ia. Territory, 1841; made 1st important exploration to Wind River, Chain of the Rockies (with Kit Carson as guide), 1842; published Report of the Exploring Expedition of the Rocky Mountains, 1843; explored West to Ore. and South to Santa Fe, N.M., 1843-44 (expdn. left early because his wife informed him that expdn. was to be recalled); made survey of Central Rockies, Gt. Salt Lake Region, also part of Sierra Nevada; participated prominently in conquest of Cal.; helped capture Los Angeles during Mexican War, 1846; apptd. civil gov. Cal., 1847; involved in Stockton-Kearny mil. quarrel, refused to obey orders, arrested for mutiny, court martialled, Washington, 1847-48, found guilty of mutiny, disobedience, conduct prejudicial to order; penalty remitted by Pres. Polk; resigned from U.S. Army to lead an expdn. subsidized by pvt. interests in Cal. to locate railraod passes from Upper Rio Grande into Cal., largely unsuccessful, 1848-49; mem. U.S. Senate from Cal. (one of 1st 2 senators from Cal.) Sept. 9, 1850-Mar. 4, 1815; led expdn. in search of So. route for Pacific R.R., 1852-54; 1st Republican and Nat. Am. (Know Nothing) Party candidate for U.S. Pes., 1856; in quartz mining bus., Mariposa, Cal.; served as maj. gen. U.S. Army in charge of Dept. of West during Civil War, removed because of his ordering of the "confiscation of rebel property" (including slaves); comdr. Mountain Dept. in Western Va., 1862; Radical Republican nominee for U.S. Pres. (withdrew before elections), 1864; pres., promoter Memphis & El Paso R.R., circa 1865-73; lost fortune in railroad ventures, 1870; territorial gov. Ariz., 1878-83; restored to U.S. Army as maj. gen., 1890; called "Pathfinder" Died N.Y.C., July 13, 1890; buried Piermont on the Hudson, N.Y.

FREMONT, JOHN CHARLES naval officer; b. San Francisco, Apr. 19, 1849; s. Maj. Gen. John Charles (U.S.A.) and Jessie (Benton) F.; grad. U.S. Naval Acad., 1872; adding expert studies in torpedoes, elec. science and ordnance; m. Sally Anderson, May 27, 1877. Promoted through various grades to rank of capt., Oct. 10, 1906. Comd. U.S.S. Pinta, 1875-77 (suppressed riots Baltimore, 1877); U.S.S. Drift, 1883-85; torpedo boat Porter in Spanish-Am. War; comdt. Cavite Navy Yard, 1899-1901; U.S.S. Calgoa, 1902-03; was comdg. U.S. monitor Florida, June 1903; 6 months' spl. duty as expert on searchlights on army bd. for coast fortification, 1902; naval attaché Paris and St. Petersburg, 1906-07; comdg. Mississippi, 1908-09. Died 1911.

FRENCH, EDWARD L(IVINGSTONE), found. exec.; b. Scunthorpe, Eng., Dec. 15, 1916; s. William M. and Elizabeth (Picken) F.; A.B., Ursinus Coll., 1938; M.A., U. Pa., 1947, Ph.D., 1950; m. Jean Parker Wingate, June 27, 1942; children—Elizabeth, Jean, Edward Livingstone. Tchr., Chestnut Hill Acad., 1938-43; chief psychologist Vineland Tng. Sch., 1949-50; dir. psychology and edn. Devereux Schs., 1950-57; trustee Devereux Found., Devon, Pa., 1954-69, pres., 1957-69; pres. Inst. Biochem. and Behavioral Research, 1964-69. Served from pvt. to sgt., AUS, 1943-46. Decorated Bronze Star medal. Fellow A.A.A.S., Soc. Research Child Devel., Am. Assn. Mental Deficiency, Orton Soc., Am. Psychol. Assn., N.Y. Acad. Sci.; member American Management Assn. Author: Child in the Shadows, 1960; How to Help Your Retarded Child, 1967; also articles, chpts. tech. books. Home: Wayne PA

FRENCH, EDWARD VINTON fire ins. co. exec.; b. Lynn, Mass., Mar. 11, 1868; s. Benjamin Vinton and Elisa (Tufts) F.; B.S., Mass. Inst. Tech., 1889; m. Mary O. Wentworth, Oct. 26, 1892; children-Helen Wentworth (Mrs. Jerome C. Greene), Margaret Vinton (Mrs. Sandford G. Gorton). Hydraulic testing, elec. engring. and spl. inspections, Asso. Factory Mut. Fire Ins. Cos., 1892-1906; v.p., engr. Arkwright Mut. Fire Ins. Co., 1906-20, pres., 1920-43, chmn. bd., 1943-46; dir. Ark. Mut. Fire Ins. Co., Brockton Edison Co.; trustee Eastern Utilities Assos. Served as maj. U.S. Army in charge fire protection work, France, World

War I. Mem. Am. Soc. M.E., Am. Soc. E.E., Am. Water Works Assn., N.E. Water Works Assn., Nat. Fire Protection Assn. Episcopalian. Clubs: Engineers. Down Town, Episcopalian, North Andover Country. Home: 20 School St., Andover, Mass. Died Dec. 19, 1957.

FRENCH, FRANCIS HENRY army officer; b. in Indiana, Sept. 27, 1857; grad. U.S. Mil. Acad., 1879, Army War Coll., 1912. Commd. 2d lt., June 13, 1879; 1st lt., Mar. 24, 1888; capt., Nov. 26, 1894; maj. 16th Inf., Feb. 28, 1901; lt. col., 12th Inf., June 25, 1906; assigned to 11th Inf., Jan. 13, 1911; col. 28th Inf., Feb. 15, 1911; assigned to 2d Inf., Nov. 23, 1912, to 21st Inf., Oct. 1, 1915; brig. gen., Sept. 30, 1916; maj. gen. N.A., Aug. 5, 1917. Duty on Mexican border, 1916, 17; apptd. comdr. Camp Jackson, Columbus, S.C., 1917; hon. disch. as maj. gen., Mar. 27, 1918. Died Mar. 10, 1921.

FRENCH, FRANK CHAUNCEY engr., educator; b. Humboldt, Ia., Feb. 20, 1876; s. David Baker and Mary Rachel (McConnell) F.; B.C.E., Ia. State Coll., 1896, C.E., 1905; m. Theo. C. Plambeck, Jan. 1, 1907; children-Frank C., Dorothy Josephine, Tom Ellis, Montana Wands, David Jerry. Served as location and constrn. engr. rys. and as asso. prof. civ. engring., Ia. State Coll., until 1906, sr. constrn. engr., with U.S. Govt., P.I., 1906-07; asso. prof. civil engring., U. Utah, 1907-09; cons. engr., Salt Lake City, 1910-11; designing engr. Butte Superior Copper Co., 1912-14; supt. constrn. Kennecott Copper Corp., Latouche, Alaska, 1915-17; supt. and chief engr. Colo. Consol. Mines & Power Co., Lake City, Colo., 1919-23; became dean Marquette U., Milw., 1924; cons. civil and mining engr. and country judge of Hinsdale County, Colo.; cons. engr. U.S. Treasury Dept., 1931-42. Commd. capt. engrs., U.S. Army, 1917, maj., 1918, lt. col. O.R.C., 1924, col. 1935. With War Dept., U.S. Army Engrs., 1942-46, ret., 1946—. Formerly mem. Am. Soc. C.E., Ia. Engrs. Soc., Milw. Engrs. Soc. Am., Assn. Cooperative Schs. (dir.). Democrat. Mason (Shriner). Home: Box D, Lake City, Colo. Died Dec. 23, 1956.

FRENCH, LEIGH HILL engineer; b. Dover, N.H., Oct. 1, 1863; s. George F. and Clara Shackford (Hill) F.; ed. Portland (Me.) High Sch.; M.D., U. of Minn., 1894. Practiced medicine in Washington, 1897. Capt. and insp. rifle practices, Washington, 1898; maj. 3d Cav. U.S.V. "Rough Riders"), 1898. Admitted to bar, 1902. Prominent in development of Alaska, building ry., and hydraulic mining waterways. Mem. Loyal Legion, Arctic Brotherhood, Am. Inst. Mining Engrs. Pres. Tex. Boy Scouts, 1920. Clubs: Cosmos, Chevy Chase, Army and Navy (Washington, D.C.); Worcester (Worcester, Mass.). Apptd. lt. comdr. U.S.N. and assigned to Am. Embassy, Paris, France, as asst. naval attaché, 1918; trans. to U.S. Army Air Service as capt., Aug. 1918. Big game hunter in India, Africa, Alaska, etc. Author: Sanitary Conditions at Camp Thomas During 1898, 1898: Nome Nuggets, 1902; Seward's Land of Gold, 1905; also medical books and brochures. Home: Flintridge, Pasadena, Calif.

FRENCH, ROY LAVERNE, journalism educator; b. Eureka, Kan., Aug. 6, 1888; s. Albert Lord and Cora Alice (Emmerson) F.; A.B., U. of Wis., 1923, M.A., 1924; Oberlander Trust fellow with study of newspapers in Germany, 1936; m. Una Odetta Meredith, Sept. 22, 1917. Instr. Sch. of Journalism, U. of Wis., 1923-24; organizer and head of dept. of journalism, Univ. of N.D., 1924-27; chmn. and organizer of dept. of journalism, U. of Southern Calif., 1927-33, dir. Sch. Journalism, 1933-53. Served as private, A.E.F. (wounded in action), 1918-19, wearer of the Purple Heart. Major A.C., 1942, on duty with 8th Bomber command hdqrs. in England, as specialist in bomber raid reporting. Intelligence Sect., 1942-43, with hdqrs. of 2d Air Force, as instr. combat intelligence, 1943-44. Vice pres. The Chalfant Press, Inc., printing the only newspapers in eastern Calif.; Inyo Independent, Inyo Register, The Owens Valley Progress-Citizen, Bridgeport Chronicle-Union. Mem. Calif. Newspaper Pubs. Assn., Assn. for Education in Journalism, National Collegiate Players, Live Oaks Tennis Assn., Am. Inst. Journalists (treas.), Assn. Accredited Schs. and Depts. Journalism (v.p.), Sigma Delta Chi (nat. pres., 1926-27), Theta Delta Chi, Phi Kappa Phi. Clubs: Greater Los Angeles Press. Home: Alhambra CA Died Mar. 23, 1968; buried San Gabriel Cemetery, San Gabriel CA

FRENCH, SAMUEL GIBBS soldier; b. Gloucester Co., N.J., Nov. 22, 1818; s. Samuel F.; grad. U.S. Mil. Acad., 1843; in U.S.A. until May 1856, when he resigned, having reached grade of capt.; served in Mexican War and took part in battles of Palo Alto, Resaca de la Palma, Monterey and Buena Vista (severely wounded); m. E. Matilda Roberts; m. 2d, Mary E. Abercrombie. Cotton planter, Greenville, Miss., 1856-78; col. and chief of ordnance, Army of State of Miss., before he joined the Confederacy; commd. brig. gen. C.S.A., Oct. 23, 1861; maj. gen., Aug. 31, 1862; served in Army of Northern Va., Oct. 1861, to June 1863; comd. Dept. of N.C. and Southern Va., July 1862 to June 1863, when he was sent in the West on the Dalton and Atlanta campaign; took part in many battles, blockaded the Potomac at Evansport, 1861-62; comd. the troops at Harrison's Landing on the James River (where he shelled McClellan's army from midnight to dawn, July 31, 1862, with 45 pieces of artillery), Kingstown, Whitehall, Rome, Tilton; fought the battle of Allatoona, Kenesaw Mountain, defeating Gen. McPherson's assault, and Jackson, Miss., on the Meridian campaign. Home: Pensacola, Fla. Died 1910.

FRENCH, WILLARD soldier; b. Boston, June 21, 1854; ed. in New Haven, Conn., Berlin and Leipzig; m. Louise J. Dutton, g.d. James King, of William, famous in the history of Cal. Extensive traveler in all prin. countries of the world; served with British Army in India, Egypt and Blue Nile, S. Africa, etc., with commn. of lt.-col.; in recent yrs. has lectured in Eng. and America. Author of several books and contbr. to leading mags. and jours. Address: Washington, D.C.

FRENCH, WILLIAM HENRY army officer; b. Balt., Jan. 13, 1815; s. William French; grad. U.S. Mil. Acad., 1837. Commd. 1st lt. U.S. Army, 1838, capt., 1848; served in Seminole and Mexican wars; commd. maj., arty. U.S. Army, also brig. gen. U.S. volunteers, 1861; served in Army of Potomac; promoted maj. gen. U.S. Volunteers, 1862, served in battles of Fredericksburg, Chancellorsville and Harper's Ferry; commanded 3d Corps, 1863, mustered out of Volunteer Service, 1864, saw no further active duty in Civil War; commd. lt. col. U.S. Army, 1864, col., 1877, ret., 1880. Died Washington, D.C., May 20, 1881.

FRERET, WILLIAM ALFRED architect; b. New Orleans, La., Jan. 19, 1833; s. William and Fanny (Salkeld) F.; ed. New Orleans and Baton Rouge, La.; m. Woodville, Miss., Dec. 23, 1865, Carrie H. Lewis of Shreveport, La. Engaged in profession of architect at New Orleans; entered Confederate army as private, 5th Company, Washington Arty., 1861, and promoted from time to time, becoming lt.-col. engrs.; served on staff Gen. Kirby Smith; asst. chief and acting chief trans-Mississippi dept. until surrender. State engr. La., 1866-68; afterward had charge construction of 16 pub. schs. of Mc Donough Fund; supervising architect U.S. Govt., 1887-90; architect in reconstruction of State House, Baton Rouge; State Univ., pineville, La., Univ. of Ala., Tuscaloosa, etc. Residence: 5520 Freret Pl., New Orleans, La.

FREW, WILLIAM pres. bd. trustees Carnegie Inst.; b. Pittsburgh, Pa., Nov. 24, 1881; s. William Nimick and Emily Wick (Berry) F.; ed. St. Paul's Sch.; A.B., Yale, 1903, LL.B., U. of Pittsburgh, 1906; LL.D., Washington and Jefferson Coll., 1944; m. Margaretta Park, 1909; children-Emily Berry (Mrs. Henry Oliver, Jr.), Margaretta Park (Mrs. Theodore H. Conderman). Admitted to Allegheny County bar, 1906; assistant district attorney, 1907-10; practiced law, 1910-17; connected with Union Trust Company, 1919-22; member firm Hill, Wright & Frew, 1922-32, merged with Moore, Leonard & Lynch, 1932, partner, 1932-43; president of the boards of trustees, Carnegie Inst., Carnegie Library; chmn. bd. trustees Carnegie Inst. Tech., Pittsburgh, Pa.; trustee Carnegie Corp., N.Y. City since 1943. Served as capt. air corps, U.S. Army, 1917-19. Member Scroll and Key. Episcopalian. Clubs: Pittsburgh, Pittsburgh Golf, Duquesne, Fox Chapel Golf, Century Assn. (N.Y.). Home: 1060 Morewood Av. Office: Carnegie Institute, Pittsburgh, Pa. Died Jan. 31, 1948.

FREY, CHARLES DANIEL advertising exec.; b. Denver, Oct. s. Daniel and Augusta Eleanora (Stone) F.; ed. pub. 9, 1886; schs.; m. Mary Ross Burch, Oct. 17, 1908 (died June 2, 1945); children, Mary Elizabeth (Mrs. Gail Borden), Charles Jr., Barbara Ross (Mrs. Eugene F. Graves, Jr.); m. 2d Charlotte Goodlett Caldwell, Feb. 18, 1950. In editorial and art dept. Chgo. Examiner, 1905-06, Chgo. Evening Post, 1906-09; organized Charles Daniel Frey Co., advt. illustrations copy, Chgo., N.Y., 1910; reorganized into advt. agency, Chgo., 1921; liquidated, 1948; dir. Chgo. Times, Inc., 1939-47. Chmn. finance com. Municipal Voters League, 1920-26. Vice chmn. bd. Am. Assn. Advt. Agencies, 1934, mem. exec. bd., 1932-35. Mem. reorgn. com. and trustee Chgo. Latin Sch., 1926-32, Girls Latin Sch. of Chgo., 1928-34. Organizer Chgo. br., 1917, and nat. dir. Am. Protective League, Dir. Chgo., Press Veterans Association; mem. Chgo. board Salvation Army; dir. Civic Music Assn., Chgo., Lyric Opera of Chgo. Trustee Chgo. Musical Coll.; mem. citizens bd., U. Chgo.; mem. bd. Chgo. U.S.O. Served as capt., Mil. Intelligence Div. Gen. Staff, Washington. World War I. Decorated Medaille de la Reconnaissance Francaise. Republican. Episcopalian. Mason. Clubs: Chicago, Commonwealth, Economic, Caxton. Casino, Farmers Tavern (Chgo.); Bohemian (San Francisco). Home: 232 E. Walton Pl., Chgo. 11. Office: 230 N. Michigan Av., Chgo. 1. Died Nov. 1959.

FREY, JOHN WALTER internal med.; b. Pittsburgh, Jan. 7, 1892; s. John and Hedwig (Feibelman) F.; B.S., U. of Pittsburgh, 1913, M.D., 1916; grad. study, Johns Hopkins, 1921; m. Annette Hirsch, Dec. 18, 1919; children-John Walter, William Arthur, Margaret Ann. Interne Allegheny Gen. Hosp., 1916-17; resident Children's Hosp., 1917; instr. in U. of Pittsburgh, 1919-22; asst. in clin. diagnosis, St. Francis Hosp., 1922-23; research work Mellon Institute, Pittsburgh, Pa., 1928, 1930, 1932; specializes in internal medicine; medical staff, Presbyterian Hospital; instructor physical diagnosis, University of Pittsburgh Medical School, 1943. Served as captain Medical Reserve Corps, World War, 1917-19, Base Hospital 114, Beau Desert, France, 1918-19. Fellow Am. Medical Assn.; member Allegheny County Med. Soc., Diabetes Assn. Pittsburgh, Phi Rho Sigma. Republican. Mason (Shriner, Past Commander Legion of Honor Syria Temple). Clubs: University. Oakland Lions (pres. 1937). Contbr. to mags. Home: 5700 Centre Av. Office: Schenley Apartments, Pitts. Died Mar. 16, 1955.

FREY, OLIVER W. congressman; b. Bucks Co., Pa., Sept. 7, 1890; A.B., Coll. of William and Mary, Williamsburg, Va., 1915; LL.B., U. of Pa., 1920; m. Jessie M. Straub, June 28, 1928. Admitted to Pa. bar, 1920, and began practice at Allentown; elected to 73d Congress, Nov. 7, 1933, and reelected to 74th and 75th Congresses (1935-39), 9th Pa. Dist. Served as commd. officer U.S. Army, 1917-19. Democrat. Home: Allentown, Pa. Died Aug. 26, 1939.

FRIED, GEORGE, master mariner; b. Worcester, Mass., Aug. 10, 1877; s. John and Augusta F.; educated pub. schs., Worcester; m. Laura Parmenter, of Cincinnati, O., Mar. 21, 1922. Served in U.S. Army, Spanish-Am. War, 1898; with U.S. Navy, 1900-18; capt. S.S. President Roosevelt; widely known for rescue of crew of British steamer Antinoe in a great storm on the Atlantic, Jan. 1926; rescued entire crew of Italian steamer Florida, Jan. 1929; comdr. S.S. Washington; now supervising insp., Bureau of Navigation and Steamboat Inspection, U.S. Dept. of Commerce. Mem. Neptune Assn., Spanish War Vets., Am. Legion, Lions Club. Protestant. Mason. Home: 516 Caligula Av., Coral Gables, FL Office: 45 Broadway, New York NY

FRIEDLANDER, ALFRED M.D., educator; b. Cincinnati, Ohio, July 5, 1871; s. Abraham Joseph and Lisette (Friedman) F.; A.B., Harvard, 1892; M.D., U. of Cincinnati, 1895; grad. study, Strassburg, Berlin, Vienna, Erlangen; m. Gertrude Hyman, Apr. 17, 1900; children—Alfred Joseph, Susie, Peggy. Began practice at Cincinnati, 1898; asso. prof. pediatrics U. of Cincinnati, 1910-17, prof. medicine, 1919—, also dean College of Medicine. Was maj. Med. Corps, U.S.A., 1917-19; lt. col. Med. O.R.C. Jewish religion. Author: Hypotension, 1927. Home: Cincinnati, O. Died May 28, 1939.

FRIEDMAN, FRANCIS LEE physicist; b. N.Y.C., Sept. 5, 1918; s. Harry George and Adele (Oppenheimer) F.; grad. Phillips Exeter Acad., 1935; B.A., Harvard, 1939, M.A., 1940; Ph.D., Mass. Inst. Tech., 1949; m. Betty Anthony, Aug. 27, 1944; children - Gweneth, Karen, Seth. Grad. asst. physics U. Wis., 1941; asst. physicist atomic energy project Nat. Bur. Standards, 1941-42; physicist Manhattan Dist. Plutonium Project, U. Chgo., 1942-46; research asso. Mass. Inst. Tech., 1946-49, A.D. Little postdoctoral fellow, 1947-50, asst. prof., 1950-54, asso. prof. physics, 1954-58, prof., 1958-, dir. sci. teaching Center, 1960 - ; guest Inst. Theoretical Physics, Copenhagen, Denmark, 1955-56; chief scientist phys. sci. study com., 1956-60; v.p. Ednl. Services, Inc., 1959 - , trustee, 1961 - ; cons. Oak Ridge, Brookhaven Nat. Labs.; cons., dir. Nuclear Devel. Corp. Am., 1948-51; participant govt. projects. Mem. Am. Phys. Soc., Am. Acad. Arts and Scis. Author articles on atomic energy; nuclear reactor theory, nuclear physics. Home: 149 Brattle St., Cambridge 38, Mass. Died July 5, 1962.

FRIEDMAN, WILLIAM FREDERICK, cryptologist; b. Kishinev, Russia, Sept. 24, 1891; s. Frederick and Rosa (Trust) F.; brought to U.S. 1893; B.S., Cornell U., 1914, grad. study, 1914-15; m. Elizabeth Smith, May 21, 1917; children—Barbara, John Ramsay. Asst. dept. genetics Cornell U., 1913-15; field asst. Sta. Exptl. Evolution, Carnegie Inst., 1913-14; dir. dept. genetics Riverbank Labs., Geneva, Ill., 1915-18, dir. dept. ciphers, 1917-21; chief cryptanalyst War Dept., Washington, 1921-47; chief Signal Intelligence Service, 1930-40; dir. communications research Army Security Agy., 1942-49; chief tech. div. Armed Forces Security Agy., 1949-50, chief tech. cons. 1950-52; spl. asst. to the dir. Nat. Security Agy. 1953-55; cryptologist Dept. Def., 1947-55, cons., 1955-69; cryptologic cons., lectr. Armed Forces Service Schools and RCA, Washington, D.C.; member sci. adv. bd. Nat. Security Agy., 1957-61. Recipient 100,000 Congressional award for cryptologic inventions and patents, 1956; Medal for Merit, 1946; National Security medal, 1955; War Dept. Exceptional Service award, 1944; (with wife) Fifth Annual award Am. Shakespeare Festival Theatre and Acad. Served as 1st lt. mil. intelligence, U.S. Army, 1918-19; capt. Signal Corps Res., 1924-26, maj., 1926-36, lt. col., 1936-51. Mem. Sigma Xi. Clubs: Cosmos, Ft. Lesley J. McNair Officers' (Washington). Author War Dept. publs.; (with wife) The Shakespearean Ciphers Examined (May 1958 selection Readers' Subscription; lit. prize Folger Shakespeare Library 1955). Contbr. sci. and lit. jours., encys. Inventor many cryptographic devices and machinery. Home: Washington DC Died Nov. 12, 1969; buried Arlington National Cemetery, Arlington VA

FRIEL, FRANCIS DE SALES civil engr.; b. Queenstown, Md., Feb. 24, 1894; s. John and Avis (Whiting) F.; C.E., Drexel Inst. Tech., 1916, D. Eng., 1949; LL.D., U. of Scranton, 1958, Pa. Military Coll., 1959; D.E. Sc., Lafayette College, 1960; D.Sc., Villanova U., 1961; m. Sarah Gertrude Scanlan, Oct. 17,

1921. Pres. Albright & Friel, Inc., cons. engrs., 1931-62, chmn. bd., 1962 - , specializing in water, sewage, indsl. wastes, power plants, incineration, city planning, hwys., bridges, airports, flood control, dams, Army and Navy installations, financial studies and reports. Registered engr., Pa. (mem. state registration bd. 1952-58), N.Y., N.J., Md., Del., Va., W.Va., N.C., Ohio. Bd. dir. Beneficial Saving Fund Bank Phila.; vice chmn. bd. trustees Drexel Inst. Tech.; member of board trustees Trinity College. Served as major C.E., U.S. Army, WW I. Recipient medal Am. Pub. Works Assn., 1948; named Engr. of Year, Engring. Socs. of Phila., 1956. Diplomate Am. Acad. San. Engrs. Mem. Am. Soc. C.E. (nat. pres. 1958-59), Am. Inst. Cons. Engrs. (pres. 1955-56), Internat. Commn. on Large Dams (v.p. 1958-61, chmn. U.S. com. 1955-58), Am. Water Works Assn. (chmn. Pa. sect. 1955-58, recipient of the Fuller award 1959), Water Pollution Control Federation (president 1946-47), American Concrete Institute Am. Public Works Assn., Pa. Soc. Profl. Engrs., Am. Pub. Health Assn., Internat. Assn. Hydraulic Research, World Power Congress, Am. Road Builders Assn., Tau Beta Pi, Chi Epsilon, Pi Kappa Phi. Papal Knight of the Holy Sepulchre, Ky. col., 1959. Clubs: Engineers, Philadelphia Country, Skytop, Union League (Phila.). Contbr. engring. jours. Home: 611 Carisbrooke Rd., Bryn Mawr. Pa. Office: 3 Penn Center Plaza, Phila. 2, Pa. Died Feb. 11, 1964; buried St. Peter's Cemetery, Queenstown.

FRIERSON, HORACE lawyer: b. Columbia, Tenn., Feb. 5, 1881; s. Horace and Jeannie (Phillips) F.; grad. Wallace U. Sch., Nashville, 1898; LL.B., Vanderbilt U., 1902; m. Julia Warfield, Oct. 20, 1909; children-Horace Jr., Chloe. Practiced at Lawrenceburg, Tenn., 1902-09; dist. atty. 11th Circuit, Tenn., 1910-17; practiced at Columbia, Tenn., 1919-34; U.S. atty. Middle Dist. of Tenn. Jan. 1934-Aug. 1947; sec., treas. Maury Drilling Co., 1930—. Trustee of the Columbia Military Academy. Served in Spanish-Am. War and Philippine Insurrection, July 1898-Nov. 1899; maj. 114th F.A. World War, June 1917-Apr. 1919; in France, May 1918-Mar. 1919. Chmn. Dem. State Exec. Com. of Tenn., mng. state campaign of Franklin D. Roosevelt, Sept. 1, 1932-Aug. 31, 1934. Mem. Tennessee (past president), Maury County (past president) bar associations. American (past commander), Kappa Alpha. Presbyn. Club: Graymere Country. Home: R.F.D. 1. Address: 810 S. Garden, Columbia, Tenn. Died Aug. 30, 1956; buried Columbia.

FRIES, AMOS ALFRED, army officer; b. Debello, Vernon County, Wis., Mar. 17,21873; s. Christian May and Mary Ellen (Shreve) F.; grad. U.S. Mil. Acad., 1898; grad. Engring. Sch., U.S. Army, 1912; m. Elizabeth Christine Wait, Aug. 16, 1899; children—Elizabeth Christine, Stuart Gilbert, Barbara Hyacinth, Carol Stephanie. Commd. 2d lt. engrs., Apr. 26, 1898; promoted through grades to lt. col., May 15, 1917; col. N.A., Aug. 5, 1917; brig. gen. and chief C.W.S., A.E.F., Aug. 16, 1918; brig. gen., July 1, 1920; maj. gen., Feb. 24, 1925; chief C.W.S., U.S. Army, 1920-29; ret. May 16, 1929. Asst. building fortifications mouth of Columbia River, 1898-99; served in Philippines, 1901-03; in charge Los Angeles River and Harbor Dist., 1906-09; laid out complete modern Los Angeles Harbor; dir. mil. engring. in Engring. School, 1911-14; in charge road and bridge constrn., Yellowstone Nat. Park, 1914-17; chief C.W.S., A.E.F., Aug. 22, 1917, to end of war. Awarded D.S.M. (U.S.); Comdr. Legion of Honor (France); Companion St. Michael and St. George (British). Fellow A.A.A.S.; life mem. Am. Soc. C.E., Am. Assn. Engrs., Am. Legion, Veterans of Foreign Wars, Mil. Order World War, National Sojourners (past nat. pres.); hon. life mem. Engrs. and Architects Assn. of Southern Calif. Republican. Episcopalian. Scottish Rite Mason 33 deg. (Shriner). Clubs: Army and Navy, Army and Navy Country; hon. life mem. Chemists Club (New York). Writer on communism and on military subjects. Editor of bulletin Friends of the Public Schools. Home: 3305 Woodley Rd. N.W., Washington 8 DC

FRITTS, CARL EMERSON, highway engr.; b. Hemlock, N.C., Jan 9, 1900; s. Elzie K. and Sevilla E. (Graybeal) F.; student Wash. State Coll., 1918-21; m. Jean Lauder, June 9, 1947; 1 son, Carl Emerson. Various positions constrn., maintenance, traffic engring., planning, adminstrn. Wash. State Hwy. Dept., 1922-42; traffic engr. Hwy. Traffic Adv. Com., War Dept., 1942; hwy. engr. Automotive Safety Found., 1946-49, dir. hwys. div., 1950, v.p. in charge engring., 1951-—. Mem. national advisory com. road test Am. Association of State Highway Ofcls. Mem. hwy. research bd. dept. econs., finance and adminstrn. Served as col. Transportation Corps, AUS, 1942-45. Decorated Legion of Merit. Registered engr., Ida., Ky., D.C., La., Me., Minn. Miss. N.M., N.D., R.I., Ore., Tenn., Va., Wash., W.Va., Montana, D.C., Province of Ontario (Canada), National Bur. of Engring. Registration. Fellow Am. Society C.E. (president of national capital section); member Inst. Traffic Engrs., Sigma Chi. Episcopalian. Club: Cosmos (Washington). Home: Silver Spring MD Died Sept. 1970.

FRITZ, LAWRENCE G(EORGE), airline exec.; b. Marine City, Mich., Aug. 7, 1896; s. John Conrad and Sophia (Holstein) F.; student Mich. State Coll., East Lansing, Mich., 1915-17; grad. Air Corps Advanced Flying Sch., 1923, command pilot, 1943; m. Ruth Merritt, Nov. 2, 1929; children—Lawrence George (dec.), James D. (stepson, dec.), John (USAF), Mary, Susan. Transport pilot, 1925; test pilot, Ford Stout Aircraft Co., 1925-27; chief pilot, Maddux Airlines, 1927-29; vice pres. in charge operations, Southwest Air Fast Express, Inc., 1929-30; div. supt. Transcontinental and Western Air, Inc., 1931-32, region supt., 1932-38, vice pres. operations, 1938; v.p. operations dept., Am. Air Lines since Jan. 1946. Served with aviation sect., Signal Corps, U.S. Army during World War I; with U.S. Air Forces, 1942-46, disch. Jan. 1946; brig. gen. since June 1944; asst. chief of staff operations, Air Transport Command, 1942-43, comdg. officer North Atlantic Wing, 1943-44, comdg. gen. North Atlantic Div. June 1944. Decorated Air Medal, Legion of Merit, D.S.M. Mem. Inst. Aeronautical Sciences Nat. Aeronautical Adv. Committee, Quiet Birdmen, American Legion, Air Force Association, Air Force Reserve Officer Association. Mason. Club: Conquistadores del Cielo. Home: Saratoga CA Died Nov. 1970.

FRITZSCHE, CARL FERDINAND army officer; b. Cleve., Mar. 27, 1903; s. Arno Enton and Louise Anna (Tilkie) F.; student Miami U., 1922-24; B.S., U.S. Mil. Acad., 1928; student Command and Gen. Staff Coll., 1940, Nat. War Coll., 1949, Army War Coll., 1951; m. Ann Elizabeth Crea, July 22, 1931; children - Barbara Ann (Mrs. R. L. Swing), Karla Louise. Commd. 2d. lt. Inf., U.S. Army, 1928, advanced through grades to maj. gen., 1951; served in China, 1932-35; instr. tactics U.S. Mil. Acad., 1935-39; asst. chief staff G-2, 1st Armored Div., Ireland, 1942; master of sword, asst. comdt. U.S. Mil. Acad., 1943-44; dep. asst. chief staff G-2, 12th Army Group and European Command, Luxembourg and Germany, 1945-48; instr., chmn. nat. policy group Army War Coll., 1950-52; asst. div. comdr. 25th Inf. Div., Korea, 1952-53; asst. comdt. The Inf. Sch., 1953-55; chief Korea Mil. Adv. Group, 1955-57; chief staff 5th Army, 1957-58; comdg. gen., 1959 - . Decorated Legion of Merit with Cluster, Bronze Star (U.S.); Legion of Honor, Croix de Guerre with palm (France; Belgium). Mem. Sigma Alpha Epsilon. Home: 687 Johnson Av., Bedford, O. Office: care Commanding General, Northern Area Command, APO 757, N.Y. Died Oct. 1960.

FROEHLIC, JACK E(DWARD), aero. engr.; b. Stockton, Cal., May 7, 1921; s. Adolph Henry and Maude Leon (Gillespie) F.; student U. Cal. at Los Angeles; B.S., Cal. Inst. Tech., 1947, M.S. in Aero. Engring., 1948, Ph.D., 1950; m. Marion Louise Crofts, June 22, 1946; children - John Howard, Mark Edward. Research engr. Jet Propulsion Lab., Cal. Inst. Tech., 1949-53, chief guided missiles engring. div., 1953-55, head design and power plants dept., 1955-59, also satellite project dir.; tech. dir. electronic systems engring. div., v.p. Alpha Corp., subsidiary Collins Radio Co., 1959-60; gen. mgr. applied sci. div. Space Electronics Corp., subsidiary Aerojet-Gen. Corp., 1960, v.p. Space-Gen. Corp. (subsidiary), 1960-62, exec. v.p., 1962 - . Mem. panel on fuels and lubricants Dept. Defense; research adv. com. chem. energy processes NASA. Served to capt. USMC, 1942-46; test pilot. Mem. Am. Inst. Aeros. and Astronautics (sr.), I.E.E.E., Armed Forces Communication and Electronics Assn., Am. Astronautical Soc., Sigma Xi. Home: 621 Foxwood Rd., Pasadena 3, Cal. Office: 9200 E. Flair Dr., El Monte, Cal. Died Nov. 24, 1967.

FRONTENAC, LOUIS DE BUADE colonial gov.; b. Paris, France, 1620; married. Became col. French Army, at age of 23, brig. gen. at age 26, served in Holland, Italy, Germany, Crete; gov. Can., 1672-82, 89-98; during 1st term as gov., built forts to control Iroquois Indians, sent La Salle to explore Mississippi River; came into conflict with many leaders when he tried to exercise more power than permitted by his office; tried to overrule missionaries' objections to liquor trade (especially with Indians); quarreled with Gov. Perrot of Montreal, finally was removed; returned to office after French had suffered disastrous defeats; sent 3 armies into N.Y., N.H. and Me., defeated the British and Iroquois Indians, also English fleet under Adm. Phipps, razed strongholds in Acadia, captured St. John's, Newfoundland; honored by French Govt. for his last successful drive against Mohawk Indians, 1696. Died Quebec, Can., 1698.

FROST, ALFRED SIDNEY soldier; b. Chicago, Feb. 5, 1858; s. Thomas and Mary (Stickley) F.; ed. pub. schs., Syracuse, N.Y.; grad. U.S. Inf. and Cav. Sch., Ft. Leavenworth, Kan., 1891; studied law and admitted to bar, 1893, Supreme Ct. of U.S., 1900; m. Florence E. Mann, Dec. 31, 1884. Pvt., corporal and sergt., Co. A, 11th Inf., Sept. 13, 1881-Aug. 6, 1884; 2d. lt., 25th Inf., Aug. 4, 1884; 1st lt., 7th Inf., July 10, 1891; transferred to 25th Inf., July 20, 1891; col. 1st S.D. Inf., May 19, 1898. Served with that regt. in Philippine insurrection and was recommended for bvts. of maj. and lt. col. U.S.A., and brig. gen., U.S.V., for gallantry in action; hon. mustered out of vol. service with regt. Oct. 5, 1899. Recd. captaincy, U.S.A., while col. of vols., Jan. 1, 1899; maj., Jan 20, 1900; retired for disability in line of duty, Feb. 14, 1900. Chief of police, Evanston, Ill., 1905-07; candidate for mayor, Evanston, 1907. On duty with organized militia of S.D., 1909-10; recruiting officer U.S.A., Memphis dist., July 1, 1914-Oct. 31, 1918; comdg. officer S.A.T.C., U. of Tenn., Nov. 1, 1918-Feb. 5, 1919; prof. mil. science and tactics, city high schs., Memphis, Feb. 6-Aug. 31, 1919, and from Apr. 7, 1921; lt. col., July 10, 1918, in active service, Sept. 1, 1919; recruiting duty Nashville Dist. May 23, 1920-Apr. 1, 1921. Comdr.-in-chief Soc. Army of the Phipippines, 1905. Republican. Died Oct. 15, 1922.

FROST, ELIOTT PARK psychologist; b. Oxford, Mass., Jan 9, 1884; s. George Benjamin and Amelia Adelaide F.; B.A., Dartmouth, 1905, M.A., 1906; Ph.D., Harvard, 1908; studied at U. of Berlin, 1908-09; m. Elizabeth Hollister, June 3, 1916; 1 son, Granger Hollister. Teacher of psychology, Princeton, 1909-10, Yale, 1910-14; head dept. of psychology and chmn. athletic council, U. of Tenn., 1914-18; dir. Industrial Management Council and Mfrs.' Council, Rochester, N.Y., 1919-22; head dept. psychology and edn., 1922—. U. of Rochester, also dir. extension div. and summer sch.; dir. Hollister Lumber Co., Hollister Real Estate Co. Enlisted in U.S. Army, Mar. 19, 1918, as psychol. expert; mil. morale officer, June 1918, at Camp Greenleaf, Ga.; inaugurated the morale work subsequently established throughout the Army; transferred to newly created morale branch of the Gen. Staff, Washington, D.C., Oct. 19, 1918, rank of capt.; hon. disch., May 17, 1919. Sec. bd. of governors Rochester Home Hosp.; pres. Social Welfare League, Tuberculosis Assn. Republican. Conglist. Home: Rochester, N.Y. Died Sept. 3, 1926.

FROST, LESLIE MISCAMPBELL, former prime minister Province of Ontario, Canada; b. Orillia, Ont., Can., Sept. 20, 1895;2s. William Sword and Margaret Jane (Barker) F.; ed. Orillia Collegiate Inst. U. Toronto, Osgoode Hall; LL.D. Queen's U., Kingston, Ont., 1946, Ottawa U., 1948, McMaster U., 1951, U. Toronto, 1952, Assumption Coll. 1954, Royal Mil. Coll., 1960, Laurentian Univ., 1961; D.C.L., U. Western Ont., 1950; m. Gertrude Jane Carew, June 2, 1926 (dec. 1972). Admitted to Ont. bar, 1921; created King's Counsel, 1933; mem. Privy Council for Can., 1961-73. Elected mem. Ont. Legislature, 1937, 43, 45, 48, 51, 55, 59; became treas. Ont. and minister of mines, 1943, pres. Provincial Mines Ministers Assn. of Can., 1944; became leader Progressive Conservative Party Ont., 1949-61; prime minister Prov. Ont., and pres. of the Council, 1949-61, treas., 1949-55; mem. law firm Frost, Inrig & Gorwill. Vice pres., dir. Victoria &Grey Trust Co., Bank of Montreal; dir. Can. Life Assurance Co., Massey-Ferguson, Ltd., Radio Station CKLV, and other firms. Chancellor of Trent U., Peterborough. Served from asst. adj. to co. comdr. Simcoe Regt., 1914-18, with 20th Canadian Inf. Bn., France and Belgium, 1917-18. Mem. Canadian Legion (Sir Sam Hughes br. past zone rep.), Bencher Law Soc. Upper Can. (hon.), Phi Delta Phi (hon.). Mem. Progressive Conservative Party. Mem. United Ch. Can. (chmn. mgmt. bd. Lindsay). Mason (Shriner, 33). Clubs: Rotary (past pres.), Lindsay Curling, Albany, Twenty. Garrison, Royal Canadian Mil. Inst., National, Granite. Author: Fighting Men. Home: Lindsay ON2Canada Died May 1973.

FROST, WALTER ARCHER author; b. Amenia, N.Y., Dec. 18, 1875; s. Simeon Taylor and Phoebe (Wheeler) F.; A.B., Harvard, 1901; LL.B., U. Wis., m. Susan Winifred McCurdy, Dec. 18, 1905 (dec. 1948); 1 dau., Georgina (Mrs. Stanley Kenneth Anderson). Engaged in practice law Green Bay, Wis., 1905-06, Boston, 1909-12; editor People's Mag., N.Y., part of 1912; asso. editor Munsey's Mag., 1912-13; fiction editor Good Housekeeping Mag., N.Y., 1913-14; asst. dir. Bur Membership, and asso. dir. Bur. of Canteen Service, A.R.C., Washington, 1915-17; mgr. syndicate dept. N.Y. Evening Post, 1920; financial sec. Charity Orgn. Soc., 1920-23; lit. asst. Young & Rubicam, Inc., N.Y., 1937-46. Enlisted in U.S. Army, June 14, 1918; commd. capt. Q.M.C.; asst. salvage officer, Ft. Sam Houston, Tex.; assigned to Chief of Transp., assigned Judge Adv. Corps 1919; hon. discharged, Oct. 27, 1919; commd. capt. Q.M. Res. Corps, U.S. Army. Fellow Am. Geog. Soc.; mem. Am. Inst. Graphic Arts, Eugene Field Soc. (hon), Am. Legion Mil. Order Fgn. Wars U.S., Psi Upsilon. Officer d'Academie, France, 1939. Awarded Palmes Acadèmique (France). Republican. Presbyn. Clubs: Hasty Pudding. Inst. of 1770 (Cambridge, Mass.); Monterey (Pa.) Country; Dutch Treat Explorers, Harvard (Washington); Union Boat (Boston); Evening Post Alumni Assn. (N.Y.C.). Author: The Man Between (novel), 1913; No Questions Asked (novel), 1926. The Marworth Mystery (novel), 1927; Cape Smoke (3 act play), prod. N.Y., 1926; No Questions Asked, The Girl Between (3 act plays); also many short stories, novelettes, and gen. articles to mags., also contbr. to leading newspapers. Traveled through Central Am., Brit. Columbia, Alaska, South Seas, Japan, China, Straits Settlements, Federated Malay States, Java, Ceylon, Egypt, Arabia, Europe, Guatemala in amateur's study of Maya relics and of Asiatic eye fold. Hon. chief Alii Oletao, Samoa. Home: Army and Navy Club, Washington. Died Mar. 11, 1964; buried Arlington Nat. Cemetery.

FROST, WESLEY foreign service; b. Oberlin, O., June 17, 1884; s. William Goodell (D.D., LL.D.) and Louise (Raney) F.; B.A., Oberlin Coll., 1907; M.A., George Washington U., 1919; m. Mary Priscilla Clapp, Dec. 21, 1909; children - Nuala Anne, Phyllis Priscilla, Sophie Jeanne. Was lit. sec. to Theodore E. Burton, 1907-08; with Bur. of Statistics, Washington, D.C., 1908-09;

statistician, U.S. Dept. of State, 1909-12, prepared official Canadian reciprocity; Consul at Charlottetown, P.E.I., - U.S. 1912-14; consul at Cork (Queenstown), Ireland, Apr. 24, 1914; reported 81 submarine attacks - Lusitania, Arabic, Hesperian, Cymric, California, etc. Lecturer on submarine warfare under Com. on Pub. Information; asst. foreign trade adviser, Department of State, 1918-19; was acting foreign trade adviser, Mar. 1, 1920-Mar. 29, 1921; consul at Marseilles, France, 1921-24, consul gen., 1924-28; consul gen., Montreal, Can., 1928-35; was counselor of Embassy and charge d'affairs Rio de Janeiro, Brazil and Santiago, Chile. U.S. minister to Paraguay, 1941-42, ambassador, Apr. 1942-Dec. 1944; retired 1944. Vis. prof., U. of Denver. First chmn. Com. Economic Liaison; mem. Am. Econ. Assn. Fgn. Service officer, Class I. Club: Union (Santiago). Author: German Submarine Warfare, 1918. Contbr. to mags. Home: 279 Elm St., Oberlin, O. Died Jan. 9, 1968.

FROTHINGHAM, CHANNING physician; b. Bklyn., May 10, 1881; s. Channing and Elizabeth (Gerrish) F.; prep. edn., Poly. Prep. Sch., Bklyn.; A.B., Harvard, 1902, M.D., 1906; m. Clara Morgan Rotch. 1907; children-Channing, Mary Eliot. Joseph Rotch, Timothy Gerrish (dec.), William Rotch, Virginia, Thomas Eliot. Began practice at Boston, 1907; mem. faculty of Harvard Med. Sch. in different capacities, 1908-33; physician to Peter Bent Brigham Hosp., 1912-33, cons. physician since 1933; physician in chief Faulkner Hosp., 1933-46, cons. physician 1946—. 1st lt.-lt. col., Med. R. C., 1917-18. Trustee Boston Psychopathic Hosp.; overseer Harvard Coll., term, 1936-42. Chmn. Com. of Physicians for Improvement of Med. Care Inc., 1941-47; chmn. Com. for the Nation's Health. Mem. Assn. Am. Physicians, Mass. Med. Soc. (pres. 1937, 38). Clubs: Tavern, Tennis and Racquet (Boston); Country (Brookline, Mass.). Home: 186 Reservoir Rd., Brookline, Mass. Office: 275 Charles St., Boston. Died Aug. 11, 1959.

FROTHINGHAM, LOUIS ADAMS lawyer; b. Jamaica Plain, Mass., July 13, 1871; s. Thomas B. and Anne Pearson (Lunt) F.; A.B., Harvard U., 1893, LL.B., 1896; m. Mary S. Ames. Admitted to bar, 1896; 2d lt. U.S. Marine Corps, serving in the Atlantic Squadron during Spanish War, 1898; resumed practice of law, Boston, 1899. Mem. Mass. Ho. of Rep., 1901-05 (speaker, 1904-05); Rep. candidate for mayor of Boston, 1905; elected lt.-gov. of Mass., Nov. 1908; Rep. nominee for governor of Mass., 1911; mem. of 67th to 70th Congresses (1921-19), 14th Mass. Dist. Overseer Harvard, 1904-10, 1912-18, 1920-26. Lecturer on Mass. govt., Harvard, 1913-15. Col. 13th Regt. Mass. State Guard, 1917; maj. U.S.A., 1918. Unitarian. Author: Brief History of the Constitution and Government of Massachusetts. Home: N. Easton, Mass. Died Aug. 23, 1928.

FROTHINGHAM, THOMAS GODDARD author; b. Boston, July 9, 1865; s. Thomas Goddard and Frances Adeline (Cook) F.; grad. Boston Latin Sch., 1883; hon. A.M., 1930; m. Eleanor Felton Whiting, Dec. 30, 1903; 1 dau., Eleanor. Trustee estates. Capt. U.S.A., World War, now capt. U.S.R. Pres. Bunker Hill Monument Assn. Mem. Copley Soc. (pres.), Bostonian Soc. (librarian), Soc. Preservation N.E. Antiquities, Mil. Hist. Soc. Mass., Mass. Hist. Soc., U.S. Naval Inst., Zeta Psi. Clubs: St. Botolph, Boston Athletic, Eastern Yacht, Myopia Hunt. Author: A Guide to the Military History of the World War, 1914-18, 1920; A True Account of the Battle of Jutland, 1920; The Crisis of the Civil War-Antietam (monograph), 1922; The Naval History of the World War-Offensive Operations, 1914-1915, 1924; The Naval History of the World War-The Stress of Sea Power, 1915-1916, 1925; The Naval History of the World War-The United States in the War, 1917-1918, 1926; The American Reinforcement in the World War, 1927; George Washington, The American Commander in Chief, 1930. Home: 74 Chestnut St. Office: 18 Tremont St., Boston. Died Mar. 17, 1945; buried Mt. Auburn Cemetery, Cambridge, Mass.

FRY, ALFRED BROOKS engineer; b. New York, Mar. 3, 1860; s. Maj. Thomas William Gardiner (U.S.V.) and Frances (Olney) F.; g.g.s. Capt. Benj. F., Continental Army; ed. pvt. schs. and Morse's Sch., New York; engring. sch. Columbia Coll.; m. Emma V., d. Brig. Gen George A. Sheridan, U.S.V., 1890; 1 son, Sheridan Brooks. Marine and mech. engr., 1879-86; acting asst. engr. U.S. Treasury service, 1886, advanced through grades to supervising chief engr., supervising engr., duty at Port of New York, 1924-26; chief inspection engr. for supervising architect U.S. pub. bldgs., etc., on Pacific Coast, Aug. 1926-Mar. 1927; consulting engr., 1927—; engr. lt. and engr. lt. comdr. naval militia, 1892-1910; comdr. and chief of staff, naval militia, New York, 1910—; acting chief engr. U.S.N., Spanish-Am. War, 1898; chief engr. and supt. constrn., etc. U.S. pub. bldgs., New York, 1899-1917; engr. aide to Admiral Burd, industrial mgr. Navy Yard N.Y., and 3d Naval Dist., Mar. 1917. Capt. U.S. N.N.V., 1917; capt., U.S.N.R., July 1, 1918; duty in Navy Yard, New York, at sea and French and English ports. Mem. bd. consulting engrs. for improvement of state canals, 1904-11; consulting engr. to Assn. for Protection of the Adirondacks, 1903—, Congressional Commn. of 1913 on mech. transmission of mails; mem. com. on waterways Merchants' Assn., New York; cons. engineer, Dept. Water Supply, Gas and Electricity, City of New York, 1914; mem. com. of engrs. representing Nat. Engring. Socs., at N.Y. Constl. Conv., 1915; mem. Special Panama Canal Commn., 1921; cons. engr. U.S.A., transport service, 1922. Commodore, comdg. Naval Militia, N.Y., 1923; retired as rear adm. Feb. 27, 1924. Mem. Harbor Com. of San Diego Chamber of Commerce, 1929; mem. City Council, Coronado, Calif., 1929-30, mayor pro tem., 1930-31; elected mayor for term, 1932-34. Pres. San Diego County League of Municipalities, 1932-33; mem. Engrs. Employment Com. of Southern Calif., 1931. Home: Coronado, Calif. Died Dec. 4, 1933.

FRY, BIRKETT DAVENPORT lawyer, army officer, cotton mfr.; b. Kanawha County, Va., June 24, 1822; s. Thornton and Eliza (Thompson) F.; attended Va. Mil. Inst., Washington (Pa.) Coll., U.S. Mil. Acad., 2 years; m. Martha Micou, 1853. Admitted to Va. bar, 1846; commd. 1st lt. inf. U.S. Army during Mexican War, 1847; moved to Cal., 1849; commd. brig. gen. during William Walker's expdn. to Nicaragua while attempting to create a state ruled by Walker with gradual introduction of slavery, 1855; had returned to Cal. to recruit more troops when Walker's regime fell, 1857; mgr. cotton mill, Tallasee, Ala., 1859; commd. col. 13th Ala. Inf. Regt., 1861; commd. brig. gen. Army of Va., 1864; pres. Marshall Mfg. Co., 1886-91. Died Jan. 21, 1891.

FRY, JAMES BARNET army officer, writer; b. Carrollton, Ill., Feb. 22, 1827; s. Jacob and Eily (Turney) F.; grad. U.S. Mil. Acad., 1847. Served in Mexican War; apptd. asst. adj. gen. U.S. Army, brevetted capt., 1861; chief of staff to U.S. Army under McDowell 1861; commd lt. col., 1862; chief of staff Gen. Buell's Army of Ohio, 1 year; 1st provost marshall gen. U.S., 1863, organized Bur. of Provost Marshall Gen.; served as brig. gen., 1864-66; brevetted maj. gen., 1868, col., brig. gen., 1865; commd. col., 1875; adj. gen. of mil. divs., Pacific, South, Atlantic, Author: Operations of the Army Under Buell from June 10th to October 30th, 1862; Sketch of the Adjutant-General's Department United States Army, from 1775 to 1875, published 1875; The History and Log of Effect of Brevets in the Armies of Great Britain and the United States, 1877; The Buell Commission, 1884; McDowell and Tyler in the Campaign of Bull Run, 1884. Contbr. to Battles and Leaders of the Civil War; also articles to North Am. Review. Died Newport, R.I., July 11, 1894; buried Phila.

FRY, JOSEPH, JR. congressman; b. Northampton (now Lehigh) County, Pa., Aug. 4, 1781; attended rural schs. Engaged in business, Fryburg (later Coopersburg), Pa.; mem. Pa. Ho. of Reps., 1816-17, Pa. Senate, 1817-21; served to col. Pa. 1Militia; mem. U.S. Ho. of Reps. (Democrat) from Pa., 20-21st congresses, 1827-31; mem. Pa. Constl. Conv., 1837, 38. Died Allentown, Pa., Aug. 15, 1860; buried Union Cemetery.

FRY, JOSHUA surveyor, educator; b. Crewkerne, Eng., circa 1700; s. Joseph Fry; ed. Wadham Coll., Oxford (Eng.) U., 1718; m. Mary (Micou) Hill, circa 1720. Came to Va., before 1720; prof. mathematics and natural philosophy Coll. William and Mary, 1731; 1st presiding justice Albemarle County; justice Ct. Chancery; county surveyor; mem. Ho. of Burgesses from Abemarle County until death; county lt., 1745; mapmaker (with Peter Jefferson) Map of the Inhabited Parts of Virginia; surveyor (with P. Jefferson) ran part of Va.-Carolina boundary, 1749; commr. to the Six Nations, 1752, aided in drawing up Treaty of Logstown; col., comdr.-in-chief of a regt. Va. Militia, started for Ohio in expdn. against French, 1754, died enroute, succeeded by George Washington. Died Ft. Cumberland, Md., May 31, 1754.

FRYE, ALEXIS EVERETT educator; b. N. Haven, Me., Nov. 2, 1859; s. Capt. E. S. and Jane (King) F.; grad. English High Sch., Boston, 1878, Cook Co. Normal Sch., Chicago, 1885; LL.B., Harvard, 1890, A.M., 1897; LL.D., U. of Redlands, Calif., 1929; m. Teresa Arruebarrena, Havana, Cuba, Jan. 1, 1901; children—Pearl Eliot (dec.), Frank Brewster, Charles (dec.), Carmen, Pearl. Teacher of methods and practice in teaching, Chicago Normal Sch., 1883-86; delivered over 1,500 ednl. lectures, 1886-90; admitted to Mass. bar, 1890; supt. schs., San Bernardino, Calif., 1891-93. Traveled extensively in Europe, Asia, Africa, 1897; supt. schs. of Cuba, 1899-1901; organized and equipped pub. sch. system of Cuba; organized and conducted Cuban teachers' expdn., bringing 1,284 native teachers to U.S., 1900. Medal of Legion of Honor of Cuba, 1900; medal of La. Purchase Expn., awarded by Pres. Taft commn., for Philippine Is. textbooks, 1903. Pres. Nat. Teachers' Assn. of Cuba, 1904-06. Capt. Co. E, 7th Calif. N.G., 1893; helped organize Harvard U. Batt., and capt. Harvard Graduates' Co., 1898; lt. Co. K, 1st Mass. Arty., 1898-99. Life fellow Am. Geog. Society. Author: Child and Nature, 1888; Brooks and Brook Basins, 1891; Geografia Elemental (Spanish), 1899; Manual para Maestros, 1899; School Law of Cuba, 1899; Grammar School Geography, 1901; First Steps in Geography, 1903; Home Geography, 1911; New Geography, Book One, 1917; The Booklet's Story, 1927. Home: Redlands, Calif. Died July 1, 1936.

FRYE, JOSEPH army officer; b. Andover, Mass., Mar. 19, 1712; s. Sgt. John and Tabitha (Farmam) F.; m. Mehitable Poor, Mar. 31, 1733. Ensign in Hale's 5th Mass. Regt., 1744-45, served in capture of Louisburg; capt. during King George's War, 1747-49; commd. maj., 1755; commanding officer Ft. Cumberland, Acadia (now Nova Scotia), Can., 1759-60; moved to new settlement, Freyeburg, Mass. Militia, 1775, brig. gen. Continental Army, favored separation of Me. from Mass., del. to conv. which met to consider the measure, 1786. Died July 25, 1794.

FRYE, WILLIAM ex-government official, writer; b. Montgomery, Ala., Jan. 9, 1908; s. William Fenner and Hattie Belle (Booth) F.; grad. Ala. Mil. Inst., Anniston, 1925; student Wabash Coll., Crawfordsville, Ind., Jan. 1928-Nov. 1929; m. Mary Atkinson, May 9, 1931; children - Alice Rowena (Madame Lucien Cohen), William Fenner, Henry Booth. Reporter Gadsden (Ala.) Times, 1926-27, Birmingham News and Birmingham Post, 1927, Nashville Tennessean, 1930-31; with Associated Press, 193-n1-45, night editor, Nashville, 1931-33, various assignments in Washington, 1933-42, charge War Dept. coverage, 1942-44, war corr., E.T.O., 1944, with British 2d Army, 1945. diplomatic corr., Paris, 1945; spl. consultant to Sec. of War, 1946. to Sec. of Defense, 1947; deputy dir. pub. information, Office Sec. Defense, 1948; asst. to sec. of defense and dir. public information, Dept. Defense, 1949-50; chief, information sect., European Coordinating Com., also attache, Am. Embassy, London, 1950-51; spl. corr. in Europe, NBC, 1951-53; asst. dir. conf. Interparliamentary Union, Washington, 1953; cons. Nat. Com. for an Effective Congress, 1954; asst. editor Army-Navy-Air Force Register, and mil. editor Aero Digest, 1954-55; dept. dir., dept. mass communication. UNESCO, Paris, 1955-56, dir. information N.Y. office, 1957-58; dir. information Nat. Council Churches, 1959-60. Awarded Certificate of Appreciation for distinguished public service to Dept. of Defense, 1950. Mem. Beta Theta Pi. Democrat. Episcopalian. Clubs: National Press (Washington); Overseas Press (N.Y.C.). Author: Marshall: Citizen Soldier, 1947. Home: Netherhill, Prattville, Ala. Died Mar. 30, 1961.

FRYER, DOUGLAS (HENRY) educator; b. Willimantic, Conn., Nov. 7, 1891; s. Henry and Nellie E. (Finley) F.; B.H., Springfield (Mass.) Coll., 1914; grad. study, Brown, 1915-16; A.M., Clark U., 1917, Ph.D., 1923; postgrad. Columbia, 1921-22; m. Katharine Homer, 1934; children - Judith Anne, Barbara, Katharine Homer, Anne Homer, Sarah Louise Tchr., 1910-11; mem. sec. Providence YMCA, 1914-16; dir. vocational dept. Bklyn. YMCA, 1920-22; sr. fellow Clark U. 1922-23; asst. prof. psychology U. Utah, 1923-24, N.Y.U., 1925-28, asso. prof. since 1928, adminstrv. chmn. dept. psychology U. Coll., 1925-40; vis. prof. Cambridge U. (England), 1931-32; collaborator. Forest Service, U.S. Dept. Agr., 1936-46; chief recruitment, selection and classification, Research Unit, Personnel Research Sect., Adj. Gen.'s Office, 1945-47; research investigator, com. on Selection and Tng. of Aircraft Pilots, N.R.C., 1940-42; on leave from N.Y.U., 1943-45; govt. service as chief. personnel research br. Civilian Personnel Div., Office Sec. of War, U.S. War Dept. Dir. Richardson, Bellows, Henry & Co., Inc. since 1945, sec. since 1948; dir. indsl. tng. in psychology N.Y.U. since 1949, adj. prof., 1952-58. Served as 2d lt. U.S. Army, and capt. A.R.C., morale officer, psychol. examiner and insp., World War I. Diplomate Am. Bd. Examiners in Profl. Psychology. Fellow Am. Psychol. Assn.; mem. Eastern Psychol. Assn. (sec.-treas., 1929-31, dir. 1936-39), Am. Assn. for Applied Psychology (pres. 1937-38; chmn. bd. editors, 1938-41; mem. bd. govs. 1937-41), A.A.A.S. (v.p., chmn. sect. I, psychology 1949-50, mem. council on human relations), Am. Assn. U. Profs., Assn. Cons. Psychologists (pres. 1930-31), Nat. Vocational Guidance Assn., Perstare et Praestare (N.Y.U.), Psi Chi, Alpha Pi Zeta. Mem. Internat. Congress Psychology, Oxford, 1923, Groningen, 1926, Yale, 1929, Internat. Conf. Tech. Psychology, Moscow, 1931. Club: Town (Scarsdale, N.Y.). Author: Vocational Self Guidance, Planning Your Life Work, 1925; General Psychology (students' study syllabus), 1927, 31; Elementary Experiments in Psychology (lab. manual), 1927, 31, 46; Measurement of Interests in Relation to Human Adjustment, 1931; co-author: Developing People in Industry, 1956; An Outline of General Psychology, 1936, 37, 41, 54; Basic Units for an Introductory Course in Vocational Guidance (edited by W. B. Jones), 1931; Fields of Psychology (edited by J. P. Guilford), 1940. Editor: Handbook of Applied Psychology (with E. R. Henry), 1950. Home: 31 Circle Rd., Scarsdale, N.Y. Died Dec. 24, 1960.

FRYER, ELI THOMPSON, marine corps officer (ret.); b. Hightstown, N.J., Aug. 22,21878; s. Samuel and Mary (Shaeffer) F.; student, Brown U., 1895-97; grad. U.S. Mil. Acad., 1899; m. Edna Ella Smith, Jan. 14, 1908. Commd. 2d lt., U.S. M.C., 1900, and advanced through grades to brig. gen., 1934; ret. from active service, Oct. 1, 1934. Awarded Congressional Medal of Honor, 1914. Home: 106 North Vermont Av., Atlantic City NJ

FUGARD, JOHN REED, architect; b. Newton, Ia., Dec. 6, 1886; s. Judson Houston and Ella (Slemmons) F.; B.S. in Architecture, U. Ill., 1910; m. Rowena Owen, June 18, 1910 (dec. 1952); 1 son, John Reed; m. 2d,

Roine Russell, June 17, 1953. Sec.-treas. Fugard Orth. & Assos., architects, Chicago, Illinois; designs hosps., hotels, office bldgs.; cons. for Guy's Hosp., London, Eng.; pres. Woodhaven Dairy, Incorporated, Robertsdale, Ala.; dir. Drake Towers, 1965-68. Chmn. Chgo. Housing Authority, 1936-37, 53-54; pres. Met. Housing Council, 1934-35; cons. zoning bd. Chicago Plan Commn. Trustee Chgo. Temple; citizens bd. trustees U. Chgo.; dir. Internat. Coll. Surgeons Hall Fame, 1962-63. Served to capt. Q.M.C., 1917-18. Fellow A.I.A. (dir. 1934-35, treas. 1937-38); mem. Chgo. Dwellings Assn. (pres. 1955), Kappa Sigma. Methodist. Mason (Shriner). Clubs: University, Tavern, Forty, Arts (all of Chicago); Lakewood Golf (Fairhope, Alabama). Home: Chicago IL Died Aug. 17, 1968; buried Memorial Park Cemetery, Evanston IL

FULLAM, JAMES EDSON ret. communications exec.; b. Brookfield, Vt., May 9, 1890; s. Frank Nelson and Frances Emma (Blakebrough) F.; B.S., U. Vt., 1911, M.E., 1922; M.B.A., N.Y.U., 1921; m. Ruth Chester Tyler, June 5, 1923; 1 dau., Margaret Louise. Engr. N.Y. Telephone Co., 1911-16, 19-21; sales mgr. Bell Telephone Securities Co., 1922; v.p. Internat. Tel. & Tel. Corp., 1930-33, v.p., 1934-48, retired; v.p. Internat. Standard Electric Corp., 1931—; chmn. bd. Shanghai (China) Telephone Co.; vice chmn. bd. China Electric Co. Served with U.S. Army; pvt. 1916-17, capt. to maj. ordnance, 1917-19; lt. col. Ordnance Res., 1928-33. Mem. exec. com. China Am. Council of Commerce and Industry; dir. China Soc.; mem. China com. Nat. Fgn. Trade Council. Mem. Am. Asiatic Assn. (exec. com.), Phi Delta Theta. Phi Beta Kappa. Club: Broad Street (N.Y.C.). Home: Newtown, Conn. Office: 67 Broad St., N.Y.C. 4, Died Feb. 21, 1951.

FULLAM, WILLIAM FREELAND naval officer; b. Monroe Co., N.Y., Oct. 20, 1855; s. N.S. and Rhoda F.; grad. U.S. Naval Acad., 1877 (head of class); m. Mariana Winder, d. late Chief Justice Robinson, Md. Court of Appeals, of Eastern Shore, Md., Apr. 15, 1885. Promoted ensign, 1880, advanced through the ranks to rear admiral, Dec. 15, 1914. Served on Trenton and Marion, European sta.; Swatara, China sta.; instr. in different depts. and head of dept. of ordnance, U.S. Naval Acad., 1883-1904; on Boston, Yorktown, Chicago, Vesuvius, Raleigh, Miantonomah and Lancaster; on bd. New Orleans in war with Spain; comd. Chesapeake and Terror, practice ships, and Marietta in W.I.; comdt. Naval Training Sta., Newport, R.I., 1907-09; comdg. Battleship Mississippi, 1q10; comdt. Naval Training, Great Lakes, Ill., 1912; aid for inspections to Sec. of Navy Meyer, 1913, and for personnel to Sec. Daniels, 1914; supt. Naval Acad., Annapolis, Feb. 7, 1914; comdr.-in-chief Pacific Reserve Fleet, Oct. 15, 1915; comdr. Patrol Force, Pacific Fleet, 1916-17; comdr. 2d Div., Pacific Fleet, and sr. officer in command in the Pacific, 1917-19; retired Oct. 20, 1919. Santiago (Sampson) medal; West India Campaign medal; Cuban Pacification medal, 1906; Mexican Service medal, 1916; Order of Rising Sun (Japan); also Victory medal and Navy Cross from U.S. Author: Handbook of Infantry and Artillery, U.S.N., 1899; Textbook of Ordnance and Gunnery, 1902; Recruits' Handbook. Home: Washington, D.C. Died Sept. 23, 1927.

FULLER, BEN HEBARD officer U.S.M.C.; b. Big Rapids, Mich., Feb. 27, 1870; s. Ceylon C. and Frances (Morrison) F.; ed. U.S. Naval Acad.; m. Katharine Offey, Oct. 26, 1892. Apptd. naval cadet, May 25, 1885; trans. to U.S.M.C. and commd. 2d lt., July 1, 1891; advanced through grades to col., Aug. 29, 1916; brig. gen. (temp.) July 1, 1918; brig. gen., Feb. 8, 1924. Served on U.S.S. Columbia, Spanish-Am. War; in Philippines, 1899-1901; with Boxer Relief Expdn. to Peking, 1900; comd. 2d Brigade, U.S. Marines in Santo Domingo, Nov. 1918-Dec. 1919, 1st Brigade, Haiti, 1924-25; apptd. maj. gen., comdt. U.S. Marine Corps, Aug. 5, 1930; retired, Mar. 1, 1934. Commended by Dept. "for gallant, meritorious and courageous conduct" in Battle of Tientsin, July 13, 1900. Home: Hamilton, Va. Died June 8, 1937.

FULLER, CHARLES E. congressman; b. Boone Co., Ill., Mar. 31, 1849; s. Seymour and Eliza A. (Mordoff) F.; ed. Wheaton Coll.; m. Sarah A. Mackay, Apr. 24, 1873. Admitted to bar, 1870, and began practice at Belvidere, Ill.; city atty., 4 yrs.; state's atty., Boone Co., 4 yrs.; mem. Ho. of Rep., 3 terms, and Senate, 2 terms, 1879-1893; judge Circuit Ct., 17th Jud. Circuit, 1897-1903; mem. 58th to 62d Congresses (1903-13) and 64th to 66th Congresses (1915-21), 68th and 69th Congresses (1923-27), 12th Ill. Dist.; chmn. Com. on Invalid Pensions, 66th and 67th Congresses. V.p. Peoples Bank of Belvidere. Raised a regt., Spanish-Am. War and commd. col., 1898. Home: Belvidere, Ill. Died June 25, 1926.

FULLER, FRANK MANLY physician; b. Keokuk, Ia., Sept. 29, 1868; s. Euclid Erastus and Cecilia (Gerard) F.: A.B., Parsons Coll., Fairfield, Ia., 1888, A.M., 1891; M.D., Keokuk Med. Coll., 1897; grad. study Met. Schs. Medicine, London, Eng., 1898; Allgemeine Krankenhaus und Policlinic, Vienna, Austria, 1901; m. Anna M. Ballinger, Sept. 2, 1897 (died 1908); children-Frank Lapsley, Madison Ballinger, John Davis; m. 2d, Caroline T. Davis, Nov. 15, 1911. Began practice at Keokuk, 1897; prof. clin. diseases of children, Keokuk Med. Coll., 1897-1908; chief staff, St. Joseph's Hosp., Keokuk, 1914-27; sec. Ia. State Bd. Med. Examiners, 1924-38, pres., 1938-41; ret. Served as 1st lt., Ia. Nat. Guard, 1889-97; capt. M.C., U.S. Army, in France, 1917-19. Mem. city council, Keokuk, 2 terms. Pres., physician Bd. Keokuk. Pres. Fedn. Med. State Examining Bds. U.S., 1943—, v.p., 1939-40, mem. bd. dirs., 1940-42. Fellow A.C.P.; mem. A.M.A., Ia. State (pres. 1925), S. Eastern Ia. (ex-pres.), Lee County (ex-pres.) med. socs., Ia. Clin. Med. Soc. (pres. 1923), Interstate Post Grad. Assembly (ex-v.p.). Republican. Presbyn. Mason. Elk. Clubs: Keokuk, Keokuk Country. Home: 217 High St., Keokuk, Ia. Died 1946.

FULLER, HECTOR journalist; b. at London, Eng., Oct. 18, 1856; s. John C. (insp. hosps., Madras Presidency) and Louisa (Lockwood) F.; ed. Needham's Acad., Ealing, Eng., Kilburn Coll., London, and H.M.S., Worcester, training ship for sons of army and navy officers, Erith, the Thames; m. at Indianapolis, a d. Col. Trusler, U.S.A., Feb. 10, 1895. Left the Worcester, 1876; at sea 4 yrs., 2 yrs. S. Africa, India, W.I., etc.; farmed in Neb.; after that in newspaper work; in 1886 went to Eng. and joined army in expectation of war; returned to U.S. to position of Indianapolis News; in 1904 corr. Russo-Japanese War; first man from outside to enter Port Arthur during siege; arrested by Russians as spy; was lit. and dramatic editor Indianapolis News; now on staff Washington Herald. Contbr. various periodicals for yrs. Author: Roach & Co., Pirates, 1900; also plays - The Mouse Trap, etc. Address: The Herald, Washington, D.C.

FULLER, J(OHN) DOUGLAS, coll. prof. b. Laurens, S.C., Oct. 30, 1899; s. Claude Stokes and Corinne (Pitts) F.; B.S., The Citadel, 1919; A.M., Johns Hopkins, 1928, Ph.D., 1932; m. Minnie Lawrence Mims, June 1, 1922; children—Minnie Jane, John Douglas. Asso. prof. history Tex. Agr. and Mech. Coll., 1928-35; teaching fellow Johns Hopkins, 1931-32; prof. history Virginia Military Institute from 1935; head departments history and econs., 1952-59, head dept. history econs. and polit. sci., from 1959. Armed Services rep., instructor history and geopolitics, Army Specialized Training Programs, lecturer in geopolitics, R.O.T.C. and O.R.C., 1948-49. Served as 2d lt. U.S. Army, World War I. Member Am. and Southern hist. assns., Am. Polit. Sci. Assn., Am. Assn. Univ. Profs., Nat. Geog. Soc. Democrat. Episcopalian. Author: The Movement for the Acquisition of Mexico, 1846-48, 1936. Co-editor Greenmount: A Virginia Plantation Family During the Civil War, 1962. Home: Lexington VA Died May 30, 1967; buried Stonewall Jackson Cemetery, Lexington VA

FULLER, JOHN WALLACE army officer; b. Cambridge, Eng., July 28, 1827; s. Benjamin Fuller; m. Anna Rathbun, 1851. Came to U.S., 1833; city treas. Utica, N.Y., 1852-54; established publishing, bookselling bus., Toledo, O., 1858; commd. col. 27th Ohio Inf., 1861; commanded Ohio Brigade or Fuller's Brigade at Battle of Iuka, 1862; defeated Gen. Nathan Bedford Forrest's cavalry at Parker's Cross Roads, 1862; captured Decatur, Ala., 1864; participated in Atlanta Campaign, including Gen. Sherman's march to the sea; commd. brig. gen. U. S. Volunteers, 1864; sr. mem. Fuller, Childs & Co., whole-sale boot and shoe mchts., 1865; collector of customs Port of Toledo, 1874-81. Died Toledo, Mar. 12, 1891.

FULLERTON, WILLIAM MORTON publicist; b. Norwich, Conn., Sept. 18, 1865; s. Bradford Morton and Julia (Ball) F.; grad. Phillips Acad., Andover, Mass., 1882; A.B., Harvard, 1886. One of founders of the Harvard Monthly; formerly on staff of the Boston Advertiser; foreign staff London Times, 1891-1911. With Gen. Staff, A.E.F., 1917-18; spl. commr. for U.S. and Can., Internat. Urban Exhbn., Lyons, France. Chevalier Legion of Honor (France), 1913, Officer, 1919, Commander, 1926. Author: in Cairo, 1891; Patriotism and Science, 1893; Terres Francaises, 1905; Problems of Power, 1913 (translated into Japanese, 191 Hesitations, 1916; Les Etats-Unis et la Guerre. Editor: Gil Blas, 1912. On staff of Figaro, Paris. Regular contbr. to English, French and Am. reviews and mags. Addresss: 8 Rue du Mont Thabor, Paris, France.

FULMORE, ZACHARY TAYLOR lawyer; b. Robeson Co., N.C., Nov. 11, 1846; s. Zachary F.; ed. public schools and in Bingham School, N.C., 1862-64 and 1865-67; studied law, Univ. of Va., 1867-70; m. Luella Robertson, April 4, 1877. Entered Confederate army April, 1864; taken prisoner of war at Fort Fisher, N.C., Jan. 15, 1865. Began practice of law in Austin, Tex., Jan., 1871; chmn. commn. to codify laws of Texas, 1891-92; Democrat. Trustee State Inst. for Blind, 1875-97; trustee public schools, Austin, Tex., 17 yrs.; fellow Tex. State Hist. Assn. Author: History of the Geography of Texas (chart). Also wrote: History Geography of Texas, June, 1897; Causes of the Mexican War with U.S., 1900; Plea for Texas Literature, 1900. Address: 310 W. 13th St., Austin, Tex.

FULP, JAMES DOUGLAS, educator; b. Fort Mill, York Co., S.C., Oct. 13, 1886; s. Richard Amasa and Lucy (Parker) F.; A.B., Presbyn. Coll. of S.C., Clinton, S.C., 1906; studied U. of London, 1919; M.A., U. of S.C., 1925; m. Daisy Wilson, of Ridgeway, S.C., Oct. 14, 1909; children—James D., Jr., John R. Prin. Mt. Zion Inst., S.C., 1906-07; supt. city schs., Ft. Mill and Abbeville, S.C., 1915-17, 1919-23; high sch. insp., S.C., 1923-26; supt. Bailey Mil. Acad., Greenwood, S.C., since 1926. Served as capt. U.S.A., 1917-19; maj. Inf. Res., 1919-25; lt. col. since 1925. Trustee Presbyn. Coll. of S.C. Mem. N.E.A. (life), Nat. Assn. High Sch. Supervisors (pres. 1926), S.C. Teachers Assn. (life; pres. 1926-27), Am. Legion, Pi Kappa Alpha. Democrat. Presbyn. Kiwanian. Home: Greenwood SC

FULTON, FRANK TAYLOR M.D.; b. Westmoreland County, Pa., Apr. 28, 1867; s. Robert and Harriet Jewett (Trussell) F.; B.S., Knox Coll., 1894, hon. D.Sc., 1924; A.B., Johns Hopkins, 1895, M.D., 1899; unmarried. Pathol. interne, Boston City Hosp., 1899-1900; pathologist, Rhode Island Hosp., 1900-09; instr. Brown U., 1903-10; consulting phys. Rhode Island, Providence City, Pawtucket Meml. Woonsocket, S. County and Westerly hosps.; cardiologist Providence Lying-in Hosp. Commd. maj., M.C.U.S.A. and was chief of med. staff, Base Hosp., Camp Devens, Mass. Mem. Assn., Am. Physicians, A.M.A., Am. Assn. Pathologists, Am. Clinical and Climatol. Assn., Am. Soc. Clin. Investigation, R.I. Med. Soc. (pres. 1929), Providence Med. Soc. (pres. 1921), N.E. Heart Assn. (pres. 1933-35), Sigma Xi, Beta Theta Pi. Presbyn. Clubs: Agawam Hunt, Hope. Author: The Story of the Heart Station at Rhode Island Hospital, 1956; also articles on tb, heart and circulatory diseases. Home: 273 Bowen St. Office: 124 Waterman St., Providence 6, Dec. Apr. 1961.

FULTON, JAMES GROVE, congressman; b. Allegheny County, Pa., Mar. 1, 1903; s. James Ernest and Emilie (Fetterman) F.; A.B., Pennsylvania State Univ., 1924; LL.D., Harvard, 1927; student Carnegie Inst. Tech. 2 yrs.; unmarried. Admitted to Pa. bar, 1928, in general practice of law, Pittsburgh, Pa., 1928-42; solicitor for Dormont Borough, 1942; state senator 45th Pa. Dist., 1939-40; mem. 79th-82d Congresses, 31st Pa. Dist., mem. 83d-91st Congresses, 27th District Pa.; mem. House Fgn. Affairs committee, chmn. sub-com. for Europe, chmn. spl. sub-com. to investigate Displaced Persons and Internat. Refugee Orgn., mem. Sci. and Astronautics com., mem. vets. affairs com. 87th; U.S. del. UN Internat. Trade Orgn. Conf., Havana, 1947-48, U.S., del. 14th Gen. Assembly UN, 1959. Co-author, Definitive study on Internat. Trade Orgn.; owner, publisher Mt. Lebanon (Pa.) News, The Boro News, and The News (Allegheny County), Chartiers Valley Times Progress, The Tribune, also The News Progress, Dormont News (both Pitts.). Chmn. Pa. Heart Fund, 1970. Bd. dirs. Pitt Sch. Engring.; bd. visitors U.S. Naval Acad., Annapolis, Md. Served as lt. USNR, 1942-45; service Pacific combat area; ret. capt. Mem. bd. dirs. Pittsburgh Playhouse, Pitts. Opera Bd. Mem. Allegheny Bd. Law Examiners, 1934-42. Rep. for President U.S. at Uruguay inauguration, 1954. Decorated by Republic of Italy, 1956; named Distinguished Grad. Pa. State U., 1970; recipient Silver Quill award, 1970; mem. Young Republican Nat. Hall of Fame; life mem. Allegheny County Young Rep. Hall of Fame. Mem. Am., Pa., Allegheny County bar assns., Vets. Fgn. Wars, Am. Legion, Phi Delta Theta. Republican. Elk, Eagle. Clubs: Civic of Allegheny County, Harvard of Western Pennsylvania, Harvard-Yale-Princeton, Duquesne, St. Clair Country, Chartiers Country, Law (Pitts.). Home: Dormont PA Died Oct. 6, 1971; buried Mt. Lebanon Cemetery.

FULTON, WALTER SCOTT ret. army officer; b. Lyndoch, Ont., Can., Mar. 23, 1879; s. James and Jennie (Grey) F.; brought to U.S., 1880; B.S., U.S. Mil. Acad., 1904; grad. Command and Gen. Staff Sch., 1925, Army War Coll., 1919; m. Helen Rose Bennet, Feb. 27, 1911; children-Helen Bennet (Mrs. Stephen W. Ackerman), Walter Scott. Commd. 2d lt. Inf., June 15, 1904, and advanced through the grades to brig. gen., 1942; retired, 1944. Home: 1815 Starke Av., Columbus, Ga. Died June 24, 1950.

FUNK, JOHN CLARENCE author, lawyer; b. Harrisburg, Pa., Jan. 29, 1884; s. David Sieber (M.D.) and Matilda (Motzer) F.; A.B., Princeton, 1905; student law dept. U. Pa., 1906; LL.B., Dickinson Coll., 1909, A.M., 1909; D.Sc., Susquehanna U., 1926; m. Ada Cynthia Pruden. May 15, 1926. Vice agt. U.S. Dept. Justice, 1912-13; dep. clerk U.S. Dist. Ct., Middle Dist. Pa., 1914; U.S. Navy law enforcement rep. Commn. on Tng. Camp Activities, portion of 1917; mem. U.S.N.R.F., 1917: supervising inspector Office Naval Intelligence, 1919; supervising field agt. U.S. Interdepartmental Social Hygiene Bd., 1920; dir. Bur. Protective Social Measures, Pa. State Dept. Health, 1921; sci. asst. USPHS, 1922, regional dir., 1936, spl. atty., 1922, later chief bur. of pub. health edn., Pa. State Dept. Health; dir. health edn., Va. State Dept. Health, 1936-46; former exec. sec. Pa. Pub. Health Assn. Lt. comdr. USNR, ret. Mem. bar Supreme Ct. Pa., Phi Delta Theta, Nat. Reciprocity Club (hon.). Presbyn. Mason. Author: Vice and Health (text book on social sanitation), 1921; So This Is America! (an Am. travel book), 1923; How to Live Longer, 1927; Stay Young and Live!, 1943. Formerly health feature writer for Western Newspaper Union and contbr. mags. Home: R.D. 1, Box 103, Fayetteville, Pa. Deceased.

FUNSTON, FREDERICK army officer; b. New Carlisle, O., Nov. 9, 1865; s. Edward Hoge and Ann Eliza (Mitchell) F.; grew up on farm in Kan.; student

U. of Kan. 2-1/2 yrs.; m. Eda Blankart, Oct. 25, 1898. Apptd. spl. agt. U.S. Dept. Agr., 1890, and as such took part in Death Valley Expdn., 1891; in Alaska and adjacent portions of British Northwest, 1892-94; crossed Alaska to Arctic Ocean and traveled from McKenzie River to Bering Sea, total journey of 3,500 miles; camped on the Klondike, winter of 1893-94; floated down Yukon alone in a canoe; resigned from Dept. of Agr. and traveled in Mexico; entered Cuban insurgent army as capt. of arty., 1896; and promoted to maj. and lt. col., participating in campaigns of Maximo Gomez and Calixto Garcia. Returned to U.S. at outbreak of Spanish-Am. War and was commd. col. 20th Kan. Vol. Inf., May 13, 1898; sent with regt. to Philippines and participated in Northern Luzon campaign of General MacArthur; for crossing Rio Grande River at Calumpit, Apr. 26, 1899, on small bamboo raft in face of heavy fire, and establishing rope ferry by means of which U.S. troops were enabled to cross and win battle, was promoted to brig. gen. vols., May 1, 1899, and awarded Congressional Medal of Honor, Feb. 14, 1900; continued in campaign at head of a brigade; wounded at Santo Tomas; assigned to comd. 4th Dist., Dept. of Northern Luzon, Jan. 1900; organized and comd. expdn. resulting in capture of Aguinaldo, the insurgent leader, Mar. 23, 1901; brig. gen. U.S.A., Apr. 1, 1901; returned to U.S., 1901, and comd. in succession Depts. of the Colo., the Columbia, the Lakes, Southwestern Div. and Dept. of Calif., and Army Service schs.; comd. Dept. of Luzon, 1911-13, Hawaiian Dept., 1913-14; apptd. comdr. 2d Div. U.S.A., at Texas City, Tex., Jan. 1914; comd. expdn. to Vera Cruz, Apr. 1914, and was mil. gov. of the city until Nov. 1914; maj. gen., Nov. 17, 1914; apptd. comdr. Southern Dept., Feb. 1915; placed in gen. command of U.S. forces along Mexican border, 1916, and also of movements of U.S. troops in Mexico, in pursuit of Villa. Home: Iola, Kan. Died Feb. 19, 1917.

FUQUA, STEPHEN OGDEN army officer; b. Baton Rouge, La., Dec. 25, 1874; s. James Overton and Jeannette M. (Foules) F.; student Tulane U., 1888-89, U. of La., 1889-92, U.S. Mil. Acad., 1892-93; distinguished grad. Inf.-Cav. Sch., 1907; grad. Army Staff Coll., 1908, A.E.F. Staff Coll., Langres, France, 1918; refresher course, Inf. Sch., 1924; m. Pauline Stafford, Apr. 25, 1906; children-Jeannette Stafford, Stephen Ogden. Commd. capt., Inf., U.S. Vols., July 8, 1898; 2d lt., U.S. Inf., Feb. 2, 1901; advanced through grades to col., (temporary) Oct. 30, 1918, (permanent) Jan. 14, 1928; became chief of inf., rank of maj. gen., Mar. 28, 1929; formerly mil. attaché Am. Embassy, Madrid, Spain; now military Affairs editor, Newsweek, New York. Awarded D.S.M. Mem. Sigma Nu. Mason. Address: War Dept., Washington, D.C. Died May 11, 1943.

FURBUSH, CHARLES LINCOLN physician; b. New York, Dec. 2, 1863; s. Silas Smith and Henrietta (Hatfield) F.; pvt. and high schs., New York; M.D., Medico-Chirurgical Coll., Phila., 1893; univs. of Berlin and Heidelberg, semesters, 1893, 94, 95; m. Persis Burnham, Oct. 19, 1904. Began practice, Phila., 1893; apptd. acting asst. surgeon U.S.A. hosp. ship quarters Dept. of Havana, Cuba, May 4, 1899; dir. Dept. of Charities and Hosp., Havana, May 11, 1899; capt. and asst. surgeon U.S. vols., Aug. 21, 1899; maj. and surgeon, Mar. 16, 1901; acting chief sanitary officer, Havana, Dec. 19, 1901; chief sanitary officer, May 20, 1902. Served in Philippine Islands, 1900, 1901. Resumed practice, Phila., Oct. 1, 1902. Chmn. Phila. Milk Commn., 1911—; del. Internat. Hygiene Expn., Dresden, Germany, 1911; dir. Pa. Soc. for Prevention of Tuberculosis; fellow Coll. of Physicians, Phila. Republican. Apptd. 1st lt. Med. R.C., U.S.A., Jan 29, 1912; apptd. Oct. 1, 1916, spl. asst. to the Am. ambassador (Gerard) to Germany. Maj., asst. surgeon Med. R.C., May 10, 1917; lt. col., M.C.U.S.A., Jan. 29, 1918; col., Apr. 30, 1918; mil. observer with A.E.F., in France, Sept. 8, 1918; hon. disch., Dec. 10, 1918; col., Med. Sect. O.R.C., Jan. 28, 1919. Mem. yellow fever commn. of Rockefeller Foundation to Central America, Dec. 12, 1918. Companion Order St. Michael and St. George (C.M.G.), hon. mem. Mil. Order 3d Class, Eng., July 18, 1919. Dir. Sept. of Pub. Health and pres. Board of Health, Phila., 1919—. Home: Philadephia, Pa. Died June 26, 1923.

FURER, JULIUS AUGUSTUS naval officer; b. Mosel, Wis., Oct. 9, 1880; s. Rev. Edmund E. and Caroline Louisa (Wedemeyer) F.; B.S., U.S. Naval Acad., 1901; M.S., Mass. Inst. Tech., 1905; m. 2d, Helen Carlin Emery, May 12, 1927; 1 dau., (by 1st marriage), Helen C. (Mrs. Clifton Toal). Commd. lt., USN, 1903, advanced through grades to rear adm. 1941; midshipman U.S.S. Indiana, U.S.S. Shubrick, 1901-03; transferred to constrn. corps, 1903; duty at navy yards, N.Y., Charleston (S.C.), Phila., Pearl Harbor (T.H.), 1905-15; planned and supervised raising of submarine F-4 from depth of 304 feet (greatest depth from which any ship has been raised). Honolulu, 1915; with Bur. Constrn. and Repair, USN Dept., designing submarine chasers and supervising building program for small craft, 1915-19; mem. staff comdr.-in-chief, Pacific fleet, 1919-21; with Bur. Constrn. and Repair, 1921-23; mem. U.S. Naval Mission to Brazil, 1923-27; mgr. Navy Yard, Cavite, P.I., 1928-30, Phila., 1930-35; tech. asst. to naval attaches, London, Paris, Berlin, Rome, 1935-58; gen. insp. Bur. Ships, USN Dept., 1938-40; head Compensation Bd., Navy Dept., 1941; coordinator research and devel. Navy Dept., 1941-45; ret. from active duty, Nov. 1945; recalled to active duty 1951 - , engaged in writing History of Adminstrn. of Navy Dept. in World War II. Cons. Brazilian govt. on laying out naval yard, Rio de Janeiro, 1923-27; tech. adviser Naval Limitations Conf., London, 1936. Trustee Naval Hist. Found., supervised constrn. naval Mus., Washington. Awarded Navy Cross, Legion of Merit, various campaign and victory medals (U.S.), Legion of Honor (France), Order of Crown (Belgium). Mem. Soc. Naval Architects and Marine Engrs., Am. Soc. Naval Engrs., U.S. Naval Inst., Chi Phi. Clubs: Chevy Chase, Army-Navy (Washington), Yacht (N.Y.C.). Contbr. numerous articles to Ency. Americana, Naval Inst., other tech. jours. Invented submersible pontoons for raising sunken ships, 1915, adopted as standard salvage equipment for submarine bases. Home: 2101 Connecticut Av Washington 8, Died June 5, 1965; Buried Nat. Cemetery.

FUREY, JOHN VINCENT brig. gen.; b. Brooklyn, May 22, 1839; s. Robert and Mary F.; ed. at Brooklyn; m. Georgianna G. Grosholz, Dec. 23, 1868. Pvt. Co. C, 84th N.Y. Inf., Apr. 18, 1861-Sept. 28, 1862; capt. asst. q.m. vols., Apr. 7, 1864; capt. asst. q.m. U.S.A., Jan. 18, 1867; maj. q.m., Nov. 11, 1887; lt. col. deputy q.m. gen., Aug. 21, 1896; col. asst. q.m. gen., Aug. 12, 1900; brig. gen. U.S.A., Feb. 25, 1903; retired, Feb. 26, 1903. Home: Brooklyn, N.Y. Died Dec. 17, 1914.

FURLONG, CHARLES WELLINGTON explorer, writer, painter, soldier, ethnologist, lectr.; b. Cambridge, Mass., Dec. 13, 1874; s. Atherton Bernard and Carletta Eleanor (Wellington) F.; student pub. schs., Boston, also pvt. schs., U.S. and Eng.; grad. Mass. Normal Art Sch., 1895; student Cornell U., Harvard Ecole des Beaux Arts, Acad. Julian (Paris), 1901-02; m. Eva C. Earll, June 20, 1899; children - Ruth Earll, Roger Wellington; m. 2d, Edith Virginia Calista Spinney, Mar. 31, 1933. Faculty Cornell U., 1896-1904, 06-10, also Clark U., Boston U.; paintings in leading Am. art exhibits, life drawings of now extinct Ona and Yahgen Indians in permanent collection Smithsonian Inst., lectr. ednl. instns. and before learned socs. in U.S. and Eng. Leader expdns. and explorations in Africa, Near East, S.A., C.A., Tierra-del-Fuego and Patagonia; discovered sunken wreck of U.S. frigate Philadelphia in Tripoli Harbor, (sunk by Lt. Decatur 1804), 1904; also new Columbus date, 1915; now cons. to Stefansson Collection Baker Library, Dartmouth Coll., Hanover, N.H. Served mil. service Army of U.S. 34 yrs.; from pvt. to maj. Gen. Staff, World War I; commd. col., 1929, expert cons. M.I., World War II, 1943; ret. from Honorary Reserve, 1943. Member American Peace delegation, Paris, 1918, special military aide to Pres. Wilson; military observer and intelligence officer in Balkans and Near and Middle East, 1919. Twice was cited for D.S.M.; recipient Croix de Gueer (Greek); Medal for Bravery (Montenegro) and other U.S. and fgn. honors, including palms of French Acad. Fellow Royal Geog. society, Mil. Order World Wars (lion, life mem., d.s.m.), Order of Lafayette, Naval Inst., Cannon Hunters Assn.; Epsilon Alpha, Sigma Xi. Clubs: Ends of Earth, Explorers, Harvard Travelers. Author: The Gateway to the Sahara, 1909. 12; Tripoli in Barbary, 1911; Let'er Buck, 1921. Contbr. to ethnol. collections various museums and edns. instns. Records of expdns. to Tierra-del-Fuego and Patagonia (including the only song, speech and hand and footprint records extant of extinct Ona and Yahgan tribes) acquired - Fuegian by Stefanson Collections, Dartmouth Coll., 1960. Address: Dartmouth Coll., Hanover, N.H. Died Oct. 9, 1967.

FURNAS, ROBERT WILKINSON farmer, gov.; b. Miami Co., O., May 5, 1824; s. William and Martha (Jenkins) F.; m. Mary E. McComas, Oct. 29, 1845 (died); celebrated golden wedding before wife's death; m. 2d, Mrs. Susannah (Emswiler) Jameson. Practical printer and editor; resident Neb., 1855—; col. 2d Neb., cav. in Civil war; gov. Neb., 1873-75. Republican. Presbyterian. U.S. commr. to expns. at Phila., New Orleans, Chicago; pres. Neb. State Bd. Agr. Mason. On retiring from public life engaged in farming and tree culture. Home: Brownville, Neb. Deceased.

FURNESS, JAMES WILSON, mining engr.; b. Phila., Pa., June 5, 1874; s. Frank and Fannie (Fassitt) F.; prep. edn., William Penn Charter Ch., Phila., 1883-91; B.S., Pa. Mil. Coll. 1895, B.M.S., 1927; m. Adeline E. Brown, Oct. 25, 1899; 1 dau., Adeline Fassitt. Assayer and metallurgist in Colo., 1895-1900; asst. to D.M. Barringer, mining engr., Phila., in examining mining properties in Can., western U.S. and Mexico, 1904-08; operator of mines, 1908-09; asso. with O.A. Robertson in chge. mining properties in Can., Calif., Colo. and Nevada, also visited mines in Belgium, 1910-18; operated mines in Colo. and Ariz., 1919-22; investigated manganese situation in Georgia, Russia, 1920; with U.S. Bur. of Mines, 1922-26; chief of mineral div. U.S. Bur. Foreign and Domestic Commerce. Dept. of Commerce, 1927-34; chief of economics br. Bur. of Mines, 1934-40; retired. Served as officer Ordance Dept., U.S. Army, Aug. 1918-Jan. 15, 1919; lieut. colonel Special Res., U.S. Army, 1937; member Minerals Advisory Com. to War Dept.; mem. Mineral Policy Committee, 1935. Mem. Washington Geol. Soc. Dem. Unitarian. Clubs: Civitan, Down Town (Asheville). Author of many government publications on mineral economics. Home: 76 North Griffing Boulevard, Asheville NC

FURNISS, EDGAR STEPHENSON, JR. educator; b. Newton, Ia., Aug. 14, 1918; s. Edgar Stephenson and Beryl Frances (Gates) F.; B.S., Yale, 1940, M.A., 1945, Ph.D., 1947; student U. Cal. at Berkeley, 1941-42; m. Georgialee Bull, June 9, 1941; children - Norman Sleeter, Jean Beryl. Intern, Nat. Inst. Pub. Affairs, 1940-41; div. asst. Office Am. Republic Affairs, Dept. State, 1944-46; teaching asst. dept. govt. Yale, 1946-47; from instr. to asso. prof. dept. politics Princeton, 1947-60, prof., 1960 - ; Mershon prof. polit. sci. Ohio State U., also dir. social sci. program Mershon Center for Edn. in Nat. Security since 1963 - ; lectr. Army, Navy, Air, Nat. War Colls.; vis. prof. Columbia, U. Pa., Johns Hopkins. Mem. Am. Polit. Sci. Assn., Internat. Studies Assn. (v.p.), Council on Fgn. Relations, Phi Beta Kappa. Author: (with Richard C. Snyder) American Foreign Policy, 1954; American Military Policy, 1957; France, Troubled Ally, 1960; De Gaulle and The French Army, 1963. Home: 2760 Welsford St., Columbus, O. Died Aug. 17, 1966.

FURRER, RUDOLPH consultant; born Union City, N.J., Apr. 14, 1893; s. Rudolph and Bertha (Hardmeier) F.; ed. in pub. schs., Union City; m. Leone Barbara Peters, Oct. 19, 1921; children - John Rudolph, Barbara Christine. With Allis-Chalmers Mfg. Co., Milwaukee, 1907-17; mech. engr., chief of field inspection, and purchasing engr. A.O. Smith Corp., Milwaukee, 1918-26, chief engr. and dir. research, 1926-32; asst. to vice presidents Nat. Tube Co., Pittsburgh, 1933-35; v.p. A. O. Smith Corp., Milwaukee, 1936-47; became v.p. American Car and Foundry Co., N.Y.C., 1947, formerly pres. Nuclear Energy Products div., pres. Advanced Products div.; v.p., dir. ACF Industries Inc., until 1959; mgmt. cons., 1959-60; spl. asst. to dir. def., research and engring., Washington, 1960; sr. cons. Lockheed Missile & Space Co., 1961-62. Member of Committee on Ordnance, Joint Research and Development Board, Washington. Served with Aviation Division, United States Naval Reserve Forces, World War I; member War Metallurgy Com., 1943-45; spl. cons. Army Ordnance Research Com., 1944-45. Awarded certificate of appreciation, Bureau of Ordnance, U.S. Navy, 1946, Ordnance Dept., U.S. War Dept., 1945. Mem. Am. Ordnance Assn. Republican. Unitarian. Mason. Clubs: Milwaukee, Milwaukee University; Oconomowoc (Wis.) Lake; Rockefeller Center Luncheon. Helped develop mass prodn. auto frames with 1st automatic auto frame system, 1920s; major role in develop. flash welding large diameter pipes; supr. design and constrn. A. O. Smith Bldg., Milw. Home: 1000 Harbor Rd., Southport, Conn. Died Jan. 19, 1965; buried Wisconsin Meml. Park, Milw.

FURST, JOSEPH investment banker; b. Boston, Aug. 31, 1900; s. Louis E. and Jennie (Smith) F.; student Rice Inst., 1917-18, 18-19, U. Tex., 1919-20, Investment dealer, 1928-38, underwriter, distbr. investment securities, 1938 - ; owner Furst & Co., 1928-48, successor firm Securities Co. of Mass., 1948-54; pres. Securities Co. of Mass., Inc., 1954 - ; pres. Investment Co. Boston, 1951 - ; pres. Income Fund Boston, Inc. 1955-65, chmn. bd., chief exec. officer, 1965 - ; pres. Boston Adminstrv. & Research Corp., 1955 - ; chmn. Boston Trust Funds, Inc., 1953 - ; investment adviser Arlington Nat. Bank, Maj. to lt. col. USAAF, 1942-46. Mem. Nat. Assn. Securities Dealers, Inc. Club: University (Boston). Home: 180 Commonwealth Av. Office: 581 Boylston St., Boston. Died May 24, 1967; buried Sharon Park, Sharon, Mass.

FURSTENBERG, ALBERT CARL, physician, dean med. sch.; b. Saginaw, Mich., May 27, 1890; s. William C. and Emma Jane (Kerr) F.; B.S., U. of Mich., 1913, M.D., 1915; m. Elizabeth Nancy Maloy, June 18, 1923; children—Nancy, Julie, William Lou. Intern U. of Mich. Hosp., 1915-16; instr. otolaryngology, U. of Mich. Med. Sch., 1918-24, asst. prof., 1924-29, asso. prof., 1929-32, prof., from 1932, dean, 1935-60. Dir. Ann Arbor Trust Co., Ann Arbor Bank. Served as 1st lt. Med. R.C., during World War; consultant, surgeon gen. U.S. Army; hon. cons. Army Med. Library. Diplomate Am. Bd. Otolaryngology. Fellow A.C.S. (2d v.p.; bd. govs., 1943-46); mem. Washtenaw Co., Mich. State med. socs., A.M.A., Am. Acad. Ophthal. and Otolaryngology (pres. 1956), Detroit Otol. Soc., Southwestern Mich. Triological Soc., Am. Laryngol., Rhinol. and Otol. Soc., Inc. (pres., 1946), Am. Otol. Soc. (pres., 1952-53), Am. Laryngol. Soc., Assn. Am. Med. Colleges (past pres.). Clubs: University of Michigan, Ann Arbor, Barton Hills (Ann Arbor); Detroit (Mich.) Athletic; Cosmos (Washington). Contbr. sci. articles to jours. Home: Ann Arbor MI Died Oct. 23, 1969.

FYAN, ROBERT WASHINGTON congressman, lawyer; b. Bedford Springs, Pa., Mar. 11, 1835; attended common schs.; studied law. Admitted to bar, 1858, began practice of law, Marshfield, Mo.; county atty., 1859; commd. lt. col. Webster County Home Guards, 1861, at start of Civil War; commd. capt., maj., 24th Regt., Mo. Volunteer Inf., then col. 46th Regt., 1861; circuit atty., 1865-66; judge 14th Jud. Circuit Mo., 1866-83; mem. Mo. Constl. Conv., 1875; mem. U.S. Ho.

of Reps. (Democrat) from Mo., 48th, 52d-53d congresses, 1883-85, 91-95. Died Marshfield, July 28, 1896; buried Lebanon (Mo.) Cemetery.

GAARDE, FRED WILLIAM physician; b. Minden, Neb., June 20, 1887; s. John Frederick and Anna Dorothy (Klith) G.; B.S., U. of Chicago, 1909; M.D., Rush Medical Coll., 1912; in practice of internal medicine, Chicago, 1913-14; instr. medicine, Rush Med. Coll., 1913-20; m. Hazel Hollman, May 20, 1915. Asso. in med., Mayo Clinic, Sept. 1920; asso. prof. med., Mayo Foundation, Univ. of Minn.; head diagnostic section in med., Mayo Clinic. Major, Med. Corps. U.S. Army; with A.E.F., World War I. Mem. Chicago Inst. Medicine, Am. Medical Assn., Central Clin. Research Club, Minn. Soc. of Internal Medicine, Am. Coll. Physicians, Sigma Xi. Author: chapter in Nelson's Loose-leaf System of Medicine, and in Blumer's Bedside Diagnosis. Contbr. about 25 articles to med. jours. Address: 102 2d Av. S.W., Rochester, Minn. Died Feb. 10, 1948.

GABRIEL, GILBERT WOLF critic, author; b. Brooklyn, N.Y., Jan. 18, 1890; s. Samuel and Anna (Lavine) G.; prep. edn., Peekskill Mil. Acad. and Polytechnic Prep. School, Brooklyn; B.A., Williams College, 1912, hon. M.A., 1937; m. Ada Vorhaus, June 3, 1918. Reporter New York Evening Sun, 1912-15, lit. editor, 1915-17, music critic, 1917-24; dramatic critic New York Telegram-Mail, 1924-25, New York Sun, 1925-29, N.Y. American, 1929-37. Cue mag. since 1949; lectr. drama, criticism N.Y.U. Served as 2d lt. inf., U.S. Army, at Plattsburg T.C., Camp Upton and Camp Lee, World War. Chief of Alaska Mission, Overseas Branch. Office of War Information, Anchorage, Alaska, 1942-43; public relations and propaganda officer, G-2, Alaska Defense Command, 1943; deputy chief publs., Psychological Warfare Division, Supreme Headquarters, London, 1944. Mem. Authors League of Am. (officer, mem. council). Clubs: Dutch Treat, Williams Coll., N.Y. Critics' Circle; Critics' Circle of London (hon.). Author: The Seven Branched Candlestick, 1916; Jiminy, 1922; Brownstone Front, 1924; Famous Pianists and Composers, 1928; I, James Lewis, 1931; Great Fortune, 1933; I Got a Country, 1943; Love from London, 1946; I Thee Wed, 1948; also stories, articles and motion pictures. Home: Brewster, N.Y. Died Sept. 3, 1952.

GADE, JOHN ALLYNE b. Cambridge, Mass., Feb. 10, 1875; s. Gerhard and Helen Rebecca (Allyne) G.; B.S., Harvard University, 1896; M.A., Columbia 1948, Ph.D., 1950; m. Ruth Sibley, November 18, 1907; children-Fredrick Herman, Margaret Durbin, Ruth Allyne. Practiced architecture in N.Y. City. Mem. Commn. of Relief for Belgium, 1916-17; naval attaché U.S. Legation, Copenhagen, Denmark, 1917-19; mem. Baltic mission; entered diplomatic service, 1919; served as rep. of State Dept. in the Baltic provinces; mem. White, Weld & Co., bankers; returned to Naval Service; capt. U.S.N.R. 1938; naval attaché U.S. Embassy, Brussels and United States Legation, Lisbon; ret. naval service, 1940. Awarded Navy Cross (U.S.). Faithful Service Medal (Navy); var. fgn. decorations. Clubs: Knickerbocker, Harvard. Author: Book Plates, Old and New 1898; Cathedrals of Spain, 1911; Charles XII, King of Sweden, 1917; Christian IV, 1928: Life of Cardinal Mercier, 1934; All My Born Days, 1942; Life and Times of Tycho Brahe, 1947. Address: 920 Fifth Av., NY

GADSDEN, CHRISTOPHER Continental congressman; b. Charleston, S.C., Feb. 16, 1724; s. Thomas and Elizabeth Gadsden; m. Jane Godfrey, Aug. 28, 1746; m. 2d, Mary Hassell, Dec. 29, 1775; m. 3rd, Anne Wragg, 1776; at least 1 child. Mem. S.C. Assembly, 1757-84; owned 2 stores in Charleston, 2 stores in rural area, also a plantation, by 1761; mem. Stamp Act Congress, 1765; leader S.C. radicals; del. 1st, 2d continental congresses, 1774-75; sr. col. in command of S.C. Militia, commd. brig. gen. Continental Army, 1776; mem. S.C. constl. convs., 1778, 90; lt. gov. S.C., 1778-80, signed surrender of Charleston to Sir Henry Clinton, 1780, imprisoned by British, exchanged, 1781; mem. S.C. Conv. which ratified U.S. Constn., 1788; S.C. presdl. elector, 1789. Died Charleston, Aug. 28, 1805.

GAFFEY, HUGH J. army officer; b. Hartford, Conn., Nov. 18, 1895; s. Peter John and Anne Elizabeth (Conley) G.; grad. Worcester (Mass.) Acad., 1916; student U. of Pa., 1916-17; grad. F.A. Sch., 1923, Command and Gen. Staff Sch., 1936; m. Eleanor Schmitt, Jan. 5, 1922; 1 dau., Eleanor Anne, Commd. 2d lt., F.A., Aug. 15, 1917, and advanced through the grades to maj. gen., Apr. 28, 1943; chief of staff 3d Army, for Lt. Gen. George Patton; comdr. 2d Armored Div., landings in Africa, Sicily; now comdr. 4th Armored Div. sent to rescue of Bastonge. Decorated Silver Star citation, D.S.M., Legion of Merit. Mem. Delta Kappa Epsilon. Home: 3207 Clearview Av., Austin, Tex. Died June 17, 1946; buried in Fort Knox (Ky.) National Cemetery.

GAFFNEY, DALE V. army officer; b. Mass., Feb. 18, 1894; grad. AC Tactical Sch., 1936, Command and Gen. Staff Sch., 1937; rated command pilot, combat and tech. observer. Pvt. advancing to agt., 5th Inf., Mass. N.G., 1916-17; pvt. aviation sect. Sigma Corps, 1917; commd. 2d lt., 1918, advanced through the grades to brig. gen. AC, 1943; dep. comdr. Air Force Proving Ground. Eglin AFB, Fla. Address: care War Dept., Washington 25. Died Mar. 28, 1950.*

GAFFNEY, JOHN J(EROME) naval officer; b. Charleston, S.C., Mar. 5, 1891; s. Patrick John and Ellen Frances (O'Conner) G.; A.B., Coll. of Charleston, 1912; student St. Lawrence U. (Brooklyn Law Sch.), 1925-26; m. Wahneta Walsh, Jan. 16, 1915; children-John Jerome, Mary Yetive (Mrs. Edward W. Bridewell), Gloria Louise (Mrs. Francis Van Dyke Andrews), Lurline Loretta (Mrs. Charles R. Eisenbach). Entered supply corps, U.S. Navy, 1912; promoted through grades to rear adm., 1943; served in Chinese waters, 1913-16; built and managed naval clothing factory, Charleston, S.C., 1917; sec. Virgin Islands, 1920-23; bought navy fuel, 1937-39; staff comdr. Aircraft Battle Force, 1939-41; headed supply work ashore, Pearl Harbor, 1941-45; comdr. Naval Supply Depot, Oakland, Calif. since Aug., 1945. Awarded Silver Star, spl. commendation letter, Sec. of Navy, Legion of Merit. Home: 11 Mill St., Charleston, S.C. Address: U.S. Naval Supply Depot, Oakland 4, Calif. Died Nov. 21, 1947.

GAFFNEY, JOHN MARSHALL, steamship co. exec.; b. Boston, Aug. 18, 1907; s. Peter Joseph and Sarah (Marshall) G.; A.B., Harvard, 1931, student Bus. Sch., 1932-33; m. Marion Mary Russell, Sept. 21, 1936 (dec. Dec. 1968); children—Sarah Jane (Mrs. Jeremy Bull), John Marshall. With U.S. Lines Co., 1933-42, 46-67, European gen. mgr., 1961, dep. European gen. mgr., 1961, v.p. Europe, 1961-67; regional dir., European gen. operations mgr. War Shipping Adminstrn., 1945-46; dir. Soc. Maritime Anversoise, Antwerp, Atlantic Transp. Co., Ltd., London, Rosskai, G.m.b.H., Hamburg, Service de Consignation Atlantique, Paris. Vice chmn. Internat. Chamber Shipping, 1966-67. Served to col., Transp. Corps, AUS, 1942-45. Decorated Legion of Merit; Legion of Honor, Croix de Guerre with palm (France). Mem. Am. C. of C. in London (dir.), Nat. Def. Transp. Assn. (life), Royal Instn. Naval Architects, Harvard Bus. Sch. Assn. Clubs: Propeller (pres.), Harvard, Royal Thames Yacht, Royal Ocean Racing, American (bd. govs.) (London); Sunningdale Golf (Berks., Eng.); Royal Corinthian Yacht (Essex, Eng). Home: London Eng Died Oct. 7, 1967; buried City of Westminster Cemetery, Mill Hill, Eng (Alekseyevich),

GAGE, THOMAS army officer, royal gov.; b. Firle, Sussex, Eng., 1721; s. Thomas (1st viscount Gage) and Benedicta (Hall) G.; m. Margaret Kemble, Dec. 8, 1758, 11 children. Commd. lt. Brit. Army, 1741, lt. col., 1751; came with his regt. to Am., 1754; served under Braddock in expdns. against Ft. Duquesne, 1755, wounded; participated in Ticonderoga expdn., 1758; commd. brig. gen., 1759; served under Amherst against Montreal, 1760; mil. gov. Montreal, 1760; commd. maj. gen., 1761; succeeded Amherst as comdr.-in-chief in N. Am. with hdqrs. in N.Y.C., reapptd., 1775; commd. lt. gen., 1773; commd. vice adm., capt. gen., gov.-in-chief Province of Mass., 1774; attempted to suppress colonial resistance to parliamentary acts, but his efforts (such as an expdn. to Concord, Mass. to seize colonial arms) resulted in open fighting, eventual war; Battles of Lexington, Bunker Hill took place during his rule; established martial law, offered amnesty to all but Samuel Adams, John Hancock, 1775; sailed from Boston to Eng., 1775; served as col. 17th, later 11th Dragoons; commd. gen. Brit. Army, 1782. Died Eng., Apr. 2, 1787.

GAILLARD, DAVID DU BOSE soldier; b. Fulton P.O., S.C., Sept. 4, 1859; s. Samuel Isaac and Susan Richardson (Du Bose) G.; ed. pvt. country sch., Clarendon Co., S.C., and Mt. Zion Sch., Winnsboro, S.C., 1872-74; apptd. from S.C. and grad. U.S. Mil. Acad., 1884, Engr. Sch. of Application, 1887; m. Katherine Ross Davis, Oct. 6, 1887. Apptd. 2d lt. engrs., June 15, 1884; 1st lt., Oct. 27, 1887; capt., Oct. 25, 1895; col. 3d U.S.V. engrs., June 7, 1898; hon. mustered out, May 17, 1899; maj., Apr. 23, 1904; lt. col., Apr. 11, 1909. Asst. to Capt. W.M. Black, and in charge various surveys and harbor improvements at St. Augustine and Tampa and Withlacoochee River, Fla., 1887-91; mem. Internat. Boundary Commn., U.S. and Mex., 1891-94; in charge Washington Aqueduct, etc., 1895-98; on staff Maj. Gen. J.F. Wade, U.S.V., Apr.-June, 1898; served in U.S. and Cuba, June 1898-May 1899; chief engr. Dept. of Santa Clara, Cuba, Feb.-Apr. 1899; asst. to engr. commr. of D.C., 1899-1901; in charge all river and harbor improvement of Lake Superior, 1901-03; mem. gen. staff corps and engr. officer Northern Div., 1903-04; on duty at Army War Coll., 1904-06; chief mil. information div., army of Cuban pacification at Marianao, Cuba, Oct. 1906-Feb. 1907; mem. Isthmian Canal Common. and dir. Panama R.R. Co., Mar. 16, 1907—. Supervising engr. in charge of dredging in harbors, building breakwaters, etc., Apr. 1, 1907-July 1, 1908; div. engr. Central Div., Gatun to Pedro Miguel, July 1, 1908—. Author: Wave Action in Relation to Engineering Structures, 1904. Died Dec. 5, 1913.

GAILLARD, EDWIN SAMUEL surgeon, editor; b. Charleston, S.C., Jan. 16, 1827; grad. S.C. Coll. (Now U.S.C.), 1845; M.D., Med. Coll. State of S. C., Charleston M.A. (hon.) also LL.D. (hon), U.N.C., 1873; m. Jane Marshall Thomas, 1856; m. 2nd, Mary Elizabeth Gibson, 1865; 4 children. Practiced medicine, Fla., 1855-57; after trip to Europe settled in Balt., 1861; became asst. surgeon 1st M. Regt., Confederated Army, 1861; mem. examining bd. Army of Va., 1861; lost right arm at Battle of Seven Pines, 1862; apptd. mem. dir. mil. hosps., Va. and N.C., 1862, insp. gen. Confederate hosps., 1863-65; prof. principles and practice medicine and gen. pathology Med. Coll. Va., Richmond, 1865; founded Richmond Med. Journal (changed name to Richmond and Louisville Med. Journal 1868), publisher, 1865-79; prof. medicine Ky. Sch. Medicine, 1868; an organizer, 1st dean, prof. gen. medicine and pathology Louisville (Ky.) Med. Coll., 1869; established Am. Med. Weekly, Louisville, 1874, editor, 1874-83; moved to N.Y.C., 1879; published Gaillards's Med. Jour., until 1883. Author numerous papers including Ozone: Its Relation to Health and Disease (received Fiske Fund prize 1861), essay on diphtheria (received Ga. Med. Assn. prize 1866). Died Feb. 1885.

GAINES, EDMUND PENDLETON Army officer; b. Culpeper County, Va., May 20, 1777; s. James and Elizabeth (Strother) G.; m. Frances Toulmin; m. 2d, Barbara Blount; m. 3d, Myra Clark, 1839. Served as lt. in co. of riflemen, 1795; commd. lt. U.S. Army, 1797; surveyed road from Nashville, Tenn. to Natchez, Miss., 1801-04; made arrest of Aaron Burr; commd. maj., 1812; served as col. in engagement at Chrysler's Field, 1813; adj. gen. in command Fort Erie, 1813; brig. gen. successfully defending Ft. Erie against a superior Brit. force, 1814; recipient gold medal U.S. Congress; commr. to treat with Creek Indians in South, 1817; participated under Jackson in Creek and Seminole wars; in command Eastern Dep. of U.S. Army; led successful campaign against Black Hawk, 1832; for his unofcl. participation in Mexican War, (in which he commanded a large force of volunteers), deprived of his command by U.S. Pres., summoned to Ft. Monroe for trial by ct. martial; successfully defended himself, proceedings were dropped; bitter enemy of Gen. Winfield Scott; at odds with War Dept. through most of his career, especially in regard to methods of frontier defense. Died New Orleans, June 6, 1849.

GAINES, GEORGE STROTHER Indian agt., mcht., planter; b. Stokes County, N.C., circa 1784; s. James and Elizabeth (strother) G.; m. Ann, 1812. Asst. factor govt. trading house, Stephens, Miss. Territory, 1805-19; Indian agt. on Spanish border; largely responsible for success of Am. trade with Spain; mem. Ala. Senate, 1825-27; mcht., Mobile, Ala., 1830-56; a promoter Mobile and Ohio R.R.; pres. Mobile br. State Bank; mem. Miss. Legislature, 1861; owned plantation, State line, Miss., retired to plantation, 1856; Gainesville (Ala.) named after him. Author: Reminiscences of Early Times in Miss. Territory, 1872. Died Miss., Jan. 21, 1873.

GAINES, JOHN POLLARD congressman, territorial gov.; b. Augusta County, Va., Sept. 22, 1795; s. Abner and Elizabeth (Mathews) G.; m. Elizabeth Kincaid, June 22, 1819; m. 2d, Margaret B. Wand, circa 1852. Admitted to Ky. bar; served in War of 1812; served as maj. gen. cavalry brigade Ky. Militia, lMexican War; mem. Ky. Legislature; mem. U.S. Ho. of Reps. (Whigs) from Ky., 30th Congress, 1847-49; apptd. gov. Ore. Territory by Pres. Taylor, 1850-55. Died Salem, Ore., Dec. 9, 1857; buried Odd Fellows Cemetery, Salem.

GAITHER, NATHAN congressman, physician; b. nr. Mocksville, N.C., Sept. 15, 1788; attended Bardstown Coll.; grad. Jefferson Med. Coll. Began practice of medicine, Columbia, Ky. served as asst. surgeon in War of 1812, mem. Ky. Ho. of Reps., 1815-18, 55-57; Democratic presdl. elector, 1829; mem. U.S. Ho. of Reps. (Democrat) from Ky., 21st-22d congresses, 1829-33; del. Ky. Constl. Conv., 1849. Died Columbia, Aug. 12, 1862; buried Columbia Cemetery.

GAITHER, P(ERRY) STOKES, life ins. co. exec.; b. Brookline, Mass., Sept. 3, 1907; s. Charles P. and Mary W. (Stokes) G.; grad. Milton (Mass.) Acad., 1925; Ph.B., Yale, 1929; student Am. Inst. Banking, 1928-33; m. Elizabeth Hamlin, Nov. 4, 1938; children—Anne M., John S. Chief investment clk. First Nat. Bank & Trust Co., New Haven, 1929-35; asst. to trust officer Second Nat. Bank, New Haven, 1935-37; asst. trust officer Merchants Nat. Bank, Boston, 1937-43; with New Eng. Mut. Life Ins. Co., Boston, 1946-67, 2d v.p., 1951-57, v.p., 1957-66, sr. v.p., 1966-67; trustee Wm. Underwood Company, Watertown, Mass.; dir. Reichhold Chemicals, Inc., North White Plains, N.Y., Baystate Corporation (Boston), McGregor-Doniger, Inc. Bd. dirs. Fed. Dorchester Neighborhood Houses, Inc.; trustee Yale Scholarship Trust of Boston, 1942-65, chmn., 1953-65. Served as lt. col. Transp. Corps, AUS, 1943-45. Mem. Nat. Inst. Social Scis. Clubs: Dedham (Mass.) Country and Polo (gov. 1957-63; pres. 1961-62); Yale of Boston (pres.), Union, Economic (Boston); Yale (N.Y.C.); Norfolk Hunt (treas.) (Dover, Mass.); The Country (Brookline, Mass.). Home: Dedham MA2Died Aug. 4, 1967.

GAITHER, WILLIAM COTTER, JR. lawyer; b. Tampa, Fla., Apr. 26, 1914; s. William C. and Monroe (Cargyle) G.; LL.B., U. Fla., 1936; m. Elaine Lucille Beisler, Dec. 28, 1943; 1 dau., Georgann. Admitted to Fla. bar, 1936; with McKay, MacFarlane, Ramsey & Jackson, Tampa, 1936-38; claims mgr., atty. Phoenix-London Ins. Group, Miami, Fla., 1938-42; mem. firm

Nichols, Gaither, Beckham, Colson & Spence, Miami, 1946 - . Pres. Colonial Arms, Inc., 1958 - ; v.p. Sea View Realty Co., 1958 - . Mem. Orange Bowl Com., 1955 - ; mem. Fla. Bd. Control, regulating instns. higher learning, 1957-59; mem. Dade County Devel. Commn., 1959 - . Past regional dir. Assn. Governing Bds. State Univs. and Allied Instns. Served from 2d lt. to capt., F.A., AUS, 1942-46; ETO. Decorated Bronze Star medal. Mem. Am., Fla., Dade County bar assns., Miami Jr. C. of C. (past pres.), Acad. Fla. Trial Lawyers, Am. Trial Lawyers Assn., Nat. Assn. Claimants Compensation Attys., U. Fla. Alumni Assn., Law Center Assn. U. Fla. (trustee), National Conference Christians and Jews (regional director). Episcopalian (sr. warden). Kiwanian (dist. lt. gov. 1962) (Coral Gables). Home: 4615 Santa Maria St., Coral Gables, Fla. Office: 1111 Brickel Av., Miami, Fla. Died Jan. 26, 1967; buried Woodlawn Cemetery.

GALATTI, STEPHEN broker; b. Monmouth Beach, N.J., Aug. 6, 1888; s. Paul Stephen and Angelique (Kessisoglov) G.; A.B., Harvard, 1910; M.A. (hon.), Yale, 1956; m. Grace S. Montgomery, Sept. 25, 1925 (dec.); 1 son, Stephen. Clk., Ralli Bros., mchts., 1911-14; with John Munroe & Co., N.Y., Munroe et Cie, Paris, 1919-30; with Jackson & Curtis brokers, 1930-43, Paine, Webber, Jackson & Curtis, brokers, 1930-43, Paine, Webber, Jackson & Curtis, brokers, 1943-54, ret. Attached U.S. Embassy, London, Eng., Aug.-Nov. 1914. Commd. capt. U.S. Army Ambulance Service, 1917, promoted maj., 1918. Served with Am. Field Service, 1915, asst. insp. gen., 1916-17; reorganized service, 1939, dir. gen. 1939 - ; trustee Saint Marks Sch. Dir. Greek War Relief, Am. Relief for France. Decorated Croix de Guerre, 1915, Chevalier Legion of Honor, 1947 (France), Comdr. (civilian) Order Brit. Empire, 1946, Medal of Freedom, 1946 (U.S.). Clubs: Knickerbocker, Racquet and Tennis (N.Y.). Home: 134 E. 40th St. Office: 113 E. 30th St., N.Y.C. Died July 13, 1964.

GALDWIN, HENRY army officer; b. Derbyshire, Eng., Nov. 19, 1729; s. Henry and Mary (Dakeyne) G.; m. Frances Berridge, Mar. 30, 1762. Commd. lt. 48th Regt., Brit. Inf., 1753; served with Gen. Braddock's expdn. to Ft. Duquesne, 1755; commd. capt. 80th Regt., Brit. Inf., 1757, maj., 1759; served in relief of St. Niagara, 1760; in command at Detroit, 1761-64, supervised successful defense of fort during Pontiac's War, 1763; commd. lt. col., 1763; dep. adj. gen. in Am., 1764-80, but returned to Eng., 1764, never returned to Am. colonies; promoted col., 1777, maj. gen., 1782. Died Chesterfield, Eng., June 22, 1791; buried Wingerworth Churchyard, nr. Chesterfield.

GALE, HENRY GORDON physicist; b. Aurora, Ill., Sept. 12, 1874; s. Eli Holbrook and Adelaide (Parker) G.; A.B., U. of Chicago, 1896, grad. student, 1896-97, fellow in physics, 1897-99, Ph.D., 1899; m. Agnes Spofford Cook, Jan. 5, 1901; 1 dau., Beatrice Gordon. Asst. in physics, 1899-1900, asso., 1900-02, instr., 1902-07, asst. prof., 1907-11, asso. prof. physics, 1911-16, prof., 1916-40, dean in Junior Colls., 1908-40, dean of science in the Colls., 1912-40, dean of Ogden Grad. Sch. Science, 1922, chmn. dept. of physics, 1925, dean div. of phys. sciences, 1931, emeritus, Univ. of Chicago. Physicist, Solar Observatory, Mt. Wilson, Calif., 1906; research associate of Carnegie Inst. at Mt. Wilson, 1909, 10, 11; editor Astrophys. Jour. since 1912. Capt. of Inf., N.A., 1917; maj. Sig. Corps, Jan. 1918, lt. col., Mar. 1919; in charge spl. service div., Tours, France, 1918-19. Cited by comdr.-in-chief A.E.F. for "especially meritorious and conspicuous service"; Chevalier Legion of Honor, France. Mem. bd. John Crerar Library. Fellow A.A.A.S. (v.p. 1934), Am. Physical Soc. (v.p. 1927-29; pres. 1929-31), Am. Optical Society; mem. Delta Kappa Epsilon, Sigma Xi and Gamma Alpha fraternities. Clubs: Quadrangle, Wayfarers, University, Lake Zurich (Ill.) Golf. Republican. Author: (with R.A. Millikan) A First Course in Physics, 1906; A Laboratory Course in Physics, 1906; Practical Physics, 1920; Elements of Physics, 1926; (with R. A. Millikan and C. W. Edwards) A First Course in College Physics, 1928. Vice chmn. div. of phys. sciences, Nat. Research Council, 1920-21, chmn., 1921-22. Home: 5646 Kimbark Av., Chicago, Ill. Died Nov. 16, 1942.

GALE, JOSEPH WASSON, physician; b. Milton, Ia., Jan. 21, 1900; s. William and May (Rhoades) G.; M.D., Washington U., St. Louis, 1924; m. Marion Sutherland Reed, Oct. 20, 1928; children—Christina May (Mrs. Michael McPhee), Margaret Reed (Mrs. David Mayer). Intern, Barnes Hosp., St. Louis, 1924-25, asst. resident in surgery, 1925-26, resident, 1926-27; asso. surgeon Wis. State Gen. Hosp.; asst. in surgery U. Wis., Madison, 1927-30, asso. in surgery, 1930-41, prof., 1941-68. Served with U.S. Army, World War I; to col., M.C., AUS, 1942-44. Diplomate Am. Bd. Surgery (founder), Am. Bd. Thoracic Surgery (founder). Fellow A.C.S.; mem. A.M.A., Wis., Dane County med. socs., Am., Central, Western surg. assns., Am. Assn. for Thoracic Surgery, Soc. Univ. Surgeons, Nat. Tb Assn. Home: Madison WI Died Oct. 26, 1968.

GALEN, ALBERT JOHN judge; b. on ranch near Three Forks, Mont., Jan. 16, 1876; s. Hugh F. and Matilda (Gillogly) G.; student Manhattan Coll., New York, 1892-93; LL.B., U. of Notre Dame, Ind., 1896; LL.B., U. of Mich., 1897; m. Ethelene Bennett, Feb. 22, 1898. Admitted to Mont. bar 1897; mem. Galen & Moore, 1897-99, Galen & Beattie, 1899-1901, Galen & Metteler, 1905-21. Atty. gen. of Mont. 2 terms, 1905-13. Served on Mont. Capitol Commn. until new bldg. was completed, 1912. Chmn. Selective Service Board, Division 1, Montana, 1917. Commd. maj., judge adv. U.S.A., Jan. 5, 1918; judge adv. 8th (regular) Div. Camp Fremont Calif., Jan.-Aug. 1918; judge adv. gen. of A.E.F., Siberia, Aug. 1918-June 1919; lt. col., Mar. 28, 1919; hon. disch., July 25, 1919; lt. col. O.R.C. Asso. justice Supreme Court of Mont., 2 terms, 1921-27 and 1927-33; resumed practice at Helena. Awarded D.S.M. (U.S.). Republican. Catholic. Home: Helena, Mont. Died May 16, 1936.

GALLOWAY, FLOYD EMERSON army officer; b. Falmouth, Ky., Sept. 11, 1890; s. Grant and Alice (Moreland) G.; student U. of Ky., 1911-14; grad., Air Service Pilots Sch., 1921. Air Service Observation Sch., 1922, Air Corps Tactical Sch., 1933, Command and Gen. Staff Sch., 1938, Army War Coll., 1941; 1 dau., Mary Ann; m. 2d, Martha Gardener, June 8, 1929; children-Mary Ann (by 1st marriage), Patton, Floyd Emerson. Fibre specialist with Philippine govt., 1914-17; commd. 2d lt., U.S. Army, June 16, 1917, and advanced through the grades to brig. gen., Nov. 4, 1942; served in World War I with A.E.F. in Siberia; has comd. Bolling Field, Washington, D.C., Maxwell Field, Montgomery, Ala., Crissy Field, San Francisco, Calif., and Albrook Field, Canal Zone; organized and comd. Air Force Service Command in the Caribbean Area. Mason. Blk. Club: Army and Navy (Washington, D.C.). Home: Glen Iris Farm, Paris, Ky. Died Sept. 19, 1955; buried Paris, Ky.

GALLOWAY, IRENE OTI'LIA army officer; b. Templeton, Ia., Sept. 1, 1908; d. Franklin and Rose Anna (Reicher) Galloway. Commd. 2d lt. WAC, 1942, advanced through grades to col.; WAC staff dir. European command, 1948-52; apptd. comdt. WAC Tng. Center, 1952; dir. WAC 1953-56; past liaison officer Continental Army Command, Washington; now chief spl. projects br. legislative affairs, Office Sec. Def., Washington. Roman Catholic. Home: Walton House, 3900 Tunlaw Rd., N. W., Washington 7. Office: Pentagon, Washington 25. Died Jan. 1963.

GALLUP, EDWARD HATTON, JR., transp. exec.; b. Boston, Jan. 16, 1898; s. Edward Hatton and Marion (Ramsey) G.; A.B., Harvard, 1920, postgrad., 1929; N.Y. U., 1930-31; m. Claire Louise Lenfestey, Dec. 18, 1924; children—Edward Hatton III, Marion Elizabeth (Mrs. Robert H. Drummond). Sales, Bird & Son, Boston, 1923-28, Ginn & Co., Boston, 1928-41; sec. Pitts. Hotels Assn., 1946-53; asst. gen. mgr. Penn-Sheraton Hotel, Pitts., 1953-59; asst. exec. dir. Port Authority Allegheny County, Pitts., 1960-69. Lectr. U. Pitts., 1946-57; cons. Pa. Dept. Labor and Industry, 1966-69. Pres. South Hills Child Guidance Assn., 1957-58; treas. Pitts. Chamber Music Soc., 1962-68; pres. Pitts. chpt. Pa. Assn. for the Blind, 1966-69, trustee, 1959. Served as lt. col. AUS, 1941-46. Mem. Mil. Order World Wars (chpt. trustee 1952-69), Sigma Alpha Epsilon. Presbyn. (trustee). Clubs: University, Longue Vue Country, Harvard-Yale-Princeton (dir. pres. Western Pa. 1951). Home: Pittsburgh PA Died Dec. 7, 1969; interred Boston MA

GALPIN, WILLIAM FREEMAN educator; b. Ishpeming, Mich., Nov. 17, 1890; s. Rev. William and Helena B. (Grisson) G.; A.B., Northwestern U., 1913, M.A., 1914; Ph.D., U. Pa., 1917; m. Gladys Anna Bixby, Dec. 20, 1917; children - Jeanne Bixby (Mrs. Fred Thomas), Harriet (Mrs. Donald Hughes). Instr. history N.Y.U., summer 1917, Carnegie Sch. of Tech., 1917-18, Jamline U., 1919-20, U. Mich., Ann Arbor, 1920-24; prof. U. Okla., Norman, 1924-26; prof. Syracuse (N.Y.) U., 1926-56, historian, 1942-56, chmn. dept. hist., 1948-56, prof. emeritus, historian emeritus, 1956 - . Served as maj., div. agts. office, 14th div. U.S. Army, 1918-19. Mem. Am. Agrl. Hist. Assn. (v.p. 1928-29), N.Y. Hist. Soc., Onondaga Co. Hist. Soc., English Speaking Union, Am. Hist. Assn. (received Herbert B. Adams Prize for book), Delta Upsilon (v.p. 1934-35, dep. since 1935). Episcopalian. Club: Syracuse U. Faculty (pres. 1932-35). Author: several books since 1926, including Central New York, 1941; contbr. articles to prof. jours. Home: 857 Livingston, Syracuse, N.Y. 13210. Died Mar. 19, 1963; buried Oakwood Cemetery, Syracuse.

GALT, ALEXANDER sculptor; b. Norfolk, Va., June 26, 1827; studied in Florence, Italy, 1848-54, 56-60. Opened studio, Richmond, Va., 1860; executed busts of several noted Americans before and during Civil War; mem. staff of gov. Va.; made many drawings for Confederate Engrs., circa 1861-63. Died of smallpox, Richmond, Jan. 19, 1863.

GALVIN, MICHAEL JOSEPH lawyer; b. Boston, Sept. 7, 1907; s. James and Bridget (Hallahan) G.; LL.B., Northeastern U., 1932; student Northeastern U. Sch. of Finance, 1933, Command and Gen. Staff Sch., U.S. Army, 1939; m. Eleanor Henrietta Stevens, June 7, 1936; children - Patricia, Noreen, Priscilla, Michael, Gail. Lawyer, Boston, Washington, 1930 - ; under sec. labor, 1949-53. Mem. Nat. Maritime Emergency Commn., 1949-50, Nat. Def. Moblzn. Bd., 1950-53, Nat. Housing Council, 1949-53. Operations chief in Gen. Patton's 6th Armored Div., 1944-45, Intelligence Chief, 1942-43; in all major battles Patton's 3rd army, France and Germany; maj. gen., comdg. gen. 94th Inf. Div., 1960. Recipient five battles stars (Bastogne, Normandy, Rhineland, Germany, and N. France). Decorated Silver Star, Legion of Merit, Bronze Star Medal, Bronze Star Cluster, European Theater, Am. Theater, Am. Def., German Occupation and Victory medals (U.S.), Croix de Guerre with gold star (France). Mem. Greater Boston Community Fund, 1936-41 (chmn. Pub. Employee Div. 1941), Patton Meml. Commn., 1946-47. Author: Manpower Limited, 1951; Manpower and National Defense, 1952; Manpower Reserves for National Defense, 1953. Home: 107 Hobart Rd., Newton Centre 59, Mass. Died Dec. 12, 1963; buried Arlington Nat. Cemetery.

GAMACHE, GEORGE PAUL, air force officer; b. Fall River, Mass., Sept. 26, 1929; s. Louis Philippe and Rose (Montplaisir) G.; student Assumption Coll., Worcester, Mass., 1947-49; B.S., Okla. State U., 1962, M.S., 1963; m. Pauline Alice Masse, June 4, 1955; children—Monique Marie, Janine Renee, Murielle Ellen, Daniel Charles. Commd. 2d lt. USAF, 1952, advanced through grades to lt. col., 1969; navigator B-29 and RB-47 in Okinawa, North Africa, O., 1952-60; student Air Force Inst. Tech., 1960-63; electronics engr., system analysis div. Hdqrs. Air Force Eastern Test Range, Patrick AFB, Fla., 1963-65; prof. aerospace studies, head dept. Mass. Inst. Tech., 1965-69; chief, sensor monitor control Task Force Alpha, Thailand, 1969-70. Decorated Air Force Commendation medal. Registered profl. engr., Fla. Mem. I.E.E.E., Phi Kappa Phi, Eta Kappa Nu. Roman Catholic. Home: McCoy AFB FL Died Mar. 31, 1972.

GAMBLE, ROBERT BRUCE surgeon; b. Mosiertown, Pa., June 28, 1871; s. William J. and Helen (Beebee) G.; A.B., Allegheny Coll., Pa., 1893, A.M., 1896; M.D., U. of Buffalo Med. Dept., 1896; m. Nella M. White, July 5, 1900. House surgeon, City Hosp., Rochester, N.Y., 1896-97; settled in Meadville, Pa., 1897; surgeon City Hosp.; dir. First Nat. Bank, Meadville. Capt. 15th Pa. Vol. Inf., Spanish-Am. War, later lt. col. 16th Inf., N.G. Pa.; lt. col. of the 112th Inf., 1917; with A.E.F., 15 months. Chevalier Legion of Honor (France). Trustee Allegheny College. Fellow Am. Coll. of Surgeons. Republican. Episcopalian. Mason. Home: Meadville, Pa. Died July 11, 1940.

GAMBLE, ROBERT HOWARD chmn. Federal Reserve Branch Bank of Jacksonville; b. Tallahassee, Florida, Dec. 18, 1888; s. Robert and Mary Margaret (Summer) G.; student Law Sch., Yale, 1911; m. Mildred Franklin, Feb. 23, 1929; children-Catharine Bruce, Robert Howard. Began as runner Redmon & Co., N.Y. City; jr. partner Prince & Whitely, N.Y. City, later sr. partner, 1919-24; member National Code Authority, 1933-35; chmn. Regional Face Brick Code Authority No. 4, Washington, D.C., Regional Structural Clay Tile Code Authority No. 5, and Regional Common Brick Code Authority No. 19, 1933-35; co-founder Structural Clay Products Inst., Washington, D.C., dir. since 1934; labor advisor for Structural Clay Products Industry, Dept. of Labor, Walsh Healey div., Washington, since 1939; dir. Federal Reserve Branch Bank of Atlanta, Ga., Dist. No. 6, Jacksonville, Fla., since 1938; chmn. Duval County-Jacksonville Defense Council; mem. Industry Committee for Clay Products Industry, Labor Department; chmn. of Board of Directors Ga. Ice Co., Savannah; pres. Gamble Holding Corp., Jacksonville, Fla., Fla. Ice & Coal Co., Fla.-Ga. Brick & Tile Co., Fla. Brick & Tile Corp., Magaba Corp. Enlisted in Am. Field Service for service with French Army; returned to U.S., Sept. 1917 and transferred to U.S. Naval Aviation; placed on inactive duty, Jan.-1919 with rank of lieutenant-commander; resumed active duty, U.S. Navy, June 13, 1942, with rank of Commander; spl. asst. to Adm. A. B. Cook, Chief Air Operational Training Command, U.S. Naval Air Sta., Jacksonville, Fla.; transferred overseas as asst. and aide to Vice Adm. Cook, 1943; asst. and aide to Vice Adm. W. R. Munroe, Comdr. Gulf Sea Frontier, 1944; now asst. and aide to W. S. Anderson, Commandant 7th Naval Dist. and Comdr. Gulf Sea Frontier. Mem. Southern Clay Products Assn. (pres.), Fla. Brick Makers Assn. (pres.). Democrat. Episcopalian. Home: New Cut Plantation, Wadmalaw Island, S.C. Died Feb. 10, 1953; buried Oak Lawn, Jacksonville, Fla.

GANDY, CHARLES MOORE army officer; b. Ocean View, N.J., Nov. 6, 1857; s. Lewis Corson and Eliza A. (Smith) G.; prep. edn. S. Jersey Inst., Bridgeton, N.J.; M.D., Jefferson Med. Coll., Phila., 1879; m. Emma R. Graham, Nov. 6, 1884; children-Charles Lewis, Lila Marguerite. Apptd. asst. surgeon, Dec. 3, 1883; capt. asst. surgeon, Dec. 3, 1888; maj. brigade surgeon vols., June 4, 1898; maj. chief surgeon, Jan. 7, 1899; hon. disch. from vols., Mar. 22, 1899; maj. surgeon U.S.A., Feb. 2, 1901; maj. med. corps, Feb. 2, 1901; lt. col., Jan. 1, 1909; col. Apr. 16, 1913. Acting chief surgeon 4th Army Corps, Oct. and Nov., 1898; surgeon and prof. mil. hygiene, U.S. Mil. Acad., 1906-10; chief surgeon Western Dept., 1910-11; asst. surgeon gen.'s office, Washington, 1912-14; chief surgeon Philippine Dept., 1915-16; comdg. Army and Navy Gen. Hosp., Hot Springs, Ark., Feb. 20, 1917-May 26, 1919; chief surgeon, Eastern Dept., Governors Island, N.Y., 1919-21; retired Nov. 6, 1921. Mason. Home: Ocean View, N.J. Died Jan. 8, 1937.

GANNON, SINCLAIR naval officer; b. Columbia, Tex Mar. 19, 1877; s. William Andrew and Nancy Clementine (Robinson) G.; grad. U.S. Naval War Coll., Newport, 1921; m. Dell Triplett Sept. 25, 1902; children-Nancy Stuart (wife Comdr. Hilyer Fulford Gearing), Mary Sinclair (Mrs. Ott Lang), commd. ensign July 1, 1902; promoted through grades to rear adm., July 1, 1933; with landing part from U.S.S. Machias, Colon, Colombia, 1901-02; participated Abyssinian Expdn. in U.S.S. Machias, 1903-04; with Atlantic Fleet world cruise in U.S.S. Glacier Kearsarge and Connecticut, 1907-09; flag sec. to comdr. in chief U.S. Asiatic Fleet in U.S.S. Saratoga, Cincinnati and Rainbow, 1911-12, and comdg. officer U.S.S. Elcano on Yantze River, 1912-14, during overthrow of Manchu Dynasty; comdg. officer U.S.S. Saranac participated in laying North Sea mine barrage, 1918; comdg. officer U.S.S. San Francisco and comdr. Mine Detachment, 1919-20; mem. War Plans Div., Office of Naval Operations, Joint Army and Navy Planning Com. and Joint Bd., 1921-23; asst. chief of staff to commander in chief U.S. Fleet in U.S.S. Seattle, 1923-25; commandant of midshipman U.S. Naval Academy, 1925-28; commanding officer U.S.S. New York, 1928-29; chief of staff to comdr. U.S. Scouting Fleet, in U.S.S. Wyoming, 1929-30; comdg. officer U.S. Naval Training Sta., San Diego, Calif., 1930-33; comdr. Aleutian Islands Survey Expdn., 1934, and comdr. Minecraft, Battle Force, in U.S.S. Oglala, 1934-35; comdr. Destroyers Scouting Force, in U.S.S. Raleigh, Dobbin, Whitney and Aylwin, 1935-36; comdt. 11th Naval Dist. and San Diego Naval Operating Base, 1936-39; sr. mem. Pacific Coast sect. U.S. Navy Bd. of Inspection and Survey, 1939-41; retired Apr. 1941. Awarded D.S.M., Victory medal, Expeditionary medal, Spanish War medal. Clubs: Army and Navy (Washington); Army and Navy (Manila); N.Y. Yacht (New York, N.Y.). Address: 14 Thompson St., Annapolis, Md. Died Oct. 21, 1948.

GANO, ROY A., retired naval officer, steamship lines executive; born Pipestone, Minnesota, December 3, 1902; s. Harry and Myrtle (Hitchcox) G.; B.S., U.S. Naval Acad., 1926, postgrad. student, 1934; m. Harriet Howard, July 18, 1929; children—Myrtle Eugenia, James A. Commd. ensign USN, 1926, advanced through grades to vice adm., 1954; assigned U.S. ships Tennessee, 1926-29, John D. Edwards, 1929-30, Edsall, 1930-31, MacLeish, 1931-32; engr. U.S.S. Dewey, 1934-37; spl. engr. Naval Research Lab., Bellevue, D.C., 1937-39; material officer comdr. Destroyer Battle Force, 1941; material officer comdr. Task Force 8, Alaska, 1941-42; comdr. U.S.S. Dyson, 1942-44; asst. dir. naval communications for adminstrn., Office Chief Naval Operations, Washington, 1944-46; comdr. Destroyer Squadron 5, also Destroyer Div. 51, Japan-Korea area, 1946-48; dir. recruiting Bur. Naval Personnel, 1948-50, dir. enlisted personnel div., 1950-51; comdr. U.S.S. St. Paul, Korea, 1951-52; chief staff, aide comdr. Service Force U.S. Pacific Fleet, 1952-54; comdr. Service Squadron 3, evacuation refugees from No. Indo-China, 1954; asst. chief staff for logistics, 1954-55; dep. chief staff operations and adminstrn. Far East, UN Commands, 1955-56; dep. comdr. Mil. Sea Transportation Service, 1956-58; commander of Amphibious Group Two, 1958-59, Mil. Sea Transp. Service, 1959-64, ret. USN, 1964; v.p. Moore-McCormack Lines, Washington, 1964-71. Decorated Bronze Star Medal with gold star, Navy Cross with gold star, Legion of Merit with Gold Star, D.S.M. Home: Falls Church VA Died Jan. 20, 1971; buried Arlington Nat. Cemetery, Washington DC

GANOE, WILLIAM ADDLEMAN, b. Mifflintown, Pa., May 14, 1881; s. Rev. William Van Devender and Cynthia Constance (Addleman) G.; grad. Dickinson Sem., Williamsport, Pa., 1898; A.B., Dickinson Coll., 1902, A.M., 1913, Litt.D., 1952; B.S. U.S. Mil. Acad., 1907; grad. Staff and Command Sch., 1925, Army War Coll., 1930; m. Honora Patton Russell; children—Constance, Mary, Honora, Rebecca; m. 2d, Rose Laeh Shelnitt. Commissioned 2d lieutenant, infantry, U.S. Army, June 14, 1907; promoted through grades to major July 1, 1920; lt. col. (temporary), World War; lt. col. (permanent), January 1931; promoted to rank of colonel, Feb. 1, 1936. Has served in Cuba and Hawaii; instr. U.S. Mil. Acad., 1911-12, asst. prof. English, 1916-18, adj., 1918-21; head bd. to edit inf. drill regulation, 1923, history sect. U.S. Inf. Sch., 1923-24; General Staff eligible list, 1925; prof. mil science and tactics, Boston U., 1930-36; comdg. Fort Screven, Ga. and Dist. F, Civilian Conservation Corps, 1936; apptd. chief of staff, 2d Mil. Area, 3d Corps Area, and all reserve units of Western Pa., 1938; dir. Public Relations Div., First Army, 1941; later comdt., U.S. Army forces, Univ. of Mich., Theater Historian, European Theater Operations, U.S. Army, 1943-46; lectr. Brit. officers' schs. including Sandhurst and Oxford. Mem. British-American Liaison Bd., London, Eng. Mem. American Legion and Phi Delta Theta. Methodist. Mason. Author: The English of Military Communications, 1918; The History of the United States Army, 1924; Ruggs—R.O.T.C., 1917 (first story to be reprinted in pamphlet form by Atlantic Monthly); also stories and articles in mags. and Atlantic Narratives. Contributor to American Year Book, 1925-29, Dictionary American Biography, 1929-33, Encyclopedia Britannica, 1925; U.S. Army editor Encyclopedia Britannica, 1929. Radio speaker Yankee Network, 1934-35. Author: Soldiers Unmasked, 1935; History of the United States Army, 1942; My Heart Remembers, 1950; MacArthur Close-Up, published 1962. Decorated Bronze Star, also Medal Legion of Merit (U.S.), Order of British Empire (Gt. Britain), Croix de Guerre with palm (France). Address: Sarasota FL Died Sept. 5, 1966.

GANSEVOORT, PETER army officer; b. Albany, N.Y., July 1749; s. Harmen and Magdalena (Douw) G.; m. Catherina Van Schaick, Jan. 12, 1778. Served with Gen. Montgomery in expdn. against Que., Can., 1775; commd. maj. 2nd N.Y. Regt., 1775, lt. col., 1776, col. 3d N.Y. Regt., 1776; comdr. Ft. George, defended Ft. Stanwix against Brit. and Indians under St. Leger for 20 days, 1777; commanded F.T. Schuyler, Rome, N.Y., 1777; in temporary command, Albany, 1777; with Sullivan in expdn. against Indian allies of British, 1779; in command, Saratoga, N.Y., 1780; commd. brig. gen. N.Y. Militia, 1781, maj. gen. 1793; accompanied Gen. Washington in tour of Northern battlefields, 1783; mil. agt. Northern Dept., U.S. Army, 1802; dir. N.Y. State Bank, 1803-12; U.S. commr. Indian affairs; regent Univ. State N.Y., 1808-12; commd. brig. gen. U.S. Army, 1809. Died Albany, July 2, 1812.

GANTENBEIN, CALVIN URSINUS judge; b. Phila., Pa., Mar. 22, 1865; s. John (D.D., M.D.) and Mary (Schwaeble) G.; grad. Royal Charles Gymnasium Stuttgart, Germany, 1885; post-grad. work, Collège de France, Paris, 4 mos., 1885; LL.B., U. of Ore., 1891; m. Winifred Watson, d. of James Finley Watson, of Roseburg, Ore., Oct. 18, 1899. Prof. ancient and modern langs., West Chester (Pa.) State Normal Sch., 1885-88; instr. German and Latin, Portland (Ore.) High Sch., 1888-92; admitted to Ore. bar, 1892, and began practice at Portland; judge Circuit Court, 4th Jud. Dist., 1906-13, and 1915—; declined appmt. as justice Supreme Court of P.I., 1899; judge Juvenile Court, Multnomah Co., Ore., 1907-09, 1909-11; dean. Sch. of Law, U. of Ore., 1903-15; dean Northwestern Coll. of Law, Portland, Ore., Oct. 1915—. Private and advanced to lt. col. Oregon N.G., 1891-98; maj. 2d Oregon U.S. Vol. Inf., 1898-99; adj. gen. State of Ore., 1899-1903; col. 3d Inf., Ore. N.G., 1903-06; v.p. Interstate N.G. Assn., 1902; commd. col. of infantry, O.R.C., 1917. Was mem. 1st Mil. Commn. in Philippines, also of Bd. of Liquidation, etc. Mem. Portland Chamber of Commerce, Republican. Mem. German Reformed Ch. Scottish Rite Mason. Author: Oregon Volunteers in Spanish War and Philippine Insurrection, 1902. Home: Portland, Ore. Died Nov. 19, 1919.

GARCIA-VELEZ, CARLOS diplomat; b. at Jiguany, Santiago, Cuba, Apr. 29, 1867; s. Gen. Calizto Garcia and Ysabel Velez de Garcia Yñiguez; grad. New York pub. schs.; studied medicine and denistry. U. of Madrid, Spain, lit. and arts, Atenco de Madrid and Circulo de Bellas Artes, Madrid, mathematics and Latin under one of fathers of Royal Chapel of Madrid; m. Amalia M. Ybor, of New York and Tampa, Fla., Feb. 19, 1900. Editor Revista Estomatologica (med. rev.), Madrid, 1894; prof. Fomento de las Artes and Centro Instructivo del Obero, Madrid, 1892-93; entered services of Cuban Junta, New York, 1895, and took active part in preparing filibustering expdns. to aid Cuban insurgents against Spain; shipwrecked off Barnegat, Jan. 27, 1896, in steamer Hawkins, loaded with arms and ammunition and bound for Cuba, under command of his father; landed in Cuba, in Mar., same yr.; commd. capt. for services in filibustering; maj. at assault and fall of Guaimaro; lt.-col. after successful operations in laying mines in the Cauto River, blowing up several gunboats, and constant fighting to prevent passage of the Spaniards up the stream; col. for deeds of bravery and prin. part taken in capturing town of Las Tunas, making 600 of the enemy prisoners; as inspr.-gen. of prisons, under Gen. Wood, reformed the prison system of Cuba, 1900-02; reapptd. to same position by Gov. Magoon, under provisional govt., 1906-09; Cuban minister to Mex., 1902-06; E.E. and M.P. from Cuba to U.S., Apr. 9, 1909-1910. Mem. Veteranos de la Indepencia of Cuba, Am. Acad. Polit. and Social Science, Nat. Geog. Soc., Am. Prison Assn. lMem. Liberal Party. Catholic. Club: Union (Havana). Wrote 1st two chapters of History of Spanish-American War, by the War Leaders, 1899. Also of pamphlets on Cuban affairs and mil. subs., - and contbr. to mags. and newspapers. Address: Havana, Cuba.

GARDEN, HUGH RICHARDSON soldier, lawyer; b. Sumter Co., S.C., July 9, 1840; s. Alester Gibbes (originally A. G. Gibbes, but changed by act of legislature), revolutionary ancestry; grad. S.C. Coll., 1860; m. 1868, Charlotteville, Va., Lucy Gordon, d. William J. Robertson, judge Supreme Court of Appeals of Va. Joined C.S. army as pvt. Co. D, 2d regt., S.C. inf., 1861; re-enlisted 1862; apptd. capt. of arty, raised and equipped a battery of field guns. Served under Gen. John B. Hood as capt. arty. through campaigns of Western Va. His battery suffered severely at battles of Antietam, Gettysburg, 2d Cold Harbor, Fts. Harrison and Suffolk; at surrender of Confederate army at Appomattox, 1865, comd. arty. of rear guard of Lee's army. At close of war began study of law, Univ. of Va.; admitted to bar, 1866; commenced practice at Columbia, S.C. Removed to Warrenton, Va., where he practiced for 15 yrs.; removed to New York winter 1882-83. Mem. Va. Bondholders' Com., 1890-92, where he was greatly instrumental in effecting a settlement of the debt of Va. Mem. New York Southern Soc. (pres., 1890-91); mem. Young Men's Dem. Club, Manhattan Club, Reform Club, Bar Assn., Lawyers' Club, Delta Kappa Epsilon Club, etc. Address: Mutual Life Bldg., New York.

GARDENER, CORNELIUS army officer; b. in Netherlands, Sept. 4, 1849; s. Rev. Wynand and Barendina (Visser) G.; grad. Holland (Mich) Acad., 1865; student Hope Coll., 1865-66 (A.M., 1892); grad. U.S. Mil. Acad., 1873; m. Bessie E. Patton, Oct. 1901. Commd. 2d lt. 19th Inf., June 13, 1873; 1st lt., June 19, 1879; capt., Feb. 24, 1891; col. 31st Mich. Inf., May 11, 1898; hon. mustered out of vol. service, May 17, 1899; col. 30th U.S.V. Inf., July 5, 1899; hon. disch., Apr. 3, 1901; major 13th U.S. Inf., Sept. 16, 1899; lt. col., 21st Inf., Feb. 18, 1903; colonel 16th Inf., Dec. 26, 1905. Served in Indian wars, 1874-80; on Rio Grande, 1881-90; Ft. Wayne, Detroit, 1891-96; instr. Mich. N.G., 1897-98; in charge Pingree potato farms, Detroit, 3 yrs.; col. 31st Mich. Vols. in U.S. and Cuba, Spanish War; in Philippines as col. 30th U.S. Vols., Oct. 1899; to Apr. 1901; gov. of Tayabas, Luzon, P.I., Mar. 1901-Mar. 1902; retired, Sept. 4, 1913, after 44-1/2 yrs.' service. Home: Claremont, Calif. Died Jan. 2, 1921.

GARDINER, ASA BIRD army officer; lawyer; b. New York, Sept. 30, 1839; s. Asa and Rebekah Willard (Bentley) G.; A.B., Coll. City of New York, 1859, A.M., 1862; LL.B., New York U., 1860; (hon. A.M., Dartmouth, 1864, Columbia, 1869; LL.D., New York U., 1875; L.H.D., Hobart, 1896); m. Mary Austen, Oct. 18, 1865 (died 1900); 2d, Harriet Isabella Lindsay, Nov. 5, 1902. 1st lt. 31st N.Y. Vol. Inf., May 14, 1861; capt. 22d N.Y. Vols., May 31, 1862; 1st lt. U.S. Vet. Reserve Corps, Feb. 11, 1865, and adj.; bvt. capt. U.S. vols., May 13, 1865, for gallant and meritorious services during the war; hon. mustered out of vol. service, Aug. 13, 1866; 2d lt. 9th U.S. Inf., July 20, 1866; 1st lt., Feb. 14, 1868; transferred to 1st Arty., April 3, 1869; maj. judge advocate U.S.A., Aug. 13, 1873; awarded Congressional Medal of Honor, Sept. 23, 1872, "for conspicuous bravery and distinguished conduct during the Gettysburg Campaign, particularly in the action at Sporting Hill, Pa., June 30, 1863, and in defense of Carlisle, Pa., July 1-2, 1863" where wounded; retired Dec. 8, 1888; lt. col. U.S.A. retired, Apr. 23, 1904. Served during Civil War in 6th Corps, Army of the Potomac, and in 8th and 23d Army Corps; participated in fight at Union Mills, nr. Fairfax C.H., Va.; battles of Blackburn's Ford and Bull Run; skirmish at Winchester, Va., Aug. 30, 1862; etc. Acting adj. gen., recruiting service U.S.A., 1866-68; a.d.c. to Maj. Gen. McDowell, and chief signal officer Dept. of the East, 1869-72; judge advocate and acting adj. gen. Mil. Div. of South, 1871-73; judge adv. Mil. Div. of the Atlantic, 1878-87; prof. law, U.S. Mil. Acad., 1874-78; acting asst. sec. of war, 1887-88; dist. atty. N.Y. Co., 1897-1900. Counsel for Generals Grant and Sheridan in the Gen. G. K. Warren court of inquiry; counsel for govt. in Freedman's Bur. investigation, and Gen. Fitz John Porter and colored cadet Whittaker cases, and in many habeas corpus damage actions and criminal causes affecting army or navy. Commandant Vet. Corps Arty. State N.Y., and bvtd. maj. gen., mil. forces of State of N.Y., under concurrent resolution of legislature of N.Y., "for gallant conduct in Gettysburg Campaign and gallant and meritorious services during the war." Trustee Am. Coll. Musicians; sachem Tammany Soc., New York; deputy Gen. Conv. P.E. Ch., 1892, 1910; deputy P.E. Conv. Diocese L.I., 1885—; mem. P.E. Gen. Conv. Standing Commn. on Archives, 1892—. Author: The Writ of Habeas Corpus as Affecting the Army and Navy, 1874; Practice and Proceedings of Courts-Martial, 1878; The Rhode Island Continental Line of the Revolution, 1885; The Order of the Cincinnati in France, 1905. Died May 28, 1919.

GARDINER, WILLIAM TUDOR ex-governor; b. Newton, Mass., June 12, 1892; s. Robert Hallowell and Alice (Bangs) G.; graduate of Groton School, 1910; A.B., Harvard, 1914; LL.D., Bates, 1929; Univ. of Maine, 1932, Bowdoin College, 1945; student Harvard Law School, 2 years; m. Margaret Thomas, Sept. 16, 1916; children-Tudor, Thomas. Margaret, Sylvester (died 1947). Admitted to Mass. bar, 1917, to Maine bar, 1919; began practice of law at Augusta; formerly mem. firm Andrews, Nelson & Gardiner; chmn. Inc. Investors, Nat. Dock & Storage Warehouse Co.; v. chmn. Pacific Coast Co.; dir. Rayonier, Inc. Enlisted as pvt., 1st Me. Heavy F. A., reorganized as 56th Pioneer Inf.; advanced through grades to 1st lt.: served in Meuse-Argonne offensive, World War I; commd. maj. U.S. Air Force, Mar. 1942, advanced to colonel; placed on inactive list, July 1945, World War II, Mem. Me. Ho. of Rep., 1921-25 (speaker of house 1925); elected governor of Me. two terms, 1929-33; vice-pres. and dir. Incorporated Investors; director U.S. Smelting, Refining & Mining Co., Northwest Airlines, Inc., Nat. Dock & Storage Warehouse Co. Mem. Am. Legion. Republican. Episcopalian. Mason (33ff). Elk, Grange, Clubs: Brookline Country, Somerset, Harvard, Tavern Union Boat (Boston); Harvard (New York). Home: Gardiner, Maine. Office: 200 Berkeley St., Boston. Died Aug. 2, 1953.

GARDNER, ARTHUR mfg. exec., diplomat; b. Omaha, Neb., Feb. 21, 1889; s. Rev. Charles Henry and Margaret Morrison (Jackson) G.; student Hill Sch.;

A.B., Yale; m. Suzanne Anderson, Oct. 10, 1925; children - Arthur Wendell, Joan Gardner (Mrs. A. Britton Browne, Jr.), Suzanne Blake (Mrs. Frank R. MacLear). With the Equitable Trust Co., N.Y.C., 1910-12; partner in firm Anderson & Gardner, Detroit, 1926-31; first v.p. Bundy Tubing Company, 1929-53, in charge Washington office, 1951-62, chmn. bd., 1962 - ; pres. Detroit Macoid Co., 1934-53; asst. sec. U.S. Treasury, 1947-48; A.E. and P. to Cuba to 1957. Staff aircraft bd. W.P.S., 1 a year, 1943-45. Served as capt. tank corps, U.S. Army, World War I. Clubs: Metropolitan (Washington); The Brook, St. Anthony (N.Y.); Yondotega (Detroit); Everglades (Palm Beach, Fla.); Misquamicut (Watch Hill, R.I.). Died Apr. 11, 1967.

GARDNER, GEORGE PEABODY corp official; b. Boston, Nov. 19, 1855; s. George Augustus and Eliza Endicott (Peabody) G.; B.A., Harvard U., 1877; m. Esther Burnett, June 11, 1884; children—Catharine, George Peabody, Jr. Pres. Provident Instn. for Savings; pres. and trustee Amoskeag Co.; dir. State St. Exchange, Am. Telephone & Telegraph Co., Union Freight R.R. Co., etc. Mem. bd. of mgrs. Mass. Eye and Ear Infirmary; trustee Mus. Fine Arts; treas. Soc. for the Relief of Aged and Disabled Episcopal Clergymen. Hon. pres. Children's Hosp. Mem. 1st Corps Cadets; capt. and a.-d.-c. 2d Brig. staff, M.V.M. Home: Boston, Mass. Died June 6, 1939.

GARDNER, GRANDISON, air force; b. Pine Valley, Utah, Sept. 18, 1892; s. John Alexander and Celestia (Snow) G.; B.S., Utah State Coll., 1914; student U. of Calif., 1915-17; M.S., Mass. Inst. Tech., 1928; m. Edith McMurrin, March 25, 1918; children—Joseph Mather, Edith Rose. Commd. 2d lt., U.S. Army, Nov. 27, 1917, and advanced through the grades to maj. gen.; commd. A.F. Proving Ground Comd., World War II; assigned to Strategic Bombing Survey, Berlin, Guam and Tokyo, 1945; assigned Headquarters U.S.A.F., 1946; dir. Joint Air Defense Board, Colo. Springs, Colo., 1951-54; ret., 1954. Awarded Legion of Merit, Distinguished Service Medal, Order of British Empire. Home: Phoenix AZ Died Jan. 19, 1973.

GARDNER, JOHN HENRY army officer; b. Meadowdale, N.Y., Oct. 10, 1893; s. John Henry and Fanny Brooks (Ostrander) G.; B.S., Union Coll., 1913; M.S. in E.E., 1915; M.S., Yale, 1924; m. Mercedee Latham Crum, Oct. 15, 1921; children-Frances Patricia, John Underhill. With Gen. Electric Co., 1913-17; commd. 2d lt. F.A., 1917 and advanced through the grades to brig. gen., 1943; with E.A., A.E.F. and Army of Occupation, 1918-21; transferred to Signal Corps in 1923 and served in various research and development activities since 1927; comdg. gen., Signal Corps Aircraft Signal Service, Wright Field, Dayton, O., 1943; asst. chief, Procurement and Distribution Service, Office Chief Signal Officer, Washington, D.C., since August 1943. Mem. Am. Inst. E.E., Chi Psi. Home: 1719 37th St. N.W., Washington. Died Oct. 11, 1944; buried Arlington National Cemetery.

GARDNER, J(OHN) HEWLAND naval architect; b. Newport, R.I., Feb. 28, 1871; s. Stephen Ayrault and Mary (Sherman) G.; B.S., Mass. Inst. Tech., 1894; m. Helen M. Douglas, Dec. 26, 1900; children- John Howland, Helen Douglas (Mrs. George W. Elkins). Vice-pres. New England Steamship Co., 1913-28, pres., 1928-31; cons. engr. and mem. bd. dirs. Keerfoot Engring Co.; dir. New England Steamship Co., Hartford-New York Transportation Co. Mem. Bd. of Survey and Cons. Engrs., World War; commr. to Peruvian govt. for purchase of German vessels seized by Peru, 1918; co-founder (at request of U.S. Shipping Bd.) U.S. Bur. of Survey, 1920; was for over twenty years chmn. joint equipment com. of President's Conf. Com. and of Bur. of Valuation of Interstate Commerce Commn. Past pres. and hon. mem. Soc. Naval Architects and Marine Engrs. (mem. of exec. com. and member of com. on applications); trustee Webb Inst. Naval Architecture (20 yrs.): Republican. Conglist. Clubs: Engineers (past pres., and mem. admission com.), India House (New York). Home: Old Lyme, Conn. Died July 7, 1944.

GARDNER, JOHN LANE army officer; b. Boston, Aug. 1, 1793; s. Robert Gardner; m. Caroline Goldsborough, 1835. Commd. 3d lt., 4th Inf., U.S. Army, 1813, 2d lt., 1814; served on Northern frontier in War of 1812; transferred to arty., 1814; commd. 1st lt., 1818; q.m. gen., stationed Washington, D.C., 1819-30; promoted capt., 1823; served in Fla. War, also on garrison duty, Fla., 1830-45; commd. maj., 1845; served under Gen. Winfield Scott in campaign from Cerro Gordo to Mexico City during Mexican War; brevetted lt. col. for services at Cerro Gordo, col. for services at Contreras, 1847; in command of dist. of Fla., 1848-50; promoted lt. col., 1852; in command of Ft. Moultrie, Charleston, S.C., 1860, replaced after vowing to defend ft. from confiscation by secessionists, 1860; commd. col., ret., 1861; brevetted brig. gen., 1865. Died Wilmington, Del., Feb. 19, 1869.

GARDNER, JOSEPH Continental congressman, physician; b. Chester County, Pa., 1752; studied medicine. Began practice of medicine; raised co. of Volunteers, 1776, commanded 4th Battalion, Chester County Militia; mem. com. of safety, 1776-77; mem. Pa. Assembly, 1776-78, Supreme Exec. Council, 1779; mem. Continental Congress from Pa., 1784-85; resumed practice of medicine, Phila., 1785-92, Elkton, Md., 1792-94. Died Elkton, 1794.

GARDNER, KARL DANA merchant; b. Warren, R.I., Jan. 23, 1892; s. Dana Leonard and Katherine Esther (Macomber) G.; A.B., Brown U., 1913; m. Laura Borden Batt, Sept. 23, 1916. Connected with W. T. Grant Co., nat. chain stores, since 1913; asst. mgr., store mgr., later dist. mgr., 1924-28; dir. of sales promotion, 1928-30; dir. of merchandising, 1930-35; v.p. and gen. mgr., 1935-37; pres. and gen. mgr., 1937-40; chmn. exec. com., May 1940-Mar. 1942. Lt. col., Army United States, dir. procurement, Army Exchange Service, Jan. 1942-July 1942, col. since July 1942. Trustee Brown University. Mem. Beta Theta Pi. Mem. Reformed Ch. Clubs: Brown (New York); Siwanoy Country. Home: 43 Greenfield Av., Bronxville, N.Y. Died Feb. 25, 1944.

GARDNER, LESTER DURAND aero, exec.; b. N.Y.C., Aug. 7, 1876; s. Harry and Frances (Scott) G.; S.B., Mass. Inst. Tech., 1898; postgrad. Columbia, 1899; LL.D., Polytech. Inst. Bklyn., 1943; m. Margaret Kettle, Sept. 2, 1913. Staff N.Y. Mail, Sun, Times, and with Everybody's and Collier's mags.; pres., 1916-27. The Gardner Pub. Co., pubs. Aviation and Acro. Engring., Who's Who in American Aeronautics; pres. The Overbrook Press, Highland, N.Y.; pres. Aero. Industries, 1928; pres. Aero. C. of C. Am., 1928; exec. Inst. Aero. Scis., 1932-36; pres. Aero. Archives, 1932-36. Private 1st Plattsburg Regiment, 1915; commd. 1st lieutenant Signal Officers R.C., Aug. 1917; capt. Aviation Sect., Signal Corps, U.S. Army, Sept. 1917; maj. Air Service, Sept. 17, 1918; comdg. officer Aviation Camp, Waco, Tex., and mem. Bd. of Control, Dept. Mil. Aeronautics; on flying status when hon. discharged Dec. 13, 1918. Flew 26,000 miles over European airways, 1926. Del. U.S. Dept. of Commerce to 4th Internat. Civil Aviation Congress, Rome, 1927; apptd. by President Coolidge del. on the part of U.S. to Internat. Conf. on Civil Aeronautics, Washington, 1928; aero. mem. com. of N.Y. Statewide Econ. Congress, 1928; mem. Nat. Panel of Arbitrators, Am. Arbitration Assn., 1928; Am. del. German Aero Expn. and Conf., Berlin, 1928; as pres. Aero C. of C. Am., presented in 1928, cooperatively with Motion Picture Producers and Distbrs. Am., hist. film of Col. Charles A. Lindbergh's flying career, to U.S. State Dept., for U.S. Govt. archives; also to M. Laurent Eynac, French minister for air, at Aero Club de France, Paris, for French Govt. archives; to M. Lippens, Belgian minister of railroads and aeronautics, at Brussels for Belgian Govt. archives; to Sir Samuel Hoare, sec. of state for air of Great Britain, at Air Ministry, London, for British Govt. archives; Am. del., British Aircraft Expn., London, 1929; guest speaker, Internat. Advt. Conv., Berlin, 1929. Flew New York-Moscow-Rome-London via Hindenburg and European airlines. Del. to Lilienthal Soc., Berlin, 1936. Recipient Diploma of Honor, Ligue Internat. des Aviateurs, 1934; Daniel Guggenheim Medal for contbns. to aviation. Del. 1st World Congress Aero Press, Rome, 1939. Mem. aviation com. N.Y. World's Fair; mem. S.A. Reed, Octavo Chanute, Lawrence Sperry, Collier Trophy bds. of award. Hon. fellow Royal Aero. Soc.; mem. Soc. Automotive Engrs., Aero Med. Assn. U.S. (hon.), Am. Soc. M.E., N.Y. Mil. and Naval Officers of World War, Mass. Inst. Tech. Alumni Assn., S.A.R., Mil. Order World War. Am. Legion, Soc. Colonial Wars, Mil. Order Fgn. Wars, Soc. War 1812, Gamma Alpha Rho. Republican. Clubs: University, Wings Club (N.Y.C.); Army and Navy (Washington); Aviation Country (L.I., N.Y.). Home: 875 West End Av., N.Y.C. 25. Died Nov. 23, 1956; buried Arlington Nat. Cemetery.

GARDNER, TREVOR mfg. exec.; b. Cardiff, Wales, Aug. 24, 1915; s. George William and Elizabeth Ann (Thomas) G.; came to U.S., 1928, naturalized, 1937; B.S. in Engring., U. So. Cal. at Los Angeles, 1937; M.A. in Bus. Adminstrn., 1939; D.Sc., U. So. Cal., 1955; m. Helen Thurn-Taxis Aldridge, March 27, 1936 (div. Aug. 22, 1958); children - Trevor Helen Ann; m. 2d, Carie Bjurling, September 20, 1958; children - George W., Lars V., Charles Michael. Student engr. Gen. Electric Co., 1937-38; engr. Milw. Gas Specialty Co., 1939-41; asst. works mgr. Plomb Tool Co., 1941-42; supvr. development engring. sect. Cal. Inst. Tech., 1942-45; gen. mgr., exec. v.p. Gen. Tire & Rubber Co. of Cal., 1945-49; pres. Hycon Mfg. Co., 1948-53, Hycon Engring. Co., 1950-53; asst. sec. of the Air Force for research and development, Washington, 1953-55; chmn. pres. Hycon Mfg. Co., 1956-63. Mem. Pres.'s Space Task Force Com., 1961, Gen. Adv. Com. U.S. Arms Control and Disarmament Agy.; chmn. U.S. Air Force Space Task Force, 1960-61; cons.-at-large USAF Scientific Adv. Bd.; bd. visitors Air Force Systems Command; bd. trustees Aerospace Corp. Bd. Systems Command; bd. trustees Aerospace Corp. Bd. trustees Cal. State Colls. Recipient Naval Ordnance award, 1944, Pres.'s Certificate Merit, 1945, Paul T. Jones award Arnold Air Soc. (posthumously), 1964. Mem. Am. Newspaper Pubs. Assn. (mem. Scientific div. Com.), Am. Ordnance Assn., Tau Beta Pi. Club: Burning Tree Golf. Home: 1750 Linda Vista Av., Pasadena, Cal. Office: 700 Royal Oaks Dr., Monrovia, Cal. Died Sept. 28, 1963; buried Washington.

GARFIELD, JAMES ABRAM 20th Pres. U.S.; b. Cuyahoga County, O., Nov. 19, 1831; s. Abram and Eliza (Ballou) G.; attended Western Res. Eclectic Inst. (now Hiram Coll.); grad. Williams Coll., 1856; m. Lucretia Rudolph, Nov. 11, 1858, at least 5 children including James Rudolph, Harry Augustus. Admitted to Ohio bar, 1860; tchr., prin. Hiram Coll., 1856-71, pres., 1856-61; mem. Ohio Senate (Republican), 1859; an organizer 42d Ohio Volunteer Inf. Regt., 1861, served as lt. col. and col.; fought at Battle of Middle Creek, 1862; promoted brig. gen. U.S. Volunteers; chief of staff under Rosencrans' Army of Cumberland, 1863; served under Buell in battles of Shiloh and Corinth; organized Div. of Mil. Information; maj. gen. U.S. Volunteers, 1863; mem. U.S. Ho. of Reps. from Ohio 38th-46th congresses, 1863-Nov. 8, 1880; gained reputation as orator and defender of sound finance; charged with having received gift of stock in Credit Mobilier, 1873, also assailed for not having prevented passage of "Salary Grab Act," a leader Republican Party, after 1874; mem. Electoral Commn., 1876, active in framing compromise legislation that settled electoral contest between Hayes and Tilden; elected to U.S. Senate, 1880, never took seat; head Ohio delegation to Rep. Nat. Conv., Chgo., 1880, nominated as dark horse candidate, broke deadlock between Blaine and Grant; elected 20th Pres. U.S., Nov. 8, 1880 (defeated Gen. Winfield Scott Hancock), became involved before inauguration in controversy with N.Y. "Stalwarts" led by Roscoe Conkling over claim to control N.Y. patronage appointments (presdl. authority upheld by Senate); shot by Charles J. Guiteau (a disappointed officer seeker of "Stalwart" faction), July 2, 1881. Died Elberon, N.J., Sept. 19, 1881; buried Lake View Cemetery, Cleve.

GARLAND, L(EO) HENRY physician, educator; b. Dublin, Ireland, Mar. 30, 1903; s. John Peter and Mary M. (Martin) G.; student Belvedere and Castleknock Coll., 1911-19; M.B., B.Chir., B.A.O., U.Coll. Med. Sch., 1924; grad. study London, Eng., 1924-25, San Francisco, 1925-27; M.D., U. Coll. Dublin, 1960; m. Edith Isabel Dohrmann, July 6, 1928; children - Edith M. (Mrs. J. Merrifield, Jr.), Isabel A. (Mrs. V. E. Caglieri), Judith M. (Mrs. R. Harrington), Michael H., Sheila E. (Mrs. E. Reeves). Came to U.S., naturalized, 1931; Intern. Richmond and Rotunda hosps., Dublin, 1924; radiologist St. Mary's Hosp., San Francisco, 1927-29; clin. instr. Stanford, 1929-32, asst. prof., 1932-43, clin. prof. radiology, 1948-60; clin. prof. radiology U. Cal., 1960 - ; cons. Armed Forces Inst. Pathology, USPHS, Army, Navy, VA. Chmn. com. cancer diagnosis therapy NRC. Served as comdr. USNR, 1942-46. Recipient distinguished service award Am. Cancer Soc., 1954; gold medal Am. Coll. Radiology, 1960; gold medal Radiology Soc. N.Am., 1961. Diplomate Am. Bd. Radiology. Past fellow Am. Coll. Radiology (pres. 1961-62); mem. Cal. Acad. Med. (pres. 1957-58), Cal. Radiol. Soc. (hon. sec.), Cal. and Am. med. Oct. 31, 1966; buried Holy Cross Cemetery, Colma, Cal.

GARLINGTON, CRESWELL army officer; b. Rock Island, Ill., June 23, 1887; s. Ernest Albert and Anna Bowers (Buford) G.; ed. St. Paul's Sch., Concord, N.H., 1902-06; B.S., U.S. Mil. Acad., 1910; grad. Engr. Sch., 1912, Ecole Supericure de Guerre, Paris, 1923; distinguished grad. Command and Gen. Staff Sch., 1925; grad. Army War Coll., 1928; m. Alexandrine Fitch, Feb. 5, 1921; children-Crewsell, Henry Fitch, Sally. Command. 2d lt., Corps of Engers., U.S. Army, 1910, and advanced through the grades to temp. brig. gen.; temp. col., Corps of Engrs., 1918; comdg. gen., Engr. Replacement Training Center, Ft. Leonard Wood, Mo., since Jan. 20, 1943. Decorated D.S.C.; Purple Heart; Officer, Order of the Crown (Belgium); Legion of Merit (posthumous). Mem. Soc. of Am. Mil. Engrs. Clubs: Chevy Chase (Md.); Army and Navy Country (Arlington, Va.). Address: Hotel General Oglethorpe, Savannah, Ga. Died Mar. 11, 1945; buried in Arlington National Cemetery.

GARLINGTON, ERNEST ALBERT brig. gen.; b. Newberry C.H., S.C., Feb. 20, 1853; s. Albert Creswell and Sally Lark (Moon) G.; collegiate edn. at U. of Ga., 1869-72; apptd. from Ga., and grad. U.S. Mil. Acad., 1876; m. Anna, d. T. J. and Grace Bowers Buford, of Rock Island, Ill., Aug. 17, 1886. Second lt. 7th Cav., June 15, 1876; promoted through grades to brig. gen. insp. gen. U.S.A., Oct. 1, 1906. Comd. Greely Relief Expdn., 1883; severely wounded in battle with hostile Indians at Wounded Knee P.O., Dec. 19, 1890; awarded Congressional Medal of Honor for distinguished gallantry in that action; mem. bd. to revise cav. drill regulations, 1894; present at battle, siege and surrender of Santiago de Cuba; insp. gen. Div. of the Philippines, 1899-1901, and May 2, 1905-June 6, 1906; gen. staff U.S.A., June 6, 1906; brig. gen. and insp. gen. U.S.A., Oct. 1, 1906. Author: Historical Sketches of the Seventh Cavalry Regiment - A Catechism; Cavalry Outposts, Advance and Rear Guards, Reconnoissance, etc. Died Oct. 16, 1934.

GARNER, JOHN NANCE former vice-pres. of U.S.; b. in Red River County, Tex., Nov. 22, 1868; s. John N. and Sara G.; had limited sch. advantages; LL.D., John Marshall Coll. Law, 1936, Baylor U., 1936; m. Ettie Rheiner, Nov. 25, 1895 (dec. Aug. 1948). Admitted to bar, 1890; mem. Tex. Ho. of Reps., 1898-1902; mem. 58th to 72d Congresses, 15th Tex. Dist.; elected Speaker Ho. of Reps., 1931; elected to 73d

Congress but resigned; elected v.p. of U.S. Nov. 1932, re-elected, Nov. 1936. Del. Dem. Nat. Convs., 1900, 04, delegate at large, 1916. Home: Uvalde, Tex. Died Nov. 7, 1967.

GARNETT, ALEXANDER YELVERTON PEYTON physician; b. Essex County, Va., Sept. 19, 1819; s. Muscoe and Maria (Battaile) G.; M.D., U. Pa., 1841; m. Mary Wise, June 13, 1848. Commd. Asst. surgeon Med. Corps, U.S. Navy, 1841; prof. clin. medicine Nat. Med. Coll., Washington, D.C., 1850-61, 67-70; served as med. officer Confederate Army in charge of 2 mil. hosps., Richmond, Va., also Pres. Davis' personal physician; considered a leading gen. practitioner; mem. bds. dirs. of charitable instns. and hosps. in Washington; pres. A.M.A., 1885-88. Author: Observations on the Sanitary Advantages of Tide-Water Virginia, 1877. Died Rehoboth Beach, Del., July 11, 1888.

GARNETT, ROBERT SELDEN army officer; b. Essex County, Va., Dec. 16, 1819; s. Robert Selden and Olympia Charlotte (DeGouges) G.; grad. U.S. Mil. Acad, 1841; m. Mary Neilson, 1857. Asst. instr. tactics U.S. Mil. Acad., 1843-44; aide-de-camp to Gen. Wood, 1845; brevetted capt. in Cattle of Monterey during Mexican War, 1846-48; aide-de-camp to Zachery Taylor, 1846-49; commd. 1st lt. with brevets of capt., maj., 1850; capt. inf., 1848-50; comdt. of cadets, intrs. inf. tactics U.S. Mil. Acad., 1852-54; commd. maj., 1855; commanded Puget Sound, also Yakima expdns. in N.W., 1856; commd. brig. gen. in command Confederate Army in N.W. Va., 1861; served in Battle of Carricks Ford, Va., covered the retreat of his force from Laurel Hill across Cheat River in face of McClellan's Army. Killed in Battle of Carricks Ford (1st gen. to fall in Civil War), July 13, 1861.

GARNETT, THEODORE STANFORD lawyer; b. Richmond, Va., Oct. 28, 1844; s. Theodore Stanford and Florentina Isidora (Moreno) G., bro. of James Mercer G.; ed. Episcopal High Sch., nr. Alexandria, 1854-61; pvt. to Capt. Army of Northern Va., C.S.A., 1861-65; a.-d.-c. on staffs Gens. J. E. B. Stuart and W. H. F. Lee; a.-a.g. on staff of Gen. Wm. P. Roberts, N.C. cav. brigade; LL.B., U. of Va., 1867; m. Emily Eyre Baker, Oct. 23, 1873; 2d, Louisa Bowdoin, July 25, 1885. In practice at Norfolk, Va., 1873—. Maj. gen. comdg. Va. Div., U.C.V., 1900-06; comdg. Army of Northern Va. Dept., U.C.V., 1912. Mem. Bd. Trustees P.E. Theol. Sem. and High Sch. in Va. Democrat. Home: Norfolk, Va. Died Apr. 17, 1915.

GARNSEY, DANIEL GREENE congressman, lawyer; b. Canaan, N.Y., June 17, 1779; attended pvt. schs.; studied law, Norwich, N.Y. Became mem. N.Y., 1810-11; admitted to bar, 1811, began practice of law, Rennsselaer and Saratoga counties; served (with rank of maj.), as aide-de-camp to maj. gen. in War of 1812; moved to Pomfret, 1866; a promoter devel. of Village of Dunkirk; commr. to perform spl. jud. duties at chambers of Supreme Ct.; surrogate Chautauqua County (N.Y.), 1813-31; brigade insp. Chautauqua County, 1817; dist. atty. Chautauqua County, 1818-26; mem. U.S. Ho. of Reps. (Jackson Democrat) from N.Y., 19th-20th congresses, 1825-29; moved to vicinity of Battle Creek, Mich., 1831; apptd. postmaster, govt. supt. public works, nr. Detroit and Ypsilanti, Mich.; served with Gen. Scott in Black Hawk War, 1836; moved to Rock Island, Ill.; receiver of public moneys at land office, Dixon, Ill. (apptd. by Pres. Harrison), 1841-43; pres. of Harrison celebration, Galena, Ill., 1840. Died (while on way to attend celebration of completion of Erie R.R.), Gowanda, N.Y., May 11, 1851; buried Pine Hill Cemetery.

GARRARD, JAMES gov. Ky., clergyman; b. Stafford County, Va., Jan. 14, 1749; s. William Garrard; m. Elizabeth Mountjoy, Dec. 20, 1769, 12 children including James. Commd. col. Stafford County Regt., Va. Militia, 1781; mem. Va. Ho. of Dels., 1779; helped organize Cooper's Run Ch., nr. Mt. Lebanon, Ky., 1787; mem. Va. Ho. of Dels. from Fayette County, 1785; rep. Fayette and Bourbon counties in convs. for establishment of Ky. statehood, 1784-90; mem. 1st Ky. Constl. Conv.; gov. Ky., 1796-1804, used great influence in adoption Ky. Resolutions of 1798; dropped from Baptist Ch. and Nat. Bapt. Assn. for possessing and spreading Unitarian views, 1803. Died Bourbon County, Ky. Jan. 19, 1822.

GARRARD, JEPTHA lawyer; b. in Ohio; A.B., Yale, 1858; LL.B., U. of Cincinnati, 1859; m. Anna Knapp, Oct. 4, 1864. Admitted to bar, 1859, and began practice at Cincinnati. Capt. 3d N.Y. Cav., Sept. 18, 1861; maj., Sept. 27, 1862; col. 1st U.S. Colored Cav., Dec. 7, 1863; bvtd. brig. gen. vols., Mar. 13, 1865, "for gallant and meritorious services"; resigned, Apr. 25, 1865. Died Dec. 16, 1915.

GARRARD, KENNER army officer; b. Ky., circa Sept. 1828; s. Zeptha Dudley and Sarah (Ludlow) G.; grad. U.S. Mil. Acad., 1851. Served frontier duty before Civil War; served as col. 146th N.Y. Volunteers in Rappahannock (Va.) and Pa. campaigns, 1861; brevetted lt. col. U.S. Army; commd. brig. gen. U.S. Volunteers, 1863; transferred to Army of Cumberland as comdr. cavalry comm. in Tenn., Ga.; in charge of Cavalry Bur., Washington, D.C.; brevetted col. for leading expdn. to Covington, Ga., 1864; commanded 2d div. XVI U.S. Army Corps, 1864-65; brevetted maj. gen., also brig. gen. U.S. Army 1865; comdg. officer Dist. of Mobile until 1865; asst. insp. gen. Dept. of Mo. until 1866; mem. Hist. and Philos. Soc. of Ohio. Died Cincinnati, May 15, 1879; buried Spring Grove Cemetery, Cincinnati.

GARRETSON, GEORGE ARMSTRONG banker; b. Columbiana Co., O., Jan. 30, 1844; s. Hiram and Margaret King (Armstrong) G.; grad. U.S. Mil. Acad., 1867; m. Anna Scowden, 1870 (died 1886); m. 2d, Emma R. Ely, Dec. 5, 1888. Enlisted Co. E, 84th Ohio Vol. Inf., May 26, 1862; served in W.Va. and Md.; hon. disch., Sept. 20, 1862; 2d lt. 4th U.S. Arty., 1867-Jan. 1, 1870 (resigned); capt. 1st Cleveland Troop (Troop A, O.N.G.), 1887-92 (resigned); brig. gen. vols., May 27, 1898; hon. disch., Nov. 30, 1898. Pres. Bank of Commerce, Cleveland, 1890—. Republican. Presbyn. Home: Cleveland, O. Died Dec. 8, 1916.

GARRETT, CAMPBELL DEANE business exec.; born Webster Groves, Mo., Sept. 8, 1900; s. Earl D. and Charlotte C. (Campbell) G.; student U. of Mo., 1918-19, Washington U., 1920-21; m. Doris M. Maull, Jan. 7, 1928. With J. C. Penney Co., N.Y. City, 1927-45; with J.P. Stevens & Co., Inc., since 1945, v.p. since 1947, dir. since 1949. Dir. Expn. Mill, Atlanta. Served as col., Office W.M. Gen., U.S. Army 1942-45. Legion of Merit. Republican. Clubs: Links Golf (Roslyn, L.I.); Cedar Creek Golf (Locust Valley, L.I.); Biltmore Forest Country (Asheville, N.C.); Lawrence Beach (Atlantic Beach, L.I.); Union League (N.Y.C.). Home: 20 Bonnie Heights Rd., Manhasset, L.I., N.Y. Office: 1460 Broadway, N.Y.C. 36. Died Feb. 2, 1961.

GARRETT, ERWIN CLARKSON author; b. Germantown, Phila., Mar. 28, 1879; s. George L. and Sophia Cooper (Gray) G.; B.S., U. Pa., 1906. Served as pvt., cos. L and G, 23d U.S. Inf., Troop I. 5th U.S. Cav., in Philippine Insurrection, 1899-1902. Made trip around world, including Central Borneo, home of the head hunting Dyaks, crossed the Emperor's closed, "sacred," red bridge at Nikko, Japan, 1908; went to France, Aug. 1917, as civilian, at own expense, so as to insure "front line" service in the World War, enlisted in Paris, Sept. 1, 1917, became pvt., Co. G, 16th U.S. Inf., 1st Div., AEF, serving until 1919 (wounded at Soissons, in 2d Battle of the Marne, 1918). Decorated Order of Purple Heart, Silver Star (U.S.), regiment and division awarded the fourragére from French Govt. Mem. Rittenhouse Astronomical Soc., Hist. Soc. of Pa., Colonial Soc. of Pa., Soc. of Colonial Wars (Pa.), S.A.R., Mil. Order Loyal Legion of U.S. (Pa.), Soc. of First Div. AEF (2d v.p., mem. bd. dirs. nat. soc.), Soc. of Deses. Continental Congress (v.p.). Plantagenet Soc. (recorder), Barons of Magna Charta (herald), Colonial Order of the Crown (justiciar). Author: Army Ballads and Other Verses, 1916; Trench Ballads and Other Verses, 1919; Jenghiz Khan and Other Verses, 1924; Io Triumphe and Other Verses, 1928. Contbr. army verse 1904—. Lectr. on astronomy. Address: 431 W. Stafford St., Germantown. Address: 1528 Walnut St., Phila. Died Oct. 1954.

GARRETT, GEORGE ANGUS, ex-ambassador; born La Crosse, Wis., Aug. 5, 1888; s. John Willis and Anna (Laughlan) G.; student Cornell, 1906-07, U. of Chicago; 1907-10; LL.D., Trinity College, Dublin, Ireland, 1950; L.H.D., Clarkson College of Technology, 1956; married Ethel Shields Darlington, Apr. 11, 1935; 1 dau. (by former marriage), Margot (Mrs. Luis Mariano de Zuberbuhler); step-children—Harry Darlington III, McCullough Darlington, Elaine Darlington (Mrs. Anderson Fowler). Began with Harris Trust and Savings Bank, Chicago, 1910; v.p. Dupont National Bank of Washington, D.C., 1913-17; general partner of Merrill, Lynch, Pierce, Fenner & Smith, investment bankers, 1939-60; dir. of the Nat. Savs. & Trust Company, Merchants Transfer and Storage Company. Appointed by President Truman, member of the Redevelopment Land Agency, Washington, D.C., Jan. 1947; appointed U.S. minister to Ireland, April 1947; apptd. U.S. ambassador to Republic of Ireland, 1950. President Federal City Council, 1954-58, then chmn. Owner, Washington Senators. Served as 1st lt. U.S. Army, World War I; OSS, World War II. Pres. Emergency Hosp., Washington, 1943-51; v.p., dir. Nat. Symphony Orch., 1930-51; chmn. ARC Fund Raising Campaign, D.C., 1952; apptd. special assistant to chairman and pres. Am. Nat. Red Cross, 1952; mem. bldg. com. Washington Cathedral; active Navy Relief Soc. Clubs: Metropolitan (pres. 1939-42), Alibi, Chevy Chase (Washington), Brook, Racquet and Tennis, Turf and Field, United Hunts, Jockey (N.Y.C.); Whites (London); The Travelers (Paris). Home: Washington DC Died Sept. 29, 1971; buried Washington Cathedral.

GARRETT, JAMES MADISON, JR., ret. army officer, ret. ofcl.; b. Montgomery, Ala., Nov. 12, 1892; s. James Madison and Lucy (Tankersley) G.; B.A., U. Va., 1913; m. Helen DeLloyd Foster, July 12, 1921; children—James Madison, Elwood, Carolyn. Employed by C.E., U.S. Army, 1913; commd. 2d. lt. F.A., Regular Army, 1917, advanced through grades to col., 1941; comd. 2d Bn., 16th F.A., 1918-20, 186th F.A. Regt., N.Y. N.G., 1941-43; mem. 4th Div. participating in campaigns of Aisne-Marne, St. Mihiel, Meuse-Argonne, Defensive Sector, World War I; exec. officer XX Corps Arty., participating in campaigns of Normandy, No. France, Rhineland, Ardennes-Alsace of World War II; ret. because of physical disability in September 1947; dir. of Civil Def., State Ala., 1951-55. Member of Sigma Alpha Epsilon. Episcopalian. Home: Montgomery AL Died Apr. 14, 1971; buried Greenwood Cemetery, Montgomery AL

GARRETT, RAY, lawyer; b. Murphysboro, Ill., Sept. 17, 1889; s. Anderson Barker and Georgia (Williams) G.; student U. Ill., 1906-08; LL.B., Ill. Wesleyan U., 1916; student Northwestern U., 1924-25; m. Mabel Marian May, Aug. 1, 1916; children—Glenn May, Ray, Martha Ann. Ofcl. stenographer Supreme Ct. Ill., Springfield, 1910-17; admitted to Ill. bar, 1916; law asso. A. M. Fitzgerald, Springfield, 1916-17; atty. Chgo. Mill & Lumber Co., 1919-21; counsel A. W. Swayne & Co., 1921-23; asso., partner Cooke Sullivan & Ricks, Chgo., 1923-34; partner Lawyer & Garrett, 1934-39; pvt. practice, 1939-42; asso., partner Sidley, Austin, Burgess & Smith, Chgo., from 1942. Pres. Midland Subsidiary Corp., 1937-39, Chgo., South Shore & South Bend R.R., 1938-39; pres., trustee Indiana R.R., 1941-51; counsel to bd. D. & R.G.W., R.R. Co., from 1970; dir. Denver and Rio Grande Western R.R. Served from lieutenant to major, infantry, U.S. Army, 1917-19; AEF. Fellow American Bar Foundation; member American Law Inst., Am. Bar Assn. (former chmn. corp. banking and bus. law), Ill., Chgo. bar assns., Newcomen Soc., Phi Delta Phi. Methodist. Clubs: Mid-Day, Univ., Law (Chgo.); Mich. Shores (Wilmette, Ill.). Co-author: Illinois. Business Corporation Act, Model Business Corporation and Non-Profit Corporation Acts. Contbr. articles legal jours. Home: Evanston IL Deceased.

GARRETT, WILLIAM ROBERTSON educator; b. Williamsburg, Va., Apr. 12, 1839; s. Dr. Robert M. and Susan (Winder) G.; ed. Williamsburg Mil. Acad.; grad. William and Mary Coll., A.M., 1858; studied law 1 yr., 1858-59, Univ. of Va.; hon. Ph.D., U. of Nashville, 1891; capt. Co. F 1st Va. regt. arty., 1861-62; adjt. 11th Tenn. cav., 1862-65; capt. Co. B, same, in Forrest's cav., 1865; m. Julia Flournoy Batte, Nov. 12, 1868. Master grammar school, William and Mary Coll., 1866-67; moved to Pulaski, Tenn., 1868; pres. Giles Coll., 1868-73; co. supt. schools, Giles Co., 1873-75; asso. prin. Montgomery Bell. Acad., Nashville, 1875-91; State supt. public instn., Tenn., 1891-93; prin. Mil. Acad., 1893-95; supt. Watkins Inst. night schs., 1887—; prof. Am. history, Peabody Normal Coll., 1895—; dean of coll., 1899—. Author: The South as a Factor in the Territorial Expansion of the United States (200 pp. in "Confederate Military History," 12 vols.); Garrett & Goodpasture's History of Tennessee, 1900; Geography of Tennessee (Supplement to Frye's Geography). Editor: Am. Hist. Mag. of Peabody Normal Coll. (quarterly), 1895-1900; etc. Home: Nashville, Tenn. Died 1904.

GARRIGA, MARIANO SIMON, bishop; b. Port Isabel, Tex., May 30, 1886; s. Frank and Elizabeth (Baker) G.; student St. Mary's (Kan.) Coll., St. Francis Sem., Wis.; LL.D., St. Edward's U., Austin, Tex., 1936. Ordained priest, R.C. Ch., 1911; asst. to chancellor, San Antonio, 1911-12; asst. pastor, Marfa and missions, 1912-15; vice-rector, St. John's Sem., 1915-16; chaplain, Tex. N.G., 1916; pastor, St. Cecelia's Parish, 1919-36; named domestic prelate, 1935, coadjutor bishop of Corpus Christi, 1936, consecrated coadjutor bishop, 1926; bishop of Corpus Christi. Trained with 144th Infantry, 36th Division, United States Army, Camp Bowie, and A.E.F.; resigned from U.S. Army, 1919. Apptd. Vicar Delegate for Army and Navy, Tex. and La., 1941-42. Pastor St. Peter's Church. Mem. Am. Legion, Vets. of Fgn. Wars, Tex. Hist. Commn., Order of Alhambra. K.C. (3d and 4th degree). Home: Corpus Christi TX Died 1965.

GARRISON, DANIEL MERSHON naval officer; b. Bordentown, N.J., May 3, 1874; s. Samuel and Hannah Gary (Mershon) G.; grad. Bordentown Mil. Inst., 1891; grad. U.S. Naval Acad., 1895; hon. D.Sc., St. John's Coll., 1923; m. Jessie Croft Kelly, Sept. 26, 1901; children—Jessie Croft (Mrs. G. F. Good), Daniel Mershon. Promoted asst. engr., July 1, 1897; ensign, Mar. 3, 1899; lt. (jr. grade), July 1, 1900; lt., July 4, 1902; commd. prof. mathematics, Oct. 27, 1906; captain, Sept. 18, 1918; head dept. of mathematics, U.S. Naval Acad., 1918-23; retired; head dept. of mathematics, St. John's Coll., Annapolis, Md., 1923—. Served on board Indiana during Spanish-Am. War; took part in bombardments of San Juan, P.R., and Santiago, Cuba; awarded Congressional Medal for battle of July 3, 1898; chief engr. Pacific Submarine Telegraph Survey which surveyed route for cable across Pacific, 1899-1900; served on Cincinnati, on guard duty at Chemulpo, Korea, and Chefo, China, during Russo-Japanese War. Episcopalian. Died Dec. 30, 1927.

GARRISON, FIELDING HUDSON col. U.S.A.; b. Washington, D.C., Nov. 5, 1870; s. John Rowzee and Jennie (Davis) G.; A.B., Johns Hopkins, 1890; M.D., Georgetown U., 1893; m. Clara Augusta Brown, Apr. 26, 1909. Asst. librarian, Surgeon General's Office, Washington, D.C., 1889-1922. Editor Index Medicus, 1903-1927; asso. editor of the Quarterly Cumulative Index Medicus, 1927-29. Commd. maj. Med. Reserve Corps, 1917; lt. colonel M.C.U.S.A., 1918; lt. col., M.C. regular army, July 1, 1920; lt. col. retired, May 19, 1930.

Librarian Welch Med. Library, Baltimore, 1930—. Author: An Introduction to the History of Medicine, 1913, 4th edit., 1928; A Physician's Anthology (with Casey A. Wood), 1920; The Principles of Anatomic Illustration before Vesalius, 1925; Medicine in Space, 1934. Died Apr. 18, 1935.

GARRISON, LINDLEY MILLER secretary of war; b. Camden, N.J., Nov. 28, 1864; s. Rev. Joseph Fithian and Elizabeth Vanarsdale (Grant) G.; bro. of Charles Grant G.; ed. pub. schs.; P.E. Acad., Phila., 2 years; Phillips Exeter Acad., 1 yr.; spl. student Harvard, 1 yr.; LL.B., U. of Pa., 1885; LL.D., New York U., 1914, Rutgers, 1915, Kenyon, 1916, Brown, 1917; m. Margaret Hildeburn, June 30, 1900. Studied law in offices of Redding, Jones & Carson, Phila.; admitted to Pa. bar, 1886; practiced with preceptors, and successors, Jones & Carson, 1883-88; admitted to N.J. bar, 1888, and practiced at Camden, N.J., until Dec. 1898; mem. Garrison, McManus & Enright, Jersey City, 1899-1904; vice chancellor of N.J., June 15, 1904-Mar. 5, 1913; sec. of war in cabinet of President Wilson, Mar. 5, 1913-Feb. 10, 1916 (resigned). Democrat. Episcopalian. Home: New York, N.Y. Died Oct. 19, 1932.

GARRISON, SIDNEY CLARENCE college pres.; b. Lincolnton, N.C., Oct. 17, 1887; s. Rufus J. and Susie Elizabeth (Mooney) G.; A.B., Wake Forest (N.C.) Coll., 1911; A.M., 1913; A.M., George Peabody Coll. for Teachers, 1916; Ph.D., 1919; m. Sara Elizabeth McCurry, Oct. 16, 1918; Children-Sidney Clarence, Lucy Fuqua, Wm. Louis, Frank McMurry, Rufus James. County supt. schools, Lincoln County, N.C., 1912-14; supt. of schs., Crouse, N.C., 1911-12; prof. psychology, 1919-33, dean Grad. School, 1933-36, pres. since 1937, George Peabody College for Teachers. Captain U.S. Army, 1918-19. Trustee Meharry Med. Coll.; mem. State Bd. of Education. Fellow A.A.A.S.; member Am. Psychol. Assn., Am. Ednl. Research Assn., Souther Soc. for Psychology and Philosophy, Phi Delta Kappa, Kappa Delta Pi. Democrat. Baptist. Co-Author: Things to Do in the Teaching of Reading, 1928; (with Karl C. Garrison) Psychology of Elementary Education, 1929; Psychology of Secondary Education, 1934. Home: Peabody Campus, Nashville, Tenn. Died Jan. 18, 1945.

GARRISON, WILLIAM HART, printing co. exec.; b. Silver Point, Tenn., Sept. 12, 1920; s. William Claud and Beatrice (Hart) G.; B.S., Wayne U., 1943; M.A., U. Mich., 1950; m. Carrie Wallach, Feb. 10, 1951; children—Roger, Bruce. Tech. writer Gen. Prec. Lab., Pleasantville, N.Y., 1952; saleman Osborne Co. div. Am. Colortype, Clifton, N.J., 1953; founder, dir., pres. Garrison House, Inc., N.Y.C., 1953-68; pres., dir. Polygraphic Co. Am., Inc., 1959-68, chmn. bd., 1962-68; pres., dir. Garrison Color Corp., Dumont, N.J., 1960-68; treas., dir. Olympic Sales Club, Inc., Windsor Locks, Conn., Friendly Card Co., Inc., North Bennington, Vt., 1965-70; v.p., dir. Brook-Parker Co., Montclair, N.Y., 1954-70; chmn., pres., chief exec. officer Garrison Corporation, 1968-70; Garrison Printing Division, Incorporated, 1968-—. vice pres., dir. Brook-Parker Co., Montclair, 1954-70. Pres. Ossining (N.Y.) Young Republican Club, 1958. Served from pvt. to capt., USAAF, 1942-51; PTO and Korea. Decorated D.F.C., 5 Air Medals. Mem. N.Y. Union League, Ossining C. of C. (pres. 1960-61). Conglist. Clubs: Mt. Anthony Country (Bennington, Vt.); Sleepy Hollow Country, Shattemuc Yacht (Ossining, N.Y.). Home: Ossining NY Died Jan. 13, 1970.

GARSIDE, CHARLES lawyer; born in Middletown, Connecticut, May 12, 1898; son of John William and Harriet (Brearley) Garside; B.S., Princeton University, 1923 (honors in history and in politics); LL.B., Cornell Law School, 1921; LL.D. (honorary), Hobart College, 1952; L.H.D. (honorary), Alfred University, 1953; married Helen Hunt Johnson, February 27, 1926; children - Charles, Jr., Grenville, Helen (Mrs. Peter B. F. Randolph). Admitted to the New York bar, 1923, also the United States Supreme Court, 1927; associate Choate, Larocque & Mitchell, New York City, 1923-27, partner 1927-3 Webster & Garside, 1936-47; dir. Harsco Corporation; adv. com. Met. branch Chase Manhattan Bank. Director of the Intercultural Publs., Inc.; dir., vice chmn. State U. Research Found.; trustee, chmn. com. on med. edn. centers State U. of N.Y., 1948-52; chmn. com. on legislation, acting pres., 1951-52. Chmn. N.Y. State Commn. Against Discrimination, 1947-49; member adv. council, Dept. Econ. and Social Instns., Princeton U., 1948-51, mem. adv. council, dept. history, 1951 - ; trustee, pres. of the board of Woodlawn Cemetery. Private United States Marine Corps, World War I; col., General Staff Corps, U.S. Army, World War II. Mem. adv. com., Ditson Fund, Columbia U. Mem. American, N.Y. State and N.Y. City bar assns., Am. Legion Mil. Order Foreign Wars, Am. Judicature Society, Order of Coif. Clubs: Edgartown (Mass.) Yacht; Norfolk (Conn.) Country; Players (N.Y.); Century, Princeton (New York City); Chevy Chase (Washington); Pilgrims. Republican candidate for Congress, 25th Congl. Dist., New York, 1946. Home: 1148 Fifth Av., New York 28; also Cobble Hill Farm, Norfolk. Died Oct. 31, 1964; buried Norfolk, Conn.

GARTELL, LUCIUS JEREMIAH congressman, army officer; b. Wilkes County, Ga., Jan. 7, 1821; s. Joseph and Miss (Boswell) G., Jr.; attended U. Ga., Randolph-Macon Coll.; m. Louisiana O. Gideon, 1841; m. 2d, Antoinette T. Burke, 1855; m. 3d, Maud Condon, circa 1888; 11 children. Admitted to Ga. bar, 1842; elected to Ga. Gen. Assembly, 1847-51, radical pro-Southern, pro-slavery leader, 1849; mem. U.S. Ho. of Reps. from Ga., 35th-36th congresses, 1857-59, strongly advocated secession; organized 7th Ga. Regt., Confederate Army, 1861; elected col.; mem. Confederate Congress, 1861; commd. brig. gen., 1864; noted criminal lawyer; leading mem. Ga. Constl. Conv., 1877; regent Smithsonian Instn. Died Atlanta, Ga., Apr. 7, 1891.

GARTON, WILL MELVILLE naval officer; b. Des Moines, Ia., Oct. 31, 1875; s. William Thomas and Minerva (Allum) G.; student Des Moines Coll., 1890-93; M.D., State U. of Ia., 1896; post grad. work Naval Med. Coll., 1906, Naval War Coll., 1922-23; hon. LL.D., Sioux Falls (S.D.) University; m. Beatrice Farquahar, 1900 (died 1923); children-Norman Farquhar (U.S. Navy), Will Melville; m. 2d, Katherine Ballou, Oct. 15, 1927. Commd. ensign Med. Corps. U.S. Navy, 1898; advanced through grades to rear adm., 1930; retired, Nov. 1, 1930. Awarded campaign medals for Spanish-Am. War, Mexican Service, World War, Haitian and Dominican campaigns. Fellow Am. Coll. Surgeons; mem. A.M.A., Phi Delta Theta. Mason (32fi, Shriner). Clubs: Metropolitan, Army and Navy, Army and Navy Country (Washington, D.C.); New York Yacht, New York Athletic, Lambs (N.Y. City). Died June 7, 1946.

GARY, HAMPSON diplomat; b. Tyler, Tex., Apr. 23, 1873; s. Franklin Newman and Martha Isabella (Boren) G.; ed. Bingham Sch., Bingham, N.C., and U. Va.; children-Mrs. Bernard A. Moran, Franklin. Admitted to Texas bar, 1894, practice of law at Tyler, Tex., until removal to Washington, 1914; was referee in bankruptcy, 4 yrs.; standing master in chancery U.S. Court, 2 yrs.; apptd. spl. counsel Dept. of State, Dec. 9, 1914, to assist in the consideration of matters arising out of war situation in Europe; advanced to regular service and made a solicitor, same, June 8, 1915; diplomatic agt. and consul gen. to Egypt, rank of minister resident, Oct. 2, 1917-Apr. 7, 1920. While serving in Cairo was in charge of Am. interests in Palestine, Syria and Arabia; at the front beyond Jerusalem with Field Marshal Allenby for a while in 1918; called to Paris, 1919, for work with Am. Commn. to Negotiate Peace; E.E. and M.P. to Switzerland, Apr. 7, 1920-June 1, 1921; in gen. law practice, Washington, 1921-32, N.Y.C., 1931-34. Mem. Fed. Communications Commn. (first chmn. radio-broadcast div.), 1934-35, gen. counsel, 1935-38; solicitor U.S. Export-Import Bank, 1938-46; retired. Capt. U.S. Vols. Spanish-Am. War, 1898; col. 3d Tex. Inf. Mem. Tex. Ho. of Reps., 1901-02; regent U. of Tex., 1909-11. Mem. Am. Bar Assn., Am. Soc. Internat. Law, U. of Va. chpt. Phi Beta Kappa, Alpha Tau Omega, Soc. Colonial Wars, S.R. Episcopalian. Clubs: Metropolitan, Chevy Chase (Washington). Home: Metropolitan Club, Washington. Died Apr. 18, 1952; buried Arlington Cemetery, Washington.

GARY, MARTIN WITHERSPOON army officer; b. Cokesbury, S.C., Mar. 25, 1831; s. Thomas Reader and Mary Anne (Porter) G.; attended S.C. Coll.; grad. Harvard, 1854. Admitted to S.C. bar, 1855; mem. S.C. Legislature, 1860; leader S.C. secession movement; commd. capt. Watson Guards, 1861; commd. lt. col. of inf. Confederate Army, col. of regt.; brig. gen., 1864, in charge troops conducting Jefferson Davis to Cokesbury where last Confederate cabinet meeting was held at Gary's mother's home; a foremost defender of 'straightout policy,' white supremacy, no compromise with negroes; opposed payment of reconstrn. debts.; mem. S.C. Senate, 1876-80. Died Apr. 9, 1881.

GASSER, LORENZO DOW army officer; b. Lykins, O., May 3, 1876; s. Frederick and Lycinda (Rhoad) G.; ed. pub. schs., Tiffin, O.; grad. U.S. Gen. Staff Coll., Langres, France, 1918; grad. Army War Coll., Washington, 1921; m. Molly Gregory Sugrue, September 5, 1904. Captain 2d Ohio Inf., 1898-99; apptd. lt. 43d U.S. Inf., 1899; commd. 2d lt. Regular Army, 1901, advanced through grades to maj. gen., 1942; dep. chief of staff, U.S. Army, retired, 1940; returned to active duty, 1941; pres. War Dept. Manpower Bd., ret. 1945. Decorated D.S.M. with two oak leaf clusters, Legion of Merit (U.S.); French Legion of Honor. Clubs: Army and Navy, Chevy Chase. Home: 36011 Connecticut Av., N.W., Washington. Died Oct. 29, 1955.

GASTON, ARTHUR LEE judge; b. Chester, S.C., Aug. 14, 1876; s. Thomas Chalmers and Adelaide (Lee) G.; A.B., Davidson (N.C.) Coll., 1896; student U. Va., 1896-97; m. Virginia Aiken, Dec. 3, 1902 (died 1907); 1 son, David Aiken; m. 2d, Edith Byrd Smith, Apr. 20, 1910; 1 dau., Sarah Elizabeth. Admitted to S.C. bar, 1897, and practiced at Chester; became mem. Gaston. Hamilton & Gaston; judge 6th Judicial Circuit of S.C., 1934-48; pvt. law practice, 1948—. Mem. S.C. Ho. of Reps., 1900-06, 30-34, chmn. judiciary com., 1932. Dem. Nat. Conv., 1920. Served as 1st lt. 1st S.C. Vol. Inf., Spanish-Am. War; lt. col., staff of Gov. R. I. Manning during World War I. Recipient citation for distinction in law Davidson Coll., 1948. Commr. to Gen. Assembly Presbyn. Ch. in U.S., 1951. Chmn. bd. regents S.C. State Hosp. 1928. Mem. Chester Bar Assn. (pres.), C. of C. (pres. 1926-27), Kappa Alpha. Democrat. Presbyn. Rotarian (past pres.). Author: Remarks and Reminiscences. Home: Chester, S.C. Died Aug. 13, 1951.

GASTON, EDWARD PAGE art writer, lecturer; b. Henry, Ill., Nov. 19, 1868; s. Alexander H. and Henrietta (Page) G.; m. Lilian Craske, of Eng., 1901; children - Alexander Page, Margaret Lilian, Kathleen Mary. Joined Hemenway Archaeol. expdn., 1888, to ruins of Ariz. and N.M.; lived among ancient tribe of Zuiu Indians; attached to Am. Embassy in City of Mexico; climbed Popocatepetl volcano, 17,775 feet; received gifts from several sovereigns and decorated by Sultan of Turkey with the Lyakat (merit), 1900; lectured extensively Europe and America; has many yrs. European mgr. for Funk & Wagnalls Co., pubs.; founder, 1909, now hon. sec. World Prohibition Federation, operating in 40 countries. Made 4 war relief expdns. during 1914-15, visiting nearly 70,000 prisoners of war held by British and Germans; was attached to Am. Embassy at Berlin; as a neutral made reports to British and German govts.; made reconnaissance of battlefields of Belgium, recovering effects of the dead and collecting information for British War Office; later advised War Dept., Washington, D.C., on welfare measures for Am. prisoners of war held by the Germans, 1917. Capt. N.Y. Guard (Reserve), 1918, and exec. sec. N.Y. Mayor's Com. Defense for Army and Navy forces, etc., 1918-19. Knight Order of Dannebrog (Danish), 1920. Fellow Royal Geog. Soc., London. Attempted recovery of long-lost remains of Princess Pocahontas of Va., at Gravesend, Eng., 1923; prevailed upon King George V. of Great Britain and President Cosgrave of Ireland to better protect the ruined Robert Burns church, at Alloway, Scotland, and Olvier Goldsmith's early home at Lissoy, Ireland, 1927. Author: The American's Rapid Guide to England (with Canadian Notes), 1925. Address: Logmore, Cheam, Surrey, Eng., and 7 Haymarket, London, S.W., Eng.

GASTON, JAMES MCFADDEN physician; b. nr. Chester, S.C., Dec. 27, 1824; s. John Brown and Polly (McFadden) G.; grad. S.C. Coll., 1843; M.D., same, 1846; (M.D. ad eundem Univ. of Brazil, 1854); m. Sue G. Brumby, Nov. 2, 1852. Practiced Chester dist., S.C., 1846-52, Columbia, S.C., 1852-61; surgeon and med. director C.S. army, 1861-65; practiced in province of São Paulo, Brazil, 1867-73, Campinas, Brazil, 1874-83; at Atlanta, Ga., 1883—. Prof. principles and practice of surgery, Southern Med. Coll., Atlanta, 1884—. Honorary mem. Am. Assn. Obstetricians and Gynecologists, Southern Surg. and Gynecol. Assn. Asso. editor Annual of the Universal Medical Sciences and Sajous' Annual and Analytical Cyclopaedia of Practical Medicine. Home: Atlanta, Ga. Died 1903.

GASTON, JOSEPH ALFRED army officer; b. Honey Brook, Pa., Sept. 2, 1856; s. Joseph (M.D.) and Agnes (Greenbank) G.; prep. edn. Wyoming (Pa.) Sem. and Commercial Coll.; grad. U.S. Mil. Acad., 1881; grad. Army War Coll., 1912; m. Lavinia, d. Brig. Gen William L. Haskin (U.S.A.), May 16, 1903. Commd. 2d lt. 8th Cav., June 11, 1881; promoted through grades to brig. gen. N.A. (temp.), Aug. 5, 1917. Engaged against Apache Indians, 1885-86, against Sioux Indians, 1890-91; served in Cuba, 1899-1902, P.I., 1908-10; supt. permanent camps, relief work, San Francisco, 1906; commandant Ft. Riley, Kan., 1913-14; on Mexican border, 1914-17; comd. 6th Cav., with punitive expdn., Mexico, 1916; brig. gen. N.A., Aug. 5, 1917; comdg. 165th Depot Brigade, Camp Travis, Tex., until Nov. 22, 1917. 90th Div., Nov. 23-Dec. 17, 1917, 11th Brigade, 6th Div., Camp Forrest, Ga., Dec. 30, 1917; trans. to 37th Div., Camp Sheridan, Ala., Mar. 1918, which comd. about 2 weeks; comdg. Camp Meade, Md., June 29, 1918-Feb. 5, 1919; resumed rank of col. of cav., U.S.A., Feb. 5, 1919; recruiting duty, Phila., Feb. 1919-20; retired. Sept. 2, 1920. Died Mar. 31, 1937.

GATCH, THOMAS LEIGH lawyer; born at Salem, Ore., Aug. 9, 1891; s. Claud and Helen (Plummer) G.; student Ore. State Coll., 1906-08; grad. U.S. Naval Acad., 1912; LL.B., George Washington U., 1922; LL.D., Willamette U., Salem, Ore., 1944; m. Nancy Dashiell, June 13, 1917; children-Nancy, Eleanor, Thomas. Entered U.S. Navy, 1908, and advanced through the grades to vice adm., 1945; judge adv. gen., 1943-45; comd. U.S.S. South Dakota in battles of Santa Cruz and Guadalcanal, 1942, wounded in action; retired from navy, 1947; member law firm of Boyd and Erwin, 1947—. Decorated Navy Cross with gold star, Purple Heart. Address: 90 Gloucester St., Annapolis, Md. Died Dec. 16, 1954; buried Ft. Rosecrans, San Diego, Cal.

GATCHELL, GEORGE WASHINGTON army officer; b. in R.I., Feb. 22, 1865; s. James Lawrence and Mary E. (Jones) G.; grad. U.S. Mil. Acad., 1887, Arty. Sch., 1898. Commd. add. 2d lt. 5th Arty., 1887; promoted through grades to brig. gen. N.A. (temp.), Dec. 17, 1917. Participated in campaign against Sioux Indians, 1890-91; prof. mil. science and tactics, Vermont Acad., Saxtons River, 1891-95; with siege arty. at Ybor City, Fla., May-Aug. 1898, Spanish-Am. War; duty with tests of mortar fire at Portland, Me., 1901-02; on march with 6th Battery, Field Arty., from Ft. Riley, Kan., to Ft. Sam Houston, Tex., Nov. 1905-Jan. 1906; comd. Ft. Rosecrans and Arty. Dist. of San Diego, 1907; comdg. Ft. Strong, Mass., 1910; insp. instr.

R.I.N.G., 1911-15; comdg. Ft. Williams, Med., and coast defenses, Portland, 1915-Feb. 1918; comd. 31st Heavy Arty. Brig., A.E.F., Feb.-Aug. 1918; chief of arty., 3d Army Corps., EA.E.F., Aug.-Oct. 1918; remanded to regular rank of col. after the armistice; comd. Camp de Souge, later Embarkation Camp, Pauillac, France, Nov. 1918-Feb. 1919; comd. Ft. Howard, Md. and coast defenses, Baltimore, Apr.-Dec. 1919; retired Dec. 6, 1919. Participated in Marne-Aisne, Oise-Aisne and Meuse-Argonne offensives. Home: San Diego, Calif. Died Feb. 4, 1939.

GATES, CLIFFORD ELWOOD, educator; b. Canastota, N.Y., Dec. 31, 1893; s. Roscoe Conklin and Minnie (Clifford) G.; A.B., Colgate U., 1915, A.M., 1917; Ph.D., Cornell U., 1925; student U. Berlin (Germany), 1925, 32, U. Innsbruck (Austria), summers 1958-59, 61; m. Florence Mae Wentzel, Aug. 14, 1918; children—Florence Mae (Mrs. Charles G. Rickard) Elizabeth Anita, Kathryn Patricia; m. 2d, Dorothy Bernice Parcels, June 22, 1962. Mem. faculty Colgate U., 1915-18, 20-64, prof. German lang. and lit., 1919-34, chmn. dept., 1934-42, head dept., 1942-64, nat. dir. univ. alumni service for vets., 1946-62; master German and Spanish, Blair Acad., 1918-20; lectr. on modern Germany; lectr. Kan. State Tchrs. Coll., Emporia, 1964-68. Served to lt. col. USAAF, World War II. Recipient Colgate U. Alumni Corp. award, 1948. Mem. Phi Beta Kappa, Theta Chi (pres. Iota chpt. 1925-57), Delta Sigma Rho. Clubs: Torch; Colgate U. Alumni (N.Y.C.). Republican. Baptist. Author: Im Herzen Europas, 1935. Editor: Tantchen Mohnhaupt, 1927; die Kapitalistinnen, 1928; Herrn Schmidt sein Dackel Haidjer, 1935. Home: Emporia KS Died July 1968.

GATES, EDMUND O., physician; b. Howard City, Mich., 1905; M.D., Northwestern U., 1933. Intern U. Chgo. Hosp., 1932; intern Cook County Hosp., Chgo., 1933-34, resident in ears, nose and throat, 1937-38; resident in eye Presbyn Hosp., Chgo., 1938; mem. staff Grace Hosp., Welch, W.Va., until 1966. Served to col., M.C., AUS 1941-45. Diplomate Am. Bd. Ophthalmology. Mem. A.M.A. Home: Welch WV Died Mar. 17, 1966; buried Woodlawn Cemetery Mausoleum, Bluefield WV

GATES, KERMIT HOYT hosp. adminstr.; b. Norwalk, Ia., June 3, 1903; B.A., Simpson Coll., Indianola, Ia., 1925; M.D.,U. Ia., 1930; grad. Med. Field Service Sch., 1934, Army Med. Sch., 1935, Army War Coll., 1946; M.P.H., U. Cal. at Berkeley, 1949; grad. course med. aspects atomic explosion, 1948, 7th Interagy. Course Hosp. Adminstrs., 1953; m. Phyllis M. Davis, Dec. 26, 1931; children - Alice Jane (lMrs. Paul J. Schwehm), Kermit Hoyt, Davis Feesenden, Jeremy Hunt. Commd. 1st lt., M.C. U.S. Army, 1930, advanced through grades to col., 1955; intern Fitzsimmons Gen. Hosp., 1930-31; surg. tng. Army Hosp., Ft. Sill, Okla., 1931-33; chief surgery Ft. Totten Army Hosp., 1934-35; comdg. officer, chief surgery Army Hosp., Carlisle Barracks, 1936-41; div. surgeon 24th Inf. Div., 1941-42; dep. theatre surgeon Mid-Pacific Area, 1943-45; comdrg. officer Hosp. Trains, U.S., 1946; dep. to comdg. gen. Letterman Gen. Hosp., 1947-48; dep., later surgeon 6th Army, 1950-51; comdg. officer Army Hosp., Ft. Jackson, S.C., 1952-53; dept. to comdg. gen. Walter Reed Hosp., 1953-55; retired, 1955; dir. dept. hosps. Dade County, Fla., also exec. dir. Jackson Meml. Hosp. and Met. Med. Center, Miami, 1955 - ; asst. prof. preventive medicine, also dir. teaching hosp. U. Miami Sch. Medicine, 1955 - . Chmn. div. United Fund, 1963 - , bd. dirs. med. research and health, 1962-64; v.p. United Health Found. Dade County, 1964 - . Bd. dirs. Blue Cross Fla., nursing dept. Dade County Jr. Coll., Dade County chpt. A.R.C. Fellow Am. Coll. Hosp. Adminstrs. (regent 3d dist.); mem. Am., Fla., Dade County med. assns., Am. (council adminstrv. practices), Fla. (bd. govs.) hosp. assns., S. Fla. Hosp. Assn. (pres. 1963-64), Am. Pub. Health Assn, Assn. Am. Med. Colls., Miami Heart Assn., Dade County Tb Assn., Delta Omega. Rotarian, Mason (Shriner). Home: 4501 Granda Blvd., Coral Gables, Fla. 33146. Office: Jackson Memorial Hosp., 1700 N.W. 10th Av., Miami, Fla. 33136. Died July 31, 1965.

GATEWOOD, JAMES DUNCAN officer Med. Corps, U.S.N.; b. Halifax Co. Va., May 24, 1857; s. Robert (D.D.) and Harriet Elizabeth (Duncan) G.; ed. Norfolk Acad. (father prin.); B.S., Va. Mil. Inst., 1876; M.D., U. of Va., 1879 (spl. certificate in chemistry); post-grad. work, N.Y. Univ. and Bellevue Hosp. Medical Coll; (hon. M.A., Va. Mil. Inst., 1916); m. Anne Wythe Mallory Critcher, June 12, 1883. Commd. asst. surgeon U.S. Navy, July 6, 1880; promoted passed asst. surgeon, July 6, 1883; surgeon, Jan. 28, 1896; med. insp., Sept. 19, 1908; med. dir., July 12, 1911; Served on Franklin, New Hampshire, Kearsarge, Dispatch (when she was lost in 1891), Dolphin, Puritan, Lancaster, Yankee, Tennessee, California; asst. to Bur. Medicine and Surgery, 1900-02; instr. naval hygiene, U.S. Naval Med. Sch., Washington, 1905-09; fleet surgeon Pacific fleet, 1909-10; pres. Naval Examining Bd., 1910-12; in command Naval Med. Sch. and Naval Hosp., Washington, 1912-16; Naval Examining Bds., 1916-17; in command Naval Hosp., Gulfport, Miss., 1917-21. Mem. mil. com. Nat. Research Council, 1917. Holds Cuban campaign medal and badge, and Victory medal. Fellow Am. Coll. Surgeons. Author: Naval Hygiene, 1909. Retired with rank of commodore, 1921. Died Feb. 27, 1924.

GATLEY, GEORGE GRANT army officer; b. Portland, Me., Sept. 10, 1868; grad. U.S. Mil. Acad., 1890; m. Bessie W. Crabb, Feb. 10, 1896. Commd. additional 2d lt. 5th Arty., June 12, 1890; 2d lt. 3d Arty., July 31, 1891; transferred to 5th Arty., Aug. 12, 1891; 1st lt. 2d Arty., Mar. 21, 1898; transferred to 5th Arty., May 4, 1898; capt. Arty. Corps, May 8, 1901; assigned to 3d Field Arty., June 6, 1907; maj. 2d Field Arty., Mar 11, 1911, to 4th Field Arty., July 21, 1913; col., May 15, 1917; brig. gen. N.A., Aug. 5, 1917. With Siege Battery K, 5th Arty., Tampa, Fla., July-Aug., 1898; organized 17th Battery and served with same in P.I., 1903-05; participated in various expdns. against the Moros and battery mentioned for "distinguished service"; in Cuba throughout 2d intervention 1906-09; organized and instructed Cuban field arty., 1909-13; Mexican border, 1913-15; Ordnance Bd., 1915-17; apptd. comdr. 55th Field Arty. Brigade, Camp Sevier, Greenville, S.C., Sept. 1917; trans. to 67th F.A. Brig., 42d (Rainbow) Div., July 1, 1918, and comd. same in Champagne-Marne defensive, and Aisne-Marne, San Mihiel, Meuse-Argonne offensive and occupation of Germany; Camp Dix, N.J., demobilization duty, May 1-Aug. 13th, 1919; comdg. 8th F.A. Brig., and Camp Knox, Ky., Aug. 1919—. Died Jan. 9, 1931.

GATLING, RICHARD JORDAN inventor; b. Hertford Co., N.C., Sept. 12, 1818. As a boy assisted his father in perfecting machine for sowing cotton-seed; later invented machine for sowing rice; adapted it to sowing wheat and patented it. Grad. Ohio Med. Coll., 1850, but never practiced. Invented, 1862, the revolving gun known as the "Gatling gun"; invented, 1886, a new gun metal, composed of steel and aluminum. Congress voted him $40,000 for proof experiments in a new method of casting cannon. Also invented hemp-breaking machine, a steam Plow, etc. Home: Hartford, Conn. Died 1903.

GAUSE, LUCIEN COATSWORTH congressman, lawyer; b. nr. Wilmington, N.C., Dec. 25, 1836; grad. U. Va. at Charlottesville; studied law; grad. Cumberland U., Lebanon, Tenn. Admitted to bar, began practice of law, Jacksonport, Ark., 1859; served from lt. to col. Confederate Army, during Civil War; mem. Ark. Ho. of Reps., 1866; commr. to represent state govt. at Washington; mem. U.S. Ho. of Reps. (Democrat) from Ark. 44th-45th congresses, 1875-79. Died Jacksonport, Nov. 5, 1880; buried pvt. burying ground nr. Jacksonport.

GAY, FREDERICK PARKER pathologist, bacteriologist; b. Boston, July 22, 1874; s. George Frederick and Louisa Maria (Parker) G.; A.B., Harvard, 1897; M.D., Johns Hopkins, 1901; Sc.D. George Washington U., 1932; m. Catherine Mills Jones, Oct. 18, 1904; children-Louisa Parker, Lucia Chapman, Frederick P. (dec.), William. Asst. on Johns Hopkins Med. Commn. to Philippines, 1899; asst. demonstrator pathology U. Pa., 1901-03; fellow Rockefeller Inst. for Med. Research, 1901-03; research student Pasteur Institute, Brussels, 1903-06; bacteriologist Danvers Insane Hosp., 1906-07; asst. and instr. in pathology Harvard Med. Sch., 1907-10; prof. pathology, U. Cal., 1910-21, prof. bacteriology, 1921-23; prof. bacteriology, Columbia, 1923—. Maj., M.C., U.S.A., 1918-19; mem. med. sct. NRC, 1917-24, chmn., 1922-23, chmn. Med. Fellowship Bd., 1922-26; C.R.B. exchange prof. to Belgian univs., 1926-27. Fellow A.M.A., A.A.A.S.; mem. Nat. Acad, Science, Assn. Am. Physicians, Am. Assn. Pathologists and Bacteriologists, Soc. Experimental Biology and Medicine Assn. Am. Bacteriologists, American Assn. Immunologists. Comdr. Order of Crown of Belgium. Republican. Clubs: Faculty (Columbia and U. Cal.); Century (N.Y.C.). Author: Studies in Immunity, 1909; Typhoid Fever, 1918; Agents of Disease and Host Resistance (with others) 1935; The Open Mind-a Life of Elmer Ernest Southard; also contbr. scientific jours. on bacteriology, immunology and pathology. Home: New Hartford, Conn. Office: 630 W. 168th St., N.Y.C. Died July 14, 1939; buried Old Town Hill Cemetery, New Hartford, Conn.

GAY, JOHN LONGDON lawyer; b. Pisgah, Cooper Co., Mo., June 28, 1866; s. Thomas C. and Mary Ann (Hill) G.; ed. Clarksburg (Mo.) Acad. and Hooper Inst., Clarksburg; m. at San Juan, P.R., Gertrude Mary Vidler, of Gravesend, Eng., Nov. 18, 1915. In U.S. Ry. service, 1887-91, seaport service, 1901-08; clk. Federal Court, Porto Rico 1908-10; corp. assessor, 1910-12; sec.-treas. and gen. mgr. P.R. Expn., 1912-13; pres. Municipal Assembly, Dist. of Darado, P.R., 1916; admitted to practice law in P.R., later in courts of U.S.; asst. U.S. atty., P.R., 1922-23, U.S. atty. since Mar. 22, 1924, reapptd. May 29, 1928. Grad. as capt. inf. 2d O.T.C., P.R., 1918; capt. adj. 374th Inf., U.S. Army, P.R., May 23, 1918; hon. discharged, Jan. 25, 1919; maj. O.R.C. Actively interested in citrous fruit industry, 1905-26. Lt. col. staff of Gov. Reily, 1921-23. Mem. Federal Bar Assn. P.R. Republican. Mason, K.P., Elk. Home: San Juan, P.R.

GAYLE, R(OBERT) FINLEY, JR. physician; b. nr. Norfolk, Va., Dec. 18, 1891; s. Robert Finley and May Jeanette (Young) G.; M.D., Med. Coll. Va., 1915; post grad. Columbia, 1921; m. Elizabeth Marshall Cole, Aug. 16, 1919 (dec. Aug. 14, 1944); children-Elizabeth Marshall (Mrs. Parke S. Rouse, Jr.), Robert Finley, III, John Cole; m. 2d, Sarah Geer Dale, Nov. 3, 1945. Intern Tucker Hosp. Richmond, Va., 1915-16, asso. chief staff, 1919-29; residency Phila. Orthopedic Hosp. and Infirmary for Nervous Disease, 1916, Neurol. Inst., N.Y. City, 1916-17; pvt. practice neurology and psychiatry since 1919; professor and chairman of the department neurology and psychiatry Medical College of Virginia since 1937, chief neurologist and psychiatrist, hosp. div., since 1937, chief neurologist and psychiatrist, hosp. div., since 1937; vis. psychiatrist Crippled Children's Hosp., Home for Incurables, Johnston-Willis Hosp., Retreat for the Sick, St. Lukes Hosp., Sheltering Arms Hosp., Stuart Circle Hosp., St. Elizabeth Hosp.; psychiatric cons. V.A. Mem. Governor's Adv. Bd. on Mental Hygiene; bd. mem. Va. Dept. Mental Hygiene and Hosps. Served as capt., 3rd div., U.S. Army, A.E.F., Army of Occupation, World War I; cons. Selective Service, World War II. Diplomate Am. Bd. Neurology and Psychiatry, Fellow A.C.P., A.M.A., Am. Neurol. Assn., Am. Psychiatric Assn. (past president), Medical Society of Virginia, American Academy Neurology, So. Psychiatric Association (past pres.): mem. A.A.A.S., So. Med. Assn. (ex-councilor), Neuropsychiatric Soc. Va. (past pres.), Richmond Acad. Medicine (past pres.). Virginia Democrat. Episcopalian. Mason. Clubs: Commonwealth, Country Club of Va., Farmington Country, Deep Run Hunt. Contbr. articles profl. jours. Home: 311 Charmian Rd., Richmond 26. Office: 414 W. Franklin St., Richmond 20, Va. Died Nov. 4, 1957; buried Richmond.

GAYLORD, HARVEY RUSSELL med. scientist; b. Saginaw, Mich., Oct. 4, 1872; s. Augustine S. and Ellen Emaline (Warren) G.; ed. Cheltenham Acad., Ogontz, Pa.; M.D., U. of Pa., 1893; m. Bessie May Ketcham, Oct. 4, 1893. Interne Phila. Hosp., 1893; asst. in pathology, U. of Göttingen, 1895-98; dir. State Inst. of Study of Malignant Disease, Buffalo, 1899—; prof. surg. pathology, U. of Buffalo, 1899-1906; surgeon to Erie Co. Hosp., 1900. Republican. Joint Author: Gaylord and Aschoff's Pathological Histology, 1901. Maj., M.C. U.S.A., May 20, 1917-Dec. 24, 1918, div. surgeon 99th Div. Home: Eggertsville, N.Y. Died June 21, 1924.

GAYOSO DE LEMOS, MANUEL colonial ofcl.; b. 1752; m. Teresa y Pereira, circa 1788; m. 2d, Margaret Watts, 1797. Lt. col. of inf. Lisbon Regt., 1783; commd. gov. Dist. of Natchez, 1787; arrived in La., 1789; commd. col., 1789; contbd. to Northward extension of Spanish frontier by building forts at Walnut Hills, 1790-92, Chickasaw Bluffs, 1795; duties included inducing Am, frontiersmen trying to settle on Spanish soil and to promote separation of West from U.S. (conspirator with Gen. James Wilkinson); persuaded Southern Indians to form confederacy and enter into defensive alliance with Spain v. U.S., 1793; commd. brig. gen., 1795; took possession of Govt. of La., 1797, excluded Americans from settlement in La., while encouraging their commerce. Died July 18, 1799.

GEARY, GEORGE REGINALD, retired; b. Strathroy, Ont., Aug. 12, 1874; s. Theophilus Jones and Mary (Goodson) G.; student, Upper-Can. Coll., 1889; Osgoode Hall, 1894, Barrister-at-law U. Toronto, 1896; m. Jessy Beatrice Caverhill, Mar. 23, 1927; children—Mary Rosalind, Richard Reginald Caverhill. Mayor, Toronto, 1910-12; mem. Can. Parliament, 1925-35, privy council, 1935; Minister of Justice, Atty. Gen. of Can., 1935; King's counsel; counsel Corp. Toronto, 1912-27. Served as lt. to maj., C.E.F., 1915-19. Awarded Order of British Empire, Mil. Cross, Legion of Honor, Mentioned in dispatches. Mem. Alpha Delta Phi, Phi Delta Phi. Clubs: York, University, Golf, Cricket (Toronto). Home: 124 Park Rd., Toronto 5 ON Canada

GEARY, JOHN WHITE gov. Pa., territorial gov. Kan.; b. Mt. Pleasant, Pa., Dec. 30, 1819; s. Richard and Margaret (White) G.; attended Jefferson Coll.; m. Margaret Logan, 1843; m. 2d, Mary Church Henderson, 1858. Admitted to Pa. bar; asst. supt. and engr. of Allegheny Portage R.R.; lt. in militia, 1835; elected first alcalde of San Francisco, 1843; served as lt. col. in Mexican War, 1846, col., 1848; apptd. 1st postmaster of San Francisco and mail agt. for Pacific Coast, 1848; also performed duties of chief civil officer of city; 1st mayor of San Francisco, 1850; active in making Cal. free state; returned to Pa., 1852; chmn. Democratic Territorial Com.; gov. of Kan. Territory, 1856; substituted U.S. troops for pro-slavery militia, organized a new territorial militia, arrested irregular bands of free-state sympathizers; resigned due to trouble with legislature and some pro-slavery ofcls., 1857; set up recruiting office in Pa., 1861; became col. 28th Pa. Volunteers, 1861, promoted brig. gen., 1862; served in Battle of Cedar Mountain, 1862, commanded div. at Chancellorsville, Gettysburg, Lookout Mountain, and in Sherman's March to the Sea; mil. gov. of Savannah after capture; brevetted maj. gen., 1865. gov. of Pa., 1867-73, tried to reduce state debt by tight monetary policies; advocated gen. railroad law, state control of ins., gas cos., safeguards for public health. Died Pa., Feb. 8, 1873.

GEDDES, JAMES LORAINE army officer, educator; b. Edinburgh, Scotland, Mar. 19, 1827; s. Capt. Alexander and Elizabeth (Careless) G.; m. Margaret Moore, Oct. 14, 1856; m. 2d, Elizabeth Evans, Apr. 14, 1876. Served as col. Canadian Cavalry, 1854-57; moved to Benton County, Ia., 1857; commd. lt. col. Co. D, 8th Ia. Inf., 1861; promoted col., 1862; commd. brig. gen. U.S. Volunteers, 1865; commanded Ia. regt., served in battles of Shiloh, Vicksburg, Jackson; in charge of a brigade, 1863; provost marshal Memphis (Tenn.); supt. Ia. Instn. for Edn. of Blind, 1867-69; became steward Ia. land-grant coll. at Ames, 1870, prof. mil. tactics, v.p., dep. treas. coll., treas., 1884, initiated mil. instrn. in a land-grant coll., became coll. land agt., 1886. Author war songs including The Soldier's Battle-Prayer, The Stars and Stripes. Died Ames, Feb. 21, 1887.

GEDDES, NORMAL BEL designer, author, theatrical producer; b. Adrian, Mich., Apr. 27, 1893; s. Clifton Terry and Lulu (Yingling) G.; student Cleve. Sch. of Art, Art Inst. Chgo.; M.A., U. Mich., 1937; LL.D., Adrian College, 1936; B.F.A., Syracuse U., 1940; m. Helen Belle Sneider, Mar. 9, 1916 (dec.); children-Joan, Barbara; m. 2d, Frances Resor Waite, Mar. 3, 1933 (dec.); m. 3d Ann Howe, 1944 (div.); m. 4th, Edith Luytens, 1953. Pioneer in Am. stage design, 1914, in present day methods of stage lighting, 1916; designer, dir., co-author or producer of more than 200 plays, musicals, operas, motion pictures, and for the circus; planner or designer numerous theatres in U.S. and Europe, including Theatre Guild, Roxy Theatre (N.Y.C.), Ukrainian State Opera House (Karov, USSR), Copa City (Miami, Fla.); designer Gen. Motors Corp. bldg. and exhibit, Futurama, N.Y. World's Fair, 1938, master plan for City of Toledo, 1941, NBC studios, 1955; asso., archtl. commn., Century of Progress Expn., Chgo., 1938; indsl. designer, 1927—; pioneer designer indsl. products, including streamlined automobiles, 1928, railways trains, 1931, ocean liner, 1932, airplane interiors, 1933, electric typewriter, 1946; originator methods and techniques for use by U.S. Army, USN, USAF, OSS, as techniques for ship identification, aircraft recognition, "natural" camouflage (Corps Engrs.,) model constrn. and photograph (USN), Mark IV submarine trainer, stop motion tng. films, rubber mat processes, psychol. warfare weapons (OSS), method, equipment and bldg. Air Force Strategic Command trainer; ofcl. record Battle of Midway (sec. of def.); mem. Inventors Council; adviser QMG, U.S. Army, also OWI. Exhibitor in museums in U.S., Europe, Africa, Asia, 1912—; represented in collections of museums in U.S., Europe, Asia. Mem. NRC, Authors League Am., United Scenic Artists Union. Illuminating Engring. Soc., Archtl. League of N.Y., U.S. Naval Inst., Mediaeval Acad. Am., Royal Soc. Arts (London), (hon.) Arquitectura de Mexico, Clubs: Players, Coffee House, North American Yacht Racing Union. Author: Theatrical Presentation of the Divine Comedy of Dante, 1923; Horizon, 1932; Magic Motorways, 1940. Contbr. encys. and mags. Address: 350 Park Av., N.Y.C. 22. Died May 8, 1958.

GEHLE, FREDERICK W. pub. relations; b. London, Apr. 9, 1886; s. Henry D. and Anna Sabina (Bauer) G.; student N.Y.U., 1905-06. Reporter N.Y. Evening Post, 1906-12, asst. financial editor, 1912-16; publicity dir. and author monthly econ. rev. Mechanics and Metals Nat. Bank, N.Y.C., 1916-22, v.p., 1922-26; v.p. Chase Nat. Bank, N.Y.C., 1926-50; dir. Union Labor Life Ins. Co. Exec. Co. Co. Exec. dir. Greater N.Y. Fund, 1949-52. Past v.p. Allied War Relief, 1940; nat. v. chmn. commerce and industry div., chmn. labor div. Brit. War Relief Soc., 1941-43. Exec. dir., state chmn. N. Y. War Finance Com. 1944-45 (heading campaigns that yielded 26 billion dollars in war bond sales). Dir. Greek War Relief Assn.; treas. Friends of Luxembourg, Austrian Relief, Belgium War Relief Soc. Awarded U.S. Treasury citation, Award of Merit, V.F.W., 1951. Decorated Officer The Crown (Belgium), Comdr. The Crown (Luxembourg). Comdr. Order White Rose (Finland), Comdr. Order of Brit. Empire. Clubs: Metropolitan, Economic, Silurians, Pilgrims, N.Y. Athletic, Nat. Republican (N.Y.). Episcopalian. Author: Steps to Victory, 1917; The World's War Debt, 1918; The World Tomorrow, 1919; Our Dubgledam Journey, 1941. Home: 120 Central Park S., N.Y.C. Died Apr. 24, 1960.

GEIS, GEORGE (SHERMAN), soldier, printer by trade; b. Grand Island, Neb., 1875; s. Col. J. and Eleanor F. G.; early life on plains and Western frontier; worked in hotels of Denver, Chicago and New York while completing ed'n. Served in Astor Battery during Spanish War, and with Gen. Merritt, 1st mil. gov. to Philippines; took part in capture of Manila, Aug. 13, 1898, and Philippine campaign; tour around world, 1902-3; war corr., 1st expd'n into Mindanao. In newspaper work since 1901; contb'r to Success and other mags. on Orient and Far East. Past comdr. Lincoln Camp, No. 7, Sons of Veterans, New York, 1901; maj. and a.-d.-c., gen. staff Sons of Veterans Reserve, 1904-7; del. at large, Calif. Div., Nat. Encampments, Sons of Veterans, 1903-4, senior vice-comdr., 1904-5. Mem. U.S. Revolver Assn., Nat. Soc. Army of Philippines, Am. Geog. Soc., New Thought Federation, United Spanish War Veterans, etc.; sec. Astor Battery Vet. Assn., New York, 1905; Nat. del. from Calif. to United Spanish War Veterans and Army of the Philippine encampments, 1905. Author: History of the Famous Astor Battery, 1905. Address: 345 Golden Gate Av., San Francisco

GEIST, SAMUEL HERBERT physician; b. New York, N.Y., July 1, 1885; s. Ralph Roger and Frances (Davis) G.; A.B., Coll. of City of New York, 1904; M.D., Coll. of Physicians and Surgeons, Columbia, 1908; grad. study, U. of Freiburg, 1911-12; m. Juliet Beecher, July 1, 1933; 1 dau., Joyce B. Interne Mt. Sinai Hosp., New York, 1908-10; mem. attending staff since 1913; gynecologist since 1936; clin. prof. of gynecology, Coll. of Physicians and Surgeons, Columbia, since 1936. Served as capt. Med. Corps. U.S. Army, 1917-19; with A.E.F., 14 months. Mem. Am. Gynecol. Soc., N.Y. Obstet. Soc., Club: Sunnydale Country (Scarsdale, N.Y.). Contbr. to textbooks on surgery and gynecology; also articles to med. jours. Home: 969 Park Av. Office: 100 E. 74th St., New York, N.Y.* Died Dec. 14, 1943.

GEMMELL, WILLIAM HENRY ry. official; b. Ottawa, Ont., Can., Nov. 25, 1866; s. John James and Harriet Amelia (Garvey) G.; ed. Collegiate Inst., Ottawa, Can.; LL.B., U. of Minn.; m. Lavinia Austin Lamb, of St. Paul, Minn., May 10, 1898; children - Kathleen (Mrs. S. W. Hartwell), John, Robert. Came to U.S., 1889, naturalized citizen, 1895. Pres. Minn. & Internat. Ry. Co. until Aug. 1933, now retired. Formerly member Canadian Militia; colonel on staff of Governors Eberhart and Burnquist of Minnesota; mem. District Draft Bd., Duluth, World War. Mem. Tuberculosis Commn. of Crow Wing-Aitkin Counties; elected by Minn. legislature, 1929, as mem. Bd. of Regents, U. of Minn. Republican. Episcopalian. Mason. Club: St. Paul Athletic. Home: Brainerd, Minn.

GENTILE, EDWARD, designer, illuminator; b. Chicago, Ill., July 20, 1890; s. Joseph and Mary (Tise) G.; student Art Inst., Chicago, 1911-12; m. Ruth R. Running, Dec. 16, 1919; children—Amadeus Edward, Urania Ruth. Commercial artist North American Newspaper, Phila., Pa., 1914; with Studio of Design and Lettering, N.Y. City, 1914-17; free lance artist, 1919-30; manuscript illuminator from 1930. Served as panoramic draftsman Balloon Corps, A.E.F., 1918-19. Paintings extensively displayed in Chicago by U.S. Treasury Dept. in war bond sales. Designs reproduced by The Inland Printer, 1925. Exhibitor at Art Inst. Chicago, Marshall Field Galleries, All-Ill. Soc., one-man show Chicago Galleries, one man exhibit, Town Club. Address: Oak Park IL Died Aug. 4, 1968.

GEORGE, CHARLES P. army officer; b. Aug. 10, 1886; grad. Mounted Service Sch., 1915, Command and Gen. Staff Sch., 1925, Army War Coll., 1927. Commd. 2d lt., Jan. 1, 1908; promoted through grades to brig. gen., Apr. 1941, major gen., 1942; served as lt. col., later col., Field Arty., World War I; served with 4th Army; retired Oct. 1946. Died Dec. 30, 1946; buried in National Cemetery, Fort Sam Houston, Tex.

GEORGE, JAMES ZACHARIAH senator, jurist; b. Monroe County, Ga., Oct. 20, 1826; s. Joseph Warren and Mary (Chamblis) G.; m. Elizabeth Young, c. 1848. Admitted to Miss. bar, circa 1848; elected reporter of Miss. Supreme Ct., 1854, 60; mem. Miss. Secession Conv., 1861; served from capt. to brig. gen. of Miss. state troops, during Civil war; published 10 vols. of Miss. Reports; prepared Digest of the Reports, 1872; became partner (with Wiley P. Harris) in law firm, Jackson, Miss., 1872; led in restoration of native white supremacy in Miss.; chief justice Miss. Supreme Ct., mem. U.S. Senate from N Miss., Mar. 4, 1881-97; led in defense of Miss. and South from fed. interference; only Democrat to play important part in framing Sherman Anti-Trust Law of 1890; mem. Miss. Constl. Conv., 1890. Author: The Political History of Slavery in the United States, published 1915. Died Jackson, Miss., Aug. 14, 1897.

GEREN, PAUL FRANCIS, diplomat, univ. president; b. El Dorado, Arkansas, Dec. 5,21913; s. Rev. Hiram Marian and Julia (Goodwin) G.; A.B., Baylor U., 1936; M.A., La. State U., 1937; M.A., Harvard, 1940, Ph.D., 1941; LL.D., St. Mary's U., San Antonio, 1962; married Elizabeth Powers, Apr. 5, 1946; children—Natasha, Juliana, Nancy Magdalene. Lectr. economics Judson Coll., U. Rangoon, Burma, 1941; vol. ambulance driver Chinese Army, Burma, 1942; escaped from Burma in Stilwell March; lectr. economics Forman Christian Coll., Lahore, 1942-43; prof. economics Berea Coll., 1946-47; apptd. v. consul career, sec. Diplomatic Service, 1947; v. consul, Bombay, India, 1948-50; internat. trade economist South Asia sect. Office of Internat. Trade, Dept. of Commerce, 1950-51; consul, 2d sec. Am. Legation, Damascus, Syria, 1951, 1st sec., 1952-54; counselor Am. Embassy, Amman, Jordan, 1954-56; exec. v.p., Baylor Univ., Waco, Texas, 1956-58; executive dir. Dallas Council on World Affairs, 1959-61; dep. dir. Office Internat. and Devel. Affairs, Department State, 1961-62; deputy director Peace Corps., 1961-62; consul gen. with rank of minister Fedn. Rhodesia and Nyasaland, Salisbury, 1962-64; dir. Office Telecommunications and Maritime Affairs, Dept. State, 1964-65; counselor econ. affairs Am. embassy, Tripoli, Libya, 1965-67; president Stetson University, DeLand, Fla., 1967-69. Candidate for U.S. Congress, 1946. Served as combat med., later intelligence officer AUS, CBI, 1943-46; disch. as 1st lt. Decorated Bronze Star Medal. Fellow Soc. for Religion Higher Edn. Baptist. Author: Burma Diary, 1943; The Pilgrimage of Peter Strong, 1948; New Voices, Old Worlds, 1958; Christians Confront Communism, 1962; also econ., religious articles profl. jours. Home: ElDorado3AR Died June 22, 1969; buried Lexington Cemetery, Lexington KY

GERHARDT, AUGUST EDWARD surgeon; b. Fayette County, Ill., Oct. 1, 1882; s. Julius and Caroline (Berg) G.; student Concordia Coll., Springfield, Ill., 1897-1900, Ill. Sch. Pharmacy, Chicago, 1903-05; M.D., Northwestern U., Chicago, 1909; m. Elizabeth Walsh, July 17, 1912. Practiced in Wenatchee, Wash., since 1915; chief of staff Deaconess Hosp., 5 yrs.; asst. div. surgeon G.N. Ry.; dir. Columbia Valley Bank. Served as maj. M.C., World War; lt. col. Med. O.R.C. Fellow Am. Coll. Surgeons, A.M.A.; mem. Wash. State Med. Soc. (trustee), Pacific Coast Surg. Assn., Puget Sound Surg. Soc., Seattle Surg. Soc., Spokane Surg. Soc. Republican. Clubs: Rainier, University (Seattle). Home: R.R. 3, Wenatchee. Office: 32 S. Wenatchee Av., Wenatchee, Wash. Died May 3, 1942.

GERLACH, ARCH C., geographer; b. Tacoma, May 12, 1911; s. William Henry and Kate Alice (Cooper) G.; A.B., San Diego State Coll., 1933, M.A., U. Cal. at Los Angeles, 1935; Ph.D., U. Wash., 1943; m. Arlene M. Schmiedeman, 1935. Geographer Los Angeles City Coll., 1939-42; acting chief map div. Dept. State, 1945-46; asso. prof. geography U. Wis., 1946-50; chief geography and map division, also incumbent chair of geography Library of Congress, Washington, 1950-67; vis. prof. in geography U. Mich., 1957-58. U.S. rep. directing council Pan-Am. Inst. Geography and History, from 1958, v.p., 1965-69; chief National Atlas project United States Geological Survey, 1962-63, staff geographer, 1963-67, chief geographer U.S. Geol. Survey, from 1967. Vice president, U.S. member commn. on nat. atlasas Internat. Geog. Union, 1964-68. Served as lieutenant, cartographer and map intelligence officer, OSS, USNR, 1942-45. Chmn. NRC adv. com. geography Dept. State, 1956-62; Co-ordinator Geographie Applications Program for Remote Sensor Data from Aircraft and Spacecraft, 1967-72. Fellow American Geographic Society (honorary); member American Congress on Surveying and Mapping, Association of American Geographers (pres. 1962-63), Nat. Council Geography Teachers, Special Libraries Association (nat. chmn., geog. and map div., 1953-55, mem. exec. board, 1956-59), Am. Soc. Photogrammetry, Pan Am. Inst. Geography and History (president 1969). Editor of The Professional Geographer, 1951-54. Home: Washington DC Died May 20, 1972; buried Gettysburg Nat. Cemetery.

GERONIMO (Indian name Goyathlay), Indian warrior; b. Ariz., June 1829; s. Taklishim and Juana. Joined Chiricahua Apaches as a youth, took part in raids led by Cochise and Mangas Coloradas; led party of warriors on raid when Apaches were moved to San Carlos Reservation, Ariz., 1876; led other raids, 1880, 82-83, captured each time and returned to reservation; made most infamous raid, May 1885-Mar. 1886, captured in Mexico by Gen. George Crook of U.S. Cavlary; escaped, later recaptured by detachment of army under Gen. Nelson A. Miles on Bavispe River, Mexico; imprisoned at Ft. Pickens, Fla., then at Mt. Vernon, Ala., finally at Ft. Sill, Okla.; became farmer on reservation; joined Dutch Reformed Ch., 1903; appeared in inaugural procession of Pres. Theodore Roosevelt, 1905; dictated his memoirs, 1906. Died Ft. Sill, Feb. 17, 1909.

GEROW, LEONARD TOWNSEND, army officer; b. Petersburg, Va., July 13, 1888; s. Leonard Rodgers and Eloise (Saunders) G.; B.S., Virginia Military Inst., 1911; m. Mary Louise Kennedy, July 28, 1939. Commd. 2d lt. Inf., U.S. Army, 1911; advanced through grades to lt. gen., Jan. 1945; served as chief of staff, War Plans Div. to Feb. 1942; comdg. gen. 29th Div., Ft. George Meade, 1942-43; comdg. gen. V Corps, European Theater, July 1943-Jan. 1945; comdg. gen. 15th Army, Jan.-Oct. 1945; comdg. gen. Ft. Leavenworth; comdt. Comd. and Gen. Staff Coll. 1945-48; commanding general 2d Army, hdqrs. Fort George G. Meade, Maryland, Jan. 15, 1948 to July 31, 1950. Decorated D.S.M. with Oak Leaf Cluster, Legion of Merit with Cluster, Silver Star, Bronze Star (U.S.); Legion d' Honneur Commander, Croix de Guerre with Palm (France); Order of Bath (Great Britain); Order of Suvorov, 2d Class (Russia); Order of Crown of Luxembourg; Order of Leopold II, Grand Officer with Palm; Croix de Guerre 1940, with Palm (Belgium) Order Military Merit (Brazil); D.S.M. (Va.), D.S.M. (Pa.). Episcopalian. Address: Fort George G Meade MD Died Oct. 1972.

GERRITY, THOMAS PATRICK air force officer; b. Harlowton, Mont., Dec. 8, 1913; s. Edward Michael and Evelyn J. (Wagner) G.; student Armour Inst., Chgo., also advanced mgmt. program Harvard; m. Margaret Briscol, May 13, 1940; children-Thomas Patrick, Rita Ann. Commnd. 2d lt. USAAF, 1940, advanced through grades to lt. gen. USAF, 1962; bomber pilot Southwest Pacific, 1941-42; chief aircraft br. Air Material Command, 1943-50; wing comdr. Strategic Air Command, 1950-53; dir. procurement and prodn. Hdqrs. USAF, Washington, 1953-55, asst. for prodn. programming, DCS Material, 1955-57; comdr. Oklahoma City Air Materiel Area, 1957-60; comdr. Ballistic Systems Div. (AFSC), Inglewood, Cal., 1960-62; dep. chief Staff Systems and Logistics Washington, 1962-. Home: Quarters 7, Bolling AFB. Office: Systems andLogistics, Hdqrs. USAF, Washington 25. DiedFeb. Died Feb. 1968.

GERSTLE, MARK LEWIS, corp. official; b. San Francisco, Calif., May 28, 1866; s. Lewis and Hannah (Greenebaum) G.; student Harvard, 1889, Harvard Law Sch., 1892; m. Genevieve Mills Bennett, Aug. 16, 1936; children—(by previous marriage to Hilda Hecht) Dr. Mark L. Jr., Louise Alice Stahl. Practiced law until 1910; pres. Arroyo Seco Gold Dredging Co., Gen. Metals Recovery Corp.; vice pres. and dir. The Emporium, San Francisco, Met. Laundry Co.; pres. Townsend Co.; dir. Yreka Dredging Co. Attended Mil. Training Camp, Monterey, Calif., in 1916; served during World War I as major. Awarded Distinguished Service Medal by U.S. Govt., 1928. Military aide to Sec. of War, IX Corps Area, since 1929. Clubs: Family; Harvard of New York. Home: 545 Powell St. Office: 310 Sansome St., San Francisco CA*

GETTY, GEORGE WASHINGTON army officer; b. Georgetown, D.C., Oct. 2, 1819; s. Robert and Margaret (Wilmot) G.; grad. U.S. Mil. Acad., 1840; m. Elizabeth Stevenson, 1848. Commd. 2d lt., 4th Arty., U.S. Army, 1840, 1st lt., 1845; served at battles of Contreras, Churubusco, Molino del Rey, Chapultepec during Mexican War; brevetted capt., 1847; served in wars against Seminole Indians, 1849-50, 56-57; promoted capt., 1853, lt. col., 1861; served in Peninsular campaign, battles of South Mountain, Antietam, Fredericksburg, also Wilderness and Shenandoah campaigns; apptd. brig. gen. U.S. Volunteers, 1862; commd. maj. U.S. Army, 1863, col., 1866; commanded post and arty. sch., Ft. Monroe, 1871-77; led troops in suppressing riots along B. & O. R.R., 1877; ret., 1883. Died Forest Glen, Md., Oct. 1, 1901.

GETTY, ROBERT N. army officer; b. Ft. Hamilton, N.Y., Jan. 17, 1855; s. Gen. C. W. and Elizabeth Graham (Stevenson) G.; grad. U.S. Mil. Acad., 1878; m. Cornelia T. Colegate, Oct. 14, 1885. Additional 2d lt. 22d Inf., June 14, 1878; promoted through grades to brig. gen., Aug. 5, 1917. Served with Casey's scouts against Sioux Indians, 1890-91, with 5th Army Corps in Cuba, 1898, participating in battles of El Caney and San Juan, and in siege of Santiago; in P.I., 1900-03, 1906-07, 1908-11; comd. Recruit Depot, Ft. Logan, Colo., 1914-17; apptd. comdr. 175th Inf. Brigade, Camp Dodge, Ia., Sept., 1917. Home: Warrenton, Va. Died Apr. 15, 1941.

GEYER, HENRY SHEFFIE senator; b. Frederick, Md., Dec. 9, 1790; s. John and Elizabeth (Sheffie) G.; m. Clarissa B. Starr, Jan. 1, 1818; m. 2d, Joanna Easton, Apr. 26, 1831; m. 3d, Jane Stoddard, Feb. 12, 1850. Began practice law, 1811; served as 1st lt. in War of 1812, became regt. paymaster 38th Regt., Md. Inf., 1813; moved to St. Louis, 1813; mem. Mo. Territorial Legislature, 1818; played principal part in struggle for statehood; mem. Mo. Ho. of Reps., 1820-24, 34-35, speaker, 1820-22, 24, effected maj. revision of Mo. statute law in legislative sessions 1825, 35; mem. U.S. Senate (Whig) from Mo., 1851-57; leading atty. for defendant slave-owner in Dred Scott case. Died St. Louis, Mar. 5, 1859.

GHEEN, EDWARD HICKMAN rear admiral; b. Delaware Co., Pa., Dec. 11, 1845; s. Edward and Phebe (Hickman) G.; grad. U.S. Naval Acad., 1867; m. Florence, d. Delos A. and Mary Edgerton Monfort, Oct. 17, 1883. Promoted ensign, Dec. 18, 1868; master, Mar. 21, 1870; lt., Mar. 21, 1871; comdr., Mar. 28, 1898; capt., June 14, 1902; retired at his own request, after 40 yrs.' service, as rear admiral, Dec. 1, 1902. Flagship "Delaware," Asiatic Sta., Oct. 10, 1867, to Nov. 28, 1870; signal duty, Washington; Mar. 15 to July 1, 1971; at different stations and on various duties to 1890; steel inspection, Pittsburgh and Thurlow, Pa., Oct. 6, 1890, to May 9, 1891; branch Hydrographic Office, Phila., May 9, 1891, to May 31, 1892; Navy Yard, Phila., Apr. 1, 1893, to Sept. 17, 1894; "Minneapolis," North Atlantic and European Stas., Dec. 13, 1894, to Oct. 27, 1896; Hydrographic Office, Washington, Jan. 5, 1897-June 20, 1898; comdg. "Frolic," June 23 to Sept. 27, 1898; Hydrographic Office, Washington, Sept. 27, 1898 to June 18, 1899; comdg. "Marietta," Asiatic Sta., June 20, 1899, to Apr. 29, 1901; "Petrel," May 4 to Sept. 7, 1901; inspector 11th Light House Dist., Detroit, Feb. 12, 1902 to Sept. 15, 1902; naval recruiting office, Chicago, Sept. 19, 1902, to Feb. 24, 1903. Died Aug. 10, 1920.

GHERARDI, BANCROFT rear admiral; b. Jackson, La., Nov. 10, 1832; entered navy from Mass. as midshipman, June 29, 1846; served on Ohio, Pacific squadron, until 1850; entered Naval Acad.; passed midshipman, June 8, 1852; master and lt., 1855; lt. comdr., July 16, 1862; comdr., July 25, 1866; capt., Nov. 9, 1874; commodore, Nov. 1884; rear adm., Aug. 1887; retired, Nov. 10, 1894. In numerous engagements in Civil war; took especially prominent part in battle of Mobile Bay. Vice-comdr. for N.Y. Mil. Order of Foreign Wars. Home: Stratford, Conn. Died 1903.

GHERARDI, WALTER ROCKWELL naval officer; b. Honolulu, H.I., Aug. 9, 1875; s. Bancroft (rear adm. U.S.N.) and Anna Talbot (Rockwell) G.; grad. U.S. Naval Acad., 1895; m. Neville Sims Taylor, June 4, 1904; children—Walter Rockwell, Harry Taylor, Neville Taylor, Bancroft II (dec.). Ensign U.S.N., July 1897; promoted through grades to rear adm., May 10, 1930. Served in Atlantic, Pacific and Asiatic waters; on U.S.S. Marblehead, Santiago Campaign, Spanish-Am. War, 1898; on U.S.S. Annapolis, Philippine Insurrection, 1900-02; naval attaché, Am. Embassy, Berlin, 1913-17; comdr. U.S.S. De Kalb and U.S.S. New Jersey, World War; attached to Am. conf. to negotiate peace, Paris, Dec. 1918-Mar. 1919; comdr. Aircraft Squadrons, Scouting Fleet, 1922-24; hydrographer of Navy, 1930-35; comdt. First Naval Dist. and Navy Yard, Boston, June 5, 1935—. Fellow Am. Geog. Society. Episcopalian. Died July 24, 1939.

GHOLSON, SAMUEL JAMESON congressman, jurist; b. Madison County, Ky., May 19, 1808; m. Miss Ragsdale, 1838. Admitted to Miss. bar, 1829; mem. Miss. Ho. of Reps., 1835, 36, 39; mem. U.S. Ho. of Reps. from Miss., 24th-25th congresses, 1836-38; judge U.S. Dist. Ct. for Miss., 1839-61; pres. Miss. Democratic Conv., 1860; mem. Miss. Constl. Conv. which passed Ordnance of Secession, 1861; capt. of Monroe Volunteers, promoted col., brig. gen. Miss. Militia, 1861, maj. gen., 1863; brig. gen. Confederate Army, 1864, commanded brigade of cavalry; mem. Miss. Ho. of Reps., 1865, speaker, 1866; mem. Miss. Legislature, 1878. Died Aberdeen, Miss., Oct. 16, 1883; buried Odd Fellows Cemetery, Aberdeen.

GHORMLEY, RALPH K. cons. surgeon orthopedic surgery- Mayo Clinic; b. Portland, Ore., Feb. 10, 1893; s. David O. and Alice M. (Irwin) G.; B.S., Whitworth Coll., Tacoma, Wash. (now in Spokane), 1914; M.D., Johns Hopkins U., 1918; m. Jean McDougall, June 25, 1924; children-Ralph M., Alice E., now (Mrs. Charles D. Baker). Served at Letterman General Hospital, United States Army Hospital, in San Francisco, California, 1919: interne Johns Hopkins Hospital and Children's Hospital, Baltimore, Maryland, 1919-20, New York Hosp., 1920-21; asst. resident surgeon, Johns Hopkins Hosp., 1921-22; assistant in orthopedic surgery, Harvard Univ., 1922-23, instr., 1923-29; with Mayo Foundation, Rochester, Minn., 1929-58, instr. in orthopedic surgery, 1929-32, asso. prof., 1932-37, prof., 1937-58, prof. emeritus 1958—; asso. in orthopedic surgery, Mayo Clinic, 1929-38, head of section, 1938-58, senior consultant in orthopedic surgery, 1955-58; cons. U.S. Naval Hospital, Oakland, California; also honorary consultant Peninsula Community Hospital, Carmel, California. Consultant Orthopedic Surg., Vets. Administrn., Washington, D.C. Certified specialist orthopedic surg. by Bd. Orthopedic Surgery. Served as pvt., lieut., capt., Med. Corps, A.E.F., 1917-19. Fellow Am. Coll. Surgeons; mem. Am. Orthopedic Assn. (sec. 1933-40, pres. 1948-49), Clin. Orthopedic Soc. (pres. 1941), Am. Acad. Orthopedic Surgeons, Am. Surg. Assn., A.M.A., Am. Bd. Orthopedic Surgery (pres. 1951-52), Western Surg. Soc., Am. Assn. for Surgery of Trauma, Robert Jones Orthopedic Society,* International Surgery Society, International Society Orthopedic Surgery and Traumology, Alpha Omega Alpha, Sigma Xi; corr. mem. Scandanavian, Belgian orthopedic socs. Club: Harvard (Boston). Author: Diagnosis in Joint Disease (with Nathaniel Allison). 1931. Home: P.O. Box 4223, Carmel, Cal. Died June 6, 1959.

GHORMLEY, ROBERT LEE naval officer; b. Portland, Ore., Oct. 15, 1883; s. David Owen and Alice Minerva (Irwin) G.; A.B., U. Ida., 1902, LL.D., 1946; B.S., U.S. Naval Acad., 1906; m. Lucile Elizabeth Lyon, Oct. 20, 1911; children-Daniel Dyer, Alice Elizabeth (Mrs. W. C. F. Robards), Robert Lee. Commd. ensign USN, advanced through grades to vice adm., 1941; asst. chief staff, U.S. Fleet, 1931-32; comd. U.S.S. Nevada, 1935-36; Fleet operations officer, 1936-37; dir. war plans div., Office Chief of Naval Operations, Navy Dept., 1938-39, asst. to chief of Naval operations, 1939-40: spl. naval observer, London, Eng., 1940-42; comdr. U.S. Naval Forces European Waters, 1942; comdr., South Pacific Force and South Pacific Area, 1942; comd. allied forces during seizure of Guadalcanal-Tulagi, 1942: comdr. Hawaiian Sea Frontier, comdt. 14th Naval Dist., 1943-44; comdr. U.S. Naval Forces, Germany, 1944; retired from active duty, 1946. Decorated: D.S.M. (Army and Navy), Nicaraguan Campaign badge, Mexican Campaign badge, Legion of Merit; Pacific and Atlantic Campaign badges. Victory medals, World Wars I and II. Mem. Phi Beta Kappa, Phi Delta Theta. Presbyterian. Club: Army-Navy (Washington). Home: 3305 Macomb St. N.W., Washington 8. Died June 21, 1958; buried Arlington Nat. Cemetery.

GIBB, FREDERICK WILLIAM, army officer; b. N.Y.C., July 24, 1908; s. Frederick Innes and Jessie Anna (Leake) G.; B.S., U.S. Mil. Acad., 1933; grad. Inf. Sch., 1938. Command and Gen. Staff Coll., 1946. Nat. War Coll., 1949; m. Delana Elizabeth Skeldon, June 13, 1933 (dec. Sept. 1959); children—Frederick William II, Jean Innes (Mrs. Fred B. Phillips), m. 2d, Ruth Gidley, Nov. 29, 1960. Commd. 2d lt. U.S. Army, 1933, advanced through grades to maj. gen., 1959; various assignments with inf. units, 1933-42; battalion comdr. 3d Bn., 16th Inf., 1st Inf. Div., 1942-43; asst. chief staff G-3, 1st Inf. Div., 1943-44; regtl. comdr. 16th Inf., 1st Inf. Div., 1944-45; chmn. attack com. Inf. Sch., Ft. Benning, Ga., 1946-48; staff mem. advanced study group dept. of army and joint staff, Joint Strategic Plans Group, Office Joint Chiefs Staff, 1949-52; dep. chief staff plans and operations, Allied Land Forces, S.E. Europe, Izmar, Turkey, 1952-54; chief army war plans br., plans div. Office Asst., Chief Staff G-3, Dept. of Army, 1954-55, asst. chief, then dir. orgn. and tng. div., Office Dep. Chief Staff Operations, 1955-56; comdg. gen. U.S. Army Combat Devel. Expt. Center, Ft. Cid, Cal., 1956-60; comdg. gen. 2d Inf. Div., Ft. Benning, from 1960. Decorated Silver Star, Legion of Merit with oak leaf cluster, Bronze Star with V device with 2 oak leaf clusters. Combat Inf. badge (U.S.); Mil. Cross, 3d class, Order of Lion (Czechoslovakia); Legion of Honor, Fourragere, Croix de Guerre with palm (France); Order of Leopold, Croix de Guerre, Forragere (Belgium). Home: Camp Springs3MD Died Sept. 1968.

GIBB, HAMILTON ALEXANDER ROSSKEEN, educator; b. Alexandria, Egypt, Jan. 2, 1895; s. Alexander Crawford and Jane Ann (Gardner) G.; M.A., Edinburgh U., 1919, LL.D., 1952; M.A., London U., 1921, Oxford, 1937; Hon. Dr., U. Algiers, 1943; A.M., Harvard University, 1955, D.Litt. (honorary), 1963; married Helen Jessie Stark, July 12, 1922; children—John A.C., Dorothy S. (Mrs. Edward J. Greenslade). Lectr. Sch. Oriental Studies, 1921-30; prof. Arabic, U. London, 1930-37; Laudian prof. Arabic, U. Oxford, 1937-55; Haskins lectr. U. Chgo., 1945; U. prof., James Richard Jewett prof. Arabic, Harvard, 1955-64. Served as capt., Royal Arty., Brit. Army, 1914-18. Decorated Knight Bachelor (United Kingdom); Comdr. Orange-Nassau (Netherlands); Legion of Honor (France). Fellow Brit. Acad.; corr. fellow Medieval Acad. Am.; hon. fgn. member of the American Acad. Arts and Sciences, American Philosophical Society. Author: The Damascus Chronicle of the Crusades, 1932; Modern Trends in Islam, 1947; (with H. Bowen) Islamic Society and the West, 1950, 57. Died Oct. 22, 1971.

GIBBINS, HENRY army officer; b. Knoxville, Tenn., May 20, 1877; s. William E. and Ellen M. (Henry) G.; ed. Holbrook Coll., Knoxville, 1894-95; grad. Mounted Service Sch. (U.S. Army), 1910, Army Sch. of the Line, 1916; m. Grace McGonigle, Jan. 19, 1907; children-Margaret, Henry, Jr. Enlisted in Tenn. N.G., 1896; 1st lt. 3d Tenn. Inf., May 1898-Jan. 1899; 2d and 1st lt., 31st U.S. Vol. Inf., 1899-1901; commd. 2d lt. cav., regular army, Feb. 2, 1901; promoted through grades to col., Aug. 31, 1929; asst. to q.m. gen., with rank of brig. gen., Feb. 6, 1935-Apr. 1, 1936; apptd. q.m. gen., with rank of maj. gen., Apr. 1, 1936; retired Apr. 1, 1940. Participated in Spanish-Am. War, Philippine Insurrection, Cuban Occupation and World War. Awarded Mexican border and Victory medals. Home: 2139 Wyoming Av. Office: 923 15th St., Washington, D.C. Deceased.

GIBBON, JOHN army officer; b. Holmesburg, Pa., Apr. 20, 1827; s. John Heysham and Catharine (Lardner) G.; grad. U.S. Mil. Acad., 1847; m. Frances Moale, Oct. 16, 1855. Served in Seminole War in Fla., 1849, commd. 1st lt., 1850; prepared The Artillerists' Manual, 1859, adopted by War Dept., 1859, published 1860; promoted capt., 1859; commanded brigade at battles of Antietam, 1862, Gettysburg, 1863; commd. brig. gen. U.S. Volunteers, 1862, maj. gen., 1864; assigned to command of Iron Brigade; commanded a draft depot., 1864; div. comdr., 1864; served in battles of Wilderness, Spatsville and Cold Harbor, 1864; commanded XXIV Corps in last operations in No. Va., 1865; a commr. designated to arrange details of surrender of South; commd. col. U.S. Army, 1866; Indian fighter; commanded column of inf.; participated in Yellowstone expdn. against Sitting Bull, 1876; promoted brig. gen., 1885; commanded Dept. of Columbia; maintained peace during threatened anti-Chinese outbreak in Seattle, 1885-86; chief of Loyal Legion, 1896. Author: Personal Recollections of the Civil War, 1885. Died Balt., Feb. 6, 1896; buried Arlington (Va.) Nat. Cemetery.

GIBBON, JOHN HEYSHAM surgeon; b. Charlotte, N.C., Mar. 16, 1871; s. Robert (M.D.) and Mary Amelia (Rogers) G.; prep. edn. Macon Sch., Charlotte; M.D., Jefferson Med. Coll., 1891; m. Marjorie G. Young, Sept. 2, 1901; children-Marjorie Young, John H. Samuel Young, Robert, Prof. surgery and clin. surgery Jefferson Med. Coll., 1907-31 (emeritus); cons. surgeon Pa., Jefferson Med. and Bryn Mawr hosps. Surgeon U.S. Vol. Engrs., Spanish-Am. War, 1898; col. M.C.U.S. Army and cons. in surgery to AEF, World War I. Fellow, ex-pres. Am. Surg. Assn., Coll. Physicians of Phila., Phila. Acad. Surgery; mem. A.M.A., Med. Soc. State of Pa., Phila. Pediatric Soc., Nat. Soc. Study and Prevention Tb, etc. Contbr. to Reference Hand-Book of Medical Sciences, Keen's System of Surgery, many articles to surg. jours. Address: Lynfield Fram, Media, Pa. Died Mar. 13, 1956; buried Old St. David's Ch., Radnor, Pa.

GIBBON, JOHN HEYSHAM, JR., surgeon; b. Phila., Sept. 29, 1903; s. John Heysham and Marjorie (Young) G.; A.B., Princeton, 1923; M.D., Jefferson Med. Coll., 1927, Ph.D.; fellow surgery Harvard, 1930-31, 33-34; fellow surg. research U. Pa., 1936-42; Sc.D., U. Buffalo,

Princeton, Dickinson Coll.; m. Mary Hopkinson, Mar. 14, 1931; children—Mary, John, Alice, Marjorie. Intern, Pa. Hosp., 1927-29, cons. surgeon, 1950-73; chief surg. service Mayo Gen. Hosp., 1945; asst. prof. surgery U. Pa., 1945-46; prof. surgery, dir. surg. research Jefferson Med. Coll., 1946-56, Samuel D. Gross prof., head dept. surgery, 1956-67, emeritus prof. surgery, 1967-73. Served as lt. col. M.C., AUS, 1943-46. Recipient Albert Lasker Med. Research award, 1968. Diplomate Am. Bd. Surgery, Am. Bd. Thoracic Surgery. Fellow A.C.S., Royal Coll. Surgeons (Eng.); mem. Am. Surg. Assn. (past pres.), Am. Assn. Thoracic Surgery (past pres.), Soc. Clin. Surgery (past pres.), Phila. Acad. Surgery (past pres.), Heart Assn. Southeastern Pa. (past pres.), Coll. Physicians Phila. (past pres.), Soc. Vascular Surgery (past pres.), A.M.A. Democrat. Contbr. articles to surg. jours. Home: Media PA Died Feb. 5, 1973.

GIBBONS, DOUGLAS real estate broker; b. Balt., Dec. 5, 1883; s. John Francis and Nora, (Hayward) G.; prep. edn. Drisler Sch., N.Y. City, 1897-1902; Ph.B., Yale, 1906; LL.D., National U., Dominion of Canada, 1960; m. Tesson Thayer, October 28, 1915; 1 dau., Marie Thayer. Civil engr. Brooklyn Union Gas Co., 1906-09; real estate, 1909-20; pres. Douglas Gibbons & Co., Inc., real estate, 1920-53, chmn. bd., 1953-57; hon. chmn. board Douglas Gibbons-Hollyday & Ives, Inc., 1957 - ; chmn. bd. Ridgely Realty Co., 1957 - ; dir. City Investing Co., Northern Insurance Company; trustee Consolidated Edison Company of New York, Incorporated. Served as seaman, U.S. Navy, 1917; served as lt. and aide to Vice Adm. Sims, 1919; lieut. comdr., U.S.N.R.; director New York Chapter American Red Cross (vice chairman, 1930-41; chairman disaster relief 1933-41); chmn. Professional and Special Services Sect. in War Loan Drives; ex-gov. Real Estate Bd. New York. Decorated Eloy Alfaro Grand Cross. Member Mil. Order Fgn. Wars, Mil. Order World War, Book and Snake (Yale). Ind. Republican. Episcopalian. Clubs: Union (past gov.), Links (N.Y.C.); Cloister, Long Island Country. Home: 550 Park Av., N.Y.C. 21, Office: 745 Fifth Av., N.Y.C. 22. Died July 7, 1962.

GIBBS, GEORGE SABIN army officer, industrialist; born in Harlan, Iowa, December 14, 1875; son of George Sabin and Della (Baughn) Gibbs; B.S., State Univ. of Iowa., 1897, M.S., 1901; grad. Army Signal School, 1912; also grad. of Army War College, 1920; m. Ruth Annis Hobby, Oct. 9, 1899; children-Jessie Louise (Mrs. George K. Perkins), Robert Henry (capt. U.S. Navy), George Wareham (lt. col. U.S. Army), David Parker (lt. col. U.S. Army). Private and q.m. sergt. Co. C, 51st Ia. Inf., and 1st class sergt. Signal Corps U.S.V., May 30, 1898-Jan. 30, 1899; commd. 2d lt. signal officer vols., Jan. 13, 1899; promoted through grades to col., May 9, 1921; col. and brig. gen. (temp.), World War, Served in the Philippines in Spanish-Am. War and Philippine Insurrection, 1898-1900; built north central sect. of the Alaska telegraph system, 1901-03. Chief signal officer, Army of Cuban Pacification, 1907-09; chief signal officer Hawaiian Dept., 1913-15, and of the El Paso Dist., 1917; assistant chief signal officer A.E.F. in France, 1917-19, with the rank of brig. general; General Staff, 1920-21; in charge of laying of new Alaska cable, 1924; chief signal officer of Army, with rank of maj. gen. for 4 years from Jan. 9, 1928; retired from active service, June 30, 1931, to become v.p. Internat. Telephone and Telegraph Corp.; became pres. Postal Telegraph-Cable Co., Oct. 15, 1931, apptd. a trustee in reorganization of the co., 1936, director, 1940; director and vice chairman Federal Telephone and Radio Corporation since 1943. Recommended "for especially gallant and meritorious conduct" in the Battle of Manila, Aug. 13, 1898. Decorated D.S.M.; Officer Legion of Honor (France); Companion of the Order of St. Michael and St. George (Great Britain); Commandeur, Ordre de la Couronne (Belgium); Commendatore dell'Ordine della Corona d'Italia (Italy). Mem. Nat. Inst. Social Sciences, Sigma Nu, Sigma Xi. Mason (K.T.). Clubs: Army and Navy, Army, Navy Country (Washington, D.C.). Home: Lime Rock, Conn. Office: 67 Broad St., New York, N.Y. Died Jan. 9, 1947.

GIBBS, ROBERT ADAMS educator; b. Fort Ann, N.Y., Oct. 6, 1871; s. Thoron Z. (M.D.) and Mary J. (Thomas) G.; student Stanford U., 1893-96, U. Cal., summer 1906; A.B., U. So. Cal., 1908; m. Della M. Page, Apr. 7, 1909 (died Feb. 10, 1937); a dau., Edith Caroline (Mrs. Earle Russell Vaughan); m. 2d, Mrs. Lillian (Clark) Schouten, May 13, 1941. Founder, 1908, head master, Page Mil. Acad., Los Angeles. Recommended by Redfield Proctor, Sec. of War, as lt., U.S. Army, 1892. Maj. Cal. N.G. Republican. Baptist. Fellow Am. Geog. Soc.; mem. Soc. Colonial Wars, S.R., N.E. Hist. and Geneal. Soc., Inst. Am. Genealogy, Assn. Ind. Schs. Los Angeles County (pres. 1939-40), Pi Gamma Mu; founder, life mem. Pacific Geog. Soc. Mason (32ff), Elk., Rotarian. Author: Western Tales, 1925; Sea Stories, 1926. Address: Page Military Academy, 1201 S. Cochran Av., Los Angeles 35. Died July 23, 1952.

GIBBS, WILLIAM FRANCIS naval architect, marine engr.; b. Phila., Pa. Aug. 24, 1886; s. William Warren and Frances Ayers (Johnson) G.; student Harvard, scientific, 1906-19; LL.B. and M.A., Columbia, 1913; E.D. (hon.), Stevens Inst. Tech., 1938, N.Y.U., 1955; D.Sc. (hon), Harvard, 1947, Bowdoin Coll., 1955; m. Mrs. Vera Cravath Larkin, 1927; children - Francis C., Christopher L.; (step-son) Adrain C. Larkin. Organizer Gibbs Bros., Inc., Feb. 1922, Gibbs & Cox, Inc., 1929 (pres.). Controller of shipbuilding WPB, Dec. 1942-Sept. 1943. Chmn. Combined Shipbulding Com. of Combined Chiefs of Staff, 1943; rep. Office War Mobilization on Procurement Rev. Bd. of Navy, 1943. Recipient Am. Design award, 1943, David W. Taylor gold medal Soc. Naval Architects and Marine Engrs., 1946. Presdl. Certificate of Merit, 1947, Holland Soc. of N.Y. Distinguished service gold medal, 1951, Franklin Medal (gold) from Franklin Inst., 1953; Elmer A. Sperry Award, 1955; Michael Pupin medal, Columbia Engring. Alumni Assn., 1959; Allied Professions medal, A.I.A., 1960; William S. Newell Meml. award, United Seaman's Service, 1962. Fellow Royal Soc. Arts. Arts, Am. Soc. M. E. (hon.), (asso.) Inst. Aeronautical Scis.; mem. Soc., N.Y. Acad. Scis., Naval Architects and Marine Engrs. (v.p.), Instn. Naval Architects, Am. Soc. Naval Engrs., Am. Bur. Shipping (tech. com.), N.E. Coast Inst. Engrs. and Shipbuilders, U.S. Naval Inst., Nat. Acad. Scis., N.Y. Bar, Phi Beta Kappa. Clubs: University, Century, Broad Street, Piping Rock, India House, N.Y. Yacht. Home: 945 5th Av. Office: 1 Broadway, N.Y.C. 4. Died Sept. 1967.

GIBBS, WILLIAM HASELL lawyer. b. Charleston, S.C., Mar. 16, 1754; s. William and Elizabeth (Hasell) G.; read law under John Rutledge; attended Inner Temple, London, Eng., 1774; m. Elizabeth Allston, Aug. 29, 1772, m. Mary Philip Wilson, Jan. 21, 1808; at least 10 children including Robert W. Signed petition protesting Intolerable Acts to Ho. of Commons, during stay in Eng., 1774; refused passport to Am. when Am. Revolution began, but managed to get to S.C.; commd. capt. lt. Ancient Arty. Co., Charleston, S.C., served in defense of Charleston and Savannah; arrested by Cornwallis, 1780, held prisoner in St. Augustine, Fla.; admitted to S.C. bar, circa 1782; master in equity S.C., 1783-25, impeached by S.C. Legislature on charges resulting from a sale of slaves, 1811, acquitted by large majority on all charges; engaged in pvt. practice of law, 1825-34. Died Charleston, Feb. 13, 1824; buried St. Philip's Churchyard, Charleston.

GIBLIN, WALTER M. investment banker; b. Aug. 3, 1901; s. John T. and Ida J.; grad. U. Chgo., 1923; m. Elizabeth Hughes, Apr. 1924; 1 son, W. Michael; m. 2d, Constance Talmadge, Oct., 1939. Vice pres. Blyth & Co., Inc.; member board directors Howard Johnson Co., Norwich Pharmacal Co., Drilling & Exploration Co., Inc.; partner Glore, Forgan & Company. Served with ambulance unit AEF, World War 1, 1918; from maj. to col., AUS, ETO, 1942-45, exec. officer OSS, 1943-44. Decorated Legion of Merit, Legion of Honor, Croix de Guerre with palm, Czechoslovak War Cross. Roman Catholic. Clubs: Meadow Brook (Westbury, L.I.); Seminole Golf, Everglades (Palm Beach); Misquamicut (Watch Hill, R.I.); Buck's (London). Home: 680 Madison Av., N.Y.C. 21. Office: 45 Wall St., N.Y.C. 5. Died May 1, 1964.

GIBSON, CHARLES LANGDON surgeon; b. Boston, Mass., May 5, 1864; s. Charles Langdon and Margarette Carter (Smith) G.; A.B., Harvard, 1886, M.D., 1889; unmarried. Prof. emeritus surgery, Cornell Med. Coll.; cons. surgeon, N.Y. Hosp., St. Luke's Memorial, State Hosp. for Deformed and Crippled Children, and Southside (Babylon) hospitals. Commanding major Medical Corps, U.S. Army; director Base Hospital 9, A.E.F., in France, 1917-18. Commander of Crown (Belgian). Fellow American Surg. Assn.; mem. Soc. Clin. Surgery, Am. Assn. Genito-Urinary Surgeons, Internat. Surg. Assn., Practioners' Soc., N.Y. Clin. Soc., N.Y. Surg. Soc., Soc. Colonial Wars, S.E., Mil. Order Foreign Wars; asso. mem. Academie de Chirurgie, Paris; corr. mem. Academie de Medecine, Paris. Club: University. Address: 1 W. 54th St., New York, N.Y. Died Nov. 24, 1944.

GIBSON, EDWIN T. univ. ofcl.; grad. Cornell U. Law Sch., 1907; m. Wilmoth Cosby, 1916; children-Edwin C., Wilmoth C. Uellendahl. Gen. Law Practice New York, 3 yrs.; trial counsel Legal Aid Soc., New York; legal dept. Nat. Biscuit Co., 1912-15; asst. to pres., sec. Am. Sugar Refining Co., 1915-26; pres. Brooklyn Cooperage Co., 1926-30; exec. vice pres. Empire Bond & Mortgage Corp., 1930-32; exec. v.p. Gen. Foods Corp., dir., 1946, member exec. com., 1950, ret., 1951; research dir. Kraft Paper Industry, 1955-59; chmn. bd. Market Research Corp. of Am., 1958—; dir., mem. exec. com. Mchts. Refrigerating Co., First Fed. Savs. and Loan Assn. Administrator D.P.A., 1951; member board governors Refrigeration Research Foundation. President Eisenhower Exchange Fellowships, Inc. Am. mem., chmn. Internat. Materials Conf., Washington, 1951; vice chmn. Mut. Security Administrn. Evaluation Group 1953—. Trustee, mem. exec. com. Cornell U. Served in A.U.S., maj., ordnance A.E.F., World War I. Decorated Order of World Wars; named Man of the Year, Nat. Assn, of Mfrs., 1953. Mem. Nat. Planning Assn., Phi Kappa Psi, Phi Delta Phi. Mem. Am. Legion. Clubs: American Yacht; Cornell University (N.Y.); Army and Navy (Washington). North Fork Country (Cutchogue, L.I.); Cavalry (Bklyn.). Home: Rt. 3, Box 341, Montgomery Rd., Savannah, Ga. Office: 149 E. 78th St., N.Y.C. Died Feb. 23, 1959; buried Kensico Cemetery, Valhalia, N.Y.

GIBSON, ERNEST WILLARD U.S. senator; b. Londonderry, Vt., Dec. 29, 1871; s. William L. and Saville (Stowell) G.; B.S., Norwich U., 1894, A.M., 1896; studied law, U. of Mich., 1898-99; m. Grace Hadley, Nov. 25, 1896 (died 1925); children-Frank Hadley (dec.), Ernest William, Doris, Preston Fullerton. Prin. Chester High Sch., 1894-98; practiced at Brattleboro, 1899—; register of probate and deputy clk. U.S. Dist. Court; mem. Vt. Ho. of Rep., 1906, Senate 1908 (pres. of Senate); del. Rep. Nat. Conv., 1912; state's atty., 1919-21; sec. civil and mil. affairs, Vt., 1921-22; mem. 68th to 73d Congresses (1923-35), 2d Vt. Dist.; apptd. mem. U.S. Senate Nov. 22, 1933, to fill vacancy occasioned by death of Hon. Porter H. Dale, elected to same office, Jan. 16, 1934, reelected, 1938. Enlisted in Vt. N.G., 1899, retired, 1908; col. insp. rifle practice, staff of Gov. Fletcher D. Proctor; returned to service, 1915, as capt. inf.; served on Mexican border and over seas; col. 172d Inf., Aug. 5, 1921-Nov. 5, 1923. Republican. Episcopalian. Trustee Diocese of Vt. Home: Brattleboro, Vt. Died June 20, 1940.

GIBSON, ERNEST WILLIAM, judge; b. Brattleboro, Vt., Mar. 6,21901; s. Ernest Willard and Grace Fullerton (Hadley) G.; A.B., Norwich U., 1923; student George Washington Law Sch., 1924-27; m. Dorothy P. Switzer, Oct. 9, 1926 (dec. Aug. 1958); children—Ernest Willard III, Grace, Robert Hadley, David Alan; m. 2d, Ann H. Haag, Jan. 21, 1961. Teacher and track coach N.Y. Mil. Acad., Cornwall-on-Hudson, N.Y., 1923-24; mathematician Coast and Geodetic Survey, 1924-27; admitted to Vt. bar, 1926, practiced law, Brattleboro, Vt., from 1927; sr. partner Gibson, Gibson & Crispe. Elected States' Atty. of Windham Co., Vt., 1928, 30; asst. sec. Vt. State Senate, 1931-33; sec., 1933-40; resigned to serve appointment in U.S. Senate on death of father; mem. Railroad Tax Commn. of Vermont, 1939-40; governor of Vt. 1947-50, resigned to accept appointment as Fed. Dist. Judge for Dist. of Vt., 1950. Elected national chairman of Com. to Defend America by Aiding the Allies, Jan. 9, 1941, succeeding William Allen White. Entered Army as captain, May 19, 1941, served overseas with combat div., September 1942 to January 1944; col., G.S.C., duty War Dept.; disch. Dec. 25, 1945. Decorated Silver Star, Legion of Merit, Purple Heart, War Dept. Citation medals. Mem. Vt. Bar Assn., Phi Delta Phi, Theta Chi. Republican. Episcopalian. Mason, Odd Fellow, Elk. Home: Brattleboro VT Died Nov. 4, 1969.

GIBSON, GEORGE army officer; b. Lancaster, Pa., Oct. 1747; s. George and Elizabeth (deVinez) G.; m. Anne West, 1772; 1 son, John Banister. Organized, commanded company of frontiersmen for service in West, 1775; negotiated purchase of powder from Spanish at New Orleans for use of Va. and Continental troops, 1776; served as col., 1777-78; in charge of Am. prison camp, York, Pa., 1779; joined Maj. Gen. Arthur St. Clair's expdn. as lt. col. in command 2d Regt., 1791; fatally wounded in battle against Miami Indians on Wabash River. Died Fort Jefferson, O., Dec. 14, 1791.

GIBSON, HARVEY DOW banker; b. North Conway, N.H., Mar. 12, 1882; s. James L. and Addie (Dow) G.; A.B., Bowdoin Coll., 1902, LL.D., 1919; LL.D., U. N.H., 1933, Northeastern, 1945; m. Carrie Hastings Curtis, June 10, 1903; m. 2d, Helen Whitney Bourne, Mar. 12, 1926. Entered employ Am. Express Co., at Boston, 1902, and became asst. mgr. financial dept. at N.Y.C.; asso. with others and purchased control Raymond & Whitcomb Co., of which was v.p.; apptd. asst. to pres. Liberty Nat. Bank. 1912, v.p., 1913-17, pres., 1917-21, when Liberty Nat. Bank was merged with N.Y. Trust Co., elected pres. of latter co.; pres. Mfrs. Trust Co. of N.Y., 1931, chmn. bd., 1931-47; chmn. bd. Nat. Bondholders Corp., Textile Banking Co.; dir. Shuron Optical Co., Huron Holding Corp., Chesapeake Ohio Ry., N.Y., N.J. & H. R.R. (exec. com.), Am. Home Products Corp., U.S. Lines Co. (exec. com.), Internat. Mercantile Marine Co., Western Electric Co. (exec. com.), Brooklyn-Manhattan Transit Corp., Distillers Corp., Seagrams, Ltd., Paramount Pictures, Inc. (exec. com.), New England Pub. Service Co., Home Ins. Co. Exec. and Finan Hershey Creamery Co. Chmn. N.Y. County chpt. A.R.C., 1917; apptd. gen. mgr. A.R.C., 1917, also mem. War Council and War Finance Com., commr. for France, 1918, and for Europe, 1919; A.R.C. commr. to Great Britain, 1942-45, commr. to Gt. Britain and Western Europe, 1944-45; nat. chmn. 1946-47 Fund Campaign, gov., mem. exec. com., 1947. Mem. N.Y. World's Fair Finance Com., Inc., chmn. 1936-41, mem. exec. com., 1936-41; chmn. bd., 1939-41; incorporator, Nat. Orgn., 1919, dir. N.Y. chpt. A.R.C.; chmn. Emergency Unemployment Relief Com., N.Y.C., 1931-33; chmn. American Com. of Short-term Creditors of Germany. Served as lt. col. to col., U.S. Army, 1919. Decorated citation by Pres. Truman; Medal of Merit, 1945; Asso. Comdr. Order of St. John (Brit.); oFFICER OF Legion of Honor (France); Comdr. Order of the Crown (Belgium); Knight Order of Vasa (Sweden); Order of the Crown (Rumania); recipient Gold Medal award; Assn. of N.Y., 1934; Curtis Bowdoin prize, 1938; certificate by Pres. F. D. Roosevelt, for service overseas, 1942; ann. award by U. N.H. of Pette Medal, 1948. Trustee and chmn. finance com. of Bowdoin Col.; pres. bd. trustees Fryburg Academy; trustee Northeastern Univ., Florence Nightingale Internat. Foundation, Am. Foundation for Blind, Helen Keller Endowment Fund; treas. Jane A.

Delano Meml. Fund; treas., dir. Beckman-Downtown Hospital; trustee, mem. exec. com. Community Service Soc. N.Y.; dir. Am. Horse Shows Assn., Am. Arbitration Assn. Mem. Piping Rock Horse Show Assn. (pres.), English Speaking Union (dir.), Greater N.Y. Fund (dir.), Newcomen Soc. of Eng., Am. br., N.Y. State C. of C. (v.p., 1947), Bond of N.Y. (mem. adv. council). Buck's (London), National Golf Links of America, Recess Travellers (Paris), Union Interalliee, Maine Society, Theta Delta Chi. Republican. Presbyn. Clubs: Bankers of America, Links, Links Golf, Nat. Golf Links, Racquet and Tennis, Turf and Field, Recess Union League, University, Piping Rock, River, Wall Street, Meadown Book, Madison Sq. Garden (pres. and gov.), The Creek (pres.), N.Y. Yacht (gov.), Meadow Brook Hounds (past master of foxhounds). Home: 52 E. 69th St., New York; (country) Locust Valley, N.Y. Office: 55 Broad St., N.Y.C. Died Sept. 11, 1950; buried North Conway (N.H.) Cemetery.

GIBSON, HORATIO GATES brig. gen. U.S.A.; b. Baltimore, Md., May 22, 1827; s. Rev. John and Elizabeth (Jameson) G.; grad. U.S. Mil. Acad., 1847; m. Harriet L. Atkinson, Mar. 16, 1863. Bvtd. 2d lt., 2d Arty., July 1, 1847; served in war with Mexico, 1847-48, Vera Cruz, Puebla and City of Mexico; 2d lt., 3d Arty., Sept. 8, 1847, 1st lt., May 26, 1851; capt., May 14, 1861; lt. col., 2d Ohio Arty., Aug. 1, 1863; col., Aug. 15, 1863; hon. mustered out of vol. service, Aug. 23, 1865; maj. 3d Arty., Feb. 5, 1867; lt. col. 2d Arty., Apr. 19, 1882; col. 3d Arty., Dec. 1, 1883; retired, May 22, 1891; advanced to rank of brig. gen. retired, by act of Apr. 23,, 1904. Bvtd.; maj., May 5, 1862, "for gallant and meritorious services in battle of Williamsburg, Va."; lt. col., Sept. 17, 1862, for same at Antietam, Md.; col., Mar. 13, 1865, for same in the field during the war. Died Apr. 12, 1924.

GIBSON, JOHN army officer, territorial ofcl.; b. Lancaster, Pa., May 23, 1740; s. George and Elizabeth (de Viner) G.; m. Ann; possibly married an Indian wife, Took part in Forbes Expdn. which won Ft. Duquesne from the French, 1758; at Ft. Duquesne as Indian trader, 1758-62; captured by Indians during Pontiac's uprising, 1763; took part in Lord Dunmores' War, 1774; aided in negotiations resulting in Treaty of Pitts., 1775; Western agt. for Va., 1775; mem. Western Pa. Com. of Correspondence; active in securing peace with Indians; served as lt. col. Continental Army, 1776, col., 1777-81; judge ct. common pleas and maj. gen. of Militia, Allegheny County, Pa., 1781; mem. Pa. Constl. Conv., 1790; helped negotiate purchase for Pa. of Erie Triangle from Iroquois Confederacy, 1789; organizer Ind. Territorial Govt., 1800-16; sec. Ind. Territory, acting gov. during War of 1812; fluent speaker of various Indian dialects. Died Braddock's Field, Pa., Apr. 16, 1822.

GIBSON, RANDALL LEE senator; b. Woodford County, Ky., Sept. 10, 1832; s. Tobias and Louisiana (Hart) G.; grad. Yale, 1853, law dept. U. La. (now Tulane U.), 1855; m. Mary Montgomery, Jan. 25, 1868, 3 sons. Served as capt. 1st Regt., La. Arty., Confederate Army, 1861; col. 13th Regt., La. Inf., 1861, brig. gen., 1864; mem. U.S. Ho. of Reps. from La., 44-47th congresses, 1875-83, influential in securing adoption of J.B. Eads plan for constructing jetties at mouth of Mississippi River, 1878, urged creation of Mississippi River Commn., 1879; mem. U.S. Senate from La., 1883-Dec. 15, 1892; 1st pres. bd. adminstrs. Tulane U., 1884-92; mem. bd. adminstrs. Howard Meml. Library, New Orleans, bd. regents Smithsonian Instn.; trustee Peabody Edn. Fund. Died Hot Springs, Ark., Dec. 15, 1892; buried Lexington (Ky.) Cemetery.

GIBSON, STANLEY physician; b. Jacksonville, Il., Apr. 9, 1883; s. George C. and Lavina (Carlisle) G.; A.B., De Pauw U., Greencastle, Ind., 1907; A.M., Northwestern U., 1912, M.D., 1913; m. Virginia Woltersdorf, Sept. 30, 1922. Practiced in Chgo., 1913—; prof. emeritus of pediatrics Northwestern U. Med. Sch.; cons. pediatrician St. Luke's Hosp., cons. in cardiology Children's Meml. Hosp. Capt. M.C., U.S. Army in World War, serving 18 mos. overseas at Base Hosp., No. 12, Camiers, France. Mem. Phi Beta Kappa, Alpha Omega Alpha, Sigma Psi. Delta Upsilon, Nu Sigma Nu. Club: University. Contbr. to med. journals. Home: 1710 Wesley Av., Evanston, Ill. 707 W. Fullerton, Chgo. Died Oct. 1956.

GIBSON, WILLIAM CAMPBELL rear admiral; b. Albany, N.Y., July 23, 1838; s. Joseph and Marion (Campbell) G.; ed. Albany, N.Y., 1838-47, Sand Lake Acad., N.Y., 1847-52; m. Aurelia A. Holbrook, Aug. 5, 1875. Clerk in hardware business, Albany, N.Y., 1853-54; went to sea in merchant service, 1855; enlisted in U.S.N., Aug. 1861; apptd. acting mate, Dec. 1862, acting ensign, Aug. 1863; promoted through grades to capt., Feb. 1900; rear admiral and retired, July 23, 1900. Served on Potomac flotilla and North and South Atlantic blockading squadrons during Civil War; subsequently served on the European, North Atlantic, Pacific and South Atlantic stations. During the Spanish-Am. war comd. Str. City of Peking, which carried part of 1st mil. expdn. to Manila, arriving there June 30, 1898; last duty, command battleship Texas, North Atlantic Station. Died 1911.

GIBSON, WILLIAM RICHIE army officer; b. Ontario, O., June 3, 1877; s. Andrew Rae and Margaret Lemon (Richie) G.; grad. Inf. and Cav. Sch., 1904; grad. Army War Coll., 1925; m. Louise G. Beatley, June 13, 1911. Cadet U.S. Mil. Acad., June 15, 1896; commd. 2d lt. inf., June 1, 1899; promoted through grades to brig. gen., regular army, and asst. to q.-m. gen., Mar. 1, 1934; retired, July 31, 1937. Served as capt. 51st Ia. Inf., Spanish-Am. War; lt. col. inf., N.A., Aug. 5, 1917; col., July 30, 1918; hon. disch. from N.A., Mar. 15, 1920. Home: Pasadena, Calif. Died Oct. 29, 1940.

GIBSON, WILLIAM WESLEY army officer; b. New Haven, Conn., June 20, 1856; s. Robert and Jemima (Carey) G.; Ph.B., Yale, 1879; grad. U.S. Mil. Acad., 1879, Arty. Sch., Ft. Monroe, Va.; m. Mary E. Manning, of Troy, N.Y., Oct. 25, 1913. 2d lt. 5th Inf., June 13, 1879; transferred to 3d Arty., July 11, 1879; 1st lt. Ordnance Dept., Jan. 10, 1887; capt., June 12, 1894; maj., Jan. 21, 1904; lt. col., Sept. 10, 1907; col., Sept. 2, 1912. Gen. Staff, 1903-07; mil. attaché in Sweden and Russia, 1905-08; rep. of War Dept. at coronation of King Haaken, of Norway, 1906; apptd. commandant Army Gun Factory, Watervliet Arsenal, N.Y., 1908; head administration div. Ordnance Dept., 1918. Clubs: University (N.Y. City); Metropolitan, Army and Navy, Chevy Chase (Washington); Union (Cleveland, O.); Troy (Troy, N.Y.); Albany (N.Y.) Country. Address: War Dept. Washington, D.C.

GIDDINGS, HOWARD ANDRUS ins. exec., author; b. Hartford, Conn., Oct. 2, 1868; s. Edwin Alden and Susan M. (Keep) G.; ed. high sch.; m. Florence Chase Starkweather, Apr. 7, 1892; children-Helen, Florence, Elizabeth. Bradford, Chase, Marion, Constance, Marston Todd. With Conn. Mut. Life Ins. Co., Hartford, 1887-1901; with Travelers Ins. Co. since 1901, now vice-pres. Maj. brig. staff Conn. Nat. Guard, 1893-1902; capt. Vol. Signal Corps, Spanish-Am. War; acting chief signal officer 7th A.C. Mem. Conn. State Council of Defense, World War; mem. Am. Liberty Loan Mission to Europe, 1918. Mem. Soc: Mayflower Descendants, The Pilgrims, Mil. Order Foreign Wars of U.S. (formerly vice comdr. gen.), Naval and Mil. Order Spanish War; fellow Royal Geog. Soc. (London). Republican. Clubs: Hartford; Explorers (New York). Author: Hand Book of Military Signaling, 1896; New Handbook of Military Signaling, 1917; Exploits of the Signal Corps in the War with Spain. Contbr. on outdoor and insurance subjects. Home: 182 Fern St. Office: 700 Main St., Hartford, Conn. Died Mar. 10, 1949.

GIDDINGS, NAPOLEON BONAPARTE congressman; b. nr. Boonsborough, Ky., Jan. 2, 1816; attended common schs., Mo.; studied law. Served as sgt. maj. of regt. in Tex. War of Independence; apptd. chief clk. auditor's office Republic of Texas, served as acting auditor until 1838; returned to Fayette, Mo., admitted to bar, 1841, began practice of law, Fayette; served as capt. Co. A, 2d Regt., Mo. Mounted Volunteers during Mexican War, 1846-47; editor Union Flag (1st paper published in Franklin County, Mo.), after Mexican War; mined gold in Cal.; then practiced law, Savannah, Mo., later in Nebraska City, Neb.; mem. U.S. Congress (Democrat) from Neb. Territory, 33d Congress, Jan. 5-Mar. 3, 1855; served as lt. col. 51st Regt., Mo. Volunteer Inf., during Civil War, 1865. Died Savannah, Mo., Aug. 3, 1897; buried City Cemetery.

GIDNEY, HERBERT ALFRED oil cons.; b. Boston, Nov. 16, 1881; s. William Henry and Susan Elizabeth (Chapman) G.; ed. high sch.; m. Corena L. Bazley, May 1, 1920; children - Mrs. Pauline V. Livingstone, Mrs. Elizabeth G. Elder, Mrs. Priscilla G. Kaiser, Herbert Alfred. Held various positions Tenney Service Cos., group of pub. utilities in New Eng., N.Y. and N.J., 1900-19; chief accounting officer Gulf Oil Corp., 1920, exec. v.p., dir. until 1951, ret., now cons. Served as maj. inf., lt. col. ordnance, 1917-18; col. Ordnance Res., served to retirement, 1947. Vice pres., dir. Am. Ordance Assn., Washington. Awarded Silver Plaque, Pitts. C. of C., 1941; Scott Gold Medal, Am. Ordnance Assn., 1946. Mem. Am. Petroleum Inst., Amateur Astron. Assn., Hist. Soc. Western Pa. Mason (32ff, Shriner, K.T.). Republican. Episcopalian. Clubs: Duquesne, Oakmont Country, Rolling Rock, Junta, Beach, Wianno, Hyannisport (pres., dir. Cape Cod), Home: Pa. Apt. C8, 4403 Center Av., Pitts. 13; (summer) P.O. Box 516, Hyannis Port, Cape Cod, Mass. Died Mar. 1963.

GIESE, OSCAR W. lawyer; b. Baltimore, Nov. 25, 1905; s. Frederick A. and Gertrude (Stolzenbach) G.; student Baltimore Poly. Inst., 1923; John Hopkins, 1925; U. of Fla., 1926; LL.B., George Washington U., 1930; m. Virginia Buell, Oct. 4, 1929: children-Ann Mather, Carr William, Robert Buell. Engr. Fla. Power and Light Co., 1926-27; law practice, Washington, D.C., 1930; private law practice Minneapolis, 1930-42; v.p. McGraw Electric Co., 1946-48; private law practice, Washington, D.C., since 1948. Served as major, chief patent officer, Q.M. Corps, U.S. Army, 1942-45. Mem. Am. Bar Assn., Am. Patent Law Assn. Nat. Assn. Mfrs. (com. on patents and research). Clubs: Minneapolis (Minn.); Army and Navy, National Press (Washington). Home: 3045 Foxhall Rd. N.W. Office: National Press Bldg., Washington. Died Dec. 12, 1956; buried Arlington Nat. Cemetery.

GIESECKE, FREDERICK ERNEST, engineer; b. Washington County, Tex., Jan. 28, 1869; s. Julius and Wilhelmine (Groos) G.; M.E., Tex. A. and M., Coll., 1890; student Cornell, 1893-94; S.B. Architecture, Mass. Inst. Tech., 1904; student Tech. Hochschule, Charlottenburg, 1906-07; Ph.D., Univ. of Ill., 1924, C.E., 1943; m. Hulda C. Gruene, Mar. 5, 1891; children—Bertram E., Alma (Mrs. McCloud B. Hodges,) Linda (Mrs. Preston M. Geren), Minnie (Mrs. Edward A. Wight). Instr. in shop work and drawing, Tex. A. and M. Coll., 1886-88, prof. of drawing 1888-1906, prof. of archtl. engring., 1906-12; prof. archtl. engring., head div. engr. research, Univ. of Tex., 1912-27; dir. expt. sta. and coll. architect, Tex. A and M. Coll., 1927-39, prof. emeritus, 1939-45; cons. engr., New Braunfels, Tex., since 1945. Served as maj. engr. reserves, U.S., 1926-42. Awarded the F. Paul Anderson medal by Am. Soc. Heating and Ventilating Engrs., 1942. Mem. Am. Soc. E.E. (charter and life mem.), Am. Soc. C.E. (life mem., past pres. Tex. sect.), Am. Soc. Heating and Ventilating Engrs. (life mem., past pres. Tex. chapter, nat. pres. 1940), Am. Soc. M.E., A.A.A.S., Am. Soc. Engring. Edn., (past pres. Tex. chapter), Tau Beta Pi, Sigma Xi. Mason (32 deg.). Author: Gravity-Circulation Hot-Water Heating Systems, 1926; Descriptive Geometry and Descriptive Geometry Problems (with A. Mitchell), 1921; Technical Drawing and Technical Drawing Problems (with A. Mitchell and H. C. Spencer), 1933; Hot-Water Heating, Radiant Heating, and Radiant Cooling, 1947. Contbr. about 75 tech. articles in engring. pubs. and bulls. Home: New Braunfels TX*

GIESY, JOHN ULRICH physician, author: b. Chillicothe, O., Aug. 6, 1877; s. William Sommers and Anna Kate Hutton (Heckerman) G.; M.D., Starling Med. Coll., Columbus, O., 1898; m. Juliet Galena Conwell, Dec. 8, 1904. Practiced at Salt Lake City, Utah, since 1898; asst. city physician, 1899. Capt. Med. Corps, U.S. Army, May 28-Dec. 23, 1918, retired lt. col. Med. R.C. Prime mover in securing officers' training camp at Ft. Douglas, Utah, 1916; gen. sec. Citizens' Mil. Training Camp Assn., Salt Lake City, 1916. Mem. Pub. Safety Com., Salt Lake City, 1917. Section leader, medical section, American Legion Alerte (Auxilliary police unit) Salt Lake Post No. 2, 1943. Examiner U.S. Recruiting and Induction Station on civilian status, Salt Lake City, 1942-43. Fellow American Medical Association; mem. Am. Congress Physiotherapy, Utah State and Salt Lake Co. med. socs., Authors League of America, Am. Legion, Am. Forestry Assn., Reserve Officcrs Assn. U.S. (past pres. Salt Lake chapter), Utah State R.O.A. (v.p.), S.A.R.; life mem. U.S. Inf. Assn. Republican. Protestant. Author: All For His Country, 1914; The Other Woman (with O.R. Cohen), 1917; Mimi, 1918. Contbr. fiction and detective stories to mags. also science articles to med. jours., Home: 207 Maryland Apts. Office: Medical Arts Bldg., Salt Lake City, Utah. Died Sept. 8, 1947.

GIGNILLIAT, LEIGH ROBINSON, educator; b. Savannah, Ga., July 4, 1875; s. William Robert and Harriet (Heyward) G.; grad. Emerson Inst., Washington, 1891, Va. Mil. Inst., Lexington, Va., 1895; M.A., Trinity Coll., 1915; Sc.D. from Colgate U., 1931; LL.D., Kenyon Coll., Gambier, O., 1935; m. Mary Seddon Fleet, Aug. 2, 1898;children—Leigh Robinson, Frederick Fleet, Henry Culver. Asst. engr. boundary line location Yellowstone Nat. Park, 1896. Comdt. Cadets, Culver Mil. Acad., 1897-1910, supt. 1910-39; pres. The Culver Ednl. Foundation 1939-42, now pres. emeritus. Coordinator, Fort Worth, Tex., area for engring. science and management War Training, 1942-45. Apptd. consultant to Secretary of War, 1941. Commd. major R.C., 1916; lt. col. 1st O.T.C., Ft. Benjamin Harrison, Aug. 1917; sr. instr. 2nd O.T.C.; apptd. Gen. Staff, A.E.F., Sept. 1918; commd. col. Feb. 1919, brig.-gen. organized reserves, Nov. 24, 1911; comdg. 168th Inf. Brigade, Reserves, 1921-39. Am. rep. Interallied Mil. Commn., Hq. Army Occupation, Coblenz, Germany, Mar.-July 1919. Pres. Private Sch. Assn. of Central States, 1913-14. Mem. Nat. Council Boy Scouts America; in comd. 300 Am. reps. at Internat. Council Boy Scouts Jamboree, London, 1920. Comdr. Dept. Ind. Am. Legion, 1920-21; mem. Am. delegation Interallied Vets'. Congress, New Orleans, 1922, Brussels, 1923, London, 1924; chmn. Am. delegation to Congress Interallied Veterans, Rome, Italy, 1925, Warsaw, 1926, Paris, 1927, Bucharest, 1929, Washington, D.C., 1930. Mem. Soc. Colonial Wars, Huguenot Society, S.C., Mil. Order World War, Mil. Order Foreign Wars, Association Military Colleges and Schools (president 1927-28), St. Fidac (vice-pres. 1927-28). Awarded D.S.M. (U.S.); Comdr. Legion of Honor (French); Knight Comdr. Order of Nicham Iftikar (Tunis); Comdr. Order of the Star (Rumania); Comdr. Order of Polonia Restituta (Poland), Order of the Crown (Italy). Clubs: Army and Navy (Washington, D.C.); Fort Worth (Fort Worth, Tex.). Author: Arms and the Boy. Home: Blackstone Hotel, Fort Worth TX*

GILBERT, EDWARD congressman, journalist; b. Cherry Valley, N.Y., circa 1819; attended public schs. Became compositor Albany Argus, 1839, later asso. editor; served as 1st lt. Co. H., Col. J.D. Stevenson's N.Y. Volunteer Regt. during Mexican War; in command of detachment, also dep. collector Port of San Francisco, 1847-48; founder, editor Alta California, 1849; mem. Cal. Constl. Conv., 1849; mem. U.S. Ho.

of Reps. (Democrat) from Cal., 31st Congress, Sept. 11, 1850-51. Killed in duel with Gen. James W. Denver, nr. Sacramento, Cal., Aug. 2, 1852; buried Lone Mountain (now Laurel Hill) Cemetery, San Francisco.

GILBERT, NEWELL CLARK physician; b. Clinton, Ill., Dec. 5, 1880; s. Newell Darrow and Elizabeth (Clark) G.; B.S., U. of Wis., 1903; student U. of Mich., 1904; M.D., and M.S., Northwestern U., 1907; m. Charlotte Louise Pettibone, Sept. 22, 1914; children-Robert Pettibone Mary Elizabeth. Interne St. Luke's Hosp., 1907-09, attending physician since 1916; prof. emeritus, past chmn. dept. of internal medicine, Northwestern U. Med. School. During World War served as capt., and later maj., Med. Corps, later lt. col. Med. O.R.C. Fellow A.A.A.S.: mem. Central Soc. for Clin. Research, Illinois State and Chicago med. socs., Chicago Soc. of Internal Medicine, Inst. of Medicine of Chicago, Am. Soc. for Clin. Investigation, Assn. of Am. Physicians, Am. Med. Assn., past chmn. sect. pharmacol. and exptl. therapeutics: past chmn. sect. on med.), S.R., Sigma Alpha Epsilon, Phi Rho Sigma, Sigma Xi, Pi Kappa Epsilon. Republican. Baptist. Club: University. Contbr. to various med. jours. editor. Home: 5740 S. Kenwood. Office: 104 S. Michigan Av., Chgo. Died Aug. 1953.

GILBERT, NEWTON WHITING lawyer; b. Worthington, O., May 24, 1862; s. Theodore R. and Ellen L. G.; ed. Ohio State U. (non-grad.); admitted to bar, 1885; LL.D., Iowa Wesleyan and U. of Philippines, 1913; m. Martha Edna Berge, Aug. 8, 1906; 1 dau., Viola. Practiced at Angola, Ind.; mem. Ind. Senate, 1896-1900; lt. gov. of Ind., 1900-04; mem. 59th Congress (1905-07), 12th Ind. Dist.; capt. Co. H, 157th Ind. Vol. Inf., May-Nov. 1898; judge Court of 1st Instance, Manila, P.I., 1906-08; mem. Philippine Commn., 1908-09; apptd. sec. pub. instrn. of P.I., 1909, and v. gov., 1909-13 (acting gov. gen. 1912-13); del. Rep. Nat. Conv., 1916. In New York, 1916—. Pres. bd. regents Philippine U., 1908-13. Fellow Royal Geog. Soc., London. Mason. Episcopalian. Home: Santa Ana, Calif. Died July 5, 1939.

GILBERT, PRENTISS BALLEY b. Rochester, N.Y., Oct. 3, 1883; s. Lt. Col. William Wallace (U.S.A.) and Mary Elizabeth (Chapman) G.; Ph.B., Univ. of Rochester, 1906, A.M., 1916; A.B., Yale Univ., 1907; studied Columbia, and El Colejio de San Carlos, Cebu, P.I.; grad. U.S. Army War Coll., 1924; m. Charlotte Jeannette Gilder, Nov. 9, 1918. Mine supt., 1907-10; travel and study in Europe, Orient, Australia, Oceania, and Central America, 1911-16; organizer, and first dir. Sch. of Extension Teaching, U. of Rochester, 1916. Spl. aide U.S.A., in Philippines, Spanish-Am. War; 1st lt., capt. and maj., Gen. Staff U.S.A., World War; was chief of Combat Sect., Div. of Mil. Intelligence; chief Div. of Polit. and Econ. Intelligence, 1919-24; chief Div. of Western European Affairs, Dept. of State, Washington, 1924-29; 1st sec. Am. Embassy, Paris, 1930; U.S. consul, Geneva, 1930-37; counselor Am. Embassy, Berlin, 1937—. First rep. of U.S. at Congress of Internat. Chamber of Commerce, Stockholm, 1927, Amsterdam, 1929; rep. of U.S. Govt. on Com. for Tech. Assistance to China. Commd. lt. col. O.R.C., U.S.A., July 31, 1923. Author: A Maid of Honor (play), adapted (from the German): Der Gute König, by Raoul Aurenheimer, play, presented by Philadelphia Civic Theatre, 1930. Home: Berlin, Germany. Died Feb. 24, 1939.

GILBERT, RUFUS HENRY physician, inventor; b. Guilford, N.Y., Jan. 26, 1832; s. William Dwight Gilbert; attended Coll. Phys. and Surg., N.Y.C.; m. Miss Maynard; m. 2d, Miss Price; 2 children. Began practice medicine, Corning, N.Y., circa 1853; went to Europe, circa 1857, became convinced that public health problems could best be solved by building rapid transp. facilities to permit urban residents to live outside cities in cleaner atmosphere; surgeon to Duryée Zouaves, 1861, later served as med. dir. XIV Corps, U.S. Army; to implement his ideas on rapid transp., became asst. supt. Central R.R. of N.J.; obtained patents for pneumatic tube system, 1870; instrumental in incorporation of Gilbert Elevated R.R. Co., 1872 (opened for travel, 1878), forced out of mgmt. of Co., circa 1878. Died N.Y.C., July 10, 1885.

GILBRETH, FRANK BUNKER cons. engineer; b. Fairfield, Me., July 17, 1868; s. John Hiram and Martha (Bunker) G.; grad. English High Sch., Boston, 1885; LL.D., U. of Me., 1920; (B.L., M.D., U. of Calif.; Ph.D., Brown U.); m. Lillian Evelyn Moller, Oct. 19, 1904. Contracting engr., Boston, 1895-1904, New York, 1904-11; consulting engr., 1911—; pres. Frank B. Gilberth (Inc.). Commd. maj., Engrs., July 1917; on active duty Gen. Staff Coll., Washington, Dec. 1917. Lecturer at 20 Am. and European univs.; dir. Summer Sch. of Management for Professors of Engineering. Psychology and Economics; organized Soc. Promotion Science of Management (afterwards Taylor Soc., the first of its kind); founder internat. museums for elimination of unnecessary fatigue of workers in the industries; inventor of the micro-motion and chronocyclegraph processes for determining fundamental units and methods of industrial edn., and of methods for fitting crippled soldiers for industrial life. Author: Field System, 1908; Concrete System, 1908; Bricklaying System, 1909; Motion Study, 1911; Primer of Scientific Management, 1911; also with wife, Time Study; Fatigue Study, 1916; Applied Motion Study, 1917; Motion Study for the Handicapped, 1919. Home: Montclair, N.J. Died June 14, 1924.

GILCHRIST, ALBERT WALLER governor; b. (during temporary absence of mother from Florida) at Greenwood, S.C., Jan. 15, 1858; s. Gen. William E. (planter, slave owner, state senator) and Rhoda Elizabeth (Waller) G.; desc. of Col. Joseph Ball, g.f. George Washington and Col. Edwin Conway, g.f. James Madison; grad. Carolina Mil. Inst., Charlotte, N.D.; cadet U.S. Mil. Acad. 3 yrs., class of *82. Civ. engr., real estate dealer, orange grower. Mem. Fla. Ho. of Rep., 1893, 95, 1903, 05 (speaker 1905); gov. of Fla., 1909-13. Democrat. Resigned as brig. gen., Fla. Militia, June 1898, and enlisted as pvt. Co. C, 3d U.S. Vol. Inf.; served in Santiago, Cuba; mustered out with rank of capt., 1899. Mason. Mem. bd. visitors U.S. Mil. Acad., 1896. Home: Punta Gorda, Fla. Died May 16, 1926.

GILCHRIST, DONALD BEAN librarian; b. Franklin, N.H., Jan. 11, 1892; s. Harry W. and Martha (Bean) G.; A.B., Dartmouth, 1913; B.L.S., N.Y. State Library Sch., 1915; m. Ella Trowbridge, June 26, 1918; 1 son, David Trowbridge. Dept. head, U. of Minn. Library, 1915-16; librarian U. of Rochester, 1919—. Served on Mexican border, 1916-17; capt. 339th F.A., U.S.A., Aug. 1917-Dec. 1918; librarian Am. Commn. to Negotiate Peace, Paris, France, 1918-19. Sec. Assn. Research Libraries. Protestant. Editor: Doctoral Dissertations Accepted by American Universities, 1933-35. Home: Rochester, N.Y. Died Aug. 4, 1939.

GILCHRIST, HARRY LORENZO army officer; b. Waterloo, Ia., Jan. 16, 1870; s. Lorenzo D. and MargaretJane (Ohl) G.; M.D., Western Res. U., 1896; honor grad. and medalist, Army Med. Sch., 1903; m. Mayme L. Morgan, June 30, 1909. Contract surgeon, U.S. Army, 1898-1900; asst. surgeon, U.S. Army, 1900-05, capt., Med. Corps, Oct. 3, 1905, maj., Jan. 1, 1909, lt. col., May 15, 1917, col., Oct. 1, 1926, maj. gen., Mar. 28, 1929. Health officer, Manila, P.I., 1900-01; experimented with X-ray in treatment of Leprosy, 1903-04; commanded 1st U.S. expdn. to Europe in World War, Lakeside Hospital Unit No. 4; comdr. British General Hosp. No. 9, Rowen, France, May-Dec. 1917; med. director Chemical Warfare Service, A.E.F., Dec. 1917-Dec. 1918; comdr. American Typhus Expdn. to Poland, 1919; chief of med. research div., Washington, D.C., and Edgewood Arsenal, Chem. Warfare Service, 1921-29; chief of Chem. Warfare Service, March 28, 1929-May 16, 1933; retired Jan. 16, 1934; editor of The Military Surgeon, 1934-Sept. 1940. Awarded D.S.M., Purple Heart (U.S.); General Service Medal (Gt. Britain); Officer Legion of Honor, Medaille d'Honneur Epidemics (France); Cross of the Valiant, Comdr. Order of Polonia Restituta (Poland); Order of Star of Abdon Calderén (Ecuador); Spanish-Am. War decoration (Cuba); campaign medals for Spanish War, Philippines, Cuba, Mexican Border, World War; cited in spl. orders by Sir Douglas Haig; cited by Gen. Pershing for "especially meritorious service with Chem. Warfare Service." Fellow Am. Coll. Surgeons; mem. Assn. Mil. Surgns. (pres. 1933-34; sec. since 1934); hon. prof. Polish Army Med. Sch.; hon. mem. Mexican Assn. Mil. Surgeons, Clubs: Army and Navy (Washington); Army, Navy and Marine Corps (Arlington, Va.). Home: 2219 California St., Washington, D.C. Died Dec. 26, 1943

GILCHRIST, JACK CECIL, educator; b. Birmingham, Ala., June 7, 1918; s. James Cecil and Ellen (Norton) G.; B.S., U. Cal. at Los Angeles, 1945, Ph.D., 1950; m. Breta Nissen, Nov. 8, 1941; children—James Carl, McKay, John Henry. Asst. prof. psychology U. Ark., 1948-50; faculty U. Wis., 1950-68, prof. psychology, 1959-68, chmn. dept., 1959-62. Served to capt. AUS, 1940-45. Fellow Am. Psychol. Assn.; mem. Psychonomic Soc., Sigma Xi. Home: Madison WI Died Aug. 12, 1968.

GILCHRIST, JOHN RAYMOND, former air force officer, financial mgmt. exec.; b. Woonsocket, R.I., May 18, 1906; s. John S. and Alice (Talbot) G.; B.S., U.S. Mil. Acad., 1928; grad. Indsl. Coll. Armed Forces, 1948; m. Mabel Moran, Nov. 7, 1930; children—Carole Jean (Mrs. Kimbrough S. Bassett), John Raymond, Robert Michael. Commd. 2d lt. U.S. Army, 1928, advanced through grades to maj. gen., 1952; chief operations Office Chief Finance, 1941-42; chief fgn. fiscal affairs War Dept., 1942-43; chief finance div. German country unit Hdqrs. SHAEF, 1944; dep. dir. econs. div. U.S. Group Control Coun. for Germany, 1944-45; alternate U.S. mem. econ. div. Allied Control Council for Germany, 1945; rep. Sec. War, Reparations Mission to Japan, 1945; chief econs. and supply br. Civil Affairs Div., War Dept. Spl. staff, 1945-47; chief projects Logistics Div., Army Gen. Staff, 1948; dep. dir. finance USAF, 1948-52; comdg. gen. AF Finance Center, 1950-52; dir. finance USAF, 1952-56, asst. comptroller USAF, comdg. gen. Air Force Finance Center, Denver, 1957, ret.; adminstrv. v.p. for orgn. planning and devel. Tidewater Oil Co., 1957-58; adminstrv. v.p., dir. Financial Indsl. Fund Mgmt. Corp., Denver, FIF Assos., Inc.; exec. v.p., dir. Financial Programs, Inc.; dir. Financial Assurance, Inc., Financial Trust Co.; v.p. Financial Indsl. Fund, Financial Indsl. Income Fund, Financial Dynamics Fund, Financial Venture Fund. Decorated D.S.M., Legion of Merit. Clubs: Army and Navy Country (Washington); Denver; Columbine Country (Littleton, Colo.). Home: Littleton CO Deceased.

GILDER, RODMAN publisher; b. N.Y.C., Jan. 8, 1877; s. Richard Watson and Helena (de Kay) G.; A.B., Harvard, 1899; m. Comfort Tiffany, Apr. 20, 1911; children-Rodman, Mrs. A. E. Treat, Mrs. A. A. Miller. Identified with monthly, daily and weekly journalism in New York. Capt., later maj., U.S. Army Air Service, 1917-19. Trustee the Art Guild. Clubs: Century Association, Harvard (N.Y.C.); Cold Spring Harbor Beach. Author: Joan, the Maiden, 1933; The Battery, New York-a History, 1935. Address: 108 E. 82d St., N.Y.C. 28. Died Sept. 30, 1953.

GILDER, WILLIAM HENRY journalist, explorer; b. Phila., Aug. 16, 1836; s. Rev. William Henry and Jane (Nutt) G. Served as pvt. 5th N.Y. Inf., 1861; commd. 2d lt. Co. H, 40th N.Y. Inf., 1862, promoted lt., capt., asst. adj. gen.; transferred to Co. D, 40th N.Y. Inf., 1863; wounded at Battle of Gettysburg, discharged; re-enlisted, 1864, wounded at Hatcher's Run, 1864; correspondent for N.Y. Herald; accompanied Lt. Frederick Schwatka on expdn. to discover bodies and records of Sir John Franklin's expdn. in No. Can., 1878-80; explored (with Lt. Robert M. Berry) for missing ship Jeannette in Bering Strait, 1881-82; correspondent in China when French took Cochin; editor Sunday Standard, Newark, N.J., Sunday Times, Trenton, N.J.; mem. staff N.Y. Journal, N.Y.C.; Author: Schwatka's Search, 1881; Ice Pack and Tundra, 1883. Died Feb. 5, 1900.

GILDERSLEEVE, HENRY ALGER lawyer; b. Dutchess Co., N.Y., Aug. 1, 1840; s. Smith James and Rachel (Alger) G.; ed. College Hill, Poughkeepsie, N.Y., and Columbia U. Law Sch.; m. Virginia Crocheron, Apr. 14, 1868. Admitted to bar, 1866; served capt. and maj. during Civil War and was bvtd. lt. col. for gallant and meritorious services in Georgia and Carolina campaigns. Judge Ct. of General Sessions, 1876-89; judge Superior Ct., 1891-94; justice Supreme Ct. of N.Y., 1894-1909, resigned. Democrat. Mem. N.G.N.Y.; capt. of co. of Am. riflemen sent to Ireland, 1875. Home: New York, N.Y. Died Feb. 27, 1923.

GILKYSON, (THOMAS) WALTER, writer; b. Phoenixville, Pa., Dec. 18, 1880; s. Hamilton Henry and Eleanor (Trego) G.; A.B., Swarthmore (Pa.) Coll., 1901, A.M., 1904; LL.B., U. of Pa., 1908; m. Bernice Kenyon, June 11, 1927. In civ. service, Philippine Islands, 1901-03; admitted to Pa. bar, 1908, and practiced at Philadelphia until 1924; mem. Johnson & Gilkyson, 1912-19, Johnson, Gilkyson & Freeman, 1919-24. Served as 1st lt., Ordnance Dept., U.S. Army, Dec. 1917-May 1918, capt., May 1918-Feb. 1919, maj. Feb.-May 1919. Arbitrator, wages and working conditions of employees, Lehigh Valley Transit Co., Pa., 1941, 1944, 1946. Trenton (N.J.) Transit Co., 1941; mem. Nat. Railway Labor Panel, Nat. Mediation Bd., Washington, D.C., from Dec. 1944. Am. sec. Internat. Mil. Tribunal, Nuremberg, Germany, 1946. Mem. Delta Upsilon, Order of the Coif, Book and Key ((Swarthmore). Club: Coffee House (New York). Author: Oil, 1924; The Lost Adventurer, 1927; Lights of Fame, 1930; Tomorrow Never Comes, 1933; Toward What Bright Land, 1947. Contbr. to mags. and Best Short Stories of America (O'Brien Collections), 1925, 1930, 1936. Home: New Hartford CT Died Nov. 7, 1969; cremated.

GILL, CHARLES CLIFFORD author, naval officer; b. Junction City, Kan., Aug. 24, 1885; s. Clifford Belcher (lt. U.S. Navy) and Sarah Stoddard (Frothingham) G.; grad. St. John's Mil. Acad., Manlius, N.Y.; grad. U.S. Naval Acad., 1906; grad. Naval War Coll., 1920; m. Helen, d. Rear Admiral W. L. Howard, U.S. Navy, Apr. 25, 1911; children - Anne Alden, Charles Howard; m. 2d, Golda Chase Munroe; m. 3d, Marie Meuffels. Passed as midshipman, 1903; was promoted through the grades to captain, September 1, 1932; commander U.S.S. Vestal, 1932; was senior member United States Naval Mission to Brazil; commanded U.S.S. Astoria, 1937-38; was professor of naval science and tactics, and commanding officer Naval Training Unit, Yale Univ. Author: Naval Power in the War 1918; The War on the Sea (vol. IV Harper's Pictorial Library of the World War), 1920 - . Edited Part I - Naval Strategy and Major Naval Operations; What Happened at Jutland, 1921. Lectures delivered at Army and Navy War Colleges in Brazil and pub. in Portuguese, 1927, Escape of the Goeben and Breslau, Army and Navy Cooperation in the Civil War, Strategic and Tactical Analysis North Sea Battles, 1936. Died Jan. 9, 1948.

GILL, HENRY Z. physician; b. on farm, Rochboro, Pa., Oct. 6, 1831; s. Henry and Mary (Fretz) G.; ed. in public schools and private acad. (A.M., McKendree Coll., 1875; LL.D., U. of Wooster, 1885); taught school, 1853-54; read medicine under physicians and at Starling Med. Coll., Phila., 1857; m. Mattie W., d. Timothy R. Carpenter, Columbus, O., April 21, 1869. Practiced at Columbus, O., until 1861; asst. surgeon 11th regt., 1861, and later surgeon 95th regt., Ohio vols.; surgeon U.S. vols. from June, 1864-65 (surgeon-in-chief 1st div., 20th army corps, during Atlanta, Savannah and Carolina campaigns); 2 yrs. in European hosps.; later 3 yrs. asst. St. Louis Eye and Ear Infirmary; lecturer on pathology,

St. Louis Med. Coll.; asso. editor and prop. St. Louis Med. and Surg. Jour.; pres. St. Louis Micros. Soc.; physician Southern Ill. penitentiary, 1881-83; prof. operative and clinical surgery, med. dept. Wooster Univ., 1883-86; resigned and removed to Kan.; some time prof. histology, microscopy and bacteriology, Kan. Med. Coll., Topeka; sec. State bd. of health, Kan., 1897-99. Author: Gill's Sanné on Diptheria, Croup and Tracheotomy. Home: Long Beach, Calif. Died 1907.

GILL, THOMAS AUGUSTUS rear admiral, U.S.N.; b. Philadelphia, Pa., Feb. 8, 1840; s. John S. and Sarah B. G.; A.B., Bucknell U., 1865, A.M., 1868, B.D., Theol. Sem., 1867, D.D., 1893; m. Miss M.A. Nevin, Apr. 8, 1875 (died 1878); m. 2d, Miss R. H. Souder, June 19, 1883. During coll. course served 2 enlistments in vol. army during Civil War; pastor Phila., 1868-71; apptd. chaplain U.S.N., from Pa. by President Grant, and commd. Dec. 22, 1874; served on various vessels, and at various stas. during period of active service; retired pursuant to personnel act of Mar. 3, 1890 with rank of rear admiral, Feb. 8, 1902. Home: Brookline, Mass. Died Aug. 2, 1926.

GILL, WILLIAM ANDREW naval officer; b. Tamaqua, Pa., June 8, 1859; grad. U.S. Naval Acad., 1879. Ensign jr. grade, Mar. 3, 1883; ensign, June 26, 1884; lt. jr. grade, June 25, 1891; lt., Oct. 10, 1895; lt. comdr., Oct. 9, 1901; comdr., Aug. 5, 1906; capt., July 1, 1910. Served on Miantonomoh, Spanish-Am. War, 1898; exec. officer Celtic, 1902-03; insp. duty, Bur. of Equipment, 1903-05; exec. officer Cleveland, 1905, Maryland, 1905-06; insp. ordnance, Midvale Steel Co., 1906-08; comd. Solace, 1908; duty Navy Yard, Mare Island, 1908-09, Navy Yard, New York, 1909; comd. receiving ship Texas, 1909-10; comd. Colorado, 1910-12; supervisor Naval Auxiliaries, 1913-14; mem. Naval Examining Bd., Washington, 1914-15; comd. Delaware, 1915-16; apptd. pres. Bd. of Inspection and Survey, Navy Dept., May 30, 1916. Home: Washington, D.C. Died Oct. 10, 1918.

GILLANDERS, JOHN GORDON judge; born Highgate, Ontario, Aug. 26, 1895; s. Angus and Helen (Learmonth) G.; ed. Ridgetown Coll. Inst., Faculty of Education, Toronto, Ontario, 1913, Osgoode Hall, 1921; m. Kathleen M. White, London, Ontario, Sept. 17, 1927; children-Ellen Jean, John Ross. Called to the bar of Ontario, 1921; created King's Counsel, 1934; practised as partner, Ivey, Elliott & Gillanders, London, 1922-34, Ivey & Gillanders from 1934-38; justice in appeal, Supreme Court of Ontario since 1938. Served in World War I, capt., R.A.F. Awarded D.F.C. Chmn., Ontario Cancer Commn., 1938. Club: London Hunt and Country (London, Eng.). Home: 24 Chestnut Park. Office: Osgoode Hall. Toronto, Ontario, Canada. Died May 15, 1946.

GILLEM, ALVAN CULLEM army officer; b. Jackson County, Tenn., July 20, 1830; s. Samuel J. Gillem; grad. U.S. Mil. Acad., 1851; m. Margaret Jones. Served in Seminole War, also on garrison duty and duty on Tex. frontier; commd. capt. U.S. Army, 1861; col. 10th Tenn. Volunteers, chief q.m. Army of Ohio during Tenn. campaign; provost marshal Nashville (Tenn.); adj. gen. Tenn. (apptd. by Gen. Andrew Johnson), 1863-65; commanded troops guarding Nashville & Northwestern R.R., 1863-64; commd. brig. gen. U.S. Volunteers, 1863, brevetted lt. col., col., brig. gen., promoted maj. gen. for gallantry at capture of Salisbury, 1865; prominent in reorgn. of Tenn. civil govt., v.p. of reorgn. conv., Jan. 1865; mem. Tenn. Legislature, 1865; commanded Dist. of East Tenn., 1865-66; commd. col. U.S. Army, 1866; commanded 4th Mil. Dist. (Miss. and Ark.), 1868-69; transferred to Tex., took part in Modoc campaign, 1873. Died Nashville, Dec. 2, 1875.

GILLEM, ALVAN CULLOM, JR., army officer; b. Nashville, Tenn., Aug. 8, 1888; s. Alvan Cullom and Lillian Courts (Cummins) G.; student U. of Ariz., 1908, U. of the South, 1908-09, Army Staff Sch., 1922-23, Army War Coll., 1925-26; m. Virginia Lucille Harrison, June 14, 1916; children—Alvan Cullom, II, Mary Virginia, Richard Douglas. Enlisted, Regular Army, Jan. 19, 1910; commd. 2d lt. U.S. Army, Feb. 11, 1911, advanced through grades to maj. gen., Inf., July 12, 1941, and assigned to command III Armored Div.; activated and took command II Armored Corps, Jan. 17, 1942; commanded Desert Training Center, Aug.-Oct. 1942, directing first U.S. Army maneuvers held solely for armored and mechanized troops; appointed comdg. gen., Armored Force, May 14, 1943, and comdg. gen., Armored Command, July 2, 1943, promoted lt. gen., 1945; comdr. XIII Corps, European Theater of Operations; Am. commr. exec. hdqrs., Peiping, China, Oct. 1946-Apr. 1947; comdg. gen. 3d Army, June 15, 1947-50. Mem. Sigma Alpha Epsilon, Omicron Delta Kappa. Episcopalian. Writer of Army notes for instructional purposes in service schs. Home: Atlanta GA Died Feb. 13, 1973.

GILLESPIE, ALEXANDER GARFIELD army officer; b. Gaines, Mich., Aug. 19, 1881; s. Alexander and Sarah (Gillespie) G.; B.S., U.S. Mil. Acad., 1906; diploma Coast Arty. Sch., 1911, Command and Gen. Staff Sch., 1924, Army War Coll., 1929; m. Mildred Hathaway Green, July 23, 1908; children-Marguerite Alice (wife of Colonel William G. Bartlett), Alexander Garfield (dec.). Served with various units of the Army in U.S., Philippines and France, 1906-19; asst. mil. attaché, Tokyo, Japan, 1920-22; corps area ordnance officer, Chicago, 1924-28; prof. of ordnance and science of gunnery, U.S. Mil. Acad., 1929-33; in command of Rock Island (Ill.) Arsenal, 1934-37; in Washington, 1937-40; in command of Watervilet (N.Y.) Arsenal, 1940-45; chief of indsl. service, Ordnance Dept., Washington, D.C., 1945-46; retired since 1947. Awarded Purple Heart, Distinguished Service Medal, Legion of Merit. Member Army Ordnance Assn. Methodist. Mason. Club: Army and Navy (Washington). Address: 3415 34th Pl. N.W., Washington 16. Died Jan. 7, 1956.

GILLESPIE, GEORGE LEWIS maj. gen.; b. Kingston, Tenn., Oct. 7, 1841; grad. U.S. Mil. Acad., 1862. Second lt. engrs., June 17, 1862; promoted through grades to maj. gen. U.S.A., Jan. 23, 1904. Breveted; maj., Aug. 1, 1864, for gallant and meritorious services during campaign before Richmond; lt. col., Apr. 9, 1865, for same in campaign from Winchester to Appomattox C.H., Va.; awarded Congressional Medal of Honor, Oct. 27, 1897, for most distinguished gallantry in action near Bethesda Ch., Va., May 31, 1864. Engr. officer on staff gen. comdg. Army of Potomac, 1862-64, participating in all the battles of that army; then chief engr. Army of Shenandoah, Gen. Sheridan commanding; present at Lee's surrender at Appomattox; was with Sheridan in New Orleans, 1865, and as chief engr. took part in reconstruction of Gulf States and the restoration of the Republic of Mexico; pres. Miss. River Commn., 1885; later mem. bd. of engrs., U.S.A., New York; mem. Lighthouse Bd., Washington; div. engr., N.E. div., Atlantic Coast from British boundary to Barnegat, N.J.; during war with Spain, 1898, assigned to command of Dept. of East for the defense of the Atlantic Coast; mem. bd. of officers to visit Puerto Rico, 1900, to set apart from the late crown lands those needed for mil. and naval purposes of U.S.; mem. bd. of ordnance and fortification of Army War Coll. Bd. and mem. joint Army and Navy Bds.; retired, June 17, 1905. Home: Washington, D.C. Died Sept. 27, 1913.

GILLESPIE, JULIAN EDGEWORTH commercial attaché; b. Brownwood, Tex., June 20, 1893; s. James and Ethel (Muse) G.; prep. edn., high sch., Dallas, Tex.; A.B., U. of Tex., 1914; student law dept. U. of Chicago; LL.B., Georgetown (D.C.) U., 1915; m. Adrian Inez Posey, Mar. 20, 1924; children—Mary Howard, Ann Muse, Julian E. Admitted to Tex. bar, 1915, and practiced at Dallas; 1st lt. and capt. with A.E.F., 1917-20; asst. trade commr. U.S. Dept. Commerce, to near East and Balkans, 1920-22 (hdqrs. Constantinople), trade commr., 1922-26; commercial attaché to Turkey, Dec. 1, 1926—. Served as economic and financial adviser to Am. observers. Allied and Turkish Peace Conf., Lausanne, Switzerland, 1922-23; to Am. delegation, Internat. Economic Conf., Geneva, May-June, 1927; del. to negotiate treaty of commerce and navigation between Turkey and U.S. at Angora, 1929. Baptist. Home: LaPlata, Md. Died June 23, 1939.

GILLET, GUY MARK, senator; born Cherokee, Ia. Feb. 3, 1879; s. Mark Dennis and Mary (Hull) G. LL.B., Drake U., 1900; LL.D., Drake University, St. Ambrose Coll.; m. Rose Freeman, June 17, 1907; 1 son, Mark Freeman. Admitted to Ia. bar, 1900, and began practice at Cherokee; city atty., Cherokee, 1906-07; county atty., Cherokee County, 1907-09. Served as sergt. U.S. Vol. Inf. Spanish-Am. War; capt. inf., U.S. Army, 1917-19. Mem. Ia. State Senate, 1912-16; mem. 73d and 74th Congresses (1933-37), 9th Ia. Dist.; elected U.S. Senate to fill unexpired term of Louis Murphy, 1936, term expiring, 1939; reelected to Senate of U.S. for term, 1939-45; re-elected Nov. 1948, for 6-yr. term; chairman Surplus Property Board, 1945. President Am. League for Free Palestine, 1945. Member Spanish War Vets., Vets Fgn. Wars, Am. Legion. Democrat. Presbyterian. Mason, K.P. Home: Cherokee IA Died Mar. 1973.

GILLET, RANSOM HOOKER congressman; b. New Lebanon, N.Y., Jan. 27, 1800; s. Capt. John and Lucy Gillet; studied law under Silas Wright, 1821; m. Eleanor C. Barhydt, 1825. Admitted to N.Y. bar, circa 1822; partner (with Silas Wright) in law firm, circa 1823; served as maj., insp. local brigade N.Y. Militia, 1827-37; postmaster Ogdensburg (N.Y.), 1830-33; mem. 1st Nat. Democratic Conv., 1832; mem. U.S. Ho. of Reps. (Dem.) from N.Y., 23d-24th congresses, 1833-37; U.S. Indian commr. for N.Y., 1837-39; mem. Dem. nominating conv., 1840, helped draw up resolutions used as platform for every Dem. conv. until 1864; U.S. register of treasury, 1845-47, U.S. solicitor of treasury, 1847-49; asst. U.S. atty. gen., 1855-58; solicitor to U.S. Ct. of Claims, 1858-60. Author: Democracy in the United States, 1868; The Federal Government, 1871; The Life and Times of Silas Wright, 2 vols., 1874. Died Washington, D.C., Oct. 24, 1876; buried Glenwood Cemetery, Washington.

GILLIAM, DAVID TOD surgeon; b. Hebron, O., Apr. 3, 1844; s. William and Mary Elizabeth (Bryan) G.; ed. pub. schs., and Bartlett's Commercial Coll., Cincinnati; M.D., Med. Coll. of Ohio, 1871; m. Lucinda E. Mintun, of Nelsonville, O., Oct. 7, 1866. Enlisted 2d Va. (Union) Cav., Aug., 1861; elected corporal Co. I; with Garfield in march against Humphrey Marshall on Big Sandy River, Ky.; sent to Wheeling, W. Va., as recruiting officer; later ascended Kanawha River and took part in many skirmishes; with Crook in battle of Lewisburg, Va.; wounded and taken prisoner nr. Gauley, Va., by Gen. Loring; escaped 5 weeks later; sent to parole camp; discharged spring of 1863. In practice of medicine, Columbus, O., since 1868; emeritus professor of gynecology, Medical Department of Ohio State University (trustee same since 1905); gynecologist to St. Anthony's and St. Francis hospitals. Originated operations for suspension of uterus, for cystocele, for incontinence of urine in the female; devised many surg. instruments and the Gilliam operating table. Hon. fellow Am. Assn. Obstetricians and Gynecologists (v.p., 1905-06); mem. A.M.A., Ohio State Med. Assn., Columbus Acad. Medicine; ex-pres. Franklin Co. Med. Soc.; hon. mem. Northwestern Ohio Med. Assn.; mem. Pan-Am. Med. Congress, World's Med. Congress, Congregationalist. Republican. Author: Pocket Book of Medicine, 1882; Essentials of Pathology, 1883; Practical Gynecology, 1903; The Rose Croix, 1906; The Righting of Richard Devereux. Collaborator, Randall & Ryan's History of Ohio, 5 vols., 1912. Home: 1819 Franklin Park, S. Office: 333 E. State St., Columbus, O.

GILLINGHAM, CLINTON HANCOCK, coll. pres.; b. Phila., Pa., Sept. 29, 1877; s. Jonathan and Henrietta (Smith) G.; B.A., Maryville (Tenn.) Coll., 1905, M.A., 1907, D.D., 1919; student Princeton Theol. Sem., 1905-06; B.D., Presbyn. Theol. Sem. of Ky., 1908; spl. studies in Palestine, Jerusalem, 1923; m. Nancy Virginia Gardner, Nov. 2, 1903 (dec.); children—George Gardner, Alice Armitage (Mrs. John C. McDowell), Samuel Wilson, Mary (Mrs. J. M. Padgette) and Jonathan (twins), Edward Clinton; m. 2d, Helen Lewis, July 14, 1935. Ordained Presbyterian ministry, September 29, 1907; with Y.M.C.A., Philadelphia, 1890-93; with Pa. Railroad Company, 1893-1901; with Maryville Coll., 1907-29, registrar, 1907-26, prof. O.T. history and lit., 1907-11, prof. English Bible and head of dept. of Bible and religious edn., 1911-29; pres. Tennent Coll. of Christian Edn., 1929-43; pres. emeritus since 1943; vis. prof. English Bible. Maryville Coll., 1945-46. Served as major inf. 4th Tenn. Regt. 1918-19; reserve officer Tenn. Nat. Guard, 1919-29. Moderator of Presbytery of Union, 1910. Mem. bd. dirs. Presbyn. Theol. Sem. of Ky., 1923-32; mem. bd. trustees Tennent Coll. of Christian Edn. since 1929; pres. 1929-44; sec.-treas. Tenn. Coll. Assn., 1924-29. Club: Kiwanis (past pres.). Home: Maryville TN

GILLIS, JAMES HENRY commodore, U.S.N.; b. Ridgway, Pa., May 14, 1831; s. James L. and Cecilia Ann (Berray) G.; grad. Naval Acad., 1854; m. Lydia A. Alexander, Sept. 21, 1854 (died 1893); 2d, Ursula Z. Canfield, Mar. 17, 1903. Passed midshipman, June 15, 1854; promoted through grades to commodore, Jan. 29, 1887. Rescued master and three of crew of an Argentine vessel that had foundered outside of the harbor of Montevideo during a terrific "pampero," Mar. 1, 1859 (received thanks from Argentine minister and many testimonials from citizens of Montevideo; also medal from citizens of Buenos Aires and officers of Argentine Navy); took part in sinking Confederate privateer Petrel, July 1861; served N. Atlantic blockading squadron, 1862; after capture of Confederate battery at junction of Dawho and S. Edisto Rivers, was ambushed at Slamm's bluff by a battery and 2 regts. of infantry, but drove them off; comd. Commodore Morris in battle of Jamestown Island, S.C., June 1862; engagement with battery, Taylor's Landing, Pamunkey River, Apr. 16, 1863; was up Red River with Admiral Porter; comd. iron-clad Milwaukee until it was sunk by torpedo during engagement with Spanish Fort, Mobile Bay, March 28, 1865; then comd. naval battery on shore at siege of fort until it fell; afterward on various stations and duties; comd. the Wateree, S. Pacific squadron, which was carried half a mile inland by tidal wave at Arica, Peru (received thanks of British govt. for assistance rendered British subjects on this occasion); comd. S. Atlantic sta. as rear admiral, 1888-90; retired May 14, 1893. Home: Melbourne Beach, Fla. Died 1910.

GILLISS, JAMES MELVILLE naval officer, astronomer; b. Georgetown, D.C., Sept. 6, 1811; s. George and Mary (Melville) G.; attended U. Va., 1833; m. Rebecca Roberts, Dec. 1837. Entered U.S. Navy, 1826; commd. midshipman, 1833; studied in Paris in 6 months, 1835, ordered back to Washington (D.C.), assigned to Depot of Charts and Instruments; in charge of depot, 1837; commd. to make astron. observations in Washington necessary for evaluation of longitude observation of Lt. Charles Wilkes' expdn., 1838; pointed out inadequacy of existing building and equipment for astron. research to Bd. Naval Commrs., 1841 (led to act of Congress providing for establishment U.S. Naval Observatory at Washington); visited Europe in interests of observatory, circa 1842-1843, authorized by Congress to go to Santiago (Chile) to observe Venus and Mars, 1849-52; became supt. U.S. Naval Observatory, 1861; mem. Nat. Acad. Sci. Died Feb. 9, 1865.

GILLMOR, HORATIO GONZALO rear adm.; b. Menomonie, Wis., Jan. 7, 1870; s. Daniel Webster and Jane (Shipman) G.; grad. U.S. Naval Acad., 1891; student Royal Naval Coll., Greenwich, Eng., 1891-94; m. Mary S. Grandy, Apr. 16, 1912 (dec. 1917); children - Wiley Grandy (dec.), Daniel Shipman; m. 2d, Grace V. Estes, Aug. 31, 1922. Commd. asst. naval constructor, lt. j.g., USN, July 1, 1893, and advanced through grades to capt., July 1, 1917; rear adm., Oct. 1, 1932. Asst. to constrn. officer Navy Yard, N.Y.C., 1894-95; served on U.S.S. New York, 1895-96; superintending constructor Herreshoff Mfg. Co., Bristol, R.I., 1896-98; with Bur. Constrn. and Repair, Navy Dept., 1898; superintending constructor Elswick Shipyard, Newcastleon-Tyne, Eng., 1898-1900; again with Bur. Constrn. and Repair, 1900-02; superintending constructor Bath (Me.) Iron Works, 1902-07; same, Fore River Shipbldg. Corp., Quincy, Mass., 1907-10; constrn. officer Navy Yard, Norfolk, 1910-15; mem. Bd. Inspection and Survey, Navy Dept., 1915-27, 1931-32; with Dept. Justice (assisting def. suits), 1927-31; naval operations Navy Dept., 1932-34; ret.; recalled to active duty as mem. Compensation Bd., Navy Dept., July 14, 1941. Mem. Soc. Naval Architects and Marine Engrs. Awarded Spanish War, World War and Nat. Def. medals. Episcopalian. Clubs: Army and Navy, Army-Navy Country, Chevy Chase. Home: 7120 N St. N.W., Washington 20036. Died Dec. 21, 1960; buried Arlington Nat. Cemetery.

GILLMORE, JAMES CLARKSON commodore U.S.N.; b. Phila., July 10, 1854; s. James Clarkson and Josephine Augusta (Hagner) G.; Pa. Mil. Acad., Chester; grad. U.S. Naval Acad., 1876; m. Mary Stuart Ball, May 12, 1882 (dec.). Promoted ensign, 1879; lt., jr. grade, 1890; lt., sr. grade, 1893; lt. comdr., 1900; comdr., 1904; capt., 1909; promoted commodore and retired at own request after 40 yrs.' service, July 1, 1911. Served as midshipman aboard Hartford, N. Atlantic Sta., Monogahela, China Sta.; returned home in alert from China, 1879; served on Jamestown in Alaska, 1879-82, Iroquois, Pacific Sta., 1882-85, comdg. gatling co. at Panama, in landing force, 1885; aboard Marion, Asiatic Sta., 1887-90, Machias, Atlantic Sta., Vesuvius, and again Machias, Asiatic Sta., 1893-97; during war with Spain was navigator U.S.S. St. Paul; comd. torpedo boat Porter; exec. officer Scorpion; navigator Solace, sailing for Manila, 1899; navigator U.S.S. Yorktown; captured by Filipinos and prisoner 8-1/2 mos.; exec. officer Franklin, Norfolk, Va., 1900-01; exec. officer, Cincinnati, 1901-07; capt. Cavite Navy Yard, P.I., and comdg. Helena; in charge naval recruiting sta., New York, 1907-09; comdg. battleship Illinois; comdg. Maryland, Pacific Sta., 1909-11. Esoteric Buddhist. Sampson medal, Philippine War medal, Congressional medal for Spanish-Am. War. Mason. Died June 14, 1927.

GILLMORE, QUINCY ADAMS army officer; b. Black River, O., Feb. 28, 1825; s. Quartus and Elizabeth (Reid) G.; grad. U.S. Mil. Acad., 1849; m. Mary O'Maher, 1849; m. 2d, Mrs. Briggs; 4 children. Commd. 2d lt. engrs. U.S. Army, 1849, 1st lt., 1856, capt., 1861; chief engr. Port Royal expdn.; brevetted lt. col. for services during capture of Ft. Pulaski, 1862; commd. brig. gen. U.S. Volunteers, 1862, maj. gen., 1863; brevetted col. U.S. Army for gallantry, 1863; commanded 10th Army Corps., then Dept. of South; wounded during defense of Washington (D.C.), 1864; pres. bd. to test wrought iron cannon; brevetted brig. gen. and maj. gen. U.S. Army for bravery; pres. Mississippi River Commn. Author various engring. works including; Practical Treatise on Limes, Hydraulic Elements and Mortars, 1863; Report on Experiments with the Seely and Bethell Processes for the Preservation of Timber, 1879. Died Bklyn., Apr. 7, 1888; buried U.S. Mil. Acad., West Point, N.Y.

GILLMORE, QUINCY ADAMS army officer; b. West Point, N.Y., Jan. 12, 1881; s. Quincy O'Mahr and Margaret (Van Kleeck) G.; pre. edn., Mohegan Lake (N.Y.) Sch. and Preston Sch., Washington, D.C.; student Colo. Sch. Mines, 1898-1900; grad. U.S. Mil. Acad., 1904; m. Frances West Hemsley, Nov. 16, 1904; children-Quincy A., Frances West, Frederick Hemsley. Commd., 2d lt., Arty., U.S. Army, 1904, resigned,1907; col., F.A., N.J. Nat. Guard, 1917, brig. gen., 1922, maj. gen., 1924; comdg. gen., N.J. Nat. Guard, and 44th Div., (N.Y. and N.J. troops), 1924-32, resigned Comd. 112th A.E.F., 1917-19. Mem. Huguenot Soc., Soc. Colonial Wars, Loyal Legion. Awarded Distinguished Service Medal, State of N.J. Republican. Episcopalian. Clubs: Rittenhouse, Racquet (Philadelphia, Pa.): Union. Racquet and Tennis, Turf and Field. Home: 840 Park Av., N.Y.C. 21. Died Jan. 5, 1956; buried West Point Cemetery, West Point, N.Y.

GILLMORE, WILLIAM E. army officer; b. Lorain, O., Nov. 29, 1876; s. Q.A. and Mary J. (Fitzgerald) G.; student U.S. Mil. Acad., 1896-99; m. Florence Edgerton Nelson, Dec. 14, 1901; children-Martha Huntington (wife of Frederick W. Huntington, U.S.A.), William N. Commd. 2d lt. U.S.A. Feb. 2, 1901; promoted through grades to lt. col., July 1, 1920; served in Air Corps, 1917-31; now retired. Successively chief of Personal Div., chief of Planning Div., exec. officer A.C., pres. Control Bd., comdg. officer Kelly Field (San Antonio, Tex.), air officer 9th Corps Area (San Francisco), and chief of Supply Div.; apptd. asst. chief A.C., July 17, 1926, rank of brig. gen., term of 4 yrs. Col. Air Service, U.S.A., Aug. 24, 1918-June 30, 1920. Mem. Nat. Aeronautic Assn., Soc. Automotive Engrs. Republican. Conglist. Clubs: Army and Navy, Columbia Country; Engineers, Dayton City, Dayton Country. Address: War Dept., Washington. Died Nov. 7, 1948.

GILLON, ALEXANDER naval officer, congressman; b. Rotterdam, Holland, Aug. 13, 1741; s. Mary Gillon; m. Mary Cripps, July 6, 1766; m. 2d, Ann Purcell, Feb. 10, 1789; 1 son, 2 daus. Commanded Brit. mcht. vessels with hdqrs. at Charleston, S.C., 1764-65; engaged in trading enterprises, 1766-76; mem. S.C. Provincial Congresses, 1775-77, strongly favored Am. independence; apptd. commodore in state navy of S.C., 1778, sent to France as financial agt. to borrow money and purchase ships; obtained from Chevalier Luxembourg frigate which he named South Carolina, 1780, took command of ship, captured prizes in North Sea, 1781, commanded expdn. which took Bahamas, 1782, his ship captured by British, 1782, lost money in the enterprise (claims for payment made by Chevalier Luxembourg continued in courts for many years); del. to Congress of Confederation, 1784; mem. S.C. Assembly, 1786-88; mem. U.S. Ho. of Reps. from S.C., 3d Congress, 1793-94. Died at estate Gillon's Retreat, Oct. 6, 1794.

GILMAN, NICHOLAS senator, congressman; b. Exeter, N.H., Aug. 3, 1755; s. Nicholas and Ann (Taylor) G.; attended common schools, Exeter. Commd. capt. N.H. Militia 1775, served with adj. gen. until 1782; returned to Exeter, 1783, active politically; commanded local militia during currency troubles, 1786; del. to Congress of Confederation, 1786-88; del. to U.S. Constl. Conv., Phila., 1787; mem. U.S. Ho. of Reps. (Federalist) from N.H., 1st-4th congresses, 1789-97; mem. N.H. Senate, 1804-05; changed allegiance to Republican Party; mem. U.S. Senate (Rep.) from N.H., 1805-14. Died Phila., May 2, 1814; buried Exeter.

GILMER, GEORGE ROCKINGHAM gov. Ga., congressman; b. Lexington, Ga., Apr. 11, 1790; s. Thomas Meriwether and Elizabeth (Lewis) G.; attended acad., Abbeville, S.C., 1804-08, pvt. law school, Lexington, 1808-circa 1811; m. Eliza Grattan, 1822. Began practice of law, Lexington, circa 1811; commanded Ga. Militia in expdn. against Creek Indians, 1813; elected to Ga. Legislature, 1818, 24; mem. U.S. Ho. of Reps. from Ga., 17th Congress, 1821-23, 20th Congress, 1826, 23d Congress, 1833-35; an adherent Troup Faction in Ga. politics and advocate slavery and states' rights; gov. Ga., 1828-31, 37-39; bequeathed Gilmer Fund to U. Ga., for teacher tng. Author: Sketches of Some of the First Settlers of Upper Georgia (recollections of early years), 1885. Died Lexington Nov. 16, 1859; buried Presbyn. Cemetery, Lexington.

GILMER, WILLIAM WIRT naval officer; b. at Chatham, Va., May 21, 1863; s. John and Eliza Williams (Patton) G.; grad. U.S. Naval Acad., 1885; m. Florence Peterson, of Germantown, Pa., June 2, 1906. Commd. ensign U.S.N., July 1, 1887; lt. jr. grade, Sept. 4, 1896; lt., Mar. 3, 1899; lt. comdr., Jan. 1, 1905; comdr., Dec. 23, 1908; capt., July 1, 1912. Served on Merrimac and Vulcan in West Indies, Spanish-Am. War, 1898; in P.I., 1900; successively on Caesar, Don Juan de Austria and Glacier, and ashore at Isabela de Basilan; comdr. 12th Naval Dist. and Training Sta., San Francisco, 1916-17; apptd. comdr. South Carolina. Atlantic Fleet, July 23, 1917; comdt. naval sta. and gov. Island of Guam, Nov. 15, 1919 -. Democrat. Episcopalian. Clubs: Army and Navy (Washington and Manila). Address: Care Navy Dept., Washington, D.C.

GILMOR, HARRY army officer; b. Balt., Jan. 24, 1838; s. Robert and Ellen (Ward) G.; tutored at home; m. Mentoria Strong; Engaged in farming in Wis. and Neb., later with father in Md., circa 1848-61, joined Confederate Army under Ashby in Va., 1861; commd. capt. 21st Va. Cavalry, 1862; served in Shenandoah Valley throughout war, captured and exchanged, 1862; commd. maj. 2d Md. cavalry, 1863; cut B. & O. R.R. during raid nr. Harper's Ferry, 1864, acquitted by Confederate court martial for robberies which occurred at that time; burned Chambersburg, Pa., 1864; leader of many raids, highly successful at guerilla style warfare; captured again, 1865; in business in Balt., 1865-74; police commr. of Balt., 1874-79. Died Balt., Mar. 4, 1883; buried Balt.

GILMORE, JOHN CURTIS brig. gen.; b. in Can., Apr. 18, 1837; s. James and Mary B.; when 6 months old went with family to Louisville, N.Y.; ed. there; LL.B., Albany (N.Y.) Law School. Capt. 16th N.Y. Inf., May 15, 1861; maj., Sept. 29, 1862, lt. col. 193d N.Y. Inf., Mar. 28, 1865; bvtd. col. vols., Nov. 14, 1865; hon. mustered out of vol. service, Jan. 18, 1866; bvtd. maj., Mar. 2, 1867, col., Mar. 2, 1867, for same, at Fredericksburg; Congressional Medal of Honor, Oct. 10, 1892, for distinguished conduct at Salem Heights, Va., May 3, 1863. Apptd. 2d lt., 12th U.S. Inf., May 11, 1866; capt. 38th Inf., Jan. 22, 1867; maj. a.-a.-g., Aug. 14, 1890; lt. col. a.-a.-g., Nov. 15, 1896; brig. gen. vols., May 27, 1898-June 12, 1899; col. a.-a.-g., Apr. 28, 1900; retired, Apr. 18, 1901; brig. gen. retired, by act of Apr. 23, 1904. Chief of staff and adj. gen. to Gen Miles, headquarters of the army in Cuba and Puerto Rico, during summer of 1898 and until retired; as mem. bd. of officers took part in preparing Infantry, Cavalry and Light Artillery Drill Regulations and Manual of Guard Duty. Home: Washington, D.C. Died Dec. 22, 1922.

GILMORE, MAURICE E. ex-commr. Public Works Adminstrn.; b. Somerset, Ky., Sept. 14, 1878: s. Cyrus Beattie and Elizabeth (MacOuarrie) G.; student Haskell Inst., 1892-94; B.S., Henry Kendall Coil, (Tulsa Univ), 1899, Mo. Univ., 1898; grad. Army War Coll., 1918; m. Mary Wells Barnes, Feb. 3, 1937; children-Maurice Eugene, George Barnes, Mfary Elizabeth. Engring. asst., 1899; engr. on allotment of Indian Reservations in Okla., Interior Dept., Indian Affairs, 1899-1906; constrn. engr. Panama Canal and Panama R.R. (levelman to supt. pulic works), 1906-13; constrn. and operation of Elec. Power Plant and St. R.R. and Municipal Development in Panama, 1913-15; with Elec. Bond & Share Co., 1915-17: R. W. Hebard & Co., Inc., in South and Central America, 1919-33; state engr. insp. N.Y., Public Works Administrn., 1933-37, regional director, region No. 1, 1937-40, commissioner 1940-44; director Department of Transportation and Economic Development; coordinator of Inter-American Affairs, 1944-47. Retired February 1947. Served in Spanish American War with Rough Riders, 1898; Mexican Campaign, 1914; commissioned capt. and advanced through grades to colonel, World War I, 1917-19. Democrat. Roman Catholic. Mem. Am. Soc. C.E., Soc. Am. Military Engrs., Am. Soc. for Testing Materials, Am. Geog. Soc. Clubs: Army-Navy (Washington, D.C.); Club Union, Country (Panama); Club International, Club Union, Country (San Salvador). Home: 5111 Moorland Lane, Bethesda, Md. Died Nov. 19, 1957; buried Arlington Nat. Cemetery.

GILMORE, PASCAL PEARL banker; b. Dedham, Me., June 24, 1845; s. Tyrrel and Mary Wood (Pearl) G.; desc. Revolutionary ancestry; ed. E.Me. Conf. Sem., Bucksport, Me.; m. Alma M. Hart, of Holden, Me., Oct. 25, 1881; 1 dau., Madge (Mrs. Raymond Fellows). Mem. Co. E, 16th Me. Vols., Civil War (not off duty a single day); wounded in face at Battle of Dabney's Mill, Feb. 6, 1865; promoted "for gallant and meritorious conduct" at battles of White Oak Road and Five Forks; present at surrender of Gen. Lee at Appomattox, Apr. 9, 1865. Insp. lumber, Mich., 1867-71; engaged in farming, 1871-91; mem. Me. Ho. of Rep., 1875, 83, Senate, 1891; state liquor commr., 1891-96; state treas., Me., 1907-11; supt. schs., Dedham, 15 yrs.; chmn. Bd. of Selectmen 10 yrs.; pres. Bucksport Nat. Bank 16 yrs. Col. on staff of comdr. in chief G.A.R., 1904-05. Republican. Conglist. Mlason (K.T., 32ff. Author: Gilmore Ancestry, 1925; Civil War Memories, 1928. Home: Bucksport, Me.

GILPATRIC, GUY author; b. N.Y.C., Jan. 21, 1896; s. John Guy and May (Smith) G.; student Columbia Grammar Sch., N.Y.C.; m. Louise Lesser, Mar. 27, 1920. Began as aviator, 1912; instr., exhibition and test pilot for various firms in U.S. and Can., 1912-17; established altitude record for U.S. (one passenger) at Dominguez, Cal. (4665 ft.), 1912; advt. and story writing, 1918-30, writing books, 1930—. Served from 1st lt. to capt. U.S. Air Service, AEF, 1917-18. Author: Scotch and Water, 1931; Half Seas Over, 1932; French Summer, 1933; Brownstone Front, 1934; Mr. Glecannon, 1935; Three Sheets in the Wind, 1936; The Glencannon Omnibus, 1937; The Gentleman with the Walrus Mustache, 1938; The Compleat Goggler, 1939; Glencannon Afloat, 1941; Second Glencannon Omnibus, 1942; Action in the North Atlantic, 1943; Mr. Glencannon Ignores the War, 1944; Guy Gilpatric's Flying Stories, 1945; The Canny Mr. Glencannon, 1947. Contbr. fiction to mags. Home: 1806 El Encanto Rd., Santa Barbara, Cal. Died July 6, 1950; buried Evergreen Cemetery, Elizabeth, N.J.

GILPIN, WILLIAM territorial gov. Colo.; b. Brandywine, Pa., Oct. 4, 1813; s. Joshua and Mary (Dilworth) G.; grad. U. Pa., 1833; attended U.S. Mil. Acad., 1834-35; m. Mrs. Julia Dickerson, Feb. 12, 1874. Served as 2d lt. U.S. Army, in Seminole War 1836, resigned as 1st lt., 1838; editor Mo. Argus, (newspaper which he made organ of Democratic Party), St. Louis, 1838; accompanied Fremont's expdn. to Pacific coast, 1843; served as maj. in volunteer Mo. regt., Mexican War, 1846-47, then engaged in Indian wars in Rockies, mustered out as lt. col. of Mo. Volunteers, 1848; lectured often on theme of establishing Denver as capital of new civilization in West in 1850's; apptd. territorial gov. of Colo., 1861, held territory for U.S. during early stages of Civil War, raised 1st Regt. of Colo. Volunteers, autumn, 1861, served until 1862 (recalled after dispute); owned interest in land devel. in N.M., 1870's; continued propagandizing on behalf econ. and polit. devel. of West in 1870's-80's. Author: The Central Gold Region, 1860; The Cosmopolitan Railway (urged uniting Asia and U.S. via railroad across Bering Straits), 1890. Died Denver, Jan. 20, 1894; buried Denver.

GINDER, PHILIP DEWITT, army officer; b. Plainfield, N.J., Sept. 19, 1905; s. Grant D. and Emma Edith (Troxell) G.; B.S., U.S. Mil. Acad., 1927; m. Martha Calvert, 1933 (div. 1945); children—Jean Calvert, Louise Calvert; m. 2d, Jean Dalrymple, Nov. 1, 1951. Commd. 2d lt., AUS, 1927, advanced through grades to maj. gen., 1953; various mil. assignments, 1927-45; sr. mil. attache at Prague, Czechoslovakia, 1949-51; comd. 6th Inf. Regt., 1951-52; asst. chief of staff Intelligence of Army Field Forces, 1952; comd. 45th inf. div., Korea, 1953; comd. 37th inf. div., 1954; comdg. gen. Fifth Army, Chgo., 1955; spl. asst. to chief of staff for Res. Components, 1955-57; dep. comdg. gen. for Res. Forces, 1958-63, ret., 1963; pres. Brazilia-Am. Import Co., 1963-68. Decorated Distinguished Service Cross, Distinguished Service Medal, Silver Star, Legion of Merit, Bronze Star with 2 oak leaf clusters, Purple Heart, Legion of Honor and Croix de Guerre with palm (France), Order of Mil. Merit (Czechoslovakia), Mil. Order of Patriotic Fight (Russia), Fourragere (Belgium), Legion of Merit (Philippines), Order of Taegu (Korea). Home: New York City NY also Danbury CTDied Nov. 1968.

GINGRICH, JOHN EDWARD retired naval officer, telephone and telegraph corp. executive; b. Dodge City, Kan., Feb. 23, 1897; s. Edward Grant and Bertha (Allen) G.; student Kan. Univ., 1915; grad. U.S. Naval Academy, 1919; m. Florence Benson, 1925; 1 son, Edward; m. 2d, Vanetta Oliphant, July 3, 1939; 1 daughter, Susan. Commissioned ensign, 1919, and advanced through grades to rank of vice adm.; served in Atlantic and Pacific Fleet; served as aide to under sec. of navy, 1940-44; comdr. U.S.S. Pittsburgh, 1944-45; chief of staff 2d Carrier Task Force, 1945; asst. chief of Naval Operations, dir. Naval Reserve, 1946-47; dir. security, Atomic Energy Commn., 1947-49; chief of staff to Comdr. to Chief. U.S. Pacific Fleet, 1949-51; comdr. Tng. Command Pacific Fleet, 1951; comdr. U.N. Blockading and Escort Force, 1952; dep. chief Naval Operations (adminstrn.). Dept. Navy, 1953-54; v. adm., chief Naval Materials, 1954, adm. ret., 1954; v.p. Internat. Tel. & Tel. Corp., N.Y.C., 1954 - ; pres. Fed. Telephone & Radio Co., 1956 - . Episcopalian. Author: (book) Navigation Tables, 1931. Home: 125 E. 84th St. Office: 67 Broad St., N.Y.C. Died May 26, 1960; buried Arlington Nat. Cemetery.

GINSBURGH, A(BRAHAM) ROBERT ret. A.F. officer; b. Warsaw (then Russian Poland), May 30, 1895; s. David and Anne (Ellion) G.; came to U.S., 1901, naturalized, 1901; A.B., Harvard, 1917, LL.B., 1936; A.M., U. of Louisville, 1922; A.M., U. of Mo., 1931; grad. Field Arty Sch., 1921, Army Indsl. Coll., 1939, Army-Navy Staff Coll., 1943; m. Elsie Bulitt Pinney, Dec. 29, 1922; children-Robert Neville, Anne and Martha, twins, Commd. 2d lt., U.S. Army, 1917, and advanced to brig. gen., 1948, ret., 1953; served as capt., F.A., in Philippines, 1919-20, France, 1933; col. Gen. Staff Corps, Southwest Pacific Theater, 1943-45, Japan, 1945-46; mem. staff F.A. Sch., 1921-25; recruiting publicity bureau, 1925-28; battery comdr. and mem. Pack Arty. Bd., 1928-30; mem. staff Sec. of War Hurley, 1931-33, asst. Sec. of War Johnson, 1937-40, Asst. and Undersec. of War Patterson, and chief indsl. services div., 1940-43, Sec. of War Patterson, 1946-47, Sec. of Army Royall, 1947-48; dep. dir. public relations U.S. Air Force, 1948-49; mem. staff. Sec. of Defense Johnson, 1949-50, mem. staff Secretary of Defense Marshall, 1950-51, Secretary of Defense Lovett, 1951-52, Sec. of Defense Wilson, 1952-53, ret. 1953; asso. editor U. S. News and World Report, 1953. Reporter for the New York World, 1925-27; admitted to D. C. bar, 1937. Decorated D.S.M., Legion of Merit Air medal, Bronze Star medal, Distinguished Service Star (Philippines). Mem. Caribou Society, Aviation Writers Association. Phi Beta Kappa. Delta Sigma Rho. Unitarian. Clubs: National Press, Army-Navy. Home: 2572 Military Rd., Arlington, Va. Office: 24th N St. N.W., Washington. Died June 27, 1958; buried Arlington Nat. Cemetery.

GIRARD, ALFRED CONRAD brig. gen.; b. Switzerland, July 31, 1841; s. Prof. C. F. (of U. of Basel) and J. (Blumer) G.; grad. U. of Würzburg, Germany, 1884; m. Annie R., d. J. P. M. Epping, U.S. marshal, of Charleston, S.C., Mar. 3, 1868. Acting asst. surgeon, Jan. 1865-67; asst. surgeon U.S.A., May 14, 1867; advanced through grades to col.; asst. surgeon-gen., June 28, 1902; brig. gen., Apr. 6, 1905; retired at own request, Apr. 7, 1905. Served in depts. of La. and Tex., 1867-82; visited hosps. in Europe and published report advocating antiseptic surgery; then served 8 yrs. on frontier in campaigns against Indians, and after another trip to Europe published an atlas of clinical microscopy; just before Spanish-Am. War represented U.S. at an internat. congress, Madrid; chief surgeon, 2d Army Corps, during Spanish-Am. War; at its close equipped Gen. Hosp. at the Presidio, Calif., where he took care of 19,000 patients in 3 yrs., mostly invalids from P.I.; chief surgeon Dept. Luzon, 1 yr., then chief surgeon Dept. Calif.; med. reference librarian, John Crerar Library, Chicago, 1907; now representing same at Washington. Died Jan. 31, 1914.

GIRARD, JOSEPH BASIL army surgeon; b. Courpiere, Puy-de-Dome, France, Dec. 26, 1846; s. Michael and Genevieve (Navarron) G.; ed. pvt. schs., France and Can.; M.D., U. of Mich., 1867; m. Louise Oury, May 17, 1875 (died 1899). Entered U.S.A. as asst. surgeon with rank of 1st lt., May 14, 1867; capt. asst. surgeon, May 14, 1870; maj. surgeon, Mar. 22, 1888; lt. col. deputy surgeon gen., Feb. 2, 1901; col. asst. surgeon gen., Sept. 7, 1902. Service has been chiefly on western plains, H.I. and P.I., where was chief surgeon Div. of the Philippines, 1904-06; chief surgeon Dept. of Tex., 1907-10; retired for age, Dec. 26, 1910. Home: San Antonio, Tex. Died Aug. 25, 1918.

GIST, MORDECIA army officer; b. Reisterstown, Md., Mar. 6, 1743; s. Thomas and Susannah (Cockey) G.; attended common schs.; m. Cecil Carnan; m. 2d, Mary Sterrett, Jan. 23, 1778; m. 3d, Mrs. Mary Cattell, 1783; 2 sons, Independent, States. Engaged in merc. pursuits, Balt., circa 1770; served as capt. Balt. volunteer unit, 1774; commd. maj., then col. 1st Md. Battalion (under Gen. Smallwood), 1776; served in Battle of Germantown, 1777; commd. brig. gen., 1779, commended for role in Battle of Camden (1779) by Congress, 1780; served in recruiting and supply depts., 1780-81. Died Aug. 2, 1792.

GIVEN, JOSIAH justice Supreme Court Iowa; b. Westmoreland Co., Pa., Aug. 31, 1828; s. Josiah and Jane (Glendening) G.; common school edn. Holmes Col., O., 1838-51; m. Elizabeth Armour, Oct. 6, 1852 (dec.). Admitted to bar, 1851; served 2 terms as State's Atty. and for 24 yrs. on nisi prius and supreme bench of Iowa; also 1 term in Iowa Ho. Reps. and 1 term postmaster Ho. Reps., 39th Congress; dept. commr. internal revenue during Grant's 1st administration. Served as drummer, private and corporal in war with Mexico, and apt., lt. col., col. and bvt. brig. gen. in the Union army. Republican. Home: Des Moines, Ia. Deceased.

GIVEN, WILLIAM BARNS, JR., manufacturing executive; born Columbia, Pa., December 7,21886; son William Barns and Mary (Bruner) G.; student Hill Sch., Pottstown, Pa., 1899-1904, Mass. Inst. Tech., 1904-07; Ph.B., Sheffield Scientific Sch. (Yale), 1908; D.C.S. (honorary), New York University, 1950; LL.D., Franklin and Marshall Coll. (Lancaster, Pa.), 1951; D.Eng. (hon.), Mo. Sch. of Mines, 1951; L.H.D., Hobart and William Smith Colls., 1957; married Dorothy Weiman, Oct. 8, 1917; children—The Reverend Davis Given, and Dorothy (Mrs. John L. Kee, Jr.). With Am. Brake Shoe Co. (company name changed to Abex Corporation), 1911-68, secretary to president, 1911-16, asst. to pres., 1916-17, asst. v.p., 1919-20, v.p., 1920-29, president, 1929-50, chmn. bd., 1950-63, honorary chairman, board of directors, 1963-68; mem. Uptown adv. com. Bankers Trust Company; director Lloyds-Brake Shoe, Ltd. (England); hon. director Mellon Nat. Bank & Trust Co. (Pitts.); trustee Dry Dock Savs. Bank. Served as 1st lt., later capt., 42d Div., AUS, WW I. Republican. Episcopalian (vestryman); dir. Episcopal Church Found., N.Y.C.; alumni trustee General Theological Sem. Clubs: Racquet and Tennis, Links, Rolling Rock, Chicago, Piping Rock, Brook (N.Y.C.). Author: Bottom Up Management, 1949, Reaching Out in Management, 1953. Home: New York City NY Died Jan. 30, 1968.

GLANCY, ALFRED ROBINSON mfr.; b. Miamiville, O., July 17, 1881; s. Augustus C. and Louise (Robinson) G.; M.E., Lehigh U., 1903, Dr. Engring., 1943; m. Lenora Courts, Nov. 14, 1906; children-Alfred Robinson, Lenora Courts (rMrs. Richard L. Hull), Louise Courts (Mrs. Inman Brandon). In mining engring., 1903-10; pres. Glancy Malleable Corp., 1922-30; chmn. bd. A. R. Glancy, Inc.; pres. Oakland Motor Car Co., 1924-30; v.p. General Motors Corp., 1926-30, ret. 1931. Chief of Ordnance, OPM, 1941. Brig. gen., U.S. Army, Dept. Chief of Ordnance. Chief, Tank-Automotive Center, Aug. 1942. Chmn. Mich. State Planning Commn.; chmn. Mich. Pub. Trust Commn. Trustee Lehigh U. Awarded Legion of Merit, U.S. Army, 1943. Mem. Theta Delta Chi. Clubs: Detroit, Detroit Country, Bloomfield Hills Country; Royal Bermuda Yacht; Capital City, Piedmont Driving (Atlanta, Ga.). Home: 3206 Arden Road, Atlanta, Ga.; (winter) Somerset Bridge, Bermuda. Died Aug. 4, 1959.

GLASCOFF, DONALD G. exec.; b. Albion, Mich., Mar. 26, 1898; s. Robert Belmont and Ida Molena (Wocholz) G.; A.B., Albion (Mich.) Coll., 1924; student U.S. Mil. Acad. 1918 (resigned because of eyesight); m. Elrose Butterworth Alexander, Oct. 25, 1941; 1 son, Donald G.; 1 step-dau., Florence Hall. Mem. editorial staff Greenville (Mich.) Daily News, 1924-26, bus. mgr., 1926-28, editor, 1928, publisher and part-owner, 1929-32. Mem. dept. publicity com. Am. Legion, 1931-32, nat. adj. (chief adminstrv. ofcl., sec. nat. exec. com., finance com. and retirement com.), 1943-48. Dir. self-regulation and spl. activities U.S. Brewers Found. N.Y.C., since Feb. 1, 1948, also sec. nat. exec. com., nat. finance com., nat. retirement com.; sec. Records for Our Fighting Men, Inc. Served as pvt., inf. U.S. Army, 1918-19. Chevalier, French Legion of Honor; Italian Cross Merito di Guerra. Chmn., Republican City Central Com., Greenville, Michigan, 1928; sec. Rotary Club, 1929-33. Mem. Am. Legion, 40 and 8, Delta Tau Delta. Mason, K.P. Clubs: Metropolitan (N.Y.); Secor Farms Riding (White Plains, N.Y.). Home: Harris Rd., Bedford Hills, N.Y. Office: 534 5th Av., N.Y.C. Died July 28, 1963.

GLASGOW, WILLIAM JEFFERSON army officer; b. St. Louis, Mo., May 18, 1866; s. Edward James and Harriet (Clark) G.; grad. U.S. Mil. Acad., 1891; grad. Army War Coll., 1921; m. Josephine Richardson Magoffin, Oct. 29, 1896. commd. 2d lt. 1st Cav. June 12, 1891; promoted through grades to col., June 19, 1920; served as brig. gen. U.S.A., Aug. 8, 1918-May 31, 1919; brig. gen. regular army, ret., May 21, 1927; personnel dir. Nichols Copper Refinery. Address: 1120 Magoffin Av., El Paso, Tex. 79901. Died Aug. 4, 1967; buried Ft. Bliss Nat. Cemetery.

GLASOE, PAUL MAURICE, educator; b. Lanesboro, Minn., Aug. 24, 1873; s. Nias Edward and Anne Kjestline (Hjelde) G.; B.A., from U. of Minn., 1897, N.S., 1898, Ph.D., 1902; LL.D. (hon.) Wittenberg Coll., Springfield, O., 1949; traveled and studied in Eng., Norway, Sweden and Denmark, 1928-29; m. Gena Annette Kirkwold, June 28, 1899 (died 1927); children—Gynther Norris, Alf Melius I (dec.), Alf Melius II. Paul Kirkwold; m. 2d, Agnes Skartvedt, 1929 (died 1931); m. 3d, Hannah Fjeldstad, 1932. Instr. in chemistry, U. of Minn., 1898-1901; instr. in physics and chemistry, St. Olaf Coll., Northfield, Minn., 1901, prof., 1902-07; pres. Spokane Coll., Wash., 1907-10; prof. chemistry, St. Olaf Coll., 1910-16; pres. Augustana Coll., Canton. S.D., 1916-18; v.p. and prof. chemistry, St. Olaf Coll., since 1918, acting pres., 1927-28. Pres. Choral Union of Norwegian Luth. Ch., 1911-47; mem. Bd. of Elementary Christian Edn. So. Minn. Dist., 1920-45; vice pres. United Temperance Movement, 1940. pres. Minn. Anti-Saloon League; mem. Minn. Leif Erickson Monument Assn. Served as capt. Minn. Nat. Guard, 1903-05. Decorated Comdr. Order of St. Olaf, by King Haakon VII, Norway. Fellow A.A.A.S.; mem. Chem. Soc., Minn. Ednl. Assn., Sigma Xi. Republican. Lutheran. Author: General Chemistry, 1913; Introduction to the Periodic System (monograph), 1925; Foundations of General Chemistry, 1927; also numerous articles on teaching of chemistry. Home: 804 St. Olaf Av., Northfield MN

GLASS, HENRY naval officer; b. Hopkinsville, Ky., Jan. 7, 1844; s. Henry and Martha K. G.; grad. U.S. Naval Acad., 1863; m. Ella M. Johnson, Mar. 15, 1881. Promoted ensign, May 28, 1863; advanced through grades to rear admiral, Oct. 9, 1901. Served in Canandaigua, S. Atlantic Blockading Squadron, 1863, Pawnee, 1863-65; participated in all gen. engagements with forts and batteries in Charleston Harbor, July-Sept., 1863; engagements with batteries in Stono River, S.C., Dec. 28, 1863, and July 3 to 11, inclusive, 1864; engagements with batteries in North Edisto River, Feb. 9, 1865; capture of Georgetown, S.C., Feb. 5, 1865; served in Powhatan and Dacotah, Pacific Squadron, 1865-68; Tuscarora, 1869; Navy Yard, Phila., 1869-70; Mohican, 1870; comd. Nyack, 1870; California, 1871-72; chief of staff Iroquois and Hartford, 1873-74; comd. nautical sch.-ship Jamestown, 1874, 1876-78; exec. officer receiving-ship Independence, 1875; spl. duty San Francisco, 1879; comd. Jamestown, 1880-81, Wachusett, 1881-82; Navy Yard, Mare Island, 1883-86; comd. Monocacy, 1886-88; Naval Acad., 1889-91; mem. Examining and Retiring Bds., 1891-92; Navy Yard, Mare Island, 1893-94; comd. Cincinnati, 1894-95, Texas, 1895-97; capt. of yard, Navy Yard, Mare Island, 1897-98; comd. Pensacola, April, 1898, capt. of port, Manila, Aug.-Oct. 1898, while comdg. Charleston; comd. Pensacola April, 1898; Charleston, May-Dec. 1898, capture of Ladrone Islands, May 1898, taking of Manila, Aug. 1898, capt. of port, Manila, Aug.-Oct. 1898, while comdg. Charleston; comd. Pensacola and comdt. naval training sta., San Francisco, 1899-1902; comdr.-in-chief Pacific Sta., 1903-04; comdt. Pacific Naval Dist., 1904-08; retired, Jan. 7, 1906. Author: Marine International Law, 1885. Home: Berkeley, Calif. Died 1908.

GLASSFORD, WILLIAM ALEXANDER II ret. naval officer, corp. ofcl.; b. San Francisco, June 6, 1886; s. William Alexander and Allie (Davis) G.; student N.M. State Normal U., 1901-02; B.S., U.S. Naval Acad., 1906; U.S. Naval War Coll., 1929-32; m. Eleanor Phelps, June 1, 1909; children-Eleanor Phelps (Mrs. Ernest von Helmburg), Thomas Phelps, Margaret Phelps; m. 3d, Henrietta Sherwood, Oct. 1946. Commd. ensign U.S. Navy, 1908, and advanced through the grades to vice adm., 1942; comdr. U.S. Naval Forces, Southwest Pacific, 1941-42; personal rep. of President, with rank of Minister, French W. Africa, 1943; deputy comdr. U.S. Naval Forces in Europe, 1944; comdr. U.S. Naval Forces, Mediterranean, 1945; comdr. U.S. Naval Forces, Germany, 1945-46; ret., 1947; now European mgr. RCA; partner Glassford Farms, Phoenix, now ret. Decorated Navy D.S.M.; awarded gold star in lieu of 2d D.S.M.; Order Orange and Nassau; Order Star of Africa; Order Crown of Italy; Order of the Bath. Episcopalian. Clubs: Army and Navy (Washington); Chevy Chase (Md.); New York Yacht, Ends of the Earth (N.Y.C.). Address: Santa Barbara, Cal. Died July 30, 1958.

GLASSMAN, OSCAR, physician; b. Evanova, Sept. 9, 1901; s. Moss and Anna Glassman; M.D., N.Y.U., 1925; m. Jeanette Bitterbaum, June 5, 1926; 1 son, George. Intern, Bellevue Hosp., N.Y.C., 1925-27, resident in obstetrics, 1927; resident in obstetrics Berwind Maternity Clinic, 1926-27; resident in gynecology Mt. Sinai Hosp., N.Y.C., 1928-29, courtesy staff, until 1970; cons. obstetrician and gynecologist Sydenham Hosp.; attending obstetrician and gynecologist N.Y. Hosp., N.Y. Lying-In Hosp.; courtesy staff Doctors Hosp.; asso. prof. obstetrics and gynecology Cornell U. Med. Sch., N.Y.C. Served from maj. to lt. col., M.C., AUS, 1942-46. Diplomate Am. Bd. Obstetrics and Gynecology. Fellow A.C.S., Internat. Coll. Surgeons, Am. Coll. Obstetricians and gynecologists; mem. A.M.A., A.A.A.S., Am. Geriatrics Soc., Assn. Mil. Surgeons U.S. Home: New York City NY Died Oct. 10, 1970; buried Kensico Cemetery.

GLAZIER, WILLARD soldier, explorer; b. Fowler, N.Y., Aug. 22, 1841; s. Ward and Mehitable (Bolton) W.; worked on farm summers, attended dist. sch. winters; at 15 a trapper in the woods, earning means for higher edn.; 2 yrs. at Gouverneur Wesleyan Sem.; later at State Normal Coll., Albany; teaching sch. at intervals; m. Harriet Ayres, 1868. Served 1861-65, pvt. to 1st lt. and bvt. capt., Harris Light (2d N.Y.) and 26th N.Y. cav.; took part in over 60 battles and engagements; 14 months in Confederate prisons, 1863-64, escaped, was recaptured and escaped a 3d time and reached Union line at Savannah after trial as spy. Toured U.S. and Can., 1865-75, gathering lit. material; rode horseback Boston to San Francisco, 1876; located 1881, and verified on 2d expdn., 1891, true source of Mississippi in a lake beyond Itasca, now known as Lake Glazier. Organized and was col. provisional regt., Ill. vols., for the Spanish war, 1898; explored coast and interior of Labrador, 1902. Lecturer. Author: Ocean to Ocean on Horseback, 1896. Home: Albany, N.Y. Died 1905.

GLEAVES, ALBERT naval officer; b. Nashville, Tenn., Jan. 1, 1858; s. Henry Albert and Eliza (Tannehill) G.; ed. U.S. Naval Acad.; m. Evalina M. Heap, June 12, 1889; children—Mrs. Anne Heap Van Metre, Mrs. Evelina Porter Cohen. Commissioned ensign U.S. Navy, Jan. 1, 1881; promoted through various grades to rear admiral, July 29, 1915; temp. vice adm. and adm. World War; reverted to rank of rear admiral after the war and later advanced to admiral on the retired list. Served in Hartford, S. Atlantic Station, in Plymouth and Texas on N. Atlantic, Mipsic on European Sta., Trenton and Monocacy on Asiatic Sta.; comd. torpedo-boat Cushing during Spanish-Am. War; served as navigator battleships Indiana and Alabama, 1900-01; comd. Dolphin and Mayflower, spl. service, 1901-04; in charge of Torpedo Sta., Newport, R.I., 1904-08; spl. service in Europe, 1907; comdg. U.S.S. St. Louis, Pacific Fleet, 1908-09; aid to asst. sec. of the Navy and mem. Gen. Bd., until July 1910; comdg. U.S.S. North Dakota, July 1910-Nov. 1911; comdt. Naval Sta., Narragansett Bay, Nov. 1911-May 1912, Navy Yard and Naval Sta., New York, June 1912-Sept. 28, 1914; comd. U.S.S. Utah, Sept. 28, 1914-July 28, 1915; comdg. destroyer Force, Atlantic Fleet, Nov. 22, 1915-July 16, 1917; comdr. convoy operations in Atlantic, May 29, 1917, and convoyed the 1st A.E.F. to France, June 1917; comdg. cruiser and transport force, Atlantic Fleet, July 16, 1917-Sept. 1, 1919; comdg. Asiatic Sta., Sept. 1, 1919-21; spl. duty, Washington, D.C., Mar.-May 1921; comdt. 1st Naval Dist. and Navy Yard, Boston; retired Jan. 1922; gov. of U.S. Naval Home, Phila., Pa., 1928-31. While in command of Dolphin discovered greatest depth in North Atlantic Ocean. Established 1st gov. torpedo factory, 1908. Awarded Victory Medal with star, and D.S.M. (both Navy and army); Mil. Medal (Czecho-slovakian); Order of Sacred Treasure, 1st Class (Japanese); Order of Weng Hu, 1st Class (Chinese); Commander Legion of Honor (French). Presented with gold and jeweled sword by citizens of Nashville, 1919; LL.D., Jefferson Coll., Pa., 1919; gold watch, Hoboken (N.J.) Chamber of Commerce, 1919. Mem. board of Mgrs. Naval History Soc., 1934—. Episcopalian. Author: Captain James Lawrence, U.S.N., 1904; History of the Cruiser and Transport Force, 1921; Life of An American Sailor-William Hemsley Emory, Rear Admiral U.S.N., 1923; Life and Letters of Rear Admiral S. B. Luce, U.S. Navy, 1925. Home: Haverford, Pa. Died Jan. 6, 1937.

GLEN, HENRY congressman; b. Schenectady, N.Y., July 13, 1739. Clk., Schenectady County, 1767-1809; served as dep. q.m. gen. in Revolutionary War; mem. 1st-3d provincial congresses, 1774-76; mem. N.Y. State Assembly, 1786-87, 1810; mem. U.S. Ho. of Reps. from N.Y., 3d-6th congresses, 1793-1801. Died Schenectady, Jan. 6, 1814.

GLENDINNING, ROBERT banker; b. Philadephia, Pa., Aug. 10, 1867; s. Robert and Ellen E. (Butcher) G.; prep. edn. Cheltenham Acad.; A.B., U. of Pa., 1888; m. Elizabeth Rodman Fisher Carpenter, Sept. 17, 1894. Mem. Robert Glendinning & Co., bankers, Phila. Served through P.R. campaign in 1st Troop, Phila. City Cav., Spanish-Am. War, 1898; founded the aviation sch. at Essington, Pa., 1917; served as lt. col. U.S. Air Service, A.E.F., for 19 mos. from June 1917. Decorated D.S.M.; Officer Crown of Italy. Home: Philadephia, Pa. Died Apr. 19, 1936.

GLENN, EDGAR EUGENE army officer; b. Kansas City, Kan., Oct. 27, 1896; s. Stephen Edgar and Rose (Scranton) G.; student, U. Ill., 1917-18; grad. Advanced Pursuit Sch., 1922, AC Tactical Sch., 1935. Command and Gen. Staff Sch., 1936; m. Ethel Foster, Oct. 13, 1921. Began as private Aero Squadron, 1917; commd. 2d lt. Aviation Sect., 1918, advanced through the grades to brig. gen., 19 instr., 1918-19; pursuit tng., 1922; observation, 1923; bombardment, 1923; Panama Canal Zone, 1923-25; on faculty Ga. Sch. Tech., 1926-27; in charge Organized Res., Colo.-Okla., 1928-29; sec. and operations officer Advanced Flying Sch., Kelly Field, Tex., 1930-33; staff, 2d Wing, 1937-40; became chief of staff First Air Force, Mitchel Field, N.Y., 1942; spl. observer, Eng. and Ireland, 1941-42; chief of staff for Maj. Gen. Claire Chennault of 14th Air Force, 1943-45; wounded in action, Apr. 28, 1943; chief of staff 1st Air Force, 1945—; rep. USAF at Korean truce negotiations, 1953. Decorated D.S.M., Legion of Merit with oak leaf cluster, Air Medal, Purple Heart (U.S.); Chinese Hero medal, Chinese Cloud Banner (China). Mem. Phi Gamma Delta. Club: Meadowbrook Hunt (Army). Home: 67 Hilton Av., Garden City, L.I., N.Y. Died Mar. 9, 1955.

GLENN, EDWIN FORBES army officer; b. nr. Greensboro, N.C., Jan 10, 1857; s. Robert Washington (M.D.) and Julia (Gilmer) G.; Lenoir Sch. for Boys, Caldwell Co., N.C., Dr. Simon's Prep. Sch., Sing Sing, N.Y.; grad. U.S. Mil. Acad., 1877; LL.B., U. of Minn., 1890; grad. War Coll., Washington, 1914; hon. degrees Union and Kenyon Colls. and Ohio, DePauw and Vt. univs.; m. Louise, d. Henry Murney Smyth, of St. Paul, Minn., Apr. 29, 1886. Second lt. 25th Inf., June 15, 1877; promoted through grades Instituted mil. training and was asst. prof. mathematics, U. of Minn., 1888; admitted to Minn. bar and was mem. Stephens, O'Brien & Glenn; judge advocate Dept. Dak., later Dept. Columbia, 1896-98; comd. exploring and relief expdns. to Alaska, 1898-99; judge advocate Dept. Visayas, P.I., 1900; comd. Columbua (O.) Barracks, 1905-07; again in P.I. with 23d Inf., 1911-13; War Coll., 1913-14; chief of staff Dept. of East, 1914-16; comd. 18th Inf. and 1st Separate Brig., Deming, N.M., 1916-17; organized Camp Sherman, O., and 83d Div., Aug. 1917-Jan. 1918; overseas for observation at various fronts, Jan.-Apr. 1918; comd. 83d Div. A.E.F., June 1918, also organized and comd. 2d Replacement Depot and Training Centre, Le Mans, Sarthe, France, and Am. Embarkation Centre there, also most extensive small arms target facilities, comd. demobilization at Camp Sherman, Feb. 1919; retired at own request, Dec. 1919. Comdr. Legion of Honor (French). Author: Glenn's International Law, 1895; Rules of Land Warfare (pub. auspices Gen. Staff), 1914. Pres. Inf. Assn., 1913-20. Home: Glendon, N.C. Died Aug. 5, 1926.

GLENN, MILTON WILLITS congressman; b. Atlantic City, N.J., June 18, 1903; LL.B., Dickinson Law Sch., 1925; m. Irma L. Lambert, 1931; children - Milton Willets, Alfred 2d, Jane B. (Mrs. Durham), Laoma E. (Mrs. Whims). Admitted to N.J. bar, 1925; mem. firm Glenn & Glenn, Margate City; mem. N.J. Gen. Assembly, 1950-57; mem. 85th-88th Congresses, 2d Dist. N.J. Served with USNR, World War II; lt. comdr. Res. Mem. Atlantic County Bar Assn., Atlantic County Republican Union League, Am. Legion, Sigma Xi. Republican. Home: 103 N. Pembroke Av., Margate City, N.J. Office: House Office Bldg., Washington. Died Dec. 14, 1967.*

GLENN, ROBERT BRODNAX governor; b. in Rockingham Co., N.C., Aug. 11, 1854; s. Chalmers L. and Annie S. (Dodge) G.; ed. Davidson Coll., N.D., U. ov Va., and Pearson's Law Sch., Richmond Hill, N.C.; m. Nina Deaderick, Jan. 8, 1878. Engaged in gen. law practice, first at Danbury, N.C., 1878; in 1886 with W. B. Glenn and in 1891 with Manly & Hendren; was asst. div. counsel for Southern Ry., atty. for Western Union Telegraph Co., etc. Was mem. legislature, 1881; solicitor for state, 1886; elector for Cleveland, 1884, 1892; U.S. dist. atty., 1893-97; gov. of N.C., 1905-09. Democrat. Presbyn. Was capt. and maj. Nat. State Guard, 1890-93. Home: Winston-Salem, N.C. Died May 16, 1920.

GLENN, THOMAS L. congressman from Idaho for term, 1901-03; b. Ballard Co., Ky., Feb. 2, 1847; s. Tyre and Barzilla J. G.; ed. in native co., and at Evansville, Ind.; attended Commercial Coll., Evansville, Ind., 1869-70; studied law at home; newsboy with Grant's army, spring, 1861, to Feb., 1863; attempted to join C.S. army, 1863, but was not enrolled because of his being too young until Feb., 1864; joined Co. F, 2d Ky. cav., Gen. John H. Morgan's brigade; in battle of Wytheville, Va., May 10, 1864; wounded in right shoulder, lft. Sterling, June 9, 1864; m. Milburn, Ky., Mar. 17, 1870, Lucretia I. Stephens; (died, Jan. 24, 1893); 2d Montpelier, Ida., 1895, Nellie Co. clerk - Ballard Co., Ky., 1874-82; State senator 2d Ky. dist., 1887-91; admitted to bar, 1890; removed to Ida.; Populist; elected on fusion ticket. Address: Montpelier, Ida.

GLENNAN, ARTHUR HENRY asst. surgeon-gen. U.S. Pub. Health Service; b. Rochester, N.Y., July 28, 1853; s. Patrick (surgeon U.S.A.) and Margaret Denver (O'Donnell) G.; B.S., St. John's Coll., D.C., 1872; M.D., Univ. Med. Coll. (New York U.), 1882. Apptd. asst. surgeon, U.S. Marine Hosp. Service, June 6, 1883; passed asst. surgeon, Sept. 7, 1886; commd. surgeon, Aug. 10, 1898; asst. surgeon gen., June 10, 1903. Comd. U.S. marine hosps. and quarantine stas. at various points, 1883-97; served in epidemic of yellow fever in South, 1897-98; sanitary insp. west coast of Fla., during Gen. Shafter's expdn. to Cuba; organized quarantine service of P.R., 1899, and apptd. mem. Superior Bd. of Health; chief quarantine officer of Cuba during yellow fever epidemic in Havana, on staff Maj. Gen. Wood, 1900-02; detailed upon sanitary mission to Cal. in cooperation with gov. and state health officials, 1902-03. Mem. A.M.A., Loyal Legion. Address: University Club, Washington, D.C.

GLENNON, JAMES HENRY naval officer; b. French Gulch, Calif., Feb. 11, 1857; grad. U.S. Naval Acad., 1878; m. Susan Davenport Blair, Aug. 12, 1884; children-Isabel Harrison (wife of M.A. Cross, U.S.A.), James Blair, Randolph Harrison (dec.), Harrison Randolph, Philip Thompson (dec.). Ensign, Feb. 4, 1882; promoted through grades to rear admiral, Aug. 19, 1916. Served on Massachusetts, Spanish-Am. War, 1898; actg. capt. of port, Havana, 1899; exec. officer and navigator Vicksburg, 1900-02; comd. General Alava, 1902; in charge Nautical Sch., Manila, P.I., 1902; exec. officer and navigator Monterey, 1902-03; exec. officer Independence, 1904; duty Bur. of Ordnance, Navy Dept., 1905-07; comd. Yorktown, 1907-08; Navy Yard, New York, 1909; comd. Virginia, 1910-11; pres. Bd. on Naval Ordnance and Joint Army and Navy Bd. on smokeless powder, 1912-13; comd. Florida, 1913, Wyoming, 1913-15; mem. Panama Fortifications Bd., pres. Bd. on Naval Ordnance and Joint Army and Navy Bd. on gun forgings, 1915; comd. Navy Yard, and supt. Naval Gun Factory, Washington, 1915-17; naval rep. Pres. of U.S. Am. spl. mission to Russia, 1917; comdr. Squadron One. Battleship Force, Atlantic Fleet, Sept. 1917; comdr. 5th Div. Atlantic Fleet, 1918; comdt. 13th Naval Dist., 1918-19, 3d Dist., 1919; retired Feb. 11, 1921. Died Dec. 24, 1927.

GLICK, GEORGE WASHINGTON governor; b. Fairfield Co., O., July 4, 1827; s. Isaac and Mary Vickers (Sanders) G.; ed. Central Coll., Ohio; m. Elizabeth Ryder, Sept. 17, 1857. Admitted to bar, 1850, and practiced in Ohio, 1850-59; apptd. col. and judge advocate gen. 17th Regt. Ohio Militia by Gov. S. P. Chase, 1857; enlisted for Mexican War, but saw no active service; went to Kan., 1859; served in Civil War short time; atty., central branch, U.P. R.R., 1867-74; engaged in farming and stock raising, 1874-1903; now retired. Mem. Kansas legislature, 1863-64, 65-66-68, 76, 82; gov. of Kan., 1883-85; U.S. pension agt., Topeka agency, 1885-92; mem. Kan. State Bd. Agr. past 32 yrs. (pres. 1902-03). Democrat. Commr. Centennial, Chicago and St. Louis expns. Mason. Home: Atchison, Kan. Died 1911.

GLIDDEN, CHARLES JASPER financier, automobilist; b. Lowell, Mass., Aug. 29, 1857; s. Nathaniel Ames and Laura Ellen (Clark) G.; ed. pub. schs. Lowell; m. Lucy Emma, d. James Cleworth, July 10, 1878. Mgr. Atlantic Pacific Telegraph Co., 1873-77; became interested in the telephone, 1876 and conducted experiments with Prof. A. Graham Bell, from Boston to Manchester, N.H., built pvt. lines in Mass. and N.H.; secured the first subscriber to an exchange system in the world, at Lowell, 1877; built 1st long distance line from Lowell to Boston, 1879; organized and was pres. and treas. several N.E. and Western telephone cos., 1876-1900; at one time controlled one-sixth of the Bell system in U.S.; retired, 1900. Interested in development of the automobile and aerial navigation; first to tour around the world in an automobile, touring 46,528 miles in 39 countries, countries, 1901-08; pres. Aerial Navigation Co. to operate a line of airships bet. Boston and New York (1st col of the kind); has made 42 balloon ascensions in U.S., 3 in France and 4 in Eng. After Completion of cable from Vancouver to Australia sent 1st telegram around the world, from Boston to Boston, etc. Commd. 1st lt., Aviation Sect., Signal O.R.C., June 12, 1917; capt., Signal Corps, U.S.A., Feb. 20, 1918; hon. disch., Aug. 19, 1919; maj., Aviation Sect., O.R.C., Oct. 3, 1919. Made 3d tour of world, Oct. 1919-June 1920, as exec. sec. of commn. which organized the 1st aerial derby around the world. Elected pres. World's Bd. Aeronautical Commrs., Inc., Mar. 24, 1921; pres. Aeronautical Digest Pub. Corp. Col. Police Reserve of N.Y. Home: New York, N.Y. Died Sept. 11, 1927.

GLOCK, CARL (EDWARD), lawyer, business exec.; b. Johnstown, Pa., Nov. 23, 1892; s. Charles Robert and Elmaretta (Swank) G.; A.B., Williams Coll., 1914; A.M., Harvard, 1915, law study, 1915-17; LL.B., U. Pitts., 1920; m. Lydia Dibert Bates, Nov. 29, 1917; children - Carl Edward, Anne (Mrs. Raymond Etienne). With Reed, Smith, Shaw & McClay, Pitts., since 1923, partner since 1935; v.p., dir. Swank Hardware Co., Johnstown, 1924 - ; adv. bd. Commonwealth Trust Co., Pitts.; dir. Bessemer & Lake Erie R.R. Co. Govt. appeal agt. SSS, 1941 -. Mem. Allegheny Co. Bd. Law Examiners. Served as capt. and adj. 316th Inf., 79th Div., U.S. Army, 1917-19, in Poland under Interallied Armistice Commn. Decorated Silver Star, Army Citation; Croix de Guerre; Silver Star Order. Mem. Phi Beta Kappa, Delta Sigma Rho, Delta Phi, Beta Theta Pi. Republican. Lutheran. lMason. Clubs: Duquesne, Longue Vue, Univ., Harvard-Yale-Princeton (Pitts.); Williams (N.Y.C.). Home: 1440 Wightman St. Pitts. 17. Office: Union Trust Bldg., Pitts. 19. Died Nov. 29, 1966; buried Grandview Cemetery, Johnstown.

GLONINGER, JOHN congressman, jurist; b. Lancaster County, Pa., Sept. 19, 1758; attended common schs. Served as subaltern officer Associaters during Revolutionary War, later commanded militia battalion; apptd. by supreme exec. council at lt. upon orgn. of Dauphin County, 1785; mem. Pa. Ho. of Reps., 1790, Pa. Senate, 1790-92; apptd. justice of peace Dauphin County, 1790; commd. asso. judge, 1791; commd. asso. judge Lebanon County, 1813; mem. U.S. Ho. of Reps. (Democrat) from Pa., 13th Congress, Mar.

4-Aug. 2, 1813 (resigned); again apptd. asso judge Lebanon County. Died Lebanon, Pa., Jan. 22, 1836; buried 1st Reformed Churchyard.

GLORE, CHARLES FOSTER investment banker; b. Eureka Springs, Ark., Nov. 16, 1887; s. Charles B. and Laura (MacAdams) G.; student Lewis Inst., Chgo., 1905-08, U. Chgo., 1910; Ellen Josephine Hixon, Sept. 11, 1915: children-Frances Hixon (Mrs. Kellogg C. Beach), Charles Foster, Robert Hixon. Identified with banking business in Chgo., 1910—; partner Glore, Forgan & Co., offices Chgo. and N.Y.C./ chmn. exec. com. and dir. The Chicago Corp., Anderson Prichard Oil Corp., mem. exec. com., dir. Continental Assurance Co., Continental Casualty Co., Libby, McNeil & Libby, Stewart-Warner Corp.; dir. The Englander Co., Inc., Studebaker Corp., Spiegel, Inc. Served as major Inf., attached to Gen. Staff, 1st Army AEF, World War I. Trustee Art Inst. Chgo., St. Luke's Hosp. Mem. Delta Kappa Epsilon. Republican. Episcopalian. Clubs: Attic Chicago, Commercial, Old Elm, Onwentsia, Shoreacres) The Links (N.Y.C.). Home: 301 N. Sheridan Rd., Lake Forest, Ill. Office: 135 S. La Salle St., Chgo. Died Oct. 6, 1950; buried Lake Forest, Ill.

GLOVER, JOHN GEORGE, educator; b. Carlow, Ireland, Jan. 6, 1895; s. John George and Annie Glover; student McGill U., U. Newark; B.C.S., N.Y.U., 1926, M.C.S., 1927, B.S., 1929, A.M., 1930, Ph.D., 1932; m. Augusta M. Behrens, July 10, 1924. Chief accountant T. A. Edison Storage Battery Co., 1920-26; member faculty N.Y.U., 1926-65, research prof. emeritus, 1965-70. Served as colonel USAF 1940-45. Mem. Acad. Mgmt., Operations Research Soc. Am., Ret. Officers Assn. (p.pres. No. N.J. chpt.), Author: Business Operations Research and Reports, 1949; Fundamentals of Professional Mgmt., rev. 1958. Home: West Orange NJ Died Sept. 23, 1970; inurned Fresh Pond Crematory, Middle Village LI NY

GLOVER, JOHN MONTGOMERY congressman; b. Harrodsburg, Ky., Sept. 4, 1822; attended Marion and Masonic Colls., Philadelphia, Mo.; studied law. Admitted to bar, began practice of law, St. Louis; practiced law, Cal., 1850-55; served as col. 2d Regt., Mo. Volunteer Cavalry, during Civil War, 1861-64; collector internal revenue 3d Dist. Mo., 1866-67; mem. U.S. Ho. of Reps. (Democrat) from Mo., 43d-45th congresses, 1873-79; engaged in agriculture. Died nr. Newark, Mo., Nov. 15, 1891; buried on his farm nr. Newark; reinterred Woodland Cemetery, Quincy, Ill.

GLUECK, BERNARD, psychiatrist; b. Poland, Dec. 10, 1884; M.D., Georgetown U., 1909; studied univs. of Munich and Berlin, 1911; m. Betty J.; children—Bernard, Ruth (Mrs. Addison). Mem. staff Govt. Hosp. for Insane, 1909-16; mental examiner of immigrants, Port of New York, 1913; dir. psychiatric clinic, Sing Sing Prison, 1915-18; dir. of mental hygiene dept., N.Y. Sch. of Social Work, and Bur. of Child Guidance, 1918-23; mem. faculty U. N.C., Chapel Hill, 1956-64; sr. psychiat. cons. John Umstead Hosp., Butner, N.C., 1956-64. Capt. Medical Corps. U.S. Army. 1918; chief of staff Stony Lodge Foundation, Ossining-on-Hudson. Mem. A.M.A., Am. Psychiatric Assn., Am. Psychopathol. Assn., Am. Psychoanalytic Assn., N.Y. Soc. Psychopathology and Psychotherapy (ex-pres.). Author: Studies in Forensic Psychiatry, 1916. Translator: (with John E. Lind) Neurotic Constitution (by Alfred Adler), 1917; Introduction to a Psychoanalytic Psychiatry (by Paul Schilder), 1927; (with Bertram D. Lewin) Psychoanalysis of the Total Personality (by Franz Alexander), 1930. Lecturer New School for Social Research. Home: Butner NC Died Oct. 5, 1972; buried Arlington Nat. Cemetery.

GLUHAREFF, MICHAEL E. aero engr., designer; b. St. Petersburg, Russia, Sept. 17, 1892; s. Eugene and Iraida (Borisoff) G.; grad. (gen. scis.) Imperial Coll. Commerce, 1910, (mech. engring.) Poly. Inst. Tech., 1914, (mil. engr.) Imperial Mil. Engring, Coll., 1916, (mil. pilot) Mil. Aviation Sch., 1917; m. Antonina Gretzkoff, Apr. 21, 1915; children - Eugene, Alexander; m. 2d Anastasia Gartwig, Oct. 1947. Came to U.S., 1924, naturalized, 1937. Began as designer, builder and test pilot sailplanes of original types, Finland, 1920-24; designer 1st non-spinnable airplane, U.S., 1925; chief engr., Sikorsky Aviation Corp., 1925-35, in charge all models in regard to gen. structural aerodynamic and hydrodynamic design, developed wings known as G.S. airfoils with which all types of Sikorsky land planes, amphibions and flying boats were equipped; chief design, Vought - Sikorsky Aircraft div. United Aircraft Corp., 1935-42, charge complete design of large flying boats which made 1st non-stop Pacific and Atlantic flights with Am. mail and passengers, inauguration of Pan-American Airways; also in charge design 1st successful helicopter, which set new world's records, 1942; chief engr. Sikorsky Aircraft Div. United Aircraft Corp., in charge design research and development, Sikorsky Helicopters, 1943-57, engring. mgr. Sikorsky Aircraft div., 1957-60, engineering consultant to the division, 1960 - . Mem. tech. adv. panel Office Asst. sec. Def., 1954-58; mem. Army scientific advisory panel, 1959-61. Awarded Certificate of Merit, American Helicopter Soc., 1948, Dr. Alex Klemin award, 1954; Chrysler Award, as outstanding world designer, 1954; Elmer A. Sperry award for transportation, 1964. Fellow Am. Inst. Aeros. and Astronautics, Soc. Automotive Engrs. (hon.), Am. Helicopter Soc. (hon.); mem. Soaring Soc. Am. Holds patent of first Dartshaped airplane. Home: Hoyden Hill Rd., Fairfield, Conn. Office: N. Main St., Stratford, Conn. Died Sept. 4, 1967; buried St. Joseph's Cemetery, Stratford, Conn.

GLYNN, JAMES naval officer; b. Phila., June 28, 1801; s. James Anthony Glynn; m. Anne Stoddard. Entered gunboat service at New Orleans, 1810; served as acting midshipman in ships General Pike and Superior, Lake Ontario, 1815; apptd. midshipman, 1815; promoted lt., 1825, comdr., 1841; commanded sloop Preble on Cal. coast, 1848; transferred to East India Squadron, 1848, took part in rescue of several Am. seamen held captive by Japanese; credited by Commodore Geisinger with 1st successful negotiation with Japan; returned to U.S., expressed view that relations could be opened with Japanese govt., 1851, published article stating this view, 1851; put on reserve list, 1855, restored and given back pay, 1858; served in ship Macedonian against Confederate raider, 1862; ret. as capt. Died New Haven, Conn., May 13, 1871.

GOBIN, JOHN PETER SHINDEL lawyer; b. Sunbury, Pa., Jan. 26, 1837; s. Samuel S. and Susan (Shindel) G.; acad. edn.; LL.D., Susquehanna U.; m. Annie M. Howe, 1866. Served in Union Army, attaining rank of bvt. brig. gen.; practiced law at Lebanon, Pa.; dir. in various industrial instns. Mem. Pa. Senate, 1884-98; comdr. a div. of Pa. N.G.; served as brig. gen. U.S.V. in war with Spain; elected lt. gov. of Pa., 1898; comd. Pa. N.G. during coal strike, 1902. Comd.-in-chief G.A.R., 1897-98; past grand master Knights Templar U.S. Address: Lebanon, Pa. Died 1910.

GODCHARLES, FREDERIC ANTES librarian, historian; b. Northumberland, Pa., June 3, 1872; s. Charles Aiken and Elizabeth (Burkenbine) G.; E.E., Lafayette Coll., Easton, Pa., 1892; Litt.D. from Susquehanna Univ., 1928; m. Mary Walls Barber, June 15, 1904. Elec. engr., city hall, Phila., Pa., 1893-95; pres. F.A. Godcharles Co., Milton Nail Works, 1895-1914; editor and pub. The Miltonian and Milton Morning Bulletin, 1910-26; dir. Pa. State Library and Museum, 1927-31. Mem. Pa. N.G., 1893-98; served with same, Spanish-Am. War, mem. staff Brig. Gen. J.P.S. Gobin; regimental insp. of rifle practice, rank of capt., 1900-10; capt. ordnance, on staff Maj. Gen. Leonard Wood, World War I. Mem. Pa. Gen. Assembly, 1900; Pa. Senate, 1904, 08; dep. sec. Commonwealth of Pa., 1915-23. Mem. A.L.A., Pa. Federation Hist. Socs. (past pres.), Pa. Hist. Soc., Northumberland County Hist. Soc. (pres.), Pa. Hist. Assn. (dir.), Eastern States Archeol. Fedn. (expres.), Pa. Soc. Archaeology (past pres., editor), Pa. Folk-Lore Soc. (v.p.), Huguenot Soc., Pa. German Soc. (dir.), Mil. Order Foreign Wars, Sons of Union Vets. of Civil War (past state comdr.), S.A.R., Am. Legion, Newcomen Soc. of Great Britain, Phi Kappa Psi. Republican. Presbyn. Mason (33ff). Clubs: Manufacturers, Rotary (ex-pres.), Acacia (Williamsport); Union League (Phila.); Explorers (New York); Tilghman Island (Md.). Author: Freemasonry in Northumberland and Snyder Counties, 1911; Daily Stories of Pennsylvania, 1924 and 1927; Pennsylvanias Past and Present, 1926; also Daily Stories of New York. Editor Ency. of Pennsylvania Biographies; Pennsylvania, Political, Governmental, Military and Civil; Chronicles of Central Pennsylvania, also writer of syndicate hist. articles. Expert marksman. Home: Milton, Pa. Died Dec. 30, 1944.

GODDARD, CALVIN HOOKER army officer, military historian, criminologist; born Baltimore, October 30, 1891; s. Capt. Henry P. and Eliz4 W. (Acheson) G.; A.B., cum laude, Johns Hopkins, 1911, M.D., 1915; honor grad. Army Med. Sch., Washington, 1917; m. Eliza Cunningham Harrison, Aug. 3, 1915; children-Eliza Cunningham (Mrs. Harry Bacas), Mary Woodbridge (Mrs. Henry Zon). Commissioned first lieutenant, Medical Corps, United States Army, Feb. 18, 1917; promoted through grades to maj., Mar. 28, 1918; served in U.S., France, Germany and Poland; resigned June 2, 1920; assistant director (business administrn.) Johns Hopkins Hospital, 1921-24; administrative dir. Cornell Clinic, New York, 1924-25; developed the science of identifying fired bullets and empty cartridge cases, now known as forensic ballistics, N.Y., 1925-29; managing director Scientific Crime Detection Lab, Northwestern Univ., 1929-33; dir. research, 1933-34, prof. police science, law faculty, 1930-34. Awarded fellowship by Guggenheim Foundation, 1935, to write book on arms identification; fellowship from Oberlaender Trust (Phila.), 1936, to permit studies in Europe. Mem. bd. dirs. Soc. American Military Engrs., 1940-42; collaborator (ordnance), National Park Service, U.S. Dept. Interior, since 1940; member board editors and advisors Encyclopedia Britannica since 1940. Recalled to active service as lt. col., U.S. Army, and assigned to hist. section Army War Coll., 1941-42; chief, hist. sect. Ordnance Dept., 1942-45; mem. hist. div., War Dept. Spl. Staff, 1945-47; mem. hist. sect. G/2 Gen. Hdqrs., Far East Command, Tokyo, Japan, to 1948, Chief of Criminal Investigation Lab., Far East Command, Tokyo, 1948-51; chief Hist. Unit, Army Med. Service, since 1951; cons. on mil. history to surgeon gen., U.S. Army; promoted to col., 1950. Awarded Legion of Merit, 1951; Order of the Crown of Italy, 1946. Mem. Soc. Am. Mil. Engrs., Assn. Mil. Surgs., Army Ord. Assn., Am. Military Inst., Am. Acad. Forensic Scis., Internat. Soc. for Detection of Deception, Internat. Assn. for Identification, Am. Hist. Assn., Soc. War 1812 (N.Y.), Veteran Corps of Arty. (N.Y.), Order Indian Wars, French Soc. for Advancement of Science, Phi Kappa Psi, and Pi Gamma Mu. Episcopalian. Club: Cosmos (Washington). Contbr. articles on ordnance and munitions, Ency. Brit., Ency. Brit. Year Book, Junior Ency. etc. Home: 3533 Quebec St. N.W., Washington 16. Died Feb. 22, 1955; buried St. Peters Episcopal Church, New Kent County, Va.

GODDARD, ROBERT HALE IVES mfr.; b. Providence, R.I., Sept. 21, 1837; s. William Giles and Charlotte (Ives) G.; A.M., Brown U., 1858; m. Rebekah B. Grosbeck. Served pvt. 1st R.I. Inf., May 1-Aug. 2, 1861; lt. and vol. a.-d.-c. to Gen. Burnside, Sept. 23, 1862; capt. a.-d.-c. vols., Mar. 11, 1863; bvtd. maj. vols., Aug. 1, 1864, for gallant and meritorious services during campaign in E. Tenn. and at siege of Knoxville; lt. col. vols., Apr. 2, 1865, for same at Ft. Steedman and in assault before Ft. Sedgwick, Va.; resigned July 3, 1865. Mem. firms Goddard Bros., and Brown & Ives, cotton mfrs.; pres. Lonsdale Co.; treas. Berkeley Co., and Hope Co.; dir. R.I. Hospital Trust Co. Rep. presdl. elector, 1896; mem. R.I. Senate, 1897-98; mem. State Bd. Charities and Correction; commr. Providence parks; nominated for U.S. senator by Dem. State Conv., 1907. Mem. bd. fellows, Brown U., 1893—. Home: Providence, R.I. Died Apr. 22, 1916.

GODDARD, WILLIAM banker, mcht.; b. Warwick, R.I., Dec. 25, 1825; s. William Giles and Charlotte (Ives) G.; grad. Brown U., 1846; m. Mary Edith Jenckes, Feb. 19, 1867. After graduation studied law; traveled extensively; engaged in mercantile and mfg. business; mem. Providence Common Council, 1852-55; was mem. 1st light inf.; maj. 1st regt. R.I. detached militia; commissioned col. vols. for gallantry at battle of Bull Run, a.d.c. on Gen. Burside's staff before Fredericksburg, Dec. 11, 1862. Head of firm of Brown & Ives, mchts., founded in 18th century; mem. firm of Goddard Bors., and pres. Providence Nat. Bank. Trustee Bworn U., 1857—, chancellor, 1888—. Home: Providence, and Warwick, R.I. Died 1907.

GODFREY, ALFRED LAURANCE, lawyer; b. Lima, Wis., Jan. 8, 1888; s. Thomas G. and Mary (Dickson) G.; A.B., U. of Wis., 1914; J.D., 1919; m. Helen Humphrey, Apr. 24, 1918; children—Thomas Grant, Richard Laurance. Prin. Westby (Wis.) High Sch., 1910-12, Stevens Point High Sch., 1914-15; admitted to Wis. bar, 1919, engaging in practice of law at Milwaukee, at Elkhorn, 1921-70; on legal staff Soo Line Ry., 1919-21; dir. and gen. counsel State Long Distance Telephone Co.; dist. atty., Walworth County, Wis., 1922-26; chmn. Walworth County Rep. Com., 1926-29; chmn. Rep. Congressional Com., 1st Dist. of Wis., 1931; sec. State Rep. Com. of Wis., 1932-34. Commd. 1st lt. 1917, resigned, 1919; later commd. capt. and maj., Reserve Corps. Chmn. Central Walworth Co. chpt. Am. Red Cross; mem. bd. govs. Wis. State Bar, 1948-51, pres. 1951-52. Fellow American Bar Found.; mem. American (house of delegates 1952-60, Wis. (past president), Walworth County (pres.) bar assns., Phi Delta Phi, Am. Legion. Republican. Conglist. Mason. Club: Kiwanis, Big Foot Country. Home: Elkhorn WI Died Apr. 11, 1970.

GODFREY, EDWARD SETTLE army officer; b. Kalida, O., Oct. 9, 1843; s. Dr. Charles Moore and Mary (Chambers) G.; ed. public schs., in Ohio, and Vermilion Inst.; pvt. Co. D, 21st Ohio Inf., Apr. 12, 1861; grad. U.S. Mil. Acad., 1867; m. Mary Pocock, June 15, 1869; children- Guy C. M., Edward S., Mary, David Ewing; m. 2d, Ida D. Emley, Oct. 6, 1892. Second lt. 7th Cav., June 17, 1867; promoted through grades to brig. gen., Jan. 17, 1907. Bvtd. maj., Feb. 17, 1890, and awarded Congressional Medal of Honor for "most distinguished gallantry" at Bear Paw Mts., against Chief Joseph and Nez Percé Indians, Sept. 30, 1877. In all the campaigns and Indian fights of his regiment, under General Custer, until Custer's death; originated "Cossack" and "Rough Riding" for Army; mem. bd. of officers that devised drill regulations for inf., cav. and arty. for the Army; served in Cuba and P.I.; retired by operation of law, Oct. 9, 1907. Former sr. vice commander-in-chief Military Order Loyal Legion U.S. (mem. Council-in-Chief). Mason (32ff, K.T.). Home: Cookstown, N.J. Died Apr. 1, 1932.

GODFREY, STUART C. army officer; b. Milford, Mass., Jan. 1, 1886; s. Charles Boker and Cora Anna (Chapin) G.; ed. Phillips Exeter Acad., 1902-04; student Mass. Inst. of Tech., 1904-05; B.S., U.S. Mil. Acad., 1909; honor grad. Command and Gen. Staff Sch., 1926; grad. Army War Coll., 1933; m. Dorothy Severeance Rich, Sept. 2, 1915; children-Dorothy Hope (Mrs. Christopher McGrath), Charles Stuart, Pearce. Commd. 2d lt., Engr. Corps, U.S. Army, June 15, 1909, and advanced through the grades to brig. gen., Mar. 1942, Air Forces. Decorated Legion of Merit, Air Medal (1944); D.S.M. of Soc. Am. Mil. Engrs.; French Order of Palms. Awarded Silver Beaver, Boy Scouts of America. Mem. Am. Soc. C.E., Soc. of Am.. Mil. Engrs. Bd. of Visitors, Civil Engring. and Mil. Science, Mass. Inst. of Tech. Club: Army and Navy (Washington). Home: 3619 O St. N.W., Washington, D.C. Died Oct. 9, 1945.

GODWIN, EDWARD ALLISON army officer; b. Kingwood, W.Va., May 18, 1850; s. Joseph Madison and Elizabeth (Royse) G.; grad. U.S. Mil. Acad., 1870; m. Elizabeth Jackson Clark, June 30, 1870. Pvt. Co. A., 1st W.Va., Cav., Feb. 13-July 8, 1865; apptd. cadet at West Point, from 2d Dist. W.Va., Oct. 17, 1865; 2d lt. 8th Cav., June 15, 1870; 1st lt., Oct. 3, 1876; capt., July 5, 1886; col. 7th U.S. Vol. Inf., May 24, 1898; hon. mustered out Feb. 28, 1899, maj. 7th Cav., July 1, 1899; col. 40th U.S. Vol. Inf., Aug. 17, 1899; hon. mustered out June 24, 1901; transferred to 10th Cav., Oct. 1, 1902; lt. col. 9th Cav., Jan. 16, 1903; col. 14th cav., June 22, 1905; brig. gen. and retired, Nov. 15, 1908, after more than 43 yrs. service. Died July 13, 1923.

GOELET, ROBERT bus. exec.; b. N.Y.C., Jan. 9, 1880; s. Ogden and Mary R. (Wilson) G.; M.A. Harvard, 1903; LL.B., N.Y. Law Sch., 1905; m. Elsie Whelen, June 14, 1904; children - Ogden, Peter; m. 2d, Fernanda Rocchi Riabouchinsky, Oct. 22, 1919; 1 son, Robert; m. 3d, Roberta Willard, Sept. 24, 1925; 1 dau., Mary Eleanor (Mrs. James Eliot Cross). Dir. Chem. Bank N.Y. Trust Co. formerly Chem. and Corn Exchange Bank; dir. City Investing Co., Lopert Films, Inc. Dir. Fifth Av. & Sixty-Sixth St. Corp. Served as capt. Inf., World War I, 77th, 82d Divs. in France, 1918-19, participated in Oise-Aisne and Meuse-Argonne offensives. Mem. St. Nicholas Soc., 82d Div. Assn. Episcopalian. Mason. Clubs: University, Knickerbocker, Racquet and Tennis, Links, Southside Sportsmen's of Long Island, Harvard. Home: 4 E. 66 St., N.Y.C. 21. Office: 608 Fifth Av. N.Y.C. 20. Died Feb. 1966.

GOERTNER, FRANCIS B(ARNES) govt. lawyer; b. Bklyn., Aug. 9, 1893; s. Francis Joseph and Rosamond (Landau) G.; A.B., Harvard, 1915; LL.B., Columbia, 1918; m. Carmen M. Philippi, July 3, 1924; children - John Francis, Thomas Grenville. Admitted to N.Y. State bar, and practiced in N.Y.C., specializing in admiralty law, 1920-33; govt. atty. since 1933, successively with A.A.A., R.F.C.; with U.S. Maritime Commn. since 1937, asst. gen. counsel, 1941-48, gen. counsel since 1948. Counsel Maritime War Emergency Bd. since 1942, acting sec., 1946-49, permanent sec. since 1949; asso. firm Coles & Goertner, Washington, 1951-60, ret., 1960. Democrat. Episcopalian. Club: National Press. Died Aug. 15, 1964.

GOETHALS, GEORGE WASHINGTON army engr.; b. Brooklyn, June 29, 1858; student Coll. City of New York, 1873-76; grad. U.S. Mil. Acad., 1880; LL.D., U. of Pa., 1913, Princeton U., 1915. Apptd. 2d lt. engrs., June 12, 1880; 1st lt., June 15, 1882; capt., Dec. 14, 1891; lt. col. chief engr. vols., May 9, 1898; hon. discharged from vol. service, Dec. 31, 1898; maj. engr. corps, Feb. 7, 1900; grad. Army War Coll., 1905; lt. col. engrs., Mar. 2, 1907; col., Dec. 3, 1909; major general, March 4, 1915; retired, Nov. 15, 1916. Instr. in civil and mil. engring., U.S. Mil. Acad., several yrs. until 1888; in charge of Muscle Shoals Canal constrn., on Tenn. River; chief of engrs. during Spanish-Am. War; mem. Bd. of Fortifications (coast and harbor defense); chief engr. Panama Canal, Feb. 26, 1907-14; 1st civil gov. Panama Canal Zone, 1914-16; apptd. state engr., N.J., 1917; apptd. chief Div. of Storage and Traffic of General Staff, Feb. 1918, and chief of Div. of Purchase, Storage and Traffic, Apr. 1918; was also mem. War Industries Bd.; relieved from active duty at own request, Mar. 1919. Received thanks of Congress, Mar. 4, 1915, for "distinguished service in constructing Panama Canal"; awarded D.S.M., 1918, "for especially meritorious and conspicuous service"in reorganizing Q.-M. Dept.; Comdr. Legion of Honor (France). 1919; medals Nat. Geog. Soc., Civic Forum and Nat. Inst. Social Sciences. Address: New York, N.Y. Died Jan. 21, 1928

GOETZ, NORMAN S., lawyer; b. New York, N.Y., Mar. 7, 1887; s. Samuel and Julia (Marx) G.; A.B. Columbia U., 1906, LL.B., 1909; m. Mildred Blout, Feb. 12, 1925 (dec. 1953); m. 2d, Beatrice J. Lane. Jan. 12, 1956. Law practice, partner of Leventritt, Riegelman, Carns & Goetz 1912-24; partner Proskauer, Rose, Goetz & Mendelsohn and predecessor firms, from 1925. Dir. Greater N.Y. Fund, 1942-64, v.p., 1945-48, pres., 1956-59, chmn. bd., 1950-51, 55-56; pres. Fedn. Jewish Philanthropies N.Y., 1945-48, chmn. bd., 1961-63, trustee-at-large, 1940-48, hon. trustee from 1948, chmn. lawyers div., 1937-38, chmn. citywide campaign, 1942-43, chmn. com. communal planning, 1951-57; former chmn. legacy com.; dir. Hosp. Council Greater N.Y., 1944-64, pres., 1948-55; trustee State U. N.Y., 1948-58, chmn. com. on med. edn., 1952-57; dir. United Hosp. Fund, 1948-57, mem.-at-large, 1961-64; director of New York Adult Edn. Council, 1941-65, Hillside Hosp., 1941-48; former dir. Welfare Council City N.Y., Council Jewish Fedn. and Welfare Funds; former mem. exec., adminstrv. coms. Am. Jewish Com. Served from pvt. to capt., non-flying AS, 1917-19. Mem. Assn. Bar City of N.Y. (v.p., 1950-52, exec. com. 1943-47), N.Y. County Lawyers Assn. (past chmn. bankruptcy com.). Internat., Am., N.Y. bar assns. Democrat. Jewish religion. Club: Ocean Beach. Home: New York City NY Died Mar. 5, 1972.

GOFF, NATHAN senator; b. Clarksburg, W.Va., Feb. 9, 1843; s. Nathan G.; ed. Northwestern (Va.) Acad., Georgetown Coll., and U. City of New York; (LL.D., Georgetown, 1889;) m. Catherine Penny, Aug. 28, 1919. Served in Union Army, lt. to maj., 1861-65; admitted to bar, 1866; mem. W.Va., 1868-81; Rep. candidate for Congress, 1870, 1874, for gov., 1876; Sec. of the Navy in cabinet of President Hayes, 1881; again U.S. dist. atty., 1881-82; mem. 48th to 50th Congresses (1883-89); elected gov. W.Va., 1888, on the face of returns by plurality of 130 votes, but election was contested by the Dem. candidate, who was seated by a majority vote of the legislature; U.S. circuit judge, 4th Circuit, 1892-1911; judge U.S. Circuit Ct. of Appeals, Jan. 1912-13; U.S. senator, 1913-19. Address: Clarksburg, W.Va. Died Apr. 24, 1920.

GOFORTH, WILLIAM physician; b. N.Y.C., 1766; s. Judge William and Catharine (Meeks) G.; studied medicine under Drs. Joseph Young and Charles McKnight, N.Y.C.; m. Miss Wood, circa 1790. Went to Ky., 1788, to Cincinnati, 1800; probably 1st to vaccinate West of Alleghanies; made 1st vaccinations in N.W. Territory, 1801; commd. surgeon-gen. 1st Div., Ohio Militia, 1804; at Big Bone Lick (Ky.) dug up collection of prehistoric fossils of interest to natural science, 1803; signed 1st med. diploma given in N.W. Ty. (given Daniel Drake), 1805; considered leading physician of Cincinnati, 1800-07; went to New Orleans as parish judge, 1807; mem. La. Constl. Conv.; served as surgeon in a volunteer regt. during Brit. attack on New Orleans. Died Cincinnati, May 12, 1817.

GOGGIN, WILLIAM LEFTWICH congressman, lawyer; b. nr. Bunker Hill, Va., May 31, 1807; grad. Tucker's Law Sch., Winchester, Va. Admitted to bar, 1828, began practice of law, Liberty (now Bedford), Va.; also engaged in agriculture; mem. Va. Ho. of Dels., 1836-37; mem. U.S. Ho. of Reps. (Whig) from Va., 26th-27th, (filled vacancy) 28th, 30th congresses, 1839-43, Apr. 25, 1844-45, 47-49; unsuccessful Whig candidate for gov. Va., 1859; del. Va. Constl. Conv., 1861; served as capt. Home Guards, Confederate Army, during Civil War. Died on his estate nr. Liberty, Jan. 3, 1870; buried Goggin Cemetery on family estate nr. Bunker Hill.

GOING, CHARLES BUXTON, writer; b. Westchester, N.Y., Apr. 5, 1863; s. Charles Henry and Eliza (Buxton) G.; Ph.B., Columbia, 1882, hon. M.Sc., 1910; m. Mary Evelyn Thompson, June 1, 1887 (died 1896); m. 2d, Marie Overton Corbin, Dec. 18, 1912 (died 1925); m. 3d, Mathilde Marie Sylvie Roux, Feb. 14, 1929. Asso. editor, New York and London, 1896-98, mng. editor, 1898-1912, editor and v.p., 1912-15, Engineering Magazine; editor Works Management Library, 1915-16 (retired); spl. lecturer, Columbia and Harvard, 1909-15; a leader in organizing Soc. Indsl. Engrs., continuing as chmn. until permanent Officers were elected, 1917. Commd. maj., Ordnance Dept., U.S.R., and on spl. duty, Washington, 1917; spl. asst. to chief ordnance officer, A.E.F., 1918; recommended for lieut. col.; disch., Apr. 1919. Cited for "specially conspicuous and meritorious service" in Ordnance Dept., A.E.F. Mem. Poetry Soc. America; corr. mem. Canadian Mining Inst. Auth: Summer-Fallow, 1892; (with Marie Overton Corbin) Urchins of the Sea, 1900, and Urchins at the Pole, 1901; Star-Glow and Song, 1909; Methods of the Santa Fe, 1909; Principles of Industrial Engineering, 1911; David Wilmot, Free-Soiler, 1924; Folklore and Fairy Plays, 1927; Precarious Paradise and other Plays, 1904; On Provencial Roads, 1936 (serial); Adventures in Statecraft, 1940 (serial). Author many songs set to music. Contbr. to mags. Home: Lei Tres Mario, Cassels-sur-Mer, B. du Rh. France

GOLAY, JOHN FORD, univ. dean; b. Warrensburg, Mo., July 29, 1917; s. Ned and Martha Aurora (Ford) G.; B.A., U. So. Cal., 1938; B.A. (Rhodes scholar), Oxford U., 1940, M.A., 1941, D.Phil., 1955; m. Leland Theodora Bailey, Mar. 7, 1950; 1 son, John Edward. Asst. to Lord Beveridge, various projects including revision Brit. social ins. system, war-time manpower survey, 1940-42; tchr. polit. sci. Pomona Coll., Claremont, Cal., 1946-48; dep. Am. sec. Allied Secretariat to Allied Mil. Govs. and High Commrs., Berlin and Bonn, Germany, 1948-52, chief Am. sect. Allied Gen. Secretariat, also sec.-gen. Allied High Commn., Bonn; exec. sec. Office U.S. High Commr. for Germany, Bonn, 1952-53; dean faculties, prof. history Roosevelt U., Chgo., 1956-60; provost, grad. dean, prof. history W.Va. U., 1961-69. Served as flight lt., Brit. R.A.F., 1942-46; air navigator. Mem. Am. Hist. Assn., Phi Beta Kappa. Author: The Founding of the Federal Republic of Germany, 1958; also textbook. Contbr. The New Republic, 1953-69. Home: Morgantown WV Died Jan. 27, 1969.

GOLDEN, CADWALLADER DAVID lawyer, mayor N.Y. C.; b. Spring Hill, L.I., N.Y., Apr. 4, 1769; s. David and Ann (Willett) C.; m. Maria Provost, 1793. Admitted to N.Y. bar, 1791; dist. atty. N.Y.C., 1798, 1810; served as col. in War of 1812; commd. maj. gen. N.Y. Militia; mayor N.Y.C., 1818-20; mem. U.S. Ho. of Reps. from N.Y., 17th Congress, 1821-23; mem. N.Y. State Senate, 1825-27. Author: Life of Robert Fulton, 1817; Vindication of the Steamboat Rights Granted by the State of New York, 1819; Memoir of the Celebration of the Completion of the New York Canals, 1825. Died Jersey City, N.J., Feb. 7, 1834.

GOLDEN, JOHN playwright, producer of plays; b. N.Y. City, June 27, 1874; s. Joel and Amelia (Tyreler) G.; family moved to Wauscon, O., 1875; ed. pub. and night schs., and New York Univ. Law Sch.; Dr. of Pub. Service, Oglethorpe Univ. Super at Harrigan Theatre, and actor in stock, repertoire and Shakespeare; comic journalist and rhymester, then studied music under Damrosch; wrote many songs (Poor Butterfly, etc.), also many short plays and lyrics; comp. the music for over a dozen mus. com. Major O.R.C., U.S. Army; maj. N.Y. Police Reserves. Mem. Am. Soc. Composers. Authors and Publishers, Moose. Clubs: New York, Lambs (shepherd), Lotos, Flushing Country, Belleclaire Golf, Lakeville Golf, Bays Yacht Club, Atlantic Yacht; Green Room (London); Coldstream Golf, Sands Point Country, Artists and Writers Club. Author or producer (plays); Turn to the Right; Lightnin' (1,291 consecutive performances, New York); Three Wise Fools; Thunder; Dear Me; The First Year; The Wheel; Spite Corner; The Seventh Heaven; Chicken Feed; The Serpent's Tooth; The Streak; The Wisdom Tooth; 2 Girls Wanted; Four Walls; Eva the 5th; Night Hostess; Let Us Be Gay; Salt Water; When in Rome-; That's Gratitude; As Husbands Go; Riddle Me This; When Ladies Meet; The Bishop Misbehaves; A Touch of Brimstone; Susan and God; Skylark; Claudia; Theatre; Counselor at Law, Three's a Family; A Place of Our Own; Made in Heaven; short plays: River of Souls; The Clock Shop. Musical comedies: The Little Colonel; Miss Print; The Hoyden; Forward March; Over the River; The Candy Shop. Shows at the Hippodrome: Hip Hip Horray, 1915-16; The Big Show, 1916-17; Cheer Up, 1917-18; Everything, 1918-19. Produced Revival of They Knew What They Wanted, 1949; The Male Animal, 1952. Member of the bd. dirs. Am. Theatre Wing War Service and N.Y.C. Center of Music and Drama; chmn. entertainment div. N.Y. Defense Recreation Com.; dir. U.S.O. camp shows; trustee United Seaman's Service; dir. Percy Williams Home, Actor's Fund Queensboro Soc. Prevention Cruelty to Children; sponsored playwriting contest for U.S. soldiers, sailors and airmen and prize play contest for Navy; originated plan for the entertainment of soldiers; twice produced Red Cross at War, for Red Cross War Fund. Received citation from War and Navy Depts., United China Relief, Finnish Relief; Army Dept. highest civilian decoration for distinguished service. N.Y.C. chmn. for observance of UN Day, 1950. Home: Bayside. L.I. Office; St. James Theatre Bldg., 246 W. 44th St., N.Y.C. Died June 17, 1955.

GOLDMAN, EDWARD ALPHONSE naturalist; b. Mt. Carroll, Ill., July 7, 1873; s. Jacob Henry and Laura Carrie (Nicodemus) G.; ed. pub. schs. and under pvt. tutors; m. Emma May Chase, June 23, 1902; children-Nelson Edward, Orville Merriam, Luther Chase. With U.S. Biol. Survey since 1892; much of time, 1892-1906, in biol. investigations in Mexico; in biol. survey of Panama, 1911-12, of Ariz., 1913-17; in charge div. of biological investigations, 1919-25; in charge div. of game and bird reservations, 1925-28; senior biologist since 1928. Fellow A.A.A.S.; mem. Am. Ornithologists' Union, Am. Soc. of Washington (pres. 1927-29), Am. Forestry Assn., Cooper Ornith. Club of Calif., Washington Biologists' Field Club. Commd. major, Sanitary Corps N.A., 1918, and with A.E.F. in France; maj. Sanitary Officers' Res. Corps, 1921-37, now retired. Clubs: cosmos (Washington), Explorers (New York). Author: Revision of Wood Rats of Genus Neotoma, 1910; Revision of Spiny Pocket Mice (Heteromys and Liomys), 1911; Plant Records of an Expedition to Lower California. 1916; Rice Rats of North America (Oryzomys), 1918; Mammals of Panama, 1920; The Wolves of North America (with Stanley P. Young); also numerous shorter papers, mainly on mammals and birds and conservation of wild life. Home: 2702 17th St. N.E. Office: U.S. National Museum, Washington, D.C. Deceased.

GOLDMAN, EDWIN FRANKS comdr., composer; b. Louisville, Ky., Jan. 1, 1878; s. David and Selma (Franko) G.; ed. pub. schs., N.Y. City; student Nat. Conservatory of Music, N.Y. City; studied cornet under Jules Levy and Carl Sohst; Mus.D. (hon.), Phillips University, 1934, Boston University, 1936, DePauw University, 1953; married Adelaide Malbrunn, Oct. 8, 1908; children-Richard Franko, Louise Elizabeth. Cornetist, Met. Opera House orchestra, 1895-1905; teacher, band instruments, 1905-18; was mem. faculty, Columbia, 1919-26; organizer, 1911, since comdr. Goldman Band; mgr. and condr. Goldman Band Free Summer Concerts (Columbia campus, later in Central Park, also on campus New York U.) since 1918; concerts in Prospect Park, Brooklyn, since 1934; Decorated Officier de l'Instruction Publique, for services in cause of French music, 1929; Cavaliere of Oroer of Crown of Italy, 1933; Order of White Lion (Czechoslovakia), 1936; gold medal from City of N.Y., 1923: 1st official gold medal, American Bandmasters Assn., 1932; medal Eastern States Exposition, 1933; Citizenship Medal from the Vets. of Fgn. Wars, 1949; Outstanding Musician medal, National Association of American Conductors and Composers, 1950; Lincoln Award for outstanding citizen of country, 1951; Ky. Col.; also awards and throughout the U.S. Organizer and 1st pres. Am. Bandmasters' Assn., elected hon. life pres., 1933. Member American Society of Composers, Authors and Publishers; honorary mem. Kappa Kappa Psi, Alpha Mu Pi, Phi Alpha Mu, Toronto (Can.) Mus.

Protective Assn., Newark (N.J.) Musician's Union, New Haven (Conn.) Musicians' Union, Pa. Bandmasters' Assn., Assn. of Mus. Instrument Dealers of New York; hon. mus. counsellor 4H Clubs of U.S., Boy Scouts of America. Made chief of Pawnee Indians, title Chief Bugle, 1935; hon. mem. Ottawa and London, Ont. Musicians Unions. Club: The Bohemians. Composer over 110 marches and numerous other compositions for band, also a large number of solos for various wind instruments, etc. Visited Philippines and Japan for USO, Oct. 1945; made report on Am. Army bands to Pres. Truman, General Eisenhower, and Secretary of War Patterson. Author of The Band Guide and Aid to Leaders, 1916; Band Betterment, 1934; The Goldman Band System for Developing Tone, Intonation and Phrasing, 1935. A pioneer in presentation of symphony music by all-wind band. Apptd. maj., city Patrol Corps, N.Y. City, 1942. Home: 1 University Pl., N.Y.C. Died Feb. 21, 1956.

GOLDSBOROUGH, LAIRD S(HIELDS) editor; b. La Fayette, Ind., Mar. 6, 1902; s. Winder Elwell and Charlotte Poole (Wallace) G.; A.B., Yale, 1924; fellow Royal Univ. of Norway; m. Forence Maconaughy in Goldsborough, Eng., June 17, 1919. Asso. editor Fortune mag., 1929-34; foreign affairs editor of Time mag., 1925-40; became spl. asst. to chmn. bd. Time, Inc., 1941. Became co-ordinating officer in New York for Counter Espionage, U.S. Army Office of Strategic Services, 1943. Clubs: Union Interalliée (Paris); Yale (New York); Elizabethan (New Haven). Home: 1200 Fifth Av. Office: 9 Rockefeller Plaza, N.Y.C. Died Feb. 14, 1950; buried Evergreen Cemetery, Gettysburg, Pa,

GOLDSBOROUGH, LOUIS MALESHERBES naval officer; b. Washington, D.C., Feb. 18, 1805; s. Charles Washington and Catharine (Roberts) G.; m. Elizabeth Wirt, Nov. 11, 1833, 3 children. Commd. midshipman U.S. Navy, 1812, lt., 1825, comdr., 1841, capt., 1855, rear adm., 1862; orginator plan for depot of charts and instruments Washington, in charge, 1830; commanded mounted volunteers in Seminole War, 1833; served in Mexican War; sr. naval mem. commn. which explored Cal. and Ore., 1849-50; supt. Naval Acad., 1853-57; commanded Brazil Squadron, 1859-61, Atlantic Blockading Squadron, 1861, N. Atlantic Blockading Squadron, 1861; cooperated with Gen. Burnside in capture of Roanoke Island, 1862; adminstrv. duties, Washington until 1865; in charge of European Squadron, 1865. Died Washington, Feb. 20, 1877.

GOLDSBOROUGH, WORTHINGTON naval officer; b. Cambridge, Md., Oct. 9, 1834. Apptd. acting asst. p.m. in vol. navy, Sept. 30, 1862; apptd. asst. p.m. in regular service, July 2, 1864; promoted p.m., May 4, 1866; pay instp., Nov. 24, 1891; retired, Oct. 9, 1896; advanced one grade and promoted pay dir. retired, with rank of capt., for service during Civil War, on the Southfield and St. Lawrence, 1862-65; Shamrock, 1866-68; Naval Acad., 1868-71; Omaha, 1872-75; accounts of vessels at Naval Acad., 1876; coast survey, 1876-80; Brooklyn, 1881-84; Navy Yard, League Island, 1885-88; navy pay office, San Francisco, 1888-90; San Francisco, 1891-92; San Francisco, fleet p.m. Pacific sta., 1892-93; Naval Acad., 1893-96; during the Spanish War was on duty at Navy Yard, Norfolk, 1898; Naval Acad., 1901-03. Home: Cambridge, Md. Died Apr. 23, 1918.

GOLDSMITH, ALAN GUSTAVUS corp. exec.; b. Milw., July 25, 1892; s. Bernard and Alpha (Smith) G.; ed. Hohenzollern Sch., Berlin; Kenyon Coll., 1911; m. Mary Boyd, Oct. 27, 1917 (dec. 1932); 1 son, John Alan; m. 2d, Josephine Bolinger, Feb. 10, 1934. Began with Am. Rolling Mill Co., 1911-17; With Supreme Econ. Council, Peace Conf. and Am. Relief Adminstrn., Central Europe and Balkans, 1919-20; chief European div. Dept. Commerce, 1920-25; lectr. Georgetown U. Sch. Fgn. Service, 1920-25; tech. expert to Dawes Com., 1923-24; sec. Mead Investment Co., 1925; treas. and sec. Mead Paperhood Corp., 1925-30; sec. Mead Corp., 1930-37, now v.p.; dir. Mead Board Sales, Inc., Mead Investment Co. Trial justice and probate judge, Killingworth, Conn. Served from lt. to lt. col. U.S. Army, World War I. Mem. Nat. Paperhood Assn. (dir.), Phi Beta Kappa, Delta Tau Delta, Delta Phi Epsilon. Mason (32ff, Shriner), Elk. Clubs: Army and Navy, Cosmos (Washington); Canadian (N.Y.C.); Tavern (Chgo.). Author: Economic Problems of Western Europe, 1925. Home: The Old Ely House, Killingworth, Conn. 06417. Deep River, Conn. Office: Dayton, O. Died Mar. 30, 1961.

GOLDSMITH, MIDDLETON surgeon; b. Port Tobacco, Md., Aug. 5, 1818; s. Dr. Alban and Talia Ferro (Middleton) Smith; attended Hanover (Ind.) Coll.; grad. Coll. Physicians and Surgeons, N.Y.C., 1840; m. Frances Swift, June 1843, 2 daus. Introduced (with his father) the practice of lithority (method of crushing bladder stones) in Am. A founder 1st Alumni Assn. Coll. Physicians and Surgeons, N.Y. Path. Soc., 1844; prof. surgery Castleton (Vt.) Med. Coll., 1844-45; pres. Vt. Med. Soc., 1851; prof. surgery Ky. Sch. Medicine, Louisvele, 1856; brigade surgeon Army of Cumberland; med. dir. U.S. Army under Gen. Buell at Battle of Shiloh; insp. hosps. under Gen. Grant at Battle Corinth; surgeon gen. Ky. and Dept. of Ohio mil. hosps.; in charge of Gen. Army Hosp., Jeffersonville, Ind.; wrote pamphlet A Report on Hospital Gangrene, Erysipelas, and Pyaemin as Observed in the Departments of the Ohio and the Cumberland: With Cases Appended, 1863; pioneer in antiseptic surgery; established Rutland (Vt.) Free Dispensary; spl. commr. to investigate state insane asylum, Vt., which resulted in its improvement and reform; drew up game laws of Vt. Died Nov. 26, 1887.

GOLDSTEIN, MAX AARON M.D., Oto-laryngologist; b. St. Louis, Mo., Apr. 19, 1870; s. William and Hulda (Loewenthal) G.; M.D., Mo. Med. Coll., 1892; LL.D.; study in oto-laryngology, Strassberg, Berlin, Vienna and London, 1893; m. Leonore Weiner, June 4, 1895; 1 dau., Helen (Mrs. Norman C. Wolff). Began practice oto-laryngology, Beaumont Hosp. Med. Coll., 1896-1900, St. Louis U., 1900-12; founder, 1914, and dir. Central Inst. for Deaf, St. Louis; dir. dept. otology and laryngology. Jewish Hosp. of St. Louis. Founder, 1896, and editor The Laryngoscope (monthly mag.); founder, 1922, and editor Oralism and Auralism (semi-annual jour.). Served as maj., Med. Corps, U.S. Army, World War; head of dept. head surgery, Camp Dodge, Ia.; mem. com. on reconstrn. for deaf and defective speech soldiers. Democrat. Mem. Jewish Ref. Ch. Author: Problems of the Deaf; The Acoustic Method for Training the Deaf and Hard of Hearing Child, 1939. Home: Clayton, Mo. Died July 27, 1941.

GOLDTHWAIT, JAMES WALTER prof. geology; b. Lynn, lMass., Mar. 22, 1880; s. James Wesley and Olive Jane (Parker) G.; A.B., Harvard, 1902, A.M., 1903, Ph.D., 1906; D.Sc. (hon.) Univ. of New Hampshire, 1945; married Edith Dunnels Richards, June 25, 1906; children-Richard Parker, Lawrence. Asst. prof. geology, Northwestern U., 1904-08; asst. prof. geology, 1908-11, prof. geology since 1911, Dartmouth. Engaged during summers in geologic field work for state surveys of Wis. and Ill., for U.S. Geol. Survey and for Geol. Survey of Can. Served as capt. U.S. Army, Apr. 8-Dec. 31, 1918, in charge of map room, Office Chief of Staff, Washington. Geologist, N.H. State Highway Dept. since 1917. Fellow Geol. Soc. America, Am. Acad. Arts and Sciences; mem. Phi Beta Kappa, Sigma Xi, Gamma Alpha fraternities. Conglist. Author: Abandoned Shorelines of Eastern Wisconsin (Wis. Geol. Survye). 1906; Physiography of Nova Scotia (Geol. Survey of Can.), 1925; Geology of New Hampshire (N.H. Acad. Science Handbook No. 1), 1925; also numerous reports and papers, dealing with extinct shorelines, earth movements, river floods, glacial and physiographic studies in N.E. and Can. Home: Hanover, N.H. Died Dec. 31, 1947.

GOLDTHWAIT, JOEL ERNEST, surgeon; b. Marblehead, Mass., June 18, 1866; s. William Johnson and Mary L. (Pitman) G.; S.B., Mass. State Coll., 1885; M.D., Harvard, 1890, and since in practice at Boston; served as house surgeon, Boston Children's and Boston City hosps.; m. Jessie S. Rand, May 16, 1894; m. 2d, Mrs. Philip Leverett Saltonstall, Apr. 30, 1936. Was formerly chief of orthopedic service, Mass. Gen. Hosp., Carney Hosp.; mem. Staff Boston Children's Hosp.; formerly asst. in orthopedic surgery, Harvard Med. Sch.; now instr. orthopedic surgery, Grad. Sch. of same. Ex-pres. Am. Orthopedic Assn.; fellow Am. Coll. Surgeons; mem. British Orthopedic Assn., A.M.A., Mass. Med. Soc. Republican. Conglist. Author numerous monographs; frequent contbr. on orthopedic surgery. Col. Med. Corps, serving 2 yrs. with A.E.F.; now brig. gen. M.R.C. Awarded D.S.M. (U.S.); Companion St. Michael and St. George (Great Britain). Home: Medfield Mass Address: 372 Marlborough St.,2Boston MA*

GOOD, HOWARD HARRISON naval officer; b. Warren, Ind., Aug. 12, 1888; s. James F. and Ola (Irwin) G.; grad. U.S. Naval Academy, 1912; m. Margaret Coffey; 1 son, Edward L. (by former marriage). Commd. ensign USN, 1912, advanced through grades to rear Adm., 1942; commd. U.S.S. Truxtun, Asiatic Sta., 1926-29, participating in operations in valley of Yangtze River, 1926-27; comd. U.S.S. New Orleans, 1941-42 (ship was under repair, with engines torn down, Pearl Harbor, Dec. 7, 1941, but crew hand-operated antiaircraft batteries and ammunition hoists, and with U.S.S. Honolulu beat off dive bombing attack on dock area; as mem. task force the New Orleans participated in Battle of Coral Sea, May 7-8, 1942, and engaged at close quarters in def. disabled U.S.S. Lexington and in rescue of her survivors); in Battle of Midway, June 1942; comdr. cruiser div. Pacific Fleet, with U.S.S. Northampton as flagship, June-Dec. 1942 (cruiser div. served on patrol, covered movement of convoys to Guadalcanal and participated in Battle of Cape Esperance; formed screen for U.S.S. Hornet, Battle of Santa Cruz; after attempt to tow disabled Hornet, Northampton stood by to fight off attacking planes until Hornet was abandoned; Northampton was sunk shortly afterward in Battle of Tassafaronga); mem. staff comdr. in chief Pacific Fleet, 1943; dir. base maintenance div. Office Chief of Naval Operations 1943-46; comdr. U.S. Naval Forces in the Philippines, 1946-48; comdr. Thirteenth Naval Dist., Seattle, 1948-50, ret. with rank vice adm., Sept. 1, 1950. Decorated Commendation Ribbon, Mexican Service, Dominican Campaign, Yangtze Service, China Service and Asiatic-Pacific Area Campaign medals, Victory Medal with destroyer clasp, Am. Def. Service Medal with fleet clasp, Legion of Merit with Gold Star, Distinguished Service Star (Philippines), Am. Area Campaign Medal, Philippine Independence Ribbon, Philippine Legion of Honor, Philippine Distinguished Service Star. Home: 824 33d Av. N. Seattle 2, Died Aug. 1963.

GOODALE, GREENLEAF AUSTIN army officer; b. Orrington, Me., July 4, 1839; s. Ephraim, Jr. and Lucinda Larned (Martin) G.; ed. E. Me. Conf. Sem., Bucksport; m. Fidelia S. Beach, June 1, 1870; 2:, Margaret Montgomery, Sept. 1, 1886. Pvt., corporal and sergt. Co. E, 6th Me. Inf., May 7, 1861-Jan. 2, 1864; hon. mustered out of vol. service, Nov. 14, 1866; 1st lt., 23d U.S. Inf., July 28, 1866; capt., June 25, 1878; maj., Apr. 26, 1898; lt. col. 3d Inf., July 19, 1899; col. 17th Inf., Apr. 1, 1901; brig. gen., Feb. 23, 1903. Bvtd.; maj., Mar. 13, 1865 for faithful and meritorious services during the war; capt., Mar. 2, 1867, for gallant and meritorious services in battle of Gettysburg. Served in Army of Potomac, 1861-63. Dept. of Gulf, 1864-66, frontier and Indian country, 1867-98; Philippines, 1898-1901; retired after 42 yrs. service, Feb. 24, 1903. Home: Wakefield, Mass. Died Feb. 17, 1915.

GOODALL, ALBERT GALLATIN engraver; b. Montgomery, Ala., Oct. 31, 1826. Served as midshipman Tex. Navy during Mexican-Texan war; went to Havana, Cuba, 1844, learned copperplate engraving; established himself as banknote engraver, Phila., 1848; asso. with a co. which merged to form Am. Bank Note Co., 1858, pres., 1874-87; visited several European and S. Am. countries to obtain fgn. contracts for firm. Died N.Y.C., Feb. 19, 1887.

GOODE, SAMUEL congressman; b. "Whitby," Chesterfield County, Va., Mar. 21, 1756; studied law. Admitted to bar, practiced law; served as lt. Chesterfield Troop of Horse, later as col. militia during Revolutionary War; mem. Va. Ho. of Dels., 1778-85; mem. U.S. Ho. of Reps. from Va., 6th Congress, 1799-1801. Died Invermay, Va., Nov. 14, 1822; buried on estate nr. Invermay.

GOODKIND, MAURICE LOUIS M.D.; b. Chicago, Ill., Nov. 14, 1867; s. Louis G.; Williams Coll., 1885-86; M.D., Coll. Phys. and Surg. (Columbia), 1889; post-grad. work, Vienna and Munich; m. Rose S. Snydacker, 1896; children-G. L., Ruth, M. Lewis. Attending physician Cook County Hosp., 14 yrs., Michael Reese Hosp., 29 yrs.; prof. clin. medicine, U. of Ill. Coll. of Medicine; specializes in internal medicine. Was chief of med. service, Base Hospital 53, U.S. Army, Langres, France; col. Med. R.C. Officier the French Acad., silver palm, for services during war. Republican. Mason. Home: Chicago, Ill. Died. Jan. 4, 1939.

GOODLOE, WILLIAM CASSIUS diplomat, legislator; b. Madison County, Ky., June 27, 1841; s. David Short and Sally Ann (Smith) G.; ed. Transylvania U.; m. Mary E. Mann, June 8, 1865, 6 children. Acting sec. of legation, St. Petersburg, Russia, 1861; served as capt. U.S. Army in Civil War; an organizer Republican Party in Ky., 1867; published Kentucky Statesman (advocating principles of Republican Party), 1867; speaker Ky. Ho. of Reps., 1871; mem. Ky. Senate, 1873; U.S. minister to Belgium, 1878-80; apptd. U.S. collector internal revenue, 1889. Died in fight with polit. enemy Armistead Swope, Lexington, Ky., Nov. 10, 1889.

GOODMAN, CHARLES surgeon; b. Hungary, June 14, 1871; s. Albert and Frances (Richman) G.; brought to U.S., 1874; M.D., Western Reserve U., 1892; post-grad. work, Berlin, Goettingen and Halle; m. 2d, Adele Frederica Prauger, July 11, 1923; 1 dau., Jane Helen. On staff Lying-in Hosp., N.Y. City and City Hosp., Blackwell's Island, 1892; mem. resident staff, surg. div., Mt. Sinai Hosp., 1893-96, chief of surg. dept., 1896-1916; attending surgeon Sydenham Hosp. 3 yrs., Montefior Hosp. 15 yrs., Beth Israel Hosp. 20 yrs.; clin. prof. surgery, N.Y. Univ. and Bellevue Hosp. Med. Coll. since 1914; cons. surgeon Rockaway Beach Hosp., Beth Member of Nobel Prize nominating committee in medicine, 1936. Successively capt. U.S. Med. Reserve Corps, comdg. officer of reinforcement of Presbyn. Hosp. (Gen. Hosp. No. 1, A.E.F.), major, head of operating team, Paschendale offensive, dir. Field Hosp. Sect., 42d Div., 1917-19; lt. col. Med. Res., U.S. Army. Cons. vascular surgeon to U.S. Veterans Facilities, II Corps Area, U.S. Veterans Hosp., No. 81. Fellow Am. Coll. Surgeons; mem. A.M.A., Acad. Medicine, Internat. Surg. Soc., N. Y. State and N.Y. Co. med. socs., Metropolitan, Harlem and Riverside med. socs., Harvey Soc., Eastern Med. Soc. (ex-pres.), Assn. Alumni of Mt. Sinai Hosp. (ex-sec.), Physicians' Mut. Aid Assn., Am. Legion, Mil. Order World War, Reserve Officers' Assn., Assn. Mil. Surgeons, Am. Public Health, Internat. Med. Club (v.p.), Union Médicale Latine. Republican. Clubs: Army and Navy, Central Park Riding, Lakeville Golf and Country. Author of 64 reprints of med. articles pub. in various scientific journals on file at N.Y. Acad. of Medicine. Home: 125 E. 72d St., New York 21. Address: 745 5th Av., New York 22, N.Y. Died May 23, 1945.

GOODMAN, JOHN FOREST army officer; b. Texas, Aug. 22, 1891; B.S., U.S. Mil. Acad., 1916; grad. Inf. Sch., field officers course, 1922, Command and Gen. Staff Sch., 1931, Chem. Warfare Sch., field officers course, 1940, Army War Coll., 1940. Commd. 2d lt.,

U.S. Army, 1916, and advanced through the grades to brig. gen., 1945. Decorated Silver Star, Purple Heart, Legion of Merit, Croix de Guerre. Address: care The Adjutant General's Office, War Department, Washington 25, D.C. Died Mar. 6, 1947.

GOODMAN, WILLIAM M. army officer (ret.); b. Norfolk, Va., Sept. 6, 1892; s. Hayman and Fannie (Kaminsky) G.; B.S., Va. Mil. Inst., 1912; grad. Command and Gen. Staff Sch., 1931. Army War Coll., 1936, Navy War Coll., 1937; m. Marjorie Whitaker, Sept. 8, 1923; 1 dau., Marjorie Frances, Commd. 2d lt. CAC, U.S., Army, 1916, and advanced through the grades to maj. gen., Feb. 21, 1944; served with AEF, France, 1918-19, with 40th Artillery Brigade (ry.) and at headquarters S.O.S.; served War Dept. Gen. Staff (supply div.) July 1937-Feb. 1942; comd. Antiaircraft Def., Los Angeles, Feb. 1942-July 1942; charge of Oversea Supply Div., N.Y. Port Embarkation, 1942-45, San Francisco Port Embarkation 1945-1946. Awarded D.S.M. Club. Army and Navy (Washington). Mason. Address: 1458 Hampton Rd., San Marino 9, Cal. Died Dec. 13, 1958; buried San Francisco Nat. Cemetery.

GOODRELL, MANCIL CLAY brig. gen. U.S. Marine Corps; b. Cambridge, O., Nov. 9, 1843; s. Stewart and Jane Priscilla (Israel) G.; ed. pub. schs. and Dr. Nash's Acad., Des Moines, Ia.; m. Emily Truxtun Read, Nov. 14, 1872. Served during Civil War in 15th Ia. Vols. Army of the Tenn.; apptd. from Ia. 2d lt. U.S. Marine Corps, Mar. 9, 1865; promoted 1st lt., Apr. 21, 1870; capt., Aug. 16, 1886; maj., 1903; brig. gen. and retired, Jan. 31, 1906. Served on flagship New York during war with Spain and after in P.I. Died May 23, 1925.

GOODRICH, CASPAR FREDERICK naval officer; b. Phila., Jan. 7, 1847; s. William and Sarah A. (Bearden) G.; grad. U.S. Naval Acad., 1864; hon. A.M., Yale, 1888; D.Sc., Princeton, 1919; m. Eleanor Milnor, Sept. 4, 1873; m. 2d, Sarah M. Hays. Ensign, Nov. 1, 1866; master, Dec. 1, 1866; lt., Mar. 12, 1868; lt. comdr., Mar. 26, 1869; comdr., Sept. 27, 1884; capt., Sept. 16, 1897; rear adm., Feb. 17, 1904; retired, Jan. 7, 1909. Commandant Naval Unit, Princeton U., 1918, and officer Material Sch. for the Pay Corps, Princeton, N.J., 1918-19. Naval del. to Historical Conv., Saragossa, Spain, 1908. Gold medalist, U.S. Naval Inst.; pres. Naval History Soc., 1914-16. Home: Princeton, N.J. Died Dec. 26, 1925.

GOODRICH, DAVID MARVIN chmn. bd. B. F. Goodrich Co.; b. Akron, O., June 22, 1876; s. Benjamin Franklin and Mary (Marvin) G.; prep. edn., Germany and France, 1886-88, St. Paul's Sch., Concord, N.H., 1888-94; A.B., Harvard, 1898; m. Ruth Pruyn, June 2, 1903; 1 dau., Anne Marvin; m. 2d, Beatrice Morgan Pruyn, Nov. 13, 1936. Chmn. bd. B. F. Goodrich Co., 1927-50; dir. Commercial Solvents Corp., Freeport Sulphur Co., Sulphur Export Corp. Served as lt., Roosevelt's Rough Riders, Spanish-Am. War; lt. col. U.S. Army, World War. Home: Mt. Kisco, N.Y. Office: 230 Park Av., N.Y. C. 17. Died May 17, 1950; buried Lakeview Cemetery, Jamestown, N.Y.

GOODRICH, DONALD REUBEN army officer; b. Marshall, Mich., Oct. 17, 1894; grad. Army Indsl. Coll., 1931, Air Corps Tactical Sch., 1938. Commd. 2d lt., Air Service, U.S. Army, 1920, and advanced through the grades to brig. gen., 1944; served as flight adjutant and supply officer, 2d Observation Squadron, Camp Nichols, Rizal, P.I., 1927-29; asst. chief, personnel div., training group, Office Chief of Air Corps, also liaison officer Adj. Gen.'s Office, 1938-40; exec. officer, military personnel div. Office Chief of Air Corps, 1940-42; comdg. officer, 3d Air Service Area Command, Atlanta, Ga., 1942-43; became chief of staff, Eighth Air Force Service Command, European Theater of Operations, Mar. 1943, assuming command of an air depot area, European Theater of Operations, Aug. 1943. Address: care The Adjutant General's Officer, War Department, Washington 25, D.C.* Died July 12, 1945.

GOODRICH, EDGAR JENNINGS, lawyer; b. Anoka, Minn., Nov. 15, 1896; s. George Herbert and Mary Anne (Funk) G.; spl. course for Am. soldiers, U. of Nancy, France, 1919; LL.B., State U. of Ia., 1922; m. Beulah E. Lenfest, Sept. 30, 1922; children—George Herbert, Mary Alice, Charles Lenfest. Admitted to bar, Ia. and Minn., 1922, W.Va., 1923, to District of Columbia bar, 1935; asst. county atty., Anoka County, Minn., 1922-23; removed to Charleston, W.Va., 1923, and asso. in practice with Price, Smith & Spilman, specialized in federal and state taxation; apptd. mem. U.S. Bd. of Tax Appeals, 1931; reentered law practice, charge Washington, D.C., office Guggenheimer & Untermeyer of New York, 1935, now Washington partner; lecturer, Practicing Law Institute, Federal Taxation. Mem. nat. panel arbitrators, Am. Arbitration Assn. Served with 3d Minn. Inf. on Mexican border, 1916; with 1st Officers Training Camp, Ft. Snelling, Minn., 1917; duty with troops, 34th Div., later staff duty; in France with 59th Field Arty. Brigade; assigned to Air Service as arty. observer 1st Aero Squadron, and served in Army of Occupation; commd. 1st lt. Mem. Am. Bar Assn. (taxation, adminstrv. law sects.), Am. Law Inst., D.C. Bar Assn., Phi Kappa Psi. Republican. Conglist. Mason Clubs: Metropolitan, Chevy Chase, National Press (Washington, D.C.); also Bohemian (San Francisco). Co-author: Procedure Before The Bureau of Internal Revenue, 1951. Contbr. numerous articles on taxation. Home: Washington DC Died Apr. 10, 1969; buried St. George's Cemetery, Lewes DE

GOODRICH, NATHANIEL LEWIS librarian; b. Concord, N.Y., Feb. 9, 1880; s. Arthur Lewis and Mary Eastman (Bachelder) G.; A.B., Amherst, 1901; B.L.S., N.Y. State Library Sch., Albany, 1904; M.A., Dartmouth Coll., 1920; Litt.D., Amherst Coll., 1941; m. Alice Lyman, July 30, 1908. Reporter Utica Press, 1901-02; in charge of order section, New York State Library, 1904-07; librarian, W.Va. U., 1907-09, U. of Tex., 19009-11, 1, Dartmouth Coll., 1912-50. Capt. Mil. Intelligence Div., Gen. Staff, July-Dec. 1918. Mem. A.L.A., Beta Theta Pi. Conglist. Clubs: Appalachian Mountain Canadian Alpine, American (Alpine) Ski Club of Gt. Britain.

GOODSPEED, CHARLES BARNETT b. Cleveland, O., Feb. 8, 1885; s. Wilbur F. and Harreitt (Howe) G.; M.E., Cornell U., 1908; m. Elizabeth Fuller. Dir. Buckeye Steel Castings Co., City Nat. Bank & Trust Co. Served as capt. 32d, 29th, 42d Division, A.E.F., World War I. President bd. managers Presbyterian Hospital. Trustee U. of Chicago, Art. Inst. Chicago, Chicago Symphony Orchestra Assn., Fourth Presbyn. Ch., Ill. Children's Home and Aid Soc.; citizen fellow Inst. Med. of Chicago. Republican. Home: 2430 Lake View Av., Chicago, Ill. Died Feb. 23, 1947; buried at Columbus, O.

GOODWIN, WILLIAM HALL surgeon; b. Lexington, Ky., Feb. 3, 1882; s. William Moore and Katherine (Hall) G.; B.A., Transylvania U., Ky., 1904; M.D., U. of Va., 1908; m. Mary Stuart Cocke, Dec. 27, 1921. Interne U. of Va. Hosp., 1908-09; mem. house staff, Bellevue Hosp., New York, 1909-10; recalled to U. of Va. as house surgeon of hosp., 1910. later prof. clinical surgery and gynecology. Commd. maj. Med. Corps U.S.A., Sept. 6, 1917; lt. col., June 27, 1918; hon. discharged, Apr. 23, 1919; was organizer and chief of surg. service, Base Hosp. 41, A.E.F., at Saint Denis, France. Citation by Gen. John J. Pershing, Apr. 19, 1919. Democrat. Presbyterian. Home: University, Va. Deceased.

GOODWYN, PETERSON congressman, lawyer; b. "Sweden," nr. Petersburg, Va., 1745; studied law. Admitted to bar, 1776, began practice of law, Petersburg; also a planter; served from capt. to maj. during Revoluntionary War; equipped his own company; promoted col. for gallantry at Battle of Smithfield; mem. Va. Ho. of Dels., 1789-1802; mem. U.S. Ho. of Reps. (Democrat) from Va., 8th-15th congresses, 1803-18. Died "Sweden," Feb. 21, 1818; buried family burying ground on his estate.

GOODYEAR, ANSON CONGER mfr.; b. Buffalo, June 20, 1877; s. Charles Waterhouse and Ella Portia (Conger) G.; A.B., Yale, 1899; LL.D., Norwich, U., 1952; D. Fine Arts, Adelphi Coll., 1958; m. Mary Forman, June 29, 1904 (div.); children - George F., Mary, Anson C., Stephen; m. 2d, Zaidee Bliss, Nov. 10, 1950. In mfg., 1900; chmn. exec. com., dir. G.M. & O. R.R.; dir. Crown Zellerbach Corp.; v.p. Goodyear Lumber Co., Buffalo, 1907-11, pres., 1911-17; pres. Norwich Lumber Co., 1911-17; other bus. enterprises. Served as dep. commr. A.R.C. Pacific Ocean areas, 1944-45; personal rep. Sec. of War, Am. Zone, Germany and Austria, 1947. Student First Officers Tng. Camp, Madison Barracks, 1917; capt. F.A., U.S. Army, Aug. 15, 1917; maj., Mar. 1918; lt. col., June 1918; col., Oct. 1918; assigned comd. Battery A, 307th F.A.; grad. Sch. of Fire, Ft. Sill, Okla., Jan. 1918; instr. at Ft. Sill, Jan.-June 1918; exec. officer, F.A. Sch., Camp Taylor, Ky., June-Oct. 1918; went to France in comd. 81st F.A.; assigned after Armistice to Transport Corps., A.E.F., as gen. insp., and later apptd. pres. Coal Commn. for Central Europe under Supreme Econ. Council; honorably discharged, Oct. 1919. Maj. gen. 1st Div., N.Y. Guard, ret. Decorated Officer, Legion of Honor (France). Recipient Chancellor's Medal, U. Buffalo, 1955. Press., ANTA, 1935-39; trustee Mus. Modern Art, N.Y.C., 1929-60, pres., 1929-39, hon. trustee, 1960-64; trustee Norwich U., trustee Buffalo Fine Arts Acad., 1911-14, 16-28, v.p., 1925-28; hon. gov. N.Y. Hosp. 1943-51. Mem. Alpha Delta Phi, Wolf's Head (Yale). Republican. Presbyn. Clubs: Saturn (Buffalo); Racquet and Tennis (N.Y.); Links Golf. Home: Old Westbury, L.I., N.Y. Office: 527 Lexington Av., N.Y.C. 17. Died Apr. 23, 1964.

GOOKIN, DANIEL colonial ofcl.; b. Kent, Eng., 1612; s. Daniel and Mary (Byrd) G.; married 3 times; m. 2d, Mary Dalling, 1639; m. 3d, Hannah Tyng, 1685; children including Nathaniel, Daniel. Mem. Va. House of Burgesses, 1641-42; captain in charge of train bands, circa 1641-42, 49-circa 1687; ardent Puritan, a signer of Nansemond Petition asking ch. elders in Mass. to send clergy to Va.; settled in Roxbury, Mass., 1644; a founder of free grammar sch., Rosbury; dep. to Mass. Gen. Ct., 1649-52, spl. magistrate, 1652; supt. of all Indians acknowledging govt. of Mass., 1656, 61; went to Eng., collector customs and Dept. Treas. at war, Dunkirk, Eng., 1658; supporter Indian Rights which made him unpopular with many colonists, 1661; sgt.-maj. Middlesex Regt., 1680; maj. gen. all forces in Mass. colony, 1681. Author: Historical Collections of the Indians of Massachusetts, written 1674, published 1792. Died Cambridge, Mass., Mar. 30, 1687.

GORDON, ARMISTEAD CHURCHILL, JR. educator; b. Staunton, Va., July 9, 1897; s. Armistead Churchill and Maria Breckinridge (Catlett) G.; A.B., Coll. of William and Mary, 1916; A.M., U. of Va., 1918, Ph.D., 1921; m. Cornelia Daniel Waddell, Aug.29, 1922; 1 dau., Ann Waddell (Mrs. Richard Henry Webster). High sch. teacher, Staunton, 1916-17; instr. English, U. of Va.. 1919-22, asst. prof., 1922-28, asso. prof., 192O-40, prof. English, 1940—. Served as pvt., Chem. Warfare Service, U.S. Army, 1918-19; lt. U.S.N.R., 1942-44; lt. comdr., U.S.N.R., 1944-46; cons. Research and Development Bd., Nat. Mil. Establishment, Dec. 1950-Feb. 1951. Mem. Pi Kappa Alpha, Phi Beta Kappa. Jeffersonian Democrat. Episcopalian. Author: Virginian Writers of Fugitive Verse, 1924. Asst. editor Southern Life and Literature, Vols. 1-3, 1941-42. Contbr. to Nat. Cyclopedia of American Biography, Dictionary of American Biography, and various noursl and revs. Home: 1844 Westview Rd., Charlottesville, Va. Died May 12, 1953: buried U. Va.

GORDON, DAVID STUART army officer; b. Franklin County, Pa., May 23, 1832; s. Alexander and Hannah (Ely) G.; ed. pub. and pvt. schs. in country and Commercial Sch., Baltimore; m. Ann E. Hughes; m. 2d, Mrs. Bell (Vedder) Fleming; step-children-Robert Vedder Fleming, Mrs. Louis F. Corea. Apptd. from Kan. 2d lt. 2d Dragoons, Apr. 10, 1861; 1st lt. 2d Cav., June 1861; capt., Apr. 25, 1863; maj., June 25, 1877; lt. col., Nov. 20, 1889; col., 6th Cav., July 28, 1892; retired May 23, 1896; advanced to rank of brig. gen. retired, by act of Apr. 23, 1904. Bvtd. maj., July 3, 1863, "for gallant and meritorious services in Gettysburg campaign"; lt. col., Feb. 17, 1890, "for gallant services in action against Indians at Miners Delight, Wyo., May 4, 1870." In Civil War served in Army of Potomac and engaged at first battle of Bull Run; taken prisoner and confined in Libby Prison, Richmond, Va., Castle Pinckney, Charleston and Columbia jails, S.C., and Salisbury, N.C.; exchanged Aug. 1862; took part in many other battles of Civ. War, including Manassas Gap, Todd's Tavern, Cold Harbor, Hawes Shop, Trevillian Sta., etc.; after war engaged in frontier service and battles with Indians as well as various other branches of service until retired. Presbyn. Home: Washington, D.C. Died Jan. 28, 1930.

GORDON, GEORGE HENRY army officer; b. Charlestown, Mass., July 19, 1823; s. Robert and Elizabeth (Carlisle) G.; grad. U.S. Mil. Acad., 1846, Harvard Law Sch., 1856; m. Mary Scott, June 1864. Served in Mexican War, brevetted 1st lt., 1847; served in Washington, D.C., then frontier duty in Kan., 1850-54; admitted to bar, 1857; raised 2d Mass. Inf., 1861; commd. col., 1861, served in Shenandoah Valley operations; commd. brig. gen., 1862, participated in battles of Winchester, Cedar Mountain and Antietam; in command of Eastern dist., 1865; brevetted maj. gen. U.S. Volunteers, 1865; a founder Mil. Hist. Soc. of Mass. Author: Brook Farm to Cedar Mountain ... 1861-2, published 1863; History of the Campaign of the Army of Virginia . . . from Cedar Mountain to Alexandria, 1862, 1879; A War Diary of Events in the War of the Great Rebellion, 1882. Died Framingham, Mass., Aug. 30, 1886.

GORDON, GEORGE WASHINGTON congressman; b. Giles County, Tenn., Oct. 5, 1836; s. Andrew and Eliza K. G.; grad. Western Mil. Inst., 1859; m. Ora S. Paine, Sept. 5, 1876. Practiced civ. engring. till outbreak of Civil War; enlisted in mil. service of Tenn. as drill master 11th Inf.; transferred to mil. service of C.S.A.; promoted capt., lt.. col., col.; in 1864 made brig. gen.; participated in every engagement fourght by his command with exception of Bentonville, N.C., being a prisoner until Aug. 1865, at Ft. Warren, Boston Harbor. Studied law Lebanon, Tenn.; practiced at Pulaski and Memphis until 1883; apptd. one of ry. commrs. of state; received apptmt. in Interior Dept., U.S., 1885; served 4 yrs. in Indian country and territories west of Rocky Mountaians. Resumed practice of law Memphis until 1892; supt. city schools of Memphis, 1892-1907; mem. 60th and 61st Congresses (1907-10), 10th Tenn. Dist. Democrat. Maj. gen. comdg. Tenn. div. U.C.V. Address: Memphis, Tenn. Died 1911.

GORDON, HIRSCH LOEB, neuropsychiatrist; b. Wilno, Lithuania, Nov. 26, 1896; s. Rabbi Elijah and Malcah (Katzenellenbogen) G.; prep. edn. Wolozhin Yeshivah Gymnasium, Odessa, Russia, 1911-14; Ph.D., in Semitic Langs., Yale, 1922; L.H.D. in Egyptology, Cath. U., 1923; A.M. in Diplomacy, American U., 1924; A.M., in Edn., Teachers Coll., Columbia, 1926; D.H.L., Jewish Theol. Sem. of Am., 1928; A.M. in Fine Arts, N.Y.U., 1928; U. Berlin, 1931; Litt.D. in Classical Archaeology, Royal U. Rome, Italy, 1931, M.D., Sc.D., Diplomate Royal Inst. of Legal Medicine, Rome, 1934; m. Tamara L. Liebowitz. Came to U.S., 1915, naturalized, 1922. Lectr. in instructor, tchrs. colls., 1920-27; with neurol. clinic of Mt. Sinai Hosp., N.Y.C., 1935, Maimonides Hosp., Bklyn., 1935-37, physician skin and syphilis clinic, Mt. Sinai Hospital, 1937-40, surgery, 1940-41; member of psychiatric staff of Pilgrim State Hosp., Brentwood, N.Y., 1941-42; Cornell Div.

Neurology, Bellevue Hospital, N.Y.C.; Kings County Psychiatric Hospital, Bklyn., 1934-44; Bellevue Psychiatric Hospital, 1944; qualified psychiat., State of New York, 1944; chief, shock therapy, U.S. Vets. Hosp., Northport, N.Y., 1944-46; chief neuropsychiat., U.S. Vets. Adminstrn., Jacksonville, Fla., 1947; neuropsychiat. consultant Div. U.S. Surgeon Gen., U.S. Army, Washington, 1947-48; sr. surgeon (comdr.) USPHS, also chief neuropsychiatry div. U.S. Marine Hosp., S.I., 1948-50; with neuropsychiat. div. Met. Hosp., N.Y.C., 1951-69, now asso. psychiatrist; asso. vis. psychiatrist Bird S. Coler Meml. Hosp., Met. Hosp.; adjunct in neuropsychiatry Beth Israel Hosp.; asso. in psychiatry, N.Y. Med. Coll.; lectr. N.Y.C. Cancer Com., 1935-69, N.Y.C. Dept. Health, 1937-69, L.I. Inst. 1951-53. Member board of appeal New York State SSS, 1951-69. Sgt. Royal Fusiliers, B.E.F., Palestine front, 39th R.F., 1918-19; maj., M.C., AUS, 1944-46. Recipient Maimonides award Michael Reese Med. Center, 1967, Am. Univ. Alumni Recognition award, 1968. Fellow Am. Geriatric Soc., Am. Psychiatric Assn., A.C.P.; mem. numerous medical, psychiatric, other orgns. Mason. Author several books, 1926-69, including Objectors to Electric Shock, 1946; Fractures in Electric Shock, 1946, 50; Shock Therapy Theories, 1946; The Maggid of Caro; Psychiatric Concepts in the Bible, Talmud and Zohar; contbr. literary and scientific monographs in Amer. and foreign reviews. Address: New York City NY Died Jan. 19, 1969; buried Cedar Park NJ

GORDON, JAMES congressman; b. County Antrim, Ireland, Oct. 31, 1739; attended local schs. Came to U.S., 1758, settled in Schenectady, N.Y.; an Indian trader; served as lt. col. Albany County (N.Y.) Militia Regt. during Revoluntionary War, captured and imprisoned in Can.; mem. N.Y. State Assembly, 1777-80, 86, 90; moved to Ballston Spa. N.Y.; mem. U.S. Ho. of Reps. (Federalist) from N.Y., 2d-3d congresses, 1791-95; trustee Union Coll., Schenectady, 1795-1809; mem. N.Y. Senate, 1797-1804. Died Ballston Spa, Jan. 17, 1810; buried Briggs Cemetery.

GORDON, JAMES senator; b. Monroe County, Miss., Dec. 6, 1833; s. Robert and Mary Elizabeth (Walton) G.; A.B., U. of Miss., 1855; m. Carolina Virginia Wiley, Feb. 7, 1856; m. 2d, Ella Narcissa Neilson, Apr. 28, 1904. Capt. Co. B, Jeff Davis Legion, Under Gen. J.E. B. Stuart, Army of Va., C.S.A.; later col. 4th Miss. Cav. Cotton planter. Appointed U.S. senator, Dec. 27, 1909, and served until Feb. 22, 1910, when legislature elected a successor to Anselm J. McLaurin, deceased. Author: The Old Plantation, and other Poems. For many yrs. contbr. to mags., especially field notes to Forest and Stream, American Field, London Field, etc. Home: Okolona, Miss. Died Nov. 28, 1912.

GORDON, JOHN BROWN gov.; b. Upson County, Ga., Feb. 6, 1832; ed. U. of Ga.; admitted to bar; m. Fanny Haralson, 1854. Served in C.S.A. capt. to lt. gen.; shot 8 times; severely wounded at Antietam; Dem. candidate for gov. of Ga., 1868, and claimed election, but his Rep. opponent, Rufus B. Bullock, obtained the office; U.S. Senator, 1873-80, and 1891-97; gov. Ga., 1887-90; comdr.-in-chief United Confederate Veterans. Home: Atlanta, Ga. Died 1904.

GORDON, WILLIAM FITZHUGH congressman; b. Germanna, Va., Jan. 13, 1787; s. James and Elizabeth (Gordon) G.; m. Mary Rootes, Dec. 12, 1809; m. 2d, Elizabeth Lindsay, Jan. 21, 1813. Admitted to Va. bar, circa 1808; atty. Commonwealth of Va., 1812; served as brig. gen., maj. gen. Va. Militia in War of 1812; mem. Va. Ho. of Dels., 1818-29; mem. Va. Constl. Conv., 1829-30; framer successful compromise measure fixing representation in the 2 houses on the mixed basis of population and taxation; mem. U.S. Ho. of Reps. (Democrat) from Va., 21st-23d congresses, Jan. 25, 1830-35, introduced bill providing for establishment of independent treasury, (1st step in separation of bank and state) 1834; leading figure in So. Conv., Nashville, Tenn., 1850. Died Albemarle County, Va., Aug. 28, 1858; buried Springfield, nr. Gordonsville, Va.

GORDON, WILLIAM W. merchant; b. Savannah, Ga., Oct. 14, 1834; s. William Washington G. and Sarah Anderson (Stites) G.; A.B., Yale, 1854; m. Eleanor Lytle Kinzie, Dec. 21, 1857. Second lt. Ga. Hussars, J.E.B. Stuart's Cav., C.S.A.; capt. and insp. Mercer's Brigade of Inf.; capt. and adj. Anderson's brigade, Wheeler's cav.; wounded at Lovejoy's Sta., Ga.; placed upon the Roll of Honor for gallantry at Frederick City, Md. After war served in Ga. cav.; 4 times in command of troops for riot duty. Engaged in cotton business, Savannah, Ga., 1854—; sr. partner W.W. Gordon & Co.; v.p. Merchants Nat. Bank, 1894-98; pres. Savannah Cotton Exchange, 1876-79, Savannah Benevolent Assn., 1890-91. Mem. Ga. Ho. of Rep., 1884-90. Brig. gen. U.S.V., May 27, 1898-Mar. 24, 1899, Spanish-Am. War; mem. Puerto Rican Evacuation Commn., Aug.-Oct., 1898. Home: Savannah, Ga. Died Sept. 11, 1912.

GORGAS, JOSIAH army officer, educator; b. Dauphin County, Pa., July 1, 1818; s. Joseph and Sophia (Atkinson) G.; grad. U.S. Mil. Acad., 1841; went abroad to study ordnance and arsenals of European armies, 1845; m. Amelia Gayle, Dec. 1853; children - William C., Jesse, Mary, Amelia, Maria, Richard H. Served as lt. Ordnance, Mexican War, 1847-48, commd. capt., 1855; commd. maj., chief of ordnance Confederate Army, 1861; established armories for making arms, Richmond, Va. and Fayetteville, N.C.; set up arsenals throughout South; responsible for founding a cannon foundry and central lab. at Macon, Ga.; brought about steady improvements in products of foundries and armories despite difficulties of Confederate system; brig. gen., by Nov. 1864; became mgr. Brierfield Iron Works in Ala. after war; became headmaster jr. dept. U. of South, Sewanee, Tenn., 1869, prof. engring., 1870, vice chancellor, 1872; pres. U. Ala., 1878-79, librarian of univ., 1879-82. Died Tuscaloosa, Ala., May 15, 1883.

GORGAS, WILLIAM CRAWFORD surgeon gen. U.S. Army; b. Mobile Ala., Oct. 3, 1854; s. Gen Josiah (C.S.A.) and Amelia (Gayle) G.; A.B., U. of the South, 1875; M.D., Bellevue Hosp., Medical College (New York U.), 1879; interne, Bellevue Hosp., 1878-80; hon. Sc.D., U. of Pa., 1903, U. of the South, 1904, Harvard, 1908, Brown, 1909, Jefferson Med. Coll. 1909; LL.D., U. of Ala., 1901, Tulane, 1911; m. Marie Cook Doughty, Sept. 15, 1885. Apptd. surgeon U.S. army, June 16, 1880; capt. asst. surgeon, June 16, 1885; maj. brigade surgeon vols., chief sanitary officer of Havena and in charge of sanitary work there, 1898-1902; applied methods of combating yellow fever which eliminated that disease in Havana; col. asst. surgeon gen., by spl. act. of Congress, for yellow fever work at Havana, Mar. 9, 1903; surgeon gen. U.S. Army, with rank of brig. gen., Jan. 16, 1914; major gen., surgeon gen., U.S. Army, Mar. 4, 1915; retired, Dec. 1, 1918; director yellow fever research, Rockefeller Foundation. Apptd. chief sanitary officer Panama Canal, Mar. 1, 1904; mem. Isthmian Canal Commn., Mar. 4, 1907—; permanent dir. Internat. Health Board of Rockefeller Foundation. Recipient of Mary Kingsley medal from Liverpool School of Tropical Medicine, May 27, 1907; gold medal Am. Museum of Safety, 1914. Awarded D.S.M., 1918; comdr. Legion of Honor (French), 1919; Grand Officer Order of the Crown of Italy, 1918. Died July 4, 1920.

GORMAN, WILLIS ARNOLD army officer, territorial gov.; b. Flemingsburg, Ky., Jan. 12, 1816; s. David L. and Elizabeth G.; LL.B. (hon.), U. Ind. Law Sch., 1845; m. Martha Stone, Jan. 1836; m. 2d, Emily Lewington, Apr. 27, 1865. Admitted to Ind. bar, 1835; clk. Ind. Senate, 1837-38, enrolling sec., 1839-40; mem. Ind. Ho. of Reps., 1841-44; commd. maj. 3d Ind. Regt. under Gen. Lane, 1846; col. 4th Ind. Regt. in Mexican War, 1847; civil and mil. gov. Puebla (Mexico), 1848; mem. U.S. Ho. of Reps. (Domcrat) from Ind., 31st-32d congresses 1849-51; gov. Minn. Territory, 1852-57; supt. Indian affairs, negotiated several treaties; responsible for Minn.'s system of taxing landgrants; del. Minn. Constl. Conv.; mem. Minn. legislature, 1859; commd. col. 1st Minn. Volunteers 1861, brig. gen., 1861; served in 1st Battle of Bull Run, 1861; commanded a brigade at battles of Savage's Station, South Mountain, Edwards Ferry, Antietam, 1862; atty. City of St. Paul (Minn.), 1869-76. Died St. Paul, May 20, 1876.

GORRELL, EDGAR STALEY industrial engr.; b. Baltimore, Md., Feb. 3, 1891; s. Charles Edgar and Pamelia Stevenson (Smith) G.; ed. Baltimore City Coll., 1904-07; B.S., U.S. Mil. Acad., 1912; M.Sc., Mass. Inst. Tech., 1917; D.Sc., Norwich Univ., Northfield, Vt., 1937; m. Ruth Maurice, Dec. 10, 1921; children-Mary (dec.), Edgar Staley; m. 2d Mary Frances O'Dowd Weidman, Feb. 22, 1945. Served in inf., 1912-14; trans. to Aviation Sect. Signal Corps (now Army Air Corps), 1914; joined 1st Aero Squadron, as lt., San Antonio, Tex., Jan. 1916; participated in Punitive Expdn., Mexico, under General Pershing; detailed to Mass. Inst. Tech., then at hdqrs., Washington, D.C.; promoted to capt., 1917; sent to Europe by Pres. Wilson, as mem. Bolling Mission; to visit Allies to determine what aerial material should be produced in United States and what purchased in Europe; served as chief engr. officer of Air Service, A.E.F.; promoted to colonel October 28, 1918; later assistant chief of staff, Air Service; representative of U.S. at more than 200 internat. confs.; participated in campaigns on all five fronts during war; chief of staff of Air Service, A.E.F., with rank of col.; resigned from arny, Mar. 1920. With the Nordyke & Marmon Co., 1920-25, vice-pres., 1923-25; with Statuz Motor Car Co., 1925-39, dir., v.p. and gen. mgr., 1925-29, dir. and pres., 1929-35, also chmn. board; pres., dir. and chmn. of bd. Edgar S. Gorrell Investment Co. since 1935; pres. and dir. Air Cargo, Inc., since 1940; apptd. mem. Air Force Service Investigating Com., Mar. 1934; now mem. Transportation Advisory Group, U.S. Army. Mem. bd. of trustees Norwich U. since 1935; pres. Air Transport Assn. of America since 1936; mem. visitors com. Mass. Inst. of Tech. since 1936; mem. com. of nat. sponsors Air Youth of America, 1940; mem. Aeronautical Advisory Council, 1940. Mem. Soc. Automotive Engineers, Nat. Aeronautic Assn.; mem. Inst. of Aeronautical Science, Am. Meterological Soc. Awards; medal, Mexican Punitive Expdn., 1916; Victory medal, 1918; Distinguished Service medal (U.S.); British D.S.O.; Legion of Honor (French). Presbyterian. Clubs: Country (Indianapolis); Racquet and Tennis, Wings (New York); The Attic (Chicago); Winter Lake (Lake Forest); Conquistadores del Cielo, New Mexico. Author of Study in Aerofoils, 1917. Member editorial board Journal of Air Law. and Commerce, Northwestern U., Jan. 1939. Home: 777 N Washington Rd., Lake Forest, Ill. Office 1515 Massachusetts Av. N.W. Washington. Died Mar. 5, 1945; ashes scattered by Army Air Corps over West Point.

GORRINGE, HENRY HONEYCHURCH naval officer; b. Barbados, W.I., Aug. 11, 1841. Entered U.S. Navy, 1862, served under Porter on Upper Mississippi River, 1862-65, commd. lt. comdr., 1869; with Hydrographic Office, Washington, D.C., prepared several volumes of sailing directions for South Atlantic, 1871-74; in charge of bringing Egyptian Obelisk Cleopatra's Needle from Alexandria to N.Y.C., 1880 resigned commn., 1883; organized, became mgr. Am. Shipbldg. Co. Author: Egyptian Obelisks; contbr. letters to N.Y. Nation. Died N.Y.C., July 6, 1885; buried Sparkill, N.Y.

GOSE, THOMAS PHELPS, lawyer; b. Walla Walla Wash., Dec. 25, 1901; s. Thomas Phelps and Clara (Crowe) G.; LL.B., U. Wash., Seattle, 1925; m. Jane Ankeny, June 29, 1928 (dec.),; children—John Ankeny, Phelps Ridpath, Jane Beclen; m. 2d, Margaret Jane Sell, June 11, 1964. Admitted to Wash. bar, 1925; practiced in Walla Walla, 1925-42, 45-70; mem. firm Gose & Gose, and predecessors, 1925-70; atty. City of Walla Walla, 1932-41. Pres., dir. Ridpath Hotel, Inc., Spokane, Wash., 1951-70; v.p., dir. Walla Walla Canning Co., 1951; mem. adv. bd. for Spokane, Seattle First Nat. Bank, 1958-70; pres., dir. Hotel Spokane, Ltd., 1961-63. Mem. jud. council State of Wash., 1941-42. Bd. regents Wash. State U., 1959-65, pres., 1963-64; dist. dir. Assn. Bds. Univs. and Colls., 1963-65; regent Gonzaga U. Spokane; trustee St. Paul's Sch. Girls, Walla Walla, 1948-68. Served to maj. AUS, 1942-45; ETO. Decorated Bronze Star. Fellow Am. Bar Found.; mem. Am., Wash. (pres. 1967-68) bar assns., Am. Judicature Soc., Eastern Wash. Hist. Soc. (trustee). Episcopalian. Home: Walla Walla WA Died Sept. 9, 1970.

GOSSETT, BENJAMIN BROWN cotton textile exec.; b. Williamston, S.C., Aug. 18, 1884; s. James Pleasant and Sallie A. (Brown) G.; Clemson (S.C.) Coll., 1899-1901; U.S. Naval Academy, Annapolis (Maryland), 1903-05: D.Sc., N.C. State Coll., Raleigh, N.C., 1939; LL.D., Presbyterian Coll. of South Caroline, 1943: m. Katharine Coleman Clayton, Dec. 19, 1906; children-James Pleasant II, Katharine Clayton (Mrs. F. Jones), Philip Clayton, Lt. U.S. Marines, 1905-07 (resigned); in cotton mfg. since 1907; v.p., asst. treas. Williamson (S.C.) Mills, 1908-28; v.p., asst. treas. Brogon Mills, 1909-22; pres., treas. Riverside Mfg. Co., 1913-28, Toxaway Mills, 1913-28; pres. Panola Cotton Mills, 1920-21, Cohannet Mills, 1919-23; pres. and treas. Chadwick-Hoskins Co., 1921-46; pres. Martinsville (Va.) Cotton Mill. Co., 1921-45; v.p., treas. Gossett Mills, 1928-36, pres., treas., 1936-46; pres., treas. Calhoun Mills, 1936-46: pres. Hoskins Corp., N.Y., 1928-40; dir. Textron, Inc., 1945-46; chmn. bd. Textron Southern, Inc., 1946; pres. Bank of Calhoun Falls, S.C., 1912-18; v.p. Citizens Nat. Bank (Anderson, S.C., 1916-21; v.p. American Trust Co., 1924-30, dir., 1919-33; dir. Republic Cotton Mills, 1926-33, Judson Mills, 1915-25. Southern Worsted Co., 1922-26, Dan River Mills, Inc., The Liberia Co., Stettinius Assos.-Liberia, Inc., Pharis Tire & Rubber Co., Carlisle Tire and Rubber Co., P. & N. Ry. Co., M.D. & S. R.R. Co., Turner, Halsey Co., Liberty Mutual Ins. Co., Fed. Fuel Adminstr. for S.C., 1917-18; chmn. commerce and industry div. of State Bd. Conservation and Development of N.C., 1927-30; mem. code authority cotton textile industry under N.R.A.; mem. N.C. Tax Classification Amendment Commn., 1937-38; mem. bd. visitors Clemson Coll.; trustee N.C. State Coll. Commd. capt., U.S. Army, 1918. Mem. Cotton Textile Inst. (dir., mem. exec. com.) Navy League Textile Inst. of U.S. (v.p. and dir. for N.C.), N.Y. Southern Soc., Am. Cotton Mfrs. Assn., Am. Legion, S.A.R., Soc. of Sons of Confederate Vets., Newcomen Soc. of Eng., United Confederate Vets. (hon. maj. gen.), Mil. Order World Wars. Dem. Mason (K.T. Shriner), Clubs: Carlotte Country, Charlotte City, Poinsett, Biltmore Forest Country, Army and Navy, Merchants (N.Y.), Execs., Ponte Vedra, Circus Saints and Sinners. Home: 912 Granville Rd. Office: 1119 Johnston Bldg., S. Tyron St., Charlotte, N.C. Died Nov. 13, 1951; buried Foest Lawn Cemetery, Charlotte, N.C.

GOSSETT, ROBERT KENNETH, sales exec.; b. Indianapolis, Sept. 19, 1921; s. Paull Leland and Leila (Hornberger) G.; B.S., Purdue, 1942; m. Kathryn Moore Bertsch, January 22, 1943 (div.); children—Carolyn (Mrs. Frank L. Sibr, Jr.), Robert Kenneth, Paull; m. 2d, Ann Harrington Bertram, Dec. 16, 1966. Sr. mfg. development engr. R.C.A. Victor Div., Indianapolis, 1942-43; mfrs. sales engring. rep., pres., Gossett-Hill Co., 1946-67; v.p., dir. Zenter Enterprises, Inc., Albion, Mich., 1966-67. Bd. dirs. Vols. America. Served as captain U.S.A.A.F., 1943-46. Mem. Soc. Plastics Engrs. Inc. (nat. pres. 1958), American Management Association, A.I.M., Ind. Soc. Chgo., Phi Gamma Delta. Club: 49'ers Country (Tucson). Home: Des Plaines IL Died Sept. 13, 1967.

GOSTELOWE, JONATHAN cabinetmaker; b. Passyank, Pa. (now part of Phila.), 1744; s. George and Lydia G.; m. Mary Duffield, June 16, 1768; m. 2d. Elizabeth Towers, Apr. 19, 1789. Made cabinets in mahogany and walnut; made clock cases for Edward

Duffield; served as maj. arty. Continental Army, 1776, later chief commissary mil. stores in Phila., capt. of a co. 3d Bn., Pa. Militia, 1783-84; lt. arty., 1787; elected chmn. Gentleman Cabinet and Chair Makers, Phila., 1788; presented carved font to Christ Ch., Phila., 1789. Died Phila., Feb. 3, 1795; buried Christ Ch. Graveyard.

GOTWALS, JOHN C. civil engr.; b. Norristown, Pa., Nov. 4, 1884; s. Abraham G. and Mary (Logan) G.; grad. Pa. State Coll., 1906, C.E., 1907; m. Muriel C. Clemens, Nov. 10, 1927; children-Katharine, Mary Muriel, Engring. work with Pa. R.R. and Catskill Aqueduct, N.Y., until 1913; commd. 2d lt. engrs., U.S.A., Mar. 8, 1913: capt., July 1, 1916; maj. (temp.), Aug. 5, 1917; lt. col. (temp.), 1918-20; maj. engrs., U.S.A., July 1, 1920. Organized and comd. 56th Engrs. in France; in charge searchlight operations, A.E.F., Aug. 1917, to close of war; apptd. chief engr. Alaska Rd. Commn., July 1, 1920; v. chmn. Alaska R.R., Apr. 1-Sept. 30, 1923, chief engr. since Oct. 1, 1923-Mar. 15, 1924; U.S. dist. engr., St. Louis, Mo., 1924-30; engr. commr. Dist. of Columbia, 1930-34; ret. as lt. col., 1934. Mem. Am. Soc. Mil. Engrs., Delta Upsilon; asso. mem. Am. Soc. C.E. Presbyn. Address: 11321 Conway Rd., St. Louis 31. Died Jan. 15, 1946; buried Calvary Cemetery.

GOUCH, LEWIS KETCHAM past comdr. Am. Legion; b. Los Angeles, Apr. 21, 1908; s. Robert Willard and Hazel (Ketcham) G.; B.S., U. So. Cal., 1931; grad. U.S. Naval War Coll., 1943; m. Marguerite Shipley, Apr. 14, 1937. Asst. to pres., pub. relations officer U. So. Cal., 1931-40, also exec. dir. alumni assn.; inheritance tax appraiser State Cal., 1949-50; v.p. Forest Lawn Meml.-Park Assn.; pres. Forest Lawn Mortgage & Investment Co. Chmn. California Vets. Bd., 1957; co-chmn. Pres. Eisenhower's People to People Com.; mem. of U.S.N. Civilian Research Commn., 1948. Served as comdr., U.S.N., 1941-45; instr. U.S. Naval War Coll., 1943-45; on staffs V. Adm. W. S. Pye and Rear Adm. I. C. Johnson; organizer, comdr. 11th Naval Dist., 11th Bn., USNR, 1946-48. Trustee U. So. Cal., 1954. Decorated Legion of Honor (France); Trojan Diamond medal, University So. Cal., 1931; Croix D'Honneur (Belgium), others. Pecipient National Distinguished Service Citation, People to People Program, 1959; USIA Distinguished Service citation, 1961; national commander's award Disabled American Veterans, 1962. Mem. Navy League United States (nat. v.p. 1953-56), Am. Legion (post comdr. 1947, dist. comdr. 1948, dept. comdr. 1949-50, World War II cons. to nat. exec. com., chmn. nat. security commns. Dept. Cal.; nat. v. comdr. 1950-51, nat. comdr. 1952-53), Gen. Alumni Assn. U. So. Cal. (pres. 1953, mem. bd. dirs.), Asso. Student Body U. So. Cal. (pres. 1931), Western Student Body Presidents Assn. (past v.p.), Native Sons of Golden West, Phi Kappa Phi, Chi Phi, Alpha Kappa Psi, Alpha Delta Sigma, Skull and Dagger, Trojan Knights, Blue Key, 40 et 8. Methodist. Mason (Shriner). Kiwanian. Home: 1840 Linda Vista Av., Pasadena 2, Cal. Office: 1712 S. Glendale Av., Glendale, Cal. Died Nov. 13, 1967.

GOULD, EDWIN b. New York, Feb. 25, 1866; s. Jay and Halen Day (Miller) G.; student Columbia, class of '88; m. Sarah Cantine, d. Dr. George F. Shrady, Oct. 27, 1892. Was mem. Troop A, and later capt. and insp. of rifle practice, 71st Regt. N.G.N.Y.; supply sergt. Troop A, Squadron A, N.Y.G., 1917-18; maj. ordnance officer, 1st Brigade, N.Y.G., 1918. Sec. St. Louis, Ark. & Tex. Ry., 1888, until reorganized, 1891, as the St. Louis Southwestern, of which was vice-pres., later pres. and chmn. bd., then sr. v.p.; organized in 1894, the Continental Match Co., which was consolidated with the Diamond Match Co., 1829; pres. Bowling Green Trust Co. of New York until merged with the Equitable Trust Co.; dir. Pine Bluff, Ark., River Ry., Paragould Southeastern Ry. Home: New York, N.Y. Died July 11, 1933.

GOULD, EDWIN MINER LAWRENCE psychologist; b. Montreal, Can., May 4, 1886; s. Edwin and Elizabeth (Whittemore) G.; B.A., McGill U., 1907; The New Church Theol. School, Cambridge, Mass., 1908-10; graduate studies New York School of Social Work and Fordham Univ., 1931-33; m. Caroline Louise Wunsch, June 14, 1910 (divorced 1932); children-Nancy Lawrence (Mrs. Robert Wood), Carol (Mrs. Robert Gilmartin); married second, Harriet Hebbard, July 14, 1932. Came to United States, 1907, naturalized citizen, 1918. Instructor classics, Urbana (Ohio) University, 1907-08; ordained ministry Church of the New Jerusalem (Swedenborgian), 1910; assistant and associate pastor, Newtonville, Massachusetts, 1910-22; pastor, Brooklyn, N.Y., 1922-32; sec. Council of Ministers of General Conv. of New Jerusalem, 1916-20; editor New Church Messenger, 1920-32; dir. New Church Press, Swedenborg Publishing Assn., 1922-36, School of Human Relations (New York), 1933-34, Chief Yeoman U.S.N.R.F., 1917-18; 1st lt. chaplain U.S. Army, 1918-19; chaplain 1st Coast Defense Command Massachusetts National Guard, 1920-22. Member of Phi Kappa Pi. Club: Leewood Golf. Democrat. Author: Problems of the New Christianity, 1924; A Modern Pilgrimage, 1925; The Business of Living, 1926; If We Were Christians, 1931, The Way to be Happy, 1948; Your Your Most Intimate Problems, 1948; Mirror of Your Mind, 1940; The Commonsense of Psychoanalysis, 1950. Now cons. psychologist, writer and author syndicated newspaper column. Mirror of Your Mind. Address: 140 E. 46th St., N.Y.C. 17. Died Dec. 26, 1952; buried Mt. Royal Cemetery, Montreal Can.

GOULD, FRANK MILLER ry. official; b. New York, N.Y., Feb. 6, 1899; s. Edwin and Sarah (Cantine) G.; student Browning Sch., N.Y. City, 1912-16, Yale to 1920; m. Florence Amelia Bacon, Nov. 16, 1924 (divorced May 1944); children-Marianne Alice, Edwin Jay; m. 2d Helen Roosen Canan, June 7, 1944. Assistant secretary St. Louis Southwestern Railway Company, 1920-24, vice president since 1924. Trustee (chairman board) Edwin Gould Foundation for Children. Mem. Yale R.O.T.C., 1917; lt. U.S. Army. 1918; lieutenant 212th Artillery, New York National Guard, 1921-22. Commissioned captain, Army Air Coprs, March 21, 1942. Mem. United Hunt Racing Assn., Virginia Gold Cup Assn. Clubs: New York Yacht. Racquet and Tennis, Turf and Field, University (New York); Jekyll Island (Ga.); Seminole Golf (Palm Beach); Sewanhaka-Corinthian Yacht (L.I.). Home: Oyster Bay, L.I., N.Y. Office: 165 Broadway New York. Died Jan. 13, 1945; buried in Woodlawn, New York.

GOULD, MOSES JOSEPH marine corps officer (ret.); b. Slonim, Russia, Jan. 22, 1887; s. Joseph William and Sarah (Miller) G.; ed. primary schs. in Russia; m. Ruth Virginia Colledge, Feb. 2, 1920; children - Virginia Ruth (Mrs. C.R. Schwenke), Joseph Charles, Robert William. Came to U.S., 1901, naturalized, Jan. 29, 1918. Various jobs, 1901-08; enlisted in U.S. Army, Mar. 27, 1908, discharged, 1911; enlisted USMC, 1911, 15; commd. 2d lt. USMCR, July 15, 1918, 1st lt. USMC, Mar. 29, 1921, and advanced through grades to brig. gen., 1946; ret. from active service, Apr. 1, 1946. awarded Navy Cross for conduct in action against bandit forces, Nicaragua, 1927. Mem. Nat. Geog. Soc., Marine Corps Assn., Ret. Officers Assn. Clubs: Army Navy (Washington), Yacht (Clearwater Beach). Home: 1566 Walnut St., Clearwater, Fla 33515. Died Aug. 23, 1958.

GOVE, AARON educator; b. Hampton Falls, N.H., Sept. 26, 1839; s. John Francis and Sarah Jane (Wadleigh) G.; grad. Ill. Normal U., 1861; hon. A.M., Dartmouth, 1878; LL.D., U. of Colo., 1888; m. Caroline Spofford, Feb. 13, 1865. Entered Union Army as pvt., Sept. 1861, elected 1st lt. 33d Ill. Inf.; left service honorably as adj., bvt. maj., Aug. 1864. In charge of schools at Normal, Ill., 1864-74; supt. schs., Denver, 1874-1904; rep. of the beet sugar industry in the arid states, 1905—. Mason. Conglist. Republican. Address: Denver, Colo. Died Aug. 1, 1919.

GOVE, CHARLES AUGUSTUS naval officer; b. Concord, N.H., July 5, 1854; s. Colonel Jesse Augustus and Maria Louise (Sherburne) G.; grad. U.S. Naval Acad., 1876; m. Minnie Webster, May 23, 1887. Ensign, Mar. 20, 1879; promoted through grades to rear adm., July 11, 1914. Served on all the principal stations, and 21 yrs. and 6 mos. at sea.; on U.S.S. Topeka during Spanish-Am. War, 1898; commandant of midshipmen, U.S. Naval Acad., 1908-09; comd. the new dreadnaught Delaware, 1910, making trip around Cape Horn, and later in comd. same ship at coronation of King George V, naval review off Spithead, the Delaware being the largest of all the war ships there; comd. U.S. Naval Training Sta., San Francisco, 1912-13; retired 1914. Episcopalian. Mason. Comdt. U.S. Naval Unit U. of Calif., 1918. Home: San Francisco, Calif. Died Sept. 11, 1933.

GOW, CHARLES R(ICE), engineering; b. Medford, Mass., Dec. 5, 1872; s. Robert M. and Cordelia (Flynn) G.; B.S., Tufts Coll., 1893, D.Sc., 1919; hon. Dr. Engring., Northeastern Univ., 1932; same, Worcester Poly. Inst., 1935; m. Jeannette A. Weaving, June 12, 1900; children—Ralph F., Arthur R., Jeannette (dec.), Charles R., Grace A. Asst. supt. water dept., Medford, 1893; asst. city engr., Medford, 1895; supt. for contractor in sewer and subway constrn., 1895; asst. engr. Boston Transit Commn., 1895-98; contractor, pub. works and engring. constrn., 1899-1922; cons. engr., Boston, 1922-30; pres. Warren Bros. Co. since 1930; chairman of the board since November 30, 1942. Lecturer on foundations, Mass. Inst. of Tech., 1912-18, prof. of humanics, 1928-30. Postmaster Boston Postal Dist. (25 cities and towns), 1929-30. Served as pvt., advancing to lt. col. engrs., Mass. Nat. Guard, 1889-1908; sergt. maj., later 2d lt. and 1st lt., 5th Mass. Vols., Spanish-Am. War; maj., later lt. col., Constrn. Div., U.S. Army, World War. Mem. commn. on water needs of cities and towns of Ipswich River Valley, 1911-12; chmn. Boston Licensing Bd., 1915-16, Joint N.E. Commn. on St. Lawrence Waterway, 1924-25, Met. Water Supply Investigating Commn., 1924-25, Met. Planning Div., 1928-34. Mem. Am. Soc. C.E., Boston Soc. C.E. (pres. 1915); pres. Associated Industries of Mass., 1921-23. Republican. Conglist. Author: Fundamental Principles of Economics, 1922; Foundations for Human Engineering, 1930; Elements of Human Engineering, 1931. Home: 1751 Beacon St., Brookline, Mass. Office: 38 Memorial Drive, Cambridge MA

GOWDY, ROBERT CLYDE physics; b. Springfield, O., Mar. 10, 1886; s. William Fishell and Rhoda Elizabeth (Vose) G.; B.A., U. of Cincinnati, 1906, M.A., 1907, Ph.D., 1909: studied Trinity Coll. (U. of Cambridge), Eng., 1909-10, College de France, Paris, 1910-11; D.Sc. (honorary), University of Cincinnati, 1947; m. Mabel Greely, Dec. 19, 1914; 1 son, William Robert. Instr. physics, Lehigh U., 1911-12; instr. physics, U. of Cincinnati, 1912-16; asst. prof., 1916-19, asso. prof., 1919-20, prof. since 1920, also acting dean Grad. Sch., 1924, asst. dean Coll. Engring. and Commerce, 1925-28 and since Sept. 1932, acting dean, 1928-32, and 1939-40, dean, Jan. 1940, to Sept. 1946, dir. Sch. Applied Arts, 1940-46, dean emeritus, Coll. of Engineering since Sept. 1946. Commd. 1st lt. Ordnance Dept., U.S. Army, Jan. 1918; capt. Chem. Warfare Service, July 1918. Mem. A.A.A.S., Am. Physical Soc., Societe Physique, Phi Beta Kappa, Sigma Xi, Tau Beta Pi, Omicron Delta Kappa, Delta Tau Delta. Republican. Presbyterian. Club: Literary. Home: 2111 Auburn Av., Cincinnati 19. Died Mar. 27, 1950.

GOWEN, JAMES BARTHOLOMEW army officer; b. N.Y.C., Sept. 25, 1872; s. Michael Duggan and Elizabeth (O'Connell) G.; grad. U.S. Mil. Acad. 1898; honor grad. Army Sch. of Line, 1912; grad. Army Staff Coll., 1916, Army War Coll., 1923; m. Helene Lily Burlinson; children-Dorothy Aline (wife of Haydon L. Boatner, U.S. Army), Helen Burlinson, Mildred Muriel (wife of W. Spencer Rockwell, U.S. Army), Elizabeth Lucille (wife of Richard G. Prather, U.S. Army), Mary Marjorie (wife of Robert H. Sanders, U.S. Army), Kathleen Constance (wife of James M. Worthington, U.S. Army), Asst. cashier Parke, Davis & Co., 1889-94; commd. 2d lt., inf., U.S. Army, 1898; advanced through grades to brig. gen., 1929. Served in Cuban and Philippine campaign against San Ildefonso, P.I., Dec. 1899; acting mil. gov. Nueva Viscaya, P.I., 1900; chief staff, 38th Div., AEF, 1917-18; duty with Gen. Staff, G.H.Q., France, 1918-19; exec. officer Army War Coll., 1919-22, chief staff. 5th Corps Area, 1927-29; comdg. 1st F.A. Brigade, Ft. Hoyle, Md., 1929-32, 11th F.A. Brig., Schofield Barracks, H.T., 1932-34; 21st Brig., Schofield Barracks, H.T., 1934-36; ret., 1936. Campaign badges for Spanish-Am. War, Philippine Insurrection. Cuban Pacification, World War. Decorated Purple Heart. Catholic. Address: care Maj. R. G. Prather, West Point, N.Y. Died Aug. 9, 1958.

GOWEN, JOHN KNOWLES, JR. editor; b. Dover, N.H., Jan. 27, 1894; s. John Knowles and Isabel Sophia (Moore) G.; ed. Barringer High Sch., Newark, N.J.; m. Dora Moise Cohen, Aug. 20, 1913; children - John Knowles III, Paul Roy. Reporter successively Elizabeth (N.J.) Times, Newark (N.J.) Star, Boston (Mass.) Journal, Boston (Mass.) American, Manchester (N.H.) Mirror and American, Charleston (S.C.) News and Courier, until 1914; telegraph editor Brockton (Mass.) Times, 1915-16; mng. editor Charleston (S.C.) American, 1916-17; sub-editor Boston American, 1917-22; make-up editor, Rochester (N.Y.) Journal, 1922; night editor Boston Daily Advertiser, 1922-24; mng. editor Boston Sunday Advertiser, 1924-31; publicity rep. Republican Nat. Com. in 1932 presdl. campaign, for 8 Eastern states; asso. Sunday editor New York American, 1933; editor and pub. "Now" (monthly), 1933-34; pub. The Microphone, 1933-38. Commd. 2d lt. U.S. Signal Corps. 1917; apptd. maj. AC, 1941, col. 1942; ETO. Pacific Theatre Operations; various public relations and command assignments, first G-2, U.S. Army Forces in Australia, 1942. G-2 for Iwo Jima, 1945, sec. to task com. of Electronics Equipment Industry Adv. Com. of Munitions Bd., 1948; Mobilization Assignment Hdqrs. Continental Air Command. Mitchel A.F.B., N.Y. 1946-54, ret. 1954; exec. Hazeltine Corp., 1946 - . Decorated Bronze Star, Legion of Merit. Mem. Am. Legion. Mason (32ff). Club: Wings (N.Y.). Soc. Silurinas. Author: Forty Years of Flying. Contbr. to mags. Home: 75 S. Middle Neck Rd., Great Neck, N.Y. Died June 25, 1961; buried Arlington Nat. Cemetery, Washington.

GOWENLOCK, THOMAS RUSSELL ret. exec.; born Clay Center, Kan., Feb. 14, 1887; s. Thomas and Emma (Allen) G.; LL.B., U. Kan., 1909; m. Marjorie Gird, Sept. 27, 1923; 1 son Thomas Russell III. Admitted to Kan. bar; writer advt., publicity, 1909-28; financial banking, oil exploration, 1828-41; coordinator Ill. law enforcement agencies, 1941-46, oil exploration, 1946 -. Served as colonel Infantry, A.E.F., World War I; asst. chief staff G-2 1st Div., G-2 1st Army Corps; chief staff 33d Div. Ill. N.G. Awarded Distinguished Service Medal, Personal Citation, 2 Unit Citations, Purple Heart; Legion of Honor, Croix de Guerre with Palm (France). Mem. Am. Legion (founder), Chgo. Hist. Soc. (trustee), Soc. First Div. A.E.F. (dir.), Beta Theta Pi. Presbyn. Clubs: Racquet, Saddle and Cycle, Casino. Author: Soldiers of Darkness, 1936. Home: 1550 N. State Pkwy., Chgo. 60610. Died May 15, 1961; buried Rosehill Cemetery.

GRABAU, MARTIN scientist; Ph.D., Harvard, 1931; married Catharine Yale Knock. Executive director committee on basic physical sciences Research and Development Bd., Dept. Defense, 1948-51; sr. staff mem. Operations Research Office U.S. Army, of Johns Hopkins, 1951-56; operations research duty with U.S. Army in Korea, 1951; also dir. operations research office, Tokyo, Japan; supr. thermodynamics sect., researcher in space problems Von Karman Hypervelocity br. Arnold Engring. and Devel. Center, also prof. Space Inst., Tullahoma, Tenn., 1956-65. Home: Point Circle, Route 2, Tullahoma, Tenn. 37388. Died Dec. 26, 1965.

GRACE, ATONZO G., educator; b. Morris, Minn., Aug. 14, 1896; s. Richard H. and Sarah Elizabeth (Murphy) G.; A.B., U. of Minn., 1917, A.M., 1921; Ph.D., Western Reserve University, 1932; Sc.D., Boston University, 1946; L.H.D., Springfield College, 1951; graduate American Musicians School, Chaumont, France, 1919; mar. Jeanette Meland, June 18, 1921; children—Alonzo Gaskell, Richard Simmons, David Harlan. Instr. U. Minn., 1920-22; professor State Tchrs. Coll., S.D., 1923-25; asst. supr., asst. dir., dir. and chmn. dept. adult edn. Cleve. Bd. Edn., 1925-30; mem. faculty, U. Rochester, 1930-38; commissioner of education, Connecticut, 1938-48; dir. edn. and cultural relations Office Mil. Govt. in Germany and Office High Commr., 1948-50; prof. edn., also chmn. dept. edn. Univ. of Chicago, 1950; prof. education and dir. Div. Advanced Studies, Sch. of Edn., N.Y.U., 1951-60, asso. dean 1952-60; dean College Edn., U. Ill., 1960-64, dean emeritus, 1964-71; instr. Yale, 1940-48; lecturer Western Reserve U., Columbia, Harvard, New York U.; dir. of school surveys, N.Y., Washington, New Orleans, etc. Served as private, corpl., sergt., 2d lt. 135th and 76th F.A., 1917-19; dir. of field operations, Pre-Induction Training Branch, U.S. Army, 1943; dir. study Armed Service Edn. and Training Program since 1946. Mem. Monroe Co. (N.Y.) Charter Commn. Trustee Rochester Sch. for Deaf. Decorated Cross of Merit (Germany Fed. Republic). Mem. A.A.A.S., Am. Soc. Pub. Adminstrn., Am. Assn. Univ. Profs., Phi Kappa Sigma. Clubs: Hartford, Yale, Faculty. Author books including: Educational Lessons from Armed Services, 1948. Home: Andover CT Died Oct. 19, 1971; buried Nathan Hale Cemetery, Coventry CT

GRACE, THOMAS L., airlines exec.; b. Neb., June 28, 1911; married; 1 dau. Supt. flight and space control Slick Airways, 1946, supt. operation, 1946-49, v.p. operation, 1949-50, v.p. operation, gen. mgr., 1950, pres., 1950-54, following consolidation with Flying Tiger Line, Inc., 1954, became exec. v.p. of new corp., then v.p. operations N.E. Airlines. pres. Ozark Air Lines, Inc., St. Louis, 1964-71. Served as pilot USAAF, 1942-46. Home: St Louis MO Died July 21, 1971; buried Rose Hills Cemetery, Whittier CA

GRACIE, ARCHIBALD army officer; b. N.Y.C., Dec. 1, 1832; s. Archibald and Elizabeth (Bethune) G.; studied in Heidelberg, Germany; grad. U.S. Mil. Acad., 1854; m. Josephine Mayo, Nov. 19, 1856. Took part in Snake River expdn., 1855; moved to Mobile Ala., 1856; capt. Washington Light Inf. Co., Mobile; commd. maj. 11th Ala. Regt., 1861; raised 43d Ala. Regt., 1862, elected col., led expdn. across Cumberland Mountains to attack and capture Ft. Cliff (Tenn.) commd. brig. gen. Confederate Army, 1862; served in engagements at Chickamauga and Beans Station; posthumously commd. maj. gen. Died Petersburg, Ky., Dec. 2, 1864; buried N.Y.C.

GRAF, HOMER WILLIAM, naval officer; b. Chicago, Ill., Feb. 16, 1894; grad. U.S. Naval Acad., 1915. Commd. ensign, U.S. Navy, 1915, and advanced through the grades to commodore, 1944; served in U.S.S. Florida with British Grand Fleet, during World War I; exec. officer U.S.S. Helena, Asiatic Station, 1921, U.S.S. New Orleans (Vladivostok, Siberia, and Kobe, Japan), 1921-22, U.S. ships Borie, Peary, Penguin and Canopus, 1924-27; exec. officer, U.S.S. Tennessee, 1940; commd. U.S.S. Cincinnati, 1941-42; aide, and officer in charge building and grounds, U.S. Naval Acad., 1942-43; chief of staff to comdr. Seventh Fleet, Southwest Pacific Area, 1943; comdr. transport squadron, transport division; participated Iowa Jima, Luzon campaigns, also occupation of Japan. Supervisor Harbor of New York, 1946-48. Decorated Legion of Merit, Victory Medal with Grand Fleet clasp, Navy Expeditionary Medal with bronze star, Am. Defense Service Medal with fleet clasp, Asiatic-Pacific Area Campaign Medal Philippine Liberation Medal, Japanese Occupation Medal, unit citation medal. Home: Sarasota FL Died Mar. 1970.

GRAHAM, CHARLES KINNAIRD naval and army officer, civil engr.; b. N.Y.C., June 3, 1824; m. Mary Graham. Commd. midshipman U.S. Navy, 1841; served with Gulf Squadron during Mexican War, 1846-48; one of surveyors employed in laying out Central Park, N.Y.C.; became constrn. engr. Bklyn. Navy Yard, 1857; commd. maj. Army of Potomac, U.S. Army, 1862, later lt. col.; apptd. col. 74th Inf.; promoted brig. gen. for services with Army of Potomac, 1863; commanded brigade of III Corps at battles of Chancellorsville and Gettysburg, captured and exchanged, 1863; comdr. gunboat flotilla under Gen. B.F. Butler on James River, took part in attack on Ft. Fisher; chief engr. dock depot, N.Y.C., 1873-75; surveyor Port of N.Y., 1878-83, naval officer, 1883-85. Died Lakewood, N.J., Apr. 15, 1889.

GRAHAM, DONALD GOODNOW, lawyer; b. Ft. Worth, Tex., Dec. 9, 1894; s. Theodore F. and Carrie (Knight) G.; B.S., Coe Coll., 1916; LL.B., Harvard, 1921; m. Juanita Fisher, Sept. 2, 1919; children—Richard Fisher, Donald Goodnow. Admitted to Wash. bar, 1921; also U.S. Supreme Ct., U.S. Fed. Cts., Wash. State Cts., U.S. Tax Ct.; practice in Seattle, 1921—; asst. U.S. atty., 1924-25; pvt. practice, 1925-73; sr. mem. Graham, Dunn, Johnston & Rosenquist, 1930-73. Dir. Fisher Flouring Mills Co., Fisher's Blend Sta., Inc., San Juan Fishing & Packing Co., West Coast Airlines, Inc., Columbia River Packers. Chmn. advance gift sect. United Good Neighbor Fund, 1936. Treas. Republican Primary campaign U.S. Senate, Janet Tourtellotte, 1950. Pres., bd. dirs. U. Wash. Arboretum Found.; bd. dirs. O.D. Fisher Charitable Found; former gov. for Wash. Nat. Aero. Assn. Served to 1st lt. USAAF, 1917-19, to col., 1942-45. Mem. Am., Wash., Seattle bar assns., Seattle C. of C. (past sect. chmn.), Order Daedalians, Am. Judicature Soc. Episcopalian. Clubs: Rainier, Sea Tennis, Sea Golf, Quiet Birdmen. Home: Seattle WA Deceased.

GRAHAM, EVARTS AMBROSE surgeon; b. Chicago, Ill., Mar. 19, 1883; s. David Wilson and Ida Anspach (Barned) G.; A.B., Princeton, 1904; M.D., Rush Med. Coll., 1907; Sc.D., Cincinnati, 1927; LL.D., Central Coll., 1927; hon. M.S., Yale, 1928; Sc.D., Princeton Univ. 1929; Sc.D., Western Reserve University, 1931; Sc.D., U. of Pa., 1940; Sc.D., U. of Chicago, 1941; Sc.D., McGill, U., 1944, Emory University, 1954, New York University, 1955; LL.D. University of Glasgow, 1951, Johns Hopkins U., 1952. Washington U., 1952, U. Leeds (England), 1954; special student chemistry, University Chgo., 1913, 14; m. Helen Tredway, January 29, 1916; children-David Tredway, Evarts Ambrose. Interne Presbyn. Hosp. Chgo., 1907-08; asst., also instructor surgery, Rush Medical College, 1909-15; asst. attending surgeon, Presbyterian Hosp., Chgo., 1912-15; mem. staff Otho. S. A. Sprague Meml. Inst., Rush, Chgo., 1912-15; chief surgeon Park Hosp., Mason City, Ia., 1915-17; professor surgery Washington U. Sch. of Medicine 1919-51, prof. emeritus since 1951; emeritus surgeon in chief Barnes Hosp. and St. Louis Children's Hosp.; mem. Presidents Commn. on Health Needs of Nation, 1952; apptd. by Rockefeller Foundation to investigate teaching of surgery in British medical school, 1922. Harvey Soc. lecturer, 1924 and 1934; Mutter lecturer, 1924; McArthur lecturer, 1926; Shattuck lecturer, 1928; Alvarez lecturer, 1930; Joyce lecturer, 1931; Bevan lecturer, 1932; Caldwell lecturer, 1933; Balfour lecturer, 1934; Judd lecturer, 1937; Lister orator, London, 1947 ; Fraser lectr., Edinburgh, 1954; surgeon in chief Peter Bent Brigham Hosp., 1925; temp. prof. surgery St. Bartholomew's Hosp., London, 1939. Mem. Nat. Research Council (med. fellowship bd.), 1925-39; chmn. com. on surgery, 1940-46. Captain Medical Corps, U.S. Army, Jan. 1918; maj. May 1918; served with Sch. of Neurol. Surgery, Chicago, later as mem. Empyema Commn., Camp Lee, Va.; spl. lab. research on empyema, at Baltimore, Md.; comdg.officer Evacuation Hosp. No. 34, in France, Sept. 1918-May 1919; hon. discharged, 1919. Mem. com. apptd. by sec. of war to study activities of Medical Department of U.S. Army, 1942. Pres. bd. trustees John Burroughs School, St. Louis, 1930-37; mem. Nat. Bd. Med. Examiners, 1924-33. Chairman Am. Board of Surgery (1937-41); fellow Am. Coll. Surgeons (pres. 1940-41); Am. Med. Assn. (chmn. sect. gen. and abdominal surgery, 1925); mem. Am. Surg. Assn. (pres. 1937), Soc. Clin. Surgery, Am. Assn. Thoracic Surgery (pres. 1928), St. Louis Assn. Surgeons (pres. 1925), Soc. for Clin. Research. Société Internationale de Chirugie; Kaiserlich Deutsche Akad. d. Naturforscher (1932); National Academy Sciences (1941), Am. Philos. Soc. (1941); hon. fellow Assn. of Surgeons of Great Britain and Ireland, Royal College of Surgeons (London, Eng.); honorary mem. Society of Thoracic Surgeons of Great Britain and Ireland, Sociedad Argentina de Cirujanos Royal Society of Sciences, Uppsala, Sweden, others; mem. Nu Sigma Nu, Alpha Omega Alpha fraternities. Author: Empyema Thoracis, 1925; Diseases of the Gall-Bladder and Bile Ducts, 1928. Editor: Surgical Diagnosis, 1930. Wrote sect., "Treatment of the Acute Empyema," for Medical and Surgical History of World War (published by Surgeon General's Office), 1924. Editor, Year Book of Surgery. Awarded Gross prize in surgery, 1920; Leonard prize by American Roentgen-Ray Society, 1925; gold medal by the American Radiol. Soc., 1925, for the development of cholecystography; gold medal and certificate of merit from St. Louis Medical Society, 1927, for development of cholecystography; gold medal by Southern Medical Association, 1934, for scientific research; John Scott medal by City of Philadelphia, 1937; received St. Louis Award, 1942; Lister Medal of Royal Coll. Surgeons, Eng., 1942; Roswell Park medal, 1949; American College Chest Physician medal, 1949; Miss. Valley Med. Soc. medal, 1949; distinguished service medal of A.M.A., 1950; Bigelow Medal of Boston Surgical Soc., 1951, Charles Mickle Fellowship, Univ., Toronto, 1943. Gave expositions of disturbed mechanics of respiration and circulation when normal intrathoracic pressures are altered; developed method for cholecystography, or the X-ray visualization of the gall-bladder; new treatment for chronic abscess of the lung; contbns. to pathology and treatment of carcinoma of bronchus, explanation of particular toxicity of choloroform and similar anaesthetic agents; etc. Co-editor Archives of Surgery, 1920-45 and of Annals of Surgery, 1935-45; editor Journal of Thoracic Surgery since 1931; editor Year Book of Surgery, 1926-27. Home: Old Jamestown Rd., R.R. 2, Box 256, Florissant, Mo. Office: Barnes Hospital, 600 S. Kingshighway, St. Louis 10. Died Mar. 4, 1957.

GRAHAM, JAMES DUNCAN army officer; b. Prince William County, Va., Apr. 4, 1799; s. Dr. William and Mary (Campbell) G.; grad. U.S. Mil. Acad., 1817; m. Charlotte Meade, July 6, 1828; m. 2d, Frances Wickham; 1 son, William M. First asst. on Maj. Stephen H. Long's expdn. to Rocky Mountains, 1819-21; served topog. duty, 1819-38; commd. maj. Topog. Engr. Corps, 1838; astronomer in surveying party that fixed boundary between U.S. and Republic of Tex., 1839; astronomer, head scientific corps in joint demarcation of Me.-Canadian boundary, 1840-43; brevetted lt. col., circa 1847; directed resurvey of Mason-Dixon line, 1848-50; astronomer and head scientific corps that surveyed part of Mexican border, 1850-51; served on Gt. Lakes, 1854-64; promoted lt. col., 1861, col., 1863; supt. engr. of sea-walls in Boston Harbor, 1864-65; Mt. Graham (Ariz.) named after him. Died Dec. 28, 1865.

GRAHAM, JAMES HIRAM coll. dean; m.; 2 daus. Served to col., U.S. Army, in charge AEF heavy constrn., France, World War I, aide to under sec. of War, World War II; dean Coll. Engring., U. Ky., Lexington, 1935-46, ret. Decorated D.S.M.; French Legion of Honor. Died June 24, 1960; buried Cave Hill Cemetery, Louisville.

GRAHAM, JOHN HUGH congressman; b. Belfast, Ireland, Apr. 1, 1835; brought to U.S., 1836; attended public schs., Bklyn. Recruited Co. A, 5th Regt., Heavy Arty., N.Y. Volunteers, during Civil War, served as capt., 3 years; commd. maj., brevetted lt. col. for services at Harpers Ferry and in Shenandoah Valley (Va.); engaged in hardware bus., Bklyn., after Civil War; mem. U.S. Ho. of Reps. (Democrat) from N.Y., 53d Congress, 1893-95. Died Bklyn., July 11, 1895; buried Greenwood Cemetery.

GRAHAM, JOSEPH army officer; b. Chester County, Pa., Oct. 13, 1759; s. James and Mary (McConnell) G.; ed. Queen's Museum, Charlotte, S.C.; m. Isabella Davidson, 1787. Joined Continental Army as enlisted man, 1778, became capt. of a company of mounted inf.; in command reserve during defense of Charlotte, 1780; organizer company of dragoon, maj., 1781; del. to N.C. Conv. that ratified, U.S. Constn., 1788; del. to N.C. Conv. that ratified Bill of Rights, 1789; mem. N.C. Senate, 1788-94, N.C. Council of State, 1814-15; an original trustee U. N.C.; stated writing series letters and articles for Archibald D. Murphy, 1820, which provide valuable record of Revolutionary times in N.C. Died Lincoln County, N.C., Nov. 12, 1836.

GRAHAM, LAWRENCE PIKE brig. gen. vols. Col. U.S. Army; b. Amelia County, Va., 1815; apptd. 2d lt., 2d dragoosn, 1837; later becoming 1st lt. and capt.; served in campaign against Seminoles, 1842; bvtd. maj. for gallantry in Mexican War; promoted maj., June 14, 1858; lt. col., 5th cav., Oct. 1861; col., 14th Cav., May 1864; bvtd. brig. gen. for meritorious services in Civil War, March 1865. Commissioned brig. gen. vols., Aug. 1861; raised, 1862, and comd. cav. brigade in Army of Potomac; mustered out of vol. service, Aug. 1865; retired as col., Dec. 1870. Home: Washington, D.C. Died 1905.

GRAHAM, ROBERT X(AVIER) univ. prof.; b. Moosic, Pa., Mar. 26, 1902; s. James and Catherine (Drexel) G.; A.B., Colgate Univ., 1925; A.M., Univ. of Wis., 1933; student, Univ. of Pittsburgh, 1935-37; m. Eleanor Kathryn Warner, Nov. 21, 1931. Instr. and asst. prof. English and journalism, Westminster Coll., 1925-35, dir. of pub. relations, 1927-35, coach of track and cross country, and asst. athletic dir., 1928-35; instr. English and journalism, Pa. Coll. for Women, 1935-36, dir. of publicity, 1935-36; dir. of pub. relations, Univ. of Pittsburgh, 1935-42, asso. prof. and head, Div. of Journalism, since 1945. Served in U.S. Naval Res., advancing from lt. to lt. comdr., 1942-45. Mem. Am. Coll. Pub. Relations Assn. (nat. editor, 1934-38; nat. pres., 1938-39), Am. Assn. Teachers of Journalism, Baker St. Irregulars, Pi Delta Epsilon, Omicron Delta Kappa, Kappa Delta Rho. Republican. Presbyterian. Author: A Bibliography in the History and Backgrounds of Journalism (privately pub.), 1940, Mechanics of Newspaper Editing, 1947; Ethics in Publicity in College Publicity Handbook, 1948; The College Newspaper (Pi Delta Epsilon), 1949. Editor of various club and assn. publs., 1935-39. Contbr. articles to trade, professional, fraternal and gen. mags. Home: 2333 McNary Boulevard, Pitts. 35. Died Feb. 4, 1953; buried Oa, Park Cemetery. New Castle, Pa.

GRAHAM, STEPHEN VICTOR, naval officer; b. Mich., Mar. 4, 1874; s. Lester and Margaret (Smith) G.; grad. U.S. Naval Acad., 1894; m. Viola Jurgens, July 8, 1927. Commd. ensign, U.S. Navy, 1896, retired as capt., 1929; commd. rear adm., retired, 1931; served as naval attache, Vienna, Austria, 1914-17; gov. of Am. Samoa, 1927-29. Decorated Distinguished Service Medal, World War I; special commendation Navy Dept. Home: 2227 Observatory Av., Hollywood CA

GRAHAM, STERLING EDWARD, newspaper pub.; b. Cleve., May 16, 1892; s. Thomas C. and Jennie (Wright) G.; A.B., Columbia, 1915; m. Jane Peterson, Feb. 26, 1921; (dec. 1965); children—Thomas R., Sterling Edward, Jane E. (Mrs. Joseph H. Champ); m. 2d, Dorothy Pratt, July 14th, 1966. Display advt. salesman Cleve. Plain Dealer, 1924-28, local advt. mgr.,

1928-31, advt. dir., 1931-43, gen. mgr., 1943-53; pres., dir. Forest City Pub. Co., pub. Cleve. Plain Dealer, 1953-63, ret. Served as captain of infantry, U.S. Army, 1917-19. Member Ohio (director), Cleveland (pres. 1950-51, dir.), chambers of commerce, American Legion. Clubs: Union, Madison Country, Automobile (dir.), Advertising, Rotary, City, Cleveland Skating (Cleve.). Home: Shaker Heights OH Died May 24, 1971.

GRAHAM, WILLIAM ALEXANDER retired army officer, author; b. Chgo., Jan. 23, 1875; s. William Robinson (maj. U.S.A.) and Martha Smith (Hawkins) G.: student Bellit Coll. Acad., 1891-93, Beloit Coll., 1893-94, Stanford U., 1894-96, LL.B., U. Ia., 1897; m. Ada Jane Houck, June 25, 1902 (dec.); 1 son, Alexander (col. U.S.A.); m. 2d, Helen Jeanette Bury, Nov. 28, 1935; 1 son, William Alexander, Jr. (midshipman U.S. Naval Acad.). Admitted to Ia. bar, 1897, in gen. practice, Cedar Falls, 1897-1902, Des Moines, 1902-16; capt. of inf., Ia. Nat. Guard, 1912-17, Mexican Border 1916-17; major, judge advocate, 88th Div., 1917-19; with A.E.F., 1918-19; commd. lt. col., Judge Advocate General's Dept., U.S. Army, 1920, col., 1931; retired, 1939. Decorated Mexican Border service medal, Victory medal with Meuse-Argonne and Defensive Sector bars. Mem. Alpha Tau Omega, Phi Delta Phi. Clubs: University, Lake Shore Athletic, Illinois Athletic (Chicago). Author: The Story of the Little Big Horn, 1926; The Custer Myth, 1953; Abstract of the Reno Court of Inquiry, 1954. Home: 555 Radcliffe Av., Pacific Palisades, Cal. Died Oct. 8, 1954; buried Arlington Nat. Cemetery.

GRAHAM, WILLIAM MONTROSE army officer; b. Washington, Sept. 28, 1834; s. Col. James Duncan and Charlotte (Meade) G. Apptd. from D.C., 2d lt. 1st Arty., June 7, 1855; promoted through grades to brig. gen., 5th Arty., May 26, 1897; maj. gen. vols., May 4, 1898; retired, Sept. 28, 1898; hon. discharged from vol. service, Nov. 30, 1898. Bvtd. maj., July 1, 1862, "for gallant and meritorious services during Peninsular campaign"; lt. col., Sept. 17, 1862, for same in battle of Antietam; col., July 3, 2963, for same in battle of Gettysburg; brig. gen., Mar. 13, 1865, for same in field during the war. Comd. Dept. of Texas, 1897; organized and comd. Dept. of the Gulf until apptd. maj. gen. of vols., May 4, 1898; organized and comd. 1d Army Corps for service in Spanish War. Mem. bd. of officers apptd. by Sec. of War to locate positions of the regular batteries of Arty. on the battlefield of Gettysburg and to prepare the inscriptions on the tablets erected to mark the same. Died Jan. 17, 1916.

GRAMMER, ELIJAH SHERMAN senator; b. Hickory County, Mo., Apr. 3, 1868; s. John W. and Sarah F. G.; ed. Bentonville (Ark.) Coll.; m. Emma Kindley, Jan 21, 1904. Logger, later gen mgr. lumber camps, Washington; in charge constrn. tramway, Chilcoot Pass, Alaska; owner logger successively of Scott & Grammer, Sisco, Wash., Grammer's Camp, Montborne, Brown's Bay Logging Co., Seattle, Admiralty Logging Co., Portland, Ore.; pres. and mgr. Grammer Investment Co.; v.p. and treas. Carlton & Coast Ry. Co. Served as maj. U.S. Army, assigned to Spruce Production Div., 1918. Apptd. mem. U.S. Senate to fill unexpired term of Senator Wesley L. Jones, dec., Nov. 22, 1932, term expiring Mar. 4, 1933. Republican. Presbyn. Mason. Home: Seattle, Wash. Died Nov. 21, 1936.

GRAND, GORDON, JR., chem. ofcl.; b. Orange, N.J., Mar. 14, 1917; s. Gordon and Emma (Dill) G.; grad. The Hill Sch., 1934; B.A., Yale, 1938; LL.D., Harvard, 1941; m. Ruth Young, Feb. 27, 1943; children—Minette, Gordon, III, Lorna, Diana, Timothy. Teacher at the Millbrook (New York) School, from 1938-39; admitted to the N.Y. bar, 1943, to practice before U.S. Supreme Ct.; lawyer Spence, Hotchkiss, Parker & Duryee, N.Y.C., 1946-48; Counsel Rep. mems. Ways and Means Com., U.S. Congress, 1948-52; clk. Ways and Means Com., 83d Congress, 1953; asst. to pres. Olin Industries, Inc., N.Y.C., 1954; sec. Olin Mathieson Chem. Corp., N.Y.C., 1954-55, corporate v.p., 1955-63, vice chmn. bd., exec. v.p., 1964-65, pres., chief exec. officer, from 1965, chmn. 1966-67; dir. Nat. Starch & Chem. Co., 1st Nat. City Bank, Prudential Ins. Co. America, Squibb Beechnut. Gov. Young Rep. Club N.Y.C., 1947-48. Trustee, vice chairman Tax Foundation, Incorporated. Served to Maj., U.S. Army Res., ret. Decorated B.S.M.; 2 croix de Guerre (France). Clubs: Metropolitan (Washington); Links, Yale (N.Y.C.). Author: Federal Legislative Process, 1951; Proposals for Revising the Tax System, 1954. Home: Greenwich CT Died Jan. 16, 1972; buried Millbrook NY

GRANGER, AMOS PHELPS congressman, businessman; b. Suffield, Conn., June 3, 1789; attended public schs. Moved to Manlius, N.Y., 1811; pres. Town of Manlius, several years; served as capt. at Sackets Harbor and on Canadian border, during War of 1812; moved to Syracuse, N.Y., 1820, engaged in various business enterprises; trustee City of Syracuse, 1825-30; delivered welcoming address when Gen. Lafayette visited Syracuse, 1825; del. Whig Nat. Conv., Balt., 1852; mem. U.S. Ho. of Reps. (Whig) from N.Y., 34th-35th congresses, 1855-59. Died Syracuse, Aug. 20, 1866; buried Oakwood Cemetery.

GRANGER, CHARLES TRUMBULL lawyer; b. Monroe County, N.Y., Oct. 9, 1835; acad. edn. at Waukegan, Ill. Taught sch. until Aug. 1862; was supt. schs., Mitchell County, Ia., 1861-62; admitted to bar, 1860, at Waukon, Ia. Twice married; now widower. Recruited, Aug. 1862, Co. K, 27th Ia. Inf.; was its capt. to close of war. After war practiced law; dist. atty., 10th Jud. Dist., Ia., 1869-72; circuit judge, 1872-86; dist. judge after change of jud. system, 1886-89; judge Supreme Ct. of Ia., 1889-1900. Address: Waukon, Ia. Died Oct. 26, 1915.

GRANGER, FRANK BUTLER M.D., b. Belmont, Nev., Aug. 22, 1875; s. Frank Clark and Alice M. (Butler) G.; A.B., Harvard, 1899; M.D., 1902; m. Clara Talbot Davis, Oct. 29, 1902. Instr. physical therapeutics, Harvard Grad. Sch. of Medicine, 1911—; lecturer on same, Tufts Coll. Sch. of Medicine, 1906-10; physician for physical therapeutics, Boston City Hosp.; neurologist Boston Dispensary. Commd. capt. Med. Corps, U.S. Army, May 17, 1918; major, September 5, 1918; honorably discharged, rank lieutenant colonel, December 5, 1919; organizer and dir. dept. of physiotherapy, Div. of Physical Reconstruction, Office of Surgeon Gen., Washington; counsellor med. council, U.S. Vets. Bur. Pres. Am. Coll. Physiotherapy. Progressive Rep. Episcopalian. Mason. Author: Technic of Physiotherapy, 1920. Home:Allston, Mass. Died Oct. 23, 1928.

GRANGER, GORDON Union soldier; b. Joy, N.Y., Nov. 6, 1822; s. Gaius and Catharine (Taylor) G.; grad. U.S. Mil. Acad., 1845; m. Maria Letcher, 1869. Soldier in Mexican War; 1st lt., 1852; stationed mostly on frontier before Civil War; capt., 1861, col., 1861; served under Gen. Nathaniel Lyon in Battle Wilson's Creek, Aug. 1861; commanded cav. brigade in Miss., 1862, brig. gen., Mar. 26, 1862; maj. gen. Vols., commanding div. in Tenn., Sept. 17, 1862; in command Army of Ky., spring 1863; most famous for aid to Gen. Thomas at Battle Chickamauga; comdr. army aiding Adm. Farragut in capture Ft. Morgan (Ala), Aug. 1864; col. inf. Regular Army, July 28, 1866; commanded Dist. N.M. Died Santa Fe, N.M., Jan. 10, 1876.

GRANGER, MOSES MOORHEAD judge; b. Zanesville, O., Oct. 22, 1831; s. James and Matilda Vance (Moorhead) G.; A.B., Kenyon Coll., 1850, A.M., 1853, LL.D., 1880; m. Mary Hoyt, d. Gen William J. Reese, Dec. 29, 1858. Practiced law at Zanesville, 1853-61 and 1865—; capt. 18th U.S. Inf., May 14, 1861; maj. 122d Ohio Inf., Sept. 10, 1862; lt. col., May 1, 1863; bvtd. col. vols., Oct. 19, 1864, for gallant and meritorious services in campaign before richmond, Va., and in Shenandoah Valley; resigned Dec. 16, 1964. City solicitor, Zanesville, O., 1865-66; pros. atty., 1866; judge Ct. Common Pleas, 8th Jud. Dist., from 1866; chief judge Ohio Supreme Ct. Commn., 1883-85. Author: The Battle of Cedar Creek, 1890; Washington versus Jefferson, The Case Tried by Battle, 1861-65, 1898; Ohio Judiciary, 1803-1903, in Ohio Centennial Celebration, 1903; A Fair Answer to the Confederate Appeal at Richmond, Va., 1907. Home: Zanesville, O. Died Apr. 29, 1913.

GRANT, ALBERT WESTON naval officer; b. E. Benton, Me., Apr. 14, 1856; grad. U.S. Naval Acad., 1877; married; children-Albert Weston, Charles Sharp, Richard Southall. Ensign, May 17, 1881; lt. jr. grade, Nov. 1, 1887; lt., May 9, 1893; promoted through grades to rear adm., Sept. 7, 1915. Served on Massachusetts, Spanish-Am. War, 1898; duty U.S. Naval Acad., 1894-97, 1900-02, 1905-07; exec. officer Oregon, 1902-03; comd. Frolic, 1903-05; comd. U.S.S. Arethusa, 1907-08; chief of staff Atlantic Fleet during cruise battleships around world, 1908-09; comd. Connecticut, 1909-10, Navy Yard, Phila., 1910-13; duty in connection with building of Texas, 1913-14; comd. Texas, 1914-15; comd. Submarine Force, Atlantic Fleet, 1915-17; apptd. comdr. Battleship Force One, Atlantic Fleet, July 1917, with rank of vice admiral, and comd. U.S. Fleet in Western Atlantic, 1918-19; Navy Yard, Washington, D.C. 1919-20; retired, 1920. Philadelphia, Pa. Died Sept. 30, 1930.

GRANT, CARROLL WALTER, educator; b. Kalamo, Mich., Nov. 14, 1900; s. Walter Merwin and Sara Eliza (Wilson) G.; B.A., Olivet Coll., 1924, D.Sc., 1960; M.A., Battle Creek (Mich.) Coll., 1927; student Marine Biol. Lab., summer 1926; Ph.D., Yale, 1931; m. Sara Ann Cline, Sept. 1, 1928; children—Linda Lee (Mrs. Robert W. Clark), David Carroll. Asso. prof. biology Battle Creek Coll., 1931; mem. faculty Bklyn. Coll., 1833-63, professor of biology, chairman of the department, 1956-63, prof. emeritus biology, 1963-69; research asso. Scripps Instn. Oceanography, La Jolla, Cal., 1941-42. Served to lt. comdr. USNR, 1942-46. Mem. Soc. Am. Bacteriologists, Acad. Microbiology, A.A.A.S., Sigma Xi. Home: Boca Raton FL Died May 15, 1969; buried Boca Raton Cemetery, Boca Raton FL

GRANT, CLAUDIUS BUCHANAN judge; b. Lebanon, Me., Oct. 25, 1835; s. Joseph and Mary (Merrill) G.; A.B., U. of Mich., 1859, A.M., 1862, LL.D., 1891; teacher and prin., Ann Arbor High Sch., 1859-62; m. Caroline L. Felch, June 13, 1863. Served in Civil War, Capt. to col., 20th Mich. Vols., 1862-65; studied law, U. of Mich., 1865-66; admitted to bar, 1866; recorder and postmaster, Ann Arbor, 1867-70; mem. Mich. Ho. of Rep., 1870-74 (speaker pro tem.); regent U. of Mich., 1872-80; practiced law, Houghton, Mich., 1873-82; pros. atty., Houghton County, 1876-77; judge Circuit Ct., 1881-89; justice, 1889-1909, chief justice, 1888, 1889 and 1908. Supreme Ct. of Mich. Republican. Retired from the bench Jan. 1, 1910, and engaged in practice of law as gen. counsel the law firm of Warren, Cady & Ladd, Detroit. Address: Detroit, Mich. Died 1921.

GRANT, DAVID NORVELL WALKER physician; b. Richmond, Va., May 14, 1891; s. Percival Stuart and Avis Barney (Walker) G.; M.D., U. Va., 1915; grad. Army Med. Sch., 1917, Sch. of Aviation Medicine, San Antonio, 1931, Air Corps Tactical Sch., 1937, Chem. Warfare Sch., 1939; Sc.D., Hahnemann Med. Coll., 1944; m. Dorothy Krayenbuhl, May 14, 1917; 1 son, David Norvell Walker. Res. officer, M.C., U.S. Army, 1916; commd. 1st lt., U.S. Army, 1917, and advanced through grades to maj. gen., 1943; ret. for physical disability, 1946; served in Panama and Occupation of Germany, World War I; became chief med. service AAF, 1939, The Air Surgeon, 1941-46, duties including responsibility for all med. research, such as devel. of oxygen equipment and clothing for altitude flight; inaugurated rehab. program (later adopted by Army and Navy); established aviation psychology program, also introduced organized air evacuation of casualties on mass scale; now med. dir., dir. blood program A.R.C. Decorated D.S.M.; hon. mem. mil. div. Order of the Bath. Fellow A.C.S.; mem. Assn. Mil. Surgeons U.S., A.M.A., Assn. Aviation Medicine, D.C. Med. Soc., Academia Brasileria de Medicina Militar, Delta Kappa Epsilon, Theta Nu Epsilon, Phi Rho Sigma. Club: Army and Navy (Washington). Contbr. articles to med. publs. Home: 3134 Ordway St. Office: care A.R.C. 17th and D Sts., Washington. Died Aug. 1964.

GRANT, FREDERICK DENT army officer; b. St. Louis, May 30, 1850; s. President Ulysses S. and Julia (Dent) G.; apptd. at-large, and grad. U.S. Mil. Acad., 1871; m. Ida M. Honoré, Oct. 20, 1874. Commd. 2d lt. 4th Cav., June 12, 1871; 1st lt., June 28, 1876; lt. col. a.-d.-c. to Lt. Gen Sheridan, Mar. 17, 1873-June 1, 1881; engr. on U.P. and Colo. Central rys., 1871; served on frontier, 1873-81; resigned Oct. 1, 1881. U.S. minister to Austria, 1889-93; police commr. of New York, 1894-98; apptd. col. 14th N.Y. Inf., May 1, 1898; apptd. brig. gen. vols., May 27, 1898; hon. discharged, Apr. 15, 1899; apptd. brig. gen. vols., Apr.15, 1899, brig. gen. U.S. Army, Feb. 18, 1901; maj. gen. U.S. Army, Feb. 6, 1906. Served in P.R. 1 yr., and after war comd. mil. dist. of San Juan; comd. 2d Brigade, 1st Div., 8th Army Corps in P.I., Apr.-Nov. 1899, 2d Brigade, 2d Div., Nov. 1899-Jan. 1900; comd. 5th dist. Northern Luzon, Jan. 1900-Apr. 1901, Southern Luzon, Oct. 1901-Apr. 1902; comd. Dept. of Tex., 1902-04, Dept. of the Lakes, Jan.-Sept. 1904, Dept. of the East, 1904-08, Dept. of the Lakes, 1908-10, Dept. of the East, July 25, 1910-July 1, 1911, Eastern Div., July 1, 1911—. Died Apr. 11, 1912.

GRANT, JOHN THOMAS railroad builder; b. Greene County, Ga., Dec. 13, 1818; s. Daniel and Lucy (Crutchfield) G.; grad. U. Ga., 1833; m. Martha Cobb, 1834, at least 1 son, William. Acquired huge tract of land, Walton County, Ga., 1844, owned largest plantation in Ga. (2000 acres and 100 slaves); executed large railroad bldg. contracts in Ga., Ala., Tenn., Miss., Tex.; mem. Ga. Senate, 1856; served with rank of col. on staff Gen. Howell Cobb during Civil War; moved to Atlanta (Ga.) after Civil War, owned large tracts of real estate, furthered railroad constrn. Died Atlanta, Jan. 18, 1887.

GRANT, LESTER STRICKLAND, mining engr.; b. New Haven, Conn., Oct. 31, 1877; s. Charles Alfred and Mary J. (Strickland) G.; E.M., Colo. Sch. of Mines, 1899; m. Chloe Ella Thornton, 1900; children—Robert Waltman, Richard Thornton. Engr. Isabella Gold Mining Co., Cripple Creek, Colo., 1899-1901, Isabella Mines Co., 1901-03; supt. Isabella Lease, 1904; engr. and assayer, Findley Consol. Mining Co., Cripple Creek, 1905-06; metallurgist and engr. Inca Mining Co., Peru, S.A., 1906-09; asst. supt. Roosevelt Drainage Tunnel, Cripple Creek, 1909-10; supt. Isabella Mines Co., 1910-13; gen. mgr. Jumper, Calif., Gold Mines. Co., Stent, Calif., and v.p. and gen. mgr. Contention Mining Co., Knight Creek, Tuolumne Co., Calif., 1913-19; treas. Ajax Mine Lease Co., Victor, Colo., 1921-22; mgr. and vice president McElroy Ranch Co., Crane, Tex., 1927-49 (ret.); v.p., dir. Franco Wyoming Oil Co., McElroy Royalty Corp. Professor mining, 1919-28, dean, 1921-28, Colo. Sch. of Mines. Served as captain, engineer, Officer Reserve Corps (now retired). Distinguished Achievement Medal, Colo. Sch. of Mines, 1949. Mem. Inst. Mining and Metall. Engrs., Am. Petroleum Inst., Theta Tau, Tau Beta Pi. Republican. Episcopalian. Mason. Clubs: Teknik (Denver); Rotary (Midland, Tex.). Home: 1613 Palmer Park Blvd., Colorado Springs, Colo. Address: P.O. Box 912, Midland TX

GRANT, LEWIS ADDISON soldier, lawyer; b. Bennington County, Vt., Jan. 17, 1829; s. James and Elizabeth (Wyman) G.; ed. Townshend and Chester, Vt.; taught sch. in Vt., N.J., and Mass., 1848-53; m. S. Augusta Hartwell, Mar. 11, 1857 (died 1859); m. 2d, Mary Helen Pierce, Sept. 9, 1863; father of Ulysses

Sherman G. Admitted to bar, 1855, and engaged in practice at Bellows Falls, Vt. Maj. 5th Vt. Inf., Aug. 15, 1861; lt. col., Sept. 25, 1861; col., Sept. 16, 1862; brig. gen. vols., Apr. 27, 1864; bvtd. maj. gen. vols., Oct. 19, 1864, "for gallant and meritorious services in campaign before Richmond and in Shenandoah Valley"; hon. mustered out, Aug. 24, 1865; Congressional Medal of Honor, May 11, 1893, for Battle of Salem Heights, Va.; wounded at battle of Fredericksburg, Dec. 14, 1862, and at battle of Petersburg, Apr. 2, 1865; apptd. lt. col. 36th Inf., U.S.A., July 1866, but declined; asst. sec. of war, Apr. 5, 1890-Dec. 1893. Republican. Home: Minneapolis, Minn. Died Mar. 20, 1918.

GRANT, ULYSSES S., III, ret. army officer; b. July 4, 1881; s. Frederick D. (Maj. Gen., U.S. Army) and Ida (Honore) G.; g.s. Pres. U. S. Grant; ed. Theresianum, Vienna, 4 yrs., and Cutler Sch., N.Y. City, 4 1/2 yrs.; student Columbia, 1898; B.S., U.S. Military Academy, 1903; graduate, U.S. Engineer School, 1908, Army War College, 1934, married Edith Root, dau. Hon. Ehihu Root, Nov. 27, 1907; children—Edith, Clara Frances, Julia. Commd. 2d lt., U.S. Army, 1903; advanced through the grades to col., Corps of Engrs., 1934; col. N.A., 1917-20; maj. gen. (temp.) 1943; various assignments U.S. and abroad 1903-42, including Cuban pacification, 1906, Vera Cruz expdn., 1914, Mex., 1916, World War I, II; chief of protection branch, Office Civilian Def., 1942-44; chmn. Nat. Capital Park and Planning Commn., 1942-49; v.p. George Washington U., 1946-51. Pres. Am. Planning and Civic Assn., 1947-49, Govt. Service, Inc.; chmn. Civil War Centennial Commn., 1957-61; comdr.-in-chief Mil. Order Loyal Legion, 1957-61; trustee Nat. Trust Historic Preservation. Decorated Distinguished Service Medal, Legion of Merit (United States) also decorations from 6 foreign countries. Mem. several vets. orgns., military service organizations, also prof. and engring socs., Columbia Hist. Soc. (pres.). Clubs: Union League, Century (N.Y.C.); Cosmos, Army and Navy, Metropolitan (Washington). Address: Washington DC Died Aug. 29, 1968; buried Hamilton Coll. Cemetery, Clinton NY

GRANT, ULYSSES SIMPSON 18th Pres. U.S.; b. Point Pleasant, O., Apr. 27, 1822; s. Jesse Root and Hannah (Simpson) G.; grad. U.S. Mil. Acad., 1843; m. Julia T. Dent, Aug. 22, 1848, 4 children including Frederick Dent, Jesse. Commd. lt. 4th Inf., U.S. Army, 1843; served under Gen. Zachary Taylor in Mexico, 1845-47; joined Gen. Winfield Scott's army 1847, active in all battles from Buena Vista to Mexico City; promoted 1st lt., brevetted capt., 1848; stationed in Miss., 1848-52; transferred to Ft. Vancouver, Ore., 1852; promoted capt., Humboldt Bay, Cal., 1853; resigned commn., 1854; unsuccessful as farmer, real estate salesman, clk. in brother's leather bus., 1854-61; commd. col. 21st Ill. Volunteers, 1861, promoted brig. gen., 1861, hdqrs. at Cairo, Ill.; 1st action was indecisive battle, Belmount, Mo., 1861; captured Ft. Henry and Ft. Donelson in Tenn. (1st major Union victory), 1862; promoted maj. gen. U.S. Volunteers; led U.S. Army Battle of Shiloh, 1862, saved from defeat by reinforcements headed by Gen. D.C. Buell; captured Vicksburg (Miss.) by siege, 1863 (gave U.S. Army complete control of Mississippi River, divided Confederacy); given supreme command U.S. Army in West, 1863; defeated Confederate Army under Gen. Braxton Bragg at Battle of Chattanooga (Tenn.), 1863; promoted comdr. in chief U.S. Army with rank lt. gen. 1864; directed Army of the Potomac in Wilderness Campaign; adopted policy of attrition, although suffering great losses at battles of Spotsylvania and Cold Harbor finally defeated Gen. Robert E. Lee by sheer force of numbers; accepted Lee's surrender at Appomattox Courthouse, Va., Apr. 9, 1865; promoted full gen. (1st since George Washington to hold rank), 1866; apptd. U.S. sec. of war by Pres. Andrew Jackson (to replace E.M. Stanton), 1867, served for 5 months, turned office back to Stanton when U.S. Senate refused to approve Stanton's removal; elected Pres. U.S. (Republican), 1868, reelected 1872, his adminstrn. characterized by corruption, scandal, gave polit. appointments to friends and relatives without regard for ability or merit; signed bill providing for specie-payment legal tender notes issued during Civil War, 1869, other bills included inflation bill of 1874 which favored indsl., comml. interests; attempted to annex Dominican Republic, 1869; backed punitive Reconstrn. measures; apparently unaware of illegal conduct of some subordinates; when his pvt. sec. Orville Babcock and Sec. of War William E. Belknap were implicated in graft scandals (1875) allowed them to resign before they could be impeached; made world tour, 1877-79; candidate for Rep. nomination for Pres., 1880, defeated by James Garfield; involved in fraudulent unsucceesful banking bus., N.Y.C., 1884; began writing his memoirs, 1884, published posthumously as Personal Memoirs, 1885. Died of cancer of the throat, Mt. McGregor, N.Y., July 23, 1885; buried Grant's Tomb, Riverside Dr., N.Y.C.

GRASS, JOHN Indian chief; b. 1837. Chief of Blackfoot Sioux Indians; received warrior name Charging Bear for bravery in battle with Crow Indians, 1854; advocated peace with white man, realizing that war would ruin his people, 1870's; chief justice Ct. of Indian Offenses at Ft. Yates, circa 1880-1918; Indian commr. at council to cede lands in S.D. to U.S. Govt., 1888, broke off original negotiations, later accepted treaty with more favorable terms for his people. Died May 10, 1918.

GRASSELLI, THOMAS FRIES, business exec.; b. Cleve., Jan. 21,21903; s. Thomas Saxton and Emilie (Smith) G.; student Cleve. U., 1922; m. Mary Allen, June 24, 1929. With Grasselli Chem. Co., Cleve., 1923-29; with E. I. duPont Co., Wilmington, Del., 1929-70, successively mfg., sales, mgmt. Dir., sec. Boys Club of Wilmington, 1948-70; nat. asso. State of Del. Boys Club of Am. Served from capt. to lt. col., AUS, 1942-46. Mem. Cleve. Mus. Art. Clubs: Wilmington Country; Concord Country. Home: Wilmington DE Died Mar. 23, 1970.

GRASSELLI, THOMAS SAXTON mfr.; b. Cleveland, O., Nov. 14, 1874; s. Caesar A. and Johanna (Ireland) G.; ed. Mt. Saint Mary's Coll., Emmitsburg, Md.; m. Emilie Smith, May 29, 1899; children-Caesar A., II, Thomas Fries, Harry Williams. Engaged in chem. mfg. since 1893; pres. The Grasselli Chemical Co., 1916-36, when co. became div. of E. I. du Pont de Nemours & Co., v.p. and dir. latter co.; retired as mem. exec. com. Nov. 1939. Captain 1st Ohio Vol. Cav., Spanish-Am. War, 1898, later capt. q.m. dept. Mem. Ohio Soc. of New York, Cleveland Chamber of Commerce. Republican. Catholic. Clubs: Union, Chagrin Valley Hunt, Kirtland Country (Cleveland); Wilmington (Del.) Club: Chemists (New York). Home: 2775 S. Park Blvd., Shaker Heights, Cleveland, O. Died Aug. 22, 1942.

GRASSHAM, CHARLES C. lawyer, corp. exec.; b. Salem, Ky., Mar. 20, 1871; s. Montgomery and Martha Elizabrth (Mahan) G.; ed. McCully and Kemp Sch, Madisonville, Ky., and Nat. Normal U., Lebanon, O.; m. Corrie Bush, Aug. 19, 1896; children-Roscoe Bush (dec.), Pauline Bush. Teacher, pub. schs., 1886-91; admitted to Ky. bar, 1891, later to practice in U.S. dist. cts. of Ky. and Ind. in U.S. Circuit Court of Appeals (6th Circuit), and before Supreme Court of U.S., 1915; began practice at Smithland, Ky., gen. counsel Ayer & Lord Tie Co., mfrs. and preservers of wood, ry. ties and bridge timers, now the Wood Preserving Corp., and Koppers Co., since 1894, gen. mgr., 1916-20; commd. spl. judge, by gov. of Ky., and chief justice of Ky. Court of Appeals; first appellate dist. judge of Special Court of Appeals of Kentucky to try judges' pension case, 1940; vice preseident and general manager Mineral Ridge Fluorspar Company, Salem, Ky., producer of Flurospar. Dem. presdl. elector, 1st Ky. Dist., 1904. Active in Woodrow Wilson campaign for pres. of U.S., 1912; served as mem. Dem. Finance Com. of McCracken County, Ky.; mem. board - representing local draft board No. 109, of McCracken County, Ky.; mem. Nat. Reemployment Com. for McCracken County. Was aide de camp, rank of col, staff of Gov. J. C. W. Beckham. Del. from Ky. to Conservation Congress, St. Paul, Minn., to Rivers and Harbors Congress, Washington, D.C. Mem. Am. Bar Assn., Ky. State Bar Assn. (v.p.), Am. Law Inst., Am. Judicature Soc. Presbyterian. Clubs: Paducah (Ky.) Country; Forest Hills County (Paducah). Home: 105 Fountain Av. Office: Citizens Savings Bank Bldg., Paduach, Ky. Died May 25, 1945.

GRASSHOFF, FRANK O. publisher; b. West Alexandria, O., Jan. 29, 1894; s. Henry and Mary (Zimmerman) G.; B.S., Wittenberg Coll., 1928, M.A., 1934; m. Norma Ludy, June 3, 1917. Supt. schs., 1919-20; dean Miami Jacobs Coll., 1929-42; sec., controller Jour. Herald Pub. Co., 1945-46, sec.-treas., 1946-48, exec. v.p., treas. since 1948, dir. since 1945; dir. Gen. Transportation & Storage Co. Served as 2d lt., U.S. Army, 1917-18; lt. col., A.C., 1942-45. Mem. Am. Newspaper Pubs. Assn., Controllers Inst. Am., Research Inst. Am., Y.M.C.A., Dayton Art Inst., Dayton C. of C., Am. Legion, Phi Delta Kappa. Methodist, Mason (Shriner), Lion. Clubs: Engineers, Miami Valley Golf, Executives. Home: 447 Cherry Dr., Dayton 2, O. Died May 8, 1952.

GRAUPNER, ADOLPHUS EARHART lawyer; b. Clinton, Ia., Feb. 3, 1875; s. Louis Carl and Mazilpha Josephine (Earhart) G.; prep. edn., Boys' High Sch., San Francisco; LL.B., U. of Calif. 1897; m. Elise Wenzelburger, Apr. 22, 1903; children-Adolphus Earhart, Eleanor Louise. Admitted to Calif. bar, 1897, and began practice at San Francisco; asst. city atty., San Francisco, 1908-13; judge Superior Court, Calif., 1913-15; pvt. practice, 1916-17; gen. counsel Calif. Industrial Accident Commn., 1919-23; mem. U.S. Bd. of Tax Appeals, Washington, D.C., 1924-26; member faculty of Hastings College of Law, Univ. of Calif., 1931-40. Member firm of Graupner, Janin & Haven, San Francisco, Calif. Served in U.S. Army, May 8, 1917-May 5, 1919; capt. 364th Inf., 91st Div.; wounded in action at battle of Meuse-Argonne, and cited for courage and efficient leadership in face of enemy. Awarded Order of the Silver Star for Valor and Order of the Purple Heart. Mem. Am. Calif. and San Francisco bar assn., Phi Alpha Delta. Am. Legion. Republican. Unitarian. Mason. Home: 209 Walnut St. Office: 1104 Mills Tower, San Francisco, Calif. Died Sept. 19, 1947.

GRAVE, CASWELL biologist; b. Monrovia, Ind., Jan. 24, 1870; s. Thomas C. and Anna (Hubbard G.; B.S., Earlham Coll., Richmond, Ind., 1895; awarded LL.D. from same college, 1928; scholar and fellow and Adam T. Bruce fellow, Johns Hopkins Univ., 1898-1901, Ph.D., 1899; m. Josephine Grave, Sept. 24, 1896; 1 son, Thomas Brooks. Temporary asst., U.S. Fish Commn., 1809-1900; asst. in zoology, 1901-02, asso., 1902-06, asso. prof., Johns Hopkins; Rebstock prof. Zoology and head dept., Washington U., 1919-40, emeritus prof. of zoology since 1940. Dir. U.S. Fisheries Lab., Beaufort, N.C., 1902-06; shellfish commr., Md., 1906-12; instr. in charge course in invertebrate zoology, Marine Biol. Lab., Woods Hole, Mass., 1912-19. Capt. Chem. Warfare Service, U.S. Army, 1918-19. Fellow A.A.A.S. (ex-v.p. sect. F); mem. Am. Soc. Zoologists (sec.-treas, 1913-18; v.p. 1920; pres. 1928), Am. Soc. Naturalists, Phi Beta Kappa, Sigma Xi, Trustee Marine Biol. Lab., 1936-40, emeritus trustee since 1940; mem. Bd. Nat. Research Fellowship in the Biol. Sciences, 1935-38. Club: University (Winter Pk.). Author scientific papers. Home: Winter Park, Fla. Died Jan. 8, 1944.

GRAVELY, JOSEPH JACKSON congressman; b. nr. Leatherwood, Va., Sept. 25, 1828; attended public schs.; studied law. Engaged in agriculture, also taught schs.; admitted to bar, practiced law; mem. State Ho. of Reps., 1853-54; moved to Mo., 1854; del. Mo. Constl. Conv., 1860; mem. Mo. Senate, 1862, 64; served as col. 8th Regt., Mo. Volunteer Cavalry, U.S. Army, during Civil War; mem. U.S. Ho. of Reps. (Republican) from Mo., 40th Congress, 1867-69; lt. gov. Mo., 1871-72. Died Stockton, Mo., Apr. 28, 1872; buried Lindley Prairie Cemetery, nr. Bear Creek, Mo.

GRAVES, ALVIN C(USHMAN) physicist; b. Washington, Nov. 4, 1909; s. Herbert C. and Clara Edith (Walter) G.; B.S., U. Va., 1931; postgrad. Mass. Inst. Tech., 1932; Ph.D., U. Chgo., 1939; m. Elizabeth Riddle, Sept. 27, 1937; children - Marilyn Edith, Alvin Palmer, Elizabeth Anne Instr. physics U. Tex., 1939-41, asst. prof., 1941, asso. prof. (on leave), 1942-60; with U. Chgo. Metall. Lab., 1942-43; staff mem. Los Alamos (N.M.) Sci. Lao., U. Cal., 1943-45, group leader, 1945-47, asso. div. leader, 1947-48, div. leader, 1948 - ; dep. sci. dir. Pacfic Proving Grounds operations, 1947-48, sci. dir., 1948-55; test dir. Nev. Proving Grounds operations, 1951-54, sci. adviser Nev. Test Site, 1955 - , Eniwatok Proving Ground operations, 1955-60. Chmn. Com. Sr. Reviewers, AEC; AEC rep. Conf. on Discontinuance Nuclear Weapons Tests, and Tech. Working Group on Detection and Identification High-Altitude Nuclear Explosions, Geneva, Switzerland, 1959-60; chmn Nev. planning bd. (AEC), 1961; mem. Pacific planning bd. (AEC), 1963, also joint nuclear test plan group, 1964; cons. Army Science Adv. Panel. Organizer, dir., chmn. bd. Los Alamos Nat. Bank, 1963 - . Mem. Past pres. Los Alamos School Board. Recipient Exceptional Civilian Service award, Air Force, 1951, Certificate of Achievement, Army, 1954; Distinguished Service award, FCDA, 1955. Fellow American Physical Society; member American Institute Physics, Sigma Xi, Gamma Alpha, Delta Sigma Phi, Tau Beta Pi. Home: 277 Andanada. Office: P.O. Box 1663, Los Alamos Sci. Lab., Los Alamos, N.M. Died July 28, 1965; buried Guaje Pines Cemetery, Los Alamos, N.M.

GRAVES, BIBB ex-gov.; b. Hope Hull, Ala., Apr. 1, 1873; s. David and Martha (Bibb) G.; B.C.E., U. of Ala., 1893; LL.B., Yale, 1896; m. Dixie Bibb, Oct. 10, 1900. Admitted to Ala. bar, 1897, and began practice at Montgomery. Mem. Ala. Ho. of Rep., 1898-99, 1900-01; city atty., Montgomery, 1901-02; chmn. Ala. State Dem. Exec. Com., 1914-18; gov. of Ala., terms 1927-31, and 1935-39. Capt. Ala. Nat. Guard, 1897-98; maj., 1898-1905; adj. gen. Ala., 1907-11; lt. col. 1st Ala. Cav., 1916, col., 1917; served as col. 117th F.A., U.S. Army, 1917-19. Trustee Bob Jones Coll. Address: Montgomery, Ala. Died Mar. 14, 1942.

GRAVES, CHARLES HINMAN diplomat; b. Springfield, Mass., Aug. 14, 1839; s. Rev. Hiram Atwell and Mary (Hinman) G.; ed. pub. schs., Boston, and Litchfield, Conn.; m. Grace Totten, May 20, 1873; m. 2d, Alice K. Tripp, Apr. 25, 1905. Sergt. 40th N.Y. Inf., June 27, 1861; 2d lt., Nov. 4, 1861; 1st lt., July 8, 1862; capt. a.-a.-g. vols., Feb. 29, 1864; maj. a.-a.-g. vols., Jan 15, 1865, for faithful and efficient services during the war, and gallant conduct in the field; bvtd. maj., U.S.A., Mar. 2, 1867, for gallant and meritorious services at Gettysburg; lt. col. U.S. Army, Mar. 2, 1867, for same at Ft. Fisher; hon. mustered out of vol. service, Sept. 1, 1866; apptd. 1st lt. 14th U.S. Inf., Nov. 29, 1865; capt. 34th Inf., July 28, 1866; hon. discharged at own request, Dec. 29, 1870. Officer on staffs, Gens. Phil. Kearney, Birney, Stoneman, A. H. Terry; served in all operations and battles Army of Potomac. Settled in Minn.; pioneer in many of the important business enterprises of Duluth. Mem. Minn. Senate, 1875-78, Ho. of Rep., 1889-91 (speaker); mayor of Duluth, 1881-83; state capitol commr., Minn., 1893-1905; U.S. minister to Sweden, 1906-14. Pres. Cottage Hosp., Santa Barbara. Republican. Companion Loyal Legion. Episcopalian. Home: Santa Barbara, Calif. Died Oct. 7, 1928.

GRAVES, HENRY SOLON forester; b. Marietta, O., May 3, 1871; s. William Blair and Luranah (Hodges) G.; A.B., Yale, 1892, A.M., 1900; spl. studies in forestry, Harvard and Univ. Munich: hon. A.M., Harvard, 1911; LL.D., Syracuse U., 1923, Yale, 1900-10; chief of U.S. Forest Service, 1910-20; dean Sch. of Forestry, Yale, 1922-39; provost of Yale U., 1923-27, prof. emeritus, 1939—. Mem. Miss. Valley Com. (P.W.A.); pres. New Haven Park Commn. Served as lt. col. Corps Engrs.,

U.S. Army, 1917; A.E.F. Hon. mem. Am. Acad. of Arborists, Royal British Arboricultural Soc., Royal Scottish Arboricultural Soc.; fellow Soc. of Am. Foresters, Am. Geog. Soc.; mem. Am. Forestry Assn., A.A.A.S., Sigma Xi, Société Forestière de Franche-Comté de Belfort, and numerous assns. for the advancement of forestry and conservation. Author: Forest Mensuration, 1906; Principles of Handling Woodlands, 1911; also various bulls. Joint Author: The White Pine, 1896; Forest Education, 1932. Home: 339 Prospect St., New Haven, Conn. Died Mar. 7, 1951.

GRAVES, SCHUYLER COLFAX surgeon; b. Kalamazoo, Mich., Mar. 6, 1858; s. Samuel (D.D.) and Mary Colfax (Baldwin) G.; M.D., U. of Mich., 1881; m. Annie M. Dryden, Oct. 9, 1883; m. 2d, Caroline Elizabeth Launt, Apr. 16, 1906. Maj. and brigade surgeon in Spanish-Am. War (chief surgeon 1st Brigade, 3d Div., 4th Corps). Home: Grand Rapids, Mich. Died July 14, 1941.

GRAVES, WILLIAM SIDNEY army officer; b. Mt. Calm, Tex., Mar. 27, 1865; s. Andrew C. and Evelyn (Bennett) G.; grad. U.S. Mil. Acad., 1889; m. Katherine Boyd, Feb. 9, 1891; children-Sidney C., Dorothy (wife of Wm. R. Orton, U.S.A.). Commd. 2d lt. 7th Inf., June 12, 1889; promoted through grades to maj. gen., July 11, 1925. Instr. small arms practice, Dept. of Columbia, 1897-99; also acting judge advocate, 1898-99, participating in various campaigns; received thanks of Gen. J. F. Bell for gallantry in action against insurgents at Caloocan, Dec. 31, 1901; again in P.I., 1904-06; at San Francisco, Apr.-May 1906, after earthquake; duty Gen. Staff, 1909-11; sec. Gen. Staff Corps, Jan. 1911-July 1912, and Sept. 3, 1914-Feb. 6, 1918; comdr. A.E.F., in Siberia, 1918-20; comdr. Ft. William McKinley, P.I., Apr.-Oct. 1920, 1st Brigade of 1st Div., Dec. 1920-Apr.1, 1925; comdr. 1st Div., Apr. 1-July 10, 1925; comdr. 6th Corps Area, Chicago, July 11, 1925-Oct. 26, 1926; comdr. Panama Canal Div., Dec. 14, 1926-Oct. 1, 1927; comdr. Panama Canal Dept., Oct. 1, 1927; retired, 1928. Awarded D.S.M., 1919; Order of Rising Sun, 2d Class, Japan; Order of the Wen Hu (Striped Tiger), China; War Cross, Czechoslovakia; Comdr. Order of Crown of Italy. Home: Shrewsbury, N.J. Died Feb. 27, 1940.

GRAY, CARL RAYMOND, JR. ret. VA ofcl.; b. Wichita, Kan., Apr. 14, 1889; s. Carl Raymond and Harriette (Flora) G.; student Western Mil. Acad., Alton, Ill.; A.B., U. of Ill., 1911; m. Gladys Beach, Oct. 16, 1911 (dec.); children-Gladys (Mrs. Maxwell Dieffenbach), and Carl Raymond III. Began with St. L.&S.F. R.R., 1911; asst. engineer Ore. Electric Ry. and S.P.&S. Ry., 1911-12; trainmaster and supt., 1912-13; asst. to gen. mgr. C., B.&Q. R.R., 1913-14; asst. to gen. supt. St.L.&S.F. R.R., 1914-15; asst. engr. Consolidated Coal Co., Baltimore, Md., 1961; pres. Peach Bottom Slate Corp., 1916-17; gen. supt. Montgomery Ward & Co., 1919-20, gen. mgr. Chicago house, 1920-21; gen. mgr. City Ice Co., Kansas City, Mo., 1922-23, v.p. and gen. mgr., 1923-25; v.p. Central Mfg. District Bank, Chicago, 1926; mgr. industrial dept. C.&N.W. Ry. and C.,St.P.,M.&O. Ry., 1928-29; gen. mgr., C.,St.P.,M.&O. Ry. at St. Paul, 1929, v.p. and gen. mgr. of operation and maintenance, 1930-37, exec. vice pres., 1937-46; v.p. Chicago & Northwestern System, 1946-48; dir. Investors Mutual, Inc., subsidiary Investors Syndicate; administrator Veterans Affairs, VA, 1947-53. Served as capt., maj. and lt. col., U.S. Army, World War I; later, col., U.S. Engr., Res.; apptd. brig. gen. in charge railway transportation Allied European Theater War, 1942: promoted maj. gen., 1945. Decorated D.S.M., Legion of Merit with oak leaf cluster, Bronze Star Medal, Army Commendation Medal (U.S.); Italian War Cross for Merit, Order Crown of Italy; Knight Comdr. Brit. Empire (Gt. Brit.); Officer Legion of Honor, Croix de Guerre with 2 palms (France); Order Crown of Belgium. Mem. Soc. American Railway Engrs., Am. Mil. Engrs., Soc. Mayflower Descendants, S.A.R., Sons Confederate Vets., Order Founders and Patriots of America, Am. Legion. Military Ry. Service Veterans, Mil. Order World War, Reserve Officers Association, Sigma Alpha Epsilon. Republican. Baptist Clubs; St. Paul Athletic, Minnesota, Midway, Transportation (St. Paul); Interfraternity, Economic, Traffic (Chicago). Home: 1021 Third St., Hudson, Wis. Died Dec. 2, 1955; buried Willow River Cemetery, Hudson, Wis.

GRAY, DAVID, writer diplomat; b. Buffalo, Aug. 8, 1870; s. David and Martha (Guthrie) G.; A.B., Harvard, 1892; Litt.D., Bowdoin Coll. 1925; m. Mrs. Maude Livingston Hall Waterbury, Oct. 13, 1914. Reporter, editorial writer Rochester Union and Advertiser, 1893; editorial writer Buffalo Times, 1894; sub-editor New York World, 1896; mng. editor Buffalo Courier, 1897; editorial writer Buffalo Enquirer, 1898-99; admitted to bar, 1899; U.S. minister to Ireland, 1940-47. Author: The Sphinx (Harvard Hasty Pudding Club Play), 1892; Gallops I and II (play produced), 1906; The Recantation of an Anit-Imperialist (in Outlook); Mr. Carteret and Others; Smith (with W. Somerset Maugham); Ensign Russell; The Bommerand (novel, based on play by V. Mapes and W. Smith); (play) The Best People (with Avery Hopwood) prod. 1923. Commd. capt., aviation sect., Signal Corps; with AEF in France; charge photographic div. Signal Corps, 1917-18; liaison officer with French 7th and 2d Corps and 10th French Army to 1919. Decorated Corix de Guerre, chevalier Legion d'Honneur, chevalier de la Couronne. Home: Sarasota FL Died Apr. 1968.

GRAY, EARLE, physician, educator; b. Wabash County, Ill., Nov. 20, 1898; s. George Washington and Martha Jane (Hancock) G.; B.S., U. of Chicago, 1925, M.D., 1929; m. Susan Eleanor Heaney, Apr. 28, 1943; 1 dau., Deborah Floy. Began practice of medicine, 1932; asst. attending physician Presbyterian Hosp., Chicago, 1932-41; asst. in medicine, Rush Med. Coll., 1932-33, instr., 1933-37, asst. clin. prof. medicine, 1937-41, acting dean, 1939-June 1942, on which date Rush Med. Coll. became part of U. of Ill. Med. Sch.; asst. clin. prof. medicine, U. of Ill. Med. Sch.; clin. prof. medicine U. Ill. Med. Sch., from 1953; clinical professor medicine, acting chief med. service Presbyn. Hosp. Served as maj. M.C. Army of the United States, 1942; promoted lt. colonel, 1943, col., 1946; col., Med. Corps Res., 1946-55, ret. Fellow A.C.P.; mem. Am. Assn. Med. Colls., A.M.A., Central Interurban Clin. Club, Am. Heart Assn., Am. Soc. Tropical Medicine, Lambda Chi Alpha, Nu Sigma Nu. Democrat. Episcopalian. Clubs: University, Caxton, Chicago Literary. Home: Chicago IL Died Aug. 4, 1967.

GRAY, HOWARD KRAMER surgeon; b. St. Louis, Mo., Aug. 28, 1901: s. Carl Raymond and Harriette (Flora) G.; B.S., Princeton U., 1923; student U. of Neb., Coll. of Med., 1923-25, D.Sc. (honorary); M.D., Harvard, 1927; M.S., in surgery, Univ. of Minn., Mayo Foundation, 1932; D.Sc. (hon.), Lafayette College; married Lila DeWeenta Conrad, September 2, 1925; children-Howard Kramer, DeWeenta Russell (Mrs. Walter I. Bones, Jr.). Fellow in surgery, Mayo Foundation, 1928-32; jr. surgeon, Mayo Clinic, 1932-35, surgeon and head of a sect. in surgery since 1935; professor, May Foundation, Graduate Sch. U. of Minn., since 1935. Captain U.S. Naval, Med. Corps Res. Fellow A.C.S., So. Surg. Assn. A.M.A.; mem. Am. Surg. Assn., Am. Assn. Thoracic Surgery, Western Surgical Assn., Soc. of Clinical Surgery, Surgeons' Club: Minn. State Med. Assn., Minn. Surg. Assn., Southern Minn. Med. Assn., Nu Sigma Nu. Independent. Baptist. Clubs: Ivy (Princeton, N.J.); Rochester Country, Rochester Tennis. Contbr. to med. jours. Home: 612 10th Av., S.W. Office: Mayo Clinic, Rochester, Minn. Died Sept. 6, 1955; buried Rochester, Minn.

GRAY, ISAAC PUSEY gov. Ind., diplomat; b. Chester County, Pa., Oct. 18, 1828; s. John and Hannah (Worthington) G.; m. Eliza Jaqua, 1850. Admitted to Ind. bar before the Civil War; served as officer in Civil War, 1862-63; col. in "minute men" emergency in Ind., 1862; mem. Ind. Senate, 1868-72; largely responsible for Ind. ratification of 15th Amendment to U.S. Constn. (Ind. was last state to vote on it and her ratification was needed); lt. gov. Ind., 1876-80; filled out term as gov. Ind., Nov. 1880-Jan. 1881; gov. Ind., 1885-89; apptd. U.S. minister to Mexico, 1893. Died Mexico City, Mexico, Feb. 14, 1895.

GRAY, JOHN CHIPMAN lawyer; b. Brighton, Mass., July 14, 1839; s. Horace and Sarah Russell (Gardner) G.; A.B., Harvard, 1859, LL.B., 1861; (LL.D., Yale, 1894, Harvard, 1895); m. Anna Lyman (Mason), 1873. Admitted to bar, 1862; served in Civil War, 1862-65; 2d lt., 3d Mass. Vol. Cav., a.d.c. to Gen. George H. Gordon; maj. and judge-advocate, U.S.V.; in practice of law in Boston, 1865—. Lecturer, 1869-71, Story prof. law, 1875-83, Royall prof. law, 1883-1913, Harvard Law Sch. Author: Restraints on Alienation, 1883, 1905; The Rule Against Perpetuities, 1886, 1906; Select Cases and Other Authorities on the Law of Property, 6 vols., 1888-92 (2d edit., 1905-08). Home: Boston, Mass. Died Feb. 25, 1915.

GRAY, JOHN HENRY economist; b. Charleston, Ill., Mar. 11, 1859; s. James Cowan and Mary A. (Mitchell) G.; ed. full course and diploma, Ill. State Normal U.; A.B., Harvard, 1887; Ph.D., U. of Halle, 1892; studied also at Paris, Vienna and Berlin; m. Helen Rockwell Bliss, June 14, 1894 (died 1922); children-James Bliss (dec.), Evelyn (Mrs. George E. Talmage, Jr., dec.). Instr. polit. economy, Harvard, 1887-89; prof. polit. and social science, Northwestern U., 1892-1907; prof. economics, U. of Minn., 1907-20, Carlton Coll., 1920-25; chief analyst and examiner, Interstate Commerce Commn. Bur. of Valuation, 1917-19, examiner valuation, 1925-28; prof. and head dept. of economics, Grad. Sch. of Am. Univ., 1928-32. Prof. economics, Univ. of Calif., summer 1914. Chmn. World's Congress Auxiliary on Polit. Science, Chicago, 1893; chmn. municipal com. Civic Fedn. of Chicago, 1894-96; expert U.S. Dept. Labor, 1902-03, to investigate restrictions of output in Great Britain; represented U.S. Commr. of Labor at Internat. Cooperative Congress, Manchester, Eng.; 1902; represented U.S. at Internat. Congress on Insp. of Laboring Men, Dusseldorf, Germany, 1902, and at Internat. Congress of Commerce and Industry, Ostend, Belgium, 1902; mem. Nat. Civic Federation Commn. on Municipal Ownership, 1905, and expert to commn. for Am. investigation; mem. exec. council dept. Nat. Civic Federation to investigate regulation of pub. service corps., 1911-14; sec. of the dept. and dir. of investigation. Published Commission Regulation, a compilation and analysis of all Am. statutes relating to regulation of public service corps. (1284 pp.), 1913; Urban Mortgages in U.S. since 1920 (with G. W. Terborgh), 1929; Regulation and Valuation of Public Utilities (with Jack Levin), 1933; also more than 100 articles in scientific journals; mem. Minnesota Efficiency and Economy Commission, 1914-15. Lt. col. U.S. Army and mem. bd. appraisers for all property commandeered for the army. Asso. editor Economic Bulletin, 1908-10, Journal of Accountancy, 1908-15. Specialist in pub. utilities and railroads. Pres. Am. Econ. Assn., 1913-14. Treas. People's Lobby since 1935. Has traveled most of the time since 1928 in Asia, Europe, Africa, the West Indies, South and Central America and the U.S. Clubs: Cosmos (Washington); University (hon. mem.; Evanston). Address: 1323 Jackson St. N.E., Washington, D.C. Died Apr. 4, 1946.

GRAYDON, JAMES WEIR engineer, inventor; b. in U.S., of American parents, Jan. 18, 1848; grad. U.S. Naval Acad.; served in vol. army in Civil War under Grant and Sherman; apptd. midshipman, 1865; served on various stations and became lt. U.S.N.; r-signed. Inventor Graydon Dynamite Gun, Graydon Gigantic Wheels (exhibited at Paris, Vienna, Madrid, Pome, Blackpool, England, etc.). Graydon Aerial Torpedo, Graydon Cable System of Torpedoes, Graydon Ry. Carriage Heater, Graydon High Volecity Projectiles, Graydon Compound Rotary Turbine Engines, etc. Address: Care Jensen & Son, 77 Chancery Lane, W.C., London.

GRAYSON, CARY TRAVERS rear adm.; b. "Salubria," Culpeper County, Va., Oct. 11, 1878; s. John Cooke (M.D.) and Adelena (Pettus) G.; William and Mary Coll., 1895-98; Ph.G., U. of the South, 1902, M.D., 1902; M.D., Med. Coll. of Va.; grad. U.S. Naval Med. Sch., 1904; hon. LL.D., William and Mary College; m. Alice Gertrude Gordon, May 24, 1916; children-James Gordon, Cary Travers, Wm. Cabell. Interne, Columbia Hosp. for Women, Washington, 1902-03; commd. act. asst. surg. U.S.N., July 14, 1903 1903; asst. surgeon, June 28, 1904; passed asst. surgeon, June 28, 1907; 1907;surgeon, Aug. 1916; med. dir. with rank of rear admiral, Aug. 29, 1916. Surgeon U.S. Naval Hosp., Washington, 1903-05, U.S.S. Maryland, 1905-07; cruise around the world, 1905-07; surgeon of the President's yacht, Mayflower, and attending and counsulting physician, Naval Dispensary, Washington, during the Roosevelt and Taft administrations; physician to President Wilson. Mem. pub. health com. of Nat. Food Administration; med. mem. Council Nat. Defense; mem. staff Emergency Hosp.; formerly mem. staff Ear, Nose and Throat Hosp. and Providence Hosp.; chmn. Am. Nat. Red Cross, 1935—; chmn. Gorgas Memorial Inst. of preventive medicine and tropical research. Retired from Navy, Dec. 30, 1928. Dir. The Warwick Memorial Clinic; med. dir. Washington Gas Light Co. Decorated; Navy Cross (U.S.), Commander Order of Leopold (Belgium), Commander Legion of Honor (France). Dir. Nat. Capitol Horse Show (Washington). Episcopalian. Home: Washington, D.C. Died Feb. 15, 1938.

GRAYSON, THOMAS JACKSON army officer; b. Mobile, Ala., May 5, 1896; m. Elizabeth Watkins; children - Mrs. walter Wildman, Mrs. William Geer. Commd. 2d lt. Inf., U.S. Army, Aug. 1917; col. Miss. N.G. July 1932, advanced to brig. gen., July 1933; active duty, Oct. 1940; dir. Miss. SSS, 1940 - . Decorated D.S.C., Purple Heart. Address: Hdqrs. SSS, Jackson, Miss. Died Apr. 1962.

GRAYSON, THOMAS WRAY M.D.; b. Meadville, Pa., Nov. 22, 1871; s. Thomas Wray and Mary Elizabeth (Green) G.; A.B., Washington and Jefferson Coll., 1892, A.M., 1897; M.D. West Penn Med. Coll. (now Med. Cept. U. of Pittsburgh), 1897; m. Mary Elizabeth Bard, June 9, 1920. Interne, West Penn Hosp., 1898. First lieut. Medical R.C., 1917; in active service, Sept. 1, 1917; at Camp Greenleaf, Ga.; gastroenterologist, Base Hosp., Camp Shelby, Miss., Nov. 20, 1917; chief med. service, rank of maj., Base Hosp. No. 77, France, and comdg. officer, Camp Hosp. No. 108, to July 1919. Trustee P.E. Diocese of Pittsburgh. Progressive. Home: Pittsburgh, Pa. Died May 17, 1933.

GRAYSON, WILLIAM army officer, Continental congressman, senator; b. Prince William County, Va., 1736; s. Benjamin and Susanah (Monroe) G.; attended Coll. of Phila. (now U. Pa.); m. Eleanor Smallwood. Commd. lt. col., a.d.c. to George Washington, 1776; promoted col., in command of a Va. Regt., 1777; took part in battles of L.I., White Plains, and Brandywine; testified at trial of Maj. Gen. Charles Lee regarding confusion prior to Battle of Monmouth; ret. from Army, 1779; commr. Bd. of War, 1780-81; mem. Va. Ho. of Dels., 1874-85, 88; mem. Continental Congress, 1875-87; mem. U.S. Senate from Va., 1789; strong supporter of So. interests; influential in procuring passage Ordnance of 1787. Died Dumfries, Va., Mar. 12, 1790.

GREATON, JOHN army officer; b. Roxbury, Mass., Mar. 10, 1741; s. John and Catherine (Lenton) G.; m. Sara Humphreys, 1760, several children including Ann, Richard. A trader; joined Sons of Liberty, 1774; commd. lt. Mass. Militia, 1774, col., 1775, served in 24th Mass. Regt., 36th Mass. Regt., 3d Mass. Regt., Continental Army; commd. col. 24th Inf., Continental Army, 1776, brig. gen., 1783; took part in expdn. to Can. Died Roxbury, Dec. 16, 1783.

GREBLE, EDWIN ST. JOHN army officer; b. West Point, N.Y., June 24, 1859; s. John Trout and Sarah Bradley (French) G.; grad. U.S. Mil. Acad., 1881, Inf. and Cav. Sch., Ft. Leavenworth, Kan., 1884, Coast Arty. Sch., Ft. Monroe, Va., 1892; m. Gertrude, d. Gen. John S. Poland, June 24, 1885. Commd. 2d lt. 2d Arty., June 11, 1881; promoted through grades to brig. gen. Oct. 13, 1916; maj. gen. (temp.) World War. Served as adj. gen. 2d Div. of the Army Corps; asst. adj. gen. Dept. of Havana, under Gen. Ludlow; in charge guard to City of Havana, taking over pub. bldgs. and barracks during evacuation by the Spaniards, under Gen. Ludlow; organized Dept. of Charities while in Republic of Cuba, under Gen. Wood; supervisor sec. of interior in the 2d intervention, Cuba; mem. Gen. Staff, in charge field arty., U.S.A., 1910-14; comdg. 6th Field Arty., 1914-16; service on Mexican border-Naco, Douglas and El Paso-Sept. 13, 1914-Aug. 22, 1917; assigned as comdr. 36th Div., N.G.; Camp Bowie, Ft. Worth, Tex., Aug. 27, 1917; retired on account of disability incurred in active service, Oct. 1918. Home: Washington, D.C. Died Sept. 20, 1931.

GREBLE, JOHN T. army officer; b. Phila., Jan. 19, 1834; s. Edwin and Susan Greble; grad. U.S. Mil. Acad., 1854; m. Sarah B. French, Aug. 4, 1858, 2 children. Commd. 2d lt. arty, U.S. Army, 1854, stationed Newport Barracks, Fla., 1854-56, explored lakes of area, served against Seminole Indians; asst. prof. ethics and English, U.S. Mil. Acad., 1856-60; promoted 1st lt., 1859; joined regt. at Fortress Monroe, Va., 1860; transferred to construct batteries and instruct volunteers in arty., Newport News, Va., 1861; ordered by Gen. Benjamin F. Butler to lead attack against Big Bethel, Va., 1861. Killed while covering retreat of his men from Big Bethel, June 9, 1861.

GREELEY, EDWIN SENECA banker; b. at Nashua, N.H., May 20, 1832; s. Seneca and Priscilla (Fields) G.; settled in New Haven, Conn., 1855; learned machinist's trade and locomotive building; m. Elizabeth, d. Daniel Corey, of Taunton, Mass., Feb. 20, 1856. First lt. 10th Conn. Inf., Oct. 22, 1862; capt., Apr. 25, 1862; maj. Mar. 4, 1863; lt.-col., Sept. 7, 1864; col., Feb. 16, 1865; bvtd. brig-gen. vols., Mar. 13, 1865, for gallant and meritorious services during the war. Mem. L. G. Tillotson & Co., elec. and ry. supplies, 1865-85, which became E. S. Greeley & Co. until discontinued, 1897; was pres. Yale Nat. Bank of New Haven; retired, 1905. Pres.-gen. Nat. Soc. S.A.R., 1903; mem. Loyal Legion, G.A.R. Pres. Grace Hosp. Soc. of New Haven; trustee Norwich Circuit, 1891, and elected to same position, 1892, humane, charitable, fraternal and mil. orgns. Clubs: Union League, Army and Navy (New York). Mason (32ff, K.T.). Address: 15 Turnbull St., New Haven, Conn.

GREELEY, WILLIAM B. forester; b. Oswebo, N.Y., Sept. 6, 1879, s. Frank Norton and Anna Cheney (Buckhout) G.; LL.B., Univ. of Calif., 1901, LL.D. (hon.), 1925; M.F., Yale, 1904, M.S., 1924; m. Gertrude Maxwell Jewett, Dec. 30, 1907; children-Molly (Mrs. J. A. Harvey, Jr.), Arthur W., Henry J., David C. With U.S. Forest Service, Cal., Hot Springs, Missoula, Mont., Washington, D.C., 1904-17, 1919-28, chief forester, 1920-28; sec.-mgr. West Coast Lumbermen's Assn., Seattle, 1928-45; bd. chmn. Am. Fore

GREELY, ADOLPHUS WASHINGTON army officer; b. Newburyport, Mass., Mar. 27, 1844; s. John Balch and Frances (Cobb) G.; grad. Newburyport High Sch., 1860; m. Henrietta H. C. Nesmith, June 20, 1878; children-Antionette, Adola, John Nesmith, Rose Ishbel, Adolphus W., Gertrude Gale. Served in Civil War, 1861-65, pvt. to capt., and bvt. maj. vols. (thrice wounded); apptd. 2d lt. 36th U.S. Inf., Mar. 7, 1867; 1st lt. 5th Cav., May 27, 1873; capt., June 11, 1886; brig. gen. chief signal officer U.S.A., Mar. 3, 1887; maj. gen., Feb. 10, 1906. First vol. pvt. soldier of Civil War to reach grade of brig. gen. U.S.A. Constructed 1,000 miles mil. telegraph in Tex., Dak., and Mont., 1876-79; in pursuanc pursuance of recommendation of Hamburg Internat. Geog. Congress (1879) was placed, 1881, in command of U.S. expdn. to establish one of a chain of 13 circumpolar stations; his party of 25 reached further north (83ff24') than any previous record; discovered new land N. of Greenland and crossed Grinnel Land to the Polar Sea; two relief expdns. failed to reach the party, which retreated S. to Cape Sabine, where, relief still failing, the party largely perished of starvation, only 7 survivors being found by 3d expdn. under Capt. Winfield S. Schley. During mil. operationa abroad (1898-1902) there were built and operated under his direction 1,000 miles of telegraph in P.R. 3,800 miles in Cuba, 250 miles in China, and 13,500 miles of lines and cables in P.I.; installed system of 3,900 miles of telegraph lines, submarine cables and wireless in Alaska, 1900-04, the wireless section of 107 miles, from Nome to St. Michael, being the first successful long-distance wireless operated regularly as part of a commercial system. Men. bd. to regulate wireless telegraphy in U.S., 1904; mem. bd. to report on coast defenses of U.S., 1905; U.S. del. Internat. Telegraph Conf., London, 1903, Internat. Wireless Telegraph Conf., Berlin, 1903. Comdg. Pacific Div. and in charge relief operations, San Francisco earthquake sufferers, Apr.-Aug. 1906; comdg. Northern Div. 1906, Dept. Columbia, 1907; retired by operation of law, 1908. Gold medalist, Royal Am. and French geog. socs., Author: Isothermal Lines of the United States, 1881; Chronological List of Auroras, 1881; Diurnal Fluctuations of Barometric Pressure, 1891; Three Years of Arctic Service, 2 vols., 1885; Proceedings of Lady Franklin Bay Expedition, 1888; American Weather, 1890; American Explorers, 1894; Handbook of Arctic Discoveries, 1896; Rainfall of Western States and Territories, 1888; Climate of Oregon and Washington, 1889; Climate of Nebraska, 1890; Climatology of Arid Region, 1891; Climate of Texas, 1891; Public Documents First Fourteen Congresses of United States, 1900; Handbook of Polar Discoveries, 1909; Handbook of Alaska, 1925; True Tales of Arctic Heroism, 1912; Reminiscences of Travel and Adventure, 1927; Polar Regions in Twentieth Century, 1928. Rep. U.S.A. at coronation of George V of England, 1911. Died Oct. 20, 1935.

GREELY, JOHN NESMITH army officer; author; b. Washington, June 6, 1885; s. Adolphus Washington and Henrietta Hudson (Nesmith) G.; ed. Phillips Acad., Andover, 1901-02; B.A., Yale, 1906; grad. F.A. School, 1913; Command and Gen. Staff Sch., 1932; grad. Army War Coll., 1936; m. Marian Chapman, Dec. 24, 1920; 1 son, John Chapman. Reporter, Boston Herald, 1905; commd. 2nd lt. U.S. Army, 1908, advanced through grades to major gen., 1941; rep. U.S. Del. to Prep. Disarmament Commn., Geneva, Switzerland, 1928-29; formerly chief of staff, Hawaiian Div., 1932-35; mil. attaché Madrid, Spain, 1939-40; cmnomdg. 2d Div. Ft. Sam Houston, Tex., 1941; chief mil. mission to Iran, 1941-42; mil. analyst, Office of Coordinator Inter-Am. Affairs, 1943 - ; spl. mil. observer Brazil, 1944, Italy, 1944. Decorated D.S.M.; Officer, Legion of Honor (France). Episcopalian. Clubs: Army and Navy, Chevy Chase (Washington). Author several books, Contbr. of fiction to mags. Address: 3503 Springland Lane, Washington 8. Died June 13, 1965.

GREEN, ADWIN WIGFALL, univ. prof.; b. Virginia, Sept. 21, 1900; s. Adwin Wigfall and Lillie May (Gray) G.; A.B., Coll. of William and Mary, 1925; LL.B., Georgetown U., 1921; A.M., U. of Va., 1927, Ph.D., 1930; m. Mary Moore (Dooley). Admitted to bar, 1921; in practice law, Washington, 1921-24; asst. prof. English, Gettysburg Coll., 1926-27; prof. English U. of Miss. 1930-66, dean of grad. sch. 1940-46; visiting prof., University of Virginia, 1938, University of Puerto Rico, 1947, Fulbright prof. University of Philippines, 1949-50. Served as chief petty officer, U.S.N.R., 1917-18; colonel, Judge Advocate Gen.'s Dept., World War II; active duty European Theater of Operations, 1942-44, head of Internat. Law Div., Philippines, Korea, and Japan. Member of bar of Supreme Court and Court of Appeals, Dist. of Columbia, bar Supreme Ct. of Miss. Mem. Mod. Lang. Assn., Phi Beta Kappa. Author: Beowulf, A Literal Translation, 1935; Complete College Composition, 1940; The Will of Alfred, King of West Saxons, 1944; Sir Francis Bacon, 1952, 66; The Epic of Korea, 1950; The Man Bilbo, 1963. Co-editor: Prose of the English Renaissance, 1952; Tudor Poetry and Prose, 1953; William Faulkner of Oxford, 1965; The Inns of Court, 1931, 65. Home: Lauderdale by the Sea FL Died June 15, 1966; buried Popano Beach FL

GREEN, CHARLES HENRY expn. dir.; b. Albion, Mich., Apr. 17, 1967; s. Henry S. and Mary E. (Ketcham) G.; ed. Homer Acad., Mich.; registered chemist in Mich.; m. Ada May Kerhaghan, July 16, 1890 (died Oct. 16, 1917); children-Lloyd Francis, Harold Clement; m. 2d, Adele Wright Drummond, Nov. 26, 1920; 1 dau., Marilynn Adele, Advt. and sales mgr. Shredded Wheat Co., Niagara Falls, N.Y., 1900-02; in expn. work as mng. dir. or pres. of over 50 trade expns., 1903-13; chief Dept. of Mfrs. and Varied Industries, Panama-Pacific Internat. Expn., San Francisco, 1913-15; U.S. commr. to Japan and China in interest of same; mem. Superior Jury Internat. Jury of Award, Panama P.I. Expn., 1915. Mng. dir. Nat. Music Show, Internat. Silk Expn., Internat. Fur Expn., Archtl. and Allied Arts Expn., Internat. Fabric Expn.; del. representing Archtl. League N.Y. to Paris Decorative and Indsl. Arts Expn., 1925. Tech. adv. N.J. Commn. N.Y. World's Fair, 1939. Veteran Co. A, 4th Regt. Mich. N.G. Received Chia Ho decoration from Pres. of China, 1916; Gold Medal of Honor, Archtl. League N.Y., 1925. Republican. Episcopalian. Home: Ridgewood, N.J. Office: 127 W. 43d St., N.Y.C. Deceased.

GREEN, FITZHUGH naval officer, author; b. St. Joseph, Mo., Aug. 16, 1888; s. Charles Edward and Isabelle Fitzhugh (Perryman) G.; grad. U.S. Naval Acad. 1909; M.Sc., George Washington U., 1913; grad. Naval War Coll., 1924; m. Natalie Wheeler Elliot, Nov. 27, 1916; children - Fitzhugh, Elizabeth Farnum, Richard Elliot; m. 2d, Margery Durant, Nov. 15, 1933. Commd. ensign, June 19, 1911; promoted through grades to comdr., Mar. 1927. Serverd 2 yrs. with Atlantic Fleet; duty Bur. of Ordnance, 1912-13; sent as engr. and physicist, 1913, to Arctic regions, with Donald B. MacMillan, in S.S. Erik, in search of Crocker Land and to explore unknown areas of Polar Sea, returning, 1916. Aide and flag lt. to Adm. Rogers in World War, in European waters; apptd. officer in charge proving and testing all ordnance material for the Navy, Mar. 1919, at Naval Proving Grounds, Indian Head, Md.; detailed as gunnery officer U.S.S. Texas, June 1921; was aide to pres. of Naval War Coll.; shifted to Naval Reserve, May 31, 1927; recommissioned in U.S. Navy, duty at Bureau of Ordnance, Navy Department, Washington, D.C., 1940, rank of lt. comdr.; transferred to staff of vice adm. Ghormley, comdg. South Pacific Area, May 1942; took part in preparation and execution of Guadalcanal Campaign. Commissioned Commander, U.S.N.R., July 19, 1942. Served on Staff of Comdr. South Pacific Area World War II. Became temporary technical film director for Richard Barthelmess, 1925; managing editor George Matthew Adams Newspaper Service, 1925-26; assistant to president Putnam Publishing Co., 1927. Fellow Am. Geog. Soc. Mem. Phi Lambda Epsilon, Phi Sigma Kappa. Democrat. Episcopalian. Clubs: Explorers', Army and Navy (New York and Washington); Racquet (Phila.); N.Y. Yacht, Knickerbocker, Dutch Treat (New York); Appawamis. Author: Arctic Duty, 1917; Clear the Decks, 1918; Won for the Fleet, 1921; The Mystery of Erik, 1923; ZR Wins, 1924; Midshipman All, 1925; Fought for Annapolis, 1925; Our Naval Heritage, 1925; History of American Navy; Life of Robert E. Peary, 1926; I'll Never Move Again, 1926; Uncle Sam's Sailors, 1926; Hold 'em Navy, 1926; Anchor's Aweigh, 1927; Famous Sea Fights (with H. H. Frost), 1927; Bob Bartlett, Master Mariner, 1929; Martin Johnson, Lion Hunter, 1928; Dick Byrd, Air Explorer, 1928; The Film Finds its Tongue, 1929. Co-author with Chas. A. Lindbergh of "We," 1927; also collaborator with Rear Adm. Richard E. Byrd, Martin Johnson, Etc. Address: Lambert Road, New Canaan, Conn. Died Dec. 2, 1947.

GREEN, FRANCIS Loyalist, philanthropist; b. Boston, Aug. 21, 1742; s. Benjamin and Margaret (Pierce) G.; grad. Harvard, 1760; m. Susannah Green, Oct. 18, 1769, 3 children; m. 2d, Harriet Matthews, 1785, 6 children. Ensign in French and Indian War, 1754; present at battles of Louisburg, 1758, Martinique and capture of Havana, 1762; capt. 3d Co. of Loyal Asso. Volunteers, 1775; apptd. magistrate, Halifax, N.S., Can., 1776; went to N.Y., 1777; banished to Eng. because of Loyalist sympathies, 1778-84; sheriff of Halifax County (N.S.), 1784-87; went to Mass., 1797; 1st joint treas. of Mass.; published many articles and translations concerning tng. of deafmutes (1st Am. writer in this field, became interested in subject because one of his children was a deaf mute); helped to establish a sch. for deafmutes, London, Eng. Author: The Art of Imparting Speech, 1782, Died Medford, Mass., Apr. 21, 1809.

GREEN, FRANCIS MATHEWS comdr. U.S. Navy; b. Boston, Feb. 23, 1835; s. Mathews W. and Margaret A. (Gilchrist) G.; ed. English High School, Boston; m. Elizabeth S. Cushing, Sept. 1, 1870. Author: The Navigation of the Caribbean Sea, 1877; Telegraphic Determination of Longitudes, 1876, 1880, 1883; List of Geographical Positions, 1883. Died 1902.

GREEN, FREDERICK ROBIN physician; b. Cameron, Mo., July 17, 1870; s. Rev. John M. and Martha (McCreary) G.; A.B., Oberlin, 1894, A.M., 1898; M.D., Northwestern U., 1898; m. Helen Hutchinson, June 30, 1923. General practice, Chicago, 1898-1905; instr. anatomy, Northwestern U. Med. Sch., 1898-1904; asst. editor, Ill. State Med. Jour., 1904-05; asst. to gen. sec. A.M.A., 1905-10; sec. Council on Health and Publ. Instruction A.M.A., 1910-22. Editor of Health Magazine, May 1922-24; sec. of Medical and Dental Arts Club. First lt. Medical Reserve Corps, 1908-17, commd. capt., June 4, 1917; ordered to active duty Med. O.T.C., Ft. Riley, Kan., Aug. 11, 1917; instr. and asst. adj., Nov. 20, 1917; commd. maj., M.C. U.S.A., Feb. 3, 1918; adj. Med. O.T.C., Ft. Riley, May 1, 1918-July 12, 1918; personnel div. S.G.O., Washington, July 17, 1918-Dec. 15, 1918; hon. discharged, Dec. 15, 1918; lt. col. Med. O.R.C., Feb. 1, 1925. Home: Chicago, Ill. Died Apr. 26, 1929.

GREEN, HORACE author, publisher; b. N.Y. City, Oct. 13, 1885; s. George Walton and Harriet Brodhead (Atwater) G.; grad. Groton (Mass) Sch., 1904; A.B., Harvard, 1908; student Harvard Law Sch.; m. Eleanor Rodman Townsend, June 4, 1915; children - Barbara Alison, Georgina Walton, Eleanor On Sheldon. staff of the New York Evening Post, 1911-14; went to Europe as corr. for New York Evening Post at outbreak of World War; taken prisoner at the front, sent to interior of Germany; released and made his way back into Antwerp; present at bombardment and capture of city; returned to U.S., Jan. 1915; corr. for Post in France and the Balkans, 1915-16; editor U.S. Air Service Magazine, and treas. Air Service Pub. Co., Washington, D.C., 1919-21; asso. editor Leslie's Weekly, 1921-22; polit. editor, The Forum short periods; with Duffield & Co. (later Duffield & Green), pubs., 1923-34, pres., 1925-34. Commd. 1st lt. U.S. Air Service, Aug. 1917; capt. Aug. 1918; licensed pilot; maj. O.P.C. Clubs: Harvard, Century Assn. (New York City); Nat. Press, Overseas Writers (Washington, D.C.). Author: The Log of a Non-Combatant, 1915; The Life of Calvin Coolidge, 1924; General Grant's Last Stand (biography), 1936; Triumph (play), 1938. Edited The Contemporary Statesman Series. Home: Cow Lane, King's Point, Great Neck, L.I., N.Y. Died Nov. 14, 1943.

GREEN, JAMES GILCHRIST naval officer; b. Jamaica Plain, Mass., June 27, 1841; s. Matthews W. and Margaret Augusta G.; ed. N.H. and Mass.; m. Cornelia F. Bond, Jan. 19, 1864. Entered U.S.N., volunteer service, as acting ensign, May 1861; transferred to regular navy at end of Civil war;

commissioned lt. comdr. July 3, 1870; comdr., Mar. 1887; capt. Mar. 3, 1900; commandant Puget Sound Station, 1898-1900; retired May 11, 1901, as rear admiral, upon own request, after 40 years service. Was commandant Havana, Cuba, Naval Station, 1900; comd. U.S.S. New Orleans, 1900-01. Died 1909.

GREEN, JOHN army officer; b. Germany, Nov. 20, 1825; s. Gottieb and Mary G.; ed. pub. schs., Crawford County, O., 1832-42; m. Dec. 8, 1878, Mary Yeager. In army as sergt. and 1st sergt. Co. B, and sergt. maj. Mounted Rifles, 1846-48 and 1852-55; apptd. 3d lt. dragoons, June 18, 1855, 1st lt., Mar. 3, 1861, capt. 2d Cav., Aug. 13, 1861, maj. 1st Cav., June 9, 1868, lt. col. 2d Cav., July 3, 1885; retired for age, Nov. 20, 1889; col., Apr. 23, 1904, act of Congress; bvtd. maj., July 3, 1863, lt. col., Apr. 15, 1865, col., Feb. 27, 1890, brig. gen., Feb. 27, 1890; awarded Congressional Medal of Honor. Died 1908.

GREEN, JOSEPH ANDREW army officer; b. Cherokee, Ia., Jan. 14, 1881; s. Joseph S. and Carrie (Conant) G.; student U. Wis., 1901-02; B.S., U.S. Mil. Acad., 1906; grad. Command and Gen. Staff Sch., Ft. Leavenworth, Kan., 1923; Army War Coll., 1926; m. Julia Hughes, Dec. 27, 1912. Commd. 2d lt., U.S. Arny, advanced through grades to maj. gen.; served at various posts in U.S. and Philippines; adj. 2nd Coastal Arty. Regt., with A.E.F., 1917; comd. 1st batt., 57th Coast Arty., 1919, in action at Chalons, Verdun, St. Mihiel and Racicourt; with 62nd Coast Arty., Fort Totten, N.Y., then with War Dept. Gen. Staff at Washington, comd. 61st Anti-Aircraft Regt. of Coast Arty., 1931-33; on Gen. Staff, 8th Corps Area, San Antonio, 1933-37; exec. officer to chief of Coast Arty., 1937-40, maj. gen., chief of Coast Arty., 1940-52; comdg. gen., Antiaircraft Command, Army Ground Forces, 1942 - . Home: 2905 Monument Av., Richmond, Va. Died Oct. 1963.

GREEN, ROBERT GLADDING prof. bacteriology; b. Wadena, Minn., Jan. 11, 1895; s. George Henry and Ella Augusta (Banta) G.; student Valparaiso (Ind.) U., 1914-16; A.B., U. of Minn., 1919, A.M., 1920, M.B., 1921, M.D., 1922; m. Beryl Bertha Sparks, Apr. 7, 1917 (died Apr. 23, 1941). Asst. in bacteriology, U. of Minn., 1918, instr., 1921, asst. prof., 1922-25, asso. prof. 1925-29, became prof. 1929, head dept. of bacteriology, Univ. of Minn. 1946-47. Served in Med. R.C., 1917, Students' Army Training Corps. 1918-19, World War I. Capt. and Med. Officer, Civil Air Patrol, Wing No. 71, Air Corps, Minnesota State Guard, 1942-43. Fellow N.Y. Zool. Soc.; mem. A.A.A.S., Soc. Am. Bacteriologists, Am. Assn. Pathologists and Bacteriologists, A.M.A., Society for Exptl. Biology and Medicine, Am. Soc. Mammalogists, Am. Assn. of Immunologists, American Legion, Sigma Xi, Alpha Omega Alpha. Republican. Episcopalian. Mason. Club: Minneapolis Athletic. Author of many scientific publs. and contbr. numerous tech. articles. Home: 3948 1st Av. S. Office: 223 Millard Hall, Dept. of Bacteriology, University of Minnesota, Minneapolis. Died Sept. 6, 1947.

GREEN, WALTON ATWATER lawyer, editor; b. N.Y. City, Nov. 4, 1881; s. George Walton and Harriet Brodhead (Atwater) G.; grad. Phillips Exeter Acad., 1900; A.B., Harvard, 1904, LL.B., 1909; m. Eleanor Munroe, June 22, 1904; 1 dau., Gloria. Editor and pub. Boston Journal, 1913-17; mem. New York Stock Exchange firm, 1919-25; chief prohibition investigator, Washington, D.C., 1925—. Sec. Mass. Spl. Commn. on Mil. Edn. and Reserve, 1915; chmn. Mass. Commn. on State Constabulary, 1916-17; mem. exec. com. Mass. Com. on Pub. Safely, 1917—. Commd. maj. inf., 1917; served in France at Gen. Staff Coll. and as batln. comdr. 108th Inf. Republican. Clubs: Union Boat, St. Botolph (Boston); Harvard (Boston and New York); Union, Rockaway Hunt (N.Y.). Home: Cedarhurst, N.Y. Died Dec. 2, 1954.

GREEN, WHARTON JACKSON congressman; b. St. Marks, Fla., Feb. 28, 1831; s. Thomas Jefferson and Sarah Angelina (Wharton) G.; ed. Georgetown Coll. and U.S. Mil. Acad.; studied law U. of Va. and Cumberland U.; m. Esther Sargent Ellery, May 4, 1858; m. 2d, Mrs. Addie Burr Davis, Oct. 29, 1888. Lt. col. C.S.A.; twice wounded and taken prisoner. Del. Dem. Nat. convs., 1868, 76; candidate for presdl. elector, 1868, mem. 48th and 49th Congresses (1883-87); propr. Tokay Vineyard in Cumberland County, N.C. Author: Recollections and Reflections, 1907. Home: Fayettevill, N.C. Died 1910.

GREENBAUM, EDWARD S., army officer, lawyer; b. New York City, N.Y., Apr. 13, 1890; s. Samuel and Selina G.; grad. Horace Mann Sch., 1907, Williams Coll., Williamstown, Mass., 1910, Columbia Law Sch., 1913; LL.D., Williams Coll., 1946; research asso. Johns Hopkins Univ.; m. Dorothea R. Schwarez, Oct. 21, 1920; children—David S., Daniel W. In practice of law, N.Y. City, 1913-17, 1919-40, 46-70; mem. firm Greenbaum, Wolff & Ernst, 1915-70; D.C., 1933; special asst. to atty. gen., 1938, counsel, Long Island Railroad Commn., 1952-53. Mem. N.Y. Judicial Conf., 1st dept., 1956-67; mem. United States delegation to UN 1956-57. Mem. N.J. Commn. on Dept. Instns. and Agys., 1958. Served in U.S. Army, 1917-19 and, 1940-46; commd. lt. col., 1940, col. 1941, brig. gen., 1943-46. Awarded Distinguished Service Medal, 1945. Mem. American Academy of Arts and Letters, American, City of New York and N.Y. State bar assns., N.Y. County Lawyers Assn. Clubs: Army and Navy (Washington); Williams. Democrat. Jewish religion. Author: The King's Bench Masters (with Leslie I. Reade), 1932; A Lawyer's Job, 1968. Home: Princeton NJ Died June 12, 1970.

GREENBAUM, SIGMUND SAMUEL dermatologist; b. Philadelphia, Pa., Mar. 17, 1890; s. Joseph and Sarah (Klein) G.; B.S., Central High Sch., Phila., 1909; M.D., Jefferson Med. Coll., 1913; certificate from U. of Paris, faculty of medicine Hosp. St. Louis Clinic of Skin Diseases and Syphilis, 1919; married Rae Refowich, Nov. 30, 1922; children-Charles, Edwin, Carol (dec.), Janet. Practiced Phila. since 1913; professor clinic dermatology and syphilology, University of Pennsylvania; graduate School of Medicine since 1935; attending dermatologist, Philadelphia General Hospital since 1922; dermatologist Graduate Hosp. University of Pennsylvania, Rush Hosp., Phila. Psychiatric Hosp., Med. Adv. Bd. 1 of Pa. Selective Service; lecturer on skin and social diseases, Phila. Occupational Sch. of Therapy; cons. dermatologist, Bamberger Home and Betty Bacharach Home, Atlantic City, N.J., Eagleville Sanitarium, Camden (N.J.) General Hospital; fellow in research, Inst. of Cutaneous Medicine; director Bankers Securities Corporation. Trustee National Farm School. Diplomate Am. Bd. Dermatology and Syphilology. Fellow Am. Acad. Dermatology and Syphilology. Served as capt. Med. Corps, U.S. Army. Mem. A.M.A., West Phila. Med. Assn., Med. Club of Phila., A.A.A.S., Northern Med. Assn. of Phila., Phila. Dermatol. Soc., Phila. Defense Council (venereal disease sub-com), Med. Soc. State of Pa., Phila. County Med. Soc. (chmn. com. on cutaneous and social diseases), Am. Coll. of Physicians, Phila. Coll. of Physicians, Am. Legion, Phi Delta Epsilon. Author (with H. Prinz) diseases of the Mouth, 1935; Dermatology in General Practice, 1947. Contbr. to med. jours. Home: 320 S. 18th St., Philadelphia. Died Oct. 3, 1949; buried Roosevelt Cemetery, Philadelphia.

GREENE, ALBERT COLLINS senator; b. East Greenwich, R.I., Apr. 15, 1791; grad. Kent Acad., East Greenwich; studied law. Admitted to bar, 1812, began practice of law, East Greenwich; mem. R.I. Ho. of Reps., 1815-25, 57, speaker, 1821-25; served as brig. gen. 4th Brigade R.I. Militia, 1816-21, maj. gen., 1821-23; atty. gen. R.I., 1825-43; mem. R.I. Senate, 1843-44, 51-52; mem. U.S. Senate (Whig) from R.I., 1845-51. Died Providence, Jan. 8, 1863; buried Grace Ch. Cemetery.

GREENE, CHARLES LYMAN M.D.; b. Gray, Me., Sept. 21, 1862; s. Dr. William Warren and Elizabeth (Lawrence) G.; ed. Portland, Me., and began course at U. of Mich., class of 1885; M.D., U. of Minn., 1890; post-grad. work in hosps. of Harvard, Johns Hopkins, London, Paris, Merne, Heidelberg; m. Jessie Rice, Oct. 6, 1886. First asst. city physician, St. Paul, 1 yr.; prof. medicine, U. of Minn., and chief dept. medicine until 1915 (resigned); med. dir. Minn. Life Ins. Co., 1892-1904; chief of staff, St. Luke's Hosp.; attending physician, Miller Memorial Hosp.; consulting physician State Hosp. for Crippled Children. War lt. col. M.C. U.S. Army; col. Med. Sect. O.R.C. Author: The Medical Examination for Life Insurance, and its Associated Clinical Methods, 1900; Medical Diagnosis, 1907, 6th edit., 1925. Home: St. Paul, Minn. Died Jan. 19, 1929.

GREENE, CHRISTOPHER army officer; b. Warwick, R.I., May 12, 1737; s. Philip and Elizabeth (Wickes) G.; m. Ann Lippitt, Jan. 6, 1757, several children. Asso. with relatives in operation of extensive mfg. works build in South br. Pawtuxet River; freeman Colony of R.I., 1759; mem. R.I. Legislature from Warwick, 1771-72; chosen lt. in Kentish Guards established by R.I. Legislature, 1774; apptd. maj. in regt. of King's and Kent County Militia under Col. James Mitchell Varnum, 1775; commd. lt. col. in command of 1st bn. R.I. Militia in Benedict Arnold's expdn. to Can., captured and imprisoned in Que. until 1777, promoted col. 1st R.I. Inf., 1777, placed in command of Ft. Mercer on Delaware River, 1777; voted sword by Continental Congress for gallant defense of fort against Col. (Count) Donop's troops; transferred to R.I., 1778, took part in Battle of R.I. commanding regiment Negro troops recruited from slaves; transferred to Westchester County, N.Y., 1781, with hdqrs. on Croton River. Killed in Westchester County, May 14, 1781.

GREENE, FRANCIS VINTON maj. gen. U.S. Vols.; b. Providence, R.I., June 27, 1850; s. Gen. George Sears and Martha (Dana) G.; apptd. from D.C., and grad. U.S. Mil. Acad., 1870; m. Belle Eugénie Chevallié, Feb. 25, 1879. Second lt. 4th Arty., June 15, 1870; transferred to engr. corps, June 10, 1872; 1st lt., Jan. 13, 1874; capt., Feb. 20, 1883. Served on Internat. Commn. for survey of northern boundary of U.S. as asst. astronomer and surveyor, 1872-76; on duty in War Dept.; mil. attaché U.S. Legation, St. Petersburg, 1877-79; was with Russian Army in Turkey, 1877-78; present at battles of Schipka, Plevna, Sophia, Philipopolis and minor engagements, receiving decorations of St. Vladimir and St. Anne and campaign medal from Emperor of Russia; afterward on U.S. engr. duties; engr. in charge of pub. works in Washington, 1879-85; prof. practical mil. engring., West Point, 1885; resigned, Dec. 31, 1886. Col. 71st N.Y. Inf., May 2, 1898; brig. gen. vols., May 27, 1898; maj. gen. vols., Aug. 13, 1898. Comd. 2d Div., 7th Army Corps at Jacksonville, Fla., Savannah, Ga., and Havana, Cuba, Oct. to Dec. 1898; resigned Feb. 28, 1899. Chmn. com. on canals, N.Y., 1899. Del. Rep. Nat. Conv., Phila., 1900; police commr., Jan. 1, 1903-04. Pres. Niagara-Lockport & Ont. Power Co. Author: The Russian Army and Its Campaigns in Turkey (2 vols.), 1879; Army Life in Russia, 1881; The Mississippi Campaigns of the Civil War, 1882; Life of Nathanael Greene, Major General in the Army of the Revolution, 1893; The Revolutionary War and The Military Policy of the United States, 1911; The Present Military Situation in the United States, 1915; Our First Year in the Great War, 1918. Home: New York, N.Y. Died May 15, 1921.

GREENE, FRANK LESTER senator; b. St. Albans, Vt., Feb. 10, 1870; s. Lester Bruce and Mary Elizabeth (Hoadley) G.; ed. pub. schs., Cleveland, and St. Albans, to 13; hon. M.A., Norwich U., 1908, LL.D., 1915; m. Jessie Emma Richardson, Feb. 20, 1895; children-Richard Lester, Dorothy, Stuart Hoadley. Began as errand boy in auditor's office Central Vt. Ry.; became stenographer, and chief clk. gen. freight dept.; reporter, 1891, editor, 1899-1912, St. Albans Daily Messenger; mem. commn. to prepare and propose amendments to state const.; chmn. Rep. State Conv., 1914; elected to 62nd Congress July 30, 1912, for unexpired term of late David J. Foster; reelected 63d to 67th Congresses (1913-23), 1st Vt. Dist.; elected to U.S. Senate 2 terms, 1923-35. Pvt. to capt., Vt. N.G., 1888-1900; a.-d.-c. staff of gov. of Vt.; raised and recruited Co. B, 1st Vt. Inf. Vols., Spanish-Am. War, and mustered into U.S. service as capt.; was adj. gen. 3d Brigade, 1st Div., 3d A.C. Regent Smithsonian Instn., Washington, 1917-23; trustee Vt. Soldiers' Home, Lyndon Inst. Mason. Home: St. Albans, Vt. Died Dec. 17, 1930.

GREENE, FREDERICK STUART civil engr.; b. Rappahannock County, Va., Apr. 14, 1870; s. Thomas Tileston and Elise Glenn Davis (Skinner) G.; C.E., Va. Mil. Inst., 1890; D.E., Syracuse U., 1929; m. Grace Emily Clapp, 1900; 1 son, Francis Thornton. Engr. on Central R.R. Ga., 1890-91; with cable rys., Washington, D.C. and New York, 1892-93; asst. engr., river and harbor work, U.S. Engrs., 1894-95; gen. supt. John Monks & Sons, dock builders, 1896-1900; with Am. Mfg. Co., 1900-05; v.p. Waterproofing Co. of N.Y. City, 1905-17; commr. of highways, State of N.Y., 1919-21; pres. Greene-Huie Co., engrs. and contractors, 1921-22; reapptd. commr. highways, 1923, and apptd. supt. works, State of N.Y. Entered Plattsburg Mil. Camp, May 7, 1917; Camp Upton, Aug. 1917; comdr. Co. B., 302d Engrs., France, Apr. 14, 1918; batt. comdr. May 25, 1918, to close of war; participated in Oise, Aisne and Argonne offensives; colonel Engineers Auxiliary. Conspicuous Service Medal, State of N.Y. Democrat. Episcopalian. Author: The Blue Book of Rope Transmission, 1901. Editor: The Grim 13, 1917. Home: Rensselaerville, N.Y. Died Mar. 26, 1939.

GREENE, GEORGE SEARS army officer, engr.; b. Apponaug, R.I., May 6, 1801; s. Caleb and Sarah (Robinson) G.; grad. U.S. Mil. Acad., 1823; m. Elizabeth Vingon, July 14, 1828; m. 2d, Martha Barrett Dana, Feb. 21, 1837; 3 children. Taught mathematics U.S. Mil. Acad., 1823-27; served in various arty. posts throughout New Eng., 1827-36; promoted 1st lt., 1829; became engr. after leaving army; engr. in charge of Croton water-works extension and Croton Reservoir, Central Park, N.Y., at outbreak of Civil War; apptd. col. 60th N.Y. Volunteers, 1862, served at Washington, D.C., 1862, apptd. brig. gen. volunteers serving in Shenandoah Valley; fought in battles of Antietam, Chancellorsville and Gettysburg (where he commanded defense of Culp's Hill); transferred to Tenn., 1863, wounded at Battle of Wauhatchie, 1863; resigned commn., 1866, resumed engring. work, N.Y.C., did notable work in other Eastern cities; planned sewerage system for Washington, extension of water system in Detroit, Troy and Yonker, N.Y.; a founder Am. Soc. C.E., pres., 1875-77; returned to U.S. Army as lt. by spl. act of Congress, placed on retired list, 1894. Died Morristown, N.J., Jan. 28, 1899; buried Warwick, R.I.

GREENE, HENRY ALEXANDER army officer; b. Matteawan, N.Y., Aug. 5, 1856; s. Edgar Gale and Margaret Dundee (Scott) G.; grad. U.S. Mil. Acad., 1879; m. Augusta B. Barlow, Dec. 21, 1881. Commd. 2d lt. 20th Inf., June 13, 1879; 1st lt., July 24, 1886; capt., Oct. 14, 1891; maj. 14th Inf., May 31, 1900; lt. col. 1st Inf., Aug. 8, 1903; col. 10th Inf., Oct. 20, 1906; brig. gen., Nov. 19, 1914; maj. gen., Aug. 5, 1917. Served in Tex.; in Mont. as lt. regtl. adj. and as organizer, and comdr. for nearly 3 yrs. of co. of Sioux Indians; comdr. of co. in Santiago Campaign, Cuba, and co. in field in Philippines, Jan. 1899-July 1900; a.-d.-c. to Maj. Gen. Otis, press censor, mem. Ct. of Claims, P.I.; mem. bd. to select 1st gen. staff of the army, 1903, and mem. and 1st sec. of staff; mem. War Coll. Bd., 1903-04; chief of staff, S.W. Div., Oklahoma City, Okla., 1904-05, Northern Div., St. Louis, 1905-07; comdr. 10th Inf. in Alaska, 1907-08, and at Ft. Benjamin Harrison, Ind., 1908-11; pres. Inf. Equipment Bd., Rock Island Arsenal, 1909-10; comd. regt. in Tex. and Panama Canal Zone to 1914; comd. Central Dept., Chicago, Apr.-Aug. 1914; comd. army service schs., Ft. Leavenworth, Kan., 1914-16; comdg. Eagle Pass dist.,

Mexican border, May-Aug. 1916, 12th Provisional Div., San Antonio, Aug. 1916-Mar. 1917, 2d Brigade, 3d Provisional Div., Douglas, Ariz., Aug. 1917; comdg. 91st Inf. Div. and Camp Lewis, Am. Lake, Wash., Aug.-Nov. 1917; observation duty with British, French and A.E.F. in France and Belgium, Dec. 1917-Feb. 1918; comdg. 91st Div., Mar. 2-June 1918; comdg. Philippine Dept., Aug. 6, 1918, until retirement from active service, Nov. 29, 1918. Episcopalian. Mason. Home: Berkeley, Calif. Died Aug. 19, 1921.

GREENE, HOWARD investment banking (ret.); b. Milwaukee, May 17, 1864; s. Thomas Arnold and Elizabeth Lynes (Cadie) G.; student Milwaukee Acad., 1877-82; Litt.B., U. of Wis., 1886; m. Louise McMynn, Oct. 27, 1890 (died 1932); children-Howard (dec.), Charles (dec.), John, Elizabeth M. (Mrs. Austin Ross), dec.; m. 2d, Carolyn Anderson, Feb. 1, 1936; children-Andrew Anderson, Abigail Carolyn, Martha Marie. With Greene and Button, wholesale druggists, 1886-94; president Fidelity Trust Company, 1902-12; became secretary Wisconsin Securities Company, 1912, now chairman board; trustee Northwestern Mutual Life Insurance Co.; director Northwestern Nat. Ins. Co., Pusey Jones Corp. (Wilmington, Del.). Served as capt. and adjutant, 4th Wis. Vol. Inf., 1898-99; maj. engr. corps, 107th Engrs., U.S. Army, 1917-19; lt. col. O.R.C. Mem. Wis. State Hist. Soc., Chi Psi. Republican. Episcopalian. Mason (32ff), K.T. Clubs: Milwaukee, University Wilmington Country, Wilmington. Home: Christiana, Del. Died July 10, 1956; buried Milw.

GREENE, JACOB L. pres. Conn. Mutual Life Ins. Co.; b. Waterford, Me., Aug. 9, 1837; ed. Freyburgh Acad., Me., and U. of Mich.; studied law; admitted to bar, 1859, and began practice in Lapeer County, Mich. Apptd. court comml., 1860; enlisted 7th Mich. Inf., - June 1861; captured and imprisoned at Libby, Macon and Charleston; paroled and exchanged, 1864, and joined staff of Gen. Custer with rank of maj., and was bvtd. lt. col.; mustered out Apr. 1866. Asst. sec. Berkshire Life Ins. Co., 1867-70; asst. sec., 1870-71, sec., 1871-78, and pres. Conn. Mutual Life Ins. Co., 1878—. Home: Hartford, Conn. Died 1905.

GREENE, JOSEPH INGHAM army officer, mil. editor; b. Watertown, N.Y., Dec. 11, 1897; s. Will Camp and Mabel (Sanford) G.; B.S., U.S. Mil. Acad., 1923; grad. Inf. Sch., Ft. Benning, Ga., 1937; Command Gen. Staff Sch., Ft. Leavenworth, 1938: m. Marjorie Kennard Hutchins, May 29, 1930. Reporter Daytona (Fla.) Daily News, 1915-18; served as private and corpl., U.S. Army, 1918-19; cadet, U.S. Military Acad., West Point, 1919-23; commd. 2d lt., U.S. Army, 1923, and advanced through grades to col., 1943; service in Panama, Philippines, China and United States; assistant editor Panama American, 1926; corr. Manila Daily Bulletin, 1931; editor Tientsin Sentinel, China, 1932; asst. editor Inf. Sch. Mailing List, 1935-36; asso. editor Infantry Jour., 1938-40, editor, 1940-50, editor, gen. mgr., 1946-50; editor U.S. Army Combat Forces Journal, 1950; retired from Army, 1945, recalled to active duty, 1945; relieved, 1946. Member panel, Council on Books in Wartime for selection of useful books, 1943. Staff mem. Bread Loaf (Vt.) Writer's Conf., 1944-46). Sec.-treas. U.S. Inf. Assn. Sec. Assn. U.S. Army, 1950. Awarded Legion of Merit, 1946. Mem. Assn. Grads. U.S. Mil. Acad., Nat. Rifle Assn., Am. Military Institute (president, 1948), Military Order World Wars, Retired Officers Assn. Clubs: Army-Navy, Cosmos, National Press, Army War Coll. Mess, (Washington, Dist. of Columbia). Author: What You Should Know About Ground Forces, 1943, Asso. editor: Living Thoughts of Clausewitz; editor, The Infantry Journal Reader, 1943. Editor of mil. books, Spl. edit. Am. College Dictionary, 1947; editor (with Elizabeth Abell) anthology, First Love, 1948. Contributor articles to Infantry Journal and other mags. Home: 3601 Connecticut Av., Washington 8. Office: 1529 18th St. N.W. Washington. Died June 25, 1953; buried Arlington Nat. Cemetery.

GREENE, JOSEPH NATHANIEL, utilities exec.; b. Ft. Logan, Colo., Feb. 1, 1893; s. Lewis Douglass and Lillian Taft (Adams) G.; B.S., U. Ill., 1915; m. Nanine W. Pond, 1917 (div. 1931); children—Joseph Nathaniel, Nicholas Misplee; m. 2d, Margaret Mordock Wright, 1938; children—William Mordock, Elizabeth Kimberly. With Astoria Importing & Mfg. Co., Long Island City, N.Y., 1922-29; officer, dir. Fed. Water Service Corp. or subsidiary firms, 1929-52; pres., dir. Ala. Gas Corp., 1940-52, chmn. bd., 1953-67. Trustee Pelham Manor, N.Y., 1925-27, mayor, 1928-29; coordinator Jefferson County Civilian Def., 1941-46; chmn. local chpt. ARC, 1949-52, chmn. com. on resolutions 1957 conv. Am. Nat. Red Cross, mem. bd. govs., 1960-66; chmn. Alabama Hall of Fame Bd., 1952-69; co-chairman Birmingham Committee of 100, 1954, chairman 1955-57. Served as captain U.S. Army, 1916-19. Member Birmigham Symphony Assn. (pres. 1958-62, chmn. bd. 1961-65, trustee), Sigma Nu. Mason. Club: Birmingham Country. Home: Birmingham AL Died June 20, 1969.

GREENE, NATHANAEL army officer; b. Warwick, R.I., Aug. 7, 1742; s. Nathanael and Mary (Mott) G.; m. Catharine Littlefield, July 20, 1774; children - George Washington, Martha Washington, Cornelia Lott, Nathanael Ray, Louisa Catherine. ep. to R.I. Gen. Assembly, 1770-72, 75; organized militia co. known as Kentish Guards, 1774; commd. brig. gen. Continental Army, 1775; present at siege of Boston, later commanded army of occupation in Boston, Mar. 1776; then commanded Continental troops in N.J.; promoted maj. gen. Continental Army, took part in fighting around N.Y., Aug. 1776; led left wing of Am. force in Battle of Trenton; served at Valley Forge, 1777-78; promoted q.m. gen., Mar. 1778; led right flank at Battle of Monmouth, June 1778; in supreme command of Continental Army during Washington's absence, Sept. 1780; pres. of bd. which condemned Maj. John André to be hanged, 1780; in command of post at West Point, Oct. 1780; in command of Army of South, 1780; noted for his strategy in the Carolinas, which ultimately forced Cornwallis, to Yorktown; lived on plantation outside Savannah, Ga., after war. Died Savannah, June 19, 1786; buried Christ Episcopal Ch., Savannah.

GREENE, OLIVER D. army officer; b. Cortland County, N.Y., Jan. 25, 1833; s. Geo. S. and Amelia Maxson G.; grad. West Point, July 1, 1854 1854; m. Kate Rich, Oct., 1859. Commd. 2d lt., 1854; lt., 1861, 2d arty.; capt. arty., Aug. 3, 1861; maj., July 17, 1862; on staff lt. col., Feb. 27, 1887; retired as brig. gen. Jan. 25, 1897. Served in border troubles in Kan., 1857-58; in Civil war as asst. adj. gen. depts. Cumberland and Ohio, 1861-62; adj. gen. 6th corps, Army of the Potomac, 1862-63, dept. of Mo., 1863-64; took part in many battles; medal of honor for distinguished gallantry at Antietam; after war in various depts. as adj. gen.; last service as adj. gen., dept. Calif., 1890-97. Address: San Francisco, Calif. Deceased.

GREENE, RALEIGH W. banker; b. Opelika, Ala., July 2, 1893; s. James and Julia (Casey) G.; student pub. schs., Opelika; m. Anne M. Kenny, Sept. 28, 1921: 1 son, Raleigh W.; m. 2d, Evelyn S. Shabbot, May 3, 1939. With Weil Bros., Montgomery Ala., 1913-17; founder First Fed. Savs. & Loan Assn., St. Petersburg, 1933, chief exec., dir. since 1933. Mem. War Price and Rationing Bd., 1941-46, chmn., 1943-46. Served as lt. col. G-1, 9th corps U.S. Army, 1917-20. Mem. Nat. (pres.), Fla. (past pres.) says, and loan leagues, St. Petersburg C. of C. (past mem. bd. govs.). Clubs: Lions (past pres.), Ambassador, Rotary, Yacht, Bahama Shores Yacht Assn. Home: 1858 Brightwaters Blvd., Sneil Isle, St. Petersburg. Office: First Federal Bldg., St. Petersburg 1, Fla. Died Apr. 28, 1954.

GREENE, SAMUEL DANA naval officer; b. Cumberland, Md., Feb. 11, 1840; s. Gen. George Sears and Martha (Dana) G.; grad. U.S. Naval Acad., 1859; m. Mary Willis, Oct. 9, 1863; m. 2d, Mary Babbitt, Nov. 8, 1876; 3 children. Entered U.S. Navy, 1855, commd. lt., 1861; only exec. officer in iron-clad Monitor during 1st battle with Merrimac, 1862, critcized for allowing Merrimac to escape, although his orders had been to keep Monitor on defensive, rather than to follow Merrimac; served in Monitor until its sinking, 1862, commended for his bravery; exec. officer ship Florida, 1863-64; promoted lt. comdr., 1865; instr. mathematics, head dept. astronomy, navigation and surveying, asst. in charge bldgs. and grounds, sr. aide to supt. U.S. Naval Acad., 1866-84; served with Pacific Squadron, 1868-71; commd. comdr., 1872; comdr. ships Juniata, 1875, Monogahela, 1876-77, Dispatch, 1882-84; exec. officer Portsmouth (N.H.) Navy Yard. Committed suicide, Portsmouth, Dec. 11, 1884.

GREENE, WARWICK b. Washington, D.C., Dec. 18, 1879; s. Gen. Francis Vinton (U.S.V.) and Belle Eugenie (Checallié) G.; A.B., Harvard, 1901, LL.B., 1905; unmarried. Dir. Bur. Pub. Works, Manila, P.I., 1910-15; dir. War Relief Commn., Rockefeller Foundation, 1916. Maj. Air Service, A.E.F., 1917-18; lt. col., 1918-19; chief of mission to Finland, Estonia, Latvia and Lithuania, 1919; pres. New England Oil Refining Co. Republican. Episcopalian. Home: New York, N.Y. Died Nov. 18, 1929.

GREENE, WILLIAM CORNELL copper miner; b. New York, N.Y., 1851. West west at 17; became govt. contractor in Colo. and Kan.; went to Ariz. and prospected around Prescott with varying success; farmed in San Pedro Valley; made success as rancher and cattleman; bought from the widow of Gov. Pesquiera of Sonora the La Cananea mines, 45 miles south of Ariz. line in Mexico; organized the Greene Consolidated Cooper Co. Pres. and dir. Greene Consolidated Gold Co., Greene Gold Silver Silver Mining Co., Greene Cattle Co., Turkey Track Cattle Cos. of Ariz., W. Va., and Sonora. Mex., Balvanera Mining Co., Belen Mining Co., Cananea Cattle Co., Cananea Realty Co., El Paso Southern R.R. Co., Guaynopita Copper Co., Internat. Ore Treating Co., Rey del Oro Mining Co., Rio Grande, Sierra Madre & Pacific R.R. Co., Santa Brigida Gold Co., Sierra Madre Land & Lumber Co.; v.p. Greene-Cananea Copper Co.; dir. Cananea Central Copper Co., Greene Land & Cattle Co. During Apaché troubles of early '80s organized and led several vol. forces against hostile Indians. Home: New York, N.Y. Died 1911.

GREENER, RICHARD THEODORE lawyer; b. Phila., Jan. 30, 1844; A.B., Harvard, 1870; LL.B., U. of S.C., 1876; (L.D., Monrovia Coll., 1882, Howard U., 1898). Taught sch., Phila. and Washington, 1870-72; editor New National Era, Washington, 1873-77; prof. metaphysics and logic, U. of S.C., 1874-77; admitted to bar, Washington, 1877; dean law faculty, Howard U., 1877-82; law clerk 1st comptroller U.S. Treasury, 1880-82; sec. Congressional Exodus Com., 1879; defended Cadet Whittaker case at West Point, 1881; demanded and obtained for Whittaker a court-martial, established in precedent that cadet at U.S. Mil. Acad. is an officer of U.S.A.; represented S.C. in Union League of America, 1875-81; life mem. (sec. 1885-92) Grant Monument Assn.; prin. examiner New York Civil Service Bd., 1885-90; took part in every nat. campaign, 1872-96; U.S. consul to Bombay, Jan.-May, 1898; consul to Vladivostok, Russia, 1898-1906. Mem. Soc. for Exploration of the Amoor, Am. Philol. Assn.; life mem. Am. Missionary Assn.; decorated, 1902, by Chinese Govt. (order Double Dragon) for services to Chinese in Siberia and to Shansi famine sufferers. During Japanese-Russian War represented Japanese and British interests in Siberia. Clubs: Commonwealth, Riverside, Republican (New York). Address: 1940 11th St., N.W., washington, D.C.

GREENFIELD, KENT ROBERTS educator; b. Chestertown, Md., July 20, 1893; s. David Lee and Kate Mathews (Roberts) G.; Washington Coll., Chestertown, 1905-07; A.B., Western Md. Coll., 1911; Ph.D., Johns Hopkins U., 1915; L.H.D., Washington Coll., 1939; unmarried. Instr. history and economics, U. of Del., 1915-16, asst. prof., 1916-19, asso. prof., 1919-20; prof. history, Rutgers summers 1916, 17; asst. prof. history, Yale 1920-30, Sterling fellow, leave of absence for research in Italy, 1929; prof. modern European history and chmn. dept., Johns Hopkins, 1930-46; chief historian, War Department, April 19 1953. Served as 2d lt., Inf., U.S. Army, 1918-19; commd. maj., Army of U.S., 1942; promoted lt. col., 1943; hist. officer Army Ground Forces, 1942-46; col., O.R.C., since 1946; chief historian, Dept. of Army, since 1947. Awarded Legion of Merit. Mem. Am. Hist. Assn. American Assn. Univ. Profs., Phi Beta Kappa. Presbyn. Clubs: Potomac Boat, 14 West Hamilton Street Club. Author several books including Economics and Liberalism in the Risogimento, 1934; The Historian and the Army, 1953. Co-author: Army Ground Forces: Organization of Ground Combat Troops, 1947. General editor, The United States Army in World War II (22 vols.) contbr. Am. Hist. Rev., Yale Rev. and Jour. Modern History, Home: The Park Lane, 2025 I St., Washington 6. Died July 25, 1967.

GREENLEAF, CHARLES RAVENSCROFT brig. gen. U.S. Army; b. Carlisle, Pa., Jan. 1, 1838; s. Rev. Patrick Henry and Margaret (Johnson) G.; M.D., Ohio State Med. Coll., 1860; m. Georgie Franck de la Roche, Sept. 10, 1862. Asst. surgeon 5th Ohio Inf., Apr. Apr. 24-July 18, 1861 (1st surgeon commd. from Ohio for Civil War); asst. surgeon U.S. Army, Aug. 5, 1861; capt. asst. surgeon, July 28, 1866; maj. surgeon, June 26, 1876; lt. col. asst. med. purveyor, Feb. 24, 1891; col. asst. surgeon gen. U.S. Army, Oct. 10, 1896; retired, Jan. 1, 1902; brig. gen. retired, 1904. Built Mower Gen. Hosp., Chestnut Hill, Phila., 1862, where he was exec. officer; on staffs of Gens. McClellan, Lew Wallace, Hancock, George H. Wright, George H. Thomas; med. dir. after battle of Antietam; served with Army of Potomac through Peninsular, Antietam and Gettysburg campaigns; chief med. officer during Pittsburgh riots, 1876; Nez Perces and Sioux Indian campaigns, 1878-79; on staff Gen. Terry, 1882-83; exec. officer surgeon gen.'s office, 1887-93; author of present system for personal identification of soldiers in U.S.A.; organized hosp. corps, U.S.A.; originated and organized ambulance service, San Francisco; chief surgeon of army in the field during Spanish-Am. War, serving in Cuba and R.P., 1898; med. insp. of army, 1898-99; chief surgeon, div. of the Philippines, on staffs of Gens. Otis and MacArthur, 1900. Prof. pub. and mil. hygiene, U. of Calif. Del. Internat. Med. Congress, Rome, 1893. Author: Greenleaf's Manual for Medical Officers; Greenleaf's Epitome of the Examination of Recruits (present standard for the army). Died 1911.

GREENLEAF, EDMUND silk dyer, army officer; b. Ipswich, Suffolk, Eng., circa 1574; s. John and Margaret Greenleaf; m. Sarah Dale; m. 2d, Sarah Hill; at least 9 children. Became silk dyeing business, Boston; admitted as freeman to Newbury, Mass., 1639, opened house of entertainment; commanded mil. co. which fought Indians, 1637-39; ensign mil. co. at Newbury, 1639-42; became lt. comdr. Mass. provincial forces under Capt. William Gerrish, 1642, capt., 1644-47; returned to silk-dyeing, Boston, 1650-71. Died 1671.

GREENLEAF, MOSES army officer; b. Newburyport, Mass., May 19, 1755; s. Jonathan and Mary (Presbury) G.; m. Lydia Parsons, Sept. 1776. Asso. with his father in ship-bldg. bus., Mass., 1781-90; served as pvt. Mass. Militia, 1775, 2d lt., 1775-76, lt., 1776, took part in siege of Boston; commd. capt., 1779; served with 11th Mass. Regt. under Col. Benjamin Tupper, 1777-81; retired from Continental Army, 1790; farmer, New Gloucester, Me., until 1812. Died New Gloucester, Dec. 18, 1812.

GREENLEE, KARL B. hosp. adminstr.; b. Lineville, Ia., Nov. 5, 1902; s. Rollo Waldo and Lynn Marie (Lovett) G.; B.S., Ia. State U., 1925; M.A., U. Ia., 1933; m. Christine Corbett, Oct. 9, 1929. Athletic coach, sch. adminstr., Ia., 1925-42; hosp. adminstr., 1942 - ; adminstr. Wilden Hosp., Des Moines, 1946 - , treas. 1947 - . Pres. Hopkins Sporting Goods, Inc., Des

Moines, 1945 - ; treas. Eastern Investors, Inc., Des Moines, 1958 - ; pres. Swift Finance Co., Inc., Des Moines, 1959 - . Chmn. Des Moines Civil Service Commn., 1955-61. Mem. Polk County Republican Finance Cmnom. Sec. bd. trustees Coll. Osteopathic Medicine and Surgery; adv. council Central Ia. Air Force Tng. Center. Served to lt. col. USAAF, 1942-46; ETO; col. Res. Decorated Bronze star; Croix de Guerre (France). Mem. Am. Osteopathic Hosp. Assn. (pres.), Am. Coll. Osteopathic Adminstrs. (past pres.), Greater Des Moines C. of C. (dir.), Am. Legion, Res. Officers Assn., Air Force Assn., Phi Delta Kappa. Mason (Shriner). Clubs: Des Moines; East Des Moines. Home: 1156 28th St., West Des Moines, Ia. Office 1347 Capital St. Des lMoines. Died July 13, 1964; buried Glendale Cemetery, Des Moines.

GREENMAN, FREDERICK FRANCIS lawyer; b. N.Y. City, Sept. 3, 1892; s. Max and Kate (Cooperman) G.; A.B. magna cum laude, Harvard (Pulitzer scholar), 1914, LL.B. cum laude, 1916; m. lMildred S. Liebman, Nov. 15, 1921; children - Barbara (Mrs. Leon M. Stier), Mimi (Mrs. George H. Grosser), Frederick Francis. Admitted to N.Y. bar, 1917; clk. Leventritt, Cook, Nathan & Lehman, 1916; mem. Cook, Nathan, Lehman & Greenman, predecessors and successors, 1922-47, Greenman, Shea, and Zimet, New York City, and Washington, since 1947; counsel financial and gen. litigations state and fed. cts.; gen. counsel Army-Navy Liquidation Commr., 1945, Fgn. Liquidation Commr., State Dept., 1945-46. Republican candidate for N.Y. State senator, 1934, for U.S. Congress, N.Y., 17th Congl. Dist., 1936; asst. to Eastern campaign mgr. for Wendell L. Wilkie, v. chmn. Eastern div. Rep. Nat. Com., 1940; mem. Pep. State Com., exec. mem. 7th Assembly Dist., N.Y., 1942-43. Chmn. bd. Menorah Assn., 1930-32; chmn. allotment com. United Jewish Appeal, 1941; trustee Jewish Inst. Religion, 1934-43, State U. N.Y. since 1948, chmn. 4-year coll. com., 1948-51, chmn. tech. sch. com. Community Coll. 1951-57, chmn. com. planning and development, 1957- ; pres. United Neighborhood Houses; chmn. joint def. appeal Am. Jewish Com. Anti-Defamation League. Trustee, v.p. Temple Emanu-El, Jewish Bd. Guardians, Citizens Housing, Planning Council; chairman executive board American Jewish Committee, 1961 - ; vice president Union Am. Hebrew Congregations, vice pres., vice chmn., 1939-50; p.p., hon. pres. N.Y. Fedn. Reform Synagogues; chmn. adv. com. on debating, Harvard Univ.; del. White House Conf.,on Education, 1955. Served as pvt. to 2d lt. F.A., U.S. Army, World War I; 2d lt. F.A. Res., 1919-34; maj. to col. Judge Adv. Gen. Dept., World War II, col. Res. since 1946; past. dep. comdr. 1568th Judge Adv. Gen. Training Group. Decorated Legion of Merit (Army); Conspicuous Service Cross (N.Y. State). Mem. Bar Assn. City N.Y., N.Y. Co. Lawyers Assn., Harvard Law Sch. Association of New York (vice president 1943), American Law Institute, American, N.Y. State bar assns., Phi Beta Kappa, Delta Sigma Rho. Clubs: Army and Navy, Woodmont Country (Washington); Harvard, Lawyers, North Shore Country, Harmonie (N.Y.C.); Harvard Faculty (Cambridge). Author: Wire Tapping and Civil Liberties, 1938. Editor Harvard Law Rev. Home: 135 Central Park W., N.Y.C. 23. Office: 1 Chase Manhattan Plaza, N.Y.C. Died June 26, 1961; buried Arlington Nat. Cemetery, Washington.

GREENOUGH, GEORGE GORDON army officer; b. Washington, Dec. 8, 1844; s. John James and Mary Frances Ascough (Cushing) G.; ed. pvt. and pub. schs. to 1857, Paris, France, 1857-60, pvt. sch., Baltimore, 1860-61; grad. U.S. Mil. Acad., 1865; unmarried. Commd. 2d lt. and 1st lt., 12th Inf., June 23, 1865; transferred to 21st Infantry; Sept. 21, 1865; assigned to 4th Arty., Dec. 15, 1870; grad. Arty. Sch., 1882; capt., Dec. 1, 1883; maj. 7th Arty., Mar. 8, 1898; lt. col., Arty. Corps, July 1, 1901; col., Feb. 21, 1903; brig. gen. and retired, Dec. 8, 1908. Instr. asst. prof. and acting prof. of French, U.S. Mil. Acad., 1868-73; served in 3d Army Corps, 1863; in Modoe Indian campaign, 1873; Nev. expdn., 1875, and in Powder River expdn., 1876-77; mil. instr. U. of Calif., 1877-78; was one of the pioneers in range-finding work, 1882-98; sharp shooter for 5 yrs.; comd. arty. defenses of Washington, 1898; served in Cuba, 1898-99, and in P.I., 1900-02. Inventor of various devices for arty. operation. Died June 27, 1912.

GREENSLADE, JOHN WILLS naval officer; b. Bellevue, O., Jan. 11, 1880; grad. U.S. Naval Acad., 1899, Naval War Coll., 1926; children-John Francis (capt. U.S. Navy), Robert Wills (Lt. U.S.N.R.), Service: Cuban and Puerto Rican campaigns, Spanish-American War, 1898; Philippines, 1899-1902; head dept. ordnance and gunnery, Naval Acad., 1917; comd. U.S.S. Housatonic, Northern Mine Barrage, North Sea, 1918; inspector of ordnance, Naval Powder Factory and Proving Ground, 1920-23; comdr. Mine Squadron 1, U.S. Fleet, 1923-25; head operations dept., Naval War Coll., 1926-28; comd. U.S.S. Pennsylvania, 1928-29; chief of staff, Battleship Divs., U.S. Fleet, 1929-30; mem. Gen. Bd., 1931-32, 1934-36, 1939-41; comdr. Submarine Force, U.S. Fleet. 1932-34; vice admiral comdr. battleships, U.S. Fleet, 1933-39; sr. mem. President's Bd. to select sites for Atlantic bases in Brit. possessions, 1940; comdt. 12th Naval Dist., 1941; comdr. Western Sea Frontier, 1942-Feb. 1944; retired; coordinator of naval logistics, Pacific Coast, 1944; resources coordinator, Western Sea Frontier, 1945. Awards (service) D.S.M., 1918, 1944; (campaign) Spanish-Am., Philippines, Cuban and Mexican Interventions, World Wars I and II; (foreign) Mexican Nat. Order of Aztec Eagle, Merito Naval; Chilean Orden del Merito; Panamanian Order of Vasco Nunex de Balboa. Address: 226 Greenwood Heights, Bellevue, O. Died Jan. 6, 1950.

GREER, FRANK U. army officer; b. Washington, D.C., Sept. 24, 1895; s. Wiliiam Alexander and Cecelia (Throckmorton) G.; student Catholic Univ., 1915-18; LL.B., George Washington Univ., 1926; grad. Inf. Sch., 1921, Chem. Warfare Sch., 1934, Command and Gen. Staff Sch., 1934, Army War Coll., 1936; hon. M. Mil. Science, R.I. State Coll., 1941; m. May Imogene Mann, December 26, 1917; children-Mary Imogene (Mrs. P. J. McCaskey), Charles Francis, Thomas Upton, Frank Upton, Rebecca Ellan. Commd. 1st lt., 1917 and advanced through the grades to brig. gen., 1943, Awarded Purple Heart, Silver Star (Africa, 1943), oak leaf cluster to both Purple Heart and Silver Star (France, 1944). Bronze Star (France, 1944) Legion of Honor, Croix de Guerre with Palm (French). Mem. Alpha Tau Gamma, Odd Fellow, K.C. Home: 859 Second Av., Gainesville, Fla. Died May 17, 1949.

GREGG, ALAN physician; b. Colorado Springs, Colo., July 11, 1890; s. James Bartlett and Mary (Needham) G.; prep. edn., Cutler Acad. Colorado Springs; A.B., Harvard, 1911; M.D., Harvard Med. Sch., 1916; m. Eleanor Agnes Barrows, July 2, 1923; children-Peter Alan, Nancy Barrows, Richard Alexander, Michael Barrows. Interne, Mass. Gen. Hosp., Boston, 1916-17; served with Royal Army Med. Corps, B.E.F., 1917-19; field staff mem. Internat. health bd. Rockefeller Foundation, 1919-22, asso. dir. div. med. edn., 1922-28, asso. dir. med. sciences, 1929-30. dir. med. sciences, 1930-51, vice pres., 1951-56. Decorated Chevalier Legion d'Honneur, 1951; recipient Lasker award Am. Pub. Health Assn., 1957. Fellow A.A.A.S., Am. Acad. Arts and Scis., N.Y. Acad. Medicine, American Coll. Surgeons; hon. member Alpha Omega Alpha, American Association Physicians; mem. Am. Philosophical Society, Phi Beta Kappa (1936). Club: Century (N.Y.C.); Cosmos (Washington). Home: Big Sur, Cal. Died June 9, 1957; buried Westwood Cemetery, Oberlin, O.

GREGG, J. A. bishop; b. Eureka, Kan., Feb. 18, 1877; s. Alexander and Eliza Frances (Allen) G.: A.B., U. of Kansas, 1902; m. Celia Ann Nelson, Aug. 20, 1900 (died 1941); m. 2d, Mrs. Alberta McFarland, Dec. 1945. School teacher, Oskaloosa, Kan., 1902-03; ordained to ministry of African Meth. Episcopal Ch.; pastor, Emporia, Kansas, 1903; missionary teacher, Cape Town, South Africa, 1903-06; pastor, Leavenworth, Kan., 1906-08, St. Joseph, Mo., 1908-13; pres. Edwards Coll., Jacksonville, Fla., 1913-20, Wilberforce U., 1920-24; elected bishop, 1924; assigned 17th Episcopal Dist., South Africa, 1924-28, 5th Episcopal Dist., 1928-36, 4th Episcopal Dist., 1936-48, 11th Episcopal District since 1948; president Bishops Council African M.E. Church since 1948. Served as sergeant, later second lieutenant, 23d Kansas Volunteers, during Spanish-American War. Pres. trustee bd. Payne Theol. Sem. (Wilberforce U.); elected pres. Howard U., 1926, but declined position. Recipient Award for Merit by sec. of Army Kenneth C. Royall, 1947; Citation by Univ. of Kan., 1948. Pres. Fla. State Teachers Assn., 1916, Nat. Assn. Preachers in Colored Schs., 1922, African Meth. Episcopal-Coll. Presidents Assn., 1922-24. Mem. Alpha Phi Alpha, Sigma Pi Phi. Mason, Knight of Pythias, Elk. Author: (pamphlets) Christian Brotherhood, 1930; Superlative Righteousness, 1944; Of Men and Of Arms, 1945. Delivered keynote address 8th Worlds Christian Endeavor, Berlin, Germany, 1930, invocation Nat. Rep. Conv., Philadelphia, 1940. By invitation of the president visited all war fronts, except Alaska, representing Fraternal Council of Negro Churches, 1943-44. Home: 1150 Washington Blvd., Kansas City 2, Kan. Office: Edward Waters College, Jacksonville, Fla. Died Feb. 1953.

GREGG, JOHN army officer; b. Lawrence County, Ala., Sept. 28, 1828; s. Nathan and Sarah (Pearsall) G.; grad. La Grange Coll., 1847; m. Mary Garth, 1856. Moved to Tex., 1852; dist. judge Freestone County (Tex.), 1856; mem. irregularly assembled secessionist conv. which voted Tex. out of Union; Tex. rep. Confederate Provisional Congress, Montgomery Ala., 1861; commd. col. 7th Tex. Inf., 1861; captured at Ft. Donelsen, 1862, later exchanged; commd. brig. gen. Confederate Army, 1862; commanded brigade of Tenn. and Tex. troops; participated in battles of Vicksburg, Chickamauga, also Campaign of 1864. Killed in battle before Richmond (Va.), Oct. 7, 1864.

GREGG, JOHN ANDREW clergyman; b. Eureka, Kan., Feb. 18, 1877; s. Alexander and Eliza Frances (Allen) G.; A.B., U. Kan., 1902; M.A., Morris Brown U., 1915; D.D., Wilberforce, 1916; m. Celia A. Nelson, Aug. 20, 1900; m. 2d, Melberta McFarland, 1946. Pres. Bethel Inst., Cape Town, S. Africa, 1903-06; pastor A.M.E. Ch., Leavenworth, Kan., 1906-08, St. Joseph Mo., 1908-13, elected bishop, Kansas City, Kan., 1924; pres. Edward Waters Coll., Jacksonville, Fla., 1913-26, Wilberforce U., 1920-24. Apptd. rep. Fraternal Council Negro Chs., vis. war fronts, 1943-44. Served six mos. in Cuba as q.m. sgt. 23d Kan. Vols., Spanish-Am. War. Recipient Award of Merit from Sec. of Army, 1947. Mem. Nat. Assn. Tchrs. Colored Schs. (pres. 1922-23), N.E.A. Republican. Mason. Club: Green Country (O.), Rifle (pres.). Author: Christian Brotherhood, 1930; Superlative Righteousness, 1944; Of Men and of Arms, 1945. Address: 1150 Washington Blvd., Kansas City, Kan. Died 1953; buried Kansas City, Kan.

GREGG, JOHN B. physician; b. Gladbrook, Ia., Sept. 28, 1888; s. Daniel and Lillie A. (Sharp) G.; A.B., State U. of Ia., 1915, M.D., 1915, M.S., 1916; M. A. Elida Bailey, Aug. 10, 1921; children-John Bailey, Charles Dan, Mary Elida, Elizabeth Ann, Margaret Jane. Sr. clinical assistant oto-laryngology; State University of Ia., 1915-17; maj. Medical Reserve Corps, U.S. Army, assigned to British Royal Army Medical Corps, 1917-19; asso. prof. oto-laryngology, State U. of Ia., 1919-20; private practice specializing in oto-laryngology, Sioux Falls, S.D., since 1920. Fellow Am. Coll. Surgeons: mem. A.M.A., S.D. State Med. Soc., Am. Acad. Ophthalmology and Oto-laryngology, Am. Laryngol., Rhinol. and Otol. Soc., Newcomen Soc. of England, Alpha Omega Alpha, Sigma Xi, Phi Rho Sigma. Decorated British Mil. Cross, 1918. Republican. Episcopalian. Mason (Shriner). Club: Minnehaha Country. Home: 309 N. Duluty Av. Office: Security Nat. Bank Bldg., Sioux Falls, S.D. Died Mar. 3, 1954; buried Woodlawn Cemetery, Sioux Falls, S.D.

GREGG, JOHN PRICE govt. official; b. Portland, Ore., Sept. 8, 1891; s. John Thomas and Eva (Price) G.: A.B., Stanford, 1913, grad. studies, law and economics, 1913-14; student Univ. of Paris (Sorbonne), 1919; m. Elizabeth Emily Dyer, Apr. 2, 1929: 1 son, Lawrence Alexander. Admitted to bar of Ore., 1915, Mont., 1917, New York, 1925. Dist. of Columbia, 1935. Regional dir. Am. Relief Adminstrn. southern and eastern European relief and famine operations, London, England, 1920-23: asst. to Sec. of Commerce, Washington, D.C., 1926-27; mgr. Am. sect. and sec. Am. Com. Internat. Chamber of Commerce, Washington, D.C., 1927-35; sec. com. for reciprocity information, State Dept., 1937-41; asst. dep. and dep. chief. Priorities, War Prodn. Bd., 1941-42; U.S. sec. combined prodn. and resources bd., Washington, D.C., 1942-43; chief staff operations, War Prodn. Bd., Washington, D.C., 1943-44; exec. dir. U.S. Assos. Internat. Chambers of Commerce, New York, 1945-46; mem. U.S. Tariff Commn. since Sept. 1946. Commd. 2d lt., U.S. Army, Nov. 1917; served overseas Mar. 1918 to hon. disch. as capt., Mar. 1920. Mem. Alpha Delta Phi Republican. Presbyterian. Clubs: Army and Navy Country. Cosmos (Washington, D.C.), University (New York, N.Y.); Devon Yacht (Amagansett, N.Y.). Home: 4313 Yuma St., Washington 16. Office: U.S. Tariff Commission, Washington 25. Died Oct. 29, 1952.

GREGG, MAXCY army officer; b. Columbia S.C., 1814; s. James and Cornelia (Maxcy) G.; grad. Coll. of S.C., 1830. Admitted to S.C. bar, 1839; commd. maj. 12th Inf., U.S. Volunteers, 1847, mem. central com. framing S.C. ordinance of secession, adopted 1860; commd. col. Confederate Army, 1861, brig. gen., commanded brigade of reserves at battle of Beavers Dam Creek, 1862, also 2d battle Manassas, 1862, battles of Mechanicsville, Cold Harbor, Frazers Farm, Malvern Hill, Cedar Mountain; held center reserve of Gen. Jackson's line at Battle of Fredricksburg, 1862. Engaged in astron.; ornithol. and bot. studies; an early advocate of So. Rights; leading mem. Conv. So. Rights Assns., Charleston; advocated reopening of African slave trade as means of separation from North. Died in Battle of Fredericksburg (Va.), Dec. 14, 1862; buried Columbia.

GREGORY, EDMUND BRISTOL army officer; b. Storm Lake, Ia., July 4, 1882; s. Frank Buckingham and Emily Hatch (Bristol) B.; B.S., U.S. Mil. Acad., 1904; M.B.A., Harvard Grad. Sch. of Business Adminstrn., 1929; Army War Coll., 1936-37; m. Verna Ellsworth Green, July 19, 1911. Commd. 2d lt. Inf., U.S. Army, 1904, advanced through the grades to col. Q.M. Corps, 1935; lt. gen., Q.M. Gen., 1945; Post Q.M. and Commissary, Philippines, 1908-10; Ft. Harrison, Mont., 1910-11; instr. history and English, U.S. Mil. Acad., 1911-12; Gen. Supply epot, Jeffersonville, Ind., 1917-21; transferred to Q.M.C., 1920; in charge Q.M. Columbus Gen. Depot, 1921; settlement War Dept. contracts, Shanghai, China, 1922-24; N.Y. Nat. Guard, 1924-27; Office Q.M. Gen., Washington, 1929-33; Hdqrs. 2d Corps Area, 1933-36; Office Q.M. Gen. 1937; Q.M. Gen., 1940-46; chmn. War Assets Corp., 1946; adminstr., War Assets Adminstrn., 1946, ret. 1946. Decorated D.S.M. (2); Legion of Honor (French); officer Brit. Empire Home: 4401 Greenwich Parkway N.W., Washington. Died Jan. 26, 1961; buried Arlington Cemetery.

GREGORY, JOHN HERBERT engineer, educator; b. Cambridge, Mass., Aug. 7, 1874; s. John Porter and Mary Clerice (Stone) G.; New England ancestry; B.S. in C.E., Mass. Inst. Tech., 1895; m. Sarah Ann James, July 16, 1900; 1 son, Richard Sears. Engr. with Boston Metropolitan Sewerage Works, 1893-94, Boston Met. Water Works, 1895-97, Albany Water Filtration Works, 1897-1900, Phila. Water Filtration Works, 1900-02, Jersey City Water Supply Works, 1902-03, N.Y. Filtration Dept. Commn. on Additional Water Supply, 1903-04; engr. in charge Improved Water and Sewerage Works, Columbus, O., 1904-09; resident engr. Passaic

Valley Sewerage Project, Newark, N.J., 1909-10; engr. Met. Sewerage Commn., New York, 1910-11; mem. Rudolph Hering & John H. Gregory, cons. engrs., New York, 1911-17; practiced alone, 1917-19; settled at Baltimore as cons. engr., 1919; also prof. civil and sanitary engring., Johns Hopkins U., 1920—. Commd. capt. U.S.A., 1918. Mem. Engineers' Advisory Board, Reconstruction Finance Corp., 1932. Awarded Thomas Fitch Rowland prize, 1910, James Laurie prize, 1930, and Rudolph Hering medal, 1935, by Am. Soc. Civil Engineers. Episcopalian. Home: Baltimore, Md. Died Jan. 18, 1937.

GREGORY, LUTHER ELWOOD b. Newark, Jan. 9, 1872; s. A. Belknap and Susan (Montrose) G.; C.E., Sch. of Mines, Columbia, 1893; hon. D.Eng., Rensselaer Polytechnic Inst., 1938; m. Anna R. Roome, Dec. 26, 1894 (dec. Feb. 1904); 5 daughters; m. 2d, Pauline E. Turner, Nov. 12, 1918 (dec. Jan. 1936); one son; m. 3d, Ethel B. Nelson, June 20, 1947. Became civil engineer, U.S. Navy, 1898; served as public works officer at U.S. naval stas.; mem. Alaskan Coal Commn., 1919; chief of Bur. Yards and Docks, Navy Dept., 1922-29; mem. bd. location San Francisco-Oakland bridge; cons. engr. Lake Washington pontoon bridge, Seattle, foundations and piers of Puget Sound Bridge, Tacoma; ret. as rear admiral. Chmn., Wash. Liquor Control Bd., 1934-42, 1945-49. Mem. Am. Soc. C. E., Soc. Am. Mil Engrs. (trustee, dir.), Mil. Order of World War (comdr. Seattle chapter), Beta Theta Pi. Mason (33ff, K.T., Shriner). Clubs: Army and Navy, National Sojourners, Rainier and Washington Athletic of Seattle. Home: 310 W. Prospect St., Seattle. Died Nov. 14, 1960.

GREGORY, THOMAS T(INGEY) C(RAVEN) lawyer; b. Sulsun, Calif., Oct. 4, 1878; s. John Munford and Evelyn Tingey (Craven) G.; A.B., Stanford U., 1899, studied law dept. same univ., 1900-01; m. Gertrude Martin, Apr. 15, 1903; children-John Munford, Gertrude Evelyn, Margaret Martin. Practiced at San Francisco, 1907—; dist. atty. Solano Co., Calif., 1903-07; dir. numerous companies. Trustee Stanford U. Capt. 144th F.A., with A.E.F., in France, World War; associated with Herbert Hoover in Europe as one of original members of Am. Relief Adminstrn.; dir. Central Europe A.R.A. and asst. to dir. of relief of Supreme Economic Council; Am. mem. Interallied Commn. Austro-Hungarian and Jugo-Slavian empires, feeding people and reinstating economic interchanges between Central and S.E. European countries. Republican. Episcopalian. Mason. Home: Stanford University, Calif. Died June 5, 1933.

GREGORY, WILLIAM EDWARD educator; b. Bianchester, O., July 3, 1901; s. William Charles and Birdie Grace (Parker) G.; B.S., Miami U., Oxford, O., 1924; grad. Field Arty. Sch., U.S. Army, 1931; M.A., U. of Mich., 1934; Ed.M. (Austin scholar), Harvard, 1935; Litt.D., Colgate U., 1940; m. Iris Beryl Hinton, of Middlesex, England, June 25, 1945. Began as educator, 1922; prin. Hanover High Sch., Hamilton, O., 1923; instr. mathematics, Culver Mil. Acad., Culver, Ind., 1924-27, tactical officer, F.A., 1927-30, asst. headmaster, 1930-33, dean, 1935-39, acting supt., 1939-40, supt. since 1940. Mem. bd. dirs. Culver Ednl. Foundation. Past president Private Schools Association. With 12th U.S. Army Group, May 1942-July 1945; colonel Headquarters, October 1943 July 1945. Awarded Legion of Merit, Bronze Star Medal with Oak Leaf Cluster (United States); Legion of Honor, Croix de Guerre with Palm (France); Croix de Guerre with Palm (Belgium); Couronne de Chene (Luxembourg). Mem. N.E.A., Am. Acad. Polit. and Social Science, Pvt. Schs. Assn. of Central States, Association of Military Colleges and Schools, Delta Kappa Epsilon, Phi Delta Kappa, Cum Laude Soc., Kappa Delta Pi, Phi Beta Kappa. Presbyterian. Clubs: University, Harvard (Chicago); Army and Navy (Washington). Address: Culver Military Academy, Culver, Ind. Died Mar. 14, 1956; buried Culver Masonic Cemetery Culver, Ind.

GREIGER, ROY STANLEY marine officer; b. Middleburg, Fla., Jan. 25, 1885; s. Marion Francis and Josephine (Prevatt) G.; student Fla. State Normal Sch., 1900-04; LL.B., John B. Stetson U., 1907; LL.D., 1940; distinguished grad., Commd. and Gen. Staff Sch., 1925; grad. Army War Coll., 1929, Naval War Coll., 1940, student advanced course, 1941; completed naval aviation course, Pensacola, Fla., 1916; m. Eunice Renshaw Thompson, July 18, 1917; children-Joyce Renshaw (wife of Lt. Col. Roger J. Johnson, U.S. M.C.), Maj. Roy Stanley, Jr. Commd. 2d lt., U.S. M.C. and promoted through grades to lt. gen., 1945; comd. Squadron A, 1st Marine Aviation Force, France, World War I; apptd. head Marine Corps Aviation, Washington, D.C., 1931; asst. naval attaché for air, London, England, 1941; directed operations of all Allied aviation activities on Guadalcanal, 1942 (1st Allied offensive, World War II); assumed command 1st Marine Amphibious Corps, 1943, seized Bougainville; comdr. 3d Marine Amphibious Corps which seized Guam, 1944, Palaus, 1944, participated in invasion and capitulation of Okinawa, 1945; comdr. U.S. 10th Army, Okinawa upon death of Lt. Gen. Simon B. Buckner; U.S. Marine rep. at formal surrender of Japan, Tokyo Bay, 1945; comdr. Fleet Marine Force, Pacific, 1945; sr. Marine rep. Bikini, during Atomic tests Able and Baker, 1946. Returned to U.S., duty Marine Corps Hdqrs., Washington, D.C., Nov., 1946. Awarded Navy Cross, Gold Star in Lieu of 2d Navy Cross, Navy Distinguished Service Medal, Distinguished Flying Cross, 2 Gold Stars in lieu of 2d and 3d D.S.lM.'s, Air Medal, Presidential Unit Citation with 2 stars, 1st Nicaraguan with stars, Victory Medal, Haitian Campaign, 2d Nicaraguan, American Defense Medal, Pacific Area Medal with 1 silver star, Nicaraguan Medal of Distinction, Dominican Medal of Merit with 2 Silver Stars. Member American Legion. Clubs: Army and Navy, Army-Navy Country Washington, D.C.). Home: Rosemont, Penscola, Fla. Died January 23, 1947; buried in Arlington National Cemetery.

GRESHAM, WALTER QUINTIN army officer, cabinet officer; b. Lanesville, Ind., Mar. 17, 1832; s. William and Sarah (Davis) G.; attended Ind. U.; m. Matilda McGrain, Feb. 11, 1858. Admitted to Ind. bar, 1854; mem. Ind. Legislature, 1860; served as div. comdr. in Gen. Blair's Corps, U.S. Army, before Atlanta, 1861; commd. brig. gen., 1863, brevetted maj. gen., 1865; U.S. dist. judge for Ind., 1869-82; U.S. postmaster gen., 1882-84; suggested as Republican candidate for presidency, did not receive nomination, 1884, 88; U.S. sec. of treasury, 1884; apptd. circuit judge 7th U.S. Jud. Dist., 1884; broke with Rep. Party over McKinley tariff; offered nomination as Populist Party candidate for Pres. U.S., 1892; supported Cleveland in 1892 election; sec. of state under Pres. Cleveland, 1893-95; advised against Hawaiian annexation treaty, settled Nicaraguan-Brit. dispute and Allianca affair between U.S. and Spain. Died Washington, D.C., May 28, 1895; buried Arlington (Va.) Nat. Cemetery.

GRIDLEY, RICHARD army officer, mil engr.; b. Boston, Jan. 3, 1711; s. Richard Gridley; m. Hannah Deming, Feb. 25, 1730, 9 children. Served as engr. during Siege of Louisbourg, 1745; drew plans for battery and other fortifications Boston Harbor, 1746; built Ft. Western (Augusta, Me.) and Ft. Halifax, 1752; commd. col. Brit. Army, served under Winslow in expdn. to Crown Point, 1756, under Amherst, 1758, under Wolfe in expdn. to Quebec, 1759; commanded Mass. arty., 1759; commd. chief engr., comdr. arty. Continental Army at Cambridge, Mass., 1775; commd. maj. gen., 1775, planned defensive works of Bunker Hill on the night before battle, 1775; commd. col., 1775; engr. gen. Eastern Dept., 1777-80. Died Stoughton, Mass., June 21, 1796.

GRIER, WILLIAM commodore U.S.N.; b. in Ireland, Oct. 5, 1816; s. William and Margaret (Hayes) G.; ed. at Baltimore; m. Margaret Watmough. Apptd. from Md. asst. surgeon U.S.N., Mar. 7, 1838; passed asst. surgeon and surgeon, Apr. 14, 1852; med. dir., Mar. 3, 1871; on board Cyane, 1838-41; storeship Erie, 1842-44; Shark, 1844-46; hospital, New York, 1848-49; Independence, 1849-52; Vincennes, as fleet surgeon, N. Pacific Surveying Expdn., 1853-56; spl. duty, 1857; Naval Acad., 1858-60; Macedonian, 1860-61; receiving ship at Baltimore, 1862; Naval hosps., Mound City, Ill., and Memphis, Tenn., 1862-65; spl. duty at Hartford, Conn., 1867; mem. Naval Examining Bd., 1868-69; spl. duty at Baltimore, 1869-71; mem. Examining and Retiring Bds., 1871-72; pres. Med. Examining Bd., 1872-76; surgeon gen. of the navy, and chief of Bur. of Medicine and Surgery, with the rank of commodore, 1877-78; retired, Oct. 5, 1876. Home: Washington, D.C. Died 1911.

GRIERSON, BENJAMIN HENRY brig. gen.; b. Pittsburgh, July 8, 1826; s. Robert and Mary (Shepard) G.; ed. Youngstown (O.) Acad.; m. Alice Kirk, Sept. 24, 1854 (died 1888); m. 2d, Mrs. Lillian Atwood apptd. maj. 6th Ill. Cav., Oct. 24, 1861; col., Apr. 12, 1862; brig. gen. vols., June 3, 1863; maj. gen. vols., May 27, 1865; hon. mustered out of vol. service, Apr. 30, 1866; col. 10th U.S. Cav., July 28, 1866; brig. gen., Apr. 5, 1890. Bvtd.; maj. gen. vols., Feb. 10, 1865; brig. gen U.S.A., Mar. 2, 1867, for gallant and meritorious services in raid through Miss. in 1863; maj. gen., Mar. 2, 1867, for same in raid through Miss. and Ala. in 1864. Home: Jacksonville, Ill. Died 1911.

GRIFFIN, ANTHONY JEROME congressman; b. N.Y. City, Apr. 1, 1866; s. James A. and Mary Ann (Zeluiff) G.; student Coll. City of New York, 1 yr.; B.S., Cooper Union, 1887; LL.B., from New York U., 1892; m. Katharine L. Byrne, Oct. 23, 1895. Practiced in New York, 1892—; founder, 1906, and editor Bronx Independent; mem. N.Y. Senate 2 terms, 1911-15; mem. State Constl. Conv., 1915; elected mem. 65th Congress, Mar. 5, 1918, to fill vacancy, 22d N.Y. Dist., for term ending 1919; reelected 66th to 73d Congresses (1919-35). Democrat. Enlisted in 12th Regt. N.G. of New York, 1888; 2d lt., 1892; 1st lt. 69th Regt., 1895; organized Co. F, 69th Inf., N.G. N.Y., 1898, and served as capt. Spanish-Am. War. Author: Speeches and Addresses, 1917; Chaos (dramatic peom, published under nom de plume of "Altair"), 1919; War and Its Aftermath, 1922. Home: New York, N.Y. Died Jan. 13, 1935.

GRIFFIN, BULKLEY SOUTHWORTH, newspaperman; b. Springfield, Mass., Aug. 16, 1893; s. Solomon Bulkley and Ida (Southworth) G.; ed. Springfield Central High Sch., 1909-12; B.A., Williams College, 1916; married Isabel Kinnear, July 8, 1926; 1 daughter, Charmain (Mrs. John Clark, Jr.). Reporter, city editor and Washington coorespondent, Springfield (Mass.) Republican, 1916-17, 1919-22; founder, owner Griffin-Larrabee News Bur., Washington, serving a group of daily newspapers, from 1922. Served in U.S. Navy and U.S. Army during World War; disch. 2d lt. Army Air Service (pilot), 1919. War corr. with 3d Army, Europe, Jan.-June 1945. Clubs: National Press, Overseas Writers, Internat. (Washington). Author: Offbeat History. Donated collection of Mark Twain books, including many in fgn. langs., to Buffalo and Erie County (N.Y.) Library. Home: Washington DC Died May 15, 1967; buried Timber Ridge Cemetery, nr. Lexington VA

GRIFFIN, CHARLES army officer; b. Granville, O., Dec. 18, 1825; s. Appolus Griffin; grad. U.S. Mil. Acad., 1847; m. Sallie Carroll, Dec. 10, 1861. Served in Mexican War; commd. 1st lt. U.S. Army, 1849; served against Navajo Indians in N. M., 1849-54; instr. in tactics U.S. Mil. Acad., 1860; organizer Battery D, 5th Arty., 1860; promoted capt., 1861; brig. gen., 1862; commanded West Point battery in 1st Battle of Bull Run served at Battle of Malvern Hill Commanded div. at battles of Antietam and Fredericksburg in Hooker's Campaign, served in Peninsular Campaign under Gen. John Pope (relieved of command after 2d Battle of Bull Run pending investigation because of remarks about Pope but restored to command), 1862; comdr. 5th Army Corps, 1865, directed by Grant to receive arms and colors of Army of North Va. after surrender at Appomattox Court House; commd. maj. gen., 1865, col., 1866, in charge Mil. Dist. of Tex., stationed at Galveston 1866-67. Died of yellow fever (after refusing to leave his duty station when epidemic broke out), Sept. 15, 1867.

GRIFFIN, EUGENE soldier, elec. engr.; b. Ellworth, Me., Oct. 13, 1855; s. George K. and Harriet J. G.; grad. West Point, 1875; m. Allie Hancock, April 24, 1880. Served 2d lt., 1st lt. and capt. corps of engrs., 1875-89; resigned Oct. 5, 18889; col. 1st U.S. col. engrs., May 24, 1898; brig. gen. vols., Jan 21, 1899. In regular army, served on various surveys until 1883; was asst. prof. civil and mil. engring. and the art of war, West Point, 1883-85, a.-d.-c. staff of Maj. Gen Winfield Scott Hancock, 1885-86; chief engr. div. Atlantic and dept. of the East, 1885-86; asst. engr., commr. Dist. of Columbia, 1886-88; in volunteer service, organized 1st regt. U.S. vols., engrs., serving with it in Puerto Rico, 1898-99. Gen mgr. ry. dept. and 2d v.p. Thomson-Houston Elec. Col, 1888-91; 1st v.p. Gen. Elec. Co., 1892—; pres. Thomson-Houston Internat. Elec. Co., 1893—; dir. British-Thomson-Houston Co. and of the Cie. Francais pour l'Exploitation des Procédés Thomson-Houston, Paris, 1893—. Home: New York, N.Y. Died 1907.

GRIFFIN, JAMES M. engr.; b. Ft. Edward, N.Y., Sept. 3, 1889; s. James J. and Sarah (Stevens) G.: B.E., Union Coll., 1912; m. Dorothy Van Valkenburgh, May 25, 1918; 1 dau., Janet (Mrs. Robert J. O'Connell). Surveyor and field engr., barge canal dept. State of N.Y., Waterford, 1912-13; with Pub. Service Commn., 1st dist., State N.Y., and successor bodies, Transit Commn. and Bd. Transportation, City of N.Y., 1913—, jr. engr., 1913-17, asst. engr., 1917-39, div. engr., 1939-45, dep. chief engr., 1945, chief engr., 1945—. Served as capt. 5th U.S. Engrs., 1917-18; maj. Engrs. Res. Corps, 1924-40. Mem. Am. Assn. Engrs. (nat. pres., 1931-32), Am. Soc. C.E., Soc. Am. Mil. Engrs.(pres., N.Y. City post). Am. Legion (post comdr.), Phi Gamma Delta. Clubs: The Engineers, N.Y. Railroad. Home: Hillcrest Av., Darien, Conn. Office: 370 Jay St., Bklyn. 1. Died Sept. 17, 1955.

GRIFFIN, LEVI THOMAS lawyer, congressman; b. Clinton, N.Y., May 23, 1837; s. Charles Nathaniel and Margary (Thomas) G.; removed with parents to Rochester, Mich., 1848; ed. Rochester Acad. and grad. Univ. of Mich., 1857. Admitted to Mich. bar, 1858; practiced at Detroit until commd. 2d lt. Mich. cav., Dec. 18, 1862; promoted lt. adj. capt., and bvtd. maj. Mar. 13, 1865; returned to Detroit after war and practiced law; Fletcher prof. law, Univ. of Mich., 1886-97; candidate for justice Supreme Court, 1887, defeated; mem. Congress to fill vacancy, Aug. 17, 1893, to Mar. 4, 1895; defeated for reelection. Democrat. Home: Detroit, Mich. Deceased.

GRIFFIN, MARTIN EUGENE army officer; b. Iowa, Dec. 18, 1900; M.D., State U. Ia., 1925; 1 son Martin Eugene (U.S. Army Medical Corps); graduate Army Med. Sch., 1927, Army Indsl. Coll., 1938. Commd. 2d lt. M.C., Organized Res. Corps., June 1925, 1st lt. M.C., U.S. Army, 1926, advanced through grades to maj. gen., 1953; now comdg. gen. Fitzsimmons Army Hosp., Denver. Decorated Distinguished Service Medal, 1953. Address: 2311 Briarwood St., San Antonio 78209. Died May 18, 1964; buried Nat. Cemetery, Ft. Sam Houston, Tex.

GRIFFIN, ROBERT STANISLAUS naval officer; b. Fredericksburg, Va., Sept. 27, 1857; grad. U.S. Naval Acad., 1878; Sc.D., Columbia, 1915; D. Engring., Stevens Inst. Tech. Promoted asst. engr., June 20, 1880; passed asst. engr., Aug. 25, 1889; chief engr., 1899; promoted through grades to rear adml., Aug. 19, 1916. Served on Mayflower, Spanish-Am. War, 1898, on Illinois, 1901-02, Chicago, 1902-03, Iowa, 1903-04; fleet engr. N. Atlantic Fleet, 1904-05; duty Bur. Steam Engring., Navy Dept., 1905-08; asst. to chief same,

1908-13; apptd. engr. in chief and chief Bur. Steam Engring., May 18, 1913, reappointed 1917; retired, Sept. 27, 1921. D.S.M. (U.S.); Comdr. Legion of Honor (France). Home: Washington, D.C. Died Feb. 21, 1933.

GRIFFIN, SAMUEL congressman; b. Richmond County, Va.; studied law. Admitted to bar, practiced law; served as col. in Revolutionary War, wounded at Harlem Heights, 1776; mem. state bd. of war; mem. Va. Ho. of Dels., 1786-88; mem. U.S. Ho. of Reps. from Va., 1st-3d congresses, 1789-95. Died Nov. 3, 1810.

GRIFFIN, SIMON GODDELL capitalist, soldier; b. Nelson, N.H., Aug. 9, 1824; s. Nathan and Sally (Wright) G.; reared on farm; became teacher; later mem. legislature; admitted to N.H. bar, 1860. Served in Union army from 1st battle of Bull Run to Appomattox, beginning as pvt. and becoming Apr. 2, 1865, bvt. maj. gen. of vols.; mustered out, Aug. 24, 1865; participated in many heavy battles. After war settled in Keene; served 5 terms in N.H. legislature, 2 terms speaker; for 2 yrs. was comdr. Mass. Commandery Mil. Order Loyal Legion; has large interests in Texas lands and cattle. Home: Keene, N.H. Died 1902.

GRIFFITH, FREDERIC RICHARDSON, surgeon; b. Phila., Sept. 17, 1873; s. David R. and Sarah Jane (Richardson) G.; ed. Friends, schs., Phila., and Camden, N.J., grad., 1892, Pa. Nautical Sch., Phila., 1892; M.D., U. of Pa., 1897; m. Lucile Andrews Menken, of New York, Dec. 12, 1900. Surgeon since 1897; surgeon Bellevue Dispensary, 1899-1904; pub. lecturer, on practical surgery, under direction New York City Bd. Edn., 1904-5; examiner First Aid to the Injured Soc., New York, since 1904; lecturer and examiner on first aid to New York City police and fire depts. since 1905. Acting asst. surgeon, 3d Regt. Inf. N.G., Pa., 1897-8. Fellow N.Y. Acad. Medicine; mem. N.Y. Hist. Soc. Sculptor since 1905; studied France, Italy; served in studio C. Daal Magelssen; executed 4 groups. Mem. Friends Meeting. Inventor; chloroform inhaler; eyed grooved dir.; modern enclosed ambulance; instruments to increase safety of anaesthetics, to increase scope of cocaine surgery, and to diagnosticate hydrocele; combination gas and liquid anaesthetizing inhaler; new surg. mallet, chisel, operating table bed, med. chart, and various other devices. Del. 13th Internat. Peace Congress, Lucerne, 1905. Author: Wounds (pamphlet), 1902; Handbook of Surgery, 1904; revised edit. Stoney's Bacteriology and Surgical Technic for Nurses, 1905. Contbr. in surgery to Internat. Clinics, and more than 150 articles in professional and scientific jours. Address: 49 E. 64th St., New York NY!5

GRIFFITH, HARRY ELMER educator; b. Galesburg, Ill., Mar. 5, 1908; s. Edward Nathan and Myrtle (File) G.; Ed. B., U. Cal. at Los Angeles, 1931, M.A. at Berkeley, 1937; Ed.D., Stanford, 1950; grad. student Claremont Coll., U. So. Cal., Washington and Lee U., U. Va., Indsl. Coll. Armed Forces; m. Alice Hay, Jan. 3, 1930; children - Alice Dolores (Mrs. Keith C. Thornton), Sheila Frances; m. 2d, Beverly M. Cresto, Aug. 4, 1947. Tchr., Riverside (Cal) city schs., 1931-39; asso. prof. Humboldt State Coll., 1939-41, prof., 1941 - , dir. athletics, chmn. div. health and phys. edn., 1940-42, prin. Campus Lab. Sch., 1946-52, dean students, 1947-48, coordinator elementary tchr. edn., 1952-53, chmn. div. edn. and psychology, 1953-57; vis. prof. Summer Sch. Edn., Victoria, B.C., 1954, 55, U. B.C., 1958. Fulbright vis. prof. Union Burma, 1950-51; del. U.S. nat. commn. UNESCO, 1958; tchr. edn. adviser Hashemite Kingdom of Jordan, 1959-61. Chmn. finance com. Humboldt council Camp Fire Girls, 1957-58; mem. Cal. Def. Com., 1940-42. Served to lt. col. USAAF, 1942-46; liaison officer Air Force Acad., 1957-59. Mem. Cal. Tchrs. Assn., N.E.A., Cal. Council Tchr. Edn., Assn. Cal. State Coll. Instrs., Assn. Student Teaching, Res. Officers Assn., Cal. Edn. Adminstrs., P.T.A., Vets Eng Wars, Air Force Assn., Theta Xi, Phi Delta Kappa. Presbyn. Author: Japanese Normal School Education, 1950. Address: P.O. Box 427, Arcata, Cal. Died Jan. 7, 1966.

GRIFFITH, JEFFERSON DAVIS surgeon; b. Jackson, Miss., Feb. 12, 1850; s. Richard and Sallie (Whitfield) G.; ed. Summerville (Miss.) Inst.; M.D., Univ. Med. Coll. (New York U.), 1871; m. Sallie Coningo, Jan. 28, 1880. House surgeon, Bellevue Hosp., New York, 1873; prof. surgery, 1890-1905, dean, 1893-98, Kansas City Med. Coll.; prof. clin. surgery, U. of Kan., 1905—; prof. oral surgery, Kansas City Dental Coll., 1886—; prof. surgery, Kansas City Women's Med. Coll., 1890—; Surgeon-gen. of Mo., 1886-90; maj. surgeon vols., May 20, 1989; chief surgeon, 3d Div., 1st Army Corps; hom. disch., Dec. 2, 1898; retired chief surgeon N.G. Mo., with rank of colonel. Gold Democrat. Episcopalian. Home: Kansas City, Mo. Died Aug. 29, 1924.

GRIFFITH, JOHN L. athletics; b. Mt. Carroll, Ill.; s. Hugh Jordan and Lucy Luella (Cummings) G.; grad. Warren (Ill.) Acad., 1898; B.A., Beloit (Wis.) Coll., 1902; m. Alice Keiley, Aug. 17, 1904; 1 son, John L., Jr. Director of athletics Yankton (S.D.) Coll., 1902-05, Morningside Coll., Sioux City, Ia., 1905-08. Drake U., Des Moines, Ia., 1908-18; commr. of athletics, Intercollegiate Conf. "Big Ten") since 1922; editor and pub. Athletic Journal, tech, mag. for coaches and athletic dirs. Athletic dir. U.S. Army, and Camp Dodge, Ia., Aug. 1917-Aug. 1918; commd. capt. and had charge of organized recreation at the camp, of 30,000 men; sent to Camp Gordon, Aug. 1918, to assist in est. a sch. of physical training and bayonets, and in Sept. 1918, to Camp Pike to take charge of physical and bayonet sch. there; aptd. exec. officer, Washington, D.C., Jan. 1919, of Athletic Div. of Commn. on Training Camp Activities; promoted maj. June 1919. Mem. Nat. Collegiate Athletic Assn. (pres.), Am. Olympic Com., Paul Reveres (gov.). Baptist. Clubs: Rotary (pres. 1934-35), Executives (dri.). Home: 717 Walden Rd., Winnetka, Ill. Office: Hotel Sherman, N. Clark and W. Randolph Sts., Chicago, Ill.* Died Dec. 7, 1944.

GRIFFITH, SAMUEL HENDERSON, surgeon U. S. N.; apptd. from Pa. asst. surgeon, Dec. 15, 1877; passed asst. surgeon, Dec. 15, 1880; surgeon, March 30, 1895; served at Museum of Hygiene, Washington, 1893-8; was assigned to U. S. S. Mayflower, March, 1898, serving in war against Spain. Rank of lt.-comdr. U. S. N. Mem. Am. Chem. Soc.; m. Ellen Coxe. Address: 1308 N. H. Av., Washington

GRIFFITH, WENDELL HORACE, scientist; b. Churdan, Ia., Nov. 7, 1895; s. George William and May Elizabeth (Fowler) G.; B.S., Greenville (Ill.) Coll., 1917; M.S., U. of Ill., 1919, Ph.D., 1923; m. Harriet Isabel Leas, Aug. 31, 1922; 1 son, Wendell Horace. Instr., Cooper Coll., Sterling, Kan., 1919-20, U. of Mich., 1922-23; dept. of biol. chemistry, St. Louis U., 1923-48, prof., 1940-48; chmn., prof. dept. biochem. and nutrition, U. Tex. Med. Sch., 1948-51; chmn., prof. dept. physiol. chemistry U. Cal., 1951-63, prof. emeritus, 1963-68; Gen. Edn. Bd. fellow, Oxford Eng., 1936-37; mil. leave absence, 1941-45; leave absence as FAO nutrition advisor in India, 1959-60, as dir. Life Scis. Research Office, Fedn. Am. Socs. for Experimental Biology, 1962-68; consultant Office Surgeon Gen., Army, 1946-68; cons. Office Surgeon Gen., USPHS, 1949-53, 55-68. Mem. Food and Nutrition board, NRC, 1950-61. Served with U.S.A., 1918-19; col. Sanitary Corps. U.S.A., 1941-46; nutrition officer, chief nutrition br., European Theater Operations, 1942-45. Decorated Legion of Merit, Bronze Star (World War II); recipient Outstanding Civilian Service award Dept. Army, 1966. Fellow Am. Public Health Assn., A.A.A.S., N.Y. Acad. Sci.; mem. Am. Soc. Biol. Chemists, Am. Inst. Nutrition (pres. 1950-51), Am. Chemical Soc., Soc. for Exptl. Biol. and Medicine. A.M.A. (council on Foods and Nutrition, 1953-59), Inst. Food Technologists, Sigma Xi, Alpha Omega Alpha, Phi Lambda Upsilon. Club: Cosmos, Asst. editor: Nutrition Reviews, 1946-50, editorial com., 1952-68. Editorial bd., Jour. Biol. Chemistry, 1949-59. Home: Bethesda MD Died Feb. 5, 1968; buried Oak Hill Cemetery, Kirkwood MO

GRIFFITHS, JOHN WILLIS naval architect; b. N.Y.C., Oct. 6, 1809; s. John Griffiths. Wrote series of articles on naval architecture in Portsmouth Advocate, 1836; delivered 1st formal lecture on naval architecture, N.Y.C.; editor American Ship, 1878-82; one of 1st to specialize in designing; designed Rainbow (1st "extreme clipper ship"); designed Sea Witch; developed improved form of rivet; invented machine for bending timber into crooked forms used in shipbldg.; designed New Era (1st ship with mechanically bent timber), 1870. Author: Treatise on Marine and Naval Architecture, 1850; Ship Builder's Manual, 1853; Progressive Ship-Builder, 1875. Died Bklyn., Mar. 30, 1882.

GRIGGS, CHAUNCEY WRIGHT lumberman; b. Toland, Conn., Dec. 31, 1832; ed. Monson Acad.; m. Martha Ann Gallup, Apr. 14, 1859. Took charge of a general store, St. Paul, Minn., 1856: served in Civil War, reaching rank of col.; afterward in banking and contracting in Minn. Alderman, St. Paul, 7 terms; mem. Minn. Ho. of Rep., 2 terms, Senate, 3 terms; removed to Tacoma, 1887; pres. The St. Paul & Tacoma Lumber Co., owning large mills and 80,000 acres of fir timber. Democratic caucus candidate for U.S. senator from Wash., 1889 and 1891. Home: Tacoma, Wash. Died 1910.

GRIGGS, EVERETT GALLUP lumberman; b. Chaska, Minn., Dec. 27, 1868; s. Col. Chauncey W. and Martha A. (Gallup) G.; B.A., Yale, 1890; m. Grace Isabel Wallace, July 6, 1895. With St. Paul & Tacoma Lumber Co., 1892-, pres., 1908-33, chairman of the board, 1933-. Pres. of the National Lumber Mfrs. Assn., 1911-13. Joined Wash. State N.G., 1890: capt., 1892: maj. coast arty. N.G. Wash., 1909-11; maj. U.S. Signal Corps, transferred to A.S.A.P., 1918-19. Home: Tacoma, Wash. Died Mar. 6, 1938.

GRIMES, DONALD ROBERT, retail food store exec.; b. Chgo., Aug. 12, 1906; s. J. Frank and Barbara (Adam) G.; A.B., U. Ill., 1928; m. Edythe Homan, Nov. 2, 1929; children—Elaine, Diane. Clk. Atlantic & Pacific Tea Co. store, 1928; warehouseman, Sprague Warner & Co., 1928; store engr. Ind. Grocers Alliance, 1929-33, supervision dept. rep., 1933-38, director supervision, 1938-40, assistant to president, 1940-52, pres., from 1952; pres., dir. Ind. Grocers' Alliance Distbg. Co. Trustee U. Ill. Served as capt. signal corps, AUS, 1943-46. Christian Scientist. Home: Evanston IL Died Mar. 26, 1972; cremated.

GRIMES, GEORGE SIMON brig. gen., U.S.A.; b. in Eng., Feb. 15, 1846. Pvt. Co. G, 116th N.Y. Inf. and sergt. maj. 89th and 93d U.S. Colored Inf., Aug. 16, 1862-Mar. 29, 1865: 2d lt. 81st U.S.C.T., Mar. 30, 1865; 1st lt., Jan. 6, 1866; hon. mustered out of vol. service, Nov. 30, 1865: apptd. from N.Y., 2d lt. 39th Inf., Jan. 22, 1867; 1st lt., July 20, 1868; transferred to 25th Inf., Apr. 20, 1869; assigned to 2d Arty., Dec. 15, 1870; grad. Arty. Sch., 1886; capt., Nov. 20, 1887; maj., Mar. 31, 1899; lt. col. Arty. Corps, Aug. 22, 1901; col., July 19, 1903; brig. gen. and retired at own request, over 40, yrs.' service, Aug. 12, 1907. Died Aug. 9, 1920.

GRIMES, WILLIAM MIDDLETON army officer: b. Ft. Barrancas, Fla., Mar. 4, 1889; s. George S. and Margaret (McArthur) G.; student Manlius (N.Y.) Sch., 1908-11, Phillips Exeter Acad., N.Y., 1906-08; grad. Cavalry Sch., 1922. Command and Gen. Staff Sch., 1925, Army War Coll., 1933: m. Mabel Lowe, Dec. 17, 1913; children-Peggy Lowe (wife of Capt. Sherbourne Whipple, Jr.), William Middleton. Commd. 2d lt., U.S. Army, Sept. 29, 1911; promoted through grades to brig. gen., 1941, maj. gen., May 1942: has been instr. The Cavalry Sch., Inf.Sch., Command and Gen. Staff Sch.; mem. War Dept. Gen. Staff, 1938-40. Awarded Silver Star citation. Episcopalian. Clubs: Army and Navy. Army-Navy Country (Washington); Potomac Hunt (Potomac, Md.). Address: Ft. Riley, Kan. Died Apr. 2, 1951.

GRIMKE, JOHN FAUCHERAUD army officer, jurist, b. Charleston, S.C., Dec. 16, 1752; s. John Paul and Mary (Faucheraud) G.; A.B., Trinity Coll., 1774; m. Mary Smith, Oct. 12, 1784, 14 children including Thomas Smith, Sarah Moore, Angelina Emily. Commd. capt. S.C. Arty., Continental Army, 1776, promoted lt. col.; dep. adj; gen. for S.C. and Ga., 1776-80. imprisoned at surrender of Charleston (S.C.), 1780, parolled, 781; mem. S.C. Ho. of Reps., 1781-86; sr. asso. of S.C. Superior Court 1799-1819; mem. S.C. Conv. which ratified U.S. Constn., 1788; presdl. elector, 1789. Died Long Branch, N.J. Aug. 9, 1819.

GRINDLEY, CHARLES VERNON naval officer; b. Logansport, Ind., Nov. 24, 1844; s. Franklin and Ann (Sholes) G.; grad. U.S. Naval Acad., 1863; m. Harriet Frances Vincent, May 1, 1872, 3 children including Ruth. Took part in Battle of Mobile Bay, 1864; commd. lt., assigned to South Pacific Squadron 1867; assigned to ship Michigan on Gt. Lakes, 1870-73, to South Atlantic stas., 1873-74; instr. U.S. Naval Acad., 1875-79; promoted comdr., 1882; navigation officer Boston Navy Yard, 1882-84; commanded vessels Jamestown and Portsmouth, 1884-86, cruiser Marion, 1892-94; commd. capt., 1897, commanded receiving ship Richmond; commanded Olympia, flagship of Commodore (later Adm.) Dewey in Asiatic Squadron, 1897, received Dewey's order "You may fire when ready, Gridley," in Battle of Manila Bay, 1898; a destroyer named in his honor, 1918. Died Kobe, Japan, June 5, 1898; buried Lakeside Cemetery, Erie, Pa.

GRINNELL, WILLIAM MORTON lawyer; b. New York, Feb. 28, 1857; s. William F. and Mary (Morton) G.; ed. Anthon's and Mohegan Lake schs., Harvard Univ., Stuttgart (Germany), Univ. of France, grad. Bachelier-és-lettres and Bachelier-en-droit; grad. Columbia Coll. Law Sch., LL.B., 1881; m. Elizabeth Lee Ernst, Dec. 8, 1898. Practiced law in Paris, France, as counsel to U.S. Legation, 1881-86; in New York, 1886-92: 3d asst. sec. of state of U.S., 1892-93; partner in banking house of Morton, Bliss & Co., 1893-1900, when firm became a trust co. under name of Morton Trust Co., resumed practice of law, acting as atty. for the co., the Mt. Morris Bank, etc., and still engaged in practice of law. Maj. U.S.V., in Spanish-Am. War, on staff Gen. Poland, 1st div., 2d army corps, Chevalier de la Légion d'Honneur, France, 1890. Dir. Illinois Central R.R. Co., Rio Grande & Sierra Madre R.R. Co., Loup Creek Coal Co., Mt. Morris Bank. Episcopalian. Republican. Home: New York, N.Y. Died 1906.

GRISCOM, LLOYD CARPENTER, b. Riverton, N.J., Nov. 4, 1872; s. Clement Acton and Frances Canby (Biddle) G.; Ph.B., U. of Pa., 1891, LL.D., 1906; studied U. of Pa. Law Sch., 1891-93, New York Law Sch., 1895; sec. to Mr. Bayard, 1st ambassador to England, 1893-94; admitted to N.Y. bar, 1896; m. Elisabeth Duer, d. Frederic Bronson, of New York (dec.); children—Bronson Winthrop, Lloyd Preston; m. 2d, Audrey Margaret Elisabeth, d. Marlborough Crosse, of South Sea, Eng. Deputy dist. atty. New York, 1897; volunteer in Spanish-Am. War; commd. capt. and asst. q.-m; served 4 months in Cuba as a.-d.-c. to Maj.-Gen. James F. Wade; recommended for promotion, but resigned to reenter diplomacy apptd. sec. legation, Constantinople, July 1899; charge d'affaires, Constantinople, 1899-1901; E.E. and M.P. to Persia, 1901-02, to Japan, 1902-06 (during Russo-Japanese War); A.E. and P. to Brazil, Jan. 29, 1906-Mar. 3, 1907, to Italy, Mar. 6, 1907-June 14, 1909. Pres. N.Y. County Rep. Com., 1910-11 and former mem. Rep. State Com., N.Y.; del. Rep. Nat. Conv., Chicago, 1912. Hon. v.p., Community Service Soc. of New York; hon. pres. Am. Asiatic Assn. Mem. Italy America Soc., Am. Soc. of Royal Italian Orders, New York Water Color Club. Clubs: Knickerbocker, Century, Republican, Piping Rock. Contbr. to Phila. Sunday Press on travels in Central America. Apptd. maj., adj. gen.'s dept., 1917; ordered on active duty,

June 26, as a.-a.-g., Eastern Dept.; made a.-a.-g. 77th Div., Nat. Army, at Camp Upton, N.Y., Aug. 1, 1917; with 77th Div. in France; later liaison officer staff of Gen. Pershing; promoted lt. col. Awarded D.S.M.; Knight Comdr. St. Michael and St. George (Brit.), 1919. Author: Tenth Avenue (stage melodrama and moving picture); Diplomatically Speaking (autobiography). Home: Luna Plantation, Tallahassee, Fla.; also Syosset, LI NY

GRISSOM, VIRGIL IVAN astronaut; b. Mitchell, Ind., Apr. 3, 1926; s. Dennis D. and Cecil (King) G.; B.S. in Mech. Engring., Purdue U., 1950; student aero. engring., Air ForceIn Inst. Tech., 1955, Test Pilot Sch., Edwards AFB, 1956; m. Betty L. Moore, July 6, 1945; children - Scott, Mark, Aviation cadet USAAF, 1944-45; commd. 2d lt. USAF, 1951, advanced through grades to lt. col.; fighter pilot 75th Fighter-Interceptor Squadron, Presque Isle, Me., 1951; combat pilot 334th Fighter-Interceptor Squadron, Korea, 1951-52; test pilot Fighter Br., Wright-Patterson AFB, 1957-59; astronaut Project Mercury, 1959 - ; made 2d Project Mercury Flight, July 1961, Gemini two-man 3 orbital flight, Mar. 1965. Decorated D.F.C., Air Medal with cluster. Home: 211 Pine Shadows, Seabrook, Tex. Office: Project Mercury Nat. Aeronautics and Space Administration, Washington. Died Jan. 27, 1967.

GRISWOLD, AUGUSTUS H. telegraph official: b. Milo, Ill., Sept. 29, 1879; s. Augustus Root and Mary (Swarthout) G.; B.S. in E.E., U. of Ill., 1901; m. Edna E. Holmes, Sept. 30, 1907; children-Janet Carter, Augustus Root. Engr. with Western Electric Co., Chicago, 1901-05; plant engr. Pacific Telephone & Telegraph Co., 1905-17; asst. chief engr. Internat. Western Electric Co., New York, 1920; asst. v.p. Am. Telephone & Telegraph Co., 1925-28; exec. v.p. Postal Telegraph and Cable Corp. and v.p. Internat. Telephone and Telegraph Corp., 1928-35; exec. v.p. Postal Telegraph and Cable Corp., 1935-38; v.p. Internat. Telephone and Telegraph Corp., 1938-. Commd. maj. Signal O.R.C., June 1917, and apptd. comdr. 411th Telegraph Battery, U.S. Army; went overseas, January 1918; apptd. dir. telephone and telegraph services, A.E.F., May 1918, in charge constrn., installation operation and maintenance of all signal corps lines of A.E.F. in Europe; lt. col., Sept. 1918; apptd. mem. Signal Corps Bd. of Adjustments, Nov. 1918, having disposition of all signal corps property in Europe: returned to U.S., Feb. 1919; hon. discharged, Mar. 4, 1919; returned to France as chmn. Am. Engring. Commn., to assist French in restoring communication in devastated areas. Cited by Gen. Pershing "for exceptionally meritorious service"; decorated Legion of Honor (French). Republican. Protestant. Home: New York, N.Y. Died Feb. 24, 1940.

GRISWOLD, DWIGHT PALMER U.S. Senator; b. Harrison, Neb., Nov. 27, 1893; s. Dwight H. and Clarissa (Palmer) G.; student Neb. Wesleyan U., 1910-12; A.B., University of Nebraska, 1914; m. Erma Elliott, Sept. 25, 1919; children-Dorothy Helen (Mrs. John H. Gayer), Dwight (dec.). Connected with First Nat. Bank, Gordon, Neb., 1914-22, successively as bank clk. asst. cashier, cashier. dir. since 1919; editor and pub. Gordon Jour., 1922-40; pres. Gering (Neb.) Natl. Bank since 1951. With mil. govt. in Germany, Jan.-June 1947; named chief Am. Mission for Aid to Greece, June 1947, resigned Sept. 1948. Mem. Neb. Ho. of Reps., 1921, Neb. St. senate, 1925, 17, 29; elected gov. of Neb. 1940, 42, 1944; elected United States senator from Neb., 1952. Served as sergt., 4th Neb. Infantry on Mexican Border Service, 1916; 1st lieut. and capt., 127th F.A., 1917-18. Mem. Neb. Press Assn. (state pres. 1931), Am. Legion (state comdr. 1930), Alpha Tau Omega. Republican. Presbyterian. Mason (Shriner). Home: Scottsbluff, Neb. Died Apr. 12, 1954: buried Scottsbluff, Neb.

GRISWOLD, OSCAR WOOLVERTON army officer: b. Ruby Valley, Nev., Oct. 22, 1886; s. Willard Smith and Margaret (Woolverton) G.; student U. of Nev., 1905-06; B.S., U.S. Military Acad., 1910; grad. Command and General Staff School, 1925, Army War College, 1929; LL.D., University of Nevada, 1946; married Elizabeth Katherine Matile, July 1, 1911; children-Mattie (wife of Lt. Col. William Lyons Porte, U.S. Army), Katherine (dec.), George Matile. Commd. 2nd lt., Inf., U.S. Army, 1910, advanced through grades to lt. gen., 1945; fgn. service in China, 1914-17; served as maj. and lt. col., A.E.F., 1918-19; on War Dept. Gen. Staff, 1929-31; in Air Corps, July to Sept., 1931; comd. XIV Corps, during recapture of Luzon, P.I., 1945, in operations from Guadalcanal to Luzon. Legion of Merit, Distinguished Service Medal with Oak Leaf Cluster, Army. Navy Distinguished Service Medals, Silver Star with Oak Leaf Cluster, Bronze Star Medal, Air Medal, Purple Heart. Episcopalian. Mason (32ff), Shriner, Retired. Home: The Broadmoor, Colorado Springs, Colo.

GRISWOLD, RETTIG ARNOLD, surgeon; b. Peru, Ind., Apr. 17, 1898; s. Edward Harvey and Georgine (Rettig) G.; A.B., Harvard Coll., 1921; M.D., U. Louisville, 1925; m. Bonita Bligh, Aug. 8, 1923; children—Rettig Arnold, Bonita, Georgine, Annalee. Grad. tng. in pathology Louisville City Hosp. and U. Louisville, 1925-27; grad. tng. in surgery Western Res. U. and Lakeside Hosp., Cleve., 1927-32; asso. prof. surgery U. Louisville Med. Sch., 1932-37, prof. and head dept. surgery, 1938-52, prof. surgery, 1952-72. Cons. surgeon St. Joseph Infirmary, Ky. Bapt., Meth. and Evang., St. Anthony hosps., Kosair Crippled Children Hosp., John W. Norton Meml. Infirmary. Served as lt. j.g., Flying Corps USN, 1917-21; naval aviator, overseas service, 10 mos.; served to col., M.C., AUS, 1942-44; cons. in surgery 4th Service Command; chief Surg. Service Walter Reed Gen. Hosp., Washington, 1943. Decorated Legion of Merit (U.S.); Mil. Order of Ayacucha (Peru); recipient Citation Navy Dept.; Surgeon's award for distinguished service to safety Nat. Safety Council, 1963. Fellow A.C.S. (2d v.p. 1957-58), Am., Central surg. assns., mem. Societe Internationale de Chirurgie, Am. Assn. for Surgery of Trauma (founder; pres. 1951-52), Am. Bd. Surgery (founders' group), Soc. Surgery Alimentary Tract (a founder), Southeastern Surg. Congress (1st v.p. 1963-64), Western, So. surg. assns., A.M.A., So. Med. Assn. Alpha Kappa Kappa, Alpha Omega Alpha. Republican. Episcopalian. Club: Pendennis. Home: Louisville KY Died May 1, 1972; buried Cave Hill Cemetery, Louisville KY

GROAT, WILLIAM AVERY physician; b. Canastota, N.Y., Nov. 9, 1876; s. Willaim Robert and Elizabeth Morgan (Avery) G.; B.S., Syracuse U., 1897, M.D., 1900; m. Sellie Nichols Bacon, Oct. 2, 1901; children-William Avery, Robert Andrews, Elsie (Wade). In practice Syracuse, N.Y., since 1901; mem. faculty, Coll. of Medicine, Syracuse U., since 1902, prof. clin. pathology since 1911; sr. attending physician and dir. Hazard Lab., Memorial Hosp.; sr. attending physician diseases of metabolism and dir. Jacobson Memorial Lab., St. Joseph Hosp.; consultant University, City and Psychopathic hosps. and Syracuse Free Dispensary. Chmn. advisory com. on pub. health, City of Syracuse. Served as capt., later maj., M.C., U.S. Army, World War; lt. col. Med. O.R.C. Mem. Am. Pharmacopoeia Convs., 1910, 20, 30, 40 (com. on constl. revision, 1940). Trustee Syracuse Univ. Fellow American College Physicians, A.A.A.S. Diplomate and member exec. committee American Board Internal Medicine, A.M.A. (delegate), N.Y. State Medical Society (chmn. bd. trustees, ex-president and member house of delegates; ex-chairman committee on scientific work; ex-president 5th district branch), American Assn. Immunologists, Am. Assn. Clin. Pathologists, Am. Assn. for Study of Coitre, Am. Assn. for Diseases of Internal Secretions, Delta Kappa Epsilon, Nu Sigma Nu, Sigma Xi, Alpha Omega Alpha, Phi Kappa Phi, Phi Kappa Alpha. Republican. Episcopalian. Clubs: Faculty, Onondaga Golf and Country, Thousand Island Park Golf; Holland Society of N.Y. (ex-v.p.). Contbr. articles and reports of reserches, particularly diseases of the blood and metabolism, to med. publs. Cons. editor N.Y. State Med. Jour. Home: 1352 Teall Av., Syracuse; (summer) Cedar Island, Fishers Landing, N.Y. Died Sept. 9, 1945.

GROESBECK, STEPHEN WALLEY army officer; b. Albany, N.Y., Nov. 26, 1840; s. Garrett E. and Elsie (Walley) G.; ed. commercial Sch., Albany, N.Y., and Mil. Sch., Phila.; m. Alice W. Thomas, Apr. 12, 1887. Enlisted 4th Ia. cav. vols., Oct. 28, 1861: mustered in as q.m. sergt., Jan. 1, 1862; apptd. 2d lt., Oct. 5, 1862; totally disabled by lodging of rifle ball in left foot, in battle Nov. 8, 1862; resigned Apr. 4, 1863; upon recovery accepted apptmt. as 2d lt., Vet. reserve corps, Sept. 16, 1864; served as such in South during reconstruction period; read law and later was admitted to bar. Apptd. 2d lt. 42d Inf., Jan. 15, 1867; transferred to 6th Inf., Apr. 22, 1869; adj. 6th Inf., 1875-80; acting judge advocate, Dept. of Mo., 1881-82; again adj. 6th Inf., 1883-86; acting judge advocate, Dept., Dakota, 1886-91; apptd. maj. judge advocate, Mar. 23, 1892: lt. col., Feb. 2, 1901; col., May 24, 1901; judge advocate 5th Army Corps during campaign against Santiago de Cuba, 1898, and of Div. of the Philippines, 1900-02. Apptd. brig. gen., U.S.A., Apr. 16, 1903; retired from active service, Apr. 17, 1903. Died 1904.

GROFF, GEORGE G. physician: b. Chester Valley, Pa., Apr. 5, 1851; s. John and Susan (Beaver) G.; M.D., L.I. Coll. Hosp., 1877: B.S., Pa. State Coll., 1897: (hon. LL.D., Judson Coll., N.C., 1887; Ph.D., Franklin and Marshall, 1898; Sc.D., Susquehanna U., 1902); m. Margaret Pusey marshall, Apr. 14, 1880. Taught in pub. schs. 3 yrs., State Normal Sch. 2 yrs.; sch. dir. 8 yrs.; prof. anatomy, Bucknell U., 1879-. Mem. State Bd. Health, 1885-99, State Bd. Agr. 10 yrs., State Med. Council, 1 yr.; surgeon N.G. Pa. 3 yrs.; organized sanitary work at Johnstown after the flood of 1889. Maj. and brigade surgeon Spanish-Am. War, 1898-99. After war in P.R. as commr. Nat. Relief Commn.; dir. of vaccination (790,000 persons were vaccinated in 3 months): sec. and treas. Superior Bd. of Health. Insane Asylum, Leper Hosp.; pres. Insular Bd. Edn.; supt. pub. instrn.; acting commr. of edn.; mem. Exec. Council, P.R. Republican. Home: Lewisburg, Pa. Died 1910.

GROSE, WILLIAM state legislator, army officer; b. Montgomery County, O., Dec. 16, 1812; s. William and Mary (Hubbel), G.; m. Rebecca Needham, Dec. 1836; m. 2d, Mrs. Martha Black, 1884. Admitted to Ind. bar, 1843, began practice of law, Newcastle, Ind., 1846; Democratic presdl. elector, 1852; mem. Ind. Legislature (Republican), 1857-59; commanded 36th Ind. Volunteer Inf. in Gen. Don Carlos Buell's army, 1861, took part in battles of Shiloh, Corinth, Chickamauga, Chattanooga, Missionary Ridge; commd. brig. gen. U.S. Volunteers, 1864, later transferred to Gen. George Henry Thomas' party; pres. of court-martial in Nashville, Tenn., June-Dec. 1865; commd. maj. gen. U.S. Volunteers, 1865; collector internal revenue 5th Dist. (apptd. by Andrew Johnson), 1866-74; mem. commn. that supervised building of 3 state hosps. for insane, 1884-86; mem. Ind. Senate, 1888. Author: The Story of the Marches, Battles, and Incidents of the 36th Regiment, Indiana Volunteer Infantry, 1891. Died Newcastle, July 30, 1900.

GROSS, MERVIN E. army officer; b. Bowyer, S.C., Feb. 16, 1900; s. Rufus Barnwell and Carrie Sutton (Kane) G.; B.S., U.S. Mil. Acad., 1922; grad. Air Service Bombardment Sch., 1924, Air Corps Engring. Sch., 1933, Tactical Sch., 1938; rated command pilot, combat observer, aircraft observer. Commd. 2d lt., Air Service, U.S. Army, and advanced through the grades to brig. gen., 1943. Instr. mathematics U.S. Mil. Acad., 1928-32; engaged in aeronautical engring. and procurement Army Air Force Material Command, 1933-Dec. 1944; chief of requirements div. Hdqrs. Army Air Forces, determining all type requirements for aircraft, aircraft accessories, organization and organizational equipment for A.A.F., Mar. 1942-Dec. 1944; acting chief of staff U.S. Forces, China Theater, Jan. 1945; comdt. Air Inst. of Technology, Wright Field, Dayton, O., April 1946. Decorated Distinguished Service Medal. Address: 1511-44th St. N.W., Washington 25, D.C. Died Oct. 18, 1946; buried at Holly Hill, S.C.

GROSSMAN, MARC JUSTIN, lawyer; b. Cleve., Sept. 1, 1892; s. Louis J. and Lillie (Meyers) G.; A.B., Harvard, 1913, student Harvard Law Sch., 1914-15; m. Carolyn Kahn, June 5, 1916; children—Marcia (Mrs. Leslie Goodfriend), Carole (Mrs. Robert Honigsfeld). Admitted to Ohio bar, 1916, practiced Cleve.; sr. partner Grossman, Familo, Cavitch, Kempf & Durkin; chmn. Cuyahoga County Relief Adminstrn., 1933-34, Cleve. Met. Housing Authority, 1933-43. Former chmn. Cuyahoga County Civilian Defense Council, Mayor's Vets. Emergency Housing Committee, Red Cross Home Service. Former trustee Citizens League, Family Welfare Association of America; past president Council Ednl. Alliance, Jewish Family Service Assn.; trustee Mt. Sinai Hosp. (Cleve.). Served as lt. col., A.U.S., 1943-45, M.T.O.U.S.A., 18 mos. Recipient European-African-Middle Eastern Medal, 2 bronze stars. Distinguished Service award, Cleve. Community Chest, 1938. Fellow Am. Bar Found., Ohio Bar Association; member Cleveland (pres., 1950-51), Am. (member ho. of dels.), Cuyahoga County bar Associ8tions, Am. Judicature Soc. (past dir.). Club: City Cleveland (past pres.). Home: Shaker Heights OH Deceased.Heights OH Deceased

GROSVENOR, CHARLES HENRY congressman: b. Pomfret Conn., Sept. 20, 1833; s. Maj. Peter and Ann (Chase) G.; went to Ohio, May 1838; attended country log schoolhouse; taught sch.; studied law; admitted to bar, 1857; engaged in practice; m. Samantha Stewart, 1858 (died); m. 2d, Louise H. Currier, 1865. Enlisted as pvt. 18th Ohio Inf., Aug. 1861; maj. Sept. 25, 1861; lt. col., June 9, 1863; col., Apr. 19, 1865; bvtd. col. and brig. gen. vols., Mar. 13, 1865, for gallant and meritorious services during the war; hon. mustered out, Oct. 9, 1865. Mem. Ohio Ho. of Rep., 1874-78 (speaker, 1876-78); presdl. elector, 1872, 1880; trustee Ohio Soldiers' and Sailors' Orphans' Home, Xenia, 1880-88 (pres. 1883-88): mem. 49th to 51st (1885-91) and 53d to 59th (1893-1907) Congresses, 11th Ohio Dist. Home: Athens, O. Died Oct. 30, 1917.

GROSVENOR, WILLIAM MASON journalist, author; s. Rev. Mason and Esther D. (Scarborough) G.; attended Yale, 1851-53; m. Ellen M. Stone, 1867; m. 2d, Ellen Sage, 1870. Editor, New Haven (Conn.) Palladium, 1859-61; enlisted in 13th Regt. Conn. Volunteers, 1861, promoted capt., 1862; commd. col. 2d Regt., La. Native Guards, 1863; editor Jour.-Courier, New Haven, 1864-66; editor St. Louis Democrat, 1866-70, 72-75, helped Carl Schurz in his election to U.S. Senate, 1872, provided evidence leading to conviction of more than 100 leaders St. Louis Whiskey Ring, 1873-74; econ. editor N.Y. Times, 1875-1900; frequently gave aid to U.S. Govt. in connection with tariff acts and other financial measures; controlled Electro Matrix Printing Co. during Panic of 1893. Author: Does Protection Protect, 1871; American Securities, 1885. Died July 20, 1900.

GROUITCH, SLAVKO Y., diplomat; b. Belgrade, Serbia, Feb. 15, 1871; s. Yevrem and Helene (Yovanovitch) G.; father was Serbian minister to Constantinople, London and Paris; grad. Lycee of Versailles, France, 1889; LL.D., U. of Paris, 1897; m. Mabel Gordon Dunlap, of Clarksburg, W.Va., Aug. 12, 1902. Began as attache of Ministry of Foreign Affairs, Belgrade, 1898; sec. of Legation, at Constantinople, Turkey, 1898-1900; charge d'affaires, Athens, 1900-2; chief of polit. sect. of Ministry of Foreign Affairs, Belgrade, 1902-4; charge d'affaires, Petrograd, 1904-7, London, Eng., 1907-14; asst. sec. of State, at Belgrade, 1914-17; minister at Berne, Switzerland, 1917-18. E.E. and M.P. from the Kingdom of the Serbs, Croats and Slovenes to U.S. since Jan. 1919. Capt. of cav. of Reserve, in army of the Serbs, Croats and Slovens.

Decorated Serbian White Eagle; Knight Comdr. British Empire, etc. Mem. Greek Orthodox Ch. Club: Metropolitan (Washington, D.C.). Address: 1339 Connecticut Av., Washington DC

GROUT, WILLIAM WALLACE congressman, lawyer; b. Compton, Quebec, of Am. parents, May 24, 1836; s. Josiah and Sophronia (Ayer) G.; academic edn.; grad. Poughkeepsie Law School, 1857; LL.D., Norwich Univ., 1897; admitted to bar, 1857; engaged in practice; served as lt. col., 15th Vt. vols., in Union army, and brig. gen., Vt. militia, at time of St. Albans raid, 1864; State's atty., 1865-66; mem. Vt. Ho. of Reps., 1868, 1869, 1870 and 1874; was mem. and pres. pro tem. of Vt. senate, 1876; mem. Congress, 1881-83, and 1885-1901, 2d Vt. dist.; chmn. Com. on Dist. of Columbia in 51st Congress, and mem. Com. on Appropriations. Republican. Chmn. Com. on Expenditures of War Dept., 55th Congress. Home: Barton, Vt. Died 1902.

GROVE, LON WOODFIN abdominal surgeon; b. Panola, Ala., Aug. 9, 1890; s. Clarence and Nina Frances (Rogers) G.; M.D., U. Ala.; postgrad. work Harvard Med. Sch.; m. Dorothy Haverty, Jan. 18, 1923; children - Dorothy Haverty (Mrs. Claiborne Van Cortlandt Glover, Jr.), Frances Lonette (Mrs. William Henry Harris). Chief surg. service S.I. (N.Y.) Hosp., 1919; pvt. practice surgery, Atlanta, 1920 - ; hon. staff Egleston Meml. Hosp. for Children; clin. asso. prof. surg. emeritus Emory U. Hosp. With M.C. U.S. Army, 1917-19, chief surg. service Base Hosp., 202, Orleans, France, 1917-19, disch. as maj. Founder mem. Am. Bd. Surgery. Fellow A.C.S.; mem. So., Ga. State med. assns., Soc. Surg. Assn., So. Soc. Clin. Surgeons, Fulton Co. Med. Soc., Atlanta Art Assn., Atlanta symphony Guild, Am. Med. Editors and Authors Assn., Alpha Omega Alpha. Clubs: Piedmont Driving, Capital City, Fifty. Home: Biltmore Apts., 14 Fifth St. N.E., Atlanta 83. Died Oct. 9, 1963.

GROVER, CUVIER army officer; b. Bethel, Me., July 29, 1828; s. John and Fanny (Lary) G.; grad. U.S. Mil. Acad., 1850; m. Susan Flint, Aug. 1, 1865; m. 2d, Ella Miller, Jan. 28, 1875. Engr. on exploring expdn. (removed many objections to feasibility of a No. Pacific railroad), 1854; commd. 1st lt. 10th Inf., U.S. Army, 1855, capt., 1858; served in expdn. against Mormons in Utah, circa 1856, apptd. provost marshall Utah Territory, circa 1857; promoted brig. gen., 1862, in command of 1st Brigade, 2d Div., 3d Corps, Army of Potomac, served in Battle of Williamsburg; brevetted lt. col., then col.; commanded 4th Div., 19th Corps; served in 2d Battle of Bull Run; took possession of Baton Rouge, La.; commanded div. 19th Corps, Dept. of Gulf, 1862-64; served in 1st Battle of Winchester, 1864; brevetted maj. gen., 1864; fought in battles of Fisher's Hill and Cedar Creek; comdr. Dist. of Savannah; 1865; commd. brig. gen., 1865, then maj. gen.; returned to frontier duty; promoted col. 1st Cavalry, U.S. Army, 1875. Died Atlantic City, N.J., June 6, 1885.

GROVER, WAYNE C(LAYTON), U.S. archivist; born Garland, Utah, Sept. 16, 1906; s. George Frederick and Mary (Clayton) G.; A.B., Univ. of Utah, 1930; A.M., Am. Univ., 1937, Ph.D. (in polit. sci. and pub. adminstrn.), 1946; LL.D., Brown U., 1956, Bucknell U., 1960, Belmont Abbey Coll., 1964; m. Esther Thomas, Nov. 8, 1935;children—Ann (Mrs. John N. Richardson), Mary Esther (Mrs. Alan H. Blumenthal), Jane (Mrs. Steve Brown), Eleanor. Archivist, Nat. Archives staff, 1935-41; technical asst. to bd. of analysts, research and analysis br. Office of Strategic Services, 1941-42; chief, records management br., Adj. Gen. Office, U.S. War Dept., 1943-47; apptd. asst. archivist of U.S., July 31, 1947, archivist, June 5, 1948-65. Consultant on Fed. records management problems, Commn. on Orgn. of Exec. Br. of Govt., 1948; cons. L.B. Johnson Library, 1965-70; member U.S. National Commn. for UNESCO, 1961-70; cons. Canadian Royal Commn. on Government Orgn. Served in AUS, advancing from capt. to lt. col., 1943-46; v.p. western hemisphere Internat. Council on Archives, mem. exec. bd., 1953-70; Awarded Legion of Merit; recipient Distinguished Service award General Services Administration, 1959, Career Service award National Civil Service League, 1961. Mem. American Polit. Sci. Assn., Am. Mil. Inst., Am. Soc. for Public Adminstrn., Soc. of Am. Archivists (president, 1953-54), Am. Hist. Assn., Pi Kappa Alpha. Club: Cosmos. Author: Records Administration Program of War Department, 1948. Contbr. articles in field. Home: Silver Spring MD Died June 8, 1970; buried Rock Creek Cemetery, Washington DC

GROVES, LESLIE RICHARD, retired army officer, business consultant; born at Albany, New York, August 17, 1896; son of Leslie Richard and Gwen (Griffith) G.; student U. of Wash., 1913-14, Mass. Inst. of Tech., 1914-16; B.S., U.S. Mil. Acad., 1918; grad. Army Engr. Sch., 1921, Command and Gen. Staff School, 1936, Army War College, 1939; LL.D. (honorary) U. Cal., Hamilton Coll., St. Ambrose; D.S.C., Lafayette, Williams, Hobart, Ripon and Pa. Military Colleges; m. Grace Hulbert Wilson, February 10, 1922; children—Richard Hulbert, Gwen (Mrs. John A. Robinson). Commd. 2d lt. U.S. Army, 1918, advanced through grades to lt. gen., 1948, retired 1948; various assignments U.S., Hawaii, Europe, Nicaragua, dep. chief construction, Corps Engrs. 1941; headed Manhattan Atomic Devel. Project, 1942-47, in responsible charge all phases of project; v.p. Remington div. Sperry Rand Corporation, 1948-61. Decorated Distinguished Service medal, Legion of Merit (U.S.); Presdl. Medal of Merit (Nicaragua); Comdr. Order of the Crown (Belgium); Hon. Companion Most Honourable Order of the Bath (British). Professional engr., D.C. Mem. Am. Soc. C.E., Am. Soc. M.E. Clubs: Army, Navy, Chevy Chase; Univ. (N.Y.). Author: Now it can be Told, The Story of the Manhattan Project. Home: Washington DC Died July 13, 1970; buried Arlington National Cemetery, Arlington VA

GROWER, ROY WILLIAM ret. army officer; b. Richland, N.Y., Jan. 27, 1890; s. William Seth and Elizabeth Ellen (Thomas) G.; E.E., Syracuse U., 1913; grad. co. Officers Course Engr. Sch. U.S. Army, 1922; 1 son, William L. Grower. Apptd. assistant supt. Bur. Gas & Elec., City of Syracuse, 1914. Served as 1st lt. O.R. with 56th Engrs. 2d Army, France, World War I; later detailed in A.C. with All-Am. Pathfinders; 1st lt. C.E. U.S. Army, 1920, advanced through grades to Brig. Gen., 1944; troop duty with 2d and 6th Engrs., R.O.T.C. and staff details; asst. C. A. engr. 1st C. A. (Boston); assistant adminstr. engineer W.P.A., New York City, 1935-36; asst. dept. engr. Panama Canal Dept., 1937-39; dist. engr., St. Louis Engr. Dist., 1939-42; base sec. engr. Eastern Base Sec. (Eng.), 1943: base sec. comdr. Eastern Base Sec. (Eng.), 1st Base Sec., Brittany Base Sec. (France), 1944: retired 1946. Decorated Legion of Honor, Grand Officer Chevalier de Tastevin (France); Croix de Guerre (Luxembourg); Legion of Merit (U.S.). Mem. Tau Beta Pi, Scabbard and Blade. Mason. Address: 40 Devon Dr., Clearwater Beach; Fla. Died Jan. 31, 1957.

GRUITCH, JERRY M., business exec.; b. Beckerek, Serbia, Aug. 16, 1904; s. Peter and Helen (Marich) G.; B.S. in Mech. Engring., U. Mich., 1933; M.M.E., M.S. Automotive Engring., Chrysler Inst. Engring., 1940; m. Ruth Storrs Lovejoy, Dec. 4, 1933; 1 dau., Judith Ellen. Successively toolmaker apprentice, labor and personnel supt. Ford Motor Co., 1921-29; chief engr., research and devel., heating and refrigeration airtemp div. Chrysler Corp., 1934-41, asst. chief engr. Dodge Div., 1946-47; v.p. engring. O. A. Sutton Corp., Wichita, Kan., 1947-48; dir. research and devel. Am. Car & Foundry div. ACF Industries, Inc., N.Y.C., 1948-57, dir. def. products, 1957-58; dir. govt. products, marketing, ACF Industries, Inc., 1959-62, corporate project mgr. Minuteman Program, 1961-62; dir. govt. products O. M. Edwards Co., Inc., Syracuse, N.Y., Excel. Corp., Elkhart, Ind., 1962-64; v.p. devel. Stanray Corp., Chgo., 1964-69. Cons. to Office Asst. Sec. Def., 1958-69; mem. steering group, adv. panel on ordnance Office Dir. Def. Research and Engring., 1959-69. Mem. tech. adv. group Air Force Armament Center, USAF Research and Devel. Command; mem. tech. adv. com. on ordnance Office Asst. Sec. Def., Research and Devel.; Nat. Strategy Seminar, Nat. War Coll., 1962. Col. USAF, 1941-46; Nat. Mil. Establishment research and devel. com. on ordnance, 1948. Awarded Commendation Ribbon with 2 Oak Leaf Clusters, Bronze Star, Legion of Merit; recipient Distinguished Alumnus citation U. Mich., 1957, sesquicentennial award, 1967; Bronze medallion Am. Ordnance Assn., 1967. Registered profl. engr., N.Y.; registered Nat. Bur. of Profl. Engrs. Fellow Am. Soc. M.E., Am. Inst. Aeronautics and Astronautics (asso.); mem. Soc. Automotive Engrs., Am. Soc. Heating, Refrigerating and Air Conditioning Engrs., Am. Ordnance Assn. (chmn. emeritus, prodn. techniques div., dir. Syracuse post, dir. N.Y. post, mem. nat. council), Assn. U.S. Army, Inst. Metals (London), Scabbard and Blade, Triangles, mem. Sigma Xi, Phi Kappa, Tau Beta Pi. Clubs: Engineers, Union League (N.Y.C.); Army-Navy (Washington); Los Alamos Civic; Century (Syracuse); Military Order of the Carabao. Contbr. to engring. jours. Home: Lake Forest IL Died Mar. 1969.

GUENTHER, FRANCIS LUTHER brig. gen.; b. Buffalo, Feb. 22, 1838; s. Rev. Francis Henry and Katharine (Knotts) G.; apptd. from N.Y., and grad. U.S. Mil. Acad., 1859; unmarried. Bvtd. 2d lt. 1st Arty., July 1, 1859; 2d lt. 4th Arty., Nov. 2, 1859; 1st lt. 5th Arty., May 14, 1861; capt., July 2, 1863; maj. 2d Arty., June 26, 1882; lt. col. 5th Arty., July 1, 1891; col. 4th Arty., June 6, 1896; brig. gen. vols., May 4, 1898, to Oct. 31, 1898; brig. gen. U.S.A., Feb. 13, 1902. Bvtd.; capt., Apr. 7, 1862, for gallant and meritorious services at battle of Shiloh; maj., Dec. 31, 1862, for same at Stone River; lt. col. and col., Mar. 13, 1865, for same during the war. In Civil War served in W.Va. and in Army of the Ohio and Army of the Cumberland; took part in many battles, including Greenbrier, Virginia, Pittsburgh Landing, Shiloh Corinth, Stone River, Tullahoma, Chattanooga, etc.: retired Feb. 22, 1902. Died Dec. 5, 1918.

GUÉRARD, ALBERT LEON author; b. Paris, France, Nov. 3, 1880; s. Marcel Theophile and Marie (Collot) G.; B.A., Paris, 1899; post-grad. studies, London and Sorbonne, Paris; Agrégé, 1906; Litt.D., Geneva College, Beaver Falls, Pa., 1936, Brandeis University, Waltham, Massachusetts, 1957; m. Wilhelmina Macartney, 1907; children-Sidney (dec.), Therina, Albert Joseph Traveling scholarship in Eng., 1901-03; jr. p prof. lt. and examiner in history Paris Normal Sch., 1904-06; instr. Williams Coll., 1906-07; asst. and asso. prof. French. Stanford, U., 1907-13, prof. gen. lit., 1925-46, emeritus, 1946-; prof. French, Rice Inst., Houston, 1913-24, U. Cal., So. br., 1924-25; prof. French, U. Chgo., Summer 1916, 20, U. Cal., 1921, 22, 26, U. Wis., 1923, U. Hawaii, 1930, U. Ore., 1931; prof. English, Harvard, summer 1949, U. Hawaii, 1950; prof. comparative lit. Brandeis U., 1950-53; lectr. French civilization New Sch. for Social Research, 1951, Radcliffe College, 1951-52; associate in Humanities, Stanford, 1957-58. Served with U.S. Army, intelligence and liaison services during world War I; with OWI, 1942-45. Mem. Phi Beta Kappa, Pi Delta Phi, Pi Sigma Alpha. Episcopalian. Decorated Chevalier of Legion of Honor (France); Crown of Rumania. Author: French Prophets of Yesterday, 1913; French Civilization in the XIX Century, 1914; Five Masters of French Romance, 1916; French Civilization from Its Origins to the Close of the Middle Ages, 1920; International Languages, 1921; The Napoleonic Legend, 1923; Honoré de Balzac (pamphlet), 1924; Beyond Hatred, 1925; Life and Death of an Ideal, 1928; L'Avenir de paris, 1929; Literature and Society, 1935; Art for Art's Sake, 1936; Preface to World Literature, 1940; The France of Tomorrow (de luxe edit), 1941. (complete), 1942; Napoleon III, 1943; Europe Free and United, 1945; France: A Short History, 1946; What the Teacher Learned (4 vols.), 1948-; Napoleon III, 1955; Napoleon I, 1956; Fossils and Presences, 1957; Joan of Arc, 1957; France: The Biography of a Nation, 1959. Address: 635 Gerona Rd., Stanford, Cal.

GUERRANT, EDWARD OWINGS clergyman; b. Sharpsburg, Ky., Feb. 28, 1838; s. Dr. Henry Ellis and Mary Beaufort Howe (Owings) G.; A.B., Center Coll. (now Central U.), Danville, Ky., 1860; Jefferson Med. Coll., Phila., 1865-66; M.D., Bellevue Med. Coll., New York, 1867; grad. Union Theol. Sem., Va., 1876; (D.D., Austin Coll., Sherman, Tex.); m. Mary J. DeVault, May 12, 1868. Practiced medicine, Mt. Sterling, Ky., 1867-73; ordained Presbyn. ministry, 1876. pastor Salem, Ky., 1876-77, Mt. Sterling, 1877-79, 1st Ch., Louisville, 1880-83, Troy and Wilmore, 1885. Served in C.S.A., pvt. to capt. and asst. adj. gen. brigade of cav., Jan. 1862-Apr. 1865. Pres. Am. Inland Mission, 1897-, and editor The Soul Winner. Democrat. Mason. Home: Wilmore, Ky. Died Apr. 26, 1916.

GUGGENHEIM, M. ROBERT diplomat; b. N.Y.C., May 17, 1885; s. Daniel and Florence (Schloss) G.; student Drisler Sch., N.Y.C., also Sch. Mines, Columbia, 1907; grad. Army War Coll., 1925; m. Rebecca Pollard, 1938; 1 son by previous marriage, M. Robert. Dir., mem. exec. com. Am. Smelting & Refining Co.; sec., v.p. U.S. Zinc Co.; dir. Daniel and Florence Aviation Safety Center, Cornell, 1952—; apptd. U.S. ambassador to Portugal, 1953-54. Dir. Nat. Symphony Orchestra Bd., Washington, Daniel Florence Guggenheim Found, 1924— (sponsor ann. summer band concerts, N.Y.C.) Served as maj. U.S. Army, World War I; staff War Dept., 1932-33; now col. Decorated Purple Heart, Silver Star; hon. col. Ecuadorean Army. Clubs: Army Navy, Army Navy Country (Washington). Home: 4400 Board Branch Rd. Office: 2800 Albermarie St., Washington. Died Nov. 16, 1959.*

GUILD, CURTIS journalist, soldier; b. Boston, Feb. 2, 1860; son of Curtis and Sarah Crocker (Cobb) G.; A.B., summa cum laude, Harvard, 1881; (LL.D., Holy Cross Coll., 1906; Williams Coll., 1908: S.T.D., U. of Geneva, Switzerland, 1909); m. Charlotte H. Johnson, June 1, 1892. After graduation made tour of Europe; entered office Commercial Bulletin, Boston, founded by his father; served from bill collector to editor, and, 1902-, sole owner of the paper; pres. Anchor Linotype Printing Co. Pres. Rep. State Conv., 1895; del.-at-large from Mass. and a v.p. Rep. Nat. Conv., 1896. Active as volunteer public speaker on Rep. side, in N.E., Central West and Southern States. Brig. gen. state militia at outbreak of Spanish War; insp. gen. 7th Army Corps (Gen. Fitzhugh Lee), and later insp. gen. Dept. of Havana, until break-up of corps in Cuba; work praised by insp. gen. of army in report. Offered colonial commn. by President, declined; offered place 1st asst. postmaster gen., declined; offered chairmanship of Nat. Civil Service Commn., declined; Roosevelt's companion on stump tour of West, campaign of 1900; lt. gov. Mass., 1902-05, gov. Mass., 1906-09; received 75 votes for Vice-Presdl. nomination, Rep. Nat. Conv., 1908; spl. ambassador to Mexico, 1910; ambassador to Russia, July 21, 1911-13. Grand Officer Crown of Italy; Grand Cordon Order St. Alexander Nevski, Russia. Mem. Boston Chamber of Commerce. Home: Boston, Mass. Died Apr. 6, 1915.

GUILD, LAFAYETTE physician, army officer; b. Tuscaloosa, Ala., Nov. 23, 1825; s. James and Mary (Williams) G.; M.D., Jefferson Med. Coll., Phila., 1848; m. Martha Aylette Fitts, 1851, 2 adopted Indian sons. Entered med. service U.S. Army as asst. surgeon, 1849; served in South and S.W.; assigned to 2d Dragoons, 1857-61; accompanied regt. in actions against Indians of No. Cal.; entered Confederate Army as surgeon, 1861, commd. maj.; insp. hosps., 1861-62; med. dir. Army of No. Va., 1862-65; pvt. practice medicine, Mobile, Ala., 1865-66; quarantine officer Port of Mobile, 1866-69; moved to San Francisco, 1869; vis. surgeon San Francisco City and County Hosp., 1869-70. Died Marysville, Cal., July 4, 1870; buried Tuscaloosa.

GUINEY, PATRICK ROBERT lawyer, army officer; b. Parkstown, Ireland, Jan. 15, 1835; brought to Portland, Me., at age 6; attended Holy Cross Coll.; m. Janet Doyle. Admitted to bar, 1856; moved to Boston; served from pvt. to brig. gen. 9th Mass. Regt. during Civil War, served in 30 engagements, was decorated; partially blinded at Battle of Wilderness; asst. dist. atty.; founder Catholic Union; mem. various civic orgns., Boston. Died Boston, Mar. 21, 1877.

GUINEY, PATRICK WILLIAM army officer; b. Fall River, Mass., Feb. 10, 1877; s. John and Johanna (Farrell) G.; ed. pub. schs., Fall River, 1884-95, U.S. Mil. Acad., 1895-99) m. Margaret Wells Buck, Feb. 24, 1906; 1 son, Patrick William. Commd. 2d lt. cav., U.S.A., 1899; advanced through grades to col., 1921; brig. gen., asst. to q.m. gen., U.S.A., 1933-. Served in China, Philippines, Mexican Border, World War. Awarded Silver Star Citation; Purple Heart with oak leaf cluster. Died Dec. 17, 1936.

GUION, LEWIS commr. Vicksburg Nat. Mil. Park; b. Parish of Lafourche, La., Aug. 28, 1838; s. George Seth and Caroline Lucretia (Winder) G.; g.s. Maj. Isaac G., U.S.A., also an officer Continental Army; St. James Coll.; A.B., U. of Miss., 1858; Law Dept. U. of Va., 1858-59; LL.B., Law Dept., U. of La., 1861; m. Mrs. Mary E. (Harris) Lanier, July 13, 1875. Admitted to La. bar, 1861; 1st lt. Co. A, 1st La. Inf., C.S.A., 1861: capt. Co. D, 26th La. Vols., 1863-65; acting asst. insp. gen. staffs of Gens. F. A. Shoup and Allen Thomas; paroled Aug. 1865. Resumed practiced after the war, also sugar planter; melter and refiner New Orleans Mint, 1893-98; mem. bd. commrs. Vicksburg Nat. Military Park, 1908-. Democrat. Episcopalian. Home: New Orleans, La. Died Jan. 12, 1920.

GULICK, JOHN W. army officer; b. Goldsboro, N.C., Nov. 8, 1874; s. James Wharton and Susan Holland (Green) G.; grad. U.S. Arty. Sch., 1905, Army War Coll., 1925; m. Florence MacMullan, July 3, 1905. Served as 1st lt. U.S. Vols., 1898; commd. 1st lt., U.S.A., Sept. 17, 1901; promoted through grades to col., Aug. 19, 1925: maj. gen., Mar. 20, 1930. Instr., Coast Arty. Sch., 1901-11; on duty with Chilean Govt., 1911-15; dir. Coast Arty. Sch., 1915-17; chief of staff, 40th Div., 1917-18; chief of staff, Army Arty., First Army, A.E.F., 1918-19; on War Dept. General Staff, 1919-24: later chief of coast artillery. D.S.M. (U.S.); Legion of Honor (France). Died Aug. 18, 1939.

GULLION, ALLEN WYANT major general, United States Army; b. Carrollton, Kentucky, Dec. 14, 1880; s. Edmund A. and Atha (Hanks) G.; A.B., Centre Coll., Ky., 1901; B.S., U.S. Mil. Acad., 1905; LL.B., U. of Ky., 1914; grad. Gen. Service Sch., Leavenworth, Kan., 1928, Army War Coll., Washington, D.C., 1931; grad. Naval War College, Newport, R.I., 1932; General Staff Corps Eligible List; hon. LL.D., University of Hawaii, 1935, Centre College, 1939, University of Kentucky, 1942; m. Ruth Mathews, September 9, 1905 (deceased); children-Ruth, Edmund, Atha, Margaret (dec.), Phillip, Allen. Commd. 2d lt. U.S. Army, June 13, 1905; promoted through grades to lt. col., Aug. 31, 1929; col., 2d Ky. Inf., Mexican Border, 1916; lt. col. (temp.) World War. Prof. mil. science and tactics, U. of Ky., 1912-14. Chief of Mobilization Div., Office of Provost Marshal Gen., Nat. Selective Service, Washington, D.C., 1917; judge advocate Third Corps, A.E.F., 1918; legal adviser to Gen. R. L. Bullard, Governors Island, N.Y., 1919-24; chief of Mil. Affairs Div., Office Judge Advocate Gen., Washington, 1928-30; sr. War Dept. rep. at Geneva, 1929, participating with representatives of 47 nations in formulation of code for prisoners of war, and in revision of Geneva Convention of 1906; sneior judge adv. Hawaiian Dept., 1932-33; sole U.S. del. to Congress of Juridical Experts, Luxembourg, 1938, addressing the conf. on the "present state of international law regarding protection of civilians against the new war technics"; senior War Dept. rep. and del. of Am. and Federal bar assns. at first convention of Inter-American Bar Assn., Havana, 1941. Deputy administrator, NRA, Territory of Hawaii, 1933-35; chief of mil. affairs div., Office of Judge Advocate Gen., Washington, D.C., 1935, asst. judge advocate gen., 1936, acting judge advocate gen., 1937, judge advocate general (major general), 1937; provost marshal general (major general), July 31, 1941-Apr. 28, 1944; overseas (France) 1944; retired as major general, December 1944. Honorary president Kentucky Soc., Washington. Awarded D.S.M. (U.S.); Oak Leaf cluster to D.S.M., 1944; legion of Merit (1944); Estralia d'Abdon Calderon (Ecuador). Clubs: Army and Navy (Washington, D.C.); Army and Navy Country (Arlington, Va.). Home: 2737 Devonshire Pl. N.W., Washington, D.C. Died June 19, 1946.

GUNDER, DWIGHT FRANCIS engineer; b. Ames, Ia., Dec. 11, 1905; s. F. E. and Catherine (Cooney) G.; B.S., Ia. State Coll., 1925, M.S., 1926; Ph.D., U. Wis., 1933; m. Kathryn Mae Lamb, 1932. Prof., Colo. A. and M. Coll., 1926-47; prof. and head dept. engring. mechanics and engring. materials Cornell since 1947-56; cons. Hercules Powder Company, Rohm & Haas Company, Project Lincoln (Massachusetts Institute of Technology), Project Rand, Rock Island Arsenal. Spl. advisor Bur. Ordnance, USN (rockets, missiles). Served as engr., U.S. A.S.F., 1943-45. Mem. Am. Soc. M.E., Am. Soc. C.E., Am. Soc. Engring. Edn., Am. Soc. for Metals, Am. Soc. Testing Materials. Math. Assn. Am., Sigma Xi, Phi Kappa Phi, Tau Beta Pi, Sigma Tau. Author: Engineering Mechanics (with D.A. Stuart), 1959. Home: 463 W. 5th St., Loveland, Colo. 80537. Died Oct. 21, 1964; buried Loveland Burial Park, Loveland, Colo.

GUNDERSON, CLARK YOUNG lawyer, educator; b. Vermillion, S.D., Nov. 4, 1908; s. Andrew Bennett and Clara (Jones) G.; A.B., U. S.D., 1931, LL.B., 1933; grad. student Northwestern U. Law Sch., 1931, Yale, 1932; m. Ethel Lyckholm, June 11, 1934; 1 dau., Karla Ann. Admitted to S.D. bar, 1932; U.S. Supreme Ct., 1941; law practice, partner, Gunderson & Gunderson, Vermillion, S.D., 1932 prof. law U. S.D., 1934 - ; legal counsel, 1946 - ; mem. state bd. examiners, 1936 - . Served to lt., Q.M.C., U.S. Army, 1 yr. overseas, E.T.O. U.S.A., chief mil affairs dept., judge adv. gen. sch., 1942-43, div. judge adv. 69th inf. div., 1943-45; relieved from duty 1946, col., judge adv. gen. div. Mem. Am. Miss., S.D. bar assns., Phi Delta Theta, Phi Delta Phi. Mason. Republican. Home: 205 E. Lewis St., Vermillion, S.D. 57069. Died Dec. 6, 1964.

GUNN, JAMES senator; b. Va., Mar. 13, 1753; attended common schs.; studied law. Admitted to the bar; began law practice, Savannah, Ga.; served in Revoluntionary War, capt. dragoons defending Savannah, 1782; col. 1st Regt., Chatham County Militia; promoted brig. gen. Ga. Militia; elected to Continental Congress, 1787, did not serve; mem. U.S. Senate from Ga., 1789-1801. Died Louisville, Ga., July 30, 1801; buried Old Capitol Cemetery, Louisville.

GUNN, JOHN W., lawyer, judge; b. Butte, Mont., June 4, 1920; s. Nelson T. and Jane (Gracey) G.; ed. Pomona Coll.; LL.B., U. Ida., 1948; m. Jean V. Gray, Nov. 7, 1943; children—John W., Laura Jean, George N. Practice law, Boise, Ida., 1949-63, Weiser, Ida., 1963-65, Caldwell, Ida., 1965-70; asst. atty. gen. State of Ida., 1949-60; chief counsel Ida. Employment Security Agy., 1949-63; city atty. Weiser, 1963, Cambridge, 1963-64; justice of peace Canyon County, Ida., 1965-70. Sub-chmn. United Fund Dr., Boise, 1955; chmn. Ida. Anti Sales Tax Com., Weiser, 1964. Served with Inf., AUS, 1943-46; maj. Res. Mem. Ida. Bar Assn., Am. Legion, Phi Alpha Delta, Sigma Chi. Episcopalian (sr. warden 1964, lay reader 1964-65). Mason, Elk, Toastmaster. Home: Caldwell ID Died May 1970

GUNN, ROSS research physicist; b. Cleve., May 12, 1897; s. Ross Delano Aldrich and Lora Arletta (Conner) G.; B.S. in E.E., U. Mich., 1920, M.S., 1921; Ph.D., Yale, 1926; m. Gladys Jeannette Rowley, Sept. 8, 1923; children - Ross, Andrew Leigh, Charles Rowley, Robert Burns. Instr. engring. physics, U. Mich., 1920-22; radio research engr. U.S. Air Service, 1922-23; instr. physics, Yale, 1923-27; research physicist U.S. Naval Research Lab., 1927-33, tech. adviser, 1933-47, supt. mechanics and electricity div. 1938-46; supt. aircraft elec. div., 1943-46; supt. physics div., 1946-47; tech. dir., Army-Navy Precipitation Static Project, 1943-46; Army-Navy Atmospheric Electricity Project, 1946-47; cons. NACA, 1943-59, NDRC, 1942-43; Research and Development Bd., 1946-48. Dir. phys. research, U.S. Weather Bur., 1947-57; also asst. chief, 1955-56; research prof. physics, Am. U., 1958 - ; cons. AEC, 1958-60; dir. Air-Force-Weather Bur. Cloud Physics Project physics, Am. U., 1958 - ; cons. AEC, 1958-60; A.F., 1948-53; cons. C.F. Kettering Found. 1951-54. Inventor instruments and specialized devices, several fundamental contbns. Served in U.S. Signal Res. Corps. World War I. Cited by sec. of navy for exceptionally distinguished service in connection with devel. of atomic bomb, 1945; Distinguished Service award, Flight Safety Found., 1951, Robert M. Losey Award, Inst. of Aero. Scis., 1956, also recipient Gold medal for Exceptional Service U.S. Dept. Commerce, 1957, Distinguished Alumnus award U. Mich., 1953. Fellow Am. Phys. Soc., I.E.E.E., Geophys. Union; mem. Nat. Acad. Scis., Am. Meterol. Soc., Sigma Xi, Tau Beta Pi. Author more than 100 sci. and tech. articles, Inventor, organizer 1st work on atomic powered submarine. Patentee in field. Address: American University, Washington. Died Oct. 15, 1966; buried Bethesda Methodist Church Cemetery.

GUNNELL, FRANCIS M. surgeon gen. U.S.N.; b. Washington, Nov. 27, 1827; s. James and Helen (Mackall) G.; A.B., Georgetown U., 1845, A.M., 1848; M.D., Columbian (now George Washington) U., 1846 (hon. A.M., 1852; LL.D., George Washington U., 1911); m. Harriet Patterson Chew. Apptd. from D.C., asst. surgeon, Mar. 22, 1849; passed asst. surgeon, Apr. 7, 1854; surgeon, Apr. 23, 1861; med. insp., Mar. 3, 1871; med. dir., Feb. 3, 1875; insp., Mar. 3, 1871; med. dir., Feb. 3, 1875; surgeon gen. U.S.N., 1884; retired with relative rank of commodore, Nov. 27, 1889; promoted to rank of rear admiral retired, June 1906. Served on various stas. and N. and S. Atlantic blockading squadrons, 1861; Naval Hosp., Washington, 1863-65, etc. Died June 10, 1922.

GUNNISON, JOHN WILLIAMS army officer, engr.; b. Goshen, N.H., Nov. 11, 1812; s. Samuel and Elizabeth (Williams) G.; grad. U.S. Mil. Acad., 1837; m. Martha A. Delony, Apr. 15, 1841, 3 children. Served with 2d Artillery as 2d lt. in Seminole War, 1837-38; aided transfer of Cherokees to Indian Territory, 1838; participated in surveys in Ga. and lake region of Northwest, 1840-49; spent winter in Salt Lake City, made study of Mormon religion; commd. capt., 1853, assigned to survey Huerfano River, Cochetopa Pass and Grand and Green valleys to Santa Clara in S.W. Utah, expdn. attacked by band of Pahvant Indians. Author: The Mormons, 1852. Killed in Indian attack, Utah, Oct. 26, 1853.

GUNNISON, ROYAL ARCH war correspondent, broadcaster, author; b. Juneau, Alaska, Feb. 7, 1909; s. Royal Arch and Helena (Cobb) G.; grad. George Washington U., Washington, D.C.; studied for U.S. Foreign Service; student The Principia, St. Louis, Mo.; Univ. of Washington, Seattle, Wash.; grad. student internat. politics and economics, U. of Geneva; m. Marjorie Hathaway, 1935. Began as fgn. corr. Associated Press, Europe, assigned to cover League of Nations, 1934; later staff corr. Christian Science Monitor, working fgn. news desk (Boston), writing front page column The World's Day, also conducting daily newscast; assigned by Monitor to West Coast News Bureau, covering Australia, New Zealand, Hawaii, Alaska, 11 western states; joined staff North Am. Newspaper Alliance, 1940, sent Alaska first Clipper flight, June 1940, to New Zealand and Australia first Pan Am. Clipper flight, Aug. 1940; remained on assignment in East Asia, Australia, Netherlands East Indies, Singapore, Malaya, free and occupied China and Philippine Islands; broadcast from Australia for M.B.S., 1941, later from Chunking, China. Became Collier's corr., in Far East prior war with Japan; caught last Clipper from Hong Kong to Manila, arriving just before Philippines attacked, Dec. 7, 1941; covered Philippines campaign for M.B.S., Collier's, North Am. Newspaper Alliance. Captured by Japanese Army in Manila, Jan. 2, 1942, repatriated to U.S. aboard M.S. Gripsholm, December 1943; correspondent for M.B.S. and Collier's covering Philippine liberation campaign, 1944-45. Now M.B.S. news analyst. Received 1942 National Headliner's Journalism award for radio reporting under combat conditions; United Nations Association, award for "unceasing effort and contribution to cause of internat. cooperation," Jan. 1944; citation from Alaska for remaining in Manila to report the invasion. Mem. Sigma Chi. Author: So Sorry - No Peace, 1944. Was in Vienna when Premier Dolfuss was assassinated: in Berlin just after first blood purge, Nazi Party. Address: care Mutual Broadcasting System, New York, N.Y. Died Sept. 25, 1946.

GUNTER, CLARENCE surgeon; b. Montgomery, Ala., Jan. 16, 1879; s. William Adams and Ellen Florence (Poellnitz) G.; prep. edn., Univ. Sch., Montgomery; M.D., Coll. Phys. and Surgeons, Columbia, 1901; m. Laurette O'Connell, June 30, 1909 (died in 1932): children-Manning, Randolph, Lovell; m. 2d, Evelyn Camilla Nolstad, Dec. 1936. Began the practice of medicine at Cananea, Sonora, Mexico. 1902; surgeon and asst. chief surgeon, S.P. R.R. of Mexico, 1900-16; div. surgeon, Ariz. Eastern R.R., 1916-24; dist. surgeon, S.P. R.R., 1924—. Served as surgeon, 18th Inf., United States Army Mexican border, 1916; capt., Med. R.C., 1917. Del. to Dem. Nat. Conv., 1924; mem. Dem. Nat. Com., 1928-32. Apptd. by Ariz. legislature mem. com. of 5 to assist in Arizona's fight on Boulder Dam in Congress, 1927. Pres. Board of Trustees Globe Schs. Fellow A.C.S.; mem. Ariz. Med. Assn. (past pres.), Gila County Med. Soc. (past pres.). Presbyterian. Clubs: Cobre Valle Country; Arizona Club (Phoenix). Address: Globe, Ariz. Died Mar. 1955.

GUNTHER, CHARLES OTTO prof. mathematics and ordnance engring.; b. N.Y.C., May 21, 1879; s. Otto and Anna (Eybel) G.; M.E., Stevens Inst. Tech., 1900, D.Sc., 1950; m. Beatrice Disbrow, Feb. 19, 1901; children-Beatrix (Mrs. Fred B. Llewellyn), Jack Disbrow. With Stevens Inst. of Tech. 1900—, as instr. in mathematics, 1900-02, asst. prof., 1902-03, asst. prof. mathematics and mech. drawing, 1903-04, mathematics and mechanics, 1904-08, prof. and head of dept., 1908-36, prof. mathematics and ordnance engring., 1936-50, emeritus prof. mathematics and engring., 1950—, dean of student activities, 1920-25, dean of sophomores, 1927-28. Served with Ordnance Dept., U.S. Army, 1918-19; now lt. col. Ordnance Dept. Army U.S., inactive duty. Recipient of Stevens Honor Award, 1947; Stevens Alumni award, 1957. Fellow A.A.A.S.; mem. Army Ordnance Assn., Assn. Mathematics Teachers of New Jersey (past president, member council), Am. Soc. Civil Engrs. (life member), Am. Society Mech. Engrs., Soc. Am. Mil. Engrs., Societe Astronomique de France, Tau Beta Pi, Sigma Nu. Club: Officers of Army and Navy (New York). Author: Integration by Trigonometric and Imaginary Substitution, 1907; The Identification of Firearms from Ammunition Fired Therein 1935. Contbr. to jours. Home: Grand View-on-Hudson, Nyack 9, N.Y. Office: Stevens Institute of Technology, Hoboken, N.J. Died June 8, 1958.

GUNTHER, ERNEST LUDOLPH naval officer; b. Louisville, Ky., Sept. 7, 1887; s. Marius Harrison and Fanny Lee (Aroni) G.; B.S., U.S. Naval Acad., 1909; m. Helen St. Goar, May 20, 1922; children-Ernest Harrison, Charles Frederick. Commd. ensign U.S. Navy, 1909, advancing through the grades to rear adm., 1942; comd. U.S.S. Jarvis (destroyer) in European waters, World War I; naval attaché to Chile, 1931-34; comd. Naval Air Station and Naval Air Center, San

Diego, Calif., 1942-43; comdr. aircraft, South Pacific Force, 1943-45; comdr. Air Force Pacific Fleet Subordinate Comd. Forward Areas, Feb. 1945-May 1946; comdr. Fleet Air, Quonset Pt. since 1946. Decorated Navy Cross, Legion of Merit (U.S.), Orden del Merito (Chile), Presidential Medal of Merit (Nicaragua), British Order of the Bath. Clubs: New York (N.Y.) Yacht; Philadelphia (Pa.) Racquet; Army and Navy (Washington, D.C.). Home: 9241 Peabody Av., Memphis. Died Mar. 27, 1948.

GURD, FRASER BAILLIE surgeon; b. Montreal, Quebec, Can., Jan. 7, 1883; s. David Fraser and Mary (Baillie) G.; B.A., McGill U., 1904, M.D., C.M., 1907; m. Jessie Gibson Newman, Jan. 4, 1910; children-Fraser Newman (M.D.), Katharine Mary (Currie), Frank Ross Newman. Instr., lecturer in pathology, Tulane U.; pathologist Touro Infirmary, New Orleans, 1909-11; lecturer in immunology, McGill U., 1911-20, consecutively demonstrator, lecturer, asst. prof., asso. prof., prof. of surgery, since 1911; asst. in surgery, Montreal Gen. Hosp., consecutively asso. surgeon, attending surgeon, chief of surgical service, suregon-in-chief, since 1911; surgeon-in-chief Grace Dart Home Hosp. (for pulmonary tuberculosis), since 1932. Served as capt., Royal Army Med. Corps, 1915-18, officer commanding dept. exptl. surgery, Alder Hey Hosp., Liverpool; surgery specialist, 22 casualty Clearing Stations; maj. Royal Canadian Army Med. Corps, officer comdg. St. Annes Mil. Hosp., 1918-21. Fellow Canadian Med. Assn., Am. Assn. of Pathologists and Bacteriologists, Am. Assn. for Tropical Medicine, A.M.A., Am. Coll. of Suregons (2d vice pres., 1938-39), Am. Assn. for Thoracic Surgeons (vice pres., 1939, pres., 1940-41), Am. Surgical Assn. Royal Coll. Surgeons of Can.; mem. Candian Assn. Clin. Surgeons (pres., 1938-40), Am. Assn. for surgery of Trauma (founders group; vice pres., 1938-39, pres., 1939-40), Am. Bd. of Surgery (founders group), Surg. Research Soc., Central Surg. Soc. (founders group), McGill regional Com. of Surgery (chmn.), Nat. Research Council of Can., Nat. Research Council (mem. subcom. on surgery, 1942-46), Phi Rho Sigma, Delta Upsilon, Sigma Xi. Mem. Conservative party. Mem. United Ch. of Canada. Clubs: Mount Royal, Unviersity, Faculty (McGill U.), Royal Montreal Golf, Rotary, Canadian (Montreal). Home: 3180 The Boulevard, Westmount 6, Quebec, Can. Office: 1538 Sherbrooke St. W., Montreal 25, Quebec. Can. Died Feb. 22, 1948; buried Mount Royal Cemetery, Montreal.

GURLEY, JOHN ADDISON congressman; b. East Hartford, Conn., Dec. 9, 1813; attended dist. schs.; studied theology. Learned hatter's trade; pastor Universalist Ch., Methuen, Mass., 1835-38; moved to Cincinnati, 1838; pastor, Cincinnati, 1838-50; owner, editor Star and Sentinel (later Star in the West), 1838-54; mem. U.S. Ho. of Reps. (Republican) from Ohio, 36th-37th congresses, 1859-63, unsuccessful candidate for re-election, 1862; served as col. and a.d.c. on staff of Gen. John Fremont during Civil War; apptd. gov. Ariz. by Pres. Lincoln, died before taking office. Died Green Twp. nr. Cincinnati, Aug. 19, 1863; buried Spring Grove Cemetery, Cincinnati.

GURNEY AUGUSTUS M. army officer; b. Oneonta, N.Y., Feb. 18, 1895; s. Louis Comstock and Florence S. (Moody) G.; B.S., U.S. Mil. Acad., 1917; M.S., Yale, 1927; m. Dora Josephine Bonbright, Aug. 5, 1919 (dec. Oct. 1944); children - Margaret Eleanor, Louise Cummings; m. 2d, Gladys Kirton, May 23, 1946. Commd. 2d lt., 1917, advanced through the grades to brig. gen., Apr. 1942; ret. 1954. Home: Hillside Rd. Southern Pines, N.C. 28387. Died Apr. 10, 1967; buried Oneonta.

GUTHNER, WILLIAM ERNEST govt. official; b. Dec. 18, 1884; s. Kaspar and Lousie (Deininger) G.; grad. Sch. of Automatic Arms, 1917; Command and Gen. Staff Sch., 1929, Gen. Officers Course, 1941; m. Hannah Barrett, 1907; 1 dau., Dorothy R. (wife of Col. Howard M. Williams); m. 2d, Alyce Maus, 1930; children-Barbara Louise (wife of 1st Lt. Richard W. Hazen, A.C.), William E., Jr. Entered U.S. Army from Colo., served as pvt., corpl. and sergt., 6th U.S. Cavalry, 1901-04; capt., 157th Inf., A.E.F., 1917-19; successively maj., lt. col. and brig. gen., U.S. N.G., 1921-40, comdg. gen., 89th inf. brigade, 45th div., 1934-42, brig. gen., U.S. Army, 1941-46, with duty as brigade comdr., provost marshal, dir. security and intelligence, VI Corps Area and Sixth Service Comd., Chicago, 1942-46. Dir. pub. safety, Denver, 1934-40, exec. sec. Highway Traffic Safety Com., 1946-49. Awarded Legion of Merit with bronze cluster, 1944. Mem. Am. Legion, U.S. War Vets., Vets. Fgn. Wars (nat. chief of staff, 1936, nat. council adminstrn., 1929-35, v.p. Nat. Home bd., 1937-39). Mason. Club: Civitan. Home: 7924 Keystone Av., Skokie, Ill. Died Jan. 24, 1951; buried Fairmount Mausoleum, Denver.

GUTHRIE, CHARLES CLAUDE physiologist; b. nr. Wentzville, Mo., May 13, 1880; s. Robert McCluer and Fannie (Hall) G.; grad. Woodlawn Inst., O'Fallon, Mo., 1897; M.D., U. Mo., 1901, Sc.D., 1962; Ph.D., U. Chgo., 1907; Sc.D., U. Pitts., 1935. Western Res. U., Cleve., 1902-03; instr. physiology, U. Chgo., 1903-06; prof. physiology and Pharmacology, Washington U., 1906-09; prof. physiology and pharmacology, U. Pitts., 1909-49, emeritus 1949-63. Served to maj. Med. Res. Corps. Dept. of War, 1917-43. Recipient award Am. Assn. Plastic Surgeons, 1962. Mem. Am. Physiol. Soc., Soc. Pharmacology and Exptl. Therapeutics, Soc. Exptl. Biology and Medicine, Sigma Xi, Alpha Omega Alpha. Author: Blood Vessel Surgery and Its Applications, 1912; also contbr. articles on physiol. and other med. problems to profl. jours. Home: 814 Hitt St., Columbia, Mo. 65201. Died June 16, 1963; buried Columbia Cemetery.

GUTMANN, ADDIS, savings and loan exec.; b. Victoria B.C., Can., Jan. 6,21901; s. Moritz and Adelaid (Hyams) G.; grad. U. Wash., 1923; m. Estelle Schlesinger, June 15, 1927; children—Addis, Alene (Mrs. Ralph Nofield). Sec. Alaska Fur Co., Seattle, 1923-40, mgr., 1940-47, pres., 1947-56; pres. Alaska Jewelry Co., 1956-60; pres., dir. Franklin Savings & Loan Assn., Seattle, 1960-71; dir. Plaza Devel. Co. Pres. Jewish Community Center, 1960. Bd. dirs. Arthritis Found.; pres. Seattle chpt. Am. Cancer Soc., 1969-71. Served to col. AUS, 1941-46; PTO, ETO. Decorated Bronze Star with cluster. Mem. Retired Officers Assn. (nat. dir. 1970-71), Am. Legion (comdr. Seattle 1959). Nat. Sojourners, D.A.V. Mason (Shriner), Elk. Clubs: Wash. Athletic, Forty Nine (Seattle); Army and Navy (Washington). Home: Seattle WA Died Oct. 29, 1971.

GUTTMACHER, MANFRED S. psychiatrist; b. Baltimore, May 19, 1898; s. Adolf and Laura (Oppenheimer) G.; student Park Sch., Baltimore, 1915; A.B., Johns Hopkins, 1919, M.D., 1923; m. Jocelyn McDonough, 1928 (div. 1940); children - Jonathan, Richard; m. 2d, Carola Blitzman, Oct. 12, 1946; children - Laurence, Alan. Emanuel Libman European fellow, 1925-27; intern Johns Hopkins Hosp., 1924-25; resident, Boston Psychopath. Hosp., 1927-28; psychiatrist, Md. Mental Hygiene Clinic, 1928-30; instr. neurology, Johns Hopkins, 1928-30; chief med. officer (psychiatric adviser), Supreme Bench Balt. from 1930; pvt. practice of psychiatry from 1928; lectr. Johns Hopkins U., U. Md., Jacob Gimbel lectr., Stanford, 1951; psychiatric cons. VA, to Surgeon Gen.; chief psychiatric cons. Second Army, Psychiatric cons. to Com. of UN Studying Crime, 1948. Lt. col., M.C., U.S. Army, 1942-46. Awarded Legion of Merit, 1945. Mem. med. adv. bd., Seton Inst., Balt. Fellow Am. Psychiatric Assn. (chmn. legal aspects of psychiatry com., 1948-51); mem. Soc. Med. Consultants World War II, Group for Advancement of Psychiatry (chmn. forensic com., 1946-49), Legal Aid Bur. (mem. bd.), lMd. Mental Hygiene Soc. (past pres.), Med. Chirurgical Faculty of Md. Author: Americas Last King (biography of King George III), 1941; Sex Offenses, 1951; Psychiatry and The Courts, 1951. Defense psychiatrist for Jack Ruby (called him insane), accused killer of Lee Harvey Oswald. Home: Stevenson, Md. Offices: 1109 Calvert St., Baltimore 2, also Court House, Baltimore 2. Died Nov. 7, 1966.

GUTTRIDGE, G(EORGE) H(ERBERT), univ. prof.; b. Hull, Eng., Aug. 6, 1898; s. Rev. Frederick William Hamilton and Eleanor Cowley (Peace) G.; B.A., Cambridge, Eng., 1920, M.A., 1924; m. Eleanor Mann, Dec. 27, 1928. Came to U.S., 1922. Scholar, St. John's Coll., Cambridge, 1919-21, Prince Consort Prizeman (Cambridge), 1922; lecturer in Brit. Empire history for Bd. of Mil. Studies, 1921-22, for economics tripos (Cambridge), 1923-24; Choate fellow, Harvard, 1922-23; asst. prof. history U. of Calif., 1925-31, asso. prof., 1931-42, prof. English history, 1942-58, Sather professor of history, 1958-64, emeritus, 1965-69. Served as 2d lt., later lt. Royal Garrison Arty., 1917-18. Fellow Royal Hist. Soc., Royal Commonwealth Soc.; mem. Hist. Assn. (London). Author books: (latest) English Whiggism and the American Revolution, 1942; Early Career of Lord Rockingham, 1952. Contbr. articles hist. jours. and Ency. Brit. (14th ed.). Editor: Burke Correspondence Vol. 3. Home: Carmel CA Died Jan. 7, 1969; buried Malvern Wells, Worcs England

GUYON, JAMES, JR. congressman; b. Richmond, N.Y., Dec. 24, 1778; s. James Guyon. Apptd. capt. 2d Squadron, 1st Cavalry Div., N.Y. Militia, 1807; mem. N.Y. State Assembly, 1812-14; promoted maj., 1814, col. 1st Regt. of Horse 1819; mem. U.S. Ho. of Reps. (Federalist) from N.Y., 16th Congress, Jan. 14, 1820-21; engaged in farming. Died Richmond, Mar. 9, 1846; buried St. Andrew's Cemetery, Richmond.

HAAN, WILLIAM GEORGE army officer; b. Crown Point, Ind., Oct. 4, 1863; s. Nicholas and Anna M. H.; grad. U.S. Mil. Acad., 1889, Army War Coll., 1905; m. Margaret H. Haan, Aug. 16, 1905. Commd. 2d lt. 1st Arty., June 12, 1889; trans. to 5th Arty., Jan. 29, 1891; 1st lt., Aug. 29, 1896; capt. actg. q.m. vols., Oct. 17, 1898; hon. disch. from vols., Mar. 23, 1901; capt. Arty. Corps, U.S.A., Feb. 2, 1901; maj., Apr. 9, 1907; lt. col. Coast Arty Corps, Dec. 6, 1911; col., July 1, 1916; brig. gen. N.A., Aug. 5, 1917. Served in Cuba and Philippines, 1898-1901; 3 times recommended for brevets "for conspicuous conduct in action"; served on Gen. Staff, 1903-06, 1912-14; was chief of staff Eastern Dept.; later mem. Panama Fortifications Bd. and Nat. Land Defense Bd.; apptd. comdr. 57th Field Arty. Brigade, Camp MacArthur, Tex., 1917, and 32d Div., N.G., Jan. 1918. Died Oct. 26, 1924.

HAAS, GUSTAV editor; b. Ludwigsburg, Wuerttemberg, Germany, July 14, 1861; s. Carl and Agnes (Binder) H.; ed. Gymnasium (Stuttgart), Royal Prussian Cadet Sch. (Berlin), War Sch. (Hanover); m. Iris Krueger, May 5, 1888; 1 son, Grant Carl. Became officer in German army, 1880; hon. disch. on application, 1883; came to U.S., 1883, natural citizen, 1890; draftsman constrn. dept. Pullman Palace Car Co., Pullman, Ill., writing also for German lang. newspapers; reporter Anzeiger, Cleveland, O., 1885; identified with Milwaukee Herold, 1886-, editor in chief, 1917-. Republican. Protestant. Author: A Book of Love (Ein Buch der Liebe), 1919. Home: Wauwatosa, Wis. Deceased.

HAAS, SAMUEL, oil co. exec.; b. Tiger Bend Plantation, Avoyelles Parish, La., Apr. 7, 1894; s. Dr. William David and Hattie (Haas) H.; B.S., Tulane U., 1915; student bus. adminstrn., Alexander-Hamilton Inst., 1923; m. Lulu Susan Haupt, July 10, 1920; children—Samuel Douglas, Joseph Marshall. Cotton buyer, bookkeeper W.D. Haas & Co., 1915-27; sec. Alexandria Compress Co., 1920-27; pres. Commercial Bank & Trust Co., 1928-33; postmaster, Alexandria, La., 1934-42; pres., gen. mgr. Avoyelles Who Gro Co., Ltd.; pres. Haas Investment Co., Inc., La. Central Land & Improvement Co., Inc., Haas Land Co., Ltd., Bunkie Lumber and Supply Company, Limited; vice president of Union Texas Natural Gas Corporation, and also Farmers Truck & Produce Co., Foster Gin Co., Coastal Hunting Club, Inc.; dir. Gen. American Oil Co. of Tex., La. & Ark. R.R. Co., Meeker Sugar Coop., Inc. Active A.R.C., Community Fund drives. Chmn civil def., Rapides Parish; commr. Alexandria Housing Authority, from 1940. Served from 2d lt. to 1st lt., F.A., U.S. Army, 1917-19; as maj. F.A., AUS, 1940-54. Decorated Verdun medal (France), 1919; recipient Red Cross of Constantine, Masonic Frat. Mem. Alexandria C. of C. (pres. 1942-43), Vets. Fgn. Wars (dep. comdr. La.-Miss. 1930-31), Am. Legion (comdr. 1923), 40 and 8, Officers Res. Corps (past pres. Alexandria), S.A.R., Wholesale Grocers Assn.(past dir., v.p.), La. Motor Transport Assn. (dir.), Nat. Postmasters Assn. (past pres. La.; nat. dir. 1934), Kappa Sigma. Methodist (steward). Mason (K.T., Shriner). Club: Alexandria Rotary (pres. 1930-31). Home: Alexandria LA Died Jan. 5, 1964; buried Hillcrest Cemetery, Dallas TX

HABERSHAM, ALEXANDER WYLLY naval officer, mcht.; b. N.Y.C., Mar. 24, 1826; s. Richard W. and Sarah (Elliott) H.; grad. U.S. Naval Acad., 1848; m. Jessie Steele, several children. Assigned to Pacific Squadron, U.S. Navy, 1848-50; served with Coast Survey, 1851-52; served in ship J. P. Kennedy in expdn. to North Pacific and China Seas as acting lt., 1853; assigned to John Hancock at Hong Kong, 1854; assigned to Phila. Navy Yard, 1855-57; assigned to ship Powhatan of East India Squadron, 1857-60, resigned to engaged in business in Japan; one of 1st Am. importers tea; returned to U.S., 1861, arrested as Southern sympathizer; became part owner firm Habersham & Barrett, importers and dealers in teas and East Indian goods, Balt., 1865; engaged in coffee and canned goods brokerage business, 1870-71-83. Author: My Last Cruise, or Where We Went and What We Saw, circa 1856. Died Annapolis, Md., Mar. 26, 1883.

HABERSHAM, JOHN Continental congressman; b. "Beverly" nr. Savannah, Ga., Dec. 23, 1754; s. James Habersham; attended Coll. of N.J. (now Princeton). Engaged as mcht.; served as 1st lt., brigade maj. 1st Ga. Regt., Continental Army during Revolutionary War, taken prisoner twice; mem. Continental Congress from Ga., 1785-86; apptd. Indian agt. by Gen Washington; commr. to Beaufort Conv. to adjust Ga.-S.C. boundary; mem. 1st bd. trustees U. Ga.; 1st sec. Ga. br. Soc. of Cincinnati; collector customs Port of Savannah, 1789-99. Died nr. Savannah, Dec. 17, 1799; buried Colonial Park Cemetery, Savannah.

HABERSHAM, JOSEPH patriot, postmaster gen.; b. Savannah, Ga., July 28, 1751; s. James and Mary (Bolton) H.; ed. Coll. of N.J. (now Princeton); m. Isabella Rae, May 1776, 10 children. An organizer firm Joseph Clay & Co., 1773; mem. Ga. Council of Safety, 1775, raised body of volunteers which captured Sir James Wright (Ga. gov.) and held him under guard in his own home for a month; mem. Ga. Provincial Congress, Savannah, July 4, 1775; commd. col. 1st Ga. Battalion, Continental Army; mem. Continental Congress, 1785-86; speaker Ga. Gen. Assembly, 1785-90; mem. Ga. Conv. which ratified U.S. Constn., 1788; mayor Savannah, 1792; postmaster-gen. U.S. under Presidents Washington, Adams and Jefferson, 1795-1801; pres. branch of Bank of U.S., 1802-15. Died Savannah, Nov. 17, 1815.

HACKER, NEWTON lawyer; b. in Green Co., Tenn., Mar. 3, 1936; s. Jacob and Sarah (Lloyd) H.; ed. public schs., Greene Co., Tenn., Tusculum Coll., Tenn., A.B., 1860; m. Antoinette Bradley, Oct. 3, 1867. Served in Union Army as pvt., 1st lt. and capt., Jan. 26, 1863-Aug., 1865; mustered out at Nashville, Tenn. Admitted to bar, 1866; mem. Tenn. legislature from Washington Co., Tenn., 1867; atty.-gen. for 1st Jud. Circuit, Tenn., 1870-78; circuit judge, same circuit, 8 yrs.; since then in practice of law at Jonesboro, Tenn. Was pres. 1st Nat.

Bank, Greenville, Tenn., several yrs. Presbyn. Republican. Address: Jonesboro, Tenn. Died Aug. 22, 1922.

HACKETT, FRANK D. army officer; b. Minn., Aug. 11, 1889; grad. Air Corps Tech. Sch., armament course, 1929. Engr. Sch., 1932, Tactical Sch., 1937. Served as 1st lt., aviation sect. Signal Officers Res. Corps, 1917-20; commd. pilot 1st lt. A.S., U.S. Army, 1920, advanced through the grades to brig. gen., 1945; ret. from USAF, 1948. Address: Hdqrs., USAF, Washington 25. Deceased.

HACKLEY, CHARLES ELIHU physician; b. Unadilla, N.Y., Feb. 22, 1836; s. Archbald and Eliza (Stott) H.; A.B., U. of Pa., 1856, later A.M., M.D., 1860; m. Emma Kent, of New York, Dec. 16, 1867, Surgeon 2d N.Y. Cav. and Surgeon-in-chief 3d cav. div., Army of Potomac, during Civil War. Physician to New York and Trinity hosps., New York Eye and Ear Infirmary. Mem. Loyal Legion. Translator: Stellwag on the Eye, 1866; Niemeyer's Practical Medicine, 1867; Billroth's Surgical Pathology, 1869. Address: S. Norwalk. Conn.

HADEN, RUSSELL LANDRAM med. educator; b. Palmyra, Va., May 22, 1888; s. Clifton James and Nicie Delima (Landram) H.; A.B., U. of Va., 1910, A.M., 1911; M.D., Johns Hopkins, 1915; m. Isabel McLeod Smith, Oct. 6, 1917; children-Russell Landram, James Coke. Resident house officer, Johns Hopkins Hosp., 1915-16; asst. resident physician, Henry Ford Hosp., Detroit, Mich., 1916-17; dir. of labs., same hosp., 1917-18, 1919-21; asso. prof. medicine, U. of Kan., 1921-23, prof. exptl. medicine, 1923-30; head of dept. medicine, Cleveland (O.) Clinic, 1930-49, ret. 1949, now consultant in medicine and research. First lt. Med. Corps, U.S. Army asst. chief med. service base hosp., Camp Lee, Va., 1918-19. Fellow Am. Coll. of Physicians; mem. A.M.A., Am. Assn. of Pathologists and Bacteriologists, Am. Soc. for Clin. Investigation, Am. Clin. and Climatol. Assn., Assn. Am. Physicians, Central Soc. for Clin. Research, Society for Experimental Medicine and Biology, American Society of Clinical Pathologists, Phi Beta Kappa, Sigma Xi, Theta Delta Chi, Nu Sigma Nu, Alpha Omega Alpha, Pithotomy, Rowfant and Pasteur clubs. Democrat. Methodist. Author: Clinical Laboratory Methods, 1923; Dental Infection and Systemic Disease, 1928; Principles of Hematology, 1939. Awarded gold medal by Radiol. Soc. America for contributions to dental roentgenology, 1929. Contbr. on diseases of the blood, focal infection and intestinal obstruction. Home: Brightberry Farm, Crozet, Va. Died Apr. 26, 1952; buried Monticello Meml. Park, Charlottesville, Va.

HADFIELD, BARNABAS BURROWS lawyer; b. Bklyn., May 31, 1906; s. Barnabas Burrows and Jane (McDermott) H.; A.B., Harvard, 1927; LL.B., Columbia, 1930; m. Mary Louise Haber, Nov. 9, 1945; children - Mary Jane, Alicia, Bridget. Admitted to N.Y. bar, 1932, since practiced in N.Y.C.; partner Hecht, Hadfield, Farbach & McAlpin, 1939-. Director of the Tidewater Oil Company, also Getty Realty Corp., Pacwest Realty Corp., Pacific Western Iran, Ltd. Served from 1st lt. to maj., USAAF, World War II. Decorated Legion of Merit Home: 929 Newfield Av., Stamford, Conn. Office: 11 Broadway, N.Y.C. 4. Died June 24, 1961; buried Longridge Union, North Stamford, Conn.

HADLEY, EDWIN MARSHALL b. Peoria, Ill., Oct. 14, 1872; s. of James Marshall and Margaret (Widenham) H.; eighth in lineal descent from Edward Fitz Randolph, from Nottinghamshire to New England, 1630; ed. Ill. Wesleyan and Northwestern units; m. Jessie Seymour McCarthy, June 21, 1904; children-James M., Edwin M., Jr., Raymond W. An organizer, 1898, of H. W. Dudley Coffee Co. and Ceylon Planters Tea Co., of which was sec., treas. and dir. until 1906; served as chmn. bd. Chicago-Cleveland Car Roofing Co., 1906-25, and as v.p. Pioneer Cast Steel Truck, Co., Sullivan Metallic Packing Co., Reliable Ry. Equipment Co. Lt. col. Ill. Nat. Guard; maj. Mil. Intelligence Res., U.S. Army; completed mil. intelligence course, Army War Coll., 1928; Ill. chmn. Civilian Aides Com., for enlistments, Army Air Forces, World War II. National president. The Paul Reveres, Inc.; member S.R., S.A.R., Order of Runnymede, Ill. Chamber Commerce, Chicago Assn. Commerce, American Coalition, American Alliance, Am. Legion, Beta Theta Pi (past pres. Chicago Alumni). Republican. Reformed Episcopalian. Mason (K.T., 32ff, Shriner). Sojourners, Grange. Clubs: Adventurers, Forty Chicago Athletic, Union League, Executives, So. Shore Country (Chicago); Army and Navy (Washington, D.C.); Green Lake Yacht; Authors' (London). Received Northwestern U. Alumni Merit Award "in recognition of worthy Achievement," 1945; Distinguished Service Citation, American Legion (Boone County), 1940. Author: Credenda, 1924; The Thoughtful Hour, 1925; Sinister Shadows, 1929; 1931; of the The Rape . - - Republic, 1935. Editor Revere sect. of Chicago Leader. Pub. speaker. Farmer Home: 690 Longwood Ave., Glencoe, Ill. Office: 11 S. LaSalle St., Chgo. Died Feb. 16, 1953; buried Rosehill Cemetery, Chgo.

HADLEY, ERNEST ELVIN psychiatrist; b. Alton, Kan., Aug. 2, 1894; s. John McCracken and Luella (Marshall) Hadley; S.B. in Medicine, U. Kan., 1918, M.D., 1920; m. Agnes Marie Hackerott, III), Virginia Lee (Mrs. Joseph D. Jeffrey). Arianne (Mrs. C. Stanley Lowell). Rotating interne Walter Reed U.S. Gen. Hosp., 1920-21; mem. psychiatric staff St. Elizabeth's Hosp., Wash., 1921-29; pvt. practice of psychiatry, 1929—. Director Washington-Baltimore Psychoanalytic Inst., 1949-52. Washington Psychoanalytic Institute, 1952—. Trustee and sec. William Alanson White Psychiat. Found., 1933-45; chmn. publs. com. and co-editor, Psychiatry, 1938-45; sec. Washington Sch. of Psychiatry, 1936-45, dir., 1936-43, dir. emeritus, 1943, fellow, 1943-45. Served as private, Enlisted Reserve Corps, U.S. Army, 1918; chmn. central examining board for neurology and psychiatry. Selective Service System, 1941; chmn. psychiatry panel, Army Induction Board, Fort Myer, Va., 1942-44. Mem. pub. health com. Washington Bd. of Trade. Fellow Am. Coll. Physicians, Am. Psychiat. Assn., George M. Kober Med. Soc. (pres. 1932-33). A.M.A.; mem. Am. Psychoanalytic Assn. (sec. 1930-36), Washington Soc. for Mental and Nervous Diseases (pres. 1930). Washington Psychopath. Soc. (pres. 1930), Psychopath Soc. (pres. 1930). Washington Psychopath. Soc. (pres. 1928), Washington Psychoanalytic Soc. (pres. 1933, 41, 53, 54—). Am. Sociol. Assn., Southern Psychiatric Assn., Am. Genetic Assn., N.Y. Acad. of Science, History of Science Soc., Phi Beta Pi. Contbr. to scientific publs. Home: 4304 Forest Lane, N.W., Washington 7. Office 1835 Eye St. N.W., Washington 6. Died Aug. 10, 1954.

HAGAN, JOHN CAMPBELL JR. investment banker; b. Richmond, Va., July 21, 1899; s. John Campbell and Alice (Nipe) H.; grad. McGuire's U. Sch., Richmond, Va., 1916; A.B., Va. Mil. Inst., 1921; m. Eliza Tabb Mason, Oct. 25, 1924; children-John Campbell, III, Anthony Mason. Tchr., asst. comdt. Castle Heights Mil. Acad., Lebanon, Tenn., 1921-22; security salesman Frederick E. Nolting, Inc., Richmond, 1922-24; v.p., mgr. investment dept. Grace Securities Corp., Richmond, 1926-29; pres., dir. Mason-Hagan, Inc., Richmond, 1929—; chmn. Eastern Life & Casualty Co., Richmond; dir. Va. Tel. & Tel. Co., Charlottesville, Va., P.C. Gwaltney, Jr. & Co., Inc., Smithfield, Va., S. H. Heironimus Co., Inc., Roanoke. Dir. Richmond Boys Club. Pres. George C. Marshall Research Found., Inc., Lexington, Va.; pres. Va. Mil. Inst. Found., 1943-46, dir., 1936—; bd. visitors Va. Mil. Inst., 1946-54, pres., 1952-54; trustee Sisters of Charity of St. Joseph Acad. and Orphan Asylum, v.p., 1942—. Served with USMC, 1918; as lt. col. USAAF, World War II. Decorated Bronze Star Medal. Mem. Investment Bankers Assn. Am. (v.p., exec. com. 1954-56), Nat. Assn. Securities Dealers (dist. chmn. 1950), Richmond C. of C. (dir. 1935—, pres. 1938), Richmond German Soc., Soc. Va. Creepers, Kappa Alpha. Clubs: Commonwealth (bd. govs.). Country of Va., Downtown (Richmond); Farmington Country (Charlottesville); City Mid-Day (N.Y.C.). Home: Weyanoke Farm, Charles City, Va. Office: 1110 E. Main St., Richmond 10, Va. Died Nov. 1959.

HAGGARD, WILLIAM DAVID surgeon; b. Nashville, Tenn., Sept. 28, 1872; s. William David and Jane (Douglass) H.; M.D., U. of Tenn., 1893; D.C.L.,U. of the South, 1931; m. Mary Laura Champe, Jan. 18, 1898 (died 1920); m. 2d, Lucile Holman, July 27, 1926. Practiced, 1893-; prof. gynecology and abdominal surgery, U. of Tenn., 1899-1912; prof. surgery and clin. surgery, Vanderbilt U. Med. Dept., 1913-; surgeon, president staff, St. Thomas Hosp.; visiting surgeon Vanderbilt U. Hosp. Served as major and lt. colonel Med. Corps, U.S.A.; surgeon Evacuation Hosp. No. 1, Toul, France, 1918-19, also consultant in surgery, Mesves Hosp. Center, France, Was chmn. med. sect. Council Nat. Defense, State of Tenn.; maj. and med. aide to gov. of Tenn.; mem. advisory bd. div. of surgery, Surgeon General's Office, Washington D.C. Fellow Am. Coll. Surgeons (regent; pres. 1933). Am. Surg. Assn. Democrat. Episcopalian. Home: Nashville, Tenn. Died Jan. 28, 1940.

HAGGERTY, MELVIN EVERETT psychologist; b. Bunker Hill, Ind., Jan. 17, 1875: s. John Wright and Phoebe Ellen (Hann) H.; A.B., Ind. U., 1902, A.M., 1907; student U. of Chicago, 1904; A.M., Harvard, 1909, Ph.D., 1910; m. Laura Caroline Garretson, June 26, 1902; children-Helen Ruth, Margaret Elizabeth (Mrs. Norman Anderson), William James. Teacher in high schs. Indiana and Massachusetts, 1902-09; asst. in philosophy, Harvard, Radcliffe, 1909-10: asst. prof. and prof. psychology, Ind. U., 1910-15; prof. ednl. psychology, U. of Minn., 1915-; lecturer on ednl. psychology, Teachers Coll. (Columbia), 1917; dean Coll. of Education, U. of Minn., 1920. Maj. Sanitary Corps, U.S. Army, Jan. 1918-Mar. 1919; stationed in Surgeon, Gen.'s Office and identified with reëducation of disabled soldiers; lt. col. O.R.C. Dir. div. of tests and measurements, Va. Edn. Commn., 1919; same, North Carolina Sch. Survey, 1920; N.Y. State School Survey, 1921; chmn. U. of Minn. Com. on Edn. Research, 1924-. Mem. bd. of trustees College of St. Catherine. Democrat. Conglist. Mason. Home: Minneapolis, Minn. Died Oct. 6, 1937.

HAGOOD, JOHNSON army officer, gov. S.C.; b. Barnwell County, S.C., Feb. 21, 1829; s. James O. and Indina (Allen) H.; grad. The Citadel, Charleston, S.C., 1847; m. Eloise Butler, Nov. 21, 1856. Admitted to S.C. bar, 1850; master in equipt Barnwell County, 1851-61; dep. adj. gen. S.C. Militia, circa 1850; served as col. 1st Regt. of S.C. under Gen. Beauregard in capture of Ft. Sumter, 1861; commd. brig. gen. Confederate Army, 1862, serving in defense of coast and siege of Morris Island; comdr. 1st brigade Gen. R.F. Hokes div. Anderson's Corps, Army of No. Va., 1864, served in battles of Walthall Junction, Swift Creek, Drewry's Bluff, Cold Harbor, the Burmuda Hundred; served under Beauregard in defense of Petersburg, 1864; 1st pres. S.C. Agrl. and Mech. Soc., 1869; v.p. S.C. Democratic Conv., 1876; comptroller-gen. S.C., 1876-80; gov. S.C., 1880-82; chmn. S.C. Bd. of Agr., twice; chmn. bd. visitors The Citadel, 14 years. Died Barnwell, S.C., Jan. 4, 1898.

HAGOOD, JOHNSON army officer; b. Orangeburg, S.C., June 16, 1873; s. Lee H.; nephew of Brig. Gen. Johnson Hagood, Confederate Army, and governor of South Carolina; student Univ. of S.C., 1888-91, LL.D., 1921; grad. U.S. Mil. Acad., 1896; m. Jean Gordon Small, Dec. 14, 1899; children-Jean Gordon (wife of Adm. J. L. Holloway, U.S.N.), Johnson (U.S. Army), Francesca (wife of A. B. Packard, U.S. Army). Commd. add. 2d lt. 2d Artillery, June 12, 1896; promoted through grades to brig. gen. N.A., Apr. 12, 1918; brig. gen. U.S. Army, July 3, 1920 (recess apptmt. exp. Mar. 4, 1921), reapptd. Apr. 27, 1921; maj. gen. Aug. 2, 1925. Garrison duty in R.I., Conn. and S.C., 1896-1901; instr. dept. of philosophy, U.S. Mil. Acad., 1901-04; asst. to chief of arty., Washington, D.C., 1905-07; mem. Gen. Staff Corps, 1908; a.d.c. Maj. Gen. J. F. Bell, 1908-10; asst. to Maj. Gen. Leonard Wood, re-detail to Gen. Staff Corps until 1912; comdr. Ft. Flagler, Wash., 1912-13; in Philippines, 1913-15; various commands, coast defense, 1915-17, detailed as commander of 7th regt. 1st Expeditionary Brigade, Coast Arty. Corps, July 16, 1917. Arrived in France, Sept. 11, 1917; duty in battlefield nr. Soissons, Sept.-Oct; organized and in comd. advance sect. Line of Communications, A.E.F., Oct. 24; in comd. Neufchateau, Nov. 1-Dec. 1; chief of staff, Line of Communications, Dec. 2; Gen. Staff, A.E.F., Jan. 10, 1918; pres. of bd. that reorganized A.E.F. staff and created S.O.S.; chief of staff S.O.S., until Armistice; rep. Am. Army in replying to address of Marshal Joffre, Paris, May 12,1918; in battle sectors along Am., French, and British fronts, June-July 1918; Meuse-Argonne offensive, Oct. 1918; designated by comdr. in chief ot be maj. gen. N.A., Oct. 20, 1918, but apptmt. failed on account of Armistice; apptd. comdr. 20th C.A. Brigade, Nov. 10, trans. to 66th F.A. Brigade, Nov. 24; crossed Raine River Dec. 31, 1918, and estab. hdqrs. at Hohr, Germany; comd. army arty. of 3d Army and corps arty. of 3d Corps until Apr. 10, 1919; sailed for U.S., May 16, 1919; assigned to comd. 30th Brigade (Ry.), C.A.C., and Camp Eustis, Va., Nov. 24, 1919; comd. South Atlantic Coast Arty. Dist., Nov. 1920-Sept. 1921; apptd. comdr. Camp Stotsenburg, P.I., Feb. 1, 1922, 2d Coast Arty. Dist., Ft. Totten, N.Y., Aug. 1924, 45h Corps Area, Oct. 5, 1925-Mar. 1927; comdg. Philippine Div., Apr. 25, 1927-June 22, 1929; comdg. 7th Corps Area Aug. 26, 1929-Oct. 2, 1933, 4th Army, Aug. 9, 1932-Oct. 2, 1933, 3d Army and 8th Corps Area, 1933-36, 2d Army and 5th Corps Area, May 1, 1936; retired, May 31, 1936. Decorated with Distinguished Service Medal, Jan. 9, 1919; Comdr. Legion of Honor (French), 1919; Comdr. Order of Crown of Italy; Grand Officer Order of the Sacred Treasure (Japanese). Member United Confederate Vets., Soc. of the Cincinnati, Am. Legion. Episcopalian. Rotarian (hon.), Clubs: Army and Navy (Washington), D.C.); Army and Navy of Manila (past pres.), Charleston. Devised Hagood tripod mount, mortar deflection board, and other apparatus connected with sea-coast defense. Author: The Services of Supply-A Memory of the Great War, 1927; We Can Defend America, 1937; Soldiers Handbook; Meet Your Grandfather, 1946; General Wood as I Knew Him, Closing the Gap in National Defense, I Had a Talk with the President (Saturday Evening Post) and other articles in leading mags. and newspapers. Home: Charleston, S.C.; also San Antonio, Tex. Died Dec. 22, 1948.

HAHN, CONRAD VELDER consulting engr.; b. Phila., Pa., May 9, 1890; s. John G. and Elizabeth (Velder) H.; B.S., U. of Pa., 1908, M.E., 1912; studied Temple U. (Phila.), D.Eng., Ph.D.; U. of San José (Costa Rica), Oxford U. (Eng.); married. Consulting practice, 1910-; mng. dir. The Hahn Co. (cons. engrs.); dir. and asso. engr. Internat. Development Co., Washington, D.C.; cons. mech. engr. Turbo Motor Co., East Radford, Va.; mem. N. T. Whitaker & Co., Washington, D.C.; mem. faculty, civ. engring, dept., Temple U., 1912-14; 1910-12, and of mech. engring. dept. U. of Pa., 1912-14; dir. mech. engring. dept. of evening schs., Drexel Inst., Phila., 1919-. 1st lt. and capt. Ordnance Dept., U.S.A., 1917-19; maj. Ordnance R.C.; spl. mention for tech. service, Am. Ordnance Base Depot, France, and Aberdeen Proving Ground, Scotland, World War. Mason. Republican. Baptist. Home: Aberdeen, Md. Died Dec. 3, 1933.

HAIGHT, CHARLES congressman; b. Colts Neck, N.J., Jan. 4, 1838; grad. Princeton, 1857; studied law. Admitted to N.J. bar, 1861, began practice in Freehold; mem. N.J. Assembly, 1860-62, speaker, 1861-62; commd. brig. gen. N.J. Militia, 1861; in command of Camp Vredenburgh, 1862-65; organized, equipped 14th, 28th, 29th N.J. regts.; mem. U.S. Ho. of Reps. (Democrat) from N.J., 40th-41st congresses, 1867-71; resumed law practice; chmn. N.J. delegation; Dem. Nat.

Conv., Balt., 1872; apptd. prosecutor of pleas; pres. atty. Monmouth County (N.J.), 1873-91. Died Freehold, Aug. 1, 1891; buried Maplewood Cemetery, Freehold.

HAINES, HENRY CARGILL officer U.S.M.C.; b. Ft. Leavenworth, Kan., Nov. 19, 1859; s. Brig. Gen. T. J. (U.S.A.) and Anne Hays (Cargill) H.; grad. U.S. Naval Acad., 1881; m. Emma Burgers, Mar. 26, 1887; children-Thomas B., John Meade; m. 2d, Helen Rockwell, Mar. 28, 1898; children-Henry R., Barbara, Helen. Apptd. 2d lt. U.S.M.C., July 1, 1883; promoted through grades to brig. gen., Jan. 14, 1920; retired 1923. In charge office of asst. adj. and insp., San Francisco, Calif., 1903-05, Berkeley, Calif., 1906; duty Marine Corps Hdqrs., 1908-12; Pacific Inspection Dist., San Francisco, 1912-14; placed in charge asst. adj. and inspector's dept., San Francisco, Apr. 1, 1914. Republican. Episcopalian. Home: Berkeley, Calif. Died Aug. 8, 1926.

HAINS, PETER CONOVER army officer; b. Phila., Pa., July 6, 1840; s. Reuben P. and Amanda M. H.: grad. U.S. Mil. Acad., 1861; m. Virginia P., d. Admiral Jenkins, U.S.N., Nov. 1864. Second and 1st lt. 2d Arty., June 24, 1861; transferred to topog. engrs., July 24, 1862, to engr. corps, Mar. 3, 1863; capt., July 18, 1863; maj., Sept. 22, 1870; lt. col., Sept. 16, 1886: col., Aug. 13, 1895; brig. gen. vols., May 27-Nov. 30, 1898; brig. gen. U.S.A., Apr. 21, 1903. Bvtd.: capt., May 27, 1862, "for gallant and meritorious services" in battle of Hanover C.H., Va.; maj., July 4, 1863, for same during siege of Vicksburg; lt. col., Mar. 13, 1865, for same during the war. Served as engr. of numerous works of harbor and river improvement: as engr. sec. Lighthouse Bd.; as engr. in charge charge Potomac Flats improvement, Washington; as engr. of numerous works of harbor defense; as mem. Bd. of Ordnance and Fortifications; as mem. Nicaragua Canal Commn., 1897-99, and as mem. of Isthmian Canal Commn., 1899-1903; retired from active service in army, July 6, 1904. Mem. Isthmian Canal Commn. (constructing commn.), 1905-07. Apptd. maj. gen. U.S.A., Nov. 1, 1916, under a special act of Congress; assigned to active duty, Sept. 18, 1917, as engr. Norfolk Harbor and River Dist.; div. engr. Eastern Div., May 28-Sept. 2, 1918, when returned to retired list. Died Nov. 7, 1921.

HAISLIP, WADE HAMPTON, army officer; b. Woodstock, Va., July 9, 1889; s. Reuben Drake and Etta (Heller) H.; B.S., U.S. Mil. Acad., 1912; student Infantry Sch., 1923-24, Command and Gen. Staff Sch., 1924-25, Ecole Superieure de Guerre, 1925-27, Army War Coll., 1931-32; m. Alice Jennings Shepherd, July 14, 1932. Commd. 2 lt., June 12, 1912; promoted through grades to general, 1949; served in Vera Cruz, Mexico, 1914; with A.E.F. and Am. Forces in Germany, 1917-21, successively with Gen. Staff, 5th Corps, Div. Machine Gun Officer, 3d Div., Gen. Staff, Am. Forces in Germany; participated in defensive operations in the Vosges, St. Mihiel and Meuse-Argonne operations; instr. U.S. Mil. Acad., 1921-23; asst. exec. Office of Asst. Sec. of War, 1928-31; instr. Command and Gen. Staff Sch., 1932-36; with 29th Inf., 1936-38; in Budget and Legislative Planning Branch, War Dept. Gen. Staff, 1938-41, asst. chief of staff for personnel, 1941; commanded 85th Inf. Div. Apr. 1942-Feb. 20, 1943; commanded XV Corps throughout campaigns of Normandy, Northern France, Ardennes, Rhineland, Central Europe; comd. 7th Army, June-Aug., 1945. Pres., Sec. of War's Personnel Bd., Sept. 1945-April 1946; sr. mem. Chief of Staff's adv. group, 1946-48; dep. chief of staff for adminstrn., 1948-49, vice chief of staff 1949-51; retired from active service, 1951; gov. U.S. Soldiers Home, 1951-66. Awarded Victory medal with 3 bars, Mexican Service medal, D.S.M. with 3 Oak Leaf Clusters, Legion of Merit, Bronze Star with oak leaf cluster, Legion of Honor (grand officer), Croix de Guerre with Palm. Clubs: Army and Navy (Washington); Army and Navy Country (Va.). Home: Washington DC Died Dec. 23, 1971; buried Arlington Nat. Cemetery, Arlington VA

HAKANSSON, ERIK GOSTA naval officer; b. Sweden, Sept. 4, 1886; came to U.S., 1909, naturalized, 1915; M.D., U. of Ill., 1915; grad. Naval Med. Sch., Washington, 1917, Gorgas Memorial Laboratory, 1937; m. Dorothy Elizabeth Dorset, June 20, 1942. Interne Cook County (Ill.) Hosp., 1915-17; commd. lt. Med. Corps, U.S. Navy, 1917, advanced through the grades to capt., 1941; comdg. Naval Med. Research Inst., Bethesda, Md., 1943-48; ret. Mem. AS. Am. Assn. Tropical Medicine, Acad. Tropical Medicine, Phi Chi, Alpha Omega Alpha. Club: Army-Navy Country (Washington). Home: R, 10, Richmond, Va. Office: Naval Medical Research Institute, Bethesda, Md. Died June 19, 1950; buried Arlington Nat. Cemetery.

HALBERSTADT, BAIRD engineer, geologist: b. Pottsville, Pa., Jan. 26, 1860; s. Andrew Howell (M.D.) and Augusta Mary (Baird) H.; U. of Pa.; Internat. Inst., Paris, France: m. Ida Ray Smith, Oct. 15, 1918; children-Lesley Richards, Anne Josephine. Aid, Geol. Survey of Pa., 1881-86; engr. and supt. Tazewell Coal & Iron Co., 1887; asst. to Dr. Charles A. Ashburner, coal expert, 1889; spl. agt. and expert, 11th U.S. Census, 1889-91; asst. geologist, Pa. Geol. Survey, 1891-93; spl. tech. corr. and representative mining jours., 1893-98; geol. expert for large coal cos. before important commns. and in local cts., 1902: consulting geologist, State Bd. Agr., 1909-19. Capt. Signal and Telegraph Corps, attached (but not mustered) Pa. N.G., 1893-95; 1st lt. and insp. 4th Regt. Inf., 1897; 1st lt. and regimental q.m. 4th Regt., 1898; 1st lt. and regimental q.m. Pa. Inf. U.S.V., Spanish-Am. War, 1898; capt. and regimental q.m. 4th Reg. Pa. N.G., 1899; maj. and a.d.c. on staff nat. comdr. Soc. P.R. Expdn. Mem. Advisory Commn. for Preservation of Pub. Records of Pa., 1918; chmn. Local (state) Armory Bd., 1916-22. Federal fuel adminstr. for Schuylkill Co., 1917-19; chmn. com. on materials and mem. com. on mil. of Com. Pub. Safety of Pa. Republican. Episcopalian. Home: Pottsville, Pa. Died Sept. 13, 1934.

HALDERMAN, JOHN A. soldier, diplomatist; b. in Ky., April 15, 1838; s. Dr. John A. and Susan Henderson (Rogers) H.; academic edn. (LL.D., Highland Univ., Kan.). Private sec. to 1st gov. of Kan.; judge probate court; mayor of Leavenworth; mem. both houses Kan. legislature. Served in Union army in Civil war as maj. and as maj. gen.; named in General Orders and Official Report for "Conspicuous Gallantry" in action; was U.S. consul, Bangkok, Siam, 1880; later consul gen., and 1882-85, minister resident in Siam. Received decorations from Kings of Siam and Cambodia and French govt. for services to civilization in Far East. Deceased.

HALE, EDWARD JOSEPH diplomatic service; b. "Haymount," near Fayetteville, N.C., Dec. 25, 1839; s. Edward J. and Sarah Jane (Walker) H.; A.B., U. of N.C., 1860 (LL.D., 1910); m. Maria Rhett Hill, Jan. 15, 1861; 2d Caroline Green Mallett, Dec. 5, 1905. A propr. and editor Fayetteville Observer, 1860-65; served pvt. to maj. and asst. adj. gen., of gen. staff, C.S.A., his last promotion being for "conspicuous gallantry and merit"; reestablished Fayetteville Observer, 1882; Am. consul at Manchester, Eng., 1885-89; presented with an "illuminated address" by leading men of England, 1889; v.p. Internat. Congress on Internal Navigation, 1800; commr. Manchester Ship Canal in N. America, 1800-91; dir. a founder. Nat. Rivers and Harbors Congress, 1899-1913; E.E. and M.P. to Costa Rica, June 21, 1913-21; detained in the U.S. by exec. order on account of revolution in Costa Rica. Trustee U. of N.C. (exec. com.). Home: Fayetteville, N.C. Died Feb. 15, 1922.

HALE, HARRY CLAY army officer; b. at Knoxville, Ill., July 10, 1861; s. T. J. and Sarah (Pierce) H.; grad. U.S. Mil. Acad., 1883, LL.D., Knox Coll., 1924; m. Elizabeth C. Smith, Dec. 2, 1886. Commd. 2d lt., June 13, 1883, and promoted through grades to col., Mar. 26, 1915; trans to China in command of 15th Inf., Nov. 30, 1915; brig. gen. R.A., 1917; maj. gen. N.A., Aug. 5, 1917. At Ft. Sully, S.D., in charge Sioux Indian prisioners of war, Jan.-June 1891; a.d.c. to Brig. Gen. Wesley Merritt, at St. Paul, Chicago, and Governor's Island, N.Y., 1893-99; adj. gen. and actg. aide to Maj. Gen. Wesley Merritt during Manila campaign, 1898; batt. comdr. 44th U.S. Vols., Philippine Insurrection, 1899-1902; comd. Bilibid Prison, Manila, 1902; acting batt. comdr. 20th U.S. Inf., Luzon Campaign, 1902; duty Gen. Staff, 1903-06; again in Philippines, 1906-09; adj. gen. Dept. of the Lakes, 1909-10, Dept. of Mo. 1910-11; Apptd. Comdr. Camp Zachary Taylor, Louisville, Ky., Sept. 1917; Comdr. 84th Div. AEF, in French, 1918; after armistace comdr. Combat Div. 26th; comdg. 2nd Brigade AF in Germany, Dec. 17, 1922-Feb. 3, 1922, promoted maj. gen., Nov. 2, 1921; comd. 1st Div., US Army, Camp Dix, N.J., Feb.-Dec. 1922; comd. 6th Corps area Chicago, 1922-25; retired, July 10, 1925. Awarded D.S.M., 1920. Home: Rockville, Md. Died Mar. 20, 1946.

HALE, IRVING brigadier-general U.S.V.; b. N. Bloomfield, N.Y., Aug. 28, 1861; s. Horace Morrison and Eliza (Huntington) H.; went to Colo., 1865; ed. common and high schs. in Colo.; grad. U.S. Mil. Acad., 1884, with the highest rank ever made at the acad. (2070.4 out of a possible 2075); (E.E., Colo. Sch. Mines, 1895); (LL.D., U. of Colo., 1899); m. Mary Virginia, d. Lt.-Col. William R. King, U.S.A., June 14, 1887. Second lt. Engr. Corps, June 15, 1884; 1st lt., Sept. 16, 1886; resigned, Apr. 1, 1890. Won 1st div. gold medal and 1st skirmish medal in div. of Atlantic rifle competition, 1888. Instr. engring. U.S. Mil. Acad., 1888-89; elec. engr. Colo. State Sch. of Mines, 1895; now mgr. and elec. engr. Gen. Electric Co. at Denver, Col. 1st Colo. Inf., May 1, 1898; brig.-gen. vols., Aug. 13, 1898, for "gallant and distinguished services"; comd. 2d Brigade, 2d Div., 8th Army Corps, at Manila, and comd. same in Filipino campaigns until return of vols., July, 1899; wounded, Meycauayan, Mar. 26, 1899; recommended for bvt. maj.-gen. for "gallant and meritorious services throughout campaign against Filipino Insurgents; particularly for skill, zeal and courage in conducting operations of his brigade from Malolos to Calumpit"; hon. discharged Oct. 1, 1899. Pres. Nat. Soc., Army of the Philippines, 1901-03 (life mem. exec. com.). Pres. Colo. Soc. S.A.R., 1899-1902 (v.p.-gen. Nat. Soc.), Colo. Scientific Soc., 1902. Denver Charter Conv., 1903. Contbr. on elec. subjects to scientific socs. and mags. Home: 1430 Franklin St., Denver, Colo.

HALE, MORRIS SMITH college dean and registrar; b. Albany, Ga., Sept. 7, 1895; s. Frank Simmons and Mary Anna (Morgan) H.; student Emory U., 1914-17; B.S., Peabody Coll., Nashville Tenn., 1928, A.M., 1931; m. Alice Lois Sellers, Aug. 20, 1919; children-Morris Smith, Robert Frank, James Morgan. Teacher pub. schs., Lee County, Ga., 1915-16; prin. high sch., Morven, Ga., 1916-17, city supt., 1918-20; supt. schs., Gore, Ga., 1920-24; pres. Sparks (Ga.) Jr. Coll., 1924-26; supt. schs., Arlington, Ga., 1926-31; supervisor, Tampa pub. schs., 1931-32, city supt., 1932-34; dean and bus. mgr., U. of Tampa, 1934-40, acting pres., 1936-37; dean and registrar, Orlando Jr. Coll., since 1941. Commd. 2d lt., U.S. Army, serving in World War, 1917. Home: 1207 Hillcrest, Orlando, Fla. Died Dec. 16, 1948.

HALE, WILLIS H. army officer; b. Kan., Jan. 7, 1893; grad. Army Signal Sch., 1920, Air Service Primary Flying Sch., 1923, advanced Flying Sch., 1923, Air Corps Tactical Sch., 1928, Command and Gen. Staff Sch., 1934, Army War Coll., 1937; rated command pilot, combat observer. With Philippine Constabulary, 1913-17; commd. 2d lt. Inf., Mar. 1917, and advanced through the grades to brig. gen., Jan. 1942, maj. gen., June 1942; served as lt. and capt. Inf., World War I; with Signal Corps, 1920-22; AS, 1922-39; Insp. Gen. Dept., 1939-40; AS since 1940; comdr. Hawaiian Bombardment Command which bombed the Jap naval force at Midway Islands, June 1942 and Central Pacific campaign since 1943; apptd. comdr. Army Air Forces, Pacific Ocean areas, Mar. 1945. Awarded D.S.M., Navy Cross, Legion of Merit, D.F.C., Air medal. Address: A.P.O. 234, San Francisco. Died Mar. 1961.

HALEY, ANDREW GALLAGHER lawyer; b. Tacoma, Nov. 19, 1904; s. Christopher Joseph and Kathleen Rose (Gallagher) H.; LL.B., Georgetown U., 1928; A.B., George Washington U., 1934; m. Delphine Delacroix, Dec. 1, 1934 (dec. Apr. 1963); children - Delphine, Andrew Gallagher. Admitted to D.C. bar, 1928, Wash. bar, 1929; pvt. law practice, Tacoma, 1929-33; counsel Fed. Radio Commn. and FCC, 1933-39; practicing lawyer, Washington, since 1939; sr. mem. firm Haley, Bader & Potts; gen. counsel Internat. Astronautical Fedn.; counsel Am. Inst. Aeros. and Astronautics; co-founder, pres., dir. Aerojet Engring. Corp., Pasadena and Azusa, Calif., 1942-45; pres., dir. Kagh, Inc., Pasadena, 1947-50; v.p., dir. Axe Sci. and Electronics Fund; adviser U.S. Senate Spl. Com. investigating Nat. Def. Program, 1945-46; legal advisor Internat. Telecommunications Conf., Atlantic City, 1947, 4th Inter Am. Radio Conf., Washington, 1949; industry adv. 3d N. Am. Regional Broadcasting Conf., Montreal, 1949, Havanna, Cuba, 1950; Am. Rocket Soc. del. to 2d Internat. Congress Astronautics, London, 1951, 3d Stuttgart, 1952, 4th, Zurich, 1953 5th Innsbruck, 1954, 6th Copenhagen, Denmark, 1955, 7th Rome, 1956, Barcelona, Spain, 1957, Amsterdam, 1958, London, 1959, Stockholm, 1960, Washington, 1961, Varna, 1962, Paris, 1963, Warsaw, 1964. Academician Acad. Astronautics; dir., gen. counsel Internat. Inst. Space Law. Served as maj. Judge Adv. Gen. Dept., Air Forces, 1942. Recipient Am. Rocket Soc. award, 1954; Grotius award, Munich, 1958. Fellow Brit. Interplanetary Soc. (medal outstanding contbrs. astronautics 1962), S. African Interplanetary Soc., Canadian Astronautical Soc. (hon.); hon. mem. Schweizerische Astronautische Arbeitsgemeinschaft, Astronautical Soc. Rep. of China; hon. corr. mem. Institut Francisco Vitoria; hon. counsellor Sociedade Interplanetaria Brasileira; mem. Soc. Comparative Legislation and Internat. Law; Internat. Astronautical Fedn. (pres. 1958-59) Inst. Aero Scis., Soc. Motion Picture and TV Engrs., Broadcast Pioneers, Am. Television Soc., Am. (vice chmn. com. space law), D.C., Internat., Inter-Am., Fed., FCC bar assns., Am. Rocket Soc. (pres. 1954, dir.). Clubs: Nat. Press, Aero, Congressional Country (Washington); Washington State Press, Nat. Aviation. Author legal articles; Rocketry and Space Exploration, 1958; Space Law and Government, 1963 (G. Edward Pendray award 1964). Home: 1026 16th St. N.W. Office: 1735 DeSales St., Washington 6. Died Sept. 10, 1966; buried Arlington Nat. Cemetery.

HALFORD, ELIJAH WALKER lt. col.; b. Nottingham, Eng., Sept. 4, 1843: s. Elijah and Maria Ann (Walker) H.: ed. pub. schs., Hamilton, O., and at acad., Newtown, O., nr. Cincinnati; became printer, journalist, Indianapolis, Ind.; m. Mary Frances Armstrong, May 1, 1866 (dec.). Edited Indianapolis Journal; then was editorial founder Chicago Inter-Ocean, Mar. 1872, to Nov. 1893; returned to Indianapolis Journal and was again its editor until 1889; pvt. sec. to President Benjamin Harrison, Mar. 1889-Mar. 4, 1893; apptd. maj. p.-m. U.S.A., Jan. 10, 1893; disbursing officer Bering Sea Arbitration Commn., Paris, 1893; lt. col. deputy p.-m. gen., Sept. 13, 1906; retired by operation of law, Sept. 4, 1907. Mem. M.E. Ch.; v. chmn. exec. com. Interdenominational and chmn. Meth. Laymen's Missionary Movement. Internat. Com. Y.M.C.A. Home: Leonia, N.J. Died Feb. 27, 1938.

HALL, CHARLES BADGER major gen. U.S.A.; b. at Portland, Me., Apr. 29, 1844; s. Charles Henry and Caroline (Page) H.; grad. Portland High Sch., 1862; widower. Commd. 2d lt. 25th Me. Vol. Inf., Sept. 29, 1862; 1st lt., Mar. 6, 1863: hon. mustered out July 10, 1863; 1st lt. 30th Me. Vol. Inf., Jan. 1, 1864; hon. mustered out, Sept. 2, 1865; apptd. to U.S.A. from Me., 2d lt. 28th Inf., Jan. 22, 1867; promoted through grades to maj. gen., Mar. 28, 1908. Bvtd.; 1st lt., Mar. 2, 1867, "for gallant and meritorious services" Battle of Sabine Cross Roads, La.; capt., Mar. 2, 1867, for same in battle of Pleasant Hill, La. Commandant Inf. and Car. Sch., Signal Sch. and Army Staff Coll., Aug. 21, 1906-Apr. 29, 1908. Episcopalian. Mason. Died May 11, 1914.

HALL, CHARLES PHILIP ret. army officer; b. Sardis, Miss., Dec. 12, 1886; s. James Gatlin and Isabel Thornton H.; student Jefferson Mil. Coll., Natchez, 1900-04, U. of Miss., 1905-07; B.S., U.S. Mil. Acad., 1911; grad. Advanced Course, Inf Sch., 1924; distinguished grad. Command and Gen. Staff Sch., 1925; grad. Army War Coll., 1930; m. Isabel Durand Mayor, Oct. 20, 1920; 1 dau., Gail Thornton. Commd. 2d lt., U.S. Army, 1911; advanced through the grades to lt. gen., 1945. Served in U.S. Army in U.S. and Philippines; with 2d Div. in France and Germany in World War I; with 3d Div., Fort Lewis, Wash., 1941; comdg., gen. 93d Inf. Div., 1942; comdg. XI corps, S.W. Pacific, 1942 until ret.; service in New Guinea and Luzon. Decorated D.S.M. with oak leaf cluster, 1945; D.S.C., silver star with three oak leaves, Bronze Star Medal, Purple Heart. Legion of Honor, Croix de Guerre, Victory medal with 5 clasps. Mem. Phi Delta Theta. Club: Army and Navy (Washington). Died Jan. 26, 1953; buried Fort Sam Houston Nat. Cemetery, San Antonio.

HALL, DANIEL lawyer; b. Barrington, N.H., Feb. 28, 1832; s. Gilman and Eliza (Tuttle) H.; A.B., Dartmouth, 1854; read law with Hon. D. M. Christie, Dover, N.H.; admitted to N.H. bar, 1860: m. Sophia Dodge, Jan. 25, 1877. Capt. and a.-d.-c. Union Army, 1862-64; served in army of Potomac, participating in its battles, 1862-63; provost marshal 1st N.H. dist., 1864, 1865; pres. N.H. Rep. State Conv., 1873; chmn. N.H. Rep. State Com., 1874-78; chmn. N.H. delegation Rep. Nat. Conv., 1876; maj. and judge-advocate N.H. militia, 1875; law reporter, N.H. Supreme Ct., 1875-76; naval officer, Port of Boston, 1877-86. Dir. Strafford Nat. Banks; trustee Strafford Savings Bank. Trustee Berwick Acad., Dover Pub. Library, Wentworth Home for the Aged (chmn. bd.), Wentworth Hosp. (all of Dover); mgr. N.H. Soldiers' Home, Tilton, N.H., 1888-1907. Republican. Home: Dover, N.H. Died 1920.

HALL, ELMER EDWARDS marine corps officer (ret.); b. Rocky Bar, Ida., Apr. 20, 1890; s. Joseph N. and Louise (Lovell) H.; E.M., U. of Ore.; student Ore. State Coll., 1 yr.; m. Emma B. Wootton, Feb. 14, 1918; 1 dau., Nancy Louise (wife of Comdr. E. J. Pawka) Began as miner in Eastern Ore.; commd. 2d lt., USMC, 1917, and advanced through grades to brig. gen., 1942; ret., 1946. Mem. Sigma Nu. Home: 6203 Waverly Av., La Jolla, Cal. Died Sept. 1958.*

HALL, GEORGE ELISHA lawyer; b. May 10, 1870; s. Elisha and Mary (Hayden) H.; grad. high sch., New Haven; LL.B., Yale, 1894; D.P.E., Arnold Coll., New Haven, 1929; m. Harriet F. Blakeslee, Dec. 4, 1908; children-William Blakeslee, George Elisha. Practiced in New Haven since 1894; served as alderman; city atty., judge of City Court, and chmn. Zoning Bd. of Appeals, New Haven; mem. Conn. State Senate, 1925-29, also Tuberculosis Commn. of Conn. Secretary, dir. New Haven Trap Rock Co., Branford Steam R.R. Co., Wilcox Crittenden & Co. Formerly pres. and trustee Arnold Coll. for Hygiene and Physical Education. Enlisted as private Conn. Nat. Guard, 1896, and advanced through grades to brig. gen.; served on Mexican border; lt. col. U.S. Army, 1917-19; col. U.S. Inf. Res., May 1, 1926; regt. comdt. 417th Inf., 1926-34, retired 1934; inactive reserve, 1934-41. Mem. Am. Bar Assn., Conn. State and County of New Haven bar assns., Internat. Law Assn., Am. Judicature Soc., Acad. of Polit. Science, Am. Museum of Natural History, New Haven Colony Hist. Soc., Edgewood Civic Assn., English-Speaking Union, National Travel Club, American National Red Cross, American Legion, Military Order World War (past comdr.), Yankee Division Vets. Assn., Reserve Officers Assn. of U.S. Republican. Universalist. Mason (32ff). Odd Fellow, Woodman. Clubs: Graduate (New Haven); Waterbury (Conn.). Home: 1 West Park Av. Office: 718 Second Nat. Bank Bldg., New Haven, Conn. Died Feb. 4, 1944.

HALL, HENRY newspaper corr.; b. Edmondsley, Eng., Oct. 13, 1851; s. John and Mary Anne (Elstob) H.; came to America with parents in infancy; ed. common schs., Pa.; unmarried. Sch. teacher, 1876-78; editor and part propr., Mercer (Pa.) Dispatch, 1881-89; editorial writer Pittsburgh Commercial Gazette, 1884-85; legislative corr., Pittsburgh Dispatch, 1891; Washington corr. Pittsburgh Times, 1893-1906, Pittsburgh Chronicle-Telegraph, 1907-. Recorder of deeds, Mercer Co., Pa., 1879-82; mem. Pa. Ho. of Rep., from Mercer Co., 1887, 89, from Pittsburgh, 1901. Lt. col. and a.-d.-c. on staffs of Govs. D. H. Hastings and W. A. Stone, of Pa., 1895-1901. Republican. Episcopalian. Home: Washington, D.C. Died Oct. 22, 1934.

HALL, HENRY B(ETHUNE) shoe mfg. exec.; b. St. Louis, Dec. 29, 1905; s. Marshall and Inez (Bethune) H.; B.S., Sheffield Sci. Sch., Yale, 1927; m. Martha H. Schuyler, Feb. 13, 1930; 1 son, Peter T. With Brown Shoe Co., Inc., St. Louis, 1927-, beginning in mdse. dept., successively asst. sec., asst. treas., 1927-53, treas., dir., 1953-. Dir. Better Bus. Bur. Served as lt. comdr. USNR, 1943-45. Republican. Presbyn. Clubs: Bellerive Country, University, Clayton (St. Louis); Yale (N.Y.C.). Home: 45 Clermont Lane, Clayton 24, Mo. Office: 8300 Maryland Av., St. Louis 5. Died July 14, 1964.

HALL, HERMAN army officer; b. at Carthage, Ill., June 6, 1864; s. Dr. George W. and Mary (McQuary) H.; grad. U.S. lMil. Acad., 1887; m. Anna Grace Jack, of Harlan, Ia., Oct. 18, 1893. Commd. 2d lt. 4th Inf., June 12, 1887; promoted through grades to col., May 15, 1917; served as brig. gen. N.A.; retired Oct. 23, 1923. For details of service see Vol. 12 (1922-23). Address: P.O. Box 532, Santa Barbara, Cal.

HALL, JOHN DEAN army officer; b. in N.H., Mar. 17, 1842; A.B., Harvard, 1863, A.M., 1866; M.D., Coll. Phys. and Surg. (Columbia), 1867. Apptd. from N.Y., asst. surgeon U.S.A., Nov. 16, 1868; capt. asst. surgeon, Nov. 16, 1871; maj. surgeon, Aug. 20, 1889; lt. col. deputy surgeon gen., Feb. 2, 1901; col. asst. surgeon gen., Feb. 13, 1903; retired by operation of law, Mar. 17, 1906. Address: War Dept., Washington.

HALL, JOSIAH NEWHALL M.D.; b. North Chelsea, Mass., Oct. 11, 1859; s. Stephen A. and Evalina A. (Newhall) H.; B.S., Mass. Agrl. Coll., 1878; M.D., Harvard, 1862; m. Carrie G. Ayres, Apr. 12, 1885; children-Sigourney D., Oliver W. (dec.). House phys., Boston City Hosp., 1882-83; practiced medicine, Sterling, Colo., 1883-92, Denver, 1892-1937; prof. medicine, med. dept., U. of Colorado; physician to Denver City and Co. St. Joseph's, St. Anthony's hosps., and Mercy Sanitarium. Pres. State Bd. Med. Examiners, Colo., 1891; pres. Colo. State Bd. Health, 1903-04. Maj. and surgeon, Med. R.C., U.S.A., 1917; was chief of med. service, Base Hosp., Camp Logan, Tex., and later consultant in internal medicine to the 16 southwestern mil. hosps. during period of the war. Republican. Mayor Sterling, Colo., 1888-89. Author: Borderline Diseases, 2 vols., 1915. Home: Denver, Colo. Died Dec. 17, 1939.

HALL, NORMAN BRIERLEY retired coast guard officer, corp. cons.; b. N.Y.C., Sept. 1, 1886; s. Thomas Stratford and Emma (Brierley) H.; B.S., U.S. Coast Guard Acad., 1906-07; m. Elizabeth Hamilton, Jan. 8, 1913 (dec. 1951); children - Norman B., Elizabeth Hamilton; m. 2d, Gladys Marsh Footner, 1954. Naval architect and marine engr., 1906, on various ships and stations, Atlantic, Pacific and Bering Sea, 1907-16; aviation duty, Coast Guard and Navy; insp. aero. material, U.S.N., 1916-20; installed machinery on N.C. flying boats, 1st transaltantic flight, 1919; asst. to engr. in chief USCG, 1924, charge aviation div., 1927-35, asst. insp. in chief, 1935, insp. in chief, 1937, chief port security div., 1941, chief Merchant Marine insp., 1945; chief insp. USCG, 1946; apptd. commodore; retired with the rank rear adm. 1947; now cons. Gen. Teleradio Corp., N.Y.C. Decorated Legion of lMerit, Am. Def., European African -Middle Eastern Area Campaign, Am. Area Campaign, World War I and II Victory medals. Asso. fellow Inst. Aero. Scis.; mem. Am. Ordnance Assn.; Vt. Hist. Soc., Lake Fairlee (Vt.) Assn. (V.P.), Am. Assn. Port Authorities, Newcomen Soc. Eng. (Am. br.). Home: 3608 Thornapple St., Chevy Chase 15, Md. Office: 218 W. Lanvale St., Balt. 17. Died Apr. 26, 1962.

HALL, OLIVER LEIGH editor, librarian; b. Rockland, Me., May 6, 1870; s. Oliver Gray and Sarah Frances (White) H.; student Coburn Classical Inst., Waterville, Me., 1887-89, Colby Coll., 1890-92; A.M., Colby Coll., 1914, U. of Me., 1927; m. Marie Agnes Bunker, June 3, 1896; children - Oliver Gray, Miriam Adelaide, Leonora Edith (lMrs. Herschel L. Good). Editor of Waterville (Me.) Sentinel, 1892-94; city editor of Rockland (Me.) Daily Star, 1895-97, editor, 1897-1900; city editor Bangor (Me.) Evening Commercial, 1905-11, editor, 1911-37 and since 1942; exec. sec. to Governor of Maine, 1937-38; state librarian, Me., 1938-41. Served as sr. lt. U.S.N.R., 1927-34. Member Bangor City Council, 1908-09, Bangor Bd. of Aldermen, 1910-11; chmn. Republican Com. of Hampden, 1928-38. Director of Port of Portland Authority, 1937-42. Editor Colby Alumnus (mag.), 1936-41. Trustee Hampden Acad. (pres. of bd.), Coburn Classical Inst., Good Samaritan Home. Past pres. of Me. Daily Newspaper Pubs. Assn., past pres. of Maine S.A.R.; mem. Reserve Officers Assn. of Bangor, patrons of Husbandry (Hampden), Society of Mayflower Descendants, Zeta Psi. Republican. Mason. Clubs: Masonic, Hampden Community Assn. Author: The Man from East Corinth, biography of Arthur R. Gould, former U.S. Senator from Me., 1941. Home: Hampden, Me. Died Nov. 17, 1946.

HALL, REYNOLD THOMAS naval officer; b. at Phila., Pa., Nov. 5, 1858: s. Edward Smyth and Katherine Piercy (Romney) H.; grad. Episcopal Acad., Phila., 1875; tech. course, Franklin Inst., Phila.; m. Anne Martin, Dec. 15, 1887. Apptd. asst. engr. U.S. Navy, Apr. 22, 1880; promoted through grades to rear adm., Dec. 12, 1914; retired, Nov. 5, 1922. Chief engr. U.S.S. Petrel, under Commodore Dewey in Battle of Manila Bay, May 1, 1898, and acting industrial mgr. of Cavite Navy Yard during Spanish-Am. War, 1898; squadron engr., Caribbean Squadron, 1903; fleet engr., European Sta., 1904; head of Dept. of Steam Engring., Navy Yard, New York, 1907, 1908. Advanced 3 numbers in rank "for eminent and conspicuous conduct in battle during Spanish-Am. War"; Dewey Medal. Mason. Home: Wynnewood, Pa. Died Feb. 10, 1934.

HALL, ROBERT HENRY brig. gen.; b. Detroit, Nov. 15, 1837; s. Benjamin F. and Catherine F. (Mullitt) H.; grad. U.S. Mil. Acad., 1860; m. Georgianna K. Foote, Feb. 7, 1866. Bvt. 2d lt. 5th Inf., July 1, 1860; commd. 2d lt. 10th Inf., Jan. 23, 1861; 1st lt., June 1, 1861; capt., Aug. 31, 1863; maj. 22d Inf., May 21, 1883; lt. col. 6th Inf., Aug. 5, 1888; col. 4th Inf., May 18, 1893; brig. gen. vols., May 27, 1898; hon. disch. from vol. service, Apr. 15, 1899; brig. gen. vols., Apr. 15, 1899-Mar. 1, 1901; brig. gen. U.S.A., Feb. 5, 1901; retired by operation of law, Nov. 15, 1901. Bvtd. maj., Nov. 24, 1863, for battle of Lookout Mountain, Tenn.; lt. col., Aug. 19, 1864, for battle on Weldon R.R. in Va. After war served on frontier until 1871; U.S. Mil. Acad., 1871-88; comd. Ft. Sheridan, Ill., 1896-98; in P.I., 1899-1900. Mason. Died Dec. 29, 1914.

HALL, WALTER PERLEY lawyer; b. Manchester, N.H., May 9, 1867; s. James Perley and Catherine (Willey) H.; grad. Worcester High Sch., 1885; student Brown U., 1885-88, LL.D., 1928; Harvard Law Sch., 1888-90; m. Anna Bigelow Davis, Dec. 4, 1893. Admitted to Mass. bar, 1891; town solicitor, Clinton; city solicitor, Fitchburg; asst. dist. atty., Middle Dist., Mass., 1905; 1st asst. atty.-gen., Mass., 1906-07; chmn. Mass. R.R. Commn., 1907-11; justice Superior Ct. of Mass., 1911-22, became chief justice, 1922. Formerly capt. Mass. Vol. Militia. Mem. Rep. State Com., 1898; presdl. elector, 1904. Unitarian. Club: St. Rotolph (Boston). Home: Fitchburg, Mass. Died 1942.*

HALL, WILLARD PREBLE gov. Mo.; b. Harper's Ferry, Va. (now W. Va.), May 9, 1820; s. John and Statica (Preble) H.; grad. Yale, 1839; m. Ann Eliza Richardson, Oct. 28, 1847; m. 2d, Ollie C. Oliver, June 22, 1864; 7 children. Admitted to Mo. bar, 1841; apptd. circuit atty. in Mo., 1843; Democratic presdl. elector, 1884; served as lt. in 1st Mo. Cavalry during Mexican War; with Col. Alexander Doniphan drew up code of laws for governing N.M. Territory; mem. U.S. Ho. of Reps. (Dem.) from Mo., 30th-32d congresses, 1847-53; mem. Mo. Constl. Conv. which made decision to remain in Union, 1861; provisional lt. gov. of Mo., 1861-64; brig. gen. Mo. Militia, 1861-63; gov. Mo., 1864-65. Died St. Joseph, Mo., Nov. 3, 1882; buried Mt. Moriah Cemetery, St. Joseph.

HALL, WILLIAM congressman, gov. Tenn.; b. Surry County, N.C., Feb. 11, 1775; attended country schs. Moved to New River, N.C., 1779, Sumner County, Tenn., 1785; engaged in farming; mem. Tenn. Ho. of Reps., 1797-1805; served as brig. gen. during War of 1812; served under Andrew Jackson in Creek War; mem. Tenn. Senate, 1821-29, speaker, 1827-29; gov. Tenn. Senate, 1821-29, speaker, 1827-29; gov. Tenn., 1829; maj. gen. Tenn. Militia; mem. U.S. Ho. of Reps. (Democrat) from Tenn., 22d Congress, 1831-33. Died "Locust Land" nr. Castalian Springs, Sumner County, Oct. 7, 1856; buried family cemetery, "Locust Land."

HALL, WILLIAM AUGUSTUS congressman; b. Portland, Me., Oct. 15, 1815; attended Yale; children include Uriel Sebree. Moved to Randolph County, Mo., 1840; admitted to Mo. bar, 1841, began practice in Huntsville; moved to Fayette, Mo., continued practice of law; Democratic presdl. elector, 1844; judge circuit ct., 1847-61; served as capt. during Mexican War; del. Mo. Constl. Conv., 1861; mem. U.S. Ho. of Reps. (Dem.) from Mo., 37th-38th congresses, Jan. 20, 1862-65; del. Nat. Dem. Conv., Chgo., 1864; resumed law practice, engaged in farming. Died nr. Darkville, Randolph County, Mo., Dec. 15, 1888; buried family cemetery.

HALL, WILLIAM BALDWIN FLETCHER, financing executive; born at Indpls., Jan. 22, 1905; s. Arthur Fletcher and Una Gladys (Fletcher) H.; grad. Lake Forest Acad., 1922; B.S., Yale, 1926; M.S. in Aero. Engring., U. Mich., 1929; m. Sarah Niezer, Dec. 26, 1932; children—Peter Vincent, Ann, Charles Niezer, Michael William. Spl. agt. Lincoln Nat. Life Ins. Co., 1926-27; aviation tng. Naval Air. Sta., Pensacola, Fla., 1929-30; naval aviator U.S.S. Texas, 1930-31; comml. pilot, 1931-32; staff mortgage loan dept. Lincoln Nat. Life Ins. Co., 1932-42, 2d v.p., mgr. mortgage loan dept., 1932-42, mem. finance com., bd. dirs., 1942-67; pres. Gen. Homes div. Sherbrook Homes, Inc., home prefabrication, Ft. Wayne, Ind., 1962-66; pres. Gen. Equity Investment Corp., 1960-66; pres. Colonial Mortgage Co., Inc., 1945-66, chmn. bd., 1966-69; pres. Industries Bldg. Corp., 1951-66; dir. Kissell Co., Springfield, O., Growth Capital, Inc., Cleve., Fox Realty Corp., Ft. Wayne. Chmn. Ft. Wayne Housing Authority, 1937-50; exec. bd. Anthony Wayne council Boy Scouts. Trustee of St. Francis Coll., Ft. Wayne. Served to comdr. USNR, 1942-45. Mem. Home Mfrs. Assn. (past pres., dir.), Appraisal Inst., Sportsman Pilot Assn., Zeta Psi. Roman Catholic. Home: Ft Wayne IN Died Oct. 22, 1969.

HALL, WILLIAM PREBLE brig. gen.; b. Mo., June 11, 1848; apptd. from Mo., and grad., U.S. Mil. Acad., 1868. Second lt., 19th Inf., June 15, 1868, 5th Cav., July 14, 1869: 1st lt., July 1, 1866; capt., Mar. 8, 1867; maj. staff a.-a.-g., Nov. 6, 1893; lt. col. staff a.-a.-g., Sept. 11,

1897; col. a.-a.-g., Apr. 18, 1901; brig. gen. a.-a.-g., Apr. 23, 1904; brig. gen., adj. gen. U.S.A., Mar. 5, 1907, with rank from Apr. 23, 1904. Served principally on frontier duty until Spanish war; was in fight with Apaches at Whitestone Mountain, Ariz., July 13, 1873; Big Horn and Yellowstone Expdn., 1876, and in action at Indian Creek, Wyo., July 17, 1876, and combat of Slim Buttes, Dak., Sept. 9-10, 1876; attacked by Indians while in command of reconnoitering party near camp on White River, Col., Oct. 29, 1879, and while going to rescue of brother officer was surrounded by about 35 warriors; awarded Congressional Medal of Honor for most distinguished gallantry on that occasion; adj. gen. dept. Puerto Rico, 1899-1900. Was mem. dept., div., army, and distinguished marksmen teams, 1879-92, and won medals upon all these teams, shooting, carbine and revolver. Retired June 11, 1912. Died Dec. 4, 1927.

HALLECK, HENRY WAGER army officer, businessman; b. Westernville, N.Y., Jan. 16, 1815; s. Joseph and Catherine (Wager) H.; A.B., Union Coll., 1837, A.M. (hon.), 1843, LL.D., 1862; grad. U.S. Mil. Acad., 1839; m. Elizabeth Hamilton, Apr. 10, 1855; 1 son, Henry Wager. Asst. prof. chemistry and engring. U.S. Mil. Acad., 1839-40; asst. to bd. of engrs., Washington, D.C., 1841-42; commd. 1st lt. U.S. Army, 1846; served as chief of staff under Col. Burton on expdn. into Lower Cal. in Mexican War; brevetted capt., 1847; author of constn. for state of Cal., 1849; lt. gov. Mazatian (Cal.); commd. capt., 1853; head of law firm Halleck, Peachy and Billings, 1854; dir.-gen. New Almaden quicksilver mine; pres. Pacific & Atlantic R.R.; maj. gen. Cal. Militia; commd. maj. gen. U.S.Army, 1861, commanded Dept. of the Missouri, 1861, Dept. of the Mississippi, 1862; commanded seizure of Corinth, 1862; assumed command as gen.-in-chief U.S. Army, hdqrs. Washington, D.C., 1862, superseded by Gen. Grant, 1864; mil. adviser to Pres. Lincoln, 1862; chief of staff to Grant, 1864-65; commanded Div. of the James, 1865, mil. div. of pacific, 1865-69, div. of South, 1869, 72; mem. Phi Beta Kappa. Author: The Science of War, 1845 Elements of Military Art and Science, 1846; A Collection of Mining Laws of Spain and Mexico, 1859; International Law, 1861. Died Louisville, Ky., Jan. 9, 1872; buried Greenwood Cemetery, Louisville.

HALLIGAN, JOHN naval officer; b. Boston, Mass., May 14, 1876; s. John and Margaret Elizabeth (Mccarthy) H.; grad. U.S. Naval Acad., 1898; m. Katrina Hoskinson Loomis, Feb. 11, 1902: 1 dau., Katherine Porter (wife of Charles Adair, U.S.N.). Rear adm. U.S. Navy; served as naval cadet, U.S.S. Brooklyn, Spanish-Am. War; with U.S. Naval Forces, France, World War; engr.-in-chief, U.S.N., 1927-29; now comdr. aircraft, U.S. Scouting Force. Officer Legion of Honor (France); D.S.M. (U.S.). Catholic. Home: Annapolis, Md. Died Dec. 11, 1934.

HALLORAN, EDWARD ROOSEVELT, ret. naval officer, pub. information exec.; b. Washington, Dec. 30, 1895; s. Matthew Francis and Mary Agnes (Beadle) H.; LL.B., Columbus U., Washington, 1932; m. Flavia Griffin, Aug. 15, 1926; 1 dau., Julia Ann (Mrs. Richard H. Rush). Admitted to D.C. bar, 1932; reorganized property and supply dept. Fed. Bd. Vocational Edn., 1921; purchasing agt. Bur. Pub. Roads, 1922-24; bus. mgr. VA Hosp., Jefferson Barracks, Mo., 1924-27; securities counselor Young Bros., St. Louis, 1927-28; pres. Halloran & Thorn, Inc., road building, St. Louis, 1929; spl. agt. Dept. Commerce, 1930-32; information specialist RFC, 1932-33; asst. comptroller, credit mgr. Washington Post, 1933-41; served with Md. N.G. on Mexican Border, 1915-17; served to maj. Signal Corps and inf., U.S. Army Res., 1917-40; commd. lt. (s.g.) USNR, 1941, advanced through grades to rear adm. USN, 1958; coordinator press censorship, officer charge overseas telephone communications censorship 12th Naval Dist., 1942-43; served in M.S. Sommels-Dijk, 1943, U.S.S. Rigel, 1943-44; comdg. officer naval beach parties 7th Amphibious Forces, 1944-45; tng. officer, liaison officer Office Pub. Information, Navy Dept., 1946-49; dist. pub. information officer 15th Naval Dist., 1949-52; officer charge fleet home-town news center, Great Lakes, Ill., 1952-57; asst. dir. civil relations Navy Dept., 1957-58; ret., 1958; counselor Richard H. Rush Enterprises, Washington, from 1958. Decorated Legion of Merit with combat V, others; Order of J. Gabriel Duque (Panama). Mem. Gamma Eta Gamma. Clubs: Washington State Press (Seattle); Army and Navy (Washington). Address: Tucson AZ Died Mar. 22, 1972; buried Arlington Nat. Park, Arlington VA

HALLORAN, PAUL JAMES, naval officer (ret.); b. Norwood, Mass., June 26, 1896; s. John Francis and Nora Frances (Knox) H.; B.S., Dartmouth Coll., 1919, C.E. and M.C.E., 1920; m. Catherine Lenihan, June 25, 1927; children—Richard Colby, David Granger, Joan. Commd. lt. (j.g.), Civil Engr. Corps., U.S. Navy, 1921, and advanced through grades to rear adm., 1942; ret., 1948; service as structural designer, supt. of constrn., civil engr.; overseas, 8 yrs.; commd. in Corps of Engrs., Rep. of Haiti; apptd. high chief Am. Samoa; comd. 6th Brigade (Constrn. Bn., 'Seabess'); comd. naval constrn. forces, Kyushu. Now vice pres. Foley Bros., Inc., internat. contractors, Pleasantville, N.Y. Decorated Legion of Merit with gold star, Presdl. Citation with one star, Navy Unit Citation with one star (U.S.), Presdl. Citation (Rep. of Haiti). Exhibits in Smithsonian Instn., Bishop and Dartmouth museums. Member Am. Soc. C.E., Am. Concrete Inst. (Wason medalist), Soc. Am. Mil. Engrs., Sigma Phi Epsilon, Gamma Alpha, Moles. Roman Catholic. Clubs: Downtown Athletic (New York). Home: Ossining NY Died Feb. 14, 1971; buried Gate of Heaven, Valhalla NY

HALSEY, WILLIAM FREDERICK naval officer; b. Elizabeth, N.J., Oct. 30, 1882; s. William Frederick and Anne Masters (Brewster) H.; student U. of Va., 1899-1900; B.S., United States Naval Academy, 1904; LL.D., Columbia University, 1947, Lehigh U., Washington University, American International College, Lafayette College, 1954; married Fanny Cooke Grandy, Dec. 1, 1909; children-Margaret Bradford Halsey Spruance, and William Frederick, III. Commissioned ensign U.S. Navy, 1906, and advanced through the grades to rear adm., 1938; rank of vice adm., June 13, 1940; rank of adm., Nov. 18, 1942, and Dec. 11, 1945 took oath as fleet adm. comdg. U.S. Third Fleet in Pacific; retired, Apr. 1, 1947. Member board of dir. Bullock's Found. Decorated Navy Cross, Distinguished Service medal with 3 gold stars, Army D.S.M., Victory Medal with Destroyer clasp, Am. Area Campaign medal, Am. Defense Service medal, Philippine Liberation Campaign ribbon with 2 stars, Gold Cross of Chevalier, Order of the Redeemer (Greece), Insignia Al Merito (1st class), Diploma (Chile), Hon. Knight Comdr. British Empire. On good will tour to S.A. in summer of 1946; awarded Order of Naval Merit (Cuba), Order of the Liberator (Venezuela), Order of Ayacucho (Peru), Grand Cross of Legion of Merit (Chile), Abdon Calderon of Balboa (Panama), Supreme Chief in the Order of the Inotzal (Guatemala), Nat. Order of the Southern Cross (Grand Cross), Brazil. Mem. Delta Psi. Episcopalian. Clubs: Army and Navy, Chevy Chase (Washington, D.C.), Military Order of the Carabao; Metropolitan, Racquet and Tennis University, The Brook (New York). Home: 530 Park Av. Office: 90 Church St., N.Y.C. 7. Died Aug. 16, 1959.

HALSTEAD, ALBERT EDWARD surgeon; b. Ottawa, Ont., Apr. 21, 1868; s. William S. and Sara (Gibbons) H.; M.D., Northwestern U. Med. Sch., 1890; m. Mary S. Cochems, Feb. 1, 1893; children-Lucile Marie Byford, Dorothy Logan. Interne Cook Co. Hosp., 1890-91, then engaged in practice in Chicago; attending surgeon Cook Co. Hosp. for 20 yrs.; formerly prof. anatomy, Northwestern U. Med. Sch.; prof. surgery, Med. Dept. U. of Ill.; attending surg. Cook Co., St. Luke's hosps. Fellow Am. Surg. Assn., Chicago Surg. Soc. Lt. col. M.C.U.S.A., with A.E.F., 1917. Home: Chicago, Ill. Died Dec. 6, 1926.

HALSTEAD, ALEXANDER SEAMAN naval officer; b. Phila., Pa., Dec. 17, 1861; s. David and Janet (Gunn) H.; A.B., Central High Sch., Phila., 1879: grad. U.S. Naval Acad., 1883; grad. Naval War Coll., Newport, R.I., 1917; unmarried. Promoted asst. engr., July 1, 1885; passed asst. engr., Sept. 11, 1895; transferred to line as lt., Mar. 3, 1899; lt. comdr., Jan. 1, 1904; commander, July 1, 1908; capt., July 1, 1911; rear admiral (tem.), July 1, 1918; rear admiral (permanent), July 1, 1919. Served on Raleigh, Spanish-American War, participating in the Battle of Manila Bay, May 1, 1898, also capture of Corregidor Island, Manila Bay, capture of Grand Island, Subig Bay, and assault on Manila, Aug. 1898; on Chicago, 1904-06; insp. ordnance, San Francisco, Calif., 1906-09; comd. Vicksburg, 1909-10, Pensacola, 1910-11; comd. California, flagship of Pacific Fleet, 1912-13, participating in operations of U.S. forces in connection with revolution in Nicaragua; supervisor New York Harbor, 1915; comdr. Utah, 1915-16, Naval War Coll., Newport, R.I., 1916-17; apptd. sr. mem. Bd. for Appraisal for Mcht. and Pvt. Vessels, N.Y. City, Apr. 2, 1917. Comdr. dist. of Brest, France, Oct. 1918-Jan. 1919; comdr. U.S. naval forces in France, hdqrs., Brest, Jan. 30, 1919; returned to U.S., Oct. 1919; comdr. Navy Yard, Portsmouth, N.H., Dec. 1, 1919-20; comdt. 12th Naval Dist. San Francisco, Oct.1920-. Holder Dewey medal, and Spanish-Am. War and Nicaragua campaign badges; awarded D.S.M., and Navy Cross; Comdr. Legion of Honor (French). Presbyn. Home: Philadelphia, Pa. Died Nov. 12, 1923.

HALSTEAD, LAURENCE army officer; b. Cin., Oct. 21, 1875; s. Col. Benton and Rowena (Smith) H.; grad. U.S. Mil. Acad., 1899; honor grad. Army Sch. of the Line, 1910; grad. Army Staff Coll., 1911, Army War Coll., 1925; m. Ann Louise Maus, Feb. 10, 1903; children-Laurence, Mervin, Commd. 2d lt. inf., U.S. Army, 1899; promoted through grades to brig. gen., 1935; with the 11th Inf., P.R., 1899-1900, 13th Inf., Philippine Islands and San Francisco, 1901-04, 6th Inf., 1905-13; chief of staff 84th Div., Camp Taylor, Ky., 1917; asst. chief of staff 1st Army, France 1918-19; instr. Army Center of Arty. Studies, Trier, Germany, 1919; with War Dept. Gen. Staff, 1922-24; comdr. 27th Inf., 1926-28; chief of staff 7th Corps Area, Omaha, Neb., 1929-31; exec., office of chief of inf., Dept. of War, Washington, 1931-34; comdr. 12th Inf., Ft. Howard, Md., 1934-35; comdr. Pacific Sector, Panama Canal, 1935-38; ret. May 31, 1938. Decorated D.S.M. (U.S.). Club: Corinthian Yacht, Army and Navy. Home: 3311 Macomb St. N.W., Washington. Died June 1, 1954.

HALSTEAD, WILLIAM congressman; b. Elizabeth, N.J., June 4, 1794; s. grad. Princeton, 1812; studied law. Admitted to N.J. bar, 1816, began practice in Trenton; reporter N.J. Supreme Ct., 1821-32; pros. atty. Hunterdon County (N.J.), 1827-29, 33-37; mem. U.S. Ho. of Reps. (Whig) from N.J., 25th, 27th congresses, 1837-39, 41-43; U.S. dist. atty. for N.J., 1849-53; organized 1st Regt. of N.J. Volunteer Cavalry for Civil War, col. until 1862. Died Trenton, Mar. 4, 1878; buried Riverview Cemetery, Trenton.

HALTOM, WILLIAM LORENZ, physician; b. Jonesboro, Ark., Oct. 22, 1904; s. William Columbus and Zepha (McColl) H.; A.B., Hendrix Coll.; B.S., M.S., U. Ala.; M.D., Duke U., 1932; m. Estelle Armstrong, June 8, 1926; children—Jan (Mrs. Everett Lanson Plyler), Martha (Mrs. William Edgar Warrick). Former curator mineralogy Mus. Natural History, U. Ala.; intern Duke U. Hosp., Durham, N.C., 1932-33, asst. resident in urology, 1933-34, resident in urology, 1935-37; resident in urology Kretschmer service Presbyn. Hosp., Chgo., 1934-35; urologist King's Daus. Hosp., Martinsburg, W.Va., until 1970. Served to maj., M.C., AUS. Diplomate Am. Bd. Urology. Mem. A.M.A. Home: Martinsburg WV Died Feb. 16, 1970; buried Martinsburg WV

HAM, CLIFFORD DUDLEY b. Detroit, Mich., Jan. 2, 1861; s. M. M. and Helen (Tucker) H.; A.B., Yale, 1882; m. Mary Barber, of Waterloo, Ia., June 28, 1892; children-Marian Barber, Clifford Dudley. Was sec. to gov. of Ia. and in newspaper work, Dubuque, Ia.; lt. col. 49th Ia. Vols., Spanish-Am. War, 1898-99; editor Dubuque Herald until 1903; in customs service, Philippine Islands, 1903-11, collector of customs, Iloilo, and surveyor of port, Manila; collector gen. of customs, Republic of Nicaragua, by appmt. of Pres. of Nicaragua, and fiscal agt. for bonded foreign loans of Nicaragua, since Dec. 1911. Episcopalian. Author of new tariff law, codification of Laws of Customs, Ports, Maritime Commerce and Vessels of Nicaragua, and map of Nicaragua. Address: Managua, Nicaragua, C. A.* Deceased.

HAMBLEN, ARCHELAUS L., army officer; born Me., July 25, 1894; B.S., U. of Me., 1916; grad. Inf. Sch., Advanced Course, 1928, Command and Gen. Staff Sch., 1934, Army War Coll., 1937. Commd. 2d lt., Inf., Nov. 1916, and advanced through the grades to brig. gen., Dec. 1942; served on Gen. Staff, 1940-41. Died Oct. 8, 1971.

HAMBLIN, JOSEPH ELDRIDGE army officer; b. Yarmouth, Mass., Jan. 13, 1828; s. Benjamin and Hannah (Sears) H.; m. Isabella Gray, Oct. 15, 1868. Served with various militia cos. before Civil War; served from lt. to maj., 65th N.Y. Volunteers (1st U.S. Chasseurs) under Gen. B.F. Butler at siege of Yorktown (Va.) and battles of Williamsburg, Fair Oaks, Glendale, Malvern Hill (Va.); commd. lt. col., assigned to 1st Brigade, 1862, col., 1863; commanded regt. at Gettysburg; served in Chancellorsville campaign, 1863; distinguished at Hazel Run, 1864; brig. gen., 1864; served with Grant's army from the Wilderness to Petersburg, with Sheridan's army in Shenandoah Valley; commanded 2d Brigade in Appomattox campaign; commd. maj. gen., 1865; adj. gen., chief of staff. N.Y. Nat. Guard 1867-70. Died N.Y.C., July 3, 1870.

HAMBRO, SIR CHARLES JOCLYN banker; b. London, Eng., Oct. 3, 1897; s. Sir Charles Eric and Sybil Martin (Smith) H.; ed. Eton Coll. and Sandhurst Royal Mil. Coll.; m. Pamela Cobbold (dec. 1932); children - Cynthia, Diana, Pamela, Charles Alexander; m. 2d, Dorothy Helen Mackay, Apr. 16, 1936; 1 dau., Sally. Dep. chmn. and mng. dir. Hambro Bank, Ltd.; dir. Bank of Eng., Union Corp., Ltd., Hambro Investment Trust, Ltd.; chmn. Bay Hall Trust, Ltd.; chmn. Hellenic & Gen. Trust, Ltd. Served as lt. Coldstream Guards, 1916-19; col. Gen. Staff, 1940-44, ret., 1944. Brit. mem. Combined Raw Materials Bd., Washington, 1946. Dep. lt. City of London. Decorated Knight Brit. Empire, Mil. Cross, Am. Legion of Merit, Order of Danneborg, Knight of St. Olaf. Clubs: White's, Turf, Guards (London). Home: Dixton Manor, Gotherington, Gloucestershire, Eng. Office: 41 Bishopsgate, London, Eng. Died Aug. 28, 1963.

HAMER, THOMAS LYON congressman; b. Northumberland County, Pa., July 1800; studied law under Thomas Morris; m. Lydia Higgins; m. 2d, Catherine Johnston, 1845. Admitted to Ohio bar, 1821; mem. Ohio Ho. of Reps., 1825, 28-30, speaker, 1829-30; mem. U.S. Ho. of Reps. from Ohio, 23d-25th congresses, 1833-39, elected to 30th Congress, 1845, died before taking office; presided over Ohio Democratic Conv., 1840; commd. brig. gen. 1st Ohio Volunteers in Mexican War; posthumously awarded sword for gallantry at Monterey, Mexico (presented by Congress to his nearest male relative). Died Monterey, Dec. 2, 1846; buried Georgetown (O.) Cemetery.

HAMILTON, ALEXANDER 1st U.S. sec. of treasury; b. Nevis, B.W.I., Jan. 11, 1757; s. James and Rachel (Faucette) H.; attended King's Coll. (Columbia), 1773-76; m. Elizabeth Schuyler, 1780, 8 children including James Alexander, Philip, John C. Worked as clk. for a time; came to Am., 1772; wrote pamphlets and newspaper articles defending colonists' against British, circa 1773-76; apptd. capt. of arty. Continental Army, 1776; sec., aide-de-camp to Gen. George Washington, 1777-81, served in battles of L.I., Yorktown; admitted to N.Y. bar, 1781; became noted lawyer in N.Y.; del. from N.Y. to Continental Congress, 1728-83, 87-88; developer and exponent of theory of stronger central govt.; mem. Annapolis Conv., 1786; mem. N.Y. Legislature, 1787; largely responsible for sending N.Y. delegation (including himself and 2 anti-constn. Clinton Democrats, Robert Yates and John Lansing) to U.S. Constl. Conv., Phila., 1787; played only a minor role in drafting U.S. Constn.; signed U.S. Constn. for State of N.Y., 1787; wrote (with John Jay, James Madison) series of articles The Federalist Papers, favoring adoption of U.S. Constn., 1787-88; attended N.Y. Conv. to ratify U.S. Constn., was highly influential in securing ratification; U.S. sec. of treasury (apptd. by Washington), 1789-95; identified with Federalist Party, became probably its main spokesman; conducted (as sec. of treasury) financial program based on paying U.S. domestic debt, founding Bank of U.S., assuming state debts, raising excise taxes and imposing protective tariffs; presented plan to Congress in series of reports (final one the famous report on manufactures), 1790, defended his plan largely through the implied powers argument of U.S. Constn.; met strong opposition, but all measures were adopted except the imposition of protective tariffs (assumption of state debts came about only because Jefferson agreed to swing votes for it in return for Hamilton's support on locating nat. capital in South); adoption of excise taxes was main cause of Whiskey Rebellion in Pa., 1794; clashed with Jefferson both personally and in policy matters (basic theory of govt., fgn. policy); his conflict with Jefferson led to development of 2-party system in Am.; resigned cabinet post, 1795, continued to attempt to advise Washington, wrote part of Washington's Farewell Address, 1796; apptd. insp. gen. U.S. Army in anticipation of of war with France, 1798 (John Adams managed to avert war, which caused break in Federalist Party ranks); put his influence on Jefferson's side during tie for presidency that developed between Jefferson and Aaron Burr, swung many Federalist votes in U.S. Ho. of Reps. to Jefferson (start of enmity between Burr and Hamilton); practiced law, N.Y.C., 1795-1804; a founder N.Y. Evening Post (1801), Bank of N.Y., influential in preventing the election of Burr as gov. N.Y., 1804; challenged to duel by Burr, mortally wounded at Weehawken Heights, N.J. Died N.Y.C., day after duel, July 12, 1804; buried Trinity Churchyard, N.Y.C.

HAMILTON, ALEXANDER, association executive; b. N.Y.C., Jan. 25, 1903; s. William Pierson and Juliet Pierpont (Morgan) H.; grad. St. Paul's Sch., 1921, Harvard, 1925; m. Elizabeth Malcolm Peltz, Dec. 26, 1935. Formerly dep. commr. N.Y. City Dept. Markets, formerly asst. to commr. Dept. Sanitation. Dir. Ramapo Land Co., Pothat Water Co. Chairman advisory board national shrines, New York City; secretary-treasurer of American Museum of Immigration. Pres., Tuxedo (N.Y.) Meml. Hosp. Served to maj. USMCR, World War II. Mem. St. Nicholas Soc. (past pres.), St. Andrew's Soc. N.Y. (v.p. 1959-60), Am. Scenic and Historic Preservation Soc. (pres.), N.Y. Young Republican Club (past pres.). Republican, Episcopalian. Clubs: Century Association; Racquet and Tennis; Harvard; Brook; Travellers (Paris, France). Home: Sloatsburg Rockland County NY Died May 29, 1970; buried St. Elizabeth's Meml. Chapel, Sloatsburg, Rockland County NY

HAMILTON, ALSTON army officer; b. nr. Oxford, N.C., Oct. 20, 1871; s. Robert Alston and Martha Elizabeth (Venable) H.; prep. edn., University Sch., Petersburg, Va.; grad. U.S. Mil. Acad., 1894; grad. Army War Coll., Washington, 1914, again 1922; m. Nancy Thompson Creel, Oct. 20, 1896; children-John Creel, Alston (dau.). Commd. 2d lt. U.S.A., June 12, 1894; promoted through grades to brig. gen., Jan. 19, 1927. Served in Cuba, Spanish-Am. War (silver star citation for gallantry at El Caney), later in Philippines (silver star for gallantry at Calamba); instr. mathematics U.S. Mil. Acad., 1899-1903, in ballistics and seacoast engring., Ft. Monroe, Va., 1904-09; mem. and pres. Arty. Bd. for a number of yrs., later mem. Ordnance Bd., Sandy Hook Proving Ground; in comd. coast defenses Eastern N.Y., 1917; went to France as col. 58th Arty., C.A.C., May 1918; participated at St. Mihiel, Sept. 116, 1918; assigned as comdr. 35th Arty. Brigade, Oct. 1918; comdr. Panama Coast Arty. Dist., 1919-21; executive of 9th Coast Arty. Dist., hdqrs. Presidio, San Francisco, 1922-26; prof. mil. science and tactics, Mass. Inst. Tech., 1926-27; assigned as comdr. 2d Coast Arty. Dist., Jan. 1927, comdr. 11th Field Arty. Brigade, Schofield Barracks, Oahu, T.H., 1927-30; comdr. 1st Coast Arty. Dist., 1930-35; retired, Oct. 20, 1935. Presbyn. Died Dec. 18, 1937.

HAMILTON, ANDREW JACKSON congressman, army officer; b. Madison County, Ala., Jan. 28, 1815; s. James and Abagail (Bayless) H.; m. Mary Jane Bowen, 1843. Admitted to Ala. bar, 1841; atty. gen. Tex., 1849; mem. Tex. Legislature, 1851-53; mem. U.S. Ho. of Reps. from Tex., 36th Congress, 1859-61; elected to Tex. Legislature, 1861, refused to take seat under Confederate States Am.; served as brig. gen. Tex. Volunteers, U.S. Army during Civil War, 1862; apptd. mil gov. Tex., 1862; provisional gov. Tex., 1865-66; justice Tex. Supreme Ct., 1866. Died Austin, Tex., Apr. 11, 1875; buried Oakwood Cemetery, Austin.

HAMILTON, ARTHUR STEPHEN neurologist and psychiatrist; b. Wyoming, Ia., November 28, 1872; s. Arthur A. and Ada O. (Fisher) Hamilton; B.S., Univ. of Ia., 1894; M.D., Univ. of Pa., 1897; m. Susanna P. Boyle, Dec. 25, 1903; 1 son, David Arthur. Asst. physician, Independence (Ia.) State Hosp., 1897-1904; instr. neuropathology, U. of Minn., 1904-12, clin. instr. and asst. prof. nervous and mental diseases, 1905-12, asso. prof., 1912-16, prof. since 1916, also chief div. since 1912; neurologist to Univ., St. Mary's, Swedish, Fariview, Abbott, New Asbury, St. Andrews and Northwestern hosps.; dir. neurol. service U.S. Vets.' Hosp. No. 68. Capt. M.C., U.S.A., 1918; maj. 1919. Mem. Am. Neurol. Soc., Chicago Neurol. Soc., Minn. Neurol Soc. (ex-pres.), Central Neuropsychiatric Assn. (ex-pres.), Am. Psychiatric Soc., Am. Med. Psychol. Assn., A.M.A. (ex-chmn. sect. nervous and mental diseases), Minn. State Med. Soc., Minn. Acad. Medicine (ex-pres.), Hennepin County Med. Soc. (ex-pres.), Phi Delta Theta, Nu Sigma Nu, Sigma Psi, Republican. Episcopalian. Clubs: Minneapolis, Campus, Minneapolis Golf Home: 1432 Minnehaha Parkway W. Office: Medical Arts Bldg., Minneapolis. Died June 2, 1940.

HAMILTON, CHARLES MEMORIAL congressman; b. Pine Creek Twp., Clinton County, Pa., Nov. 1, 1840; grad. Columbia (Pa.) Law Sch. Enlisted as pvt. U.S. Army during Civil War, 1861; captured at Battle of Fredericksburg, imprisoned in Libby Prison, Richmond, Va., until 1863; exchanged, 1863; commd. ensign, transferred to Vets. Res. Corps; promoted 1st lt., later capt.; judge advocate of gen. ct. martial, gen. pass officer for Army of Potomac; mem. staff of mil. gov. Washington (D.C.), transferred to Marianna, Fla., 1865; admitted to Fla. bar, 1867, began practice in Marianna; mem. U. S. Ho. of Reps. (Republican) from Fla., 40th-41st congresses, July 1, 1868-71; apptd. sr. maj. gen. - 1871; postmaster of Jacksonville (Fla.)., 1871-72; collector of customs Key West (Fla.), 1873. Died Pine Creek Twp., Oct. 22, 1875; buried Jersey Shore Cemetery, Pa.

HAMILTON, CHARLES SMITH army officer; b. Oneida County, N.Y., Nov. 16, 1822; s. Zane A. and Sylvia (Putnam) H.; grad. U.S. Mil. Acad., 1843; m. Sophia Shepard, Feb. 1849. Served in Mexican War, brevetted capt. for gallantry; served in Indian Wars, resigned commn., 1853, settled in Fond Du Lac, Wis.; commd. col., recruited and organized 3d Wis. Volunteers, 1861; commd. brig. gen., served under Gen. Banks during Shenandoah campaign, 1861; commd. maj. gen. on recommendation of Gen. Grant, 1862, transferred to Army of W. Va., primarily responsible for success of Battle of Corinth; command of XVI Army Corps and dist. of Tenn., in command of left wing of Grant's Army, 1863; resigned his commn. in 1863 because he thought his mil talents were not duly recognized U.S. marshal at Milw., 1869; pres. Hamilton Paper Co., 1878; mem. bd. regents U. Wis., 1866-75, pres. bd. 1869-75. Died Milw., Apr. 17, 1891.

HAMILTON, HENRY army officer; b. England. Served in Canada and West Indies during French and Indian Wars; apptd. lt. gov. of Detroit, 1775; served in West during Am. Revolution; became notorious for inciting Indians to attack Am. frontier settlements; accused of paying Indians for Am. scalps which were brought to him; captured (with his command) by George Rogers Clark, Vincennes (now Ind.), 1779, exchanged; held various imperial adminstry. posts until death. Died 1796.

HAMILTON, JAMES ALEXANDER, actuary; b. Kingston, Ont., Can., Sept. 12, 1906; s. John Rennie and Clara (Howlett) H.; B.S., Queens U., 1927; M.S., U. Chgo.; M.A., Pa. State U.; m. Geraldine Lucy Boyce, June 21, 1930; children—Margaret Lynne, Nancy Lee. Came to U.S., 1927, naturalized, 1940. Instr. math. Pa. State U., 1928-33; research Met. Life Ins. Co., 1933-43; with Wyatt Co., also Wyatt Actuaries, Inc., Washington, 1946-69, pres., chmn. bd., 1961-69; cons. actuary, 1969-73; dir. Fidelity Nat. Bank, Arlington, Va. Served to maj. AUS, 1943-46; actuary, then chief life sect., contract ins. br. Office Chief of Finance. Fellow Soc. Actuaries Conf. Actuaries in Pub. Practice; mem. Fraternal Actuarial Assn., Internat. Assn. Cons. Actuaries (vice chmn.), Internat. Congress Actuaries. Author: (with D.C. Bronson) Pensions. Home: Punta Gorda FL Died Feb. 27, 1973.

HAMILTON, PAUL gov. S.C., sec. of navy; b. St. Paul's Parish S.C. Oct. 16, 1762; s. Archibald and Rebecca (Branford) H.; m. Mary Wilkinson, Oct. 10, 1782. Fought in Revolutionary War; justice of peace, St. Paul's Parish, 1786; mem. lower house S.C. Legislature, 1787-89, S.C. Senate, 1794, 98-99; comptroller S.C., 1800-04; gov. S. C. 1804-06, although a slave-owner, urged S.C. Legislature to prohibit African slave trade; U.S. sec. of navy, 1809-13, hampered throughout adminstrn. by lack of funds, but helped secure act for constrn. of naval hosps., 1811, endeavored to enforce govt. embargo policy at beginning War of 1812. Died Beaufort, S.C., June 30, 1816.

HAMILTON, ROBERT PATRICK, prof. law; b. Petersburg, Va., Nov. 23, 1896; s. Robert P. and Sally Parke (Wellford) H.; B.A., U. of Va., 1917; B.A. in Jurisprudence (1st class honours), Oxford Univ., 1922, B.C.L., 1923, M.A., 1928; LL.B., Columbia Univ., 1924; student Caen Univ., France, 1919; Rhodes Scholar 1920-23; grad. U.S. Army Sch. of Mil. Government, 1943; m. Portia Goulder, June 5, 1926 (divorced, Aug. 29, 1947); 1 dau., Portia Virginia. Admitted to Va. State bar, 1920; associate law firm, Root, Clark, Buckner, Howland & Ballantine, N.Y. City, 1924-29; asso. prof. law, Columbia, 1929-37, prof. law since 1937; mem. Alien Enemy Hearing Bd., South Dist. N.Y., 1941-43; govt. appeal agt., Selective Service System, 1942-43. Served as lt. col., on active service, 1943-45, col. 1945-46, col. SA-Res. U.S. Army; overseas July 1943-Apr. 1946; mem. gen. staff corps with troops, 1944-46; Asst. Chief of Staff, G-5, U.S. Administrative Staff, British 21, Army Group, then Seine Sect., Com. Z., E.T.O., 1944-45; dep. comdg. officer, 176th staff and adminstrn. group, O.R.C., 1946-49; special mission to Germany, 1948; special staff, Department of the Army, 1949. Decorated Legion of Merit, Bronze Star Medal, Purple Heart (with Oak Leaf Cluster), Victory Medal with 3 battle clasps, World War I, Victory Medal, World War II. E.T.O. medal with 2 battle stars, Chevalier, French Legion of Honor Croix de Guerre with Silver Star (1914-18), Croix de Guerre with 2 Palms (1939-45). Mem. Am. Bar Assn., Assn. Am. Rhodes Scholars, Res. Officers Assn., Phi Beta Kappa, Phi Delta Phi. Democrat. Episcopalian. Club: Men's Faculty of Columbia Univ. Co-author: Cases on Business Organization (2 vols.). Home: New York City NY Died July 1970.

HAMILTON, SCHUYLER soldier; b. New York, July 25, 1822; s. John Church H.; g.s. Alexander H., the statesman; grad. U.S. Mil. Acad., 1841; served on frontier as lt., 1st inf.) was asst. instr. tactics. West Point; served with distinction through Mexican war, especially at battle of Monterey and at Mil Flores, where he overcame a number of Mexicans in hand-to-hand encounter, winning praise in official report of Gen. Scott; was a.d.c. to latter, 18 New York. Entered Union army as pvt., 1861, but soon after was on staff of Gen. B. F. Butler; later mil. sec. Gen. Scott, until latter retired, Oct. 31, 1861; promoted col. and asst. chief of staff to Gen. H. W. Halleck; brig. gen. vols., Nov. 12, 1861; took leading part in campaigns of armies of the Tenn. and Cumberland; for services at Island No. 10 and at battle of New Madrid, promoted maj. gen. vols., Sept. 17, 1862; comd. reserve at battle of Farmington, but Feb. 27, 1863, retired because of failing health. Was hydrographic engr., dept. of docks, New York, 1871-75. Died 1903.

HAMILTON, WILLIAM HENRY, naval officer; b. Chestnut Hill, Phila., Pa., Oct. 21, 1899; s. William Henry and Elizabeth Ada (Young) H.; B.S., U.S. Naval Acad., 1923; student Torpedo Sch., Newport, R.I., 1924; m. Marjorie Elvira Powell, July 24, 1926; children—William Henry, Frank Powell. Commd. ensign, U.S. Navy, 1923, and advanced through the grades to commodore, 1943; served in U.S.S. Utah, 1923-24, U.S.S. Hopkins, 1925; flight instr. Naval Air Sta., Pensacola, Fla., 1925; with torpedo squadron two (VT-2), 1926-29; flight instrn., 1929-31; fighting squadron one, U.S.S. Saratoga, 1931-33; supt. engine overhaul Naval Air Sta., Norfolk, Va., 1933-35; observation squadron three, U.S.S., New Mexico and Idaho, 1935-37; fighting squadron four, U.S.S. Ranger, 1937-38; patrol squadron three (later VP-32), 1938-40; mem. staff comdr. aircraft Atlantic Fleet, 1940-41; Bureau of Aeronautics, Washington, D.C., 1941-43; comdr. Fleet Air Wing Seven, 1943-45; comdr. Naval Air Bases 7th Naval Dist., 1945-46; comdg. offices U.S.S. Antretam, 1946-47; dir. plans and policy bd., office of Sec. of Defense since 1948-49; comdr. Naval Air Bases 5th Naval Dist. since 1949. Decorated Legion of Merit (U.S.); Order Comdr. British Empire, Croix de Guerre. Address: Norfolk VA Died 1969.

HAMILTON, WILLIAM PETER editor; b. Great Britain, Jan. 20, 1867; m. Georgianna Tooker, June 20, 1901 (died 1916); m. 2d, Lilian Hart, May 19, 1917. Began newspaper work 1890; was on staff Pall Mall Gazette, under William T. Stead; traveled as corr. principal parts of world; served as lt. British auxiliary forces, Royal Engrs.; war corr. 1st Matabele War, S. Africa, 1893-94 (medal); came to America, 1899; editor Wall Street Journal., Jan. 1, 1908-. Catholic. Home: Brooklyn, N.Y. Died Dec. 9, 1929.

HAMILTON, WILLIAM REEVE army officer; b. Fond du Lac, Wis., June 13, 1855; s. Charles Smith (maj. gen. U.S.A.) and Sophia J. (Shepard) H.; student U. of Wis., 1871-72; apptd. from Wis., and grad. U.S. Mil. Acad., 1876; grad. Arty. Sch., 1894; (hon. M.S., Asbury, now De Pauw U., 1882); m. Jane H. Bond, June 21, 1902. Second lt. 5th Arty., June 15, 1876; promoted through grades to col. Coast Arty. Corps, Jan. 14, 1909; retired. Prof. mil. science and tactics, Asbury U., 1879-83; instr. N.G.S.N.Y., 1888-90; prof. mil. science and tactics, U. of Nev., 1894-97; served at Ft. Slocum, N.Y., Willetts Pt. Arty. Sub-post, and Tampa, Fla., in siege arty. train during Spanish-Am. War; comd. Ft. Schuyler, N.Y., 1899-1901, Ft. Terry, N.Y., 1901-03; stationed at

Ft. Moultrie, S.C., 1903-05; on gen. recruiting duty, St. Louis, 1905-07. Statistician of mil. and naval tables, New York World Almanac, 1887-. Died Sept. 16, 1914.

HAMILTON, WILLIAM THOMAS trapper, scout; b. Eng., Dec. 6, 1822; married, 1850. Came to U.S., 1825; mem. trapping party going to Northwest, 1842-45; served in Rogue River War, 1855, Modor War, 1856; traded with Blackfoot, Crow, other Indians in Walla Walla (Wash.) area to determine and report on their activities to Col. George Wright, 1857; sheriff Missoula County, 1861; marshal for Crow Indians, 1837; scout for Gen. George Crook in Sioux War, 1876-77. Author: My Sixty Years on the Plains, 1905; My Experiences in Montana (unpublished). Died May 24, 1908.

HAMLET, HARRY GABRIEL U.S. Coast Guard officer; b. Eastport, Me., Aug. 27, 1874; s. Oscar Charles and Annie (Holland) H.; student Mass. Inst. Tech., 1892-93; grad. U.S. Coast Guard Acad., 1896; m. Francel Allen Hastings, Apr. 26, 1905; 1 dau., Jean Hastings. Ensign. Apr. 27, 1896; promoted through grades to vice-adm., comdt., June 14, 1932; retired. Awarded Gold Life Saving Medal (U.S.); Silver Star (U.S.N.); Victory Medal; Comdr. Crown of Italy. Mem. Mil. Order World War, Am. Legion, Vets. Fgn. Wars, Mil. Order of Carabao, Sigma Alpha Epsilon, Pi Gamma Mu. Episcopalian. Mason (32ff), Elk. Clubs: Army and Navy (Washington); Army and Navy (Chicago); Army and Navy (San Francisco); Jibboom (New London, Connecticut). Home: 7110 Beechwood Dr., Chevy Chase 15, Md. Died Jan. 24, 1954.

HAMLIN, CHARLES lawyer; b. Hampden, Me., Sept. 13, 1837; s. Hannibal (V.P. of U.S., 1861-65) and Sarah Jane (Emery) H.; A.B., Bowdoin, 1857, A.M., 1859; (LL.D., U. of Me., 1909); admitted to bar, 1858; m. Sarah P. Thompson, Nov. 28, 1860. Maj. 1st Me. Arty., Aug. 21, 1862; asst. adj. gen. U.S.V., 1863; bvtd. lt. col. and brig. gen. vols., Mar. 13, 1865, "for faithful and meritorious services" during the war; early Civil War engaged in recruiting service; asst. adj. gen. of 2d div., 3d corps, Army of the Potomac; asst. insp. arty. U.S.A., 1864-65; took part in battles of Gettysburg, Kelly's Ford, Locust Grove, Mine Run, Harper's Ferry, etc.; hon. mustered out, Sept. 14, 1865. Resumed practice at Bangor, Me.; city solicitor, 1867-68; register in bankruptcy, 1867-78; U.S. commr., 1867-1909; reporter decisions Supreme Judicial Ct., 1885-1905; lecturer in Coll. of Law, U. of Me., 1899-; mem. Me. Ho. of Rep., 1883-85); Republican. Chmn. exec. com. Me. Gettysburg Commn.) trustee Penobscot Savings Bank, 1868-; pres. Eastern Me. Gen. Hosp., 1892. Author: Insolvent Laws of Maine, etc. Home: Bangor, Me. Died 1911.

HAMLIN, CHAUNCEY J. civic service; b. Buffalo, Jan. 11, 1881; s. Harry and Grace (Enos) H.; A.B., Yale, 1903; LL.B., Buffalo Law Sch., 1905; LL.D., Alfred U., 1954; m. Emily Gray, Apr. 4, 1905 (dec. Sept. 25, 1933); children - Chauncey J., Martha (wife of Dr. Franciscus Vissre't Hooft), Mary King Goodwin; m. 2d, Elizabeth Wilkeson Freeman, Nov. 26, 1934 (dec. Mar. 27, 1951); m. 3d, Ella Gayle Hand, Mar. 20, 1952. Clk. law offices Rogers, Locke & Milburn, Buffalo, 1905; opened office on own account, 1907; U.S. referee in bankruptcy until 1912; mem. O'Brian & Hamlin, later O'Brian, Hamlin, Donovon & Goodyear; spl. partner Wood, Trubee & Co., investment securities, 1937-, Landgon B. Wood & Co., 1940-41, Hamlin & Lunt, 1941-; mem. N.Y. Stock Exchange, 1941-; dir. Buffalo, Rochester & Pitts. Ry. Co., 1931. Chmn. Erie County Com. of Progressive Party, 1912; candidate for lt. gov. of N.Y., 1914. Commd. 2d lt. 65th Inf., N.Y. N.G.; regt. called to Fed. service, served from 1st lt. to capt., Mexican border, 1916; U.S. Army, AEF, 1917-19. Endowment founder mem. Buffalo Soc. Natural Scis.; 1937, mem. bd. mgrs., 1915, v.p. 1919, pres., 1920-48; instrumental in creation Allegheny State Park mem. commn., 1921-, chmn. 1943-46; mem. council Am. Assn. Museums, 1921-50, hon. v.p., 1921-23, pres., 1923-29; mem. N.Y. State Council Parks, 1943-46; bd. dirs. Buffalo Fine Arts Acad., 1912-14, 22-27, life fellow, 1940-; mem. N.Y. State Planning Bd.; chmn. Nat. GuardConf. on Outdoor Recreation, 1924-30, Niagara Frontier Planning Bd., 1925-47; bd. dirs. Buffalo City Planning Assn., pres., 1920-27; bd. dirs. Niagara Frontier Planning Assn., Am. Civic Assn., Buffalo Legal Aid Bur.; chmn. Niagara Frontier Com. for Def. Am.; mem. council Yosemite Mus. Assn. (adv. council), Nat. Econ. League; mem. hon. adv. council Roosevelt Wildlife Sta.; Pres. Buffalo Chamber Music Soc., 1934-55; vice chmn. Buffalo Philharmonic Soc., 1936, mem. bd. dirs. 1937-; asso. life mem. Buffalo council Boy Scouts Am., 1936-. Life mem. N.Y. State Hist. Assn., Am. Forestry Assn., Rochester Mus. Arts and Scis.; mem. Alpha Delta Phi, Phi Beta Kappa, Skull and Bones. Awarded Chancellor's medal U. Buffalo 1931; Cornelius Pugsley medal Am. Scenic and Historic Preservation Soc. 1933; Distinguished Service award Am. Assn. Museums, 1947; Officer, French Legion of Honor, 1947; medal of the Order of King George (Greece), ú 1946; Officer of Legion of Honor and Merit (Haiti), 1950; awarded medal Swedish Museums Assn.; Chauncey J. Hamlin Hall Buffalo Mus. Sci., named in his honor. Trustee Am. Mus. Natural History, N.Y., State Roosevelt Meml., Am. Scenic and Historic Preservation Soc., Internat. Council Museums (founder and pres. 1946-53), Isaac Walton Conservation Found.; mem. Cult White Buffalo (hon.). Republican. Episcopalian. Clubs: Country, Automobile, Buffalo, Thursday (Buffalo); Century Assn., Links (N.Y.); Cosmos (Washington); Sierra; Cypress Point (Pebble Beach, Cal.). Home: 580 Park Av., N.Y.C. 10021. Office: Buffalo Museum of Science, Humboldt Park, Buffalo 11. Died Nov. 23, 1963; buried Forest Lawn Cemetery, Buffalo.

HAMMER, JOHN SCHACKELFORD U.S. officer; b. Maysville, Ky., July 13, 1842; s. George and Panophy H.; common school edn.: m. Belle Sanders, June 30, 1869 (died 1889); m. 2d, Ella C. Sloat, 1896. Served all grades private to col. 16th Ky. vol. inf., 1861-65; as 2d and 1st lt., 19th U.S. inf., 1866-73; deputy U.S. marshal, 3d div., U.S. Court, Ind. Ty., 1889-92; postmaster Ardmore, Ind. Ty., 1892-96; 1st mem. Nat. Rep. Com. from Ind. Ty., 1892-96; U.S. marshal, southern dist. Ind. Ty., 1897-1902; U.S. clerk, Ada, Ind. Ty., from Nov. 1, 1902. Dept. comdr. G.A.R. for Ind. Ty., 1901-02. Mem. mil. order Loyal Legion. Mason. Deceased.

HAMMOND, CHARLES HERRICK, architect; b. Crown Point, N.Y., Aug. 8, 1882; s. Charles Lyman and Mary Electa (Stevens) H.; ed. pub. schs.; grad. Chicago Manual Training Sch.; B.S. in Architecture, Armour Inst. Tech., 1904; winner Traveling Scholarship, Chicago Architectural Club; studied in Paris; m. Marion Eugenie Rogers, Oct. 4, 1911 (died Apr. 2, 1933); 1 dau., Marion Rogers; m. 2d, Mrs. L. K. Stout, February 22, 1934; 1 stepson, Richard H. Stout, U.S.N.R. Practiced at Chicago since 1907; member Chatten &Hammond, 1907-27, Perkins, Chatten & Hammond, 1927-33, Burham & Hammond since Oct. 28, 1933. Supervising architect, State of Illinois, since 1929. Served as maj. res. mil. aviator, Air Service, World War I, Chief Architect 6th Corps Area U.S. Army World War II. Former trustee Foundation for Architecture and Landscape Architecture; former vice-pres. Chicago Assn. Commerce; U.S. del. Internat. Congress Architects, 1937. Fellow A.I.A. (pres. 1928-30; past pres. Chicago chpt.); mem. Ill. Soc. Architects (past pres.); corr. mem. Royal Inst. of British Architects; U.S. del. Pan-Am. Congress Architects (Havana, Cuba), 1950. Mem. Congl. Ch. Clubs; University, Indian Hill, Country, Arts, Chicago Curling. Home: Winnetka IL Died Jan. 1969.

HAMMOND, CREED CHESHIRE army officer; b. Eugene, Ore., Oct. 9, 1874; s. James Gilmore and Sarah Elizabeth (Cheshire) H.; ed. U. of Ore.; m. Mrs. Bertha Lois Titus, Apr. 6, 1917; stepson, Bruce Linville Titus. Mercantile business and realty broker, Eugene, 1900-11 ; chief dep. sheriff, Eugene, Oregon; dir. and assistant cashier Bank of Commerce, Eugene, 1911-17; dir. and cashier Portland (Oregon) National Bank, 1919-20. Served with U.S. Vols., Philippine Islands, Spanish-American War; colonel C.A.C., U.S.A., July 25, 1917-Apr. 19, 1919; on General Staff and in Militia Bureau, 1920-25; appointed major general and chief of Militia Bur. for 4 yrs. from June 29, 1925; insular auditor of Philippines, 1929-33. Republican. Episcopalian. Home: Portland, Ore. Died Apr. 2, 1940.

HAMMOND, EDWIN POLLOCK lawyer; b. Brookville, Ind., Nov. 26, 1835; s. Nathaniel and Hannah (Sering) H.; LL.B., Asbury (now De Pauw) U., Ind., 1857; (LL.D., Wabash Coll., Ind., 1892); admitted to bar, 1858, and began practice at Rensselaer, Ind.; m. Mary V. Spitler, Mar. 1, 1864. Served as 1st lt. Co. G, 9th Ind. Vol. Inf., Apr.-July 1861; capt. Co. A, 87th Ind. Inf. and maj. and lt. col. Same regt., 1862-65. Resumed law practice, 1865; judge 30th circuit, Ind., 1873-83, 1890-92; asso. justice Supreme Ct. of Indiana, 1883-85; mem. Stuart, Hammond & Simms, Lafayette, Ind. Republican. Home: Lafayette, Ind. Deceased.

HAMMOND, GRAEME MONROE neurologist; born Phila., Feb. 1, 1858; s. William A. and Helen (Nisbet) H.; Sch. of Mines (Columbia), 1874-77; M.D., Univ. Med. Coll. (New York U.), 1881; LL.B., New York Law Sch., 1900; m. Louise Elsworth, Apr. 27, 1881. Interne, N.Y. Post-Grad. Med. Sch. and Hosp., 1881, since been identified with that instn., now prof. nervous diseases; frequently called as expert in insanity cases. Served maj. Med. R.C., Apr. 1917-Feb. 1919. Mem. Am. Neurol. Assn. (sec. and treas. 25 yrs., pres. 1911-12), Am. Psychiatric Assn., A.M.A., New York Psychiatric Soc., New York Neurol. Soc. Home: 145 E. 52d St. Office: 140 E. 54th St., New York. Died Oct. 30, 1944.

HAMMOND, ROBERT HANNA congressman, army officer; b. Milton, Pa., Apr. 28, 1791; attended acads., Milton. Engaged in merc. business; brig. gen. Pa. Militia; enlisted as lt. U.S. Army, 1817, resigned; register, recorder Northumberland County (Pa.); postmaster Milton, 1833-37; mem. U.S. Ho. of Reps. (Van Buren Democrat) from Pa., 25th-26th congresses, 1837-41; commd. paymaster U.S. Army during Mexican War, wounded and ordered home on sick leave; sailed on steamship Orleans for New Orleans, 1847. Died on the high seas, June 2, 1847; buried Milton Cemetery.

HAMMOND, ROLAND orthopaedic surgeon; b. Bellingham, Mass., July 29, 1875; s. Roland and Mary Lucinda (Rockwood) H.; A.B., Tufts Coll., 1898, hon. A.M., 1939; M.D., Harvard, 1902; m. Jane M. Macomb, Jan. 19, 1911 (dec. June 1923); m. 2d, Jane Elizabeth Moore, Sept. 3, 1925. Ex-terne orthopedic surgery dept., R.I. Hosp., 1905-07, asst. orthopedic surgeon, 1907-13, surgeon, 1913-36, cons. orthopedic surgeon since 1936; asst. orthopedic surgeon St. Joseph's Hosp., 1907-16, cons. since 1916; orthopedic surgeon Pawtucket Meml. Hosp. 1916-46, cons. since 1946; cons. orthopedic surg. Roger Williams Gen. Hosp. USNRF, Apr. 1917-June 1919; mem. M.C. U.S. Naval Hosp., Queenstown, Ireland, Sept. 1918-Feb. 1919, naval hdqrs., London, Feb.-May 1919; lt. comdr. lM.C., USNR; hon. ret., 1938. Fellow A.C.S. (chmn. 1935-46, R.I. Com. on Fractures); mem. Am. Orthopedic Assn. (v.p. 1919, 35), Am. Acad. Orthopedic Surgeons, A.M.A. (del. from R.I. 1924-34), R.I. Med. Soc. (pres. 1935-36), Providence Med. Assn. (pres. 1926), Boston Orthopedic Club (pres. 1926), Am. Assn. History Medicine (del. from Providence lMed. Hist. Club). Republican. Unitarian (non-mem.). Clubs: Providence Art, Players (Providence); Harvard (Boston). Address: 41 Boylston Av., Providence 02906. Died June 11, 1956.

HAMMOND, SAMUEL army officer, congressman; b. Richmond County, Va., Sept. 21, 1757; s. Charles and Elizabeth (Steele) H.; m. Rebecca (Elbert) Rae, 1783; m. 2d, Eliza A. O'Keefe, May 25, 1807. Served as volunteer during Lord Dunmore's War, 1774; commd. capt. Va. Volunteers, 1775; commd. capt. Continental Army, 1779, maj. LeRoy Hammond's Regt., 1780; participated in battles of Kings Mountain, Cowpens, Eutaw, others in S.C. and Ga.; commd. lt. col. at end of Revoluntionary War; mem. Ga. Legislature from Chatham County; fought against Creek Indians, 1793; surveyor gen. Chatham County; mem. U.S. Ho. of Reps. from Ga., 8th Congress, 1803-05; col. mil. and civil comdt. No. part of Dist. of La., 1804-06; judge Ct. Common Pleas, Dist. of La., 1811; pres. Territorial Council of Mo., 1813; surveyor gen. S.C., 1827; sec. State of La., 1831-35. Died Hamburg, S.C., Sept. 11, 1842.

HAMMOND, WILLIAM ALEXANDER army officer, physician; b. Annapolis, Md., Aug. 28, 1828; grad. U. City N.Y., 1848; m. Helen Nisbet, 1849; m. 2d, Esther D. Chapin, 1886. Commd. 1st lt. U.S. Army, 1849, advanced through grades to brig. gen.; served as asst. surgeon, 1849-60, surgeon gen., 1862-64, court-martialed, 1864, honorably restored to rank, 1878; prof. anatomy, physiology U. Med., 1860-62; established practice medicine N.Y., circa 1864; prof. diseases of mind, nervous system Balt., N.Y. med. colls. Amateur ornithologist, Hammond's flycatcher named in his honor. Home: Washington. Died 1900.

HAMPTON, WADE congressman, army officer, planter; b. Halifax County, Va., 1752; s. Anthony and Anne (Preston) H.; m. Mrs. Martha Epps Howell, 1783; m. 2d, Harriet Flud, 1786; m. 3d, Mary Cantey, 1801; 2 children including Wade. Commd. lt. col. Continental Army, 1781, served with distinction under Gen. Thomas Sumter in Revolutionary War; mem. Va. Legislature, 1782-92; justice of peace Richmond County; mem. conv. which ratified U.S. Constn., 1788; sheriff Camden Dist.; mem. U.S. Ho. of Reps. (Republican) from Va., 4th Congress, 1795-97, 8th Congress, 1803-05; presdl. elector, 1801; commd. col. U.S. Army, 1808, brig. gen., 1809; in charge of fortification of Norfolk, Va., 1812-13; commd. maj. gen., 1813, in command of army on Lake Champlain in Mil. Dist. 9, repulsed in attack on Sir George Prevost at Chateaugay, and in expdn. against Montreal, 1813; owner cotton plantation, Richland County, S.C., also sugar plantations, Ark. and Miss.; reputed to have been wealthiest planter in Am. at time of death. Died Columbia, S.C., Feb. 4, 1835; buried Trinity Churchyard, Columbia.

HAMPTON, WADE soldier, U.S. senator; b. Columbia, S.C., 1818; s. Col. Wade H., g.s. Gen. Wade H.: grad. Univ. of S.C.; studied law, but never practiced, devoting his attention to managing his plantations in S.C. and Miss. Was mem. S.C. legislature before war, and made notable speech against reopening of the slave trade; m. Margaret, d. Gen. Francis Preston; m. 2d, d. of Senator George McDuffie of S.C. Enlisted at beginning of Civil war as pvt., but soon after raised command of inf., cav. and arty. known as Hampton's Legion, which distinguished itself at Bull Run, in Peninsula campaign, and many others, especially at Gettysburg; became maj. gen. Aug. 3, 1863; checked Sheridan at Trevillian's Station, 1864; was made comdr. Lee's cav., Aug. 1864, with rank of lt. gen.; later detached to command Gen. Joseph E. Johnston's cav.; several times wounded; cotton planter after war; gov. S.C., 1877-79; U.S. senator, 1879-91. Democrat, but advocate of the gold standard. Home: Columbia, S.C. Died 1902.

HAMTRAMCK, JOHN FRANCIS army officer; b. Ft. Wayne, Ind., Apr. 19, 1798; s. Col. John Francis and Rebecca (Mackenzie) H.; grad. U.S. Mil. Acad., 1819; m. Miss Williamson; m. 2d, Ellen Selby; m. 3d, Sarah Selby; several children including Selby Mackenzie. Left under guardianship of William Henry Harrison at death of his father, 1803; served as sgt. 1st inf. under Zachary Taylor in War of 1812; commd. 2d lt. of arty., 1819, stationed at Ft. McHenry, Balt., resigned 1822; U.S. Indian agt. (apptd. by Pres. John Q. Adams) to Osage

Indians, 1826-31; planter, nr. Shepherdstown, Va. (now W. Va.), 1831-46; apptd. col. 1st Va. Volunteer Regt., 1846; joined Zachary Taylor in Mexico; mil. gov. of Saltillo (Mexico); mustered out 1848; mayor Shepherdstown, justice Jefferson County (Va.) Ct., 1854-58. Died - Apr. 21, 1858.

HANCOCK, WINFIELD SCOTT soldier, presdl. candidate; b. Montgomery Square, Pa., Feb. 14, 1824; s. Benjamin Franklin and Elizabeth (Hoxworth) H.; grad. U.S. Mil. Acad., 1844; m. Almira Russell, Jan. 24, 1850; 2 children. Served as 2d lt. U.S. Army during Mexican War, 1846, distinguished at battles of Contreras and Churubusco, brevetted 1st lt., 1847; regimental q.m. and adj. on Upper Missouri, 1848-55; served as q.m. with rank capt. under Gen. Harvey during Seminole War, 1855; accompanied Gen. Harvey expdn. to Utah; commd. brig. gen., organized and trained newly assembled Army of Potomac, 1861; served under McClellan in Peninsular Campaign at battles of Antietam and Fredericksburg, 1862, commanded a corps at Battle of Gettysburg, 1863, and at Spottsylvania Ct. House, where he took 4000 prisoners, 1864; commd. maj. gen., 1862; in command of II Army Corps, 1863; commd. brig. gen. U.S. Army, 1864, maj. gen., 1866; command of Central Mil. Dept., 1867 commanded Dept. of La. and Tex., 1867; commanded Dept. of Dakota, 1870-72, Div. of the Atlantic, 1872-86, and Dept. of East; unsuccessful Democratic candidate for U.S. Pres., 1880. Died Governors Island, N.Y., Feb. 9, 1886; buried Norristown, Pa.

HAND, EDWARD physician, army officer; b. Kings' County, Ireland, Dec. 31, 1744; s. John Hand; ed. Trinity Coll.; m. Catharine Ewing, Mar. 13, 1775. Served as surgeon's mate Brit. Navy, came to Phila., 1767; lt. col. of brigade under Gen. William Thompson Continental Army, 1775, took part in seige of Boston, battles of L.I., Trenton, Princeton; Lancaster County Associators, col. riflemen, 1776; commd. brig. gen., 1777; brevetted maj. gen. Pa. Militia, 1783; mem. Continental Congress from Pa., 1784-85; mem. Pa. Assembly, 1785-86; presdl. elector, 1789; mem. Pa. Constl. Conv., 1789-90; maj. gen. provisional U.S. Army, 1798; U.S. insp. revenue, 1791-1801. Died "Rockford," Lancaster, Pa., Sept. 3, 1802.

HANDLEY, HAROLD WILLIS, gov. Ind., advt. agy. exec.; b. LaPorte, Ind., Nov. 27,21909; s. Harold Lowell and Lottie (Brackbill) H.; A.B., Ind. U., 1932, LL.D., Valparaiso U., 1957, Indiana U., 1957, Tri-State College (Angola, Indiana), 1958; married Barbara Jean Winterble, Feb. 17, 1944; children—Kenneth David, Martha Jean. Sales rep. Unagusta Furniture Corp., Hazelwood, N.C., 1940-53; v.p. Darling Motion Picture Sales, 1949-53; Midwest sales rep. John Sutherland Prodns., Hollywood, Cal, 1952; Ind. State senator, 1941, 49-52; lt. gov., State Ind., 1953-57, gov., 1957-61; chmn. bd. Handley-Miller, Indpls. Served with Armed Forces, 1942-46; lt. col. Inf., O.R.C. Mem. Am. Legion, Delta Tau Delta. Republican. Presbyn. Elk, Mason. Eagle, Moose. Club: Lions. Home: Indianapolis IN Died Aug. 30, 1972.

HANES, FREDERIC MOIR physician; b. Winston-Salem, N.C., Sept. 18, 1883; s. John Wesley and Anna (Hodgin) H.; A.B., Univ. of N.C., 1903; A.M., Harvard, 1904; M.D., Johns Hopkins, 1908; m. Elizabeth Peck, Dec. 16, 1913. Interne. Johns Hopkins Hosp., 1908-09; asso. prof. of pathology, Columbia, and pathologist, Presbyn. Hosp., New York, 1909-12; asso. Rockefeller Inst., 1912-13; asso. prof. of medicine, Washington U. Med. Dept., 1913-14; asst. in neurology Queen Square Hosp., London, 1914; prof. of therapeutics, Med. Coll. of Va., 1914-16; internist., Winston-Salem, N.C., 1918-31; physican Duke Hosp., 1931, prof. of medicine since 1933. Served as lt. col., Med. Corps, U.S. Army, Comdg. Base Hosp. 65, A.E.F., 1917-19. Fellow Am. Coll. Physicians; mem. Assn. Am. Physicians, A.M.A., Clin. and Climatol. Assn., N.C. State Med. Soc., Sigma Alpha Epsilon, Nu Sigma Nu, Phi Beta Kappa, Alpha, Omega Alpha. Contbr. to med. jours. Home: Campus Road, Durham, N.C. Died Mar. 25, 1946.

HANES, ROBERT MARCH banker; b. Winston-Salem, N.C., Sept. 22, 1890; s. John Wesley and Anna (Hodgin) H.; student Woodberry Forest Sch., Orange, Va., 1907; A.B., University of North Carolina, 1912, LL.D., 1945; student Harvard University School of Business Administrn., 1912-13; m. Mildred Borden, July 3, 1917; children-Frank Borden, Sara Anne. Sec., treas. Crystal Ice Co., Winston-Salem, 1913-17; v.p. Wachovia Bank & Trust Co., Winston-Salem, 1920-31, pres., 1931-56, hon. chmn., 1956—: dir. So. Ry. Co., P. H. Hanes Knitting Co., Hanes Dye & Finishing Co., Security Life & Trust Co., R. J. Reynolds Tobacco Co., Borden Mfg. Co., Chatham Mfg. Co., Piedmont Nat. Gas Co., Piedmont Pub. Co., Carolina Power & Light Co. Chief E.C.A. Mission to Belgium and Luxembourg, 1949; dir. Economic Affairs for Western Germany, 1949-50; mem. bus. adv. council for sec. of commerce; civilian aide to sec. of army; chmn. commerce and industry div. N.C. Dept. Conservation and Development; pres. Gov.'s Research Triangle Com. of N.C. Mem. N.C. Gen. Assembly, 1919, 1931, Senate, 1933. Trustee Morehead Found., U. N.C. Served from 1st lt. to maj., arty., U.S. Army, 1917-18, AEF. Selected as Man of Year in N.C. by Newcomen. Mem. Am. (pres.), N.C. (pres.) bankers assns., C. of C. (pres.), Assn. Reserve City Bankers (pres.), Sigma Alpha Epsilon, Democrat. Methodist. Clubs: Twin City, Forsyth Country, Old Town, Dunes, Rotary (pres.), Lint Head Shoot, Rainbow Springs, Coral Bay. Home: 140 Stratford Rd., Winston-Salem, N.C. Died Mar. 10, 1959; buried Winston-Salem.

HANFORD, CHARLES BARNUM actor and mgr.; b. Sutter Creek, Calif., May 5, 1859; s. Levi and Lucy (Barnum) H.; grad. Washington (D.C.) High Sch., 1881, followed by short time each in collegiate and law depts. Columbian U.; m. Mariella Twaddell Bear, June 30, 1885. Was in U.S. Pension Office, 1880-82; pvt. sec. Hon. H. F. Page, M.C., Calif., 1880-82. Began 1st season as actor at New London, Conn., Sept. 1882, with William Stafford, playing Shakespearean plays; with Thomas W. Keene, 1883-85, with Robson and Crane as AEgeon in "Comedy of Errors," 1885-86, with Edwin Booth, 1886-87, Booth and Barrett, 1887-89 (prin. success as Marc Antony to Booth's Brutus and Barrett's Cassius), Booth and Modjeska, 1889-90, Julia Marlowe, 1890-92; 1st starring tour, 1892-93, as Marc Antony in Julius Caesar and in Ingomar; sub-star and mgr. with Thomas W. Keene, 1896-98, joint star with Louis James and Kathryn Kidder as James, Kidder & Hanford Co., 1899-1900, later starring with own co.; season 1910 and 11, engaged for Appius, in Maeterlinck's "Mary Magdalene," at the New Theatre, New York, with Miss Olga Nethersole; lecture tours with Captain Scott South Pole Expedition, motion pictures, 1913, 14, 15. Engaged for part of "King Duncan," by James K. Hackett, Criterion Theatre, New York, production of Macbeth, 1915-16; joint star with John E. Kellerd in Shakespearean plays, 1916-17. Enlisted June 19, 1917, as chief yeoman, U.S.N.R.F., and assigned to office of Naval Intelligence; detailed to duty with Thomas A. Edison, later as an editorial writer in hist. sect., Navy Dept. Mason. Died Oct. 16, 1926.

HANFORD, FRANKLIN rear adm. U.S.N.: b. Chili, N.Y., Nov. 8, 1844; s. William Haynes H., Jr., and Abbey (Pixley) H.; apptd. from N.Y., and grad. U.S. Naval Acad., 1866: m. Sara A. Crosby, Nov. 6, 1878 (died 1915); children-Mary Crosby (dec.), John Munn, Ruth Crosby. Promoted ensign Apr. 1868; master 1869; lt., 1870. lt. comdr., Oct.1885; comdr., Sept., 1894; capt., Jan. 29, 1901; rear adm. Jan. 3, 1903. Served on various stas. and duties; circumnavigated the globe while attached to flagship Pensacola as navigator, 1881-84, taking observations for determination of the variations of the compass. protected Am. interests during revolutions in Ecuador and Nicaragua while comdg. U.S.S. Alert, 1895-97; comdt. U.S. Naval Sta., Cavite, P.I., 1900-02; retired after 40 yrs.' service, Jan. 3, 1903. Farming since retirement. Home: Scottsville, N.Y. Died Feb. 8, 1928.

HANLEY, JOSEPH RHODES lawyer; b. Davenport, Ia., May 30, 1876; s. John R. and Katherine (Rhodes) H.; LL.B., State U. Ia. Coll. Law, 1900; hon. D.D., Ia. Wesleyan Coll.; hon. LL.D., Houghton Coll., N.Y.; m. Henrietta Victoria Robertson, Oct. 31, 1900; children - James Robertson, Josephine Georgia (Mrs. Kenneth Edgar Wilcox), Julian Richard. Admitted to Ia. bar, June 1900; ordained Meth. ministry Ia. Conf., June 1900; lectr., Chatauqua and Lyceum, 1912; entered Presbyn. ministry, Genesee Presbytery, N.Y., 1924; elected N.Y. State legislature, 1926; elected majority leader Senate, 1939; lt. gov., 1943-51; admitted to N.Y. bar, 1931; mem. law firm, Hanley & Hanley; spl. counsel N.Y. Div. Vets. Affairs. Served in Spanish Am. War, 50th Ia. Vol. Inf.; chaplain 157th Inf., World War I; comdr. in chief U.S. War Vets. Am. Mason (32ff). Home: 21 W. Erie St. Address: 11 N. Pearl St., Albany, N.Y. Died Sept. 1961.

HANLEY, THOMAS JAMES, JR., air force officer; b. Coshocton, O., Mar. 29, 1893; s. Thomas J. and Mary (O'Connor) H.; stu. U.S. Mil. Acad., 1911-15; grad. Air Corps Tactical Sch., 1921, Command and Gen. Staff Sch., 1930; Dr. Mil. Science, St. Vincent's College, Latrobe, Pa.; B.S., U.S.M.A., West Point, N.Y. LL.D., Duquesne University, Pittsburgh, Pa.; married Cecelia Meilleur, June 12, 1917; children—Thomas J., Dexter Long, Cecile Marie. Commd. 2d lt., U.S. Army, 1915, and advanced through the grades to brig. gen (temp.), May 22, 1942, major gen., June 1943; comdg. gen. S.E. Air Force Training Center, Maxwell Field, Ala., 1943-44; comdg. gen Air Service Comd., India-Burma Theater, 1944-45, Army Air Forces, India-Burma Theater, 1945-46, 11th Air Force 1946-48; chief mil. personnel Procurement Service Div., AGO, 1948-52; Decorated Distinguished Service Medal, Legion of Merit with Oak Leaf Cluster, Air Medal; Hon. Companion of the Bath (Brit.); Spl. Collar Ornament Yun Hui (China). Clubs: Army and Navy (Washington); Army-Navy Country (Va.). Home: Chevy Chase MD Died Mar. 1969.

HANLON, LAWRENCE WILSON, coll. dean, physician; b. Wellsburg, N.Y., Nov. 15, 1914; s. James F. and Lula (Halstead) H.; A.B., Cornell U., 1935, M.D., 1938. Intern, then asst. resident Rochester (N.Y.) Gen. Hosp., 1938-40; asst. resident 2d med. div. Bellevue Hosp., N.Y.C., 1946-49; asst. dean Cornell U. Med. Col., 1949-55, asso. dean, 1955-70, sec. faculty, 1962-70. Served to lt. col., M.C., AUS, 1941-45. Mem. Assn. Am. Med. Colls. (chmn. Northeastern region group student affairs 1959-65), Harvey Soc., A.A.A.S. Club: Griffis Faculty (pres.) (Cornell U. Med. Coll.). Home: New York City NY Died Sept. 1970.

HANN, CHARLES lawyer; b. Montgomery, Ala. Feb. 7, 1888; s. Charles and Annie (Sykes) H.; A.B., Harvard, 1911. Carnegie Found. fellow in internat. law, 1912-13, A.M., LL.B., Columbia, 1915. Admitted to N.Y. bar, 1915, and later to bar U.S. Supreme Ct.; admitted to Cal. bar, 1932; began practice in N.Y.C.; dep. atty. gen. of N.Y., 1920; sr. mem. Hann and Hann; dir. Anderson Die Casting & Engring. Corp.; v.p. treas. Canadian U.S. Knitting Co. of St. Hyacinthe, Que. Served in USN, 1917-19, advancing to lt. comdr.; put U.S.S. Edorea in commn.; organized and directed Officers' Material Sch. (deck) and in charge sea tng. 4,250 naval officers for troop and cargo transports operated by U.S. Navy (4 mos. tng. for commns. instead of customary 2 yrs. for licenses). Named by Gov. Miller to represent state of N.Y. at ceremonies incident to burial of Unknown Soldier, at Arlington, Va., 1920. Del. to Internat. Congress of Interallied Veteran's Fedn., Warsaw, 1926, London, 1927, Bucharest, 1928, Belgrade, 1929, Lisbon, 1932 (chmn.), Casablanca, 1933 (chmn.). Trustee Am. Seamen's Friend Soc.; nat. v.p. Bundles fo Am. and Bundles for Bluejackets. Mem. Am., N.Y. State bar assns., N.Y. County Lawyers' Assn., Harvard, Columbia law sch. assns., Maritime Law Assn. U.S., Rep. County Com., Am. Legion (comdr. N.Y. County, 1936, 1st dist. 1922), Navy League U.S. (v.p.), Mil. Order World Wars (past comdr.-in-chief), Naval Order U.S. (comdg. gen.), Soc. Mil. and Naval Officers World Wars (perpetual). Mil. Order Fgn. Wars (registrar), Soc. Am. Wars (past commander-general), Army and Navy Union U.S.A. (past comdr.) F I D A C (v.p. 1932-35), 40 and 8 (avocat), Rep. Service League (treas.), Am. Soc. French Legion of Honor (dir.), Bolivarian Soc. (dir.), 1937 N.Y. Nat. Conv., Am. Legion Corp., (ex-com), Am. Nautical Cadets (pres.), Am. Emergency Vol. Ambulance Corps (treas.). Decorated Officer Legion of Honor (French); Order of Crown (It.); Polonia Restituta (Polish); Gen. Haller Swords; Macedonian (Greek); Bolivarian; Columbia Conspicious Service; Victory; N.Y. State, c.-in-c.'s Medal, M.O.W.W.; Medal of Army, Navy, Air Force Veterans in Can. Episcopalian. Clubs: Bankers of Am., Harvard, Delta Kappa Epsilon, Economic, Ends of Earth, N.Y. Yacht, University, Embassy, Nat. Republican. Propeller, Harvard Varsity, Columbia C. The Pilgrims, Church, English Speaking Union; Phi Sigma Omega (hon.), Sigma Phi Upsilon, Pershing Hall (Paris). Presented with loving cup by Harvard football players, 1912, by undergrads of Columbia, 1914. Homes: 536 Hardee Rd., Coral Gables 46. Florida; and S. Sea Av., West Yarmouth. Cape Cod, Mass. Office: 12 E. 41st St., N.Y.C. 17. Died June 5, 1957.

HANNA, JOHN ANDRE congressman; b. Flemington, N.J., 1762; grad. Coll. of N.J. (now Princeton), 1782; studied law. Admitted to Lancaster County (Pa.) bar, 1783, began practice in Lancaster, Pa.; moved to Harrisburg, Pa., admitted to Dauphin County (Pa.) bar, 178S; del. Pa. Conv. to ratify U.S. Constn., 1787; sec. Anti-Federal Conf., 1788; mem. Pa. Ho. of Reps., 1791; elected lt. col. 3d Battalion of Dauphin County, 1792; apptd. brig. gen. Dauphin County Brigade, 1793, in command during Whiskey Rebellion, 1793; apptd. maj. gen. 6th Div. of Dauphin and Berks counties, 1800; mem. U.S. Ho. of Reps. (Anti-Federalist) from Pa., 5th-9th congresses, 1797-1805. Died Harrisburg, July 23, 1805; buried Mt. Kalmia Cemetery, Harrisburg.

HANNA, MATTHEW ELTING diplomatic service; b. Gillespieville, O., Mar.9, 1873; s. Robert and Eliza (Corken) H.; grad. U.S. Mil. Acad., 1897; honor grad. Inf. and Cav. Sch., 1906. honor grad. Staff Coll., 1907; m. Helen Richards, Nov. 12, 1902; children-Matthew Elting, Barbara; m. 2d, Gustava von der Tann née Baroness von Rheinbaben, Apr. 28, 1925. Second lt., 1st lt. and capt. cav., 1897-1913. Served on western frontier, 1897-98, in 2d Cav.; in Santiago Campaign, Spanish-Am. War; recommended for brevet for gallantry at Battle of San Juan Hill, July 1-3, 1898; a.d.c. to Maj. Gen. Leonard Wood, 1898-1902; mil. attaché, Havana, 1902-04; with 3d Cav., 190 United States in Panama, 1909; War Coll., 1910; capt. on Gen. Staff, U.S.A., 1910-12: spl. rep. of U.S. At German Imperial Maneuvers, 1911; resigned from army, 1913. In mfg. business, 1912-17; insp. gen. Mass. N.G., 1912-14; vol. asst., Am. Embassy, Mexico, Feb.-Aug. 1917; 3d 2d and 1st sec. Am. Embassy in Berlin, 1924-25: apptd. foreign service insp. for Latin America, Nov. 1925, for Europe, May 1927; apptd. counselor of Am. Embassy, Lima, Peru, Nov. 1927; sec. 6th Internat. Conf. of Am. States, at Havana, Jan. 16-Feb. 20, 1928; charge d'affaires at Am. Legation, Managua, Nicaragua, May-Dec. 1929; apptd. E.E. and M.P. to Nicaragua, May-Dec. 16, 1929; apptd. E.E. and M.P. to Guatemala, Aug. 11, 1933. Developed pub. sch. system of Cuba, 1900-02. Decorated Service Medal, Santiago Campaign, Spanish-Am. War; Presidential Medal of Merit, Nicaragua, for services following earthquake at Managua, Mar. 31, 1931. Died Feb. 19, 1936.

HANNAH, HARVEY HORATIO lawyer; b. Louisville, Aug. 30, 1868; s. John H. and Lillie L. (Gerding) H.; ed. mil. coll.; LL.B., Univ. of Tenn., 1891; unmarried. Began practice at Oliver Springs, Tenn.,

1891; pvt. sec. to Gov. Robert L. Taylor; Dem. presdl. elector, 1896; U.S. commr.; state railroad commr. since Jan. 1, 1907. Served as capt. Tenn. N.G.; lt. col. 4th Tenn. Vols., Spanish-Am. War; adj. gen. Tenn., 1903-07. Presbyterian. Mem. Sigma Nu. Residence: Oliver Springs, Tenn. Address: Nashville, Tenn. Died Nov. 8, 1936.

HANRAHAN, EDWARD MITCHELL surgeon; b. Binghamton, N.Y., Oct. 16, 1892; s. Edward M. and Julia (Stack) H.; A.B., Cornell, 1915; M.D., Johns Hopkins, 1919; m. Evelyn Barton Randall, Feb. 3, 1923; children-Julia Stack, Edward Mitchell. Intern, asst. resident Johns Hopkins Hosp., 1919-21; asst. resident Union Meml. Hosp., Balt., 1921-22; grad. study surgery, Vienna, Austria, 1922: instr. surgery and anatomy med. sch., Johns Hopkins, 1923-26, asso. surgery, 1936-45, asst. prof., 1945-49, asso. prof. plastic surgery since 1949; vis. surgeon plastic surgery Johns Hopkins Hosp., 1926-49, plastic surgeon in charge since 1949; vis. plastic surgeon Union Meml. Hosp., Balt. City Hosp., U.S. Marine Hosp., Balt.; cons. plastic surgery Hanover (Pa.) Gen. Hosp. Served with S.A.T.C., Med. Officers Res. Corps, Diplomatic Am. Bd. Surgery (fdr.), Am. Bd. Plastic Surgery. Fellow A.C.S.; mem. A.M.A., So. Surg. Assn., Brit. Assn. Plastic Surgeons, So. Med. Assn., Am. Soc. Plastic and Reconstrn. Surgery. Alpha Delta Phi Democrat. Episcopalian. Club: Halsted. Contbr. to med. books and encys., also articles to jours. Home: Cambridge Arms Apt., Balt. 18. Office: 1201 N. Calvert St., Balt. Died 1952.

HANSCOM, JOHN FORSYTH rear adm.; b. Eliot, Me., May 21, 1842. Served in vol. army, Sept. 10, 1862-July 17, 1863: apptd. from Mass., asst. naval constr. U.S.N., July 29, 1875; promoted naval constr., Oct. 10, 1888. On duty at navy yards, Boston and League Island, Pa., Bur. Constrn., Navy Dept. advisory bd., Chester, Pa., 1883-87, and New York, 1887-88; mem. Bd. Inspection and Survey, 1889-91, 1895-97; supt. constrn., Alabama and Maine, 1898-1893; sr. mem. bds. on hull changes for ships building on Atlantic Coast: retired with rank of rear admiral, May 4, 1904. Died Sept. 30, 1912.

HANSEN, CARL W. educator; b. Russell, Minn., Dec. 9, 1901; s. Peter and Carrie K. (Petersen) H.; B.S., U. Mfinn., 1926, Ph.D., 1943; A.M., U. Chicago, 1930; m. Kathryn B. Hatheway, Sept. 13, 1930 (dec. Feb. 1958); 1 dau., Karen G.; m. 2d, Martha B. Riebel, Sept., 1959. Teacher history, Jr. High Sch., Wausau, Wis., 1926-30; prin., Madison Elem. and Jr. High Sch., Quincy, Ill., 1930-39, supervisor, Office of Supt. of Schs., 1940-41; asonso. prof. edn., Teachers Coll., U. Cincinnati, 1946-48, prof. edn. since 1948, dir. student teaching and placement since 1947. Res. officer, U.S. Army since 1926, dir. instrn., Adj. Gens. Sch., 1942-43; commandant U.S. Armed Forces Inst., Madison, Wis., 1943-45; col., U.S.A.R. since 1945. Mem. Am. Assn. Univ. Profs. Co-author (with Margaret McKim and William L. Carter). Learning to Teach in the Elementary School, 1959, Learning To Teach in the Secondary School, 1962. Home: 2728 Erie Av., Cin. 8. Died May 21, 1961; buried Vine Street Cemetery, Cin.

HANSON, MURRAY, lawyer, assn. exec.; b. Balt., Dec. 19, 1904; s. John M. and Maude L. (Rowe) H.; student U. Del., Harvard Law Sch. With Baker, Hostetler & Patterson, Cleve., 1930-42, as sec. and asst. to Newton D. Baker, 1930-34; legal service Nat. Assn. Securities Dealers, 1935-42; gen. counsel Investment Bankers Assn. Am., Washington, 1946-54, managing director, general counsel, 1954-66, consultant, 1966-71. Served from 1st lieutenant to col. AUS, 1942-46, asst. exec. officer Asst. Sec. War for Air, 1943-46. Clubs: Burning Tree, Metropolitan, University (Washington); Lunch (N.Y.C.); Farmington Country (Charlottesville, Va.). Home: Washington DC Died Dec. 5, 1971.

HANSON, NORWOOD RUSSELL educator; b. N.J., Aug. 17, 1924; s. Samuel Norwood and Hannah Helen (Proper) H.; music student Curtis Inst., 1941; B.A., U. Chgo., 1946; B.Sc. (E.W.S. Johnstone scholar), Columbia, 1948, A.M., 1949; B.Phil. (Fulbright scholar, Fulbright fellow), Oxford (Eng.) U., 1951, D.Phil., 1955, research student Nuffield Coll.; M.A. (fellow St. John's Coll.), Cambridge (Eng.) University, 1952, Ph.D., 1956; also M.A., Yale U., New Haven, Conn., 1963; m. Frances Fay Kenney, Aug. 14, 1948; children - Trevor Russell, Leslie Fay. Univ. lecturer philosophy of science, Cambridge U., 1952-57; prof. philosophy Ind. U., 1957-62, prof. of history and logic of sci., 1962-63, chmn. dept. history and logic of sci., 1960-62; prof. philosophy Yale U., 1963 - ; visiting lecturer at Oxford U. Internat. Congress History 1961; Silliman lectr. Yale, 1961. Served to maj. USMCR, 1942-45. Nuffield Found. fellow for study Inst. Advanced Study, Princeton, N.J., Cal. Inst. Tech., Ford Found. fellow, 1957; Am. Council Learned Socs. fellow, 1958; Rockefeller fellow, 1959; research fellow U. Minn. Center philosophy of Sci., 1959; grantee Am. Philos. Soc., 1961; Distinguished Alumni award Columbia, 1962. Carnegie fellow, 1967. Fellow A.A.A.S. (v.p. 1961). Author: Patterns of Discovery, 1958; The Concept of the Positron, 1962. Contbr. articles to learned jours. Home: 47 Deepwood Dr., Hamden, Conn.

HANSON, ROGER WEIGHTMAN army officer; b. Winchester, Ky., Aug. 27, 1827; s. Samuel and Matilda (Calloway) H. Served as 1st lt. U.S. Army in Mexican War, 1846-48; mem. Ky. Legislature, 1853-55; col. Ky. State Guards, regt. formed nucleus of 2d, 3d, 4th and 5th Ky. Regts.; held Confederate right wing at Ft. Donelson repulsing 2 attacks, 1862; commanded 2d Ky. Inf., then 1st Brigade (2d, 4th, 6th, 9th, Ky. inf. regts.), 1862; brig. gen., 1862; under Gen. J. H. Morgan in expdn. against Hartsville, 1862, captured and destroyed Union force of 2,000 men with loss of only 68 Confederate soldiers. Died Battle of Stone's River, Jan. 4, 1863; buried Nashville, Tenn., reinterred, Lexington, Ky.

HANSON, THOMAS GRAFTON army officer; b. San Rafael, Calif., May 1, 1865; s. Thomas Hawkins and Carlotta (Milewater) H.; grad. U.S. Mil. Acad., 1887, Inf. and Cav. Sch., 1891; m. Pauline De Forest, Sept. 13, 1893; children-Thomas Grafton, Elizabeth D. (Mrs. B. R. Alexander). Commd. 2d lt., 19th Inf., June 12, 1887; 1st lt., June 7, 1894; capt., Mar. 2, 1899; maj. 8th Inf., Mar. 24, 1910; maj. Q.-M. Corps, May 11, 1917; brig. gen. N.A., Aug. 5, 1917. Served in Spanish-Am. War, 1898, Philippine Insurrection, 1899-1901; asst. prof. modern langs., U.S. Mil. Acad., 1901-05; sr. instrn. modern langs., Army Sch. of the Line, and Army Staff Coll., Ft. Leavenworth, Kan., 1910-12; assigned to comd. 178th Inf. Brigade, 89th Div., Camp Funston, Kan., Aug. 1917; comd. 178th Brig., 89th Div., in Am. capture of St. Mihiel salient, operations beginning Sept. 12, 1918, and in final Am. assault, Nov. 1-Nov. 9, 1918, Meuse-Argonne. Retired at own request, Jan. 4, 1919. Home: Union League Club, San Francisco. Died May 23, 1945.

HARADEN, JONATHAN naval officer, privateer; b. Gloucester, Mass., Nov. 11, 1744; s. Joseph and Joanna (Emerson) H.; m. Hannah Deadman, June 8, 1767; m. 2d, Mrs. Eunice (Diman) Mason, Mar. 11, 1782; m. 3d, Mrs. Mary Scallon, Oct. 12, 1797. Lt. in sloop (later brigantine) Tyrannicide of Mass. Navy 1776, comdr., 1777; together with another ship he sailed around Brit. Isles and France searching for prizes; cruised in W.I., 1777; comdr. privateering ship General Pickering, 1778, engaged and captured 3 ships at one time, encountered larger ship Brit. privateer Achilles, 1780, forced Achilles to run off; captured with General Pickering at St. Eustatius, W.I., 1781; commanded privateer Julius Caesar after obtaining freedom, 1782. Died Salem, Mass., Nov. 23, 1803.

HARALSON, HUGH ANDERSON congressman; b. nr. Penfield, Ga., Nov. 13, 1805; grad. Franklin Coll. (now U. Ga.), 1825; studied law. Admitted to Ga. bar, 1825, began practice in Monroe; moved to Lagrange, Ga., 1828, practiced law; engaged in farming; mem. Ga. Ho. of Reps., 1831-32; Ga. Senate, 1837-38; served as maj. gen. Ga. Militia, 1838-40; mem. U.S. Ho. of Reps.(Democrat) from Ga., 28th-31st congresses, 1843-51; resumed practice of law. Died Lagrange, Sept. 25, 1854; buried Hill View Cemetery, Lagrange.

HARBACH, ABRAM ALEXANDER army officer; b. Pa., Aug. 14, 1841. Sergt. Co. E, 1st Ia. Inf., May 7-Aug. 20, 1861; pvt. and corporal, Co. H, 11th U.S. Inf., Dec. 7, 1861-June 20, 1862; 2d lt. 11th Inf., June 11, 1862; 1st lt., July 2, 1863; transferred to 20th Inf., Sept. 21, 1866: capt., Jan. 22, 1867; maj. 18th Inf., Mar. 12, 1894; lt. col. 3d Inf., Aug. 8, 1897; served in Santiago campaign in Cuba, 1898, and P.I., 1900; col. 1st Inf., July 19, 1899) brig. gen. U.S.A., Mar. 16, 1902: retired, May 28, 1902, at his own request, after 40 yrs.' service. During Civil War was engaged in many battles, and bvtd. capt., July 2, 1863, "for gallant and meritorious services at Gettysburg." Home: Santa Barbara, Calif. Died Nov. 22, 1933.

HARBER, GILES BATES rear adm.; b. Youngstown, O., Sept. 24, 1849; s. Joseph and Ann Eliza (Darrow) H.: apptd. from Ohio, and grad. U.S. Naval Acad., 1869; m. Jeannette Thurston Manning, Apr. 25, 1889. Promoted ensign July 12, 1870; master, July 12, 1871; lt., Sept. 19, 1874; lt. comdr., Sept. 4, 1896: comdr., Sept. 25, 1899; capt., Sept. 30, 1904; rear adm., Nov. 12, 1908. Served on Sabine and Franklin, European sta., 1869-71; Iroquois and Monocacy, China sta., 1872-75; Omaha, S. Pacific sta., 1875-78; Tennessee and Alarm, N. Atlantic sta., 1879-82; Saratoga and Tallapoosa, W.I. and S. Atlantic stas., 1885-88; Hassler (coast survey), in Alaska, 1892-95; aboard Texas, W.I., during Spanish-Am. War, 1898-99; New Orleans, China sta., 1903-05; comd. Independence, Mare Island Navy Yard, 1905-07, comd. 3d Squadron Pacific Fleet, 1907-10; comdr.-in-chief Pacific Fleet, Feb. 19-Nov. 1, 1910; pres. Naval Examining and Retiring Bds., Dec. 1910-Oct. 1911; retired by operation of law, Sept. 24, 1911. Was in commd. of expdn. sent to search for survivors of the Jeannette Polar Expdn., 1882-84, and brought home bodies of DeLong and nine of his companions; naval attaché U.S. embassies, France and Russia, 1900-03. Promoted 5 numbers, Aug. 10, 1898, for "eminent and conspicuous conduct in battle." Died Dec. 30, 1925.

HARBORD, JAMES GUTHRIE army officer, hon. chmn. Radio Corp. of America; b. Bloomington, Ill., Mar. 21, 1866; s. George W. and Effie Critton (Gault) H.; B.S., Kan. State Agrl. Coll., Manhattan, Kan., 1886. M.S., 1895; grad. Inf. and Cav. Sch., 1895, Army War College, 1917; LL.D., Trinity College, 1924, Colgate, 1926, Marietta College, 1927, Yale, 1928; Washington and Jefferson College, 1938; m. Emma Yeatman Ovenshine, Jan. 21, 1899 (died May 29, 1937); m. 2d, Mrs. Anne Lee Brown, Dec. 31, 1938. Pvt., corpl. and sergt. and q.-m. sergt. 4th Inf., 1899-91; commd. 2d lt. 5th Cav., July 31, 1891; maj. 2d Vol. Cav., May 24, 1898; hon. mustered out vols., Oct. 24, 1898; 1st lt. 10th U.S. Cav., July 1, 1898; capt. 11th Cav., Feb. 2, 1901; assigned to 1st Cav., Jan. 1, 1914; maj. Dec. 10, 1914; lt. col. Gen. Staff, May 15, 1917; brig. gen. N.A., Aug. 5, 1917; maj. gen. N.A., June 26, 1918; brig. gen. U.S. Army, Nov. 30, 1918; maj. gen. U.S. Army, Sept. 8, 1919. Served as asst. chief Philippine Constabulary with rank of col., Aug. 18, 1903-Jan. 1, 1914; chief of staff, A.E.F., in France, May 15, 1917-May 6, 1918; com. Marine Brigade nr. Chateau Thierry, June-July 1918; comd. 2d Div. in Soissons offensive, July 18, 19, 1918; comd. Service of Supply, July 29, 1918-May 26, 1919; re-apptd. chief of staff, A.E.F., May 25, 1919; dep. chief of staff, U.S. Army, July 1, 1921-Dec. 29, 1922; retired lieutenant general, U.S. Army July 9, 1942; pres. Radio Corp. of America, Jan. 1, 1923-30, chmn. bd., 1930-47; honorary chairman and director since July 1947; chairman board RCA Communications, Inc.; director and member exec. com. A.T.&S.F. Ry..; mem. exec. com. N.Y. Life Ins. Co., Employers Liability Assurance Corp., Ltd. (London); dir. Bankers Trust Co., Nat. Broadcasting Co., New York Life Insurance Company. Chief of American Mil. Mission to Armenia, 1919. Hon. chmn. Am. Red Cross. N.Y. Chapter. Awarded D.S.M. of both Army and Navy; Comdr. Legion of Honor, Croix de Guerre, two palms (French); Knight Comdr. St. Michael and St. George (British); Grand Officer Order of the Crown (Belgina); Comdr. St. Maurice and St. Lazarus (Italian); Order of Prince Danilo (Montenegrin); Order of La Solidaridad (Panamanian); Grand Officer Order Polonia Restituta (Polish); gold medal of 2d Div. Mason (32ff, Knights Templar). Clubs: Army and Navy (Washington, D.C.); Knickerbocker. Nat. Republican, Century (New York); Army and Navy (Manila); Apawamis(Port Chester, N.Y.). Home: Dogwood Lane, Rye, N.Y. Office: 30 Rockefeller Plaza, New York, N.Y. Died Aug. 20, 1947; buried in Arlington Nat. Cemetery.

HARDEE, WILLIAM JOSEPH army officer; b. Camden County, Ga., Oct. 12, 1815; s. John and Sarah (Ellis) H.; grad. U.S. Mil. Acad., 1838; m. Mary Lewis, Jan. 1863, 1 child. Commd. 1st lt. 2d Dragoons, 1839, capt., 1844, accompanied Gen. Taylor across Rio Grande, commd. lt. col., 1848; published Rifle and Light Infantry Tactics (known as Hardee's Tactics, adopted as textbook by Army), 1855; sr. maj. 2d Cav., 1855; lt. col., comdt. of cadets U.S. Mil. Acad., 1856; commd. brig. gen. Confederate Army, 1861, maj. gen., 1861; commanded corps at Battle of Shiloh, 1862; commanded left wing Confederate Army at Battle of Perryville, 1862; organized original Ark. Brigade (known as Hardee's Brigade); commd. lt. gen., 1862; commanded mil. depts. of S.C., Ga. and Fla., 1864; commanded army defending Savannah (Ga.) against Gen. Sherman, 1864. Died Wytheville, Va., Nov. 6, 1873; buried Selma, Ala.

HARDEMAN, THOMAS, JR. congressman; b. Eatonton, Ga., Jan. 12, 1825; grad. Emory Coll., 1845; studied law. Admitted to Ga. bar, 1847; engaged in warehouse and commn. bus.; mem. Ga. Ho. of Reps., 1853, 55, 57; mem. U.S. Ho. of Reps. (Democrat) from Ga., 36th, 48th congresses, 1859-Jan. 23, 1861, 83-85; capt. Floyd Rifles; maj. 2d Ga. Battalion during Civil War, later col. 45th Ga. Inf., Confederate Army; mem. Ga. Ho. of Reps., 1863 64, 74, speaker; del. Nat. Dem. Conv., Balt., 1872; pres. Ga. Dem. Conv., also chmn. Ga. Dem. Exec. Com., 4 years. Died Macon, Ga., Mar. 6, 1891; buried Oak Hill Cemetery, Macon.

HARDESTY, FREDERICK A(RCHIBALD) naval officer (ret.), tchr.; b. Astoria, Ore., Jan. 16, 1893: s. Millard Fillmore and Nettie Blanche (Harriman) H.; A.B., U. Ore., 1915; student Harvard, 1917, Ensign's Sch., 1918, Submarine Sch., 1922, Naval War Coll., 1926-27, USN, Postgrad. Sch., 1931-33; m. Hannah Florence Kelly, Oct. 4, 1923 (dec. Feb. 14, 1930); 1 son, John Frederick; m. 2d, Elizabeth Fuller Collingwood, June 17, 1931; 1 son, William Harriman. Tchr. high sch., Ore., 1915-17; entered USNR, 1917; commd. ensign USN, 1918, advanced through grades to capt., 1943; ret. as rear adm., 1947. Served in U.S.S. Ohio. World War I; exec. officer, U.S.S. Heywood, 1940-42, comdg. officer U.S.S. Schuylkill, 1943-44, U.S., Rocky Mount, 1944-45. Decorated with World Wars I and II medals, Bronze Star, Philippine Liberation medal, various campaign and battle ribbons and stars. Mason. Club: Players' (Swarthmore, Pa.). Home: Moylan, Pa. Died June 6, 1956; buried Arlington Nat. Cemetery.

HARDIE, JAMES ALLEN army officer; b. N.Y.C., May 5, 1823; s. Allen Wardwell and Caroline (Cox) H.; grad. U.S. Mil. Acad., 1843; m. Margaret Hunter, 1851, 5 children. Asst. prof. geography, history and ethics U.S. Mil. Acad., 1844-46; served as maj. N.Y. Volunteers, 1846-48; became Roman Catholic; helped raise money to build 1st cathedral ch. in San Francisco during Mexican War; commd. 1st lt. 3d Arty., U.S. Army, 1848; adj. gen. Dept. of Oregon; lt. col. on staff Gen. McClellan during Peninsular and Md. campaigns, 1861, on staff Gen. Ambrose Burnside in battles around

Fredericksburg (in controversy between Burnside and William Franklin over responsibility for disaster on the Rappahannock, 1862, both contestants agreed to use his accurate field dispatches as true record of events); asst. adj. gen. Army of Potomac; commd brig. gen. Volunteers, 1862; carried secret personal message making George Meade comdr. in place of Joseph Hooker just before Gettysburg, 1863; asst. sec. to U.S. Sec. of Army Edwin W. Stanton; judge advocate gen. Army of Potomac, 1863; promoted maj. U.S. Army, 1863, maj., 1865; maj. chief of Insp. Gen.'s Office, 1865. Died Washington, D.C., Dec. 14, 1876.

HARDIN, JOHN army officer, Indian fighter; b. Fauquier County, Va., Oct. 1, 1753; s. Martin Hardin; m. Jane Davies, before 1786, at least 1 son, Martin D. Ensign in Dunmore's Indian campaign, 1774; served with Daniel Morgan's Riflemen at Saratoga during Revoluntionary War; lt. col. Ky. Militia in Wabash expdns. led by George Rogers Clark, 1786, then served with every U.S. Expdn. into Ky. Indian territory except that of Gen. Arthur St. Clair; fought Indians in Western Pa., 1786-92; col. in charge of Nelson County (Ky.) Militia; 1788, 89; commd. brig. gen. Ky. Militia; Hardin County (O.), (formed 1792) named in his honor, also Hardin County (Ky.); killed by Indians while on peace mission to Miami tribes Died Hardin County, O., Apr. 1792.

HARDIN, MARTIN D. army officer; senator; b. in Southwestern Pa., June 21, 1780; s. John and Jane (Davies) H.; ed. Transylvania Sem.; m. Elizabeth Logan, 1 son, Col. John J. Hardin. Family moved to Ky., 1786; mem. Ky. Ho. of Reps., 1805, 19-20, speaker, 1819-20; published Reports of Cases Argued and Adjudged in the Court of Appeals, Kentucky, 1810; sec. of state Ky., 1812; served as maj., in a Ky. regt. during War of 1812; mem. U.S. Senate from Ky. (Democrat), 1816-17; known as a nationalist, favored liberal interpretation of U.S. Constn. Died Frankfort, Ky., Oct. 18, 1823.

HARDIN, MARTIN D. brig. gen.; b. Jacksonville, Ill., June 26, 1837; s. Gen. John J. H., of Ill. (killed at battle of Buena Vista, Mex.); grad. U.S. Mil. Acad., 1859: bvt. 2d lt. 3d U.S. Arty., July 1, 1859; Artillery School, Ft. Monroe, Va., 1859-60; on staff Col. R. E. Lee during John Brown raid at Harper's Ferry; crossed continent with Blake Expdn., May-Oct. 1860; stationed at Ft. Umpqua, Ore., Oct. 1860 to Oct. 1861; returned to east with Gen. Sumner's expdn., via Panama; served with U.S. arty., Army of Potomac, 1861-62; present at siege of Yorktown and 7 days' battles before Richmond, Va.; lt. col. 12th Pa. reserves, April 1, 1862; col., July 8, 1862, comd. regt. at Harrison's Landing; served in Pope's campaign; comd. 12th regt. Pa. reserves; present at Rappahannock Sta., battle of Groveton, Aug. 29, 1862 (slightly wounded); comd. 3d brigade Pa. reserves 2d Bull Run (severely wounded); comd. 12th Pa. reserves at Gettysburg and Falling Waters: 3d brigade same in Rapidan campaign, Sept.-Dec., 1863; comd. 2 regts. inf. and troop of cav. guarding O.&A. R.R., Dec. 1863; severely wounded by guerrillas, Dec. 14, 1863; comd. draft rendezvous Pittsburgh, to May 15, 1864; comd. 1st brigade Pa. reserves Spottsylvania, North Anna, Bethesda Church. Brig. gen. U.S. vols., comdg. Hardin's div., defenses north of the Potomac, Washington, July 1864-Aug. 1865; present at attack of Early's forces on Washington; comd. dist. Raleigh, N.C., 1865-66; maj. 43d U.S. Inf., July 26, 1866; retired as brig. gen. U.S.A. on account of wounds, Dec. 15, 1870. Admitted to Ill. bar, Sept. 1870, and began practice at Chicago. Home: Lake Forest, Ill. Died Dec. 12, 1923.

HARDING, ABNER CLARK congressman, army officer, financier; b. East Hampton, Conn., Feb. 10, 1807; s. Nathan and Philena Sears (Clark) H.; m. Mrs. Rebecca L. (Laybricks) Byers, Jan. 30, 1829; m. 2d Susan A. Ickes, June 30, 1835; 2 children. Admitted to Pa. bar, 1828; county sch. commr., 1847-49; mem. Ill. Ho. of Reps., 1848-50; organizer 2d Nat. Bank Monmouth (Ill.); engaged in constrn. of Peoria & Oquawka R.R.; mem. 1st bd. trustees Monmouth (Ill.) Coll., 1853, later endowed a professorship; commd. brig. gen. U.S. Volunteers, 1863; mem. U.S. Ho. of Reps. from Ill., 39th-40th congresses, 1865-69. Died Monmouth, July 1874; buried Monmouth Cemetery.

HARDING, CHESTER army officer: b. Enterprise, Miss., Dec. 31, 1866; s. Horace and Eliza Procter (Gould) H.; B.E., U. of Ala., grad. U.S. Mil. Acad., 1889, U.S. Engr. Sch. of Application, Willetts Point, N.Y., 1S92; m. Flora Krum, July 15, 1895. Commd. add. 2d lt. engrs., June 12, 1889; advanced through grades to lt. col., Feb. 27, 1913; brig. gen. and retired, Apr. 1, 1920. Served as asst. to engr. commr. of D.C., 1901-06; div. engr., Gatun Locks Div., Panama Canal, 1907-08; asst. div. engr., Atlantic Div., Panama Canal, 1908-13; engr. commr. of D.C., 1913-14; engr. of maintenance, Panama Canal, 1915-17; gov. Panama Canal, Jan. 1917-Mar. 1921. Unitarian. Home: Vineyard Haven, Mass. Died Nov. 11, 1936.

HARDING, EDWIN FORREST, army officer; b. Franklin, O., Sept. 18, 1886; s. Clarence Henry and Lilly (Woodward) H.; B.S., U.S. Military Acad., 1909; grad. The Inf. Sch. (advanced class), 1928, Command and Gen. Staff Sch., 1929, Army War Coll., 1934; m. Eleanor Hood, Sept. 23, 1913; children—Davis Philoon, Elinore Hood (wife Lt. Col. James O'Hara, U.S. Army), Edwin Forrest, Jr., Anne Woodward. Commd 2d lt., Inf., U.S. Army, 1909, advanced through ranks to maj. gen., 1942; instr. English, Hist. and Econs. at U.S. Military Acad., 1919-23; instr. The Infantry Sch., 1929-33; sec. U.S. Inf. Assn and editor of The Inf. Jour., 1934-38; commd 27th Inf. at Schofield Barracks, T.H., 1938-40; asst. to div. comdr., 9th Inf. Div., 1941; comd. 32d Inf. Div., Feb.-Dec. 1942, and during early phases of Buna campaign in New Guinea; comdg. Mobile Force Panama Canal Dept., Mar. 1943-Aug. 1944; comdg. Antilles Department, Aug. 1944-45; dir. hist. div. Office Chief of Staff, U.S. Army, 1945-46; ret., 1946. Awarded Silver Star for gallantry in action, Legion of Honor; Order of Abder Calderon, Ecuador; Gran Official del Order Militar de Ayucucho, Peru; Gran Official de la Orden del Condor de los Andes (Bolivia). Co-author and editor Infantry in Battle, 1934. Home: Franklin OH Died June 5, 1970; buried Franklin OH

HARDING, GEORGE M. artist; b. Phila., October 2, 1882; s. Joseph and Charlotte Elizabeth (Matthews) U.; brother Charlotte Harding Brown; ed. Pa. Acad. Fine Arts, and with Howard Pyle, 1902-03; studied architecture; m. Anita Cotheal Nisbett, 1916 (dec.); children-Anita N. (Mrs. John Kistler), George M. Sent to northern ice fields, West Indies by Harper's, 1908, 10, 11; spl. artist, Harper's Mag., on journey around the world, working in Australia, New Guinea, Arabia, Dutch East Indies, Malay States, China, 1912-13. Mem. faculty Pa. Acad. of Fine Arts, dept. mural decoration. Mural decorations in First Nat. Bank, Corn Exchange Nat. Bank (Phila.), Germantown Trust Co.; war decoration State of Pa. Winner competition for mural decorations in U.S. Custom House., Phila., 1935, 2 panels in Post Office Bldg., Washington, D.C., 1936, murals in Phila. Post Office 1937, mural in Legislative Hall, U.S. Government Building, New York World's Fair, 1339; murals in main hall of new Municipal Court, Phila., 1940; Murals in Common Please Court No. 7, City Hall, Philadelphia; five murals Montgomery Country Court House; mural designer for interior of Audubon Shrine Mus. 1st home of John James Audubon, Montgomery Co., Pa. Pictures in permanent collections of Pa. Academy Fine Arts and Chrysler collection and many private collections. Member board directors Pennsylvania Academy Fine Arts, 1958-59. Awarded E. T. Statesbury prize Pa. Acad. Fine Arts, 1938, Gold Medal of Honor, 1953. Fine Arts award, A.I.A., 1953, gold medal for mural painting, Architectural League New York, 1953. Drawings shown in United States, England and Australia. Commanding captain engineers, U.S. Army, 1918, and apptd. one of official artists of A.E.F.; made sketches and covered Château Thierry defense, Marne offensive, St. Mihiel offensive, Argonne-Meuse offensive, besides all American sectors from Amiens to Baccarat; accompanied Army of Occupation through Lorraine, Luxembourg and Germany; disch. May 1919; U.S. Marine Corps, June 1942, served as major in New Georgia Vella la Vella, Bougainville Emerau and Guam invasions. Dir. Abbey Scholarship Found. Mem. Acad. Natural Scis., U.S. Naval Inst., Soc. Am. Mil. Engrs., Pa. Art Commn., Nat. Soc. Mural Painters, Pa. Hist. Society; fellow Royal Geog. Soc.; National Academy; hon. mem. Tau Sigma Delta. Clubs: Century (N.Y.); Racquet. Home and Studio: Wynnewood, Pa. Died Mar. 26, 1959; buried St. David's Churchyard, Radnor, Pa.

HARDING, SETH naval officer; b. Eastham, Mass., Apr. 17, 1734; s. Theodore and Sarah (Hamilton) H.; m. Abigail Doane, Apr. 27, 1753; m. 2d, Ruth Reed, Nov. 24, 1760. In his youth served on mcht. vessels to West Indies, also during French and Indian War; assumed command brig Defence at start of Revolutionary War; consummated most brilliant Am. naval feat up to that time by forcing 2 Brit. armed transports in Mass. Bay to surrender, 1776; commanded Continental frigate Confederacy, 1778; became comdr. Diana, engaged in commerce raiding and convoy service between Am. and W.I. until captured, 1781; was exchanged in 1782, became 2d in command ship Alliance under John Barry; in mcht. service after war; ret. on capt.'s half-pay, 1807. Died Schoharie, N.Y., Nov. 20, 1814.

HARDING, WILLIAM BARLCAY investment underwriter, broker; b. N.Y.C., Nov. 16, 1906; s. J. Horace and Dorothea (Barney) H.; grad. Groton Sch., 1926; student Yale, 1926-29; m. Constance Fox, May 30, 1929 (div. 1943); children - Dorothea, James H., Timothy F.; m. 2d Mary Reed Dodge, Aug. 11, 1943. With Chasen. D. Barney & Co., investment bank and stock brokers, 1929-35, partner, 1935; through merger, partner, Smith, Barney & Co., Inc., 1938-, now chmn.; dir. ELTRA (Toledo). Mem. aviation research adv. com. Harvard Sch. Bus. Adminstrn., 1942-; trustee Groton Sch.; gov. Flight Safety Found., 1951-. Served as lt. (j.g.) USNR, 1941-42; capt. to col. AUS, 1942-45. Decorated Legion of Merit. Mem. Transp. Assn. Am. (dir.), N.Y. Stock Exchange. Clubs: Metropolitan (Washington); The Links, River, Rumson Country. Home: Holmdel, N.J. Office: 20 Broad St., N.Y.C. 5. Died June 30, 1967.

HARDING, WILLIAM WHITE publisher; b. Phila., Nov. 1, 1830; s. Jesper and Maria (Wilson) H.; m. Catharine Hart, 6 children. Clk. bookstore of George S. Appelton, Phila., 1846-49; made partner in his father's publishing business, 1856; Sole propr. Pa. Inquirer and father's hugh Bible-publishing bus., 1859, changed paper's name to The Phila. Inquirer; served as col. on staff of Gov. James Pollack during Civil War; maintained circulation to armies during war; his paper became a sch. for journalists; established paper mill, Manayunk Pa., 1864; 1st attempted to make paper out of wood (by permission of the inventor), received medal for this at Phila. Centennial Expn., 1876; ret. from active mgmt. of Inquirer, 1889. Died Phila., May 15, 1889.

HARDISON, OSBORNE BENNET ret. naval officer; b. Wadesboro, N. C., Dec. 22, 1892; s. William Cameron and Harriett Eleanor (Bennett) H.; A.B., U. of N.C., 1911; grad. U.S. Naval Acad., 1916; m. Ruth Morgan, Nov. 28, 1926; children-Osborne Bennett, William Gerry Morgan. Commd. ensign, USN, 1916, advancing through the grades to rear adm., 1942; served on U.S.S. Texas, 1916-20, operating in association and cooperation with British Grand Fleet during World War I; exec. officer U.S.S. Wickes, 1920-21, later serving on destroyers Claxton and Parrott: assigned to presdl. yacht U.S.S. Mayflower, 1922; became naval aviator, 1923, joining aircraft squadron, Scouting Fleet, 1923; observer, army air station, Selfredge Field, Mt. Clemens, Mich., 1925; instr. in dept. engring. and aeros., U.S. Naval Acad., 1925-27; comdg. officer, fighting squadrons based on U.S.S. Lexington, 1927-29; on duty, Navy Dept. Washington, 1929-32; operations officer on staff Rear Adm. John Halligan, Jr., U.S.S. Lexington; comdr. aircraft, Battle Force, U.S.S. Saratoga, 1932-34; navigator, U.S., Langley, 1934-35; with Bur. Aeros, and Bur. of Navigation, 1935-36; aviation officer Office of Chief of Naval Operations, 1936-38; exec. officer U.S. Ranger, 1938-39; aviation officer on staff Adm. James O. Richardson. comdr. in chief U.S. Fleet, 1939-40; comdg. officer naval air station, Anacostia, D. C., also on duty Bur. Aeros., 1940; aide to asst. sec. of navy for air, 1941-42; comdg. officer U.S.S. Enterprise, 1942-43, engaging in battles of Santa Cruz and Solomon Islands and other operations in vicinity of Solomons; comdr. Fleet Air in South Pacific, 1943-44; became chief of naval air primary tng., 1944 (with hdqrs. Kansas City, Kan., removed to Glenview, Ill., July 1944); dir. Pan-Am. Affairs, Office, Chief of Naval apropriations, now ret. Decorated Navy Cross, Legion of Merit, with star. Presidential Unit Citation. Mem. Phi Delta Theta. Clubs: Chevy Chase (Washington); Glen View (Glenview, Ill.). Home: 3315 Rowland Pl. N.W. Office: Navy Dept., Washington. Died Mar. 1959.*

HARDON, JOHN J. congressman, army officer; b. Frankfort, Ky., Jan. 6, 1810; s. Martin and Elizabeth (Logan) H.; grad. Transylvania U., Lexington, Ky.; m. Sarah Smith, Jan. 13, 1831, 4 children including Martin D. Maj. gen. Ill. Militia during Blackhawk War, 1832; mem. Ill. Gen. Assembly from Morgan County, 1836-42; mem. U.S. Ho. of Reps. from Ill., 28th Congress, 1843-45; comdr.-in-chief Ill. Militia, 1845, conducted campaign against Mormons, inducing them to leave Ill. peacefully; col. 1st Regt., Ill. Volunteers during Mexican War, 1846-47, joined army of occupation under Gen. Zachary Taylor. Killed in Battle of Buena Vista, Feb. 23, 1847; buried East City Cemetery, Jacksonville, Ill.

HARDY, DAVID PHILLIP business mgr.; b. Petaluma, Calif., May 24, 1890; s. Henry and Louise (Daum) H.; B.S. in M.E., U. of Cal., 1912; m. Roena Vina Hinkle, Santa Cruz, Mar. 3, 1918; children-Charles Edward, James Herbert. Tchr. San Rafael Military Acad., Cal., 1912-16; high sch. tchr., prin., San Francisco Pub. Schs., 1916-24: dept. supt. schs., 1924-45 (leave for army service); asst. supt. of schs., San Francisco, 1945-48. With Cal. N.G., 1914—, beginning as private; served on Mexican border, 1916; capt. C.A., U.S. Army, 1917-19; col. 250th C.A., U.S. Army, 1940; brig. gen., 1941; now brig. gen. Cal. Def. and Security Corps. Mem. Am. Legion, Pi Kappa Phi. Republican. Club: Commonwealth of California. Address: 500 Rivera St., San Francisco. Died Sept. 17, 1957; buried San Francisco Nat. Cemetery.

HARE, JAMES MADISON, clergyman; b. Huntingdon, Pa., Oct. 22, 1859; s. David and Margaret (Kemp) H.; Ph.B., Bucknell U., 1884, D.D., 1922; studied theology, Rochester Theol. Sem. and Union Theol. Sem., 1885-87; m. Anne Appleton Griffin, of Phila., Pa., July 19, 1887; 1 dau., Myrtle (dec.). Ordained Bapt. ministry, 1881; student pastor various chs. to 1888; pastor East Ch., Elizabeth, N.J., 1888-89, Phoenixville, Pa., 1889-92, Burlington, N.J., 1892-98, Parmly Memorial Ch., Jersey City, 1899-1902, Linden Ch., Camden, 1902-05, Parmly Memorial Ch., Jersey City, 1906-14, Scotch Plains, 1914-24, Huntingdon, 1924-28, retired. Capt. chaplain, N.J.N.G., with 6th, 3d and 4th Regts., 1895-1917; with 1st and 3d N.J. Col. Inf., 1898-99, Spanish-Am. War; with 4th N.J. Col. Inf. Mexican border, 1916-17; in World War with same regt., in France, also 104th Engrs., 29th Div., sr. chaplain 29th Div., A.E.F. July 1918-May 1919; retired with rank of maj., 1922. Awarded Croix de Guerre (Fr.); holder expert rifle and revolver medals. Mem. United

Spanish War Vets., Mil. Order Foreign Wars (served as nat. chaplain of both), Vets. Foreign Wars, Am. Legion. Clubs: Huntingdon; Clergy (New York); Chaplains' Club of North Bapt. Conv. Home: Pocono Lake, Pa.†

HARGRAVE, HOMER PEARSON broker, banker; b. Danville, Ind., Apr. 30, 1895; s. Charles Allan and Nettie (Pearson) H.; B.S., Central Normal Coll., Danville, Ind., 1914; A.B., Ind. U., 1917; m. Leah Loso, June 3, 1922 (died Nov. 1933); children - Homer P., Judith Lynn; m. 2d, Colleen Moore, May 19, 1937. Broker with William H. Colvin & Co., Chicago, Ill., 1919-26; with E. A. Pierce & Co., 1926-40; gen. partner in charge Chicago offices, Merrill Lynch Pierce Fenner and Beane, brokers, 1940 - (now Merrill Lynch, Pierce, Fenner, and Smith). Chairman Chgo. Stock Exchange, 1947-49; chairman Midwest Stock Exchange, 1949-53; dir. Chgo. Bd. Trade, 1945-51; mem. Chgo. Merc. Exchange, Chicago Board of Trade, Midwest Stock Exchange, also the Detroit Stock Exchange. Trustee Glenwood Sch. for Boys; dir. Ill. Inst. Tech., Inst. Psychiatric Research, Inc. (Ind.). Served as capt. A.U.S., World War I. Mem. Ind. Society (president 1949), Chgo. Assn. Commerce and Industry (dir.), Chgo Better Business Bur. (vice chmn. 1953-56), S.A.R., Am. Legion, Phi Gamma Delta. Republican. Mason. Clubs: Chicago Economics, Executives, Midday, Glen View, Casino, Old Elm, Bond (pres. 1958), Commercial; Question (Detroit). Home: 1320 N. State St. Office: 141 W. Jackson Blvd., Chgo. Died Feb. 3, 1964.

HARGRAVE, THOMAS JEAN chmn. Eastman Kodak Co.; b. Wymore, Neb., Dec. 5, 1891; s. Thomas Pyle and Adelaide (Cromwell) H.; A.B., U. of Nleb., 1912, LL.D., 1941; LL.B., Harvard U., 1915; LL.D., Hobart and William Smith Colleges, 1955; m. Catherine Forbes Davidson, Dec. 1, 1917; children - Jean Hargrave Farnham, Alexander J., Catherine Hargrave Sykes. Richard Davidson, Margaret Hargrave Frame. Admitted to N.Y. bar, 1915; mem. firm of Hubbell, Taylor, Goodwin, Nixon & Hargrave, 1921-35; sec. Eastman Kodak Co., 1928-41, vice-president, 1932-41, president, 1941-52, chmn., 1952-; chairman board Lincoln Rochester Trust Co., 1944-53, now dir.; dir., mem. executive com. Westinghouse Electric Corp.; dir. Rochester Gas & Electric Corp., Gannet Co., Inc., Timely Clothes, Inc., Kodak Ltd. of London, Kodak-Pathe of Paris, Canadian Kodak Co., Toronto, Chmn. Army and Navy Munitions Bd., 1947; chmn. Munitions Board, 1947-48. Presidential Certificate of Merit, 1947. Served as Captain Company C, 309th Machine Gun Bn., 78th Div., World War I. Decorated D.S.C. (l).S.), Croix de Guerre (France), Chevalier in the French Legion of Honor. Trustee, mem. exec. com. U. Rochester; trustee George Eastman House, Rochester, Nat. Fund for Medical Education. Member N.A.M. (former v.p., dir.), N.Y. State Rochester bar assns., Phi Beta Kappa. Republican. Presbyn. Clubs: Country, Genesee Valley, Rochester (Rochester). Home: 65 Sandringham Rd. Office: 343 State St., Rochester 4, N.Y. Died Feb. 21, 1962.

HARGREAVES, JOHN MORRIS air force officer; b. La Moille, Ill., Feb. 26, 1901; s. John Robert and Bessie (Kay) H.; A.B., Macalester Coll., 1920; B. S., U. Minn., 1921, M.G., 1924, M.D., 1925; m. Hartie Noel Mickel, Mar. 31, 1929; children-John Joaquin, Hardy Mickel. Intern Letterman Gen. Hosp., San Francisco, 1925-26; commd. 1st lt. M.C., U.S. Army, 1925, and advanced through grades to major gen., 1949; assigned to various Air Force and Ground Force hosps., Philippine Islands, 1927-30; dir. eye, ear, nose and throat, Sch. of Aviation Med., Randolph Air Force, Tex., 1935-40; asst. air surgeon Office of the Air Surgeon, Washington. 1940-42; command surgeon Air Material Command. 1942-45; surgeon 8th Air Force, Okinawa, Aug.-Dec. 1945; command surgeon hdqrs. Pacusa, Jan.-Oct. 1946; dep. air surgeon Air Surgeons Office, USAF, Washington, 1946-49; became air surgeon Continental Air Command, 1949. Decorated am. Defense Service, World War II Victory, Legion of Merit and Bronze Star medals. Fellow A.C.S.; mem. A.M.A., Aero Med. Assn., Assn. Mil. Surgeons. Clubs: Army-Navy, Manila University, Manila Polo, Belle Haven Country. Author treaties: protection Against Night Blindness, 1938; Testing of Hearing with Audiometer, 1939; Aviation Deafness, 1940; Ophthalmological Factors Selections of Military Aviators, 1940; Transportation of Patients by Airplane, 1942. Address: USAF. Died June 1959.

HARING, CLARENCE MELVIN prof. veterinary science; b. Freeville, N.Y., June 1, 1878; s. Purley Work and Ellen Augusta (Ainsworth) H.; student Colgate Acad., 1897-98; D.V.M., N.Y. State Vet. Coll., Cornell U., 1904; m. Grace E. Moody, Aug. 22, 1908. Asst. in vet. anatomy, Cornell U., 1903-04; instr. vet. science, 1904-06, asst. prof., 1906-10, veterinarian and bacteriologist at Agrl. Expt. Sta. U. of Calif., 1910-13, dir. same, 1920-24; prof. veterinary science, U. of Calif., since 1913. Dir. Calif. anti-hog cholera serum lab., 1911-18. Consultant Calif. State Dept. Pub. Health since 1928; consultant War Manpower Commission, 1942-45. Second lieut. Vet. R.C., Feb.-Apr. 1918; 1st lt., Vet. Corps N.A., Apr.-June 1918; capt., Vet. Corps U.S. Army, July Vet. Med. Assn. (sec. 1915-16), Soc. Am. Bacteriologists, Sigma Xi, Alpha Zeta, Delta Omega, Phi Zeta. Mason. Club: Faculty. Contbr. to agrl. and vet. publs.; investigator of animal diseases. Home: 2405 Hillside Av., Berkeley 4, Cal. Died July 9, 1951; buried Riverside, Cal.

HARKNESS, WILLIAM astronomer, rear admiral U.S.N.; b. Ecclefechan, Scotland, Dec. 17, 1837; s. James and Jane Weild H.; studied Lafayette Coll., Pa., 1854-56, Rochester Univ., 1856-58, A.B., 1858, A.M., 1861, LL.D., 1874, Rochester (A.M., Lafayette, 1865); studied medicine, New York, M.D., 1862. Served as surgeon, U.S. army, at second battle of Bull Run; also during attack on Washington, July 1864. Apptd. from N.Y. as aide U.S. Naval Observatory, Aug. 1, 1862; commd. prof. mathematics, with relative rank of lt. comdr., Aug. 24, 1863; served at Naval Observatory until Oct. 4, 1865. Served on U.S. monitor Monadnock, 1865-66; attached to U.S. Hydrographic Office, 1867; discovered the coronal line K 1474, during total solar eclipse of Aug. 1869; mem., 1871, and from 1882 exec. officer U.S. Transit of Venus Commn.; had charge of transit of Venus parties in 1874 at Hobart, Tasmania, and in 1882 at Washington, D.C. In 1879, discovered the theory of the focal curve of achromatic telescopes, now universally adopted. Attached to U.S. Naval Observatory most of the time from Aug. 1862; designed most of its large instruments; astron. dir. Naval Observatory, 1894-99, and dir. U.S. Nautical Almanac, 1897-99. Attained relative rank of comdr., May 31, 1872, capt., April 17, 1878, rear admiral, Dec. 15, 1899; unmarried. Home: Jersey City, N.J. Died 1903.

HARKNESS, WILLIAM HALE investments; b. Cleveland, July 13, 1900; s. William Lamon and Edith (Hale) H.; student Browning Sch., New York, 1910-13; student St. Paul's Sch., Concord, N.H., 1913-18; B.A., Yale, 1922; LL.B., Harvard, 1925; m. Elisabeth Grant, June 13, 1932 (divorced Dec. 1945); 1 dau., Anne; m. 2d, Rebekah West Pierce, Oct. 1, 1947; 1 dau. Edith Hale. Admitted to New York bar, 1927, asso. in practice of law Murray, Aldrich & Webb, 1926-30; kept own office for management of investments, 1930—. Dir. Hoving Corp., Va. Hot Springs, Inc., Republic Foil & Metal Mills Inc., The New York Trust Co. Served in Yale unit S.A.T.C., 1918, 2d lt., O.R.C., 1918-20. Served as lt. col., U.S. Army Air Force in Washington, D.C., Mar.-July 1942, hdqrs. 8th Fighter Command. Watford, Eng., and Charleroi, Belgium, July 1942-July 1945. Decorated Bronze Star medal, Croix de Guerre avec Etoile de Vermeil, European, African, Middle Eastern Ribbon with 5 battle stars (Germany, Air Offensive Europe, Normandy, Northern France, Central Europe). Mem. Am. Geog. Soc. (v.p.), Am. Mus. Natural Hist. (trustee), Boys' Club of N.Y. (v.p.), Presbyn. Hosp. in the City of New York (v.p.), Episcopalian. Clubs: Downtown Assn., The Links Madison Square Garden, New York Yacht, Racquet and Tennis, River, University, Yale (New York City); Yeamans Hall (Charleston, S.C.). Home: 778 Park Av. Office: 654 Madison Av., N.Y.C. 21 . Died Aug. 12, 1954; buried Woodlawn Cemetery, N.Y.C.

HARL, MAPLE TALBOT business exec.; b. Marshall, Mo., Feb. 4, 1893; s. Baldwin Evans and Maxcy Jane (Campbell) H.: A.B., William Jewell Coll., Liberty, Mo., 1914 LL.D., 1952; U. of Chgo. Law Sch., 1916-17; m. Maybelle Mayfield, July 12, 1920; 1 dau., Suzanne. Former pres. Denver Safe Deposit Co.; v.p. Englewood Colo. State Bank, 1923-25; state bank commr. Colo., 1939-45; dir. F.D.I.C. (chmn. bd. dir. 1945-53); bd. dirs. United Am. Life Ins. Co., D.&R.G.W. R.R. National Commander Disabled American Veterans of the World War, 1937. Former director Denver Chamber of Commerce, Salvation Army, Denver chapter American Red Cross. Enlisted as private U.S. Army, 1917; commd. 2d lt. and advanced through grades to maj., 1918, with A.E.F., 1918-19; hon. disch. 1919. Trustee. Colo. Women's Coll. Former vice pres. Nat. Assn. State Bank Supervisors. Mem. Am. Legion, Vets of Fgn. Wars, D.A.V., Forty and Eight Soc., Phi Gamma Delta, Phi Delta Phi, Beta Gamma Sigma. Baptist. Mason (32ff, K.T., Shriner). Clubs: Kiwanis of Denver (past pres., gov. Rocky Mt. Dist.). Metropolitan, National Press, Army and Navy (Washington); Denver, Denver Country (Denver). Home: 800 Ogden St., Denver 18; also The Westchester, Washington. Office: National Press Bldg., Washington. Died Apr. 17, 1957; buried Fairmont Mausoleum, Denver.

HARLAN, AARON congressman; b. Warren County, O., Sept. 8, 1802; attended publ schs.; studied law. Admitted to Ohio bar, began practice in Xenia, 1825; mem. Ohio Ho. of Reps., 1832-33, Ohio Senate, 1838, 39, 49; moved to a farm nr. Yellow Springs, O., 1841, continued law practice; presdl. elector, 1844; del. Ohio Constl. Conv., 1850; mem. bd. trustees Antioch Coll., 1852; mem. U.S. Ho. of Reps. (Whig) from Ohio, 33d-35th congresses, 1853-59; served as lt. col. 94th Regt., Ohio Minutemen during Civil War, 1862; moved to San Francisco, 1864. Died San Francisco, Jan. 8, 1868; buried Laurel Hill Cemetery, San Francisco.

HARLAN, JOHN MARSHALL, asso. justice Supreme Ct. of U.S.; b. Chgo., May 20, 1899; s. John Maynard and Elizabeth Palmer (Flagg) H.; A.B., Princeton, 1920, LL.D., 1955; B.A., M.A. (Rhodes Scholar), Balliol Coll., Oxford U., 1923, hon. fellow, 1955; LL.B., N.Y.L.S., 1924, LL.D., 1955; LL.D., Columbia, Brandeis U., Oberlin Coll., Evansville College; married Ethel Andrews, November 10, 1928; 1 daughter, Eve (Mrs. Frank Dillingham). Admitted to N.Y. bar 1925, Circuit Court Appeals, 1925, U.S. Dist. Ct., 1925, U.S. Supreme Court, 1945; asst. U.S. atty. So. Dist. N.Y., 1925-27; spl. asst. atty. gen., N.Y., 1928-30, 1951-53; mem. firm Root, Ballantine, Harlan, Bushby & Palmer, N.Y. City, 1931-54; judge U.S. Ct. of Appeals, 2d Circuit, 1954-55; associate justice Supreme Court of U.S., 1955-71; chief counsel, gen. counsel N.Y. State Crime Commn., 1951-53. Served as col. USAAF, 1943-45, chief operations analysis section, 8th Air Force, Eng. Decorated Legion Merit, Croix de Guerre (France), Croix de Guerre (Belgium). Mem. Am., N.Y. State bar assns., Assn. Bar City of N.Y., N.Y. Co. Lawyers Assn. Clubs: Century Assn., University (N.Y.C.); Country (Fairchild, Conn.); Ivy (Princeton, N.J.). Home: Washington DC Died Dec. 29, 1971.

HARLAN, JOSIAH army officer, adventurer; b. Newlin Twp., Pa., June 12, 1799; s. Joshua and Sarah (Hinchman) H.; m. Elizabeth Baker, May 1, 1849, 1 child. Journeyed to Far East, 1823; asst. surgeon East India Co.; med. officer Col. George Pollock's Bengal Arty. in 1st Burmese war; left army, 1826, became friend of Sha Shooja-ool-Moolk (ex-king of Kabul), apptd. secret agt. to start revolution in Afghanistan, 1828 (unsuccessful); became friend of Maharajah Ranjit Singh (sovereign of Punjab), apptd. gov. of Goozerath; unable to dethrone Sha Shooja successfully, and returned to U.S. after Brit. intervention, 1841; raised Pa. regiment known as Harlan's Light Cavalry during Civil War, 1861; commd. col. and served in Army of Potomac until 1862. Died San Francisco, Oct. 1871.

HARLLEE, WILLIAM CURRY, marine corps officer; b. Manatee, Fla., June 13, 1877; s. John Waddell and Mary Ellen (Curry) H.; student S.C. Mil. Acad. (The Citadel), 1891-93, U. of N.C., 1893-94, U.S. Mil. Acad., 1897-99; grad. Army War Coll., 1926, Naval War Coll., 1928; m. Ella Florence Fullmore, July 30, 1903; children—John (officer U.S. Navy), Ella Fulmore. Served as pvt., cpl., sergt. and 1st sergt., Co. F, 33d U.S. Vol. Inf., Philippine Insurrection, 1899-1900; comd. 2d lt., U.S. Marine Corps, 1900, advancing through the grades to brig. gen., 1942, retired since 1935. As senior aide and asst. to Maj. Gen. George F. Elliott, comdt. U.S.M.C., devised and established methods of marksmanship training in Marine Corps, 1908-10; asst. dir. gunnery exercises and engring. performances, Navy Dept., 1914-20; established Marine Corps Inst., for extending ednl. and vocational training throughout Marine Corps, Quantico, Va., and removed it to Marine Barracks, Washington, D.C., 1920; comd. 15th Regt., U.S.M.C., and Eastern Dist. under mil. (naval) govt. of Dominican Republic, 1921-22; exec. officer div. of operations and training Hdqrs. U.S.M.C., 1924-25; brig. gen., chief of staff and asst. comdt. Gendarmerie d'Haiti, 1926-27; Fleet Marine Officer, U.S. Fleet, 1929-30. Decorated Comdr. Order of Honor and Merit (Haiti). Formerly dir. and vice pres. Nat. Rifle Assn.; formerly mem. and recorder Nat. Bd. for Promotion of Rifle Practice. Mason. Clubs: Racquet (Philadelphia); Army and Navy, University, Chevy Chase, National Press (Washington, D.C.); New York (N.Y.) Yacht. Author and publisher: Kinfolks, a geneal. treatise and record of early Am. families and their progeny, Vol. I, 1934, Vol. II, 1935, Vol. III, 1937; also of Marine Corps scorebooks and Rifleman's Instructor (1910), and of manuals of instruction and U.S. Navy Small Arms Firing Regulations, 1914-18. Home: 1753 Lamont St. N.W., Washington 10 DC*

HARLOW, WILLIAM PAGE physician: b. Dixon, Ill., Nov. 14, 1867; s. William Francis and Martha Samson (Besse) H.; M.D., U. of Mich., 1899; A.B. in geology, U. of Colo., 1907; post-grad. work, Johns Hopkins, Vienna, Berlin and Harvard, 1902-03; m. Jean Hoatson, Dec. 26, 1898. Engaged in copper mining in Mich., Mont. and Ariz., 1887-95; mine and ry. surgeon, Greenland, Mich., 1890-1902; prof. med. diagnosis, 1906-15, dean med. sch., 1907-15 and dean emeritus, 1916-. U. of Colorado. Republican. Fellow Fedn. of State Med. Bds. Mason. Capt., Med. R.C., May 21, 1918; maj., M.C., Aug. 7, 1918; chief med. service, Gen. Hosp. No. 8, Otisville, N.Y.; comdg. officer Gen. Hosp. No. 21, Denver, Aug. 27, 1918; lt. col., M.C., U.S.A., Apr. 28, 1919; hon. disch., June 19, 1919; lt. col., Med. Sect. O.R.C., Aug. 11, 1919; col. Med. O.R.C., Oct. 12, 1922. Home: Boulder, Colo. Died May 11, 1924.

HARMAN, HARVEY JOHN, found. exec. b. Selingsgrove, Pa., Nov. 5, 1900; s. Henry Elias and Cora (Jarrett) H.; B.A., U. Pitts., 1922; M.A., U. Pa., 1928; m. Wilhelmina Hamilton Eakin, July 5, 1922. Head football coach Haverford (Pa.) Coll., 1922-29, U. South, Sewanee, Tenn., 1930, U. Pa., 1931-37, Rutgers U., 1938-41, 46-55; exec. sec. Nat. Football Found. and Hall of Fame, New Brunswick, N.J., 1956-58, exec. dir., from 1958. Mem. Lambert Cup and Trophy Com., from 1958, Liberty Bowl Selection Com., from 1961. Mem. New Brunswick Recreation Com., 1947-62; treas. Raritan Valley (N.J.) United Fund, 1950-58. Borough councilman, Narbeth, Pa., 1934-38. Served with U.S. Army, 1918, as comdr. USNR, 1942-46. Recipient Stagg award Football Coaches Assn., 1960. Mem. Am. Football Coaches Assn. (pres. 1949), Druid, Phi Gamma Delta, Omicron Delta Kappa, Phi Delta Kappa. Mem. Reformed Ch. Am. (deacon 1956-58, elder from 1960). Mason, Kiwanian. Home: Highland Park NJ Died Dec. 17, 1969; buried Mercer PA

HARMAR, JOSIAH army officer; b. Phila., Nov. 10, 1753; m. Sarah Jenkins, Oct. 19, 1784. Served as maj. 3d Pa. Regt., 1776, lt. col. 6th Pa. Regt., 1777; served in Continental Army under Washington, 1778-80, Greene's div. in South, 1781-82; commd. col., 1783; Indian agt. for N.W. Territory, took part in Treaty of Ft. McIntosh, 1785; commd. brig. gen., 1787; commanded expdn. against Miami Indians, not entirely successful, 1790 (court of inquiry held, did not find against him); adj. gen. Pa., 1793-99. Died Phila., Aug. 20, 1813.

HARMON, HUBERT REILLY air force officer; b. Chester, Pa., Apr. 3, 1892; s. Millard Fillmore and Madelin (Kendig) H.; B.S., U.S. Mil. Acad., 1915; grad. Army Flying Sch., 1917; m. Rosa-Maye Kendrick, Feb. 19, 1927; children-Eula Wulfjen, Kendrick. Served in Air Arm of Army or in USAF, 1917—; apptd. lt. gen. USAF, 1945; comd. 6th Air Force, 13th Air Force, also den. comdt. aircraft, S. Pacific Theater, World War II; USAF Rep. UN Mil. Staff Com., also U.S. del. Inter-Am. Def. Bd. and spl. asst. to Chief of Staff USAF, for Air Force Acad. matters, 1947-53, ret. June 1953, recalled to active duty 1953; supt. USAF Acad., 1954-56, ret. Decorated D.S.M. (with Oak-Leaf Cluster), 2d, D.S.M. (with two Oak-Leaf Clusters), 1956. Legion of Merit, Distinguished Flying Cross (U.S.); also fgn. decorations. Rated command pilot, combat observer and aircraft observer. Clubs: Army and Navy (Washington); Chevy Chase (Md.); San Antonio (Tex.) Country; Cherry Hills, Denver Country (Denver). Home: 312 Westover Rd., San Antonio. Died Feb. 22, 1957; buried Cemetery at USAF Academy, Colorado Springs, Colo.

HARMONY, DAVID BUTTZ rear admiral U.S.N.; b. Easton, Pa., Sept. 3, 1832; s. William J. and Ebba (Herster) H.; apptd. from Pa., acting midshipman, 1847; passed midshipman, June 10, 1852; promoted through grades to rear admiral, Mar. 26, 1889. Served successively on the Brandywine, Ohio, Falmouth at Naval Acad., on the relief and receiving-ship Baltimore, Decatur and receiving-ship at New York; during the Civil War was exec. officer of the Iroquoisat; participated in bombardment and passage of Fts. Jackson and St. Philip, Chalmette batteries and at capture of New Orleans, at engagements at Vicksburg, and with Confederate ram Arkansas, 1861-62; on Nahant at engagements at Charleston, 1863; comd. Tahoma, and Sebago, W. Gulf Blockading Squadron, 1884-85; at the capture of Mobile, 1865; served at Navy Yard, New York, 1865-67; comd. Frolic, European Sta., 1867-69; Navy Yard, New York, 1869-72; comd. Portsmouth and Kearsarge, 1872-75: recruiting duty, New York, 1876; comd. Plymouth, Powhatan, Tennessee, and receiving-ship Colorado, 1878-83; spl. duty Navy Dept., 1883-84; chief Bur. of Yards and Docks, 1885-89; chmn. Lighthouse Bd., 1889-91; comdr.-in-chief Asiatic Sta., 1892-93; retired, June 26, 1893. Died Nov. 2, 1917.

HARNEY, WILLIAM SELBY army officer; b. Haysboro, Tenn., Aug. 22, 1800; s. Thomas and Margaret (Hudson) H.; m. Mary Mullanphy, 1833; m. 2d, Mrs. St. Cyr; 3 children. Served as 2d lt. 10th U.S. Inf., 1818; participated in Seminole War; commd. lt. col., 1836; brevetted col., 1840; served as col. during Mexican War, 1846; brevetted brig. gen. for bravery, ranking cavalry officer, 1847; defeated Sioux Indians at Sand Hill on the Platte River, 1855; brig. gen. in command Dept. of Ore., 1858; as consequence of his mil. seizure of Island of San Juan (claimed by Brit. as part of Brit. Columbia), dispute with Gt. Britain led to his recall from Ore., 1860; commanded Dept. of West, 1861; ret. as maj. gen., 1863. Died Orlando, Fla., May 9, 1889.

HARPER, FOWLER VINCENT educator; b. Germantown, O., July 21, 1897; s. Ellahue A. and Cora A. (Rudy) H.; A.B., Ohio No. U., 1921, LL.B., 1923; A.lf., U. Ia., 1925; S.J.D., U. Mich., 1927; m. Grace Gill, 1925 (div. 1950); 1 dau., Constance; m. 2d, Miriam Cohen, Dec. 14, 1950. Professor of law U. N.D., 1926-28, U. Ore., 1928-29, Ind. U., 1929-46; prof. law Yale, 1947-57, Simeon F. Baldwin prof. law, 1957-; Fulbright lectr. law Lucknow U., Delhi U., India, 1956-57; vis. prof. law University of Puerto Rico Law School, 1956, Miami U. Law Sch., 1963, 64. Gen. counsel FSA, 1939-40; dep. chmn. War Manpower Commn., 1941-43; solictor Dept. Interior, 1943-45; with Dept. of State Specialist Program, East and West Africa, 1960-61. Cadet AS, 1918; capt. Judge Adv. Gen. Dept., AUS, 1938-41. Recipient Holmes-Weatherly award Unitarian Fellowship for Social Justice, May 1961. Member of the American Law Inst., Nat. Lawyers Guild, Conn. Bar Assn. Author: Harper on Torts; Problems of the Family; Harper and James on Torts; (with Fleming James, Jr.) The Law of Torts, 3 vols., 1957; also case books on law. Editor: Bohlen's Cases on Torts, 5th edit., 1954. Home: 809 Whitney Av., New Haven. Died Jan. 8, 1965.

HARPER, GEORGE WASHINGTON FINLEY banker; b. Lenoir, N.C., July 7, 1834; s. James and Caroline Ellen (Finley) H.; ed. Classical Schs., Lenoir, 1847-53; Davidson Coll., N.C., 1885-6: m. Ella A. Rankin, June 14, 1859 (dec. 1909); children-George F. Ellen (Mrs. Bernhardt). In mercantile business at Lenoir, 1853-61 and 1865-94; built sect. of Chester & Lenoir R.R. from Lenoir to Hickory, 1873-9, and Inter pres. same; pres., gen. mgr. Carolina & Northwestern Ry. Co., 1893-1900; pres. Bank of Lenoir since its orgn., 1893; pres. Green Park (N.C.) Improvement Co.; v.p. Lenoir Cotton Mill; partner Benhardt-Seagle Hardware Co.; etc. Served in C.S.A. under Gens. Bragg, Johnston and Hood; was wounded and disabled at Battle of Resaca, Ga., May 15, 1864; advanced to maj. 58th N.C. Regt., which comd. at Battle of Bentonville, N.C., Mar. 19 and 20, 1865; surrendered at Greensboro, N.C., May, 1865. Co. register and justice of peace Caldwell Co., N.C., 1856-62; mem. N.C. Ho. of Rep., 1860-1; del. Dem. Nat. Conv., St. Louis, 1888, Trustee Davidson Coll., 1900-12, Western N.C. State Hosp. for Insane, 1893-01. Democrat. Presbyn. Comdr. Confederate Vets. Camp Lenoir. Author: Caldwell County, N.C., in the Great War of 1860-65, 1910. Home: Lenoir, N.C. Died Mar. 16, 1921.

HARPER, JAMES CLARENCE congressman; b. Cumberland County, Pa., Dec. 6, 1819; attended common schs., Ohio Moved to Darke County, O., 1831, to Lenoir, N.C., 1840; land surveyor, civil engr., draftsman; laid out Town of Lenoir, 1841; engaged in merc. bus., later in mfg. cotton and woolen goods; served as col. N.C. Militia; mem. N.C. Ho. of Commons, 1865-66; mem. U.S. Ho. of Reps. (Conservative) from N.C., 42d Congress, 1871-73. Died nr. Patterson, N.C., Jan. 8, 1890; buried Cemetery at Harpers Chapel, Patterson.

HARPER, JAMES PATTERSON JR. dentist; b. Fort Madison, Ia., Nov. 9, 1863; s. James Patterson and Elizabeth Bradford (Durfee) H.; ed. Indianapolis High Sch.; D.D.S., Chicago Coll. of Dental Surgery (Lake Forest U.), 1895; m. Elizabeth Pike, June 23, 1900; 1 son, James Durfee. Practiced in St. Louis, 1895-; prof. pathology and histology, Marion-Sims Dental Coll., 1895-1916: dean St. Louis U. Sch. of Dentistry, 1912-; mem. visiting staff St. Louis City Hosps., 1910-; mem. Bd. of Edn., St. Louis, 1911- (pres. 1915-16). Trustee Mo. Bot. Garden (Shaw's Garden). Democrat. Presbyn. Commd. 1st lt., D.R.C., U.S.A., Aug. 1917; maj., Mar. 1q18; lt. col., Aug. 1919; col., Feb. 1923. Home: St. Louis, Mo. Died Feb. 13, 1934.

HARPER, ROBERT GOODLOE senator; b. Fredericksburg, Va., Jan. 1765; s. Jesse and Diana (Goodloe) H.; grad. Princeton, 1785, LL.D., 1820; m. Catherine Carroll, May 1801. Admitted to S.C. bar, 1786; mem. U.S. Ho. of Reps. from S.C., 3d-6th congresses, Feb. 9, 1795-1801, elected as Republican, became a leader in Federalist Party, chmn. Ways and Means Com., 1799-1801; organizer Balt. Exchange Co.; maj. gen. Md. Militia, 1814; mem. U.S. Senate from Md., 1816-22; unsuccessful candidate (Federalist) for vice pres. U.S., 1816; an original mem. Am. Colonization Soc. Died Balt., Jan. 14, 1825; buried Greenmount Cemetery, Balt. Died pr. 15, 1825.

HARRAL, JARED ALPHONSO retired mcht.; b. Russelville, Ala., Sept. 27, 1842; s. Whitfield and Louisa Graham (Hotchkiss) H.; ed. Hernando (Miss.) Male Coll. and at Gonzales, Tex., to 1857; m. Mrs. Lavinia Brown Foster, of Galveston, Tex., Jan. 20, 1866 (died m. 2d, Feb., 1870); Lydia Eliza Strong, of Selma, Ala., June 20, 1871. Enlisted for 6 mos. in Gillespie's Co., 6th Tex. Inf., C.S.A., Sept. 1861; later received commn. to raise a co. for Waul's Tex. Legion, in which was successful, but, being a minor, waived captaincy in favor of B. J. Hogue; continued in service to close of war, under Gens. Forrest, Lee and others. Became mem. firm of W. Harral & Sons, 1859; entered commn. bus., New Orleans, 1866; mem. of Harral & Woodruff, and Harral & Clay, wholesale groceries, Selma, Ala., 1873-78; returned to commn. and importing business, New Orleans, 1878. Democrat. Episcopalian. A.-d.-c. to comdr.-in-chief U.C.V., 11 yrs.; pres. Veteran Cav. Assn. U.C.V., 3 yrs.; chmn. design com. Beauregard Monument Assn. Mason. Clubs: Pickwick, Highland Lake, Church. Home: 3026 St. Charles Av. Office: 317 Carondelet St., New Orleans.†

HARRIES, GEORGE HERBERT major gen. (Aux.) U.S.A.; b. Haverfordwest, S. Wales, Sept. 19, 1860; s. John and Sarah (Davies) H.; ed. Haverfordwest Grammar Sch.; hon. A.M., Howard U., Washington, D.C., in recognition of lectures on Colonial history; LL.D., Ky. State U.; m. Elizabeth Langley, Apr. 23, 1884 (died May 29, 1925); children-Herbert Langley (lt. col. U.S.A.), Warren Godwin (1st lt. U. S. A., killed in France, 1918): m. 2d, Alice Loveland, Jan. 11, 1927. Printer, newspaper reporter and syndicate writer: mem. staff, later asso. editor Washington (D.C.) Evening Star; pres. Metropolitan R.R. Co., Washington, 1895-96; v.p. Washington Ry. & Electric Co. and of all cos. in that combination, 1900-11; on staff, 1911-12, v.p., Oct. 1912-, H. M. Byllesby & Co., Chicago. Vol. aide to Gen. Nelson A. Miles in Wounded Knee Campaign, S.D., 1890-91; active mem. Sioux Commn. which established boundary line between Pine Ridge and Rosebud Indian reservations and removed northern Cheyennes to old home on Lame Deer, Mont., 1891-92; brig. gen. comdg. militia (mil. and naval) of D.C., Nov. 30, 1897-May 8, 1915, by presdl. commn.; promoted maj. gen., May 18, 1915, and retired upon own request, May 26, 1915; col. 1st D.C. Inf., U.S.V., 1898, serving before Santiago de Cuba, during siege of that city and in Cuban Army of Occupation; mem. War Dept. Bd. on Promotion of Rifle Practice many yrs.; brig. gen. comdg. 1st Brig. Neb. N.G., June 25, 1917; brig. gen. U.S.A., Aug. 5, 1917-Sept. 30, 1919; comd. successively, 59th Depot Brig., 186th Inf. Brig. (13th Corps, 2d French Army), Base Sect. No. 5, A.E.F., 173d Inf. Brig.; chief U.S. Mil. Mission, Berlin, Germany, Dec. 3, 1918-Sept. 30, 1919, brig. gen. O.R.C., Dec. 28, 1920; maj. gen. (Aux.) Sept. 16, 1924. Awarded D.S.M. Army, and D.S.M. Navy; comdr. Legion d'Honneur (for constrn. and operation Port of Brest, etc.); also decorated by 8 other European govts. for mil. services. V.p. Bd. of Edn., Washington, D.C., 1895-1903; pres. Washington (D.C.) Bd. Trade, 1910-11. Nat. comdr. Order Indian Wars, U.S., 1912; comdr. in chief Mil. Order World War, 1920-25, declined reelection; v.p. Soc. Army of Santiago de Cuba, 1924-25, pres. 1926-27. Fellow Am. Inst. E.E. Republican. Methodist. Home: Washington, D.C., and Bel Air, Los Angeles, Calif. Died Sept. 28, 1934.

HARRIGAN, NOLAN banker; b. N.Y.C., Feb. 26, 1894; s. Edward and Annie T. (Braham) H.; grad. Germantown Acad., 1912; B.S., Princeton, 1916; m. Grace Furey, Apr. 28, 1917 (dec. Mar. 1962); children - Edward J., Nolan, Jr., m. 2d, Grace Regina Englehardt, May 4, 1963. With Irving Trust Co. since 1920, sr. v.p., 1950-59; chairman Republic Industrial Corp., 1959-; dir. Am. Creosoting Co., Inc., Sperti Products, Sunrise Coal Co., Republic Indsl. Corp., Revco, Stanley Drug Co. Served as capt. C.A.C., U.S. Army, 1917-20. Clubs: Princeton, University. Home: 32 Wellesley Rd., Rockville Centre, L.I., N.Y. 11570. Office: 1 Wall St., N.Y.C. 10015. Died Apr. 2, 1966; buried Holy Rood Cemetery, Westbury, L.I.

HARRIMAN, EDWARD AVERY, lawyer (retired); b. Framingham, Mass., Dec. 31, 1869; s. Charles Franklin and Mary White (Conant) H.; A.B., Harvard, 1888; studied U. of Va. and Cincinnati Law Sch.; LL.B., Boston U., 1891; married Bertha Cornwall Ray, Aug. 31, 1897 (died Oct. 1941). Admitted to Mass. bar, 1891; practiced in Kansas, 1891-92; professor law, Northwestern University, 1892-1901, and member Chicago bar; practiced in Conn., 1901-20, Washington, D.C., 1920-39; lecturer, Yale Law Sch., 1906-17, Boston University Law Sch. Mem. S.C.W., Harvard Chapter Phi Beta Kappa (1887-88); 1st president Harvard Club of Connecticut, 1908-09; pres. N.E. Federation Harvard Clubs, 1912-13; v.p. Associated Harvard Clubs, 1915-16; pres. Harvard Club, Washington, D.C., 1936-38; pres. Church Club Diocese of Conn., 1916-18. Trustee of donations and bequests for ch. purposes, 1917-18; pres. Churchmen's League of D.C., 1924-26; pres. Nat. Federation of Ch. Clubs, 1926-27; trustee Episcopal Eye, Ear and Throat Hosp., and House of Mercy; pres. Finance Reserve Officers' Assn., 1924-26; treas. Reserve Officers' Assn of U.S., 1925-29. Maj. judge advocate U.S. Army, and counsel to the dir. of finance, U.S. Army, 1919. Lt. col. Q.M.R.C., 1920-21; lt. col. finance R.C., 1921-25, promoted col., 1925. Spl. counsel Interdepartmental Bd. of Contracts and Adjustments, 1922; counsel Am. Economic Assn., 1923-29, and of R.O.T.C. Assn. of U.S., 1929-39; lecturer internat. law, George Washington U. Law Sch., 1923-27; v.p. Am. Society of Foreign Law, 1937-39. Episcopalian. Republican. Clubs: University (Pasadena); Harvard (New York). Author: Law of Contracts, 1896, 1901. Editor: Greenleaf on Evidence, vols. II and III (16th edit.), 1899; The Constitution at the Crossroads, 1925. Fingerprint operator, Office of Civilian Defense, Altadena, 1942. Address: 1226 E. Foothill Blvd., Altadena CA

HARRIMAN, JOHN WALTER, economist, educator; b. Providence, July 8, 1898; s. John W. and Mary (Jones) H.; Ph.B., Brown U., 1920; M.B.A., Harvard, 1925, D.C.S., 1932; M.A., Dartmouth, 1938; m. Ingeborg Sophie Rathe, Oct. 13, 1945; children—Mary (Mrs. Robert C. Young), Joan (Mrs. John C. Watson). Mem. faculty Grinnell Coll., also U. Rochester, 1925-28; head research dept. Russell, Berg & Co., Boston, also instr. bank mgmt. Harvard Bus. Sch., 1928-32; prof. finance Dartmouth, 1932-46; prof. bus. adminstrn. Syracuse U., 1946-53, dean Bus. Sch., 1950, Grad. Sch., 1952; prof. finance N.Y.U. Grad. Sch. Bus. Adminstrn., 1953-64, prof. emeritus, 1964-72, vice dean, 1953-72; research cons. J.R. Williston & Co., 1955-57; economist Union Service Corp. (Tri-Continental Corp. and Union Service Funds), 1958-68; dir. Atlantic Bank N.Y., Guardian Park Av. Fund Inc.; cons. Whitney Goadby, Inc. Head priorities specialist OPM and WPB, Washington, 1941-42; fgn. service officer ECA and Mut. Security Adminstrn., Washington, Paris, London, Belgrade, 1949-52, dep. chief mission to UK., 1950-51. Bd. mgrs. Am. Bible Soc. Served from capt. to col. USAAF, SHAEF, 1942-46. Mem. Am. Finance Assn., Am. Econ. Assn., Nat. Assn. Bus. Economists, Am. Assn. U. Profs., N.Y. Soc. Security Analysts, Phi Beta Kappa, Delta Upsilon, Beta Gamma Sigma. Conglist. Clubs: Lawyers, N.Y. University. Home: New York City NY Died Oct. 21, 1972; buried Bangor ME

HARRIMAN, WALTER army officer, gov. N.H.; b. Warner, N.H., Apr. 8, 1817; s. Benjamin Evans and Hannah (Flanders) H.; m. Apphia K. Hoyt, Sept. 1841; m. 2d, Almira Andrews, Oct. 1844; 3 children. Ordained to ministry Universalist Ch., minister, 10 years; mem. N.H. Ho. of Reps., 1849-51, 53-54, 58-59; mem. commn. for classification of Indian lands in Kan., 1856; mem. N.H. Senate, 1859-61; editor, part owner Union Democrat (renamed Weekly Union) in N.H.,

1861; commd. col. 11th N.H. Volunteers, 1862-65; served at 1st Battle of Fredricksburg, 1862; commanded a brigade at Battle of Petersburg; brevetted brig. gen. U.S. Volunteers, 1865; sec. of state N.H., 1865; gov. N.H. (Republican), 1867-68; U.S. naval officer for Port of Boston, 1869-77; mem. N.H. Legislature, 1881. Author: History of Warner, N.H., 1879. Died Concord, N.H., July 25, 1884.

HARRINGTON, FRANCIS CLARK commr. of work projects, army officer; b. Bristol, Va., Sept. 10, 1887; s. William Clark and Victoria (Gauthier) H.; B.S., U.S. Mil. Acad., 1909; student Engr. Sch., U.S. Army, 1910-11, Gen. Staff Sch., 1927-28, Army War Coll., 1928-29, Ecole Superieure de Guerre, 1933-35; m. Eleanor Crosier Reyburn, June 30, 1915 (died 1938), children-William Stuart, Mary Eleanor. Commissioned 2d lt., Corps of Engrs., U.S. Army, 1909, and advanced through the grades to col., 1938; during World War was instr. in officer training camps, also with 603d Engrs. and comdg. 215th Engrs. and special duty Hdqrs., A.E.F.; has served as asst. prof. of mathematics at U.S. Mil. Acad., dir. Engr. Sch. of U.S. Army, dist. engr., Baltimore, asst. engr. of maintenance at Panama Canal and on War Dept. Gen. Staff. assigned asst. adminstr. Works Progress Administration, 1935, apptd. adminstr., Dec. 24, 1938, commissioner of work projects, July 1, 1939; dir. Panama R.R. Co. Home: Washington, D.C. Died Sept. 30, 1940.

HARRINGTON, PURNELL FREDERICK rear admiral U.S.N.; b. Dover, Del., June 6, 1844; s. Hon. Samuel M. and Mary (Lofland) H.; apptd. to U.S. Naval Acad., from Del., 1861; m. Mia N. Ruan, of St. Croix, D.W.I., Aug. 5, 1868; children-Helen Nelthrop, Ethel, Samuel Milby, Frederick Littell (dec.). Promoted ensign, Oct. 1, 1863; advanced through grades to rear adm., Mar. 21, 1903. Served on Ticonderoga, N. Atlantic Blockading Squadron, 1863; Monongahela, W. Gulf Blockading Squadron, 1864-65: participated in operations against defenses at mouth of Mobile Bay, and battle Mobile Bay, 1864; on bd. Monongahela, North Atlantic Squadron, 1865-68; at Naval Acad., 1868-70; California, 1870-73; Naval Acad., 1873-76; exec. officer Hartford, 1877-79; Naval Acad., 1880-83; comd. practice-ship Dale during the cruises of 1881 and 1882; comd. Juniata, 1883-85: Naval Acad., 1886-89; comd. practice-ship Constellation during cruises of 1888 and 1889; light-house insp. 4th dist., 1890-93; comd. Terror, 1896-97, Puritan, 1897-98; capt. of yard, Navy Yard, Portsmouth, 1898-1901, Navy Yard, New York, 1902-03; commandant, Navy Yard, Norfolk, 1903-06: retired, June 6, 1906; duty in connection with Jamestown Expn., 1906-07. Comdr.-in-chief, Loyal Legion, 1925-27. Home: Yonkers, N.Y. Died Spet. 20, 1937.

HARRINGTON, SAMUEL MILBY Marine Corps officer; born, Md., Nov. 13, 1882; commd. 2d lt., Marine Corps, 1909, and advanced through the grades to brig. gen., Mar. 1941; pres. Naval Examining Bd. Address: U.S. Marine Corps Headquarters, Washington, D.C.* Died Mar. 31, 1948.

HARRINGTON, STUART WILLIAM, surgeon; b. Blossburg, Pa., Apr. 20, 1889; s. John C. and Jeanette (Dunsmore) H.; student Pa. State Coll., 1908-09; M.D., U. of Pa.; 1913; M.S., U. of Minn., 1920; m. Gertrude Jones, Nov. 17, 1922. Fellow in surgery Mayo Clinic, 1915, head of sect. on gen. surgery, 1920, became head sect. on thoracic surgery, 1925, asso. prof. surgery, U. of Minn., 1925-36, prof. surgery, 1936, emeritus prof., Lt. Med. Corps, during World War I. Mem. Minn. and Olmsted County med. socs., A.M.A., Southern Minn. Med. Assn., Am. Coll. of Surgeons, Alumni Association Mayo Clinic, American Association for Thoracic Surgery, Am. Surg. Assn., Western Surg. Assn., Southern Surg. Assn., Internat. Soc. of Surgery, Am. Board of Surgery, Sigma Alpha Epsilon, Sigma Xi, Republican. Presbyterian. Mason. Clubs: University Country, Gun. Home: Rochester MN Died Mar. 8, 1973.

HARRINGTON, VINCENT FRANCIS congressman; b. Sioux City, Ia., May 16, 1903; s. Thomas Francis and Maria (O'Leary) H.; student Trinity Coll., Sioux City, Ia., 1917-21; A.B., U. of Notre Dame, 1915; m. Catherine O'Connor; children-Catherine Tim, Patricia Ann. Instr. history, economics, and athletic dir., U. of Portland (Ore.), 1925-26; v.p., gen. mgr., Continental Mortgage Co., Sioux City, since 1927; mem. Iowa State Senate, 1933-37; mem. 75th to 77th Congresses (1937-43), 9th Ia. Dist. (resigned). Entered Army Air Force (U.S.) as major, May 1943, assigned I Troop Carrier Command, Hdqrs., Stout Field, Indianapolis (asst. A-3). Democrat. Catholic, K.C., Elk, Eagle. Clubs: Country (Sioux City), Monogram (U. of Notre Dame). Home: Warrior Hotel, Sioux City, Ia. Address: 320 E. Maple Rd., Indianapolis, Ind. Died Nov. 29, 1943.

HARRIS, BRAVID WASHINGTON bishop; b. Warrenton, N.C., Jan. 6, 1896; s. Bravid Washington and Margaret O. (Burgess) H.; grad. St. Augustine's Coll., Raleigh, N.C., 1917; B.D., Bishop Payne Div. Sch., Petersburg, Va., 1922; spl. work Berkeley Div. Sch., Middletown, Conn., summer 1920; D.D., Va. Theol. Sem., Alexandria, 1946; m. Flossie M. Adams, May 23, 1918. Ordained to ministry P.E. Ch., Dec. 21, 1921; rector All Saints Ch., Warrenton, N.C., 1922-24, Grace Ch., Norfolk, Va., 1924-44; archdeacon Negro work, Diocese So. Va., 1937-44; sec. Negro Work, Nat. Council P.E. Ch., N.Y., 1944-45; missionary bishop of Liberia since Feb. 1945. Mem. Joint Commn. Negro work, Gen. Conv. P.E. Ch., 1937-43. Served as 1st lt. U.S. Army, 365th Inf., 92d Div., Oct. 1917-May 1919; active duty in France. Cited in gen. orders for Meritorious Service, Moselle sector, France, Nov. 1918. Trustee Bishop Payne Div. Sch. Pres. bd. City Beach Corp., Norfolk, 1934-44. Pres. Norfolk Community Hosp., 1934-44; dir. Norfolk Community Fund (resigned 1943); former chmn. dist. com. Boy Scouts; hon. v.p. Evang. Edn. Soc. Democrat. Author: Study of Our Work, 1937. Died Nov. 1965.

HARRIS, CHARLES TILLMAN, JR. army officer; b. Mexia, Tex., Mar. 31, 1884; s. Charles Tillman and Cornelia Jane (Womack) H.; student U. of Tex., 1902-03; B.S., U.S. Mil. Acad., 1907; grad. Army War Coll., 1924, Army Industrial Coll., 1926; m. Kate Alexander Marvin, June 15, 1907. Commd. 2d lt. C.A.C., U.S. Army, 1907, advanced through grades to rank of major gen., 1941; served as lt. col. and col., Ordnance Dept., Nat. Army, in ammunition production during World War I; dir. Planning Branch, Office of Asst. Sec. of War, 1934-38; comd. Watertown Arsenal, 1937; asst. chief of ordnance, in charge industrial service, Ordnance Dept., 1938-42; comdg. gen., Aberdeen Proving Ground, Md., 1942-46; retired from active duty, July 1, 1946. Decorated D.S.M. (World War I), D.S.M. with oak leaf cluster, Legion of Merit (World War II). Mem. Army Ordnance Assn. (awarded Rice gold medal for notable contribution to ordnance progress, 1944), Sigma Chi. Home: 3224 Cleveland Av. N.W., Washington, D.C. Died Dec. 24, 1961; buried Arlington Nat. Cemetery.

HARRIS, CHRISTOPHER C. banker; b. at Mt. Hope, Lawrence Co., Ala., Jan. 28, 1842; s. William and Nancy L. (Stovall) H.; ed. common schs. and under pvt. teachers; m. Julia Wert, of Moulton, Lawrence Co., Ala., Feb. 16, 1869 (died Dec. 21, 1913). Enlisted as pvt. in Co. F, 16th Ala. Inf., 1861, later commd. lt.; participated in battles of Fish Creek, Shiloh, Perryville, Murfreesboro, Chickamauga, Missionary Ridge and in all battles from Dalton to and around Atlanta, and at Franklin, Tenn.; wounded 4 times; prisoner in Camp Chase, Ohio, until close of war. Clk. Circuit Court of Lawrence Co., Ala., 1865-67; admitted to Ala. bar, 1868; began practice in Moulton; removed to Decatur, 1872; organizer and pres. 1st Nat. Bank, Decatur, 1887-13; organizer, 1913, and pres. Bank of Commerce; pres. Decatur Land Co.; dir. Decatur Ice & Coal Co. Was for many yrs. active in politics and mem. Dem. State Exec. Com.; elected mem. 63rd Congress, May 11, 1914, to fill vacancy, 8th Ala. Dist., caused by death of Hon. William Richardson. Pres. Bd. of Control, Carnegie Library. Methodist. Mason; K. of P.; Elk; etc. Address: Decatur, Ala.†

HARRIS, DUNCAN G., real estate exec.; b. N.Y. City, July 1, 1878; s. Richard Duncan and Annie (Gibert) H.; student Cutler's Sch., N.Y. City; A.B., Harvard, 1900; m. Alice Abell, June 18, 1913. Asso. with Astor Estate, 1901; pres., Harris & Vaughn, 1906, Harris, Vought & Co., 1910; v.p., Brown, Wheelock, Harris, Vought & Co., 1925; chmn. bd. Brown, Harris, Stevens, Inc.; member board of directors Fidelity Phoenix Insurance Co.; mem. adv. board Chemical Bank and Trust Co.; trustee Title Guarantee & Trust Co. Served as major, 305th Infantry, World War I; lt. col., Officers Res. Corps. Awarded D.S.C., Purple Heart (U.S.), Chevalier Legion of Honor, Croix de Guerre (France). Roman Catholic. Clubs: Union, Knickerbocker Racquet and Tennis, Harvard, Brook, Catholic (N.Y.C.). Home: New York City NY Died Dec. 13, 1970.

HARRIS, EUGENE DENNIS, writer; b. Chgo., Jan. 4, 1911;2s. Edward and Fay (Carr) H.; B.S., U. Ill., 1937; grad. student U. Chgo., 1938; m. Janet Corinne Sasserath, June 19, 1957; 1 dau., Deirdre Moira; 1 stepdau., Corinne. Asst. to v.p. Scott Radio Labs., 1939-42; commd. pvt. U.S. Army, 1942, advanced through grades to lt. col., 1962; served in campaigns in Africa, Italy, Korea; 1st radio corr., Korea, 1950; chief Armed Forces Korea Network, 1957-58; retired, 1964; asso. editor Nat. News-Research, Washington, 1964-71; treas. Electronic Advt. Corp., 1966-71. Decorated Purple Heart, Army Commendation medal; recipient certificate appreciation Boys' Nation, 1956; certificate commendation A.R.C., 1957; commendation Republic Korea, 1952. Member Institute of Electrical and Electronic Engineers, Retired Officers Assn., Pi Kappa Phi, Gamma Theta Phi. Club: Nat. Press (Washington). Author: Non-Commissioned Officers' Guide, 1962; Company Administration and the Army Personnel System, 1963; Interviewing Guide and Rating System for WAC Applicants, 1963; A Handbook on Questionnaire Preparation; A Handbook on Questionnaire Administration; (in Japanese) A Primer of Television Production, 1953. Home: Chevy Chase MD Died June 4, 1971; buried Arlington Nat. Cemetery.

HARRIS, FREDERIC ROBERT retired rear adm.; b. N.Y. City, Apr. 10, 1875; s. Siegmund and Rose (Leeberg) H.; M.E., Stevens Inst. Tech., Hoboken 1896, hon. E.D., 1921; m. 2d, Dena Sperry, Mar. 4, 1931 (died July 21, 1945). Engineering practice, 1896-1903; commissioned lieutenant (j.g.) Navy Corps, civil engineers, January 3, 1903; promoted through grades to chief Bur. Yards and Docks of Navy, temp. rear adm., 1916; permanent rear adm., Aug. 1916; retired Feb. 1927. In charge navy war construction, shore program in the U.S. and abroad, 1915-17; general manager Emergency Fleet Corp., U.S. Shipping Bd., in charge war emergency merchant marine constrn.; rep. Emergency Fleet Corp., U.S. Shipping Bd.; cons. and mng. engr., specializing in harbor and river work, bridges, etc.; pres. Frederic R. Harris, Inc.; consulting engr. U.S. Navy, 1939-45; designed water-front facilities, floating drydocks (including largest in world); cons. engr. Brit. admiralty. Mem. Am. Soc. Civil Engrs., Soc. Naval Architects and Marine Egnrs., Naval Inst., Soc. Am. Mil. Engrs., N.Y. State Soc. Professional Engrs. and Land Surveyors, N.J. Soc., Am. Legion. Clubs: Army and Navy, University Washington, D.C.); Union League (hon.), Collectors (New York); City Midday; Nat. Sojourners; Royal Philatelic (London). Asso. editor Am. Civ. Engrs'. Handbook, River and Harbor Works. Home: 420 Park Av. Address: 27 William St., New York. Died July 22, 1949; buried in Arlington National Cemetery.

HARRIS, HENRY TUDOR BROWNELL rear admiral U.S.N.; b. Hartford, Conn., Mar. 10, 1845. Apptd. acting asst. p.m. in vol. navy, Nov. 1, 1864; hon. disch. Sept. 13, 1865: apptd. asst. p.m., from New York, Feb. 21, 1867: promoted passed asst. p.m., Feb. 17, 1869; p.m., Jan. 18, 1881; pay insp., Aug. 29, 1899; pay dir., June 13, 1902; paymaster gen. retired with the rank of senior rear admiral, Mar. 10, 1905. Served during the Civil War on the Napa, 1864-65; Nyack, 1867-69; Supply, 1871-72: Frolic, 1873-74: in charge of stores at Honolulu, 1875-77, at Rio de Janeiro, 1878-79; on various duties to 1897; receiving-ship Vermont, 1897-1900; fleet p.m., Asiatic Fleet, 1900-01, European Fleet, 1901-02: Navy Yard, League Island, 1902-03: paymaster gen. U.S.N., and chief of Bur. of Supplies and Accounts, with rank of rear admiral, 1903-06. Participated in N. China campaign and Philippine insurrection, 1900-01. Died July 12, 1920.

HARRIS, ISHAM GREEN senator, gov. Tenn.; b. Tullahoma, Tenn., Feb. 10, 1818; s. Isham Green and Lucy (Davidson) H.; m. Martha Travis, 1843, 8 children. Admitted to Tenn. bar, 1841; mem. Tenn. Senate, 1847-48; mem. U.S. Ho. of Reps. from Tenn., 31st-32d congresses, 1849-53; gov. Tenn., 1857-63, strongly advocated secession and alignment with Confederacy; served as aide-de-camp to generals Albert Sidney Johnston, G. T. Beauregard, Braxton Bragg, Joseph E. Johnston, Joseph B. Hood, participated in all Civil War battles in Tenn. and N. Ga., 1862-65; mem. U.S. Senate from Tenn., 1877-97, pres. pro. tem, 1893-95. Died Washington, D.C., July 8, 1897; buried Elmwood Cemetery, Memphis, Tenn.

HARRIS, JOHN congressman; b. Harris Ferry (now Harrisburg), Pa., Sept. 26, 1760; moved to Aurelias, N.Y., 1789; operated 1st ferry across Cayuga Lake; Indian interpreter; opened 1st store and tavern in Cayuga County (N.Y.), 1789; apptd. col. N.Y. State Militia, 1806; mem. U.S. Ho. of Reps. from N.Y., 10th Congress, 1807-09; commanded 158th N.Y. Regt. during War of 1812. Died Bridgeport, N.Y., Nov. 1824; buried local cemetery.

HARRIS, JOHN AUGUSTUS adjutant gen. of Mo.; b. Centralia, Mo., Mar. 4, 1890; s. Edwin Ruthyen and Mary (Gillaspy) H.; student Univ. of Mo., 1911-12; m. Susan Luella Chambers, May 31, 1913; children-John Robert, Ann Elizabeth. Sec. State Supt. of Pub. Schs., Jefferson City, Mo., 1915-19; chief advisor for 4-state area, Mo., Kan. Ia., Neb., rehabilitation div., Fed. Bd. Vocational Edn. (forerunner of Vets. Adminstrn.), 1919-20; industrial journalist and publisher since 1920; member board dirs. of National Guardsman Pub. Co. Enlisted F.A., 1918; attended O.T.S., F.A., Camp Taylor, Ky.; organized Hdqrs. Co., 4th Mo. Inf., M.S.G., Columbia, Nov. 1940, capt. and advanced through the grades to maj. gen., April 1945; adj. gen. of Mo. since Apr. 18, 1945; comdg. gen. Mo. N.G. and all state's mil. forces, Mar. 1946; apptd. dir. Selective Service for Mo., 1948; apptd. mem. Army's Com. on Civilian Components, 1949. Member National Guard Assn. of U.S. (mem. exec. com.), Am. Legion. Democrat. Baptist. Mason (Shriner). Clubs: Scabbard and Blade. Rotary, Jefferson City Country. Member of the 9th generation of family founded, Jamestown, Va., in 1630's by Robert Harris, son-in-law of Sir William Claiborne, 1st sec. Colony of Va. Home: Jefferson City Mo. Office: Adj. Gen. Office: Jefferson City, Mo. Died Oct. 20, 1951.

HARRIS, JULIAN LAROSE editor; b. Savannah, Ga., June 21, 1874; s. Joel Chandler and Esther (LaRose) H.; ed. Gordon lMil. Inst., Atlanta; studied French, St. Ephrem d'Upton, Can.; m. Julia Florida Collier, Oct. 26, 1897. Asst. to Sunday editor Chgo. Times-Herald, 1896; right editor Atlanta Constn., 1896-97, city editor, 1897-98, mng. editor, 1898-1904; mng. editor Atlanta Daily News, 1904-05, Tri-Weekly Constn., 1905-07; bus. mgr. Uncle Remus Home Mag., 1907-09, editor and gen. mgr., 1909-11, editor, 1911, advt. mgr., 1912; Sunday editor N.Y. Herald, 1914; advt. mgr. N.Y. Evening Telegram, 1915; editor European edit. N.Y. Herald, 1916, asst. to editor N.Y. Herald, 1918, Paris corr., later editor and gen. mgr.

European edit., 1919; gen. mgr. Columbus (Ga.) Enquirer, 1920-22, editor Enquirer-Sun, 1923-29; pres. Enquirer-Sun Pub. Co., 1923-30; state news editor Atlanta Constn., 1930, news dir., 1931-32. Apptd. advt. dir., 1933; exec. editor Chattanooga Times, 1935-42; so. corr. N.Y. Times, Atlanta, 1942-45. Commd. 1st lt., 1917, capt. M.I. Div., U.S. Army, 1918. Mem. adv. bd. Sch. Journalism, Columbia; mem. So. Commn. on Study of Lynching; elected mem. So. Edn. Found., 1941-45. Democrat. Awarded Pulitzer prize ($500.00 gold medal) "for most disinterested and meritorious public service" rendered by an Am. newspaper in 1925 for fight against K.K.K., against law barring teaching of evolution, and for justice for the Negro. On the Nation's roll of honor, 1927. Home: 835 Myrtle St. N.E., Atlanta 5. Died Feb. 9, 1963.

HARRIS, LOUIS MARSHALL naval officer; b. Mineola, Tex., Dec. 24, 1900; s. William Milton and Mary Lucy (Jenkins) H.; B.S., U. of Texas, 1926; M.D., U. of Ark.; M.Sc. in Med., U. of Pa., 1939, D.Sc., 1949; m. Fannie Muriel Coltharo, Apr. 9, 1926; children-Frances, Barbara (Mrs. R.S. Stallings). U.S. Navy, 1931, advanced through the grades to capt., Med. Corps, 1945; regimental surg. 9th Marines and comdg. officer 1st Corps Medical Bn., Fleet Marine Force, Southwest Pacific, 1942-44; medical officer in charge appointments and reserve personnel, V-12 medical tng. program. Bureau of Medicine and Surgery, Navy Dept., Washington, 1944-45; now chief department obstetrics and gynecology National Naval Medical Center, Bethesda, Maryland with additional duty BuMed and Navy Dispensary. Associated obstetrics and gynecology Northwestern U. Sch. Medicine since 1946. Served with 3d Marine Div., Bougainville and Solomon Islands campaigns. Decorated Purple Heart, Bronze Star Medal with combat citation. Commendation (Bougainville campaign), Commendation Ribbon (from sec. of navy). Certified by Am. Bd. Obstetrics and Gynecology, 1945. Fellow A.C.S., Am. Assn. Obstetricians Gynecologists and Abdominal Surgeons, A.M.A., American Academy Obstetrics and Gynecology; mem. Assn. Mil. Surgeons Phi Chi. Mason. Presbyn. Author articles in profl. jours. Address: 1805 Melody Lane, Garland, Tex. Died Nov. 11, 1955; buried Arlington Nat. Cemetery.

HARRIS, PETER CHARLES army officer; b. Kingston, Ga., Nov. 10, 1865; s. Charles Hooks and Margaret (Monk) H.; grad. U.S. Mil. Acad., 1888; honor grad. Inf. and Cav. Sch., 1895; Army War Coll., 1908; m. Mary Gughrie, Sept. 30, 1894 (dec.). Commd. 2d lt., 13th Inf., 1888, promoted through the grades to col., adj. gen., 1917; brig. gen. N.A., 1917; adj. gen. of Army, rank of maj. gen., 1918; retired 1922. In Battle of San Juan Hill and siege of Santiago de Cuba, 1898; in active operations against Philippine insurgents, 1899-1900; rep. of War Dept. at Buffalo Expn., 1901; again in Philippines, 1905-07, 12-15; duty Gen. Staff, 1907-11; duty in office of Adj. Gen., Washington, 1916-22. Nominated by Pres., bvt., capt., for gallantry in battle at Santiago de Cuba, 1898. Decorated D.S.M. (U.S.); Comdr. Legion of Honor (France); Comdr. Order of the Crown (Italy). Democrat. Presbyn. Clubs: Army and Navy (Washington and Manila). Home: The Highlands, Washington. Died Mar. 18, 1951.

HARRIS, ROBERT ALFRED, assn. exec.; b. Beloit, Wis., Mar. 28, 1905; s. William L. and Florence (Marlatt) H.; student N.M. Mil. Inst., 1924-26; grad. Engring. Mech., U. Notre Dame, 1926-28; m. Marguarite G. Gleeson, Dec. 28, 1929; children—Marguerite G. (Mrs. George Main), Rose Mary (Mrs. Gerard Gunter), Robert Alfred. Commd. 2d lt. U.S. Cavalry, 1928, advanced through grades to capt., 1933; tranferred to USAAF, 1933, advanced through grades to lt. col., 1946; transferred to USAF, 1947, advanced through grades to col., 1954; ret., 1958; mgr. Lake Worth (Fla.) C. of C., 1961-69. Bd. dirs. Community Fund, Lake Worth, 1964-69, Salvation Army, Lake Worth, 1964-69. Bd. dirs. Rehab. Center, Palm Beach County. Decorated Legion of Merit. Kiwanian (lt. gov. 1963-64). Home: Lake Worth FL Died Apr. 4, 1969; buried Palm Beach Meml. Gardens

HARRIS, SEALE physician; born Cedartown, Ga., Mar. 13, 1870; s. Charles Hooks and Margaret Ann (Monk) H.; U. Ga.; M.D., U. Va., 1894; grad. study N.Y. Polyclinic, 1898; U. Chgo., 1904, Johns Hopkins, 1906, U. Vienna and other European clinics, 1906; hon. LL.D., U. Ala.; m. Stella Rainer, on April 28, 1897 (dec. 1940);children-Seale (deceased 1943), Josephine Anne (Mrs. John J. Keegan). General private practice medicine, Union Springs, Ala., 1894-1906; physician-in-chief Mobile (Ala.) City Hosp., 1906-13; prof. medicine U. Ala., 1906-13, now prof. emeritus med. coll.; founder, dir. Seale Harris Clinic, 1922-56, ret. Served as maj., M.C. Res., U.S. Army, 1917; staff Surgeon Gen. Gorgas Hosp., 1918-19; sec. research com. A.R.C., France, 1918-19; investigated food conditions and nutritional diseases in Italy, Austria and Germany, Jan.-Feb. 1919; cons. physician Pres. Wilson's Party, Italy, Jan. 1919; col. (ret.), M.C. Res. Recipient Distinguished Service Medal, A.M.A., Research Medal, So. Med. Assn. for discovery (1923) of hyperinsulinism, 1949; citation by Gen. Pershing for conspicuous and meritorious service in France. Fellow A.C.P., Am. Geriatrics Soc., mem. Jefferson Co. Med. Soc., Ala. Med. Assn., So. Med. Assn. (past pres. and sec.), A.M.A., Am., Ala. diabetes assns., Jefferson Co. Diabetes Soc., Am. Therapeutic Soc., Am. Gastroenterological Assn., Am. Medical Editors Assn. (past pres.), Sigma Alpha Epsilon, Phi Chi. Independent Presbyn. Club: Mountain Brook. Author: Clinical Pellegra, 1940; Banting's Miracle, 1946; Woman's Surgeon, 1950. Editor-owner Southern Medical Journal, 1910-22; editor War Medicine, Paris, France, during World War I. Home: 3822 Jackson Blvd., Birmingham 13. Office: 2219 Highland Av., Birmingham, Ala. Died Mar. 16, 1957; buried Elmwood Cemetery, Birmingham.

HARRIS, THOMAS LANGRELL congressman; b. Norwich, Conn., Oct. 29, 1816; grad. Washington (now Trinity) Coll., Hartford, Conn., 1841; studied law. Admitted to the bar, 1842; began practice of law, Petersburg, Menard County, Ill.; sch. commr. Menard County, 1845; raised and commanded a co. during Mexican War, joined 4th Regt., Ill. Volunteer Inf., later elected maj. of the regt.; elected mem. Ill. Senate (in absentia), 1846; presented with sword by State of Ill. for gallantry at Battle of Cerro Gordo; mem. U.S. Ho. of Reps. (Democrat), from Ill. 31st, 34th-35th congresses, 1849-51, 55-58. Died Springfield, Ill., Nov. 24, 1858; buried Rose Hill Cemetery, Petersburg, Ill.

HARRIS, URIAH ROSE rear admiral; b. Columbus, Ind., Sept. 14, 1849; s. John and Abigail (Rose) H.; grad. U.S. Naval Acad., 1869; m. Sophia Ann Simonton, Feb. 8, 1878. Midshipman, June 4, 1869; ensign, July 12, 1870; master, Jan. 1, 1872: lt., Feb. 11, 1875; lt. comdr., Feb. 25, 1897; comdr., Dec. 31, 1899; capt., Feb. 21, 1905; rear admiral, Jan. 7, 1909. Served on bd. Sabine, 1869-70; Ossipee, 1871-72; Frolic, 1873; Narragansett, 1874-75; coast survey schooner Earnest, 1876; navy yard, Mare Island, Calif., 1877; coast survey schooners Earnest and Yukon, 1877-78; Shenandoah, 1879-82; Naval Obs., 1882-84; navy yard, Mare Island, 1884-87, Ranger, 1887-90; Naval Acad., 1890-94; Ranger, 1895; Adams, 1896-97; navy yard, Boston, 1898; Chicago, 1899; light house duty, St. Louis, 1900-01; comdt. naval sta., Olongapo, P.I., 1902; Wilmington, 1903-04; navy yard, Boston, 1905-06: comdt. naval stas., Olongapo and Cavite, P.I., 1907-08; comdt. navy yard, Phila., May 27, 1909-Mar. 21, 1910; gov. Naval Home, Phila., to Sept. 14, 1911; retired, Sept. 14, 1911. Episcopalian. Home: Washington, D.C. Died June 20, 1930.

HARRIS, WALTER ALEXANDER lawyer; b. Macon, Ga., Nov. 17, 1875; s. Nathaniel Edwin and Fannie (Burke) H.; A.B., U. of Georgia, 1895, LL.B., 1896, also LL.D., 1928; m. Emily Williamson, Jan. 9, 1901 (died June 5, 1936). Admitted to Ga. bar, 1896, and practiced in Macon. mem. Harris, Russell, Weaver & Watkins. Mem. Bibb County Bd. of Edn., 1905-12. Pvt., 1st lt. and capt., 3d Ga. Vols., May 1, 1898-Apr. 22, 1899; served in Cuba with Army of Occupation; comd. Ga. Brig. U.S. Nat. Guard. on Mexican border, 1916-17; comdg. 61st Inf. Brig., 31st Div., 1917-18; comdg. 31st Div., A.E.F., Sept. 28-Nov. 14, 1918; returned in command 174th Inf. Brig., 87th Div., Jan. 10, 1919: hon. disch., Jan. 21, 1919. Maj. Gen. Ga. N.G. (ret.). Mem. Am., Ga. bar assns., Macon Bar Assn., Macon Hist. Soc. (pres.), Soc. for Ga. Archaeology (mem. exec. com.). Trustee emeritus Wesleyan Coll. Mem. Chi Phi, Phi Beta Kappa, Comdr. Ga. Dept. Am. Legion, 1919. Democrat. Episcopalian. Club: Kiwanis. Author: Emperor Brim, 1937. Home: 644 College St. Office: Persons Bldg., Macon, Ga. Died Mar. 15, 1958.

HARRISON, DESALES, sales exec.; b. Atlanta, July 13, 1899; s. James Lawrence and Kathleen (Mecaslin) H.; student Marist Coll., 1913-16; Oglethorpe U., 1917-18; m. Virginia Wyatt Pegram, June 6, 1923; children—DeSales, Virginia (Mrs. Jack Friling), Robert Pegram, Nancy Knight (Mrs. Keith S. Latimore). Salesman various cos., 1919-20; head advt. dept. The Coca-Cola Co., Atlanta, 1925-30, regional mgr. Southeastern Region, New Orleans, 1930-33, v.p. Central Region, Chgo., 1933-34, v.p. in charge of Fountain Sales Div. U.S., 1934-41; chmn. adv. com., dir. Coca-Cola Bottling Co. (Thomas), Inc.; dir. other cos., The Alabama Gt. So. R.R. Interstate Life & Accident Ins. Co., Am. Nat. Bank & Trust Co. Pres. YMCA Chmn. Bd. dirs. Meml. Hosp., Community Found. Greater Chattanooga, Inc.; trustee Benwood Found., Inc. Served to comdr. USNR, 1942-45, H.I., Okinawa, Mem. Am. Soc. Sales Execs., Newcomen Soc. N. Am., Kappa Alpha. Episcopalian. Clubs: Nine O'Clocks, The Fifty Club, Piedmont Driving (Atlanta); Mountain City, Lookout Mountain-Fairyland. Rotary (Chattanooga). Home: Lookout Mountain TN Died Feb. 21, 1973.

HARRISON, FRANCIS BURTON ex-gov.-gen. P.I.; b. New York, Dec. 18, 1873; s. Burton and Constance (Cary) H.; A.B., Yale, 1895; LL.B., New York Sch. of Law, 1897; m. Mary Crocker, June 7, 1900 (died 1905); m. 2d, Magel Judson, 1907; m. 3d, Elizabeth Wrentmore, May 15, 1919 (divorced), 1927); m. 4th, Margaret Wrentmore, Apr. 8, 1927. Instructor in New York night law school, 1897-99; admitted to bar, 1898; private Troop A, N.Y. Vol. Cav., and capt. and adj.-gen. U.S. Vols., Spanish-Am. War, June 20, 1898-Jan. 31, 1899; mem. 58th Congress (1903-05), 13th N.Y. Dist., 60th, 61st, 62d Congresses (1907-13), 16th Dist., and 63d Congress (1913-15), 20th Dist.; resigned from 63d Congress, 1913; gov.-gen. P.I., 1913-21. Dem. candidate for lt.-gov. of N.Y., 1904. Home: Teaninich, Alness, Scotland. Died Nov. 21, 1957.*

HARRISON, GEORGE PAUL ex-congressman; b. at Monteith Plantation, 12 miles from Savannah, Ga., Mar. 19, 1841; s. Gen. George P. and Adelaide (Guinn) H.; (lineal descendant Benjamin Harrison of Va., signer Declaration of Independence); m. Sara Nunnally, of LaGrange, Ga., Nov. 20, 1900. Grad. Ga. Mil. Inst. with first honors and as capt. Co. A; entered C.S.A., 2d lt., 1st Ga. regulars; successively promoted 1st lt., maj., col., and brig.-gen.; being youngest brig.-gen. commissioned by Confed. govt.; was col. before he was 20 yrs. old, brig.-gen. before he was 22. After war removed to Ala.; for several yrs. was a planter, 1 yr. commandant cadets, Agrl. and Mech. Coll., Auburn, Ala.; studied law; began practice, 1817. Del. Ala. Constl. Conv., 1875; mem. Ala. Senate, 1876-84 (pres. 1882-84); del. Dem. Nat. Conv., Chicago, 1892; elected to 53d Congress, Nov. 6, 1894, for unexpired term (1894-95) of W. C. Oates, resigned; elected to 54th Congress (1895-97); declined renomination, 1896; del. Ala. Constl. Conv., 1900; mem. Ala. Senate, 1900-04; gen. counsel 2 rys. for 20 yrs. Grand Master Grand Lodge of Ala., A.F. & A.M., 1894-96; prominent layman M.E. Ch., South; mem. Sigma Alpha Epsilon; maj.-gen. comdg. Ala. Div., U.C.V.; pres. Ala. State Bar Assn., 1905-06. Address: Opelika, Ala.†

HARRISON, IKE H(ENRY), univ. dean; b. San Marcos, Tex., Dec. 20, 1909; s. Ike Henry and Jessie (O'Bannon) H.; A.B., Southwest Tex. Tchrs. Coll., 1929; B.B.A., U. Tex., 1933, M.B.A., 1934; Ed.D., N.Y.U., 1942; M. Anne Randolph, Aug. 25, 1939; 1 son, Ike Henry III. Asst. prof. bus. East Tex. State Coll., 1935-36; prof. bus. adminstrn. Houston State Tchrs. Coll., 1936-46; dean Sch. Bus. U. Houston, 1946-47, Tex. Christian U., 1955-71; vis. prof. N.Y.U., 1937-38, Harvard Graduate School Bus. Administrn., 1962. Served as colonel USAAF, 1942-46, 47-54. Mem. Am. Mgmt. Assn., Am. Marketing Assn., Am. Statis. Assn., Am., So. econs. assns., So. Case Writers, Am. Soc. Quality Control, Sigma Nu. Co-author: Business Policy Cases with Behavioral Science Implications. Home: Ft Worth TX Died Feb. 15, 1971.

HARRISON, RAYMOND LEYDEN merchant, army officer; b. Excelsior, Minn., Apr. 4, 1896; s. Amos and Mary (Leyden) H.; ed. pub. schs. of Excelsior, Minneapolis; m. Sarah Helen Tracy, Nov. 29, 1919 (div. Sept. 1947); children - Raymond, Gloria, Loretto, Sally; m. 2d. Katharine Henkel Allen, July 5, 1949; children - Edward, Robert, Thomas, John. Established own business under name R. L. Harrison Co., Albuquerque, N.M., pres. since 1921, also pres. Tri-State Equipment Co., El Paso, Texas, since 1934; vice pres. Carbonic Chemicals Corp., Solano, N.M. since 1937, Commodity Credit Corp., U.S. Dept. Agrl., 1945-47. Served as sergt. maj. U.S. Army in transportation corps. 1917-18; served as colonel U.S. Army gen staff corps, 1942-47; disch. rank of col. Home: 1000 Grandview Dr. S.E. Office: R. L. Harrison Co. Inc., Albuquerque, N.M. Died Jan. 20, 1960; buried Arlington Nat. Cemetery.

HARRISON, WILLIAM, JR., Continental congressman; b. Md.; s. William Harrison. Mem. Continental Congress from Md., 1785-87; engaged in shipbldg., St. Michaels, Md., 1810; served as 1st lt. Ind. Light Dragoons, 9th Cavalry Regt., Md. Militia, 1812, later capt., comdr. troop; justice ct. at St. Michaels, 1813.

HARRISON, WILLIAM BENJAMIN business exec.; b. Louisville, Ky., July 28, 1889; s. William and Virginia L. (Trezevant) H.; B.L., U. of Va., 1910; m. Margaret W. Allis, June 4, 1912; children-William H., Winston P., Penelope A. Dixon, Margaret T. Reynolds, Dorothy F. Seelbach. Adjuster, Travelers Ins. Co., Louisville, Ky., 1910-12; asst. mgr. Am. Surety Co. of New York, 1912-17; sec., treas. Foundry Products Co., 1919-22; pres. Ky. Refrigerating Co., 1922-30; pres. Louisville Indsl. Foundation since 1934; chmn. Mengel Co.; dir. B. F. Avery & Sons Co., Puritan Cordage Mills, Wheatley Foods, Inc., Porcelain Metals Corp., Morton Packing Co., Castlewood Mfg. Co. Dir. Louisville Bd. of Trade. Mayor of Louisville, 1927-33. Served as capt. F.A., U.S. Army, 1917-19. Mem. Louisville Area Development Assn., Zeta Psi. Republican. Presbyterian. Clubs: Pendennis, Louisville Country. Home: 1460 St. James Ct. Office: Columiba Bldg., Louisville, Ky. Died July 13, 1948.

HARRISON, WILLIAM HENRY 9th Pres. U.S.; b. "Berkeley," Charles City County, Va., Feb. 9, 1773; s. Benjamin and Elizabeth (Bassett) H.; attended Hampden-Syndey Coll., 1787-90; studied medicine under Dr. Benjamin Rush, Phila., 1790-91; m. Anna Symmes, 1795, 6 sons including John Scott (father of Benjamin Harrison, 23d Pres. U.S.), Col. William Henry, 4 daus. Apptd. ensign 1st Inf., U.S. Army, 1791; served on frontier duty old N.W. Territory; promoted capt., 1797; in command at Ft. Washington (now Cincinnati), 1797-98; resigned commn., 1798; sec. N.W. Territory, 1798-99, del. to U.S. Congress, 1799-1800; gov. and Indian commr. for Territory of Ind., 1800-13; defeated Indian confederation under Tecumseh and Elskwatawa (the Prophet) at Battle of Tippecanoe, Nov. 6-7, 1811; brevetted maj. gen. U.S.

Volunteers and brig. gen. U.S. Army, 1812, comdg. gen. Army of N.W.; commd. maj. gen., 1813; victor in Battle of Thames (assured Am. control of N.W.), 1813, brought about pacification of most of Indians at death of Tecumseh; resigned commn., 1814; mem.U.S. Ho. of Reps. from Ohio, 14th-15th congresses, Oct. 8, 1816-19; mem. Ohio U.S. Senate from Ohio, 1825-28; U.S. - - minister to Colombia, S. Am., 1828-29; unsuccessful Whig candidate for U.S. Pres., 1836; elected 9th Pres. U.S. after extensive popular campaign (included slogan "Tippecanoe and Tyler too"), 1840, served from Mar. 4-Apr. 4, 1841 (1st pres. to die in office). Died of pneumonia, Washington, D.C., Apr. 4, 1841; buried Harrison Tomb, opposite Congress Green Cemetery, North Bend, O.

HARRISON, WILLIAM HENRY communications engr.; b. Bklyn., June 11, 1892; s. John and Ann (Terahin) H.; student Pratt Inst., 1913-15; D. Engring. (hon.), Polytech. Inst. Bklyn., 1938; LL.D. (hon.), Notre Dame U., 1939. Hofstra Coll., 1951; D. England (honorary) Renssalaer Poly. Inst., 1946, Manhattan College, 1950; Master of Procurement (hon.), Signal Supply Sch., Ft. Horabird, Md., 1952; married Mabel Gilchrist Ouchterloney, Apr. 14, 1915, children-William Henry, John Grant. Repairman and wireman, N.Y. Telephone Co., 1909-14; in engring. dept., Western Electric Co., New York, N.Y., 1914-18; engineer equipment and bldg. engr., and plant engr., Am. Telephone and Telegraph Co., N.Y. City, 1918-33: v.p. and dir. The Bell Telephone Co. of Pa. and The Diamond State Telephone Co., 1933-37; asst. v.p., Am. Telephone and Telegraph Co., N.Y.C., 1937-38; v.p. and chief engr., 1938-45, v.p. department operational engineering, 1945-48, pres., dir., 1948—; chmn. divs. of Internat. Tel. & Tel. Corp., subsidiaries; dir. subsidiary cos. Chief Shipbuilding, Construction and Supplies Branch, Office of Prodn. Management, 1941-42; dir. of Production, W.P.B., 1942. Apptd. brig. gen. U.S. Army, 1942, maj. gen., 1943; director construction division National Defense council, 1940; dir. of procurement and distribution service, Office of Chief Signal Officer, 1943-45; adminstr. N.P.A., 1950-51, D.P.A., 1951. Awarded D.S.M., 1945; Hon. Comdr. Order British Empire, 1946; Hoover Medal, 1946; Cross French Legion of Honor (Officer) 1947. Dir. Nassau Hosp.; mem. bd. gov. N.Y. Hospital; trustee Pratt Institute, Manhattan Coll. Mem. Am. Inst. Electric Engrs. (ex-president), Newcomen Society, Eta Kappa Nu, Tau Beta Pi. Clubs: University, Downtown Athletic (New York); North Fork Country (Cutchogue, N.Y.); Garden City Golf, Cherry Valley (Garden City); Chevy Chase (Wash.); India House; Chgo. Home: 120 Kensington Rd., Garden City, N.Y. Office: 67 Broad St., N.Y.C. 4. Died Apr. 21, 1956.

HARROLD, CHARLES COTTON surgeon; b. Americus, Ga., Dec. 9, 1878; s. Uriah Bullock and Mary Elizabeth (Fogle) H.; grad. high sch., Americus, 1895; B.S., U. of Ga., 1898; A.M. Columbia, 1902, M.D., 1902; m. Helen Sophia Shaw, Oct. 23, 1906; children-Helen Shaw (Mrs. Sinclair Alfred Frederick), Mary Fogle (Mrs. John Emory Seals), Charles Cotton. Began practice. Macon, 1904; limited to surgery since 1911; pres. Middle Ga. Hosp. since 1925; dir. Citizens & Southern Nat. Bank since 1929; v.p. Macon Federal Savings & Loan Assn. since 1930 Served in Ga. Nat. Guard, 1904-16; maj. U.S.M.C. 1916-19, World War. Fellow Am. Coll. Surgeons A.A.A.S.; mem. A.M.A., Am. Soc. for Control of Cancer, Soc. for Ga. Archaeology (pres.), Phi Beta Kappa, Phi Delta Theta. Democrat. Episcopalian. Mason. Clubs: Kiwanis, Idle Hour Country. Contbr. surg. articles. Home: 550 Orange St. Office: 700 Spring St., Macon, Ga. Died Oct. 11, 1948.

HARROP, LESLIE DEVOTTIE lawyer, pharm. mfr.; b. Ashland, Ky., Feb. 9, 1901; s. Arthur Henry and Myrtle (Carman) H.; A.B., Albion Coll., 1922; J.D., U. Detroit, 1934; m. Catherine Woodena Tench, May 21, 1926; 1 dau., Helen Carman (Mrs. James M. Canon). Newspaper reporter, Detroit, Lorain, O. and Greenville, Mich., 1922-26; bus. mgr. Manistee (Mich.) News Advocate, 1926-28; corr., bus. rep., bur. mgr. U.P., 1928-34; admitted to Mich. bar, 1934; asst. atty. gen., Mich., 1935-36; gen. counsel Upjohn Co., Kalamazoo, 1937-, v.p., dir., 1950. Gen. counsel Am. Drug Mfrs. Assn., Washington, 1938-54; dir. Health Information Found., 1951-. Vice chmn. trustees Kalamazoo Inst. Arts. Served as lt. col., San. Corps, AUS, 1942-44. Mem. Am., Mich., N.Y. State bar assns., Am. Judicature Soc., Sigma Chi, Delta Theta Phi, Delta Sigma Rho. Home: 1201 Short Rd. Office: The Upjohn Co., Kalamazoo, Mich. Died Dec. 5, 1964.

HART, FRANKLIN AUGUSTUS ret. MC officer; b. Cuthbert, Ga., Sept. 16, 1894; s. Samuel Beall and Florence (Smith) H.; B.S. in Mining Engring., Sch., field officers course Marine Corps Sch., Chm. Warfare Sch., Army War Coll.; m. Katherine Killeen Costello, Apr. 19, 1924; 1 son, Franklin Augustus. Commd. 2d lt., U.S. Marine Corps, 1917, advancing through the grades to general, 1954; served with marine detachment, U.S.S. Vermont, Atlantic Fleet, 1917-18; with Co. B, 5th Brigade, Machine Gun Bn., France, 1918-19; on staff Comdr. U.S. Naval Forces in Europe, with additional duty as liaison officer, Chief Combined Operations, London, 1941-42; participated in Dieppe operations, 1942, offensives in Marshall Islands, Feb. 1944, Saipan, June-July 1944, Tinian, Iwo Jima (comd. 24th Marines, 4th Marine Div.), July-Aug. 1944; comdg. gen., Fleet Marine Force, Pacific, 1952-54, ret. 1954; now v.p., dir. Porter Internat. Co. Decorated Navy Cross Legion of Merit, Bronze Star, Presdl. Unit Citation, Navy Unit Citation, Victory Medal with star and Maltese Cross, Marine Corps Expeditionary Medal with 2 stars, Mex. Border Medal, Nicaragua Campaign Medal, Am. Defense Service Medal, Asiatic-Pacific Area Medal with 2 stars, European Area Medal with 1 star (U.S.), Order of Honor and Merit Medal, Distinguished Service Medal, Mil. Medal of Merit (Republic d'Haiti), Mil. Merit Taiguk Korea; Korean Presdl. unit citation. Mem. Am. Inst. Mining, Metall., Petroleum Engrs., Soc. Am. lfil. Engrs. Club: Army and Navy (Washington). Home: 1919 23d St., Washington 8. Office: 1025 Connecticut Av. N.W., Washington. Died June 1967.

HART, HENRY HERSCH, b. San Francisco, Calif., Sept. 27,21886; s. Henry and Etta (Harris) H.; A.B., U. of Calif., 1907, J.D., 1909; studied Chinese and Japanese under native teachers; m. Alice Patek Stern, 1912 (deceased, September 18, 1936); children—Peggy H. (deceased April 7, 1952), and Alice Virginia (Mrs. Virginia H. Page, dec.); m. 2d, Helen K. Ach, Aug. 21, 1941. Practiced law in San Francisco, Calif., 1909-19; asst. city attorney, San Francisco, 1911-18; collected Oriental art for collectors, 1922-37; lecturer on Chinese and allied subjects and on comparative religion and literature since 1915, at San Francisco State College, since 1960; lectr. on Chinese art and culture U. Cal., 1933-36; lectr. U. Cal. Extension Div., 1932-60; U. Cal., 1960-68; lectr. on circuit W. Colston Leigh, Inc. since 1950; radio and TV; vis. lectr. numerous orgns., clubs, and univs. on oriental fields, traveled extensively in Far East; mem. executive board Temple of Religion, Golden Gate Internat. Exposition, 1940-41. With U.S. Postal Censorship, 1942; on active duty maj. corps Military Police, A.U.S., service in U.S.A., Africa and India, 1943; special adviser, Office War Information, 1944. Recipient several decorations, 1923, including: Chevalier Order White Elephant of Cambodia (France), 1923; collar and gold medal of mem. Instituto de Coimbra (Portugal), 1941. Licenciate in pharmacy, Cal. Fellow Royal Geog. Society, London, Royal Asiatic Soc.; mem. Hispanic Soc. Am. (corr.), profl. sci. and cultural socs. and assns., U.S., several fgn. countries including Linschoten Vereeniging (Amsterdam), Friends of the Library, San Francisco (pres. 1951-58). Clubs: Faculty (University of Calif.); Commonwealth, Roxburgh (San Francisco); Calif. Writers. Author and translator numerous works relating to China and Portugal, latest being: Sea Road to the Indies (voyages of the Portuguese), 1950. English edit. 1952, German and Polish transls., 1960; Poems of the Hundred Names, 1954; Venetian Adventurer (Marco Polo) in Bantam Biographies, 1956, Spanish, German and Polish transls., 1960; Luis De Camoens and the Epic of the Lusiads, 1962. Joint author: Tamalpais—Enchanted Mountain, 1946. Contbr. articles to Asia, Japan. Home: San Francisco CA Died Dec. 18, 1968.

HART, THOMAS CHARLES, naval officer; b. at Davidson, Mich., June 12, 1877; s. John Mansfield and Isabella (Ramsay) H.; grad. U.S. Naval Acad., 1897, Navy War Coll., 1923, Army War Coll., 1924; m. Caroline Brownson, Mar. 30, 1910; children—Isabella, Roswell Roberts, Thomas Comins (died 1945), Caroline Brownson, Harriet Taft. Commd. ensign U.S. Navy, 1899, and advanced to captain, Apr. 1, 1918; rear admiral, Sept. 1929. Served in Cuban waters, Spanish-Am. War; comdr. submarines, waters of British Isles and Azores, World War; in Office of Operations, Navy Dept., 1919-20; comdr. U.S.S. Beaver and Asiatic Submarine Flotilla, 1920-22; capt. U.S.S. Mississippi, 1925-27; supervisor N.Y. Harbor and comdr. Torpedo Sta., Newport, R.I., 1927-29; comdr. submarines, Atlantic and Pacific, 1929-31; supt. U.S. Naval Acad., 1931-34, comdr. cruisers Scouting Force, 1934-36; mem. Gen. Bd., 1936-39; comdr. in chief Asiatic Fleet, July 1939-June 1942; comd. allied naval forces in Far East, Jan.-Feb. 1942; retired for age, being 1 yr. overtime, June 30, 1942, and recalled to active service Gen. Bd., July 1942; on inactive list, Feb. 1945. Apptd. U.S. senator from Conn.; served until Dec. 1946, did not stand for election. Awarded Distinguished Service Medal (U.S.), 1918 and again 1942. An Act of Congress, June 1942, provided for retention of rank of adm. when retired. Clubs: University, Adirondack League, New York Yacht (New York); Sharon (Conn.) Country; Army and Navy (Washington); Chevy Chase (Md.). Home: Sharon CT Died July 4, 1971; buried Arlington Nat. Cemetery, Arlington VA

HART, WILLIAM H. army officer; b. Winona, Minn., Mar. 20, 1864; s. John and Mary (Murphy) H.; grad.U.S. Mil. Acad., 1888; unmarried. Commd. 2d lt. 20th Inf., June 11, 1888; promoted through grades to col. Q.M.C., May 2, 1917; maj. gen., q.m. gen., Aug. 28, 1922. Q.m. 7th Cav., Ariz., 1896-98; adj. same, Cuba, 1899-1900; depot commissary, Manila, P.I., 1901-02; asst. com. gen., Washington, D.C., 1903-09; depot com., Honolulu, 1909-11, San Francisco, 1911-16, also supt. Army Trans. Service, 1913-16; base q.m., Base Sec. 1, St. Nazaire, France, 1918-19; depot q.m., New York, 1920-22; apptd. q.m. gen., Aug. 28, 1922. Initial Gen. Staff Corps Eligible List; awarded D.S.M. (U.S.); Officer Legion of Honor (French). Died Jan. 2, 1926.

HART, WILLIAM LEE medical officer U.S. Army; b. Yorkville (now York), S.C., Jan. 27, 1881; s. George Washington Seabrook and Ellen Almene (Hackett) H.; M.D., Univ. of Md., 1906; LL.D., Baylor Univ., May 28, 1945; L.H.D., Southwestern Med. Foundation, June 10, 1946; grad. Army Medical School, 1908, Command and General Staff Sch., 1926, Army Industrial Coll., 1927, Army War Coll., 1931; m. Mariana Catherine Franklin, June 30, 1920; children-William Lee II, Mariana Catherine II. Pvt. practice, 1906-07; with Medical Corps, U.S. Army, 1908—. Served as pvt. to capt. S.C. Militia and N.G., 1898-1908; 1st lt., advancing to col., U.S. Army, 1908-34; promoted to brigadier general, March 16, 1945; now brigadier general, United States Army, retired. Served as chief Overseas Div., Office of Surgeon General; with A.E.F. and with Army in France and Germany; various stations in the United States and P.I.; commanded 12th Med. Reg. in Philippines; pres. 7th C.A. Medical Research Board. Dean, South- western Medical College, 1946-49; dean S.W. Med. Sch. U. of Tex., 1949-50, dean emeritus, 1950—; professor pub. health, Southwestern Med. Coll., 1948-49, S.W. Med. School U. of Texas, 1949-50. Made researches in Philippines, in cholera; helminthology, and effects of tropical light on white people, also researches in typhoid fever, smallpox, etc., in U.S. Decorations from Bolivia, Ecuador, Serbia, Poland, France, Montenegro, Panama, etc. Awarded Founders' Medal by Assn. Mil. Surgeons of U.S., 1942. Ho Din, Southwestern Med. Foundation, 1944. Co-founder Celsus Soc. of San Antonio. Fellow A.M.A., Am. Coll. Phys., Am. Coll. Surg., A.A.A.S., Am. Pub. Health Assn., Scientific Soc. of San Antonio (pres. 1940-41); hon. mem. York County (S.C.) Med. Soc.; mem. Texas Acad. Science, Soc. of the Cincinnati, Geog. Soc. of Mexico, Pi Delta Upsilon, Nu Sigma Nu, Theta Nu Epsilon, Pi Gamma Mu, Upsilon Pi, Alpha Omega Alpha, Sigma Xi, Dem. Episcopalian. Clubs: Cosmos, Army and Navy (Wash.); Lambs (N.Y.). Compiler: History of Base Hospital No. 53. Contbr. on med. and scientific subjects. Address: 133 E. Mulberry Av., San Antonio 12. Died Dec. 22, 1957; buried York, S.C.

HARTE, HOUSTON, newspaper pub.; b. Knobnoster, Mo., Jan. 12, 1893; s. Edward Stettinius and Elizabeth (Houston) H.; student U. of Southern Calif., 1912-13; B.J., U. Mo., 1915; LL.D., Austin Coll., 1950, Tex. Technol. Coll., 1958; m. Caroline Isabel McCutcheon, Mar. 26, 1921; children—Edward Holmead, Houston Harriman. Reporter Los Angeles (Calif.) Examiner, 1912-13; pub. Knobnoster Gem, 1914; business mgr. Mo. Republican, Boonville, 1915, editor and pub., 1916-20; pub. San Angelo (Tex.) Evening Standard, 1920-62, San Angelo Standard-Times, 1928-62; mem. Harte, Hanks & Co. (pubs. San Angelo Standard (Morning), San Angelo Standard-Times (Evening), Abilene Reporter-News, Corpus Christi Times, Corpus Christi Caller, Paris Evening News, Big Spring Herald, Marshall News-Messenger), Denison Herald, Greenville Herald-Banner, San Antonio Express and Evening News; dir. Times Pub. Co., Wichita Falls, Bryan Daily Eagle, Corsicana Daily Sun, Commerce Jour., Huntsville Item. Mem. Texas Industrial Commission. Pres. Concho Valley Council Boy Scouts Am., 1932-35; mem. Tex. Relief Commn., 1933-35; v.p. Asso. Press, 1935-36, dir. 1937-43, 1st v.p., 1943-46; pres. Texas Pubs. Assn., Inc. Served as 2d lt., later 1st lieutenant and discharged as captain inf., U.S. Army, 1918-19. Dir. Texas Tech. Coll., 1926-33. Mem. West Tex. C. of C. (pres. 1931), Alpha Delta Sigma, Sigma Delta Chi, Delta Upsilon. Awarded medal of honor, Sch. of Journalism, U. of Mo., 1931. Democrat. Presbyn. Clubs: San Angelo Country, San Angelo, River. Editor: In Our Image. Home: San Angelo TX Died Mar. 13, 1972.

HARTIGAN, CHARLES CONWAY naval officer; b. Middletown, N.Y., Sept. 13, 1882; s. William C. and Minnie (Conway) H.; B.S., U.S. Naval Acad., 1906; m. Margaret Thompson, May 5, 1910; children-Margaret Alden (Mrs. James A. B. Barton), Charles Conway (lt., U.S. Navy). Commd. ensign, U.S. Navy, 1906, and advanced through the grades to rear admiral, 1941; retired July 1941; served in Mexican campaign, 1913; comd. U.S.S. Cassin (destroyer), June 1918-Mar. 1919; mem. U.S. Naval mission to Brazil, 1919-21, 1925-27; comd. Destroyer Div. 25 (U.S.S. Isherwood, flagship), 1927-29; U.S. naval attaché, Peking, China, 1929-32; comd. U.S.S. Oklahoma, 1937-39; Office Chief of Naval Operations, 1939-41. Awarded Medal of Honor, 1913; Mexican campaign, World War, Dominican campaign and Yangtse campaign medals. Clubs: Chevy Chase; Army and Navy; New York Yacht. Home: Edgewater, Ann Arundel County, Md. Died Feb. 25, 1944.

HARTLEY ROLAND H. ex-gov. Wash.; b. Shogomoc, York County, N.B., Can., June 26, 1864; s. Rev. Edward Williams and Rebecca Barker (Whitehead) H.; student pub. schs. and Mpls. Acad.; m. Nina M. Clough, Aug. 22, 1888; children-Edward Williams, David Marston, Mary. Settled at Brainerd, Minn., 1878; served as pvt. sec. to Gov. Clough, 1897, 98; moved to Everett, Wash., 1903, and engaged in lumber business; mayor of Everett, 1910, 11: mem. Wash, Ho. of Reps., 1915, 16; gov. of Wash., 1925-33. Served with Gen. Staff Minn. N.G., 8 yrs.; capt. O.R.C., U.S. Army. Republican. Mason (Shriner), Elk. Home: 2320 Rucker Av., Everett, Wash. Died Sept. 21, 1952; buried Everett.

HARTLEY, THOMAS congressman; b. Colebrookdale Twp., Pa., Sept. 7, 1748; s. George Hartley; m. Catherine Holtzinger. Admitted to Pa. bar, 1769, U.S. Supreme Ct. bar (1st Pa. lawyer admitted), 1791; dep. Pa. provincial confs., Phila., 1774-75; elected lt. col. 6th Battalion, Pa. Regt., Continental Army, 1776, commanded Pa. brigade, 1777; mem. Pa. Council of Censors, 1783-84; mem. U.S. Ho. of Reps. from Pa. 1s-6th congresses, 1789-Dec. 21, 1800; Federalist. Died York, Pa., Dec. 21, 1800; buried St. John's Churchyard, York.

HARTNEY, HAROLD EVANS tech. adviser in aviation; b. Packenham, Ont., Can., Apr. 19, 1888; s. James Harvey and Annie Evans (Cuthbert) H.; B.A., U. of Toronto, 1911; grad. U. of Saskatchewan, 1912; student Law Soc. of Saskatchewan, 1911-14; married to Irene McGeary, November 11, 1914; children-Mrs. Frederick Yeager, Mrs. Robert Gensel, Harold Evans (killed in action May 13, 1944), James Cuthbert. Came to United States, 1917, naturalized, 1928. Began with Royal Flying Corps, Canada; comdg. 1st Pursuit Group, U.S. Army Air Service, with A.E.F., 1917-19; chief of training, Washington, D.C., 1919-21; discharged with rank of lt. col. (reserve); organizing sec. and 1st gen. mgr. Nat. Aeronautic Assn., 1921-23; tech. adviser to several aeronautic corps; tech. adviser to U.S. Senate Com. on Air Safety, 1935-38; tech. adviser Civil Aeronautics Adminstrn., 1938-41; active duty Ferry Command Air Corps (lt. col.); mgr. Washington Bureau, Ziff-Davis Publicans, 1941-42; has been active in efforts to make air power recognized in war and industry. Decorated Distinguished Service Cross, Silver Star, Purple Heart (U.S.); Legion of Honor, Croix de Guerre (France); Silver Medal for Valor (Italy); Service Decoration (Brit.); Victory medals U.S. and Great Brit. Mem. Early Birds, Quiet Birdmen, Inst. Aeronautical Sciences, Am. Legion (past comdr. Aviators Post), Nat. Aeronautic Assn. Episcopalian. Author: Up and At 'Em, 1940; Complete Flying Manual, 1940; Aircraft Spotters' Guide, 1942; What the Citizen Should Know about the Air Force, 1942. Home: 3130 16th St., N.W., Washington, D.C. Died Oct. 5, 1945.

HARTRANFT, JOHN FREDERICK army officer, gov. Pa.; b. Fagleysville, Pa., Dec. 16, 1830; s. Samuel Engle and Lydia (Bucher) H.; grad. Union Coll., 1853; m. Sallie D. Sebring, Jan. 26, 1854, 3 children. Admitted to Pa. bar, 1860; commd. col. 51st Regt., Pa. Inf., U.S. Army, 1861; commd. brig. gen. U.S. Volunteers, 1864, served in 2d Battle of Bull Run, battle of Chantilly, South Mountain and Fredericksburg; led famous charge which captured stone bridge at Antietam, (one of most brillant achievements of war); a comdr. Army of West, 1863, engaged in battles of Campbell's Station, Vicksburg, Knoxville, brevetted maj. gen. U.S. Volunteers, 1865; auditor gen. Pa. (Republican), 1865-68; gov. Pa. (Rep.), 1872-74; comdr. Pa. Nat. Guard, 1879-89; postmaster Phila., 1879; collector Port of Phila., 1881-35. Died Norristown, Pa., Oct. 17, 1889.

HARTS, WILLIAM WRIGHT army officer; b. Springfield, Ill., Aug. 29, 1866; s. Peter Wilde and Harriet (Bates) H.; student Princeton, 1884-85 (hon. M.A. 1913); B.S., U.S. Mil. Acad., 1889, Engr. Sch. of Application, 1892, Army War Coll., 1912 and 1921; Navy War Coll., 1913; Field Arty. School of Fire, 1923; Coast Arty. Sch., 1924; m. Martha Davis Hale, Oct. 27, 1898; children - Mary Hale, Clement Bates Ellery, William W., Cynthia Prudden. Commd. 2d lt. Corps of Engrs., 1889; promoted through grades to brig. gen. N.A., 1917, brig. gen. U.S. Army, 1924. Served with Corps Engrs., 1889-1917, in a large variety of constrn. projects, including river and harbor improvements, locks and dams, army camps and meml. projects, student and instructor United States Army War College, Washington, D.C., 1911-13; mil. aide to President Wilson, 1913-17; comdg. 6th U.S. Engr. Regt., 1917, served with French and with British; comdg. U.S. brig. with British, 1918; chief Am. Mission, British G.H.Q., 1918; comdg. Dist. of Paris, 1918-19; mil aide to Pres. Wilson while in Europe, Dec. 1918-June 1919; chief of staff, Army of Occupation, Germany, 1919-20, 22-23; military attaché Am. Embassy, Paris, 1926-30. Awarded numerous prizes and decorations, 1902 - , including: D.S.M. (U.S.); K.C.M.G. (British); Commander Légion d' Honneur (French); Ordre de la Couronne (Belgian). Mem. Am. Soc. C.E., Soc. Mil. Engrs., S.R., Mil. Order Loyal Legion, Am. Legion, Instn. C.E. (London). Presbyn. Clubs: Army and Navy (Washington); University (New York); Madison (Conn.) Country, Madison (Conn.) Beach; Cercle Interalliee (Paris). Address: Madison, Conn. Died Apr. 21, 1961. Died Apr. 21, 1961; buried Arlington Nat. Cemetery.

HARTSTUFF, GEORGE LUCAS army officer; b. Tyre, N.Y., May 28, 1830; grad. U.S. Mil. Acad., 1852; m. Sarah Maine, Dec. 11, 1858. Participated in Seminole War, severely wounded; asst. instr. tactics U.S. Mil. Acad., 1856-59; asst. adj. gen. during Civil War; commd. capt., 1861; served at Ft. Pickens, Fla., 1861; served under Rosecrans in W. Va., 1861-62; in command Abercrombie's brigade at battles of Cedar Mountain and Antietam; commd. brig. gen. U.S. Volunteers, 1862, promoted maj. gen., 1862; commanded XXIII Army Corps in Ky., Tenn., 1863; brevetted brig. gen., also maj. gen., 1864; ret. as maj. gen. U.S. Army. Died N.Y.C., May 16, 1874.

HARTSUFF, ALBERT army officer; b. New York, Feb. 4, 1837; M.D., Castleton Med. Coll., Vt. Apptd. from Mich., asst. surg. U.S.A., Aug. 5, 1861; capt. asst. surg., July 28, 1866; maj. surg., June 26, 1876; lt. col. dep. surgeon gen., Dec. 4, 1892; col. asst. surg. gen., Apr. 28, 1900; retired by operation of law, Feb. 4, 1901; advanced to rank of brig. gen. retired, by act of Apr. 23, 1904. Bvtd. capt. and maj., Mar. 13, 1865 for services during the war; lt. col., Nov. 26, 1866, for services during cholera epidemic in New Orleans. Died 1908.

HARTZOG, JUSTIN R. cons. city and regional planner; b. Ada, O., July 13, 1892; s. William B. and Caroline (Richardson) H.; B.S., Denison U., 1914; Master Landscape Design, Cornell U., 1917; m. Margaret McCafferty, Aug. 29, 1940. Summer asst. Arnold Arboretum, Boston, 1916; student asst., dept. of landscape design, Cornell U., 1916-17; professional study and travel in Europe, 1921-22; planning asst. John Nolen, city planner, Cambridge, Mass., 1922-25, asso. in city plans and reports for Roanoke, Va., Little Pock, Ark., San Diego, Calif., and Dubuque, Ia., 1926-37; cons. city and regional planner, Cambridge, Mass., Fayetteville, O., 1937-. Con. Nat. Resources Bd., state planning cons. N.H. and R.I., 1933-43; tech. consultant, Me. State Planning Bd., 1934; mem. bd. consultants New England Regional Planning Commn., 1934-35; chief town planner U.S. Resettlement Adminstrn. for Greenhills, O., 1935-37; town planning consultant Farm Security Adminstrn., 1938-40; city planning consultant U.S. Housing Authority, 1938-42; regional coordinator (New England) Office of Defense Housing Coordinator, advisory com. Council of National Defense, 1940-41, special consultant for studies of Hampton Roads, New Orleans, Detroit, Los Angeles, 1941-42; consultant Fed. Pub. Housing Authority, 1942-43; chief consultant, city planning, Nat. Housing Agency, 1942-43; state planning consultant, R.I. State State Planning Bd., 1943-48; visiting critic in city planning Mass. Inst. Tech. 1938-43. Served as officer, U.S. Army, 1917-19; asst. to officer in charge of camp planning, War Dept., and to Constructing Quartermaster, Camp Travis, Tex., 1919-20. Fellow American Society of Civil Engineers, American Society Landscape Architects, Royal Soc. Arts, London; mem. Am. Inst. of Planners (mem. bd. govs., pres. N.E. chpt. 1948-49), Mass Fedn. Planning Bds. (chmn.), Am. Soc. Landscape Architects (bd. trustees; sec. exam. bd.), A.S. C.E., Boston Soc. Landscape Architects, Am. Soc. Planning Ofcls., Am. Planning and Civic Assn., Cambridge (Mass.) Planning Bd. (chmn.), Beta Theta Pl. Home: 83 Brattle St. Office: 5 Boyleston St., Harvard Sq., Cambridge, Mass. Died Dec. 22, 1963.

HARVEY, BASIL COLEMAN HYATT educator; b. Watford, Ont., Can., Jan. 16, 1875; s. Dr. Leander H. and Anne (Wilson) H.; A.B., U. Toronto, 1894; M.B., 1898; M.D., 1928; grad. Normal College of N.S., 1895; member College of Physicians and Surgeons, Ontario, 1898; student U. Basel, Switzerland, 1903; m. Janet Hinsdill Holt, Sept. 1, 1904. Demonstrator of anatomy U. Toronto, 1895-97: practiced medicine, Watford, Ont., 1898-1901; asst. in anatomy U. Chgo., 1901-02, asso., 1902-04, instr., 1904-08,asst. prof., 1908-11, asso. prof., 1911-17, prof., 1917-40, emeritus, 1940—, dean med. students, 1923-40, dean students of biol. science div., 1931-40; recalled as acting dean of med. students and students in biol. sciences, 1943-44. Served as maj. Med. Dept., U.S. Army, AEF, during World War. Treas. Assn. Am. Med. Colls., 1933-35. Vice pres. Inst. Medicine (Chicago), 1933; mem. Assn. Am. Anatomists, A.A.A.S., Sigma Xi, Alpha Kappa Kappa. Clubs: Quadrangle, University, Olympia Fields Country. Translator: The Inheritance of Acquired Characters, Rignano. Author: The Nature of Vital Processes According to Rignano; Simple Lessons in Human Anatomy. Asso. editor Anat. Record, 1928-40; Papers on Anatomy; article on anatomy, Ency. Britannica. Home: 1326 E. 58th St., Chgo. 37. Died Feb. 15, 1958.

HARVEY, JAMES MADISON senator, gov. Kan.; b. nr. Salt Sulphur Springs, Va. (now W. Va.), Sept. 21, 1833; attended common schs. Civil engr.; engaged in farming; served as capt. 4th and 10th regts. Kan. Volunteer Inf., U.S. Army, during Civil War, 1861-64; mem. Kan. Ho. of Reps., 1865-66, Kan. Senate, 1867-68; gov. Kan., 1868-72; mem. U.S. Senate (Republican) from Kan., Feb. 2, 1874-77; govt. surveyor in N.M., Utah, Nev. and Okla. Died nr. Junction City, Kan., Apr. 15, 1894; buried Highland Cemetery, Junction City.

HARVEY, PHILIP FRANCES colonel U.S.A.; b. Thorneville, O., Dec. 12, 1844; s. Philip and Elizabeth Mary (Hodge) H.; ed. Bapt. U., Burlington, Ia., U. of Mich.; M.D., U. of Ia., 1864; M.D., Bellevue Hosp. Med. Coll. (New York U.), 1866; married. Apptd. from Iowa, asst.surgeon, U.S.A., Nov. 16, 1868; capt. asst. surgeon, Nov. 16, 1871; maj. surgeon, Feb. 9, 1890; lt. col. chief surgeon vols., July 8, 1898; resigned from vol. service, July 31, 1898; lt. col. deputy surgeon-gen., Feb. 2, 1901; col. asst. surgeon gen., Aug. 6, 1903. Served in med. dept. U.S.A. during Civil War, med. dept. U.S.A. during Sioux Indian wars, 1876, 1890-91, and during Spanish-Am. War and Philippine insurrection; prof. surgery, Nat. U., Washington, 1886-88; retired. Dec. 12, 1908. Unitarian. Republican. Home: Denver, Colo. Died July 7, 1922.

HARVEY, SAMUEL CLARK surgeon; b. Washington, Conn., Feb. 12, 1886; s. Calvin Ferry and Ellen Sophia (Clark) H.; Ph.B., Yale, 1907, M.D., 1911; Sc.D., Western Res. U., 1931; m. Katharine Kingsley Farnam, June 29, 1921; children-Elizabeth Kingsley, Louise Farnam, Samuel Clark. Instr. surgery Yale, 1919-21, asso. prof., 1921-24. William H. Carmalt prof. surgery, 1924-47, prof. surgery (oncology), 1947-52, ret. and continued research in field. Served as lt. to maj. Med. O.R.C., U.S. Army, 1917-18; active service in France, Fellow A.C.S.; mem. N.E. Surg. Soc., Soc. Clin. Surgery, Soc. Neurol. Surgery, A.A.A.S., A.M.A., Am. Surg. Assn., Am. Assn. for Thoracic Surgery, Sigma Xi. Clubs: Graduate (New Haven); Century, Yale (N.Y.C.). Home: 211 Highland St., New Haven 11; (summer) Race Hill Rd., Madison, Conn. Died Aug. 23, 1953; buried Grove St. Cemetery, New Haven.

HARVEY, WILLIAM EDWIN soldier and lawyer; b. Kirkwood, Mo., Aug. 6, 1871; s. William Egbert and Martha Bates Beach H.; LL.B., Columbian, 1893, LL.M., 1894; m. Katherine E. Heydrick, Feb. 12, 1896. Practiced law in Washington, D.C., 1893-1919, as mem. King & King and asso. of its predecessors. Enlisted in D.C.N.G., 1890, and served through all grades; apptd. brig. gen. comdg. militia D.C., June 4, 1915; commd. brig. gen. N.A., Aug. 22, 1917, and assigned to command 75th Inf. Brigade, at Camp Shelby, Hattiesburg, Miss., trans. to command 1st Prov. Brig. Army Troops; hon. disch., May 9, 1918. Episcopalian. Home: Chevy Chase, D.C. Died Jan. 13, 1922.

HARWOOD, ANDREW ALLEN served in suppression of slave trade and piracy in W.I., 1818-23; commd. lt., 1827, capt., 1855; insp. of ordnance, 1858-61; promoted commodore, 1862, rear-adm. on ret. list, 1869. Died Marion, Mass., Aug. 28, 1884.

HASBROUCK, ALFRED army officer; b. Poughkeepsie, N.Y., Nov. 1, 1858: s. Alfred and Margaret Anne (Manning) H.; grad. U.S. Mil. Acad., 1883, Army War Coll., 1913. Commd. 2d lt. 14th Inf., June 13, 1883; 1st lt. 13th Inf., Feb. 24, 1891; trans. to 14th Inf., July 20, 1891; capt. of inf., July 2, 1898; assigned to 14th Inf., Jan. 1, 1899; maj. 29th Inf., July 2, 1906; trans. to 14th Inf., Aug. 29, 1906; lt. col. 18th Inf., Nov. 27, 1911; col. of inf., Oct. 24, 1915; col. 20th Inf., Dec. 10, 1915. Prof. mil. science and tactics, Riverview Mil. Acad., Poughkeepsie, N.Y., 1895-98; went with regt. to Philippines, 1898; in China during Boxer troubles; again in Philippines, 1903-5 (in field against Pulajanes, Jan.-Mar. 1905) and 1908-10. Home: Poughkeepsie, N.Y. Died Aug. 19, 1920.

HASBROUCK, HENRY CORNELIUS brig. gen. U.S.A.; b. Newburgh, N.Y., Oct. 26, 1839; s. William Cornelius and Mary Elizabeth (Roe) H.; apptd. from N.Y., and grad. U.S. Mil. Acad., 1861; m. Laetitia Viele Warren, Oct. 26, 1882. Apptd. 2d lt. 4th Arty., May 6, 1861; 1st lt., May 14, 1861; capt., July 26, 1866; maj., Mar. 5, 1887; lt. col., Oct. 29, 1896; brig. gen. U.S.V., May 27, 1898; hon. discharged, June 12, 1899; col. 7th U.S. Arty., Feb. 13, 1899; brig. gen., Dec. 1, 1902. Bvtd.; capt., Oct. 25, 1862, "for gallant and meritorious services" in action at Blackwater Bridge, Va.; maj., Feb. 27, 1890, "for gallant services" in action against Indians at Sorass Lake, Cal., May 10, 1873. Commandant cadets U.S. Mil. Acad., 1882-88; mem. of bd. that prepared inf., cav. and arty. drill regulations for use in U.S.A.; comd. 2d Brigade, 2d Div., 7th Army Corps and Dept. of Pinar del Rio, Cuba, 1898-99; retired at own request, over 40 yrs. service, Jan. 5, 1903. Home: Newburgh, N.Y. Died 1910.

HASCALL, MILO SMITH brig. gen. U.S. vols.; b. Le Roy, N.Y., Aug. 5, 1829; s. Amasa Hascall; went to Goshen, Ind., 1846; grad. West Point, 1852; served in garrison, 1O52-53; resigned; practiced law in Ind.; pros. atty., 1856-58; clerk of court, 1895-61; served private to brig. gen. vols., 1861-64; at Stone River was the only gen. officer who held his ground and saved the day after the defeat and rout of Union army on the 1st day of the battle; took part in siege at Atlanta; resigned Commn. Oct. 27, 1864; after war banker at Goshen, Ind.; real estate operator, Chicago, 1890-. Home: Oak Park, Ill. Died 1904.

HASE, WILLIAM FREDERICK army officer; b. Milwaukee, Wis., Aug. 31, 1874; s. Henry and Minnie (Bergeler) H.; LL.B., U. of Wis., 1897; grad. Coast Arty. Sch., 1902, advanced course, 1909, Sch. of the Line, 1920, Gen. Staff Sch., 1921, Army War Coll., 1922; m. Pearl Newman, June 6, 1906; children-Mary Elizabeth (wife of H. A. Brusher, U.S.A.), Hilda Houghton. Began as lawyer, 1897; commd. 2d lt. 6th Arty., July 9, 1898, advanced through grades to col., Feb. 1918; maj. gen., chief of coast arty., Mar. 1934-. Decorated D.S.M. (U.S.). Lutheran. Home: Washington, D.C. Died Jan. 20, 1935.

HASELTINE, HERBERT sculptor; b. of American parents, Rome, April 10, 1877; s. William Stanley and Helen (An(Marshall) H.; student Collegio Romano, Rome; Harvard, Class 1899; hon. M.A.; studied art Royal Acad., Munich, also at Rome and under Aime Morot, Paris; m. Madeleine Keith, 1911; children - Heather (Toggenburg), William Marshall Known for equestrian statues and statues of horses and other animals, latest being equestrian monument of George

Washington for Washington; exhibited in large exhbns. and famous galleries in U.S., abroad, 1906-; also numerous one-man shows. Represented by works on permanent exhbn. throughout the world. Recipient hon. mention Paris Salon, 1906; Speyer memorial prize, 1934; gold medal Paris Worlds Fair, 1936. Decorated Chevalier Legion of Honor. Attached to Am. Embassy, Paris, 1914-15; served as capt., engrs., U.S. Army, AEF, 1916-19; organizer Am. camouflage section in France. Mem. Nat. Inst. of Arts and Letters. Nat. Sculpture Soc., Institute de France, Academie des Beaux Arts (foreign member), National Academy Design (academician). Clubs: Century (N.Y.C.); Buck's (London, England); The Travellers, Polo de Paris, University (Paris). Home: 20. Impasse Raffet, rue Raffet, Paris XVIe. Studio: 200 Central Park S., N.Y.C. 19; 20 Impasse Raffet, Paris XVIe, France, Died Jan. 8, 1962; buried Rome, Italy.

HASKELL, HARRY LELAND army officer; b. in Me., Sept. 24, 1840. Served as pvt. Co. A, and sergt. maj. 125th N.Y. Inf., Aug. 26, 1862-Mar. 16, 1863; 2d lt., Mar. 16, 1863; capt., Dec. 7, 1863; hon. mustered out, Sept. 22, 1864; commd. capt. 7th U.S. Vet. Inf., May 10, 1865; hon. mustered out, Apr. 27, 1866; apptd. from N.Y., 2d lt., 12th U.S. Inf., Aug. 30, 1867; 1st lt., June 30, 1877; capt., Jan. 2, 1888; maj. Mar. 2, 1899; transferred to 30th Inf., July 17, 1901; lt. col. 20th Inf., Sept. 27, 1901; transferred to 12th Inf., Oct. 15, 1901; col. 27th Inf., July 31, 1903; transferred to 3d Inf., Sept. 10, 1903: brig. gen., Jan. 20, 1904; retired at own request over 30 yrs.' service, Jan. 21, 1904. Died 1908.

HASKELL, LLEWELLYN FROST soldier, mcht.; b. Belleville, N.J., Oct. 8, 1842; s. Llewellyn and Mary Anna H.; ed. Eagleswoods sch., Perth Amboy, N.J., 1856-60; Heidelberg Univ., Oct., 1860, to Jan., 1861; m. Orange, N.J., June 4, 1868, Emmeline A. Gilmore. Enlisted Apr. 23, 1861; pvt., 14th N.Y. militia; apptd. 2d lt. Independent Co. of Engrs., St. Louis, Sept. 17, 8n1861; a.-d.-c. on Gen. Anselm Asboth's staff, Jan. 1862; post commissary, Rolla, Mo., May, 1862; a.d.c. and asst. insp.-gen. on staff Gen. Henry Prince, 1862; severely wounded at battle Cedar Mountain, Va., Aug. 9, 1862; recommended for colonelcy of the 1st class by Gen. Casey's bd., Sept., 1863; apptd. lt.-col., 7th U.S., colored troops, at his own request, Oct. 28, 1863; col., 41st U.S. colored troops, Nov. 1, 1864; bvtd. brig.-gen. vols., U.S.A., Mar. 13, 1865; honorably mustered out in Tex., Sept. 30, 1865; after war associated with his father in development of Llewellyn Park, Orange, N.J.; removed to San Francisco, 1877; since then engaged as mfr. of furniture, also in mining and oil development. Residence: San Rafael, Calif. Office: 2084 Bush St., San Francisco.

HASKELL, WILLIAM EDWIN JR. newspaper exec.: b. Mpls., Mar. 28, 1889; s. William Edwin and Olga (von W.) H.; prep. edn. Shattuck Mil. Acad. (Faribault, Minn.), Haverford (Pa.) Sch., Worcester (Mass.) Acad.; student Dartmouth Coll., 1906-08; m. Elizabeth Lewis Osgood, Dec. 19, 1934. With Boston Herald, 1908-10; sales, adv. and promotion mgr. N.Y. dept. stores, 1911-14; advt. mgr. N.Y. Herald and Telegram, 1914-16; mem. advt., promotion and circulation staffs N.Y. Tribune (now N.Y. Herald Tribune), 1919—, asst. to pres., 1931—; pres. Philosopher Tobacco Co. Trustee Northern Dispensary, N.Y.C. Lecturer and writer on journalism. Awarded Gold Key by Columbia Scholastic Press Assn. in recognition of service, 1939. Served as capt. inf., World War I, AEF, 2 yrs. Decorated Croix de Guerre. Mem. Sigma Delta Chi. Republican. Unitarian. Mason (32ff). Home: Putman Valley, N.Y. Address: New York Herald Tribune, 230 W. 41st St., N.Y.C. Died Aug. 28, 1953.

HASKELL, WILLIAM NAFEW army officer; b. Albany, N.Y., Aug. 13, 1878; s. William and Sarah (Churchill) H.; grad. U.S. Mil. Acad., 1901; distinguished grad. Inf. and Cav. Sch., 1904; grad. Army and Staff Coll., 1905; grad. Staff College, Langres, France, 1918; LL.D., Georgetown, 1925; m. Winifred Farrell, July 3, 1901: children-John H. F., William N. (dec.), Joseph F., Mary. Commd. 2d lt., Feb. 18, 1901; promoted through grades to lt. col., Sept. 17, 1920; retired with rank of lieutenant general, 1942. Served in the Philippine Islands, 1901-02, 1906-07, 1912-14; commanded regt. on Mexican border, 1916-17; arrived in France, Feb. 1918; asst. chief of staff, 77th Div., and with 4th A.C.; participate as chief of operations, St. Mihiel offensive, also assisted in operations south of Metz; deputy chief staff and chief of operations 2d Am. Army; detailed as head of Am. Relief Mission to Rumania, under U.S. Food Administration, and later apptd. allied high commr. to Armenia, representing Great Britain, France, Italy and U.S., and dir. gen. all relief in the Caucasus; apptd. by Herbert C. Hoover as chief of Am. Relief Mission to Russia, leaving U .S. with staff, Sept. 3, 1921, and returning 1923; also Red Cross Commr. in Greece, in charge relief work incident to the Smyrna disaster, 1922-23. Apptd. maj. gen. N.Y. Nat. Guard, 1916. On active duty as maj. gen. comdg. the 27th Div. U.S. Army, stationed at Fort McClellan, Ala., 1940-41. Organized Army Emergency Relief, hdqrs. in Washington, D.C., Feb.-May 1942; dir. Civilian Protection, State of N.Y., May-Dec. 1942; apptd. mem. staff in charge of field operations by Dir. of Office of Fgn. Relief and Rehabilitation Operations, State Dept., Washington, D.C., Jan. 1, 1943. Apptd. National Dir. Office Civilian Defense, February 28, 1944. Executive director Cooperative for American Remittances to Europe, Inc., Europe, Inc., Jan. 1946-Apr. 1947, cons. to Oct. 1947; v.p. Save the Children Fedn., since March 1947. Awarded D.S.M. (United States); Officer Legion of Honor (France); Comdr. of Crown (Rumania); Comdr. Polonia Restituta (Poland); Comdr. Cross of the Redeemer (Greece); Order of Regina Maria, 1st class and Grand Officer of the Crown (Rumania); Order of White Lion (Czechoslovakia); U.S. Certificate of Merit. Conspicuous Service medal, State of N.Y. Catholic. Clubs: Union (New York). Century, Army and Navy (Washington). Home: 20 Church St., Greenwich, Conn. Died Aug. 13, 1952; buried U.S.A. Cemetery, Westpoint, N.Y

HASKELL, WILLIAM T. congressman; b. Murfressboro, Tenn., July 21, 1818; attended U. Nashville (Tenn.). fought in Seminole War, 1836; admitted to Tenn. bar, 1838, began practice in Jackson; mem. Tenn. Ho. of Reps., 1840-41; served in Mexican War; apptd. col. 1st Brigade, 2d Regt., Tenn. Volunteers, 1846; mem. U.S. Ho. of Reps. (Whig) from Tenn., 30th Congress, 1847-49. Died in an asylum, Hopkinsville, Ky., Mar. 12, 1859; buried Riverside Cemetery, Jackson.

HASKIN, WILLIAM LAWRENCE brig. gen. U.S.A.; b. Houlton, Me., May 31, 1841; s. Gen. Joseph Abel and Rebecca E. (Sprague) H.; ed. Mexico Acad., Oswego Co., N.Y., 1852-57; C.E., Rensselaer Poly. Inst., 1861; m. Annie L. Davis, Apr. 26, 1865. Apptd. 2d lt. and 1st lt., 1st U.S. Arty., Aug. 5, 1861; promoted through grades to brig. gen., July 28, 1903. Bvtd. capt., July 8, 1863, "for gallant and meritorious services in capture of Port Hudson, La."; maj., Mar. 13, 1865, "for good conduct and gallant services during the war." After Civil War served in N.Y., S.C., Me., Calif., Ore., and Conn. Sent in command of regt. to Cuba, Dec. 1898, and in 1902 was designated to command U.S. troops still remaining there; retired at own request after 40 yrs.' service, July 29, 1903. Home: New London, Conn. Died Sept. 24, 1931.

HASLUP, LEMUEL A(LLEN) prof. law; b. near Laurel, Md., July 23, 1896; s. James P. and Annie (Gaither) H.; student Charlotte Hall (Md.) Mil. Acad., 1911-14; B.S., Univ. of Md., 1917; LL.B., George Washington Univ., 1934; m. Mildred Motts, June 5, 1923; children-Allen Lee. Commd. 2d lt., in the United States Marine Corps, 1917, and advanced through grades to cap.; served in Haiti, Dominican Republic, Nicaragua, Guam, China and at sea; legal aide to comdt. Norfolk Navy Yard, 1934-38; retired for phys. disability, 1938, recalled to active duty, June 1941; lt. col., ret. list, Marine Corps, since 1946; on active duty, court martial rev. sect. Office of Judge Adv. Gen., Navy Dept., Washington, 1941-46. Admitted to D.C. bar, 1934, Supreme Ct. of U.S., 1938; lecturer in law, John B. Stetson U., 1938, dean and prof. of law Coll. of Law since 1946; asst. prof. Law Sch., U. of Miami, 1939-41; professorial lecturer, Law Sch., George Washington U., 1946. Mem. Am., Fla. State bar assns., Maritime Law Assn. of U.S., Am. Acad. Polit. and Social Sci., Am. Law Inst. (hon.), Am. Legion, Delta Sigma Phi. Episcopalian. Mason. Club: Rotary. Home: Box 116, Deland, Fla. Died Aug. 9, 1953; buried Arlington Nat. Cemetery.

HASSELTINE, HERMON ERWIN, USPHS ofcl.; b. Bristol, Vt., Aug. 13, 1881; s. Erwin Amos and Jennie (Searles) H.; student Middlebury (Vt.) Coll., 1898-99, U. of Kan., 1899-1900; M.D., Baltimore Med. Coll., 1904; student U.S. Army Med. Sch., 1905-06; D.Sc., Middlebury Coll., 1937; m. Bertha M. Mohl, June 6, 1905; children—Lee Luther, Catherine Luther Jennie, Margery Searles; married 2d, Gertrude A. Kendall, Dec. 26, 1948. Interne Manhattan State Hosp., N.Y., 1904-05; contract surgeon, U.S. Army, 1905-08, lt. Med. Res. Corps, 1908-09; commd. asst. surgeon U.S.P.H.S., 1909, passed asst. surgeon, 1913, surgeon, 1920, sr. surgeon, 1930, med. dir., 1935, dir. U.S. Leprosy Investigation Sta., Honolulu, 1921-24; in charge Psittacosis Research Lab., Pasadena, 1932-35, U.S. Leprosarium, Carville, La., 1935-40; in charge stream pollution investigations, Cincinnati, O., 1940-42, U.S. Quarantine Sta., Boston, Mass., 1942-45; Mem. A.M.A., Am. Pub. Health Assn., Assn. Mil. Surgeons, Am. Soc. Tropical Medicine, Internat. Leprosy Assn., Phi Chi. Republican. Episcopalian. Mason. Nat. Sojourner. Contbr. to jours. Address: Bristol VT Died June 8, 1968; buried Bristol VT

HASTINGS, THOMAS WOOD, M.D., retired; b. St. Louis, Mo., Sept. 29, 1873; s. Samuel Weston and Frances (Wood) H.; ed. pub. schs. and Morris Acad., Morristown, N.J.; A.B., Johns Hopkins, 1894, M.D., 1898; m. Athenia Agnes Belknap, of Yonkers, N.Y., Oct.6, 1909; children—Thomas Wood, John Frazee. House officer Johns Hopkins Hosp., 1898-99; apptd. lt. surgeon Hosp. Ship Maine, 1899; with British Expeditionary Forces, S. African War, 1899-1900, British China Expdn., Boxer Rebellion, 1900-01; instr. in clin. pathology, Cornell U. Med. Coll., 1901-06, prof., 1906-18; substitute clin. pathologist Presbyn. Hosp., 1902-04; asst. visiting phys. Cornell Med. Coll. Dispensary, 1901-07, Bellevue Hosp., 1908-17, acting visiting phys., 1917-21; mem. cons. staff Nassau County Hosp., 1919-22; cons. staff St. Bartholomew's Clinic and Hosp., 1920-21. Lt. Med. R.C., U.S.A., 1910-17; maj., 1917-18; retired as maj., June 6, 1928. Fellow A.A.A.S.; mem. Mil. Order World War, Phi Kappa Psi, Sigma Chi, Alpha Omega Alpha; formerly mem. A.M.A. and many other socs. Republican. Presbyn. Extensive contbr. on med. subjects. Home: Kinderhook NY

HATCH, EDWARD army officer; b. Bangor, Me., Dec. 23, 1832; s. Nathaniel and Mary (Scott) H.; attended Norwich (Vt.) U., 2 years; m. Evelyn Barrington. Served as capt. troop 2d Iowa Cavalry, U.S. Army, 1861, commd. col., 1862, commanded 2d Ia. Cavalry in Grant's western campaign; served in battles of Corinth, Franklin, Nashville, also Grant's Miss. campaign; in command of cavalry div. Army of Tenn.; commd. brig. gen. 1864, in command of cavalry div. participating in actions at Florence, Lawrenceburg, Campbellville, Spring Hill, Franklin; brevetted maj. gen. U.S. Volunteers, 1864; commd. col. 9th U.S. avalry, 1866, brevetted brig. gen. and maj. gen. U.S. Army, 1867; commanded Dept. of Ariz. and N.M., 1866-67. Died Ft. Robinson, Neb., Apr. 11, 1889.

HATCH, EVERARD E. army officer; b. Montville, Me., July 18, 1859; s. Enos M. and Kate A. (Newham) H.: grad. U.S. Mil. Acad., 1884, Army War Coll., 1915; m. Mellie S. Rowe, Aug. 7, 1884: m. 2d, Annie K. Spring, Sept. 12, 1899. Second lt. 18th Inf., June 15, 1884; promoted through grades to brig. gen. N.A., Aug. 5, 1917. Duty U. of Me., 1888-91, Clinton Liberal Inst., Ft. Plain, N.Y., 1894-95: participated in assault and capture of Manila, P.I., Aug. 13, 1898; with regt. at capture of Iloilo, Feb. 11, 1899, and at engagement at Jaro, Feb. 12, 1899; again in Philippines, 1903-04 and 1907-09. Organized and trained 158th Inf. Brig., Aug. 1917-June 1918; comd. 154th Depot Brig., June-Nov. 1918, and in charge instrn. and training same, Nov. 1918-Mar. 1919, comd. same, Mar.-June 1919; with A.E.F., June-Aug. 1919; hon. disch. as brig. gen. N.A., May 24, 1918; comd. Fort Benjamin Harrison, Ind., Aug, 1919-. Episcopalian. Deceased.

HATCH, HENRY JAMES army officer; b. Charlotte, Mich., Apr. 28, 1869; s. Hiram F. and Sarah J. H.; B.S. in C.E., U. of Mich., 1891; grad. Arty. Sch., 1903; Army War Coll., 1925; m. Alice E. Hill, June 26, 1893; children-Walter A., Melton A. Cashier Farmers Nat. Bank, Arkansas City, 1891-97; commd. 2d lt. arty., U.S.A., July 9, 1898; promoted through grades to col., Feb. 6, 1918; brig. gen. N.A., June 26, 1918; col., C.A.C., July 1, 1920, brig. gen., Sept. 5, 1927. Chief of heavy arty. sect. of staff of chief of arty., A.E.F., 1918-19; comdr. Ry. Arty., 2d Army, Oct. and Nov. 1918; later comdr. coast defense of Los Angeles, Calif., later comdr. Harbor Defenses, Manila and Sobig Bay; now comdr. 2d Coast Artillery Dist. Decorated D.S.M. (U.S.); Officier Legion d'Honneur, France. Home: Washington, D.C. Died Dec. 31, 1931.

HATCH, JOHN PORTER col. U.S.A., retired Jan. 9, 1886; b. Oswego, N.Y., Jan. 9, 1822, desc. in 7th generation from Thomas Hatch Freeman of Mass. Colony, 1635; mother was Hannah, d. Otis Reed, Salina, N.Y.; grad. West Point, 1845: served in Mexican war; bvtd. 1st lt. and later capt. for gallantry; capt., Oct. 13, 1860; brig. gen. vols., Sept. 28, 1861; took part in many battles; twice wounded; reached bvt. rank of brig. gen., U.S.A., and maj. gen. vols.; apptd. maj., 4th cav., at end of war; col., 3d cav., 1881-86; m. Adelaide, d. Christian J. Burckle, Oswego, N.Y., June 14, 1851. Home: New York, N.Y. Deceased.

HATCH, ROBERT SEYMOUR, marine corps exec., lawyer; b. Jamestown, N.Y., July 6,21907; s. Frank Delos and Aura (Lowell) H.; B.A., Ohio U., 1929; LL.B., Ohio State U., 1931; LL.M., George Washington U., 1943; m. Zetta Collins, Dec. 22, 1928; children—Robert Neil, Margaret Ann. Admitted to Ohio bar, 1931; practice in New Philadelphia, O., 1932-41; sec. to Congressman Thom, 1941-42; atty. Bituminous coal div. Dept. Interior, 1942-43; asst. gen. counsel Solid Fuels Adminstrn. War, 1943-46; asst. counsel Coal Mines Adminstrn., 1946-47; counsel Bur. Naval Personnel, 1947-53, Navy Purchasing office, Los Angeles, 1953-55; counsel for comdt. USMC, from 1955. Mem. Fed. Bar Assn., Phi Alpha Delta. Methodist. Mason (Shriner). Home: Chevy Chase MD Died Sept. 10, 1968; interred Park Lawn Meml. Park.

HATCH, WILLIAM HENRY congressman; b. Georgetown, Ky., Sept. 11, 1833; s. Rev. William and Mary (Adams) H.; m. Jennie Smith; m. 2d, Thetis Hawkins, 1861. Admitted to Ky. bar, 1854; circuit atty. 16th Jud. Dist. Mo., 1858-62; served as lt. col. Confederate Army during Civil War; mem. U.S. Ho. of Reps. from Mo., 46th-53d congresses, 1879-95, proposed and sponsored act to create Bur. of Animal Industry, 1884, 1st oleomargarine act, 1886; author Hatch Act calling for fed. aid to encourage study of scientific agr. (passed 1887), meat inspection act, 1890. Died Hannibal, Mo., Dec. 23, 1896; buried Riverside Cemetery, Hannibal.

HATCHER, JULIAN SOMMERVILLE author, army officer; b. Winchester, Va., June 26, 1888; s. Lindley Lovett and Ada (Sommerville) H.; B.S. and honor grad. U.S. Naval Acad., 1909; m. Eleanor Dashiell, Oct. 19, 1910; children - Julian Somerville,

Eleanor (Mrs. Charles Edward Robertson), Robert Dashiell. Served 14 months as naval officer, then transferred to Army, 1910; promoted through grades to maj. gen., 1944. Invented breech mechanism for Army, 1914. Established and headed Army Machine Gun Schs., Mexican Border and Springfield Armory, 1916-17. Lt. Col., Chief of Machine Gun and Small Arms Engrng. and Design, Washington, 1918; later at Hdqrs. A.E.F., Chaumont, France. Had charge of Rifle Mfg., Springfield Armory, 1919-21; Ammunition Mfg., Frankford Arsenal, 1923-28. Chief, Small Arms Div. Ordnance, 1929-33; head Ordnance Sch., later Chief of Ordnance Tng., 1937-42. Chief of Ordnance Field Service, 1943-45 inclusive; in Pacific Ocean Arenas, Saipan, Guam, 1944, and in Europe, 1945; awarded D.S.M., Legion of Merit. Mag. writer and editor; expert rifle and pistol shot; authority and writer on firearms. Distinguished Pistol Shot, U.S. Army, gold medal Mgr., U.S. Internat. Rifle Teams, Switzerland, 1925, Rome, 1927, Antwerp, 1930. Capt. U.S. Internat. Rifle Team, and winner the Webley & Scott Pistol Match with Brit. Empire Record of 100x100, Bisley, 1931. Life Mem. Nat. Rifle Assn. Am., U.S. Revolver Assn. Mem. Army Ordnance Assn., Rocks and lfinerals Assn. Episcopalian. Club: Army and Navy Country (Washington). Author: Pistols and Revolvers and Their Use, 1927; Textbook of Pistols and Revolvers, 1935; Textbooks of Firearms Investigation, Identification and Evidence, 1935; Hatcher's Notebook, 1947; The Book of the Garand, 1948; co-author: Machine Guns, 1917, 2d ed., 1918. Asso. editor Arms and the Man, 1922-23, The American Rifleman, 1923-31. Ret. as maj. gen. for phys. disability, 1946. Now tech. editor Am. Rifleman; dir. tech. services Nat. Rifle Assn. Am.; Mem. Nat. Bd. for promotion Rifle Practice. Mem. U.S. Olympic Com. Home: 6039 Brook Dr., Falls Church, Va. Died Dec. 4, 1963; buried Arlington Nat. Cemetery.

HATCHER, ROBERT ANTHONY congressman; b. Buckingham County, Va., Feb. 24, 1819; attended pvt. schs., Lynchburg, Va.; studied law. Admitted to Ky. bar; began practice of law, New Madrid, Mo., 1847; circuit atty.; mem. Mo. Ho. of Reps., 1850-51; served to maj. Confederate Army during Civil War; mem. Confederate Congress, 1864-65; mem. U.S. Ho. of Reps. (Democrat) from Mo., 43d-45th congresses, 1873-79. Died Charleston, Mo., Dec. 4, 1886; buried Odd Fellows Cemetery, Charleston.

HATFIELD, CHARLES ALBERT PHELPS army officer; b. Dayton, Ala., Dec. 9, 1850; s. Henry Phillips and Stella (Phelps) H.; ed. Eutaw Acad., Ala., and Onderdonk's Acad., Baltimore; grad. U.S. Mil. Acad., 1872; m. at Ft. Garland, Colo., Frances E. Blackmore, Oct. 7, 1880. Commd. 2d lt. 4th U.S. Cav., June 14, 1872; 1st lt., June 28, 1878; capt., Nov. 26, 1884; maj. 8th Cav., Oct. 16, 1898; lt.-col. 5th Cav., Apr. 29, 1901; col. 13th Cav., Mar. 2, 1903-July 10, 1914; retired, Dec. 1914. Brevetted maj., Feb. 27, 1890, "for gallantry in action against Indians in attack on Geronomo's camp in Santa Cruz Mountains, Mex., May 16, 1886." Served in Southwest, 1872-90, in Cuba, 1899-1901, in P.I., 1901-05; comdg. Ft. Myer, Va., 1905-09; in P.I., 1909-11, comdg. Dept. Luzon, 1910-11; comdg. Dept. of Mo., Omaha, Neb., May and June, 1911; comdg. 13th Cav., Ft. Riley, Kan., July, 1911-Sept., 1912; on duty on Mexican border, N.M. and Ariz., Sept., 1912-Dec., 1914; comdg. 2d Cav. Brigade and patrol dist. from El Paso, Tex., to Yuma, Cal., Apr.-Dec., 1914; retired by operation of law, Dec. 9, 1914. Address: War Dept., Washington.†

HATHAWAY, FORREST HENRY brig. gen. U.S.A.; b. in Vt., Oct. 7, 1844. Enlisted as pvt. Co. G, 16th Vt. Inf., Sept. 4, 1862; hon. disch., Aug. 10, 1863; commd. capt. 107th U.S.C.T., June 30, 1864; bvtd. maj., July 25, 1866: hon. mustered out, Feb. 20, 1867; apptd. from Vt., 2d lt. 41st U.S. Inf., Mar. 7, 1867; transferred to 40th Inf., Nov. 27, 1867; assigned to 5th Inf., Dec. 17, 1869; 1st lt., Sept. 4, 1878; capt. asst. q.m., Feb. 13, 1882; maj. q.m., Sept. 12, 1894; lt. col. q.m. vols., Sept. 3, 1898-Mar. 2, 1899; lt. col. deputy q.m. gen., Aug. 12, 1900; col. asst. q.m. gen., Apr. 12, 1903; brig. gen., Jan. 29, 1904; retired at own request, after 40 yrs.' service, Jan. 21, 1904. Bvtd. 1st lt., Mar. 7, 1867, for battle of Fair Oaks, Va.; capt., Mar. 7, 1867, battle of Newmarket, Va. Died July 29, 1912.

HATHAWAY, KING cons. engr.; b. San Francisco, Calif., Apr. 9, 1878; s. John Dudley and Susan (King) H.; ed. pub. schs. of San Francisco, Calif.; m. Ethel Cramer, in Paris, France, Aug. 12, 1929; children-Pierre, Taylor, Joan. With Midvale Steel Works, Phila., 1896-1901; supt. Payne Engine Co., 1902-04; supt., v.p., mgr. Tabor Mfg. Co., 1904-16; asso. with Dr. F. W. Taylor, 1904-15; lecturer on scientific management, Harvard Grad. Sch. of Business Adminstrn., 1912-17, Wharton Sch., U. of Pa., 1921-22; cons. engr. in foundry operation Industrial Assn. of San Francisco, 1923-26; gen. mgr. Schlage Lock Co.,1927-28; cons. work in Japan and Europe, 1929; cons. engr. Manning, Maxwell & Moore and gen. mgr. Consol. Ashcroft Hancock Co., 1930-32; consultant in orgn. and management, 1906-17, 1919-22, and since 1932; also cons. prof. of scientific management, Stanford U., since 1937. Served as capt. and lt. col. Ordnance Dept., U.S. Army, with A.E.F., 1917-18. Decorated Offcier de l'Ordre de l'Etoile Noir. Mem. Massaryk Acad. of Work (Prague), Soc. for Advancement of Management, Am. Soc. Mech. Engrs. Republican. Episcopalian. Contbr. articles to professional societies and jours. Home: 200 Lowell Av., Palo Alto, Calif. Died June 12, 1944.

HATHAWAY, ROBERT JOSEPH surgeon; b. Ovid, Mich., Jan. 21, 1874; s. Joseph Obed and Martha (House) H.; student med. dept. U. of Mich., 3 yrs.; M.D., College of Medicine, University of Illinois, 1902; post-grad. work, University of Paris, University of Vienna; married Myrta A. Bement, 1897 (died 1901); 1 son, Robert J. Began practice at Glendive, Mont., as health officer Dawson County, 1902; chief surgeon Grace Hosp., 1905-17; capt., maj. and lt. col. Med. Corps, U.S. Army, World War; in France with A.E.F.; resumed practice at Glendive, 1919; supt. State Hosp., Warm Springs, Mont., 1921-25; settled at Evanston, Ill., 1926. Del. World Peace Conf., London, 1918. Fellow Am. Coll. Surgeons, A.M.A.; mem. Chicago Med. Soc., Chicago Soc. Industrial Medicine and Surgery. Mason (32ff, K.T., Shriner), Sovereign Master Red Cross of Constantine; Grand Master of Masons of Mont., 1920. Office: Glendive, Mont. Died July 15, 1955; buried Middlebury Cemetery, Ovid, Mich.

HATHAWAY, SAMUEL GILBERT congressman; b. Freetown, Mass., July 18, 1780; studied pub. schs. Moved to Chenango County, N.Y., 1803, Cincinnatus, N.Y., 1805, engaged in farming; justice of peace, 1810-58; mem. N.Y. Assembly, 1814, 18; moved to Solon, N.Y., 1819; mem. N.Y. Senate, 1822; served as maj. gen. N.Y. Militia, 1823-58; mem. U.S. Ho. of Reps. (Democrat) from N.Y., 23d Congress, 1833-35; Dem. presdl. elector, 1852; del. Dem. Nat. Conv., Charleston, S.C., 1860. Died Solon, May 2, 1867; buried family cemetery nr. Solon.

HATHORN, JOHN congressman; b. Wilmington, Del., Jan. 9, 1749. Surveyor, sch. tchr.; capt. N.Y. Colonial Militia; apptd. col. 4th Orange County (N.Y.) Regt., 1776, served throughout Revoluntionary War; commd. brig. Gen. Orange County Militia, 1786, maj. gen. N.Y. State Militia, 1793; mem. N.Y. Assembly, 1778, 80, 82-85, 95, 1805, speaker, 1783-84; mem. N.Y. Senate, 1786-90, 99-1803; mem. council of appointment, 1787, 89; elected to Continental Congress, Dec. 1788, no further sessions held; mem. U.S. Ho. of Reps. (Federalist) from N.Y., 1st, 4th congresses, 1789-91, 95-97. Died Warwick, N.Y., Feb. 19, 1825; buried cemetery on family estate, reinterred Warwick Cemetery.

HATHORNE, WILLIAM colonial ofcl.; b. Binfield, Eng., circa 1607; s. William and Sara Hathorne; m. Anne. Came to Am., 1630; mem. bd. selectmen Dorchester (Mass.), 1634; dep. Mass. Gen. Ct., 1635-37; speaker, 1644-50; served to ranks capt. and maj. Mass. Militia; mem. Mass. Bd. of Assts., 1662-69; 1 of 5 principal citizens of Mass. ordered to Eng. by Charles II, 1666. Died 1681.

HATTON, ROBERT HOPKINS congressman; b. Steubenville, O., Nov. 2, 1826; grad. Cumberland U., Lebanon, Tenn., 1847, attended law sch., 1848-49. Tutor, Cumberland U., 1847-48, trustee, 1854-62; prin. Woodland Acad., Sumner County, Tenn., 1849-50; admitted to Tenn. bar, 1850, began practice in Lebanon; mem. Tenn. Ho. of Reps., 1855-57; unsuccessful candidate for gov. Tenn., 1857; mem. U.S. Ho. of Reps. (Am. Party rep.) from Tenn., 36th Congress, 1859-61; commd. col. 7th Regt., Tenn. Volunteer Inf., 1861, brig. gen. Confederate Army, 1862; assigned to command 5th Brigade, 1st Corps, Army of Va. Killed in Battle of Seven Pines, nr. Richmond, Va., May 31, 1862; buried Cedar Grove Cemetery, Lebanon.

HAVARD, VALERY surgeon U.S.A.; b. Compiégne, France, Feb. 18, 1846; grad. Inst. of Beauvais, France, 1865, Manhattan Coll., New York, 1869; M.D., Univ. Med. College, New York, 1869; m. Agnes J. Hewitt, Nov. 1885; children-Eugene P., Aline, Valery. Asst. surgeon, Nov. 10, 1874; capt. asst. surgeon, Nov. 10, 1879; maj. surgeon, Feb. 27, 1891; lt. col. chief surgeon vols., Aug. 1-Nov. 5, 1898; lt. col. deputy surgeon gen., Oct. 24, 1901: col. asst. surgeon gen., Apr. 26, 1904. Chief surgeon 5th Corps under Gen. Shafter in Santiago de Cuba, 1898, and of Dept. of Cuba under Gen. Wood, 1900-01; mil. attaché to the Russian Army in Manchuria, Nov. 16, 1904-May 1, 1905; chief surgeon Dept. of the East, 1905-06; pres. Army Med. Sch. and in charge of Library and Museum Division, Med. Dept. U.S.A., 1906-10; retired by operation of law, Feb. 18, 1910. Recalled to active duty, Sept. 22, 1917, and ordered to Havana to reorganize med. dept. Cuban Army and Navy; relieved from Cuban service, May 1923. Author of Manual of Military Hygiene (pub. under authority and with approval of Surgeon Gen. U.S.A.). Home: Fairfield, Conn. Died Nov. 6, 1927.

HAWES, HARRIET BOYD (MRS. CHARLES HENRY HAWES) archaeologist; b. at Boston, Oct. 11, 1871; d. Alexander and Harriet Fay (Wheeler) Boyd; A.B., Smith Coll., 1892. M.A., 1901, L.H.D., 1910; student, 1896-97, fellow, 1898-1900, Am. Sch. of Classical Studies, Athens, Greece; m. Charles Henry Hawes, Eng., Mar. 3, 1906; children-Alexander Boyd, Marv Nesbit. Began archaeol. explorations in Greece, 1896. under fellowship of Am. Sch. of Classical Studies. Athens; excavated citadel and tombs of Iron Age (1000 B.C.) at Kavousi, Crete, 1900; as rep. am. Exploration Soc., Phila., discovered and excavated town and palace of Bronze Age (1600 B.C.) at Gournia, Crete, 1901, 03, 04. Red Cross nurse in Turko-Grecian War, 1897. Spanish-Am. War, 1898; conducted relief work among Serbians, in Corfu, 1915-16; organizer and first dir. of Smith College Relief Unit in dept. of Somme, France, 1917. Life mem. Archaeol. Inst. America. Red Cross decoration from Queen Olga of Greece. Episcopalain. Author: Gournia, Vasiliki and Other Prehistoric Sites on the Isthmus of Hierapetra, Crete (with others), 1908; Crete, the Foierunner of Greece (with C. H. Hawes), 1909. Lecturer in pre-Christian art. Wellesley Coll., 1920-36; active in work for New Economics, 1937-. Home: 2 Belfield Rd., Alexandria, Va. Died Mar. 31, 1945.

HAWES, HARRY BARTOW ex-senator; b. Covington, Ky., Nov. 15, 1869; s. Smith Nicholas and Susan Elizabeth (Simrall) H.; LL.B., St. Louis Law Sch. (Washington U.), 1896; m. Eppes Osborne Robinson, Nov. 15, 1899; children-Mrs. Peyton Hawes Dunn, Eppes Bartown (Mrs. William Fahnestock, Jr.). Began practice of law, St. Louis, 1896; represented the Republic of Hawaii during annexation to the U.S., 1898; mem. Mo. Ho. of Rep., 1916-17; pres. Bd. Police Commrs., St. Louis, 4 yrs.; mem. 67th to 69th Congresses (1921-27), 11th Mo. Dist.; mem. U.S. Senate, 1927-33, resigned, Feb. 3, 1933; was candidate for gov.; now in practice of law at Washington and St. Louis, Major U.S. Army, and apptd. to mil. intelligence bur.; mil. attaché, Madrid, World War. Democrat. Episcopalian. Mem. Am., Mo., D.C. and St. Louis bar assns., Am. Soc. Internat. Law, Am. Geog. Soc., Am. Econ. Assn., Mo. Hist. Soc., Soc. of St. Louis Authors, Am. Soc. Polit. and Social Science, Chamber of Commerce, Isaak Walton League, Am. Game Assn., Audubon Soc., Am. Forestry Assn., Nat. Rifle Assn., Reserve Officers Assn., S.A.R., Sons Confederate Vets., Am. Legion. Mil. Order World War. Clubs: St. Louis, Racquet, Noonday, Miss. Valley Kennel (pres. many yrs.). Mo. Athletic (St. Louis); Chevy Chase, Metropolitan, National Press (Washingon); Lotos (New York); pres. Jefferson Islands Club (Sherwood, Md.); Camp Fire of America, Corinthian Yacht. A leader in behalf of good roads; author of the State Highway Law of Mo., known as the "Hawes Law"; ex-pres. Federated Roads Council of St. Louis and Mo. Good Roads Federation which directed campaign for $1,000,000 road bond issue; an organizer Lakes to Gulf Deep Waterways Assn.; joint author of Hawes-Cutting bill giving Philippines independence; counsel for Philippine Commonwealth. Author: My Friend the Black Bass, 1930; Philippine Uncertainty-An American Problem, 1932; Fish and Game, Now or Never, 1935; also of brochures on "The Dog," and "Conservation." Counselor for great game orgns. of America; apptd. mem. representing U.S. Senate, on Migratory Bird Conservation Commn. Home: 4822 Quebec St. N.W. Office: Transportation Bldg., Washington, D.C. Died Aug. 1, 1947.

HAWKINS, GEORGE SYDNEY congressman, jurist; b. Kingston, N.Y., 1808; grad. Columbia; studied law. Admitted to N.Y. bar, practiced law; moved to Pensacola, Fla.; served as capt. during Seminole War, 1837; mem. Legislative Council of Territory of Fla.; apptd. dist. atty., 1841; apptd. U.S. dist. atty. for Apalachicola dist., 1842; asso. justice Fla. State Supreme Ct., 1846-60; judge circuit ct., 1851; mem. Fla. Ho. of Reps., Fla. Senate; collector of customs Port of Apalachicola; mem. U.S. Ho. of Reps. (Democrat) from Fla., 35th-36th congresses, 1857-Jan. 21, 1861; judge dist. ct. under Confederacy, 1862-65; commd. by Fla. Legislature to prepare a digest of state laws, 1877. Died Marianna, Fla., Mar. 15, 1878; buried St. Luke's Episcopal Cemetery, Marianna.

HAWKINS, HAMILTON SMITH brig. gen.; b. Ft. Moultrie, S.C., Nov. 13, 1834; s. Maj. Hamilton Smith (surgeon U.S.A.) and Ann Alicia (Chifelle) H.; m. Annie Gray, Dec. 3, 1868. Apptd. from N.Y., and cadet U.S. Mil. Acad., July 1, 1852-Jan. 31, 1855; commd. 2d lt. 6th Inf., Apr. 26, 1861) 1st lt., May 14, 1861; capt., Sept. 20, 1863; maj. 10th Inf., Oct. 31, 1883; lt. col. 23d Inf., Feb. 17, 1889; col. 16th Inf., Aug. 13, 1894; brig. gen. vols., May 4, 1898; maj. gen., July 8, 1898; brig. gen., U.S.A., Sept. 28, 1898; hon. disch. from vol. service. Nov. 30, 1898. Bvtd. maj., Oct. 11, 1865 (declined). Commandant cadets, U.S. Mil. Acad., 1888-92; commandant Inf. and Cav. Sch., 1894-98; participated in battle of San Juan, 1898; retired at own request after 40 yrs.' service, Oct. 4, 1898. Gov. Soldiers' Home. Washington, Jan. 10, 1903-. Died 1910.

HAWKINS, HAMILTON SMITH ret. army officer; b. Dakota, Ty., Sept. 25, 1872; s. Brig. Gen. Hamilton Smith (U.S. Army) and Annie (Gray) H.; grad. U.S. Mil. Acad., 1894; distinguished grad. Army Sch. of Line, 1911; grad. Army Staff Coll., 1912. Commd. add. 2d lt. 4th Cav., 1894; promoted through grades to brig.gen., 1928. Detailed as mem. Gen. Staff Corps, 1918; chief of staff 35th Div., Argonne-Meuse offensive, 1918-19; asst. comdt. Cav. and Mounted Service Schs., Ft. Riley, Kan., 1919-23: comdg. Ft. Myer, Va., 1923-26; chief of staff Philippine Div., 1926-28; comdg. 14th Inf. Brigade, Ft. Omaha, Neb., 1928-29; comdg. 1st Cav. Brigade, Ft. Clark, Tex., 1929-34, 1st Cav. Div., Ft. Bliss, Tex.,

1934-36; retired, 1936. Contbd. articles to cav. jour. Address: 3508 Lowell St., Washington. Died Oct. 19, 1950; buried Cemetery West Point, N.Y.

HAWKINS, ISAAC ROBERTS congressman, army officer; b. nr. Columbia, Tenn., May 16, 1818; attended common schs.; studied law. Admitted to Tenn. bar, 1843, began practice in Huntingdon; served as lt. during Mexican War; resumed law practice; del. from Tenn. to Washington (D.C.) Peace Conf., 1861; elected to conv. for consideration of fed. relations; judge circuit ct., 1862; commd. lt. col. 7th Regt., Tenn. Volunteer Cavalry, U.S. Army, 1862, captured at Union City, Tenn., 1864, imprisoned, one of officers who were placed under fire at Charleston (S.C.); exchanged, 1864, in command of cavalry force in Western Ky. until end of Civil War; declined appointment as chancellor of Tenn., 1865; del. Republican Nat. Conv., Chgo., 1868; mem. U.S. Ho. of Reps. (Rep.) from Tenn., 39th-41st congresses, July 24, 1866-71. Died Huntingdon, Aug. 12, 1880; buried Hawkins family burial ground, nr. Huntingdon.

HAWKINS, J(OHN) E(RSKINE) educator; b. Media, Pa., May 17, 1899; s. John Howard and Anna Augustine (Wright) H.; A.B., U. Pa., 1919, B.S. in Chem. Engring., 1922, M.S., 1924, Ph.D., 1927; m. Trella Esther Yoder, Feb. 6, 1927; 1 dau., Mary Diane, Asst. in chemistry U. Pa., 1921-22, instr., 1922-32; plant supr., chief chemist P. J. Ritter Co., Bridgeton, N.J., 1932-33; head chemistry dept. U. Tampa, 1933-35; acting head chem. engring. U. Fla., 1935-36, asst. prof. chemistry, asso. dir. naval stores research, 1936-37, asso. prof. chemistry, 1937-45, prof. chemistry, 1945-, dir. naval stores research, 1946-, also asst. head chemistry; collaborator So. Utilization and Development div. Dept. Agr. Served as pvt. U.S. Army, World War I; capt. inf., U.S. N.G., 1920-38. Recipient award for contbns. development of chemistry in Southeast, Am. Chem. Soc., 1959. Fellow A.A.A.S., Am. Inst. Chemists; mem. Am. Legion, Am. Chem. Soc. (sec.-treas. Fla. sect. 1938-41, chmn. 1943, councilor 1945, 46), Fla. Acad. Sci. (chmn. phys. sci. div., pres. 1949), Am. Assn. U. Profs. (mem. nat. council 1952-54), Am. Edn. Assn., Council Basic Edn., Sigma Xi, Sigma Gamma Sigma, Gamma Sigma Epsilon (grand keeper of cult 1941-46). Club: Gainesville Golf and Country. Contbg. author Ency. of Chem. Tech., vol. 13, Contbr. articles sci. jours., Congl. Record. Home: 530 N.E. 10th Av., Gainesville, Fla. Died July 22, 1961; buried Gainesville.

HAWKINS, JOHN PARKER brig. gen. U.S.A.; b. Indianapolis, Sept. 29, 1830; s. John and Elizabeth (Walter) H.; student Wabash Coll., Ind., 2 yrs.; apptd. from Ind., and grad. U.S. Mil. Acad., 1852; m. Jane B. Craig, Oct. 10, 1867. Bvt. 2d lt. 6th Inf., July 1, 1852; apptd. 2d lt. 2d Inf., June 23, 1854; 1st lt., Oct. 12, 1857; capt. commissary subsistence, Aug. 3, 1861; lt. col. vols., Nov. 1, 1862-Apr. 13, 1863; brig. gen., Apr. 13, 1863; hon. mustered out, Feb. 1, 1866; maj. commissary subsistence, June 23, 1874; lt. col. asst. commissary gen., Sept. 3, 1889; col., Mar. 12, 1892; bri. gen. commissary gen. subsistence, Dec. 22, 1892; retired by operation of law, Sept. 29, 1894. Bvtd.; maj., Mar. 13, 1865, "for gallant and meritorious services during siege of Mobile," lt. col. and col., Mar. 13, 1865, for same during the war; brig. gen. and maj. gen., Mar. 13, 1865, for same in the field during the war; maj. gen. vols., June 30, 1865, for same during the war. Home: Indianapolis, Ind. Died Feb. 7, 1914.

HAWKS, FRANK MONROE aviator; b. Marshalltown, Ia., Mar. 28, 1897; s. Charles Monroe and Ida Mae (Woodruff) H.; grad. high sch., Long Beach, Calif., 1917: also grad. U.S. Sch., of Mil. Aeronautics; student U. of Calif., 2 years; m. Newell Lane, Aug. 16, 1918 (divorced); 1 dau., Dolly; m. 2d, Edith Bowie, Oct. 26, 1926. Began as aviator, Mar. 1916; entered U.S. Air Service, Apr. 1917, serving as instr. until Mar. 1919. Lt. comdr. U.S. Navy Reserve Air Force. Awarded Harmon trophy as outstanding aviator in U.S. for year 1930; French Aero Club decoration; Swiss Aero Club decoration; also Italian, Swedish, Norwegian, Danish and English decorations. Established transcontinental record of 12 hrs., 25 min., 3 seconds, west to east, Aug. 13, 1930, and east to west record of 14 hrs., 50 min., 43 seconds, Aug. 6, 1930, non-stop transcontinental record 13 hrs., 27 min., 15 seconds, June 2, 1933. Has established 214 city to city records in U.S., Europe, South America, Mexico and Cuba, Vice-pres. Quinn Aircar Co., Buffalo. Mem. advisory bd. Roosevelt Aviation Sch., Roosevelt Field, L.I., N.Y.; mem. advisory bd. Guggenheim Sch. of Aeronautics, New York Univ. Dir. Junior Birdmen of America. Author: Speed, 1931; Once to Every Pilot. Made hon. chief of Sioux Indian Tribe, Aug. 12, 1931. Home: Redding, Conn. Died Aug. 23, 1938.

HAWLEY, JOHN BALDWIN congressman; b. Hawleyville, Conn., Feb. 9, 1831; attended Jacksonville (Ill.) Coll.; studied law. Admitted to Ill. bar, 1854, began practice in Rock Island; state's atty., 1856-60; served as capt. Co. H., 45th Regt., Ill. Volunteer Inf. during Civil War, ret. because of injuries, 1862; apptd. postmaster of Rock Island, 1865, removed from office by Pres. Johnson, 1866; mem. U.S. Ho. of Reps. (Republican) from Ill., 41st-43d congresses, 1869-75; asst. sec. of treasury U.S., 1877-80; resumed law practice, Chgo., 1880; gen. atty. for Western brs. Northwestern R.R. Co., Omaha, Neb. Died Hot Springs, S.D., May 24, 1895; buried Prospect Hill Cemetery, Omaha.

HAWLEY, JOHN MITCHELL rear admiral U.S.N.; b. Northampton, Mass.,July 28, 1946; grad. U.S. Naval Acad., 1868; m. Ella S. Moore, June 17, 1874. Promoted through all grades to capt., Mar. 15, 1904; rear admiral and retired, June 30, 1907. Has served at sea 22 yrs., 6 of which were in coast survey; during early career in navy was connected with 3 interoceanic surveys; exec. officer of U.S. ship Nipsic during Samoan hurricane, 1889, and received thanks of State of Mass. for services there; first officer to establish recruiting stations in West with view of bringing Western men into service; had charge of all recruiting stas. in West and Southwest during the war with Spain, enlisting about 1,900 men; comdr. Hartford, training ship for landsmen, 1899-1901; insp. 5th light house dist. at Baltimore, 1902-4; comd. flagship Brooklyn, Apr. 21, 1904; comdr.-in-chief S. Atlantic Squadron, Nov. 23, 1904-Jan. 12, 1905; comdg. Wabash, 1906-07. Presented with a jeweled sword by Ill. Naval Militia, 1898. Died Feb. 9, 1925.

HAWLEY, PAUL RAMSEY army officer and medical adminstr. ret.; b. West College Corner, Indiana, January 31, 1891; son of William Harry and Sabina Cora (Ramsey) H.; A.B., Indiana University, 1912; M.D., University of Cincinnati, 1914; Dr. P.H., Johns Hopkins, 1923; grad. Army Med. Sch., 1917 and 1921, Command and Gen. Staff Sch., 1936, Army War Coll., 1939; LL.D., U. Cin., U. Birmingham (England), Indiana U., Syracuse U., Georgetown U., Sc.D. (hon.) Miami Univ., Wayne Univ., Union Coll.; m. Lydia W. Wright; children - Barbara (Mrs. T. G. Tousey, Jr.), William Harry. Intern, Cincinnati Gen. Hosp., 1914-15, house physician, 1915; commd. 1st lt., U.S. Army Med. Corps, Oct. 11, 1916, and advanced through the grades to maj. gen., 1944; Chief Med. Dir., U.S. Veterans Adminstrn., 1945-47; chief exec. officer Blue Cross and Blue Shield Comms., 1948-50; bd. dirs. Ohio Natural Life Ins. Co. Bampton lectr., Columbia Univ., 1949. Recipient Gorgas Award, 1947; Spl. Award, Nat. Rehabilitation Council, 1947; Lasker Award, 1948; received the Irving S. Cutter Medal in 1950. Decorated Distinguished Service Medal, Legion of Merit, Bronze Star (U.S.); Presidential Medal of Merit (Nicaragua); Companion of the Bath, Order of St. John of Jerusalem (Eng.); Officer Legion of Honor, Comdr. Order of Pub. Health, Croix de Guerre with Palm (France); Comdr. Order of Crown (Belgium); Commander Order of St. Olaf (Norway); Officer Order of Carlos Finlay (Cuba). Fellow A.C.P., A.C.S. (dir. 1950-61), So. Surgical Assn., Royal College Phys. (England), Royal College Surgeons (Edinburgh) (Eng.) (hon.), Royal Soc. Medicine (London), Am. Coll. Hosp. Adminstrs. (hon.); mem. A.M.A., l'Acad. de Chirurgie (France) (hon.), Am. Psychiat. Assn. (hon.), Southeastern Surg. Congress, Col. Med. Assn., Delta Omega, Phi Delta Theta (nat. pres. 1956-58), Phi Rho Sigma. Mfason. Club: Army and Navy Washington). Home: Shady Side, Md. 20867. Died Nov. 24, 1965; buried Arlington Nat. Cemetery, Arlington, Va.

HAY, MALCOLM, lawyer, judge, N.G. officer; b. Pitts., May 19, 1907; s. Southard and Eleanor (Humbird) H.; grad. Phillips Acad., Andover, Mass., 1925; A.B., Yale, 1930; LL.B., U. Pitts., 1933; m. Martha Verner Leggate, June 4, 1931; children—Eleanor Anne (Mrs. Leon Thomson), Malcolm, Thomas Southard; m. 2d, Mary Otis Mather, Dec. 16, 1943; m. 3d, Jessie F., May 1968. Admitted to Pa. bar, 1933, practiced in Pitts.; partner firm Miller, Hay & Entwisle, from 1957; instr. U. Pitts. Sch. Social Work, 1948-52; judge orphans ct. div. Ct. Common Pleas, Allegheny County, 1968-72. Commd. 2d lt. O.R.C., U.S. Army, 1931, advanced through grades to capt., 1941; active duty in ETO, World War II; col. Res., 1946-61; comdt. Pitts. U.S. Army Res. Sch., 1950-61; adj. gen., Pa., maj. gen. N.G., from 1961; maj. gen. AUS, from 1961. Lay dep. Triennial Conv. P.E. Ch. U.S., 1953-61, mem. com. canons, from 1955; mem. Community Chest Allegheny County, from 1959; Pa. Citizens Assn., from 1959. Chancellor P.E. Diocese Pitts., from 1951, trustee from 1937; trustee St. Margaret Meml. Hosp., Pa. Mental Health Inc.; trustee Family and Childrens Service Allegheny County, from 1947, pres., 1956-57; dir. United Mental Health Service Allegheny County, from 1958. Decorated Legion of Merit. Mem. Pitts. C. of C. (dir., gen. counsel from 1959), Res. Officers Assn. U.S. (pres. Pa. 1955-56, nat. judge adv. 1950-51, nat. council 1951-52, nat. v.p. 1956-57) Am. Legion, Mil. Order World Wars, Assn. U.S. Army, S.A.R., Am., Pa., Allegheny County bar assns., Phi Delta Phi. Mason (320, Shriner). Clubs: Fox Chapel, Pittsburgh, Harvard-Yale-Princeton, University (Pitts.). Home: Pittsburgh PA Died Feb. 4, 1972.

HAY, WILLIAM HENRY army officer; b. Fla., July 16, 1860; grad. U.S. Mil. Acad., 1886, Inf. and Cav. Sch., 1891, Army War Coll., 1913; married; children- Thomas Robson, William Wren, Edward Northup, Richard Carman. Second lt. 3d Cav., July 1, 1886; 1st lt. 10th Cav., July 21, 1893; capt. a.q.m. vols., Nov. 26, 1898; hon. discharged volunteers, March 15, 1901; capt., U.S.A., Feb. 2, 1901; advanced through grades to the rank of col., July 1, 1916; brig. gen. N.A., Oct. 31, 1917; maj. gen. N.A., Oct. 1, 1918; brig. gen. regular army, Apr. 11, 1922; maj. gen., Nov. 5, 1923; retired, Nov. 6, 1923. Apptd. comdr. 15th Cav., Manila, P.I., 1916; comdr. 184th Brig., 92d Div., Nov. 5, 1917-Oct. 24, 1918; comdg. 28th Div., Oct. 25, 1918-Apr. 17-1919; demoted grade of col. regular U.S. Army, Mar. 15, 1920; insp. gen., July 1920; Gen. Staff and chief of staff, Am. Forces in Germany. May 9, 1921-Apr. 25,-1922; comdr. 1st Cav. Brig., 1st Cav. Div., Aug. 18-Nov. 17, 1922. Campaigns: St. Die sector, vosgres, Pont-a-Mousson sector, Thian-court sector, Meuse-Argonne offensive, offensive of 2d Army. Awarded D.S.M. (U.S.); Croix de Guerre with two palms, and Comdr. Legion of Honor (French); Comdr. Black Star; Comdr. Order of Leopold (Belgian). Address: War Dept., Washington. Died Dec. 17, 1946.

HAYDEN, CARL (TRUMBULL), former U.S. senator; b. Hayden's Ferry, now Tempe, Ariz., Oct. 2, 1877; s. Charles Trumbull and Sallie Calvert (Davis) H.; grad. Normal Sch. of Ariz., Tempe, 1896; attended Leland Stanford U., 1896-1900; LL.D., U. Ariz., 1948, Ariz. State U., 1959; m. Nan Downing, Feb. 14, 1908 (dec.). Mem. Tempe Town Council, 1902-04; treas. Maricopa County, 1904-06; sheriff Maricopa County, 1907-12; maj. inf., U.S.N.A., 1918; Member of Congress from Arizona, 1912-27; United States Senator from Arizona, 1927-69, (pres. pro tempore 1957-69); during his Congl. serv. specialized on legislation relating to irrigation of arid lands and Federal aid for hwys.; chmn. Senate com. on appropriations; mem. interior and insular affairs com. Democrat. Mason. Home: Tempe AZ Died Jan. 25, 1972; buried Twin Butte Cemetery, Tempe AZ

HAYDEN, EDWARD EVERETT naval officer; b. Boston, Apr. 14, 1858; s. William and Lousie Annie (Dorr) H.; grad. U.S. Naval Acad., 1879; m. Kate Reynolds, Dec. 12, 1882; children-Reynolds, Herbert Bainbridge, William (dec.), Dorothy, Alfred Dorr, Mary Bainbridge. Promoted through grades to rear adm., retired, June 30, 1921. Asst. geologist, U.S. Geol. Survey, 1885; marine meteorologist, U.S. Hydrographic Office, and editor pilot chart, 1886-92; in charge Naval Obs., Mare Island, Calif., 1898, branch hydrographic office, Manila, 1899; in charge, dept. chronometers and time service, U.S. Naval Obs., Washington, 1902-10, comdt. U.S. Naval Sta., Key West, Fla., 1910-15; pres. Gen. Court Martial, Navy Yard, Norfolk, Va., 1916-21. Republican. Episcopalian. Died Nov. 17, 1932.

HAYDEN, JOHN LOUIS army officer; b. in Ill., Nov. 2, 1866; grad. U.S. Mil. Acad., 1888; grad. Arty. Sch., 1898. Commd. 2d lt. 1st Arty., June 11, 1888; 1st lt., Oct. 2, 1894; capt. Arty Corps, Feb. 10, 1901; maj., Jan. 25, 1907; lt. col. Coast Arty. Corps, Oct. 5, 1911; col., July 1, 1916; brig. gen. N.G., Aug. 5, 1917. Participated in campaign against Sioux Indians in S. Dak., 1890-91; in action at Wounded Knee, Dec. 29, 1890, and at White Clay Creek, Dec. 30, 1890; prof. mil. science and tactics, U. of Wash., 1892-96; apptd. comdr. 56th Field Arty. Brigade, Camp Wheeler, Macon, Ga., Sept. 1917. Died Feb. 22, 1936.

HAYES, CARLTON JOSEPH HUNTLEY historian; b. Afton, N.Y., May 16, 1882; s. Dr. Philetus A. and Permelia M. (Huntley) H.; A.B., Columbia, 1904, A.M., 1905, Ph.D., 1909, Litt.D., 1929; LL.D., U. of Notre Dame, 1921, Niagara U., 1936, Fordham U., 1946, Mich. State U., 1955; L.H.D., Marquette U., 1929, Williams Coll., 1939, Det. U., 1950, Georgetown U., 1953; married Mary Evelyn Carroll, Sept. 18, 1920; children - Mary Elizabeth (Mrs. William D. Tucker, Jr.), Carroll Joseph. Lecturer in history, 1907-10; assistant professor, 1910-15, associate professor, 1915-19, professor, 1919-35, Seth Low prof., 1935-50, emeritus Columbia, 1950-; vis. prof. several univs., 1911-. U.S. ambassador to Spain, May 1942-March 1945. Served in World War as captain U.S. Army, Military Intelligence ivision, General Staff, 1918-19; major, O.R.C., 1928-33. Mem. nat., state and local profl. hist. and philos. socs., has served as officer several. Clubs: Columbia University, Round Table, Faculty. Awarded annual Laetare Medal, 1946; Cardinal Gibbons Medal, 1949; Alexander Hamilton Medal, 1952; Knight of Malta, Grand Cross Order of Alfonso the Wise. Author many history books, including studies of modern nationalism; and also Spain, 1951; Modern Europe to 1870, 1953; Contemporary Europe since 1870, 1958; Christianity and Western Civilization, 1954. Co-author numerous books, latest; History of Western Civilization, 1962. Editor: Social and Econ. Studies Post-War France. Contbr. to mags. and revs. and 11th edit. Ency. Britannica. Home: Jericho Farm, Afton, N.Y.; 88 Morningside Dr., N.Y.C. 27. Died Sept. 3, 1964; buried Afton.

HAYES, EDWARD ARTHUR lawyer; b. Morrisonville, Ill., Jan. 5, 1893; s. Michael Patrick and Mary Ellen (Bray) grad. St. Theresa's Parochial Sch., 1910; LL.B., St. Louis U., 1915; m. Margaret M. Muleady, Sept. 10, 1918. Admitted to Ill. bar, 1915, and practiced in Decatur, Ill., mem. firm Hayes & Downing, 1915-40; mem. firm Damon, Hayes White & Hoban, Chicago, since 1945; one of the gen. counsel, Bowser, Inc., since 1945; pres. Defense Identification Service, Inc., since 1951. Served as apprentice seaman, U.S. Navy, 1917, ensign U.S.N.R., aide to Adm. Moffett, 1918-19; comd. lt. comdr., U.S. N.R., 1933. Mem. Am. Legion (dep. comdr., Ill. dept., 1929-30; nat. comdr., 1933-34 mem. nat. exec. com., since 1931), Am., Ill. and

Chicago bar assns. Republican. Mem. Americans for America (nat. chmn.), K.C. (4ff). Clubs: Chicago Athletic Association. Home: 2130 Lincoln Park West, Chicago 14. Office: 33 LaSalle St., Chgo. 2. Died Apr. 1, 1955.

HAYES, EDWARD MORTIMER brig. gen.; b. in N.Y., Dec. 28, 1842. Enlisted in U.S.A., Aug. 28, 1855; served 2d Cav. in Tex., under Col. Lee and Capt. Kirby Smith, until Aug. 28, 1860; 1st lt. 10th Ohio Cav., Jan. 15, 1863; capt., Mar. 24, 1864; hon. mustered out, July 24, 1865; apptd. from N.J., 2d lt. 5th U.S. Cav., Feb. 23, 1866; promoted through grades to brig. gen., Jan. 1903; retired, Jan. 26, 1903. Served on frontier in many Indian campaigns, in Cuba and P.I. Bvtd.; maj. vols., Mar. 13, 1865, "for gallant and meritorious services during campaign in Ga. and the Carolinas," maj., Feb. 27, 1890, "for gallant services in action against Indians at Beaver Creek, Kan., Oct. 25, 26, 1868." Home: New York, N.Y. Died Aug. 15, 1912.

HAYES, HAROLD M. lawyer; b. Foxcroft, Me., Feb. 2, 1894; s. Charles Webster and Lola Belle (Whittier) H.; A.B., Bowdoin Coll., 1914; student U. Me. Coll. Law, 1915-17, 17-18; m. Mabel Marion MacFadyen, July 17, 1918; children - Stuart Edward, Lendall Whittier. Instr. physics Bowdoin Coll., 1914-15; admitted to Me. bar, 1918, since practiced in Dover-Foxcroft, gen. real estate and probate law; member of firm C. W. & H. M. Hayes; recorder Piscataquis Municipal Ct., 1919-20; county atty., Piscataquis County, 1921-22; judge Municipal Ct., 1922-34; dir. Selective Service, Me., 1944-47. Mem. 94th, 95th Me. Legislatures. Served from pvt. to 2d lt., inf., U.S. Army, 1917; capt. to lt. col., AUS, 1943-46. Decorated Legion of Merit. Mem. Am., Me. (pres. 1959-60) bar assns., Soc. Mayflower Descendants, S.A.R., Am. Legion, 40 and 8, Phi Beta Kappa, Zeta Psi. Conglist. Mason. Home: 108 Lincoln St. Office: 5 Lincoln St., Dover-Foxcroft, Me. Died Oct. 30, 1963; buried Dover-Foxcroft.

HAYES, HENRY REED financial consultant; b. Boston, Mass., Mar. 26, 1879; s. John J. and Caroline L. (Raymond) H.; grad. Roxbury (Mass.) Latin Sch., 1897; A.B., Harvard, 1901; m. Yvonne Stoddard, Oct. 24, 1917: children-Henry Reed, Holland, David, Philip. With Stone & Webster, Boston, 1901-10, later New York, in investment banking div., 1912-27; v.p. Stone & Webster, Inc., 1925-30; v.p. and dir. Stone & Webster and Blodget, N.Y.C., 1927-33. Served as major, later lt. col., U.S. Army, World War. Chmn. Rep. Town Com., Dedham, Mass., 1909-12; mem. exec. com. Mass. Rep. State Com., 1912. Pres. Investment Bankers Assn. of America, 1927. Dir. Better Business Bureau of N.Y.C., New York Sch. for the Deaf; trustee, mem. exec. com. Teachers Ins. and Annuity Assn. of America; dir. The Columbia Gas System, Inc., General Public Utilities Corp. Episcopalian. Clubs: Harvard, The Players (New York). Home: Dan's Highway, New Canaan, Conn. Office: 74 Trinity Pl., N.Y.C. 6. Died June 29, 1955.

HAYES, ISAAC ISRAEL physician, explorer; b. Chester County, Pa., Mar. 5, 1832; s. Benjamin and Ann (Borton) H.; M.D., U. Pa., 1853. Surgeon, 2d Arctic Expdn. of Elisha Kent Kane, 1853; explored unknown coast of Ellismere Land northwest of Cape Sabine; organized new expdn. to determine extent of Arctic Ocean (financed largely by Am. Geog. Soc. and Henry Grinnell), sailed from Boston, 1860, expdn. helped open way to North Pole; in charge Satterlee Hosp., West Philadelphia, during Civil War; promotted maj., then col. U.S. Army; made 3d voyage to Arctic, 1869; attended Iceland millennial as correspondent for N.Y. Herald, 1874; mem. N.Y. Assembly (Republican); a promoter Hudson River Tunnel. Author: The Open Polar Sea, 1876; The Land of Desolation (sketch of Greenland), published London, 1871, N.Y.C., 1872. Died N.Y.C., Dec. 17, 1881.

HAYES, JOSEPH soldier, mining engr.; b. S. Berwick, Me., Sept. 14, 1835; s. William Allen H.; ed. S. Berwick, Me., and Phillips Acad., Andover, Mass.; grad. Harvard, 1855; unmarried. Apptd. maj., 18th Mass. Regt., July 26, 1861, lt.-col., Aug. 25, 1862, col., Nov. 20, 1862, brig.-gen. vols., lMay 12, 1864; comd. 1st div., 5th Army Corps; taken prisoner by Confederates, and confined for several months in Libby Prison; apptd. U.S. commr. of supplies in seceded States, Jan., 1865; bvtd. maj.-gen. vols., Mar. 13, 1865; mustered out of service, Aug. 24, 1865. Later engaged as mining engr.; introduced Am. system of hydraulic mining into United States of Colombia, 1877. Address: Care J. E. Kelly, 318 W. 57th St., New York.

HAYES, PHILIP army officer; b. Portage, Wis., June 16, 1887; B.S., U.S. Mil. Acad., 1909; grad. F.A. Sch., 1923; distinguished grad. Command and Gen. Staff Sch., 1924; grad. Army War Coll., 1930. Commd. 2d lt., Inf., 1909, transferred to F.A., 1915, and advanced through the grades to major gen., Jan. 17, 1944; instr., U.S. Mil. Acad., 1912-17; with 2d F.A., Camp Stotensburg, P.I., 1917-18, F.A., Camp Grant, Jan.-July 1918; with War Plans Div., War Dept. Gen. Staff, Washington, D.C., 1918-19; exec. for athletics, U.S. Mil. Acad., 1919-22; instr., F.A. Sch., Ft. Sill, 1924-27; exec. of F.A. Sch., 1927-29; instr., Command and Gen. Staff Sch., Ft. Leavenworth, Kas., 1930-35; comdr., 19th F.A. Fort Benjamin Harrison, Ind., 1935-37; asst. chief of staff, G-3 (Operations and Training), Hawaiian Dept., Ft. Shafer, Hawaii, 1937-39, chief of staff, 1939-41; prof. mil. science and tactics, Harvard U., Dec. 1941-Mar. 1942; chief of staff, hdqrs. 1st Corps Area (1st Service Command), Boston, Mar. 1942-May 1943; exec. for Deputy chief of staff for Service Commands, May-Aug. 1943; acting deputy chief of staff for service commands to Nov. 30, 1943; commanding general. Third Service Command, Army Service Forces, since December 1, 1943. Retired as major general U.S. Army May 31, 1946. President, Tower Realty Co. since 1946. Home: 10 St. Martins Rd., Baltimore 1S. Office: American Bldg., Baltimore 2, Md. Died Nov. 25, 1949.

HAYES, PHILIP CORNELIUS congressman: b. Granby, Conn., Feb. 3, 1833; s. Gaylord and Mary (Goodrich) H.; A.B., Oberlin, 1860, A.M., 1863; grad. Oberlin Theol. Sem., 1863; m. Amelia E. Johnson, Jan. 25, 1865. Capt. 103d Ohio Inf., July 16, 1862; lt. col., Nov. 18, 1864; apptd. col. but not mustered in; bvtd. brig. gen. vols., Mar. 13, 1865, "for gallant and meritorious services during the war"; hon. mustered out, June 12, 1865. Actively engaged in journalism, 1866-95; mem. 45th and 46th Congresses (1877-81). Home: Joliet, Ill. Died July 13, 1916.

HAYES, RUTHERFORD BIRCHARD 19th Pres. U.S.; b. Delaware, O., Oct. 4, 1822; s. Rutherford and Sophia (Birchard) H.; grad. Kenyon Coll., Gambier, O., 1842, LL.D. (Hon.), 1868; grad. Harvard Law Sch., 1845; LL.D. (hon.), Harvard, 1877, Yale, 1880, Johns Hopkins, 1881; m. Lucy Webb, Dec. 30, 1852, children - Birchard Austin, Webb Cook, Rutherford Platt, Joseph T., George C. Frances, Scott R., Manning F. Admitted to Ohio bar, 1845; mem. Literary Club of Cincinnati; city solicitor Cincinnati, 1858; commd. maj. 23d Regt., Ohio Volunteers, 1861; in command of Gen. George Crook's 1st Inf. Brigade, 1863-64; promoted brig. gen., 1864; brevetted maj. gen. U.S. Volunteers, 1865; mem. U.S. Ho. of Reps. from Ohio, 39th-40th congresses, 1865-June 20, 1867 (resigned), sided with radical Republicans in U.S. Congress; gov. Ohio (Rep.), 1868-72, 75-77, obtained reforms in treatment of insane, helped create Ohio Geol. Survey; Republican candidate for Pres. U.S. (Against Democrat Samuel J. Tilden), 1876, elected (after disputed Electoral Commn. results) by spl. electoral commn. created by Congress; Pres. U.S., 1877-81, withdrew last fed. troops from South, attempted to reform Civil Service, opposed free and unlimited coinage of silver as legal tender; pres. Nat. Prison Assn., 1883-93; trustee Peabody Edn. Fund, Slater Fund. Died Fremont, O., Jan. 17, 1893; buried Spiegel Grove Park, Fremont.

HAYES, WADE HAMPTON banker; b. Norfolk, Va., May 12, 1879; s. William Arnold and Emma (Mathews) H.; Norfolk Academy; special course in political science, Columbia, 1899-1900; m. Julia Florence Yard, Dec. 14, 1905; 1 daughter, Sally. Sunday editor New York Tribune, Feb. 1908-14; member Hayes & Lord, investment bankers, and vice-president Chase Securities Corporation, investment bankers; now chairman Edmundsons Electricity Corp., Ltd.; dir. English Electric Co., Ltd., Utilities Corp. (Poland), Ltd., Marconi's Wireless Tele[graph Co., Ltd., Marconi Instruments, Ltd., D. Napier & Son, Ltd., Edmundsons Electricity Corp., Ltd., and various other electric cos. in Eng. Enlisted 4th Regt. Va. Nat. Guard, 1896, and with same regt. in Spanish-Am. War as chief of couriers, staff of Maj. Gen. Fitzhugh Lee, Fla., Ga. and Matanzas, Cuba; mustered out, Nov. 1899; served as col. 107th Regt., N.Y. Nat. Guard, until 1931; was lt. col. 107th Regt., N.Y. Nat. Guard, until 1931; was lt. col. 107th U.S. Inf., service in France, 1917-19; on staff of Gen. Pershing in operations section Gen. Staff. Gen. Hdqrs., A.E.F., June 1918-Feb. 1919; now brig. gen. retired: comdg. 1st American Squadron (Home Guard, Great Britain). Past comdr. Am. Legion. Dept. N.Y. Comdr. Legion d'Honeur (France); Comdr. Order British Empire. Mem. Southern Soc., Va. Soc., S.C. Soc., S.C.V., 7th Regt. Vet. Assn. Democrat. Clubs: Salmagundi, Down Town (New York); Carlton, City Athenaeum, American, Turf (London). Home: 48 Ennismore Gardens, London, S.W. 7. Office: 30 Gillingham St., S.W. 1, London, Eng. Died Sept. 4, 1956.

HAYES, WEBB COOK mfr.; b. Cincinnati, O., Mar. 20, 1856; s. Rutherford Birchard (19th President of U.S.) and Lucy Ware (Webb) H.; student Cornell U., 1872-75; m. Mary Otis Miller, Sept. 30, 1912. Sec. to father, 1875-81; joint organizer, 1881-1901, and treas. Whipple Mfg., Nat. Carbon Co., Union Carbide Co. Served as maj. First Ohio Cav., later adj. gen., Spanish-Am. War, serving in Cuba and Puerto Rico; wounded at crossing of San Juan River, Cuba; served as lt. col., U.S. Vols., Philippine Insurrection, Island of Mindanao; attached to staff Gen. Chaffee, China Relief Expdn., Boxer uprising, 1900; served on Mexican border, 1911, 13, 16; dispatch bearer between Am. ambassadors in Paris, London and Berlin, World War, 1916; served with Brit. and French brigades on Italian front, 1917-18; regional commr. A.E.F. in France and North Africa, 1918. Donated Spiegel Grove, 25-acre Hayes Homestead, to State of Ohio, building Hayes Memorial Library and Museum ($500,000 endowment) in memory of parents. Awarded Congressional Medal of Honor for "distinguished gallantry pushing through the enemy's lines alone on the night of Dec. 4th, 1899, from the beach to our beleagured force at Vigan, P.I., and returning the following morning to report the condition of affairs to the Navy and get assistance." Decorated by Marshall Lyantey for the Sultan of Turkey, Aug. 15, 1918. Home: Fremont, O. Died July 26, 1934.

HAYES, WEBB COOK II naval officer; b. Toledo, O., Sept. 25, 1890; s. Birchard Austin and Mary (Sherman) H.; B.S., U.S. Naval Acad., 1911; LL.D. (hon.), Bowling Green State U.; m. Martha Baker, Apr. 29, 1919: children-Webb Cook III, Arthur Baker, Scott Birchard, Commd. ensign, U.S. Navy, 1911, and advanced through the grades to rear adm., 1954; served on destroyer, U.S.S. Trippe, World War I; transferred to U.S.N.R., 1928; recalled to active duty, 1941; dir. recruiting and induction, Navy Dept., 1941-44; comd. U.S.S. West Point (Am.), 1944-45. Pres., dir. Pemiscot Land & Cooperage Co., 1930—; dir. and chmn. exec. com. Baker Brothers Machine Tool Co., 1933-51. Trustee Ohio Hist. Soc., Meml. Hosp. of Sandusky County, O., Birchard Library, Fremont, O.; pres., trustee Rutherford B. Hayes Found. Awarded B.S.M. by Pres. U.S.; Commendation with ribbon by Sec. of Navy (U.S.); Order of Avis (Portugal). Clubs: Army and Navy, Chevy Chase (Washington); New York Yacht; Toledo Country, Toledo (O.); Everglades (Fla.). Address: Spiegel Grove, Gremont, O. Died July 10, 1957.

HAYHOW, EDGAR CHARLES hosp. dir.; b. N.Y.C., July 21, 1894; s. Henry Herbert and Lina Caroline (Buehlmater) H.; B.S., Fordham U.; B.C.S., M.A., Ph.D., N.Y.U.; also postgrad Columbia. Successively asst. supt. Presbyn., St. Luke's and Lenox Hill hosps., N.Y.C., 1916-24; supt. New Rochelle (N.Y.) Hosp., 1924-27; hosp. cons., 1927-30; supt. Paterson (N.J.) Gen. Hosp., 1930-46; dir. East Orange (N.J.) Gen. Hosp., 1946—; lectr. on instnl. mgmt. N.Y.U., 1924-28. Mem. lay council Tchrs. Coll. Columbia; expert examiner Municipal Civil Service Commn., N.Y.; mem. Hosp. Survey of New York, 1937 (member gen. com.); mem. bd. trustees Am. Hosp. Assn., 1940-43 (1st v.p. 1939; chmn., mem. several councils); mem. Joint Com. of Edn. of Am. Hosp. Assn. and Am. Coll. Hosp. Adminstrs. Mem. Nat. Com. Mental Hygiene; chmn. com. on hosps. and instns. Midcentury White House Conf. Children and Youth. Served with Hosp. Service, BEF, later AEF, 1916-17; capt. Med. Administrv. Res. Corps, U.S. Army. Fellow Am. Coll. Hosp. Adminstrs. (regent 1938-52, pres. 1947-48); asso. fellow N.Y. Acad. Medicine; mem. adm., Internat., Inter-Am., N.Y., N.J. (pres. 1937) hosp. assns., Am. Acad. Polit. and Social Science, Lambda Sigma Phi, Phi Delta Kappa. Republican. Methodist. Clubs: Army and Navy, Railroad and Machinery (N.Y.C.). Contbr. to hosp. and social service mags. Home: 283 S. Center St., Orange, N.J. Address: East Orange General Hospital, East Orange, N.J. Died Aug. 23, 1957.

HAYMOND, THOMAS SHERWOOD congressman; b. nr. Fairmont, Va. (now W.Va.), Jan. 15, 1794; attended Coll. William and Mary; studied law. Served as pvt. during War of 1812; admitted to Va. bar, 1815, began practice in Morgantown, Va. (now W. Va.); mem. U.S. Ho. of Reps. (Whig) from Va., 31st Congress, Nov. 8, 1849-51; served as brig. gen. Va. Militia; commd. col. Confederate Army, 1861, served throughout Civil War. Died Richmond, Va., Apr. 5, 1869; buried Palatine Cemetery, nr. Fairmont.

HAYNE, ARTHUR PERONNEAU senator, army officer; b. Charleston, S.C., Mar. 12, 1790. Engaged in bus.; served as 1st lt. at Sackets Harbor, during War of 1812, maj. of cavalry on St. Lawrence River, insp. gen., 1814; brevetted lt. col. for gallantry at Battle of New Orleans; admitted to the bar, practiced law; served as comdr. Tenn. Volunteers during Fla. War; ret., 1820; mem. S.C. Ho. of Reps.; Democratic presdl. elector, 1828; U.S. naval agt. in Mediterranean for 5 years; declined Belgian mission; mem. U.S. Senate from S.C., May 11-Dec. 2, 1858. Died Charleston, Jan. 7, 1867; buried St. Michael's Churchyard, Charleston.

HAYNE, ISAAC planter, army officer; b. Colleton Dist., S.C., Sept. 23, 1745; s. Isaac and Sarah (Williamson) H.; m. Elizabeth Hutson, July 18, 1765, 2 children. Planter and breeder of fine horses in S.C., before Am. Revolution; served as capt. Colleton Militia, during Revolutionary War; swore allegiance to Crown after fall of City of Charlston (S.C.), with assurance that mil. service would not be required of him, later ordered to join Brit. Army; considering this a release from his oath of allegiance, joined S.C. Militia, captured Gen. Andrew Williamson. Captured by Col. Nisbet Balfour, July 1781, hung at Charleston, Aug. 4, 1781.

HAYNES, EVAN lawyer; b. St. Louis, Missouri, July 23, 1895; s. Edgar Allan Poe and Cora Idella (Schwinn) H.; A.B., U. of Calif., 1922, J.D., 1924; m. Irene Whitford, July 23, 1928; children-Diana, Duncan. Admitted to Calif. bar, 1924, practiced law in San Francisco with Garret W. McEnerney, 1924-27; teacher Sch. of Jurisprudence, U. of Calif., 1927-29, 1930-35, 1936-42, acting dean, 1941-42; teacher, Columbia Law Sch., 1929-30; practiced law with Brobeck, Phleger & Harrison, 1935-36: head of Compliance Sect.; Office of Price Administrn., Washington, D.C., 1942; regional rent exec., Pacific Coast Region, 1942-43; various posts in Foreign Economic Administration, Washington,

D.C., 1943-44; partner Brobeck, Phleger & Harrison, San Francisco, since 1945. Served as private lt., and capt., 58th Inf., 4th Div., 1917-19. Mem. State Bar of Calif., Am. Bar Assn., Sigma Pi, Phi Alpha Delta. Author: Selection and Tenure of Judges (Nat. Conf. Judicial Councils 1944), articles in legal periodicals. Home: Rt. 1, Box 30, Calistoga, Cal. Office: 111 Sutter St., San Francisco 4. Died Mar. 18, 1955; buried Mountain View Cemetery, Oakland, Cal.

HAYNES, IRA ALLEN ret. army officer; b. in Ky., Sept. 10, 1859; grad.U.S. Mil. Acad., 1883; grad. Arty Sch., 1888. Commd. 2d lt. 3d Arty., 1883; promoted through grades to col. C.A.C., 1912; brig. gen. N.A., 1917; brig. gen., regular army, 1923. Duty with Va. State Militia at Richmond, Va., 1893; at Washington Barracks, D.C., 1893-95; at Honolulu, Hawaii, 1899; comdt. Coast Arty. Sch., 1913-16; apptd. comdr. 64th F.A. Brigade, camp Beauregard, Alexandria, La., 1917; served in France, 1918-19; later comdr. 9th Coast Arty. Dist., San Francisco, retired, 1923. Home: 47 Hamilton Court, Palo Alto, Cal. Died Feb. 25, 1955.*

HAYS, ALEXANDER army officer; b. Franklin, Pa., July 8, 1819; s. Samuel and Agnes (Broadfoot) H.; grad. U.S. Mil. Acad., 1844; m. Annie Adams McFadden, Feb. 19, 1846. Served with U.S. Army on frontier in La. after 1844; brevetted 1st lt. for services at battles of Palo Alto and Resaca-de-la-Palma in Mexican War; resigned commn., 1848; prospected for gold in Cal., 1849-51; engaged in constrn. bus. in Pa., 1851-61; returned to U.S. Army with rank of capt. 16th Inf., 1861; promoted to col. 63d Pa. Regt. in defense of Washington (D.C.), 1861; served in Army of Potomac, 1862-64; brevetted maj. for services at battles of Fair Oaks, Peach Orchard and Glendale (Va.); brevetted lt. col. after Battle of Malvern Hill, 1862; wounded at Battle of Manassas; given command of div., 1863; brevetted col. for conduct in Battle of Gettysburg. Killed on 2d day of Battle of Wilderness, May 5, 1864.

HAYS, CHARLES congressman; b. "Hays Mount" nr. Boligee, Ala., Feb. 2, 1834; attended U. Ga., U. Va. Cotton planter; del. Democratic Nat. Conv., Balt., 1860; served as maj. Confederate Army; mem. Ala. Constl. Conv., 1867; mem. Ala. Senate, 1868; mem. U.S. Ho. of Reps. (Republican) from Ala., 41st-44th congresses, 1869-77. Died "Myrtle Hall," Greene County, Ala., June 24, 1879; buried family cemetery, "Hays Mount."

HAYS, HARRY THOMPSON lawyer, army officer; b. Wilson County, Tenn., Apr. 14, 1820; s. Harmon and Elizabeth (Cage) H.; grad. St. Mary's Coll., Balt.; m. Elizabeth Cage, circa 1859. Served in Mexican War; formed successful legal practice with W.C. Harmon, New Orleans, 1848; del. to Whig Nat. Nominating Conv., 1852, Scott ticket presdl. elector, 1852; commd. col. 7th La. Regt., Army No. Va., 1861; brig. gen., 1862, maj. gen., 1865; sheriff Orleans Parish, 1866. Died New Orleans, Aug. 21, 1876; buried Washington St. Cemetery, New Orleans.

HAYS, JOHN COFFEE army officer; b. Wilson County, Tenn., Jan. 28, 1817; s. Harmon and Elizabeth (Cage) H.; m. Susan Calvert, 1857, 6 children. Went to Tex., 1836; served in Texan Army against Indians and Mexicans, 1836-40; capt. Tex. Rangers, serving in the region between Rio Grande and Nueces rivers, 1840-47; col. Tex. Volunteer Ca., Mexican War; moved to Cal., 1849; sheriff San Francisco County, 1850-53; apptd. surveyor-gen. Cal., 1853; engaged in real estate, banking, indsl. affairs. Died Apr. 28, 1885.

HAYS, SAMUEL congressman; b. County Donegal, Ireland, Sept. 10, 1783. Came to U.S., 1792; treas. Vemango County (Pa.), 1808, sheriff, 1808, 20, 29, 33; mem. Pa. Ho. of Reps., 1813, 16, 23, 25, Pa. Senate, 1822, 39; trustee Allegheny Coll., Meadville, Pa., 1837-61; served as brig. gen. in command 1st Brigade, 7th Div., Pa. Militia, 1841-43; mem. U.S. Ho. of Reps. (Democrat) from Pa., 28th Congress, 1843-45; mfr. of iron, nr. Franklin, Pa.; apptd. U.S. marshal for Western dist. Pa., 1847; asso. judge dist. ct., 1856. Died Franklin, July 1, 1868; buried Old Town Cemetery, Franklin, Reinterred, New Franklin Cemetery.

HAYS, SILAS B. A.R.C. exec.; b. St. Paul, Feb. 18, 1902; s. Willet M. and Ellen B. Hays; B.S., State U. of Ia., 1925. M.D., 1928; m. Marjorie Murtagh, July 19, 1928; children - Ellen, James. Interne, Letterman Gen. Hosp., San Francisco, 1928-29; commd. 1st lt., M.C., U.S. Army, 1929, and advanced through grades to maj. gen., 1952; chief, supply div., Office of Surgeon Gen. U.S. Army, Washington, 1945-50; surgeon Japan Logistic Command, 1950-51; dep. surgeon gen. U.S. Dept. Army 1951-55, surgeon gen. U.S. Army, 1955-59; med. dir. Eastern area Am. Nat. Red Cross, 1959-. Member of Theta Delta Chi, Phi Rho Sigma, Alpha Omega Alpha. Home: 1813 N. Herndon St., Arlington, Va. Office: Am. Nat. Red Cross, 615 N. St. Asaph St., Alexandria, Va. Died July 24, 1964; buried Arlington Nat. Cemetery.

HAZELWOOD, JOHN naval officer; b. Eng., circa 1726; m. Mary Edgar, Aug. 10, 1753; m. 2d, Esther Fleeson. Came to Pa.; in command various mcht. ships; apptd. to Pa. Com. of Safety in constrn. of warships, floating batteries, fire rafts, 1776; supt. fleet of rafts, 1776; commodore Pa. Navy, 1777, full command, 1777, successfully defended fleet against Brit. in Port of Phila.; commr. purchases Continental Army, Phila., 1780; receiver provisions Pa. Militia, 1780; port warden Phila., 1785; owner or part owner vessels engaged in fgn. trade; a founder St. George Soc., Phila. Died Phila., Mar. 1, 1800.

HAZEN, MOSES army officer; b. Haverhill, Mass., June 1, 1733; s. Moses and Abigail (White) H.; m. Charlotte de la Saussaye, Dec. 1770. Served in French and Indian Wars, other Colonial wars, as lt. in expdns. against Crown Point, N.Y., 1756, against Louisbourg, French stronghold on Cape Breton Island, N.S., Can., 1758; with Gen. James Wolfe's expdn. against Quebec, Can., 1759; settled in Que.; British seized his property at outbreak of Revolutionary War because he was suspected of loyalty to colonies, 1776; joined colonial side; formed 2d Canadian Regt. known as Hazen's Own, col., 1776; took part in battles of Brandywine and Germantown with Continental Army under Washington; began constrn. of mil. road to Canadian border, 1779; commd. brig. gen., 1781. Died Troy, N.Y., Feb. 3, 1803.

HAZEN, WILLIAM BABCOCK army officer; b. West Hartford, Vt., Sept. 27, 1830; s. Stillman and Sophrona (Fonno) H.; grad. U.S. Mil. Acad., 1855; m. Mildred McLean, 1 child. Commd. capt. inf. U.S. Army, 1861; col. 41st Ohio Volunteers, 1862, maj. gen., 1865; commanded 15th Corps, Army of Tenn., 1865, comdr. division in Sherman's march to the sea, opened up communications between army and fleet; served at battles of Shiloh, Corinth, Perryville, Stone River, Chickamauga, Chattanooga; commd. col. U.S. Army, 1868, responsible for forcing Custer not to attack friendly Kiowa Indian camp, 1868; mil. observer with German armies in War of 1870; wrote articles in N.Y. papers pointing out corruption in adminstrn. of post-trader system of West and false claims of railroad promoters regarding real value of their land; 1872; chief signal officer U.S. War ept., 1880; organized scientific expdn. under Lt. Greely sent to Layd, ú Lady, ú Franklin's Bay, 1881; reprimanded for criticizing what he felt to be negligent inaction in War Dept. in sending relief expdns. to Ft. Greely, 1885. Died Washington, D.C., Jan. 16, 1887.

HAZEN, WILLIAM LIVINGSTON educator; b. Elizabeth, N.J., May 4, 1861; s. Aaron Coursen and Sarah (Young) H.; A.B., Columbia, 1883, LL.B., 1885; LL.D., Manhattan Coll., N.Y. City, 1933; m. Olive Starr, Oct. 23, 1889; children-Starr (dec.), Eleanor (dec.), Elizabeth Starr (Mrs. Burritt Alden Cushman, Jr.). Began as teacher, 1883; founder Barnard Sch. for Boys, N.Y. City, 1886, and since headmaster; founder Barnard Sch. for Girls, 1896, and since headmaster; founder Camp Iroquois for Boys, Mallett's Bay, Vt., 1899, and since pres.; founder Camp Barnard for Girls, Mallett's Bay, 1902, and since dir. Served as capt. Co. 5, 71st Regt. Inf. N.Y. Vols., Spanish-Am. War, 1898; participated in Santiago campaign. Pres. mem. Schoolmasters Assn. of New York and Vicinity; mem. Country Day Sch. Assn. of U.S., Vets. (Dept. of New York), Soc. of Army of Santiago de Cuba, Phi Gamma Delta (pres. 1889), Phi Delta Phi, Phi Beta Kappa. Awarded Columbia U. Medal for Service, 1933, medal for conspicuous Columbia alumni service, 1938. Republican. Baptist. Clubs: Columbia Univ., Phi Gamma Delta. Home: 440 Riverside Drive. Office: Barnard School for Boys, W. 244th St., New York. Died Apr. 13, 1944; buried, Newton, N.J.

HAZLETT, HARRY FOUTS army officer; b. Deersville, O., Apr. 17, 1884; s. Thomas Bone and Emma Amelia (Fouts) H.; Ph.B., Mt. Union Coll., 1904, LL.D. (hon.), 1944; grad. Inf. Sch., 1926, Comd. and Gen. Staff Sch., 1927, Army War Coll., 1933; m. Ona Estelle Douglass, Aug. 23, 1906; children - Robert Thomas, Paul Frederick, Ruth Emma (Mrs. Russell Lynn Hawkins). Began as athletic dir. and coach, 1906; commd. 1st lt. Ohio N.G., 1904, and advanced through the grades to maj., 1919; commd. maj., Regular Army, July 1, 1920, and advanced through grades to brig. gen., Sept 9, 1942, major gen., Mar. 18, 1943; served with 10th Ohio Inf., 134th Machine Gun Bn., 135th Machine Gun Bn., and div. machine gun officer, 37th Div., 1917-19; chief of staff, Replacement and Sch. Command, Army Ground Forces, 1942-43; command of replacement and school command, Army Ground Forces, Birmingham, Ala., Mar. 1943-June 1946. Comdr. 86th Inf. Div. and Philippine Ground Force Comd. 1946-47; comd. 2d Major Port, Mar.-June 1947; ret. Oct. 1947. Decorated Belgian War Cross, D.S.M. Mem. Sigma Nu. Home: Crestline, Cal. Died Sept. 27, 1960.

HEAD, WALTON O., ins. co. exec.; b. Stephenville, Tex., June 5, 1909; s. William Burres and Lulu Rose (O'Hara) H.; B.A. cum laude, Dartmouth, 1929; LL.B. with highest honors, U. Tex., 1932. Admitted to Tex. bar, 1932; asso. Worsham Rollins, Burford, Ryburn & Hincks, Dallas, 1932-36; with Employers Casualty Co., 1936-72, dir. 1938-72, pres., 1962-72, chmn. bd., 1967-72; with Employers Nat. Inc. Co., 1954-72, dir., 1954-72, pres., 1962-72, chmn. bd., 1967-72; dir. Employers Nat. Life Ins. Co., 1961-72, pres., 1962-72, chmn. bd., 1967-72; with Tex. Employers Ins. Assn., 1936-72, dir., 1956-72, pres., 1962-72, chmn. bd., 1967-72. Served to lt. col. USAAF, 1942-46. Decorated Legion of Merit. Mem. Am. Judicature Soc., Am. Inst. Property and Liability Underwirters, Am., Tex., Dallas bar assns., Internat. Assn. Ins. Counsel. Home: Dallas TX Died June 11, 1972; interred Grove Hill Meml. Park, Dallas TX

HEADLEY, CLEON lawyer; b. Fairmont, Minn., Nov. 14, 1887; s. Charles Wesley and Sara (Sherman) H.; B.S., Beloit (Wis.) Coll., 1909; LL.B., Harvard, 1914; m. Gertrude Knight. Dec. 10, 1917; children-David K., Richard K., Beth. Admitted to N.Y. bar, 1915; asso. Elkus, Gleason & Proskauer, N.Y. City, 1914-16; admitted to Minn. bar, 1917 and since practiced in St. Paul; mem. Morgan, Headley, Raudenbush & Morgan and predecessor firms since 1923. Pres. St. Paul Community Chest, 1943-44; mem. bd. Minn. div. Am. Cancer Soc. Served as capt., U.S. Army Inf., World War I. Mem. Am., Minn. State and Ramsey Co. (pres. 1937-38) bar assns. Clubs: Minnesota, Athletic (St. Paul). Home: 1173 Davern St., St. Paul 5. Office: First Nat. Bank Bldg., St. Paul 1. Died Jan. 1, 1954.

HEALY, DANIEL WARD, JR., educator; b. Bklyn., Oct. 9, 1915; s. Daniel W. and Ada (Owen) H.; B.S., Bowdoin Coll., 1937; M.A., Harvard, 1946, M.E.S., 1948, Ph.D., 1951; m. Barbara Reade, Sept. 2, 1939; children—Michael Reade, Sally Claire. Tchr. pvt. sch., 1937-41; asst. prof. physics and elec. engring. USS Naval Postgrad. Sch., 1946-48; asso. prof. elec. engring. Syracuse U., 1951-58; mem. faculty U. Rochester, 1958-69, prof. elec. engring., chmn. dept., 1958-69. Served to lt. comdr. USNR, 1941-45. Mem. I.E.E.E., Am. Soc. Elec. Engring., Am. Assn. U. Profs., Am. Phys. Soc., Sigma Xi. Home: Victor NY Died Oct. 9, 1969.

HEALY, ROBERT WALLACE soldier; b. Chicago, Oct. 22, 1836; s. Robert and Ann (Wallace) H.; A.B., U. of Notre Dame, Ind., 1859, A.M., 1865, LL.D., 1908; took course Sloan's Commercial Coll., Chicago; entered mercantile life; del. Dem. State Conv., Springfield, Ill., 1869; m. Sarah J. Nolan, Oct. 1, 1862; m. 2d, Jeannette Cooke, Oct. 25, 1899. Enlisted 58th Ill. Inf., Sept. 25, 1861; capt., Dec. 25, 1861; maj., Oct. 20, 1864; lt. col., Apr. 10, 1865; col., Oct. 3, 1865. Bvtd. maj., Mar. 26, 1865, "for faithful and meritorious services during campaign against Mobile"; brig. gen. vols., Mar. 13, 1865, for same during the war; hon. mustered out, April 1, 1866. Served at Ft. Donaldson, Shiloh, Corinth, Iuka, Meridian, on Banks' Red River Expdn. at Ft. DeRussy, Pleasant Hill, Yellow Bayou, etc.: comdg. regt.; also in various engagements in A. J. Smith's campaign against Gen. Forest and Oxford, Miss.; transferred to Mo., serving under Rosecrans against Price; comdg. regt. in battle of Nashville and pursuit of Hood, Dec. 1864; apptd. insp. gen. 2d Div., 16th Army Corps, Mar. 1865; took part in the campaign against Mobile and battle of Blakely, Apr. 9, 1865; returned to command of regt., July 1865, and garrisoned Montgomery, Ala., after Lee's surrender. Cotton planter in Ala. after the war; purchasing agt. Erlanger Syndicate, operating Queen & Crescent system of railroads, until Jan. 1892, when he became pres. Ross-Meehan Foundry Co. U.S. marshal middle and southern judicial dists. of Ala., 1867-77; chmn. Ala. Rep. State Exec. Com., 1872-74; del. Rep. Nat. Conv., 1876; candidate for presdl. elector, 1876. Dir. Carnegie Library; mem. Loyal Legion, Soc. Army of Tenn. Home: Chattanooga, Tenn. Died Nov. 2, 1912.

HEANEY, JOHN WILLIAM lawyer; b. San Francisco, Calif., Jan. 14, 1891; s. William Peter and Mary L. (Hayes) H.; LL.B., University of Calif., 1913; m. Matilde A. Coffield, December 17, 1917 (div.); children-Sally, John William; m. 2d Viola C. Glaister, Jan. 17, 1949. Admitted to California bar, 1913 and practiced in San Francisco, 1913-15 in Santa Barbara since 1915; founder Richards, Carrier & Heaney, now Heaney, Price, Postel & Parma; director First Nat. Trust & Savings Bank. Served in Batt. C, 144th F.A., Sept. 1917; 1st lt. May 1918; capt., Sept. 1918; hon. disch. Dec. 1918. Rep. U.S. Army on Lumber Commodity Com., War Prodn. Bd. Chmn. com. to restore St. Francis Hosp., destroyed in 1925; chmn. advisory com. on restoration Santa Barbara Mission destroyed in 1925. Attended joint meeting British-Canadian-Am. Bar, London, 1924. Mem. Am., Nev. State and Santa Barbara County bar assns., State Bar of Calif., bar of U.S. Supreme Court. Mem. Am. Legion, Phi Alpha Delta. Republican. Clubs: Valley (charter mem.), Santa Barbara, (hon. mem.). Home: 2441 Garden St., Santa Barbara, Cal. Died Aug. 12, 1953; buried Santa Barbara Cemetery.

HEAP, SAMUEL DAVIES diplomat, naval officer; b. Carlisle, Pa., Oct. 8, 1781; s. Judge John and Margaret (Kerr) H.; m. Margaret Porter, 1810, 5 children. Commd. surgeon's mate U.S. Navy, 1804, promoted surgeon, 1808; stationed at New Orleans, Norfolk, Boston, Phila., 1808-17; in charge of hosp. of Am. Mediterranean fleet, 1817-23; chargé d'affaires, Tunis, 1823-24, Am. consul to Tunis, 1824-53. Died Oct. 2, 1853; buried Protestant Cemetery, Tunis.

HEARD, JAMES DELAVAN, physician; b. Pittsburgh, Jan. 9, 1870; s. James B. and Emilie Lucretia (Delavan) H.; Western U. of Pa. 2 yrs.; M.D., U. of Pa., 1891, Sc.D., 1938, post-graduate work, 1891; universities of Leipzig and Vienna, 1892-93; m. Edith van Rensselaer McIlvaine, Dec. 27, 1910. Intern, German Hosp., Phila., 1891-92; asso. prof. medicine,

1910-12, prof. since 1912, U. of Pittsburgh. During the war was lt. col., M.C. U.S. Army in charge med. service. Base Hosp. 27, A.E.F.; col. M.R.C., gen. Hosp. No. 27, 1924. Episcopalian. Mem. A.M.A., Assn. Am. Physicians, Pittsburgh Acad. Medicine, Med. Soc. State of Pa., Biol. Soc. U. of Pittsburgh. Mason (32 deg.). Clubs: University, Pittsburgh Golf (Pittsburgh); Pot and Kettle (Bar Harbor, Me.). Home: 5720 Aylesboro Av., Pittsburgh, Pa.; (summer Bar Harbor, Me.). Office: 121 University Pl.,2Pittsburgh PA

HEARN, CLINT CALVIN army officer; b. Weston, Tex., Mar. 29, 1866; s. Levi A. and Margaret Adelaide (Routh) H.; grad. U.S. Mil. Academy, 1890; Artillery School, 1894, School of Submarine Defense, 1908, Army War College, 1912. General Staff College, 1920; m. Laura Wright Overaker, Dec. 2, 1897. Commd. add 2d lt., 4th Arty., June 12, 1890; promoted through various grades to rank of colonel, May 15, 1917; brig. gen. N.A., Aug. 5, 1917-June 15, 1919; chief of staff Non-Divisional Group, Reserve Units, 3d Corps Area (reorganized reserves), Harrisburg, Pa., Apr. 10, 1922-. Died Feb. 11, 1928.

HEATH, FERRY KIMBALL asst. sec. of Treasury; b. Grand Rapids, Mich., Oct. 23, 1876; s. Lewis Wadsworth and Jane Sophia (Worcester) H.; ed. U. of Mich.; unmarried. Asst. sec. of the Treasury, June 26, 1929-Apr. 17, 1933; became resident partner Harriman & Co., brokers, 1933, later Harriman & Keech. Pvt., U.S. Vol. Inf., Spanish-Am. War; maj., F.A., U.S.A., World War. Republican. Home: Grand Rapids, Mich. Died May 27, 1939.

HEATH, WILLIAM army officer; b. Roxbury, Mass., Mar. 2, 1737; s. Samuel and Elizabeth (Payton) H.; m. Sarah Lockwood, Apr. 19, 1759. Mem. Mass. Gen. Ct., 1761; joined Ancient and Honorable Arty. Co. of Boston, 1765; mem. Mass. Provincial Congress, 1774-75; commd. brig. gen., organized forces at Cambridge before Battle of Bunker Hill, 1774; served as brig. gen. Continental Army under Washington, 1775-76; commd. maj. gen., 1776; in charge of unsuccessful attack on Ft. Independence (N.Y.), 1777; severely reprimanded by Washington, received no more field commands from then until close of war, restricted mainly to staff duty; in command Eastern Mil. Dist., 1777-78, Dist. of Lower Hudson, 1779; mem. Mass. Conv. which ratified U.S. Constn., 1788; mem. Mass. Senate, 1791-92; judge Probate Ct., Norfolk, Mass. 1792; elected lt. gov. Mass. but declined to serve. Died Roxbury, Mass., Jan. 24, 1814.

HEAVEY, JOHN WILLIAM army officer; b. Vandalia, Ill., Feb. 19, 1867; s. Patrick and Susan (Mahan) H.; grad. U.S. Mil. Acad., 1891. Command and Staff Sch., 1912, Army War Coll., 1913, Inf. Sch., 1923; m. Julia Baggette, Apr. 19, 1894; m. 2d, Katherine Theresa Sullivan, Jan. 19, 1915; children-William Francis, Thoams Jackson, Wade Hampton. Commd. 2d lt. Inf., U.S. Army, June 12, 1891, and advanced through grades to col., Aug. 15, 1917; retired with rank of brig. gen., Feb. 28, 1931. Mem. Mil. Order Carabao. Republican. Catholic. Clubs: Army and Navy (Washington); Union League. Penn Athletic (Philadelphia); Army and Navy (Manila). Died Nov. 18, 1941.

HEBERT, PAUL OCTAVE army officer, gov. La.; b. Iberville Parish, La., Dec. 12, 1818; s. Paul Gaston and Mary (Hamilton) H.; grad. Jefferson Coll., 1836, U.S. Mil. Acad., 1840; m. Cora Vaughn, Aug. 2, 1842; m. 2nd Penelope Lynch Andrews, Aug. 3, 1861. Asst. prof. engring. U.S. il. Acad., 1840-42; chief engr. of La., 1845; lt. col. 14th Inf., U.S. Army, participated in all important battles of Mexican War; brevetted col., 1848; mem. La. Constl. Conv., 1852; gov. La., 1852; commd. brig. gen. Confederate Army, 1861; commanded Dept. of Tex., in charge of defenses of Galveston; commanded sub-dist. of North La.; engr. State of La., 1873; commr. and civil engr. of Mississippi levees. Died New Orleans, Aug. 29, 1880; buried Bayou Goula, La.

HECK, NICHOLAS HUNTER hydrog. and geodetic engr.; b. Heckton Mills. Pa., Sept. 1, 1882; s. John Lewis and Mary Frances (Hays) H.; B.A., Lehigh, 1903, C.E., 1904, D.Sc., 1929; D.Sc., Fordham University, New York, N.Y., 1941. With U.S. Coast Survey, 1904-45; in charge wire drag parties, Atlantic Coast, 1906-16, comdr. schooner Mathiess, 1917; lt. and lt. comdr. USNRF, New London, Conn., London, Eng., 1917-19, in charge location of submerged forest in Lake Washington, nr. Seattle, 1919-20; comdr. steamer, Explorer, 1920-21; chief div. geomagnetism and seismology Coast and Geodetic Survey, 1921-42, asst. to dir., 1942-45, ret. 1945. Recipient William Bowie medal, Am. Geophys. Union. 1942. Fellow A.A.A.S., Am. Geog. Soc., Philos. Soc. Washington (pres. 1938), Washington Soc. Engrs., Wash. Acad. Sci., Am. Geophys. Union (chmn. 1935-38), Geol. Soc. Am.; mem. Am. Soc. C.E., Geol. Soc., Washington, Seismol. Soc. Am. (pres. 1936-39), Soc. Am-Mil. Engrs., Internat. Seismol. Assn. (pres. 1936-45), Tau Beta Pi, Phi Beta Kappa, Sigma Xi. Presbyn. Club: Cosmos. Author: Earthquakes; also govt. publs. concerning wire drag and sweep work of Coast and Geodetic Survey; compensation of the magnetic compass; velocity of sound in sea water; radio acoustic method of determining position in hydrography; earthquake history of U.S. and articles relating to magnetism and seismology. Home: 3421 Northampton St., Washington 15. Died Dec. 21, 1953; buried Arlington Nat. Cemetery.

HECKER, FRIEDRICH KARL FRANZ army officer; b. Eichtersheim, Baden, Germany, Sept. 28, 1811; attended U. Heidelberg (Germany); LL.D., U. Munich (Germany); m. Josephine Eisenhardt, 5 children. Practiced law, Mannheim, Germany, 1835-42; mem. 2d Chamber of Baden, 1842-47; expelled from Prussia because he opposed German incorporation of Schleswig-Holstein area, 1845; agitated Germans in Lake Dist. to fight for German Republic which he had proclaimed, defeated by Gen. Von Gagern, 1848, fled to Sweden; came to U.S., 1849, successful farmer in St. Clair County, Ill., 1849-61; enlisted as pvt. under Gen. Sigel, 1861, became col. 24th Ill. Volunteers; led 82d Ill. Volunteers for greater part of war; served in battles of Chattanooga, Missionary Ridge and Chancellorsville; returned to farm, St. Clair County, 1866; active in Liberal Republican Movement of 1872; visited Germany, St. Clair County, Mar. 24, 1881.

HEDGES, BENJAMIN VAN DOREN, assn. exec.; born Plainfield, N.J., June 8, 1907; s. Dr. Benjamin Van Doren and Adele Cutts (Williams) H.; student Loomis Sch., 1922-26; grad. Princeton, 1930; student N.Y. U.; m. Alice-Marian Hecht, Feb. 22, 1947; children—Ann Sportswood, Benjamin Van Doren. Personnel adminstr. Bankers Trust Co., 1920-48; nat. dir., exec. v.p. Big Bros. of Am., Inc., 1948-69. Mem. quota com., nat. budget com. Community Chests and Councils; mem. atty. general's nat. conf. on citizenship; mem. com. individual agencies, ad hoc com. social security Welfare Council N.Y.C. Dir. Plainfield Y.M.C.A., 1931-32. Served as comdr., air combat intelligence, U.S.N.R., 1942-45. Awarded Presdl. Unit Citation, Aircraft Carriers 13 Battle Stars. Mem. Nat. Welfare Assn. (mem. coms.), Nat. Conf. Social Workers, Nat. Soc. Welfare Assembly, Alumni Assn. Loomis Sch. (trustee, past pres.). Presbyn. Clubs: Princeton Cap and Gown, Princeton. Home: New York City NY Died Dec. 1969.

HEFFERAN, THOMAS HUME, lawyer, corp. exec.; b. Grand Rapids, Mich., Nov. 2, 1908; s. George and Ella (Backus) H.; grad. Taft Sch., 1927; A.B., Yale, 1931; LL.B., U. Mich., 1934; m. Constance Howard, Dec. 19, 1942; children—Thomas Howard, Roger Littlefield. Admitted to Mich. bar, 1934; asso. atty. Warner, Norcross & Judd, Grand Rapids, 1934-42; asst. v.p., trust officer Mich. Nat. Bank, Grand Rapids, 1946-51; real estate developer, builder, Spring Lake, Mich., 1952-58; dir. real property mgmt. Dept. Def., Washington, 1958-61; pres. Thomas H. Hefferan & Sons, Inc., Arlington, Va., from 1962; admitted to D.C. bar, 1967. Served from lt. (j.g.) to lt. comdr., USNR, 1942-45. Mem. Am., Mich. bar assns., Zeta Psi, Phi Delta Phi, Episcopalian. Clubs: Yachting of Am., Yale. Home: Alexandria VA Died Mar. 28, 1969.

HEG, ELMER ELLSWORTH physician; b. Waupun, Wis., Feb. 23, 1861; s. Col. Hans C. and Cornelia Elinong (Jacobson) H.; ed. Beloit (Wis.) Coll., 1876-80; M.D., Bellevue Hosp. Med. Coll. (New York U.), 1887; m. May Thornton, of Seattle, Aug. 13, 1890. Removed to Wash., 1888; mem. Wash. State Bd. Health, 1897-98, and 1902-(sec. 1897-98 and 1903-11, and president 1912 and 1916), Seattle Bd. of Health, 1900-02; state commr. of health, Wash., Apr. 3, 1909-Oct. 1, 1911; med. dir. Pulmonary Hospital of Seattle, May, 1909 - . Surgeon Wash. N.G., 1896-98; maj. brigade surgeon U.S. vols., July 8, 1898-May 12, 1899, on staff Maj.-Gen. J. C. Bates in Cuba. U.S. del. 14th Internat. Congress on Hygiene, Berlin, 1907. Mem. A.M.A. (sec. sect. hygiene and sanitary science, 1905-07), Wash. State Med. soc. (sec. 1891-92), King Co. Med. Soc. (pres. 1904-05). Home: Riverton Heights. Office: Cobb Bldg., Seattle, Wash.†

HEILBRUNN, LEWIS VICTOR, biologist; b. Bklyn., Jan. 24, 1892; s. Victor and Matilda (Biedermann) H.: A.B., Cornell U., 1911; Ph.D., U. Chgo., 1914; m. Marion Applebee Kerr, Jan. 13, 1923 (dec.); 1 dau., Constance; m. 2d, Ellen Donovan, June 3, 1932. Asso. in zoology, U. Chgo., 1914-16: instr., U. of Ill., Med. Sch., 1916-17; instr. of zoology, U. of Mich., 1919-21, asst. prof., 1921-29; Guggenheim Meml. Found. fellow, 1927-28; asso. prof. zoology, U. Pa., 1929-43, prof. 1943—. Mem. Nat. Research Council (Div. of Biology and Agriculture), 1935-38; trustee Marine Biol. Lab., Woods Hole, Mass., 1931—. Served as 1st lt. Air Service U.S. Army, 1917-19; later capt., Air Corps Res., 1919-29. Awarded Silver Star with 2 oak leaf clusters. Fellow A.A.A.S.; mem. Am. Soc. Zoologists (v.p. 1932), Am. Soc. Naturalists, Amer. Physiol. Soc., Soc. for Exptl. Biology and Medicine, Soc. Gen. Physiologists (pres., 1946). Author: The Colloid Chemistry of Protoplasm, 1928: An Outline of General Physiology, 1937; 2d ed., 1943. Former mng. editor Protoplasm monographs; mem. editorial bd. Physiol. Zoology. Address: Zool. Laboratory, Univ. of Pa., Phila. 4. Died Oct. 1959.

HEILEMAN, FRANK A. aircraft corp. exec.; b. St. Louis, Mar. 13, 1891; s. August and Emily (Meis) H.; B.S. in Mech. Engring., U. Mo., 1914; grad. Command and Gen. Staff Sch., 1931, Army War Coll., 1940; m. Margaret Armel Hawkins, Dec. 25, 1919; 1 dau., Margaret Frances (Mrs. George Mayo, Jr.). Commd. 2d lt., inf., U.S. Army, 1917, advanced through grades to maj. gen., 1945; transferred Engr. Corps, 1923, Gen. Staff Corps, 1940; dir. supply ASF, 1943; asst. chief staff G-4, Army Forces Western Pacific, 1945; asst. chief transportation Dept. Army, 1947, chief transportation, 1948-53; ret., 1953; dir. advanced research, mem. bd. dirs. Hiller Helicopters, Palo Alto, Cal. (now Hiller Aircraft Corp.). Decorated D.S.M., Legion of Merit, Bronze Star medal. Mem. Am. Soc. Mil. Engrs., Am. Helicopter Soc., Nat. Def. Transportation Assn., Acacia, Tau Beta Pi. Episcopalian. Mason. Home: 19 Vernon Terrace, Alexandria, Va. Office: 1350 Willow Rd., Palo Alto, Cal. Died Sept. 24, 1961; buried Arlington Nat. Cemetery.

HEIMANN, HENRY HERMAN exec. mgr. Nat. Assn. of Credit Men; b. Aviston, Ill., Sept. 26, 1891; s. Bernard Henry and Mary Ann (Peek) H.; student St. Mary's (Kan.) Acad., 1905-08; LL.B., St. Louis U., 1914; m. Florentine Catherine Giller, July 25, 1915; children-Olivia Martha, Henry Herman (dec.). Began as an accountant, 1915; auditor Kawneer Co., 1917-19, asst. treas. and credit mgr., 1919-21, treas., 1921-27, v.p. same, and 4 affiliated cos., 1927-31; exec. mgr. Nat. Assn. of Credit Research Foundation. Chmn. safety bd., Niles, Mich.; chmn. Dem. State Com. of Mich., 1928-30; del. Dem. Nat. Conv., Houston, Tex., 1928, Chicago, Ill., 1932; mem. exec com. of Business Advisory and Planning Council for U.S. Dept. of Commerce; vice-chmn. industrial com. NRA; dir. U.S. Shipping Bd., Jan. 1-June 1, 1934. Capt. U.S.N.R. Chmn. Com. of Causes and Remedies Accident Prevention Conf., Natural Business Year Council; pres. The Service Corp. of Nat. Assn. of Credit Men. Chmn. bd. Citizens Com. for Army, Navy and Air Force, Inc., Democrat. Catholic. Clubs: Rotary, Union League (New York); Wykagyl Country (New Rochelle): Orchard Hills Country; Piping Rock Locust Valley, L.I.); Bohemian (San Francisco). Author: America's Balance Sheet; numerous mag. articles. Home: 1219 Cedar St., Niles, Mich. Office: 229 4th Av., N.Y.C. Died Sept. 12, 1958; buried Silver Brook Cemetery, Niles.

HEIN, OTTO LOUIS author, army officer; b. Georgetown, D.C., May 1, 1847; s. Charles Samuel Frederick Ernest and Henrietta Sara (Simpson) H.; student Georgetown Coll., D.C.; grad. U.S. Mil. Acad., 1870; m. Sallie Lee Ross, of Washington, D.C., May 3, 1883; children - Herbert Ross, Celeste Marie (Mrs. Lewis M. Adams). Commd. 2d lt. 1st Cav., June 15, 1870; promoted through grades to lt. col., Aug. 5, 1903; retired, July 28, 1904. Active duty against hostile Indians; recommended for bvt. by Gen. Crook, "for gallant conduct" in campaign against Tonto Apaches, 1873 and 1875; instr. tactics U.S. Mil. Acad., 1874-79; mil. attaché, U.S. Legation, Vienna, Austria, 1889-94; comdt. cadets, West Point, 1897-1901. Mem. Assn. Graduates U.S. Mil. Acad., U.S. Cav. Assn., Order Indian Wars of U.S., Order of Caraboa, Order of Foreign Wars. Catholic. Author: Memories of Long Ago, 1925. Home: 752 S. Mariposa Av., Los Angeles, Calif.†

HEINTZELMAN, SAMUEL PETER soldier; b. Manheim, Pa., Sept. 30, 1805; s. Peter and Ann (Grubb) H.; grad. U.S. Mil. Acad., 1826; m. Margaret Stewart, Dec. 5, 1844. Commd. capt. U.S. Army, 1838; served in battles of Pasolos Ovejas, Huamantla and Atexco in Mexican War, 1846-48; brevetted maj., 1847; promoted to maj. 1st Inf., in Cal., 1855; founder Ft. Yuma (Ariz.); commd. col. 17th Inf., 1861, brig. gen. U.S. Volunteers, 1861; commanded 3rd Div., U.S. Army under Gen. Irvin McDowell at 1st Battle of Bull Run; commanded III Corps. right wing of army under Gen. John Pope, 2d Battle of Bull Run, 1862; took part in Peninsula campaign, battles of Malvern Hill and Seven Days; promoted maj. gen. U.S. Volunteers, 1862, participated in battles of Williamsburg, Seven Pines and Fair Oaks assigned to defenses of Washington, D.C., 1862-63; sent to command No. (Central) States Dept., 1864; command 17th Inf. in Tex., 1865-69; promoted gen., ret. 1869. Died Washington, D.C., May 1, 1880.

HEINTZELMAN, STUART army officer; b. N.Y. City, Nov. 19, 1876; s. C. S. (U.S. Army) and Emily (Bailey) H.; g.s. of S. P. Heintzelman (U.S. Army); grad. U.S. Mil. Acad., 1899; honor grad. Inf. and Cav. Sch., 1905; grad. Army Staff Coll., 1906, Army War Coll., 1920; hon. M.A., Princeton, 1917; m. Rubey Bowling, Mar. 14, 1910. Commd. 2d lt. cav., Feb. 15, 1899; promoted through grades to brig. gen., Dec. 29, 1922; major general, Dec. 1, 1931. Served in Nat. Army as lt. col., col. and brig. gen., World War. In Philippines, 1900-02, 1907-09; China Relief Expdn., 1900; instr. Army Service Schs., 1909-12, 1914-16; instr. Princeton Univ., 1916-17; arrived in France, July, 1917; operation sect., G.H.Q., until Jan., 1918 chief of operation, 1st Corps, to June, 1918; chief of staff, 4th Corps, to Sept. 1918; chief of staff, 2d Army, until demobilized, Apr. 1919; returned to U.S. July, 1919; dir. Army War Coll., 1919; asst. chief of staff, 1921-24; comdt. Command and Gen. Staff Sch., Ft. Leavenworth, Kan., 1929-35. Holder of Philippine, China, Mexican border and Victory campaign badges; awarded D.S.M.; Croix de Guerre with Palm, and Comdr. Legion of Honor (France); Comdr. Order of Crown (Italy). Died July 6, 1935.

HEISEN, AARON JONAH, physician; b. Huntington, W.Va., 1917; M.D., U. Pa., 1942, postgrad., 1951-52. Intern, Fitkin Meml. Hosp., Neptune, N.J., 1942-43, med. resident, 1943-44; fellow cardiology Grad. Hosp. U. Pa.; asso. cardiologist, Mercer Hosp., Trenton, N.J., 1954-70, attending in med., 1960-70, dir. out patient dept. also chmn. internship and ednl. com., 1963-69, pres. med. staff, 1969-70. Served to capt. M.C. AUS, 1944-46. Diplomate Am. Bd. Internal Medicine. Fellow A.M.A., Am. Heart Assn., A.C.P.; mem. Aero. Med. Assn., Flying Physicians Assn., FAA Aviation Med. Examiners. Home: Trenton NJ Died Dec. 24, 1970.

HEISS, GERSON KIRKLAND, govt. ofcl; b. Timmonsville, S.C., Sept. 18, 1896; s. Samuel and Lillie (Welch) H.; grad. Porter Mil. Acad., Charleston, 1912; B.S. Clemson (S.C.) A. and M. College, 1916; grad. Army Indsl. Coll., 1938; m. Anna M. Milchsack, July 14, 1918; children—Gerson Kirkland, Elizabeth Ann. Chem. and ins. with British Ministry of Munitions, U.S.A., 1916-19; supt. Apex Chemical Co., 1919-21; asso. chemist, Piccatinny Arsenal, 1921-22; served with U.S. Army since 1923, beginning as 2d lt., Ordnance dept., promoted through the grades to brigadier general, Jan. 1946. Awarded D.S.M., U.S. Legion of Merit with Oak Leaf Cluster, Commendation ribbon with two Oak Leaf Clusters. Mem. Army Ordnance Assn., Washington, D.C., Clemson Coll. Alumni Assn. (Washington chapter); Clemson Iptay Club. Mason. Home: Largo FL Died Jan. 1971.

HEISTAND, HENRY OLCOT SHELDON army officer; b. on farm nr. Richmond, O., Apr. 30, 1856; s. Henry Olcot Sheldon and Lavina (Irwin) H.; grad. U.S. Mil. Acad., 1878; m. Mary J. Rippey, Sept. 19, 1878. Additional 2d lt. 11th Inf., June 14, 1878; 2d lt., June 28, 1878; 1st lt., June 1, 1886; capt., Mar. 19, 1891; maj. asst. adj. gen., Sept. 11, 1897; lt. col., Apr. 28, 1900; col. asst. adj. gen., July 22, 1902; col. adj. gen., Mar. 5, 1907. Apptd. govt. insp. and instr. Ohio N.G., May 19, 1892; confidential sec. to Maj. McKinley during presdl. campaign, 1896; a.d.c. to President McKinley, 1897-1900; U.S. mil. commr., Paris Expn., 1900; adj. gen. and chief of staff, China Relief Expn. for relief of Peking, 1900; adj. gen. Div. of the Philippines until Oct. 1902, Dept. of the East to Dec. 1909, Div. Philippines to Feb. 15, 1912; on duty in office of adj. gen. of the army, Feb., 1912-Dec., 1914; adj. gen. Central Dept., Chicago, Dec., 1914-Sept., 1917; adj. gen. Camp Grant, Rockford, Ill., and 86th Div., Sept. 1917-Apr. 3, 1918; dept. adjt. Central Dept., Chicago, Apr. 3, 1918-Apr. 30, 1919, Eastern Dept., Governors Island, N.Y., May 1, 1919-. Home: Richwood, O. Died Aug. 8, 1924.

HEITMAN, CHARLES EASTON b. McLean County, Ky., Nov. 12, 1874; s. John and Isabel (Moore) H.; ed. pub. schs.; studies law; C.S.B., Mass. Metaphysical Coll., Boston, 1923: m. Mary Elizabeth Sproul. Dec. 1, 1906. Hudson-Fulton commr. 1909: financial editor Cassiers Mag., New York, 1910-13; mem. N.Y. City Real Estate Bd., 1911-23; first reader, 2d Ch. of Christ. Scientiest, N.Y. City, 1918-21; mem. Christian Science Com. on Publication, State of N.Y., 1922-26: pres. The Mother Ch. Boston, 1923-24 asso. editor Christian Science Monitor, 1926-27: former mem. editorial bd., Christian Science Monitor, and mgr. Christian Science Publishing Soc., now dir. The Mother Church, 1st Ch. of Christ, Scientist, Boston. Trustee Gifts and Endowments Fund of the Mother Ch., 1926-27. Served as corporal 1st Vol. Cav., U.S. Army (Roosevelt's Rough Riders), Spanish-American War. Mem. Am. Arbitration Soc. (trustee), Columbia Univ. Acad. Polit. Science. Republican. Mason (32ff, K.T.). Clubs: University (Boston): Bankers (New York); National Press (Washington). Home: 8 W. Cedar St. Office: 107 Falmouth St., Boston, Mas

HEIZMANN, CHARLES LAWRENCE army officer; b. in Pa., Apr. 15, 1846; A.B., Georgetown Univ., 1864; M.D., Univ. of Pa., 1867. Apptd. from Pa. asst. surgeon U.S.A., May 14, 1867; capt. asst. surgeon, May 14, 1870; maj. surgeon, Nov. 18, 1886; lt. col. deputy surgeon-gen., Apr. 28, 1900; col. asst. surgeon-gen., Apr. 7, 1902. Pres. Army Med. Sch., Washington, 1904. Address: War Dept., Washington.

HELLER, EDWARD HELLMAN corp. exec.; b. San Francisco, Calif., Mar. 15, 1900; s. Emanuel S. and Clara (Hellman) H.; grad. U. of Calif., Class of 1921; student Harvard Law Sch., 1921-23; m. Elinor Raas, lMay 26, 1925; children - Clarence E., Alfred E., Elizabeth. With Wells Fargo Bank & Union Trust Co., 1924-25, partner, Schwabacher & Co., San Francisco, 1925-; dir. Permanente Cement Co., Siegler Corporation, Pacific Industries, Incorporated, State Guaranty Corp., Riches Research, Inc., U.S. Leasing Corp., Allied Properties, Pacific Intermountain Express Company, Raychem Corporation, Quinn River-Sonora Co. Regent U. Cal. Mem. Surplus Property Bd., Wash., 1945; adv. bd. Hoover Inst. War, Revolution and Peace, Stanford U., 1956-. Served with U.S. Army, World War I; commd. maj. finance dept., 1942, lt. col., 1943, inactive status, 1944-. Vice chmn. Cal. Commn. Golden Gate Internat. Expn., 1939-40. Chmn. War Finance Com. No. Cal., 1941-42. Mem. Security Analysts San Francisco, World Affairs Council No. Cal. Clubs: Olympic, Stock Exchange, Commonwealth (San Francisco); Palo Alto (Cal.). Home: 99 Faxon Rd., Atherton, Cal. Office: 100 Montgomery St., San Francisco. Died Dec. 18, 1961.

HELLER, JOSEPH MILTON M.D., surgeon; retired; b. Staunton, Va., Jan. 29, 1872; s. Jonas and Pauline (Frank) H.; prep. edn., Emerson Inst., Washington, D.C.; M.D., Georgetown U., 1896; post-grad. study, New York Polyclinic Sch. and Hosp.; m. Renee V. Manning, Mar. 31, 1923. Demonstrator of anatomy, Georgetown Med. Sch., 1896-98; in pvt. practice, Washington, 1903-17; mem. dispensary staff, Emergency and Garfield hosps., Washington, 1896-98; prof. tropical medicine, George Washington U. Med. Sch., 1904-10. First volunteer accepted for Spanish-Am. War; apptd. asst. surg. U.S. Army, Apr. 18, 1898; served as surg. 3d Cav., P.I., 1899; detailed regtl. surgeon 5th Cav., 1901; commd. major and surgeon by President McKinley; in charge water supply, Manila, during cholera epidemic, 1902 (commended by William Howard Taft, then gov. gen. of Philippines; post surgeon Governor's Island, N.Y.; commd. maj. M.R.C., U.S. Army, May 11, 1917; served as div. sanitary inspector and acting chief surgeon, 90th Div., later comdg. officer Base Hosp., Ft. Riley, Kan., Gen. Hosp. No. 23, Hot Springs, N.C., and No. 22, Phila, Pa.; lt. col. Med. Corps, U.S. Army, 1918-22; col. Med. R.C. Participated in Gen. Lawton's advance in Northern Luzon and was surgeon of Maj. Batchelor's "Lost Battalion." Recommended for Congl. Medal of Honor, 1915. Fellow A.M.A., Am. Coll. Physicians; mem. Med. Soc. D.C., Assn. Mil. Surgeons U.S. Army, Internat. Med. Club, Assn. Oldest Inhabitants (D.C.), Mil. Order Foreign Wars (surgeon 1917-23), Naval and Mil. Order of Spanish-Am. War. Mil. Order of the Carabao (nat. comdr. 1929; nat. sec. since 1910), Mil. Order World War (surgeon gen. since 1938, Assn. War Surgeons, Am. Legion, United Spanish War Veterans. Received citation and silver star, War Dept., for attending wounded under fire, Battle of Naguilan, Northern Luzon, Feb. 7, 1899. Mason. Clubs: Army and Navy, Nat. Sojourners, Nat. Press, Alfalfa, Congressional Country, Army Navy Country. Address: 1028 Connecticut Av. N.W., Washington, D.C. Died Oct. 11, 1943.

HELMICK, ELI ALVA army officer; b. in Ind., Sept. 27, 1863; s. Hiram T. and Matilda Ann Helmick; graduate U.S. Military Academy, 1888; grad. Army Sch. of the Line, 1909; Army War Coll., 1910; LL.D., Kan. State Agrl. Coll.; m. Elizabeth Allen Clarke, Nov. 20, 1889; children-Charles Gardiner, Florence (Mrs. John Macaulay), George Randall, Apptd. add. 2d lt. 11th Inf., June 11, 1888; promoted through grades to brig. gen. Mar. 5, 1921. Duty in Idaho during Coeur d'Alene riots, Sept.-Nov. 1892; at Chicago Expn., 1893; duty Hillsdale (Mich.) Coll., 1894-96; participated in expdn. at Santiago de Cuba, 1898; comd. Ft. Reno, Okla., 1898-99; provost marshal and insp. rural guard of Cuba, 1900-01; comd. Puerto Princessa, P.I., 1901-02; comd. prov. batln. against Moros, in Mindanao, 1902; recruiting, Springfield, Mass., 1903-06; comd. Fort Liscum, Alaska, 1906-07; on Mexican border, 1910-11; insp. gen., 1911-14; comdg. bn. 17th Inf., 1914-15; comdg. troops, Donna, Tex., on Mexican patrol, 1915-16; duty Insp. Gen.'s Dept., as lt. col., col. and brig. gen. (temp.), Aug. 26, 1918-Sept. 30, 1919, comdg. 8th Div., Sept.-Nov. 1918, comdg. Base Sect. 5, Service of supplies, at Brest, France, Nov. 23, 1918-Aug. 24, 1919; detailed to General Staff and chief of staff, Central Dept., Aug. 22, 1919-May 10, 1921; apptd. insp. gen. of the Army, rank of maj. gen., Nov. 7, 1921, reapptd. insp. gen. Nov. 7, 1925; retired Sept. 27, 1927. Awarded D.S.M. Home: 2746 Ferdinand Av., Honolulu, T.H. Died Jan. 13, 1945; buried in Arlington National Cemetery.

HELMSLEY, WILLIAM Continental congressman; b. Clover Fields Farm nr. Queenstown, Md., 1737; Engaged in planting; provincial treas. of Eastern Shore (Md.), 1773; surveyor Talbot County (Md.); col. 20th Battalion, Queen Annes County Militia, 1777; justice of peace Queen Annes County, 1777; mem. Md. Senate, 1779-81, 86, 90, 1880; Mem. Continental Congress from Md., 1782-84. Died Queen Annes County, June 5, 1812; buried Clover Fields Farm Cemetery.

HEMINGWAY, ALLAN, physiologist, biophysicist; B. Leeds, Eng., Jan. 25, 1902; s. Arthur and Eleanor (Eastwood) H.; B.A., U. B.C., 1925; Ph.D., U. Minn., 1929; Sterling fellow, Yale, 1936-37; m. Gayle Shirey, Nov. 9, 1929, (dec.); 1 dau., Eleanor; m. 2d Claire Conklin Carr, July 5, 1951. Instr., asst. prof. physiol. chemistry U. Minn., 1930-36, asst. prof., asso. prof. physiology, 1936-48, prof. physiology 1948-51; prof. physiology Med. Sch., U. Cal. at Los Angeles, 1951-72; chief cardiopulmonary lab. San Fernando VA Hosp. (Cal.). Served as maj. USAAF, 1943-45; chief lab. biophysics Sch. Aviation Med., Randolph Field, Tex., 1942-45. Mem. Am. Physiol. Soc., Am. Phys. Soc., Am. Chem. Soc., Soc. Exptl. Biology and Medicine, Am. Assn. U. Profs., Sigma Xi, Gamma Alpha, Phi Beta Pi. Contbr. articles to physiol. and biochem. jours. Home: Los Angeles CA Died Apr. 22, 1972.

HEMINGWAY, ERNEST author; b. Oak Park, Ill., July 21, 1899; s. Clarence Edmonds and Grace (Hall) H.; ed. pub. schs.; m. Hadley Richardson, Sept. 3, 1921; 1 son, John; m. 2d, Pauline Pfeiffer, 1926; children - Patrick, Gregory; m. 3d, Martha Gellhorn, 1940; m. 4th, Mary Welsh, Mar. 21, 1946. Author: Three Stories and Ten Poems, 1923; In Our Time, 1924; The Torrents of Spring, 1926; The Sun Also Rises, 1926; Men Without Women, 1927; A Farwell to Arms, 1929; Death in the Afternoon, 1932; Winner Take Nothing, 1933; Green Hills of Africa, 1935; To Have and Have Not, 1937; The Fifth Column and the First Forty-Nine, 1938; Spanish Earth, 1938; For Whom the Bell Tolls, 1940; Across the River and Into the Trees, 1950; The Old Man and the Sea (Scribners), 1952. Contributor leading magazines. Covered Spanish Civil War for North American Newspaper Alliance, 1937, 1938; war corr. China, 1941; war corr. E.T.O. and Western Front, 1944, 1945 accredited R.A.F.; Third U.S. Army; Fourth U.S. Infantry Division. Decorated Medalia D'Argento Al Valore Militare, Croce de Guerra (2), Bronze Star Orden de Carlos Manuel de Cespedes (Cuban) and others. Recipient Pultizer Price in fiction, 1953, Nobel Prize in Literature, 1954. Hon. Game Warden, Kenya, 1953. Clubs: Gun, Vedado Tennis. Home: San Francisco de Paula, Cuba. Died July 2, 1961.

HEMLEY, SAMUEL, educator; b. N.Y.C., Feb. 8, 1898; s. David and Hannah (Brunner) H.; D.D.S., Columbia, 1918; m. Clara Bernstein, Nov. 24, 1920. Asst. oral surgery Vanderbilt Clinic, Columbia, 1919-25; asst. surgeon L.I. Coll. Hosp., 1924-26; instr. orthodontics coll. dentistry, N.Y.U., 1929-33, asst. prof., chmn. dept. orthodontics, 1933-34, asso. prof., 1934-37, prof., chmn. dept., 1947-66. Served with U.S. Army, 1918, as lt. comdr. USNR, 1936-51. Diplomate Am. Bd. Orthodontics. Mem. Northeastern Soc. Orthodontists, Research Soc. Am. Fellow A.A.A.S., American Coll. Dentistry, Am. Assn. Orthodontics, Internat. Assn. Dental Research, N.Y. Acad. Scis.; mem. Am. Dental Assn., Omicron Kappa Upsilon. Author: Fundamentals of Occlusion, 1944; Orthodontic Theory and Practice, 1953; Myths in Science; A Text on Orthodontics. Contbr. articles profl. jours. Home: Lake George NY Died Aug. 29, 1970; buried Mt. Ararat Cemetery, Farmingdale NY

HEMPHILL, JOSEPH NEWTON rear admiral; b. Ripley, O., June 18, 1847; s. Samuel and Sarah (Campbell) H.; entered U.S. naval acad., Sept. 1862; cruised after Alabama, summer of 1863; grad. June 1866; m. Oro E. Stark, Dec. 1873 (died, Oct. 1886); m. 2d, Mrs. Dora A. Hancock, of Dubuque, Ia., Aug. 1893. Was on the Monongahela, wrecked in W. Indian earthquake Nov. 1867; promoted ensign, Mar. 12, 1868; master, Mar. 26, 1869; lt., Mar. 21, 1870; lt. comdr., Jan. 26, 1887; comdr., June 1895; capt., Mar. 3, 1901; rear admiral, Aug. 6, 1906. At Manila during Philippine outbreak and at Venezuela during the Andrade-Castro revolution; comdg. Kearsarge and chief of staff of North Atlantic Fleet, 1902-04; capt. New York Navy Yard, 1904-06: pres.Bd. of Inspection and Survey, 1906-07; comdg. Asiatic sta. and fleet, 1907-08; pres. Naval Examining and Retiring Boards, 1908-09; retired, June 18, 1909. Died July 8, 1931.

HENCH, PHILIP SHOWALTER physician; b. Pitts., Feb. 28, 1896; s. Jacob Bixler and Clara John (Showalter) H.; A.B., Lafayette Coll., 1916, Sc.D., 1940; M.D., U. Pitts., 1920, Sc.D., 1951; post grad. study U. Freiburg and Ludwig-Maximilians-Universitat, Munich, 1928-29; M.S. in Internal Medicine, U. lfinn., 1931; Sc.D., Lafayette Coll., 1940, Washington and Jefferson Coll., 1940, Western Res. U., Nat. U. Ireland, 1950, University of Pittsburgh, 1951; LL.D., Middlebury (Vt.) Coll., 1951; m. Mary Genevieve Kahler, July 14, 1927; children - Mary Showalter, Philip Kahler, Susan Kahler, John Bixler. Intern. St. Francis Hosp., Pitts., 1920-21; with Mayo Found., Mayo Clinics, Grad. Sch., U. Minn., 1921-; cons., head sect. rheumatic diseases, Mayo Clinic, 1926-; prof. medicine Mayo Found. and Grad. School, University of Minnesota, 1947-. Vice president Kahler Corporation, Rochester, Minn. Chmn. arthritis and rheumatism study sect. Nat. Insts. of Health, U.S.P.H.S., 1949-50; mem. adv. council Nat. Inst. Arthritis and Metabolic Diseases, U.S.P.H.S., 1950-53; mem. med. and sci. com. Arthritis and Rheumatism Found.; mem. adv. com. Nat. Research Council. Vice pres. bd. mgrs. Walter Reed Meml. Assn. Chmn. Am. com. of Ligue Internat. Contre le Rheumatisme; titulate to Central Com. of Pan. Am. League Against Rheumatism. Recipient Heberden Medal (London), 1942, spl. citation Am. Rheumatism Assn., 1951, Pa. Ambassador award Pa. State C. of C., 1951, Northwestern U. Centennial award, 1951; recipient (with Edward C. Kendall, Ph.D.) Lasker award Am. Pub. Health Assn., 1949, Page One award Newspaper Guild of N.Y. (for discovery and development of cortisone), 1950, Passano Found. award, 1950.n, Award of Merit of Masonic Found. Med. Research and Human Welfare, 1951, Criss Award, 1951, spl. citation from Regents of U. Minn., 1951; recipient (with Prof. George Thorn, Harvard) scientific award Am. Pharm. Mfrs. Assn., 1950; recipient (with E. C. Kendall and Tadeus Reichstein) Nobel prize for physiology and medicine, 1950, honor award Miss. Valley Med., Soc., 1952; decorated Order of Carlos Finlay, Orden Nacional de Merito Carlos Manuel de Cespedes (Cuba). Served with Med. Enlisted Res. Corps, 1917-19; from lt. col. to col., AUS, 1942-46; on active duty, expert civilian cons. to surgeon gen. U.S. Army, 1946-. Fellow A.M.A., A.C.P.; mem. internat., nat., state and local profl. socs. and assns.; fgn. mem.

of foreign corr. Several profl. assns. Republican. Presbyn. Chief editor Am. Rheumatism Reviews (Am. Rheumatism Assn.), 1932-48; asso. editor Annals of Rheumatic Diseases (London). Contbr. about 200 articles to med. jours. Home: 517 Fourth St. S.W. Address: Mayo Clinic, Rochester, Minn. Died Mar. 30, 1965; buried Oakwood Cemetery Rochester.

HENDEE, GEORGE ELLSWORTH rear admiral: b. Roxbury, Mass., June 30, 1841; s. Charles J. and Adeline (Davis) H.; ed. pub. and pvt. schs.; m. Elsie S. Lewis, Apr. 21, 1870. Entered U.S.N. as paymaster's clerk, Oct.10, 1861; promoted asst. p.m., Mar. 25, 1864; passed asst. p.m., July 26, 1866; p.m., Feb. 21, 1869: pay dir., Sept. 1, 1899; retired, June 30, 1902, with rank of rear admiral. Served in U.S.S. Brandywine, Pinola, Ossipee, Richmond, Saranac, Independence, and Philadelphia. Home: Brookline, Mass. Died Sept. 10, 1916.

HENDERSON, ALEXANDER ISELIN lawyer; born New York, New York, May 11, 1892; s. Edward Cairns and Helen (Iselin) H.; A.B., Harvard Coll., 1913; student Trinity Coll., Cambridge, Eng., 1912-13; LL.B., cum laude, Harvard Law School, 1916; m. Priscilla Alden Bartlett, June 2, 1922. Partner, Cravath, Swaine & Moore. Asso. with Nat. Defense Adv. Council, Office Prodn. Management, 1940-41; dir. Materials Div., W.P.B., 1942; gen. counsel ECA, 1948-49; dir. Vis. Nurse Services, N.Y., Am. Field Service, Inc. Former trustee Smith Coll. Served as 1st lt. to captain 7th F.A., 1st Division, A.E.F., colonel to A.U.S., 1942-45. Awarded Legion of Merit, Croix de Guerre, Fourragére. Member American, N.Y. State, N.Y. County and New York City bar assns. Clubs: Century, University (New York); Metropolitan (Washington); Piping Rock. Office: Cravath, Swaine & Moore, 15 Broad St., N.Y.C. 5. Died July 22, 1961.

HENDERSON, EDWARD, physician; b. Hendersonville, N.C., Dec. 16, 1896; s. Edward Everett and Muriel Lee (Bell) H.; M.B., B.Chir., M.D., Glasgow U., 1922; Ph.D., Oxford U., 1932; postgrad. Yale, 1937-38; diploma tropical medicine, Tulane U., 1944; m. Kathryn Silverthorne, 1944; children—Edward Bell, Susan Lee (Mrs. Catani). Intern Royal Infirmary, 1922-23; med. officer sci. expdns. Malay archipelago, 1927, China, India, 1929, Central Africa, 1935, Amazon region, 1938-39; med. research div. Schering Corp., Bloomfield, N.J., 1939-62, sec., 1940-52, v.p., 1952-62, dir., 1940-43, dir. div. clin. research, 1945-62; cons. tropical medicine Med. Soc. N.J., 1945; research cons. Mound Park Hosp. Found., St. Petersburg, Fla., from 1955; pres. Ellis Bell & Co., Inc., N.Y.C., from 1967, Bansen, Inc., N.Y.C., from 1967, Henderson Safety Closure Co., Inc., N.Y.C., from 1969; chmn. bd. Elbesa Ltd., London, Eng., from 1970. Bd. dirs. Liberian Inst., Am. Found. Tropical Medicine, 1951; trustee Aging Research Inst., Inc., from 1953, pres., from 1953; pres. Pneumonia Research Found., from 1969. Served as lt., inf., U.S. Army, 1917, capt. Intelligence Corps, 1918. Recipient Willard O. Thompson award, 1961; Malford W. Thewlis gold medal award, 1967. Mem. Internat. Soc. Tropical Dermatology, Pan Am. Med. Assn. (pres. sect. geriatrics and gerontology from 1967), A.A.A.S., Am. Soc. Tropical Medicine, Endocrine Soc., Gerontological Soc., Am. Geriatrics Soc. (dir. from 1952, pres. 1955, editor-in-chief jour. from 1954, exec. dir. from 1962), Am., N.J. rheumatism assns., Assn. Med. Dirs. (pres. 1949-50), N.Y. Acad. Scis. Clubs: New York Athletic; Graduates (New Haven); Columbia University (N.Y.C.). Author: Sixteenth Century Literature and Its Influence on Modern Civilization, 1932; Disorders of Calcium Metabolism, 1952; Section on Cholera, Clinical Tropical Medicine, Gradwohl, Benitex Soto, Felsenfeld, 1951. Contbr. articles sci. jours. patentee chemistry, sci. instruments, safety devices. Home: New York City NY Died Jan. 5, 1973; buried Mill Hill, London England

HENDERSON, ELMER LEE surgeon; b. Garnettsville, Ky., Mar. 23, 1885; s. Jonas and Henrietta (Lewis) H.; M.D., U. Louisville, 1909; m. Laura Bell Owen, April 4, 1911; children-William Owen, Henrietta Marie. In practice of gen. surgery, Louisville, 1911—; mem. staff Ky. Bapt. Hosp., St. Joseph Infirmary; mem. cons. staff S. S. Mary and Elizabeth Hosp.; courtesy staff all other pvt. hosps., Louisville; spl. surg. cons. to air surgeon's office. U.S. Army, 1942—. Chmn. 5th Service Command Com. Procurement and Assignment Service for Physicians, Dentists and Vets., 1942-46. Served from lt. to maj., M.C., World War I; with AEF, 9 mos.; lt. col. Med. R.C., 1919-20. Mem. bd. overseers U. Louisville. Mem. mission to Japan to make survey and recommendations on Social Security, med. edn., med. service, 1948. Mem. bd. govs. Kosair Crippled Children's Hosp.; bd. trustees Nat. Soc. Crippled Children and Adults. Diplomate Am. Bd. Surgery. Hon. fellow Societe Piedmontese Di Chirurgia, Internat. Coll. Surgeons, Japanese Med. Assn.: fellow A.C.S.; mem. Southeastern Surg. Cong. (pres. 1946-47, mem. exec. com., 1947—), So. Med. Assn. (councillor from Ky., 1938-42; chmn. surg. sect. 1942-44; pres. 1946-47; trustee, 1947—), A.M.A. (bd. trustees, 1938—, chmn., 1947-). World Med. Assn. (mem. council, del. from A.M.A., 1948; pres., chmn. bd. U.S. Com. Inc.). Alumni Assn. U. of Louisville (pres. 1938-41), Ky. Med. Assn. (pres. 1941-42), Jefferson County Med. Soc. (pres. 1918), Am. Legion, Alpha Omega Alpha. Mason (33ff, Shriner), De Molay. Clubs: Pendennis, Filson, Big Spring Golf (Louisville). Home: 87 Valley Rd. Office: 606 S. 4th St., Louisville. Died July 30, 1953.

HENDERSON, JAMES PINCKNEY senator, gov. Tex.; b. Lincoln County, N.C., Mar. 31, 1808; s. Lawson and Elizabeth (Carruth) H.; attended U. N.C., did not graduate; m. Frances Cox, Oct. 1839. Admitted to N.C. bar, 1829; col. N.C. Militia; commd. brig. gen., 1836; appointed atty. gen. Republic of Tex., 1836, sec. of state, 1836-37; diplomatic agt. to Eng. and France with power to secure recognition of Tex. independence and to effect treaties of commerce, amity and navigation, 1837-1840, in Eng. negotiated informal comml. trading arrangement between Eng. and Tex., in France made similar treaty, 1838, signed, 1839; special envoy to U.S. to assist with Tex. annexation, 1844; del. to Tex. Constl. Conv. 1845; 1st gov. of Tex. (Democrat), 1845-47; took command of 4 regts. furnished by Tex., commd. brig. gen. U.S. Volunteers during Mexican War, 1846; mem. U.S. Senate (Dem.) from Tex., 1857-58. Died Washington, D.C., June 4, 1858.

HENDERSON, JOSEPH physician, congressman; b. Shippensburg, Pa., Aug. 2, 1791; grad. Jefferson Med. Coll., Phila., 1813. Commd. 1st lt. 22d Regt., Pa. Volunteers during War of 1812, promoted capt.; brevetted maj., given command of a regt., 1814; participated in battles of Chippewa and Lundy's Lane, Siege of Ft. Erie; practiced medicine, Browns Mills, Pa.; mem. U.S. Ho. of Reps. from Pa., 23d-24th congresses, 1833-37; practiced medicine, Lewistown, Pa., 1850-63. Died Lewistown, Dec. 25, 1863; buried St. Mark's Cemetery, Lewistown.

HENDERSON, LEON N(ESBIT) univ. prof.; born Baker, Fla., Feb. 22, 1906; s. Jerry Matt and Eliza Jane (Griffith) H.; AnB.A.E., U. of Fla., 1929; A. M., neorge Peabody Coll. for Teachers, 1939; Ed. D., Columbia, 1948; m. Elma Haddon Copeland, June 5, 1937; children - Elma Copeland, Leon Nesbit. Rural sch. teacher near Baker, Fla., 1922-26; teacher of social studies Henry B. Plant Sr. High Sch., Tampa, 1929-40; asso. prof. and coordinator Sloan project in applied econs. U. of Fla., 1940-43, professor of education, 1956-; vis. mem. faculty, summer session Columbia, officer Navy V 12 Unit, Univ. Miami, 1943-4 standards and curriculum div. Bur. Naval Personnel, Washington, 1945; to inactive status 1945; lt. comdr. USNR, 1946-; commanding officer Res. Research Co. 6-4, 1957-59. Member Assn. for Higher Edn., Am. Edn. Pesearch Assn., Am. Assn. Jr. Coll., Soc. Advancement of Edn., Fla. Edn. Assn., Fla. Classroom Teachers Assn. (pres. 1937-38, 1938-39), Fla. West Coast Edn. Assn. (prsnes. 1936-37), Hillsborough Co. Teachers Assn. (pres. 1934-36) Democrat. Baptist. Home: 1524 N.W. 12th Rd., Gainesville, Fla. 32601. Died Feb. 7, 1960; buried Hillcrest Meml. Park, Gainesville.

HENDERSON, ROBERT naval officer; b. Albany, N.Y., Oct. 15, 1878; s. William and Isabella (Simpson) H.; B.S., U.S. Naval Acad., 1902; LL.B., George Washington U., 1925; grad. U.S. Naval War Coll., 1920, U.S. Army War Coll., 1927; m. Margaret Tyson Ellicott, May 25, 1905: children-Robert Ellicott (U.S.N.R.), Carroll Ellicott (wife of Dr. Eilif C. Hanssen). Entered U.S. Navy, Spanish War, 1898, served successively through all grades to rear adm., 1947; ret. voluntarily, 1929; served in Spanish War, West Indies Revolution; comdr. troop transports to France, World War I; served on active duty in Alaska, India and Navy Dept., World War II. Vice pres., dir. So. Cal. Asso. Newspapers (a subsidiary of Copley Press) 1929—. Nominated Rep. candidate to Congress, 18th Cal. Dist., 1931; del. from Cal. to Cleveland Rep. Nat. Conv., 1936. Decorations; Navy Cross, Spanish War Service medal; World War I Service medal with service bars and stars for Battleship Fleet, W.I. Campaign, Army Armed Guard Service, Cruiser and Transports Force: World War II Service medal; Royal Norwegian Order of Saint Olaf (rank of commodore), Chinese Spl. Breast Order of Yun Hui with ribbon; Order of Polish Restituta Officers Cross; Czechoslovak medal of Merit First Class with silver star; War Dept. Letter of Commendation for World War I Services. Baptist. Clubs: Chevy Chase, Army and Navy (Washington); Yacht (N.Y.C.); Athletic (Los Angeles). Home: 126 S. Lucerne Blvd., Los Angeles. Office: 801 Moraga Dr., Bel Air, Cal. Died Feb. 5, 1956; buried Arlington Nat. Cemetery.

HENDERSON, ROBERT MILLER lawyer; b. N. Middletown Twp., Pa., Mar. 12, 1827; s. William Miller and Elizabeth (Parker) H.; ed. pub. schs., Carlisle, Pa., Dickinson Coll., A.B., 1845 (A.M., LL.D.); m. Margaret Ann Webster, June 7, 1853. Admitted to bar, Aug. 25, 1847; mem. Pa. legislature, 1851-53: capt. Pa. Reserves (7th Pa.), 1861, 36th Pa. Vol. Inf., attached to 2d brigade McCall's Div., Army of Potomac; judge-advocate of div., 1861-June 1862; wounded at Charles City Cross Roads, June 30, 1862; promoted (on recommendation of Brig. Gen. Seymour) for "brilliant gallantry" to lt. col.,July col., July 4, 1962; severely wounded, Aug. 30, 1862, at 2d Bull Run; apptd. insp. gen. of div., June 2, 1863; provost-marshal, 15th Pa. dist., Apr. 18, 1863: hon. disch., November 10, 1865; bvtd. col. and brig. gen. U.S.V., for gallantry, Mar. 13, 1865. Apptd. Apr. 1874, and elected Nov. 1874, additional law judge, 12th jud. dist., Pa., and in Jan., 1882, became pres. judge of dist.; subsequently resigned and resumed practice. Original mem. and officer Pa. State Bar Assn.; 1st pres. Cumberland Co. Bar Assn.; pres. Carlisle Deposit Bank; pres. bd. trustees Metzgar Coll.; trustee Carlisle Indian Industrial Sch. Presbyterian. Republican. Home: Carlisle, Pa. Died 1906.

HENDERSON, THOMAS physician, army officer, congressman; b. Freehold, N.J., Aug. 15, 1743; s. John and Ann (Stevens) H.; grad. Coll. of N.J. (now Princeton), 1761; m. Mary Hendricks, Sept. 23, 1767; m. 2d, Rachel Burrowes, Jan. 2, 1778; 7 children. Mem. N.J. Com. of Safety, 1774; mem. Freehold Com. of Observation and Inspection, 1774; lt. local militia in N.J., 1775; maj. Minutemen, 1776; commd. maj. Continental Army, 1776; surrogate Monmouth County (N.J.), 1776; lt. col. Forman's Additional Continental Regt., 1777; mem. N.J. Provincial Council, 1777, N.J. Assembly, 1780-84; became mem. local com. of retaliation, 1780; mem. N.J. Gen. Assembly, 1780-84; judge of common pleas, 1783, 99, master of chancery, 1790; mem. N.J. Council, 1793-94; 1812-13, v.p., 1794; acting gov. N.J., 1794; mem. U.S. Ho. of Reps. (Federalist) from N.J., 4th Congress, 1795-97; mem. N.J. Died Freehold, Dec. 15, 1824; buried Old Tennent Cemetery, Freehold.

HENDERSON, THOMAS JEFFERSON congressman; b. Brownsville, Tenn., Nov. 29, 1824; ed. Brownsville Male Acad., 1835-36; State U. of Ia., 1845-46; m. Henrietta Butler, May 29, 1849. Practiced law in Ill., 1852-75; clerk co. commrs. court Stark co., Ill., and co. court, same, 1847-52; mem. Ill. Ho. of Rep., 1854-56: Senate, 1856-60. Col. 112th Ill. Inf., Sept. 22, 1862; bvtd. brig. gen. vols., Nov. 30, 1864, "for gallant and meritorious services during the campaign in Ga. and Tenn." Presdl. elector, 1868; mem. 44th to 53d Congresses (1875-95). Republican. Was mem. bd. of mgrs. Nat. Home for Disabled Vol. Soldiers; mgr. Danville (Ill.) branch Nat. Home; now mem. Bd. Ordnance and Fortification, War Dept. Home: Princeton, Ill. Died 1911.

HENDERSON, WILLIAM THOMAS, justice, Court of Appeal of Ont.; b. Stratford, Ont., Sept. 17, 1874; s. Thomas and Catherine (Collins) H.; student Stratford Collegiate Inst., Osgoode Hall, Toronto; m. Victoria White, Jan. 10, 1914. Read law with the Hon. Mr. Justice Idington, Supreme Court of Can.; called to bar, Ont., Nov. 1894; city solicitor, Brantford, 1898-1934; King's counsel, Nov. 1910; appointed to the Bench, Supreme Court of Ontario, 1934; appointed a Justice in Appeal of the Supreme Court of Ontario, 1935. Served with 54th Battery, C.E.F., World War I; became major, Jan. 1916. Clubs: University (Toronto), Toronto Golf (Long Branch, Ont.), Brantford Golf and Country (Brantford, Ont.). Conservative. Home: 127 Brant Av., Brantford, Ont. Address: Osgoode Hall, Toronto OT Canada*

HENDREN, PAUL naval officer; b. nr. Statesville, N.C., Nov. 10, 1889; s. John J. and Sarah Pearl (Linney) H.; B.S., U.S. Naval Acad., 1913; grad. U.S. Naval War Coll., 1932, U.S. Indsl. Coll., 1933; m. Elizabeth Bryson Pettit, Feb. 4, 1922; children-Constance Pettit (Mrs. H. M. Nicholson, Jr.), Paul M.: m. 2d, Emma B. Williamson, June 1, 1957. Commd. ensign U.S. Navy, 1913, advanced through grades to vice adm., 1949: participated in occupation Vera Cruz, Mexico, 1914, in World Wars I and II; commanded cruiser U.S.S. Philadelphia in invasion of N. Africa, of Sicily, and at Salerno, 1943; ret. Aug. 1949. Awarded Legion of Merit (3), gold star in lieu of 4th; Military medal 1st class: diploma from Chile; British Distinguished Service Order. Episcopalian. Clubs: Army-Navy (Washington); Army-Navy Country (Arlington, Va.); N.Y. Yacht; Cape Fear (Wilmington, N.C.). Contbr. articles to New York Times, Sat. Ev. Post, U.S. Naval Inst. Proc. Home: 616 Market St., Wilmington, N.C. Died Nov. 28, 1958: buried Arlington Nat. Cemetery.

HENDRICKSON, ROBERT C. former anbassador; b. Woodbury, N.J., Aug. 12, 1898; s. Daniel F. and Emma R. (Mergary) H.; LL.B., Temple U., Phila., 1922; LL.D., Temple Univ., Bloonfield College and Seminary; married Olga Bonsal, 1919; children - Claire (Mrs. Ivor Macfarlane), Olga (Mrs. Willard Lloyd Nyburg), Marguerite (Mrs. Donald Brewer), Robert C., Jr., June (Mrs. Donald Nolte). Admitted to New Jersey bar, 1922; in practice of law, Woodbury, N.J., 1922-; corp. counsel and solicitor, City woodbury, 1931-; elected to fill unexpired term of state senator, Gloucester County, N.J., 1934; re-elected 1938, 1941, pres. State senate, 1939; elected state treas., 1942, re-elected 1946; vice chmn. Commn. on Delaware River Basin; mem. bd. mgrs. Council of State Govts., 1940, chmn. 1941; U.S. Senator, N.J., 1948-53; U.S. Ambassador to New Zealand, 1955-56. Mem. Nat. Com. Support Pub. Sch.; trustee Nat. Com. U.S.O. Served as pvt., U.S. Army, 1918-19; lt. col., sr. legal officer of Am. Mil. Govt., U.S. Army, 1943-46. Awarded Medal of Verdun, Unit Citation, Letters of Commendation, Army Commednndation Ribbon, Allied Mil. Govt. Medal, Fifth Army. Mem. Am. Legion (comdr. 1929), Soc. Cin. (hon.), Gloucester County Bar Assn. (past pres.; treas.). Episcopalian. Rotarian. Author: Youth in Danger. Home: 325 Cooper St. Office: 21 Cooper St., Woodbury, N.J. Died Dec. 8, 1964.

HENKLE, CHARLES ZANE banker; b. Chgo., Aug. 16, 1892; s. William H. and Mary F. (Zane) H.; student Cornell U., 1911-12; m. Rita J. Guignon, Nov. 11, 1922; 1 son, Charles Zane (dec.). Solicitor, Commonwealth Edison Co., Chgo., 1912-13; div. contract agt. Pub. Service Co. of No. Ill., Evanston, Ill., 1914-15. salesman Councilman & Co., investment bankers, Chgo., 1916-17, Ill. Trust & Savs. Bank, Chgo., 1920-21; municipal buyer, bond dept. Merchants Loan & Trust Co., 1922; corp. buyer, bond dept. Ill. Merchants Trust Co., 1923-29; 2d v.p. Continental Ill. Co., 1929-32, 2cp2d v.p. Continental Ill. Nat. Bank & Trust Co., 1932-40, v.p. 1941—. Served as 1st lt., 166th Inf., capt., 359th Inf., AEF, 1917-19; col., on active duty, dep. dir. personnel Gen. Staff Corps, hdqrs. 6th Service Command, 1942-44. Vice chmn. Chgo.-Cook County 6th War Loan Com.; treas., mem. nat. exec. com. Mil. Training Camps Assn. of U.S., 1944-49. Trustee Ravinia Festival Assn., 1940-49. Chmn. Red Cross Fund Chgo., 1948, chmn. Chgo. chpt. A.R.C., 1918-50. Mem. Am. Banking Inst., Mil. Order World War, Am. Legion. Republican. Clubs: Union League (pres. 1946-47), Commercial Exmoore Country, Bankers, Caxton. Awarded Silver Star, Purple Heart, Army Commendation ribbon. Home: 17 Brittany Rd., Highland Park, Ill. Office: 231 S. LaSalle St., Chgo. 90. Died Oct. 3, 1949.

HENLEY, ROBERT naval officer; b. Williamsburg, Va., Jan. 5, 1783; s. Leonard and Elizabeth (Dandridge) H.; attended Coll. William and Mary, before 1799; married, no children. Obtained midshipman's warrant to U.S. Navy, 1799; served in ship Constellation in war with France, circa 1800; studied navigation and naval science, Williamsburg, Va., 1806-07; commd. lt. U.S. Navy, 1807; commanded brig. Eagle at Battle of Lake Champlain in War of 1812; captured pirate schooner Moscow off Santo Domingo, 1821; promoted capt., 1825; stationed at Naval Sta., Charleston, S.C., 1825-28. Died Sullivan's Island, Charleston, Oct. 6, 1828.

HENMON, VIVIAN ALLEN CHARLES educator; b. Centralia, Wis., Nov. 27, 1877; s. Joseph Jonas and Minnie (Ekelund) H.: A.B., Bethany Coll., Kan., 1895, A.M., 1898: Ph.D., Columbia, 1905; m. Katharine Porter Vilas, June 9, 1914. Prin. schs., Lincoln, Mo., 1895-97; instr. pedagogy, 1898-1900, prof., 1900-05. Bethany Coll.; lectr. on psychology Columbia, 1905-07; prof. psychology. edn., 1907-10, acting dean Coll. Liberal Arts, 1909-10. U. Colo.; asso. prof. edn., 1910-13, prof., 1913-26, dir. Sch. of Edn., 1916-26, prof. psychology U. Wis., 1927-48, emeritus, 1948—; prof. ednl. psychology Yale, 1926-27; prof. summer sessions, Columbia, Harvard, Yale. Adv. in ednl. psychology Modern Lang. Study, 1925-29; mem. Com. on Modern Langs., 1920-43. Supr. psychol. research, Civil Aeros. Authority, 1939-40. Pres. Aviation Exam. Bd., Syracuse, N.Y. Capt. Aviation Sect., Signal O.R.C., 1917-19; maj., 1919-31. Republican. Lutheran. Fellow A.A.A.S. (v.p. and chmn. sect. L, 1919-; mem. Am. Psychol. Assn., Soc. Coll. Tchrs. Edn. (pres. 1926), Am. Edn. Research Assn., Soc. Advancement Edn., Phi Beta Kappa. Sigma Xi, Alpha Tau Omega, Phi Kappa Phi, Phi Delta Kappa. Home: 4205 Hillcrest Drive, Madison 5, Wis. Died Jan. 10, 1950.

HENNINGS, THOMAS CAREY, JR. U.S. Senator; b. St. Louis, June 25, 1903; s. Thomas Carey and Sarah Pouillain (Wilson) H.; A.B., Cornell U., 1924; LL.B., Washington U., 1926; LL.D., Central Coll., Fayette, Mo., 1954, Westminster Coll., 1958; m. 2d Elizabeth Stallcup. Admitted to the Missouri State bar, 1926 and to bars of U.S. Supreme Court, also U.S. Federal Court and various state courts; mem. firm Green, Hennings, Henry & Evans; asst. circuit atty., St. Louis, 1929-34; mem. 74th to 76th Congresses, 11th Mo. Dist., resigned from Congress to become circuit atty., St. Louis, 1940-41; lectr. in criminal jurisprudence, Benton Coll. of Law, St. Louis, 1931-35, U.S. senator from Mo., 1950-; chmn. committee on rules and administration; chairman or mem. some fifteen coms. or sub-coms.; mem. Dem. steering com., Dem. policy com., sec. Dem. conf. Del. Inter-Parliamentary Union, Vienna, 1954, Helsinki, 1955. Commd. lt. comdr. U.S.N.R., 1940; called to active duty, July 1941, served in Atlantic and Pacific areas, hon. disch. from active duty 1944 for phys. disability incurred in line of duty. Hon. pres., past pres., now nat. dir. Big Brother Organization (National Big Brothers of 1956); past dir. Urban League, Navy League of U.S.; trustee Mo. Hist. Soc.; v. chmn. Mo. Basin Survey Commn. Charter mem. U. Investment Syndicate, St. Louis. Mem. Am., Mo., St. Louis bar assns., Cornell Law Assn., Am. Legion, Veterans of Foreign Wars, American Judicature Society, St. Louis Chamber of Commerce, Order of Coif, Delta Kappa Epsilon, Phi Delta phi. Democrat. Clubs: Missouri Athletic, Cornell, Racquet, University, Noonday (St. Louis), 1925 F Street, Burning Tree (Washington), Cornell, Mexico Pilgrims (New York). Home: 220 N. Kingshighway, St. Louis; also 4201 Cathedral Av. N.W., Washington. Office: Boatman's Bank Bldg., St. Louis, Mo. and U.S. Senate, Washington. Died Sept. 13, 1960; buried Arlington Nat. Cemetery.

HENNINGSEN, CHARLES FREDERICK army officer, author; b. Brussels, Belgium, Feb. 21, 1815; m. Williamina (Belt) Connelly. Entered service of Carlists in Spain, 1834; knighted, made capt. Lancers in Spain, 1835-36; came to U.S. with Louis Kossuth, (leader of Hungarian freedom movement), after fighting with Hungarians against Austrians, 1851; joined expdn. to Nicaragua as brig. gen. in charge of arty. under William Walker, 1856; col. 59th Regular Va. Inf., Confederate Army, 1861-62; an accomplished linguist. Author: Revelations of Russia (gave Americans 1st idea of Russia through a book), 1844; The White Slave, 1845; Eastern Europe and the Emperor Nicholas, 3 vols., 1846; Sixty Years Hence, 1847; Analogies and Contrasts, 2 vols., 1848; The Past and Future of Hungary, 1852. Died Washington, D.C., June 14, 1877; buried Congressional Cemetery, Washington.

HENRICI, ARTHUR TRAUTWEIN bacteriologist; b. Economy, Pa., Mar. 31, 1889; s. Jacob Frederick and Viola (Irons) H.; M.D., U. of Pittsburgh, 1911; m. Blanche Ressler, Aug. 7, 1913; children-Carl Ressler, Ruth Elizabeth, Hazel Jean. Pathologist St. Francis Hosp., Pittsburgh, 1912-13; instr. in pathology and bacteriology, U. of Minn., 1913-16, asst. prof. bacteriology, 1916-20, asso. prof., 1920-25, prof. since 1925; Walker-Amers Prof., U. of Wash., 1941. Served as capt. Med. Corps, U.S. Army, 1917-19. Mem. Soc. Am. Bacteriologists (pres. 1939), Soc. Exptl. Biology and Medicine, Limnological Soc. of America, Mycological soc. of Am., Sigma Xi, Gamma Alpha, Alpha Omega Alpha. Author: Morphologic Variation and the Rate of Growth of Bacteria, 1928; Molds, Yeasts and Actinomycetes, 1930; The Biology of Bacteria, 1934, 2d edit., 1939. Contbr. to bacteriological jours. Home: 130 Arthur Av. S.E., Minneapolis, Minn. Died Apr. 23, 1943.

HENRICKS, COLEMAN BRESEE, physician; b. Portland, Ore,, June 4, 1907; s. Andrew O. and Fawn (Galbraith) H.; M.D., U. So. Cal., 1937; m. Opal Marie Campbell, Feb. 19, 1935; children—Coleman Bresee, Jon Andrew. Intern Los Angeles County Gen. Hosp., 1937, resident in internal medicine, 1937-39, later sr. attending staff; chief teaching resident in internal medicine Los Angeles County Gen. Hosp and U. So. Cal. Sch. Medicine, 1939-40; practiced medicine specializing in internal medicine; vis. staff Hosp. Good Smaritan. Served to maj. M.C., AUS, 1942-46; CBI. Diplomate Am. Bd. Internal Medicine. Mem. A.M.A., Am. Soc. Investigative Medicine, Alpha Omega Alpha. Republican. Home: Los Angeles CA Died Mar. 17, 1969; buried Forest Lawn Cemetery, Glendale CA

HENRIQUES, ROBERT DAVID QUIXANO author; b. In London, Eng., Dec. 11, 1905; s. Maj. Julian Quixano and Margaret (Beddington) H.; student Rugby Sch., 1919-23, New Coll., Oxford, 1923-26 (honors in modern history); m. Vivien Doris Levy, Oct. 11, 1928; children - David Vivian Quixano, Veronica Esme, Michael Robert Quixano, Penelope Jane. Served as subaltern, Regular Army, Royal Artillery, 1926-33, Territorial Army, 1933; formed one of first commando troops, 1940; participated in raid on Vaagso; with Hdqrs. Combined Operations, 1942; lent to Gen. Patton's staff, U.S. Army, and participated at Casablanca, North Africa, and in Sicilian assaults with U.S. Army forces; promoted lt. col., 1943, col., 1944. Awarded Mem. Order British Empire (Gt. Britain), Silver Star, Bronze Star Medal (U.S.). Made big game trip from Blue Nile to Dinder River, 1928; engaged in pub. business, 1933-37; lion hunting in Darfur, 1937. Won "All Nations" prize novel competition, 1939. Vice pres. British Assn. for Jewish Youth, World Fedn. Y.M.H.A.'s. Mason. Jewish Religion. Clubs: Garrick, Cavalry, Savile (London); Vale of White Horse Hunt (Gloucestershire). Author several books before 1945, later publs. include: The Cotswolds; Too Little Love (U.S.), 1950, under title Through the Valley (Eng.) (awarded James Tait Black Mleml. prize for best novel of 1950); A Stranger Here, 1953; Red over Green, 1956; 100 Hours to Suez, 1957; Maruncus Samuel, First Viscount Bearsted and Founder of Shell, 1960. Home: Winson Mill Farm, Winson, Cirencester, Gloucestershire, Eng. Died Jan. 23, 1967.

HENRY, DOUGLAS SELPH, lawyer; b. Nashville, Dec. 30, 1890; s. Robert Allison and Emily James (Selph) H.; A.B., Vanderbilt U., 1911, LL.B., 1916; m. Kathryn Craig, Apr. 24, 1924; children—Douglas Selph, Margaret Sinclair (Mrs. Harry A. J. Joyce). Admitted to Tenn. bar, 1915, practiced in Nashville, 1916-49; v.p., gen. counsel Nat. Life & Accident Ins. Co., Nashville, from 1950, also dir.; v.p., gen. counsel WSM, from 1950, also dir. Mem. bd. edn. Davidson Co., Tenn., 1939-42; state senator Davidson Co., 1927-28; mayor City Belle Meade, Tenn., 1938-40. Member board of trustees of the Tennessee Teachers Retirement System, 1945-57. Served as capt. F.A., U.S. Army, 1917-19. Mem. Assn. Life Ins. Counsel, Am., Tenn., Nashville bar assns., Phi Delta Theta. Methodist. Clubs: Belle Meade Country, Colemere, Cumberland (Nashville). Home: Nashville TN Died Sept. 3, 1971.

HENRY, GUY VENOR army officer; b. Ft. Robinson, Neb., Jan. 28, 1875; s. Guy Vernor and Julia (McNair) H.; grad. U.S. Mil. cad., 1898, U.S. Cav. Sch., 1904, 24, French Cav. Sch., 1907, Army War Coll., 1921; honor grad. Sch. of the Line, 1922; grad. Gen. Staff Sch., 1923; m. Mary Ingraham Rogers, Oct. 29, 1910; children - Mary Ingraham, Patricia Vernor. Second lt. inf., U.S. Army, Apr. 26, 1898; promoted through grades to col.; apptd. chief of cav., rank of maj. gen., Mar. 21, 1930, to March 20, 1934; brig. gen., March 26, 1934. Participated in Spanish-American War; brig. gen., World War; commandant of cadets U.S. Mil. Acad., 1916-17; retired with rank of major general, 1939; recalled to active service, September 1941; on duty Italian and European Theaters, June-July, 1944. on duty as head Inter-Allied Personnel Bd. and sr. army mem. U.S. Can. and Mexican Defense Commissions; relieved from active duty Oct. 1948. Chairman of U.S.-Can. Defense Bd., since Dec. 1948. Cited for gallantry in Philippine Insurrection. Received Distinguished Service Medal. Decorated by French, Swedish, German, British and Mexican governments. Episcopalian. Clubs: Chevy Chase, Army and Navy, Army Navy Country (Washington); Polo, Army and Navy (Manila); Astec. Home: 6 Kennedy Drive. Kenwood, Chevy Chase, Md. Died Nov. 29, 1967.

HENRY, GUY VERNOR brig. gen. U.S.A.; b. Fort Smith, Indian Ty., Mar. 9, 1839; grad. West Point, May 5, 1861; served through Civil war and Indian wars as lt., capt., maj., lt. col. and brig. gen. Successive bvts. for gallantry in various battles: bvtd. brig. gen. for gallantry at Rose Bud, Mont., where he was shot through the face fighting Indians; received medal of honor from Congress for distinguished gallantry at Cold Harbor; later col. 10th cav.; bvt. brig. gen., commanding Fort Assinniboine, and May 1898, promoted brig. gen. vols.; brig. gen. U.S.A., Oct. 1898, and maj. gen. vols., Dec. 1898, serving in the war against Spain. Military gov. Puerto Rico, Dec. 1898, to May 1899-. Home: Washington, D.C. Died 1899.

HENRY, HETH army officer; b. Chesterfield County, Va., Dec. 16, 1825; attended Georgetown Coll., 1837; grad. U.S. Mil. Acad., 1847; m. Harriet Selden, 3 children. Brevetted 2d lt., 1847, served in Mexican War; promoted 1st lt., 1853, capt., 1855, served against Sioux Indians; joined Confederate Army, 1861, organized Floyd's command for W.Va., Fall 1861; commd. brig. gen. in command of mil. dist. around Lewisburg, Va., 1862; post and div. comdr. in Bragg's Army during expdns. into Ky.; transferred to Army of No. Va., 1863; commd. maj. gen. 1863; his most conspicuous action was at Battle of Gettysburg (which he precipitated by engaging U.S. Army early); civil engr. for U. S. Govt., 1880-84; spl. agt. Office of Indian Affairs, 1884-98. Died Washington, D.C., Sept. 27, 1899.

HENRY, NELSON HERRICK federal officer; b. Staten Island, N.Y., Apr. 27, 1855; s. Joshua J. and Maria C. H.; A.B., Coll. City of New York, 1877; M.D., Coll. Phys. and Surg. (Columbia), 1879; m. Mrs. Sarah B. Rodgers Sloan, Apr. 30, 1901. Practiced in New York; surgeon 12th Regt. N.G.S.N.Y., 1883; asst. surgeon gen. state of N.Y., 1893; chief surgeon, N.G.S.N.Y., 1898, reappointed, 1900; maj. Spanish-Am. War, 1898-99; mem. N.Y. Ho. of Rep., 1899-1901; adj. gen. N.Y., 1902-10; brevet maj. gen. N.G.S.N.Y., 1910; U.S. surveyor port of New York, 1910-. Republican. Episcopalian. Home: New York, N.Y. Died Mar. 15, 1933.

HENRY, PATRICK gov. Va., Continental congressman; b. Hanover County, Va., May 29, 1736; s. John and Sarah (Winston) H.; m. Sarah Shelton, 1754; m. 2d, Dorothea Dandridge, 1776. Licensed to practice law, 1760; elected to Va. Ho. of Burgesses, 1765; claimed legislative independence for Va. in response to Stamp Act, 1765; gave one of his most famous speeches against Stamp Act, contained phrase "If this be treason, make the most of it;" organized (with Thomas Jefferson and Richard Henry Lee) Com. of Correspondence, 1773; mem. 1st Continental Congress from Va., 1774-75, offered resolution providing that "this Colony be immediately put into a position of defense" (contained famous phrase, "give me liberty or give me death"); took seat in 2d Continental Congress, May 18, 1775, participated in legislation by which Continental Army was organized; resigned commn. as col. Va. Militia, 1776; elected mem. 3d Va. Revoluntionary Conv., 1776, took decisive part in drafting new Va. constn., too, part in urging passage of resolutions authorizing Congress to declare independence and to appeal to France for aid; gov. Va., 1776-79, 84-86, sent George Rogers Clark to Illinois County to expel Brisith from N.W. Territory, 1778; del. to Va. Conv. to ratify U.S. Constn., 1788, opposed ratification, largely responsible for addition of Bill of Rights; elected to Va. Ho. of Dels. (Federalist), 1799, died before taking office. Died Va., June 6, 1799; buried Red Hill Plantation, Staunton River, Va.

HENRY, PATRICK ex-congressman, lawyer; b. Madison Co., Miss., Feb. 12, 1843; ed. Miss. Coll., Clinton, Miss., Madison Coll., Sharon, Miss., and Nashville, Tenn., Mil. Coll.; left latter, 1861, to enter 6th Miss. inf., C.S.A.; served through war until surrendered, April 26, 1895; maj. 14th (consolidated) Miss. regt., m. Margie E. Cocke, Feb. 10, 1874. Farmed, 1866-73; since then in law practice at Brandon, Miss.; mem. Miss. legislature, 1878, 1890; del. at large to State Constitutional Conv., 1890; mem. Congress, 1897-1901, 7th Miss. dist.; mem. Miss. senate, 1903-07. Democrat. Address: Brandon, Miss. Died May 18, 1930.

HENRY, ROBERT LLEWELLYN, JR., judge; b. Chicago, Ill., Nov. 4, 1882; s. Robert Llewellyn and Ada Camille (Badger) H.; Ph.B., U. of Chicago, 1902, J.D., 1907; Rhodes scholar at Worcester Coll., Oxford, Eng., 1904-07, B.C.L., Oxford, 1907, D.C.L., 1926; m. Elaine

Goodale Read, June 30, 1908 (dec.); children—Robert L., Alvan Read, McClelland. Prof. law, La. State U., 1907-11; asst. prof. law, U. of Ill., 1911-12; prof. law and dean Coll. of Law, U. of N.D., 1912-14; prof. law, U. of Calif., summer, 1914; prof. law, State U. of Ia., 1914-16. Capt. inf., O.R.C., Nov. 13, 1916; maj., Mar. 8, 1919; instr. officers training camps and schs., Ft. Sheridan, Ill., Camp Grant, Ill., Camp Lee, Va., May 1, 1917-Mar. 8, 1919; mem. constrn. demobilization com., Gen. Staff, Washington, D.C., Mar. 8-Aug. 1, 1919; mem. War Dept. Bd. Contract adjustment, Washington, D.C., 1919-20; lecturer at Oxford U., 1921-22; later judge Mixed Court, Alexandria, Egypt. Democrat. Mem. Chi Psi, Phi Delta Phi. Author: Liens and Pledges, 1913; Consideration in Contracts, 601 A.D. to 1520 A.D. (article), 1917; Anglo-Saxon Contracts (article), 1917; Contracts in the Local Courts of Medieval England, 1926. Home: Louisville KY Died May 1969.

HENRY, ROBERT SELPH, ry. exec.; b. Clifton, Tenn., Oct. 20, 1889; s. Robert Allison and Emily James (Selph) H.; A.B., LL.B., Vanderbilt Univ., 1911; post grad. work Queens' Coll., Cambridge, Eng., 1919; Litt.D., U. Chattanooga, 1950; m. Lura Temple, Oct. 30, 1929; children—Elizabeth Temple (Mrs. N. B. Musselman), Roberta Selph (Mrs. George B. Vest, Jr.). Began career as newspaper reporter, 1907-13; pvt. sec. to gov. of Tenn., 1913-15; admitted to Tenn. bar, 1911, and practiced in Nashville, 1915-21, asst. to v.p. N.C.&St.L. Ry., 1921-34; asst. to pres. Assn. Am. R.R.'s., 1934-37, v.p., 1947-58. Served as capt. F.A., U.S. Army, 1917-19; maj. and lt. col., Field Artillery Res. Chmn. bd. trustees Ladies Hermitage Assn., Nashville, Tenn., 1926-34; trustee Vanderbilt University. Member Am., So. (v.p. 1956, pres. 1957) hist. assns., Soc. Am. Historians, Phi Beta Kappa, Phi Delta Theta, Phi Delta Phi. Presbyterian. Clubs: Army and Navy, National Press Club, Cosmos (Washington, D.C.). Author: The Story of the Confederacy, 1931; Trains, 1934; On the Railroad, 1936; Portraits of the Iron Horse, 1937; The Story of Reconstruction, 1938; This Fascinating Railroad Business, 1942; "First With the Most" Forrest, 1944; Headlights and Markers (with Frank P. Donovan, Jr.), 1945; The Story of the Mexican War, 1950; As They Saw Forrest (editor), 1956; The Armed Forces Institute of Pathology: Its First Century, 1862-1962, 1964. Contbr. articles to profl. jours. Home: Alexandria VA Died Aug. 18, 1970; buried Mt. Olivet Cemetery, Nashville TN

HENRY, SIDNEY MORGAN shipping exec.; b. Staten Island, N.Y., Dec. 2, 1878; s. James B. and Louisa (Anderson) H.; B.S., U.S. Naval Acad., 1901; M.S., Mass. Inst. Tech., 1905: m. Julia B. Persons, Sept. 11, 1907 (dec. 1933); children-Sidney Morgan, Julia P. (dec.); m. 2d, Katherine E. Crabbs, Oct. 25, 1948. Commd. naval cadet U.S. Navy, 1897, advanced through grades to capt., 1918) served in Spanish-Am. War and World War I; resigned, 1920; asst. to pres., later v.p. Balta Dry Docks & Shipbldg. Co., also v.p. Clavert Navigation Co., 1920-21; comml. mgr., later v.p. U.S. Shipping Bd. Emergency Fleet Corp., 1921-25; with firm Edward P. Farley & Co., shipping, 1926-34: financial v.p. Munson Steamship Line, 1928; pres. J. B. Inderrieden Co., 1933-35; gen. mgr. for trustees Munson Steamship Line and affiliated cos., 1934-39; dir. Glen Falls Ins. Co., 1949-58. Asst. to dep. chief Office Procurement and Materials. Navy Dept., 1942-43. Decorated Spanish-Am. War medal, Sampson medal. Victory medal. Mem. Soc. Naval Architects and Marine Engrs., Chi Phi. Republican. Episcopalian. Clubs: Army and Navy, Chevy Chase (Washington); India House (N.Y.C.). Address: 35 Fifth Av., N.Y.C. 3. Died Mar. 16, 1959; buried U.S. Naval Acad. Cemetery, Annapolis, Md.

HENRY, WILLIAM M (BILL), columnist, war corr., radio analyst; born at San Francisco, August 21, 1890; s. John Quincy Adams and Margaret (Weddell) H.; ed. various schools in U.S. and abroad; grad. Los Angeles High Sch., 1909; student Sydney U., Australia, 1910, A.B., Occidental Coll., Los Angeles, 1911-14, Litt.D., 1947; Litt.D., University of Redlands, 1957; married Corinne Stanton, 1914; children—Margaret (Mrs. Fred Stichweh), Patricia (Mrs. Yeomans), Mary Virginia (Mrs. Blum) (dec.). With Los Angeles Times, 1911-70; Times and CBS war corr. with R.A.F. in France, 1939; war corr., South Pacific, 1942; news analyst on NBC, until 1970. Adminstrv. Aide to V.P. Nixon on round-the-world Goodwill trip, 1956, spl. asst. to Nixon on African tour, 1957; member President's Com. Fitness for Youth, 1956. Pres. Radio Corr. Assn., Washington, 1947. Chmn. Radio-TV Arrangements Com. for Rep.-Dem. polit. convs., 1948, 52, 56, 60, 64. Mem.-at-large U.S. Olympic Com., 1962; pres. So. Cal. Com. for Olympic Games, 1962-66. Recipient Nat. Headliners Award for 1943 as outstanding columnist; received Headliners Award for radio reporting in 1948; Freedoms Found. Spl. Achievement Award, 1951-52; The Olympic Diploma by Internat. Olympic Com., Helsinki, Finland, 1952; Presdl. Medal of Freedom, 1970. Fellow Sigma Delta Chi for outstanding service to journalism, 1954; Printers Devil award, Theta Sigma Phi, 1957; M and M award for outstanding contbn. to pub. understanding of U.S. Econ. and Political System, 1964. Author: An Approved History of the Olympic Games, 1948. Home: Chatsworth CA Died Apr. 13, 1970; buried Oakwood Memorial Park, Chatsworth CA

HENSHAW, DAVID state polit. leader, sec. of navy; b. Leicester, Mass., Apr. 2, 1791; s. David and Mary (Sargent) H. With assos. established Boston Statesman, 1821; established in ins. co., 1824; incorporator Western R.R.; dir. Boston and Worcester R.R.; collector Port of Boston, 1827; recognized as Democratic boss of Mass.; mem. Mass. Legislature, 1839; U.S. sec. of navy, 1843-1884. Author: Remarks Upon the Rights and Powers of Corporations, 1837; Letters on Internal Improvements and Commerce of the West, 1839. Died Leicester, Nov. 11, 1852.

HENSHEL, HARRY DAVIS watch mfr.; b. Rochester, N.Y., June 29, 1890; s. Morris Jacob and Sarah Ellen (Davis) H.; student Walworth Bus. Inst., Bulova, Apr. 22, 1918; 1 son, Harry Bulova. Clk., stenographer, sec. to v.p. Erie R.R. Co., 1906-12; sec. Eugene Meyer, 1912-13; conducted Direct Mail Advt. Agy., 1913-18; with Bulova Watch Co., Flushing, N.Y., 1918-, v.p., 1930-, also dir., vice chmn. Chmn. N.Y. State Democratic Finance Com., 1949, mem. Nat. Dem. Finance Com., 1952; dir. finance Nat. Dem. Senatorial Com., 1956. Chmn. armed services com. Nat. Jewish Welfare Bd.; fgn. relations com. Amateur Athletic Union of U.S.; chmn. U.S. Olympic Basketball Com., 1952-56, N.Y.C. Com. 1952, 56, 60 Olympic Games; nat. bd. dirs. USO. Served from maj. to lt. col. USAAF and AUS, 1942-45. Decorated Bronze Star. Clubs: Army-Navy (Washington); Old Oaks Country (Purchase, N.Y.); Nat. Democratic, Harmonie (N.Y.C.). Home: 25 Central Park W., N.Y.C. Office: 630 Fifth Av., N.Y.C. 20. Died May 15, 1961; buried Arlington, Va.

HENSLEY, RICHARD GIBSON librarian; b. Tenn., June 16, 1903; s. John Wm. and Blanche (Dromgoole) H.; A.B., Columbia, 1929; Columbia Sch. of Library Service, summer 1929; grad. study Harvard, 1929-32; m. Henrietta Barr, Mar. 14, 1927. Reference asst. Library of Congress, 1920-27, N.Y. Pub. Library, 1927-29; with Boston Pub. Library since 1929 as asst. to dir., 1929-33, asst. librarian, 1933-34, chief librarian of the reference div. since 1934, lecturer library training class since 1929. Lt. col., Corps Engineers, U.S. Army; with staff, Chief of Engrs., Washington, D.C., 1942-43; Staff and Faculty, The Engineer Sch., Ft. Belvoir, Va., 1943-44; with U.S. Group Control, Austria, and Allied Commn., 1945-46. Mem. Am. Library Assn., Bibliog. Soc., America, Bibliog. Soc. of London (Eng.), Res. Officers Assn., Soc. Am. Mil. Engrs., Spl. Libraries Assn., Assn. Coll. and Reference Libraries, Res. Officers Assn. (mem. council Mass. dept., 1947-49; mem. exec. bd., Boston chap., 1946-49), Charitable Irish Soc., Hancock, (New Hampshire) Hist. Society, Am. Legion, Mil. Order World Wars, Vets. Foreign Wars. Clubs: Appalachian Mountain, Harvard (Boston); Peterborough (N.H.) Golf. Home: Bonds Corner Rd., Hancock, N.H. Died Nov. 7, 1959.

HENSLEY, WILLIAM NICHOLAS, JR. army officer; b. Columbia, Neb., Oct. 18, 1881; s. William N. and Margaret Anna (McAllister) II.; grad. U.S. Mil. Acad., 1905, Mounted Service Sch. (Ft. Riley, Kan.) Sch. of the Line, 1922, Gen. Staff Sch., 1923, Army War College, 1926; G.S.C. eligible list; m. Matie Merle Manard, July 10, 1908; children-William Nicholas III, Gertrude Barbara. Commanding 2d lt. cav., June 13, 1905; promoted through grades to maj. regular army, July 1, 1920; organized div. of Philippine N.G., 1917; col. and chief q.m., Philippine N.G., 1917; col. Air Service, U.S.A., Aug. 24, 1918-June 30, 1920; comdr. army balloon sch., Pasadena, Calif., 1918-19; apptd. comdr. U.S.A. Air Service Sta., at Mitchel Field, L.I., July 17, 1923 First Am. to make non-stop flight, U.S. to Europe by air, as U.S. observer on return trip of R-34 from Eng., July 1919; made study of Zeppelin Airship Line in Germany, 1919, training as airship pilot; furnished War Dept. first detailed authentic information on the L-72, the giant dirigible build at Friedrichshafen for the bombing of N.Y. City the dirigible being practically completed when armistice was signed. Free balloon pilot, kite balloon pilot, and observer, airship pilot, airplane pilot, and distinguished marksman. Episcopalian. Mason. Home: Ft.Sam Houston, Tex. Died Mar. 21, 1929.

HEPBURN, ARTHUR JAPY naval officer; b. Carlisle, Pa., Oct. 15, 1877; s. Samuel and Marie (Japy) H.; Dickinson Coll., 1892-93; LL.D., 1938; grad. USN Acad., 1897; m. Louisa Lowndes Roman, June 15, 1899 (dec. 1933); children - Arthur Japy, Philip Roman; m. 2d, Agnes McMahon, June 3, 1950. Ensign, June 1899; promoted through grades to rear adm., June 1929. Asst. chief Bur. Engring., Navy Dept., 1919-22; chief of staff Naval Forces in Turkey, 1922-24, of U.S. Fleet, 1929-30; promoted adm., 1936; comdr.-in-chief U.S. Fleet, 1936-38; comdt. 12th Naval Dist. and Naval Operating Base, San Francisco, Feb. 1938-41; dir. pub. relations Navy Dept., May 1941, chmn. gen. bd., Aug. 1942-45; mem. naval staff at Limitation of Arms Conf., Geneva, 1927, London, 1930, Geneva, 1932. Del., Dumbarton Oaks Conversations, 1944. Sr. naval adviser UN Conf., San Francisco, 1945. Mem. Am. Soc. Naval Engrs., Theta Delta Chi. Clubs: Army and Navy (Washington); Chevy Chase (Md.); New York Yacht. Address: 2800 Woodley Rd., Washington 20008. Died May 31, 1964; buried Arlington Nat. Cemetery.

HERBERT, HILARY ABNER secretary of the navy; b. Laurensville, S.C., Mar. 12, 1834; s. Thomas E. and Dorothy Teague (Young) H.; family moved to Ala., 1846; student Univ. of Ala., 1853-54, Univ. of Va., 1854-56; (LL.D., Tulane Univ., and Univ. of Ala.); m. Ella B. Smith, Apr. 23, 1867. Admitted to bar, and practiced at Greenville, Ala., 1857-72; capt. to col. 8th Ala. Vols., C.S.A., 1861-64; moved to Montgomery, Ala., 1872; mem. 45th to 52d Congresses (1877-93); sec. of the navy in cabinet of President Cleveland, 1893-97. Democrat. In practice at Washington, 1897-: sr. mem. Herbert & Micou. Editor: Why the Solid South? or, Reconstruction and Its Results, 1890; The Abolition Crusade and Its Consequences, 1912. Grand marshal Confed. Vets. Reunion. Washington, June 1917. Home: Washington, D.C. Died Mar. 6, 1919.

HERBERT, JOHN KINGSTON, magazine exec.; b. Winthrop, Mass., Feb. 10, 1903; s. John William and Mary E. (Brickley) H.; m. Lucretia Reiner, Jan. 27, 1928; children—Sheila, John Kingston. Salesman, Standard Oil Co. of N.Y., Boston, 1921-28; cotton broker Cooper & Brush, New Bedford, Mass., 1928-31, Jones, Gardner & Beal, 1931-32; salesman Esquire mag., N.Y.C., 1932-38; New Eng. Mgr. Good Housekeeping mag., Boston, 1938-43, eastern advt. mgr., N.Y., 1945-47; gen. advt. mgr., v.p. Hearst Mags., Inc., 1947-50; v.p. in charge radio network sales NBC, N.Y.C., 1950-52, v.p. charge radio and TV sales, 1952, v.p. charge radio and television, 1953-54; exec. pub. N.Y. Jour.-American, 1954-55; pub. The Am. Weekly and Puck, The Comic Weekly, 1955-61; pres. Mag. Pubs. Assn., N.Y.C., 1961-69; pres. Microfragrance Div. John B. Lanigan & Assos., Inc., N.Y.C., 1971-72; v.p., marketing dir. Hearst Mags., 1972. Served as capt. aviation br. USMCR, 1943-45; lt. col. Res., ret. Clubs: Fifth Avenue (N.Y.C.); Everglades, Seminole (Palm Beach); Nat. Golf Links Am. Home: Southampton NY Died Sept. 24, 1972.

HERBERT, LOUIS army officer, engr.; b. La., Mar. 13, 1820; s. Valéry and Clarisse (Bush) H.; grad. Jefferson Coll., 1840, U.S. Mil. Acad., 1845; m. Malvina Lambremont, 1848, 3 children. Asst. engr. in constrn. of Ft. Livingston, La., 1845-47; served as maj. La. Militia, 1847-50, col., 1858-61; mem. La. Senate, 1853-55; chief engr. La., 1855-59; served as col. 3d La. Inf., Confederate Army, from 1861, commd. brig. gen., 1862; editor Iberville South, Plaquemine, La., 1866-circa 1870; taught sch., Iberville and St. Martin Parish, La., 1870-1901. Died Jan. 7, 1901.

HERBERT, PHILEMON THOMAS congressman; b. Pine Apple, Ala., Nov. 1, 1825; attended U. Ala.; Moved to Mariposa City, Cal., circa 1850; mem. Cal. Assembly, 1853-54; mem. U.S. Ho. of Reps. (Democrat) from Cal., 34th Congress, 1855-57; moved to El Paso, Tex., circa 1859, practiced law; served as lt. col. 7th Tex. Cavalry, Confederate Army, during Civil War; fatally wounded at Battle of Mansfield, 1864. Died Kingston, La., July 23, 1864; buried Evergreen Cemetery, Kingston.

HERKIMER, NICHOLAS army officer; b. in what is now Herkimer, N.Y., 1728; s. Johan Jost and Katharine Herkimer; m. Lany Tygert; m. 2d, Myra Tygert. Served as lt. N.Y. Militia during French and Indian Wars; comdr. Ft. Herkimer, 1758; chmn. Com. of Safety of Tyron County (Mohawk Valley), N.Y.; brig. gen. N.Y. Militia in charge of defense against Indian and Tory attacks (because of large Loyalist following in Mohawk Valley), 1776; in charge of relief expdn. to Ft. Stanwix which was besieged by British, ambushed by Tories and Indians at Oriskany, forced to retreat; although it appeared to be a Brit. victory, its adverse effect on larger Brit. strategy of Gen. Burgoyne was influential to overall Am. cause. Died nr. Little Falls (N.Y.) of wounds received in Battle of Oriskany, Aug. 16, 1777.

HERNANDEZ, JOSEPH MARION territorial del.; b. St. Augustine, Fla., Aug. 4, 1793. Transferred his allegiance from Spain to U.S.; del. to U.S. Congress from Territory to Fla., Sept. 30, 1822-23; mem. presiding officer Fla. Territorial Ho. of Reps.; apptd. brig. gen. volunteers in Seminole War; served with U.S. Army, 1835-38; commanded expdn. which captured Indian chief Oceola, 1837; apptd. brig. gen. Mounted Volunteers, 1837; unsuccessful Whig Candidate for U.S. Senate, 1845; moved to Cuba, engaged as planter in Dist. of Coliseo, nr. Matanzas. Died "Audaz," Dist. of Coliseo, Matanzas Province, June 8, 1857; buried Junco family vault, San Carlos Cemetery, Matanzas.

HERNDON, THOMAS HORD congressman; b. Erie, Ala., July 1, 1828; grad. U. Ala., 1847; attended Harvard Law Sch., 1848. Admitted to Ala. bar, 1849, began practice in Eutaw; editor Eutaw Democrat, 1850; moved to Mobile, Ala., 1853, practiced law; mem. Ala. Ho. of Reps., 1857-58; trustee U. Ala., 1858-59; mem. Ala. Secession Conv., 1861; served as maj. lt. col., then col. 36th Regt., Ala. Inf., Confederate Army, during Civil War, twice wounded in battle; volunteered to command troops at evacuation of Spanish Fort after Civil War, credited with saving hundreds of lives; resumed law practice, Mobile. Unsuccessful candidate for gov. Ala., 1872; mem. Ala. Constl. Conv., 1875; mem. Ala. Ho. of Reps. 1876-77; mem. U.S. Ho. of

Reps. (Democrat) from Ala., 46th-48th congresses, 1879-82. Died Mobile, Mar. 28, 1883; buried Magnolia Cemetery, Mobile.

HERNDON, WILLIAM LEWIS naval officer; b. Fredericksburg, Va., Oct. 25, 1813; s. Dabney and Elizabeth (Hull) H.; m. Frances Elizabeth Hansbrough, Mar. 9, 1836, 1 child. Became midshipman U.S. Navy, 1828; commd. lt., 1841; commanded ship Iris in Mexican War, 1847-48; stationed at Naval Observatory, Washington, D.C., 1848-51; head of Amazon River exploration trip, 1851-53; promoted comdr., 1855; commanded Pacific Mail steamer Central America, 1855-57; a naval destroyer named for him, 1919. Author: Exploration of the Valley of the Amazon, 2 vols., 1853-54. Died Sept. 25, 1857.

HERO, ANDREW, JR. army officer; b. New Orleans, La., Dec. 13, 1868; s. Andrew and Otweana R. (Pugh) H.; Tulane U., New Orleans, 3 yrs., Columbia. 1 yr.; grad. U.S. Mil. Acad., 1891, Arty. Sch., 1896; m. Fanny Caroline, d. Capt. J. M. K. Davis, July 14, 1897; children-Jacklyn (wife of H. W. Brimmer, U.S. Army), Prentice, Elinor Kelso (Mrs. T. G. Murrell), Andrew. Commissioned 2d lt., 12th Infantry. June 12, 1891; promoted through grades to col., Coast Arty. Corps, May 15, 1917; brig. gen. N.A., Aug. 5, 1917. Special work in electricity, Arty. Sch., 1896-98; with 3d Div., 1st Army Corps, Chickamauga Park, 1898-99, Matanzas, Cuba, Jan.-May 1899; instr. in drawing, U.S. Mil. Acad., 1899-1902; editor Jour. U.S. Arty., 1902-07; asst. to chief Coast Arty., 1909-11; brigade adj., 1st Separate Brigade, Galveston, Tex., Mar.-June 1911; adj. S. Atlantic Coast Arty. Dist., Charleston, S.C., 1913-15. comd. 1st Federal Training Camp for Boys, Ft. Terry, N.Y., July 6-Aug. 10, 1916; comd. 154th F.A. Brig., 79th Div., Sept. 17, 1917-Dec. 9, 1918, and Feb. 1-May 25, 1919, Camp Meade, Md., training to July 14, 1918, Liverpool, Eng., July 31, 1918, firing schools, France, Aug. 8,-Nov. 19, 1918; with 153d F. A. Brig., Meuse-Argonne offensive, Nov. 1, 1918; on duty G.H.Q., A.E.F., Dec. 9, 1918-Jan. 31, 1919; army center of arty. studies, Treves, Germany, Feb. 16-Apr. 2, 1919; brigade joined div., Dec. 1918; left France, lfay 15, 1919; comd. 39th Arty. Brig. (C.A.C.), May 25, 1919-Oct. 4, 1921; staff, 2d C.A. Dist., Oct. 1921-Nov. 1922; Coast Defense, Manila and Subic Bays, Jan. 1923-Mar. 1925; comd. 4th C.A. Dist., June-Dec. 1925; chief C.A.C., rank of maj. gen., Mar. 1926-Mar. 1930; maj. gen. retired, May 1930. Republican. Episcopalian. Home: Washington, D.C. Died Feb. 7, 1942.

HERRICK, CHARLES JUDSON univ. prof.; b. Minneapolis, Oct. 6, 1868; s. Rev. Henry Nathan and Anna (Strickler) H.; B.S., U. Cin., 1891, Sc.D., 1926; M.S., Denison U., 1895, Sc.D., 1930; Ph.D., Columbia, 1900, Sc.D., 1931; m. Mary Elizabeth Talbot, Aug. 17, 1892; 1 dau., Ruth. Instr. natural sciences, Granville Acad., 1891-92; prof. natural sciences, Ottawa U., 1893-93; fellow in biology, 1893-95, instr., 1895-96. Denison U.; univ. scholar biology, Columbia, 1896; asso. in comparative neurology, Pathol. Inst. of N.Y. State Commn. in Lunacy, 1897-1901: prof. zoology, Denison, 1898-1907; prof. neurology, U. Chgo., 1907-34, emeritus in residence, 1934-37, emeritus 1937, chmn. dept. anatomy, 1933; visiting prof. anatomy, emeritus, U. Mich., 1942. Fellow A.A.A.S. (secretary zool. sect. 1902-07, chmn. 1908); pres. Ohio Acad. Science, 1903. Author many books and papers on biol. and neurol. subjects. Editor Journal Comparative Neurology since 1894. Commd. maj., Sanitary Corps, N.A., 1918. Mem. Nat. Acad. Sciences, Kan. Akademic von Wetenschappen to te Amsterdam, Norwegian Acad. of Science and Letters; Royal Acad. Science of Sweden; honorary member American Neurol. Assn., Société Scientifique "Antonio Alzate," Mexico; corr. mem. Academie Royale de Medicine de Belgique. Home: 236 Morningside Drive, Grand Rapids 6, Mich. Died Jan. 29, 1960.

HERRICK, CURTIS JAMES, ret. army officer; b. Fordville, N.D., Aug. 12, 1909; s. James O. and Lillian Madeline (Connolly) H.; B.S., U.S. Mil. Acad., 1931; grad. Command and Gen. Staff Coll., 1942, Army-Navy Staff Coll., 1944, Indsl. Coll. Armed Forces, 1949, Fgn. Service Inst., 1963; m. Alice Milnor Reasoner, Mar. 3, 1936; children—Curtis James, Robert M., Alice (Mrs. Larry J. Reynolds), Mary R. (Mrs Robert P. Moltz). Commd. 2d lt. U.S. Army, 1931, advanced through grades to maj. gen., 1961; various inf. and armor assignments, 1931-42; battalion comdr. and staff positions 11th Armored Div., 1942-44; dep. chief logistics U.S. Army Forces, Pacific, 1944-47; rear echelon comdr. Joint Task Force 7, 1947-48; operations staff officer, chief deployments br. operations, gen. staff Dept. Army, 1949-52; regtl. comdr., asst. div. comdr. 11th Airborne Div., 1952-53; regtl. comdr. 223d Inf. Regt., Korea, 1953; sr. adviser III ROK Corps, Korea, 1953-54; dep. comdr., then comdr. 187th Airborne Regtl. Combat Team, 1954-55; chief staff XVIII Airborne Corps, also dep. comdg. gen. XVIII Corps, 1955-57; asst. div. comdr. 25th Inf. Div., 1957-59; dep. for adminstrs. USARPAC, 1959-60; chief staff 3d U.S. Army, 1960-61; comdg. gen. XI Corps, 1961-63; chief JUSMMAT, 1963-65; comdg. gen. Mil. Dist. Washington, U.S. Army, 1965-67. Decorated D.S.M., Silver Star, Legion of Merit with oak leaf cluster, Bronze Star, Combat Inf. badge, Sr. Parachutist badge; Ulchi Distinguished Service medal with silver star (Korea). Home: Honolulu HI Died Feb. 9, 1971; buried Arlington National Cemetery, Arlington VA

HERRINGTON, ARTHUR WILLIAM SIDNEY, tech. adviser U.S. Mission to India; b. Coddenham, Eng., Mar. 30, 1891; s. Arthur and Mary Matilda (Pottinger) H.; brought to U.S., 1896; ed. Stevens Prep. Sch. and Stevens Inst. Technology, hon. M.E., 1943; honorary Engr. Dr., Rose Polytechnic Inst., 1943; m. Nell Ray Clarke, Feb. 12, 1926; 1 son, Arthur Clarke. Served with U.S. Army, Oct. 1917-Sept. 1919; with motorcycle companies, 7th and 4th infs., Tex.; Motor Transport Corps, Washington, D.C., 2d div. supply train, A.E.F., 1st Army hdqrs., G-4; hon. discharged as capt. Motor Transport Corps. Asso. with various motor car companies and cons. engr. U.S. Army and Marine Corps, 1921-31; designed several types of mil. trucks with 4- and 6-wheel drives, also track laying tractors; vice pres. and chief engr., Marmon-Herrington Co., 1931, pres. 1931-42, chmn. bd., 1940-60; member board directors Gabriel Corporation, Cleve.; economic adviser to government of Pakistan, 1949-50. Director, American Medical Center for Burma, Inc., Phila. Appointed technical adviser to Louis Johnson, head of American Mission to India, 1942. Mem. Soc. Automotive Engrs. (nat. pres. 1942), Soc. Am. Mil. Engrs. (dir.), Army Ordnance Assn. (dir.), Newcomen Soc. Episcopalian. Mason (32 deg., Shriner). Clubs: Indianapolis Service, Indianapolis Athletic, Columbia, Woodstock Country (Indianapolis); Bohemian (San Francisco); Gibson Island (Md.) Yacht, Tred Avon (Md.) Yacht; University, Yacht, Metropolitan (N.Y.C.); Automobile Old Timers (pres.); Cruising Am.; Quisset (Mass.) Yacht. Home: Indianapolis IN Died Sept. 6, 1970.

HERRMANN, ERNEST EDWARD naval officer; b. Memel, Germany, July 17, 1896; s. Albert Edward and Friedrieka (Wiechmann) H.; came to U.S., 1897, naturalized, 1905; student Coll. City of New York, 1914-15; B.S., U.S. Naval Acad., 1918; m. Jean Simpson Stewart Hughes, June 8, 1918: 1 dau. Margot Jean. Commd. ensign U.S. Navy June 6, 1918, and advanced through grades to rear adm., March 4, 1944; on duty, Cruiser Transport Force, World War I; served in various capacities, chiefly gunnery, in Atlantic and Pacific Fleet ships, 1918-39; battle force gunnery officer, 1939-40, U.S. Fleet gunnery officer, 1940-41; instr. in ordance and gunnery U.S. Naval Acad., 1924-26, 29-31, 34-37; coordinator for antiaircraft matters, Bur. of Ordnance, Navy Dept., Washington, D.C., 1941-43 dir. of plans, 1943-44; commanded heavy cruiser U.S.S. Boston, from Marianas campaign to beginning Okinawa campaign, 1944-45; chief, logistic plans, Office of Chief of Naval Operations, Navy Dept., 1946; comd. cruiser Div. 3, U.S. Pacific Fleet, 1947, Div. 13, 1948-49; supt. U.S. Naval Postgrad. Sch. since 1950. Awarded 3 Legions of Merit for service World War II. Episcopalian. Author: Exterior Ballistics, 1926, 1930, 1935 (official text books on subject, U.S. Naval Acad.). Address: Supt. U.S. Naval Postgraduate School, Monterey, Cal. Died Nov. 19, 1952; buried Arlington Nat. Cemetery.

HERRON, CHARLES DOUGLAS, army officer (ret.); b. Crawfordsville, Ind., Mar. 13, 1877; s. William Park and Ada (Patton) H.; prep. edn., Wabash Coll., Crawfordsville, 1892-96, A.M., 1908; grad. U.S. Mil. Acad., 1899; attended Gen. Service Sch., 1906-08; distinguished grad. Army Sch. of the Line, 1907; grad. Army Staff Coll., 1908; attended Army War Coll., 1919-20, Field Arty. Sch., 1923-24; m. Louise Milligan, Nov. 12, 1912; children—William Milligan, Louise. Entered army, 1899; advanced through grades to maj. gen., 1937; in operation against Philippine Insurgents, 1899-1901; instr. U.S. Mil. Acad., 1908-10; comd. 313th F.A., 1917-18, Gen. Staff Gen. Hdqrs., 1918; chief of staff of 78th Div., Sept. to Dec. 1918; War Dept. Gen. Staff, 1919, 1920-23; chief of Staff Philippine Dept., 1927-29; exec. for Res. Affairs, War Dept., 1930-35; comdg. Hawaiian Dept., 1938-41; retired Mar. 31, 1941. On active duty with War Dept. Gen. Staff since Sept. 1941; ret. 1946. Decorated with medals, Spanish-Am. War, Philippine Islands, Mexican Border; D.S.M.; Officer Legion of Honor (France); La Solidaridad (Panama). Mem. Beta Theta Pi. Presbyn. Club: Army and Navy. Author: War Dep. Gen. Staff Manual, 1923. Home: Bethesda MD

HERSEY, HENRY BLANCHARD meteorologist and balloonist; b. Williamstown, Vt., July 28, 1861; s. Joel and Recta Wheelock (Blanchard) H.; B.S., Norwich U., Vt., 1885, M.S., 1906; course at U.S. Signal Service Tech. Sch., Va.; m. Mrs. Laura A. Saunier, Mar. 13, 1926 (died 1940). Service of U.S. Weather Bur., 1885-1932. Maj. 1st U.S. Vol. Cav. ("Roosevelt's Rough Riders"), Spanish-Am. War; exec. officer Wellman Chicago Record-Herald Polar Expdn., 1906-07; experienced meterologist and balloonist, being a licensed aeronautic pilot of the Aero Club of France, and of the Aero Club of America. Assisted Lt. Frank P. Lahmn, U.S. Army, in the internat. balloon race at Paris, 1906, helping to win the James Gordon Bennett cup; sailed the balloon "United States" in the internat. race at St. Louis, 1907, crossing lakes Michigan, St. Clair and Erie, and landing in Canada. Apptd. maj., Aviation Sect., Signal Corps. May 1917, and placed in command U.S. Army Balloon Sch., Ft. Omaha, Neb.; rated as jr. mil. aeronaut, July 24, 1917; promoted lt. col. Signal Corps, U.S. Army, Sept. 27, 1917; served with balloon div., Air Service, in France, Oct. 1918-Mar. 1919. Fellow Royal Meteorol. Soc., London; mem. Southern Calif. Acad. Sciences, A.A.A.S., etc. Elected permanent non. comdr. Los Angeles Bd. No. 4, Am. Balloon Corps Vets. Mason (32ff). Club: Cosmos (Washington). Contbr. on aeronautical subjects to Century Mag. Home: 135 East Laurel Av., Sierra Madre, Calif., Died Sept. 24, 1948.

HERSEY, MARK LESLIE army officer; b. Stetson, Me., Dec. 1, 1863; s. George L. and Olive (Hodsdon) H.; A.B., Bates Coll., Me., 1884; grad. U.S. Mil. Acad., 1887; A.M., Bates Coll., 1902, LL.D., 1919; LL.D., U. of Me., 1921; m. Elizabeth Noyes, Sept. 16, 1887; children-Mark Leslie, Dorothy, Alice Elizabeth. Add. 2d lt. 19th Inf., June 12, 1887; promoted through grades to col., 58th Inf., July 27, 1917; brig. gen.; N.A., Aug. 28, 1917; maj. gen., Oct. 15, 1918; returned to grade of col. U.S.A., Aug. 31, 1919; brig. gen. (temp.), July 15, 1920-Mar. 4, 1921; reapptd. brig. gen., confirmed Mar. 5, 1921; maj. gen., Sept. 20, 1924; retired Nov. 2, 1924 Supt. supplies, City of Boston, Oct. 1925-26. Detached service at U. of Me., 1891-1805, with the Philippine Constabulary, 1905-14, chief of Mindanao Constabulary, 1909-14; assigned as comdr. 155th Inf. Brigade, Camp Dix, N.J., Aug. 29, 1917; comd. 155th Inf. Brigade in St. Mihiel offensive and defensive and at Bois des Loges in the Meuse-Argonne, until Oct. 29, 1919, when assigned to command 4th Div.; comd. 4th Div. on march to the Rhine and throughout service with Army of Occupation. returned to U.S. with 4th Div., July 31, 1919. Decorated D.S.M. (U.S.); officer Legion of Honor and Croix de Guerre with palm (France). Democrat. Episcopalian. Home: Washington, D.C. Died Jan. 22, 1934.

HERSHMAN, OLIVER SYLVESTER editor, publisher; b. Pittsburgh, Pa., July 2, 1859; s. Henry Logan (killed in Union Army, Civil War) and Lucy (Buhoup) H.; pub. sch. edn.; m. Belle C. Boyd, May 24, 1904. Entered business office Pittsburgh Evening Telegraph, 1873, becoming business mgr.; consolidated this paper with the Evening Chronicle, forming Chronicle Telegraph, 1884; pub. same until 1900, when he bought The Press, later acquiring Daily News, which he merged with The Press; pres. and treas. The Press Pub. Co. Republican. Apptd. a.d.c. on staff of Gov. Stuart of Pa., 1907, with rank of lt. col., and reapptd. by Govs. Tener and Brumbaugh. Mem. Pittsburgh Chamber Commerce. Home: Pittsburgh, Pa. Died July 9, 1930.

HERVEY, HARCOURT, retired banker; b. Los Angeles, Sept. 2, 1892; s. Edward King Blades and Browning (Clarke) B.; A.B., U. Cal. at Berkeley, 1916; m. Ruth Brown, June 18, 1917; 1 son, Harcourt. Various positions Security 1st Nat. Bank, Los Angeles, 1920-52, v.p., until 1952. Served from 2d lt. to col., U.S. Army, 1917-19; participated all actions of 1st Division, AEF; apptd. lt. col. ORC; apptd. lt. col. Cal. N.G., 1922, advanced through grades to maj. gen., overseas duty, 1942-45; participant all action of 40th Inf. Div. and Korea occupation, ret., 1947. Decorated Silver Star, Legion of Merit, Air Medal, Purple Heart (U.S.); Croix de Guerre, Fouragerye of Croix de Guerre, Verdun medal (France); Comdr. Philippine Legion of Honor; Medal of Merit with oak leaf cluster (State of Cal.); Cal. N.G. service medal with diamond clasp (25 years). Mem. S.R., Soc. Colonial Wars, Am. Legion, Soc. of First Div., U.S.O. (hon. v.p.), Psi Upsilon, Phi Delta Phi. Episcopalian. Mason (32 degree). Home: Pasadena CA Died Dec. 28, 1970.

HERVEY, HARCOURT, JR., banker; b. Los Angeles, May 14, 1920; s. Harcourt and Ruth (Brown) H.; student U. Cal. at Berkeley, 1939-41; m. Constance B. Smith, Jan. 3, 1946; children—Harcourt III, Robert Rhodes, John Kendall. Loan officer The John M. C. Marble Co., Los Angeles, 1946-52, sec., 1952-60; v.p. The Marble Co., Pasadena, Cal., 1952-68, dir., 1950-68; dir. O. K. Earl Constrn. Co., Pasadena, 1961. Served to maj., inf., AUS, 1941-46; to lt. col., 1950-52. Decorated Bronze Star with two oak leaf clusters, Philippine Medal of Merit. Mem. Pasadena C. of C. (mem. Am. enterprise com.), Soc. Colonial Wars, S.R., Psi Upsilon. Republican. Episcopalian. Mason (32 degree). Clubs: Valley Hunt (Pasadena); Balboa Angling (Newport Beach, Cal.); San Pasqual (pres.) (Pasadena, Cal.). Home: Pasadena CA Died Dec. 30, 1968.

HESS, ELMER physician; b. Millville, N.J., May 31, 1889; s. Frederick and Mary (Theise) H.; prep. edn. Peddie Sch., Hightstown, N.J., 1903-07; M.D., U. of Pa. Med. Sch., 1911; grad. study, Johns Hopkins U., 1919-21; grad. study in Europe, 1919, 1925; D.Sc., Allegheny Coll., Meadville, Pa., 1956; m. Edna Africa, June 26, 1911; children - Celeste Remle (wife of Capt. P. W. Cann, USN, ret.), Hope (Mrs. John W. Luther). Physician Indian Service U.S., 1911-12, in pvt. practice of medicine and surgery at Erie, Pa., 1912-, specializing in urology, 1920-; consultant urologist numerous hospitals Pennsylvania. Surveyed med. installations in Israel for Hadassah, 1956. Chmn. health resources adv. com. Office Civil and Def., Exec. Office of President, Washington. Served from lt. to capt. M.C., U.S. Army, 1917-19, with 15th F.A., 2d Div., A.E.F. Decorated Croix de Guerre, Verdun medal, Chateau Thierry medal (France); 3 army citations (Silver Star), Victory medal with 5 clasps (U.S.). Pep. nominee for mayor, Erie, 1919; pres. Erie Boys Club, 1919-39; mem. bd. trustees, pa. Soldiers and Sailors Home 1940-56; mem. Pa. State Board of Medical Education and Licensure, 1946-57. Mem. of governing com. Gorgas Memorial Inst. Certified by Am. Bd. Urology, 1935. Fellow Am. Coll. Surgeons, Internat. Coll. Surgeons, Academy-Internat. of Medicine; member A.M.A. (pres. 1955-56), Pa. State Medical Society (pres., 1947-48), Erie County Med. Soc. (pres. 1938), Am. Urol. Assn. (pres. 1952), Western N.Y. and Ontario l)rol. Assn. (pres. 1941), Canadian Urol. Assn., World Med. Assn., Pan-Am. Urol. Assn., Pan.-Am. Med. Assn. (trustee since 1937; pres. urol. sect. 1937), Newcomen Soc. of England, Am. Legion, Forty and Eight; hon. mem. Detroit Urol. Soc., Western Branch Soc. Am. Urology Assn.; corr. mem. Cuban and Argentine urol. soc.; hon. mem. Colegio Brasileiro de Urologistas. Republican. Episcopalian. Mason. Clubs: Erie, Kahkwa, Rotary (pres. 1943-44), Lake Shore Golf, Aviation Country. Contributor medical jours.; urol. editor Cyclopedia of Medicine, Revision Service for Sajou's System of Medicine, 1933-40, 1942-54. Home: 4819 Highview Blvd. Office: 8 E. 12th St., Erie, Pa. Died Mar. 29, 1961; buried Wintergreen Gorge Cemetery, Erie.

HESS, HARRY HAMMOND, geologist; b. N.Y.C., May 24, 1906; s. Julian S. and Elizabeth (Engel) H.; B.S., Yale, 1927; Ph.D., Princeton, 1932; D.Sc. (hon.), Yale, 1969; m. Annette Burns, Aug. 15, 1934; children—George Burns, Frank Deming Mather. Geologist Loangwa Concessions, Ltd., N. Rhodesia, 1928-29; geologist gravity measuring cruises U.S. submarines S-48 and Barracuda, 1931, 36; asst. instr. Rutgers U., 1932-33; research asso. geophys. lab. Carnegie Instn., Washington, 1933-34; instr. Princeton U., 1934-37, asst. prof., 1937-46, asso. prof., 1946-48, prof., 1948-69, Blair prof. geology, 1964-69, chmn. dept., 1950-66; vis. prof. U. Cape Town, 1949-50, Cambridge U., 1965. Chmn. Space Science Bd., 1962-69; mem. U.S. nat. com. geology Internat. Union Geol. Scis., 1961-69, chmn., 1961-62; mem. div. com. math., phys. and engrng. scis. NSF, 1960-64; cons. U.S. Navy Oceanographic Office, 1966-69, Nat. Council Marine Resources and Engring. Devel., 1967-69; mem. Pres.'s Com. Nat. Medal Sci., 1967-69; mem. sci. and tech. adv. com. manned space flight NASA, 1964-69, mem. lunar and planetary missions bd., 1967-69, mem. lunar sample analysis planning team, 1967-69. Served comdr. USNR; commanding officer U.S.S. Cape Johnson, 1945; rear adm. USNR. Recipient Penrose medal Geol. Soc. Am., 1966; Feltrinelli prize Accademia Nazionale dei Lincei, 1966; Distinguished Pub. Service medal NASA, 1969. Fellow Geol. Soc. Am. (pres. 1962), Mineral Soc. Am. (pres. 1954-55); mem. Nat. Acad. Sci. (chmn. sect. geology 1960-63), Mineral Soc. London, Geol. Soc. S. Africa, Soc. Econ. Geologists, Am. Geophys. Union (pres. sect. geodesy 1951-53, pres. sect. tectonophysics 1956-58), NRC (chmn. division of earth sciences 1956-58, chmn. committee on disposal radioactive waste 1955-62), Geol. Soc. London, Am. Soc. Oceanography (dir. 1966-69), Sociedad Venezolana de Geologos (hon.), Am. Philos. Soc., Accademia Nazionale dei Lincei, Am. Acad. Arts and Scis. Clubs: Cosmos (Washington); Nassau (Princeton). Author articles in science journals. Discoverer greatest depth in oceans, 1945. Home: Princeton NJ Died Aug. 25, 1969; buried Arlington National Cemetery, Arlington VA

HESSER, FREDERIC WILLIAM naval officer; b. Hinsdale, Mont., Dec. 2, 1904; s. William Hewey and Jessie Marie (Lemon) H.; B.S., U.S. Naval Acad., 1927; M.B.A., Harvard, 1932; grad. Army Indsl. Coll., 1938; m. Annah Clarke Day, Apr. 11, 1930; 1 dau., Joann Patricia. Commd. ensign. Supply Corps, U.S.N., 1927, advanced through grades to rear admiral, 1953; associate professor Harvard, 1943-45; exec. officer Navy Supply Corps Sch., 1942-45; staff supply officer Western Sea Frontier, 1945-48; fleet supply officer Pacific Fleet 1948-49; Gen. Stores Supply officer, Phila., 1949-53; dir. Navy Cost Inspection Service, 1953. Recipient Navy Commendation Ribbon. Clubs: University (Washington); Bohemian (San Francisco). Home: care H. D. Walter, 1275 Greenwich St., San Francisco 9. Office: Bur. Supplies and Accounts (OT) Navy Dept., Washington 25. Died Apr. 1, 1954; buried Arlington Nat. Cemetery.

HESTER, CLINTON MONROE, lawyer; b. Des Moines, Ia., Apr. 16, 1895; s. John Kenton and Sarah Hannah (Hamilton) H.; grad. Phillips-Exeter Acad., 1916; A.B., George Washington U., 1920; LL.B., Georgetown U., 1922; m. Margaret Lee Bixby, July 30, 1965; children—Todd McCane, and Jean Hamilton. Admitted to practice before Dist. of Columbia bar, 1922; atty. Dept. of Interior, 1922; asst. counsel U.S. Shipping Bd. and U.S. Shipping Bd. Emergency Fleet Corp., 1922-27; counsel Office U.S. Alien Property Custodian and special assistant to Attorney General of United States, 1927; chief attorney U.S. Dept. of Justice, 1927-34, U.S. Dept. of Treasury, 1934-35; asst. gen. counsel Dept. of Treasury, 1935-38; adminstr. CAA, 1938-40, supervised construction of Washington National Airport; apptd. mem. Nat. Advisory Com. for Aeronautics, Aug. 23, 1938; resumed private practice of law Oct. 1, 1940. Mem. James Madison Meml. Commn., 1960-71; chmn. exec. com. 1961. Served with 301st Engrs., 76th Div., AUS, 1918-19. Mem. American, District of Columbia bar associations, Phi Gamma Delta. Mason. Owns historic estate Bath Alum, Hot Springs, Va. Pioneered survey airplane flights for comml. passenger service across Atlantic and South Pacific. Home: Washington DC Died July 1971.

HESTER, JOHN KENTON air force officer; b. Plains, Mont., Nov. 7, 1916; s. John Kenton and Anna Pearl (McMillan) H.; B.S. in Ceramics, U. Ill., 1938; grad. Air Force Flying Sch., 1939, Air War Coll., 1949; m. Helen Vivian Singer, Nov. 29, 1941; children - Virginia Randall, John Kenton. Commd. 2d lt., Air Corps, U.S. Army, 1939, advanced through grades to maj. gen. USAF, 1960; assigned Albrook Field, C.Z., 1939-41, Craig Field, Ala., 1941-43, CBI, 1943-45; mil. aide to sec. air force, 1945-48; assigned Armed Forces Spl. Weapons Project, 1949-50; comdr. 22d Air Base Group, March AFB, Cal., 1950; dep. comdr. 43d Bomb Wing, Davis-Monthan AFB, Ariz., 1951, comdr. 303d Bomb Wing, 1952-54; dir. operations 15th Air Force, March AFB, 1954-55; comdr. 806th Air Div., Lake Charles, La., 1955-57; chief staff 2d Air Force, Barksdale AFB, La., 1957-59; dep. dir. operations Hdqrs. USAF, Washington, 1959-62, asst. vice chief of staff, 1962-64; commander of the 17th Air Force, 1964-. Decorated Legion of Merit with Oak Leaf cluster, D.S.M. Episcopalian (vestry, lay reader). Address: Comdr. 17th Air Force, APO 12, N.Y.C. Died Apr. 8, 1965; buried Arlington Nat. Cemetery.

HETERICK, ROBERT HYNTON med. dir. USPHS (ret.); b. Georgetown, O.; s. Robert Grand and Martha Bell (Cooper) H.; student U. Cin., M.D., Med. Coll. of Ohio, 1906; grad. U.S. Army Med. Sch., 1911; m. Frances Susan Felker, Feb. 8, 1908. Resident physician Ohio Maternity Hosp., 1906, Hosp. of Good Samaritan, Cin., 1907; commd. 1st lt., Med. Dept., U.S. Army, 1909; commd. asst. surgeon, US PHS, 1911, passed asst. surgeon, 1915, surgeon, 1923, sr. surgeon, 1931; served in Iloilo, Manila, Batan, P.I., 1912-15; instr. pub. health U. of Philippines, 1914-15; assigned to U.S. Naval Forces in European waters during World War I; med. dir., 3d Dist. U.S. Indian Service, 1935-36, commd. med. dir., 1937; formerly sr. med. officer Ellis Island Hosp., exec. officer Marine Hosps. at Chgo., Cleve. and San Francisco; former comdg. officer Vineyard Haven, Savannah and Louisville Marine hosps. and UASP Cal. Hosp., French Hosp., Cal. and Hollywood hosps., Los Angeles; chief quarantine officer, Port of Los Angeles, 1941-46; supr. ports of Hueneme, Port San Luis, Santa Barbara, Newport, San Diego, Quarantine affairs; dist. med. officer, War shipping Administrn., Los Angeles Dist., 1944-45; cons. in pub. health and sanitation to port surgeon, U.S. Army, Los Angeles, to sr. med. officer of U.S. Naval Bases at San Diego and Terminal Island, 1941-45; cons. in pub. health to State of N.M., City of Albuquerque; lecturer in pub. health U. So. Cal. Med. Sch., U. of N.M. Recipient medal S.A.R., 1948; hon. mem. Indian Medical Service, third district. Fellow A.C.S.; mem. A.M.A., Med. Officers of World War Vets. Fgn. Wars of America, Assn. Mil. Surgeons, S.A.R., Wanderers and Sojourners. Omega Upsilon Phi. Mason (32ff, Shriner). Author: articles on public health in various med. jours.; Health Hints for Primary Teachers, 1949. Also short stories for children. Address: 605 Ridgecrest Dr., Albuquerque, N.M. Died Sept. 14, 1957.

HEUBER, WILLIAM HENRY colonel U.S.A.; b. St. Louis, Mar. 2, 1843; s. Henry and Margaret (Wrede) H.; apptd. from Mo., and grad. U.S. Mil. Acad., 1865; unmarried. First lt. Engr. Corps, June 23, 1865; capt., Sept. 22, 1870; maj., Mar. 17, 1884; lt.-col., Jan. 29, 1900; col., June 11, 1904. Early service on surveys in Cal.; later on surveys of Union and Central Pacific rys.; on duty at Key West, Fla., New Orleans, New York and Phila.; afterward light house engr., and in charge of defenses, river and harbor improvements, etc., principally on Pacific Coast; retired by operation of law, Mar. 2, 1907; consulting engr. at San Francisco, 1907-17; recalled to active service, Apr. 1917, at San Francisco. Home: 1235 5th Av., San Francisco.†

HEUER, GEORGE J. surgeon; b. Madison, Wis., Feb. 6, 1882; s. George H. and Louisa (Zehnter) H.; B.S., U. Wis., 1903; M.D., Johns Hopkins, 1907: hon. LL.D., U. Cincinnati, 1932; m. Juanita Reid, July 18, 1925; children-George J., Reid. Intern Johns Hopkins Hosp., Baltimore, 1907, asst. resident surgeon, 1908-11, resident surgeon, 1911-14; asso. prof. surgery. Johns Hopkins, 1914-22; prof. Surgery, U. Cincinnati, 1922-31. Cornell U. Med. Coll., 1931-47, prof. emeritus since 1947. Surgical dir. Cincinnati Gen. Hosp., 1922-31; surgeon in chief New York Hosp., 1931-47, now cons. surgeon. Served as major, Med. Corps, U.S., in France, June 1917-Feb. 1919. Fellow Am. Coll. Surgeons, A.A.A.S.; mem. A.M.A., Am. Surg. Assn., Soc. Clin. Surgery, So. Surg. Assn., Am. Soc. Thoracic Surgery, Neuro Surg. Soc., N.Y. Surg. Soc., N.Y. Acad. Medicine, Med. Soc. State of N.Y. (mem. com. med. research), Harvey Soc. of N.Y., Am. Genetic Assn., N.Y. Acad. Science, Osler Soc. of N.Y.; hon. fellow Chicago Surg. Soc.; hon. mem. Soc. of Univ. Surgeons; corr. hon. mem. Academy Science, Med., Physical and Natural, U. of Havana, Cuba. Mem. Founders Group, Am. Bd. of Surgery. Mem. adv. bd. Cushing Brain Tumor Registry of Yale U. Sch. of Medicine. Clubs: University (New York); Megantic Fish and Game (Quebec and Me.). Contbr. to surg. jours. and chapters on surgery of thorax to Keen's Surgery, Lewis's Surgery. Nelson's Loose Leaf Surgery. Home: 2900 N.E. Center Av., Fort Lauderdale, Fla. Died Dec. 15, 1950; buried, Finecastle, Va.

HEWETT, HOBART army officer; b. Mass., Mar. 21, 1900; B.S., U.S. Mil. Acad., 1918; grad. Coast Arty. Sch., Advanced Gunnery Course, 1930, Command and Gen. Staff Sch., 1936, Army War Coll., 1939; m. Myrtle Bickmore, 1921; children - Hobart B., Paul C., Everett B. Commd. 2d lt., C.A.C., 1918, advanced through grades to major C.E., 1942, maj. gen. 1954; served on Gen. Staff, 1940-51; asst. commdt. Arty. Sch., Ft. Bliss, Tex., 1952; comdg. gen. 3d div. arty., Korea, 1953; mem. UN Mil. Armistice Com., Korea, 1954; comdg. gen. 6th Regional A.A. Command, Ft. Baker, Cal., 1954-56; dep. comdr. in chief REUR, 1958-59; with Hdqrs. 6th Army, San Francisco, 1960; ret. 1960. Decorated D.S.M.; Comdr. Mil. Div. Order Brit. Empire. Address: 3040 26th Av., San Francisco 94132. Died Mar. 18, 1967; buried San Francisco Nat. Cemetery, The Presidio.

HEWITT, H. KENT, naval officer (ret.); b. Hackensack, N.J., Feb. 11, 1887; s. Robert Anderson and Mary (Kent) H.; ed. U.S. Naval Acad., 1903-06, (B.S.), Naval War Coll., 1928-29; LL.D., Middlebury Coll., m. Floride Louise Hunt, Aug. 23, 1913; children—Floride Hunt (wife of Capt. Le Roy T. Taylor, U.S.N. ret.), Mary Kent (wife of Capt. Gerald S. Norton, U.S.N. ret.). Commd. ensign U.S.N., 1908, and advanced through grades to adm., 1945; comdr. U.S. 8th Fleet, also U.S. Naval Forces Northwest African Waters, 1943-45; comd. landings Morocco, Nov. 8, 1942, Sicily, July 10, 1943, Salerno, Sept. 9, 1943, South Coast of France, Aug. 15, 1944; comdr. U.S. 12th Fleet and U.S. Naval Forces in Europe, Aug. 1945-Sept. 1946; U.S. rep. U.N. mil. staff com., N.Y.C.; retired from service 1949. Decorated Navy Cross with gold star, D.S.M. with gold star (Navy); D.S.M. with oak leaf cluster (Army) (U.S.), Knight Comdr. of Bath (Great Britain); Order of Kutuzov, First Class (Russia), Legion of Honor, Croix de Guerre with palm (France), Order of Southern Cross (Brazil), Order of Abdon Calderon (Ecuador), Order of Nichan-Iftikar (Tunis); Order of King George I (Greece), Order of SS. Maurice and Lazarus (Italy), Order of Orange-Nassau (Netherlands), Order of Leopold, Croix de Guerre with Palms (Belgium). Mem. U.S. Naval Inst. Episcopalian. Clubs: Army-Navy, Army-Navy Country (Washington), University, Century (New York). Home: Orwell VT Died Sept. 15, 1972; buried U.S. Naval Acad. Cemetery, Annapolis MD

HEWITT, LELAND HAZELTON ret. army officer; b. Northwood, Ia., Oct. 11, 1894; s. Leland G. and Frances S. (Hazelton) H.; B.S., U.S. Mil. Acad., 1918; B.S. in Civil Engring., Mass. Inst. Tech., 1921; grad. Engr. Sch., 1928, Command and Gen. Staff Sch., 1936; m. Birdie A. Krupp, Apr. 27, 1926; 1 dau., Margaret K. (Mrs. Robert B. Bolt). Commd. 2d lt. C.E., U.S. Army, 1918, advanced through grades to col., 1942; instr. U.S. Mil. Acad., 1918-20; dist. engr., Washington, 1933-34, Galveston, Tex., 1939-42, Seattle, 1946-49; organized 52d Combat Engr. Regt., 1942; comdr. 4th Engr. Aviation Unit Tng. Center, 1943; div. engr. New Eng. Div., 1952-54; exec. officer engr. sect. Gen. McArthur's Hdqrs., 1943; air engr. 5th Air Force, New Guinea, 1944; chief engr. Far East Air Force, 1944-46; army engr. U.S. Army in Caribbean, 1949-52; ret., 1954; mem. U.S. Beach Erosion Bd., intermittently, 1930-54, pres., 1953-54; U.S. commr. Internat. Boundary and Water Commn., U.S. and Mexico, 1954-62; mem. U.S. Sect. Internat. Park and Forestry Commn., U.S. and Mexico, 1956-62. Decorated Silvet Star, Legion of Merit, Purple Heart, Cross of Fundacion Internacional EEnlay Alfaro. Mem. Soc. Am. Mil. Engrs. Clubs: Army and Navy (Washington and Manila, P.I.); Army and Navy Country (Arlington, Va.). Rotarian. Home: 919 E. Kerbey St., El Paso, Tex. 79902. Died Mar. 31, 1964; buried Nat. Cemetery, Fort Bliss, Tex.

HEWITT, RICHARD MINER, medical editor; b. New London, Conn., Aug. 20, 1892; s. Richard Wheeler and Carie (Miner) H.; A.B., Wesleyan U. (Conn.), 1914; M.A., Princeton U., 1917; M.D., George Washington U., 1924; m. Dr. Edith Lillian Swartwout, Aug. 19, 1925. Teacher English, Sanford Sch., Redding Ridge, Conn., 1914-16; interne, Gorgas Hosp. Canal Zone, 1924-25; asst. editor, Jour. A.M.A., Chicago, 1925-28; asso. editor div. of publs., Mayo Clinic, Rochester, Minn., 1928-33, head of div., 1933-49, senior consultant, 1949-57, member emeritus staff, 1957-70; instructor in medical lit. Mayo Found. Grad. Sch., U. Minn., 1934, assistant professor, 1935-55, associate professor, 1955-57, emeritus, 1957-70; Alfred P. Sloan visiting prof. Menninger Sch. Psychiatry, Topeka, Kan., 1958. Served in U.S. Army, 1917-19, engaged in clin. pathology and writing Med. Dept., Surgeon Gen.'s Office. Fellow Am. Med. Writers Assn. chmn. ednl. com., 1951-54; distinguished service award, 1954, pres. 1955-56; mem. A.M.A. (asso.), Coffman Memorial Union (life), Alumni Assn. of the Mayo Foundation Member com. on information, Div. of Med. Sciences, National Research Council, 1940-44; mem. sub-com. on information, procurement and assignment service for physicians, dentists and veterinarians, Office Defense Health and Welfare, Fed. Security Agency (later under War Manpower Commn.), 1941-44; expert consultant to Preventive Med. Div., Surgeon General's Office, U.S.

Army, 1943-44; Minn. State Med. Assn., Delta Tau Delta, Phi Chi, Phi Beta Kappa, and Phi Beta Kappa Associates, Sigma Xi, American Legion. Republican. Baptist. Recipient Alumni Achievement Award. George Washington U., 1944, also from Wesleyan University (Connecticut), 1963. Author: The Physician-Writer's Book, pub. 1957. Joint editor: Collected Papers of the Mayo Clinic and the Mayo Foundation (annual vols.), 1928-57; gen. manuscript editor National Research Council series of 12 Military Surgical Manuals, 6 vols., 1942-43, mem. editorial bd. War Medicine, 1941-42, and its sponsoring com., 1942-44, The Am. Illustrated Med. Dictionary, 22d, 23d edits. Contbr. med. jours. Home: Rochester MN Died June 4, 1970; buried Cedar Grove Cemetery, New London CT

HEWLETT, A(LBION) WALTER physician; b. Petaluma, Calif., Nov. 27, 1874; s. Frederick and Cleora Melissa (Whitney) H.; B.S., U. of Calif., 1895; M.D., Johns Hopkins, 1900; studied in Germany, 1902-03; m. Louise Redington, June 12, 1907. House officer, New York Hosp., 1900-02: asst. instr. and asst. prof. medicine, Cooper Med. Coll., San Francisco, 1903-09: prof. internal medicine and dir. Clin. lab., U. of Mich., 1908-16: prof. medicine, Leland Stanford Jr. Univ., 1916-. Lt. comdr., M.C.U.S.N.R.F., 1917-. Republican. Episcopalian. Translator; Krehl's Clinical Pathology, 1905. Author: Functional Pathology of Internal Diseases, 1916-22. Died Nov. 10, 1925.

HEYDON, HENRY DARLING capitalist; b. Coventry, R.I., Dec. 25,1851; s. David and Remima Cordelia (Johnson) H.: ed. Mt. Pleasant Acad., Providence, R.I.; m. Charlotte Amanda Booth, Mar. 16, 1881. Began in mercantile business at Olneyville, R.I., 1871; formed partnership with Daniel W. Batchelder, 1874, and for over 30 yrs. operated gen. store at Crompton; now pres. Central Real Estate Co., Providence. Mem. R.I. Gen. Assembly, 1879-80, 1888-1902; mem. staff of Gov. Royal C. Taft of R.I., 1888-89, and of Gov. Herbert W. Ladd, 1889-92, rank of col.; served as chmn. State Armory Commn. and mem. Camp Ground Commn. for State Militia. Pres. bd. trustees R.I. Inst. for the Deaf; mem. bd. mgrs. Home for Aged Men and Aged Couples, Providence; mem. bd. dirs. Providence Lying-In Hosp. Republican. Episcopalian. Mason. Home: Providence, R.I. Died Jan. 8, 1925.

HEYMANS, CORNEILLE (JEAN) (FRANCOIS), educator; b. Ghent, Belgium, Mar. 28, 1892; s. Jean-Francois and Marie-Henriette (Henning) H.; M.D., University of Ghent, 1920; post grad. work, College of France (Paris), Universities of Lausanne and Vienna, University College (London), Western Res. Univ. Med. School; M.D. hon. University of Utrecht, 1938, Univ. of Louvain, 1940, M.D. (hon.), University of Montevideo, 1948, U. of Montpellier, 1953, U. of Torino, 1954, U. Santiago, Univ. Lima, U. of Bogota, 1958, University of Paris, 1959, U. Alger, 1959, U. Munster, U. Toulouse, U. of Bordeaux, U. Rio de Janeiro; m. Bertha May, Jan. 18, 1921; children—Marie-Henriette, Pierre, Jean, Berthe. Lecturer in pharmacology U. of Ghent, 1923-30, prof. pharmacology, 1930-66; emeritus professor of pharmacology, 1966-68; also lecturer in other large univs. throughout world. Served as lieutenant, F.A. Belgian Army, 1914-18. Head of medical department Belgian Relief Com., 1940-44. Awarded Nobel prize for physiology and medicine (for studies on physiology and pharmacology of respiration), 1939; prizes from Royal Acad. Medicine (Belgium), Pontifica Academia Scientiarium, Academie medecine de Paris, Institut de France, Acad. of Science (Bologna), U. of Berne, and others. Decorated Comdr. Order of Leopold, Officer Order of Crown, Cross of War. Mem. Royal Acad. of Medicine of Belgium, Pontificia Academia Scientiarium, Physiol. Soc. of Gt. Britain, Soc. for Exptl. Biology and Medicine, Societe belge de biologie, Nederlandsche Vereeniging voor Physiologie en Pharmacologie, Vlaamsche Chemische Vereening, Biol. Soc. Paris, French Soc. Endocrinology, Biol. Soc. Barcelona, Biol. Soc. Argentina, Societa Italiana biologia sperimentale, N.Y. Acad. Medicine, Am. Med. Assn., Acad. Medicine of Buenos Aires, Med. Soc. Argentine, Pharmacol. Soc. Argentine, Soc. Biol. Montevideo, Alpha Omega Alpha. Author: Le Sinus Carotidien, 1933. Contbr. articles on physiol. and pharmacol. problems sci. publs. Home: Ghent Belgium Died July 18, 1968.

HEYSINGER, ISAAC WINTER physician; b. Fayetteville, Franklin Co., Pa., Mar. 27, 1842; s. Jacob and Catharine (Stahl) H.; Dartmouth Coll.; A.B., Union U., 1863, A.M., 1866; U. of Mich., 1865-66; M.D., Jefferson Med. Coll., Phila., 1867; m. Laura A. Downey, of Fayetteville, Pa., Oct., 1869. Pvt. to capt., 7th Squadron R.I. Cav.; 19th Pa. Cav.; 45th U.S.C.T. Vols., Civil War, 1862-65. Practiced in Phila., July, 1867-. Has taken out over 100 patents; pres. Phila. Novelty Mfg. Co., 1884-, mfg. own inventions. Mem. Pa. State Insane Hosp. Commn. (now building hosp. for insane that has cost, so far, $2,250,000). Mem. Soc. for Psychical Research, London, Hist. Soc. Pa., Loyal Legion, Zeta Psi, etc. Author: The Source and Mode of Solar Energy Throughout the Universe, 1894, 2d edit., 1901; The Battle against Prosperity, 1896; Scientific Basis of Medicine, 1897; Spirit and Matter Before the Bar of Modern Science, 1910; The Mechanism of Conversion, 1912; The Military Life of Gen. George E. Pickett, 1912; Antietam and the Maryland and Virginia Campaigns of 1862, 1912. Translator: The Light of China (literal translation of the Tao Teh King, from the Chinese), 1903; also many translations from Persian, Hebrew and American native langs. Has written verse, and works on astronomy, psychology, comparative religions, and many other subjects. Connoisseur of art and has valuable collection of pictures (mostly by old masters) and many thousand valuable prints. Holds commn. as capt. signed by President Lincoln; was present at surrender of Gen. R. E. Lee, Apr. 8, 1865, and was made div. officer of the day, comdg. line of pickets for 3 miles. Home: 1521 Poplar St., Philadelphia.†

HEYWARD, THOMAS army officer, jurist; b. St. Helena's Parish, S.C., July 28, 1746; s. Daniel and Mary (Miles) H.; m. Elizabeth Mathewes, Apr. 20, 1773; m. 2d, Susanna Savage, May 4, 1786. Admitted to S.C. bar, 1771; elected to S.C. Ho. of Commons, 1772; del. S.C. Provincial Conv., Charleston, 1774; mem. 1st, 2d S.C. provincial congresses, Charleston, 1775; mem. S.C. Council of Safety; served on Com. of 11 to prepare Constn. for S.C., 1776; mem. 2d Continental Congress, 1776-78; signer Declaration of Independence, 1776; circuit judge, 1778-79, 84-89; capt. arty. battalion S.C. Militia in Charleston, 1780, served in Battle of Port Royal Island, 1779, defense of Charleston, 1780; mem. S.C. legislature from Charleston, 1782-84; a founder, 1st pres. Agrl. Soc. of S.C., 1785. Died St. Luke's Parish, S.C., Mar. 6, 1809; buried St. Luke's Parish.

HEYWOOD, CHARLES major general U.S. Marine Corps; b. Waterville, Me., Oct. 3, 1839; s. Lt. Charles (U.S.N.) and Antonia H.; m. Caroline Bacon, Oct. 25, 1866. Apptd. 2d lt. from N.Y., Apr. 5, 1858; promoted through grades to maj. gen., July 1, 1902. Saw service in quelling quarantine riots, Staten Island, N.Y., Sept. 1858; then on spl. service taking captured Africans back to Africa: later at Greytown, Nicaragua, looking after the filibuster, Walker; served in U.S.S. Cumberland, Sept. 1860, until it was sunk, with flag flying, in battle with Merrimac, March 8, 1862; took part in battle of Hatteras Inlet, and capture Forts Clark and Hatteras, Aug. 1, 1861; was on Hartford, battle of Mobile Bay; also at capture Forts Gaines, Morgan, Powell, and capture ram Tennessee, and steamers Gaines and Morgan; bvtd. maj. and lt. col. "for distinguished gallantry in presence of the enemy." Had comd. battalion of marines at Baltimore, Phila. and Reading during labor riots, and was hon. mentioned by Maj. Gen. Hancock; organized and equipped, 1885, battalion to open transit and protect Am. lives and property at Panama. Comdt. U.S. Marine Corps, 1891-1903; retired Oct. 3, 1903. Died Feb. 26, 1915.

HIBBEN, SAMUEL GALLOWAY, engr. elec. illumination; b. Hillsboro, O., June 6, 1888; s. Joseph M. and Henriette (Martin) H.; B.Sc., Case Institute Tech., 1910, E.E. (hon.), 1915, D.Eng., 1952; student U. of Paris, Sorbonne, France, 1918; m. Ruth Rittenhouse, April 14, 1923; children—Eleanor Rittenhouse, Stuart Galloway, Barry Cummings, Craig Rittenhouse. Began as electrician, 1906; illuminating engineer Macbeth Evans Glass Company, Pittsburgh, Pennsylvania, 1910-15; consulting engr., Pittsburgh, 1915-16; with Westinghouse Lamp Co. from 1916, dir. of lighting from 1933. Served as 2d and 1st lt. U.S. Army, searchlight design Washington, D.C., and capt. sound ranging, A.E.F., World War I; U.S. Strategic Bombing Survey, Germany, World War II. Mem. Am. Inst. E.E., Soc. Am. Mil. Engrs., Illuminating Engring. Soc. (p. pres), Am. Soc. Agrl. Engrs., Illuminating Engrs. London, Sigma Nu. Republican. Presbyn. Clubs: Engineers, Ohio Soc. of New York. Contbr. tech. articles. Credited with designing 1st mobile anti-aricraft searchlight, 1917; pioneered marine illumination; designed floodlight displays illuminating Washington Monument, Holland Tunnel, Natural Bridge and Endless Caverns in Va., Carlsbad Caverns, N.M., Crystal Cave, Bermuda. Home: Montclair NJ Died June 9, 1972.

HIBBS, LOUIS E., army officer; b. Washington, D.C., Oct. 3, 1893; s. Frank Warren and Janette (Nelson) H.; student Culver Military Acad., 1909-11; B.S., U.S. Mil. Acad., 1916; m. Margaret Hayes, Feb. 17, 1923; children—Louis Emerson. Commd. 2d lt., 1916 and advanced through the grades to major gen., 1943; combat duty with artillery, 1st Div. and 2d Am. Corps. 1917-18; adj. and aide to Gen. Douglas MacArthur, 1919-22; staff and command duties, 1922-40, at Ft. Sill, Okla., Ft. Leavenworth, Kans., Hawaii, Ft. Bragg, N.C., Washington, D.C., West Point, N.Y.; comdg. 63d Infantry Division, May 1943-46; Comdg. Field Art. Sch., Aug. 1945-June 1946; comdg. 12th Inf. Div., P.I., 1946, ret. from active duty. Decorated Distinguished Service Medal, Silver Star, Purple Heart with Oak Leaf Cluster. Home: Mirror Lake NH Died Apr. 28, 1970; buried Post Cemetery, U.S. Military Acad., West Point NY

HICHBORN, PHILIP rear adm. U.S.N.; b. Charlestown, Mass., 1839; grad. Boston High Sch.; was 5 yrs. shipwright apprentice, Boston Navy Yards; took course of spl. instruction in ship construction, calculation and design, by direction of Navy Dept. Went from Boston to Calif., 1860; entered Mare Island Navy Yard, becoming master shipwright, 1862; entered navy, 1869, as asst. naval constructor, becoming, 1875, after competitive exam., full constructor; chief constructor, 1893-1901; retired, Mar. 4, 1901. Hon. mem. Instn. Naval Architects, Eng. Mason. Invented Franklin Life Buoy, Hichborn Balanced Turrets. Died 1910.

HICKAM, JOHN BAMBER, physician, educator; b. Manila, Philippines, Aug. 10, 1914; s. Horace Meek and Helen J. (Bamber) H.; B.; A.B., Harvard, 1936, M.D., 1940; m. Mary Margaret Kennedy, May 12, 1945; children—Helen Kennedy, Thomas Bamber. Med. intern, asst. resident Peter Bent Brigham Hosp., Boston, 1940-42; chief med. resident Grady Hosp., Atlanta, 1942-43; instr. medicine Emory U. Sch. Medicine, 1946-47; from asso. in medicine to prof. medicine Duke Sch. Medicine, 1947-58; prof. medicine, chmn. dept. Indiana U. Sch. Medicine, 1958-70. Mem. aero-med. panel of sci. adv. bd. to chief of staff USAF, 1952-56, chmn., 1955-56; mem. cardiovascular study sect. Nat. Insts. Health, 1958-63, chmn., 1959-63; chmn. spl. med. adv. group VA, 1966-70. Trustee, Thomas Alva Edison Found.; Mem. Harvard Med. Alumni Council. Served to capt., M.C., AUS, 1943-46. Recipient exceptional service award USAF, 1957. Diplomate Am. Bd. Internal Medicine (mem. bd. 1965-70), Nat. Bd. Med. Examiners (exec. com., vice chmn.). Fellow A.C.P., Am. Coll. Cardiology; mem. A.M.A., Am. Federation Clin. Research, So., Central societies clinical research, American Physiol. Society, American Society Clinical Investigation, American Clin. and Climatological Association, Assn. Am. Physicians (sec. 1966-70), Am. Profs. Medicine (pres. 1969-70), Marion County Med. Soc., Phi Beta Kappa, Alpha Omega Alpha. Author papers cardiopulmonary physiology and disease. Home: Indianapolis IN Died Feb. 9, 1970; buried Indianapolis IN

HICKENLOOPER, ANDREW engr., soldier; b. Hudson, O., Aug. 10, 1837; s. Andrew and Abigail H. (Cox) H.; removed to Cincinnati 1844; ed. Woodward Coll.; practiced as civ. engr.; was chief engr., City of Cincinnati; entered army, 1861; capt. 5th O. battery; promoted to brig. gen., comdg. 3d brigade, 4th div., 17th army corps. For 5 yrs. U.S. marshal, Southern dist., O.; lt. gov. O., 1880-81; pres. Cincinnati Gas Light & Coke Co., 1872-. Author: Street Lighting, 1899; Fairy Tales, or Romance of an Arc Electric Lamp, 1901; Competition in the Manufacture and Delivery of Gas, 1881; Incandescent Electric Lights for Street Illumination, 1886. Home: Cincinnati, Ohio. Died 1904.

HICKENLOOPER, BOURKE BLAKEMORE, U.S. Senator; b. Blockton, Ia., July 21, 1896; s. Nathan Oscar and Margaret Amanda (Blakemore) H.; B.S., Ia. State Coll., 1920; J.D., U. of Ia., 1922; LL.D., Parsons Coll., 1942, Lorcas Coll., 1943, Coe Coll.; D.C.L., Elmira Coll.; m. Verna Eileen Bensch, Nov. 24, 1927; children—Jane Carroll (Mrs. Russell Oberlin), David Bourke. Admitted to Ia. bar June, 1922, and since practiced in Cedar Rapids; with Johnson, Donnelly & Lynch, 1922-25; private practice, 1925-35; formed firm Hickenlooper & Mitvalsky, 1935-42; mem. Ia. House of Representatives, 1935-39; lt. gov. of Iowa, 1939-43, gov., 1943-44; U.S. senator from Iowa, 1945-69. Served as 2d lieutenant, 339th F.A., A.E.F., World War I. Mem. Am., Linn County and Ia. State bar assns., Am. Legion, Phi Delta Phi, Sigma Phi Epsilon. Methodist. Mason (Shriner), Odd Fellow, Elk, Moose. Home: Cedar Rapids IA Died Sept. 4, 1971.

HICKEY, JAMES BURKE brig. gen.; b. in Md., May 8, 1848. Surgeon steward U.S.N., Apr. 4, 1864-May 15, 1865; grad. U.S. Mil. Acad., 1871; 2d lt. 8th Cav., June 12, 1871; 1st lt., Apr. 23, 1879; capt., Jan. 20, 1890; maj. a.-a.-g. vols., Sept. 5, 1899-Feb. 2, 1901; maj., 11th U.S. Cav., Feb. 2, 1901: transferred to 1st Cav., Nov. 29, 1904; lt. col., Nov. 30, 1904; mil. sec. U.S.A., Mar. 16, 1905; col. of cav., Nov. 15, 1908; brig. gen. retired, after 40 hrs.' service, Mar. 23, 1909. Home: New York, N.Y. Died Jan. 19, 1928.

HICKEY, PRESTON MANASSEH roentgenologist; b. Ypsilanti, Mich., Dec. 3, 1865; s. Rev. Manasseh and Sarah (Bush) H.; A.B., U. of Mich., 1888; M.D., Detroit Coll. Medicine, 1892; m. Grace Maley, Nov. 3, 1897. Practiced at Detroit, 1892-1922; prof. roentgenology, Detroit Coll. of Medicine, 1909-22; was roentgenologist Children's Harper and Receiving hosps.; lt. col. Med. Dept. U.S.A., consultant in roentgenology, A.E.F., in France, 1917-19; prof. roentgenology, U. of Mich., 1922-. Democrat. Methodist. Home: Ann Arbor, Mich. Died Oct. 30, 1930.

HICKOK, JAMES BUTLER (known as Wild Bill Hickok), army officer, scout, U.S. marshall; b. Troy Grove, Ill., May 27, 1837; s. William and Polly (Butler) H.; m. Mrs. Agnes Lake, Mar. 1876. Went to Kan., 1855, took part in border wars of area; constable Monticello Twp. (Kan.), 1856, fought McCanles gang at Rock Creek Station, Neb., killing McCanles and 2 of gang, 1861; stage driver on Sante Fe Trail, later on Oregon Trail; served as scout and spy for U.S. Army during Civil War; dep. U.S. Marshal Ft. Riley (Kan.), 1866; U.S. marshal Hays City (Kan.), 1869; marshall Abilene (Kan.), 1871; toured East with Buffalo Bill,

1872-73; went to Deadwood, Dakota Territory, 1874; known as good shot, frontier legends (pro and con) grew up around him. Shot by Jack McCall, Deadwood, Aug. 2, 1878. buried Mt. Moriah Cemetery, Deadwood.

HICKS, LEWIS EZRA college pres.; b. Kalida, O., Mar. 10, 1839; s. Ezra and Julia Anna (Lincoln) H.; B.A., Denison U., 1868, M.A., 1871, Ph.D., 1833; post-grad. Harvard, under Prof. Agassiz, 1869-70; (LL.D., Brown, 1912); m. Frances E. Edens, of Richmond, Ind., Mar. 12, 1864 (died 1884); 2d, Hattie A. Brown, of Cleveland, June 6, 1887. Lt.-col. 69th Ohio Inf., 1861-65; in all campaigns Army of the Cumberland; led assault on Reed's Bridge, Battle of Chickamauga; comd. regt. on "March to the Sea"; thrice wounded. Prof. science, Denison U., 1870-84; prof. geology, U. of Neb. (and state geologist), 1884-91; prof. physics, 1894-1905, pres., 1905-11, pres. emeritus, 1911-, Rangoon (Burma) Bapt. Coll. Fellow A.A.A.S.; charter member Geol. Soc. America, G.A.R., Loyal Legion. Associate editor Am. Geologist. Republican. Author of Critique of Design Arguments, 1882; and numerous scientific papers in periodicals and in state and govt. reports. Address: 6032 Harwood Av., Oakland, Cal.†

HICKS, THOMAS HOLIDAY ret. naval officer; b. Sept. 8, 1869; entered USN, 1892, and advanced through the grades to rear adm., 1925; retired 1933. Deceased.

HIGGINS, CHARLES H. architect; b. Southington, Conn.; s. Joseph and Catherine Ridley (Houchin) H.; grad. Cheshire Mil. Acad., 1898; C.E., Princeton, 1903; postgrad. Columbia, 1910-11; m. Claire Trumbull Van Lennep, Dec. 14, 1918; children - Trumbull, Anita (Townsend), Faith (McCurdy). Engaged on various bldgs., 1903-12; in practice as C. H. Higgins, architect, since 1912 (with Delano, Aldrich & Higgins, 1918-22). Various bldgs. including: Lab. for Research for IBM, Office bldg., present home of IBM, Corp., N.Y. Children's Home for Christian Herald, Dormitories, Valeria Home. United States Bldg., Paris Fair, 1937. Residences, including Finch House, Middletown, N.J., Hower House, New Canaan, Conn.; indsl. bldgs. including Endicott, N.Y., Charlestown, W. Va., lMem. Signal Corps., N.J. Nat. Guard, 1904-18; Plattsburg Mil. Camp, 1916; maj. Ordnance U.S. Army, 1918; lt. col. inactive, U.S. Army; pres. Manhattan Chpt. Res. Officers Assn. U.S., 1939-40. Received certificate Nat. Council Archtl. Registration Bd.; diplome de Grand Prix, Decerne a Public Architecture. Sec. Am. Fine Arts Soc., 1923-29. Mem. A. I.A. (past pres. N.Y. chpt.), France-Am. Soc. (dir.). Presbyn. Clubs: University, Military and Naval, Princeton (N.Y.C.); Southampton Bathing, Edgartown Yacht. Bathing (L.I.). Contbr. articles to Archtl. and tech. mags. Home: 755 Park Av. Office: 901 Park Av., N.Y.C. Died July 26, 1961.

HIGGINS, FRANCIS G. lawyer; b. nr. Missoula, Mont., Dec. 28, 1862; grad. Phillips Exeter Acad., 1884; Univ. of Mich. Law School, 1886 (LL.B.). First native born Montanian admitted to the bar; mem. 1st State legislature, 1889; mayor, Missoula, 1891; delegate Dem. Nat. Conv., 1892; during Spanish-Am. war, capt. Troop F, 3d U.S. vol. cav. (Grisby's regt. rough riders). Address: Missoula, Mont.†

HIGGINS, ROBERT BARNARD naval officer. b. Rockville, Md., Sept. 16, 1868; grad.U.S. Naval Acad., 1882. Promoted asst. engr., July 1, 1884; passed asst. engr., Jan. 15, 1895; transferred to the line as lt., Mar. 3, 1899; lt. comdr., Oct. 11, 1903; comdr., Jan. 30, 1908; capt., July 1, 1911. Served on Amphitrite, Spanish-Am. War, 1898, on Atlanta, 1904; fleet engr., S. Atlantic Squadron, 1904-05; duty at U.S. Naval Acad., 1905-07; fleet engr., Atlantic Fleet, 1907-18; at Navy Yard, N.Y. City, 1908-09; apptd. insp. engring. material, Conn. Dist., Sept. 1909. Died Jan. 6, 1928.

HIGGINSON, FRANCIS JOHN rear admiral, U.S.N.; b. Boston, Mass., July 19, 1843; s. Stephen and Agnes Gordon (Cochrane) lt.; apptd. from Mass., and grad. U.S. Naval Acad., 1861; m. Grace Glenwood Haldane, Jan. 5, 1878. Promoted lt., July 1, 1862; lt. comdr., July 25, 1866; comdr., June 10, 1870; capt. Sept. 27, 1891; commodore, Aug. 10, 1898; rear admiral, Mar. 3, 1890. Served on Colorado, W. Gulf Blockading Squadron, 1861-62; wounded in boat attack privateer Judity, Pensacola Harbor; participated in bombardments and passage of Fts. Jackson and St. Philip; engagements with Chalmette batteries, and capture of New Orleans; served Vixen, 1862, Powhatan, 1862-64, S. Atlantic Blockading Squadron; participated in bombardment of Ft. Sumter. exec. officer Housatonic when she was blown up by a torpedo of Charleston; Naval Acad., 1864-65; Hartford, Asiatic Squadron, 1865-68; Franklin, 1868-69; Richmond, 1873-74, Dictator, 1874; comd. naval rendezvous, Boston, 1874-75; exec. officer receiving ship Ohio, 1875; Torpedo Sch., Newport, 1875; Bur. Ordnance, 1875-77; on various duties to 1894: capt. of yard, Navy Yard, Mare Island, 1894-95; comd. Monterey, Feb.-Sept. 1895; spl. duty, Navy Yard, New York, 1895-96; capt. of yard, Navy Yard, New York, 1896-97; comd. Massachusetts, 1897-98, during war with Spain; advanced 3 numbers in rank for eminent and conspicuous conduct in battle, during Spanish-Am. War; chmn. Lighthouse Bd., 1898-1901; comdr.-in-chief N. Atlantic Fleet, 1901-03: comdt. Navy Yard, Washington, 1903-05; retired, July 19, 1905. Home: Kingston, N.Y. Died Sept. 13, 1931.

HIGHTOWER, LOUIS VICTOR, army officer; b. Union Springs, Ala., Aug. 11, 1909; s. Louis Victor and Annie Jean (Pippin) H.; student U. Tex., 1926-27; B.S. in Mech. Engring., U.S. Mil. Acad., 1931; grad. Nat. War Coll., 1952; m. Aug. 16, 1931; children—Gretchen B., Anne Ellen, Julia T., Louis Victor III (U.S. Army); m. 2d, Virginia Lovell, July 28, 1970. Commd. 2d lt., F.A., U.S. Army, 1931, advanced through grades to maj. gen., 1958; various assignments F.A. units and schools, U.S., 1931-41; assigned 1st Armored Div., ETO, 1941-42; comdr. rank battalion 1st Armored Regt., 1942-43, comdr. regt., 1943-44; pres. Armored Bd., Armored Center, Ft. Knox, Ky., 1944-46, Army Ground Forces Bd. 2, 1946-48; armored adviser, asst. chief U.S. Army Mission to Argentina, 1948-51; research and development coordinator Office Chief Staff, Dept. of Army, 1952-53; chief staff 2d Inf. Div., also comdg. officer 9th Inf. Regt., Korea, 1953-54; comdg. officer 40th Inf. Div., 1954; chief orgn. and tng. div. G3, operations, Dept. of Army, 1954-56; dep. comdg. gen. U.S. Army Carribbean, Ft. Amador, C.Z., 1956-57; chief staff Hdqrs. Caribbean Command, Quarry Heights, C.Z., 1957-58; sr. army mem. weapons systems evaluation group Office Dir. Def. Research and Engring., 1958-60; chief staff combined mil. planning orgn. Central Treaty Orgn., Ankara, Turkey, 1960-61, dep. comdg. gen. U.S. Army Ryukyus Islands, IX Corps, 1961-62, Continental Army Command, Ft. Monroe, Va., 1962-63; ret. D.S.C., Silver Star with oak leaf cluster, Legion of Merit with oak leaf cluster, Bronze Star medal with oak leaf cluster. Purple Heart with 5 oak leaf clusters. Clubs: University, Army-Navy (Washington). Home: Washington DC Died July 30, 1972; buried Arlington Nat. Cemetery, Arlington VA

HIGLEY, ALBERT MALTBY, bldg. contractor; b. Cleve., Feb. 2, 1895; s. Frank and Carrie (Maltby) H.; B.S., C.E., Case Institute of Technology, 1917; m. Mildred Schuch, September 11, 1926; children—Ann (Mrs. Joseph F. Kelley), Albert Maltby. Employed by contractor, 1920-25; organized, chmn. Albert M. Higley Co., 1925-69; dir. Central Nat. Bank Cleve., Land Title Guarantee & Trust Co. Chmn. Cleve. chpt. A.R.C., 1945-48; bd. govs. Am. Nat. Red Cross, 1951-54; trustee Denison U., 1954-60, Cleveland Development Found., Cast Inst. Tech. Served as 1st lt. AUS, 1917-19. Mem. C. of C. (dir., past chairman of the board). Clubs: Rotary (past pres.), Union, University, Mayfield Country (Cleve.). Home: Shaker Heights OH Died Dec. 30, 1969.

HILDRETH, HAROLD MOWBRAY psychologist; b. Franklin, Neb., Aug. 17, 1906; s. Carson and Flora Nowbray (Stockton) H.; A.B., U. Neb., 1927; student U. Chgo. and Chgo. Theol. Sem., 1927-30; Ph.D., Syracuse U., 1935; m. Jane Dibble Morgan, Feb. 18, 1949; 1 dau., Jacquelyn M. Chief psychologist Syracuse (N.Y.) Psychopathic Hosp., 1932-36; from instr. to prof. Syracuse U., 1936-46; br. chief clin. psychologist VA, San Francisco, 1946-48, chief clin. psychology div. Dept. Medicine and Surgery, Washington, 1948-56; cons. psychologist USPHS, 1956-. Served from lt. (j.g.) to lt. comdr. USNR, 1942-46. Mem. Am. (pres. div. cons. psychology 1951, pres. div. clin. psychology1n 1955, pres. div. psychologists in pub. service 1957, council of reps. 1949-52, 53-56, policy and planning bd., bd. dirs., 1956-59), Va. psychol. assns., Am. Public Health Assn., A.A.A.S., Am. Assn. U. Profs., Sigma Xi. Contbr. A Survey of Clinical Practice in Psychology, 1954. Author articles sci. jours. Home: 6230 Lakeview Dr., Falls Church, Va. Office: Nat. Inst. Mental Health, Bethesda 14, Md. Died Nov. 2, 1965.

HILDRETH, MELVIN ANDREW lawyer; b. Watertown, N.Y., Oct. 27, 1859; s. Curtis L. and Sarah Ann (Luther) H.; ed. Whitestown (N.Y.) Sem.; m. Luella Davis, Feb. 13, 1889. Began practice at Watertown, 1883; removed to Fargo, N.D., 1888; spl. asst. atty. gen., N.D., 1892; city atty., Fargo, 1892-94, 1902-04; asst. U.S. atty., N.D., 1913-14, U.S. Atty., 1914-24; now atty. in Cass County for Home Owners Loan Corp. Enlisted in Nat. Guard N.D., Oct. 1890; mem. 1st N.D. Vols., Spanish-American War; service as colonel, Philippine Insurrection, 1898-99; detailed as judge advocate by Maj. Gen. Otis; mem. commn. under treaty, 1899, to settle mil. affairs with Spanish Govt. in Philippines; brig. gen. N.D. N.G., 1908. Awarded Congressional Medal of Honor for active service. Life mem. Am. and N.D. State bar assns. Democrat. Presbyterian. Mason (K.T., Shriner). Home: 300 8th St. S, Office: 11 Broadway, Fargo, N.D. Died Jan. 13, 1944.

HILL, AMBROSE POWELL army officer; b. Culpeper, Va., Nov. 9, 1825; s. Maj. Thomas and Fannie (Baptist) H.; grad. U.S. Mil. Acad., 1847; m. Kitty Morgan, May 1859, 4 children including Lucy. Served in Mexican War, 1846-48, in Seminole War in Fla., 1849-50; commd. 1st lt., 1851; commd. col. 13th Va. Inf., Confederate Army, 1861, brig. gen., 1862; maj. gen., 1862, served in 3 engagements in Battle of Seven Days, 1862; served with Stonewall Jackson at battles of Cedar Mountain, 2d Bull Run, 1862; directed Confederate attack at Battle of Chancellorsville after Jackson was wounded, until he himself was wounded; promoted lt. gen., 1863; directed Confederate action of 1st day at Battle of Gettysburg, July 1, 1861; served in Battle of Wilderness, also in actions from North Anna and Cold Harbor; killed during last Union attack on Petersburg, (Va.), 1865; served in all great battles of Civil War in Va., considered one of ablest Confederate gens., famed for ability to move troops rapidly. Killed in Battle of Petersburg, Apr. 2, 1865; buried Richmond, Va.

HILL, ARTHUR DEHON lawyer; b. Paris, France, June 25, 1869; s. Adams Sherman and Caroline Inches (Dehon) H.; spl. student, Harvard, 1888-90, LL.B., 1894; m. Henriette Post McLean, June 20, 1895. Practiced at Boston, since 1894; dist. atty., County of Suffolk, 1908-09; mem. firm Hill, Barlow, Goodale & Wiswall; mem. corp. Provident Instn. for Savings Prof. law, Harvard, resigned in 1916; corp. counsel City of Boston, 1919-23. Commd. maj., Judge Advocate's Dept., U.S. Army, Dec. 27, 1917; lt. col., Apr. 23, 1919; hon. discharged July 7, 1919. Served in France, Jan. 1918-June 1919. Mem. Am. Bar Assn., N.Y. Bar Assn., Mass. Bar Assn., Assn. Bar City of Boston, Am. Legion. Mason, Elk. Clubs: Somerset, Union, Tavern, Union Boat; Harvard (Boston). Home: 61 Mount Vernon St., (summer) Portsmouth, N.H. Office: 53 State St., Boston, Mass. Died Nov. 29, 1947.

HILL, ARTHUR MIDDLETON, transportation exec.; b. Charleston, W.Va., Mar. 23, 1892; s. Arthur Edward and Ellen Dickinson (Middleton) H.; ed. Central Mo. State Coll.; Dr. of Engring. (honoris causa), Drexel Inst. Tech., 1948. married Caroline Quarrier Staunton, June 29, 1918; children—Frederick Staunton, Caroline Quarrier; m. 2d, Mary McDowell Ellis, Dec. 4, 1944. Former chmn., mem. exec. com., director The Greyhound Corporation and subsidiaires, retired, 1965; director, member executive committee Internat. Tel. & Tel.; pres., chmn. Charleston Transit Co. (formerly Charleston Interurban R.R. Co.); dir., pres. Kanawha City Co.; dir. Kanawha Banking & Trust Co., Greenbrier Valley Bank, Diamond Ice & Coal Co.; adv. dir. Riggs Nat. Bank, Washington. Mem. Rep. Nat. Finance Com. Served as 2d lt., advancing to capt., asst. chief of staff, 77th Div., AUS, WW I; grad. Army Gen. Staff College, Langres, France. Chairman National Association Motor Bus Owners; director U.S. C. of C., 1935-48; member bd. govs. Nat. Highway Users Conf. Chmn. Motor Bus Code Authority, N.R.A., 1933-35; spl. asst. to sec. of navy, 1942-45; chairman Nat. Security Resources Bd., 1947-48; member of the National Security Council. Awarded Medal for Merit World War II. Republican. Episcopalian. Mason (32 deg., Shriner). Clubs: Metropolitan, Burning Tree, Chevy Chase (Washington); Racquet and Tennis, Links (New York City); Seminole Golf, Bath and Tennis, Everglades (Palm Beach, Florida); Royal and Ancient Golf of St. Andrews (Scotland). Home: Washington DC Died Sept. 6, 1972; buried Lewisburg WV

HILL, CARLTON, lawyer; b. Hart, Mich., May 8, 1894; s. John and Margaret E. (Corcoran) H.; B.S., U. Mich., 1917; LL.B., Chicago Kent Coll. of Law, 1922; m. Janet O'Connor, Sept. 6, 1921; 1 dau., Sue Page (Mrs. George R. Keller). Admitted to Ill. bar, 1922, lawyer, specializing in patents, Chicago, from 1919. Served with U.S.M.C. and Res., 1917-49, active duty world wars I and II; retired as lt. col. Mem. Ill. Mfrs. Assn. (tech. adv. patent and trade mark com.), Am. Ill. State, Chicago bar assns., Am., Chicago (past pres.) patent law assns., Soc. Automotive Engrs., Tau Beta Pi, Phi Delta Phi. Home: Chicago IL Died Dec. 28, 1971; buried All Saints Cemetery, Des Plaines IL

HILL, DANIEL HARVEY army officer, coll. pres.; b. York Dist., S.C., July 12, 1821; s. Solomon and Nancy (Cabeen) H.; grad. U.S. Mil. Acad., 1842; m. Isabella Morrison, Nov. 2, 1852. served as 2d lt. U.S. Army in every important battle in Mexican War, 1846-48; prof. mathematics Washington Coll., 1849-54, Davidson (N.C.) Coll., 1854-59; pres. N.C. Mil. Inst., 1859-61; commd. brig. gen. Confederate Army, 1861, maj. gen., 1862, held the pass in Blue Ridge nr. Boonesboro until Stonewall Jackson had captured Harper's Ferry and Lee had crossed Potomac River during Md. Campaign, 1862; promoted lt. gen., 1863, in command of corps under Gen. Braxton Bragg at Battle of Chickamauga; publisher mag. The Land We Love, 1866-77; pres. U. Ark., 1877-84; directed Ga. Mil. Coll., 1885-89. Author: A Consideration of the Sermon on the Mount, 1858; The Crucifixion of Christ, 1860; The Elements of Algebra. Died Charlotte, N.C., Sept. 24, 1889; buried Davidson Coll.

HILL, FREDERICK THAYER, physician; b. Waterville, Me., June 14, 1889; s. James Frederick and Angie (Foster) H.; B.S., Colby Coll., Waterville, Me., 1910, D.Sc., 1936; M.D., Harvard, 1914; D.Sc. (honorary) University of Maine, 1942; m. Ruby Winchester Choate, June 16, 1924; children—Virginia, Barbara, Joan, Marjorie. Resident in otolaryngology, Mass. Eye and Ear Infirmary, Boston, Mass., 1915-16, mem. staff, 1919-20; engaged in pvt. practice as otolaryngologist, Waterville, Me., from 1920; mem. staff Sisters Hosp. (Waterville), 1920-30; mem. staff Thayer Hosp. since 1930; mem. cons. staff Central Maine Gen. Hosp., St. Marie's Hosp. (Lewiston), Augusta (Me.) Gen. Hosp., Gardiner (Me.) Gen. Hosp., Redington Hosp. (Skowhegan), Knox County Hosp. (Rockland), Waldo County Hosp. (Belfast), Miles

Memorial Hosp. (Damariscotta), St. Andrews Hosp. (Boothbay Harbor), Central Maine Sanatorium (Tb); v.p. planning and devel. Trayer Hospital; member consulting staff, Bath Memorial Hospital, Franklin Co. Hosp., Farmington, U.S. V.A. Hosp. Togus. Served as lt. Med. Corps, U.S. Army, 1918-19; instr. Army Sch. of Otolaryngology, Gen. Hosp. No. 14. Mem. Council for Health and Welfare, State of Maine; chmn. Me. Adv. Hosp. Commn. Dir. Am. Bd. Otolaryngology (pres., 1953-54); past mem. Federal Hospital Council; past president of Me. Hosp. Assn.; mem. bd. of directors Me. Heart Assn. Former trustee Colby Coll. Recipient Newcomen award American Laryngological Association, 1953, Roaldes award, 1961; received Roselle W. Huddilston award Me. Tb Association. Fellow A.C.S., Am. College of Hospital Administrators (hon.); mem. Am. Laryngol. Assn. (pres. 1948), Internat. Congress Otolaryngology (treas. 1957), Me. Med. Assn. (past pres.), New England Otolaryngol. Soc. (past pres.), Am. Otol. Soc. (pres. 1953), N.E. Hospital Assembly (pres. 1953), Am. Laryngol., Rhinol. and Otol. Soc., Am. Broncho-Esophol. Assn., American Academy of Ophthalmology and Otolaryngology (1st v.p. 1961), Am. Coll. Chest Physicians, Am. Cancer Soc., Zeta Psi, Alpha Kappa Kappa, Mason (33 deg.), Rotarian. Club: Harvard (Boston). Mem. editorial bd. Annals of Otology, Rhinology and Laryngology. Contbr. to Military Surgical Manual, Otolaryngology, 1942; also numerous articles to professional jours. and med. publs. Home: Waterville ME Died April 1969.

HILL, GEORGE ALFRED, JR. pres. Houston Oil Co. of Tex.; b. Corsica Tex., Jan. 12, 1892; s. George Alfred and Julia (McHugh) H.; student U. of Tex., 1907-11; m. Mary Van Den Berge, June 24, 1916; children-Joanne (Mrs. Pieter Cramerus), George Alfred, Raymond Monroe. Admitted to Tex. bar, 1911; assistant general attorney, I.G.N. Railroad, 1911-17; partner Kennerly, Williams, Lee & Hill, 1917-32; vice president and general counsel Houston Pipe Line Company, 1925-32, pres. since 1932; vice president and gen. counsel Houston Oil Co. of Texas, 1930-32, pres. since 1932; v.p. Houston Natural Gas Corp., 1928-32. Capt., Troop C, 7th Tex. Cav., during World War. Dir. gen., Houston Community Chest, 1933; dir. gen., Endowment Fund Campaign (1934) Mus. of Fine Arts, Houston, and pres. and trustee of mus., 1935-38; vice-pres. for production, Am. Petroleum Inst., 1934-46; vice-pres. San Jacinto Centennial Assn., Oil World Expn.; pres. San Jacinto Museum of History (1938-47), pres. The Philos. Society of Tex.; chmn. City of Houston Water Dept. Bd.; chmn. U. of Tex. Development Bd.; mem. Business Advisory Council of Dept. of Commerce; adv. to Am. Delegation, London, 1945, in re Anglo-American Oil Treaty. Director of Federal Reserve Bank of Dallas. Chmn. exec. com. S. Tex. C. of C. Dir. Houston Chamber of Commerce. Mem. Petroleum Industry War Council. Mem., chmn. Agenda Com., Nat. Petroleum Council; Chmn. Facilities Security Com. of Petroleum Administrator for War. Received Distinguished Service Award, 1946, Tex. Mid-Continent Oil and Gas Assn. Director Am. Petroleum Inst., Independent Pet. Assn., Mid-Continent Oil and Gas Assn.; mem. Tex. Petroleum Council, Am. Inst. Min-assns., Tex. State Hist. Soc. (vice pres. and fellow), Texas Folk-Lore Society, Yanaguana Society, Sociedad Bibliographia de Mexico, Kappa Alpha, Phi Delta Phi. First Knight of the Order of San Jacinto of the Sons of the Republic of Texas. Democrat. Episcopalian. Clubs: Houston Country, Bayou, River Oaks, Tex., Corinthian Yacht., Texas, University (Austin). Home: 1604 Kirby Drive. Office: Petroleum Bldg., Houston, Tex. Died Nov. 2, 1949.

HILL, HARRY W., naval officer; b. Oakland, Calif., Apr. 7, 1890; s. John Clayton and Ida Belle (Miller) H.; B.S., U.S. Naval Acad., 1911; grad. Army Chem. Warfare Sch., 1923, Navy War Coll., 1938; m. Margaret Harwood Hall, Oct. 8, 1913; children—Elizabeth Stockett, John Clayton (capt. USN ret.). Commissioned ensign, United States Navy, 1912, and advanced through grades to 4 star admiral, 1952; commanded U.S.S. Wichita, February 1942, serving in North Atlantic, Marmansk convoy, and with British Home Fleet. Commanded naval task force in South Pacific area, November 1942-Sept. 1943. Ordered to command Amphibious Group 2, U.S. Pacific Fleet, Sept. 1943; comd. assault and capture of Tarawa Atoll, Nov. 1943, and occupation of Apamama Atoll, Gilbert Islands, Nov.-Dec. 1943; comd. occupation force at Majuro Atoll, Marshall Islands, Jan. 31, 1944, where first American flag to fly over pre-war Japanese territory was hoisted. Comd. force which assaulted and captured Eniwetok Atoll, Marshall Islands, Feb. 17-22, 1944. Second in command of assault force which captured Saipan, Marianas Islands, June 15-July 9, 1944. In command of assault force which captured Tinian, Marianas Islands, July 24-Aug. 1, 1944. Second in command Assault Force, Iwo Jima, February-March, 1945. Promoted to vice admiral in command Fifth Amphibious Force, April 1945. In comd. Amphibious Force, Okinawa, May 17-July 1, 1945; in occupation of southwestern Japan, September-October 1945. Founder, comdt. National War College, Washington, 1946-49. Member United States Canadian Permanent Joint Bd. on Defense, 1940-42. Superintendent U.S. Naval Academy, 1950-52; gov. Naval Home, 1952-54. Bd. dirs. Hammond-Harwood House. Decorations: Distinguished Service Medal with Gold Stars in lieu of second and third award, Russian Order of Kutozov (2d Class), British Distinguished Service Order, Companion of the Order of the Bath (Great Britain); Legion of Honor (France). Campaign medals: Mexican, First Nicaraguan, American Defense, American Area, European Area, Asiatic-Pacific Area; expert pistol medal; mem. Helms Hall of Fame for basketball. Mem. Historic Annapolis, Potomac Chrysanthemum Soc. Episcopalian. Clubs: Army and Navy (Washington, D.C.); South River, Annapolis Yacht. Author: Maryland's Colonial Charm Portrayed in Silver, 1938. Home: Annapolis MD Died July 19, 1971; buried U.S. Naval Acad. Cemetery.

HILL, JAMES army officer, shipbuilder, legislator; b. Kittery, Me., Dec. 20, 1734; s. Benjamin and Mary (Neal) H.; m. Sarah Coffin; m. 2d, Sarah Hoyt; m. 3d, Martha Wiggin; 17 children. Patricipated in expdn. against French at Crown Point (N.Y.), 1755; shipwright on warship Achilles to Jamaica and Eng.; served as capt. under Gen. John Sullivan; Continental Army; in Revolution, 1775; signer of "Association Test", 1776; lt. col., 1777; served as brig. gen. N.H. Militia, 1788-93; fought with Gates against Burgoyne; mem. N.H. Provincial Congress, 1775; mem. 1st session N.H. Legislature under new N.H. Constn., 1784. Died Aug. 22, 1811.

HILL, JOHN A(RTHUR) wool specialist; b. nr. Carrollton, O., June 10, 1880; s. James Ross and Mary (Marshall) H.; B.S., University of Wyoming, 1907, Doctor of Laws (hon.), 1948; m. Evelyn Cornell, June 30, 1911; children-Robert Morris, John Marshall, Ross Corthell, Nellis Eugene, Sally Evelyn. Special work in wool, Philadelphia Textile Sch., Philadelphia, 1907; wood specialist University of Wyoming Expt. Station since 1907: prof. textile industry, Wyo. Agrl. Coll. since 1912; dean Agrl. Coll. and dir. Expt. Sta., U. of Wyo., 1923-50; chmn. bd. of deans for adminstrn. purposes, 1941-50; v.p. U. Wyo., 1950-51; cons. in animal husbandry. U.S. Bureau Animal Husbandry, 1928-32; judge of wool at Chicago International Live Stock Exposition, 1932, 33, 34, and at San Francisco World's Fair, 1940, at American Royal Livestock Exposition, 1947, 48, mem. advisory com. to study Nat. Live Stock Marketing Conditions, 1940-45; mem. wool advisory board, U.S. Dept. Agriculture. Awarded medal, Casper (Wyo.) Kiwanis, for distinguished service to state, 1943; named Outstanding Livestockman of U.S. for 1949 by Am. Soc. Animal Prodn. and portrait hung in Saddle and Sirloin Club, Chicago. Served as captain 166th Depot Brigade, World War I; commd. to Infantry Sec. O.R.C., United States Army, since 1923, now lt. col. (retired since June 30, 1944). Mem. Wyoming State Board Agr., Am. Soc. Animal Production (Western v.p. 1930-31; pres. 1932), N.E.A., Colo. Wyo. Acad. Science, Wyo. Farm Bureau, Reserve Officers Assn., Wyo. Pioneers Assn., Am. Legion, Sigma Xi, Epsilon Sigma Phi, Phi Beta Kappa, Phi Kappa Phi, Lambda Gamma Delta, Alpha Zeta; fellow A.A.A.S. Republican. Club: Lions. Coauthor: Range Sheep and Wool (with Fred S. Hultz), 1931. Writer and lecturer on wool production; contbr. to Nat. Wool Grower, Wyo. Stockman Farmer, Wyo. Wool Grower, etc. Mem. editorial bd. Jour. of Am. Soc. Animal Production, 1941-45. Home: 264 N. 9th St., Laramie, Wyo. Died Mar. 10, 1951; buried Laramie.

HILL, J(OHN) B(OYNTON) P(HILIP) CLAYTON lawyer; b. Annapolis, Md., May 2, 1879; s. Charles Ebenezer and Kate Watts (Clayton) H.: A.B., Johns Hopkins Univ., 1900; LL.B., Harvard Univ., 1903; m. Suzanne Howell, d. late John Howell and Mary Grafton (Rogers) Carroll, Oct. 28, 1913; children-Suzanne Carroll Clayton (Mrs. Phillips Huntington Clarke), Elise Bancroft Clayton, Catherine Coleman Clayton. Practiced at Boston, 1903-04, Baltimore and Washington, 1904-17; was mem. Hill, Randall & Leser (withdrew from firm 1925, because of congl. duties); resumed practice, 1927, Howe, Hill & Bradley, later Hill, Ross & Hill, Baltimore, Washington and New York; U.S. atty. Dist. of Md., 1910-15; counsel for Baltimore and State of Md. in N.J.-N.Y. Lighterage, Boston, Baltimore and Phila. Differential cases, 1930-33; spl. counsel State of Md. in Albany Port Differential, Pres. Artesian Water Co.; Rep. nominee Congress, 4th Md. Dist., 1908; Rep. candidate for nomination for mayor of Baltimore, 1915, 1915; pvt. Battery A, Mass. V.M., 1904; 2d lt., 1st lt., capt. 4th Inf., Md. N.G.; mil. observer 11th German Army Corps maneuvers, Sept. 1911; maj., judge adv. gen., Md. N.G., 1910-17; judge adv. 15th Div. Mexican border service, Aug. 26-Dec. 15, 1916: active duty, Aug. 3, 1917; mem. staff, 29th Div., Aug. 25, 1917-Dec. 10, 1918, then judge adv. and asst. G-3, Gen. Staff, 8th Army Corps, A.E.F., until its dissolution: liaison officer 17th French Army Corps during offensive north of Verdun, Oct. 1918; promoted lt. col., Oct. 22, 1918. Served in defense of center sector, Haute Alsace, July 25-Sept. 23, and Meuse-Argonne offensive, north of Verdun, Oct. 8-30, 1918; hon. disch., May 9, 1919; col. R.C., comdg. 306th Cav. Member Am. Battle Monuments Commn.; military observer 1st and 2d cavalry brigades, Interbrigade Maneuvers, British Army, Salisbury Plains, Sept. 1933; apptd. mem. Md. Tercentenary Commn., 1934; apptd. brig. gen. the asst. adj. gen. State of Md., June 8, 1935. Decorated D.S.M. (U.S.); Legion of Honor (French); Croix de Guerre, with silver star, for "most distinguished services in the operations north of Verdun." Oct. 1918; La Solidaridad (Panama); Polonia Restituta (Poland); The Star of Abdon Calderon, 1st class (Ecuador). Mem. 67th Congress (1921-23), 3d Md. Dist.; reelected to the 68th and 69th Congresses (1923-27), same dist.; not candidate for reelection to House but candidate for Rep. senatorial nomination, 1926, 193 lecturer on Am. Government, Johns Hopkins, various periods to 1924, and at Harvard, 1924. Author: Hill and Padgett's Annotated Public Service Commission Law of Md., 1913; The Federal Executive, 1916; National Protection-Policy, Armament and Preparedness, 1916. Homes: Annapolis, Md.; and Army and Navy Club, Washington, D.C. Died May 23, 1941.

HILL, LAMAR lawyer; b. Atlanta, Ga., May 27, 1885; s. Abner Welborn and Lucy Cobb (Erwin) H.: grad. Boys' High Sch., Atlanta, 1901; student U. of Ga., class of 1904; m. Adelaide Jaudon Singleton, Dec. 11, 1919; children-Adelaide Jaudon, Ellen Cobb. Admitted to Ga. bar, 1905, and began practice at Atlanta; removed to N.Y. City, 1919; counsel Continental Ins. Co. and its affiliated companies, 1922-, v.p. and general counsel of same companies, 1924-. Served as lt. col. adj. gen., A.E.F., World War; lt. col. adj. gen., O.R.C. Pres. Young Men's Dem. League of Ga., 1906-08; v.p. Citizen's Independent Democracy of New York, 1920-22. Episcopalian. Mason. Home: New York, N.Y. Died June 24, 1937.

HILL, REUBEN L(ORENZO) coll. prof., chemist; b. Ogden, Utah, Mar. 24, 1888; s. George Richard and Elizabeth Nancy (Burch) H.; student Brigham Young U., 1908-11; B.S., Utah State Agrl. Coll., 1912; Ph.D., Cornell U., 1915; m. Mary Theresa Snow, Oct. 11, 1911; children-Reuben Lorenzo, Cornelia (Mrs. Mac Novak), Richard Snow, Theresa Marie (Mrs. Donald Ashdown), Wesley Sherwin, Alwyn Spencer, Edward Eyring, Carl David. Instr. in biochem. Cornell U., 1914-16; biochemist, Bureau of Chemistry, U.S. Dept. Agr., Washington, 1916; biochemist Md. Agr. Expt. Sta., 1916-18; head dept. chemistry Utah State Coll. of Agr. since 1919, human nutritionist, expt. sta., 1919-41. Commd. 1st lt., San. Corps, U.S.A., 1918; in Med. Officers Training, Camp Greenleaf, 1918, 2 mos.; nutrition officer, Camp Upton, L.I., 1918-19, 6 mos.: capt. Gen. Res. Corp. U.S. Army, 1927-41; recalled to active duty as maj., U.S. Army, 1941; completed Army Nutrition course, Army Med. Center, Washington, 1941, 2 mos.; nutritionist and chief Nutrition Service, 5th Service Command, U.S. Army, 1941-44, 34 mos.; apptd. lt. col., San. Res. Corps, 1946. Mem. Am. Chem. Soc., Am. Assn. Univ. Profs., A.A.A.S., Utah Acad. Arts, Sci. and Letters, Res. Officers Assn., Sigma Xi. Republican. Mem. Ch. of Jesus Christ of Latter-Day Saints. Author of research papers and bulls. on milk secretion, soft curd milk. Holder patent on original equipment used in Hill Curd Test. Home: 645 N. 8th East St., Logan, Utah. Died Jan. 22, 1953; buried Logan (Utah) City Cemetery.

HILL, ROLLA BENNETT pub. health officer; b. Franklin, Ill., Oct. 2, 1891; s. Charles Robert and Lulu (Morgan) H.; B.S., Whitman Coll., 1912; M.D., U. Pa., 1917; Dr. P.H., Johns Hopkins, 1931: m. Martha Claire McDowell, June 18, 1923; children-Martha Lyle (Mrs. Randolph Renda), Helen McDowell (Mrs. Winslow S. Caughey), Rolla Bennett. Staff, Rockefeller Found., 1920-56, field staff, then regional dir., 1920-51, asst. dir. med. edn. and pub. health, 1952-56; dir. Malaria Inst. of Portugal, 1935-38; mem. Malaria Commn. of Cuba, 1941-42; staff Pub. Health Tng. Sta., Jamaica, 1942-45. Served as capt., M.C., U.S. Army, 1917-19. Decorated govts. Venezuela, Portugal. Mem. Am. Pub. Health Assn., Am. Soc. Tropical Medicine and Hygiene, Royal Soc. Tropical Medicine and Hygiene, Am. Mosquito Control Assn. Home: 3575 Saint-Gaudens Rd., Coconut Grove 33, Fla. Died May 30, 1963.

HILL, TOM BURBRIDGE ret. naval officer; born Ft. Worth. Dec. 12, 1898; s. Benjamin Felix and Norma (Burbridge) H.; student Colo. Sch. of Mines, 1916-17; B.S., U.S. Naval Acad., 1922; student U.S. Naval Postgrad. Sch., 1927-28; M.S., U. of Mich., 1929; m. Lillian Jamison. Nov. 3, 1924; children-Thomas Burbridge, Emma Patricia (Mrs. Wm. Truman Smith), Norma Lillian (Mrs. John M. Redfield). Commissioned ensign United States Navy, 1922, and advanced through grades to vice admiral, retired; gunnery officer U.S.S. California and U.S.S. North Carolina. World War II; mem. staff of comdr. in chief Pacific, 1942-45; comd. U.S.S. Wyoming, 1945, U.S.S. Missouri, 1946-47; dep. dir., div. of atomic energy Office of Chief of Naval Operations, Washington, 1947-48, dir., 1949; mem. Mil. Liaison Com. to Atomic Energy Commn., 1949; amphibious task force commander Far East, 1951; chief of staff Pacific Fleet, 1952; superintendent naval gun factory, 1952; also comdt. Potomac River Naval Command, 1953. Awarded Legion of Merit, Bronze Star Medal, World War I Victory medal. American Defense medal with fleet clasp, Asiatic Pacific Area Campaign and World War II Victory medals. Member Naval Institute, Sigma Alpha Epsilon, Iota Alpha. Episcopalian. Clubs: New York Yacht; Army and Navy Country (Washington); Army and Navy. Home: 3803 Everett St., Kensington, Md. Died Oct. 21, 1957; buried Arlington Cemetery.

HILL, WILLIAM ironmaster, army officer; b. North Ireland, 1741; m. Jane McCall, 6 children. Came to Am., circa 1761, settled in Pa.; moved to S.C., 1762, acquired extensive land grants nr. Bowers's Mill Creek, before Am. Revolution; began iron works (with Isaac Hayne), Allison's Creek, S.C., 1776; supplied most of cannonballs used at siege of Charleston (S.C.), 1780; works burned by British, 1780; commd. lt. col. S.C. Militia, distinguished in several battles; mem. S.C. Legislature after Am. Revolution; justice Camden Dist., S.C., 1783, York County (S.C.) Ct., 1785-99; rebuilt iron furnace, 1787, built another in 1788 but paid his employees in iron. Died. Dec. 1, 1816; buried Presbyn. Churchyard, York, S.C.

HILLEBRAND, HAROLD NEWCOMB author, educator; b. Washington, Jan. 1, 1887; s. William Francis and Martha May (Westcott) H.; student Cornell U., 1905-06; A.B., Harvard, 1909, A.M., 1910. Ph.D., 1914. Sheldon traveling fellow Harvard, doing research work in London, 1911-12; asst. in English, Harvard, 1912-14; with U. Ill., 1914—, prof. English, 1931—, head dept. English, 1939-46. Served as 1st lt. inf. U.S. Army, 1917-18, capt., Camp Grant, Ill., and Camp Lee, Va., 1918-19. Unitarian. Author: Writing the One-Act Play, 1925; The Child Actors of the Sixteenth and Seventeenth Centuries, 1926; Edmund Kean, 1933; Troilus and Cressida. 1953. Editor New Variorum Shakespeare, 1946. Died Jan. 26, 1953.*

HILLES, FREDERICK VANTYNE HOLBROOK, ret. naval officer; b. Chgo., Apr. 18, 1908; s. John Adolphus and Grace (Holbrook) H.; B.S. in Elec. Engring., U.S. Naval Acad., 1930; student U.S. Naval Postgrad. Sch., 1937-38, U.S. Naval War Coll., 1948-49; m. Genevieve McKinley Brown, Dec. 19, 1934; 1 dau., Genevieve Diane (Mrs. Jack D. Clay). Commd. ensign U.S. Navy, 1930, advanced through grades to rear adm., 1958; assigned battleship U.S.S. Idaho, 1930-32, destroyers U.S.S. Hamilton, 1932-33, U.S.S. Barry, 1933-34, ammunition ship U.S.S. Nitro, 1934-35, light cruiser U.S.S. Omaha, 1935-37, destroyers U.S.S. Balch, 1939-41, U.S.S. Maury, 1941-42; comdg. officer destroyer U.S.S. Putnam, 1944-45; comdr. Destroyer Div. 132, 1945-46, gunnery officer 2d Fleet, 1949-51; comdg. officer attach transp. U.S.S. Calvert, 1954-55; comdr. Transp. Div. 52, 1955-56, Amphibious Squadron 5, 1956, Destroyer Flotilla 4, 1960-61; dir. strike warfare div. Office Chief Naval Operations, 1958-60; asst. chief Bur. Naval Weapons (astronautics), 1962; chmn. ship, characteristics bd. Office Chief Naval Operations, 1962-64, comdr. mil. sea transp. service Pacific aera, 1964-65, ret., 1965. Mem. exec. bd. San Francisco Bay Area council Boy Scouts Am., also chmn. sea explorer com. Decorated Bronze Star with V, numerous area and unit ribbons; Navy Legion of Merit. Mem. of the Am. Ordnance Assn., U.S. Naval Acad. Alumni Assn. (trustee 1959-62), U.S. Naval Inst., Nat. Geog. Soc. Episcopalian. Clubs: Propeller (Annapolis, Md.); Army-Navy Country (Arlington, Va.); Commonwealth of California (San Francisco). Author naval manual. Home: San Francisco CA Died Apr. 16, 1969; buried Arlington National Cemetery.

HILLHOUSE, JAMES senator; b. Montville, Conn., Oct. 21, 1754; s. William and Sarah (Griswold) H.; grad. Yale, 1773, LL.D. (hon.), 1823; m. Sarah Lloyd, Jan. 1, 1774; m. 2d, Rebecca Woolsey, Oct. 10, 1782; 5 children including James Abraham. Admitted to Conn. bar, 1773; lt. co. New Haven (Conn.) Volunteers, 1776; capt. Gov.'s Foot Guards when New Haven attacked by British under Tryon, 1779; mem. Conn. Ho. of Reps., 1778-85; mem. U.S. Ho. of Reps. from Conn. 2d-4th congresses, 1791-96; mem. U.S. Senate from Conn., Dec. 6, 1796-June 10, 1810, pres. pro tem, 1801-10; commr. Conn. sch. funds, 1810-25; treas. Yale Coll., 1782-1832. Died New Haven, Dec. 29, 1832; buried Grove St. Cemetery, New Haven.

HILLIARD, ISAAC, stock and bond broker; b. Louisville, Oct. 10, 1879; s. John James Byron and Maria Louisa (Henning) H.; grad. Lawrenceville Sch., 1898; A.B., Princeton, 1902; m. Helen Cochran Donigan, Nov. 1, 1910 (dec. 1932); children—Helen (Mrs. Peter E. Spalding, Jr.), James Henning; m. 2d, Elizabeth Haldeman Campbell, June 15, 1934 (dec. 1955). With J.J.B. Hilliard & Son (now J.J.B. Hilliard, W.L. Lyons & Company), Louisville, 1901-70, sr. partner, member Midwest Stock Exchange, 1905-70; past dir. Citizens Union Nat. Bank, Louisville Cement Co., Stearns Coal and Lumber Co., Ohio River Sand Co. Commnr., Jefferson County, 1933-35. Served to capt. U.S. Army, World War I. Clubs: Louisville Country, Pendennis, River Valley (Louisville). Home: Louisville KY Died May 16, 1970.

HILLIS, DAVID pioneer, state ofcl.; b. Washington County, Pa., Nov. 1788; s. William and Jane (Caruthers) H.; m. Ealia Werden, 1812; m. 2d, Margaret Burk; 5 children. Moved to Ind. Territory, 1808, became one of largest landowners in the area; commd. lt. col. 6th Regt., Ind. Militia, War of 1812, lt., 1813-14; asso. judge Ind. Circuit Ct., 1816-18; mem. Ind. Gen. Assembly, 1823-32, Ind. Senate, 1832-35; lt. gov. Ind., 1837-40; mem. Ind. Ho. of Reps., 1842-44. Died Jefferson County, Ind., July 8, 1845.

HILLMAN, JAMES FRAZER, business exec.; b. Pitts., Oct. 10, 1888; s. John Hartwell and Sallie Murfree (Frazer) H.; B.S., Yale, 1912; Doctor of Laws, University of Pitts., 1965; m. Marguerite Cabell Wright, Nov. 25, 1914; children—Constance Cabell (Mrs. John Oliver, Jr.), Marguerite (Mrs. Richard Purnell), Audrey (Mrs. Thomas Hilliard, Jr.), Sally Frazer (Mrs. J. Mabon Childs). Pres., dir. Harmon Creek Coal Corp. and affiliates since 1934; trustee Dollar Savs. Bank, Pittsburgh, Pa., director of Pitts. Chmn. Allegheny Conf. Community Development, 1950-52; pres. Pitts. Park and Playground Soc.; trustee Carnegie Inst.; dir. Civic Light Opera Assn.; vice president of Carnegie Library; mem. fine arts com. Carnegie Mus.; mem. adv. com. Home Crippled Children. Served as capt. inf., 82d Div. U.S. Army, 1918-19. Mem. Pitts. C. of C., Chi Phi. Episcopalian (trustee Pitts. diocese). Clubs: Duquesne, Pittsburgh Golf, Rolling Rock, Fox Chapel Golf, Elizabethan. Home: Pittsburgh PA Died May 1972; buried Homewood Cemetery, Pittsburgh PA

HILTON, DAVID CLARK surgeon; b. Saline County, Neb., Apr. 22, 1877; s. John Bulin Whitehead and Mary Elizabeth (Redgate) H.; A.B., U. of Neb., 1900, A.M., 1901; M.D., Rush Med. Coll., Chicago, 1903; m. Sarah Luella O'Toole, Aug. 23, 1900; children-Blossom Virginia (Mrs. Harold Stanley Gish), Ruth Acacia (Mrs. Woodward Burgert), Hiram David (M.D.). Practice Lincoln, Neb., since 1903; head of science depts., Cotner U., 1904-05; demonstrator in anatomy, U. of Neb., 1903-05; attending surgeon St. Elizabeth's Hosp. since 1905; attending surgeon Bryan Memorial Hosp. since 1926; consultant-surgeon U.S. Vets. Bur. Hosp. since 1930. Served as captain Med. Corps. U.S. Army, World War; col. comdg. 110th Med. Regt., Neb. N.G. 1925-40; div. surgeon, 35th Div., N.G., 1927-40; brig. gen. of the line, Neb. N.G., since Sept. 1940 (unassigned). U.S. del. to 5th Internat. Congress of Mil. Medicine and Pharmacy, Warsaw, Poland, 1927, VIth, London, Eng., 1929. Awarded cross of the Army Med. Sch. (Poland), 1927. Fellow A.A.A.S., Am. Coll. Surgeons; mem. A.M.A., S.A.R., Soc. Colonial Wars, Lancaster County Medical Soc., Inter-Professional Men's Inst., Neb. Ornithol. Union, The Audubon Soc., Neb. General. Soc., Lincoln Chamber of Commerce, Acacia, Sigma Xi. Republican. Anglican. Mason (33ff, K.T., R.C. of Constantine). Author of various papers on med., mil. and ornithol. subjects. Home: 2500 Woodscrest Blvd. Office: Continental Bldg., Lincoln, Neb. Died Dec. 12, 1945.

HIMSTEAD, RALPH E(BNER) educator, editor; b. Blue Mound, Ill., Jan. 31, 1803; s. Christopher and Carolyn (Ellrich) H. H., A.B. U. of Ill., 1916; LL.B., Northwestern U., 1921, A.M. 1924, J.D., 1924; S.J.D., Harvard, 1929: LL.D., Cornell College, 1946; married Dorothy Scott, September 7, 1918; children-James (dec.), Scott. Teacher English, Central High Sch., Omaha, Neb., Jan.-June 1919; prof. pub. speaking, Cornell Coll., Mt. Vernon, Ia., 1919-23, professor political science, 1923-24; Harris fellow in political science, Northwestern University, 1922-23; prof. of law, Syracuse U., 1924-36; gen. sec. Am. Assn. Univ. Profs., Washington, D.C., since 1936; research fellow Harvard Law Sch., 1928-29; prof. polit. science, Pa. State Coll., summers, 1925, 26; prof. law, Northwestern U. Sch. of Law, summer 1927. Mem. U.S. Office of Edn. Wartime Commn., 1941-43; mem. U.S. National Commn. for UNESCO. Served as private, advancing to rank of 1st lieut., U.S. Army, 1917-19; instr. Central O.T.C. June-Dec. 1918. Mem. Am. Polit. Science Assn., Am. Soc. Internat. Law, Am. Assn. Univ. Profs., Phi Delta Phi, Phi Kappa Phi, Delta Sigma Rho, Acadia. Methodist. Clubs: Cosmos, Federal Schoolmen's (Washington, D.C.), Manor Country (Norbeck, Md.). Author Elec. Utilities: The Crisis in Public Control (with W. E. Mosher); and articles and reports in edn. journals. Editor Bull, Am. Assn. Univ. Profs. since 1937. Home: 4110 Rosemary St., Chevy Chase, Md. Office: 1785 Massachusetts Av., Washington 6. Died June 9, 1955; buried Arlington Nat. Cemetery.

HINCKLE, WILLIAM lawyer; b. Riverside, Cal., Nov. 8, 1906; A.B., Stanford, 1927, J.D., 1930; student Harvard Law Sch. Admitted to Cal. bar, 1930; practice in Los Angeles; mem. firm Mitchell, Silberberg & Knupp. Served to comdr. USNR, 1942-45. Mem. State Bar Cal., Los Angeles County Bar Assn., Phi Delta Phi. Office: 6399 Wilshire Blvd., Los Angeles 48. Died Mar. 1961.

HINCKS, CARROLL CLARK judge; b. Andover, Mass., Nov. 30, 1889; s. Edward H. and Elizabeth Tyler (Clark) H.; prep. edn., Phillips Acad., Andover; A.B., Yale, 1911, LL.B., 1914, LL.D., 1952; m. Edith Walker Ney, Jan. 26, 1926. Law practice, New Haven, 1914-16, Waterbury, Conn., 1919-31; judge U.S. Dist. Ct., Dist. of Conn., 1931-53; judge U.S. 2d Circuit Ct. of Appeals, 1953-. Asso. fellow Branford Coll., Yale. Capt. F.A., Conn. N.G., 1916; capt. F.A., U.S. Army, 1917-19, Episcopalian. Clubs: Graduate (New Haven); University (Waterbury); Yale, Century (N.Y.C.). Home: Cheshire, Conn. Office: P.O. Bldg., New Haven. Died Sept. 30, 1964.

HINDMAN, THOMAS CARMICHAEL army officer, congressman; b. Knoxville, Tenn., Jan. 28, 1828; s. Thomas and Sallie (Holt) H.; m. Mary Biscoe, Nov. 11, 1856; 1 son, Biscoe. Served as lt. U.S. Army in Mexican War, 1846-48; admitted to Miss. bar, 1851; mem. Miss. Legislature, 1854; moved to Ark.; mem. U.S. Ho. of Reps. from Ark., 36th Congress, 1859-61, reelected, 1860, but declined seat to join Confederate Army; commd. maj. gen., enforced Jefferson Davis' western policy; served at Battle of Praire Grove, 1862, in fighting around Chattanooga and against Gen. Sherman; moved to Mexico, 1865, returned to Ark., 1867. Assassinated for opposition to Reconstrn., Helena, Ark., Sept. 27, 1868; buried Maple Hill Cemetery, Helena.

HINDS, THOMAS congressman; b. Berkeley County, Va., Jan. 9, 1780. Moved to Greenville, Miss., served as maj. cavalry during War of 1812, distinguished at Battle of New Orleans, brevetted brig. gen. for gallantry; unsuccessful candidate for gov. Miss., 1820; mem. U.S. Ho. of Reps. (Democrat) from Miss., 20th-21st congresses, Oct. 21, 1828-31. Died Greenville, Aug. 23, 1840.

HINES, CHARLES army officer; b. Salt Lake City, Dec. 25, 1888; B.S., U.S. Mil. Acad., 1910; grad. Coast Arty. Sch., 1929, Command and Gen. Staff Sch., 1931; Army War Coll., 1937. Commd. 2d lt. Coast Arty., 1910, and advanced through the grades to brig. gen., Apr. 1941; served as sec. Army and Navy Munitions Bd., 1939-42; dir. resources div., Services of Supply since Mar. 1942. Died Oct. 1966.

HINES, FRANK THOMAS army officer; b. Sale Lake City, Utah, Apr. 11, 1879; s. Frank L. and Martha J. H.; LL.D., Agrl. Coll. of Utah, 1920; LL.D., Lincoln Memorial U., 1927. U. ofAla., 1932; honor grad. Coast Arty. Sch., 1904; grad. C.A. Sch., 1911; LL.D., Bethany College, West Virginia, 1944; m. Nellie M. Vier, Oct. 4, 1900; children-Mrs. Viera H. Kennedy (dec.), Frank T. Jr. Sergt., 1st sergt. Battery B, Utah Light Arty., May 9, 1898-Mar. 22, 1899; commd. 2d lt. Utah Light Arty., 1899; hon. mustered out vols., Aug. 16, 1899; comd. 2d lt. Arty. Corps, U.S. Army, Sept. 20, 1901; promoted through grades to brig. gen. N.A., Apr. 18, 1918. Served in 24 engagements P.I., recommended for Congl. Medal of Honor; was in Europe, 1914, and assisted in returning 3,100 Am. citizens to U.S., after opening of World War; assigned to ofice of chief of staff as asst. in Embarkation Service, Aug. 5, 1971; 1917; apptd. chief of embarkation, Jan. 26, 1918; apptd. chief of Transportation Service, U.S. Army, 1919. With Secretary of War Baker represented U.S. at Interallied Transport Council, London, Sept. 1918; again in England also in France, January 1919, to represent War Department in adjustment of transport matters with allied nations; recommended by Pres. Wilson for permanent appmt. as brig. gen., Dec. 3, 1919; appmt. confirmed, Jan. 7, 1920; resigned from Army, Aug. 31, 1920; apptd. brig. gen. O.R.C., Sept. 7, 1920; dir. U.S. Vets.' Bur., Washington, 1923-30; administrator Vets.' Affairs, 1930-44; retraining and re-employment adminstrn., 1944-45; retired as brig. gen., 1944. Apptd. ambassador to Panama. 1945-48. Former mem. Am. Society Mechanical Engrs. Awarded D.S.M. (both Army and Navy); Companion Order of the Bath (British); Grand Officer Ordre de Léopold (Belgina); Legion of Honor (French); Order of Sacred Treasure, 2d class (Japanese); War Cross (Czechoslovakian). Clubs: Congressional Country, Sulgrave, Army-Navy (Washington, D.C.); Bonneville (Salt Lake City).Home: 3900 Cathedral Av. N.W., Washington 16, D.C. Died Apr. 3, 1960.

HINES, JOHN FORE, naval officer; b. in Ky., Sept. 22, 1870; grad. U.S. Naval Acad., 1892; Naval War Coll., 1910; m. Mary Dudley Breckinridge, Oct. 1898. Promoted ensign, July 1, 1894; lt. jr. grade, Mar. 3, 1899; lt., July 1, 1900; lt. comdr., July 1, 1906; comdr., Dec. 14, 1911; capt., July 1, 1917. Served on Dorothea during Spanish-Am. War, 1898; on Cincinnati, 1905-7; duty U.S. Naval Acad., 1907-10; exec. officer North Carolina, 1910-12; comd. North Carolina, 1912, Petrel, 1912-13; at U.S. Naval Acad., 1913-16; comd. Chattanooga, 1916-17, Cleveland, 1917; apptd. comdr. Minneapolis, Aug. 1917; comd. Charleston, 1917-18; chief of staff to comdr. Newport News div. cruiser and transport service, Sept. 1918, comdr. same, Jan. 1919; comd. Louisiana, Oct. 1919. Awarded D.S.M., 1919. Home: Bowling Green KY

HINES, JOHN LEONARD, army officer; b. White Sulphur Springs, W.Va., May 21, 1868; s. Edward and Mary (Leonard) H.; grad. U.S. Mil. Acad., 1891; m. Rita S., d. Gen. William M. Wherry, U.S. Army, Dec. 19, 1898; children—Alice Grammer (wife of J.R.D. Cleland, U.S. Army), John Leonard (col. U.S. Army). Commd. 2d lt. inf., June 12, 1891; promoted through grades to colonel (temp.), Aug. 5, 1917; colonel 16th Inf., Nov. 1, 1917; brig. gen. N.A., Apr. 12, 1918; maj. gen. U.S. Army, Aug. 8, 1918 (temp.); brig. gen. regular army, Nov. 30, 1918; major general, Mar. 5, 1921; general, U.S. Army, ret., June 15, 1940. Served at Ft. Omaha, Neb., 1891-96; acting q.m. 2d Inf., at Tampa. Fla., and Santiago de Cuba, 1898; Cienfuegos, Cuba, 1899, 1900; in Philippines, 1900-01, 1903-05, 1911-12, 1930-32; chief q.m. Camp of U.S. Troops Jamestown Expn. 1907; asst. to chief q.m. Dept. of Mo., 1908-09; Nagasaki, Japan, 1910, 11; adj. Punitive Expedition into Mexico, 1916-17; asst. adj. gen. A.E.F., May-Oct. 1917; arrived in France, June 13, 1917; col. 16th Inf., Nov. 1, 1917, apptd. comdr. 1st. Brig. Infantry, 1st Div., A.E.F., May 4, 1918; assigned to 4th Div., Aug. 25, 1918; apptd. comdr. 3d Army Corps, Oct. 11, 1918; comdr. 4th Div., Nov. 21, 1919; comdr. 5th Div., Sept.

25, 1920; comdr. 2d Div., July 11, 1921; comdr. 8th Corps Area, Oct. 6, 1921; dep. chief of staff, U.S. Army, Dec. 5, 1922; chief of staff, Sept. 13, 1921; apptd. comdr. 9th Corps Area, Dec. 31, 1926; apptd. comdr. Philippine Dept., Oct. 2, 1930; ret. from active service, May 31, 1932. Awarded D.S.M., 1919, "for services as regimental, brigade, division and corps comdr."; D.S.C., "for service in Soissons drive,"; Silver Star Medal for service in Cuba, 1898; Comdr. Legion of Honor and Croix de Guerre (French), 1918; Comdr. Order of Leopold (Belgian), 1918; Knight Comdr. of St. Michael and St. George (English), 1919; Order of the Crown (Italian), 1919; Medal of the Solidaridad (Panamanian), 1919; Grand Officer Kingdom of Cambodia (France), 1931; Distinguished Service Medal, State of W.Va., 1941. Mem. Soc. Santiago de Cuba. Home: 3740 Military Rd., N.W., Washington

HINKLEY, JOHN lawyer; b. Baltimore, Mar. 1, 1864; s. Edward Otis and Anne M. (Keemie) H.; A.B., Johns Hopkins, 1884; LL.B., U. of Md., 1886; unmarried. Sec. Am. Bar Assn., 1893-1909, mem. com. on professional ethics and grievances, 1923-34; dir. Baltimore National Bank; mem. Hinkley, Burger & Singley, Mem. Md. State Bd. Law Examiners, 1906-16. Capt. 5th Md. Inf. in Spanish War, May 14-Oct. 22, 1898; col. 5th Md. Inf., June 4, 1913-Feb. 28, 1917; Mexican border service, July 1, 1916-Feb. 24, 1917. One of Md. commrs. on Uniform State Laws, 1912-, mem. com. on uniform commercial acts, 1921-. Dir. Md. Sch. for the Blind. Home: Baltimore, Md. Died July 18, 1940.

HINMAN, DALE DURKEE army officer; b. Cherokee, Ia., Nov. 4, 1891; s. Frank Melvin and Ida Emerita (Durkee) H.; E.M., Colo. Sch. of Mines, 1915; grad. Command and Gen. Staff Sch., 1927, War Coll., 1934; m. Mrs. Elizabeth H. Kirkpatrick, Jan. 2, 1940; children (by 1st marriage)-Georgiana M., Frank M. Mining engr., 1915-16; commd. U.S. Army, Nov. 30, 1916, advanced through the grades to brig. gen. (temp.), 1941; comdg. gen. 38th Coast Arty. Brigade, 1941-42; Office of Chief of Coast Arty., 1942—. Mem. Tau Beta Phi, Beta Theta Pi. Presbyn. Club: Army and Navy (Washington). Address: Office, Chief of Coast Artillery, War Dept., Washington. Died Dec. 26, 1949.*

HINMAN, ELISHA naval officer; b. Stonington, Conn., Mar. 9, 1734; s. Capt. Andrew and Mary (Noble) H.; m. Abigail Solbear, Mar. 1, 1777. Commd. lt. Continental Navy, served as capt. sloop Cabot also frigate Alfred, 1777; captured, imprisoned, 1778; became privateer in command ships Deane, later Marquis de Lafayette; became mcht. after Revolutionary War. Died Stonington, Aug. 29, 1805.

HINSDALE, JOHN WETMORE lawyer: b. Buffalo, N.Y., Feb. 4, 1843; s. Samuel Johnston and Elizabeth (Christopher) H.: acad. edn. at Fayetteville, N.C., and Yonkers, N.Y.; student, U. of N.C., 1858-61, Columbia Law Sch., 1865-66; m. Ellen, d. Maj. John Devereux, 1869. Served in C.S.A., 1861-65; adj. gen. of Gens. Pettigrew and Pender and Lt. Gen. T. H. Holmes; took part in many battles; comd. as col. 72d N.C. Regt. in battles of Kinston and Bentonville, N.C.; surrendered with Johnston's army at High Point, N.C. In practice at Raleigh, 1866-. Has been before Supreme Ct. of U.S. in important cases; retained by state in various tax suits. Was author of the Nonsuit Act and Equity Reference Act of N.C., as adopted by state legislature; also annotation of Winston's N.C. reports. Home: Raleigh, N.C. Died Sept. 15, 1921.

HINSHAW, (JOHN) CARL (WILLIAMS) congressman: b. Chicago, Ill., July 28, 1894; s. William Wade and Anna (Williams) H.; C.E., Princeton U., 1916; grad. student Sch. of Business, U. of Mich., 1916-17; m. Helen Frances Veeder, June 24, 1924 (died Jan. 12, 1929); 1 son, John Veeder; m. 2d, Wilberta Ripley, Jan. 1, 1932; 1 son, William Ripley. Began with Mercury Mfg. Co., Chicago, 1920-23; salesman Walker Vehicle Co., Motor trucks, Chicago, 1923-26; asst. dist. sales mgr., 1924-26; salesman Halsey-Stuart Co., investments, Chicago, 1927-28; with corp. buying dept. Continental Nat. Co., investments, Chicago, May-Oct. 1928; real estate investments, Tucson, Ariz., 1928-29; real estate and insurance, Pasadena, Calif., and Hinshaw Huston Co., 1929-32, Morse-Hinshaw Co., 1932-39; mem. 76th and 77th Congresses (1939-43), 11th Cal. Dist., 78th to 84th Congresses from the 20th Cal. Dist.; mem. House Com. on Interstate and Foreign Commerce; mem. Joint Commn. on Atomic Energy; vice chmn. Congressional aviation policy bd. of 80th Congress, President 47th District. Republican Assembly, California, 1934: vice president Los Angeles County Republican Assembly, 1935-36; mem. Republican State Central Com., 1934, 36, 38; Rep. nominee for rep. in Congress, 1936; vice chmn. Rep. Nat. Congl. Com., 1945. Director, Pasadena Realty Bd., 1933-36; dir. Calif. Real Estate Assn. since 1935, exec. chmn. Arroyo-Seco-Parkway Assn. since 1934; v.p. Carmelita Civic Grandstand Assn., Inc., 1937-39; dir. Pasadena C. of C., 1938; mem. Pasadena Tournament of Roses Assn.; chmn. highway legislation coms., Calif. Chamber of Commerce. Served in U.S. Army, May 1917-Sept. 1919; commd. 1st lt., 16th Engrs. (Ry.): with A.E.F., 1 year; disch. as capt. Corps Engrs. Awarded Wright Brothers Meml. Trophy, 1953. Mem. Am. Legion, Vets. Fgn. Wars, World War Engrs. Assn., Soc. Automotive Engrs., S.A.R. (life); mem. American Soc. Civil Engrs.; mem. Inst. Aero. Scis., Astron. Soc. Pacific, Congl. Flying Club (dir. 1945), Princeton Terrace Club, Zeta Psi. Methodist. Mason (32ff), Elk. Clubs: Columbia Country (Washington); Overland (Pasadena). Home: 1401 S. Oak Knoll Av., Pasadena, Cal. Office: 1511 House Office Bldg., Washington. Died Aug. 5, 1956.

HINTON, HAROLD B. author, journalist; b. Frederick, Ill., June 9, 1898; s. Harlan and Emma (Boaz) H.; grad. Sewanee Mil. Acad., 1914; A.B., U. of the South, 1917; A.M., Vanderbilt U., 1920; m. Eva Robertson, Nov. 23, 1920; 1 son, Harold Clendenin. Began in newspaper work, 1919; successively with New York World Washington Bur., Nashville Tennessean and N.Y. Times; mem. editorial staff N.Y. Times, Paris and London, 1923-32, assigned to Washington Bur., 1932; asst. to J. P. Kennedy at Am. Embassy, London, 1938; asst. to sec. of Def. James Forrestal, 1948-49. Enlisted Air Service, Apr. 1917; commd. 1st lt., 1918; served with A.E.F., 16 mos.; called to active duty with Air Corps, Apr. 28, 1941, and assigned as asst. intelligence officer, 3d Air Force, Tampa, Fla., with rank of major; asst. chief of staff, Intelligence, Hdqrs. 12th Air Force in Italy, as colonel; reverted inactive duty, March 28, 1946. Awarded Legion of Merit, Army Commendation Ribbon, Croix de Guerre, with Palm (France). Democrat. Episcopal. Clubs: Nat. Press (Washington), Chevy Chase. Author: America Gropes for Peace, 1937; Cordell Hull, 1942; Air Victory; The Men and The Machines, 1948. Articles on futility of "Neutrality policy" which was written into law appeared in North American Review, New York Times Mag. and elsewhere, 1936-41. Home: 1425 34th St. N.W. Address: New York Times, 1701 K St. N.W., Washington. Died Mar. 12, 1954; buried Arlington Nat. Cemetery.

HIRE, CHA(RLE)S prof.; b. Whitley Co.,Ind., Dec. 1, 1887; s. Simon W. and Anna Catharine (Seymour) H.; A.B., Ind. U., 1915, M.A., 1917, Ph.D., 1927; m. Frances Willard Swain, June 13, 1920; children-Helen Margaret (Mrs. Herbert Neal Drennon), Eleanore Ann. Rural sch. teacher, Whitley County, Ind., 1907-08, 1909-10 high sch. prin., Churubusco, Ind., 1912-14; physics lab. asst., Ind. U., 1915-17, physics instr., 1919-23, asst. prof. physics, 1923-25, prof. physics, since 1943, supervisor physics instrn., A.S.T.P., 1943-44, acting chmn. dept. physics, 1944-45; head dept. phys. sciences, Murray State Coll., 1925-43, dir. summer session, 1931, dir. and coordinator civilian pilot training, 1940-43. Served as capt. ordnance dept. A.E.F., 1917-19. Fellow A.A.A.S.; mem. Am. Phys. Soc., Am. Assn. Physics Teachers, Am. Assn. Univ. Profs., Sch. and Soc., Sigma Xi. Republican. Methodist. Mason. Author: Laboratory Studies in College Physics, College Physics for General Education. Home: 215 E. 8th St. Office: Indiana University Bloomington, Ind. Died Sept. 8, 1952.

HIRSCH, GUSTAV cons. engr.; b. Columbus, O., Nov. 4, 1876; s. Leonhard and Charlotta (Meyer) H.; M.E., in Elec. Engring., Ohio State U., 1897; m. Aletta Kremer, Aug. 12, 1899; 1 dau., Irene Dorothea, Cons. engrs., builder or engr. of utility properties in all states, 1902—; v.p. and dir. Conneaut Telephone Co.; pres., dir. Warren Telephone Co., Gustave Hirsch Orgn., Skyway Broadcasting Co.; v.p., dir. Mansfield Telephone Co., United Utilities, Inc.: dir. Elyria Telephone Co., Cosmo Investors Corp., Jaeger Machine Co. Dir. Ohio Mental Health. Served from pvt. to capt. O.N.G., 1893-96, 1899-1901; 2d lt., Signal Corps, U.S. Army, Spanish-Am. War; maj. and lt. col., Signal Corps, U.S. Army, 1917-19, now lt. col. U.S. Army retired. Decorated French Verdun medal. Registered engr., Ohio. Fellow Am. Geog. Soc.; mem. Am. Soc. M.E., Am. Inst. E.E., Am., Ohio socs. profl. engrs., A.A.A.S., Ind. Telephone Pioneers, Am. Legion, U.S. Veteran Signal Corps Assn., United Spanish War Vets, (dir.), Ohio Independent Telephone Assn., Independent Telephone Pioneers of America, Tau Beta Pi. Elk. Clubs: Columbus Athletic, Scioto Country, Columbus Riding (Columbus). Home: 2459 Tremont Rd. Office: 1347 W. 5th Av., Columbus 12. O. Died Jan. 7, 1959; buried Green Lawn Cemetery, Columbus.

HIRST, ROBERT LINCOLN army officer; b. in Pa., Dec. 17, 1864; s. John and Margaret (MacCartney) H.; grad. U.S. Mil. Acad., 1886. Commd. 2d lt. 11th Inf., July 1, 1886; 1st lt., Sept. 19, 1890; capt. 12th Inf., Apr. 26, 1898; maj. 29th Inf., July 20, 1905; lt. col. 1st Inf., June 1, 1911; col. of Inf., Nov. 20, 1914; assigned to 3d Inf., Feb. 10, 1915. Instr. mathematics, U.S. Mil. Acad., 1891-95. Served in P.R., Aug.-Dec. 1898; in Philippines, 1899-1902; recruiting duty, 1902-03; again in Philippines, 1904-05; staff duty, Washington, Mfay-June, 1907; chief of staff Dept. of Colo., 1907-11: served in H.I., 1912-14; retired for disability, Aug. 27, 1917. Clubs: Army and Navy (Washington and New York). Address: Care Adjutant General U.S.A., Washington†.

HITCH, ARTHUR MARTIN educator; b. Cuba, Mo., Feb. 26, 1875; s. Charles R. and Ruth E. (Martin) H.; student Mo. Sch. Mines, Rolla, Mo., 1892-93; A.B., U. Mo., 1897, B.S. in Edn., 1907, A.M., 1934; LL.D., Westminster College, 1944; m. Bertha Johnson, June 27, 1908; children-Charles Johnston, Thomas Kemper. Began teaching, 1897; with Kemper Military Sch., 1899—, v.p. and prin., 1907-27, supt. 1927-49, pres., 1934—, Lt. col. O.R.C. Vice pres. N. Central Assn. Colleges and Secondary Schs., 1933-34; pres. Assn. of Mil. Colls. and Schs. U.S., 1923-33; pres. Am. Assn. Junior Coll., 1933-34. Regent Central Mo. State Tchrs. Coll., 1937-49, pres. bd., 1942—. Mem. N.E.A. Republican. Presbyn. Mason. Rotarian (gov. 134th dist. internat. 1944-45). Author: Cadet Days of Will Rogers. Home: 601 3d St., Boonville, Mo. Died Feb. 20, 1956; buried Walnut Grove Cemetery, Boonville.

HITCHCOCK, FRANK HARRIS postmaster-gen.: b. Amherst, O., Oct. 5, 1869; s. Henry Chapman and Mary Laurette (Harris) H.; A.B., Harvard, 1891; LL.B., Columbian (now George Washington) U., 1894, LL.M., 1895: admitted to D.C. bar, 1894: Supreme Ct. of U.S., 1897; unmarried. Chief Div. Foreign Markets, Dept. Agr., 1897-1903; chief clerk Dept. Commerce and Labor, 1903-04; mem. Govt. Expn. Bd., 1903-04; mem. Keep Commn., 1905-06: 1st asst. postmaster-gen., 1905-08: postmaster-gen., in cabinet of President Taft, March 5, 1909-March. 4, 1913; established postal savings banks and parcel post and started the first air mail service; resumed law practice, New York, 1913. Asst. sec. Rep. Nat. Com., 1904-08: mgr. Mr. Taft's campaign for presdl. nomination, 1908; chmn. Rep. Nat. Com., 1908-09, and managed presdl. campaign, 1908; managed campaign for nomination of Charles E. Hughes for President, 1916. Mem. Rep. Nat. Advisory Com., 1916; now mem. Rep. Nat. Committee. Col. O.R.C., Air Coprs. Gov. for Ariz. of Nat. Aeronautic Assn.; mem. Am. Econ. Assn. Home: Tucson, Ariz. Died Aug. 5, 1935.

HITCHLER, WALTER HARRISON dean of law; b. Plymouth, Pa., Feb. 20, 1883; s. Adolph Frederick and Alice Carey (Harman) H.; B.L., U. of Va., 1905; D.C.L., Dickinson Coll., 1932; LL.D., Saint Francis Coll., Loretta, Pa., 1932, Muhlenberg Coll., 1939. Albright College, Reading, Pa., 1943. Editor Michie Pub. Co., Charlottesville, Va., 1905-06; tchr. Dickinson Sch. of Law, Carlisle, Pa., 1906-17; editor Statuatory Law of Pa., 1919-23: tchr. Dickinson Sch. of Law, 1919-30, dean of sch., 1930-54. Chmn. Pa. Liquor Control Bd., 1939-40; chmn. Alien Enemy Hearing Bd., U.S. Dept. of Justice, 1941—. Admitted to bars of Pa. and Va. Served as 2d lt. inf., U.S. Army, 1918-19; 1st lt. O.R.C., 1919-23, capt., 1923—. Mem. Am., Pa. bar assns., Raven Soc. (U. of Va.), Am. Law Inst., Episcopalian. Mason. Clubs: Rotary, Carlisle Country; Penn Athletic (Phila.). Contbr. to Dickinson Law Review. Home: Sadler Curtilage, Carlisle, Pa. Died Feb. 5, 1959.

HOAD, WILLIAM CHRISTIAN engineer; b. Lecompton, Kan., Jan. 11, 1874; s. Francis Dearing and Gertrude Millicent (Evans) H.; B.S., Lane Univ., 1896; B.S. in C.E., U. of Kansas, 1898; m. Louise Green, August 7, 1901; children - Hortense (Mrs. John Russell) (dec.), William Marvin, John Green. Engaged in railroad location and maintenance, 1898-1900; assistant prof., associate prof. and prof. civil engineering, University of Kansas, 1900-12; chief engr. Kan. State Bd. of Health, 1907-12; prof. municipal and san. engring., U. of Mfich., 1912-37, prof. civil engring., 1937-44, prof. emeritus since 1944; mem. firms Hoad and Decker; Hoad, Decker, Shoecraft and Drury; Drury, McNamee and Porter; mem. engring. firm McNamee, Porter & Seeley, consultants in gen. field of municipal and sanitary engring. since 1912; has served more than fifty cities and industries in solving major problems related to water supply, sanitation, drainage, stream control, etc. Maj. and lt. col. engring. div. Sanitary Corps, U.S. Army, 1918-19; lt. col. Engr. R.C., 1919-26. Fellow Am. Pub. Health Assn.; mem. American Society C.E., American Water Works Association, N.E. Water Works Association, Sigma Xi, Theta Xi. Republican. Presbyn. Clubs: Union, Potary. Author reports and articles in field. Home: 2114 Devonshire Rd., Ann Arbor, Mich. Died July 2, 1962.

HOBBS, CHARLES WOOD army officer; b. Albany, N.Y., Feb. 2, 1842; s. George W. and Sarah (Boggs) H.; ed. pub. and pvt. schs., Albany (N.Y.) Classical Inst., Bryant and Stratton Business Coll.; m. Kate Beresford Potts, Nov. 25, 1874; children-Horace P., Mrs. Mary L. H. Pfeil, Charles W. Commd. 2d lt. 113th N.Y. Vol. Inf., Aug. 19, 1862; promoted to maj. in Civil War and entered regular army as 2d lt. 3d Arty., Sept. 21, 1867; promoted through grades to brig. gen., Apr. 12, 1905, and retired following day, Bvtd.; 1st lt., Sept. 21, 1867, "for gallant and meritorious services in battle of Spottsylvania, Va.": capt., Sept. 21, 1867, for same in battle of Cold Harbor, Va.; also breveted lt. vol. N.Y. vols. Wounded in hand and leg at battle of Cold Harbor, June 3, 1864, with loss of part of left hand. Participated in campaigns in Spanish-Am. War and Philippine insurrection, July 1898-June 1900, wounded before Manila. July 31, 1898. Retired at own request after 40 yrs. service, Apr. 13, 1905. Home: Washington, D.C. Died Dec. 21, 1929.

HOBBS, GUSTAVUS WARFIELD JR. clergyman, editor; b. Washington, D.C., Aug. 29, 1876; s. Rev. Gustavus Warfield and Jeannettee Dawson (Richardson) II.; A. B., Baltimore City Coll., 1896; D.D., U. of South; m. Augusta Richardson Kent, of Baltimore, Md., Oct. 18, 1902; children-Gustavus Warfield III, Mary Richard (Mrs. Wilfred B. Fry). City staff, Baltimore American, 1897; Spanish-Am. War corr., 1898-99; Washington corr., city editor, mng.

editor. Phila. Pub. Ledger, 1903-16; art dir. Cyrus II. K. Curtiss Newspaper Publs., 1914-16; ú editor Baltimore Sunday Sun. 1916-23. Ordained deacon, 1923, priest, 1925, P.E. Ch.; editorial sec. Nat. Council P.E. Ch., 1923; editor The Spirit of Missions and Church at Work; exec. sec. dept. of Publicity Nat. Council. P.E. Ch., 1926; now retired; chaplain Md. chpt. Sons Colonial Wars. Capt. chaplain 107th Inf., Nat. Guard, New York. Club: Nat. Arts Author: The Japan-Russian War, 1905; (with Dr. Ralph S. Tarr) The Geology of the San Francisco Disaster, 1906. Pen name, Sydney Tyler. Address: McKinsey Rd., Severna Park, Md. Died April 24, 1957; buried Loudon Park Cemetery, Balt.

HOBBS, ICHABOD GOODWIN rear admiral U.S.N.; b. North Berwick, Me., Mar. 13, 1843; s. Wilson and Sarah Eliot (Goodwin) H.; bro. of John Edward H.; A.B., Dartmouth, 1864, A.M., 1865; m. Helen M. Hazard, June 29, 1882. Acting asst. p.m. U.S.N., 1864-65) asst. p.m., 1867-69; passed asst. p.m., 1869-78; p.m., 1879-98; pay insp., 1898-1902; pay dir., 1902-05; retired with rank of rear admiral, Mar. 13, 1905. Served on bd. U.S.S. Unadilla, 1864-65, Tallapoosa, 1867-71, Navy Dept., 1871-72; on bd. Tuscarora, 1872-75, Dispatch, 1876-78; Torpedo Sta., 1879-82; on bd. Juniata, 1882-85; Training Sta. and Torpedo Sta., Newport, 1886-89; on bd. Boston, 1890-93: Training Sta., Newport, 1894-96; on bd. Brooklyn, 1896-99, Kearsarge, 1900; navy pay office, Newport, R.I., 1900-05. Home: Newport, R.I. Died Dec. 2, 1918.

HOBBS, LELAND STANFORD army officer; b. Gloucester, Mass., Feb. 24, 1892; s. Willard Knowles and Alnina Sybil (Perkins) H.; B.S., U.S. Mil. Acad., 1915; grad. Inf. Sch., advanced course, 1928, Command and Gen. Staff Sch., 1934, Army War Coll., 1935, Naval War Coll., 1940; m. Lucy Davis Berger, Jan. 3, 1916. Commd. 2d lt., U.S. Army, June 1915; and advanced through the grades to maj. gen. Sept. 1942; chief of staff Third Army, 1937-39, Trinidad Sector, 1941-42; now comdr. 30th Inf. Div. Decorated Mexican Border, Mexican Service, and World war I medals. Clubs: Chevy Chase (Md.); Minneapolis; St. Paul Athletic. Home: 1169 Morton Av., Rutledge, Pa. Died Mar. 1966.

HOBSON, RICHMOND PEARSON rear adm.; b. Greensboro, Ala., Aug. 17, 1870; s. James Marcellus and Sarah Croom (Pearson) H.; educated in private school, 1878-82, Southern U., 1882-85; graduate U.S. Naval Acad., 1889; student École National Superieur des Mines; grad. Ecole d'Application du Genie Maritime, Paris, 1893; LL.D., Southern U., 1906; M.S., Washington and Jefferson Coll., 1898; m. Grizelda Houston Hull, May 25, 1905; children-Richmond P., Lucia Houston, George Hull. Midshipman cruise with White Squadron in Mediterranean and South Atlantic, 1889-90; duty Navy Department, 1894-95; on flagship New York, with North Atlantic Squadron, summer 1895; Navy Yard, New York, 1895-96; at Newport News in construction of battleships, 1896-97; organized and conducted post-grad. course for officers destined for construction corps, at U.S. Naval Acad., 1897-98: with N. Atlantic Squadron, taking post-grad. students, Mar. 1898; served as constructor with fleet: prin. work on stability and fire systems of vessels in action, on flagship New York in blockade duty, in bombardment of Mantanzas, in expdn. against San Juan de Puerto Rico. Was commissioned collier Merrimac and with a crew of 7 volunteers sunk her in Santiago harbor; was held prisoner in Spanish fortress, June 3, to July 6, 1898. Insp. of Spanish wrecks; in charge of operations to save same: success with Teresa; on duty in far East, 1899-1900; directed reconstruction at Hong-Kong of 3 Spanish gunboats-Isla de Cuba,Isla de Luzon and Don Juan de Austria; in charge construction dept., Cavite, P.I.; spl. rep. Navy Dept., Buffalo Expn., 1901, Charleston Expn., 1901-02; superintending naval constrn., Crescent Shipyard, Elizabeth, N.J., May-June 1902; resigned from U.S.N. Feb. 6, 1903. Presdl. elector-at-large from Ala., 1904; mem. 60th to 63rd Congresses (1907-15), 6th Ala. Dist. Lecturer, speaker, writer, advocating Am. naval supremacy and Am. leadership in internat. movement for peace. Advocating nation-wide and world-wide prohibition; first to introduce in Congress and advocate prohibition amendment to Constitution for total prohibition; for long-time process of alcohol education for the nation to grow out of the drinking habit; organizer, 1921, and gen. sec. Am. Alcohol Edn. Assn.; organized, 1923, and pres. Internat. Narcotic Edn. Assn.; organized, 1926, World Conf. on Narcotic Education, of which is sec. gen. and chmn. bd. govs.; founder, pres. World Narcotic Defense Assn., 1927; founder, pres. Constl. Democracy Assn., 1935. Author Alcohol and the Human Race for Truth Inoculation of Society, 1919; Narcotic Peril, 1925; The Modern Pirates-Exterminate Them. 1931; Drug Addiction, a Malignant Racial Cancer, 1933. Awarded Congressional Medal of Honor, 1933, for sinking the Collier Merrimac, 1898; made rear adm. by act of Congress, 1934. Home: New York, N.Y. Died Mar. 16, 1937.

HOBSON, WILLIAM HORACE army officer (ret.); b. Somerville, Tenn., Sept. 5, 1888; s. Horace Pullian and Sarah M. (Walker) H.; B.S., U.S. Mil. Acad., 1912; distinguished grad. Command and Gen. Staff Sch., 1924, Army War Coll., 1935; hon. D. Mil. Sci., Georgetown U., 1922; m. Frances Josephine Bingham, Oct. 30, 1913; 1 dau., Mary Josephine. Commd. 2d lt. U.S. Army, 1912, advanced through the grades to brig. gen., 1944; served in Panama C.Z., P.I., during World War I; prof. mil. sci. Georgetown U., 1919-23, 1929-33; instr. Inf. Sch., Fort Benning, Ga., 1939-40, chief tactical group, July-Oct. 1940, dir. tng., Oct. 1940-July 19 comdt., July-Oct. 1941; comdg. officer, 30th Inf., Oct. 1941-Aug. 1942; mem. Munitions Assignments Bd., Washington, 1942-43; comd. Ft. Benning, Ga., 1946, ret. Award. D.S.M. Dir. Georgetown U. Alumni Assn.; mem. Outdoor Writers Assn. Am. Club: Monterey Peninsular Country (Pebble Beach, Cal.). Contbr. to outdoor mags. Address: 1024 San Carlos Rd., Pebble Beach, Cal. 93953. Died July 4, 1960; buried Presidio of San Francisco.

HOCHE, HERMAN EMANUEL orgn. ofcl., hosp. cons.; b. Chgo., Feb. 7, 1913; s. Herman Anand Elizabeth (Haenold) H.; M.H.A., U. Minn., 1951; M.B.A., Harvard, 1956; m. Edna Byrnece Have, Apr. 21, 1934; children - Linda Marie, Cristine Barbara. Enlisted in U.S. Navy, 1930, commd. Med. . Service Corps, 1944, advanced through grades to comdr., 1960; served in U.S.S. Nevada, Pearl Harbor, also U.S.S. Massachusetts, 1943-45; tng., exec. officer U.S. Naval Sch. Hosp. Adminstrn., Bethesda, Md., 1956-58; retired, 1960; mem. faculty program hosp. adninstrn. U. Minn., also mem. firm James A. Halnmilton Assos., hosp. cons., Mpls. 1960-. Mlem. Toastmasters Internat., 1948-, gov. Dist. 30, 1953, mem. nat. bd. dirs., 1957-63, 2d v.p., 1959-60, 1st v.p., 1960-61, internat. pres., 1961-62. Mem. Am. Hosp. Assn., Am. Coll. Hosp. Adminstrs., U. Minn. Program Hosp. Adminstrn. Alumni Assn., Harvard Bus. Sch. Alunni Assn. Methodist (tchr. adult Sunday sch. classes). Mason (Shriner). Home: 408 E. Minnehaha Pky., Mpls. 19. Office: 425 Harvard St. S.E., Mpls. 14. Died Sept. 21, 1963; buried Arlington Nat. Cemetery.

HOCHMUTH, BRUNO ARTHUR Marine corps officer; b. Houston, May 10, 1911; s. Walter Edward and Amelia Elizabeth (Geidel) H.; B.S., Tex. A. and M. Coll. 1935; grad. Marine Corps Staff and Command Sch., 1943, Indsl. Coll. Armed Forces, 1951; m. Mary Elizabeth Stovall, July 12, 1937; children - Joan (Mrs. Robert L. Rutz), Mary Lynn. Commd. 2d lt. USMC, 1935, advanced through grades to maj. gen., 1963; staff officer Saipan and Tinian operations, also comdg. officer Okinawa Campaign, World War II; staff officer Hdqrs. USMC, 1947-51; comdr. 2d Marine Regt., 1951-52; instr. Canadian Army Staff Coll., 1953-55; asst. chief staff G-4, 3d Marine Div., 1955-56; chief staff Marine Corps Recruit Depot, San Diego, 1957-59; chief research and devel. Hdqrs. USMC, 1960-63; comdg. gen. Marine Corps Recruit Depot, San Diego, 1963-67; comdr. of 3d Marine Division, Vietnam, 1967-. Bd. dirs. San Diego chpts. A.R.C., Navy Relief Soc., United Community Fund, YMCA, USO, Salvation Army, also San Diego Symphony Assn. Decorated Legion of Merit with combat V, Navy Commendation medal. Presdl. Unit citation. Kiwanian, Mason (Shriner). Home: 3530 Browning St., San Diego 92106. Office: Hdqrs. Marine Corps Recruit Depot, San Diego 92140. Died Nov. 14, 1967.

HODES, HENRY IRVING army officer; b. Washington, Mar. 19, 1899; s. Harry Ketcham ndand Mary Sophia (Shaw) H.; B.S., U.S. Mil. Acad., 1920; grad. Cav. Sch. basic course, 1921, advanced equitation course, 1928, Command and Gen. Staff Sch., 1937, Army War Coll., 1940; m. Laura Celeste Taylor, July 9, 1925; children - John Taylor, Jean Marie, Laura Celeste. Commd. 2d lt., U.S. Army, 1920, advanced through grades to gen., 1956; served as Army comdr., overseas; comdg. gen. 7th Army, 1955-56; comdr-in-chief U.S. Army, Europe, 1956-59. Decorated D.S.M. with oak leaf cluster, Legion of Merit with oak leaf cluster, Silver Star with oak leaf cluster, Bronze Star medal with oak leaf cluster, Purple Heart with oak leaf cluster, Combat Inf. Badge (U.S.); D.S.O. (Gt. Britain), Order of Mil. Merit Taiguk (Korea). Address: Hdqrs. U.S.Army, Europe, APO 403, N.Y.C. Died Feb. 14, 1962; buried Nat. Cemetery, Fort Sam Houston, Tex.

HODGDON, ANDERSON DANA foreign service officer; b. Baltimore, Md., May 8, 1890; s. Dr. Alexander Lewis and Lillian Dana (Coolbaugh) H.; student Charlotte Hall Mil. Sch., 1902-08; A.B., Washington and Lee Univ., 1911; LL.B., U. of Md., 1914; grad. work, Johns Hopkins, 1912-14; m. Virginia May Lehrs, July 17, 1935; children (by former marriage), Anderson Dana, Jr., Alpheus Hyatt, Samuel Carter (deceased). Admitted to Md. bar, 1913; with trust company, 1913-14; law practice, 1914-17, 1919-23; with U.S. Foreign Service since 1923; appointed vice consul of career, June 21, 1923; vice consul, Prague, 1923, Stuttgart, June 1924; foreign service officer unclassified, 1924-27; vice consul, Windsor, June 1927; consul, Windsor, Aug. 1927; Dept. of State, Mar. 1928; asst. chief Visa Office, Feb. 29, chief, July 1930; detailed to attend consular conferences at London, Stuttgart and Warsaw in connection with enforcement of laws and regulations relating to issuance of visas, 1930; chief Visa Div., Jan. 1931; sec. in Diplomatic Service and consul Jan. 15, 1934; foreign service officer at Moscow, Feb. 7, 1934, consul, Moscow, Feb. 1934, Riga, Oct. 1934; consul, Berlin, June 1936, and 2d sec., Berlin, May 1939; consul, Naples, December 6, 1940, Rome, February 1941; secretary, Rome, April 1941; relieved of duties as consul July 1941 and continued as sec. of Embassy; class 4, June 1942; assigned to Dept. of State, June 19, 1942, following the exchange of Diplomats in May 1942, between U.S. and Italy; asst. to the liaison officer, Dept. of State with War and Navy Depts., Mar. 1943; also duty with Joint Intelligence Staff, Sept. 1943; chief liaison office, Dept. of State with War and Navy Depts., June 1, 1944; first sec. Am. embassy, London and consul gen. for duty S.H.A.E.F., Aug. 1944; mem. staff polit. advisor, U.S. Group, Control Council for Germany, June 18, 1945, hdqrs., Berlin, later office polit. affairs. Office Mil. Govt., U.S.-Berlin, in charge consular affairs; consul general (temp.), Hamburg, Feb. 1946, Stuttgart, March 1946. Mem. bd. trustees Charlotte Hall Mil. Sch. (founded 1774). Served with Md. Naval Militia, 1914-17, Nat. Naval Vols., 1917, U.S. Naval Res. Force, 1918-19, lt. comdr. (at sea World War I, 1917-19). Vice comdr. Dept. of Md., Am. Legion, 1920-22. Mem. Am. Foreign Service Assn., Am. Bar Assn., Md. Hist. Soc., Phi Gamma Delta, Phi Beta Kappa, Am. Legion, Mil. Order of the World Wars. Clubs: Maryland, Bachelors (Baltimore): Army and Navy, Chevy Chase (Washington, D.C.). Home: "Brambly," Maddox P.O., St. Mary's County, Md.; 2905 32d St. N.W., Washington 8, D.C. Address: Dept. of State, Washington, D.C. Died July 12, 1948.

HODGE, EDWARD BLANCHARD surgeon; b. Burlington, N.J., Aug. 21, 1875; s. Edward Blanchard and Alice C. (Van Rensselaer) H.; A.B., Princeton, 1896; M.D., U. of Pa., 1899; m. M. C. Gretchen Greene, Feb. 10, 1904; children-Edward Blanchard, Mary Stewart (wife of C. Alexander Hatfield, M.D.). Asst. surgeon, Childrens Hosp., Phila, 1902-07, surgeon, 1907-25; asst. surgeon, Pennsylvania Hosp., Phila., 1903-20, asso. surgeon since 1920; asst. surgeon, Presbyterian Hosp., Phila., 1903-10, surgeon, 1910-41, cons. surgeon since 1941; surgeon, Germantown Shop., 1925-41, cons. surgeon since 1941; chief surgeon, Chester County Hosp., West Chester, Pa., 1927-44, cons. surgeon since 1944. Served as capt., Med. Corps, U.S. Army, World War I; with Base Hosp. 10, overseas, 1917-19; disch. with rank of lt. col. Charter trustee Princeton U.; trustee Princeton Theol. Sem. Mem. bd. mgrs. Children's Hosp. (Philadelphia), Children's Seashore House (Atlantic City, N.J.). Mem. bd. dirs., bd. of Christian education, Presbyterian Ch. of U.S.A. Mem. Am. Surg. Assn., A.M.A., Am. Bd. Surgery (founders group), Phila. Acad, Surgery, Coll. of Physicians of Phila. (vice pres.). Club: Princeton (Philadelphia). Home and office: 2019 Spruce St., Philadelphia 3, Pa. Died June 19, 1945.

HODGE, HENRY WILSON civil engr.; b. Washington, Apr. 14, 1865 ; s. John Ledyard and Susan Savage (Wilson) H.; C.E., Rensselaer Poly. Inst., 1885; m. Sarah Cunningham Mills, Dec. 14, 1897. Asst. engr. Phoenix Bridge Co., Phila., 1885-91; chief engr. Union Iron Works, New York, 1891-93; mem. Boller, Hodge & Baird, consulting engrs., 1899-; pres. The Porterfield Construction Co. Designed municipal bridge over Miss. River, at St. Louis, G.N. R.R. bridge, Duluth, Minn., C.,R.I.&P. bridge, Little Rock, Ark., all bridges for Choctaw, Okla. & Gulf R.P., Nat. R.R. Co. of Mex., and for Wabash-Pittsburgh Terminal Co., including the large cantilever bridges over Monongahela River and Ohio River, the former the largest R.R. bridge in U.S. Engr. for City of New York for Melrose Av. viaduct, 96th St. bridge; commr. for Blackwell's Island bridge and Manhattan Suspension bridge over East River; cons. engr. for Brooklyn Rapid Transit Co., N.Y. and N.J. Interstate Bridge and Tunnel Commn., and many other corps., etc. Apptd. pub. service commr., State of N.Y., Jan. 1916, resigned July 1917; commd. major Engr. R.C.U.S.A., and dir. of rys. in France, July 1917-. Presbyn. Republican. Home: New York, N.Y. Died Dec. 21, 1919.

HODGE, JOHN R. army officer; b. n. Golconda, Ill., June 12, 1893; s. John Hardin and Melissa Caroline (Steagall) H.; student So. Ill. Tchrs. Coll., 1912-13, U. Ill., 1917; LL.D., Seoul U. (Korea), 1948, So. Ill. U., 1954; m. Lydia Gillespie Parsons, Oct. 6, 1917; 1 dau., Barbara Anne. Commd. 2d lt. 1917, advanced through grades to gen., 1952; served in France, 1918-19, PTO, 1942-48; attended Army Inf. Sch., Chem. warfare Sch., Command and Gen. Staff Sch., Army War Coll., Air Corps Tactical Sch.; on War Dept. Gen. Staff, 1936-41; comdr. 24th Corps from activation, Apr. 1944 to Aug. 1948; comdr. U.S. Army Forces in Korea, 1945 until Korean Govt. formed in 1948; comdg. Third Army 1950-52, chief of army field forces, 1952-53, now gen. U.S. Army, ret. Decorated D.S.M. with 2 oak leaf clusters, Navy D.S.Ml., Legion of Merit, Air medal, Purple Heart (U.S.); comdr. Legion of Honor (France); comdr. Legion of Honor (Republic Philippines); various campaign medals with battle stars for actual combat in World Wars I and II. Mem. Triangle, Scarab, Sigma Tau, Tau Beta Pi. Address: 1515 Twin Oak Dr., Fayetteville, N.C. Died Nov. 12, 1963; buried Arlington Nat. Cemetery.

HODGES, CAMPBELL BLACKSHEAR army officer, univ. pres.; b. Bossier Parish, La., Mar. 27, 1881; s. Campbell Bryan and Luella Virginia (Sockwell) H.; prep. edn. Mount Lebanon (La.) College, and Louisiana Polytechnic Institute, Ruston; grad. U.S. Mil. Acad., 1903; A.M., La. State U., 1913; LL.D., Naval U., 1941; La. Coll., Pineville, 1943; unmarried. Commd. 2d lt. inf.,

U.S.Army, June 11, 1903; advanced through grades to maj. gen., 1940. Lieut. col. 1st La. Inf., N.G., 1916-17; col. (temp.), 1918-20. Served in Philippines, 1903-05, 1908-09, with A.E.F., France, 1918-19, Am. Forces in Germany, 1921. Prof. mil science and tactics, La. State U., 1911-12; detailed for duty on Gen. Staff, Militia Bur., Bur. Insular Affairs; mil. attaché to Spain and Portugal, 1923-26; comdt. of cadets, West Point, 1926-29; mil. aide to President of U.S., Mar. 1929-June 1933; with 14th Inf., Canal Zone, 1933-36; chief of staff 4th Corps Area, Atlanta, Ga., Aug.-Dec. 1936; in command 14th Brigade and Fort Snelling, Minn., 1936-39; comdg. 5th Div., Oct. 1939-May 1940; 5th Corps Area, May-Oct. 1940; 5th Army Corps, 1940-41; retired from active military service, June 30, 1941; pres. La. State U. since July 1, 1941. Awarded D.S.M. (U.S.). Address: University Station, Baton Rouge, La. Died Nov. 23, 1944; buried at West Point, N.Y.

HODGES, CHARLES LIBBENS brig. gen. U.S.A.; b. Providence, R.I., Mar. 13, 1847; ed. pub. and pvt. schs.; m. Anna L. Borden, Aug. 5, 1879. Served as pvt., corporal and sergt., cos. H. E. and G. and sergt. maj. 65th N.Y. Inf., Aug. 20, 1861-July 17, 1865; pvt., corp., sergt. and 1st sergt. Co. D. and sergt. maj. 18th U.S. Inf. and pvt. and corporal gen. service, Nov. 17, 1869-Feb. 13, 1875; commd. 2d lt. 25th Inf., Jan. 20, 1875; 1st lt., June 1, 1880: capt., Nov. 1, 1891; maj. 17th Inf., July 13, 1900; transferred to 23d Inf., Aug. 28, 1901; lt. col., Aug. 12, 1903: col. 24th Inf., Jan. 1, 1907; brig. gen. U.S.A., Apr. 30, 1907. Died 1911.

HODGES, COURTNEY H. army officer; b. Perry, Ga., Jan. 5, 1887; student U.S. Mil. Acad., 1904-05; grad. F.A. Sch., Ft. Sill, 1920, Command and nen. Staff Sch., Ft. Leavenworth, 1925, Army War Coll., 1934. Enlisted as pvt. U.S. Army, 1906; commd. 2d lt. Inf., Nov. 13, 1909, advanced through grades to brig. gen., Apr. 1, 1940, maj. gen., May 31, 1941, lt. gen. Feb. 1943, gen. (temporary) Apr. 1945; permanent maj. gen., Feb. 1941, advanced to gen., ret. list, 1949. With 17th Inf., Fort McPherson, Ga., 1906-09; served successively Ft. Leavenworth, San Antonio, Philippines and El Paso, 1909-16; with Gen. Pershing's Punnitive Expdn., Mexico, 1916-17; sailed as maj. 6th Inf., A.E.F., spring 1918; participated in St. Mihiel and Meuse-Argonne offensives; was with Army of Occupation, Germany, 1919; with 6th Inf., Camp Gordon, na., 1919-20; duty at U.S. Mil. Acad., 1920-24; instr. Inf. Sch., Ft. Benning, 1925-26; instr. AC Tactical Sch., Langley Field, Va., 1926-29; mem. Inf. Bd., Ft. Benning, 1929-33; exec. officer, 7th Inf., Vancouver Barracks, 1934-36; Hdqrs. of Philippine Dept., Manila, 1936-38; asst. comdt. Inf. Sch., Ft. Benning, 1938-40, comdt., 1940-41; Chief of Inf., Washington, May 31, 1941-Mar. 1942; cmdg. gen. Replacement and Sch. Command, Mar. 9-May 15, 1942 (organizer); comdg. gen. 10th Army Corps, 1942-43; comdg. gen. 3d Army, 1943-44, 1st Army, France, Germany, 1944-49, ret. 1949. Campaigns World War II: invasion of continent, Normandy, No. France, Ardennes, Rhineland, Central Europe. Awarded D.S.C., Silver Star, 1918, D.S.M. with 2 oak leaf clusters, Bronze Star medal. Home: San Antonio. Ret. Died Jan. 16, 1966; buried Arlington Nat. Cemetery.

HODGES, GILBERT TENNENT publisher; b. Monroe, Wis., June 29, 1872; s. Gilbert Tennent and Anna (Banks) H.; LL.B., U. of Wis., 1895; Master Commercial Science, Bryant Coll., 1931; m. Edith Martin, June 21, 1906. Admitted to Ill. bar, 1895, practiced at Chicago, 1895-1905; mem. advertising dept. Frank A. Munsey Co. Chicago, 1905-12; western advertising mgr., 1912-17; advertising mgr. New York Sun, 1917-18; advertising mgr. Frank A. Munsey Co., 1918-25; mem. exec. com. The N. Y. Sun since 1925, chmn., 1935-50; staff executive The Wall Street Journal since 1950; dir. Munsey Trust Company, Washington, Mohican Co. (N.Y.). Apptd. lt. col., U.S. Army Res., 1931, 36. Decorated French Legion of Honor, 1937, U.S. Selective Service Medal, 1946; recipient Award of Merit, N.Y. Alumni Assn. Wis. U., 1956; Award of Merit, Advt. Club of N.Y., 1956. Past pres. and chairman Advt. Fedn. of Am.; honorary member U. of Wis. Research Foundation; mem. Phi Delta Theta. Independent Republican. Clubs: Union League, University, Advertising, Economic, Sleepy Hollow Country. Sales Executives, Lawyers (N.Y.); Army and Navy (Washington); Seigniory (Quebec); Thirty of London (hon. mem). Home: 29 Washington Sq., N.Y. City 11. Office: 44 Broad St., N.Y.C. 4. Died July, 1959.

HODGES, HARRY FOOTE army officer: b. Boston, Mass., Feb. 25, 1860; s. Edward Fuller and Anne Frances (Hammatt) H.: Boston Latin Sch. and Adams Acad., Quincy, Mass.; grad.U.S. Mil. Acad., 1881; m. Alma L'Hommedieu Raynolds, Dec. 8, 1887 (died 1926); children-Antoinette (dec.), Frances (widow of Col. A. H. Acher), Alma Louise (Mrs. G. L. Dickson), Duncan. Additional 2d lt., June 11, 1881; promoted through grades to maj. gen. N.A., Aug. 5, 1917; maj. gen. regular army, Dec. 21, 1921; retired Dec. 22, 1921. Lt. col. 1st U.S. Vol. engrs., June 10, 1898; col., Jan. 21, 1899; hon. mustered out Jan. 25, 1899. Served with battalion of engrs. and on river and harbor duty, 1881-88; instr. and asst. prof. engring., U.S. Mil. Acad., 1888-92; river and harbor, and fortification duty, 1892-98; in field in P.R., 1898-99; river and harbor duty, 1899-1901: chief engr. Dept. of Cuba, 1901-02; in office of chief of engrs., U.S.A., 1902-07; gen. purchasing officer, asst. chief engr. and mem. Isthmian Canal Commn., 1907-14: in charge design of locks, dams and regulating works, Panama Canal; engr. of maintenance, Panama Canal, 1914-15; given thanks of Congress and advanced in rank Mar. 4, 1915: comdg. N. and Middle Atlantic Coast Arty. dists., 1915-17; comdg. 76th Div., U.S.A., Aug. 25, 1917-Jan. 1, 1919, at Camp Devens, Mass., and with A.E.F. in France; comdg. 20th Div., Camp Sevier, S.C., and Camp Travis, Tex., Jan. 1-July 1, 1919; comdg. N. Pacific and 3d Coast Arty. districts, July 1, 1919-Dec. 21, 1921. Awarded D.S.M. Episcopalian. Home: Lake Forest, Ill. Died Sept. 24, 1929.

HODGES, HARRY MARSH captain U.S.N.; b. Carrollton, Ill., June 1, 1855; s. Judge Charles Drury and Ellen (Hawley) H.; apptd. to U.S. Naval Acad. from Ill., 1870, grad. 1875; m. New York, Sept. 5, 1901, Laura George Muir-Drew (Née Chapman). Promoted midshipman, June 21, 1875; ensign, July 11, 1877; jr. grade, Aug. 24, 1883; lt., Sept. 9, 1889; lt.-comdr., lfar. 3, 1899; comdr., Aug. 24, 1904; retired voluntarily as capt., June 30, 1905. Served on Swatara, 1875; Richmond, 1875-77; Constellation and St. Louis, 1878; Wyoming, 1878-81; Alarm, 1881-82; Passaic, Enterprise, 1883-86; Michigan, 1886-87; Quinnebaug, 1887-89; Portsmouth, 1890-92; Vermont, 1892; Atlanta, 1892-93; Chicago, 1893-95; exec. officer. St. Mary's, 1895-97; Detroit, 1897-98; exec. officer Arethusa, 1898-99; Nero, 1899; comd. Nero, 1899-1900; completed survey for Trans-Pacific sumbarine cable, 1900, and discovered the greatest depth ever found and took the deepst sounding, that of 5,269 fathoms; supervisor New York harbor, 1900-02; exec. officer Chicago, 1902-03; hydrographer of the navy, 1904-06. Had the longest, most continuous man-of-war sea service of any officer on the naval list; in less than 25 yrs. after graduation was in 23d year of actual sea service. Communication officer, Am. Embassy, Rome, Italy, 1917-18. Decorated with Cross Santi Maurizzio e Lazzaro (Italy). Mem. Naval Order of U.S., Permanent International Assn. of Navigation Congresses (Brussels), Nat. Geog. Soc. Clubs: University, New York Yacht, Manhattan, Larchmont Yacht (New York), Metropolitan, Army and Navy (Washington). Address Navy Dept., Washington.†

HODGES, HENRY CLAY brig. gen. U.S.A.; b. in Vt., Jan. 14, 1831. Grad. U.S. Mil. Acad., 1851; bvtd. 2d lt., 4th Inf., U.S.A., July 1, 1851, and promoted 2d lt., Aug. 1, 1852: promoted through grades to col. a.q.m. gen., Oct. 19, 1888; retired, Jan. 14, 1895; advanced to brig. gen. retired, Apr. 23, 1904. Bvtd. maj. and lt. col., Mar. 13, 1865, "for faithful and meritorious services during the war." Early service on frontier, and, 1853-54, on Pacific R.R. explorations; in Civ. War served in equipping troops and later as q.m. Army of the Cumberland, on staff Maj. Gen. Rosecrans in Tenn. campaign; depot q.m. at Ft. Leavenworth, Kan., and at last part of war chief q.m. at Mobile, Ala., and New Orleans; after war in various duties as dept. q.m. and as a.q.m. gen. until retired. Died Nov. 3, 1917.

HODGES, JOSEPH GILLULY, lawyer; b. Denver, Apr. 30, 1909; s. William Vanderveer and Mabel (Guilluly) H.; grad. Hotchkiss Sch., 1926; A.B., Yale, 1930; LL.B., Harvard, 1933; m. Elaine Chanute, Mar. 31, 1939; children—Elaine M. (Mrs. Duval Edward Harvey), Joseph Gilluly, Ann V. Admitted to Colo. bar, 1933, later practiced in Denver; dep. dist. atty. Denver County, 1933-34; mem. firm Hodges, Wilson & Vidal, 1934-36; partner Hodges, Wilson & Vidal and Hodges, Vidal & Goree, 1936-53; partner Hodges, Silverstein, Hodges & Harrington and Hodges, Silverstein & Harrington, 1953-69, Hodges, Harrington, Kerwin & Otten, also Hodges, Kerwin, Otten & Weeks, 1970-72. Dir. Colo. Nat. Bank Denver, Colo. Nat. Bankshares, Inc. Pres. Denver Water Bd., 1963-64. Bd. dirs. Childrens Hosp. Assn., Denver, 1969-72; trustee Denver Mus. Natural History, Colo. Hosp. Service. Served to maj. USAAF, 1942-45. Fellow Am. Bar Found., Am. Law Inst.; mem. Am. (past del.), Colo. (past pres.), Denver bar assns., Denver C. of C. (past dir.), Alpha Delta Phi. Episcopalian. Rotarian. Home: Denver CO Died Nov. 24, 1972; buried Fairmount Cemetery, Denver CO

HODGSDON, DANIEL BASCOME officer U.S. Coast Guard; b. New York City, Feb. 4, 1836: s. George and Catharine (Evans) H.; ed. pub. and pvt. schs.; m. Georgia M. Smith, Oct. 26, 1869. Served in U.S. merchant marine, 1849-61: entered U.S. Revenue Service, Nov. 12, 1861, as 3d lt.; promoted 2d lt., July 14, 1863; first lieutenant July 11, 1864; captain, September 14, 1868; senior captain, April 16, 1908, by act of Congress "for a creditable record during the Civil War." During the Civil War on duty on lower Chesapeake Bay and its tributary waters; blockading duty in cooperation with the U.S.N. served in Alaskan waters at the time that Territory was transferred to the U.S. Govt., 1867; comd. revenue training schoolship S. P. Chase, 1897-91; spent about 25 yrs. on Atlantic coast stas., 10 on lakes and 3 on the Pacific; ordered, Nov. 1897, to comd. cutter McCulloch, which he took through Suez Canal, reaching Singapore, Apr. 8, 1898, reported to Commodore Dewey at Hongkong, Apr. 17, 1898, joined his squadron and took part in the battle of Manila Bay; later comd. cutter Fessenden; retired on full duty pay by joint resolution of Congress, May 3, 1900, "for efficient and meritorious service at battle of Manila Bay." Asst. insp. 10th and 11th Life Saving dists., 1902-05. Died Sept. 10, 1916.

HODGSON, FRED GRADY surgeon; b. Athens, Ga., Sept. 25, 1878; s. Edward R. and Mary V. (Strahan) H.; student U. Ga., 1894-97; M.D., Columbia, 1901; m. Margaret Fassett, Oct. 4, 1904; children - Martha E. (Mrs. Rutherford Ellis), Jennie C. (Mrs. Ed van Winkle), Fred G., Sloat F., Newton C., Bryant F., Margaret F. (Mrs. Hubert C. Hoff). Interne, St. Luke's Hosp., N.Y.C., 1901-03; began practice at Atlanta 1904; prof. orthopedic surgery Emory U., since 1915; attending surgeon Emory U. Hosp., Grady Meml., Eggleston hosps. Served as maj. M.C., U.S. Army, 10 months in France, World War. Fellow A.C.S.; mem. Am. Orthopedic Assn., Kappa Alpha. Clubs: Atlanta Athletic, Capitol City. Home: 851 Clifton Rd., N.E., Atlanta 30307. Office: Med. Arts Bldg., Atlanta. Died Dec. 5, 1965.

HOEHLING, ADOLPH AUGUST rear adm. U.S.N.; b. Phila., Mar. 5, 1839. Apptd. asst.surgeon U.S.N., Aug. 14, 1861; passed asst. surgeon, Apr. 24, 1865; surgeon, Oct. 2, 1867; med. insp., Jan. 31, 1865; med. dir., May 11, 1893; retired, June 14, 1895: advanced to rank of rear adm. retired, June 29, 1906. Served on various vessels and at various stas. during Civil War; in charge Naval Hosp., Washington, 1888-90; mem. various bds. Home: Washington, D.C. Died Apr. 25, 1920.

HOEING, FREDERICK WALDBRIDGE ednl. adminstr.; b. Rochester, N.Y., Nov. 7, 1907; s. Charles and Augusta (Laney) H.; B.A., Amherst Coll., 1929, M.A. (hon.), 1949; M.A., Harvard, 1930, Woodbury Lowery travelling fellow, 1935-36. Asst. history Harvard, 1931-35, 36-37; instr. history Coll. William and Mary, 1937-40; with British Am. Ambulance Corps, 1940-41; lt. col. Am. Field Service, attached to British Army, 1941-45; lectr. history U. Rochester, 1946; field rep. N.Y. State Commn. Against Discrimination, 1946-48; first adminstr. N.Y. State Fair Edn. Practices Act, 1948-51; spl. asst. to pres. Hofstra Coll., 1952-55; with Am. Field Service, 1955-, also mem. bd. dirs. Trustee Hampton Inst. Decorated hon. officer Order British Empire. Mem. Am. Hist. Assn., Am. Assn. U. Profs., Phi Beta Kappa, Alpha Delta Phi. Clubs: Harvard (N.Y.C.); Genesee Valley, University (Rochester, N.Y.). Address: 25 Tudor City Pl., N.Y.C. 17. Died Aug. 25, 1962.

HOFF, JOHN VAN RENSSALAER army officer; b. Mt. Morris, N.Y., Apr. 11, 1848; s. Bvt. Col. Alexander H. and Ann Eliza (Van Rensselaer) H.; A.B., Union U., N.Y., 1871, A.M., 1874; M.D., 1871; M.D., Coll. Phys. and Surg. (Columbia), 1874; U. of Vienna, 1886; (LL.D., Bucknell, 1907, Union, 1912); m. Lavinia, d. Gen. Hannibal Day, U.S.A., June 22, 1875. Apptd. from N.Y., 1st lt. asst. surgeon, Nov. 10, 1874; capt. asst. surgeon, Nov. 10, 1879; maj. surgeon, June 15, 1891; lt. col. chief surgeon vols., May 9, 1898; hon. disch. Nov. 5, 1898; lt. col. deputy surgeon gen., U.S.A., Jan. 1, 1902; col. asst. surgeon gen., Jan. 19, 1905. Organized the first detachment of the hosp. corps in U.S.A. at Ft. Reno, Ind. Ty., 1887, and the first co. of instrn. hosp. corps, at Ft. Riley, Kan., 1891; chief surgeon 3d corps, Spanish-Am. War, 1898, P.R., 1898-1900; organizer and pres. Superior Bd. of Health and Bd. of Charities, P.R.; in charge of hurricane relief work following disaster of Aug. 1899; chief surgeon China Relief Expdn., Aug. 1900; detailed as observer with Russian Army, 1905, Russo-Japanese War; chief surgeon Dept. of the Mo., 1906, P.I., 1907, Dept. of Lakes, 1909, Eastern Div., 1911; retired, 1912. Instr. ophthalmology, etc., U. of Cal., 1885; prof. Army Med. Sch., 1901-02; instr. in mil. hygiene, Gen. Service and Staff Coll., 1903-05; prof. mil. sanitation, U. of Neb., 1906. Acting editor The Military Surgeon. Pres. bd. dirs. The Lenthall Home: chmn. exec. com. Garfield Memorial Hosp.: vestryman Ch. of the Epiphany, Washington. Assigned to active duty July 10, 1916, in office of Surg. Gen. U.S.A. Home: Washington, D.C. Died Jan. 14, 1920.

HOFF, WILLIAM BAINBRIDGE naval officer; b. Phila., Feb. 11, 1846; s. Rear Adm. Henry Kuhn and Louisa Alexina Wadsworth (Bainbridge) H.; prep. edn. Episcopal Acad., Phila.; entered U.S. Naval Acad., 1860; ordered into active service, Sept. 1863: m. Juliet A. Potts, Jan. 6, 1869. While midshipman he at one time comd. yacht America; promoted ensign Oct. 1, 1863; attached to steam frigate Niagara, 1864; served on E. Gulf Blockading Squadron, 1864-65; took part in expdn. to capture St. Marks, Fla., which terminated in battle of Natural Bridge. After war promoted master, May 10, 1866, lt., Feb. 21, 1867, lt. comdr., Mar. 12, 1868, comdr., Aug. 7, 1881, capt., May 10, 1895; retired for physical disability, Mar. 13, 1897; served on various duties and stations; was naval commr. to London for World's Columbian Expn., 1892-93; originated system of tactics officially adopted in navy, 1890. Home: Washington, D.C. Died 1903.

HOFFMAN, HAROLD GILES ex-gov.; b. South Amboy, N.J., Feb. 7, 1896; s. Frank and Ada Crawford (Thom) H.; grad. high sch., South Amboy, 1913; m. Lillie Moss, Sept. 20, 1919 children-Ada Moss, Lillie Moss (dec.), Hope. Director N.J. Division of Employment Security since February 1938. Enlisted as pvt., 3d N.J. Inf., 1917; promoted through grades to capt. Hdqrs. Co., 114th Inf.; participated in Meuse-Argonne campaign; major, U.S. Reserve since 1925; active service United States Army 1942-46, lt. col. Transportation Corps; disch. colonel. Awarded the Legion of Merit and the Verdun Medal. Mem. N.J. Ho. of Assembly, 1923-24; mayor of South Amboy, 1925-26; mem. 70th and 71st Congresses (1927-31); 3d N.J. Dist.; commr. of motor vehicles, N.J., 1930-35; gov. of N.J., 3 yrs., 1935-37. V.p. Nat. Safety Council. Mem. Jr. Order U.A.M., Patriotic Sons America, Am. Legion, Vets of Foreign Wars. Republican. Methodist. Mason, Elk, Eagle; mem. Royal Arcanum. Clubs: Lambs, Circus Saints and Sinners (pres.), N.Y. Athletic. Author: Mile a Minute Men; Getting Away with Murder; The Crime The Case, The Challenge. Home: 178 Broadway, South Amboy, N.J. Office: Div. Employment Security, Trenton, N.J. Died June 4, 1954.

HOFFMAN, HUGH FRENCH T(HOMASON) army officer; b. Van Buren, Ark., Nov. 27, 1896; s. Bert and Dora (Thomason) H.; B.S., U.S. Mil. Acad., 1918; grad. Cav. Sch., basic course, 1920, regular course, 1937, Command and Gen. Staff Sch., 1941; m. Winifred Gurney, July 19, 1924; children-Hugh French Thomason, Richard Gurney. Commd. 2d lt., U.S. Army 1918, advancing through grades to maj. gen., 1951; with Army of Occupation, Germany, 1919; with 13th Cav., 1920-24; academic instr. U.S. Mil. Acad., 1924-28; with 1st Cav., 1928-31, 12th Cav., 1931-36, 6th Cav., 1937-40, 5th Cav. including Admiralties Campaign), 1940-44: comdg. 2d Cav. Brigade (7th and 8th Cav.), 1944-45, Japan, 1945-49; comd. 1st Cavalry Div., Luzon, 1945. Chief of Staff, 4th U.S. Army, Fort San Houston, Tex., 1949—. Address: Chief of Staff, Hdqrs. 4th Army, Fort Sam Houston, Tex. Died Apr. 19, 1951.

HOFFMAN, ROY, lawyer, soldier; b. Neosho County, Kan., June 13, 1869; s. Peter S. and Julia (Hakins) H.; ed. Kan. Normal Coll., Ft. Scott, Kan.; m. Estelle Conklin, Oct. 5, 1898; children—Dorothy (Mrs. Hubert R. Hudson), Margaret (Mrs. Chas. A. Vose), Roy, Edgar Peter. Founded Guthrie Daily Leader, 1889; admitted to Okla. bar, 1892; dist. judge 10th Dist., 1908-12; U.S. atty., Okla., 1903-07; mem. Miley, Hoffman, Williams, France & Johnson, Okla. City. Past pres. Okla. State Press and Bar Assns.; dir. First Nat. Bank & Trust Co. and other banks and oil cos. Enlisted Spanish-Am. War; capt. Co. K. 1st Vol. Inf., 1898; lt. col. 1st Okla. Inf., 1900; col. same, 1901-16; in comd. same. Mexican Border service, 1916-17; brig. gen. U.S. Army, Aug. 5, 1917, and comd. Ft. Sill, Okla., and 61st Depot Brig., Camp Bowie, Tex.; assisted in orgn. 36th Div.; comdr. 93d Div. (colored), Dec. 3, 1917; organized 93d Div., Newport News, Va.; took same overseas, Feb. 1918, and now in continuous front line service under commd. French; attached to 1st Div. in Battle of Cantigny; comd. Camp Shelby, Miss.; hon. disch., Mar. 1919; brig. gen. O.R.C., U.S. Army, Apr. 1920; assigned as comdr. 95th Div.; retired as maj. gen. comdg. 45th Div., Nat. Guard (states Ariz., N.M., Colo., Okla.). Decorated by Marshall Foch; Comdr. Legion of Honor (French); Comdr. Nichan Iftikhar (Tunis); Comdr. of the Crown (Italian, Rumanian, Belgian). Awarded D.S.M., State of Okla. Nat. charter mem. and organizer Am. Legion (nat. exec. com. 3 terms), also dept. comdr. Am. Legion, and chmn. Nat. Defense Com.; national v.p. American Legion Founders; pres. Nat. Reserve Officers' Assn., 3 terms. Chmn. Nat. Will Rogers Memorial Commn. Now and for 18 yrs. continuously, civilian aide to Sec. of War. Mem. Oklahoma's Hall of Fame. Mason (hon. 33deg.), Odd Fellow, K.P. Clubs: Men's Dinner, Oklahoma, University, Country, Army and Navy. First chmn. and organizer State Bd. of Affairs. Home: 1414 N. Hudson Av. Office: First National Bldg., Oklahoma City OK

HOFFMAN, WICKHAM army officer, diplomat, b. N.Y.C., Apr. 2, 1821; s. David Murray and Frances (Burrall) H.; grad. Harvard, 1841; m. Elizabeth Baylies, May 14, 1844. Admitted to N.Y. bar, practiced law until Civil War; a.d.c. to Gov. Edwin Morgan, also insp. of N.Y. troops at Fortress Monroe, 1861; commd. asst. adj. gen. U.S. Volunteers, 1862, assigned to staff of Brig. Gen. Thomas Williams in expdn. at Baton Rouge, La.; ordered to Gen. W. T. Sherman's staff as asst. adj. gen., 1862-63; with Maj. Gen. W. B. Franklin in Red River Campaign, 1863; on Maj. Gen. Quincy Gillmore's staff in Va.; asst. adj. gen. of E. Va. and N.C. dist.; ordered to New Orleans as adj. gen. and chief of staff to Maj. Gen. Edward Canby, 1865; commd. col. U.S. Volunteers for meritorious service in war, 1865; asst. sec. U.S. legation in Paris, France, 1866, 1st sec. of legation, 1867-74; sec. legation, London, Eng., 1874-77, St. Petersburg, Russia, 1877-83

HOGAN, FRANK J. lawyer; b. Brooklyn, N.Y. Jan. 12, 1877; s. Maurice and Mary E. (McSweeney) H.; ed. pub. schs.; LL.B., Georgetown U., 1902; hon. LL.D., Georgetown U., 1925, Litt.D., 1939; hon. D.C.L., U. Southern Calif., 1939; hon. LL.D., Manhattan Coll., 1939; hon. LL.D., Laval U., Quebec, Can., 1939; m. Mary Cecil Adair, Feb. 14, 1899; 1 dau., Dorothy (Mrs. John W. Guider). Sec. to chief quartermaster, U.S.Army, Cuba, 1898-99; to quartermaster general, Washington, D.C., 1899-1902; to chief of staff of The Army, 1904; began practice of law at Washington, D.C., 1902. Lecturer on law of wills, evidence and partnership, Sch. of Law, Georgetown U., 1912-19. Mem. Prog. Nat. Com., 1912-16; del. Rep. Nat. Conv., 1916, 20. Pres. D.C. Bar Assn., 1932-33, Washington Lawyers Club, 1930-31; prs. Am. Bar Assn., 1938-39, mem. exec. com. and bd. of govs., 1933-36, mem. house of delegates, 1937-39; pres. Georgetown Alumni Assn., 1925-39; v.p. Shakespeare Assn. of America. Catholic. Clubs: Metropolitan. Nat. Press, Blue Ridge Rod and Gun (Washington); California, Zamorama (Los Angeles); Bohemian (San Francisco); Grolier (New York). Book collector. Home: 2320 Massachusetts Av. N.W. Office: Colorado Bldg., Washington, D.C. Died May 15, 1944.

HOGAN, JOHN PHILIP engr.; b. Chgo., June 12, 1881; s. Dennis John and Mary A. (Duhey) H.; grad. Chgo. U. Sch., 1899; A.B., Harvard, 1903, S.B., 1904; hon. D. Engring., N.Y. U., 1940; m. Helen Scott Fargo, Oct. 4, 1929. Engr. N.Y. Rapid Transit Commn., 1904-06; asst. and div. engr. constrn. Catskill Aqueduct, 1916-17; acting dep. chief engr. N.Y. Bd. Water Supply, 1919-20; dir. N.Y. Water Power Investigation under William Barclay Parsons, 1920-23; cons. engr. Parsons, Klapp, Brinckerhoff & Douglas, now Parsons Brinckerhoff, Hogan & MacDonald, 1923-25, mem. firm since 1926; chief engr. and dir. constrn., then v.p. and chief engr. N.Y. World's Fair 1939; chmn. constrn. adv. com. Army and Navy Munitions Bd., 1940. Served in U.S. Army, May 1917-July 1919. two yrs. in France, grades from capt. engrs. to lt. col. Gen. Staff Staff. Trustee United Engring. Socs. Mem. John Fritz Medal Bd. of Award. Mem. Am. Soc. C.E. (past pres., past. v.p.), Am. Soc. M.E., Am. Inst. E.E., Soc. Am. Mil. Engrs. (1st v.p.), Harvard Engring. Soc., A.A.A.S.; gen. chmn. Constn. League of U.S.; mem. Tau Beta Pi. Awarded D.S.M., Purple Heart (U.S.); citation A.E.F.; Conspicuous Service Cross (N.Y. State); Chevalier Legion d'Honneur (French); Officer of Order of Crown of Home: 225 E. 73d St. Office: 142 Maiden Lane, N.Y.C. Died June 1966.

HOGAN, WILLIAM RANSOM, educator; b. Toledo, Nov. 23, 1908; s. Lemuel Ransom and Irene (Logan) H.; A.B., Trinity U., 1929; A.M., U. Tex., 1932; Ph.D., 1942; m. Mrs. Jane Carpenter Ogg, June 20, 1949; stepchildren—Mary (Mrs. Randolph Farenthold), Thomas, Jon. Tchr. Ranger (Tex.) Jr. Coll. and High Sch., 1929-31; regional historian Southwestern Nat. Park Service, Dept. Interior, 1935-38; asst. archivist La. State U., 1938-41, asso. archivist, 1941-42, head dept. archives, 1946; asso. prof. history U. Okla., 1946-47; asso. prof. history Tulane U., New Orleans, 1947-49, prof., 1949-71, chmn. dept., 1953-68, faculty adminstrv. chmn. Archive New Orleans Jazz, 1958-65. Served from pvt. to capt. M.I., AUS, 1942-45. Recipient Guggenheim fellowship, 1962-63. Fellow Tex. Hist. Assn.; mem. Am., Miss. Valley, So. hist. assns., La. Hist. Assn., Philos. Soc. Tex., Phi Beta Kappa (hon.). Author: The Texas Republic, 1946; The Barber of Natchez (with E. A. Davis), 1954. Editor: Guide to Manuscript Collections in the Department of Archives, Louisiana State University, 1940; William Johnson's Natchez: The Ante-Bellum Diary of a Free Negro (with E.A. Davis), 1951; (with Jane Hogan) Tales from the Manchaca Hills, 1960. Contbr. to hist. and lit. jours. Home: New Orleans LA Died Sept. 26, 1971.

HOGUN, JAMES army officer; b. Ireland; m. Ruth Norfleet, 1 child. Came to N.C., 1751; rep. from Halifax County to N.C. Militia by N.C. Provincial Congress, 1776; assigned to command N.C. Brigade, Continental Army under Washington, fought at battles of Brandywine, Germantown; assigned by Washington to command Phila., 1779; in charge of brigade in defense of Charleston, S.C., 1780; captured by British, offered pardon, but elected to stay with men of his brigade. Died as result of strain of imprisonment, Haddrell's Point, S.C., Jan. 4, 1781.

HOHENBERG, A(DOLPH) ELKAN cotton exec.; b. Wetumpka, Ala., Oct. 26, 1899; s. Adolphe and Helen (Elkan) H.; A.B., U. Ala., 1919; M.A. in Econs., U. Pa., 1921; m. Dorothy Kayser, June 7, 1922; children - Julien Jefferson, Helen (Mrs. Rudi E. Scheidt). Entered cotton bus. with M. Hohenberg & Co., Wetumpka, 1921, became mng. partner, 1929; pres. Hohenberg Bros. Co., successor co., Memphis, N.Y.C., Atlanta, Dallas, Lubbock, Texas, Fresno, Cal. and Phoenix, Selma, Ala., 1946-; pres., chmn. bd. First Nat. Bank of Wetumpka, 1930-45; director Algondonera Hohenberg S.A. de C.V. Mexico City, Hohenberg S.A. Comercio Algodaoe, Sao Paulo, Brazil; mem. N.Y., New Orleans, Memphis, Dallas cotton exchanges. Mem. nat. council Boy Scouts American mem. exec. board Chickasaw Council); member National Council of National Pal Planning Bd., 1956-; mem. pres. council Southwestern College, 1958-; pres. Memphis-Shelby Co. Community Chest, 1953, hon. life dir.; mem. 14th American Assembly. Served from capt. to maj., USAAF, 1942-44. Mem. Am. Cotton Shippers Assn. (pres. 1935), Nat. Cotton Council Am. of America (dir.), Liverpool Cotton Association, Phi Beta Kappa, Omicron Delta Kappa. Home: 54 S. White Sta. Rd. Office: 266 S. Front St., Memphis 1. Died July 6, 1961.

HOHMAN, LESLIE B., physician; b. Columbia, O., July 23, 1891; s. Lee and Hennie (Schlesinger) H.; A.B., U. Mo., 1912; M.D., Johns Hopkins, 1917; grad. student U. Vienna, 1924. Psychiat. tng. and residency Phipps Clinic, Johns Hopkins Hosp., 1917-22; instr. psychiatry Johns Hopkins Med. Sch., 1920-22, asso. psychiatry, 1922-43, asst. prof., 1943-46; prof. of psychiatry sch. medicine Duke, 1946-60, prof. psychiatry emeritus, 1960-72, director child guidance clinic, 1946-53; pvt. practice psychiatry, 1924-72; cons. dept. of psychiatry Duke Medical Center, Veterans Administration, U.S. Army, U.S.N. Served as 1st lt. M.C., U.S. Army, 1917-19; comdr. M.C., U.S.N., 1943-46. Mem. Am. Acad. Cerebral Palsy (past pres.), Am. Psychiat. Assn., A.A.A.S., A.M.A., Am. Neurol. Assn., Am. Psychopath. Association (councillor, past president), North Carolina, Southern medical assns., So. Psychiat. Assn. Author: As the Twig is Bent, 1939. Contbr. articles popular mags., profl. jours. Home: Durham NC Died Jan. 28, 1972; buried Druid Ridge Cemetery, Baltimore MD

HOIDALE, ELNAR lawyer, ex-congressman; b. Tromso, Norway, Aug. 17, 1870; s. Andrew and Dorothea (Lund) H.; brought to U.S., 1879; LL.B., U. Minn., 1898; m. Martha Skjel, Mar. 7, 1912; children-Elsa, Sherwood, Jean. Began as newspaper pub., Dawson, Minn.; began practice of law at New Ulm, Minn., 1898; 73d Congress, Minn. at large. Judge advocate, maj. Minn. N.G., 1900-08. Mem. Theta Chi. Democrat. Club: Minneapolis Athletic. Home: Leamington Hotel. Office: McKnight Bldg., Mpls. Died Dec. 5, 1952.

HOKE, ROBERT FREDERICK soldier, ry. official; b. Lincolnton, N.C., May 27, 1837; s. Michael and Frances (Burton) H. Maj., 1st N.C. inf., early in 1861; later maj., lt.-col., and col., 33d N.C. inf.; col., 21st N.C.; apptd. brig.-gen., C.S.A., Jan. 17, 1863; maj.-gen., Apr. 20, 1864. His brigade served in Army of Northern Va., in Gen. Early's Div.; comd. div. at battle of Cold Harbor; comdr. dist. of N.C., 1865; surrendered with Johnston at Durham Sta., N.C., Apr. 26, 1865. Engaged in business in N.C., and became pres. Seaboard Air Line system. Address: Raleigh, N.C. Died July 3, 1912.

HOLABIRD, JOHN AUGUR architect; b. Evanston, Ill., May 4, 1886; s. William and Maria (Augur) H.; grad. Hill Sch., Pottstown, Pa., 1903, U.S. Mil. Acad., 1907, Engers. Sch., Washington Bks., 1909, Ecole des Beaux, Arts, Paris, 1913; m. Dorothy Hackett, May 12, 1917; children-John Augur, Christopher. Mem. firm Holabird & Root; firm designed Palmolive, Daily News and Board of Trade bldgs., Chicago, Ill., also Ramsey County Court House, St. Paul, Minnesota, Lafayette Building, Statler Hotel, Washington, D.C. Commd. 2d lt. Engrs., U.S. Army, 1907; capt. Ill. Nat. Guard, 1914-17; maj., later lt. col. F.A., U.S. Army, Aug. 1918-Mar. 1919. Awarded D.S.M. Trustee Art Institute, John Crerar Library, Newberry Library, Morton Arboretum. Fellow Am. Inst. Architects. Republican. Episcopalian. Mason (32ff). Clubs: University, Commercial, Chicago Saddle and Cycle, Glen View Golf, Tavern. Home: 2236 Lincoln Park W. Office: 333 N. Michigan Av., Chicago, Ill. Died May 4, 1945.

HOLABIRD, SAMUEL BECKLEY brig. gen., U.S. Army, retired, 1890; b. Canaan, Conn., June 16, 1826; s. H. N. and A. M. (Beckley) H.; grad. West Point, 1849; 1st lt., May 1855; adj. at West Point, 1859-61; served in northern Va. and Md. campaigns with Army of Potomac, 1861-62; chief q.m. gen., Dept. of the Gulf, Dec. 1862 to July 1865; bvtd. brig. gen. for services in war. After war promoted regularly until July 1, 1883, became brig. gen. and q.m. gen.U.S. Army. Translator: Gen. Jomini's Treatise on Grand Military Operations of Frederick the Great, 1865 V1. Died 1907.

HOLBROOK, JOHN, ins. co. exec.; b. Yonkers, N.Y., May 25, 1909; s. Harry and Eleanore (Williams) H.; B.A., Yale, 1931; m. Alice Doubleday, June 6, 1936; children—John, David D., Phyllis, Peter M. Exec. v.p., dir. Marsh & McLennan, Inc., 1931-63, president, director, 1963-66, chairman executive committee, 1966-67, also dir.; member board trustees Seamen's Bank for Savs. Mem. United Republican Finance Com., State of N.Y., 1954. Trustee No. Westchester Hosp. Served from capt. to 1t. col., USAAF, 1942-45. Decorated Legion of Merit. Episcopalian (trustee). Clubs: Downtown Assn., Racquet and Tennis, Links (N.Y.C.); Bedford (N.Y.) Golf and Tennis; Blind Brook (Rye, N.Y.); Stanwich (Stamford, Conn.). Home: Bedford Hills NY Died Dec. 25, 1970.

HOLBROOK, LUCIUS ROY, army officer (ret.); b. Arkansaw, Wis., Apr. 30, 1875; s. Willard Francis and Mary (Ames) H.; grad. U.S. Mil. Acad., 1896; distinguished grad. Inf. and Cav. Sch., 1905; grad. Staff Coll., 1906; m. Henrietta Coffin, June 7, 1899; children—Frank Coffin, John Ames, Lucius Roy. Commd. add. 2d lt. 4th Cav., June 12, 1896; promoted through grades to lt. col., May 15, 1917; brig. gen. (temp.) Aug. 16, 1918; brig. gen. regular army, Oct. 20, 1925; promoted to rank of maj. gen., Dec. 28, 1933. Duty at Boise Barracks, Ida., 1896-98; in Philippines, 1899-1900 and 1901, 03; organized the training sch. for bakers and cooks, Ft. Riley, Kan., 1907, 11; developed the army field bakery and cooking equipment; attended the French Sch. of Supply, Paris, 1911-13; went to France with the 1st F.A. Brig., July 15, 1917; returned from France, May 1919; senior instr. arty. Command and Staff Coll., 1919-20; mem. Gen. Staff, 1920-24, Inspector Gen. Dept., 1925; comdg. gen. Ft. Douglas, Utah, 1925-26; comdg. Camp Stotsenburg, P.I., 1926-

29, Ft. Bragg, N.C., 1919-30; comdr. 1st Division; hdqrs. Ft. Hamilton, N.Y., 1930-36, Philippine Dept. and Troops in China, 1936-38; retired, Jan. 31, 1939. Specially cited for bravery in P.I., 1900; also "for skillfully handling artillery" in Cantigny operations and during 2d Battle of the Marne; decorated D.S.M.; Legion of Honor, and Croix de Guerre (French); silver medal for bravery and cross of Prince Danilio (Montenegrin). Episcopalian. Home: McCall ID

HOLBROOK, WILLARD AMES army officer; b. Arkansaw, Wis., July 23, 1860; s. Willard F. and Mary (Ames) H.; grad. U.S. Mil. Acad., 1885; honor grad. Inf. and Cav. Sch., Ft. Leavenworth, Kan., 1891; grad. Army War Coll., Washington, 1912; m. Josephine Stanley, Oct. 6, 1909. Commd. 2d lt. 1st Cav., June 14, 1885; 1st lt. 7th Cav., Dec. 17, 1891; capt. a.a.g. vols., May 12, 1898; vacated, Apr. 11, 1899; capt. a.q.m., Apr. 1, 1899; maj. 38th U.S. Inf., Aug. 17, 1899; capt. 5th Cav., U.S. Army, Oct. 18, 1899. hon. discharged vols., June 30, 1901; maj. 8th Cav., Mar. 3, 1911; q.m., Dec. 10, 1911; assigned to 10th Cav., Apr. 12, 1912; lt. col. cav., Nov. 26, 1914; col., July 1, 1916; brig. gen. N.A., Aug. 5, 1917; maj. gen. N.A., Apr. 16, 1918; hon. discharged from N.A., Aug. 15, 1919. Aide to Gen. D. S. Stanley, 1891-92; tactical officer, U.S. Mil. Acad., 1892-96; in Cuba, Spanish-Am. War; participated in subduing Philippine insurrection, 1899-1901; civil gov. Province of Antique, Panay, 1901-02; on duty at Pa. Mil. Coll., 1905-09; dir. Army Staff Coll. and Sch. of the Line, Ft. Leavenworth, 1913-16; in comd. squadron of cav., after beginning of coal miners' strike, Trinidad, Colo., 1914; apptd. comdr. 165th Inf. Brigade, Camp Sherman, O., Aug. 25, 1917; comd. Southern Dept. and in charge of Mexican border, May 3-Sept. 26, 1918; comd. 9th Div., Camp Sheridan, Ala., Sept. 26, 1918, until demobilization of div., Feb.1919: comd. Camp Grant demobilization center, Feb. 28-May 25, 1919; overseas service, May 1919; later chief of staff Southern Dept.; chief of cavalry, with rank of major gen., July 1, 1920: retired July 23, 1924. Died July 18, 1932.

HOLCOMB, THOMAS marine officer; b. New Castle, Del., Aug. 5, 1879; s. Thomas and Elizabeth Hindman (Barney) H.; grad. Western High Sch., Washington, 1897, Command and Gen. Staff Sch., 1925, Navy War Coll., 1931, Army War College, 1932; LL.D., Hobart Coll.; hon. D.C.L., U. Del.; hon. LL.D., John Marshall Coll.; hon. D. Mil. Sci. Georgetown U.; m. Beatrice Miller Clover, Nov. 11, 1916; 1 son, Franklin Porteous. Commd. 2d lt. USMC, 1900 and promoted through grades to brig. gen., 1935, lt. gen., Jan. 1942; apptd. maj. gen. comdt. USMC, 1936; ret. from active duty with rank of gen., Dec. 31, 1943; on active duty with Navy, Jan.-Apr. 1944; E.E. and M.P. to Union of South Africa since Apr. 1944; served in various marine corps posts in U.S., P.I. and China; comd. 2d Bn. 6th Marines, A.E.F., 1918, and participated in Chauteau Thierry-Soissons offensives; advanced to 2d in comd. 6th marines, 1918, and participated in St. Mihiel, Meuse-Argonne offensives; with Army of Occupation, 1918; on duty in U.S. and Cuba, 1919-27; comd. marines at Am. Legation, China, 1919-27; comd. marines at Am. Legation, China, 1927-30; commandant Marine Corps Schs.; Quantico, 1935-36. Awarded Navy D.S.M., Navy Cross, Chevalier French Legion of Honor, Croix de Guerre with 3 palms; Purple Heart, Silver Star medal with 3 oak leaf clusters, Naval Order of Merit (Cuba); Knight Grand Cross, Order of Orange-Nassau, with swords. Mem. Marine Corps Assn. Episcopalian. Clubs: Army and Navy, Army and Navy Country (Washington); New York Yacht, Corinthian Yacht, Gibson Island; Chevy Chase (Md.). Address: care State Department, Washington. Died May 1965.

HOLCOMBE, AMASA MAYNARD, lawyer; b. Winchester, Mass., Oct. 27, 1882; s. Frank Gibbons and Inez Norman (Maynard) H; B.S., Mass. Inst. Tech., 1904; law student George Washington U., 1908-10; m. Eleanor Pearl Marshall, Sept. 9, 1909 (dec. 1932); children—Priscilla, Marshall Maynard; m. 2d Violet Strong Gillett, March 10, 1934 (divorced 1946); married 3d, Martha Ellicott Ramey, Feb. 19, 1952. Machine designer Waterbury (Conn.) Farrell Foundry & Machine Co., 1904-05; asst. to treas. Pope Mfg. Mfg. Co., Hartford, Conn., 1905-07; asst. examiner U.S. Patent Office, Washington, 1907-10; admitted to D.C. bar, 1910, Mo. bar, 1913; practicing lawyer, specializing in patent law, asso. Carr & Carr, St. Louis, 1910-17; mem. Emery, Booth, Janney & Varney, Washington, 1919-29, Emery, Booth, Varney & Holcombe, 1929-33, Emery, Holcombe & Miller, 1933-42, Holcombe, Wetherill & Brisebois, from 1953; director Kistner Lock & Appliance Co., Power Condenser & Elec. Corp. Spl. asst. to atty. gen., 1920-24; cons. Dept. Justice, 1946-50; chief patent prosecution sect. Office Allen Property Custodian, Washington, 1942-46. Mem. com. of 100 nat. capitol Am. Civic Assn.; del. Fedn. Citizens Assn., 1926-34. Served as maj., U.S. Army, 1917-19; capt., O.R.C. Mem. Am. Bar Assn., Am. Patent Law Assn., Patent Inst. of Can., Assn. Internat. Protection Industrial Property (Am. sect.), Am. Soc. Mil. Engrs., Washington Soc. Engrs., Am. Ordnance Assn., Am. Soc. M.E., Washington Bd. Trade, S.A.R. Republican. Unitarian (past chmn. bd. trustees). Clubs: Rotary, University (Washington); Columbia Country (Chevy Chase, Md.); Montgomery Sycamore Island (Glen Echo, Md.). Holder patent. Home: St Petersburg FL Died May 14, 1971.

HOLCOMBE, JOHN LAVALLEE govt. ofcl.; b. North Platte, Neb., Aug. 28, 1911; s. John Henry and Eleanor (Lavallee) H.; A.B. in Econs., U. Cal. at Berkeley, 1932; LL.B., George Washington U., 1936; m. Frances McGuire, Sept. 16, 1934; 1 dau., Ann (Mrs. Ralph D. Fertig). Asst. regional dir. U.S. Bur. Employment Security, 1937-41; div. dir. readjustment allowance service, VA, 1946-48; asst. dir. budget div. Dept. Def., 1949-53, chmn. NATO llil. Budget Committee, 1951-52, deputy comptroller, 1953-56, dir. Office Programming and Control, 1956-59; commr. Bur. Labor-lfgmt. Reports Dept. Labor, 1960-. Served as col. AUS, 1941-46. Decorated Legion of Merit. Author: MAP for Security, 1957. Home: Box 144, Route 1, Springfield, Va. Office: U.S. Dept. Labor, Washington 25. Died Feb. 28, 1964; buried Golden Gate Nat. Cemetery, San Francisco.

HOLDEN, CARL FREDERICK naval officer; b. Bangor, Me., May 25, 1895; s. William F. and Mary Ellen (Riley) H.; B.S., U.S. Naval Acad., 1917; M.S. (elec. communication engring.), Harvard, 1924; m. Cordelia Folsom Carlisle, Nov. 27, 1919; children-Jean, Carl Frederick. Commd. ensign U.S. Navy, 1917, and advanced through grades to rear adm., 1945; duty in destroyers, Queenstown, Ireland and Brest, France, 1917-19, as exec. officer, navigator, engring. officer, 1919-22; on staff of comdr., destroyer scouting force, Atlantic, 1924-27; mem. U.S. Naval mission to Brazil, Rio de Janeiro, 1927-30; communication officer, U.S.S. Arizona, 1931-32; comdr. U.S.S. Tarbell, 1932-34; dist. communication officer, 14th Naval Dist., Honolulu, T.H., 1934-36; navigator U.S.S. Idaho, comdg. officer; U.S.S. Ramapo, 1936-38; in charge of radio shore activities, office of dir. of naval communications, U.S. Navy Dept., 1938-40; exec. officer, U.S.S. Pennsylvania, 1940-42; communication officer, U.S. Fleet, 1942, dir. of naval communications, 1942-43; comdg. officer, U.S.S. New Jersey, Task Force 38 and 58, Pacific, 1943-45; comdr. cruiser div., Pacific, 1945; comdr. training command, Atlantic fleet, 1946-52; comdr., U.S. Naval base, N.Y., 1948-52, ret. 1952; pres. Fed. Telecommunication Labs., Inc., 1952—. Awarded Legion of Merit with gold star in lieu of 2nd with V for combat, bronze star with gold star in lieu of 2nd with V for combat, victory medal with star, World War I, Occupation Germany Medal, World War I, China Service Medal, following World War II medals; Am. defense medal with star. Asiatic Pacific with 11 stars, Am. area, Victory, Naval occupation service, Phillippine Liberation with 2 stars. Republican. Roman Catholic. Clubs: Army Navy. Army Navy Country (Washington), N.Y. Yacht, India House (N.Y. City), Racquet and Tennis (N.Y. City), Union (N.Y.C.). Home: Greenfield, N.H. Office: Federal Telecommunication Laboratories, Inc., 500 Washington Av., Nutley 10, N.J. Died May 18, 1953; buried Arlington Nat. Cemetery.

HOLDEN, JAMES STANSBURY, real estate; b. Detroit, Mich., June 12, 1875; s. Edward G. and Jean M. (Stansbury) H.; grad. high sch., Detroit, 1894; student Mich. Agrl. Coll., East Lansing, 1890-91; LL.B., Detroit Coll. of Law, 1897; m. Lynelle Anderson, June 10, 1916. Bookkeeper, 1893-98; began in real estate business, 1898; pres. and dir. James S. Holden Co., Grand Lawn Cemetery; director of the Detroit Manufacturers Railroad, Autopulse Corp., First Liquidating Corporation. Served as major, General Staff, U.S. Army, 1918. President of the Detroit Board of Estimates, 1905-08; member of Detroit Common Council, 1917-18, City Plan Commn., 1919-20, Detroit Zool. Park Commn. since 1924. Trustee Grace Hosp. Republican. Unitarian. Clubs: Detroit, Yondotega, Detroit Athletic, Country, Grosse Pointe Club, Prismatic, Witenagemote, Bloomfield Hills Country. Home: 320 Washington Rd., Grosse Pointe 30, MI Office: Buhl Bldg., Detroit MI

HOLDEN, THOMAS STEELE business exec.; b. Dallas, Tex., May 5, 1886; s. Thomas Steele and Mary Helen (Wylie) H.; A.B., U. of Tex., 1907, A.M. in Mathematics, 1911; B.S. in Architecture, Mass. Inst. of Tech., 1916; m. Anne Stratton, Aug. 17, 1922; 1 son, Clay Stratton. Mathematics instr., U. of Tex. and Mass. Inst. Tech., 1909-14; archtl. practice, Boston, Mass., and Akron, O., 1916-18; spl. econ. investigator, U.S. Dept. of Labor, Jan.-June 1919; with F. W. Dodge Corp., pubs. constrn. and archtl. information, New York, since 1919, chief statistician, 1919-27, v.p. in charge statistics and research, and dir. 1927-41, pres., 1941-53, vice chairman board, 1953—; member board dirs. Fired Federal Savs. and Loan Assn., New York, Hon. mem. Bus. Adv. Council for Dept. of Commerce; pres., gov. N.Y. Bldg. Congress, Inc., 1935-40; dir. Commerce and Industry Assn. N.Y.; v.p., dir. Regional Plan Assn., Inc.; v.p., trustee John B. Pierce Found., 1954—. Served as 1st lt. Engring. Div., Ordnance Dept., U.S. Army, 1918; capt. Ordnance Res. Corps, 1919-22. Mem. N.A.M., A.I.A. (hon. member nat. and N.Y. chapters). Archtl. League of New York, Phi Gamma Delta and Phi Beta Kappa. Episcopalian. Clubs: Century Engineers (New York); Tokeneke (Darlen, Conn.); Nat. Press (Washington, D.C.). Contbr. of articles on constrn. industry economics, housing etc., to publs. Lecturer to real estate bds., trade assns. Home: Rock Meadow, 27 Tory Hole Rd., Darlen, Conn. Office: 119 W. 40th St., N.Y.C. 18. Died Nov. 3, 1958.

HOLDERBY, ANDREW ROBERDEAU clerygyman; b. Petersburg, Va., Jan. 25, 1838; s. Andrew S. and Mary Caroline (Nichols) H.; Hampden-Sidney Coll., Va., 1856-59; med. student, 1859-60; (D.D., Presbyn. Coll., S.C., 1893); enlisted in Co. E, 12th Va. Regt., C.S.A., Apr. 21, 1861; served in field and mil. hosps., Petersburg, Va.; wounded June 16, 1864, in 2d battle of Petersburg; surrendered at Greensboro, N.C., Sept., 1865; m. Hattie Smith, of Prince Edward Co., Va., July 24, 1866. Ordained Presbyn. ministry, 1869; pastor Tuskegee, Ala., 1869-80, Louisville, Ky., 1880-82, in Tenn., 1882-84, Richmond, Va., 1884-90, Moore Memorial Ch., Atlanta, Ga., 1890-1915. M.D., Southern Med. Coll., Atlanta, 1893. Organizer, 1893, and chief of staff Free Med. Ch. Dispensary; pres. trustees Presbyn. Hosp., Atlanta, 1901-09; trustee Atlanta Sch. of Medicine; Surgeon-gen. on staff Gen. B. H. Young, U.C.V. Mason. Active for many years in Anti-Saloon League of Ga. Author: The Pastor and His Elders. Address: Box 45, College Park, Ga.†

HOLLAND, ELMER JOSEPH, congressman; b. Pitts., Jan. 8,21894; s. Thomas and Margaret (Keelan) H.; student Duquesne U., 1913-14, U. Montpelier, France, 1919; m. Emily Jane Wilson, June 30, 1941; children—Jane, Christine. Dist. sales mgr. Macbeth Evans Glass Co., St. Louis, 1914-17; sales and advt. mgr. Consol. Lamp & Glass Co., Corapolis, Pa., 1921-30; v.p. Neon Sign Co., Pitts., 1930-32; mem. gen. assembly Commonwealth of Pa., 1934-41, senate, 1942-56; mem. 77th Congress, and 84th-87th Congresses, 30th Pa., mem. 88th-90th Congresses 20th Pa. Dist. Mem. United Steelworkers Am., AFL-CIO. Served as 1t. F.A., U.S. Army, 1917-20; as maj., AUS, World War II; ETO. Mem. Vets. Fgn. Wars (comdr.), Am. Legion. Democrat. Home: Pittsburgh PA Died Aug. 9, 1968; buried Arlington National Cemetery, Arlington VA

HOLLAND, JOHN PHILIP inventor; b. Liscanor, County Clare, Ireland, Feb. 29, 1840; s. John and Mary (Scanlon) H.; m. Margaret Foley, Jan. 17, 1887, 4 children. Taught sch., Ireland, 1858-72; came to U.S., 1873, taught sch., Paterson, N.J.; offered design of submarine to U.S. Navy, 1875 (offer rejected); constructed his 1st submarine with financial backing of revolutionary Fenian Soc. (sank on 1st trial, 1878; launched Fenian Ram, 1881 (proved impractical); contracted to build submarine Plunger for U.S. Navy, 1895, but his designs were radically altered; launched his own submarine the Holland, 1898 (1st submarine equipped to move underwarer by electric power and on surface by gasoline engine; 1 of 1st designed to dive by inclining its axis); sold Holland, with 6 sister ships, to U.S. Navy, 1900; also built submarines for Russia, Japan, Gt. Britain; invented repirator for escape from disabled submarines, 1904. Died Newark, N.J., Aug. 12, 1914.

HOLLAND, SPESSARD LINDSEY, senator; b. Bartow, Fla., July 10, 1892; s. Benjamin Franklin and Fannie Virginia (Spessard) H.; Ph.B., Emory Coll. (now Emory U.), 1912, LL.D., 1943; LL.B., U. Fla., 1916, D.C.L., 1953; LL.D., Rollins Coll., Fla. So. Coll., 1941, Fla. State University, 1956, University of Miami, 1962; H.H.D., University Tampa, 1956; m. Mary Agnes Groover, Feb. 8, 1919; children—Spessard Lindsey, Mary Groover, William Benjamin, Ivanhoe. High sch. teacher, Warrenton, Georgia, 1912-14; teacher in sub-Freshman dept. U. of Fla., 1914-16; admitted to bar, 1916, and since in practice at Bartow, Fla. Prosecuting atty., Polk County, Fla., 1919-20, county judge, 1921-29; mem. Fla. State Senate, 1932-40; served as governor of Florida, term 1941-45; apptd. by Gov. of Fla. to succeed the late Charles O. Andrews in U.S. Senate, Sept. 25, 1946; U.S. senator from Fla., from 1946, mem. com. on agr. and forestry, com. on appropriations, com. on aero. and space scis. Served with C.A.C., all grades through capt., U.S. Army, World War I; 24th Squadron Air Corps, in France. Awarded Distinguished Service Cross, 1918. Trustee of Florida Presbyterian Coll., Fla. So. College, Emory U.; bd. visitors U.S. Air Force Acad. Mem. S.A.R., U. of Fla. Alumni Assn. (member exec. council since 1922; pres. 1931), Am. Legion, Vets. of Fgn. Wars, Phi Beta Kappa, Phi Kappa Phi, Alpha Tau Omega, Phi Delta Phi. Democrat. Methodist. Mason (33 deg., Shriner). Elk. Kiwanian. Home: Bartow FL Died Nov. 6, 1971.

HOLLAND, THOMAS LEROY army officer; born Ind., Aug. 10, 1879; LL.B., St. Lawrence U., 1906, LL.M., 1907. Commd. capt. Q.M. Sect., O.R.C., Apr. 1917; called to active duty, May 1917, and advanced to lt. col., 1940; retired June 1942; recalled to active duty July 1942; made brig. gen., Mar. 1943. Address: Quartermaster Corps, Atlanta, Ga. Died Aug. 19, 1944.

HOLLIDAY, HOUGHTON, dentist; b. Sanborn, N.D., July 9, 1889; s. William and Marilla (Hancock) H.; A.B., U. of Minn., 1915, D.D.S., 1917; hon. D.D.S., U. Montreal, 1944; grad. work Columbia, U. of Chicago, New York U.; m. Ellen Hope Wells, Dec. 8, 1917 (dec. June 29, 1945); children—Paul Houghton, Robert William; m. 2d Irmgard Oesterreich Menke, Mar. 9, 1950. Fellow Mayo clinic, 1918-19; supt. coll. dentistry, U. of Minn., 1919-22, asst. prof. dental surgery, 1920-25; dental surgeon Earl clinic, Mound Park Sanitarium and Midway Hosp., 1923-25; asso. in surgery Peking Union Med. Coll. (China), 1925-27; exodontia practice,

Minneapolis, Minn., 1927-28; supt., Sch. of Dental and Oral Surgery, Columbia, and instr. in x-ray and periodontia, in charge x-ray div., 1928-30, asso. dean, 1936-45, prof. of dentistry, 1936-54; head of the radiology division, Columbia, 1928-54; attending dental surgeon Presbyn. Hospital 1930-54; engaged in private practice, New York City, 1929-54. Served as 1st lieutenant Army dental reserve corps, 1918; lt. comdr. U.S.N.R. since 1932. Mem. bd. dirs. Am. Bur. Med. Aid to China, Inc.; mem. of dental advisory com. of Community Service Soc. of New York; mem. of Dean's Screening Com. for Navy V-12 program; consultant on dental admissions com. of Army Specialized Training Program. Fellow Am. Coll. of Dentists; mem. First District Dental Soc., N.Y. Acad. of Dentistry, N.Y. State Dental Soc., Am. Dental Assn., A.A.A.S., Internat. Assn. of Dental Research, N.Y. Acad. of Science, Am. Acad. Periodontology, Federation Dentaire Internationale, Sigma Xi, Omicron Kappa Upsilon. Protestant. Author: Dental Radiology Handbook, 1935. Contbr. to dental jours. Home: Oakhurst CA Died Nov. 1972.

HOLLINS, GEORGE NICHOLS naval officer; b. Balt., Sept. 20, 1799; s. John and Janet (Smith) H.; m. twice, the Steritt sisters; 2 children. Apptd. midshipman U.S. Navy, 1814; served under Capt. Stephen Decatur during War of 1812 and in Tripolitan War; promoted lt., 1825, comdr., 1845, capt., 1855, resigned, 1861; commd. capt. Confederate States Navy, 1861; captured steamer St. Nicholas and converted it into gunboat, capturing several Union trading vessels; promoted commodore, 1861; commanded Confederate Naval Station, New Orleans, 1861-62; commanded Confederate forces on Upper Mississippi River, 1862; served in battles of Columbus, New Madrid, Island Number 10, Ft. Pillow, and Memphis. Died Balt., Jan. 18, 1878.

HOLLMANN, HARRY TRIEBNER physician; b. Phila., Pa., Dec. 13, 1878; s. Harry and Mary (Thomas) H.; M.D., Medico-Chirurg. Coll., Phila., 1898; m. Amelia Thomas Duncalfe, Apr. 17, 1900; m. 2d, Bonita Clarke, July 12, 1929; children-Bonita L., Pamela Jane, Harry Triebner. Instr. in pathology, Medico-Chirurg. Coll., 1903-05; physician to Dept. of Charities, Phila., 1903-06; asst. eye, ear, nose and throat surgeon, Phila. Gen. Hosp., 1905-06; with U.S. Public Health Service, 1907-18. on Duty at Leprosy Investigation Sta., Honolulu, 1907-18; med. supt. Kalihi Hosp.; supt. Queen's Hosp., 1918, 19. Chmn. Territorial Radio Commn. (Hawaii). First lt. Med. Corps, Hawaiian Nat. Guard. Mem. Ky. State Med. Soc., Hawaiian Territorial Med. Soc., W. E. Hughes Med. Soc. Baptist Mason, Odd Fellow. Club: Commercial. Author of various bulls. setting forth original reserach on leprosy; specialist in diseases of the skin. Home: 2154 Atherton Road. Office: 1124 Miller St., Honolulu, T.H. Died Dec. 13, 1942.

HOLLYDAY, RICHARD CARMICHAEL rear-admiral U.S.N.; b. Easton, Md., Nov. 13, 1859; s. Richard Carmichael and Marietta Fauntleroy (Powell) H.; ed. Shenandoah Valley Acad., Washington and Lee U.; m. Mary Holton King, of Newark, O., Apr. 28, 1894. Commd. civ. engr., U.S.N., with rank of lt. jr. grade, Mar., 1894; lt., Aug. 1897; comdr., Feb., 1907; apptd. chief Bur. of Yards ocks with rank of rear-admiral, Apr. 1, 1907. Home: Dresden Apts., Washington, D.C.

HOLMES, EDWARD MARION, JR., physician, govt. ofcl.; b. Norfolk, Va., Aug. 4, 1907; s. Edward M. and Emma (Ehrmantraut) H.; grad. St. Mary's Male Acad., Norfolk, 1924; A.B., Georgetown U., 1928, M.A., 1929, M.D., 1933; M.P.H. (Rockefeller fellow), John Hopkins, 1936; m. Sarah Daily Walsh, Apr. 27, 1935; children—Edward M. III, Sarah Daily (Mrs. Venable Lane Stern, Jr.). Engaged as asst. state epidemiologist Va. State Dept. Health, 1934-35; med. dir. Fairfax County Health Dept., Fairfax, 1936-39; dir. bur. veneral disease control, 1939-47; asst. dir. pub. health Richmond City Health Dept., 1947-49; dir. pub. health, 1949-57; asso. prof. pub. health Med. Coll. Va., 1947-52, dir. dept. pub. health medicine, 1949-59, prof. head dept. community medicine, 1952-58, vis. prof. preventive and social medicine, cons. med. edn., All India Inst. Med. Sci., New Delhi, 1958-63; cons. in med. edn. AID, Washington, 1963-64; asso. regional rep. health and med. affairs Vocational Rehab. Adminstrn., Dept. of Health, Education and Welfare, Atlanta, 1964-67; cons. for med. affairs Social and Rehab. Service, Dept. Health, Edn. and Welfare, 1967-69; dir. Rehab. Programs and Research and Tng. Center 19, U. Ala. Med. Center, Birmingham, 1969-71; with dept. phys. med., rehab. N.Y. U. Sch. Med., 1963-71; cons. med. affairs Soc. and Rehab. Service, 1968-69. Past mem. bd., exec. com. Richmond Area Community Council; mem. Richmond Bd. Cath. Charities; mem. Pan-Am. Sanitary Com. U.S.-Mexican Border Veneral Disease Control Commn., 1942-44. Served from captain to lieutenant colonel Medical Corps, USAAF. World War II. Diplomate AM. Bd. Pub. Health and Preventive Medicine (founder). Fellow Am. Public Health Assn., Royal Society Health; mem. Assn. Tchrs. Preventive Medicine (dir.), Am. Assn. Pub. Health Physicians (sec., editor bull.), Acad. Medicine, American Congress of Physical Medicine and Rehabilitation, Southern Medical Association, Am. Heart Assn., Med. Soc. Va., Soc. Va. Creepers, Phi Chi Fraternity. Clubs: The Club (Birmingham); Country of Virginia Commonwealth (Richmond); Delhi Gymkhana (New Delhi, India). Author: (with Ruth Benson Freman) The Administration of Public Health Services, 1960. Editor: Selected Writings of Marvin Pierce Rucker, 1957. Contbr. to Textbook of Preventive Medicine (Leavell and Clark), 1953; articles profl. jours. Home: Birmingham AL Died Feb. 26, 1971; buried Hollywood Cemetery, Richmond VA

HOLMES, EDWIN FRANCIS capitalist; b. Orleans Co., N.Y., Aug. 8, 1843; s. Asel Heth and Harriet (Sturges) H.; practically self ed.; m. Jennie Carleton, of St. Clair, Mich., Sept. 13, 1870 (died, 1894); 2d, Mrs. Susanna Bransford-Emery, of Salt Lake City, Utah, Oct. 12, 1899. Enlisted as pvt. in Union Army Feb. 7, 1862, and served as corporal, sergt. Maj., 1st lt. and adj., and capt. until mustered out, July, 1865; participated in many battles and skirmishes; recommended for bvt. commission at close of war. Engaged with John L. Woods, of Lexington, Mich., in lumber business, 1865; was taken into partnership, 1870, business being conducted under various names, as Woods & Co., Pack, Woods & Co., etc.; has also been pres. mining cos., steamship cos., etc., but has been connected with nothing in the nature of a "trust"; retired from active business, 1898; pres. Galigher Machinery Co., Salt Lake City; v.p. Yosemite Dredging & Mining Co.; extensively interested in ranching, and in irrigated lands in Ida. Republican. Congregationalist. Pres. 11th Nat. Irrigation Congress, 1902-03. Mason (32ff); mem. Loyal Legion, G.A.R. Clubs: Union League (Chicago); University, Alta, Commercial (ex-pres.), Country (Salt Lake City). Takes great interest in art and is the owner of a valuable collection of pictures at "Amelia Palace," Salt Lake City. Home: 141 N. Grand Av., Pasadena, Cal.†

HOLMES, GEORGE ROBERT newspaper corr.; b. Tippecanoe County Ind., Jan. 28, 1895; s. George Fox and Rose Lincoln (Beaver) H.; grad. high sch., New Richmond, Ind., 1911; student U. of Wis., 1911-13; m. Mary Catherine Early, Apr. 23, 1921; children-Mary Catherine, Kathryn Early. Began as reporter Indianapolis Sun. 1914; with United Press, N.Y. City, 1914; reporter New York Evening Mail, 1915; with Internat. News Service, Washington, D.C., 1916-, chief of Washington Bur., 1920-. Commd. 2d lt. cav., U.S.A., 1917; served as asst. adj., 78th Div., A.E.F., and aerial observer, 258th Aero Squadron, World War. Received hon. mention in Pulitzer prize award for account of burial of Unknown Soldier, Arlington Cemetery. Chief polit. writer for Internat. News Service in all Presidential campaigns, 1916-; weekly news commentator on polit; events in Washington for Nat. Broadcasting Co. Home: Washington, D.C. Died Feb. 12, 1939.

HOLMES, JULIUS CECIL, U.S. ambassador; b. Pleasanton, Kan., Apr. 24, 1899; s. James Reuben and Louella Jane (Trussell) II; student U. of Kan., 1917-22; m. Henrietta Allen, Apr. 26, 1932; children—Henry Allen, Elsie Jane, Richard Peyton. Served in cav. and inf., Nat. Guard and Reserve, 8 years; major, U.S. Army, Feb. 1942, and advanced to brig. gen., July 1943. Began in ins. business, 1923-25; entered foreign service, 1925; vice-pres., New York World's Fair, charged with relations with Fed. Govt., Foreign Govts. and State Govts., 1937-40; president Gen. Mills, do Brasil, 1941-42, director since 1942; served as asst. sec. of State, resigning Aug. 1945; became vice pres. Transcontinental Western Air, Inc., Dec. 1945; president Taca Airways, S.A., Apr. 1946; appointed U.S. fgn. service officer, 1948; minister Am. Embassy, London; with Department of State, 1953; diplomatic agt., minister, Morocco, 1955-56; spl. asst. to sec. of state for NATO affairs, 1956-59; consul gen., Hong Kong, 1959-61; ambassador to Iran, Tehran, 1961-65 chief U.S. delegation to Internat. Telecommunications Conf., Montreux, Switzerland, 1965; head Joint State-Def. Study of Middle East and Mediterranean, 1967. Mem. China adv. panel Dept. of State 1966-67. Decorated D.S.M., Officer Legion of Merit, United States Army; Commander Crown of Yugoslavia; Comdr. Order of the Foenix, Greece; Lebanese Order of Merit; Officer Southern Cross of Brazil; Officer French Legion of Honor, Croix de Guerre with Palm; Comdr. Oussam Alaouite, Morocco; Grand Officer Nishan Iffticar, Tunisia; Comdr. Crown of Rumania; Comdr. Order Brit. Empire; World War I, N. African, European campaign medals. Fellow Am. Geographic Inst.; mem. Am. Foreign Service Assn., Acad. of Polit. Sci. Clubs: Chevy Chase, 1925 F Street, Army and Navy; Metropolitan (Washington); Whites, Travelers London. Home: Washington DC Died July 14, 1968; buried Arlington Nat. Cemetery.

HOLMES, RALSTON SMITH naval officer (ret.); b. Yonkers, N.Y., June 5, 1882; s. Cornelius Schneck and Harriet Phelps (Smith) H.; B.S., U.S. Naval Acad., 1903; hon. Sc.D., U. So. Cal., 1943; m. Rachel Bond, Oct. 14, 1911; 1 dau., Sally (Mrs. Irving L. Camp). Commd. ensign USN, 1905, advanced through grades to rear adm., 1936; duty afloat and ashore, 1899-1945; ret. from active service, Dec. 30, 1945. Home: Huntington Hotel, Pasadena 15, Cal. Died Jan. 1966.

HOLMES, THEOPHILUS HUNTER army officer; b. Sampson County, N.C., Nov. 13, 1804; s. Gov. Gabriel H. and Mary (Hunter) H.; grad. U.S. Mil. Acad., 1829; m. Laura Wetmore, 1841. Served as 2d lt. U.S. Army on frontier duty in La., Ark. and Indian lands, 1830-36; served in Mexican War; in command of recruiting Governor's Island, N.Y., 1859-61; commd. brig. gen. Confederate Army, in command of brigade at Aquia Creek, Va., June 5, 1861; in command brigade at 1st Battle of Bull Run; fought in N. Va. campaign; maj. gen. in command div. under Magruder's command in Battle of Seven Days before Richmond; served as lt. gen. at Battle of Vicksburg, 1862. Died nr. Fayetteville, N.C., June 21, 1880.

HOLMES, WILLIAM HENRY educator, curator; born Augusta, Me., Sept. 13, 1874; s. William Henry and Emma Augusta (Penney) H.; A.B., Colby Coll., 1897; Ph.D., Clark U., 1910; spl. courses in edn., New York U. and Teachers Coll. (Columbia); m. Louise Macdonald, July 19, 1898; 1 son, Lt. Richard M. Prin. Israel Putnam Grammar Sch., Putnam, Conn., 1897-98, Putnam High Sch., 1898-99; supt. schs., Grafton and Upton, Mass., 1899-1903, Westerly, R.I., 1903-13, Mt. Vernon, New York, 1913-40; restorer, curator "Victoria Mansion" Museum, Portland, Me., 1941, best standing example of early Victorian Art and Architecture in Northeastern U.S. Lecturer on sch. adminstrn., Dartmouth Coll., summer 1913, Pa. State Coll., summer, 1924, Bates Coll., summers, 1926, 27; lecturer on school publicity, Pa. State Coll., 1927; surveyor N.Y. City Sch. Survey, 1915. Asst. in charge of personnel and chmn. com. on extension lectures under Army Ednl. Commn., A.E.F., Paris, Nov. 1918-Apr. 1919; gen. field supervisor Army Ednl. Corps U.S. Army, Beaune, France, Apr.-July 1919. Life member N.E.A. (N.Y. state dir. 1926-29; v.p. 1930-31), Nat. Parent Teacher Assn., National Association of School Administrators; member American Institute Instruction (vice-pres.), World Federation of Ednl. Associations, Delta Upsilon. Republican. Author: School Organization and the Individual Child, 1912; Key to Number, 1929. Co-author: Key to Reading, 1928; Along the Way (school poems), 1938. Wrote nat. shc. songs, "We'll Carry On" and "Stand By the Schools." Editor of Educational Work (mag.), 1906. Contbr. to ednl. jours. Home: The Eastland, Portland, Me. Died Jan. 6, 1948; buried Augusta, Me.

HOLSTEIN, OTTO geographer; b. Lexington, Ky., Jan. 14, 1883; s. Otto and Emilie Octavia (Gilman) H.; ed. pub. schs., Bourbon County, Ky., and S. Am. univs.; m. Ester San Martin, Aug. 20, 1911; children-Otto, Ester (dec.), Marion. With Panama R.R., 1908, Cerro de Pasco Ry., Peru, 1908-09; supt. of transportation and gen. supt. Central Ry. of Peru and supt. transportation, Guayaquil & Quito Ry., Ecuador, 1909-14; econ. survey in Brazil for Mercantile Bank of the Americas, 1920; with Northern Peru Mining & Smelting Co., 1922-27; sec. Am. Chamber Commerce of Mexico, 1927-31; prof. extraordinary of geography, Nat. U. of Mexico, 1927-. Served as lt. Philippines Constabulary, 1904-07; capt. Signal Corps, later F.A., U.S.A., later maj., F.A., 1915-19; spl. duty in Balkans, 1919-20; maj. Officers Res. Corps; grad. of Army War College, 1932; col. and aide de camp, staff of gov. of Ky. Fellow Royal Econ. Soc. (London), Royal Asiatic Soc., Royal Geog. Soc. (London), Royal Scottish Geog. Soc. (Edinburgh), Awarded Philippine Constabulary Service Medals, Mexican Border and World War Medals (U.S.), 4 war medals, Italy, 2 war medals, France; decorated Grand Officer Order of St. Stanislas, 2d Class, Order St. Anne, 2d Class, Order Vladimir, 4th Class (Russia); Comdr. Order Star of Rumania, with Swords; Comdr. Order of Prince Danilo I (Montenegro): Comdr. Order Polonia Restituta (Poland); Officer Order of St. Sava, 4th Class (Serbia); Officer Order Condor of the Andes (Bolivia); Order of Abdon Calderon, 2d Class (Educador); etc. Contbr. articles to 13th edit. Ency. Brit. Died Mar. 23, 1934.

HOLT, ANDREW HALL prof. civil engring.; b. Sunderland, Vt., Aug. 23, 1890; s. Winfield Selah and Effie Ida (Andrew) H.: student Burr & Burton Sem., Manchester, Vt., 1904-08; B.S. in C.E., U. of Vt., 1912, C.E., 1922; M.S., State U. of Ia., 1920, J.D., 1931; m. Ruth E. Brownson, Jan. 1, 1915; children-Elisabeth Ursula, Barbara Ruth, Winfield Andrew, Nancy Fay. Began 1911, surveying and engring., summer work with Am. Bridge Co., Ia. Ry. & Light Corp., U.S. Dist. Engr. and others; engr. in chg. river improvements, Iowa City: instr. U. of Vt., 1912-14; instr. civil engring., State U. of Ia., 1914-17, asst. prof., 1919-21, asso. prof., 1921-34, prof., 1934-37; prof. civil engring. and head of dept. of civil engring., Worcester Poly. Inst., since 1937. Served as capt. engrs., U.S. Army, A.E.F., World War I; col., Corps Engineers, commanding 361st Engineer Regiment, Pacific and European Theaters, World War II; Colonel, Corps of Engineers Reserve, ret. Member Iowa, Massachusetts and Federal bars. Member Am. Soc. Civil Engrs., Am. society for Engineering Edn., Soc. American Military Engrs., Worcester Society of Civil Engineers, Scabbard and Blade. Order of Coif, Phi Beta Kappa, Tau Beta Pi, Sigma Xi, Theta Tau, Alpha Tau Omega. Republican. Conglist. Mason. Author: Manual of Field Astronomy, 1916, 2d edit., 1927; (with B. J. Lambert) Elementary Structures in Steel and Concrete, 1929; also papers on surveying and the law of boundaries. Home: 10 Germain St., Worcester, Mass. Died Nov. 22, 1956; buried Ira Allen Cemetery. Sunderland, Vt.

HOLT, JOSEPH judge adv. gen.; b. Breckenridge County, Ky., Jan. 6, 1807; s. John and Eleanor (Stephens) H.; ed. St. Joseph's Coll., Centre Coll.; m. Mary Harrison, 2d, Margaret Wickcliffe. Commonwealth's atty. for 4th Louisville (Ky.) dist., 1833-35; U.S. commr. patents, 1857-59; U.S. postmaster gen., 1859-61; apptd. U.S. sec. of war, 1861; judge adv. gen. U.S. Army, 1862-75, prosecuted Clement Vallandigham, John Wilkes Booth and compatriots for assassination of Pres. Lincoln. Died Washington, D.C., Aug. 1, 1894.

HOLTHUSEN, HENRY FRANK, lawyer; b. New York, N.Y., Aug. 3, 1894; s. Henry and Barbara (Schindler) H.; A.B., Columbia Coll., 1915; LL.B., Columbia, 1917; m. Lenore Adeline Sutter, Oct. 10, 1953. Asso. Cadwalader, Wickersham & Taft, 1917; practiced law with offices in New York City and Norfolk, Va., 1920-24; spl. asst. atty. gen. U.S., Washington, 1924-26; partner House & Holthusen & McCloskey practicing gen., Corporate and admiralty law, New York City, 1927-34; apptd. Envoy Extraordinary and Minister Plenipotentiary to Czechoslovakia, 1931; partner House, Holthusen & Pinkham, New York City, 1934-37, partner Holthusen & Pinkham, 1937-51; staff Bur. Municipal Research. Conducted negotiations with Mexican Govt. for Economic Survey of Mexico by joint U.S.-Mexican Econ. Commn., 1944; visited 23 European countries as consultant to Fgn. Relations Sub-committee of U.S. Senate, 1947; chief of Telecommunications Mission to Japan, Turkey and other countries, 1951-52; counsel and cons. Foreign Relations Subcom. on Overseas Information Programs, 1953; chief Communications Mission for Egypt, 1953; general counsel committee on banking and currency U.S. Senate Study of Internat. Bank and Export-Import Bank U.S., 1954; cons. fgn. relations committee Tech. Cooperation Program, 1955; cons. spl. com. U.S. Senate to study Fgn. Aid Program, 1956; cons. fgn. relations com. U.S. Senate, Latin Am. study, 1958; American specialist U.S. State Department, 1959; cons. fgn. relations com. U.S. Senate, 1962-63; pub. mem. insp. U.S. Foreign Service, 1968; insp. Foreign Service of U.S., Portugal, 1968, France, 1969, Senegal and Gambia, 1970, Switzerland, 1971. Served as major U.S. Army, World War I. Del. Judicial Conv., N.Y. State, 1926. Counsel Protestant Unity League, 1932-34. Member Phi Kappa Psi. Protestant, Episcopalian (formerly vestryman Church of the Ascension). Club: National Republican (chmn. bd. govenors, New York Young Republican Club, 1929). Author: James W. Wadsworth, Jr., 1926; Turning the Hour Glass, 1928. Home: New York City NY Died Sept. 19, 1971.

HOLTON, EDWIN LEE educator; b. Scott County, Ind., Dec. 15, 1876; s. William Henry and Mary Hannah (Crist) H.; diploma Ind. State Normal Sch., Terre Haute, Ind., 1900; A.B., Ind. U., 1904; studied Columbia 1909-10; 1916-17 Ph.D. 1927; studied U. Paris 1919; m. Anna Carr, Aug. 4, 1904 (died Aug. 1, 1908); 1 dau., Ruth; m. 2d, Lillian Beck, June 1, 1911; 1 dau., Mary. Prin. twp. high schs., Henryville and Lapel, Ind., and supt. schs., Holton, Kan., and Noblesville, Ind., until 1908; supr. Indsl. Schs., N.Y.C., 1908-09; prof. edn. and dean of summer school Kan. State Coll. of Agr. and Applied Science, 1910—. Dir. of farm project instrn. U. Minn., 1925-26. Deputy commr. A.R.C. in France, 1918-19, was in charge reeducation and rehabilitation of the disabled soldiers and sailors of U.S. in France; with assimilated rank of major in U.S. Army, rep. U.S. as mem. of Inter-Allied Com. on Reeducation and Rehabilitation of war-disabled men. Mem. N.E.A., Soc. Coll. Tchrs. Edn., Phi Beta Kappa, Phi Kappa Phi, Phi Delta Kappa, Pi Gamma Mu.; pres. Kansas State Tchrs. Assn., 1923. Republican. Methodist. Mason (32ff). Clubs: Country, Rotary (dist. gov. internat. 1930-31) (Manhattan); Kansas Schoolmasters', Kansas Authors'. Author: (with Dr. W. E. Grimes) Modern Agriculture; Training Teachers of Vocational Agriculture. Home: Manhattan, Kan. Died July 7, 1950.

HOLTON, WINFRED B., JR. b. Oct. 27, 1888: s. Winfred Byron and Lula C. (Glover) H.; A.B., Wesleyan U., 1910; m. Elizabeth Curran, Dec. 4, 1920; children-Nancy E. (Mrs. G. B. M. Walker), Patricia C. (Mrs. Claud Morris), Winfred B, III. With Bur. Municipal Research, N.Y.C., 1910-16, asst. dir., 1915-16; asst. dir. N.Y. State Budget Com., 1916; engaged in survey examinations and preparation of reports on pub. works and pub. utility projects and taxation in various states, municipal and provincial govtl. depts. in U.S. and Canada, 1912-17; mng. dir. San Francisco Bur. of Governmental Research, 1916-17; U.S.S.B. Emergency Fleet Corp., chmn. contracts, claims and cancellations bd. and acting v.p., 1918-19; pres. Holton, Richards & Co., Inc., 1920-49; pres. and chmn. exec. com. Walworth Co., mfrs. valves, pipe fittings and tools, 1935-51, chmn. bd., 1951—; dir. Westcott Valve Co., Walworth Internat. and Cal. cos., Copper Recovery Corp. (subsidiary RFC Metals Reserve Corp.); trustee Susquehanna Silk Mills. Mem. valve mfrs. adv. com. WPB, 1941-45, prodn. cons., 1943-45; Valve and Fitting Industry, 1943-45. Served as capt. Ordnance, U.S. Army, 1917-18. Trustee Wesleyan U., 1935; hon. life mem. Wesleyan U. Alumni Council (chmn. 1926-31) Pres. and dir. Valve Mfrs. Assn., 1938-50; v.p. and dir. Pipe Fittings Mfrs. Assn., 1937-49; chmn. bd. trustees Navy Indsl. Assn., 1944-46. Mem. N.A.M., Am. Petroleum Inst., U.S. and N.Y. State C.'s of C., Psi Upsilon. Republican. Clubs: Pelham Country (pres. 1940-45, chmn. bd. govs. 1945-50, mem. bd., 1950—), University, Uptown (N.Y.); Faculty (Middletown); Blind Brooke (Portchester, N.Y.). Home: 98 Rockledge Dr., Pelham Manor, N.Y. Office: 60 E. 42d St., N.Y.C. Died July 12, 1957; buried Beechwood Cemetery, New Rochelle, N.Y.

HOLTZWORTH, BERTRAM ARTHUR, army officer; b. Huntington, W.Va., Apr. 3, 1904; s. Arthur Nicholas and Nettie Belle (Hunt) H.; student Va. Poly. Inst., 1921-23; B.S., U.S. Mil. Acad., 1927; m. Caroline Van Duyn Dorwin, June 25, 1932. Commd. 2d lt. F.A., U.S. Army, 1927, advanced through grades to maj. gen., 1952; successively battery officer, battery comdr., bn. comdr. various field arty. regts., 1927-43; gen. staff 12th U.S. Army Group, United Kingdom, France, Germany, 1943-45; chief staff Armor Center, 1945-47; mem. Dept. Army Gen. Staff, 1948-50; faculty Army War Coll., 1950-52; asst. chief staff J-4, Alaskan Command, 1952-54; asst. chief staff G-4, Continental Army Command, 1954-56; dep. chief staff Army Forces Far East, 1956-57; dep. chief staff programs, comptroller U.S. Army Pacific, 1957-59; chief of staff Sixth U.S. Army, 1959-61, deputy commanding general, 1961-63, ret., 1963. Decorated Distinguished Service medal, Legion of Merit, Bronze Star Medal; Order Brit. Empire; Legion of Honor, Croix de Guerre with palm, Croix de Guerre with gold star (France); Croix de Guerre with palm (Belgium). Methodist. Clubs: Army-Navy (Washington); Army and Navy Country (Arlington, Va.). Home: Washington DC Died Oct. 31, 1971; buried Arlington Nat. Cemetery, Arlington VA

HOMAN, PAUL THOMAS, economist; b. Indianola, Ia., Apr. 12, 1893; s. Fletcher and Kate (Wilson) H.; A.B., Willamette U., 1914; B.A., Oxford, England, 1919; Ph.D., Brookings Grad. Sch. of Economics and Govt., 1926; m. Christine Chittenden, June 10, 1924. Mgr. credit dept. Commonwealth Nat. Bank, Kansas City, Mo., 1921-23; instr. in economics, Washington U., St. Louis, 1923-25; asst. prof. of economics, U. of Calif., 1926-27; asst. prof. econ., Cornell, 1927-29, prof., 1929-47; staff, Council of Econ. Advisers to the President, 1947-50; prof. econs. U. of Calif., Los Angeles, since 1950; member research staff Brookings Instn., 1933-35 and 1937-38; economic advisor, O.P.M., 1941-42, W.P.B., 1942-44, W.A.A., 1945-46; dir. supply coordination div., U.N.R.R.A., London, 1944-45; member Com. on War Studies, S.S.R.C., since 1943; U.S. Commn. UNESCO, 1946-47. Served with Mesopotamia Expeditionary Forces, 1916-17; 2d lieut. Air Service, United States Army, with A.E.F., 1918-19. Awarded Rhodes scholarship, Oxford, 1914-16, and 1919-20. Mem. Am. Econ. Assn. (mem. exec. com. 1938-41); fellow Royal Econ. Soc. Author: Contemporary Economic Thought, 1928. Co-author: American Masters of Social Science, 1927; The National Recovery Administration, 1935; The Sugar Economy of Puerto Rico, 1938; Government and Economic Life, 1940. Contbr. to Encyclopedia of the Social Sciences and professional jours. Mng. editor Am. Econ. Review since 1941. Address: Los Angeles CA Died July 3, 1969; cremated.

HOMER, JOHN L. army officer; b. Mount Olive, Ill., Sept. 16, 1888; B.S., U.S. Mil. Acad., 1911; LL.D. (hon.), Blackburn Coll., 1948; m. Olive Kennedy, September 15, 1921 (dec. 1959); grad. Coast Arty. School, 1924, Army Industrial College, 1935. Command and Gen. Staff Sch., 1925, Army War Coll., 1939. Commd. 2d lt., Coast Arty., 1911, and advanced through the grades to brig. gen., Apr. 1941, major gen., Aug. 1942; comd. 61st Coast Arty. (anti-aircraft), Fort Sheridan, Ill., June 1939-Apr. 1941; comd. 40th C.A. Brigade since Apr. 1941; served overseas Sept. 1941 to Sept. 1942; commanded New York-Phila. Sector and Southeastern Sector, Eastern Defense Command, to April 1944; commanded 4th Anti-aircraft Command, to Dec. 1944; deputy commander, Panama Canal Dept., Jan.-Sept. 1945; comdg. gen. A.A. and G.M. Center, Ft. Bliss, Tex., 1946-50) exec. Ill. Defense Agency, 1950-59. Awarded Legion of Merit for service in Iceland; D.S.M. for service in Panama; Order of Vasco Nuñez de Balboa (Panama); Star of Abdon Calceron, First Class, Al Merito Gran Oficial (Ecuador); Order Al Merito (Gran Official de Chile); Medal Mil. Merit 1st class (Mexico). Home: 81 E. Van Buren St., Chgo. Died Sept. 27, 1962; buried Post Cemetery, U.S. Mil. Acad., West Point, N.Y.

HONAN, WILLIAM FRANCIS surgeon; b. Maysville, Ky.; s. Anthony and Anna Eliza (Bryan) H.; M.D., New York Home. Med. Coll. and Hosp., 1889; m. Annette Newdecker Dickey. Practiced in New York, 1889-; prof. clin. surgery N.Y. Home. Med. Coll. and Flower Hosp.; attending surgeon Met. Hosp. Dept. of Public Welfare; visiting surgeon Flower Hosp.; consulting surgeon 5th Av. Hosp., Carson C. Peck Memorial Hosp. Colonel M.R.C.; comdg. officer Gen. Hosp. 81. Catholic. Home: New York, N.Y. Died Oct. 7, 1935.

HONEY, SAMUEL ROBERTSON lawyer; b. Eng., 1841; s. William and Sarah Waynman (Robertson) H.; ed. in Eng.: taught sch. 2 yrs.; came to America, 1860; m. Mary Edwards; m. 2d, Frances H. Arkless, Feb. 21, 1906. Served pvt., corpl., sergt. and sergt. maj., 2d Batt., 15 U.S. Inf., Aug. 20, 1860-Aug. 13, 1862; 2d lt., Aug. 13, 1862: 1st lt. and adj., 1st Batt., 15th U.S. Inf., Feb. 17, 1863; capt. 33d Inf., Nov. 1, 1866; bvtd. capt., Sept. 1, 1864, "for gallant and meritorious services during Atlanta Campaign and at Battle of Jonesboro, Ga." (severely wounded); participated in Chickamauga, Missionary Ridge and Atlanta campaigns; acting asst. judge advocate gen. staffs of Generals Pope and Meade, 1867-68; hon. discharged at own request, Oct. 7, 1870. Read law with Judge W. P. Chilton, of Montgomery, Ala.; admitted to bar, 1869, to U.S. Supreme Court, 1887; retired from practice, Dec., 1905. Chief of staff to Gov. Van Zandt, 1877-79; lt. gov. of R.I., 1887-88; mayor of Newport, 1891-92; mem. Dem. Nat. Com., 1888-96; del. Dem. Nat. Convs., 1892, 1904; leader of Ho. of Rep., R.I., 1893-94. Mason. Home: Newport, R.I. Died Feb. 17, 1927.

HONEYCUTT, FRANCIS WEBSTER army officer; b. San Francisco, Calif., May 26, 1883; s. John Thomas (capt. U.S.A.) and Jennie (Webster) H.; B.S., U.S. Mil. Acad., 1904; hon. grad. Command and Gen. Staff Sch., Ft. Leavenworth, Kan., 1923; grad. Army War Coll., Washington, D.C., 1929; m. Margaret Harmon, Aug. 28, 1910: children-John Thomas (U.S.A.), Margaret (wife of Donald P. Graul, U.S.A.), Jane. Commd. 2d lt., Arty. Corps, U.S. Army, June 15, 1904, and advanced through the grades to brig. gen., June 1, 1938; assigned to field arty., 1907; served as lt. col. and col., field arty., with A.E.F., 1917-19. Decorated Victory Campaign Medal. Mason. Presbyterian. Inter-collegiate fencing champion, 1903, 1904, capt. Am. Olympic Fencing Team, Antwerp, 1920; nat. foil champion, 1921: capt. Am. Fencing Team vs. British, in U.S., 1921, in England, 1923. Died Sept. 20, 1940.

HOOD, CHARLES CROOK army officer; b. Somerset, O., Aug. 28, 1841; s. Thomas and Sarah H.; ed. pub. schs. of Somerset; m. Frances Skinner, Sept. 14, 1876. Pvt., corporal and sergt. Co. G, 31st Ohio Inf., Aug. 20, 1861-Feb. 3, 1864; 1st lt., Feb. 3, 1864; capt., Oct. 26, 1864, hon. mustered out of vol. service, July 20, 1865; capt. 41st U.S. Inf., July 28, 1866; transferred to 24th Inf., Nov. 11, 1869; maj. 7th Inf., July 4, 1892; lt. col., 19th Inf., Jan. 28, 1897; col. 16th Inf., May 5, 1899: brig. gen. U.S.A., Oct. 18, 1962; retired at own request, after 40 yrs.' service, Nov. 25, 1902. Wounded in skirmish with Roddy's Cav., Apr., 1863 and at battle of Chickamauga, Sept. 20, 1863. Served 4 yrs. in P.R. and P.I. Address: New York, N.Y. Died June 13, 1927.

HOOD, GEORGE E. congressman; b. Wayne County, N.C., Jan. 27, 1875; s. Edward B. and Edith (Bridgers) H.; ed. pub. schs.; m. Julia Annie Flowers, Sept. 23, 1903. Admitted to N.C. bar, 1896, and practiced in Goldsboro; sec. Dem. Exec. Com., Wayne Co., 1896; treas. Wayne Co., N.Y., 1897-9; mem. N.C. Ho. of Rep., 1901: mayor of Goldsboro, 1901-7; Dem. presdl. elector, 1912; mem. 64th and 65th Congresses (1915-19), 3d N.C. Dist. Capt. Co. B., N.C.N.G., 1901-5; lt. col., insp. general's dept., 1905-7; retired, 1909, rank of col. Mem. Goldsboro Bar Assn. Methodist. Home: Goldsboro, N.C. Died Mar. 1960.

HOOD, JOHN naval officer; b. Florence, Ala., Dec. 3, 1859; s. John Murray and Mary Cornelia (Heslep) H.: grad. U.S. Naval Acad., 1879; m. Rosalie, d. Thomas Thompson Caswell, Jan. 28, 1890. Commd. midshipman, June 10, 1881; promoted through grades to rear admiral, Aug. 29, 1916. Wrecked with the Kearsarge, Feb. 2, 1894; blown up on Maine, Feb. 15, 1898; comd. Hawk during Spanish-Am. War, carried information of arrival of Spanish Squadron at Santiago to comdr. of Flying Squadron at Cienfuegos, and delivered orders for him to proceed to Santiago, May 23, 1898; made survey for Pacific Cable, 1899-1900, and prepared charts and data by which cable was laid; comd. Elcano in Chinese waters during Russo-Japanese War, 1903-05; comd. Tacoma, 1907-09, regulating Haitian and Central Am. revolutions and elections; comd. ships at Naval Acad., 1909-10; comd. Rhode Island, Atlantic Fleet, 1910-11; comd. Delaware, Atlantic Fleet, 1911-12, and won battle efficiency pennant: mem. Gen. Bd. of Navy, 1912-15; comd. Texas, Atlantic Fleet, 1915-16, won the battle efficiency pennant and gunnery trophy for the year and awarded the "Red E" for excellence in engring. efficiency; comd. reserve force, U.S. Atlantic Fleet, Oct. 30, 1916-Apr. 6, 1917; ordered to command 4th Div., Atlantic Fleet, on mobilization of reserve for war, Apr. 6, 1917. Home: Florence, Ala. Died Feb. 11, 1919.

HOOD, JOHN BELL army officer; b. Bath County, Ga., June 1, 1831; s. Dr. John and Theodocia (French) H.; grad. U.S. Mil. Acad., 1853; m. Anna Marie Hennen, 1868, 10 children. Cavalry instr. U.S. Mil. Acad., 1859-60; commd. 1st lt. in charge of cavalry under Gen. John B. Magruder, Confederate Army, 1861; brig. gen. in command of Tex. Brigade, led at battles of Gaine's Mill, 2d Bull Run and Antietam, 1862; wounded at Battle of Gettysburg, 1863; directed corps and 3 divs. Army of Tenn. at Battle of Chickamauga; commd. lt. gen. in command of corps under Joseph E. Johnston, 1864; tried to stop Sherman, but lost in battles at Atlanta, Franklin and Nashville; gave up his command, Jan. 1865, surrendered, May 1865; became commn. mcht., New Orleans, after Civil War. Died New Orleans, Aug. 30, 1879; buried New Orleans.

HOOD, J(OSEPH) DOUGLAS biologist; b. Laramie, Wyo., Nov. 29, 1889; s. Thomas Henry and Eva Maria Josephine (Dickson) H.; A.B., U. Ill., 1910; M.A., George Washington U., 1913; Ph.D., Cornell U., 1932; m. Helen Madge Hincher, 1930; 1 dau., Barbara. Asst. instr. in mil. sci. and tactics, U. Ill., 1909-10; instr. biology U. Rochester, 1922-25, asst. prof., 1925-28, prof., 1928-37; Cornell U. resident dr., 1937-38, asst. prof., biology, 1939-43, asso. prof. 1943, prof., 1948; cons. U. Fla. Brevet capt. Ill. N.G., 1910; served as 2d lt. D.C. N.G., Mexican Border, 1916-17; 1st lt. Ordnance Dept., U.S. Army, 1917-18, capt., 1918-20; supervised procurement all gun carriages for ry., seacoast and improvised field arty., World War. Fellow A.A.A.S., Entomol. Soc. Am. (charter mem.), Royal Entomol. Soc. London; mem. N.Y. Entomol. Soc., Entomoly Soc. Washington, Bklyn. Entomol. Soc., Bol. Soc. Washington, Natural History Soc. C.Z. (hon.), Entomol. Soc. Brazil, Sigma Xi, Phi Kappa Phi, Alpha Sigma Phi (nat. sec. 1910-13), Theta Nu Epsilon, Scabbard and Blade (nat. sec. and treas. 1910-13). Republican. Unitarian. Mason. Rifle and pistol expert; mem. D.C. rifle team, 1914, 15, U.S. N.G. team, 1915; winner 2d pl. Boyle Match and Reading Matches, Sea Girt, N.J., 1914. Contbr. articles to sci. jours. Home: 207 Cobb St., Ithaca, N.Y. Died Oct. 22, 1966.

HOOGEWERFF, JOHN ADRIAN naval officer; b. Howard County, Md., Nov. 27, 1860; s. Samuel Evans and Mary Elizabeth (Duval) H.; student Pa. Mil. Acad., 1875-76; grad. U.S. Naval Acad., 1881, Naval War Coll., 1913-14; m. Edwardine L. Hiester, Oct. 10, 1889. Ensign jr. grade, July 1, 1883: promoted through grades to capt., Mar. 4, 1911; temporary rear admiral, Aug. 31, 1917: permanent rear admiral, July 1, 1918. Landed with U.S. force at Alexandria, Egypt, after bombardment by British. 1882; at U.S. Naval Obs. with Prof. Asaph Hall, 1883-85; in charge Magnetic Obs., 1889-92: instr. electricity, etc., U.S. Naval Acad., 1895-98, 1901-04: served on Cincinnati, Spanish-Am. War, 1898; head Dept. Ordnance and Gunnery, U.S. Naval Acad., 1908-09: comd. Kansas, 1911-13; supt. U.S. Naval Obs., 1914-17; comd. Pennsylvania, Apr.-Sept. 1917; apptd. comdr. Mine Force, Atlantic Fleet, Sept. 1917; comdg. Battleship Div. One, Atlantic Fleet, Nov. 1917-Feb. 1919; supt. U.S. Naval Obs., Mar. 1919-June 1921; comdt. Navy Yard, Puget Sound, Wash., June 1921-Oct. 1924; retired Nov. 27, 1924. Medals for engagement at Matanzas, and for West Indian Campaign, Spanish-Am. War; Victory Medal and Navy Cross, World War. Episcopalian. Author: Magnetic Observations, 1891. Died Feb. 13, 1933.

HOOKER, CHARLES EDWARD ex-congressman; b. Union Dist., S.C., 1825; LL.B., Harvard, 1846; m. Fannie C. Sharkey, 1851. Admitted to bar, and since in practice at Jackson, Miss.; mem. Miss. Ho. of Rep., 1859-61; served in C.S.A., 1861-65, becoming col. of cav.; atty.-gen. Miss., 1865-68; removed by mil. authorities; was associated with Charles O'Connor and James Lyons in Jefferson Davis' trial for treason. Mem. 44th to 47th (1875-83), 50th to 53d (1887-95) and 57th(1901-03) Congresses, 7th Miss. Dist.; Democrat. Address: Jackson, Miss.

HOOKER, EDWARD comdr. U.S.N.; b. Farmington, Conn., Dec. 25, 1822) s. Edward and Elizabeth (Daggett) H.; ed. Farmington Acad.; m. Esther Ann Battey, May 11, 1851 (died 1896). Sailor and officer in merchant service, 1837-61) entered U.S. Navy, July 19, 1861; acting master on gunboat Louisiana; severely wounded, Oct. 5, 1861 (the 1st acting master wounded in the war); exec. officer of "Louisiana." Stationed at Washington, N.C., in unexpected absence of comdg. officer; comd. the ship in the fight of Sept. 5, 1862; promoted acting vol. lt. for gallantry in that action; comd. steamer Victoria, 1863, on Wilmington blockade, and captured brig. Minna and steamer Nicholai I: comd. boats on Rappahannock during advance of Gen. Grant and cleared the river of torpedoes; promoted, through various grades, to comdr. U.S.N., retiring 1884. Address: Brooklyn, N.Y. Died 1903.

HOOKER, HENRY STEWART lawyer; b. San Francisco, Calif., Sept. 21, 1879; s. Richard Campbell and Elizabeth (Stewart) H.; A.B., Yale, 1902; LL. B., N.Y. Law Sch., 1904; m. Madeleine Forrest Burke, May 7, 1918 (div. Apr. 22, 1930). In practice of law at N.Y.C., 1904-; mem. Marvin, Hooker & Roosevelt (F.D.), 1910-18. g Personal rep. of Pres. with rank of ambassador at unveiling of Roosevelt Memorial, London, Eng., 1948; now Hooker, Alley & Duncan (since May 1, 1944). Former mem. Squadron A, N.Y. Nat. Guard; attended 1st Plattsburg T.C., 1915, Plum Island T.C., 1916; commd. maj. U.S. Army, 1917, and assigned to staff of Gen. Leonard Wood; went to France, May 1918, as asst. div. adj. 33d Div., A.E.F.; acting div. adj. at British front, May-Aug. 1918, battles of Hamel and Gressaire Wood; served with 33d Div. at St. Mihiel, Argonne-Meuse offensive, and in Troyon sector. Cited for "exceptionally meritorious and conspicuous services," also for "gallantry in action." Chevalier of the Legion of Honor (France); Chevalier Order of the Crown (Belguum); Conspicuous Service Cross (New York); Order of the Purple Heart and Medal of Silver Star (U.S.). Mem. Assn. Bar City of N.Y., Scroll and Key (Yale). Democrat. Episcopalian. Clubs: Knickerbocker, Racquet and Tennis, Piping Rock, Down Town Association. Captain Yale Freshman Crew, 1899; mem. Yale U. Crew, 1901. Home: 825 Fifth Av., N.Y.C. 21. Office: 50 Broadway, N.Y.C. Died May 17, 1964; buried Arlington Nat. Cemetery.

HOOKER, JOSEPH (nickname Fighting Joe), army officer; b. Hadley, Mass., Nov. 13, 1814; s. Joseph and Mary (Seymour) H.; grad. U.S. Mil. Acad., 1837; m. Olivia Groesbeck, 1865. Served with U.S. Army in campaigns under Taylor and Scott in Mexican War, 1846-48; served in Florida War, 1836-43; supt. mil. roads in Ore., 1858-59; commd. col. Cal. Militia, 1859-61; commd. brig. gen. U.S. Volunteers, aided in defense of Washington (D.C.), 1861; leader div. in Peninsular Campaign, 1862; in command 1st Corps in Md. Campaign, 1862, wounded at Battle of Antietam, promoted brig. gen. U.S. Army, fought at Battle of Fredricksburg; comdr. Army of Potomac, 1863, failed to take initiative at Battle of Chancellorsville, resulting in Union retreat, 1863; brevetted maj. gen. U.S. Army at Battle of Lookout Mountain, Nov. 24, 1863; comdr. 11th and 12th Corps under Gen. Thomas and Gen. Sherman, battles of Mill Creek Expdn., Pasaca, Cassville, New Hope Church, Pine Mountain and siege of Atlanta; in command No. Dept., Cincinnati, 1864, Dept. of East, N.Y.C., 1865, Dept. of the Lakes, Detroit, 1866. Died Garden City, N.Y., Oct. 31, 1879; buried Laurel Grove Cemetery, Cincinnati.

HOOPER, BEN W. ex-gov. Tenn.; b. Newport, Tenn., Oct. 13, 1870; grad. Carson and Newman Coll., Jefferson City, Tenn., 1890; m. Anna B. Jones, Sept. 25, 1901; children-Anna B., Ben Jones, Randolph, Janella, Lemuel W., Newell Sanders. Admitted to Tenn. bar, 1894; asst. U.S. atty. Eastern Dist. Tenn., 1906-10; gov. of Tenn., 1911-13, 13-15; resumed practice as mem. firm Hooper, Cate & Greer. Baptist. Rep. nominee for U.S. senator, 1916, 34; elected judge Chancery Ct., 1920, resigned, 1921; became mem. U.S. R.R. Labor Bd., Chicago, serving as chmn., 1922-26; mem. Great Smoky Mountain Park Commn., 1927-28, chief land buyer for park, 1928-29; became mem. law firm Hooper, Crawford and Hurd. Served as Capt., Spanish-Am War, 1898-99; served in Puerto Rico. Home: Newport, Tenn. Died Apr. 18, 1957.

HOOPER, STANFORD CALDWELL rear admiral USN, ret., electronics consultant; b. Colton, Cal., Aug. 16, 1884; s. William Swayze and Mary (Caldwell) H.; B.S., U.S. Naval Academy, 1905; m. Margaret Nye, May 27, 1915; 1 dau., Elizabeth. Commd. ensign, USN, 1907, advanced through grades to rear adm., 1938; first U.S. Fleet radio officer, 1912; head of Radio Div., Navy Dept. during 3 tours of shore duty beginning 1915; comd. destroyer Fairfax during World War I; chief engr. Fed. Radio Commn., 1927-28; dir. Naval Communications, 1928-34; dir. Tech. Div., Naval Operations, and chmn. Naval Research Com., 1934-39; dir. Radio Liaison Div., 1940-43, ret. Hooper Trophy awarded annually to outstanding electronics div. USNR. Decorated World War I medal Navy Cross, Mexican Campaign medal (United States); Legion of Honor (France); awarded gold medal Institute Radio Engineers, 1934, Marconi Medal of Merit, 1939, Elliot Cresson Medal (Franklin Institute), 1945, U.S. delegate to International Radio Confs. at The Hague, Bucharest, Lisbon, Cairo, Chile. Episcopalian. Clubs: Army and Navy, Army and Navy Country, Chevy Chase, Sulgrave (Washington, D.C.); New York Yacht; Bath (Miami Beach, Fla.). Editor of Robinson's Manual of Radio Telegraphy and Telephony. Address: 4425 Garfield Street N.W., Washington; also 6320 Alton Rd., Miami Beach, Fla. Died Apr. 6, 1955; buried Arlington Nat. Cemetery.

HOOPINGARNER, NEWMAN LEANDER cons. business psychologist; b. University Place, Neb., May 1, 1891; s. Noah Leander and Dora Emma (Stallsmith) H.; A.B., U. of Tex., 1913, A.M., 1915; grad. study Columbia, Carnegie Inst. Tech. and N.Y.U.; m. Ethel Barron, June 24, 1917; 1 son, Newman Avery. Tutor in psychology and asst. to dir. extension dept., U. of Tex., 1912-15; instr. psychology and history of edn., Southwest Tex. State Teachers Coll., summer 1914; mgr. edn. exhibits and lecturer on sch. improvment, U. of Tex., 1915-17; major research fellow in applied psychology, Bur. of Salesmanship Research, Carnegie Inst. Tech., Pittsburgh, Pa., 1917-18; asso. prof. applied psychology and field rep. Bur. Personnel Research, same inst., 1919-20; dir. service methods, Bus. Training Corp., N.Y.C., 1920-21; lecturer on business psychology and management, N.Y.U., 1922-26, Brooklyn Edison Sch., 1922-25, Brooklyn Inst. Arts and Sciences, 1922-26; organizer, and dir. Bur. of Business Guidance, 1923—; asst. prof. business psychology, Sch. Commerce, N.Y.U., 1926, asso. prof., 1927-31, prof., 1931—. Personnel adj. Ordnance Training Camp, Camp Hancock, Ga., 1918-19; 2d lt., ordnance, Feb. 1, 1918, 1st lt., Nov. 1, 1918; capt., A.G.D., 1919-29. Mem. A.A.A.S., Winconna Assn., Inc. (dir.), Personnel Research Fed., Phi Delta Kappa, Pi Gamma Mu; fellow, American Geographical Society of New York. Methodist. Mason. Club; City. Author: (in collaboration) Modern Production Methods, 1921; Self Measurement Tests for Executive and Business Ability, 1923; Personality and Business Ability Analysis, 1927. Originated and developed a method of analyzing and developing personality which may be applied in education and in business; organized the first credit course in personality improvement offered in any college or university. Home: 14 Dartmouth St., Rockville Center, L.I., N.Y. Died Jan. 1958.

HOOTON, MOTT army officer; b. Phila., Apr. 16, 1838; s. Mott and Ann Eliza (Carpenter) H.; acad. edn., West Chester, Pa.: unmarried. First sergt. to capt. 1st Pa. Reserve Vols., June 4, 1861-June 13, 1864; apptd. from Pa., 2d lt. and 1st lt., 13th Inf., Feb. 23, 1866; transferred to 31st Inf. Sept. 21, 1866 to 22d Inf., May 15, 1869; capt., Aug. 5, 1872; maj., 25th Inf., May 1, 1896; lt. col., 5th Inf., Oct. 4, 1898; col. 28th Inf., Feb. 2, 1901; brig. gen., Apr. 15, 1902. Bvtd.; maj. vols., Mar. 13, 1865, "for gallant and meritorious services in Wilderness campaigns"; maj. U.S.A., Feb. 27, 1890, "for gallant services in action against Indians at Spring Creek, Mont., Oct. 15 and 16, 1876." Participated in campaigns of 7 days before Richmond, with Pope's army at Warrenton, Va., 2d battle of Bull Run (severely wounded), Gettysburg, Wilderness, etc.; after Civil War served in 13th U.S. Inf., 1866-67; 31st Inf., 1867-71; recruiting service, 1871-73; Yellowstone Expdn., 1873; New Orleans, 1874-75; Sioux campaigns, 1875-77; served in Mich., Texas, Colo., Mont., until Spanish-Am. War; served 9 mos. in Cuba; organized 28th Inf. and served in Philippines; retired by operation of law, Apr. 16, 1902. has traveled extensively in Europe and the Far East. Home: West Chester, Pa. Died May 30, 1920.

HOOVER, DONALD DOUGLAS, advt. and pub. relations exec.; Indpls., Jan. 6, 1904; s. Samuel Carpenter and Martha Belle (Stinson) H.; student pub. schs.; m. Pauline Holmes, May 28, 1927; 1 dau., Cynthia. Began newspaper career, Indpls., 1921; with Asso. Press Bur., Washington, 1926-28; city desk Indpls. News, 1928-33; advt. pub. relations Bozell & Jacobs, Inc., 1933-41, 48-69, pres. N.Y. Corp., 1950-64, chmn. bd., chief exec. officer, 1964-69; associate editor Indpls. Times, 1946-47. Past pres. Pogakon council Boy Scouts Am., mem. committee; president Indpls. Community Relations Council; bd. mem. of Greater New York Safety Council. Mem. of bd. govs., nat. exec. com. U.S.O., 1958-65. Civilian advisory bd. pub. relations U.S. Military Academy. Served from 1st lt. to col. M.I., Gen. Staff Corps, World War II. Decorated Order Brit. Empire; Philippine Liberation Medal with two stars; seven battle stars; Legion of Merit; recipient Pulitzer prize for Indpls. News, 1931. Mem. Bd. Fundamental Edn., Ind. Soc. (past pres. N.Y.C.), Am. Assn. Advt. Agys. (mem. com. on govt. and pub. relations), Soc. Silurians (v.p.), Conn. Society Prevention of Blindness (director), National Soc. Prevention Blindness (bd. 1959-62), Pub. Relations Soc. Am., Sigma Delta Chi (trustee endowment fund; recipient Wells Meml. Key 1961). Conglist. Clubs: Nat. Press (Washington); Society of Silurians, Advertising, Overseas Press (N.Y.C.); Indianapolis Press (past pres.). Author: Copy!, 1931. Home: New York City NY Died Feb. 1969.

HOOVER, HERBERT thirty-first U.S. Pres.; b. West Branch, Ia., Aug. 10, 1874; s. Jesse Clark and Hulda Randall (Minthorn) H.; A.B. in Engring., Stanford, 1895; hon. degrees from 81 instns. in U.S. and abroad; 296 medals, awards, honors including 61 gold medals from Am., fgn. orgns. and socs. Hon. citizen of 24 European cities; 56 hon. memberships in sci. and tech. socs.; m. Lou Henry, 1899 (died Jan. 7, 1944); children - Herbert, Allan Henry. Profl. work in mines, r.r.'s, metall. works, U.S., Mexico, Can., Australia, Italy, Gt. Britain, South Africa, India, China, Russia, etc., 1895-1913. Represented Panama-Pacific Internat. Expn., in Europe, 1913-14; chmn. Am. Relief Com., London, Eng., 1914-15; chmn. Commn. for Relief in Belgium, 1915-19; U.S. food adminstr., June 1917-July 1, 1919; served as mem. War Trade Council; was chmn. U.S. Grain Corp., U.S. Sugar Equalization Bd., Interallied Food Council, Supreme Econ. Council, European Coal Council; chmn. Am. Relief Adminstrn. since 1919; v. chmn. Pres. Wilson's 2d Indsl. Conf., 1920; chmn. European Relief Council since 1920; apptd. sec. commerce by Pres. Harding, Mar. 5, 1921, reapptd. by Pres. Coolidge. Chmn. Pres.' Conf. on Unemployemnt, Sept. 20, 1921; mem. adv. com. Limitation of Armaments Conf., Nov. 1921, World War Debt. Com., etc.; chmn. Colo. River Commn.; chmn. Spl. Miss. Flood Relief Commn., 1927; Pres., U.S., term 1929-33; renominated for Pres., Rept. Nat. Conv., 1932. At request of Pres. Truman undertook coordination of world food supplies of 38 countries, March-June 1946; at request of Pres. Truman, undertook a study of econ. situation in Germany and Austria, 1947; chmn. Commn. On Orgn. Exec. Br. of Govt., 1947-49, also chmn. second commn., 1953-55; guest of Fed. Rep. of Germany at invitation Chancellor Adenauer, 1954; mem. adv. bd. World Bank Reconstrn. and Devel. Trustee Stanford U., Mills Coll., Carnegie Inst. of Wash., Henry E. Huntington Library and Art Gallery; chmn. C.R.B. Ednl. Fund, Am. Children's Fund, Boys' Clubs of Am., Finnish Relief Fund, Inc., Robt. A. Taft Meml. Found.; hon. mem. Woodrow Wilson Centenniel Celebration Commn.; hon. chmn. Nat. Fund lMed. Edn., Hlth. Information Found. Recipient John O'Hara Cosgrave gold medal award Dutch Treat Club of N.Y.; Gold medal Internat. Benjamin Franklin Soc., 1954. Mem. Am. Inst. Mining and Metall. Engr. (pres. 1920), Am. Engring. Council (pres. 1921), Am. Child Health Assn. (pres. 1922). Author: Am. Individualism, 1922; The Challenge to Liberty, 1934; America's First

Crusade, 1941; The Problems of Lasting Peace, 1942; Addresses on American Road, 7 vols.; 1938-55; Memoirs, Vols. I, II, III, 1951-52; The Ordeal of Woodrow Wilson, 1958. Translator (with Mrs. Hoover) Agricola de Ré Metallicca. Home: Waldorf Astoria Towers, N.Y.C. Died Oct. 1964.

HOOVER, JOHN HOWARD, naval officer; b. Seville, O., May 15, 1887; s. Benjamin Franklin and Claudia Irene (Crawford) H.; student U.S. Naval Acad., 1903-06; m. Helen Branconier Smith, Dec. 26, 1916; children—Jacqueline, William Howard, Jean. Commd. comdr. U.S. Navy, 1918, and advanced through grades to rear admiral, 1941, vice adm., 1942. Formerly comdr. Caribbean Sea Frontier, Comdr. Forward Area Central Pacific and Comdr. Mariannas; became dep. comdr. in chief, Pacific Fleet, July 1945. Awarded Navy Cross, 1919, Distinguished Service Medal with two stars, 1944-45. Club: N.Y. Yacht (N.Y.C.). Home: Bethesda MD Died Dec. 3, 1970.

HOPE, JAMES HASKELL, state supt. schs.; b. Hope Station, S.C., Sept. 22, 1874; s. James Christian and Martha Fletcher (Miller) H.; graduated Newberry (S.C.) College, received degrees, A.B., and LL.D.; student Clemson Agricultural College 2 years, Winthrop Normal Coll. 5 summers; 1 son, James Donald; m. 2d, Wilhelmina Grimsley, Mar. 5, 1921; children—Martha Louise, James Haskell, John Christian, Stuart Cromer. Teacher rural schs. 6 yrs., supt. schs. 12 yrs., supt. city schs. 5 yrs.; state supt. edn., S.C., 1923-47, ret. Capt. S.C.N.G. 2 yrs. Mem. County Bd. Edn., Union County, 1900-16; county supt. edn., Union County, 1916-22. Life mem. N.E.A., S.C. State Teachers Assn. Democrat. Baptist. Mason (Shriner), K.P. Jr. Order United Am. Mechanics. Club: Lions. Home: 129 Walker St., Columbia SC

HOPKINS, ESEK 1st comdr.-in-chief Continental Navy; b. Scituate, R.I., Apr. 26, 1718; s. William and Ruth (Wilkinson) H.; m. Desire Burroughs, Nov. 28, 1741, 10 children. Privateer during French and Indian Wars; brig. gen. in charge all mil. forces of R.I., 1775; became comdr.-in-chief Continental Navy, 1775, met difficulties in equipping and manning the few Am. ships available, censured by Congress for failure, 1776, suspended from command, 1777, dismissed 1778; dep. to R.I. Gen. Assembly, 1779-86; collector imposts, 1783; trustee Brown U., 1782-1802. Died North Providence, R.I., Feb. 26, 1802.

HOPKINS, JAY PAUL, army officer (ret.); b. Mattawan, Mich., Nov. 2, 1875; s. Josiah and Elvira (Mains) H.; student Hillsdale Coll., 1892-93; B.E., U.S. Military Academy, 1900; married Jeannette Ward, Aug. 7, 1900; 1 daughter; married 2d, Jessie Howell Zook, Nov. 29, 1927. Commander 2d lieutenant, artillery, 1900, advanced through grades to brigadier gen.; retired as col., C.A.C., 1930, brig. gen. (ret.), 1940; instr. Coast Arty. Sch., 1908-12; chief of antiaircraft service, 1918. Now dir. and pres. First Nat. Bank of Cassopolis, Mich. Awarded Distinguished Service Medal (U.S.), Legion of Honor (France). Republican. Presbyterian. Mason. Clubs: Union League (Chicago); Rotary (Dowagiac, Mich.). Home: 530 E. State St., Cassopolis MI

HOPKINS, JOHN BURROUGHS naval officer; b. Providence, R.I., Aug. 25, 1742; s. Esek and Desire (Burroughs) H.; m. Sarah Harris, Oct. 2, 1768. Took part in burning of Brit. ship Gaspee, 1772; apptd. capt. ship Cabot, 1775; took command ship Warren, 1777; captured Brit. ships Jason and Hibernia, 1779, dismissed from command because of irregularities in his conduct on this cruise; commanded privateers, 1780-81. Died Dec. 5, 1796.

HOPKINS, JOSEPH GARDNER physician; b. Brooklyn, June 30, 1882; s. George Gallagher and Alice (Gardner) H.; student Adelphi Acad., Brooklyn, 1890-98; A.B., Columbia, 1902; M.D., Johns Hopkins, 1907; unmarried. Interne Johns Hopkins Hosp., 1907-08; resident pathologist St. Luke's Hosp., New York 1908-10; bacteriologist, 1910-13; asst. instr. clinical pathol. Columbia, 1911-13, asso. in bacteriol., 1913-14, asst. prof. bacteriol., 1915-17, asso. instr. in dermatology, 1920-26; prof. dermatol., 1925-47, prof. emeritus since 1947; dir. Dermatology Vanderbilt Clinic, 1926-47, Presbyn. Hosp., 1936-47; practicing physician New York City since 1921. Served as bacteriol. Am. Red Cross Commn. to Serbia, 1915. Served as lt., capt. U.S. Army Med. Corps, 1917-19; investigator com. on med. research. Office Scientific Research Development, 1941-46, tech. observer, consultant Office of Field Service, 1945-46; civilian cons. to surgeon gen. (Army), 1945-46; cons. Veterans Hosp., Bronx, N.Y., since 1946. Mem. Am. Bd. Dermatol. and Syphilol., 1938-47. Mem. Am. Dermatol. Assn., Am. Acad. Dermatol., Soc. Investigative Dermatol., New York Dermatol. Soc., Am. Soc. Pathol. and Bacteriol., Soc. Am. Bacteriol., Am. Mycological Soc., Torrey Botanical, Soc. Pithotomists, Royal Soc. Medicine, Austrian Dermatol. Soc. (hon. mem.), Swedish Dermatol. Soc. (corr. mem), Phi Beta Kappa, Alpha Omega Alpha. Republican. Clubs: Century Assn., Columbia University. Home: 217 Haven Av., New York 33. Office: 102 E. 78th St., N.Y. City 21. Died Feb. 27, 1951; buried Washington St. Cemetery, Geneva, N.Y.

HOPKINS, SAMUEL congressman, army officer; b. Albemarle County, Va., Apr. 9, 1753; s. Dr. Samuel and Isabella (Taylor) H.; m. Elizabeth Branch Bugg, Jan. 18, 1783. Fought under George Washington at battles of Trenton, Princeton, Monmouth, Brandywine and Germantown during Am. Revolution; served as lt. col. 10th Va. Regt. at seige of Charleston; original mem. Soc. of Cincinnati; moved to Ky., 1796; chief justice 1st Ct. Criminal Common Law and Chancery Jurisdiction in Ky., 1799-1801; mem. Ky. Ho. of Reps., 1800, 01, 03-06, Ky. Senate, 1809-13; commd. maj. gen. U.S. Army, 1812; comdr.-in-chief Western frontier; led 2000 volunteers against Kickappo Indian villages on Illinois River, 1812; mem. U.S. Ho. of Reps. from Ky., 13th Congress, 1813-15, Died Henderson, Ky., Sept. 16, 1819; buried family burial plot "Spring Garden" nr. Henderson.

HOPKINS, WALTER LEE lawyer; b. Rocky Mount, Va., Dec. 26, 1889; s. Wm. Leftwich Turner and Mary Ella (Hancock) H.; student William and Mary Coll., 1908-11; spl. work U. of Va., summer 1911; A.B., Washington and Lee U., 1912, LL.B., 1914. Admitted to Va. bar, 1914; editor and mgr. Franklin Chronicle, 1916-17; with Hairston, Woodrum and Hopkins, 1914-16; mem. Hopkins and Hopkins, Richmond, 1920—. In U.S. Army, 1917; commd. lt. inf. and assigned to 318th Regt., 80th Div.; in charge Cable Sect. Bur., War Dept., from Nov. 17, 1918, until hon. disch., Mar. 10, 1919; asst. chief atty. Board of Contract Adjustment, War Dept., 1919 (asso. mem. 1919-20); apptd. mem. staff of Gov. John Garland Pollard of Va., 1930, by Gov. Ruby Laffoon of Ky., 1933 (a.d.c. with rank of col.), Gov. Eugene Talmadge of Ga., June 5, 1934 (a.d.c. with rank of lt. col.), Gov. Wm. H. Murray, of Okla., May 28, 1934 (a.d.c. with rank of col.); commd. by Gov. J. M. Futrell, of Ark., in Ark. Res. Militia, with rank of col., May 25, 1934, and assigned as aide-de-camp on his staff; reapptd. by Gov. Talmadge as mem. staff (a.d.c. with rank of lt. col.), to rank from Jan. 16, 1935; apptd. to staff of Gov. James V. Allred of Tex., May 17, 1935 (a.d.c. with rank of lt. col.); commd. hon. col. in the Nat. Guard of U.S. and State of Miss., Aug. 23, 1935, by Gov. Sennett Conner; apptd. mem. of staff of Gov. Olin D. Johnston, of S.C. (a.d.c with rank of lt. col.), 1938; reappointed mem. of staff of Gov. Johnston, Feb. 1, 1943; appt. mem. of staff of Gov. James H. Davis of La. (a.d.c. with rank of col.), Oct. 28, 1944; asst. adj. gen. U.C.V., 1927, 28, with rank of brig. gen. apptd. judge adv. gen. on staff of comdr. in chief, U.C.V., 1935 (with rank of brig. gen.). Mem. Va. House of Dels., 1940—. Mem. or former mem. Am., Va. State and Richmond City bar assns., Va. State bar, Va. Society of Colonial Wars, S.R., S.A.R., La Société Nationale, 40 and 8, Am. Legion (post comdr. 1919; post adj. 1921; mem. state exec. com., 1920-22), Sons of Confederate Vets. (camp comdr. 1921-22; judge advocate in chief, 1921-22; state comdr. 1922-23; mem. nat. exec. council, and 1933-35; adj. in chief, 1923-33, 1935-44; comdr. in chief 1933-35); mem. Am. Acad. Polit. and Social Science, Am. Geog. Soc., Repeal Associates, Va. Commn. on Inter-racial Co-operation, Nat. Com. for Protection of Child, Family, School and Church (mem. exec. com.), Va. Hist. Soc., Phi Alpha Delta, Kappa Chi, Omicron Delta Kappa. Mem. bd. visitors R. E. Lee Camp, Soldiers' Home (pres.), Eightieth Div. Vets. Assn., Bd. Pension Commrs. of Richmond City (chmn.), Manassas Battlefield Foundation Com., Beauvoir, Jefferson Davis Memorial Home Com., Appomattox Hist. Park Assn. (v.p.; mem. bd. dirs.); Manassas Battlefield Confed. Park, Inc. (bd. dirs.), pres. bd. dirs. of R. E. Lee Camp Confed. Memorial Park; mem. bd. trustees, Booker T. Washington Birthplace Memorial (member executive committee). Democrat. Member State Central Democratic Committee and vice chairman third Congressional District Com. Episcopalian. Mason (32ff, Shriner), Odd Fellow, Elk. Awards of S.C.V.; gold medal and Certificate of Distinction, "for unusual and extraordinary achievement in perpetuating the history of the South and Nation"; gold medal, Southland Star, "for distinguished and meritorious service in historical and patriotic work." Clubs: Westmoreland, Commonwealth. Author: Hopkins of Virginia and Related Families, 1931; Leftwich-Turner Families of Va. and Their Connections, 1932. Editor S.C.V. year book, 1926, 27. Contbr. various hist. publs. Home: 1017 Park Av. Office: Law Bldg., Richmond, Va. Died July 12, 1949.

HOPLEY, RUSSELL JAMES public utilities; born in Blue Island, Ill., Apr. 28, 1895; son of John Barnes and Mary Elizabeth (Russell) Hopley; educated in public schools and business college of Fort Madison, Ia.; married Helen Joyce Kreymborg, February 6, 1931; children-Russell J., Jr., John K. Collector Northwestern Bell Telephone Co. (formerly Iowa Telephone Co.), Fort Madison, Ia., 1915-17, manager offices-McGregor and Waterloo, Ia., 1919-22, gen. staff Omaha, Neb., 1922-23, mgr. Des Moines, 1923-25, dist. mgr. Des Moines, 1925-29, commercial operations-supervisor, Omaha, 1929-37, gen. mgr. states of Neb. and S.D., 1937, v.p. of operations, dir. and mem. exec. com. 1937-42, pres. since 1942; pres., dir. and mem. exec. com. The Tri-State Telephone and Telegraph Co.; vice pres., dir. and mem. exec. com. Dakota Central Telephone Co., Omaha, 1937-42; dir. Neb. Savings & Loan Assn. and United States Nat. Bank, Omaha; mem. proxy com. Northwest-Bancorporation, Minneapolis. During World War I (1917-19), served with Field-Signal Battalion, A.E.F. (Haute-Alsace, Meuse-Argonne), during World War II (1941-45), served as civilian adv. army air serivce. Trustee United Seamans Service; vice chmn. United War and Community Fund. Member Omaha C. of C. (chmn. finance com. 1943-44; post war planning bd., municipal tax com.); international vice president Int'l dir. Conopos Clubs, 1926-29; trustee U. of Neb. Foundation; trustee Children's Memorial Hosp.; vice president and trustee World War II Memorial Park Association; Salvation Army Advisory Bd.; gen. chairman Mayors City-Wide Planning Commission. Mem. Newcomen Soc. of Eng., Telephone Pioneers of Am. Am. Legion, Neb. Table Tennis Assn. (hon. vice pres.). Republican. Presbyterian. Mason (32ff, Shriner, Jesters), Clubs; Country, Omaha, Athletic, Engineers (Omaha); University (Lincoln); Minneapolis (Minneapolis, Minn.); Minnesota (St-Paul); Des Moines (Des Moines, Ia.). Home: 725 N. 57th St., Omaha 3. Office: 118 S. 19th St., Omaha 2, Neb. Died Nov. 23, 1949.

HOPPIN, WILLIAM WARNER lawyer; b. N.Y. City, Dec. 13, 1878; s. William W. and Katharine (Beekman) H.; A.B., Yale, 1901; m. Mary Gallatin, Mar. 31, 1902. Began practice at N.Y. City, 1906; of counsel to alien property custodian; asst. U.S. atty. gen. in charge of customs cases, June 16, 1921-Nov. 15, 1925; resigned to resume pvt. practice; apptd. city magistrate, Apr. 1940. Mem. Mayor Mitchel's Com. of Defense, World War; govt. appeal agt. in first draft; enlisted in U.S. Army for service in Field Arty.; former capt. O.R.C. City Magistrate of City of N.Y. Mem. bd. mgrs. Ruptured and Crippled Hosp., secretary New York Assn. for the Blind. Director Florence Crittenton League. Member Field Artillery Reserve Assn. (dir.), First Av. Assn. (dir.), St. Nicholas Soc. Republican. Clubs: Union, Yale, Nat. Republican. Home: 53 E. 66th St., New York, N.Y. Died May 27, 1948.

HOPPING, ANDREW DANIEL army officer; b. Lima, O., Jan. 3, 1894; s. Harvey Platt and Carrie (Lockette) H.; A.B., Butler U., 1917; M.B.A., Harvard, 1935; grad. French Tank Sch., 1929, Q.M.C. Sch., 1931, Army Indsl. Coll., 1940; m. Gabrielle Decaux, Aug. 17, 1918; children-Andree Charlotte (wife of Lt. Peter P. Shills, Jr., U.S.M.C. Res.), Daniel Henri (officer U.S. Army), Gabrielle Louise (widow of Lt. George C. Oertel, Jr., killed in action, 1944), Harvey Charles, Mary Jane, Martha Caroline. Served with machine gun co., 151st Inf., Ind. N.G., 1917; commd. 2d lt., inf. U.S. Army, 1918; served with 38th Div., AEF, France; commd. 2d lt., U.S. Army, 1920, advanced through grades to brig. gen., 1945; with Army of Occupation, Germany, 1920-22; trans. Q.M.C., 1933; with supply div. War Dept. Gen. Staff, 1940-42; staff officer A.S.F., Washington, 1942-44; dep. q.m. gen. for supply planning and operations 1944-46; chief q.m. Philippines-Ryukus Command, Manila, P.I., 1946-47; q.m. Far East Comd., Tokyo, Japan, 1947—. Decorated Legion of Merit with oak leaf cluster. Mem. Q.M. Assn., Mil. Order of World War. Clubs: Army and Navy, Harvard Business School Alumni (Washington). Address: care Adjutant General's Office, Dept. of Army, Washington. Died Jan. 11, 1951.

HOPWOOD, HERBERT GLADSTONE naval officer; b. Mt. Carmel, Pa., Nov. 23, 1898; s. Kendrick Isaiah and Anna Mary (Williams) H.; B.S., U.S. Naval Acad., 1919; m. Jean Fulton, Sept. 12, 1931. Comd. ensign USN, 1919, advancing through grades to rear adm., 1945; dir. budget and reports, Navy Dept., 1946-50; dep. comptroller Navy 1950-52; comdr. cruiser destroyer Pacific Force, 1952; chief of staff Pacific Fleet, 1953; vice adm. comdr. First Fleet, 1955; dept. chief Naval Operations (logistics), 1956; adm., comdr. in chief U.S. Pacific Fleet, 1958; v.p. Grace Line, Inc., N.Y.C. Presbyn. Mason. Address: Grace Line, Inc., 3 Hanover Sq., N.Y.C. 4. Died Sept. 15, 1966; buried Arlington Nat. Cemetery.

HORN, TIEMANN NEWELL army officer; b. Brooklyn, N.Y., Jan. 18, 1868; s. Daniel Tiemann and Frances (Capron) H.: grad. U.S. Mil. Acad., 1891. Arty. Sch., 1898, Sch. of Submarine Defense, 1903; honor grad. Army Sch. of the Line, 1911; grad. Army Staff Coll., 1912; m. Myra Rivers, Nov. 28, 1894. Commd. 2d lt. 3d Cav., June 12, 1891; trans. to 2d Arty., Dec. 15, 1891; 1st lt. 1st Arty., Oct. 7, 1898; promoted through grades to col. 9th F.A., July 1, 1917; brig. gen., Feb. 6, 191S. Dist. ordnance officer and arty. engr. Southern Arty. Dist. of N.Y., 1903-06; duty at Jamestown Expn., 1907; in Philippines, 1913-15, Hawaii, 1915-18; as brig. gen. comd. 7th F.A. Brigade, 7th Div., during war period. Mason. Episcopalian. Home: Plainfield, N.J. Died May 5, 1923.

HORNBOSTEL, HENRY architect; b. Bklyn., Aug. 15, 1867; s. Edward and Johanna (Cassebeer) H.; B.A., Columbia, 1891; M.A. (hon.), 1907; student Ecole des Beaux Arts, Paris, 1893-97; m. Martha Armitage, 1899 (dec.); children - Lloyd, Caleb; m. 2d, Mabelle Sylvester Weston, May 14, 1932. Architect, works include Carnegie Inst. Tech., Soldiers and Sailors Meml. Hall (Pitts.), Ednl. Bldg., Albany, N.Y., city halls in Oakland, Cal., Wilmington, Del., Hartford, Conn., Pitts., Meml. City Hall, Cedar Papids, Ia., gen. plans for Northwestern U., Harding Meml. Tomb, Rodef Scholan Synagogue, Pitts., U. Pitts., Hell Gate Bridge, N.Y., Queensborough Bridge, Emory U., Aluminum Research

Bldg., Pitts., and others; prof. architecture Columiba, also Carnegie Inst. Tech. Served as maj. C.W.S., U.S. Army, World War I; France. Fellow A.I.A.; mem. Am. Legion, Soc. Ecole des Beaux Arts (pres. 1915-16). Home: Pine St., Melbourne Beach, Fla. 32951. Died Dec. 13, 1961.

HORNE, FREDERICK JOSEPH admiral; b. N.Y.C., Feb. 14, 1880; s. George Edward and Marguerite Agnes (Cooper) H.; grad. U.S. Naval Acad., 1899; m. Alma Beverly Cole McClung, Aug. 4, 1903. Served on U.S.S. Texas and participated in battle of Santiago, Cuba, 1898; comd. ensign, 1901: advanced through grades to admiral; served as naval attache at Am. Embassy, Tokyo, Japan, 1915-19, receiving Navy Cross for distinguished and meritorious services during this period; became asst. to chief of Naval Operations, Navy Dept., Washington, D.C., 1941; apptd. vice chief of Naval Operations with rank of vice adm., 1942; promoted admiral, 1944; retired, 1946. Decorations: Navy Cross, Distinguished Service Medal, Army Legion of Merit, Navy Unit Commendation, Spanish Campaign, Santiago, Philippine Campaign, Comdr. of Legion of Honor (French); Grand Officer Order of Polonia Restituta (Polish): Grand Cordon Chinese Order Yellow Banner; Grand Officer Order Leopold with Palm, Croix de Guerre with Palm (Belgium); Brazillian Order of Naval Merit, Bank of Grand Cross; Knight Commander of Military Division of Order of British Empire, Club: Army and Navy. Home: 601 Margarita Av., Corondao, Cal. Died Oct. 1959.

HORNER, BERNARD JUSTINE, newspaper pub.; b. Uvalde, Tex., July 13, 1895; s. Herman and Clara H.; student Draughons Bus. Coll.; La Salle Extension U.; m. Nov. 20, 1920; children—Madelyn, Bernard Gentson. Entire career with Light Pub. Co., San Antonio, Tex.; advt. dir., 1919-Mar. 1942, became pub., Aug. 1946, editor, vice-pres. Board of directors San Antonio Symphony Soc. Military service with 36th inf. div., 1917; disch. capt. inf., 1919; re-entered mil. service as lt. col. with III Corps, Mar. 1942; overseas duty as col., G-2 III Corps; disch., 1946. Awarded Army Legion of Merit, Bronze Star, Commendation ribbon, Cross of War with Palms (Belgium). Mem. Res. Officers Assn., Tex. Pub. Assn., Am. Legion, San Antonio C. of C. (dir.). Independent. Episcopalian. Mason (Scottish Rite). Rotarian. Clubs: Patio; St. Anthony. Home: San Antonio TX Died Sept. 1968.

HORNER, LEONARD SHERMAN elec. engr.; b. Marshall, Va., Mar. 26, 1875; s. Frederick (U.S. Navy) and Maria Elizabeth H.; prep. edn. Bethel Mil. Acad., Warrenton, Va.; E.E., Lehigh U., 1898; m. Julia Stuyvesant Barry, Nov. 8, 1902; children-H. Mansfield, Helen N. Began with engr. constrn. dept., Am. Telephone & Telegraph Co., New York, 1898; with Corcker-Wheeler Co. as sales engr. and mgr. for Conn., 1900-08; v.p. Acme Wire Co., 1908-26, now dir.; pres. Niles-Bement-Pond Co., 1926-30; v.p. and dir. The Bullard Co. Cohmn. com. on census of mfrs., Dept. Commerce, 1931-32, chmn. Nat. Research Council Com., 1929-30, in preparation of aircraft prodn. study and report, which study covered factors affecting increased output and reduced cost of prodn. and embodied recommendations in methods, etc.; dep. adminstr. National Recovery Administration, 1933-34; now active in estate management and supervision of investments; also active on indsl. surveys and as indsl. advisor to mfrs. With troop A, New York Cavalry, in Puerto Rico, Spanish-Am. War, 1898; with Air Service at Washington, D.C., World War, 1917-18, as chief of staff, Bureau Aircraft Production, rank of maj.; promoted to lt. col. Mem. U.S. Chamber Commerce (dir. 1929, 30), Chamber Commerce of New Haven (v.p.; dir.). Mem. Nat. Industrial Conf. Bd., Nat. Assn. Mfrs., New England Council, Va. Hist. Soc., New Haven Host. Soc., Sigma Chi, Am. Legion. Republican. Episcopalian. Clubs: Graduate, New Haven County (New Haven); Army and Navy (Washington, D.C.). Home: 870 Prospect St., New Haven, Conn. Died Aug. 1, 1943.

HORNEY, ODUS CREAMER ret. army officer; b. Lexington, Ill., Sept. 18, 1866; s. James W. and Josephine (Creamer) H.; B.S., U.S. Mil. Acad., West Point, N.Y., 1891; m. Kezia Bryan, July 29, 1891; children-Ruth (Mrs. T. G. M. Oliphant), Grace (Mrs. E. Louis Ford) (dec.), Esther (Mrs. Francis J. Gillespie), Odus C. With inf., U.S. Army, 1891-94; with ordnance dept., 1894-1930; ret. as brig.-gen.; designed, developed Springfield rifle, caliber 30; pioneered 16 inch rifle in U.S., built and put into operation pioneer Army Smokeless Powder Plant. Mem. Mil. Order of the World Wars, Nat. Sojourners. Mason (32ff). Clubs: Engineers (Philadelphia), Army-Navy (Washington, San Francisco). Home: 452 Hillcrest Rd., San Mateo, Cal. Died Feb. 16, 1957: buried Presidio of San Francisco.

HORNSBY, JOHN ALLEN M.D.) b. St. Louis, Mo., Dec. 19, 1859; s. Doddridge Christopher and Elizabeth Matilda (Pim) H.; M.D., Washington U. Sch. of Medicine, 1882; m. Edith Primm, Sept. 18, 1883: children-Edith Marie, Hubert Primm. Interne St. Louis City Hosp., 1882-83; asst. supervising surg., M.P. Ry., 1883-84; coroner, St. Louis County, 1884-85; surgeon White Pass and Yukon Ry., Alaska, 1898-1900; spl. officer, Nome, Alaska, under U.S. Pub. Health Service, 1900-01; supt. Michael Reese Hosp., Chicago, 1907-014; supt. U. of Va. Hosp. and prof. Med. Sch. U. of Va. until 1931. Commd. 1st lt. M.R.C., U.S.A., 1911; maj. M.C., U.S.A., 1917; in active service throughout World War; promoted to lt. col., Apr. 1918; was chief of Hosp. Div., U.S.A., chief insp. of mil. hosps. and confidential adviser to Secretary of War Newton D. Baker. Author: (text book) The Modern Hospital: The Small Community Hospital; etc. Home: Washington, D.C. Died June 4, 1939.

HORRAX, GILBERT neurosurgeon; b. Glen Ridge, N.J., Apr. 9, 1887; s. Edwin and Mary Alice (Gilbert) H.; A.B., Williams Coll., 1909, Sc.D., 1936; M.D., Johns Hopkins, 1913; m. Geraldine Kemmis Martin, June 29, 1921 (dec.); children-Trudeau Martin, Elizabeth Daintry; m. 2d, Helen Anne Pagenstecher (Mrs. S. S. Tregellas), July 19, 1938; 1 step-son, S. Staley Tregellas. House officer Peter Bent Brigham Hosp., Boston, 1913-14, neurol. resident, 1915-16, jr., later sr. asso. in neurol. surgery, 1919-32; Arthur Tracy Cabot fellow Harvard Med. Sch., 1914-15, successively asst., instr., faculty instr. and asst. prof. surgery, 1919-32, instr. in neurology courses for graduates, 1935-41; resident surgeon Mass. Gen. Hosp., 1916-17; neurosurgeon N.E. Deaconess and N.E. Bapt. Hosps., 1932—; in charge dept. neurosurgery The Lahey Clinic, Boston, 1932—; cons. to U.S. Vets. Hosp., W. Roxbury, Mass., 1944-46: cons. in neurosurgery Cushing Gen. Hosp., Framingham, Mass. Served from 1st lt. to maj. M.C., U.S. Army, France, 1917-19; USPHS Res., 1944—. Diplomate Am. Bd. of Surgery and Am. Bd. Neurol. Surgery. Fellow A.C.S.; mem. Soc. Neurol. Surgeons (pres. 1937-39), Am. Neurol. Soc. (v.p. 1940-41), Assn. for Research in Nervous and Mental Diseases (v.p. 1936), Am. Surg. Assn., N.E. and Boston surg. socs., Harvey Cushing Soc., Boston Soc. Psychiatry and Neurology (pres. 1939), Mass. Med. Soc., A.M.A., Royal Soc. of Med. (hon. mem. sect. of neurology): corrs. mem. Société de Neurol., France; hon. mem. La Societe de Neuro-chirurgie de la langue Francaise; mem. Phi Delta Theta, Gargoyle. Trustee Met. State Hospital (Waltham, Mass.), Lawrence Acad. (Groton, Mass.). Clubs: Harvard (Boston); Williams (N.Y.C.); The Country, Longwood Cricket (Brookline, Mass.); Orleans Fish and Game (Quebec, Can.). Contbr. numerous sci. articles to med. and surg. publs. Home: 30 Cedar Rd., Chestnut Hill. Mass. Office: 605 Commonwealth Av., Boston 15. Died Sept. 28, 1957; buried Forest Hills Cemetery.

HORSFALL, FRANK LAPPIN, JR., physician; b. Seattle, Dec. 14, 1906; s. Frank L. and Jessie Laura (Ludden) H.; B.A., U. Wash., 1927; M.D., C.M., McGill U., 1932; Ph.D., Uppsala Univ., 1961; LL.D., U. Alberta, 1963; D.Sc., McGill University, 1963; m. to Norma E. Campagnari, July 1, 1937; children—Frank III, Susan, Mary. House officer pathology Peter Bent Brigham Hosp., Boston, 1932-33; resident physician Royal Victoria Hosp., Montreal, 1933-34; resident surgeon Montreal General Hosp., 1934; asst. The Rockefeller Inst., 1934-37, member, 1941-57, mem., prof., 1957-60, v.p. clin. studies, 1955-60, asst. resident physician Hosp. The Rockefeller Inst., 1934-36, resident physician, 1936-37, physician, 1941-55, physician-in-chief, 1955-60; staff mem. Internat. Health Div., The Rockefeller Found., 1937-41; pres., dir., trustee Sloan-Kettering Institute Cancer Research, 1960-71; director research Memorial Sloan-Kettering Cancer Center, 1965-71, Memorial Hospital Cancer and Allied Diseases, 1965-71; professor of medicine Cornell U. Med. Coll., 1960-71, dir., prof. microbiology Sloan-Kettering Div. Grad. Sch. Med. Scis., 1960-71; cons. to Surgeon Gen. U.S. Army, mem. commn. immunization Army Epidemiol. Bd., 1947-55; cons. USPHS, 1948-53; mem. nat. research council com. adv. U.S. Army Chem. Corps, Washington, 1957-59; chmn. research and engring. adv. panel Def. Dept., 1960-61, vice chmn., 1959-60, mem.-at-large Def. Sci. Bd., 1957-62; vice chmn. Biol. and Chem. Def. Planning Bd., 1959-61; mem. U.S. Panel, U.S.-Japan com. Sci. Coop., 1962-63, Human Cancer Virus Task Force, NIH, 1962-64, Pres.' Commn. Heart Disease, Cancer, Stroke, 1964-65. Chmn. vis. com. Med. Dept. Brookhaven Nat. Lab., Upton, L.I., N.Y., 1955-57; mem. sci. adv. comm. Inst. Microbiology Rutgers U., 1955-62; mem. expert adv. panel virus diseases WHO, Geneva, Switzerland, 1956-71; director of Public Health Research Institute City of New York, Incorporated, 1956-71, chairman research council, 1956-57; special cons. N.Y.C., Dept. Health, 1956-71; member nat. adv. com. Okla. Med. Research Found., Oklahoma City, 1957-71; mem. bd. sci. dirs. Roscoe B. Jackson Meml. Lab., Bar Harbor, Me., 1958-61; mem. exec. com. Health Research Council City N.Y., 1958-68, vice chairman, 1962-66; member panel of advisers New York State Committee for Medical Edn., 1962-63; sci. adv. com. Inst. Cancer Research, 1962-71; sci. adv. council N.Y. State Legislature, 1963-71; mem. Commn. Health Services City New York, 1959-71; member committee respiratory diseases, National Tb Association, 1959-60; chairman program committee 5th Internat. Poliomyelitis Conf., Denmark, 1960; gen. chmn. 2d Internat. Conf. Congenital Malformations. N.Y. 1963; mem. com. virus research and epidemiology Nat. Found., 1956-58, com. on research basic scis., vaccine adv. com., 1959-71; adv. com. electronic computers biology and medicine Nat. Acad. Scis.-NRC, 1959-60; com. sci. and pub. policy Nat. Acad. Scis., 1963-66. Trustee Internat. Med. Congress, Ltd., 1959-71, v.p., 1962-71; trustee Internat. Poliomyelitis Congress Ltd., 1959-71, So. Research Inst., 1960-71, Memorial Sloan-Kettering Cancer Center, N.Y., 1960-71, bd. govs. Weltzmann Inst. Sci., Rehovoth, Israel, 1964-71; trustee Med. Library Center N.Y., 1959-71. Served to comdr. M.C., USNR, 1942-46. Recipient Banting research fellow, McGill U. Med. Sch., 1930-32; Holmes gold medal, 1932; Eli Lilly award bacteriology and immunology, 1937; Casgrain and Charbonneau award in medicine McGill U., 1942; John F. Lewis prize Am. Philos. Soc., 1959; Alumnus Summa Laude Dignatus award Alumni Assn. U. Wash., 1962; gold medal award Peter Bent Brigham Hosp., 1963. Fellow Montreal Medico-Chirurgical Soc.; mem. Am. Assn. Immunologists (councillor 1962-66, v.p. 1966-67, pres. 1967-68), A.M.A., Am. Philos. Soc., Am. Pub. Health Assn. (mem. Lasker awards committee 1958-60), Assn. of Am. Cancer Insts. (president 1968-71), Royal Society Medicine (affiliate), National Institutes Health (member virus and rickettsial study section 1948-53), International Board Editors Excerpta Medica (U.S. sect. rep.), American Soc. Clin. Investigation (past v.p.), N.Y. Acad. Medicom. 1957-58, editorial bd. Bull. 1969-71), Nat. Acad. Scis., Assn. Am. Phys., A.A.A.S., Harvey Soc., Practitioners' Soc. (president 1969-71), Am. Assn. Cancer Research, American Assn. Pathologists and Bacteriologists, Am. Soc. Microbiology, Soc. Exptl. Biology and Medicine, Am. Acad. Arts and Scis., Royal Coll. Physicians and Surgeons Can. Mem. bd. editors Jour. Immunology, 1950-62; asso. editor Virology, 1954-60, co-editor, Journal of Experimental Medicine, 1958-60, adv. editor, 1963-71; mem. editorial bd. World Wide Abstracts Gen. Medicine, 1958-71, Am. Jour. Pub. Health, 1958-60; mem. editorial adv. bd. Med. World News, 1959-61. Home: New York City NY Died Feb. 1971.

HORTON, GEORGE TERRY civil engr., mfr.; b. Waupun, Wis., 1873; s. Horace E. and Emma (Babcock) H.; C.E., Rensselaer Poly. Inst., 1893; m. Hazel Heath, Nov. 27, 1907; 1 dau., Florence (Mrs. Arnold Gillatt). Became identified with the Chicago Bridge & Iron Works, 1893, pres. and mgr. since 1912. Chairman Chicago Plan Commission.; life trustee Rensselaer Poly. Inst. Lt. comdr. U.S.N.R., retired. Mem. Am. Soc. C.E., Western Soc. Engrs., Chicago Hist. Osc., Am. Welding Soc. (pres.), Am. Soc. for Testing Materials, Soc. naval Architects and Marine Engrs., Chicago Engrs., New Eng. Historic General. Soc., Art Inst. of Chicago, Am. Petroleum Inst., Am. Water Works Assn., Delta Kappa Epsilon. Clubs: Engineers', University, South Shore Country, Commercial Club, Aero Club of Illinois (Chicago). Home: 4940 Woodlawn Av. Office: 1305 W. 105th St., Chicago, Ill. Died Mar. 19, 1945.

HORTON, J(OSEPH) WARREN, acoustical engr.; b. Ipswich, Mass., Dec. 18, 1889; s. Benjamin R. and Susan Elizabeth (Tower) H.; B.S. in Electrochemistry, Mass. Inst. Tech., 1914, D.Sc. in Elec. Engring., 1935; m. Adelina C. Doucet, Sept. 4, 1916; 1 son, Peter. Asst. physics and electrochemistry Mass. Inst. Tech., 1914-16, research asso., 1933-37, asso. prof. biol. engring., 1937-45, asso. prof. elec. communication, dept. elec. engring., 1945-49; tech. staff Bell Telephone Labs., N.Y.C., 1916-28; chief engr. Gen. Radio Co., Cambridge, Mass., 1928-33; tech. expert Naval Expt. Sta., Nahant, Mass., also Naval Hdqrs., London, 1917-18; spl. adviser Nat. Def. Research Com., also OSRD, 1941-45; chief research cons. U.S. Navy Underwater Sound Lab., New London, Conn., 1949-59, technical director, from 1959; lecturer in electrical engineering University Conn., from 1950. Trustee, mem. corp. Cable Meml. Hosp., Ipswich, Mass., from 1940. Served as lt. comdr. USNR, inactive, 1936-51. Recipient best research of year award Am. Inst. E.E., 1927, distinguished civilian service award U.S. Navy, 1958. Fellow A.A.A.S., Acoustical Soc., Am. Inst. E.E. (bd. examiners from 1950), Inst. Radio Engrs. (adminstrv. com. profl. group ultrasonics engring. from 1958), Am. Phys. Soc.; mem. N.E. Soc. Anesthetists (hon.), Newcomen Soc., Audio Engring. Soc. (hon.), Sigma Xi, Eta Kappa Nu. Club: Thames (New London). Author: Fundamentals of Sonar, 1957. Contbr. tech. articles profl. jours. Drafted safe practice recommendations operating rooms for Nat. Fire Protection Assn. Holder 56 patents, including submarine detectors, frequency standardizing systems, picture transmission and TV systems, carrier current and radio secrecy systems. Home: New London CT Died May 10, 1967.

HORTON, WILLIAM EDWARD army officer; b. Washington. D.C., June 28, 1868; s. William Edward and Josephine Julia (Clarke) H.: grad. high sch., Washington, 1886; LL.B., Georgetown U., 1892, LL.M., 1893; unmarried. Commd. 1st lt. and adj. 1st D.C. Inf., U.S.A., May 11, 1898; advanced through grades to col., July 1, 1920; apptd. asst. to q.m.g., in charge constrn. service, rank of brig. gen. for 4 yrs. from Aug. 2, 1927; retired, 1929, and has practiced law since at Washington. Served in Spanish-American War, participating in charge of San Juan Hill; in campaigns against Aguinaldo, 1899, and Malvar, 1901-02. Philippine Islands; builder of Ft. William McKinley and Malate Bks., P.I.; in 2d intervention in Cuba, 1906-07; served as chief q.m., advance sect., and asst. to chief q.m., A.E.F., Tours, France, World War. Decorated D.S.M., Spanish Campaign Medal, silver star (citation for gallantry in action, Santiago, Cuba, July 1, 1898), Cuban Occupation Medal, Philippine Campaign Medal, silver star (citation for gallantry in action, Taboatin Bridge, P.I., Dec. 3, 1899), Cuban Pacification Medal, Victory Medal, World War (all U.S.): Officer Legion of Honor and Grand Cross Order Nichan El Anouar (France); companion of order St. Michael and St. George (Eng.); comdr. order Leopold II (Belgium); comdr. Order of Crown of Italy: officer Order of White Eagle (Serbia): Comdr. Order of Crown of Rumania: Grand officer Order Prince Danilo I (Montenegro): officer Mil. Medal La Solaridad (Panama): Grand Dignitary (Grand Cross) of order of Crown of Charlemagne: Grand Official Assn., also of Nat. Albanian order of Skanderbeg. Comdr. Polonia. Restituta (Poland); War Cross (Montenegro): Croix d' Honneur du Croix de Merite (France): Star of Royal Acad. Hispano-Americana of Sciences and Arts (Spain). Hon. Mem. Arts, Sciences, Letters. Societe d' Education and D'Encouragement de tres.: pres. and tres. Soc. of Am. Friends of Albania: Mason. Mem. Baronial order of Runnemede. Home: Washington D.C. Died Sept. 13, 1935.

HOSKINS, JOHN DEANE CHARLES brig. gen.; b. Potosi, Mo., Jan. 19, 1846; s. late Lt. Charles (U.S.A.) and Jennie (Deane) H.; grad. U.S. Mil. Acad., 1868; m. Bianca Guiteras, of Matanzas, Cuba, Feb. 7, 1871. Second lt. 1st Inf., June 15, 1868; transferred to 3d Arty., May 13, 1869; grad. Arty. Sch., 1874; 1st lt. Dec. 20, 1875; capt. June 7, 1897; maj. Arty. Corps, July 1, 1901; lt. col. Mar. 22, 1905; col., June 22, 1906; brig. gen. U.S.A., Dec. 27, 1908, and retired at own request after 44 yrs.' service. Episcopalian. Mason. Died Mar. 1, 1937.

HOSKINS, JOHN M(ADISON) naval officer; b. Pineville, Ky., Oct. 22, 1898; s. Thomas Jefferson and Lucy (Renfro) H.; B.S., U.S. Naval Acad., June 1921; m. Susne Waters, Oct. 13, 1928; children - John M., Renfro W., Mary Sue. Commd. ensign USN, 1921, advanced through grades to rear adm., Dec. 31, 1946; participated in Second Battle of Philippine Sea; lost right foot in action; hospitalized, Oct. 1944-July 1945; later restored to active duty; comd. U.S.S. Princeton, 1945-46; comd. Carrier Div. 3, U.S.S. Valley Forge (flagship), Mar-Dec. 1950; participated in Korean campaign, 1950; comd. Pacific Div. of Mil. Air Transport Services, 1951-54; later comdr. Fleet Air Quonset, Quonset point, R.I.; pres. Naval Examining Bd., Phys. Disability Bd., Washington, fron 1957; ret. with rank vice adm.; dir. declassification policy Office Asst. Sec. Def., 1958-. Awarded Navy Cross, Legonion of Merit, Purple Heart, Victory medal World Wars I and II, Am. Def., Am. Theatre, African-European Theatre, Pacific Theatre, Philippine Liberation nedal, Philippine Medal of Mil. Merit, D.S.M., Silver Star, UN Service Medal and Pibbon, Korean Service Medal. Methodist. Clubs: Army and Navy, Army-Navy Country (Washington); Racquet (Phila.). Home: Pineville, Ky. Address: 3804 Lakeview Terrace Falls Church, Va. 22041. Died Mar. 27, 196 Cemetery.

HOSTETLER, ERWIN CASE, adj. gen. Ohio; b. Alden, Ia., Apr. 1, 1904; s. Christopher R. and Elizabeth Lee (Jones) H.; student Roanoke Coll., Salem, Va., 1922-23; m. Una Ratcliff, Feb. 2, 1945; stepchildren-Helen Virginia (Mrs. Dale E. McMath), Russell McVay, With B.F. Goodrich Co., 1923-63, sr. specification editor aerospace and def. div., 1954-63; enlisted as pvt. Ohio N.G., 1923, advanced through ranks and grades to maj. gen., 1963; active duty World War II, also Korean War; regimental comdr. 145th Inf., Ohio N.G., 1959-63; adj. gen., also dir. civil def. Ohio, 1963-68, also dir. emergency planning. Mem. Adjs. Gen. Assn., Ohio N.G., Assn. (pres. 1962), Assn. U.S. Army (pres. Buckeye chpt. 1962), 37th Div. Assn. (life; pres. Akron chpt. 1948), Sojourners. Mason (32 deg., Shriner). Home: Columbus OH Died May 7, 1968; buried Rose Hill Cemetery, Akron OH

HOTCHKISS, CLARENCE ROLAND soldier, lawyer; b. Bradford County, Pa., June 5, 1880; s. Charles Frederick and Melissa (Taylor) H.; ed. acad., Owego, N.Y., Eastman Coll. of Bus. Administration (Poughkeepsie), 1903, Realty Inst. (New York), 1909; LL.B., U. of Ore., 1911; grad. various service schs., U.S. Army, including Tank Sch., 1930, War Coll., 1931; m. Grace Evangeline North, July 2, 1908. Organized C. R. Hotchkiss Co., Stewart-Hotchkiss Co., Realty & Mortgage Co., Portland, Ore., of which was pres., 1911-17; mem. Rep. Nat. Conv. 1916; presdl. elector and sec. Rep. State Central Com., Ore., 1920; U.S. marshal, District of Oregon, 1921-30. Admitted to Oregon bar, 1911, Federal Ct., 1928, U.S. Supreme Ct., 1937; practiced Portland, Oregon, 1911-17, 1920-21, 1938-41. Expediter and control supervisor Kaiser Shipbldg. Co., 1942-43; inventory auditor, Comml. Iron Works, 1944-45; counsel, National Mortgage & Bond Co., 1946. Served as pvt. 9th Pa. Inf., Spanish-Am. War; non-commd. officer, Co. A, 21st Inf. and Arty. Corps, U.S. Army, Philippine Insurrection: capt. and adj. 3d Ore. Inf., and dist. adj. on Mex. border; capt. Co. E, 162d Inf., World War, 30 mos., 20 mos. with A.E.F.; hon. disch. as maj., Oct. 1919; lt. col. Inf. Res., U.S. Army, 1923, col. 1932; mem. War Dept. Gen. Staff, 1933-37. Retired, 1948. Decorated D.S.M. Fellow Am. Geog. Soc., Am. Geneal. Soc.: mem. Fed. Bar Assn., Ore. State bar, Am. Legion, Vets. Fgn. Wars, United Spanish War Vets. (past camp comdr.; past dept. comdr.; nat. v-comdr.), Mil. Order World War (past chapter comdr.; state comdr.; mem. gen. staff), Reserve Officers' Assn. of U.S. (past state pres.; mem. nat. council Nat. exec. com.; awarded Armed Forces Res. medal with 4 hourglasses), S.A.R., Nat. Soc. of Puritan Descendants, Genealogical Soc. Colonial Wars. Founders and Patriots of America, Soc. War of 1812, Delta Theta Phi, Pi Gamma Mu, Scabbard and Blade. Conglist. Mason (32ff, Shriner, K.C.C.H., Grotto, K.T., Sojourners), Clubs: Mazama Mountaineering (Portland): Army and Navy (Washington, D.C.). Author: Around the World As a Soldier, 1903; History of Third Oregon Infantry, 1914: England's Inns and Courts of Chancery (monograph), 1919; The Knight Hospitallers, 1933; Samuel Hotchkiss of the New Haven Colony and Some of His Descendants (booklet), 1933-39, 46. Editor Oregon Veteran, 1920-22. Home: 2632 S.E. Harrison St., Portland, Ore. Died Sept. 17, 1952; buried Arlington Nat. Cemetery.

HOTCHKISS, H(ENRY) STUART b. New Haven, Conn., Oct. 1, 1878; s. Henry L. and Jane (Trowbridge) Hotchkiss; Ph.B., Yale University, 1900; m. Elizabeth Wyndham Washington, Oct. 9, 1907; children-Henry, Mary Bolling Washington, Stuart Trowbridge, Joseph Washington. With L. Candee & Co., a subsidiary of U.S. Rubber Co., 1901-30, advancing to vice-pres. of latter; pres. Cambridge Rubber Co., 1937-40, now chmn. bd.; devoted much time to development of rubber plantations in Sumatra and the Malay Peninsula; chmn. bd. General Rubber Co. and subsidiaries until 1930; pres. U.S. Rubber Plantations, Inc., and subsidiaries until 1930; chmn. bd. General Latex & Chemical Corp.; director Union & New Haven Trust Co.; member board of management U.S. Govt. Synthetic Rubber Plant, Baytown, Texas. Representative in Europe of trustee in bankruptcy of International Match Corporation, 1932-33; industrial advisor to Swedish liquidators of Kreuger & Toll, 1934-35. Member Connecticut Naval Reserve, 1899-1901; apptd. chmn. Com. on Rubber, Council of Nat. Defense, Apr. 1917; commd. capt. S.C., Oct. 25, 1917; maj., Jan. 28, 1918; lt. col. Air Service, Oct. 8, 1918; served as asst. chief insp. equipment div. and as sr. asst. mil. attaché, Am. Embassy, London; with A.E.F. in France, and as chief of raw material production, Air Service, Washington, D.C. Trustee Bermuda Biol. Sta. for Research; asso. fellow of Silliman College, Yale. Mem. Am. Council, Inst. of Pacific Relations, Am. Geog. Soc. (v.p.; chmn. council), Mayflower Soc., Soc. Colonial Wars, Conn. Soc. (ex-gov.), Delta Psi; fellow Royal Geog. Soc., London. Conglist. Mason (32ff). Clubs: Century Assn., Yale, St. Anthony (New York); Graduate, New Haven Lawn (New Haven, Conn.). Home: "Wyndham," East River, Conn. Office: 205 Church St., New Haven, Conn.; and 748 Main St., Cambridge, Mass. Died Sept. 16, 1947.

HOUGH, ALFRED LACEY soldier; b. Springfield Twp., N.J., Apr. 23, 1826; s. Jonathan and Jane Chapman (Lacey) H.; ed. local county sch., Juliustown, Burlington Co., N.J., and T. D. James Acad., Phila.; m. Mary Jane Merrill, Feb. 11, 1857 (dec.). In mercantile business till Apr. 18, 1861, then to 17th Pa. vols. as pvt. and sergt. on upper Potomac until June 29, 1861, when discharged to accept apptmt. as capt. 19th U.S. Inf.; served as such with regt. and on staff of Maj. Gen. George H. Thomas in Army of Cumberland through the war; a.d.c. to Maj. Gen. Thomas, 1867, till his death, 1870; capt. 13th U.S. Inf., serving in Utah until 1874; maj. 22d U.S. Inf., serving in Northern Mich., Mont., in Pa. against rioters, in Colo., Ind. Ty. and Tex. until 1882; lt. col. 16th U.S. Inf., serving in Tex., in New York as supt. of recruiting service, again in Texas and in Utah till 1888; col. 9th U.S. Inf., serving in Ariz. till Apr. 23, 1890, when retired for age; brig. gen. retired, 1904. Bvtd. maj., 1863, lt. col., 1865, col., 1865. Episcopalian. Republican. Home: Princeton, N.J. Died 1908.

HOUGH, HENRY HUGHES naval officer; b. St. Pierre, Miquelon (island nr. Newfoundland), Jan. 8, 1871; s. Charles Thacher and Sarah (Hughes) H.; grad. U.S. Naval Acad., 1891; m. Flaurence Oliphant Ward, Apr. 16, 1901. Ensign, July 1, 1893; promoted through grades to rear adm. Sept. 16, 1924. Served on Morris, Spanish-Am. War, 1898, Cleveland, 1903-06; duty Office of Naval Intelligence, Navy Dept., 1907-08; ordnance officer Idaho, 1908-09; navigator same, 1909; exec. officer Virginia, 1909-10; with Office Naval Intelligence, Navy Dept., 1910; naval attaché, Paris, France, and St. Petersburg, Russia, 1911-14; comd. Wilmington, 1914-15; assigned to duty U.S. Naval Acad., 1915; dist. comdr. Brest, France, 1918; commr. Prisoner of War Conf., Berne, Switzerland, 1918; comdg. U.S.S. Utah, 1919-21; comdg. receiving ship New York, 1921-22; governor Virgin Islands of the U.S., 1922-23; dir. Naval Intelligence, 1923-25; comdr. Yangtse (China) Patrol Force, 1925-27; mem. General Board, 1928-30; comdt. 15th Naval Dist. and Naval Operating Base, Canal Zone, 1930-31; Commander Base Force, U.S. Fleet, 1931-33; Commandant 1st Naval Dist. and Navy Yard, Boston, Mass., 1933-35; retired, Feb. 1, 1935. Decorated Officer of the Legion of Honor (French). Episcopalian. Clubs: Army and Navy, Chevy Chase (Washington); New York Yacht (New York). Address: Navy Dept., Washington, D.C. Died Sep. 9, 1943.

HOUGHTELING, JAMES LAWRENCE financial cons.; B. Chgo., Nov. 6, 1883; s. James Lawrence and Lucretia Ten Broeck (Peabody) H.; B.A., Yale, 1905; married Laura Delano, May 26, 1917; children - James Lawrence, Margaret Stuyvesant (Mrs. John O. Neustadt), Frederic Delano, Louise Delano. Member, 1909-18, vice president, 1918-20, Peabody, Houghteling & Co., bankers, Chicago, Illinois. With N.Y. Evening post, 1920, Chicago, Daily News, 1921; joined staff, Chicago Evening Post, April 1, 1921, as head editorial writer; joined editorial staff Chicago Daily News, 1923; v.p. and treas., 1926-31; dir. Chicago Times, 1931-47. lMem. and sec., Ill. Adv. Board, Federal Emergency Adminstrn. of Public Works, 1933-34; apptd. U.S. commr. of immigration and naturalization, July 22, 1937-July 31, 1940; asst. to sec. of Treasury, Jan. 1941, div. dir. War Finance Div., Treasury Dept., 1941-46; chmn. Fair Employment Bd., Civil Service Commn. 1949-52. Served as captain Battery A, 103d F.A., A.E.F., World War; took part in Argonne and Meuse offensive; spl. attaché An. Embassy, Petrograd, Russia, Jan.-Apr. 1917, during overthrow of czar. Mem. Brotherhood of St. Andrew (nat. council; pres. 1938-40), Psi Upsilon. Episcopalian. Democrat. Clubs: Yale (New York); Chevy Chase, Cosmos, Metropolitan (Washington). Author: A Diary of the Russian Revolution, 1918. Address: 2431 Kalorama Road, Washington 8. Died April 8, 1962; buried Fairhaven, Mass.

HOUGHTON, SHERMAN OTIS lawyer; b. New York, Apr. 1828; s. Abijah and Eliza (Farrand) H.; acad. edn.; m. Mary Martha Donner, Aug. 29, 1859 (died May, 1860); 2d, Eliza Poor Donner, of Springfield, Ill., Oct. 10, 1861. Enlisted, June, 1846, in 1st regt. N.Y. vols. for Mexican war; went with regt. to Cal. via Cape Horn, 1846, and from there, 1847, to Mex.; apptd. lt. and adj. 1847; served until close of war; returned to Cal., Oct. 14, 1848; mined for gold, 1848-49; practiced law since 1857; pres. city council, 1854; mayor, 1855-56, San Jose, Cal. In Civil war as ordnance officer, lt.-col. on staff Maj.-Gen. H.W. Halleck. Mem. Congress, 1st Cal. dist., 1871-73, from 4th dist., 1873-75; apptd. by Pres. Arthur on commn. to investigate U.S. Mint, 1881. Address: Hynes, Los Angeles Co., California.†

HOUK, LEONIDAS CAMPBELL congressman, jurist; b. Boyds Creek, Tenn., June 8, 1836; a son, John Chiles. Admitted to Tenn. bar, 1859; enlisted as pvt. U.S. Army, 1861; promoted lt. 1st Regt., Tenn. Volunteer Inf., col. 3d Regt., 1862-63; mem. Tenn. Constl. Conv., 1865; judge 17th Jud. Circuit of Tenn., 1866-70; mem. Tenn. Legislature, 1873-75; mem. U.S. Ho. of Reps. from Tenn., 46th-52d congresses, 1879-91. Died Knoxville, Tenn., May 25, 1896; buried Old Gray Cemetery, Knoxville.

HOUSTON, EDWIN SAMUEL naval officer: b. Lancaster, Pa., May 13, 1845; s. William Houston and Mary Henderson H.; grad. U.S. Naval Acad., 1865. Promoted ensign Dec. 1, 1866, master, Mar. 12, 1868, lt., Mar. 29, 1869, lt. comdr., Mar. 1881, comdr., Sept. 27, 1891, capt., Mar. 3, 1899, rear admiral, Apr. 18, 1902, and retired, 1902, after 40 yrs. service on many duties and stas. Was capt. League Island Navy Yard, 1896-98; comd. U.S. Gunnery Training ship Amphitrite, 1899-1902. Home: Washington, D.C. Deceased.

HOUSTON, SAMUEL pres. Republic of Tex.; b. Timber Ridge Church, nr. Lexington, Va., Mar. 2, 1793; s. Maj. Samuel and Elizabeth (Paxon) H.; ed. Maryville (Tenn.) Acad. (now Maryville Coll.); m. Eliza Allen, Jan. 22, 1829; m. 2d, Margaret Lea, 1840; 8 children. Adopted by Chief Jolly of Cherokee Indians, circa 1806; enlisted as pvt. 39th Inf. Regt., U.S. Army, 1813, promoted ensign, 1813; served as sgt. 7th Inf. Regt. under Gen. Andrew Jackson during Creek War; promoted lt., 1814; admitted to Tenn. bar, 1818; dist. atty. Nashville (Tenn.), 1819; adj. gen. Tenn., 1820; commd. maj. gen. Tenn. Militia, 1821; mem. U.S. Ho. of Reps. from Tenn., 18th-19th congresses, 1823-27; gov. Tenn., 1827-29; moved to Cherokee Indian territory, 1829, to Tex., 1833; mem. San Felipe de Austin Conv. to establish separate statehood for Tex., 1833; mem. Tex. Constl. Conv., 1835; became comdr-in-chief Tex. Army, 1836, routed Mexican forces and captured Santa Anna at Battle of San Jacinto, Apr. 21, 1836; 1st pres. Republic of Tex., 1836-38, 3d pres., 1841-44; mem. Tex. Congress, 1838-40; mem. U.S. Senate from Tex., Feb. 21, 1846-57; gov. Tex., 1859-61, deposed because he refused to take oath of allegiance to Confederate States of Am., Mar. 18, 1861; Houston (Tex.) named for him. Died Huntsville, Tex., July 26, 1863; buried Oakwood Cemetery, Huntsville.

HOUSTON, VICTOR STEUART KALEOALOHA, naval officer; b. San Francisco, Calif., July 22, 1876; s. Edwin Samuel and Caroline Poor Kahikiola (Brickwood) H.; prep. edn. Real Schule, Dresden, Coll. Cantonal, Lausanne, Force Sch., Washington, D.C.; grad. U.S. Naval Acad., 1897; m. Pinao G. Brickwood, July 19, 1910 (died Sept. 27, 1936). Commd. U.S. Navy, July 1, 1919; advanced through grades to comdr., June 30, 1926 (retired); recalled to active duty in U.S. Navy, Dec. 7, 1941. Served as naval cadet, Spanish-Am. War; lt. comdr. later comdr., World War. Del. to Congress from H.Ty., 3 terms, 1927-33. Republican. Mason. Clubs: University, New York Yacht. Home: 448 Lewers St., Honolulu HI

HOUSTON, WILLIAM CHURCHILL Continental congressman; b. S.C., circa 1746; s. Archibald and Margaret Houston; A.B., Coll. of N.J. (now Princeton), 1768; m. Jane Smith, 4 children. Prof. mathematics and natural philosophy Coll. of N.J., 1771-83; capt. Somerset County Foot Militia, 1776-77; mem. Continental Congress from N.J., 1775-76, 79-82, 84-85, dep. sec., 1775, 76; mem. N.J. Assembly, 1776, mem. com. to settle public accounts, clk. pro tem; mem. N.J. Council of Safety 1778; admitted to N.J. bar, 1781; clk. N.J. Supreme Ct., 1781-88; receiver Continental taxes in N.J., 1782-85; del. to Annapolis (Md.) Conv., also U.S. Constl. Conv., Phila. did not sign U.S. Constn. Died Frankford, Pa., Aug. 12, 1788.

HOVEY, ALVIN PETERSON gov. Ind., jurist, army officer; b. nr. Mt. Vernon, Ind., Sept. 6, 1821; s. Abiel and Frances (Peterson) H.; m. Mary Ann James Nov. 24, 1844; m. 2d, Rosa Smith, 1863; 5 children. Admitted to Ind. bar, 1842; 1st lt. company of volunteers, during Mexican War; mem. Ind. Constl. Conv. 1850; circuit judge, 1851-54; mem. Ind. Supreme Ct., 1854-56; pres. Democratic State Conv., 1855; U.S. dist. atty. for Ind., 1856-58; served as col. 1st regt. Ind. Legion and col. 24th Ind. Inf. in Civil War, promoted Brig. gen., 1862, fought at Battle of Shiloh, brevetted maj. gen. U.S. Volunteers, 1864, in command Dist. of Ind., 1864-65; U.S. ministr to Peru, 1865-70; mem. U.S. Ho. of Reps. from Ind., 50th Congress, 1887-89; gov. Ind., 1888-91. Died Indpls., Nov. 23, 1891.

HOVEY, CHARLES EDWARD educator, army officer; b. Thetford, Vt., Apr. 26, 1827; s. Alfred and Abigail (Howard) H.; grad. Dartmouth, 1852; m. Harriette Spofford, Oct. 9, 1854, 3 children including Richard. Prin. free high sch., Framingham, Mass., 1852-54; 1st prin. boys' high sch., Peoria, Ill., 1854-56; supt. Peoria pub. schs., 1856-57; elected pres. Ill. State Tchrs. Assn., 1856; mem. 1st Ill Bd. Edn., 1857; editor Illinois Teacher, 1856-58; founder Ill. State Normal U., 1857, apptd. prin., served as col. of regiment largely composed of students and tchrs. of the univ. in Civil War; commd. col. 33d Ill. Volunteer Inf., 1861, brig. gen., 1862; brevetted maj. gen. for gallant battle conduct, Sept. 5, 1862 particularly at Ark. Post, 1863; commd. maj. gen. U.S. Volunteers, 1865; practiced law, Washington D.C., until 1897. Died Washington, Nov. 17, 1897.

HOWARD, BENJAMIN territorial gov., congressman; b. Va., 1760; s. John Howard. Mem. Ky. Legislature, 1801-02; mem. U.S. Ho. of Reps. from Ky., 10th - 11th congresses, 1807 - Apr. 1810; resigned to become gov. Dist. of La. (later Territory of Mo.), 1810 commd. brig. gen. 8th Mil. Dept., U.S. Army, 1813; Howard County (Mo.) named for him, 1816. Died St. Louis, Sept. 18, 1814; buried Bellefontaine Cemetery, St. Louis.

HOWARD, BENJAMIN CHEW army officer, congressman; b. "Belvedere" nr. Balt., Nov. 5, 1791; s. Col. John Eager and Peggy (Chew) H.; B.A., Coll. of N.J. (now Princeton) 1809. M.A., 1812; m. Jane Grant Gilmore, 1818. Served as capt. Mech. Volunteers of Balt. during War of 1812; participated in Battle of North Point, 1814; admitted to Md. bar, circa 1816; elected mem. Balt. City Council, 1820; mem. Md. Ho. of Dels., 1824; mem. 1829-33, 35-39, chmn. fgn. relations com.; mem. U.S. Ho. of Reps., 21st-22d, 24th-25th congresses, Md. Senate, 1840-41; reporter U.S. Supreme Ct., 1843-61, wrote 24 vols. of Supreme Court Reports; unsuccessful candidate for gov. Md., 1861; del. Washington (D.C.) Peace Conf. from Md., 1861. Died Balt., Mar. 6, 1872; buried Green Mount Cemetery, Balt.

HOWARD, CHARLES PAGELSEN pub. ofcl., lawyer; b. Tewksbury, Mass., Dec. 26, 1887; s. Herbert Burr and Emily (Pagelsen) H.; A.B., cum laude, Harvard, 1909, A.M., 1910, LL.B., 1914; m. Katherine Montague Graham, Sept. 15, 1921; children - Margaret, Herbert Graham. Asst. dept. govt. Harvard, 1914-16; in practice of law, Boston, 1914-25, 38-43, 58-66. Served to capt. U.S. Army, World War (St. Mihiel and Meuse-Argonne offensives); to col. AUS, World War II; SHAEF, Allied Force Hdqrs., hdqrs. U.S. Forces, Austria. Decorated Bronze Star medal, Legion of Merit. Selectman, town counsel and moderator, Reading, Mass.; mem. Mass. Constl. Conv., 1917, offered amendment consolidating 101 adminstrv. depts. State govt.); mem. Mass. State Senate, 1923-25; alternate del. Rep. Nat. Conv., 1924, del. to conv., 1928; budget commr. Mass., 1926-28; chmn. Commn. on Adminstrn. and Finance, Mass., 1925-38; mem. Mass. Emergency Pub. Works Commn., 1933-38, 40-47; coordinator and fiscal agt. Mass. state projects Civil Works Adminstrn., 1933-34, Emergency Relief Adminstrn., 1935-38; cons. Grad. Sch. Pub. Adminstrn., Harvard, 1937-39, 41-43; treas. Middlesex County, 1938-55; pres. Blackstone Savs. Bank (Boston) 1940-43. Mem. Mass. Pub. Bldg. Commn., 1947-51, chmn. since 1948; pres. Greater Boston adv. bd. Salvation Army, 1954-57, Age Centre New Eng., 1954-57, 60-62, Mass. Civic League, 1961-66, Neighborhood Assn. Back Bay, 1962-66. Mem. Civil Service Assembly U.S. and Can. (v.p. 1937-38). Am. Polit. Sci. Assn., Am. Soc. for Pub. Adminstrn., Mil. Govt. Assn. (pres. Boston chpt., 1949-50), Am. Legion (judge adv. dept. Mass. 1932-34). Mason (Shriner). Clubs: Eastern Yacht, Union, Boston City (pres. 1938-40), Meadow Brook Golf (pres. 1920-22); hon. mem. Rotary Internat. Home: 186 Summer Av., Reading, Mass. Office: Court House, East Cambridge, Mass. Died July 2, 1966.

HOWARD, CLINTON WILBUR army officer; b. Campello, Mass., Nov. 27, 1890; s. Ernest Clinton and Ida Palmer (Legge) H.; B.S., U.S. Mil. Acad., 1915; grad. Army Service Engring. Sch., 1921; M.S. and Sc.D. in aeronautics, Mass. Inst. of Tech., 1923; grad. Army Indsl. Coll., 1936, Army War Coll., 1937; rated command pilot, combat and tech. observer. Commd. 2d lt., U.S. Army, 1915, and advanced through the grades to brig. gen.; chiefly in research, experimentation and development of aeronautical equipment for the Air Corps; became comdg. gen. Air Service Command, Sacramento, Calif., June 1943. Retired as brig. gen., U.S. Army, 1946. Mgr. Markwart Industries, Inc., since 1946, Sacramento, Calif. Mem. A.A.A.S., Soc. of Automotive Engring., Inst. Aeronautical Science, Aircraft and Engine Development. Home: 3360 H St., Sacramento, Calif.; died Sept. 22, 1949; buried in Arlington National Cemetery.

HOWARD, FREDERIC HOLLIS, prof. physiology; b. Newburyport, Mass., Sept. 3, 1876; s. Eugene and Susan Ella (Nash) H.; M.D., U. of Pa., 1898; m. Mary Malleville McClellan, of Lakewood, N.J., Apr. 9, 1901; children—Edgerton McClellan, Paul Malleville, Caroline. Began teaching at U. of Pa. (med. dept.), 1899; prof. physiology, Williams Coll., since 1900. Mem. A.M.A. Conglist. Mem. M.C.U.S.A., June 1, 1917. maj., Sept. 3, 1918; with A.E.F., Jan. 7, 1918-Apr. 18, 1919; hon. discharged, May 6, 1919; now lt. col., Med. R.C. Address: Williamstown MA

HOWARD, GRAEME KEITH automotive mfg. co. exec.; b. Los Angeles, Mar. 4, 1896; s. Burt Estes and Sarah (Gates) H.; A.B. in Econs., Stanford, 1917; grad. student Harvard Grad. Sch. Bus. Adminstrn., 1920-21; m. Margaret Evans Mar. 16, 1922; children - Reese, Sally Ann, Graeme K. With Gen. Motors, 1920-47, mgr. Gen. Motors Export Co., Bombay, India, 1923-24, mng. dir. Gen. Motors Internat., Copenhagen, Denmark, 1924-25, mng. dir. Gen. Motors, Ltd., London, 1925-26, regional dir. Far East Gen. Motors Export Co., 1926-29, regional dir. for Europe, Gen. Motors Export Co., 1929-30, gen. mgr. Gen. Motors Export Div., N.Y.C., 1930-35; gen. mgr. overseas operations Gen. Motors Corp., 1935-39, v.p., 1939, v.p. charge overseas operation, 1940-42, v.p. charge Europe, 1945-47; v.p., dir. internat. div. Ford Motor Co., 1948-50. Chmn. Cocoa Beach Planning and Zoning Bd., Citizens Com. for Better Govt., Norfolk Plan Commn. Fla. alternate del. Republican Nat. Conf., 1956; treas. Norfolk Rep. Town Com. Trustee Norfolk Library. Served as capt., 23d Machine Gun Bn., U.S. Army, 1917-19; AEF; col. ordnance dept., AUS, 1942; head U.S. element SHAEF mission to Norway, 1944, chief eoncon. div. U.S. Group Control Council, Germany, 1944-45. Decorated Legion of Merit; King Haakon Liberation medal Policy Assn. Episcopalian (sr. warden). Clubs: The Leash (N.Y.C.); Norfolk Country, Norfolk Curling, Doolittle (Norfolk); St. Cloud Country (Paris, France). Author: America and a New World Order, 1940. Home: Roughland, Norfolk, Conn. Died Dec. 6, 1962; buried Center Cemetery, Norfolk.

HOWARD, JOHN EAGER army officer, senator, gov. Md.; b. Baltimore County, Md., June 4, 1752; s. Cornelius and Ruth (eager) H.; m. Peggy Chew May 18, 1787; 1 son, Benjamin Chew. Commd. capt. in Col. Carvil Hall's "Flying Camp," 1776, served at Battle of White Plains, Oct. 28, 1776; commd. maj. 4th Md. Regt., 1777; lt. col. 5th Md. Regt. at Battle of Camden, Mar. 11, 1778 led charge at critical moment in Battle of Cowpens, Jan. 17, 1781, received gold medal and thanks of Continental Congress; del. to Continental Congress, 1787-88; gov. Md., 1788-91; mem. U.S. Senate from Md., 1796-1803; commd. brig. gen. U.S. Army, 1803; Federalist candidate for vice pres. U. S., 1816. Died Belvedere, Md., Oct. 12, 1827.

HOWARD, NATHANIEL LAMSON corp. official; b. Fairfield, Ia., Mar. 9, 1884; s. Elmer A. and Mary (Lamson) H.; grad. U.S. Mil. Acad., 1907; m. Marie Blaul, June 3, 1915. Began as civil engr. C.B.&Q. Ry. Co., 1907, trainmaster, at Centerville, Ia., 1910, successively asst. supt. at Galesburg, Ill., and supt. of Burlington div., till 1916; supt. Hannibal div., 1916-17; asst. to federal mgr., C.B.&Q. Ry. Co., May-Nov. 1919, gen. supt. Mo. dist., at St. Louis, 1919-24; gen. mgr. Chicago Union Sta. Co., 1924-25; pres. C.G.W. R.R., 1925-29; chmn. bd. and pres. North Am. Car Corp., 1930-36. Lt. col. 13th Ry. Engrs. U.S. Army, May-Aug. 1917; duty with dir. gen. of transportation in France, Aug. 1917 to spring 1918; comdr. 13th Ry. Engrs., Verdun sector; col. July 8, 1918. Decorated Officer Legion of Honor and Croix de Guerre (French). Mason (K.T., Shriner), Clubs: Commonwealth, Commercial, University, Indian Hill. Adventures. Home: 715 Sheridan Rd., Winnetka, Ill. Died May 6, 1949; buried at Burlington, Ia.

HOWARD, OLIVER OTIS army officer; b. Leeds, Me., Nov. 8, 1830; s. Rowland Bailey and Eliza (Otis) H.; attended dist. schs. and acads.; grad. Bowdoin Coll., 1850, A.M., 1853, West Point, 1854; (LL.D., Waterville Coll., 1865, Shurtleff Coll., 1865, Gettysburg Theol. Sem., 1866, and Bowdoin Coll.); m. Elizabeth Ann Waite, Feb. 14, 1855. Bvt. 2d lt. ordnance, July 1, 1854; apptd. 2d lt., Feb. 15, 1855; 1st lt., July 1, 1857; resigned, June 7, 1861; col. 3d Me. Inf. U.S.V., June 4, 1861; brig. gen., Sept. 3, 1861; maj. gen., Nov. 29, 1862; hon. mustered out of vol. service, Jan. 1, 1869; apptd. brig. gen. U.S.A., Dec. 21, 1864; maj. gen., Mar. 16, 1886; retired by operation of law, Nov. 8, 1894. Bvtd. maj. gen., Mar. 13, 1865, for gallant and meritorious services at battle of Ezra Church and during campaign against Atlanta; received thanks of Congress, Jan. 28, 1864, for Gettysburg; awarded medal of honor, Mar. 29, 1893, for distinguished bravery of battle of Fair Oaks, Va., June 1, 1862, where was twice severely wounded in right arm, necessitating its amputation. Served in Seminole campaign in Fla.; instr. and asst. prof. mathematics, West Point, 1857-61; comd. brigade at Bull Run, July 21, 1861; participated in many great battles; apptd. July 1864, comdr. Army and Dept. of Tenn. Was largely instrumental in establishing Howard Univ., Washington, which was named in his honor and was its pres., 1869-73, then trustee; commr. Freedmen's Bureau, 1865-74; peace commr. to Indians of Ariz. and N. Mex., 1872, in addition to bureau work; then dept. and div. comdr., successively the Columbia (where comd. Nez Perces campaign, 1877, and Bannock War, 1878); supt. Mil. Acad., 1881-82; comd. depts. of the Platte, the Pacific and the Atlantic, 1882-88. Founder, 1895, and pres. bd. dirs. Lincoln Memorial Univ. (Coll., Normal and Industrial Sch.), Cumberland Gap, Tenn. Chevalier Legion of Honor, France, 1884. Author: Isabella of Castile; Fighting for Humanity; Henry in the War; Our Wild Indians; Autobiography, 2 vols. Home: Burlington, Vt. Died 1909.

HOWARD, ROBERT MAYBURN surgeon; b. Morgantown, Ky., Aug. 17, 1878; s. John Woodville and Belle (Harreld) H.; grad. Central State Normal Sch., Edmond, Okla., 1897; M.D., U. lMich., 1901; m. Dolores Brockus, Sept. 18, 1907. Physician and surgeon, Oklahoma City, 1910-17; practice limited to surgery since 1919; chief of staff St. Anthony Hosp. since 1907; prof. clin. surgery U. Okla., 1919-34, prof. surgery, 1933-44, emeritus prof. surgery, 1944-47; dir. Fidelity Nat. Bank, Oklahoma City. Maj., lf.C., U.S. Army, 1917-19; lt. col. M.C. U.S. Army Res., 1919-27. Fellow A.C.S., A.M.A.; mem. Founders Group Am. Bd. of Surgery, 1937-47; mem. Am. Assn. for Study of Goiter (pres. 1933-34), Okla City Acad. of Medicine, Phi Beta Pi. Democrat. Mason (Shriner). Elk. Clubs: Oklahoma Club, Oklahoma City Golf and Country Club. Home: 815, N.W., 15th St., Oklahoma City 73106. Office: 1200 N. Walker St., Oklahoma City. Died Feb. 22, 1963; buried Meml. Park Cemetery, Oklahoma City.

HOWARD, THOMAS BENTON rear admiral U.S.N.; b. Galena, Ill., Aug. 10, 1854; s. Bushrod Brush and Elizabeth (Mackay) H.; apptd. by President Grant, and grad. U.S. Naval Acad., 1873; m. Anne J. Claude, May 13, 1879. Promoted through the various grades to rear admiral, Nov. 14, 1910. Navigator, U.S.S. Concord, Manila Bay, May 1-Aug. 13, 1898; in Charleston and Monadnock during Philippine insurrection, Feb. 1890-May 1900; comd. caravel Pinta from Barcelona to Havana, 1892-93; comd. Chesapeake, 1901, Nevada, 1903-05, Olympia and Naval Acad. Squadron, 1907, Tennessee, 1907. Battleship Ohio, Admiral Sperry's fleet, on cruise around the world, 1908-09; mem. General Bd., 1909-10; comdg. 4th div. Atlantic Fleet, Oct. 1910-Jan. 1912, 3d div. Atlantic Fleet, Jan.-Apr. 1912; pres. Naval Examining and Retiring Bds., Apr. 1912-Dec. 1913; comdr.-in-chief Pacific Fleet, Feb. 1914-Sept. 1915, receiving rank of admiral the last 6 mos. of this service; pres. Naval Examining and Retiring Bds., Sept. 1915-Aug. 10, 1916, when retired by operation of law. Ordered on active duty as supt. U.S. Naval Obs., 1917-19. Was on duty at U.S. Naval Acad. at various times, as instr. in mathematics, applied mathematics and physics and chemistry; was twice head of dept. of ordnance and gunnery. Died Nov. 10, 1920.

HOWARD, WILLIAM EAGER, JR., ret. naval officer; b. Wash., June 15, 1906; s. William E. and Katherine (Tufts) H.; B.S., U.S. Naval Acad., 1928; M.S., Mass. Inst. Tech., 1933; grad. Naval War Coll., 1952; m. Frances Bacon, May 14, 1930; children—William Eager III, Richard B. Commd. ensign U.S. Navy, 1928, advanced through grades to rear adm., 1956; assigned Phila. Naval Shipyard, 1933-35; with Bur. Constrn. and Repair Navy Dept., 1936-40; material officer on staff comdr. service force Atlantic Fleet, 1940-42; mem. staff comdr. amphibious force S.W. Pacific, also staff comdr. in chief U.S. Fleet, 1942-43; supt. design, ship-bldg. and hulls, also indsl. engr. officer Mare Island Naval Shipyard, 1943-47; indsl. engring. officer, planning and estimating supt., repair supt. Norfolk Naval Shipyard, 1947-51; asst. chief staff logistics, maintenance officer Atlantic Fleet, 1952-55; comdr. Boston Naval Shipyard, 1955-59; asst. chief plans and adminstrn. Bur. Ships, also insp. gen. bur., 1959-60; comdr. Norfolk Naval Shipyard, 1960-63; director of admissions and registration, dir. financial aid Old Dominion Coll., from 1963. Decorated

Commendation ribbon with star, numerous others. Mem. Soc. Naval Architects and Marine Engrs., Am. Soc. Naval Engrs. Club: Columbia Country (Chevy Chase, Md.). Author naval tech. bulls. Home: Portsmouth VA Died June 14, 1972; buried Arlington Nat. Cemetery.

HOWARD, WILLIAM LAURISTON naval officer; b. Plainfield, Conn., Jan. 10, 1860; s. George F. and Mary (Phillips) H.: grad. U.S. Naval Acad., 1882; m. Louise G. Alden, Nov. 23, 1886; 1 dau., Helen. Ensign, July 1, 1884; promoted through grades and retired with rank of rear adm., Dec. 1919. Home: Newport, R.I. Died Feb. 3, 1930.

HOWE, ALBION PARRIS army officer; b. Standish, Me., Mar. 25, 1818; s. Dr. Ebenezer and Catherine (Spring) H.; grad. U.S. Mil. Acad., 1841; m. Elizabeth Mehaffey, 1859. Asst. prof. mathematics U.S. Mil. Acad., 1843-46; served with 4th Arty. Regt., U.S. Army, in Mexican War; brevetted capt. for service in battles of Contreras and Churubusco, 1847; sent with his battery to help restore peace at Harper's Ferry after John Brown's Raid, 1859; served in Civil War campaigns and battles including W. Va. and Peninsular campaigns, battles of Manassas, S. Mountain, Antietam, Fredericksburg, Gettysburg; commanded arty. depot, Washington, D.C., 1864-66; a guard of honor after Lincoln's assassination; mem. Arty. Bd., U.S. Army, 1866; mem. Bur. of Refugees, Freedmen and Abandoned Lands; retired, 1882. Died mbridge, Mass., Jan. 25, 1897; buried Mt. Auburn Cemetery, Cambridge.

HOWE, GEORGE AUGUSTUS army officer; b. circa 1724; s. Emanud and Maria (von Kielmansegge) H. Mem. Brit. Parliament from Nottingham borough, 1747-58; became ensign Grendadier Guards, 1745, promoted lt. col., 1749; col. 3d Battalion of Royal Americans, 1757; col., then brig. gen. 55th Battalion, Upper N.Y., 1757; 2d in command of Abercromby's Ticonderoga expdn., 1758. Killed in skirmish with French nr. Lake George, July 6, 1758; buried St. Peter's Ch., Abany, N.Y.

HOWE, HARRISON ESTELL chemist, editor; b. Georgetown, Ky., Dec. 15, 1881; s. of William James and Mary (Scott) H.; B.S., Earlham Coll., Ind., 1901; U. of Mich., 1901-02; M.S., U. of Rochester, 1913, Sc.D., 1927; LL.D., Southern Coll., 1934; Eng.D., Rose Poly. Inst. 1936, S.D. State Sch. of Mines 1939; m. May McCaren, Oct. 17, 1905; children-Mary, Betty. Chemist, Sanilac Sugar Refining Co., Corswell, Mich., 1902-04; chemist, office mgr. and editor Bausch & Lomb Optical Co., Rochester, N.Y., 1904-16; chem. engr. with Arthur D. Little, Inc., Boston, 1916; asst. to pres., Arthur D. Little, Ltd., Montreal, Can., 1916-17; mgr. commercial dept. Arthur D. Little, Inc., Cambridge, Mass., 1917-19; chmn. div. research extension, Nat. Research Council, 1919-22; editor Industrial and Engineering Chemistry, Washington, since Dec. 1, 1921. Trustee Science Service; mem. Purdue Research Foundation; chmn. Chemicals Group, and chmn. Chemicals Priority Com., Priorities Div., Office of Production Managment, Feb.-July 1941, now chmn. adv. com. Chemical Sect. Cons. chemist nitrate div., Ordnance Bureau, U.S. Army, World War; col. R.O.C., C.W.S. Fellow A.A.A.S.; mem. Am. Chem. Soc., Am. Inst. Chem. Engrs. (div., and its rep. in Am. Engring. Council 1921-32), Am. Engring. Council (treas. 1923-30); round table and gen. conf. leader Inst. of Politics, Williamstown, Mass., 1926-29. Decorated Officer Crown of Italy, 1926. Republican. Baptist. Mason (K.T.). Clubs: Cosmos, Rotary, Torch, Chemists' (New York). Author: The New Stone Age, 1921; Profitable Science in Industry, 1924; Chemistry in the World's Work, 1926; Chemistry in the Home (with F.M. Turner), 1927; Series of six Nature and Science Readers (with E.M. Patch). Editor: Chemistry in Industry, Vol. I, 1924, Vol. II, 1925. Contbr. numerous articles in scientific jours.; a leader in organizing industrial groups for research. Home: 2702 36th St. N.W., Washington, D.C. Office: 1155 16th St. N.W., Washington, D.C., and 332 W. 42nd St., New York. Died Dec. 10, 1942; buried in Ft. Lincoln Cemtery, Washington.

HOWE, MARK DE WOLFE lawyer; b. Boston, Massachusetts, May 22, 1906; s. Mark Antony De Wolfe and Fanny Huntington (Quincy) H.; A.B., Harvard, 1928. LL.B., 1933; m. Mary Manning, Feb. 19, 1935; children - Susan, Fanny, Helen. Sec. to Justice O. W. Holmes, 1933-34; admitted to Mass. bar, 1933, practiced in Boston with Hill, Barlow, Goodale & Wiswall, 1933-37; prof. law U. Buffalo Sch. Law, 1937-45, dean, 1941-45; prof. law Harvard, 1945-. Served as maj., AUS, 1943, disch. col., 1945. Awarded Legion of Merit, D.S.M. Mem. Mass. Hist. Soc., Colonial Soc., Selden Soc. (v.p. U.S.A.), Phi Beta Kappa. Democrat. Editor: Holmes Pollock Letters (correspondence of Mr. Justice Holmes and Sir Frederick Pollock, 1874-1932), 2 vols., 1941; Touched with Fire (Civil War Letters of O. W. Holmes Jr.), 1946; Readings in American Legal History, 1949; Holmes-Laski Letters, 1916-1935, 2 vols. 1953; Holmes: The Common Law, 1963. Author: Mr. Justice Holmes: The Shaping Years, 1841-1870, 1957; Justice Holmes: The Proving Years, 1870-1882, 1963. Contbr. legal jours. Address: 58 Highland St., Cambridge, Mass. Died Feb. 28, 1967.

HOWE, ROBERT army officer; b. Bladen County, N.C., 1732; s. Job and Sarah (Yeamans) H.; m. Sarah Grange. Justice of peace Bladen, 1756, Brunswick County, N.C., 1764; mem. N.C. Assembly, 1764-75; in command of Ft. Johnston, 1766-67, 69-73; commd. col. Arty.; mem. N.C. Colonial Assembly, 1772-73; del. to Colonial Congress, New Bern, N.C., 1774; mem. N.C. Com. of Correspondence; commd. col. 2d N.C. Regt., 1775, with Gen. Woodford at Norfolk, Va. drove Lord Dunmore out of that part Va.; commd. brig. gen. Continental Army, 1776; in command of So. Dept.; commd. maj. gen., 1777; commanded Savannah, 1778, later West Point, N.Y.; elected to N.C. Ho. of Commons, 1786, died before taking seat. Died Brunswick County, Dec. 14, 1786.

HOWE, STANLEY H(ART) publicist; b. Howell, Mich., May 30, 1890; s. George Franklin and Eleanora (Hart) H.; A.B., Albion (Mich.) Coll., 1911; m. Helen Gregg, Jan. 31, 1913. Spl. investigator N.Y. Assn. for Improving Condition of Poor, 1911; organizer, and sec. Pub. Charities Assn. Pa., 1912; dep. commr. Pub. Charities under Mayor Mitchell N.Y.C., 1913-17; sec. N.Y. Pub. Welfare Com., 1917; exec. dir. Nat. Budget Com., which was largely instrumental in securing budget system for U.S. Govt. Served as capt., Q.M.C., U.S. Army, World War I; after armistice was with Ednl. Corps, AEF, Beaune, France. Vice chmn. finance com. Honest Ballot Assn., Actors' Nat. Meml. Fund Com.; organizer, v.p., sec. Home Community Corp. (for building moderate-priced homes under laws of State of N.Y.). Mem. Acad. Polit. Science, Nat. Conf. Social Work, Delta Sigma Rho, Sigma Nu. Republican. Clubs: City, Lions, New York Young Republican. Winner Nat. Intercollegiate Oratorical Contest, at Johns Hopkins U., 1911. Home: Otisville, Pa. Died Mar. 30, 1955.

HOWE, WALTER brig. gen.; b. in Ind., Dec. 31, 1846; s. James Montgomery Allison Higgins and Mary Frances (Graham) H.; grad. U.S. Mil. Acad., 1867; m. Elizabeth Dunn, Sept. 21, 1869. Second lt. 4th Arty., June 17, 1867; 1st lt., Sept. 1, 1872; grad. Arty. Sch., 1873; capt., July 1, 1891; col. 47th U.S. Inf. Vols., Aug. 17, 1899-July 2, 1901; maj. Arty. Corps, Feb. 2, 1901; lt. col., Dec. 20, 1902; col., May 20, 1904; brig. gen. U.S.A., Jan. 11, 1910. Participated in the Modoc war, 1873, and Powder River expdn., under General Crook, 1876; comd. provinces of Alboy and Sorsogon while on duty in the P.I.; retired, Dec. 31, 1910. Died Nov. 8, 1915.

HOWE, WALTER ex-ambassador; b. Washington, June 10, 1907; s. Ernest and Anne G. (Wilson) H.; A.B., Yale, 1929; A.M., Harvard, 1931, Ph.D., 1938; m. Mary Jane Wild, Nov. 14, 1936; children - Jonathan, Peter Massie, Timothy Brigham, Walter Robins. Research in Latin Am. history, Mexico, 1932-34; prof. Am. history U. Mexico, 1933-34; dir. First Nat. Bank of Litchfield; treas., dir. Litchfield Enquirer Publ. Co.; dir. U.S. Fgn. Operations Mission to Bogota, Colombia, 1954-56; U.S. ambassador to Chile, 1958-61; hist. researcher and lectr. on Latin Am., 1961-; adviser U.S. delegation 5th consultative meeting Fgn. Ministers Am. Republics. Mem. Conn. Gen. Assembly, 1934-42, speaker Ho. of Reps., 1939-40. Pres. Com. Forest and Park Assn.; mem. Conn. Pub. Welfare Council, 1947-50. Mem. Republican Town Com. of Litchfield. Chmn. Natural Resources Council of Conn., 1952-, Litchfield County 4-H Found., 1945-; trustee Conn. Jr. Republic, U. Conn., Harvard Found. Advanced Study and Research; mem. adv. council sch. Advanced Internat. Studies, Johns Hopkins, 1963-. Served from lt. (j.g.) to comdr. USNR, 1941-46, 50-51. Pecipient medal of merit Nat. U. Colombia. Mem. Conn. Antiquarian and Landmarks Soc. (trustee 1946-50), N.Y. State Soc. Cin., Litchfield County Farm Bur. (exec. com. 1950-). Episcopalian. Clubs: University Century, Grolier (N.Y.C.); Metropolitan (Washington); Graduates (New Haven). Author: The Mining Guild of New Spain, 1949. Address: Red Horse Farm, Barboursville, Va. Died Apr. 8, 1966.

HOWE, WALTER BRUCE lawyer; b. N.Y.C., Nov. 18, 1879; s. Walter and Mary Bruce (Robins) H.; A.B., Yale, 1901; LL.B., Harvard, 1904; m. Mary Carlisle, Jan. 16, 1912; children-Bruce, Calderon, Mary. Began practice at N.Y.C., 1905; dept. asst. dist. atty., N.Y. County, 1906-09; practiced in Washington, 1912—; asst. U.S. atty., Washington, 1913; counsel to U.S. Senate Select Commn., Haiti and Dominican Republic, 1921-22, Am. Electoral Commn. Nicaragua, 1928, counsel to U.S. Senate Select Commn. of Inquiry and Concilation, Bolivia-Paraguay, 1929; arbitrator of Harrah Claim, U.S. vs. Cuba, 1929-30. Served as capt. inf. U.S. Army, 1917-19, sec. operations sect. Gen. Staff, G.H.Q., AEF, 1918-19. Mem. Recorder Roberts Pearl Harbor Commn., 1941-42. Mem. Assn. Bar City N.Y. Republican. Protestant. Clubs: Metropolitan, Alibi (Washington); Racquet and Tennis (N.Y.). Home: Berry Hill, Newport, R.I. Office: 1819 H St. N.W., Washington 6. Died Feb. 20, 1954.

HOWE, WILLIAM army officer; s. Emanuel Scrope and Mary (Sophia) H.; m. Frances Conolly, June 4, 1765, no children. Cornet in Duke of Cumberland's Light Dragoons, 1746, promoted lt., 1747; capt. Lord Bury's Regt., 1750; maj. 60th Foot, Brit. Army, 1756; took part in capture of Louisbourg in French and Indian War, 1758; served under Gen. James Wolfe in capture of Quebec, 1759; apptd. col. 46th Foot in Ireland, 1764; mem. Parliament for Nottingham, 1768-80; commd. maj. gen., 1772; came to Am. with Gen. Gage, 1775; created knight of Bath, commd. lt. gen., 1775; succeeded Gage in command in Am., 1775; defeated Washington at L.I., N.Y., captured N.Y.C., 1776; resigned his command, 1778; charges on his conduct in Am. brough before Ho. of Commons but without result either way, 1779. Died Plymouth, Eng., July 12, 1814.

HOWE, WILLIAM FRANCIS army officer; b. Dorchester, Mass., Dec. 16, 1888; s. William Francis and Alice (Tusley) H.; Ph.B., Yale, 1913; m. Margaret Allen, May 21, 1921; children-William F., Elizabeth, Margaret. Apprentice wool scouring and carbonizing plant, 1913, foreman, 1915-17: bond salesman, office mgr., 1920-37: asst. dir. Commonwealth Mass. Unemployment Compensation, 1938-41. Capt. F.A., 26th Div., commdg. battery C, 102d F.A., France, 1917-19; capt., Mass. N.G., 1920, advanced to brig. gen., 1939; in Federal Service 1941—; comdg. 51st F.A. Brigade, 26th Div., 1941-42; apptd. col., detailed as comdt. Army Schs., prof. mil. sci. and tactics Yale, 1943; asst. dir. Mass. Div. of Employment Security, 1948—. Decorated Croix de Guerre, 1918. Mem. St. Anthony, Delta Psi (Yale). Clubs: Union Boat (Boston); Weston Golf, New Haven Lawn, Yale Graduate. Home: 38 Lincoln St., New Haven. Died Nov. 9, 1952.

HOWELL, DANIEL LANE army officer; b. in Ia., Aug. 30, 1853; grad. U.S. Mil. Acad., 1875. Commd. 2d lt. 7th Inf., June 13, 1879; 1st lt., Apr. 23, 1889; capt., Apr. 26, 1898; maj. 18th Inf., Nov. 24, 1903; lt. col. 19th Inf., Mar. 3, 1911; col. of inf., Aug. 27, 1913; assigned to 1st Inf., July 2, 1914. Prof. mil. science and tactics, U. of Wyo., 1891-92; in Cuba, 1898, participating in Battle of El Caney, July, and in siege of Santiago; comd. Port of Mariveles, P.I., 1903-04; duty at Ft. Bumpus, Leyte, P.I., 1904-05; recruiting officer Memphis, Tenn., 1907; duty on Mexican border, 1917. Address: War Dept., Washington, D.C.†

HOWELL, JOHN ADAMS rear admiral U.S.N.; b. Bath, N.Y., Mar. 16, 1840; s. William and Frances A. (Adams) H.; apptd. from N.Y., and grad. U.S. Naval Acad., 1858; m. Arabella E. Krausé, of St. Croix, W.I., May 1867. Passed midshipman, Jan. 19, 1861; promoted through grades to rear adm., Aug. 10, 1898. Served on Macedonian, Mediterranean Squadron, 1858-59; Pocahontas and Pawnee, 1860; store-ship supply, 1861; Montgomery, 1862; Ossipee, W. Gulf Blockading Squadron, 1864-65; participated in battle of Mobile Bay, Aug. 5, 1864; served De Soto, spl. service, 1865-67; Naval Acad., 1867-71; coast survey, 1872-74; Naval Acad., 1875-79; comd. Adams, 1879-81; asst. Bur. of Ordnance, 1881; Navy Yard, Washington, 1882-84; mem. Advisory Bd., 1882-88; comd. Atlanta, 1888-90; pres. Steel Bd., 1891-94; comdt., Navy Yard, Washington, 1893-96, Navy Yard, League Island, 1896-98; comdr.-in-chief, European Squadron, Feb.-Apr. 1898; comd. Northern Patrol Squadron, Apr.-Oct. 1898; pres. Naval Examining and Retiring Bds., 1898-1902; retired, Mar. 16, 1902. Invented and patented a fly wheel torpedo, a disappearing gun carriage and an amphibious vehicle; originated the gyroscopic steering torpedoes, etc. Died Jan. 10, 1918.

HOWELL, REESE M. army officer; b. Wellsville, Utah, Oct. 9, 1889; s. Joseph and Mary Elizabeth (Maughan) H.; U. Utah, 1909-11; B.S., U.S. Mil. Acad., 1915, grad. Battery Officers Course, F.A. Sch., 1921, Field Officers Course, 1929; Command and Gen. Staff Sch., 1931; Chem. Warfare Sch., 1940; Army War Coll., 1940; m. Mary Lilian Curry Aug. 20, 1917. Commd. 2d lt. U.S. Army, 1915; advanced through grades to brig. gen., 1943; Gen. Staff duty, 1931-35. Address: War Dept., Washington. Died Mar. 1967.

HOWELL, RICHARD army officer, gov. N.J.; b. Newark, Del., Oct. 25, 1754; s. Ebenezer and Sarah (Bond) H.; m. Keziah Burr, Nov. 1799, 9 children. Mem. Greenwich (N.J.) tea party on ship Greyhound, 1774; commd. capt. N.J. Militia, serving at battles of Ticonderoga and Quebec, 1775; wounded in Battle of Brandywine, 1777; served as maj. of a brigade; licensed atty., 1779; succeeded William C. Houston as clk. N.J. Supreme Ct., 1788; gov. N.J., 1793-1801, commanded right wing of troop sent to put down Whiskey Rebellion in Pa.; mem. Soc. of Cincinnati, Died Burlington, N.J., Apr. 28, 1802.

HOWES, ROYCE B., writer; b. Minneapolis, Jan. 3, 1901; s. George R. and Alice M. (Bucknam) H. ed. pub. schs. Minneapolis; m. Dorothy Jane Chandler, May 17, 1924; children—Geoffrey C., Jane B. (Mrs. Jerry Flint). Mem. staff bus. office Detroit News, 1924-26; with Detroit Steel Products Co. as editor house publs., 1926-27; mem. editorial staff, Detroit Free Press, 1927-65, editorialist, columnist, 1942-55, asso. editor, 1955-62, editorial dir., 1962-65; instr. journalism Wayne State U., 1931-41. Entered United States Army, rank of capt., 1942; served as officer in charge Army News Service, Army Dept. Spl. Staff; released active service rank of lt. col., 1946. Awarded Bronze star; Pulitzer prize for editorial writing, 1955, award for editorial writing, Nat. Headliners Club, 1955. Mem. Am. Soc. Newspaper Editors, Detroit Hist. Soc., Friends of Detroit Pub. Library. Clubs: Nat. Headliners; Detroit Press. Author: Death on the Bridge, 1935; The Callao Clue, 1936;

Night of the Garter Murder, 1937; Death Dupes a Lady, 1937; Murder at Maneuvers, 1938; Nasty Names Murders, 1939; Death Rides A Hobby, 1939; Case of the Copy Hook Killing, 1945; Edgar A. Guest, a biography 1953. Address: Highland Park MI Died Mar. 1973.

HOWEY, BENJAMIN FRANKLIN congressman; b. Pleasant Meadows, nr. Swedesboro. N.J., Mar. 17, 1828; attended acads., Swedesboro and Bridgeton, N.J. Engaged as flour and grain commn. mcht., Phila., 1847, later in quarrying and mfg. slate; served as capt. Co. G, 31st Regt., N.J. Volunteers during Civil War, 1862-63; sheriff of Warren County (N.J.), 1878-81; mem. U.S. Ho. of Reps. (Republican) from N.J., 48th Congress, 1883-85. Died Columbia, N.J., Feb. 6, 1895; buried Trinity Ch. Cemetery, Swedesboro.

HOWISON, HENRY LYCURGUS rear admiral U.S.N.; b. Washington, Oct. 10, 1837; s. Henry and Juliet Virginia (Jackson) H.; grad. U.S. Naval Acad., 1858; m. Hannah J. Middleton, Oct. 3, 1865. Warranted midshipman, June 11, 1858; passed midshipman, Jan. 19, 1861; promoted through grades to rear adm., Sept. 30, 1898. During Civil War was present at many important engagements, including skirmish with enemy's cav. while comdg. detachment of men and howitzer from U.S.S. Pocahontas, Clouds' Mills, Va., June-July 1861; battle of Port Royal, S.C.; engagements with rams off Charleston, 1862; engagements Forts Moultrie, Sumter and Wagner, 1863-64; battle of Mobile Bay, etc. After war in various branches of service; mem. 1st advisory bd., 1881; comd. Pacific Squadron, 1886; pres. Steel Inspection Bd., 1888-90; mem. Light House Bd., 1890-92; comdt. of Navy Yard, Mare Island, Calif., 1893-96; commissioned the battleship Oregon, as her first capt., July 15, 1896; comdt. Navy Yard, Boston, 1897-99; comdr.-in-chief South Atlantic Sta. until retired, Oct. 10, 1899. Home: Yonkers, N.Y. Died Dec. 31, 1914.

HOWLAND, CHARLES ROSCOE army officer; b. Jefferson, O., Feb. 16, 1871; s. William Perry and Esther Elizabeth (Leonard) H.; student Oberlin (O.) Coll., 1890-91, hon. A.M., 1912; B.S., U.S. Mil. Acad., 1895; LL.B., Nat. U. Law Sch., Washington, D.C., 1909; hon. grad. Army Sch. of the Line, Fort Leavenworth, Kan., 1920; grad. Army Gen. Staff Sch., Fort Leavenworth, 1921, Army War Coll., Washington (D.C.) Barracks, 1927; Army refresher courses, 1928; unmarried. Commd. 2d lt., U.S. Army, June 12, 1895, advancing through the grades to brig. gen., Dec. 25, 1927; ret. as brig. gen. comdg. 2d Div., Feb. 28, 1935. Capt. 28th Inf., U.S. Volunteers, July 5, 1899-1901; col. of infantry Nat. Army, Aug 5, 1917-Aug. 21, 1919. commander 343d, later 165th, Infantry; comdr. 14th Inf., 1923-26; chief of staff 3d Division, 1927; comdr. 3d Arty. Brig. to 1929; comdr. 4th Brigade, 1929-31; 3d Brigade, Ft. Sam Houston, Tex., 1932-34; 2d Div., 1934-35. Served as a.d.c. to Gen. Loyd Wheaton, 1898-1902; adj. gen., 1st Division, 4th and 7th Army Corps, 1898; a.d.c. to General Arthur MacArthur, 1903; assistant judge adv. gen., 1907-12. Organized and trained machine gun detachment, 1897; installed civil gvt., Dagupan, P.I., 1899; selected location for target range, San Francisco Area, 1903; planned and constructed Safe Protective Range, 1904; prevented spread of war south in Island of Leyte, P.I., 1906; as recorder tried Brownsville Shooting Affray Case, before Congl. Ct. of Inquiry, 1909-10; comdr., Alcatraz Island Mil. Prison (changed to Disciplinary Barracks), San Francisco Bay, Calif., 1914-17; instr. in mil. history and strategy, Army Gen. Service Schs., Fort Leavenworth, 1922-23; comdr. invading army in joint Army-Navy training exercises, May 1927; chief of staff 3d Div., 1927. Recommended for brevet promotion 6 times for gallantry in action, D.S.M., Medal of Honor; decorated 3 Silver Star citations with 2 Oak Leaf clusters; U.S. gold life saving medal; Spanish-Am. War badge; Philippine Insurrection badge; World War I Victory medal. Mem. Mil. Order of Carabao, Am. Legion, Mil. Order World War, The Pilgrim John Howland Soc., New Eng. Hist. and Genealogical Soc., Vermont and Western Reserve Hist. Socs. Conglist. Mason. Clubs: Army and Navy (Washington); University (Cleveland). Author: Digest of Opinions of the Judge Advocate General of the Army, 1912; Military History of the World War, 1923. Home: University Club, 3813 Euclid Av., Cleveland 15. Died Sept. 21, 1946; buried in Arlington National Cemetery.

HOWZE, ROBERT LEE army officer; b. Rusk Co., Tex. Aug. 22, 1864; s. James Augustus and Amanda Hamilton (Brown) H.; A.B., Hubbard Coll., Tex., 1883; grad. U.S. Mil. Acad., 1888; m. Anne Chifelle, d. late Hamilton S. Hawkins, Feb. 24, 1897; children-Harriot, Robert Lee, Hamilton Hawkins. Commd. 2d lt. 6th Cav., July 7, 1888; promoted through grades to brig. gen. vols., June 20, 1901; hon. disch. vols., June 30, 1901; maj. Puerto Rico provisional regt. of inf., Oct. 9, 1901-June 20, 1901; hon. disch. vols., June 30, 1901; maj. Puerto Rico provisional regt. of inf., Oct.9, 1901-June 30, 1904; comdt. cadet, U.S. Mil. Acad., with rank of lt. col., 1905-09; lt. col. comdg. Puerto Rico Regt. and Mil. Dist. of P.R., Feb. 1909-Aug. 1912; maj. 4th Cav., Nov. 18, 1911; transferred to 11th Cav., Dec. 21, 1911; lt. cav., July 1, 1916; detailed to Gen. Staff Sept. 1916; col. of cav., May 15, 1917; chief of staff 10th Provisional Div. and cav. div.; assigned chief of staff Northeastern Dept., June 1917; brig. gen. N.A., Dec. 1917, and assigned to command 2d Cav. Brig., Ft. Bliss, Mexican border duty; maj. gen. U.S.A., Aug. 8, 1918; comd. 38th Div. and overseas duty; served in Meuse-Argonne: comd. 3d (Marne) Div., marched to the Rhine and comd. that div. in Army of Occupation in Germany until Aug. 14, 1919; returned to U.S. in command of 3d Div. and assigned to Mexican border duty in command of the Dist. of El Paso, comdg. First Cav. Div.; maj. gen., regular army, Dec. 1922. Comd. detachment of 34th Vols. in rescue of Lt. Comdr. Gilmore, U.S.N., and 27 other Americans who had been prisoners of insurgents in Philippines 10 mos. or more; under Gen. Pershing performed distinguished service in Mexico while comdg. a selected squadron of 11th Cav. Awarded Congressional Medal of Honor, July 25, 1891, "for gallantry in repulsing attacks of Sioux Indians in S.D., Jan. 1, 1891." Awarded D.S.M. (U.S.), Croix de Guerre with palm, and Officer Legion of Honor (French). Home: Washington, D.C. Died Sept. 10, 1926.

HOXIE, RICHARD LEVERIDGE army officer; b. New York, Aug. 7, 1844; s. Joseph and Jacqueline (Barry) H.; ed. in N.Y., Pa., Italy, 1851-58; Ia. State U., 1858-61; grad. U.S. Mil. Acad., 1868; m. Vinnie Ream, May 28, 1878 (died Nov. 20, 1914); 1 son, Richard Ream; m. 2d, May Ruth Norcross, Apr. 30, 1917. Bugler, pvt., corporal Co. F., 1st Ia. Cav., June 13, 1861-June 9, 1864; cadet, West Point, 1864-68; 2d lt. Engr. Corps, June 15, 1868; 1st lt., Sept. 22, 1870; capt., June 15, 1882; maj., Mar. 21, 1895; lt. col., Apr. 23, 1904; col. June 9, 1907; brig. gen., Aug. 7, 1908 (retired). In engr. work in constrn. of defenses, improvements of rivers and harbors, the light house establishment, etc.; asst. on Western explorations under Lt. Wheeler, 1872-74; mem. bd. of pub. works, D.C., and engr., D.C. 1874-78, and asst. to engr. commn., D.C., 1878-83, etc. Home: Washington, D.C. Died Apr. 30, 1930.

HOYLE, ELI DUBOSE army officer; b. Canton, Ga., Jan. 19, 1851; s. George Summers and Margaret Amanda (Erwin) H.; grad. U.S. Mil. Acad., 1875; grad. U.S. Arty. Sch., 1880; m. Fanny DeRussy, d. late Bvt. Brig. Gen. R. E. DeRussy, U.S. Army, Dec. 11, 1878. Commd. 2d lt., 2d Arty., June 16, 1875; 1st lt., Oct. 28, 1883; maj. and chief ordnance officer, U.S. Vols., July 18, 1898; hon. disch., May 12, 1899; capt. 1st Arty., Sept. 18, 1898; maj. Arty. Corps, Aug. 10, 1903; lt. col. field arty., Jan. 25, 1907; col., Mar. 3, 1911; brig. gen., Sept. 24, 1913; retired (age limit), Jan. 19, 1915. Adj. U.S. Mil. Acad., 1882-85; adj. 2d Regt. Arty., 1885-89; served on staff Maj. Gen. James H. Wilson, in Puerto Rican Campaign, 1898; on staff Brig. Gen. Geo M. Randall, 1898-99, and on staff of Major Gen. James H. Wilson as chief ordnance officer and provost marshal gen., Dept. of Matanzas, Cuba, until May 1899; asst. to insp. gen., Dept. of East, 1900-02; pres. bd. for preparation of drill regulations for rapid fire gun, 1903-06: pres. Field Arty. Bd., 1906-07; comd. recruit depot, Ft. Slocum, N.Y., 1907-08; comd. 6th Regt. Field Arty., 1908-11 and 1911-13; comdg. Central Dept. (Chicago), Mar.-June, 1913, Dist. of Luzon, P.I., 1913-14, Ft. William McKinley, Rizal, P.I., May-Dec. 1914. On active duty and comdg. Eastern Dept. hdqrs. Governors Island, N.Y., Aug. 25, 1917-Jan. 15, 1918. Medal Spanish-Am. War. Episcopalian. Died July 27, 1921.

HOYNES, WILLIAM lawyer, university dean; b. nr. Callan, Co. Kilkenny, Ireland, Nov. 8, 1846; s. Patrick and Catherine (Kennedy) H.; came to America in early childhood matriculated as student, U. of Notre Dame, Apr. 2, 1868, A.M., 1878, LL.D., 1888; LL.B., U. of Mich., 1872; unmarried. Learned printing trade with LaCrosse (Wis.) Republican. Enlisted June 9, 1862, Co. A. 20th Wis. Vol. Infantry; severely wounded at battle of Prairie Grove, Ark., Dec. 7, 1862; participated in capture of Van Buren on the Ark. River; participated in siege and capture of Vicksburg: discharged from service on account of wound, but reenlisted and joined Co. D. 2d Wis. Cav., participating in all actions and skirmishes with latter command; treated for wound in Adams St. Hosp., Memphis, in winter of 1865: returned with regt. from Austin, Tex., to Wis. at close of war; mustered out of U.S. service at Madison. Became editor New Brunswick (N.J.) Daily Times, 1873, and later associated with M. M. ("Brick") Pomeroy in editorial work at Chicago; editor Peoria (Ill.) Daily Transcript, 1881-82; practiced law at Chicago, 1882-83; admitted to Supreme Court of Mich., Apr. 10, 1872, U.S. Circuit Court, Apr. 11, 1872, Supreme Ct. of U.S., 1875, Supreme Ct. of Ill., 1877; prof. law and dean of law faculty, U. of Notre Dame, 1883-1918 (dean emeritus). Was organizer and commanded the University Light Guards, 1887. Rep. candidate for Congress, 1888; declined nomination for Congress, 1904; appointed U.S. commr. to treat with Turtle Mountain (N.D.) Indians, Oct. 4, 1890; apptd. three times to serve on state commns. Catholic. Apptd. Knight of St. Gregory, by Pope Pius X, 1912. Died Mar. 28, 1933.

HOYT, COLGATE business exec., gov. official; b. Yonkers, N.Y., Aug. 1, 1883; s. Colgate and Lida (Sherman) H.; grad. Westminster Sch., 1901; A.B., Brown U., 1905; m. Jeannette Myers, June 1912; children-Sherman, Jeannette, Barbara; m. 2d, Muriel Williams Williamson, Dec. 1924; 1 son, Coleman Williams; 3 stepsons, Clement W., Maclean, Charles P. Williamson. Partner, Colgate Hoyt & Co., 1908-26, Bramley & Smith, 1926-28; sr. partner Stokes Hoyt & Co., 1928-42, partner since 1942. Mem. N.Y. Stock Exchange, 1908-42; dir. U.S. Pipe & Foundry Co. since 1911. Chmn. Selective Service local bd. 15, N.Y. City, and Selective Service adviser to Mayor LaGuardia, 1940-42. Served with U.S. Army, 1916-18; on active duty, U.S. Army, 1942-46; ret. with rank lt. col.; mem. staff of Gen. Hershey, Nat. Hdqrs. Selective Service, Washington, and Selective Service officer, Army Separation Center, Fort Dix, N.J., liaison with 30 Army gen. hosps.; asst. chief Veterans Personnel Div., Selective Service Nat. Hdqrs., 1946-48, adminstrv. officer N.Y. Hdqrs., 1948-, and chief occupational deferment div. Decorated Army Commendation Citation, N.Y. State Conspicuous Service Cross. Mem. bd. mgrs. Army YMCA. Mem. Ex-Mems. Assn. Squadron A, Inc. (pres.), Loyal Legion (pres.), Alpha Delta Phi (past chmn. exec. council). Republican. Mason (32ff). Clubs: Union (former gov. and asst. sec.), Army and Navy (Washington); Pilgrims of U.S. Home: Union Club, 701 Park Av., N.Y.C. 21. Office: N.Y. City Hdqrs. Selective Service, 205 E. 42d St., N.Y.C. 17. Died Sept. 1963.

HOYT, HENRY MARTYN gov. Pa.; b. Kingston, Pa., June 8, 1830; s. Ziba and Nancy (Hurlbut) H.; A.B., Williams Coll., 1849, A.M., 1865; LL.D. (hon.), U. Pa., 1881, Lafayette Coll., 1881; m. Mary Loveland, Sept. 25, 1855, 1 son, Henry Martin. Admitted to Pa. bar, 1853, served with U.S. Army, from lt. col. to brig. gen. Army of Potomac, 1861-63, in battles of Bottom's Bridge, Seven Pines, Fair Oaks, Morris Island, Ft. Wayner; apptd. temporary judge Luzerne County (Pa.), 1867; became collector internal revenue for Luzerne and Susquehanna counties (Pa.), 1869; chmn. Pa. Republican Com., 1875; gov. Pa., 1878-82; v.p. Nat. Prison Assn.; mem. Pa. d. Public Charities; served as gen. sec. and mgr. Am. Protective Tariff League during presdl. campaign of 1888. Died Wilkes-Barre, Pa., Dec. 1, 1892.

HOYT, RALPH WILSON brig. gen. U.S.A.; b. Penn Yan, N.Y., Oct. 9, 1849; s. Benjamin L. and Celestia U. (Mariner) II; grad. U.S. Mil. Acad., 1872; m. Mary C. Cravens, Jan. 17, 1878 (died 1910); m. 2d, Cora McK. Harbold. Commissioned 2d lt. 11th Inf., June June 14, 1872; 1st lt., June 7, 1879; regtl. q.m. June 7, 1879-May 31, 1886; capt., Sept. 19, 1890; maj. 10th Inf., May 16, 1899; lt. col. 14th Inf., May 28, 1902; transferred to 10th Inf., Oct. 18, 1902; assigned to adj. gen. dept. Feb. 4, 1903; col. 25th Inf., Dec. 3, 1903; brig. gen. U.S.A., Mar. 18, 1910; retired by operation of law, Oct. 9, 1913. Home: Penn Yan, N.Y. Died Nov. 3, 1920.

HUBBARD, CHARLES J. explorer; b. Kansas City, Mo., June 25, 1902; s. Charles J. and Alice (Davis) H.; A.B. cum laude, Harvard, 1924, S.B. magna cum laude, 1925; m. Anna Fuller, 1925; 1 son, Charles J.; m. 2d, Dorothy Speare, 1934; m. 3d, Harriet Bissell, Jan. 18, 1943; children-Aries B., Hamal, Dana. Engr. Stone & Webster, Inc., 1925-28; v.p. George B. H. Macomber Co., Boston, 1929-31; made aerial surveys with N. Labrador Expn. of Forbes and Grenfel, 1931-35; freelance exploration and journalism, 1935-40; now chief Arctic Sect. U.S. Weather Bur., mng. U.S. interests in network internat. Arctic sci. stas. Served as lt. comdr. USNR, 1941-42; lt. col. USAAF, 1942—. Comdr. surveys and airfield construction in Greenland, N. Labrador, Hudson Bay area, etc., in development of northern airways through Greenland and eastern Canadian arctic for U.S. Army Air Transport Command; established first Arctic weather sta. network by airplane. Recipient medal. U.S. Dept. Agr., 1950. Mem. Am. Geographical Soc. Geophys. Inst. Clubs: Explorers, Cruising Club of America, Delphic, Varsity (Harvard). Contbr. articles and fiction to numerous popular mags. Navigator, aviator, comml. license, Office: Arctic Section. U.S. Weather Bureau, Washington. Killed in air crash at Alert, Ellesmere Island, July 31, 1950; buried Alert Ellesmere Island, N.W.T., Can.

HUBBARD, JOHN naval officer: b. S. Brewick, Me., May 19, 1849; s. John and Eleanor Augusta (Tucker) H.; grad. U.S. Naval Acad., 1870. Promoted ensign, 1871; master, 1873; lt., 1878; lt. comdr., 1898; comdr., 1901; capt., July 8, 1905; rear adm., 1909; retired May 19, 1911. In command U.S.S. Nashville and naval force on Isthmus of Panama during revolution of Nov. 1903, which resulted in independence of State of Panama; comd. U.S.S. Minnesota on cruise of the battleship fleet around the world; later on spl. duty Navy Dept. and mem. Gen. Bd.; comdr.-in-chief Asiatic Fleet, 1910. Home: Washington, D.C. Died May 28, 1932.

HUBBARD, JOHN CHARLES physicist; b. Boulder, Colo., Apr. 16, 1879; s. James Edwin and Rhoda Maude (Duke) H.; B.S., U. of Colo., 1901; Ph.D., Clark Univ., 1904; LL.D., Loyola Coll., Baltimore, 1938; m. Gertrude L. Pardieck, Feb. 9, 1929. Instr. in physics, at Simmons Coll., Boston, 1904-05; asst. prof. physics, New York U., 1905-06. Clark U., 1906-11; prof. physics Clark Coll., 1911-16; prof. and head of physics dept., N.Y. Univ., 1916-27; prof. same. Johns Hopkins Univ., 1927-46; physicist. Radiation Lab., Johns Hopkins Univ., 1946-47; research prof. physics, Catholic U. of Am., 1947—. Dir. summer work in physics, New York Univ., 1906, U. of Colo., 1912, 14; research engr., Western Electric Co., summer, 1917. Commd. capt. Signal Corps, U.S.R., Div. Research and Insp., Sept. 29,

1917; active service in France, information sect. Office of Chief Signal Officer, A.E.F.; official historian. Signal Corps, A.E.F.; maj., Oct. 4, 1918; discharged, May 20, 1919. Awarded Mendal medal, Villanova College, 1946. Officier d'Académie Instruction Publique, 1919. Fellow A.A.A.S., Am. Acad. Arts and Sciences, Am. Physical Soc.; mem. Beta Theta Pi, Phi Beta Kappa, Sigma Xi; rep. of Am. Inst. of Physics on Am. Engring. Standards Com.; mem. at large Div. of Physical Sciences of Nat. Research Council, 1931-33; sec. member National Defense Research Committee. Clubs: Johns Hopkins (Baltimore); Andiron (New York). Author various papers giving results of original physical research. Asso. editor Physical Rev., 1933-35. Roman Catholic. Address: 4304 13th Place N.E. Washington. Died Aug. 2, 1954; buried Richmond, Ind.

HUBBARD, LUCIUS FREDERICK governor; b. Troy, N.Y., Jan. 26, 1836; s. Charles F. and Margaret (Van Valkenberg) H.; acad. edn., Granville, N.Y.; learned tinner's trade; went to Minn., 1857; m. Amelia Thomas, Apr. 17, 1868. Newspaper publisher at Red Wing, 1859-61; register of deeds, Goodhue Co., Minn., 1858-60; pvt. Co. A, 5th Minn. Inf., Dec. 19, 1861; capt., Feb. 4, 1862; lt. col., Mar. 24, 1862; col., Aug. 30, 1862; bvtd. brig. gen. vols., Dec. 16, 1864, "for gallant and distinguished services in actions before Nashville," hon. mustered out, Sept. 6, 1865. In grain and milling business at Red Wing, 1866-84; built Midland R.R. in Minn., 1877-78; pres. Cannon Valley R.R., 1878-81; built; and operated Duluth, Red Wing & Southern R.R., 1888-1902. Mem. Minn. Senate, 1872-76; gov. of Minn., 1882-87. Brig. gen. vols., May 27-Oct. 31, 1898, in Spanish-Am. War; comd. 3d Div., 7th Army Corps. Mason. Home: St. Paul, Minn. Died Feb. 5, 1913.

HUBBARD, RICHARD BENNETT senator, gov. Tex.; b. Walton County, Ga., Nov. 1, 1832; s. Richard Bennett and Serena (Carter) H.; grad. Mercer Coll., 1851; LL.B., Harvard, circa 1853; m. Eliza Hudson; m. 2d, Janie Roberts. U.S. dist. atty. western dist. of Tex., 1858-60; del. Democratic Nat. Conv., Charleston, S.C., 1860, supported John C. Breckinridge against Stepehn A. Douglas; organizer, served to rank of col. 22d Tex. Inf., Confederate Army, 1860-65; del. Dem. Nat. Conv., 1872; gov. Tex., 1873-76; mem. U.S. Senate (Dem.) from Tex., 1876-82; temporary chmn. Dem. Nat. Conv., Chgo., 1884; E.E. and M.P. to Japan, 1884-88. Author: The United States in the Far East, 1899. Died July 12, 1901.

HUBBARD, THOMAS HAMLIN lawyer; b. Hallowell, Me., Dec. 20, 1838; s. John and Sarah Hodge (Barrett) H.; A.B., Bowdoin, 1857, A.M., 1860 (LL.D., 1894); LL.B., Albany Law Sch., 1861; admitted to Me. bar, 1860, N.Y., 1861, Supreme Ct. of U.S., 1870; 1st lt. adj. 25th Me. Inf., Sept. 20, 1862; lt. col., 30th Me. Inf., Dec. 19, 1863; col., June 2, 1864: bvtd. brig. gen. vols., July 13, 1865 "for meritorious services"; resigned, July 23, 1865, "for meritorious services"; resigned, July 23, 1865: m. Sibyl A. Fahnestock, Jan. 28, 1868. Mem. Butler, Stillman & Hubbard, New York, 1875-96; v.p. and dir. S.P. Co., 1896-1900; pres. Mexican Internat. R.R. Co., 1897-1901, Houston & Tex. Central R.R., 1894-1901; pres. Guatemala Central R.R. Co., 1901-12. Internat. Bank, 1905-; dir. Nat. Bank of Commerce; dir. and chmn. exec. com. Toledo, St. Louis & Western R.R. Co., Am. Light & Traction Co.; dir. and mem. exec. com. Wabash R.R. Co., Western Union Telegraph Co.; dir. and mem. finance com. Met. Life Ins. Co. Trustee Bowdoin Coll., Albany Law School. Died May 19, 1915.

HUBBELL, FREDERICK WINDSOR pres. Equitable Life Ins. Co. of Ia.; b. Des Moines, Ia., Nov. 24, 1891, s. Frederick Cooper and Mary (Windsor) H.; A.B., Harvard, 1913; m. Helen L. Clark, June 19, 1915; children-Frederick Windsor (deceased), Helen Ann. Asst. treas. Equitable Life Ins. Co. of Ia., Des Moines, 1913, successively treas., v.p. and pres. since 1939. Served as capt. F.A., U.S. Army, 1918. Home: Route No. 6. Office: Equitable Bldg., Des Moines, Ia. Died Mar. 14, 1959.

HUDDLESTON, GEORGE, JR., ex-congressman; b. Birmingham, Ala., Mar. 19, 1920; s. George and Bertha (Baxley) H.; A.B., magna cum laude Birmingham-Southern Coll., 1941; LL.B., U. of Ala., 1948; married to Alice Jeane Haworth; children—George III, Margaret, Nancy. Admitted to Alabama bar, 1948, D.C. bar, 1965; dep. circuit solicitor 10th Judicial Circuit, 1948-49; asst. U.S. atty. No. Dist. Ala., 1949-52; practice of law, Birmingham, Alabama, 1952-54; member of 84th-87th Congresses, ninth District of Alabama, member 88th Congress at large, Ala.; asst. to v.p. N.Am. Rockwell Corporation, 1964-71. Served comdr. USN, World War II. Mem. Am. Legion (dept. comdr. Ala. 1950-51), Phi Beta Kappa, Phi Delta Phi. Editor: Index to Official Proceedings of Alabama Constitutional Convention of 1901, 1948. Home: Potomac MD Died Sept. 1971.

HUDSON, JAY WILLIAM professor of philosophy, author, lecturer; b. Cleveland, O., Mar. 12, 1874; s. William Ingersoll and Emma (Bratt) H.; student Hiram Coll., 1893-95; Oberlin College, 1895; A.B., University of California, 1905; A.M., 1906; A.M., Harvard, 1907, Ph.D., 1908; m. May Bernard Small, August 11, 1909 (died 1915); m. 2d, Germaine Sansot, April 14, 1918. Assistant in philosophy, Univ. of California, 1904-06, Harvard, 1907-08; asst. prof. philosophy, U. of Missouri, 1908-11, asso. prof., 1912-13, prof. 1913-44, John Hiram Lathrop prof., 1930-44, prof. emeritus since 1944; lecturer, Insts. of Internat. Understanding for Rotary Internat., 1944-45; prof. Washington U., St. Louis, summer 1945; visiting professor, U. of Kansas City, 2d semester and summer, 1945-46; vis. prof., Stephens Coll., 1945-51, sabbatical year of philos. research in Europe, 1930-31. Dir. education department Massachusetts Peace Soc.; spl. lecturer American Sch. Peace League, 1914-15; prof. philosophy, George Peabody Coll. for Teachers, various summer quarters; speaker for Nat. Com. on Pub. Information and Mo. Council of Defense, 1917-18; commd. capt., Am. Red Cross in France, 1918. Mem. Nat. advisory bd., World Court League; mem. Nat. Com. Friends of Democracy; mem. Am. Philos. Assn. (chmn. board of officers, 1939), Western Philos. Assn. (pres. 1939), Mo. Academy of Science, Am. Assn. Univ. Profs., Phi Mu Alpha, Phi Kappa Phi, Alpha Pi Zeta, Phi Beta Kappa (pres. Alpha of Mo. chapter, 1940; mem. 20th Triennial Council, united chapters, San Francisco, 1940). Mason (grand orator, grand Lodge of Mo., 1929, 44, 45). Clubs: Faculty, Rotary. Author: The Treatment of Personality by Locke, Berkeley and Hume, 1911; America's International Ideals, 1915; The College and the New America, 1920; The Truths We Live By, 1921; Abbé Pierre's People, 1928 (awarded prize as best novel of 1928 by Catholic Press Assn.); Morning in Gascony, 1935; Why Democracy?, 1936; The Old Faiths Perish.,, 1939; Prayers of Aspiration, 1959; Life and Logic, 1950. Co-author: Religious Liberals Reply, 1947. Contbr. to philos. jours. Home: 216 Edgewood Av., Columbia, Mo. Died May 11, 1958; buried Columbia.

HUDSON, JOSEPH KENNEDY soldier, editor; b. Carrollton, O., May 4, 1840; s. John and Rebecca (Rothacker) H.; ed. Salem, O.: m. Mary W. Smith, Apr. 5, 1863. Served, pvt. to maj., in Mo., Ark., Indian Ty., La. and Tex., Civil War; farmer and stockraiser, 1865-73; regent State Agrl. Coll.; mem. Kan. legislature, 1871; editor Kansas Farmer, 1873; was independent candidate for Congress, 1874, and one of leading candidates for U.S. senator, 1874; founder, and for yrs. editor and propr., Topeka Daily Capital; editor Topeka Daily Herald, July 1901-; State printer, Kan., 1895-97; apptd. brig. gen. U.S. vols., May 27, 1898, for war with Spain. Home: Topeka, Kan. Died 1907.

HUDSON, MILLARD FILLMORE naval med. officer; b. Madisonville, Tenn., Dec. 17, 1889; s. Millard Fillmore and Esther Ann (Magill) H.; Pharm. D., Univ. of Va., 1910; M.D., Vanderbilt Univ., 1971; m. Ollie Mae Sanford, March 6, 1918 (dec. Oct. 9, 1944); m. 2d, Helen O'Rourke, Feb. 19, 1946. Interne, U.S. Naval Hosp., Norfolk, Va., 1917; commd. lt. (j.g.), 1917, and advanced through grades to capt. 1941; specialized in internal medicine pres., med. examining bd., U.S. Navy, since 1947; mem. U.S. Navy Retiring Bd., also U.S. Navy Marine Corps Retiring Bd. Awarded various mil. decorations and commendation medals from Navy and Army, World Wars I and II. Diplomate Am. Bd. Internal Medicine. Mem. A.M.A., Kappa Psi. Democrat. Presbyterian. Home: 2480-16th St., N.W. Office: U.S. Naval Retiring Board, Washington 25. Died Mar. 29, 1951.

HUDTLOFF, MARTIN JOHN, govt. ofcl.; b. Butte, Mont., Nov. 10, 1902; s. Martin David and Julia (Detloff) H.; A.B., U. Mont., 1925; m. Ruth Hewitt, Jan. 10, 1939 (dec. 1965); son, Martin John. Employee Anaconda (Mont.) Copper Mining Co., 1925-32; controller Mont. Relief Commn., Helena, 1932-35, N.M. Relief Adminstrn., Santa Fe, 1935; commr. accounts, accountant in charge field offices Treasury Dept., 1935-42; joined Dept. Agr., 1946, dir. transportation and storage services division Commodity Stabilization Service, 1949-63; deputy director fiscal division Agriculture Stabilization Service, Department Agr., from 1963; controller Commodity Credit Corp., 1947-49. Served as col. Office Fiscal Dir., War Dept., A.U.S., 1942-46. Decorated Am. Theatre ribbon; European, African, Middle East ribbon; Victory medal; Occupation medal; Commendation ribbon. Mem. Alpha Tau Omega. Presbyn. Home: Kensington MD Died Apr. 1969.

HUEBNER, CLARENCE R., army officer; b. Bushton, Kan., Nov. 24, 1888; s. Samuel G. and Martha (Rishel) H.; grad. business coll., Grand Island, Neb., 1909; grad. Inf. Sch., Advanced Course, 1923; honor grad. Command and Gen. Staff Sch., 1925; grad. Army War Coll., 1929; m. Florence Barrett, December 28, 1921; one daughter, Mary Juliette (Mrs. Richard J. Buck); m. 2d, Anna Imelda Matthews, Oct. 19, 1968 Enlisted, 18th Inf., U.S. Army, 1910-16; commd. 2d lt., Inf., November 26, 1916, and advanced through grades to lt. gen., March 1947; served as capt., major and lt. col., A.E.F., World War I; mem. War Dept. Gen. Staffs Corps, 1940-42; became dir. training, Services of Supply, Jan. 1942. Comdg. gen. 1st Inf. Div., Western Front, 1944; later comdr. 5th Army Corps; dep. comdr.-in-chief European Command and comdg. gen., U.S. Army, Europe, 1947; acting Am. Mil. Gov. in Germany and acting comdr. United States Armed Forces in Europe, 1949-50; director N.Y. Civil Def. Commn., Sept. 1951-72; director National Association of State and Territorial Civil Defense, 1957-58, president, 1958-72. Decorations: Distinguished Service Cross with oak leaf cluster. Distinguished Service Medal with two oak leaf clusters, Silver Star; Legion of Merit; Bronze Star Medal; Purple Heart with oak leaf cluster; Victory medal with 5 battle clasps; French Legion of Honor; French Croix de Guerre with palm; Italian War Cross; Comdr. Order Leopold I (Belgium); Order Sivurov 2d class (Russia); Croix de Guerre with palm (Belgium); Order White Lion 2d class (Czechoslovakia), Grand Officer de la Conronne de Chene (Luxembourg); Companion Order of Bath (Eng.). Retired 1950. Home: Washington DC Died Sept. 23, 1972; buried Arlington Nat. Cemetery, Arlington VA

HUFFMAN, LATON ALTON photographer; b. Castalia, Ia., Oct. 31, 1854; s. Perrin Cuppy and Chastina (Baird) H.; learned photography from his father; married, at least 1 dau., Ruth. Opened studio, Postville, Ia., 1875; traveled and photographed western frontier, Indians, Rocky Mountains, 1875-1919; army post photographer Ft. Keogh, Mont., 1878; commr. Custer County (Mont.), 1886; mem. Mont. Ho. of Reps., 1893; advocate of conservation; served as hunting guide; left large collection of photographs of Old West. Died Billings, Mont., Dec. 28, 1931.

HUGER, ALFRED lawyer; b. Charleston, S.C., Oct. 10, 1876; s. Thomas Bee and Caroline Banks (Smith) H.: prep. edn. Porter Mil. Acad., Charleston; LL.B., Cornell U., 1903; pres. sr. Law Class, 1903; m. Margaret, d. Wilhelmus Mynderse, Apr. 17, 1906; children-Thomas Bee (dec.), Margaret, Wilhelmus Mynderse (dec.), Jeanne, Alfred. Chief passenger clk. S.C. Ry. Co., later asst. to div. passenger agt. Southern Ry. Co. until 1899; pvt. sec. in Europe, 1903-04, to Andrew D. White (first pres. Cornell U. and U.S. ambassador to Germany); in law office of Henry W. Sackett, New York, 1904, and with Butler, Notman & Mynderse, 1905-07; mem. Huger & Wilbur, Charleston, 1907, now Huger, Wilbur, Miller & Mouzon; first admiralty counsel U.S. Shipping Bd., June 1917-Apr. 1918. Former mem. Squadron A Cav., N.Y.N.G.; maj. O.M.C., World War; assigned to 1st Sect. Gen. Staff, S. of S., Tours, France, chief of Div. of Staff representing Am. Shipping Control Com.: maj. O.R.C. Citation from Gen. Pershing; awarded Cross Legion of Honor (French); Order of Purple Heart (U.S.A.). Former member State Bd. Law Examiners of S.C.; trustee S.C. Med. Coll. 3 yrs.; dir. Internat. Chamber Commerce: pres. Charleston Chamber Commerce. Mason. Democrat. Episcopalian. Home: Charleston, S.C. Died May 18, 1936.

HUGER, BENJAMIN army officer; b. Carleston, S.C., Nov. 22, 1805; s. Francis Kinlock and Harriott (Pickney) H.; grad. U.S. Mil. Acad., 1825; m. Elizabeth Pickney, Feb. 17, 1831, 5 children. Commd. 2d lt. arty., U.S. Army, 1825, capt. of ordnance, 1832, commanded arsenals at Fortress Monroe, Pikesville, Md. and Charleston, S.C., armory at Harpers Ferry; mem. ordnance bd. Dept. of War, 1839-46, sent abroad to study European mil. methods, 1840; chief of ordnance U.S. Army under Gen. Scott, in charge of seige of trains at Vera Cruz during Mexican War, 1846; brevetted maj., lt. col., col.; commd. col. arty. Confederate Army, 1861; commd. brig. gen. Provisional Army of Confederate States, 1861, commanded troops from S.C. at Norfolk, later all troops and defenses around Norfolk, 1861; relieved of command after Battle of Malvern Hill (under charge of failing to cut off McClellan's retreat after Confederate victory), 1862; became an insp. arty. and ordnance, 1862. Died Charleston, Dec. 7, 1877.

HUGER, DANIEL ELIOTT senator, jurist; b. S.C., June 28, 1779; s. Daniel and Sabina (Elliott) H.; A.B., Coll. of N.J. (now Princeton), 1798, A.M., 1801; m. Isabella Middleton, Nov. 6, 1800, 10 children. Admitted to S.C. bar, 1799; mem. S.C. Legislature, 1804-19, 38-42 (protested against states rights doctrine); commd. brig. gen. S.C. Militia, 1814; circuit judge S.C. Ct. Appeals, 1819-30; became reconciled with Calhoun, adopted moderate states rights position; mem. U.S. Senate from S.C. (States Rights Democrat, replacing John C. Calhoun), 1843-45. Died Sullivans Island, S.C., Aug. 21, 1854.

HUGER, FRANCIS KINLOCH physician, army officer; b. Charleston, S.C., Sept. 17, 1773; s. Benjamin and Mary (Kinloch) H.; studied in London under surgeon John Hunter; M.D., U. Pa., 1797; m. Harriet Lucas Pinckney, Jan. 14, 1802. Served on med. staff Brit. Army, Flanders, 1794-95; unsuccessfully attempted (with Dr. Justus Eric Bollman) to liberate Lafayette imprisoned at Olmutz, Vienna, circa 1796; returned to Am., 1796; served as capt. U.S. Army, 1798-1801, lt. col. arty. during War of 1812; moved to Pendleton, S.C., 1826; lived in Charleston, S.C., circa 1854-55. Died Charleston, Feb. 14, 1855.

HUGER, ISAAC army officer; b. S.C., Mar. 8, 1742; s. Daniel and Mary (LeJan) H.; m. Elizabeth Chalmers, Mar. 23, 1762, 8 children. Mem. S.C. Provincial Congress, 1755, 1778; served as lt. S.C. Militia during Cherokee War, 1760, lt. col. 1st Regt., 1775; col. 5th Regt., Continental Army, 1776; brig. gen. So. Army, 1779, fought at battles of Stone Ferry, Charleston, Guilford Court House (in command Virginians), Hobkirk's Hill; defeated by Tarleton and Webster at

Battle of Monk's Corner, 1780; mem. S.C. Gen. Assembly, 1782; v.p. S.C. br. Soc. of Cincinnati, 1783. Died Charleston, S.C. Oct. 17, 1797.

HUGGINS, ELI LUNDY brig. gen.; b. Schuyler Co., Ill., Aug. 1, 1841; s. Alexandre Gilliland and Lydia (Pettijohn) H. Pvt. and corporal Co. E. 2d Minn. Inf., July 5, 1861-July 14, 1864; pvt. Co. K, 1st Minn. Arty., Feb. 16-Feb. 28, 1865: 1st lt., Mar. 1-Sept. 27, 1865; apptd. from Minn., 2d lt. 2d U.S. Arty., Feb. 23, 1866; 1st lt., Dec. 24, 1866; trans. to cav., 1870: promoted through grades to brig. gen., Feb. 22, 1903; retired Feb. 23, 1903. Awarded Congressional Medal of Honor "for most distinguished gallantry" in action against Ogalalla Sioux Indians, Mont., Apr. 1, 1880; received surrender of Rain-in-the-Face, the slayer of Custer, and 800 other Sioux Indians, Oct. 1880. Author: Winona, a Dakota Legend, and Other Poems. Home: San Diego, Calif. Died Oct. 22, 1929.

HUGHES, AARON KONKLE rear adm., U.S.A. retired, March 1884; b. Elmira, N.Y., March 31, 1822; apptd. acting midshipman, Oct. 30, 1838; promoted to passed midshipman, May 28, 1844: master, 1853; lt., Aug. 1853; lt. comdr., July 16, 1862; comdr., Nov. 16, 1862: capt., Feb. 10, 1869; commodore, Feb. 4, 1875; rear adm., July 2, 1882. Served in S. Atlantic and Gulf squadrons during Civil war. Home: Washington, D.C. Died 1906.

HUGHES, CHARLES EVANS, JR. lawyer; b. N.Y. City, Nov. 30, 1889; s. Charles Evans (late retired Chief Justice of United States) and Antoinette (Carter) H.; grad. Collegiate Sch., N.Y. City, 1905; A.B., Brown, 1909, LL.D., 1937; LL.B., Harvard, 1912; m. Marjory Bruce Stuart, June 17, 1914; children-Charles Evans 3d, Henry Stuart, Helen, Marjory Bruce. Editor in chief Harvard Law Review, 1911-12; admitted to N.Y. bar, 1913, and began practice at N.Y. City; with Byrne & Cutcheon, 1912-13; law sec. to Justice Benjamin N. Cardozo, 1914; with Cadwalader, Wickersham & Taft, 1914-16; mem. Hughes, Rounds, Schurman & Dwight, later Hughes, Schurman & Dwight, 1917-29 and 1930-37, and Hughes, Richards, Hubbard & Ewing, now Hughes, Hubbard & Ewing, since 1937. Solicitor General of the United States June 1, 1929-Apr. 1930 (resigned upon apptmt. of father as Chief Justice of the United States). Director N.Y. Life Ins. Co., 1930-34. Private, batt. sergt. maj. and 2d lt. F.A., U.S. Army, 1917-29. Mem. N.Y. City Charter Revision Commn., 1935-36; Gov. Lehman's Preparatory Com. on State Constitutional Conv., 1937-38. Chmn. War Com. of Bar of City of N.Y. 1942-46. Chmn. Mayor's Com. on Unity, 1944-48. Fellow Brown University; trustee of Teachers College, N.Y. City. Mem. Am and N.Y. State bar assns., Assn. Bar City, New York, N.Y. County Lawyers Assn. (pres. 1936-38), Phi Beta Kappa, Delta Upsilon. Republican. Episcopalian. Clubs: University, Century Assn., Harvard, Brown, St. Andrews Golf, Down Town (New York). Home: 5040 Independence Av., Riverdale-on-Hudson, N.Y. City 63. Office: 1 Wall St., New York 5, N.Y. Died Jan. 21, 1950.

HUGHES, CHARLES FREDERICK naval officer; b. Bath, Me., Oct. 14, 1866; s. John and Lucy Maria (Delano) H.; U.S. Naval Acad., 1884; m. Caroline Russell Clark, Jan. 31, 1898; 1 dau., Louisa Russell (wife of Otto Nimitz, U.S.A.). Promoted ensign, July 1, 1890; lt. jr. grade, Apr. 27, 1898; lt., Mar. 3, 1899; lt. comdr., July 1, 1905; comdr., Jan. 9, 1910; capt., July 10, 1904; rear adm., Oct. 10, 1918. Served on Monterey, Spanish-Am. War, 1898, and participated in Battle of Manila; duty Bur. of Equipment, Navy Dept., 1904-06; recorder Bd. of Inspection and Survey, Navy Dept., 1909-11; comd. Birmingham, 1911-12, Des Moines, 1912; was at Vera Cruz, Mexico, during Diaz revolution, 1912, and again when the city was captured, 1914; chief of staff, Atlantic Fleet, 1913-14; mem. Gen. Bd., Navy Dept., 1914-16; comd. New York, 1916-18; served with British Grand Fleet in the North Sea, Nov. 1917-Oct. 1918; comdt. Navy Yard, Phila., 1918-20; comdr. 2d Battleship Squadron, Atlantic Fleet, 1920-21, divs. 7 and 4, U.S. Battle Fleet, 1921-June 25, 1923; comdt. Naval War Coll., July 1, 1923-July 1, 1924: dir. fleet training, July 1, 1924-Oct. 10, 1925: later comdt. in chief U.S. battle fleet and chief of naval operations, retired, Nov. 1, 1930. Conglist. Died May 28, 1934.

HUGHES, EVERETT S. ret. army officer; b. S.D., Oct. 21, 1885; B.S., U.S. Mil. Acad., 1908; grad. Ordnance Sch. Tech., 1912, Sch. of the Line, 1922, Gen. Staff Sch., 1923, Army War Coll., 1928. Commd. 2d lt. F.A., 1908; 1st lt. Ordnance Dept., 1911; capt. F.A., 1916; major, Ordnance Dept., 1917, advanced through grades to maj. gen., 1943; became chief Equipment Div., Office of Ordnance, 1940; chief ordnance officer S.O.S.E.T.O., 1942, chief of staff, 1942; dep. chief of staff E.T.O., 1942; dep. theater comdr. N.A.T.O.U.S.A., 1943; spl asst. to theater comdr. E.T.O., 1944, inspector gen., 1945, chief of Ordnance, 1946; retired 1949. Decorated Comdr. Legion of Honor (France); Legion of Merit, D.S.M., Bronze Star (U.S.); Comdr. Nichan Iftikhas; Comdr. Order of Crown of Palm; Commander de l'Ordre de la Couroune avec Palm (France); Croix de Guerre (Russia). Address: The Westchester, Washington. 1940 avec Palm (France); Order of Fatherland Class. Died Sept. 5, 1957; buried Arlington (Va.) Cemetery.

HUGHES, FRANCIS MASSIE Naval officer; born June 27, 1899; m. Helen Rooney Lovelace; children-Eynon, Francis Massie; step-children-Helen Sally Lovelace, Donald A. Lovelace. Entered USN, 1923, advanced through grades to rear adm., 1951; comdr. Anti-submarine Force, Atlantic Fleet, 1956-57, comdt. 5th Naval Dist., Norfolk, Va., 1957-. Home: Bay Colony Dr., Virginia Beach, Va. Office: Commandant Fifth Naval District, Naval Base, Norfolk 11, Va. Died Dec. 1960.

HUGHES, GEORGE WURTZ congressman, engr.; railroad exec.; b. Elmira, N.Y., Sept. 30, 1806; s. John and Anna (Konkle) H.; attended U.S. Mil. Acad.; m. Ann Sarah Maxey. Became civil engr. for U.S. Govt.; commd. capt. Topog. Engrs., U.S. Army, 1838; served in Mexican War, promoted maj. later col.; mil. gov. Jalapa Province for a time; railroad surveyor employed by W. H. Aspinwall and J. C. Stevens to run line across Panama, 1848-49; resigned commn., 1850; pres. Balt. & Susquehanna R.R., 1854-57, continued as pres. after merger into No. Central R.R., q.m. gen. of Md., 1857-59; mem. U.S. Ho. of Reps. (Democrat) from Md., 36th Congress, 1858-61; engaged as planter and cons. engr. Died West River, Md., Dec. 3, 1870; buried West River.

HUGHES, MERRITT YERKES, prof. of English; b. Phila., Pa., May 24, 1893; s. Adoniram Judson and Annabelle (Yerkes) H.; A.B., Boston U., 1915, A.M., 1916; Doctor of Letters (honorary), 1954; M.A., University of Edinburgh, 1918, Litt.D., 1950; Ph.D., Harvard, 1921; student U. of Paris, 1921-22; m. Grace J. Dedman, Aug. 10, 1923;children–David Yerkes, Elspeth Baillie. (Mrs. John F. Benton). Instr. English, Boston U., 1919-20; asst. prof. English, U. of Calif., 1922-26; asso. prof., 1926-36; prof. English, U. of Wis., 1936-63, professor emeritus, 1963-71; chairman department English, 1938-41, 42-43, 46-48, 52-55; Taft lecturer, University of Cincinnati, 1962; summer instr. various univs.; vis. fellow Folger Shakespeare Library, Washington; 1964-65; vis. mem. Inst. Advanced Study, Princeton, 1965-66. Awarded fellowship Am. Field Service, 1921-22, fellowship John S. Guggenheim Meml. Found., 1925-26; fellowship Henry E. Huntington Library and Art Gallery, San Marino, Cal., 1941-42, 66-67; Fulbright grantee U. London, Brit. Mus., 1949-50; research grantee Lon., Am. Philos. Soc., 1968-69. Delivered Tudor-Stuart Lecture at Johns Hopkins U., 1943. Served as sgt. inf. Intelligence Corps. U.S. Army, A.E.F., 1918-19; maj. to lt. col., as field historian, G-5, Third U.S. Army, France, Luxembourg, and Bavaria, 1943-46. Fellow American Academy of Arts and Sciences; mem. Modern Lang. Assn. Am. (council 1948-52). Renaissance Soc. America (council 1958-60), Modern Humanities Research Assn., Am. Assn. U. Profs. (council 1954-57, chpt. pres. 1957-58), Wis. Acad. Scis. Arts and Letters (pres. 1960-61), Internat. Assn. Univ. Profs. English (exec. 1956-65). Mem. Soc. of Friends. Clubs: University (Madison, Wis.); Tudor-Stuart. Author: Ten Perspectives on Milton, 1965. Editor: Milton Complete Poems and Major Prose, 1957; vol. III The Complete Prose Works of John Milton, 1962. Contbr. to scholarly jours. Home: Madison WI Died May 12, 1971; buried Lawnview Cemetery, Philadelphia PA

HUGHES, ROBERT PATTERSON army officer; b. in Pa., Apr. 11, 1839; ed. Jefferson Coll., Pa. Enlisted as pvt. Co. E, 12th Pa. Inf., Apr. 25, 1861; hon. disch., Aug. 5, 1861; commd. 1st lt. 85th Pa. Inf., Oct. 11, 1861; capt., May 20, 1862; hon. mustered out, Dec. 6, 1864; lt. col. 199th Pa. Inf., Dec. 7, 1864; bvtd. col., Apr. 2, 1865; mustered out, June 28, 1865; apptd. from Pa. capt. 18th U.S. Inf., July 28, 1866; assigned to 3d Inf., July 5, 1870; maj. insp. gen., Feb. 19, 1885; lt. col., Mar. 11, 1885: col., Aug. 31, 1888; brig. gen. vols., June 3, 1898; hon. disch., Apr. 16, 1899; brig. gen. vols. Apr. 16, 1899; maj. gen. U.S.A., Apr. 1, 1902; retired Apr. 11, 1903. Bvtd. maj., Mar. 2, 1867, for assault on Ft. Gregg, Va. Provost marshal gen., Manila and suburbs, 1898; comd. 1st Mil. Dist., P.I., 1899, Dept. Visayan Islands, 1900. Died 1909.

HUGHES, RUPERT author; b. Lancaster, Mo., Jan. 31, 1872; s. Felix Turner and Jean Amelia (Summerlin) H.; brother of Felix Hughes; A.B., Adelbert Coll. (now Western Reserve Univ.), 1892, A.M., 1894; A.M., Yale U., 1899; Litt.D., Western Reserve U., 1936; m. 3d, Elizabeth Patterson Dial, Dec. 31, 1924 (died lMar. 23, 1945). Asst. editor Godey's Mag., Current Lit. and The Criterion; in London, May 1901-Nov. 1902, New York till 1905, with Ency. Britannica Co. Mem. Phi Beta Kappa, Delta Upsilon. Served pvt. to Capt. N.G.N.Y., 1897-1908; capt., Mexican border service, 1916; asst. to adjutant general, N.Y., 1917; capt. Inf., Jan. 7, 1918; maj. Sept. 4, 1918; hon. disch. Jan. 15, 1919; maj. Reserve Corps, Apr. 3, 1919; lieut. col., Mar. 10, 1928: active in formation of California State Guard, 1940; colonel commanding 2d Regiment. July 1, 1941, resigned Jan. 1943. Decorated with Order of Polonia Restituta (Polish), 1923. Author: The Lakerim Athletic Club, 1898; American Composers; 1900; Gyges Ring (verse), 1901; The Whirlwind, 1902; Live Affairs of Great Musicians, 1903; Zal, 1905: Miss 318, 1911; The Old Nest, 1912; What Will People Say?, 1914; Music Lovers' Cyclopedia, 1914; Empty Pockets, 1915; Clipped Wings, 1916; The Thirteenth Commandment, 1916; In a Little Town, 1917; we Can't Have Everything, 1917; Unpardonable Sin, 1919; Long Ever

Ago (Irish stories), 1919; Cup of Fury, 1919; Fairy Detective (for children), 1919; What's the World Coming To?, 1920; Beauty, 1921; Momma, 1921; Souls for Sale, 1922; Within These Walls, 1923; Golden Ladder, 1924; Destiny, 1925; The Old Home Town, 1926; We Live but Once; 1927; The Patent Leather Kid, 1927; The Lovely Ducklings, 1928; Mermaid and Centaur, 1929; Ladies' Man, 1930; No One Man, 1931; Static, 1932; The Uphill Road, 1933; Love Song, 1934; The Man Without a Home, 1935; Stately Timber, 1939; City of Angels, 1941; Gyges' Ring and Other Verse, 1949; The Complete Detective, The Giant Wakes, 1950; The Triumphant Clay, 1951; The War of the Mayan King, 1952; other publs. include (biography) George Washington, 1926, 27, 30; Attorney for the People, the Story of Thomas E. Dewey, 1940; (plays) Alexander the Great (toured U.S. 1903-04); All for a Girl (produced 1908); The Bridge (produced 1909, later revived as The Man Between); The Transformation (prod. 1909, later revised as Two Women); Excuse Me (prod. 1911; 4 cos. toured U.S., 1911-12, 2 cos. 1912-14, prod. in Australia, 1913, London, 1915); Uncle Zeb (prod. 1913); The Cat Bird (prod. 1910); (dramatizations) Tess of the Storm Country (prod. 1911); vaudeville sketches, including "Miss 318," 1912-14. Composed A Riley Album, "Cain," and other songs. Has written and directed many motion pictures; radio commentator, author, many radio sketches. Home: 204 N. Rossmore Av., Los Angeles 4. Died Sept. 9, 1956; buried Forest Lawn Meml. Park, Glendale, Cal.

HUGUS, WRIGHT lawyer; b. nr. Wheeling, W.Va., Nov. 8, 1890; s. Thomas J. and Annie V. (Wright) H.; A.B., Dartmouth, 1913; LL.B., Harvard, 1916; m. Martha Majesky, Dec. 27, 1927; children-Mary Anne, Wright. Admitted to W.Va. bar, 1916, and began practice at Wheeling; mem. Schmidt, Hugus & Laas; gen. counsel Wheeling Steel Corp.; mem. W.Va. Ho. of Del., 1921-23, 1943-44, state Senate (chmn. judiciary com., 1925, floor leader), 1923-30; mem. and sec. W.Va. Constl. Commn., 1930; mem. bd. govs. W.Va. U. 1935-41. Served in World War 27 mos. as 1st lt. inf., later capt., A.G.D. and maj. A.G.D., overseas 14 mos. Mem. Am. Wheeling, W.Va. (pres. 1935-36) bar assns. Sigma Chi. Republican. Methodist. Mason. Clubs: Twilight, Ft. Henry, Wheeling Country (Wheeling); Dartmouth (N.Y.). Home: Forest Hills, Wheeling, W.Va. 26003. Died Apr. 23, 1958.

HUIDEKOPER, FREDERIC LOUIS military writer; b. Meadville, Pa., Mar. 8, 1874's. Frederic Wolters and Anna Virginia (Christie) H.; A.B., cum laude., Harvard, 1896; English lit. and law, Christ Ch., Oxford, 1896-96; Law Sch. Columbian (now George Washington) U., 1898-1900; admitted to bar, 1900; m. Helena K., d. late John Stuart and Helena F. (Ellis) Elliott. Sept. 14, 1916; children-Stuart Elliott, Frederic Fitz-James Christie; m. 2d, Anne Marie Amélie Debrinay de Montmort, dau. late Maj. A. A. G. Debrinay, June 7, 1933. Treas. The Disston Land Co., 1900-01; treas. United Land Co. of Fla., 1901-08, v.p., 1908-10; head of investment dept. W. B. Hibbs & Co., Washington, D.C., 1920-25. Has made extensive researches, 1897-, in archives of war offices at Paris, Vienna and St. Petersburg, being one of few Americans ever granted such permission, also given access to important pvt. archives; sec. Am. delegation to Internat. Opium Conf., The Hague, 1911-12. A founder Washington br. Nat. Cav. and Arty. Remount Assn. of U.S., 1912; founded, Apr. 3, 1912, and organized Army League of U.S.; sec. and dir. Nat. Remount Assn., 1913-14, v.p., 1914; one of founders of Nat. Security League, 1914, v.p., mem. army com. and pres. D.C. br., 1916-17. Commd. major, adjutant gen. sec., O.R.C., May 16, 1917, to rank from May 14, 1917; asst. to dept. adj., Southeastern Dept., Charleston, S.C., June 13-Aug. 23, 1917; div. adj. 33d Div. Ill. N.G., Aug. 28, Mar. 9, 1919; grad. Army Gen. Staff Coll., Langres, France, 1918; promoted lt. col. Sept. 25, 1918; served on British front and participated in Meuse-Argonne offensive; temporarily attached to presdl. party, Am. peace Commn., Feb. 1919; hon. disch., Apr. 1, 1919. Cited, in G.O., 33d Div., "for gallantry in action against the enemy," and by Gen. Pershing "for exceptionally meritorious and conspicuous services as div. adj., 33d Division, France"; awarded D.S.M. (U.S.), 1921; Chevalier Legion of Honor, 1923, Médaille de Verdun (France), and silver star (U.S.), all for services in front of Verdun, Meuse-Argonne offensive. Wrote: Military Studies (Internat. Mil. Series), 1904; The Military Unpreparedness of the United States, with introd. by Maj. Gen. Leonard Wood, 1915; 33rd Division, A.E.F., 1919; The Thirty-third Division, in Vol. I of Ill. in the World War, 1921; The History of the 33rd Division, A.E.F. (3 vols. and portfolio of maps), officially published by State of Ill., 1921; Huidekoper, American Branch 1928; The American Ancestry of Frederic Louis Huidekoper and Reginald Shippen Huidekoper of Washington, D.C., 1931. Episcopalian. Home: Washington, D.C. Died Mar. 7, 1940.

HUIDEKOPER, HENRY SHIPPEN soldier; b. Meadville, Pa., July 17, 1839; s. Edgar and Frances (Shippen) H.; A.B., Harvard, 1862, A.M., 1872; m. Emma G. Evans, Oct. 26, 1864. Served in Civil War, July 1862-Mar. 1864; lt. col. comdg. 150th Pa. Regt., at Gettysburg, where he was twice wounded and lost right arm; received Congressional Medal of Honor "for gallantry in battle." After war was 15 yrs. brig. gen. and maj. gen. N.S. of Pa.; comd. 7th div. during railroad riots of 1877; postmaster of Phila., 1880-85. Overseer of Harvard, 1898-1910. Home: Philadelphia, Pa. Died Nov. 9, 1918.

HUIDEKOPER, REGINALD SHIPPEN lawyer; b. Meadville, Pa., Pa., May 24, 1876; s. Frederic Wolters and Virginia (Christie) H.; A.B., Harvard 1898; studied law at Trinity Coll. (Oxford U.), Eng., 1898-1900, and Columbian Univ., 1900-01; admitted to bar, 1901; m. Bessie Cazenove du Point, Jan. 24, 1917; children-Henry Shippen, Ann du Pont, Elizabeth Gardner, Peter Galloway. Practiced law, Washington, D.C.; asst. U.S. dist. atty., D.C., 1909-14; mem. Wilson, Huidekoper & Lesh, 1914-24; dir., mem. exec. com. Nat. Savings & Trust Co.; dir. St. Jo Paper Co.; trustee and v.p. Nemours Foundation; co-executor and co-trustee Estate of Alfred I. du Pont. Retired. Commissioned major, judge advocate U.S. Army, Nov. 15, 1917; lt. col., Oct. 25, 1919; over 6 months duty at G.H.Q., A.E.F., France; hon. disch., June 25, 1919. In 1917 assisted in Provost Marshal Gen.'s office in preparation of the "Rules and Regulations" and the "Forms of Proof of Claims for Exemption and Discharge" promulgated by the President to put the Selective Service Act into operation. Mem. Bd. of War Contract Adjustment, War Dept., Nov. 1, 1919-July 1, 1920. Mem. Am. Law Inst. Clubs: Alibi, Grasslands, Chevy Chase (Washington); Patuxent; Leander (England). Home: 2934 Edgevale Terrace N.W., Washington, D.C. Died Sep. 28, 1943.

HUIDEKOPER, RUSH SHIPPEN physician; b. Meadville, Pa., May 3, 1854; s. Edgar and Frances (Shippen) H.; ed. Philips Acad., Exeter; grad. med. dept. Univ. of Pa., 1877; veterinarian, Nat. Veterinary School, Republic of France, Alfort, France, 1882, and following yr. in laboratories of Virchow, Koch, Chauveau and Pasteur; m. Anne P. Morris, 1877. Physician Phila. Dispensary; outpatient physician Children's Hosp.: asst. surgeon hosp., Univ. of Pa.: coroner's physician of Phila.; U.S. commr. gen., Agrl. Expn., Hamburg, Germany, 1883; dean veterinary dept. Univ. of Pa., and prof. internal pathology and contagious diseases, zootechnics and hygiene, prof. comparative anatomy and veterinary surgery, New York Coll. Veterinary Surgery; maj. and a.d.c. Nat. Guard, Pa., 1874-78: maj. and brig. surgeon Nat. Guard Pa., 1878-91; acting asst. q.m. gen. Nat. Guard Pa., 1888 (Johnstown flood); late lt. col. and surgeon-in-chief, Nat. Guard Pa.; lt. col. and chief surgeon U.S. vols., 1898; chief surgeon 1st army corps and chief surgeon Puerto Rico; Pennsylvania Republican. Editor: Journal of Comparative Medicine and Veterinary Archives, Phila., 1889-. Died 1901.

HULEN, JOHN AUGUSTUS ry. ofcl.; b. Centralia, Mo., Sept. 9, 1871; s. Harvcey Harvey and Fanny (Morter) H.; grad. Marmaduke Mil. Acad., Sweet Springs, Mo., 1891; m. Frankie L. Race, Feb. 14, 1893. In real estate and ins. business, Gainesville, Tex., 1891-98; city passenger agt. Frisco Lines, Houston, 1907-08, later gen. agt. R.I.-Frisco Lines; apptd. gen. freight and passenger agt. Trinity & Brazos Valley R.R. Co., 1910, pres. and receiver, 1919, also pres. Galveston Terminal Ry. Co.; apptd. traffic mgr. Ft. Worth & Denver City and Wichita Valley ry. cos., 1920, v.p. of both, 1930-42; ret. Oct. 1, 1941; also retired as pres. Burlington, Rock Island R.R.; Co., Houston, Belt and Terminal Ry. Co., v.p. Union Terminal Co. Dallas, Ft. Worth & Denver Terminal Ry. Co. Dir. Ft. Worth Nat. Bank, Second Nat. Bank of Houston. Commd. lt. Tex. N.G., 1889, advanced to lt. gen. ret. 1935; served Philippine Insurrection, 1899-1901, comd. 6th Separate Brigade, Tex. border; served as brig. gen. U.S. Army, AEF, 1918-19 Awarded silver star "for gallentry in action," Philippine Insurrection: D.S.M. (U.S.); Croix de Guerre (France); recommended for Medal of Honor and twice for brevet maj. Mason (32ff, Shriner), K.P. Clubs: Ft. Worth, River Crest Country (Ft. Worth). Home: Palacios, Tex. Died Sept. 13, 1957.*

HULICK, GEORGE WASHINGTON lawyer, ex-congressman; b. Batavia, O., June 29, 1833; s. Lott and Rhoda (Dimmitt) H.; grad. Farmers' Coll., Ohio, July 9, 1855; m. Josephine W. Harrison Oct. 16, 1861. In charge Pleasant Hill Acad., 1855-8: studied law; admitted to bar Mar., 1857, practiced Batavia, O.; sch. examiner Clermont Co., O., 1856-9; Rep. candidate for pros. atty., 1858. Served capt. Co. E. 22d Ohio inf., Apr. 14 to Aug. 16, 1861; probate judge Clermont Co., 1864-7; mem. bd. ed'n Batavia, 9 yrs.; del. Rep. Nat. Conv., 1868; Hayes and Wheeler elector, 1876: mem. Congress, 6th Ohio dist. 1893-7. Republican. Address: Batavia, O. Died Aug. 13, 1907.

HULINGS, GARNET naval officer; b. Oil City, Pa., Mar. 6, 1889; s. Gen. Willis James and Emma (Simpson) H.; grad. U.S. Naval Acad., 1912; m. Salena Shumard Carden, Aug. 14, 1913; children-Carol Carden, Isabel Simpson. Commd. midshipman, U.S. Navy, 1912, and advanced through grades to lt. commander; retired 1927; v.p. and gen. mgr. Continental Steamship Co., 1927-. Served on U.S.S. Texas, Occupation of Vera Cruz, 1914; comdr. Submarine C-4, Panama, 1914-17, comdr. Submarine AL-4, patrol of Irish coast, World War; naval attaché, Tokyo, Japan, 1921-24; comdr. U.S.S. Billingsley, 1925-27. Awarded Navy Cross (U.S.). Home: Cockeysville, Md. Died Apr. 1932.

HULINGS, WILLIS JAMES congressman; b. Clarion Co., Pa., July 1, 1850: s. Marcus and Margaret H.: ed. as C.E.; admitted to bar, Pa., Ariz. and W.Va.; m. Emma Simpson, Apr. 28, 1874; engaged in mining and petroleum business, 1874-. Mem. Pa. Ho. of Rep., 1881-87, Senate, 1887-1911; mem. 63d Congress (1913-15), 28th Dist., Pa. (Progressive), and 66th Congress (1919-21). Republican. Served pvt. to brig. gen. Pa. N.G., 1876-1912; col. 16th Pa. Vol. Inf., Spanish-Am. War; promoted brig. gen. vols., "for meritorious conduct in action," Aug. 9, 1898; disch. from vols., Jan. 1, 1899; comd. 2d Brigade N.G.Pa., 1907-13. Was 1st comdr.-in-chief Nat. Assn. Spanish-Am. War Vets., 2 yrs. Home: Oil City, Pa. Deceased.

HULL, GORDON FERRIE physicist; b. Garnet, Haldimand County, Ont., Oct. 7, 1870; s. John and Jane (Moore) H.; A.B., U. Toronto, 1892, fellow in physics, 1892-95; fellow and asst. in physics U. Chgo., 1895-97, Ph.D., 1897; Cambridge U., 1905-06; studied at English and German univs., 1928-29; m. Wilhelmine Brandt, Sept. 5, 1911; 1 son, Gordon Ferrie. Taught in Hamilton Collegiate Inst., 1890-91; instr. physics U. Chgo., 1897-98, and summers 1898-99; prof. physics Colby Coll., 1899-1903, prof. 1903-40, prof. meritus, 1940—, active service, 1941-44; prof. physics Columbia, summer sessions 1909-15. Maj. Ordnance Dept., U.S. Army, 1918-19, head math, and dynamics sect., staff Ordnance Dept., 1919-20, cons. physicist, tech. staff, 1920—. Fellow Am. Acad. Arts and Sciences, A.A.A.S.; mem. Am. Phys. Soc., etc. Author: Survey of Modern Physics, 1936; Elementary Modern Physics, 1948. Contbr. various sci. jours. on radiation. Home: 5 Parkway, Hanover, N.H. Died Oct. 7, 1956.

HULL, ISAAC naval officer; b. Huntington, Conn., Mar. 9, 1773; s. Lt. Joseph and Sarah (Bennet) H.; m. Anna Hart, Jan. 2, 1813, no children. Commanded 1st ship before age of 21, 1793; commd. lt. U.S. Navy, 1798; served on frigate Constitution during naval war with France; commanded ships Enterprise and Argus during war with Tripoli; promoted comdr., 1804; assisted Gen. William Eaton in attacking and seizing Derna in Libya, 1805; commd. capt., 1806; in command of Constitution, 1810. 1810, noted for defeating and compelling surrender of Brit. frigate Guerrier during War of 1812 (1st important naval action of war); commanded Boston Navy Yard, Portsmouth Navy Yard, 1812-15; apptd. naval commr., resigned to return to Boston Navy Yard; commanded Pacific Station; commd. commodore; comdt. Washington (D.C.) Navy Yard, 1829-35; chmn. Bd. of 1838; in command Mediterranean Station, 1839-41. Died Phila., - Feb. 13, 1843; buried Laurel Hill Cemetery, Phila.

HULL, JOHN ADLEY army officer, lawyer; b. Bloomfield, Ia., Aug. 7, 1874; s. John Albert Tiffin and Emma Gertrude (Gregory) H.; Ph.B., State U. of Ia., 1895, LL.B., 1896; m. Norma Bowler King, Sept. 21, 1919 (divorced 1934); 1 son, John Bowler. Admitted to Ia. bar, 1896, and practiced law at Des Moines, Ia.; while serving as capt. Ia. Nat. Guard apptd. lt. col. judge adv. vols., May 9, 1898; hon. disch. Apr. 17, 1899; maj. judge adv., Apr. 17, 1899, vacated, Apr. 4, 1901; maj. judge adv., U.S. Army, Feb. 2, 1901; lt. col., Apr. 16, 1903; col., Feb. 15, 1911; apptd. judge adv. gen. with rank of maj. gen., Nov. 15, 1928; legal adviser to gov. gen., P.I., 1930-32; asso. justice Supreme Court of P.I., 1932-36. Served in World War as judge advocate, S. of S., also as dir. Rents, Requisition and Claims Service and finance officer A.E.F., in France. Awarded D.S.M. (United States); Comdr. St. Michael and St. George (Great Britain); Officer Legion of Honor (France); Order of St. Peter (Serbia); Royal Aman (Indo-China). Mem. Phi Kappa Psi. Mason. Clubs: Alfalfa, Army and Navy, Chevy Chase (Washington). Address: Army and Navy Club, Washington, D.C. Died Apr. 17, 1944.

HULL, ROGER BENTON lawyer: b. Greenfield, Mass., Feb. 18, 1885; s. Arthur Norton and Frances Roe (Benton) H.; A.B., Yale, 1907; LL.B., Harvard, 1911; married Miriam Marsh, Sept. 23, 1913: children-Beverly Marsh and Nancy Norton; m. 2d, Amelia Goodyear Crim, June 25, 1937. Admitted to New York bar, 1911; asst. atty. gen. of Puerto Rico, 1911-14; spl. counsel to the Insular Pub. Service Commn., 1912-14; spl. asst. to the atty. gen. of U.S., 1914-17; asso. Chadburne, Babbitt and Wallace, 1919-24; gen. atty. New York Rys. Corp., 1925-27; gen. counsel Nat. Assn. of Life Underwriters, 1927-. Awarded Thatcher prize, Demosthenes and De Forest medals (Yale), 1907. Republican. Conglist. Home: New York, N.Y. Died Jan. 23, 1942.

HULL, WILLIAM territorial gov., army officer; b. Derby, Conn., June 24, 1753; s. Joseph and Eliza (Clark) H.; grad. Yale, 1772, A.M. (hon.), 1779; A.M., (hon.) Harvard, 1787; m. Sarah Fuller, 1781, 1 adopted son, Isaac (naval hero). Admitted to Conn. bar, 1775; joined Continental Army as capt. Derby Militia, 1775, advanced through grades to maj., lt. col.; served in battles of White Plains, Trenton, Princeton, Saratoga, Monmouth and Stony Point; helped suppress Shay's Rebellion, 1787; judge Mass. Ct. Common Pleas, circa 1790; mem. Mass. Senate, 1790-1805; an organizer Soc. of Cincinnati; gov. Mich. Territory (apptd. by Pres. Jefferson), 1805-12; brig. gen. U.S. Army in command of defense of Mich. and attack on upper Can., 1812; surrendered to Gen. Isaac Brock after Futile attack upon British in upper Can., at Detroit without even giving battle 1812; court martialed, found guilty of cowardice and neglect of duty, sentenced to death; vindicated, 1824. Died Newton, Mass., Nov. 29, 1825.

HUMBER, ROBERT LEE, lawyer; b. Greenville, N.C., May 30, 1898; s. Robert Lee and Lena Clyde (Davis) H.; A.B., Wake Forest, 1918, LL.B., Rhodes scholar from N.C., Oxford (Eng.) U., 1923; 1921, LL.D., 1949, M.A., Harvard, 1926; B. Litt. Am. field service fellow, U. of Paris, 1926-28; LL.D., U. N.C., 1958; H.H.D., Duke, 1967; m. Lucie Berthier, Oct. 16, 1929; children—Marcel Berthier, John Leslie. Admitted to N.C. bar, 1920; tutor dept. of govt. history and economics Harvard, 1919-20; lawyer and bus. exec., Paris, France, 1930-40. Founded at Davis Island, N.C., Dec. 1940, Movement for World Federation whose principles and objectives were embodied in a resolution, approving World Federation, that has been passed by 16 State Legislatures of U.S. Rep. Southern Council on Internat. Relations, UN Orgnl. Conf., San Francisco 1945. Co-founder, United World Federalists, 1947, v.p., 1947-50, mem. nat. exec. council, 1947-49, mem. exec. council N.C. br., 1949-70, pres. N.C. br., 1960-66; mem. adv. bd. Am. Freedom Assn., 1953-66, bd. dirs., 1966-70 v.p. N.C. Bapt. State Conv., 1947; mem. N.C. Gov.'s Study Com. in Vocational Rehab., 1967-69; state chmn. UN Day, 1969; mem. Pitt County Good Neighbor Council, 1969-70, N.C. Council on Prevention of Crime and Delinquency, 1968-69; trustee, Meredity Coll., 1947-50; trustee Wake Forest Coll., 1951-54, 59-60, pres. bd., chmn. exec. com., 1960, hon. life trustee, 1969-70; chmn. N.C. Art Commn., 1951-60; chmn. N.C. Arts Council, 1964-67; pres. N.C. Mus. Art Found., 1969-70; mem. N.C. Mus. Bldg. Commn., 1967-70; pres. Tar River Basin Assn., 1965-70; bd. dirs. Am. and Fgn. Christian Union, Inc., 1941-70, Pitt County chpt. A.R.C., 1957-70; mem. adv. bd. Raleigh Historic Sites Found., 1966-68; mem. cultural and lit. centennial adv. com. N.C. State Coll., 1961-62; mem. Pitt. County Devel. Commn., 1959-70, N.C. Rhodes Scholarship Com., 1946-60, 63, Greenville Com. of 100, N.C. Commn. on Interstate Cooperation, 1959-60; bd. dirs. Pitt County United Fund, 1965-70, pres., 1964-65; co-chmn. Greenville Citizens Awareness Com., 1970; mem. cultural arts adv. council N.C. Dept. Pub. Instrn., 1970; mem. Sir Walter Raleigh Commn., 1947-70, chmn. exec. com., 1952-60; mem. exec. com. N.C. Council on World Affairs, 1966; mem. adv. com. N.C. State Library-Community Project, 1958-60, Topographic Mapping of N.C., 1963; mem. com. on art, lit. and music N.C. Planning Bd., 1944; mem. Adv. Com. on Hwy. Safety, 1950; past chmn. Prudential Com. Am. Ch. in Paris; mem. Edenton Hist. Commn., chmn., 1962-70; bd. dirs. Coastal Plains Planning and Devel. Commn., 1962-65, 69-70 chmn., 1962-64; chmn. bd. trustees N.C. Mus. Art, 1961-70; mem. N.C. Conservatory Com., 1962-63, N.C. State Capital Planning Commn., 1962-65, Heritage Sq. Commn., 1962-67; trustee N.C. Symphony; 1955-70, mem. exec. com., 1963-65, 67-70; mem. Tryon Palace Commn., 1956-70; trustee Pitt County Indsl. Edn. Center, 1963-64; chmn. bd. Pitt Tech. Inst., 1964-70. Mem. N.C. Senate, 1959-64. as 2d lt., F.A., U.S. Army, 1918. Recipient World Govt. News medal for most outstanding service by an individual to World Fedn., 1948, Am. War Dads prize for greatest single contbn. toward world peace, 1948; certificate of merit Thomas Gilcrease Inst. Am. History and Art, 1955; Citizen of Month award for meritorious service N.C. Joint Council on Health and Citizenship, 1961; Salmagund: Art Achievement medal, 1966; Peace award Am. Freedom Assn., 1967; N.C. award for public service, 1968. Mem. Am., N.C., Pitt County bar assns., Am. Judicature Soc., Am. Soc. Internat. Law, Am. Acad. Polit. and Social Sci., Acad. Polit. Sci. (life), Nat. Forensic League (hon.), N.C. Farm Bur., Internat. Platform Assn., Am. Legion, Greenville C. of C. and Mchts. Assn., N.C. Music Soc., East Carolina U. Alumni Assn. (life), Pitt County Hist. Soc. (pres. 1964-68), East Carolina Art Soc. (dir. 1956-64), N.C. Soc. for Preservation Antiquities (life), Nat. Trust for Historic Preservation, Pitt County Execs. Club (pres. 1961-63), N.C. Art Soc. (dir. 1945-70, exec. com. 1947-61, chmn. 1949-61, pres. 1955-61; certificate of merit and achievement 1956 N.C. Trustees Assn. Community Edn. Instns. (pres. 1968-70), N.C. Lit. and Hist. Assn. (pres. 1950-51), Roanoke Island Hist. Assn. (dir. 1955-61, chmn. 1955-59), Phi Beta Kappa, Omicron Delta Kappa, Sigma Phi Epsilon, Phi Delta Phi, Epsilon Pi Tau, Sigma Pi Alpha. Democrat. Baptist. Clubs: Greenville Music; Rotary; Watauga (Raleigh, N.C.); Harvard, Century Assn., Salmagundi (N.Y.C.); American resolution: The Declaration of the Federation of the World. (Paris, France). Author of Home: Greenville NC Died Nov. 10, 1970; buried Cherry Hill Cemetery, Greenville NC

HUMBERT, JEAN JOSEPH AMABLE army officer, adventurer; b. Rouvray, France, Nov. 25, 1775. Entered French Army, 1792; gen. of brigade, 1794; aided in suppressing Vendée Revolt; fought for Irish, 1798; served in Santo Domingo; came to U.S., 1814; took part in Battle of New Orleans on U.S. side; fought in Mexico on various filibuster expdns. Died New Orleans, Jan. 2, 1823; buried St. Louis Cemetery, New Orleans.

HUMBIRD, JOHN ALEXANDER lumberman; b. Hudson, Wis., May 29, 1888; s. Thomas Jacob and Agnes (Hyslop) H.; student Northwestern Mil. and

Naval Acad., Lake Geneva, Wis., 1902-06, Princeton, 1907-09; m. Hedvig Pearson, Nov. 19, 1920; children-Dorothy Jane (Mrs. James D. Donlon), Virginia (Mrs. Julian A. Dickey), Jerry, James. Various positions with the Humbird Lbr. Co., 1904-10, assistant manager, 1911-17, general mgr., 1919-23; v.p. gen. mgr. Victoria Lumber Co., 1924-50; pres., dir. Seaboard Lumber Sales, Seaboard Shipping Co., 1935-46; v.p. Potlatch Forests, 1957, also dir.; dir. Victoria Lumber & Mfg. Co., 1924-50, Gen. Ins. Co., 1923-, Gen. America Co., 1920-, First Nat. Ins. Co., 1923-, SafeCo. Ins. Co., 1954-. Trustee John A. Humbird Estate, 1954-. Served from 1st lt. to capt., 26th Div., U.S. Army, 1917-19; AEF. Decorated Purple Heart, D.S.C., Silver Star; Legion of Honor, Croix de Guerre (France). Home: 491 Eastcot Rd., West Vancouver, B.C., Can. Died Feb. 25, 1963.

HUME, DAVID, lawyer; b. Eagle Pass, Tex., Oct. 2, 1915; s. David E. and Lupita (James) H.; B.A., U. Tex., 1937; student Temple U. Sch. Law, 1939-41; LL.B. with honors, So. Meth. U. Sch. Law, 1939-41; LL.B. with honors, So. Meth. U., 1946; m. F. Arlee Eaton, Aug. 28, 1943 (div.); children—David III, Stephen; m. 2d, Margaret Williams, June 19, 1966; 1 dau., Marge Ann. Admitted to Tex. bar, 1946, D.C., Md. bars, 1954, U.S. Supreme Ct., 1948, also Ct. Mil. Justice, FCC, ICC; trial atty. U.S. Dept. Justice, 1947, spl. asst. to atty. gen. U.S., 1948; with firm Steptoe & Johnson, Washington, 1954-58; mem. firm Hume & Stewart, Washington, 1958-65, Hume & Hume, Eagle Pass, Tex., 1965-72. Hon. cons. to Consulate of Republic of Mex., 1970. Rep. Am. Bar Assn., 12th Inter-Am. Bar Assn. conv. Bogota, Colombia, 1961. Mem. Md. Bd. Natural Resources. Chmn. Democratic Party So. Md., 1958, treas., 1958-60; mem. Dem. Nat. Adv. Council, 1958-60; candidate for Gov. Md., 1962. Bd. dirs. Balt. Civic Opera. Served with Submarine Service, USNR, World War II, Korean War; capt. Res. Decorated Bronze Star. Mem. Am., Inter-Am., Md. bar assns., Tex. Trial Lawyers Assn., State Bar Texas, Border Bar Assn. (dir.), Judge Adv. Assn. Am. Vets. Com., Am. Legion, Navy League, S.A.R., Md. Hist. Soc., Izaak Walton League. Clubs: Terrapin (U. Md.); Jefferson Island (St. Mary's County, Md.); Marlboro Hunt (Prince George's County, Md.); Taylor's Landing Rod and Gun (Washington County, Md.); Hawthorne Country (Charles County, Md.). Author numerous articles on conservation, govt. and agrarian reform, Latin Am. Home: Eagle Pass TX Died Oct. 7, 1972.

HUME, EDGAR ERSKINE army officer; b. Frankfort, Ky., Dec. 26, 1889; s. Enoch Edgar (M.D.) and Mary (South) H.; B.A., Centre Coll., Ky., 1908, M.A., 1909; M.D., Johns Hopkins, 1913, Dr.P.H., 1924; D.M., U. Munich, 1914, U. Rome, 1915; 1st honor grad. Army Med. Sch., 1917; M.P.H., Harvard and Mass. Inst. Tech., 1921; D.T.M., Harvard, 1922; grad. U.S. Infantry Sch., 1928; hon. degrees from Centre Coll., U. Ky., Georgetown U., William and Mary, Hampden-Sydney, Washington and Lee, Transylvania U., Dickinson, Louisville, Washington and Jefferson, univs. of Naples, Rome, Florence, Bologna, Modena, Milan, Pisa, Slena, Chile, San Marcos (Peru), Paris, Madrid, and Leon (Nicaragua); grad. U.S. Army Medical Field Service Sch., 1936; m. Mary Swigert Hendrick, 1918 (deceased); 1 son, Edgar Erskine. Commd. 1st lt. Med. Corps, U.S. Army, 1916: promoted through grades to maj. gen., 1949. Staff Johns Hopkins Hosp., 1913-14; med. dir. Am. Relief Expdn. to Italy after earthquake, 1915: dir. dept. sociology, Disciplinary Barracks, Ft. Leavenworth, Kan., 1917; executive, Div. of Sanitation in Surgeon Gen.'s Office, 1917-18; Cocomdg. officer U.S. Army Hospitals, with Italian Army; with Brit. Expeditionary Forces, 1918; at Meuse-Argonne, St. Mihiel and Vittorio-Veneto (wounded): chief med. officer (dir. typhus fever campaign) and Am. Red Cross Commr. for Serbia, 1919-20; in charge Army Lab. for N.E., Boston, 1920-22; editor Index Catalog Army Med. Library, Washington, 1922-26; med. insp. Infantry Sch., Ft. Benning, Ga., 1926-30; insp. Mass. and N.H. Nat. Guards, 1930-32; librarian Army Med. Library, 1932-36: dir. of adminstrn. Med. Field Service Sch., Carlisle, Pa., 1937-42; comdg. officer, Winter Gen. Hosp., Topeka, Kan., 1942-43: in African, Sicilian and Italian invasions (wounded): chief of public health, Sicily, 1943; chief Allied Mil. Govt., 5th Army, Italy, 1943-45; chief Mil. Govt. U.S. Zone, Austria, 1945-47; chief reorientation br. Dept. of Army, 1947-49; chief surgeon Far East Command, 1949-51, U.N., Korea, 1950-51; ret. for age, Dec. 31, 1951. Editor Mil. Surg., 1922; lectr. in med. history Georgetown Univ. and Univ. of Kan.; U.S. Army del. to Internat. Congress of Mil. Medicine, Paris, 1925, London, 1929, The Hague, 1931, Madrid, 1933, Brussels, 1935, Mexico, 1936, Bucharest, 1937, Washington, 1939, Basle, 1947. Stockholm, 1948 (nat. corr. for these congresses). Awarded D.S.M. (three), Silver Star (four), Legion of Merit, Purple Heart (four) Bronze Star (four), Soldier's Medal, Commendation ribbon (four), Air Medal (two), Typhus Medal (U.S.); also decorations from France, Gt. Britain, Belgium, China, Turkey, Philippines, Jugoslavia, Brazil, Russia, Bolivia, Sweden, Ecuador, Bulgaria, Tunis, Nicaragua, Denmark, Peru, Lithuania, Colombia, Norway, Haiti, Vatican, Esthonia, Cuba, Hungary, Chile, Netherlands, Finland, Venezuela, Latvia, Italy, Serbia, Panama, Poland, Spain, Greece, Czechoslovakia, Portugal, lMontenegro, Luxembourg, Roumania, Korea; Bali Grand Cross of Soverign Mil. Order of Malta; Sir Henry Wellcome prize, 1933; Oberlaender fellow to Germany, 1937; Gorgas Medal, 1948; hon. prof. U. Warsaw; hon. col. Royal Serbian Army; hon. cpl. French Army; hon. citizen of 40 Italian and Austrian cities. Mem. Soc. of Cincinnati (pres. gen.), Aztec Club (pres), Kappa Alpha, Phi Beta Kappa, Sigma Xi, Alpha Omega Alpha, Delta Omega (founder; nat. pres. 1926), Omicron Delta Kappa, etc.; fellow Am. Acad. Arts and Sciences, Royal Soc. of Edinburgh, Royal Soc. Tropical Med. and Hygiene, Am. Coll. Surgeons, Am. Pub. Health Assn., Am. Coll. Physicians, Royal Italian Soc. Hygiene, Soc. Antiquaries of Scotland, academies of science of Spain, Mexico and Philadelphia, Assn. of Mil. Surgeons (pres.), academies of medicine of Rome, Washington (charter), Mex., Rio, Lima, Madrid, Swedish Soc. Anthropology, Royal Soc. of Naples, Accademia Pontiniana (Naples). Diplomate Am. bds. Neurology, Preventive Medicine and Internal Medicine. Clubs: Union (Tokyo, Japan); Army and Navy, Cosmos, Chevy Chase (Washington); Lambs, Metropolitan, Union, Explorers (N.Y.); Pithotomy (Baltimore): St. Botolph (Boston): Caccia (Rome); Cercle Militaire (Paris); Royal Soc. (London). Author of about 400 books and papers, including The Med. Book of Merit; Pettenkofer's Theory; Military Operations on the Italian Front (also Italian transl.): A Colonial Scottish Jacobite Family; Sanitation in War Planning; various papers on the Soc. of Cincinnati, Fighting Typhus Fever in Serbia; Preparation of Potable Water for Field, Heros von Borcke, Italy's Part in World War, Theodore O'Hara, Sandfly Fever, History and Work of Army Med. Library, Med. Service inCombined Army and Navy Operations, Med. Work of Knights Hospitallers, Ornithologists of Army Med. Corps, General Washington's Correspondence, Victories of Army Medicine, War and Medicine, Vesuvius Eruption of 1944, Medicine Goes to War, etc. Asso. editor Annals of Medical History. Contbr. to Ency. Brit., Ency. Am., Tice's Practice of Medicine, Dictionary of Am. Biography. Believed to be most decorated soldier in U.S. history. Home: Frankfort, Ky. Address: care Soc. of the Cincinnati, 2118 Massachusetts Av., Washington 8. Died Jan. 24, 1952; buried Arlington Nat. Cemetery.

HUMPHREY, CHARLES congressman; b. Little Britain, N.Y., Feb. 14, 1792; attended Newburgh (N.Y.) Acad.; studied law. Entered U.S. Army at beginning of War of 1812, served as capt. 41st Regt., U.S. Inf.; admitted to N.Y. bar, 1816; moved to Ithaca, N.Y., 1818, practiced law; mem. U.S. Ho. of Reps. (Democrat) from N.Y., 19th Congress, 1825-27; pres. Village of Ithaca, 1828-29; surrogate of Tompkins County (N.Y.), 1831-34; mem. N.Y. Assembly, 1834-35, 42, speaker, 1835-56; clk. N.Y. Supreme Ct., 1843-47. Died Albany, N.Y., Apr. 17, 1850; buried City Cemetery, Ithaca.

HUMPHREY, CHARLES FREDERIC maj. gen.; b. New York, Sept. 2, 1844. Pvt. corporal, sergt. and 1st sergt. Co. E, 5th Arty., Mar. 17, 1863-June 28, 1866; commd. 2d lt. 5th Arty., May 8, 1866: transferred to 4th Arty., Oct. 23, 1866; 1st lt., May 21, 1868; grad. Arty. Sch., 1874: capt. asst. q.-m., June 23, 1879; maj. q.-m., Dec. 11, 1892; lt. col. deputy q.-m. gen., Oct. 15, 1897; col. q.-m. vols., July 7-Sept. 20, 1898; brig. gen., Sept. 21, 1898; hon. disch. from vol. service, June 12, 1899; col. asst. q.-m. gen., Oct. 26, 1901; brig. gen. q.-m.-gen. U.S.A., Apr. 12, 1903; maj. gen. and retired after over 44 yrs.' service, July 1, 1907. Served in following Indian campaigns; Nez Percé, 1877; Snake Bannock, 1878; Sioux, 1890-91; Shoshone-Snake, 1895. Bvtd. capt., Feb. 27, 1890, "for gallant service in action against Indians" at the Clearwater, Ida., July 11, 1877; awarded Congressional Medal of Honor, Mar. 22, 1897, "for most distinguished gallantry" in action at the Clearwater, Ida., July 11, 1877, when he voluntarily and successfully conducted, in the fact of a withering fire, a party which recovered possession of an abandoned howitzer and 2 Gatling guns lying between the lines and within a few yards of the Indians, while serving as 1st lt., 4th U.S. Arty. Was chief q.-m. Santiago de Cuba Expdn., 1898, Div. of Cuba, 1898-99, Chinese Relief Expdn., 1900-01. Philippines, 1901-03. Home: Washington, D.C. Died June 4, 1926.

HUMPHREY, CHARLES FREDERICK, JR., army officer; b. Washington, D.C., Aug. 11, 1876; s. Charles Frederick and Juanita DaCosta (Foster) H.; ed. in pub. schs.; grad. Sch. of the Line, 1921, Gen. Staff Sch., 1922, Army War Coll., 1923; m. Helen Kingsbury, Sept. 16, 1903; 1 dau., Helen Elizabeth. Entered U.S. Army as 2d lt. inf., July 20, 1898; advanced through grades to brig. gen., Aug. 9, 1935; served as col. inf., Nat. Army, A.E.F., World War. 1917-19; mem. Gen. Staff Corps, 1923-27, and 1929-33; retired Mar. 31, 1940. Episcopalian. Home: San Antonio TX Died Jan. 1968.

HUMPHREY, EVAN H., army officer; b. Calif., Mar. 5, 1875; grad. U.S. Military Acad., 1899; commd. 2d lt. Cavalry, 1899; advanced through grades to brig. gen., Feb. 7, 1935; retired Mar. 31, 1939. Address: 136 Harrigan Court, San Antonio TX

HUMPHREYS, ANDREW ATKINSON engr., soldier, scientist; b. Phila., Nov. 2, 1810; s. Samuel and Letitia (Atkinson) H.; grad. U.S. Mil. Acad., 1831; LL.D. (hon.), Harvard; m. Rebecca Hollingsworth, 1839, 4 children. Commd. lt. arty., U.S. Army, 1831, served as civil engr. in Corps Topog. Engrs.; planned Delaware River fortifications and harbor works, 1837-38; commd. lt. Corps Topog. Engrs., 1838; assigned to duty in Coast Survey, 1844; commd. capt., 1848, maj. on McClellan's staff, 1861; commd. maj. gen., chief of staff Army of Potomac, 1863-64; commd. brig. gen. U.S. Volunteers, chief Topog. Engrs., fought at battles of Fredericksburg and chancellorsville, commanded Union div. at Battle of Gettysburg and corps in operations around Gettysburg, 1864-65; commd II Army Corps, 1864; chief C.E. with rank brig. gen., 1866-79, brevetted col. Battle of Fredericksburg, brig. gen. Battle of Gettysburg, maj. gen. Battle of Sailor's Creek. Mem. Am. Philos. Soc., Am. Acad. Arts and Scis.; incorporator Nat. Acad. Scis. Died Washington, D.C., Dec. 27, 1883.

HUMPHREYS, BENJAMIN GRUBB army officer, gov. Miss.; b. Clairborne County, Miss., Aug. 24-26, 1808; s. George Wilson and Sarah (Smith) H.; ed. U.S. Mil. Acad.; m. Mary McLaughlin 1832; m. 2d, Mildred Hickman, Dec. 1839; 14 children. Mem. Miss. Legislature from Claiborne County, 1838-40, Miss. Senate, 1840-44; commd. capt. 21st Miss. Regt., Confederate Army, 1861; col., led regt. through major battles of Army N. Va.; achieved distinction at Gettysburg and Fredericksburg; brig. gen. commanding 21st, 3, 17th, 18th Miss. regts. McLaw's Div., Longstreet's Corps, Army No. Va., 1863; gov. Miss. 1865-68 (famous Black Code passed during this period, effecting his removal and downfall of local govt.). Died Ita Bena, Miss., Dec. 20, 1882; buried Port Gibson, Miss.

HUMPHREYS, FRANK LANDON chaplain, author; b. Auburn, N.Y., June 16, 1858; s. Dr. Frederick and Frances M. (Sperry) H.; A.M., St. Stephen's Coll., 1883, Mus. Doc., 1888; S.T.D., Hobart Coll., 1894; LL.D., U. of Maryland, 1915; m. Jean Todd, Apr. 29, 1886; children-Landon, Malcolm, George, David. Deacon, 1879, priest, 1883, P.E. Ch.; asst. Ch. of Heavenly Rest, New York, 1879-81; rector Short Hills, N.J., 1883-85; precentor in charge Cathedral of Incarnation, Garden City, 1885-90; canon Cathedral St. John the Divine, New York, 1900-06. Acting chaplain U.S. Mil. Acad., 1897; gen. sec. Ch. Univ. Bd. of Regents, 1894-1900; sec. Parochial Fund, Diocese of New York, 1898. Chaplain Soc. of the Nazarene; gen. chaplain Soc. of the Cincinnati, 1896-; chaplain Naval Order of U.S., Soc. of 1812, 1895-. Naval Reserves (U.S.S. Portsmouth); staff chaplain Naval Reserve rank comdr., World War, -, also was comdr. in the line, N.J. Naval Militia, Spanish-Am. War; chaplain N.Y. Soc. S.R. 27 yrs.; chaplain for spl. service, U.S. Naval Res.; historian Soc. Colonial Wars 15 yrs.; pres. Soc. of Cincinnati in N.J. 10 yrs. Officer Legion of Honor (France), 1921; medal Reconnaissance (France); Officer French Acad., decorated with palms; Knight Comdr. Order St. George, 1929; Comdr. of Order of St. Lazare (Italy); Commander of our Lady of Bethlehem. Mayor of City of Boynton, Fla. Author: What We Owe to France, 1915; Life and Times of David Humphreys, 1917; Ce Que Nous Devoir a la France, 1922; France and America (are our present negotiations worthy of American traditions?), 1926. Home: New Canaan, Conn., and Boynton, Fla. Died July 18, 1937.

HUNDLEY, JOHN ROBINSON, JR., steel co. exec.; b. St. Louis, Jan. 29, 1917; s. John Robinson and Emily (Shewell) H.; B.Sc. in Bus. Adminstrn., Washington U., St. Louis, 1939; m. Shirley Conrad, May 2, 1941; children—John Robinson III, Nancy Conrad (now Mrs. William F. Hecker), Stephen Thomas. Asst. v.p. Stouffer Corp., 1945-47; personnel dir. Owens-Ill. Glass Co., 1939-42; dir. indsl. relations Granite City Steel Co. (Ill.), 1947-63, v.p., 1963-72; dir. Cemrel, Inc. Mem. Ill. Gov.'s Com. on Unemployment, 1961; pub. mem. Ill. Commn. Aged and Aging, 1958-62; adv. com. Mo. Manpower Tng. and Devel. Act, 1962-72; chmn. Civil Service Commn. Met. Sewer Dist. St. Louis and St. Louis County; mem. citizens adv. com. Ill. State Bd. Higher Edn. chmn. Tri Cities United Fund., 1964-65. Bd. dirs. Washington U., 1958-61, Works Opportunities Unltd.; adv. bd. So. Ill. U. Served to col. USAAF, World War II. Decorated Air medal; recipient spl. merit award for outstanding community service St. Louis Indsl. Relations Club, 1959. Mem. Am. Iron and Steel Inst., Indsl. Relations Club St. Louis (past pres.), Ill. C. of C., Newcomen Soc. Presbyn. (elder). Clubs: Mo. Athletic, Old Warson Country. Home: St Louis MO Died Apr. 8, 1972.

HUNGERFORD, CLARK railroad exec.; b. Jackson, Tenn., Dec. 22, 1899; s. Homer Leslie and Lizzie Phillips (Clark) H.; grad. Porter Mil. Acad., Charleston, S.C., 1917; C.E., Princeton University, 1922; LL.D., University of Arkansas, 1950; Drury Coll., 1950; E.D., U. Mo., 1954; advanced mgmt. program U. Hawaii, 1954; m. Augusta Cannon, Nov. 3, 1926; children-Clark, Richard, Betty (Mrs. Jefferies M. Arrick). With So. Ry. Co., 1918-46, starting as transitman, served as gen. mgr. western lines, Cin., 1939-46; v.p. operations and maintenance Assn. of Am. Railroads, Washington, 1946; pres. St. Louis, San Francisco Ry. Co., St. Louis, San Francisco and Tex. Ry. Co., 1947-; chmn. board subsidiary roads; dir. subsidiary and affiliated ry. cos., also Merc. Trust Co., Merc.-Commerce Nat. Bank. Mem. grad. council Princeton U., trustee Princeton U., 1955-59. Pres. Municipal Theatre Assn., 1959-61, chmn., 1961-. Col. Transp. Corps, U.S. Army, 1950, brig. gen. U.S. Army Res., 1956-59, comdg. gen. 3d Transportation Command, 1956-59. Mem. several sometime officer profl. engring., ry. assns. Presbyn. Mason (32ff, K.T., Shriner). Clubs: Birmingham Traffic and Transportation, Downtown (Birmingham, Ala.); Cincinnati Traffic; Round Table, Mo. Athletic, St. Louis Traffic. St. Louis Country, Bogey, Princeton, Bellerive Country, Racquet, Noonday (pres. 1957). University (St. Louis); National Press, Metropolitan, Burning Tree (Washington); Saddle & Sirloin (Kansas City); Western Railway (Chicago). Home: 14 The Orchards, St. Louis 63132. Died Oct. 18, 1962; buried Oak Grove Cemetery, St. Louis.

HUNGERFORD, JOHN PRATT congressman; b. Leeds, Va., Jan. 2, 1761; studied law. Admitted to the bar, practiced law; served in Revolutionary War; mem. Va. Ho. of Dels., 1797-1801, 23-30, Va. Senate, 1801-09; mem. U.S. Ho. of Reps. from Va., 18th-14th congresses, 1813-17; served as brig. gen. Va. Militia during War of 1812. Died "Twiford," Westmoreland County, Va., Dec. 21, 1833; buried Hungerford Cemetery, Leedstown, Va.

HUNKER, JOHN JACOB rear admiral U.S.N.; b. Pittsburgh, Pa., June 12, 1844; s. Andrew and Margaret (Donaldson) H.; ed. Toledo High Sch. to 1861; grad. U.S. Naval Acad., 1866; m. Mary Monroe, Dec. 22, 1875. Served as pvt., Co. H, 1st Ohio Arty., for 7 months, 1861-62, in Civil War; midshipman, Naval Acad., 1862-66; ensign, Apr. 1868; master, Mar. 26, 1869; lt., Mar. 21, 1870; lt. comdr., Oct. 1870; comdr., Sept. 1894; capt., Dec. 11, 1900; rear admiral, June 6, 1906. Organized and comd. transport fleet and convoys assembled at Tampa, Fla., June 1898, to carry Shafter's army to Santiago, Cuba, during Spanish-Am. War; comdr. expdn. capturing Nipe Bay, Cuba, July 21, 1898, in Spanish-Am. War; advanced 3 numbers "for eminent and conspicuous conduct in battle"; retired, June 12, 1906. Home: Put-in-Bay, Ohio. Died Dec. 16, 1916.

HUNT, ERNEST LEROL surgeon; b. Abington, Mass., Nov. 11, 1877; s. Washington and Mary (Nickerson) H.; desc. Enoch Hunt, Newport, R.I., 1638; student Mass. Coll. of Pharmacy, Boston, 1894-95; M.D., Harvard, 1902; m. Isabel Girling, June 4, 1907 (dec.); children-Isabel (Mrs. James A. Dawson), Ethel Dorothy (Mrs. Joseph Navas), Mildred Elizabeth (Mrs. Charles Andrew Hall); m. 2d, Charlotte Alling; 1 son, Roger Alling. Practiced in Worcester since 1903; asst. pathologist, 1903-30, and dir. div. surgery Worcester City Hospital, 1919-33; consultant surgeon Worcester City Hospital, Worcester Memorial Hospital, Worcester State Hospital, Holden Hosp., Harrington Memorial Hosp., Day-Kimball Hosp.; surgeon-in-chief to Fairlawn Hosp.; pathologist U.S. Veterans' Hosp. 89, 1922-31; chmn. and chief of staff Worcester Cancer Clinic, 1929-46. Medical member Division 4, Worcester, U.S. Selective Service, 1918; captain Medical Corp, United States Army, active service, July 1918-March 22, 1919; lt. colonel Med. Res., U.S. Army, inactive since Nov. 11, 1941; formerly asso. med. examiner 11th Worcester Dist., resigned 1942; med. div. head, Region 3, Mass. Com. Public Safety, 1941. (Member governing bd. ednl. div. Worcester Y.M.C.A. (formerly Worcester Div. Northeastern U.) 1928-46; member board directors Worcester Free Pub. Library, 1938-42. Fellow Am. Coll. Surgeons, A.M.A., Mass. Med. Soc. (pres. Worcester District 1931-32; member New England Surgical Society (v.p. 1940-41), Massachusetts Medico-Legal Soc. (pres. 1926-28), N.E. Cancer Soc. (pres. 1939-40), Mass. Div. Am. Cancer Soc., Inc. (dir. 1943-48), Worcester Hist. Soc., The Gov. and Co. of Mass. Bay Colony in New England; mem. bd. dirs. Worcester chapter Am. Red Cross (chmn. 1930-35). Republican. Universalist. Mason, Odd Fellow. Clubs: Harvard (Boston & Worcester), U., Economic. Contbr. to surg. jours. Home: 20 Kenilworth Rd., Worcester; (summer) Saybrook, Conn. Office: 28 Pleasant St., Worcester, Mass. Died Jan. 17, 1948.

HUNT, HENRY JACKSON army officer; b. Detroit, Sept. 14, 1819; s. Lt. Fanuel Wellington and Julia (Herrick) H.; grad. U.S. Mil. Acad., 1839; m. Emily de Russy; 1 dau., Mary Craig. Commd. 2d lt. 2d Arty., U.S. Army, 1839, served in Mexican War; commd. capt., 1852; revised light mil. tactics, 1856; commd. maj. 5th Arty. and chief of arty. of Washington (D.C.) defenses; commd. col. in charge tng. arty. res. Army of Potomac, 1861; commd. brig. gen. U.S. Volunteers for his participation as arty. expert in Peninsular Campaign; helped break Pickett's charge by concentration of arty. fire at Battle of Gettysburg; in charge of siege of Petersburg; commd. col. 5th Arty., 1869; in command of Dept. of South, 1880-83; gov. Solider's Home, Washington, D.C., 1885. Died Washington, Feb. 11, 1889.

HUNT, JAMES RAMSAY M.D.; b. Phila., Pa., 1874; s. William R. and Eva (Ramsay) H.; M.D., U. of Pa., 1893, hon. Sc.D., 1931; studied Vienna, Berlin and Paris; m. Alice St. John Nolan, Sept. 26, 1908; children-James Ramsay, Alice St. John. Asso. prof. nervous diseases, Columbia, 1910-15; clin. prof. nervous diseases, Columbia, 1924; prof. clin. neurology, 1931-; director neuropsychiatric division, New York Neurol. Institute; cons. neurologist Psychiatric Inst., the Babies', N.Y. Eye and Ear and Lenox Hill hosps., and Letchworth Village for Mental Defectives; formerly cons. psychiatrist to Lying-In Hosp., New York Hospital and Randall's Island institutions. Consulting neuropathologist to Craig Colony for epileptics. Lt. Col. Medical Corps, U.S.A., World War; consultant in neuropsychiatry with A.E.F. Home: New York, N.Y. Died July 22, 1937.

HUNT, JAMES STONE, land developer; b. Detroit, Dec. 23, 1897; s. Charles F. and Ina F. (Simpson) H.; student Mich. Mil. Acad., 1913-16; Detroit Coll. Law, 1923-24; LL.D. (hon.), U. Miami (Fla.) 1962; m. Bessie C. Bidigare, May 7, 1924; children—James Stone, John Patrick. Automobile dealer, Detroit, 1924-45; chmn. bd. Coral Ridge Properties, developer, Ft. Lauderdale, Fla.; mng. dir. Royal Amsterdam N.V.; chmn. bd. Bank of Commerce, Ft. Lauderdale, 1962-72, Bank. of Fla., Ft. Lauderdale, 1963-72, also Atlantic Bond and Mortgage Co., Financial Life Ins. Co., Intercoastal Dredging Co., Financial Fire & Casualty Co., Royal Continental Hotels Corp.; dir. Alleghany Corp. (N.Y.C.), N.Y. Worlds Fair 1964-65 Corp., Investors Diversified Services (Mpls.), N.Y. Central R.R., N.Y.C. Commnr. Detroit Street Ry., 1930; price stabilizer for Pacific, 1947; dir. Fla. Devel. Commn. Chmn. Broward dist. Boy Scouts Am. 1954-55; hon. mem. lay adv. bd. Holy Cross Hosp., Ft. Lauderdale. Served with British Flying Corps, 1916-21; as comdr. USCG, 1941-45; rear adm. (ret.) Res., 1959. Decorated Silver Star; Distinguished Flying Cross (Great Britain); Croix de Guerre (France); Order St. Stanislas, Order St. Anne (N. Russian Expdn.); recipient Citizens award Ft. Lauderdale Daily News, 1953. Mem. Fla. C. of C. (dir.), Coast Guard League (comdr. 1948), War Birds of Royal Air Force. Mason (32 deg., Shriner). Clubs: Metropolitan (Washington); Circumnavigators, N.Y. Athletic, Metropolitan (N.Y.C.); Coral Ridge Yacht, Coral Ridge Country (Ft. Lauderdale); Coral Harbour Yacht (dir.) (Nassau, Bahamas); Nautico, Bankers San Juan, P.R.). Home: Fort Lauderdale FL Died 1972.

HUNT, LEROY PHILIP marine corps officer; b. Newark, N.J., Mar. 17, 1892; s. Philip Macedon and Charlotte Marsh (Hand) H.; student U. of Cal., 1911-13, Marine Corps Schs., 1929-30, Naval War Coll., 1938-39; m. Hazel Alma Orr, Nov. 7, 1914; 1 son, LeRoy Philip Jr. Joined U.S.M.C., 1917 as 2d lt., advanced through grades to lt. gen., 1949; served in France and Germany, World War I; U.S. fleet, Nicaragua, China, Iceland, Alaska, Panama, New Zealand, W.I., T.H., U.S., 1919-48; participated in campaigns on Guadalcanal, Saipan. Okinawa and occupation of Japan, World War II; comdg. gen., dept. of the Pacific, San Francisco, 1947-49; now comdg. gen. Fleet Marine Force, Atlantic. Awarded Navy Cross, D.S.C., Legion of Merit, Silver Star, Bronze Star, Purple Heart, Presidential unit citation, Croix de Guerre, Fourragere (France), Medal of Distinction (Nicaragua). Mem. Phi Gamma Delta. Home: 535 Dillingham Blvd., Naval Base, Norfolk 11, Va. Died Feb. 8, 1968.

HUNT, LESTER CALLAWAY U.S. senator: b. Isabel, Ill., July 8, 1892; s. William and Viola (Callaway) H.: student Ill. Wesleyan U., Bloomington, Ill., 1912-13; D.D.S., St. Louis U., 1917; post grad., Northwestern U., 1920; LL.D., University of Wyoming, 1950; married Emily Nathelle Higby, February 38, 1918: children-Elise Nila, Lester Callaway. Dentist, Lander, Wyo., 1917-34; sec. of state, Wyo., 1935-43, gov., 1943-49, U.S. senator from Wyoming, January 1949—. Chmn. governor's conf., 1948-49. Served as first lieutenant, captain and major, Dental Corps., United States Army, 1917-19. Pres. State Bd. Dental Examiners, 1924-28. Dir. U. Wyo. Named Dentist of Year, 1951. Fellow International (hon.), Am. colls. dentists; mem. Pierre Fauchard Acad., Mem. Am. Dental Assn., State Dental Soc. (pres., 1927), Am. Legion, Psi Omega Tau Kappa Epsilon. Mason (32ff, Shriner), Elk, Eagle. Sponsor Wyoming Guide, 1941. Sponsor Wyoming Hist., Blue Book, 1946. Originated and designed Wyoming's unique "bucking horse" license plate, 1936. Home: 5105 Linnean. Office: 304 Senate Office Bldg., Washington. Died June 19, 1954; buried, Cheyenne, Wyo.

HUNT, LIVINGSTON naval officer; b. New Orleans, La., Nov. 3, 1859; s. William Henry and Elizabeth Augusta (Ridgely) H.; prep. edn., Hopkins Grammar Sch., New Haven, Conn.; student Harvard 1 yr., class of '81; m. Catharine Howland Hunt, July 7, 1921; 1 son, Livingston. Apptd. by President Arthur to Pay Corps, U.S. Navy, 1881; on U.S.S. New Orleans, Spanish-Am. War; promoted through grades to rank of rear adm. (by selection), July 7, 1921; retired June 1, 1923. Clubs: Clam Bake (Newport, R.I.); Army and Navy (New York). Contbr. articles on naval history. Home: 80 Catherine St., Newport, R.I. Died Jan. 18, 1943.

HUNT, O(RA) E(LMER), army officer (ret.); b. nr. Napa, Calif., June 26, 1872; s. Frank Martin and Mary Ellen (Southard) H.; B.S., U.S. Mil. Acad., West Point, N.Y., 1894; distinguished grad. Inf. and Cav. Sch. (1906) and Staff Coll. (1907), Ft. Leavenworth, Kan.; m. Eva B. Smith, Jan. 1, 1896 (div. Aug. 18, 1927); children—Ora Leland, Edna Virginia (Mrs. Colin T. Penn), Margaret (Mrs. M. H. Pringle); m. 2d, Josephine W. Guion, Mar. 16, 1929; 1 dau., Katherine Guion. Commd. 2d lt. Inf., U.S. Army, June 12, 1894 and advanced through grades to brig. gen., Apr. 12, 1918; assigned to Vancouver (Wash.) Barracks, 1894-98; served in Philippines during Spanish War and Philippine Insurrection, 1898-1904; instr. dept. English and history, and dept. modern langs, U.S. Mil. Acad., West Point, N.Y., 1908-10, asst. prof. dept. modern langs., 1910-12, asso. prof. dept. modern langs., 1914-17; with troops at Texas City, Tex., enroute to Mex., 1912-14; sr. instr. Inf. tactics Officers Training Camp, Ft. Myer, Va., 1917; col. 320th Inf., 80th Div., Camp Lee, Va. 1917-18; brig. gen. comdg. 165th Brig., 83d Div., 1918; comdg. gen. 6th Brig., 3rd Div., in St. Mihiel and Meuse-Argonne offensives 1918 and in Army of Occupation, Germany, 1918-19; comdg. gen. 3d Div. Camp Pike, Ark., 1919; assigned to Inspector General's Dept., Washington, D.C., 1919-23; ret. 1923; mem. U.S. mission in Nicaragua supervising presidential elections, 1928. Awarded distinguised service medal, 1918, and silver star citation for services against Germany; U.S. Marine Corps medal for service in 2d Nicaraguan campaign. Mem. West Point Alumni Foundn. (New York). Republican. Presbyterian. Editor Vol. V, Photographic History of the Civil War (Review of Reviews Co., 1911); contbr. to this publ. Home: 443 Kentucky Av., Berkeley 7 CA

HUNT, RALPH HUDSON M.D.; b. Camden, Me., Dec. 9, 1869; s. Abel and Evelina (Knight) H.; A.B., Bowdoin, 1891, A.M., 1893; M.D., Med. Sch. of Me. (Bowdoin), 1894; m. May Williams, June 6, 1903; 1 dau., May Hayward. Began practice, Portland, Me., 1894; removed to East Orange, N.J., 1899; attending phys., Orange Memorial Hosp., and phys.-in-chief to tuberculosis dispensary of same; mem. East Orange Bd. of Health, 1907-; pres. Essex Co. Mosquite Extermination Commn. Hosp. steward, Essex Troop 1st Troop, N.G.N.J., 1905-09; commd. capt., Med. R.C., May 15, 1917; Med. O.T.C., Camp Greenleaf, Ft. Oglethorpe, Ga., Aug. 2, 1917; maj., M.C., U.S.A., Jan. 15, 1918; lt. col., May 2, 1919; regtl. surgeon 22d Cav. to Nov. 20, 1917, 80th F.A. to June 20, 1919; overseas service, Aug. 22, 1918-June 20, 1919; pres. med. bd., Camp Merritt, N.J., to Sept. 12, 1919. Unitarian. Fellow Am. Coll. Phys. Mason. Home: East Orange, N.J. Died July 9, 1928.

HUNT, WESTLEY MARSHALL otolaryngologist; b. Auburn, Me., Sept. 1, 1888; s. Edward Everett and Ellen Matilda (Anderson) H.; B.S., Dartmouth, 1910, M.D., 1913; grad. St. Luke's Hosp. and S.I. Hosp., N.Y.C.; post-grad. study, Vienna; m. Emily H. Callaway, Feb. 27, 1920. Instr. N.Y.U. and Bellevue Med. Coll., 1920-22, lectr., 1922-25, clin. prof. otology, 1925-30; dir. dept. otolaryngology Fifth Av. Hosp., 1924-35; attending otolaryngologist and bronchopist St. Luke's Hosp., N.Y.C.; surgeon, director Manhattan Eye, Ear, and Throat Hosp.; cons. otolaryngologist Woman's Hosp., Huntington Hosp., S.I. Hosp., Nat. Hosp. for Speech Disorders, Ruptured and Crippled Hosp. Dir. Am. Bd. of Otolaryngology. Served as lt. (s.g.) USNRF, and maj. U.S. M.C., comdg. head surgery operating team, France, 1917-18. Past pres. New York League for the Hard of Hearing. Fellow A.C.S., N.Y. Acad. Medicine (past chmn. otolaryngology sect.); mem. A.M.A., Am. Laryngol. Assn., Am. Otol. Soc., Am. Broncho-Esophogological Assn. Am. Laryngol., Rhinol. and Otol. Soc. (v.p. eastern sect.), Clin. Research Soc. (pres. 1924), New York Bronchoscopic Club (pres. 1932), N.Y. Laryngol. Soc. (pres. 1942), Am. Acad. Ophthalmology and Oto-Laryngology, N.Y. Oto-Laryngol. Soc. (pres.), Soc. Colonial Ward (Lt. governor), S.R., - Officers World War, Assn. Mil. Surgeons of U.S., Order Founders and Patriots (past gov.), Soc. Mayflower Descendants of N.Y., (past gov.), Am. Legion (past comdr. Fiji Post), Alpha Kappa Kappa, Phi Gamma Delta. Republican. Conglist. Mason. Clubs: Ouill (pres. 1942), Sleepy Hollow, Megantic Fish and Game, Home: Northport, L.I. Office: 907 Fifth Av., N.Y.C. 21, Died June 28, 1950; buried Cathedral St. John Divine, N.Y.C.

HUNT, WILLIAM HENRY sec. of navy, diplomat; b. Charleston, S.C., June 12, 1823; s. Thomas and Louisa (Gaillard) H.; ed. Yale; m. Frances Ann Andrews, Nov. 16, 1848; m. 2d, Elizabeth Ridgely, Oct. 14, 1852; m. 3d, Sarah Harrison, 1864; m. 4th, Mrs. Louise Hopkins, June 1, 1871; 7 children. Admitted to La. bar, 1844; prof. civil law U. La. Law Sch. (Now Tulane U.), 1866; apptd. atty. gen. La., 1876, asso. judge U.S. Ct. Claims, 1878; U.S. sec. of navy under Pres. James Garfield, 1881-82; U.S. minister to Russia, 1882-84. Died St. Petersburg, Russia, Feb. 17, 1884; buried Oak Hill Cemetery, Washington, D.C.

HUNTER, ALFRED M. army officer; b. in Ill., Jan. 21, 1864; s. Nelson F. and Elizabeth (Williamson) H.; grad. U.S. Mil. Acad., 1887, grad. Arty., Sch., 1896, Army War Coll., 1909; m. Elizabeth Martin, Oct. 19, 1904. Commd. 2d lt. 5th Cav., June 12, 1887; trans. to 4th Arty., Apr. 3, 1888; 1st lt. 1st Arty., Mar. 22, 1894; promoted through grades to col. Coast Arty. Corps, Aug. 25, 1915. With siege train 5th Army Corps, campaign against Santiago, Cuba, 1898; comd. Ft. Mott, N.J., 1899-1901; observer for Bd. of Ordnance and Fortification, at Sandy Hook, N.J., and Ft. Riley, Kan., 1901-02; comdr. Ft. Fremont, S.C., 1903-04, Ft. Rodman, Mass., 1906-07, Ft. Constitution, N.H., and Arty. Dist. of Portsmouth, 1907-08, Army War Coll., 1908-09, Ft. Mott, N.J., 1909-10; duty hdqrs. Dept. of the Gulf and hdqrs. Eastern Dept., 1910-14; Ft.

Winfield Scott, Calif., 1914-16; comdg. coast defense of Oahu, Honolulu, 1916-17; comd. S. Pacific Coast Arty. Dist., San Francisco, Sept. 1917-Jan. 1919. Died May 12, 1929.

HUNTER, CROIL, airlines exec.; born Fargo, N.D., Feb. 18, 1893; s. John Croil and Emma (Schulze) H.; student Yale U., Sheffield Sci. Sch., 1915; m. Helen Floan, Feb. 24, 1923; children—Andrea (Mrs. Jeremiah Milbank, Jr.), John Croil. Treas. Fargo Merc. Co., 1915-28; N.Y. mgr. First Bancredit Corp., 1928-32; traffic mgr. Northwest Airlines, Inc., 1932, v.p., gen. mgr., 1933-37, pres., gen. mgr., 1937-53, chmn. bd., 1953-70. Served as 1st lt. and capt. F.A., U.S. Army, 1917-19, in active service overseas. Clubs: Book and Snake, Cloister, Minnestoa, Somerset (St. Paul); Burning Tree (Washington). Home: St Paul MN Died July 21, 1970.

HUNTER, DAVID army officer; b. Washington, D.C., July 21, 1802; s. Rev. Andrew and Mary (Stockton) H.; grad. U.S. Mil. Acad., 1822; m. Maria Kinzie, circa 1829. Commd. 2d lt. 5th Inf., U.S. Army, 1822; capt. 1st Dragoons, 1833; maj., paymaster U.S. Army, 1842; col. calvary, 1861; commd. brig. gen. U.S. Volunteers, in command 2d div. U.S. Army under Gen. McDowell, 1861, served at 1st Battle of Bull Run; comdr. Western Dept., (succeeding Fremont), 1861; assumed command of South, 1862, issued order emanicpating all slaves in Union custody in his dept., 1862, sanctioned liberation of all slaves in area, 1862; in command operations in Shenandoah Valley, 1864, won Battle of Piedmont, took Lynchburg (Va.); retreated before Early's troops, enabling Confederate comd. to threaten Washington (D.C.) by way of Shenandoah Valley; served court martial duty, 1865 until end of Civil War; pres. mil. commn. which tried Lincoln's assassins; pres. spl. claims commn. Cavalry Promotion Bd.; brevetted brig. gen. and maj. gen. meritorious conduct during war; ret. as col., 1866. Died Washington, Feb. 2, 1886.

HUNTER, EDWARD colonel U.S.A.; b. Gardiner, Me., Nov. 1839; s. John Patten H.; ed. Gardiner, Me., 1847-59; apptd. from Me., and grad. U.S. Mil. Acad., 1865; m. San Francisco, Caroline Clay Hoff, Mar., 1870. Mem. bar, State of Cal., and admitted to practice before U.S., circuit and dist. courts for State of Wash. Second and 1st lt. 12th Inf., June 23, 1865; transferred to 1st Cav., Feb. 19, 1870; capt., Aug. 21, 1879; maj. judge advocate, Dec. 10, 1888; lt.-col. deputy judge advocate gen., Jan. 3, 1895; col. judge advocate, May 21, 1901; lt., 12th Inf., June 23, 1865; on garrison duty, 1865-67; a.-d.-c. and acting asst. adj.-gen. to Gen. Getty, Santa Fe, N.M., 1867-69; took part in campaign against hostile Indians, winter, 1868-69; on various garrison and frontier duties in Cal. and Wash. 1869-86; served on Nez Perces Expdn., 1877; on duty examining claims of States and Territories; judge advocate Div. of Pacific and Dept. Cal., 1889-95; in Dept. of Dak. until May, 1898, when he accompanied Gen. Brooke to P.R. as judge advocate and mustering officer; in charge civ. affairs, Dist. of Guayama, P.R., Aug. 1-Sept. 1, 1898; sec. and recorder of commn. on evacuation by Spain of P.R. and adjacent islands, Aug. 29-Oct. 18, 1898; judge advocate dept., P.R. until Oct., 1898; later judge advocate, Dept. of the East; retired Nov. 22, 1903. Address: Mt. Vernon, N.Y.

HUNTER, GEORGE BOWDITCH army officer (ret.); b. Ft. Fetterman, Wyo. Sept. 26, 1879; s. Brig. Gen. George King and Mary Elizabeth (Hinman) H.; B.S., U.S. Mil. Acad., 1904; honor grad. Command and Gen. Staff Sch., 1923; grad. Army War Coll., 1926; m. Reba Ballou, July 19, 1912; 1 son, George Bowditch; m. 2d, Opal Phelps, July 14, 1937. Commd. 2d lt. U.S. Army, 1904, advanced through grades to brig. gen., Mar. 27, 1942; served as comdr. U.S. Sch. Mil. Aeros., Berkeley, Cal., and in office of Chief of AC, World War I; exec. for the 3d Mil. Area, New Orleans, 1940-41; comdr. New Orleans Port of Embarkation from July 1941 to Sept. 1943. Ret. from active duty Mar. 1944. Club: Army and Navy (Washington). Home: 833 Hamilton Av., Palo Alto, Cal. Died Sept. 1965.

HUNTER, GEORGE KING army officer; b. Lancaster, O., Apr. 6, 1855; s. Henry B. and Josephine L. (King) H.; grad. U.S. Mil. Acad., 1877; m. Mary E. Hinman, Dec. 17, 1878. Commd. additional 2d lt., 4th Cav., June 15, 1877; promoted through grades to brig. gen. N.A., Aug. 5, 1917. Participated in numerous Indian campaigns; wounded at Battle of San Juan Hill, Cuba, July 1, 1898; actively engaged in subduing Philippine Insurrection, 1899-1903; assigned in duty Camp Funston, Kan., 1917; retired, Feb. 1, 1918; comd. Jefferson Barracks, Mo., Feb. 22, 1918-July 28, 1919. Mem. Loyal Legion, Soc. Foreign Wars, Mil. Order Carabao, S.A.R. Episcopalian. Home: Cleveland, O. Died Feb. 2, 1940.

HUNTER, HOWARD OWEN assn. exec.; b. Darien, Ga., July 25, 1895; s. Thomas Marshall and Sallie (Owen) H.; B.A., La. State U., 1917; m. Mary E. Jackson, Dec. 23, 1920; children-Howard O., Mary Kate; m. 2d, Marjory Lichty, Oct. 27, 1932; m. 3d, Edna McNabb, Aug. 14, 1945. Exec. Community Chest, 1925-33; dep. adminstrn., nat. adminstr. Works Projects Adminstrn., 1933-42; dep. adminstr. food distbn. War Food Adminstrn., 1942-44; pub. relations exec., 1944-49; pres. Am. Inst. of Baking, 1949-; pres. Research and Ednl. Inst. Served as capt., Sanitary Corps, U.S. Army, 1917-19. Mem. Nat. Assn. Social Workers, North Mich. Av. Assn. (dir.). Club: University (Chgo.). Home: 3200 N.E. 36th St., Ft. Lauderdale, Fla. Died Feb. 22, 1964; buried Baton Rouge.

HUNTER, KENT A. correspondent; b. Omaha, Neb., Feb. 7, 1892; s. William Howard and Anna May (White) H.; ed. Bellevue (Neb.) Acad., 1908-09; B.A., St. Thomas Coll., St. Paul, Minn., 1909-12; m. Ruty Taylor, Apr. 11, 1953. Reporter Mpls. Tribune, 1912, Chgo. Inter-Ocean, 1913-15, Chgo. Examiner, 1915-17 and 1919-21, Los Angeles Examiner, 1921-24, Chicago Herald-American, 1924-28, N.Y. Journal-Am., 1928-41; corr. Washington bur., Hearst Newspapers, King Features Syndicate, 1945-51; special writer New York Journal-American; founded Facts. Evaluated, research service, 1954. Served as private to captain, 122d F.A., U.S.N.G., World War I; O.R.C., 1922-41; maj. to col., including staff Gen. Patton, in France, Luxembourg, Germany, World War II. Decorated Silver Star with 2 Oak Leaf Clusters, Bronze Star, Legion of Merit. Mem. Am. Legion, Mil. Order World Wars, Club: Army and Navy (Washington). Author of: Strategy and Tactics World Communist, Part 1, Senate Internal Security Committee, 1954; Symposium Soviet Total War, Vol. II, 1956; The Communist Drive for Africa, 1957. Home: 1026 16th St. Washington 6. Died Aug. 26, 1958; buried Arlington Nat. Cemetery.

HUNTER, MORTON CRAIG congressman; b. Versailles, Ind., Feb. 5, 1825; grad. law dept. Ind. U., 1849, Admitted to Ind. bar, practice law; mem. Ind. Ho. of Reps., 1858; Republican presdl. elector, 1860; enlisted in U.S. Army during Civil War, 1862; commanded 1st Brigade, 3d Div., 14th Army Corps; with Sherman's march to the sea; brevetted brig. gen. U.S. Volunteers; discharged, 1865; mem. U.S. Ho. of Reps. (Republican) 40th, 43d-45th congresses, 1867-69, 73-79; - operated a limestone quarry in Ind. Died Bloomington, Oct. 25, 1896; buried Rose Hill Cemetery, Bloomington.

HUNTER, ROBERT royal gov.; b. Hunterston, Scotland; s. James and Margaret (Spalding) H.; m. Elizabeth Orby. Fought at Blenheim, 1704; served as lt. col. Brit. Army until 1707; apptd. lt. gov. Va., 1708, captured on way to Am., exchanged by French for Bishop of Quebec; capt. gen. and gov.-in-chief N.Y. and N.J., 1709-19, arrived to begin his adminstrn., N.Y.C., 1710, one of colonial America's most successful govs., played prominent part in orgn. colonial def. against French in N.Am.; gov. Jamaica, B.W.I., 1727-34. Author: (with Lewis Morris) Androborus (satire, 1st play published and written in Am.). Died Jamaica, Mar. 1734.

HUNTINGTON, ARTHUR FRANKLIN, naval officer; b. Brooklyn, N.Y., Feb. 24, 1877; s. Charles Lathrop and Elizabeth Franklin (Bache) H.; student U.S. Naval Acad., 1894-97; m. Mary E. Klink, Jan. 16, 1907; 1 son, Seymour Franklin (dec.). Asst. paymaster (rank of ensign), U.S. Navy, 1898, advanced through grades to rear admiral, S.C., 1938, filing usual assignments afloat and ashore; retired (statutory age) March 1, 1941; remained on active duty to August 1942. Awarded West Indian Campaign medal, 1898; Sampson medal, 1898; Philippine Campaign medal, 1901; Victory medal, 1918. Mem. U.S. Naval Institute, Naval Hist. Foundation, Naval Acad. Alumni Assn., Nat. Sojourners, Mil. Order of the Carabao. Presbyterian. Mason. Clubs: New York Yacht (N.Y. City); Army and Navy (San Francisco); City Commons (Berkeley). Home: 107 Parkside Dr., Berkeley, CA*

HUNTINGTON, EBENEZER congressman; b. Norwich, Conn., Dec. 26, 1754; grad. Yale, 1775. Served to lt. col. Continental Army, during Revolutionary War; commd. brig. gen. U.S. Army, 1798; discharged, 1800; mem. U.S. Ho. of Reps. (Whig) from Conn., 11th, 15th congresses, Oct. 11, 1810-11, 17-19. Died Norwich, June 17, 1834; buried Norwichtown Cemetery.

HUNTINGTON, EDWARD VERMILYE mathematician; b. Clinton, Oneida County, N.Y., Apr. 26, 1874: s. Chester and Katharine Hazard (Smith) H.; A.B., Harvard, 1895, A.M., 1897; Ph.D., U. of Strassburg, Germany, 1901; hon. Sc.D., U. of San Marcos, Lima, Peru, 1925; m. Susie Edwards Van Volkenburgh, July 6, 1909. Instr. mathematics, Harvard, 1895-97, Williams Coll., 1897-99; in Europe, 1899-1901; instr. mathematics, 1901-05, asst. prof. 1905-15, asso. prof., 1915-19, prof. mechanics, 1919-41, emeritus since 1941, Harvard U. Western Exchange prof. from Harvard to Beloit, Carleton, and Knox Colls., 1925. Consultant, Nat. Defense Research Com. since 1942. Major, Gen. Staff, on statis. duty at Washington, 1918-19. Editor Annals of Mathematics, 1902-11. Fellow Am. Acad. Arts and Sciences (chmn. com. of pub., 1914-19), A.A.A.S. (vice pres. and chmn. section A, 1926), Am. Inst. of Math. Statistics; mem. Am. Philos. Soc., Am. Math. Soc. Statistics; mem. Am. Philos. Soc., Am. Math. Soc. (v.p. 1924; rep. on National Research Council, 1923-26), Math. Assn. America (pres. 1918), Am. Statistical Assn., Am. Standards Assn. (mem. sectional com.; chmn. sub-committee on math. symbols, 1928), Assn. for Symbolic Logic, American Academy Political Science. Honorary member of Phi Beta Kappa. Author: Four-Place Tables of Logarithmus and Trigonometric Functions, arranged for decimal division of the degree, 1907; Monograph IV on "The Fundamental Propositions of Algebra," in work entitled "Mathematical Statistics" (edited by H. L. Rietz), 1924; Survey of Methods of Apportionment in Congress (Senate Doc. No. 304), 1940. Contbr. to math. journals. Congregationalist. Devised the method of apportioning representatives in Congress which became law Nov. 15, 1941. Home: 48 Highland St., Cambridge 38, Mass. Died Nov. 25, 1952.

HUNTINGTON, HENRY ALONZO soldier; b. Chicago, Mar. 23, 1840; s. Alonzo and Patience Lorain (Dyer) H.; ed. Phillips Acad., Andover, Mass.; m. Frances S. Tucker, Began study of law in father's office at 19; raised a troop of cav. and was commd. 2d lt. 9th Ill. Cav., Oct. 9-Nov. 6, 1861; 2d lt. 4th U.S. Arty., Oct. 24, 1861; 1st lt., May 3, 1863; apptd. a.-d.-c. to Maj. Gen. Hallock, July 12, 1865; resigned Nov. 19, 1869. Bvtd. 1st lt., Apr. 7, 1862, for gallant and meritorious services at battle of Stone River, Tenn.; maj., Mar. 13, 1865, for same during the war. One of founders Chicago Civ. Service Reform League and for 2 yrs. v.p. Nat. Reform League. Mem. Am. Art Assn. (life), L'Association pour l'Encouragement des Etudes Greques en France (both of Paris). Died 1907,

HUNTINGTON, JEBEZ army officer, jurist; b. Norwich, Conn., Aug. 7, 1719; s. Joshua and Hannah (Perkins) H.; grad. Yale, 1741; m. Elizabeth Backus, Jan. 20, 1742; m. 2d, Hannah Williams, 1746, children - Jedediah, Andrew, Joshua, Ebenezer. Justice of peace, New London, Conn.; mem. Conn. Assembly from Norwich, clk., 1757; speaker Conn. Ho. of Reps., 1760; commd. capt. troop of horse 3d Regt., Conn. Militia, 1754, lt. 1st company 5th Pegt., 1760, capt., 1764; made assistant by Conn. Assembly, 1764; lt. col. 3rd regt. Conn. Miltiia, 1765; apptd. probate judge for Norwich Dist., 1773; moderator of large meeting assembled "to take into consideration the melancholy situation of our civil constitutional liberties, rights and privileges," Norwich, June 6, 1774; mem. Conn. Council of Safety, 1775-1779; apptd. one of 2 maj. gens. from Conn., 1776, maj. gen. entire Conn. Militia, 1777. Died Oct. 5, 1786.

HUNTINGTON, JEDEDIAH army officer; b. Norwich, Conn., Aug. 4, 1743; s. Gen. Jabez and Elizabeth (Backus) H.; grad. Harvard, 1763; m. Faith Trumbull; m. 2d, Ann Moore; 2 sons, Joshua, Daniel. Commd. ensign 1st Norwich Co. by Conn. Assembly, 1769, lt., 1771, capt., 1774; col. 20th Regt., Conn. Militia, 1774, col. 8th Regt., 1775, 17th Inf. Regt., Continental Army, 1776, fought at Battle of L.I.; col. 1st Conn. Regt., 1777; commd. brig. gen. Continental Army, 1777, brevetted maj. gen. at close of Revolutionary War; sheriff New London (Conn.); del. to Conn. Constl. Conv.; treas. Conn.; apptd. collector customs Port of New London by Pres. Washington, 1789. Died New London, Sept. 25, 1818.

HUNTON, EPPA lawyer; b. Faruquier Co., Va., Sept. 22, 1822; chiefly self-taught; studied and practiced law; m. Lucy C. Weir, Commonwealth atty. Prince William Co., 1849-62; mem. Va. conv., 1861; col. 8th Va. Inf., 1861-63, brig. gen., 1863-65, C.S.A.; prisoner of war at Ft. Warren, April 6 to July 1865. Mem. Congress, 1873-81; U.S. senator from Va. for unexpired term, 1892-95. Democrat. Home: Richmond, Va. Died 1908.

HURD, EUGENE surgeon; b. Ft. Atkinson, Wis., July 7, 1881; s. Samuel Curtis and Emily Ann (Wilds) H.; M.D., West Coast Coll. Medicine and Surgery, San Francisco, 1905; m. Baroness Nella von Hochstetter, Aug. 20, 1913; 1 son, John Gavin. Began practice at Seattle, Washington, 1906; mem. of Washington House of Representatives, 1913. Apptd capt. Russian Army, Oct. 14, 1914; lt. col., Feb. 2, 1915; col. Sept. 1, 1915; capt. Med. Corps, U.S. Army, Aug. 26, 1917; hon. disch., July 22, 1918. Served as med. officer at the front with the Russian Army, in numerous engagements; surgeon to Root Commn. from Petrograd, Russia, to Washington, D.C., 1917; with Am. Army in France, Dec. 1917-July 1918. Corr. on Russian front for Chicago Tribune. Decorated Order of St. Stanislaus; Order of St. Anna, 3d and 2d degrees with crossed swords; Order of St. Vladimir, 3d degree; Order St. George, 3d degree; Order St. Nicolis, 2d degree. Mason. Republican. Episcopalian. Home: Auburn, Calif. Died May 19, 1941.

HURLBUT, STEPHEN AUGUSTUS congressman, army officer, diplomat; b. Charleston, S.C., Nov. 29, 1815; s. Martin Luther and Lydia (Bunch) H.; m. Sophronia R. Stevens, May 13, 1847. Admitted to S.C. bar, 1837; adj. S.C. Regt. during Seminole War, 1835-43; moved to Ill., 1845; mem. Ill. Constl. Conv. from Boone and McHenry counties, 1847; mem. Ill. Gen. Assembly, 1858-61; commd. brig. gen. U.S. Army, 1861, comdr. 4th Div. at Battle of Shiloh; promoted maj. gen., 1862; stationed Memphis, Tenn., 1862-63; in charge of XVI Army Corps, 1863, defense of Memphis during Vicksburg campaign, 1863; served with Gen. Sherman at Mobile (Ala.), 1864; commanded Dept. of Gulf, 1864; discharged from U.S. Army, 1865; 1st comdr.-in-chief Grand Army of Republic, 1866-68; U.S. minister to Colombia, S.Am., 1869-72; mem. U.S. Ho. of Reps. from Ill., 43d-44th congresses, 1873-77; U.S. minister to Peru, 1881-82. Died Lima, Peru, Mar. 27, 1882; buried Belvidere (Ill.) Cemetery.

HURLEY, PATRICK JAY lawyer, mining co. exec.; b. Choctaw Indian Terr. (now Okla.) Jan. 8, 1883; s. Pierce and Mary (Kelly) H.; A.B., Indian U. (now Bacone Coll.), Indian Terr., 1905; LL.B., Nat. U., Washington, 1908; LL.D., George Washington U., 1913; LL.D. Okla. A. and M. Coll. (hon.); m. Ruth Wilson, Dec. 5, 1919; children - Patricia, Ruth, Wilson, Mary. Admitted to Okla. bar 1908, and began practice law in Tulsa; admitted to Supreme Ct. U.S. 1912; nat. atty. Choctaw Nation 1912-17; under-sec. war, Mar.-Dec., 1929, sec. war, Dec. 9, 1929-Mar. 4, 1933. Served successively as pvt., corpl., sgt., H., capt. Indian Terr. Vol. Cav., 1902-07; capt. Okla. N.G., 1914-17; maj., lt. col., col., U.S. Army, World War I; participated in Aisne-Marne, Meuse-Argonne and St. Mihiel offensives and defensive sector A.E.F.; negotiated agreement between Gov. of Grand Duchy of Luxembourg and AEF, 1919; col. inf. U.S. Res., assigned to duty as col., advanced to brig. gen. outbreak World War II; assigned active duty Far East Theater Operations, Jan. 1942; personal rep. chief of staff, Gen. Marshall, in Far East; running blockade P.I., Jan.-Mar., 1942. Minister to New Zealand, Apr. 1942; personal rep. Pres. of U.S. to Soviet Union, Nov.-Dec., 1942, and to Egypt, Syria, the Lebanon, Iraq, Iran, Palestine, Trans-Jordan, Saudi Arbia, Afghanistan, India and China, 1943; drafted Iran Declaration, Teheran Conf., Dec. 1, 1943; maj. gen. and personal rep. of Pres. in China, Aug.-Dec., 1944; ambassador to China, Dec. 1944; pres. Uranium Inst. Am., 1957-58. Mem. nat. council Boy Scouts Am.; dir. Boys Clubs Am. Okla. del.-at-large Republican Nat. Conv., 1924; chmn. Rep. State Conv., Okla., 1926; assisted in orgn. U.S. C. of C., 1912; chmn., U.S. War Policies Commn., 1931-33; negotiated agreement between Republic of Mexico and 5 expropriated oil cos., 1940; del. Rep. Nat. Conv. 1952, 1956; Rep. nominee for U.S. senator in N.M., 1946, 1948; 1952. Decorated D.S.M. with oak leaf cluster, Silver Star, D.F.C. Purple Heart Aztec Eagle (Mexico), 1943; Medal of Merit, 1946; Order of Yun Hwei (cloud banner) Spl. Grand Cordon, Chinese Nat. Govt. Mem. Am., Okla., N.M. bar assns., Am. Legion, V.F.W., D.A.V., Nat. C. of C. Sigma Chi, Phi Beta Kappa. Home: P.O. Box 9, Santa Fe. Died July 30, 1963; buried Nat. Cemetery, Santa Fe.

HUSE, HARRY PINCKNEY naval officer; b. at West Point, N.Y., Dec. 8, 1858; s. Caleb and Harriet (Pinckney) H.; B.S., U.S. Naval Acad., 1878, Naval War Coll., 1916; m. Mary S. Whitelock, Sept. 15, 1886; 1 dau., Jean Stockton. Midshipman, June 4, 1880; promoted through grades to rear admiral, Aug. 29, 1916; promoted to vice admiral, retired, June 21, 1930. Pres. Naval Examining Bd., Washington, D.C., Sept. 29, 1916; comdr. Atlantic Fleet Train (flagship Columbia), Jan. 24, 1919; spl. duty, London and Paris, Dec. 13, 1919; comdr. U.S. Naval Forces in European waters, rank of vice adm., June 25, 1920; comdt. 3d Naval Dist., New York, Feb. 5, 1921; mem. Gen. Bd. of Navy, July 26, 1921-Dec. 3, 1922 (retired). Advanced 5 numbers "for eminent and conspicuous conduct in battle," while serving on bd. Gloucester, commanded landing force from Gloucester at Guanica, Puerto Rico, July 25, 1898; secured landing place for Army, hauled down Spanish flag and hoisted first American flag over Puerto Rico. Awarded Congressional Medal of Honor for "distinguished conduct in battle," engagement of Vera Cruz, Humane Soc., for going overboard in his uniform from his flagship to rescue one of his crew. Member (Washington); New York Yacht. Author of "The Descendants of Abel Huse of Newbury (1602-1690)" Home: 2400 16th St., Washington, D.C. Died May 14, 1942.

HUSSEY, CHARLES LINCOLN rear admiral; b. Rochester, N.H., Aug. 18, 1870; s. George D. and Mary J. (Foss) H.; grad. U.S. Naval Acad., 1892; Naval War Coll., 1920; m. Mrs. Harriet Brownson Tooker, Dec. 21, 1908; 1 dau., Faith. Ensign U.S.N., July 1, 1894; promoted through grades to capt., July 1, 1917; rear admiral, June 4, 1926. Served on Oregon, Spanish-Am. War, 1898; comd. expdn. to Abyssinia, 1903; duty Bur. of Navigation, Navy Dept., 1906-08; navigator New Hampshire, 1908-10; exec. officer, Georgia, 1912-13; duty Gen. Bd., Navy Dept., 1914-17, and mem. commn. on Navy Yards and Naval Stas., 1916-17; comdr. Birmingham, World War, 1917-19; comd. Idaho, 1920-21; naval attaché to American Embassy, London, 1922-24; comd. train, Scouting Fleet, 1925-27; retired Oct. 1, 1927. Awarded Navy Cross (U.S.); decorated Companion Order St. Michael and St. George; Star of Ethiopia. Conf. leader Williamstown Inst. Politics, 1929. Presbyn. Author: (with Sir Norman Angell and Carl Russell Fish) The United States and Great Britain, 1931. Home: Litchfield, Conn. Died Dec. 4, 1934.

HUSSEY, RAYMOND physician; b. Greensboro, N.C., Dec. 26, 1883; s. John Bryant and Sue Ann (Mallard) H.; M.D., U. of Md., 1911: A.M., (hon.) Yale, 1927; m. Edith Woodward, June 14, 1917. Resident physician Municipal Tuberculosis Hosp., Baltimore, Md., 1911-12, Md. Tuberculosis Sanatorium, 1912-14; in gen. practice of medicine, Baltimore, 1912-15, also vol. asst., med. clinic, Johns Hopkins Hosp. Outpatient Clinic. 1914-15, med. clinic Phipps Tuberculosis Clinic, Johns Hopkins Hosp., Outpatient Clin. and dept. pathology, Johns Hopkins Med. Sch., 1915-16; asst. in pathology, Johns Hopkins Med. Sch., also resident pathologist, Baltimore City Hosps., 1916-17; associate in pathology and biophysics, Rockefeller Inst. Med. Research, New York, N.Y., 1919-22; asst. prof. pathology, Sch. of Medicine, Cornell U., 1922-24; asso. prof. pathology, Sch. of Medicine, Yale, 1924-27, prof., 1927-35; asst. attending physician, cardiology, Baltimore City Hosps., 1937-39, cardiologist, 1939-45; in practice of medicine, field of cardiac diseases, Baltimore, Md., also asso. prof. medicine, U. of Maryland, instr. medicine, Johns Hopkins Med. Sch., mem. visiting staff Union Memorial Hosp., Church Home and Infirmary, attending physician University Hosp. (Baltimore), 1937-45; physician in chief, St. Joseph's Hosp., Baltimore, 1940-41 (on leave from all civilian activities); dean, Sch. of Occupational Health, Wayne U., Detroit, Mich., 1945-49; sci. dir. Council on Indsl. Health, A.M.A., since 1950. Vice chmn. and acting chmn. div. med. sciences Nat. Research Council, 1918-19. Spl. investigator Md. Tuberculosis Commn., 1938-39; chmn. med. bd. adminstrn. of occupational disease law, Md., 1939-45. Served as lt., advancing to major, Med. Corps, U.S. Army, 1917-19; lt. col., Med. Reserve Corps, 1919-24; lt. col., Med. Corps, U.S. Army, 1943-45: assigned as sci. dir. Army Indsl. Lab., Baltimore, Md., Feb.-June 1943, comdg. officer and dir., 1943-45. Vice chmn. com. on blood transfusion Baltimore chapter Am. Red Cross, 1938-40, mem. bd. dirs. and mem. exec. com., 1939-44, chmn. Am. Red Cross Blood Donor Center, 1940-41. Mem. bd. govs., Am. Acad. Compensation Med., 1948. Mem. com. indsl. health Md. State Med. Soc., 1938-45, v. chmn., 1938-39, chmn., 1939-44; mem. med. com. Indsl. Hygiene Foundation America Mellon Inst., Pittsburgh, Pa., since 1942; mem. professional adv. com. on physical restoration, Office Vocational Rehabilitation, Fed. Security Agency, since 1943. Fellow A.A.A.S., Am. Coll. Physicians, American Public Health Assn., Gerontological Society, Am. Med. Assn. (mem. council indsl. health since 1941); mem. Illinois State and Chicago med. socs., Am. Soc. Exptl. Pathology, Soc. Exptl. Biology and Medicine, Sigma Xi, Phi Sigma Kappa. Contbr. numerous articles to med. publs. Home: 105 E. Delaware Pl., Chicago 11. Office: 535 N. Dearborn, Chgo. 10. Died Apr. 15, 1953; Buried Balt.

HUTCHESON, GROTE army officer; b. Cincinnati, O., Apr. 1, 1862; s. Ebenezer E. and Therese C. (Turpin) H.; grad. U.S. Mil. Acad., 1884; m. Rosalie E. St. George, Jan. 16, 1900 (died Feb. 20, 1942); m. 2d, Anne Holt Pegram, Dec. 11, 1943. Commd. 2d lt. 9th Cav., June 15, 1884; colonel, 1916; brig. gen. N.A., Aug. 24, 1917; maj. gen. (temp.) Aug. 27, 1918; brig. gen., regular army, July 3, 1920; maj. gen., July 19, 1924; retired July 20, 1924. Participated in campaigns in Okla., 1884-85, in campaigns against the Sioux Indians in S.D., 1890-91; duty railroad strikes, 1894; campaign against Bannock Indians, July-Sept. 1895; adj. gen., Puerto Rican expdn., 1898; adj. gen. and judge advocate Dept. of Mo., 1899-1900; with China-Relief Expdn., 1900, as adj. gen., later insp. gen. and judge advocate; participated in advance to Peking; mil. sec. to mil. gov. of P.I., 1901-02; judge adv. Dept. of the East, New York, 1903-04; mem. Gen. Staff Corps, 1904-08; duty Office Chief of Staff, 1904-08; mem. spl. mission to witness maneuvers of French Army, 1905; in Philippines, 1901-02, 1908-10, 1915-16; Mexican border, 1911-12, 1916-17; organized Recruit Depots at Ft. San Houston, Tex., and Ft. Thomas, Ky.; created and organized Port of Embarkation, Newport News and Norfolk, Va.; comd. 14th Div., Camp Custer, Mich., and Camp Meade, Md.; comdg. New York Gen. Intermediate Depot, reducing war activities and co-ordinating supply services in and around N.Y. City, 1921-23; comdg. 11th Field Arty. Brig., Schofield Barracks, Hawaii, 1923-24. Awarded D.S.M. (U.S.), "for especially meritorious and conspicuous services in administration of Port of Embarkation," 1918; also Navy D.S.M. for service, World War. Mem. Order of Dragon, Order of Carabao, Soc. Foreign Wars. Episcopalian; dir. gen. Cathedral Foundation, Washington, 1925-27. Clubs: Army and Navy (Washington, D.C.); Union League (San Francisco). Address: Saratoga, Calif. Died Dec. 28, 1948; buried in Arlington National Cemetery.

HUTCHINS, CHARLES THOMAS rear admiral U.S.N.; b. Kingston, Pa., Feb. 5, 1844; s. Richard and Emily (Little) H.; grad. U.S. Naval Acad., 1866; m. Marion Clementine Borup, Nov. 17, 1876. Ensign, 1868; master, 1869; lt., 1870; lt. comdr., 1887; comdr., 1896; capt., 1901; rear admiral and retired, June 30, 1905. Served on sailing-ship Relief on voyage to France with supplies for starving French, 1871; served as navigator of Wyoming, with Comdr. Cushing, when he went to Santiago de Cuba to retake Virginius; was watch officer and navigator, flagship Lancaster, European Sta., at bombardment of Alexandria, Egypt, and in command of fleet landing party on shore for 5 days; personally thanked by Kings of Sweden and Norway; at Kronstadt, Russia, coronation of the Czar, 1884; comd. several vessels, 1893-1900; comdg. U.S.S. Buffalo, spl. service carrying recruits to China and training landsmen, 1900-02; naval sec. Lighthouse Bd., 1902-04; comdg. new U.S. battleship Maine, 1904-05. Episcopalian. Home: Washington, D.C. Died Aug. 9, 1920.

HUTCHINS, FRANK FRAZIER M.D., educator; b. Indianapolis, Feb. 9, 1870; s. Hezekiah Sharpe and Mary Elizabeth (Lemon) H.; student Butler Univ.; M.D., Indiana Medical Coll., 1892; special work several yrs., New York Post-Grad. Sch., Vienna, Berlin, Zurich, Paris and London; m. Luella McWhirter, June 12, 1907. Instr. Butler U. and Ind. Med. Coll., 1892-95; resident physician Eastern Hosp. for Insane, Richmond, Ind., 1895-1901; asst. prof. psychology and psychiatry, Central Coll. Physicians and Surgeons, Indianapolis, 1903-05; prof. mental and nervous diseases, State Coll. Physicians and Surgeons, 1906-08; prof. mental and nervous diseases, Ind. U. Sch. of Medicine, 1908-37; now emeritus; cons. City Hosp., Long Hosp., City Dispensary and Riley Memorial Hosp. for Children. Pres. Lemona Farm Stock Co.; dir. Peoples State Bank. Served as maj. and lt. col., M.C., World War; instr. Med. Officers' Training Corps, Ft. Benjamin Harrison and Ft. Oglethorpe; Neyropsychiatrist 8th Div. Reg., later Base Sect. 5, France; chief neuropsycihiatric service Walter Reed Gen. Hosp., Washington, D.C.; clin. dir., neuropsychiatry U.S. Vets.' Bur., June 1922-July 1923; dean Neuropsychiatric Sch. of U.S. Vets.' Bur.; col. M.R.C., U.S. Army, Mem. Nat. Com. for Mental Hygiene. Republican. Methodist. Mem. A.M.A., Ind. State Med. Assn., Indianpaolis Med. Soc., Am. Psychiatric Assn., Mil. Order of Foreign Wars, Am. Legion, Delta Tau Delta, Alpha Omega, Nu Sigma Nu. Mason (32ff, Shriner). Clubs: Service, Army and Navy (Washington, D.C.). Home: 3824 N. Delaware St., Indianapolis, Ind. Died Feb. 22, 1942.

HUTCHINSON, MYRON WELLS, JR. naval officer; b. Bismarck, N.D., Dec. 29, 1892; s. Myron Wells and Gertrude G. (Griffin) H.; student Mich. State Coll., 1910-11; B.S., U.S. Naval Acad., 1915; M.S., Columbia, 1922; m. Heather P. Baxter, Apr. 20, 1918; children-Ronald B., David M., Kenneth F. Command. ensign USA of staff Hawaiian Sea Frontier and 14th Naval Dist., Pearl Harbor, T.H., 1945—. Decorated Bronze Star medal, Gold Star in lieu of 2d Bronze Star, spl. letter of commendation with ribbon and combat device. Victory medal, Am. Defense medal, China campaign medal, Haitian campaign medal, Am., European and Asiatic Theatre Medals, Mem. Am. Soc. Naval Engrs., Naval Inst., S.A.R. Presbyterian. Clubs: Army and Navy (Washington, D.C.). Home: Six Acton Pl., Annapolis, Md. Office: Chief of Staff, Hawaiian Sea Frontier and 14 N.D., Pearl Harbor, T.H. Died Oct. 1959.

HUTCHISON, MILLER REESE inventor, engr.; b. Montrose, Baldwin County, Ala., Aug. 6, 1876; s. William Peter and Tracie (Magruder) H.; student Marion Mil. Inst., 1889-91, Spring Hill Coll., 1891-92, University Mil. Inst., Mobile, 1892-95; B.S. in E.E., Ala. Poly. Inst., 1897, E.E., 1913; Ph.D., Spring Hill Coll., 1914; attended Ala. Med. Coll.; m. Martha J. Pomeroy, May 31, 1901. Chief elec. engr. U.S. Light House Establishment, 7th and 8th dists., during Spanish-Am. War, engaged in laying submarine mines and cables, Gulf Harbors; established Hutchison Laboratory, New York, 1899; invented and marketed many elec. and mech. appliances among which are "Acousticon" for the deaf, "Dictograph," "Klaxon Horn"; has been granted serveral hundred patents. Presented with spl. gold medal by Queen of Eng. for exceptional merit in the field of invention, 1902 present at Coronation Edward VII and Alexandra, Westminster Abbey, 1902; awarded gold medals, St. Louis Expn., 1904 for Acousticon and commercially operated wireless telephone. Became associated with Thomas A. Edison, 1910, in spl. work on storage batteries; apptd. chief engr. Edison Laboratory and all affiliated Edison interests, chief engr. to and personal rep. of Thomas A. Edison, 1913, and in addition adv. mgr. Edison Storage Battery Co., 1912-17; engr. adviser Thomas A. Edison, 1917-18; formed Miller Reese Hutchison, Ind., Jan. 1, 1917, to act as sole distributors Edison Storage Batteries for all govt. purposes all nations, of which became pres.; sold rights back to Edison Co., June 5, 1918, to devote entire time to govt. service for period of war; propr. Hutchison Laboratory. Hon. commr. of Dept. of Electricity, St. Louis Expn., 1904; mem. Internat. Elec Congress, St. Louis, 1904, Internat. Engring. Congress, San Francisco, 1915; mem. Naval Consulting Bd. Mem. Am. Acad. Polit. and Social Science, A.A.A.S., Am. Inst. E.E., Am. Inst. Radio Engrs., Am. Soc. M.E., Am. Soc. Naval Engrs., Nat. Inst. Social Sciences, Navy League U.S., New York Elec. Soc., Soc. Automotive Engrs., Nat. Geog. Soc., Soc. Am. Mil. Engrs., U.S. Naval Inst., Optical Soc. Am., Kappa Alpha (Southern), Accademia Internazionale di lettre e Scienze (Napoli), Royal Soc. for Encouragement of Arts, Manufacture and Commerce (London). Awarded diploma of academic corr. by Internat. Acad. Letters and Science, Naples, 1922, also Cross of Honor "for scientific and literary achievements," by same, 1925. Address: Box 1703, 180 Central Park South, New York, N.Y. Died Feb. 16, 1944.

HUTCHISON, RALPH COOPER coll. pres.; b. Florissant, Colo., Feb. 27, 1898; s. Joseph Cooper and Estelle Katherine (Mosier) H.; student Sterling (Kan.) Coll., 1914-16; A.B., Lafayette Coll., 1918, D.D., 1930; M.A., Harvard, 1919; Princeton Theol. Sem., 1919-22; Ph.D., U. Pa., 1925; LL.D., Otterbein Coll., 1941, U. Pitts., 1942, Rutgers U., 1946, Jefferson Med. Coll., 1947; Sc.D., Lincoln U., 1953; L.H.D., Lehigh U., 1945; Litt.D., Mo. Valley, 1951; d. Internat. Law, Parsons Coll., 1955; D.C.L., Emporia (Kan.) Coll., 1960; m. Harriet Sidney Thompson, Jan. 2, 1925; children-Mary Elizabeth (Mrs. E. J. Clark), Wm. Robert. Ordained ministry Presbyn. Ch., 1922; dir. religious edn. 1st Presbyn. Ch., Norristown, Pa., 1922-24; sec. young peoples work Presbyn. Bd. Christian Edn., Phila., 1924-25; prof. philosophy and religion Alborz Coll. of Teheran, Persia, 1925-26, dean 1926-31; pres. Washington and Jefferson Coll., 1931-45; pres. Lafayette Coll., 1945-57; chancellor Abadan (Iran) Inst. Tech., 1957-60; ednl. adviser Oil Consortium of Iran, 1957-59; ednl. adviser Nat. Iranian Oil Co., 1959-60; exec. dir. Nat. Presbyn. Ch. Center, 1960, dir. Studies in Higher Education, Phila., 1960-; dir. Acacia Mut. Life Ins. Co. of Washington. Chmn. Def. Savs., Washington County, 1941-43; exec. dir. Civilian Def. for Pa., 1943-45; vice chmn. Pa. Aeros. Commn., 1943-56; v.p., Pa. United War Fund 1942-44; dir. Pa. Commn. Higher Edn., 1945-50; dir. Am. Friends of Middle East; ednl. adviser Iran Found.; dir. Middle East Relief. Mem. Pa. State Adv. Com. on sci., engring., and specialized personnel. Served as aviator U.S. Naval Aviation, World War I. Pres. bd. trustees Alborz Coll., 1933-45; dir. Princeton Theol. Sem.; v.p., Pa. State YMCA, 1945-50. Pres. Pa. Fedn. Ind. Colls., 1956. Awarded Yorktown medal Soc. of Cin., 1942, Meritorious Service medal Commonwealth of Pa., 1946; Certificate of Merit, U.S. Govt., 1947; Notable Service to Nation medal Ulster Irish Soc., 1953; Sigma Alpha Epsilon Distinguished Service award, 1953; Distinguished Salesmanship award Easton Area execs., 1954; Knight Comdr. Liberian Order African Redemption, 1955; Legion Honor, French Republic. Mem. Sigma Alpha Epsilon, Pi Delta Epsilon, Alpha Phi Omega. Mason (33ff), Rotarian. Clubs: University (N.Y.C.); Metropolitan (Wash.); Pomfret (Easton, Pa.); Union League (Phila.). Author study reports various colls. and univs. Contbr. to mags. Home: 840 Montgomery Av., Bryn Mawr, Pa. Office: 1616 Walnut St., Phila. Died Mar. 8, 1966; buried Easton (Pa.)

HUTTON, JOHN EDWARD physician, congressman; b. Polk County, Tenn., Mar. 28, 1828; grad. Pope's Med. Coll., St. Louis; studied law. Taught sch.; began practice of medicine, Warrenton, Mo., 1860; commd. col. 59th Regt., Mo. Volunteer Inf., U.S. Army, during Civil War; admitted to Mo. bar, 1864, began practice of law Warrenton; moved to Mexico, Mo., 1865, practiced law, 1865-73; became owner, publisher Intelligencer (a Democratic newspaper), 1873; mem. U.S. Ho. of Reps. (Dem.) from Mo., 49th-50th congresses, 1885-89; resumed practice Died Mexico Mo., Dec. 28, 1893; buried Elmwood Cemetery, Mexico.

HUXLEY, HENRY MINOR patent lawyer; b. Newton, Mass., Jan. 21, 1880; s. Edward Charles and Alice Jane (Haley) H.; A.B., Havard, 1899, A.M., 1902; LL.B., Chgo. Kent Coll. Law, 1911; m. Carroll Coleman, Apr. 16, 1913; 1 dau., Margaret Carroll (Mrs. Robert L. Dick). Operating dept. Am. Steel & Wire Co., Worcester, Mass., 1903-07; with Duplex Metals Co., N.Y.C., 1907-08, Brown & Williams, patent lawyers, Chgo., 1908-09, Linthicum, Belt & Fuller, 1909-14; admitted to Ill. bar, 1911; mem. firm Bell & Huxley, 1914-15, Wilkinson & Huxley, Byron & Hume, Chgo., 1946—; pvt. practice, 1915-16; lectr. patent law Northwestern, 1928-29. Trustee Northwestern Mil. and Naval Acad, Seabury-Western Theol. Sem. dir. Freyn Engring. Co. Served as capt. 11th Ill. Inf., 1917, capt., maj. ordnance dept., Army U.S. 1918-19; 1st lt. inf. Ill. N.G., 1920-21, capt. tank corps, 1921-22; lt. col. ordnance dept., Army U.S., 1942-43; lt. col. hon. ret., 1947. Mem. Am. Bar Assn. (chmn. patent sect. 1928-30), Ill. State, Chgo. bar assns., Am. Patent Law Assn., Patent Law Assn. Chgo. (pres. 1932), Internat. Assn. Protection Indsl. Property (pres. Am. group 1931-32), Delta Upsilon, Delta Theta Phi. Republican. Episcopalian. Clubs: Law; Univ., Adventurers (Chgo.); Univ (Evanston); Glen View; Chevy Chase; Farmington Country. Home: 1625 Judson Av., Evanston, Ill. Office: First National Bank Bldg., Chgo. 3. Died Aug. 19, 1954; buried Mt. Auburn Cemetery, Cambridge, Mass.

HYATT, FRANK KELSO ret. pres.; b. Chester, Pa., Nov. 19, 1885; s. Gen. Charles Eliot and Keziah West (Dyer) H.; father pres. Pa. Mil. Coll. many yrs.; student Gilbert's Acad., 1902, Swarthmore Prep. Sch., 1903; student Pa. Mil. Coll., 1903, LL.D., 1930; B.S. in Engring., Swarthmore Coll., 1907; m. Blanche L. Cramp, June 1, 1909 (dec. Oct. 1, 1950); 1 son (died in infancy); m. 2d, Mabel E. Cramp, Dec. 26 1951. With Pa. Mil. Coll. since 1907, asst. prof. Mathematics, 1909-12, prof., 1912-29, treas. since 1916, v.p., 1917-30, succeeded father as pres., 1930, also trustee, president emeritus since 1952. Organizer, and captain Troop G, Pennsylvania National Guard, 1910, lt. col. inf., 1917, col., 1930. Republican. Presbyterian. Mason (K.T.). Clubs: Union League, Pickering Hunt; (hon. mem.) Kiwanis (Philadelphia) Chester. Address: 701 E. 14 St., Chester, Pa. Died July 13, 1958.

HYDE, JAMES FRANCIS CLARK army officer; b. Newton Highlands, Mass., April 29, 1894; s. Frank C. and Blanche E. (Bean) H.; student Mass. Inst. of Tech., 1912-14; B.S., Colo. Coll., 1916; m. Marie S. Spink, Jan. 10, 1918; 1 son, James F. C., Jr. Commd. army engr. officer, U.S. Army, June 1916, and advanced through the grades to brig. gen., Sept. 13, 1942. Awarded World War, Army of Occupation, Defense Period, Am., European and Asiatic theater medals. Mem. Mil. Engrs., Theta Chi. Clubs: Army and Navy (Washington, D.C.); Engineer Mess (Ft. Belvoir, Va.). Home: Marlyn Apts., 39th and Cathedral, N.W., Washington, D.C. Died Aug. 7, 1944.

HYDE, JOHN BACHMAN, ry. ofcl. (ret.); b. St. L., Mo., Apr. 28, 1890; s. Charles R. (clergyman) and Anne Rea (Bachman) H.; A.B., U. of Va., 1912; LL.B., Chattanooga Coll. of Law, 1914; m. Willa Ker Foster, Jan. 5, 1916; 1 dau., Rose Foster (Mrs. Herbert P. Fales). Admitted to Tenn. bar and practicing atty., Chattanooga, Tenn., 1914-26; solicitor law dept. Southern Ry. Co., 1926-30, gen. atty., later gen. solicitor, 1930-32, v.p. in charge finance, corporate relations, purchases, ins., real estate 1932-56 (ret.); engaged in historical research. Enlisted as private in the U.S. Army, promoted through grades to 2d lt., adj., 1st Bn., 308th Inf., 77th Division, A.E.F., 1918. Mem. Washington Society of Investment Analysts, American Legion, American Bar Association, Sigma Alpha Epsilon, Delta Theta Phi. Republican. Episcopalian. Clubs: Metropolitan, Chevy Chase (Washington); Mountain City (Chattanooga). Author: Second Supplement Legal History Southern Railway Company, 1958. Home: Washington DC Died Mar. 30, 1970.

HYDE, JOHN MCEWEN brig. gen. U.S.A.; b. New York, Nov. 1, 1841; s. Joseph and Catherine Maria (McEwen) H.; m. Katharine Hubbard, Oct. 21, 1885. Pvt. Co. A, 71st Regt., N.G.S.N.Y., June 16, 1861; disch., July 30, 1861; 2d lt. 38th N.Y. Inf., Jan. 11, 1862; promoted through grades to lt. col. deputy q.m. gen., Apr. 12, 1903; brig. gen., July 9, 190 13, 1865, "for gallant and meritorious services in battle of Cold Harbor, Va"; col. vols., Mar. 13, 1865, for same in front of Petersburg, Va. Wounded in battle of Bull Run; was in siege of Yorktown and at 2d Bull Run, where was again wounded, and at Fredericksburg; served at Chancellorsville in Miles' Div., 2d Corps, Army of Potomac, in action of Morton's Ford, battles of the Wilderness, Po River, Spottsylvania C.H., North Ann, Tolopotomoy Creek, Cold Harbor, Petersburg. Surveying expdn. N.P. R.R., 1872; served in Wyo., Ariz., Nev., Ida. and Calif., 1874-83; on recruiting service, New York, 1883-84; 1883-85; took part in Bannock campaign, 1878, in Chimehueva troubles in Ariz., 1880, and Cibicu troubles, 1881; adj. 8th Inf., 1886; capt. and asst. q.-m., 1889; at Davids Island, New York Harbor, 1889-92; Jefferson Barracks, Mo., 1892-93; Vancouver Barracks, Wash., 1893-96; at Boston, 1896-99, adding to q.-m. work that of purchasing commissary during Spanish War; ordered to Manila, Oct. 1899; sent to Nagasaki, Japan, where established depot; was depot q.-m. when expeditionary force went to Peking; chief q.-m. Dept. of Visays, at Iloilo, Panay, Sept., 1901-September 1902; assigned to Portland, Oregon, Jan. 1903; chief q.-m. Dept. of Calif., May 1903; chief of q.-m. Dept. of Dakota, at St. Paul, Aug. 1903; retired at own request after 40 yrs.' service, July 10, 1904. Episcopalian. Died Oct. 25, 1916.

HYLAND, WILLIAM A. surgeon; b. Grand Rapids, Mich., Apr. 26, 1892; s. Michael and Sophia Hyland; B.S., M.D., Georgetown U.; m. Edith Goodspeed, Oct. 20, 1923; 1 son, William Goodspeed. Pvt. practice, E. Grand Rapids, Mich. Mem. SSS med. adv. bd., Mich., World War II; nat. bd. Am. Cancer Soc. Dir. Lansing and Grand Rapids bds. Mich. Nat. Bank. Served to maj., M.C., U.S. Army, World War II. Mem. A.C.S., A.M.A. (chmn. constn. and by laws com.), Central Surg. Soc., Am. Goiter Soc. Author papers abdominal and surgery of thyroid gland. Home: 2311 Wealthy S.E. Office: Ramona Med. Bldg., East Grand Rapids, Mich. Died July 18, 1966.

HYMAN, ALBERT SALISBURY, cardiologist; b. Boston, Mass., Apr. 6, 1893; s. John Jacob and Caroline (Greenwood) H.; A.B., Harvard, 1915, M.D., 1918; Med. Sc.D., U. London, 1924; med. deg. cardiology U. Vienna, 1925; m. Lillian Edyth Levenson, Jan. 29, 1967. Resident physician Boston City Hosp., 1919-20; med. supt. Mt. Sinai Hosp., Phila., 1920-23; med. dir. Jewish Maternity Hosp., Phila., 1922-23; med. supt. Beth David Hosp., N.Y.C., 1923-24; cons. cardiologist VA, N.Y. City Hosp. div. Mt. Sinai Hosp., Manhattan Gen. Hosp. div. Beth Israel Hosp., Richmond Meml. Hosp. (S.I.), Hosp. for Aged (Bronx); cons. cardiologist Wolffe Clinic, Phila., U.S. Naval Hosp., St. Albans, N.Y., Valley Forge (Pa.) Heart Inst. and Hosp., Beth David Hosp., Jewish Meml. Hosp., N.Y.C. Hosp. at Elmhurst, Long Beach Meml. Hosp.; attending physician N.Y. City Hosp.; dir. Daitz Cardiovascular Research Fund, N.Y. Dir. Witkin Found. for Study and Prevention Heart Disease, Cordiosonic Research Found. Examiner, Nat. Bd. Med. Examiners, 1948. Founders trustee Am. Coll. Cardiology; pres. Am. Coll. of Sports Medicine. Served from lt. comdr. to capt., USN, 1934-46; PT., and base hosps. Received Presidential Unit Citation (1st Marine Div.), Navy Commendation Ribbon. Diplomate Am. Bd. Internal Medicine. Fellow A.C.P.; mem. numerous nat., state, local profl. socs. and affiliated orgns., former pres. several. Clubs: Harvard (N.Y.C.); Rod and Gun, Outboard (Fairfield, Conn.). Medical editor Greenwood Collegiate Press. Author several books in field of cardiology latest being: Practical Cardiology, 1958; Acute Medical Syndromes, 1959. Co-author: Medical Care of the Athlete. Editor: The Medical Emergencies, 1957; Practical Cardiology, 1958; Functional Capacity of the Heart in Health and Disease, 1959. Editor: Ency. of Sports Medicine. Contbr. articles to sci. publs. Inventor artificial pacemaker for resusciatation of dying heart and other life-saving apparatus. Home: New York City NY Died Dec. 7, 1972; buried L.I. Nat. Cemetery, Farmingdale NY

HYMAN, IRVING neurologist, educator; b. Buffalo, Aug. 12, 1908; s. Max and Rose (Dickman) H.; B.S., U. Buffalo, 1929, M.D., 1935; m. Irma Cohen, Dec. 31, 1937; children-Susan (Mrs. Franklin E. Koven). Lisbeth, Mark. chief neurology and electroencephalography, attending neurologist Millard Fillmore Hosp.; Buswell research fellow, prof. neurology U. Buffalo, 1959-61. Buswell prof. neurology, chmn. dept., 1959-. Served to lt. col., M.C., AUS, 1942-45. Fellow Am. Psychiat. Assn.; mem. A.A.A.S., Am. Assn. Research Nervous and Mental Disease, Am. Acad. Neurology, Eastern Assn. Electroencephalographers. Jewish religion. Contbr. sci. articles to profl. publs. Home: 96 Leicester Rd., Tonawanda, N.Y. Office: 100 High St., Buffalo 3. Died Mar. 7, 1961.

HYPES, SAMUEL L. mcht.; b. Evanston, Ill., May 10, 1894; s. William F. and Fanny Edgerton (Loomis) H.; A.B., Princeton, 1916; m. Charlotte Parmelee, March 12, 1921; children-Barbara (Mrs. Blair A. Hellebush), William Parmelee, Jean. Dept. mgr. Marshall Field & Co., Wholesale, Chgo., 1916-36; mdse. mgr. Wieboldt Stores, Inc., Chgo., 1936-41, v.p., dir., 1941-43, pres. since 1943. Served as capt. U.S. Army, 1917 to 1919; with AEF. pres. Chgo. YMCA, mem. nat. and internat. bd. Republican. Presbyn. Clubs: Commercial, University (Chgo); Skokie Country. Home: 566 Washington Av., Glencoe, Ill. Office: 106 S. Ashland Blvd., Chgo. Died Oct. 1963.

HYRNE, EDMUND MASSINGBIRD army officer; b. Jan. 14, 1748, son of Col. Henry Hyrne. Served as capt. 1st S. C. Continental Regt., promoted to major 1779, dep. adj-gen. souther dept., 1778-83, received congressional notice for bravery, 1780; aide-de-camp to Gen. Nathanael Green, 1781-82, mem. Jackson borough; S.C. legislature 1782. Died on his plantation; Ormsby St. Bartholomew's Parrish, S.C., Dec. 1783.

IDE, GEORGE ELMORE naval officer; b. Zanesville, O., Dec. 6, 1845; s. Dr. William E. and Angelina (Sullivan) I.; grad. U.S. Naval Acad., 1865; m. Alexandra Louise Bruen, July 28, 1899. Served on various ships, including Juniata in Greenland after Polaris survivors, 1873; brought home Virginius filibusters from Santiago, 1873; comd. U.S.S. Justin, off Santiago, in Spanish-Am. War, 1898; took U.S.S. Yosemite to Guam, 1899, and surveyed harbor; comd. U.S.S. New Orleans in Manila, 1900, thence capt. navy yard, Mare Island, Calif., until retired as rear admiral U.S. Navy, Sept. 26, 1901, after 40 yrs.' service. Address: New York, N.Y. Died Feb. 12, 1917.

IDE, JOHN JAY aeronautics; b. Narragansett Pier, R.I., June 26, 1892; s. George Elmore (rear adm. U.S. Navy) and Alexandra Louise (Bruen) I.; grad. Browning Sch., New York, 1909; Certificate of Architecture, Columbia, 1913; studied Ecole des Beaux Arts, Paris, 1914; LL.D. (honorary), Hanover College, 1952; married Dora Browning Donner, February 12, 1940. Architect with H. T. Lindeberg, N.Y., 1916-17 and 1920-21; tech. asst. in Europe of Nat. Adv. Com. for Aeronautics, at American Embassy, Paris, 1921-40, 1949-50; consultant for Nat. Adv. Com. for Aeros., 1950-58; on active duty in Bur. Aeronautics, Navy Dept., Wash., D.C., 1940-43. Ensign lt. (j.g.) and lt. United States Naval Reserve Flying Corps, 1917-20. Assigned to staff, commander U.S. Naval Forces (Europe) as Tech. Air Intelligence Officer, 1943-46; temporary duty with Combined Intelligence Objectives subcom., Paris, Aug. 1944, U.S. Strategic Bombing Survey, Germany, June 1945; apptd. asst. Naval attaché for Air, Am. Embassy, London, Aug. 1945, advanced to capt. U.S.N.R., Nov. 1945; ended fgn. duty, Nov. 1946; del. Anglo-Am. Air Conf., 1947-59; spl. mission Europe USAF, 1951. Trustee French Institute of the United States, Museum of the City of N.Y.; fellow Pierpont Morgan Library. Awarded Commendation Ribbon by Commander of Twelfth Fleet. Recipient gold medal NACA, 1952; Chevalier Legion of Honor (France). Hon. fellow Smithsonian Instn., Washington; fellow Inst. Aero. Scis.; mem. Society Colonial Wars, Soc. Automotive Engrs., Nat. Aero. Assn., Council Fgn. Relations (dir.), Fedn. French Alliances in U.S. (pres. 1959-60), Naval Order U.S., Huguenot Soc., France-Am. Soc. (dir.), Am.-Italy Soc. (dir.), Pilgrims of U.S.; hon. mem. Royal Aero. Society (London); vice pres. Internat. Aero. Fedn., 1948-50, 58-60. Republican. Episcopalian. Clubs: Union, River, St. Nicholas, Wings (N.Y.C.); Metropolitan (Washington); Everglades, Bath & Tennis (Palm Beach). Author: Georgian Country Houses in Ireland, 1959. Home: 485 Park Av., N.Y.C. 10022. Died Jan. 12, 1962; buried Jay Cemetery, Rye, N.Y.

IGLAUER, SAMUEL otolaryngologist; b. Cincinnati, O., Dec. 28, 1871; s. Arnold and Delia (Fechheimer) I.; B.S., U. of Cincinnati, 1895; M.D., Med. Coll. of Ohio, 1898; intern and house phys. Cincinnati Hosp., 1898-99; studied Vienna Hosp., 1900; m. Helen S. Ransohoff, Apr. 19, 1906; children-Helen, Charles (dec.), Josephine. Asst. in Throat Dept., Ohio Med.

Coll. Dispensary, 1901-05; laryngologist and aurist to Jewish Hospital, 1901-22, Cincinnati General Hospital, 1910-17; director of laryngology Cincinnati Gen. Hosp., 1917-31; director of Oto-laryngology, Jewish Hosp., since 1922; Cincinnati General and Children's hospitals since 1931; asso. prof. otology, rhinology and laryngology, 1904-16, prof. laryngology, 1916-30, prof. oto-laryngology since 1930, College of Medicine of U. of Cincinnati, Mem. Charter Commn., 1918. Fellow Am. Coll. Surgeons; mem. A.M.A., Ohio State Med. Assn., Am. Laryngol., Rhinol. and Otol. Soc., Am. Acad., Ophthalmology and Otolaryngology, Am. Laryngol. Soc. Ex-pres. Am. Broncho-Esophagological Soc.; mem. Cincinnati Anti-Tuberculosis League, Cincinnati Acad. Medicine, Cincinnati Oto-Laryngol. Soc., Sigma Xi. Capt. M.C. U.S. Army, 1918-19. Clubs: University, Cincinnati Country, Losantiville Country. Home: 162 Glenmary Av. Office: 707 Race St. Bldg., Cincinnati, O. Died June 23, 1944.

IGLEHART, DAVID STEWART pres. W.R. Grace & Co.; b. New Albany, Ind., Sept. 4, 1873; s. Ferdinand Cowle (clergyman) and Nannie Dorsey (Stewart) I.; A.B., Columbia U., 1894; m. Aida Birrell, April 29, 1909 (died Nov. 26, 1933); children-Stewart Birrell, Philip Lawrence Birrell, Wendy (Mrs. Douglas A. McCrary). With W. R. Grace and Company since 1894; representative in S.A., 1901-15; returned to New York office, 1915, pres. since 1929; also pres. Grace Line and dir. subsidiaries; director Grace National Bank. Mem. Bus. Advisory Council for U.S. Dept. of Commerce. Served as lt. 112th Regt., U.S. Army, Spanish-Am. War; capt. and aide-de-camp on staff of late Theodore Roosevelt when gov. of N.Y. Decorated with Order of the Sun (Peru); Order of Merit (Chile); Order of Merit (Ecuador); Condor de los Andes (Bolivia). Clubs: Knickerbocker, Racquet and Tennis, India House, Down Town Association (New York); Meadow Brook (L.I.); Gulf Stream Golf (Fla.). Home: Westbury, L.I., N.Y.; (winter) "LaCentinela." Delray, Fla. Office: 7 Hanover Sq., New York, N.Y. Died May 14, 1946.

IJAMS, FRANK BURCH business exec.; b. Terre Haute, Dec. 3, 1886; s. William P. and Sallie (Warren) I.; student Phillips Exeter Acad., 1904-06; A.B., Yale, 1909; m. Helen Fairbanks, Sept. 15, 1915; children-Edward Burch, Emily Alice (Mrs. John H. Williams). Chmn. bd. Alton Box Bd. Co.; pres., dir. Tribune-Star Pub. Co.; dir. Terre Haute First Nat. Bank, Ind. Coke & Gas Co., Terre Haute Gas Co. Served with CAC, 1917-18; disch. as maj. Mem. Am. Legion, Elk. Clubs: Clear Lake Outing (pres.) (Topeka, Ill.); Indiana Society (Chgo.); Country (Terre Haute). Home: Allendale, Terre Haute. Office: Terre Haute House, P.O. Box 511, Terre Haute, Ind. Died Mar. 1966.

IJAMS, GEORGE EDWIN born at Baltimore, September 29, 1888; s. Dr. George Edgar and Helen Elizabeth (Jordan) I.; ed. Baltimore grade schs. and Baltimore City Coll.; m. Mary Rawlings Addison, Feb. 7, 1912; children-George Edwin, Virginia (Mrs. Tracy C. Coleman), Barbara Ann (Mrs. Robert S. Whitmore). Enlisted in Maryland Cavalry, 1908; served on the Mexican border in First Maryland Cav., Nat. Guard, 1916; enlisted as pvt. A.U.S., subsequently entered R.O.T.C., Fort Myer, Va., 1917; served as capt. of inf., U.S. Army; assigned to A.E.F., detachment of War Risk Ins. Bur.; drafted plan of soldier ins., used in the field; apptd. war risk ins. officer of 1st Div.; in that capacity wrote $20,000,000 ins. at the front, some of it under fire for which cited by Gen. Pershing for "exceptionally meritorious and conspicuous service"; joined staff of Brig. Gen. Charles G. Dawes, rendering service in Eng., Spain, Portugal, Switzerland, Italy and N. Africa, coöperating with mil. missions of allies; promoted to maj. and lt. col.; given spl. duties with demobilization and peace conf.; on return to U.S. apptd. asst. dir. Bur. War Risk Ins.; sent to Europe to negotiate reciprocal agreements with foreign countries for care disabled vets., 1921; dir. U.S. Vets. Bur. during its last year; was assistant adminstr. Vet. Adminstrn. since orgn., in charge med. and domiciliary care, constrn. and supplies. Mem. Commn. to study econ. conditions in P.I., created by Japanese occupation, May 1945, which resulted in establishment War claims Commission, 1948. Resigned from gov. Mar. 1, 1946, to serve as dir., Nat. Rehabilitation Service, Vets. Fgn. Wars to 1954. Served 3 terms as comdr. in chief Mil. Order World Wars, its membership doubling during his adminstrn. Decorated Purple Heart (U.S.); Officer Order of Crown of Italy; Officer French Acad. (gold palms); Chevalier Legion of Honor (France); Order of Lafayette (France). Member of the Veterans of Foreign Wars, American Legion Founders (past pres.), Soc. War 1812, Am. Legion, Heroes of '76, R.O.T.C. Assn. of U. S., Nat. Soujourners. Mason (K.T., Shriner). Home: 218 Shaw Av., Silver Spring, Md. Died Mar. 22, 1964; buried Loudon Park Cemetery, Balt.

ILLINGWORTH, SIR CYRIL GORDON commodore Cunard White Star Line; b. Kendal, Westmoreland, Eng., April 28, 1884; s. George R. and Ada I.; ed. privately; m. Grace Watt, Nov. 9, 1917 (div. 1950); children-James, David; m. 2d, Marie Randall Caldwell, July 11, 1950. Cadet, the Sierra Line of squarerigger ships, 1901, served in sailing deep water ships 6½ years; with Cunard Line 1910-49, comd. Queen Mary 1942-49, comd. Queen Elizabeth; comd. Queens, Aquitania, Manretania, Laconia, Lancastria; commodore Cunard White Star fleet 1947-49. Served as capt. with Royal Navy Reserve, 1934, promoted commodore 2d class and commodore of Ocean Convoys, 1940. Knighted, 1949. Decorated Order Merit, Rank Comdr. U.S.A. 1949, Chevalier de L'Ordre, Maritime, France. Mem. Freeman of City of London, Honorable Co. of Master Mariners (Freeman and livery-man). Clubs: Devonshire (London); Southampton Yacht. Home: Longwood Towers, Brookline, Mass. Office: Cunard White Star, Ltd., 25 Broadway, N.Y.C. Died Aug. 7, 1959.

IMBODEN, JOHN DANIEL army officer; b. Augusta County, Va., Feb. 16, 1823; s. George William and Isabella (Wunderlich) I.; attended Washington Coll., 1841-42; m. Eliza McCue; m. 2d, Mary Wilson McPhail; m. 3d, Edna Porter; m. 4th, Anna Lockett; m. 5th, Mrs. at least 5 children. Taught sch., also - - practiced law, Staunton, Va.; mem. Va. Legislature, 2 terms; organized and commanded Staunton Arty. which aided in Confederate capture of Harper's Ferry; promoted col. Confederate Army, brig. gen., 1863; served under gens. Jackson and Lee; involved in railroad promotion for most of life after Civil War. Died Damascus, Va., Aug. 15, 1895; buried Hollywood Cemetery, Richmond, Va.

IMES, BIRNEY, SR. newspaper pub.; b. Gloster, Miss., Feb. 18, 1889; s. Lemuel J. and Mary E. (Whittington) I.; ed. pub. schs., Columbus, Miss.; grad. Miss. Coll., Clinton, Miss., 1907; student army orientation course Command and Gen. Staff Sch., Ft. Leavenworth, Kan., 1943; m. Eunice Tanner, Mar. 1912; 1 son, Birney. Engaged in newspaper work since 1912; editor and publisher Commercial Dispatch, Columbus, Miss., since 1920; owner Columbus Broadcasting Co. since 1943; dir. First Columbus Nat. Bank. Exec. sec. bd. of trustees Univ. of Colls. of Miss., 1925; mem. 1st Fed. P.W.A. bd., Miss., 1933; mem. commn. to study expdn. of Hernando DeSoto in discovery of Miss. River, 1936; mem. Miss. Unemployment Commn., 1936; mem. U.S. delegation (asst. to Sec. of State Hull) to Conf. of Ministers of Fgn. Affairs of Am. Republics, Havana, Cuba, 1940; chmn. Columbus Airbase Com., 1940-41. Organizer and pres. of Columbus Rotary Club, 1922, director, 1943; Governor of Rotary International, 1928. Pres. rep., Inter-American Conf., Mexico City, 1945, and at United Nations Conf., San Francisco, 1945. Mem. Miss. Press Assn. (pres. 1930, mem. bd. govs. 1943), Southern Newspapers Pubs. Assn. (dir. 1943), Miss. Automobile Assn. (dir. 1943), Columbus Chamber of Commerce (pres. 1933, dir. 1943). Apptd. col. on staff Gov. Hugh White, 1936, Govt. Thomas L. Bailey, 1944. Home: 803 College St. Office: Main St., Columbus, Miss. Died June 18, 1947.

IMLAY, JAMES HENDERSON congressman; b. Imlaystown, Monmouth County, N.J., Nov. 26, 1764; grad. Coll. of N.J. (now Princeton), 1786; studied law. Tutor, Coll. of N.J.; admitted to N.J. bar, 1791, practiced law; maj. Monmouth County Militia, during Revolutionary War; mem. N.J. Assembly, 1793-96, speaker, 1796; mem. U. S. Ho. of Reps. from N.J., 5th-6th congresses, 1797-1801; a mgr. apptd. to conduct impeachment proceedings against William Blount (senator from Tenn.), 1798; postmaster of Allentown (N.J.), 1804-05; resumed practice of law, Allentown. Died Allentown, Mar. 6, 1823; buried Presbyn. Ch. Cemetery, Allentown.

IMPERATORI, CHARLES JOHNSTONE physician; b. N.Y.C., Jan. 20, 1878; s. Carlo and Sarah (Johnstone) I.; M.D., N.Y.U., 1899; m. Olga Gilbert, 1902; children-Charles Johnstone, Olga (Mrs. W. R. Wolfinbarger), Sarah (Mrs. William F. Farrell). Sub-extreme Bellevue Hosp., 1899-1900, vis. surgeon, 1917-21, 30-35; prof. laryngology N.Y. Post-Grad. Med. Sch. and Hosp., Columbia, 1922-38; clin. prof. otolaryngology N.Y.U., 1932-35; cons. laryngologist Nyack (N.Y.) Gen. Hosp., Harlem Hosp., N.Y.; cons. bronchoscopist Manhattan Eye, Ear and Throat Hosp.; mem. div. med. scis. NRC, 1941-44. Served as lt. col., C.O. 309th Med. Regt., 84th Div., U.S. Army, 1917-19, AEF. Decorated Medaille D'Honneur Des Epidemies (France). Mem. Am. Laryngol. Assn. (pres. 1942-44), Am. Bronchoscopic Soc. (pres. 1928), N.Y. Acad. Med., Am. Rhinol. Otol. and Laryngol. Soc., A.M.A., A.C.S. (bd. govs. 1942-49), Alpha Delta Sigma, Phi Alpha Sigma. Republican. Episcopalian. Author: Diseases of Nose and Throat (with Dr. H. J. Burman), 1935, 2d edit., 1939, Spanish Am. edition, 1942. Address: Block House, Essex, N.Y. Died June 15, 1949.

INCH, RICHARD naval officer; b. Washington, June 20, 1843; s. Philip and Mary (O'Neil) I.; ed East Washington Sem. and Washington Sem. Apptd. 3d asst. engr. U.S. Navy, Sept. 8, 1863; promoted 2d asst. engr., Oct. 15, 1865; passed asst. engr., Sept. 28, 1874; chief engr., Aug. 3, 1892; comdr., Mar. 3, 1899; capt., Nov. 12, 1902; retired as rear admiral, June 29, 1905. Served on Lancaster and Powhatan, 1863-67; Navy Yard, New York, 1867-68; Nyack, 1868-70; Triana, 1871-72; Richmond, 1872-73; Tallapoosa, 1873; Gettysburg, 1873-74; Navy Yard, Washington, 1875-77; Wyoming, 1877-81; Passaic, 1881; spl. duty Exec. Mansion. Washington, 1881; Passaic, 1881-82; Pinta, 1883; Yantic, 1884-86; Navy Yard, Washington, 1887-90; Lancaster 1891-92; Marion, 1892-94; Navy Yard, Mare Island, 1895-97; Concord, 1897; Boston, 1898; Charleston, 1898-99; naval sta., Cavite, P.I., 1899; insp. machinery. Newport News, 1900-05; advanced 3 numbers on the comdrs. list, Feb. 11, 1901, "for eminent and conspicuous conduct in battle." Address: Washington, D.C. Died 1911.

INGALLS, JAMES MONROE army officer, author; b. Sutton, Vt., Jan. 25, 1837; s. James and Mary (Cass) I.; prep. edn. Evansville (Wis.) Sem., 1859-63; grad. Artillery Sch., Ft. Monroe, Va., 1872; m. Eliza H. Niles, July 29, 1860; children-Arthur Niles, Hilda Eliza; m. 2d, Harriet Elizabeth Thurston, July 17, 1877; 1 dau., Fanny Thurston. Pvt. and corporal Co. A, 1st Battalion, 16th Inf., and commissary sergt. and q.-m. sergt. 16th Inf., Jan. 2, 1864-May 21, 1865; commd. 2d lt. and 1st lt., May 3, 1865; transferred to 2d Inf., Apr. 17, 1869, to 1st Arty., Jan. 1, 1871; capt. July 1, 1890; maj., June 1, 1897; transferred to 5th Arty., Oct. 28, 1899; lt. col. 3d Arty., Oct. 5, 1900; retired, Jan. 25, 1901; advanced to rank of col.; retired, by act of Apr. 23, 1904. Participated in Atlanta campaign and was engaged in reconstruction duty in South until Jan. 1, 1871. Founded Dept. of Ballistics at U.S. Arty. Sch., Ft. Monroe, 1882; was prin. instr. until school suspended operations, Apr. 1898, at outbreak of war with Spain. Author: Exterior Ballistics, 1883, 85, 86; Ballistic Machines, 1885; Handbook of Problems in Exterior Ballistics, 1890, 1901; Interior Ballistics, 1894, 1911; Ballistic Tables, 1891, 1900; Ballistics for the Instruction of Artillery Gunners, 1893. Wrote: Articles Gunnery Gunpowder, Johnson's Universal Cyclopaedia, 1894; article Ballistics in New Internat. Ency., 2d edit., 1915. Home: Providence, R.I. Died May 1, 1927.

INGERSOLL, ROYAL RODNEY rear admiral U.S.N.; b. Niles, Mich., Dec. 4, 1847; s. Harmon W. and Rebecca A. (Deniston) I.; grad. U.S. Naval Acad., 1863; m. Cynthia Eason, Aug. 26, 1873; 1 son, Royal Eason. Has served as naval officer in all parts of the world; commd. capt., Mar. 21, 1903; rear admiral, July 11, 1908. Comd. U.S.S. Supply during Spanish-Am. War; comdg. Maryland, 1905; chief of staff Atlantic Fleet, voyage from Hampton Roads to the Pacific; mem. Gen. Bd. of the Navy; retired, Dec. 4, 1909. Pres. spl. bd. on naval ordnance, July 9, 1917-Jan. 2, 1919. Presbyterian. Author: Textbook of Ordnance and Gunnery, 1887; Exterior Ballistics, 1891; Elastic Strength of Guns, 1891. Home: LaPorte, Ind. Died Apr. 21, 1931.

INGRAHAM, DUNCAN NATHANIEL naval officer; b. Charleston, S.C., Dec. 6, 1802; s. Nathaniel and Louisa (Hall) I.; m. Harriot Horry Laurens, 1827, 3 sons, 5 daus. Apptd. midshipman U.S. Navy at age 9 years, 1812; served in ships Congress and Madison during War of 1812; promoted lt., 1825, comdr., 1838; served in Mexican War; participated in Koszta affair (his most celebrated act), 1853; chief Bur. Ordnance, 1856-60; entered Confederate Navy, 1861; chief ordnance, Richmond, Va.; commanded Confederate naval forces on S.C. coast; commanded 2 iron clads, 1863; on shore duty, 1863-65. Died Charleston, Oct. 16, 1891.

INGRAHAM, PRENTISS soldier, author; b. Adams County, Miss., Dec. 22, 1843; s. Rev. Prof. J. H. I. and Mary (Brooks) I.; ed. private tutor, St. Timothy's Mil. Acad., Md., and Jefferson Coll., Miss.; studied medicine, Mobile Med. Coll., but left to enter C.S.A., Apr. 1861; m. Rosa Langley, 1875. Served in light arty., Withers' Miss. Regt.; wounded and captured at Ft. Hudson; also served on staff as lt. and in Ross' brigade, Texas cav., commdr. of scouts; wounded at battle of Franklin; served after Civil war in Mexico under Juarez; also in Austria, in war with Prussia; in Crete and in Africa; extensive traveler in Eastern lands; served afloat and ashore in Cuban ten years' war for independence, with ranks of capt. of navy and col. of cav.; was tried as filibuster and condemned to death by Spaniards; escaped. Entered upon literary career in London, England, 1870; later in New York. Democrat. Author: Zuleikah: A Story of Crete, 1887; Darkie Dan, 1888; In Golden Fetters, 1888; Cadet Carey, of West Point, 1890; Red Rovers on Blue Waters, 1890; In Satan's Coll. 1890; An American Monte Cristo, 1891; The Vagabond, 1891; Wandering Jew of the Sea, 1891; Given for Gold, 1893; Trailing with Buffalo Bill; Land of Legendary Lore, 1899; Girl Rough Rider, 1903; Satan's Slave, 1903; and over 600 novels. Home: Chicago, Ill. Died 1904.

INGRAM, JONAS HOWARD mfg. exec., ret. naval officer; b. Jeffersonville, Ind., Oct. 15, 1886; s. William Thomas and Anna I. (Howard) I.; student Culver (Ind.) Mil. Acad., 1902-03; B.S., U.S. Naval Acad., 1907; grad. U.S. Naval War Coll., 1940; m. Jean Fletcher-Coffin, July 14, 1914; children-William Thomas II, Mary-Birch (wife L. C. Hays, U.S.M.C.). Commd. ensign, U.S.N., 1909, advanced through grades to admiral, 1944; football coach U.S. Naval Acad., 1909-12, head coach, 1915-17, dir. athletics, dir. football, 1926-30; chief staff 9th Naval Dist., Great Lakes, Ill., 1921-23; comdr. U.S.S. Stoddert, 1924-26; exec., acting comdr. U.S.S. Pennsylvania, 1930-33; pub. relations officer Navy Dept., naval aide to sec. navy, 1933-36; comdr. Destroyer Sqdn. Six, U.S. Battle Fleet, 1936-37; capt. N.Y. Navy Yard, 1937-39; comdr. U.S.S. Tennessee, 1940, cruisers U.S. Atlantic Fleet, 1941,

Allied Forces in South Atlantic, 1942; comdr.-in-chief Atlantic Fleet, 1944-46, ret. Apr. 1, 1947; commr. football, pres. All-Am. Football Conf., 1947-49; v.p., dir. Reynolds Metals Co., Richmond, Va., since 1949; pres. Acme Fuel Co., Jeffersonville, since 1947; dir. summer schs. Culver (Ind.) Mil. Acad. 1952. Hon. mem. Princeton, 1915. Trustee U.S. Naval Acad. Alumni Assn., Inc. Clubs: New York (N.Y.) Yacht; Annapolitan (Annapolis, Md.); Racquet Phila.,); Army-Navy Country (Washington); Pendennis (Louisville); San Diego (commr.), University (San Diego, Cal.); Maxinkuckee Yacht (Culver, Ind.). Address: 330 Eighth St., Coronado 18, Cal. Died Sept. 10, 1952; buried Arlington Nat. Cemetery.

INMAN, ARTHUR CHARLES corp. ofcl.; b. Star Lake, Wis., June 30, 1901; s. Charles and Anna (Ludewig) I.; A.B., U. Wis., 1923, LL.B., 1925; m. Winona Cherry, Mar. 2, 1929; 1 dau., Ann I. Martin. Admitted Wis., Ida., Utah bars; practiced, Milw., 1925, Salt Lake City, 1927-28; asst. atty. Utah Power & Light Co., 1928-37; v.p., sec., gen. counsel, dir. Idaho Power Co., Boise, 1937-. Director Boise YMCA. Served as maj., Judge Advocate Gen. Department Reserve. Mem. Beta Theta Pi, Phi Alpha Delta, Delta Sigma Rho, Beta Gamma Sigma, Order of Coif. Episcopalian. Mason (33ff, Shriner). Home: 3149 Grover Ct. Office: 1220 Idaho St., Boise, Ida. Died Feb. 1, 1966.

INMAN, GEORGE army officer; b. Boston, Dec. 3, 1775; s. Ralph and Susanna (Speakman) I.; grad. Harvard, 1772; m. Mary Badger, Apr. 23, 1778, 4 daus. Served with British at Bunker Hill, 1775; took part in capture of Am. intelligence officers at Battle of L.I. (perhaps decisive in Am. defeat), 1776; commd. ensign 17th Inf., 1776, served in battles of Princeton, Brandywine, Germantown, Monmouth; exiled in Eng., 1780-88. Died circa Feb., 1789.

IRBY, NOLEN MEADERS coll. pres.; b. Green Forest, Tex., July 27, 1887; s. Henry Wiley and Fannie Lou (Meaders) I.; A.B., U. Ark., 1916; A.M., George Peabody Coll. for Tchrs., Nashville, 1926, Ph.D., 1930; m. Nell Cole, Nov. 27, 1919: children-Nell Cole (wife of Major George A. Barron, Jr.), Mary Charles (Mrs. Lee Yarbrough). Supt. schs., Bearden, Ark., 1919-22; prin. North Little Rock High Sch., 1922-23; supt. schs., Marianna, Ark., 1924-27; prof. psychology Ore. State Coll., 1928-29; state agt. for rural schs. Ark., 1930-38; dir. field service U. Ga., 1938-41; pres. Ark. State Tchrs. Coll., Conway, Ark., 1941—. Served as capt. U.S. Army, 1918-19. Mem. Rural Com. Edn., A.E.R.A., Phi Beta Kappa, Kappa Delta Pi, Phi Delta Kappa. Rotarian. Home: 140 Donaghey Av., Conway, Ark. Died Nov. 1, 1958; buried Conway.

IRELAND, CHARLES THOMAS, JR., lawyer; b. Boston, Apr. 14, 1921; s. Charles Thomas and Margaret (Keough) I.; A.B. summa cum laude, Bowdoin Coll., 1942; LL.B., Yale, 1948; wife Dorothy; children—Anne, Claire, Stephen, Allan. Admitted to New York bar, associate of White and Case, New York City, 1948-51; sec. N.Y.C. R.R., 1954-59; senior v.p. Internat. Tel. & Tel. Corp.; dir. Investors Diversified Services, Inc., Levitt & Sons, Inc., Sheraton Corp. Am.; dir., mem. Mid-Town adv. bd. Chem. Bank N.Y. Trust Co. Member board overseers Bowdoin Coll.; bd. dirs. Grand Central branch YMCA, New York City. Served as captain USMC, 1942-46. Decorated Silver Star, Bronze Star, Purple Heart. Mem. A.I.M., Am. Bar Assn. Bar City of N.Y., Am. Mgmt. Assn., Phi Beta Kappa, Theta Delta Chi. Home: Chappaqua NY Died June 1972.

IRELAND, JOHN army officer, gov. Tex.; b. Millerstown, Ky., Jan. 1, 1827; s. Patrick and Rachel (Newton) I.; m. Matilda Wicks, 1854; m. 2d, Anna Penn, 1857. Dep., Hart County, Ky., 1847-50; admitted to Ky. bar, 1852; 1st mayor Sequin, Tex., 1858; del. to conv. which abrogated articles of annexation between Tex. and U.S., 1861; argued for secession; commd. lt. col. Confederate Army, served in campaigns in Trans-Miss. Dept., 1862; mem. Tex. Ho. of Reps., 1872; mem. Tex. Senate, 1873-75; asso. justice Tex. Supreme Ct., 1875-76; gov. Tex. (Democrat), 1882-86. Died Sequin, Mar 15, 1896.

IRELAND, MERRITTE WEBER former surg. gen. U.S. Army; b. Columbia City, Ind., May 31, 1867; s. Martin and Sarah I.; M.D., Detroit Coll. Medicine, 1890; M.D., Jefferson Med. Coll., 1891, LL.D., 1919; A.M., U. Mich., 1920; LL.D., Gettysburg Coll., 1922, Wayne U., 1939; m. Elizabeth Liggett, Nov. 8, 1893; 1 son, Paul Mills. Apptd. asst. surgeon U.S. Army, 1891; capt. asst. surgeon, 1896; maj. surgeon 45th U.S. Inf., 1899; hon. disch. vols., 1901; maj. surgeon U.S. Army, and maj. M.C., 1903; lt. col., May 1, 1911; col., May 15, 1917; brig. gen. N.A., May 16, 1918; asst. surgeon gen. with rank of maj. gen. (temp.), Aug. 1918; surgeon gen., 1918-31 (ret.). Was in Santiago Campaign; in Philippines during insurrection; chief surgeon AEF in France until Oct. 12, 1918. Decorated D.S.M. (U.S.); Legion of Honor and Med. Epidemie (France); Order of the Bath (Gt. Britain); Polonia Restituta (Poland). Pres. A.C.S. Lutheran. Clubs: Army and Navy, Army and Navy Country. Address: War Dept., Washington. Died July 5, 1952.*

IRELAND, R.W., air transportation; b. Chicago, July 6, 1892; s. A.D. and Ella May (Strouse) I.; ed. high school Pace Inst., Washington; m. Nell Otis, Nov. 14, 1913; 1 son, James R. Ticket agent Erie Railroad, 1912; civilian chief of div. Office of Chief of Engrs., U.S. Army, 1913-21; sec. War Dept. sub-com. on appropriations U.S. Ho. of Reps., 1921-26; became dist. traffic mgr. and gen. traffic mgr. United Air Lines, and predecessor companies, 1926, vice pres., 1945, v.p. traffic adminstrn., until 1957; dir. Air Cargo Inc.; adminstr. Defense Air Transport Adminstrn., Washington, from 1952. Pres. Air Traffic Conf. of America, 1940, chmn. various commns. on air traffic confs., 1939-42; mem. panel Am. Arbitration Assn. Served as col., U.S.A.A.F., asst. chief of staff and dept. chief of staff Air Transport Command, July 1942-Nov. 1945; brig. gen. U.S.A.F.R. D.S.M., Legion of Merit, O.B.E. Mem. Air Nat. Defense Transportation Assn. (v.p.). Home: Hendersonville NC Died Jan. 26, 1968; buried Hendersonville NC

IRELAND, THOMAS SAXTON, lawyer, author; b. Cleveland, O., Dec. 16, 1895; s. Paul F. and Lucretia (Bailey) I.; A.B., Princeton U., 1918; LL.B., Boston U., 1923, Harvard U., 1927; m. Mildred Locke, Aug. 3, 1932; children—Patricia, Ruth, Tom III, Bill, John, Fred. Admitted to O. bar, 1926; practiced in N.Y. City, later returning to Cleveland; elected judge of Municipal Court of Cleveland, short term, 1937. Grad. Inf. Sch., Ft. Benning, Ga., 1935; on active duty with U.S. Army, Ft. Benjamin Harrison, Ind., 1941-43; capt. inf., reception center, Co. G, comdg. officer, May 1942-June 1943; orientation lecturer, 1942; post defense counsel, courts martial, 1943. Nominated for assembly, 1934, 36; led Cuyahoga County legislative ticket for Rep State Senate nomination, 1938; nominated for State Senate, 1940; led Rep. slate for short term U.S. Senate nomination, Cuyahoga County, 1946; Rep. candidate for mayor of Cleve., 1959. radio news commentator, station WJAY (now WCLE), 1936-38, WTAM, Cleveland, 1938, WACD, Akron, 1941; spl. corr. Cleveland Plain Dealer, Germany, France, 1948. Columbus Dispatch, Europe, Asia, S.A., 1955-58. Mem. Ohio Bar Assn. (member of citizenship committee), Ohio Society New York, Amvets World War II, American Legion. Republican. Mason (32 deg., Shriner), Sojourner. Clubs: Rowfant, Mayfield Country, Ripon, Ocean of Fla. Author: The Greater Lakes—St. Lawrence Deep Waterway to the Sea, 1934; War Clouds in the Skies of the Far East, 1935; Child Labor as a Relic of the Dark Ages, 1937; Ireland Past and Present, 1942; The Great Lakes-St. Lawrence Seaway and Power Project, 1946. Contributing editor: Irish-American Quarterly, 1946-46. Speaks French, German, Spanish, Italian. Reportorial tours Russia, Poland, Czechoslavakia, Yugoslavia, 1955-56. Home: Shaker Heights OH Died Mar. 25, 1969; buried Lakeview Cemetery, Cleveland OH

IRISH, EDWIN M. lawyer; b. Gorham, Me., June 11, 1848; s. Marshall I.; attended Gorham Sem., grad. Law School, Univ. of Mich., 1872. Practiced law in Kalamazoo, Mich., since 1872; pros. atty., Kalamazoo Co., 1874-80; has been city atty. and mem. Kalamazoo common council. Served 12 yrs., various grades, Mich. Nat. Guard; col. 2d inf. 6 yrs.; adj.-gen. Mich., 1897-98; col. 35th Mich. vols., June 6, 1898; served in Spanish-Am. war; mustered out with regt., Mar. 31, 1899; m. July, 1902, Elisabeth C. Vannerson. Address: Kalamazoo, Mich.†

IRONS, JAMES ANDERSON army officer; b. Phila., Pa., Feb. 21, 1857; s. James R. and Sarah M. (Anderson) I.; grad. Central High Sch., Phila., 1875, U.S. Mil. Acad., 1879, Inf. and Cav. Sch., 1885; m. Florence Farrell, June 7, 1888. Commd. 2d lt. 20th Inf., June 13, 1879; 1st lt., May 14, 1887; capt., Aug. 25, 1893; maj. engr. vols., June 13, 1898; hon. discharged vols., Feb. 16, 1899; maj. U.S.A., Feb. 2, 1901; insp. gen., Feb. 28, 1901; assigned 16th Inf., Mar. 1, 1905; lt. col. 14th Inf., Apr. 9, 1905; col. 20th Inf., June 26, 1909; brig. gen. N.A., Aug. 5, 1917. Served in campaign against Santiago, Cuba, 1898, engaging in actions at El Caney, San Juan and siege of Santiago; with regt. to Philippines, 1899; in action at Guadaloupe, Pasig, Cainta, Mar. 1899; insp. gen. Dept. of Colo., 1901-03; mem. Gen. Staff Corps, 1903-05; mil. attaché Am. Embassy, Tokyo, Japan, 1907-10, 1914-17; mil. observer at Tsingtao, China, during Japan-German campaign, 1914; with Japanese mission to U.S., Aug. 13-Oct. 12, 1917; apptd. comdr. 166th Depot Brigade, Camp Lewis, American Lake, Wash., Sept. 1917; comdr. 5th Inf. Brigade, Camp Greene, N.C., Dec. 23, 1917. Died July 20, 1921.

IRVINE, JAMES army officer; b. Phila., Aug. 4, 1735; s. George and Mary (Rush) I. Commd. ensign 1st Bn., Pa. Provincial Regt., 1760, capt., 1763; del. Provincial Conf., Phila., 1775; commd. lt. col., 1775; commd. rank of col. on charge of 9th Pa. Regt., 1776; served in Can. campaign, 1776; commd. brig. gen. Pa. Militia, 1777, given command of 2d Brigade; commanded right flank of Am. line at Battle of Germantown; mem. Supreme Exec. Council of Pa. (Constitutionalist), 1782-85, v.p. council, 1784-85; mem. Pa. Assembly, 1785-86; maj. gen. Pa. Militia, 1782-93; mem. Pa. Senate, 1795-99. Died Phila., Apr. 28, 1819.

IRVINE, WILLIAM army officer, congressman; b. Enniskillen, Ulster Province, Ireland, Nov. 3, 1741; ed. Trinity Coll., Dublin, Ireland; m. Anne Calender, Children include Calender, Col. William N., Capt. Armstrong. Served as surgeon on Brit. ship of war during Seven Years War; came to Am., 1763; mem. Pa. Provincial Conv., Phila., 1774; commd. col. 6th (later 7th) Pa. Regt., 1776; participated in Battle of Three Rivers, 1776; commd. brig. gen. Continental Army, 1779; participated in Lord Stirling's expdn. against Staten Island, also unsuccessful attack at Bull's Ferry with Gen. Wayne, 1780; del. from Pa. to Continental Congress, 1786-88; del. Pa. Constl. Conv., 1790; mem. U.S. Ho. of Reps. from Pa., 3d Congress, Dec. 2, 1793-95; pres. Pa. br. Soc. of Cincinnati, 1801-04. Died Phila., July 29, 1804.

IRVINE, WILLIAM congressman; b. Whitneys Point, N.Y., Feb. 14, 1820; attended common schs.; studied law. Admitted to N.Y. bar, 1849, began practice in Corning; mem. U.S. Ho. of Reps. (Republican) from N.Y., 36th Congress, 1859-61; an organizer, lt. col. 10th Regt., N.Y. Volunteer Cavalry, 1861; wounded at Battle of Beverly Ford (Va.), taken prisoner, imprisoned in Libby Prison; honorably discharged, 1864; brevetted col. and brig. gen. U.S. Volunteers, 1865; adj. gen. on staff of Gov. Fenton of N.Y., 1865-66; moved to Cal., practiced law. Died San Francisco, Nov. 12, 1882; buried Elmira (N.Y.) Cemetery.

IRVING, FREDERICK CARPENTER physician; b. Gouverneur, N.Y., May 30, 1883; s. Andrew and Nina Frances (Carpenter) I.: grad. Phillips Exeter Acad., N.H., 1902; A.B. cum laude, Harvard, 1906, M.D. cum laude, 1910; m. Mary Amanda Chapman, June 25, 1912; children-Frances, Mary Brewster, Frederick Carpenter, Rebecca, Colin Franklin Newell. Began practice, Boston, 1910; William Lambert Richardson prof. Emeritus obstetrics, Harvard Med. Sch.; cons. obstetrician Boston Lying-In Hosp., Newton-Wesley Hosp.; cons. obstetrician and gynecologist Faulkner Hosp.; cons. surgeon N.E. Bapt. Hosp. Served from 1st lt. to maj. M.C., U.S. Army, France and Italy, World War I. Fellow A.C.S., Am. Gynecol. Soc. (v.p.); mem. Va. Obstet. and Gynecol. Soc., Sociedade Brasileira Gynecologia, So. Atlantic Obstet. and Gynecol. Soc., Mass. Charitable Fire Soc. Rep. Episcopalian. Club: Harvard (Boston, Mass.). Author: A Textbook of Obstetrics; The Expectant Mothers Handbook; Safe Deliverance, a Life-in-America Prize Book; also many articles and jours. Home: 26 Edge Hill Rd., Brookline. Office: 1180 Beacon St., Brookline 46, Mass. Died Dec. 24, 1957.

IRWIN, GEORGE LE ROY army officer; b. Fort Wayne, Mich., Aug. 26, 1868; s. Brig. Gen. Bernard John Dowling and Antoinette Elizabeth (Stahl) I.; grad. U.S. Mil. Acad., 1889, Coast Arty. Sch., 1894, Army War Coll., 1910; m. Maria Elizabeth Barker, Apr. 30, 1892. Commd. additional 2d lt. 5th Arty. June 12, 1889; 2d lt. 3d Arty., Feb. 11, 1890; 1st lt. 5th Arty., Sept. 23, 1897; capt. a.q.m. vols., July 13, 1899; hon. discharged vols., Mar. 21, 1901; capt. Arty. Corps, U.S. Army, Feb. 28, 1901; promoted through grades to major gen., Mar. 1928. Served in Philippines, 1899-1901, Cuba, 1906-09, later in Panama, C.Z.; comdr. 161st F.A. Brigade, Camp Grant, Ill., 1917; sailed for France in command 41st Inf. Div., Dec. 12, 1917; comd. 66th, 2d, and 57th F.A. brigades, and (Nov. 1918-Feb. 1919) the Saumur Arty. Sch.; served on Verdun front, Alsace front, in Marne-Aisne offensive and in the Oise-Aisne and Meuse-Argonne offensives; returned to U.S., May 1919. Comdr Field Arty Sch., Ft. Sill, Okla., 1923. Officer Legion of Honor (France). Episcopalian. Died Feb. 19, 1931.

IRWIN, JARED congressman; b. Ga., Jan. 19, 1768. Apptd. commr. for valuation of lands and dwellings and enumeration of slaves for 2d Div. of Ga., 1798; engaged in merc. bus., Milton, Pa.; postmaster of Milton, 1802-03; sheriff of Northumberland County (Pa.), 1808-12; mem. Pa. Ho. of Reps., 1811; served as col. 5th Rifle Regt., War of 1812; mem. U.S. Ho. of Reps. (Democrat) from Pa., 13th-14th congresses, 1813-17; moved to S.Am.

IRWIN, JOHN rear admiral U.S. Navy, retired Apr. 15, 1894; b. Pa., Apr. 15, 1832; apptd. to navy, Sept. 4, 1847; passed midshipman, June 10, 1853; master 1855; lt., Sept. 6, 1855; lt. comdr., July 16, 1862; comdr., July 25, 1866; capt., May 15, 1875; commodore, Mar. 1886; rear admiral, May 19, 1891. Served on frigate "Wabash" in Civil War; participated in capture of forts at Hatteras Inlet and of Forts Walker and Beauregard; also in battle of Port Royal and capture of Fort Pulaski, 1862. Died 1901.

IRWIN, NOBLE EDWARD naval officer; b. Greenfield, O., Sept. 29, 1869; s. Henry Wilson and Lavina Ann (Rogers) I; grad. U.S. Naval Acad., 1891; m. Elma Natalie Norris, Sept. 26, 1896; 1 dau., Phyllis Natalie. Ensign, July 1, 1893; promoted through grades to rear adm., Dec. 1924. Served aboard U.S.S. Newark at Rio de Janeiro during Brazilian Revolution, 1893-94; wounded while serving on U.S.S. Baltimore at Battle of Manila Bay, May 1, 1898; participated in Philippine Campaign; in comd. at Tientsin, China, during Boxer trouble; as comdr. destroyer Barry, accompanied first flotilla to Philippines; comdr. U.S.S. New Orleans, West Coast of Mexico, 1913-15, and in charge during Turtle

Bay incident; first dir. naval aviation, May 1917-May 1919, also arranged for trans-Atlantic flight; comdr. U.S.S. Oklahoma, 1919-21; comdt. Naval Yard, Portsmouth, N.H., 1921-22; comdt. 15th Naval Dist., Canal Zone, 1923-25; comdg. Destroyer Squad., Scouting Fleet, 1925-27; chief of naval mission, Brazil, 1927-30; comdt., 15th Naval Dist., Canal Zone, 1931-33, retired. Medals: Battle of Manila Bay. Spanish-American War, Philippine Campaign, Chinese Campaign. Mexican Campaign. World War; Navy Cross; Officer Legion of Honor (French). Died Aug. 10, 1937.

IRWIN, STAFORD LEROY army officer; b. Fort Monroe, Va., Mar. 23, 1893; s. Maj. Gen. George LeRoy and Maria Elizabeth (Barker) I.; B.S. U.S. Mil. Acad., 1915; grad. F.A. Sch., 1926, Command and Gen. Staff Sch., 1927, Army War Coll., 1937; m. Helen Hall 1921 (died 1937); 1 son, Francis LeRoy; m. 2d, Clare Moran, May 20, 1941; 1 son, Stafford D'Arcy. Commd. 2d lt., F.A., 1915, advanced through the grades to lt. gen., 1950; now comdg. gen. U.S. Forces in Austria, Mem. Army and Navy Country Club. Home: Asheville, N.C. Office: Hdqrs. USFA, Salzburg, Austria. Died Nov. 23, 1955.

IRWIN, WALLACE author; ú b. Oneida, N.Y., Mar. 15, 1875; s. David S. and Edith E. (Greene) I.; grad. Denver High Sch., 1895; student Stanford, 1896-99; m. Trace Luce, Mar. 22, 1901 (died 1914); m. 2d. McDonald, Jan. 5, 1916; children-Donald McDonald, Wallace. Spl. writer, San Francisco Examiner, 1900; editor Overland Monthly Mag., 1902; revue writer Republic Theatre, San Francisco, 1903; writer topical verse, N.Y. Globe, 1904-05; on staff Collier's Weekly, 1906-07. Life hon. editor Harvard Lampoon, 1912. Mem. Com. Pub. Information, 1917-19. Hon. mem. Fijian Soc. Lt. comdr. USNR, 1926. Clubs: Players, Dutch Treat, Coffee House (N.Y.C.). Author: The Love Sonnets of a Hoodlum, 1902; The Rubaiyat of Omar Khayyam, Jr., 1902; Fairy Tales Up to Now; Nautical Lays of a Landsman; At the Sign of the Dollar, 1904; Chinatown Ballads, 1905; Random Rhymes and Odd Numbers, 1906; A Yankee Tourist (light opera, with Richard Harding Davis), 1907-08; Letters of a Japanese Schoolboy, 1909; Mr. Togo, Maid of All Work, 1913; Pilgrims into Folly, 1917; Venus in the East, 1918; The Blooming Angel, 1919; Suffering Husbands, 1920; Seed of the Sun, 1921; Lew Tyler's Wives, 1923; The Golden Bed, 1924; Mated, 1926; Lew Tyler and the Ladies, 1928; The Days of Her Life, 1931; The Julius Caesar Murder Case, 1935; Young Wife, 1936. Collaborator, Yankee Doctor in Paradise (with Dr. S. M. Lambert), 1940-41. Contbr. to mags. Home: (winter) Southern Pines, N.C.; (summer) 1 Summit Av., Larchmont, N.Y. Office: care Bankers Trust Co. 16 Wall St., N.Y.C. Died Feb. 14, 1959; buried Cave Hill Cemetery, Louisville.

ISERMAN, MICHAEL, physician; b. N.Y.C., Sept. 29,21898; s. Samuel and Dorothy Iserman; M.D., Cornell U., 1923; m. Marian V. Hayman; 1 dau., Susan (Mrs. Edwin Sunshine). Intern, Montefiore Hosp., N.Y.C., 1923-24, resident in Tb, 1925-26; intern Bklyn. Jewish Hosp., 1924-25; postgrad. in cardiology and internal medicine Columbia Coll. Phys. and Surg., 1936-41; clin. asst. cardiologist Mt. Sinai Hosp., N.Y.C. Served to comdr. M.C., USNR, 1942-46. Diplomate Am. Bd. Internal Medicine. Mem. A.M.A., Am. Heart Assn. Home: New York City NY Died Jan. 4, 1971; buried New York City NY

ISHAM, ASA BRAINERD physician; b. Jackson C.H. O., July 12, 1844; s. Chapman and Mary A. I.; ed. schs. of Jackson until 1857; Marietta Coll., 1857-59 (A.M., 1889); M.D., Med. Coll. of Ohio, 1869; m. Mary Hamlin Keyt, of Cincinnati, Oct. 10, 1870. Compositor and asso. editor Lake Superior Journal, Marquette, Mich., 1860-62; city reporter, Detroit Daily Tribune, 1862; enlisted pvt. 7th Mich. Cav., fall, 1862; promoted sergt. Co. I; severely wounded in action nr. Warrenton Junction, Va., May 14, 1863; promoted 1st lt. Mar. 21, 1864; slightly wounded and captured Yellow Tavern, Va., May 11, 1864; prisoner 7 months; paroled for exchange Dec. 11, 1864; hon. discharged on account of wound received in action Apr. 14, 1865; prof. physiology, materia medica and therapeutics, Cincinnati Coll. Medicine and Surgery, 1876-80; trustee Cincinnati Hosp.; pres. bd. med. dirs. Cincinnati Hosp. Expres. Cincinnati Acad. Medicine; mem. A.M.A., Ohio State Med. Assn., G.A.R., 7th Mich. Cav. Assn., Custer's Mich. Cav. Brigade Assn.; comdr. Ohio Commandery Loyal Legion. Author: Prisoners of War and Rebel Prisons, 1890; Historical Sketch of the Seventh Michigan Volunteer Cavalry, 1893. Editor; Sphygmography and Cardiography, by Alonzo T. Keyt, M.D., 1887. Has written a number of papers in Sketches of War History (vols. 1, 2, 4 and 5); also many articles in med. jours. Address: 849 Oak St., Walnut Hills, Cincinnati.

ISHAM, RALPH HEYWARD collector books and manuscripts; b. N.Y.C., July 2, 1890; s. Henry Heyward and Juliet Calhoun (Marsh) I.; student Cornell U., 1908-09. Yale, 1910-11; married; children-Heyward, Jonathan Trumbull. Pres. Trumbull Securities Corp.; v.p. New England Water Power Co. Vol. British Army; served 3 yrs.; on staffs Field Marshal Sir William Robertson and Lord Haig, 1918-19. Decorated Comdr. Order British Empire, for war services; granted permanent rank of lt. col. Fellow Royal Geog. Soc. Clubs: Grolier, Union League, Garrick, Elizabethan (Yale), Royal Socs., Hurlingham (London). Owner large collection of books and manuscripts, acquiring in 1927 the "Boswell Papers," Office: 342 Madison Av., N.Y.C. Died June 13, 1955.*

ISHERWOOD, BENJAMIN FRANKLIN commodore U.S. Navy; b. June 6, 1822. Entered U.S. Navy. May 23, 1844, as 1st asst. engr.; promoted chief engr., Oct. 31, 1848; was engr.-in-chief U.S. Navy, 1861-69; afterward at Mare Island Navy Yard, Calif., and on spl. duties; retired by operation of law, June 6, 1884, with relative rank of commodore. Address: New York, N.Y. Died June 19, 1915.

IVES, HERBERT EUGENE physicist; b. Phila., Pa., July 31, 1882; s. Frederic Eugene and Mary Elizabeth (Olmstead) I.; B.S., U. of Pa., 1905; Ph.D., Johns Hopkins, 1908; hon. Sc.D., Dartmouth and Yale, 1928, Pa., 1929; m. Mabel Agnes Lorenz, Nov. 14, 1908; children-Ronald Lorenz, Barbara Olmstead (Madame Charles Beyer), Kenneth Holbrook. Asso. with Ives Kromskop Company, Phila., 1898-1901; physicist, Bur. of Standards, Washington, 1908-09; physicist, Nat. Electric Lamp Assn., Cleveland, O., 1909-12, United Gas Improvement Co., Phila., 1912-18, Bell Telephone Laboratories, New York, 1919-47. Commissioned capt., Aviation Sect. Signal Corps, Jan. 1918, in charge exptl. work in airplane photography; discharged, 1919, and commd. maj. R.C. Contbg. editor Lightning Journal, New York, 1913-15; asso. editor Jour. of Optical Soc. America. Fellow A.A.A.S. (v.p. Sect. B, 1938), Am. Inst. E.E.; mem. Am. Philos. Soc., Am. Phys. Soc., Optical Soc. Am. (v.p. 1922-23, pres. 1924-25), Am. Astron. Soc., Franklin Inst., Am. Numis. Soc. (pres. 1942-47), Nat. Acad. Sciences, Phys. Soc. of London, Phi Beta Kappa, Sigma Xi; pres. Physics Club of Phila., 1917-18; v.p. Illuminating Engring. Soc., 1911-12; corr. mem. British Illuminating Engring. Soc., 1911-12; corr. mem. British Illuminating Engring. Soc. Section head, NDRC, 1941-46. Medals from Franklin Inst. for diffraction color photography, artificial daylight and studies of Welsbach mantle; John Scott medal and award, 1927, for electric telephotography and television; medal of the Optical Society for distinguished work in optics, 1937, U.S. Medal for Merit, 1948, Rumford Medal from Am. Acad. Arts and Sci., 1951. Inventor apparatus for testing visual acuity, various photometric instruments, illuminating devices, means for producing artificial daylight, relief pictures, electrical photoengraving apparatus for transmission of pictures over telephone lines; in charge of experimental and development work culminating in first demonstration of television by wire and radio, 1927; developed scientific trichromatic palette for artists' use. De Forest lecturer, Yale, 1928; Lowell lecturer, Boston, 1932; Thomas Young orator Physical Society, London, 1933; Traill-Taylor memorial lecture, Royal Photographic Soc., 1933. Clubs: Cosmos (Washington); Century, (New York). Author: Airplane photography, 1920. Contbr. to scientific journals, Ency. Britannica, etc. Home: 32 Laurel Pl., Montclair, N.J. Died Nov. 13, 1953; buried Litchfield, Conn.

IVES, JAMES EDMUND physicist; b. London, Eng., Sept. 19, 1865; s. James Thomas Bostock and Mary Collins (Johns) I.; U. of Pa., 1888-89; Harvard U., 1894; U. of Cambridge, Eng., 1896; Ph.D., Clark U., Mass., 1901; m. Georgiana Luvanne Stone, June 25, 1903; 1 dau., Elizabeth Laura (Mrs. Ives Lowe). Asst. curator, Acad. Natural Sciences, Phila., 1887-93; instr. physics, Drexel Inst., 1893-97; scholar and fellow in physics, Clark U., 1897-1901; instr. physics, U. of Cincinnati, 1901-03; scientific expert with the DeForest Wireless Telegraph Co., New York , 1903-05; asst. prof. physics, 1905-09, asso. prof., 1909-12, U. of Cincinnati; lecturer and research asso. in physics, Clark U., 1912-21; physicist U.S.P.H.S., on duty with the Office of Industrial Hygiene and Sanitation, 1921-31, sr. physicist, 1931-36. Asso. physicist Dept. Terrestrial Magnetism, Carnegie Instn., Washington, June-Aug. 1921. In charge dept. electricity and signals of U.S. Naval Aviation Detachment, Mass. Inst. Tech., 1917; lt., 1918, capt., 1919, Signal Corps, U.S. Army; capt. Signal R.C., U.S. Army, 1921; capt. Auxiliary R.C., U.S. Army, 1926 and 1931; capt., inactive, 1935. Awarded silver medal, St. Louis Expn., 1904, for work in wireless telegraphy. Episcopalian. Fellow Am. Acad. Arts and Sciences; mem. Acad. Natural Science Phila., Am. Phys. Soc., Illuminating Engring. Soc., Optical Soc. of America, Washington Acad. of Sciences, Philos. Soc. of Washington. Clubs: Cosmos, Chevy Chase (Washington). Author: An Annotated List of Experiments in Physics, 1912; also many papers in scientific journals and reviews. Address: care Cosmos Club, Washington, D.C. Died Jan. 2, 1943.

IVES, JOHN HIETT, air force officer; b. Delphi, Ind., Aug. 29, 1906; s. George R. and Josephine (Cartwright) I.; A.B., U. Ill., 1928; student Nat. War College, 1946-47; married Katherine Sullivan, January 2, 1936 (deceased, 1955); children—John Hiett, Katherine C.; m. Judith McGowan, Apr. 19, 1958; 1 dau., Laura K. Commissioned second lieutenant, USAF, 1930, and advanced through grades to maj. gen. USAF, 1953; served hdqrs. A.A.C. and PTO, World War II; dep. sec. Joint Chiefs of Staff, 1947-50; chief staff Air Univ., 1950-52; dep. dir. mil. personnel USAF, 1952-53; dir. mil. personnel policy div. Office Asst. Sec. Def. for Manpower and Personnel, 1953-56; chief staff, Continental Air Command, Mitchel Air Force Base, N.Y., 1956-57, comdr. First Air Force, 1957-58; dep. comdr. Third Air Force, 1958-61, comdr., from 1961, also chief Mil. Assistance Adv. Group, United Kingdom. Decorated Legion of Merit (with oak leaf cluster), Bronze Star Medal, D.S.M. Mem. Beta Theta Pi. Home: San Antonio TX Died Mar. 14, 1965; buried Fort Sam Houston Nat. Cemetery, San Antonio TX

IVES, JOSEPH CHRISTMAS army officer; b. N.Y.C., 1828; grad. U.S. Mil. Acad., 1852. Asst. to lt. A. W. Whipple, U.S. Topog. Engrs., to survey Pacific R.R. route, 1853-54; promoted 1st lt. U.S. Army, 1857; in charge of expdn. to explore Colorado River, 1857-58; engr., architect Washington Nat. Monument, 1859-60; commr. to survey border between Cal. and U.S. territories, 1860-61; declined appointment as capt. U.S. Army, 1861; commd. capt. engrs. Confederate Army; chief engr. Southeastern States, 1861; fortified defenses of Savannah and Charleston, 1861-62; commd. col. Confederate Army, 1862; a.d.c. to Jefferson Davis, 1863-65; adviser to Gen. Beauregard in defense of Charleston, 1864. Author: Memoir to Accompany a Military Map of the Peninsula of Florida, South of Tampa Bay, 1856; Military Maps of the Seat of War in Italy, 1859. Died N.Y.C., Nov. 12, 1868.

IZARD, GEORGE army officer, territorial gov.; b. Richmond, Eng., Oct. 21, 1776; s. Ralph and Alice (DeLancey) I.; m. Elizabeth Farley, June 6, 1803, 3 children. Took part in actions along N.Y. border during War of 1812; commd. 2d lt. U.S. Army, 1812, sent to N.Y. as brig. gen. by Sec. John Armstrong, 1812; promoted maj. gen., 1814, became sr. officer in command N.Y. on Canadian border; apptd. gov. Ark. Territory by Pres. Monroe, 1825-28; mem. Am. Philos. Soc.; Izard County (Ark.) named for him. Died Little Rock, Ark., Nov. 22, 1828.

JACKSON, ANDREW 7th Pres. U.S.; b. Waxhaw, S.C., Mar. 15, 1767; s. Andrew and Elizabeth (Hutchinson) J.; read law, Salisbury, N.C.; m. Rachel (Donelson) Robards, 1791 (again in Dec. 1794); 1 adopted son, Andrew, Jr. Served in Battle of Hanging Rock during Am. Revolution, was captured by British and imprisoned at Camden, S.C.; admitted to N.C. bar, 1787; moved to Nashville, Tenn., 1788; apptd. pros. atty. for S.W. Territory under Gov. William Blount, 1791; judge advocate Davidson County (Tenn.) Militia Regt., 1791; del. Tenn. Constl. Conv., 1796; mem. U.S. Ho. of Reps. from Tenn., 4th Congress, Dec. 5, 1796-97; mem. U.S. Senate from Tenn., Mar. 4, 1797-Apr. 1798, 1823-Oct. 14, 1825; judge Tenn. Supreme Ct., 1798-1804; elected maj. gen. Tenn. Militia, 1802; defeated Creek Indians at Horseshoe Bend, Ga., Mar. 1814; apptd. maj. gen. U.S. Army, May 1814; defeated British at Battle of New Orleans, Jan. 8, 1815 (after signing of peace treaty at Ghent); became major hero of War of 1812 because of totality of this victory; sent to punish Seminole Indians who were raiding on Fla. border, 1818, misinterpreted his orders, crossed border into Fla., captured Pensacola (which belonged to Spain) and hung 2 Brit. subjects (gunrunners) who were inciting the Seminoles (incident placed U.S. in danger of war with Spain and Gt. Britain); his actions were defended by John Q. Adams who placed the blame on Spain (only mem. of Pres. Monroe's cabinet to take Jackson's side); was not chastized, but instead apptd. 1st gov. of Fla. Territory (ceded from Spain 1820), Mar. 10, 1821, resigned July 18, 1821; Democratic candidate for Pres. U.S., ran against Henry Clay, John Q. Adams, William Crawford, 1824 (no candidate received majority in Electoral Coll., election went to U.S. Ho. of Reps.); lost election in Ho. of Reps. when Clay threw his support to Adams; defeated Adams in election of 1828 to become 7th Pres. U.S., Mar. 4, 1829-Mar. 3, 1837; considered to be father of "spoils system"; his cabinet became split as result of Peggy O'Neill (wife of Soc. of War John Eaton) incident, basically brought about by polit. differences between Sec. of State Van Buren and Vice Pres. Calhoun; surprised supporters of John C. Calhoun by strength of his support of Union during nullification crisis, 1832; at this time made famous statement: "Our Federal Union! it must and shall be preserved"; became further alienated from Calhoun upon William Crawford's publication of Calhoun's attempt to censure Jackson for his conduct in Seminole campaign of 1818, chose Van Buren to succeed Calhoun as vice pres.; votoed bill calling for constrn. of road from Maysville to Lexington (Ky.) on grounds it was a matter of local concern, 1830 (polit. rebuff to Clay); vetoed bill for rechartering Bank of U.S. (passed on Congress with Clay's aid), 1832, Bank question thus became leading issue of election of 1832; initiated Dem. Party nat. nominating conv. (replacing previous caucus system), 1832; favored the conv. (ostensibly introduced to better reflect will of the people) as means of getting Van Buren nominated for vice presidency; defeated Clay in presdl. election of 1832 (won by greater margin than in 1828); initiated Force Bill of 1833 in retaliation to S.C.'s decision to P ú prohibit ú collection of duties within the state, threatened to use force to execute the law if necessary (crisis was eased by Compromise Tariff of 1833); supported states-rights position of Ga. in removal of Cherokee Indians; removed funds from Bank of U.S. and placed them in "pet" state banks; removed Sec. of Treasury McLane for refusing to make this transfer of Funds, replaced McLane with James Duane (who also refused); replaced Duane with R. B. Taney, who made the transfer; rewarded Taney for his loyalty by appointing him to U.S. Supreme Ct., 1836; raised power of exec. br. of govt. to new high through use of patronage and veto, and refusal to implement Supreme Ct. decisions; supported Van Buren for Pres. U.S., 1836, 40, James K. Polk, 1844; advocated annexation to Tex. Died "Hermitage," nr. Nashville, June 8, 1845; buried "Hermitage."

JACKSON, ED ex-gov. Ind.; b. Howard County, Ind., Dec. 27, 1873; s. Presley E. and Elizabeth (Howell) J.; m. Lida Beaty. Admitted to Ind. bar, 1898, began practice at Newcastle; pros. atty. Henry County, Ind., 1903-05; apptd., 1909, by governor, judge Circuit Court of Henry County, to fill vacancy, and elected to same office; defeated for sec. of state, 1914, but elected 1916; resigned, 1917, to enter army; apptd. to fill vacancy as sec. of state, 1918, and elected to same office 1918, 20; gov. of Ind., 1925-28. Enlisted as pvt. U.S. Army, 1917; attended 2d O.T.C., Ft. Benjamin Harrison, Ind.; commd. capt., later maj. Republican. Home: Fairhill, Orleans, Ind. Died Nov. 20, 1954; buried Green Hill Cemetery, Orleans.

JACKSON, FREDERIC ELLIS architect; b. Tarrytown, N.Y., Apr. 14, 1879; s. Frederick Harvey and Anne Blanchard (Ellis) J.; B. Arch., Cornell U., 1900, grad. student, 1901; Diplomé par le Couvernement, Pecole des Beaux Arts, Paris, 1909; m. Eliza Greenough Fiske, June 1, 1904 (died May 2, 1935); children-Elise Greenough (Mrs. Charles Richard Steedman), Anne Blanchard (wife of Lt. Comdr. Arthur Watson Cocroft, U.S.N.R.); m. 2d, Marianne Learned Olcott Henry, Apr. 3, 1943. Mem. firm Hilton & Jackson, architects, 1902-11, Jackson, Robertson & Adams, Providence, R.I., since 1912; instr. architecture R.I. Sch. of Design, Providence, 1912-13. Architectural works of office include: R.I. State Office Bldg., Providence County Court House, Myron Taylor Hall at Cornell U., adminstrn. bldg. and library, R.I. State Coll., College St. Bldg., R.I. Sch. of Design, Burriluille Town Project, R.I. Nat. Guard Hangar, Hillsgrove, R.I.; World War I Memorial, Cornell Univ. (with Charles Z. Klauder). Served with Battery A, Light Field Arty., R.I.N.G., 1910-13; capt. liaison service, U.S. Army, 1918-19. Mem. R.I. Hosp., Butler Hosp., Hosp. (Providence), Lying-in - Providence Dist. Nursing Assn., St. Mary's Home for Children, R.I. Hosp., Peoples Savings Bank, Providence Inst. for Savings, R.I. Sch. of Design, Coll. of Architecture Council, Cornell U., since 1940. Mem. ednl. advisory com. architecture, R.I. Sch. of Design, since 1930; vice chmn. zoning bd. of review, Providence, 1923-26. Chmn. adv. bd. Providence City Planning Commn., 1931-44; architectural adviser R.I. Home Owners Loan Corp., 1934-41; mem. adv. com. Met. Homes Registration Office, State Council of Defense, 1943-44; chmn. property maintenance com. Community Fund since 1941; chmn. program com. Providence Postwar Planning, 1943-44; mem. bipartisan state com. on coordination and execution of postwar planning, 1943-46; state agent R.I. chapter France Forever since 1946. Member Providence com. N.Y. Museum Modern Art since 1937. Regional dir. Cornell Alumni Assn., 1938-44; exec. com., 1942-44. Mem. nat. adv. com. N.Y. World's Fair, 1939. Trustee The Annmay Brown Memorial since 1941. Fellow A.I.A. (v.p. R.I. chapter, 1919-21, pres. 1921-23, 1935-37); dir. A.I.A. 1925-28; mem. jury of fellows 1937-41; member committee on National Capital since 1943; associate member National Academy of Design; mem. Kappa Alpha. Ind. Republican. Episcopalian. Clubs: Agawam Hunt, Art, Hope, University (Providence); Century, Cornell (New York); Edgartown Yacht (Edgartown, Mass.). Recipient silver medal 5th Congress of Pan-Am. Architects, 1940; Roger award, Providence, 1944. Home: 244 Irving Av., Providence 6. Office: Turks Head Bldg., Providence 3, R.I.* Died Feb. 9, 1950.

JACKSON, GEORGE congressman; b. Cecil County, Md., Jan. 9, 1757; studied law; children include John George, Edward Brake. Served to col. during Am. Revolution: ú Revolution; ú admitted to Va. bar, 1787, began practice in Clarksburg, Va. (now W.Va.); justice of peace, 1784; mem. Va. Ho. of Dels., 1785-91, 94; mem. Va. Conv. which ratified U.S. Constn., 1788; mem. U.S. Ho. of Reps., from Va., 4th, 6th-7th congresses, 1799-1803; moved to Zanesville, O., circa 1806, engaged in farming; mem. Ohio Ho. of Reps., 1809-12, Ohio Senate, 1817-19. Died Zanesville, May 17, 1831; buried Falls Twp., nr. Zanesville.

JACKSON, HENRY army officer; b. in Eng., May 31, 1837. Pvt. and corporal Co. A, 14th Ill. Cav., and sergt. maj. 5th U.S.C.T., Dec. 28, 1863-May 13, 1865; commd. 2d lt., 5th U.S. Cav., May 14, 1865; 1st lt., Dec. 28, 1865; hon. mustered out, Mar. 16, 1866; apptd. from Ill., 2d lt. 7th U.S. Cav., July 28, 1866; 1st lt., July 31, 1866; capt., June 25, 1876; maj. 3d Cav., Aug. 27, 1896; lt. col. 5th Cav., Jan. 23, 1900; col. 3d Cav., Apr. 29, 1901; retired by operation of law, May 31, 1901; advanced to rank of brig. gen. retired, by act of Apr. 23, 1904. Deceased.

JACKSON, HENRY ROOTES jurist, diplomat; b. Athens, Ga., June 24, 1820; s. Henry and Martha (Rootes) J.; grad. Yale, 1839; A.M. (hon.), U. Ga., 1848, LL.D. (hon.), 1893; m. Cornelia Davenport; m. 2d, Florence King; 4 children. Admitted to Ga. bar, 1840; U.S. dist. atty. for Ga., 1842; served as col. of a Ga. regt.; editor Georgian, Savannah, 1848-49; judge Superior Ct. of Eastern Circuit, 1849-53; U.S. charge d'affaires Austria, 1853-54, minister resident, 1854-58; mem. Ga. Secession Conv., 1861; judge Confederate cts. of Ga.; commd. maj. gen. of a div. Ga. Militia, 1861; commd. brig. gen. Confederate Army, 1864; U.S. minister to Mexico, 1885, resigned, 1886; pres. Ga. Hist. Soc.; trustee peabody Edn. Fund. Author: Talulah and Other Poems, 1850. Died Savannah, Ga., May 23, 1898.

JACKSON, JAMES senator, gov. Ga.; b. Moreton-Hampstead, Eng., Sept. 21, 1757; s. James and Mary (Webber) J.; m. Mary Young, 5 children. Came to Am., 1772; mem. 1st Ga. Constl. Conv., 1777; commd. lt. col. Continental Army, 1782; commd. col. Chatham County (Ga.) Militia, 1784, brig. gen. 1786; declined governship of Ga., 1788; mem. U.S. Ho. of Reps. from Ga., 1st Congress, 1789-91; mem. U.S. Senate from Ga., 1793-95; 1801 - Mar. 19, 1806; gov. Ga., 1798-1801. Died Washington, D.C., Mar. 19, 1806; buried Congressional Cemetery, Washington.

JACKSON, JAMES congressman, jurist; b. Jefferson County, Ga., Oct. 18, 1819; s. William H. and Mildred (Cobb) J.; grad. U. Ga., 1837; m. Ada Mitchell, 1853; m. 2d, Mrs. Mary Schoolfield, 1870. Admitted to Ga. bar, 1839; mem. Ga. Ho. of Reps., 1845-47; judge Ga. Superior Ct., 1846-59; mem. U.S. Ho. of Reps. from Ga., 35th-36th congresses, 1857-Jan. 23, 1861; served as judge adv. Confederate Army on staff of Gen. Thomas (Stonewall) Jackson, 1861-65; justice Ga. Supreme Ct., 1875-87, chief justice, 1879-87. Died Atlanta, Ga., Jan. 13, 1887; buried Rose Hill Cemetery, Macon, Ga.

JACKSON, JAMES KIRKMAN lawyer; b. Montgomery, Ala., Dec. 15, 1900; s. James Kirkman and Helen (Gunter) J.; A.B., U. Ala., 1921; LL.B., Harvard, 1924; m. Margaret Crawford, Dec. 20, 1933; children-Gordon, James Kirkman. Admitted to Ala. Bar, 1923; asso. McClellan, Rice & Stone, Birmingham, 1925-27; asso. London, Yancey & Brower, 1927-30, partner, 1930-36; partner Jackson, Rives, Pettus & Peterson, Birmingham, 1936-58; pvt. practice, 1958-66. Dir. Employers Ins. Co. of Ala., Employers Life Ins. Co. Bd. dirs. Jefferson County chpt. A.R.C. Served as lt. col. USAAF, 1942-45. Decorated Officer Order Brit. Empire. Mem. Ala. State Bar (pres. 1959-60), Am., Birmingham (Past pres.) bar assns., Bar Assn. City N.Y. Democrat. Episcopalian. Clubs: Birmingham Country, Mountain Brook (Birmingham); Army-Navy Country (Washington). Author articles profl. publs. Home: 2603 Park Lane Ct. N., Mountain Brook, Birmingham. Office: Jackson Bldg., Birmingham 3, Ala. Died Mar. 16, 1966; buried Elmwood Cemetery, Birmingham, Ala.

JACKSON, JAMES STRESHLY congressman; b. Fayette County, Ky., Sept. 27, 1823; attended Centre Coll., Danville, Ky.; grad. Jefferson Coll., Pa., 1844; grad. law dept. Transylvania U., Lexington, Ky., 1845. Admitted to the bar; began practice in Greenupsburg, Ky., 1845; enlisted as pvt. 1st Ky. Cavalry during Mexican War, commd. 3d lt., 1846, resigned, 1846; moved to Hopkinsville, Ky., 1859; mem. U.S. Ho. of Reps. (Unionist) from Ky., 37th Congress, Mar. 4-Dec. 13, 1861; commd. col. 3d Regt., Ky. Volunteer Cavalry, U.S. Army, Dec. 13, 1861; commd. brig. gen. U.S. Volunteers, 1862. Killed in Battle of Perryville, Oct. 8, 1862; buried Riverside Cemetery, Hopkinsville.

JACKSON, JOSEPH COOKE lawyer, brig. gen.; b. Newark, N.J., Aug. 5, 1835; s. lion, Hon. John P. and Elizabeth (Huntington Wolcott) J.; A.B., Yale, 1857, A.M., 1860; LL.B., New York U., 1859; LL.B., Harvard, 1860. Admitted to N.Y. bar, 1860, and began practice at New York. Del. Rep. Nat. Conv., Chicago, 1861. Volunteered on fall of Ft. Sumter and was ordered to staff of Gen. Robert Anderson, U.S.A.; commd. 2d lt. 1st N.J. Vols., and assigned to staff Gen. Philip Kearny; promoted to div. staff of Maj. Gen. Franklin, Oct. 11, 1861; commd. capt. and a.d.c. vols., Aug. 20, 1862, "for gallantry during Seven Days' Battles before Richmond," and assigned to Sixth Corps staff as a.d.c. to Gen. Franklin; commd. lt. col. 26th N.J. Inf., Dec. 2, 1862; served in nearly 30 engagements of war as a.d.c. on staffs of Generals Anderson, Kearny, Franklin, Meade and Wool, U.S.A., in campaigns of McDowell, McClellan, Pope, Burnside and Meade; bvtd. col. vols., Mar. 13, 1865, "for gallant and meritorious conduct at battle of Fredericksburg, Va.," Sept. 13, 1862; a.d.c. to Gen. Wool, U.S.A., quelling July riots, 1863; bvtd. brig. gen. vols., Mar. 13, 1865, "for faithful and meritorious services in the field"; resigned, Jan. 5, 1863. While holding present commn. of brig. gen. U.S.V. was also commd. a.d.c. to Gov. Marcus L. Ward, N.J., in Reconstruction period. During war was apptd. by Secretary Stanton special War Dept. commr. U.S. Naval Credits, and established 1,900 naval enlistments, which were credited to quota of troops from N.J., and thereby rendered a draft unnecessary and saved nearly $1,000,-000 to the state. Admitted to U.S. Supreme Court, 1864; del. Ship Canal Conv., Chicago, 1864; resumed general law practice, New York, near close of war and for nearly 30 yrs. was atty. and counsel for railways, banks, express and other corps.; m. Katharine Perkins, d. Hon. Calvin and Catherine (Seymour) Day, Oct. 12, 1864. Apptd. by President Grant, asst. atty., Southern Dist. N.Y., 1870; was counsel for Soc. of Polit. Reform which created first Com. of 70; counsel for removal police commrs.; also N.Y. Bar Assn. and N.Y. Supreme Ct. in their proceedings to purify N.Y. bar; active in Law Inst. and com. of bar assn.; retired from office engagements, 1890. Organizer by request of N.Y. Rep. Club and grand marshal of citizen night parade of over 60,000 Republican voters assembled from different states, in New York City, 1889; campaign and convention speaker and liberal contbr. to Rep. measures. Was an original founder of the earliest Am. coll. local alumni assn. (Yale); its treas., v.p., and mem. exec. com. many years; trustee and v.p. De Milt Dispensary 15 yrs. Home: New York, N.Y. died May 22, 1913.

JACKSON, JOSEPH HENRY editor; b. Madison, N.J., July 21, 1894; s. Herbert Hallett and Marion Agnes (Brown) J.; prep. edu., Peddie Sch., Hightstown, N.J.; student Lafayette Coll., 1915-17; Litt.D. (honorary), U. So. Cal., 1950; m. Charlotte E. Cobden, June 21, 1923; 1 dau., Marion (Mrs. David Skinner). Asso. editor Sunset Mag., 1920-23, mng. editor, 1924-26, editor, 1926-28; lit. editor San Francisco Argonaut, 1929-30, San Francisco Chronicle since 1930; broadcaster of "Bookman's Guide," over Nat. Broadcasting Co., Pacific Coast network, 1924-43. Mem. bd. dirs. Book Club of Cal. Served with Ambulance Corps, U.S. Army, 1917-18; 2d lt. infantry, United States Army, 1918-19. Mem. Cal. Hist. Soc., Society of American Historians, Phi Kappa Psi. Democrat. Presbyterian. Clubs: Bohemian (San Francisco); University (N.Y.). Author: Mexican Interlude, 1936; Notes on a Drum, 1937; Tintypes in Gold, 1939; Extra! Extra! (with Scott Newhall), 1940; Anybody's Gold, 1941. The California Story, 1949; Bad Company, 1949; The Christmas Flower, 1951; My San Francisco, published in 1953; The Girl in the Belfry, published in the year 1955. Editor: Tale of Soldiers and Civilians, 1941; Continent's End, 1944; Portable Murder Book, 1945; San Francisco Murders, 1947; The Gold Rush Album, 1949; Western Gate: A San Francisco Reader, 1952. Contbr. to newspapers, mags., revs. Mem. bd. of judges O. Henry Memorial Award (short story annual) 1935, 1942, 1951 and of Harper Prize Novel Contest, 1947, 1949; mem. Pulitzer Prize fiction jury, 1949-51; mem. editorial bd. The Pacific Spectator. Home: 2626 Buena Vista Way, Berkeley, Cal. Office: San Francisco Chronicle, 5th and Mission Sts., San Francisco. Died July 15, 1955.

JACKSON, PHILIP LUDWELL newspaper pub.; b. Portland, Ore., Oct. 18, 1893; s. Charles Samuel and Maria Foster (Clopton) J.; Litt.B., Princeton, 1915; M.B.A., Harvard, 1917; m. Alice D. Strowbridge, Mar. 15, 1922 (dec.); m. 2d, Ella R. Tenney, Nov. 21, 1931 (dec.); married 3d, Esma P. Ransom, June 11, 1951. Publisher of the Oregon Journal, Portland, Ore., since 1924; president of the Journal Co., president KO Corps, U.S. Army, 1917-18, capt., 1918-19. Mem. bd. dirs. Chamber of Commerce (pres. 1934-35); pres. Pacific Coast div. Bur. Advt.; sec. Ore. Princeton Alumni Assn.; mem. Sigma Delta Chi. Democrat. Episcopalian. Clubs: University, Multnomah, Waverley Country, Portland Hunt, Racquet, National Press, Press Club of Oregon, Oregon Advertising; Princeton (N.Y.); Union League (San Francisco). Home: 11522 S.W. Riverwood. Address: Oregon Journal, Portland 7, Ore. Died Feb. 14, 1953.

JACKSON, RICHARD HARRISON, naval officer; b. Tuscumbia, Ala., May 10, 1866; s. George M. and Sarah (Perkins) J.; grad. U.S. Naval Acad., 1887, Naval War Coll., 1920; M.D., U. of Va.; m. Catharine, d. Rear Admiral W.T. Sampson, U.S. Navy, Jan. 6, 1897 (dec. 1924). Hon. discharged from U.S. Navy, June 30, 1889; restored to service, July 1, 1890, by spl. act of Congress "for conspicuous gallantry on occasion of wreck of the Trenton, at Apia, Samoa, Mar. 27, 1889"; promoted lt. jr. grade, July 3, 1898; promoted through grades to rear admiral. Served in the Spanish-Am. War, 1898; nagivator Colorado, 1905-07; exec. officer same, 1907-08; in charge naval proving ground, Indian Head, Md., 1908-10, Naval Sta., Cavite, P.I., 1910-11; comd. Albany, 1911-12, Helena, 1912; sr. officer in comd. gunboats on Yangtse River during Chinese Revolution; at U.S. Naval Acad., 1912-13; duty with Gen. Bd., Navy Dept., 1913-15; comd. Virginia, 1915-17; spl. rep. Navy Dept. at Ministry of Marine, Paris, and naval attache, Paris, June 1917-Nov. 1918; commandant Base 24, Bermudas, Jan.-Mar. 1919; comdr. spl. detachment, Azores, and Base 13, Apr.-Oct. 1919; mem. Gen. Bd. Navy Dept., 1921; rear adm. comdg. Battleship Div. 3, 1922; asst. chief naval operations, 1923; vice adm. comdg. Battleship Divs., 1925; admiral, commander-in-chief of Battle Fleet, 1926; mem. General Board, 1927-30; retired. Awarded Navy War Cross (U.S.); Officer Legion of Honor (France); Order of Avis (Portugal); medal for Spanish-Am. War, Philippine Insurrection, Boxer Campaign. Life mem. U.S. Naval Inst. (gold medals essayist). Episcopalian. Clubs: Army and Navy (Washington); Chevy Chase (Md.); New York Yacht. Home: Coronado CA Died Oct. 3, 1971.

JACKSON, THOMAS HERBERT brig. gen.; b. Westmeath, Ont., Can., Jan. 18, 1874; s. Noah Willard and Pauline (Adams) J.; brought to U.S., 1880; grad. U.S. Mil. Acad., 1899, Engr. Sch. of Application, Washington Bks., D.C., 1902; m. Maude Edgar Jurich,

Aug. 24, 1912.Commd. add. 2d lt., Corps Engrs., U.S. Army, Feb. 15, 1899; advanced through grades to col., May 11, 1921; brig. gen., June 10, 1928. Served in Philippines, 1903-05; served as engr. dist. officer, San Francisco, Calif., 1907-11, Dallas, Tex., 1911-14, Wheeling, W.Va., 1914-17; engr. supply officer, France, 1917; sect. engr., Advance Sect., 1918; chief engr., Am. Forces in France, July-Nov. 1919; div. engr., San Francisco, 1926-28, St. Louis, Mo., 1928, Norfolk, Va., 1932-34, San Francisco, 1934-; pres. Miss. River Commn., 1928-32. Decorated D.S.M. (U.S.); Officer Legion of Honor (France); Comdr. Order of Leopold II (Belgium). Author of flood control plan for Sacramento River, 1907-10. Home: San Francisco, Calif. Died 1937.

JACKSON, THOMAS JONATHAN (NICKNAME STONEWALL) army officer; b. Clarksburg, Va. (now W.Va.), Jan. 21, 1824; s. Jonathan and Julia (Beckwith) J.; grad. U.S. Mil. Acad., 1846; m. Eleanor Junkin, 1853; m. 2d, Mary Anne Morrison, July 16, 1857. Entered U.S. Army; served at battles of Vera Cruz, Cerro Gordo and Chapultepec during Mexican War, 1846-48; brevetted maj., 1847; served at Ft. Columbus and Ft. Hamilton (N.Y.), 1849-51; resigned commn., 1851; prof. artillery tactics and natural philosophy Va. Mil. Inst., 1851-61; commd. brig. gen. Confederate Army, 1861; received nickname Stonewall at 1st Battle of Bull Run; commd. maj. gen., 1861; in command of Shenandoah Valley dist. Dept. of No. Va.; withdrew from Winchester, Va., 1862, beginning Shenandoah Valley campaign which prevented 2 Northern armies from joining attack on Richmond (Va.); made a series of brilliant marches and battles, 1862, including Kernstown, Staunton, Front Royal, Winchester, Cross Keys, Port Republic; fought under Robert E. Lee in Seven Days Campaign, 1862 (including Battle of Gaines Mill); captured Manassas Junction, Aug. 27, defeated (with Lee) Union Army at 2d Battle of Bull Run, Aug. 30, captured Harper's Ferry, Sept. 15, Antietam, Sept. 17, Fredericksburg, Dec. 13, (all 1862), commd. lt. gen., 1862; accidentally shot by his own men after routing Union right wing at Battle of Chancellorsville, May 2, 1863; considered best and most famous Confederate gen. after Lee. Died Fredericksburg, Va., May 10, 1863; buried Lexington Lexington, Va.

JACKSON, THOMAS WRIGHT, army surgeon; b. at Akron O., Aug. 21, 1869; s. Andrew and Lucy Ann (Wright) J.; grad. Akron High Sch., 1887; spl. scientific course, Amherst Coll., 1887-9; M.D., Jefferson Med. Coll., Phila., 1892 (gold medalist); m. Mell V. Odiorne, of Nutley, N.J., Sept. 12, 1894; 2d, M. Louise Odiorne, of Phila., June 1, 1905. Practiced at Akron, O., and Phila., 1892-8; apptd. acting asst. surgeon U.S.A., 1898, and later capt. and asst. surgeon U.S.V., serving in Southern camps, Cuba and P.I.; med. reserve corps U.S. Army since 1908; phys. Bur. of Health for P.I., 1912—. Lecturer on tropical diseases, Jefferson Med. Coll., 1905-7. Mem. Am. Soc. Tropical Medicine, Manila Med. Soc., P.I. Med. Assn. (v.p. 1913-14), Beta Theta Pi. Clubs: Army and Navy (Manila and Washington), Authors' (London). Author: Tropical Medicine, 1907 (used as text-book in U.S.A.). Contbr. to Modern Treatment, Vol. I, 1910. Address: Manila PI

JACKSON, V(ESTUS) T(WIGGS) chemist; b. Sandersville, Ga., Jan. 29, 1889; s. Vestus and Jennie Irene (Beasley) J.: A.B., B.S., Mercer U., 1912; M.S., U. Chgo., 1916, Ph.D. cum laude, 1921; post-grad. work on photochemistry U. Wis., summer 1935; m. Josephine Louise Stenhouse, Sept. 12, 1918; 1 dau., Betty (Mrs. John Stanley Livingstone, Jr.). Asst. in physics Mercer U., 1910-11, asst. in chemistry 1911-12; instr. chemistry Okla. A. and M. Coll., 1912-16; chmn. research Lindsay Light Co., Chgo., 1916-19; 2d rank, chemistry dept. Catholic U. of Am., 1921-22; chem. research Western Electric Co., 1922-23; acting head, dept. chemistry Heidelberg U., Tiffin, O., 1924; asst. prof. chemistry U. Fla., 1924-27, asso. prof. 1927-35, prof., 1935—. Active duty tng., Ft. Benning, summer 1932; instr. chem. warfare, Ft. Bragg, summer 1936; Edgewood Arsenal, 1940; major (inactive) C.W.S., U.S. Army, Res. Officers Assn. Recipient Blalock Science medal (Mercer U.). Mem. Am. Chem. Soc. (past pres. Fla. sect.), Sigma Xi, Gamma Sigma Epsilon, Delta Sigma Phi, Phi Kappa Phi. Democrat. Club: Athenacum (U. Fla.; past sec. and treas. and pres.). Author numerous articles on chem. subjects. Home: 515 Boulevard, Gainesville, Fla. Died Nov. 25, 1950; buried Oakwoods, Cemetery, Chg.

JACKSON, WILLIAM army officer, sec. to Pres. U.S.; b. Cumberland, Eng., May 9, 1759; m. Elizabeth Willing, Nov. 11, 1795. Served as lt. in expdn. against St. Augustine (Fla.), 1778; maj., aide to Gen. Benjamin Lincoln; U.S. asst. sec. of war, 1782-84; sec. U.S. Constl. Conv. Phila., 1787; admitted to Pa. bar, 1788; sec. to Pres. George Washington, 1789-91; U.S. surveyor of customs, Phila., 1796-1801; sec. Soc. of Cincinnati, 1800-28; founder, editor Polit. and Comm. Register, Phila., 1801-17. Died Phila., Dec. 18, 1828; buried Christ Church Cemetery, Phila.

JACKSON, WILLIAM H(ARDING), lawyer, investment banker, b. Nashville, Tenn., Mar. 25,21901; s. William Harding and Anne Davis (Richardson) J.; grad. St. Mark's Sch., Southborough, Mass., 1920; A.B., Princeton, 1924; LL.B., Harvard, 1928; m. Elisabeth Lyman, Oct. 31, 1929; children—William H., Richard Lee; m. 2d, Mary Leet Pitcairn, Feb. 10, 1951; children—Bruce, Howell; m. 3d, Irma M. Hanly, May, 1970. Began with Cadwallader, Wickersham & Taft; admitted New York bar, 1932; employe Carter, Ledyard & Milburn, 1930, partner, 1934-47; partner J. H. Whitney & Co., investment banking firm, 1947-56. Adv. council Woodrow Wilson Sch. Internat. Affairs. Chairman of President's Com. on Internat. Information Activities, 1953; special assistant to the secretary of state, 1955, to Pres., 1956; mem. bd. cons. Nat. War Coll. Served with U.S. Army, 1942-45; assigned as dep. G-2 on staff Gen. Omar Bradley, E.T.O., 1944; disch. with rank of col. Dep. dir. or Central Intelligence, Washington, 1950-51. Pres. N.Y. Hosp., 1940-49, mem. bd. govs. Mem. Episcopalian. Clubs: Metropolitan (Washington). Home: Tucson AZ Died Sept. 28, 1971; buried Nashville TN

JACKSON, WILLIAM HICKS soldier, stock man; b. Paris, Tenn., Oct. 7, 1836; served in C.S.A., 1861-65, becoming brig. gen.; stock-raiser; partner of Richard Croker in the Belle Meade stock farm in Tenn. Home: Nashville, Tenn. Died 1903.

JACOB, RICHARD TAYLOR soldier; b. Oldham County, Ky., Mar. 13, 1825; s. John Jeremiah and Lucy Donald (Robertson) J.; joined emigrant party leaving Missouri River, May 11, 1846, for Calif.; chosen 2d in command of Republican Fork of Blue at Ft. Laramie; reached Calif. Sept. 9, 1846, with 8 of his party; found Californians in rebellion; raised company, becoming its capt. and joined Fremont, serving under him until surrender of the Mexican army to Col. Fremont, 40 miles from Los Angeles. Returned to Ky., raised a vol. co. for Mexican war, which was not accepted; went to Washington as witness in Fremont courtmartial; m. 1st, Sarah, 3d d. Senator Thomas H. Benton, Jan. 17, 1848 (died 1863); m. 2d, Laura, d. Dr. Wilson, June 6, 1865 (died 1895). Lived on farm in Mo., 1848-54; returned to Ky.; Breckenridge elector, 1860; representative from Oldham County in Ky. legislature, 1857-61; drafted com. report in favor of remaining loyal to Union, which was adopted. Raised, 1862, and was col. 9th Ky. vols.; served in Ky., driving Scott's brigade and the Secession govt. out of Frankfort; lt. gov. Ky., 1863-67; supported McClellan, 1864; opposed enlistment of Negro troops in Ky.; was arrested by Gen. Burbridge and escorted across enemy's lines; appealed to President Lincoln who directed his return to his home. Park Commr. Louisville, 1895-99. Home: Louisville, Ky. Died 1903.

JACOBS FERRIS, JR. congressman; b. Delhi, N.Y., Mar. 20, 1836; s. Ferris Jacobs. Grad. Williams Coll., 1856; studied law. Admitted to N.Y. bar, 1859, began practice in Delhi; served in U.S. Army during Civil War; commd. capt. 3d N.Y. Cavalry, 1861, maj., 1863, lt. col., 1864, mustered out, 1864; commd. lt. col. 26th N.Y. Cavalry, 1865; brevetted brig. gen. U.S. Volunteers, 1865, mustered out, 1865; resumed law practice Delhi; elected dist. atty., 1865, 66; del. Republican Nat. Conv., Chgo., 1880; mem. U.S. Ho. of Reps. (Rep.) from N.Y., 47th Congress, 1881-83. Died White Plains, N.Y., Aug. 30, 1886; buried Woodland Cemetery, Delhi.

JACOBS, FENTON STRATTON army officer; b. Gordonsville, Va., Apr. 17, 1892; grad. Cav. Sch., troop officers course, 1923, advanced course, 1932, Command and Gen. Staff Sch., 1935; m. Sophia Schroeder. In fed. service wtih Va. Nat. Guard, 1916-17; commd. 2d lt., U.S. Army, 1917, and advanced to brig. gen., 1944. Decorated Legion of Merit, D.S.M., Legion of Merit with Oak Leaf Cluster, Bronze Star, Mexican Border, Victory Medal of World War I with one star, Army of Occupation (World War I), Am. Def. Ribbon, Am. Theater, European Theater with two stars, Asiatic-Pacific Theater with one star, World War II Victory Medal; Comdr. of British Empire; French Legion of Honor, Grade of Chevalier; Croix de Guerre with Palm; Belgium Order Leopold II, Grade of Comdr.; Philippine Liberation Ribbon with one star. Home: R.F.D. 1, Box 507, Carmel, Cal. Address: care Dept. Army, Washington 25. Died June 20, 1966.

JACOBS, JOSHUA W. soldier; b. in Ky., June 24, 1843. Entered mil. service as pvt. Co. K, and sergt. maj. 4th Ky. Vol. Inf., Nov. 10, 1861-Sept. 25, 1862; commd. 1st lt. 4th Ky. Vol. Inf., Sept. 25, 1862; capt., Sept. 1, 1863; maj. 6th Ky. Vols., July 1, 1865; hon. mustered out of vol. service, Aug. 17, 1865. Apptd. 2d lt. 18th U.S. Inf., June 28, 1866; transferred to 36th Inf., Sept. 21, 1866; capt. and a.-q.-m., Mar. 8, 1882; maj. q.m., Dec. 31, 1894; lt. col. deputy q.-m. gen., Nov. 1, 1900; col. a.-q.-m. gen., 1903; brig. gen., 1904, and retired after 40 yrs. service Deceased.

JACOBS, RANDALL naval officer (ret.); b. Danville, Pa., Dec. 12, 1885; s. William Frederick and Jane (McCoy) J.; B.S., U.S. Naval Acad., 1907; hon. degrees, D. Eng., Northeastern U., 1942, Worcester Inst. Tech., 1944; LL.D., U. Pitts., 1943, Bucknell U., 1943, Franklin and Marshall Coll., 1943, So. Meth. U., 1945, Northwestern U., 1945, Trinity Coll., 1944; D.C.L., U. South, 1944; doctor naval sci. Holy Cross Coll., 1944; m. Emily Hamor Voris, Aug. 27, 1913; children-Randall, Mary Jane. Commd. ensign U.S. Navy, 1907, and advanced through grades to vice adm., 1946; service in battleships, destroyers, cruisers, auxiliaries; comd. battleships, target and repair ships, Yangtze river gunboat, cruiser; tng. comdr., Atlantic fleet, 1941; chief of naval personnel, 1941-45; comdt. 13th Naval Dist., 1945-46; ret. Nov. 1, 1946; returned to active duty as gov., Naval Home, Phila., 1946. Awarded D.S.M., Cuban Pacificiation medal, Victory medal (World War I), various service, campaign and area medals. Mason. Clubs: Army Navy, Army Navy Country (Washington). Home: Danville, Pa. Office: U.S. Naval Home, Philadelphia 46. Died June 19, 1967.

JACOBSON, GABE lawyer; b. Meridian, Miss., June 16, 1875; s. Julius and Bertha (Schulberr) J.; B.S., Miss. State Coll., 1894; LL.B., U. of Miss., 1902; unmarried. Admitted to Miss. bar, 1902, and in practice of law in State and U.S. Courts and in adminstrn. proceedings and hearings; sr. mem. Jacobson, Snow & Covington, Meridian, Mississippi, 1940; now practicing law alone in Meridian; vice-president Stonewall (Mississippi) Cotton Mills since 1936. U.S. Referee in bankruptcy, Meridian, 1910-13; former department inspector U.S. War Vets. of Mississippi. Served as 1st lt., 1st Miss. Vol. Inf., Spanish-Am. War, 1898. Former mem. Board of State Bar Examiners; mem. Miss. State Bar Assn. (pres. 1920-21), Am. Bar Assn., Rotary Internat. (past pres. Meridian Club). Phi Delta Theta. Democrat. Jewish religion. Mason (33ff). Contbr. to Comml. Law Jour. and Miss. Law Jour. Home: Lamar Hotel. Office: Threefoot Bldg., Meridian, Miss. Died Aug. 9, 1944.

JADWIN, EDGAR army officer; b. Honesdale, Pa., Aug. 7, 1865; s. Hon. C. C. and Charlotte E. (Wood) J.; student Lafayette Coll., Easton, Pa., 1884-86; grad. head of class, U.S. Mil. Acad., 1890; grad. Engr. Sch. of Application, 1893; hon. Dr. Engring., Lafayette, 1925; m. Jean Laubach, Oct. 6, 1891; children-Charlotte (Mrs. Thomas G. Hearn), Cornelius C. (U.S. Cav.). Apptd. add. 2d lt. engrs., June 12, 1890; promoted through grades to lt. col., Oct. 12, 1913; col. N.A., July 6, 1917; brig. gen. (temp.), Dec. 17, 1917-Oct. 31, 1919; col. engrs., Sept. 10, 1919; apptd. asst. to chief of engrs. with rank of brig. gen., 1924, chief of engrs. with rank of major gen., 1926; retired Aug. 7, 1929. In charge improvements, Ellis Island, 1890-91; duty, Office Chief of Engineers, Washington, D.C., 1897-98, Panama Canal, 1907-11, Office Chief of Engrs., Washington, D.C., 1911-16; dist. engr. to various engring. dists.; organized and comd. 15th U.S. Engrs. (Ry.), the first Am. regt. to pass under arms through England, 1917; dir. light rys. and roads, A.E.F., in France, later dir. constrn. and forestry, in charge gen. construction program, working 160,000 men in dredging, building railroads, barracks, hosps., warehouses, roads, lumbering, etc.; mem. Am. Mission to Poland, 1919; observer in Ukraine, 1919; engr. 8th Corps Area, San Antonio, Tex., 1920-22; div. engr. Southeast Div., Charleston, S.C., 1922-24; div. engr. Southeast Div., Charleston, S.C., 1922-24. Served as sr. mem. Am. sect. Joint Engring. Bd. St. Lawrence Waterway Project and as sr. mem. Bd. of Engrs. for Rivers and Harbors; was mem. tech. advisory com. of Federal Oil Conservation Bd., and mem. Am. delegation to Internat. Conf. on Oil Pollution of Navigable Rivers; served as chmn. Nat. Capital Park and Planning Commn.; supervised, 1927, plan which was adopted by congress for control of floods in Mississippi Valley, etc.; appointed 1929, chmn. Interocean Canal Bd. Presbyn. Awarded D.S.M. (U.S.); Companion Order of the Bath (British); Comdr. Legion of Honor (French). Home: Honesdale, Pa. Died Mar. 2, 1931.

JAFFE, LOUIS ISAAC newspaper editor; b. Detroit, Feb. 22, 1888; s. Philipand Lotta Maria (Kahn) J.; A.B., Trinity Coll. (now Duke U.), 1911; m. Margaret Stewart Davis, Dec. 8, 1920; 1 son, Christopher; m. 2d, Alice Cohn Rice, 1942; 1 son, Louis Isaac, Junior. Member staff Durham Sun, 1911; reporter and asst. city editor Richmond (Va.) Times-Dispatch, 1911-17; editor Virginian-Pilot, Norfolk, Va., since Nov. 1919; mem. board of dirs. Norfolk Newspapers, Inc. Student R.O.T.C., Fort Myer, Va.; commd. 2d lt. F.A., Nov. 1917; re-commd. Air Service, Kelly Field, Texas, December, 1917. Served in A.E.F., April 1918-March 1919; honorably discharged in France, Mar. 29, 1919; with Am. Red Cross Commn. to the Balkans, Apr.-July 1919; dir. Am. Red Cross News Service at Paris, July-Oct. 1919. Mem. Norfolk Council Com. on Higher Edn.; mem. adv. bd. Norfolk Div., Va. State Coll. for Negroes; dir. Norfolk General Hosp.; mem. bd. trustees Norfolk Museum of Arts and Sciences. Awarded Pultizer prize for best newspaper editorial, 1929. Mem. Phi Beta Kappa. Omicron Delta Kappa. Democrat. Clubs: National Press (Washington), Virginia (Norfolk). Office: Norfolk Newspapers, Inc., 1950 W. Brambleton Av., Norfolk, Va. Died Mar. 12, 1950.

JALLADE, LOUIS EUGENE architect; b. Montreal, Can., Feb. 16, 1876; s. Ettiene and Georgenia (Roger) J.; brought to U.S., 1877, naturalized, 1897; student New York Latin Sch., 1886-92, Met. Museum of Art Schs., 1892-96, Archtl. Ateliers of Beaux Arts Soc., 1896-99, Ecole des Beaux Arts, 1901-03; m. Eugenie M.-L. Pinquet, Feb. 2, 1901; children-Louis Eugene, 2d (dec.), Louis Eugene, 3d, John Henry, Architect, 1904—; asso. with Paul DuBoy, 1904, Allan & Collins, Boston, in charge of construction of Union Theol. Sem., N.y., N.Y., 1906; practiced alone, 1906 (designed Naval YMCA, Norfolk, Va., as first commission); tchr. architecture Columbia extension courses, 1906-09; bldg. consultant to nat. bd. YWCA, Soc. of Dirs. of Phys. Edn. in Colls., Playground and Recreation Assn.,

Russell Sage Found., Boys Club of America; cons. engr. for Dept. of Correction in remodeling Riders Island Penitentiary; dir. Staten Island Investment Service Corp., Upanin Hotels, Inc.; pres. Midridge Realty Corp.; now his 2 sons asso. with him. Works: YMCA bldgs. at Newport, R.I., West Side, New York, Roanoke, Va., Worcester, Mass., Allentown, Pa., McKeesport, Pa., also 124th St. and Lenox Av., N.Y.C., Hartford, Conn., Passaic, N.J., etc.; churches, Flatburh Congl., Bklyn., Broadway, Presbyn., N.Y.C., First Presbyn., Jamaica, N.Y., Mariemont (O.) Community, Metropolitan Temple, New York, etc.; colleges; Women's Coll. at U. Del., Recreation Bldg. at Skidmore, Skidmore Coll., Internat. House., New York, etc.; clubs; Town Hall and Phi Delta Gamma Club of New York, etc.; hospitals: Kings County Hosp., Addition, Red Hook-Gowanus Health Center, Hosp. Addition, Inst. Pediatry, N.Y., Coney Island Bklyn., Outpatient Dispensary Bldg. for Welfare Island, N.Y.C., Luch Hasting Hosp., Manchester, N.H.; also factory bldgs., hotels, garages, residences, schs., libraries, etc. Registered architect Conn., N.Y., N.J., Pa.; cons. engr. in N.Y. Served in N.Y. N.G., 1914-29, in all ranks from pvt. to maj., 11th Inf., and lt. col. 369th Inf.; brig. gen. N.Y. N.G. (ret.). Past pres. N.Y. Soc. Architects; mem. Archtl. League, Beaux Arts Soc., Beaux Art Inst. of Design. Ind. Republican. Episcopalian (former warden). Club: Army and Navy (Washington). Contbr. to profl. mags. Home: 22 E. 36th St. Office: 597 Fifth Av., N.Y.C. Died Feb. 26, 1957.

JAMERSON, G(EORGE) H., army officer (ret.); b. Martinsville, Va., Nov. 8, 1869; s. Thomas J. and Louisa C. (Salmons) J.; student Ruffner Inst., Martinsville, 1882-87, Va. Agrl. and Mech. Coll., Blacksburg, 1888-89; B.S., U.S. Mil. Acad., 1893, grad. Army War Coll., 1910, 1922; m. Elsie T. Barbour, Oct. 20, 1897; 1 son, Osmond T. Commd. 2d lt., inf., U.S. Army, 1893, and advanced through the grades to maj. gen., 1942; retired, 1933; prof. mil. science and tactics Va. Poly. Inst., 1906-09; with A.E.F., France, 1918-19. Decorated D.S.M., Silver Star, Victory Medal with 4 clasps, Spanish War, Cuban Occupation, Philippine Insurrection and Mexican Border campaign medals. Mem. Va. Hist. Soc. Presbyterian. Clubs: Army and Navy (Washington); Current Events (Richmond). Home: Prestwould Apts., Richmond 20 VA

JAMES, EDWARD DAVID, architect; b. Indpls., Oct. 14, 1897; s. David John and Evangeline (Crull) J.; B.Arch., Cornell U., 1923; m. Catharine Lewis, Mar. 26, 1927; children—David Lewis, Stephen Edward. With archtl. offices Price & McLanahan, 1926-29; partner Burns and James, architects, Indpls., 1926-49; pres. Edward D. James Architect, Inc., Indpls., 1949-56; pres., chmn. bd. James Assos., Inc., architects and engrs., Indpls., 1956-69; dir. Brown County Fed. Savs. & Loan Assn.; prin. works include univs., air terminal facilities, elementary and high sch. facilities, hosps., banks, comml. and indsl. installations, residences. Chmn. Ind. Bd. Registration Architects, 1962-64. Pres. Beck Chapel Guild, Ind. U., 1957-69; organizer, fund raiser summer camp Wheeler City Rescue Mission, Indpls., 1958-69. Bd. dirs. Historic Landmarks Found.; adv. bd. Historic Madison (Ind.); ex-mem. Cornell U. Council. Served to 1st lt., Air Corps, U.S. Army, World War I; to lt. col. USAAF, World War II. Recipient award merit from Instns. mag. for design Student Union Bldg., Ind. U. Med. Center, 1946, for Men's Residence Hall, Ind. U., 1952, for Meml. Union Bldg., Ind. U., 1959; hon. mention award Ch. Archtl. Guild Am. for design St. Marks Meth. Ch., Bloomington, Ind., 1958; A.I.A. citation merit for Eastgate Christian Ch., Indpls., 1959. Fellow A.I.A. (past nat. vice chmn. com. preservation historic bldgs., past chmn. com. religious bldgs.), Internat. Inst. Arts and Letters; member Indiana Soc. Architects (past preservation officer Ind.), Ind. C. of C., Newcomen Soc. N.Am., English Nat. Trust, Nat. Trust Historic Preservation, Soc. Archtl. Historians, Art Assn., Gargoyle Archtl. Scholastic Frat., Delta Tau Delta. Clubs: Columbus, Indpls. Service. Author book revs. Home: Indianapolis3IN Died Mar. 1969.

JAMES, MARQUIS author; b. Springfield, Mo., Aug. 29, 1891; s. Houstin and Rachel (Marquis) J.; educated public schools of Enid, Oklahoma; m. Bessie Williams Rowland, June 25, 1914 (div.); 1 dau., Cynthia (Mrs. John Hugh Norwood); married 2d, Jacqueline Mary Parsons, Jan. 9, 1954. Began bus. career as reporter Enid (Okla.) Eagle, Kansas City (Mo.) Jour., St. Louis Globe-Democrat, Chicago Inter Ocean, St. Louis Republic, New Orleans Item, etc, 1909-13; copy reader, Chicago Tribune, 1914; asst. city editor Chicago Daily Journal, 1915; rewrite man, N.Y. Tribune, 1916; nat. dir. publicity, Am. Legion, 1919-23; member editorial staff of The New Yorker, 1925, American Legion Monthly, 1923-32. Was 1st lt., later captain infantry, United States Army, 19 mos. with A.E.F., France, 1917-19. Awarded Pulitzer prize for biography, 1930 and 1938. Member National Institute of Arts and Letters, Society of American Historians. Clubs: American Yacht (Rye, N.Y.); Nat. Press (Washington). Author: books including: A History of the American Legion, 1923; The Raven, A Biography of Sam Houston, 1929; Andrew Jackson, The Border Captain, 1933; They Had Their Hour, 1934; Andrew Jackson; Portrait of a President, 1937; Mr. Garner of Texas, 1939; Alfred I. duPont: The Family Rebel, 1941; Biography of a Business, 1791-1942 (a history of Insurance Co. of North America), 1942; The Cherokee Strip, 1945; The Metropolitan Life Insurance Co., 1953; Biography of a Bank (with B. R. James), 1954. Contbr. to mags. and radio. Home: Rye, N.Y. Died Nov. 19, 1955; buried Greenwood Union Cemetery, Rye, N.Y.

JAMIESON, CHARLES CLARK army officer, cons. engr.; b. Glover, Vt., Nov. 3, 1866; s. Williams S. and Isabella A. (MacDowell) J.; grad. U.S. Mil. Acad., 1892; m. Frances Floyd, June 12, 1894; children-Floyd M., Eleanor; m. 2d, Anne Uezzell, July 12, 1930. Commd. 2d lt. 15th Inf., June 11, 1892; 1st lt. ordnance, Apr. 9, 1895; capt., Feb. 7, 1901; maj., June 25, 1906; retired on account of disability in line of duty, Oct. 12, 1910; recalled to active service Apr. 13, 1919; col. N.A., Jan. 11, 1918; brig. gen. (temp.), Oct. 1, 1918; discharged as brig. gen., at his own request, Jan. 3, 1919; resumed business as v.p. firm George W. Goethals & Co., Inc., New York; consulting industrial engineer; pres. Asfalterra Co., Jacksonville, Fla., Duty Ft. Sheridan, Ill., 1892-95, Sandy Hook Proving Ground, 1897-1900; instr. U.S. Mil. Acad., 1900-03; duty Rock Island Arsenal, 1903-05, Watervliet Arsenal, N.Y., 1905-10; duty Washington, D.C., World War, as asst. to chief of production and spl. asst. to chief of ordnance until appmt., Dec. 1918, as dir. of sales of property acquired by War Dept. after Apr. 6, 1917. Presbyn. Address: Ocala, Fla. Died Aug. 21, 1935.

JAMISON, CHARLES LASELLE univ. prof.; b. Rochester, Pa., Feb. 17, 1885; s. Curtis Alexander and Elizabeth (Erdice) J.; A.B., U. Wis., 1913, A.M., 1924; Ph.D., U. Chgo., 1930; m. Anne Hutchison, June 28, 1949; 1 son, Robert Scott. Sec., treas. A.M. Byers Co., Pitts., 1913-21; lectr. U. Minn., 1921-22; successively asst. prof., asso. prof., and prof. bus. adminstrn., U. Wis., 1922-29; prof. policy, U. Mich., 1929-. Served as capt. Q.M.C., U.S. Army, assigned to dir. finance, 1918-19. Am. Econs. Assn., Soc. for Advancement Mgmt., Am. Assn. Univ. Profs. (mem. Nat. Council, 1941-43), Phi Beta Kappa, Beta Gamma Sigma, Alpha Kappa Psi. Republican. Presbyterian. Clubs: Ann Arbor Golf and Outing, University (pres. 1943-44), Barton Boat (Ann Arbor). Author: Finance, 1927; Management of Unit Banks, 1931; Managing Finances, 1931; Trading on the Equity by Industrial Companies, 1934; Economic Problems in a Changing World (with others), 1939. Contbr. articles on econs. and bus. to jours. Home: 1060 Baldwin Av., Ann Arbor, Mich. Died May 23, 1965.

JANNOTTA, ALFRED VERNON, ret. naval officer, corporation exec.; b. Chgo., Dec. 13,21894; s. Alfredo A. and Stella (Skiff) J.; B.A., Cornell U., 1917; D.Sc., Detroit Institute of Technology, 1961; m. Mary Brokerick Lamm, Aug. 20, 1918; children—Mary Frances, Shirley Skiff (Mrs. Henry C. Nickel), Diane Broderick (Mrs. Wallace B. Mallu). With Jewel Tea Co., Inc., from 1919, mem. salary and profit sharing, stock options and audit coms., from 1934, also dir.; with Lehman Bros., investment bankers, N.Y.C., 1926-27; pres., dir. Motor Inst. Am., Chgo., 1927-32, Tapp, Inc., Chgo., 1932-42; mng. trustee two investment trusts, 1933-42; pres., dir. Consol. Trading Corp., Chgo., 1947-49; cons., dir. Mayfair, Inc., Albany, also Porters, Inc., retail home furnishings, Racine, Wis., from 1949; dir. Western Lithograph Co., Los Angeles, Quality Park Envelope Co., St. Paul, Quality Park Box Co., St. Paul, J. D. Jewell, Inc.; with Standard Packaging Corp., N.Y.C., from 1955, vice chmn. of bd. dirs., also dir., mem. exec. com. Served from seaman to lt. (j.g.) U.S. Navy, 1917-19, from lt. comdr. to comdr., 1942-46; mem. Res., from 1946, rear adm., 1954. Decorated Navy Cross, Silver Star, Bronze Star with V (2), Purple Heart. Mem. Nat. Retail Tea and Coffee Merchants Assn. (dir.), Furniture Mfrs. Assn. (dir.), Navy League, Military Order of Loyal Legion United States, Legion of Valor, Order Lafayette (v.p., dir.), Res. Officers Assn., Soc. Mayflower Descendants, Sigma Nu. Clubs: Savage (Ithaca, N.Y. and London, Eng.); Chicago Athletic Assn.; Bob-O-Link Golf (Highland Park, Ill.); University (Albany, N.Y.); Everglades (Palm Beach, Fla.); Manalapan (Fla.). Home: Lantana FL Died May 31, 1972; buried Arlington Nat. Cemetery, Arlington VA

JAQUES, CHARLES EVERETT mfr.; b. Chgo., Dec. 24, 1873; s. Frank F. and Annie L. (Everett) J.; student Chgo. Manual Tng. Sch.; m. Annie C. Champlin, Aug. 9, 1899; children-Hallie M., Annie Laurie. Began with F. F. Jaques & Co., Kansas City, Mo., mfrs. K.C. baking powder; on organization, 1891, of Jaques Mfg. Co., became dir. and treas., and in 1895 moved to Chicago, in charge of Chgo. br., now the main office and factory of the co. Commd. by President Wilson maj. in Q.M. Corps, U.S.R., Oct. 30, 1916; on active duty at Plattsburg, N.Y., 1917: lt. col., U.S. Army, 1918-19; hon. discharged June 1919; now col., O.R.C. Republican. Mason (32ff, K. T., Shriner). Home: 6314 Sheridan Rd., Chgo. Died 1955.

JARDINE, JOHN EARLE, JR., investment exec.; b. Pasadena, Cal., July 31, 1899; s. John Earle and Mary Chater (Peck) J.; student U. Cal. at Berkeley; m. Laura Blair Synder, Oct. 21, 1922 (dec. Sept. 1966);children—John Earle III, Lauris Earle (Mrs. James Albert Phillips III); m. 2d, Alice Ayer Ellis, May 15, 1967. With William R. Staats and Co., Los Angeles, 1922-72, gen. partner charge syndicate buying, 1951-72, sr. v.p., sec.; sr. v.p., dir. Glore Forgan, Wm. R. Staats; v.p. du Part Glore Forgan, Inc. Past chmn. Los Angeles chpt. A.R.C., chmn. fund campaign, 1955, exec. com., dir. Los Angeles chpt., vice chmn. nat. conv., St. Louis, 1956. Bd. dirs., So. Cal. Area Bldg. Fund, AID-United Givers; treas., bd. dirs. Braille Inst. of Am., Inc.; pres., bd. dirs. San Gabriel Cemetary Assn.; bd. govs. Am. Nat. Red Cross. Served as 2d lt. U.S. Army, World War I; as lt. col. AUS, World War II. Mem. Soc. Colonial Wars (gov. for Cal.) S.R., Investment Bankers Assn. Am. (past v.p., past gov.), Assn. Stock Exchange Firms (past gov.), Los Angeles C. of C. (past dir., v.p.), Phi Delta Theta. Clubs: Bond (pres. 1948-49), Municipal Bond (past pres.) (Los Angeles); California; Stock Exchange (dir. past pres.); Valley Hunt. Home: Pasadena CA Died Oct. 16, 1972.

JARMAN, PETE ex-ambassador; b. Greensboro, Ala., Oct. 31, 1892; s. Peter Bryant and Hunter Elizabeth (Gordon) J.; student So. Univ., Greensboro, Ala., 1907-11; A.B., U. of Ala., 1913; certificate, J. of Montpelier (France), 1919; LL.D., University of Melbourne, 1952; married Beryl Bricken, February 25, 1930. Chief clk. in Probate Office, Sumter (Ala.) County, 1913-17; asst. examiner of accounts State of Ala., 1919-31; sec. of State of Ala., 1931-35; asst. comptroller State of Ala., 1935-37: mem. 75th to 80th Congresses (1937-49), from 6th Ala. District; A.E. and P. of U.S. to Australia, 1949-53. Served as 2d lt., later 1st, 327th Inf., A.E.F., U.S. Army, World War; maj. Ala. N.G., 1922-24, lt. col., 1924-40. Mem. Am. Legion (comdr. dept. of Ala., 1927-28). Vets. of Foreign Wars, D.A.V.; Mil. Order of World War, Forty and Eight, Sigma Alpha Epsilon; Skulls, Key Ice (U. of Al.). Democrat. Methodist. Mason. Home: Livingston, Ala. Died Feb. 17, 1955; buried Arlington Nat. Cemetery.

JARMAN, SANDERFORD army officer (ret.): b. Boatner, La., Nov. 24, 1884; s. James Sanderford and Emily Amanda (Tullos) J.; student La. State U., 1901-04; B.S., U.S. Mil. Acad., 1908; m. Dorothy Donald, Apr. 20, 1910; children-Katharine Lea (Mrs. E. E. Clark, Jr.), Dorothy Schuyler (wife of Harvey Jablonsky, U.S. Army). Commd. 2d lt., C.A.C., U.S. Army, Feb. 14, 1908, and advanced through the grades to maj. gen., Oct. 1940; served as maj. of field arty. and lt. col. of coast arty. during World War I; mem. Gen. Staff; 1934-38; became comdr. 64th Coast Arty., Hawaii; organized and commanded Coast Artillery and Anti-aircraft Command, Panama Canal Zone, 1939-41; comdg. gen., Camp Stewart, Ga., Sept.-Dec. 1941, anti-aircraft Arty. Command, Eastern Defense Command, Dec. 1941-44, Saipan, 1944-45; ret., 1945. Decorated D.S.M. with 2 oak-leaf clusters (U.S. Army), D.S.M. (USN), Legion of Merit, Mason. Club: Army and Navy (Washington). Address: 3915 Oliver St., Chevy Chase, Md. Died Oct. 15, 1954.

JARVIS, THOMAS JORDAN senator; b. Jarvisburg, N.C., Jan. 18, 1836; s. Rev. B. H. and Elizabeth J.; grad. Randolph-Macon Coll., 1860; served in C.S.A., 1861-64, pvt. to capt.; right arm shattered by bullet and compelled to leave service; m. Mary Woodson, Dec. 23, 1874. Mem. State Constl. convs., 1865 and 1875; admitted to bar, 1868, and began practice; presdl. elector, 1868, 1872; mem. Legislature, 1868-69 and 1870-71 (speaker last term); lt. gov., 1877; became gov. on election of Gov. Vance to U.S. Senate, 1879; elected gov. for term, 1881-85; U.S. minister to Brazil, 1885-89; elected to fill Senator Vance's term on latter's death, 1894, serving until 1895; del.-at-large to Dem. Nat. Conv., 1896. Address: Greenville, N.C. Died 1915.

JASPER, WILLIAM patriot, army officer; b. probably Georgetown, S.C., circa 1750. Enlisted as sgt. in co. recruited by Francis Marion, 1775, company assigned to Ft. Johnson, S.C., 1775-76, assigned to Ft. Sullivan (now Ft. Moultrie), 1776, awarded sword by Gov. John Rutland for bravery during bombardment by Brit. lines in Ga.; used in Black Swamp after capture of Savannah by Brit.; accompanied Benjamin Lincoln's assault upon Savannah, 1799. Killed trying to plant colors of 2d S.C. Inf. upon Spring Hill Redoubt, Oct. 9, 1779.

JAY, JOHN chief justice U.S.; b. N.Y.C., Dec. 12, 1745; s. Peter and Mary (Van Cortlandt) J.; grad. Kings Coll. (now Columbia), 1764; m. Sarah Livingston, Apr. 28, 1774, 7 children, including Peter Augustus, William. Admitted to N.Y.C. bar, 1768; sec. royal commn. to settle boundary between N.Y. and N.J., 1773; del. to Continental Congress, 1774-1779, pres., 1778-79; N.Y. Provincial Congress (helped draft a state constn.), 1776; chief justice of N.Y., 1776-78; commd. col. N.Y. Militia; minister plenipotentiary to Spain, 1779; called to Paris by Benjamin Franklin as joint commr. for negotiating peace with Gt. Britain, 1782; U.S. sec. fgn. affairs, 1784-89, tried to settle boundary disputes with commerce with Morocco and Prussia wrote (with James Madison and Alexander Hamilton) Federalist Papers (written as argument in favor of adoption of U.S. Constn. by N.Y. State), 1787-88; 1st chief justice U.S., 1789-95, wrote Chisholm vs. Ga. decision which resulted in 11th Amendment to U.S. Constn.; formulated Jay Treaty with Gt. Britian, 1794, settling outstanding disputed matters such as debts, navigation of the Mississippi River, boundaries; gov. N.Y., 1795-1801; pres. Westchester Bible Soc., 1818, Am. Bible Soc., 1821. Died Bedford, N.Y., May 17, 1829.

JAY, NELSON DEAN, banker; b. Elmwood, Ill., Mar. 7, 1883; s. Fred Dean and Elizabeth (Buchanan) J.; A.B., Knox College, Galesburg, Illinois, 1905, LL.D. (honorary degree), 1960; m. Anne Augustine, June 23, 1910; children—Nelson D., George A. (dec.), Robert Dean. With Milw. Trust Co., 1907-10, mgr., bond dept., 1910; v.p. First Nat. Bank, Milw., 1911-15; mgr. bond dept. Guaranty Trust Co., N.Y.C., 1915-16, v.p., 1916-20; partner Morgan & Cie, Paris, France, 1920-45; chmn. Morgan & Cie, Incorporated, Paris, France, until 1955; member of directors advisory com. Morgan Guaranty Trust Co. Chmn. adminstrv. com. A.R.C., 1943-44; chmn. bd. Am. Hosp. Paris, 1937-57; trustee of Knox Coll. Served from capt. to lt. col., U.S. Army, World War I; asst. gen. purchasing agt. AEF. Decorated D.S.M. (U.S.); Order of Honor with Star (Austria); comdr. Legion d'Honneur (France); officer de l'Ordre de Leopold (Belgium). Clubs: Metropolitan (Washington); Knickerbocker, Century (N.Y.C.); Travellers, Union Interallee (Paris). Address: New York City NY NY also Syosset NY Died June 6, 1972; buried Elmwood ILElmwood IL

JAY, WILLIAM lawyer; b. New York, Feb. 12, 1841; s. John and Eleanor (Field) J.; A.B., Columbia, 1895, A.M., 1863, LL.B., 1867; m. Lucy Oelrichs, June 12, 1878. Served as capt., gen. staff, U.S.V. in Civil War; bvtd. maj., Aug. 1, 1864, "for faithful and meritorious service in the field," and lt. col. vols., Apr. 9, 1865, "for gallant and meritorious services during operations resulting in fall of Richmond and surrender of Gen. Lee"; resigned, Mar. 29, 1865. Practiced in New York, 1869-; mem. firm of Jay & Chandler; pres. New York Herald Co., Valley Farms Co.; dir. Commercial Cable Co., Manhattan Storage & Warehouse Co., New York Mortgage & Security Co. Atty. Trinity Corp. and sr. warden and clerk Trinity Ch. Home: Bedford House, nr. Katonah, N.Y. Died Mar. 28, 1915.

JAYNE, JOSEPH LEE naval officer; b. Brandon, Miss., May 30, 1863; s. William McAfee and Julia Hamilton (Kennon) J.; grad. U.S. Naval Acad., 1882; studied Johns Hopkins, 1885-88 (certificate in applied electricty for which awarded B. engring. degree, 1927); courses Torpedo Station and Naval War Coll.; m. Elizabeth Tilton Eastman, Dec. 5, 1894; children-John Kennon, Anna Morwell. Ensign, July 1, 1884; promoted, through grades to rear adm., Oct. 15, 1917; retired May 1921. Comd. Torpedo boat Rodgers during Spanish-Am. War, blockade duty, Cuban coast; comd. various vessels, including armored cruisers Colorado and New York; has served as mem. Naval and Inter-Departmental Wireless Telegraph bds. and sec. Gen. Bd. of Navy; supt. Naval Obs., Oct. 16, 1911-14; comd. U.S.S. New Jersey and U.S.S. Mississippi, 1914-17; comd. Naval Air Sta., Pensacola, Fla., Apr.-Oct. 29, 1917; comd. Mississippi to Jan. 31, 1918; comd. div. 3, Battleship Force 1, Atlantic Fleet, Feb. 1-Sept. 13, 1918; comdt. 12th Naval Dist., 1918-20; comdr. Train Pacific Fleet, 1920-21. Methodist. Home: Newton, Miss. Died Nov. 24, 1928.

JEFFERS, WILLIAM NICHOLSON naval officer; b. Gloucester County, N.J., Oct. 16, 1824; s. John Ellis and Ruth (Westcott) J.; grad. U.S. Naval Acad., 1846; m. Lucy Smith, Sept. 17, 1850, 2 children. Apptd. midshipman U.S. Navy, 1840; served in ship Vixen during Mexican War; instr. U.S. Naval Acad., 1848-49; served in Gulf of Mexico in ship Honduras on survey for interoceanic ry., 1852-53, 57; commanded Water Witch in Brazil Squadron surveying Parana and LaPlata rivers, 1853-56; promoted lt., 1855; hydrographer in survey for canal route across Chiriqui Isthmus, Honduras, 1859-60; commanded ship Philadelphia in Potomac River, 1861; served in ship Roanoke in Atlantic blockade; commanded gunboat Underwriter in N.C. sounds, 1862; commanded ironclad Monitor, 1862; promoted lt. comdr., 1862; insp. of ordnance Washington (D.C.) Navy Yard, 1863-65, chief of ordnance, 1873-81; promoted capt., 1870, commodore, 1878; introduced system of bronze and steel boat howitzers, 1875; converted smooth-bore guns used on ships to breech-loaded rifles for all calibers up to 12-inch. Author: Nautical Rules and Stowage, 1849; A Concise Treaties on the The úTheory úand Practise of Naval Gunnery, 1850; Nautical Surveying, 1871; Care and Preservation of Ammunition, 1874; editor Ordnance Instructions for the U.S. Navy, 4th edit., 1866, 5th edit., 1880. Died Washington, D.C., July 23, 1883; buried Naval Cemetery, Annapolis, Md.

JEFFERSON, THOMAS 3rd Pres. U.S.; b. "Old Shadwell," Goochland (now Albemarle County), Va., Apr. 13, 1743; s. Peter and Jane (Randolph) J.; grad. Coll. William and Mary, 1762; studied law under George Whyte; m. Martha Wayles Skelton, Jan. 1, 1772; 6 children (only 2 daus., Martha and Marie, attended maturity). County lt. Albemarle County, 1770, county surveyor, 1773; admitted to bar, 1776; mem. Va. Ho. of Burgesses, 1769-75; mem. com. which created Va. Com. of Correspondence; introduced (with others) resolution for a fast day in Va. in sympathy with Boston Port Bill (resolution resulted in dissolution of Ho. of Burgesses); wrote A Summary View of the Rights of British America, 1776 (not adopted by Va. Ho.); mem. Continental Congress, 1775-76; mem. com. of 5 to draw up Delcaration of Independence, personally wrote most of declaration with minor changes by John Adams and Benjamin Franklin and by Congress as finally adopted); mem. Va. Ho. of Dels., 1776-79; signed Declaration of Independence, Aug. 2, 1776; gov. Va., 1779-81, instrumental in abolishing primogeniture and in finally achieving separation of church and state (much of his work finished under Madison, 1784-89); his conduct as gov. investigated because of war and Brit. invasion Va., but vindicated; went into semi-retirement and finished his scientific work Notes on the State of Virginia (published in France, 1784-85); mem. Va. Ho. of Dels., 1782; again mem. Continental Congress, 1783-84, drafted law that established decimal system of coinage based on the dollar, also proposed ordinance for N.W. Territory (not adopted, but became basis of famous N.W. Ordinance of 1787); succeeded Benjamin Franklin as minister to France, 1785-89; 1st U.S. sec. of state under new constn., 1790-93 (during this period polit. parties as we know them were developed largely through growing polit. differences of Jefferson and Sec. of Treasury Alexander Hamilton); became leader of Anti-Federalist forces (Republicans); resigned, retired to Monticello, 1793; vice pres. U.S., 1796-1801; wrote Ky. Resolutions in answer to Alien and Sedition Acts which grew out of Am.-French trouble of the time, 1798; Pres. U.S., 1801-09; his 1st adminstrn. marked by decision in Marbury vs. Madison, 1803, and La. Purchase, 1803; sent Lewis and Clark to explore new territory; his 2d adminstrn. beset with troubles stemming from English-French wars on the Continent; maintained Am. neutrality largely through econ. measures such as Non-Importation Act, 1806, Embargo Act, 1807; forced by econ. distress to partially ease embargo through Non-Intercourse Act, 1809; retired to Monticello for remainder of his life, 1809; an architect of renown, partly planned City of Washington (D.C.), designed and built Monticello; a prin. founder U. Va., mem. 1st bd. visitors, a rector (1819-26), also designed number of univ.'s bldgs.; pres. Am. Philos. Soc., 1797-1815; maintained scientific interests which led him into studies and writings on paleontology, ethnology, geography and botany; writings include: An Essay Towards Facilitating Instruction in the Anglo-Saxon and Modern Dialects of the English Language, published 1851. Died Monticello, Albemarle County, July 4, 1826; buried Monticello.

JEFFERY, WILLIAM PRENTISS lawyer; b. Brooklyn, N.Y., Feb. 24, 1878; s. Reuben and Emma (Lord) J.; student Denison U., 1896-98, N.Y. Law Sch., 1898-1900; m. Idelle Scott, Feb. 2, 1918; children-William Prentiss, Scott Wellington, Carleton, Janet Idelle. Admitted to N.Y. bar, 1901, and since practicing at New York; now member of Jeffery and Murray; director Container Corp. of America. Served as capt., later maj., Ordnance Dept. U.S. Army, World War. Formerly dir. and pres. Greenwich Country Day Sch. Formerly trustee Greenwich (Conn.) Acad. Mem. Am. Bar Assn., Assn. of Bar City of N.Y., Beta Theta Pi. Republican. Episcopalian. Clubs: Round Hill, Field (Greenwich). Home: 155E. 72d St. Office: 50 Broadway, N.Y.C. 4. Deceased.

JEFFREY, FRANK RUMER lawyer; b. Parkersburg, W.Va., Oct. 22, 1889; s. Thomas P. and Sarah (Grossfield) J.; student arts and science, George Washington U., 3 yrs., LL.B., 1913; m. Ray 13, 1919; 1 son, Frank Rumer. Formerly newspaper reporter; pvt. sec. to U.S. Senator W. L. Jones; began practice of law at Kennewick, Wash. 1914, as mem. Moulton & Jeffrey; apptd. U.S. atty. for Eastern Dist. of Wash., by President Harding, Oct. 10, 1921, resigned Mar. 2, 1925. Served 2 yrs., World War; maj. 146th F.A., 66th F.A. Brigade, A.E.F., 18 mos.; cited "for gallantry in action," Meuse-Argonne offensive. First State comdr. Am. Legion of Wash.; mem. Delta Sigma Rho. Sigma Phi Epsilon. Republican. Presbyterian. Mason (32ff, Shriner), Royal Order of Jesters, Elk. Clubs: Broadmoor Golf, Rainier, Wash. Athletic, Seattle Golf. Office: Dexter Horton Bldg., Seattle, Wash. Died Feb. 10, 1940.

JEFFREY, WALTER ROLAND, civil engr.; b. Ainsworth, Ia., July 25, 1892; s. William Riley, Jr. and Jessie (Brenhoits) J.; student Willamette U., 1912-16; m. Mildred Keith Honey. June 8, 1918 children—Judith Anne (Mrs. Burr E. Lee, Jr.), John Roland. Resident engr., chief estimating engr. Sinclair Refining Co., 1920-24; mgmt. engr. Bus. Research Corp., Chgo., 1924-28; pvt. cons. mgmt. engr., 1929-39; area mgr. Ill. and Ind., U.S. Bur. Census, 1940; exec. accountiant OPS, Chgo., 1951-53; supervisory auditor 5th Army Area, Army Audit Agy., 1953-56; bus. adviser to comdr., staff and suppliers Hdqrs. Def. Subsistence Supply Center, Chicago, Illinois, 1957-63, consultant, from 1964; president, chmn. bd. Analytical Tabulating Mgmt., Inc., Chgo., from 1928; v.p. Bills Realty, Inc., Chgo., 1946-47. Dir. Army Emergency Relief, Chgo., 1942; soldiers bonus div. Office Ill. Auditor, 1947-48. Served as pvt. Mexican Border, 1916; to capt. U.S. Army, 1917-19, as col., 1941-45, 49-51. Registered profl. engr., Ill. Recipient certificate outstanding performance Mil. Subsistence Supply Agy., 1961. Mem. Am. Assn. Engrs. (pres., sr. mem.), Soc. Am. Mil. Engrs. (charter mil. mem., past pres. Chgo.), Fed. Govt. Accountants Assn. (past pres. Chgo.), Am. Soc. Mil. Comptrollers (pres. Chgo. 1963), Midwest Joint Small Bus Council (chmn. from 1961), Am. Legion, Res. Officers Assn., Mil. Order World Wars, Retired Officers Assn., Assn. U.S. Army. Def. Supply Assn. (v.p., chmn. membership com., recipient meritorious civilian service award 1963). Republican. Methodist. Club: Union League (Chgo.). Home: Chicago IL Died Jan. 19, 1971.

JEFFS, CHARLES RICHARDSON naval officer; b. Bklyn., Jan. 20, 1893; s. Charles Frederick and Eliza (Boulton) J.; student Naval Acad. Post Grad. Sch., 1926-27: M.Sc., Columbia, 1928; m. Harriet Herring, Apr. 30, 1918; children-Charles R. (ensign U.S. Navy), Thomas Lee, Harriet Elizabeth. Entered U.S. Navy, 1911, commd. ensign, 1918, and advanced through grades to commodore, U.S.N., 1946; destroyer duty, U.S.S. Cushing, World War I; submarine service, 1922-31; asst. engr. then engr. officer battleship California, 1933-36; machinery supt., Mare Island Navy Yard, 1933-37; Yangtze patrol gunboats, 1938-41; staff Naval War Coll., 1942-43; comd. U.S.S. Appalachian, Guam, Leyte, Lingayen, 1944-45; dep. comdr. Naval Forces, Germany Land (State). Bremen, 1948-49: ret. as Rear Admiral, 1950; land commr. Bremen under High Commr. and Dept. of State, 1949—. Episcopalian. Home: 8186 San Gabriel Av., South Gate, Calif. Office: Deputy dir. Mil. Government Land Bremen, Bremen, Germany (A.P.O. 751). Died Oct. 1959.

JENCKES, JOSEPH colonial gov.; b. Pawtucket, R.I., 1656; s. Joseph and Esther (Ballard) J.; m. Martha Brown; m. 2d, Alice (Smith) Dexter, 1727; 9 children. Dep. to R.I. Gen. Assembly, 1891, 98, 1700-08, speaker, 1698-99, 1707-08; maj. of mainland R.I. Militia, 1707-11; asst. on R.I. Gov.'s Council, 1708-12; dep. gov. R.I., 1715-27, gov. 1727-32. Died Providence, R.I., June 15, 1740.

JENKINS, ALBERT GALLATIN congressman, army officer; b. Cabell County, Va., Nov. 10, 1830; s. Capt. William and Janetta (McNutt) J.; grad. Jefferson Coll., 1848, Harvard Law Sch., 1850; m. Virginia Bowlin, 1858. Admitted to Va. bar 1850; del. Democratic Nat. Conv., Cincinnati, 1856; mem. U.S. Ho. of Reps. from Va., 35th-36th congresses, 1857-61; del. Confederate Provisional Congress, 1861; commd. brig. gen. Confederate States Army, 1862; led brigade on 500 mile raid into Ohio, 1862; led advance guard into Pa., 1863; wounded at battles of Gettysburg, 1863, Cloyd's Mountain, 1864. Killed in Battle of Wilderness, May 9, 1864; buried at home, Green Valley, W.Va.

JENKINS, C(LAUDIUS) BISSELL officer corps.; b. Summerville, S.C., June 3, 1865; s. Septimus Hamilton and Annie Manson (Gautier) J.; ed. Rockville Sch., Wadmawlaw Island, S.C.; m. Lula Thomas, June 25, 1889: 1 son, River T. Gen. mgr. Cameron & Barkley Co. at 20, vp. at 22, pres., 1898—; organizer Gen. Asbestos & Rubber Co., 1901, also pres. Formerly maj. Charleston Militia. Mem. Huguenot Soc. Am., N.E. Soc., S.C. Hist. Soc., St. Cecilia Soc., etc. Democrat. Presbyn. Mason. Clubs: Carolina Yacht, Wappoo Country. Home: 52 Boulevard. Office: 27 Cumberland St., Charleston, S.C. Died Jan. 21, 1940.

JENKINS, JOHN MURRAY ret. army officer: b. York, S.C., Nov. 5, 1863; s. Micah and Caroline Harper (Jamison) J.; grad. U.S. Mil. Acad., 1887, U.S. Inf. and Cav. Sch., Ft. Leavenworth, Kan., 1891; m. Lucretia Dwinelle Flowe, Flower, Nov. 30, 1916. Commd. 2d lt. 5th Cav., 1887; promoted through grades to maj. gen., 1927; now ret. With Punitive Expdn., Mexico, 1916; organized and comd. trains, 2d Div., AEF; insp. 42d div. and 6th Corps; in campaigns, Champagne-Marne, Aisne-Marne, St. Mihiel; comd. 30th Inf., Meuse-Arganne (gassed); comd. 11th Cav., 1920-23; insp. gen., 1923. Decorated D.S.C. (U.S.) for extraordinary heroism in action near Cunel, France, Oct. 14, 1918; La Solidaridad (2d Class). Episcopalian. Home: The Dresden, 2126 Connecticut Av., Washington. Died Apr. 30, 1958; buried Arlington Nat. Cemetery.

JENKINS, JOHN S., JR., business exec.; b. Portsmouth, Va., Nov. 17, 1895; s. John Summerfield and Mary MacKenzie (Judkins) J.; grad. Woodberry Forest Sch., 1913; A.B., U. of Va., 1916; m. Marjorie Hope Aull, July 26, 1919; children—Marjorie (Mrs. Edward A. Mitchell), Alice H. (Mrs. Stephen P. Mallett), Jean McK. Joined John S. Jenkins & Co., cotton merchants, 1919; organizer and treas. Dixie Jute Corp., Norfolk, Va., 1922-69; dir. and mem. exec. com. Bank of Commerce; dir. Va. Elec. & Power Co., Planters Mfg. Co., Carolinas Ginners Assn. Mem. Norfolk City Sch. Bd., 1932-42, City Recreation Commn., 1944-45, Norfolk Port Authority, 1948; trustee Norfolk Museum of Arts; chmn. Norfolk Community Chest, 1941-43; pres., Norfolk Gen. Hosp., 1946-48; served on Regional War Labor Bd. Panel, adv. draft bds., W.P.B. adv. com., 1941-45. Commd., U.S. Army, 1917, resigned as capt., Coast Arty. A.A., 1918. Mem. Am. Legion. Methodist. Clubs: Norfolk Yacht, Norfolk Country, Rotary. Contbr. articles to trade mags. Home: Norfolk VA Died July 26, 1969.

JENKINS, MICAH army officer; b. Edisto Island, S.C., Dec. 1, 1835; s. Capt. John and Elizabeth (Clark) J.; grad. S.C. Mil. Acad., 1854; m. Caroline Jamison, 1856, 4 children, including Maj. Micah, Maj. Gen. John M. A founder King's Mountain Mil. Sch., Yorkville, S.C., 1855; an organizer, col. 5th S.C. Regt.; commanded a brigade in 7 days battle around Richmond, Va.; commanded a brigade at Battle of Seven Pines; brig. gen. at 2d Battle Bull Run, 1862;

commanded Hood's Div. at Battle of Chickamauga; accompanied Gen. Longstreet to Tenn. Killed at Battle of Wilderness, Mar. 6, 1864.

JENKINS, PAUL BURRILL clergyman, writer; b. Joliet, Ill., Aug. 25, 1872; s. Hermon Dutilh and Harriet Newell (Burrill) J.; A.B., Princeton U., 1891, A.M., 1907; grad. Princeton Theol. Sem., 1897; D.D., Carroll Coll., Wis., 1907; m. Gertrude M. Halbert, Nov. 23, 1897; 1 son, Halbert Dutilh. Ordained Presbyn. ministry, 1897; asst., Vermilye Chapel, New York, 1897; pastor, Linwood Ch., Kansas City, Mo., 1897-1907, Immanuel Ch., Milwaukee, 1907-23. Mem. standing com. V. and S. Gen. Assembly Presbyn. Ch. U.S.A., 1912-23; del. World's Presbyn. Council, Edinburgh, 1913; mem. Presbyn. Nat. Service Com. and Social Service Commn. Gen. Assembly Presbyn. Ch. U.S.A., 1917. Sergt. Co. L, 9th Training Regt., Plattsburg, N.Y., Aug. 1916; chaplain U.S. Base Hosp. 22 and 2d U.S. Arty. Aerial Observn. Sch., A.E.F., 1917-18; attached U.S. Evac. Hosp. 41, St. Mihiel campaign; chaplain (capt.) Hdqrs., 101 Div., O.R.C., U.S.A., 1924-34; chaplain Northwestern Mil. and Naval Acad., Lake Geneva, Wis., 1933— Historian of Geneva Lake Centennial, 1931; mem. outdoors advisory staff, Milwaukee Journal. Author: The Battle of Westport, 1906; The Book of Lake Geneva, 1922; History and Indian Remains of Lake Geneva, Wis., 1930. Co-author: Church Advertising, 1917. Contbr. on travel and nature subjects. Asst. editor Outdoor Recreation, 1915-27; editor catalog Nunnemacher Firearms Collection, Milwaukee Pub. Museum (3,000 specimens), 1927, advisor on arms, same, 1927-. Adopted into Wis. Pottawatomi Indian tribe, 1927. Lecturer, "Book-Talks," Lake Geneva, Wis., Pinehurst and Southern Pines, N.C., and Milwaukee, 1924-. Home: Williams Bay, Wis. Died Aug. 4, 1936.

JENKINS, THORNTON ALEXANDER naval officer, govt. ofcl.; b. Orange County, Va., Dec. 11, 1811; s. William Jenkins; m. Annie Powers, 1835; m. 2d, Elizabeth Tornton, 1849; 5 children. Apptd. midshipman U.S. Navy, 1828, lt., 1839; sec. 1st temporary lighthouse bd., 1850-52, framed law of 1852 for adminstrn. lighthouse service, sec. permanent bd., 1852-58, 61-62; served in Mexican War, also on West Indies duty; capt. in command ship Oneida, 1862, sr. officer, 1862; Farragut's flag capt. on the Mississippi River commanding ship Hartford, 1863, commanded div. blockading entrance to Mobile Bay, 1863-64; chief Bur. Navigation, 1865-69; commd. rear adm., 1870, commanded Asiatic Squadron, 1872-73, ret., 1873. Died Washington, D.C., Aug. 9, 1893.

JENKS, ALMET writer; b. Bklyn., Apr. 18, 1892; s. Almet Francis and Lena Barré J.; grad. Bklyn. Latin Sch., 1906; Hotchkiss Sch., 1910; A.B., Yale, 1914; LL.B., Columbia, 1917; m. Charlotte Williams Fenner, Dec. 4, 1923. Practiced law, N.Y.C. 1919-27. Served in World War as 1st lt. Cav., U.S. Army, with A.E.F., 1918-19. On active duty as maj. USMCR, 1942-45; staff III Amphibious Corps, Okinawa Operation, 1945. Mem. Delta Kappa Epsilon, Skull and Bones (Yale). Clubs: Racquet and Tennis (N.Y.C.). Author: The Huntsman at the Gate, 1952; The Second Chance, 1959. Contbr. to Sat. Eve. Post, Harper's Bazaar, Harper's and other publs. Home: 230 Clarke Av., Palm Beach, Fla. Died Feb. 2, 1966.

JENNE, JAMES NATHANIEL M.D., educator; b. Berkshire, Vt., Dec. 21, 1895; s. John Gilbert and Charlotte (Woodworth) J.; M.D., U. of Vt., 1881, M.S., 1924; grad. study N.Y. Post-Grad Sch. and Hosp. (6 weeks annually), 1890-95, Ecolé de Médecin, Paris, 1896; m. Abbie Cushman, Sept. 19, 1883. Began practice of medicine and surgery in Ga., 1881; surg. dir. Central Vt. R.R., 1891-1901; adjunct prof. materia medica, U. of Vt., 1891-93, prof., 1894-99, prof. therapeutics and clin. medicine, 1900-31, dean of Coll. of Medicine and mem. of univ. council, 1926-; dir. U. of Vt. Coll. of Medicine Dispensary; cons. physician Mary Fletcher Hosp.; cons. surgeon Bishop De Goesbriand Hosp., Burlington, Vt., Fanny Allen Hosp., Winooski, Vt. Mem. bd. trustees U. of Vt. Surgeon gen. Vt. N.G.; maj.-chief-surgeon U.S.A., Spanish-Am. War. Republican. Home: Burlington, Vt. Died Sept. 9, 1937.

JENNINGS, B. BREWSTER, trustee; b. New York, N.Y., June 9, 1898; s. Oliver Gould and Mary Dows (Brewster) J.; grad. St. Paul's Sch., Concord, N.H., 1916; A.B., Yale, 1920; m. Kate deForest Prentice, June 18, 1923; children—Mary Brewster (Mrs. Paul J. Chase), Kate de Forest (Mrs. George Seemann), John Prentice. With marine department, Standard Oil Co. of N.Y., 1920-27, purchasing agent, 1927-29, mgr. real estate dept., 1929-35; asst. to pres. Socony Vacuum Oil Co., 1935-39, dir. from 1939, on leave of absence for govt. service, 1942-44, pres. and chmn. exec. com., 1944-55, chmn. Socony-Mobil Oil Co. (co's name changed), 1955-58; trustee of Central Savings Bank, N.Y. Trust Co. Trustee of The Avalon Foundation, director The Greater New York Fund. Served with USNR, 1917-19; commd. ensign, 1917; exec. officer and in command U.S.S.C. 131, overseas. Dir. tanker operations and asst. dep. adminstr. for tanker operations U.S. Maritime Commn. and War Shipping Adminstrn., Washington, D.C., 1942-44. Decorated Navy Cross. Dir. Meml. Hosp., N.Y. Fellow Yale Corp.; mem. Psi Upsilon. Scroll and Key. Clubs: Links, Yale (N.Y.C.); Sewanhaka Yacht (Oyster Bay, N.Y.); Piping Rock (Locust Valley, N.Y.). Address: Glen Head LI NY Died Oct. 2, 1968; buried Oaklawn Cemetery, Fairfield CT

JENNINGS, JOHN army officer, jurist; probably born Phila.; circa 1738; probably son of Solomon Jennings. Sheriff, Northampton County (Pa.), various times 1761-78; became prominent in Pennamite War by ejecting Conn. settlers from Wyoming Valley; became pvt. 3d Regt., Continental Army, 1783; elected q.m. 1st Co., 2d Battalion, Northampton County Militia, 1784; moved to Phila., became sec. (or clk.) Mut. Assurance Co.; clk. to commrs. of bankrupts, Phila., 1791; dep. U.S. marshall for dist. of Pa., 1794; alderman Phila., 1796; asso. justice Mayor's Ct., Phila., 1796-1802. Died Jan. 14, 1802.

JENSEN, BEN FRANKLIN, congressman; b. Marion, Ia., Dec. 16, 1892; s. Martin and Gertrude Anna (Anderson) J.; attended Exira (Ia.) High Sch.; m. Charlotte Elizabeth Hadden, Dec. 13, 1917; 1 dau., Betty Lorraine (Mrs. Donald G. Fitzpatrick). With Green Bay Lumber Co., Exira, 1914-38, yard manager, 1919-38, member 76th-88th Congresses, 7th Ia. District Commd. 2d lt., U.S. Army, Camp Pike, Ark., 1918. Past 7th Dist. comdr. American Legion, 1936-37. Republican. Lutheran. Mason. Home: Exira IA Died Feb. 5, 1970; buried Exira IA

JENSEN, LESLIE gov. of S.D.; b. Hot Springs, S.D., Sept. 15, 1892; s. Christian L. and Lillie May (Haxby) J.; student Culver Mil. Acad., 1912-13; LL.B., U. S.D., 1926; m. Elizabeth Ward, Dec. 19, 1925; children-Leslie Ward, Natalie, Karen. Lineman, 1913-16; collector U.S. Internal Revenue Dist. of S.D., 1922-34; pres., gen. mgr. Peoples Tel. & Tel. Co., 1934-; gov. of S.D., 1937-38. Served in U.S. Army, Mexican border, 1916-17; capt., A.E.F., U.S. Army, 1917-19. Col., comdg. 147th F.A. with the Armed Forces in service, 1941-45; relieved from active duty, Mar. 26, 1945. Awarded the Edwin Mitchell law prize, U. S.D., 1926. Mem. Am. Legion, Hot Springs C. of C., V.F.W., Beta Theta Pi, Phi Delta Phi. Republican. Episcopalian. Mason. Club: Kiwanis. Home: 346 N. 17th St. Office: 1504 National Av., Hot Springs, S.D. Died Dec. 14, 1964.

JEPSON, WILLIAM surgeon; b. of Am. parents at Aarhus, Denmark, June 29, 1863; s. Neils and Wilhelmina (Hostmark) J.; M.D., State U. of Ia., 1886, Jefferson Med. Coll., 1891, U. of Pa., 1891; B.S., Morningside Coll., Sioux City, Iowa, 1899; L.R.C.P. and L.R.C.S., Edinburgh, 1897; A.M., U. of S.D., 1908; LL.D., Morningside College, Sioux City, Ia., 1943; m. Beatrice Baker, Dec. 21, 1886; children-William Roscoe, Weir Agnew, Florence (Mrs. Thomas Briggs), Beatrice; m. 2d, Mary S. Ohge, Oct. 15, 1917. Began practice at Oakland, Neb., 1886; moved to Sioux City, 1886; professor surgery, Sioux City College of Medicine, 1891-1901. State University of Iowa, 1902-13; in general surgery practice, Sioux City, since 1886; president Wilmar Investment Company, Sious Interstate Investment Co. Ex-pres. Ia. State Bd. Med. Examiners; past state chmn. Am. Soc. for Control of Cancer. Maj. Med. Corps, U.S. Army, Mexican border service, 1916-17, chief of surg. staff, Base Hosp., Camp Bowie, nr. Ft. Worth, Tex., 1918-19. Ex-pres. Tri State Med. Soc., Ia. State Med. Soc., Med. World War Vets. of Ia., Nat. Professional Men's Assn.; mem. A.M.A. Ia. Coin. Surg. Soc. (ex-pres.), Sioux Valley Med. Soc., Mo. Valley Med. Soc., Western Surg. Soc., Sigma Xi, Nu Sigma Nu, Alpha Omega Alpha; fellow Am. Coll. Surgeons, Internat. Coll. of Surgeons (Geneva). Mason (32ff). Founder, Jepsonian Institute of Natural Sciences. Office: 2000 Jackson St., Sioux City, Ia. Died Nov. 7, 1946.

JEROLOMAN, JOHN lawyer; b. in N.J., 1845; ed. Princeton and at Albany Law Sch. Served in Civil War, capt. N.J. Cav.; with Gen. Sheridan in Shenandoah Valley in Gen. Custer's brigade; badly wounded at battles of West Point, Guntown (Miss.) and Dinwiddie C.H., Va. Mem. law firm of Jeroloman & Arrowsmith until 1905; sch. insp. 9th and 16th wards, 1885-88; justice Civil Ct., 8th Jud. Dist., and pres. Bd. of Alderman, 1895-98; Democrat. Home: 305 W. 102d St. Office: 229 Broadway, New York.†

JERVEY, HENRY army officer; b. in Va., June 5, 1866; s. Henry (M.D.) and Helen Louise (Wesson) J.; C.E., U. of the South, 1884, LL.D., 1920; grad. U.S. Mil. Acad., 1888, Engring. Sch. of Application, 1891, Army War Coll., 1916; m. Katherine Erwin, Nov. 14, 1895 (died 1929); 1 son, William Wesson; m. 2d, Henrietta Postell Jersey, Mar. 19, 1930. Add. 2d lt. engrs., June 11, 1888; promoted through grades to brigadier general, 1920; promoted major general; retired, 1930. In charge 4th Dist. Mississippi River Improvement, 1898-99; charge rivers and harbors on west coast of Fla., and defenses of Tampa Bay, 1899-1900; in Philippine Islands, 1901-03; instr. and asst. prof. U.S. Mil. Acad., 1903-05; charge rivers, harbors and defenses, Mobile Dist., 1905-10; in charge river improvements Cincinnati Dist., 1910-15; apptd. comdr. 66th Field Arty. Brigade, Camp Greene, Charlotte, N.C., Sept. 1917; chief div. of operations, Gen. Staff, Feb. 1918; comd. 41st Div., Camp Greene and Camp Mills; comd. 11th Brig. F.A., Hawaii, 1921; retired Apr. 10, 1922. Awarded D.S.M. "for especially meritorious and conspicuous services as director of operations, Gen. Staff, and as asst.chief of staff during the war"; Comdr. Legion of Honor (French); Grand Officer Order of Leopold (Belgian); Companion of the Bath (British); Order of Crown of Italy. Author: Warfare of the Future, 1917. Address: War Dept., Washington, D.C. Died Sep. 30, 1942.

JERVEY, JAMES POSTELL army officer; b. Powhatan County, Va., Nov. 14, 1869; s. Henry and Helen Louise (Wesson) J.; grad. U.S. Mil. Acad., 1892; m. Jean B. Webb, June 27, 1894; children-Jean P. (Mrs. A. S. Quintard), James P., Darrell E. Comd. 1st lt., engrs., June 11, 1892; promoted through grades to brig. gen., and retired, Sept. 22, 1920. Duty with Engrs'. Sch., New York Harbor, 1892-95; fortification work, Pensacola, Fla., 1895-99; instr. and asst. prof. U.S. Mil. Acad., 1899-1905; comdg. engr. co. P.I., 1905-07; dir. civ. engr., U.S. Engr. Sch., 1907-08; at Panama Canal, in charge constrn. Gatun Locks, 1908-13; dist. engr. Wheeling, W.Va., 1913-14, Norfolk, Va., 1914-17; mobilization camp and France, 1917-18; dist. engr., Wilmington, Del., 1919; dist. and div. engr., Baltimore, Md., 1920; city mgr., Portsmouth, Va., 1920-26; prof. mathematics, U. of the South, Sewanee, Tenn., since 1926. Served in Spanish-Am. War, in Philippines, in World War as div. engr. 79th Div., chief engr. 7th Corps, and asst. to chief engr. A.E.F. Awarded D.S.M.; citation by div. comdr. and comdg. gen. A.E.F. Democrat. Episcopalian. Address: University of the South, Sewanee, Tenn. Died Mar. 12, 1947.

JESSUP, EVERETT COLGATE, physician; b. Bklyn., Sept. 11, 1887; s. Benjamin A. and Mary Caroline (Nesmith) J.; B.S. cum laude, Princeton, 1911; M.D., Coll. Physicians and Surgeons, Columbia, 1916; m. Helen Batho Castle, June 2, 1919; children—Mary (Mrs. C. Ogden Amonette), John Batho, Richard Nesmith, Joan (Mrs. John Kean, Jr.). Practiced gen. medicine, internal medicine, Roslyn, L.I., N.Y., 1919-62; instr. medicine Coll. Physicians and Surgeons, 1923-29, asst. prof. clin. medicine, 1929-33; cons. physician North County Community Hosp., Glen Cove, Nassau Hosp., Mineola, South Nassau Hosp., Rockville Centre, North Shore Hosp., Manhasset, Manhasset Med. Centre Hosp., Meadowbrook Hosp. Hempstead; attending physician Green Vale Sch. Mem. exec. council C. W. Post Coll., L.I. U.; dir. Nassau County chpt. A.R.C., Nassau Tb, Heart and Pub. Health Assn.; dir., ex-pres. Soc. Prevention Cruelty to Children; mem. Bd. Health, Nassau County. Entered Plattsburg Tng. Camp 1916; served as lt. and capt., M.C., U.S. Army, AEF, attached to B.E.F., 1917-19; maj. Med. Res. Corps to 1930. Pres. 2d Dist. br. Med. Soc. State N.Y., 1946-47. Diplomate Am. Bd. Internal Medicine. Fellow A.C.P., N.Y. Acad. Medicine; mem. Nassau County Med. Soc. (pres. 1934), A.M.A., Sportsmanship Brotherhood (dir.). Baptist. Clubs: Princeton (N.Y.); Seawonhaka Yacht (Oyster Bay. N.Y.); Lake Placid (N.Y.). Contbr. med. jours. Holds U.S. Interscholastic record for 50 yds., 5-3/5 seconds, made at St. Louis, 1904. Address: Roslyn LI NY Died July 1, 1968; buried Greenwood Cemetery, Brooklyn NY

JESTER, BEAUFORD HALBERT governor of Tex.; b. Corsicana, Tex., Jan. 12, 1893; s. George T. and Frances (Gordon) J.; A.B., Univ. of Tex., 1916, LL.B., 1920; m. Mabel Buchanan, June 15, 1921; children-Barbara (Mrs. Howard Burris), Joan, Beauford. Admitted to bar of Tex., June 1920, gen. practice of law, Corsicana, 1920-42; railroad commr. of Tex., hdqrs., Austin Tex., Aug. 1942-Nov. 1946; governor of Tex. since Jan. 21, 1947. Chairman Interstate Oil Compact Commission, 1948. Commd. capt. inf., 1st O.T.C., 1917; assigned to and comdr. Co.D., 357th Inf., 90th div. from orgn. to demobilization; participant in St. Mihiel and Meuse-Argonne offensives and in Army of Occupation; disch., July 1919. Mem. bd. regents Univ. of Tex., 1929-35 (chmn., 1933-35), hon. state chmn. United Service to China, Inc.; regional advisor Am. Commn. for Living War Memorials; mem. Nat. Youth Adminstrn. of Texas (dir.), Good Neighbor Foundation (hon. v.p., 1946-47), State Bar Assn. (dir. 1940-41), Navarre Co. Bar Assn. (pres. 1925-39), Texas Safety Assn., Inc., Am. Legion (hon. mem. distinguished guests com.; post comdr. Corsicana, 1923-24), Texas Resource-Use Com., 36th Div. Memorial Com., Chamber of Commerce (East Tex., Austin), 90th Div. Assn. (past pres.), 1st Officers Training Camp Leon Springs Assn. (past pres.), Reserve Officers Assn., Sons of Republic of Texas, S.A.R., Y.M.C.A. (pres. Corsicana 1939-42), Kappa Sigma (nat. pres., 1941-43), Sigma Delta Chi. Democrat. Methodist. Mason (Shriner), Elk. Clubs: Rotary, Lions International, Rancheros Vistadores. Home: 1508 Sycamore St., Corsicana, Tex. Office: Executive Department, State Capitol, Austin 11, Texas. Died July 11, 1949.

JESUP, THOMAS SIDNEY army officer; b. Berkeley County, Va. (now W.Va.), Dec. 16, 1788; s. James Edward and Ann (O'Neill) J.; m. Ann Croghan. Commd. 2d lt. 7th Inf., U.S. Army, 1808, 1st lt., 1809; served as brigade maj. and adj. gen. during War of 1812; commd. capt. and maj. of inf., 1813; brevetted lt. col. for bravery at Battle of Chippewa, 1814; brevetted col. for services at Battle of Niagara, 1814; full lt. col., 1817; adj. gen. U.S. Army with rank of col., 1818; q.m. gen. with rank of brig. gen., 1818; maj. gen., 1828; brig. gen.

in command army in Fla., 1836; resumed duties as q.m. gen. 1838-60. Died Washington, D.C., June 10, 1860; buried Arlington (Va.) Nat. Cemetery.

JEWELL, THEODORE FRELINGHUYSEN rear admiral; b. Georgetown, D.C., Aug. 5, 1844; s. Thomas and Eleanor (Spencer) J.; grad. U.S. Naval Acad., 1864; m. Elizabeth Lindsay, d. Rear Admiral C. H. Poor, U.S.N., June 15, 1871. Acting midshipman, Nov. 28, 1861; comd. naval battery of field howitzers in defense of Washington, June and July 1863; commd. ensign, Nov. 1, 1866; promoted through grades to rear adm., Mar. 15, 1904; retired, Nov. 22, 1904. Served on all foreign stas.; comd. Naval Torpedo Sta., 1890-93; supt. naval gun factory, 1893-96; comd. U.S. protected cruiser Minneapolis through war with Spain, on scouting service in W.I.; also comd. armored cruiser Brooklyn serving in the P.I.; mem. Naval Examining Bd.; comdr.-in-chief, European Squadron, 1904. Author numerous pamphlets and articles on professional subjects. Companion Mil. Order Loyal Legion. Home: Washington, D.C. Died July 26, 1932.

JEWETT, DAVID naval officer; b. New London, Conn., June 17, 1772; s. David Hibbard and Patience (Bulkley) J.; m. Mrs. Eliza Lawrence McTiers, 1827. Served as comdr. U.S. Navy, 1799-1801; in service of United of the Rio de la Plata (Argentina), commanded the Invincible, 1815; sailed for Port Soledad in command the Heroina; landed and took possession in the name of United Provinces, 1820; commd. capt. Brazilian Navy, 1822, promoted to div. chief, 1823. Died July 26, 1842.

JEWETT, JOHN HOWARD author; b. Hadley, Mass., Jan. 19, 1843; s. Edwin and Elizabeth (Jones) J.; grad. Hopkins Acad., Hadley, 1861; entered army, Apr. 26, 1861, Co. C, 10th Mass. Inf.; resigned, Aug. 1864, with rank of lt. and brigade a.-q.-m. and ordnance officer; m. Sarah Hart Phelps, Oct. 1, 1867. Editor and business mgr. Holyoke (Mass.) Transcript, 1867-73; business mgr., 1873-96, pub. 1896-99, Worcester Gazette; editor "The Profession" mag., New York, 1901-02; mng. editor the Craftsman mag., 1905-06; in spl. lit. work, 1906-. Has written popular verse over own name and nom de plume "Hannah Warner." Author: The Bunny Stories, 1890; More Bunny Stories, 1900; The Easter Story, 1901; Christmas Stocking Stories (5 vols.), 1905-07; Little Mother Stories (10 vols.), 1906; Grandmother Goose Stories (4 vols.), 1907; Friends of the Hunted, 1909; also juvenile stories, army songs, poems, etc. Died Sept. 18, 1925.

JOCELYN, STEPHEN PERRY army officer; b. Brownington, Vt., Mar. 1, 1843; s. William and Abigail Nims (Wilder) J.; ed. Brownington Acad. to 1855 People's Acad., 1858-62; m. Mary Chamberlain Edgell, Feb. 2, 1886. Enlisted in 6th Vt. Vols., Aug. 22, 1863, serving to July 6, 1864; 1st lt. 115th U.S. Vols., Aug. 1, 1864-Feb. 10, 1866; entered regular army as lt. 6th Inf., Feb. 23, 1866; capt. 21st Inf., May 19, 1874; maj. 19th Inf., June 27, 1897; lt. col. 25th Inf., Mar. 31, 1899; col. 14th Inf., Feb. 28, 1901; brig. gen., June 16, 1906. Bvtd. maj., Feb. 27, 1890, "for conspicuous gallantry in action against Indians at the Clearwater, Ida., July 11, 12, 1877." During Civil War served in Army of the Ohio and Army of the James, being present at the fall of Richmond; served on Rio Grande border of Tex., 1865-66; in numerous Indian campaigns west of the Miss. River, 1867-91; participated in Spanish-Am. War and in P.I., 1898-1901; comd. forces in Samar, 1903, and Dept. of the Visayas, 1904; mem. Gen. Staff U.S. Army and chief of staff Pacific Div., 1904-06; comd. Dept. of the Columbia, 1906-07. Episcopalian. Home: Burlington, Vt. Died Mar. 8, 1920.

JOHN, MURRAY army officer; b. Pitts., Apr. 27, 1835; s. John T. and Sarah (Murray) C.: entered U.S. Mil. Acad., 1853; m. Ellen F. Prince, Dec., 1856; m. 2d Frances McNeil, 1882: 2 children. Commd. maj. 6th Ia. Inf., 1861, lt. col. U.S. Volunteers, 1862, col., 1863, brig. gen., 1863; insp. gen. U.S. Army under Gen. Sherman, 1864; collector internal revenue Chgo., 1866 postmaster, Boston, 1885. Died Winchester, Mass., Apr. 27, 1893; buried Burlington, Ia.

JOHNSON, ADAM RANKIN soldier, land dealer; b. Henderson, Ky., Feb. 8, 1834; s. Dr. Thos. J. J.; ed. Henderson, Ky.; m. Burnet, Tex., Jan. 1, 1861, Josephine Eastland. Moved to Texas in 1854, Burnet being then extreme frontier, and while surveying had several conflicts with Indians; joined C.S.A. spring of 1861 at Hopkinsville, Ky. (Gen. Forrest's command); raised, mounted and equipped 2,200 men in Union, Henderson and other counties in Ky. Comd. one of Morgan's brigades on the Ohio raid; reorganized and comd. men while he was in prison; comd. them at battle of Chickamauga; ordered back to pay dept., Ky., July, 1864; wounded Aug. 21, 1864, having had both eyes entirely shot out; was sent to prison at Fort Warren, Boston Harbor, Nov., 1864; returned to Tex., 1865; resumed business as land agt.; laid off the town of Marble Falls, 1887. Address: Burnett, Tex.†

JOHNSON, ANDREW 17th Pres. U.S.; b. Raleigh, N.C., Dec. 29, 1808; s. Jacob and Mary (McDonough) J.; m. Eliza McCardle, May, 17, 1827; children - Martha, Charles, Mary, Robert, Andrew. Moved to Greeneville, Tenn., 1826, employed as a tailor; alderman Greeneville, 1828-30, mayor, 1830-34; mem. Tenn. Senate, 1835-37, 39-41; mem. U.S. Ho. of Reps. from Tenn., 28th-32d congresses, 1843-53, supported 1st homestead bill which granted land to settlers gratis or at nominal price, 1858 (vetoed by Pres. Buchanan), reintroduced bill and continued support until passage of Homestead Act of 1862; gov. Tenn., 1853-57; mem. U.S. Senate from Tenn., Oct. 8, 1857-Mar. 4, 1862; voted for Jefferson Davis' resolution to permit citizens to take slaves into new territories, 1860; apptd. mil. gov. Tenn. with rank of brig. gen. U.S. Volunteers, 1862; organized provisional govt. for Tenn., held Nashville against Confederate Army; vice pres. U.S., Mar. 4-Apr. 15, 1865; after Lincoln's assassination became Pres. U.S., Apr. 15, 1865-Mar. 3, 1869; issued 2 proclamations continuing Lincoln's reconstrn. policy, May 29, 1865; vetoed Freedmen's Bur. extension act, also Civil Rights act, 1866; vetoed Tenure of Office act, 1867 (act passed over his veto); suspended Edwin M. Stanton as U.S. sec. of war, 1867 (Senate refused the suspension, 1868); impeachment proceedings started against him by Thaddeus Stevens and John A. Bingham, Feb. 1868; acquitted in subsequent impeachment, (Mar. 5-May 11, 1868) by 35 to 19 vote in U.S. Senate; vetoed reconstrn. legislation passed by Congress during completion of presdl. term; during his adminstrn. French were forced from Mexico and Alaska was purchased from Russia; unsuccessful candidate for U.S. Senate, 1869, for U.S. Ho. of Reps., 1872; mem. U.S. Senate from Tenn., 1875. Died nr. Elizabethon, Cartar County, Tenn., July 31, 1875; buried Andrew Johnson Nat. Cemetery, Greeneville.

JOHNSON, BASCOM assn. exec.; b. Washington, Jan. 17, 1878; s. Joseph Taber and Edith Maude Bascom J.; A.B., Yale, 1900; LL.B., U. Pa., 1903; m. S. Frances Adams, June 11, 1904; children-Bascom, Margaret, Joseph Taber. Admitted to Pa. bar, 1903 and in practice at Phila., 1903-09; law officer for Fed. Indian Bur., Washington, 1909-11; sec. Recreation Comms. of N.Y.C., 1912-13; with Am. Social Hygiene Assn., N.Y., 1913—, asso. dir., 1919—; spl. cons. for USPHS, 1938—; apptd. dir. Div. of Legal and Social Protection in the Office of the Coordinator of Health, Welfare, and Related Defense Activities, FSA, Washington, 1941; on project with state and local agys. of Cal. dealing with conditions of Panama Pacific Expn. and in City of San Francisco, 1915-17; dir. of investigations for the special body of experts, apptd. by the Council of the League of Nations, to study internat. traffic in women and children, 1924-27, chmn. Commn. of Three to make similar study in 20 countries of the Near, Middle and Far East; mem. Adv. Commn. on Protection and Welfare of Children and Young Persons, of the League of Nations, 1925—; cons. in N.M. for U.S. Indian Bur., 1935; an organizer and dir. campaign of pub.health edn. for San Antonio C. of C., 1937. Served as maj. San. Corps U.S. Army, 1917-19; assigned as dir. law enforcement division of Army and Navy Comms. of Tng. Camp Activities. Since 1941, dir. of legal and protective measures, Am. Social Hygiene Assn., and legal cons. of USPHS, temporarily assigned to 8th Service Command, U.S. Army, with hdqrs. at Dallas, 1941-45; resumed position asdir. of legal and protective services, Am. Social Hygiene Assn., ret. 1947. Called from retirement to rep. the Internat. Union Against Venereal Diseases, in orgn. citizen activities on both sides of Mexican border, Jan.-Apr. 1949. Mem. of Internat. Com. of Am. Social Hygiene Assn. and accredited representative of latter to ECOSOC. Home: 7 Clinton St., Pleasantville, N.Y. Office: 1790 Broadway, N.Y.C. Died Oct. 21, 1954.

JOHNSON, BUSHROD RUST army officer; b. Belmont County, O., Oct. 7, 1817; grad. U.S. Mil. Acad., 1840; 1 child. Served as 2d lt. 3d Inf., U.S. Army, commd. 1st lt., 1844; served in Mexican War, 1847; commissary duty, Vera Cruz Mexico, 1847; resigned commn., 1847; instr. philosophy chemistry, Western Mil. Inst., Georgetown, Ky., 1847, instr. natural philosophy, mathematics, engring., supt., 1851-55; commd. lt. col. Ky. Militia, 1849-51; col., 1851-54; col. Tenn. Militia, 1854-61; supt. Mil. Coll., U. Nashville, 1855; commd. col. of engrs. Confederate Army, 1861, brig. gen., 1862; commanded a div. in Battle of Shiloh, in Bragg's invasion of Ky. at Perryville, 1862, Stone's River, 1863, Battle of Chickamauga in siege of Knoxville, 1863; promoted maj. gen., 1863; commanded a S.C. div., surrendered with Lee at Appomattox; chancellor U. Nashville, 1870. Died Brighton, Ill., Sept. 12, 1880; buried Miles Cemetery, Brighton.

JOHNSON, CAMPBELL CARRINGTON, army officer, social worker; b. Washington, Sept. 30, 1895; s. Rev. William Henry and Ellen Berry (Lee) J.; B.S., Howard U., 1920, LL.B., 1922; spl. work, Columbia, 1927-28; m. Ruby Etta Murray, Nov. 2, 1918; 1 son, Campbell Carrington. Chief of sect. handling ins. and compensation claims Bureau War Risk Ins., Washington, 1919-23; admitted to N.C. and D.C. bars, 1922; practiced law in Washington as mem. firm Love, Johnson, Mazyck, 1922-26; exec. sec., Y.M.C.A., Washington, 1923-40; instr. in social scis. Howard U., 1932-47; exec. asst. to dir., Selective Service, Washington, 1940-47; exec. asst. to dir. Office Selective Service Records, 1947-48, asst. to dir. Selective Service System since June 1948. Dir. Indsl. Bank of Wash. Mem. D.C. Bd. Parole since 1939, chmn. since 1946. An organizer Washington Community Chest, 1928, trustee 1928-41; an organizer Southeast House, 1929, Southwest Community House, 1929, Northwest Settlement House, 1934, serving as dir. until 1947; organizer Washington Urban League, 1938, dir., 1940-43; organizer Girl and Boy Scouts among Negro children. Lecturer, provisional course, Jr. League of Wash. since 1938. Commd. 1st lt., inf., 1917, and advanced through grades to col., 1943; organized and comd. Battery A., 350th F.A., 1917-18; organized R.O.T.C., Howard U., 1919, served as prof. mil. sci. and tactics, 1919-20; mem. O.R.C., 1920-41, active duty as major, 1941. Decorated D.S.M., Army Commendation ribbon; recipient Howard Univ. 1st alumni award for distinguished post-grad. achievement, 1943; Wash. Fedn. Chs. award for most outstanding layman in City of Washington, 1944; Omega Psi Phi nat. achievement award, 1945; scroll for distinguished and humanitarian service from 48 civic, social welfare, ednl. and religious orgns. of Washington, 1947. Sec. Chesapeake Summer Sch. Assn., 1923-32, pres., 1932-41. Mem. orgn. com. and mem. adv. com. U.S. Employment Service for D.C., 1933-37; mem. com. to reorganize Juvenile Ct. of D.C., 1934-35; mem. steering com. Atty. Gen.'s Juvenile Delinquency Conf., 1947-49; dir. Family Service Assn., 1934-46, Washington Council Social Agencies, 1934-48 (v.p. 1947-48), Washington Housing Assn. since 1935 (v.p. since 1947), Washington Self-Help Exchange since 1938, Bur. Rehabilitation, 1940-47; Wash. Fedn. Chs. (assisted in gaining admission of Negro chs. to fedn.; mem. com. and dirs., 1936-68; v.p. 1947-49). Mem. survey com., reorgn. Pub. Child Welfare Program for D.C., 1938-39. Mem. Nat. Assn. Housing Officials (vice chmn. Potomac chapter, 1945-46, mem. exec. com. 1945-46), Am. Legion, Am. Vets Com. Americans for Dem. Action (award for outstanding contbns. to Washington, 1949), United Community Service (mem. orgn. com. 1948; by-laws and constitution com. 1948-49, exec. com. and trustee since 1948). Citizens Council for Community Planning, Community Chest Fedn. for Nat. Capital Area (trustee since 1946), apptd. by Pres. Truman mem. Nat. Housing Authority, 1950; mem. Nat. Study Commn. Y.M.C.A., 1950-68. Mem. Am. Acad. Polit. and Social Sci., Omega Psi Phi, Sigma Pi Phi. Baptist (trustee). Mason, Elk. Contbd. articles to jours. Home: Washington DC Died Aug. 22, 1968.

JOHNSON, CHARLES G(EORGE) surgeon; born St. Louis, Mar. 13, 1899; s. Charles George and Lulu (Harris) J.; student McKendree Coll. Lebanon, Ill., 1919-22; B.S., Washington U., 1926, M.D., 1926; student U. of Mich. 1924, U. of Freiburg 1933-34; M.S., U. of Pa. (Nat. Research Council fellow in med. sci. 1926-28; Harriet M. Frazier fellow in surgery, 1928-36), 1928; m. Mary Esther Geitz, Sept. 7, 1922; children-Charles George (killed in action, World War II), James Harlock. Interne, internal medicine, Presbyn. Hosp. New York, 1928-29; asso. in surgery, U. Pa. 1935-36; prof. surgery Wayne State U. Coll. of Medicine since 1936; dir. surgery, Detroit Receiving Hosp. since 1936; chief of surgery Dearborn V.A. Hosp. since 1947; cons. surgeon Jennings Meml. Hosp., Det. Meml. Hosp.; private practice surgery, Phila., 1933-36, Detroit, 1936. Entered M.C., U.S. Navy, 1942, commd. lt. 1942-44, active duty, as med. officer, 1942-44. Mem. Am. Coll. Surgs., Am. Assn. for Surgery of Trauma (pres.), A.M.A., Am. Physiol. Soc., Am. Surg. Assn., Am. Diabetic Assn., Central Surg. Assn., Central Soc. for Clin. Research, Soc. Exptl. Biology, Western Surg. Assn., Wayne Co. Med. Soc., Physiol. Soc., Detroit Surg. Assn., Societe Internationale de Chirurgie; Alpha Omega Alpha, Phi Rho Sigma, Xi. Independent. Methodist. Research in gastro-intestinal physiology, liver and bile ducts. Home: 7945 St. Paul, Detroit 14. Office: 1401 Rivard, Detroit 48207. Died June 3, 1960; buried St. Louis.

JOHNSON, CHARLES SPURGEON univ. pres.; b. Bristol, Va., July 24, 1893; s. Charles Henry and Winifred (Branch) J.; A.B., Va. Union U., 1917, Litt.D., 1928; Ph.B., U. Chgo., 1918; L.H.D., Howard U., 1941; Litt.D., Columbia, 1947; LL.D., Harvard, 1948, U. Glasgow, 1952; m. Marie Antoinette Burgette, Nov. 6, 1920; children-Charles Spurgeon, Robert Burgette, Patricia Marie, Jeh Vincent. Dir. research and investigations Nat. Urban League, 1921; editor Opportunity, a jour. of negro life, 1923-29: dir. dept. social sci. Fisk U., 1928-47, pres., 1946—, also established Academic Development Program with headmasters and tutorial system plus closed circuit TV system; dir. Inst. Race Relations, Swarthmore Coll., 1933, co-dir., 1934-38. Am. mem. commn. apptd. by League of Nations to investigate forced labor in Liberia, 1930; sec. com. on negro housing Pres. Hoover's Conf. on Home Bldg. and Home Ownership, 1931; mem. sociology com. TVA, 1934; mem. exec. com. So. Commn. on Study of Lynching, So. Regional Council; mem. Pres.' Com. on Farm Tenancy, Tech. Com. on Tenancy, Commn. on Health Needs of Nation; mem. Nat. Manpower Council; mem. adv. bd. Nat. Youth Administrn. of Tenn., 1941; mem. exec. and planning com. White House Conf. on Children in a Democracy, 1940; dir. so. rural div. Negro Youth Study for Am. Youth Commn. and Council on Edn.; mem. Fulbright Bd. Fgn. Scholarships. Trustee Julius Rosenwald Fund, Nat. Urban League; dir.-at-large Bd. Home Missions Congl. Christian Chs.; del. 1st Assembly World Council Chs., Amsterdam, Holland; dir. race relations program Am. Missionary Assn., 1943-48; co-dir. race relations program Julius Rosenwald Fund, 1942-48; cons. John

Hay Whitney Found., 1950-56. Mem. U.S. Edn. Mission to Japan, 1946; mem. exec. com. U.S. Commn. for UNESCO; mem. U.S. delegation to 1st UNESCO Conf., Paris, 1946; chmn. UNESCO Conf. on Race Relations in Paris, also lectr. for Am.-Scandinavian Found. at univs. of Stockholm, Oslo and Copenhagen, 1955; Am. corr. mem. UNESCO project for sci. and cultural history and mankind. Served as regtl. sgt. maj. inf. U.S. Army, AEF, World War I, participated Meuse-Argonne offensive. Recipient William E. Harmon gold medal for distinguished achievement among negroes in sci. for yr. 1930; cited for distinguished pub. service U. Chgo. Alumni Assn., 1945. Mem. Sociol. Research Assn. (sec.-treas. 1943-46), Am. Social Hygiene Assn. (v.p.), Nat. Tb Assn. (dir.), Am. Adult Edn. Assn. (v.p. 1956, chmn. 15th symposium on sci. philosophy and religion at Columbia), Am. (exec. com.), So. (pres. 1945) sociol. socs., Social Sci. Research Council, N.E.A., Nat. Planning Assn., Alpha Phi Alpha. Conglist. Author: The Negro in American Civilization 1930; Economic Status of the Negro, 1933; Shadow of the Plantation, 1934; Preface of Racial Understanding, 1936; The Negro College Graduate, 1936 (Anisfield award 1938); Growing Up in the Black Belt, 1941; Statistical Atlas of Southern Counties, 1941; Patterns of Negro Segregation, 1943; To Stem This Tide, 1943; Into the Main Stream, 1946; Education and the Cultural Crisis, 1951; (with others) The Negro in Chicago, 1922; Race Relations, 1934; the Collapse of Cotton Tenancy, 1935. Editor: Ebony and Topaz, 1927; Education and the Cultural Process, 1944. Co-editor: Race and Culture, 1950. Home: 1700 Meharry Blvd., Nashville. Died Oct. 29, 1956; buried Greenwood Cemetery, Nashville.

JOHNSON, CRAWFORD TOY, business exec.; b. Chattanooga, Tenn., Oct. 22, 1898; s. Crawford Toy and Anne Caroline (Acree) J.; student Lawrenceville (N.J.) Sch., 1913-17; B.S., Yale, 1920; Yale, 1920; m. Mary-Stuart Snyder, Apr. 30, 1921 (dec. May 1963); children—Crawford Toy, Frederic Stuart; m. 2d Mary Nauman Bartow, Nov. 4, 1965. Clk. Birmingham Coca-Cola Bottling Co. (Ala.), 1920-24, sales mgr., 1924-26; v.p. Crawford Johnson & Co., Inc., 1926-42, pres., 1942-56, chmn. bd., 1956-65, also dir.; pres., chmn. or dir. numerous Coca-Cola Coca-Cola Bottling Cos.; dir. 1st Nat. Bank of Birmingham, Ala. Metal Industries Corp. Served as chief Q.M., Naval Aviation, World War I; lt. col. Fiscal Div., U.S. Army, 1942-45. mem. Book and Snake Soc. Republican. Episcopalian. Clubs: Augusta (Ga.) Nat. Golf; Racquet and Tennis, Links, Leash, River (N.Y.C.); Birmingham Country (pres. 1938), Mountain Brook Country (pres. 1947) (Birmingham); Minneapolis, Woodhill (Mpls.); Louisiana (New Orleans); Rolling Rock (Ligonier, Pa.); Royal and Ancient Golf of St. Andrews (Scotland); Somerset Hills Country, Essex Hunt. Home: Excelsior MN Deceased.

JOHNSON, EARLE GEORGE physician and surgeon; b. Bellwood, Neb., May 30, 1887; s. Edmund and Harriet Opal (Arasmith) J.; student Neb. Wesleyan U., 1905-08; A.B., U. Neb., 1910, M.A., 1911; M.D., Rush Med. Coll., Chgo. U., 1913; post grad. in surgery, Vienna, Austria and London, Eng., 1927; m. Laura Melvina Huyck, June 19, 1915; children - E. George, Beatrice Elizabeth (Mrs. Harold Albert Meedel). Intern Akron City (O.) Hosp., 1913-14, practiced medicine, surgery, Grand Island, Neb., 1914-; local and div. surgeon U.P. R.R., Grand Island 1915-32; mem. surg. staff St. Francis and Gen. hosps., Grand Island, Luth. Hosp., St. Francis Hosp.; cons. surgeon VA Hosp., Grand Island, 1950-57. Mem. adv. council Neb. Hosp., 1948-49. Regent U. Neb., 1951-57, pres. bd. regents, 1956-57; chmn. exec. com. Assn. Governing Bds. of State Univs. and Allied Instns., 1956; pres. Mid-State Reclamation Dist., Neb., 1948-51; pres. Grand Island Bd. Edn., 1936-58. Mem. rent adv. board Grand Island Def. Rental Area, 1948-49; president Nebraska Medical Examiners, 1942-55. Member board dirs. Grand Island Community Chest, 1948-50; chmn. exec. com. Salvation Army, 1921-22. Active Boy Scouts Am. Served as capt. M.C., U.S. Army, 1917-18. Recipient Distinguished Service Medal University of Nebraska; Certificate Nebraska Alumni Association, 1958; Congressional Medal, Selective Service. Methodist. Fellow A.C.S. (pres. Neb. chpt. 1936-53; life); mem. American Association Railway Surgeons, Neb. Reclamation Assn., Nebraska Medical Assn. (pres. 1946-47, bd. trustees, 1940-52), C. of C., Am. Legion, Hall Co. Med. Soc. (pres. 1920-21), Sigma Xi, Nu Sigma Nu, Sigma Alpha Epsilon. Republican (chairman Hall Co. central com. 1941-42). Methodist. Mason (Shriner, K.T., 32). Rotarian. Owner, operator 500 acre farm, Merrick Co., Neb. Address: 1402 W. Division St., Grand Island, Neb. Died Mar. 12, 1964; burid Grand Island, Neb.

JOHNSON, EBEN SAMUEL bishop; b. Warwickshire, Eng., Feb. 8, 1866; s. William and Catherine (Sidwell) J.; teachers' training course, Eng.; engaged in newspaper work in London; came to U.S., 1889; A.B., A.M., Morningside Coll., Ia.; studied Oxford U., Eng.; D.D., Syracuse; ú m. Sarah Tisley. Ordained M.E. ministry, 1889; pastor in Ia. for many yrs., also dist. supt.; elected missionary bishop of Africa, 1916, bishop, 1920. Del. and Journal sec. 9en. Conf. M.E. Ch., 1904, 08, 12, 16; secretary and publisher minutes Northwest Ia. Conf. 13 yrs.; chmn. Conf. Bd. Examiners 10 yrs.; pres. Northwest Ia. Conf. Bd. of Edn. 8 yrs.; was trustee Morningside Coll. Chaplain Ia. N.G. 18 yrs.; chaplain 52d Ia. Vols., Spanish-Am. War 1898; on Mexican border with 2d Ia. Regt., 1916. Extensive missionary travels in Africa, including journey across the wilds of Angola and Belgian Congo, 800 miles of which was accomplished on foot, 1919; traveled by motor car through southern and northern Rhodesia, Belgian Congo and Angola and back to Cape Town, over 8,000 miles, 1927, and more extensive journeys in succeeding years. Mason (Past Grand Prelate, Grand Commander K.T. of Ia.). Address: New York, N.Y. Died Dec. 9, 1939.

JOHNSON, EDGAR AUGUSTUS JEROME, economist; b. Orion, Ill., Jan. 31, 1900; s. Klaes August and Hannah Charlotte (Carlson) J.; B.S., U. of Ill., 1922, A.M., Harvard, 1924, Ph.D., 1929; LL.D., Johns Hopkins, 1972; m. Virginia Gravelle, Aug. 8, 1922; 1 son, Edgar Augustus Jerome. Instr. economics U. of Okla., 1922-23; asst. prof. and asso. prof. various schs., 1924-31; assistant professor economics Cornell, 1931-37, associate professor economic history New York Univ., 1937-41, prof. economic history, 1941-43; vis. prof. of economics U. of Cal., summer 1951, U. Md., U. Pa., 1955-56; prof. internat. econs. Johns Hopkins Sch. Advt. Internat. Studies, 1956-62, professor of economic history, 1962-69; sr. specialist East-West Center, Honolulu, 1968-69. Director of Dept. of Commerce of the S. Korean Interim Govt., 1946, civil adminstr. of the S. Korean Interim Govt., 1946-47, chief adviser to the Govt. of Korea, 1947-48, dir. div. Korea program, E.C.A., Washington, 1948-51; econ. adviser E.C.A. mission to Greece, 1951-52 deputy chief M.S.A. Mission to Yugoslavia 1952-55; cons. Gen. Motors, 1940-41, Govt. India, New Delhi, 1964-65, AID, India, 1966-67. Res. officer (Cavalry), 1922-37; entered active duty, U.S. Army, 1943; served with C.O.S.S.A.C., London, with S.H.A.E.F., London, Allied Land Forces Norway, Oslo, and U.S.F.E.T., Frankfort; disch. rank lt. col., 1946. Decorated: Order of the British Empire, Cross King Haakon the 7th, Bronze star. Mem. Econ. History Assn. (pres. 1960-62). Clubs: Harvard (N.Y. City); Cosmos (Washington, D.C.). Author: American Economic Thought in the Seventeenth Century, 1932; Some Origins of the Modern Economic World, 1935; Predecessors of Adam Smith, 1937; An Economic History of Modern England, 1939; (with Herman Krooss) The American Economy, Its Origin, Development and Transformation, 1960; Market Towns and Spatial Development in India, 1964; The Organization of Space in Developing Countries; American Imperialism in the Image of Peer Gynt; Dimensions of Freedom (pub. posthumously). Translator: Pioneers of American Economic Thought. (Ernst Teilhac), 1935. Editor: The Dimensions of Diplomacy; also 34 vols. of Prentice-Hall Econ. Series; Jour. Econ. History, 1940-43. Interested in Buddhist iconography. Home: Washington DC Died Aug. 17, 1972; buried Arlington Nat. Cemetery, Arlington VA

JOHNSON, EDWARD army officer, farmer; b. Salisbury, Va., Apr. 16, 1816; s. Dr. Edward Johnson; ed. U.S. Mil. Acad., 1838. Commd. 1st lt. U. S. Army, 1839; brevetted capt., 1847, maj., 1848; participated in siege of Veracruz during Mexican War, 1847, skirmish of Amazoque, 1847, Battle of Churubusco, 1847; storming of Chapultepec, 1847, Molina del Rey, Sept. 18, 1847, also at assault and capture of city of Mexico; commd. capt. 6th Inf., U.S. Army, 1851; col. 12th Ga. Volunteers, Confederate Army, 1861, served as brig. gen. at Battle of McDowell (Va.), commanded div. in battles of Winchester, Martinsburg Pike, 1861; maj. gen., 1863; participated in battles of Carlisle, (Pa.), Gettysburg, 1863; led div. at Battle of Payne's Farm, 1863; participated in battles of Wilderness and Spotsylvania, 1864, taken prisoner; fought under Hood at Nashville, Tenn., again captured, 1864; returned to farming, Chesterfield County, Va. Died Ford's Hotel, Richmond, Va., Mar. 2, 1873; buried Hollywood Cemetery, Richmond.

JOHNSON, EDWARD ROBERTS corp. officer; b. Aurora, Ill., Sept. 10, 1882; s. Lucius Elisha and Ella (Parker) J.; ed. Allegheny Inst., Roanoke, Va., and Purdue; m. Edith Grace Carson, Jan. 16, 1905; children-Lucius Carson, Ruth. Sec. and treas. H. T. Wilson Coal Co., Detroit, Mich., 1905-10; pres. E. R. Johnson Coal Mining Co., and Borderland Coal Sales Co., Cincinnati, 1911-13; gen. mgr. Jas. C. Cassell, contractor, Roanoke, Va., 1913-16; pres. Va. Supply Company, Roanoke, 1916-36; director of Johnson-McReynolds Corporation; director Roanoke Indsl. Loan Co., Valley Ins. Agency, Inc., Norfolk & Western Ry., Pocahontas Land Co., Va. Holding Corp., First Nat. Exchange Bank, Commonwealth Discount Corporation, Roanoke, Va.; director Life Insurance Company of Delaware. Member war work council Y.M.C.A., 1917; served as capt., later maj., Q.M.C., U.S. Army, 1918-19. Pres. Rotary Internat., 1935-36; mem. U.S. C. C.; mem. Roanoke C. of C. (pres. 1928), Virginia State C. of C. (v.p.), member Fort Lauderdale C. of C., Phi Delta Theta. Decorated Officer Legion of Honor (France); Order of Red Cross (Estonia). Republican. Presbyterian. Mason (K.T., Shriner), Elk. Clubs: Shenandoah, Beach, Lauderdale Yacht (Fort Lauderdale, Fla.). Home: 2241 Brambleton Av. S.W. Office: 22 Franklin Rd. S.W., Roanoke, Va. Died Apr. 12, 1960; buried Sherwood Burial Park, Salem, Va.

JOHNSON, FRANKLIN WINSLOW coll. pres.; b. Jay, Me., Aug. 17, 1870; s. John Sullivan and Elizabeth Williams (Winslow) J.; grad. Wilton (Me.) Acad., 1887; A.B., Colby Coll., Me., 1891, A.M., 1894, L.H.D., 1916: LL.D., U. Me., Brown U., 1933; D.C.L., Acadia U., 1938; studied U. Chgo., Columbia; m. Carolyn May Lord, July 15, 1896; m. 2d, Imogene Donovan Hall, Nov. 9, 1919. Prin. Calais (Me.) High Sch., 1891-94. Coburn Classical Inst., Waterville, Me., 1894-1905, Morgan Park (Ill.) Acad., 1905-07; asst. prin. U. Chgo. High Sch., 1907-09, prin. 1909-19; prof. edn. Tchrs. Coll. (Columbia), 1919-29; pres. Colby Coll., Waterville, Maine, 1929-42, pres. emeritus, 1942—. Lectr. on secondary school adminstrn. U. Chgo., 1913-19; courses in secondary edn. Tchrs. Coll., 1916. Served as maj. San. Corps, U.S. Army, rehabilitation service, 1918-19. Mem. N.E.A., Religious Edn. Assn., Delta Kappa Epsilon, Phi Beta Kappa. Baptist. Mason. Club: University (Boston). Author: Problems of Boyhood, 1914; Administration and Supervision of the High School, 1925; also numerous articles on edn. in mags. Home: Mayflower Hill Dr., Waterville, Me. Died Feb. 19, 1956.

JOHNSON, HARRY MILES psychologist; b. Nelson, Mo., May 16, 1885; s. Daniel H. and Virginia (Reeder) J.; A.B., Mo. Valley Coll., Marshall, 1909; fellow Johns Hopkins, 1911-12, Ph.D., 1912, LL.D., 1947; grad. study U. Chgo., 1911; m. Mary Ethel Johnston, Aug. 21, 1912. Asst. psychologist Nela Research Lab., Cleve., 1912-13, asso. psychologist, 1914-16, psychologist, 1916-18; research with B. F. Goodrich Co., Akron, 1920-21; lectr. psychology U. Minn., 1921-23; asst. prof. psychology Ohio State U., 1923-25; sr. fellow. Mellon Inst. U. Pitts., 1925-32; prof. psychology Grad. Sch., Am. U., Washington, 1931-36; asso. Hwy. Research Bd., NRC, 1936-38; prof. and chmn. dept. psychology, Tylane U., 1938-47, John Madison Fletcher research prof. psychology, 1947-50, prof. emeritus, research consultant indsl. psychology, 1950—; vis. prof. summers. U. Va., 1932-33, 1935, U. Cal., Los Angeles, 1941, U. of N.C., 1947, Cornell, 1948, U. Pitts., 1949. Served from lt. to capt. San. Corps, U.S. Army, 1918-20, chief of psychology sect. AS Med. Research Lab., 1919-20. Mem. A.A.A.S., Am. Psychol. Assn., Nat. Inst. Psychology, Soc. Exptl. Psychology, Am. Assn. for Applied Psychology, Am. Statis. Assn., So. Soc. for Psychology and Philosophy (pres. 1931-32), Nat. Research Council (served as mem. various committees; chmn. com. on psychology of the highway, 1934-40). Democrat. Episcopalian. Author: Audition and Habit-formation in the Dog, 1913; Principles of Applied Psychology, 1951. Cooperating editor Am. Jour. Psychology. Contbr. many tech. articles to Am. psychol. jours. and popular sci. articles to Harper's Mag., Forum, Colliers, etc. Research on fatigue and sleep for Simmons foundation, on human causes of highway accidents, and on selection and training of aircraft pilots. Clubs: Cosmos, Round Table. Home: 7837 Freret St., New Orleans 18. Address: Tulane University, New Orleans 18. Died Aug. 15, 1953.

JOHNSON, HUGH S. b. Ft. Scott, Kan., Aug. 5, 1882; s. Samuel and Elizabeth (Mead) J.; grad. Okla. Northwestern Teachers Coll., 1901; B.S., U.S. Mil. Acad., 1903; A.B., U. of Calif., 1915; J.D., 1916; m. Helen d. Col. H. S. Kilbourne, U.S. Army, Jan. 5, 1904; 1 son, Maj. Kilbourne Johnston (U.S. Army), Advanced from 2d lt., 1903, U.S. Army, to brig. gen., 1918; resigned from mil. service, Feb. 25, 1919; brig. gen. O.R.C. V.p., general counsel and asst. gen. mgr. Moline Plow Co., 1919; organizer, and chmn. bd. Moline Implement Co., 1925-29; associated with Bernard M. Baruch, N.Y. City, 1927-33. Served as q.-m. for refugees, San Francisco fire, 1906; in Philippines, 1907-09; exec. officer Yosemite Nat. Park, 1910-12; supt. Sequoia Nat. Park, 1911; judge advocate under Gen. Pershing, Punitive Expdn., Mexico, 1916; asst. to law officer, Bur. Insular Affairs, Oct. 1, 1916-Apr. 1, 1917; dep. provost marshal gen., Washington, 1917; apptd. col. Gen. Staff, Mar. 20, 1918, brig. gen. and chief of Purchase and Supply Bur., Gen. Staff Army; mem. War Industries Bd., Apr. 1918, asst. chief of Purchase, Storage and Traffic Div., U.S. Army, July 18, 1918; comdr. 15th Brigade, 8th Div., Camp Fremont, Calif., Sept. 1-18, 1918; comdr. 8th Div., Oct.-Nov. 1918, Camp Lee, Va., Nov. 1918-Jan. 1, 1919. Originated plan for selective draft, 1917, also rules and policies of same, and was exec. in charge, 1917-18; proposed organization of Purchase, Storage and Traffic Div. of Gen. Staff in effect Aug. 1918, to close of war. Holder of Mexican Campaign, and World War medals; awarded D.S.M. "for work on selective draft." Mem. Phi Delta Phi, Phi Beta Kappa. Democrat. Administrator NRA, June 16, 1933-Oct. 15, 1934; works progress adminstr., N.Y. City, Aug.-Oct. 1935. Editorial commentator for Scripps-Howard and many other newspapers and radio since 1934. Home: Okmulgee, Okla. Office: 1636 K St. N.W., Washington, D.C. Died Apr. 15, 1942.

JOHNSON, ISAAC CURETON naval officer; b. Evergreen, Avoyelles Parish, La., June 20, 1881; s. Isaac Cureton and Alzine (Marshall) J.; ed. La. State U., 1897-1900; B.S., U.S. Naval Acad., 1904; grad. Naval War Coll., 1923. Naval Submarine Sch., 1928; m. Sheila Helena Allen, Sept. 10, 1934. Promoted through grades to rear-adm., 1942 (retired). Decorated Navy Cross, French Legion of Honor, Mexican Service Medal, World War Victory Medal, Am. Defense Bar. Mem.

Sigma Alpha Epsilon. Clubs: New York Yacht; Army and Navy (Washington, D.C.). Home: 2193 W. 25th St., Los Angeles, Cal. Died Apr. 3, 1960.*

JOHNSON, JAMES army officer, congressman; b. Orange County, Va., Jan. 1, 1774; s. Robert and Jemima (Suggett) J.; at least 3 children. Served as lt. col. Ky. Volunteers under command of his brother (Col. Richard M. Johnson) during War of 1812; served at Battle of Thames, 1813, led right wing of U.S. forces against combined forces of British and Indian allies led by Tecumseh; outmaneuvered British at Thames, largely responsible for U.S. success; contractor for supplying U.S. troops on Mississippi and Missouri rivers, 1819-20; mem. U.S. Ho. of Reps. (Democrat) from Ky., 19th Congress, 1825-26. Died Great Crossings, Ky., Aug. 13, 1826.

JOHNSON, JOHN P.E. clergyman; b. Charleston, S.C., Dec. 25, 1829; s. Joseph J. (M.D.) and Catharine (Bonneau) J.; ed. U. of Va.; D.D., U. of the South; LL.D., Charleston Coll.; m. Floride Cantey, Dec. 1865. Civil engr. on surveys, construction and operation of railways, 1847-57; then went to U. of Va.; served lt., capt. and maj. of engrs., Confederate army, 1861-65, in the Carolinas and Ga. Was 15 months engr. in charge of Fort Sumter during the heavy and prolonged bombardments; twice wounded there; present at battles of Averysboro and Bentonville, N.C. Ordained to P.E. ministry, 1866; in charge Grace Ch., Camden, S.C., 5 yrs.; rector St. Philip's Ch., Charleston, 1871-; repeatedly deputy to Gen. Conv., P.E. Ch. Author: The Defense of Charleston Harbor, 1863-65, 1890. Home: Charleston, S.C. Died 1907.

JOHNSON, SIR JOHN Loyalist, supt. Indian affairs, b. Johnstown, N.Y., Nov. 5, 1742; s. Sir William and Catharine (Weisenberg) J.; m. Mary Watts, June 30, 1773, 1 son, Sir Adam Gordon. Capt. company N.C. Militia, 1760, col. regt. of horse; created knight in Eng., 1765, baronet, 1774; commd. maj. gen. N.Y. Militia, 1774; commd. lt. col. during Revolutionary War, served as Battle of Oriskany, 1777; supt. gen. of Six Nations of Indians in Province of Que., 1782, renewed, 1791; made home in Can., 1783, was given tract of land to compensate for N.Y. Seizure of Am. lands, became me. Que. Provincial Council; commd. col. Brit. Army. Died Montreal, Que., Can., Jan. 4, 1830.

JOHNSON, JOHN MONROE civil engr., r.r. exec.; b. Marion, S.C., May 5, 1878; s. John Monroe and Emma Crider (Richardson) J.; student U. of South Carolina, 1895-96, Furman U., 1896-97; m. Helen Barnwell, Nov. 15, 1900. In practice as civ. engr., mem. Johnson & Roberts, Marion, S.C., since 1898; prin. projects, Cow Castle Drainage Dist., Dillon, S.C., Mars. Bluff Bridge, Pee Dee, S.C., Society Hill (S.C.) Bridge, Godfreys Bridge, Gresham, S.C. Served as sergt. arty., U.S. Vols., Spanish-Am. War; maj., lt. col. and col., chief engr. Rainbow Div., U.S. Army, World War I; participated in all campaigns of the div. and was with Army of Occupation. Chief engr. and chmn. Marion County (S.C.) Highway Commn., 1912-14; chmn. S.C. State Highway Commn., 1916-17; apptd. boundary commr., S.C., 1928; asst. sec. of Commerce, 1935-40; apptd. mem. Interstate Commerce Commn., June 1940; apptd. Dir. Office of Defense Transportation, April 4, 1944; renominated by President Truman as interstate commerce commr., Jan. 1949, confirmed by Senate, Feb., term, 1949-55, chmn. 1950, 1953-56; became assistant to president A.C.L. R.R., 1956. Mem. Am. Soc. C.E., Am. Soc. Mil. Engrs. (pres. 1940-41), Mil. Order of World Wars, Am. Legion (mem. nat. exec. com. 1919-36), Sigma Nu, Omicron Delta Kappa. Awarded D.S.M. (U.S.); Verdun Medal, Legion of Honor (France), Order of Leopold II (Belgium). Received from President Truman, Medal for Merit, Mar. 8, 1946, in recognition of services to U.S. as dir. Office of Defense Transportation, Certificate of Appreciation, U.S. Navy, Sept. 12, 1946, in recognition of meritorious personal service during World War II. Mem. Newcomen Soc. in N.A., Order of Lafayette. Democrat. Baptist. Mason. Clubs: Army and Navy, Burning Tree, Post Mortem (Washington). Home: 3040 Idaho Av. N.W., Washington 25. Office: ACL R.R. Co., 1000 Connecticut Av. N.W., Washington. Deceased July 1, 1964.

JOHNSON, KEEN, ex-gov. of Kentucky; b. Lyon County, Ky., Jan. 12, 1896; s. Robert and Mattie Davis (Holloway) J.; student Central Coll., Fayette, Mo., 1914-17; A.B., U. of Ky., 1922; LL.D., (hon.), University of Kentucky, June 1940; m. Eunice Lee Nichols, June 23, 1917; 1 dau., Judith Keen. Editor Elizabethtown (Ky.) Mirror, 1919-21, Lawrenceburgh (Ky.) News, 1922-25; editor Richmond (Ky.) Daily Register since 1925; pres. Richmond Daily Register Co. With Reynolds Metals Co. asst. to pres.; assigned to Washington office, 1944, vice pres., 1945-46, v.p. for pub. affairs, 1947-70, director, 1949-70. Lt. gov. of Ky., 1935-39, gov. 1939-43; under sec. of labor, 1946-47; president Louisville Safety Council. Bd. regents Eastern Kentucky State Coll. Entered 1st R.O.T.C., Ft. Riley, Kan., May 1917; commd. 2d lt., later 1st lt.; served with 354th Infantry, 89th Div., 1917-19; with A.E.F., 1 year. Mem. Ky. State Press Assn. (former pres.), Public Relations Soc. America, U. of Ky. Alumni Assn. (past pres.), Am. Legion, Vets. Fgn. Wars, 40 et 8, Sigma Alpha Epsilon, Alpha Delta Sigma, Omicron Delta Kappa. Democrat. Methodist. Mason, Elk. Clubs: Metropolitan, National Press (Washington), Pendennis, Rotary (Louisville). Home: Richmond KY Died Feb. 7, 1970; buried Richmond Cemetery, Richmond KY

JOHNSON, KENNETH D(EWEY) lawyer, educator; b. Quincy, Mass., Sept. 5, 1898; s. John Louis and Charlotte M(atilda) (Almquist) J.; A.B., Brown U., 1921; LL.B., Harvard, 1924; m. Ethel G. Mayo, Aug. 14, 1930; children-Mayo, Charlotte Dallas. Admitted to Mass. bar, 1924, and practiced as asso. firm of Goodwin, Proctor, Field & Hoar, Boston, 1924-30, individually, 1930-42; dean N.Y. Sch. of Social Work, Columbia, 1949-58, emeritus, 1958—; judge, Dist. Ct., Quincy, (also presiding judge Juvenile Ct.), 1930-38. Enlisted with Bn. C. 103th F.A., 26th Div., U.S. Army, Jan. 1917; with A.E.F., 1917-19; entered active duty with rank of maj., 1942, promoted col., 1945; chief labor officer. Signal Corps, Washington, 1942-45; chief, spl. labor mission to E.T.O., Jan. 1945; legal adviser to mil. govt., Germany, 1945-46; spl. asst. to sec. of war, 1946-47; gen. counsel Nat. Security Resources Bd., 1947-49. Mem. bd. of selectman, Milton, Mass., 1924-31, chmn., 1928-31; chief of rubber prodn. team, Office of Sec. of War, 1943-45; alternate mem. Pres.'s spl. commn. on employee loyalty, 1947-48. Recipient Silver star, Legion of Merit, Commendation ribbon with 2 clusters. Pres. Mass. Conf. of Social Work, 1936; pres. Habit Clinic for Child Guidance of Boston, 1936-41; dir. Citizens Com. on Children of N.Y.C., 1951—, chmn., 1954—; dir. National Travelers Aid Assn., 1950—, U.S.O., Inc., 1951—, Big Brothers Am., 1952--, N.Y. Chpt. A.R.C., United Neighborhood Houses, 1951—, Greater N.Y. Council for Fgn. Students, 1952—, pres., 1952-54; pres. N.Y. State Welfare Conf., 1956—; exec. gd. Internat. Social Service, 1949—; trustee Columbia U. Press, 1949—. Nat. Probation and Parole Assn., 1950—. Chmn. health and welfare adv. com. to AFL-CIO Community Services Com. Home: Barley Neck Rd., Orleans, Mass.; also 130 E. 75th St., N.Y.C. 21. Office: 2 E. 91st St., N.Y.C. 28. Died Nov. 6, 1958; buried Orleans, Mass.

JOHNSON, LEE PAYNE naval officer; b. Concord, N.C., Oct. 26, 1886; s. Daniel Dudley and Mattie Lee (Hilton) J.; student Trinity Coll., Durham, N.C.; grad. U.S. Naval Acad., 1909; grad. U.S. naval War Coll.; m. Emily Edelin Tilley, Dec. 12, 1911; 1 dau., Emily Williamson (Mrs. James Leon Price). Commd. ensign, U.S. Navy, 1911, and advanced through the grades to commodore, 1943; comd. destroyer with Adm. Sims Force based on Queenstown, Ireland, during World War I; became Chief of Staff, Amphibious Force, U.S. Atlantic Fleet, 1942, Comdr. Rear Echelon, 1942; Comdr. Amphibious Tng. Command U.S. Atlantic Fleet, 1943-44; ret. for phys. disability, 1944; on active duty as comdr. Naval Ordnance Plant, York, Pa., 1944-. Decorated Navy Cross, Legion of Merit with gold star, Special Commendation by Sec. of Navy, ribbons of World War I, Mexican Border, European-African Theater, Am. Theater, Am. Def. Methodist. Club: Army-Navy Country (Washington). Address: Naval Ordnance Plant, York, Pa. Died Apr. 5, 1964; buried Naval Acad. Cemetery, Annapolis, Md.

JOHNSON, LEIGHTON FOSTER otolaryngologist; b. Hingham, Mass., Nov. 30, 1891; s. Rev. Samuel F. and Dora Alice (Beicher) J.; M.D., Boston U., 1915; post grad. Harvard Med. Sch., 2 yrs.; m. Harriet Woodman, Nov. 28, 1917; children-Leighton Foster, David Stanton. Engaged in practice as physician, otolaryngologist, Boston, Mass., since 1923; prof. and head of dept. otolaryngology, Sch. of Medicine, Boston U., 1941-45; surgeon in chief, ear, nose, throat dept. Mass. Meml. Hosp., since 1941, pres. staff, 1952-53; consultant to Fitchburg, Natick, Norwood, Cape Cod, Marthas Vineyard and Nantucket hospitals; lecturer Wellesley College. Consultant to Guild for Hard of Hearing. Served as captain, Fourth Division, Medical Reserve Corps, United States Army, during World War I. Fellow American College Surgeons; mem. A.M.A. (Pres. Norfolk Dist., 1935-36), Am. Bd. Otolaryngology, Am. Acad. Otolaryngology, Am. Bronchoscopic Soc., Am. Triological Soc., N.E. Otolaryngol. Soc. (pres.), Boston Surgical Soc., Am. Brocho-Aesophological Soc. (president elect), Psi Upsilon. Clubs: Algonquin (Boston); Wellesley (Mass.) Country; Wellfleet (Mass.) Country. Contbr. numerous articles to nat. sci. jours. Home: Longwood Towers, Brookline, Mass. Office: 203 Commonwealth Av., Boston. Died July 21, 1953.

JOHNSON, LOUIS ARTHUR b. Roanoke, Va., Jan. 10, 1891; s. Marcellus A. and Katherine Leftwich (Arthur) Johnson; LL.B., U. Va., 1912; LL.D., Salem Coll., 1938, Kenyon Coll., 1939, Creighton Coll., 1949, Villanova Coll., 1949, Marietta Coll., 1949, W.Va. U., 1949, Pa. Mil. Coll., 1950; m. Ruth F. Maxwell, Feb. 7, 1920; children-Lillian Maxwell, Ruth Katherine. Began practice at Clarksburg, W.Va., 1912; mem. Steptoe and Johnson, Clarksburg and Charleston, W.Va., Washington; dir. Union Nat. Bank, Community Savs. & Loan Co. (both Clarksburg); sec. of def., Washington, 1949-50. Became civilian aide to Sec. of War, State of W.Va., 1933; mem. fed. adv. council U.S. Employment Service under Dept. of Labor; asst. sec. of war, 1937-40; personal rep. of pres. in India, 1942. Served as capt. inf., overseas 1 yr., World War; lt. col. Inf. Res. Decorated Commdr. Legion of Honor (France); Medal of Merit (U.S.); recipient W.Va.'s Distinguished Service edal, 1961. Mem. W.Va. Ho. of Reps., 1917 (chmn. jud. com.; majority floor leader). Nat. comdr. Am. Legion, 1932-33. Del. to Democratic Nat. Conv., 1924; nat. chmn. Dem. Advisory Com., 1936-40. Chmn. Nat. Finance Com., Dem. Nat. Com., 1948. Mem. Am., Fed., W.Va. State, Harrison Co. bar assns., Assn. Bar City N.Y., Nat. Soc. S.A.R., Res. Officers Assn. of U.S., F.I.D.A.C. (v.p. for U.S. 1933-34), Delta Chi, Delta Sigma Rho, Tau Kappa Alpha, Raven. Democrat. Episcopalian. Mason. Elk. Clubs: Metropolitan, Army and Navy, Burning Tree, Chevy Chase, 1925 F. St. (Washington); Rotary, Clarksburg Country; University; Metropolitan, Midday, Drug and Chemical, Recess (N.Y.C.); Bohemian (San Francisco). Offices: Union Nat. Bank Bldg., Clarksburg, W.Va.; Kanawha Valley Bldg., Charleston, W.Va.; Shoreham Bldg., Washington. Died Apr. 1966.

JOHNSON, MAX SHERRED army officer; b. Greenville, Pa., Oct. 16, 1902; s. William M. and Effie L. (Sherred) J.; grad. Culver Mil. Acad., 1922; student Thiel Coll., 1922-23; B.S., U.S. Mil. Acad., 1927; B.S. in Civil Engring., Cornell U., 1929; grad. Engr. Sch., 1932, Command and Gen. Staff Coll., 1938, Nat. War Coll., 1949; student Ecole Superieure de Guerre, Paris, France, 1939; LL.D., Dickinson Coll., 1957, Thiel Coll., 1957; m. Helen Pendleton Manley, Oct. 20, 1934; children-Helen Sherred (Mrs. Robert Lee Myers, III), Max Sherred. Commd. 2d lt., Corps of Engineers, U.S. Army, 1927, advanced through grades to maj. gen., 1955; various assignments U.S., P.I., France, Greece, 1927-43; chief staff 80th Inf. Div., 1943-44, Europe, Invasion of Normandy, Battle of Bulge, 1944-45; chief strategy sect. operations div. War Dept. Gen. Staff, 1945-46; army dir. Joint War Plans Com., Office Joint Chiefs Staff, 1946-47; engr. hdqrs. USARPAC, Ft. Shafter, T.H., 1949-51; asst. comdt. Command and Gen. Staff Coll., Ft. Leavenworth, Kan., 1951-53; asst. div. comdr. 40th Inf. Div., Korea, 1953; dep. chief staff, plans and combat operations Hdqrs. 8th Army, Korea, 1953-54; asst. comdg. gen., chief staff Engr. Center, Ft. Belvoir, Va., 1954-55; comdt. Army War Coll., Carlisle Barracks, Pa., 1955-. Decorated Silver Star, Legion of Merit with clusters, Bronze Star medal (U.S.); Croix de Guerre with palm (France); Order Mil. Merit Taeguk (Republic of Korea); Ulchi Distinguished Mil. Service Medal with gold star (Korea). Mem. Newcomen Soc. N.A., Inst. Am. Strategy (dir.), Assn. U.S. Army, Am. Soc. Mil. Engrs. Clubs: Army-Navy, Army-Navy Country (Washington); Kiwanis, Rotary (Carlisle, Pa.). Address: Quarters 1, Army War Coll., Carlisle Barracks, Pa. Died Jan. 1968.

JOHNSON, MORTIMER LAWRENCE rear admiral U.S.N.; b. Nahant, Mass., June 1, 1842. Apptd. from Mass. and grad. U.S. Naval Acad., 1862; promoted ensign, Sept. 16, 1862; lt., Feb. 22, 1864; lt. comdr., July 25, 1866; comdr., Apr. 26, 1878; capt., May 9, 1893; rear admiral, Jan. 29, 1901. Served on Mississippi, 1861; Susquehanna, 1861; Sabine and Wabash, 1862-63; S. Atlantic Blockading Squadron, and was in all engagements under Admiral Du Pont and Dahlgren, 1863-64; served on Colorado, 1864-65, participated in both attacks on Ft. Fisher; comd. Estrella, W. Gulf Blockading Squadron, 1865; Dacotah, 1866-88; Kenosha and Plymouth, 1869-70; Navy Yard, Portsmouth, 1870-71; Worcester, 1871; Wyoming, 1872-73; exec. officer receiving-ship Sabine, 1873-74, Powhatan, 1874-75; served on receiving ship Wabash, 1875-78; Navy Yard, Portsmouth, 1878-79; comd. Ashelot, 1879-81; spl. duty, 1882-83; Navy Yard, Boston, 1884-87; comd. Monocacy, 1889-91; Naval War Coll., 1892; Navy Yard, Portsmouth, 1893; comd. receiving ship Franklin, 1894-95; comd. Cincinnati, 1895-97. San Francisco, 1897; comd. Miantonomoh during Spanish War, 1898; Navy Yard, Boston, 1898-1901; commandant, Naval Sta., Port Royal, 1901; commandant, Navy Yard, Boston, 1901-04; retired, June 1, 1904. Address: Portsmouth, N.H. Died Feb. 14, 1913.

JOHNSON, RAY PRESCOTT business exec.; b. Muncie, Ind., July 31, 1907; s. Ray Prescott and Anna Crawford (Davis) J.; student Boys Prep. Sch., Indianapolis, 1920-22, Asheville (N.C.) Sch., 1922-24; B.A., Wabash Coll., 1928; Harvard Grad. Sch., 1929; m. Mary Katherine Healy, Apr. 11, 1936 (div.); children-Ray P., Wendy K.; m. 2d, Alice Boyd Boa, Apr. 7, 1956; 1 son, Boyd Davis. Mem. accounting dept. Warner Gear Co., Muncie, Ind., summers 1925, 27; with Borg-Warner Corp., 1929-, adminstrv. asst. to pres., 1949-52, dir. sales research, 1953-59; now chmn. bd., dir. Warner Chem. Products, Inc., Warner Machine Products, Inc., Muncie; v.p., director Roscoe Turner Aeronautical Corp., Indpls., 1938-; v.p. Borg-Warner Internat., 1952-58. Morse Chain Co., Ithaca, 1946-58; v.p., dir. Glascock Corp., Muncie, Ind., 1933-60; director Phoenix Towers, Incorporated. Served as engineering counsel for Wash. office of Ill. Council of Defense, Feb.-Sept. 1942. Commd. capt., Office Chief of Ordnance, 1942, served as officer in charge, Industry Integration Com. for Half-tracks, sta. White Motor Co., Cleveland, 1943; advanced to major and served as dep. chief, wheeled vehicle sect. O.C.O., Detroit, 1944, hon. disch., 1945; maj., O.R.C., U.S. Army, 1945-53. Life mem. Am. Ordnance Assn.; member Natl. Alum. Assn. of Wabash Coll. (v.p. 1942-46, pres. 1946-48); Soc. Automotive Engrs., Reserve Officers Assn., Sigma Chi.

Clubs: Harvard; Country (Detroit); Athletic, Economic, Chicago, Racquet, Columbia Yacht (Chgo.); Scottsdale Country (Phoenix); Glenview Country, Ind. Soc. Chgo. (v.p., trustee). Asst. starter Indpls. 500 mile race, 1946-51, judge 1952-. Home: 209 Lake Shore Dr., Chgo. 60611. Died Mar. 27, 1964; buried Beech Grove Cemetery, Muncie, Ind.

JOHNSON, RICHARD MENTOR vice pres. U.S.; b. Beargrass, Ky., Oct, 17, 1781; s. Robert and Jemima (Suggett) J.; never married; 2 children by Julia Chinn (Slave). Admitted to Ky. bar, 1802; mem. Ky. Ho. of Reps., 1804-07, 1850 drafted law forbidding imprisonment of debtors, 1819; mem. U.S. Ho. of Reps. (Democrat) from Ky., 10th-15th, 21st-24th congresses, 1807-19, 29-37, chmn. com. on mil. affairs; served as col. Ky. Volunteers, 1812-13; commanded U.S. forces in Battle of Thames, 1813, killed Indian chief Tecumseh during the battle; mem. U.S. Senate from Ky., 1819-29; vice pres. U.S. under Martin Van Buren, 1837-41, failed to get majority of electoral votes, only vice pres. ever elected by Senate, unsuccessful candidate for reelection 1840; founder, trustee Georgetown (Ky.) Coll. Died Frankfort, Ky., Nov. 19, 1850; buried State Cemetery, Frankfort.

JOHNSON, RICHARD W. army officer; b. Smithland, Ky., Feb. 7, 1827; s. Dr. James L. and Jane (Leeper) J.; grad. U.S. Mil. Acad., 1849; m. Rachel Steele, 1855; m. 2d, Julia McFarland, 1894; 4 children. Commd. lt. col. 3d Ky. Cavalry, 1861; commd. brig. gen. U.S. Volunteers, 1861; assigned to Gen. Buell's army in engagements at Shiloh, Tenn., siege of Corinth, Miss.; commanded a div. of Army of Ohio in Tenn. campaign; commanded 12th div. Army of Cumberland in battles of Stones River, Chickamauga, Missionary Ridge, New Hope Ch., Ga. brevetted lt. col. for service at Battle of Chickamauga, 1683, col. for Battle of Chattanooga, 1863, maj. gen. U.S. Volunteers; commanded a div. of cavalry in Battle of Nashville, 1864 subsequently brevetted brig. gen. 1865; commd. maj. gen. U.S. gen. U.S. Army; ret. with rank of maj. gen., 1867; prof. mil. sci. U. Mo., later at U. Minn. Author: A Memoir of Gen. George H. Thomas, 1881; Manual for Colt's Breech-Loading Carbine, 1886. Died St. Paul, Apr. 21, 1897.

JOHNSON, ROBERT WOOD, industrialist; born New Brunswick, New Jersey, Apr. 4, 1893; son Robert Wood and Evangeline (Armstrong) J.; educated at Lawrenceville Sch. and by pvt. tutors; LD.D. (honoris causa), Rockhurst Coll., 1948, Rutgers Univ., 1950, Northwestern, 1952, University of Dallas, 1962; D.Sc. (honorary), Philadelphia College Pharmacy and Sci., 1960; m.; children—Robert W., Sheila; m. 3d Evelyne Vernon, Aug. 1943. Entered family firm Johnson & Johnson, mfrs. of surg. dressings, 1910, v.p., 1918-30, v.p. and gen. mgr., 1930-32, pres., 1932-38, chairman of the board, 1938-63, dir., chmn. finance com., 1963-68. Mem. Borough Coun. of Highland Pk. N.J., 1918-19, mayor, 1920-22. Pres. Middlesex Gen. Hosp., New Brunswich, 1921-27. Entered Ord. Dept., U.S. Army. May 4, 1942, promoted col., May 29, 1942; promoted to rank of brig. gen., May 17, 1943; apptd. chief N.Y. Ordnance Dist., Sept. 14, 1942. Apptd. vice chmn. War Production Board and chmn. Smaller War Plants Corp., 1943. Pub. Interest Award, Pub. Relations Soc. Am., Inc., 1949; Human Relations award, Soc. Advancement Management, 1950; The Charles Parlin Memorial award, 1953, People to People, Inc. award from Pres. Eisenhower, 1957, Brotherwood award Nat. Conf. of Christians and Jews, 1958, N. Am. Industrialist of Year, Soc. Indsl. Realtors, 1959, Gold medal of merit V.F.W., 1959, Distinguished Service award Arthritis and Rheumatism Found., 1964, Gold medal internat. Oceanographic Found., 1964, Exec. of Year award Am. Coll. Hosp. Adminstrs., 1965. Hon. fellow A.C.S., Am. Coll. Hosp. Adminstrs. Patron Am. Mus. Natural History. Episcopalian. Mem. Am. Ord. Assn., Am. Legion. Mason. Clubs: Racquet and Tennis, N.Y. Yacht, Cruising; Surf; Indian Creek County (Surfside, Florida). Author: But, General Johnson (pvtly. pub.); Or Forfeit Freedom (received Franklin D. Roosevelt Memorial Award); Robert Johnson Talks It Over, (Certificate of Merit, 1949 Awards Jury of Freedom Found.); Human Relations in Modern Business (with others). Home: Princeton NJ Died Jan. 30, 1968.

JOHNSON, WALDO PORTER senator; b. Bridgeport, Va., Sept. 16, 1817; grad. Rector Coll., Pruntytown, Va., 1839; studied law. Admitted to Va. bar; began practice in Harrison County, Va., 1841; moved to Osceola, Mo., 1842, practiced law; served with 1st Regt., Mo. Mounted Volunteers, during Mexican War; mem. Mo. Ho. of Reps., 1847; circuit atty., 1848; judge 7th Jud. Circuit, 1851-52; mem. Washington (D.C.) Peace Conf., 1861; mem. U.S. Senate (Democrat) from Mo., Mar. 17, 1861-Jan. 10, 1862 (expelled); served to lt. col. 4th Mo. Inf., Confederate Army, during Civil War; wounded twice in Battle of Pea Ridge, 1862; engaged in recruiting troops for Gen. Price's army; filled vacancy as mem. Confederate States Senate; resumed practice of law, Osceola, 1866; pres. Mo. Constl. Conv., 1875. Died Osceola, Aug. 14, 1885; buried Forest Hill Cemetery, Kansas City, Mo.

JOHNSON, SIR WILLIAM army officer, supt. Indian affairs; b. Smithtown, County Meath, Ireland, 1715; s. Christopher and Ann (Warren) J.; m. Catharine Weisenberg, circa 1739; m. 2d, Molly Brant; children - John, Mary, Nancy. Connected with fur trading, Oswego, N.Y., 1743; erected flour mills nr. Amsterdam (N.Y.), 1744; one of his majesty's justices of the peace for Albany County (N.Y.), 1745; commissary of N.Y. for Indian affairs, 1746; responsible for supply of English garrison, Oswego, 1746; attended Albany Council, 1746; col. of Six Nations involved in transferring conduct of Indian affairs to Gov. Clinton, 1746; commanded 14 cos. of N.Y. Militia, for defense of frontiers, 1748, col. Albany Regt., 1748; mem. Council of N.Y., 1750-74; mem. Albany Congress, 1754; commanded expdn. sent against Crown Point; supt. Indian affairs, responsible for mgmt. and direction of affairs of Six Nations and their allies; maj. N.Y. Militia; created baronet, 1755; col. Six Nations, their confederates and affairs, 1756; commanded force which captured Niagara, 1759; mem. Am Philos. Soc., 1769; trustee Queen's Coll. (now Rutgers U.), 1770; aided in opening up Mohawk Valley to settlement; helped to drive French power from N. Am.; commd. maj. gen., 1772. Died Johnstown, N.Y., July 11, 1774.

JOHNSTON, ALBERT SIDNEY army officer; b. Washington, Ky., Feb. 2, 1803; s. Dr. John and Abigail (Harris) J.; grad. U.S. Mil. Acad., 1826; m. Henrietta Preston, Jan. 20, 1829; m. 2d, Eliza Griffin, Oct. 3, 1843; 5 children. Brevetted 2d lt. 2d Inf., U.S. Army, served at Sackett's Harbor, N.Y., 1826; commd. 2d lt., 6th Inf. at Jefferson Barracks, Mo., 1827; adjutant in Black Hawk War; resigned commn., 1834; adj. gen. Army of Tex., 1836, sr. brig. gen., 1837; sec. of war Republic of Tex., 1838-40; col. 1st Tex. Rifle Volunteers and insp. gen. at Monterrey (Mexico) during Mexican war; paymaster U.S. Army for Tex., comdr. Dept. of Tex., 1856-58; led expdn. against Mormons, 1857; comdr. Dept. of Utah, 1858-60; commd. brig. gen. U.S. Army, 1858; comdr. Dept. of Pacific , 1860; joined Confdedrate Army as gen. in charge of operations in West; loss of Ft. Donelson forced him to retreat, 1862; concentrating his army around Corinth (Miss.) attacked Grant at Pittsburg landing (known in North as Shiloh), Apr. 6, 1862 (a So. victory); Killed in Battle of Shiloh, Apr. 6, 1862; buried Austin, Tex.

JOHNSTON, ERIC A. motion picture association exec., diplomate; b. Washington, Dec. 21, 1895; s. Bertram Allen and Ida Fazio (Ballinger) J.; student U. of Wash., 1913-17 (LL.B., 1917); hon. LL.D.; Whitworth Coll. (Spokane, Wash.), Whitman College (Walla Walla, Wash.), 1943, Rhode Island State College, Boston U., 1943; Lafayette Coll., 1944; Tufts Coll., 1945; U. of So. Calif. 1946, Wash. State U., 1947, U. lMd., 1950; S.C.D., New York U., 1950; hon. B.A., U. Wash., 1943; Doctor Humane Letters, Hahnemann Med. Coll.; m. Ina Harriet Hughes, Oct. 25, 1922; children - Harriet Ballinger (Mrs. William Carlin Fix), Elizabeth Hughes (Mrs. Fred Hanson). Organized Brown- Johnston Company, electrical retail business Spokane, 1923; organized the Columbia Electric & Manufacturing Co., Spokane, 1933, pres., 1933-49, chmn. bd. since 1949; pres. Motion Picture Assn. Am., Inc., 1945-; director Hot Shoppes, Inc., Washington McCormick & Co., Inc., Olympic S.S. Co., Seattle First Nat. Bank, Farmers New World Life, Spokane and Eastern Trust Co., United Air Lines, Bank of Am., Am. Security & Trust Co., Motion Picture Assn., Motion Picture Export Assn., Mass Mut. Life Ins. Co. Dir. U.S. C. of C. Served as capt. U.S. Marine Corps, 1917-22. Pres. Spokane Chamber of Commerce, 1931-32; director Chamber of Commerce of United States, 1934-41, president 1942 to May, 1946 (4 terms); president Inland Empire Mfrs. Assn., 1929; chmn. Wash. State Progress Commn., 1937-42; chmn. Eastern Wash. Welfare, 1931-33; chmn. Inter-Am. Econ. Development Com.; mem. Econ. Stabliization Bd., 1943; mem. Econ. Development Com., under Paul G. Hoffman; mem. War Manpower Commn. and Com. for Drafting of Fed. Employees, 1943; mem. John Steelman's War Mobilization and Reconversion Committee; mem. Defense Mobilization Board, 1951; adminstr. Economic Stblzn. Agy., Washington, 1951; chairman International Development Board, 1952-; special rep. of President of U.S. with personal rank of ambassador to Middle East, 1953-. Awarded Medal for Merit, 1947; fgn. medals Japan, Belgium, Italy, Germany, others. Dir. Am. Cancer Soc., Jan., 1946, chmn. bd., 1946. Mem. Pub. advisory board, Economic Co-op. Administration, 1948. Trustee Whitman Coll. Republican candidate for U.S. senator from Wash., 1940. Mem. Am. Legion, Theta Delta Chi. Clubs: Bohemian, Calif. Rainier (Seattle); Spokane, Kiwanis (Spokane); Metropolitan, Alfalfa, Chevy Chase, Army-Navy (Washington). Home: E. 615 16th Av., Spokane, Wash. 99203. Office: 1600 Eye St., Washington 20006. Died Aug. 22, 1963; buried Greenwood Meml. Cemetery, Spokane, Wash.

JOHNSTON, GEORGE DOHERTY soldier; b. Hillsboro, N.C., May 30, 1832; s. George Mulhollan and Mary Eliza (Bond) J.; early edn. at Marion, Ala.; A.B., Howard Coll., Ala., 1849, later A.M.; LL.B., Lebanon (Tenn.) Law Sch.; LL.D., U. of Ala.; m. Euphradia Poellnitz, 1854; m. 2d, Maria Barnett, 1865; m. 3d, Stell a Search, 1876. Entered C.S.A. as 2d lt. 4th Ala. Regt., Apr. 15, 1861; maj. 25th Ala., Jan. 27, 1862; lt. col., Apr. 6, 1862; col., Sept. 9, 1863; brig. gen. C.S.A., July 24, 1864, serving to close of war; wounded at Murfreesboro and at Atlanta. Commandant of cadets, U. of Ala., 1871-73; supt. S.C. Mil. Acad., 1885-90; U.S. civil service commr., 1892-93; mem. Ala. Senate, 1900-06, Democrat. Presbyterian. Lectured on Memories of the Old South, The Confederate War, Jefferson Davis and Women of the Confederacy. Address: Tuscaloosa, Ala. Died 1910.

JOHNSTON, GORDON army officer; b. Charlotte, N.C., May 25, 1874; s. Gen. Robert Daniel (C.S.A.) and Elizabeth Johnston (Evans) J.; A.B., Princeton, 1896; hon. grad. Inf. and Cav. Sch., 1903; grad. Gen. Staff Coll. A.E.F., June 1918; m. Anna Julia, d. Dr. Robert W. Johnson, May 25, 1904. Sergt. Co. M, 2d Miss. Inf. and pvt. Troop M, 1st U.S. Vol. Cav. (Rough Riders), June 8-Sept. 15, 1898, Spanish-Am. War; commd. 2d lt. 43d U.S. Inf., Aug. 17, 1899; 2d lt. cav., Aug. 5, 1901; maj. N.A., Aug. 21, 1917; lt. col., June 1918; col., Oct. 1918; promoted through various grades in regular army to lt. col., July 1, 1920. Served Philippine Insurrection, Cuban occupation, on Mexican border, and with A.E.F., in France; chief of staff, 82d Div., Oct. 1918; later acting chief of staff, 7th Army Corps, chief of staff, 7th Regular Div., and asst. chief of staff, 2d Army; selected by Maj. Gen. Wood as mem. Wood-Forbes Mission to P.I., and as asst. to gov. gen., 1921. Decorated Congressional Medal of Honor for "extraordinary gallantry in action at Bud Dajo, Sulu, P.I.," Mar. 1906; D.S.M. (U.S.); Officer Legion of Honor (France). Presbyn. Died Mar. 8, 1934.

JOHNSTON, JOHN ALEXANDER army officer; b. Allegheny, Pa., Feb. 22, 1858; s. Alexander and Sarah R. J.; grad. U.S. Mil. Acad., 1879; honor grad. Inf. and Cav. Sch., Ft. Leavenworth, Kan., 1883; m. Henrietta V. Vandergrift, 1888. Commd. 2d lt., June 13, 1879; 1st lt., Jan. 20, 1886; capt., Jan. 3, 1895; maj. a.a.g., May 19, 1898; lt. col. a.a.g., Feb. 21, 1901; brig. gen., Jan. 7, 1903; resigned Jan. 15, 1903. Frontier service in Tex., 1879-82, 1885-87, in S.D., 1891-93, and 1895-97; instr. art of war and engring., Inf. and Cav. Sch., 1883-85; instr. history, law and tactics, U.S. Mil. Acad., 1887-91; in charge mounted instrn., Cav. Depot, Jefferson Barracks, Mo., 1893-95. Duty in office of adj. gen. in charge of orgn. and muster in and out of all vol. forces raised during Spanish-Am. War, 1898, and the vols. raised for the Philippines 1898-1901; in charges reorgn. of gen. recruiting service U.S.A., incident to army increase; prepared reports upon German Army maneuvers, 1902; was commr., Dist. Govt., D.C.; apptd. comdr. Northeastern Dept., U.S. Army, Boston, 1917. Address: Washington, D.C. Died Jan. 5, 1940.

JOHNSTON, JOSEPH EGGLESTON army officer, congressman; b. "Cherry Grove", Prince Edward County, Va., Feb. 3, 1807; s. Peter and Mary (Wood) J.; grad. U.S. Mil. Acad., 1829; m. Lydia McLane, July 10, 1845. Commd. 2d lt. 4th Arty., U.S. Army, 1829, 1st lt., 1836, resigned, 1837; commd. 1st lt. Topog. Engrs., 1838, capt., 1846; served in Mexican War, 1846-48, in battles of Vera Cruz, Contreras, Churbusco, Molino del Rey, Mexico City; wounded twice at Battle of Cerro Gordo, 3 times in Battle of Chapultepec; promoted lt. col. 1st Cavalry , U.S. Army, 1855, brig. gen. and q.m., 1860, resigned to serve with Confederate Army, 1861; atd maj. gen. Va. Militia, then brig. gen. Confederate Army, 1861; served at 1st Battle of Bull Run, 1861; 4th ranking gen. of Confederate Army, 1861-75; wounded at Battle of Fair Oaks; in command of Southwest forces, 1863; engaged in futile effort to reinforce Vicksburg, 1863; in command of Army of Tenn., 1863; defeated Gen. William T. Sherman at Battle of Kenesaw Mountain, June 1864; relieved of command because he retreated before Sherman's advance to Richmond (Va.), July 1864; reinstated (after his successor, Gen. Hood, had lost most of Army of Tenn. trying to stop Sherman) by Gen. Lee to command Army of Tenn. and all forces in Fla., S.C. and Ga. to drive back Sherman, 1865; surrendered to Sherman, 1865; railroad pres., Ark., 1866-69; moved to Richmond, 1877; mem. U.S. Ho. of Reps. from Va., 46th Congress, 1879-81; U.S. commr. of railroads, 1887-91. Author: Narrative of Military Operations, 1874. Died Washington, D.C., Mar. 21, 1891; buried Greenmount Cemetery, Balt.

JOHNSTON, KILBOURNE, forest products company executive; born in Fort Clark, Texas, on April 17th, 1907; the son of Hugh Samuel and Helen (Kilbourne) J.; B.S., U.S. Mil. Acad., 1928; LL.B., Columbia, 1932; m. Dorothy May Ward, June 30, 1928; 1 son, Hugh Samuel. Commd. 2d lt., inf., U.S. Army, 1928, advanced through grades to col., 1942; asst. gen. counsel NRA, 1933-35; asst. adminstr. WPA, N.Y.C., 1935-36; with Judge Adv. Gen. Dept., 1936; mem. gen. staff G-1 Sect., 1939; asst. dir. Nat. Selective Service System, 1940; asst. sec. Army Navy Munitions Bd., 1941; dep. dir. control div. ASF War Dept., 1942-44; base comdr. S.W. Pacific Area, 1944; asst. G-4 Pacific Ocean Areas, 1945; dir. post war planning, legislative liaison div. War Dept. Gen. Staff, 1946; dir. mgmt. div. WDGS, 1947; asst. comptroller U.S. Army, 1948-50; ret., 1950; asst. dir. CIA, 1950-53; mgmt. cons., Washington, 1953-55; chmn. bd. Silverlith Corp., Washington, 1951-65; with Champion Papers, Inc., Hamilton, O., 1955-56, group exec. planning, adminstrv. services, 1961, v.p., group exec. mgmt. services, 1962-65, staff v.p., 1965-66; spl. asst. to chairman U.S. Plywood-Champion Papers, Incorporated, 1966-72. Decorated Legion of Merit with oak leaf cluster, Bronze Star medal with combat V. Mem. Tech. Assn. Graphic Arts, Am. Mgmt. Assn., Ret. Officers Assn. Clubs: Army and Navy, Internat. (Washington); Army-Navy Country (Arlington, Va.). Home: Santa Cruz CA Died Jan. 12, 1972.

JOHNSTON, MARBURY naval officer; b. Alabany, Ga., Dec. 2, 1860; s. Thomas Henry and Laura Camilla (Hill) J.; grad. U.S. Naval Acad., 1878; unmarried. Promoted ensign, July 1, 1884; promoted through grades to capt., June 14, 1911; temporarily apptd. rear admiral, Aug. 31, 1917; rear admiral (permanent), Nov. 28, 1918; retired Dec. 2, 1924. Served on New Orleans and Cassius, Spanish-Am. War, 1898; comd. 2d Torpedo Flotilla, 1903-05, Navy Yard, N.Y. City, 1906-07, Albatross, 1907-08, Galveston, 1908-09, Navy Yard, Puget Sound, 1909-10; capt. of yard, Navy Yard, Portsmouth, N.Y., 1901-11; comd. Georgia, 1911-13; at Naval War Coll., Newport, R.I., 1913-14; comd. Naval Sta., New Orleans, 1915-17; comd. Squadron Four, Patrol Force, 1917; apptd. comdr. Div. Three and Four, Cruiser Force, 1917. Home: Cuthbert, Ga. Died Mar. 15, 1934.

JOHNSTON, PETER army officer, jurist; b. Osborne's Landing Va., Jan. 6, 1763; s. Peter and Martha (Butler) Rogers Johnson; m. Mary Wood, June 23, 1788; m. 2d, Ann Bernard, Dec. 13, 1828; 10 children including Joseph Eggleston. Commd. lt. cavalry Continental Army under command Lt. Col. Henry Lee, 1781; adj., capt. light corps, later brig. gen. militia; mem. Legislature, 1792; speaker, Va. Ho. of Dels., 1805-06, 06-07; rep. from Va. on commn. to settle Tenn. boundary question, 1802; judge Va. Gen. Ct., 1811. Died Dec. 8, 1831.

JOHNSTON, ROBERT BORN, banker; b. Rock Falls, Ill., June 21, 1910; s. Robert Ewer and Alda Halderman (Born) J.; S.B., Harvard, 1932, M.B.A., 1934; student Kent Coll. Law. With First Nat. Bank of Chgo., 1934-67, v.p., 1959-67; pres., dir. Johnston Lumber Co., Annawan, Ill., 1944-67; dir. 40-50 W. Schiller St. Corp.; chmn. Midwest Stock Exchange Clearing Corp. Served as pvt. AUS, 1941; to lt. comdr. USNR, 1942-46. Mem. Transportation Association of America (mem. board dirs.). Clubs: Harvard, Harvard Business, Racquet (past pres., gov.), Attic (Chgo.); Shoreacres Lake Bluff, Ill. Home: Chicago IL Died June 5, 1967.

JOHNSTON, ROBERT DANIEL soldier; b. Mt. Welcome, Lincoln Co., N.C., Mar. 19, 1837; s. Dr. William and Nancy (Forney) J.; brother of Joseph Forney J. (q.v.); A.B., U. of N.C., 1857; LL.B., U. of Va.; served pvt., 2d lt., lt.-col. and brig.-gen. C.S.A., 1861-65; participated in all battles of Army of Northern Va.; wounded at Seven Pines (twice), Spottsylvania C.H., Gettysburg and Hare's Hill, Va.; m. Lizzie Johnston Evans, d. Gov. John M. Morehead, of N.C., Nov. 1, 1871. Admitted to bar, 1866; practiced at Charlotte, N.C., 1867-87; pres. Birmingham (Ala.) Nat. Bank, 1888-95; register U.S. land officer, Montgomery, Ala., until 1908; now promoting investments in mineral and other lands. Address: 1721 Av. L, Birmingham, Ala.

JOHNSTON, W(ILLIAM) DAWSON librarian; b. Cincinnati, Oct. 19, 1861; s. William Hartshorne and Mary (Neele) J.; student Washington U., 1876-79, LL.B., 1897; honor grad. Inf. and Cav. Sch., Ft. Leavenworth, Kan., 1887; Army War Coll., Washington, D.C., 1907-08; grad. Gen. Staff Coll., 1920; m. Lucille Barat Wilkinson, June 27, 1888 (died 1917); m. 2d, Isabelle Gros, Mar. 17, 1923. Pvt., corpl. and sergt., Lafayette Guard, St. Louis, 1878-81; 1st l5. Prescott Rifles, Co. B, Ariz. Territorial Militia, 1881-82; commd. 2d lt. 16th Inf., U.S.A., Oct. 10, 1883; promoted through grades of vol. service to maj. 46th U.S. Inf. Vols., Aug. 17, 1899; hon. mustered out vols., May 31, 1901; maj., Philippine Scouts, Apr. 1904-Oct. 6, 1906; col. June 12, 1916; brig. gen. N.A., Aug. 5, 1917; maj. gen., Aug. 8, 1918-July 31, 1919; brig. gen., U.S.A., Apr. 30, 1921; maj. gen., Nov. 3, 1924. Gov. Province of Isabela, 1901-02; comd. 1st Bn., Philippine Scouts, campaign against Pulajanes, 1905-07; mem. Gen. Staff Corps, Army War Coll., 1914-17; organized, and comd. 180th Inf. (Texas) Brig., Aug. 25, 1917-Aug.27, 1918; served with Texas Brig., 90th Division, 1st Army Corps, in Toul sector, Aug. 1918; maj. gen. U.S.A. and assigned to the 91st Div., Aug. 1918; comd. 91st Div. in St. Mihiel offensive, Sept. 12-13, Meuse-Argonne, Sept. 26-Oct. 15, and with the French Army in Belgium in the Group of Armies of Flanders, under command King of Belgians, during the Ypres-Lys campaign in Belgium, Oct. 19-Nov. 11, 1918. Served at Camp Lewis, Wash., during demobilization of 91st Div., Gen. Staff Coll., Aug. 1919-July 1920; with Am. Forces in Germany from Aug. 18, 1920; chief of Staff A.F. in G., Aug. 25, 1920-May 11, 1921; comdg. 1st Brig., July 1, 1921-Apr. 6, 1922; gen. liaison officer French Army of the Rhine, Apr. 1922-Jan. 1923; sr. mil. adviser Am. Delegation Commn. of Jurists, studying rules of war at The Hague, Dec. 1, 1922-Mar. 1923; comdg. 4th C.A. Dist., Ft. McPherson, Ga., July 15, 1923-Nov. 15, 1924; comdg. 3d Div., Dec. 3, 1924-Oct. 19, 1925; retired, Oct. 19, 1925. Awarded silver star citation, Philippine Insurrection, 1900; D.S.C. "for extraordinary heroism in action" during Meuse-Argonne; D.S.M. "for distinguished services in command of 91st Div. in Meuse-Argonne and in Belgium"; Victory medal (three major offensives, one defensive sector); Comdr. Legion of Honor, Croix de Guerre with palm. Comdr. Order of Leopold I of Belgium. Died Feb. 19, 1933.

JOHNSTONE, ERNEST KINLOCH physician; b. Devon, Eng., Dec. 21, 1871; s. Charles and Mary Frances (de Beaumont) J.; brought to U.S. in infancy (father an American); ed. Trinity Coll., Glenalmond, and Wellington Coll., Eng., U. of Edinburgh and U. of Calif; M.D., U. of Calif. Med. Sch., 1898; licentiate of Royal Colleges of Physicians and Surgeons, Edinburgh and Glasgow, Scotland; hosp. work, Paris, London, Vienna and Berlin; m. Belle Shiels, 1898. Began practice at San Francisco, 1898; served as asst., chair of surgery, Post-Grad. Dept., U. of Calif., and lecturer hygiene and med. jurisprudence, same univ.; jr. demonstrator anatomy, Royal Coll. Surgeons, Edingurgh; gold medalist in clin. surgery, same. ice-pres. San Dimas Co. Apptd. acting asst. surgeon U.S. Army, Spanish-Am. War, 1898; mustered out as maj. surgeon, U.S.V.; served through World War (with British from 1914 to entry of U.S.); chief surgeon U.S. Army Ambulance Service, with French Army, 1918-19; col. Med. Res., U.S. Army; div. surgeon 91st pres. Res. Officers Assn. Decorations: Spanish War Medal, Philippine Insurrection Medal, Victory World War Medal, 2 stars, Silver Star Medal (U.S.); Reconnaissance Francaise and Médaille Commemorative (French); war service medals "as special case" (British); Veterani della Guerra (Italian). Republican. Episcopalian. Mason. Club: Army and Navy (Washington, D.C.). Author of brochures and articles on med. and mil.-med. subjects. Home: St. Francis Hotel, San Francisco. Died May 23, 1948.

JONAH, FRANK GILBERT railway official; b. Albert County, N.B., Oct. 6, 1864; ed. high sch., Moncton, N.B., and privately. Began in office of chief engr. Intercolonial Ry., 1882; asst. engr. in charge constrn. govt. lines in Nova Scotia, 1887-89; asst. engr. Intercolonial Ry., 1889-90; asst. engr. St. Louis Merchants Bridge Terminal Ry., 1890-94; resident engr., St. L., Peoria & Northern Ry., 1894-99; engr. maintenance of way, C.&A.R.R., 1899-1901; chief engr., Blackwell, Enid & S.W. Ry., 1901-03; asst. engr. New Orleans Terminal Co., Mar.-June 1903; chief engr., St. L., Brownsville & Mexico Ry., 1903-04; locating engr., St.L&S.F. R.R., 1904-05; terminal engr. N.O. Terminal Co., 1905-10; chief engr. constrn., St.L.&S.F. R.R., at St. Louis, 1910-13, chief engr., since Mar. 1, 1913; also chief engr. Ft. Worth & Rio Grande R.R., K.C., Clinton & Springfield R.R. Served as maj. 12th Regt. Ry. Engrs.; chief engr. Dept. of Ligh Rys., in France, Oct. 1917-Dec. 1918, with rank of lt. col. Home: 5355 Pershing Av. Office: Frisco Bldg., St. Louis. Died Dec. 7, 1945.

JONES, ALBERT MONMOUTH army officer; b. Quincy, Mass., July 20, 1890; s. Frederick L. and Alice (Richardson) C.; grad. Thayer Acad., 1909; student Mass. Inst. Tech., 1909-11; hon. grad. Command and Gen. Staff Sch., 1924, Army War Coll., 1932; m. Barbara Viola Levatte, June 4, 1912; children-Barbara Alberta, Robert Summer, Tom, Jack Jean, Bud Levatte. Commd. 2d lt. inf., Oct. 7, 1911, advanced through the grades to maj. gen., March 12, 1942; (temp.); permanent maj. gen., Regular Army, Aug. 27, 1944; in Panama Canal Zone, 1912-15, Mexican Border, 1916, Alaska, 1917-18; comdt. div. inf. Sch. of Arms, Camp Lewis, Wash., 1918; comdr. Ft. George Wright, Spokane, 1919; prof. mil. sci. and tactics, Ore. Agrl. Coll., 1920; comdr. 19th Inf. Presidio, San Francisco, 1921-22; gen. staff, 2d div., Ft. Sam Houston, Tex., 1924-28; exec. officer 5th brigade Vancouver Barracks, 1929-31; gen. staff 9th corps area. Presidio, San Francisco, 1932-36; sr. instr. Mass. N.G. and 26th div., 1936-40; comdr. 31st U.S. Inf., Manila, P.I., 1940-41; comdg. gen. 51st div. Philippine Army and 1st Philippine corps, S. Luzon and Bataan, 1941-42; participant in death march and spent 40 months in Japanese prison camps in P.I., Formosa and Manchuria, liberated by Russians 1945; comdg. gen. Camp Beale, Calif., 1946; chief U.S. Mil. Adv. Group to Rep. Philippines, 1946-49; pres. Army Personnel Bd., O.S.A., 1949-51; dir. ARBCOSA since 1951. Decorated D.S.C., D.S.M., Silver Star, with oak leaf cluster, Bronze Star medal with oak leaf cluster, Commendation Ribbon, D.U. badge, 3 oak leaf clusters (U.S.); L.II., D.C.S., D.SS., D.U. Badge (Philippines). Episcopalian. Mason (32ff, Shriner). Address: A.R.B.C. Office: Sec. Army, The Pentagon, Washington 25. Died May 1967.

JONES, ANSON pres. Republic of Tex.; b. Great Barrington, Mass., Jan. 20, 1798; s. Solomon and Sarah (Strong) J.; M.D., Jefferson Med. Coll., 1827; m. Mrs. Mary McCrory, May 17, 1839. Practiced medicine, Phila., 1827-32, New Orleans Brazoria, Tex., 1833; Physician Tex. Army under Sam Houston, 1836; chmn. mass meeting which drew up resolutions in favor of Declaration of Independence of Tex., Dec. 1835; judge adv. gen. in war of Tex. independence, 1836-37; rep. in 2d Tex. Congress, 1837; Tex. minister to Washington (D.C.), 1837-39; elected to Tex. Senate; v.p. ex officio Republic of Tex., 1840, sec. of state, 1841-44, last pres., 1844-47; unsuccessful candidate for U. S. Senate, 1857; Committed suicide at Capital Hotel, Houston, Tex., Jan. 9, 1858.

JONES, BUELL FAY lawyer; b. Spain, S. Dak., Nov. 25, 1892; s. Even N. and Ellen (Hughes) J.; LL.B., S. Dak. U., 1914; m. Florence I. Bockler, June 21, 1914; children-Quentin B., Jamie R., Dorothy F. Admitted to S. Dak. bar, 1914, and began practice at Britton; state's atty. Marshall County, S. Dak., 1919-23; mem. Gardner & Jones, 1919-22, alone since 1922; atty. gen. S. Dak., 3 terms, 1923-29; Rep. nominee for governor of S. Dak., 1929, gen. atty. Standard Oil Co. of Ind., 1930-40, v.p., 1945 and gen. counsel since 1940. Was mem. ex-officio S. Dak. State Game Commn., State Bd. of Pardons, etc. Organized vol. troops of cav. for World War, June 1917; entered U.S. Army as pvt., June 15, 1917; with 34th Div., at Camp Cody, N.M., later with 307th Cav.; hon. disch. as capt., Dec. 21, 1918. Mem. Am., Ill., S. Dak. and Chicago bar assns., Delta Theta Pi, Am. Legion. Republican. Presbyterian. Mason (32ff, Shriner), Odd Fellow. Home: 9425 N. Hamlin Av., Evanston, Ill. Office: 910 S. Michigan Av., Chicago. Died Nov. 17, 1947.

JONES, CALVIN physician; b. Great Barrington, Mass., Apr. 2, 1775; s. Ebeneezer and Susannah (Blackmer) J.; m. Temperance Williams, 1819. Licensed to practice medicine in Mass., 1792; practiced medicine, Great Barrington, 1792-95, Smithfield, N.C., 1795, Raleigh, N.C., 1803-32; a founder N.C. Med. Soc., 1799; mem. lower house N.C. Legislature, 1799, 1802, 07; co-owner newspaper Star, Raleigh, 1808-15; adjutant gen. N.C. Militia, 1808, maj. gen. N.C. Militia during War of 1812, organized coastal defenses of state; one of 1st physicians in state to urge use of inoculation against smallpox; active Freemason; retired, 1832, moved to estate nr. Bolivar, Tenn. Died at estate Pontine, nr. Bolivar, Sept. 20, 1846.

JONES, CARL H(ENRY) ret. naval officer; b. Jones Mill. Ala., June 17, 1893; s. Sidney Morgan and Mary Jane (Whittle) J.; B.S., U.S. Naval Acad., 1914: student Columbia, 1919-20) m. Elizabeth Stockton Dorsey, July 31, 1941. Commd. ensign USN, 1914, advanced through grades to rear adm., 1946, ret.; advanced to vice adm. on retired list. Commended for performance duty in action against enemy on Tarawa, Nov. 1943. Qualified to command submarine, 1917. Club: Army and Navy (Washington). Home: R.F.D. 3, Box 360, Annapolis, Md. Died Sept. 1, 1958; buried U.S. Naval Acad. Cemetery, Annapolis.

JONES, CATESBY AP ROGER navy officer; b. Fairfield, Va., Apr. 15, 1821; s. Roger and Mary Ann Mason (Page) J.; m. Gertrude Tartt, Mar. 23, 1865, 6 children. Apptd. midshipman U.S. Navy, 1836, served on ships including frigate Columbia and schooner Shark, passed midshipman, 1842; asst. in surveying Tampa Bay, 1843; served in Pacific Squadron during Mexican War, seeing no active service; lt., 1849; assisted John A. Dahlgren in perfecting Dahlgren gun while on ordnance duty, Washington, D.C., 1853; resigned U.S. commn., became capt. Va. Navy, 1861; lt. Confederate Navy, 1861; exec. officer on ironclad Virginia (known in North as Merrimac), acting comdr. during famous fight with Monitor, 1862; became comdr. ship Chattachooche, 1862; commanded naval gun foundry and ordnance works, Selma, Ala., 1863; comdr. Confederate Navy, 1863; became businessman after Civil War. Shot by J.A. Harral during a quarrel, Selma, June 30, 1877.

JONES, CLAUD ASHTON rear admiral; b. Fire Creek, W.Va., Oct. 7, 1885; s. John H. and Lillian H. Jones; ed. U.S. Naval Acad., 1903-07; M.S., elec. engring., Harvard, 1912-13; Annapolis, 1911; hon. D.Sc., W.Va. U., 1942; m. Margaret Cox, Apr. 15, 1913; children-Frank C., Margaret B. Served on Indiana, New Jersey, Severn, North Carolina, Franklin, 1906-11; New York, 1913-15; engr. officer North Dakota, later Tennessee, 1916; engring. duty on elec. machinery for Tennessee at Westinghouse plant, Pittsburgh, 1917 (also asst. insp. engring. materials, Pittsburgh Dist.); attached to Indsl. Dept., N.Y. Navy Yard, 1918-20; on duty Bur. Engring., Washington, D.C., 1920-23; asst. naval attaché to American Embassies in London, Paris, Rome, Berlin, The Hague, 1923-25; on duty Bur. Engring., 1925-29; aide on staff, Comdr. Battleship Divisions, Battle Fleet with added duty as Divisions Engr. Officer, 1930; transferred to staff, Comdr.-in-Chief, Battle Fleet as Fleet Engr. with Bur. Engring., 1931-35; insp. Groton shipyards, 1935-40; head Shipbldg. Div., Bur. Ships, 1940-42; later asst, chief; asst. chief in charge of prodn., Office of Procurement and Material to Sept. 1944; dir. Naval Engr. Exp. Sta., Annapolis, Md., 1944-46; retired, June 1946. Decorated Medal of Honor (citation for extraordinary heroism as engineer officer on board U.S.S. Memphis during Santo Domingo hurricane), Cuban Pacification medal, 1906, Mexican Service medal (Vera Cruz), Dominican Campaign medal, Victory medal (World War Services), Expert Rifleman medals; Legion of Merit, 1944; mem. Am. Soc. Naval Engrs. (past pres.), Soc. Naval Architects and Marine Engrs. (vice pres.), U.S. Naval Inst., Newcomen Soc. Home: 15 Grosscup Rd., Charleston 4, W.Va. Died Aug. 8, 1948; buried in Arlington National Cemetery.

JONES, DANIEL FISKE surgeon; b. Minneapolis, Minn., June 2, 1868; s. George Edward and Emma Maria (Hall) J.; A.B., Harvard, 1892, M.D., 1896; m. Mary Haughton Richardson, May 1, 1898- House officer, Mass. Gen. Hosp., 1896-97; cons. surgeon Mass. Gen. Hosp; hon. cons. surgeon N.E. Deaconess and Palmer Memorial hosps. Surgeon-in-chief Harvard Surg. Unit, with British Forces in France, Sept.-Dec. 15, 1916, rank of lt. col. (temp.); commissioned maj. M.C., U.S.A., July 1918; lt. col. Med. Corps, U.S.A., May 1919; served in France; hon. discharged, May 21, 1919. Regent Am. College of Surgeons, 1921-24; overseer Harvard U., 1932-. Republican. Episcopalian. Home: Boston, Mass. Died Sept. 11, 1937.

JONES, DAVID RUMPH army officer; b. Orangeburg Dist., S.C., Apr. 5, 1825; s. Donald Bruce and Mary (Rumph) J.; grad. U.S. Mil. Acad., 1846; m. Rebecca Taylor. Served as 2d lt. 2d Inf., U.S. Army during Mexican War; brevetted 1st lt. for bravery at battles of Contreras, Churubusco, 1852; served in Adj. Gen.'s Dept. on Pacific Coast, also St. Louis; commd. maj. Confederate Army, Chief of staff to Gen. Beauregard besieging Ft. Sumter, 1861; assigned to command 3d brigade in Army of Potomac; brig. gen. comdg. brigade in Battle of Bull Run, 1861; commd. maj. gen., 1862; participated in Battle of Fair Oaks, 1862; fought under Longstreet at 2d Battle of Bull Run, Battle of Antietam. Died Richmond, Va., Jan. 15, 1863.

JONES, EDWARD FRANC scale mfr.; b. Utica, N.Y., June 3, 1828; s. Lorenzo Baldwin and Sophronia (Chapman) J.; ed. schs. and acad., Leicester, Mass.; m. Sarah Antoinette Tarbell, May 1850; m. 2d, Susan Annie Brown, May 1863, Col. 6th Regt. Mass. Vol. Militia-first regt. in Civil War; attacked in Baltimore and reached Washington Apr. 19, 1861; met on arrival by President Lincoln. Col. 26th Mass. Inf., Oct. 18, 1O61; bvtd. brig. gen. vols., Mar. 13, 1865, "for meritorious services during the war." Mem. Mass. Legislature, 1865; has held several municipal offices in Binghamton; lt. gov. of N.Y., 1886-91. Democrat. Conducted Jones Scale Works at Binghamton, N.Y., under corporate name "Jones of Binghamton," 1865-; originator of phrases "He pays the freight," and "Do it now." For past several yrs. has been totally blind. Mason. Author of "Origin of the Flag," "Richard Baxter," "Uncle Jerry." Address: Binghamton, N.Y. Died Aug. 14, 1913.

JONES, EDWIN WHITING army officer; b. Huntsville, Ala., Dec. 7, 1896; s. George Walter and Elva Lena (Moore) J.; B.S., U. Ala., 1918; m. Katherine Hickman Simmerman, June 2, 1928; children-Nancy Woodson, Barbara Tannahill. Partner firm G. W. Jones & Sons, civil engrs., 1919. Served as 2d lt. C.E., Officers Res. Corps, 1918-22; commd. 1st lt., Ala. Nat. Guard, 1922, and advanced through the grades to col., Engr. Regt., 1941; called to active service, 1941; brig. gen. U.S. Army, 1942-. Awarded Ala. Nat. Guard Faithful Service medal, Legion of Merit, 1944. Mem. Soc. Am. Mil. Engrs. Mason (K.T.). Club: Rotary (Huntsville, Ala.). Home: 609 E. Clinton St., Huntsville, Ala. Died June 7, 1956.

JONES, E(RNEST) LESTER hydrographic and geodetic engr.; b. E. Orange, N.J., Apr. 14, 1876; s. Charles Hopkins and Ada (Lester) J.; mem. class of 1898, Princeton, A.M., 1919; m. Virginia Brent Fox, Sept. 28, 1897; children-Mrs. Elizabeth Brent Barker, Cecil Lester. Business, research and secretarial work 10 yrs.; U.S. dep. commr. fisheries, 1913-15; apptd. supt. U.S. Coast and Geod. Survey, Apr. 1915, title changed to dir., 1919, and commd. dir., 1920. Commr. Internat. Boundary bet. U.S. and Can. (Alaska and Can.); mem. first Aerial Coastal Patrol Commn.; mem. Federal Bd. Surveys and Maps, Federal Personnel Bd. Served pvt. to maj., D.C. Militia; commd. lt. col. Signal Corps U.S.A., World War, later col. Div. Mil. Aeronautics; served with A.E.F. in France and Italy. An organizer and incorporator Am. Legion; organizer, 1st comdt. 1st American Legion Post (Pioneer Post) and 1st Am. Legion Dept. Diploma of Honor, Aerial League America; decorated Officer Order S.S. Maurizio e Lazzaro, by King of Italy, and Fatigue de Guerre (Italy); Officer Legion of Honor (France); Verdun medal. Cited for D.S.M. Author: Alaska Investigations, 1914; Hypsometry, 1915; Elements of Chart Making, 1915; Neglected Waters of the Pacific, 1916; Safeguard the Gateways of Alaska, 1917; Aerial Surveying, 1919; Earthquake Investigation in United States, 1925; Tide and Current Investigations of the U.S.C. and G.S., 1926-all Govt. publs.; Surveying from the Air, 1922; The Evolution of the Nautical Chart, 1924; Science and the Earthquake Perils, 1926. Called first meeting, Feb. 5, 1919, and first caucus World War Vets., at Washington, D.C., Mar. 7, 1919; wrote first draft Preamble and Constn. of Am. Legion, and presented same, St. Louis Conv., May 1919. Home: Rixeyville, Va. Died Apr. 9, 1919.

JONES, GEORGE naval chaplain; b. York, Pa., July 30, 1800; s. Robert and Elizabeth (Dunnman) J.; grad. Yale, 1823; m. Mary Silliman, 1837. Taught sch., Washington D.C., 1823-25; sec. to comdr. of ship Brandywine, U.S. Navy, 1825-28; tutor Yale, 1828-30; rector Episcopal ch., Middletown, Conn., 1830-31; ordained to ministry Episcopalian Ch., 1830; served as chaplain U.s. Navy in ship United States, later in Delaware, 1832-36; chaplain Norfolk (Va.) Navy Yard, 1836-40; chaplain several vessels including Columbus and Constitution, 1840-45; prof. English, U.S. Naval Acad., Annapolis, Md., 1845-50, chaplain, 1857-61; accompanied Commodore Matthew C. Perry on expdn. to Japan, aided in writing ofcl. report of journey, 1851-56; retired from Navy, 1862; served in mil. hosps. as chaplain and nurse during Civil War, Washington, D.C., also Annapolis. Author: Narrative of an American Squadron to the China Seas and Japan, 1856; Life Scenes from the Old Testament, 1868. Died Phila., Jan. 22, 1870; buried Phila.

JONES, HAROLD WELLINGTON physician, ex-army officer, editor; b. Cambridge, Mass., Nov. 5, 1877; s. Frank Henry and Elizabeth Cook (Towne) J.; ed. Mass. Inst. Tech., 1894-97; M.D., Harvard, 1901; Army Med. Sch., 1905-06 (honor grad.), Army Med. Field Service Sch., 1930; LL.D., Western Res. U., 1945; m. Eva Ewing Munn, Jan. 1, 1910 (died 1936); m. 2d, Mary Winifred Morrison, May 1, 1937; 1 dau., Helen (Mrs. Clifford M. Esler); 1 stepson, Frank A. McGurk. Physician, Boston, 1901; house surgeon Children's s Hosp., Boston, 1902-03; practicing physician, St. Louis, 1903-05; asso. prof. orthopedic surgery St. Louis U. Med. Sch., 1904-05; entered M.C., U.S. Army, 1906, capt., 1909 (temp. col. and col., 1918-19), col., 1932; served in Philippines, 1906-08, 20-23; charge of ambulance and evacuation service. Mexican campaign, 1916; prof., sec. faculty Army Med. Sch., 1917-18; comdr. Beau Desert Hosp. Center, AEF, France, 1918-19; chief surg. service Gen. Hosp. 41, N.Y., 1920, Ft. Sam Houston Hosp., 1927-33; comdg. officer Tripler Gen. Hosp., Hawaii, 1933-36; librarian Army Med. Library, Washington, 1936-43, dir., 1944-46. Sec. gen. 10th Internat. Congress Mil. Medicine, 1939; chief U.S. del. 9th Internat. Congress Mil. Medicine, Rumania, 1937; mem. Commn. Naval Experts revising Hague and Geneva Convs. (Red Cross), Geneva, 1937; v.p. Internat. Congress Air Relief, Budapest, 1937; hon. curator Osler Library, Montreal, 1936-46. Decorated Chevalier, Legion of Honor (France), 1918; Officer, l'ordre de la Sante Publique (France), 1939; Cross of Order of Merit (Poland), 1939; Rumania, 1940; Legion of Merit (U.S.) 1945; Philippine Insurrection, Mexican Expdn. and World War medals. Recipient Marcia C. Noyes award Med. Library Assn., 1956. Fellow A.C.S., A.A.A.S.; hon. fellow Cleve. Med. Library Assn., Beaumont Med. Club; hon. mem. Mexican Assn. Mil. Surgeons, Med. Library Assn. (pres. 1940, 41); mem. Boylston Med. Soc., A.C.S. (mem. com. on library). Unitarian. Clubs: Harvard (N.Y.C.); Army and Navy (Washington). Author: Green Fields and Golden Apples. Editor: Proceedings of 10th International Congress Mil. Medicine, 1939; Bulletin of Medical Library Assn., 1941-42; New Gould Medical Dictionary, 1946-56. Contbg., med. editor Ency. Americana. Contbr. about 600 articles to med. and hist. Jours. Mayo Found. lectr., 1942. Home: 1303 Chichester Av., Orlando, Fla. Died Apr. 5, 1958.

JONES, HILARY POLLARD, naval officer; b. Va., Nov. 14, 1863; m. Virginia Lippincott, Oct. 2, 1917. Grad. U.S. Naval Acad., 1884; ensign, July 1, 1886; promoted through grades to rear admiral, Dec. 24, 1917; vice admiral, July 1, 1919; adm., July 1, 1921. Served on Dorothea, Spanish-Am. War, 1898; comd. Scorpion, 1904-06, Navy Yard, Washington, 1906-09; exec. officer on Idaho, 1909; at Naval Sta., Cayite, P.I., 1909-10, Navy Yard, Washington, D.C., 1910-11; commanded Birmingham, 1911, Tennessee, 1911, Rhode Island, 1911-12; comd. Navy Yard and supt. Naval Gun Factory, Washington, D.C., 1913-14; comd. Florida, 1914-16; at Naval War Coll., 1916-17; comd. Squadron One, Patrol Force, Atlantic Fleet, Apr.-July 1917; apptd. comdr. Div. One, Cruiser Force raider guard, Atlantic Fleet, July 17, 1917; comdr. Newport News div. cruiser and transport force, Apr. 1918-Jan. 1919; dir. naval overseas transportation, Jan.-July 1919; vice admiral comdg. 2d Battleship Squadron Atlantic Fleet, 1921-22; adm., comdr. in chief Atlantic Fleet, 1921-22; comdr. in chief U.S. Fleet, Dec. 1922-Aug. 1923; apptd. to Gen. Bd., Aug. 1923. E.E. and M.P. on special mission to Brazil 1922; naval adviser on Am. delegation to Preparatory Commn. for Limitation of Armaments, Geneva, 1926-27; del. to Conf. for Limitation of Naval Armaments, Geneva, 1927; retired from active service, Nov. 14, 1927; commd. admiral on retired list, Oct. 15, 1930. Home: Doswell, Va. Died Jan. 1, 1938.

JONES, JACON naval officer; b. Smyrna, Del., Mar. 1768; s. Jacob Jones; m. 1st, Miss Sykes; m. 2d, Ruth Lusby, 1821; 6 children, including Richard Clk., Del. Supreme C.; commd. midshipman U.S. Navy, served on frigate United States, 1799; promoted lt., 1801; 2d. lt. on ship Philadelphia grounded and captured off Tripoli, 1803; comdr. Wasp. 1810; awarded gold medal by U.S. Congress; captured Frolic (a Brit. sloop of war, under Capt. Whingates), 1812; commd. capt., given command of ship Macedonian in Stephen Decatur's squadron operating in Mediterranean Sea, 1813, comdr. Mediterranean Squadron, 1821-23; navy commr. Pacific Squadron, 1826-29; in charge of Phila. Naval asylum, until 1850. Died Phila., Aug. 3, 1850.

JONES, JAMES SUMNER soldier, mcht.; b. Wheeling, W.Va., Apr. 23, 1881; s. Henry and Anna (Stone) J.; grad. Linsly Inst., Wheeling, 1896; student Washington and Jefferson Coll., 1897-99, hon. D.Sc., 1938; grad. U.S. Mil. Acad., 1903; m. Marguerite Westinghouse Sands, Oct. 4, 1905; children-Wilbur Stone, Pearson Sands. Commd. 2d lt. Cav., U.S.A., 1903; 1st lt., 1911; resigned Oct. 1913; maj., lt. col. and col. Adj. Gen.'s Dept., U.S.A., staff of Gen. Pershing, June 1917-July 1919; brig. gen. Adj. Gen.'s R.C. 1923-. With Stone & Thomas, Inc., dept. store. Wheeling, 1913-, except 1917-19, later pres. and gen. mgr.; pres. Security Trust Co.; dir. M. Marsh & Son, Inc., Ohio Valley Drug Co., Clarksburg Drug Co., Stone & Thomas, Inc., Hazel Atlas Glass Co., U.S. Stamping Co., Sterling Products, Inc., Wheeling & Belmont Bridge Co., Wheeling Tile Co. Member Wheeling (W.Va.) Park Com. Awarded D.S.M. (U.S.); Legion of Honor (French); Order of The Crown (Italian). Republican. Episcopalian. Mason. Home: Wheeling, W.Va. Died Aug. 17, 1940.

JONES, JAMES TAYLOR congressman; b. Richmond, Va., July 20, 1832; grad. Princeton, 1852; grad. Law Sch., U. Va., 1855. Admitted to the bar, 1856; began practice of law, Demopolis, Ala.; enlisted as pvt. 4th Ala. Regt., Confederate Army, during Civil War, elected capt. Co. D., 1862; judge advocate Confederate War Dept., 1864-65; del. Ala. Constl. Conv., 1865; mem. Ala. Senate, 1872-73; mem. U.S. Ho. of Reps. (Democrat) from Ala., 45th, 48th-50th congresses, 1877-79, Dec. 3, 1883-89; judge 1st Jud. Circuit of Ala., 1890-95. Died Demopolis, Feb. 15, 1895; buried Lyon Cemetery, Demopolis.

JONES, JOHN B. army officer; b. Fairfield, S.C., Dec. 22, 1834; s. Henry and Nancy (Robertson) J.; grad. Mt. Zion Coll., Winnsboro, S.C., circa 1855; m. Mrs. A. J. Anderson, Feb. 25, 1879. Rancher, Navarro, Tex., circa 1856-61; adjutant Tex. 15th Inf., Confederate Army, 1861-63; capt. Tex. Inf. brigade, 1863-65; elected mem. Tex. Legislature, 1868, denied seat by reconstrn. regime; maj. Frontier Battalion of Tex. Rangers, 1874-79, suppressed Indian violence Western borders of state, pursued outlaws in interior regions; pacified mob in El Paso (Tex.) during "Salt War," 1877; adjutant gen. of Tex., 1879-81. Died Austin, Tex., July 19, 1881; buried Austin.

JONES, JOHN PAUL, naval officer; b. Kirkcudbrightshire, Scotland, July 6, 1747; s. John and Jean (Macduff) Paul. First mate on slave ship Two Friends, 1766; commanded mcht. ship John, on two voyages to West Indies, 1769-70; added Jones to his name, 1773; master ship Betsey of London, 1773; commd. lt., 1775; sr. 1st lt., 1st Continental Navy, 1775, 1st ranking officer in list chosen from colonies south of Pa.; hoisted flag of Colonial Am. on board the Alfred, 1775 (displayed for 1st time); commanded ship Providence, later chosen capt.; commanded sloop Ranger, 1777; made successful offensive cruise in waters around Brit. Isles, captured Drake (1st Brit. warship to surrender to a Continental vessel); commanded French ship Duras, forty guns, renamed Bonhomme Richard, 1779, defeated Brit. ship Serapis, Sept. 23, 1779; received Cross of Instn. of Mil. Merit which entitled him to be called "Chevalier," 1781; unanimously elected to command the America, 1781; presented with Gold medal by U.S. Congress, 1787; served as rear adm. with Russian Navy on Black Sea, 1788-90; decorated Order of St. Ann; resided in Paris, France, 1790-92; remembered for attributed saying (when asked if he was surrendering): "Sir, I have not yet begun to fight." Died Paris, France, July 18, 1792; remains brought to U.S., 1905; buried U.S. Naval Acad., Annapolis, Md.

JONES, JOHN SILLS lawyer; b. Champaign County, O., Feb. 12, 1836; grad. Ohio Wesleyan, 1855; admitted to bar, 1857; pros. atty. Delaware County, 1860-61; served in Union army 1861-65, pvt. to col., 174th Ohio regt., and bvt. brig. gen. vols.; mayor Delaware, O., 1866; pros. atty. Delaware County, 1866-71; presidential elector, 1872; congressman, 1877-79; mem. Ohio legislature, 1879-84. Republican. Address: Delaware, O. Died 1903.

JONES, LEWIS HOWEL, lawyer, judge, b. Brigham, Utah, Feb. 22, 1900; s. Brigham Howel and Melvina (Christensen) J.; student pub. and pvt. schs.; m. Lucille Reeves, May 28, 1929; children—Betty, Ann, Patty, Lewis Howel. Admitted Nev. bar 1922; practiced Brigham, Utah, 1922-36; county atty. Box Elder Co., 1929-36; dist. judge, Utah, 1937-69. Served as pvt. inf., U.S. Army, 1918; col., AUS, 1941-48. Mem. Am., Utah, Nev. bar assns. Democrat. Elk. Mem. Ch. Jesus Christ-Latter Day Saints. Rotarian. Home: Brigham UT Died Sept. 11, 1969.

JONES, LLOYD E. army officer; b. Columbia, Mo., June 17, 1889; s. Dr. John Carleton and Clara Field (Thompson) J.; student U. of Mo., 1909-11; grad. Sch. of Fire, Ft. Still, Okla., 1915, Army Center of Arty. Studies (A.E.F.), 1919, Command and Gen. Staff Sch., Ft. Leavenworth, 1924, Army War Coll., 1930; m. Elizabeth Herriot Rembert, May 17, 1919; children-Lloyd Edmonstone, John Carleton, Anne Iredell. Commd. 2d lt., Field Arty., 1911; promoted through grades to brig. gen. (temp.), May 1941; served as lt. col. (temp.) Regimental Exec., 5th F.A., with A.E.F.; mem. operations and training branch Gen. Staff Corps, 1930-34; exec. of tactics with rank of lt. col., Field Arty. Sch., 1935-38; prof. mil. science and tactics, U. of Mo., 1939-40; col., chief of staff, 1st Army Corps, Columbia, S.C., 1940-41; became comdr. 76th Field Arty. Brigade, Ft. F. E. Warren, Wyo., Apr. 1941; assumed comd., Cold

Bay, Aleutian Islands, June 1942; directed occupation of Amchitka Island (Aleutians), Jan. 1943; trained 10th Mountain Div., Camp Hale, Colo., July 1943; duty A.G.F. War Coll., Dec. 1944; retired, Apr. 30, 1946. Awarded Distinguished Service Medal, Aug. 1943; Victory medal, 1919. Mem. U.S. Field Arty. Assn., Am. Legion, Beta Theta Pi. Scabbard and Blade. Mem. Knights of St. Patrick. Club: Army-Navy (Washington). Author: Field Artillery Applied Mathematics, 1922. Address: War Dept., Washington, D.C. Died Jan. 3, 1958.

JONES, LOUIS R., ret. marine corps officer; born Philadelphia; s. William F. and Katharine (Reeder) J.; married Rhita Wilmer Thomas, Aug. 8, 1917; children—Virginia Thomas (wife of Lt. Col. Edwin C. Godbold, U.S.M.C.), Robert Alexander (2d lt., U.S.M.C.), Mary Elizabeth. Enlisted U.S.M.C., Dec. 14, 1914, commd. 2d lt., July 5, 1917, and advanced through the grades to maj. gen., ret., 1949; pres. Marine Corps Equipment Board, Decorated Silver Star with oak leaf cluster, Purple Heart, Navy Cross, Legion of Merit with gold star and oak leaf cluster (U.S.), Croix de Guerre (France), Cloud and Banner (China). Mason. Mem. National Sojourners. Club: Army-Navy (Washington). Home: Arlington VA Died Feb. 2, 1973.

JONES, MORTON TEBBS ins. official; b. Kansas City, Mo., July 3, 1892; s. Richard Bacon and Sally (Cloon) J.; student University of Missouri, 1910-12; married Pauline Perry, February 28, 1922; 1 dau., Paula Perry (Mrs. Eugene S. Taylor). Began with R. B. Jones & Sons Inc., 1912, chmn., mng. dir., 1931-60, pres., mng. dir., 1960-; organized Kansas City Fire & Marine Ins. Co., 1929, since pres., dir. City Nat. Bank & Trust Co. (Kan. City), Minnesota Av., Inc., Black, Sivalls and Bryson, Inc. 1st O.T.C., Ft. Riley, Kan., 1917; commd. capt., serving with 354th Inf., 89th Div.; promoted to major. Trustee, v.p. and gov. Kansas City Art Inst., 1938-41; mem. Mo. State Council of Defense, 1941, State Social Security Commn., 1941; adv. trustee Citizen's Bond Com. of Kansas City. V.p. and dir. Kansas City Chamber of Commerce, 1922, pres., 1940-41; pres. Mo. Ins. Council, 1939-40, 89th Div. War Soc., 1940-41; comdr. Mil. Order World War, 1937; comdr. Bland Post of Am. Legion, 1920; mem. Sigma Alpha Epsilon, Phi Alpha Delta. Republican. Mem. St. Paul's Episcopal Church. Clubs: River, Kansas City Country, University, Saddle and Sirloin. Home: 5049 Wornall Rd., Kansas City 64112. Office: 301 W. 11th St., Kansas City, Mo. Died Dec. 17, 1962.

JONES, NELSON EDWARDS physician; b. Liberty Twp., Ross County, O., Sept. 20, 1821; s. Henry and Rachel (Corkin) J.; ed. at home and at an acad. at Chillicothe, O.; entered coll. at Augusta, Ky.; grad. Cleveland Med. Coll., 1846; m. Virginia Smith, June 9, 1846. Practiced at Circleville, O., 1852-. Commd. May 4, 1864, surgeon Bd. of Enrollment, 12th dist. of Ohio, serving to end of war. Served 31 yrs. as examining surgeon for pensions. Author: The Squirrel Hunters of Ohio; or Glimpses of Pioneer Life, 1896. Home: Circleville, O. Died 1901.

JONES, OWEN congressman; b. nr. Ardmore, Pa., Dec. 29, 1819; grad. U. Pa.; studied law, Phila. Admitted to the bar, Montgomery County, Pa., 1842, began practice in Ardmore; mem. U.S. Ho. of Reps. (Democrat) from Pa., 35th Congress, 1857-59; raised a troop of cavalry during Civil War, served from capt. to col., 1861-63; resumed law practice. Died nr. Ardmore, Dec. 25, 1878; buried Laurel Hill Cemetery, Phila.

JONES, ROBERT OTIS banker; b. nr. Balt., Oct. 2, 1894; s. Edgar Godman and Ellis B. (Hood) J.; A.B., St. John's College (Annapolis) and University of Maryland, 1916; married Mrs. Helen Barnes Bailey, May 19, 1928 (deceased December 1957). Joined Wood, Struthers & Co., N.Y.C., 1920, becoming head of investment advisory dept.; in same capacity joined J. P. Morgan & Co., N.Y.C., 1935; with Union Trust Co., Pitts., 1941-59, v.p. (since merger in 1946) Mellon Nat. Bank & Trust Co., 1946-59, ret., 1959. Served in Md. Nat. Guard, Mexican Border, 1916; lt. and capt. inf., U.S. (Regular) Army, 1916-19; with 5th Div., A.E.F., France, and Army of Occupation. Former mem. adv. bd. Protestant Home for Incurables, Pitts.; mem., chmn. finance com., Bd. of Visitors and Govs., St. John's Coll. Mem. Newcomen Soc., Kappa Alpha (Southern). Republican. Episcopalian. Club: Merchants (Balt.). Home: Wyman Park Apts., Balt. 21211. Died Dec. 12, 1960.

JONES, ROBERT TYRE, JR. (BOBBY JONES), golf champion; b. Atlanta, Mar. 17, 1902; s. Robert P. and Clara (Thomas) J.; prep. edn., Tech. High Sch., Atlanta; B.S. in M.E., Ga. Sch. of Tech., Atlanta, 1922; B.S., Harvard, 1924; studied law, Emory U., 1926-27; m. Mary Malone, June 17, 1924; children—Clara Malone Black, and Robert Tyre III, Mary Ellen (Mrs. Carl Hood, Junior). Admitted to Georgia bar, 1928, practiced in Atlanta; partner law firm Jones, Bird & Howell; v.p. Spalding Sales Corp., Chicopee, Mass. So. amateur golf champion, 1917, 20, 22; national amateur champion, 1924, 25, 27, 28, 30; British amateur champion, 1930; nat. open champion, 1923, 26, 29, 30; open champion of Gt. Britain, 1926, 27, 30; first official champion in nat. open championships of Gt. Britain and U.S. in the same season, and won both championships same season twice, 1926, 30. Served as lt. col. USAAF, 1944. Clubs: Capital City, Athletic, Piedmont Driving, Royal and Ancient, St. Andrew's; Augusta (Georgia) National Golf (pres.); Peachtree Golf. Author: Down the Fairway (with O. B. Keeler), 1927; Gold is my Game, 1960; Bobby Jones on Golf, 1966; Bobby Jones on the Basic Golf Swing, 1969. Office: Atlanta GA Died Dec. 18, 1971.

JONES, SAMUEL FOSDICK surgeon; b. Cincinnati, O., Aug. 4, 1874; s. Maj. Frank J. and Frances Dering (Fosdick) J.; ed. The Hill Sch., Pottstown, Pa.; B.S., Mass. Inst. Tech., 1898; M.D., Columbia, 1902; m. Mary Catherine Cordes, Dec. 3, 1910. Began practice in N.Y. City, 1902; moved to Denver, 1906; prof. orthopedic surgery, Med. Dept. U. of Colo., 1919-31, now emeritus prof.; ex-pres. St. Lukes' Hosp. Staff of Denver; retired from active practice. Served as maj. Med. Corps. U.S. Army, Apr. 6, 1917-Jan. 13, 1919; with A.E.F. in France 8 mos. Fellow Am. Coll. Surgeons; mem. Am. Orthopedic Assn., Western Surg. Assn., New York Pathol, Soc., Soc. Mayflower Descendants, Loyal Legion, Veterans of Foreign Wars, Delta Psi; asso. mem. Calif. Inst. Tech. Republican. Episcopalian. Clubs: Denver Club, Cactus, Mile High (Denver); California (Los Angeles); University, The Athenarum (Pasadena); St. Anthony (New York); Cosmos (Washington); Santa Barbara. Home: Huntingdon Hotel, Pasadena 15, Calif. Died Mar. 24, 1946.

JONES, THOMAS AP CATESBY naval officer; b. Westmoreland County, Va., Apr. 24, 1790; s. Maj. Catesby and Lettice (Turberville) J.; m. Mary Carter, July 1, 1823, 4 children. Entered U.S. Navy as midshipman under Isaac Hutland and Stephan Decatur, 1805; commd. lt., 1812, master commandant, 1820, capt., 1829; helped suppress slave trade in Gulf of Mexico, 1808-12; comdr. South Seas Surveying and Exploring Expdn., 1836; comdr. Pacific Squadron, 1842, and prematurely seized Monterey, Cal., thinking war had been declared between U.S. and Mexico; commanded Pacific Squadron for 3d time, 1844. Died Sharon, Fairfax County, Va., May 30, 1858.

JONES, THOMAS GOODE judge; b. Macon, Ga., Nov. 26, 1844; s. Samuel G. and Martha Ward (Goode) J.; grad. Va. Mil. Inst., 1862; m. Gena C. Bird, Dec. 20, 1866. Served C.S.A. of Northern Va. as staff officer under Gen. John B. Gordon, attaining rank of maj.; was several times wounded; carried a flag of truce, sent out by Gordon, to Sheridan's lines to Appomattox C.H., Apr. 9, 1865. Established law practice, Montgomery; reporter decisions Supreme Ct. of Ala., 1870-80; alderman, 1875-84; mem. Ala. Legislature, 1884-88 (speaker, 1886-88); gov. of Ala., 1890-94; U.S. dist. judge, Middle and Northern dists. of Ala., 1901-. Del. Ala. Constl. Conv., 1901. Democrat. Col. 2d Regt. Ala. state troops, 1880-90; chmn. relief com. yellow fever epidemic, 1897; pres. Ala. State Bar Assn., 1901. Compiled 18 vols. of Alabama Supreme Court Reports; author of Code of Ethics Ala. State Bar Assn. and also of state laws regulating employment of military in enforcement of law and suppression of riots. Address: Montgomery, Ala. Died Apr. 28, 1914.

JONES, WILIE banker; b. Hillsboro, N.C., Oct. 17, 1850; s. Cadwallader and Annie Isabella (Iredell) J.; ed. high schs.; Ebenezer, S.C., and Raleigh, N.C.; m. Annie Reaux Caldwell, of Columbia, S.C., May 20, 1886. Began as clk., Carolina National Bank, 1870, and continued for 36 yrs., advancing to v.p.; pres. Palmetto National Bank, Columbia, 1906-17. Enlisted in N.C.S.C., 1874; retired as maj. gen., 1915; col. 2d S.C. Regt., Spanish-Am. War, 1898; served in Cuba under Gen. Fitzhugh Lee. Mem. S.C. Constl. Conv., 1895; chmn. Dem. State Com., S.C., 15 years. Episcopalian. K.T. Club: Columbia. Office: Palmetto Nat. Bank, Columbia, S.C.

JONES, WILLIAM army officer, gov. R.I.; b. Newport, R.I., Oct. 8, 1753; s. William and Elizabeth (Pearce) J.; m. Anne Dunn, Feb. 28, 1787, 1 dau., Harriet. Received commn. as lt. from R.I. Gen. Assembly, 1776, capt., 1776; served as capt. of marines on brig. Providence, 1778; justice of the peace, Providence, R.I.; rep. R.I. Gen. Assembly, 1807-11; presented a petition against the Embargo Act, 1808; speaker R.I. Gen. Assembly, 1809, 10; gov. R.I., 1811-17; mem. Soc. of Cincinnati; pres. Peace Soc., also R.I. Bible Soc., Am. Bible Soc.; trustee Brown U. ied Providence, Apr. 9, 1822.

JONES, WILLIAM sec. of navy, congressman; b. Phila., 1760. Served with Continental Army in Revolutionary War; participatd in battles of Trenton, 1776, Princeton, 1777; served as 3d lt. in ship St. James; commd. 1st lt. U.S. Navy, 1781; mem. U.S. Ho. of Reps. from Pa., 7th Congress, 1801-03; U.S. sec. of navy under Pres. Madison, 1813-14; pres. Bank of U.S., 1816-19; collector of customs Phila., 1827-29. Died Bethlehem, Pa., Sept. 16, 1831; buried St. Peter's Churchyard, Phila.

JONES, WILLIAM ALBERT brigadier gen. U.S. Army; b. St. Charles, Mo., June 26, 1841; s. Stilman and Ann J. (Perkins) J.; grad. U.S. Mil. Acad., 1864; m. Louisa V. Test, Nov. 25, 1873. Commd. 1st lt. engrs., June 13, 1864; capt., Mar. 7, 1867; maj., June 30, 1882; lt. col., Oct. 2, 1895; col., Apr. 21, 1903; brig. gen. and retired by operation of law, June 26, 1905. Asst. prof. civil and mil. engring., law and ethics, and instr. practical mil. engring., and comdg. Co. A Battalion of Engrs., also treas., U.S. Mil. Acad., 1864-66; served in 6th Corps, Army of the Potomac, Civil War; comd. U.S. Army exploring expdn. in northwestern Wyo. and Yellowstone Park, 1873; discovered Two Ocean Pass, Togwotee Pass and Shoshone Mountains; served on constrn. of fortifications, harbors and lighthouses on Atlantic coast and Great Lakes, on improvement of rivers in northwest, Yellowstone Park, etc.; mem. commn. to investigate salmon fisheries of Columbia River; div. engr. of the Chesapeake, etc.; consulting engr. location and construction rys., mining and treating ores, bldg. dams and water works in various localties; consulting engr. state of Calif., Golden Gate Park, San Francisco; consulting engr. Commonwealth of Mass., Marine Park, Charles River Dam. Owner and manager 2,000 acres oyster plantation on eastern shore of Va. Protestant. Author: Report of Exploration of Northwestern Wyoming and Yellowstone Park, 1874; The Salmon Fisheries of the Columbia River. Home: Ft. Monroe, Va. Died Nov. 10, 1914.

JONES, WILLIAM RICHARD engr., steel co. exec.; b. Hazelton, Pa., Feb. 23, 1839; m. Harriet Lloyd Apr. 14, 1861, 4 children. Journeyman machinist, 1853; with Cambria Iron Co., Johnston, Pa., 1859; served with Co. A, 133d Pa. Volunteers, 1862-63, served in battles of Fredericksburg and Chancellorsville; served as capt. Co. F., 194th Pa. Regt. of Emergency Men (which he raised), 1864-65; gen. supt. Edgar Thomson Steel Co., Braddock, Pa., 1875-89; cons. engr. Carnegie, Phipps & Co., 1888-89; inventor and patentee numerous devices connected with prodn. steel, most important was Jones mixer (mixed molten iron from blast furnaces for converter), 1889; 1st American to be invited to see Krupp steel works at Essen. Died Pitts., Sept. 28, 1889.

JONES, WILLIAM RUSSELL, physician; b. Orange County, Va., Jan. 18, 1870; s. Thomas Scott and Lillie Clark (Coleman) J.; M.D., U. of Va., 1892; Ph.G., Univ. Coll. of Medicine, Richmond, Va., 1894; m. Jane Taylor Fisher, Jan. 5, 1905 (died 1918). Began practice Richmond, 1892; prof. chemistry, toxicology and med. jurisprudence, Univ. Coll. of Medicine, Richmond, 1897-1906, lecturer in clin. medicine and asso. prof. practicing medicine, 1906-12; visiting physician Virginia Hosp., 1897-1912; visiting physician Retreat for the Sick Hosp.; chief med. adviser, chief surgeon Richmond, Fredericksburg & Potomac R.R., Co. In charge med. and surg. relief and suppression of influenza, U.S. Munition Bag Loading Plant, Richmond, World War I; cons. med. officer U.S. War Risk and Veterans' Bur., 1918-22; chief surgeon, maj. Med. Corps, Va. Nat. Guard, 1926. Mem. A.M.A., Med. Soc. Va., Richmond Acad. Medicine and Surgery, Assn. Ry. Chief Surgeons, Chesapeake & Ohio Assn. Ry. Surgeons, Assn. of Mil. Surgeons of U.S. Democrat. Episcopalian. Author: Abstract Lectures on Chemistry, 1899; A Textbook of Chemistry for Students of Medicine, Dentistry and Pharmacy, 1905. Home: 2701 Grove Av., Richmond VA

JOPSON, JOHN HOWARD surgeon; b. Phila., Dec. 28, 1871; s. William and Elizabeth S. (Thomas) J.; A.B., Phila. High Sch., 1888; Biol. Sch. U. Pa., 1890; M.D., U. Pa., 1893; m. Susanna B. Michener, June 7, 1909; children-Harry Gorgas Michener, Frances Leslie. Resident physician Univ. and Children's hosps., Phila., 1893-95; surgeon, Children's Hosp., 1900-29, Presbyn. Hosp., 1905-34; emeritus prof. surgery, Grad. Sch. Medicine, formerly clin. prof. surgery, Med. Sch., U. Pa.; cons. surgeon, Children's Hosp., Bryn Mawr Hosp. Maj. Med. R.C., 1917; lt. col., M.C., U.S. Army, Nov. 11, 1918. Fellow Am. Surg. Assn., A.C.S., Coll. Physicians Phila., Phila. Acad. Surgery (hon.); Soc. Clin. Surgery; Internat. Soc. Surgery. Author articles on Peritonitis, Intubation and Tracheotomy in Diphtheria, in Musser and Kelly's Handbook of Practical Treatment, 1911-12, 1917; also contbr. to Nelson's Loose-Leaf Surgery and med. jours. Home: Rutherfordton, N.C.; University Club, Phila. Died 1954.

JORDAN, DAVID FRANCIS prof. finance; b. Watervliet, N.Y., July 21, 1890; s. Thomas Henry and Ellen (Tierney) J.; B.C.S., N.Y. Univ., 1919; m. Edith Irene Wilson, Dec. 27, 1922 (died 1924); m. 2d, Frances Marion Reinken, May 24, 1927; children-Eleanor Irene, David Francis, Nancy Ellen, Thomas Dietrich. Mem. faculty N.Y. U. since 1919, prof. finance since 1928; economist Gen. Electric Co., 1922-25. In Chem. Warfare Service, U.S. Army, 1918-19; vet. Co. G, 7th Regt., N.Y.N.G. Pres. Fedn. Coll. Catholic Clubs, 1923-24. Mem. Am. Econ. Assn., Albany Soc. of New York, Delta Mo Delta, Alpha Kappa Psi. Catholic. Author: Jordan on Investments, 1919 (22d printing 1941), Business Forecasting, 1921; Practical Business Forecasting, 1926; Economic Principles and Problems (with others), 1932; Managing Personal Financers, 1936; Problems in Investment Principles and Security Analysis, 1937. Home: 136 Shorewood Drive, Great Neck, N.Y. Office: Washington Sq., New York, N.Y. Died Aug. 20, 1942.

JORDAN, G(ERALD) RAY clergyman, educator; b. Kinston, N.C., Nov. 11, 1896; s. Charles Marion and Sophia (Faulkner) J.; A.B., cum laude, Trinity Coll.

(now Duke), 1917; B.D., Emory U., 1920; A.M., Yale, 1921; D.D., Duke, 1935; Litt.D., Lincoln Meml. U., 1950; m. Caroline Moody, Mar. 7, 1922; children-Gerald Ray, Terrell Franklin. Ordained to ministry, M.E. Ch., S., 1921; pastor Black Mountain M.E. Ch., 1921-23, Chestnut St. M.E. Ch., Asheville, N.C., 1923-24, College Pl. M.E. Ch., Greensboro, 1924-26, Dilworth M.E. Ch., Charlotte, 1926-30, Wesley Meml. M.E. Ch., High Point, 1930-33, Centenary Ch., Winston-Salem, 1933-40, First Meth. Ch., Charlotte, 1940-45; prof. homiletics and chapel preacher Sch. Theology, Emory U., 1945-60, Charles Howard Candler prof., 1960-. At Camp Zachary Taylor, Louisville, 1918; commd. 2d lt. F.A.R.C. Trustee Scarritt Coll. for Christian Workers, High Point Coll., Children's Home, Winston-Salem. Mem. to unite Davenport and Greensboro Colls.; mem. Gen. Bd. Christian Edn. of Meth. Ch., 1939-48, mem. Youth Commn., Peach Commn., also Interboard Com. on Missionary Edn., 1940-48, Western N.C. Conf. Commn. (Meth.) uniting Rutherford and Weaver colls.; attended ministers' conference, Union Sem., N.Y., various summers, also conf., U. Chgo., 1932; one of seven reps., M.E. Ch., S., to World Conf. on Faith and Order, Edinburgh, Scotland, 1937; asso. del. World Conf. on Life and Work, Oxford, Eng., 1937; del. Gen. Conf. of M.E. Ch., S., Birmingham, Ala., 1938; del. Uniting Conf. of the M.E. Church, M.E. Ch, S and M.P. Church, Kansas City, 1939; del. gen. conf. Meth. Ch., 1940, Atlantic City, N.J.; del. Jurisdictional Conf., South Eastern Jurisdiction, 1940, Asheville, N.C.; del. gen. conf. Kansas City, 1944, Boston, 1948; Jurisdictional Conf., Atlanta, 1944, Columbia, S.C., 1948, Roanoke, Va., 1952; spl. preacher at various colls., univs. and confs. Bd. dirs. A.R.C. (Charlotte). Mem. Am. Assn. U. Profs, Assn. Sem. Profs. in Practical Field, Phi Beta Kappa Assoc., Kappa Alpha, Omicron Delta Kappa, Pi Gamma Mu, Theta Phi Beta Kappa. Democrat. Mason (grand orator N.C. Grand Lodge 1936). Clubs: Atlanta Athletic; East Lake Country. Author: What Is Yours?, 1930; Intimate Interests of Youth, 1931; The Intolerance of Christianity, 1931; Courage That Propels, 1933; Faith That Propels, 1935; We Face Calvary-and Life, 1936; Adventures in Radiant Living, 1938; Why the Cross?, 1941; Look at the Stars!, 1942; We Believe: A Creed that Sings, 1944; The Supreme Possession, 1945; The Emerging Revival, 1946; The Hour Has Come, 1948; You Can Preach, 1951; Perkins Lectures, 1947; Wilson Lectures, 1947; Brown Lectures, 1949. Contbr. to After Pentecost What?, 1930; These Prophetic Voices, 1942; Talks to Youth, 1949; The Pulpit in the South, 1950; Communion Addresses, 1950; Beyond Despair, 1955; Prayer that Prevails, 1958; Religion that is Eternal, 1960; Preaching During a Revolution, 1962; Christ Communion and the Clock, 1963; Life-Giving Words, 1964; Contbr. to The Spirtual Diary; Christian Century, Christian Century Pulpit, Church Management, Christian Advocate, The Pastor, Christian Herald, The Upper Room Pulpit, Evangelism in the Sunday School, 1929; The Upper Room, Church School Literature. Contbg. editor to Through the Bible; Expositor (editor homiletic dept. 1931), Am. Pulpit Series, 1945-46. Lit. editor The Pulpit Digest, 1941-45. Home: 1733 E. Clifton Rd., N.E., Emory U., Atlanta 30307. Died Nov. 15, 1964; buried Decatur (Ga.) Cemetery.

JORDAN, RICHARD HENRY, army officer; b. Haymarket, Va., Sept. 8, 1877; s. Charles Edward and Alice Melville (Moore) J.; student Va. Poly. Inst., 1893-97, C.E., 1919; student U.S. Mil. Acad., 1897-99; grad. Coast Arty. Sch., Fort Monroe, 1910; m. Frances Bell, Feb. 29, 1920. Commnd. 2d lt. Coast Arty., 1901, and promoted through grades to brig. gen., 1936; had charge of gold star mothers pilgrimage to Am. cemeteries in Europe, 1932-33; mil attache to Brazil, 1919-20; chief of Transportation Div., O.Q.-M.G., 1936-40. Awarded D.S.M. for World War service. Mem. Mil. Order of the World War, Mil. Order of Carabao. Democrat. Episcopalian. Clubs: Army and Navy, Army and Navy Country. Home: Washington DC Died Jan. 30, 1971; buried Arlington National Cemetery, Arlington VA

JORDAN, THOMAS army officer, editor; b. Luray, Va., Sept. 30, 1819; s. Gabriel and Elizabeth (Silbert) J.; grad. U.S. Mil. Acad., 1840; m. Miss Kearney, 2 children. Commd. lt. 3d Inf., U.S. Army, served in Fla. War; 1st lt., 1846; served as capt., q.m. in Mexican War, 1847; served as staff q.m. in 2d Seminole uprising, 1848-50; served on Pacific Coast, and against Indians in Wash., 1850-60; introduced steam navigation on Columbia River above Ft. Dalles, Ore., and initiated successful irrigation project, 1856-60; commd. lt. col. Va. Militia, Confederate Army, 1861; served as adj.-gen., 1st Battle of Bull Run, 1861; promoted brig. gen., 1862; contbr. article attacking Jefferson Davis to Harper's Magazine, aroused widespread interest; editor Memphis (Tenn.) Appeal, 1866; chief of staff, later comdr. Cuban insurgents, 1869; founder, editor Financial and Mining Record of N.Y. Author: The South, Its Products, Its Commerce, and Resources, 1861; The Campaigns of Lieutenant-General N.B. Forrest, 1868. Died N.Y. N.Y.C., Nov. 27, 1895.

JORDAN, WEYMOUTH TYREE, educator; b. Hamlet, N.C., Oct. 31, 1912; s. William Daniel and Mary (Utley) J.; B.S., N.C. State Coll., 1933; M.A., Vanderbilt U., 1934, Ph.D., 1937; m. Louise Elizabeth Riggan, Aug. 11, 1935; children—Weymouth Tyree, Elizabeth H. Markowski, William Royster. Fellow history Vanderbilt U., 1934-37; prof. history, head dept. N.C. Indian Coll., 1937-38; from instr. to asso. prof. history, head dept. Judson Coll., 1938-42; asst. prof., then asso. prof., research prof. Auburn U., 1942-49; prof. history Fla. State U., 1949-68, head dept., 1954-64; vis. prof., head dept. history Transylvania Coll., 1936; tchr. summers Blue Mountain Coll., 1938, Stetson U., 1939, U. Okla., 1941, U. Mo., 1958. Regional asso. Am. Council Learned Societies, 1957-59; adv. bd. Guggenheim Meml. Found., 1959-68; Fulbright-Hays prof. U. Erlangen (Germany), 1964-65. Recipient C.M. McClung award E. Tenn. Hist. Soc., 1939, 41; fellow Social Sci. Research Council, 1940, 41, 47, 50. Gen. Edn. Bd., 1947-48; Guggenheim fellow, 1957-58. Served to lt. comdr. USNR, 1943-45. Mem. Agrl. History Soc. (exec. council 1948-49, 59-67, pres. 1962-63), Fla. Hist. Soc., Am., Miss. Valley So. (chmn. membership com. 1948, program com. 1961, exec. council 1953-55) historical assns., Kappa Sigma, Kappa Phi Kappa, Phi Alpha Theta, Sigma Pi Alpha. Democrat. Episcopalian. Author: Hugh Davis and His Alabama Plantation, 1948; George Washington Campbell of Tenneessee, 1955; Ante Bellum Alabama, Town and Country, 1957; Rebels in the Making, Planters Conventions and Southern Propaganda, 1958; Herbs, Hoecakes and Husbandry, 1960; The United States, 1783-1861: From Revolution to Civil War, 1964; also articles. Editor: The Purchase of Florida (H.B. Fuller), 1964; bd. editors E. Tenn. Hist. Soc. Publs., 1947-52, Ala. Rev., 1948-50, Fla. State U. Studies, 1950-54, Agrl. History, 1957-62, Fla. Hist. Quar., 1959-63, Jour. So. History, 1961-64, So. Humanities Rev., 1966-68; co-editor Fla. State U. Studies, 1950-52, editor, 1952-54. Home: Tallahassee FL Died Nov. 22, 1968; buried Roselawn Cemetery, Tallahassee FL

JOSTES, FREDERICK AUGUSTUS physician and surgeon; b. St. Louis, Mo., Aug. 14, 1895; s. Clemense and Appolonia (Niederberger) J.; B.S., Washington U., St. Louis, 1918, M.D., 1920; grad. student, orthopedic clinics, Eng., France, Germany, Austria, Switzerland, Ireland, Italy, 1925-26; m. Barbara Mary Donohoe, Dec. 4, 1945. Interne, Barnes Hosp., St. Louis, 1921, asst. resident surgeon, 1922, surgical pathologist, 1923; resident fellow, med. sch., Washington U., 1924; resident surgeon, orthopedics, Shriner Hosp. for Crippled Children, St. Louis, 1925; prof. clinical orthopedic surgery, U. of Mo., 1927-29; asst. prof. clin. orthopedic surgery, Washington U., since 1935; mem. staff Barnes, Childrens, Maternity, Deaconess, Jewish, City, County, Barnard Skin and Cancer hosps., St. Louis. Served with U.S. Navy, chief of surgery at Naval Air Station, San Diego, Calif., Jan.-July, 1942; exec. officer, Mobile Hosp. No. 2, July-Nov. 1942; sr. med. officer, U.S.S. Mt. Vernon, Nov. 1942-Feb. 1944; with bur. medicine and surgery, Office of Rehabilitation, Feb.-Sept. 1944; chief orthopedic surgery, U.S. Naval Hosp., St. Albans, Long Island, N.Y., Sept.-Nov. 1944; chief surgery and orthopedics, U.S. Naval Hosp., Great Lakes, Ill., Nov. 1944-Feb. 1946; dist. med. office, 12th Naval Dist., San Francisco; rank of capt., Naval Reserve. Member of the Baruch Committee on Phys. Medicine, Certified by Am. Bd. Orthopedic Surgery, 1934. Fellow Am. Coll. Surgeons; mem. St. Louis, Mo. State, Am. Southern and Miss. Valley med. assns., Clin. Orthopedic Assn., Am. Acad. Orthopedic Surgeons, Am. Orthopedic Assn., St. Louis Surg. Soc., Acad. Internat. of Medicine, La Societe Internationale de Chirurgie Orthopedique et de Traumatologie. Contbr. of articles to med. jours.; author chpts. in med. books. Home: River's Arm, St. Ferdinand de Fleurissant, St. Louis County, Mo. Office: 3720 Washington, St. Louis 8. Died May 19, 1952.

JOUETT, JAMES EDWARD rear admiral U.S. Navy, retired, 1800; b. Lexington, Ky., Feb. 27, 1828; s. Matthew Harris J. (artist) and Margaret H. (Mamer) J.; m. Galena Stockett, 1852. Entered U.S.N. as midshipman, 1841; fought in Mex. war; grad. U.S. Naval Acad., 1847; served in Paraguay expdn. and in Berriby war, 1845; promoted to passed midshipman; became master and lt., 1855. For services on expdn. into Galveston harbor, 1861, when he destroyed Confederate war vessel "Royal Yacht, " he was given command of U.S.S. "Montgomery." Promoted to lt. comdr., July 16, 1862; took prominent part in entrance to Mobile bay under Farragut, Aug. 1864; promoted in course to rear admiral and comd. North Atlantic squadron. In 1885, when rebels closed the transit across the Isthmus of Panama, he opened the transit and restored peace, for which he was thanked by pres. of the United States of Colombia. Home: Orlando, Fla. Died 1902.

JOUETT, JOHN state legislator; b. Albermarle County, Va., Dec. 7, 1754; s. Capt. John and Mourning (Harris) J.; m. Sallie Robards, Aug. 20, 1784, 1 son, Matthew Harris. Signer oath of allegiance to Va. Commonwealth, 1779; capt. Va. Militia; remembered for daring ride over 40 miles to save Gov. Jefferson and Va. Legislature from capture; mem. Va. Assembly from Lincoln County, 1786-87, Mercer County, 1787-88, 90; a leading mem. Danville Conv., influential in organizing Ky. as separate state; mem. Ky. Legislature from Mercer County, 1 term, from Woodford County, 3 terms. Died Mar. 1, 1822.

JOY, CHARLES TURNER naval officer; b. St. Louis, Feb. 17, 1895; s. Duncan and Lucy (Turner) J.; B.S., U.S. Naval Acad., 1916; M.S. (grad. work in explosive engring.), U. Mich., 1922; m. Martha Ann Chess, Oct. 16, 1924; children-Charles Turner, David Duncan, Mary Martha. Commd. ensign USN, 1916, and advanced through the grades to vice adm., 1949; served in U.S.S. Pennsylvania, 1916-20; exec. officer U.S.S. Pope, 1925-26; in U.S.S. California, 1928-31; comd. U.S.S. Litchfield, 1933-38; exec. officer U.S.S. Indianapolis, 1940-41; operations officer, staff of Vice Adm. Wilson Brown, 1941-42; comd. U.S.S. Louisville, 1942-43; on duty comdr. in chief hdqrs., 1943-44; comd. Cruiser Div. 6, 1944-45; comdg. Amphibious Group 2, 1945, Task Force 73 in Chinese waters, 1945-46; comdg. Naval Proving Ground, 1946-49; comdr. Naval Forces, Far East, 1949-52; sr. del. UN commd. delegation to Korean Armistice Conf., 1951-52; supt. U.S. Naval Acad., 1952—. Decorated Legion of Merit with 3 gold stars, Commendation Ribbon; D.S.C., D.S.M. (Army), D.S.M. (Navy) Bronze Star; Comdr. British Empire. Clubs: Chevy Chase (Md.); Army and Navy (Washington); New York Yacht (N.Y.C.). Address: U.S. Naval Acad., Annapolis, Md. Died June 1956.

JOY, HENRY BOURNE automobile mfr.; b. Detroit, Nov. 23, 1864; s. James Frederick and Mary (Bourne) J.; grad. Phillips Acad., Andover, Mass., 1883; Sheffield Scientific Sch. (Yale), jr. yr., 1886; m. Helen Hall Newberry, Oct. 11, 1892. Began as office boy, Peninsular Car Co., and became clk., p.m. and asst. treas.; in mining business in Utah, 1887-89; asst. treas., dir. Fort St. Union Depot Co., Detroit, from 1889; pres. Detroit Union Depot Co., 1896-1907; receiver C.&G.T. Ry. Co., 1900-03; dir. Federal Res. Bank of Chicago, 1913-14; pres., mgr. and dir. Packard Motor Car Co., 1901-18; former pres. Detroit Union Railroad Depot & Station Co.; former treas. and sec. Fort Street Union Depot Co. Pres. Lincoln Highway Assn.; v.p. Navy League of U.S.; dir. Chamber Commerce, U.S.A., Am. Protective Tariff League, Am. Fair Trade League; dir. Detroit Bd. of Commerce, 1914-15, v.p., 1915-16 and 1922-23. Republican. Presbyn. Mem. State Naval Militia, Mich., 9 yrs.; served in U.S. Navy during Spanish-Am. War as chief boatswain's mate U.S.S. Yosemite; capt. and lt. col. U.S.A., World War. Home: Grosse Pointe Farms, Mich. Died Nov. 6, 1936.

JOYCE, CHARLES HERBERT lawyer; b. in Eng., Jan. 30, 1830; s. Charles and Martha E. J.; grad. Northfield Acad., 1851; read law; admitted to bar of Vt., 1852; Supreme Ct. of U.S., 1885; m. Rouene M. Randall, of Northfield, Vt., Feb. 21, 1853 (died May 26, 1902). State librarian of Vt., 1854-55; state's atty., Washington Co., Vt., 1856-57; maj. and lt.-col., 2d Vt. Inf.; mem. Vt. Ho. of Rep., 1869-71 (speaker, 1870-71); mem. 44th to 47th Congresses (1875-83); retired from legal practice, 1895. Address: Rutland, Vermont.

JOYCE, J(AMES) WALLACE, engr.; b. Cranston, R.I., July 8, 1907; s. James and Annie Josephine (Malkin) J.; B.Eng., Johns Hopkins, 1928, Ph.D., 1931; m. Edith Mae Clagett, June 25, 1932; 1 son, James Wallace. Applied geophysical prospecting U.S. Bur. Mines, 1931-35; observer-in-charge U.S. Coast and Geodetic Survey, Tucson Magnetic Obs., 1935-37, head magnetic sect., 1937-41; elec. engr. U.S. Naval Ordnance Lab., 1941-42; engr. Bur. Areonautics (electronics) U.S. Navy Dept., 1947-51; spl. assignments to Dept. State; mutual def. assistance program, Apr.-June 1949, internat. science policy survey group, 1949-50; deputy science adviser Department of State, 1952-53; asst. dir. electronics and guided missiles Office Sec. Def., 1953-55; head Office for the International Geophysical Year, Nat. Science Foundation, Washington, 1955-58, head Office Special International Programs, 1958-61; spl. asst. to the dir. of foundation, 1961-63; officer in charge general sci. affairs Office Internat. Sci. Affairs, Dept. State, 1963-65, acting dep. dir. internat. sci. and technol. affairs, 1965-67, dep. dir. internat. sci. and technol. affairs, 1967-70. Entered active duty as lt. USNR, 1942; discharged to inactive duty as comdr., 1947. Mem. Internat. Assn. Terrestial Magnetism and Electricity (sec. 1948-51), Am. Geophys. Union (pres. sect. terrestial magnetism and electricity, 1950-53), Seismol. Soc. Am., Washington Academy of Science, Sigma Xi, Tau Beta Pi. Club: Cosmos. Contbr. articles geophysical prospecting (magnetic methods) in pubs. Home: Washington DC Died Jan. 6, 1970.

JOYCE, KENYON ASHE army officer; b. N.Y.C., Nov. 3, 1879; s. Charles Malcom and Norma McLeod (Kenyon) J.; distinguished grad. Infantry and Cavalry Sch., 1905; Army Staff Coll., 1906; Army War Coll., 1930; m. Helen E. Jones, Nov. 15, 1910 (dec. 1951-: m. 2d, Mrs. Mary Kane Drury, March 27, 1953. Commd. 2d lt. cav., U.S. Army, 1901; advanced through grades to maj. gen. 1939. Participated in operations at Santiago, Cuba, Spanish-Am. War, 1898, in Northern Luzon and Cavite Province, Philippine Insurrection, 1900-01; operations against Ute Indians, Mont., 1906; during World War I served as chief of staff 87th, 83d divs., and Embarkation Center, Le Mans, France; participated in Meuse-Argonne offensive; on War Dept. gen. staff and gen. staff with troops; mil. attaché Am. Embassy, London, 1924-27; comdt. 3d U.S. Cavalry and Fort Myer, Va., 1933-36; comdr. 1st Cavalry Div., Fort Bliss,

Tex., 1938-40; in command of Ninth Army Corps, Fort Lewis, Wash., 1941; comdg. 9th Service Command, 1943. Pres. Allied Control Commn. for Italy, 1943-44; ret. Nov. 30, 1943; mem. Cal. Crime Commn., 1947-50; mem. Pres. Com. Nat. Armed Forces Mus., 1957-60. Awarded D.S.M. on two occasions, Purple Heart (U.S.); Officer Legion of Honor and Croix de Guerre with palm (France); Knight Grand Cross, Order Crown of Italy; Order Aztec Eagle (Mexico). Clubs: Pacific Union, Burlingame, Bohemians (San Francisco); Army and Navy (Washington). Address: 1000 Mason St., San Francisco. Died Jan. 11, 1960; buried Arlington Nat. Cemetery.

JOYES, JOHN WARREN army officer; b. Waterloo, N.Y., Apr. 17, 1870; s. James J. and Charlotte L. (Stratton) J.; grad. 5th in class of 52, U.S. Mil. Acad., 1894; m. Georgiana M. Butler, June 14, 1904; children - John Warren, Georgiana Butler, Charlotte P. Commd. 2d lt. 5th Arty., June 12, 1894; promoted through grades to col., May 15, 1917, asst. chief of ordnance, with rank of brig. gen., 1923-27; chief of ordnance field service, 1925-27; at Army Indsl. Coll., 1927-28. In ordnance dept. of U.S. Army since 1897; served as chief ordnance officer Southern, Philippines and Western depts., 2d Corps Area, etc.; chief of nitrate div., World War, in charge government's work in fixation of nitrogen, including Muscle Shoals; toured Europe, 1919, to investigate status of nitrogen fixation; apptd. chief of tech. staff, Ordnance Office, 1921. Mem. Army Ordnance Assn., Loyal Legion. Episcopalian. Club: Chevy Chase. Home: 2405 Waterside Drive N.W. Address: care Adjutant: General, U.S. Army, Washington. Died Sept. 24, 1945.

JUDAH, NOBLE BRANDON lawyer; b. Chicago, Ill., Apr. 23, 1884; s. Noble Brandon and Kate (Hutchinson) J.; grad. Chicago Manual Training Sch., 1900; A.B., Brown U., 1904, LL.D., 1929; law study, Northwestern U., 1907; m. Dorothy Patterson, May 12, 1917 (divorced, 1933); twin daughters-Katharine Patterson, Ann Patterson (adopted). Admitted to Ill. bar, 1907, and began practice at Chicago with Judah, Willard, Wolf & Reichmann; mem. Judah, Reichmann, Trumbull, Cox & Stern; dir. Chicago Title & Trust Co. Mem. 1st Ill. F.A., I.N.G., 1915-17, lt., later capt., in service on Mexican border, 1916; served as capt., maj. and lt. col., F.A., U.S.A., and as asst. chief of staff 42d Div., World War; took part in Champagne offensive, 2d Battle of the Marne, St. Mihiel offensive and Meuse-Argonne offensive; col., F.A., O.R.C. Mem. Ill. Ho. of Rep., 1911-12; ambassador to Cuba, 1927-29. Trustee Brown U. Decorated D.S.M. (U.S.); Croix de Guerre with Palm and Legion of Honor (France). Republican. Home: Chicago, Ill. Died Feb. 26, 1938.

JUDD, JOHN WALTUS lawyer; b. Sumner Co., Tenn., Sept. 6, 1839; s. Rev. John Waltus and Lydia (Stark) J.; ed. pub. schs. and acads.; read law in office of Judge Joseph C. Stark, Springfield, Tenn.; m. Mrs. Lee Miller, of Springfield, May, 1870; 2d, Eliza H. Bayless, of Springfield, Jan., 1881. Enlisted, 1861, in Co. C, 49th Tenn. Inf., and taken prisoner with regt. at fall of Ft. Donelson, Feb. 16, 1862; exchanged Sept., 1862, and volunteered for 3 yrs. or during the war; transferred to 9th Tenn. Cav., spring of 1863, and was with Morgan on his raid into Ohio; was in battles of Chickamauga and Missionary Ridge, and Wytheville, Va.; severely wounded at Mt. Sterling, Ky., June 9, 1864; again captured and confined at Camp Chase, O., until near close of war. Practiced with Judge Joseph C. Stark until 1878 and with Hon. Lewis T. Cobbs, 1886-88; asso. justice Supreme Ct. of Utah, by apptmt. of President Cleveland, 1888-89, resigned; formed law partnership with Judge Jabez B. Sutherland, 1889; U.S. dist. atty. Dist. of Utah, 1893-98; located at Nashville, Tenn., 1898; apptd. asst. counsel L.&N.R.R. for Tenn., 1899; retired from active practice Jan., 1907; prof. law, Vanderbilt U. Law Sch. in Porto Rico 8 mos., 1910-11, straightening out pub. franchises and pub. utilities at request of Sec. of War; Democrat. Methodist. Mem. Tenn. State Bar Assn. (pres., 1886-87), Ala. State Bar Assn. (hon.), Phi Delta Phi. Mason (K.T., Shriner). Home: Gallatin, Tennessee.

JUDSON, CLAY lawyer; b. Lexington, Ky., Feb. 6, 1892; s. William Voorhees and Alice (Clay) J.; student Milwaukee Acad., 1905-09; A.B. cum laude, Harvard Coll., 1914; J.D. cum laude, U. of Chicago Law Sch., 1917; student U. of Paris, Faculté de Droit, 1919; m. Sylvia Van Doren Shaw, Sept. 3, 1921; children-Alice (Mrs. Edward L. Ryerson,III), Clay, Jr. Admitted to Ill. bar, 1917; instr. U. of Chicago Law Sch., 1919-20; asso. Winston Strawn & Shaw, Chicago, 1920-24; mem. firm Elting & Judson, Chgo., 1924-28; mem. Wilson & McIlvaine, Chgo., 1928-. Served as capt., inf., World War I. Mem. Price Adjustment Bd., Chgo. Ordnance Dist., World War II. Recipient War Dept. award for meritorious civilian service, 1945. Trustee United Charities Chgo., 1935-52 (chmn. legal and com.); mem. exec. com. Chicago Council Fgn. Relations, 1928-38, pres. 1928-29; trustee Francis Parker Sch., 1934-53, pres. 1938-49, chmn. 1945-53; mem. bd. governors Internat. House, 1932-48, pres., 1936-39; bd. dirs. America First Com., 1940-41; hon. pres. bd. trustees Chicago Zool. Soc. Mem. Chicago Bar Assn. (bd. mgrs. 1936-38), Ill. and Am. bar assns., Law and Legal Club of Chicago, Order of Coif. Pres. Harvard Club of Chicago, 1936-37; mem. Harvard Fund Council, 1939-44; mem. bd. dirs. Harvard Alumni Association, 1948-51. Member Society of Friends. Clubs: Commercial, Chicago, University, Tavern, Attic, Literary and Wayfarers (Chicago); Onwentsia (Lake Forest, Ill.). Author: Validity of Transactions of the Board of Trade, Illinois Law Review, 1925; The Renegotiation of Government War Contracts, Law Review of U. of Chicago, Jan. 1943. Home: 1230 Green Bay Rd., Lake Forest, Ill. Office: 120 W. Adams St., Chgo. Died Nov. 28, 1960; buried Graceland Cemetery, Chgo.

JUDSON, WILLIAM VOORHEES col. Corps Engrs. U.S.A.; b. Indianapolis, Ind., Feb. 16, 1865; s. Charles E. and Abby (Voorhees) J.; ed. Harvard, 1882-84, M.A., 1911; grad. U.S. Mil. Acad., 1888, U.S. Engr. Sch. of Application, 1891; m. Alice Carneal Clay, Apr. 21, 1891. Additional 2d lt. Engr. Corps, June 11, 1888; 2d lt., July 23, 1888; 1st lt., May 18, 1893; capt., July 5, 1898; maj., Mar. 2, 1906; lt. col., Mar. 2, 1912; col., May 15, 1917; brig. gen. N.A., 1917-19. Recorder board of engineers U.S.A.; mem. U.S. bd. of engrs. for rivers and harbors; harbor improvements at Galveston, etc.; river improvements, Miss. River, etc.; instr. mil. engring., U.S. Engr. Sch.; asst. to chief of engrs.; mil. attaché with Russian Army during Russo-Japanese War; in charge of harbor improvements and light house constrn. on Lake Michigan; engr. commr. of D.C.; on duty with Panama Canal Commn.; in charge of river and harbor improvements, Chicago and vicinity. With Root mission to Russia, 1917; detached therefrom and remained in Russia as mil. attaché and chief of Am. Mil. Mission to Russia until spring 1918. Comd. 38th Div., Camp Shelby, Miss., until Aug. 1918; thereafter until after Armistice comd. Port of Embarkation, New York; div. engr., Northwestern Div. Awarded D.S.M. Address: Chicago, Ill. Died Mar. 29, 1923.

JUIN, ALPHONSE HENRI French Army Officer; b. Bone, Algeria, Dec. 16, 1888; ed. Algerian high sch.; grad. St. Cyr Mil. Acad., France, 1911; m. Cecile Bonnefoy; 2 son, Pierre, Michel. Served as lt., Moroccan Div., Western Front, World War I; wounded in right arm making it useless; served in North Africa, after the war; command 15th Motorized Div., French Army, in Belgium, World War II; comdr. French Expeditionery Force in Italy, 1943-44; chief of staff Nat. Def., 1944-47; resident gen. of Morocco, 1947-51; pres. of com. of Joint Chiefs of Staff, and insp. gen. French Armed Forces, 1951-5 Allied Land Forces, Central Europe, 1953-. Marshall of France, 1952. Home: 26 Ave. Kleber, Paris 16e. Office: 138 Rue de Greuelle, Paris 7e, France. Died Jan. 27, 1967.

JUNKERSFELD, PETER engineer; b. Champaign County, Ill., Oct. 17, 1869; s. Peter J. and Josephine (Schmitz) J.; B.S., U. of Ill., 1895, E.E., 1907; m. Anna Boyle, June 19, 1901; children-Florence Rita, Josephine. In charge engring. dept. Chicago Edison Co. and its successor, Commonwealth Edison Co., 1895-1909, asst. to v.p. same, 1909-17; engring. mgr. Stone & Webster, Boston, 1919-22; mem. firm McClellan & Junkersfeld, Inc., engrs. Commd. maj. engrs., U.S.R., Feb. 23, 1917; called to active service June 7, 1917, as supervising officer cantonment and other war constrn., hdqrs., Washington, D.C.; lt. col. Feb. 1918; col., Mar. 1918; hon. discharged, Mar. 4, 1919. Awarded D.S.M., Aug. 1919. Pres. Assn. Edison Illuminating Cos., 1916-17. Home: Scarsdale, N.Y. Died Mar. 18, 1930.

JUNKIN, FRANCIS THOMAS ANDERSON lawyer; b. Falling Spring, Va., Feb. 3, 1864; s. William Finney (D.D.) and Anna Aylett (Anderson) J.; A.B., Kenyon, 1884, A.M., 1890; LL.B., Columbia, 1887; LL.D., Kenyon, 1913, Washington and Lee, 1913; m. Mrs. Emily Sprague (Hutchinson) Crane, Apr. 30, 1913. Admitted to N.Y. bar, 1887; practiced, N.Y. City, 1887-98; gen. atty. A.,T.&S.F. Ry. System, 1898-1915 (retired). Identified with reorganization of many large ry. systems, 1893-97, notably the N.P. Ry., Erie Ry., Central Ry. of Ga., Ore. Ry. & Nav. Co., U.P. Ry., Chicago & N.P. Ry., etc. Lt. col. U.S.A. and mem. Bd. Contract Adjustment P.S. and T. Div., Gen. Staff, 1919-. Trustee Kenyon Coll., Western Theol. Sem. Democrat. Vestryman and sr. warden Trinity P.E. Ch., Chicago. Address: New York, N.Y. Died May 6, 1928.

KABRICH, WILLIAM CAMILLUS army officer; b. Pocahontas, Va., Sept. 19, 1895; s. William Sisiastel and Sarah Isolena (Wilburn) K.; B.S., Va. Poly. Inst., Blackburg, Va., 1917; grad. Coast Arty. Sch., 1925, Chem. Warfare Sch., 1930; S.M., Mass. Inst. of Tech., 1933; m. Beulah B. Hinkle, May 1, 1920. Commd. 2d lt., Coast Arty. Corps., U.S. Army, Aug. 15, 1917, and advanced through the grades to brig. gen., Dec. 4, 1942; transferred to Chem. Warfare Service, 1929; chief tech. div., Office of Chief, C.W.S., and comdg. gen. of C.W.S. Tech. Command, Edgewood Arsenal, Med., 1942-45; in charge of design of plants mfg. chem. agents; supervised development of smoke screen devices for large areas. Chmn. of tech. com. for control of research chem. warfare material for C.W.S. and Nat. Defense Research Com. Supervised development of chemical warfare weapons, munitions, agents and protective equipment now comdg. gen. Pine Bluff Arsenal, Arsenal, Ark. Decorated Victory, Am. Defense Service. Am. Theater of Operations medals. European Theater of Operations, African and Mediterranean Medal, Legion of Merit, Army Commendation Citation, Honorable Commander, Order of the British Empire, World War II Victory Medal, Mem. Am. Chem. Soc., Am. Inst. of Chem. Engrs., Alpha Chi Sigma. Clubs: Army and Navy, Army and Navy Country (Washington, D.C.). Home: 300 N. Mountain Av., Montclair, N.J. Died Jan. 27, 1947.

KAEMMERLING, GUSTAV naval officer; b. Cincinnati, O., May 15, 1858; grad. U.S. Naval Acad., 1881. Promoted asst. engr., July 1, 1883; passed asst. engr., Aug.10, 1893; transferred to the Line as lt., Mar. 3, 1899; promoted through grades to rear adm., July 1, 1919. Served on Olympia, Spanish-Am. War, 1898; insp. engring. material, Mass. Dist., 1905-08; duty Bur. Steam Engring., Navy Dept., 1908-09; insp. engring. material, Chester Dist., 1909-12; with Bur. Steam Engring., 1912-15; assigned as insp. machinery, Camden, N.J., Jan. 5, 1915; sr. insp. for Navy Dept., at New York Shipbuilding Corp., Camden, N.J., during the war; sr. insp. of Engring. Dept. at Cramp's Shipyard, Phila., 1920-22; retired, May 15, 1922. Died Aug. 30, 1934.

KAISER, LOUIS ANTHONY, naval officer; b. at Kirkwood, Ill., Apr. 1, 1870; grad. U.S. Naval Acad., 1889. Promoted ensign, July 1, 1891, lt. jr. grade, Dec. 25, 1898; lt., Mar. 3, 1899; lt. comdr., July 1, 1905; comdr., Sept. 22, 1910; capt., Aug. 29, 1916. Served on Concord, Spanish-Am. War, 1898; with Bur. of Equipment, Navy Dept., 1904-6; sr. engr. on the Washington, 1906-8; navigator Colorado, 1908-9; with Bur. of Equipment, 1909-10, Bur. Steam Engring., 1910-12; comd. Montgomery, 1912-14, Boston Navy Yard, 1914-15; at Naval War Coll., 1915-16; comd. New Jersey, June 26, 1916-Aug. 21, 1917. Home: Monmouth, Ill. Address: Navy Dept., Washington DC

KALB, JOHANN army officer; b. Huttendorf, Bavaria, June 29, 1721; s. Johan Leonhard and Margarethe Seitz (Putz) K.; m. Anna Van Robais, Apr. 10, 1764. Known as "Baron de Kalb"; served as lt. in Count Loewendal's Regt., French Inf. under name "Jean de Kalb", capt., adj. officer of detail, 1747; commd. maj. during Seven Years' War, 1756; secret agt. of French Govt. in Am., 1768; returned to Am. to enter patriot cause, 1776; maj. gen. Continental Army, served with Washington at Valley Forge; joined Gen. Gates nr. Camden, S.C., 1780, their combined forces attacked British under Cornwallis and Rawdon, Aug. 1780. Died from wound received in battle at Camden, Aug. 19, 1780.

KALBFUS, EDWARD CLIFFORD naval officer; b. Mauch Chunk, Pa., Nov. 24, 1877; s. Daniel and Mary Electra (Jones) K.; grad. U.S. Naval Acad., 1899; m. Syria Florence Brown, May 13, 1905. Commd. ensign, USN, 1901; promoted through grades to rear adm., 1931; permanent rank of admiral on retired list, 1942. Participated in Spanish-Am. War, 1898, Philippine Insurrection, 1900-01, Cuba Pacification, 1905, Mexican occupation, 1914; capt. U.S.S. Pocahontas, World War I, later capt. U.S.S. Iowa, Trenton, California; mem. staff Naval War Coll., 1927-29; chief of staff Battleship Divs., Battle Fleet, 1930; dir. War Plans, Navy Dept., 1931; comdr. Destroyers, Battle Force, U.S. Fleet, 1931-34; pres. Naval War Coll., 1934-36, 39-42; vice adm., comdr. Battleships, Battle Force, U.S. Fleet, 1937; adm., comdr. Battle Force, U.S. Fleet, 1938-39, mem. Gen. Bd., 1942-45. Dir. of Naval History, 1944-45; mem. Am. Battle Monuments Commn., 1947-52. Mem. Military Order of Carabao. Episcopalian. Clubs: Army and Navy (Washington); hon. mem. Cruising Club of America. Home: Restmere, Newport, R.I. Died Sept. 6, 1954; buried Arlington Nat. Cemetery.

KALKSTEIN, MENNASCH, physician; b. Bklyn., Aug. 24, 1907; s. Joseph and Jennie (Weinberg) K.; M.D., St. Andrews (Scotland) U., 1933; m. Claire Weininger, Dec. 28, 1940; children—Janet (Mrs. Paul L. Plansky), Stephen W., Helen L. Postgrad. instr. Columbia, 1938-40; intern Harlem Hosp., N.Y.C., 1933-34, resident in pneumonia service, 1934; intern, also resident internal medicine Bellevue Hosp., N.Y.C., 1934-37, admitting physician, 1937-38, later asso. vis. physician; phys. pneumonia N.Y.C. Dept. Health, 1938-40, clin. physician Tb, 1938-42; mem. cardiology staff L.I. Jewish Hosp. Asst. clin. prof. medicine N.Y. U. Served to lt. col. M.C., AUS. Diplomate Am. Bd. Internal Medicine. Fellow Am. Heart Assn., A.C.P.; mem. A.M.A., Am. Thoracic Soc., Am. Fedn. Clin. Research, Home: New York City NY Died Mar. 12, 1971; buried Beth-El Cemetery, Westwood NJ

KAMAIAKAN Indian chief; b. at what is now Lewiston, Ida., circa 1800; s. Jayayaheha and Kaenoxnith. Chief, Yakima Indians; helped obtain establishment of mission in Yakima Valley, 1847; influenced other tribes not to war with whites; failed in efforts to prevent cessions of land in Treaty of 1855, aroused most of Northwest tribes to fight, defeated, 1858 (his defeat brought outbreak to end). Died circa 1880.

KANE, ELISHA KENT naval officer, surgeon, explorer; b. Phila., Feb. 3, 1820; s. John Kintzing and Jane (Leiper) K; attended U. Va., 1838-39; grad. Med. Dept., U. Pa., 1842. Asst. surgeon U.S. Navy in ship Brandywine, 1843; served as surgeon in China, 1844, African coast, 1846, Mexico, 1848, in Mediterranean, 1849; attached to U.S. Coast Survey, served as surgeon in Advance; sailed for Arctic in Grinnell Expdn. sent by U.S. Govt. in search of English expdn. under Sir Franklin (which had been lost since 1845), 1850-51; sailed for No. seas in command 2d Grinnell Expdn. (with rank of passed asst. surgeon), 1853-55; abandoned ship, hiked to Upernauik, May 1855, arrived, Aug. 6, 1855, returned home, Oct. 1855; brig. entered unknown waters now called Kane Basin. Author: The U.S. Grinnell Expedition in Search of Sir John Franklin, 1853; Arctic Explorations: The Second Grinnell Expedition in Search of Sir John Franklin in the Years 1853, 1854, 1855, published 1856. Died Havana, Cuba, Feb. 16, 1857.

KANE, HOWARD FRANCIS obstetrician; b. Machias, Me., May 14, 1887; s. George Wesley and Cora (Leighton) K.; grad. Worcester Acad., 1905; A.B., Bowdoin, 1909; M.D., George Washington U., 1912; m. Clara Bailey, Jan. 28, 1920. Mem. house staff successively of George Washington, Children's Columbia hosps., Washington, D.C., and New York Lying-In Hosp., 1912-16; mem. teaching staff George Washington U. Sch. of Medicine since 1916, prof. of obstetrics and gynecology since 1932; mem. attending staffs George Washington, Gallinger, Garfield hosps. Served as 1st lt. and capt. M.C., U.S. Army, with B.E.F., 1917-19; maj. Med. Res. Corps, U.S. Army, 1919-28; lieut. comdr. U.S. Naval Res., 1937-40; comdr. since 1940; consulting obstetrician United States Naval Hosp., San Diego, Calif., 1943-44; retired. Decorated Military Cross (British), 1917. Diplomate American Bd. Obstetrics. Fellow Am. Coll. Surgeons, Internat. coll. of Anesthetists, fellow Am. Assn. Obstetricians, Gynecologists and Abdominal Surgeons; mem. A.A.A.S., Am. Legion, Mil. Order of Foreign Wars. Zeta Psi, Alpha Kappa Kappa, Sigma Xi. Republican. Conglist. Mason (K.T., Shriner). Clubs: Cosmos, Metropolitan (Washington, D.C.); Gibson Island (Md.); Columbia Country (Md.); Chevy Chase Club (Md.). Contbr. many articles to med. jours. Home: Machias, Maine. Died July 21, 1946.

KANE, JAMES JOHNSON chaplain U.S.N.; b. Ottawa, Ont., Oct. 18, 1837; s. Capt. Clement (Royal Navy) and Barbara (Price) K.; student Chambale Coll. 1 yr. and Montreal Coll. 1 yr.; Stonyhurst Coll., Eng., 1847-51; studied medicine in Toronto (A.M.). On account of ill health went to sea, 1853, and became comdr.of coastwise vessel; entered U.S.N. as vol. officer, 1861; comd. a dispatch gunboat, under Admiral Farragut, 1862, who promoted him for spl. services; served under Admiral Porter, 1864-65; participated in both battles of Ft. Fisher; at close of war declined appmt. in regular navy, and resigned to enter U. of Lewisburgh (now Bucknell), Pa., grad. theol. dept. same, 1867; student Harvard Law Sch., 1869-70; chaplain U.S.N., 1868; served in various vessels and stas.; retired with rank of capt., 1896; rear admiral retired, Dec. 1906, for services during Civil War. Was chaplain pro tem. of U.S. Senate at various times. Mason. Died Mar. 10, 1921.

KANE, PAUL V. army officer; b. Worcester, Mass., July 19, 1892; s. John and Johanna (Power) K.; student Mass. State Coll., 1911-12; B.S., U.S. Mil. Acad. 1916; grad. Army War Coll., 1937; m. Lillian Mary Reilly, Dec. 26, 1921; children-William Spooner, Walter Reilly, John Power. Commd. 2d lt., U.S. Army, 1916, advanced through the grades to brig. gen., 1942; assigned to 96th Inf. Divs., 1942; left the 96th Div., 1944, was assigned to Hdqrs. III Army Corps: formerly at Camp Polk, La. under same assignment; comd. Task Force Frigid, Alaska; ret. 1949. Decorated Legion of Merit, Bronze Star, Silver Star, D.S.M. (U.S.); Legion of Honor (France); Distinguished Service Order (Gt. Britain); Croix de Guerre with palm. Club: Lions (Norman, Okla.). Home: P.O. Box 163, Forest Grove, Ore. Died July 1, 1959; buried Post Cemetery, West Point, N.Y.

KANE, THOMAS LEIPER army officer; b. Phila., Jan. 27, 1822; s. John Kintzing and Jane (Leiper) K.; m. Elizabeth Ward, Apr. 21, 1853. Admitted to the Pa. bar, 1846; clk. U.S. Dist. Ct. for Eastern dist. Pa.; U.S. commr. Eastern dist., Pa.; chmn. Pa. Central com. Free Soil Party, 1848; became friend of Brigham Young, helped end Mormon War, 1857-58; organizer regt. of woodsmen and hunters known as Bucktails, col. regt., 1861, then. lt. col.; commd. brig. gen. U.S. Volunteers, 1862; comdr. 2d brigade 2d div. XII Army Corps, at Battle of Chancellorsville; brevetted maj. gen., 1865; 1st pres. Pa. d. State Charities; mem. Am. Philos. Soc. Died Phila., Dec. 26, 1883.

KANE, WILLIAM T. clergyman, educator; b. Chicago, Ill., Oct. 20, 1880; s. Lawrence and Elizabeth (McCarthy) K.; M.A., St. Louis U., 1905; Ph.D., D.D., Colegio de Ona, Spain, 1914. Mem. faculty, Detroit Coll., 1905-06, St. Xavier Coll., Cincinnati, O., 1906-08, St. John's Coll., Belize, Brit. Honduras, 1908-10, Creighton U., Omaha, 1916-17, Loyola U., Chicago, 1919-24; prof. philosophy and edn., St. Xavier Coll., Cincinnati, 1924-27; research work, 1927-30; librarian E. M. Cudahy Memorial Library, Loyola U., 1930-46. Served as chaplain 35th Div., U.S. Army, 1918-19, World War; cited "for bravery in action." Author: For Greater Things, 1915; Life of William Stanton, 1918; An Essay Toward a History of Education, 1935; Some Principles of Education, 1938; Catholic Library Problems, 1939; The Education of Edward Cudahy, 1941; Life of Cornelius Shine, 1945; Paradise Hunters, 1946. Address: Loyola University, Chicago. Died Dec. 29, 1946.

KARAPETOFF, VLADIMIR elec. engr.; b. St. Petersburg, Russia, Jan. 8, 1876; s. Nikita Ivanovitch and Anna Joakimovna (Ivanova) K.; C.A., Inst. of Ways of Communication, St. Petersburg, 1897, M.M.E., 1902; Technische Hochschule, Darmstadt, Germany, 1899-1900; hon. Mus. Doc., N.Y. College of Music, 1934; hon. D.Sc., Poly. Inst. Brooklyn, 1937; m. Frances Lulu Gillmor, Aug. 2, 1904 (died 1931); m. 2d, Rosalie Margaret Cobb, Nov. 25, 1936. Consulting engr. for Russian Govt., and instr. elec. engring. and hydraulics in 3 colls., St. Petersburg, 1897-1902; spl. engring. apprentice with Westinghouse Electric & Mfg. Co., E. Pittsburgh, Pa., 1903-04; prof. elec. engring. Cornell U., 1904-39; prof. emeritus since 1939; visiting prof. for grad. students, Poly. Inst. of Brooklyn, 1930-32; lecturer Stevens Inst. Technology, 1939-40. Cons. engr. and patent expert to various enterprises; with J. G. White & Co., Inc., engineers and contractors, 1911-12. Inventor and patentee of several elec. devices and of five-stringed cello. Awarded Montefiore prize, 1923, and Elliot Cresson gold medal, Franklin Inst., 1927, both for kinematic models of elec. machinery. Lt. comdr. U.S. Naval Res. since 1933, assigned to engring duties for spl. service. Mem. bd. trustees, Ithaca Coll., 1932-39, chmn., 1933-36. Mem. U.S. Naval Inst., U.S. Naval Reserve Officers' Assn., International Jury Awards, Panama P.I. Expn., San Francisco, 1915; mem. advisory bd. U.S. Naval Acad., 1916. Christian. Fellow Am. Inst. E.E., A.A.A.S., Am. Physical Soc.; mem. Am. Assn. Univ. Profs. (charter), Am. Math. Soc., Math. Assn. America, Franklin Inst., Sigma Xi.; hon. mem. Eta Kappa Nu, Tau Beta Pi, Phi Mu Alpha (Sinfonia), Theta Xi. Author: Ueber Mehrphasige Stromsysteme, 1900; Resistance of Ships to Propulsion (in Russian), 1st part 1902, 2d part 1911; Experimental Electrical Engineering, 2 vols., 1908; The Electric Circuit, 1910; The Magnetic Circuit, 1911; Engineering Applications of Higher Mathematics, part I, 1911; parts II to V, 1916; Rhythmical Tales of Stormy Years (poems), 1937; also numerous articles in engring. mags. and trans. Research editor of the Electrical World, 1917-26. Gave several series of public piano recitals; developed five-stringed cello and plays it in public; lecturer on engring., and on moral and psychol. topics. Chmn. com. on physics of Conf. on Electrical Insulation, National Research Council, 1928-35, chmn. com. on monographs, 1935-38. Consultant to U.S. Bd. of Economic Warfare, 1942-43; consultant to Bethlehem Steel Co. since 1944. Home: 39 Claremont Av., Apt. 84, New York 27. Died Jan. 11, 1948; buried in East Lawn Cemetery, Ithaca, N.Y.

KARIG, WALTER ret. naval officer, author; b. N.Y.C.; ed. pvt. and pub. schs. of N.Y. and N.J.; art edn., N.Y. Sch. Fine and Applied Art, 1917; military scholarship student, Julian Academy, 1919; married to Eleanor Keating Freye, 1920; children-Patricia Mary (Mrs. Richard L. Ruffner, Junior), Keating Victoria (Mrs. Francis A. Carrier). Began as sports writer, Norfolk Virginian-Pilot, 1919; editor Elizabeth City (N.C.) Herald, 1920; editorial writer and artist Newark Evening News, 1921-42; chief editorial writer, 1933, chief of Washington bur. since 1934; mem. editorial bd. Liberty mag., 1938-42; U.S. Columnist London Star and Allied British newspapers, 1939-42; teacher journalism, Knights of Columbus Sch. for U.S. Vets., Newark, 1922. Served in French and Polish Armies; advanced from pvt. inf. to capt. motor transport, 1918-19; lt. comdr. U.S.N.R., 1942, comdr., 1944, capt., 1946; spl. asst. to Chief of Naval Operations, 1947-50; special deputy chief of information 1950; special assistant to the Secretary of the Navy, 1952-54; 1st v.p., del. to 1st Pan-American Press Congress, Mexico. Member bd. trustees, St. Agnes Episcopal Sch., Alexandria, Va. Mem. Military Order of Carabao, U.S. Naval Institute Mem. U.S. Mission to Philippines, 1935. Award Haller D.S.C. (Poland), Legion of Merit awarded by the United States Navy. Clubs: Nat. Press (bd. of govs. 1941-44), Overseas Writers, Gridiron, Cosmos. Author: (also illustrator): The Magic Acorn (with wife), 1928; Asia's Good Neighbor, pub. 1937; War in the Atomic Age, published 1946; The Fortunate Islands, History of Micronesia, 1948; novels, The Pig in the Parlor (with wife and daus.), 1949; Caroline Hicks, 1951: Battle Submerged (with Adm. Harley Cope), 1951; Neely, 1953; Don't Tread On Me, 1954; co-author "Battle Report," vol. I, 1944, vol. II, 1945: vol. III, 1945; vol. IV, 1948, vol. V, 1949; vol. VI, 1951; also author of four series of popular juvenile mystery stories. Home: Seminary Hill Post Office. Alexandira, Va. Died Sept. 30, 1956; buried Arlington Nat. Cemetery.

KARRER, ENOCH research physicist; b. Rich Hill, Mo., May 23, 1887; s. Frank Xavier and Theresa (Braun) K.; A.B., U. of Wash., 1911, A.M., 1912; Ph.D., Johns Hopkins U., 1914; m. Ethel Walther, Aug. 2, 1919; children-Enoch, Aurora, Ethelds, Rathe. Research asst. with United Gas provement Co., Phila., 1914-18; chief searchlight sect. U.S. Bur. of Standards, 1919-21; in General Electric Co.'s research lab., Cleveland, O., 1921-26; research associate Cushing Laboratory for Exptl. Medicine, Western Reserve U., Cleveland, 1923-31; research physicist B. F. Goodrich Co., 1926-31; cons. research engr., 1931-36; economics and govt. research, Washington, D.C., 1934-35; research biophysics Smithsonian Instn., 1935; tech. consultant Am. Instrument Co., 1936; sr. physicist, U.S. Dept. of Agr. since 1936, at Southern Regional Research Lab., New Orleans, since 1941. Served as pvt. 1st sergt. Med. Corps, 345th Engrs., later master engr., 447th Engrs., U.S. Army, World War; now capt. Engrs., O.R.C. Awarded James A. Moore prize in physics, Seattle, 1913, Longstreet medal (co-winner), Franklin Inst., 1918. Mem. Washington Philos. Soc., Sigma Xi, Phi Beta Kappa, and several tech. socs. Author 70 publications in sci. field. Holder of 6 patents. Contbr. of papers to tech. jours. Home: 7003 Broad Place. New Orleans 18. Died Mar. 27, 1946; buried in Garden of Memories, New Orleans.

KARSNER, HOWARD, pathologist; b. Phila., Pa., Jan. 6, 1879; s. Charles W. (M.D.) and Martha M. (Wright) K.; B.S., Central High Sch., Phila., 1897; Phila. Sch. of Pedagogy, 1899; M.D., Univ. of Pa., 1903; LL.D., Western Reserve University, Cleveland, 1949; m. Audrey W. Stanwood, Dec. 11, 1912 (died 1944); m. 2d Daisy Stanley-Brown, Mar. 12, 1946 (died 1949); married 3d Jessie Spencer Beach, July 5, 1950. Demonstrator pathology, Univ. of Pannsylvania, 1908-11; asst. prof. pathology, Harvard Med. Sch., 1911-14; prof. pathology, Western Reserve U., 1914-49; med. research adviser to Bur. Medicine and Surgry, U.S. Navy, from 1949; dir. Inst. Pathology, 1929-49; dir. Pathology, University Hosps.; div. chief of labs., City Hosp., 1914-49; cons. to Surg. Gen., U.S.A. Mem. sci. adv. bd. Armed Forces Inst. Pathology, adv. med. bd. Leonard Wood Meml. for Eradication Leprosy. Served as capt., Med. R.C., with A.E.F. in France, 1917-Feb. 11, 1918. Awarded W.W. Gerhard Medal, Phila. Path. Soc., Centennial Award, Northwestern U., 1951; Capt. Robert Dexter Conrad award, U.S. Navy, 1961. Fellow Aero. Med. Assn. (hon.), N.Y. Acad. Scis.; mem. Nat. Bd. Med. Examiners (pres. 1951-54), A.M.A., Assn. American Physicians, Am. Coll. Physicians, Am. Soc. Exptl. Pathol., Internat. Soc. Geog. Path. (vice president, Assn. Pathologists and Bacteriologists Society Exptl. Biology and Med., A.A.A.S. (v.p. Sect. N, 1931), Sigma Xi, Alpha Omega Alpha; corr. mem. various orgns. Rep. Club: Army and Navy. Author: Human Pathology, 1926, 55. Editor Year Book of Pathology, 1941-53. Contbr. tech. jours. Chmn. div. med. sciences, Nat. Research Council, 1927-28, chmn. com. on Pathology 1948-58; consultant in pathology, Army Air Forces, Army Med. Mus. and Office Scientific Research and Development, 1943-46; spl. cons. Secretary of War, 1946. Home: Washington DC Died Apr. 8, 1970; buried Beiliel Cemetery, Beiliel MD

KASTEN, WILLIAM HENRY retired army officer, insurance executive; born at Schenectady, New York, July 15, 1891; son of Charles Henry and Josephine (Smith) K.; B.S., U. of Ill., 1916; m. Ethel Lavonia Brown, July 9, 1938; 1 dau. (by former marriage), Allys Josephine (wife of Col. William E. Riggs A.A.F.). Commd. 2d lt., Cavalry, U.S.A., 1916, and advanced through grades to maj. gen.; chief of finance, 1945-49, maj. gen. U.S. Army, ret. 1949; treasurer Miltary Personnel Buying Service, Inc. (Virginia); dir. Charlesfred Corp., Inc., Am. Investment Fund, Inc.; mem. mil. adv. bd. Bank of Services and Trusts, Dallas, Am. Life Ins. Co., Birmingham; mem. organizing group Nat. Bank of Benning, Ga. Decorated D.S.M. Founder Armed Forces Relief and Benefit Assn. (sec., treas. 1941-57); Co-founder, mem. adv. bd. Officer's Benefit Assn. Mason. Home: 3417 Fulton St. N.W., Washington 20007. Died Dec. 19, 1963; buried Arlington Nat. Cemetery, Washington.

KATZENTINE, A(RTHUR) FRANK lawyer; b. Talladega, Ala., Jan. 16, 1902; s. Siegfried Zach and Elizabeth (Rayfield) K.; LL.B., Vanderbilt U., Nashville, Tenn., 1924; m. Ucola Collier, June 11, 1928. Admitted to Florida bar, 1928, practiced in Miami, 1928-; judge Municipal Ct., 1928; mayor, 1932-34; owner Radio Sta. WKAT, WKAT-FM, Muzak, Melody, Inc., Serenade, Mayan Recordings, Inc. Pres., Crime Commission of Greater Miami. Served as lt. col., U.S.A. A.F., World War II. Awarded medal for outstanding community service by U.S. Jr. Chamber of Commerce, 1935. Apptd. lt. col. staff of Gov. of Fla. and col. staff Gov. of Ky., 1934; apptd. col. staff of Gov. of Fla., 1941. Chmn. Organizational com. Inter-Am. Cultural & Trade Center. Mem. S.A.R., Sigma Nu. Democrat. Baptist. Clubs: Com. of 100 (bd. govs.), Surf, Army and Navy (Wash., D.C.); La Gorce Country. Home: 4745 Pine Tree Drive. Office Du Pont Bldg., Miami, Fla. Died Mar. 27, 1960.

KAUFMANN, GORDON BERNIE architect; b. London, Eng., Mar. 19, 1888; s. Gustav and Matilde (Cook) K.; ed. Whitgift Sch., Croyden, 1899-1904, Polytechnic, London, 1904-08; m. Eva Macfarlane, May 1911; children-Kenneth Macfarlane, Cecil St. Denis (Mrs. Thomas E. Dawson); m. 2d, Elsie Bryant Jenvey, Aug. 4, 1933. Came to U.S., 1914, naturalized, 1934. Partner Johnson, Kaufmann & Coate, architects, Los Angeles, 1920-24; practiced under own name 1924-42; Sr. partner Kaufmann, Lippincott and Eggers, 1945-47; currently in partnership with J. E. Stanton; director of the Union Bank and Trust Company. Los Angeles. Works: newspaper plant of Los Angeles Times; Santa Anita race track, L.A. Turf Club; Scripps Coll., Claremont, Calif.; Dormitories and Athenaeum,

California Institute of Technology; Vultee Aircraft, Inc.; Consolidated Steel Company; Basic Magnesium, Inc. U.S. Army Chemical Warfare Service, Lt. Col., Col., 1942-45. Awarded Legion of Merit. Awarded Gold medal French Exposition, 1937. President Los Angeles Area Boy Scouts of America. Fellow American Institute Architects. Episcopalian. Club: California (Los Angeles); Bohemian (San Francisco); Cosmos (Washington, D.C.). Address: 627 S. Carondelet St., Los Angeles, Calif. Died Mar. 1, 1949.

KAUTZ, ALBERT rear admiral U.S.N., retired Jan. 29, 1901; b. Georgetown, O., Jan. 29, 1839; s. George and Dortha (Lewing) K.; entered navy, acting midshipman, Sept. 25, 1854; grad. Naval Acad., and apptd. midshipman, June 11, 1858; promoted passed midshipman, Jan. 19, 1861; master, Feb. 23, 1861; lt., April 21, 1861; prisoner of war in N.C. and Richmond, Va., June-Oct. 1861; served as Farragut's flag lt. on board Hartford at capture of New Orleans, April 1862; personally hauled down the "Lone Star" flag from the city ball (which Mayor Monroe refused to strike), and hoisted "Stars and Stripes" on custom-house; served on Hartford during engagements with the Vicksburg batteries, June and July, 1862; afterwards on various stations and duties; promoted lt. comdr., 1865, comdr., 1872, capt., 1885, commodore, 1897, rear admiral, Oct. 1898; placed in command of Pacific sta.-flagship Philadelphia; was in command at Apia, Samoa, March and April 1899, during the troubles of the native chiefs, and was commended for his conduct on that occasion. Died 1907.

KAUTZ, AUGUST VALENTINE army officer; b. Ispringen, Baden, Germany, Jan. 5, 1828; s. George and Doratha (Lalwing) K.; grad. U.S. Mil. Acad., 1852; m. Charlotte Tod, Sept. 1865; m. 2d, Fannie Markbreit, 1872; 3 children. Enlisted in 1st Ohio Inf., Mexican War, 1846; assigned to 4th Inf. at Vancouver Barracks, Wash., 1852; commd. 1st lt., 1855; commissioned capt. 6th Cavalry, U.S. Army in Civil War, 1861, participated in Peninsular War, 1862; promoted to col., 1862; chief of cavalry XXIII Army Corps; commd. brig. gen. U.S. Volunteers, 1864; chief of cavalry Dept. of Va.; brevetted maj. U.S. Army, 1863, lt. col. and col., 1864, brig. gen. and maj. gen., 1864; brevetted maj. gen. U.S. Volunteers; comdr. 1st Div. XXV Corps (Negro), 1865, entered Richmond; lt. col. 34th Inf., 1866; col., 1874, placed Mescalero Apaches back on their reservation; promoted brig. gen., 1891; commanded Dept. of Columbia, 1891-92. Author: The Company Clerk, 1863; Customs of Service for Non-Commissioned Officers and Soldiers, 1864; Customs of Service for Officers, 1866. Died Sept. 4, 1895.

KAVANAGH, MARCUS A. judge b. Des Moines, Ia., Sept. 3, 1859; s. Marcus and Mary (Hughes) K.; grad. Niagara U., 1876; LL.B., State U. of Ia., 1878; LL.D., Univ. of Notre Dame, Niagara Univ., Loyola Univ.; m. Mrs. Herminie Templeton, d. Maj. George McGibney, of Longford, Ireland, Aug. 19, 1905 (died 1923); m. 2d, Jeanne Velma Latour, Nov. 8, 1934. Admitted to Ia. bar, 1878; elected city atty. of Des Moines, 1880; reelected 1882; elected dist. judge of the 9th Jud. Dist. of Ia., 1885, but resigned in 1889; moved to Chicago, 1889, becoming a partner with John Gibbons, under firm name of Gibbons & Kavanagh, later Gibbons, Kavanagh & O'Donnell, and after the election of Judge Gibbons to the bench, title changed to Kavanagh & O'Donnell and so continued until 1888; judge Superior Court of Cook Co., 1898-1935. Was maj. and lt. col. 3d Inf. Ia. N.G.; elected lt. col. 7th Regt., I.N.G., 1894, col., 1896; served in Spanish-Am. War as Col. 7th Ill. Vol. Inf. Republican. Known generally for work in law reform; apptd., 1923, with Charles S. Whitman of New York and Wade H. Ellis, of Washington, to make study of European legal procedure and report upon same. Author: The Criminal and His Allies, 1928; You Be the Judge. Home: Ocean Grove, N.J. Died Dec. 31, 1937.

KAVANAUGH, JOHN MICHAEL, fgn. service officer; b. Clay, La., Mar. 1, 1918; s. Joseph Michael and Mary Ruth (Kendall) K.; B.A., La. Polytech. Inst., 1937; M.A., La. State U., 1937; m. Virginia Ware Gaines, Dec. 30, 1942; children—Michael G., Kathleen V. Asst. prof. English, La. Polytech. Inst., 1937-42; joined U.S. fgn. service, 1946, vice consul, Munich, Germany, 1946-49, Halifax, Can., 1949-50; consul, St. John, N.B., Can., 1950-52; officer charge Australian and New Zealand affairs State Dept., 1952-58; polit. officer Am. embassy, The Hague, Netherlands, from 1958. Served to maj. USAAF, 1942-46; ETO. Decorated Air medal with 6 battle stars. Mem. Sigma Tau Delta, Kappa Delta Phi. Home: Clay LADeceased.

KEALY, PHILIP JOSEPH civil engr., ex-pres. Kansas City Rys. Co.; b. Bloomington, Ill., July 2, 1884; s. Patrick J. and Mary Agnes (Ryan) K.; Lewis Inst., Chicago; U. of Ill., 1905-09; m. Josephine Dynan, 1909 (dec.); 1 dau., Coaina A.; m. 2d, Josephine Helen Crowley, 1917 (dec); 1 son, J. Gerald; m. 3d, Joyce M. Hutchins, 1925; children - Hutchins D., Philip H. With Bd. Supervising Engrs., Chicago, 1909-10, Bion J. Arnold, Chicago, 1910-13, receivers of Traction Co., Kansas City, Mo., 1913-15; pres. Kansas City Rys., 1915-21; City mem. Board of Supervising Engrs. Chicago Traction, 1934-42, chmn. since 1942; dir. Lewis Sch. of Aeronautics, Cath. Youth Orgn. Lt. col. 3d Mo. Infantry, 1915, col., 1916-17; col. 138th Inf., U.S. Army, 1917-18. Mem. Memorial Assn. of Kansas City. Mem. Am. Soc. Civil Engrs., Am. Legion, Delta Upsilon. K.C. Club: Chicago Athletic Assn. Home: 37 Indian Hill Rd., Winnetka, Ill. Office: 231 S. LaSalle St., Chicago, Ill. Died Aug. 26, 1944.

KEAN, JEFFERSON RANDOLPH ret. army officer; b. Lynchburg, Va., June 27, 1860; s. Robert G. H. and Jane Nicholas (Randolph) K.; g.g.s. Thomas Jefferson: student Episcopal High Sch., Bellevue H.S.; M.D., U. Va., 1883; studied New York Polyclinic; m. Louise Hurlbut Young, Oct. 10, 1894 (dec. 1915): children-Martha Jefferson, Robert Hill; m. 2d, Cornelia Knox, Mar. 24, 1919. Commd. lt. asst. surgeon, 1884; promoted through grades to col., 1914; retired, 1924; brig. gen. (temp.), 1918-19. Served on Western frontier 8 yrs.; took part in winter campaign of 1890-91 against the Sioux; then stationed 5 yrs. in Fla.; in Spanish War assigned to duty with 7th Army Corps; served in Cuba, 1898-1902, as dept. chief surgeon under Gen. Fitzhugh Lee and supt. dept. of charities under Gen. Wood; on return to U.S. in 1902 made asst. to surgeon-gen.; adviser dept. of sanitation for Provisional Govt. of Cuba, 1906-09; in charge sanitary div. surgeon gen.'s office, 1909-13. Author of laws organizing sanitary depts. of Cuba and P.R. and first Res. Corps, U.S. Army. Dir. gen. and organizer dept. of mil. relief of A.R.C., 1916-17; chief U.S. Ambulance Service with French Army, 1917-18; then deputy chief surgeon, AEF to end of war. Apptd. by President, mem. U.S. Commn. for construction of Nat. Expansion Memorial, at St. Louis, 1934, and mem. U.S. Commn. to erect Permanent Memorial to Thomas Jefferson, 1938. Pres. Assn. Mil. Surgeons of U.S., 1914-15 (sec. and editor same, 1924-34); mem. Phi Beta Kappa. Awarded D.S.M. (U.S.); Officer Legion d'Honneur; Grand Cross Order of Merit, Carlos J. Finlay (Cuba); awarded Gorgas medal by Assn. Mil. Surgeons of U.S., 1942. Home: 2804 N St. N.W., Washington 7. Died Sept. 4, 1950; buried Monticello, nr. Charlottesville, Va.

KEARNEY, ERICK WILSON, engr.; b. Franklinton, N.C., Feb. 26, 1906; s. Isaac Henry and Ozella (Williams) K.; B.S., N.C. State U., 1928; certificate pub. health U. N.C., 1936; M. Margaret Louise Lewis, Nov. 23, 1932; children—Erick W., William Lewis, Kay (Mrs. Jerry Gilbert), City clk. Town of Franklinton, N.C., 1929; supt. water plant Town of Mt. Airy, N.C., 1929-36; asst. san. engr. State of N.C., 1936-41; gen. engr. U.S. VA, 1946-69. Served to maj. AUS, 1941-46. Registered profl. engr., N.C. Mem. Tau Beta Pi. Democrat. Baptist. Mason. Home: Jackson MS Died Sept. 18, 1969.

KEARNY, LAWRENCE naval officer; b. Perth Amboy, N.J., Nov. 30, 1789; s. Michael and Elizabeth (Lawrence) K.; m. Josephine Hall, Jan. 2, 1834, 2 children. Apptd. midshipman U.S. Navy, 1807, commd. lt., 1813; commanded schooners Caroline, Ferret, Nonsuch during War of 1812; promoted master commandant, 1825; in service against Mediterranean pirates, 1825; promoted capt., 1832; commanded East India Squadron, 1840-43; obtained promise from China that U.S. would be allowed same trading privileges with China as England and Japan; pres. bd. examiners of midshipman, 1846; commandant Norfolk Navy Yard, 1847; gen. supt. ocean mail steamships at N.Y.C., 1852; retired, 1861; promoted commodore, ret., 1867; mayor of Perth Amboy, 1848-49. Died Perth Amboy, Nov. 29, 1868.

KEARNY, PHILIP army officer; b. N.Y.C., June 1, 1814; s. Philip and Susan (Watts) K.; grad. Columbia, 1833; m. Diana Bullett, June 24, 1841; m. 2d, Agnes Maxwell, 1858; 4 children. Commd. 2d lt. 1st U.S. Dragoons, 1837; sent to France to study tactics in cavalry sch. at Saumur, 1839; served with Chausseure Afrique in Algiers, 1840; a.d.c. to Gen. Alexander Macomb (comdr.-in-chief U.S. Army), later Gen. Winfield Scott, 1840-46; lead advance to City of Mexico in Mexican War, 1846; resigned from U.S. Army, 1851; returned to France as mem. staff Gen. lforris, French Army, 1859; command of cavlary of guard under Napoleon II in Italian Wars; decorated cross Legion d'Honneur by French Emperor; commd. brig. gen. 1st N.J. brigade U.S. Volunteers in Gen. Franklin's div. Army of Potomac during Civil War; promoted maj. gen., 1862, in command of 1st div. 3d Corps. Died Chantilly, Va., Sept. 1, 1862; buried Nat. Cemetery, Arlington, Va.

KEARNY, STEPHEN WATTS army officer; b. Newark, N.J., Aug. 30, 1794; s. Philip and Susannah (Watts) K.; attended Columbia, 1811; m. Mary Radford, Sept. 5, 1830. Served as 1st lt. 13th Inf., U.S. Army during War of 1812; commd. capt., 1813; brevetted maj., 1823; participated Gen. Atkinson's expdn. to mouth of the Yellowstone River, 1825; assumed command of Ft. Crawford, Prairie du Chien, Wis., 1828; maj., 1829; lt. col. dragoons, 1833; commanded 3d Mil. Dept., 1842; leader expdn. to South Pass, 1845; began bldg. 1st Ft. Kearny, Nebraska City, Neb., 1846; commanded Army of West during Mexican War, 1846; commd. brig. gen., 1846; conquered N.M., 1846, mil. gov., 1846; helped draw up code of laws for N.M., 1846; defeated by Mexicans at San Pascual, Cal., 1846; brevetted maj. gen., 1847; leading role in conquest of Cal.; civil gov. Vera Cruz, 1847. Author: Carbine Manual, 1837. Died St. Louis Oct. 31, 1848.

KEEFER, FRANK ROYER med. officer U.S. Army; b. Venango County, Pa., Oct. 10, 1865; s. John Brua and Caroline Rebecca (Royer) K.; Ph.B., Dickinson Coll., 1885, A.M., 1901, Sc.D., 1935; M.D., U. of Pa., 1889; m. Mary Cornelia Terrell, Feb. 18, 1903. Entered Army Med. Corps, 1890; advanced through grades to col. in 1916; brig. gen., asst. surg. gen., 1927, retired, 1929. Prof. Mil. Hygiene, U.S. Military Academy, 1910-14; comdg. mil. hosps., 1915-19; chief, med. div., Provost marshal gen. office, Washington, 1918; chief surgeon, Am. Forces in Germany, 1920-22; same, 2d Corps Area, N.Y. City, 1922-27; decorated officer French Legion of Honor. Chmn. D.C. Chapter Am. Red Cross, 1930-42; now chmn. emeritus; fellow Am. Med. Assn. and Am. Coll. Surgeons. Mem. Chi Phi. Presbyterian. Clubs: Army and Navy; Chevy Chase; Army and Navy Country (Washington); University (Phila.). Author: Alcoholic Drinks and Narcotics; Military Hygiene and Sanitation. Address: 2800 Woodley Rd., Washington. Died May 15, 1954.

KEEHN, ROY DEE lawyer; b. Ligonier, Ind., Nov. 7, 1877; s. Jonathan N. and Harriet (Shobe) K.; student De Pauw U., Ind. U.; Ph.B., U. of Chicago, 1902, J.D., 1904; m. 2d, Ellen Henderson, Apr. 1922; children-Roy D., Kay, Kent. Asst. corp. counsel of Chicago, 1905-07. Served as maj. World War I; major judge advocate 33d Div., 1924-27; maj. gen. comdr. 33d Div. Ill. Nat. Guard and attached troops, 1927-41; cited and retired as lt. gen. Aug. 1942; pres. Nat. Guard Assn. of U.S., 1934-35. Chmn. Ill. Commerce Commn., 1941-42; mem. Ill. Athletic Commn. since 1942. Decorated Order of the Crown of Italy. Mem. Am., Ill. State and Chicago bar assns., Chicago, Law Inst., Art Inst. Chicago, Phi Kappa Psi, Phi Delta Phi. Clubs: University, Racquet. Home: Ken-Ro-Ka Farm, Lake Forest, Ill. Office: 208 S. La Salle St., Chicago. Died Feb. 21, 1949.

KEEL, ELMO W., 1st nat. comdr., AMVETS; b. Jonesville, Va., Aug. 11, 1914; s. Walter J. and Myrtle (Adkinson) K.; grad. Pennington High Sch., 1929-33, New England Air Craft Sch., 1941-42, Columbia Tech. Inst., 1942; B.S., George Washington U., 1947; m. Polly March, Jan. 27, 1942 (divorced); m. 2d Jessie Howell, June 1950 (dec. 1961); children—Margaret Ann Keel Pollock, Mary Louise; m. 3d, Nora E. Palm Hall, 1963. Public relations work, salesman N. American Cement Corporation. County surveyor in Lee County, Virginia; building inspector 9th Congl. Dist., Va., founder of Am. Vets (Am. Vets of World War II), became nat. exec. committeeman; dist. mgr. Ohio Hoist Mfg. Co., Cleveland; sales engr. Safway Steel Products Co. of Milwaukee. Joined Army Air Corps as private, 1939; became master sergeant; flight engr. in Burma-China Theater; discharged, 1943. Mem. Society for Advancement of Indsl. Management; student mem. Am. Inst. of Electrical Engrs. Awarded Purple Heart Citation, Asiatic-Pacific Theater ribbons. Mem. Goerge Washington U. Veterans Club. Home: Oxon Hill MD Died Jan. 15, 1969; buried Jonesville VA

KEENAN, ALBERT JOSEPH, JR., transportation exec.; b. Bklyn., Apr. 15, 1913; s. Dr. Albert J. and Helen M. (Reichmann) K.; A.B., Dartmouth, 1935; LL.B., Bklyn. Law Sch., 1939; m. Katherine C. Lee, June 20, 1942; children—Albert J. III, Gail Lee, Barbara Lee. Admitted to N.Y. bar, 1939; asso. editor U.S. Code Annotated, 1939-40; with Moore-McCormack Lines, Inc., N.Y.C., 1945-68, gen. passenger traffic mgr., 1954-57, v.p., 1957-68. Mem. travel adv. com. U.S. Travel Service. Served as maj., M.I., AUS, 1941-45. Mem. Defense Orientation Conference Association, Maritime Association of Port of New York, Am. Soc. Travel Agts. (chmn. Western Hemisphere com. 1956-57). Am. Merchant Marine Inst., Vets. 7th Regt. N.Y., S.Am. Travel Orgn. (pres. 1966-68), Inst. Certified Transportation Agts. (founder, trustee), Sigma Nu, Phi Delta Phi. Episcopalian (vestry 1954-60). Clubs: New York Skal, Downtown Athletic, Bon Vivants (N.Y.C.); Propeller U.S. (nat. exec. com. 1957); Travel Executives. Home: New York City NY Died Aug. 14, 1968; buried at sea.

KEENAN, JOSEPH BERRY lawyer; b. Pawtucket, R.I., Jan. 11, 1888; s. Bernard A. and Sarah (Berry) K.; A.B., M.A., Brown U., 1910; LL.B., Harvard, 1913; m. Charlotte Quigley, July 7, 1920; children-William Quigley, Joseph Berry, Betty Jean, John David. Admitted to Ohio bar, 1913, and since in practice at Cleve.; mem. firm Day, Day & Wilkin, 1919; apptd. spl. asst. to atty. gen. of Ohio to investigate crime, 1919; formed firm Keenan & Butler, 1930; apptd. spl. asst. to atty. gen. of U.S., to investigate crime, July 1933, asst. atty. gen. of U.S., in charge of criminal division of Dept. of Justice, Oct. 1933, asst. to the atty. gen., 1936-39; pvt. practice, Washington, 1939—. U.S. chief of counsel for prosecution in trials of Japanese war criminals, Tokyo, Japan, 1946. Served with cav. Mexican border, 1916; with 137th F.A., AEF, 1917; commd. 1st lt. judge adv. gen.'s dept. Cited by Gen. Pershing "for meritorious service"; cited by French govt. "for distinguished service." Mem. Am.Ohio, Cuyahoga County, Cleve. bar assns. Democrat. Roman Catholic Home: 10 Hesketh St., Chevy Chase, Md. Office: Woodward Bldg., Washington. Died Dec. 8, 1954.*

KEENEY, PAUL ALOYSIUS, physician; b. Wilkes Barre, Pa., June 6, 1903; M.D., U. Pitts., 1931; M.P.H., Johns Hopkins, 1940; m. Ann F.W. Keeney; children—

Cormac W., Ann F., Sean. Intern, St. Francis Hosp., Pitts., 1931-32, chief resident in medicine, 1932-33; comdg. officer Bermada Base Hosp., Waltham (Mass.) Regional Hosp., Murphy Gen Hosp., Waltham; dir. med. edn. St. Mary and St. Elizabeth Hosp., Louisville; clin. dir. Williamson (W.Va.) Regional Hosp. Served to col. AUS, 1943-55. Diplomate Am. Bd. Preventive Medicine. Fellow A.C.P., Am. Pub. Health Assn., Am. Coll. Preventive Medicine; mem. A.M.A., Alpha Omega Alpha. Home: Louisville KY Died July 17, 1970; buried Arlington Nat. Cemetery.

KEEP, OLIVER DAVIS publisher; b. N.Y.C., Dec. 17, 1903; s. Oliver Terry and Lucille Christine (Davis) K.; A.B.; Williams Coll., 1925; m. Helen R. Whitcomb, Dec. 26, 1925 (div.); 1 dau., Mary Whitcomb; m. 2d, Nelle Ruton Hoagland, Aug. 11, 1939 (div.); 1 son, Oliver Hoagland; m. 3d, Emily Dobie Pobinson, Nov. 29, 1953. Promotion mgr. Time Mag., 1925-30, Conde Nash Publs., 1930-33, Fortune, 1933-35; pub. Cue Mag., 1936-42, Fortnight Mag. since 1946. Served as capt. USMC, 1943-45. Mem. Gargoyle Soc., Psi Upsilon. Republican. Clubs: Williams (N.Y.C.). Home: 1543 Sunset Plaza Dr. Office: 7971 Melrose Av., Los Angeles 46. Died Feb. 1965.

KEIFER, J(OSEPH) WARREN lawyer, soldier; b. Clark County, O., Jan. 30, 1836; s. Joseph and Mary (Smith) K.; ed. Antioch Coll.; m. Eliza Stout, Mar. 22, 1860 (died 1899); children-Joseph Warren, William White, Horace Charles (dec.). Margarette Eliza (dec.). In law practice at Springfield, O., 1858; pres. Lagonda Nat. Bank, 1873-1927. Maj. 3d Ohio Inf., Apr. 27, 1861; lt. col., Feb. 12, 1862; col. 110th Ohio Inf., Sept. 30, 1862; bvtd.; brig. gen. vols., Oct. 19, 1864, "for gallant and meritorious services in battles of Opequan, Fisher's Hill and Middletown, Va."; maj. gen. vols., Apr. 9, 1865, for same, during campaign ending with surrender of Gen. Lee; wounded 4 times; hon. mustered out, June 27, 1865; apptd. lt. col., 26th U.S. Inf., Nov. 30, 1866, but declined; maj. gen. vols., June 9, 1898-May 12, 1899, Spanish-Am. War. Mem. Ohio Senate, 1868-69; mem. 45th to 48th (speaker 47th, 1881-83) Congresses (1877-85), and 59th to 61st Congresses (1905-11), 7th Ohio Dist. Trustee Ohio Soldiers' and Sailors' Orphans' Home, 1870-78, 1903-04, Antioch Coll., 1873-. Nat. mem. Perry's Victory Centennial Commn., 1911-; life member interparliamentary Peace Conf. of the World, Paris, 1912. Author: Slavery and Four Years of War, 1900. Home: Springfield, O. Died April 22, 1932.

KEIM, WILLIAM HIGH congressman; b. nr. Reading, Pa., June 13, 1813; attended Mt. Airy Mil. Sch. Served to maj. gen. Pa. Militia; mayor of Reading, 1848; mem. U.S. Ho. of Reps. (Democrat) from Pa., 35th Congress, Dec. 7, 1858-59; surveyor gen. of Pa., 1860-62; commd. maj. gen. Pa. Volunteers, U.S. Army, 1861; commd. brig. gen. U.S. Volunteers, 1861. Died Harrisburg, Pa., May 18, 1862; buried Charles Evans Cemetery, Reading.

KEISER, LAURENCE BOLLON, army officer; b. Philadelpha, June 1, 1895; s. Elmer Edgar (M.D.) and Jeanie (Deans) K.; B.S., U.S. Mil. Acad., 1917; grad. Inf. Sch., co. officers class, 1923, field officers class, 1933. Command and Gen. Staff Sch., 1939; m. Marion Polk, Mar. 20, 1926. Commd. 2d lt., 6th U.S. Inf., 1917, advancing through the grades to brig. gen., 1944; with 5th U.S. Inf., Div., A.E.F., France, 1918-19; served in Philippine Islands and China, 1920-22; tractical officer Corps of Cadets, U.S. Mil. Acad., 1924-28; comd. 29th Inf., Ft. Benning, 1941-42; chief of staff, 3d Army Corps, Apr. 1942-Sept. 1943; chief of staff, 6th Army Corp., (italy), Sept. 1943-Mar. 1944; dep. chief of staff, 5th Army, Mar.-Apr., 1944; became chief of staff, 4th Army, 1944. Decorated Silver Star, Legion of Merit, Address: Washington DC Died Oct. 1969.*

KEITH, HAROLD CHESSMAN shoe mfr.; b. Brockton, Mass., June 18, 1884; s. George E. and Anna G. (Reed) K.; grad. Lawrenceville (N.J.) Sch., 1904; B.A., Amherst, 1908; m. Ethel Middlebrook Bowne, Apr. 12, 1910; children-Barbara Bowne (dec.), Jean Reed, Anne Middlebrook. Identified with shoe mfg. bus., 1909-; chmn. bd. Geo. E. Keith Co., Brockton, Brockton Nat. Bank; dir. United Shoe Machinery Corp., Eastern Corp. Served as capt. Q.M.C., Washington, World War. Mem. Chi Phi. Republican. Conglist. Mason (32ff). Clubs: Union (Boston); Union League (New York); The Country (Brookline, Mass.). Home: P.O. Box 907, Falmouth, Mass. Died Sept. 1961.

KEITH, LAWRENCE MASSILLON congressman, army officer; b. Orangeburg Dist., S.C., Oct. 4, 1824; s. George and Mary (Wannamaker) K.; grad. S.C. Coll. (now U. S.C.), 1843; m. Susanna Sparks, 2 children. Admitted to S.C. bar, 1845; mem. U.S. Ho. of Reps. from S.C., 33d-36th congresses, 1853-July 16, 1856, re-elected to fill vacancy caused by his own resignation, Aug. 6, 1856-Dec. 1860; mem. Provisional Congress of Confederacy, Montgomery, Ala., later Richmond, Va., 1861; organized, commd. col. 20th Regt., S.C. Volunteers, later brig. gen.; mortally wounded at Battle of Cold Harbor (Va.), June 1, 1864. Died Cold Harbor, June 2, 1864; buried family cemetery nr. St. Matthews, S.C.

KEITT, GEORGE WANNAMAKER, plant pathologist; b. Newberry County, S.C., June 11, 1889; s. Thomas Wadlington and Annie Selina (Wannamaker) K.; B.S., Clemson Coll., 1909, Sc.D., 1937; M.S., U. of Wis., 1911, Ph.D., 1914; m. Carol Seaver Keay, Aug. 30, 1927; children—George Wannamaker, Jr., John Keay, Alan Seaver. Asst. in botany and plant pathology, S.C. Agrl. Expt. Station, 1909-10; spl. agt. fruit disease investigations, U.S. Dept. Agr., 1910, and scientific asst., summers; scholar in plant pathology U. of Wis., 1911, lectr., 1912-14, asst. prof., 1914-17, asso. prof., 1917-20, prof., 1920-59, emeritus prof., 1959-69, part-time research professor, 1959-61, chairman dept. plant pathology, 1930-55; lecturer Mycol. Soc. of Am., 1956. Served as 1st lt. and capt. U.S. Army, World War; instr. Sch. of Arms, Camp Lee; asst. div. gas officer, 32d and 37th divs., div. gas officer 36th div., and asst. gas officer 1st Army, in France; maj. C.W.S., O.R.C. Fellow A.A.A.S.; mem. Am. Soc. Naturalists, Am. Phytopathol. Soc. (v.p. 1934, pres. 1937), Exptl. Bot. Soc. America, Mycol. Soc. of America, Soc. Exptl. Biology and Medicine, Wis. Acad. Sciences, Arts and Letters, American Assn. University Professors (pres. Wis. chapter 1943-44), Indian Phytopathological Society, Nederlandse Plantenziektenkundige Vereniging; 7th Internat. Bot. Cong. (v.p. phytopathol. sect., 1950); guest speaker Brit. Assn. Advancement Sci., Edinburgh, 1951), Phi Sigma (honorary), Sigma Xi (president Wisconsin chapter, 1928-29), Gamma Alpha, Phi Kappa Phi (president Wisconsin chapter 1936-37), Chaos Club. Episcopalian. Club: University. Author of bulletins, contributor to professional journals. Mem. editorial bd. Am. Jour. Botany, 1935-44. Co-discoverer antimycin. Home: Cambridge MA Died Nov. 18, 1969; buried Old St. David's Churchyard, Radnor PA

KELIHER, JOHN army officer (ret.), state ofcl.; b. Boston, Mar. 19, 1891; s. Thomas Joseph and Esther (Graham) K; B.S., U.S. Mil. Acad., 1915; grad. F.A. Sch., battery officers course, 1921, Command and Gen. Staff Sch., 1932; m. Margaret Graham; 1 son, John Graham. Commd. capt. U.S. Army, 1915; advanced through grades to brig. gen., 1945; comdg. officer, 8th F.A. Regt., 1940. Operations Officer, Pacific areas, 1943-45; operations officer USARPAC, Hawaiian area, and mem. planning bd. CincPac, 1946-49; insp. gen. 6th Army, 1949-50; chief of staff amphibious operations, Miki, 1949; asst. dir. Civilian Def., Cal., 1951-57; territorial ofcl., Hawaii, 1957-61. Pres. West Point Soc. Hawaii. Decorated D.S.M., Legion of Merit, Army Commendation ribbon. Home: 90 Niuiki Circle, Honolulu 16. Died June 8, 1964; buried Nat. Cemetery of Pacific, Honolulu.

KELLEY, FRANCIS ALPHONSUS clergyman; b. Cohoes, N.Y., Apr. 19, 1888; s. John Francis and Mary Annette (Mulvihill) K.; ed. St. Michael's Coll., Toronto, Ont., Can., Toronto U.; philosophy and theology, St. Bernard's Sem., Rochester, N.Y. Ordained priest R.C. Church, 192 1912; asst. pastor St. Joseph's Church, Albany, St. Mary's, Troy; now pastor church of the Sacred Heart, Cairo, New York. Commd. chaplain 10th Inf., N.G.N.Y., May 16, 1916; served on Mexican border; called out with same regt., Feb. 4, 1917; trans. to 104th Machine Gun Batt., 27th Div., U.S.A., Dec. 19, 1917; sailed for France Apr. 18, 1918; trans. to Hdqrs. 27th Div., July 13, 1918; returned to U.S., Feb. 27, 1919; hon. disch., Apr. 1, 1919. Decorated D.S.C. (U.S.); Mil. Cross (British); cited in gen. orders by Gen. Rawlinson, comdr. 4th Brit. Army, Sept. 20, 1918; cited in gen. orders, U.S.A., "for gallantry on field of battle," Sept. 29 and Oct. 17, 1918. First nat. chaplain, 1919, Am. Legion. Now mem. Com. of Relief of Disabled Vets., N.Y. City. Mem. K. of C., Elks. Toured Pacific Coast, May 1919, in interest of Victory Loan. Home: Cairo, N.Y. Died Oct. 15, 1931.

KELLEY, FRANK HARRISON naval officer (ret.); b. New Haven, Feb. 26, 1889: s. Frank Harrison and Jean (Richardson) K.; S.B., U.S. Naval Acad., 1910; m. Claire Parmelee, May 12, 1912; children-Janet Claire (Mrs. Joe S. Pearson), Frank Harrison, Edmund Parmelee, Archie Parmelee, Helen Patricia. Commd. ensign USN, 1912, advanced through grades to rear adm., 1946: served on all oceans and in all types naval ships; comdg. officer U.S.S. West Point, 1941-43: comdr. U.S. Naval Tng. Center, Farragut, Ida., 1943-46; ret. from active service, Dec. 1, 1946; pres., bd. dirs. Farragut Coll. and Tech. Inst., Sept. 1946—. Decorated Bronze Star Medal. Home: House 11-C-12. Farragut College and Technical Inst., Farragut, Ida. Died Nov. 19, 1953.

KELLEY, JAMES DOUGLAS JERROLD commander U.S.N., author; b. New York, Dec. 25, 1847; ed. pvt. and pub. schs. and Seton Hall Coll., N.J.; apptd. to navy by Pres. Lincoln; entered Oct. 5, 1864; grad. U.S. Naval Acad., 1868; m. Isabel de P. Morrell. Ensign, 1869; master, 1870; lt., 1872; lt. comdr., 1893; comdr., 1899. Served on many duties and stations; prize essayist and gold medalist U.S. Naval Inst., 1881; mem. and chmn. Bd. Auxiliary Vessels, 1898; insp. merchant vessels at New York; senior aid to comdt., Navy Yard, New York; in command of Resolute, West Indies, and again insp. merchant vessels; retired, Apr. 1, 1901. Co-author: Modern Ships of War; the Barbary Corsairs; The Army and Navy. Home: New York. Died Apr. 30, 1922.

KELLEY, SAMUEL WALTER M.D., surgeon; b. Adamsville, O., Sept. 15, 1855; s. Walter and Selina Catherine (Kaemmerer) K.; M.D., Western Reserve U., Cleveland, 1884; also studied in hosps. of London; m. Amelia Kemmerlein, July 2, 1884; children-Walter Paul (dec.), Katherine Mildred. Chief dept. of diseases of children, Polyclinic, Western Reserve U., 1886-93; prof. diseases of children, Cleveland Coll. Phys. and Surg. (Ohio Wesleyan U.), 1893-1910; surgeon to the children St. Luke's Hospital, sr. staff; secretary med. staff Cleveland City Hosp., 1891-99, pres., 1899-1902; pediatrist City Hosp., 1893-1910. Entered service as civilian surgeon, Spanish-Am. War; recommended for "efficiency in the field under most trying circumstances"; commd. brigade surgeon of vols. with rank of maj., Aug. 17, 1898. Editor: Cleveland Medical Gazette, 1885-1901. Pres. Ohio State Pediatric Soc., 1896, 97; chmn. sect. on diseases of children A.M.A., 1900-01; pres. Assn. Am. Teachers of Diseases of Children, 1907-08; fellow Am. College of Surgeons; mem. governing com. Gorgas Memorial Institute. Republican. Author: About Children, 1897; In the Year 1800, 1904; Surgical Diseases of Children, 1909, 2d edit., 1914; The Witchery o' the Moon and Other Poems, 1919; Lo Studente, 1925. Home: Cleveland, O., Died Apr. 20, 1929.

KELLOGG, EDGAR ROMEYN brig. gen.; b. New York, Mar. 25, 1842; s. Moses Curtis (M.D.) and Elizabeth (Swartwout) K.; pub. sch. edn.; m. Mary E. Wickham, Feb. 13, 1866. Served as sergt. Co. A, and sergt. maj. 24th Ohio Inf., Apr. 22-July 23, 1861; commd. 2d lt. 24th Ohio Inf., July 23, 1861; resigned, Oct. 28, 1861; prvt. Co. B, and sergt. maj. 1st battalion, 16th U.S. Inf., Nov. 29, 1861-Aug.1, 1862; apptd. from N.Y. 2d lt. 16th Inf., Apr. 7, 1862; 1st lt., May 3, 1862; capt., Feb. 16, 1865; transferred to 25th Inf., Sept. 21, 1866, to 18th Inf., Apr. 26, 1869; maj., Dec. 26, 1888; lt. col. 10th Inf., Sept. 16, 1892; col. 6th Inf., June 30, 1898; brig. gen. vols., Oct. 1, 1898; hon. disch. from vol. service, Feb. 24, 1899; brig. gen. U.S.A., Dec. 5, 1899; retired at own request, over 30 yrs.' service, Dec. 16, 1899. Bvtd.; capt., Dec. 31, 1862, for battle of Murfreesboro, Tenn.; maj., Sept. 1, 1864, for Atlanta campaign and battle of Jonesboro, Ga. Home: Toledo, O. Died Oct. 7, 1914.

KELLOGG, FRANCIS WILLIAM congressman; b. Worthington, Mass., May 30, 1810; attended common schs. Moved to Columbus, O., 1833, Grand Rapids, Mich., 1855; engaged in lumber bus., Kelloggville, Kent County, Mich.; mem. Mich. Ho. of Reps., 1857-58; mem. U.S. Ho. of Reps. (Republican) from Mich., 37th-38th congresses, 1859-65; organizer several regts. during Civil War, served as regtl. col.; collector of internal revenue So. Dist. of Ala., 1866-68; mem. U.S. Ho. of Reps. (Rep.) from Ala., 40th Congress, July 22, 1868-69. Died Alliance, O., Jan. 13, 1879; buried Fulton St. Cemetery, Grand Rapids.

KELLOGG, WALTER GUEST lawyer; b. Ogdensburg, N.Y., Apr. 23, 1877; s. John Morris and Henrietta Powers (Guest) K.; student Union Coll., 1895-96) A.B., Columbia, 1899 (sr. class poet); student New York Law Sch.; LL.D., St. Lawrence U., 1917, Columbia University, 1920; Doctor of Letters, Union College, 1949; married Mary Peronne Hall, 1906; m. 2d, Agnes Lauriha, 1942. Practiced law, Ogdensburg, 1901—; special counsel General Electric Co., 1922—. Elected regent University of State of N.Y., 1914, reelected, 1916, for term of 12 yrs., resigned 1929; apptd. hon. fellow in English, Union Coll., 1934. Maj., judge adv. gen.'s dept., U.S. Army, 1918-19; apptd. by Sec. of War chmn. Bd. of Inquiry on Conscientious Objectors. Mem. Sigma Phi, Am. Legion. Republican. Episcopalian. Author: The Conscientious Objector, 1919; Parish's Fancy (novel), 1929. Contbr. to mags. Home: 10757 Weyburn Av., Los Angeles 24. Died June 22, 1956: buried Ogdensburg, N.Y.

KELLS, CLARENCE HOWARD army officer; b. Kennockee, Mich., Oct. 9, 1892; grad. Inf. Sch., Ft. Benning, Ga., 1925, advanced course, 1931; grad. Command and Gen. Staff Sch., Ft. Leavenworth, Kan., 1936, Q.M. Sch., Phila., 1937. Enlisted as private, C.A.C., 1917; commd. 2d lt. Inf., 1917, advanced through the grades to brig. gen., 1943; instr. 8th Inf., Chgo., 1933; adj. Hawaiian Q.M. Depot, Ft. Armstrong, Hawaii, 1937-39; instr., O.M. Sch., Phila., 1939-40; with Water Transport br. Transportation Div., Office Q.M. Gen., Washington, 1940-41, chief of br., 1941—. Address: Office of Chief, Transportation Service, War Dept., Washington. Died Mar. 24, 1954.*

KELLY DENNIS FRANCIS mcht.; b. Chicago, Ill., Aug. 23, 1868; s. John and Mary (Murphy) K.; ed. St. Mary's Sch., Chicago; LL.D., De Paul University, 1923; LL.D., U. of Notre Dame, 1930; m. Irene E. Sullivan, Jan. 4, 1894; 1 dau., Eileen Glassbrook (Mrs. Charles P. Vogel). Started as a boy with Mandel Brothers, dept. store, Chicago, 1879, supt. of store, 1888-1901, gen. mgr., 1901-23; v.p. and gen. mgr. The Fair, 1923-24, pres. and gen. mgr., 1925-38, dir.; dir. Kresge Dept. Stores,Inc. Incorporator and trustee Century of Progress Expn., Chicago, 1933-34. President Catholic Charities of Chicago from Organization, 1918. Commissioned by Gov. Lowden, lt. col. Ill. Res. Militia.

Knight Order of St. Gregory, 1920, Knight Comdr., 1925; Knight of Malta, by Pope Pius XI, 1931. Home: Lake Forest, Ill. Died July 23, 1938.

KELLY, JAMES KERR lawyer, U.S. senator; b. Centre County, Pa., Feb. 16, 1819; grad. Coll. of N.J. (Princeton), 1839, A.M., 1842; m. Mary Buchanan Millar, Nov. 26, 1863. Admitted to Pa. bar, 1842; deputy atty. gen. for Mifflin Co., Pa., 1847-49; went to Calif., 1849, to Portland Ore. Ty., 1851; one of com. of 3 apptd. 1852 to draw up set of laws for Ty.; lieut. col. 1st regt. Ore. mounted vols., and served against Yakima Indians, 1855-56; mem. Territorial Council, 1853-56; one of framers of Ore. constitution, 1857; mem. State Senate, 1860-64; U.S. Senator from Ore., 1871-77. Democrat. Chief justice Supreme Court Ore., 1879-81. Died 1903.

KELLY, JOHN GRANT newspaper pub.; b. Peoria, Ill., July 16, 1872; s. William and Sarah Ann (Roberts) K.; grad. Central High Sch., Kansas City, Mo., 1892; m. Martha V. Miller, June 22, 1900; children-Norman M., Eugene A. (dec.), Virginia, Laura. Began newspaper work at Kansas City, 1892; with Kansas City and Omaha newspapers until 1910; owner, pub. and gen. mgr. Walla Walla (Wash.) Daily Bulletin since 1910; and Walla Walla Daily Union, 1934-; chmn. bd. Walla-Walla Union-Bulletin, 1955-. Member Missouri National Guard 10 yrs.; served as 1st lt., Co. G, 3d Mo. Vol. Inf., Spanish-Am. War; mem. Wash. State Council of Defense, World War I, also of Co. A, 4th Inf. Batt., Wash. Nat. Guard; mem. Wash. State Defense Council World War II under Gov. Arthur B. Langlie. Mem. Asso. Press. Mem. Walla Walla C. of C. Conglist. Mason. Rotarian. Home: 5930 Franklin Av., Los Angeles 90028. Died May 1, 1962; buried Walla Walla, Wash.

KELLY, LUTHER SAGE (YELLOWSTONE KELLY) scout; b. Geneva, N.Y., July 27, 1849; s. Luther and Jeannette (Sage) K.; m. Alice May Morrison, 1885. Served as pvt. U.S. Army, in the West, 1865-68; became hunter and trapper, Wyo., Mont., Dakotas; later served as dispatch bearer U.S. Army; guide to Gen. George A. Forsyth's expdn. to upper Missouri River and Yellowstone area, 1873; chief army scout for Gen. Nelson A. Miles in campaigns against Sioux and Cheyenne Indians, 1876-78; regular army scout in Colo., 1880; later served as clk. War Dept., Chgo., also Pension Bur., Washington, D.C.; guide to Capt. Edwin Glenn's exploring expdn. to Alaska, 1898, to Harriman expdn., 1899; capt. U.S. Volunteers in Philippines, 1900; treas. Province of Surigao (Philippines), 1903-04; Indian agt., San Carlos Reservation, Ariz., 1904-08; operated fruit ranch, Paradise, Cal., 1915-28. Author: Yellowstone Kelly: The Memoirs of Luther S. Kelly, 1926. Died Paradise, Dec. 17, 1928; buried Kelly Mountain, Billings, Mont.

KELLY, MONROE naval officer; b. Norfolk, Va., July 30, 1886; s. William Armstead Lane and Alice (Reid) K.; student Norfolk Acad., 1902-04; B.S., U.S. Naval Acad., 1909; student U.S. Navy Postgrad. Sch., 1912-14; m. Lucy Winder Lamb, Sept. 23, 1914; children-Monroe, Lucy Lane. Commd. ensign USN, 1911, and advanced through the grades to rear adm., 1941; comdt. 3rd Naval Dist., 1944-48, ret. as vice adm.; served on U.S. naval mission to Brazil, 1927-31; U.S. naval attaché to the Netherlands, 1938-40; naval aide to Queen Wilhelmina, Aug. 1942; comdt. N.Y. Navy Yard, 1943-Nov. 1944. Decorated D.S.M. (Navy), World War I. Defense, N. Atlantic, and African Campaign medals; Grand Officer, Order of Orange-Nassau of the Netherlands. Comder. Order Brit. Empire; Commendador Orden Al Merito (Chile). Home: Landfall, Linkhorn Park, Virginia Beach, Va. Died Aug. 29, 1956; buried Forest Lawn Cemetery, Norfolk, Va.

KELLY, ROBERT MORROW lawyer; b. Paris, Ky., Sept. 22, 1836; s. Thomas and Cordelia (Morrow) K.; ed. pvt. schs.; taught sch. several yrs.; admitted to bar, 1860; capt. to col. 4th Ky. Inf., U.S.V., 1861-65; m. Harriet Holley Warfield, June 27, 1867. Resumed law practice at Paris, Ky.; collector internal revenue, 7th Ky. Dist., 1866-70; with brief intermission, had charge of Louisville Daily Commercial, 1870-97; U.S. pension agt., 1873-86. Republican. Home: Louisville, Ky. Died Dec. 27, 1913.

KELSO, JOHN RUSSELL congressman; b. nr. Columbus, O., Mar. 23, 1831; grad. Pleasant Ridge Coll., Mo., 1859. Served as capt. of a co. Mo. Militia during Civil War; brevetted maj., lt. col., and col.; mem. U.S. Ho. of Reps. (Independent Radical) from Mo., 39th Congress, 1865-67; prin. Kelso Acad., Springfield, Mo., 1867-69; moved to Modesto, Cal., 1872, to Longmont, Colo., 1885; author, lectr. Died Longmont, Jan. 26, 1891; buried on his estate nr. Longmont, later cremated and ashes scattered.

KELTON, JOHN CUNNINGHAM army officer; b. Delaware County, Pa., June 24, 1828; s. Robert and Margaretta (Cunningham) K.; grad. U.S. Mil. Acad., 1851; m. Josephine Campbell, Apr. 30, 1870; 7 children. Commd. 1st lt. U.S. Army, 1855; commanded a brigade of Pope's div., 1861; served as asst. adj. gen. under Gen. Lyon, 1861; col. 9th Mo. Volunteers, 1861; asst. adj. gen. Dept. of Mo., 1862; aide-de-camp to Gen. Halleck (comdr. Mil. Div. of Janus), 1862-65; brevetted lt. col., col., brig. gen., 1865; chief of appointment bur. Adj. Gen.'s Office, Washington, D.C., 1865-70; commd. lt. col., 1866; prin. asst. to adj. gen., 1885-89; adj. gen. U.S. Army, 1889-92; gov. U.S. Soldier's Home, Washington, D.C., 1892; invented many improvements for service rifle, revolver. Author: Manuel of the Bayonet, 1861; Information for Riflemen, 1884. Died U.S. Soldier's Home, July 15, 1893; buried U.S. Soldiers Home.

KEMPER, JAMES LAWSON gov. Va.; b. Madison County, Va., June 11, 1823; s. William and Maria (Allison) K.; B.A., Washington Coll., 1842; m. Cremora Cave, July 4, 1853, 5 children. Commd. capt. U.S. Volunteers, 1847; mem. Va. Ho. Dels., 1853-63, speaker, 1861-62; commd. col. 7th Regt. Va. Volunteers, Confederate Army, 1861, brig. gen., 1862, maj. gen. in command Conscript Bur., 1864; supported Horace Greeley for Pres. U.S., 1872; gov. Va., 1874-77, urged full recognition of civil rights for Negroes; chmn. bd. visitors Va. Mil. Inst. Died Gordonsville, Va., Apr. 7, 1895.

KEMPER, JOHN MASON, headmaster; b. Fort D.A. Russel, Wyoming, Sept. 1, 1912; s. James Brown and Mercer (Mason) K.; B.S., U.S. Mil. Acad., 1935; M.A., Columbia, 1942; L.H.D., Williams College, 1948, Colby College, Waterville, Maine, 1958; Litt.D., Tufts College, 1952; LL.D., Harvard University, 1962; m. to Sylvia Mayo Pratt, June 9, 1936 (dec. Sept. 1961); children—Cecily Thomson, Lucy Ord, Rosamond Pratt; m. 2d, Abby Locke Castle, Dec. 27, 1963. Commissioned 2d lt., U.S. Army, 1935 advancing through the grades to col., 1944; chief historical br. War Dept. World War II; headmaster Phillips Acad., Andover, Mass., 1948-71. Decorated Legion of Merit (2). Member Headmasters Assn., Nat. Assn. of Ind. Schools (chairman 1955-57). Clubs: Century Assn., University (N.Y.C.); Tavern (Boston). Home: Andover MA Died Dec. 4, 1971.

KEMPFF, CLARENCE S(ELBY) naval officer; b. Cal., May 31, 1874; m. Alice Brigham. Commd. ensign, 1897, and advanced through grades to capt., June 3, 1921; commd. rear adm., June 5, 1930; promoted to vice adm., 1935; ret., June 1938. Address: 1027 F Av., Coronado, Cal. Died Feb. 10, 1959.

KEMPFF, LOUIS rear admiral U.S.N.; b. nr. Belleville, Ill., Oct. 11, 1841; s. Friedrich and Henrietta K.; apptd. to U.S. Naval Acad., from Ill., 1857; m. Cornelia R. Selby, July 16, 1873. Promoted lt., Aug. 1, 1862; lt. comdr., July 25, 1866; comdr., Mar. 9, 1876; capt., May 19, 1891; rear admiral, Mar. 3, 1890. Served on Vandalia, Atlantic Blockading Squadron, 1861; captured, and took to New York schooner Henry Middleton, of Charleston; participated in battle of Port Royal, S.C., Nov. 7, 1861; served on Wabash, Atlantic Blockading Squadron, 1861-62; capture of Fernandina, Fla., St. Mary's, Ga., Jacksonville, Fla., and St. Augustine, Fla.; Susquehanna, West Gulf Blockading Squadron, part of 1862, and 1863; bombardment of Sewell's Point, Va., May 1862, and reoccupation of Norfolk, May 10, 1862; Sonoma, June and July 1863; Connecticut, 1863-64; Suwanee, Pacific Squadron, 1865-66; training-ship Portsmouth, 1867-68; receiving-ship Independence, 1868-70; exec. officer Mohican, on eclipse expdn. to Siberia, 1869; Pacific Squadron, 1870-73, as exec. officer Mohican, 1871-72, Saranac, 1872, California, 1872-73; Naval Rendezvous, San Francisco, 1873-74; light house insp., 13th dist., 1874-76; sr. aid to commandant, Navy Yard, Mare Island, 1877-78; equipment officer, Navy Yard, Mare Island, 1878-80; comd. Naval Rendezvous, San Francisco, 1880-81; comd. Alert, 1881-82; ordnance officer, Navy Yard, Mare Island, Calif., 1883-85; comd. Adams, 1885-88; Navy Yard, Mare Island, 1888-90; mem. Bd. of Inspection, San Francisco, 1890-93; comd. Monterey, 1893-95; Naval War Coll., 1895; mem. Naval Examining and Retiring Bds., 1895-90; comd. receiving-ship Independence, 1896-99; comdt., Navy Yard, Mare Island, 1899-1900; squadron comdr., Asiatic Fleet, 1900-02; declined to join foreign admirals in firing on Taku forts, 1900, but after U.S.S. Monocacy was struck by a shot from the Chinese forts, joined in with forces at hand for protection of life and property of Americans; comdt. Pacific Naval Dist., 1902-03; retired, Oct. 11, 1903; special duty, 1904-05. Home: San Francisco, Calif. Died July 29, 1920.

KENDALL, JAMES, chemist; b. Surrey, Eng., July 30, 1889; s. William Henry and Rebecca (Pickering) K.; A.M., B.Sc., Edinburgh U., 1910, Sc.D., 1915; student at Heidelberg, Stockholm and Petrograd; m. Alice Tyldesley, of Victoria, B.C., Sept. 13, 1915; children—James Tyldesley, Isabella Jean, Alice Rebecca. Vans Dunlop scholar in chemistry, Edinburgh U., 1909-12, also 1851 exhibitioner in chemistry, 1912-13; instr. chemistry, 1913-15, asst. prof., 1915-16, asso. prof., 1916-22, prof., 1922-26, Columbia; prof. and chmn. dept. Washington Square Coll. (New York U.), 1926-27, also dean Grad. Sch., New York U., 1927-28; prof., U. of Edinburgh, since 1928. Acting prof. chemistry, Stanford, 1919, 23, U. of Calif., 1923, Pa. State Coll., 1927. Lt. U.S.N.R.F., 1917-19; spl. duty for Bur. of Ordnance as liaison officer with allied navies on Naval Gas Warfare. Lt. comdr. U.S.N.R.F., 1924-26. Fellow Royal Soc., Royal Soc. Edinburgh, A.A.A.S.; mem. Am. Chem. Soc. (chmn. New York sect., 1925), Am. Inst. Chemists (chmn. New York sect. 1926), London Chem. Soc., London Soc. Chem. Industry, Faraday Soc., Phi Beta Kappa, Sigma Xi, Alpha Chi Sigma, Phi Lambda Upsilon. Clubs: Century, Chemists'. Revised and rewrote Smith's Intermediate Chemistry, Smith's College Chemistry, Smith's Elementary Chemistry, Smith's Inorganic Chemistry, and lab. outlines of each, 1922-26. Author: College Chemistry Companion, 1924; Intermediate Chemistry Companion, 1925; General Chemistry and Laboratory Outline, 1927; At Home Among the Atoms, 1929. Home: 14 Mayfield Gardens, Edinburgh Scotland

KENDRICK, CHARLES, b. San Francisco, Calif., son of Thomas and Catherine (Marron) K.; educated public schools and private tutors; LL.D. (hon.), University of San Francisco, 1961; married Marie Canepa, Sept. 15, 1905 (died Dec. 2, 1911); children—Marie, Marron; m. 2d, Kathryn Clarke, Apr. 21, 1914; children—Charles, Geraldine, Kathryn, Barbara. Admitted to bar, 1902; chmn. bd. Schlage Lock Co. of Cal. Trustee San Francisco War Memorial, 1920-38; mem. adv. com. San Francisco Water System, 1923-26; mem. San Francisco Planning Commn., 1924-30; member San Francisco Relief Committee, 1932-34; v.p. Golden Gate Internat. Expn., 1938; trustee Phelan Found.; hon. trustee Mills Coll.; mem. adv. bd. Hoover Inst. Stanford U.; chmn. bd. regents U. San Francisco; mem. bd. govs. San Francisco Opera Assn., San Francisco Art Museum; pres. Pan Am Soc., San Francisco; 1942-43; pres. El Buen Vecino, 1944; mem. San Francisco Civilian War Council, 1940-45; member adv. bd. of the San Francisco Ordnance District, 1940-45, member adv. com. War Production Board, World War II. Served as capt. 26th Div., later maj. 5th Army Corps, U.S. Army, World War I. Decorated Silver Star, Order Purple Heart (U.S.); Order of St. Olav (Norway); Officier Legion of Honor (France); Bernardo O'Higgins (Chile); Gold Medal of Pan American Society (New York City); Grand Cross of the Order of Merit (Peru); Papal night of St. Gregroy the Great. Clubs: Bohemian Club, Pacific Union, Press, Menlo Country, Burlingame Country, San Francisco Golf. Home: San Francisco CA Died Aug. 3, 1970; buried Holy Cross Cemetery, San Bruno CA

KENDRICKS, EDWARD JAMES air force med. officer; b. Alpena, Mich., May 27, 1899; s. George Washington and Mary (Lees) K.; student U. Mich., 1915-19; M.B., M.D., Northwestern, 1922; grad. U.S. Army Med. Sch., 1931, U.S. Army Med. Field Service Sch., 1932; flight surgeon U.S. Army Sch. Aviation Medicine, 1934; m. Wanda Hunt, May 5, 1942. Med. practice, Mich., 1923-30; surgeon U.S. Army Transport Republic, 1932-34; gen. flight surgeon duty, 1934-37; dir. dept. neuropsychiatry U.S. Army Sch. Aviation Medicine, 1937-42; surgeon 9th A.A.F., Middle East and E.T.O., 1942-45; surgeon personnel distbrs. command, 1945-46; chief Aeromed. Lab., 1946-49; dir. med. staffing and edn. Office Surgeon Gen., USAF, 1949-53; commandant of USAF School of Aviation Medicine, 1953—; promoted through ranks to brig. gen. Decorated Legion of Merit with oak leaf cluster, Soldiers medal, Bronze Stars, Presidential Unit Citation; various campaign medals (U.S.); Legion of Honor (France); Croix de Guerre (Belgium and Luxembourg); Keber Lecture award, 1951. Mem. A.M.A., Aeromed. Assn., Assn. Mil. Surgeons, Author articles in med. jours. Home: 163 First Av., Alpena, Mich. Office: of The Surgeon Gneeral. Hdqrs. USAF, Washington 25. Died Feb. 17, 1956; buried Arlington Nat. Cemetery.

KENNEBECK, GEORGE ROBERT, air force ofcr.; b. Carroll, Ia., June 5, 1892; s. George and Elizabeth (Gleason) K.; D.D.S., State U. of Ia., 1916; m. Elizabeth Scales, June 1, 1927; children—Elizabeth V., George Robert. Commd. 1st lt., Dental Corps, U.S. Army, 1917, and advanced through grades to maj. gen., 1949; chief of dental service, Camp Davis, N.C., 1941-42, chief of dental service U.S. Air Force, Hdqrs. U.S. Air Force, Washington, since 1942; officer U.S. Air Force. Recipient Legion of Merit, Commendation Ribbon, Fellow Am. Coll. Dentists; mem. Am. Dental Assn., Internat. Coll. Dentists. Home: Silver Spring MD Died Apr. 29, 1969; buried Arlington Nat. Cemetery.

KENNEDY, CHASE WILMOT army officer; b. Portsmouth, O., Jan. 4, 1859; s. Milton and Josephine Barclay (Hutchinson) K.; grad. U.S. Mil. Acad., 1883, Army War Coll., 1914; m. Elizabeth Lord Jewett, Nov. 13, 1889. Commd. 2d lt. 3d Inf., June 13, 1883; promoted through grades to brig. gen., May 15, 1917; maj. gen. (temp.), World War; promoted maj. gen., retired, June 21, 1930. Served in Cuba, Philippines, Alaska, France and Panama; comdg. 78th and 85th Divs. to Mar. 31, 1919; comdg. Panama Canal Dept., Apr. 28, 1919-May 23, 1921; comdg. 9th Coast Arty. Dist. and 9th Training Center, Nov. 1, 1921-Nov. 30, 1922; retired. Nov. 30, 1922. Awarded badges Indian Wars, Spanish-Am. War, Philippine Insurrection, Cuban Occupation and war with Germany. Home: Washington, D.C. Died Nov. 23, 1936.

KENNEDY, FOSTER neurologist; b. Belfast, Ireland, Feb. 7, 1884; s. William Archer and Hessie Foster (Dill) K.; ed. Queen's Coll., Belfast; M.D., Royal University of Ireland, 1906; married Katherine Caragol de la Terga; 1 daughter, Hessie Juana Dill and 1 daughter by previous marriage, Isabel Ann Foster. Resident med. officer Nat. Hosp., London, 1906; became chief of clinic New York Neurol. Inst., 1910; now prof. neurology

Cornell U. Med. Coll., New York; consulting physician in neuropsychiatry. Bellevue Hosp.; consulting physician Neurol. Inst.; attending neurologist to New York Hosp.; cons. neurologist to Gen. Memorial, Lennox Hill, Women's, Monmouth (Long Branch, N.J.) Nassau (Mineola, L.I.), Vassar Bros. hosps. Chmn. com. neurology, National Research Council, Washington, D.C. Chairman Federal Medical Com., Ellis Island. Served medecinchef Hop. Militaire, V.R. 76, France; commd. lt. Royal Army M.C., Brit. Army in France; promoted capt. and maj. and mentioned in dispatches, Fellow Royal Soc. Edinburgh, Royal Soc. of Medicine, London; mem. Am. Neurol. Assn. (past pres.), N.Y. Acad. Medicine, N.Y. Neurol. Soc. (pres.), N.Y. Command Brit. Great War Vets. Am. (past pres.); hon. mem. Neurol. Soc. of Paris, Hungary, Cuba, Mexico and Sweden. Decorated Conflere la condecoracion de la Orden Nacional de Merito, Carlos F. inlay en el grado de Oficial, Cuba; Chevalier Legion of Honor (France). Protestant, Clubs: Century, River, Coffee House, Pilgrims. Contbr. to tech. jours. on neurol. and psychiat. subjects. Home: 14 Sutton Sq. Office: 410 E. 57th St., N.Y.C. 22. Died Jan. 7, 1952; buried Pendleton Hill Cemetery, R.I.

KENNEDY, JAMES MADISON med. officer U.S.A.; b. Abbeville Co., S.C., Dec. 4, 1865; s. Archibald Boggs and Mary (McCaslan) K.; student Erskine Coll., Due West, S.C.; A.B., S.C. Coll., Columbia, S.C., 1884; M.D., Med. Coll. and Coll. Phys. and Surg. U. of Maryland, 1892; LL.D., Univ. of S.C., 1928; m. Mary Edith Baldwin, Apr. 16, 1898; children-Laurence Baldwin, Katharine (Mrs. William B. Kean), Archibald Boggs. Apptd. asst. surgeon U.S.A., May 12, 1893; advanced through grades to col., May 15, 1917; apptd. brig. gen., asst. to surgeon gen., U.S.A., Mar. 3, 1927. Comdr. ambulance train, Port Tampa, Fla., and Santiago, Cuba, Spanish-Am. War; dist. surgeon and comdg. officer base hosp., Calamba, Luzon, P.I., 1900, in office chief surgeon, Div. of Philippines, 1900-02; assigned U.S.A. Gen. Hosp., Presidio, San Francisco, Calif., 1902-10, comdg. hosp. during San Francisco earthquake and fire, 1906; surgeon and comdg. officer Dept. Hosp., Ft. Shafter, T.H., 1910-12, operating and attending surgeon, 1912; surgeon and sr. recruiting officer Jefferson Barracks, 1913-16; gen. sanitary insp. Ariz. sect., Mexican border, July 1916-May 1917; comdg. officer Base Hosp., Ft. Bliss, Tex., May-July 1917; surgeon, Port of Embarkation, Hoboken, N.J., 1917-19; comdg. officer Letterman Gen. Hosp., San Francisco, 1919-22; surgeon, Philippine Dept., Manila, P.I., 1922-24; comdg. officer Letterman Gen. Hosp., 1924-26; comdg. general Army Med. Center, Washington, D.C., 1926; retired, Dec. 4, 1929. Fellow Am. College Surgeons. Presbyn. Awarded D.S.M., Navy Cross; Spanish-Am. War, Philippine Insurrection, Cuban Occupation and Victory Campaign medals; War Dept. citation-all of U.S. Died Oct. 15, 1930.

KENNEDY, JOHN DOBY diplomat; b. Camden, S.C., Jan. 5, 1840; s. Anthony M. and Sarah (Doby) K.; studied S.C. Coll., 1855-57; m. Elizabeth Cunningham, 1857; m. 2d, Harriet Boykin, 1882. Admitted to S.C. bar, 1861; became capt. Company E., 2d S.C. Pegt. in Civil War, col., 2d Regt., 1862, brig. gen., 1864; elected to U.S. Ho. of Reps., 1865, denied seat when he refused to take oath; mem. Dem. Nat. Conv., St. Louis, 1876; mem. La. Democratic Exec. Com., 1876, chmn., 1878; mem. lower house S.C. Legislature, 1878-79; lt. gov. S.C., 1880-82; U.S. consul gen., Shanghai, China, 1885-89. Died Camden, Apr. 14, 1896.

KENNEDY, JOHN FITZGERALD 35th Pres. U.S.; b. Brookline, Mass., May 29, 1917; s. Joseph Patrick and Rose (Fitzgerald) K.; B.S. cum laude, Harvard, 1940, LL.D., 1956; LL.D., U. Notre Dame, 1950, Tufts Coll., 1954, Boston U., Assumption Coll., 1955, Loras Coll., Rockhurst Coll., Boston Coll., Northeastern U.; D.Sc., Lowell Tech. Inst., 1956; m. Jacqueline Lee Bouvier, Sept. 12, 1953; children-Caroline Bouvier, John Fitzgerald, Patrick Bouvier (dec.). Mem. 80th-82d Congresses (1947-53), 11th Mass. Dist.; U.S. senator from Mass., 1953-61; Pres. U.S., 1961-63. Mem. bd. overseers Harvard, 1957. Served with USN, 1941-45. Decorated Navy and Marine Corps medal, Purple Heart. Democrat. Author: Why England Slept, 1940; Profiles in Courage, 1956 (Pulitzer prize for biography 1957); Strategy of Peace, 1960; To Turn the Tide, 1961. Assassinated at Dallas, Nov. 22, 1963; buried Arlington Nat. Cemetery.

KENNEDY, ROBERT MORRIS rear admiral Med. Corps; b. Mahanoy City, Pa., June 21, 1867; s. George Washington and Elizabeth Cunningham (Morris) K. Midshipman, U.S. Naval Acad., 1885-87; M.D., U. of Pa., 1890; post grad. courses New York Polyclinic Med. Sch. and Hosp., 1893, 1901; m. Bessie Marsden Murdaugh, Aug. 3, 1898; 1 dau., Elizabeth Morris. Commd. ensign Med. Corps. U.S. Navy, June 26, 1890, and advanced through grades to rear adm. Mar. 2, 1929; asst. surgeon, June 18, 1890; passed asst. surgeon, June 18, 1893, surgeon, Oct. 20, 1901. Served in Spanish-Am. War, Philippine Insurrection, Boxer trouble in China, disturbances in Haiti and Santo Domingo, Mexican Border, World War. Comdr. Naval Hosp., San Juan, P.R., and on surg. staff Presbyn. Hosp., 1909-11; comdr. U.S. Hosp. Ship Solace, 1915-17, and naval hosps., Washington, D.C., 1917-19, Annapolis, 1922-27. Instr., Naval Med. Sch., Washington, 1911-12; insp. med. dept. activities, U.S. Navy, 1919-21 and 1929-30; pres. Bd. Med. Examiners and naval med. examining bds., 1921-22; mem. Naval Retiring Bd., 1921-22, 1927-30; retired July 1, 1931. Awarded Navy Cross; recommended for D.S.M. "for distinguished and meritorious service in World War." Fellow Am. Coll. Surgeons; mem. A.M.A., Mil. Order World War. Episcopalian. Address: Navy Dept., Washington. Died June 16, 1946; buried in Arlington National Cemetery.

KENNEDY, ROBERT PATTERSON lawyer; b. Bellefontaine, O., Jan. 23, 1840; s. William G. and Mary E. (Patterson) K.; student Yale, and Geneva Coll., class of 1861; m. Maria L. Gardner, Dec. 29, 1862; m. 2d, Mrs. Emma (Cowgill) Mendenhall, Sept. 4, 1894. Second lt. 23d Ohio Inf., June 11, 1861; capt. asst. adj. vols., Oct. 7, 1862; maj., Nov. 16, 1864; resigned, Apr. 8, 1865; col. 196th Ohio Inf., Apr. 14, 1865; bvtd. lt. col. vols., Mar. 13, 1865, "for gallant and meritorious services during campaign in W.Va. and in Shenandoah Valley"; bvtd. brig. gen. vols., Mar. 13, 1865, "for distinguished gallantry during the war"; hon. mustered out, Sept. 11, 1865. Admitted to bar, 1866, and practiced at Bellefontaine, O.; U.S. internal revenue collector, 1878-83; lt. gov. of Ohio, 1885-87; mem. 50th and 51st Congresses (1887-91); mem. U.S. Insular Commn., to investigate conditions and formulate a code of laws for Cuba and P.R., 1899-1900. Republican. Died May 6, 1918.

KENNELLY, MARTIN H. ex-mayor Chgo.; b. Chgo., Aug. 11, 1887; s. Jeremiah and Margaret Kennelly; ed. De La Salle Inst., Chgo.; LL.D., Ill. Inst. Tech., 1948; LL.D., Loyola U., 1949, Northwestern U., 1947, DePaul U., 1959. Entire bus. career connected with storage warehousing and trucking; became co-organizer and pres. Fort Dearborn Storage Warehouse Co., 1919; with assos. purchased control Werner Bros. Fireproof Storage Co., now Werner Kennelly Co., 1923; past pres. Allied Van Lines, Inc.; dir. Wilson & Co. Co-trustee Consumers Co. (under Fed. Dist. Ct.), 1935-37, chmn. exec. bd., following reorgn. co., 1937-41. Commr. Lincoln Park Bd., 1933-34; apptd. mem. Chgo Park Dist., 1934. Elected mayor Chgo., Apr. 1947-55. Chmn. Am. Red Cross campaigns, Chgo.; nat. vice chmn. A.R.C. Fund, 1949. Dir. Chgo. Assn. Commerce. Past pres. U.S. Conf. Mayors. Past pres. Nat. Furniture Warehousemen's Assn., Ill. Furniture Warehousemen's Assn. Pres. Army Emergency Relief Aux., Chgo. area, 1942. Served with U.S. Army, 1918-19, advancing through the grades from pvt. to capt.; with Q.M.C., Washington, 1919. Democrat. Roman Catholic. Clubs: Traffic (ex-pres.), Chicago Athletic Assn. (ex-pres.); Evanston Golf (past pres.). Home: 5555 Sheridan Rd., Chgo. 60640 Died Dec. 6, 1961.

KENNER, ALBERT WALTON army officer; b. Holyoke, Mass., Dec. 15, 1889; Ph.D., George Washington, U., 1910, M.D., 1915; grad. Army Med. Sch., Washington, 1917; m. Mlle. Raymonde Minard, Feb. 2, 1921 (dec. Apr. 1959); 1 son, Albert W. Commd. 1st lt. Med. R.C., 1916, regular army, 1917, and advanced through the grades to major gen., 1943; regimental surg., 26th Inf., 1st Inf. Div., World War I. Instr. U.S. Mil. Acad., West Point, N.Y., 1920-22. Gen. surg. service, Walter Reed Gen. Hosp., 1923-27; post surgeon Med. Field Service Sch., Carlisle Barracks, Pa., 1927-31; chief Surg. Service, Fort Banks, Mass., 1931; surgeon Harbor Def., Boston, 1931-32; chief surg. service, Ft. Banks, 1932-34; chief med. service, Sternberg Gen. Hosp., Manila, P.I., 1934-36; surg. duties, Ft. Myer, Va., 1936-17, post surgeon, 1937-41; Surgeon Armored Force, Fort Knox, Ky., 1941-42; chief surgeon Western Task Force Landing at Casa Blanca, Morocco, 1942; overseas, 1942-43; then with Army Group, Washington, 1942-43; chief of tng. inspections, Surgeon Gen. Office, Washington, 1943-49, ret. maj. gen.; chief med. officer S.H.A.E.F., European Theatre, 1944-45; chief surgeon for U.S. Forces, European Theatre, 1945-46; mem. sec. of War's personnel bd. 1946-49; med. dir. Columbia Hosp. for Women, Wash. Decorated D.S.C., D.S.M. with oak leaf cluster, Silver Star with two oak leaf clusters, Legion of Merit, Purple Heart (U.S.), Officer Legion of Honor, Croix de Guerre with palm, comdr. Order Sante Publique (France), Companion of the Bath (Gt. Britain), Grand Officer Assouam Alouette (Morocco), Comdr. Order of Crown, Croix de Guerre with palm (Belgium). Fellow Am. Coll. Surgeons. Club: Army-Navy (Washington). Home: 4925 Rodman St., Washington 16. Office: Columbia Hosp. for Women, 25th and L St. N.W., Washington. Died Nov. 12, 1959; buried Arlington Nat. Cemetery.

KENNER, FRANK TERRY coast guard officer; b. Riverton, Va., Jan. 18, 1904; s. Wilson T. and Bertha M. (Bricker) K.; B.S., USCG Acad., 1925; m. Elizabeth S. Ware, September 10, 1927. USCG, 1924, advanced through grades to rear adm., 1954; served afloat, 1924-35; assigned Hawaiian dist., 1935-41, USN, Iceland, 1942-43, New Caledonia, New Guinea, Philippines, 1943-45, USCG Hdqrs., Washington, 1945-53; comdr. 14th Coast Guard Dist., 1953-56; chief operations USGC Hdqrs., 1956-. Acting field rep. Dept. Interior, adminstrn. Am. Equatorial Islands, 1939-41. Clubs: Propellor, Army and Navy (Washington); Belle Haven Country (Alexandria, Va.). Home: 38 Niuiki Circle, Honolulu, Hawaii. Office: care USCG, Washington 25. Died Mar. 1961.

KENNERLY, WESLEY TRAVIS lawyer; b. Henry County, Tenn., Aug. 29, 1877; s. Charles M. and Sarah A. (Travis) K.; LL.B., U. of Tennessee, 1901; M. Ola D. Robertson, Mar. 15, 1906 (died Dec. 9, 1934); children - Robert Travis, Warren Wesley. Began practice at Knoxville, 1900; chairman Knox County Dem. Exec. Com., 1906-10; mem. Dem. State Exec. Com., 2d Dist. of Tenn., 1910-18 and 1922-24; city atty., Knoxville, 1912-16; U.S. atty., Eastern District of Tenn., 1917-21, mem. Kennerly & Key. Lecturer on Federal Pleading, Practice and Criminal Law, U. of Tenn.; special Justice Supreme Court of Tenn., 1939. Hon. col. staff of Gov. of Tenn., 1939-43. Del. to Dem. Nat. Convention, 1932 and 1940; Dem. elector 2d Congl. Dist., 1932. Served as 1st sergt. Co. L, 1st Tenn. Inf., Spanish-Am. War. Mem. bd. trustees U. of Tenn. Pres. Alumni Assn. of U. of Tenn., 1925-26; mem. Am. (v.p. 1921-22) and Tenn. bar assns., Knoxville Bar Assn. (ex-pres.), Am. Judicature Soc., S.R., United Spanish War Vets. (comdr. Dept. of Tenn., 1926), Tenn. Hist. Soc., East Tenn. Hist. Soc., Sons of Confederate Vets., Phi Kappa Phi, Phi Delta Phi. Methodist. Mason (K.T., Shriner), K.P., Elk. Clubs: Izaak Walton League of America, Knoxville Rod and Reel. Home: 2016 Ogden Av., Knoxville, Tenn; (summer) Kenrock Lodge on Norris Lake (Tenn.). Office: 625 Market St., Knoxville, Tenn. Died Jan. 29, 1944.

KENNON, LYMAN WALTER VERE army officer; b. Providence, R.I., Sept. 2, 1858; s. Charles Henry Vere and Adelaide (Hall) K.; Grad. U.S. Mil. Acad., 1881, Army War Coll., 1910; m. Anne Beecher Rice, Apr. 3, 1883. Commd. add. 2d lt. 1st Inf., June 11, 1881; promoted through grades to brig. gen. N.A., Aug. 5, 1917. Served in Indian War, in Cuba during Spanish-Am. War. Cuban occupation and Philippines; explorations and surveys in Central American for Intercontinental Ry.; constructed the Benquet Road to Baguio, the Summer capital of Philippines, for which was complimented by Pres. Roosevelt. Apptd. comdr. 86th div., N.A., Camp Grant, Rockford, Ill., Nov. 1917. Author: Manual of Guard Duty, 1891. Died Sept. 9, 1918.

KENNY, ALBERT SEWALL rear adm. U.S.N.; b. Van Buren Co., Ia., Jan. 19, 1841; s. Sewall and Mary (Strong) K.; A.B., U. of Vt., 1861; m. Ellen Barnes, Oct. 27, 1874. Commd. asst. p.m. U.S.N., Mar. 19, 1862; p.m., Mar. 9, 1865; pay insp., July 31, 1884; pay dir., Sept. 26, 1867; p.m. gen., May 5, 1889; with rank of rear adm., Dec. 13, 1809. Served in S. Atlantic blockading squadron, 1862-63; N. Atlantic blockading squadron, 1864-65; present at both attacks on Ft. Fisher. After Civil War, service on west coast of Africa, San Francisco, in cruising ships, at Naval Acad. and at New York Navy Yard; retired, Jan. 19, 1903; relieved from duty as p.m. gen., July 1, 1903; treasurer Isthmian Canal Commn., May 1901-May 1905. Died May 17, 1930.

KENT, EDWARD MATHER, physician; b. Syracuse, N.Y., May 2, 1907; s. Edward Enos and Eunice (Mather) K.; B.S., Pa. State Coll., 1929; M.D., Syracuse U., 1932; M.Sc. in Surgery, U. Pa., 1940; m. Dorothy Jean Dearborn, June 17, 1935; children—Jean (Mrs. Jean McNutt), Brian Mather, Beth Anne. Intern, St. Mary's Hosp., Rochester, N.Y., 1932-33; postgrad. in gen. surgery Grad. Sch. U. Pa., 1934-37; resident in surgery Abington (Pa.) Meml. Hosp., 1935-37; resident in thoracic surgery Norwich (Conn.) State Tb Sanatorium, 1937-39; fellow in thoracic surgery Washington U., Barnes Hosp., St. Louis, 1939-40; resident Tb Sanatorium, Glendale, Md., 1941-42; attending surgeon Allegheny Gen. Hosp., Pitts., chmn. surg. div. med. staff, 1965-69, pres. staff, 1968; area cons. thoracic surgery VA, Pitts.; cons. staff Columbia, St. Francis, St. Margaret's, South Side hosps., also others; asst. prof. surgery U. Pitts. Sch. Med., 1946-51, asso. prof., 1951-54, clin. prof. surgery, 1954-70; mem. exec. com., 1959. Kellogg Meml lectr. in surgery George Washington U., 1952; Trudeau Meml. lectr. Trudeau Sanatorium, Saranac Lake, N.Y., 1954; mem. med. adv. bd. Heart House. Bd. dirs. Allegheny County unit Am. Cancer Soc., 1956-59. Served to comdr., M.C., USNR, 1942-46. Diplomate Am. Bd. Surgery, Am. Bd. Thoracic Surgery (founder mem., dir. 1955-60). Fellow A.C.S. (past gov.); mem. A.M.A., Pa., Allegheny County med. socs., Am. (council 1963-67, 69-70, pres. 1968-69), Pa. assns. thoracic surgery, Am. Coll. Chest Physicians (v.p. Pa. chpt. 1956), Am., Central surg. assns., Soc. Internationale de Chirurgie (titulaire), Am. Coll. Cardiology, Soc. Thoracic Surgeons, Pitts. Acad. Medicine, Pitts. Surg. Soc. (pres. 1963), Western Pa. Heart Assn. (dir.). Republican. Roman Catholic. Contbr. articles to med. jours., chpts. to books. Home: Wexford PA Died June 6, 1970; buried Syracuse NY

KENT, JACOB FORD brig. gen.; b. Phila., Sept. 14, 1835; s. Rodolphus and Sarah (Deily) K.; ed. at Samuel Crawford's Sch., Phila. and Mt. Pleasant Mil. Acad., Sing Sing, N.Y.; grad. U.S. Mil. Acad., 1861; m. Mary M. Eaton, June 3, 1885. Commd. 2d lt. 3d Inf., May 6, 1861; promoted through grades to brig. gen. vols., May 4, 1898; maj. gen. vols., July 8, 1898; brig. gen. U.S.A., Oct. 4, 1898; retired at own request, after 40 yrs.' service, Oct. 15, 1898; hon. disch. from vol. service, Nov. 30, 1898. Bvtd.; maj., May 3, 1863, "for gallant and meritorious services in battle of Marye's Heights, Va."; lt. col., May 12, 1864, for same in battle of

Spottsylvania, Va.; col. vols., Oct. 19, 1864, "for faithful and meritorious services during campaign before Richmond, Va." Home: Troy, N.Y. Died Dec. 22, 1918.

KENT, R(OBERT) H(ARRINGTON), ballistician; born Meriden, Connecticut, July 1, 1886; s. Silas William and Mary Elizabeth (Chapman) K.; A.B., Harvard 1910, A.M., 1916, Sc.D. (hon.), 1953. Asst. instr. physics, part-time instr. maths. Harvard, 1910-16; instructor electrical engineering University Pa., 1916-17; civilian engaged in experimental and theoretical work in ballistics Office Chief Ordnance, Washington and Aberdeen (Md.) Proving Ground, 1919-36; asso. dir., ballistic research labs. Aberdeen Proving Ground, Ordnance Dept., U.S. Army, 1936-48, asso. tech. dir. 1948-56, consultant 1956-. Served from first lieutenant to captain Ordnance Department, U.S. Army, 1917-19, Offices Chief Ordnance and of Chief Ord. Officer, A.E.F., France. Decorated Medal for Merit; awarded Potts medal, Franklin Inst., 1947, Air Force Exceptional Civilian Service Medal, American Ordnance Association, Campbell Medal, Army Exceptional Civilian Service Medal. Fellow A.A.A.S., Am. Phys. Soc.; member Nat. Acad. Scis., Phi Beta Kappa. Home: 307 S. Union Av., Havre de Grace. Office: Ballistic Research Laboratories, Aberdeen Proving Ground, Md. Died Feb. 3, 1961.

KENTON, SIMON Indian fighter; b. Culpeper (now Fauquier) County, Va., Apr. 3, 1755; s. Mark and Mary (Miller) K.; m. Martha Dowden, Feb. 15, 1787; m. 2d, Elizabeth Jarboe, Mar. 2,n7, 1798. Served as scout in Lord Dunmore's War, 1774; apptd. scout by Daniel Boone, leading participant in local encounters with Indians around Ky., Ill.; helped to quell Indian riots in Ill. region during Revolutionary War, 1777; capt. of a volunteer co., helped drive British and Indians out of Ky. region, 1779; served as maj. in Wayne's expdn., 1794; brig. gen. Ohio Militia, 1805; a town in Ohio, also a county in Ky. named after him; fought in Can. during War of 1812. Died Bellefontaine, O., Apr. 29, 1836; buried Urbana, O.

KENYON, GEORGE HENRY physician; b. Providence, Apr. 1, 1845; s. George Amos and Isabella Green (Brown) K.; prep. edn. Friends Sch., Providence; grad. Brown, 1864, A.M., 1867; M.D., Univ. of Vt., 1866. Pvt. 10th R.I. vols., 1862; mem. R.I. militia, in which attained rank of brig.-gen.; surgeon-gen. R.I. since 1894; mem. U.S. Examining Bd. for pensions, Providence, since July, 1897; active mem. Supreme Council 33ff Northern Masonic Jurisdiction of U.S., and its deputy for R.I. Mem. Am. Med. Assn., R.I. Med. Soc., Providence Med. Assn. Residence: 440 Smithfield Av. Office: 290 Westminster St., Providence.

KERCHEVILLE, F(RANCIS) M(ONROE), educator; b. Pearsall, Tex., Feb. 18, 1901; s. Richard and Laura (Long) K.; A.B., Abilene Christian Coll., 1924; M.A., U. Wis., 1927, grad. fellow, 1929, Ph.D., 1930; post grad. study or spl. research Nat. U. Mexico, 1924, Sorbonne, U. Paris, 1926, U. Madrid, 1935, U. Chile (Inst. Internat. Edn. fellow), 1941; m. Christina Johnson, Aug. 25, 1927; 1 dau., Francina. Teaching asst. U. Wis., 1924; asso. prof., acting head dept. Spanish, U. S.D., 1930; became prof. modern langs., head dept., U. N.M., 1931; vis. prof. U. Guadalajara (Mexico), 1955, 58, 61; ofcl. cons. Spanish, N.M. Dept. Edn., 1955-64; prof., dept. head fgn. langs. Texas College of Arts and Industries, Kingsville, Tex., 1964-69, adviser, coordinator Inter-Am. Studies, 1966; ednl. dir. fgn. travel N.M. Ednl. Assn., Dept. Edn., 1956-58; dir. Com. Subversive Research, 1955-56. Mem. orgn. com. Inst. do Literatura Ibero-Americano, 1947-49; N.M. chairman of Revolving Student Loan Fund higher edn., 1960-61; civilian advisor 4th Army, 8th Corps Area, 1961-62; Armed Forces Adv. Commn., 1962. Recipient Internat. Sertoma award for citizenship, 1955, state silver citation annual award for Americanism, 1955; Army Civilian Service citation in field of edn., 1962. Served as capt., Mil. Intelligence, U.S. Army, World War II. Mem. Army Adv. Com., 1945-69. Mem. International Council of Inter-American Studies, New Mexico Art League (past pres.), Am. Assn. Tchrs. Spanish and Portuguese (past nat. pres.), Modern Lang. Assn. Am., Rocky Mountain Modern Lang. Assn. (co-founder, co-pres. 1947), Am. Assn. U. Profs., Am. Legion, Phi Kappa Phi, Phi Sigma Iota. Mason (32 deg., K.T., Shriner). Author, co-author or co-editor of books relating to field, 1934-69. Author of poetry vol.: The White Thorn, 1966. Editor, chief cons. Joint Publs. Americanism series, joint com. Am. Legion-N.M. Edn. Assn., 1955; editor: Practical Spoken Spanish, 25th anniversary rev. edit. 1959-60; also syndicated newspaper series Dialogues of Don Placido, 1960-61. Lectr.; writer in fields of interest. Home: Kingsville TX Died Oct. 9, 1969; buried Sandia Gardens, Albuquerque NM

KERN, MAXIMILIAN endocrinologist; b. Stanislau, Austria, Jan. 16, 1890; s. Disrael and Rosalie (Shleifer) K.; ed. Royal Imperial Gymnasium Stanislau; M.D., Long Island Coll. Hosp., Brooklyn, N.Y., 1911; M.D., Chicago Coll. Medicine and Surgery (now Med Sch. Loyola U.), 1915; m. Elaine Frances Hoexter, Mar. 10, 1923 (dec.); 1 dau., Janet R. Came to U.S. 1907, naturalized citizen 1912. Practiced, Chicago, 1916-, specializing in internal medicine; prof. of endocrinology, Gen. Med. Foundation Med. Coll., Chicago, since 1922; formerly attending internist John B. Murphy Hosp., now attending internist and sec. of staff Edgewater Hosp., Chicago, and Oak Park, (Illinois) hospitals. Served as first lt. M.C., U.S. Army, 1917; med. consultant U.S. Marine Hosp. Hon. pres. Med. Round Table, Chgo. Fellow American Geriatric Society Am. Coll. Cardiology; m. A.M.A., Ill., Chgo. med. socs., U.S.P.H. Assn., Soc. for Study of Goiter, Endocrine Society Am. Heart Assn., Am. Med. Writers Assn., Zeta Mu Phi, Phi Gamma Mu (nat. social science honor soc.). Author: (monographs) Psychology and Daily Life; Blindness of Pituitary Origin; Role of Endocrinology in Epilepsy, 1923; Endocrines in Ophthalmology and Otolaryngology, Crime and the Endocrines, 1924; Les Glandes Endocrines avant la Puberté (Paris), 1925; Studies of Endocrine Types, 1926; The Sella Turcica in Relation to Endocrinology, 1927; Endocrines and Physiotherapy, 1927; Relation of the Sella Turcica to Endocrine Disturbances, 1927; Dermagraphia in Relation to Dysthyrodism, 1927; The Status of Physical Therapy in the Treatment of Obesity, 1928; The Thyroid Gland and Menstrual Disorders, 1928; Obesity and the Endocrines, 1928; Further Studies in the Problems of Obesity, 1930; Pituitary Tumors, 1931; Hemolytic Streptococcus Bacteremia with Endocarditis and Arthritis Following Scarlet Fever, 1931; Clinical Application of Testosterone Propionate, 1940. A Quantitative Study of Saliva Glucose (co-author) 1945. The Role of Carbohydrates in Management of Obesity, 1946. Home: 925 Bluff, Glencoe, Ill. Office: 55 E. Washington St., Chgo. 60602 Died July 31, 1964.

KERNAN, FRANCIS JOSEPH army officer; b. Jacksonville, Fla., Oct. 19, 1859; s. John A. and Elizabeth C. (Kernan) K.; grad. U.S. Mil. Acad., 1881; Army War Coll., 1914; m. Ella M. McCaffrey, Mar. 18, 1898; children - Francis Morgan, Katharine, George Morgan, Philip McCaffrey. Commd. 2d lt. 21st Inf., June 11, 1881; promoted through grades to brig. gen., Mar. 23, 1917; maj. gen. N.A., Aug. 5, 1917; major general Regular Army, Oct. 14, 1919. On staff Gen. MacArthur in the Philippines, 1898; judge advocate Dept. Santa Clara, Cuba, and at Cienfuegos, 1899; again aide to Gen. MacArthur in P.I., 1900-03; mem. Gen. Staff Corps, Washington, D.C., 1905-09; in P.I., 1909; comd. 8th Inf. Brigade, El Paso, Tex., Apr. 1917; acting asst. chief of staff, May-Aug. 1917, and drew up official instructions for Gen. Pershing (approved by Sec. of War Baker and President Wilson); apptd. comdr. Camp Wheeler, Macon, Ga., Sept. 1917; organized and comd. Service of Supply in France, Nov. 30, 1917-July 28, 1918. Mem. Am. mission to negotiate convention for treatment, exchange, etc., of prisoners of war and detained civilians with Germans, Berne, Switzerland, July 29-Nov. 11, 1918; tech. mil. adviser to Am. Commn. to Negotiate Peace, Paris, Nov. 23, 1919-Mar. 6, 1922; retired, Dec. 1, 1922. Clubs: Army and Navy (Washington, D.C.); San Antonio (Tex.). Address: War Dept., Washington, D.C. Deceased.

KERR, CLARENCE D(ILWORTH) lawyer; b. Fairfield, Pa., Aug. 15, 1878; s. Thomas Bakewell and Clara (Dilworth) K.; grad. Lawrenceville Sch., 1897; A.B., Princeton, 1901; LL.B., Columbia, 1904; m. Janet Brinckerhoff, April 17, 1906; children-John Brinckerhoff, Harold Brinckerhoff, Clarence Dilworth, Mary Mason, William Dilworth. Admitted to N.Y. State bar, 1903; practiced with White & Case, N.Y.C., 1904-07, with Thomas W. Bakewell, 1907-09; mem. firm Fish, Richardson & Neave, N.Y.C., 1910—, specializing in patent law. Admitted to practice N.Y. Ct. of Appeals, 1903, U.S. Dist. and Circuit Cts., 1907, U.S. Supreme Ct., 1918. Served as capt. chem. warfare U.S. Army, 1918. With council Nat. Defense and War Industries Bd. later with gen. staff under Gen. Hugh Johnson, as $1 a yr. man, 1917-18. Pres. Englewood council Boy Scouts of Am., 1919-21; mayor Englewood, N.J., 1922-23; pres. Englewood Free Pub. Library, 1924-30; mem. bd. govs. Englewood Hosp. Assn., 1928—, pres., 1930-35; mem. bd. mgrs. Englewood Community Chest, 1936-42, chmn., 1939-41; pres. Lawrenceville Sch. Alumni Assn., 1926-27, mem. bd. trustees, 1927-47; pres. 1943-47; mem. Princeton Grad. council, 1921—, twice pres. Princeton Alumni Assn. No. N.J. Presbyn. Clubs: Commodore Clayton (N.Y.) Yacht, 1941-45, University, Down Town Assn., Princeton (N.Y.C.); Englewood, Englewood Field (Englewood, N.J.); Knickerbocker Country, Cap and Gown, Nassau (Princeton). Home: 217 Cedar St., Englewood, N.J. Office: 20 Exchange Pl., N.Y.C. 5. Died Sept. 20, 1957.

KERR, JAMES TAGGART army officer; b. in Ohio, Apr. 22, 1859; grad. U.S. Mil. Acad., 1881; honor grad. Inf. and Cav. Sch., 1897. Commd. 2d lt. 17th Inf., June 11, 1881; promoted through grades to brig. gen., Oct. 2, 1917. Address: War Dept., Washington. Died Apr. 13, 1949.

KERR, JOHN BROWN army officer; b. nr. Lexington, Ky., Mar. 12, 1847; s. John and Rachel (Fry) K.; grad. U.S. Mil. Acad., 1870; m. Eva Paddock, June 7, 1894. Apptd. 2d lt., 6th U.S. Cav., June 15, 1870; promoted through grades to brig. gen. U.S.A., Apr. 13, 1908; retired, May 20, 1909. Engaged in mil. duty on frontier in Tex., Ind. Ty., Kan., Ariz. and N.M., 1870-88, and active in movements against and engagements with Indians; hon. mentioned in gen. orders, June 25, 1888, "for meritorious conduct in defeating attempt made by Navajo Indians to rescue from custody Indian prisoners, between Fts. Wingate and Gallup, N.M."; engaged in campaign against Sioux Indians, under Gen. Miles, 1890-97; awarded medal of honor "for distinguished bravery while comdg. his troop against Sioux on White River, S.D., Jan. 1, 1891"; comd. 2d squadron, 6th Cav., in Spanish-Am. War, and in campaign against Santiago de Cuba, and wounded in assault of San Juan Ridge, July 1, 1898; mil. attaché to Germany, 1900-02; asst. adj. gen., July 15, 1902; chief of staff, Philippines Div., 1903-04, Atlantic Div., 1904-06. Won many medals for marksmanship; won Army gold medal in Army Competition, 1890. Died Feb. 27, 1928.

KERR, ROBERT SAMUEL ex-governor, U.S. senator; born Ada, Oklahoma, Sept. 11, 1896; s. William Samuel and Margaret Eloda (Wright) K.; student East Central Normal School, Ada, 1909-11 and 1912-15. Oklahoma Bapt. U., Shawnee, 1911-12, U. of Okla., 1915-16; m. Reba Shelton, Dec. 5, 1919 (died Feb. 12, 1924); m. 2d, Grayce Breene, Dec. 26, 1925; children-Robert Samuel, Breene Mitchell, Kay, William Grayeen. Admitted to Okla. bar, 1922, and practiced in Ada.; mem. firm Kerr, Lambert & Conn. Drilling contractor and oil producer, 1926 - ; chmn. bd. Kerr-McGee Oil Industries, Inc., 1944-; partner Kerr-McGee & Co.; gov. Okla., 1943-47; U.S. senator from Okla., 1949-; dir. Republic Supply Co. Keynoter Democratic Nat. Convention, 1944. Spl. justice Okla. Supreme Court, 1931; mem. Unofficial Pardon and Parole Bd. of Okla., 1935-38; pres. Okla. County Juvenile Council, 1935-36; chmn. bd. West Central Broadcasting Co.; pres. Oklahoma Baptist Gen. Conv., 1944; chmn. Okla. Baptist Orphans Home Com., Interstate Oil Compact Commn., 1946. Mem. Dem. Nat. Com., Okla., 1940-44-48. Mem. exec. com. Nat. Governors Conf., 1945-46; chmn. Southern Governors Conf., 1945-46. Served as 2d lt. field arty., U.S. Army, 1917-19; 2d lt. O.R.C., 1919; capt. field arty., Okla Nat. Guard, 1921-25, maj., 1925-29. Mem. Am. Legion (post comdr., 1924; judge advocate State Dept. Okla., 1925; state comdr. 1926). Mem. Mid-Continent Oil and Gas Assn. (pres. Kan.-Okla. div. 1936-41); mem. Forty and Eight Club, Last Man's Club. Democrat. Missionary Baptist. Mason. Clubs: Beacon (Oklahoma City); Tulsa (Tulsa). Home: 327 N.W. 18th St., Oklahoma City. Address: Senate Office Bldg., Washington. Died Jan. 1, 1963.

KERRICK, HARRISON SUMMERS, army officer; b. Minonk, Woodford Co., Ill., Oct. 13, 1873; s. Josiah and Margaret (Hollenbeck) K.; student Ill. Wesleyan U., 1890-92; B.S., Northern Ill. Normal Sch., Dixon, 1894; grad. Arty. Sch., Ft. Monroe, Va., 1906; m. Lena May Clark of Urbana, Ill., Oct. 21, 1903. Teacher and prin. pub. schs., Ill., 1892-98, div. supt. schs., P.I., 1901, enlisted Co. G, 2d Ill. Vol. Inf., June 18, 1898, and advanced through grades to capt. 30th Vol. Inf., 1899; apptd. 2d lt. arty. corps, regular army, July 1, 1901; promoted through grades to col., Mar. 20, 1926. Served in Cuba, 1898-99, Philippines, 1899-1901, and 1925-27; in France with A.E.F., 1918; comdt. Heavy Arty., 7th French Army (Haute Alsace), Aug.-Oct. 1918; served as supt. Water Transp., Port of New York; pres. Hoboken Shore R.R.; asst. for Water Transp. Embarkation Service, 1919-20; transp. officer of Dept., Chicago, 1921; comdg. officer Columbus (Ohio) Gen. Reserve Depot, 1922-25; instr. Coast Arty. Res. Regiments, N.E. States, 1928; coordinator under chief coordinator and Bur. of the Budget, 6th Area, Kansas City, Mo., Apr. 1, 1929-Feb. 1, 1933; inspector harbor defenses, Manila and Subic Bay, 1933; staff officer Dept. of P.I., July-Oct. 1934; retired Oct. 31, 1934. Fellow Am. Geog. Soc.; mem. Mil. Order Foreign Wars, Mil. and Naval Order Spanish-Am. War, Nat. Sojourners, Sigma Chi, Pi Gamma Mu; mem. nat. exec. com. Am. Legion, Dept. Philippine Islands, 1928-36. Methodist. Mason (32 deg.). Clubs: Army and Navy, Army, Navy and Marine Corps Country (Washington, D.C.); Hamilton Club (Chicago). Author: Military and Naval America, 1916; The Flag of the United States, 1925. Lectures: (illustrated) The Evolution of the United States Flag; Flags Famous in American History. Prize essayist Mil. Service Instn., silver medalist, 1908, gold medalist, 1913. Home: Minonk, IL Address: War Dept., Washington DC

KERSHAW, JOSEPH BREVARD army officer, jurist; b. Camden, S.C., Jan. 5, 1822; s. Col. John and Harrietta (Du Bose) K.; m. Lucretia Douglas, 1844, 5 children. Admitted to S.C. bar, 1843; commd. lt. Palmetto Regt., 1843, served in Mexican War; mem. S.C. Legislature, 1852-56; mem. S.C. Secession Conv., 1860; commd. col. 2d S.C. Volunteers, Confederate Army, 1861, brig. gen., 1862, maj. gen., 1864; participated in battles of Bull Run, Chickamauga, prominent in operations in Va. and Md., including battles of Fair Oaks, Savage Station, Malvern Hill, 2d Bull Run, South Mountain, Antietam, distinguished at Battle of Fredericksburg, 1862; pres. S.C. Senate, 1865; judge 5th Circuit Ct. S.C., 1877-93. Died Camden, Apr. 13, 1894.

KESSING, OLIVER OWEN naval officer; b. Greensburg, Ind., Dec. 6, 1890; s. Edward and Rose (Moffett) K.; B.S., U.S. Naval Acad., 1914; m. Jane Moffett, Aug. 21, 1918; children-Thomas Edward (officer USNR), Oliver Owen (officer USN), Jonas Warren. Commd. ensign USN, 1914, advanced through the grades to commodore, 1945. Commr. and pres. All-

Am. Footbal Conf., 1949. Decorated Legion of Merit with two gold stars, Bronze Star medal, Navy Marine Corps medal, Sec. of Navy Commendation ribbon with star, Victory medal with star, Mexican Campaign Medal, Asiatic Campaign ribbon, Am. Def. Medal, Combat medal. Democrat. Roman Catholic. Clubs: Army and Navy, Army-Navy (Washington). Home: Greensburg, Ind. Address: care Navy Dept., Washington 25. Died Feb. 1963.

KESSLER, ALFRED AUGUST JR. army officer; b. Union Hill, N.J., Aug. 3, 1898; s. Alfred A. and Jane (Demorest) K.; B.S., U.S. Mil. Acad., 1922, M.S., Mass. Inst. Tech., 1932; grad. Air Service Primary Flying Sch., 1923. Advanced Flying Sch. 1924 Air Corps Engr. Sch., 1929, Tactical Sch., 1939; m. Polly Jane Crane, July 16, 1924; 1 son, Alfred A. III. Commd. 2d lt., U.S. Army, 1922; advanced through the grades to brig. gen., 1944; served with heavy bomber groups and as wing comdr. 8th Air Force, England, Apr. 1943-Mar. 1944; comdg. gen. Am. Air Force in Russia (shuttle bomber bases), Mar. 1944-Oct. 1944; wing comdr. 8th Air Force, England; mil. attache, Am. embassy, Stockholm, Sweden, Oct. 1944-47; dir. procurement and indsl. planning hdqrs., U.S. Air Force, Washington, 1947-50; deputy dir. maintenance, supply and services, 1950-51: director of supply and services, Washington, 1951-52; comdg. gen. 4th Air Force, September, 1952—. Decorated Legion of Merit, Silver Star, Distinguished Flying Cross, Air Medal with cluster, Distinguished Service Medal. Norwegian Order of St. Olay, Belgian Croix d'Guerre with palm, USSR Order of Suvorov, Swedish Silver Medal, Swedish Order of the Sword. Address: 1207 W. 4th St., North Platte, Neb. Died Nov. 30, 1956; buried The Presidio, San Francisco.

KETCHAM, DANIEL WARREN army officer; b. nr. Burns City, Ind., May 1, 1867; s. Seth L. and Almira (Benham) K.; grad. U.S. Mil. Acad., 1890, Arty. Sch., 1894, Sch. of Submarine Defense, 1904; m. Edith Varnum Smith, Oct. 9, 1897. Commd. add. 2d lt. 2d Arty., June 12, 1890; promoted through grades to col., Coast Arty Corps, May 15, 1917; brig. gen. (temp.), Oct. 1, 1918; returned to grade of col., May 15, 1919; retired from active service May 24, 1919, on own application, after more than 32 yrs.' service. Duty at Ft. Warren, Mass., 1895-97, Boston, 1899; at Honolulu, 1899-1901, Ft. Hamilton, N.Y., 1902-03, Ft. Totten, N.Y., 1903-04, Presidio, San Francisco, 1904-09; in Philippines, 1909-11; at Forts Strong and Warren, Mass., 1911-12; on Gen. Staff, Washington, D.C., 1912-14; at Ft. DuPont, Del., 1915, Ft. Monroe, Va., as pres. Arty. Bd., 1916-17; mem. Ordnance Bd., 1917; on Gen. Staff, Washington, D.C., 1917-18; arrived in France, June 17, 1918; grad. Gen. Staff Coll., Langres, Sept. 1918; comdr. 34th Brigade, C.A.C., Sept. 1918-Feb. 1, 1919; comdr. Camp Taylor, Ky., Mar.-May 1919. Died July 19, 1935.

KETCHAM, JOHN, congressman, farmer; b. Dover, N.Y., Dec. 21, 1832; academic edn.; engaged in farming. Town supervisor, 1854-55; mem. N.Y. assembly, 1856-57; State senator, 1860-61; served, col. 150th N.Y. vols., 1861-65; promoted brig. gen. and bvtd. maj. gen.; commr. of D.C., 1874-77; mem. Congress, 1865-73, 1877-93, and 1897-1903, 18th N.Y. dist., and 1903-07, 21st dist. Republican. Home: Dover Plains, N.Y. Died 1906.

KETCHAM, JOHN HENRY congressman, farmer; b. Dover, N.Y., Dec. 21, 1832; academic edn.; engaged in farming. Town supervisor, 1854-55; mem. N.Y. assembly, 1856-57; State senator, 1860-61; served, col. 150th N.Y. vols., 1861-65; promoted brig. gen. and bvtd. maj. gen.; commr. of D.C., 1874-77; mem. Congress, 1865-73, 1877-93, and 1897-1903, 18th N.Y. dist., and 1903-07, 21st dist. Republican. Home: Dover Plains, N.Y. Died 1906.

KETCHUM, ALEXANDER PHOENIX lawyer; b. New Haven, Conn., May 11, 1839; s. Edgar and Elizabeth (Phoenix) K.; grad. with honors, Coll. City of New York, 1858 (M.A.); tutor there, 1858-59; grad. Albany Law School, 1860, and admitted to bar; m. Clara McFarland Dwight, June 10, 1870 (dec.). Served in Civil War in Dept. of South, and as staff officer of Gen. Rufus Saxton, mil. gov. of S.C.; transferred to staff of Maj. Gen. O. Howard, 1865; served as A.A.A.G., in Charleston and Washington; resigned from army Sept. 1867, with rank of bvt. col.; apptd., 1869, assessor Internal Revenue, 9th dist., N.Y.; later collector same; gen. appraiser and chief appraiser Port of New York, 1874-85; from then engaged in practice of law, N.Y. City. One of founders, and 1st pres. Mt. Morris Bank; 2 yrs. pres. Presbyn. Union, New York; prominent in Y.M.C.A.; was for 4 yrs. mem. bd. education. Republican. Deceased.

KEY, ALBERT LENOIR naval officer, life ins.; b. Loudon Co., Tenn., July 30, 1860; s. David McKendree and Elizabeth (Lenoir) K.; grad. U.S. Naval Acad., 1882; m. Grace Condit Smith, of Washington, Apr. 7, 1898 (died Feb. 20, 1918); children-David McKendree, Albert Lenoir (dec.). Served in U.S.N. through grades of ensign, lt. (jr. grade), lt., lt.-comdr., comdr. and capt.; voluntarily retired as commodore, June 30, 1912. Formerly chmn. bd. Volunteer State Life Ins. Co., Chattanooga. West Indian and Philippine naval campaign medals, Spanish-Am. War. Clubs: University, N.Y. Yacht (New York); Metropolitan, Army and Navy (Washington); Mountain City (Chattanooga). Chief of staff 1st Naval Dist., 1917-18; chief of staff to commandant Boston Navy Yard, Mar. 1-Dec. 23, 1918. Spl. letter of commendation from Navy Dept. for services rendered during World War. Home: Chattanooga, Tenn.

KEY, DAVID MCKENDREE jurist; b. Green Co., Tenn., Jan. 27, 1824; grad. Hiwassee Coll., Tenn., 1850 (A.M., LL.D., also LL.D., Univ. of Tenn.); practised law in Tenn.; lt. col. in Confederate army during Civil War; member Constl. Convention, Tenn., 1870; chancellor, 3d Chancery dist., Tenn., 1870-75; U.S. senator from Tenn., 1875-77; U.S. postmaster general, 1877-80; U.S. dist. judge, 1880-95; resigned latter year; m. Elizabeth J. Lenoir, July 1, 1857. Home: Chattanooga, Tenn. Died 1900.

KEY, WILLIAM SHAFFER oil investments; b. Dudleyville, Ala., Oct. 6, 1889; s. Callie R. and Hadassah (Fargason) K.; ed. high sch., Opelika, Ala., LL.B., Oklahoma City University, 1951: married Irene Davis, May 5, 1914; children-William Shaffer, Irene Genevieve (Mrs. Wm. Lee Harper), Robert Carleton. Began in hardware business, Wewoka, 1911; moved to Oklahoma City, 1927, and since engaged in oil bus.; pres. Key Bldg. Corp.; dir. Mutual Savs. & Loan Assn., Oklahoma Natural Gas Co. Works Progress Adminstr. for Okla., 1935-37. Candidate for Gov. of Okla., 1938. Was capt. infantry, U.S. Army, on Mexican border, 1916-17: successively capt., maj. and lt. col. U.S. Army 17 mos. overseas, World War I; maj. gen. 45th Div., Nat. Guard of U.S.; in Federal service Sept. 1940-Nov. 1946; became provost marshal gen. of European Theater of Operations with hdqrs. in London, Oct. 1942, comdg. all U.S. troops in Iceland, June 1943-Dec. 1944; head U.S. Military Control Commn., Hungary, Dec. 1944-July 1946, ret. Oct. 1949. Civilian aide to Sec. Army in Oklahoma. Decorations: Distinguished Service Medal with Oak Leaf Cluster, Legion of Merit, Bronze Star Medal, Commendation Ribbon; Order of Bath (British); Order of Falcon (Icelandic), Distinguished Service Medal (Oklahoma). Warden Oklahoma State Penitentiary, 1924-27. Chmn. Oklahoma Pardon and Parole Board, - 1928-1930. Trustee, Okla. City University. Pres. Oklahoma Historical Society, Masonic Foundation; member Supreme Council Scottish Rite. Mem. Am. Legion, Democrat. Baptist. Mason (33ff). Clubs: Rotary, Men's Dinner. Comd. Okla. City Mil. Dist. during state-wide martial law, Sept.-Oct. 1923. Home: 600 Culbertson Dr. Office: Oklahoma Natural Bldg., Oklahoma City. Died Jan. 5, 1959; buried Oklahoma City.

KEYES, EDWARD LOUGHBOROUGH urologist; b. Elizabeth, N.J., May 15, 1873; s. Edward Lawrence and Sarah M. (Loughborough) K.; A.B., Georgetown (D.C.) U., 1892, Ph.D., 1901; M.D., Coll. Phys. and Surg. (Columbia), 1895; m. Emma W. Scudder, Nov. 17, 1898; children-Edward Lawrence, Emma Willard, Elizabeth Hewlett, Alexander Loughborough; m. 2d, Bessie Potter June 1919. Lecturer on urology, Georgetown Med. 1902-06; - - adj. prof. urology New York Polyclinic Med. Sch., 1903-08; lecturer on surgery, Cornell U. Med. Sch., 1904-10; surgeon St. Vincent's Hosp., 1905-20, urologist, 1920-32; urologist, N.Y. Hosp., 1932-37; prof. urology, Bellevue Med. Sch., 1910-11, Cornell U. Med. Sch., 1911-37; urologist Bellevue Hosp., 1910-24; surgeon Gen. Memorial Hosp., 1914-17; formerly cons. urologist Memorial, Bellevue, New York, St. Vincent's hosps.; retired 1939. Maj. Med. R.C., 1917, and dir. Base Hosp. No. 1; lt. col. M.C.N.A., and col. M.C., 1918, and consultant in urology, A.E.F.; col. M.R.C., 1919. Decorated Officer Legion of Honor (France), 1935. Fellow American Coll. Surgeons; hon. fellow Royal Coll. Surgeons (London); hon. member English College Surgeons, 1936; mem. Am. Assn. of Genito-Urinary Surgeons (pres. 1912), Soc. Sanitary and Moral Prophylaxis (pres. 1913-14), A.M.A., Internat. Urol. Soc. (pres. 1927-36), Clin. Urol. Assn. (pres. 1923-24), Am. Urol. Assn. (pres. 1915), Am. Social Hygiene Assn. (pres. 1923-25), New York Acad. Medicine (v.p. 1921-23). Clubs: Century, Charaka; Southside Sportsman's (Islip, L.I.). Author: Genito-Urinary Diseases, 1903, 10; Urology, 1917; A Sea Change, 1939. Contbr. to med. jours. Home: 33 W. 67th St., N.Y. City. Died Mar. 16, 1949; buried Gate of Heaven Cemetery, White Plains, N.Y.

KEYES, ERASMUS DARWIN army officer, businessman; b. Brimfield, Mass., May 29, 1810; s. Justus and Elizabeth (Corey) K.; grad. U.S. Mil. Acad., 1832; m. Caroline Clarke, Nov. 8, 1837; m. 2d, Mary (Laughborough) Bissell, Nov. 22, 1862; 10 children including Edward Lawrence. Commd. 2d lt., 3d Arty., U.S. Army, 1833, capt., 1841; a.d.c. to Gen. Winfield Scott, 1837-38, 38-41; instr. field arty. and cavalry U.S. Mil. Acad., 1844-48; served primarily on West Coast, 1851-60; commd. maj. 1st Arty., 1858; mil. sec. to Gen. Scott with rank of lt. col., 1860-61; commd. col. 11th Inf., 1861; commd. brig. gen. U.S. Volunteers, 1861, maj. gen., 1862, brig. gen. U.S. Army, 1862; pres. Maxwell Gold Mining Co., 1867-69; v.p. Cal. Vine-Culture Soc. for Napa County; v.p. Humboldt and Savs. and Loan Socs., 1868-70. Author: Fifth Years' Observations of Men and Events, 1884. Died Nice, France, Oct. 14, 1895; buried West Point, N.Y.

KEYES, GEOFFREY army officer; b. Fort Bayard, N.M., Oct. 30, 1888; grad. U.S. Mil. Acad., 1913, staff course, Army War Coll., Washington, D.C., 1918. Advanced Course, Cavalry Sch., Ft. Riley, Kans., 1925, Command and Gen. Staff Sch., Ft. Leavenworth, Kans., 1926; grad. Ecole Superieure de Guerre, Paris, 1933, Army War Coll., Washington, 1937. Commd. 2d lt. Cav., 1913, and advanced through the grades to lt. gen., Apr. 1945, chief dept. of tactics, Cavalry Sch., Ft. Riley, Kans., 1933-36; exec. officer 13th Cav., Ft. Knox, Ky., and 7th Cav. Brigade, 1938-39; chief of supply and transportation branch, supply div., War Dept. Gen. Staff, Washington, D.C., 1939-40; chief of staff, 2d Armored Div., Ft. Benning, Ga., 1940-42; comdg. gen. combat command 3d Armored Div., Camp Polk, La., 1942, 9th Armored Div., Ft. Riley, Kans., June-Sept. 1942; dep. comdr. I Armored Corps hdqrs. N. Africa, 1942-43, 7th Army, Sicily, July 1943; comdr. II Corps, Sicily, Italy, Austria, 1943-45; comdg. gen. 7th Army 1945-46, Third Army, 1946-47; comdg. gen. and U.S. High Commr. in Austria since Apr. 1947. Decorations: D.S.M. with 2 oak leaf clusters; Legion of Merit; Silver Star with one cluster, Bronze Star Medal; and eight foreign decorations. Died Sept. 17, 1967.*

KIBLER, A. FRANKLIN army officer; b. Stanton, Va., July 10, 1891; s. Green Markwood and Almira (Fishburne) K.; student Augusta Mil. Acad., Ft. Defiance, Va., 1906-08; B.S., Va. Mil. Inst., 1912; post grad. work U. Wis., 1914-15; grad. Signal Corps Sch., 1921, F.A. Sch., 1923. Command and Gen. Staff School, 1935, Army War College, 1938; married to Clara Fickel, September 23, 1918; children-Virginia Claire (Mrs. Samuel L. Obenschain), Robert Franklin. Commd. 2d lt., F.A., U.S. Army, Aug. 1917, and advanced through the grades to maj. gen. 1944; comd. battery of F.A. during World War I; mem. President's Econ. and Social Mission to B.W.I., 1940; sr. Army mem. U.S. Mil. Mission to French W. Africa, 1942. Mem. War Dept. Gen. Staff, 1939-42; comdg. 78th Div. Arty., 1942-43; 13th Corps Arty., Sept., Oct. 1943; asst. chief of staff, G-3, 12th Army Group, 1943-45, chief G-3 Div., Theater Gen. Bd., ETO, 1945-46; den. AUS rep. UN Mil. Staff Com., 1946-48; chief U.S. del. to Mil. Com. of the Western Union, 1948-49; dir. Joint Am. Mil. Adv. Group, Europe, 1949—. Decorated D.S.M. with oak leaf cluster, Legion of Merit. Bronze Star Medal, Army Commendation Ribbon (all U.S.); Officer Legion of Honor, Croix de Guerre with Palm (French); Comdr. Order of British Empire; Comdr. Order Orange-Nassau (Netherlands); Comdr. Order Leopold II, Croix de Guerre with Palm (Belgium) Comdr. with Crown, Order Civil and Military Merit of Adolph of Nassau, Croix De Guerre (Luxembourg); War Cross (Czechoslovakia). Mason. Club: Army and Navy (Washington). Address: 45 Orchard Rd., Staunton, Va. Died Jan. 24, 1955; buried Arlington Nat. Cemetery.

KIBLER, RAYMOND SPIER, physician; b. East Aurora, N.Y., Nov. 8, 1917; s. Michael and Rose (Spier) K.; M.D., U. Buffalo, 1941; M.Sc. in Medicine, U. Ill., 1948; m. Diana Duszynski, Mar. 8, 1943; 1 dau., Jacqueline Louise (Mrs. Byledbal). Intern, Buffalo Gen. Hosp., 1941-42, asst. resident in internal medicine, 1942-43, resident in internal medicine, 1943, jr. clin. med. asst. in hematology and clin. pathology, 1957-69; practice medicine, specializing in nuclear medicine, Buffalo; Med. fellow U. Buffalo, 1946-47, U. Ill., 1947-48; sr. cancer research intern dept. nuclear medicine Roswell Park Meml Inst.; instr. State U. N.Y. at Buffalo. Served from 1st lt. to capt. AUS, 1943-46. Diplomate Am. Bd. Internal Medicine. Mem. A.M.A., Am. Soc. Clin. Pathologists, Soc. Nuclear Medicine, Am. Soc. Hematology. Home: Buffalo NY Died June 4, 1969; buried Mt. Calvary Cemetery, Cheekborough NY

KIDD, ISAAC CAMPBELL naval officer; b. Cleveland, O., Mar. 26, 1884; s. Isaac and Jemima (Campbell) K.; B.S., U.S. Naval Acad., 1906; attended Naval War Coll., 1936-38; m. Inez Gillmore, Apr. 29, 1911; children-Nereide (dec.), Isaac Campbell (midshipman, U.S. Navy). Became midshipman, 1902; served as passed midshipman on cruiser Columbia, which carried Marine Expeditionary Force to Canal Zone, and participated in Cuban Pacification, 1906; on U.S.S. New Jersey during round-the-world curise of fleet, 1907-09; 1st lt., U.S.S. Pittsburgh, during Mexican disturbance, 1913-14; on staff comdr.-in-chief Pacific Fleet, 1914-16; promoted to comdr. and served as gunnery officer on U.S.S. New Mexico, later on staff of comdr.-in-chief Atlantic Fleet, during World War; exec. officer U.S.S. Utah, 1925-26; comdg. officer U.S.S. Vega, 1926-27; on duty at Panama Canal, 1927-30, serving as capt. of Port of Cristobal, chmn. Bd. of Inspection and Survey, and actg. marine sup. Panama Canal; promoted to capt., 1930; chief of staff Base Force, U.S. Fleet, 1930-32; officer personnel assignments with Bur. of Navigation, Navy Dept., 1932-35; comdr. Destroyer Squadron One, U.S. Fleet, 1935-36; comdg. officer U.S.S. Arizona, 1938-39; selected rear admiral, 1939; chief of staff, Battleships, U.S. Fleet, 1940-41; comdr. Battleship Div., U.S. Fleet, since 1941. Served as Asso. Press corr., 1914-15, 1916; editor Proceedings, U.S. Naval Inst., 1917. Awarded Cuban Pacification Medal, 1906, Mexican Campaign Medal, 1916, World War Victory Medal with bronze star and bar, 1919. Mem. U.S. Naval Inst. Episcopalian. Clubs:

New York Yacht; Los Angeles Athletic, Jonathan (Los Angeles); Pacific Coast (Long Beach, Calif.). Killed in action Pearl Harbor, Hawaii, Dec. 7, 1941.

KIDDER, BENJAMIN HARRISON naval officer; b. Edgartown, Mass., Jan. 23, 1836. Apptd. asst. surgeon U.S.N., Sept. 30, 1861; passed asst. surgeon, June 28, 1865; surgeon, Mar. 2, 1868; med, insp., Jan. 30, 1887; med. dir., Aug. 21, 1893; retired Jan. 23, 1898; advanced to rank of rear admiral retired, June 29, 1906, for services during Civil War. Home: Malden, Mass. Died 1909.

KIEFER, ANDREW R. congressman; b. Marlenborn, nr. Mainz, on the Rhine, Germany; ed. there; came to U.S., 1849; to St. Paul, 1855; organized on Lincoln's first call, 1861, and comd. Co. G, 2d Minn. vol. inf.; took part in several battles; apptd. provost marshal, 1863; commissioned col. 32d regt., State militia, 1864; served in State legislature; elected clerk dist. courts, 1878; mem. Congress, 1893-97; mayor of St. Paul, Jan. 1, 1899; to Jan. 1, 1901. Republican. Retired to country villa, "Marlenborn," Lake Gervais, nr. St. Paul, Minn. Died 1904.

KIEFER, DIXIE naval officer; b. Apr. 4, 1896; entered U.S. Navy, 1915, and advanced through the grades to capt., 1942; later commodore (temporary); naval aviator. Decorated Navy Cross, D.S.M. (navy). Died in airplane crash, Nov. 11, 1945.*

KIEL, EMIL CHARLES, air force officer; b. Manitowoc, Wis., Sept. 25, 1895; s. Henry and Katharine (Reis) K.; student Stout Inst., Menomonie, Wis., 1915-17; m. Elizabeth F. Cass, Nov. 1, 1919; children—Betty Frances, Margaret Anne. Commd. 2d lt. Kelly Field, Tex., 1918; promoted through grades to brig. gen. (temp.), 1943; chief of staff, 4th Air Force, Dec. 1941-June 1944; deputy comdr., 8th Air Force, Nov. 1944-July 1945, chief of staff, July-Oct. 1945; commanding general, 8th Frontier Command, Oct. 1945-Feb. 1946; commander 40th Bomb Wing, Mar.-Dec. 1946; pres. War Crimes Court, Dachau, Germany, Jan.-Aug. 1947. Comdg. gen., Scott Air Force Base, Ill., 1947-49, Sheppard Air Force Base, Wichita Falls, Tex., 1949-50; comdg. gen. Caribbean Air Comd., Albrook AFB, C.Z., from 1950; ret. Decorated Air Medal, 1943, Legion of Merit, 1945; D.S.M., Bronze Star; Comdr. British Empire, Belgian Croix de Guerre. Home: San Francisco CA Died Nov. 1971.

KIERNAN, LOYD JULIAN, ret. r.r. ofcl.; b. Vicksburg, Miss., Sept. 12, 1895; s. Thomas and Margaret Elizabeth (Hartman) K.; Master of Accounts, Holy Cross Coll., New Orleans, 1909; m. Jennie P. Howard, June 29, 1921; children——Loyd J., Frances Margaret (Mrs. Wm. A. Ries). With I.C. R.R., 1911-37; with Equitable Life Assurance Soc., 1938-42, Assn. Am. R.R.'s, Washington, 1942-55; exec. v.p., chief exec. officer B. & M. R.R., 1955; cons. transportation U.S. Govt., other countries, 1956-61, Sec.-gen. 8th Pan-Am. Ry. Congress, Washington, 1953. Served from pvt. to 1st lt., 155th Inf., U.S. Army, 1916-19; capt. O.R.C. ret. Episcopalian, Club: Army and Navy (Washington). Contbr. articles to profl. publs. Home: Miami FL Died Mar. 27, 1972.

KIERSTED, ANDREW JACKSON rear admiral; b. New Point Comfort, Va., Dec. 25, 1832; s. Luke and Catharine Sophia (Myer) K.; ed. schs. of Va. and Me.; m. Isabella Stuart Henderson, Jan. 25, 1866. Apptd. asst. engr. U.S.N., June 26, 1856; promoted 1st asst. engr., Aug. 2, 1859; chief engr., Nov. 12, 1861; retired, Dec. 25, 1904; advanced to rank of rear admiral in recognition of services during Civil War, June 29, 1906. Served on spl. duty during Civil War; mem. Naval Examining Bd., Mar. 18-Aug. 28, 1873, and Apr. 18-Nov. 9, 1878, pres. same, Feb, 4-July 27, 1875; fleet engr. N. Atlantic Squadron, Sept. 19, 1881-Aug. 7, 1882, Pacific Sta., June 19, 1888-Apr. 15, 1889. Home: Philadelphia, Pa. Died 1910.

KILBOURNE, CHARLES EVANS author, ret. army officer; b. Fort Whipple, Va., Dec. 23, 1872; s. Charles E. and Ada (Coolidge) K.; grad. Va. Mil. Inst., 1894; honor grad. Arty. Sch., 1903; grad. Gen. Staff Coll., 1920; m. Elizabeth Gordon Egbert, June 9, 1900. Commd. 2d lt., May 20, 1898; promoted through grades to maj. gen., July 9, 1935; brig. gen. temp., Oct. 15, 1918-June 1, 1919. Served in Spanish-Am. War; in campaign ending in capture of Manila; in subduing Philippine Insurrection, operations in Cavite, Laguna and Bulucan provinces; in Boxer Campaign, China, and relief of legation, Pekin, and in op Honor "for distinguished gallantry" at Paco Bridge, P.I., Feb. 5, 1899; D.S.C., "for extraordinary heroism in action" nr. Thiacourt, France, Sept. 12, 1918; D.S.M. "for services in 89th Div. and 36th Arty. Brigade"; Croix de Guerre (French) "for reconnaissances preparatory to assault on St. Mihiel Salient," and Legion of Honor; Philippine and Victory medals (U.S.); Royal Order of St. Olav (Norway). Chief of staff Army of No. Va., United Confed. Vets., 1939. Republican. Episcopalian. Club: St. Nicholas (N.Y.C.). Author: Army Boy Series (4 vols.), 1913-16; Baby Animal Books (10 vols.), 1913-17. Editor Nat. Service Library (5 vols.), 1917. Address: 1 pendleton Pl., Lexington, Va. Died Nov. 1963.

KILBOURNE, JAMES mfr.; b. Columbia, O., Oct. 9, 1842; s. Lincoln K., g.s. Col. James K., Ohio pioneer; A.B., Kenyon Coll., 1862, A.M., 1864 (LL.D., 1910); LL.B., Harvard, 1868; enlisted as pvt. 84th Ohio Vols. in Civil War; 2d lt., 1st lt. and capt. 95th Ohio Vols. to end of war; on staffs Gen. J. M. Tuttle, comdg. 3d Div., 15th Army Corps, and Gen. John McArthur, comdg. 1st Div., 16th Army Corps, Army of the Tenn.; bvtd. maj., lt. col. and col. vols., "for gallant and meritorious services during the war"; m. Anna B., d. Gen. George B. Wright, Oct. 3, 1869. Admitted to bar and practiced at Columbus; founder and pres. the Kilbourne & Jacobs Mfg. Co.; dir. Columbus, Hocking Valley & Toledo Ry. Co., Columbus, Cincinnati & Midland R.R. Co., Hayden-Clinton Nat. Bank, First Nat. Bank. Dem. nominee for gov. of Ohio, 1901. Pres. Ohio Centennial Commn., 1898; pres. trustees Columbus Pub. Library, 10 yrs.; organized Columbus Children's Hosp., and pres. 5 yrs.; mem. bd. mgrs. Associated Charities; mem. Columbus Bd. Trade (dir. 1887-91, pres., 1891). Home: Columbus, O. Deceased.

KILBURN, CHARLES LAWRENCE soldier; b. Lawrenceville, Tioga Co., Pa., Aug. 9, 1819; grad. U.S. Mil. Acad., 1842; apptd. lt. artillery, served through Mexican war, including battles of Monterey and Buena Vista; promoted capt. and commissary of subsistence; maj., May 11, 1861; lt. col. and asst. commissary-gen., Feb. 9, 1863; col., June 29, 1864; bvt. brig. gen. at close of war; after war chief commissary Dept. of Atlantic and later of Dept. of Pacific, until retired, May 20, 1822. Home: Germantown, Pa. Died 1899.

KILGORE, HARLEY MARTIN senator; b. Brown, W. Va., Jan. 11, 1893; s. Quimby and Laura Jo (Martin) K.; LL.B., W.Va. U., 1914; m. Lois Elaine Lilly, May 10, 1921; children-Robert Martin, Elinor Stuart (Mrs. Albert T. Young, Jr.). Admitted to West Virginia bar, 1914; in practice at Beckley, West Virginia, 1914-17 and 1920-32; became judge Criminal Court. Raleigh County, W.Va., 1932-40; mem. U.S. Senate, W.Va., 1940—; mem. special senate com. to investigate Nat. Def. Program, 1941-46, chmn., 1946, chmn. Senate Judiciary Com. In 1st O.T.C., Fort Benjamin Harrison, Ind., 1917; successively 2d lt., 1st lt., capt., U.S. Army, 1917-20; officer W. Va. Nat. Guard, 1921-53, ret. col. Mem. Am. Polit. Sci. Assn., W.Va. Hist. Soc., S.A.R. Mem. Christian Ch. Democrat. Am. Legion, Mason, Moose, Elk, Delta Tau Delta. Address: 3834 Macomb St., N.W., Washington Office: Senate Office Bldg., Washington. Died Feb. 28, 1956.

KILMER, THERON WENDELL physician; b. Chicago, Ill., Mar. 7, 1872; s. Chauncey and Antoinelle (Wendell) K.; student Coll. City of New York, 1889-92; M.D., Coll. Physicians and Surgeons (Columbia), 1895; m. Angie Ransom, Jan. 5, 1898; children-Gladys Kilmer, Theron Wendell Kilmer, Jr. Practicing medicine in New York since 1895. Asst. attending physician out-patient dept., St. Vincent's Hosp., 1895; asst. attending surgeon, St. Bartholomew's Clinic, and of Met. Throat Hosp., 1895; attending physician, diseases of children, West Side Dispensary, 1901; asso. prof. diseases of children, N.Y. Sch. Clin. Med., 1901; asso. prof. pediatric dept., N.Y. Polyclinic Med. Sch. Hosp., 1902; attending physician Halsey Day Nursery, 1902, Summer Home of St. Giles the Cripple, Garden City, N.Y., 1903; asst. attending phys. out-patient dept., Babies' Hosp., 1902; asst. attending physican Suydenham Hosp., Dispensary (dept. diseases of children), and adj. attending pediatrist to Suydenham Hosp., 1905. Lecturer, Dept. of Edn., New York, 1898-1921; medical dir. of Soc. of First Aird to the Injured, New York. Commd. surgeon (rank of maj.), 22d Regt., Nat. Guard, N.Y., 1906. Police surgeon of Hempstead, L.I., N.Y.; mem. Nassau County Police Conf. Mem. Assn. Mil. Surgeons U.S., Nat. Assn. Police and Fire Surgeons, A.M.A., Nassau County and N.Y. State med. assns., Alpha Delta Phi; surgeon N.Y. State Assn. Chiefs of Police; associate mem. Internat. Assn. Chiefs of Police. Episcopalian. Republican. Club: Union League (N.Y.) Author: Practical Care of the Baby, 1903; Physical Examination of Infants and Young Children, 1905. Address: Hempstead, N.Y. Died July 31, 1946.

KILNER, WALTER GLENN army officer; b. Shelby, N.Y., July 8, 1888; s. Charles Windsor and Mary Elizabeth K.; B.S., U.S. Mil. Acad., 1912; m. 2d, I. M. Givenwilson, Oct. 10, 1924. Commd. 2d lt. Inf., June 12, 1912; transferred to Aviation sect. Signal Corps, 1915, and advanced through the grades to brig. gen., Air Corps, 1938; served with 1st Aero Squadron on Punitive Expdn. into Mexico, 1916; comdr. Aviation School, Mineola, L.I., N.Y., Mar.-Oct. 1917; with A.E.F. in France, Oct.1917-Jan. 1919, as organizer and comdr. U.S. Aviation Center at Issoudun, and in charge of training of flying personnel for the front; exec. officer Army Air Service, 1924-25. Mem. Nat. Advisory Com. for Aeronautics. Decorated D.S.M., 1919; Companion Order of St. Michael and St. George (British); Officer Legion of Honor (French). Author: Cantonment Manual, 1917. Died Aug. 30, 1940.

KILPATRICK, HARRY COLMAN banker; b. Philadelphia, Feb. 7, 1907; s. James Lester and Mary (Colman) K.; grad. Lehigh U., 1929; m. Barbara Park, Sept. 15, 1934; 1 dau., Barbara Gail. With Pease and Elliman, 1929-33; with Mfrs. Trust Co. since 1933, asst. vice pres., 1937-38, vice pres. in charge of mortgage dept., 1938-47, vice pres. in charge of mortgage dept., 1938-47, vice pres. and asst. to pres., 1947-50, exec. v.p. and dir. since 1950; pres. and dir. 261 5th Av. Corp.; dir. and mem. executive com. N.Y. Dock Trade Facilities Corp., N.Y. Dock Co.: dir. Bing and Bing, Inc., Interstate Dept. Stores Inc., New Yorker Hotel Corporation, 500 5th Avenue, Inc.; trustee Harlem Savings Bank. Served with Corps of Engrs., U.S. Army, advancing from capt. to lt. col., 1942-45; exec. officer to chief of engrs. Awarded Legion of Merit. Mem. Chamber of Commerce of State of N.Y. mem. Newcomen Soc. of Eng., Psi Upsilon. Clubs: Wall Street (New York); Apawamis (Rye, N.Y.). Home: 955 5th Av. Office: 55 Broad St., N.Y. City 15. Died Nov. 1, 1952.

KILPATRICK, HUGH JUDSON army officer, diplomat; b. Deckertown, N.J., Jan. 14, 1836; grad. U.S. Mil. Acad., 1861; m. Alice Nailer, May 6, 1861. Commd. 2d lt. 1st Arty., U.S. Army, 1861; capt. 5th N.Y. Volunteers, 1861; lt. col. 2d N.Y. Calvary, 1861; commd. brig. gen. U.S. Volunteers, 1863, served in battles of Aldie and Gettysburg; brevetted maj. and col. U.S. Army, then brig. gen. and maj. gen., 1865; one of noted Union cavalry leaders in Civil War; U.S. minister to Chile, 1865-81; dir. U.P. R.R.; del. to Republican Nat. Conv., 1880. Died Valparaiso, Chile, Dec. 2, 1881.

KILPATRICK, JOHN REED business exec.; b. N.Y.C., June 15, 1889; s. Frank James and Manie (Patterson) K.; grad. Phillip's Acad., Andover, Mass., 1907; B.A., Yale, 1911; m. Stephanie d'Hengster, Oct. 25, 1919; 1 dau., Frances Reed. Began as constrn. timekeeper Thompson Starrett Co., 1911, v.p., 1919; v.p. Internat. Coal Products Corp., 1919-23; v.p. George A. Fuller Co., 1923-33; pres. Madison Sq. Garden Corp., 1933-55. Enlisted as pvt. N.Y. State N.G., Oct. 1912, advancing to 2d lt.; maj. Nat. Army, June 1917, advancing to col., Gen. Staff, AEF and chief regulating officer, AEF; hon. discharged Mar. 1919; recalled to active service, Mar. 13, 1942, made brig. gen., U.S. Army, Aug. 10, 1942. Released from active duty Oct. 1, 1945; chmn. bd. Madison Sq. Garden Corp. Decorated Chevalier Legion of Honor, Croix de Guerre with palm (France); comdr. Crown of Italy; Distinguished Service medal with Oak Leaf Cluster (U.S.). Mem. Phi Beta Kappa, Psi Upsilon. Home: 200 E. 66th St., N.Y.C. 21. Office: 307 W. 49th St., N.Y.C. 19. Died May 7, 1960; buried Old Tennents' Cemetery, Englishtown, N.J.

KILPATRICK, WALTER KENNETH navy officer; b. N.Y. City, Oct. 29, 1887; s. Walter Fisher and Margaret Humphrey (Holmes) K.; B.S., U.S. Naval Acad., 1908, Naval War Coll., 1922-23; Army War Coll., 1927-28; m. Ethel Studley, Nov. 30, 1925. Promoted from midshipman, 1908, through grades to rear adm., 1942; served in Asiatic, Atlantic, and Pacific fleets; comd. U.S.S. Doyen, Hatfield, Bushnell, Chester; on duty with Navy Dept. Boston, New York, Hawaii, San Francisoc; flag sec. Asiatic fleet; chief of staff, 14th Naval Dist., 12th Naval Dist. Western Sea Frontier, Atlantic Fleet. Awarded Distinguished Service Medal, Legion of Merit with two stars; Nicaragua. World War, Haitina, Yangtze, Atlantic Area campaign medals. Home: 404 Rochampton Rd., Hillsborough, Calif. Died Sept. 26, 1949.

KIMBALL, AMES SAMUEL army officer; b. Lawrence, N.Y., July 14, 1840; s. James and Sophia (Taft) K.; grad. State Normal Sch., Albany, N.Y., 1859; m. Hattie F. Crary, 1861. Commissioned Nov. 1861, 1st lt. 98th N.Y. vol. inf.; served in Army of Potomac to Nov. 1862, including McClellan's peninsular campaign; afterward in Carolinas with Hunter and Heckman; acting q.-m. Roanoke Island, N.C.; capt. and a. q. m. vols. Apr. 7, 1864, in charge water transportation Ft. Monroe; later q. m. at Newbern, N.C., during yellow fever epidemic, where he became ill with the disease; ordered to New York, Apr., 1865; bvtd. capt., maj., lt. col. and col. by State and apptd. maj. vols. by bvt. and asst. q. m. U.S.A. Served under Sheridan in Indian campaign, 1868-69; field q. m. with Gen. Miles in Ariz. campaign against Geronimo, etc.; assigned to charge of gen. depot, New York, 1897, and during Spanish war, 1898, distributed over $8,000,000 in 4 months; promoted col. Nov. 13, 1898, and brig. gen. U.S.A., Oct. 1902; retired. Died 1909.

KIMBALL, DAN A., ex.-sec. navy; b. St. Louis, Mar. 1, 1896; s. John H. and Mary (Able) K.; ed. pub. schs., St. Louis; m. Dorothy Ames, June 22, 1925; married second Doris Fleeson, August 1958. Began Los Angeles manager, General Tire & Rubber Co., 1920, v.p., 1942-69; chmn., president Aerojet-General, El Monte, Cal.; chmn. bd. Bank of Sacramento; director Frontier Airlines. Served with A.A.C., advancing to rank of 1st lt., World War I. Apptd. assistant secretary of navy of air, Mar. 1949, under sec. navy, 1949-51, sec., 1951-53. Named Home Study Man of Year, Internat. Correspondence Schs., 1968. Conglist. Democrat. Clubs: Los Angeles Country, Jonathan (Los Angeles); Metropolitan, Burning Tree (Washington). Home: Washington DC Died July 30, 1970; buried Arlington Nat. Cemetery, Arlington VA

KIMBALL, HARRY SWIFT indslist., b. Brockton, Mass., Jan. 14, 1875; s. Rufus Henry and Louise (Swift) K.; grad. U.S. Naval Acad., 1896; m. Adele C. Corner, Jan. 19, 1898. Resigned from U.S. Navy, 1896; pres. Am. Zinc, Lead & Smelting Co., Boston, 1902-16; pres. Remington Arms-Union Metallic Cartridge Co., 1916-20; v.p. and mgr. Gaston, Williams & Wigmore, Inc., N.Y.C., 1920-21; v.p., in charge finance, U.S. Shipping Bd. Emergency Fleet Corp., 1921-2; mem. firm Kimball & Co. Served as lt. comdr.,USNR, Apr. 1917-Apr. 1921. Republican. Swedenborgian. Clubs: University. Union League, Bankers'. Home: Portchester, N.Y. Died Mar. 10, 1957.

KIMBALL, JOHN WHITE soldier; b. Fitchburg, Mass., Feb. 27, 1828; s. Alpheus and Harriet (Stone) K.; ed. Fitchburg Acad.; m. Almira Melissa Lesure, July 15, 1851. Entered army, capt. Co. B, 15th Mass. Vols., June 28, 1861; maj., Aug. 1, 1861, lt. col., Apr. 29, 1862, col., 53d Mass. Vols., Nov. 12, 1862; bvtd. brig. gen. vols., Mar. 13, 1865, "for gallant and distinguished services during the war." Mem. Mass. Legislature, 1864, 65, 1872, 1888, 89, 1890, 91; auditor Commonwealth of Mass., 1892-1900; custodian Bur. of Engraving and Printing, Treasury Dept., Washington, 1877-78; postmaster, Fitchburg, 1879-87. Trustee and auditor Fitchburg Savings Bank many yrs. Republican. Mason. Home: Fitchburg, Mass. Died 1910.

KIMBALL, NATHAN army officer; b. Fredericksburg, Ind., Nov. 22, 1823; s. Nathaniel and Nancy (Furgeson) Kimball; attended DePauw U., 1839-41; m. llartha Ann McPheeters, Sept. 23, 1845. Raised a company and served as capt. 2d Ind. Regt. in Mexican War, 1846; commd. capt. Ind. Militia, 1861; helped raise 14th Ind. Regt., became col.; commd. brig. gen. U.S. Volunteers, 1862; in command V Army Corps at battles of Kernstown, Antietam, Fredericksburg; had commanding division at siege of Vicksburg, 1863, Battle of Franklin, 1864; mustered out of service, 1865; fought at Atlanta, Franklin and Nashville in charge IV Army Corps; brevetted maj. gen., 1865; helped organize Grand Army of Republic in Ind., became comdr.; elected treas., State of Ind., 1866, 68; mem. Ind. Legislature, 1872; surveyor gen. Utah, 1873. Died Ogden, Utah, Jan. 21, 1898.

KIMBALL, WILLIAM WIRT rear admiral; b. Paris, Me., Jan. 9, 1848; s. Brig. Gen. William King and Frances Freeland (Rawson) K.; grad. U.S. Naval Acad., 1860; m. Esther Smith Spencer, July 18, 1882. Ensign, 1870; promoted through grades to rear admiral, Dec. 17, 1908. Served on N. and S. Atlantic, European, Asiatic and Pacific stas.; mem. of the first class of officers at the Torpedo Sta., 1870; assisted in capture of Am. steamers in the Orinoco, 1872; torpedo officer of the first two torpedo craft of the navy, 1874; engaged in development of magazine and machine guns in the early 80's; designed, constructed, and operated the first armed cars used by U.S. forces and assisted in occupation of Isthmus of Panama, 1885; reported to Congress progress of work on Panama Canal, 1886; exec. officer Detroit in the affair of Enchadas in Rio harbor, 1894; engaged in development of submarine boats in early 90's (John P. Holland, inventor of the Holland boats, wrote of him, "Submarining owes more to him than to any other living man."); organized first torpedo boat flotilla of U.S.N., and comd. Atlantic Torpedo Boat Flotilla in war with Spain; comd. Caesar, Glacier, Supply, Vixen, Concord, Wheeling, Abarenda, Alert and New Jersey; on bds. of Construction, Examination and Retirement, 1907-09; selected for command of Nicaraguan expeditionary squadron, Dec. 1, 1909; retired by operation of law, Jan. 9, 1910, but retained in active command afloat until withdrawal of squadron from Nicaraguan waters, Apr. 1910; relieved from active duty, June 1, 1910; recalled to active duty during the World War as pres. bd. for the examination of officers, and officer in charge of hist. sect., Office of Operations, Navy Dept. Sr. officer present at and awarded medal for 2d action at Matanzas bar for Santiago; medal for Spanish-Am. War. Home: Paris, Me. Died Jan. 26, 1930.

KIMBERLY, LEWIS ASHFIELD rear admiral U.S.N.; b. Troy, N.Y., Apr. 2, 1830; apptd. to navy from Ill., Dec. 8, 1846, acting midshipman; grad. U.S. Naval Acad., passed-midshipman. June 8, 1852; master, Sept. 15, and lt., Sept. 16, 1856; comdr., July 16, 1862; comdr., July 25, 1866; capt., Oct. 3, 1874; commodore, Nov. 27, 1884; rear admiral, Sept. 4, 1887; retired Apr. 2, 1892. Served on frigate Potomac, 1861-62; then exec. officer on the Hartford, Admiral Farragut's flagship, participating in actions of Port Hudson, Grand Gulf, Warrington, Mobile Bay, etc. Was in expdn. to Korea and comd. the force which landed and captured the forts. Was comdr.-in-chief of Pacific station; was in the great hurricane of Mar. 15 and 16, 1889, at Apia, Samoa; was commended by the sec. of the navy for his conduct of affairs there. Home: West Newton, Mass. Died 1902.

KIMES, RUSSELL A. mfg. exec.; b. Phila., Feb. 26, 1912; s. George R.C. and Elizabeth (Astfalk) K.; B.S. in Elec Engring., Drexel Inst., 1934; m. Helen Shuman, Sept. 5, 1936; children - Russell A., Mary E. Requirements specialist engr. Western Electric Co., 1934-46; with Am. Machine & Foundry Co., 1946 - , dir. gen. engring. labs., 1956-59, div. v.p. govt. products group, 1959-62, corporate v.p., 1962-63. Served to lt. col. Signal Corps, AUS, World War II, PTO. Mem. Am. Ordnance Assn., Armed Forces Chem. Assn., I.R.E. Home: Canoe Hill Rd., New Canaan, Conn. Office: 11 Bruce Pl., Greenwich, Conn. Died Apr. 10, 1963; buried Lakeview Cemetery, New Canaan.

KIMM, NEAL EDWIN ret. fgn. service officer; b. Norway, Ia., Nov. 15, 1917; s. Jacob Carl and Pearl Louella (Primrose) K.; student Hamilton U., 1934-36, George Washington U., 1939-41, Am. U., Washington, 1947-48; m. Rosamond Eileen Knight, Sept. 17, 1938; 1 dau., Donna Kay; m. 2d, Julia Frances McAllister, Feb. 12, 1949; children-James Craig Kimm (foster son), Julia Frances, Neal Edwin. Staff div. communications and records Dept. of State, 1938-44, 46-47, adminstrv. officer Office Departmental Adminstrn., 1947-50, exec. officer Bur. German Affairs, 1950-51; asst. chief operating facilities div. U.S. High Commr. for Germany, 1951-53, spl. asst. to chief adminstrv. services div., 1953-54, budget officer, 1954-55; gen. services officer Am. Embassy, London, 1955-56, 1st sec., consul, 1956; chief property mgmt. br. Div. of Supply Mgmt. Dept. of State. 1956-60; mgmt. analyst Office Personnel, 1959-60, ret., 1960. Participant in 4th Exec. Mgmt. Program, Pa. State U., 1958. Served as 2d lt. USAAF, 1944-46. Home: 402 S.W. 7th Terrace, Boca Raton, Fla. Died Apr. 6, 1962; buried Arlington Nat. Cemetery, Washington.

KIMMEL, HUSBAND EDWARD, naval officer; b. Henderson, Ky., Feb. 26, 1882; s. Manning Marius and Sibbie (Lambert) K.; student Central U., Richmond Ky., 1899-1900; B.S. in Engring., U.S. Naval Academy, 1904; hon. Doctor of Law, Centre College, 1941; m. Dorothy Kinkaid, January 31, 1912; children—Manning Marius (U.S. Navy), Thomas Kinkaid (U.S. Navy), Edward Ralph. Commd. ensign, U.S. Navy, 1906, and advanced through the grades to rear adm., 1937, admiral, Feb. 1, 1941; comdg. Cruisers Battle Force, U.S. Fleet, 1939-41; command U.S. Pacific Fleet and the combined U.S. Fleet, 1941; retired, 1942. Decorated Cuban Pacification, Mexican, Grand Fleet World War campaign badges. Mem. Sigma Alpha Epsilon. Club: Army and Navy (Washington, D.C.). Address: New London CT Died May 15, 1968.

KINCAID, ROBERT LEE coll. pres.; b. Blairsville, Ga., May 17, 1893; s. James R. and Virginia A. (Wild) K.; A.B., Lincoln Meml. U., 1915, LL.D., 1937; student Sch. Journalism, U. Mo., 1915-16; D.Litt., U. Chattanooga, 1956; m. Beula C. Chance, May 24, 1917; children-Helen (Mrs. M.K. Henry), Robert Hugh (dec.). Sec. Lincoln Meml. U., 1916-22; mng. editor Middlesboro (Ky.) Daily News, 1923, 1926-37; bus. mgr. Grafton (W.Va.) Sentinel, 1924; v.p. Lincoln Meml. U., 1937-47, dir., chmn. exec. com., 1927-47, pres., 1947-58. Mem. bd. Grace Nettleton Home for Girls, Cumberland Gap Nat. Hist. Park Assn. (pres.); mem. Tenn. Hist. Commn. since 1951. Vice chmn. Ky. Nat. Park Commn., 1943-46; pres. Citizens News Co., Middlesboro, Ky. Sgt. maj. coast arty., U.S. Army, 1917-18. Mem. Am. Legion, Alumni Assn. Lincoln Meml. U. (past prspes.), Tau Kappa Alpha. Republican. Baptist. Clubs: Kiwanis (past pres.); Filson. Author: Jinny and Jim, 1941; Joshua Fry Speed, 1943; The Wilderness Road, 1947. Home: Harrogate, Tenn. Died May 21, 1960.

KINDELBERGER, JAMES HOWARD aviation executive; b. Wheeling, W.Va., May 8, 1895; s. Charles Frederick and Rose Ann (Riddle) K.; student Carnegie Inst. Tech., 1956; LL.D., Howard U., 1958; m. Thelma Beatrice Knarr, Apr. 26, 1919 (div. 1945); children-Ruth Joan, Howard Byron (dec.); m. 2d, Helen Louise Allen, Dec. 20, 1946 (div. 1960). Apprentice-engr. National Tube Company, Wheeling, 1911; jr. draftsman and insp. U.S. Army Engr. Corps, 1913-16; designer and chief draftsman, Glenn L. Martin Co., Cleveland, 1919-25; v.p. and chief engr. Douglas Aircraft Co., Santa Monica, Calif. 1925-34; pres. Gen. Aviation Mfg. Corp.; Baltimore, 1934; pres., dir. and gen. mgr. North Am. Aviation, Inc., aircraft mfrs., Los Angeles, 1935-48, now chmn. bd. and chief exec. officer. Dir. Hosp. Good Samaritan; mem. adv. com. St. John's Hosp. Served as 2d lt., Air Corps, AUS, World War I. Mem. development com. Case Inst. Tech., 1952-; member Air Force Historical Foundation. Decorated Chevalier Legion of Honor France), 1951; Comdr. Order Al Merito della Republica Italiana, 1954; Companion Exalted Order White Elephant (Thailand), 1956; recipient Alumni merit award Carnegie Inst. Tech., Presdl. Certificate of Merit for War Contbn., 1948; exceptional civilan service award, Dept. Air Force, 1953; Collier trophy, 1954; Fedn. Aeronautique Interntionale diploma, 1955; Golden Knight award, Nat. Mgmt. Assn., 1958; achievement award, Alumni Fedn., Carnegie Inst. Tech., 1958; General William E. Mitchell award, 1959. Fellow Inst. Aero. Scis. (pres. 1950, hon. fellow 1953-); mem. Mfrs. Aircraft Assn. (v.p.), Aerospace Industries Assn. Am. (gov.), Cal. C. of C. (dir.), Air Force Assn., Soc. Automotive Engrs., American Legion, Am. Soc. French Legion Honor, Delta Upsilon. Mason. Office: North American Aviation, Inc., 1700 E. Imperial Hwy., El Segundo, Cal. 90246. Died July 27, 1962.

KINDLEBERGER, DAVID medical dir. U.S.N.; b. Smithville, O., Sept. 2, 1834; s. T. J. (M.D.) and Katherine (Newcomer) K.; A.B., Wittenberg Coll., Springfield, O., 1857; m. Olivia M. Bishop, Mar. 10, 1906. Entered U.S. Naval service, 1859; advanced through various grades to med. dir. with rank of capt.; retired, Sept. 2, 1896, on account of age limit advanced to rank of rear adm. retired June 29, 1906. Served on African coast on U.S.S. San Jacinto, 1859-61; participated in all the battles of Admiral Farragut's squadron in Civil War except Vicksburg; fleet surgeon Asiatic Squadron, 1877-80, S. Pacific Squadron, 1882; comd. U.S. Naval Hosp., Phila., 1892-96. In command naval hosp., Guam, 1914. Died Mar. 25, 1921.

KING, CAMPBELL army officer; b. Flat Rock, N.C., Aug. 30, 1871; s. Alexander Campbell and Mary Lee (Evans) K.; attended Charleston Coll.; hon. M.A., Harvard, 1920; distinguished grad. Inf., and Cav. Sch., 1905; grad. Army Staff Coll., 1906; grad. Army War Coll., 1911; grad. Gen. Staff Coll., 1920; m. Harriott Laurens King, December 19, 1907: children-Duncan Ingraham, Barbara. Private and corporal cavalry, July 1897-July 1898; commd. 2d lieut. 1st Infantry, July 9, 1898; promoted through grades to brig. gen., July 23, 1924; brig. gen. (temporary) during the World War; maj. gen., May 1, 1932; retired, 1933. Served in Cuba, Philippines, Hawaii, China, and on Mexican border; arrived in France with 1st Div., June 25, 1917; chief of staff, 1st Div., Dec. 1917-Sept. 1918; brig. gen. and chief of staff, 7th A.C. and 3d A.C., Oct. 1918-July 1910. Served in following sectors of the line in France; Somervillier, Ansauville, Montdidier, Saizerais and Vosges Mountains. Participated in following battles: Verdun, Aug. 1917, Cantigny, Montdidier-Noyon, Aisne-Marne, St. Mihiel, Meuse-Argonne. Took part in march to the Rhine and occupation of Cobienz bridgehead. Awarded D.S.M. (U.S.); Croix de Guerre with palm and silver star, Officer Legion of Honor (French); Comdr. Order of the Crown (Italian). Was first Am. officer, with Col. George B. Duncan, to receive French Croix de Guerre, awarded by Gen. Deville, comdg. 42d French Div., to which he was attached during French Verdun offensive, Aug. 1917. Home: Flat Rock, N.C. Died Oct. 16, 1953; buried Church of St. Johns in the Winderness, Flat Rock.

KING, CHARLES soldier, author; b. Albany, N.Y., Oct. 12, 1844; s. Rufus and Susan McKown (Eliot) K.; grad. U.S. Mil. Acad., 1866; m. Adelaide Lavander, d. Capt. Yorke, of Carroll Parish, La., Nov. 20, 1872; children - Adelaide Patton (dec.), Carolyn Merritt, Elinor Yorke, Rufus. Second lt. 1st Arty., June 18, 1866; 1st lt., May 15, 1870; transferred to 5th Cav., Dec. 31, 1870; regimental adj., 1876-78; capt., May 1, 1879; retired for wounds, June 14, 1879. Insp. and instr. Wis. Nat. Guard, 1882-89; col. comdg. regt., 1890; adj. gen., 1895; brig. gen. vols., May 27, 1898-Aug. 2, 1899; served in P.I. under Gen. Lawton. Supt. Mich. Mil. Acad., 1901. Author: Famous and Decisive Battles; Between the Lines; The Colonel's Daughter, 1883; Marion's Faith, 1885; Captain Blake, 1892; The General's Double, 1897; The Iron Brigade, 1902; A Conquering Corps Badge, 1902; Medal of Honor, 1905; and others. Home: Milwaukee, Wis. Died Mar. 18, 1933.

KING, CYRUS congressman; b. Scarboro, Mass. (now Me.), Sept. 6, 1772; attended Phillips Acad., Andover, Mass.; grad. Columbia, 1794; studied law. Pvt. sec. to Rufus King (his half brother; U.S. minister to Eng.), 1796; admitted to the bar, 1797, began practice in Saco, Mass. (now Me.); served as maj. gen. 6th Div., Mass. Militia; a founder Thornton Acad., Saco.; mem. U.S. Ho. of Reps. (Federalist) from Mass., 13th-14th congresses, 1813-17. Died Saco, Apr. 25, 1817; buried Laurel Hill Cemetery, Saco.

KING, EDGAR, med. officer U.S. Army; b. Van Buren, Ark., Aug. 1, 1884; s. Lilburn Henderson and Minnie Bauregard (Childress) K.; M.D., U. of Ark., 1906; grad. Army Med. Sch., 1907; m. Susan Nickerson Moody, Jan. 28, 1910; children—Susan Childress (Mrs. Frederick J. Dau), Dorothy Moody (Mrs. Victor B. Geibel). Interne St. Vincent's Infirmary and Parlaski County Hosp., Little Rock, Ark., 1903-04 and 1906; commd. 1st lt., U.S. Army, 1907, and advance through grades to brig. gen., 1942; retired from active service as brig. general, 1948. Special work in mental diseases and their relation to mil. service disciplinary problems. Decorated D.S.M., Legion of Merit. Mem. A.M.A. Address: Reno NV Died Oct. 17, 1970; buried Ft. Leavenworth Nat. Cemetery.

KING, EDWARD LEONARD army officer; b. Bridgewater, Mass., Dec. 5, 1873; s. Francis Dane and Mary Ann (Malloy) K.; grad. U.S. Mil. Acad., 1896; distinguished grad. Army Sch. of the Line, 1913; grad. Army Staff Coll., 1914; Army War Coll., 1917-22; m. Nancy Vose Sumner, Jan. 18, 1898; 1 dau., Nancy Sumner (Mrs. Chas. Lee Andrews). Commd. 2d lt. 9th Cav., Dec. 22, 1896; promoted through grades to brig. gen., Dec. 4, 1922; promoted to major general, U.S.A., Oct. 1, 1931. Participated in Spanish-Am. War, and Philippine Insurrection; a.d.c. to Gen. H. W. Lawton; chief of staff 28th Div., and comdr. 65th Inf. Brigade, A.E.F., World War; comdr. Cav. Sch., Ft. Riley, Kan., July 1, 1923-June 30, 1925; comdt. Gen. Service Schs., Ft. Leavenworth, Kan., 1925-29; asst. chief of staff, War

Dept. Gen. Staff, 1929-32; commander Fourth Corps Area, Feb. 1932-. Decorated D.S.C. and D.S.M. (U.S.); Officer Legion of Honor and Croix de Guerre with palm (French). Conglist. Mason. Died Dec. 27, 1933.

KING, EDWARD POSTELL JR. army officer (ret.); b. Atlanta, July 4, 1884; s. Edward Postell and Mary Montgomery (Edwards) K.; B.L., U. of Ga., 1903; grad. Sch. of Fire for Field Arty., 1912; Command and Gen. Staff Sch., 1923, Army War Coll., 1930, Naval War Coll., 1937; m. Elizabeth McLaws, Dec. 26, 1912 (dec. 1954); m. 2d, Pauline T. King Beutell, 1956. Commd. 2d lt., 6th Field Arty., U.S. Army, 1908, promoted through grades to maj. gen., 1941; instructor Command and Gen. Staff Sch., 1930-35, Army War College, 1937-40: retired 1946. Awarded D.S.M. with oak leaf cluster. Mem. Phi Delta Theta. Episcopalian. Mason. Clubs: Army and Navy (Washington); Army and Navy Country (Arlington, Va.); Savannah (Ga.) Golf. Prisoner of war of Japanese Govt.; released Aug. 1945. Address: Sea Island, Ga. Died Aug. 31, 1958, Brunswick, Ga. Buried Church Yard of St. John in the Wilderness, Flat Rock, N.C.

KING, ERNEST JOSEPH naval officer; b. Lorain, O., Nov. 23, 1878; s. James Clydesdale and Elizabeth (Keam) K.; grad. U.S. Naval Acad., 1901; student U.S. War College, 1932-33; hon. LL.D., College of William and Mary, 1942; LL.D., Columbia U., 1947; Princeton Univ., 1946, Miami Univ., 1946; D.Sc., Bowdoin College, Harvard Univ. and Northwestern U., 1945; D.C.L., Oxford University, 1945; m. Martha Rankin Egerton, October 10, 1905; children-Elizabeth Egerton (wife of Col. Oliver W. Van den Berg, U.S. Army), Eleanor Calvert (Mrs. Eleanor King Hempstead), Martha Stuart (wife of Lt. Gen. Frederic H. Smith, Jr., U.S.A.F.), Clara Clydesdale (Mrs. J. M. B. Howard), Florence Beverly, Mildred Wilson (Mrs. J. O. McReynolds), Ernest Joseph (lt. comdr. U.S.N.). Served as midshipman U.S.N., Spanish-American War; commd. ensign, U.S. Navy, June 6, 1903; advanced through grades to rear admiral, Nov. 1, 1933, admiral, 1941; asst. chief Bureau Aeronautics, 1928-29, chief, 1933-36; vice adm., comdg. Aircraft Battle Force, U.S. Fleet, 1938-39; mem. gen. bd., Navy Dept., 1939-40; then comdr. in chief, U.S. Atlantic Fleet; apptd. comdr. in chief U.S. Fleet, Dec. 1941, chief of naval operations, Mar. 1942-Dec. 1945. Apptd. Fleet Admiral, Dec. 17, 1944. Awarded Navy Cross, D.S.M., D.S.M. with 2 gold stars, Sampson medal, Spanish Campaign badge, Mex. Service medal, Victory Medal (1918) with bronze star, Am. Defense Service medal (1941), American Area Campaign medal, Order of Crown of Italy (Grand Ufficiale), Order Vasco Nunez de Balboa, Commander (2d degree) Panama, First Rank (Grand Cross) Moroccan Ouissam Alaouite Cherifian, French Morocco, Naval Order of Merit, 1st Class (Cuba, Am. Legion D.S.M., Star of Estrella Abdon Calderon, 1st Class, Ecuador, Order of Naval Merit (Gran Cruz) Brazil; Order of the Bath, Croix de Guerre, Grand Cross Legion of Honor (France), Order of Tripod (China): Grand Cross, Order George I (Greece), Knight Grand Cross, Order Orange Nassau (Netherlands), Order of Crown, Croix de Guerre (Belgium), Grand Cross, Mil. Order Italy, Gold Medal U.S. Congress. Clubs: Army and Navy, Army and Navy Country (Washington). Home: 2919 43d St. N.W., Washington. Died June 25, 1956; buried U.S. Naval Acad. Cemetery, Annapolis, Md.

KING, HENRY LORD PAGE army officer; b. Macon, Ga., Apr. 17, 1895; s. Richard Cuyler and Henrietta Dawson (Nisbet) K.; B.S. in E.E., Ala. Poly. Inst., 1916; m. Sarah Brumley Evans, Sept. 6, 1919; children-Henry Lord Page, May Lindsay (Mrs. Warren Duncan). Commd. 2d lt., June 9, 1917, and advanced through the grades to brig. gen., Dec. 1942; apptd. officer in charge, Mil. Personnel Div., Nov. 1941. Mason (Scottish Rite). Home: 1026 Crest Court, Neosha, Mo. Died Oct. 29, 1952.

KING, HORATIO COLLINS lawyer; b. Portland, Me., Dec. 22, 1837; s. Horatio (Postmaster Gen., 1861) and Anne (Collins) K.; reared in Washington; A.B., Dickinson Coll., 1858, A.M., 1863; (LL.D., Allegheny Coll., 1897); admitted to bar, 1861; m. Emma C. Stebbins, Oct. 1862 (died 1864); m. 2d, Esther A. Howard, June 14, 1866, Capt. and a.q.m. vols., Aug. 19, 1862; maj. q.m., Feb. 20-May 19, 1865; bvtd.: maj. vols., Mar. 13, 1865, "for meritorious services during war," and lt. vol. and col. vols., May 19, 1865, "for faithful and meritorious services"; Congressional Medal of Honor "for distinguished bravery nr. Dinwiddle C.H., Va., Mar. 29, 1865." Practiced law, 1865-71, and 1877-; asso. editor New York Star, 1871-73; publisher Christian Union and Christian At Work, 1873-77. Maj. 13th Regt. N.G.S.N.Y., 1877; judge advocate 11th Brigade, 1880; judge advocate gen. of N.Y., 1883; mem. Brooklyn Bd. Edn., 1883-94; trustee N.Y. State Soldiers' and Sailors' Home, 1894-1900; trustee Dickinson Coll., 1896-; chmn. Fredericksburg Nat. Park Assn., 1898. Dem. nominee for sec. of state, N.Y., 1895; Progressive Republican, 1900-; mem. state commn. on law's delays; mem. N.Y. State Monument Commn. Author; History of Dickinson College, 1896; Sketch of Army of potomac, 1896; Songs of Dickinson, 1901; Souvenir of Poems and Compositions, 1908. Mason, Elk. Home: Brooklyn, N.Y. Died Nov. 15, 1918.

KING, RAYMOND THOMAS, lawyer, b. Springfield, Mass., Aug. 15, 1893; s. Thomas Edward and Anna (Davis) K.; A.B., Dartmouth, 1915; LL.B., Harvard, 1919; m. Olive Geran King, Oct. 19, 1918; children—Joan (Mrs. Eugene Loveland), Nancy (Mrs. Hobart Swan), Lucy, Raymond T., Mary (Mrs. Charles Whelan). Admitted to Mass. bar, 1919; pvt. practice law, Springfield, 1921-71; mem. Ely, King, Kingsbury & Corcoran; city solicitor City of Springfield, 1936-37, spl. counsel, 1939-40. Dir. Legal Aid Soc., 1942-71; mem. Cath. Scholarships for Negroes, Inc., 1948-71; dir. Springfield Community Chest, 1936-40; organizer, dir. War Chest, 1941-43, United Fund Greater Springfield, Inc., 1950-51; mem. Mass. White House Conf. on Youth, 1950; area chmn. Easter Seal campaign Bay State Soc., 1956; pres. Concert Association of Springfield, 1933-48; Springfield chmn. Am. Aid for Children to Palestine, 1948, Children's Med. Center, Boston, 1949. Served as capt. inf. U.S. Army, 1917-19. Recipient citation for work among Boys Clubs Am., 1955. Mem. Am., Mass., Hampden County (pres. 1942-43) bar assns., Harvard Law Sch. Assn., Am. Legion. K.C. Clubs: University, Dartmouth (Springfield); Dartmouth (N.Y.C.). Home: Springfield MA Died Feb. 20, 1971.

KING, RUFUS army officer, editor, diplomat; b. N.Y.C., Jan. 26, 1814; s. Charles and Eliza (Gracie) K.; grad. U.S. Mil. Acad., 1833; m. Ellen Eliot, 1836; m. 2d, Susan Eliot, 1843; 3 children including Gen. Charles. Commd. lt. of engrs. U.S. Army, 1833, resigned commn., 1836; asst. engr. Erie R.R., 1836; editor Albany (N.Y.) Daily Advertiser, 1839-41, Albany Evening Jour., 1841-45; adj. gen. N.Y. State, 1839-43; part owner Milw. Sentinel and Gazette, 1845-57,e1845-47, editor, 1845-61; mem. 2d Wis. Constl. Constn., 1846, adopted, 1848; mem. bd. regents U. Wis., 1848-54; mem. bd. visitors U.S. Mil. Acad., 1849; supt. schs. Milw., 1859-60; commd. brig. gen. U.S. Army, 1861; organized Iron Brigade and which fought at Gainesville; U.S. minister to Rome, Italy, 1861, 63-68; resigned from active service, 1868; dep. collector of customs N.Y.C., 1869. Died N.Y.C., Oct. 13, 1876.

KING, SAMUEL WILDER gov. of Hawaii; b. Honolulu, T.H., Dec. 17, 1886; s. James Anderson and Charlotte Holmes (Davis) K.; student pub. schs., Honolulu; grad. U.S. Naval Acad., 1910; m. Pauline Evans, Mar. 18, 1912; children-Charlotte K., Samuel Pailthorpe, Davis Mauliola, Evans Paliku, Pauline Nawahine, Mem. bd. supervisors city and county Honolulu, 1923-24; pres. Samuel W. King, Ltd. (real estate, ins.) since 1924; T.H. del. 74th, 75th, 76th congresses, 1935-41; governor of Hawaii until 1957, resigned in 1957. Served as lt. comdr. United States Navy, 1910-24. Member of Honolulu Realty Board, United States Naval Inst., U.S. Naval Acad. Grads. Assn., Order of Kamehameha, Am. Legion, Vets. Fgn. Wars. Republican. Club: Commercial. Home: Halekon, Kaneohe, Oahu, T.H. Office: Governor's House, Honolulu, Hawaii. Died Mar. 24, 1959.

KING, WILBURN HILL lawyer, farmer, public official; b. Cullodenville, Ga., June 10, 1839; s. Alexander and Mary (Douglas) K.; ed. Americus, Ga., 1846-55; studied medicine and law and practiced law; m. Lucy Furman, Dec. 1867. Served 4 yrs. in C.S.A. as pvt., 1st lt., capt., maj. lt. col., col., brig. gen. and acting maj. gen. Has served as mayor of Sulphur Springs, Tex.; mem. Texas legislature 4 yrs.; adj. gen. of Texas nearly 10 yrs. Democrat. Home: Sulphur Springs, Tex. Died 1910.

KINGMAN, JOHN J. army officer; b. Omaha, Neb.; s. Brig. Gen. Dan C. Kingman (former Chief of Engrs., U.S. Army) and Eugenia (Jennings) K.; B.S., U.S. Mil. Acad., 1904; grad. Engr. Sch., U.S. Army, 1907; m. Adelaide Lewis Warren, Aug. 22, 1911; children-Jean, Ann Warren. Commd. 2d lt. Corps Engrs., U.S. Army, 1904, and advanced through the grades to brig. gen., 1938; served in Philippines, 1907-10; on War Dept. Gen. Staff and chief of staff 90th Div., A.E.F. in France and Germany, during World War; War Dept. Gen. Staff to 1924; command 1st Engrs., 1924-26; dist. engr., Milwaukee, 1926-30; chief of River and Harbor Div., Office Chief of Engrs., 1930-33; dist. engr., Boston, 1933-36; div. engr., South Pacific div., San Francisco, 1936-38; asst. chief of engrs., 1938, until retired Nov. 1941; returned to active duty throughout World War II. Episcopalian. Address: Office Chief of Engineers, War Dept., Washington, D.C. Died July 21, 1948.

KINGMAN, MATTHEW HENRY Marine Corps officer; born Iowa, Mar. 1, 1890. Commd. 2d lt., Marine Corps, and advanced through the grades to col., Sept. 1938; retired, Apr. 1940; called to active duty and advanced to brig. gen., Aug. 1942. Awarded Purple Heart, Silver Star.* Died Nov. 16, 1946.

KINGSBURY JEROME dermatologist; b. Boston; s. Alden Newell and Mary Jerome K.; M.D., N.Y.U. and Bellevue Hosp. Med. Coll., 1897. Interne N.Y. hosps. special work in pathology, dermatalogy, obstetrics, and post grad. study, London and Paris, 1897-1900; practided in N.Y. City since 1900; chief dept. skin diseases, Presbyn. Hosp. Dispensary, 1900-17; attending phys. N.Y. Skin and Cancer Hosp., 1912-22 and 1928-35; visiting dermatologist N.Y. City Hosp., 1920-36; prof. dermatology Polyclinic Med. School and Hosp.; dir. dermatology, Midtown Hosp.; cons. dermatologist Harlem Eye and Ear and N.Y. City hosps. Trustee Bronx Savings Bank. Trustee Northern Dispensary. Served in 7th Regt., Nat. Guard N.Y., 5 yrs.; with 1st Training Regt., Plattsburg, N.Y., 1915; 1st Medico-Mil. Train. Camp (1st lt.), Plattsburg, 1916; suregon with 1st Provisional Regt., 1971; entered Army as capt. Med. Corps and served with A.E.F. in France; now col. Med. Res. Surgeon Veteran Corps Arty. since 1917. Mem. A.M.A., Am. Dermatol. Assn. N.Y. Dermatol. Soc., N.Y. Acad. of Medicine, Alumni Presbyn. Hosp., Alumni Skin and Cancer Hosp. (pres.), S.C.W. (surg.) S.R., Naval Order of U.S. (comdr.), Mil. Soc. War of 1812, Mil. Order World War, Soc. Am. Wars (surg. gen.), N.Y. Soc. Mil. Naval Officers World War (surg.), Res. Officers Assn. of U.S. (pres. Manhattan chapter), Vet. 1st Provisional Regt. (pres.), U.S. Revolver Assn. (life). Surgeon, N.Y. City Petrol Corp. with rank col. on staff Maj. Gen. R. M. Danford. Mem. med. advisory board and panel of specialists, Selective Service. Democrat. Mason. Licensed balloon pilot (Federation Aeronautique Internationale); has compete in nat. and internat. balloon races; formerly chmn. balloon com. Aero Club of America; charter mem. Am. Inst. Aeronautic Engrs.; mem. Early Birds. Clubs: New York Athletic, Metropolitan, Camp Fire Club of America; Army and Navy (Washington, D.C.). Address: 471 Park Av., New York, N.Y. Died July 15, 1944.

KINKAID, THOMAS CASSIN, naval officer; b. Hanover, N.H., Apr. 3, 1888; s. Thomas Wright and Virginia Lee (Cassin) K.; grad. U.S. Naval Academy, 1908; m. Helen Sherburne Ross, Apr. 25, 1911. Promoted through grades to admiral. Tech. advisor to Am. del., Gen. Disarmament Conf., Geneva, Switzerland, Jan.-July 1932; naval attache Am. Embassy, Rome (Italy), Nov. 1938-Mar. 1941; additional duty naval attache Belgrade, Yugoslavia, 1939-41; promoted rear adm., 1941; now adm.; comd. cruiser group action off Bougainville, Feb. 20, 1942; Salamaua-Lae raid, Mar. 10, 1942; Battle of Coral Sea, May 4-8, 1942; Battle of Midway, June 3-6, 1942; comd. Enterprise carrier group, Guadalcanal-Tulagi landings, Aug. 7-9, 1942; battle of Eastern Solomons, Aug. 25, 1942, Santa Cruz Islands, Oct. 26, 1942; Guadalcanal, Nov. 15, 1942; comdr. North Pacific Force in Aleutian campaign, Jan.-Oct. 1943; promoted vice adm., June 1943; comdr. 7th Fleet, and comdr. Allied Naval Forces, Southwest Pacific Area, Nov. 1943-Sept. 1945, New Guinea and Philippine campaigns, including battle for Leyte Gulf, Oct. 25, 1944; promoted admiral, Apr. 1945; landed 24th Corps in Korea, Sept. 1945, and with Lt. Gen. Hodge, took surrender of Japanese Army and Navy in Seoul; landed Am. Marines under Maj. Gen. Rockay at Taku and at Tsingtao, China; transported 5 Chinese armies from Haiphong, Kowloon and Ningpo, landed them at Formosa, Chingwantao and Tsingtao; detached 7th Fleet Nov. 19, 1945; took comd. Eastern Sea Frontier and Atlantic Res., Jan. 16, 1946; retired from active duty May 1, 1950. Vice chmn. Am. Battle Monuments Commn. Mem. Nat. Security Training Commn. Decorations; Navy D.S.M. with 3 gold stars, Army Legion of Merit, Army D.S.M. Presidential Citation, Victory Medal, Atlantic Clasp, American Defense Service Medal, Asiatic-Pacific Campaign Medal (10 battle stars), W.W. II Victory Medal; Companion Order of the Bath (British); Grand Officer Order Orange Nassau with Swords (Netherlands); Order Al Merito, Gran Official (Chilean); Grand Officer Order of Leopold with Palm, Croix de Guerre with Palm (Belgian). Mem. Soc. Cincinnatus in State N.H. Clubs: Chevy Chase, Army-Navy, Aibi (Washington), Union (N.Y.). Home: Washington DC Died Nov. 17, 1972; buried Arlington Nat. Cemetery, Arlington VA

KINKAID, THOMAS WRIGHT naval officer; b. Cincinnati, O., Feb. 27, 1860; s. William P. and Susan (Monahan) K.; grad. U.S. Naval Acad., 1880; m. Virginia Lee Cassin, Apr. 3, 1883. Promoted asst. engr., June 10, 1882; passed asst. engr., Nov. 11, 1892; transferred to the line as lt., Mar. 3, 1899; lt. comdr., Nov. 2, 1902; comdr., July 1, 1907; capt., Mar. 1, 1911; rear admiral, Oct. 15, 1917. Served on Machias, Spanish-Am. War, 1898; on Oregon, 1901-04; fleet engineer Asiatic Fleet, 1904; duty at Navy Yard, Norfolk, Va., 1904-06; fleet engr. Pacific Squadron, 1906-07; insp. engring. material, Chester, Pa., 1907-08; head of dept. steam engring., Navy Yard, Norfolk, 1908-09; at Engring. Expt. Sta., U.S. Naval Acad., 1909-10; apptd. head of engring., Expt. Sta., Annapolis, Md., Sept. 26, 1910. Home: Annapolis, Md. Died Aug. 11, 1920.

KINKEAD, CLEVES playwright; b. Louisville, Ky., Mar. 4, 1882; s. Robert C. and Julia (Grimstead) K.; spl. studies, Centre Coll., Ky., later at Harvard (non-grad.); studied law, U. of Louisville; m. Kathleen Patch, Dec. 14, 1917. Formerly newspaper reporter with St. Louis Republic, New York Press, Louisville Post; practiced law, Louisville, 1905-13; mem. Ky. Ho. of Rep., 1908. Commd. 1st lt. inf., World War. Mem. Kappa Alpha. Mason. Clubs: Pendennis, Louisville Country, River Valley (Louisville); Players, Harvard (New York). Author: (play) Common Clay, first prod. Boston, Republic Theatre, New York, season 1915-16, pub. as novel, 1917. Address: Pendennis Club, Louisville 2. Died Oct. 1955.

KINKEAD, EUGENE F. banker; b. Buttevant, Ireland, 1876; s. Thomas C. and Nora (Barrett) K.; brought to U.S., 1880, naturalized, 1897; A.M., LL.D., Seton Hall Coll., 1895; LL.D., St. Peters College, Jersey City, N.J.; married Anne O'Neill, Sept. 29, 1909; children-Eileen, Jean (Mrs. Layng Martine), Anne (Mrs. Lemuel Skidmore, Jr.). Chmn. exec. com., dir. Colonial Trust Co., N.Y. City, 1920 - ; mem. board of directors of AmerIca Corporation, Chesapeake Industries. Served as major M.I. Department, World War I. Mem. N.Y. Soc. Mil. and Naval Officers World Wars. Democrat. Roman Catholic. Clubs: Rockefeller Center, Touchdown, Lotos (N.Y.C.); Orange Lawn Tennis. Home: 273 Scotland Rd., South Orange, N.J. Office: 1230 6th Av., N.Y.C. 10020. Died Sept. 6, 1960; buried Gate of Heaven Cemetery, Hanover, N.J.

KINLOCH, FRANCIS Continental congressman, army officer; b. Charleston, S.C., Mar. 7, 1755; grad. Eton Coll., Eng., 1774; studied law Lincoln's Inn, London, Eng. Admitted to the bar, London; traveled and studied in Paris, France and Geneva, Switzerland, 1774-77; served as volunteer, lt. and capt. during Revolutionary War, 1778-81; participated in Battle of Beaufort, defense of Charleston; mem. staffs of gens. Moultrie and Huger, and Gov. Rutledge; wounded in attack on Savannah, 1779; mem. S.C. Ho. of Reps., 1779, 86-88; mem. Continental Congress from S.C., 1780-81; rice planter, "Kensington," Georgetown Dist., S.C.; del. S.C. Conv. which ratified U.S. Constn., 1788; warden City of Charleston, also justice of peace and quorum, 1789; mem. S.C. Legislative Council, 1789, S.C. Constl. Conv., 1790; traveled in Europe, 1790, 1802-06. Died Charleston, Feb. 8, 1826; buried St. Michael's Ch. Cemetery, Charleston.

KINNEY, COATES writer; b. Kinney's Corners, N.Y., Nov. 24, 1826; s. Giles and Myra (Cornell) K.; removed to Ohio, 1840; ed. common schools, acad. and 1 term Antioch Coll.; admitted to bar, 1856; m. Hanna Kelly, 1851; m. 2d, Mary C. Allen, 1862. Edited Xenia Torchlight, Cincinnati Daily Times, Springfield Daily Republic, etc.; was maj. and paymaster U.S.A. during Civil war; mustered out with bvt. rank of lt. col.; mem. Ohio senate, 1881-82. Author: Keuka, 1855; Lyrics, 1888; Mists of Fire and Some Eclogues, 1899. The famous lyric, "Rain on the Roof," is included in this last volume. Home: Xenia, O. Died 1904.

KINTNER, EDWIN G., naval officer; b. Harrison County, Ind., May 5, 1881; s. James P. and Anna (Montgomery) K.; U.S. Naval Acad., 1898-1902; M.S., Mass. Inst. Tech., 1908; m. Susie Grice, Sept. 6, 1906 (dec.); children—Edwin G., James G., Susan B. Entered U.S. Navy, 1898; advanced to capt., 1925; served on Olympia, Marietta, Prairie, and Atlanta, 1902-05; Norfolk Navy Yard, 1908-11; inspector, Phila., 1911-15; Norfolk, 1915-1919; Panama, 1919-21; Portsmouth, 1921-23; Camden, 1923-28; Navy Dept., 1928-32; mgr. Norfolk Naval Shipbldg. Yard, 1932-36; Navy Dept. 1936-46. Sr. mem. Compensation Bd., U.S. Navy. Mem. Soc. Naval Architects. Home: Washington DC Died Feb. 5, 1971; buried Arlington Nat. Cemetery, Arlington VA

KIRBY, ABSALOM naval officer; b. Washington, D.C., Mar. 16, 1837; s. John and Georgianna (Eslin) K.; ed. pub. schs., Washington; m. Sarah Watson Hogg, July 16, 1862. Was engr. of the steamboat "Mt. Vernon," which carried Col. Ellsworth and his regt. to Alexandria the morning he was killed, May 24, 1861; apptd. 3d asst. engr., Oct. 3, 1861; promoted through all the grades; retired Feb. 15, 1898. Chief engr. of ships, Navy Yard, inspr. of machinery and fleet engr. on the blockade, 1861-65; participated in battle of Port Royal, Nov. 7, 1861, battle of Mobile Bay, Aug. 5, 1864; cruised in different parts of the world. Trustee Trinity M.E. Ch., Washington; mem. bd. dirs. Washington City Bible Soc. Republican. Home: Washington, D.C. Died Jan. 23, 1924.

KIRBY, GEORGE HUGHES psychiatrist; b. Goldsboro, N.C., Feb. 9, 1875; s. George L. and Mary C. (Green) K.; B.S., U. of North Carolina, 1896; LL.D., from same univ., 1929; M.D., L.I. Coll. Hosp. Med. Sch., 1899; m. Jeanette Kruszewska, Apr. 29, 1912; 1 dau., Jeanette Vincenta. Specialist in mental and nervous diseases; asst. phys., Worcester (Mass.) State Hosp., 1899-1902; asso. in clin. psychiatry, Psychiatric Inst., New York, 1902-08; dir. clin. psychiatry, Univ. and Bellevue Med. Coll., 1914-17; dir, N.Y. Psychiatric Inst., 1917-31; prof. psychiatry, Cornell U. Med. Coll., 1917-27, Coll. Phys and Surg. (Columbia), 1927-32; attending physician New York Hospital. Chief consulting psychiatrist, N.Y. City Dept. of Correction; mem med. advisory com. N.Y. State Hosp Development Commn. Editor Am. Journal of Psychiatry. Commissioned major, M.C., U.S.A., July 26, 1918; attached to staff of surgeon of Port of Embarkation, New York; later apptd. chief of neuro-psychiatric service, U.S.A. Hosp. 1; assisted in organization of spl. unit for care of returning soldiers suffering from mental or nervous disorders; hon. discharged, Mar. 28, 1919. Consultant in neuropsychiatry U.S. Pub. Health Service, with rank of sr. surg., 1919-; apptd. by sec. of treasury, member Board of Consultants to Develop Hospital Facilities Throughout the Country for Ex-soldiers, 1921; mem. med. council. U.S. Veterans' Bur., Washington, D.C. Home: New York, N.Y. Died Aug. 11, 1935.

KIRBY, WILLIAM MAURICE soldier; b. Bridgeport, Seneca Co., N.Y., Dec. 2, 1842; s. William Austin and Elizabeth C. (Maurice) K.; ed. pub. schs., Buffalo; m. June 26, 1867, Sophia E. Miller. Served in Civil war, pvt. 3d N.Y. vol. arty., Jan. 1, 1862; 3d lt., Mar. 10, 1862; 1st lt., July 3, 1863; capt., Feb. 17, 1865; honorably discharged, July 8, 1865; wounded, Dec. 16, 1862; prisoner of war, Feb. 2, 1864, escaped, Jan. 13, 1865. Lt.-col. 3d Regt., N.Y. Vol. Inf., May 17 to Dec. 10, 1898, in Spanish-Am. War. In N.G.S.N.Y., 1st lt. and adj. 49th Regt., Nov. 29, 1876; lt.-col., Feb. 10, 1880; supernumerary, Aug. 28, 1880; capt. 2d separate co., May 11, 1881; bvt. lt.-col., Aug. 10, 1881; gen. insp. rifle practice S.N.Y. of grade of brig.-gen., Jan. 1, 1897; insp. small arms practice and ordnance officer on staff maj.-gen. comdg. Nat. Guard, of grade of maj., Dec. 31, 1898, and bvt. maj.-gen. Senior vice-comdr. Assn. of Spanish-Am. War Veterans. Address: Auburn, N.Y.

KIRCHNER, ARTHUR ADOLPH physician; b. Sargeant, Minn., Aug. 30, 1903; s. Charles Henry and Edith Ida (Zander) K.; B.S., Northwestern U., 1925, M.D., 1929; m. Madelyn Doris Burnett, Sept. 22, 1928; children-JoAnn Doris (Mrs. Charles W. Johnson), Arthur Burnett. Rotating intern San Diego County Gen. Hosp., 1928-29; pvt. practice, San Fernando, Cal., 1929-31, Los Angeles, 1931-; res. gastroenterology U. Chgo., 1937, U. Pa., 1939; mem. staff Meth. Hosp. So. Cal., 1931-55, Queen of Angels Hosp., 1937-, Hosp. Good Samaritan, 1957-; instr. medicine U. So. Cal., 1932-37, asst. clin. prof. medicine, 1958-. Founder, 1954, since pres. Los Angeles Physician Retirement Assn.; dir. Los Angeles Physician Aid Assn., 1953-. Engaged in citrus ranching Coachella Valley, Cal., 1954-; sec.-treas., dir. Absentee Desert Ranchers Assn., 1954-; sec., dir. Am. Auto Stores, Inc., 1949-; partner Burtnett Variety Stores, 1948-56. Served to lt. col. AUS, 1942-46. Recipient Meritorious Service citation Northwestern U., 1946, Alumni Service award, 1958. Fellow Am. Coll. Gastroenterology (pres. 1956, chmn. bd. 1957); mem. Am. (alternate del., then del. 1953-, chmn. com. nursing 1962-65), Cal. (councillor 1951-62, del. 1948-), Los Angeles County (Councillor 1951-62) med. assns., Am., Los Angeles socs. internal medicine, So. Cal. Soc. Gastroenterology, Am., So. Cal. proctologic assns., Am. Endoscopic Assn. Republican. Methodist. Mason (Shriner), Lion (pres. Los Angeles 1935). Home: 531 S. Hauser Blvd., Los Angeles 90036. Office: 2007 Wilshire Blvd., Los Angeles 90057. Died Jan. 3, 1966; buried Forest Lawn Cemetery, Hollywood Hills, Cal.

KIRK, ALAN GOODRICH U.S. ambassador; b. Phila., Pa., Oct. 30, 1888; s. William Thompson and Harriet (Goodrich) K.; Bachelor of Science, United States Naval Academy, 1909; married Lydia S. Chapin, Sept. 14, 1918; children-Marian (Mrs. John W. Appel), Deborah (Mrs. Peter Solbert), Roger K. Commd. ensign, U.S. Navy, 1911, advanced through grades to rear adm., 1941; midshipman Atlantic Fleet, 2 years; served on gunboat U.S.S. Wilmington at Canton, China, during Sun Yat-sen Revolution, later lt. U.S.S. Saratoga; returned to the U.S. and served on U.S.S. Utah; ordered to Naval Proving Ground, Indian Head, Maryland, 1916, and served there as proof and experimental officer throughout World War I; gunnery officer on U.S.S. Connecticut and U.S.S. North Dakota, and asst. gunnery officer on U.S.S. Arizona, 1919-22; exec. officer and navigator of the Mayflower, presdl. yacht, during final months of President Wilson's 2d term and beginning of President Harding's term; in Bur. of Ordnance, 1922-24, and gunnery officer, U.S.S. Maryland, 1924-26, Scouting Fleet until 1928; student (1 yr.), on staff (2 yrs.), Naval War Coll., 1928-31; comdg. U.S.S. Schenck, destroyer, 1931-32, exec. officer U.S.S. West Virginia, 1932-33, receiving letter of recommendation from sec. of navy for winning Battle Efficiency, Gunnery, Engineering, and Communication trophies; asst. dir. ship movements, Office of Naval Operations, 1933-36; comd. U.S.S. Milwaukee, 1936-37; detached from duty on staff, Battle Force, Jan. 29, 1938, and ordered to duty as operations officer, U.S. Fleet; U.S. Naval Attaché and Naval Attaché for Air, Am. Embassy, London, Eng., 1939-41; director of Naval Intelligence, 1941; escort, North Atlantic, 1941; chief of staff for comdr. Naval Forces in Europe, London, 1942-43; comdr. Amphibious Force, U.S. Atlantic Fleet, 1943; apptd. vice admiral, Sept. 1944; comdr. U.S. Naval Forces, France, Sept. 1944. Comd. Task Force, invasion of Sicily, July 1943; comdg. U.S. Naval Task Forces, invasion of Normandy, 1944; retired from Navy with rank of admiral, Feb. 1946; apptd. ambassador to Belgium and minister to Luxembourg; March 1946; United States representative on United Nations special Committee on Balkans, 1947-48; appointed U.S. A.E. and P. to 1949-52, and to Republic of China, Taiwan, 1962-; chairman of American Committee for Liberation of Russian Peoples, 1952; chairman of the board, Mercast Corp., 1954-58; dir. N.Y. World's Fair, 1964-65. Awarded Legion of Merit, August 1943; D.S.M. (Army), 1944, (Navy), 1951; Knight Commander of the Bath (England); commander de la Legion d'Honneur (France). Officer Order of the Crown, Croix de Guerre with Palm, Grand Cordon, Order of Leopold (Belgian). Episcopalian. Clubs: Metropolitan, Chevy Chase, Army-Navy (Washington); Ends of the Earth (N.Y.C.). Contbr. on ballistics to Naval Institute Proceedings. Address: Am. Embassy Taipei, APO 63, care Post Master, San Francisco. Died Oct. 15, 1963; buried Arlington Nat. Cemetery, Washington.

KIRK, NORMAN THOMAS army officer; b. Rising Sun, Md., Jan. 3, 1888; s. Thomas and Anna (Brown) K.; grad. Tome Sch., 1906; M.D., U. Md., 1910; grad. Army Med. Sch., 1913, Med. Field Service Sch., 1931; Sc.D. (hon.), Davidson Coll., 1944, U. Md., 1944; LL.D., Columbia, 1947; m. Anne M. Duryea, Sept. 21, 1917; children-Ann Kirk Willard, Jane Kirk Kimbrell. Commd. 1st lt. M.C., U.S. Army, May 1912, advancing through grades to maj. gen., surgeon gen. U.S. Army, June 1, 1943-May 31, 1947; ret. as maj. gen., July 31, 1947; served in Vera Cruz, Mexico, with Field Hosp. 3, 1914; temp. lt. col., World War 1, 2 tours of duty in Philippines; chief surg. service Letterman Gen. Hosp., 1936-41, Walter Reed Gen. Hosp., 1941-42; comdg. officer, Percy Jones Gen. Hosp., 1942-43. Dir. Am. Found. for Tropical Medicine. Decorations: D.S.M., Legion of Merit; Comdr. Order Brit. Empire (hon.); Comdr. Order Crown of Italy; Cross of Legion of Honor, Degree of Comdr. (France); Royal Order of No. Star, comdr. 1st class (Sweden). Diplomate Am. Bd. Surg., Am. Bd. Orthopaedic Surgery; fellow A.C.S. (gov.), hon. fellowship A.C.S., 1946, A.C.P., So. Surg. Assn.; hon. fellow So. Psychiat. Assn., Am. Hosp. Assn.; mem. Am. Surg. Assn., A.M.A., Am. Orthopaedic Assn., Am. Assn. for Surgery Trauma, Am. Acad. Orthopaedic Surgeons, U.S. Typhus Commn., Pan Am. Med. Assn., Nat. Com. for Mental Hygiene, Nu Sigma Nu; hon. life mem. Washington Orthopaedic Soc.; hon. mem. Acad. Medicine, Washington. Med. Soc. D.C., Alpha Omega Alpha. Mason. Author: Amputations (Dean Lewis' Looseleaf Surgery); Tetanus (Nelson's Looseleaf Surgery); Cineplastic Amputations and Prosthesis (Cyclopedia of Medicine, Surgery and Specialties); Prosthesis (Christopher Textbook of Surgery, by American authors); numerous articles on surgical subjects; Amputations (monograph). Home: Montauk, L.I., Died Aug. 13, 1960; buried Arlington Nat. Cemetery.

KIRK, RAYMOND ELLER chemist; b. Hamilton County, Neb., June 24, 1890; s. Joseph Alexander and Virginia Eads (Eller) K.; student Neb. State Normal, Kearney, 1910-13; B.S., U. of Neb., 1915; M.S., Ia. State Coll., 1917; Ph.D., Cornell, 1927; student U. of Chicago, summer 1919; m. Beth Sibley, June 30, 1920; children-Virginia, Josephine Alvira. Instr. in chemistry, Ia. State Coll., 1917-20; asst. prof. chemistry, U. of Minn., 1920-27, asso. prof., 1927-29; prof. and head dept. of chemistry, Mont. State Coll., and state chemist, 1929-31; prof. and head dept. of chemistry, Poly. Inst., Brooklyn, N.Y., 1931-55; dir. Shellac Research Bureau, 1936-42; also dean of the graduate school, 1944—. Served as civilian insp. Ordnance Dept. United States Army, 1917-18; captain Ordnance Reserve, 1923-30, major, 1930-42. Fellow Am. Inst. Chemists, A.A.A.S., mem. Am. Chem. Soc., Am. Assn. Univ. Profs., Sigma Xi, Phi Lambda Upsilon, Alpha Chi Sigma, Phi Kappa Phi, Gamma Alpha, Delta Sigma Rho. Author: Laboratory Manual in Inorganic Chemistry (with M. C. Sneed), 1927. Co-editor Encyclopedia of Chemical Technology (15volumes), 1947-56. Medical bd. editors Inorganic Synthesis, 1939. Contbr. to sci. jours. Home: 9269 Shore Rd., Bklyn. 9. Died Feb. 6, 1957.

KIRKLAND, JOSEPH army officer, author; b. Geneva, N.Y., Jan. 7, 1830; s. William and Caroline M. (Stansbury) K.; m. Theodosia Burr Wilkinson, 1863, 4 children. Served from pvt. to maj. U.S. Army in Civil War, 1861-63; with U.S. Revenue Service, 1875-80; admitted to Ill. bar, 1880; spl. correspondent reviewer, literary editor Chgo. Tribune, 1890; influenced literary devel. of Hamlin Garland. Author: Zury: The Meanest Man in Spring County, 1885; The Captain of Company K, 1891; The McVeys; The Story of Chicago. Died Chgo., Apr. 29, 1894.

KIRKLIN, BYRL RAYMOND radiologist; b. Gaston, Ind., Sept. 22, 1888; s. John Walter and Sarah Lavina (McCreery) K.; B.S., Indiana U., 1926, M.D., 1914; m. Gladys Marie Webster, June 3, 1915; children-John Webster, Mary Webster. Radiologist Muncie (Ind.) Home Hosp. and private practice, 1916-25: radiologist Mayo Clinic, Rochester, Minn., 1926-54, chmn. sects. on Radiology, prof. radiology, Mayo Foundation, Univ. of Minn., 1936-54. Served as 1st lt., M.C., United States Army, World War I; col., M.C., U.S. Army sr. X-ray consultant Office of Surgeon Gen., World War II; ret. col. M.C. Res.: sr. cons. to surgeon gen., U.S. Army and to USAF. Past pres. Muncie Home Hosp. staff Diplomate and mem. bd. trustees Am. Bd. Radiology (sec.-treas); mem. adv. bd. med. specialties (sec.-treas.). Fel. Am. Coll. Radiology (pres. 1942-43), Am. Coll. Physicians, A.M.A., hon. fel. Internat. Coll. Surgeons; mem. Am. Roentgen Ray Society (pres. 1937-38), Radiol. Soc. North America, Minn. State and Olmsted County med. assns., Minn. Radiol. Soc. (pres. 1930), Am. Assn. Gastro-enterologists, Central Soc. Clin. Research, Am. Assn. Ry. Surgeons, Southern Minnesota Medical Association; corresponding mem. Academia Nacional de Medicina Republic de Colombia; hon. mem. Die Deutsche Rontgen-Gesellschaft (Germany), Royal Soc. Medicine (Eng.) Assn. Gastroenterologists of Paris (France), Soc.

Columbiana de Radiologia, Soc. Mexicana de Radiologia y Fisioterapia, Soc. de Radiologia y Fisioterapia de Cuba, Chicago Roentgen Soc., St. Louis Med. Soc., Muncie Acad. Medicine (pres. 1921,22), Dallas Southern Clin. Soc., Miss. Valley Med. Assn.: mem. Sigma Chi, Phi Rho Sigma, Sigma Xi. Republican. Methodist. Mason. Clubs: Univ., Rochester Country, Rotary (Rochester, Minn.): Army and Navy (Washington), Contbr. to med. jours. Home: 725 11th St., S.W. Office: Kahler Hotel Bldg., Rochester, Minn. Died Mar. 2, 1957; buried Rochester.

KIRKMAN, HAROLD LAURENS DUNDAS plastic surgeon; b. Norfolk, Eng., Mar. 24, 1887; s. Frederick William and Delphine (Laurens) K.; ed. Bedford Modern Sch. (Eng.) and Junior Local, U. of Oxford; M.D., U. of Tex., 1909; m. Frida Julia Buchel, Feb. 8,-1911 (died 1927); children-Harold Buchel, Doris Buchel (Mrs. Charles A. Brokaw); m.2d, Margaret Shelton Shimin, Apr. 1, 1933; children-Margaret, Elizabeth. Came to U.S., 1904, naturalized, 1918. Interne, St. Joseph's Infirmary, Houston, Tex., 1909; prof. plastic surgery, Baylor U., Houston, Tex., since 1943; plastic surgeon, Southern Pacific R.R., Meth. Hosp., Jefferson Davis Hosp. (all Houston, Tex.). Serving as capt., Med. Corps V9S). U.SN.R.; chief of dept. of plastic surgery U.S. Naval Hosp., San Diego, Calif.; organizer Med. Specialist Unit. No. 48, U.S.N.R. Diplomate Am. Bd. Surgery (Founders Group); fellow Am. Coll. Surgeons; mem. Am. Bd. Plastic Surgery, Am. Assn. Plastic Surgeons (past pres.). Tex. Surg. Soc. (past pres.), Southern Surg. Soc. Republican. Episcopalian. Clubs: Rotary, Braeburn Country (Houston). Home: 2241 Sunset Blvd., Houston, Tex. Office: 3603 Audubon Pl., Houston, Tex. Died Mar. 18, 1949; buried Forest Park Cemetery, Houston, Tex.

KIRKPATRICK, GEORGE HOLLAND, physician; b. South Thomaston, Me., Dec. 20, 1880; s. George and Emma (Bartlett) K.; student U. of Vt., 1897-98, M.D., 1906; m. Mary Lovejoy, July 30, 1923; 1 step-son, Herbert V. Olds. Intern, Lynn Hosp., 1906, house officer, 1906-07; out-patient surgeon, 1907-15, asst. vis. surgeon, 1915-25, vis. surgeon, 1925-1938, former president of visiting staff, honorary staff since 1938. Served as capt., med. corps 104th inf., 26th Division. U.S. Army, World War I. Decorated Silver Star medal. Mem. bd. governors Lynn Home for Aged Women. Mem. Lynn and Mass. State med. socs., Am. Med. Assn., Lynn Hist. Soc., S.A.R., Am. Legion, Yankee Div. Vets. Orgn., Mass. Audubon Soc. Episcopalian. (vestryman, St. Stephen's Church, Lynn, 20 yrs.). Mason. Clubs: Eastern Yacht (Marblehead, Mass.); Whiting, Harvard (Lynn). Address: Lynn MA Died Aug. 23, 1968.

KIRKPATRICK, SANFORD congressman; b. Madison Co., O., Feb. 11, 1842; s. Minor and Hannah (Godfrey) K.; emigrated with parents to Wapello Co., Ia., 1849; ed. dist. sch., 1854-58; m. Nellie Metcalf, of Nashville, Tenn., Feb. 11, 1888. Enlisted in Co. K, 2d Ia. Inf., 1861, and served 4½ yrs.; hon. discharged as 1st lt.; connected with mercantile business, coal mining and farming; identified with secret service U.S. internal revenue dept. for 27 yrs. and visited 41 states and tys.; shot 3 times, one eye shot out and the other severely injured; mem. 63d Congress (1913-15), 6th Ia. Dist.; Democrat. Address: Ottumwa, Ia.

KIRKPATRICK, SIDNEY DALE, chem. engr., cons.; born Urbana, Ill., Apr. 2, 1894; s. Frederick Dilling and Virginia Mae (Hedges) K.; B.S., U. of Ill., 1916, grad. study, 1916-17; Sc.D., Clarkson Coll. of Tech., 1946; D. Engring., Polytechnic Institute, Brooklyn, 1948; m. Bonnie Jean Hardesty, Aug. 6, 1919; children—Mary (Mrs. A. H. Gable), S. Dale, Chemist and editor Ill. State Water Survey, 1916-17; chem. adviser U.S. Tariff Commn., 1917-18, spl. expert with same, 1919-21; with McGraw-Hill Pub. Co., N.Y.C., 1921-59, as asst. editor Chemical & Metall. Engineering (mag.), 1921-25, asso. editor, 1925-28, editor, 1928-50; editorial dir. Chem. Engring. and Chemical Week, 1950-59; v.p., McGraw-Hill Book Co., ret. 1959; director General Aniline & Film Corp., Mich. Chem. Corp., 1960-61, Carus Chem. Co., Roger Williams Tech. & Econ. Services, Inc.; cons. engr., 1959-73. Served as 2d lt. and lst lt. S.C., A.E.F., 1918-19; chem. advisor Am. Commn. to Negotiate Peace, 1919; mem. referee bd., Office of Prodn. Research and Development, War Prodn. Bd., 1942-45; cons. on engring., W.M.C., 1942-45; member advisory bd. U.S. C.W.S., 1935-62; consultant on research to U.S.Q.M.C., 1943-45, to tech. indsl. intelligence com. investigating Germany, 1945, to sec. of war, Operations Crossroads, Bikini, 1946; consultant U.S. Atomic Energy Commission, 1950-55; chmn. AEC, adv. com. on information for industry, 1950-55, Recipient Founders award, Am. Inst. Chem. Engrs., 1958; Meml. award, Chem. Market Research Assn., 1959, Fellow Am. Institute Chemists, 1949, hon. member, 1952; mem. Am. Inst. Chem. Engrs. (dir. 1932-39, 1946-49; v.p. 1940-41; pres. 1942), Am. Electrochem. Soc. (dir. 1933-35; v.p. 1931-35; pres. 1944-45), Am. Chem. Soc. (councillor), Society Chemical Industry Great Britain (dir. 1942-44; chmn. 1946-47), A.A.A.S., Am. Soc. Engring. Edn., Sigma Xi, Phi Lambda Upsilon, Alpha Chi Sigma, Sigma Delta Chi, Pi Delta Epsilon, Omega Chi Epsilon, Theta Delta Chi. Awarded silver anniversary medal American Institute Chemical Engineers, 1932; Chemical Industry medalist, 1945. Republican. Methodist. Clubs: Chemists (trustee), Western Universities. Editor: Twenty Five Years of Chemical Engineering Progress. 1933. Co-editor: Perry's Chemical Engineers' Handbook, 1963; cons. editor Chem. Engring. series (36 titles). Contbr. to Chem. Engring. Address: Short Hills NJ Died Feb. 1973.

KIRKPATRICK, THOMAS LE ROY lawyer; b. Mecklenburg County, N.C., May 3, 1877; s. James Watt and Martha Ann (Griffith) K.; prep. edn., Sharon Acad.; student Erskine Coll., Due West, S.C., 1894-98; certificate of completion, U. of N.C. Law Sch., 1900; m. Eva Chalmers, Oct. 9, 1907; children-Thomas Le Roy, Carolyn Chalmers, Nancy Reynolds. Admitted to N.C. bar, 1900, and since practiced at Charlotte; adlerman, Charlotte, 1907-11; v. mayor, Charlotte, 1911-17, mayor, 1915-17; chmn. Local Exemption Board, 1917-18; state senator 20th Senatorial Dist., 1933-35. Organizer and 1st pres. Wilmington, Charlotte, Asheville Highway Assn., also Citizens' Highway Assn. of N.C.; drafted Good Roads bill and successfully promoted $1,000,000 road bond issue for N.C.; chmn. bd. Bankhead Nat. Highway Assn.; pres. Chamber of Commerce, Charlotte; pres. U.S. Good Roads Assn., also mem. exec. com., representing N.C.; proponent of $1,000,000,000 bond issue for U.S. Govt. to build internat. system of interstate highways; mem. Sesquicentennial Commn., Phila., 1926. Mem. Queen City N.G., 1892-98; asst. judge advocate gen. N.C.N.G., 1905-09, rank of lt. col.; judge advotate gen., 1913-17, rank of col. Mem. Am., N.C. State and Mechlenburg bar assns., Chamber Commerce of U.S. (mem. council), Charlotte Chamber Commerce (ex-pres.). Democrat. Elder Asso. Reformed Presbyteriain Ch.; supt. S.S. Mem. Woodmen of World, Modern Woodmen, Elks, Jr. Order United Am. Mechanics; served as dist. gov. Lions of N.C. and as pres. Lions Club of Charlotte, N.C.; past dictator of the Moose Lodge of Charlotte. Home: "Chal Kirk Manor," Park Rd., Charlotte, R.F.D. 2. Office: First Nat. Bank Bldg., Charlotte, N.C. Died Feb. 4, 1946.

KIRKPATRICK, WILLIAM HUNTINGTON, judge; b. Easton, Pa., Oct. 2, 1885; s. of Hon. William S. (former atty. gen. of Pa.) and Elizabeth H. (Jones) K.; A.B., Lafayette Coll., 1905, LL.D., 1944; student law dept., U. of Pa., 1905-06, LL.M., 1937; m. Mary Stewart Wells, May 17, 1913; children—William S., Miles. Admitted to Pa. bar, 1908; mem. 67th Congress (1921-23), 26th Pa. Dist.; U.S. dist. judge for Eastern District of Pa., 1927-58, sr. dist. judge, 1958-70. Trustee Lafayette Coll. Lt. col. Judge Adv. Gen.'s Dept., and mem. Bd. of Review of Courts Martial. World War. Republican. Presbyn. Home: Harwood MD Died Nov. 28, 1970.

KIRTLAND, FRED DURRELL, naval officer; b. Salina, Kan., Nov. 6, 1892; s. Charles Byron and Elizabeth (Dohmyer) K.; S.B., U.S. Naval Acad., 1916; B.S., Columbia, 1922; m. Mary Adikes, Sept. 14, 1921; 1 son, Robert A. Commd. ensign U.S. Navy, 1916, and advanced through grades to rear adm., 1943; served on U.S.S. Wyoming and Brit. Grand Fleet, 1917-18; sea service in battleships, cruisers, destroyers and shore duties, 1919-39; comdg. officer and div. comdr., destroyers, N. Atlantic neutrality patrol, 1939-40; squadron comdr., Atlantic convoy and anti-submarine duty, 1941-42; comdr. U.S.S. Ala., with Brit. Home Fleet, 1943, S. and Central Pacific to Japan, 1943-44; comdt., Naval Operating Base, Okinawa, 1945-46; comdr. Amphibious Training Command, U.S. Atlantic Fleet, with hdqrs. at Little Creek, Va., from 1946. Awarded Legion of Merit, commendation ribbon. Presbyterian. Clubs: Army Navy Country (Washington), Manhasset Bay Yacht (L.I., N.Y.). Home: New Cambria KS Died Oct. 1972.

KIRWIN, THOMAS JOSEPH urologist; b. Frederick, Md., 1891; s. James John and Margaret Mary (Surplus) K.; Ph.C., B.S., U. Mich., 1910; grad. student U. Wis. 1912-13; M.D., Tulane, 1916. Cornell, 1917; M.A. in anatomy, Columbia, 1923; M.S. in surgery, Yale, 1929; m. Margaret Hughes, Sept. 8, 1917; 1 dau., Ruth Ann (Mrs. William S. McLean). Instr. in urology, Cornell Med. Coll., 1920-22; instr. in embryology, histology, Columbia, 1921-23; chief of clinic, adjunct vis. urologist James Buchanan Brady Found., Dept. Urology, N.Y. Hosp.; attending genito-urinary surgeon, N.Y.C. Hosp., Welfare Island; cons. urologist Coney Island Hosp. (Bklyn.), Benedictine Hosp. (Kingston), Monmouth Meml. Hosp. (Long Branch, N.J.), South Nassau Communities Hosp.; prof. urology N.Y. Med. Coll.; dir. of urology Flower and Fifth Avenue Hosp., Met. Hosp.; dir. Bird S. Coler Hosp. Served as capt. M.C., U.S. Army, France, World War I (Arsne-Marne, Orse-Arsne, Saint Mihiel, Meuse-Argonne, Ypres-Lys). Certified by Bd. Urology. Fellow N.Y. Acad. Medicine, Am. Coll. Surgeons, Internat. Coll. Surgeons; mem. A.M.A., N.Y. State and County med. socs., Am. Urol. Soc., Italian Urol. Soc., Societa de Obstetrica Gynecology et Urology (Rumania), Internat. Urol. Soc., Societas Japonica Urologiac (hon.), Delta Tau Delta, Nu Sigma Nu, Sigma Zi. Clubs: University, Yale, University of Michigan (N.Y.C.). Author: (with Dr. O. S. Lowsley) Textbook of Urology, 1926, Urology for Nurses, 1936, Clinical Urology (2 vols.), 1940. Author Chpt. Oxford Loose Leaf Surgery; chpt., Diseases of the Ureter, in Ency. of Medicine; Diseases of the Ureter, in Cyclopedia of Medicine. Contbr. numerous articles on surg. subjects to sci. jours. Devised instruments known as the Kirwin vesical neck resector, Kirwin prostatic resector, Kirwin Lithrotrite, Kirwin radon seed implanter, Kirwin measuring device for bladder tumor, Kirwin Automatic resectoscope, Kirwin cystoscope. Home: 21 E. 90th St., N.Y.C. 28. Office: 1 E. 63d St., N.Y.C. 21. Died Aug. 18, 1959.

KITCHELL, JOSEPH GRAY artist, writer; b. Cincinnati, Apr. 25, 1862; s. Joseph S. K.; educated in Cincinnati and New York: m. Caroline Lincoln Jacobs, Oct. 1890; 1 son, Joseph William. Introduced first bicycle (high in Cincinnati, imported from Scotland, organizer and pres. of Cincinnati Bicycle Club; dir. League of Am. Wheelmen. Photographic editor Quarterly Illustrator; publisher L'Art du Monde; invented method and apparatus for first scientific composite photograph. In 1900 produced the Kitchell Composite Madonna, a merging of the most important madonnas painted by the great masters during 300 yrs., which attracted wide attention in America and Europe; invented, 1915, and patented new method of reproducing pictures known as "Sub-Chromatic Art," examples of which were accepted by Metropolitan Museum, N.A.D., Congressional Library, British Museum, Bibliotheque Nationale, Paris. Pres. the Ethridge Co., 12 yrs. Recruited and capt. Co. F, 6th Regt. Conn. H.G.; apptd. head of personnel unit, gen. control, gun div. Ordnance Dept., Washington, with rank of capt., Nov. 1917; later headed personnel branch, engring. div. Ordnance Dept.; delivered lectures to stimulate munitions production in N.Y. dist.; made maj., Apr. 1918; pres. Commd. Officer's Exam. Bd., Gen. Staff, stationed in New York; after armistice transferred to Washington in morale br., Gen. Staff; discharged, Apr. 1919. Produced official Red Cross allegorical picture, "Thine Is the Glory," 1919, which was given to War Dept. and presented by sec. of war to Red Cross Hdqrs., Washington. Mem. Conn. State Council Defense, Army Ordnance Assn. Comdr. Military Order Foreign Wars; fellow Royal Soc. Arts (Great Britain); hon. officer, Los Angeles Police Dept. Mason. Club: Manhattan (New York City). Author: American Supremacy, 1901; Earl of Hell, 1923; 25,000 Days; also econ. features and scientific writings in mags. and newspapers. Home: Hollywood Hotel, Hollywood, Calif. Died June 1, 1947.

KITTELLE, SUMNER ELY WETMORE Naval officer; b. Peekskill, N.Y., June 14, 1867; s. George Wetmore and Marie Louise (Geer) K.; grad. U.S. Naval Acad., 1889; m. Anna Lockwood, d. late Adm. Charles D. Sigsbee, Mar. 22, 1897; children-Anna Louise (wife of C. J. Moore, U.S. Navy), Elsa (dec.), Mary Sigsbee (wife of Lester A. Dessez, U.S. M.C.), Sumner Sigsbee, John, Nancy; m. 2d, Elizabeth R. Delaney (widow Gen. Delaney). Ensign, July 1, 1891; promoted through grades to rear adm., June 1921. Served on Dolphin, Spanish-Am. War, 1898; sec. Gen. Bd., Navy Dept., 1905-07; duty with the building of the Mississippi, 1907-08; served on Mississippi, 1908-09; exec. officer same, 1909-10; at Navy Yard, Boston, 1910-13; comd. Wheeling, 1913-14; at Naval War Coll., Newport, R.I., 1914; comd. Albany, 1914, Maryland, 1915; at Naval War Coll., 1915-17; apptd. comdr. Georgia, Jan. 5, 1917; sr. mem. Alaskan Coal Commn., 1919; mem. Bd. of Inspection and Survey, 1920; apptd. gov. of Virgin Island, by President Harding, Apr. 1921; comdr. Destroyer Squadrons of Scouting and Battle Fleets, 1922-24; comdt. Eighth Naval Dist., 1924; pres. Naval Examining Bd., 1925; comdt. Naval Dist. of P.I., 1926-28; comdr. Fleet Base Force, U.S. Fleet, 1928-29; pres. Bd. of Inspection and Survey, 1920-31, retired. Home: 2229 California St., N.W., Washington. Died Dec. 29, 1950.

KITTREDGE, FRANK ALVAH U.S. Nat. Park Service; b. Glyndon, Minn., Mar. 29, 1883; s. Charles Brigham and Katherine (Forbes) K.; B.S. in C.E., U. Wash., 1912, C.E., 1915; m. Catharine Mears, Mar. 11, 1915; 1 dau., Catharine Jane (Mrs. Robert Andrews). With Alaska Central Ry., 1905-07; engr. in charge constrn., Wash. State Highway Commn., 1907-11; div. engr. Ore. State Highway Commn., 1913-15; sr. highway engr. Bur. Pub. Rds., 1917-27; chief engr. Nat. Park Service, U.S. Dept. of Interior, 1927-37, regional dir. Region Four, 1937-40, supt. Grand Canyon Nat. Park, 1940-41, supt. Yosemite Nat. Park, 1941-47, chief engr. U.S. Nat. Park Service, 1947-51. Served as 1st lt. Engr. Corps, U.S. Army, 1918; capt. Rd. and Bridge Engrs. in France, 1918-19. Mem. Am. Soc., C.E. (life mem.), Soil Conservation Soc., Wilderness Soc., Am. Planning and Civic Assn. Save the Redwoods League. Presbyn. Mason. Clubs: Sierra Mountaineers, Cosmos, American Legion. Address: 1961 Waverley St., Palo Alto Cal. Died Dec. 11, 1954; buried Alta Mesa, Los Altos, Cal.

KITTS, JOSEPH ARTHUR cons. engr. and concrete technologist; b. Nevada City, Calif., Apr. 14, 1881; s. James and Mary Alice (Rafford) K.; student U. of Calif., 1900-03, 1908-09; m. Alberta Waldo Hawley, Sept. 10, 1912; children-James Waldo, Mary Elisabeth, Jean Josephine. Mining, surveys and constrn., Nevada City Mines, 1900-05; engr. of constrn., Panama Canal, 1905-06; engr. and supt. constrn., C. A. Meusdorfer, Couchot & O'Shaughnessy and Union Constrn. Co., San Francisco, 1906-10; engr. of surveys, concrete tests, design and constrn., Panama Canal, 1910-15; resident and field engr. U.S. Steel Co., Sonoma County Highway Commn., Calif. Highway Commn., Portland Cement Co., 1915-24; cons. concrete technologist, operating as Joseph A. Kitts Co., San Francisco, since 1924. Served as capt. Engr. Corps, U.S. Army, in France, 1917-19. Mem. Alpha Tau Omega (pres. Gamma Iota Asso.), Calif. Alumni Assn., Am. Concrete Inst., Am. Legion, Am. Red Cross. Awarded Roosevelt Panama Canal medal and bars; Victory medal with France bar. Author: Coordination of Basic Principles of Concrete Mixtures, 1933; Specifications for Structural Concrete, 1937. Contbr. to Concrete (Mag.). Inventor erosion control, water conservation, irrigation system, in use in exptl. project, Town Talk, Calif., since 1944. Home: Nevada City, Calif. Office: Rialto Bldg., San Francisco. Died March 1947.

KITTS, WILLARD AUGUSTUS, 3RD corp. exec.; b. Oswego, N.Y., Apr. 14, 1894; s. Willard Augustus, Jr., and Augusta Belle (Cook) K.; B.S., U.S. Naval Acad., 1916; student Naval Post Grad. Sch., 1920-21; B.S., Mass. Inst. Tech., 1922; m. Fredrika Burlingame Jones, Dec. 27, 1917; children-Willard, David Burlingame, Susanna Burlingame. Commd. ensign USN, 1916, advancing through grades to rear adm., 1943; served in Grand Fleet during World War I, in various Pacific campaigns during World War II (fleet gunnery officer, comdg. officer Northampton, Nevada); asst. chief, Bur. of Ordnance, Washington, 1944-45; comdr. Naval Proving Ground, Dahlgren, Va.; ret. with rank vice adm., 1951. With Gen. Electric Co., Schenectady, mgr. ordnance engring. sec., now mgr. Indsl. Atomic Products Study. Decorated Navy Cross, Legion of Merit, Condr. Order Brit. Empire. Clubs: Army and Navy, Army-Navy Country (Washington); N.Y. Yacht. Home: 19 Front St., Schenectady 12305. Office: Atomic Products div. Gen. Electric Co., Schenectady. Died Nov. 21, 1964; buried Arlington Nat. Cemetery.

KLECKNER, MARTIN SELER surgeon; b. Allentown, Pa., Apr. 14, 1890; s. Francis and Amelia Isabella (Seler) K. B.S., Muhlenberg Coll., Allentown, Pa., 1910; M.D., Univ. of Pa., 1914; postgrad. study, Univ. of Pa., 1920-21, Postgrad. Hosp., N.Y.C., 1923-24, Cornell Med. Sch., 1926-28; m. Florence Street, Nov. 25, 1920; children-Martin Seler, Donald S., Francis S. Interne, chief resident German Hosp. (now Lankenau), 1914-16; surgeon Allentown Hosp., 1917-18; practice gen. surgery, Allentown, 1920-24, practice limited to diseases of the rectum and colon since 1924, cons. proctologist Sacred Heart Hosp., Allentown, St. Luke's Hosp., Bethlehem, Pennsylvania, Allentown State Hospital. Captain United States Army, World War I, 1918-20. Certified diplomate surgery and proctology. Fellow A.P.S., A.C.S. (counsellor State of Pennsylvania, 1934-38). Founder-fellow International College of Surgeons. Mem. A.M.A. (chmn. sect. gastroenterology and proctology, 1946-47), Am. Proctologic Soc. (pres. 1939-40), Pa. State Cancer Commn. (chmn. 1946-49; pres. Lehigh Co. Unit since 1949), Wainwright Tumor Clinic Assns. (chmn. 1947, 1952, Pres., dir. 1951-52), Postgrad. and Phila. proctologic Socs. (p.p. both socs.), Lehigh Co. Med. Soc. (pres. 1950), Lehigh Valley Medical Association (president 1939), Am. Cancer Society (bd. dirs., Lehigh Co.). Invitation lectr. proctology, Univ. of Pa. Medical School. American Legion, Y.M.C.A. (director), Chi Phi, Alpha Kappa Kappa, Alpha Omega Alpha. Rep. Lutheran, Mason (Shriner), Elk. Clubs: Livingston, Lehigh Country, Maskenozha Hunting and Fishing; Union League (Phila.). Author articles on proctologic subjects and cancer in medical jours. Home: Dorneyville, 3110 Hamilton Blvd. Office: 202 N. 8 St., Allentown, Pa. Died May, 1958.

KLEIN, GERALD BROWN, lawyer; b. North Liberty, O., Nov. 7, 1902; s. William and Ida (Brown) Kleinknecht; student Tulsa U., 1920-21; B.A., Miami U., Ohio, 1924; LL.B., Cumberland U., 1928; m. Marjorie Abbott, Aug. 29, 1927; 1 son, Tomas Abbott. Admitted to Okla. bar, 1928, U.S. Supreme Ct., 1950; practice in Tulsa, 1928-68; mem. firm Houston, Klein & Davidson, 1945-68. Gen. counsel Home Fed. Savs. & Loan Assn., Tulsa; sec., counsel General Television, Inc.; dir. Hanna Lumber Co. Faculty Okla. Sch. Bus., 1936-42, U. Tulsa Law Sch., 1946-58. Active U.S.O., A.R.C., Community Fund. Pres. Okla. Bar Found., 1957-58; trustee Okla. N.G. Armory of Tulsa. Served from capt. to lt. col., USAAF, 1942-45. Fellow American Bar Foundation, American College of Probate Counsel. Winner of dramatic teachings contest Readers Digest, 1941. Mem. Am., Fed., Okla. (pres. 1946, chairman of judicial appointments committee 1965), Inter-Am., Tulsa County (pres. 1940), Tulsa County Jr. (pres. 1932) bar assns., Internat. Assn. Ins. Counsel, Am. Judicature Soc., Tulsa C. of C. (chmn. civic dept. 1947), Phi Kappa Tau, Sigma Delta Kappa, Tau Kappa Alpha, Pi Kappa Delta. Republican. Presbyn. Clubs: The Tulsa (pres. 1957), Southern Hills Country, University (Tulsa); Nat. Lawyers (gov. Washington 1963-68). Home: Tulsa OK Died Sept. 23, 1968; buried Rose Hill Mausoleum.

KLEIN, HARRY THOMAS lawyer; b. Bellevue, Ky., Mar. 22, 1886; s. John Henry and Carrie(Gauckler) K.; LL.B., McDonald Law Inst., Cin., 1908; D.C.S. (hon.), N.Y. U., 1950. Admitted to Ohio bar, 1909; in practice, Cin., 1909-17; spl. counsel to U.S. Liquidation Commn., 1919-20; asso. gen. counsel Tex. Co., 1921-25, gen. counsel since 1925, dir. since Jan. 1, 1933, v.p., mem. exec. com. 1933-40 exec. v.p., gen. counsel 1940-44, pres. 1944-52, mem. exec. com. 1952-53; dir. Tex. Co., Seaboard Oil Co.; chmn. Am. Petroleum Industries Com., 1932-43. Served as 1st lt., later maj. and lt. col., judge adv., chief requisition officer AEF, World War I. Awarded D.S.M. (U.S.); Chevalier and Officer Legion of Honor (France). Mem. Am. Petroleum Inst. (dir.). Mem. Ohio, Ky., N.Y., Am. bar assns., Assn. Bar City N.Y., U.S. C. of C., N.A.M. Lutheran. Republican. clubs: Cloud (pres.); Links (N.Y.); Pacific Union (San Franciso); Queen City (Cin.). Home: 870 Burney Lane Rd., Watch Hill, Cin. Office: 135 E. 42d St., N.Y.C. 17. Died Jan. 1965.

KLINE, GEORGE WASHINGTON naval officer; b. Flemington, N.J., Jan. 4, 1864; grad. U.S. Naval Acad., 1885. Promoted ensign, July 1, 1887; lt. jr. grade, Mar. 12, 1896; lt., Mar. 3, 1899; lt. comdr., Sept. 13, 1904; comdr., Aug. 1, 1908; captain July 1, 1912; now retired with rank of rear adm. Served on Annapolis, Spanish-Am. War, 1898; exec. officer, Raleigh, 1904-05; duty Navy Recruiting Sta., N.Y. City, 1905-07; exec. officer Georgia 1907-09; comd. Castine, 1909-10; insp. ordnance, Phila., Pa., and Camden, N.J., 1910-12; comd. Naval Sta., Guantanamo, Cuba, 1912-13; comd. Idaho, 1913, Vermont, 1913-15; apptd. mem. Bd. Inspection and Survey, Navy Dept., Dec. 24, 1915. Home: Bound Brook, N.J. Died June 28, 1922.

KLINE, JACOB army officer; b. Lebanon, Pa., Nov. 5, 1840; s. Levi and Bella M. (Ebert) K.; ed. Pa. Coll.; m. Leila Cassell, Oct. 4, 1871. Apptd. from Pa., 1st lt. 16th Inf., Sept. 9, 1861; promoted through grades to brig. gen. vols., May 27, 1898; hon. disch. from vol. service, Mar. 15, 1899; brig. gen. U.S.A., Jan. 23, 1904; retired at own request after 40 yrs.' service, Jan. 24, 1904. Bvtd. capt., Apr. 7, 1862, for battle of Shiloh, Tenn.; maj., Sept. 1, 1864, for Atlanta campaign. Instr. art of war and in dept. of inf., at Inf. and Cav. Sch., Ft. Leavenworth, Kan., 1887-92. Home: Lebanon, Pa. Died 1908.

KLOTZ, ROBERT congressman; b. Northampton (now Carbon) County, Pa., Oct. 27, 1819; attended county schs. First register and recorder Carbon County, 1843; served from pvt. to lt. and adj. 2d Pa. Volunteers during Mexican War, 1846-47; mem. Pa. Ho. of Reps., 1848-49; moved to Pawnee, Kan., 1855; mem. Topeka (Kan.) Constl. Conv., 1855; 1st sec. of state under Topeka Constn.; served as brig. gen. under Gov. Robinson of Kan.; moved to lMauch Chunk, Pa., 1857; treas. Carbon County, 1859; served as col. 19th Pa. Emergency Militia, U.S. Army during Civil War; trustee Lehigh U., Bethlehem, Pa., 1874-82; mem. U.S. Ho. of Reps. (Democrat) from Pa., 46th-47th congresses, 1879-83; agt., dir. Laflin-Rand Powder Co., N.Y.C. Died Mauch Chunk, May 1, 1895; buried City Cemetery, Mauch Chunk.

KLUSS, CHARLES LAVERNE paper mfg. co. exec.; b. Postville, Ia., Aug. 28, 1912; s. Verni and Nina Gertrude (Rush) K.; B.S., U. Ia., 1932; post-grad. U. Chgo., Northwestern U., 1935-39; m. Madeline Riddell, Nov. 11, 1933; 1 dau., Carol (Mrs. Peter Walker). With Continental Ill. Nat. Bank & Trust Co., Chgo., 1932-33; v.p. Shea & Co., Chgo., 1933-35; with Conn. Mut. Life Ins. Co., Chgo., 1935-27; founding partner Hewitt Assos., mgmt. cons., Chgo., 1937-59; v.p., dir. exec. resources Champion Papers. Inc., Hamilton, O., 1959-. Served to lt. comdr. USNR, 1942-45. Club: Union League (Chgo.). Home: 1747 Woodridge Dr. Office: Champion Papers, Inc., Hamilton, O. Died Sept. 1967.

KNAPP, FRANCIS ATHERTON, printing co. exec.; b. Mpls., July 2, 1907; s. Albert Henry and Laura Anna (Bean) K.; A.B., Stanford, 1929; student San Diego State Coll., 1925-27; m. Alice Royal McCarthy, Dec. 17, 1933; 1 son, David Atherton. Office mgr. Cal. Art & Engraving Co., 1929-32; prodn. mgr. Lederer, Street & Zeus Co., Berkeley, Cal., 1932-69; pres. Asso. Printing Industries, Oakland, Cal., 1956-69. Commr., Cal. Apprenticeship Council, 1960-69, chmn., 1966-67. Mem. trade adv. com. Peralta Colls., 1946-69; mem. Greater E. Bay Apprenticeship Com., 1946-69. Mem. Alameda-Contra Costa County Com. for Equal Opportunity in Employment and Tng., 1965-69; active Nat. Found.; chmn. Typog. Welfare Trust Fund, 1955-69; mem. com. Cal. Jr. Coll. Assn., 1966-69. Bd. dirs. Printing Industry Pension Fund. Served from lt. to lt. comdr. USNR, 1942-46. Mem. Printing Industries No. Cal. (dir.). Clubs: Commonwealth of Cal. (San Francisco); San Francisco Press; Outlook (Berkeley); Berkeley Breakfast. Home: Berkeley CA Died May 24, 1969.

KNAPP, GEORGE journalist; b. Montgomery, N.Y., Sept. 25, 181 s. Edward and Frances (Flood) K.; m. Eleanor McCartan, Dec. 22, 1840, 12 children. With newspaper Mo. Republican, 1836-83, part propr. book and job printing dept., 1836, then editor (made it one of leading newspapers in U.S.), 1837-83; an organizer of volunteer militia St. Louis Legion, served as capt. and lt. col., Mexican War; organizer, capt. company called Mo. Republican Guards, 1862; largely responsible for building 1st bridge over Mississippi in St. Louis. Died in S.S. Pennland while returning to U.S. from European trip, Sept. 18, 1883.

KNAPP, HARRY SHEPARD naval officer; b. New Britain, Conn., June 27, 1856; s. Fredric and Mary Eunice (Burritt) K.; grad. U.S. Naval Acad., 1878; unmarried. Midshipman, 1880; ensign, 1882; lt. jr. grade, 1889; lt., 1894; lt. comdr., 1902; capt., 1909; rear admiral, Aug. 13, 1916. Served on various ships at sea and at Naval Acad. and Naval War Coll.; Army War Coll., winter, 1906-07; chief of staff, Pacific Fleet, 1907-08; comdg. Charleston, 1908-09, Tennessee, 1910-11, Florida, 1911-12; mem. Gen. Bd. of Navy, 1909-10 and 1912-16; mil. gov. Santo Domingo, 1917-18; duty with Peace Conf., 1919; comdr. U.S. Naval Forces in European waters, 1919-20, retired. Conglist. Home: Hartford, Conn. Died Apr. 6, 1923.

KNAPP, JOHN JOSEPH naval officer; b. St. Louis, Oct. 29, 1857; s. John and Virginia (Wright) K.; grad. U.S. Naval Acad., 1878; m. Lilias Harrison, July 31, 1884. Commd. ensign, June 26, 1884; promoted through the various grades to capt., July 1, 1910. Served on U.S.S. Ouinnebaug, 1878-80; Wachusett, 1881-84; New Hampshire, 1884-85; Alert, 1887-90; Baltimore, 1892-93; Patterson, 1896-97; flag lt. to Rear Admiral Howell, on U.S.S. San Francisco, Feb.-Oct. 1898; detached duty and comd. torpedo boat Somers, Mar.-Apr. 1898, and comd. Topeka, Apr.-May 1898, comd. Sylph. July-Sept. 1899; in P.I., 1900-01; on Petrel and comd. Wompatuck; supt. Nautical Sch., Manila, 1901-02; on Solace, 1904-05; comd. Celtic, 1905-06, Cheyenne, 1908-09; hydrographer, Bur. Navigation, Navy Dept., 1910-. Medal for W.I. campaign during Spanish-Am. War; Spanish War and Philippine campaign badges. Home: Washington, D.C. Died Sept. 28, 1915.

KNAPP, LYMAN ENOS lawyer; b. Somerset, Vt., Nov. 5, 1837; s. Hiram K.; grad. Middlebury Coll., 1862 (A.M.; also LL.D., Whitman Coll., 1893); m. Martha A. Severance, Jan. 23, 1865. Entered army, 1862, as capt.; engaged in 14 of the historic battles from Gettysburg to the capture of Petersburg; 3 times wounded; bvtd. for gallantry by President Lincoln and retired at close of war as lt. col., comdg. regt. Editor Middlebury. Vt., Register, 1865-78; editorial contributor to Am. Law Register and Chicago Inter Ocean; corr. Associated Press, etc. Practiced law, 1876-. One of clerks Vt. Ho. of Reps., 1872-73; judge of probate, Addison dist., Vt., 1879-89; mem. Vt. Ho. of Reps., 1884-85; gov. of Alaska, 1889-93; engaged in law practice at Seattle, Wash. Home: Seattle, Wash. Died 1904.

KNEELAND, YALE, JR., physician; b. Rumson, N.J., July 18, 1901; s. Yale and Anna Ilsley (Ball) K.; A.B., Yale, 1922; M.D., Columbia, 1926; m. Deborah Dyer, Jan. 4, 1930; children—Hopeton Drake, Deborah Van Dyck, Yale, III, Anne Ball. Interne Presbyn. Hosp., New York City, 1926-28; asst. in medicine Coll. of Physicians and Surgeons, Columbia, 1928-31, instr. medicine, 1931-34, asso. in medicine, 1934-39, asst. prof. medicine, 1939-47, asso. prof. 1947-58, professor, 1958-67, professor of medicine, 1967-70; attending physician Presbyn. Hosp., N.Y. City, 1945-70; clin. dir. Columbia service Goldwater Memorial Hosp., N.Y. City; consulting physicians Sharon (Conn.) Hosp., St. Francis Hospital, Poughkeepsie, N.Y.; civilian expert cons. to War Dept. Served as col. med. corps U.S. Army, 1942-45, sr. consultant infectious disease, E.T.O.; cons. in medicine United Kingdom base. Fellow Am. Coll. Physicians; mem. Am. Soc. Clin. Investigation, Assn. Am. Physicians, Phi Beta Kappa, Alpha Omega Alpha. Republican. Protestant Episcopalian. Clubs: Union, Century Association (president 1964-68), Grolier (New York City, N.Y.). Contributor of articles on infectious diseases to med. jours. Home: Millbrook NY Died Dec. 15, 1970.

KNIGHT, AUSTIN MELVIN admiral U.S. Navy; b. Ware, Mass., Dec. 16, 1854; s. Charles Sanford and Cordelia (Cutter) K.; grad. U.S. Naval Acad., 1873; m. Alice Phinney Tobey, 1878 (died 1879); 1 dau., Alice Austin (Mrs. W. L. Pryor); m. 2d, Elizabeth Harwood Welsh, Apr. 29, 1886 (died 1911); children-Dorothy Knight, Richard Harwood. Commd. ensign, July 1874; promoted through grades to rear admiral, Jan. 20, 1911. Served on board the Tuscarora, Pacific Station, 1873-74; Kearsarge, Palos, and Saco, Asiatic Station, 1874-75; Naval Acad., 1876-78; Quinnebaug, European Station, 1878-79; Galena European and South Atlantic Stas., 1880-83; ordnance proving ground, Annapolis, Md., 1883-85; in charge same, 1885-89; Flagship Chicago, North Atlantic, European and South Atlantic stas., 1889-92; Naval Acad., 1892-95; Lancaster and Castine, South Atlantic station, 1895-97; Puritan, North Atlantic station, 1897-98; engaged in blockade on north coast of Cuba, and in Puerto Rican expdn. during the Spanish-Am. War; head of dept. of seamanship, Naval Academy, 1898-1901; comd. Newport, summer practice cruise, 1900; War College, summer, 1901; comd. Yankton, surveying on south coast of Cuba, 1901-03; comd. Castine, N. Atlantic Squadron, 1903-04; pres. special board on naval ordnance and pres. joint army and navy board on smokeless powders, 1904-07; comd. Washington, Oct. 7, 1907, to May 1, 1909; pres. special board on naval ordnance and of joint army and navy board on smokeless powders, 1909; later comd. Narragansett Bay (R.I.) Naval Sta.; comdt. same and pres. Naval War Coll., Dec. 1913-Feb. 1917; comdr.-in-chief Asiatic Fleet with rank of admiral, Apr. 1917-Dec. 9, 1918; retired, Dec. 16, 1918. Pres. Board to Award

Decorations for War Service, 1918-19. Author: Modern Seamanship, 1901. Home: Washington, D.C. Died Feb. 26, 1927.

KNIGHT, HARRY EDWARD, army officer; b. Elizabeth, N.J., July 9, 1876; s. Henry Warren and Tressa (Taylor) K.; grad. Montclair (N.J.) Mil. Acad., 1895; student Lehigh U., 1895-98; grad. Infantry and Calvary Sch., 1904, Army War Coll., 1928; m. Celeste Foote, Dec. 12, 1905. Enlisted as pvt., U.S. Army, 1898; apptd. 2nd lt. inf., 1898; advanced through grades to maj. gen.; retired May 31, 1938. Mem. Mil. Order of World War, Psi Upsilon. Conglist. Club: Army and Navy (Washington). Home: 2126 Connecticut Av., Washington DC*

KNIGHT, MILTON, banker; b. Toledo, Aug. 18, 1906; s. W. W. and Edna S. (Ford) K.; A.B., Yale, 1928, LL.B., 1931; m. Dorothy Gardner, Nov. 7, 1941; children—William G., Barbara Ross, Milton Ford. Admitted to Ohio bar, 1931; with law firm Marshall, Melhorn, Marlar & Martin, Toledo, 1931-36; asst. sec. to v.p. Libbey-Owens-Ford Glass Co., from 1936, sec., v.p. charge Spl. Products div., until 1942, chmn. bd., exec. com., 1965-71, dir., 1940-71; pres., dir. First Nat. Bank of Toledo, 1946-62, chmn. bd., 1962-66, chairman trust investment com., 1966-71; dir. Wyandotte Chemicals Corp., Toledo Scale Corp., until 1968. Pres. Toledo Community Chest, 1949; mem. adv. council Civil Aeros. Authority, 1940. Trustee, Toledo Mus. Art, Toledo council Boy Scouts Am., Jr. Achievement, Boys Clubs Toledo. Served as lt. comdr. USNR, 1942-45; PTO; MTO. Mem. Res. City, Am. bankers assn., Ohio Bar Assn. Home: Perrysburg OH Died Nov. 10, 1971.

KNIGHT, SAMUEL lawyer; b. San Francisco, Dec. 28, 1863; s. Samuel and Elizabeth (Stuart) K.; A.B., Yale, 1887; Yale Law Sch., 1887-88; LL.B., Columbia, 1889; m. Mary Hurd Holbrook, Oct. 8, 1895. Admitted to N.Y. bar, 1889; asst. U.S. atty, Northern Dist. of Calif., 1893-95; U.S. atty., same, 1896-97; mem. firm of Knight, Boland & Riordan; former trustee Hillsborough, San Mateo County, Calif. Maj., Judge Advocate General's Dept., U.S. Army, 1918-19. Hon. mem. central com. Am. Red Cross. Mem. San Francisco, Calif. State and Am. bar assns., Am. Soc. Internat, Law, Delta Kappa Epsilon, Skull and Bones, Phi Beta Kappa (Yale). Republican. Presbyn. Clubs: Pacific-Union, Commonwealth (San Francisco); Burlingame Country; Monteciot (Santa Barbara); University (New York); Elizabethan (New Haven); Metropolitan (Washington). Home: 2234 Forest View Rd., Burlingame, Calif.; also 151 Buena Vista Rd., Santa Barbara, Calif. Office: 444 California St., San Francisco, Calif. Died Jan. 28, 1943.

KNIGHT, WEBSTER banker; b. Providence, R.I., Aug. 10, 1854; s. Robert and Josephine L. (Webster) K.; A.B., Brown U., 1876; m. Sarah Waldo Lippitt, Jan. 27, 1881; children-Robert Lippitt, Adelaide. Mem. B. R. & R. Knight, mfrs. sheetings and shirtings, 1897-1921; chmn. bd. Peoples Savings Bank, Phoenix Nat. Bank. Mem. staff Gov. Charles Warren Lippitt, rank of col., 1895; asst. q.m. gen. R.I. N.G., 1897-1911. Mem. Warwick (R.I.) Town Council 11 yrs. (pres. 4 yrs.); Rep. presdl. elector, 1904. Trustee Homeopathic Hosp. of R.I. Mem. Providence Chamber Commerce. Episcopalian. Home: Natick, R.I. Died June 30, 1933.

KNISKERN, LESLIE ALBERT corp. exec.; born Muskegon, Mich., Oct. 25, 1900; son Dr. Emory Leroy and Nellie (Butler) K.; B.S. U.S. Naval Acad., 1922, grad. study, 1924-25; M.S., Mass. Inst. Tech., 1927; grad. study Ecole d'Application du Genie Maritime, Paris, France, 1934-35; m. Mary Porter Poyer, Sept. 24, 1924; 1 son, John Poyer. Commd. ensign, U.S.N., 1922, advanced through grades to rear adm., 1951; charge all ship design Bur. Ships, 1944-46; atom bomb tests Bikini, 1946; prodn. officer Puget Sound Naval Shipyard, 1946-49; commander Phila. Naval Shipyard, 1946-49; commander Phila. Naval Shipyard, 1949-52; USN shipbuilding rep., Europe, 1952-55; inspector gen. Bur. ships, San Francisco, 1955-56; commander of New York Naval Shipyard, 1956-58, retired; v.p. Gibbs & Cox, Inc., N.Y. City, 1958-. Decorated Legion of Merit (Navy); Sec. Navy Letter of Commendation with ribbon; Comdr. Mil. Div. Order of Brit. Empire. Mem. Soc. Naval Architects and Marine Engrs., Am. Soc. Naval Engrs., St. Nicholas Soc. N.Y., Academie de la Marine (France). Clubs: Chevy Chase (Chevy Chase, Md.); New York Yacht, University, India House (N.Y.C.). Home: 761 Park Av, Manhasset, NY Office: 1 Broadway, N.Y.C. 10004. Died Mar. 19, 1961; buried Arlington Nat. Cemetery, Arlington, Va.

KNISKERN, PHILIP WHEELER real estate, loans, appraising; b. Hastings, Mich., Mar. 25, 1889; s. Albert Decatur (brig. gen. U.S. Army) and Estelle (Wheeler) K.; B.C.E., U. of Mich., 1911; m. Karine Nessen, Sept. 4, 1917; children-Karen (Mrs. Robert E. White, Jr.), Philip Nessen. With Thompson-Starrett Co., engrs., N.Y., 1912-15, Kniskern Co., Chicago, 1915-17 and 1919-20; appraiser and negotiator, real estate loan dept. Chicago Trust Co., 1921-22; examiner and appraiser, city loan div. Metropolitan Life Ins. Co., New York, 1923; mgr. real estate loan dept. Reliance State Bank, Chicago, 1924; v.p. Nat. Surety Co., New York, 1925-27; pres. Nat. Reserve Corp., 1927-29; v.p. and gen. mgr. Continental Mortgage Guarantee Co., 1929-32; pvt. appraisal practice since 1932; appraisal adviser to Federal Home Loan Bank Bd., Washington, D.C., 1933-35; pres. First Mortgage Corp. (Phila.), 1935-56; now principal Philip W. Kniskern & Associates, real estate consultants and appraisers, Philadelphia; chmn. board 1st Federal Savings & Loan Assn. of N.Y. Village trustee Bronxville, N.Y., 1932-34; trustee Urban Land Inst., Washington (pres. 1951-52). Was capt. Engr. O.R.C., World War I, on constrn. chem. plants and in charge purchase, storage and distribution of forage for Army in U.S. First pres. Am. Inst. Real Estate Appraisers; pres. (1941) Nat. Assn. Real Estate Bds. (pres. 1951-52), Am. Soc. Real Estate Councilors (pres. 1956-57), Urban Land Inst.; mem. exec. com. Appraisal Com. Phila. Real Estate Bd.; life mem. Am. Soc. C.E. (asso.), Society Indsl. Realtors, Nat. Assn. Home Builders, Beta Theta Pi. Republican. Presbyn. Mason. Club: Union League. Speaker and writer on real estate appraisal and financial subjects. Home: 507 Riverview Rd. Office: 100 Park Av., Swarthmore, Pa. Died May 19, 1961; buried Hastings, Mich.

KNOPF, S. ADOLPHUS M.D.; b. Halle-on-the-Saale, Germany, Nov. 27, 1857; s. Adolphus and Nanina (Bock) K.; A.B., U. of Paris (Sorbonne) 1890; M.D., Bellevue Hosp. Med.Coll. (New York University), 1888; Faculty of Medicine, Univ. of Paris, 1895; m. Perle Nora Dyar, Oct. 19, 1889 (died 1931); m. 2d, Julia Marie Off, Oct. 6, 1935; children-Gertrude, Lucille, Adolphus. Professor of medicine, department physiotherapy N.Y. Post-Grad. Med. School, Columbia U., 1908-20; sr. visiting phys. Health Department's Riverside Tuberculosis Hosp., 1906-22; hon. dir. Gaylord Farm Sanitorium, Wallingford, Conn.; hon. pres. med. bd. Bruchesi Tuberculosis Inst., Montreal; attending tuberculosis specialist, ranking as maj., U.S.P.H.S., 1920-22; consulting phys. to Riverside Hosp. (N.Y.), St. Gabriel's (N.Y.) Sanatorium for Consumptives, West Mountain Sanatorium, at Scranton, Pa., etc. Fellow N.Y. Acad. Medicine, Assn. Mil. Surgeons U.S., Soc. Med. Jurisprudence, Am. Heart Assn., Am. Soc. for Psychical Research; hon. member Am. Assn. for Thoracic Surgery, Am. Tuberculosis Assn.; hon. vice pres. Brit. Congress on Tuberculosis; govt. del. Internat Prison Congress, Budapest, Internat. Tuberculosis Congress, Paris; v.p. sect. V of Tuberculosis Congress, Washington, 1908; official del. 4th Internat. Congress on Sch. Hygiene, Buffalo, 1913; laureat French Inst. of Paris, 1896, Coll. Physicians of Phila., 1898, Internat. Congress for study of how best to combat tuberculosis as a disease of the masses, 1900, Institut de France, 1900, Internat. Tuberculosis Congress, Washington, 1908; apptd. rep. U.S. International Union Against Tuberculosis, The Hague, 1932. Founder N.Y. City and Nat. Tuberculosis Assns. Capt. Med. R.C., U.S. Army, 2917 1917; maj. M.O.R.C. Mason. Home: New York, N.Y. Died July 15, 1940.

KNOTT, THOMAS ALBERT prof. English; b. Chicago, Ill., Jan. 12, 1880; s. George John and Sarah Jane (Carlisle) K.; A.B., Northwestern U., 1902; student Harvard, 1909; Ph.D., U. of Chicago, 1912; m. Myra Celinda Powers, 1908; children-John Russell, Carlisle (Mrs. Karl J. Klapka). Teacher of English, Northwestern Academy, 1901-02, high school., Coshocton, Ohio, 1902-03, Bradley Polytechnic Institute, 1903-05, Northwestern University, 1905-06, Stevens Point (Wisconsin) Normal School, 1907; instructor and asso. prof. of English, U. of Chicago, 1907-20; prof. of English, State U. of Iowa, 1920-26; gen. editor Webster's Dictionaries, 1926-35; prof. of English and editor Middle English Dictionary, U. of Mich., since 1935. Served as capt., Mil. Intelligence Div., Gen. Staff, Washington, D.C., 1918-19. Fellow A.A.A.S. Mem. Modern Lang. Assn. of America, Nat. Council Teachers of English, Linguistic Society, Philol. Society, Mediaeval Acad., Mich. Acad. Sciences, Arts and Letters, Dialect Soc., Mich. Schoolmasters Club, Am. Assn. University Profs. Phi Beta Kappa, Phi Kappa Phi Republican. Conglist. Clubs: Michigan Union, University, Quadrangle, Research (University of Michigan). Author: Elements of Old English (with S. Moore), 1919, 9th edit., 1942. General editor of Webster's New International Dictionary, 2d edit., 1934. Asso. editor Philological Quarterly, 1922-26. Contbr. articles on lang. and medieval lit. to Modern Philology, Modern Lang. Notes, Philol. Quarterly, Quarterly Jour. of Speech, Am. Speech, Manly Anniversary Studies. Home: 1504 Brooklyn Av., Ann Arbor, Mich. Died Aug. 16, 1945.

KNOTTS, HOWARD C(LAYTON) lawyer and transportation consultant; born Girard, Illinois, Aug. 25, 1895; s. Edward Clay and Elizabeth (Routzahn) K.; student Blackburn College, Carlinville, Illinois, 1912-15; A.B., Knox College, 1916; LL.B., Harvard, 1912; 1921; m. Charlotte Ann Sterling, June 25, 1921; children-Howard Clayton, Elizabeth Ann. Admitted to Illinois bar, 1921; staff U.S. district atty., Southern Ill. Dist., 1921-23; mem. Knotts and Knotts, 1923-33; mem. firm Knotts & Dobbs since 1933; editor of Jour. of Air Law and Commerce, pub. by Air Law Inst., Northwestern U. Sch. of Law, since 1937; lecturer on air transportation, Sch. of Commerce, and on public utility law. Sch. of Law, Northwestern U.; Aviation supervisor Illinois Commerce Commn. since 1931; formerly cons. expert Bureau of Air Commerce, Dept. of Commerce and Civil Aeronautics Authority; formerly general counsel Nat. Aeronautic Assn.; counsel Am. Assn. Airport Executives. Commd. 2d lt. and pilot, U.S. Army, and served with 17th U.S. Aero Squadron, A.E.F., 1917-19; twice wounded and officially credited with 8 enemy aircraft. Awarded D.S.C., Purple Heart (oak leaf cluster), Silver Star medal (U.S.), Distinguished Flying Cross (British). Mem. Sangamon County, Ill. State and Am. bar assns.; Quite Birdmen Episcopalian. Mason. Club: Sangamon and Illini Country (Springfield). Author of aeronautical regulations, enactments and published articles. Home: 1303 S. 6th St. Office: 205 S. 6th St., Springfield, Ill. Died Nov. 23, 1942.

KNOWLTON, THOMAS army officer; b. West Boxford, Mass., Nov. 1740; s. William and Martha (Pinder) K.; m. Anna Keyes, Apr. 5,, 1759. Served in Brit. Army during Seven Years War; farmer, Ashford, Mfass., 1762-75; elected capt. of an Ashford Company, 1775, served in Battle of Bunker Hill; commd. maj. 20th Inf., Continental Army, 1776; promoted to lt. col. Durkees' Regt. by Continental Congress, 1776, served in Battle of L.I. Killed in Battle of Harlem Heights (N.Y.), Sept. 16, 1776.

KNOX, DUDLEY WRIGHT naval officer; b. Ft. Walla Walla, Wash., June 21, 1877; s. Thomas Taylor and Cornelia Manigault (Grayson) K.; grad. U.S. Naval Acad., 1896, Naval War Coll., 1913; m. Lily Hazard McCalla, May 18, 1908; 1 son, Dudley Sargent. Commd. ensign, May 6, 1898; advanced through grades to commodore, 1945; ret. from active list, 1921, but continued on duty Navy Dep.; served in Spanish Am. War; fleet ordnance officer. Pacific Fleet and Atlantic Fleet, 1909-12; on staff Adm. W. S. Sims, 1918-19; faculty U.S. Naval War Coll., 1919-20; naval editor Army and Navy Jour., 1920-23; naval corr. Balt. Sun, 1924-29, N.Y. Herald Tribune, 1929; mem. adv. council Living Age, Am. Neptune and Americana Inst. Awarded Navy Cross, Legion of Merit (U.S.); comdr. St. Michael and St. George (British), St. Maurice and St. Lazarus (Italian); gold medal essayist U.S. Naval Inst., 1914, 15 Pres., Naval Hist. Found. Episcopalian. Mason. Clubs: Army and Navy, Army and Navy Country. Author: The Eclipse of American Sea Power, 1922; The Naval Genius of George Washington, 1932; A History of the United States Navy, 1936, 48; Naval Sketches of the War in Calif., 1939. Contbr. articles on naval subjects to various jours. Home: 2122 California St., Washington. Died June 11, 1960; buried Arlington Nat. Cemetery.

KNOX, HARRY naval officer; b. Greenville, O., July 2, 1848; s. John Reily and Isabel Southgate (Briggs) K.; grad. U.S. Naval Acad., 1867; m. Mary Gard, Sept. 7, 1875. Promoted ensign, 1868; master, 1870; lt., 1871; lt. comdr., Jan. 1888; comdr., Oct. 1896; capt., Sept. 22, 1901; rear admiral, and retired, June 20, 1905. Comd. Vesuvius, 1894-95, Thetis, 1895-96, Princeton, 1899-1901, Concord, 1901; comd. Brooklyn, 1903-04. Died Aug. 29, 1923.

KNOX, HENRY army officer, sec. of war; b. Boston, July 25, 1750; s. William and Mary (Campbell) K.; m. Lucy Flucker, June 16, 1774, 12 children. Started London Book Store, 1771; 2d in command Boston Grenadier Corps, 1772; commd. col. in charge arty. Continental Army, 1775; brought arty. equipment from Ft. Ticonderoga, forcing Brit. out of Boston; in charge of arty., N.Y.C., also L.I., 1776; field comdr., Trenton, N.J., 1776; commd. brig. gen., 1776; started govt. arsenal, Springfield, Mass., 1777; led at battles of Brandywine and Germantown, 1777, Monmouth, 1778; prin. founder mil. acad. which became U.S. Mil. Acad., 1779; on ct. martial duty, one of tribunal to try and condemn to death Maj. Andre for treason, 1780; commanded, placed arty. for Siege of Yorktown, 1781; commd. maj. gen., 1781; in command West Point, 1782-85; conceived, organized Soc. of Cincinnati, 1783, 1st sec., v.p., 1805; elected 1st sec. of war U.S. by Continental Congress, 1785, served, 1785-94; founder (with Thomas Jefferson) U.S. Navy; settled in Me.; 1796, became brickmaker, cattle-raiser, shipbuilder, lumber-cutter; close friend, adviser George Washington. Died Thomaston, Me., Oct. 25, 1806; buried Thomaston.

KNOX, (WILLIAM) FRANKLIN Sec. of Navy, newspaper publisher; b. Boston, Mass., Jan. 1, 1874; s. William Edwin and Sarah Collins (Barnard) K.; A.B., Alma (Mich.) Coll., 1898, LL.D., 1936; LL.D., U. of N.H., 1933; Litt.D., Rollins Coll., Winter Park, Fla., 1937; LL.D., Harvard, 1942, Dartmouth, 1941, Northwestern, 1943, Williams, 1943, Colgate, 1943, Bethany Coll., 1943; m. Annie Reid, Dec. 28, 1898. Reporter, city editor, mgr. circulation, Grand Rapids (Mich.) Herald, 1898-1900; publisher Sault Ste. Marie (Mich.) News, 1901-12, Manchester (N.H.) Leader, Sept. 1912-13, Manchester Union and Leader since July 1913; also pub. Boston American, Boston Daily Advertiser and Boston Sunday Advertiser, 1927-31; gen. mgr. Hearst newspapers until Jan. 1, 1931; with Theodore T. Ellis purchased controlling interest in Chicago Daily News, becoming pub., 1931. Mem. Troop D. 1st U.S. Vol. Cav. (Rough Riders), Spanish-Am. War. Apr.-Sept. 1898; maj. on staff of gov. of Mich., 1908-10; apptd. maj. on staff of gov. of N.H., 1913. Chmn. Rep. State Central Com., Mich., 1910-12; apptd. by President Taft mem. Board of Indian Commrs., 1911. Commd. capt., F.A., U.S. Army, Aug.

14, 1917; assigned to staff of 78th Div.; promoted to maj., Dec. 1, 1917; served with 153d Arty. Brig., 78th Div., overseas May 26, 1918-Feb. 10, 1919; col. 365th F.A., Res.; now retired. Chmn. delegation from N.H. to Rep. Nat. Conv., Chicago, 1920; chmn. State Publicity Commn. of N.H., 1922-24; chmn. Nat. Campaign to Combat Hoarding, 1932. Republican nominee for Vice-President of U.S., 1936; apptd. Sec. of Navy, July 11, 1940. Conglist. Mason. Clubs: Derryfield Country (Manchester, N.H.); Army and Navy, Burning Tree (Washington, D.C.); Chicago, Commercial, Old Elm, Union League (Chicago); Advertising (New York). Home: 4704 Linnean Av. N.W. Office: Navy Department, Washington, D.C. Died Apr. 28, 1944.

KOBBE, WILLIAM AUGUST major general U.S.A.; b. New York, May 10, 1840; s. William A. and Sarah Lord (Sistare) K.; ed. N.Y. City until 1854; Wiesbaden, Germany, until 1857; studied mining engring., Freiburg, and Clausthal, Germany, until 1862; grad. U.S. Arty. Sch., 1873; m. Isabella Hoffman, June 26, 1867; children-Ferdinand Walter, Sarah Perry, Rolf (dec.), William Hoffman, Herman, Eric (dec.); m. 2d, Margaret Carnes, 1916. Pvt. Co. K, 7th N.Y. State Militia, June 5-Sept. 5, 1862; pvt. Co. G, 178th N.Y. Inf., May 29, 1863; 1st lt., Oct. 18, 1863; promoted through grades to maj. gen., Jan. 19, 1904; retired at own request after 40 yrs. service, Jan. 20, 1904. Bvtd. maj. and lt. col. vols., Mar. 13, 1865, "for distinguished and faithful services during the war"; capt., Mar. 2, 1867, "for gallant and meritorious services at battle of Nashville, Tenn."; maj., Mar. 2, 1867, for same at capture of Ft. Blakely, Ala. Mil. gov. of the Hemp ports, and mil. gov. and dept. commr. of Mindanao and Jolo in P.I.; instr. at U.S. Arty. Sch., 1885-96; comd. Dept. of Dakota, 1902-04. Citations for "gallantry in action" against insurgent forces near Manila, P.I., Feb. 5, 1899, and against insurgent forces at Tulihan River, Luzon, P.I., Mar. 25, 1899. Home: Pasadena, Calif. Died Nov. 18, 1931.

KOBE, KENNETH ALBERT chem. engr.; b. Osakis, Minn., Mar. 19, 1905; s. Albert M. and Mildred (Stillwell) K.; B.S., with distinction, Univ. of Minn., 1926, M.S., 1928, Ph.D., 1930; m. Jeneva K. Holm, July 6, 1932; children-Donald, Jean. Chem. engr. Dupont Ammonia Corp., Wilmington, Del., 1930; instr. Univ. of Wash., Seattle, 1931-34, asst. prof. chem. engring., 1934-39, asso. prof., 1939-41; prof. chem. engring., Univ. of Texas, since 1941, asso. director Bur. of Indsl. Chemistry, 1946-54; ednl. advisor Petroleo Brasileiro, Brazil, So. Am., 1951-. Served as major, C.W.S., 1942-44, now lt. col. USAF Reserve. Recipient outstanding achievement award U. Minn., 1955. Mem. Am. Inst. Chem. Engrs., Am. Soc. Engring. Edn., Am. Chem. Soc., Sigma Xi, Tau Beta Pi, Phi Lambda Upsilon, Alpha Chi Sigma, Gamma Alpha, Omega Chi Epsilon (national pres., 1955-). Author: Process Industries, 1948; Petroleum Refining With Chemicals, 1956; Chemical Engineering Reports, 1957; associated editor Journal Chem. Education, 1947-; co-editor Advances in Petroleum Chemistry and Refining, vol. I, 1958. Contbr. many articles to scientific, technical and trade publications. Holder several patents on tear gas, submerged combustion, recovery of manganese and sodium sulfate. Specialist in submerged combustion processes, unit chem. processes, thermo-dynamics. Home: 3305 Bowman Rd., Austin 78703. Office: Dept. of Chemical Engineering, U. Texas, Austin, Tex. Died Nov. 2, 1958; buried Sunset Meml. Park, Mpls.

KOCH, CHARLES RUDOLPH EDWARD b. Birnbaum, Polish Prussia, Apr. 24, 1844; s. Augustus and Josephine (Von Lutz) K.; brought to America in infancy; student in dental office of Dr. Kennicott, Chicago, until Aug. 1862, when enlisted as pvt. 72d Ill. Inf., serving in Northern Miss. campaign, Yazoo Pass expdn., Vicksburg campaign and siege; detailed chief clk. Gen. Ransom's hdqrs., Nov. 1863; apptd. capt. 49th U.S.C.T.; detailed on staff of Lorenzo Thomas, adj. gen., organizing colored troops in southwest; rejoined command Feb. 1864, serving with it in La. until May 1865; provost marshall, Yazoo City, Miss., May-Aug. 1865, western dist. of Miss., Vicksburg, Aug. 1865-Mar. 1866, when was mustered out; m. Sylvia Bigelow, d. Hon. Otis Adams, of Grafton, Mass., June 25, 1868. Rejoined Dr. Kennicott, 1866, and later his partner in practice of dentistry until 1871, then practiced alone until 1898; sec. dental dept., Northwestern U., Jan. 1904-; lecturer on dentistry. Organized and was capt. of a co. of Union Veterans, serving in labor riots of 1877, and when I.N.G. was organized, enlisted as pvt. in 1st Inf., I.N.G., Aug. 1877; became capt. Co. I, Oct. 1877; maj., Apr. 1886; lt. col., Feb. 1888; col. Apr. 1889; voluntarily retired, Nov. 1893. Organized regt., at breaking out of Spanish-Am. War, 1898, which was accepted by the State and maintained at his own expense over disch. by act of legislature. Mem. George H. Thomas Post No. 5 G.A.R.; pres. Ill. Grand Army Memorial Hall Assn.; past post comdr., past insp. gen., past adj. gen., Dept. of Ill., adj. gen. G.A.R., 1913. Secretary and editor annual publs. of the Chicago Dental Soc., 1871-75; pres. Ill. State Dental Soc., 1877; mil. editor Chicago Inter Ocean, 1880-82; sec. and pres.Ill. State Bd. of Dental Examiners, 1886-91. Received hon. degree D.D.S. from Washington U., 1888. Home: Evanston, Ill. Died July 20, 1916.

KOCH, GEORGE PRICE, Naval officer; b. Cresson, Pa., June 21, 1910; s. Edward Louis and Mary (Price) K.; B.S., U.S. Naval Acad., 1933; m. Virginia Vredenburgh, June 5, 1937; children—George Price, James Peter, Alexander Richard, Virginia Cabell. Commd. ensign U.S.N., 1934, advanced through grades to rear adm., 1961; designated naval aviator, 1934; various assignments in ships and ashore, 1934-42; comdg. officer Hdqrs. Squadron 5, 1942-43; mem. staff comdr. in chief U.S. Fleet, 1943-44; comdg. officer U.S.S. Humboldt, 1944-45; navigator, operations officer U.S.S. Leyte, 1945-47; grad. Naval War Coll., 1948; exec. officer Naval Air Tech. Tng. Center, Memphis, 1948-50. Naval Sta., Kodiak, Alaska, 1950-52; operations officer, then chief staff on staff comdr. Fleet Air Wings, Atlantic, 1952-53; head, war plans br. Office Chief Naval Operations, 1953-55; comdr. Naval Air Sta., Barbers Point, Hawaii, 1955-57; chief staff to comdr. Fleet Air, Quonset Point, R.I., 1957-58; comdr. Fleet Air Wing 3, 1958-59; comdg. officer Naval Air Sta., Norfolk, Va., 1959-61; comdr. Carrier Div. 18, 1961-62, Fleet Air Wings Atlantic, 1962-63; chief, Naval Air Res. Tng., 1963-65; comdr. Carrier Task Force, Mediterranean, 1965-67; comdr. Naval forces So. Command, comdt. 15th Naval Dist., Canal Zone, 1967-69; comdt. Naval Dist., Washington, 1969-72. Decorated numerous unit, battle and area ribbons. Home: Tingey House Washington DC Died Sept. 17, 1972; buried U.S. Naval Academy, Annapolis MD

KOCHAN, EDWARD JOHN, oral surgeon; b. Bridgeport, Conn., Nov. 24, 1922; s. John and Julia (Fekete) K.; student U. Va., 1942-44; D.D.S., U. Pa., 1948; m. Anna Epifano, Jan. 6, 1949; children—Edward John, Jeffrey, Kenneth. Intern, resident Bellevue Hosp., N.Y.C., 1948-49, clin. visiting, 1950-53; practice oral surgery, Bridgeport, 1949-69; lectr. Fones Sch. Hygiene, St. Vincents Hosp. Sch. Nursing; chief dept. dentistry, oral surgery St. Vincents Hosp.; mem. staff Bridgeport Hosp., Park City Hosp. Served with USNR, 1943-44; to capt. USAF, 1953-54. Diplomate Am. Bd. Oral Surgery. Mem. Am., Conn., Bridgeport (pres.) dental assns., Am., Conn. (past pres.), New Eng. socs. oral surgeons, N.Y. Soc. Oral Surgery, Kappa Sigma, Delta Sigma Delta. Lion. Contbr. articles to profl. jours. Home: Easton CT Died June 16, 1969.

KOLB, LOUIS JOHN mfr.; b. New York, June 25, 1865; s. John Gotlieb and Sarah Elizabeth (Kaiser) K.; grad. Rugby Academy, Phila.; A.B., U. of Pa., 1887; LL.D., Juniata Coll.; m. Caroline Kaiser, Mar. 20, 1895. V.p. Pa. Sugar Co. and Real Estate Trust Co.; dir. Keystone Telephone Co., Internat. Equities, Phila. Mfrs. Mut. Fire Ins. Co. Lt. col. and a.d.c. on staff Gov. Brumbaugh of Pa. Pres. Hahnemann Hosp.; mem. bd. dirs. Graduate Hosp., U. of Pa., St. Luke's Hosp., Children's Homeopathic Hospital. Republican. Presbyn. Mason. Home: Philadelphia, Pa. Died July 1, 1941.

KOLSETH, J. HAROLD, mgmt. cons., corp. exec.; b. Schenectady, May 4, 1904; B.A., Union Coll., 1928; student Universite de Dijon (France), 1928; M.A. in Bus. Adminstrn., Harvard, 1931; m. Adele Rouyon Mackey, 1940; children—Sandra (Mrs. David F. Mawicke), Karen (Mrs. James P. Brossard). Faculty, Union Coll., 1928-29; with Atlas Supply Co., 1931-51, dir. research and devel., 1947-51; exec. v.p., dir. Devoe & Raynolds Co., N.Y.C., 1951-55; v.p. Anheuser Busch Inc., St. Louis, 1956-57; parnter, v.p. Barrington Assos., N.Y.C., 1957-58; prin. Kolseth & Partners, Greenwich, Conn., 1958-—; mgmt. cons. Mem. WPB, 1942-43; dir. operations Smaller War Plants Corp., 1944; cons. Dept. of State, Chile, 1957, Cuba, 1958, Ecuador, 1960, Brazil, 1961, Spain, 1961, Jamaica, 1962. V.p. Council Internat. Progress in Mgmt., 1966-67, also bd. directors. Served lt. comdr., USNR, 1944-45. Mem. Phi Beta Kappa; Pi Gamma Mu. Clubs: Indian Harbor Yacht, Harvard, Sky (N.Y.C.); Army and Navy (Washington); Greenwich Country. Contbr. articles to various mags. Home: Greenwich CT Died May 31, 1972.

KOMP, WILLIAM H. WOOD entomologist; b. Yokohama, Japan, Mar. 16, 1893; s. Frederick and Carrie Joanna (Wood) K.; brought to U.S., 1895; derivative citizenship; student Miss. State Coll., 1911, N.Y.U., 1912; B.S., Rutgers U., 1916, M.S., 1917, D. Sc., 1955; fellow in agr. Cornell, 1917; m. Mildred Crowell, Sept. 1, 1944; 1 dau., Anita (Mrs. Harry M. Williams), Ensign, USPHS, 1918, advanced through grades to capt., 1944, malaria control; vis. staff mem. Gorgas Meml. Lab., Republic of Panama, 1931-47; traveling rep. Pan-Am. San. Bur., 1937; research in malaria, 1921—; loaned to Rockefeller Found. Internat. Health Div. for research on yellow fever, Colombia, 1936; consultant to Creole Petroleum Co., Venezuela, 1936. United Fruit Co., tropical divs., 1924-30, Inst. Inter-Am. Affairs (consultant malaria), 1942—. Chmn. com. on entomology Pan-Am. San. Conf., Rio, 1942. Fellow A.A.A.S., Am. Soc. Tropical Medicine and Hygiene; mem. Am. Mosquito Control Assn., Nat. Malaria Soc., Sociedad Venezolano de Ciencias Naturales (corr. mem.), Am. Acad. Tropical Medicine, Isthian Med. Soc. (Panama), Entomol. Soc. Wash., Washington Acad. Medicine, Chi Psi. Author: The Anopheline Mosquitoes of the Caribbean Region, bull., 1941; discovered Anopheles Darlingi (malaria mosquito) in Central Am., 1940. Home: 6906 Dartmouth Av., College Park, Md. Office: National Institutes of Health, Bethesda, Md. Died Dec. 7, 1955; buried Elmwood Cemetery, New Brunswick, N.J.

KOPETZKY, SAMUEL JOSEPH surgeon; b. N.Y. City, Aug. 1, 1876; s. Joseph and Lena (Bernhardt) K.; student Coll. City of N.Y., 1894-96; M.D., Coll. Physicians and Surgeons (Columbia), 1898; m. Anah Doob, Apr. 2, 1903; children-Karl, Yvonne K. (Mrs. Robert Sterling). Prof. otology N.Y. Polyclinic Med. Sch. and Hosp. since 1920; cons. otolaryngologist, Beth Israel Hosp.; dir. of otolaryngology, United Israel Zion Hosp. (Brooklyn); cons. otologist Nyack (N.Y.) Hosp., Newark (N.J.), Beth Israel Hosp., Vassar Bros. Hosp. (Poughkeepsie, N.Y.). Served in Spanish-Am. War and World Wars I and II; colonel Med. Corps. Received the Legion of Merit and the Silver Star; Chevalier of the Legion of Honor (France). Fellow Am. Coll. Surgeons, A.M.A., New York Acad. Medicine, Am. Acad. Ophthalmology and Otolaryngology, Am. Rhinol., Laryngol. and Otol. Soc. (pres. 1937-38), Med. Soc. of State of N.Y. (pres. 1941-42); corr. Société Laryngologie des Hospiteaux de Paris; formerly speaker House of Delegates, Medical Society State of N.Y. Author: Surgery of the Ear, 1908; Otologic Surgery, 1925, 2d edit., 1929; Deafness, Tinctus and Vertigo, 1948. Editor of New York Medical Week since its establishment 1920-36; editor Surgery of the Ear. Home: 300 E. 57th St. Office: 30 E. 60th St., N.Y. City 21. Died Nov. 13, 1950.

KOPPER, SAMUEL KEENE CLAGGETT lawyer; born New York City, July 7, 1914; s. John Matthias and Sarah Genevieve (Claggett) K.; A.B., Princeton, 1937; LL.B., U. Va., 1940; grad. law student George Washington U., 1946-47: Diploma, Acad. de Drott Internat. de la Haye, 1953; m. Elizabeth Duke Lee, Sept. 1, 1941; children-Elizabeth Marshall, Samuel Keene Claggett, Richard Henry Lee, Robert Brooke, Law clk. Davies, Auerbach, Cornell & Hardy, N.Y.C., 1939; rsrch. sec. Fgn. Affairs Coun., Cleve., 1940-41; admitted to Ohio bar, 1941; asst. to counsel Lake Carriers Assn., Cleve., 1941: officer div. export controls Dept. of State, Washington, 1941; jr. exec. officer Bd. Econ. Warfare, 1941-42, staff office internat. security affairs, 1945-47, staff Bur. Nr. Eastern, S. Asian and African Affairs, 1947-49, dep. dir. Office of Near Eastern Affairs, 1950-52, resigned, 1952; dep. publicity dir. Nat. Volunteers for Stevenson, Chgo., Sept.-Dec. 1952; cons. to asst. secretary state for Near Eastern, S. Asian and African Affairs, 1952; counsel Arabian Am. Oil Co., 1953—, assistant to the chairman of the board, 1956—. Admitted to D.C. bar, 1953. Adviser to U.S. delegation UN Security Council, 1946-48, Gen. Assembly, 1947-49; rep. Internat. Law Assn. 18th-22 session UNECOSOC Geneva; N.Y., 1954-56, 12th session UN Econ. Commn. Asia and Far East, 1956; rep. Nat. Assn. Mfgrs. to 11 session UN Econ. Commn. Europe, Geneva, 1956. Chmn. Men's Com., Mayor's UN Hospitality Com., 1956—; adv. council Dem. Nat. Com. Served as lt. comdr. USNR, 1942-45. Mem. Am. (chmn. com. on Nr. East law), Internat. (chmn. com. internat. restrictive bus. practices Am. br. 1954), D.C. bar assns., Am. Soc. Internat. Law (exec. council 1956—), Middle East Inst. (bd. govs., 1956—), Am. Petroleum Inst., Société de Legislation com. paree, Fgn. Service Assn., Council Fgn. Relations. Episcopalian, Clubs: Princeton (N.Y.C.); Army and Navy (Washington); Farmington Country (Charlottesville, Va.), Larchmont Shore. UN corr. Middle East Jour., 1956. Author profl. articles. Home: 85 Willow Av., Larchmont, N.Y. Office: 505 Park Av., N.Y.C.: also Shoreham Bldg., Washington. Died June 1957.

KOREN, WILLIAM JR. fgn. service officer; b. Princeton, N.J., Apr. 8, 1909; s. William and Adelaide Louise (Thornell) K.; grad. Phillips Exeter Acad.; A.B., Princeton, 1930; B.S., Oxford U., 1933, B.Litt., 1934; M.A., Harvard, 1937; m. Isabelle Gilbert Johnston, May 4, 1935. Research staff Fgn. Policy Assn., 1934-35; instr. history Princeton, 1935-36, 39-41; asst. history Harvard, 1937-38; Social Sci., Research Council fellow for study in France, 1938-39; asst. to dir. research Office of Coordinator of Information (later OSs0, 1941-42; div. asst. Dept. of State, 1942-43, research analyst, 1945-47, chief Western European sect. div. research for Europe, 1947-48; fgn. service officer, 1948—; 2d sec., consul. Paris, 1948-52, 1st sec., consul. 1952-53, detailed to Def. Coll., Paris, 1951--. 52; 1st sec., consul, Teheran 1953—, with temp. rank of counselor, 1954—. Served from lt. (j.g.) to lt. USNR, 1943-45, ETO. Mem. Phi Beta Kappa. Home: 1419 36th St., Washington 7. Office: Dept. of State, Washington 25. Died Feb. 6, 1956; buried Princeton, N.J.

KORZYBSKI, ALFRED HABDANK (SKARBEK) scientist, author; b. Warsaw, Poland, July 3, 1879; s. Ladislas Habdank K. and Countess Helena (Rzewuska) K.; e.d Warsaw Realschule and Warsaw Poly. Inst.; grad. study in Germany, Itay., U.S.; m. Mira Edgerly, Jan., 1919. Came to U.S. 1916, naturalized, 1940. Managed family estates in Poland; teacher of mathematics, physics, French and German in Warsaw, Poland; served with cav. and bodyguard heavy arty., also attached to Intelligence Dept., Russian Gen. Staff; sent to U.S. and Canada as artillery expert; sec. Polish-French Mil. Commn. in U.S., 1918; recruiting officer Polish-French Army, U.S. and Can., 1918; war lecturer for U.S. Govt.; sec. Polish Commn. (labor Sect.), League of Nations, 1926; writer and lecturer; became pres. and dir. Inst. of General Semantics, Chicago, 1938, now Lakeville, Conn. Fellow American Assn. Advancement Sci.; member Am. Math. Soc., Chicago Soc. for Personality Study, Assn. for Symbolic Logic, N.Y. Acad. Sciences, Soc. for Applied Anthropolgy. Author: Manhood of Humanit-The Science and Art of Human Engineering, 1921; Science and Sanity, An Introduction to Non-aristotelian Systems and General Semantids, 1933, 3d edit., 1948; also many scientific papers. Address: Institute of General Semantics, Lakeville, Conn. Died Mar. 1, 1950.

KOSCIUSZKO, TADEUSZ ANDRZEJ BONAWENTURA (Americanized as Thaddeus Kosciuszko), army officer, Polish patriot; b. Palatinate of Breescin Grand Duchy of Lithuania, Feb. 12, 1746; grad. with rank of capt., Royal Sch., Warsaw, Poland, 1769. Capt., Polish Army, 1769; came to Am., 1775; commd. col. of engrs. Continental Army, 1776; advised Horatio Gates to fortify Bemis Heights which resulted in victory of Saratoga; in charge bldg. fortifications U.S. Mil. Acad., 1778-80; charge of transp. during Greene's campaign in South, 1781, adjutant to George Washington, 1779; apptd. brig. gen. by Continental Congress, 1782; a founder Soc. of Cincinnati; maj. gen. Polish Army, 1789; vowed to fight for Polish freedom from Russia until his death; head Polish Army against Russians, 1792; led rebellion of 1794; imprisoned, 1794-96; continued efforts for a free Poland until death. Died Switzerland, Oct. 15, 1817; buried Cracow, Poland.

KOSER, RALPH B., ret. advt. exec. b. Williamsport, Pa., Nov. 27, 1909; s. Ralph S. and Clara (Russell) K.; student Bucknell U., 1927-30; m. Helen Gould, Aug. 11, 1934; 1 dau., Marcie E. (Mrs. Richard Henry Greenwell). With N. W. Aver & Son, 1930-33, J. M. Mathes, Inc., 1933-37; with McCann-Erickson, Inc., 1937-60, v.p., 1949-60; sr. v.p., dir. McCann-Erickson (USA), 1960; exec. v.p., dir. McCann-Marschalk Co., Inc., N.Y.C., 1960-64, ret.; currently engaged free-lance writing. Trustee Scarborough Country Day Sch., 1955-61. Recipient ann. writing awards Freedom Found., Sat. Rev., others. Served to 1st lt., inf., AUS, World War II. Mem. Sigma Alpha Epsilon. Presbyn. Club: Sleepy Hollow Country (Scarborough, N.Y.). Home: Naples FL Died Apr. 28, 1969.

KOSZALKA, MICHAEL FRANCIS, physician; b. Bklyn., May, 25, 1911; s. John and Mary (Wojtas) K.; B.S., St. Bonaventure Coll., 1935; M.D., Georgetown U., 1938; m. Helen Charlotte Groniak, Aug. 14, 1942; children—Michele (Mrs. Gustav Massee), Michael Francis, Pamela. Intern, Kings County Hosp., Bklyn., 1938-40; practice medicine specializing in internal medicine, Woodhaven, N.Y., 1940-41; resident in internal medicine Norwalk (Conn.) Gen. Hosps., 1941-42, Mpls., 1949-50; resident in internal medicine VA Hosp., Wood, Wis., 1946-48, chief sect. gastroenterology, 1948-49; chief med. service VA Hosp., Fargo, N.D., 1950-69, chief staff, Hosp., 1969-70; teaching asst. Marquette U. Sch. Medicine, Milw. 1948, clin. instr. med., 1949; clin. asst. dept. medicine U. Minn., Mpls., 1949-50; asso. teaching staff U. N.D. Sch. Medicine, Fargo, 1954-68, asst. clin. prof. medicine, 1969-70, asso. prof. clin. medicine, 1970; adj. prof. pharmacology N.D. State U., 1969. Mem. Fargo-Moorhead Fed. Exec. Council, 1968-70; mem. med. subcom. N.D. Council for Safety, 1961; chmn. bus. sect. Cass County chpt. Am. Cancer Soc., 1963; mem. N.D. Com. on Mental Health with Spl. Interest in Alcoholism, 1969. Bd. dirs. Fargo VA Employees Credit Union, 1962-70, v.p., 1963, pres., 1963-70; trustee United Fund of Fargo, 1963-65. Served to maj., M.C., AUS, 1942-46. Diplomate Am. Bd Internal Medicine. Fellow A.C.P.; mem. A.M.A., Am. Soc. for Gastrointestinal Endoscopy, Am. Gastroscopic Soc., Am. Thoracic Soc., 1st Dist. Med. Soc. N.D. (asso.), Assn. U.S. Army, Res. Officers Assn., Am. Legion, Catholic War Vets. Elk. Contbr. articles to med. jours. Home: Fargo ND Died Nov. 11, 1970; buried Nat. Cemetery Ft Snelling St Paul MN

KOVACH, GEORGE STEPHEN govt. ofcl.; b. Debrecen, Hungary, Mar. 24, 1904; s. Eugene Elizabeth (Ratz) K.; student Hungarian Royal Gymnasium, Budapest, 1921, Columbia, 1925; grad. Sch. Mil. Govt., U. Va., 1943, Command and Gen. Staff Sch., 1947, Strategic Intelligence Sch., Washington, 1951, Psychol. Warfare Sch., 1951, Armed Forces Information Sch., 1953; married to Ilona de Döry, Dec. 30, 1947. Came to U.S., 1921, naturalized, 1927. Draftsman, jr. engr., 1921-28; asst. mgr., mgr., then gen. mgr. and v.p. hotel cos., 1928-42, 48-51, 53-55; chief of mission, CARE, to Hungary, 1947; pub. relations cons., 1951-53; regional tourism adviser Middle East and South Asia, ICA, Am. embassy, Beirut, Lebanon, 1955-. Served with N.Y.N.G., 1926; to col. Gen. Staff, AUS, 1942-47; liaison officer Hungarian Govt., Am. Mil. Mission, Budapest, 1945-46. Decorated Bronze Star (U.S.); Legion of Honor, Croix de Guerre, Medaille d'Argent de la Reconnaissance (France); Croix de Merit d'Argent with swords (Poland); Order of Merit 1st Class (Lebanon); comdr. Souverian Order of Grand Constantin. Mem. 7th Regt. Vets. Assn. N.Y., Res. Officers Assn. Roman Catholic. Clubs: Metropolitan (N.Y.C.); University (Mexico City); Skal (Beirut). Home: care Metropolitan Club, 1 E. 60th St., N.Y.C. Office: American Embassy, Beirut, Lebanon. Died Sept. 18, 1960; buried U.S. Mil. Cemetery at Pine Lawn, Farmingdale, L.I., N.Y.

KRAMER HERMAN FREDERICK army officer; b. Lincoln, Neb., Nov. 27, 1892; s. Frank and Sophia (Rosenfeld) K.; B.S., U. Neb., 1914; grad. Inf. Sch., 1927, Command Gen. Staff, 1931-33, Kriegs-Akademie, Berlin, 1937-39; m. Frances I. Pratt, Mar. 28, 1917; 1 dau., Betty (Mrs. James M. Hall.) Served with Neb. N.G., 1910-17; commd. 2d lt., inf. U.S. Army, 1917, advanced through grades to maj. gen., 1943; asst. div. comdr. 104th (Timberwolf) Div., 1942-43; comdr. 66th (Black Panther) Inf. Div., 1943-45; comdr. Allied Forces, Atlantic Coast Sector, 12th Army Group, Brittany, consisting of 66th Div., 19th and 25th French Divs., Detachment French Navy, 1944-45; mil. gov. Province of Coblenz, Germany, 1945; comdr. 97th (Trident) Inf. Div., on occupation of island of Honshu, Japan, 1945-46, 87th (Black Hawk) Div. Philippine Ground Forces, 1946-47, ret. Awarded War Dept. Gen. Staff medal, Bronze Star with Oak Leaf Cluster, Legion of Merit, D.S.M., French Legion of Honor, Croix de Guerre with palm. Mem. Alpha Sigma Phi. Home: 129 Luther Dr., San Antonio 12. Died Oct. 1964.

KRAMER, EDWIN WEED engineer; b. Louisville, Ky., Mar. 4, 1877; s. William Paul and Jean (Mobley) K.; C.E., Cornell U., 1905; m. Ruth Edwards, June 22, 1905; children-Ruth (Mrs. Joel Magnes Popper), Edwin Weed, Jean Mobley (Mrs. Samuel Harper Berry), Paul, Margaret (Mrs. David Purcell Mealiffe). Engr. with N.Y. state barge canal, 1905; construction engr., Construction Q.M. Dept., New London, Conn., 1905-07; engr. U.S. Forest Service, Missoula, Mont., and San Francisco, Calif., 1907-36; regional engr., U.S. Forest Service, San Francisco, 1929-36; mem. Calif. power bd., Federal Power Commn., 1924, regional dir. San Francisco regional office since 1936. Served as corp., U.S. Army, Spanish-Am. War. Represented Federal Power Commn. on Hoover-Young Commn. to investigate Calif. Central Valley project, 1929. Mem. Am. Soc. C.E., S.A.R. Author: Construction of Fish Dams for Water Storage in California, 1935. Co-author of reports Uses of the Stanislaus River and Uses of the American River. Prepared curves for determining Cain formula factors for arches with fixed ends. Home: 142 Capra Way. Office: 300 Phelan Bldg., San Francisco, Calif. Died Oct. 31, 1941.

KRAMER, HANS cons. engr.; b. Magdeburg, Germany, Dec. 12, 1894; s. Adolf and Toni Kramer; came to U.S., 1902, naturalized, 1913; student U. Mich., 1912-13; B.S. U.S. Mil. Acad., 1918; grad. Engr. Sch., 1927, 1929; M.S., U. Pa., 1928; D.Eng., Tech. U. of Dresden, Germany, 1932; m. Alice Elizabeth Harvey, May 20, 1939; 1 son, Hans Harvey. Commd. 2d lt. C.E., U.S. Army, 1918, advanced through grades to brig. gen., 1942, ret. from service, 1945; now in practice as cons. engr. Recipient Freeman Traveling Scholarship, Am. Soc. C.E., 1930-31. Mem. Soc. Am. Mil. Engrs., Am. Soc. C.E., Permanent Internat. Assn. Nav. Congresses, Am. Geophys. Union, Am. Inst. Cons. Engr., Internat. Assn. Hydraulic Structures Research. Tau Beta Pi. Rep. U.S. on Ark. River Compact between Colo. and Kans.; mem. bd. of cons. engrs. for the Panama Canal. Author: Modellgeschiche and Schleppkraft, 1932. Address: 462 Nevada Av., San Mateo, Cal. Died Feb. 16, 1957; buried Golden Gate Nat. Cemetery, San Bruno, Cal.

KRAMER, SIMON PENDLETON surgeon; b. Cincinnati, Jan. 1, 1868; s. Jacob and Emma (Bloom) K.; grad. Woodward High Sch., Cincinnati, 1885; M.D., Med. Coll. of Ohio, 1888; post-grad. work U. of Göttingen, 1889, U. of Berlin, 1890, Univ. Coll., London, 1893; m. Minnie Halle; children-Victor Horsley, Simon Paul. Engaged in practice of medicine, Cincinnati, 1888-; prof. principles of surgery, U. of Cincinnati Hosp., Nov. 1910-. Maj. and brigade surgeon, U.S.V., in Spanish-Am. War, Aug. 11, 1898-Oct. 31, 1899; served in Havana, during Am. occupation as comdg. officer Mil. Hosp., etc. Pres. Acad. Medicine of Cincinnati, 1904-05; 1st pres. Cincinnati Soc. Med. Research; mem. Am. Neurol. Assn. Author: of various memoirs on Surgery and Physiology of Central Nervous System. Maj. M.C., U.S.A., World War. Office: 826 Glenwood Av., Cincinnati, Ohio.

KRAUS, WALTER MAX neurologist; b. N.Y. City, Aug. 25, 1889; s. Max William and Carrie May (Adler) K.; B.A., Harvard, 1910 as of 1909; M.D., Johns Hopkins, 1913; M.A., Columbia, 1914; studied U. of Paris Med. Sch., 1923-24; m. Marian Florance Nathan, May 5, 1917 (divorced); children-John Walter, Fancis Va. Praag; m. 2d. Ines Heffes Adé, Dec. 29, 1924 (died 1931); m. 2d, Victoria Rowe, Dec. 20, 1935. Admitted to practice, N.Y., and Conn., 1913, D.C., 1938; interne Bellevue Hosp., 1914-16; instr. biology, Coll. Phys. and Surg. (Columbia), 1915-16, adjunct assistant neurologist, 1916-23; clin. assistant in neurology, Cornell Medical School Dispensary, 1917; war service Bellevue Hospital, also in Europe and at U.S. General Hospital No. 11, Cape May, New Jersey; honorably discharged as capt. Med. Corps., June 20, 1919; major Medical Reserve Corps, 1925-35; major, Medical Corps, Army of U.S., 1943. Served in various capacities with College of phys. and Surg., Mt. Sinai, Montefiore, French and Bellevue hosps., etc.; asso. neurologist Cornell U., 1926-32; sec. Med. Bd. Montefiore Hosp., also of exec. com., 1927-30; asso. neurologist Neurol. Inst., 1929-32. Companion, Soc. of Am. Wars, Mil. Order of Fgn. Wars. Mem. Am. Assn. Advancement Science, Am. Genetic Assn., Research Council on Problems of Acohol, New York General and Biog. Society. Military Order World War (charger mem.), Am. Economic Assn., N.Y. Soc. Mil. and Naval Officers of World Wars, Authors League of America, Am. acad. Polit. and Social Sciences, Am. Legion. Fellow and mem. many Am. and fgn. med. socs. Club: Military-Naval (New York). Contbr. numerous articles, alone and with others, on med. subjects, reviews of books, etc. Address: The Military Naval Club, 4 W. 43d St., New York, N.Y. Died Aug. 18, 1944.

KRAUTHOFF, CHARLES RIESECK army officer; b. St. Louis, Mo., Oct. 6, 1863; enlisted as pvt. in Light Battery F, 2d F.A., Aug. 13, 1884; apptd. 2d lt., 14th Inf., July 31, 1891; grad. Inf. and Cav. Sch., 1895. 1st lt. 14th Inf., Apr. 26, 1898; promoted through grades to brig. gen. O.M.C., Oct. 1, 1918; retired Dec. 7, 1922. Asst. q.m. gen., July 15, 1919. D.S.M. (U.S.A.); Comdr. Order of the Crown (Belgium); Officer Legion of Honor (France); Officer Order of the Crown (Roumania); Officer Order of the White Eagle (Serbia); Order of St. Sava (Serbs, Croates and Slovens); medal for bravery (Montenegro). Died Feb. 24, 1936.

KREGER, EDWARD ALBERT army officer, lawyer; b. nr. Keota, Ia., May 31, 1868; s. William and Johanna H. K.; B.Sc., Iowa State College 1890; studied law, State University of Iowa, and Iowa Coll. of Law, Drake U.; graduate of U.S. Inf. and Cav. Sch., 1905; grad. U.S. Army Staff Coll., 1906; m. Laura Mae Roddis, 1891; 1 dau., Vera Mae (wife of Colonel J. Huntington Hills, U.S. Army). High school prin., 1891-93; supt. schools, Cherokee, Ia., 1894-96; admitted to bar of Ia., Jan. 1897; D.C., 1930; Hawaii, 1932; U.S. Supreme Court, 1912. Began practice of law at Cherokee. Cadet, private through grades to major, Ia. State Coll. Cadet Corps, 1887-90; capt. and maj. Iowa, N.C., 1893-98; capt. 52d Ia. Vol. Inf., Apr.-Oct. 1898; 1st lt. and capt. 39th U.S. Vol. Inf., 1899-1901; commd. 1st lt. inf., U.S. Army, Feb. 2, 1901; promoted through grades to col., June 4, 1920; brig. gen. (temp.), Feb. 1918-June 1920; apptd. maj. gen., judge adv. gen., U.S. Army, Nov. 16, 1928; retired from active mil. service Feb. 28, 1931. Served with 39th Inf. in Luzon, Philippine Islands, 1899-1901; with 28th Inf. in Luzon and Mindanao, 1901-04; instr. law, U.S. Army Staff Coll., 1906-08; asst. supervisor, Dept. of State and Justice, and chief Bureau of Elections, Provisional Govt. of Cuba, 1907-09; judge advocate, Dept. of Colo., 1909-11; assistant in judge advocate general's office, War Department, 1911-14; professor law, U.S. Military Academy, 1914-17; assistant provost marshal gen. of U.S., May 1917-Feb. 1918; acting judge advocate gen. for A.E.F. in Europe, Mar. 1918-Mar. 1919; acting judge advocate gen., U.S. Army, Mar. 1919-Oct. 1921; asst. judge advocate gen., U.S. Army, 1921-24; judge advocate 3rd Corps Area, 1924-25; legal adviser, Am. Delegation, Plebiscitary Commn., Tacna-Arica Arbitration, S. America, 1925-27; judge advocate 2d Corps Area, 1927-28; judge advocate gen. U.S. Army, 1928-31. Drafted the Electoral Law of Cuba, 1908. Compiled Cases on Martial Law, 1910; supervised preparation of Manual for Courts-Martial, U.S. Army, 1920, and Military Laws of the United States, Annotated, 1921. Contbr. to National Encyclopedia, 1932. Decorated D.S.C. "for heroism" in action nr. Bay, Laguna, P.I., Mar. 10, 1900; D.S.M. "for exceptionally meritorious and distinguished services" as acting judge advocate gen., A.E.F., World War. Mem. Am. Bar Assn., Fed. Bar Assn., Am. Mil. Inst., State His. Soc. of Ia., Am. Soc. Internat. Law. Presbyterian. Clubs: Army and Navy, Congressional Country (Washington, D.C.). Address: 405 Genesco Rd., San Antonio. Died May 24, 1955; buried Fort Sam Houston Nat. Cemetery, San Antonio.

KREGER, HENRY LUDWIG FLOOD lawyer; b. Benton, Me., Aug. 2, 1892; s. William Robert and Jennie Paulina (Flood) K.; student Coburn Classical Inst., 1909; grad. Philips Exeter Acad., 1912; A.B., Harvard, 1916, LL.B., 1920; m. Mary Chloe Stoddard, Sept. 16, 1922; children-Charles Stoddard, Paulina Chadwick. Admitted to Mass. bar, 1920, Ohio bar, 1926; asso. Herrick, Smith, Donald & Farley, 1920-26; asso. Squire, Sanders & Dempsey, Cleve., 1926-32, partner 1932-. Dir. Midwest Forge Co., Ohio Bronze Powder Co., Wilson McBride & Co., Macco Chem. Co. Council, Harvard Law Sch. Assn., 1952-, pres., 1963-65; trustee Phillips Exeter Acad., 1954-56. Served with Signal Corps, U.S. Army, 1917-18; res. pilot AC, 1920-40; from capt. to lt. col. USAAF, 1941-45. Decorated Legion of Merit. Mem. Am., Ohio, Cleve. bar assns., Nat. Pilots Assn., Quiet Birdmen, Phi Beta Kappa, Phi Beta Kappa Associates (life member). Clubs: Harvard (Boston, Cleve., N.Y.C.); Kirtland Country, Skating, Tavern, Union (Cleve.); Army and Navy (Washington); Eastward Ho. (Catham, Mass.) Home: 2283 Chatfield Dr., Cleveland Heights 6, O; also Sears Point Rd., Chatham, Mass. Office: Union Commerce Bldg., Cleve. 14. Died Oct. 27, 1966; buried Lakeview Cemetery, Cleve.

KRESS, JOHN ALEXANDER army officer; b. Tioga Co., Pa., Nov. 4, 1839; s. Benjamin and Margaret Ann (Wilcox) K.; early edn. in schs. of Tioga Co., Pa., and

Laporte Co., Ind.; m. Annie A. Muhlenberg, Sept. 1, 1887. Entered U.S. Mil. Acad., 1858; resigned Oct. 31, 1861, to accept apptmt. by Gen. James S. Wadsworth of New York as 1st lt. 25th N.Y. Vol. Inf. and a.-d.-c. to Gen. Wadsworth; maj. 94th N.Y., July 1862; lt. col., Nov. 1862; comd. regt. in battle of Fredericksburg; detailed as insp. gen. 1st div. 1st corps; apptd. 2d lt., ordnance dept., U.S.A., and later chief ordnance Officer, Dept. of the James; lt. col., 117th U.S.C.T., and insp. gen. 25th Army Corps; assigned to Rock Island Arsenal, 1865; U.S. Arsenal, Pittsburgh, 1867; Vancouver, Wash., 1871; San Antonio, Tex., 1882; Indianapolis, 1883; St. Louis Powder Depot, 1886; Benicia, Calif., Arsenal, 1887; St. Louis Powder Depot, 1890; assigned as chief ordnance officer U.S.A., encamped at Chickamauga, Tenn., 1898; served in Cuba as chief ordnance officer 1st army corps, and chief ordnance officer, entire Island of Cuba, on staff Maj. Gen. Brooke; again comdr. St. Louis Powder Depot, 1899, until promoted brig. gen. U.S.A., and retired Aug. 17, 1903. Baptist. Home: Merion, Pa. Died July 4, 1933..

KRESS, WALTER JAY, lawyer; born at Johnstown, Pa., May 21, 1893; the son of Jacob Fronheiser and Myrtle L. (Zimmerman) K.; grad. Lawrenceville (N.J.) Sch., 1911; B.S. in Econs., U. Pa., 1920; mem. Princeton, class 1915, Cornell U. Coll. Law, class 1918; student Oxford (Eng.) U., 1919, U. Pa. Law Sch., 1920-23; m. Arline Mae Hill, Oct. 11, 1924. Admitted to Pa. bar, 1924; practiced in Johnstown, 1924-29, Harrisburg, 1937-39; sec. Pa. Bd. Finance and Revenue, 1929-37; head revenue dept. Commonwealth Pa., 1939-42; head Pa. Corp. Taxes, 1945-47; mem. Pa. Tax Equalization Bd., 1947-56; mem. program com. Nat. Tax Assn., 1955, bank tax com., 1951-57, exec. dir. assn., hdqrs. Harrisburg, 1956-66. Chmn. Cambria County (Pa.) Rep. Com., 1926-28; mem. exec. com. Pa. Rep. Com., 1934-36; sec.-treas. Rep. Nat. War Vets., 1940-42. Served from 2d lt. to col. World Wars I and II; brig. gen. (ret.) Pa. N.G. Decorated Army Commendation ribbon with oak leaf cluster; recipient J in Life, Johnstown Jr. Chamber of Commerce, 1942; commd. Kentucky Colonel, 1962. Member of American, Pa., Dauphin County bar assns., Pa., Harrisburg chambers commerce, Am. Legion (comdr. Pa. 1936-37, chmn. nat. rehab. com. 1937-38), Mil. Order World Wars (past Pa. comdr.), Princeton Alumni Assn. Central Pa. (v.p. 1960-64), Nat. Tax Assn. (hon.), Pa. Soc. of N.Y., Harrisburg Execs. Club (past pres.), Sigma Chi, Phi Delta Phi. Lutheran (past Vestry). Rotarian, Mason (Shriner). Clubs: Vesper (Phila.): Officers (various posts). Author numerous articles on taxes. Home: Harrisburg PA Died Apr. 25, 1968; buried Franklin NH

KROMER, LEON BENJAMIN army officer; b. Grand Rapids, Mich., June 25, 1876; s. N. B. and Rosetta (Suddick) K.; grad. U.S. Mil. Acad., 1899; m. Jane Miller Stotsenburg, Mar. 20, 1907 (div.); children-Rosetta Suddick (dec.), John Stotsenburg, Leon Benjamin, Jane Statsenburg, William Annesley (killed in action). Entered U.S. Army as 2d lt. and promoted through grades to col.; apptd. chief of cav., rank of maj. gen., for 4 yrs. from Mar. 1934-38; ret. with rank of maj. gen., June 30, 1939; returned to active duty with rank of Col., Jan. 7, 1941, relieve Sept. 30, 1941. Decorated D.S.M. (U.S.); Distinguished Service Order (British); Officer, Legion of Honor (French). Episcopalian. Clubs: Army and Navy, Army and Navy Country (Washington). Address: Northfield, Vt. Died Oct. 1966.

KRUEGER, WALTER army officer; b. Flatow, Germany, Jan. 26, 1881; s. Julius O. H. and Anna (Hasse) K.; student Cin., Tech. Sch., 1896-98; distinguished grad. Inf.-Cav. Sch., 1906; grad. Gen. Staff Coll., 1907, Army War Coll., 1921, Naval War Coll., 1907, Army War Coll., 1921, Naval War Coll., 1926; Doctor of Laws (hon.) Trinity U.; m. Grace Aileen Norvell, Sept. 11, 1904 (dec. May 1956); children-James Norvell, Col. Walter, Junior (Army United States), Dorothy Jane (Mrs. Aubrey Dewitt Smith). Served as pvt., corporal, sergt., U.S. Army, 1898-1901; commd. 2d, lt., 30th Inf., 1901, and promoted through grades to brig. gen., Oct. 1, 1936, maj. gen., Feb. 1, 1939; lt. gen., May 16, 1941, and promoted to the rank of full gen. Mar. 5, 1945; served in Spanish-American War in Cuba, 1898, Philippine Insurrection, participating in numerous engagements, 1899-1903, Mexican border, 1916, World War overseas, 1918-19; Asst. Chief of Staff, G-3, 84th and 26th Divs., Chief of Staff, Tank Corps, A.E.F., 1918, and Asst. Chief of Staff, G-3, VI and IV Corps, 1919; instr. Sch. of the Line and Gen. Staff Coll., 1909-12, Army War Coll., 1921-22, Naval War Coll., 1928-32; mem. War Plans Div. War Dept. Gen. Staff, 1922-25, 1934-36; chief War Plans Div. War Dept. Gen. Staff and mem. Joint Army and Navy Bd., 1936-38; comd. 6th Inf. and Jefferson Barracks, Mo., 1932-34, 16th Inf. Brig. and Ft. Geo. G. Meade, Md., Sept. 1938-Mar. 1939, 2d Div. and Ft. Sam Houston, Mar., 1939-Oct. 1940, VIII Corps, Oct. 1940-May 1941, Third Army and Southern Defense Command, May 1941-Jan. 1943, Sixth Army in Southwest Pacific Theater, 1943-46, in operations in New Britain, Admiralty Islands, New Guinea, Biak, Noemfoor, Morotai, and Leyte, Samar, Mindoro and Luzon, P.I., occupation of Japan; retired as gen., July 1946. Decorations: Distinguished Service Cross (Army); D.S.M. with two oak leaf clusters (Army): D.S.M. (Navy); Legion of Merit; Order of Aztec Eagle (Mexican); Grand Officer, Order of Orange-Nassau with swords (Netherlands), Philippine Distinguished Service Star; Grand Officer Order of Leopold with palm and Croix de Guerre with palm (Belgium). Lutheran. Mason. Clubs: Army and Navy, San Antonio Country. Author: From Down Under to Nippon, The Story of the Sixth Army in World Regimental War Game (Immanuel), 1907; Infantry Tactics (Black), 1911; Calvalry and Artillery Tactics (Black) 1914; Tactics and Technique of River Crossings (Mertens), 1918. Home: 112 Ridgemont Av., San Antonio 9. Died Aug. 20, 1967

KUNZIG, LOUIS A. army officer; b. Altoona, Pa., Jan. 6, 1882; grad. U.S. Mil. Acad., 1905, Sch. of Line, Ft. Leavenworth, Kan., 1922. Command and Gen. Staff Sch., 1926, Army War Coll., Washington, 1931. Commd. 2d lt. Inf., 1905, advanced through the grades to brig. gen., 1942; with 12th Inf., Ft. Washington, Md., 1931-34; 3d Corps Area, hdqrs. Balt., 1934-37; commd. 11th Inf., Ft. Benjamin Harrison, Ind., 1937-40; prof. mil. sci. and tactics U. Pa., 1940; with Inf. Replacement Center, Spartansburg, S.C., 1940-41; commd., Camp Blanding, Fla., 1941-44; ret. as brig. gen., 1944; bus. mgr. Mich. Kiquor Control Commn., 1944—. Awarded Legion of Merit. Address: Michigan Liquor Control Commission, Lansing, Mich. Died Aug. 7, 1956.

KURTZ, THOMAS RICHARDSON naval officer; b. Mpls., Oct. 31, 1881; s. Thomas Crofts Wright and Anna Zehring (Richardson) K.; B.S., U.S. Naval Acad., 1901; m. Irene Van Arsdale, Sept. 16, 1908; children-Thomas Richardson, Irene Virginia (Mrs. William Scott Von Stein). Commd. ensign, USN, 1901, and advanced through the grades to commodore, 1945; retired from navy at own request, 1929; recalled to active duty, Feb. 1942; serving as chief of staff Eastern Sea Frontier. Mgr. of operations, Shell Oil Co., 1930-41. Decorated Navy Cross, Office Legion of Honor Clubs: Chevy Chase (Md.); Army and Navy (Washington and New York); Bay Head (N.J.) Yacht. Home: 350 W. 86th St., N.Y.C.; also Bayhead, N.J. Office: 90 Church St., N.Y.C. Died Mar. 1956.

KUTZ, CHARLES WILLAUER, army officer; b. Reading, Pa., Oct. 14, 1870; s. Allen and Emily (Briner) K.; grad. U.S. Mil. Acad., 1893; Engr. Sch. of Application, 1896; m. Elizabeth Randolph Keim, June 25, 1895; children—Mrs. W.G. Bingham, Mrs. L.T. Ross, C.R. Commd. add. 2d lt. engrs., June 12, 1893; 2d lt. Oct. 2, 1895; promoted through grades to col., June 1, 1920; served as col., later brig. gen. N.A., 1917-20. Duty Willets Pt., N.Y., 1893-96; fortification, river and harbor work, Baltimore, Md., 1896-1900, Portland, Me., 1900-01; asst. to chief of engrs., Washington, D.C., 1903-06; instr. mil. engring., U.S. Mil. Acad., 1906-08; fortification, river and harbor work, Seattle, Wash., 1908-11; chief engr. officer, Philippines Dept., 1911-14; engr. commr. Dist. of Columbia, 1914-17; in France, 1 yr., 1917-18; assigned to comd. engr. camp. at Camp Humphreys, Va., Aug. 1918; engr. commr., Dist. of Columbia, 1918-21; div. engr., Central Div., Cincinnati, 1921-28; mem. Mississippi River Commn., 1925-28; dept. engr. Hawaiian Dept., 1928-29; retired with rank of brig. gen., 1929; active as engr. commr., Dist. of Columbia, since May 1941. Mem. Am. Soc. C.E. Universalist. Club: Army and Navy. Home: 2028 Allen Pl. N.Y., Washington DC*

KUTZ, GEORGE FINK rear admiral U.S.N.; b. Wilkes-Barré, Pa., June 14, 1835; s. Jacob and Rosanna (Fitzgerald) K.; ed. Wilkes-Barré Acad. and Wyoming Sem.; m. Mrs. Katherine Makee Bennett, Oct. 1, 1874. Apptd. 3d asst. engr., June 26, 1856; 1st asst. engr., Aug. 2, 1859; chief engr., Nov. 10, 1861. Served in Frigate Niagara, Atlantic cable expdn., 1857-58; Atlanta, on Paraguay expdn., 1858-59; in Saginaw, Asiatic sta., 1859-62; Pawnee, S. Atlantic sta., 1862; Monongahela, West Gulf squadron, 1862-65; participated in battles of Port Hudson, College Point, Donaldsonville and Mobile Bay; in Ticonderoga, European sta., 1865-69; mem. Examining Bd., 1869-72; in Pensacola and Benicia, Pacific sta., 1872-74; fleet engr. Asiatic sta., 1876-77; at Mare Island Navy Yard, Calif., 1878; fleet engr. Pacific sta., 1881-83; chief engr. of yard, Mare Island, 1883-88; insp. machinery Cramp's Ship Yard, 1888-89, Union Iron Works, San Francisco, 1889-93; chief engr. Mare Island, 1893-96; retired after 40 yrs.' service, June 26, 1896; advanced to rank of rear admiral retired, June 29, 1906, for services during Civil War. Insp. torpedo boats building at Portland, Ore., 1908. Home: Oakland, Calif. Died Aug. 9, 1921.

KYLE, JOHN JOHNSON physician; b. Aurora, Ind., May 27, 1869; s. Thomas M. and Anna (Johnson) K.; M.D., Miami Med. Coll., 1899; unmarried. Began practice at Marion, Ind., 1892; prof. rhinology, laryngology and otology, Ind. University Med. Coll. (Ind. U.), 1900-12; prof. same, Coll. Physicians and Surgeons, U. of Southern Calif., 1913-. Maj. and surgeon 160th Ind. Inf. in Spanish-Am. War; served in Cuba, 1898-99; commd. maj. Med. R.C., 1917; hon. disch., Jan. 1, 1918. Author: Compend of Diseases of the Ear, Nose and Throat, 1903; Manual of Diseases of the Ear, Nose and Throat, 1911. Home: Los Angeles, Calif. Died Aug. 29, 1920.

KYSTER, OLAF HEIGESEN, JR. army officer; b. N.Y.C., Sept. 5, 1903; s. Olaf Helgesen and Nathalia (Thomsen) K.; B.S., U.S. Mil. Acad., 1927; grad. Nat. War Coll., 1948; m. Mary Holabird Cruikshank, May 7, 1932; 1 dau., Mary Elizabeth (Mrs. Gilbert T. Scott). Commd. 2d lt. U.S. Army, 1927, advanced through grades to maj. gen., 1957; chief staff 82d Fighter Wing, 1944; chief operations br. Office Dir. Plans and Statistics, Army Forces Western Pacific, 1946; chief moblzn. br. orgn. and tng. div. Dept. Army, 1948, dep. chief, 1948-50; exec. officer to asst. sec. army, later exec. officer under-sec. army, 1950-52; sr. rep. army Lincoln Labs., Mass. Inst. Tech., 1954; comdg. gen. 47th A.A., Brigade, 1955-57; chief staff UN Command Mil. Armistice Commn., 1957, sr. mem. 1957-58, spl. asst. for armistice affairs, Korea, 1957-58; comdg. gen. 5th Region, Army Air Def. Command, Ft. Sheridan, Ill. 1958-. Decorated Legion of Merit (U.S.); Order Mil. Merit Taeguk (Korea). Address: Comdg. General 5th Region, U.S. Army Air Defense Command, Ft. Sheridan, Ill. Died Sept. 14, 1959; buried Arlington Nat. Cemetery, Arlington, Va.

LABRUM, J. HARRY, lawyer; born at Philadelphia, Pennsylvania; s. Thomas Joseph and Mary Theresa (Conlen) LaB.; LL.B., Georgetown U., 1925; postgrad. work, Cambridge U., England; LL.D., St. Josephs College, 1956; HH.D. (honorary), Philathea Coll., London, Ont., 1958; m. Catharine Agatha Foley, June 29, 1921; 1 dau., Agatha Mary (Mrs. Paolo Clemente). Admitted to Pa., D.C. bars, 1925; mem. LaBrum & Doak. Member board dirs. Hemphill Ferguson Company, Inc., John D. Grover & Sons, Inc., Polychrome Corp. Pa., Polychrome Corp., ER & T Sta. WHYY, Georgetown Textile & Manufacturing Co., Inc.; spl. dep. atty. gen. Commonwealth, Pa., 1936-37; mem. Pa. State Welfare Commn., 1954-55; pres. Phila. Bd. Pub. Edn. 1953-65; pres. Phila. council Boy Scouts America 1956-58, hon. pres., 1958-59; pres. Fedn. Ins. Counsel, 1957-58, chmn. bd., 1959; trustee PMS Colls.; pres. Fedn. of Ins. Counsel Found., from 1962. Served as brig. gen. U.S. Army, Signal Corps Res. Decorated Legion of Merit (U.S.); Order of The Crown of Italy; Knight Comdr. Order White Rose (Finland); recipient star and cross acad. honor Am. Internat. Acad., 1958; Distinguished Service Medal, Pa. dept. Am. Legion, 1968; George W. Yancey Meml. award, Internat. Assn. Ins. Counsel, 1968; John Carroll award, Georgetown University Alumni Association, 1968. Fellow Am. Bar Found., Am. Coll. Trial Lawyers; Internat. Acad. Trial Lawyers (dir. 1962-65, from 1967); mem. Am., Pa., Philadelphia bar associations (various coms. of each), Pa. State Chamber of Commerce (dir. 1965-69), Phi Alpha Delta (distinguished service chpt.), and many other nat., state and local profl. and civic orgns. and assns.; has served as officer of several, active in coms. of many; has served as mem. several govtl. coms. Clubs: Nat. Press, The Army and Navy (Washington), India House (N.Y. City); Union League, Racquet, Downtown, Philadelphia Country, Lawyers', Pen and Pencil (Phila.); and others. Contbr. articles in profl. jours. Home: Philadelphia PA Deceased.

LA CAUZA, FRANK EMILIO educator; b. Novara di Sicilia, Italy, Nov. 22, 1900; s. Carmelo and Angelina (Bertolami) LA G.; B.S., Harvard, 1923, M.S., 1924, M.A., 1929; grad. student Mass. Inst. Tech., 1926-27; grad. Sperry Gyro Sch., N.Y., 1930; m. Mary Ann Hunter, Mar. 16, 1935. Came to U.S., 1905, naturalized, 1926. Mem. engring. test dept. Gen. Electric Co., Schenectady, 1924; instr. elec. engring. Harvard, 1924-26; asst. prof. U.S. Navy Postgrad. Sch., Annapolis, 1929-39, asso. prof., 1939-45, prof., 1945-47; organized elec. engring., mathematics depts. Naval Schs. Gen. Line, Newport, R.I., Monterey, Cal., 1946-47, prof., head dept. elec. engring., mathematics Gen. Line Sch., Monterey, 1947-58, academic chmn. U.S. Gen. Line and Naval Sci. Sch., 1958-59. Vice president Interservice Fund. Member United States Naval Postgrad. Sch. Selection Bd., 1961. Mem. bd. trustees Monterey Library, 1956-57; mem. planning commn., Monterey, 1958-59; mem. City Council, Monterey, Cal., 1959-61. Served from lt. to lt. comdr., USNR, 1942-45; capt. Res. Decorated Knight Officer, Order of Crown (Italy), 1930. Profl. engr., Md., Cal. Mem. Am. Inst. E.E., Am. Soc. Engring. Edn., Am. Assn. U. Profs., Naval Res. Assn. (pres. Monterey chapt. 1961-62). Clubs: Officers, University, Harvard (Annapolis); Officers (Postgrad. Sch., Monterey). Contbr. Gyro Compass sect. Knights Modern Seamanship. Contbr. articles profl. publs. Home: 110 Monte Vista Dr., Monterey, Cal. 93940. Died July 25, 1964; buried Arlington Nat. Cemetery.

LACEY, JOHN army officer, public ofcl.; b. Buckingham, Pa., Feb. 4, 1755; s. John and Jane

(Chapman) L.; m. Anastasia Reynolds, Jan. 18, 1781, 4 children. Commd. capt. of a volunteer co., 1776; organized co., Bucks County, Pa.; served with 4th Pa. Regt. in Canadian campaign of 1776; commd. lt. col. Bucks County Militia, 1777, brig. gen., 1778; sub.-lt., also commr. of confiscated estates for Bucks County; mem. Pa. Assembly from Bucks County, 1778; mem. Provincial Council of Pa., 1779-81; mem. Pa. Supreme Exec. Council, 1779-82, on leave as comdr. of a militia brigade, 1780-81; apptd. justice of the peace, 1801; mem. N.J. Assembly. Died New Mills, N.J., Feb. 17, 1814.

LACKEY, HENRY ELLIS naval officer; b. Norfolk, Va., June 23, 1876; s. Oscar Hamilton and Clara Caroline (Stone) L.; student Potomac Acad., Alexandria, Va., 1889-93; grad. U.S. Naval Acad., 1899; m. Katherine Peck, July 20, 1901; children-Anne Lockwood (Mrs. Augustus Lowell Putnam), Katherine de Montalant, Caroline Hamilton. Served as naval cadet, U.S.S. New York, Spanish-Am. War; commd. ensign, 1901, advanced through grades to rear adm., 1932. Decorated Sampson Medal, Navy Cross (U.S.); Spanish Order Naval Merit; Greek Order of Savior. Club: Army and Navy (Washington). Deceased.*

LADD, EUGENE F. army officer; b. Thetford, Vt., Sept. 19, 1859; s. George A. and Louise H. L.; grad. U.S. Mil. Acad., 1884; m. Miss Norman, May 30, 1888; 1 dau., Katharine Louise. Commd. 2d lt. 9th Cav., June 24, 1884; promoted through grades to col. adj. gen., Aug. 17, 1914; retired account of disability in line of duty, Oct. 1, 1915; brig. gen. N.A., Oct. 6, 1917. Home: Cohasset, Mass. Died Apr. 23, 1927.

LADD, JESSE A. ret. army officer; b. Bradner, O., Sept. 21, 1887; s. Jonathan Elmore and Adda (Jennings) L.; B.S., U.S. Mil. Acad., 1911; m. Florence Von Kanel, Oct. 21, 1913; children-Jesse A. (dec.), Jonathan Frederic, James Von Kanel. Commd. 2d lt., Inf., 1911, promoted through grades to brig. gen., 1941; assigned Port Richardson, Alaska, 1941, later comd. 9th Inf. Div. in Germany, ret. 1947. Mason. Home: 316 W. Wooster St., Bowling Green, O. Died Dec. 14, 1957.

LADUE, LAURENCE KNIGHT army officer; b. Mo., June 14, 1903; B.S., U.S. Mil. Acad., 1924; grad. Cav. Sch., troop officers course, 1930, advanced equitation course, 1931. Command and Gen. Staff Sch., 1941. Commd. 2d lt., U.S. Army, 1924, advanced through the grades to brig. gen., 1945. Address: War Dept., Washington 25. Died May 24, 1951.

LAFAYETTE, MARQUIS DE (MARIE JOSEPH PAUL YVES ROCHE GILBERT DU MOTIER) army officer; b. Auvergne, France, Sept. 6, 1757; s. Gilbert (Marquis de Lafayette) and Marie Louise Julie de la Riviere; attended Collège du Plessis, Paris, France, 1768-72; m. Marie Andrienne Francoise de Noailles, Apr. 11, 1774, at least 1 son, George Washington. Served with 2d Co., King's Musketeers, French Army, 1771-73, transferred to regt. commanded by Louis, Vicomte de Noailles, became 2d lt., 1773, promoted capt., 1774; entered Continental Army (volunteered to do so at own expense) during Revolutionary War, 1777, commd. maj. gen. by vote of Continental Congress, July 1777, placed in command of div. of Va. light troops by vote of Congress, Dec. 1777; spent furlough in France, advancing Am. cause, 1778-80; served in Va., took part in Battle of Yorktown, 1781; became mem. Soc. of Cincinnati; an intimate asso. of George Washington; returned to France, Dec. 1781; visited U.S., 1784, 1824-25; became mem. French Assembly of Notables, 1787, French Nat. Assembly, 1789; an organizer Nat. Guard of France; designer of French tri-color flag; a founder Club of the Feuillants (conservative liberals who wished to establish constl. monarchy), 1790; commanded French Army in War with Austria, 1792, fled to Flanders, captured and imprisoned by Austrians; returned to France after 7-year exile, 1799; mem. Chamber of Deputies, 1815, 18-24; commander French Nat. Guard in July Revolution, 1830; voted ⅜,424 for his part in Am. Revolution by U.S. Congress, 1794, given 11,520 acres of land in La., 1803; named hon. citizen of U.S. Died May 20, 1834; buried Picpus Cemetery (grave covered wtih earth from Bunker Hill), Paris.

LA FOLLETTE, PHILIP FOX lawyer; b. Madison, Wis., May 8, 1897; s. Robert Marion and Belle (Case) LaF.; A.B., U. Wis., 1919, LL.B., 1922; m. Isabel Bacon, Apr. 14, 1923; children-Robert Marion III, Judith Bacon (Mrs. Sorem), Isabel Bacon (Mrs. Zabrinskie). Began practice at Madison, 1922; dist. atty., Dane County, Wis., 1925-27; lectr. law U. Wis. Law Sch., 1926-30; gov. Wis., terms 1931-33, and 1935-39; dir. Hazeltine Corp., Little Neck, N.Y., 1947-. Curator, Wis. State Hist. Soc., 1962. Served as 2d lt., inf., U.S. Army, World War I; volunteered for active service World War II; commd. capt., later col. inf., S.W. Pacific. Home: 410 N. Pinckney St., Madison, Wis. Died Aug. 18, 1965.

LA GARDE, LOUIS ANATOLE surgeon U.S.A.; b. Thibodaux, La., Apr. 15, 1849; s. Jules Adolph and Aurelia (Daspit) L.; student Louisiana Mil. Acad., 1866-68; M.D., Bellevue Hosp. Med. Coll., 1872; m. Frances Neely, Mar. 4, 1879. Interne Roosevelt Hosp., New York, 1872-74; apptd. actg. asst. surgeon U.S.A., Apr. 1, 1874; asst. surgeon, June 6, 1878; capt. asst. surgeon, June 6, 1883; maj. surgeon, Nov. 13, 1896; lt. col. dep. surgeon gen., and lt. col., Med. Corps., Mar. 17, 1906; col., Jan. 1, 1910; retired Apr. 15, 1913; recalled to active duty and served during World War. Participated in Sioux Indian War, 1876; comd. Divisional Reserve Hosp., 5th Army Corps, Siboney, Cuba, 1898; in charge evacuation of sick and wounded to Northern hosps.; prof. mil. surgery, New York U., 1900-; comdt. U.S. Army Med. Sch., 1910-13; mem. Nat. Bd. Med. Examiners. Mutter lecturer, Coll. Physicians, Phila., 1902. Author: (text book) Gunshot Injuries, 2d edit., 1916. Has carried on extensive research work with septic bullets and septic powders; demonstrated ineffective material not destroyed by firearms. Home: Washington, D.C. Died Mar. 7, 1920.

LA GUARDIA, FIORELLO H. lawyer, writer, commentator; b. N.Y. City, Dec. 11, 1882; LL.B., New York University, 1919, LL.D., 1938; LL.D., St. Lawrence University, 1938, Yale, 1940, Washington and Jefferson College, 1942; married Marie Fisher, Feb. 28, 1929. With Am. Consulate, Budapest, Hungary, and Trieste, Austria, 1901-04; consular agt. at Fiume, Hungary, 1904-06; interpreter at Ellis Island, N.Y., 1907-10; began law practice New York, 1910; dep. atty. gen. of N.Y., 1915-17; mem. 65th and 66th Congresses (1917-19), 14th N.Y. Dist., and 68th to 72d Congresses (1923-33), 20th N.Y. Dist.; mayor of New York City, term 1934-37, reëlected 2 terms, 1938-45. President Board of Aldermen of N.Y. City, 1920-21; apptd. dir. Office of Civilian Defense, May 20, 1941. Pres. U.S. Conf. of Mayors, 1936-45; chmn. Am. Sect. of Permanent Joint Defense Bd. (Canada-U.S.). Spl. Ambassador to Brazil, 1946. Dir. gen. UNRRA, Apr.-December, 1946. Commissioned U.S. Air Service, August, 1917, held rank first lt., capt., major; commanded 8th Centre Aviation Sch. and Am. Flying Force, Italian front; attached to night and day bombing squadrons there. Decorations: World War I Victory; Knight Comdr. Order of Crown of Italy, Italian War Cross; Blue Order of Jade (China); Order of Redeemer (Greece); Order of Merit (Chile); Simon Bolivar Medal (Venezuela); Medal of Honor (Haiti); Order of Honor and Merit-Commendador (Cuba); Order of St. Olav (Norway); Comdr. Legion of Honor (France); Delaware Award (Sweden); Order of Orange-Nassau (Netherlands); Lithuanian Aid Medal; Order of White Lion (Czech.); Polonia Restituta, First Class (Poland); Medal of Merit (U.S.A.); Grand Comdr. of Greek Order of Phoenix. Address: 30 Rockefeller Plaza, New York 20, N.Y. Died Sept. 20, 1947.

LAHEY, FRANK HOWARD surgeon; b. Haverhill, Mass., June 1, 1880; s. Thomas and Honora Frances (Powers) L.; M.D., Harvard, 1904; hon. Sc.D., Tufts, 1927; Boston University, 1943, Northwestern U., 1947; LL.D. (honorary) University of Cincinnati 1951; m. Alice Wilcox, Apr. 15, 1909. Surgeon Long Island Hosp., 1904-05, Boston City Hosp., 1905-07; resident surgeon Haymarket Sq. Relief Sta., 1908; instr. in surgery, Harvard Med. Sch., 1908-09, 1912-15; asst. prof., later prof. surgery, Tufts Med. Sch., 1913-17; prof. clin. surgery, Harvard Medical School, 1923-24; surgeon in chief N.E. Baptist hospitals; director of surgery The Lahey Clinic, Boston. Served as major, Medical Corps, U.S. Army, World War; dir. surgery Evacuation Hosp. No. 30, A.E.F.; now hon. consultant to Medical Dept., U.S.N. Fellow Am. Coll. Surgeons (bd. govs.); honorary fellow Royal Coll. of Surgeons, England; mem. Am. and Internat. surg. assns., Am. Assn. for Study of Goitre, A.M.A. (pres. 1942), Société des Chirurgiens de Paris, Theta Delta Chi. Republican. Mason. Clubs: Harvard, Algonquin. Author of Lahey Clinic Number (Surg. Clinics of N. America), pub. yearly. Contbr. numerous articles on surg. subjects. Chmn. Procurement and Assignment Service for Med. Personnel for the Armes Forces. Home: 118 Bay State Rd. Office: 605 Commonwealth Av., Boston. Died June 27, 1953.

LAHM, FRANK PURDY, army officer; b. Ohio, Nov. 17, 1877; grad. U.S. Mil. Acad., 1901; grad. Mounted Service Sch., 1911; m. Gertrude Jenner, Oct. 18, 1911. Commd. 2d lt. 6th Cav., Feb. 18, 1901; capt. Aviation Sect. Signal Corps, Apr. 1, 1916; lt. colonel, July 2, 1920; promoted colonel Air Corps, Oct. 7, 1931. Made many experiments with balloons for war purposes and participated in nat. and internat. races; won James Gordon Bennett cup in Internat. Balloon Race, Paris, France, Sept. 30-Oct. 1, 1906. Organized aviation service in Philippine Islands, 1912, conducting training on airplanes and seaplanes there, 1912-13; sec. Signal Corps Aviation Sch., North Island, San Diego, Calif., 1916-17; ordered to command Balloon Sch., Ft. Omaha, Neb., Apr. 1917, to England, Aug. 1917, thence to France, inspecting balloon services; organized Lighter than Air Service in A.E.F.; on duty Hdqrs. Chief of Air Service to Feb. 1918, Hdqrs. Zone of Advance Air Service to May 1918, Hdqrs. First Army Air Service to July 1918; air officer in G-3, 1st Army, to Oct. 1918; organized and commanded 2d Army Air Service, Oct. 1918; disbanded May, 1919; spl. student Army War Coll., 1919-20; G-3, War Dept. Gen. Staff, 1920-24; 9th Corps Area Air Officer, 1924-26; apptd. brig. gen. for period of 4 yrs., and asst. to chief of Air Corps, to organize and command Air Corps Training Center, 1926-30; air officer 9th Corps Area to July, 1930; apptd. air attache, Am. Embassy, Paris, France, July 1931. Awarded D.S.M. First airship pilot and first balloon pilot in U.S. Army. Address: War Department, Washington DC. Died July 1963.

LAKE, GEORGE BURT med. editor, publisher and writer, psychiatrist; b. Topeka, Kan., Nov. 26, 1880; s. George Burt and Helen Luthera (Marsh) L.; student U. of Mich., 1898-1901; M.D., Rush Med. Coll., Chicago, 1902; grad. Army Med. Sch., Washington, D.C., 1911; m. Mary Lee Blossom, Dec. 25, 1902; children-Helen Lee Blossom (Mrs. Ray J. Cox), George Burt, Jr. Asst. surgeon Mexican Central Ry., 1902-04; general practice, Wolcottville, Ind., 1904-10, town health officer, 1907-08; special lecturer in hygiene and sanitation, Purdue U., 1908-10; editor Clinical Medicine and Surgery (now Clinical Medicine) since 1924; now also owner and pub. same; attending internist American Hosp., 1927-34; editor Bull. Med. Round Table of Chicago, 1928-34. Mem. Med. Corps, U.S. Army, 1910-24, advancing to maj.; served in campaign against Moros, Sulu, P.I., 1913, in Mexican Punitive Expdn., 1916; lt. col., camp surgeon, Camp Grant, Ill., later comdg. officer, Gen. Hosp., Indianapolis, World War; now col., Med. R.C. (inactive). Fellow A.M.A.; mem. Assn. Mil. Surgeons, Med. Round Table of Chicago (pres. 1925-27; sec. 1941), Art Inst. Chicago, Bookfellows, A.A.A.S., Miss. Valley Med. Editors Assn. (pres. 1941), Am. Physicians' Art Assn., Miss. Valley Med. Soc. (bd. dirs. 1940-41), Am. Assn. of History of Medicine, Ill. Acad. Science, Chicago Poetry Center of Poetry Soc. of London (pres. 1940). Reserve officers Assn.; asso. Coll. Physicians. Liberal Catholic priest. Clubs: Saturday Evening Club, Chicago Motor Club. Author: (verse) An Apostle of Joy, 1928; (verse) Hilltops, 1932; (verse) Eros and the Sage, 1935; A 5,000 Year Plan; Parental Therapy (with Dr. W. F. Dutton); also several hundred articles. Home: 330 Bloom St., Highland Park, Ill. Office: Medical and Dental Arts Bldg., Waukegan, Ill. Died Mar. 2, 1943.

LAMAR, MIRABEAU BUONAPARTE pres. Republic of Tex., army officer; b. Louisville, Ga., Aug. 16, 1798; s. John and Rebecca (Lamar) L.; m. Tabeta Jordan, Jan 1, 1826; m. 2d, Henrietta Maffett, 1851, Pvt. sec. to Gov. George M. Troup of Ga., 1823; editor Columbua (Ga.) Enquirer, 1826; went to Tex., 1836; served as comdr. Tex. Cavalry at Battle of San Jacinto; atty. gen., then sec. of war in Pres. Burnet's provisional cabinet, 1836; v.p. Republic of Tex., 1836; pres., 1838-41; a founder City of Austin (Tex). 1840; fought in Mexican War, participated in Battle of Monterey, 1846; U.S. minister to Argentina, 1855-56; became strong advocate of Southern rights; Lamar State Coll., Tex., named for him. Died Richmond, Tex., Dec. 19, 1859.

LAMAR, WILLIAM HARMONG lawyer; b. Auburn, Ala., Dec. 11, 1859; s. William Harmong (M.D.) and Ann M. (Glenn) L.; A.B., Ala. Polytechnic, Auburn, 1881; LL.B., Georgetown U., D.C., 1884, LL.M., 1885; m. Virginia Longstreet, d. Justice L.O.C. Lamar of the U.S. Supreme Court, June 21, 1887; children-Mrs. Virginia Longstreet Matthews, Mrs. Gussie Glenn Lyttle, Lucius Q. C., William H. Began practice at Washington, D.C., Md., 1885; mem. Md. Ho. of Rep., 1894; asst. atty., Dept. of Justice (U.S.), 1906-13; asst. atty. gen. and solicitor Post Office Dept., 1913-21; in practice of law with his son, Lucius Q. C. Lamar firm Lamar & Lamar, 1921-. Capt., U.S.V. Signal Corps, Spanish-Am. War, and served in P.R. campaign. Mem. U.S. Wire Control Bd. while telegraph and telephone properties were operated by Govt., 1918-19. Democrat. Methodist. Author of ann. reports of solicitor, 1913, 34, 15, 16, pub. by Post Office Dept. Home: Rockville, Md. Died Feb. 10, 1928.

LAMB, ALBERT RICHARD prof. emeritus; b. Waterbury, Conn., Apr. 22, 1881; s. George Burton and Idabelle (Johnson) L.; prep. edn., Taft Sch., Watertown, Conn., 1895-99; A.B., Yale, 1903; M.D., Coll. Physicians and Surgeons, Columbia, 1907; m. Helen Foster, Jan. 4, 1910; children-Mary Nightingale, Albert Richard, Priscilla Foster, Helen. Interne Presbyn. Hosp., N.Y.C., 1908-10, resident bacteriologist, 1910-11, resident pathologist, 1911-13, chief of out patient dept. and asst. visiting physician, 1913-17, visiting physician since 1918; instr. of medicine, Coll. Physicians and Surgeons, 1913-18, became prof. clin. medicine, 1918, now prof. emeritus; pres. med. board Presbyn. Hosp., 1940-46; now consulting physician; cons. physician Englewood (N.J.) Hosp. Chmn. Med. Adv. Bd. No. 22, N.Y.C.; mem. emergency med. service Office Civilian Def., N.Y. Served as maj., M.C., U.S. Army, World War; attached to Am. Commn. to Negotiate Peace. Recipient D.S.M., Columbia U., 1956. Fellow A.C.P.; mem. A.M.A., Soc. Internal. Medicine,

N.Y. Acad. Medicine, N.Y. State Med. Soc., N.Y. Clin. Soc., Cosmopolitan Med. Club, Psi Upsilon, Skull and Bones. Republican. Episcopalian. Club: Century. Home: Pine Orchard, Conn. Office: Presbyn. Hosp., 622 W. 168th St., N.Y.C. Died Nov. 1959.

LAMB, JOHN revolutionary patriot, army officer; b. N.Y.C., Jan. 1, 1735; s. Anthony Lamb; m. Catherine Jandine, Nov. 13, 1765; Joined Sons of Liberty, 1756; commd. capt. arty. co., July 1775; maj. in command No. Dept., Continental Army; taken prisoner by British, exchanged apptd. col. 2d Continental Arty, 1777; commanded arty. at U. S. Mil. Acad., 1779-80; participated in siege and battle of Yorktown, 1781; brevetted brig. gen., 1783; apptd. collector of customs Port of N.Y., 1784; mem. N.Y. Legislature; an original mem. Soc. of Cincinnati. Died May 31, 1800.

LAMB, WILLIAM mcht., soldier; b. Norfolk, Va., Sept. 7, 1835; s. William Wilson Lamb and Margaret Kerr (Wilson) L.; grad. William and Mary Coll., B.P., LL.B., 1855; LL.D., St. Lawrence U., 1899; m. Sarah Chaffee, 1857. Editor Daily Southern Argus, 1856-61; mem. Nat. Dem. Conv., 1856; presidential elector, 1860 on Breckenridge ticket; capt. Woodis Rifles, mil. co. of Norfolk, Va., for several yrs. before war; with his co. joined Va. troops Apr. 1861; served in Confederate army, capt. to col.; had charge defenses at New Inlet on Cape Fear; built and had command Fort Fisher until its fall, Jan. 15, 1865; was wounded and walked on crutches seven yrs. After war in shipping business in Norfolk, leader in building up foreign trade of city; mem. Nat. Dem. Conv., 1876; joined readjusters, 1879; Hancock elector, 1880; headed Harrison and Morton electoral ticket, 1888; chmn. Rep. State Com., 1895-97; del. Rep. Nat. Conv., 1896. Consul for Germany, v.-consul for Sweden at Norfolk. Mayor Norfolk, Va., 1880-86. Pres. Lower Norfolk Coke & Gas Corp. Address: Norfolk, Va. Died 1909.

LAMBERT, GERARD BARNES corp. official; b. St. Louis, Mo., May 15, 1886; s. Jordan Wheat and Lily (Winn) L.; grad. Smith Acad., St. Louis, 1904; Litt.B., Princeton U., 1908; student Columbia Architectural Sch., 1908-10; m. Rachel Lowe, June 25, 1908; children-Rachel, Gerard B., Lily; m. 2d, Grace Lansing Mull, Apr. 18, 1936 .Pres. Gerard B. Lambert Co., lumber and cotton, 1912-28; gen. mgr. Lambert Pharmacal Co., 1921-23, pres., 1923-28; pres. Lambert & Feasley, 1922-28; pres. The Lambert Co., 1926-28, dir., 1926-55; dir. Warner-Lambert Pharm. Co., 1955-56; pres. Gillette Safety Razor Co., 1931-34, dir., chmn. exec. com., 1934-36. Adviser Federal Housing Adminstr., Washington, June 1938-Feb. 1939. In exec. office of chmn., War Production Bd., Washington, D.C., Mar. 1942-Oct. 1944. Served as 1st lt. Air Service, U.S. Army, England and France, World War; captain Air Service Reserve Corps, 1918-20. Formerly chmn. vis. com. Dept. Art and Archaeology, Princeton. Mem. Archaeological Inst. Am. So. Soc. (N.Y.C.). Republican. Episcopalian. Clubs: Knickerbocker, Coffee House, Racquet and Tennis, New York Yacht, Eastern Yacht (Boston); permanent hon. mem. Royal Thames Yacht and Lymington Yacht (London, Eng.). Home: Princeton, N.J. Author: Yankee in England; Murder in Newport; All Out of Step. Office: 250 Park Av., N.Y.C. Died Feb. 25, 1967.

LAMBERTON, BENJAMIN PEFFER rear adm.; b. Cumberland County, Pa., Feb. 25, 1844; s. James Finlay and Elizabeth (Peffer) L.; apptd. from Pa., and grad. U.S. Naval Acad., 1864; m. Lilla Stedman, Feb. 25, 1873. Promoted ensign, Nov. 1, 1866; master Dec. 1, 1866; lt., Mar. 12, 1868; lt. comdr., Apr. 27, 1869; comdr., June 2, 1885; capt., May 11, 1898; rear adm. Oct. 11, 1903. Summer of 1864 was attached to the America, in pursuit of the Confederate steamers Florida and Tallahasse; comd. Jamestown, 1889-91; at Bur. of Yards and Docks, 1891-94; light house insp. 5th dist., 1894-98; chief of staff of admiral Dewey at battle of Manila Bay, May 1, 1898, and was advanced 7 numbers in rank "for eminent and conspicuous conduct" in this battle; comd. Olympia, Admiral Dewey's flag-ship, 1898-99; mem. Naval Examining and Retiring Bds., 1900; Lighthouse Bd., 1900-03; comdr.-in-chief S. Atlantic Squadron, 1903-04; Naval War Coll., 1904; chmn. Lighthouse Bd., 1905-06; retired, Feb. 25, 1906. Home: Washington, D.C. Died June 9, 1912.

LAMONT, PETER T., oil co. exec.; b. Rotterdam, The Netherlands, Apr. 8, 1900 (parents U.S. citizens); s. John George and Florence Louise (Theobald) L.; grad. The Hill Sch., Pottstown Pa., 1918; B.S. in Petroleum Engring., Mass. Inst. Tech., 1922; m. Dorothy Hogencamp, June 14, 1924; 1 dau., Louise Florence. Tng. in oil prodn., refining and marketing Standard Oil Co. (N.J.), 1922-25, marketing asst. in Germany, 1925-30, mem. various bds. of European affiliates, 1930-41, marketing advisor for Central Europe, 1946-48, transferred to N.Y. as asst. marketing coordinator (world wide), 1948, marketing coordinator (world wide), 1949-54, v.p., dir., 1954-61. Served as comdr., USNR, 1942-45. Decorated Legion of Merit; Croix de Guerre with Gold Star; comdr. Order Merit Republic Italy; comdr.'s cross Order Orange Nassau (Netherlands). Mem. Theta Xi. Clubs: University (N.Y.C.); American (London); Greenwich (Conn.) Country. Home: Greenwich CT Died Nov. 25, 1970; buried Putnam Cemetery, Greenwich CT

LAMONT, ROBERT PATTERSON ex-sec. of Commerce; b. Detroit, Mich., Dec. 1, 1867; s. Robert and Isabella (Patterson) L.; B.S. in C.E., U. of Mich., 1891; m. Helen Gertrude Trotter, Oct. 24, 1894; children—Robert Patterson, Gertrude (Mrs. Matthew Jones), Dorothy (Mrs. Chauncey Belkan). Engineer, Chicago Exposition, 1891-92; sec. and engr. Shailer & Schinglau, contractors, 1892-97; 1st v.p. Simplex Ry. Appliance Co., 1897-1905; 1st v.p. Am. Steel Foundries, 1905-12, pres., 1912-29; Sec. of Commerce in Cabinet of President Hoover, 1930-32; pres. Am. Iron and Steel Inst., 1932-33. Commd. major N.A., Feb. 1918; chief Procurement Division Ordnance Dept., Washington, D.C., Oct. 16, 1918-Feb. 1919 with rank of col. Clubs: Century, University (New York). Home: 330 Park Av., New York. Died Feb. 19, 1948.

LAMONT, THOMAS STILWELL banking; b. Englewood, N.J., Jan. 30, 1899; s. Thomas William and Florence Haskell (Corliss) L.; grad. Phillips Exeter Acad., 1917; A.B., Harvard, 1921; student Trinity Coll., Cambridge, Eng., 1921-22; m. Elinor B. Miner, Apr. 14, 1923; children-Thomas William II (lost on submarine Snook, Apr. 8, 1945), Edward Miner, Lansing, Elinor Branscombe (Mrs. Andrew Anderson-Bell). With J.P. Morgan and Co., 1922-40, partner, 1929-40; v.p., dir. J. P. Morgan & Co., Inc., 1940-53, sr. v.p., dir., 1953-55, vice chmn. bd. dirs., 1955-58, chmn. exec. com., 1959; vice chmn. bd. dirs., Morgan Guaranty Trust Co., 1959-64, now dir.; dir. Phelps Dodge Corp., Tex. Gulf Sulphur Co., Morgan Guaranty Internat. Finance Corp., Morgan Internat. Banking Corp. Trustee Phillips Exeter Acad., 1935-61, pres. bd. trustees, 1946-56; trustee Carnegie Found. Advancement Teaching, Am. Sch. Classical Studies at Athens; mem. corp. Harvard Coll. Served as pvt. U.S. Army, World War; lt. col. AAF, overseas, 1942-44. Mem. Pilgrims U.S. Clubs: Century Assn., Links, Harvard, Down Town Assn. (N.Y.C.); The Creek (Glen Cove, L.I.). Home: 101 E. 72d St. Office: 23 Wall St., N.Y.C. 10015. Died Apr. 10, 1967.

LAMPTON, WILLIAM JAMES newspaperman; b. Lawrence County, O.; s. William H. Oampton; ed. Ohio Wesleyan U. and Marietta (O.) Coll.; hon. A.M. Marietta Coll., 1891; unmarried. Began newspaper work as editor of a Republican paper in Ky., 1877-78; consecutively reporter Cincinnati Times, paragrapher Steubenville Herald, on staff Louisville Courier-Journal, editor Merchant Traveler, Cincinnati; staff of Critic and Evening Star, Washington (originated "Shooting Stars" dept., latter), and Detroit Free Press; spl. contbr. of current verse to New York newspapers; mag. writer, prose and verse. Apptd. col. and a.-d.-c. on staff Gov. Willson of Ky., Mar. 1910. Author: Yawps and Other Things; Confessions of a Husband; The Trolley Car and the Lady, 1908; Mrs. Brown's Opinions, 1886; Jedge Waxem's Pocket Book of Politics, 1908; Tame Animals Have Known, 1912. Home: New York, N.Y. Died May 30, 1917.

LAND, EMORY SCOTT, naval officer; b. Jan. 9, 1879; s. Scott E. and Jennie Taylor (Emory) L.; B.S., M.A., U. of Wyo., 1898; grad. U.S. Naval Acad., 1902; M.S., Mass. Inst. Tech., 1907; LL.D., U. of Wyo., 1939, Calif. Maritime Acad., 1940; Dr. Engring., N.Y. U., 1944; LL.D., Columbia, 1947; m. Elizabeth C. Stiles, Apr. 15, 1909. Commd. midshipman, U.S. Navy, 1901; naval constructor since 1904; asst. chief Bur. of Aeronautics, Navy Dept., 1926-28; chief of Bur. of Construction and Repair, 1932-37; commr. United States Maritime Commission, 1937-38, chairman, 1938-46. Appointed administrator, War Shipping Administration, February 9, 1942. Served as member staff Admiral Sims, World War I. Vice-pres. and treas. Daniel Guggenheim Fund for Promotion of Aeronautics, 1928-29. Pres. Air Transport Assn. of America since 1946. Mem. Society Naval Architects and Marine Engrs. (pres. 1940-42), Inst. Aeronautic Sciences, Brit. Inst. Naval Architects, Royal Aero Soc. Decorated Navy Cross (U.S.); Spanish Campaign Badge; Victory Medal, World War I; Army of Occupation of Germany Medal; Arthur Williams Memorial Award; Gold Medal of Bolivar-San Martin of Pan-Am. Soc.; D.S.M., Army, Navy; Knight Comdr., Mil. Div., Order of the British Empire; Grand Officer in the Order of Orange-Nassau (Netherlands); Order of Polonia Restituta (Poland); Comdr. Legion of Honor (France); Cross of Comdr. of the Order of Leopold (Belgium); Commanders Cross with star, Royal Order of St. Olav (Norway), 1948. Clubs: Army and Navy, Metropolitan, Army-Navy Country, Chevy Chase, Alibi (Washington); New York Yacht; Engineers' (Phila.). Home: Washington DC Died Nov. 1971.

LANDAIS, PIERRE naval officer; b. St. Malo, Brittany, France, 1731. Served as officer French Navy; mem. French exploratory voyage around the world with Louis Bougainville, 1766-69; commd. capt. Continental Navy, 1777; commanded mcht. ship Flamand, delivered supplies from France to Portsmouth, N.H.; commanded frigate Alliance, 1778; became naturalized citizen of Mass., 1778; assigned to fleet of John Paul Jones, 1779; ct. martialed, convicted of insubordination during battle with Brit. ship Seraphis, 1781, expelled from U.S. Navy; commd. rear adm. French Navy, 1792; returned to N.Y., 1797. Died N.Y.C., Sept. 17, 1820.

LANDER, EDWARD jurist; b. Salem, Mass., Aug. 11, 1816; s. Edward and Eliza (West) L.; grad. Harvard, 1835, A.M., 1838, LL.B., 1839. Removed to Ind., 1841; was pros. atty. for 8 counties (including Indianapolis); raised company and served 14 mos. as capt. 4th Ind. Vols. in Mexican war; apptd. 1850 by Gov. Wright and at next session legislature elected for full term judge court common pleas; apptd. Mar. 17, 1853, chief justice Supreme Court Wash. Ty. by Pres. Pierce, declined renomination 1857, intending to practice law in San Francisco, but received injury to spine from which he did not recover for yrs.; counsel for Hudson Bay Co. in case before Internat. Commn. at Washington, 1865-70; afterward practiced there. Pres. Harvard Soc. of Washington. Address: Washington, D.C. Died 1907.

LANDER, FREDERICK WEST explorer, army officer; b. Salem, Mass., Dec. 17, 1821; s. Edward and Eliza (West) L.; m. Jean Davenport, Oct. 1860. Civil engr. during survey of No. Pacific R.R. route, 1853; headed party of exploration to report on feasibility of railroad from Puget Sound to Mississippi River, 1854; supt., chief engr. overland wagon road, 1855; led or participated in 5 transcontinental surveys; served as aide on Gen. McClellan's staff; commd. brig. gen. U.S. volunteers, 1861; commanded a brigade in Gen. C. P. Stone's div. on Upper Potomac, 1861; wrote patriotic poems during Civil War. Died Va., Mar. 2, 1862.

LANDERS, GEORGE FOREMAN army officer; b. in Md., Aug. 17, 1865; grad. U.S. Mil. Acad., 1887, Arty. Sch., 1892; Army War Coll., 1916. Commd. 2d lt. 4th Arty., June 12, 1887; 1st lt., Nov. 14, 1893; capt. Arty. June 12, 1887; 1st lt., Nov. 14, 1893; capt. Arty. Corps, Feb. 2, 1901; maj., Jan. 25, 1907; lt. col. Coast Arty. Corps, Apr. 1, 1911; col., Nov. 2, 1914. Served in Chicago and vicinity during railroad strikes, 1894; recruiting service, 1897; instr. in chemistry, mineralogy and geology, U.S. Mil. Acad., 1897-1901; dist. ordnance officer, Southern Arty. Dist. of N.Y., 1905-07; dist. comdr., Arty. Dist. of Charleston, S.C., 1908; at Naval War Coll., 1916-17. Died Jan. 23, 1939.

LANDERS, WILBUR NELSON naval officer; b. Boston, Mass., Feb. 15, 1902; s. Dana Wilbur and Jean (Christie) L.; A.B., Harvard, 1921; grad. U.S. Naval Acad., 1925; M.S., Mass. Inst. Tech., 1930; m. Thora Struckmann, Sept. 7, 1926; 1 son, Dana Struckmann. Commd. ensign U.S. Navy, 1925, and advanced through the grades to capt., 1945, served on U.S.S. Utah, 1925-27; apptd. asst. naval contractor, 1928; asst. hull supt., Navy Yard, N.Y. City, 1930-34; asst. design supt. (hull) Norfolk Navy Yard, 1934-39; apptd. naval constr., 1938; asst. superintending constr., Bath Iron Works Corp., 1938-39, asst. design supt. (hull), New York Naval Shipyard, 1938-45, design supt., Apr. 1945-Sept. 1946; ordered home, Nov. 1946. Sec. Society Naval Architects and Marine Engrs. Jan. 1, 1947-64. Dec. 2d Nicaraguan Campaign medal, Am. Defense medal, Am. Theatre ribbon, World War II Victory medal, Sec. of Navy Citation ribbon; mem. British Empire (hon. mem. mil. div.) award. Mem. Am. Soc. Naval Engrs., Soc. Naval Architects and Marine Engrs. (sec.). Assn. Harvard Chemists. Presbyterian. Clubs: University (New York). Home: 257 Milbourne Av., Mamroneck, N.Y. Office: Soc. Naval Architects and Marine Engrs., 74 Trinity Pl., N.Y.C. 6 Died Mar. 25, 1965; buried Mt. Auburn Cemetery, Cambridge, Mass.

LANDIS, HARRY DEWITT judge; b. Sterling, Ill., July 17, 1878; s. Elam Hershey and Alice Narcissa (Eshleman) L.; B.S., U. of Neb., 1899, LL.B., 1901, J.D., 1919; m. Alice Mabel Cattle, June 27, 1907 (died Oct. 2, 1932); children-Harry DeWitt, Walter Elam, John Cattle, Frank Eshleman, Alice Mabel, George Edward. Admitted to Neb. bar, 1901, and practiced at Seward until 1925; mem. Norval Bros., 1919-25; acting county judge, Seward County, 1914-19; judge Dist. Court, 5th Neb. Dist., since 1925. Member Governor's Penal Investigating Committee. State chmn. 4-minute men, chairman Seward County 4-minute Victory speakers, and chmn. War Savings Stamps drive, Seward County, World War; lt. col. Judge Advocate Gen. Res. Regent U. of Neb. since 1917 (pres. bd. 1923, 28); trustee Hastings Coll., U. of Neb. Foundation, dir. Neb. Tuberculosis Assn.; pres. Social Welfare Soc., 1917-20; pres. Neb. Council for Crime Prevention. Mem. Am. and Neb. State bar assns., Res. Officers Assn., Civil Legion, Heroes of '76, Phi Delta Phi, Sigma Chi, Innocents (U. of Neb.), Pi Gamma Mu. Presbyterian. Mason, O.E.S., Odd Fellow, Elk; mem. Sons of Hermann. Clubs: University (Lincoln); Rotary, Sojourners. Home: 34 Lincoln St. Office: Court House, Seward, Neb. Died Apr. 23, 1956; buried Seward.

LANDMAN, ISAAC rabbi, editor; b. Sudikov, Russia, Oct. 24, 1880; s. Louis Hyamson and Ada (Gedaliah) L.; brought to U.S., 1890; B.A., U. of Cincinnati, 1906; rabbi, Hebrew Union Coll., Cincinnati, 1906; post-graduate work, University of Pa.; D.D., Hebrew Union College, 1943; m. Beatrice Eschuer, Sept. 3, 1913; children-Amos, David, Louise. Asst. rabbi Temple Keneseth Israel, Philadelphia, 1906-16; rabbi Temple Israel, Far Rockaway, N.Y., 1917-28; editor American Hebrew, 1918-37; rabbi Congregation Beth Elohim, Brooklyn, since 1931. Organized religious services among Jewish men on Mexican border, 1916; 1st rabbi chaplain in U.S. Army on foreign soil (Mexico), 1916; organized sch. for training Jewish workers in U.S. forces at home and abroad, for Jewish Welfare Bd., 1917. Exec. sec. Nat. Farm Sch., 1906-16; corr. sec. Central Conf. Am. Rabbis, 1915-17, mem. exec. com., 1915-18;

chmn. Jewish Welfare Bd. of the Rockaways, 1918; sec. Isaac M. Wise Centenary Fund, Union of Am. Hebrew Congregations in N.Y., 1919; sec. N.Y. Exec. Com. of Am. Hebrew Congs., 1919-30; rep. Union of Am. Hebrew Congregations and Central Conf. Am. Rabbis at Peach Conf., Paris, to introduce clause for universal religious liberty into Covenant of League of Nations, 1919; launched movement of good will and better understanding between Christians and Jews, 1920; del. Central Conf. Am. Rabbis at World Union for Progressive Judaism, London, 1926; organized Permanent Commn. on Better Understanding among Catholics, Protestants and Jews in America,1927; presided at good-will conf. at the Palace of the Bishop of Tobasco, Mexico City, 1927; editor in chief Universal Jewish Encyclopedia, 1928-43. Founder Academy for Adult Jewish Education, Brooklyn, N.U., 1931; organizer annual Institutes on Judaism for Christian Clergymen since 1935; founder of farmer colony of Jews, Utah, 1911. Mem. con. on Jewish Edn. of Union of Am. Hebrew Congregations, 1943; mem. Central Conf. Am. Rabbis, Am. Oriental Soc., New York Bd. Jewish Ministers, Assn. Reform Rabbis, Am. Acad. for Jewish Research, Jewish Hist. Soc., Religious Edn. Assn. of U.S. and Can. (v.p. 1932-39; mem. bd. dirs. since 1932), N.Y. Alumni of U. of Cincinnati (pres. 1933-34). Mason. Author: Moses Hyam Luzatto, First Hebrew Playwright, 1907; Stories of the Prophets, 1912; A Course of Instruction for Jewish Religious Schools, 1921; Christian and Jew - A Symposium on Better Understanding, 1929; Status of Adult Jewish Education, 1931; the Average Man and the Bible, 1916; (play) Man of Honor; also other plays (with brother, Dr. Michael L.). Compiler of Prayer Book for Jewish Soldiers, 1916. Address: 50 Plaza St., Brooklyn, N.Y.* Died Sep. 3, 1946.

LANDON, CHARLES RAEBURNE, air force officer; b. Auburn, Ill., May 4, 1900; s. Charles and Margaret Alberta (Wyatt) L.; B.S., U.S. Mil. Acad., 1924; student Inf. Sch., 1927-28, Tank Sch., 1928-29, Command and Gen. Staff Sch., 1935-36; m. M. Elizabeth Shufflebarger, Nov. 19, 1929; children—Frances Elizabeth, Charles Raeburne. Pvt., later corpl. U.S. Marine Corps, 1918-19; Inf., U.S. Army, 1924-35; Adj. Gen. Dept., 1936-49; assigned duty with Air Force, Air Def. Command, 1946; trans. to Air Force, 1949; dir. Statis. Services since 1950; promoted through grades to maj. gen. Decorated Legion of Merit, Bronze Star, Commendation Medal, Marine Corps Good Conduct, Victory Medal (2). Am. Def. with star, Am. Theatre, E.T.O. with five stars, Occupation medal (U.S.); Officer Coronne de Chene, Croix de Guerre (Luxembourg); Officer Order Brit. Empire (Gt. Britian); Legion of Honor, Croix de Guerre with palm (France); Officer Order of Leopold with palm, Croix de Guerre with palm (Belgium); War Cross (Czechoslovakia). Mem. Nat. Sojourners, Am. Legion. Mason. Home: Arlington VA Died Sept. 1970.

LANDON, THOMAS DURLAND educator; b. Belvidere, N.J., May 18, 1865; s. Rev. Thompson Hoadley (D.D.) and Sarah (Durland) L.; ed. Centenary Collegiate Inst., Hackettstown, N.J.; Wesleyan Acad., Wilbraham, Mass.; Field Officers' Sch., Fort Sam Houston, Tex.; Army Sch. of the Line, Langres, France; m. Margaret Adams Reese, June 29, 1892. Began, 1885, as asst. to father, Bordentown Mil. Inst., now propr. and pres. Enlisted as pvt. Co. A, 6th Inf. N.G. N.J., Dec. 3, 1885; promoted through grades to col., 1913; capt. and maj. 3d N.J. Inf., Spanish-Am, War, 1898; col. in World War, 3d N.J. Inf., 114th Inf., A.E.F.; comdt. Base Training Schs., 41st Div., and comdr. 163d Inf.; hon. discharged Mar. 11, 1919; col. comdg. 309th Inf., O.R.C.; commd. brevet brig. gen. (Ret.), Nat. Guard N.J., 1933. Decorated Officer Order of Black Star, by President of France, 1919. Republican. Home: Bordentown, N.J. Died Oct. 29, 1934.

LANDRUM, WILLIAM WARREN clergyman; b. Macon, Ga., Jan. 18, 1853; s. Sylvanus (D.D.) and Eliza (Warren) L.; Mercer U., Macon, Ga.; A.B., Brown U., 1872; grad. Southern Bapt. Theol. Sem., Louisville, Ky., 1874; D.D., Washington and Lee, 1875; m. Lottie Baylor, July 15, 1868; children-Grace Warren, Margaret L. (Mrs. F. Watkins), Eliza Marshall (Mrs. Fitzhugh Scott), Baylor, Ida D. (Mrs. W. G. McGowan), Mary K. (Mrs. Stanley B. Johnson). Ordained Bat. ministry, 1874; pastor Shrevport, La., 1874-76, 1st Ch., Augusta, Ga., 1876-82; 2d Ch., Richmond, Va., 1882-96, 1st Ch., Atlanta, Ga., and Broadway Ch., Louisville, Ky.; prof. philosophy, Bethel College, Russellville, Ky. Served as capt. and chaplain 1st Regt. Cav. Ga. N.G.; brig. gen. Ky. Div. United Boys' Brigades of America. Trustee Southern Bapt. Theol. Sem. Pres. Home Mission Bd. of Southern Bapt. Conv.; sec. Bapt. Edn. Soc. of Ky.; mem. exec. com. Bapt. World Alliance; pres. Bapt. Edn. Commn. of Ga. Democrat. Mason. Author: Use and Abuse of the Baptist Message; Settled in the Sanctuary, 1925. Home: Russellville, Ky. Deceased.

LANE, CLARENCE GUY physician; b. Billerica, Mass., Oct. 21, 1882; s. Albert Clarence and Estella Josephine (David) L.; A.B., Harvard, 1905, M.D., 1908; m. Mary Rivers McHarry, May 31, 1919; 1 son, Robert. Intern Worcester City Hosp., 1908-10; in gen. practice, Woburn, Mass., 1910-14; specializing in dermatology, Boston, 1914—; mem. dept. dermatology Mass. Gen. Hosp., 1920-47, chief of dept., 1936-47, teaching in dept. dermatology Harvard Med. Sch., 1922-47, head of dept., 1936-47; clin. prof. dermatology, 1939-47, emeritus, 1947—. On editorial bd. N.E. Jour. of Medicine, Archives of Dermatology and Syphilology; cons. in dermatology at a number of hosps. Served from lt. to capt. M.C., U.S. Army, 1918-19. Awarded Cutter medal, Phi Rho Sigma, 1948. Mem. A.M.A. (mem. council on planning and chemistry), Am. Bd. Dermatology and Syphilology (dir. and sec., 1932-43; pres. 1944-45; sec. Adv. Bd. for Med. Specialties 1941-43), Nat. Com. on Indsl. Dermatoses, Am. Dermatol. Assn. (dir. 1927-35, pres. 1935, sec. 1925-30), N.E. Dermatol. Soc., N.Y. Acad. of Medicine. Republican. Protestant. Mason (K.T., Shriner). Clubs: Harvard (Boston); Faculty. Editor: Vol. X of Practitioners Medical Library, 1935; contbr. about 70 articles to med. jours. Lecturer on dermatology A.M.A., 1949. Home: 220 Marlborough St., Boston. Died Mar. 12, 1954; buried Mt. Auburn Cemetery, Cambridge, Mass.

LANE, RUFUS HERMAN officer U.S.M.C.; b. Bellatre, O., Oct. 31, 1870; grad. U.S. Naval Acad., 1891. Commd. 2d lt. U.S.M.C., July 1, 1893; promoted through grades to adjutant and inspection with rank of brig. gen., Jan. 2, 1936. Served on New York during Spansih-Am. War, 1898; asst. adj. and insp. Marine Corps at hdqrs., Washington, D.C., 1903-04; adj. and insp. 1st Brigade Marines, Manila, P.I., 1906; in charge office of asst. adj. insp., San Francisco, 1908; acting asst. q.m. in charge of office at San Francisco, 1908; duty at hdqrs., Washington, D.C., 1914; apptd. adj. gen. 2d Provisional brigade of Marines, Santo Domingo, 1916; apptd. to administer affairs of Dept. of Foreign Relations,and of Justice and Pub. Instrn., Dominican Republic, 1917; mem. staff of mil. gov. of Santo Domingo, 1918 to 1920; was head of Adj. and Insp. Dept., U.S. Marine Corps; retired. Nov. 1, 1934. Address: Falls Church, Va.* Died Apr. 20, 1948.

LANE, WALTER PAYE army officer; b. County Cork, Ireland, Feb. 18, 1817; s. William and Oliva Lane. Came with family to U.S., 1821, went to Tex., 1835; fought under Sam Houston in Tex. War for Independence, 1836; fought against Indians in Tex., privateer in Gulf of Mexico; served as capt. under Gen. Zachary Taylor in No. Mexico, under Gen. Winfield Scott at Battle of Veracruz, Mexican War, 1846; mined for gold in Cal., Nev. Ariz., Peru; served as lt. col. 3d Tex. Cavalry in battles around Bentonville (Ark.) during Civil War; participated also in Atchafalya Raid, conflicts at Fort Defiance, Donaldsonville, LaFourche, Berbeaux, under Gen. Richard Taylor in No. La., 1864; rose to brig. gen. Confederate Army. Died Marshall, Tex., Jan. 28, 1892.

LANE, WILLIAM PRESTON, JR. ex-gov.; b. Hagerstown, Md., May 12, 1892; s. William Preston and Virginia Lee (Cartwright) L.; B.L., U. Va., 1915; LL.D., U. Md., 1947; m. Dorothy Byron, Jan. 17, 1922; children-Dorothy Byron (Mrs. Campbell), Jean Cartwright (Mrs. Goddard). Admitted to Md. bar, 1916; atty. gen. Md., 1930-34; became pres. Herald-Mail Co., 1923; dir. Fairchild Engine & Airplane Corp. Gov., Md., 1947-51. Mem. Pres.' Com. White House Conf. Edn. Mem. bd. visitors U.S. Naval Acad., 1948-49; mem. bd. mgrs. Council State Govts. Trustee Johns Hopkins Hosp. Served as capt., later maj. and asst. div. advj., 29th Div., U.S. Army, World War; received Silver Star decoration. Del. to Dem. Nat. Conv., Houston, 1928. Chgo., 1932, 1940-44, Phila., 1948; presdl. elector from Md., 1936; Dem. Nat. committeeman for Md., 1940-50. Chmn., So. Gov.'s Conf., 1947; chmn. Nat. Gov's. Conf., 1948; pres. Council of State Govts., 1948. Episcopalian. Clubs: Brook, Blind Brook (N.Y.C.); Md., Merchants, University, Elkridge (Balt.); Nat. Press (Washington). Home: 943 The Terrace, Office: Herald-Mail Co., Hagerstown, Md. Died Feb. 7, 1967; buried Rose Hill Cemetery, Hagerstown.

LANG, ARTHUR H., fgn. service officer; b. N.Y.C., Sept. 17, 1909; s. Louis and Jennie (Huler) L.; B.S. in Mech. Engring., Tri-State Coll., Angola, Ind., 1931; grad. work sch. and pub. adminstrn., Temple U., 1938-41, Yale, 1933-37; m. Sarah Stamm, November 1932 (divorced July 1941); one son, D. Baer; married second, Dorothy A. Hart, September 23, 1949; children—Jennie H., Louis H. With New Haven Bd. Edn., 1932-37, Del. Bd. Edn., 1937-41, U.S. Department Interior, 1941-42, War Manpower Commn., 1942; chief job skills tng., indsl. personnel div., Army Service Forces, Army Dept., 1942-44; regional coordinator Office Chief Ordnance, U.S. Army, 1944-46; chief orgn. and methods div. War Assets Adminstrn., 1947-48; dir. div. adminstrn. NLRB, 1948-58; pub. adminstrn. adviser U.S. Operations Mission to Afghanistan, Kabul, 1959-61; chief pub. services div. U.S. Operations Mission to Korea, Seoul, 1961-63; spl. asst. to chmn. NLRB, Washington, 1963-64; mgmt. cons. to Pres.'s Com. on Equal Employment Opportunity, 1963-64; dir. office mgmt. systems Manpower Adminstrn., U.S. Dept. Labor, Washington, 1964-71; mgmt. adviser Office of Gov. S.C., Columbia, 1971-72. Recipient award Pres. South Korea, 1963; Distinguished Achievement award U.S. Sec. Labor. Mem. Am. Soc. Pub. Adminstrn., Internat. Assn. Machinists, Am. Acad. Polit. and Social Sci. Lion, Elk. Author state and govt. publs. Home: Lexington SC Died July 9, 1972.

LANGDON, LOOMIS LYMAN army officer; b. Buffalo, N.Y., Oct. 25, 1830; s. George W. and Sarah (Russell) L.; pub. and pvt. schs. and grad. U.S. Mil. Acad., 1854. Bvt. 2d lt. 4th Arty., July 1, 1854; 2d lt. 1st Arty., Aug. 31, 1854; 1st lt., July 13, 1860; capt. Aug. 28, 1861; maj. 2d Arty., Mar. 20, 1879; lt. col., Dec. 1, 1883; col. 1st Arty., Jan. 25, 1889; retired by operation of law, Oct. 25, 1894; advanced to rank of brig. gen. retired, by act of Apr. 23, 1904. Bvtd. maj., Feb. 20, 1864, for gallant and meritorious services in battle of Olustee, Fla.; lt. col., Sept. 29, 1864, for same in attack on Ft. Gilmer, Va. Occasional corr. for newspapers; studied painting, Nat. Gallery, London, 1903-04. Author of sketches, stories, etc. Address: Brooklyn, N.Y. Died 1910.

LANGDON, RUSSELL (CREAMER), army officer (ret.); b. Brooklyn, N.Y., June 20, 1872; s. Brig. Gen. Loomis Lyman and Hattie Molleson (Creamer) L.; B.S., U.S. Mil. Acad., West Point, N.Y., 1896; Army Sch. of the Line, Ft. Leavenworth, Kan., 1908, Army Signal Sch., Ft. Leavenworth, 1909, Army War Coll., Washington, D.C., 1922; m. Adria Maude Semple, Apr. 10, 1907 (dec. Oct. 13, 1947); 1 step-son, Comdr. Eduard-Semple Moale; married 2d, Lois Alene Demorest, November 19, 1950. Commd. 2d lt. U.S. Army, 1896, and advanced through grades to col., 1936; served in campaign against Santiago de Cuba, Spanish Am. War, 1898, Philippine Insurrection, 1899-1901; inf. officer, 1st, 2d and 32d divs., World War I; prof. mil. sci. and tactics, N.Y. Univ., 1925-28; assigned to office of adj. gen., Washington, D.C., 1919-21; advanced to brig. gen. by spl. act. of Congress, 1940; liaison between bd. of edn. of city N.Y. and Armed Services, war industries training program for nat. defense, World War II. Awarded commendation for organizing native municipal govt. in Pueblo de Bulacan and for influence with natives during Philippine Insurrection, 1899-1901; distinguished service cross, distinguished service medal, silver star with oak leaf cluster, N.Y. state conspicuous service cross, Officer of the Legion of Honor (France), Croix de Guerre with Palm, Croix de Guerre with Gilt Star. Mem. Am. Legion, United Spanish War Vets., Army and Navy Legion of Valor U.S. Independent. Conglist. Club: Army and Navy (Washington). Author articles in field. Home: 12 W. 95th St., New York City

LANGFITT, WILLIAM CAMPBELL army officer; b. Wellsburg, Va., Aug. 10, 1860; s. Obadiah and Virginia (Tarr) L.; grad. U.S. Mil. Acad., 1883, Engr. Sch. of Application, Willetts Point,N.Y., 1886; m. Anne St. John Bemis, Dec. 4, 1886; 1 dau., Dorothy. Commd. 2d lt. engrs., June 13, 1883; brig. gen. N.A., Aug. 5, 1917; maj. gen. N.A., Dec. 17, 1917; major gen. U.S.A., retired, June 21, 1930. Engr. office Dept. of Columbia, 1886-88; river and harbor improvements, Galveston, Tex., 1888-93; improvement of Ohio River and tributaries, 1893-95; instr. Engr. Sch., 1895-98; comd.U.S. forces in H.L. 1898-99; in charge river and harbor improvements, defenses, and engr. 13th Light House Dist., Portland, Ore., 1899-1905; comdr. Engr. Sch. and Depot, Washington Barracks, D.C., 1905-06 and 1907-10; chief engr. Army of Cuban Pacification, 1906-07; river and harbor improvements and water supply, Washington, D.C., 1910-14; river and harbor improvements and div. engr., S.E. Div., Savannah, Ga., 1914-16; chief engr. officer, Southern Dept., including ry. operations, 1916-17; organized 13th Engrs., May-Aug. 1917; joined A.E.F. in France, Aug.1917; chief of staff, Aug. 24, 1917; apptd. mgr. light rys., Sept. 14, 1917; in charge of all Am. forces on duty with British Army, Oct. 15, 1917; chief of utilities, in charge of transportation, Dept.of Constrn. and Forestry, Dept. of Light Rys, and Roads, and Motor Transportation Dept., Mar. 12, 1918; chief engr. A.E.F., in charge of mil. engring. and engr. supplies, constrn. and forestry, light rys. and roads, July 10, 1918; dist. engr., 2d N.Y. Dist. and Puerto Rico Dist., Aug. 5, 1919; div. engr., N.E. Div., N.Y. City, Aug. 14, 1919-20. D.S.M. (U.S.); Comdr. Legion of Honor (French); Companion Most Honorable Order of the Bath (English); Comdr. Order of Crown (Belgian). Home: Geneva, N.Y. Died Apr. 20, 1934.

LANGFORD, MALCOLM SPARHAWK lawyer; b. Jackson, Mich., Apr. 19, 1906; s. Theron Sparhawk and Katreena Stewart (MacLean) L.; B.A., Amherst Coll., 1927; J.D., U. Mich., 1930; m. Marian Samson Whaley, June 1, 1935; children-Malcolm Sparhawk, Stephen Arthur, Stewart MacLean. Admitted to N.Y. bar, 1932, D.C. bar, 1946; asso. Cadwalader, Wickersham & Taft, N.Y.C., 1930-42; staff gen. counsel Office Lend-Lease Adminstrn., Washington, 1942-43; mem. Cox Langford, Stoddard & Cutler, Washington, 1946-. Mem. Washington Home Rule Com., Inc. Bd. govs. Middle East Inst., Washington, 1951-60, secretary, 1953-60, life member; trustee and secretary George C. Keiser Foundation, Washington. Served from lt. to lt. commander USNR, air combat intelligence officer, 1943-46. Mem. Am., D.C., City N.Y. bar assns., Am. Judicature Soc., Amherst Alumni Assn. of Washington, Washington Fgn. Law Soc., Am. Austrian Soc., Psi Upsilon, Phi Beta Kappa, Phi Delta Phi, Order of Coif. Episcopalian. Clubs: National Aviation, Univ. Mich. Home: 3754 Jenifer St., Washington 15. Office: 1625 Eye St., Washington 6. Died Nov. 18, 1962; buried Arlington Nat. Cemetery.

LANGHORNE, GEORGE TAYLOE army officer; b. Henry County, Ky., July 5, 1867; s. John Deval and Anne Catherine (Tayloe) L.; grad. U.S. Mil. Acad., 1885, Army War Coll., 1913. Commd. add. 2d lt. 5th Cav., Sept. 1, 1885; 2d lt. 3d Cav., Aug. 31, 1889; 1st lt. Dec. 11, 1896; served as capt. 27th vols. and maj. 39th vols., Spanish-Am. War; promoted through various grades in regular army to col., June 22, 1917. Served in Tex., until 1893; a.d.c. to Gen. Wheaton, 1893-97; mil. attaché U.S. Legation, Brussels, Belgium, 1897-98; a.d.c. to Gen. Davis, Puerto Rico, May-Oct., 1899; in Philippines with regt., Aug., 1899-1901; again in Philippines, 1902-08; participated in Lake Lanas Expdn., Jolo Campaign; acting gov. Maro Province 18 mos.; accompanied Gen. Wood to Switzerland, France, Germany and Spain, 1908; mil. attaché Am. Embassy, Berlin, 1913-15; duty in Tex. and on Mexican border. Medals for Spanish-Am. War, Philippine Insurrection, Mexican border campaigns. Decorated Legion of Honor, France. Mem. Sigma Chi. Clubs: University, Metropolitan. Army and Navy, Chevey Chase, Riding and Hunt (Washington); Army and Navy of America (N.Y.C.); Casino, University, Tavern (Chgo.). Address: 1120 Lake Shore Dr., Chgo. Died Jan. 25, 1962.

LANGLEY, JAMES MCLELLAN, publisher; b. Hyde Park (Boston), Mass., Oct. 11, 1894; s. Frank Elmer and Mary Bradford (McLellan) L.; grad. high sch., Barre, Vt., 1913; B.S., Dartmouth Coll., 1918; m. Florence May Granger, July 1, 1918; children—James M., Joyce; m. 2d, Lois Hammond, June 29, 1947; children—Jane, Jeremy, Jill. Pub., Concord Monitor, N.H. Patriot, 1923-61, editor, 1961-68; ambassador to Pakistan, 1957-59. Chmn. U.S. delegation Philippine Trade Negotiations, 1954. Chmn. N.H. Planning and Development Commn., 1934-41; pres. Concord Hosp. 1944-50. Served as captain, inf., U.S. Army, World War. Mem. N.H. Constl. Conv., 1930, 38, 41, 56; pres. N.H.-Vt. Hospitalization Service, 1942-57. Independent Republican. Home: Concord NH Died June 23, 1968; cremated.

LANGLIE, ARTHUR BERNARD ex-gov. Wash.; b. Lanesboro, Minn., July 25, 1900; s. Bjarne Alfred and Carrie (Dahl) L.; B.A., LL.B., U. Wash., 1926; LL.D. (hon.), Whitman Coll., Walla Walla, Wash., 9142, Seattle Pacific Coll., 1942, Pacific Luth. Coll., 1955; D.Sc. in Govt. (hon.), Coll. Puget Sound, 1952; L.H.D., Dickinson Coll., 1958; d. Pub. Services, Bethany W.Va. Coll., 1964; m. Evelyn P. Baker, Sept. 15, 1928; children-Arthur Sheridan, Carrie Ellen (Mrs. John R. Vasko, Junior). Admitted Wash. bar, 1926; in practice with Shank, Balt & Rode, Seattle, 1926-35; city councilman, Seattle, 1935-38; mayor, City of Seattle, 1938-41; elected gov. State of Wash., Nov. 1940, inaugurated Jan. 1941. Sr. mem. law firm Langlie, Todd & Nickell, 1946-48; gov. State Wash., 1941-45, 49-57; pres., chief exec. officer McCall Corp., 1957-61, chmn. bd., 1961-65, dir., 1965-66 U.S. del. ILO Conf., Geneva, Switzerland, 1954; mem. Pres.' Com. Traffic Safety, 1955; chmn. Nat. Gov.'s Conf., 1955-56, Pacific N.W. Gov.'s Power Policy Com., 1956; mem. Nat. Civil Def. Adv. Council, 1954-58; exec. com. Atty. Gen.'s Conf. on Ct. Congestion and Delay in Litigation, 1956. Lt. (J.g.) USNR, 1937-, lt. active duty USN, 1945-. Decorated royal Order of St. Olaf (Norway); Grand Officer Order of Merit (Italy). Recipient Salvation Army Order of Distinguished Aux. Service award, 1962; grand officier de l'Ordre de la Couronne de Chene, Luxembourg; Silver Antelope award, 1951. Mem. Royal Arcanum, Am. Legion, Vets. fgn. Wars, Council State Govts. (pres. 1956), Nat. Com. Development Scientists and Engrs., Nat. Municipal League (v.p.), Phi Kappa Sigma, Phi Alpha Delt. Republican. Presbyn. Clubs: Seattle Golf; Rainier of Seattle Home: 1100 University St., Seattle 98101 Died July 24, 1966.

LANGMUIR, DEAN investment counsel; b. Elmsford, N.Y., June 18, 1886; s. Charles and Sadie (Comings) L.; graduated De Witt Clinton High Sch., N.Y. City, 1904; A.B., Williams Coll., 1910 (Clark prize scholarship); m. Ethel M.Ivimey, 1911 (dec. 1945); children-Robert Vose, Evelyn; m. 2d Mary Shattuck Fisher, 1946. Accountant for Western Electric Co., 1910-11; dept. comptroller City of Schenectady, N.Y., 1912; expert accountant N.Y. Pub. Service Commn., 1912-16, New Republic, 1914-15; field investigations of corps. for banking interests, 1916-21; with Irving Trust Co., and other banks, liquidating and administering various corps., 1921-22; with Equitable Trust Co. of New York, 1922-26; in charge research, Scudder, Stevens & Clark, 1926-28; with Lazard Freres, 1929-30; v.p. in charge of research, Distributors Group, Ind., 1930-33; own investment counsel practice since 1933; trustee in liquidation Reynolds Realization Corp., pres. 1943-45; executor Estate Lester N, Hofheimer since 1943. Served as maj. U.S. Army Signal Corps.; also B America (gov. 1940-46), Nat. Indsl. Conf. Bd., N.Y. Chamber Commerce, N.Y. Security Analysts, Menninger Foundation; Soc. of New York Hosp., Phi Beta Kappa, Phi Gamma Delta. Clubs: Players, University, India House, Am. Alpine, Appalachian Mountain. Contbr. to financial publs. Home: 148 E. 48th St. Office: 90 Broad St.,New St., New York, N.Y. Died Jan. 8, 1950.

LANING, HARRIS naval officer; b. Petersburg, Ill., Oct. 18, 1873; s. Caleb Barrett and Mary Esther (Harris) L.; prep. edn., Peekskill Mil. Acad.; grad. U.S. Naval Acad., 1895; m. Mabel Clare Nixon, July 24, 1900; 1 dau., Hester Marie. Commd. ensign, U.S.N., May 19, 1891; advanced through grades to rear adm. Served on U.S.S. Philadelphia, Oregon and Mohlean, 1895-98; served on U.S.S. Monadnock and comdr. U.S.S. Panay, Philippine Insurrection; with dept. English and law, U.S. Naval Acad., 1900-02; on U.S.S. Dolphin, 1902-05; in dept. ordnance and gunnery U.S. Naval Acad., 1905-07; navigation officer U.S.S. Nebraska in cruise around world with Battle Fleet, 1907-10; in charge athletics and head of dept. of navigation, U.S. Naval Acad., 1910-13; comdr. U.S.S. Cassin and Reserve Destroyer Flotilla, 1913-16; with chief of Naval Operations, later in charge officer personnel div., Bureau of Navigation, asst. chief of bureau and acting chief, World War; chief of staff, Destroyer Force, U.S. Fleet, 1919-21; student, later head of dept. of tactics, Naval War Coll., 1921-24; comdr. U.S.S. Pennsylvania, 1924-26, U.S. Naval Training Sta., San Diego, Calif., 1926-27; appt. apptd. chief of staff, U.S. Battle Fleet, 1927; comdr. Battleship Div., Two, U.S. Fleet, 1928-30; pres. U.S. Naval Training Sta., San Diego, Calif., 1926-27; apptd. chief of staff, U.S. Battle Fleet, 1927; comdr. Battleship Div. Two, U.S. Fleet, 1928-30; pres. U.S. Naval War Coll., 1930-33; comdr. cruisers, U.S. Fleet, with rank of vice admiral, 1933-35, comdr. Battle Force, with rank of admiral, 1935-36; comdt. Third Naval Dist. and comdt. United States Navy Yard, New York, 1936-37; retired, 1937; gov. U.S. Naval Home, Phila., 1937-. Decorated with Navy D.S.C.; campaign medals, Spanish-Am. War, Philippine Campaign, China Relief Expdn., Mexican Campaign, Dominican Campaign, World War (all U.S.); Order of Avis (Portugal); gold medal, as capt. of the United States Rifle Team winning first place in the Olympic Games, Stockholm, 1912. Episcopalian. Mason. Home: Petersburg, Ill. Died Feb. 2, 1941.

LANING, R(ICHARD) H(ENRY) ret. naval officer;, Physician; b. Osaka, Japan (of Am. parents), Sept. 25, 1883; s. Henry and Belle Tevis (Michie) L.; A.B., Kenyon Coll., 1904; M.D., U. of Mich., 1908; m. Marguerite Comegys Boyer, Feb. 5, 1917; children-Richard Boyer, Virginia Belle (Mrs. Edward Dominic Hogg), Robert Comegys, George Henry, Edward Arthur. Intern and resident, Northern Pacific Hosp., 1908-10; asst. health officer, Peiree Co. (Wash. state), 1910-11. Entered U.S. Army as med. officer, rank of lt. (j.g.), 1911, and advanced through grades to rear adm., 1943; pub. health officer, Dept. of North, Haiti, 1922-26; comdg. officer, U.S. Naval Hosp., Charleston, S.C., 1926-29; chief of surg., U.S. Naval Hosp. Ship Relief, 1929-31, U.S. Naval Hosp., Mare Island, Calif., 1931-35; med. officer of several ships; chief surgeon, U.S. Naval Hosp., San Diego, Calif., 1938-39; exec. officer U.S. Naval Hosp., Portsmouth, Va., 1939-41; naval observer, Iceland and United Kingdom, 1941-42; comdg. officer, U.S. Naval Hosp., Phila., 1942-43; dist. med. officer, 1st Naval Dist., 1943-44, 3d Naval Dist., 1945, 12 th Naval Dist., 1945-46; insp. Med. Dept. activities, Pacific Ocean areas, 1944-45; retired, 1946; health officer, Amherst-Nelson health dist., 1947-56. Fellow A.M.A., Am. Coll. Surgeons, Am. Public Health Assn.; mem. Acacia, Phi Beta Kappa, Alpha Kappa Kappa. Episcopalian. Home: Amherst, Va. Died Apr. 9, 1963; buried Arlington Nat. Cemetery.

LANKERSHIM, JAMES BOON capitalist; b. on farm nr. St. Louis, Mar. 24, 1850; s. Isaac and Annis Lydia (Moore) L.; family removed to Cal., 1854; ed. pub. schs. San Francisco; m. Caroline Jones, of Los Angeles, 1881. Engaged in stock-raising and grain growing; acquired 44,000 acres of land, and organized Los Angeles Farming & Milling Co.; erected the Lankershim office building, Los Angeles, 1898; pres. Main Street Savings Bank, Los Angeles, 1886-1900; owner Hotel Lankershim, Los Angeles. Retired from active business, 1900. Was organizer, 1897, and capt. Los Angeles Cav. Troop; lt.-col. on staff gov. Cal., 1900, 32ff Mason. Clubs: California (Los Angeles). Bohemian, Union League (San Francisco). Address: Lankershim Bldg., Los Angeles, Cal.

LANMAN, JOSEPH naval officer; b. Norwich, Conn., July 11, 1811; s. Peter and Abigail (Trumbull) L.; m. Ann Williams, Sept. 20, 1842; 4 children. Commd. midshipman, U.S. Navy, 1825, lt., 1835, served in Pacific Squadron, 1847-48, commd. comdr. 1855, commodore, 1862; comdr. Washington Navy Yard, 1855-56. In command steam frigate Minnesota, 1864; joined N. Atlantic Blockading Squadron; commd. rear adm., 1867; head Portsmouth Navy Yard, 1867-69; in command of South Atlantic Squadron, 1869-71. Died Norwich, Mar. 13, 1874.

LANNEAU, JOHN FRANCIS college prof.; b. Charleston, S.C., Feb. 7, 1836; s. Charles Henry and Sophia (Stephens) L.; grad. S.C. Mil. Acad., Charleston, 1856; A.M., Baylor U., Waco, Texas, 1869; (LL.D., Furman University, S.C., 1915); m. Louise Skinner Cox, of Greenville, S.C., 1869. Tutor mathematics, 1857, prof. physics and chemistry, 1858-61, Furman U., Greenville, S.C.; capt. cav., then lt. and capt. engrs., 1861-64; teacher pvt. sch., 1865; prof. mathematics and astronomy, Furman U., 1866-68; prof. mathematics, William Jewell Coll., Mo., 1869-73; pres. Alabama Central Female Coll., Tuscaloosa, 1873-79, Bapt. Female Coll., Lexington, Mo., 1879-88, Pierce City Bapt. Coll., Mo., 1888-90; prof. physics and applied mathematics, 1890-99; applied mathematics and astronomy since 1899, Wake Forest Coll., N.C. Mem. N.C. Acad. Science, N.C. Nature Study Soc., Astron. Soc. Pacific. Invented, 1907, the cosmoid (a model of the celestial sphere, easily adjusted to illustrate astron. conceptions and motions). Address: Wake Forest, N.C.

LANNON, JAMES PATRICK naval officer (ret.); b. Alexandria, Va.; Oct. 12, 1878; s. John and Johanna Valentine (Reddy) L.; B.S., U.S. Naval Acad., 1902; Commd. ensign U.S. Navy, 1904, advanced through grades to rear adm., 1942; served at sea and shore stas., U.S., Europe, Asia, 1902-45; ret. from active service, 1937. Awarded Congressional Medal of Honor, Navy Cross, Purple Heart, Navy War Cross (Italy). Roman Catholic. Address: Chevy Chase Club, Chevy Chase 15, Md. Died Mar. 13, 1953; buried Arlington Cemetery.

LANTAFF, WILLIAM C. (BILL), ex-congressman; b. Buffalo, July 31, 1913; s. Walter R. and Charmaine (Brooks) L.; A.B., U. of Fla., 1934, LL.B., 1936; m. Betty Wilcox, May 11, 1938; children—W. Courtland, Kent, Cathy. Admitted to Fla. bar, 1936, and practiced in Miami, 1936-41, and 1945-70; member firm Walton, Lantaff, Schroeder, Carson & Wahl; city judge, Miami Beach, 1938; mem. Fla. State Legislature, 1946-50; mem. 82d-83d Congresses, 4th Dist., Fla.; dir. City National Bank of Miami. Entered Armed Services as 1st lt., Fla. N.G., 1941; service with Gen. Staff Corps; disch. to res. as lt. col., 1945; asst. chief of staff G/2, 51st Inf. Div., Fla. N.G., 1945-50; col. M.I. Div., Dept. Army. Pres. Dade County Community Chest 1957, chmn. drive, 1955-56; president Orange Bowl Committee, 1967; president United Fund, 1962, chmn. bd., 1963; chairman board Dade Foundation, 1967, 68. Delegate Democratic Nat. Conv., 1956, 60; pres. Dade Co. Young Dems., 1947-48. Elected 1 of 5 outstanding citizens Fla. by C. of C., 1948. Mem. Am. Legion, Mil. Order World Wars, Am., Fla., Dade County bar assns., Miami Beach Jr. C. of C. (pres. 1938), Phi Alpha Delta, Phi Kappa Tau. Mason (Shriner, Jester). Clubs: Metropolitan (Washington); Lions, Miami (gov. 1964), Country Miami. Home: Miami Springs FL Died 1970.

LANZA, ANTHONY JOSEPH physician; b. N.Y.C., Mar. 8, 1884; s. Manfredi and Clara (Hammond) L.; M.D., George Washington U., 1906; m. Laura Kate Thomas, Nov. 18, 1913; children-Mary Bianca (Mrs. W. Gregory Maue, Jr.), Elizabeth (Mrs. Gordon H. Felton). With USPHS, 1907-20; spl. staff mem. Rockefeller Found., adviser to Commonwealth Govt. of Australia on indsl. hygiene, 1921-24; exec. sec. Nat. Health Council, N.Y.C., 1924-26; asso. med. dir. Met. Life Ins. Co., 1926-49; chmn. Inst. Indsl. Med., Bellevue Med. Center; prof. indsl. medicine, 1947-54, prof. emeritus, 1954-64. Chief surgeon U.S. Bur. Mines, 1914-19; 1954-64. Chief surgeon U.S. Bur. Mines, 1914-19; med. cons. Gen. Motors Corp., 1931-32. Served as sr. surgeon in charge indsl. hygiene USPHS, during World War I; col. M.C., AUS, 1942-45; dir. div. occupational health, preventive medicine service Office of Surgeon Gen. Decorated Legion of Merit. Recipient Adolph Kammer Merit-in-Authorship award Indsl. Med. Assn. Trustee Trudeau Found., N.Y. U. Mem. A.M.A. (mem. council on indsl. health), N.Y. Acad. Medicine (chmn. com. on indsl. health), Am. Pub. Health Assn., Nat. Tb Assn., Am. Social Hygiene Assn., N.Y. to and Health Assn., Kappa Sigma, Alpha Kappa Kappa, Sigma Xi. Clubs: Cosmos (Washington); Sleepy Hollow Country (N.Y.). Editor: Siliconsis and Asbestosis, 1938; Industrial Hygiene (with Jacob Goldberg), 1939; The Pneumoconioses, 1963; editor-in-chief Modern Monographs in Industrial Medicine; adv. editorial bd. History of Preventive Medicine in World War II. Contbr. articles on indsl. medicine and hygiene to med. publs. Establishment by N.Y. U. of Anthony J. Lanza Research Labs., 1964. Home: 441 E. 20th St., N.Y.C. 16. Office: 550 1st Av., N.Y.C. 16. Died Mar. 23, 1964; buried Arlington Nat. Cemetery.

LAPHAM, J(ACK) H. rancher, oil exec.; b. N.Y.C., July 4, 1885; s. Lewis H. and Antoinette (Dearborn) L.; B.A., Williams Coll.; m. Lucy Jane Thomas, Nov. 11, 1940; children-David, John, Julie, Jean. Dir., mem. exec. com. Texas Co., 1907—; co-owner Park Motel, San Antonio, Flying L Ranch, Bandera, Tex.; pvt. pilot, 1926—. Served as maj., F.A., U.S. Army, World War I; col. AAF, 1942-45. Mem. Sportsmen's Pilot Assn., Nat. Soc. Arts and Letters, Alpha Delta Phi, Order of Alamo. Clubs: Country, Meadowbrook, Matagorda, Williams (San Antonio). Address: 333 E. Summit Av., San Antonio. Died Aug. 2, 1956; buried New Canaan, Conn.

LAPHAM, ROGER DEARBORN industrialist; b. N.Y.C., Dec. 6, 1883; s. Lewis Henry and Antionette (Dearborn) L.; A.B., Harvard, 1905; m. Helen B. Abbot, Oct. 30, 1907; children-Lewis A., Carol (Mrs. Ophuls), Edna (Mrs. H. J. E. Van Oosten), Roger Dearborn. Successively agt., traffic mgr., treas., pres., chmn. bd. Am. Hawaiian S.S. Co., 1907-43, dir., 1950-54; dir. Am. Trust Co., San Francisco. Chief E.C.A. mission to China, Shanghai, 1948-49, mission to Greece, Athens, 1950-52; employer mem. Nat. Def. Mediation Bd., 1941; mem. Pres. Management-Labor Conf., Washington, 1942; mgmt. rep. Nat. War Labor Bd., 1942-43; dir. bus. adv. council Dept. Commerce. Organizer San Francisco Employers Council dir. C. of C. U.S.; mayor of San Francisco, 1944-48. Mem. bd. overseers Harvard, 1943-49; mem. bd. trustees Asia

Foundation, San Francisco. Served as capt., 305th Inf., 77th Div., U.S. Army, World War I; in charge transportation U.S. Food Adminstrn., London, Eng. Clubs: Bohemian, Golf, Pacific-Union (San Francisco); Harvard (San Francisco and N.Y.C.); Country (Burlingame, Cal.); Cypress Point (Monterey, Cal.); Links (N.Y.C.). Home: 3680 Jackson St., Office: 215 Market St., San Francisco. Died Apr. 1966.

LAPHAM, SAMUEL, architect; b. Charleston, S.C., Sept. 23, 1892; s. Samuel and Annie Grey (Souie) L.; A.B., Coll. Charleston, 1913; B.S., Mass. Inst. Tech., 1916; m. Lydia LaRoche Thomas, July 8, 1926; children—Anne Souie Blevins, Samuel Thomas (dec. 1943), Samuel Peyre. Draftsman, Fay, Spofford & Thorndike, Boston, 1916; designer Carmichael Constrn. Co., Akron, O., 1917, C. F. Warner Co., Cleve., 1919; partner Simons, Lapham, Mitchell & Small, architects, Charleston, 1920-72; works of firm include: plantation house Chelsea, for Marshall Field III; Windsor for P.D. Mills; post-office and post exchange, Parris Island; monuments, restorations, residential and ednl. bldgs. Partner, chief architect Housing Architects Asso. and Housing Authority Architects, Charleston, 1935-41, 67-71; acting prof. engring. Coll. of Charleston, 1925-26, 29-30; dist. officer S.C. historic Am. bldgs. survey, Nat. Park Service, U.S. Dept. Interior, 1933-42. Served with U.S. Army, 2d lt., CAC, 61st arty., 33d arty. brigade, 1st Army AEF, France, 1917-19; lt. to lt. col. C.A.C. Res. Corps, 1923-41; lt. col. (C.A.C.), insp. gen. dept., Insp. gen. 4th service command, 1942-45; col. U.S. Army, 1945; col. C.A.C. Res., 1946, ret. 1952. Fellow A.I.A. (past pres. S.C. chpt.); mem. Bldg. Council of S.C., Soc. for Preservation of Old Dwellings (hon.), Alumni Assn. of Coll. Charleston (past pres.), St. Cecilia Soc., S.C. Soc., Soc. Mayflower Descs. In S.C., Soc. Colonial Wars S.C. (dep. gov.-gen.), Charleston Ancient Arty. Soc. Democrat. Episcopalian. Mason Clubs: Charleston, Old Town, Carolina Yacht. Author and editor: (with Albert Simons) Charleston, S.C., Vol. 1 of Octagon Library of Am. Architecture, 1927; The Early Architecture of Charleston, 1970. Editor: (with Editor: (with Albert Simons) Plantations of the Carolina Low Country, 1938, 6th edit., 1970. Contbr. articles to archtl. and hist. publs. Home: Charleston SC Died Oct. 2, 1972; buried Magnolia Cemetery, Charleston SC

LAPRADE, LLOYD STONE editor; b. Franklin County Va., Feb. 22, 1902; s. George Washington and Mary Elizabeth (Muse) L.; student Lynchburg Coll., 1919-22; A.B., Duke U., 1925; studied U. of Va. and Duke U., summer, 1926-27; Duke U. Law Sch., 1 term; m. Rhoda Kathleen Thomas, Aug. 8, 1936. Teacher Orlando (Fla.) High Sch., 1925-26, Maury High Sch., Norfolk, Va., 1926-27; reporter Durham (N.C.) Herald, 1929-31; legislative corr. Asso. Press, Jan.-May 1931; reporter Durham Herald, 1931-32, editor, 1932-43. Tech. editor USPHS, Atlanta Editorial Branch. Served as maj. U.S. Army, A.M.G. service, Dec. 1943-Sept. 1946. Decorated French Croix de Guerre with Palm, Belgian Croix de Guerre with Palm. Democrat. Mem. Christian (Disciples) Ch. Club: Kiwanis. Home: 105 Kathryn Av., Decatur, Ga. Office: John Silvey Bldg., Atlanta. Died Nov. 5, 1953; buried Woodlawn Cemetery, Ocala, Fla.

LARDNER, JAMES LAWRENCE naval officer; b. Phila., Nov. 20, 1802; s. John and Margaret (Saltar) L.; m. Margaret Wilmer, Feb. 2, 1832; m. 2d, Ellen Wilmer, June 23, 1853; 7 children. Apptd. midshipman U.S. Navy, 1820, lt., 1828; navigating officer on the Vincennes, 1828-31; lt. in command of receiving ship at Phila., 1844-48; commd. comdr., 1851; fleet capt. West India Squadron, 1855; commd. capt., 1861; comdr. Susquehanna of N. Atlantic Squadron aiding in capture of Port Royal and blockading of S.C. and Ga. coasts; in command East Gulf Blockading Squadron, 1862; commodore in command East Coast Squadron, 1862; comdr. West India Squadron, 1863; commd. rear adm., 1866; gov. Naval Asylum, Phila., 1869-72. Died Phila., Apr. 12, 1881; buried Frankford, Pa.

LARIMER, EDGAR BROWN, naval officer; b. Tipton, Mo., Aug. 12, 1876; s. George and Laura Bennett (Ferguson) L.; grad. U.S. Naval Acad., 1899; m. Mary Bradford Burwell, July 21, 1906; 1 dau., Mary Burwell. Ensign U.S. Navy, Jan. 28, 1901; promoted through grades to rear adm., Oct. 1, 1932. Served on Indiana, Spanish-Am. War, 1898; in Philippine Insurrection, 1902; comd. Paul Jones and Perry, 1907-09, Niagara and New Orleans, 1917-20; comd. Naval Torpedo Station, Alexandria, Va., 1921-23; chief of staff, Scouting Fleet, 1923-24; comd. Naval Torpedo Station, Newport, 1925-27; comd. U.S.S. New Mexico, 1927-29; asst. to chief Bur. of Navigation, 1929-31; chief Bur. of Ordnance, 1931-34, retired, Nov. 1, 1934. Awarded Navy Cross (U.S.); War Cross of Czechoslovakia. Clubs: Chevy Chase, Army and Navy, New York Yacht. Home: 32 Altamont Apts., Charlottesville VA

LARKIN, THOMAS B., army officer; b. Louisburg, Wis., Dec. 15, 1890; s. Thomas and Dorothy (Donders) L.; B.A., summa cum laude, Gonzaga U., Spokane, 1910., hon. D.Sc., 1936; B.S., U.S. Mil. Acad., 1915; grad. Engr. Sch., 1916, Army Industrial Coll., 1927, Command and Gen. Staff Sch., 1929, Army War Coll., 1938, Naval War Coll., 1939; m. Mary Regina Irwin, April 16, 1917; children—Thomas B., Elizabeth Barbour, Harrison, Mary Virginia. Commd. 2d lt. Engrs. Corps, 1915; promoted through grades to lt. gen., 1949; on Mexican campaign, 1916-17; overseas, 1917-19; with Office Chief of Engrs., Washington, 1920-21; asst. mil. attache, Tokyo, 1921-23; asst. dist. engr., Pittsburgh, 1923-25; with Office Chief Engrs., 1925-28; asst. dist. engr. and engr., Vicksburg, Miss., 1929-33; in charge Ft. Peck Project, Mont., 1933-37; in charge 3d Locks Project, Panama Canal, 1939-42; chief engr. and chief of staff, Services of Supply, 1942-43; comdg. gen. Services of Supply and Communications Zone, N. Africa, 1943-44; Commd. hdqrs., dep. comdr. and chief of staff, Communications Zone, ETO 1943-44; comdg. gen., 2d Service Comd., Govs. Isl., N.Y., 1945-46; Q.M.G., rank of Major General; dir. logistics div., Gen. Staff, Dept. Army, 1949-52, ret., 1952; made econ. survey Dominican Republic, 1953; asst. in econ. survey West Berlin, 1953; cons. to asst. sec. def. on facilities assistance progress, Europe and Near East, 1953-60; dir. mut. weapons devel. team Dept. Def., 1955-60; project dir. transp. survey Argentine Govt.-World Bank, 1960-62; cons. Blauvelt Engring. Co., N.Y.C., 1962, Colfax Chem. Co., Cal., 1962-68. Decorated Silver Star (three bronze stars), Distinguished Service Medal (two oak leaf clusters), Legion of Merit, Bronze Star, Brazilian Military Order of Merit, Grand Officer, Order of Crown of Italy, Comdr. Honorable Order of the Bath; Grand Officer, Order of Ouissan Alouit Cherifils (Sultan of Morocco, 1945); Grand Officer 1st class, Order of Nichantan Ikhar (Bey of Tunis, 1945); Comdr. French Legion of Honor, Croix de Guerre with Palms (1945). Mem. Am. Soc. Civil Engrs., Soc. Mil. Engrs. Clubs: Chevy Chase; The American (London). Contbr. to engring. jours. Home: Washington DC Died Oct. 17, 1968; buried Arlington Nat. Cemetery, Arlington VA

LARRABEE, C(HARLES) R(OLLIN) govt. official; b. Chicago, Feb. 8, 1898; s. Rollin North and Bertha (Curtis) L.; A.B., Harvard Coll., 1919, LL.B., 1923; m. Paula Tully, June 15, 1935. Gen. practice of law, Chicago, 1923-33; asst. corp. counsel, City of Chicago, 1926-27; service of Fed. Govt., since 1933; asst. gen. counsel Fed. Emergency Adminstrn. of Pub. Works, 1938-39; chief trial examiner Bituminous Coal Div., Dept. of the Interior, 1940-41; mem. War Contracts Price Adjustment Bd., 1947-48; office of general counsel. R.F.C., 1943-50; office of general counsel Nat. Prodn. Authority, 1951-53; assistant gen. counsel Department of the Air Force, 1954-. Served with F.A. Central O.T.S., 1918. Mem. Chgo. Bar Assn., Harvard Law Sch. Assn. Democrat. Episcopalian. Home: 4701 Connecticut Av., Washington 20008. Died July 6, 1964; buried Arlington Nat. Cemetery.

LARSEN, HENRY LOUIS ret. marine corps officer, born Chicago, Dec. 10, 1890; s. Andrew A. and Ida (Hansen) L.; grad. Army and Navy Acad., Washington, 1913, Inf. Sch., 1925, Ecole Superieure de Guerre, Paris, France, 1934; m. Elizabeth Ammons, Nov. 25, 1919. Commd. 2d lt. U.S. Marine Corps, 1913, advanced through grades to lt. gen., 1946; expdn. duty, Cuba, 1914-16, Haiti, 1914-16, Santo Domingo, 1914-16, Mexico, 1915, Nicaragua, 1928-30; served with AEF, 1917-19; electoral mission, Nicaragua, 1929-30; mil. gov., comdg. gen. def. forces, Samoa, 1942-43; island comdr., mil. gov., Guam, 1944-46; comdg. gen. Dept. Pacific, 1946; retired, 1946; chmn. Colo. Planning Commn., 1947-48; dir. Colo. Civil Def., 1951-59. Decorated D.S.M. (Navy, twice), D.S.C. (Navy, twice), Silver Star (Army, 3 times), Medal of Merit (twice), Bronze Star, Commendation ribbon; comdr. Legion of Honor, Croix de Guerre with palm (France); Presdl. Medal of Merit (Nicaragua); Fouragerre and 12 campaign ribbons. Mem. Nat. Assn. State and Territorial Civil Def. Directors (pres. 1953-54), Soc. Am. Mil. Engrs. (dir.). Clubs: Denver Country, Denver, Mile High (Denver); Army and Navy (Washington); Army and Navy Country (Arlington, Va.); Chevy Chase (Md.). Home: 836 E. 17th Av., Denver 80218. Died Oct. 2, 1962; buried Arlington Nat. Cemetery.

LARSEN, WILLIAM, clergyman; b. Racine, Wis., May 19, 1909; s. Martin P. and Margarethe (Andersen) L.; B.A., Dana Coll., Blair, Neb., 1933; B.D., Trinity Theol. Sem., Blair, 1936; M.A., Boston U., 1936-40, grad. student, 1951-52; D.D., Wartburg Theol. Sem., 1957; student Harvard, 1940-43, U. Minn., 1946-47; m. Inga M. Schultz, June 12, 1936; children—William A., Ellen M., Nancy E. Ordained to ministry United Evangel. Lutheran Ch., 1936; pastor Bethany Luth. Ch., Boston, 1936-43; Luth. pastor to students U. Minn., 1946-47, Ohio State U., 1947-48; exec. dir. Luth. Student Found. Minn., 1948-56; pres. United Evangel. Luth. Ch., 1956-61; vice president American Lutheran Ch., executive director for division theological edn., 1967-71; secretary to Luth. Council United States Am. Chmn. Joint Union Com. Served as chaplain USNR, 1943-46; capt. Res. Author: We Believe, 1947. Home: Minneapolis MN Died Aug. 5, 1971.

LARSON, RANDELL lawyer; b. N.D., Apr. 11, 1893; s. Louis A. and Carrie (Walsted) L.; A.B., U. N.D., 1913; LL.B., George Washington U., 1916; m. Agnete Klitgaard, Jan. 1946; 1 dau., Linnie. Admitted to D.C. bar, 1916, Cal. bar, 1924; practice of law, San Francisco, 1926-; mem. firm Severson, Zang, Werson, Berke & Larson, 1956-; trial counsel FTC, 1920-25. Served to col. AUS, 1941-45. Fellow Am. Coll. Probate Counsel; mem. Am. Bar Assn., Bar Assn. San Francisco, State Bar Cal., Phi Delta Phi. Office: 433 California St., San Francisco 4. Died Jan. 8, 1966.

LASBY, WILLIAM FREDERICK, dean emeritus; b. Castle Rock, Minn., Oct. 25, 1876; s. Walter and Lavinia (Freeman) L.; B.S., Carleton Coll., Northfield, Minn., 1900; D.D.S., U. of Minn., 1903; m. Genevieve P. Adams, June 9, 1904 (died May 28, 1921); 1 dau., Helen Adams (Mrs. Robert N. Jeffrey); m. 2d, Rachel Mae Griffith, May 22, 1922 (died 1945); married 3d, Irma G. Lowe. Practicing dentist, Fairmont, Minnesota, 1903-08; instructor, University of Minnesota School of Dentistry, 1908-10, asst. prof., 1910-12, asso. prof., 1912-19; prof. and chmn., prosthetic dentistry, 1919-27, dean, 1927-45, now dean emeritus; v.p. and director University Nat. Bank, Minneapolis. Maj. Dental Res., U.S. Army, 1924; lt. col. (inactive) since 1934. Fellow Am. Coll. Dentists (v.p., 1935; regent 1939-1944); mem. Am. Dental Assn., Minn. State and Minneapolis Dist. Dental Socs. (life), Am. Assn. Dental Schs. (ex-pres.), Internat. Assn. for Dental Research, A.A.A.S., Minn. Acad. Science, Phi Beta Kappa, Omicron Kappa Upsilon (past nat. pres.), Xi Psi Phi. Republican. Congregationalist. Mason (32 deg., Shriner), Eastern Star. Clubs: U. of Minn. Campus; Kiwanis; U. of Minn. Golf. Contbr. Papers to dental jours. and professional socs. Home: 425 Walnut St. S.E., Minneapolis MN

LASSITER, HERBERT CARLYLE rear adm. USN. Address: care Bureau of Naval Personnel, Dept. of Navy, Washington. Died 1950.*

LASSITER, WILLIAM army officer; b. Petersburg, Va., Sept. 29, 1867; s. D.W. and A. H. Lassiter; grad. U.S. Mil. Acad., 1889, Arty. Sch., 1894; m. Jeannette Johnson, Oct. 5, 1935. Commd. add. 2d lt. 4th Arty., 1889; promoted through grades to col., 1916; brig. gen. Nat. Army, 1917; maj. gen., 1918; from brig. gen. to maj. gen. regular army, 1920-22. Served with battery at attack and capture of Santiago, Cuba, July 1898; asst. instr. tactics, U.S. Mil. Acad., 1898-1901; comd. 7th Battery, F.A., Ft. Riley, Kan., 1901-03; on Bd. Pres. F.A. Drill Regulations, 1903-08; duty Office Inspector Gen. U.S. Army, 1908-09; duty Gen. Staff, 1911-13; duty as mil. attaché Am. Embassy, London, Eng., 1916; apptd. comdr. 51st F.A. Brigade, Boston, 1917; chief arty., 1st Corps, May 1918 (Aisne-Marne Offensive), 4th Corps, Aug. 1918 (St. Mihiel offensive), 2d Army, Oct. 1918 (Toul sector); comdg. 32d Div., Nov. 20, 1918-Apr. 19, 1919 (march to Rhine and occupation of Coblentz bridgehead); chief arty., 3d Army, Apr. 19, 1919; returned to U.S. Aug. 6, 1919, assigned as col. to Gen. Staff Corps; Comdr. Camp Knox, Ky., Sept. 1920-Sept. 1921; asst. chief staff in charge operations and tng., 1921-23; apptd. comdr. Panama Div., 1923, Panama Dept., 1924; succeeded Gen. Pershing as head Tacna-Arica Plebiscite Commn., 1926; comd. 6th Corps Area, hdqrs., Chgo., 1927-28; comd. Philippine Dept., Apr.-Oct. 1928; comd. 8th Corps Area, 1928-30; comd. Hawaiian Dept., Sept. 1920-31, ret. 1931. Decorated D.S.M. (U.S.); Knight Comdr. Order of St. Michael and St. George (British); Comdr. Légion d'Honneur; Croix De Guerre, 2 palms (French). Address: 174 Miramar Av., Santa Barbara, Cal. Died Mar. 1959.

LATCH, EDWARD BIDDLE chief engr. U.S.N.; b. Lower Merion Twp., Pa., Nov. 15, 1833; s. Gardiner and Henrietta (Wakeling) L.; ed. pub. schs.; studied mech. engring. Norris Locomotive Works, Phila., 1851-57; unmarried. Began service as asst. engr. U.S.N., Sept. 20, 1858; chief engr. with rank of comdr., Mar. 21, 1870; retired, Nov. 22, 1878. During Civil War was attached to the flagship Hartford (Admiral Farragut); took part in engagements at Fts. Jackson and St. Philip and Confederate fleet Mississippi River, Chalmette, New Orleans, Vicksburg, Port Hudson, Grand Gulf, Warrenton, Grand Gulf and Fts. Morgan, Gaines and Powell; also with the ram Tennessee at the battle of Mobile Bay. Developed the Mosaic system of chronology. Extensive writer of elucidations of scripture and universal history by the Mosaic system of chronology. Editor The Greater Light (Phila. monthly). Author: A Review of the Holy Bible, 1884; Indications of the Book of Job, 1889; Indications of Genesis, 1890; Indications of Exodus, 1892; also serials in The Greater Light-Indications of Romans, 1900-01; Indications of the Revelation of St. John the Divine, 1901-03; Indications of Leviticus, 1905; Indications of Numbers, 1906-07; etc. Address: Academy P.O., Pa. Died 1911.

LATHROP, JOHN judge; b. Boston, Feb. 8, 1835; s. Rev. John P. and Maria Margaretta (Long) L.; A.B., Burlington (N.J.) Coll., 1853. A.M., 1856; LL.B., Harvard, 1855; LL.D., Williams, 1906; m. Eliza Davis Parker, June 24, 1875. Admitted to bar, 1856; lt. and capt. 35th Mass. Inf., 1862-63; practiced at Boston, 1856-88; reporter decisions Supreme Ct., 1874-88; justice Superior Ct., 1888-91; justice Supreme Jud. Ct. of Mass., 1891-1906; resigned. Lecturer Harvard Law Sch., 1871-73, Boston Law Sch., 1873, 1880-83. Address: Boston, Mass. Died 1910.

LATHROP, PALMER JADWIN business exec.; b. Scranton, Pa., Nov. 24, 1909; s. Henry Ridgway and Charlotte Hope (Jadwin) L.; student Brooklyn Poly. Prep., 1921-23, Hotchkiss Sch., Lakeville, Conn., 1924-27; A.B., Princeton, 1931; m. Caroline Marsha Kinsey, Feb. 3, 1933; 1 son, James Palmer. Various positions with Bristol-Meyers Co., N.Y. City, 1931-48; prodn. mgr., mfg. plant, Hillside, N.J., 1935-48, vice pres. in charge prodn., 1948; asst. to pres. Cameron Machine Co., Brooklyn, 1948-49, president since 1949, dir. and member executive com. since May 1947. Served with U.S. A.F. as glider pilot, later with Alaskan Division, Air Transport Command; disch. rank of major, 1945. Mem. Summit (N.J.) Bd. of Health. Mem. Soc. for Advancement of Management. Republican. Presbyterian. Clubs: Cap and Gown, Triangle (Princeton, N.J.); Baltusrol Golf (Summit, N.J.). Home: 77 Hillcrest Av., Summit, N.J. Office: 61 Poplar St., Bklyn. 2. Died Dec. 26, 1953.

LATIMER, JULIAN LANE naval officer; b. Shepherdstown, W.Va., Oct. 10, 1868; s. Thomas Wilmer and Mary Josephine (Quigley) L.; grad. U.S. Naval Acad., 1890; m. Laura Singer Richardson, Dec. 9, 1898; children-Mary Richardson (Mrs. Rupert R. Deese), Laura Towne, Elizabeth Josephine (Mrs. Robert C. Thaxton), Julian Lane. Ensign, July 1, 1892; promoted through grades to rear adm.,Nov. 13, 1923, Served on Winslow, Spanish-Am. War, 1898; with Bur. of Ordnance, Navy Dept., 1903-06; on Virginia, 1906-07; comd. Vesuvius, 1907; exec. officer and navigator Montgomery, 1907-09; insp. ordnance and in charge Naval Magazine, Hingham, Mass., 1909-11; comd. Culgoa, 1911-12; exec. officer Vermont, 1912-13; comd. Alabama, 1913-14; insp. engring. material, Mass. Dist., 1914-16; comd. Rhode Island, 1916-19; at War Coll., 1919-20; comdt. 7th Naval Dist. and Naval Sta., Key West, 1920-21; judge advocate gen. of Navy, 1921-25; comdr. Spl. Service Squadron, 1925-27; comdt. 4th Naval Dist. and Navy Yard, Phila., 1927-30, retired. Home: Clearwater, Fla. Died June 4, 1939.

LATTA, SAMUEL WHITEHILL physician; b. at Parkesburg, Pa., July 23, 1848; s. William Sutton and Margaret Eckert (Whitehill) L.; A.B., Lafayette Coll., 1867; M.D., U. of Pa., 1868; m. Anna Abel, of Easton, Pa., Sept. 25, 1873. Asst. surgeon U.S.N., 1868-73; practiced in Phila. since 1876; chief med. examiner, Pa. R.R., 1886-1918; mem. State Bd. Med. Examiners, 1894-99. Mem. A.M.A., Med. Soc. State of Pa., Phila. Med. Soc., Am. Pub. Health Assn., Pa. R.R. Surgeons' Assn. (pres. 1917), Phila. Med. Club. Democrat. Presbyn. Author of many med. brochures. Dir. John Wanamaker Life Foundation for Employees. Home: 3602 Powelton Av., Philadelphia, Pa.

LAUCHHEIMER, CHARLES HENRY officer U.S. Marine Corps; b. Baltimore, Sept. 22, 1859; s. Meyer Henry and Babette L.; grad.Baltimore City Coll., 1877; grad. U.S. Naval Acad., 1881; LL.B., George Washington U., 1894; unmarried. Officer U.S. Marine Corps, 1883-; promoted through the various grades to rank of brig. gen., Aug. 29, 1916. Also adj. and insp. U.S. Marine Corps. Author: Forms of Procedure for Naval Courts and Boards, 1896, 1902. Died Jan. 14, 1920.

LAUER, WALTER ERNST army officer; b. Bklyn., June 29, 1893; s. Albert and Anna (Rehlmeyer) L.; student Cornell U., 1915-17, Sch. Small Arms, 1917-18; grad. Inf. Sch., 1927, Command and Gen. Staff Sch., 1938; m. Lily Grace Hunter, June 9, 1918; children-Helen Ivy, Hunter. Commd. 2d lt. (Res.) U.S. Army, Aug. 15, 1917, regular army, Oct. 26, 1917, advanced through the grades to maj. gen., (temp.), 1944; served in French and Am. Army of Occupation in Germany, 1918-23; African Theater of Operations, c/s 3d Inf. Div., 1943; comdg. gen. 99th Inf. Div. (Battle Babies), 1943-45, 66th Inf. Div., 1945, 80th Inf. Div., 1945, all ETO; ret. as maj. gen., 1946. Mem. UNRRA European Region Office, 1946. In charge of all surplus property in Europe. Decorated D.S.M., Silver Star with oak leaf cluster, Legion of Merit, Bronze Star with 2 oak leaf clusters, Purple Heart; comdr. Royal Crown, Croix de Guerre with Palm (Belgium); Legion de Honneur, Croix de Guerre with Palm (French); Order of Red Banner (Russina); War Cross (Order of White Lion), 1939 (Czechoslovakia); Army Commendation and many service ribbons. Mem. Scabbard and Blade, 1st Div. Soc., 99th Inf. Organization. Mason. Contbr. articles to profl. jours. Home: P.O. Box 461, Monterey, Cal. Died Oct. 13, 1966.

LAURENS, JOHN army officer, diplomat; b. Chalreston, S.C., Oct. 28, 1754; s. Henry and Eleanor (Ball) L.; m. Martha Manning, Sept. 16, 1776. Admitted to Middle Temple, London, 1772; joined Washington's staff as volunteer aide, 1777, served in every battle Washington was in, including battles of Brandywine (1779), Monmouth, Germantown, Savannah, Charleston; commd. lt. col. by Continental Congress; mem. S.C. Assembly, 1779; commd. envoy extraordinary by Congress to France to obtain aid for colonies, 1780; helped organize plan for siege of Yorktown, received Lord Cornwallis' sword at Yorktown, 1781; mem. Jacksonborough Legislature, 1782. Died Aug. 27, 1782.

LAURGAARD, OLAF consulting engr.; b. Ekne, nr. Trondhjem, Norway, Feb. 21, 1880; s. Olaf Christenson and Marie Cecelia (Leinhardt) L.; brought to U.S. in infancy; B.S., in C.E., U. of Wis., 1903, M.S., in C.E., 1914; m. Goldie May-Sherer, Nov. 29, 1908; children-Helen, Glenn Olaf. Asst. engr. U.S. Reclamation Service, 1903-10; chief engr. Ore., Wash & Ida. Finance Co., 1910-13; div. engr. Pacific Power & Light Co., Jan.-June 1913; project engr. State of Ore., 1913-15; cons. engineer, Portland, Ore., 1915-17; city engr. Portland, 1917-34 (in charge of expenditure of about $55,000,000 in pub. works of Portland); engr. with U.S. Bur. of Reclamation, 1934-36, services as constrn. engr., Parker Dam on Colorado River and engr. in enver office, 1934-36; with Tenn. Valley Authority as gen. office engr. Engring. and Constrn. Depts., 1936-37, constrn. engr. on Hiwassee Dam in N.C., 1937-40; consulting engr., Portland, Ore., 1940-42, including principal engr. War Dept., U.S. Engrs. on defense projects, Anchorage, Alaska; resident plant engr., U.S. Maritime Commission on shipbuilding, Alameda, California, since 1942. Member Oregon legislature, 1917, prepared and introduced Ore. highway and irrigation codes. Mem. Ore. State Bd. Engring. Examiners, 1919-35, pres. 1919-30; pres. Nat. Council State Bds. of Engring. Examiners, 1933. Capt. Engr. Res. Corps, U.S. Army, 1918, 23. Life mem. Am. Assn. Engrs. (ex pres. Ore. chapter); mem. Am. Soc. C.E. (life), Am. Soc. Municipal Engrs., City Ofcls., Div. Am. Road Builders Assn., Am. Soc. Mil. Engrs., Professional Engrs. of Ore. (life mem.), N.W. Soc. Highway Engrs. (past pres.), Tau Beta Pi, Chi Epsilon. Mason (32ff, K.T.); mem. Elks, Woodmen of the World. Member Portland Auld Lang Syne Soc., East Bay Engineers, Clubs: Alameda Forum (Calif.), Portland City. Contbr. on engring. subjects. Home: Portland, Ore. Address: 2308 Webster St., Alameda, Calif. Died June 23, 1945.

LAVALLE, JOHN, artist; b. Nahant, Mass., June 24,-21896; s. John and Alice Cornelia (Johnson) L.; student, St. Paul's Sch., Concord, N.H., 1909-14, Boston Mus. Sch., 1919-23, Julian's Acad., Paris, France, 1925; A.B., Harvard, 1918; m. Ellen Tufts, Oct. 4, 1919 (died Jan. 8, 1932); children—Alice (dec.), Mary Dean (dec.), John Edward, Ellen; m. 2d, Virginia Wilson, Sept. 15, 1932; (divorced 1947); 1 dau., Virginia; m. 3d, Martha Nicholson Hoyt, Jan. 3, 1948. Exhibited Pa. Acad., Nat. Acad. of Design (New York); Boston Tercentenary Expn., Art Institute (Chicago); Corcoran Gallery of Art; Carnegie Inst. (Pittsburgh); Salon des Artistes Francais; and others; painted portraits in Europe and America. Represented in Boston Museum and Brooklyn Museum. Mem. Jury of Admission and Awards, Pa. Acad., 1929, Boston Tercentenary Expn., 1930. Mem. R.O.T.C., Plattsburg, N.Y., 1916; enlisted in Aviation Sect., S.O.R.C., 1917; trained overseas with Royal Flying Corps; commd. 1st lt., Mar. 1918; served with 33d Wing, Royal Air Force, as bombing pilot, World War I; hon. disch., Dec. 1918. Commd. Capt., Air Corps, 1942. Served as Camouflage Officer with Air Force Camouflage Sch., Hamilton Field, Calif., Engineer Board, Ft. Belvoir, Va., and Africa-Middle East Wing in preparation for N. African landings. Camouflage Officer for 12th Air Force for Sicily invasion. Maj. 1944, Pub. Relations Officer for 12th Air Force in Italy. Painted over 100 portraits & landscapes for Mediterranean Allied Air Force which were exhibited in London; at National Gallery, Washington, D.C.; and Metropolitan Mus., N.Y. Hon. discharge, Sept., 1945. Recipient hon. mention, Century, 1948, Lynch award, Providence Art Club, 1952, Bronze Medal of Honor, National Arts Club, 1954. Mem. Guild Boston Artists, Boston Soc. Water Color Painters, Copley Soc. of Boston (sec. 1926-28), Grand Central Art Gallery Assn., Rockport Art Assn., North Shore Arts Assn., American Veterans Society of Artists, American Watercolor Soc. Republican. Episcopalian. Clubs: St. Botolph, Badminton and Tennis (Boston); Harvard Century Assn., Coffee House, Knickerbocker, Brook, Southampton, Salmagundi (N.Y.); Providence Art. Contbr. to magazines. Drawings for "Bay Window Ballads," Scribner, 1935; Air Force paintings reproduced in "Mediterranean Sweep," Duell, Sloan & Pearce, 1945. Home: New York City NY Died Nov. 13, 1971; buried Providence RI

LAW, EVANDER MCIVER soldier; b.Darlington, S.C., Aug. 7, 1836; s. E. Augustus and Elizabeth (McIver) L.; grad.S.C. Mil. Acad. of Charleston, 1856; admitted to bar, Yorkville, S.C., 1868; m. Jane E. Latta, Mar. 9, 1863. Prof. history and belles lettres, King's Mountain Mil. Acad., 1857-60; entered C.S.A., Apr. 1861, as lt. col. 4th Ala. Inf.; col. same, Oct. 1861; brig. gen., Oct. 3, 1862; maj. gen., Mar. 20, 1865. Supt. S. Fla. Mil. Inst., 1894-1903. Comdr. Florida Div. U.C.V., 1899-1903, hon. comdr. for life, 1903-. Democrat. Address: Bartow, Fla. Died Oct. 31, 1920.

LAWLER, THOMAS G. comdr.-in-chief G.A.R., 1894-95; b. Liverpool, England, April 7, 1844; brought to Ill. in childhood; enlisted as private Co. E, 19th Ill. inf., June 1861; became sergt. and was elected 1st lt., but was not commissioned; comd.his co. for 2 months during Atlanta campaign; was col. 3d Ill. inf. 7 yrs.; organized, 1876. Rockford Rifles; postmaster of Rockford, 1877-85, 1889-93 and 1897-. Republican. Coal and lumber mcht. Address: Rockford, Ill. Died 1908.

LAWRANCE, CHARLES LANIER aircraft engr.; born Lenox, Mass., Sept. 30, 1882; s. Francis Cooper and Sarah Eggleston (Lanier) L.; A.B., Yale, 1905, hon. A.M., 1927; grad. Ecole des Beaux Arts, Paris, 3 yrs.; hon. D.Sc., Tufts, 1928; hon. A.M., Harvard, 1929; m. Emily M.G. Dix, 1910; children-Emily, Margaret, Francis Cooper. Engaged in engineering since 1915, with special interest in development of aircraft engines; founder, 1917 and pres. until 1923, Lawrance Aero Engine Corp, N.Y. City; corp. merged with Wright Aeronautical Corp., 1923, pres., 1925-28, v.p., 1928-30; organized Lawrance Engineering & Reserach Corp., pres. and chief engr. until 1944; chmn. bd. of dirs. and dir. of engine research, 1944-46; now chief engineer and chmn. of board, Power Industries, Inc., N.Y. City; pres. C. L. Lawrance Corp. (realty); dir. and pres. Nitralloy Corp. Ensign N.Y. Naval Militia, 1916-17; assigned by Navy Dept. to aeronautical research, World War I, Fellow Royal Aeronautical Soc., Eng.; fellow Inst. of Aeronautical Sciences (pres. 1934-35); member Society Automotive Engrs., Aeronautical Chamber of Commerce of America (pres. 1931-32), Sons of the Revolution, Society of the Cincinnati. Decorated Chevalier Legion of Honor (France). Swarded Collier trophy, 1928. Pres. Emergency Shelter, N.Y. City. Republican. Episcopalian. Clubs: Yale, Brook. Home: 151 E. 63rd St., N.Y. City 21; and East Islip, L.I., N.Y. Office: Power Industries, 22 E. 42d St., N.Y. City 17. Died June 24, 1950; buried Locust Valley Cemetery.

LAWRENCE, FLORUS FREMONT Surgeon; b. Wadsworth, Medina Co., O., Mar. 16, 1863; s. Oman and Camilia (Liggett) L.; B.Sc., Baldwin U., Berea, O., 1880; D.Sc., 1890; studied med. dept. Wooster U., Cleveland, 1881-84, Columbus Med. Coll., 1884-85, M.D., 1885; postgrad. work in Phila., New York, Boston, Baltimore, London and Edinburgh; asst. to Lawson Tait, Birmingham, Eng., 1894; LL.D., Wooster, 1902; m. Cora Estelle Peirce, of Berea, Jan. 1, 1885; children-Gerald Peirce, James Cooper, Elizabeth Camilla (Mrs. Victor I. Montenyohl). Began practice at Columbus, 1885; prof. surg. Anatomy and clin. surgery, Ohio Med. U., 1892-93; clin. lecturer abdominal pelvic surgery, Starling Med. Coll., 1900, until union with Ohio Med. U., 1906; clin. lecturer on surgery, Coll. of Medicine, Ohio State U., until reorganization of faculty, 1916; chief of staff and surgeon, Lawrence Hosp., 1900-21, McKinley Hosp., 1920-25; surgeon White Cross Hosp. since 1925. Surgeon Base Hosp. No. 4, U.S. Army, Eagle Surgeons; mem. A.M.A., Ohio State Med. Soc., Central Ohio Med. Soc. (ex-pres.), Columbus Acad. Science, Phi Beta Pi, etc. Mem. Officers' Res. Corps, U.S.A. Republican. Methodist. Mason (33ff, Shriner). Clubs: Automobile, Aero. Extensive writer on surg. subjects. Address: 201 16th Av., Columbus, O.

LAWRENCE, JAMES naval officer; b. Burlington, N.J., Oct. 1, 1781; s. John and Martha (Tallman) L.; m. Jula Montaudevret, 1808, 2 children. Apptd. midshipman U.S. Navy 1798, acting lt. on ship Adams, 1800; promoted to sailing master, 1801; served in Tripoli War, 1801-05, 1st lt., comdr. ship Enterprise and Gunboat Number 6; 1801-02; comdt. ship Hornet, captured Brit. ship Peacock, 1813; promoted capt., 1813; in command Navy Yard, N.Y.C., 1813; comdr. Chesapeake during War of 1812, fatally wounded in engagement against Brit. frigate Shannon; known for his dying words "Don't give up the ship!" Died June 4, 1813; buried Trinity Churchyard, N.Y.C.

LAWRENCE, JAMES PEYTON STUART captain U.S.N.; b. Phila., Aug. 6, 1852; s. Edward and Aramintha Margaret Annie Peyton (Stuart) L.; student Episcopal Acad., Phila.; M.E., Lehigh U., 1873; spl. chem. course, Towne Scientific School of Univ. of Pa., 1878-79; m. Frank Isabelle, d. Dr. George O. Glavis, of Washington, July 17, 1901. In machine shops John Roach & Sons, Chester, Pa., 1874-75; asst. engr. U.S.N., 1875; passed asst. engr., June 16, 1883; chief engr., 1898; lt.-comdr., 1899; comdr., Oct., 1903; capt. and retired, June 30, 1905. Extensive sea service on China and Pacific stas. and 3 cruises around the world; steel insp. for govt. at Homestead, Pa., 1894; in Spanish-Am. war, 1898 (on gunboat Wilmington), taking part in battles of Cardenas and Manzanillo, Cuba. Mem. Am. Soc. Mech. Engrs., A.A.A.S., Franklin Inst. Clubs: Pittsburgh (Pittsburgh). Fort Monroe (Va.), Racquet, Art (Philadelphia). Address: The Art Club, Philadelphia.

LAWRENCE, ROBERT H., JR. astronaut; b. Chgo., 1935; s. Robert H. and Gwendolyn Lawrence; B.S. in Chemistry, Bradley U., 1956; Ph.D., Ohio State U., 1965; m. Barbara H. Cress, 1957; 1 son, Tracey. Joined USAF, 1956, advanced through grades to maj., 1967; assigned Pilot Instrn. Sch., Craig AFB, Ala., 1957, then USAF base, Furstenfeldbruck, W. Germany; grad. Aerospace Research Pilot Sch., Edwards AFB, Cal., 1967; astronaut Manned Space Program, NASA, 1967 -. Home: 854 E. 52d St., Chgo. Died Dec. 8, 1967.*

LAWRENCE, WILLIAM jurist author; b. Mt. Pleasant, O., June 26, 1819; grad. Franklin Coll., 1838; Cincinnati Law School, 1840; A.M., Franklin; L.L.D. from 3 Ohio colleges; m. Caroline M. Miller, Mar. 20, 1845. Admitted to bar, 1840; pros. atty. Logan County, 1845-46; mem. legislature, 1846-48; State senator, 1849, 1850, 1854; editor Logan Gazette, 1845-47; reporter Ohio Supreme court, 1851; judge, court of common pleas and district court, 1857-64; one of editors Western Law Monthly. Col. 84th Ohio vols. serving in Md., 1862; mem. Congress, 1865-77; 1st comptroller U.S. Treasury, 1880-85; advocate of and writer on protective tariff; pres. Ohio Wool Growers' Assn., 1891-; press. Nat. Wool Growers' Assn., 1893-; trustee Ohio Wesleyan U., 1878-; lay delegate to Gen. Conference M.E. Ch., 1872, 1876, 1880 and 1892.

Author: Ohio Reports, Vol. 20; Law of Claims Against Governments; Law of Religious Societies; The Treaty Question; Constitutional Law; Memorials to Congress for Wool Tariff (10 vols.); numerous other minor works. Address: Bellefontaine, O. Died 1899.

LAWS, ELIJAH rear admiral U.S.N.; b. in Pa., Mar. 20, 1833. Apptd. 3d asst. engr. U.S.N., Mar. 19, 1858; 2d asst. engr., Dec. 1, 1860; 1st asst. engr., July 25, 1866; chief engr., 1870; retired Mar. 20, 1895; advanced to rank of rear admiral, June 29, 1906, and given a medal for services during Civil War.Home: Morristown, N.J. Died Sept. 25, 1926.

LAWS, GEORGE WILLIAM naval officer; b. Channahon, Ill., Feb. 11, 1870; s. William and Mary (West) L.; grad. U.S. Naval Acad., 1891; Naval War Coll., 1913-14. Asst. engr., July 1, 1893; passed asst. engr., Feb. 16, 1898; trans. to line as lt. jr. grade, Mar. 3, 1899; promoted through grades to rear adm., June 4, 1925. Served on Justin, Spanish-Am. War, 1898; aide on staff comdr. in chief Asiatic Fleet, 1906; head Dept. of Ordnance, Naval Sta., Cavite, P.I., 1906-07; at U.S. Naval Acad., 1907-10; comdr. Dolphin, 1910-13; at Naval War Coll., 1913-14; exec. officer Louisiana, 1915; U.S. Naval Acad., 1915-18; command U.S.S. Michigan, 1918-20; command U.S.S. Wyoming, 1922-24, comdt. 16th Naval Dist., also comdt. Navy Yard, Cavite, 1924-26; comdg. Battleship Div. 2, Scouting Fleet, Oct. 4, 1926-28; comdt. Navy Yard, Mare Island, Calif., 1928-32, 12th Naval Dist., 1932-34; retired Feb. 28, 1934. Deceased.

LAWSON, LAURIN LEONARD army officer; b. St. Peter, Minn., Mar. 11, 1876; s. Magne and Hannah L.; ed. pub. schs., LaCrosse, Wis.; m. Mabel Shaw Halliday, May 10, 1906. Pvt. cons. D. and B, 1st Wash. Inf., 1898-99; commd. 1st lt. 39th U.S. Inf., 1899; hon. mustered out 1901, 1st lt., 1903; assigned to 3d F.A., June 6, 1907; capt. 4th F.A., Aug. 12, 1907; maj., May 15, 1917; lt. col. (temp.), Aug. 5, 1917; col. Nat. Army, Feb. 6, 1918; brig. gen. (temp.), Oct. 1, 1918. Served in Philippines thrice; at Vera Cruz, Mexico, 1914; with punitive expdn. into Mexico, 1916; comdt. Sch. Fire for Field Arty., Ft. Sill, Okla., 1918; comd. 15th F.A. Brigade, at Camp Stanley, Tex. 1919. Address: War Dept., Washington. Died Jan. 28, 1938.

LAWSON, THOMAS army officer; b. Va., 1781. Apptd. from Va. as surgeon's mate U.S. Navy, 1809; 1005d. garrison surgeon's mate U.S. Army, 1811, promoted surgeon 6th Inf., 1813, remained in position throughout War of 1812; apptd. surgeon gen. U.S. Army, 1836, twice had line commands, once commanded a regt.; served as q.m. and adj.; brevetted brig. gen., 1848. Author: Report on Sickness and Mortality, U.S. Army 1819-1839, published 1804; Meteorological Register 1826-30, published 1848; Appendix for 1822-1825, published 1840. Died Norfolk, Va., May 15, 1861.

LAWTON, ALEXANDER ROBERT army officer, diplomat; b. St. Peter's Parish, Beaufort Dist., S.C., Nov. 4, 1818; s. Alexander James and Martha (Moses) L.; grad. U.S. Mil. Acad., 1839, Harvard Law Sch., 1842; m. Sarah Alexander, Nov. 5, 1845; 4 children. Commd. 2d lt. 1st Arty., 1839, resigned, 1841; pres. Augusta & Savannah R.R., 1849-54; mem. Ga. Ho. of Reps., 1855-56, Ga. Senate, 1860; col. 1st Volunteer Regt. of Ga., commd. brig. gen., 1861; fought in Seven Days, 2d Manassas, Sharpsburg engagements; took charge Ewell's div., commanded its advance into Md.; became q.m. gen. Confederacy, 1863; served in lower house Ga. Legislature, 1870-75; chmn. Ga. Electoral Coll., 1876; mem., pres. pro tem Ga. Constl. Conv. of 1877; unsuccessful candidate for U.S. Senate, 1880, elected pres.; Am. Bar. 1882; minister to Austria, 1887-89. Died Clifton Springs, N.Y., July 2, 1896.

LAWTON, ALEXANDER ROBERT, lawyer; born Savannah, Ga., Aug. 16, 1884; s. Alexander Rudolf and Ella Stanly (Beckwith) L.; ed. St. Paul's Sch., Concord, N.H., 1898-1902; Ph.B., Sheffield Scientific Sch. (Yale), 1905; U. of Ga. Law Sch., 1906; U. of Va. Law Sch., 1908; m. Elizabeth Wallace Shotter, Dec. 5, 1911 (deceased July 8, 1956); children—Alexander Robert III, Spencer. Admitted to Ga. bar, 1909; mem. firm Lawton, O'Donnell, Sipple & Chamlee; chmn. bd. Chatham Savings Bank; dir. Colonial Oil Industries, Lieut. col., National Guard Ga., Mexican border service, 1916; lt. col. 118th F.A., U.S. Army, World War; hon. disch., 1919. Mem. Ga. Gen. Assembly, 1925-26; mem. Alumni Adv. Bd., Yale U., 1927; mem. com. to draft Constn. for State of Ga., 1931. Ex-pres. Telfair Acad. of Arts and Science. Mem. Savannah Bar Assn. (pres. 1941), Union Soc. Savannah (pres. 1937-39), Ga. Hist. Soc., Delta Psi. Dem. Episcopalian. Clubs: St. Anthony (New York); Oglethorpe, Savannah Golf, University (Savannah). Home: Savannah GA Died Sept. 25, 1963.

LAWTON, HENRY W. maj. gen. U.S.V.; lt. col. U.S.A.; b. Ohio; apptd. to army from Ind.; joined army as sergt. Co. E, 9th Ind. vols., April 1861; discharged July 1861, to enter 30th Ind. regt. as 1st lt.; promoted capt., May 17, 1865; entered regular army as 2d lt. 41st inf., July 28, 1866; captain, March 1879; maj., 188-; lt. col., Feb. 12, 1889. Apptd. maj. gen. U.S. vols., July 8, 1898; afterward on duty in inspector-gen.'s dept. and in 1899, corps commander in Philippines. Died 1899.

LAWTON, LOUIS BOWEN, army officer; b. Independence, Iowa, Mar. 13, 1872; s. Albert Wheeler and Mary (Vorhis) L.; prep. ed'n at Owasco and Auburn, N.Y.; grad. West Point, 1893; m. Auburn, N.Y., July 26, 1893, Theresa Emily Kelsey. Apptd. 2d lt. June 12, 1893, 1st lt. Apr. 26, 1898, 9th inf.; capt., Feb. 2, 1901, 26th inf., U.S.A.; maj., Jan., 1903; served in battles of Santiago, Cuba; Guadalupe Ridge, Japote River, Calulut, Bamban and many minor engagements in Philippines; battle of Tientsin, China (wounded), 1900; recommended for promotion in many battles; awarded medal of honor "for most distinguished gallantry" at Tientsin, China, July 13, 1900. Commandant Shattuck Sch., 1901. Retired Jan., 1903, wounds. Address: Care War Dept., Washington

LAWTON, SAMUEL TILDEN lawyer, army officer; b. Peoria, Ill., Apr. 1, 1884; LL.B., John Marshall Law Sch., Ill., 1905; commd. 1st lt. Cav. Ill. N.G., May 1912, capt. 1913; Fed. Service, 1916-19; made maj., Ill. N.G., Nov. 1920, advanced to brig. gen., Mar. 1936, maj. gen., June 1940; became comdg. gen. Fed. Service, 33rd Inf. Div., Camp Forrest, Tenn., Mar. 5, 1941; comdg. gen., Gt. Lakes Sector, Central Def. Command, hdqrs. Chicago, Ill., Apr. 1942; comdg. gen. Sault Ste. Marie Mil. Area, 1943-44; mem. War Dept. Dependency Bd. since 1944. Died Jan. 1961.

LEA, HOMER author; b. Denver, Nov. 17, 1876; s. Alfred Erskine and Hersa (Coberly) L.; descendant of early Colonial ancestry of Va.; student Occidental Coll., U. of the Pacific, and Stanford U.; unmarried. Undertook relief of Kwang Emperor of China, 1900, 1901; raised and comd. 2d Army Div., 1904, holding rank of lt. gen. over these forces. Author: Vermillion Pencil (novel), 1908; The Valor of Ignorance (mil. work in 2 vols.), 1909; The Crimson Spider (drama), 1909. Home: Los Angeles, Calif. Died Nov. 1, 1912.

LEA, LUKE ex-senator; b. Nashville, Tenn., Apr. 12, 1879; s. Overton and Ella (Cocke) L.; A.B., U. of the South, 1899, A.M., 1900, LL.D., 1915; LL.B., Columbia Univ., 1903; m. Mary Louise Warner, Nov. 1, 1906 (now dec.); children-Luke, Percy W.; m. 2d, Percie Warner, May 1, 1920; children-Mary Louise, Laura, Overton. Began practice at Nashville, 1903; organized Nashville Tennesseean, 1907, now publisher; prs. Tennessee Publishing Co.; U.S. senator, from Tenn., 1911-17. Organized and became lt. col. 114th F.A., May 1917, and col. Oct. 8, 1917; with A.E.F. in France, 10 mos.; participated in Toul sector, Aug. 23,-Sept. 11; St. Mihiel offensive Sept. 12-16; Meuse-Argonne offensive Sept. 26-Oct. 8, and Woëvre sector, Oct. 11-Nov. 8, 1918. Awarded D.S.M., U.S. Mem. Alpha Tau Omega, Phi Delta Phi. Democrat. Episcopalian. Office: Tennesseean Bldg., Nashville, Tenn. Died Nov. 18, 1945.

LEACH, CHARLES NELSON, physician; gov. A.R.C.; b. Burlington, Vt., July 2, 1884; s. Horatio Nelson and Phylinda (Clark) L.; A.B., Stanford, 1909, M.D., 1913; M.P.H., Johns Hopkins, 1921; m. Florence Dixon, Sept. 11, 1922; children—Carolyn Worden (Mrs. William H. Gorman II), Nancy Murchison (Mrs. H.A. Sackett), Charles Nelson. Intern Lane Hosp., San Francisco, 1914; with Rockefeller Found., 1921-49, asst. dir. internat. health div., 1947-49. Nat. bd. govs. A.R.C., 1954-60; trustee U. Vt., 1961-67. Mem. Commn. for Relief in Belgium, 1915-18, Am. Relief Adminstrn., 1919-21. Mem. exec. com. Belgian Am. Ednl. Found. Served as capt., M.C., U.S. Army, World War I. Decorated Order of Crown (Belgium); Polonia Restituta (Poland). Fellow Am. Coll. Preventive Medicine, Am. Soc. Tropical Medicine, Royal Soc. Tropical Medicine and Hygiene; mem. A.A.A.S., Am. Pub. Health Assn., Die Gesellschaft der Aerzte in Wien. Address: Newfane VT Died Apr. 3, 1971.

LEACH, GEORGE E. ex-mayor Mpls.; b. Cedar Rapids, Ia., July 14, 1876; s. William Benton and Mary Cook (Hammond) L.; student U. Minn., 1894-95; m. Ella Van Vorous, Oct. 9, 1903; m. 2d, Anita M. Churcher, Jan. 22, 1923. Insurance business at Mpls., 1898—. Mayor of Mpls., 1921-29, elected to 5th term, 1937, 6th term, 1939. Pres. N.G. Assn. of Am., 1937. Served in World War as col., 151st Regiment, F.A., 67th Brig., 42d Div., 1st A.C., AEF; participated in 5 major engagements; served as brig. gen. in comd. 59th F.A. Brigade, Minn. N.G.; apptd. chief N.G. Bur., War Dept., 1931, with rank of maj. gen. for 4 yrs., ret. as maj. gen., comdg. 34th Div., 1941; now pres. George E. Leach, Inc. Decorated D.S.C., D.S.M. (U.S.); Legion of Honor, Croix de Guerre with 3 palms and star (France); Comdr. Crown of Italy; Medal of Merit (Minn.). Club: Army and Navy; Minneapolis Athletic. Home: 2101 W. Franklin Av. Office: 605 8th Av. S., Mpls. Died July 17, 1955; buried Ft. Snelling Meml. Cemetery.

LEACH, J(OSIAH) GRANVILLE lawyer; b. Cape May C.H., N.J., July 27, 1842; s. Joseph S. and Sophia (Ball) L.; LL.B., U. of Pa., 1866; m. Elizabeth T. Whildin, Oct. 5, 1866. In newspaper work prior to Civil War; sergt., sergt. maj. and lt. 25th N.J. Vols., 1862-63; received first promotion "for gallant conduct at battle of Fredericksburg." In law practice, 1866-; mem. Pa. Legislature, 1876. Republican. Commissary gen. of Pa., with rank of col., 1887-90; appraiser port of Phila., 1889-90. pres. Geneal. Soc. Pa.; hon. pres. of Pa. Soc. S.R.; pres. Colonial Soc. of Pa.; deputy gov. gen. Soc. Mayflower Descendants. Author and editor various books on geneal. subjects. Home: Philadelphia, Pa. Died May 27, 1922.

LEACH, W(ALTER) BARTON, educator; b. Boston, Jan. 6, 1900; s. Walter Barton and Grace Winifred (Wise) L.; A.B., cum laude, Harvard U., 1921; grad. student Universite de Grenoble, summer 1920; LL.B. cum laude, Harvard U. Law Sch., 1924; m. Florence T. Malcolm, June 14, 1924 (divorced 1941); children—Barbara, Richard Malcolm; m. 2d, Jane McIlwraith, Mar. 10, 1944 (dec. 1963); 1 son, David; m. 3d, Blanche C. Bartlett, Jan. 3, 1964. Sec. to Jus. Oliver Wendell Holmes, U.S. Supreme Ct., 1924-25; admitted to Mass. bar, 1925, and engaged in gen. prac. of law at Boston, asso. with firm Warner, Stackpole & Bradlee, 1925-30; instr. law, Harvard U. Law Sch., 1929, asst. prof. law, 1930, prof. law, 1931-69; prof. Harvard grad. sch. pub. adminstrn., 1954; vis. prof. Oxford U., 1952; mem. editorial board, Law Book Dept., Little Brown & Co., from 1938; Cons. to USAF, from 1947. Served as pvt. inf., U.S. Army, 1918; commissioned major, Army of United States, June 1942; lt. col. Air Corps, Jan. 1943; col. Air Corps, Aug. 1944; brig. gen. U.S. Air Force Reserve, 1949. Legion of Merit, 1945; Exceptional Civilian Service award, 1949, Meritorious Civilian Service award, 1966. Mem. Am., Mass. bar assns., Pi Eta Soc., Lincoln's Inn Society, Universalist. Clubs: Harvard, Weston Golf (Boston, Massachusetts). Author of: Cases on Future Interests, 1935; Cases on Mass. Law of Evidence, 1935; Cases on Wills, 1939, revised edition, 1960; Handbook of Massachusetts Evidence, 1940, fourth edition (with Paul J. Liacos), 1968; Cases and Text on Property (with A. James Casner), 2d edit., 1969; The Rule Against Perpetuities (England, with J. H. C. Morris), 1955; The Rule Against Perpetuities (U.S., with Owen Tudor), 1957; (with J.K. Logan; Cases and Text on Future Interests and Estate Planning, 1961; Property Law Indicated, published, 1967; also author articles in legal and other periodicals; co-author of Am. Law of Property, 1952. Home: 295 Meadowbrook Rd., Weston MA Address: Cambridge MA Died Dec. 15, 1971; buried Cambridge MA

LEAHY, LAMAR RICHARD ret. naval officer; b. Buffalo, Feb. 11, 1880; s. Michael and Elizabeth (King) L.; ed. U. Buffalo Law Sch., 1897-98; B.S., U.S. Naval Acad., 1903; Naval War Coll., 1927-28; m. Margery Hamilton Clinton, Sept. 17, 1919. Commd. ensign USN, 1905, advanced through grades to rear adm., 1939; served in Cuban pacification and Mexican occupation; comd. U.S. Noma, operating off French Coast, during World War; Naval attache, Am. Legation, The Hague, 1925-27; ret. 1939; dir. Internat. Hydrographic Bur., Monte Carlo, Monaco, Apr. 1939-41; returned to active duty, U.S. Navy, Sept. 1941. Decorations: Cuban Pacification, Mexican Occupation, Victory Medal, Navy Cross, Order of Brit. Empire, Legion of Honor (France), Comdr. Order of White Lion (Czechoslovakia), Comdr. Order of Orange Nassau (Netherlands), Mil. Order 2d class (Mexico), Comdr. Knights of Order Polonia Restituta. Trustee Woods Hole Oceanographic Inst., Mus. City of N.Y., Marine Mus. of City of N.Y. Mem. Am. Georg. Union. Clubs: Union, University, New York Yacht, Knickerbocker (N.Y.C.); Tuxedo (Tuxedo Park, N.Y.); Army and Navy, Chevy Chase (Washington); University (Buffalo); Newport Reading Room. Address: 910 Park Av., N.Y. City. Died Oct. 10, 1958.

LEAHY, WILLIAM D. fleet admiral; b. Hampton, Iowa, May 6, 1875; s. Michael Arthur and Rose (Hamilton) L.; grad. high sch., Ashland, Wis., 1892; grad. U.S. Naval Acad., 1897; m. Louise Tennent Harrington, Feb. 3, 1904 (died April 21, 1942); 1 son, William Harrington. Commissioned ensign, U.S. Navy, 1899; and advanced through the grades to capt., July 1, 1918; chief bur. of ordnance, rank of rear adm., 1927-31; rear adm., Apr. 6, 1930; comdr. Destroyers Scouting Force, 1931-33; chief of Bureau of Navigation, 1933-35. Vice admiral commanding battleships of Battle Force, 1935-36; admiral commanding Battle Force, 1936-37; admiral, chief of Naval Operations, 1937-39; retired Aug. 1, 1939; apptd. gov. of Puerto Rico, 1939; ambassador to France, 1940-42; chief of staff to the Commander-in-Chief of the Army and Navy of the U.S. 1942-49. Apptd. Fleet admiral of the U.S. Navy, Dec. 15, 1944. Served in Spanish-Am. War, Philippine Insurrection, Boxer trouble; chief of staff, Nicaraguan Occupation, 1912, Haitian compaign, 1916; command of U.S.S. Dolphin, Mexican Punitive Expdn., 1916; served as comdr. World War I. President Navy Historical Found., 1950—. Awarded D.S.M., Navy Cross, also Santiago, Spanish Campaign, Philippine Service, Nicaraguan Campaign, Dominican Campaign, Mexican Campaign, Victory, American Defense Service, American Area Campaign medals, Comdr. Mil. Order of Aviz (Portugal), Estrella de Abdon Calderon, 1st class (Ecuador), Cravat Tripod Medal, Special Class (China), Knight Grand Cross of Polonia Restituta (Poland), Grand Cross of Legion of Honor, Croix de Guerre with Palms (France); the Knight Grand Cross Military Division Order of Bath (Britian); Grand Cross Order of Fasco Nunez de Balboa (Panama); Grand Cross, Order of Merit (Brazil); Knight Grand Cross

Order of Orange-Nassau (Netherlands); Grand Cross Order of Crown with palm, Croix de Guerre with palm (Belgium); Grand Cross Military Order of Italy. Club: Army and Navy. Author: I Was There, 1950. Address: Main Navy Bldg., Constitution Av., Washington 25. Died July 20, 1959; buried Arlington Nat. Cemetery.

LEAKE, JOSEPH BLOOMFIELD lawyer; b. Deerfield, N.J., Apr. 1, 1828; s. Lewis and Lydia L.; removed to Cincinnati, Nov. 1836; A.B., Miami U., 1846, A.M., 1849, LL.D., 1910; m. Cordelia M. Scott, Oct. 4, 1854 (died 1858); m. 2d, Mary P. Hill, Nov. 28, 1865. Admitted to bar, 1850; removed to Davenport, Ia., 1856; mem. Iowa Ho. of Rep., 1861-62; elected state senator, 1862, but resigned after 1st session to become capt. 20th Ia. Vols.; lt. col., 1862-65; bvtd. col. and brig. gen. U.S.V., 1865; elected state senator, 1866, but again resigned; co. atty. Scott Co., Ia., 1866-71; pres. bd. edn., Davenport, 1868-71; moved to Chicago, Nov. 1871; U.S. atty. Northern Dist. of Ill., 1879-84; atty. Bd. Edn., Chicago, 1887-91. Congregationalist. Home: Chicago, Ill. Died June 2, 1913.

LEALE, CHARLES AUGUSTUS physician; b. N.Y. City, Mar. 26, 1842; s. Capt. William Pickett and Anna Maria (Burr) L.; studied science; received pvt. instruction from Dr. Austin Flint, Sr., Bellevue Med. Coll., in diseases of the heart and lungs, and from Dr. Frank H. Hamilton, in gunshot wounds and surgery; attended med. and surg. clinics in N.Y. City; M.D., Bellevue Hosp. Med. Coll., 1865; m. Rebecca Medwin Copcutt, Sept. 3, 1867; children-Annie (dec.), Lilian, Medwin, Marion, Loyal, Helen (Mrs. James Harper). Apptd. and served full term as med. cadet U.S.A.; later acting asst. surgeon U.S.A. and asst. surgeon U.S. Vols.; took charge of ward for wounded officers and was exec. officer U.S.A., Gen. Hosp., Armory Sq., Washington, 1865; first surgeon to reach President Lincoln after he was shot, Apr. 14, 1865, and was placed in charge of the President by Mrs. Lincoln; prolonged his life and remained continuously with him until he died, Apr. 15, 1865; hon. mustered out of service, Jan. 20, 1866; brevetted capt. U.S. vols.; studied Asiatic cholera in Europe, 1866; in practice, N.Y. City, 1866-. In charge of children's class, Northwestern Dispensary, 1866-71; physician Central Dispensary 2 yrs.; pres. St. John's Guild, 1891, 92; chmn. Floating Hosp. Com.; reorganized Children's and Seaside hosps. President Alumni Assn. Bellevue Hosp. Med. Coll., 1875, Northwestern Med. and Surg. Soc., 1872, New York County Med. Assn., 1885, 86, New York Soc. for Relief of Widows and Orphans of Med. Men. 1895-96. Companion, 1st Class, Mil. Order Loyal Legion; del. London Internat. Med. Congress, 1881; mem. Council Phila. Internat. Med. Congress, 1887; etc. Home: New York, N.Y. Died June 13, 1932.

LEALE, MEDWIN M.D.; b. N.Y. City, Aug. 26, 1873; s. Charles A. and Rebecca Medwin (Copcutt) L.; A.B., Columbia, 1894, post-grad. course in philosophy, M.D., Coll. Phys. and Surg. (Columbia), 1896; studied in Europe, 1900; m. Matilda Howard Marvin; children-Bianca Marvin, Rosalind, Interne Roosevelt Hosp., later phys. Children's Hosps. of St. John's Guild, 1912-13; cons. phys. Nassau, North Country Community and St. John's hospitals. Joined Squadron A, N.G.N.Y., 1892; 1st lt. asst. surgeon, 1897; surgeon N.Y. Vol. Cav. Spanish-Am. War, accompanying expdn. to Puerto Rico; surgeon U.S. Cav. in Southern P.R. and attending phys. Gen. Miles' hdqrs.; later capt. surgeon, serving until 1903; mem. exam. bd. for med. officers attached to N.Y. State hdqrs., 1902-03. Episcopalian. Home: New York, N.Y. Died June 30, 1934.

LEAMY, FRANK ASHTON coast guard officer; b. Phila., May 13, 1900; s. Frank H. and Luara M. (Weckerly) L.; student U. Del., 1920-22; B.S., USCG Acad., 1924; grad. USN Flight Sch., Pensacola, Fla., 1936; m. Helen B. Butterworth, Apr. 22, 1937; children-Frank Ashton, David Arthur. Commd. ensign USCG, 1924, advanced through grades to rear adm., 1954; miscellaneous assignments cutters, destroyers, bases and air stations 1924-50; chief of staff, 8th C.G. Dist., New Orleans, 1950-51, comdr., 1951-54; comdr. 9th C.G. Dist., Cleve., 1954-57; supt. USCG Acad., 1957. Recipient D.F.C., several area and campaign medals. Mem. U.S.Naval Inst., Newcomen Soc. N.Am., Sigma Nu. Presbyn. Clubs: Propeller of U.S., U.S. Power Squadrons. Home: Qtrs. 1, USCG Acad., New London, Conn. Died June 1966.

LEAR, BEN army officer; b. Hamilton, Ont., Can., May 12, 1879; s. Ben and Hannah (Senden) L.; came to U.S., 1881; grad. Mounted Service Sch., 1911, Sch. of the Line, 1922, Gen. Staff Sch., 1923, Army War Coll., 1926; m. Grace Russel, Oct. 6, 1906. Sgt. 1st Colo. Vol. Inf., 1898-99; apptd. 2d lt. U.S. Vols., 1899; commd. 2d lt. cav. U.S. Army, 1901, promoted through grades to lt. gen., 1940, reapptd., May 1943. Served through Spanish-War, Philippine Insurrection, World War; became comdr. 2d Army, 1940; comdr. Army Ground Forces (1943-45, dep. comdr. to Gen. Eisenhower, Jan. 1945. Ret. Dec. 31, 1945. Decorated D.S.M.; French Legion of Honor; Silver Star. Episcopalian. Mason (33ff). Clubs: Army and Navy (Washington); Memphis, Memphis Country. Home: 1859 Overton Park Av., Memphis. Died Nov. 1966.

LEARNARD, HENRY GRANT army officer; b. Wright City, Mo., Aug. 19, 1867; s. James E. and Ellen G. (Packard) L.; grad. U.S. Mil. Acad., 1890; m. Florida Lyon, Nov. 7, 1901; chidlren-Henry Grant, Catharine Florida. Commd. 2d lt. inf., U.S.A., June 12, 1890; advanced through grades to col., Apr. 2, 1918; brig. gen., Mar. 21, 1926; retired Aug. 31, 1931. Served with 3d Exploring Expdn., in Alaska, Mar.-Nov. 1899; in Philippines, 1899-1901, except 4 mos. with China Relief Expdn., 1900; wounded in action, June 10, 1898. Awarded D.S.M. "for efficient performance of duty," World War; Silver Star citation "for gallantry in action," at Peking, China, Aug. 14, 1900; awarded Purple Heart. Died Mar. 7, 1937.

LEARNED, EBENEZER army officer; b. Oxford, Mfass., Apr. 18, 1728; s. Col. Ebenezer and Deborah (Yaynes) L.; m. Jerusha Baker, Oct. 5, 1749; m. 2d, Eliphal Putnam, May 23, 1800. Served as capt. of Rangers to relieve Ft. Henry in French and Indian War, capt. in company in Col. Ruggles' Regt.; del. to Mass. Provincial Congress, Concord, 1774, Cambridge, 1775; served with Mass. Militia at Battle of Bunker Hill; commd. col. 3d Inf., Continental Army, 1776, brig. gen., 1777; in command brigade at Saratoga; mem. Mass. Constl. Conv. from Oxford, 1779; mem. Mass. Legislature, 1783; chmn. Mass. Constl. Conv., 1789. Died Oxford, Apr. 1, 1801.

LEARY, HERBERT FAIRFAX ret. naval officer; b. Washington, May 31, 1885; s. Rear Adm. Richard Philipps and Augusta Neville (Irwin) L.; B.S., U.S. Naval Acad., 1905; m. Marion Barnes Bryant, Apr. 28, 1909; children-Herbert Fairfax, Neville Carlysle (Mrs. George K. Crozer, III). Commd. ensign USN, 1905, advanced through the grades to rear adm., 1938, vice adm., 1942; has served as gunnery officer, Battle Force; staff Naval Hdqrs., London; mem. Allied Naval Armistice Commn., naval attaché, Paris; liaison officer French Fleet; dir. fleet tng., naval operations; comdr. Eastern Sea Frontier, 1945; ret. Jan. 16, 1946; supt. N.Y. State Maritime Coll., 1946-51, ret. Decorated Navy Cross, Victory and Cuban campaign medals (U.S.), Legion of Honor (France). Episcopalian. Clubs: Chevy Chase Country (Chevy Chase, Md.); New York Yacht (N.Y.C.). Address: Villanova, Pa.; also Jamestown, R.I. Died Dec. 3, 1957.

LEARY, MONTGOMERY ELIHU, physician; b. Rochester, N.Y., July 9, 1868; s. Daniel and Caroline W. (Montgomery) L.; A.B., U. of Rochester, 1892; M.D., U. of Pa., 1895; m. Caroline A. Tegg, Aug. 6, 1896 (died Oct. 30, 1936); m. 2d, Norma C. Shaughnessy, May 16, 1941. Coroner's physician, Rochester, 1898-1902; lecturer on physiology and biology, Mechanics' Inst., Rochester, 1898-1904; sec. Rochester Acad. of Science 1898-1904; health officer, Gates, N.Y., 1896-1920; sec. and managing dir. Rochester Pub. Health Assn., 1896-1910, v.p., 1911-18; organized first open air school for pre-tubercular pupils in State of New York, 1908, founder, supt., sec. and treas. Iola Sanatorium (tuberculosis hosp.), 1910-17; sec. Supts. and Mgrs. of Tuberculosis Hosps., 1914-17; trustee and sec. Children's Hosp.; etc. Mem. A.M.A., Medical Society State of New York, Rochester Pathological Society, Monroe County Medical Society, Rochester Medical Assn., Academy of Medicine, Assn. Military Surgeons, Am. Sanatorium Assn., Nat. Tuberculosis Assn., Am. Pub. Health Assn., N.Y. State Sanitary Officers' Assn. (ex-pres.), Delta Kappa Epsilon, Am. Legion (comdr. Memorial Post, 1922-23; v. comdr. Monroe County Legion, 1927-29, 1948-49); comdr. Rochester Chap. Mil. Order World War, 1921-22, 1923-26; pres. Rochester Chapter No. 61, National Sojourners' (mem. com. of 33 since 1934); nat. surgeon of National Sojourners, 1936-47. Commissioned captain Medical R.C., U.S. Army, June 11, 1918; maj. M.C., Oct. 11, 1918; served at Gen. Hosp. No. 16, New Haven, Conn., Gen. Hosp. No. 18, Waynesville, N.C., and Base Hosp., Camp Jackson, S.C.; disch., 1918; col. M.C., O.R.C. Called to active duty, U.S. Army, as med. officer in charge of med. care of personnel in Rochester Area, June 1, 1943-Aug. 1, 1945. Spl. citation for war services, 1947. In charge for Monroe County, N.Y., of Citizens' Mil. Training Camps since 1921. Mem. Rochester Council Boy Scouts America, 1923-29. Republican. Presbyn. Mason (32 deg., K.T., Shriner; mem. service and rehabilitation com. of N.Y. Grand Lodge), K.P. Rotarian. Adopted, Oct. 3, 1915, into Seneca Indian Tribe, Beaver Clan, and given name of Hah-yah-dah-ga-has ("Great Benefactor"); adopted, Mar. 29, 1941, by same tribe, Snipe Clan, and given name of Ha-dey-jehs-go-wah ("Great Medicine Man"). Home: 827 W. Main St., Rochester 11 NY

LEARY, PETER JR. army officer; b. Baltimore, Sept. 15, 1840; s. Cornelius Lawrence Ludlow and Jane Maria (Phillips) L.; ed. in pvt. schs. and acads.; grad. U.S. Arty. Sch., 1880; m. Ellen Morgan, Oct. 23, 1872. Was student of law when Civil War began; entered Alexander's Battery, Md. vols., July 1862, as 2d lt. with rank dated from Aug. 11, 1862; promoted 1st lt., Apr. 6, 1865, and hon. mustered out, June 17, 1865; took part in battles of the Gettysburg campaign, 1863, at Berryville, Opequan Creek, Winchester and Stevenson's Sta., Va., and in the Md. campaign, 1864; engaged at Middletown, Frederic, and Monocacy, Md.; pvt. sec. and a.d.c. to Gov. Swann, of Md., Jan. 1, 1866-June 30, 1867. Apptd. 2d lt., July 2, 1867; promoted through grades to brig. gen., July 7, 1904. Served in Arapahoe War, Dec. 1869, Modoc War, 1873, Nez Perces War, 1877, and War with Spain, 1898. Bvtd. capt. for gallantry, in Lava Beds campaign, Calif., Apr. 15-16, 1873. First comdr., Md. Commandery, Loyal Legion; pres. Soc. War of 1812 in Md. Republican. Chmn. Sewerage Commn. of Baltimore. Home: Baltimore, Md. Died 1911.

LEARY, RICHARD PHILLIPS naval officer; b. Baltimore; grad. Naval Acad., 1860; promoted ensign, Oct. 1863; master, May 1866; lt., Feb. 1867; lt. comdr., Mar. 1868; comdr., June 1882; capt., Apr. 1897. Attached to blockading squadrons off Charleston, S.C. 1863-65; Later on various duties and stas.; comd. Adams, Pacific sta., 1888-89; senior officer at Samoa during the revolution of 1888, when Tamasese govt. was overthrown; was voted a gold medal by the Md. legislature for courageous services to govt. at that time; comd. cruiser San Francisco, 1897-98; convoyed the New Orleans, bought from Brazil; was stationed at Boston Navy-Yard after Spanish-Am. war; apt apptd. capt., Jan. 1899, and was for short time naval gov. Guam. Died 1901.

LEAVENWORTH, HENRY army officer; b. New Haven, Conn., Dec. 10, 1783; s. Jesse and Catharine (Conkling) L.; m. Elizabeth Morrison; m. 2d, Electra Knapp, 1810; m. 3d, Harriet Lovejoy, circa 1813. Admitted to N.Y. bar, 1804; commd. capt. 25th Inf., U.S. Army, 1812, maj. 9th Inf., 1813; brevetted col. for services at Battle of Chippewa, 1814, lt. col. for services at Battle of Niagara, 1814; mem. N.Y. Legislature, 1815; commd. lt. col. 5th Inf., 1818, trans. to 6th Inf., made comdt. at Ft. Atkinson (Calhoun), 1821; brevetted brig. gen., 1824; commd. col. 3d Inf., 1824; built post Ft. Leavenworth (now Leavenworth, Kan.), 1827; post comdr. Jefferson Barracks, 1829; comdr. South Western Frontier, 1834. Died Camp Smith, Kan., July 21, 1834; buried Ft. Leavenworth.

LEAVITT, HALSEY B. business exec.; b. Essex Junction, Vt., July 25, 1878; s. Julius A. and Isabel (Brown) L.; ed. Ewing Coll.; m. Elizabeth Elder, Oct. 4, 1906; children-Halsey Brown, Jr., Martha Elder (Mrs. Edward Homer Nelson). Reporter, editor, corr. newspaper, Havana, Cuba, 1899-1920; pres. Leavitt Ins. Co., Inc., Asheville, N.C., 1921 - . Sergt., 9th Ill Inf., Spanish-Am. War. Mem. N.C. Gen. Assembly, 1929-30; Rep. candidate for Congress, 1934, lt. gov., 1940; U.S. Senate, 1950; Rep. candidate presidential elector, 1952. Dir. Asheville-Biltmore Coll., 1949-58. Awarded gold medal by Am. Ambassador to Cuba, for meritorious service as publicity dir. 4th Liberty Loan, World War I. Comdr.-in-chief, United Spanish War Veterans, 1945-46 (mem. nat. com. on legislation and its adminstrn.; ú Samaritan ú mem. bd. Masonic Temple Co.; treas. Good Mission; hon. dir. Uncle Sam's 1-2-3 Boys. Hon. mem. Naval and Mil. Order of Spanish-Am. War; mem. Society of Mayflower Descendants. Mason (33ff). Clubs: Optimist (past president, International district gov.), Wild Life. Author: Tourist-Havana, 1917. Contbr. editor Asheville News, 1948-55; editor Take It or Leavit Column. Awarded Cuban medal Spanish-Am. War, 1954. Home: Chestnut Hill. Albemarle Park, Asheville. Office: 44 Patton Av., Asheville, N.C. Died May 26, 1960; buried Calvary Episcopal Churchyard, Arden, N.C.

LEAVITT, SCOTT ex-congressman; b. Elk Rapids, Mich., June 16, 1879; s. Roswell and Annie C. (Lawrence) L.; student U. Mich., 1899-1900; m. Elsie E. Frink, Sept. 27, 1903; children-Anna J. (dec.), Roswell, Homesteading and teaching, in Ore., 1901-07; ranger U.S. Forest Service, 1907; supr. Lewis & Clark Nat. Forest in Mont., 1910, Jefferson Nat. Forest, 1913-18 (resigned); mem. 68th to 72d Congresses (1923-33), 2d Mont. Dist.; nominated as Republican for U.S. Senate, 1934; reinstated U.S. Forest Service, chief Div. of Information and Edn., N. Central Region, Milw., 1935-41; ret. Corp. Co. L, 33d Mich. Inf. Vols., Spanish-Am. War; served in Santiago Campaign; Fed. State dir. U.S. Employment Service and of Pub. Service Res., Mont., World War I. Mem. United Spanish War Vets. (ex-comdr. Mont., nat. sr. vice comdr.-in-chief 1936-37). Mason. Club: Rotary (pres. 1943-44, Newberg, Ore.; gov. dist. Rotary Internat. comprising State of Ore. and 4 counties in State of Wash., 1947-48). Address: 1212 E. Hancock St., Newberg, Ore. Died Oct. 19, 1966; buried Willamette Nat. Cemetery, Portland, Ore.

LE BLANC, THOMAS JOHN prof. preventive medicine; b. Cheboygan, Mich., June 28, 1894; s. Louis John and Mary (McGurn) Le B.; A.B., U. of Mich., 1916, M.S. in pub. health, 1919; D.Sc., Johns Hopkins, 1923; m. Anna Gurklis, June 11, 1927; 1 dau., Diana. Scientist Rockefeller Inst., 1919-20; field scientist Rockefeller Foundation, 1920-21, statistician U.S. Pub. Health Service, Washington, D.C., 1924-25; head of Inst. of Human Biology, Tohoku Imperial U., Sendai, Japan, 1927-28; asso. prof., 1925-34, and prof. and head dept. of preventive medicine, Coll. of Medicine, Cincinnati, O., since 1935. Served as constrn. officer, U.S. Naval Ry. Batteries, with A.E.F., during World War. Decorated medal by Mexico for work in yellow fever; received scroll from Japanese Emperor; received citation and Silver Star (U.S.) for service at Front in World War. Mem. Am. Pub. Health Assn., Am. Soc. for

Tropical Medicine. Club: Cincinnati Power Squadrons of U.S. Power Squadrons. Home: 409 Warren Av., Cincinnati, O. Died. Sept. 9, 1948.

LEBO, THOMAS COVERLEY army officer; b. Potters Mills, Pa., Nov. 17, 1842; s. Jacob G. and Susannah (Coverley) L.; ed. Phila. pub. schs.; m. Grace F. Hawks, Oct. 8, 1902. Apptd. 2d lt., Apr. 26, 1861; mustered out, July 31, 1861; 2d lt., Nov. 28, 1861; 1st lt., Feb. 12, 1863; capt., Dec. 13, 1864; mustered out, Aug. 7, 1865; apptd. 1st lt., June 12, 1867; advanced through grades to brig. gen., June 22, 1905. Asst. adj. gen. 1st Brigade, 2d Cav. Div., Army of the Potomac, Dec. 1864-June 1865; twice wounded during Civil War; served almost continuously on the frontier, 1867-94, where participated in many of the Indian campaigns and engagements; was thrice mentioned in General Orders "for good judgment, energy and conspicuous gallantry in action with Indians"; comd. 6th U.S. Cav. at battle of San Juan Hill in Spanish-Am. War, where was recommended for a bvt. "for gallantry in action." Home: Albuquerque, N.M. Died 1910.

LECHNER, CARL BERNARD, physician; b. Erie, Pa., Dec. 11, 1908; s. Bernard Joseph and Katherine Mary (Klang) L.; M.D., Western Res. U., 1935; m. Dolores Barbara Tellers, July 22, 1936; children—Carl Bernard, Richard J., Brenda (Mrs. Dana F. Bigelow), Mark D. Intern, St. Vincent's Hosp., Erie, 1935-36, asst. radiologist, until 1970, head radiology, 1965-70; postgrad. in radiology U. Pa., 1939-40, Drs. Putts and Bacon, 1940-42; asst. radiologist Hamot Hosp., Erie. Pres., United Fund Erie County, 1961-62; mem. law adv. bd. Mercyhurst Coll., 1968-70; mem. Erie Arts Council. Served to maj., M.C., AUS, 1942-45. Diplomate Am. Bd. Radiology. Fellow Am. Coll. Radiology, Am. Roentgen Ray Soc., Am. Med. Writers Assn.; mem. A.M.A., Pa. (pres.-elect 1969-70), Erie County (pres. 1956-57) med. socs., Radiol. Soc. N.Am., Alpha Omega Alpha. Roman Catholic. Med. editor: Pa. Medicine, 1958-70. Home: Erie PA Died Oct. 13, 1970; buried Trinity Cemetery, Erie PA

LEDERER, FRANCIS LOEFFLER, surgeon; b. Chgo., Sept. 18, 1898; s. Jacob and Frances (Loeffler) L.; S.B., U. Chgo., 1918; M.D., Rush Med. Coll., 1921; postgrad. U. Berlin and U. Vienna, 1925; m. Anne Pollock, Mar. 4, 1925; 1 son, Francis II. Practiced in Chgo., 1921-73; emeritus prof., former head dept. otolaryngology U. Ill.; mem. sr. staff Michael Reese, Grant, Columbus hosps.; former chief otolaryngol. service Research and Ednl. Hosps., and dir. otolaryngol. service Ill. Eye and Ear Infirmary, Hines Hosp. (sr. cons.); cons. emeritus Presbyn.-St. Luke's Hosp.; cons. otolaryngology VA; nat. cons. surgeon gen. USAF. Served with U.S. Marines, World War I; captain M.C. (S) USNR, World War II; chief eye, ear, nose and throat service, chief aural rehab. U.S. Naval Hosp., Phila., 1942-46. Cons. otolaryngology U.S. Naval Hosp., Great Lakes, Ill. Fellow A.C.S., Internat. Coll. of Surgeons (hon.); mem. A.M.A., Ill., Chgo. med. socs., Inst. Med., Chgo. Lryngol. and Otol. Soc., Am. Otol. Soc. (past pres.), Chgo. Path. Soc., Am. Acad. Ophthalmology and Otolaryngology (past pres.), Am. Otol., Rhinol. and Laryngol. Soc., Am. Laryngological Assn., Am. Bronchoesophagol Assn., Am. Coll. Chest Physicians, Am. Assn. Mil. Surgeons, Sigma Xi, Alpha Omega Alpha, Phi Delta Epsilon, others. Mason (32, Shriner). Jewish religion. Author: Diseases of the Ear, Nose and Throat, 6th edit., 1953. Co-author: Atlas of Otorhinolaryngology and Bronchoesophagology, 1968. Contbr. to jour. and books on subjects pertaining to ear, nose and throat splty. Home: Chicago IL Died Apr 3, 1973.

LE DUC, WILLIAM GATES U.S. commr. of agr.; b. Wilkesville, O., Mar. 29, 1823; s. Henry Savary L.; A.B., Kenyon Coll., 1848; admitted to bar, 1849; settled at St. Paul, Minn., July 1850; m. Mary E. Bronson, 1851. Commr. to World's Fair, New York, 1853; active promoter rys. and immigration; laid out W. St. Paul; protected co. which built Wabasha St. bridge, St. Paul (first to span Miss. River); removed to, and laid out Hastings, Minn., and engaged extensively in farming. Capt. to bvt. brig. gen. U.S. vols. in Civil War. Returned to Minn.; projected and in part constructed Hastings & Dak. Ry. U.S. commr. of agr., 1877-81; established tea-farm, Summerville, S.C., and introduced from foreign countries olives, tea, Japanese persimmons and other plants now acclimated in U.S.; organized what now are the Bur. of Animal Industry and the Div. of Forestry; in service Treasury dept. in N.C., 1890-95. Home: Hastings, Minn. Died Oct. 30, 1917.

LEE, ALBERT LINDLEY soldier; b. Fulton, Oswego Co., N.Y., Jan. 16, 1834; s. M. Lindley and Ann L.; A.B., Union Coll., 1853. Practiced law at New York, 1855-57; removed to Kan., 1857; judge Supreme Ct. of Kan., 1860-61; maj. 7th Kan. Cav., Oct.29, 1861; col., May 17, 1862; brig. gen. vols., Nov. 29, 1862; resigned, May 4, 1865. Mem. firm Robert Goodbody & Co., bankers, 1890-1-01. Republican. Home: New York, N.Y. Died 1907.

LEE, BURTON JAMES surgeon; b. New Haven, Conn. Feb. 4, 1874; s. James Howard and Susan Mar (Hoyt) L.; Ph.B., Yale, 1894; M.D., Coll. of Phys. and Surg. (Columbia), 1898; m. Louise Freeman, Mar. 20, 1919. Clin. prof. surgery, Cornell U. Med. Coll. Commd. capt. M.C., U.S.A., Apr. 1917; maj., June 1918; lt. col., Nov. 1918; active service in France, Aug. 7, 1917-Jan. 25, 1919. Decorated D.S.M. (U.S.); Croix de Guerre (French). Mem. Am. Surg. Assn. Republican. Home: New York, N.Y. Died Nov. 12, 1933.

LEE, CHARLES army officer; b. Dernhall, Cheshire, Eng., 1731; s. John and Isabella (Bunbury) L. Ensign in father's regt., 1747; lt. 44th Regt. 1751; with Gen. Bradstock's expdn. to Ft. Duquesne, 1755; served under Amherst in capture of Montreal, 1760; maj. 103d Regt., 1761, lt. col., 1762; served under Burgoyne in Portugal in resistance to Spanish invasion, 1762; accompanied Polish embassy to Turkey, 1764; gen. and adjutant Polish Army, 1769; returned and settled in Am., 1773; author "Strictures on a Friendly Address to All Reasonable Americans in Reply to Dr. Myles Cooper" (an incitement to colonial rebellion), 1774; commd. 2d. maj. gen. Continental Army, 1775, in command So. Dept., 1776, played prin. part in victory of Charleston; fought rear guard action in Washington's retreat from N.Y.C.; ambitious to become comdr.-in-chief, became severe critic of Washington, notably in letter to Gen. Gates; captured by British, 1776, while prisoner submitted secret plan to Gen. Howe for defeating Americans; released in prisoner exchange, 1778, put in command of planned attack on Monmouth, retreated instead of attacking and was halted by arrival of Washington, Greene, Steuben and forces; courtmartialed, found guilty of disobedience, misbehavior before enemy and disrespect to comdr.-in-chief, resulting in suspension from command; continued his abuse of Washington, was dismissed from army, 1780. Died Phila., Oct. 2, 1782; buried Christ Ch. Graveyard,Phila.

LEE, CHARLES HAMILTON hydraulic and sanitary engr.; b. Oakland, Cal., Feb. 1, 1883; s. Rev. Hamilton and Genevieve (Littlejohn) L.; B.S., U. Cal., 1905; m. Katherine Newhall, Jan. 17, 1911; 1 son, Charles Hamilton; m. 2d, Evelyn May Grundy, Oct. 1, 1921; children-Allan Eustace, Constance Evelyn. Hydrographer U.S. Geol. Survey, 1905-06; with engring. staff Los Angeles Aqueduct, 1906-12; in charge underground water investigations of Cal. State Conservation Commn., in So. Cal., 1912; pvt. practice, 1912-17; pres. State Water Commn. of Cal., Oct. 1, 1919-June 30, 1921; chief of Div. of Water Rights, Dept. of Pub. Works, Cal., July 1921-Dec. 1921; practiced as consulting engr., San Francisco, 1921-; sr. partner Lee & Praszker, cons. engrs., 1958-; dir. Pacific Hydrologic Lab. since 1929; chief Div. Water Supply and Sanitation, Dept. of Works, Golden Gate Internat. Expn., 1936-39. Lecturer in civil engring., U. Cal., 1923. Served with A.E.F. in France as 1st lt. and capt. of engrs.; with Water Supply Service on line of communications, 9 mos.; on active front 8 mos., serving with First Army during St. Mihiel and Argonne offensives. Engring. cons. on naval and military construction, World War II. Mem. Am. Water Works Assn., Am. Geophys. Union, Am. Soc. C.E. (awarded Norman Medal for special contribution to engring. sci. 1939), Kappa Sigma. Clubs: Sierra, Commonwealth of California, Engineers (San Francisco). Author: Divine Direction or Chaos? 1952. Home: 1988 San Antonio Rd., Berkeley 7, Cal. Office: 58 Sutter St., San Francisco 4. Died May 4, 1967.

LEE, DAVID B., san. engr.; b. Douglasville, Ga., Sept. 23, 1907; s. W. A. and Mollie (Smith) L.; B.S., U. Fla., 1932, D.Sc. (hon.), 1968; M.S., Harvard U., 1937; married Billie Rawls, July 28, 1939; children—David B., and Susan Rawls. With Fla. State Bd. of Health 1932-68, field engr., 1934-35, dist. engr., 1935-37, malaria control engr., 1938-41, dir. Bur. San. Engring., 1941-68; pres. David B. Smith Engrs., Inc., Gainesville, 1968. Loaned by U.S. Army to Inst. of Inter-Am. Affairs specialist in malaria control engring; spl. consultant U.S.P.H.S. on san. engring. problems 1948-68, engring. dir. res.; vis. lectr. U. Fla., 1959-60; permanent chairman Fla. com. on water supply and sewerage edn., U. Fla.; registered prof. engr. State of Fla. Adv. to U.S. World Health Orgn.; mem. delegation 2d World Health Assembly, Rome, 1949; conferred with A.E.C. on radioactive indsl. waste disposal; served on panel of environmental sanitation of the President's Commn. on Health Needs of the Nation, 1952; mem. Nat. Research Council's Commission on san. engineering and environment. Served as maj. San. Corps, Med. Dept., U.S. Army, 1942-45. Received Kenneth Allen award Fedn. Sewage Works Assns., 1948; award Fla. Engring. Soc. for exeptional service to engring. profession State of Fla., 1949; Man of Year award, Am. Soc. San. Engring., 1954; Centennial award U. Fla., 1953; Fuller award Am. Water Works Assn., 1954; Meritorious award Fla. Pub. Health Assn., 1964. One of Ten Top Men Yr., 1961, Am. Pub. Works Assn.; Gold Merit award notable achievement state govt. service Asso. Industries Fla., 1965; Charles Alvin Emerson medal meritorious service Water Pollution Control Federation, 1966. Fellow of the Fla. Engring. Society (secretary 1946-50, president 1952-53), Am. Pub. Health Association; member Nat. Assn. Sanitation (hon.), Nat. Soc. Profl. Engrs. (dir.), Fedn. Sewage and Indsl. Waste Assns. (pres. 1954-55) Conf. State San. Engrs. (chairman 1948-49), Am. Water Works Assn. (nat. dir. 1948-51; vice chmn. Fla. sect., 1957-58, chmn. 1958-59), Newcomen Soc. N.A. (mem. Fla. com.), Acad. Sanitary Engrs. Council Cons., Nat. Sanitation Found., Harvard Pub. Health Alumni Assn., Fla. Water and Sewage Works Operators Assn. (life), Fla. Pub. Health Assn. (pres. 1950-51), Fla. Anti-Mosquito Assn. (pres. 1946-47), Am. Soc. C.E., Fla. Pollution Assn. (pres. 1941-42, hon. mem. 1956), Nat. Swimming Pool Inst., Water Pollution Control Federation (honorary), Sigma Tau. Episcopalian (sr. warden). Club: Kiwanis (pres. 1953). Home: Jacksonville FL Died Oct. 31, 1968; buried Pensacola FL

LEE, ELMER physician; b. Piqua, O., Mar. 12, 1856; s. Jonathan and Nancy L.; A.B., Ohio Wesleyan, 1877, A.M., 1880; M.D., Washington U., St. Louis, 1882; Ph.B., St. Louis U., 1886; unmarried. Practiced medicine, St. Louis, 1882-88, Chicago, 1888-96, since then in New York; visited Europe in 1892; studied cholera in Russia and Germany; lecturer on health, New York Bd. of Edn. Inventor of liquid soap and holder; designed improved tenements and apartments providing outside light and ventilation for each room of every dwelling; also improved plans for hosps. and country villas; writer on diet and natural treatment of disease. Mem. com. U.S. Pharmacopoeia, 1890-1900; acting asst. surgeon U.S.A. war with Spain. Officer Am. Academy Medicine, A.M.A., Am. Social Science Assn. Author: The Health Culture Books (12 vols.), 1924. Founder Health Culture Hotel and Hosp. (New York) and Health Culture School, for edn. in right living. Editor, Health Culture Mag. Address: 140 W. 58th St., New York, N.Y.

LEE, FITZHUGH army officer; b. Clermont, Fairfax Co., Va, Nov. 19, 1835; s. Commodore Sydney Smith L. U.S.N., and Anna Maria (Mason) L.; grad. U.S. Mil. Acad., 1856. Severely wounded in a fight with Indians; instr. of cav., West Point, 1860-61; resigned commission, 1861; was adj. gen. Ewell's brigade, C.S.A., until Sept. 1861; lt. col. and col. 1st Va. cav., participating in all battles of Army of Northern Va., 1861-62; brig. gen., July 25, 1862; maj. gen., Sept. 3, 1863; had 3 horses shot under him and was himself severely wounded at Winchester, Va., Sept. 19, 1864; comd. whole cav. corps Army of Northern Va., Mar. 1865, until he surrendered to Gen. Meade at Farmville; gov. Va., 1886-90. Democrat. U.S. consul to Havana from 1893 until declaration of war with Spain; apptd., May 1898 maj. gen. U.S. vols.; placed in command 7th army corps; after war became mil. gov. Havana, Jan. 1, 1899; later in command dept. of Mo., U.S.A. Home: Richmond, Va. Died 1905.

LEE, FREDERIC PADDOCK, lawyer; b. Lincoln, Neb., Jan. 6, 1893; s. George Sterling and Maud Maria (Paddock) L.; Ph.B., Hamilton Coll., Clinton, N.Y., 1915, LL. D., 1964; M.A., Columbia, 1916, LL.B., 1918; m. Marian A. Armstrong, June 22, 1918; children—Eleanor (Mrs. Frederick R. Ahmuty), Sterling, Barbara (Mrs. Walker B. Blincoe), Richard Curry. Began as assistant legislative counsel United States House of Representatives, 1919-23; legislative counsel, U.S. Senate, 1923-30; mem. law firm of MacCracken & Lee, Washington, 1930-34; spl. counsel Sec. of Agr., 1933; member board and gen. counsel Federal Alcohol Control Adminstrn., 1934-35; mem. law firm Alvord & Alvord, Washington, D.C., 1935-49; mem. law firm Lee, Toomey & Kent 1950-61, ret., 1961; prof. law Georgetown University, 1929-35; dir. Garlock, Inc., 1952-62. Lectr. on law, polit. sci. at various times Williams Coll., Harvard, Brookings Instn., U. Va., Am. U. Columbia U. President County Council for Montgomery County, Md., 1949-50, Montgomery County (Md.) Civic Fed., 1931-33; mem. Maryland Nat. Capital Park and Planning Commn., 1934-35; chmn. Montgomery Co. (Md.) Charter Bd., 1942-44; mem., chmn. adv. council Nat. Arboretum, 1946-68. Trustee Hamilton Coll., 1942-63, emeritus, 1963-68; trustee Schwarzhaupt Found., 1937-68, Washington Center for Met. Studies, 1961-68. Served as private inf., 1918; 2d lt. inf. O.R.C., 1918-23; capt. judge advocate, 1924-29. Mem. Am., D.C. bar assns., Assn. Bar City N.Y., Am. Soc. Internat. Law, Am. Hort. Soc. (dir. 1951-68, 1st v.p. 1947-50, Gold medal 1959), Am. Rhododendron Soc. (gold medal for hort. achievement 1964), N.Am. Lily Soc., Am. Daffodil Soc., Am. Holly Soc., Am. Assn. Bot. Gardens and Arboretums, Internat. Soc. Plant Taxonomy, Royal Hort. Soc. Democrat. Clubs: Cosmos, Columbia Country. (Washington). Author: The Azalea Book, 1958. to profl. jours. Home: Bethesda MD Died Oct. 2, 1968; buried Hamilton College, Clinton NY

LEE, GENTRY petroleum exec., lawyer; b. Center Point, Ark., Feb. 20, 1903; s. William Franklin and Mattie (Gentry) L.; student So. Meth. U., 1918-20; LL.B., U. Okla., 1924; m. Wilma Elliott, June 16, 1934; 1 son, William Gentry. Admitted to Okla. bar, 1924; asst. atty. Okla. State Banking Dept., 1925-27; partner Harper & Lee, Tulsa, 1928-37, Conner, Winters, Lee & Randolph, 1946-51; staff atty. Barnsdall Oil Co., 1937-45; gen. counsel, v.p., dir. Cities Service Petroleum Co., Bartlesville, Okla., 1951-, made sr. v.p.; dir. Union Nat. Bank (Bartlesville). Mem. adv. bd. Internat. Oil and Gas Ednl. Center, S.W. Legal Found. Served with Judge Adv. Gen. Corps, U.S. Army, 1942-46; disch. Res. lt. col. Decorated Commendation ribbon. Fellow of the American Bar Foundation; mem. Mid-Continent Oil & Gas Assn. (dir., chmn. finance com., vice chmn. legal com.), Ind. Natural Gas Assn. Am., Inter-Am., Fed., Fed. Am., Okla., - Tulsa County (pres. 1950),

Washington County bar assns., Am. Petroleum Inst., Okla. U. Coll. Law Assn. (pres. 1960), Okla. U. Alumni Assn. (life), Order of Coif, Sigma Alpha Epsilon, Phi Delta Phi. Presbyn. Mason. Clubs: Rotary, Hillcrest Country (Bartlesville, Okla.); So Hills Country, Tulsa (Tulsa); Cherokee Yacht. Home: 1110 S. Cherokee St. Office: Cities Service Bldg., Bartlesville, Okla. Died June 15, 1965.

LEE, GEORGE WASHINGTON CUSTIS univ. pres.; b. Fortress Monroe, Va., Sept. 16, 1832; s. Gen. Robert Edward (C.S.A.) and Mary Ann Randolph (Custis) L.; acad. edn. in Va.; grad. U.S. Mil. Acad., 1854; LL.D., Tulane U., 1887; unmarried. Did important mil. engring. work in Fla. and Calif.; during Civil War was a.d.c. on staff Jefferson Davis; rose to rank of maj. gen. and was captured at Sailor's Creek; prof. civ. and mil. engring., Va. Mil. Inst., 1865; succeeded his father, 1871, as pres. Washington and Lee U., until 1897, pres. emeritus, 1897-. Address: Burke, Va. Died Feb. 18, 1913.

LEE, HARRY officer U.S.M.C.; b. Georgetown, D.C., June 4, 1872; s. Jesse Washington and Laura Rose (Collings) L.; ed. pub. schs., Georgetown; m. Henrietta Mercedes Saltmarsh, June 25, 1912; 5 children. Commd. in U.S.M.C., Aug. 2, 1898; promoted through grades to brig. gen., June 5, 1920. Comd. 6th Regt. Marines, June 6, 1918-Aug. 13, 1919; participated in Chateau-Thierry, Soissons, Mabache sector, St. Mihiel, Blanc Mont, Meuse-Argonne operations and with Army of Occupation, Coblenz bridgehead, Germany. Apptd. comdr. 2d Brig. U.S.M.C., Santo Domingo, D.R., Aug. 8, 1921, military gov. same, 1923-24; later comdg. Marine Barracks, Pariss Island, S.C. Decorated D.S.M., both Army and Navy (U.S.); Officer Legion of Honor and Croix de Guerre with 2 palms (French). Died May 13, 1935.

LEE, JAMES GRAFTON CARLETON brigadier gen. U.S.A.; b. nr. Hamilton, Ont., Aug. 13, 1836; s. Samuel and Anna (Shafer) L.; grad. Victoria U., Cobourg, Can.; m. Sarah J. Loomis, Apr. 25, 1861; m. 2d, Maud Cromelien, Aug. 12, 1902. Apptd. from civil life, Ohio, capt. a.q.m. vols., Nov. 26, 1862; capt. a.q.m. U.S.A., July 2, 1864; maj. q.m., July 2, 1879; lt. col. deputy q.m. gen., Dec. 11, 1892; col. asst. q.m. gen., Feb. 18, 1897; retired, Aug. 12, 1900; advanced to rank of brig. gen. retired, by act of Apr. 23, 1904. Bvtd. maj. and lt. col., July 31, 1865, "for faithful and meritorious services." In Civil War served at headquarters Army of Potomac and at several supply depots in Va., acting chief q.m. during Gettysburg campaign, and in charge depot, Alexandria, Va.; comd. right wing of defenses of Alexandria, Va., 1864; after was in various depts. and duties until retired as chief q.m. Dept. of Lakes; pres. bd. in Cuba to prepare for landing U.S. forces, 1898. Dir. Chicago Inst., 1900-01; mil. instr. Northwestern Mil. Acad., 1901-03. Mason. Address: Hague-on-Lake-George, N.Y.; and Ft. Sam Houston, Tex. Died July 26, 1916.

LEE, JESSE MATLOCK maj. gen. U.S.A.; b. Putnam County, Ind., Jan. 2, 1843; s. John W. and Effey W. L.; ed. Greencastle, Ind.; m. Lucy W. Hathaway, Dec. 23, 1868. Pvt. Co. B, and sergt. 59th Ind. Inf., Nov. 13, 1861; 2d lt., Oct. 13, 1862; 1st lt., Feb. 14, 1863; capt., Aug. 11, 1863; hon. mustered out, July 17, 1865; capt. 38th, U.S.C.T., Aug. 23, 1865; hon. mustered out of vols., Jan. 25, 1867; apptd. 2d lt. 39th U.S. Inf., July 28, 1866; 1st lt., Jan. 7, 1867; capt., May 1, 1879; maj., Apr. 26, 1898; col. 10th U.S. Inf. Vols., May 31-July 8, 1898; lt. col. 6th U.S. Inf., Oct. 9, 1900; col. 30th Inf., Nov. 8, 1901; brig. gen., June 17, 1902; maj. gen., Sept. 18, 1906; retired Jan. 2, 1907. Home: Greencastle, Ind. Died Mar. 26, 1926.

LEE, JOHN CLIFFORD HODGES army officer; b. Junction City, Kan., Aug. 1, 1887; s. Charles Fenlon and John Clifford (Hodges) L. (mother given her father's name); B.S., U.S. Mil. Acad., West Point, N.Y., 1909; student Army Engring. Sch., U.S. Army Staff Coll., France, 1918, Army War Coll., Washington, D.C., 1931-32, Army Indsl. Coll., 1932-33; hon. LL.D., Bristol University; Sc.D. (hon.), Des Moines College Osteopathy and Surgery; m. Sarah Ann Row, Sept. 24, 1917 (died Aug. 25, 1939); 1 son, Colonel John Clifford Hodges, Jr.; married 2d, Eve B. Ellis, Sept. 1945 (dec. 1953). Commd. 2d lt. C.E., U.S. Army, 1909, advancing through ranks to lieut. general (temp.), 1944; permanent major general, 1945; served, Panama Canal, 1909-10; 3d Battalion Engrs., 1911-13; mil. survey of Guam, 1913-14, of Luzon, 1914-15, Ohio River improvement, 1915-17; on staff Gen. Leonard Wood, 1917-18, 1919-20; with 89th Div., A.E.F. in France and Germany, 1918-19; Gen. Staff Corps (6th Corps Area and Philippine Dept.), 1920-23; in Office Chief of Engrs., 1923-26; dist. engr., Vicksburg, 1926-31; with Civic Works Authority, and dist. engr., Washington, D.C., 1934; mem. bd. engrs. for rivers and harbors, 1934-35; dist. engr. Phila., 1934-38; div. engr. N. Pacific Div., 1938-40; temp. duty, Air Corps, May-Aug. 1939; comd. San Francisco Port of Embarkation, Ft. Mason, Calif., 1940-41; comd. 2d Inf. Div., Nov. 1941-May 1942; comdg. Services of Supply and Communication Zone, E.T.O., May 1942-Jan. 1946; dept. theatre comdr., Jan. 1944; comdg. Mediterranean Theatre Operation, Jan. 1946-Sept. 1947; ret. as lt. gen. for disability, Dec. 31, 1947. Awarded Distinguished Serv. Medal (Army and Navy), Silver Star, Croix de Guerre; Grand Officer Legion of Honor; Knight Comdr. British Empire; also Belgian, Luxembourg and Italian decorations. Mem. Soc. Am. Mil. Engineers, Society of the Cincinnati, Scabbard and Blade. Episcopalian. Clubs: Army-Navy (Washington). Author: Manual for Topographers, 1915. Home: 182 Highland Rd., Southwood Hills. Address: Brotherhood of St. Andrew, 709 W. Market St., York, Pa. Died Aug. 30, 1958; buried Arlington Nat. Cemetery.

LEE, JOSEPH (WALLACE) newspaperman; born Donnellson, Ill., July 3, 1908; s. Oscar Benjamin and Mary Ola (Ashcraft) L.; student Grinnell Coll., 1926-27; A.B., U. Okla., 1931; m. Mary Frances Douglas, May 5, 1935. Free lance writer, 1931-34; mgr. radio sta. KADA, Ada., Okla., 1934-37, KTOK, Oklahoma City, 1937-38, KGEF, Shawnee, 1938-44; mng. dir. Okla. Network, 1937-38, pres., 1942; chief editorial writer Topeka State Jour. since 1944, editorial editor, 1946-. Served as seaman, U.S. Navy, World War II. Member American Society Newspaper Editors, Phi Beta Kappa, Delta Chi. Home: 2231 Washburn Av. Office: Topeka State Journal. Topeka. Died Nov. 26, 1960; buried Mt. Hope Mausoleum, Topeka.

LEE, LANSING B. lawyer; b. Augusta, Ga., June 20, 1887; s. John Corbett and Martha G. (Bothwell) L.; A.B., U. of Ga., 1906; LL.B., Harvard, 1910; m. Bertha Barrett, Mar. 1, 1919; children-Lansing B., Bertha B., Thomas Barrett D'Antignac (stepson). Admitted to Ga. bar, 1910; asso. firm Lamar & Callaway, 1910-14; mem. firm Alexander & Lee, 1914-24; sr. partner Lee, Congdon & Fulcher since 1924; pres. Ga.-Carolina Warehouse & Compress Co.; dir. Citizens & Southern Nat. Bank, Southern Mutual Ins. Co., Graniteville Co. Served on Augusta (Ga.) Sinking Fund Commn. since 1934. Maj. gen. staff 82d Div., A.E.F., World War. Pres. Tuttle Newton Home; trustee Augusta Free Sch. J.B. White Foundation, Gertrude Herbert Memorial Inst. of Art. Mem. Am, Ga. State and Augusta (ex-pres.) bar assns., Sigma Alpha Epsilon. Independent Democrat. Baptist. Clubs: Augusta National, Augusta Country. Home: 820 Fleming Av. Office: Southern Finance Bldg., Augusta, Ga. Died Apr. 8, 1944.

LEE, RAYMOND ELIOT ex-army officer; b. St. Louis, Mar. 26, 1886; s. Joseph Milton and Emma Susan (Lowe) L.; B.S. in Civil Engring., U. of Mo., 1909; grad. Command & Gen. Staff Sch., 1923; Army War Coll., 1927; m. Jeanette Baker, July 7, 1923; 1 dau., Susan Jenifer. Commd. 2d lt. U.S. Army, 1909, advanced through grades to brig. gen. (temp.), 1940; served Mexican Border, 1917, 2d Regular Div., 15th Field Artillery, World War, 1917-18, War Dept., 1918-22, P.I., 1923-26, Gen. Staff Corps, 1928-32; mil. attaché, London, 1935-39, 40-41; ret. Feb. 28, 1946. Decorated D.S.M. Mem. Beta Theta Pi. Episcopalian. Clubs: Chevy Chase, Army and Navy, Metropolitan (Washington). Home: 1344 30th St., N.W., Washington and St. Brandans, Paris, Va. Died Apr. 7, 1958.

LEE, ROBERT CORWIN, shipping company executive; born Central City, Nebraska, Aug. 30, 1888; s. William A. and Molly (Foulks) L.; ed. U.S. Naval Acad.; m. Elsie Calder, June 15, 1918; children—Katherine Calder, Lee Keenan, Mary Anne Foulks, Lee Llerena, Elsie Calder Lee Brothers, Robert Corwin Jr. Officer, USN, 1906-20; captain Destroyer Wainwright, and U.S. Naval Port Officer at Nantes, France, during World War I. Pres. Foreign Shipping Service Co. and R.C. Lee, Inc., 1920; asst. treas. Moore & McCormack Co., Inc., 1921, now dir. and ret. chmn. bd., also ret. chmn. of all asso. cos.; v.p. Am. Scantic Line, Inc., from 1927; pres. Am. Scantic Line in Poland, from 1930, also dir. Served as capt. to commodore, spl. asst. Naval Trans. Service; with Admiral Nimitz staff in Pacific, Adm. Stark and Gen. Eisenhower in Europe; rear adm. USN. Received Cruzeiro do Sul of Brazil (Grande Oficial), Oficial do Merito Naval (Brazil), ship-owners delegate for U.S. to 21st and 22nd Maritime Sessions Internat. Labor Conf. at Geneva; member maritime section International Labor Conf., Geneva, Soc. of Naval Architects and Marine Engrs., Maritime Exchange, Knight Order of Polonia Restituta. Mason. Clubs: Somerset Lake and Game, Army-Navy, India House, Downtown Athletic (Washington); Morristown (N.J.); Nat. Republican. Home: New York City NY Died Sept. 1, 1971; buried Arlington National Cemetery, Arlington VA

LEE, ROBERT EDWARD comdr.-in-chief Confederate Army; b. "Stratford," Westmoreland County, Va., Jan. 19, 1807; s. Henry (Light Horse Harry) and Ann (Carter) L.; grad. U.S. Mil. Acad., 1829; m. Mary Ann Curtis, June 30, 1831, 7 children including George Washington Custis, William H. Fitzhugh. Brevetted 2d lt. Corps Engrs., U.S. Army; asst. engr. Ft. Monroe, Va., 1831-34; asst. in chief engr.'s office, Washington, D.C., 1834-37; aided in running Ohio-Mich, boundary line, 1835; promoted 1st lt., 1836; supt. engr. for St. Louis harbor, upper Mississippi and Mo. rivers, 1837-41; promoted capt., 1838; stationed Ft. Hamilton, N.Y., 1841-46; asst. engr. U.S. Army, San Antonio, Tex., 1846; served in Mexican War, 1846-48, brevetted col. U.S. Army for gallantry, 1848; in charge of constrn. Ft. Carroll, Baltimore harbor, 1848-52; supt. U.S. Mil. Acad., 1852-55; promoted lt. col. 2d U.S. Cavalry, 1855; commanded detachment which suppressed John Brown's raid at Harper's Ferry, 1859; commanded Dept. of Tex., 1860-Feb. 1861; promoted col. 1st Cavalry, Mar. 1861; declined field command of U.S. Army (privately offered by Francis P. Blair, head of Ho. Com. on Mil. Def.); resigned from U.S. Army, Apr. 20, 1861 (resignation accepted Apr. 25, 1861); accepted command of Va. forces, Apr. 23, 1861; apptd. mil. adviser (with rank of gen.) to Pres. Jefferson Davis, Confederate States Am.; organized defenses of South Atlantic seaboard, Nov. 1861-Mar. 1862; placed in command of Army of No. Va., June 1, 1862; defeated McClellan in Seven Days' Battle, June 25-July 1, 1862; defeated Pope at Battle of 2d Manassas, Aug. 30, 1862; started campaign into Md., was checked at Battle of Antietam (Md.), Sept. 1862; defeated Burnside at Battle of Fredericksburg. (Va.), Dec. 1862; defeated Hooker at Battle of Chancellorsville May 1863; lost Battle of Gettysburg, July 1-4, 1863; promoted comdr.-in-chief of all Confederate Armies, Feb. 6, 1865; conducted (with interior forces) defensive operations against Gen. Grant, including battles of Spotsylvania and Cold Harbor, siege of Richmond, May 1864-Apr. 1865; surrendered to Gen. Grant at Appomattox Court House, Va., Apr. 9, 1865; pres. Washington Coll., Lexington, Va., 1866-70 (name later changed to Washington and Lee U. in his honor); spent his last years advocating acceptance of defeat and rebuilding of South; his estate "Arlington" is now site of Arlington Nat. Cemetery. Died Lexington, Oct. 12, 1870; buried Washington and Lee University.

LEE, ROBERT EDWARD farmer; b. Arlington House, Va., Oct. 27, 1843; s. Gen.-Robert Edward (C.S.A.) and Mary Ann Randolph (Custis) L.; ed. pvt. schs. in Va., and at U. of Va., 1860; m. Juliet Carter, Mar. 8, 1894. Enlisted in Army of Northern Va., C.S.A.,- until Apr. 9, 1865, becoming capt.; after Civil War engaged in farming. Episcopalian. Author: Recollections and Letters of General Robert E. Lee, by His Son, 1904. Address: West Point, Va. Died Oct. 19, 1914.

LEE, ROGER IRVING physician; b. Peabody, Mass., Aug. 12, 1881; s. William Thomas and Mary Emily (Farnsworth) L.; B.A., Harvard, 1902, M.D., 1950, LL.D., 1954; m. Ella Lowell Lyman, Feb. 26, 1919; children-Roger Irving, Arthur Lyman, William Thomas. Practiced in Boston, 1905-14; vis. physician Mass. Gen. Hosp., 1912-23; Henry K. Oliver prof. hygiene Harvard, 1914-24; returned to practice medicine, 1924; cons. internal medicine. Overseer, Harvard, 1930-31, fellow, 1931-54. Commd. maj. Med. Res. Corps, Apr. 5, 1917; lt. col. M.C., U.S. Army, June 6, 1918; service in France with Base Hosp. 5, and cons. in medicine to 3d Corps AEF, 1917-19; hon. discharged, Feb. 10, 1919. Mem. Pub. Health Council State of Mass., 1921-34; sec. Mass. Tb Commn., 1910. Trustee Boston Symphony Orch., 1934-50. Fellow Royal Coll. Physicians, London, Eng.; mem. Assn. Am. Physicians, Soc. Clin. Investigation, A.C.P. (pres. 1941), Am. Acad. Arts and Scis., A.M.A. (chmn. bd. trustees, pres. 1945-46), Mass. Med. Soc. (pres. 1943-44). Clubs: Somerset, Harvard (Boston). Author: Health and Disease, 1917; The Fundamentals of Good Medical Care (with Lewis W. Jones); The Happy Life of a Doctor, 1956; A Doctor Speaks His Mind, 1958; Letters From Roger I. Lee, 1962. Home: 446 Walnut St., Brookline, Mass. 02146. Died Oct. 28, 1965.

LEE, SAMUEL PHILLIPS naval officer; b. Fairfax County, Va., Feb. 13, 1812; s. Francis Lightfoot and Jane (Fitzgerald) L.; m. Elizabeth Blair, Apr. 27, 1843, 1 child, Francis Preston. Apptd. midshipman U.S. Navy, 1825, on coast survey duty, 1842-55, in command coast survey brig. Washington during Mexican War; commanded ship Dolphin, 1851, ship Oneida in Farragut's expdn. against New Orleans, 1862; acting rear adm. in command N. Atlantic blocking squadron off Va. and N.C., 1862; comdr. Mississippi Squadron, 1864; head Signal Service, 1870; promoted rear adm., 1870, commanded N. Atlantic Squadron, 1870-72. Died Silver Spring, Md., June 5, 1897; buried Arlington (Va.) Nat. Cemetery.

LEE, STEPHEN DILL commr. of Vicksburg Nat. Mil. Park, 1899-; b. Charleston, S.C., Sept. 22, 1833; s. Dr. Thomas and Caroline (Allison) L.; grad. West Point, 1854; LL.D., Tulane U., La.; 1st lt. 4th arty., U.S.A., 1854-61, and 3 yrs. regimental q. m. in same; became capt. in C.S.A.; afterward served in C.S.A. as capt., maj., lt. col., col., brig. gen., maj. gen. and lt. gen. Took part in battles around Richmond, 1862; in 2d Bull Run, Sharpsburg, Vicksburg campaign; comd. Confederates at Chickasaw Bayou, Miss., when Sherman was defeated, and in battles of Tupelo, Miss.; Atlanta, Ga.; Jonesborough, Ga.; Franklin, Nashville, etc. Was planter in Miss. after war; m. Regina Lillie Harrison, Feb. 9, 1865. State senator, 1870; mem. Constitutional Conv., Miss., 1890. Chmn. hist. com. Assn. of United Confederate Veterans; lt. gen. comdg. Army of Tenn. Dept. United Confederate Veterans; pres. Miss. Hist. Soc.; pres. Miss. Agrl. and Mech. Coll., 1880-99. Elected gen. comdg., U.C.V., 1904. Address: Columbus, Miss. Died 1908.

LEE, WILLIAM C. army officer; b. Dunn, N.C., Mar. 12, 1895; s. Eldridge and Emma Jane (Massengill) L.; student Wake Forest (N.C.) Coll., 1913-15; B.S., N.C. State Coll., 1917; grad. company officers course, Inf.

Sch., 1922. advanced course, 1933; grad. Tank Sch., Fort Meade, Md., 1930; Tank Sch., Versailles, France, 1934; grad. Command and Gen. Staff Sch., 1938; m. Dava Johnson, June 5, 1918. Commd. 2d lt., U.S. Army, 1913, and advanced through the ranks to brig. gen., 1942, major gen., Aug. 18, 1942; served in A.E.F., France, World War I; comdg. Am. parachute troops, 1941-42; comdg. airborne troops, 1942-45; retired 1945. Mem. Sigma Nu. Mason. Home: 209 W. Divine St. Address: Box 471, Dunn, N.C. Died June 25, 1948.

LEE, WILLIAM ERWIN govt. ofcl.; b. Madison County, N.C., Jan. 27, 1882; s. Reuben Francis and Althea (West) L.; A.B., U. of Ida., 1903; studied law, U. of Wash., 1903-04; LL.B., Nat. U. Law Sch., 1906; m. Mary Madeline Shields, July 1, 1914; children-William Shields, Richard McGowan, Mary Madeline, Flavia Ann, Charles Steele. Clerk to U.S. senators and congressmen during parts of each yr., 1904-08; admitted to Ida. bar, 1905, and began practice at Moscow; mem. firm Orland & Lee, 1913-23; asso. justice Supreme Court, Ida., 1923-26, chief justice, 1926-30; mem. Interstate Commerce Commn. 1930—, chmn., 1934. Capt., Idaho Nat. Guard, 1911-13; capt., Q.M.C., U.S. Army, 1918-19. Mem. Phi Beta Kappa, Phi Delta Theta. Republican. Elk. Home: 5422 Moorland Lane, Edgemoor, Bethesda, Md. Office: Interstate Commerce Commn., Washington. Died Dec. 5, 1955; buried Arlington (Va.) Cemetery.

LEE, WILLIAM HENRY FITZHUGH army officer, congressman; b. Arlington, Va., May 31, 1837; s. Gen. Robert Edward and Mary Ann (Custis) L.; grad. Harvard, 1857; m. Charlotte Wickham, 1859; m. 2d, Mary Boling, 1867. Served as 2d lt. 6th Inf., U.S. Army, 1857-59; commd. capt., then maj. of cavalry Confederate States Army, 1861; chief of cavalry in W. Va. Campaign, 1861; lt. col., then col. 9th Va. Cavalry, 1861-62, under command of Gen. J. B. Stuart; participated in 2d Battle of Manassas, Battle of Turner's Pass, raid on Chambersburg (Pa.), 1862; commd. brig. gen., commanded brigade at Battle of Chancellorsville, 1862, also in Fredericksburg, Gettysburg campaigns; promoted maj. gen. cavalry, 1864; pres. Va. Agrl. Soc.; mem. Va. Senate 1875-79; mem. U.S. Ho. of Reps. from Va., 50th-52d congresses, 1887-91. Died Alexandria, Va., Oct. 15, 1891; buried Lee Mausoleum, Lexington, Va.

LEE, WILLIS AUGUSTUS, JR. naval officer; b. Natlee, Ky., May 11, 1888; grad. Naval War Coll. senior course. Entered U.S. Navy, 1904, advanced to capt., 1936, rear adm., 1942, vice admiral Dec. 1944. Served as asst. chief of Staff to comdr. in chief, U.S. Fleet, to Feb. 1942; apptd. commdr. task force S.W. Pacific, Feb. 1942; in command when 5 Japanese ships were sunk in Naval engagement in Solomon Island, Nov. 1942. Decorated Navy Cross, Legion of Merit, Distinguished Service Medal, Died Aug. 25, 1945.

LEEDS, CHARLES TILESTON consulting engr.; b. Newton, Mass., May 14, 1879; s. Benjamin Ingersoll and Martha (Knapp) Huse L.; grad. (rank 2d in class) U.S. Mil. Acad., 1903; B.S., Mass. Inst. Tech., 1906; m. Amy Lee Shapleigh, Jan. 12, 1905; children-Charles Tileston, Alice Shapleigh (Mrs. E. H. Hunting), Eleanor Huse (Mrs. W. E. Fenzi), Elizabeth Chandler (Mrs. D. B. Myers, Jr.). Commd. 2d lt. A.U.S., June 11, 1903, advancing to capt. Engr. Corps, Feb. 27, 1911; exploration, rd. constrn. and port development, Mindanao, P.I., 1903-04; spl. studies at Mass. Inst. of Tech., 1905-06; post engr. ofcr. and asst. q.m., Fort Bayard, N.M., 1906-08; asst. U.S. dist. engr., Los Angeles, Calif., 1908-09, U.S. district engr., Los Angeles, Calif., 1909-12; mem. Calif. Debris Commn., 1909-12; retired (physical disability incurred in line of duty), 1912; mem. Leeds & Barnard, cons. engrs., Los Angeles, 1912-30, Quinton, Code, Hill, Leeds & Barnard, 1930-40, Leeds, Hill, Barnard & Jewett, 1940-46; Leeds, Hill & Jewett 1946-; has served as cons. engr. on harbors, water ways, sea coast protection, water supply, several govtl. agencies in Cal.; cons. engr. on seacoast protection for State of Calif., 1931-; cons. engr., Los Angeles Dept. Water & Power 1947-; tech. adv. Internat. Boundary and Water Commn., 1952-. Active duty, U.S. Army, 1917-19, maj. Engr. Corsp, 1918; lt. col. Engr. R.C., 1925-30. Mem. nat. state and local profl. socs. including: Am. Soc. C.E., Soc. Am. Mil. Engrs. Republican. Presbyn. Clubs: University, Engineers, (Los Angeles); Twilight (Pasadena); Newport Harbor Yacht. Home: 640 La Loma Rd., Pasadena, Cal. Office: 609 S. Grand Av., Los Angeles 17. Died Mar. 20, 1960; buried Mountain View Cemetery, Pasadena.

LEFFINGWELL, FORREST EMMETT, physician; b. Severy, Kan., Apr. 21, 1904; s. Howard Gordon and Etta (Warner) L.; A.B., Union Coll., Lincoln, Neb., 1926; M.D., Loma Linda U., 1933; m. Shirley Nicola, Aug. 3, 1926. Intern, Glendale (Cal.) Sanitarium and Hosp., 1932-33; pvt. practice, Montebello, Cal., 1934-40; resident anesthesiology White Meml. Hosp., Los Angeles, 1940-41, dir. dept. anesthesiology, 1946-68; sr. attending anesthesiologist Los Angeles County Hosp., 1955-69; prof. anesthesiology, chmn. dept. Loma Linda U., 1955-66. Served to lt. col., M.C., AUS, 1941-46; PTO. Diplomate Am. Bd. Anesthesiology (sec.-treas. 1958-69, bd. dirs. 1955-69, pres. 1969). Mem. Am. (speaker ho. dels. 1953-60, bd. dirs. 1950-69, pres. 1961-62), Cal. (pres. 1949), socs. anesthesiologists, Am., Cal., Los Angeles County Med. assns., Internat. Anesthesiology Research Soc., Internat. Coll. Surgeons, Los Angeles Acad. Medicine. Acad. Anesthesiology, Alpha Omega Alpha. Address: Pasadena CA Died Oct. 28, 1919; buried Rose Hills, Whittier CA

LEFFLER, CHARLES DOYLE b. Smithland, Ky., Aug. 12, 1868; s. Charles Henry and Mary Frances (Bibb) l.; ed. Horner Sch., Oxford, N.C., U. of the South, Sewanee, Tenn., Eastman Business Coll., Poughkeepsie, N.Y.; m. Hannah May Martin, Feb. 12, 1891; children-Cornelia, Lt. Comdr. Charles Doyle; m. 2d, Mrs. Bernice Horton Houser, June 26, 1935. With Plant Steamship Line until 1892; in retail grocery business, Sanford, Fla., 1892-1900, Miami, 1900-09; commn. agt. Gulf Refining Co., 1908-; pres. Florida Dairies, Linda Lee, Inc., Miami Laundry Co.; dir. Belcher Oil Co. City Commr., 1923-26. Served as 1st lt., U.S.A., Spanish-Am. War; lt. col. Fla. N.G. Served as chmn. Bd. Pilot Commrs. Port of Miami and chmn. Bd. Public Works; mayor of Miami, 1921-23. Mem. Miami Chamber Commerce (pres. 1936-17). Democrat. Home: Miami, Fla. Died Apr. 27, 1939.

LEFFLER, CHARLES DOYLE naval officer (ret.); b. Sanford, Fla., May 24, 1897; s. Charles Doyle and Hannah May (Martin) L.; B.S., U.S. Naval Acad., 1918; grad. U.S. Submarine Sch., 1924, Naval Postgrad. Sch., 1929, Jr. Naval War Coll., 1930; m. Bernice Thompson, May 10, 1929; 1 dau., May Martin (Mrs. Stewart D. Allen). Commd. ensign USN, 1918, and advanced through grades to rear adm., 1945; patrol duty in armored cruisers, 1918-19; qualified submarine comdr., 1925; served in destroyers, plane tenders, gun boats, submarines, 1920-41; comdr. U.S.S. Monrovia and Omaha, 1943-44; instr. U.S. Naval Acad. 1923-24; mem. Naval Staff Office, London, Eng., 1921; served at submarine base, Pearl Harbor, T.H., 1933-37; Bur. of Naval Personnel, Washington, 1939-42, 1944; ret. from active duty, Apr. 1, 1945; pres. Senate Bldg., Inc., Miami, since 1945; v.p. Leffler Properties, Inc., Miami, since 1945; dir. Belcher Oil Co., Belcher Towing Co., 1st Nat. Bank of Miami, Fla. Dairies Co. Chmn. bd. trustees, Jackson Meml. Hosp., Miami; trustee YMCA, Miami; chmn. aviation div. Miami C. of C. Awarded Legion of Merit, So. Cross (Brazil). Democrat. Methodist. Clubs: Biscayne Bay Yacht (Miami); Bath (Miami Beach). Home: 1625 South Bayshore Dr., Miami, Fla. Died Jan. 2, 1961; buried Woodlawn Cemetery, Miami.

LEFFLER, WILLIAM SKILLING cons. engr.; b. Stockton, Cal., Mar. 14, 1894; s. William H. and Mary L. (Skilling) L.; M.E., E.E., U. Cal., 1914. postgrad., 1915; m. Rita Wanamaker, Mar. 31, 1934. Asst. to gen. mgr. Great Western Power Co., San Francisco, 1915-17; sec., treas. Elec. Sales Service Corp., 1916-19; organizer Leffler, McLaughlin & Moore, 1919-22; dir. Bur. Rate Research, Bklyn. Edison Co., 1922-26; mem. Lacombe & Leffler, 1926-32; cons. engr., head firm William S. Leffler Engrs. Asso., Darien, Conn., 1932-. Served as aviator lt. AS U.S. Army, 1917-19; comdr. USCG Res. and Auxiliary, World War II. Mem. Am. Inst. E.E., Soc. Advancement Mgmt., Nat. Soc. Profl. Engrs., S.A.R. Soc. Aeroantique (brevet 1918), Society of Colonial Wars. Presbyterian. Clubs: Darien (Conn.) Cruising; University (Hartford, Conn.); Stamford (Conn.) Yacht. Inventor elec. water header, jellified gasoline for napalm bombs videorama. Pioneered techniques utility cost analysis. Home: 17 Baywater Dr., Darien, Conn. Died July 31, 1964; buried Springgrove, Darien.

LEGGE, BARNWELL R. army officer; b. Charleston, S.C., July 9, 1891; s. Claude Lascelles and Elizabeth Judd (Hutchinson) L.; B.S., Citadel, 1911; m. Phillis B. Gray; 1 son, Barnwell Ingraham. Commd. 2d lt., 1916; lt. col., 1st Div., World War I, 1917-20; comdg. 1st Bn., 26th Inf.; adjt. 1st Div., Grad. Inf. Sch., 1923; Ecole Superieure de Guerre, 1925; hist. sec., Army War Coll., 1927-29; student Comd. and Gen. Staff Sch., 1929; mem. Inf. bd., 1929-31; in comd. 3d Bn., 15th Inf., Am. Barracks, Tientsin, China, 1933-35; Army War Coll., 1936; instr. Comd. and Gen. Staff Sch., 1936-39; became U.S. mil. attaché, Bern, Switzerland, 1939. Advanced to brig. gen., May, 1942. Decorated D.S.C., D.S.M., Silver Star with 3 oak leaf clusters, Legion of Merit, Purple Heart, French Croix de Guerre with two palms, French Legion of Honor, Comdr. of Brit. Empire. Mem. Kappa Alpha (Southern). Address: American Legation, Berne, Switzerland. Died June 7, 1949.

LEGGE, LIONEL KENNEDY, justice; b. Charleston, S.C., Dec. 11, 1889; s. Claude Lascelles and Elizabeth Judd (Hutchinson) L.; A.B., Coll. of Charleston, 1909, LL.D., 1955; m. Dorothy Haskell Porcher, Dec. 9, 1920; children—Dorothy Porcher (Mrs. Frederick Deane, Jr.), Elizabeth Lascelles (Mrs. John W. Littlefield). Admitted to S.C. bar, 1913; practicing atty., 1913-54; asso. justice Supreme Ct. S.C., from 1954. Served as capt., inf., AEF, 1917-19. Mem. Am., S.C. bar assns., S.C. Soc., Soc. of Cin. Home: Charleston SC Died July 22, 1970; buried St. Philip's Churchyard, Charleston SC

LEGGE, ROBERT THOMAS, physician, prof.; b. San Francisco, Calif., July 16, 1872; s. Robert and Anna (Stelljes) L.; Ph.G., U. of Calif., 1891, M.D., 1899; diploma, U. of Vienna, 1924; m. Rene Farjeon, Nov. 23, 1903; children—Robert Farjeon, Margery Ann, Herbert William. Interne St. Luke's Hosp., San Francisco, 1899; chief surgeon McCloud River R.R. and Hosp., 1900-14; prof. hygiene and univ. physician, U. of Calif., 1915-42, emeritus. Lecturer on industrial medicine, U. of Calif. Med. Sch.; specialist in industrial hygiene and surgery. Dir. of Ernest V. Cowell Meml. Hosp., U. of Calif., ret. Was capt. Med. Corps, U.S. Army, 1917-18; lt. col. Med. O.R.C. Recipient of William S. Knudsen Award, 1950-51. Member Alameda County Instns. Commn. Mem. permanent Internat. Com. on Indsl. Medicine. Mem. adv. council Calif. State Bd. Vocational Edn. (rehabilitation). Past pres. Western Assn. of Indsl. Physicians and Surgeons. Diplomate Am. Bd. Pub. Health and Preventive Medicine. Fellow Am. Coll. Surgeons; mem. A.M.A., A.A.A.S., Am. College Health Assn. (Pacific dir.), Acad. Occupational Med. (hon.), Pan Am. Med. Assn. (emeritus), Calif. Heart Assn., Calif. Council Agencies for Handicapped, Calif. Academy Med. Calif. State Med. Soc., Alameda Co. Medical Assn., Sigma Xi, Delta Omega, Alpha Kappa Lambda, Nu Sigma Nu, Ramazzini Soc., Scabbard and Blade; hon. mem. Am. Indsl. Physicians, Am. Assn. U. Profs. Republican. Episcopalian. Mason (K.T.). Clubs: Faculty, City Commons (Berkeley); Bohemian (San Francisco). Asso. editor Industrial Medicine and Surgery. Home: 6 Roble Rd., Berkeley 5 CA

LEGGETT, MORTIMER DORMER supt. schs., army officer, electric co. exec.; b. Ithaca, N.Y., Apr. 19, 1821; s. Isaac and Mary (Strong) L.; studied Willoughby Med. Coll.; m. Marilla Wells, July 9, 1844; m. 2d, Weltha Post, 1879; 1 child. Admitted to bar, 1844; founder 1st free grade sch. system west of Alleghany Mountains, Akron, O., 1846, supt. schs., 1846-49; supt. schs., Warren, O., 1849-55; prof. law and pleading Ohio Law Coll., 1856; supt. schs., Zanesville, O., 1857; commd. col. 18th Ohio Volunteers; served as brig. gen. in command brigade in fight along the Mississippi River, 1862; brevetted maj. gen., 1863; fought at battles of Corinth. Shiloh, Vicksburg, Atlanta; marched with Sherman through South; commd. maj. gen. U.S. Volunteers, resigned 1866; U.S. patent commr., 1871-74; 1st pres. Brush Electric Co. (later absorbed into Gen. Electric Co.), 1884. Died Jan. 6, 1896.

LEHMAN, ROBERT, investment banker; b. New York, N.Y., Sept. 29, 1891; s. Philip and Carrie (Lauer) L.; prep. education, Hotchkiss Sch. Lakeville, Conn. 1905-09. A.B., Yale, 1913; married Lee Anz Lynn, July 10, 1952; 1 son by previous marriage, Robert Owen. Partner Lehman Bros., investment bankers, N.Y.; chmn. bd., chief exec. officer Lehman Corp. (investment trust); dir. Asso. Drygoods Corp., So. States Land & Timber Co., Gimble Brothers, United Fruit; dir. and mem. exec. com. 20th Century Fox Films Corp., Pan-Am. World Airways, Inc. Dir. Met. Opera; trustee assos. fine arts, gov. bd. art gallery, Yale U.; adv. com. Inst. Fine Arts, mem. bd., council N.Y.U.; chmn. bd. Met. Mus. Art; mem. vis. com. Fogg Art Mus. Trustee Mt. Sinai Hosp.; chmn. Hertz Found. Amassed one of most important pvt. art collections ever assembled, exhibited at Louvre, 1957, and donated to Met. Mus. Art, 1969. Served as capt. 318th F.A., U.S. Army, AEF, World War I. Mem. Council Fgn. Relations, French Legion of Art, N.Y. Stock Exchange, Delta Kappa Epsilon. Clubs: Yale, Turf and Field. Home: New York City NY Died Aug. 9, 1969.

LEHMANN, FREDERICK WILLIAM JR. lawyer; b. Des Moines, Dec. 10, 1883; s. Frederick William, Sr., and Nora (Stark) L.; student Smith Acad., St. Louis, 1901; A.B., Harvard, 1905; LL.B., St. Louis Law Sch., 1907; m. Margaret Mills, Oct. 26, 1912; children-Webster Mills, Janet (Mrs. Arthur S. Chenal). Admitted to Mo. bar, 1906, practiced St. Louis, 1906-09, Des Moines since 1909, in Kansas City, 1919-21; chairman board Pioneer Hi- Bred Corn Co.; owner, operator several Ia. farms; dir. Petrolite, Corporation. Administrator Polk County Emergency Relief, 1939; treas. Community Chest, 1935; dir. or atty. charitable agys. Served in U.S. Army, 1917-19, in France, 1918-19, disch. as capt. F.A. Dir. Am. Petroleum Inst., 1921. Mem. Am. Seed Trade Assn., Am. Ia., Polk Co. bar assns. Club: Des Moines. Home: 2410 Park Av. Office: Paramount Bldg., Des Moines 50309. Died Dec. 30, 1961.

LEHRBAS, LLOYD ALLAN govt. ofcl.; b. Montpelier, Ida., Oct. 15, 1896; s. Louis A. and Marjorie (Morris) L.; student U. Ida., 1915, U. Wis., 1916-17. Reporter successively with Salt Lake Tribune, San Francisco Chronicle, Chgo. Am., Chgo. Tribune; then asst. city editor Chgo. Evening Am.; fgn. corr. Internat. News Service, Japan, China, P.I.; news editor Fox Movietone News; fgn. affairs writer A.P. Washington; war corr. A.P., China, Poland, France, Italy, Spain, Rumania, Turkey. Hon. mention for Pulitzer prize for fgn. corr., 1939. Dir. Office Internat. Information, State Dept., 1948-49; spl asst. to undersec. of state since 1949. Served as flying lt. AS, U.S. Army, 1917-18; col., aide to Gen. MacArthur, Mar. 1942-Mar. 1946, spl. cons. to Gen. Ridgeway, SHAPE, 1952-53; spl. asst. to sec. of army and to chief of staff, 1953-58. Decorated Legion of Merit, Bronze Star. Mem. Sigma

Delta Chi. Episcopalian. Mason. Clubs: Nat. Press, Army and Navy (Washington). Exec. editor World Report, 1946-48. Contbr. mags. Address: 3636 16th St. N.W., Washington. Died Oct. 30, 1964.

LEIDY, JOSEPH II M.D.; b. Phila., Pa., Apr. 11, 1866; s. Philip (M.D.) and Penelope Fontaine Maury (Polk) L.; A.B., Phila. Central High Sch., 1884, A.M., 1885; M.D., U. of Pa., 1887; m. Helen Redington Carter; children-Cornelia Carter (Mrs. J. Hamilton Cheston), Philip Ludwell, Carter Randolph, Joseph (dec.), Physician University Hosp., 1887-89, Pa. Gen. Hosp., 1889-91, Pa. Hosp. for Insane; surgeon Howard Hosp., 1891; Hamilton and Phila. Dispensary; phys. to Med. Clinic. Pa. Hosp., 1893-1903; asst. demonstrator pathology, anatomy and morbid histology, U. of Pa., 1892, and of anatomy, 1894. Fellow Coll. of Physicians, A.A.A.S. Acad. Natural Sciences. Official del. from U.S. Govt. and juror on hygiene, Paris, 1900; decorated Officier de l'Instruction Publique, France, 1900;- official del. from U.S. Govt. to the Internat. Congress of Hygiene and Demographie, 1900; represented A.A.A.S. at transfer of home of Charles Darwin to British Nation, 1929. Served as lt. col. Med. Corps, U.S.A.; instr. and med. dir. of gas defense, 30th Div., staff officer U.S.A., 1917-19, World War; lt. col. Med. Res. U.S.A. Republican. Home: Philadelphia, Pa. Died July 7, 1932.

LEIGH, RICHARD HENRY naval officer; b. Panola County, Miss., Aug. 12, 1870; s. Elbridge Gerry and Susan (Gattis) L.; grad. U.S. naval Acad., 1891; grad. Naval War Coll., 1925; m. Minnie Hartwell Barksdale, Feb. 15, 1897. Ensign, July 1, 1891; promoted through grades to admiral, Sept. 15, 1931. Served on U.S.S. Princeton, Spanish-Am. War; comd. Pampanga, Philippine Campaign, Minneapolis, Cuban Pacification; on Oregon, Boxer troubles; in charge anti-submarine work, staff of Vice Adm. Sims, World War; chief of staff, Adm. Sims, to close of war; comd. dreadnaught Tennessee; chief of staff, U.S. Fleet; chief of Bur. of Navigation, Navy Dept.; comdr. battleships, Battle Force; comdr. Battle Force, U.S. Fleet; comdr. in chief U.S. Fleet; chmn. Gen. Board; retired for phys. disability, 1934. Naval adviser Am. delegation, Disarmament Conf. Geneva, 1933, London, 1934. Mem. Soc. Naval Engrs. Awarded D.S.M. (U.S.); decorated by British and Belgian govts., World War. Democrat. Baptist. Clubs: Army and Navy Chevy Chase (Washington); New York Yacht (New York). Home: 2316 Tracy Place, Washington, D.C. Died Feb. 4, 1946.

LEIGH, TOWNES RANDOLPH univ. prof., dean, v.p.; b. "Fair Oaks," Panola County, Miss., Oct. 26, 1880; s. Elbridge Gerry and Susie (Gattis) L.; B.S., Iuka (Miss.) Institute, 1901; A.B., Lebanon (O.) University, 1902; Ph.D., cum laude, U. of Chicago, 1915; D.Sc. (hon.), Stetson U., 1941; m. Blanche Baird Winfield, March 24, 1907. V.P.; later pres., Mary Connor Coll., Paris, Tex., 1903-08; pres. Tex. Mil. Acad., 1904-06; head dept. science, Ouachita (Arks) Coll., 1907-09; head dept. chemistry, Woman's Coll. of Ala., Montgomery, Ala., 1910-14; fellow U. of Chicago 1914-15; asst. prof. chemistry, Carleton Coll., Northfield, Minn., 1915-17; head dept. of chemistry, Georgetown (Ky.) Coll., 1917-20; head dept. of chemistry, U. of Fla., since 1920, dean Coll. of Pharmacy, 1923-33, dean Coll. Arts and Sciences including Sch. of Pharmacy, 1933-48, acting v.p. 1934-46; vice pres., 1946-48. State chemist, Fla., 1931. Inventor of Leigh fog screen for protection of vessels against submarines. Mem. orgn. com. Fla. Farm Chemuric Council, Lieut, colonel Inactive Reserve. President local sector, Association Army of the U.S., 1923-25. Former mem. Res. Officers Assn. of Fla. (ex-pres. Gainesville chapter). Mem. Revision Com. U.S. Pharmacopeia CI, Am. Assn. of Colleges of Pharmacy (pres. 1931-32, mem. exec. com. 1932-34, chmn. com. on curriculum and teaching methods, 1928-31); fellow Am. Inst. Chemists; mem. Am. Council on Pharm. Edn. 1932-46. Am. Pharm. Assn. Fla. State Pharm. Assn. (hon.); Ala. Anthropol. Soc. (hon.), Am. Chem. Soc. (former dir. 4th dist.; former chmn. Fla. sect., also Lexington (Ky.) sect.; mem., com. reconsideration local Boundaries, 1935-37, Hertz Medalist, 1932), Ky. Acad. Sci. (corr.), Fla. Acad. Sci., Sigma Xi, Sigma Chi, Phi Kappa Phi (pres. Fla. chap. 1923-24), Gamma Sigma Epsilon (nat. pres. 1927-31), Sigma Tau, Alpha Epsilon Delta, Scabbard and Blade, Rho Chi, Herty medalist, 1942. Democrat. Baptist. Clubs: Antheneum (sec. 1924-25), Kiwanis (local pres. 1930), Propeller clClub of U.S. Fellow Royal Soc. of Arts, London, Eng., 1949. Author of chem. and hist. pamphlets. Home: Gainsville, Fla. Died Feb. 15, 1949.

LEIGHTON, FRANK THOMSON naval officer; b. Tunkhannock, Pa., Sept. 2, 1885; s. James Gardner and Maria (Ackley) L.; student Phillips Andover, 1904-05; grad. U.S. Naval Acad., 1909, post-grad., 1914-15; M.S., Columbia Univ., 1916; M.Mech. Engring., Cornell, 1917; grad. U.S. Naval War Coll., 1934; m. Elizabeth Roby Ohler, Nov. 6, 1912; children-Elizabeth Roby, Marian Katharine (Mrs. Walter J. Whipple), Frank Ohler, James Gardner, David Tent. Midshipman, 1905; promoted through grades to rear adm., 1942; comdorganized and comd. Mine Sweeping Squadron, 5th Naval Dist., 1917-18, exec. U.S.S. Savannah, 1918-19, U.S.S. Cleveland, 1919; commd. Claxton, 1919-20; asst. insp. naval machinery, N.Y. Shipbuilding Corp.,

Camden, N.J., 1920-23; radio material officer, 12th Naval Dist. and Trans-Pacific Circuit, 1926-29; exec. officer, Marine Engring. Dept., U.S. Naval Acad., 1931-33; comdr. Destroyer Div. 5, 1934-36; in Office Chief Naval Operations, Washington, D.C., 1936-38, 1940-42; comdr. U.S.S. Louisville, 1938-40; in Hdqrs. Comdr. in Chief, 1942; comdt. 8th Naval Dist. (Hdqrs. New Orleans) Apr. 1942-Mar. 1943. Address: Jamestown, R.I. Died Nov. 21, 1943.

LEIGHTON, GEORGE E. capitalist, lawyer; b. in Mass.; s. Eliot L.; ed. in Cincinnati; when 23 yrs. old located as lawyer in St. Louis; m. Isabella, d. Hon. Hudson E. Bridge, Oct. 1862. Served in Union army, 1861-65, under Gens. Lyon, Halleck, Curtis and Schofield, reaching rank of col.; atty. for Mo. Pacific Ry., 1865-73; retired from practice to engage in mfg. banking and other enterprises. Was 4 yrs. pres. Commercial Club, St. Louis; pres. Mo. Hist. Soc. and Univ. Bd., Washington Univ. Delivered speech at Trans-Missouri Congress in opposition to free coinage of silver, of which 150,000 copies were distributed. Apptd. by exec. com. Indianapolis Monetary Conf., 1897, as mem. Monetary Commn. Home: St. Louis, Mo. Died 1901.

LEITCH, JOSEPH DUGALD army officer; b. Montague, Mich., Mar. 5, 1864; s. Dugaid and Sarah (Furgeson) L.; grad. U.S. Mil. Acad., 1889, Army War Coll., 1914; m. Margaret, d. Col. F. M. Crandal, U.S.A., Oct. 1, 1891. Commd. 2d lt. 24th Inf., June 12, 1889; advanced through grades to col., July 18, 1917; brig. gen. N.A., Feb. 6, 1918; major gen. (temp.), Oct.1, 1918; maj. gen. regular army, Nov. 6, 1927. Duty at various posts in the Southwest and West until 1898; participated in various engagements at San Juan, and siege of Santiago, Cuba, 1898; in Philippines, 1900-02, 1907-10, and 1916-17; with American expdn. to Vera Cruz, Mem., May 1-Nov. 23, 1914; Gen. Staff, Washington, Jan. 25, 1910-Aug. 31, 1913, and Oct. 1, 1917-Feb. 15, 1918; comd. 15th Brig., Camp Fremont, Calif., Feb. 20-Oct. 5, 1918, 13th Div., Camp Lewis, Wash., Oct. 7, 1918-Mar. 8, 1919; apptd. insp. gen. and chief of staff, A.E.F., in Siberia, 1919-1920; retired Mar. 5, 1928. Decorated D.S.M. (U.S.). Died Oct. 26, 1938.

LEJEUNE, JOHN ARCHER officer, U.S.M.C.; b. Pointe Coupée Parish, La., Jan. 10, 1867; s. Ovide and Laura Archer (Turpin) L.; La. State U., 1881-84; grad. U.S. Naval Acad., 1888, Army War Coll. 1910; m. Ellie Harrison Murdaugh, Oct. 23, 1895; children-Mrs. James B. Glennon, Laura T., Eugenia D. At sea as naval cadet 2 yrs.; shipwrecked on U.S.S. Vandalia, in hurricane at Apia, Samoa, Mar. 1889; commd. 2d lt. U.S. Marine Corps, July 1, 1890; promoted through grades to brigebrig. gen., Aug. 29, 1916, maj. gen., July 1, 1918. In command marines on board Cincinnati, Spanish-Am. War, 1898; comd. battalion marines, Isthmus of Panama, 1930-04; comd. brigade, P.I., 1908-09; comd. brigade marines during capture of Vera Cruz, Mex., Apr. 1914, and of regt. marines as part of army of occupation of that city, Apr.-Dec. 1914; asst. to commandant Marine Corps, Washington, 1915-17; apptd. comdr. Marine Barracks, Quantico, Va., Sept. 27, 1917; arrived at Brest, France, June 8, 1918; duty with 35th Div., in Wesserling, Alsae sector, Vosges Mts., June 19-July 4, 1918; comd. 64th Brig., 32d Div., then in Suarce sector on Swiss border, July 5-25, 1918, 4th Brig. (marine), July 25-28, 1918, 2d Div. A.E.F., July 28, 1918-Aug. 8, 1919; participated in occupation of Marbache sector (near Metz), battles of St. Mihiel, Blanc Mont Ridge (Champagne offensive), Meuse-Argonne, march to the Rhine, Nov. 17-Dec. 13, 1918, and occupation of Coblenz bridgehead, Dec. 13, 1918-July 15, 1919; returned to U.S. in comd. 2d Div., Aug. 1919; comd. Marine Barracks, Quantico, Va., Oct. 23, 1919-June 30, 1920; maj. gen. in command Marine Corps, July 1, 1920-Mar. 5, 1929; retired; supt. Va. Mil. Inst., Lexington, 1929-37, supt. emeritus since 1937. Mem. Marine Corps Assn., 2d Div. Assn. Episcopalian. Address 540 Pembroke Av., Norfolk, Va. Died Nov. 20, 1942; buried in Arlington National Cemetery.

LELAND, LESTER mfr.; b. Boston, Mass., July 20, 1864; s. Lester and Mary E, (Babcock); ed. English High Sch. and business coll.; m. Frances Eugenia Converse, Oct. 25, 1892. Began with C. A. Richards, pres. Met. St, Ry. Co., Boston; later treas. Boston Heating Co.; supt. bldgs. and purchasing agt. Met. Telephone Co., New York; asst. treas., 1893, treas., 1895, Boston Rubber Shoe Co., absorbed, 1898, in U.S. Rubber Co., of which was made dir. and mem. exec. com.; v.p. U.S. Rubber Co., 1901, vice chmn. and mem. exec. com., 1918-24; officer of dir. First Nat. Bank, Old Colony Trust Co.; Arkwright Mutual Fire Ins. Co. (Boston), Atlantic Coast Lumber Corp., United Timber Co. (New York). Second lt. Co. C, 5th Mass. Inf., U.S.V., Spanish-Am. War; detailed July 6, 1898, as a.d.c. on staff of Brig. Gen. William A. Bancroft; hon. discharged Aug. 20, 1898. Home: Boston, Mass. Died July 30, 1933.

LELAND, ORA MINER univ. dean, civil eng.; b. Grand Haven, Mich., June 28,21876; s. George Spencer and Harriett Elizabeth (Perkins) L.; B.S. in C.E., U. of Mich., 1900, C.E., 1920; m. Mary Yoeckel, June 28, 1906 (died Oct. 2, 1913); children—Mary Louise (Mrs. Bruce L. Clark), Walter Perkins; m. 2d, Lottie Susan Potts, Aug. 5, 1914; children—Miriam Irene (Mrs. William C. Kahle), Paul Miner. Chief clerk and

draftsman, office of surveyor-gen. of Fla., 1898-99; in Gen. Land Office (div. of surveys), Washington, D.C., 1900, 03; aid and computer, U.S. Coast and Geod. Survey, in U.S., Alaska and P.R., 1900-03; mem. faculty Coll. Civ. Engring., Cornell U., 1903-20, head dept. of topographic and geodetic engineering, 1911-20, prof. geodesy and astronomy, 1916-20; engring. supervisor, J.G. White Engring. Corp., 1920; dean colls. of engring., architecture, and chemistry, U. of Minn., 1920-36; dean of adminstrn., University of Minnesota, Inst. of Technology, 1936-44; dean emeritus since 1944. Surveyor and chief of party to United States commissioner for demarcation of boundary between Alaska and Canada, 1904-11; mem. Commn. of Engrs. in Costa Rica-Panama Boundary Arbitration, 1911-13, Demarcation Commn., 1921. In service U.S. Army, as capt., maj. and lt. col. engrs., Apr. 1917-June 1919; with 303d Engrs., 78th Div., A.E.F., until Nov. 1918; with 314th Engrs., 89th Div., A.E.F., Nov. 1918-June 1919; colonel commanding 313th Engr. Regt., 88th Div., 1922-40; colonel inactive since 1940. Fellow A.A.A.S.; mem. Am. Soc. C.E., Am. Assn. Engrs., American Society Engring. Edn. (ex-president). Am. Astron. Soc., Soc. Am. Mil. Engrs. (dir.), Engrs. Club of Minneapolis, Am. Legion, Sigma Xi, Tau Beta Pi, Chi Epsilon (nat. hon.), Scabbard and Blade, Phalanx, Triangle. Author: Practical Least Squares. Home: 911 Fifth St., S.E., Minneapolis 14 MN

LEMANN, ISAAC IVAN M.D.; b. Donaldsonville, La., Feb. 8, 1877; s. Bernard and Harriet (Friedheim) L.; A.B., Tulane U., 1895, M.D., 1900; A.B., Harvard, 1896; grad. study, Johns Hopkins Hosp., Baltimore, 1903, U. of Strassburg, 1904-05, U. of Vienna, 1905, U. of Berlin, 1905; m. Stella Hirsch, Oct. 3, 1904; children-Paul Bernard, Richard Berthelot. Began practice at New Orleans, 1900; instr. in medicine, Tulane U., 1906-10, asst. prof. medicine, 1910-14, prof. clin. medicine, 1914-; visiting physician Charity Hosp., 1900-25, consultant in medicine, 1925-, visiting physician Tonor Infirmary, 1907-19, chief of med. service, 1919-. Service as capt. Med. Corps, U.S.A., 1917-19; chief of med. service, Base Hosp. 76, Vichy, Frances, Oct. 1918-Jan.1919; formerly lt. col. Med. R.C., chief med service Tulane unit. Jewish religion. Home: New Orleans, La. Died Sept. 1938.

LEMLY, HENRY ROWAN major U.S.A.; b. Bethania, N.C., Jan. 12, 1851; s. Henry Augustus and Amanda Sophia (Conrad) L.; grad. U.S. Mil. Acad., 1872; m. Katharine Palmer, Dec. 1, 1874. Apptd. 2d lt. 3d Cav., 1872; transferred to 3d Arty., 1878; 1st lt., 1880; capt. 7th Arty., 1898; retired at own request, over 30 yrs.' service, Apr. 20, 1899. Comd. light Battery C, 7th Arty., in P.R. campaign in Spanish-Am. War. Took part in Indian combats on Tongue River, Rosebud, Slim Buttes and Belle Fourche. Many yrs. dir. Nat. Mil. Sch., Bogota, Columbia, with local rank of col.; commr.-gen. for Colombia at World's Columbian Expn. Author: Who Was El Dorado?; Among the Arapahoes; The Story of Feather-Head; Santa Fe de Bogota; A West Point Romance; Padre Anselmo; Uncle 'Man; A Queen's Thoughts; also Spanish trans, of Upton's Infantry Regulations, English trans. of a French Manual of Strategy. Ordered to duty in office of q.m. gen. U.S.A., May 7, 1917; maj.O.M. Corps, Apr. 22, 1918; retired Mar. 11, 1920. Home: Washington, D.C. Died Oct. 12, 1925.

LEMMON, WALTER S. radio engr.; b. N.Y.C., Feb. 3, 1896; s. Myron T. and Bertha (Stedecker) L.; E.E., Columbia, 1917; m. Virginia Chandler, June 18, 1932; m. 2d, Ann Handschuh, Dec. 9, 1958. Trowbridge research fellow Columbia, 1917; commd. lt. U.S. Navy, and served as signal officer; also in charge of training of radio operators and engring. officers at various naval schools, 1917-19; div. sales mgr. SKF Industries, 1919-23; pres. Malone-Lemmon Labs., Inc., 1923-28; pres. Radio Industries Corp., 1928-33; gen. mgr. radiotype div. IBM, 1933-45; founder, pres. Greenwich Broadcasting Corp. (WGCH0, (Conn.), 1947-. Spl. radio officer on staff of Pres. Wilson during Peace Conf., 1919. Founded internat. Radio Sta. WRUL; founder World Wide Broadcasting Found. (engaged in internat. edn. and devel. of good will programs); pioneer in devel. and mfr. of radio typewriter for comml. purposes; invented single-dial tuning control for radio sets. Mem. Century Assn., Tau Beta Pi, Sigma Xi. Christian Scientist. Awarded Columbia U. medal of conspicuous service 1942; Order of Cristobal Colon by Dominican Republic, 1943; civilian citation by U.S. Signal Corps., 1944; King Haakon Peace Medal (Norway), 1946; Officer, Order of Orange-Nassau (Netherlands). 1947; King Christian X Denmark Medal of Liberation, 1947; Star of Solidarity (Italy), 1949. Mem. Am. Peace Soc. (Washington) (dir.), Newcomen Soc. Eng. Clubs: University (N.Y.); Cosmos (Washington). Home: 9 Quintard Av., Old Greenwich, Conn. Office: 1 E. 57th St., N.Y.C. Died Mar. 18, 1967.

LEMON, HARVEY B. physicist; born Chicago, Apr. 23, 1885; s. Henry Martyn and Harriet Ella (Brace) L.; B.A., U. of Chicago, 1906. M.S., 1910. Ph.D., 1912; m. Louise M. Birkhoff. Dec. 25, 1907; children-Harriet Birkhoff (Mrs. D. S. Moir), Doctor Henry Martyn. Began as assistant in physics, Univ. of Chicago, 1911, now prof. emeritus Dir. sci. and edn., Mus. of Science and Industry, since 1950. Trustee Lewis Institute and Illinois Institute Tech., 1930-42; advisor in physical science to editors Encyclopedia Britannica, 1944-. Research principles charcoal activation, 1914. Served as captain Ordnance Dept., U.S. Army, 1918. Chief physicist Ballistic Lab., Aberdeen Proving Grounds, 1942-43. Fellow Am. Physical Society; mem. A.A.A.S., Am. Assn. Physics Teachers (pres. 1939-40), Delta Upsilon, Phi Beta Kappa, Sigma Xi, Sigma Pi Sigma. Unitarian. Clubs: Quadrangle (past pres.). Chicago Literary (past pres.). Author: From Galileo to Cosmic Rays, 1934; Cosmic Rays Thus Far, 1936; Analytical Experimental Physics (with M. Ference, Jr.), 1943; What We Know and Don't Know about Magnetism, 1945; From Galileo to the Nuclear Age. 1946. Home: 5801 Dorchester Av., Chgo. 37. Died July 3, 1965; buried 1st Unitarian Ch., Chgo.

LEMONNIER, ANDRÉ French naval officer; b. 1896; grad. War Naval Sch. With French Marines, Dardanelles, World War I; comdr. naval antiaircraft batteries, Paris, beginning World War II; organized Mcht. Marine, 1942, active in North African Ports; comdr. in chief Free French Navy, Aug. 1943; commd. debarkation operations in Corsica and Provence, 1943-44; landed with Sec. of Navy Forrestal, Frejus, France, 1944; chief French Naval Staff, 1945-47; advanced to adm., 1952; apptd. dep. naval comdr. SHAPE by Gen. Eisenhower, 1951, ret., 1956. Address: French Ministry of Marine, Paris, France, Died May 30, 1963.

L'ENFANT, PIERRE CHARLES army engr., city planner; b. Paris, France, Aug. 2, 1754; s. Pierre and Marie (Leullier) L'E. Brevetted lt. French Colonial Forces, commd. 1st lt. engrs., 1776; came to Am. with Lafayette, 1777, joined Continental Army, commd. capt. engrs., 1778; maj. by spl. resolution of Congress, 1783; surveyor and planner new fed. city of Washington, D.C., forced to resign because his plans were so expensive, 1792 (govt. began remodeling city along his original lines, 1901); employed to lay out "Capital scene of manufactures" for Soc. for Useful Manufactures, 1792; temporary engr. at Ft. Mifflin on Mud Island in Delaware River, 1794; engr. at Ft. Washington on Potomac River, 1812; mem. Soc. of Cincinnati. Died Prince George's County, Va., June 14, 1825; buried Arlington (Va.) Nat. Cemetery.

LENIHAN, MICHAEL JOSEPH ret. army officer; b. Hopkinton, Mass., May 1, 1865; s. James and Catherine (Granger) L.; grad. U.S. Mil. Acad., 1887, Inf. and Cav. Sch., 1891, Army War Coll., 1917, Naval War Coll., 1921; LL.D., Holy Cross Coll., Mass., 1925; m. Mathilde O'Toole, 1891 (died Aug. 29, 1934); children-Eleanora (Mrs. Douglass Taft Greene), Catherine (Mrs. Paul James Halloran); m. 2d, Mina Ward, 1938. Commd. add. 2d lt. 25th Inf., 1887, promoted through grades to col. 1917; brig. gen. Nat. Army, 1917, brig. gen. regular army, 1925. Prof. mil. sci. and tactics, Seton Hall Coll., South Orange, N.J., 1893-97; in Cuba, 1899, Philippines, 1899-1902; mem. Gen. Staff Corps, 1906-10; in Hawaii, 1913-16; at Army War Coll., 1916-17; comdr. 83d Inf. Brig., 1917; comdr. 153d Inf. Brig., 1918; in France, 1917-19; Army instr. Naval War Coll., 1921-24; comd. 3d Div., 1928-29; ret. 1929. Decorated Comdr. Legion of Honor and Croix de Guerre with 3 palms (French); Order of the Purple Heart with Oak Leaf Cluster. Home: Hopkinton, Mass. Died Aug. 13, 1958.

LENTZ, BERNARD author, army officer; b. Theresa, Wis., Jan. 23, 1881; s. Henry and Mary (Harth) L.; grad. U.S. Mil. Acad., 1905; m. Hays Vosburgh, Aug. 18, 1909. Commd. 2d lt. inf., June 13, 1905; advanced through grades to temp. lt. col. World War, and to maj. regular army, July 1, 1920. Mem. Gen.Staff, Feb. 1, 1918-Feb. 1, 1921; duty Gen. Service Sch., Ft. Leavenworth, Kan. Originator devel. bns. for tng. soldiers unfit for field mil. duty but capable of being fitted for limited service; in connection with N.Y. Victory Loan organized and supervised "Panorama of Victory," parade; originated recruit ednl. centres for tng. illiterate and non-English speaking soldiers. Republican. Mem. Am. Legion. Author: The Cadence System of Close Order, 1919. Contbr. numerous articles on mil. topics. Address: Adj. Gen. U.S. Army, Washington. Died Dec. 1961.

LEONARD, HENRY lawyer; b. Washington, D.C., July 31, 1876; s. Charles Henry and Willa (Kain) L.; LL.B., Columbian U., 1891, LL.M., 1898; m. Ellen Warder, July 27, 1914. Practiced law, Washington, D.C., and in Colo., 1911-17 and since 1921; dir. and mem. discount com. Nat. Metropolitan Bank of Washington. Mem. Rep. Nat. Com., Rep. Post War Adv. Council. Rep. State Com. for Colo. 2d lt. Marines, 1898; retired 1911, re-entered 1917, went on retired list again 1921; commd. lt. col. 1942; served in China, Panama, Spanish-Am. War. Boxer Rebellion, World War. Decorated Order of the Dragon (China); Purple Heart; twice promoted for "eminent and conspicuous conduct in battle." Mem. Am. and D.C. bar assns. Episcopalian. Clubs: Metropolitan (Washington); El Paso, Cheyenne Mountain Country (Colorado Springs); N.Y. Yacht, Potomac Hounds. Home: Elkhorn Ranch, Colo. Springs, Colo.; and 3038 N. St. N.W., Washington, D.C. Office: Investment Bldg., Washington, D.C. Died May 6, 1945.

LEONARD, JOSEPH ALEXANDER consul; b. Cambridge, Md., Dec. 24, 1830; s. Rev. William and Harriet (Laverty) L.; M.D., Phila. Med. Coll., 1851; studied law, and admitted to bar, 1858; m. Kate Cowles, Oct. 30, 1861. Practiced medicine in Mich. and Wis., 1852-54; editor Whitewater (Wis.) Gazette, 1854-56, Waukesha (Wis.) Republic, 1857; practiced law, Rochester, Minnesota, 1858-64; postmaster Rochester, 1861-64; captain commissary 1st div. 16th corps; part owner and later owner and editor Rochester (Minn.) Post till 1899; state senator, 1869-70; register U.S. Land Office at Jackson and Worthington, Minn., 1874-75; U.S. consul at Edinburgh, 1881-83; consul-gen. at Calcutta, 1884, at Shanghai, 1889-93; judge of probate, 1897-1903. Comdr. Custer Post, G.A.R., 3 terms; insp. state dept. G.A.R., 1 term; judge advocate same, 1 term. Pres. Minn. Editorial Assn., 1868-69, Minn. Rep. Press Assn., 1896-97. Home: Rochester, Minn. Deceased.

LEONARD, WARREN H(ENRY), agronomist; b. New Sharon, Ia., July 5, 1900; s. Edward James and Zilla (Miller) L.; B.S., Colo. A. & M. Coll., 1926; M.S., U. of Neb., 1930; Ph.D., U. of Minn. 1940; m. Editha Todd, June 4, 1930; 1 dau., Kay. Asst. extension agronomist, Colo. A. & M. Coll., 1926-27, asst. editor publs., 1928; grad. asst. U. of Neb., 1928-29; asst. prof. of agronomy Colorado State Univ., 1929-34, asso. prof., 1934-42, prof., 1946-48, since 1949; asst. agronomist, asso., agronomist Colo. Agrl. Experimental Sta., 1929-42, 46-48, 49-66. Survey U. of Peshawar, Pakistan for Fgn. Operations Adminstrn. and Colorado State Univ., 1954; cons. agrl. prodn. Mission to Libya International Bank Reconstruction and Development, 1959. Member adv. bd. Am. Inst. Crop Ecology, Washington, 1952; ofcl. del. 6th Nat. Conf. UNESCO, San Francisco, 1957. Served as first lieut., captain, major C.A.C., U.S. Army, 1942-46; chief (as maj.), Agrl. Div., Natural Resources Sect., G.H.Q., Supreme Comdr. for the Allied Powers, Tokyo, Japan, 1945-46, chief (civilian) 1948-49; 1st. col. United States Army Reserve, retired. Decorated Legion of Merit by Gen. Douglas MacArthur, July 22, 1946; Department of the Army commendation for Meritorious Civilian Service, 1949; fellow Population Reference Bureau, Washington, 1956; profl. achievement award, Colo. State U., 1957. Fellow A.A.A.S., American Society of Agronomy; mem. Bot. Soc. of Am., Am. Genetics Assn., Genetics Soc. of Japan, Genetics Soc. of America, American Statis. Assn., Biometric Soc., Am. Soc. of Sugar Beet Technologists, Japanese Society of Breeding (hon. member), Sigma Xi, Phi Kappa Phi. Author: Civil Affairs Handbook: Japan: Agrl. (War Dept., Army Service Forces Manual No. 354-7A). 1945; Field Plot Technique (with Andrew Clark) 1939; Principles of Field Crop Prodn. (with John H. Martin), 1949; Field Crops in Colorado (with R. S. Whitney), 1950; (with John H. Martin) Cereal Crops, 1963; other technical works on barley genetics, applied statistics, corn breeding, gen. field crops, and Japanese agr. Home: Ft Collins CO Died Aug. 23, 1966; buried Grand View Cemetery, Ft Collins CO

LEONARD, WILLIAM ANDREW bishop; b. Southport, Conn., July 15, 1848; s. William Boardman and Louisa (Bulkley) L.; ed. Phillips Academy, Andover, Mass.; St. Stephen's Coll., Annandale, N.Y.; grad. Berkeley Div. Sch., Middletown, Conn., 1871; D.D., St. Stephen's Coll., 1870, Washington and Lee U., 1885; LL.D., Kenyon Coll., Gambier, O., 1919; m. Sarah L. Sullivan, Apr. 17, 1873. Deacon, 1871, priest, 1873, P.E. Ch.; asst. Holy Trinity, Brooklyn, 1871-72; rector Ch. of the Redeemer, Brooklyn, 1872-80, St. John's, Washington, 1880-89; consecrated bishop of Ohio, 1889. Chaplain 23d Regt. N.G.S.N.Y., 1876-80. Ohio Soc. of New York, 1889. Mem. Soc. Colonial Wars (chaplain gen.). Author: Via Sacra. or Footprints of Christ., 1875; History of the Christian Church, 1878; A Faithful Life, 1888; New York Church Club Lectures, 1893; Bedell Oectures, "Witness of American Church to Christianity," 1894; Biography of Stephen Bank Leonard, 1909. Died Sept. 21, 1930.

LERCH ARCHER LYNN army officer, Judge Advocate General's Dept.; b. Sumner, Neb., Jan. 12, 1894; s. Herman H. and Maud R. (Stevens) L.; A.B., U. of Calif., 1917; LL.B., George Washington U., 1942; grad. Infantry Sch., Fort Benning, Ga., 1922, Command and General Staff Sch., Fort Leavenworth, 1937; orders Army War Coll., revoked account declaration of emergency 1941; m. Florence M. Wentworth, Feb. 5, 1918; children-Mrs. D. W. Rush, Capt. Archer Lynn. Commissioned 2d lt. Infantry, Apr. 28, 1917, Officers Reserve Corps, U.S. Army, Oct. 25, 1917; promoted through grades to brig. gen. (emp.), December 3, 1942; major gen. (temp.), May 31, 1944; 11th Division Sch. Det., A.E.F., World War I; instructor Arkansas National Guard, 1922-24; 31st Infantry, Manila, P.I., 1924-26; assistant prof. Mil. Science tactics and adjutant, U. of Calif., Berkeley, 1926-31; asst. staff judge advocate, Honolulu, T.H., 1931-33; legal advisor to Gen. B. H. Wells, Fort Shafter, T. H., 1933-34; asst. dep. administrator, NRA, Territory Hawaii, 1934-35; also legal advisor PWA, Territory Hawaii, 1933-35; 5th Inf., Ft. Williams, Me., 1935-36; asst. prof. mil. science and tactics, U. of Fla., 1937-38; exec. officer, Judge Advocate General's Dept., Washington, 1939-40; deputy provost marshal gen., ashington, 1941-42; commandant, P.M.G. School Center, Fort Oglethorpe, Ga., and comdg. officer P.M.G. Training Center, Ft. Custer, Mich., June-Dec. 1942; asst. provost marshall gen. (brig. gen.) Dec. 1942, maj. gen., provost-marshal gen., May 31, 1944; mil. gov. of Korea since Jan. 1946. Prosecuted Grover Cleveland Bergdoll before Army court-martial, 1939; admitted to practice before bars of Fla., Korea and Supreme Court of U.S. Mem. Federal, Am. bar assns. and Nat. Bar Assn. of Korea. Mem. Mil. Order World Wars (D.C. chapt.), Army and Navy Union, Am. Legion (Geo. Washington Post); hon. mem. Internat. Assn. of Chiefs of Police, bd. of dirs. The Judge Adv. Gen. Assn. Club: Army and Navy (Washington, D.C.). Decorations: Distinguished Service Medal; Legion of Merit; Honorary Member French Foreign Legion. Mason. Methodist. Home: 6315 Broad Branch Rd., Chevy Chase, Md. Address: Munitions Bldg., Washington 25, D.C. Died Sept. 11, 1947.

LERRIGO, CHARLES HENRY physician, Author; b. Birmingham, Eng., Sept. 12, 1872; s. George and Mary Olive (Watkins) L.; pub. schs., Eng.; came to U.S., 1886; M.D., Homoe Med. Coll. of Mo., St. Louis, 1900; m. Annabel Barry, Apr. 16, 1895; children-Marion Olive, Ruth Annabel, Frank Charles, George Angus. Practiced in Topeka since 1900. First lt., capt. and maj. M.C., U.S. Army, Aug. 1917-May 1919. Mem. Kan. State Bd. of Health, 1905-24 (pres. 1909-10); state registrar of vital statistics for Kan., 1919-22; exec. sec. Kan. State Tuberculosis Assn., 1922-48; sec. emeritus, 1948. Health editor, Capper Farm Press. Fellow American Pub. Health Assn., A.M.A., Am. Geriatrics Soc., hon. mem. Nat. Conf. Tuberculosis Workers, American Pub. Health Assn., American Trudeau Society. Author: Doc Williams, 1913; The Castle of Cheer, 1916; The Boy Scout Treasure Hunters, 1917; Boy Scouts to the Rescue, 1919; Boy Scouts on Special Service, 1922; Boy Scouts of Round Table Patrol, 1924; The Merry Men of Robin Hood Patrol, 1927; The Kidnapped Doctor, 1929; The Sea Is His, 1932; A Son of John Brown, 1937; The Better Half of Your Life, 1951. Address: 1403 Fillmore St., Topeka, Kan. Died Dec. 4, 1955; buried Mt. Hope Cemetery, Topeka.

LESLIE, FRANK ELLIOTT physician; b. Woburn, Mass., July 21, 1873; s. Freeman Francis and Sarah Jane (Russell) L.; prep. edn. Ayer (Mass.) High Sch., and Winthrop (N.Y.) Acad.; student Mass. Coll. Pharmacy, Boston, 1893-94; M.D., Med. Sch. Me. (Bowdoin), 1901; m. Nellie Vitella Ripley, June 2, 1903. Hosp. steward, Marine Hosp. Service, 1894-97; began gen. practice medicine, Andover, Me., 1901; mgr. Glenellis Sanitarium, Andover, 1905; mgr. VA Facility, Northampton, Mass., 1933-39, Mendota, Wis., 1939-43; psychiatrist USPHS, 1919-43. Served as maj. M.C., U.S. Army Med. Res.; ret. Aug. 1, 1943. Diplomate Am. Bd. Psychiatry and neurology. Mem. A.M.A., Me. Med. Soc., Am. Psychiatric Assn., N.E. Soc. Psychiatry, U.S. Mil. Surgeons, Mil. Order World War. Unitarian. Mason. Club: University (Winter Park, Fla.). Home: Eastland Hotel, Portland, Me. (winter) St. Petersburg, Fla. Died Mar. 27, 1951; buried Arlington Nat. Cemetery.

LESLIE, NORMAN HENRY coast guard officer; b. Chicago, Aug. 15, 1898; s. Henry T. and Myrtie (Oliver) L.; B.S., U.S. Coast Guard Acad., New London, Conn., 1918; m. Unis Frazier, Sept. 25, 1926. Enlisted Coast Guard as ordinary seaman, June 1918, hon. discharged, July 1918; appointed cadet, Aug. 1918; commd. ensign, 1921, and advanced through grades to rear adm., 1950; served on ships; Seneca, N.Y. City, 1921; Tuscarora, Milwaukee, 1921; Unalga, Juneau, Alaska, 1922-26; Seneca, 1927; Ericsson, New London, Conn., as exec. officer, 1927-28; comd. Fanning, New London, Conn., 1928-30; assigned to Coast Guard Depot, Curtis Bay, Md., 1930-33; comd. Cahokia, Eureka, Calif., 1933-35; comd. Base Six, Fort Lauderdale, Fla., 1935-39; personnel officer and res. dir., Jacksonville (Fla.) Dist., 1939-41; comd. Haida, serving escort duty in Aleutians, 1941-42; chief of staff to dist. Coast Guard officer, 8th Naval Dist., New Orleans, 1942-44; dist. Coast Guard officer, 17th Naval Dist., Ketchikan, Alaska, 1945-46, comdr., 1946-47; comdr. 7th Coast Guard dist., Miami, 1947-49; chief office of personnel, Coast Guard Headquarters, Washington, 1949-51; comdr. 13th Coast Gurad Dist., Seattle, since 1951. With international ice patrol (Seneca), 1921, Bering Sea Patrol (Unalga), 1922-26, (Haida) 1941. Served as dep. U.S. Marshal in Alaska while on Unalga; U.S. Commr. in Alaska while on Haida. Awarded Victory Medal without clasp for participation in World War I; commended for assistance rendered to crashed Navy Airship Akron, 1933; commended for assistance with establishment and conduct of Mounted Beach Patrol, 8th Naval dist., New Orleans; received commendation ribbon for war service on Haida. Mason (Shriner). Clubs: Propeller, Raninier, Arctic, Seattle Yacht. Home: 110 W. Highland Dr. Office: 618 2d Av., Seattle. Deceased.

LESTER, JAMES A. ret. army officer; b. Prosperity, S.C., Oct. 13, 1891; s. Allen and Rosaline Imogene (Ridgell) L.; B.S., The Citadel, Charleston, S.C., 1911; B.S., U.S. Mil. Acad., 1915; grad. F.A. Sch., 1926, Command and Gen. Staff Sch., 1927, Ecole de Guerre, France, 1929, Army War Coll., 1940; m. Mildred Minor White, July 1, 1925. Commd. 2d lt., U.S. Army, 1915, and advanced through the grades to maj. gen., 1945; served with A.E.F., France, 1918, with Army of Occupation, Germany, 1919; asst. mil. attaché, Paris, 1932-36; asst. comdt. F.A. Sch., comdr. div. arty., 1942-

53; overseas Pacific Theater, 1942-48; comd. 24th Div., Arty., Hollandia operation, XIV Corps Arty., Bougainville, Luzon, Manila; on Gen. MacArthur's staff, Philippines, as provost marshal gen., 1945, and comdg. gen. Philippine Constabulary to Dec. 1945; comdg. 24th Inf. Div., Japan, 1945-48; comdg. gen. San Francisco port embarkation, 1948-53, ret. 1953. Decorated D.S.M. (U.S.); Officer Legion of Honor (France). Home: 2710 Preston St., Columbia, S.C. Address: Fort Mason, Cal. Died Mar. 10, 1958; buried Arlington Nat. Cemetery.

LESTER, JAMES WESTCOTT lawyer, soldier; b. Saratoga Springs, N.Y., Sept. 8, 1859; s. Charles S. and Lucy L. (Cooke) L.; A.B., Union Coll., 1881, L.H.D., same, 1931; law dept. Columbia, 1880-81; m. Bertha N. Dowd, June 13, 1888; children-James Dowd, Charles W. Dudley Gove, Ralph Westcott. Enlisted as pvt. 22d Separate Co., N.G., Nov. 25, 1884; promoted through grades to brig. gen., June 6, 1911; bvt. maj. gen., Jan. 7, 1913. Served as maj. 2d Regt. N.Y. Vols., Spanish-Am. War, May 9-Nov. 25, 1898; in U.S. service as brig. gen. on Mexican border, June 18, 1916-Mar. 7, 1917; also in service, July 18-Aug. 5, 1917; brig. gen. N.A., Aug. 5, 1917; apptd. comdr. 54th Inf. Brigade, Camp Wadsworth, S.C., Sept. 30, 1917; hon. discharged for physical disability, as brig. gen. N.A., Apr. 6, 1918; assigned to duty as brig. gen. N.Y.N.G., Apr. 30, 1919; apptd. comdg. gen. N.Y.N.G., Dec. 17, 1921; resigned and granted hon. discharge, May 28, 1923; then engaged in law practice. Republican. Presbyn. Elk. Home: Saratoga Springs, N.Y. Died Nov. 13, 1932.

LESTER, ROBERT MACDONALD, educational exec.; b. Center, Ala., Nov. 7, 1889; s. Rev. Samuel Robert and Ann Virginia (Watson) L.; A.B., Birmingham-Southern College, 1908; A.B., Vanderbilt Univ., 1911; Buhl fellow in classics U. of Mich., 1911-12; A.M., Columbia, 1917; Litt.D., Birmingham-Southern Coll., 1931; D.C.L., Acadia U., Can., 1933; LL.D., Univ. of N.M., 1936, Tulane U., 1940, Duke U., 1941, St. Francis Xavier, Canada, 1953, University of North Carolina, 1958, University of Chattanooga, 1960; L.H.D., Southwestern at Memphis, 1954, U. Ala., 1962; D.C.L., U. of South Sewanne, Tenn., 1943; m. Memory Aldridge, Jan. 30, 1915; 1 son, Robert MacDonald. Instr. Greek, Birmingham-Southern Coll., 1907-08; teacher English and dir. athletics, Byars-Hall High Sch., Covington, Tenn., 1912-16, asst. prin., 1912-14, prin., 1914-16; mem. Columbia U. library staff, 1916-17, and 1921; supt. pub. schs. Mayfield, Ky., 1917-18, Covington, Tenn., 1919-21; mem. Columbia U. dept. English, 1921-26; instr. Columbia Coll., 1922-24, administrative officer for men univ. undergrads, 1923-26, asst. to dir. univ. extension, 1924-26; asst. to pres. Carnegie Corp. 1926-34, sec., 1934-54; asso. sec. Carnegie Found. for Advancement of Teaching, 1947; sec., 1949-54; exec. dir. So. Fellowship Fund, 1954-69; dir., v.p. Home Trust Co., 1934-54. Cons. Council of So. Universities, Inc., 1964-69. Trustee Am. U., 1941-65. Served as pvt. U.S. Inf., World War I; served in 7th Regt. N.Y. Guard, through grades to captain, 1942-45. Mem. Assn. Am. Colls. (exec. com. 1935-36), Am. Library Assn. (hon. life), Kappa Sigma, Phi Beta Kappa. Democrat. Methodist. Clubs: Century; Men's Faculty (Columbia); Cosmos (Washington); Rotary. Compiler (with others) The Diffusion of Knowledge, 1935. Author of Forty Years of Carnegie Giving, 1941; A Thirty Year Catalog of Grants, 1942; A Summing Up, 1964; also spl. reports and revs. of Carnegie Corp. activities, pub. under gen. title The Audit of Experience. Home: Chapel Hill3NC Died Feb. 21, 1969.

LETCHER, MARION foreign service; b. Macon County, Ala., Sept. 4, 1872; s. Francis Marion and Claudia Caroline Clanton (Howard) L.; A.B., U. of Ala., 1894; m. Marilu Ingram, Nov. 7, 1901; children—Marion Louise (Mrs. John M. Woodburn), Adele Fournie (Mrs. Donald G. Goddard), Margaret Billingslea (Mrs. Preston Watson). Pres. Douglasville (Ga.) Coll., 1900-01; supt. schs., Conyers, Ga., 1901-03; employed in Bur. of Edn., Washington, 1903-09; consul at Acapulco, Mex., 1909-11, Chihuahua, 1911-16; acting foreign trade adviser, Dept. of State, Washington, June 10, 1916; counsul gen., Apr. 8, 1918; consul gen. at Christiania (now Oslo), Norway, 1918-20, at Copenhagen, Denmark, 1920-28, at Antwerp, Belgium, 1928-34; retired for disability, fgn. service officer, class II, 1924, fgn. service officer, class I, 1930. Was lt. Co. A, 5th Vol. Inf., Spanish-Am. War, serving at Santiago and Baracoa, Cuba; comd. company, Sept. 5, 1898-May 3, 1899. Mem. D.C. Soc. S.A.R., Sigma Nu. Democrat. Clubs: University (Washington); Union (Rome). Address: 35 Via Ludovisi, Rome, Italy. Died July 24, 1948.

LETT, SHERWOOD judge; b. Iroquois, Ont., Aug. 1, 1895; s. Rev. Francis Graham and Ann Jane (Sherwood) L.; B.A., U. B.C., 1916, LL.D., 1945; Rhodes Scholar, U. Oxford, 1919-22, B.A. Juris, 1922; grad. Staff Coll. Camberly Eng., 1941; m. Evelyn Story, Oct. 23, 1928. Admitted to B.C. bar, 1922; chancellor U. B.C., 1951-57; chief justice Supreme Ct. B.C., 1955-. Served with Canadian Army, 1914-18, brig. gen., 1939-44; comdr. 4th inf. brigade, 1942; dep. chief gen. staff, Ottawa, 1943-44; hon. co.-comdt. Royal Canadian Corps, Inf., 1948-56. Decorated Military Cross, Efficiency Decoration, Distinguished Service Order, Commander Order British Empire, C.D. Member Canadian Institute International Affairs. Phi Kappa Pi. Mem. United Ch. Can. Clubs: Vancouver, Union (Victoria, B.C.); University, Faculty. Home: 1728 West 40th Av., Vancouver 13. Office: The Law Cts, Vancouver, B.C. Died July 24, 1961; buried Forest Lawn Cemetery, Vancouver.

LETTERMAN, JONATHAN army officer, surgeon; b. Canonsburg, Washington County, Pa., Dec. 11, 1824; s. Jonathan Letterman; grad. Jefferson Coll., 1845; M.D., Jefferson Med. Coll., 1849; m. Mary Lee, Oct. 1863. Asst. surgeon U.S. Army, serving on Western and Southwestern frontiers, 1849-61; assigned to Army of Potomac, 1861; surgeon, maj., 1862, apptd. med. dir. Army of Potomac; organizer system of field med. service featuring mobile hosps. and ambulance service which became standard for entire U.S. Army. Died Mar. 15, 1872.

LEUSCHNER, ARMIN OTTO astronomer; b. Detroit, Jan. 16, 1868; s. Otto Richard and Caroline (Humburg) L.; grad. Royal Wilhelms-Gymnasium, Cassel, Germany, 1886; A.B., U. Mich., 1888; Sc.D. (hon.), 1913; grad. student Lick Obs., U. Pitts., 1900; LL.D., U. Cal., 1938; m. Ida Louise Denicke, May 20, 1896 (died Nov. 15, 1941); children-Erida Louise, Richard Denicke, Frederick Denicke (died Dec. 8, 1941). Inst. mathematics U. Cal., 1890-92, asst. prof., 1892-94, asst. prof. astronomy and geodesy, 1894-98, asso. prof., 1898-1907, dir. Student Obs., 1898-1938, prof. astronomy and chmn. dept., 1907-38, dean Grad. Sch., 1913-18, 20-23, prof. of astronomy and dir. Students Observatory, emeritus, 1938—. Mem., sec. Cal. Earthquake Commn., 1906-10. Spl. expert U.S. Shipping Board, 1917; in charge U. Cal. Naval Tng. activities, 1917-18; chmn. scientific com. and com. on occupational selection Cal. Council of Defense, 1918; maj. C.W.S., U.S. Army, 1918-19. Awarded Watson gold medal, Nat. Acad. Sciences for researches in astronomy, 1916; Knight Order of the North Star (Sweden), 1924; Bruce gold medal, Astron. Soc. Pacific, 1936; Rittenhouse medal, 1937. Halley lectr. U. Oxford, 1938. Fellow Cal. Acad. Scis., A.A.A.S. (pres. Pacific div. 1931-32), Seismol. Soc. Am., Internat. Geophys. Union, Astron. Soc. Pacific (pres. 1908, 36, 43); mem. Nat. Acad. Sciences, NRC, Am. Philos. Soc., Am. Math. Soc., Astronomische Gesellschaft, Am. Astron. Soc., Washington Acad. Sciences, Am. Assn. U. Profs. (pres. 1923-25), Delta Tau Delta, Sigma Xi, Phi Beta Kappa; fgn. asso. Royal Astron. Soc. of London; foreign mem. Royal Physiographical Soc., Lund, Sweden. Exec. Sec. Nat. Research Council; and acting chmn. div. of physical sciences, 1919; chmn. com. on comets and minor planets, Internat. Astron. Union, 1919-38, hon. chmn., 1938—. Clubs: University (San Francisco); Faculty (Berkeley); Cosmos (Washington); Authors' (London). Special field of investigation, theoretical astronomy; also perturbations of the Watson asteroids; improvement in the methods of determining preliminary orbits of comets and planets; perturbations of the Hecuba group of minor planets. Author: Beitraie zür Kometenbahnestimmung, Berlin, 1897; Short Methods of Determining Orbits from Three Observations; Tables of Minor Planets Discovered by James C. Watson; Research Surveys of 1091 Minor Planets; also papers on astron. subjects. Died Apr. 22, 1953.

LEUTZE, EUGENE HENRY COZZENS naval officer; b. Dusseldorf Prusia, Nov. 16, 1847; s. Emanuel and Julia L.; apptd. to U.S. Naval Acad. by President Lincoln from D.C., 1863, grad. 1867; m. Julia Jarvis McAlpine, Mar. 1873; children-Mary Eugenia (dec.). Trevon Wm., Marion Alice (wife of J. G. Rowcliff, U.S.N.). Promoted ensign, Dec. 18, 1868; master, Mar. 21, 1870; lt., Mar. 21, 1871; lt. comdr., Mar. 26, 1889; comdr., Jan. 5, 1897; capt., Oct. 9, 1901; rear admiral, July 6, 1907. On various ocean survey expdns.; comd. Michigan, 1896-97, Alert, 1897-98, Monterey, May 1898-Dec. 1899, and participated in taking city of Manila; commandant Navy Yard, Cavite, P.I., 1898-1900; supt. naval gun factory, Washington, 1900-02; comd. Maine, 1902-04; mem. Bd. Inspection and Survey, 1904-05; commandant Navy Yard, Washington, and supt. naval gun factory, 1905-10; retired by operation of law, Nov. 16, 1909, but continued on active duty; commandant Navy Yard and Sta., New York, 1910. Died Sept. 15, 1931.

LEUTZE, TREVOR WILLIAM, naval officer; b. Santa Barbara, Calif., Oct. 13, 1877; s. Rear Adm. E.H.C. and Julia Jarvis (McAlpine) L.; (grandson of Emanuel Leutze who painted Washington Crossing the Delaware); student Hartford High Sch., Washington High Sch., U.S. Naval Acad., Corcoran Scientific Sch., Washington, D.C.; m. Leobelle S. Wilfert, Apr. 7, 1927. Commd. ensign, Pay Corps, U.S. Navy, advanced through the grades to rear adm., 1928; relieved from active duty, Nov. 1, 1942. Decorated Spanish War, Marine Campaign (Panama) and Mexican Campaign medals, World War I medal with Silver Star, Am. Defense Medal, World War II Medal, Commendatory Ribbons from both Army and Navy, Al Merito 1st class (Chile). Home: 1169 Lakeview Dr.,2Winter Park FL

LEVIERO, ANTHONY HARRY newspaperman; b. Bklyn., Nov. 24, 1905; s. Anthony Faustino and Thomasina (Lepore) L.; student Columbia, 1926-27, Col. City of N.Y., 1927-28; m. Fay Harrison, Aug. 29, 1936; 1 dau., Toni Harrison. Office boy, clk., auditor maritime ins. and steamship firms, 1925-26; police reporter N.Y. American, 1926-28; gen. assignments reporter Home News, Bronx, N.Y., 1928; mem. reportorial staff N.Y. Times since 1929; covered crimes, criminal, civil and constl. litigation, mil. activities, U.S. Congress, White House. Enlisted 106th Inf., N.Y. N.G., 1923; 2d lt., M.I. Res., 1935; capt., A.U.S., G-2, E.T.O., G-2 Eastern Assault Force and AFHG, North Africa, 1942-43; GSC, M.I. Div., War Dept. Gen. Staff, 1943-45, advancing from maj. to lt. col.; also chief publs. br., G-2, WDGS. Recipient War Dept. Commendation Medal, 1946. Awarded Pulitzer prize for reporting nat. affairs, 1951. Mem. White House Correspondents Assn. (pres. 1954), Nat. Audubon Soc., Audubon Soc. D.C. Club: National Press (Washington). Home: 2445 Porter St., Washington 8. Office: 1701 K St N.W., Washington 6. Died Sept. 3, 1956; buried Arlington Nat. Cemetery.

LEVINE, HARRY HARVEY, physician; b. Bklyn., Apr. 6, 1919; s. Philip F. and Henrietta Levine; M.D., Middlesex U., 1943; M.P.H., Columbia, 1958; m. Anita Weintraub, Mar. 4, 1943; children—Gloria, Richard, Amy. Intern, Cumberland Hosp., Bklyn., 1943-44; resident Sea View Hosp, 1944-45, Richmond Boro Contagious Hosp., 1944-45; resident tng. N.Y.C. Dept. Health and Health Ins. Plan Greater N.Y., 1957, 58; v.p. Health Ins. Plan Greater N.Y., until 1969; past pres. med. bd. La Guardia Hosp., Queens, N.Y.; adj. clin. prof. preventive medicine Albert Einstein Coll. Med., Yeshiva U. Served to comdr., M.C., USNR, 1945-46, 55-56. Diplomate Am. Bd. Preventive Medicine. Fellow Am. Pub. Health Assn.; mem. A.M.A., Group Health Assn., Brit. Med. Assn. Home: Brooklyn NY Died Feb. 3, 1969; buried Mt. Ararat, Long Island NY

LEVINE, VICTOR EMANUEL biochemist, nutritionist, explorer; b. Minsk, Russia, Aug. 4, 1892; s. Israel and Eva Leah (Meisels) L.; brought to U.S., 1898; B.A., Coll. City New York, 1909; M.A., Columbia, 1911, Ph.D., 1914; grad. study, Johns Hopkins, summers 1919, 20, 21; U. of Toronto (insulin div.), summer 1923; M.D., Creighton U., 1928; unmarried. Asst. in biol. chemistry, Coll. Phys. and Surg., Columbia, 1913-15, instr. in same, 1915-16; asst. prof. organic chemistry, Fordham, 1915-16; dir. chem. lab., Beth Israel Hosp., N.Y. City, 1916-17; dir. Chem. and Path. Labs., N.Y. City, 1917-18; asst. prof. biol. chemistry, Sch. of Medicine, Creighton U., 1918-20, prof. biol. chemistry and nutrition and head of dept. since 1920, advisory dir. Grad. Sch. of Chemistry 1928-; cons. USPHS, 1927-38 and summer 1939; vis. Fulbright prof. Univs. Madrid and Valencia, 1960-62; dir. health dept. Dwarfies Corp., Council Bluffs. Served as maj., M.C., A.U.S., 1942-45, lt. col., 1945-46; now lt. col., Med. Dept. Res. Leader sci. expdn. to Arctic for Office of Naval Research, U.S. Navy, hdqrs., Arctic Research Lab., Point Barrow, Alaska. 1948. Fellow A.A.A.S., Am. Geog. Soc., Am. Inst. Chemistry, N.Y. Acad. Scis., Am. Pub. Health Assn., Royal Soc. Arts and Scis. (Gt. Britain), Brit. Inst. Philosophic Studies, Royal Anthrop. Institute Gt. Brit. and Ireland, Internat. Dental Research Assn., Am. Med. Writers Assn., mem. nat., state and local profl. and scientific assns. and orgns. in med. and nutrition fields; has served as officer of several Elk Clubs: Professional Men's (dir. 1931-33). Spanish Club; Explorers. Arctic explorer primarily for biol. studies 1921 - . Awarded honorary scroll by Columbia Graduate School Alumni Assn., 1937. Author and co-author several books 1929-35; (with C. P. Stewart and A. Stolmna) Toxicology, 2 vols., 1961; Introducción a Toxicologia (Spanish), 1962. Contbr. articles on biology aspects of the Eskimo to Ency. Arctica. Address: School of Medicine. Creighton U., Omaha, Neb. Died Sept. 29, 1963; buried Mt. Lebanon Cemetery, Bklyn.

LEVIS, WILLIAM EDWARD glass mfr.; b. Alton, Ill., Dec. 14, 1890; s. Charles and Harriet (Parker) L.; student Culver Mil. Acad., 1906-08; LL.B., U. of Ill., 1913; m. Margaret Harris, June 29, 1915. Began with Ill. Glass Co., Alton, and continued through various depts., becoming asst. sec. and treas., v.p. and gen. mgr., and made pres., 1928; upon merger of the co. (1929) with the Owens Bottle Co., of Toledo, O., title of latter changed to Owens-Ill. Glass Co., of which was v.p. and gen. mgr., then president, 1930-41, chmn. bd., 1941-50; dir. Owens-Ill. Glass Co. Mem. Bus. Council. Student O.T.C., 1917; served as 2d lieutenant British Army and with 30th Inf., 3d Div., U.S. Army, in France; maj. O.R.C. Awarded D.S.C. (U.S.) for "extraordinary heroism in action," France, July 15, 1918. Asst. to chmn. War Prodn. Bd., World War II, 1941-42, 1944-45. Awarded Medal for Merit. Mem. Sigma Chi. Republican. Episcopalian. Clubs: Toledo, Carranor Hunt and Polo, Toledo Country (Toledo); Chevy Chase (Washington); The Brook, The Links (N.Y.C.); Rolling Rock (Ligonier, Pa.). Home: 77 Locust St., Perrysburg, O. 43551. Office: Owens-Illinois Bldg., Toledo 1. Died Nov. 7, 1962; buried Alton, Ill.

LEVITT, ALBERT, lawyer; born Woodbine, Md., March 14, 1887; son of Thomas Reeve and Ida Alice L.; B.D., Meadville Theol. Sch., 1911; B.A., cum magnis honoribus, Columbia, 1913; LL.B., Harvard, 1920; J.D., Yale, 1923; m. Elsie Mary Hill, Dec. 24, 1921; 1 dau., Leslie Hill-Levitt. Lecturer in philosophy, Columbia, 1913-14; acting prof. philosophy, Colgate, 1915-16; asst. prof. law, George Washington U., 1920-21; prof. law, U. of N.D., 1921-22; lecturer on med.

jurisprudence, Johns Hopkins Med. Sch., 1924; prof. law, Washington and Lee U., 1924-27; prof. law, Brooklyn Law Sch. of St. Lawrence U., 1927-30; lecturer law of finance, Sch. of Commerce, New York University, 1939; professor of law, Hastings College of the Law, University of California, 1942-43; special asst. to attorney general of U.S., 1923-24, 1933-35, 1936-37; judge U.S. Dist. Ct. of V.I., 1935-36. Mem. U.S. Assay Commn., 1921; rep. of U.S. Dept. of Justice on committee of Advisors on Codification of Nationality Laws of the U.S.; spl. advisor to Office of Production Management, Priorities Div., 1941. Candidate of Independent Rep. party for gov. of Conn., 1932; Republican candidate U.S. Senator, Cal., 1950. Served as private and sergeant Hospital Corps., U.S. Army, 1904-07, in Philippines, 1906-07; with Am. Ambulance, French Army, at the front, 1915; regtl. sergt. maj. Harvard R.O.T.C., June-Sept. 1917; chaplain U.S. Army, 1917-Jan. 1919, overseas after Apr. 1918; in Baccarat sector, Oise-Aisne and Meuse-Argonne offensives; wounded and gassed. Mem. Am. Inst. Criminal Law and Criminology, Internat. Assn. Penal Law, Phi Beta Kappa, Delta Sigma Rho. Republican. Unitarian. Author: Code of International Criminal Law, 1928; An Outline Digest of the Criminal Law of New York, 1930; The Public Utilities of Connecticut, 1931; Community Property Law of California, 1951. Contbr. numerous articles on legal subjects; associate editor Central Law Journal, St. Louis, 1921-30. Home: Redding CT Died June 1968.

LEVY, ERNEST COLEMAN sanitarian; b. Richmond, Va., Aug. 11, 1868; s. Abraham and Rachel Cornelia (Levy) L.; M.D., Med. Coll. of Va.; post-grad. work, Coll. Phys. and Surg. (Columbia), Mass. Inst. Tech.; m. Elisabeth Detwiler, June 19, 1912. House phys., Mt. Sinai Hosp., New York, 1890-92; prof. histology, pathology and bacterilogy, Med. Coll. of Va., 1897-1900; editor Medical Register, 1897-1900; chief health officer, Richmond, 1906-17; dir. pub. welfare. Richmond, 1919-24; prof. preventive medicine, Medical Coll. of Vienna, 1925; city health officer, Tampa, Fla., 1925-28. Commd. capt. M.C., U.S.A., Aug. 1918; maj., Oct. 1918; hon. discharged, Jan. 1919. Made original investigations in origin of Southern typhoid fever, 1907-08; research in breeding and control of house fly, resulting in invention of the maggot trap, 1911; research in infantile diarrhea. Charter fellow Am. Pub. Health Assn. (pres. 1923); mem. La Société de 40 Hommes et 8 Chevaux; comdr. Richmond (Va.) Post No. 1, Am. Legion, 1925 (resigned). Democrat. Jewish religion. Died Sept. 29, 1938.

LEVY, ROBERT otolaryngology; b. Hamilton, Ont., Can., May 30, 1864; s. Mandel and Rebecca (Elsner) L.; student U. of Denver, 1880-81; M.D., Bellevue Hosp. Med. Coll., N.Y. City, 1884; m. Rebecca Goldsmith, Aug. 27, 1889; children-Leona, Marion. Began practice at Denver, 1884; prof. otolaryngology, U. of Colo., 1889-1930, emeritus, 1930-44; cons. otolaryngologist St. Joseph's Hosp., Nat. Jewish Hosp. of Denver, Children's Hospital, St. Anthony's Hosp. Maj., Med. Corps, U.S. Army, 1918. Fellow Am. Coll. Surg.; mem. Am. Laryngol., Rhinol. and Otol. Soc (ex-pres.), A.M.A. (ex-chmn. sect. otolaryngology), Colo. State Med. Soc. (ex-pres.), Am. Acad. Ophthalmology and Otolaryngology, Am. Laryngol. Assn., Denver Clin. and Path. Soc. (ex-pres.), Sigma Xi, Phi Delta Epsilon, Alpha Mu Pi Omega. Republican. Jewish religion. Mason (32ff). Contbr. chapter on endolaryngeal operations to Loeb's Operative Surgery of Ear, Nose and Throat; also articles in med. jours. on laryngology, tuberculosis, etc. Home: 1215 Detroit St. Office: Metropolitan Bldg., Denver, Colo. Died July 1, 1945.

LEWIN, PHILIP orthopedic surgeon; born Chgo., June 18, 1888; son Marks Lewin; B.S., University Chicago, 1909; M.D., Ruch Medical College, 1911; postgrad. Univ. of Paris France; married Merriel Abbott, May 26, 1921; 1 son, Frank. Intern Children's Meml. Hosp., 1911-12, St. Luke's Hosp., 1912-14; in practice, Chgo., 1914-; cons. orthopedic surgeon, Cook County Hosp.; sir. attending orthopedic surgon and past chmn., dept. of bone and joint surgery Michael Reese Hosp.; cons. orthopaedic surgery Highland Park Found.; past chmn. dept., professor emeritus of bone and joint surg., Northwestern U. Med. Sch.; prof. Orthopedic surg., Cook County Grad. Sch. of Medicine; cons. Municipal Contagious Diseases Hosp., Chicago. Mem. med. adv. com. Nat. Foundn. for Infantile Paralysis; mem. Professional Adv. Com., Div. Services for Crippled Children. Internat. Soc. Orthopedic Surg. and Traumatology; mem. adv. com. Commn. for Handicapped, State of Ill.; mem. adv. com. on Infantile Paralysis, Ill. Dept. Pub. Health. Served as captain medical corps, United States Army, 1917-19; major M.O.R.C. Colonel M.C. A.U.S., chief of orthopedic surgery Mayo Gen. Hosp., Galesburg, Ill., and commdg. officer 16th Evac. Hosp., Camp Blanding, Fla., 1942-46. Diplomate Am. Bd. Orthopedic Surgery. Founder fellow, Internat. Coll. Surg., U.S. chapter. Fellow Am. Coll. Surgs.; mem. A.M.A., Ill. State and Chicago med. socs., Am. Orthopedic Assn., Clin. Orthopedic Soc., Am. Assn. for Study and Control of Rheumatic Diseases, Am. Acad. Orthopedic Surgeons (a founder-sec. 1931-36). Chicago Orthopedic Soc. (formerly pres.); mem. (hon.) Italian Orthopedic Surg. Congress, Rome, Italy, 1948. Author numerous sci. publs. in field, latest: The Back and Its Syndrome, 1953. Home: 91 Sycamore Pl., Highland Park, Ill. Office: 55 E. Washington St. Chicago 2. Died May 1960.

LEWIS, ANDREW army officer; b. Donegal, Ireland, 1720; s. John and Margaret (Lynn) L.; m. Elizabeth Givens, 6 children. Served as maj. in Ohio campaigns commanded by Washington, 1754-55; led Sandy Creek expdn., 1756; county lt. of Augusta County, Va.; justice of peace; rep. Botecourt County Legislature; aided in Indian Treaty of Ft. Stanwix; defeated Indians at Battle of Point Pleasant in Lord Dunmore's War, 1774; mem. Revolutionary Colonial Convs. of Va. 1775; commd. brig. gen. Continental Army in command Am. forces stationed at Williamsburg, Va., 1776; defeated British under Lord Dunmore at Gwynn's Island, 1776; resigned from Continental Army, 1777; mem. Va. Exec. Council, 1776-81. Died Bedford County, Va., Sept. 26, 1781.

LEWIS, CLARENCE IRVING educator; b. Stoneham, Mass., Apr. 12, 1883; s. Irving and Hannah Carolyn (Dearth) L.; A.B., Harvard, 1906, Ph.D., 1910; L.H.D., U. Chgo., 1941; m. Mabel Maxwell Graves, Jan. 1, 1907; children-Irving Maxwell (dec.), Margaret Maxwell (dec.), David Edson, Andrew Kittredge. Tchr. high sch., Quincy, Mass., 1905-06; instr. in English U., Colo., 1906-08; instr. philosophy U. Cal., 1911-14, asst. prof., 1914-20; lectr. philosophy Harvard, 1920-21, asst. prof. philosphy, 1921-24, asso. prof., 1924-30, prof., 1930-46, Edgar Pierce prof. philosophy emeritus, 1946-53; vis. prof., philosophy Columbia, 1923, 27, 29; tchr. Stanford, Mich. State U., U. So. Cal. Served as pvt., later capt., assigned to instrn. U.S. Army, Fortress Monroe, Va., 1918. Awarded Butler medal in Gold, Columbia, 1950; recipient Am. Council Learned Socs. prize, 1961. Mem. Am. Philos. Assn., Am. Acad. Arts and Scis., Am. Philos. Soc., Brit. Acad. (corr. fellow). Phi Beta Kappa. Author: Survey of Symbolic Logic, 1918; Mind and the World-Order, 1929; Symbolic Logic (with C. H. Langford), 1932; An Analysis of Knowledge and Valuation, 1946; The Ground and Nature of the Right, 1955; Our Social Inheritance, 1957. Home: 23 Oakland St., Lexington 73, Mass. Office: Emerson Hall, Cambridge 38, Mass. Died Feb. 3, 1964.

LEWIS, EDMUND HARRIS, lawyer; b. Syracuse, N.Y., Aug. 30, 1884; s. Ceylon H. and Jennie M. (Heffron) L.; A.B., Yale U., 1907, LL.D., 1954; LL.B., Syracuse U., 1909, LL.D., 1937; LL.D. Colgate U., 1940, Middlebury Coll., 1948, Hamilton Coll., 1954; m. Laura R. Strong, June 1, 1910; children—Mary Strong (dec.), Janet L. Dickson, Katharine Strong (dec.), Margaret L. Crosman. Admitted to N.Y. bar, 1909, and began practice at Syracuse; dep. atty. gen. of N.Y., 1915-18; corp. counsel Syracuse, 1920-22; elected justice Supreme Ct. of N.Y., 1929; asso. justice Appellate Div., 4th Dept., Oct., 1933-Jan. 3, 1940. Apptd. by gov. asso. judge Ct. of Appeals, Jan. 3, 1940, elected full term, Nov. 1, 1940; chief judge N.Y. Ct. Appeals, 1953-54; with Mackenzie, Smith, Lewis, Mitchell & Hughes, 1955-—. Chmn. mng. bd. Syracuse Community Chest, 1928-29. Mem. bd. trustees Syracuse U. Maj., Judge Adv. Gen.'s Corps, U.S. Army, 1918. Mem. N.Y. State Bar Assn. (pres. 1955), Onondaga County Bar Assn. (pres. 1929), Assn. Bar City New York, Syracuse C. of C. (pres. 1928-29), Delta Kappa Epsilon, Phi Delta Phi. Republican. Presbyn. Clubs: University of Syracuse (pres. 1926-27); Century (Syracuse); Skaneateles Country. Home: Skaneateles NY Died July 30, 1972.

LEWIS, EDWARD MANN army officer; b. New Albany, Ind., Dec. 10, 1863; s. William Henry and Julia Frances (Snively) L.; grad. U.S. Mil. Acad., 1886; studied DePauw U. and U. of Calif.; LL.D., DePauw U., Greencastle, Ind., 1919; m. Hattie Russell Balding, June 12, 1888; children-Henry Balding, Mrs. Adelaide Palmer McMullen, Thos. Edward. Commd. 2c lt. 11th Inf., July 1, 1886; promoted through grades to col., Mar. 23, 1917; brig. gen. N.G., in federal service, July 8, 1916; brig. gen. N.A., Aug. 5, 1917; maj. gen., June 28, 1918; brig. gen. regular army, Jan. 9, 1920; maj. gen., Dec. 2, 1922. Prof. mil. science and tactics, DePauw U., 1892-96; served in Cuba as adj. 20th Inf., Spanish-Am. War, 1898; same capacity during Philippine Insurrection, 1899-1901; duty San Francisco, following earthquake and fire, 1906; prof. mil. science and tactics, U. of Calif., 1908-12; with expdn. to Vera Cruz, 1914, comdg. 19th Inf., adj. 5th Brigade and under detail as treas. Mil. Govt.; sr. insp. instr., Ill. N.G., 1915-17, and officer in charge mil. affairs at hdqrs. Northeastern Dept., Boston, 1917; apptd. comdr. 13th Provisional Div. and Camp Llano Grande Tex., July 11, 1916; comd. 76th Inf. Brig., N.A., Aug.-Nov., 1917; comd. U.S. troops, Paris, Dec. 1, 1917-May 5, 1918; comd. 3d Brig., 2d Div. to July 13, 1918, 30th Div., July 15, 1918-Mar. 15, 1919; office of Chief of Staff, G.H.Q. and pres. Inf. Bd. to June 17, 1919; comd. Camp Gordon, Ga., to Dec. 20, 1919; comd. Douglas, Ariz. Dist., to Jan. 4, 1920; comd. 3d Div. and Camp Pike, Ark., to Sept. 15, 1921; comd. 2d Div. and Camp Travis, Tex., Sept. 15, 1921-Nov. 20, 1922; comd. 8th Corps area Nov. 1922-Aug. 1924; comd. Hawaiian Div. and Schofield Barracks, Sept. 16, 1924-Jan. 1925; comd. Hawaiian Dept., Jan. 13, 1925-Aug. 1925; comd. Hawaiian Dept., Jan. 13, 1925-Aug. 27, 1927; retired Dec. 10, 1927. Decorations: D.S.M.; Comdr. Legion of Honor and croix de Guerre with two palms (French); Comdr. Order of Leopold, Croix de Guerre (Belgian): Knight Comdr. Order of St. Michael and St. George (British); Grand Officer Order of Danilo (Montenegrin). Mem. S.R., Soc. Army Santiago de Cuba, Phi Beta Kappa. Presbyterian. Clubs: Union League (San Francisco); Faculty (U. of Calif.). Home: 89 Parkside Drive, Berkeley, Calif. Died July 27, 1949; buried in National Cemetery, Presidio of San Francisco.

LEWIS, EDWARD MCEHINEY pub. relations ofcl.; b. St. Louis, Jan. 26, 1884; s. Edward Simmons and Pattie (Cooke) L.; ed. Smith Acad., St. Louis; Yale, 1902-04; m. Katherine Richardson, Aug. 19, 1919. Customers' Man, stock broker's office, 1905; farmer on own irrigated farm nr. Santa Maria, Tex., 1907-13; polit. reporter, St. Louis Star, 1914-21; Washington corr., The Am. Legion, 1922-36; Rep. Congl. Com., 1936; with VA, 1937, now dir. pub. relations. Enlisted U.S. Army 1917, attended 1st officers T.C., commd. 1st lt., promoted capt., hdqrs. troop, 10th div., staff Maj. Gen. Wood; disch., 1919. Mem. Book and Snake Soc. (Yale), Nat. Press Club Post, Am. Legion, S.R., War of 1812, Colonial Wars. Club: National Press (Washington). Home: 3133 O St., Washington 7. Office: Veterans Administration, Vermont and H St., Washington 25. Died Aug. 8, 1954; buried Arlington Cemetery, Washington.

LEWIS, GILBERT NEWTON chemist; b. Weymouth, Mass., Oct. 23, 1875; s. Frank W. and Mary B. (White) L.; U. of Neb., 1890-93; A.B., Harvard, 1896; A.M., 1898, Ph.D., 1899; univs. of Leipzig and Göttingen, 1900-01; hon. D.Sc., U. of Liverpool, 1923, U. of Wis., 1928, U. of Chicago, 1929, U. of Pa., 1938; Dr. Hon. Caus., U. of Madrid, Spain, 1934; m. Mary Hinckley Sheldon, June 20, 1912; children-Richard Newton, Margery, Edward Sheldon. Instr. chemistry, Harvard, 1899-1900, 1901-06 (on leave of absence, in charge weights and measures, P.I., 1904-05); asst. prof. chemistry, 1907-08, asso. prof., 1908-11, prof., 1911-12, Massachusetts Institute of Technology; professor phys. chemistry, University of Calif., since July 1, 1912; Silliman lecturer, Yale, 1925. Maj. U.S. Army, 1918; lt. col., 1919; chief of defense div. Gas Service, A.E.F. Decorated D.S.M. (U.S.); Chevalier Legion of Honor (French); awarded Nichols, Gibbs and Davy medals, 1929; Soc. Arts and Sciences medal, 1930; Richards medal, 1938; Arrhenius medal, 1939. Mem. American Philosophical Society, American Chemistry Society, American Physics Soc.; fellow Am. Acad. Arts and Sciences; hon. fellow London Chem. Soc., Royal Instn. of Great Britain, Indian Acad. Sciences; hon. mem. Swedish Acad., Danish Acad., Royal Soc., Franklin Inst. of Pa. Author: Thermodynamics and the Free Energy of Chemical Substances (with M. Randall), 1923; Valence and the Structure of Atoms and Molecules, 1923; The Anatomy of Science, 1926. Home: 948 Santa Barbara Rd., Berkeley, Calif. Died Mar. 23, 1946.

LEWIS, IRVING STANTON, fgn. service officer; b. Columbus, O., Dec. 11, 1919; s. William Vermylee and Viola (Nickels) L.; student Ohio State U., 1941-42, 46-47; B.A., Western Res. U., 1948; M.A., Georgetown U., 1950; m. Patricia Jean Claflin, June 7, 1947; children—Patricia H., Paul N., Penelope J., Philip H., Peter M. With Cleve. Council World Affairs, 1947-48; legislative ref. asst. to mem. U.S. Congress, 1949-50; dir. Binational Cultural Center, LaPaz, Bolivia, 1950-54, Guatemala City, Guatemala, 1954-57; joined U.S. Fgn. Service, 1957; cultural affairs officer Am. embassy, San Salvador, El Salvador, 1957-62; desk officer, Mexico, C.Am., Panama, U.S. Information Agy., Washington, 1962-65; pub. affairs officer Am. Embassy, Managua, Nicaragua, 1965-69, Montevideo, Uruguay, 1969-70; with USIA, Washington, 1970-71. Served to 2d lt., Med. Adminstrv. Corps, AUS, 1942-46. Mem. Am. Polit. Sci. Assn. Home: Silver Spring MD Died Feb. 14, 1971.

LEWIS, ISAAC NEWTON army officer; b. New Salem, Pa., Oct. 12, 1858; s. James H. and Anne (Kendall) L.; grad. U.S. Mil. Acad., 1884; m. Mary, d. Richard Wheatley, D.D., of N.Y. City, Oct. 21, 1866; children-Richard Wheatley, Laura Anne, George Fenn, Margaret Kendall. Commd. 2d lt. 2d Arty., June 15, 1884; promoted through grades to col., Aug. 27, 1913; retired on account of disability incurred in line of duty, Sept. 20, 1913. Mem. bd. on regulation of coast arty. fire, New York Harbor, 1894-98; recorder Bd. of Ordnance and Fortification, Washington, 1898-1902; instr. and dir. Coast Arty. Sch., Ft. Monroe, Va., 1904-11. Made study of methods of mfr. and supply of ordnance materials, in Europe, 1900, resulting in complete re-armament of field arty. of U.S.; orginator of plan for modern corps orgn. for artillery which was adopted by Congress, 1902. Inventor of the Lewis machine gun which was in general use by all the allies throughout of World War; also inventor of numerous mil. instruments and devices in general use, including the first, successful arty. range and position finder, a replotting and relocating system for coast batteries, time interval clock and bell system of signals, quick firing field gun and mount, quick reading mech. verniers, electric car lighting and windmill electric lighting systems, etc. Republican. Methodist. Home: Montclair, N.J. Died Nov. 9, 1931.

LEWIS, JAMES HAMILTON senator, lawyer; b. Danville, Va.; taken to Ga.; ed. Houghton Coll., Ga., and U. of Va.; studied law, Savannah, Ga.; LL.D., Ohio Northern U. and Baylor U.; m. Rose Lawton Douglas, of Ga. Admitted to bar, Seattle; served as mem. Wash. Senate; congressman at large, State of Wash., 1896-1900; chosen by Democracy of Wash. for vice-pres. of U.S., 1900, and endorsed by Pacific Coast States, with U.S. Senator Stephen White, of Calif.; served in Spanish-Am. War; named on staff of Gen. Brooke, in Cuba, as insp. gen.; transferred to staff of Gen. F. D. Grant, commr. for War Dept. and President of U.S., in matters touching prosecution of war; reported in France to Gen. Pershing and later assigned to Gen. George Bell as soldier aide; on return to U.S. on ship Mt. Vernon, in charge of wounded soldiers, torpedoed at sea, put back to Brest, and later resumed his war duties. Tendered ambassadorship to Belgium (declined). Knighted by King of Belgium and King of Greece; made mem. Knights of the Round Table, London, King of England presiding on the occasion. Served in behalf of Am. interests at internat. confs., Genoa, Italy, and Lausanne, Switzerland. Author: (or joint author) Hand Book on Election, 1912; Constitutions, Statutes and Their Construction (with A. H. Putney); Two Great Republics-Rome and the United States; Removal of Causes from State to U.S. Courts; Lewis and Spelling on Injunctions. Home: Chicago, Ill. Died Apr. 9, 1939.

LEWIS, JAMES MALCOLM army officer; b. Moundsville, W.Va., Feb. 17, 1898; s. Edgar Malcolm and Marie (McClune) L.; B.S., U.S. Mil. Acad., 1920; grad. F.A., Basic Sch., Fort Knox, Ky., 1921, Command and Gen. Staff Sch., 1936. Commd. 2d lt. F.A., U.S. Army, 1920, advanced through grades to maj. gen., 1954. Decorated Legion of Merit, Bronze Star. Home: 515 Tenth St., Moundsville, W.Va. Office: care, The Adjutant General's Office, War Dept. Washington 25. Died Apr. 19, 1954.

LEWIS, JOHN F., JR. lawyer; b. Phila., Pa., May 29, 1899; s. John Frederick and Anne Henrietta Rush Baker L.; student Episcopal Acad., 1915-16; A.B., U. of Pa., 1920; student U. of Pa. Law Sch., 1921-23; D.F.A., Moore Inst.; LL.D., Temple U., U. Pa.; m. Ada Haeseler, June 20, 1925; children-Anne Rush, John F., 3d, Howard Haeseler. Admitted to Pa. bar, 1925; became associated with firm Lewis, Adler & Laws, 1915; partner in firm, Lewis, Wolff & Gourlay 1932-; pres. Northern Liberties Gas Co., 1936-56. Chmn. Phila. Com. Russian War Relief, 1941-45. Commd. 2d lt. Med. Corps, A.U.S. Res., 1941. Pres. Phila. Art Alliance, 1935-49, now dir., dir. Phila. Art Commn. Fairmont, Park Art Assn.; past pres. Pa. Acad. Fine Arts, Am. Acad. Music, 1932-50, Union Library Catalogue, Mercantile Library, 1932-48; v.p. Athenaeum Library, Free Library Phila., Moore Coll. Art; dir. Phila. Zool. Soc., So. Home for Children, Fine Arts Dept. of U. of Pa., University of Pennysivania Museum, Philadelphia Bourse; treas. Atwater Kent Museum. Dem. presidential elector 1940. Mem. A.I.A. (hon.), Am. Philos. Soc., Phi Beta Kappa, Alpha Chi Rho, Delta Sigma Rho. Clubs: Art Alliance, Franklin Inn (Phila.); Philobiblon. Home: 1916 Spruce St. Office: 1940 Delancey St., Phila. 3. Died Sept. 5, 1965; buried Laurel Hill Cemetery, Phila.

LEWIS, LAWRENCE lawyer, congressman; b. St. Louis, Mo., June 22, 1879; s. Thomas Addison and Melissa Ann (Lewis) L.; student U. of Colo., 1897-99; A.B., Harvard, 1901, LL.B., 1909, unmarried. Editor and mgr. Camp and Plant (weekly mag. of Colo. Fuel & Iron Co.), 1901-04; asst. instr. in English, Harvard, 1906-09; in practice of law at Denver since 1909. Mem. Colo. Civ. Service Commn., 1917-18; legal adviser to Selective Service Bd., Denver, and to adj. gen. of Colo., World War; pvt. field arty. and attended F.A. Central O.T.S., Camp Zachary Taylor, Ky. Mem. 73d to 78th Congresses (1933-45), 1st Colo. Dist. Mem. Am., Colo. State and Denver bar assns., State Hist. Soc. of Colo. (dir., sec.), Harvard Law Sch. Assn., Denver Art Museum, Am. Legion (comdr. Denver City, 1927-28), Sigma Alpha Epsilon, Democrat. Episcopalian. Mason. Clubs: University, Democratic Rocky Mountain Harvard (ex-pres.); Harvard (New York). Author: The Advertisements of the Spectator, 1909. Home: 1673 Sherman St. Office: Equitable Bldg., Denver, Colo. Died Dec. 9, 1943.

LEWIS, LLOYD GRIFFITH surgeon; b. Remsen, N.Y., Nov. 10, 1902; s. John Griffith and Nettie (Griffith) L.; A.B., Hamilton Coll., 1924; M.D., Johns Hopkins, 1928; m. Lois Falconer, Aug. 16, 1930 (div. Feb. 3, 1959); 1 son, John Richard; m. 2d, Frances Carter Frick, Feb. 14, 1959. Intern, asst. res., resident urology Johns Hopkins Hosp., 1928-33; instr., asst., asso. prof. Johns Hopkins, 1930-46; associate prof. urology med. sch. Georgetown U., 1946-48, prof. urology, 1948-53, prof. clin. urology, 1953; staff Doctors Hosp., Georgetown University Hosp.; consultant urology Walter Reed Army Hosp., Nat. Inst. Health, Bolling Field United States Air Force Hosp. Served as maj. to col., med. corps U.S. Army, 1942-46; chief sect. urology Walter Reed Gen. Hosp. Trustee of Hamilton College. Diplomate American Board of Urology. Member of Am. Medical Assn., Am. Urological Assn. (chmn. com. visual edn.). Contbr. med. jours. Address: Kennedy-Warren Apts., Washington. Died Mar. 2, 1959; buried Arlington Nat. Cemetery.

LEWIS, REUBEN ALEXANDER, JR. pub.; b. Birmingham, Ala., Aug. 29, 1895; s. Reuben Alexander and Martha Louise (Ives) L.; A.B., Washington and Lee U., 1916; spl. course, Harvard U. Grad. Sch. of Bus. Adminstrn., 1930; m. Sarah Stewart Briggs, Jan. 7, 1925 (divorced 1944); children-Barbara Stewart, Reuben Alexander III, Mitchell Ives; m. 2d, Catherine Mohan Richardson, Mar. 24, 1944. Reporter, Birmingham Age-Herald, 1911-13, sporting editor, 1913-14; sec. Southeastern League (baseball), 1915; shipping editor, N.Y. Jour. of Commerce, 1920-21, chief Washington corr., 1921-23; asso. editor Am. Bankers Assn. Jour., 1923-28; dep. mgr. in charge trust co. div., Am. Bankers Assn., 1928-30; 2d v.p. Continental Ill. Bank & Trust Co., Chicago, 1930-37; exec. vice-pres. Metropolitan Trust Co., Chicago, 1937-41; now publisher of Finance Magazine. Member Pub. Relations Council, Am. Bankers Assn., 1939; mem. Assn. of Reserve City Bankers, 1934-37. Mem. first O.T.C., Fort McPherson, Ga., May 1917, asst. adj., 20th F.A. Brig., U.S. Army, 1918, aide de camp to comdg. gen., 1918. Mem. Phi Beta Kappa, Omicron Delta Kappa, Alpha Tau Omega. Democrat. Methodist. Clubs: Executives, Electric (Chicago); National Press (Washington, D.C.). Author: (brochures) Our Changing Investment Habits; The Big Money Makers of America; Main Street Finances Wall. Street. Home: 900 N. Michigan Av. Office: 20 N. Wacker Dr., Chicago. Died May 4, 1948.

LEWIS, SPENCER STEEN naval officer; b. Calvert, Tex., Jan. 8, 1888; s. James Berry and Mary Elizabeth (Meredith) L.; B.S., U.S. Naval Acad., 1910; m. Jensy Yerger Loop, 1914 (died 1942); children-Mary Meredith (Mrs. William C. Rodgers), Harriette Loop (Mrs. Arkie C. Hauck); m. 2d, Amy Joan Micklam, 1944. Commd. ensign USN, 1910, advanced through grades to rear adm., 1942; ret. vic adm. 1947, Decorated Navy Cross, D.S.M., Legion of Merit (U.S.); Companion of the Bath (Gt. Britain); Legion of Honor, Croix de Guerre (France). Episcopalian. Clubs: Army and Navy, Army-Navy Country (Washington). Home: Calvert, Tex. Office: Navy Dept., Washington 25. Deceased.

LEWIS, WALTER OLIVER clergyman, educator; b. Stanberry, Mo., Feb. 22, 1877; s. Benjamin D. and Laura Florence (Coffey) L.; A.B., William Jewell Coll., 1898; Th.D., So. Bapt. Theol. Sem., 1904; student univs. Berlin, Erlangen, Halle and Leipzig, Germany, 1906-08; Ph.D., Erlangen, 1908; m. Maggie Rogers, Sept. 8, 1903 (died Apr. 1904); m. 2d, Jessie C. Thompson, Sept. 26, 1907; children - Frank David, Robert Edward. Ordained ministry Bapt. Ch., 1897; served as pastor following chs. in Mo., West Park Ch., St. Louis, Wyatt Park Ch., St. Joseph, Compton Heights Ch., St. Louis; prof. philosophy and religion William Jewell Coll., 1910-22; European rep. Am. Bapt. Fgn. Mission Soc., 1922-39; with Am. Relief Adminstrn. in Russia autumn 1922 and spring 1923; asso. sec. Bapt. World Alliance; dir. Bapt. Relief in Europe. Served as chaplain 360th U.S. Inf., World War; was in St. Mihiel and Meuse-Argonne offensives, and with Army of occupation in Germany. Address: 4 Southampton Row, London, W.C. 1, Died Aug. 1965.

LEWIS, W(INFORD) LEE chemist; b. Gridley, Butte County, Calif., May 29, 1878; s. George Madison and Sarah Adeline (Hopper) L.; A.B., Stanford, 1902; A.M., U. of Wash., 1904; Ph.D., U. of Chicago, 1909; m. Myrtilla Mae Lewis, Sept. 1907; children-Mrs. Miriam Lee Reiss, Mrs. Winifred Lee Harwood. Asst. and instr. chemistry, U. of Washington, 1902-04; prof. chemistry, Morningside College, Sioux City, Ia., 1904-06; fellow U. of Chicago, 1907-09; instr. chemistry, Northwestern U., 1909, asst. prof., 1914, asso. prof., 1917, prof. and head of dept., 1919-24. Asst. chemist U.S. Dept. Agr., 1908-10; city chemist, Evanston, 1912-18; consulting practice; dir. dept. of scientific research Inst. Am. Meat Packers since 1924. Capt. Chem. Warfare Service, U.S. Army, 1917-18; maj. U.S.R., 1919; lt. col., 1924; col., 1933. Fellow A.A.A.S., mem. Am. Chem. Soc., Alpha Chi Sigma, Sigma Xi, Kappa Sigma, Chemists Club, Sword and Scabbard. Republican. Episcopalian. Clubs: Originalists, Chaos, Union League (Chicago); University, Rotary (Evanston). Home: 2323 Central Park Av., Evanston, Ill. Office: 59 E. Van Buren St., Chicago, Ill. Died Jan. 20, 1943.

LEYDON, JOHN KOEBIG, investment banker; born in the city of Philadelphia, Pennsylvania, Oct. 14, 1916; s. John William and Dorothy (Koebig) L.; B.S., U.S. Naval Acad., 1938; M.S., Cal. Inst. Tech., 1945; m. Elizabeth Martin Rivinus, July 11, 1940;children—John Koebig, Edward Rivinus, Lisa Martin, Christopher Francis. Commd. ensign U.S. Navy, 1938, advanced through grades to rear adm., 1964; designated naval aviator, 1941; engring. assignments, 1945-59; comdr. U.S. Naval served in U.S.S. Ranger, 1941-43; various areo. Air Turbine Test Sta., Trenton, N.J., 1959-61; dep. chief naval material Navy Dept., 1963-64, chief naval research, 1964-67; partner Paine, Webster, Jackson & Crutis, 1967-71. Dir. Access Crop., Laser Diode Labs., Inc. Clubs: Army Navy Country (Washington); City Midday (N.Y.). Home: Lahaska PA Died Feb. 2, 1971; buried Arlington Nat. Cemetery, Arlington VA

LEYS, JAMES FARQUHARSON naval officer; b. Delaware County, Pa., Dec. 26, 1867; s. James F. and Rachel (West) L.; M.D., U. of Pa., 1890; m. Gwendoleyne Mary Wigley, 1897; children-Katharine Mary, James Farquharson, Gwendoleyne Mary, Martha Francesca. Apptd. asst. surgeon U.S.N., 1893; promoted through grades to rear adm. and retired for age, Jan. 1, 1932, with advancement to vice adm. for service on construction of Panama Canal, 1907-10, being the first officer of any staff corps in the Navy to attain that rank. Served afloat on U.S.S. Chicago, Alliance, Helena, Vesuvius, Essex, New York and Flagship Wyoming (aide and fleet surgeon); comd. naval hosps. at Newport and Boston. Medals: Santiago, Spanish Campaign, Vera Cruz, Panama, Victory (with special commendation). Wrote First Sect., Vol. II, American Practice of Surgery. Collaborator in Reference Handbook of Med. Sciences. Home: Bryn Mawr, Pa. Died Jan. 12, 1938.

LEYSHON, HAL IRWIN publicist; b. Mountain Ash, Ky., Sept. 12, 1900; s. Howell Ulysses and Alice (Richards) L.; ed. Maryville (Tenn.) Preparatory Sch., 1915-17, Maryville Coll., 1917-19; m. Margaret Sullivan, June 25, 1935; m. 2d, Marion Elizabeth Pollard, Aug. 22, 1942; one son, Hal Richards. Reporter Knoxville (Tenn.) News Sentinel, 1919-21, Knoxville Jour., 1921-22, Mobile (Ala.) Register, 1922; city editor Knoxville News Sentinel, 1923-25; Sunday editor Miami News, 1925-28, news editor, 1928-30, mng. editor, 1931-35, editor 1935-41; foreign corr. Consol. Press Assn., 1930; now pres. Hal Leyshon & Associates, Inc., public relations counsel, N.Y.C. Editor of Miami News during period for which it won Pulitzer medal for public service, 1939. Served overseas with U.S. Army Air Forces; now on inactive list as lt. col. Mem. Sigma Nu Epsilon. Democrat. Presbyn. Clubs: National Press (Washington); Overseas Press, Advertising, St. Davids Soc. (N.Y.C.); American (London). Co-author: Skyways to Berlin; Front Page Deadline. Office: 122 E. 42 St., N.Y.C. 17. Died July 9, 1967.

LIBBEY, WILLIAM univ. prof.; b. Jersey City, N.J., Mar. 27, 1855; s. William and Elizabeth (Marsh) L.; A.B., Princeton, 1877, A.M., Sc.D., 1879; m. Mary E. Green, Dec. 7, 1880; children-Mrs. W. Lester Glenney, Mrs. W. Thayer Field. Asst. prof. physical geography, 1882, histology, 1883-98, phys. geography and dir. mus. of geology and archeology, 1883-1923, Princeton, emeritus. Pres. Princeton Savings Bank; v.p. First Nat. Bank. Capt. Co. L, 2d Regt. N.G. of N.J., 1900-06; lt. col. asst. insp. gen. rifle practice, 1906, col., 1917. Maj., Ordnance R.C.U.S.A., Feb. 20, 1918; asst. chief instr., Small Arms Firing Sch., May 13, 1918; lt. col. inf., Sept. 8, 1918; chief rifle demonstrator, Oct. 1, 1918; discharged, Mar. 20, 1919. Officier d' Academie, France. Fellow and foreign sec. Am. Geog. Society. Mem. numerous Am. and fgn. societies. Author: Jordan Valley and Petra (with Dr. Franklin E. Hoskins), 1905. Home: Princeton, N.J. Died Sept. 6, 1927.

LIBBY, ARTHUR STEPHEN educator; b. Corinna, Me., Mar. 9, 1877; s. Clements Coffin and Estelle D. (Allen) L.; Ph.B., Bowdoin Coll., 1902; A.B., U. of Me., 1903; A.M., Sorbonne, Paris, 1903; A.M., Brown, 1904; Ph.D., U. of Paris, 1906; studied law depts. U. of Me. and Columbia; m. Prof. Cora M. Steele, Aug. 20, 1907. Prin. high schs. in Me., several yrs.; instr. French, Brown U., 1903-04; prof. modern langs., Converse Coll., Spartanburg, S.C., 1904-12; pres. of Southern Travel-Study Bur., Spartanburg, since 1911. Lecturer for Dept. of Edn., San Francisco Expn., 1915; traveled extensively in India, South Seas, Siberia, Africa, 1912-14; lyceum and chautauqua lecturer on travel, exploration, history and world politics since 1941; actg. prof. history and polit. science, Wofford Coll., 1917-19; dean Sch. of Commerce and prof. polit. science and internat. law, Oglethorpe U., 1919-30; founder, 1930, and pres. Libby Grad. Sch. of Business Administration and Finance (first grad. professional school of business in Southern States); founder, 1931, and pres. U. of Robert E. Lee (embracing Libby Grad. School as one of its depts.); prof. psychology at Grady Hosp. Training Sch., 1934. Served as dir. language instrn., Army Y.M.C.A., with 27th Division, and ednl. dir. and lecturer Army Camps, World War army interpreter and staff officer, rank of maj.; also speaker for Am. Red Cross and War Loan campaigns. Mem. Am. Hist. Assn.; del. from S.C. to Internat. Congress of Edn., Brussels, Belgium, 1910; founder and dir. Southern Bur. of Business Research. Lecturer economics and law, Am. Inst. of Banking. Mayor N. Atlanta, Ga., since 924. Mem. N.E. Club, Ga. Soc. Certified Pub. Accountants, Nat. Assn. of Teachers of Marketing and Advertising, Am. Legion, Kappa Alpha, Phi Kappa Delta, Phi Beta Sigma. Democrat. Presbyn. Mason. Home: Oglethorpe University, North Atlanta, Ga. Died Sept. 24, 1948; buried in Willow Valley Cemetery, Mooresville, N.C.

LIDDELL, FRANK AUSTIN lawyer; b. Hinds Co., Miss., 1892; s. James Washington and Susan (Austin) L.; grad. Ala. Presbyn. Coll., 1912; m. Virginia Roby, Sept. 22, 1927; 1 son, Frank Austin. Admitted to Tex. bar, 1915, since practiced in Houston; with Liddell, Austin, Dawson & Sapp, Houston, 1919-, partner, 1920-; v.p., dir. Western Natural Gas Co., 1934-; gen. counsel, dir. El Paso Natural Gas Company, National Bank of Commerce. Member of the board managers Jefferson Davis Hospital. Served from lt. to capt. inf., U.S. Army, 90th and 77th Divs., A.E.F., 1917-19. Citation for gallantry action. Mem. Am., Tex., Houston bar assns., U.S. Maritime Commn. Methodist. Mason.

Clubs: Houston, River Oaks. Home: 2917 Avalon, Houston 19. Office: Gulf Bldg., Houston 2. Died July 16, 1964; buried Glenwood Cemetery, Houston.

LIEBEL, WILLARD KOEHLER army officer; b. Covington, Ky., Mar. 28, 1901; s. George John and Ida (Koehler) L.; B.S., U.S. Mil. Acad., 1924; grad. Inf. Sch., 1935, Command and Gen. Staff Coll., 1936, Armed Forces Staff Coll., 1946; m. Helena Wiegand, June 16, 1927; children-John P. (colonel U.S. Air Force), Margot-Helene (Mrs. Robert H. Overby). Served with Ohio N.G., 1917-19; commd. 2d lt., inf. U.S. Army, 1924, advanced through grades to maj. gen., 1955; officer 1st Inf., Ft. Sam Houston, Tex., 1924-26, a.d.c. Brig. Gen. Harold B. Fisk, 1926-27, Brig. Gen. F. C. Bolles, 1927-34, 35; col. staff duty, Ft. Douglas, Utah, 1937-39; a.d.c. Brig. Gen. Walter Prosser, Camp Jackson, S.C., 1939-40, Ft. Benning, Ga., 1940, Ft. Clayton, C.Z., 1940-41; chief combat intelligence sect. Gen. Hdqrs., Washington, 1941-42, chief theater intelligence, intelligence div. War Dept., 1942-43; chief staff 17th Airborne Div., Camp McCall, N.C., 1942-43, asst. div. comdr., 1943-45; asst. chief staff G-2, later provost marshal 4th Army, 1945-46; sr. airborne instr. Armed Forces Staff Coll., Norfolk, Va., 1946-47; comdr. 7821 Composite Group, 1947-48, provost marshal, Austria, 1948-50; acting asst. div. comdr. 10th Inf. Div., Ft. Riley, Kan., 1950; comdr. 86th Inf. Regt., 1950-51, asst. div. comdr. 10th Inf. Div., 1951, 52; chief support plans br. J-3 Div., Hdqrs. European Command, 1952-54; chief U.S. Mil. Aid Adv. Group, Portugal, 1954-56; comdg. gen., Ft. Devens, Mass., 1956-57. Decorated Silver Star, Legion Merit, Bronze Star medal with cluster; Courrone de Cheme-Luxembourg; Croix de Guerre with palm (Belgium); Merito Militar (Portugal). Home: 218 Laramie Dr., San Antonio. Died Aug. 1, 961; buried Fort Sam Houston Nat. Cemetery.

LIGGETT, HUNTER army officer; b. Reading, Pa., Mar. 21, 1857; s. James and Margaret (Hunter) L.; grad. U.S. Mil. Acad., 1879; LL.D., U. of Calif., 1921; m. Harriet R. Lane, June 30, 1881. Commd. 2d lt. 5th U.S. Inf., June 13, 1879; promoted through grades to maj. gen., Mar. 6, 1917; retired as maj. gen., U.S.A., Mar. 21, 1921; restored to A.E.F. rank of lt. gen., U.S.A.; retired, 1930. For details of career see Vol. 12 (1922-23). Home: San Francisco, Calif. Died Dec. 30, 1935.

LIGHT, RUDOLPH ALVIN, surgeon; b. Kalamazoo, Sept. 21, 1909; s. Stellar Rudolph and Rachel Winifred (Upjohn) L.; Ph.B., Yale, 1931; B.A. in Physiology, Oxford (Eng.) U., 1934, M.A., 1937; M.D., Vanderbilt U., 1939; m. Ann Bonner Jones, June 8, 1932 (div. 1960); one daughter, Deborah Ann (Mrs. Peter J. Perry); m. second, Helen Ann Rork, Mar. 25, 1960. Began as junior intern, then sr. intern surgery, Lakeside Hosp., Cleve., 1939-41; asst. resident, then resident surgery, Vanderbilt Hosp., 1941-43, 46-47; asst. chief surgery VA Hosp., Nashville, 1947-48, dir. research, 1947-49, acting chief surgery, 1948; asso. prof. surgery Vanderbilt U. Sch. Medicine and Hosp., 1948-57, dir. surg. research, 1949-57, dir. rehab. service, 1956-57; vis. surgeon Nuffield dent. surgery Oxford U., 1958-62. Dir. Upjohn Co., Kalamazoo. Mem. exec. bd. Middle Tenn. council Boy Scouts Am., 1949-58, later member of the National council and member of the national executive board; pres., dir. Nashville Civic Music Assn., 1951-53; pres. Nashville Ednl. Television Found., 1953-57, Light Found., Kalamazoo, from 1958; exec. com. Tenn. Heart Assn., 1955-58, dir., 1956-58, sec., 1956-57; pres., trustee Rudolph A. Light Scholarship Found., from 1966; trustee Nashville Children Mus.; dir. Middle Tenn. Heart Assn., 1950-53, 56-58. Hon. fellow St. Catherine's Coll., Oxford U., Eng.; trustee Vanderbilt U.; Senior Citizens, Inc., Nashville. Served to capt., M.C., AUS, World War II; PTO. Decorated Bronze Star medal; hon. comdr. Most Excellent Order of British Empire; recipient Silver Beaver award Boy Scouts Am. Diplomate Am. Bd. Surgery. Mem. A.C.S., Soc. Univ. Surgeons, So. Surg. Assn., Am. Fedn. Clin. Research, Southeastern Surg. Congress, A.A.A.S., N.Y. Academy Sciences, A.M.A., Tennessee State Medical Society, Sigma Xi, Alpha Chi Rho, Phi Chi. Clubs: Yale (N.Y.C.); University (Chgo.); Belle Meade Country (Nashville); Farmington Country (Charlottesville, Va.); Tryall Country, Half Moon Rose Hall Country (Jamaica, W.I.); Metropolitan (N.Y.C.); Lost Tree, Lost Tree Village (North Palm Beach, Fla.) Cumberland (Nashville). Author articles. Address: Nashville TN Died Jan. 1970.

LIGHTBURN, JOSEPH A. J. clergyman; b. Westmoreland Co., Pa., Sept. 21, 1824; common school edn.; m. Oct. 14, 1855, Miss H. E. Whittlesey. Served in U.S.A. 9 yrs.; served through the Mexican and Civil wars; resigned commn. as big. gen. U.S. vols., June 22, 1865; ordained Bapt. minister, 1869. Republican. Home: Lightburn, W.Va. Died 1901.

LILIENTHAL, HOWARD surgeon; b. Albany, N.Y., Jan. 9, 1861; s. Meyer and Jennie (Marcus) L.; A.B. cum laude, Harvard Univ., 1883, M.D., Harvard Medical School, 1887; McLean Asylum, br. Mass. Gen. Hosp., 1886; grad. Mt. Sinai Hosp., New York, 1888; m. Mary Harriss d'Antignac, Oct. 19, 1891 (died Mar. 4, 1910); children-Mary d'Antignac (Mrs. Thomas Lawrence), Howard (dec.); m. 2d, Edith Strode, Nov. 7, 1911. Lecturer on surgery, N.Y. Polyclinic, 1888; now cons. surgeon N.Y. Polyclinic; surgeon, Mt. Sinai Hosp., 1892-1940, Bellevue Hosp., 1909-40; now retired from active practice; prof. clin. surgery, Cornell U. Med. Coll. for some years from 1917. Commd. 1st lt. Med. Reserve Corps, 1911 (resigned); maj. M.R.C., Apr. 26, 1917; lt. col., M.C., U.S. Army, June 21, 1918; dir. Base Hosp. 3, at Monpont sur l'Isle; served Meuse-Argonne and St. Mihiel as head of operating term 39, at Evacuation Hosp. 8, also base hosps. 101 and 34; hon. disch. Jan. 4, 1919; cited for D.S.M., May 1, 1921. Fellow American College of Surgeons (Founders Group), and American Board of Surgery, A.A.A.S.; member American Society Control of Cancer, A.M.A., American Surg. Association, American Soc. Thoracic Surgery (ex-pres.), N.Y., Soc. for Thoracic Surgery (ex-pres.) (ex-pres.), New York Surg. Soc. (ex-pres.), Med. Soc. Co. of N.Y. (ex-pres.), New York Acad. Medicine, Société Internat. de Chirurgie, Mil. Order World Wars (ex-surg. gen.), Am. Legion, Beta Theta Pi; corr. mem. Académie de Chirurgie. Republican. Clubs: University (Winter Park, Florida); Harvard. Author: Imperative Surgery, 1900; Thoracic Surgery, 1925. Contbr. to Binnie's Treatise on Regional Surgery, 1917, and Ochsner's Surgical Diagnosis and Treatment, 1920; more than 300 contbns. to surg. literature. Advisory editor Jour. of Thoracic Surgery. Home: 20 W. 77th St., New York 24, N.Y. Died Apr. 30, 1946.

LILIENTHAL, JOSEPH LEE, JR. physician; b. N.Y. City, Nov. 1, 1911; s. Joseph Leo and Edna (Arnstein) L.; B.S., Yale, 1933; M.D., Johns Hopkins, 1937; m. Katherine Arnstein, June 25, 1937; children-Julia, Nina. Clinical Clerk, National Hospital, Queen's Square, London, England, 1937; house officer Presbyterian Hospital, New York City, 1938-40; resident physician Johns Hopkins Hospital, 1940-42, physician since 1946; asso. prof. medicine Johns Hopkins, since 1946, prof. environmental medicine since 1950; reserach neuromuscular and respiratory physiology. Cons. Nat. Science Found.; mem. com. aviation medicine and com. naval med. research Nat. Research Council. Mem. med. bd. Nat. Muscular Dystrophy Assn. Cons. to Sec. of Def., Research and Development Bd., 1948-53. Office of Naval Research, 1951—. Surgeon Gen. Dept. Army, 1950-53, clin. center Nat. Inst. Health. Mem. Nat. Bd. Med. Examiners, chmn. medicine test com. Physiol. Study Sect. Nat. Inst. Health USPHS, 1953—. Served as lt. comdr., U.S. N.R., 1942-46. Fellow N.Y. Academy Sci.; mem. Am. Institute Biological Sciences, American Clinical Climatological Association, Society of Medical Consultants to Armed Forces, Association of American Physicians, Am. Soc. Clin. Investigation, Am. Physiol. Society, Society Exptl. Biology and Medicine (mem. nat. council). Interurban Clinical Club, American Federation Clinical Research, Sigma Xi, Phi Beta Kappa, Alpha Omega Alpha, Phi Gamma Delta. Club: 14 W. Hamilton St. Home: 6203 Blackburn Lane, Baltimore 12. Office: Johns Hopkins Hospital, Balt. 5. Died Nov. 19, 1955.

LILLARD, WALTER HUSTON, educator; b. Paris, Ill., Nov. 20, 1881; s. David Irvine and Emma Ada (Huston) L.; B.S., Dartmouth, 1905, A.M., 1910; studied Oxford U., Eng., 1909-10; Litt.D., Hobart College, Geneva, New York, 1935; m. Ethel Augusta Hazen, Sept. 5, 1907; children—Walter Huston, Virginia, Barbara Ann, Jane Hazen. Sec. Dartmouth Coll. Club, also grad. student, Dartmouth, and grad. mgr. athletics, 1905-07; instr., later asst. to headmaster, Phillips Acad., Andover, Mass., 1907-16; was first faculty coach of football at Phillips Acad.; headmaster Tabor Acad., Marion, Mass., since June 1916; developing Tabor Acad. as a prep. sch., with nautical training; coordinator for education in Mass., 1941; chief of personnel sect. (G-1), Mass. State Mil. Staff, 1941; dir. Sch. Munitions Technology, National Fireworks, Inc., West Hanover, Mass., since 1942; Am. Rep. in Germany of Intergovernmental Committee on Refugees, 1945; chief resettlement div., Austria, Internat. Refugee Orgn., 1947. Lecturer 1949; director of Civil Defense from 1950. Member Selective Service State Staff. United States guard, Paris Exposition, 1899-1900; enlisted in Battery D, 1st Mass. Field Artillery, Feb. 1916; commd. lt. Co. L, 8th Mass. Inf., Apr. 1916; served on Mexican border, June-Aug. 1916; capt. Co. D, 17th Regt. Inf., Mass. State Guard, May 26, 1917; apptd. comdt. Camp Cleveland (jr. naval training sch.), Marion, Mass.; field supervisor of development bns., Adj. Gen.'s Dept. U.S. Army, Sept. 1918; commd. capt. and assigned as div. personnel adj., Oct. 1918; lt. col., O.R.C. Acting chief seascout, Boy Scouts of America, 1922. Chmn. Internat. Schoolboy Fellowship; regent dist. 2 Cum Laude Soc. Mem. Headmasters Assn., N.E. Assn. Colls. and Prep. Schs., Delta Kappa Epsilon, Casque and Gauntlet. Republican. Conglist. Home: Cohasset MA. Died June 30, 1967.

LILLIE, ABRAHAM BRUYN HASBROUCK officer U.S.N.; b. In N.Y.; entered U.S. Naval Acad. from N.Y., Sept. 24, 1862; grad. 1866. Promoted ensign, Apr. 1868; master, Mar. 26, 1869; lt., Mar. 21, 1870; lt. comdr., Jan. 1887; comdr., Sept. 1895; capt., Mar. 3, 1901. Served on various duties and stations, spending 19 yrs. 3 months at sea, and 18 yrs. and 7 months on shore and other duty, and was commandant U.S. Naval Sta. at Key West, Fla., 1901-03; retired Mar. 6, 1903, with rank of rear admiral. Died 1905.

LILLY, JOSIAH KIRBY corp. exec.; b. Indpls., Sept. 25, 1893; s. Josiah Kirby and Lilly (Ridgley) L.; student Hill Sch., Pottstown, Pa., 1910-12; Ph.C., U. Mich., 1914; m. Ruth Marie Brinkmeyer, Oct. 15, 1914; children-Josiah Kirby III, Ruth (Mrs. Guernsey Van Riper, Jr.). Dir. efficiency div. Eli Lilly & Co., Indpls., 1914-17, dir., 1916-, mgmt. group, 1919-23, v.p., 1923-44, exec. v.p., 1944-48, pres., 1948-53, chmn., dir., 1937-. Served as capt. Med. Supply Service, AEF, 1917-19. Mem. Am. Pharm. Assn., Mil. Order Fgn. Wars U.S., Loyal Legion, Bibliog. Soc. Am., Nat. Soc. Autograph Collectors, Art Assn. Indpls., Chi Psi. Republican. Episcopalian. Clubs: Indianapolis Athletic, Columbia (Indpls.); Grolier (N.Y.C.). Home: Oldfields, Woodstock Dr. Office: 740 S. Alabama St., Indpls. 6. Died May 5, 1966.

LIN, PIAO, def. minister People's Republic China; b. Ungkung, Hupeh Province, Central China, 1906; student Whampoa Mil. Acad., Canton; m. Liu Hsi-hing, 1937; 1 son, 1 dau. Mem. Koumintang (Nationalist party), 1922-27; defected to join Chinese People's Liberation Army, 1927; upon defeat joined Mao Tse-Tung and aided in formation Fourth Workers and Peasants Red Army, 1927; comdr. 4th F.A., 1929-32, 1st Army Corps, 1932, Eastern Front Army, 1932-35; pres. Mil. Acad., Yenan, 1936-37, 1941; comdr. 115th Div. 8th Route Army, 1937; seriously wounded at Pinghsing Pass, went to USSR for treatment and remained until 1941; mem. central com. Chinese Communist Party, 1945-72; organizer army in Manchuria which took Peking, 1948; comdr. Chinese force during Korean War; mem. Central People's Govt. Council and People's Revolutionary Mil. Council, 1949-54, chmn. Central S. China Adminstrv. Com., 1953-54; vice premier State Council, also vice chmn. Nat. Def. Council, 1954-59; named marshal, elected to Chinese Communist party's Politburo, 1955; named to central com., 1956, vice chmn. party, mem. Politburo standing com., 1958; minister of nat. def., 1959-72. Author mil. tng. manuals. Address: Peking China Died Sept. 12, 1971.*

LINCOLN, ABRAHAM 16th Pres. U.S.; b. nr. Hodgen's Mill, Hardin County (now part of Larue County), Ky., Feb. 13, 1809; s. Thomas and Nancy (Hawks) L.; m. Mary Todd, Nov. 4, 1842; children-Robert Todd, Edward Baker, William Wallace, Thomas (Tad). As a youth lived hard pioneer life with family in Ky.; moved to Ind. with family, 1816; took flat boat trip down Mississippi River to New Orleans, 1828; moved to Macon County (Ill.) with family, 1830; moved alone to New Salem (Ill.), 1831; resided there, 1831-37, storekeeper, county surveyor, odd jobber, studied law in spare time; served in Black Hawk War, 1832; mem. Ill. Legislature (Whig), 1834-41; licensed as atty., 1836; moved to Springfield (Ill.), 1837, practiced law in partnership with J. T. Stuart, later with Stephen T. Logan, then with William H. Herndon (author of a biography of Lincoln); mem. U.S. Ho. of Reps. (Whig) from Ill., 30th Congress, 1847-49, opposed Mexican War; resumed law practice, Springfield; reentered polit. life by opposing Kan.-Neb. Bill (1854) and other policies of Stephen A. Douglas; unsuccessful Whig candidate for U.S. Senate; joined newly formed Republican Party, 1836, received 110 votes for the vice presdl. nomination at Rep. Nat. Conv., 1856; unsuccessful Rep. nominee for U.S. Senate in opposition to Stephen A. Douglas, 1858, gave acceptance speech in which he said "a house divided against itself cannot stand," campaign highlighted by Lincoln-Douglas Debates; Rep. candidate for U.S. Pres., 1860, won election because of split in Democratic Party, inaugurated, Mar. 4, 1861; conservative regarding abolition, but definitely opposed to extension of slavery into territories; Confederate States Am. formed in opposition to his election, 1861; called for volunteers to preserve Union when Ft. Sumter was fired upon, Apr. 1861 (beginning of Civil War); resorted to conscription, suspension of writ of Habeus Corpus, prosecution of So. sympathizers in North, hampered by cabinet dissension, inadequate mil. leaders; issued Emancipation Proclamation, Jan. 1863; delivered Gettysburg Address, July 1863; won re-election over Dem. nominee George B. McClellan, 1864; gave inaugural address which included memorable phrase "with malice toward none, with charity for all," 1865; began reconstrn. policy when he pardoned certain Confederate ofcls. who would swear allegiance to Union and formed loyal So. state govts.; gen. plan of reunion and reconstrn. was one of forgiveness, but abolition of slavery was a prime requisite (plan opposed by Congress); assasinated by John Wilkes Booth at Ford's Theatre, Washington, D.C., Apr. 14, 1865. Died Washington, Apr. 15, 1865; buried Oak Ridge Cemetery, Springfield, Ill.

LINCOLN, BENJAMIN army officer, sec. of war; b. Hingham, Mass., Jan. 24, 1733; s. Benjamin and Elizabeth (Thaxter) L.; M.A. (hon.), Harvard; m. Mary Cushing, Jan. 15, 1756, 11 children. Town clk. Hingham, 1757, justice of peace, 1762; mem. Mass. Legislature, 1772-73; mem. Mass. Provincial Congress, 1774-75, sec., mem. com. on supplies, 1774-75, pres., 1775; adj. 3d regt. (Suffolk County), Mass. Militia nr. Boston, 1776; commanded militia regts. to reinforce Continental Army, N.Y.C., 1776; maj. gen. Contiental Army in command militia in Vt., 1777; in command So. Dept., Continental Army, 1778, captured with his forces at Charleston by Clinton, 1779; U.S. sec. of war,

1781, resigned after Treaty of Peace; Mass. commr. to deal with Penobscot Indians on land purchases, 1784, 86; led Mass. Militia to suppress Shay's Rebellion; 1789; apptd. to negotiate with Creek Indians on borders of So. states, 1789, with Indians North of the Ohio, 1793; mem. Am. Acad. Arts and Scis., Mass. Hist. Soc.; wrote essays on Indian tribes. Died Boston, May 9, 1810.

LINCOLN, CHARLES PEREZ lawyer; b. Quincy, Mich., Oct. 7, 1843; s. Perez and Harriet Patty (Hopkins) L.; lived on farm in boyhood; ed. Hillsdale (Mich.) Coll.; m. Mary Lawrence Price, 1864 (died 1896); m. 2d, Lizabeth De Vore Allen, May 15, 1899. Orderly sergt. 1st Mich. Inf., Apr. 1861; at Alexandria and Bull Run, Va., May and July 1861; capt. 19th Mich. 1862-64; prisoner of war at Libby, 1863; col. N.G., 1871. Admitted to bar, 1871; asst. assessor internal revenue and chancery court clerk, Granada, Miss., 1871-75; consul at Canton, China, 1875-81; post-grad. Nat. Law U., Washington, 1883; deputy commr. of pensions, U.S., 1889-93; atty. for Kiowa, Comanche and Apache tribes of Indians, 1898-99; now in ins. business at El Reno, Okla. Mayor of El Reno, 1903-. Comdr. dept. of the Potomac, G.A.R., 1888. Home: El Reno, Okla. Died 1911.

LINCOLN, CHARLES SHERMAN army officer; b. Boone, Ia., Feb. 11, 1875; s. James Rush and Priscilla (Hicks) L.; B.E., Ia. State Coll. of Agr. and Mechanic Arts, 1894; grad. Army Sch. of the Line, 1909, Army Staff Coll., 1910; student Army War Coll., 1911 and 1920; m. Cora Thompson, Sept. 15, 1898. Enlisted in U.S. Army, Jan. 5, 1895; commd. 2d lt., Apr. 12, 1898; promoted through grades to brig. gen., Dec. 1, 1931; apptd. chief of staff, Gen. Staff Corps, 1935; now retired. Awarded D.S.C. (U.S.); Legion of Honor (France); Cross of Order of Leopold (Belgium). Episcopalian. Home: Ames, Ia. Died May 18, 1941.

LINCOLN, GATEWOOD SANDERS naval officer; b. Liberty, Mo., Aug. 5, 1875; s. James Edwin and Margaret Pixley (Bird) L.; student William Jewell Coll., Liberty, Mo.; grad. U.S. Naval Acad., 1896; m. Enfield C. Stogdale, June 10, 1900. Served from ensign to capt. USN, 1898-1918; on New Orleans in Adm. Sampson's fleet, off Santiago, Cuba, and in West Indies, Spanish-Am. War, 1898; engr. officer Navy Yard, Mare Island, Cal., 1912-14; comd. Dolphin, 1915; head Dept. Elec. Engring. and Physics, U.S. Naval Acad., 1915-17; comd. Powhatan, transporting troops to France, 1917-18, St. Louis, escorting troop convoys to English Coast, Sept.-Nov. 1918, and comd. U.S.S. St. Louis until Oct. 1919. Mem. Am. Soc. Naval Engrs., Kappa Alpha. Episcopalian. Club: N.Y. Yacht. Address: Navy Dept., Washington. Died Oct. 15, 1957.

LINCOLN, JAMES RUSH brigadier-general U.S.V.; b. Feb. 3, 1845; grad. Pa. Mil. Coll.; m. Lottie C. Hicks, of Three Rivers, Mich., 1872. Served in C.S.A. during Civil War; apptd. U.S.V. at outbreak of Spanish-Am. War. Prof. Mil. science and tactics, and mining engring., Ia. State Coll. Address: Ames, Ia.

LINCOLN, J(OSEPH) FREEMAN editor; b. Hackensack, N.J., July 16, 1900; s. Joseph Crosby and Florence (Sargent) L.; A.B., Harvard, 1923; m. Virginia Cross, Sept. 12, 1925; children-Anne, Crosby (Mrs. David Dodsworth). Writer, editor Curtis Pub. Co., 1924-28; free lance fiction writer, 1928-41; asso. editor Fortune Mag., Time, Inc., 1946-52, bd. editors since 1953. Served as lt. col. OSS, U.S. Army, 1941-45. Home: 20 E. 74th St., N.Y.C. 21. Office: Time & Life Bldg., Rockefeller Center, N.Y.C. 20. Died Feb. 1962.

LINCOLN, SUMNER H. brig. gen.; b. Gardner, Mass., Dec. 21, 1840; s. Rev. Sumner and Gratia (Eliza) L.; ed. Gardner, Mass., Winchendon Acad., Norwich U., Vt.; m. Ruth A. Goodin, Oct. 1, 1874. Enlisted as pvt. Co. B, 1st Vt. Inf., May 2, 1861; disch. Aug. 15, 1861; served as corporal Co. B, 6th Vt. Inf., Oct. 15, 1861-Feb. 21, 1863; 1st lt. adj., 6th Vt. Inf., Feb. 21, 1863-Oct. 28, 1864; maj. 6th Vt. Inf., Nov. 10, 1864; lt. col., Feb. 6, 1865; col. 6th Vt. Vols., June 1865; hon. mustered out, June 26, 1865; apptd. 2d lt. and 1st lt. 17th U.S. Inf., Feb. 23, 1866; promoted through grades to brig. gen. U.S.A., May 29, 1902; retired at own request after 40 yrs.' service, June 9, 1902. Died Apr. 1928.

LINDBERG, DAVID OSCAR NATHANIEL chest specialist; born at Quincy, Mass., Oct. 9, 1891; m. Olaf P. and Anna (Johnson) L.; student Adams Acad., Quincy, Mass., 1903-07; M.D., Boston U. Sch. of Medicine, 1915; married 1917; one son, David Nathaniel; married second M. Helen Gray, Sept. 19, 1941; children-Richard Oscar, Donald Everett. Began practice of med., 1915; clinical dir., U.S. Public Health Service, 1921-28; sanatorium directorships since 1928; former assistant clinical professor of medical Univ. of Utah Sch. of of Med. Flight surgeon, AEF, Army, retired 1921. Fellow American College Physicians, American College of Chest Physicians; mem. National Tuberculosis Association (past vice pres.), A.M.A., American Thoracic Society, Phi Alpha Gamma. Membro Coorespondente Sociedade Brasileira de Tuberculose. Titulaire membre Internal Union Against Tuberculosis. Invitational studies Tokyo and Moscow authorities; other spl. research and study, Stockholm; Leysin and Schatzalp, Switzerland; Copenhagen; Hamburg; Paris; Oslo; Lisbon; Rio de Janeiro. Introduced fluorophotography to the U.S., 1937. Author: A Manual of Pulmonary Tuberculosis; Atlas of Thoracic Roentgenology and Contributions to med. literature. Died July 31, 1964; buried Golden Gate Nat. Cemetery, San Bruno, Cal.

LINDEMAN, FRANK, JR. oil co. exec.; b. Fontanelle, Ia., Nov. 6, 1909; s. Frank and Maria A. (Marlay) L.; M.E., Colo. Sch. Mines, 1933; grad. Advanced Mgmt. Program, Harvard, 1950. With Pan Am. Petroleum Co., 1933-58, v.p. prodn., 1953-58; v.p., dir. United Carbon Co., also exec. v.p. United Producing Co., Inc. and dir. United Rubber & Chem. Co., 1958-63; v.p., dir. Ashland Oil & Refining Co., 1963-. Served to lt. col. AUS, 1941-46. Mem. Am. Petroleum Inst., Am. Inst. Mining, Metall. and Petroleum Engrs. Home: 19400 Hermann Dr., Houston 4, Office: Ashland Oil & Refining Co., Box 1503, Houston 77001. Died Nov. 25, 1963.

LINDSAY, HAL lawyer; b. Cedar Grove, N.C., June 11, 1891; s. Henry and Susan (Link) L.; grad. Cedar Grove Acad., 1907; LL.B., Atlanta Law Sch., 1913; student Sch. Commerce, Ga. Inst. Tech., 1914-16, Lamar Sch. Law, Emory U., 1916-17; m. Catharine Childers, Nov. 30, 1916. Admitted to Ga. bar, 1913, since practiced in Atlanta; lectr. fed. law and procedure, Atlanta Law Sch., 1940, law of evidence Woodrow Wilson Coll. Law, 1944; asst. U.S. atty. No. Dist. Ga., 1921-22, 29-34; practice fed. trial, adminstrv. and appellate law since 1934. Served as 2d lt. to 1st U.S. Army, A.E.F., 1917-19; judge adv. 1st Army Corps., 1919. Member of the Georgia, Atlanta (chmn. com. atty.-acct. coop. 1951). Stone Mountain bar assns., Atlanta Lawyers Club. Ind. Democrat. Presbyn. Home: 1803 Ridgewood Dr. N.E., Atlanta 30307. Office: Healey Bldg., Atlanta 30303. Died May 4, 1965; buried Eno Cemetery, Cedar Grove, N.C.

LINDSAY, MARRILL KIRK orthopedic surgeon; b. Topeka, May 20, 1884; s. William Sharp and Helen (Smith) L.; student U. Kan., 1903-05, Kan. Army Med. Sch., 1922; grad. study in orthopedic surgery Harvard, 1925-26; m. Mary Louise Ryan, Jan. 25, 1914; 1 son, Merrill Kirk. House officer N.Y.C. Hosp., 1910-12; pvt. practice, Topeka, 1912-17 and 1924; instr. surgery Yale, 1926-27, asst. clin. prof. orthopedic surgery, 1927-30, asso. clin. prof., 1930-38. Med. Officer U.S. Army, 1917-23; comdg. Gas Hosp. No. 1, 1st Army in France, 1918; served with Army of Occupation in Germany, 1918-20, in U.S. Army, stationed in Washington, disch. 1946; now in Bur. Medicine and Surgery, VA, Washington regional office. Fellow A.C.S., A.M.A.; mem. Am. Orthopedic Assn., Conn. State and New Haven County med. socs. Contbr. to med. texts and jours. Died May 24, 1960; buried Mount Hope Cemetery, Topeka.

LINDSAY, WILLIAM U.S. senator; b. Rockbridge Co. Va., Sept. 4, 1835; s. Andrew and Sallie (Davidson) L.; settled in Clinton, Ky., Nov. 1854; commenced practice of law, 1858; m. Eleanor, d. late Dr. George N. Holmes. Served C.S.A., pvt. to capt., 1861-65; resumed practice; State senator, 1867-70; judge Ky. Court of Appeals, 1870-78; chief justice, 1876-78; then established practice at Frankfort, Ky.; State senator for Frankfort dist., 1889; mem. World's Columbian Commn. from organization to Feb. 20, 1893; declined appmt. on Interstate Commerce Commn.; elected U.S. senator, 1893, to fill vacancy caused by resignation of John G. Carlisle; reelected, 1894, for term, 1895-1901; U.S. Commr. St. Louis Expn., 1904; mem. law firm Lindsay, Kalish & Palmer, Frankfort, Ky. Trustee Carnegie Instn. Died 1909.

LINDSEY JULIAN ROBERT army officer; b. Irwinton, Ga., Mar. 16, 1871; s. John W. and Julia F. (Tucker) L.; grad. U.S. Mil. Acad., 1892, Gen. Staff Sch., 1920, Army War Coll., 1921; m. Hannah Broster, June 11,1904 (died Mar. 29, 1905); 1 son, Julian Broster. Commd. 2d lt., cav., U.S. Army, June 11, 1892, and advanced through grades to col., July 1, 1920; brig. gen. (temporary), April 1918-June 1919; brig. gen., Jan. 1, 1932. Was comdg. gen. Ft. Knox, Ky.; promoted major gen. (retired). Served in China, P.I., Cuba (2d occupation), Mexico (1916-17). Awarded D.S.M. Clubs: Army and Navy, Columbia Country (Washington). Address: Army and Navy Club, Washington. Died June 27, 1948; buried at U.S. Military Academy, West Point.

LINDSLEY, HENRY DICKINSON past nat. comdr. Am. Legion; b. Nashville, Tenn., Feb. 29, 1872; s. Philip and Louise (Dickinson) L.; ed. pvt. schs.; admitted to Tex. bar, 1893. Engaged in banking and many other businesses in Dallas; pres. Southwestern Life Ins. Co., 1908-10; chmn. bd. Dallas Trust & Savings Bank, 1914-18; pres. Citizens Assn. of Dallas, 1905-09; mayor of Dallas, 1915-17; pres. Henry D. Lindsley Co. (New York), 1924-28; dir. City Nat. Bank of Dallas. Commd. maj. U.S. Army, 1917; joined A.E.F., Dec. 1917; commd. col. U.S.A., Aug. 1918; col. O.R.C., 1921-; dir. Bur. War Risk Ins., Washington, D.C., 1919. Permanent chmn. Am. Legion Caucus, St. Louis, Apr. 1919, permanent chmn. 1st Nat. Conv., Minneapolis, Nov. 1919, elected past nat. comdr., Nov. 1919 life mem. exec. com.; vice comdr. in chief Mil. Order of World War; elected v.p. for U.S. of Fedn. Interalliée des Anciens Combattants (FIDAC), 1926, chairman of delegation to annual congress, 1927; designated Initial General Staff Eligible List U.S.A., Dec. 1920. Decorations: D.S.M. (U.S.); Past National Commander's Medal, The American Legion; Officer Public Instruction Order University Gold Palms (France); Officer Legion of Honor (France); Commander Order of the Crown (Belgium). Treas. Am. Republics Corp., 1920-23, retired. Charter founder Roosevelt Memorial Assn., 1919. Democrat. Mason. Home: Dallas, Tex. Died Nov. 18, 1938.

LINEBARGER, PAUL MYRON ANTHONY writer, educator; b. Milw., July 11, 1913; s. Paul Myron Wentworth and Lillian (Bearden) L.; student Punaho Acad. Honolulu, 1919-20, Brit. Cathedral Sch., Shanghai, 1920-22, Oberrealschule, Baden-Baden, Germany, 1923-24, Kaiser Wilhelms Sch., Shanghai, 1926, U. Nanking, 1930, N. China Union Lang. Sch., 1930; A.B., Geo. Washington U., 1933; student Am. U., Washington, 1934, Chgo., 1935; Ph.D., John Hopkins, 1936; student U. Mich., 1937; Litt.D., Universidad Interamericana, 1964; D.C.L. (hon.), Nat. Chebgchi U., Taipei, 1965; m. Margaret Snow, Sept. 7, 1936 (div. 1949); children-Johanna Lesley, Marcia Christine; m. 2d, Genevieve Collins, Mar. 20, 1950. Pvt. sec. to legal adv. Nat. Govt. of China, Nanking and Washington, 1930-36; instr. in govt. and tutor in div. of history, govt. and econs. Harvard, 1936-37; instr. polit. sci. Duke, 1937-38, asst. prof., 1938-45, asso. prof. polit. sci. in charge Far East 1946; participated in formation O.W.I. as Far Eastern specialist Operation Planning and Intelligence Bd., 1942; lectr. Sch. Advanced Internat. Studies, 1959; vis. prof. internat. relations U. Pa., 1954-55, Australian Nat. U., 1957; cons. numerous agys. fed. govt. Comd. 2d lt. U.S. Army, 1942, advanced through grades to maj. in gen. staff 1945; col. Res. Awarded Bronze Star medal, War Dept. Commendation ribbon. Mem. several profl. assns., Am. Peace Soc. (pres. 1962-64). Episcopal. Club: Cosmos (Wash.). Author, co-author numerous works on China, Sun Yat Sen and related items; latest being: Government and Politics of the Far East, 1954, and also in field of Psychol. Warfare (1948, 55; Japanese, 1954, Chinese, 1953, Vietnamese, 1956, Spanish, 1949, German, 1960, Russian 1962). Home: 2831 29th St., Washington 20008. Office: 1740 Massachusetts Av. N.W., Washington 20036. Died Aug. 6, 1966; buried Arlington Nat. Cemetery.

LINEN, JAMES A. JR. exec.; b. Scranton, Pa., Oct. 11, 1884; s. James Alexander and Anna (Blair) L.; grad. Lawrenceville Sch., 1902; A.B., Williams Coll., 1907; m. Genevieve Tuthill, Oct. 22, 1908; children-James Alexander, Harriet Tuthill, Mary, Sally Strong. Receiver for Scranton (Pa.) Steam Pump Co., 1910-13; v.p. and treas. Scranton Pump Co., 1913-16; trea. United Service Co., 1920-23; pres. Lincoln Trust Co., 1923-38; chmn. bd. Internat. Corr. Sch. and affiliated instns., 1928-37; pres. Internat. Ednl. Pub. Co., 1937-51; now chmn. Internat. Correspondence Schs. World Ltd., Inc.; chmn. bd. Internat. Correspondence Schs., Ltd., London, Capetown, Cairo, Bombay, Australasia, New Zealand; dir. Centro Espanol; de Ensenanza por Correspondencia, S.A., Madrid; Internat. Schs. Co. Latin Am., Argentine Co., Escuelas Internaciolales de la America del Sud; Women's Inst. Domestic Arts and Scis., Ltd., Haddon Craftsmen, Wessel Mfg. Col., Internat. Textbook Col., Internat. Correspondence Schs. World, Ltd., Inc.; Conservator Union National Bank, Pennsylvania, 1933. Member Scranton City Council, 1913-16, president, 1915-16; chairman Red Cross Flood Disaster Drive, Lackawanna County, 1936; chairman Scranton chapter American Red Cross, 1938-41; pres. Scranton Community Chest,

LINK, JOHN EPHRAIM physician; b. New Albany, Ind., Aug. 14, 1839; ed. there and at Paris, Ill.; entered Rush Med. Coll., 1860; but left, April, 1861, to join army; served as hosp. steward, asst. surgeon and surgeon in Ill. vols.; m. Nov., 1862, Mary La Foe, of Lexington, Ky.; grad. Chicago Med. Coll., 1865; has since practiced Terre Haute; formerly prof. anatomy, Coll. Phys. & Surg., Indianapolis. Mem. Am. Med. Assn., Internat. Med. Congress, etc. Address: Terre Haute, Ind.

LINNEMAN, HERBERT F., fgn. service officer; b. Buffalo, Oct. 22, 1914; s. Frederick and Loretta (Reisch) L.; LL.B., Southeastern U., 1940; m. Luisa Coll., Oct. 23, 1943; children—Elena Christina (Mrs. Patrick J. Miliffe), Douglas Luis. Admitted to D.C. bar; radio actor, announcer, 1934-35; adminstrv. asst. Treasury Dept., 1936-40; field examiner U.S. Civil Service Commn., 1940-42; sr. legal cons. U.S. Bd. Vets. Appeals, 1946-49; dep. dir. Office of Security, Dept. State, 1949-53; dep. asst. dir. USIA, 1953-54; attache and exec. officer Am. embassy, New Delhi, India, 1954-56; program and policy officer USIA, 1957-58; 1st sec., dep. pub. affairs officer Am. embassy, Tehran, Iran, 1958-60, counselor for pub. affairs, 1960-63; dir. Am. Cultural Center, Brazzaville, Congo, 1963-65; exec. officer Am. embassy, Karachi, Pakistan, 1966-67; 1st sec. Am. embassy, Tokyo, Japan, 1967-69. Served from ensign to lt. USCGR, 1942-46. Mem. Sigma Delta Kappa. Home: Miami Beach FL Died July 25, 1971; interred Miami FL

LINTHICUM, GEORGE MILTON surgeon; b. Anne Arundel Co., Md., Aug. 17, 1870; s. Sweetser and Laura Ellen (Smith) L.; student St. John's Coll., Annapolis,

Md., 1887-89, A.M., 1893; A.B., Johns Hopkins, 1891; M.D., U. of Md., 1893; m. Lillian Noyes Howland, Apr. 12, 1898; children-Howland, Lillian (Mrs. John Scott Keech, dec.). Began practice at Baltimore, 1893; prof. of physiology and proctology, Baltimore Med. Coll., 1895-1907; v. p. med. and chirurg. faculty, 1908-09, pres., 1909-10; prof. diseases of colon and rectum, U. of Md., 1913-; proctologist Univ. of Md., Md. Gen., W. Baltimore Gen. and Baltimore City hosps.; consultant in diseases of colon and rectum, U.S. Vets. Hosp., Hosp. for Consumptives of Md. (chmn. exec. com.). U.S. Marine Hosp.; consultant Baltimore City Health Dept.; medical examiner Fidelity Life Insurance Co. of Am America. Served as capt. Med. Corps, Md. N.G., Mexican Border, 1916; lt. col. Med. Corps, U.S.A., 1917-19, and comdg. officer U.S. Base Hosp. 113, France; col. Med. R.C. Fellow Am. Coll. Surgeons. Democrat. Episcopalian. Mason. Home: Roland Park, Baltimore, Md. Died July 18, 1935.

LINTON, RALPH anthropologist; b. Phila., Pa., Feb. 27, 1893; s. Isiah Waterman and Mary Elisabeth (Gillingham) L.; B.A., Swarthmore Coll., 1915; M.A., U. of Pa., 1916; Ph.D., Harvard, 1925; m. Adelin M. Hohlfeld, Aug. 31, 1934; 1 son, David Hector. Field work in archaeology, N.M., 1912, 17; Guatemala, 1913, N.J., 1915, Ill., 1916, Colo., 1919, Marquesas Islands, 1920-21, Ohio, 1924, Wis., 1932-33; in ethnology, Polynesia, 1920-22, Madagascar, 1925-27, South Africa, 1928, Okla., 1934. Asst. curator of ethnology, Field Museum of Natural History, 1922-28; prof. anthropology, U. of Wisconsin, 1928-37; prof. anthropology, Columbia U., 1937-39; chmn. dept. of anthropology, 1939-43; Sterling prof., anthropology, Yale U. since 1946. Editor Am. Anthropologist, 1939-44. Corpl. Battery D, 149th F.A., U.S. Army, Rainbow Div., 1917-19. Awarded Viking medal, 1952; Huxley Meml. medal, 1954. Mem. Am. Anthrop. Assn. (pres. 1946), A.A.A.S. (v.p. 1937), National Academy Sciences (chmn. div. anthropology 1949-51), Phi Beta Kappa, Sigma Xi, Alpha Kappa Delta; honorary member Académie Malgache. Hon. fellow Royal Anthrop. Inst. Gt. Britain. Mem. Nat. Research Council, 1931-32, 1940-45; mem. Social Science Research Council, 1932-39, American Council of Learned Societies, 1947-50. Quaker, Author: The Material Culture of the Marquesas Islands, 1924; Use of Tobacco Among North American Indians, 1924; The Archaeology of the Marquesas Islands, 1925; Guide to the Polynesian and Micronesian Collections, Field Museum, 1925; The Tanaia, A Hill-Tribe of Madagascar, 1932; The Study of Man, an Introduction, 1936; Acculturation in Seven American Indian Tribes, 1940; Cultural Background of Personality, 1945; editor, The Science of Man in the World Crisis, 1945; The Tree of Culture, 1955. Editor: Most of the World, 1949. Address: Dept. of Anthropology, Yale Univ., New Haven. Died Dec. 24, 1953.

LIPPITT, FRANCIS JAMES lawyer; b. Providence, R.I., July 19, 1812; s. Joseph F. and Caroline S. L.; grad. Brown, 1830 (A.M.). Capt. 1st N.Y. vols. in Mexican war; served in Civil war as col. 2d Calif. inf. and bvt. brig. gen. U.S. vols.; m. Mrs.Pickering Dodge, Sept. 25, 1865. Counsel for U.S. in Dept. of Justice, 1877-82. Was guest of Lafayette at La Grange, 1832; sole survivor of the few who stood by his grave at his burial, 1834; assisted De Toqueville in preparation of La Democratie aux Etats Unis, 1834; attached to Am. Legation, Paris, 1834-35; mem. (chmn. com. of whole) State Constl. Conv., Calif., 1849. Lecturer at Boston Univ. Law School, 1873-74, before Naval War Coll., Newport, 1896, 1897, 1900. Ret. Died 1902.

LISCUM, EMERSON H. brig. gen. U.S. vols. lt. col. 24th inf. U.S. Army; b. Vt.; served as corporal 1st Vt. vol. inf., May to Aug. 1861; private to sergt. 12th inf., Feb. 1, 1862, to Mar. 22, 1863, when he became 2d lt.; 1st lt., May 4, 1863; later in 30th inf.; capt. 25th inf., Mar. 26, 1867, 19th inf., July 5, 1870; maj. 22d inf., May 4, 1892; lt. col. 24th inf.; May 23, 1896. Bvtd. capt., Aug. 18, 1864, for gallant services in battle of North Anna River, Va.; apptd. brig. gen. U.S. vols., 1898, for Spanish-Am. war; disch. from vol. service Dec. 31, 1898. Died 1900.

LISLE, ROBERT PATTON rear admiral U.S.N.; b. Phila., Aug. 28, 1842. Apptd. acting asst. p.-m. U.S.N., Nov. 2, 1863; asst. p.-m., July 2, 1864; passed asst. p.-m., May 4, 1866; p.-m., Dec. 11, 1867; pay insp., Jan. 19, 1892; pay dir., June 6, 1899; retired Nov. 3, 1903, with rank of rear admiral for services during Civil War. Home: Philadelphia, Pa. Died 1911.

LITCH, ERNEST WHEELER naval officer; b. Boston, Mass., Nov. 22, 1897; s. Ernest W. and Anna Wall (Burgess) L.; B.S., U.S. Naval Acad., 1919; m. Leslie Cooke, May 10, 1930; 1 son, Ernest Wheeler 3d. Commd. ensign, U.S. Navy, 1919, and advanced through the grades to rear adm., 1945; designated naval aviator, 1924, and since on active flight. Decorated Legion of Merit (4 times), special commendation, and various Navy area medals. Home: Farm St., South Weymouth, Mass. Died Feb. 1967.

LITTELL, ISAAC WILLIAM army officer; b. Elizabeth, N.J., Dec. 5, 1857; s. Isaac William and Elizabeth (Ball) L.; student Stevens Inst. Tech., 2 yrs.; grad. U.S. Mil. Acad., 1883; m. Julia, d. Capt. Gregory Barrett, U.S.A., Jan. 22, 1885. Commd. 2d lt. 10th Inf., June 13, 1883; promoted through grades to brig. gen. Q.M. Corps, Oct. 9, 1917; retired, Feb. 19, 1919. In charge of constrn. of N.A. cantonments and nat. guard camps, 1917; sec. and treas. U.S. Soldiers' Home, Washington, resigned 1922. Episcopalian. Home: Staunton, Va. Died May 1, 1924.

LITTLE, ARTHUR W. printer; b. New York, N.Y., Dec. 15, 1873; s. Joseph James and Josephine (Robinson) L.; ed. pvt. schs. and business coll., New York; m. Marguerite Lanier Winslow, Apr. 19, 1897 (died Mar. 21, 1926); children-Winslow, Arthur W.; m. 2d, Charlotte Houston Fairchild, Apr. 27, 1927 (died Sept. 2, 1927); m. 3d, Army Alice Van Nest Barney, June 30, 1928 (died Apr. 18, 1939). Joined father's company, J. J. Little & Co., printers, 1891; now chmn. bd. J. J. Little & Ives Co. Served pvt. and corpl. Co. I, 7th Regt. N.G.N.Y., 1891-98; capt. Co. D, 171st Regt. N.G.N.Y., 1898; 1st lt. Co. I, 71st Regt., 1899; capt. and a.d.c. to Gen. George Moore Smith, 1900-10; maj. insp.-gen. 1st Brigade, 1910-12. Served in World War with 15th N.Y. Inf., colored, later 369th U.S. Inf.; capt. Co. F, regtl. adj., and maj. 1st Batn., Apr. 13, 1917-Feb. 28, 1919; in all actions with Gouraud's 4th Army (French), bet. Apr. 7, 1918, and armistice, Nov. 11, 1918; wounded in action, Sept. 12, 1918. Chevalier Legion of Honor and 4 Croix de Guerre (2 palms, one gold star, one silver star); U.S. Silver Star citation for gallantry; Comdr. Order of Black Star (French); Order of Purple Heart (U.S.). Colonel 15th Inf. (colored), N.Y.N.G., Jan. 5, 1921; bvt. brig. gen., Dec. 31, 1922; resigned Apr. 8, 1925. Episcopalian. Mason (life), Elk. Mem. Business Advisory and Planning Council of U.S. Dept. of Commerce, 1933-34; mem. Industrial Advisory Board of NRA, 1934; chmn. Mayor's Advisory Bd., N.Y. City, since 1939. Mem. S.R., Sons of Vets., Am. Legion, Vets. of Foreign Wars, Nat. Farmers Union (life hon.). Home: 810 Park Av., New York, N.Y. Office: 435 E. 24th St., New York, N.Y. Died July 18, 1943.

LITTLE, EDWARD CAMPBELL congressman; b. Newark, O., Dec. 14, 1858; s. Theophilus, Jr. and Sarah Elliott (Taylor) L.; A.B., U. of Kan., 1883, LL.B., A.M., 1886; admitted to bar, 1886; m. Edna M. Steele, at Topeka, Kan., Nov. 29, 1899. Was diplomatic agent and consul gen. with rank of minister resident to Egypt, 1892-93. Lieutenant colonel 20th Kan. Vols. in P.I., 1898-99; Congressional Spanish War and Filipino campaign medals for services in Philippines. Del. at large Rep. Nat. Conv., 1892; defeated by narrow margin for U.S. Senator, 1897, and for justice Supreme Ct., 1914; mem. 65th to 68th Congresses (1917-25), 2d Kan. Dist.; chmn. Revision of Laws Com. and Codifier of the Federal Statutes, Grand Cordon of the Medjidieh, from Sultan of Turkey for diplomatic service. Home: Kansas City, Kan. Died June 27, 1924.

LITTLE, GEORGE naval officer; b. Marshfield, Mass., Apr. 15, 1754; s. Lemuel and Penelope (Eames) L.; m. Rachel Rogers, June 24, 1779, at least 1 son, Edward Preble. Commd. 2d lt. Mass. Navy, 1778, promoted 1st lt., 1779; served as 1st officer in Hazard, 1779; promoted capt. in charge of Winthrop, 1782; discharged, 1783; apptd. capt. U.S. Navy, 1799; in command of Boston, 1799-1800, captured several prizes including Danish ship Flying Fish, French ships Deux Anges and Bercean; discharged, 1801. Died Weymouth, Mass., July 22, 1809.

LITTLE, GEORGE geologist; b. Tuscaloosa, Ala., Feb. 11, 1838; s. John and Barbara (Kerr) L.; A.B., U. of Ala., 1855, A.M., 1856 (LL.D., 1905); Ph.D., U. of Gottingen, 1859; m. Caroline Patillo Doak, May 13, 1869. Prof. natural science, Oakland Coll., Miss., 1860-61; pvt. Lumsden's Battery, Army of Tenn., C.S.A.; capt. arty., ordnance duty on staffs of Generals Clayton, Bate, Brown, Cleburne, Cobb, Hill, Breckenridge, Cheatham, Bragg; lt. col. arty., chief ordnance officer. Hardee's corps until 1865. Prof. geology, U. of Miss.; 1866-74, 1881-89; state geologist of Miss., 1870-74, of Ga., 1874-81; geol. expert, Chattanooga, Tenn., 1889-92; druggist, Tuscaloosa, Ala., 1892-1902; geol. reporter on clays, Geol. Survey of Ala., 1903, on mines and railroads, 1904-18. Trustee Pontotoc (Miss.) Presbyn. Collegiate Inst. Democrat. Home: Tuscaloosa, Ala. Died May 15, 1924.

LITTLE, HERBERT SATTERTHWAITE, lawyer; b. Manchester, Eng., Oct. 6, 1902; s. George Henry and Jessie Milton (Gearing) L.; migrated to U.S. 1914, naturalized, 1920; J.D., U. Wash., 1923, A.M., 1927; m. Katharyn Stubbs, Sept. 30, 1939 (div. 1970); children—Anne Tucker, Nancy Wardell, Gwendolyn Gearing, Kathy Milton. Admitted to Wash. bar, 1923; asso. firm Stratton and Kane, Seattle, 1923-35; mem. firm Stratton, Leader, Little & Stratton, 1935-36, Little & Stratton, 1935-36, Little & Leader, 1936-41, sr. partner successor firms until retirement, 1969. Dir. Sheetwood Products Co., Gosspulp Corp., Am. Pacific Dairy Products, Inc. Vis. lectr. Am. diplomacy and internat. relations, Oriental Summer Coll., Tokyo and Kyoto Imperial univs., Japan, 1931; chmn. Am. Found. World Court Com. for Wash., 1930-34; Am. del. internat. conf. Inst. Pacific Relations, 1936, 47, 50; lectr. internat. law Inst. World Affairs, Riverside, Cal., 1939, 40. Chmn. Seattle chpt. Com. to Defend America by Aiding the Allies, 1941; mem. Wash. br. Commn. to Study Orgn. of Peace, 1941. Bd. dirs. Wash. Assn. Mental Health, Near East Found.; chmn. Northwest br. Am. Council Inst. Pacific Relations, 1946-47, trustee, 1946-49; bd. regents U. Wash., 1960-65, pres., 1964-65; trustee YMCA, Wesley Found., 1930-40, Seattle Symphony Orch. (exec. com.), 1946-50; pres. Japanese Internat. Trade Fair, Seattle, 1951; dir. Internat. Trade Fair, Inc., 1951-60; mem. Nat. Adv. Com. Internat. Jud. Procedure; dir. Am. Com. United Europe, 1950. Maj., Army of U.S., Office Undersec. War, 1942-43, OSS, 1943-46; then lt. col., chief br. Decorated Bronze Star, 1945; recipient Civic award Seattle, 1946. Mem. council sect. internat. and comparative law, Council Fgn. Relations N.Y. mem. Internat., Inter-Am., Fed., Am., Seattle, Wash., bar assns., Am. Soc. Internat. Law (exec. council, v.p.), U. Wash. Alumni Assn. (pres. 1935-36), Japan, China, Philippines Socs. of Seattle (dir.), Phi Alpha Delta, Tau Kappa Alpha, Pi Sigma Alpha. Clubs: Rainier (Seattle); Bohemian (San Francisco). Contbr. law and internat. jours. Home: Seattle WA Died Dec. 15, 1972; buried Acacia Meml. Park, Seattle WA

LITTLE, JOHN DOZIER lawyer; b. Talbotton, Ga., Apr. 17, 1871; s. William Augustus and Sarah Virginia (Dozier) L.; prep. edn., Slade's Sch., Columbus, Ga., 1880-85; A.B., U. of Ga., 1888. LL.B., 1890; m. Ilah Dunlap Jordan, June 16, 1906. Admitted to Ga. bar, 1890, and practiced at Columbus until 1902, Atlanta, 1902-; mem. Little, Powell, Reid & Goldstein. Capt., later maj. Ga. Nat. Guard, 1893-1902. Speaker of Ga. Ho. of Rep., 1808-1901. Home: Leesburg, Ga., and Atlanta. Died Feb. 9, 1934.

LITTLE, LOUIS MCCARTY officer Marine Corps; b. N.Y.C., Jan. 16, 1878; s. William McCarty and Anita Maria (Chartrand) L.; ed. Rensselaer Poly. Inst., 1895-99; grad. Advance Base School, 1910; grad. Navy and Army War Coll., 1922-23; m. Elsie Monro Cobb, June 24, 1923. Commd. 2d lt. USMC, July 15, 1899; promoted through grades to brig. gen., Jan. 1, 1934, to maj. gen. July 27, 1935. Served successively in Philippines, Boxer Campaign, V.I., Isthmus of Panama, Expdn. to Honduras, voyage of Battle Fleet around World; with Am. Legation, Peking; staff comdr. Asiatic Fleet; with Naval Planning Sect., London, World War; comdr. troops and brigade in Haiti; comdr. Am. Legion Guard, Peking; became asst. to comdt. USMC, May 1935; then comdr. Marine Barracks, Quantico, Va.; retired Feb. 1, 1942. Mem. Delta Phi. Episcopalian. Clubs: Army and Navy, Alibi, Chevy Chase, Metropolita, Racquet (Washington); Metropolitan, New York Yacht (N.Y.); University, Racquet (Phila.). Home 3010 O St., N.W. Address: U.S. Marine Corps Hdqrs., Washington. Died July 1960.

LITTLE, WILLIAM NELSON, 2D rear adm.; b. Newburgh, N.Y., Dec. 31, 1852; s. of William Nelson and Margaret (Thall) L.; grad. U.S. Naval Acad., 1875; m. Kate Sewell, of Brooklyn, Nov. 23, 1876. Commd. asst. engr., 1877; passed asst. engr., 1886; lt. comdr., 1890; chief engr., 1898; comdr., 1904; capt., 1908; rear adm., Mar. 13, 1913; retired Dec. 31, 1914. Served two cruises on N. Atlantic Sta., one on Asiatic Sta.; chief engr. of base at Key West and afloat in Philippines during Spanish-Am. War, 1898; gen. duties, Philippines, and in China waters during Boxer Rebellion; in two engagements with Philippine insurgents and assisted in searching out and destroying vessels engaged in contrabrand trade with insurgents around the coast of Luzon; insp. of machinery, ordnance and navigation material, 1904-14; inspection duty, Bur. Steam Engring., during World War. Home: Mountain Lakes, N.J. Died Jan. 4, 1925.

LITTLEFIELD, GEORGE W. ranchman, banker; b. Panola Co., Miss., June 21, 1842; s. Fleming and Mildred M. (Satterwaite) L.; pub. sch. edn.; m. Alice P. Tiller, Houston, Tex., Jan. 14, 1863. Enlisted, 2d sergt., Co. I, 8th Tex. Cav., C.S.A., 1861; wounded, 1863; resigned as capt., 1864. Farmer, 1865-71; cattle and land owner since 1871; organized, 1890, and since pres., Am. Nat. Bank, Austin, Texas. Home: Austin, Tex.

LITZENBERG, HOMER LAURENCE marine corps officer; b. Steelton, Pa., Jan. 8, 1903; s. Homer Laurence and Bertha Dayett (Rambo) L.; grad. Inf. Sch., Ft. Benning, Ga., 1933, Command and Gen. Staff Sch., Ft. Leavenworth, Kan., 1938, Nat. War Coll., 1949; m. Bessie Margarete Leech, June 30, 1925 (dec. Feb. 1946); children-Homer Laurence III (USMC), Betty Lee; m. 2d, Alice Dorothy Quinn, Jan. 6, 1947. Served with Pa. N.G., 1920-22; began mil. career as pvt., USMC, 1922, commd. 2d lt., 1925, advanced through grades to maj. gen., 1954; assigned Marine detachments U.S.S. Idaho, U.S.S. Augusta, U.S.S. Arkansas, U.S.S. Arizona, U.S.S. New Mexico, also in Nicaragua, East coast U.S.; adviser, instr. Marine bn., Phila., 1933-35; aide to gov. Guam, head police dept., inspector-instr. Guam Militia, 1935-37; staff war plans sect. Chief Naval Operations, Comdr. in Chief U.S. Fleet, Joint Chiefs Staff, Washington, 1938-43, 44-46; assigned Eng., Casablanca, French Morocco, 1942; organizer, comdr. 3d Bn., 24th Marines, 4th Marine Div., later exec. officer in assault on Roi-Namur, Kwajalein Atoll, Marshall Islands; asst. operations officer 5th Amphibious Corps, Saipan, Tinian operations, 1944; 7th Fleet liaison officer Gen. of the Army Marshall and Chinese Ministry Def., Nanking, 1946-47; plans officer staff Comdr. Naval Forces Western Pacific, 1947-48; comdr. 6th Marine Regt., 2d Marine Div., Camp Lejeune, N.C., 1949-50, 7th Marine Regt. Combat

Team, Korea, 1950-51; legal aide, legislative counsel Comdt. Marine Corps Hdqrs., Washington, 1951; dir. Marine Corps Development Center, Quantico, Va., 1952; asst. div. comdr. 3d Marine Div., Japan, later asst. Force Comdr. Fleet Marine Force Atlantic; inspector-gen. USMC, Washington, 1954-55; comdg. gen. Marine Corps Base, Camp Lejeune, N.C., 1955-56, Marine Corps Recruit Depot, Parris Island, S.C., 1956-57; sr. mem. UN Command Mil. Armistice Commission, Korea, 1957; inspector general Marine Corps., Washington, 1957-59; retired as lt. general USMC; vice pres. Birely and Company Investment Securities, 1960-62. Decorated Navy Cross, D.S.C. (Army), Silver Star Medal (3), Legion of Merit, Presdl. Unit citation (U.S.); Order of Yun Hui (China); Presdl. Unit citation with cluster (Korea). Member Retired Officers Association (president 1961-62), Nat. Sojourners (past pres. Quantico chpt.). Methodist Episcopal. Mason. Died June 27, 1963; buried Arlington Nat. Cemetery.

LIVERMORE, NORMAN BANKS, engr.; b. Oakland, Calif., July 20, 1872; s. Horatio P. and Mattie H. (Banks) L.; student U. of Calif.; C.E., Cornell U., 1899; m. Caroline Sealy, Jan. 5, 1910; children—Norman B., George S., John S., Horatio P., Robert. Began as U.S. asst. engr., fortifications and harbors; later engr., water and power works; cons. engr., San Francisco, since 1908; dir. Calif. Packing Corp. since 1915, Pacific Gas & Electric Co. since 1916, Crocker First Nat. Bank since 1930 (also mem. exec. com.), Firemans Fund Indemnity Co. since 1930, Natomas Co. since 1920 and others. Lt. col., U.S. Army, World War I; awarded French Legion of Honor. Pres. bd. trustees Calif. Acad. Sciences. Mem. various engring. and scientific socs. Contbr. to jours. Travel and exploration (agrl. investigation and studies) in Africa and Orient. Home: Ross, Marin County, Calif. Office: 216 Pine St., San Francisco 4

LIVERMORE, RUSSELL B. lawyer; b. Yonkers, N.Y., Mar. 22, 1894; s. Arthur L. and Henrietta J. (Wells) L.; A.B., Dartmouth Coll., 1915; LL.B., Columbia, 1921; m. Josephine S. Lanier, Aug. 2, 1928. Admitted to N.Y. bar, 1922; partner law firm Livermore & Lanier, chmn. exec. com. and dir. Link Belt Co. Mem. N.Y. State Assembly, 1922-23. Served as 1st lt., A.E.F., World War I; col., A.A.F., Office of Strategic Services, World War II. Awarded Distinguished Service Cross, Silver Star, Legion of Merit, Purple Heart. Clubs: Union League (New York); Dartmouth College. Home: 455 E. 51st St. Office: 501 Fifth Av., N.Y.C. Died May 21, 1958, buried Arlington Nat. Cemetery.

LIVERMORE, WILLIAM ROSCOE colonel U.S.A.; b. Cambridge, Mass., Jan. 11, 1843; s. George L.; freshman class, Harvard; grad. U.S. Mil. Acad., 1865; m. Augusta Keen, Jan. 18, 1883. First lt. engrs., June 23, 1865; promoted through grades to col. engrs., Apr. 23, 1904. Has been connected with fortification work at Key West, Tortugas, Baltimore, Newport and New Bedford; chief engr., Dept. of Tex. and Dept. of the East, survey of N. and N.W. lakes, improvement of Missouri River, river and harbor improvement in Mass., R.I., Conn., N.Y. and N.J.; lighthouse engr., making many improvements in the fog-signal system; mil. attaché Copenhagen and Stockholm, May 1899-June 1902; mem. bd. engrs. for fortifications, 1902-07; retired by operation of law, Jan. 11, 1907; returned to active duty, May 10, 1917, and on spl. duty with Chief of Engrs., U.S.A. With sir Charles Bright, laid 1st Am. cabble from U.S. to Havana, 1868; with Col. A. H. Russell, U.S.A., invented several mag. and automatic guns, including the method of loading by clips, patented 1880; author of "Am. Kriegspiel," a method of practicing the art of war on a map. Fellow Am. Acad. Arts and Sciences. Home: Washington, D.C. Died Sept. 26, 1919.

LIVINGSTON, JOHN WILLIAM naval officer; b. N.Y.C., May 22, 1804; s. William and Eliza (Livingston) Turk (changed name from Turk to Livingston, 1843); commd. midshipman U.S. Navy, 1823, lt., 1832; served in Mexican War; promoted comdr., 1855; in command ship St. Louis on African coast, 1856-58, steamer Penguin during Civil War; comdt. Norfolk (Va.) Navy Yard, 1862, naval station, Mound City, Ill., 1864; commd. capt., 1861, commodore, 1862, rear adm., 1868. Died N.Y.C., Sept. 10, 1885.

LIVINGSTON, PHILIP lawyer; b. N.Y. City, Nov. 9, 1861; s. Livingston and Mary Celia (Williamson) L.; A.B., Harvard, 1884; LL.B., Columbia, 1887; m. Juliette Turner Benedict, Jan. 5, 1910; children-Philip, Benedict. Practiced with Davies & Rapallo, later Turner, McClure & Rolston, and the Lawyers Title Ins. Co.; mem. Livingston & Van Amringe, 1896-1900, retired. Member Company K, 7th Regiment, N.G.N.Y., 1885-92; lieut. and capt. 12th Regiment, 1909-11; office of adj. gen., 1917; capt. and insp. small arms practice 12th Regt. and 23d Engrs., maj. Insp. Gen.'s Dept., N.G.N.Y., 1918-20, now on Reserve List. Ex-officer and mem. council Soc. Colonial Wars 15 yrs., S.R. 25 yrs. Republican. Episcopalian. Home: New York, N.Y. Died June 24, 1938.

LLEWELLYN, WILLIAM H. H. lawyer; b. Monroe, Wis., Sept. 9, 1854; s. Joseph Howard and Louisa (Fry) L.; Tabor (Ia.) Coll.; studied law 3 yrs., Omaha, Neb., and 4 yrs. Las Cruces, N.M.; m. Ida M. Little, Mar. 9, 1878. Admitted to N.M. bar, 1886; mem. law firm Rynerson, Wade & Llewellyn, 1886-93, Bonham & Llewllyn, 1901-04, Llewellyn & Llewellyn, 1908-10, Llewellyn & Medler, 1911—; dir., atty. several mining and other cos.; atty. Western Union Telegraph Co. for N.M. U.S. Indian agt. for Apache Indians of N.M., 1881-85; mem. N.M. Territorial Ho. of Reps., 1897, speaker 1901, 03, chmn. Judiciary Com. both sessions; mem. 1st State Legislative Assembly, N.M., 1912—; territorial atty., 3d Dist., 1901-15; U.S. atty., 1905-08; spl. asst. to U.S. atty.-gen., 1908—, in prosecutions of violations of neutrality laws of Congress and smuggling Chinese persons into U.S. from Mexico; also dist. atty. 8th Dist., 1909—. Prosecuted for U.S. A.F.&S.F. Ry. Co. and Colo. Fuel & Iron Co. for violation of Sherman law, 1906. Capt. Troop G, 1st U.S. Vol. Cav. (Roosevelt's Rough Riders), 1898, Spanish-Am. War; promoted maj. in field, siege of Santiago de Cuba, July, 1898; on Gov. Otero's staff 5 yrs. and Gov. Hagerman's staff about 2 yrs., to 1906, with rank of col. and judge advocate-gen. N.M. N.G. Del. Rep. Nat. Conv., 1884, 96, 1900, 04, 08. Episcopalian. Mason (K.T., Shriner). Home: Las Cruces, N.M. Deceased.

LLOYD, EDWARD VIII naval officer; b. Baltimore, Md., July 20, 1857; s. Edward II and Mary Lloyd (Howard) L.; ed. Bishop's Sch., Easton, Md.; grad. U.S. Naval Acad., 1878; m. Elizabeth Robinson, Oct. 12, 1887; 1 son, Edward IX. Commd. ensign, U.S. Navy, 1878, and advanced through the grades to commodore, 1911, retired, 1911. Club: Officers' (Annapolis, Md.). Home: "Wye Lodge," 203 Prince George St., Annapolis, Md. Died Feb. 5, 1948.

LLOYD, HENRY DEMAREST, bus. exec.; born Boston, Oct. 18, 1907; s. Henry Demarest and Elizabeth McEwen (Mason) L.; A.B., Harvard, 1929, grad. study, 1930-32; m. Norah Alice Keating, June 23, 1934;children—Dorothy Elizabeth, Shelia Andrea. With Ont. Paper Co., Ltd., Thorold, Ont., 1932-34, dir. since 1947; classified advt. Chicago Tribune, 1934-39; office mgr. and sch. coordinator airport operation Civil Pilot Tng. Program, Civil Air Patrol, Northbrook, Ill., 1939-42; dir. Tribune Co., Chicago Tribune Bldg. Corp., radio stas. WGN, Inc. and WPIX, Inc., Que. North Shore Paper Co., Manicouagan Power Co., News Syndicate Co., Inc., Que. & Ontario Transportation Co., Ltd., Ill. Atlantic Corp., Marlhill Mines Ltd., Chicago Tribune-New York News Syndicate, Inc.; trustee Henry D. Lloyd, Watch House Trust, Elizabeth Mason Lloyd Ins. Trust. Mem. corp. St. Andrews Sch., West Barrington. Served as lt. and lt. comdr., USNR, 1942-46. Mem. Harvard Bus. Sch. Assn., R.I. Audubon Soc. Clubs: Harvard (Boston and R.I.); Turks Head (Providence); R.I. Country, Automobile (R.I.) Died Aug. 26, 1970; buried Forest Chapel Cemetery, Barrington RI

LOBDELL, HAROLD E(DWARD) educator; b. Watervliet, N.Y., Sept. 3, 1896; s. Edward and Kathryn (Moore) L.; student Mass. Inst. Tech., 1913-17; m. Ma. Conchita Zambrano de la Garza, Mar. 29, 1954. With Mass. Inst. Tech., 1919-, asst. dean, 1921-29, dean of students, 1929-46, exec. v.p., Alumni-. Chmn. Tech. Loan Fund Bd., 1930-55. Served 2d lt. to 1st lt., U.S. Army, 1917-19. Fellow Postal Historians (London), Asso. U.S. Naval Institute. Member National Association of Deans and Advisers of Men (president 1933-34), Royal Philatelic Soc. (fellow) (London), Pi Delta Epsilon (past nat. sec. and v.p.), Phi Kappa Sigma (nat. v.p., 1933-49), Postal History Soc. (London). Mason. Clubs: Engineers; St. Botolph (Boston, Lincolnshire, Eng.); Army and Navy (Washington); East India and Sports (London). Author: Hongkong and the Treaty Ports (with A. E. Hopkins). Home: 100 Memorial Dr., Cambridge 42. Office: Massachusetts Institute of Technology, Cambridge 39, Mass. Died Jan. 1, 1963; buried Monterrey, Mexico.

LOCHRIDGE, P. D. army officer; b. nr. Bexar, Ala., Dec. 2, 1863; s. John and Permelia (Stout) L.; student Miss. Coll., 1880-83; grad. U.S. Mil. Acad., 1887. U.S. Inf. and Cav. Sch., 1893; m. Carlotta Rawolle, Feb. 20, 1889; 1 son, Rawolle. Commd. 2d lt. cav., U.S.A., June 12, 1887, and advanced through grades to col., July 1, 1916; brig. gen. Nat. Army, Dec. 17, 1917; retired for disability in line of duty, Nov. 10, 1919; brig. gen. U.S.A., retired, June 21, 1930. Served in West, Cuba, Puerto Rico. Philippine Islands, Mexican Border, France; mem. Gen. Staff U.S.A., 1915-19; paymaster of Cuban Census and in charge engring. enterprises, 1899-1900. Treas. and dir. Marx & Rawolle, shellac, N.Y. City and Montreal, 1920-26; organizer Calcutta Traders, Ltd., 1921, shellac factories at Purulia and Mirzapur, India, 1922, retired 1926. Awarded D.S.M., Spanish-am. War, Cuban Occupation and Puerto Rican occupation medals and Victory medal (U.S.); comdr. Legion of Honor (France); companion mil. Order of the Bath (England); Comdr. Order of Crown (Italy); Italian War Cross. Home: Washington, D.C. Died June 17, 1935.

LOCKE, FRANK LOVERING social service; b. Boston, Mass., July 14, 1865; s. James Lovering and Sarah Maria (Swallow) L.; S.B., in civ. engring., Mass. Inst. Tech., 1886; m. Mary Brodhead Kendall, Jan. 16, 1901; children-John Lovering, Eleanor Brodhead, Francis Kendall (dec.), Nancy Lovering. Instr. drawing and civ. engring., Mass. Inst. Tech., 1886-87; in engring. dept., City of Boston, 1887-95; spl. engring. work, asst. supt. and supt., Boston Rubber Shoe Co., 1895-1907; pres. Boston Young Men's Christian Union, 1907-27; personnel dir. Mass. Institute Tech., 1928-. Trustee Norfolk State Hosp.; Corp. Malden Hosp.; mem. Corp. Mass. Inst. Tech. Enlisted Troop D, 1st Cav. Mass. Vol. Militia, 1885; sergt. and sergt. maj., 1st lt. and adj., 1889-97; col. and asst. insp. gen., 1897-1900, staff of gov. (retired 1901). Mem. Cambridge Industrial Assn. Republican. Unitarian. Home: Boston, Mass. Died Nov. 23, 1934.

LOCKE, VICTOR MURAT, JR., Indian service; b. Ft. Towson, Okla., Mar. 23, 1876; s. Victor Murat and Susan Priscilla (McKinney) L.; ed. Austin Coll. (Sherman, Tex.) and Drury Coll. (Springfield, Mo.); married; 1 dau., Rose Ba-Nat-ima. Mem. by blood relationship of Choctaw Tribe of Indians; served as pvt. Spanish Am. War; maj. inf. U.S.A., World War. Principal chief Choctaw Tribe, 1911-18; now supt. under U.S. Govt. for Five Civilized Tribes. Mem. S.A.R., Am. Legion. Republican. Catholic. Home: Antlers, Okla. Address: Muskogee OK

LOCKETT, JAMES army officer; b. in Georgia, Oct. 31, 1855; grad. U.S. Mil. Acad., 1879. Commd. 2d lt. 4th Cav., June 13, 1879; 1st lt., Mar. 1, 1886; capt., Apr. 14, 1894; col. 11th Vol. Cav., Aug. 10, 1899; hon. mustered out vols., Mar. 13, 1901; maj. U.S.A., Jan. 30, 1903; insp. gen., Mar. 30, 1905; assigned to 4th Cav., Apr. 20, 1905; lt. col., Jan. 19, 1911; col. of cav., Aug. 28, 1912; assigned to 11th Cav., Mar. 12, 1913. Aide to Gen. MacArthur in Philippines, 1899; took comd. forces (about 2,000) after death of Gen. Lawton, Dec. 19, 1899, and directed successful assault on insurgents; drove insurgents out of Mabatobato, June 14, 1900; comd. 3d Dist., Dept. Southern Luzon, July-Oct. 1900; again in P.I., 1905-07; at various times in charge of Moro affairs; duty Ft. Sam Houston, Tex., 1971. Address: War Dept., Washington, D.C.

LOCKMAN, JOHN THOMAS lawyer; b. New York, N.Y., Sept. 26, 1834; s. Isaac Paul and Mary (Kennedy) L.; ed. pub. and pvt. schs., New York; LL.B., Columbia, 1867; m. Harriet Hall, Oct. 14, 1862. Apptd. 1st lt. 83d N.Y. Inf., May 27, 1861; capt., Nov. 25, 1861; resigned, Sept. 22, 1862; appt. lt. col., 119th N.Y. Inf., Oct. 16, 1862; col., May 3, 1863; seriously wounded 1st day of Battle of Gettysburg; bvtd. brig. gen. vols., Mar. 13, 1865, "for meritorious conduct in campaign ending with occupation of Atlanta"; hon. mustered out, June 7, 1865. Admitted to bar, 1867, and entered practice at New York; now mem. DeWitt (George G.), Lockman & DeWitt. Officer or dir. in various corps. Home: New York, N.Y. Died Sept. 27, 1912.

LOCKWOOD, BENJAMIN CURTIS brig. gen.; b. in Ky., Feb. 28, 1844. Enlisted as pvt. Co. F, 6th Ky. Inf., Oct. 2, 1861; discharged, Apr. 7, 1863; commd. 2d lt. 54th Ky. Inf., Sept. 30, 1864; hon. mustered out, Sept. 1, 1865; 2d lt. 31st U.S. Inf., Mar. 7, 1867; promoted through grades to brig. gen. U.S.A., 1908; retired by operation of law, Feb. 28, 1908. Bvtd. capt., Feb. 27, 1890, "for gallant services in action against Indians at Spring Creek, Mont., Oct. 15 and 16, 1876." Died Jan. 22, 1926.

LOCKWOOD, CHARLES ANDREWS, JR. naval officer; b. Midland, Va., May 6, 1890; s. Charles Andrews and Flora (Campbell) L.; B.S., U.S. Naval Acad., 1912; m. Phyllis Natalie Irwin, Jan. 30, 1930; children- Charles Andrews, Edward Irwin, Phyllis. Commissioned ensign U.S. Navy, June 1912, and advanced through grades to rear admiral, May 16, 1942, vice adm., Oct. 1943; served in Submarines, 1914-28; mem. U.S. Naval Mission to Brazil, 1929-31; comd. Submarine Div. 13, 1935-37; chief of staff for comdr. submarines, U.S. Fleet, 1939-41; naval attaché, London, 1941-42; comdr. submarines S.W. Pacific Force, 1942-43; comdr. submarines Pacific Fleet, Feb. 1943-Dec. 1945; naval inspector general, Apr. 1946-July 1947. Decorated D.S.M. with 2 stars, Legion of Merit, Commendation Ribbon, Victory, Defense, European and Asiatic campaign medals (U.S.), Order of Orange Nassau (Netherlands), Companion of Bath (Gt. Britain). Mason. Clubs: Army and Navy, Army-Navy Country (Washington). Home: 18234 Daves Av., Monte Serno, Cal. 95030. Died June 6, 1967; buried Golden Gate Nat. Cemetery.

LOCKWOOD, CHARLES DANIEL surgeon; b. Effingham, Ill., Jan. 22, 1868; s. John H. and Ruth (Locke) L.; Kan. Wesleyan U.; A.B., Northwestern U., 1893, M.D., 1896; post-grad. work, U. of Vienna, 1906, 11; m. Clara M. Sanford, Sept. 5, 1898. Interne, Chicago Lying-in and Cook Co. hosps., 1896-97; asst. in surgery, Northwestern U. Med. Sch., 1897-99; alternate mem. Calif. State Bd. Med. Examiners, 1901-02; prof. surgery, Coll. of Dentistry U. of Southern Calif., 1902-; sr. surgeon Pasadena Hosp.; attdg. chest surgeon Olive View Sanitarium. Organized Red Cross Ambulance Co. 1, 1916-17; commd. maj. M.C.U.S.A.; in France, Dec. 1917-Jan. 1919, 5 months at the Western front; now lt. col. Med. Reserve, U.S. Army. Mem. Union Liberal Ch. Fellow Am. Coll. Surgeons. Mason. Home: Pasadena, Calif. Died June 11, 1932.

LOCKWOOD, DANIEL WRIGHT colonel U.S.A.; b. Wilson, N.Y., Sept. 21, 1845; s. Harry and Mary J. L.; ed. N.Y. dist. schs.; grad. U.S. Mil. Acad., 1866; m. Edith Lockwood, of Toledo, O., Apr. 20, 1878. Commd. 2d lt., June 18, 1866; 1st lt., Mar. 7, 1867; capt., June 30, 1879; maj., July 23, 1888; lt.-col., Feb. 20, 1903; col., June 27, 1906. Served on engring. works at Portsmouth, N.H., Boston, New York Harbor, San Francisco, Washington, Detroit, New Orleans, Grand Rapids, Cincinnati, Newport, R.I., St. Paul, also in Ariz. and Nev., and mem. Lighthouse Bd.; retired by operation of law, Sept. 21, 1909. Club: Chevy Chase. Address: 508 Colorado Bldg., Washington.

LOCKWOOD, HENRY HAYES prof. U.S.N.; retired Aug. 1876; b. Kent Co., Aug. 17, 1814; grad. U.S. Mil. Acad., West Point, 1836; - assigned to artillery; m. Annie, oldest dau. Chief Justice Booth of Delaware, Oct. 1845. Served against Florida Indians, 1837; resigned and farmed on Del. until 1841. Apptd., 1841, prof. mathematics U.S. Navy; served at sea with Pacific squadron; took part in capture of Monterey, Calif., Oct. 1842; served at Naval Asylum, Phila., until founding, 1845, of U.S. Naval Acad.; prof. natural philosophy there, 1845; prof. field arty. and inf. tactics, 1845-61; also astronomy and gunnery, 1851-61. In Civil war as col. 1st Del. regt. and, after Aug. 8, 1861, as brig. gen. vols.; commanded at Point Lookout and defenses of lower Potomac; commanded brigade of 12th corps at Gettysburg; later commanded middle dept., with headquarters at Baltimore; mustered out at close of war. Prof. natural philosophy U.S. Naval Acad., 1865-71; served at Nat. Observatory, 1871-76. Died 1899.

LOCKWOOD, IRA HIRAM physician; b. Storm Lake, Ia., Nov. 29, 1885; s. Eli and Adelia (Day) L.; B.S., Buena Vista College, Storm Lake, Iowa, 1905, Doctor of Laws, 1956; student at the Univ. of Iowa, 1905-07; M.D., General Med. Coll. of Chicago, 1909; m. Jessie King, June 8, 1915. Interne and resident Flower Hosp., N.Y. City, 1901- 1909-11; engaged in med. practice, Lincoln, Neb., 1911-17 and 1919-24; in practice of radiology, Kansas City, Mo., since 1924; dir. radiology Research Hosp., Kansas City; radiologist and dir. Research Clinic; cons. radiologist Kansas City Municipal hosps. 1 and 2; radiologist Children's Mercy Hosp., Fitzgibbon Memorial Hosp. (Marshall, Mo.), Olathe Community Hosp., Kan., Cushing Meml. Hosp., Leavenworth, Kan., Bothwell Meml. Hosp., Seadlia, Mo., Smithville Community Hosp., Miss., Kelling Clinic, Waverly, Mo. Served as maj. Med. Corps U.S. Army, during World War I; chief of X-ray dept. Evacuation Hosp. No. 1, A.E.F.; later head of X-ray service II army, A.E.F. Pres. Research Clinic, Blue Shield (Kansas City, Mo.); commn. mem. Dist. 9 Blue Shield Med. Care Plans; area cons. V.A. Trustee Am. Bd. Radiology (president); chairman board chancellors, Am. Coll. Radiology (gold medal award, pres.). Trustee Blue Cross-Blue Shield (Kansas City, Missouri), Frederick C. Narr Fellowship Foundation. Diplomate Am. Bd. Radiology. Fellow International College of Surgeons, American College of Radiology; mem. Am. Roentgen Ray Soc., Radiol. Soc. of N.A. (recipient award of merit for original sci. investigation or roentgenol. examination of the brest; past pres.), A.M.A., So. Med. Association American Radium Society (honorary), Am. Legion, Vets. Fgn. Wars. Clubs: Kansas City, Rotary (Kansas City, Mo.). Contbr. of numerous articles on radiol. subjects to sci. publs. Home: 4607 Jefferson. Office: Argyle Bldg., Kansas City, Mo. Died July 28, 1957; buried Forest Hill Abbey, Kansas City.

LOCKWOOD, JOHN ALEXANDER army officer; b. of Am. parents, Dresden, Germany, Oct. 30, 1856; s. John Alexander (surgeon U.S.N.) and Julia (MeLane) L.; grad. U.S. Coast Guard Acad., 1879, Inf. and Cav. Sch., U.S.A., 1883; M.S., Mich. State Coll., 1887; unmarried. Commd. 2d lt. inf., U.S.A., 1880; advanced through grades to col. on retired list, 1918. Served in campaign against Sioux Indians, 1890-91, campaign in Philippine Islands, comdg. Troop M, 4th U.S. Cavalry, 1899-1900; retired from active service on account of physical disability incurred in line of duty, 1900; detailed on active duty as prof. military science and tactics, La. State U., 1900-03, Fordham U., 1903-06, also lecturer, N.Y. State Bd. of Edn., 1904-06. Served as adj., Fort Leavenworth, Kan., later asst. to comdg. officer, Plattsburg, N.Y., and comdg. officer S.A.T.C., Hahnemann Med. Coll., Phila., World War. Author: Cadet's Handbook, 1902. Deceased.

LODOR, RICHARD brig. gen. U.S.A.; b. New York, Oct. 29, 1832; s. Daniel and Mary Ann (Seyfert) L.; grad. U.S. Mil. Acad., 1856; m. Margaret M. Quintin, Nov. 27, 1856. Bvtd. 2d lt. 4th Arty., July 1, 1856; commd. 2d lt., Oct. 31, 1856; promoted through grades to col. 2d Arty., July 1, 1892; retired by operation of law, Oct. 29, 1896; advanced to rank of brig. gen. retired, by act of Apr. 23, 1904. Bvtd. maj., Dec. 31, 1862, for battle of Stone River, Tenn.; lt. col. and col., Mar. 13, 1865, for services during the war. Instr. in ordnance, gunnery, engring. and law, Arty. Sch., Ft. Monroe, Va. Home: New York, N.Y. Died May 9, 1917.

LOEB, ARTHUR JOSEPH, paper co. exec.; b. Phila., Apr. 27, 1914; s. Adolf and Hortense (Huntsberry) L.; grad. Mercersburg Acad., 1932; B.A., Yale, 1936; m. Kathleen Vachreau, Nov. 12, 1941; children—Barbara H., Joan M., M. Kathleen. With Olin Mathieson Chem. Corp., and predecessors, 1936-68, v.p., gen. mgr. Ecusta paper div., 1964-68. Chmn. trustees Transylvania Community Hosp., 1963-68. Served to capt. USAAF, 1942-45; PTO. Mem. Writing Papers Mfrs. Assn. (chmn. thin paper group), Soc. Advancement Mgmt. Elk. Club: Yale (N.Y.C.). Home: Brevard NC Died Dec. 5, 1968; buried Brevard NC

LOGAN, ALBERT J. mfr.; b. Pittsburgh, Pa., July 7, 1857; s. James and Lavira (Gill) L.; ed. Pa. Mil. Coll., 1874-76; m. Susan E. Murphy, Nov. 16, 1882. Established, 1882, firm of A. J. Logan & Co., mfrs. of mattresses and bedding, inc., 1908, as A. J. Logan Company, of which was president. Formerly chairman City Planning Commn.; dir. Chamber of Commerce of U.S.A., 1912-13; dir. Chamber of Commerce of Pittsburgh, Western Pa. Hosp. Enlisted in Co. F, 18th Inf. (Duquesne Greys) N.G. Pa., Mar. 1876; promoted through grades to col. 17th Regt., 1898; commissary gen. of Pa., 1902; col. 18th Inf., 1909; brig. gen., in comd. 2d Brig., 1912-17; Mexican border service, June 1916-Jan. 1917; brig. gen. N.A., 1917-18; comd. 56th Inf. Brig., World War, July 15, 1917-Jan. 29, 1918- hon. disch. because of physical disability, Jan. 29, 1918. Mem. Armory Bd. State of Pa.; comdr. Pittsburgh Chapter Mil. Order World War. Republican. Presbyn. Home: Pittsburgh, Pa. Died Dec. 27, 1934.

LOGAN, BENJAMIN army officer, legislator; b. Augusta County, Va., 1743; s. David and Jane Logan; m. Ann Montgomery, 1773/4, 8 children including William. Served as sgt. in Gen. Henry Bouquet's expdn. against Shawnee Indians, 1764; commd. lt. of a co. Va. Militia, 1774; county lt. Lincoln County (Va.), 1781; mem. Va. Gen. Assembly from Lincoln County, 1781-82, 85-87; mem. Ky. Constl. Constn., 1792; mem. Bod. of War in the West, also brig. gen. Ky. Militia, 1790; mem. Ky. Ho. of Reps. from Lincoln County, 1793-94, from Shelby County, 1795. Died Dec. 11, 1802; buried Shelbyville, Ky.

LOGAN, JAMES ADDISON JR. banker; b. Phila., Pa., Nov. 11, 1879; s. Judge James A. and Elizabeth (Marehand) L.; student Haverford (Pa.) Coll. 1 yr.; grad. Army War Coll., 1912; LL.D., Haverford, 1925; m. Esther Tone Griswold, May 22, 1925. Pvt. Battery A, Pa. Vols., Spanish-Am. War, 1898; capt. vols. Philippine Insurrection 1899-1900; entered U.S. Army as capt., 1901; chief Am. Mil. Mission with French Army, Sept. 1914-June 1917; col. Gen. Staff, asst. chief of staff G.H.Q., A.E.F. Principal asst. to Herbert Hoover in relief operations in Europe after Armistice; European rep. U.S. Grain Corp., also in charge coordinating operations of tech. advisers to various new states of Central and Eastern Europe; Am. rep. financial sect., Supreme Economic Council, also of communications sect. same; adviser to Am. Relief Administration in connection with Russian Relief, June 1921-June 1923; resigned from Army, July 15, 1922. Asst. Am. unofficial del. to Reparation Commn., Dec. 1919-July 1, 1923; Am. unofficial del. to same, Aug. 1, 1923-May 31, 1925; Am. unofficial rep., London Conf. of Prime Ministers, 1924. Finance Ministers' Conf., Paris, 1925. Associated with Dillon, Read & Co., bankers, June 1925-. Protestant. Home: Bala, Montgomery Co., Pa. Deceased.

LOGAN, JOHN ALEXANDER senator, army officer; b. Jackson County, Ill., Feb. 9, 1826; s. Dr. John and Elizabeth (Jenkins) L.; grad. U. Louisville, grad. law dept., 1851; m. Mary Simmerson Cunningham, Nov. 27, 1855, 2 children. Served as lt. 1st Ill. Inf. in Mexican War, 1846-48; admitted to Ill. bar, 1852; mem. Ill. Ho. of Reps., 1852, 53, 56, 57; pros. atty. 3d Jud. Dist. Ill., 1853-57; mem. U.S. Ho. of Reps. from Ill., 36th-37th congresses, 1859-Apr. 2, 1862, 41st-42d congresses, 1867-71, apptd. a mgr. to conduct impeachment proceedings against Pres. Andrew Johnson, 1868; commd. col. 21st Ill. Inf., U.S. Army, 1861; commd. brig. gen. Ill. Volunteers, 1862, maj. gen., 1862-65; an organizer Soc. of Army of Tenn., circa 1865, Grand Army of Republic, circa 1865 (3 times pres.); declined appointment as minister to Mexico, 1865; conceived idea of Meml. Day (inaugurated May 30, 1868); mem. U.S. Senate from Ill., 1871-77, 79-86. Author: The Great Conspiracy: Its Origin and History, 1886; The Volunteer Soldier of America, With Memoir of the Author and Military Reminiscences from General Logan's Private Journal, 1887. Died Washington, D.C., Dec. 26, 1886; buried Rock Creek Cemetery, Washington.

LOGAN, JOHN ALEXANDER JR. maj. U.S.A., adj. gen.'s dept.; b. in Ill., July 24, 1865 (only son of late Gen. John A. Logan); m. Edith Andrews, Mar. 22, 1887; served through campaign in Cuba on staff of Maj. Gen. J.C. Bates; recommended for promotion to rank of bvt. lt. col. and col. for gallantry in the field. Author: Joyful Russia. Home: Washington, D.C. Died 1899.

LOGAN, LEAVITT CURTIS rear adm. U.S.N.; b. Medina Co., O., Jan. 30, 1846; s. Samuel Sheldon and Hannah Hall (Curtis) L.; grad. U.S. Naval Acad., 1867; m. Elizabeth C. Porter, May 9, 1877. Promoted ensign, Dec. 18, 1868; master, Mar. 21, 1870; lt., June 12, 1871; lt. comdr., Dec. 16, 1891; comdr., May 1, 1898; capt., July 11, 1902; rear admiral, Jan.-Sept. 1871; Wabash, flag-ship European Sta., 1871-73; torpedo duty, 1874; Tennessee, Asiatic Squadron, 1875-77; Naval Acad., 1877-80; Powhatan, spl. service, 1880-81; training ships Portmouth, 1881-83, New Hampshire, 1883-84; Naval War Coll., 1884-87; Ossipee, N. Atlantic Sta., 1887-89; recorder Board inspection, 1889-92; Phila., 1892-94; Training Sta., Newport, R.I., 1894-98; comd. Armeria during Spanish War, Machias, 1898-1900; on duty under Bureau of Equipment, 1900-04; comd. Ohio, 1904-06; comdt., Navy Yard, Pensacola, Fla., Feb. 15, 1907; retired by operation of law, Jan. 30, 1908. Died Nov. 23, 1921.

LOGAN, THOMAS MULDRUP financier; b. Charleston, S.C., Nov. 3, 1840; s. Judge George William L.; grad. S.C. Coll., 1860; joined Washington Light Inf. of Charleston; served with it as pvt. during siege of Fort Sumter, 1861; after fall of Sumter became 2d lt., Co. A, Hampton's Legion; promoted through regular grades until he was commd. brig. gen. C.S.A., Dec. 1864, the youngest of that rank in the C.S. service; was at 1st battle of Manassas; wounded at Gaines' Mill, nr. Richmond, 1862; comd. his co. at 2d Manassas; frequently served on reconnoissance duty to ascertain the enemy's strength; shot from his horse and seriously wounded while endeavoring to delay the Federal advance on the morning that Gen. Grant crossed the Chickahominy; comd. Butler's brigade in Johnston's army until the surrender at Greensboro; m. Kate V. Cos, May 25, 1865. After war studied law; practiced at Richmond, Va., about 12 yrs.; became interested in railroads; organized, 1878, a syndicate of Richmond and New York capitalists which consolidated various Southern railroads into the Richmond & Danville system, now the Southern Ry.; pres. Gray Nat. Telautograph Co.; chmn. Dem. exec. com. of Va., 1879, and of the Gold Dem. party of Va., 1896. Home: Howardsville, Va. Died Aug. 11, 1914.

LOGAN, WILLIAM HOFFMAN GARDINER oral surgeon; b. Morrison, Ill., Oct. 14, 1872; s. Robert E. and Melvina (McCoy) L.; D.D.S., Chicago Coll. Dental Surgery, 1896; M.D., Chicago Coll. Medicine and Surgery, 1905; LL.D., Loyola Univ., 1926; M.S., U. of Mich., 1930; L.D., National Univ. of Ireland (Dublin), 1940; m. Florence, d. Dr. Truman W. Brophy, June 20, 1900; 1 dau., Jean Brophy (Mrs. Donald L. LaChance). Member attending staff of St. Joseph's, Michael Reese and Cook County hospitals; dean and prof. plastic and oral surgery, Chicago Coll. Dental Surgery since 1920. Maj. Medical Res. Corps, Aug. 1917; chief of dental div. Surgeon General's Office, Washington, D.C., Aug. 1917; commd. lt. col., Feb. 1918, col. May 1918; hon. disch. Feb. 12, 1919. Apptd. chmn. com. on legislation and enrollment and com. on dentistry, Gen. Med. Bd. of Council of Nat Defense, 1917. Chmn. Foundation for Dental Research of Chicago Coll. Dental Surgery since 1935; mem. Gorgas Memorial Inst. of Tropical and Preventive Medicine (sec. 1929-33); mem. bd. govs. since 1933), 3d Australian Dental Congress (v.p. 1914), 7th Internat. Dental Congress (pres. 1926). Fellow Am. Coll. Surgeons (mem. bd. govs. since 1928); mem. Nat. Dental Assn. (pres. 1917-18), Ill. State Dental Soc. (pres. 1913-14), Chicago Dental Soc. (pres. 1909-10), A.M.A., Ill. State Med. Soc., Chicago Med. Soc. (pres. North Side Branch 1940-41), Am. Assn. Oral and Plastic Surgeons, Am. Bd. Plastic Surgery, Internat. Dental Federation (v.p. 1926-36; pres. since 1936). Am. Assn. Dental Schs., Omicron Kappa Upsilon, Pi Gamma Mu, Delta Sigma Delta; hon. mem. Am. Dental Soc. of Europe, Ky. State Med. Soc. Mason. Clubs: Chicago Athletic, Press, Army and Navy. Writer of many articles on dental edn., cleft palate and lip and oral surgery. Home: 179 Lake Shore Drive. Office: 55 E. Washington St., Chicago, Ill. Died Apr. 6, 1943.

LOHR, LENOX RILEY, pres., Mus. of Sci. and Industry; b. Washington, Aug. 15,21891; s. Gustavus Peter and Margaret (Bean) L., M.E., Cornell, 1916 (honor grad.); grad. Army Gen. Staff Coll., Langres, France, 1918; Clare Coll., Cambridge U., Eng., 1919; D. Eng. (hon.), Ill. Inst. Tech. 1949; LL.D. (hon.), Knox Coll., 1950, Bradley U., 1955, Loyola U., Chgo., 1956, De Paul U., 1958, Northwestern, 1962, C.E., Rensselaer Polytech. Inst., 1952; D.Sc. (honorary), Shurtleff College, 1954; married Florence Josephine Wimsatt (M.A., M.D.), November 18, 1924; children—Margaret Priscilla (Mrs. R.L. Brown), Patricia (Mrs. James K. Rocks), Mary Josepha, Lenox Riley, Donald. Member board directors, exec. secretary Soc. Am. Mil. Engrs. 1922-29, editor The Mil. Engr., awarded its D.S.M., 1930, pres. 1954; mem. Com. on War Memorial to Am. Engrs. at Louvain U., Belgium, 1928; gen. mgr. A Century of Progress Expn. Chicago, 1929-35; pres. N.B.C., Inc., 1935-40; president of the Museum of Science and Industry, Chicago, Illinois, 1940-58, trustee, 1935-68. Bd. mem. Met. Fair and Expn. Authority, chmn., 1952-57. Fellow Inst. Medicine of Chicago, Pres. Chicago R.R. Fair 1948-49. Dir. Civil Def. State of Ill., 1950-52; pres. Centennial of Engring., 1952, Inc.; chmn. Higher Edn. Commn. of Ill., 1954-59; hon. trustee Mary Thompson Hosp. (pres. 1952-55), Heart Assn., Chgo. La Rabida Jackson Park Sanitarium, Chgo., Thomas Alva Edison Found., N.Y.C., Air Force Mus. Found.; chmn. U. Ill. Citizens Com.; mem. U. Chicago Citizens Bd. and Northwestern U. Assos.; member citizens board Loyola University. Pres. committee Notre Dame. Mem. Sec. of Navy's Civilian Adv. Com., 1946-48. Served as 2d and 1st lt. C.A.C.,

U.S.A., 1916; capt. to maj. Corps Engrs., 1917-29, resigned 1929; co. comdr. and topog. officer 4th Engrs.; Brigade Adj. 57th Inf. Brigade, 29th Div.; participated in Alsace defensive sector, Meuse Argonne, returned to U.S., July 13, 1919; in Office of Chief Engrs. Decorated Silver Star medal, citation; Navy Distinguished Pub. Service award, 1954 (U.S.); Officer Order Ouissam Alaouite Cherifien of Morocco. Recipient Deutsches Museum citation, 1960; Rosenberger medal; citation U. Ill., 1964. Mem. Am. Soc. C.E., Inst. Am. Strategy (pres. 1958-62, dir.), Soc. Am. Mil. Engrs., Assn. U.S. Army, Navy League U.S., Sigma Phi Sigma (gen. pres. 1916; hon. key 1936), Phi Sigma Kappa, Chi Epsilon. Clubs: Economic, Chicago, Commercial, Antique Auto, Nat. Press. Author: Magazine Publishing, 1932; Television Broadcasting, 1940; Fair Management, 1952; Centennial of Engineering, 1953. Home: Evanston IL Died May 28, 1968.

LOKRANTZ, SVEN M.D., public health administr.; b. Stockholm, Sweden, Sept. 22, 1892; s. Axel Wilhelm and Elizabeth (Baroness Von Duben) L.; grad. Unman's School of Swedish Gymnastics, and School of Commerce, Stockholm, Sweden; grad. Coll. Preceptors, 1912, M.D., Tufts Coll., 1918; grad. study Boston Dispensary and U. of Calif.; m. Carolina Anthony Winston, 1923; 1 son, Sven Winston. Came to U.S., 1914, naturalized citizen, 1920. Began practice at Boston, 1918; served as orthopedic surgeon, Boston Dispensary, also as director corrective physical education depts. of same, and at Cambridge Hosp.; lecturer Tufts Coll., 1918; moved to Los Angeles, Calif 1918; supervisor of the department corrective physical education, depts. of same, and at Cambridge Hosp.; lecturer Tufts Coll., 1918; moved to Los Angeles, Calif., 1918; supervisor of the department corrective physical education, city schools, Los Angeles, 1918-24, med. dir. city schs., 1924-; former lecturer U. of Calif.; mem. staff California Hosp., Anita Baldwin Hosp. for Babies, Children's Hosp.; consultant Orthopedic Hosp. Sch.; dir. Likrantz School of Swedish Gymnastics, Boston, Mass. Lt. comdr. U.S.N. Res. Medical Corps; retired. Founder and chmn. bd. govs. Ling Foundation; med. dir. Tenth Olympic Games; mem. bd. dirs. Am. Red Cross. Knight Order of Vasa, 1st class (Sweden), 1930; Knight Order of the North Star Sweden, 1933; officer Order of Orange Nassau (Holland), 1933. Author: Notes in Corrective Physical Education, 1928; Health Supervision of Kindergarten Children. Died Mar. 11, 1940.

LOMAX, LUNSFORD LINDSAY soldier; b. Newport, R.I., Nov. 4, 1835; s. Maj. Mann Page and Elizabeth (Lindsay) L.; prep. edn. Norfolk, Va.; grad. U.S. Mil. Acad., 1856; m. Elisabeth Winter Payne, Feb. 20, 1873. Served in U.S.A. as 1st lt. U.S. cav., 1856-61; resigned Apr. 22, 1861; entered Confederate service and attained the rank of maj. gen., comdg., div. of cav. Army of Northern Va., until 1865. Home: Warrenton, Va. Died May 28, 1913.

LONG, ANDRES THEODORE naval officer; b. in Iredell County, N.C., Apr. 6, 1866; grad. U.S. Naval Acad., 1887; m. Mrs. Viola V. Fife, Mar. 3, 1928. Promoted ensign, July 1, 1889; promoted through grades to rear admiral, Sept. 15, 1918. Served on Minneapolis, Spanish-American War, 1898; exec. officer Dolphin, 1904-05; comd. Mayflower, 1905-07; exec. officer Illinois, 1907-09; duty Officer of Naval Intelligence, Navy Dept., 1909; naval attaché, Rome and Vienna, 1909-12; comd. Des Moines, 1912-14; supervisor naval auxiliaries, 1914-16; apptd. capt. Connecituct, Oct. 25, 1916, Nevada, Feb. 1918; naval attaché Paris, France, staff rep., Paris; now rear adm. (perm.); comdr. div., Atlantic Fleet, 1929; dir. of naval intelligence, Navy Dept., 1920-21; chief of staff, Atlantic Fleet, 1921-22; comdr. U.S. Naval Forces in Europe, 1922-23; chief Bur. of Navigation, 1923-24; became mem. Gen. Board, Navy Dept., 1924-30, retired; dir. of Internat. Hydrographic Bur., Monte Carlo, 1930-37. Address: care Am. Security & Trust Co., Washington, D.C.* Died May 21, 1946.

LONG, ARMISTEAD LINDSAY army officer; b. Campbell County, Va., Sept. 3, 1825; s. Col. Armistead and Calista (Cralle) L.; grad. U.S. Mil. Acad., 1850; m. Mary Heron Sumner, 1860. Brevetted 2d lt. U.S. Army, 1850, commd. 1st lt., 1854, stationed chiefly in Indian Territory, Kan. and Neb., until 1860; a.d.c. to Gen. Sumner, 1861; resigned commn., 1861; Robert E. Lee's mil. sec. with rank of col. until 1863; commd. brig. gen. arty., chief engr. of a Va. canal company 1863. Author: Memoirs of Robert E. Lee, His Military and Personal History, 1886. Died Charlottesville, Va., Apr. 29, 1891.

LONG, AUGUSTINE V. judge; b. Lake City, Fla., May 14, 1877; s. Thomas T. and Annie Mariah (Pemberton) L.; ed. pub. schs., and Fla. Agrl. Coll., about 2 yrs.; studied law in attorneys' offices 3 yrs.; m. Ruby May Brownlee, Sept. 12, 1899; children-Ella May (Mrs. F. A. Canova), Augustus C., Annie E. (Mrs. Marcus Conant). Admitted to bar, 1898, and began practice at Starke, Fla.; admitted to practice before Supreme Ct. Fla., 1899, and later before Supreme Ct., U.S.; mem. Fla. Ho. of Reps., 1903; apptd. state's atty., 1907 and state's atty., 8th Jud. Circuit, 1910, serving until 1921; judge Circuit Ct., 1921-34; judge U.S. Dist. Ct. for No. Dist. Fla., 1934—. Served in Fla. N.G., 15 yrs., ret. as capt.; 1st lt. vols., Spanish-Am. War. Democrat. Presbyn. Mason. Home: Gainesville, Fal. Address: U.S. District Court, Gainesville, Fla. Died May 20, 1955; buried Gainesville.

LONG, CHARLES GRANT officer U.S. Marine Corps; b. South Weymouth, Mass., Dec. 14, 1869; s. John and Eliza (Regan) L.; grad. U.S. Naval Acad., 1889, Army War Coll., 1912; m. Edith M., d. Rear Adm. Charles J. Barclay, U.S. Navy, Sept. 1, 1903; 1 dau., Nancy Barclay, Commd. 2d lt. U.S. Marine Corps, 1891; promoted through grades to brig. gen., Nov. 1918; retired Dec. 31, 1921. Participated in campaigns in Cuba, 1898, Philippines, 1899-1900, Boxer campaign, 1900, Nicaragua campaign, 1914, at Vera Cruz, Mexico, 1915-16; served as chief of staff hdqrs., U.S. Marine Corps, Washington, 1917-20, having charge of personnel, and its distribution during the war; apptd. comdg. gen. 2d Brig., U.S. Marine Corps, Santo Domingo, D.R., Oct. 1920. Bvtd. capt. for services at Guantanamo, Cuba, 1898; mentioned in orders for spl. services as comdr. 2d Batn. Marines at Tientsin, China, during Boxer campaign; recommended for D.S.M. for services World War but awarded Navy Cross. Home: South Dartmouth, Mass. Died Mar. 5, 1943.

LONG, ELI brig. gen. U.S.A., retired Aug. 1867; b. Woodford Co., Ky., June 16, 1837; grad. Frankfort, Ky., Mil. School, 1855; apptd. 2d lt., 1st U.S. cav., 1856; served against Indians; 1st lt. and capt., 1861; col. 4th Ohio cav.; served at Tullahoma, Murfreesboro, Chickamauga and in Atlanta campaign; comd. cav. brigade; comd. div. at Selma, Ala., April 1865, capturing the place; 5 times wounded; bvtd. maj. gen. vols. and U.S.A.; mustered out of vol. service Jan. 15, 1866; retired as maj. gen.; reduced to brig. gen. by Act of March 3, 1875; m. Jane I. Lane, Sept. 5, 1865. Home Plainfield, N.J. Died 1903.

LONG, JAMES mil. officer; b. N.C., circa 1793; m. Jane Wilkinson, 1815. Moved with family to Rutherford, Tenn.; served as physician in War of 1812, 1812-15; attempted unsuccessfully to practice medicine in Tenn., 1815-17; became mcht., Natchez, Miss., 1817; selected by Natchez townsmen to lead expdn. intended to open Tex. to Am. settlement, 1819, gathered 300 men in this cause and marched to Nacogdoches, Tex., established republic, apptd. himself pres. of supreme council and comdr.-in-chief; declared Tex. independence, 1819; negotiated with Jean Laffite to become gov. of new territory, 1819, driven out of Tex. by Spanish militia; went to New Orleans, gained support of John Austin and Ben Milam; gave presidency of republic to E. W. Ripley; entered alliance with Jose Trespalacios (Am. revolutionist), 1820; attacked La Bahia, Mexico, 1820, defeated by Perez, captured and sent to Mexico City. Shot in Mexico City, Apr. 8, 1822.

LONG, JOHN DAVIS secretary of the navy; b. Buckfield, Me., Oct. 27, 1838; s. Zadoc and Julia Temple (Davis) L.; A.B., Harvard, 1857; prin. Westford Acad., Mass., 1857-59; studied law in Harvard Law Sch. and pvt. law offices, 1861; (LL.D., Harvard, 1880, Tufts, 1902); admitted to bar, 1861; practiced at Buckfield, Me., 1861-62, then at Boston; m. Mary Woodward Glover, Sept. 13, 1870; 2d Agnes, d. Rev. Joseph D. Pierce, May 22, 1886. Mem. Mass. Ho. of Rep., 1875-78 (speaker 1876-78); lt. gov. of Mass., 1879; gov., 1880-83; mem. 48th to 50th Congresses (1883-89), 2d Mass. Dist.; declined renomination, 1888; was for several yrs. on Statehouse Construction Commn. of Mass. Sec. of the navy, in cabinets of Presidents McKinley and Roosevelt, Mar. 6, 1897-May 1, 1902; resigned. Sr. of law firm of Long & Hemenway, Boston. Pres. Bd. of Overseers Harvard Coll. Fellow Am. Acad. Arts and Sciences, Presented town of Buckfield, Me., the Zadoc Long Free Library, 1901. Author: The Republican Party-Its History, Principles and Policies, 1898, 1900; The New American Navy, 2 vols. Home: Hingham, Mass. Died Aug. 28, 1915.

LONG, MITCHELL lawyer; b. Pulaski, Tenn., Nov. 15, 1889; s. W. B. and Eliza (McGoldrick) L.; legal study under Gen. Charles T. Cates, Jr., 1911-14; m. Kathrine Lockett, Feb. 20, 1923; 1 son, Mitchell Long (dec.). Admitted to Tenn. bar, 1914; pvt. practice of law, Knoxville, Tenn., since 1914. Dir., chmn. bd. and gen. counsel Sterchi Bros. Stores, Inc.; dir. and gen. counsel Jefferson Woolen Mills; gen. counsel Hamilton Nat. Bank; mem. Cates, Smith & Long, 1921-45; Cates, Fowler, Long & Fowler, since 1945. Chairman State Democratic exec. com., 1937-38; del. State-at-Large to Dem. Nat. Convs., 1928, 1944. Served as capt. 114th field arty. A.E.F., World War I. Mem. commn. uniform state laws, 1930-49; Tenn. constitutional revision commn., 1945-46. Mem. Am. Bar Assn. (house dels. 1940-48; bd. govs. 1945-48; chmn. com. on aeronautical law, 1941-42), Tenn. and Knox Co. bar assns., Am. Law Inst. Presbyterian. Club: Cherokee Country. Home: 1704 Kingston Pike, Knoxville 16. Office: Hamilton National Bank Bldg., Knoxville 2, Tenn. Died Apr. 2, 1953.

LONG, OSCAR FITZALAN army officer; b. Utica, N.Y., June 16, 1852; s. William W. and Eva E. E.; grad. U.S. Mil. Acad., 1876; m. Amy Requa, 1896; children-Amy, Sally. Apptd. 2d lt. 5th U.S. Inf., June 15, 1876; brig. gen., July 10, 1904. Served against hostile Indians in Mont., and in fight against Sitting Bull and Crazy Horse at Wolf Mountain, Jan. 8, 1877, Lame Deer Creek, May 6, 1877; on Nez Perces Expdn., 1877, and was in fight at Bear Paw Mountain against Chief Joseph, Sept. 30, 1877; received the Congressional Medal of Honor for "most distinguished gallantry" in this action; organized and was gen. supt. of the army transport service in San Francisco during the Spanish-Am. War and Filipino Insurrection; retired at own request, over 30 yrs.' service, July 11, 1904. Pres. Calif. Wire Cloth Co. (Oakland). Home: Piedmont, Calif. Died Dec. 22, 1928.

LONG, PERRIN HAMILTON physician; b. Bryan, O., Apr. 7, 1899; s. James Wilkinson and Wilhelmina Lillian (Kautsky) L.; B.S., U. Mich., 1924, M.D., 1924; M.D. (Hon. Caus.) U. Algers, 1944; F.R. C.P., 1946; D.Sc., Trinity Coll., 1955; m. Elizabeth D. Griswold, Sept. 6, 1922; children-Perrin Hamilton, Jr., Priscilla Griswold, Resident physician Torndike Meml. Lab., Boston City Hosp., 1924-25, interne fourth med. service, 1925-27; vol. asst., Hygienic Inst., Freiburg, Germany, 1927; asst. and asso. Rockefeller Inst. for Med. Research 1927-29; asso. in medicine Johns Hopkins Med. Sch., 1929-37, asso. prof. 1937-40, prof., preventive med., 1940-51; physician Johns Hopkins Hosp., 1940-51; chmn. and prof., dept. medicine, coll. medicine State U. N.Y., N.Y.C., 1951-61;, now emeritus; dir. u. div. med. service Kings Co. Hosp. Center, Bklyn., 1951-61, cons., 1961-, also chief dept. medicine; cons. V.A., F.D.A., P.H.S., Dept. of Army. Med. advisor O.C.D. Planning, 1948. Trustee Martha's Vineyard Hosp.; dir. Am. Field Service, 1959-64, Physicians's Club, 1964-. Served Am. Field Service, 1917; pvt. AS, U.S. Army, 1917-19, with AEF, col. M.C., AUS, 1942-45, brig. gen. ret., cons. medicine N.A.T.O. and M.T.O. Awarded Croix de Guerre, Chevalier Legion of Honor, (both France); Legion of Merit, hon. officer (mil. div.) Order Brit. Empire. Fellow Royal Coll. Physicians; mem. Am. Soc. Clin. Investigation, Harvey Soc., Soc. Am. Bacteriologists, A.M.A., Assn. Am. Physicians, Zeta Psi, Alpha Omega Alpha, Sigma Xi, Presbyn. Club: 14 West Hamilton Street (Balt.), Author: Clinical and Experimental Use of Sulfanilamide, Sulfapyridine and Allied Compounds (with Eleanor A. Bliss), 1939; ABC'S of Sulfonamide and Antibiotic Therapy, 1948. Contbr. many med. articles to jours. Editor-in-chief Resident Physician, Medical Times. Address: Edgartown, Mass. 02539. Died Dec. 17, 1965; buried Chappaquidick Island, Edgartown.

LONGCOPE, WARFIELD THEOBALD physician; b. Balt., Mar. 29, 1877; s. George von S. and Ruth (Theobald) L.; A.B., Johns Hopkins, 1897; M.D., Johns Hopkiins, 1901; LL.D., St. John's Coll., 1934, Johns Hopkins U., 1951; D.Sc., U. Rochester, 1941; Docteur "honoris causa," U. Paris, 1945; m. Janet Percy Dana, Dec. 2, 1915; children-Barbara, Duncan, Mary Lee, Christopher. Resident pathologist of Pa. Hosp. Phila., 1901-14; dir. Ayer Clin. Lab., same, 1904-11; asst. prof. applied medicine, U. Pa., 1901-11; asso. prof. practice of medicine, 1911-14, Bard prof., 1914-21, Columbia; asso. vis. physician, 1911-14, dir. med. service Presbyn. Hosp., N.Y., 1914-21; prof. medicine Johns Hopkins Med. Sch. and physician in chief Johns Hopkins Hosp., 1922-46. Commd. maj., Med. O.R.C., 1917; on active duty med. div., Office of Surgeon Gen. U.S. Army, Washington, Aug. 1917-July 1918; col., Medical Corps, U.S. Army, A.E.F., July 1918-Jan. 1919. Fellow (hon.) Coll. Physicians (Phila). Mem. Assn. Am. Physicians, A.M.A., Soc. Exptl. Biology and Medicine, Am. Soc. Clin. Investigation, Am. Soc. Exptl. Pathology, A.A.A.S., N.Y. Acad. Medicine, N.Y. Clin. Soc., Am. Clinic and Climatological Soc., Harvey Soc., Medico Chirurg. Faculty of Med., Balt. City Med. Soc., Nat. Acad. Scis.; fellow Am. Coll. Phys., Am. Acad. Arts and Scis.; hon. mem. Royal Soc. of Medicine, Société des Hûpital, Paris, Hon. Fellow Scandanavian Congress for Int. Med. Extensive investigations in clin. medicine and in pathology. Home: "Cornhill Farm," Lee, Mass. Died April 25, 1953.

LONGINO, OLIN HARRINGTON army officer (ret.); b. Atlanta, June 27, 1887; s. Thomas Dick and May (Harrington) L.; B.S. in Elec. Engring., Ga. Sch. Tech., 1907; student Coast Arty. Sch., 1914, Command and Gen. Staff Sch., 1925-26, Army War Coll., 1934-35; m. Lila Evans, Aug. 28, 1913; children-Frances May (wife of Lt. Col. Edw. Sigerfoos, U.S. Army), Thomas Dick, II. Commd. 2d lt. U.S. Army, 1908; promoted through grades to brig. gen., 1941; sailed for France, 1917; as capt., comdg. H Battery, 8th Regt., Coast Arty.; participated in St. Mihiel and Meuse-Argonne offensives; returned to U.S. at lt. col., 1919; served in Eng. and Alaska, also comd. anti-aircraft tng. centers, Camp Edwards, Mass., Ft. Sheridan, Ill., during World War II; ret. 1945. Home: College Park, Ga. Died Sept. 7, 1955.

LONGNECKER, EDWIN naval officer; b. Cumberland Co., Pa., Feb. 19, 1844; grad. U.S. Naval Acad., 1865; married. Promoted ensign, Dec. 1, 1866; master (Lt. jr. grade) Mar. 12, 1868; lt., Mar. 26, 1869; lt. comdr., Aug. 30, 1881; comdr., Oct. 2, 1891; capt., Mar. 3, 1899; rear admiral, July 8, 1905; retired by operation of law, Feb. 19, 1906. Served on America during Civil War; on Richmond 1890-91; comd. Passaic, 1892; comd. 1892-94; Navy Yard, Washington, D. C., 1895; Naval War Coll., Newport, R.I., 1895; insp. ordnance, Navy Yard, League Island, 1895-99; comd.

New Orleans, 1899-1900; Navy Yard, Boston, 1900-01; Naval Sta., Port Royal, S.C., 1901-03, serving as commandant, Apr. 12, 1902-June 14, 1903; comdt.Naval Sta., Charleston, 1903-04; Navy Yard, Norfolk, 190 retired on account of age, Feb. 19, 1906, and as rear admiral of sr. nine in recognition of service during Civil War. Home: Wernersville, Pa. Died Nov. 13, 1923.

LONGSTREET, HELEN DORTCH (MRS. JAMES LONGSTREET) author, journalist; b. Franklin County, Ga.; d. James Speed and Mary (Pulliam) Dortch; ed. Brenan Coll., Gainesville, Ga. and Notre Dame Convent, Balt.; m. Gen. James Longstreet, of Confederate Army, Sept. 8, 1897 (dec.). Editor daily and weekly newspapers in Ga.; apptd. by Gov. William Y. Atkinson, to State Library of Ga., 1894-97 (1st woman in Ga. to hold office under state govt.); apptd. postmaster Gainesville, Ga., by Pres. Theodore Roosevelt, 1904, reapptd. by him on record in office, in 1908 and confirmed by U.S. Senate, without reference to com., served until 1913; had supervision of erection of Post-Office bldg. at Gainesville, and was apptd. disbursing agt. by George B.Cortelyou, sec. treasury, for constrn. of bldg. Del. to Progressive Party conv. which nominated Theodore Roosevelt for pres.; leader in fight for recovery by State of Tallulah Falls, in Ga. mountains, which had been appropriated by a waterpower trust; three years asso. editor Farmers's Nat. Mag.; made transcontinental speaking tour sponsored by mag. in interest of econ. justice for agr. and labor; dist. mgr. two years, life and fire ins. agy., Gainesville, conducted stock and dairy farm in N. Ga.; actively supported bill passed by Ga. legislature establishing Ga. State Coll. for women; in change Longstreet Meml. Assn. Exhibit, N.Y. World's Fair, 1939, Golden Gate Expn., 1940. Mem. Champions of Civil Rights, Gettysburg Hist. Soc., Nat. Geog. Soc., League Am. Pen Women, Longstreet Meml. Assn., U.D.C., patriotic orgns. Awarded Nat. League of Am. Pen Women prize for brochure on Racial Relations, 1948. By order Gov. Ala. named hon. col. Ala. State Militia, and Sweetheart N.G. Ala. Catholic. Progressive Republican. Author: Lee and Longstreet at High Tide, 1904; short Stories. After exhaustive Study of conditions in V.I. became champion of dominion form of govt. for Islands. Elected Dau. of Regt., 71st C.A., U.S.A., apptd. col. on staff of Gen. J. R. Jones, Confederate States Army. Made speaking tour, 1943, in summer of war effort; entered Bell Aircraft plant, Marietta, Ga., 1943 to aid in bldg. bombers for war; awarded silver trophy B.F. Goodrich Co., 1943, for distinguished service in World War II. Her portrait by Charles Carson given State Capitol of Ga., by Ams. N. and S.; accepted by Gov. Ellis Arnall, unveiled by Gen. Julius T. Howell, 1947. Champion civil rights. Home: Savannah Beach, Ga. Died May 1962.

LONGSTREET, JAMES soldier, U.S. commr. of Pacific railroads, Nov. 2, 1897-; b. in Edgefield Dist., S.C., Jan. 8, 1821; s. James L.; grad. West Point, 1842; served in Mexican, Indian and Civil wars; won title of major at battle of Molino del Rey, Sept. 8, 1847, served in C.S.A. as brig. gen. and maj. gen.; as lt. gen. comd. 1st corps Army of Northern Va. in 1862-65; a short period in the Army of Tenn. under Bragg; returned to Lee's army in 1864. Comd. in many battles, and was wounded by the fire of his own troops at the Wilderness, May 1864; was included in the surrender at Appomattox, April 9, 1865. After war became a Republican; was apptd. surveyor of customs at New Orleans by President Grant; later was supervisor of internal revenue; postmaster at Gainesville, Ga.; U .S. minister to Turkey, and U.S. marshal for dist. of Ga.; m. Helen Dortch, Sept. 8, 1897. Home: Washington, D.C. Died 1904.

LONGSTRETH, CHARLES mfr.; b. Philadelphia, Pa., 1868; s. Edward and Anna P. (Wise) L.; ed. Swarthmore Coll.; m. M. Gertrude Heyer, 1891; children-Edward, Ellanor L. Sharp. With Baldwin Locomotive Works, Philadelphia, 1886-91; gen. supt. Pa. Warehousing & Safe Deposit Co., 1891-96; v.p. 1892-1904, pres. since 1904, U.S. Packing Co., railraod supplies; pres. Am. Locomotive Sander Co., 1899-1911. Commd. lt.-comdr. U.S.N.R.F., Feb. 1917, and on active duty from Apr. 1917, until after Armistice. Mem. Am. Soc. Mech. Engrs., Am. Soc. Naval Architects and Marine Engrs., Am. Soc. Naval Engrs., Franklin Inst. Clubs: Racquet, Corinthian Yacht (Phila.); New York Yacht (New York). Author: Rules of the Road at Sea by Diagram, 1914; Elementary Seamanship and Plan for Nautical Troops, Boy Scouts, 1915. Address: 611 A Av., Coronado, Calif. Died Mar. 1, 1948.

LONSDALE, JOHN TIPTON geologist; b. Dale, Ia., Nov. 8, 1895; s. John Dye and Eva Mary (Connor) L.; A.B., U. of Ia., 1917, M.S., 1921; Ph.D., U. of Va., 1924; m. Edna Gertrude Van Arnam, Aug. 13, 1921. Asst. prof. geology U. of Va., 1921-24; asst. prof. of geology, U. of Okla., 1924-25; geologist Bur. Econ. Geology, U. of Tex., 1925-28; prof. geology and head dept., A. and M. Coll. of Tex., 1928-35; prof. and head dept. Ia. State Coll., 1935-45; dir. bur. econ. geology and prof. geology U. of Tex. since 1945. Served as 1st lt., U.S. Army, 1917-19; lt. col. and col., Gen. Staff Corps, U.S. Army, 1942-45; col. A.U.S. Res., ret. 1953. Mem. Geological Society of America, Society of Economic Geologists, Mineralogical Society of America, Assn. American State Geologists (vice pres. 1959), Am. Assn. Petroleum Geologists, Am. Inst. Mining and Metall Engrs., A.A.A.S., Am. Geophys. Union, Sigma Xi, Gamma Alpha, Sigma Gamma Epsilon, Delta Tau Delta. Author bulls., sci. papers and articles on mineralogy, petrology, mineral resources, and ground water geology mainly of Tex. areas. Home: 2105 Meadowbrook, Austin, Tex. 78703. Died Oct. 5, 1960; buried Arlington Nat. Cemetery.

LOOKER, THOMAS HENRY rear admiral; b. Cincinnati, O., Nov. 2, 23, 1829; s. James H. and Rachel H. L.; ed. J.S. Naval Acad. and by tutors; m. Lucilia S. Brigham, Brigham, May 19, 1857. Apptd. midshipman to Naval Acad., Nov. 6, 1846; resigned Nov. 24, 1852; apptd. purser U.S.N., Aug. 31, 1853; promoted pay dir., Mar. 3, 1871; retired, June 29, 1906, with rank of rear admiral, for creditable services during Civil War. Asst. to Sec. of Navy, Mar. 16, 1877; in charge navy pay office, Washington, 1883-88; gen. insp. pay corps, 1889-90; p.m. gen. U.S.N., Mar.-May 1890. Home: Washington, D.C. Died 1910.

LOOMIS, ALFRED F(ULLERTON), (pseudonym Spun Yarn), author; b. Flatbush, New York, on August 23d, 1890; the son of Charles Battell and May Charlotte (Fullerton) L.; ed. pub. schs. and Mt. Pleasant Mil. Acad., Ossining, N.Y., 1906-07 (non-grad.); m. Priscilla Lockwood (Barnard, 1913), June 5, 1922; children—Alfred W., Robert L., Sarah W. (Mrs. Ward C. Campbell). Harvey B. Member of the editorial staff of Country Life (magazine), 1907-12; asso. editor Motor Boating, New York, 1913-17. Enlisted in U.S.N.R.F., May 6, 1917; assigned to Adriatic detachment of 110-foot sub.-chasers; commd. ensign, at Spalato, Dalmatia, December 12, 1918; commd. lieutenant commander, U.S.N.R., Jan. 17, 1941, comdr. Aug. 1942, capt. Nov. 1945. Navigated 28-foot yawl Hippocampus from New York to Panama and Pearl Islands, 1921; navigated 58-foot schooner, Pinta, in Transatlantic race for Queen of Spain's cup, 1928; navigated 61-foot schooner Brilliant to England, 1933, and the J-class cutter Yankee, 1935; known for long distance small-boat cruising and racing; lectr. yachting subjects. Clubs: Royal Ocean Racing, Lloyd's, Royal Thames, Ocean Cruising (England); Off Soundings, Los Angeles Yacht. Transpacific Yacht, Cruising of America, Cold Spring Harbor Beach; Coconut Grove Sailing, Cayman Yacht, The Windjammers; The Coffee House, The Century (New York); Royal Swedish Yacht. Author: The Cruise of the Hippocampus, 1922; Fair Winds in the Far Baltic, 1928; Hotspur's Cruise in the Aegean, 1931; Yachts Under Sail, 1933; Paradise Cove, 1933; Millions for Defense (with Herbert L. Stone), 1934; Ocean Racing, 1936, rev. 1946; Ranging the Maine Coast, 1939; The Hotspur Story, 1954; What Price Dory (with Chon Day), 1955; author (juveniles) The Sea Bird's Quest, 1923; The Bascom Chest, 1926; Walt Henley, D.S.M., 1927; Sea Legs, 1927; Walt Henley Overseas, 1928; Walt Henley, Skipper, 1929; Troubled Waters, 1929; Tracks Across the Sea, 1932; also contbr. mags. asso. editor Yachting, from 1934, Yachts and Yachting (Eng.), 1947-66. Lecturer. Home: New York City NY Died Mar. 26, 1968; buried Litchfield CT

LOOMIS, HAROLD FRANCIS, army officer; b. Rockville, Conn., June 19, 1890; s. Harry Merrifield and Mattie (McLean) L.; B.S., U.S. Mil. Acad., 1914; grad. Coast Arty. Sch., 1925, Command and Gen. Staff Sch., 1928, Ecole Superieure de Guerre, 1934, Army War Coll., 1939; m. Bessie Oler Kimberly, Sept. 8, 1915. Commd. 2d lt. Coast Arty. Corps, U.S. Army, 1914, advanced through grades to brig. gen. (temp.), Oct. 31, 1941; served on War Dept. Gen. Staff, 1939-41; with Allied Force Headquarters and Supreme Headquarters Allied Expeditionary Force. Clubs; Army and Navy (Washington, D.C.). Retired as brig. gen. Address: Washington DC Died Oct. 21, 1970; buried West Point NY

LOOMS, GEORGE author; b. Louisville, Ky., Nov. 22, 1886; s. George W. and Kate (Farrell) L.; B.Litt., Princeton, 1908; m. Laura C. Doub, May 17, 1921; 1 dau., Katherine. Dramatic critic Denver Express, 1922-23; music critic Rocky Mountain News, 1924; book editor same, 1925. Enslited in U.S. Army, Aug. 26, 1917; commd. 1st lt. Inf., Nov. 27, 1917; capt. Sept. 1918; no overseas service. Author: Stubble, 1922; John-no-Brown, 1933; The Caraways, 1925. Home: Denver, Colo. Died Dec. 24, 1926.

LOOPER, EDWARD ANDERSON otolaryngologist; b. Silver City, Ga., Dec. 16, 1888; s. John Anderson and Jennie (Stewart) L.; M.D., U. of Md., 1912; Emory U., 1908-10; Ophthal.D., U. of Colo., 1913; m. Lola Patenall, Jan. 15, 1920; children-Edward A., Lola Elise, Sybil Ann. Began practice as specialist in eye, ear, nose and throat, Baltimore, Md., 1913; prof. diseases of nose and throat, U. of Md., since 1921; laryngologist, Univ. Hosp. since 1921; surgeon, Baltimore Eye, Ear and Throat Hosp., since 1930; mem. exec. com. and mem. staff Woman's Hosp. since 1931; oto-laryngolist Md. State Sanatorium for Tuberculosis since 1922; otolaryngologist, Endowood Sanatorium for Tuberculosis since 1920; laryngologist, Md. Gen., St. Agnes, Franklin Square, West Baltimore Gen., and Nurses and Child's Hosps.; mem. staff, Union Memorial and Mercy Hosps.; cons. laryngologist Kernan Hosp. for Crippled Children; bronchoscopist and esophagoscopist, University Hosp. and U.S. Marine Hosp.; const. otolaryngologist, Provident Hosp.; otolaryngologist Baltimore City Hosps. for Tuberculosis, Edward McCready Memorial Hosp., Crisfield, Md.; and Havre de Grace Hosp., Md. Served as 1st lt. Med. Reserve Corps, U.S. Army, 1918; instr. and capt., Ft. Oglethorpe; in France 2 yrs.; maj., Med. Reserve Corps, Fellow Am. College Surgeons (mem. advisory council com. for otolaryngology); mem. American Bronchoscopic Society (vice-pres.), Am. Rhinol., Laryngol. and Otol. Soc., Am. Acad. Ophthalmology and Otolaryngology, Am. Laryngol. Assn., Internat. Coll. of Surgeons (past state regent) Med. and Chirurg. Faculty of Md., Baltimore City Med. Soc., Southern Med. Soc. (past councillor); asso. mem. Am. Coll. Chest Physicians. Democrat. Baptist. Clubs: Baltimore Country, Gibson Island Country. Author: The Diagnosis and Treatment of Laryngeal Tuberculosis, 1937; also about 30 articles related to subjects in specialty. Home: 504 Overhill Rd., Roland Park, Baltimore. Office: 104 W. Madison St., Balt. Died Jan. 14, 1953.

LORD, HERBERT MAYHEW army officer; b. Rockland, Me., Dec. 6, 1859; s. Sabin and Abbie (Swett) L.; A.B. from Colby Coll., Me., 1884, A.M. from same coll., 1889, LL.D., 1920; LL.D., Tufts Coll., 1929; m. Annie Stuart Waldo, Sept. 9, 1885. Newspaper work, and served as clerk, ways and means com. of Ho. of Rep., Washington, D.C., until 1898; apptd. maj. add. p.-m. vols., May 17, 1898; hon. discharged, May 7, 1901; capt. p.-m., U.S.A., Feb. 5, 1901; promoted through grades to brig. gen. U.S.A., July 15, 1919; retired June 30, 1922. Apptd. asst. to Maj. Gen. Goethals, title dir. of finance, Oct. 1918; chief of finance, U.S.A., July 1, 1920; served as Army Liberty Loan officer during World War; dir. Bur. of the Budget July 1, 1922-May 31, 1929. Awarded D.S.M., "for exceptionally meritorious and conspicuous service" as asst. to q.-m. gen. and as dir. of finance. Republican. Christian Scientist. Home: Washington, D.C. Died June 2, 1930.

LORD, JOHN NORTON food distbr.; b. Detroit, Aug. 18, 1910; s. Herbert Ivory and Mary (Norton) L.; grad. Hotchkiss Sch., 1930; student Princeton, 1930-33; m. Rhoda Newberry, Dec. 15, 1934; children-Charles Newberry, David Hill, Richard Stanton, Edith Norton. Dir. Lee & Cady, Detroit, 1935-, successively asst. treas., v.p. and treas., exec. v.p., 1935-52, pres., 1952-; dir. Temprite Products, 1937-; chmn. adv. bd. Nat. Bank of Detroit in Gross Pointe, Michigan 1955. Bank. Vice President of the Detroit area council, also member regional exec. bd., nat. exec. bd. Boy Scouts Am.; adv. com. United Found.; mem. bd. Vis. Nurse Assn.; trustee Grace Hosp.; pres. Mich. Hosp. Service (Blue Cross), 1954-. Served from lt. to lt. comdr. USNR, 1942-45. Clubs: Detroit Athletic, Detroit, Country of Detroit, Princton of Michigan (Detroit); Gross Pointe (Mich.); St. Clair Flats Shooting Company (Algonac, Mich.). Home: 235 Touraine Rd., Gross Pointe Farms 36, Mich. Office: Penobscot Bldg., 645 Griswold St., Detroit 26. Died June 19, 1962; buried Detroit.

LORD, JOHN PRENTISS surgeon; b. Dixon, Ill., Apr. 17, 1860; s. John L. and Mary Louise (Warner) L.; M.D., Rush Med. Coll., Chicago, 1882; post-grad. study, New York Post-Grad. Coll., 1886; m. Minnie L. Swingley, Oct. 20, 1886; children-Frances Louise, Upton Prentiss. Practiced at Creston, Ill., 1882-86; settled at Omaha, 1886; surgery, exclusively, 1893-; prof. anatomy, 1892, prof. surgery, 1893-1913, Creighton Med. Coll.; prof. orthopedic surgery, Med. Dept. U. of Neb., 1913-; orthopedic surgeon to Clarkson U., Methodist and St. Catherine's hosps.; attending orthopedic surgeon, Lord Lister Hosp.; chief surgeon of Neb. Orthopedic Hosp.; cons. orthopedic surgeon Convalescing Home for Crippled Children; dist. surgeon I.C. Railroad; cons. surgeon of C.,R.I.&P. Railway. Pres. Omaha Midwest Clin. Assn., 1935. Fellow Am. Coll. Surgeons; mem. numerous professional societies. Dir. Y.M.C.A. Maj. M.C., U.S.A.; chief instr. mil. orthopedic surgery, Med. Officers Training Camp. Ft. Riley, Kan., 1918. Conglist. Home: Omaha, Neb. Died Mar. 3, 1940.

LORD, KENNETH PRINCE army officer, ret.; b. Rockland, Me., Dec. 11, 1888; s. Brig. Gen. Herbert Mayhew and Annie Stuart (Waldo) L.; B.Sc., Tufts Coll., 1929; grad. Field Arty. Sch., Battery Officers' Course, 1922, advanced Course, 1928. Command and Gen. Staff Sch., 1930, Army Indsl. Coll., 1931; m. Helen Elizabeth Cooper, Sept. 6, 1913; children-Kenneth Prince, Herbert Mayhew II. Commd. 2d lt., Cavalry, U.S. Army, Dec. 30, 1911; transferred to Field Arty., July 1, 1920; promoted through grades to brig. gen., U.S. Army, Oct. 3, 1941; retired, 1946. Served with Punitive Expdn. in Mexico; participated in Aisne-Marne, St. Mihiel and Meuse-Argonne offensives and with Army of Occupation in Germany, World War I; chief of staff, Eastern Defense Comd., World War II. Awarded Silver Star Citation for Gallantry in action in Meuse-Argonne Offensive, 1918; Legion of Merit with Oak Leaf Cluster, and Army Commendation Ribbon. Rep. Christian Scientist. Mason. Home: Rockland, Me., Office: 100 Beech St., Rockland, Me. Died Apr. 28, 1957.

LORD, ROYAL BERTRAM ret. army officer, business cons.; b. Worcester, Mass., Sept. 19, 1899; s. Edgar Harold and Elena (Lupine) L.; B.S., Brown U., 1919; B.S., U.S. Military Academy, 1923; graduate Engineering Sch., Fort Belvoir, Va., 1924; M.S. in Engring., University of California, 1927; hon. LL.D., Brown University, 1946; married Elizabeth Richardson, June 7, 1928; 1 son, Willard Richardson. Served in U.S. Navy, World War; commd. 2d lt., U.S. Army, 1923, and advanced through the grades to maj. gen., 1944; served in Philippines, later comd. 2d Batn. 3d Engrs., Hawaii, 1923-26; asst. dist. engr. San Francisco, 1926; instr. engring., grad. mgr. athletics, in charge constrn., U.S. Mil. Acad., 1927-31; comd. co. A., 6th Engrs., Fort Lawton, Wash., 1931-33; asst. dist. engr. St. Louis, 1933-35; in charge constrn. and operations, Passamaquoddy Tidal Bay Power Project, Eastport, Me., 1935-36; coordinator of Resettlement Adminstrn. and chief engr. and coordinator of Farm Security Adminstrn., Washington, D.C. (detail from Army; in charge design constrn. of housing and farm structures, 100,000 bldgs.), 1936-38; comd. 2d Batn., 3d Engrs., Schofield Barracks, Hawaii, 1939, 9th Engrs. Squadron, Fort Riley, 1940; dep. dir., later dir., Bureau Pub. Relations, War Dept., 1941; chief of operations, Bd. Economic Warfare, Sept. 1941-Apr. 1942, asst. dir. since Apr.-Aug. 1942; assigned to E.T.O., later chief of staff for communications zone European Theater Operations, France, 1943-45; deputy chief of staff for Gen. Eisenhower, Feb. 1944 to May 1945; comdg. gen. for assembly area commd, France, redeployment of troops and material, 1945-; Theatre Gen. Bd., Versailles, France, 1945-46; ret.; now bus. cons. Awarded Legion of Merit, Bronze Star; officer, Legion of Honor, Croix de Guerre with Palm (France); Comdr. of the Bath (Brit.), Distinguished Service Medal. Awarded the Cross of Rhode Island as distinguished citizen of that state. Inventory of Lord portable steel emplacement and Lord portable military cableway, now in general use, U.S. Army. Orignator and mem. Com. on Cargo Planes for U.S. Govt.; mem. Lighter Than Air Transportation Com. Episcopalian. Clubs: Sleepy Hollow Country; Nat. Press, Army and Navy (Washington). Contbr. articles nat. mags. Made hon. citizen Reims, France, 1945; hon. mem. French Forces of the Interior, 1945. Home: Box 375, Rancho Santa Fe, Cal. 92067. Died Oct. 21, 1963.

LORD, WILLIAM PAINE governor; b. Dover, Del., 1838; A.B., Fairfield Coll., N.Y., 1860; LL.B., Albany Law Sch., 1866, Capt. 1st Del. Inf., Sept. 8, 1862; maj., Apr. 18, 1864; hon. mustered out of vol. service, June 26, 1865; 2d lt. 2d U.S. Arty., Sept. 4, 1867; resigned, May 28, 1868. Practiced law at Salem, Ore.; was city atty.; mem. Ore. Senate, 1878; justice Supreme Ct., 14 yrs.; gov. of Ore., 1895-99; E.E. and M.P. to Argentine Republic. 1899-1993. Republican. Home: Salem, Ore. Died 1911.

LOREE, JAMES TABER, corp. official; b. Logansport, Ind., Apr. 6, 1888; s. Leonor Fresnol and Jessie (Taber) L.; B.A., Yale, 1909; m. Miriam G. Collins, Mar. 23, 1927. Began as file clerk, K.C.S. Ry., 1909; became traveling auditor and chief travelling auditor, same road; signal department Pa. Lines west of Pittsburgh, 1910-11; head of party on constrn. and location S.P. Lines in Ore., Feb.-June 1911; chief tunnel insp. same rd., June-Sept. 1911; draftsman for construction engr. D.&H., at Colonie, N.Y., Sept.-Nov. 1911; spl. mission studying English railroad practices, Dec. 1911-June 1912; asst. div. engr., S.P. Co., 1912-13; with D.&H. Co. 1913-38, successively as asst. trainmaster, trainmaster to 1914, supt. Susquehanna div., 1914-15, asst. gen. supt. transportation, 1915-16, gen. mgr., 1917-23, became v.p. in charge of operation, 1923; officer or dir. many cos. Served as enlisted man, 2d lt., 1st lt. and capt. N.Y.N.G., 1915-17; maj., lt. col. and col. U.S. Army, 1917-20; served on Mexican border; later with 27th Div. and 80th Div. in France and as chief of staff Am. Mission, Interallied Mil. Mission to Hungary and as dep. U.S. commr. Decorated D.S.M. (U.S.); Legion of Honor and Croix de Guerre (French); Order Crown of Roumania; Order Crown of Italy; Order of Leopold (Belgian); Order of Simon Bolivar; Order of Danilo. Mem. Beta Theta Pi. Republican. Catholic. Clubs: University. Ft. Orange, Albany Country, Schuyler Meadows (Albany); Mohawk Golf (Schenectady); University, Yale (New York). Home: Albany NY Died Apr. 1973.

LORENZ, WILLIAM FREDERICK psychiatrist; b. N.Y. C.; Feb. 15, 1882; s. Herman and Elise (Kuenzlen) L.; student N.Y.U., 1898-99; M.D., Bellevue Hosp. Coll., 1903; m. Ada Holt, May 21, 1915; children-Adrian Holt Vanderveer, William Frederick, Thomas Holt, Paul Kuenzlen, Joseph Dean. Med. interne Gen. N.Y.C., 1903-05; med. staff Manhat . tan State Hosp., 1906-10; clin. dir. Wis. State Hosp., 1910-14; spl. expert, reserach investigation of Pellagra, USPHS, 1914-15; dir. Wis. Psychiat. Inst., 1915—; prof. psychiatry, U. Wis., 1915—. Pres. Wis. Service Recognition Bd., 1921-24; mem. Med. Council U.S. Vets.' Bur., 1923—; pres. Wis. State Bd. Control, 1923-25; pres. Wis. Rehabilitation Bd., 1925; chmn. State Bd. Mental Hygiene, 1938—. Served in Spanish-Am. War 7 mos., 1898; maj. in comd. Field Hosp. Co. 127; with 32d Div., A.E.F., 1919-19. Decorated D.S.M.; citation by Gen. Pershing. Mem. A.M.A., Am. Psychiat. Assn., Assn. Research in Newvous and Mental Diseases, Central Psychiat. Soc., Milw. Neuro-psychiat. Soc., Sigma Xi, Phi Alpha Sigma, Sigma Delta Chi, Alpha Omega Alpha. Republican. Mem. Christian Ch. Contbr. new remedies for treatment of syphilis of central nervous system (with Dr. A.S. Loevenhart), 1920-25. Notable work in promoting rehabilitation of disabled ex-service men; also investigations in use of carbon dioxide gas in treatment of psychoses. Col. M.C., Wis. N.G. and U.S. Res. Home: Route 2, Madison 5, Wis. Died Feb. 18, 1958; buried Forest Hill Cemetery, Madison.

LORING, CHARLES chief justice; b. Kinnickinnic, Wis., Nov. 26, 1873; s. Lyman and Eugenie (Hutchinson) L.; student State Tchrs. Coll., Moorhead, Minn., 1888-91, Phillips Exeter (N.H.) Acad., 1891-92; LL.B., U. Minn., 1898; m. Bertha Darrow, Oct. 3, 1900; children-Helen (Mrs. Charles B. Bryant), Genevieve; m. 2d, Frances Nye, Mar. 1, 1933. Law clk. C. A. Nye, Moorhead, 1899-1900, office Halvor Steenerson, Crookston, Minn., 1900-03; partner Steenerson & Loring, later Loring & Youngquist, Crookston, 1903-18; maj. judge adv. U.S. Army, Aug. 1918-June 1919, lt. col. judge adv., Oct. 1920-Nov. 1926, judge adv. Am. Forces in China, 1925-26; mem. Loring & Hougen, Crookston, 1926-30; Supreme Ct. commr., Minn., Aug.-Nov. 1930; justice Supreme Ct. commr., Minn., Nov. 1930-44, chief justice since Jan. 1944, chmn. Jud. Council, 1943-44. Mem. Am. and Minn. State bar assns. Republican. Unitarian. Mason. Home: 1598 Ridgewood Lane. Office: 223 State Capitol, St. Paul. Died Mar. 1961.

LORING, CHARLES GREELY dir. Museum of Fine Arts, Boston; b. Boston; s. Charles G. L.; grad. Harvard, 1818 (A.M.); m. Mary Hopkins. Commissioned capt., Dec. 1861; lt. col. and asst. insp. gen. 9th army corps, July 22, 1862; resigned July 1865; trustee Museum Fine Arts, 1873, exec. officer, 1876-. Fellow Am. Acad. Arts and Sciences. Breveted maj. gen. U.S. Volunteers. Died 1902.

LORING, WILLIAM WING army officer; b. Wilmington, N.C., Dec. 4, 1818; s. Ruben and Hannah (Kenan) L.; ed. Georgetown Coll. Commd. 2d lt., 2d Fla. Volunteers, U.S. Army, 1837; mem. Fla. bar; mem. Fla. Legislature, 3 years; capt. Mounted Rifles, 1846, maj., 1847, brevetted lt. col., 1847; commd. col. U.S. Volunteers, 1847, lt. col., 1848; commanded mil. dept. Ore., 1849-51; col. U.S. Army, 1856, commanded Dept. Mexico, 1860-61; resigned from U.S. Army, 1861, maj. gen., 1862; surrendered to Gen. Sherman, 1865; joined mil. service of Khedive of Egypt, 1st insp. gen. with rank brig. gen., in command defenses of Alexandria and all Egyptian coast, 1870, gen. of div.; decorated Egyptian orders Osman and Medjidie. Died N.Y.C., Dec.30, 1886.

LOTHROP, SAMUEL KIRKLAND anthropologist; b. Milton, Mass., July 6, 1892; s. William Sturgis Hooper and Alice (Bacon) L.; prep. end., Groton (Mass.) Sch.; A.B., Harvard, 1915, Ph.D., 1921; m. Rachel Warren, 1914; children-Samuel K., Joan, John Warren; married second, Eleanor Bachman, 1929; married third, Joy Mahler, 1958. Field work and exploration for Andover Mus., at Pecons, N.M., 1915; for Harvard U., in Puerto Rico, Guatemala and Honduras, 1915-17, Panama, 1933, 1940, 51; Cosa Rica, 1948, 49; for Carnegie Inst. in Guatemala, Yucatan, 1923; Guatemala, 1932-33; for Museum of American Indian, Heye Foundation, at Ketchipaun, New Mexico, and Central America, 1924; in Tierra del Fuego, Parana River, Argentina, Peru, 1924-25, Central America, 1926, Guatemala, 1928, Chile, 1929; in Peru for Institute of Andean Research, 1941-44; ret. curator Andean Archeol., Peabody Mus. Served as 2d lt., Military Intelligence Dept., U.S. Army, World War I. Recipient Kidder Medal for achievement Am. archaeology, 1957; Huxley Memorial Medal, 1960; Wenner-Gren Found. medal in archaeology, 1961. Honorary fellow of Royal Anthropol. Inst.; mem. Am. Anthorpological Assn., Wash. acad. Sci., Nat. Acad. Scis., Soc. of Cin., Soc. des Americanistes de Paris, Soc. Chilena de Historia Natural, Society for American Archaeology, A.A.A.S., Society Argentina de Antropologia; Society Georgrafica de Lima, Academia Panameña de Historia. Clubs: Union Boat (Boston, Massachusetts); Harvard (New York City). Author: Tulum, an Archaeological Study of Eastern Yucatan, 1924; Pottery of Costa Rica and Nicaragua, 1926; Pottery Types and Their Sequence in El Salvador, 1927; Indians of Tierra del Fuego, pub. 1928; Indians of the Paraná Delta, Argentina, published 1931; Atitlan, An Archaeological Study of the Borders of Lake Atitlan, Guatemala, 1933; Zacualpa, A Study of Quiché Artifacts, 1936; Coclé, an Archaeological Study of Central Panama, Part I, 1937, Part II, 1941; Inca Treasure as Depicted by Spanish Historians, 1938; Archaeology of Southern Veraguas, Panama, 1947; The Cenote of Sacrifice, Chichen Itza-Metals, 1951; (with Joy Mahler) Chancay Style Grave at Zapallan, Peru, 1957; (with Joy Mahler) Late Nazca Burial in Chaviña, Peru, 1957; (with F. J. Fosag and Joy Mahler) Pre-Colombian Art, 1957; Archaeology of the Diquis Delta Costa Rica, 1963. Home: 65 Partridge Lane, Belmont, Mass. Died Jan. 10, 1965.

LOTT, ABRAHAM GRANT, army officer; b. Gettysburg, Pa., June 21, 1871; s. Jacob and Joanna (Houghtlin) L.; grad. high sch., Abilene, Kan., 1889, U.S. Mil. Acad., 1896, Army Sch. of the Line, 1911, Army Staff Coll., 1912, Army War Coll., 1923; m. Clara Buel Mercur, 1897. Commd. additional 2d lt. cav., U.S. Army, June 12, 1896; advanced through grades to brig. gen., Dec. 20, 1927; retired June 30, 1935. Served on the Western plains, in Cuba, the Philippines, Panama, France and Hawaii. Awarded D.S.M. (U.S.). Club: Army and Navy (Washington). Address: 1510 W. Huisache Av., San Antonio 1 TX

LOUIS, ANDREW, educator; b. Bklyn., July 5, 1907; s. Rudolf and Julia (Jurgens) L.; Ph.B., Wesleyan U., Middletown, Conn., 1929; student U. Marburg (Germany), 1929-30; Ph.D., Cornell U., 1935; m. Virginia O'Dell Gooch, Mar. 23, 1940 (div. May 1965); children—Andrew David, Julia Caroline. Instr. German, Cornell U., 1932-34, Colgate U., 1934-37; from instr. to asst. prof. German, U. Tex., 1937-46; mem. faculty Rice U., 1946-67, prof. German, chmn. dept., 1947-61, dir. modern langs. labs., 1962-66; vis. prof. U. Houston, 1961, 65. Served to capt. USAAF, World War II. Decorated Bronze Star. Mem. Modern Lang. Assn. Am., S. Central Modern Lang. Assn. (exec. sec. 1966-67), Am. Assn. Tchrs. German, Houston Council Tchrs. Fgn. Langs., Houston Philos. Soc., Phi Beta Kappa, Delta Sigma Rho, Delta Phi Alpha, Sigma Nu. Episcopalian. Author: German Grammer: An Approach to Reading, 1954. Home: Houston TX Died Sept. 20, 1967; buried Veteran's Cemetery, Houston TX

LOUTTIT, CHAUNCEY MCKINLEY psychologist; b. Buffalo, N.Y., Oct. 9, 1901; s. William Henry and Susan (Bruman) L.; B.S., Hobart Coll., Geneva, New York, 1925; Ph.D., Yale Univ., 1928; married Laura Talcott, August 23, 1926; children-Robert Irving, Richard Talcott. Research fellow, Training Sch., Vineland, N.J., 1925; instr., Yale, 1925-28; research asso., psychol. clinic, U. of Hawaii, 1928-30; asst. prof., Ohio U., 1930-31; asst. prof. psychology, Indiana University, 1931-38; asso. prof., 1938-40; director psychological clinic, 1931-40; with United States Naval Medical School, 1940-41; asst. chief of psychology div., Office of Coordinator of Information, 1941-42; asst. officer in charge, quality control section, training div., Bureau of Naval Personnel, 1942-44; comdg. officer Naval Training Sch. (Indoctrination), Camp Macdonough, Plattsburgh, N.Y., Feb.-Oct., 1944; comdg. officer, service sch. command, Naval Training Center, Bainbridge, Md., 1944-45; prof. psychology, Ohio State University, 1945-46; dean of faculty, Sampson College, 1946-47; exec. dean, Galesburg Undergrad, Div., U. of Illinois, 1947-49, assistant to the provost 1949-54. Visiting professor University of Oregon, summer of 1937, Ohio State U., 1939; professor chairman department psychology, Wayne U., 1954—. Mem. Ind. Society Mental Hygiene (bd. dirs., 1939-41), Ind. State Conf. Social Work (bd. dirs., also exec. com., 1937-40). Fellow A.A.A.S., Am. Psychol. Assn. (mem. council, 1943-46); mem. Am. Assn. for Applied Psychology (exec. sec., 1940-42; pres., 1943; chmn. mil. psychology sect.), Phi Beta Kappa, Sigma Xi, Lambda Pi. Author: Bibliography of Bibliographies in Psychology, 1900-27, 1928; Handbook of Psychological Literature, 1933; Clinical Psychology, 1936, rev. edit., 1947. Editor: Directory of Applied Psychology, 1st edit., 1941, 2d edit., 1943; Psychological Abstracts, 1947; Professional Problems (with R. S. Daniel), 1953. Address: 631 W. Oakridge, Ferndale, Mich. Died May 24, 1956.

LOUTZENHEISER, JOE L. army officer; b. Canton, O., Feb. 5, 1899; s. Oren Henry and Mary Dora (Clay) L.; grad. U.S. Mil. Acad., 1924, Army Advanced Flying Sch., 1927, Air Corps Tactical Sch., 1937, Command and Gen. Staff Sch., 1938; m. Eleanor Cook, Aug. 15, 1931; 1 son, Joe L. Commd. 2d lt., cav., U.S. Army, 1924, advancing through the grades to brig. gen., 1944; chief, operational plans div. hdqrs., Army Air Forces since 1942. Home: 2420 16th St. N.W. Office: Hdqrs. Army Air Force, Washington, D.C. Missing after air crash in Guam, Oct. 7, 1945.

LOVE, ALBERT GALLATIN, med. officer U.S. Army; b. Trezevant, Tenn., July 31, 1877; s. Albert Gallatin and Rosa L. (Patton) L.; A.B., U. of Miss., 1899; M.D., Memphis Hosp. Med. Coll., 1904; hon. grad. and medalist, U.S. Army Med. Sch., Washington, D.C., 1906; grad. Advanced Course, same, 1927; D.P.H., Johns Hopkins U., 1928; grad. Advanced Course, U.S. Army Med. Field Service Sch., Carlisle Barracks, Pa., 1930; m. Alice T. Stone, Dec. 3, 1906; children—Alice Elizabeth, Rosa Margaret, Albert Gallatin. Contract surgeon U.S. Army, Sept. 22, 1905; 1st lt. M.C., June 20, 1906; promoted through grades to col., June 20, 1932; lt. col. (temp.), 1918-20; brigadier general (temp.), October 1940-June 1941; active duty, August 1941-March 1946; promoted to brig. general retired August 16, 1948. Fellow Am. Coll. Surgs.; mem. A.M.A., Assn. Mil. Surgeons, Delta Omega. Democrat. Presbyterian. Mason. Author: Physical Examination First Million Draft Recruits—Methods and Results (with Charles B. Davenport), 1919; Defects Found in Drafted Men (with same), 1920; Army Anthropology (with same), 1921; Medical and Casualty Statistics of the United States Army in the World War, 1925; War Casualties, Their Relation to Medical Service and Replacements, 1931; Physical Measurements—Their Relation to Health, 1932; The Geneva Red Cross Movement, European and

American Influence on Its Development, 1942; all Govt. publs. Home: 2709 Wisconsin Av., Washington 7 DC

LOVE, JAMES SPENCER textiles manufacturing exec.; b. Cambridge, Mass., July 6, 1896; s. James Lee and Julia (Spencer) L.; A.B., Harvard, 1917; m. Sara Elizabeth Love, Jan. 25, 1922 (div. 1940); children-James Spencer, Robert Lee, Richard, Julian; m. 2d, Martha Eskridge, July 23, 1944; children-Charles, Martin, Cornelia, Lela. Began as textile mfr., 1919; with Burlington Mills, Inc., since 1924; pres. Burlington Mills Corp. and affiliated mills, 1930-48, chmn. 1948-; chmn., pres. Burlington Industries, 1955-. Maj., inf., AEF, World War I; cited by Gen. Pershing "for exceptionally meritorious and conspicuous services." Dir. textile, clothing and leather bureau, W.P.B., Oct. 1943-Dec. 1944. Former pres. Nat. Rayon Weavers Assn.; former dir. N.C. Cotton Mfrs. Assn. Trustee U. N.C., Bus. Found. U. N.C., Davidson Coll. Mem. vis. com. N.C. State Coll., Harvard Grad. Sch. Bus. Adminstrn.; mem. bus. adv. council Dept. Commerce. Clubs: Harvard, River, University, Economic (New York City); Greensboro (North Carolina) Country; Everglades Club, Seminole, Bath and Tennis Club (Palm Beach); Metropolitan. Chevy Chase (Washington); Pinnacle (N.Y.C.). Home: 1610 Granville Rd. Office: 301 N. Eugene St., Greensboro, N.C. Died Jan. 1962.

LOVEJOY, JOHN MESTON, petroleum corp. executive; b. N.Y.C., July 1889; s. John F. and Abbie (Babson) L.; E.M., Columbia School of Mines, 1911; hon. D.Sc., Colby Coll., 1937; m. Leslie Mackintosh, Nov. 1920; children—Leslie (Mrs. John Scott Paine), John Stuart. Began business career as mining engineer; in oil business with Standard Oil Company, 1914, as geologist; v.p. and gen. mgr. Amerada Petroleum; was geologist Tex. Oil Co.; chmn. and pres. Seaboard Oil Co, of Del., 1930-54; director Drilling and Exploration Co., Inc. 1st lt., later capt. F.A., United States Army, 1917-19. Director, treasurer Nat. Multiple Sclerosis Society. Member American Inst. Mining and Metall. Engrs. (dir. and past pres.), Am. Petroleum Inst. (dir.), Am. Assn. of Petroleum Geologists, Nat. Petroleum Council. Clubs: University, Mining (New York); Round Hill, Indian Harbor Yacht (Greenwich); Petroleum (Dallas). Home: Greenwich CT Died Nov. 1968.

LOVEJOY, PHILIP ednl. adminstr., bus. exec.; b. Portland, Me., May 6, 1894; A.B., U. Mich., 1916, A.M., 1925; LL.D., Midwestern U. (Wichita Falls, Tex.), 1950; m. Marie Dole, May 1, 1918; children-Phyllis (Mrs. Richard Kurtzwell), Marjorie (Mrs. F. W. Stanton, Jr.). Tchr. math., Benton Harbor, Mich., 1916, tchr. sociology, econ., 1919-23; prin. high sch., Marshall, Mich., 1923-24, Mt. Clemens, Mich., 1924-27; asst. supt. pub. schs., Hamtramck, Mich., 1927-30; 1st asst. sec. Rotary Internat., 1930-42, sec. 1942-52; exec. dir. Children's Home Soc. of Fla., 1952-53; lectr., 1953-66. Mem. com. on relationships Nat. Boy Scouts Am. Served as 2d lt. 114th F.A., AEF, 1917-18; 1st lt., F.A. Officers Res. Corps., 1919-29. Hon. Chief Sermeroyet Nahnah Nermerdoeh Comanche Tribe, Okla., 1944. Recipient King Christian X Medal of Liberation (Denmark), 1946; Comendator "La Order al Mérito Bernardo O'Higgins" (Chile), 1952. Mem. Am. Ednl. Research Assn., Phi Beta Kappa, Phi Delta Kappa, Acolytes. Mason. Clubs: Rotary (past dir.), Chicago (Chgo.); Rotary (Daytona Beach, Fla.); Men's Educational. Contbr. articles ednl. jours., Rotarian mag. Home: 111 Dawn Dr., Ormond Beach, Fla. 32074. Office: First Nat. Bank Bldg., Utica, N.Y. Died June 29, 1966.

LOVELACE, WILLIAM RANDOLPH, II surgeon; b. Springfield, Mo., Dec. 30, 1907; s. Edgar Blaine and Jewell (Costley) L.; A.B., Washington U., St. Louis, Mo., 1930, M.D., Harvard, 1934; student (flight surgeon), Sch. of Aviation Medicine, Randolph Field, Tex., 1937; studied surgery in Europe (J. William White Scholarship), 1939; M.S. in Surg., U. Minn., 1939; m. Mary Moulton, Sept. 15, 1933 (dec.); 3 daus., Mary C., Sharon L., Jacqueline. Interne, Bellevue Hosp., N.Y.C., 1934-36; Fellow, Mayo Foundn. for Med. Edn. and Research, 1936-39; 1st asst. Dr. Charles W. Mayo, Mayo Clinic, 1939-40, asst. surgeon, 1940-41, chief of a surg. sect., Mayo Clinic, 1941-46. Maj. then col., A.A.F.; chief Aero Med. Lab., Wright Field, 1943-45; now col. Med. Res. Surg. staff, co-chmn. bd. govs., Lovelace Clinic, since 1946; mem. staff Bataan Meml. Meth. Hospital, St. Joseph's Hosp. and Sanatorium, Presbyn. Hosp. and Sanatorium, VA Hosp., Sandia Base Hosp (all at Albuquerque, N.M.), Los Alamos (New Mexico) Medical Center. Mem. board directors The Garrett Corporation. Medical officer, United States Public Health Service. Chmn. med. panel, Internat. Air Transport Association; mem. aviation med. panel Adv. Group for Aero Research and Development to NATO, 1952-64; mem. spl. com. space tech. NACA, 1957-59; chmn. flight medicine and biology com. Office Life Sci. Programs, 1958-61; spl. com. Life Scis. Project Mercury, 1959-63; sr. cons. NASA, 1963-64, dir. space medicine Manned Space Flight, 1964-; cons. or mem. adv. com. several airlines, univs., assns., other govt. agys. Trustee, pres. Lovelace Found. Mem. Edn. and Research; dir. Woodrow Wilson Rehabilitation Center Foundation, Incorporated, Fisherville, Virginia, 1960-64; trustee Aerospace Edn. Found., 1958-, chmn., 1961-64; trustee Air Force Academy Foundation, 1962-. Recipient Sci. award, Air Force Assn., 1959; spl. aerospace honor citation A.M.A., 1962 Boynton award Am. Astronautical Soc., 1962; Outstanding Achievement award U. of Minnesota, 1964. Diplomate Am. Bd. Surgery, Am. Bd. Aviation Medicine, Fellow Am. College Surgeons, Institute Aeronautical Sciences (1944), Aero Med. Assn. (pres. 1942-43); mem. A.M.A., Space Edn. Found., African Research Found., Air Force Assn. (past pres.), Conf. S. W. Found. (past pres.), other nat., state and spl. profl. sci. assns. and orgns. Clubs: Lotos (N.Y.C.); Univ. (Rochester, Minn.); Cosmos (Washington). Co-winner (with Dr. W. M. Boothby and Col. H. G. Armstrong) Collier Trophy Award, 1940; Jeffries Award, 1948. Awarded Flying Cross for exptl. parachute descent from 40,200 ft. Awarded Legion of Merit, Army Commendation Ribbon; Royal Order of Sword, First Class (Sweden). Awarded Air Medal and 3 combat stars. Home: 2815 Ridgecrest Dr. S.E. Office: Lovelace Clinic, 5200 Gibson Blvd. S.E., Albuquerque 87108. Died Dec. 12, 1965.

LOVELL, ALFRED HENRY educator; b. Hamilton, Ont., Can., July 13, 1884; s. Henry Theodore and Emma (Reinbolt) L.; student Niagara Falls Collegiate Inst., 1900; B.S. in E.E., U. Mich., 1909; M.S. in E.E., 1914; m. Grace Gibson, Sept. 3, 1913; children-Alfred Henry, Robert Gibson. Identified with various engring. cos., U.S., Can., 1900-11; with U. Mich. since 1911, successively instr. in elec. engring., asst. prof. and asso. prof. until 1919, prof. since 1919, asst. dean Coll. Engring. 1930-44 and sec., 1933-44; chmn. dept. elec. engring. since 1945; also served as designing, valuation or investigation engr. for various corps., U.S. and abroad, Officer entrs. U.S. Army, May 1917-Jan. 1919; served at Fort Sheridan, Fort Leavenworth, Camp Custer, and with 310th Engrs. in Eng., France, and as col. 3d Engr. Tng. Regt., Camp Humphreys, Va. Fellow Am. Inst. E.E. (dir. 1932-36, v.p. 1938-40); mem. Engring. Soc. Detroit (sec., dir. 1941-43); Am. Soc. for Engring. Edn., Sigma Xi, Tau Beta Pi, Phi Kappa Phi. Episcopalian. Clubs: University, Ann Arbor Golf. Author: Generating Stations-Economic Elements of Electrical Design, 1930, 4th edit., 1951. Home: 3000 Geddes Av., Ann Arbor, Mich. Died Oct. 26, 1960.

LOVELL, JOSEPH physician, army officer; b. Boston, Dec. 22, 1788; s. James and Deborah (Gorham) L.; A.B., Harvard, 1807, M.D., 1811; m. Margaret Mansfield, 11 children including Mansfield. Surgeon, 4th Infantry, U.S. Army, 1812-14; dir. U.S. Army Hosp., Williamsvile, N.Y., 1814-17; chief med. officer No. dept. U.S. Army, 1817; surgeon gen. U.S. Army, 1818-36, head new Army med. dept. Died Oct. 17, 1836.

LOVETTE, LELAND PEARSON, ret. naval officer, author; b. Greeneville, Tenn., Dec. 11,21897; s. Oscar Byrd and Lillie (Fowler) L.; student Tusculum Coll., 1913-14; B.S., U.S. Naval Acad., 1917; certificate Naval War Coll., 1928; student Georgetown U. Sch. Fgn. Service, 1928-29; student langs. Berlitz and Sanz schs.; LL.D., Tusculum College, 1959; m. Charmian K. Brietson, May 26, 1925. Commissioned ensign USN, 1917, advanced through grades to vice admiral; served on staffs commander mine force, commander battle ship divisions, commander battle force, comdr.-in-chief Asiatic fleet; commander subchasers, mine-sweeper, gunboats, destroyers and battle cruiser, World War II; officer charge pub. relations Navy Dept., 1937-40; comdg. squadron leader and destroyer div., 1940; dir. pub. relations USN, 1942-44; chief of United States Naval Mission to Brazil, 1946-48; ret., 1949; dir. pub. relations Vets. Fgn. Wars, 1949-55, cons. Pres. United Cerebral Palsy chpt. Washington; mem. sr. bd. govs. U.S.O., Washington. Trustee Jackson Meml. Lab. for Cancer Research. Decorated Legion of Merit (2); Order Brit. Empire; grand officer Naval Merit (Brazil); Medal Merite Combattant (France); recipient gold medal U.S. Naval Inst.; nat. citation Veterans of Foreign Wars, United Cerebral Palsy. Member Presbyn. Ch. Clubs: New York Yacht (N.Y.C.); Army-Navy (Manila, P.I.); Army-Navy, Cosmos, Nat. Press (Washington); Friends of Lafayette. Author: Naval Customs, Traditions and Usage, 1934; School of the Sea; Annapolis Tradition in American Life, 1941, also numerous articles. Home: Alexandria, VA Died July 10, 1967; buried Arlington Nat. Cemetery.

LOVINS, WILLIAM THOMAS judge; b. Wayne County, W.Va., Aug. 27, 1887; s. James Harvey and Josephine (Sink) L.; LL.B., Washington and Lee U., 1914; m. Grace Huff, Dec. 31, 1925 (dec.); 1 s., Walter McCallister. Admitted to W.Va. bar, 1914; practiced law Wayne Co., 1914-17, Huntington, W.Va., 1919-41; dir. First Nat. Bank, Kenova, 1930-40, pres. 1935-40; judge Supreme Court of Appeals of the State of W. Va. since Jan. 1, 1941. Served as 2d lt. and capt., U.S. Army, 1917-18. Chmn. State Judicial Council, State Army Adv. Com. Mem. Am., W. Va. assns., Reserve Officers Assn., Am. Legion, Delta Theta Pi, Brotherhood of R.R. Trainmen. Democrat. Baptist. Mason, Elk. Home: 1565 Virginia St. E. Office: State Capitol, Charleston, W.Va. Died Dec. 11, 1957.

LOW, BENJAMIN ROBBINS CURTIS lawyer, author; b. Fairhaven, Mass., June 22, 1880; s. William Gilman and Lois Robbins (Curtis) L.; B.A., Yale, 1902; LL.B., Harvard, 1905; m. Virginia Wagner, Feb. 15, 1922; children-Caroline Davison, Malcolm Scollay. Began practice at New York, 1905; mem. Hoes, Low & Miller, 1923-28; gen. counsel Home Life Ins. Co. Commd. capt. O.R.C., July 12, 1917; maj. U.S.A., Feb. 18, 1918; served at Washington, D.C., equipment and procurement divs., Ordnance Dept.; hon. disch. Dec. 20, 1918. Republican. Episcopalian. Author: The Pursuit of Happiness, 1919; Broken Music, 1920; Darkening Sea, 1925; Winged Victory, 1927; To the Funeral Pyre of Shelley, 1929; Roland, 1930; Child on Bronze Horse, 1931; Off Soundings, 1932; King Philip, 1933; Brooklyn Bridge, 1933; Turn of the Road, 1933; Seth Low (biography), 1925; Symphony in D Minor, 1937. New York, N.Y. Died June 22, 1941.

LOW, FRANCIS STUART naval officer; b. Albany, N.Y., Aug. 15, 1894; s. William Franklin and Anna (Stuart) L.; B.S., U.S. Naval Acad., 1915; m. Andrena LeMassena, Jan. 10, 1918; 1 son, John Stuart; m. 2d, Alice Regua Filmer, July 16, 1949. Commd. ensign, 1915, advanced through grades to rear adm., 1942, vice adm., 1947; apptd. to conduct spl. survey of U.S. Navy's anti-submarine program; dep. chief naval operations (logistics) 1951-54; comdr. Western Sea Frontier, 1953-. Awarded campaign medals and decorations. Club: Army and Navy (Washington). Address: Bur. Naval Personnel, Navy Dept., Washington. Died Jan. 1964.

LOWE, CLEMENT BELTON physician; b. Salem, N.J., Apr. 30, 1864; s. Samuel and Harriet Newell (Belton) L.; Ph.B., Bucknell U., 1865; student Poly. Coll., Phila.; Ph.G., Phila. Col. Pharmacy, 1884; M.D., Jefferson Med. Coll., 1887; m. at Phila., Abbie A. Allen, of Bridgeport, N.J., Mar. 17, 1869. Mem. Co. A, 28th Pa. Militia (U.S.V.), 1863; mounted orderly sergt. attached to Gen. Couch's staff, 1864. After war engaged as pharmacist; physician, since 1887; prof. materia medica, Phila. Coll. Pharmacy, since 1885. Pres. Pa. Pharm. Assn., 1907-08; 1st v.p. Am. Pharm. Assn., 1909-10; prs. Alumni Assn. Phila. Coll. Pharmacy; mem. Phi Kappa Psi. Independent Republican. Baptist; pres. Bapt. S.S. Supts. Assn., 1895-96. Author: Syllabus Botanical Natural Orders, 1892. Editor: Plants of the Philippines, 1901. Home: 150 E. Washington Lane. Office: 145 N. 10th St., Philadelphia.

LOWE, FRANK E., army officer; b. Springfield, Mass., Sept. 20, 1885; s. George and Mary (Jackson) L.; B.S., Worcester (Mass.) Poly. Inst., 1908; m. Rachel Lowell, Nov. 22, 1911. Veteran of World Wars I and II. Maj. gen Officers Res. Corps. Mem. Reserve Officers Assn. of U.S. Am. Legion, Phi Gamma Delta. Clubs: Cumberland (Portland, Me.); Army and Navy (Washington, D.C.). Address: Harrison ME Died Dec. 27, 1968; buried Hope Cemetery, Worcester MA

LOWE, JOHN naval officer; b. Liverpool, Eng., Dec. 11, 1838; s. John and Mary (Blinston) L.; ed. Liverpool and Columbus, O.; studied engring.; m. Josephine L., d. George B. Dyer of Washington, Nov. 5, 1867. Enlisted pvt. 2d Ohio Regt., 1861 (No. 15 on Ohio's roll); apptd. to U.S.N., Aug. 1861, by Hon. S. S. Cox, M.C.; wounded in 1st battle Bull Run; served through Civil, Corean and Spanish wars; mem. Greely Relief Expdn., 1884, and on various stas. and duties in peace times; in 1898 was 1st naval officer of any nationality to have submarine service in submarine torpedo boat, and made 1st report ever presented to sec. of the navy upon that topic; retired, Dec. 11, 1900. In Oct. 1901, participated in decisive experiment, with 6 other men, in a submarine torpedo boat, submerged to the bottom of Peconic Bay for 15 hours. Medal conferred by Act of Congress for "meritorious service." Home: Washington, D.C. Died Aug. 18, 1930.

LOWE, THOMAS MERRITT army officer; b. Buena Vista, Ga., Mar. 2, 1901; s. Marcus L. Sr., and Ida (Merritt) L.; student N.Ga. Agr. Coll., 1917-19; B.S., U.S. Mil. Acad., 1923; grad. Air Corps Tactical Sch., 1936, Command and Gen. Staff Sch., 1940; m. Etta W. Edwards, Mar. 26, 1926. Commd. 2d lt., U.S. Army, 1923, advanced through grades to brig. gen., 1945; served with hdqrs. Army Air Forces, 1941-43; dep. chief of staff 8th Air Force, 1943-44; dep. chief of staff Army Air Forces, M.T.O., Jan. 1944-Sept. 1945; comdg. gen., Lowry Field, Denver, Nov. 1945-May 1947; comdg. gen. Westover Field, Mass., 1947-48; ret., June 30, 1948. Decorated Legion of Merit, Bronze Star. Mem. Pi Kappa Alpha. Home: 301 30th Av. N., St. Petersburg, Fla. 33704. Died Sept. 23, 1962.

LOWEN, CHARLES JULES, JR. govt. ofcl.; b. Denver, June 15, 1915; s. Charles J. and Bernice T. (Duffy) L.; student U. Colo., 1934-38; m. Helen Muriel Stokes; children-Carol M., Barbara E., Charles S., Ellen C. Propr. base operation for chartering and selling of aircraft 1938-42; dir. overseas, asst. dir. domestic operations, Capital Airlines, 1946-48; dir. aviation City and County of Denver, 1948-51, mgr. safety and excise, 1954; dealer automobiles, Lowen-Thomson-Brown, Denver, 1951-54; dep. adminstr. CAA, 1955, adminstr., 1955—. Served as maj. USAAF, 1942-45; exec. officer Air Transport Command Group. Mem. Am. Legion, Vets. Fgn. Wars, Chi Psi. Clubs: Denver, Denver Country, Denver Athletic, Mile Hi, Cactus, Press (Denver); Nat. Aviation (Washington). Home: 2630 E. Cedar Av., Denver; also 4801 Dexter Terrace,

Washington. Office: Civil Aero. Adminstrn., 16th and Constitution Av., Washington 24. Died Sept. 5, 1956; buried Mt. Olivet Cemetery, Denver.

LOWER, WILLIAM EDGAR surgeon; b. Canton, O., May 6, 1867; s. Henry and Mary (Deeds) L.; M.D., Western Reserve U., Med. Dept., 1891; m. Mabel Freeman, Sept. 6, 1909; 1 dau., Mary. Practiced in Cleveland since 1892; asso. surgeon, Lakeside Hosp., 1910-31; attending surgeon, Lutheran Hosp. since 1896; dir. surgery, Mt. Sinai Hosp., 1916-24; asso. prof. genito-urinary surgery, Western Reserve U., 1910-1931. A founder, dir. Cleveland Clinic Foundation since 1921; surgeon Cleveland Clinic Hosp. since 1924. Acting asst. surgeon. U.S. Army, in the Philippines, 1900; maj. Med. Reserve Corps, 1917; asst. surg. dir. Lakeside Base Hosp. Unit, U.S. Army, in service with B.E.F. in France, May-Dec. 1917, comdg. officer, Dec. 1917-May 1918; lt. col., June 1918. Mem. Am. Urol. Assn. (pres. 1914-15). Am. Assn. Genito-Urinary Surgeons (pres. 1922), Ohio State Med. Soc. (pres. 1915), Acad. of Medicine, Cleveland (pres. 1909-10), Clin. Soc. of Genito-Urinary Surgeons (pres. 1922), Interurban Surg. Soc. (pres. 1926-27), Soc. of Clin. Surgery, Société Internationale de Cirurgie Urologie; fellow A.M.A., Am. Surg. Assn., Am. Coll. Surgeons, Southern Surgical Assn. Club: Union. Author: Anoci-Association (Crile and Lower), 1914; Surgical Shock and the Shockless Operation through Anoci-Association, 2d edit., 1920; Reontgenographic Studies of the Urinary System (Lower and Nichols), 1933. Home: 12546 Cedar Rd., Cleveland Heights, O. Office: Cleveland Clinic, Euclid at E. 93d St., Cleveland. Died June 17, 1948.

LOWNDES, CHARLES HENRY TILGHMAN, physician, naval officer (ret.); b. Baltimore, Md., July 7,21866; s. Dr. Charles and Mary Catherine (Tilghman) L.; student Johns Hopkins U.; M.D., U. of Md.; m. Mary Lucien Baker, Feb. 21, 1900; 1 son, Charles Lucien. Began as physician, 1888; entered in service of Med. Corps, U.S. Navy, as asst. surgeon, 1889, advanced through various grades to appt. as rear adm., Med. Dept., 1919; retired, 1929. Democrat. Catholic. Club: Army and Navy (Washington). Author: Reports on Results of Indian Conditions on Various Reservations; contbr. articles to med. publs. Home: Easton, Md. Office: The Fairfax, Washington DC*

LOWRY, FRANK J(ACOB) ret. naval officer; b. Cresco, Ia., Feb. 15, 1888; s. Jacob John and Jennie (Mullen) L.; student St. Johns Mil. Acad., Delafield, Wis., 1905-06; B.S., U.S. Naval Acad., 1911; Naval War Coll., 1925-26; m. Julia Kessel, Dec. 18, 1940. Promoted through grades to vice adm., 1950, ret.; served with task force participating in Battle of Coral Sea, Battle of Midway; comd. Moroccan Sea Frontier Forces, 1943, later the 8th Amphibious Forces at Anzio (Italy) and Toulon (France) landings; also participated in Operations Crossroads, the first test of the atom bomb at Bikini atoll. Decorated Navy Cross, D.S.M., Legion of Merit and Gold Star (U.S.); Campanion Order of the Bath, Oak Leaf (British); Legion of Honor, Croix de Guerre with Palms (French); Grand Officer, Ouissam Alaouite Cherifien (Morocco); Grand Officer, Nichan Iftikar (Tunisia). Campaign medals: Nicaraguan (1912), Mexican, Victory, American Defense, Asiatic-Pacific, European-African, American. Clubs: Army and Navy (Washington), Columbia Country (Chevy Chase, Md.). Mason (K.T.). Home: 5134 Coombsville Rd., Napa, Cal. Died Mar. 27, 1955.

LUBBOCK, FRANCIS RICHARD gov. of Texas; b. Beaufort, S.C., Oct. 16, 1815; s. Henry W. and Susan Ann (Saltus) L.; ed. Beaufort and Charleston, S.C.; m. Adele Baron, Feb. 5, 1835; 2d, Mrs. A. A. Porter, nee Sarah E. Black, Dec. 1883; 3d, Lue Scott, Aug. 12, 1903. Began mercantile life quite young; went to Texas, 1836; has held offices of comptroller and other offices under republic of Texas; lt. gov., 1856, and gov. of Texas, 1861-63 (and known as the "War Governor"); state treas. for 12 yrs.; has held other offices under the state govt. Democrat. After term as gov. entered C.S.A.; was lt. col. and col. cav.; a.d.c. to President Davis; captured with him; imprisoned at Ft. Delaware nearly 8 months in solitary confinement. Author: Six Decades in Texas, Austin, 1900. Home: Austin, Tex. Died 1905.

LUCAS, JIM GRIFFING, reporter; b.Checotah, Okla., June 22, 1914; s. Jim Bob, Jr., and Effie Lincoln (Griffing) L.; student U. Mo., 1932-33. Reporter, feature writer Muskogee (Okla.) Daily Phoenix and Times-Democrat, 1934-38; news broadcaster, sta. KBIX, Muskogee, 1936-38; reporter, feature writer Tulsa Tribune, 1938-42; Marine combat corr. battles Guadalcanal, New Georgia, Russell Islands, Tarawa, Saipan, Tinian, Iwo Jima, 1942-45; corr. Scripps-Howard Newspaper Alliance Washington, 1945-70. 1st lt. USMC, World War II. Decorated Bronze Star. Recip. Nat. Headliners award best combat reporting, 1943; George Polk Meml. award, 2 Ernie Pyle awards, Omar Bradley Gold Medal; Pulitzer Prize; Korean Nat. Medal; Marine Corps Res. Officers Assn. award; 1st annual Fourth Estate award Am. Legion, 1958; First Annual Mark Watson award, 1968. Mem. Amvets (charter mem.), White House Corrs. Assn., Assn. U.S. Army, Nat. Headliners, Air Force Association, Sigma Delta Chi. Methodist. Clubs: Nat. Press (Washington); Overseas Press. Author: Combat Correspondent, 1944; Battle for Tarawa (with Capt. Earl J. Wilson, Sgts. Samuel Shaffer, Cyril Peter Zurlinden), 1944; Dateline-Vietnam, 1966. Home: Alexandria VA Died June 1970.

LUCAS, JOHN PORTER army officer; b. Kearneysville, W.Va., Jan. 14, 1890; s. Charles Craighill and Francis Thomas (Craighill) L.; B.S., U.S. Mil. Acad., West Point, N.Y., 1911; attended The Field Artillery Sch., 1920-21, advanced course, 1922-23, Command and Gen. Staff Sch., 1923-24; M.S., Colorado State Coll., 1927; student Army War Coll., 193132; m. Sydney Virginia Wynkoop, Aug. 23, 1917; children-John Porter, Jr., Mary Brooke. Commd. 2d lt., Cav., 1911, advanced through ranks to maj. gen., (temp.), 1941; maj. (temp.), Signal Corps, 1918, trans. to Field Artillery, 1920; assigned to command 3d Inf. Div., Fort Lewis, Wash., July 1941; later made comdg. gen. 3d Army Corps. Served with 7th U.S. Army as personal rep. of C. in C. (General Eisenhower) with combat troops during Sicilian Campaign, July-August, 1943; commanded II Corps in Sicily, Sept., 1943; comd. VI Corps during Italian Campaign Sept., 1943, to Feb. 1944; later comdr. Fort Sam Houston to July 1945. Awarded D.S.M. with oak leaf cluster, D.S.M. (Navy), Silver Star, and Order of The Purple Heart, Order of Saints Maurice and Lazarus. Mason (K.T.). Episcopalian. Home: Charlestown, W. Va. Died Dec. 24, 1949.

LUCAS, SCOTT WIKE ex-U.S. senator; b. Chandlerville, Ill., Feb. 19, 1892; s. William D. and Sarah Catherine (Underbrink) L.; B.L., Ill. Wesleyan U., 1914; m. Edith Biggs, 1 son, Scott W. Admitted to Ill. bar, 1915 and began practice at Havana; state's atty. of Mason County 1920-25; chmn. Ill. State Tax Commn., 1933-35; mem. 74th to 75th Congresses (1935-39), 20th Ill. Dist.; elected to U.S. Senate, Nov. 8, 1938, for term ending Jan. 3, 1945; reelected Nov., 1944; elected minority whip of the Senate, Jan., 1947; elected majority leader of the Senate. Jan. 1949. Entered U.S. Army as pvt., World War I, discharged as lt.; in O.R.C., 1918-34, judge advocate gen. Ill. N.G., 1934-42. Comdr. Am. Legion, Dept. Ill., 1926; nat. judge advocate, Am. Legion, for 4 terms. Delegate Democratic Nat. Convention, 1932, 1940, 1944,1 1944, 1948 and 1952. Chmn. of Midwestern Regional Headquarters of Dem. Nat. Com., 1940. Was one of three members of the delegation representing the U.S. at the Refugee Conference, Bermuda, Apr. 1943. Democrat. Home: Havana, Ill. Offices: 1025 Connecticut Av., Washington 6; 231 S. LaSalle St., Chgo. 4; Myers Bldg., Springfield, Ill. Died Feb. 22, 1968; buried Havana, Ill.

LUCAS, THOMAS JOHN army officer; b. Lawrenceburg, Ind.; Sept. 9, 1826; s. Frederick and Letitia (Netherly) L.; ed. Lawrenceburg, Ind.; m. Ann Eliza Munson, Sept. 24, 1848. Learned jewelry trade with father and engaged in business. Served, pvt. to adj., Co. C, 4th Ind. vols., in Mexican war, participating in battles of Broken Bridge. Cerro Gordo, Huamantha, Ecliso, Pueblo, etc. In Civil war helped raise 2 cos.; raised 3d, becoming capt.; col. 16th Ind. vols., which met Kirby Smith at Richmond, Ky., losing 200 men; fought under Grant in all the operations about Vicksburg; regt. joined 13th army corps and captured Arkansas Post; later took part in all battles in and around Vicksburg until surrender; promoted brig. gen. and entered on Mobile campaign; bvtd. maj. gen., and at head of independent command, under Canby, raided Western Fla., Ga. and Ala., destroying railroads and munitions of war; after war in New Orleans until mustered out, Jan. 1866. Was in internal revenue service 4 yrs.; postmaster of Lawrenceburg, 1881-85, 1889-93; was candidate for Congress, 1886, defeated. Republican. Home: Lawrenceburg, Ind. Deceased.

LUCE, HARVEY GARDNER business exec.; b. Grand Rapids, Mich., Sept. 10, 1900; s. Hiram Gardner and Belle (Parsons) L.; student U. Mich., 1919-21; m. Lois Wickerts, Aug. 13, 1926. Joined MacManus, John & Adams, Inc., 1935, exec. v.p., 1947—, also asst. to pres. Served as maj. M.I. Div. WDGS, 1944-45. Home: Box 163. Office: MacManus, John & Adams, Inc., Bloomfield Hills, Mich. Died Nov. 24, 1955.

LUCE, HENRY ROBINSON editor, pub.; b. Am. parentage, Shantung Province, China, Apr. 3, 1898; s. Henry Winters and Elizabeth Middleton (Root) L.; prep. edn., Hotchkiss Sch., Lakeville, Conn.; B.A., Yale, 1920, hon., M.A., 1926; studied Oxford U., Eng.; hon. LL.D., Rollins, 1938, Grinnell, 1942; Colgate, 1948; Litt.D., Boston U., 1941, Syracuse U., 1945, Rutgers U., 1949, U. Ariz, 1961; L.H.D., Hamilton, 1942; H.H.D., Coll. Ida., 1951, Coll. of Wooster, 1962; LL.D., Lafayette, 1952; Dir. Journalism, Temple U., 1953; LL.D., Occidental Col., 1954, St. Louis U., 1955, Springfield Coll., 1962, Adelphi U., 1963, Williams Coll., 1965, Yale, 1966, also Westminster College (posthumously), 1967; m. Lila Hotz, Dec. 22, 1923; children-Henry III, Peter; m. 2d, Clare Boothe Brokaw (writer), Nov. 23, 1935. Founder (with Briton Hadden) of Time, 1923; founder Fortune, 1930, Life, 1936; Sports Illus., 1954; editor-in-chief Time, Life, Fortune, Archtl. Forum, Sports Illustrated, House & Home until 1964, editorial chmn. 1964-67; dir. Time, Inc. Organized United China Relief, 1940; initiated Commn. on Freedom of Press, 1944. Dir. Union Theol. Sem.; mem. United Bd. Christian Higher Edn. in Asia; trustee China Inst. in Am., Am. Heritage Found., Met. Mus., Roosevelt Hosp. Served as 2d lt. F.A., U.S. Army, World War I. Decorated Chevalier Legion of Honor (French), 1937; Order of Auspicious Star (China), 1947; Comdr. Order of Orange-Nassau (Netherlands); Comdr., Order of Cedars of Lebanon; Comdr. Royal Order George I (Greece); Comdr.'s Cross Order Merit (Fed. Republic of Germany); Henry Johnson Fisher award Mag. Pubs. Assn., 1965. Mem. N.Y. C. of C., Phi Beta Kappa, Omicron Delta Kappa, Alpha Delta Phi. Presbyterian. Clubs: University, Cloud, Yale, Union, Racquet and Tennis, Century Assn., Links, River (N.Y.C.); Chicago. Home: N.Y.C. Office: Time & Life Bldg., Rockefeller Center, N.Y.C. Died Feb.28, 1967.

LUCE, STEPHEN BLEECKER rear admiral; b. Albany, N.Y., Mar. 25, 1827; s. Vinal and Charlotte (Bleecker) L.; apptd. midshipman from N.Y., Oct. 19, 1841; served on many stations and circumnavigated the globe; served on the Pacific coast during Mexican War; went to Naval Acad. for promotion to passed midshipman, 1848; promoted master, Nov. 15, 1855; lt., Sept. 16, 1855; lt. comdr., July 16, 1862; comdr., July 25, 1866; capt., Dec. 28, 1872; commodore, Nov. 25, 1881; rear admiral, U.S.N., Oct. 5, 1885. During Civil War was lt. of frigate Wabash, comdr. of monitor Natucket and the double-ender Sonoma, the Canandaigua and the Pontiac; served in N. Atlantic Blockading Squadron; in active service after war until retired, Mar. 25, 1889. Founded Naval War Coll., 1884; was mainly instrumental in establishment of naval training system. Commr. gen., Columbian Hist. Expn., Madrid, 1892. Author: Naval Songs, 1889; Seamanship, 1898, 1905. Home: Newport, R.I. Died July 28, 1917.

LUDEWIG, JOS(EPH) W(ILLIAM) ret. naval officer, educator; b. Washington, June 2, 1904; s. Joseph Gottlieb and Louise (Zimmerman) L.; B.S., U.S. Naval Acad., 1925; M.S., Carnegie Inst. Tech., 1933; student, U.S. Naval Postgrad. Sch., 1931-32, 33-34; m. Minerva Lorraine Damon, May 12, 1928. Commd. ensign U.S. Navy, 1925, and advanced through grades to rear adm., 1947; served in cruisers, destroyers, gunboats, battleships and on U.S. Fleet and Task Force staffs; combat duty Nicaraguan campaign, 1928, and World War II; progress officer, U.S. Naval Gun factory, Washington, 1943-44; ret. as rear adm., Jan. 1, 1947; asso. prof. dept. metal engring., Carnegie Inst. Tech., 1947—. Awarded Legion of Merit combat order, (twice), Bronze Star (combat), Pacific and World War II campaign medals, Nicaraguan campaign medal. Mem. U.S. Naval Inst., Am. Soc. Engring. Edn., Am. Soc. Metals, Order World Wars, Phi Kappa Phi. Republican. Episcopalian. Clubs: Army-Navy Country (Washington), Butler Country, Univ. (Pitts.). Home: Stonecrest, Middle Rd., Glenshaw, Pa. Office: Carnegie Inst. of Technology, Pitts. Died Mar. 17, 1958.

LUDINGTON, MARSHALL INDEPENDENCE major general; b. Smithfield, Pa., July 4, 1839; s. Zalmon and Lovila (Hagans) L.; m. Harriet Foote Marvin, Oct. 18, 1871. Commd. capt. asst. q.m. vols., Oct.20, 1862; maj. q.m., Aug. 2-Oct. 23, 1864; col. q.m., Oct. 24, 1864-Jan. 1, 1867; bvtd. maj., lt. col. and col. vols., Mar. 13, 1865, "for faithful and meritorious services during the war," and brig. gen. vols., Mar. 13, 1865, and lt. col. U.S.A., Mar. 2, 1867, "for faithful and meritorious services in q.m. dept. during the war." Apptd. from Pa., maj. q.m. U.S.A., Jan. 18, 1867; lt. col. deputy q.m. gen., Mar. 15, 1883; col. asst. q.m. gen., Dec. 31, 1894; brig. gen. q.m. gen., Feb. 3, 1898; maj. gen., Apr. 12, 1903; retired at own request after 40 yrs.' service, Apr. 13, 1903. Home: Skaneateles, N.Y. Died July 29, 1919.

LUDLOW, HENRY HUNT army officer; b. Easton, Pa., Apr. 15, 1854; s. Dr. Jacob Rapelyea and Ann Mary (Hunt) L.; grad. U.S. Mil. Acad., 1867, torpedo course, Willet's Point, N.Y., 1885, Arty. Sch., 1888; m. Amanda J. Armistead, Apr. 14, 1904. Apptd. 2d lt., 3d arty., June 15, 1876; 1st lt., Nov. 3, 1882; capt. 6th arty., Mar. 18, 1898; maj. arty. corps, Apr. 14, 1903; lt. col. coast arty. corps, Jan. 25, 1907; col. Dec. 27, 1908. Instr. mathematics, U.S. Mil. Acad., 1879-83; prof. mil. sci. and tactics, Miss. Agrl. and Mech. Coll., 1903-06. Mem. Am. Math. Soc., A.A.A.S., Am. Geog. Soc, Am. Forestry Assn. Loyal Legion. Club: Army and Navy (N.Y.). Author: Elements of Trigonometry with Tables, 1890. Ret. by operation of law, Apr. 15, 1918. Home: 1113 Massachusetts Av. N.W., Washington. Now deceased.

LUDLOW, JACOB LOTT engineer; b. Spring Lake, N.J., Dec. 20, 1862; s. Samuel and Nancy (Johnson) L.; C.E., Lafayette Coll., Easton, Pa., 1885, later M.S.; m. Myra M. Hunt, Jan. 5, 1887. Began practice at Winston-Salem, N.C., 1890; pres. The Ludlow Engrs., Inc.; mem. and cons. engr. N.C. State Bd. of Health, 1890-1920; mem. Engring. Bd. of Review, Sanitary Dist. of Chicago, 1924, 25. Has served as cons. engr. various Southern cities, on water supply and sewerage projects, valuation of pub. utilities, etc. Col. and chief of engrs., N.C.N.G., 1908-16; supervising engr. on constrn. camp cantonments, World War, also supervising sanitary engr. U.S. Shipping Bd. for S. Atlantic and Gulf states. Democrat. Presbyn. Home: Winston-Salem, N.C. Died Aug. 18, 1930.

LUDLOW, NICOLL rear admiral U.S.N.; b. Riverside Islip, L.I., N.Y., Sept. 11, 1842; s. Gen. William H. and Frances Louisa L.; apptd. from N.Y., and grad. U.S. Naval Acad., 1863; m. Frances Mary Thomas, May 1870; m. 2d, Mary McLean Bugher, Feb. 1897. Promoted ensign, Oct. 1, 1863; advanced through grades to rear adm., Nov. 1, 1899; retired. Served on Wachusett, Brazilian Squadron, 1863-64; participated in capture of Confederate cruiser Florida in Harbor of Bahia, Brazil, Oct. 7, 1864; served on monitor Dictator, 1865; Monadnock, 1865-66, making passage from New York to San Francisco; Iroquois, Asiatic Squadron, 1867-70; Naval Acad., 1870-73; exec. officer Monongahela, 1873-75; Brooklyn, 1876; torpedo duty, 1876-77; exec. officer Trenton, European Squadron, 1877-80; insp. ordnance, West Point Foundry, South Boston Iron Works and Midvale Steel Works, 1880-83; comd. Quinnebaug, European sta., 1883-86; spl. duty, New York, 1886-87; light house insp., 12th dist., 1887-90, 9th dist., 1891-92; insp. ordnance, Navy Yard, Mare Island, 1892; comd. Mohican, Bering Sea Squadron, 1893; leave 1894; Naval War Coll., 1895; comd. Monterey, Pacific Squadron, 1896; mem. Naval Retiring Bd., Jan.-July 1897; comd. Terror, Atlantic Fleet, 1897-98, Massachusetts, Atlantic Fleet, 1898-99; retired, Nov. 1, 1899; gov. Naval Home, Phila., 1904-07. Died 9, 1915.

LUDLOW, WILLIAM brig. gen. U.S.A., Jan. 21, 1900; b. Riverside, Islip, L.I., N.Y., Nov. 27, 1843; s. William Handy and Frances Louisa (Nicoll) L.; ed. Burlington Coll., N.J., and N.Y. Univ., 1853-60; grad. West Point, June 20, 1864; commissioned 1st lt., corps of engrs.; m. Genevieve Almira Sprigg, 1866, Chief engr. 20th army corps, under Gens. Hooker and Slocum, in Atlanta campaign, 1864; chief engr., left wing Gen. Sherman's army in Savannah and the Carolinas campaign, 1864-65; comdg. Co. E, engr. battalion, Jefferson barracks, Mo., 1865-67; capt. engrs. U.S.A., March 7, 1867; chief engr., Dept. of Dak., in Black Hills and Yellowstone expdns.; in charge of various works of fortifications, rivers and harbors, on Atlantic coast from New York to St. Augustine, Fla.; chief engr. Phila. water dept. by election of city councils and spl. joint resolution of Congress, 1883-86; maj. engrs.,June 30, 1882; engr. sec. light house bd., Washington, 1882; engr. commr. of D.C., 1886-88; charge river and harbor and light house work on Great Lakes, 1888-93; mil. attaché U.S. Embassy, London, 1893-96; lt. col. engrs., Aug. 13, 1895; pres. U.S. Nicaragua Canal Commn., 1895; brig. gen., U.S.V., May 4, 1898; chief engr. armies in the field, May, 1898; comdg. 1st brigade, 2d div., Shafter's corps, Santiago campaign; battles of Caney and San Juan and investment of Santiago June-Sept., 1898; maj. gen. U.S.V., Sept. 7, 1898; pres. bd. to organize Army Sea Transport Service, Sept.-Oct., 1898. Mil. gov. Havana, Dec. 12, 1898, to May 1, 1900; comdg. Dept. Havana, Dec. 1898-May 1, 1900; pres. War Coll. Bd., May 1, 1900-. Died 1901.

LUEDDE, WILLIAM HENRY ophthalmologist; b. Warsaw, Ill.; s. Henry J.M. and Emilie M. (Naumann) L.; M.D., Washington U., St. Louis, 1900; vol. asst. eye clinic Royal U., Kiel, Germany, 1904-05; student Laboratoire d'Ophthalmologie, Sorbonne, Paris, 1906; m. Nettie B. Shryock, Mar. 24, 1909 (died Nov. 2, 1946); children-Philip S., Fullerton W., Henry W.; m. 2d, Irene E. Garbarino, Jan. 2, 1948. Asst. to Drs. Green, Post and Ewing, 1901-04; in pvt. practice, St. Louis, 1906—; asst. surgeon, Eye Clinic, Washington U., 1908-12; ophthalmic surgeon, St. Louis Eye, Ear, Nose and Throat Infirmary, 1912-16; prof. opthalmology St. Louis U., 1921—; ophthalmologist in chief Firmin Desloge Hosp., St. Mary's Hosp. and Infirmary; oculist Mo. Bapt. Sanitarium; attending ophthalmologist U.S. Marine Hosp.; cons. in ophthalmology St. Louis City, St. Louis County and St. Johns hosps. Recipient Gill prize (disease of children) by Washington U., 1900, Leslie Dana medal (prevention of blindness), 1933. Served from capt. to maj. M.C., U.S. Army, World War I; col. AUS, 1931-41. Dir. St. Louis Society for the Blind. Fellow A.M.A., A.A.A.S.; mem. many national, internat. and fgn. med. and ophthal. assns., S.R., Alpha Omega Alpha. Conglist. Mason (K.T.). Club: University. Home: 139 N. Tunbridge Dr., Stoneleigh Towers, St. Louis Country 24. Died Mar. 19, 1952.

LULL, CABOT, physician; b. Wetumpka, Ala., June 21, 1874; s. Cabot and Sarah Graham (Foster) L.; M.D., U. of Mich., 1899; m. Dorothy Eaves, June 25, 1913 (died 1934); children—Dorothy, Mary. Intern, Lakeside Hosp., Cleveland, O., 1899-1901; in private practice at Birmingham, Alabama, since 1901; consulting physician at the Jefferson Sanitorium; visiting phys. St. Vincent's Hospital. Major Medical Corps, U.S. Army, 1917-19, in France, 1918. Mem. A.M.A., Southern Med. Assn., Med. Assn. State of Ala., Jefferson County Med. Soc., Nat. Tuberculosis Assn. Democrat. Presbyn. Club: Birmingham Country. Home: Highland Plaza, 2250 Highland Av., Birmingham AL

LULL, EDWARD PHELPS naval officer; b. Windsor, Vt., Feb. 20, 1836; s. Martin Lull; grad. U.S. Naval Acad., 1856; m. Elizabeth F. Burton, circa 1863; m. 2d, Emma Gillingham Terry, Nov. 5, 1873. Served as midshipman U.S. Navy in ships Congress (1855-58), Colorado, Roanoke; promoted warranted master, 1858; prof. English, ethics, fencing U.S. Naval Acad., 1860-61, prof. mathematics, Spanish, 1866-69; promoted lt., 1860, lt. comdr., 1862, master of ship John Adams, 1863; promoted comdr., 1870; commanded ship Guard on Darien Surveying Expdn., 1870-71; headed Nicaragua Exploring Expdn., 1872-73; hydrographic insp. Coast and Geodetic Survey, 1875-80; promoted capt., 1881; served duty at Boston and Pensacola navy yards. Author: History of the United States Navy-Yard at Gosport, Virginia, 1874. Died Mar. 5, 1887.

LUNG, GEORGE AUGUSTUS naval officer; b. Canandaigua, N.Y. Dec. 21, 1862; s. Rev. A. H. and Catherine (Deck) L.; A.B., U. of Rochester, 1883, A.M., 1891; M.D., U. of Pa., 1886; m. Helen Van Courtland de Peyster, Apr. 28, 1908. Apptd. asst. surgeon U.S.N., Aug. 18, 1888; passed asst. surgeon, Aug. 18, 1892; surgeon, Nov. 1900; rank of lt. comdr., Apr. 9, 1908; medical director, June 1917. Served with Sampson's difficulty, in which his courageous conduct was commended by the Sec. of Navy; with China Relief Expdn., 1900; senoor med. officer with 1st Regt. U.S. Marines to Peking and return, Oct. 1900; dist. surgeons Peninsula of Cavite, P.I., 1901; spl. duty Washington, 1902-03; comdg. U.S. Naval Hosp., Brooklyn, Oct. 1916-. Died July 26, 1921.

LUSK, JAMES LORING army officer; b. Pittsburgh, Pa., Feb. 1, 1855; s. Amos (M.D.) and Agnes Sterret (Clow) L.; grad. West Point, 1878; m. Mary E. Webster, Oct. 16, 1883. Apptd. 2d lt. June 14, 1878, 1st lt. June 14, 1881, capt. June 15, 1888, maj. July 5, 1898, corps of engrs., U.S.A.; lt. col. and chief engr., U.S. Vols., May 9, 1898, to Dec. 7, 1898. Served in various duties of corps engrs., and as asst. instr. and instr. mil. engring. at West Point. Mem. U.S. Bd. Geographic Names, Mar. 21, 1899-; asst. to Chief of Engrs., U.S.A., Sept. 19, 1898-. Died 1906.

LUSTMAN, SEYMOUR LEONARD, physician, educator; b. Chgo., Apr. 23, 1920; s. Irving and Anna (Lee) L.; B.S., Northwestern U., 1941; Ph.D., U. Chgo., 1949; M.D., U. Ill., 1954; m. Katherine L. Ritman, June 1941; children—Jeffrey S., Susan T. Intern U. Ill. Research and Edn. Hosp., 1954-55; resident Yale, 1955-58; practice medicine, specializing in psychiatry, New Haven, 1958-71, asso. prof. psychiatry Child Study Center, Yale, 1958-64, prof. psychiatry, dir. research, 1964-71, master Davenport Coll., 1971; cons. div. research grants Nat. Inst. Mental Health, 1963-67, also adv. com. clin. research br.; chmn. Task Force IV, Joint Commn. on Mental Health of Children. Fellow Center for Advanced Psychoanalytic Studies, Princeton, 1963-71. Dir. Robert Knight Research Fund. Served to capt., adj. gen. dept., AUS, 1942-46. Recipient Chandler prize, 1954, David Papaport prize, 1962; Commonwealth Fund fellow, 1954-57; fellow Davenport Coll., Yale, 1967—. Mem. Am. Psychoanalytic Assn. (sec. bd. profl. standards), Am. Psychiat. Assn., Am. Orthopsychiatric Assn., Western New Eng. Inst. for Psychoanalysis, Pi Epsilon Pi. Editor: The Psychoanalytic Study of the Child, 1968. Contbr. articles profl. jours. Home: New Haven CT Died Aug. 5, 1971.

LUTHER, WILLARD BLACKINTON lawyer; b. Attleborough, Mass., Oct. 19, 1879; s. George Edward and Ella Maria (Fisher) L.; A.B., Yale, 1902, A.M., 1905; LL.B., Harvard, 1905; m. Josephine Crocker, Dec. 6, 1924; children-Willard, Joan, Michael, Crocker, Anne. Admitted to Mass. bar, 1905, and since practiced in Boston, with Peabody, Arnold, Batchelder & Luther, partner since 1909; commr. on Uniform State Laws Mass. (mem. exec. com.) since 1934; war corr. Boston Jour. in Holland, Belgium and Germany, 1914. Served with U.S. Army, 1916-19, on Mexican Border, 1916, in France, 1917-19; disch. as lt. col. F.A. Decorated D.S.M. Mem. Northeastern U. Corp., Boston; trustee Tabor Acad.; dir. and counsel Boston Met. chpt. A.R.C. Mem. Am. Law Inst., Am. (past del.), Mass. (past mem. exec. com.), Boston (past pres.) and Middlesex Co. bar assns. Clubs: Yale (past pres.), Union (past pres.) (Boston); Yale (N.Y.C.); Oakley Country (past pres. Watertown, Mass.); Kittansett (Marion, Mass.); Country (gov. Brookline, Mass.). Home: 7 Longfellow Park, Cambridge 38, Mass. Office: 10 State St., Boston 9. Died Jan. 1962.

LUTZ, BRENTON REID biologist; b. Woodlawn, N.S., Can., June 2, 1890; s. Spurden Reid and Sarah Jane (Ogilvie) L.; S.B., Boston U., 1913, A.M., 1914, Ph.D., 1917; teaching fellow Harvard, 1914-16; m. Edna Baldwin, Oct. 2, 1918. Instr. biology Boston U., 1914-22, instr. exptl. physiology Sch. Medicine, 1919-21, asst. prof. physiology, 1921-30, asso. prof., 1930-40, asst. prof. biology Coll. Liberal Arts, 1922-27, prof. since 1927. Served as 1st lt. San Corps, U.S. Army, 1918-19; capt. San. Res. Corps., 1925-30. Fellow A.A.A.S.; mem. Am. Physiol. Soc., Am. Soc. Zoologists, Am. Acad. Arts and Scis., Am. Assn. Anatomists, N.Y. Acad. Scis., Sigma Xi, Phi Beta Kappa, Beta Theta Pi. Mason. Author or co-author 48 research papers in field physiology. Co-producer sci. motion picture films on small blood vessel activity. Home: 49 Laurel St., Melrose, Mass. 02176. Office: 725 Commonwealth Av., Boston 15. Died June 22, 1960.

LYDECKER CHARLES EDWARD lawyer; b. New York, May 26, 1851; s. John A. and Julia (Kent) L.; B.S., Coll. City of New York 1871; LL.B., Columbia, 1873. Instr. Coll. City of New York, 1875-80; pub. administrator, N.Y. City, 1889-93; active practice of law, corp. work, will contests, administration of estates, reference and counsel duties. Printed and distributed ballot securing vote for State Constl. Convention, 1894. Major 7th Infantry, N.G. New York, 1901-09; bvt. lt. col. N.G. New York; mem. council U.S. Mil. Service Inst., 1903-; pres. Nat. Guard Assn., 1906; a founder Nat. Security League (elected president 1918). Trustee Coll. City of New York, 1913-. Democrat. Home: New York, N.Y. Died May 7, 1920.

LYDECKER, GARRETT J. brig. gen. U.S.A.; b. Englewood, N.J., Nov. 15, 1843; s. John R. and Elizabeth (Ward) L.; student Coll. City of New York; grad. U.S. Mil. Acad., 1864; m. Della W. Buel, Sept. 21, 1869. Commd. 1st lt. engrs., June 13, 1864; promoted through grades to col., Apr. 3, 1901; brig. gen. and retired by operation of law, Nov. 15, 1907. Bvtd. capt., Apr. 2, 1865, "for gallant and meritorious services in siege of Petersburg, Va." Has been engaged in river and harbor work at Galveston, Michigan City, Ind., New Orleans, Chicago, Detroit, etc. Died July 9, 1914.

LYFORD, OLIVER SMITH exec. and cons. engr.; b. Cleve., Mar. 21, 1870; s. Oliver Smith and Lavinia A. (Norris) L.; Ph.B., Yale, 1890; post-grad. Cornell U.; m. Frances Lyman Meigs, Jan. 1896; children-Mrs. Margaret Sheldon, Olive Meigs. Chief engr. Westinghouse Electric & Mfg. Co., 1897-99, v.p., gen. mgr. Siemens & Halske Electric Co., 1899-1901; cons. engr., mng. engr. Westinghouse, Church, Kerr & Co., 1902-12; pvt. practice, 1923; v.p., gen. mgr. Lawrence Investing Co., and Lawrence Park Heat, Light & Power Co., 1924-26; v.p. Brooklands, Inc., 1927—; v.p. Santa Clara Lumber Co. Served from maj. to lt. col. Ordnance Dept., U.S. Army, 1917-18. Fellow Am. Inst. E.E.; mem. Berzelius soc. (Yale), Kappa Alpha (Cornell). Republican. Presbyn. Club: Yale (N.Y.C.). Home: 54 Dana Pl., Englewood, N.J. Died Mar. 5, 1952; buried Delhi, N.Y.

LYLE, HENRY HAMILTON MOORE surgeon; b. Connor, Ulster, Ireland, Nov. 15, 1874; s. Samuel (D.D.) and Elizabeth (Orr) L.; med. prep. end., Cornell U., 1896; M.D., Coll Physicians and Surgeons (Columbia), 1900; m. Clara Schlemmer, May 17, 1910 (died Jan. 8, 1916); m. 2d, Jessie Benson Pickens, Apr. 16, 1919. Practiced at N.Y. City since 1900; prof. clin. surgery, Coll. Phys. and Surg., 1913-19; asst. prof. surgery, Cornell University Medical Sch., 1919-31, prof. of clinical surgery since 1931; attending surgeon at St. Luke's Hosp.; dir. of cancer service, New York Skin and Cancer Hosp.; attending surgical specialist U.S. Veteran's Bureau, Dist. No.2; cons. surgeon to Elizabeth A. Horton Memorial Hosp., Middletown, N.Y., N.Y. State Reconstruction Home, W. Haverstraw, Cornwall (N.Y.) Hospital; consultant St. Luke's Hospital, Newburgh, N.Y. Médecin chef Am. Ambulance Hosp., B, Juilly Seine et Marne, France, 1915; chirurgien chef Ambulance Longueil Annel, Oise, France, 1916; commd. maj. O.R.C., U.S. Army, Apr. 26, 1917; active duty, May 30, 1917; organized and took abroad Evacuation Hosp. No. 2; lt. col., June 6, 1918; apptd. cons. surgeon 77th div., Sept. 1918; apptd. to field staff of the chief surgeon 1st Army, in charge of western sect. of the evacuation of wounded for the 1st Army, Meuse-Argonne offensive; chief consultant surgeon 1st Army; mem. Gas Warfare Bd., A.E.F.; col. Oct. 23, 1918. Engagements-Oise-Aisne, Aisne-Marne, St.Mihiel, Meuse-Argonne, defensive sector. Decorated D.S.M. (U.S.); British War Medal and British Victory Medal, N.Y. State Service Medal, Liberty Service Medal of Nat. Inst. Social Services; awarded hon. testimonial for life saving by Royal Canadian Humane Assn., 1895. Fellow Am. Coll. Surgeons; mem. Am. Surg. Assn., New York Surg. Soc., Am. Soc. Clin. Surgeons, Internat. Surg. Soc. of Brussels, A.M.A., Acad. Medicine (New York), N.Y. State Soc. of Indsl. Medicine, Nat. Inst. Social Sciences, Am. Legion, Military Order of the World War, Kappa Alpha. Republican. Presbyterian. Clubs: Eclat, Charaka Club. Home: 1217 Park Av. Office: 33 E. 68th St., New York, N.Y. Died Mar. 11, 1947.

LYMAN, CHARLES HUNTINGTON, III, naval officer; b. Phila., Nov. 24, 1903; s. Maj. Gen. Charles Huntington and Anne Blaine (Irvine) L.; B.S., U.S. Naval Acad., 1926; grad. student ordnance engring., USN Postgrad. Sch., 1934-37; grad. Nat. War Coll., 1948, Naval War Coll., 1953; m. Marjorie Leigh Young, June 30, 1928; 1 dau., Marjorie Anne (Mrs. Arthur P. Miller, Jr.). Commd. ensign USN, 1926, advanced through grades to rear adm., 1953; comd. destroyers in Pacific, participated amphibious operations for recapture of Philippines, during war; operations officer Operations Crossroads, Bikini atomic tests, 1946, Atlantic Fleet, 1946-48; with Bur. Ordnance, 1949-51; comdr. Destroyer Squadron 24, Pacific, Caribbean and Mediterranean, 1951-52; head dept. strategy and tactics Naval War Coll., 1952-53; USN attache, London, 1953-56; comdr. destroyer Flotilla, U.S. Atlantic Fleet, 1956-57, chief of staff Naval War College, 1957-59, commandant Fourth Naval District, Philadelphia, 1959-61; commander destroyers Atlantic Fleet, 1961; commandant 8th Naval District, 1962-65, ret. 1965; field asst. to Presidents of U.S. Nat. Navy League, Washington, 1966-72. capt. USN Academy tennis team, mem. Navy Leech Cup tennis teams, 1926, 27,

28, 35. Decorated Legion of Merit with gold star; Order of Almirante Padilla (Republic Colombia). Mem. Royal Soc. St. George. Club: Army-Navy Country (Arlington, Va.). Home: Bethesda MD Died Dec. 28, 1972; buried U.S. Naval Acad. Cemetery, Annapolis MD

LYMAN, HARRY WEBSTER, otolaryngolist; b. Cedar Rapids, Ia., Mar. 10, 1873; s. James Edward and Martha Elona (Day) L.; M.D., St. Louis Coll. of Physicians and Surgeons, 1895; m. Sarah Elizabeth Long, Dec. 12, 1900; children—Elizabeth Mary (Mrs. Allan E. Clark), Edward Harry. Interne St. Louis Woman's Hosp., 1895-96; gen. practice of medicine, St. Louis, Mo., 1896-1900, specialist in otolaryngology since 1900; demonstrator and prof. of anatomy, St. Louis Coll. of Phys. and Surgs., 1900-06; volunteer asst. dept. of otolaryngology, Washington Univ., Sch. of Medicine, St. Louis, 1910-14, asst. in otolaryngology, 1914-17, instr., 1917-21, asso. clin. otolaryngology, 1921-24, asso., 1924-26, asst. prof., 1926-34, asso. prof., 1934-40, prof., 1940-43, prof. emeritus since 1943. Consultant in otolaryngology U.S. Vets. Hosp., U.S. Marine Hosp. Served as capt. med. corps, U.S. Army, 1917-19. Mem. A.M.A., Am. Coll. Surgs., Am. Acad. Ophthalmology and Otolaryngology (vice pres.), Am. Laryngological, Rhinological and Otolaryngological Soc. (pres. 1946-47), Am. Laryngological Assn., Am. Otol. Soc., Southern and Mo. State Med. Assns., St. Louis Med. Soc., Phi Beta Pi. Conglist. Mason. Contbr. about 40 articles on otolaryngology to various med. jours. Home: 6224 Washington Av., St. Louis 5 MO Office: 308 N. Sixth St., St Louis 1 MO

LYMAN, PHINEAS colonial legislator, army officer; b. Durham, Conn., 1715; s. Noah and Elizabeth Lyman; grad. Yale, 1738; m. Eleanor Dwight, Oct. 1742. Tutor, Yale, 1738-42; dep. from Suffield in Conn. Colonial Assembly, 1749-52, also 2 terms, circa 1772, assistant, 1752-59; provincial gen. Conn. in Northern colonies during 7 Years War; served as maj. gen., 2d in command of Lake George Expdn., 1755; served in battles of Crown Point, Ticonderoga, Montreal and in expdn. against Havana. Died Natchez, Miss., Sept. 10, 1744.

LYMAN, THEODORE physicist; b. Boston, Nov. 23, 1874; s. Theodore and Elizabeth (Russell) L.; A.B., Harvard, 1897, Ph.D., 1900. Instr. physics Harvard, 1902-07; asst. prof., 1907-17, dir. Jefferson Physical Lab., 1910-47, prof. physics, 1917-26, Hollis prof. emeritus, 1926—. Capt. Aviation Sect., Signal R.C., 1917; maj. Engr. Corps, U.S. Army, 1918; service with AEF, flash and sound ranging, 1917-19. Recipient Rumford medal Am. Acad. Arts and Scis.; Elliott Cresson medal Am. Philos. Soc.; Frederick Ives medal Optical Soc. Am. Fellow Am. Acad. Arts and Sciences (past pres.). Unitarian. Club: Somerset (Boston). Discoverer Lyman series. Home: 105 Heath St., Brookline, Mass. Died Oct. 11, 1954.

LYNCH, CHARLES officer U.S.A.; b. Syracuse, N.Y., Mar. 5, 1868; s. Andrew Jackson and Louise (Van Loon) L.; grad. Syracuse High Sch., 1885; Harvard U.; M.D., Syracuse U., 1891; m. Rosamond Rust. of Syracuse, May 8, 1893. Apptd. asst. surgeon U.S.A., May 12, 1893; capt. asst. surgeon, May 12, 1898; maj. surgeon U.S.V., Apr., 1901-Dec., 1902; maj. Med. Corps U.S.A., Apr. 2, 1906; lt. col., Apr. 23, 1914; col., May 15, 1917. Participated in Philippine campaign; Gen. Staff U.S.A., 1904-08; mil. attaché Am. Legation at Tokio, Japan; with troops in the field during Russo-Japanese War; dept. surgeon, Southern Dept., 1917; surgeon, Port of Embarkation, Newport News, Va., 1918-19. Clubs: Army and Navy (Washington), Harvard (New York). Address: War Dept., Washington, D.C.

LYNCH, GEORGE ARTHUR army officer; b. Blairstown, Pa., Mar. 12, 1880; s. Patrick Henry and Mary (Early) L.; student State U. Ia., 1897-98; grad. U.S. Mil. Acad., 1903, Army War Coll., 1930; m. Gladys Mona Chynoweth, June 16, 1906; children-George Edward, Gladys Mona (Mrs. Howell Hopson Jordan), Bradford Chynoweth, James Henry; married second to Mildred Pelzer, 1952. Entered U.S. Army as 2d lt. 1903, advanced through the grades to col., Sept. 1935; mem. gen. staff corps, 1917-23, 1925-29, 1933-35; emergency officer with advanced rank, World War, 1917-20; awarded D.S.M., Officer d'Académie Silver Palms. Adminstrv. officer and actg. adminstr. NRA, Washington, Apr.-Nov. 1934. Commanded U.S. Army Troops in China, 1935-37; maj. gen., chief of infantry, May 24, 1937; ret., Apr. 30, 1941. Club: Army and Navy, Washington. Author: Infantry Drill Regulations, A.E.F., 1919; Field Service Regulations, U.S. Army (with Gen. J. L. DeWitt), 1923; Infantry Field Manual (with Gens. Ridgeley Gaither, Jr., and Richard G. Tindall), 1940. Editor: U.S. Infantry Journal, 1914-16. Address: 812 Lake Formosa Drive, Orlando, Fla. Died Aug. 10, 1962.

LYNCH, JAMES DANIEL author; b. Mecklenburg Co., Va., Jan. 6, 1836; grad. Univ. of N.C., 1859; removed to Miss., 1860; capt. of cav. in Confederate army; wounded at Lafayette, Ga.; was afterward taken prisoner while making a charge near Rome, Ga.; escaped at Resaca, while on the way to Johnson's Island. After war practised law at West Point, Miss.; retired from bar on account of impairment of hearing. Author: Kemper County Vindicated, or Reconstruction in Mississippi; The Bench and Bar of Mississippi; The Bench and Bar of Texas. Also wrote the poem "Columbia Saluting the Nations," adopted by the Columbian Commission as the welcome of the U.S. to the nations of the world, 1893. Now living in Indian Territory writing a History for the Indians of the Five Civilized Tribes; m., Feb., 1861, Hettie M. Cochran, Loundes Co., Miss. Address: Tahlequah, Ind. Ty.

LYNCH, JEROME MORLEY surgeon; b. Ireland; s. Daniel and Jane (Browne) L.; student Queen's Coll., Cork, Edinburgh U.; M.D., Rush Medical Coll., Chgo., 1895; m. Harriet Louise Husted; Jan. 1, 1901. Chief surgeon St. Bartholomew's Hosp., N.Y.C.; prof. proctology N.Y. Polyclinic Hosp.; cons. surgeon Doctor's Hosp., N.Y.C. Served as lt. comdr. USN, 1917; surgeon at Naval Hosp., Bklyn., and at sea, U.S.S. America, Diplomate Am. Bd. Surgery. Fellow A.C.S., Royal Society of Medicine (Honorary); member A.M.A., New England Proctologic Soc., Am. Gastronenterological Assn., Am. Proctologic Soc. (pres. 1917-18), Mil. Order Fgn. Wars. Author: Diseases of Rectum and Colon, 1914; Tumors of Colon and Rectum, 1925; Know Your Patient, 1943. Contbr. to Johnson's Surgery, Woods Handbook of the Medical Sciences, Tice's Practice of Medicine. Clubs: Union (N.Y.C.); Author's (London, Eng.). Home: Carmel, Cal. Died Apr. 22, 1951.

LYNCH, JOHN ROY b. Concordia Parish, La., Sept. 10, 1847; s. Patrick and Catharine L.; m. Ella W. Somerville, Dec. 18, 1884; m. 2d, Mrs. Cora E. Williamson, 1911. Lived in Adams County, Miss., 1863; mem. Miss. Ho. of Rep., 1869-73 (speaker 1871-73); mem. 43d and 44th Congresses (1873-77) and 47th Congress (1881-83), 6th Miss. Dist.; chmn. Rep. Exec. Com. of Miss., 1871-89; 4th auditor Treas. Dept., 1889-93; del. Rep. Nat. Convs., 1872, 84, 88, 92, 1900 (temporary chmn. 1884); one of leading colored Republicans in the South. Apptd. maj. p.m. U.S.V., July 1898, and served through Spanish-Am. War after which apptd. capt. and p.m. U.S.A.; promoted maj. and p.m., Sept. 13, 1906; retired Sept. 10, 1911. Admitted to bar in Miss., 1896, D.C., 1897, Ill., 1919. Home: Chicago, Ill. Died Nov. 2, 1939.

LYNCH, JOSEPH BERTRAM naval officer; b. Cambridge, Mass., Mar. 11, 1893; s. Albert Edward and Mary Elizabeth (Carty) L.; A.B., Harvard, 1914; m. Kathleen Whittle, Nov. 8, 1940. Commd. ensign USN, 1918, advanced through grades to commodore, 1945; flight instr. and squadron comdr. Naval Air Station, Miami, Fla., 1917-19; peace-time duties concerned with orgn., instrn., tng. aeros. orgn. USNR, including service as flight instr. Naval Air Station, Pensacola, Fla., exec. officer Naval Res. Aviation Base, Squantum, Mass., comdg. officer Naval Res. Aviation Base, Miami, Fla., mem. bur. aeros. Navy Dept., Washington, and duty in U.S.S. Wright and U.S.S. Ranger; assigned as officer in charge naval res. aviation personnel and tng., bur. nav. Navy Dept., Washington, 1935; aided in establishment with Bur. Naval Personnel until 1943; served in U.S.S. Yorktown, Atlantic and Pacific areas, 1943; comdg. officer Naval Air Tech. Tng. Center, Jacksonville, Fla., 1943-45; Flag officer with Fleet Air Wings One and Eighteen, Asiatic Pacific Area, 1945; comdr. Naval Air Bases, P.I. 1946-47; comdr. Naval Air Bases, 9th Naval Dist., 1947-48; Bur. Naval Personnel, 1949-50; ret. July 1059; now on active duty Office Sec. of Def. Res. Nat. Def. Service, Am. Area Campaign, Asiatic-Pacific Area Campaign, World War II Victory and Naval Res. medals. Clubs: Harvard (N.Y.C., Boston); Army-Navy Country (Washington). Home: 74 Garfield St., Cambridge, Mass. 02138. Died June 27, 1961.

LYON, EDWIN BOWMAN, army officer; b. Las Cruces, N.M., Dec. 8, 1892; s. William Braden and Corie (Bowman) L.; student State Coll., Mesilla Park, N.M., 1904-10; B.S., U.S. Mil. Acad., 1915; grad. Air Service Tactical Sch., 1924; distinguished grad. Command and Gen. Staff Sch., 1927; grad. Army War Coll., 1932; m. Elsa Franzen. Commd. 2d lt. cav., U.S. Army, 1915, and advanced through the grades to major gen.; transferred to Aviation Sect., Signal Corps, 1917, to Air Service, 1920; rated command pilot and combat observer. Comdr. 6th Bomber Command, Moffett Field, Calif., 1941; dir. sect. Air Force Personnel Council. Episcopalian. Home: Washington DC Died Aug. 1971.*

LYON, GEORGE ARMSTRONG rear adm.; b. Erie, Pa., Dec. 23,1837; s. Rev. George A. and Mary (Sterrett) L.; ed. Dartmouth Coll., class of 1858; admitted to bar of Pa., 1861; m. Rose Vincent, June 21, 1877. Apptd. asst. p.-m. U.S.N., June 11, 1862; promoted p.-m., Jan. 23, 1866; pay insp., Sept. 15, 1888; pay dir., Mar. 15, 1898; retired, Dec. 23, 1899, with rank of rear adm. for services during Civil War. Died Mar. 6, 1914.

LYON, HENRY WARE rear admiral U.S.N.; b. in Mass. Grad. U.S. Naval Acad., 1866; promoted ensign, Apr. 1868; master, July 26, 1869; lt., Mar. 21, 1870; lt. clmdr., Nov. 1884; comdr., Oct. 1, 1893; capt., Mar. 27, 1900; rear admiral, Feb. 19, 1906. First sea service, 1866-67, was with the Sacramento, which was lost off the coast of India; comd. U.S.S. Olympia 1901; commandant Navy Yard, Mare Island, Calif., 1906-07; retired, Nov. 8, 1907. Home: Paris, Me. Died Nov. 22, 1929.

LYON, JAMES ALEXANDER cardiologist; b. Broome County, N.Y., Feb. 28, 1882; s. Henry and Catherine (Murray) L.; student pub. schools and pvt. tutoring, Ohio U., Syracuse U.; M.D., Md. Med. Coll., Galt., 1906; grad. study Harvard Med. Sch., Univ. Coll. Hosp. and Nat. Hosp. for Disease of Heart (London), U. Vienna; m. Irene Elizabeth Moore (dec.); 1 dau., Elizabeth Moore. Intern Bay view Hosp., Balt., 1906-07; asst. physician Loomis Sanatorium, Liberty, N.Y., 1907-09; asst. supt.; and sr. physician Mass. State Hosp. for Tb. Rutland, Mass., 1909-16; prof. clin. cardiology Georgetown U., 1929-40; cardiologist and mem. cardiac com. The Doctors Hosp., Inc.; cons. cardiologist and mem. med. bd. Children's Hosp.; cons. cardiologist Homeopathic, and Columbia hosps.; asst. physician Out-Patient Dept., Johns Hopkins' Hospital, 1925-26; attending cardiologist and chief of cardiac clinic, Emergency Hosp., 1929-40; post grad. study, Nat. Hosp. for Diseases of Heart, London, 1923, U. ov Vienna, 1924, Mass. Gen. Hosp., Boston, 1926. Mem. bd. dirs. Washington Loan and Trust Co., Inter-Am. Horse Show Assn., Inc., Community Chest of D.C.; mem. medical advisory board Civilian Defense Met. Area, D.C.; mem. nat. med. council U.S. Veterans Bureau. Served from lt. to maj. M.C., U.S. Army, 1916-25; Mexican border service, 1916-17; joined AEF, 51st brig., 26th Div., 1917; organized and commanded Camp Hosp. No. 4, Neufchateau, France, 1917, Evacuation Hosp. No. 19, Soisson Sector (French), 1918; grad. U.S. Army Sanitary Sch., Longue, France, 1918; bn. surgeon 104th U.S. Inf., 26th Div., 1918-19; asst. chief med. service U.S. Base Hosp., Camp Devens, Mass.; chief med. Service Base Hosp., Camp Shelby, Miss., and Gen. Hosp. No. 8, Otisville, N.Y., 1919; asst. to attending surg. U.S.A. Dispensary, Washington, 1919-23; detached service Med. Dept., U.S. Army, London and Vienna, 1923-24; post surgeon, Fort Wayne, Detroit, Mich., 1924-25; resigned 1925, to enter pvt. practice in Washington. As bn. surgeon 104th U.S. Inf., participated in battles Champagne-Marne, Aisne-Marne, Meuse-Argonne, St. Mihiel, Ile de France, Lorraine, defense of Toul; citations; French Army Corps, Army of the East (Verdun), and in gen. orders Nos. 28 and 74, 26th Div., U.S. Army (Aisne-Marne, Meuse-Argonne, Decorated Croix de Guerre with Gold Star, Grande Guerre, Victoire Apparaint Chateau Thiery, Verdun; Abdon Caldern (Ecuador); Purple Heart, Silver Star, Victor Medal with 5 campaign clasps, Mexican Border Service Campaign medal (U.S.); Mil. Order of Carabao (U.S.). Diplomate Am. Bd. Internal Medicine. Fellow A.M.A., A.A.A.S., N.Y. Acad. Medicine, Am. Coll. Physicians (life mem.); mem. D.C. Med. Soc., So. Med. Soc., Am. Therapeutic Society (ex-pres.), Am., Washington (ex-pres. and sec.) heart assns., Assn. Mil. Surgeons U.S., Mil. Order Fgn. Wars (surgeon gen. of Nat. Commandery; past comdr. Washington Commandery), Pan-Am. Med. Assn. (trustee; mem. regional adminstrs.; ex-pres. Washington chapter, Internat. Med. Soc. (ex-treas.; mem. bd. dirs.), Am. Inst. Banking, Washington Med. and Surg. Soc., Mil. Order of Purple Heart, Am. Assn. History Medicine, Mil. Order World War (life (life mem.), Mil. Order of Carabao, Nat. Sojurner's, Heroes of '76, Am. Legion Founders (Paris, 1918, life member nat. adv. council), 104th U.S.A. Inf. Regt. Vets. Assn.; ex-mem. Gen. Staff, Nat. Commandery, ex-comdr. D.C. Commandery, Nat. Geog. Soc., The Hippocrates-Galen Society of Washington, Ohio U. Alumni Assn., (D.C. Chapter), English-Speaking Union (dir., mem. exec. com. D.C. chapter), Phi Delta Theta (nat. ex-pres. D.C. alumni club), Phi Chi. Clubs: Army and Navy (ex-mem. bd. goves.), Metropolitan, Chevy Chase, Woodmont (Md.) Rod and Gun (mem. bd. govs.). Home: Glenview Farm, Baltimore Blvd., Rockville, Md.; also 1028 Connecticut Av., Washington D.C. Office: Washington Med. Bldg., 1801 I St. N.W., Washington. Died Aug. 4, 1955.*

LYON, LEROY SPRINGS army officer; b. Petersburg, Va., Oct. 15, 1866; s. John and Margaret M. (Springs) L.; A.B., Richmond Coll., 1886 (LL.D., 1919); grad. U.S. M.A., 1891, Coast Arty. Sch., Ft. Monroe, Va., 1898, Sch. of Submarine Defense, Ft. Totten, N.Y., 1903; m. Harriette Amsden, Dec. 1, 1902. Commd. 2d lt. 7th Cav., June 12, 1891; promoted through grades to col. May 15, 1917; brig. gen. N.A., Aug. 5, 1917; major general N.A., Apr. 12, 1918. A.d.c. to Gen. Royal T. Frank, 1898-99, serving at Chickamauga Park, Ga., Anniston, Ala., and hdqrs. Dept. of Gulf; with light battery and 2d Arty., in Cuba, 1899-1900; dist. arty. engr., Ft. Barrancas, Fla., 1903-06; in P.I., 1906-07, participating in expdn. against hostile Moros; served in Canal Zone, 1916-17; at El Paso, Tex., Aug. 1917; comd. 65th Field Arty. Brigade, Camp Kearny, Calif., Aug. 25, 1917-May 1918; comd. 31st (Dixie) Div., Camp Wheeler, Ga., and in France, May-Nov. 1918, 90th Div., Nov.-Dec. 1918; in France, Sept. 29, 1918-May 13, 1919; participated in Meuse-Argonne offensive, Oct. 11-Oct. 18, 1918; comd. Camp Bowie, Tex., May-July 15, 1918; returning to regular rank of col. F.A., July 15, 1918, comd. Field Arty. Basic School, Camp Taylor, Ky., July 26, 1919-. Died Feb. 23, 1920.

LYON, NATHANIEL army officer; b. Ashford, Conn., July 14, 1818; s. Amasa and Keziah (Knowiton) L.; grad. U.S. Mil. Acad., 1841. Commd. 2d lt. inf. U.S. Army, assigned to 2d Regt during Seminole War, 1841; served in Mexican War, 1846-48, distinguished himself at battles of Vera Cruz, Cerro Gordo, Conteras and

Churubusco; commd. capt., 1851; commd. brig. gen. in supreme command U.S. Army forces in St. Louis, 1861; brig. gen. 1st brigade U.S. Mo. Volunteers, 1861; captured Jefferson City and Boonville, 1861. Killed in battle at Wilson's Creek, Mo., Aug. 10, 1861.

LYON, WILLIAM PENN judge; b. Chatham, N.Y., Oct. 28, 1822; s. Isaac and Eunice (Coffin) L.; ed. in dist. schools of native town; studied law at intervals; admitted to bar, 1846; (LL.D., U. of Wis., 1873); m. Adelia Caroline Duncombe, of St. Thomas, Ont., Nov. 18, 1847. Dist. atty. Racine Co., Wis., 1853-59; mem. and speaker Wis. Assembly, 1859-60; capt. Co. K, 8th Wis. Vols. 1861; col. 13th Wis. Vols., 1862-65; bvtd. brig. gen., 1865. Judge 1st circuit, Wis., 1866-71; justice Supreme Ct., 1871-94 (chief justice, 1892, 1893); mem. 1896-1903, pres. 1898-1903, State Bd. of Control of State Charitable, Penal and Reformatory Institutions. Republican. Died Apr. 4, 1913.

LYONS, TIMOTHY AUGUSTINE capt. U.S.N.; b. in Ireland, Mar. 25, 1845; grad. U.S. Naval Acad., 1865; m. Marie Blanche Humbert, Sept. 14, 1871. Promoted through the various grades to comdr.; retired on account of disability, May 15, 1897; advanced to rank of capt.; retired, June 29, 1906. Served on various ships of N. Atlantic, European, Pacific and Asiatic squadrons, 1865-92, with intervals of duty at Naval Acad., Navy Dept. and New York; comd. U.S.S. Monongahela, 1892-93, U.S.S. Alliance, 1893-94. Author: Meteorological Charts of North Pacific Ocean, 1878; The Magnetism of Iron and Steel Ships, 1884; Treatise on Electro-magnetic Phenomena and on the Compass and Its Deviations Aboard Ship (2 vols.), 1901-03. Home: New York, N.Y. Died 1919.

LYSTER, THEODORE CHARLES M.D., surgeon; b. Fort Larned, Kan., July 10, 1875; s. William John and Martha Guthrie (Doughty) L.; grad. high sch., Detroit, Mich., 1893; Ph.B., U. of Mich., 1897, M.D., 1899; m. Lua Withenbury, Theodore Charles. Pvt. and acting hosp. steward, Hosp. Corps, U.S.A., June 1898-Feb. 1899; served with Med. Corps, U.S.A., June 1898-Feb. 1899; served with Med. Corps, U.S.A., advancing from 1st lt. to col., 1900-19; asst. surgeon, Manhattan Eye and Ear Hosp., New York, 1901-04; chief of eye, ear, nose and throat, Ancon Hosp., Canal Zone, 1904-09; chief of eye service, Philippine Univ., Manila, 1911; chief health officer, Vera Cruz, Mexico, during Am. occupation, 1913; chief of aviation and professional services, Surgeon-General's Office 1917-18, in France, winter 1917-18; retired as col., 1919 (brig. gen., retired, spl. act of Congress, Aug. 16, 1930); a dir. of yellow fever elimination, Rockefeller Foundation, 1918-22; in practice at Los Angeles, Calif., mem. firm Lyster and Jones, 1920-. Fellow Am. Coll. Surgeons, Am. Laryngol., Rhinol. and Otol. Society. Awarded D.S.M. "for exceptionally meritorious and conspicuous service," 1919. Republican. Episcopalian. Home: Los Angeles, Calif. Died Aug. 5, 1933.

LYTLE, WILLIAM HAINES army officer, poet; b. Cincinnati, Nov. 2, 1826; s. Robert and Elizabeth (Haines) L.; grad. Cincinnati Coll., 1842. Served from 1st lt. to capt., 2d Ohio Inf., Mexican War; mem. Ohio Legislature (Democrat), 1852-5 speaker house; appted. maj. gen. in command 1st div. Ohio Militia, 1857; commd. col. 10th Ohio Inf., 1861; in command 17th Brigade, 3d Div., U.S. Army under Gen. Buell, Huntsville, Ala., 1862; commd. brig. gen., 1863. Author poetry including Antony and Cleopatra (best known lyric); works collected in Poems of William Haines Lytle, published 1894, 1912. Killed in Battle of Chickamauga (Tenn.), Sept. 20, 1863; buried Cincinnati.

MAAS, MELVIN JOSEPH business exec.; b. Duluth, Minn., May 14, 1898; s. Frank Newton and Rose (Brady) M.; grad. Coll. of St. Thomas, St. Paul, 1919, LL.D., 1954; student U. Minn., 1919-20; m. Katherine Bole, Oct. 9, 1920; children-Marianne Rose, Patricia, Katherine; m. 2d. Katherine Endress, Dec. 1, 1934; 1 son, Melvin Joseph Jr. Salesman, Nat. Surety Co. of N.Y., Ft. Worth, 1921, mgr., Omaha, Office, 1921-24, mgr. bond dept. Northwest, 1924-26; mem. and mgr. Dwyer-Maas Co., St. Paul, 1926-27, v.p., 1926-; dir. Maas-Keefe Co. asst. to chmn. bd. Sperry Corp., N.Y., 1946-50. Chmn. Pres.'s Com. on Employment Physically Handicapped, Washington, 1954. Mem. 70th to 72d and 74th to 78th Congresses, 4th Minn. Dist. Served with Aviation br. USMC, 1917-18, 21 mos.; active duty S., Pacific, 1942; participated at capture Guadalcanal and Battle of Milne Bay (New Guinea); comd comd. 2 marine air bases Okinawa; now maj. gen. USMCR, (ret.); served with Office Sec. Def. during Korean crisis. Decorated Silver Star, Legion of Merit, Purple Heart; recipient Carnegie medal for disarming maniac in Ho. of Reps., Dec. 1932. Nat. comdr. in chief Mil. Order World Wars; nat. pres. SMCR Officers Assn.; sr. v.p. USNR Officers Assn.; v.p. Res. Officers Assn. U.S.; Minn. gov. Nat. Aero. Assn., 1937; nat. comdr. D.A.V., 1956-57. Republican. Catholic. K.C., Modern Woodman, Moose, Eagle. Club: Army-Navy (Washington). Home: 4714 Essex St., Chevy Chase, Md. Died Apr. 13, 1964; buried Arlington Nat. Cemetery.

MABEY, CHARLES R., ex-governor; b. Bountiful, Utah, Oct. 4, 1877; s. Joseph Thomas and Sarah Lucretia (Tolman) M.; U. of Utah, 1893-96, U. of Chicago, 1908-09; m. Afton Rampton, 1905; children—Rendell N., Charles Pace, Robert Burns, Edward Milo. Began in banking business, 1906; was cashier of Bountiful State Bank, 1906-21; pres. and manager Builders Finance Corp.; president and dir. Bountiful State Bank. Was councilman and mayor of Bountiful; mem. Utah Ho. of Rep., 1913-15; gov. of Utah, term 1921-25. Captain Utah Nat. Guard; private, corpl. and sergt. Utah Light Arty., Spanish-Am. War, serving in Philippines; vol. World War and mustered in as capt. 145th F.A.; maj. F.A., U.S. Army, 1918. Received Silver Star Citation, May 14, 1899. Department comdr. American Legion, Utah, 1932-33, nat. vice-comdr., 1933-34. State Adminstr. War Bond Staff for Utah since 1941. Mem. Poets of the Pacific (pres.), S.A.R. League of U.S. (v.p.), Utah State Hist. Soc. Republican. Mormon. Author: Utah Batteries, a History; The Pony Express; Our Father's House, a Biographical History. Club: Commercial. Home: 6405 Orchard Dr., Bountiful, UT Office: Continental Bank Bldg., Salt Lake City UT

MAC ARTHUR, ARTHUR lt. gen. U.S.A.; b. Springfield, Mass., June 2, 1845; s. Arthur and Aurelia (Belcher) M.; ed. pub. schs., Milwaukee, and pvt. tutors, m. Mary Pinkney Hardy, May 19, 1875. Commd. 1st lt. adj. 24th Wis. Inf., Aug. 4, 1862; maj., Jan. 25, 1864; lt. col., May 18, 1865; hon. mustered out, June 10, 1865; apptd. from Wis. 2d lt. and 1st lt. 17th U.S. Inf., Feb. 23, 1866; transferred to 26th Inf., Sept. 21, 1866; capt. 36th Inf., July 28, 1866; assigned to 13th Inf., July 5, 1870; maj. a.-a.-g., May 26, 1896; brig. gen. vols., May 27, 1898; maj. gen., Aug. 13, 1898; brig. gen. U.S.A., Jan. 2, 1900; maj. gen., Feb. 5, 1901; lt. gen., Sept. 15, 1906. Bvtd.: lt. col. vols., Mar. 13, 1865, for battles of Perryville, Ky., Stone River, Missionary Ridge and Dandridge, Tenn.; col. Mar. 13, 1865, for battle of Franklin, Tenn., and Atlanta campaign; awarded Congressional Medal of Honor, June 30, 1890, "for seizing colors of regt. at critical moment and planting them on captured works on the crest of Missionary Ridge, Nov. 25, 1863." Participated in battles of Perryville, Stone River, Dandridge, Missionary Ridge, Resaca, Adairsville, New Hope Ch., Kenesaw Mountain (wounded), Peach Tree Creek, Jonesboro, Lovejoy's Sta., Atlanta, Franklin (wounded); comd. brigade, independent div., 8th Army Corps, June 12, 1898, and 3d expdn. to Manila, June-July, 1898; comd. 1st Brigade, 1st Div., 8th Army Corps, in advance on Manila, July-Aug., and battle of Manila, Aug. 13, 1898; comd. 2d Div., 8th Army Corps, Aug. 1898-Feb. 1899, Dept. of Northern Luzon, Apr. 1, 1899-May 5, 1900, Div. of the Philippines, and mil. gov. May 5, 1900-July 4, 1901; comd. Dept of Colo., Dec. 30, 1901-Mar. 27, 1902, Dept. of the Lakes, Mar. 29-July 19, 1902, Dept. of the East, July 21-Nov. 8, 1902, Dept. of the Lakes, Nov. 10, 1902-Mar. 23, 1903, Dept. of Calif., Apr. 1, 1903, Pacific Div., Jan. 15, 1904-Apr. 30, 1907; retired by operation of law, June 2, 1909. Address: Milwaukee, Wis. Died Sept. 5, 1912.

MAC ARTHUR, ARTHUR newspaper pub.; b. Troy, N.Y., July 24, 1850; s. Charles Fafayette and Susan (Colegrove) M.; grad. Troy Acad., 1868; Rensselaer Poly Inst., Troy, 1868-72; m. Ella Elizabeth Griffin, Jan. 9, 1877 (died 1907). Pub. Troy Northern Budget,1875-; sole surviving partner of C. L. Mac Arthur & Son; dir. Union Nat.Bank. County treas. Rensselaer County, 1906-11; trustee Troy Acad., Troy Pub. Library, Y.M.C.A. Served as mem. Citizens' Corps, Troy; was mem. staff Maj. Gen. J. B. Carr, N.G.N.Y., staffs of Gov. Levi P. Morton, with rank of col. and Gov. Frank S. Black, as asst. p.-m.-gen. Republican. Presbyn. Mason (33ff); Grand Comdr. of K.T., State of N.Y., 1888; Grand Master of Grand Encampment, K.T., U.S.A., 1913-16; has had many offices in the order. Home: Troy, N.Y. Died Dec. 27, 1914.

MACARTHUR, CHARLES author, playwright; b. Scranton, Pa., Nov. 5, 1895; s. Rev. William T. and Georgiana (Welstead) MacA.; ed. Wilson Memorial Acad., Nyack, N.Y.; m. Helen Hayes, Aug. 17, 1928; children-Mary (dec.), James. Reporter Chicago Herald and Examiner, Chicago Tribune and N.Y. American, 1914-23; spl. writer Hearst's Internat. Magazine, 1924; writer and produced motion pictures and plays, 1929—. Vice pres. Oancaster & Chester Railroad. Served as trooper 1st Ill. Cav., Mexican Border, 1916; pvt. 149th F.A. (Rainbow Div.) A.E.F., 1917-19; assistant to Chief of Chem. Warfare Service, Washington, D.C., with rank of Lt. Col., 1942-45. Clubs: River, Coffee House; The Tavern (Chicago). Author: War Bugs, 1926; (plays) Lulu Belle (with E. Sheldon), 1926; Salvation (with S. Howard), 1927; The Front Page (with Ben Hecht), 1933; Ladies and Gentlemen (with Ben Hecht), 1939; Johnny on the Spot, 1941; Swan Song (with Ben Hecht), 1946; also numerous motion pictures. Contbr. fiction. Home: Nyack, N.Y. Died Apr. 21, 1956; buried Oak Hill Cemetery, Nyack, N.Y.

MACARTHUR, DOUGLAS general of the army; b. Ark., Jan. 26, 1880; s. Lt. Gen. Arthur and Mary P. (Hardy) MacA.; grad. U.S. Mil. Acad., 1903, Engr. Sch. of Application, 1908; D.M.Sc., Pa. Mil. Coll., 1928, D. Int. L., 1946; LL.D., U. Md., 1928, U. Western Md. Coll., 1929, U. Pitts., 1932, U. Philippines, 1938, U. Wis., 1942, U. Queensland (Australia), U. Santo Tomas (Philippines), 1945, Harvard, U. Seoul (Korea), 1946, Mo. Valley Coll., Columbia U., 1947, M.M.S., Norwich U., 1935; D.C.L., U. Hawaii, 1946; S.T.D., Midwestern Coll. (Australia); m. Jean Faircloth; 1 son, Arthur. Commd. 2d lt. Engrs. Corps, U.S. Army, 1903, and advanced through grades to gen., 1930; general of the army, 1944; chief of staff 42d (Rainbow) Div., 1917, comdg. gen., 1918; also comd. 34th Brigade, 1918; with Army of Occupation, Germany, 1918-19; participated in Luneville, Baccarat, and Esperance-Souain sectors, also at Champagne; in Champagne-Marne and Aisne-Marne defensives, St. Mihiel, Essey Pannes, Meuse-Argonne, Sedan offensives; supt. U.S. Mil. Acad., 1919-22; mil. adviser Commonwealth Govt. of Philippines, 1935; field marshal of Philippine Army, 1936-37; comdr.-in-chief U.S. and Filipino Forces, during invasion of Philippines by Japanese, (1941-42; comdr. U.S. Armed Forces in Far East, 1941-51; supreme comdr. Allied Forces in Pacific, 1942; apptd. supreme comdr. to accept surrender by Japan, 1945; comdr. occupational forces in Japan, 1945-51; comdr. in chief UN Forces in Korea, 1950-51. Chmn. bd. Remington Rand Inc., 1951-55, Sperry Rand Corp., 1955-. Decorated Congl. Medal of Honor, D.F.C., D.S.C. with 2 oak leaf clusters, D.S.M. with 6 oak leaf clusters, Purple Heart with oak leaf cluster, Silver Star with 6 oak leaf clusters, D.S.M. (Navy), Bronze Star Medal, Air Medal (U.S.), also highest honors and decorations from Gt. Britain, France, Belgium, Italy, Poland, Hungary, Czechoslovakia, Yugoslovakia, Rumania, Mexico, Ecuador, Australia, China, Greece, Guatemala, Netherlands, Philippines. Comdr.-in-chief Mil. Order World War, 1927; hon. pres. Soc. Am. Legion Founders; pres. Am. Olympic Com., 1928. Died Apr. 5, 1964; buried MacArthur Meml., Norfolk, Va.

MACAULEY, EDWARD naval officer: b. Washington, Aug. 13, 1875; s. Edward and Frances (Steele) M.; grad. U.S. Naval Acad., 1896; m. Jean Oliver, Feb. 8, 1913; children-Barbara (Mrs. Macauley Brown), Edward, Geo. Oliver (dec.), John Arnot, Michael. Promoted ensign USN, 1898, through grades to capt., 1918. On board Brooklyn, battle of Santiago, etc., Spanish-Am. War, 1898; duty with Evacuation Commn., P.R.; on staff Adm. Dewey in P.I., spl. shore duty with army; comdr. Scorpion, 1913; in Turkey for end of 1st and 2d Balkan wars and until Mar. 1915; duty in Office Naval Intelligence, Washington, Sept. 1915, asst. dir., Mar. 1916-July 1918; spl. duty abroad, several months; comdg. U.S.S. George Washington, Oct. 1918-Nov. 1919, taking Pres. Wilson to France for Peace Conf. and return twice, also bringing King and Queen of Belgium for visit to U.S. and return. Comdg. U.S.S. Huntington, 1919-20; comdg. Mine Force, Pacific Fleet, 1920-21; asst. comdt. 12th Naval Dist., 1921-22; ret., Nov. 14, 1922; mem. Hibbs & McCauley, naval architects, marine engrs., San Francisco, 1924-30, dir. Emergency Relief, San Mateo County, Cal., 1932-33; adminstr. Fed. Civil Works Adminstrn. for Cal., 1933-34; mem. Nat. Longshoremen's Bd., 1933-35; mem. U.S. Maritime Commn., 1941-46; dep. adminstr. War Shipping Adminstrn., 1942-46. Awarded Spanish-Am. War, West Indian and Philippine campaign medals, Victory Medal, Navy Cross; Officer Legion of Honor (France); Officer Order of Leopold (Belgium). Mem. Loyal Legion, Descs. of Signers. Episcopalian. Clubs: New York Yacht (New York); Pacific Union (San Francisco; Metropolitan, Alibi (Washington). Home: 40 Florence St., San Francisco 11. Died May 1964.

MACBRAYNE, LEWIS E. author; b. New Britain, Conn., Nov. 1, 1871; s. William S. and Mary S. (Slate) M.; grad. Lowell High Sch.; traveled in Europe; m. Sarah E. Thurlow; Aug. 27, 1903; children-Elinor, Thurlow, Elizabeth, Frances. With Lowell (Mass.) Courier-Citizen as reporter and editor 27 yrs. Regional dir. for State of N.Y. on spl. war work with Dept. of Interior, 1918-19; field sec. Mass. C. of C. in 1919. Gen. mgr. Safety Council, 1921; state dir. safety, Federal Works Projects, 1934-36. Republican. Conglist. Author: The Men We Marry, 1910; One More Chance (with James P. Ramsay), 1916; An Engaging Position (play). Contbr. to mags. Home: 45 Glendale Road, Belmont, Mass. Office: 80 Federal St., Boston. Died Dec. 29, 1954; buried Lowell, Mass.

MACCHESNEY, NATHAN WILLIAM lawyer, jud. officer, diplomat, soldier; b. Chgo., June 2, 1878; s. Alfred Brunson (M.D., lieutenant colonel United States Army) and Henrietta (Milsom) MacChesney; brother of Chester M. MacChesney; A.B., Coll. of Pacific, 1898; spl. student Stanford, 1896-99; student Northwestern Law Sch., 1899-1900; LL.B., U. of Mich., 1902; LL.M., Northwestern Univ., 1922; hon. LL.D., Coll. of Pacific, 1926, U. of Mich., 1934; m. Lena Frost, Dec. 1, 1904; children-Alfred Brunson III, Gordon. Senior member MacChesney & Becker, Chicago; special assistant attorney general of United States, 1911-12; special asst. state's atty., 1912; spl. asst. atty. gen., Ill., 1913-33; spl. counsel City of Chicago, 1924; gen. counsel Nat. Assn. Real Estate Bds.; apptd. U.S. minister to Canada by President Hoover, 1932-33; high commr. for Canada, Century of Progress Exposition, Chicago, 1933-34; counsul general for Thailand (Siam), 1924—; appointed U.S. referee in bankruptcy, 1943. Life member National Conference Commissioners on Uniform State Laws (president 1922-25); of counsel for United States Senate in investigation of U.S. War Vets. Bur. and of Rent Control in D.C. and for War Dept. in U.S. Supreme

Court, 1914-17; counsel Nat. Child Labor Com. and draftsman many acts for social, uniform and progressive legislation; lecturer U. of Ill., 1908-16; mem. exec. com. Chicago Plan Commn.; mem. Air Bd. of Chicago; mem. Chicago Crime Commn.; trustee Northwestern U., 1913-48, life trustee, 1948—; trustee Nat. Alumni Council U. of Mich., Carson Long Inst., Pub. Health Inst.; chairman Bd. Salvation Army, life mem. Com. 15. Served in Ill., Calif. and Ariz. N.G., 1893-1917 and as judge advocate gen. of Ill., 1911-17; served with 33d Div. and G.H.Q., A.E.F. in France on staffs of Sec. of War Baker, Gens. Crowder, Ansell, Carter, Barry, Wood, Kreger, Bell, Bethel and Pershing, 1917-19; assigned active duty, U.S. Army, June 27, 1917; dep. judge advocate, Central Dept. U.S. Army, 1917-18; judge advocate, G.H.Q., A.E.F., in France, brig. gen. Ill. N.G., col. U.S. Army. Presented with commenorative sabre; recommended for D.S.M.; awarded citation by Gen. Pershing "for exceptionally meritorious and conspicuous services, A.E.F." Mil. Order of Purple Heart and Victory Medal with citation (U.S.); also U.S. Army Commendation medal with 2 stars; United Nations and French Commemorative medals; Comdr. Order of the White Elephant conferred by King of Siam; Chevalier Order Crown of Italy; Officer French Legion of Honor. On active duty with United States Army, 1942-43. Mem. American Bar Assn. (v.p. 1925-26; chmn. sect. Internat. and Comparative Law, 1934-35; chmn. sect. Real Property, Probate and Trust Law, 1936-38; House of Dels. 1939); mem. Ill. State Bar Assn. (life; pres. 1915-16), Chicago Bar Assn (bd. mgrs., 1943-45), Association Bar City of New York, Conference of Bar Association Delegates (chmn. Am. Law Inst. (charter mem), Am. Inst. Criminal Law and Criminology (pres. 1910-11), Am. Soc. Internat. Law, S.A.R., Soc. War of 1812 (pres. 1912-14, Sons of World Wars (past comdr.), Phi Kappa Psi, Phi Beta Kappa, Pi Gamma Mu, Phi Delta Phi, Order of the Coif (nat. pres. 1910-13), Northwestern U. General Alumni Assn. (president 1922-24, awarded Alumni Medal, 1947), Northwestern University Foundation (rnpres. 1926-28); honorary member Chicago Council of Foreign Relations; English-Speaking Union; member Alliance Francaise (treas., director), Italy-American Society, hon. life mem. Chicago Hist. Soc.; hon. mem. Md., Neb., Iowa, Minn., Ohio, Pa., Tex., Tenn. state bar assns., Chicago Assn. Commerce. Mem. exec. com. Rep. Nat. Conv., 1908-20; active in Theodore Roosevelt, 1912, and Leonard Wood, 1920 campaigns; dir. organization bur., Hoover, Rep. Nat. Com., 1928-32. Pres. Nat. Rep. Lawyers League, 1928-40. Presbyterian. Mason. Clubs: University, Chicago, Union League, Chicago Law, Chicago Literary, Knollwood, Michigan Union, Lawyers (Ann Arbor); Metropolitan (Washington). Author: (or editor) Abraham Lincoln, The Tribute of a Century, 1909; The Significance of the War of 1812; Uniform State Laws; Challenge to American Ideals; French Contribution to American Life; Military Policy and Laws of the U.S.; Principles of Real Estate Law; Law of Real Estate Brokerage. Home: 710 Lake Shore Drive, Chicago; (summer) Riverhill Farm, Belvidere Rd. and Desplaines River, Libertyville, Lake County, Ill. Office: 225 S. Clark St., Chgo. Died Sept. 25, 1954; buried Oak Woods Cemetery, Chicago.

MAC COLL, WILLIAM BOGLE textile mfr.; b. Pawtucket, R.I., Oct. 26, 1886; s. James Roberton and Agnes (Bogle) M.; grad.St. Paul's Sch., Concord, N.H., and New Bedford, Textile School, 1905; m. Mabel Coats, Oct. 16, 1923; children-Jean, William B. With Lorraine Mfg. Co., Pawtucket, 1908-10, gen. supt., 1910-12, asst. treas., 1912-19, treas. and sec. 1919-32, pres., 1932-; treas. Lortex Co., Lorraine Mfg. Co. of N.Y.; dir. Slater Trust Co., Industrial Trust Co., Mfrs. Mutual Fire Ins. Co.; trustee Peoples Savings Bank. Commd. maj. U.S. O.M.C., and served as asst. chief purchasing officer, Paris, World War. Pres. R.I. Boy Scouts of America, 1926-27; pres. Pawtucket and Blackstone Valley Community Chest; regional dir. Liberty Mutual Ins. Co., Mill Associates. Decorated Order of Leopold (Belgium), 1918. Republican. Episcopalian. Home: Bristol, R.I. Died Nov. 7, 1941.

MAC CONNELL, CHARLES JENKINS naval officer; b. Falls Twp., Bucks County, Pa., Dec. 14, 1837; s. William and Ann S. (Jenkins); grad. Model Inst. and State Normal Sch., Trenton, N.J.; m. Louisa B. Small, Dec. 13, 1863. Served apprenticeship in Phila. as mech. engr. and builder; prof. drawing and civil engring., State Normal Sch., Trenton; served in Co. A, N.J.N.G. for 3 mos. at outbreak of Civil War; apptd. from N.J. by Pres. Lincoln, 3d asst. engr. U.S.N., Oct. 29, 1861; 2d asst. engr., Sept. 1863; 1st asst. engr., Oct. 1866; chief engr., Dec. 5, 1885; comdr., June 5, 1896; capt., Aug. 10, 1898; retired, Jan. 19, 1899, on account of disabilities received in line of duty; promoted to rank of rear admiral retired, June 29, 1906. Served on Miss. River on Gulf coast and on Atlantic coast during Civil War, and in principal parts of the world later; participated as fleet engr. N. Atlantic Sta., on flagship New York, in naval operations of Spanish-Am. War; received war medal for conspicuous conduct and bravery in battle; consulting engr. for various mining cos., etc. Home: Brooklyn, N.Y. Died 1909.

MACCONNELL, JOHN WILSON surgeon, educator; b. McConnellsville, S.C., Jan. 11, 1878; s. John Daniel and Sarah Amanda (Jaggers) MacC.; B.S., Davidson (N.C.) Coll., 1902; M.A., 1906; M.D., U. Md., 1907; studied U. Edinburgh; m. Agnes Haig Doyle, July 28, 1909 (dec.); 1 son, John Courtney. Resident surgeon Presbyn. Hosp., Balt., 1907-08; practiced at Davidson, 1908—; organized dept. of biology Davidson Coll., prof. biology, 1908-19, prof. physiology and hygiene, dir. student Health service, now emeritus; dir. Bank of Davidson. Served as 1st lt. M.C., U.S. Army, Mexican border, 1916; capt. Base Hosp., Camp Jackson, 1917; maj. to lt. col. AEF, 1918-19, col., 1925; hon. disch. 1919; retired 1929, as lt. col. E.O.R. Sec. N.C. Bd. Med. Examiners; surgeon So. Ry. Fellow A.M.A.; mem. Med. Society State of N.C., Tri-State, So. med. assns., Nat. Fedn. Medical Bds. (v.p.). Am. Legion, Mil. Order of World War, Sigma Alpha Epsilon, Nu Sigma Nu, Phi Beta Kappa, Omicron Delta Kappa. Democrat. Presbyn. Mason, K.P. Home: Davidson, N.C. Died Sept. 26, 1950; buried Davidson, N.C.

MACCORMACK, DANIEL WILLIAM banker; b. Wick, Scotland, Apr. 9, 1880; s. John G. and Sara (McCann) MacC.; came with parents to U.S., 1889; ed. prep. depts., Boston (Mass.) Coll., Robert Gordon's Coll., Aberdeen, Scotland, and St. Laurent's Coll., Montreal, Can.; m. Mary Hyde, d. Dr. Christopher Seymour, Dec. 23, 1920. Served with 26th Inf., U.S.A., Philippine Insurrection, 1899-1901; with Panama Canal orgn., 1905-17, staff div., meteorology and river hydraulics, later supt. mfg. plants and acting gen. mgr. commissary dept.; capt., later lt. col. Transportation Corps, U.S.A., World War, serving as asst. exec. officer Army Transport Service, Port of N.Y., exec. officer Shipping Control Com., and gen. insp. in charge reorgn. Army Transport Service in France; on mission to Russia for Peace Conf., 1919; resigned as capt. O.M.C., regular army, 1922; mem. Am. Financial Mission to Persia, 1922-27, serving as dir. internal revenue of Persian Govt., dir. alimentation during famine period, 1925-27; mem. Russo-Persian Tariff Commn., and assigned to visit capitols of Europe to increase Persian exports; represented Persia in council and assembly of League of Nations, 1927; organized and administered receivership dept., Irving Trust Co., N.Y. City, Jan. 1929-June 1930; pres. Fiduciary Trust Co. of New York and The Fiduciary Corp., June 1930-Mar. 1933; commr. gen. of immigration, Apr.-Aug. 1933; commr. of immigration and naturalization, Dept. of Labor, Washington, 1933-. Comdr. Order of Crown of Italy; Officer Order of the Black Star (France). Mem. advisory bd. Yorkville Music Sch. Democrat. Catholic. Home: Washington, D.C. Died Jan. 1, 1937.

MACCRACKEN, WILLIAM PATTERSON, JR., lawyer; b. Chicago, Sept. 17, 1888; s. William P. and Mary Elizabeth (Avery) MacC.; prep. edn., Montclair (N.J.) High Sch., South Side Acad. and Univ. High Sch., Chicago; Ph.B., U. of Chicago, 1909, J.D., 1911; LL.D., Norwich U., Northfield, Vt., 1936; m. Sally Lucile Lewis, Sept. 14, 1918; children—Wm. Lewis, Nell Elizabeth. Admitted to Ill. bar, 1911, and began practice in Chicago; asst. atty. gen of Ill., 1923; asst. state's atty. Cook County, 1924; asst. sec. of commerce for aeronautics, U.S., Aug. 11, 1926-Oct. 1, 1929; resigned to enter pvt. practice; now member firm MacCracken, Collins & Hawes; secretary Am. Bar Assn., 1925-36, life mem. house delegates; vice pres., dir. National Aviation Center, Inc. Chairman of Pan-Am. Commercial Aviation Conf., Washington, 1927; v. chmn. Internat. Civil Aeronautics Conf., Washington, 1928; head U.S. delegation to Internat. Conv. for Air Navigation, Paris, 1929. Served in Air Service, U.S., 1917-18; mem. Nat. Advisory Com. for Aeronautics, 1929-38; chmn. Joint Airport Users Conf., Civil Aviation Joint Legislative Com. Decorated Officer Order of Crown of Italy. Alumni Citation Award, University of Chicago; Elder Statesman of Aviation, 1955, Wright Brothers Memorial Trophy, 1959. Fellow of American Bar Found.; mem. Am., Ill., Fed., Chgo., D.C., Can. (hon.) bar assns., Am. Optometric Found. (life), Am. Law Inst., Am. Patent Law Assn., Nat. Aeronautic Assn. (gen. gounsel), Inst. Aeronautical Sciences, American Legion, Psi Upsilon, Phi Delta Phi, Legal Club, Law Club. Republican. Clubs: Nat. Press, Metropolitan, Chevy Chase Capitol Hill (Washington). Asso. editor U.S. Aviation Reports. Home: Washington DC Died Sept. 1969; buried Washington DC

MACDONALD, BYRNES petroleum exec.; b. N.Y. City, Jan. 1, 1908; s. George and Belle (Byrnes) MacD.; student Newman Sch., Lakewood, N.J., 1918-25; Hill Sch., 1925-28; A.B., Princeton, 1932; m. Aleta Morris, Feb. 2, 1935; 1 son, George Morris. With N.R.A., 1935; dep. police commr., N.Y. City, 1936-37, dep. commr. Dept. Welfare, 1938-39, sec. to mayor, 1939-41; asst. to pres. Sinclair Oil Corp. since 1946. Mem. bd. Andrew Freedman Home; mem. nat. exec. bd. Boy Scouts Am. since 1934. Served as lt. comdr. U.S.N.R., 1941-45, Pacific Theatre. Mem. Florence Crittenton League, Girls Service League, Irish Hist. Soc., Am. Legion, Mil. Order Fgn. Wars, Navy League. Roman Catholic. Elk, Knight of Malta, Knight of Holy Sepulchre. Clubs: Newport Country, Reading Room, Spouting Rock (Newport, R.I.); Meadowbrook (Westbury, L.I.); The Brook, Racquet and Tennis (N.Y.C.); Links, U. Cottage (Princeton). Author: Italo-Vatican Accord, 1932. Home: 895 Park Av., N.Y.C. 21; (summer) Chepstow, Narragansett Av., Newport, R.I. Office: 600 Fifth Av., N.Y.C. 20. Died Oct. 1959.

MACDONALD, MILTON TENNY business exec.; b. Brookline, Mass., Oct. 22, 1895; s. Robert and Ada (Tenny) MacD.; A.B., Harvard, 1918; grad. sch. banking, Rutgers U., 1943; m. Ethel Murray, Sept. 28, 1929; 1 son, Milton. Vice pres. North Atlantic & Western S.S. Co., Boston, 1919-25, William M. Hotchkiss Co., New Haven, 1926-32, Trust Co. of N.J., Jersey City, 1932-52; chmn. T. B. O'Toole, Inc., Wilmington, Del., 1952-64; cons. Wilmington Trust Co.; mem. bd. mgrs. Farmers Mut. Fire Ins. Co., Wilmington; dir. Trust Co. of N.J. Faculty adv. com. Wharton Sch., U. Pa. Served as ensign USNR, 1917-19; personal aide to Rear Adm. Spenecer Spencer S. Wood. Trustee Tchrs. Ins. & Annuity Assn. Am. (N.Y.C.). Mem. Mortgage Bankers Assn. of Am. (mem. bd. govs., since 1943, mem. exec. com., 1945-46, 47-48, 51-52, chmn. exec. com., v.p. 1949-50, pres., 1950-51). Republican. Conglist. Clubs: Riverside (Conn.) Yacht; Harvard (N.Y.C.); Round Table (Jersey City); Mory's Assn., Lawn (New Haven); University (Wilmington) Inst. of 1770, Hasty Pudding. Home: Georgetown, Conn. Office: DuPont Bldg., Wilmington, Del. Died Oct. 15, 1967.

MACDONALD, WILLIS GOSS surgeon; b. Cobleskill, N.Y., Apr. 11, 1863; s. Sylvester M.; grad. Cobleskill Free Acad., 1878, and N.Y. State Normal Sch.; student Cornell; M.D., Albany Med. Coll., 1887; U. of Berlin, 1889-90; unmarried. Resident surgeon, 1887, surgeon, 1891, Albany Hosp.; lecturer on surgery, 1892, adj. prof. surgery, 1895, Albany Med. Coll.; surgeon Albany Hosp., 1896; prof. abdominal surgery and gynecology, Albany Med. Coll., 1900. Maj. and surgeon U.S. Vols., 1898, and in charge of surgical div. of depot hosp. at Ft. McPherson, Ga., during Spanish-Am. War; mem. N.Y. State Tuberculosis Commn., 1900-; pres. bd. trustees N.Y. State Hosp. for Treatment of Incipient Pulmonary Tuberculosis. Republican. Mem. Pan-Am. Med. Congress, 10th, 11th, 12th, Internat. Med. Congresses. Home: Albany, N.Y. Died 1910.

MACDONALL, ANGUS (PETER)painter, illustrator; b. St. Louis, Apr. 7, 1876; s. John A. and Virginia C. (Van Steenkist) M.; ed. Christian Bros. Coll., St. Louis Sch. of Fine Arts; m. Catherine Agnes Walsh, Oct. 24, 1900; children-Lucille Blair, Patricia Claire, Frances Helen, Donald Angus. Worked in architects' offices, St. Louis, and with various engraving cos. to 1900; illustrator and cartoonist for Life, Scribner's American, Red Cross Mag., Ladies' Home Journal, Harper's, etc., also illustrator of books and lecturer on art. Catholic. Home: Westport, Conn. Died Dec. 19, 1927.

MACDOUGALL, CLINTON DUGALD soldier; b. Glasgow, Scotland, June 14, 1839; s. Dugald and Margaret (MacKendrick) M.; grad. Jordan Acad., 1853; m. Eva Sabine, Jan. 23, 1867 (died 1875); m. 2d, Marianna Cook, Nov. 28, 1878. Capt. 75th N.Y. Inf., Sept. 16, 1861; lt. col. 111th N.Y. Inf., Aug. 20, 1862; col., Jan. 3, 1863; bvtd. brig. gen. vols., Feb. 25, 1865, "for gallant and meritorious services"; hon. mustered out, June 4, 1865; comd. brigade and div. Army of Potomac; comd. 1st Div., 2d Army Corps, at Grand Review, Washington, May 1865. Postmaster Auburn, N.Y., 1869-73; mem. 43d and 44th Congresses (1873-77); U.S. marshal, Northern Dist., New York, 1877-85; offered, 1878, by President Hayes, choice of consul general positions at London or Paris-declined both; presdl. elector, 1888; declined treasurership of U.S. and positions of commr. internal revenue and commr. of patents in 1876; U.S. marshal, Northern Dist. of N.Y., 1901-11; retired. Republican. Address: Auburn, N.Y. Died May 25, 1914.

MACDOUGALL, WILLIAM DUGALD naval officer; b. Auburn, N.Y., June 20, 1868; s. Clinton Dugald and Eva (Sabine) MacD.; grad. U.S. Naval Acad., 1889; m. Charlotte Sackett Stone, 1898; children-Charlotte (Mrs. Henrik de Kauffmann), Zilla (Mrs. Philip Mason Sears). Promoted ensign, July 1, 1891; lt. jr. grade, Nov. 15, 1898; lt., Mar. 3, 1899; lt. comdr., July 1, 1905; comdr., July 1, 1910; capt., June 13, 1916. Served on San Francisco, Spanish-Am. War, 1898; comd. Villalobos, 1905-06; at Naval War Coll., Newport, R.I., 1906-07; ordnance officer Virginia, 1907-08; navigator Louisiana, 1908-09; exec. officer New Jersey, 1909-10; comdr. Wolverine, 1910; duty with Gen. Bd., Navy Dept., 1910-12; comd. Nashville, 1912-13, Mayflower, 1913-14, at Naval War Coll., 1915; duty Naval Obs., 1915-16; naval attaché Am. Embassy, London, Eng., Sept. 18, 1916 Dec. 1917; comd. Tacoma and North Carolina during World War; comd. Nevada, 1919-20; duty Navy Dept., 1920-21; supt. Naval Observatory, Washington, 1922-23; promoted to Rear Admiral June 8, 1923. Comdr. Train Squadron One, U.S. Fleet Base Force, Oct. 8, 1923; comdr. Battleship Div. Four, June 22, 1925, during U.S. fleet cruise to Australia and New Zealand. Comdt. Navy Yard, Portsmouth, N.H., Nov. 1925, 16th Naval Dist., Philippine Islands, Nov. 1928; comdr. Base Force, U.S. Fleet, 1930; comdt. 5th Naval Dist., Hampton Roads, Va., 1931; retired, July 1, 1932. Address: Navy Dept., Washington, D.C. Died Mar. 5, 1943.

MACDOWELL, THAIN WENDELL mining exec.; b. LaChute, Que., Sept. 16, 1890; s. Rev. John Vincent and Eleanor (Ireland) MacD.; B.A., U. Toronto, 1914, M.A. (hon.), 1919; m. Norah Jean Hodgson, July 25, 1929;

children-Thain Hodgson, Angus John. President of the Bordulac Mines, Ltd., Spirit Lake Mines, Ltd., Ouebelle Mines, Ltd., Kimset Mines, Ltd. Private secretary to the Canadian Minister Nat. Def., 1923-28. Served with 38th Bn. C.E.F., 1914-19, lt. col., 1932. Awarded Distinguished Service Order, 1916, Victoria Cross, 1917 (Eng.). Mem. Canadian Inst. Mining and Metallurgy, Psi Upsilon. Mem. United Ch. of Can. Clubs: U. Toronto. Home: 354 Cote Saint Antoine Rd., Westmount, Que., Can. Died Mar. 29, 1960; buried Brockville, Ont.

MACE, HAROLD LORING army officer; b. Lake Helen, Fla., Oct. 10, 1907; s. Loring Poole and Eleanor (Morrish) M.; student U. of Florida, 1926-28; grad. Air Corps Primary Flying Sch., 1929, Advanced Flying Sch., 1929, Tech. Sch., 1932; m. Virginia French Griggs, June 28, 1933; children-Barbara Virginia, Stephen Griggs. Commd. 2d lt., Air Res., 1929, 2d lt., Air Corps, U.S. Army, 1930, advanced through grades to brig. gen., 1944; serving overseas since Jan. 1944. Decorated Air Medal with 2 oak leaf clusters, Distinguished Flying Cross; Legion of Merit (U.S.); Croix de Guerre with Palm (Fr.); Croix de guerre with Palm (Belgium). Mem. Sigma Phi Epislon, Quiet Birdmen. Home: 138 Stetson Av., Deland, Fla. Address: care The Adjutant General's Office; War Dept., Washington 25. Died Jan. 20, 1946; buried at Manila, P.I.

MAC ELROY, ANDREW JACKSON author; b. Homeworth, O., Sept. 14, 1875; s. William and Elizabeth (Dennison) M.; B.S., Cornell U., 1898; m. 2d, Mrs. Jeanette Wells, Sept. 19, 1925; children-Webster Wells, Hetty Wells (Mrs. F. W. Finn). High sch. prin., 1898-1904; with Ginn & Co., 1905-07; with editorial and sales depts. Appleton Co., 1908-19; leave of absence, 1909, making trip around the world as rep. N.Y. American, crossing Siberia; with Popular Sci. Monthly, 1919-20; field dir. Iroquois Pub. Co., 1928-32; pres. Acorn PuB. Co. Cadet Cornell U., 1894-96; pvt., 2d lt. and 1st lt. 47th N.Y. Inf., 1915-17; capt. AS, 1917; maj., 1919; rated as res. mil. aviator (pilot); was attached to RAF as U.S. AS insp., 1918, mem. hist. sect. Gen. Staff, U.S. Army, AEF, 1919. Mentioned in orders and awarded D.S.O. (Brit.). Mem. Acad. Polit. Sci. Sigma Alpha Epsilon, Pi Gamma Mu. Republican. Presbyn. Mason. Clubs: Cornell, Fraternities, Masonic, Adventurers, Army and Navy (N.Y.); Rockville Country (Rockville Centre, N.Y.). Author: Cantonment Manual, 1917; Manual of Military Maps, 1918; Fascinating France, 1921. Home: Rockville Centre, N.Y., and Old Field, East Moriches, L.I. Address: 23 Vassar Pl., Rockville Centre, L.I., N.Y. Died July 1963.

MACFADYEN, ALEXANDER pianist, composer; b. Milwaukee, Wis., July 12, 1879; s. Archibald and Jennie Louise (Carter) MacF.; ed. pub. schs. and under pvt. tutors; studied music under Julius Klauser and Wm. Borchert, Milwaukee, and Rudolph Ganz, Arthur Friedheim, Felix Borowski, Herman Devices and Dr. Louis Falk, Chicago; Mus.B., Chicago Musical Coll., 1905; winner Marshall Field diamond medal for post-grad. work; Mus.D., Chicago Conservatory of Music, 1932; unmarried. Debut at Auditorium, Chicago, as piano soloist, 1905; was soloist with orchestra conducted by Hans von Schiller and toured with Leonora Jackson Concert Co.; appeared as soloist with Chicago Symphony Orchestra under Frederick Stock, and has toured as soloist widely in U.S.; served as mem. faculty Internat. Conservatory (New York) and Chicago Conservatory; teacher of piano, Wis. Coll. of Music, 1922-29; pres. Badger Music Pub. Co. Rebpulican. Presbyterian. Composer of more than 100 songs, piano pieces, etc.; best known songs, Inter. Nos. Love Is the Wind, Spring Singing, Cradle Song and Day Break. Sonata, composed by him, performed by Josef Hofmann, in his All-American program, in Carnegie Hall, N.Y. City. Home: Milwaukee, Wis. Died June 6, 1936.

MACFARLAND, LANNING, banker, pub.; b. Chicago, Jan. 15, 1898; s. Henry J. and Lina Wheeler (Cook) M.; A.B., Harvard, 1919; m. Elizabeth Stuckslager, Nov. 22, 1923; children—Lanning Willard C., David B., Mary Elizabeth. Clk., No. Trust Co., Chicago, 1921, v.p., 1931-53; vice pres., dir. Law Bulletin Pub. Co., Chicago, pub. Chicago Daily Law Bull.; dir. Intermountain Lumber Co., Missoula, Mont., Bear Brand Hosiery Co., Chgo. Life trustee Chgo. Wesley Meml. Hosp. Served with Am. Ambulance Field Service, France, 1916-17; with Am. Relief Commn. and A.R.C., Balkans, 1918-19; lt. col., A.U.S., World War II. Recipient Order of White Eagle (Serbia), Order of Redeemer (Greece), Legion of Merit (United States). Trustee of Cornell College, Mount Vernon, Ia., Chicago Meml. Hosp., Chicago Child Care Soc. Republican. Episcopalian. Clubs: Chicago, Union League, Harvard (Chicago); Indian Hill Country (Wilmette, Ill.); Bohemian. Home: Winnetka IL Died Oct. 12, 1971.

MACFARLANE, JOSEPH ARTHUR surgeon, univ. ofcl.; b. Lanark, Ont., Can., Apr. 28, 1893; s. Joseph and Catherine (Gemmel) MacF.; B.A., U. Sask., 1916, LL.D., 1949; M.B., U. Toronto, 1922; student (Rhodes Scholar), Oxford, U., 1922-23; M.D. (hon.) Laval U., 1952; Hon. Doctor's degree U. Brazil; LL.D., U. Western Ontario, 1960; m. Marguerite Walker, Sept. 22, 1926; 1 son, Andrew. Staff Toronto Gen. Hosp., 1926; faculty medicine U. Toronto, 1926, dean faculty medicine, 1946-, chmn. med. scis. adv. council, 1961-; cons. surgeon Dept. Vets. Affairs, 1945-. Served with 11th Field Ambulance Royal Canadian Army, 1916-18, lt. col., 15th gen. hosp., 1939-41; cons. surgeon, brig. Canadian Army Overseas, 1945-1-45. Decorated Officer Order Brit. Empire; Legion of Merit (U.S.); comdr. bro. Order of St. (Edinburgh, Can., Eng.), Assn. Surgeons Gt. Britain; mem. Am. Surg. Assn., Surgeons Gt. Britain; mem. Am. Surg. Assn., Canadian Soc. Clin. Surgeons, Nu Sigma Nu. Home: 58 Bernard Av., Toronto 5, Ont., Can. Died Apr. 1966.

MACFEELY, ROBERT brig. gen. U.S.A., retired, July 8, 1890; b. July 8, 1828; grad. West Point, 1850; served as inf. lt. against hostile Indians in Oregon; staff capt., May 11, 1861; commissary for State of Ind., then of the Army of Ohio, and later of Army of Tennessee; maj., Feb.9, 1863; received two brevets in May 1865 for faithful service; advanced after war to chief commissary of subsistence, with rank of brig. gen. Died 1901.

MAC GILVARY, PATON engineer; b. Berkeley, Calif., June 28, 1896; s. Prof. Evander Bradley and Elizabeth Allen (Paton) M.; B.S. in E.E., U. of Wis., 1916; unmarried. Chief engr. and supt. gas, works, Waukesha (Wis.) Gas & Electric Co., 1916; power specialist, Milwaukee Electric Ry. and Light of New England, 1919-; dir. Curtiss Northwest Airplane Co. Joined Air Service, U.S. Army, May 1917; went abroad, July 1917, training in Italy; successively chief pilot, adjutant and comdg. officer, Camp Ovest, Foggia; engr. attached to representative in Italy of Joint Army and Navy Aircraft Bd.; on Italian Front, June 1918 till close of war, as adj. of Combat Div.; hon. discharged, Dec. 30, 1918. Decorated by King of Italy with Croce di Guerre; awarded Bronzino and two citations while at the front. Republican. Home: Boston, Mass. Died May 10, 1921.

MACGOWAN, DAVID BELL, foreign service; b. Memphis, Tenn., June 5, 1870; s. Evander Locke and Mary Jane (Burrow) M.; A.B., Washington and Lee U., 1890; univs. Halle and Berlin 2 yrs.; m. Emma Birkhead Woods, of Memphis, Apr. 5, 1894. Reporter and spl. corr., Chicago Tribune, 1896-98, and corr. in Berlin, 1899-1900; corr. Associated Press, St. Petersburg, 1901-03, Berlin, 1903; corr. London Standard, at St. Petersburg, 1904-08; editor Knoxville (Tenn.) Sentinel, 1908-14; corr. Associated Press in Galicia, Armenia, Persia and the Caucasus, Turkey, 1915, St. Petersburg, 1915. After examination apptd. Am. consul, Oct. 18, 1915; detailed to Moscow, Jan. 1, 1916; consul at Vladivostock, Sept. 1, 1920-22; first sec. of legation, Riga, Reval and Kovno, 1922-32; assigned as consul to Bern, Dec. 22, 1931, as consul gen., Mar. 27, 1935; retired, June 30, 1935. Unitarian. Home: 106 Madison St., Lynchburg VA

MACGOWAN, JOHN ENCIL journalist; b. in Mahoning County, O., Sept. 30, 1831; s. Samuel MacG.; ed. pub. schs., Mahoning Country, O., and Mt. Union and Hiram colls.; m. Maria Malvina Johnson, 1854 (died 1896). Entered U.S.A., 1861, as pvt. and was mustered out as col. 1st U.S. arty. vols. at Chattanooga, March 31, 1866. Read law and practiced in Ohio and Ind. before war, and in Tenn. after war; then engaged in newspaper work. Address: Chattanooga, Tenn. Died 1903.

MACGREGOR, FRANK SILVER, publisher; b. Lunenburg, Nova Scotia, Jan. 13, 1897; s. Charles William and Rhoda (Silver) MacG.; A.B., Harvard U., 1918. Asst. purchasing agent, Newport Co., Milwaukee, Wis., 1919-21; entered publishing business as college traveler, 1921-24; head of coll. dept., Harper Brothers, 1924-43, v.p. 1930-42, exec. v.p. 1942-45, sec. 1943-45, president, 1945-55, chairman of the board, 1955-62. Served with the United States Navy, 1918-19. Mem. local bd. Selective Service System, World War II. Mem. Am. Hist. Assn. Clubs: Dutch Treat, Century Association, West Hamilton Street (Baltimore). Home: New York City NY Died Jan. 11, 1971.

MACK, JULIAN ELLIS physicist; b. La Porte, Ind., Apr. 26, 1903; s. Charles Samuel and Laura Gordon (Test) M.; A.B., U. Mich., 1924, A.M., 1925, Ph.D., 1928; Nat. Research fellow Princeton, Mich., Minn. and Uppsala univs., 1928-30; m. Mary Brackett, on June 11, 1932; children-Newell Brackett, Cornelia. Asst., U. Mich., 1924-25, instr., 1925-28, lectr., summer 1931; summer positions Nat. Bur. Standards, 1925, 1926; faculty U. Wis. since 1930, prof. physics since 1950; vis. asst. prof. Princeton, 1941-42, physicist uranium project, 1942-43; physicist Los Alamos Lab., 1943-46; John Simon Guggenheim Meml. fellow, 1950-51; pres. Design, Inc. Mem. NRC com. on line spectra of elements; Nat. Acad. Sci. adv. panel atomic physics Nat. Bur. Standards, 1965-; cons. USAF, Project Matterhorn, Los Alamos Sci. Lab.; sci. adviser Am. Embassy, Stockholm, Sweden, 1959-61. Pres. Madison Art Assn. 1956-57. Mem. Fedn. Am. Scientists (nat. council 1954-55). Home: 3501 Sunset Dr., Shorewood Hills, Madison 5, Wis. Died Apr. 14, 1966.

MACK, RICHARD ALFRED govt. ofcl.; b. Miami, Fla., Oct. 2, 1909; s. Charles D. and Allie Mae (Simons) M.; B.S. in Business Adminstration at University of Florida, 1932; m. Susan Marguerite Stovall, Sept. 10, 1936; 1 dau., Susan Stovall. Salesman Gen. Ins. Co., 1932-35; credit mgr. Gen. Motors Acceptance Corp., 1935-40; with Hector Supply Co., 1939-41; mem. Fla. R.R. and Pub. Utilities Commn., 1947-55, FCC, 1955-. Vice pres., mem. exec. com. Nat. Assn. R.R. and Utilities Commnrs. Served as lt. col. AUS, 1941-47; mem. Res. Mem. Sigma Nu, Blue Key. Democrat. Episcopalian. Kiwanian. Home: 1535 Dorado Av., Coral Gables, Fla. Office: Fed. Communications Commn., New Post Office Bldg., Washington 25. Died Nov. 20, 1963.

MACKEACHIE, DOUGLAS CORNELL govt. official; b. Brooklyn, N.Y., Dec. 4, 1900; s. Samuel Stevenson and Jane Adele (Cornell) M.; grad. Ridgewood (N.J.) High Sch., 1917; student Colgate U., 1917-19; m. Martha Hoagland Bade, 1939; 1 dau., Nancy Jane. With Atlantic & Pacific Tea Co. since 1919, successively as office employe, buyer and purchasing dir., dep. dir. of purchases, Office of Production Management, Oct. 1940-Aug. 1941, dir. Aug. 1941; dep. dir. Procurement and distribution, Services of Supply, War Dept. (as civilian), Feb. 1942; commd. col. and sent overseas to be U.S.A. gen. purchasing agent for European Theatre of Operations, May 1942; pres. Atlantic & Pacific Co. of Vt. Dir. New Eng. Council. Clubs: Longwood Cricket (Brookline, Mass.); Algonquin (Boston); Metropolitan (Washington, D.C.). Home: Millbrook Pan-Am. Poets' League of N. Am., 1943. Given nat. testimonial on 70th birthday, announcing his Tetralogy for the Theatre; The Mystery of Hamlet, King of Denmark, comprising the four plays: The Ghost of Elsinore, The Fool in Eden Garden, Odin Against Christus, The Serpent in the Orchard, 1945. Edited The Journal (1898-1939) of Marion Mores MacKaye, 1946. Home Cornish, N.H. P.O. Windsor, Vt. Died Feb. 1943.

MACKENZIE, ALEXANDER major gen. U.S.A.; b. Potosi, Wis., May 25, 1844; s. Donald Alexander and Mary Ann (Conner) M.; ed. Platteville (Wis.) Acad., grammar and high schs., Dubuque, Ia.; grad. U.S. Mil. Acad., 1864; Sc.D. U. of Pa., 1906; widower. Apptd. 1st lt. engrs., June 13, 1864; capt., Mar. 7, 1867; maj., Apr. 5, 1882; lt. col., Feb. 3, 1895; col., May 3, 1901; brig. gen. chief of engrs. U.S.A., Jan. 23, 1904; maj. gen., 1908. Bvtd. captain, Mar. 13, 1865, "for gallant and meritorious services during the war." Served as asst. engr., Dept. of Ark., 1864-65; as asst. engr. on various improvements, 1865-66; harbor improvement of Lake Mich., 1866-68; comd. engr. co. Willetts Point, N.Y., 1868-74; asst. engr. on Louisville and Portland canal, etc., 1874-77; on works under Maj. Weitzel, 1874-79; in charge river and harbor improvement, Miss. River, 1879-95; mem. Mo. River Commn., 1884-95; 1st asst. to chief of engrs., 1895-1903; mem. Lighthouse Bd., 1895-1904; mem. Bd. Ordnance and Fortification from 1904, bd. commrs. of Soliders' Home from 1904; retired by operation of law, May 25, 1908. Active duty, 1917-19. Home: Washington, D.C. Died Feb. 23, 1921.

MACKENZIE, KENNETH ALEXANDER J. surgeon; b. Cumberland House, Manitoba, Can., Jan. 13, 1859; s. Roderick and Jane M.; Nest Acad., Jedburgh, Scotland; high sch., Montreal, Can.; Upper Can. Coll., Toronto; M.D., C.M., McGill U., 1881; L.R. C.P. and L.R.C.S., Edinburgh 1882; also studied univs. of London, Berlin, Paris, Vienna; m. Cora Hardy Scott, 1885 (died, 1901); m. 2d, Marion Higgins Brown, Apr. 1905. In practice at Portland, Ore., 1882-; prof. theory and practice of medicine, 1887-1907, operative and clin. surgery, 1907-, U. of Ore. Surgeon St. Vincent's Hosp., 1883-; chief surgeon in Ore. and Wash. of Ore. R.R. & Navigation Co., 1895-; 1st lt. U.S.A. Medical Reserve Corps. Dir. U.S. National Bank. Head of relief corps of physicians and nurses under auspices of Citizens Relief Com. of Portland, San Francisco, 1906; organized and in charge Harbor View relief sta., under Gen. Torney, U.S.A.; dir. and med. dir. Lewis and Clark Expn.; dir. Portland Free Dispensary; dean Med. Dept., U. of Ore. Republican. Episcopalian. Fellow Am. Surg. Assn., Portland Acad. Medicine (Pres. 1909-10); v.p. A.M.A., 1906-07. Mason. Home: Portland, Ore. Died Mar. 16, 1920.

MACKENZIE, MORRIS ROBINSON SLIDELL rear admiral U.S.N.; b. N.Y.; grad. U.S. Naval Acad., 1866. Promoted ensign, Apr. 1868; master, Mar. 26, 1869; lt., Mar. 21, 1870; lt. comdr., Dec. 1884; comdr., Apr. 16, 1894; capt., July 1, 1900; rear admiral, May 13, 1906. Served on the various stas. an duties; comd. Prairie, 1898-1900, U.S.S. New York, 1901, Navy Yard, Portsmouth, N.H., 1903; insp. in charge, 3d light house dist., 1905; retired. June 28, 1906. Address: Morristown, N.J. Died Jan. 16, 1915.

MACKENZIE, RONALD SLIDELL army officer; b. Westchester County, N.Y., July 27, 1840; s. Alexander Slidell and Catherine (Robinson) M.; grad. U.S. Mil. Acad., 1862. Served as 1st lt. corps engrs. Army of Potomac, 1863, participated in Md. campaign, Rappahannock campaign (battles of Fredericksburg, Chancellorsville, 1863), Pa. campaign (Battle of Gettysburg), Rapidan campaign, 1863-64; commd. capt., comdr. engr. co. in battles of the Wilderness and Spottsylvania, 1863; took part in siege of Petersburg, 1864; commd. col. 2d Com. Heavy Arty. Volunteers, 1864, brevetted col., brig. gen. U.S. Army; commd. maj. gen. U.S. Volunteers; commd. col. 4th Cavalry, participated in campaigns of early 1870's against marauding Indians in W. Tex., along Rio Grande River; as a result of his army services large areas were opened to permanent settlement; held brevet rank of maj. gen. U.S. Volunteers, from 1865; ret. from U.S. Army, 1884, with rank brig. gen. Died New Brighton, Staten Island, N.Y., Jan. 19, 1889.

MACKLIN, JAMES EDGAR brigadier gen. U.S.A.; b. in N.Y., Oct. 18, 1846. Served as pvt. and corporal Co. B, 16th Ind. Inf., Apr. 22, 1861-May 23, 1862; pvt. Co. K, 16th Ind. Inf., June 1, 1862; discharged, Aug. 18, 1862; commd. 2d lt. 16th Ind. Inf., Aug. 19, 1862; 1st lt., Mar. 1, 1863; capt., Dec. 20, 1864; hon. mustered out, June 30, 1865; apptd. from Ind., 2d lt. 31st U.S. Inf., Aug. 9, 1867; assigned to 22d Inf., July 14, 1869; 2d lt. 11th Inf., Jan. 12, 1877; 1st lt., Apr. 24, 1886; capt. 11th Inf., Feb. 25, 1891; maj. 24th Inf., Oct. 19, 1899; transferred to 11th Inf., Feb. 17, 1900; lt. col. 3d Inf., Apr. 20, 1902; col. 4th Inf., May 8, 1906; brig. gen.U.S.A. and retired at own request, over 40 yrs.' service, Dec. 2, 1906. Died Dec. 16, 1925.

MACKLIN, W(ILLIAM) A(LEXANDER) STEWART, naval officer; b. Manchester, Md., July 23, 1897; s. Capt. Charles Fearns and Emily Slaughter (Stewart) M.; B.S., U.S. Naval Acad., 1917; m. Eleanor Keith, Sept. 15, 1920 (div. July 1932); m. 2d Mary Margaret Allen, Nov. 5, 1933; children-Margaret Ann, Stewart Allen. Commd. ensign USN, 1917, advanced through grades to rear adm., 1947; served in U.S.S. Virginia, 1917, U.S.S. O'Brien, 1918-19; instr. U.S. Naval Acad., 1923-25, 28-30; exec. officer gunboat Asheville, Central Am. and China coast, 1930-33; comd. gunboat Oahu, Yangtze River, 1933-35; attached to Navy Dept. Hydrographic Office, 1935-37; navigator U.S.S. Idaho, 1937-38; exec. officer U.S.S. Dobbin, 1938-39; dist. intelligence officer 5th Naval Dist., Norfolk, Va., 1939-41; comdr. destroyer div. 62, North Atlantic, and escort comdr. for convoys between Can. and Eng., 1941-42; comdr. Eastern Sea frontier escort vessels, 1942-43; comdr. U.S.S. Richmond, North Pacific, 1943-44; exec. officer, U.S. Naval Tng. Sta., Newport, R.I. 1944-46; retired, 1947. Decorated Legion of Merit with combat citation. Home: Wolford P.O., Md. Died Oct. 5, 1957; buried Arlington Nat. Cemetery.

MACLACHLAN, JAMES A. educator; b. Ann Arbor, Mich., Aug. 15, 1891; s. Prof. Andrew Cunningham and Lois Thompson (Angell) McLaughlin (name changed to Maclachlan by decree of court, 1948); A.B., U. Mich., 1912; LL.B., Harvard, 1916; m. Mary Jane Carrier, 1928; children-Helen Campbell, David Blair, Bruce Birge, James Angell, Rhoda Wilson. High sch. tchr., coach, Bay City, Mich., 1912-13; practiced law, Chgo., 1916-17, 19-24; asst. prof. law Harvard Law Sch., 1924-27, prof., 1927-60, now prof. emeritus; prof. law Hastings Coll. Law, San Francisco, 1960-; vis. prof. Rutgers Law Sch., 1964, U. Cin. Law Sch., 1964-65, Washington U., St. Louis, 1966. On leave, 1942-45; spl. counsel OPA, Washington, 1942; Contract Renegotiation U.S. Maritime Commn., 1943-45. Served as capt. 333d Heavy Arty., U.S. Army, 1917-19, on detached service with French Arty. Information, Oct.-Nov. 1918. Mem. Nat. Bankruptcy Conf. Mem. Fed. Union, Atlantic Union Community Council, Phi Beta Kappa, Psi Upsilon. Editor: Cases on the Federal Anti-Trust Laws of the United States, 1930, 33; on Creditors Rights (with John Hanna), 1939, 2 vol. revision, 1948-49, consol. edit., 1951, supplemented by annotated edits. of Nat. Bankruptcy Act, 1939, 47, 49, 51, 53, 57; as mem. Nat. Bankruptcy Conf. formulated substantial amendments to the Bankruptcy Act chiefly those embodied in the Chandler Act, 1938 and the amendment to the law of preferences in 1950; contbg. editor Comml. Law Jour., 1960-. Author: Text on Bankruptcy, 1956. Contbr. to legal periodicals. Home: 2117 Devonshire Rd., Ann Arbor, Mich. 48104. Died Apr. 17, 1967; buried Forest Hill Cemetery, Ann Arbor.

MACLAY, EDGAR STANTON author; b. Foochow, China, April 18, 1863; grad. Syracuse Univ., New York, 1885 (A.M.); m. Dec. 22, 1893, Katherine Koerber. Reporter Brooklyn Times, 1886-90; New York Tribune, 1891-93; editorial staff Tribune, 1893-94; editorial staff New York Sun, 1894-95; became lighthouse keeper, Old Field Point, 1895; apptd. to New York Navy Yard, Sept. 7, 1900. Contributor leading mags. Editor of "William Maclay's Journal" (senator from Pa., 1789-91). Author: The History of the United States Navy; Reminiscences of the Old Navy; Life and Adventures of Jack Philip, Admiral U.S.N.; Life of Moses Brown, Captain, N.S.N.; The History of American Privateers. In Vol. III of his History of U.S. Navy made charges against Admiral Schley's conduct at Santiago, which led to an official injury by Navy Dept. Retired from service, Dec. 22, 1901. Address: 1224 Hancock St., Brooklyn, N.Y.

MACLAY, WILLIAM WALTER civil engr.; b. N.Y.C., Mar. 27, 1846; s. Dr. Archibald and Julia Anne (Walker) M.; grad. U.S. Naval Acad., 1863; A.M., N.Y.U., 1868, C.E., 1872; m. Marian Bensel, Sept. 16, 1874. Commd. ensign, 1863; master, 1865, advanced through grades to lt. comdr., 1868; participated in both attacks on Ft. Fisher; after war made cruise of 3 yrs. around the world with Commodore John Goldsborough, as his navigating officer; apptd. by Japanese govt. to survey and designate sites for light houses, 1868; apptd. acting fleet capt. to Commodore Goldsborough, comdg. U.S. Asiatic Squadron, 1868; asst. prof. mathematics U.S. Naval Acad., 1868-69; resigned from Navy to study civil engring., 1871; asst. engr. and 1st asst. engr. N.Y. dept. of docks, 1873-93; now cons. engr.; pres., mgr. Glens Falls Portland Cement Co., 1893-1905. Mem. Inst. Civil Engrs., London, Am. Soc. C.E. (Norman gold medal, 1877), Internat. Soc. for Testing Materials; corr. mem. N.Y. Hist. Soc. Club: University (N.Y.C.). Author: Notes and Experiments on the Use and Testing of Portland Cements, 1877; Portland Cement for Engineering Works, 1892. Home: Lee, Mass. Office: 220 W. 57th St., N.Y.C. Deceased.

MACLEAN, BASIL CLARENDON hospital cons.; b. Oshawa, Ontario, Dec. 24, 1895; s. Daniel and Amelia Jane (Wigg) M.; M.D., C.M., McGill University, 1927; M.P.H., Johns Hopkins University, 1942; came to United States, 1930, naturalized, 1938; m. Caroline A. M. Davis, May 19, 1930; 1 dau., Jean Davis (Mrs. James E. McKelvey). Served as medical supt. of Montreal General Hospital, 1927-30; supt. Touro Infirmary, New Orleans, La., 1930-35; dir. Strong Memorial Hosp and professor hospital administration, U. of Rochester (N.Y.), 1935-54; commissioner of hospitals, New York City, 1954-57; president Blue Cross Association, N.Y.C., 1957-60, cons., 1960-; adj. professor Columbia University. Hospital consultant and surveyor; member American Coll. of Hosp. Administrators (charter fellow; pres. 1936-37), Rochester Hosp. Service Corp. (mem. bd. and exec. com. 1935-54); director Companion Life Insurance Company. Chairman New York State Commn. on Med. Care, 1944-45. Consultant to Children's Bureau, Dept. Labor, Sec. Navy, Commonwealth Fund and Kellogg Foundation. Trustee Trudeau (N.Y.) Sanatorium; b.d dirs. numerous N.Y. hosp. and med. organizations. Served as lieutenant col. Med. Corps, U.S. Army, 1943-44. Award of Merit, American Hospital Association, 1953. Diplomate American Board Preventive Medicine and Pub. Health. Mem. White House Com. on Integration Med. Services, 1945-46; cons. Commn. on Orgn. Exec. Br. Govt., 1948. Mem. Am. hosp. Assn. (chmn. Commn. on Hosp. Service, 1936-41; pres. 1941-42), Blue Cross Commn., N.Y. State Hosp. Assn. Rochester Vis. Nurse Assn. (mem. bd. 1935-50; pres. 1940-41), exec. com. adv. bd. Am. Red Cross Health Services (chmn. Hosp. Div.), A.A.A.S., Am., N.Y. State (charter mem.) public health associations, Society Medical Administrators, Rochester Academy of Medicine, Am. Assn. Hospital Cons., N.Y. State, N.Y. County med. socs., Canadian Society (member board directors), St. Andrew's Society, Alpha Kappa Kappa. Clubs: Genesee Valley (Rochester); Johns Hopkins Faculty (Baltimore); U. (Washington and Montreal); Lake Placid (N.Y.); University (N.Y.); Coral Beach (Bermuda). Author numerous articles for med. and hosp. jours. Mem. editorial bd. Modern Hosp., Pub. Health Reports. Address: 36 Sutton Pl. S., N.Y.C. 22. Died Feb. 14, 1963.

MACLEAN, MUNROE DEACON, educator; b. Quincy, Mass., June 1, 1907; s. Daniel J. and Mary Jane (Munroe) MacL.; B.S., West Chester State Coll., 1931; M.A., Columbia, 1934; postgrad. Boston U., 1951; m. Clara Elizabeth Schatz, June 16, 1934; children—Jean Ann, Mary Carol (Mrs. J. Noel Heermance). Tchr. Hazleton (Pa.) High Sch., 1931-34, West Chester (Pa.) State Coll., 1934-36, P.S. duPont High Sch., Wilmington, Del., 1936-37, Quincy (Mass.) High Sch., 1937-51, asst. dir. health, phys. edn., athletics, 1951-59, coach, dir., health, phys. edn., health services, athletics, 1959-69. Participant in President's Phys. Fitness Conf., Washington, 1962; mem. Mass. state basketball tournament com., 1961-69. Bd. dirs. YMCA, 1952-69, chmn., phys. edn. com., 1963-65, v.p.; bd. dirs. A.R.C., 1959-69, chmn. first aid. Served to lt. comdr., USNR, 1943-46. Recipient citations for work with youth, Amvets, 1962, Am. Legion, 1955, Boy Scouts Am., 1958; named Man of Year, Montclair Men's Club, 1962; 1st mem. inducted into Mass. Basketball Coaches "Hall of Fame", 1964. Mem. Mass., Quincy tchrs. assns., Mass. Athletic Dirs. Assn., Mass. Coaches Assn., Am. (chmn. city and county dirs. 1965), Mass. assns. health, phys. edn., recreation, Am. Legion, Amvets. Elk, Lion. Author: Curriculum Guide in Health Education, 1961, Curriculum Guide in Physical Education, 1963. Assisted in writing U.S. Navy Phys. Fitness Manual, 1962. Home: Quincy MA Died Jan. 24, 1969.

MACLEOD, COLLN MUNRO, educator; b. Nova Scotia, Can., Jan. 28, 1909; s. John Charles and Lillian (Munro) MacL.; M.D., McGill U., 1932; m. Elizabeth Randol, July 2, 1938; 1 dau., Mary. Came to U.S., 1934, naturalized, 1941. Intern Montreal Gen. Hosp., 1932-34; resident in medicine, Rockefeller Inst. Hosp., 1937-38; asst. to asso. in medicine Rockefeller Inst. for Med. Research, 1934-41; prof. microbiology New York University College Medicine, 1941-56; professor research medicine University Pa. School Medicine, 1956-60, prof. medicine N.Y.U. Sch. Medicine, 1960-66; mem. Pres.'s Sci. Adv. Com., 1961-64; chmn. Life Scis. Panel; exec. com. div. med. scis. Nat. Research Council, 1952-56; dir. Commn. on Pneumonia Army Epidemiol. Bd., 1941-46; chief preventive medicine sect. Com. Med. Research Office Scientific Research and Development, 1944-46; pres. Armed Forces Epidemiol. Bd., 1947-55; mem. panel mil. and field medicine Com. Med. Scis. Nat. Mil. Establishment, 1948-52; adv. panel on med. scis. to Asst. Sec. Def. for research and devel., 1952-56; chmn. com. on research in influenza USPHS; member Army Sci. Adv. Panel, 1958-61; chmn. sci. adv. com. Walter Reed Army Inst. Research, 1957-61; chmn. Health Research Council N.Y.C., from 1960; deputy director Office Sci. and Tech., 1963-64; v.p. med. affairs Commonwealth Fund, from 1966; consultant President's Sci. Adv. Com., from 1964; U.S. chmn. U.S.-Japan Coop. Med. Sci. Program, 1965-72; pres., sci. dir. Okla. Med. Research Found., 1970-72; mem. sci. adv. com. Hosp. for Sick Children, Toronto; vis. com. biology Harvard; adv. bd. chemistry Princeton. Dir., Merck & Co.; trustee Merck Co. Found., Sloan-Kettering Inst. for Sci. Research. Recipient Bristol award Infectious Disease Soc., 1971. Mem. Nat. Acad. Scis., Am. Epidemiol. Soc., Am. Assn. Immunologists (pres. 1951-52), Soc. Am. Bacteriologists, Assn. Am. Physicians, Soc. Clin. Investigation, N.Y. Acad. Medicine, Am. Philos. Soc., Am. Acad. Arts and Scis., Harvey Soc. (pres. 1955-56). Club: Century Association. Contbr. articles med. jours. Home: Oklahoma City OK Died Feb. 12, 1972.

MACMILLAN, WILLIAM DUNCAN mathematician, astronomer; b. LaCrosse, Wis., July 24, 1871; s. Duncan D. and Mary Jane (MacCrea) MacM.; studied Lake Forest Coll., Ill., 1888-90, Sc.D., 1930; studied U. of Va., 1895; A.B., Ft. Worth U., 1898; A.M., U. of Chicago, 1906, Ph.D., 1908; Sc.D., Lake Forest Coll., 1930; unmarried. Research asst. in geology, U. of Chicago, 1907-08, asst. in mathematics and astronomy, 1908-09, instr. astronomy, 1909-12, asst. prof., 1912-19, asso. prof., 1919-24, prof., 1924-36, prof. emeritus since 1936. Maj. Ordnance Dept., U.S. Army, 1918. Fellow A.A.A.S., Royal Astron. Soc.; mem. Am. Math. Soc., Math. Assn. America, Astron. and Astrophys. Soc. Am., Socieété Astronomique de France. Clubs: Quadrangle, University. Author: Statics and the Dynamics of a Particle, 1927; Theory of the Potential, 1930; Dynamics of Rigid Bodies, 1936; and many scientific memoirs. Home: Marine on St. Croix, Minn. Died Nov. 14, 1948.

MAC MULLAN, RALPH A., state ofcl.; b. Detroit, Sept. 2, 1917; s. A.B. in Zoology, U. Mich., 1939, Ph.D., 1960. Game research biologist Mich. Dept. Natural Resources, Rose Lake Wildlife Sta., 1946, pheasant research, Lansing, 1947-50, head Houghton Lake Wildlife Expt. Sta., 1950-56, head game research, Lansing, 1956-62, asst. chief game div., 1962, dep. dir. in charge of staff, 1963, dir. dept., 1964-72. Mem. Nat. Adv. Com. Oceans and Atmosphere, 1971; liaison and protocol officer Mich. Sister-State Relationship with Shiga Prefecture, Japan, Belize and Dominican Republic; active Mich. Natural Resources Council, Greater Mich. Found. Served to maj. USAAF, World War II. Recipient Nat. Outdoor Life Conservation award, 1969; named Mich. State Conservationist of Year Nat. Wildlife Fedn., 1970. Mem. Internat. Assn. Game, Fish and Conservations Commrs. (pres.), Wildlife Soc. (v.p.), Nat. Assn. State Outdoor Recreation Liaison Officers (past pres.), Mich. Assn. Conservation Ecologists. Author: Life and Times of Michigan Pheasants (Wildlife Soc. award), 1956. Contbr. articles to mags., profl. jours. Address: Lansing MI Died Sept. 1972.

MACNAIR, JAMES DUNCAN clergyman; b. Trout River, Que., Can., May 26, 1874 (father, Civil War vet.); s. James and Christina (Mitchell) MacN.; came to U.S., 1890; student Boston U. Sch. of Theology, 1898-1901, S.T.B., 1905; A.B., Boston U. Coll. of Liberal Arts, 1905, D.D., 1937; m. Grace Eunice Tibbetts, June 12, 1907. Teacher pub. sch., Burke, N.Y., 1895; agent Prudential Ins. Co., Hartford, Conn., 1895-96; asst. mgr. and mgr. E. P. Charlton Syndicate, Hartford, Conn., and Biddeford, Me., 1896-98; ordained deacon in M.E. Ch., 1902, received into E. Me. Conf., 1905; pastor Union Ch., Swans Island, Me., 1905-06; ordained elder, 1906; chaplain Craig Colony, Sonyea, N.Y., 1906-09; commd. chaplain with rank of lt. j.g., U.S. Navy, 1909; commd. lt., 1916, lt. comdr., 1919, comdr., 1919, capt., 1920; served at Naval Training Sta., Norfolk, Va., 1909, on U.S.S. Ga., 1909-11, U.S.S. Va., 1911, U.S.S. Ga., 1911-12, at Navy Yard, Mare Island, Calif., 1912-14, on U.S.S. Md., 1914-16, U.S.S. Pittsburgh, 1916, U.S.S. Ariz., 1916-17, with 6th Regt., U.S. Marines, in France, 1917-18, at Navy Yard, Boston, 1918-19, Naval Training Sta., Newport, R.I., 1919-21, Navy Yard, Phila., 1921-23, on U.S.S. Wyo. as fleet chaplain Atlantic Scouting Fleet, 1923-25, at Naval Home, Phila., 1926, Navy Yard, Phila., 1926-30; retired for physical disability, Sept. 1, 1930; commd. rear adm. and thus became senior ranking chaplain, U.S. Navy, retired, 1936; pres. Quick Maturity Bldg. & Loan Assn.; National Chaplain, 1941-42, Nat. Assn. of Legions of Honor; mem. Me. Conf. of Meth. Ch. Awarded Mexican Medal, 1914; Victory Medal, 1918; Navy Cross for extraordinary heroism in actual combat with enemy during World War, 1919. Mem. Am. Acad. of Polit. and Social Science, Pa. Historical Society, Benjamin Franklin Institute, American Legion, Military order of the World War, Hon. Navy League Army and Navy Union, St. Andrews Soc. of Phila., Old Guard of the City of Phila., Nat. Sojourners, Jewish Legion of Honor (hon.). Theta Delta Chi. Republican. Methodist. Mason (33ff, K.T., Shriner; Legion of Honor of Lulu Temple, Phila.), Odd Fellow, Eastern Star. Clubs: Union

League, Fellowship, One Hundred, Boston University Alumni, Shrine Luncheon (Phila.); Wardroom (Boston); Optimist (Upper Darby, Pa.). Author occasional articles. While on active duty was editor and mgr. of ships' and Stations' papers. Home: 329 Brookline Blvd., Brookline, Upper Darby, Pa. Died May 4, 1946; buried in Laurel Hill Cemetery, Saco, Me.

MACNAMARA, ARTHUR JAMES government official; b. Bracondale, Ont., Can., March 4, 1885; s. John MacNamara; ed. pub. schs. of Toronto and Montreal; LL.D. (hon.) Univ. of Manitoba, 1944; m. Myrtle Card, June 30, 1917. Dep. minister of pub. works, Province of Manitoba, 1929-36, 1936-40; associate deputy minister of labour, 1940, deputy minister of labour since 1943; acting chief commr., Unemployment Ins. commn., Jan. 1941-42; dir. Nat. Selective Service for Can., 1942; advisor on civilian employment Nat. Def., 1953; past chmn. adv. com. Unemployment Ins. Fund; mng. dir. Canadian Assn. Equipment Distbrs., 1955-. Decorated Companion St. Michael and St. George, 1946. Mem. Ch. of England. Clubs: Manitoba, Rotary (Winnipeg). Home: 72 Bronson. Office: 237 Queen St., Ottawa, Ont., Can. Died Oct. 5, 1962; buried Beechwood Cemetery, Ottawa.

MACNEAL, WARD J. bacteriologist; b. Fenton, Mich., Feb. 17, 1881; s. Edward and Jane Elizabeth (Pratt) MacN.; A.B., U. of Mich., 1901, Ph.D., 1904, M.D., 1905, hon. Sc.D., 1939; m. Nabel Perry, Dec. 28, 1905; children-Edward Perry (dec.), Herbert Pratt, Perry Scott, Mabel Ruth. Asst. and fellow in bacteriology, U. of Mich., 1901-04, instr. histology, 1905-06; instr. in anatomy and bacteriology, W. Va. U., 1906-07; asst. chief in bacteriology, Ill. Agrl. Expt. Sta., 1907-11; asst. prof. bacteriology, U. of Ill., 1908-11; lecturer on pathology and bacteriology, 1911-12, prof. and asst. dir. labs., 1912-15, prof. and dir. of labs., 1915-22, prof. and dir. dept. pathology and bacteriology, 1922-24 and 1930-39, prof. bacteriology since 1939, prof. and dir. labs., 1924-30, mem. bd. trustees, 1921-24; v. chmn. Med. Bd., 1924-29, N.Y. Post-Grad. Med. Sch. and Hosp.; asst. to pres. Josiah Macy Jr. Foundation, 1931-36. Mem. Ill State Pellagra Commn., 1909-12; mem. Thompson-McFadden Pellagra Commn., Am. Trench Fever Commn., France, 1918. Capt., Med. R.C., 1917; lt. col., M.R.C. U.S. Army, 1919; col., 1925; with A.E.F. in France to Feb. 1919. Fellow A.A.A.S.; mem. Soc. Am. Bacteriologists, Am. Assn. Pathologists and Bacteriologists (council 1929-35, pres. 1932), Assn. for Cancer Research (council 1925-33; pres. 1934), Nat. Assn. Tuberculosis, A.M.A., Soc. Exptl. Biology and Medicine, N.Y. Acad. Medicine, N.Y. Pathol. Soc. (pres. 1922-23; trustee 1925-30, 1932-37 and since 1940), N.Y. State Soc. of Pathologists (v.p. 1941, pres. 1942-45), Harvey Soc., Sigma Xi, Author: Studies in Nutrition, Volumes I to V (with H. S. Grindley), 1911-29; Pathogenic Microörganisms, 1914, 2d edit., 1920. Contbr. to Marshall's Microbiology, 1917, 20, etc. Editor Third Report Thompson Pellagra Commission, 1917. Home: 301 E. 21st St., New York 10, N.Y. Office: 303 E. 20th St., New York 3, N.Y. Died Aug. 15, 1946.

MACNIDER, HANFORD mfr.; b. Mason City, Ia., Oct. 2, 1889; s. Charles Henry and May (Hanford) M.; grad. Milton (Mass.) Acad., 1907; A.B., Harvard, 1911; M.M.S., Norwich, 1926; LL.D., Syracuse, 1932, Simpson Coll., 1962; m. Margaret McAuley, Feb. 20, 1925; three sons- Tom, Jack, Angus (dec.). Chmn. bd. Northwestern States Portland Cement Co. State comdr. Am. Legion, 1920-21, nat. commander, 1921-22; asst. sec. of war, 1925-28; U.S. Minister to Canada, 1930-32; mem. Geo. Washington Bicentennial Commn., 1925-30, trustee Grinnell Coll., 1929-39; overseer Harvard Coll., 1946-52. Mexican Border service, 2d Inf. Ia. N.G., 1916-17; World War I, 2d lt., lt. col., 9th U.S. Inf., 2d Div., A.E.F., 1917-19; World War II, colonel, brig. general, G.H.Q., S.W.P.A., 32d Div., 1st Cav. Div., 158 R.C.T. (Bushmasters), Jan. 1942-Feb. 1946; maj. gen. 103d Inf. Div. (OR) 1946-51; retired lt. gen. 1956. Decorations: D.S.C. with 2 clusters, D.S.M., Silver Star with 2 clusters, Legion of Merit, Bronze Star with cluster, Air Medal, Purple Heart with cluster, Bronze Arrowhead, Distinguished Unit Badge with 2 clusters (U.S.); Comdr. Legion of Honor, Croix de Guerre, five citations, Fourragere, C. de G. (France); Croce al Merito di Guerra (Italy); Comdr. Legion of Honor (Philippines). Del. at large, Rep. Nat. Conv., 1924, 1948; endorsed for presdl. nomination by Rep. State Conv., Des Moines, Ia., 1940. Mason. Home: Mason City, Ia. Died Feb. 18, 1968.

MACNULTY, WILLIAM K. marine corps officer, ret.; b. May 22, 1892; advanced through grades to brig. gen., 1942, ret., 1946. Address: Marine Corps Hdqrs., Washington. Died Aug. 3, 1964; buried Golden Gate Cemetery, San Bruno, Cal.

MACOMB, ALEXANDER army officer; b. Detroit, Apr. 3, 1782; s. Alexander and Catharine (Navarre) M.; grad. U.S. Mil. Acad., 1802; m. Catherine Macomb, July 23, 1803; m. 2d, Harriet Balch, 1826; numerous children. Sec. to commr. apptd. to treat with Indians of S.E., 1801-02; commd. 1st lt. Corps Engrs., U.S. Army, 1802, capt. 1805; chief engr. charge coast fortifications in Carolinas and Ga., 1807-12; promoted maj., 1808, lt. col. 1810, adj. gen., 1812; transferred to arty.; commd. col., 1812; sent to N.Y. to raise regt. brig. gen., 1814; defeated British at Battle of Plattsburg; breveted maj. gen., 1819; head Corps Engrs., 1821; sr. maj. gen. and commanding gen. U.S. Army, 1828-41; partly responsible for abolition of whiskey ration in army, 1830. Author Treatise on Martial Law and Court Martials, 1809; The Practice of Court Martial, 1840. Died Washington, D.C., June 25, 1841.

MACOMB, AUGUSTUS CANFIELD army officer; b. Detroit, Mich., Oct. 17, 1854; s. of Col. John Navarre (U.S. Engrs.) and Ann (Rodgers) M.; cadet midshipman U.S. Naval Acad., 1872-76; Army War Coll., 1915; m. Ella C. McKelden, of Washington, D.C., Mar. 10, 1881. Commd. 2d lt. 4th Inf., Jan. 23, 1878; trans to 5th Cav., June 3, 1879; 1st lt., Mar. 11, 1887; capt., June 2, 1897; maj. 9th Cav., Apr. 10, 1905; lt. col., Mar. 11, 1911; assigned to 9th Cav., Mar. 15, 1913; col. of cav., Sept. 2, 1914; assigned to 14th Cav., Aug. 5, 1915. Participated in Crow Indian campaign, summer and fall 1878; northern Cheyenne Indian campaign, winter 1879; Ute Indian campaign, 1879; Spanish war, active service in Porto Rico, recommended for two brevets; in Philippines, 1901-03, and 1907; in 2d punitive campaign in Mex., May 1916. Episcopalian. Club: Army and Navy. Home: 1508 21st St. N.W., Washington, D.C.

MACOMB, DAVID BETTON rear admiral U.S.N.; b. in Fla., Feb. 27, 1827. Apptd. 3d asst. engr., U.S.N., Jan. 11, 1849; 2d asst. engr., Feb. 26, 1851; 1st asst. engr., June 26, 1856; chief engr., Sept. 21, 1860; retired list, Feb. 27, 1889; advanced to rank of rear admiral retired, June 29, 1906, for services during Civil War. Served in Civil War on spl. duty and on Canonicus; fleet engr. N. Atlantic Fleet, May 17-Dec. 16, 1871; pres. bd., Navy Yard, Portsmouth, N.H., Sept. 15, 1882-July 26, 1883. Died 1911.

MACOMB, MONTGOMERY MEIGS brigadier gen. U.S.A.; b. Detroit, Oct. 12, 1852; s. John Navarre and Nannie (Rodgers) M.; grad. Hughes High Sch., Cincinnati, 1869; Yale, 1 yr.; apptd. cadet Sept. 1, 1870, from Ill., and grad. number 4 in class, U.S. Mil. Acad., 1874; grad. Arty. Sch., 1886; m. Mrs. Caroline Luce Walter, Oct. 7, 1908. Commd. 2d lt. 4th Arty., June 17, 1874; 1st lt. Sept. 6, 1879; capt. 7th Arty., Mar. 8, 1898; maj. Arty. Corps, Nov. 4, 1901; lt. col., Mar. 26, 1906; col. Apr. 5, 1907; assigned to 6th Field Arty., June 6, 1907; brig. gen. U.S.A., Nov. 15, 1910. Served frontier duty, Ft. Wrangel, Alaska, Jan.-June 1875; on duty in Europe, a.-d.-c. to Gen. M. C. Meigs 1875-76; with U.S. geog. explorations west of 100th meridian (Wheeler Survey), 1876-83; at Arty. Sch. and duty with regt., 1884-87; instr. in mathematics and asst. prof. drawing, U.S. Mil. Acad., 1887-91; on special duty under Intercontinental Railway Commission in charge surveys and explorations in Central America and making report on same, 1891-96; duty with regt., Ft. Riley, Kan., 1896-98; comdg. Light Battery M. 7th Arty., in Puerto Rico, Spanish-Am. War; and in Philippines, 1900-02; mem. bd. reporting upon defense of prin. harbors of P.I., 1902; recalled to U.S. Aug. 1902, and detailed as mem. Ordnance Bd. and Bd. of Ordnance and Fortification; mem. War Dept. Gen. Staff, Aug. 15, 1903-Mar. 26, 1906, and May 23, 1908-Nov. 14, 1910; mil. attaché with Russian armies in Manchuria during Russo-Japanese War, 1904-05, and present at battles of Liaoyang, Sha River and Mukden; comdg. Arty. subpost Ft. Riley, Kan., Oct. 1, 1906-June 15, 1908; also pres. Field Arty. Examining Bd. and of bd. to determine best type of field-guns and field-works; organized 6th Regt. Field Arty. (Horse), June 1907, and commanded same to June 15, 1908; comdg. District of Hawaii, Jan. 12-Sept. 30, 1911; comdg. Dept. of Hawaii, Oct. 1, 1911-Feb. 14, 1913, and Hawaiian Dept., Feb. 15-Apr. 3, 1913, also Jan. 23-Mar. 12, 1914; comdg. 1st Hawaiian Brigade, Feb. 15, 1913-Feb. 25, 1914; mem. bd. of officers on defense of Oahu, 1912-14; pres. Army War Coll., Apr. 23, 1914-Oct. 12, 1916, and mem. Gen. Staff, June 3-Oct. 12, 1916; retired by operation of law, Oct. 12, 1916. On active duty, Oct. 30, 1917-Mar. 22, 1918; comdg. post, Fort Sill, Okla., Nov. 1, 1917-Mar. 19, 1918. Episcopalian. Home: Washington, D.C. Died Jan. 19, 1924.

MACOMBER, ALEXANDER cons. engr.; b. Newton, Mass., May 21, 1885; s. James and Mary Elizabeth (Simmons) M.; B.S., Mass. Inst. Tech., 1907; m. Alfrieda Terry, Aug. 15, 1929. Elec. engr. No. Cal. Power Co., 1907-10; engr. with Chas. H. Tenney & Co., mgrs. pub. utilities, 1910-17; mem. Macombet & West, cons. engrs. and mgrs. pub. utilities, 1920-50, pres. Nantucket Gas & Elec. Co., Manchester Elec. Co., Gas Service, Inc.; mng. dir. Portland Gas Light Co., Community Pub. Service Co., Northeast Gas Transmission Co. Pres. Franklin Found. Commr. Port of Boston Authority. Served as Gas Div., W.P.B., Washington, 1942-46. Served as maj. C.E., U.S. Army, 1917-19. Trustee Old South Church, Boston. Mem. Am. Gas Assn., Alpha Tau Omega (nat. treas.). Republican. Conglist. Club: Union, Algonquin, Engineers (Boston), Nashua Country, Peterbough Country (N.H.). Contbr. to tech. publs. Home: 401 Beacon St. Office: 110 State St., Boston. Died Mar. 14, 1956; buried Mount Auburn Cemetery, Cambridge.

MAC PHERSON, EARLE STEELE engr., motor vehicle mfg. exec.; b. Highland Park, Ill., July 6, 1891; s. Arthur Grant and Emma (Eckhardt) Mac P.; B.S. in Mech. Engring., U. Ill., 1915; m. Florence Lucille Jones, Mar. 11, 1941; 1 dau., Sandra Lucille. Exptl. lab. engr. Chalmers Motor Co., 1915-17; asst. chief engr. Liberty Motor Car Corp., 1919-22; design engr., asst. chief engr. Hupp Motor Car Co., 1930-34; asst. to v.p. engring., chief engr. Chevrolet-Cleveland, chief engr. product study 6, Gen. Motors Corp., 1935-47 (all Detroit); exec. engr. Ford Motor Co., Dearborn, Mich., 1947-49; chief engr., 1949-52, v.p. engring., mem. adminstrn com., 1952—. Served as capt., A.S., A.E.F., 1917-19; engr. Bolling Mission, France. Mem. Soc. Automotive Engrs. Inc., Engring. Soc. of Detroit, Coordinating Research Council, Inc., Phi Delta Theta, Tau Beta Pi. Mason. Clubs: Detroit Athletic; Red Run Gold (Huntington Woods, Mich.). Home: 8775 Lincoln Dr., Huntington Woods. Office: Ford Motor Co., Dearborn, Mich. Died Jan. 28, 1960.

MACQUEEN, PETER lecturer; b. Wigtonshire, Scotland, Jan. 11, 1865; s. Hugh and Janet (MacHarg) M.; came to America, 1881; student Hamilton Coll., N.Y., 1883; A.B., Princeton, 1887 (hon. A.M., 1903); grad. Union Theol. Sem., 1890. Ordained to ministry, 1890; pastor Bronxville, N.Y., 1890-93, Day St. Ch., West Somerville, Mass., 1893-1900, Harvard Ch., Charlestown, 1900-07; lecturing on travel, 1898-. Has travled over 250,000 miles in various countries; was corr. Spanish-Am. War, 1898, Philippine campaign, 1899, S. African War, 1900; traveled in Russia on pass from the Czar, 1901; was in Battle of Marne, 1914, with Gen. Foch and 9th French Army; corr. for Leslie's Weekly with French Army, 1915; corr. Nat. Magazine and Leslie's Weekly at Peace Conf., Paris, 1919. Republican. Chaplain 5th Regt. Mass. Vol. Militia, 1905-; mem. Mil. Order of Pretoria, Hellenic Brotherhood, Spanish War Vets. (honorary). Author: Around the World with the Flag, 1889; Campaigning in the Philippines, 1900; in Wildest Africa, 1909; The New South America, 1914. Home: East Boothbay, Me. Died Jan. 11, 1924.

MACQUIGG, CHARLES ELLISON college dean; b. Ironton, O., Jan. 19, 1885; s. Charles Bridwell and Rosa (Ellison) MacQ.; E.M., Ohio State U., 1909; hon. Eng.D., Clarkson Coll. of Tech.; m. Lillian Rodgers, Dec. 25, 1912; children-Rodger Ellison, Charles Harrison, David Ellison. Civil engr. Santa Fe Ry., 1909-10; asst. engr. of tests Anaconda Cooper Mining Co., 1910-12; head dept. metallurgy, Pa. State Coll., 1912-17; research and development work Union Carbide and Carbon Co., research labs., 1919-37; dean Coll. Engring., Ohio State U., since 1937; dir. Engring Expt. Sta. of Ohio State U. Research Found.; mem. Ohio Water Resources Bd. Morehead medalist, Internat. Acct. Assn. Capt. Ordnance Dept. U.S. Army, 1917-19; now lt. col. ordnance, O.R.C. Mem. Am. Inst. Mining and Metall. Engrs.; mem. Am. Soc. for Engring. Edn. (pres. 1947-48), Am. Soc. Mech. Engrs., Ohio Acad. Science (fellow), Newcomen Soc., Am. Assn. Advancement of Sci., Am. Soc. for Metals, Sigma Xi, Tau Beta Pi. Republican. Episcopalian. Mason. Contbr. tech. articles to jours. Home: 393 W. 8th Av., Columbus, O. Died Apr. 24, 1952; buried Ironton, O.

MACVEAGH, (ISAAC) WAYNE Attorney-Gen. of U.S.; b. nr. Phoenixville, Chester Co., Pa., Apr.19, 1833; s. Maj. John and Margaret (Lincoln) M.; A.B., Yale, 1853; LL.D., Amherst, 1881. U. of Pa., 1897, Harvard, 1901; m. Letty Miner Lewis, May 22, 1856; m. 2d, Virginia Rolette Cameron, Dec. 27, 1866. Admitted to bar, 1856; dist. atty., Chester County, Pa., 1859-64; capt. of inf., 1862, and of cav., 1863, when invasions of Pa. were threatened; chmn. Rep. State Com. of Pa., 1863; U.S. minister to Turkey, 1870-71; mem. Pa. Constl. Conv., 1872-74; head of "MacVeagh commn." sent to La., 1877, by President Hayes to amicably adjust disputes of contending parties there; Atty.-Gen. of U.S. in cabinet of President Garfield, 1881, but resigned on accession of President Arthur, resuming law practice at Phila. Was chmn. Civ. Service Reform Assn. of Phila., and of Indian Rights Assn. Supported Cleveland for President, 1892; ambassador to Italy, 1893-97; chief counsel of U.S. in the Venezuela arbitration before The Hague Tribunal, 1903. Address: Bryn Mawr, Pa. Died Jan. 11, 1917.

MACVEAGH, LINCOLN, publisher, diplomat; b. Narragansett Pier, R.I., Oct. 1,21890; s. Charles and Fanny Davenport (Rogers) MacV.; student Groton Sch., 1903-09; A.B., Harvard, 1913; student at Sorbonne, Paris, 1913-14; Ph.D. (honorary), Athens University; married to Margaret Charlton Lewis, Aug. 17, 1917 (died Sept. 9, 1947); 1 dau., Mrs. Samuel E. Thorne; married 2d, Virginia Ferrante Coats, May 12, 1955; stepchildren—Colin MacVeagh, Mrs. Hugh Reynolds, Gloria MacVeagh, Sec. to dir. Boston Art Mus., 1912-13; with United States Steel Products Company, 1914-15, Henry Holt Company, 1915-17, 1919-23; pres. Dial Press, Inc., 1923-33; E.E. and M.P. to Greece, 1933-41; to Iceland, 1941; to Union of South Africa, 1942; ambassador to Greece and Yugoslavia, 1943, to Greece, 1944, Portugal, 1948, to Spain 1952-53. Served as 1st lieutenant, later capt. and maj., Army Expeditionary Force, World War I; cited by Gen. Pershing "for exceptionally meritorious and conspicuous services;" Grand Cross of George the First of Greece, 1954. Decorated Grand Cross Mil. Order Christ (Portugal), 1960. Hon. Citizen Athens; trustee Am. Sch. of Classical Studies; hon. fellow Archaeol.

Society of Athens; member Society Mayflower Descendants, Stewart Society of Edinburgh, Council Fgn. Relations, Am. Legion, P.E.N., Phi Beta Kappa. Democrat. Episcopalian. Clubs: Jefferson Islands Country; Century, University (N.Y.C.); Metropolitan (Washington), New Canaan Country. Editor: New Champlin Cyclopedia for Young Folks, 1924, 25, 30, Poetry from the Bible, 1925. Author: (with Margaret MacVeagh) Greek Journey, 1937. Address: Estoril Portugal Died Jan. 15, 1972.

MACY, EDITH DEWING (MRS. EDWARD WARREN MACY) orgn. officer; b. London; ed. schs. of England; children-Edward A., Molly E. (dec.). Chmn. adult edn. com. Central Branch Y.W.C.A., Bklyn.; mem. nat. bd. YWCA, 1938-, pres., 1952-55; also trustee; 2d v.p., mem. exec. com.; 1st v.p., vice chmn. exec. com.; chmn. Nat. Services div. nat. bd.; chmn. U.S.O. div.; mem. exec. com. Nat. U.S.O. Bd. Dirs.; chmn. interpretation and support com. nat. board; chmn. nat. exec. com. of Round the World YWCA Reconstrn. Fund; cons. on religious resources Nat. Urban League, 1957-66. Mem. Clothing Allocation Com., Pres.'s War Relief Control Bd.; bd. dir. exec. com. Nat. Women's Adv. Service of FCDA; nat. adv. com. U.S. for UN Day. Mem. N.Y. State and N.Y.C. League of Women Voters (past chmn. govt. and child welfare coms. both brs.). Mem. bd. and exec. com. Maternity Centre, Bklyn. Episcopalian. Clubs: Civitas, Ihpentonga, Brooklyn. Home: 128 Willow St., Brooklyn Heights, N.Y. 11201. Died July 6, 1967.

MACY, EDWARD WARREN welfare exec.; b. Fitchburg, Mass., Aug. 7, 1893; s. Edward Jenkins and Helen Elizabeth (Macy) M.; student Worcester Acad.; Mass. Inst. Tech., 1916; M.A. hon., Coll. Ozarks, 1932; m. Edith Dewing, Aug. 24, 1914; children-Edward Arthur, Molly Edwina (dec.). Sociologist Swarthmore Child Guidance Clinic, 1915-17; gen. sec. Savannah Social Service Fedn., 1922-24; exec. asst. Nat. Child Labor Com., 1924-26; dir. A.R.C. Disaster Relief (Ill. cyclone, 1927, N.J. fires, 1930, Conn. flood, 1936); dir. pub. dept. Marts & Lundy, Inc., philanthropic financing, 1926-31; director Bklyn. Children's Aid Soc., 1931-48; now director orgn. L.I. Symphony Society. Licensed minister Am. Evangelical Church, 1956. Director N.Y. Heart Assn., 1949-50, Sister Elizabeth Kenny Found., 1950-54, United Def. Fund-U.S.O., 1952-54. Formerly: asso. judge Juvenile Ct., Savannah; pres. Ga. Assn. Family Welfare Agencies; mem. Ga. State Commn. on Dependent, Neglected and Disabled Children; sec. So. Regional Child Welfare Conf.; mem. bd. dirs. Child Welfare League Am.; com. member Nat. Conf. Social Work and Welfare Council of N.Y.C. Mem. com. which reorganized children div. N.Y.C. Dept. of Welfare. Served as maj., then col. Inf. U.S. Nat. Army, 1917-18; field dir. A.R.C., 1919-21; Commander USCG Reserves, World War II, captain USCG Auxiliary, 1948-56, chaplain, 1956—. Decorated French Commenorative, French Victory, Verdun, St. Mihiel, Chateau Thierry medals, World War I; Am. Def. award, Atlantic Theatre medal, Navy Commendation (2 citations), World War II. Awarded 3d prize seascape painting, 1951 (one-man shows Art League of Nassau Co., L.I. Hist. Soc. 1951). Mem. French War Vets. (hon. life), Vets. Fgn. Wars (past comdr.), Am. Assn. Social Workers, Army and Navy Union U.S.A., Mil. Order Indian Wars, U.S. Soc. War 1912, Sons of Union Vets., Am. Legion, Alpha Delta Tau. Rep. Episcopalian. Clubs: Art League of Nassau County. Author various articles newspapers and mags. Built, operated one of the 1st wireless stas., 1907; built, flew one of the 1st heavier than air machines, 1910. Home: 128 Willow St., Bklyn.; also Oceanside, L.I., N.Y. Died Oct. 19, 1958.

MACY, JOSIAH, JR., airline exec.; b. Morristown, N.J., Apr. 20, 1910; s. Josiah and Elizabeth Wyatt (Wise) M.; grad. Taft Sch., 1928; A.B., Princeton, 1932; student U. Munich (Germany), 1930; LL.B., U. Pa., 1935; m. Mary Charlotte Emerson, July 3, 1939; children—Josiah III, Thomas Truxtun, Deborah Wright, Michael Emerson Fitzgerald. Admitted to N.Y. bar, 1936, N.J. bar, 1946; gen. practice of law, N.Y.C., 1935-41; asso. Shanley & Fisher, Newark, 1945-48; sec. Mut. Ins. Adv. Assn., N.Y.C., 1948-51; atty. Daystrom, Inc., Murray Hill, N.J., 1951-52; asst. sec. Pan Am. World Airways, Inc. N.Y.C., 1952-60, sec., 1960-72; sec. Intercontinental Hotels Corp., 1960-72, also sec., dir. affiliated hotel cos. Former adv. mem. Morristown Plan Bd. Candidate N.J. Senate, 1949. Past chmn. Morristown Assn.; trustee New Vernon (N.J.) Cemetery Assn.; past bd. dirs. Morristown chpt. A.R.C.; sec. U.S.-Nigerian Found. Served to maj. AUS, 1941-45; ETO. Decorated Bronze Star. Episcopalian. Clubs: Colonial (Princeton), Shakespeare (past pres.) (Morristown). Home: Morristown NJ Died Aug. 24, 1972.

MADDEN, JAMES LOOMIS, lawyer; b. N.J., July 5, 1892; s. James Thomas and Jane (O'Neill) M.; A.B., Washington Coll., Chestertown, Md., 1911, A.M., 1916, LL.D., 1951; J.D., N.Y. U., 1917; LL.D., Middlebury Coll., 1952; m. Irma Twining, Jan. 12, 1920; children—Mary Carolyn, James E., Richard B., Robert T. Admitted to N.Y. bar, 1917, U.S. Supreme Ct., 1926; 2d v.p. Met. Life Ins. Co., 1927-63; mem. adv. bd. Lumbermans Mut. Casualty Co.; dir. Mueller Corp., Metropolitan Fire Ins. Co. Acting chancellor N.Y. U., 1951-52, vice chmn. trustees, 1952-62, mem. faculty Law School, 1936-47; v.p., dir. Law Center Found., N.Y. U.; fellow Ins. Inst. Am.; trustee Kempner Found., Duke; Brackett lectr. Princeton, 1950; lectr. Mgmt. Inst., Oxford U. (Eng.), 1949; past trustee, treas., chmn. finance com. Nat. Indsl. Conf. Bd., also sr. mem. Pres. North Pond Assn. Capt. ordnance, U.S. Army, World War I; civilian mem. U.S. Army Gen. Staff, Manpower Bd., also mem. adv. bd. to surgeon gen. U.S. Army, and mem. adv. com. representing banking and ins. Management-Labor Bd., War Manpower Commn., World War II. Life mem. Am. Mgmt. Assn. (past treas., chmn. finance com.), Transp. Assn. Am. (past chmn. bd. dirs., chmn. exec. com.); mem. U.S. C. of C. (past dir., chmn. tax com. 1952-56), Marketing Execs. Soc., Newcomen Soc., Phi Delta Phi, Beta Gamma Sigma (hon.), Knight of Malta, Knight Order Holy Sepulchre. Roman Catholic. Author: Wills, Trusts and Estates in Relation to Life Insurance; also various papers. Home: Short Hills NJ Died May 30, 1972.

MADDEN, JOHN FITZ army officer; b. Sacramento, Calif., Mar. 30, 1870; s. Jerome and Margaret Eveline (Evans) M.; prep. edn., St. Matthews Hall, San Mateo, Calif.; U. of Calif., 1890-91; grad. Inf. and Cav. Sch., Fort Leavenworth, Kan., 1897, Army War Coll., Washington, 1921, Gen. Staff Sch., Fort Leavenworth, 1922, Naval War Coll., Newport, R.I., 1923; married (divorced); 1 son, John FitzPatrick. Commd. 2d lt. inf., U.S. Army, Oct. 7, 1891, and advanced through grades to colonel, Apr. 15, 1920; brig. gen. National Army, Oct. 1918-Mar. 1919; brig. gen. U.S. Army, March 6, 1931; retired account of physical disability in line of duty, March 31, 1934. Served in Spanish-Am. War, Cuban Occupation, Philippine Insurrection; chief q.m., Punitive Expdn. into Mexico, 1916; asst. q.m. 1st Div., A.E.F., and asst. to chief q.m., A.E.F., June 1917-Feb. 1919. Decorated Officer Legion of Honor (France). Episcopalian. Clubs: Army and Navy (Washington); Lambs, (New York); West Point Army Mess; Army and Navy (Manila, P.I.). Home: 89 N. Arlington Av., East Orange, N.J. Died May 19, 1946.

MADDOCK, WALTER GRIERSON surgeon; b. Toronto, Ont., Can., Nov. 26, 1901; s. Walter Richard and Jessie Helen (Liddell) M.; grad. Detroit Central, 1921; A.B., U. Mich., 1924, M.D., 1927, M.S. in surgery, 1934; children-Walter Munro, William Robert, Bruce C., Janet; m. Jeanne Turner Bowman, Oct. 1961. Instr. in surgery, 1929-32, assistant, asso. prof. surgery, dept. of surgery and post grad. med., 1932-46, U. of Mich. Med. Sch.; Elcock prof. surgery Northwestern U. Med. Sch., Ranson lectr. surgery, 1941; consultant in surgery Fifth United States Army; also surgeon Chicago Wesley Memorial Hospital, Chicago and chmn. department, 1952-. Served as lt. col., later col., M.C., U.S. Army, July 1942-Nov. 1945; cons. in surgery, southern base sect. European theatre of operations; commanding officer 298th Gen. Hosp. (affiliated unit U. of Michigan), European theatre of operations. Awarded Legion of Merit, 1945. Fellow A.C.S.; mem. A.M.A. (chmn. sect. on surgery, gen. and abdominal, mem. conf. com. on grad. training in surgery), Am. Assn. Surgery of Trauma, Ill. state med. soc. American Surg. Assn., Soc. Clin. Surgeons, Western Surgical Assn., Central Surg. Assn. (founder; mem. bd. 1952), Royal Soc. Medicine (London), Detroit Acad. Surgery, Chgo. Surg. Soc. (pres.), Am. Heart Assn., Am. Federation Clin. Research, Internat. Soc. Surgery, Fred A. Coller Society, Soc. Vascular Surgery (fdr. mem.), Alpha Omega Alpha, Phi Kappa Phi, Sigma Xi, Phi Chi. Republican. Author: (with Barry J. Anson) Callander's Surgical Anatomy; also of numerous papers on surg. subjects. Editorial bd. Archives of Surgery; Am. Jour. of Surgery. Home: 229 E. Lake Shore Dr. Office: 251 E. Chicago Av., Chgo. Died Oct. 26, 1962; buried Toronto.

MADDOX, LOUIS WILSON army officer; b. Lamar Mo., Apr. 22, 1891; s. John Walter and Judith M.; grad. high sch., 1908; Inf. Sch., 1927; Coast Arty. Sch., 1928; Army Finance Sch., 1934; m. Naomi Barnhouse, July 17, 1922; 1 dau., Jean. Commd. 2d lt. U.S. Army, 1917, advanced through grades to brig. gen., 1945; fiscal dir. Hdqrs. Gen. MacArthur. Decorated campaign and battle stars for World Wars I and II, D.S.M. Mason. Elk. Home: 1558 Hamilton Av., Palo Alto, Cal. Died July 1, 1956; buried Presidio Cemetery, San Francisco.

MADDOX, WILLIAM PERCY, fgn. service officer; b. Princess Anne, Md., Nov. 21, 1901; s. Robert Franklin and Ella Virginia (Hoblitzell) M.; A.B., St. John's Coll., Md., 1921; B.A., Oxford, Eng., 1925; Ph.D., Harvard, 1933; LL.D. (hon.), Pratt Inst., 1968; m. Louise Shaw Hepburn, June 15, 1945; 1 dau., Alexandra Cortelyou. Reporter on Baltimore Evening Sun, 1921-22; instr. polit. sci. U. of Ore., 1925-27, asst. prof., 1927-28; acting asso. prof. polit. sci. U. of Va., 1928-29; instr. in govt. Harvard U., 1930-36; asst. prof. politics Princeton, 1936-38; asso. prof. polit. sci. U. of Pa., 1938-46 (on leave 1942-46); asst. to pres. Fgn. Policy Assn., 1942; chief div. of tng. services Dept. of State, 1946-47, dir. Fgn. Service Inst., 1947-49; counselor of embassy at Lisbon, Portugal, 1949-52; consul gen. Port of Spain, Trinidad, 1952-55; Counselor of embassy, Pretoria, Union of South Africa, 1955-59; consul gen., Singapore, 1959-61; staff adviser U.S. Arms Control and Disarmament Agy., 1962-65; dir. Midtown Internat. Center N.Y.C., 1965; v.p. for acad. affairs Pratt Inst. Bklyn., 1965-66, acting pres., 1967-68, cons., 1968-70. Served with Office of Strategic Services, A.U.S., in E.T.O. and M.T.O., 1942-45, advancing to rank of col. Decorated Legion of Merit with oak leaf cluster (U.S.), Hon. Officer Mil. Div. Order Brit. Empire, Chevalier Legion of Honor (France), Polonia Restituta (Poland). Mem. Council Fgn. Relations, Phi Sigma Kappa. Club: Harvard (N.Y.C.). Author: Foreign Relations in British Labor Politics, 1934. Contbr. profl. jours. Home: Rocky Hill NJ Died Sept. 27, 1972; buried St. David's Episcopal Ch. Cemetery, Radnor PA

MADISON, JAMES 4th Pres. U.S.; b. Port, Conway, Va., Mar. 16, 1751; s. James and Eleanor (Conway) M.; A.B., Coll. of N.J.; admitted to Va. bar; mem. Com. of Safety for Orange County (Va.), 1774; del. to Williamsburg (Va.) Conv., 1776, mem. com. which framed constn. and declaration of rights for Va.; mem. 1st Gen. Assembly of Va., 1776, Va. Exec. Council, 1778; mem. Continental Congress from Va., 1780-83, 86-88, kept notes on debates of congress from 1782-83 (useful as supplement to ofcl. Journal), advocated fed. revenue to be raised on imports for 25 years; wrote instrns. to John Jay (U.S. minister to Spain) concerning U.S. rights to navigation of Mississippi River, 1780; proposed "/ Compromise" before Congress to break deadlock on changing basis of state contbns. from land values to population by counting 5 slaves as 3 free people; returned to Va., 1783, began study of law and natural history of U.S.; mem. Va. Ho. of Dels. from Orange County, 1783-86, completed disestablishment of Anglican Ch. in Va. (begun by Thomas Jefferson), 1779, favored admission of Ky. to statehood, inaugurated series of surveys for improvement of transmountain communications, urged power to be granted Congress to regulate commerce, leader in effecting a series of interstate confs.; del. from Va. to Annapolis Conv., 1786; published "Vices of the Policital System of the United States"; made proposals incorporated in Virginia or Randolph Plan (Drafted by Edward Randolph), including change in principle of representation to give larger states more influence, uniform nat. laws, a fed. veto on state legislation, extension of nat. authority to a judiciary dept., a 2 house fed. legislature with differing terms of office, a nat. exec., an article guaranteeing defense fo states by fed. govt., ratification of amendments to U.S. Constn. by people as well as legislature; described as "the masterbuilder of the constitution;" del. from Va., chief recorder U.S. Constl. Conv., 1787, kept records published in Journal of the Federal Constitution, 1840; asso. with Alexander Hamilton and John Jay in writing essays known as The Federalist (published under signature Publius), 1788, described constl. system of govtl. checks and balances, emphasized protection of pvt. property; largely responsible for ratification of U.S. Constn. by Va., 1788; mem. U.S. Ho. of Reps. from Va., 1st-4th congresses, 1789-97, participated in passage of revenue legislation, creation of exec. depts., framing of Bill of Rights; a leader of Democratic-Republic Party which opposed creation of U.S. Banks and pro-British sympathies; published series of letters under name "Helvidius" in Gazette of the United States, Aug. 24-Sept. 18, 1793, criticized George Washington's neutrality proclamation; declined mission to France and post of U.S. sec. of state, 1794; wrote Va. Resolutions against Allen and Sedition Acts, expressed opinion that states could declare acts of Congress unconstl.; U.S. sec. of state under Pres. Jefferson, 1801-09, faced with problems of Anglo-French war, sought peace with both countries, protested against impressment of U.S. sailors by Eng., supported Jefferson's Embargo Act of Dec. 22, 1807, repealed, Mar. 1, 1809; elected 4th Pres. U.S. (Democratic-Republic; defeated Charles Cotesworth Pinckney), 1808, inaugurated, Mar. 4, 1809, re-elected, 1812; authorized by Congress to revive non-intercourse with either Eng. or France, tricked by Napoleon Bonaparte, proclaimed non-intercourse against Gt. Britain, Nov. 2, 1810; involved in feud with Sec. State Robert Smith, Apr. 1811, dismissed him and apptd. James Monroe; advised declaration of war against Gt. Britain because of continued impressment of seamen, interference in U.S. trade, incitement of Indians on U.S. borders, June 1, 1812, declared war, June 18, 1812; accepted offer of mediation by Russian Czar, Mar. 1813 (rejected by Eng.); forced to flee White House when British invaded and burned much of Washington, D.C., 1812; instructed U.S. Commrs. at Ghent to seek only surrender to U.S. territory occupied by Brit., 1814 (Treaty of Ghent signed Dec. 24, 1814); signed bill providing for 2d Bank of U.S., 1816, Tariff Act of 1816; enrolled in soc. for encouragement of Am. mfrs., 1816; left office, Mar. 3, 1817; became rector U. Va. (succeeded Jefferson), 1826; del. Va. Constl. Conv., 1829; ret. to "Montpellier," Orange County. Died "Montpellier," June 18, 1836; buried "Montpellier."

MAGEE, CLARE, congressman, lawyer; b. near Livonia, Mo., Mar. 31, 1899; s. James Wallace and Dora Amelia M.; student Kirksville State Normal Sch., summer 1916; U. of Mo., 1917-22; m. Mary Frances Sheets, Sept. 7, 1927; (died. Aug. 1945); 1 daughter, Marjorie Lee; m. 2d, Mrs. Ruth Rixey, Homesteaded in Big Horn Basin, Wyo., 1920-21; laborer U.S. Reclamation Service, Deaver, Wyo., 1920-21; owner and operator farm near Livonia since 1932; admitted to Mo. state bar, 1922, and practiced in Unionville; postmaster, Unionville, 1935-41. Rep. from 1st Mo. Dist., U.S. Congress, 1949-52. Pres. Unionville Park Bd., 1945-46. Served as apprentice seaman to 1/c seaman, U.S. Navy, 1918; pvt. F.A., U.S. Army, 1942; capt., A.A.F., 1942-44. Hon. mem. Vets. Fgn. Wars; mem. Am. Judicature Soc., Am. Legion, Mo. Bar Assn., Mo. Archeol. Soc., C. of C. (past pres.); Phi Delta Phi. Democrat. (chmn. central com. of Putnam County, 1926-32; mem. state speakers bur., and orgn. bur.; del. to state convs., chmn. 1st dist. caucus, 1930-32). Protestant. Odd Fellow. Eagle. Mason (O.E.S., 32 deg., Shriner). Clubs: Quo Vadis (past pres.), Rotary (past pres.), Young Democrats Jefferson (past pres.). Home: Unionville MO Died Aug. 1969.

MAGILL, ROSWELL (FOSTER) lawyer; born Auburn, Ill., Nov. 20, 1895; s. Hugh Stewart and Amina (Foster) M.; A.B., Dartmouth, 1916, LL.D., 1940; J.D., U. of Chicago, 1920; m. Katherine Biggins, Sept. 7, 1918; children-Catherine, Hugh Stewart. Admitted to Ill. bar, 1920, N.Y. bar, 1928, practice of law at Chicago to 1926; N.Y. City since 2928; counsel Dunnington, Bartholow & Miller, 1938-43; mem. Gravath, Swaine & Moore since 1943. Instructor law. U. of Chicago, 1921-23; asst. prof. law, asso. prof. and prof., Columbia, 1924-52. Spl. atty. and chief atty. U.S. Treasury Dept., 1923-25; assistant to secretary of Treasury, 1933-34; under secretary of the Treasury, 1937-38; adviser tax Commn., Porto Rico, 1925, 1938-29; adviser Cuban Treasury, 1938-39; pub. gov. N.Y. Stock Exchange, 1940-41; chairman, Connecticut Tax Survey Commission, 1948; mem. Conn. Tax Study Commission, 1958; trustee of the Mutual Life Ins. Co. of N.Y., Seamen's Bank for Savs. Trustee Macy Found., Dartmouth; chmn. Tax Found. Served to capt., Inf., U.S. Army, 1917-19. Member American, N.Y. State bar associations, Assn. Bar City of New York, Am. Philos. Society, Phi Beta Kappa, Kappa Sigma. Episcopalian. Clubs: Century Assn., Down Town Assn., Union, University, (New York City); Metropolitan (Washington). Author: Taxable Income (2d edition, 1945); Cases on Taxation (with J. M. Maguire) (4th edition 1947); The Cuban Fiscal System, 1939; The Impact of Federal Taxes, 1943; (with others) A Tax Program for A Solvent America, 1945; Cases on Federal Taxation, 1950; Financing Defense, 1951; Federal Finances, 1954. Contributor articles to the Columbia Law Rev., Harvard Law Rev., Saturday Evening Post, Readers' Digest, and others. Home: 31 E. 79th St., N.Y.C. 10021. Address: 1 Chase Manhattan Plaza, N.Y.C. 5. Died Dec. 17, 1963.

MAGINNIS, MARTHA congressman; b. Wayne County, N.Y., Oct. 27, 1841; s. Patrick and Winifred (Devine) M.; Jesuit Coll., LaSalle, Ill., and Hamline U., Minn., 1856-61; pvt. 1st Minn. Inf., Apr. 18, 1861; 2d lt., Aug. 1861; 1st lt., Sept. 1862; capt., July 1863; maj. 11th Minn. Inf., Sept. 1, 1864; engaged in all battles of Army of Potomac; twice promoted for gallantry; one of the 47 survivors of the famous charge of the 1st Minn. at Gettysburg; m. Louise E. Mann, Mar. 11, 1868. Removed to Mont., 1866; editor Helena Daily Gazette; later in mining and real estate business. Mem. 43d to 48th Congresses (1873-85); in 1890, when 2 rival legislatures each elected 2 U.S. senators, he was one of the Democratic senators, but the senate, then Republican, seated his opponent; also received votes for U.S. senator, 1899; apptd. U.S. senator by Gov. Smith, May 1900, until legislature met. Was mem. Dem. Nat. Com., 30 yrs., and del. and chmn. Mont. delegation to most of nat. convs. during that period; active in nat. campaign, 1912; pres. board mgrs. Mont. Soldiers' Home; pres. Mont. Pioneers' Assn., 1913. Address: Helena, Mont. Died Mar. 27, 1919.

MAGLIN, WILLIAM HENRY army officer; b. N.Y.C., May 4, 1898; s. Jeremiah Joseph and Margaret (Hock) M.; B.S., U.S. Mil. Acad., 1924; m. Kathryn Swint, May 9, 1950. Served as pvt. and corpl. Troop L, 5th U.S. Cav., 1917-18; commd. 2d lt. Inf., 1924, advanced through grades to maj. gen., 1953; provost marshal Allied Forces N. Africa, 1942-43, organizer, dir. Korean Nat. Police, 1945-47, apptd. provost marshal gen., U.S. Army, 1953; retired, 1957. Awarded Legion of Merit with oak leaf cluster, Army Commendation ribbon and campaign medals, Korean Military Order of Teaguk, 1953, Distinguished Service Medal, 1957; William Freeman Snow medal for distinguished service to humanity, Am. Social Hygiene Assn., 1956. Referred amateur and professional boxing, New York City and Honolulu, 1934-37; asso. coach U. Md. Boxing team, 1937-39. Home: Route 1, Box 101-B, Pelican Dr., Melbourne Shores, Melbourne, Fla. Died Jan. 11, 1958; buried Arlington Nat. Cemetery.

MAGOFFIN, RALPH VAN DEMAN coll. prof.; b. Rice County, Kan., Aug. 8, 1874; s. Thomas Clarence and Martha Elizabeth Van Deman (Gillespie) M.; A.B., U. of Mich., 1902; Ph.D., Johns Hopkins, 1908, studied Marburg, Berlin, Am. Sch. of Classical Studies in Bone 1906-07; LL.D., Washington Coll., 1922; m. Lily Buckier, June 18, 1910 (died Feb. 14, 1917); m. 2d, Kate Hampton Manning, Feb. 3, 1920; 1 son, Ralph Manning. Successively instr., asso., asso. prof. classical history and instr. archaeology, Johns Hopkins, 1908-23; prof. and head dept. classics, New York U., 1923-39, prof. emeritus since 1939, Teacher summer schs. various universities; prof. in charge Sch. of Classical Studies, American Academy in Rome, 1920-21. Recorder Archaeol. Inst. America, 1914-21, pres. 1921-31, honorary pres. since 1931, trustee since 1930; sec. Baltimore Society same, 1910-20, and v.p., 1920-23, Pvt., corpl., 31st Mich. Vol. Inf., Spanish-Am. War; grad. 1st course Div. Staff Officers, Army Coll., Washington, D.C., and served as capt., maj. and lt. col. Q.M.R.C. and G.S., Camp Jackson, S.C., Camp West Point, Ky., Camp Devens, Mass., and Camp Wheeler, Ga., World War. Mem. American Historical Assn., Am. Philological Assn., Am. Classical League (pres. 1926-31; hon. pres, since 1931), Classical Assn. of Middle West and South, Classical Assn. Atlantic States, Classical Club of New York City, Classical Association of Great Britain, Spanish War Veterans, Am. Legion, Phi Beta Kappa. Omicron Delta Kappa, Eta Sigma Phi, Pi Gamma Mu; Socie Corrispondente Comitato Permanente per l'Etruria, since 1927; corr. mem. Internat. Mediterranean Research Assn. of Rome, pres. Am. nat. com. of same, since 1929. Commendatore-della Corona d'Italia; Knight Order of the Savior (Greece); Socius d. Arch. Inst. d. Deutschen Reiches; dir. Aeneid-Cruise and Vergilian Pilgrimage, Bimell, Verg. 1930; national vice chairman American Hellenic Committee since 1930; advisor Master Institute of United Arts, New York. Republican. Presbyn. Mason (32ff, K.T., Shriner). Clubs: Baltimore Classical; New York University. Author: The History and Topography of Praeneste, 1908; The Quinquinnales, 1913; The Roman Forum, 1928; The Lure and Lore of Archaeology, 1930; 5000 Years Ago, 1937. Joint Author. A Handbook of the Economic Agencies of the War of 1917, 1917; An American Guide Book to France and Its Battlefields, 1920; Latin First Year; Miliaria in Via Latina; Lucerna Pedibus Nostris; Magic Spades, the Romance of Archaeology; The Vergilian Pilgrimage and Cruise of 1930; Ancient and Medival History, 1934. Translator; The Freedom of the Seas (by H. Grotisu), 1916; The Sovereignty of the Sea (by. C. V. Bynkerrhock), 1924. Editor The Climax Series of Latin Books for High Schools; asso. editor Am. Jour. Archaeology, 1924-31, Art and Archaeology, 1914-25. Home: 1324 Bull St., Columbia, S.C. Died May 15, 1942.

MAGRUDER, BRUCE army officer; b. in D.C., Dec. 3, 1882; grad. advance course Inf. Sch., 1923; grad. Command and Gen. Staff Sch., 1927. Enlisted as pvt. CAC, 1904; commd. 2d lt., Inf., 1907, advanced through grades to maj. gen., 1940; served as lt. col. Inf., 1918-10; comdg. 1st Armored Div., 1940; comdg. officer Inf. Replacement Training Center, Camp Wolters, 1942-45, ret. Decorated D.S.M., Legion of Merit. Address: Orlando, Fla. Died July 23, 1953.

MAGRUDER, DAVID LYNN brigadier gen. U.S.A.; b. Frederick, Md., Apr. 23, 1825; s. Jonathan Wilson and Mary Galloway (Lynn) M.; ed. acad. Cumberland, Md., Coll. of St. James nr. Hagerstown, Md.; M.D., U. of Md., 1849; m. Mary Cuthbert Larkin, Oct. 15, 1863. Apptd. from Va. asst. surgeon U.S.A., Feb. 1, 1850; capt. asst. surgeon, Feb. 1, 1855; maj. surgeon, Apr. 16, 1862; lt. col. surgeon, June 30, 1882; col. surgeon, July 26, 1886; retired by operation of law, Apr. 23, 1889; advanced to rank of brig. gen. retired, by act of Apr. 23, 1904. Bvtd. lt. col., Mar. 13, 1865, "for faithful and meritorious services during the war." Served in N.M., 1850-54, Fts. Pierre, Lookout and Randall, Dak., 1854-60; in charge Infirmary Hosp., Washington, to June 1861; med. dir. Gen. McDowell's army, 1861-62 (present at battle of Bull Run); at Phila., to Feb. 1863; med. dir. Dept. of Mo., to Oct. 1893; chief med. purveyor of the West, at Louisville, 1863-66; med. dir. Dept. of the Platte, Mar.-June 1866; surgeon at various posts, 1866-73; med. dir. Dept. of Ariz., 1873-77, at St. Louis, 1877-80; med. dir. Dept. of Mo., Ft. Leavenworth, Kan., 1880-84; attending surgeon, Phila., 1884-89. Episcopalian. Home: Bryn Mawr, Pa. Died 1910.

MAGRUDER, JOHN ret. army officer; b. Woodstock, Va., June 3, 1887; s. John Williams and Mary Louise (nee Donaldson) M.; student Massanutten Acad., 1903-05; B.S., Va. Mil. Inst., 1909; distinguished grad. Command and Gen. Staff Sch., 1926; grad. Army War Coll., 1931; m. Helen Schurman, Mar. 4, 1922; children-Barbara, Malcolm, Munro. Commd. 2d inf. U.S. Army, 1910; transferred to field arty., 1911; advanced through grades to brig. gen., 1940. Served in P.I., 1913-15; with AEF in France, 1918-19; asst. mil. attaché, Peking, China, 1920-24, mil. ataché 1926-30; comdt. Va. Mil. Inst., 1932-35; mil. attaché, Bern, Switzerland, 1935-38; chief Intelligence Br., War Dept. Gen. Staff, 1938-41; comd. arty., 1st Div., 1941; chief Mil. Mission to China, 1941-42; dep. dir. OSS, 1943-45; dir. Strategic Services, Unit W.D. 1945-46. Home: 1061 Thomas Jefferson St., Washington 7. Died Apr. 30, 1958; buried Arlington Nat. Cemetery.

MAGRUDER, JOHN BANKHEAD army officer; b. Winchester, Va., Aug. 15, 1810; s. Thomas and Elizabeth (Bankhead) M.; grad. U.S. Mil. Acad., 1830. commd. 1st lt. U.S. Army, 1836, advanced to lt. col. during Mexican War, 1848; commd. col. Confederate Army, comdr. troops on Va. Peninsula, 1861; won Battle of Big Bethal, (one of 1st battles of Civil War), 1861; brig. gen. in command all forces on Va. Peninsula, with hdqrs. at Yorktown; commd. maj. gen., distinguished himself at Malvern Hill, also all of Seven Days' battles before Richmond, 1861; transferred to command Dist. of Tex., 1862, later N.M., Ariz.; served as maj. gen. under Prince Maximilian in Mexico; returned to U.S., settled in Tex., 1869. Died Houston, Tex., Feb. 18, 1871.

MAGRUDER, JOHN H., JR. naval officer, business exec.; b. Washington, July 1, 1889; s. John H. and Sarah A. (Slough) M.; ed. Friends schs., Washington, Cloyne, Newport, R.I.; B.S., U.S. Naval Acad., 1911; m. Esther Hosmer, July 10, 1918; children-John H. 3d, Agnes (Mrs. Phillips), Esther (Mrs. P.C. Brooks). Commd. ensign USN, 1912, and advanced through grades to commodore, 9143; cmdg. officer USS Fairfax, 1921, USS Breck, 1924-27; naval attache The Hague, Netherlands, 1931-33; comdg. officer USS Nokomis, 9135-36, USS Augusta Flagship U.S. Asiatic Fleet, 1939-41; chief of staff Caribbean Sea Frontier, 1943-44; dep. comdr. forward areas Central Pacific, Marianas, 1944-45; took surrender Bonin Islands 1945; ret., 1946. Chmn. of bd., Magruder, Inc., 1946-63. Awarded Legion of Merit, Navy Commendation, Mexican Service mdeal, othrs. Mem. Am. Clan Gregor Soc. (chieftain 1951-54). Home: Goshen Point, Waterford, Conn. Died Aug. 20, 1963; buried Arlington Nat. Cemetery.

MAGRUDER, THOMAS PICKETT naval officer; b. Yazoo County, Miss., Nov. 29, 1867; s. Lawson William and Jessie M. (Kilpatrick) M.; grad. U.S. Naval Acd., 1889, Naval War Coll., Newport, R.I., 1916; m. Rose Boush, May 29, 1893; 1 dau, Adele (wife of S. O. Greig, U.S. Navy). Ensign, July 1, 1891; lt. jr. grade, Oct. 9, 1898; lt., Mar. 3, 1899; lt. comdr., July 1, 1905; comdr., July 1, 1910; capt., Aug. 6, 1915; temp. grade rear adm., Apr. 25, 1920; perm. rear adm., June 5, 1921. Was wrecked on Kearsarge, Roncador Reef, Feb. 4, 1894; served on Nashville, Spanish-American War, 1898; advanced 5 numbers "for gallantry" at Cienfuegos, Cuba, May 11, 1898; duty U.S. Naval Acad., 1905-06; navigator of Iowa, 1906-07; exec. officer Alabama, 1907-09; insp. machinery, Phila., Pa., 1909-11; duty at Naval Sta., Cavite, P.I., 1911-13; comd. Albany, 1913, Raleigh, 1913-15; in charge Div. Naval Affairs, Navy Dept., 1916-17; apptd. comdr. Squadron Four, Patrol Force, Atlantic Fleet, Aug. 1917; wrecked on Guinevere, west coast of France, Jan. 25, 1918; comd. U.S.S. Nevada, 1919; naval attaché Am. Embassy, Paris, 1920-21; special duty, 1921; comdt. 8th Naval Dist. and Naval Sta., New Orleans, La., Dec. 1921-Jan. 1,1924; comdr. light cruisers Scouting Fleet, 1924-26; comdt. 4th Naval Dist. and Navy Yard, Phila., to Nov. 5, 1927; became comdr. Base Force of U.S. Fleet, Aug. 1929; retired from active service. Guarded Army World Flight, Scotland to Boston, 1924; rescued Italian aviator, Locatelli, near Greenland, Aug. 25, 1924; comd. light cruisers on visit of U.S. Fleet to Australia, 1925. Commended for gallantry on U.S.S. Charleston, at San Francisco, Calif., May 11, 1890; presented a gold mounted sword by fellow citizens of Vicksburg, Miss., after Spanish-Am. War. Awarded D.S.M. (U.S.); Comdr. Legion of Honor (France); Commenda Mauriziana (Italy). Presbyn. Home: Greenville, Miss. Died May 26, 1938.

MAGSAYSAY, RAMON Pres. of Rep. of the Philippines; b. Iba, Zambales, P.I., Aug. 31, 1907; s. Exequiel and Perfecta (del Fierro) M.; student Coll. Liberal Arts, U. Philippines, 1927-31, Coll. Engring., 1927-28, Ll.D., 1955; B.S.C., José Rival Coll., 1933; LL.D., Quezon College, 1951, Fordham University, 1952, Nat. University, 1954; E.D. (hon.), Feati Inst. of Technology, 1954; L.H.D. (hon.), Far Eastern U., 1954; D.S.P.H., (hon.), Manila Central U., 1954; married Luz Banzon, June 10, 1933; children-Teresita, Milagros, Ramon. Engaged in automotive work until Dec. 1941, becoming branch mgr., later gen. mgr.,Yangco Transportation Company, 1941; worked in motor pool, 31st Inf., 31st Div., U.S. Army, 1941-42; joined in orgn. Western Luzon Guerilla Forces, of which commd. capt., 1942; hdqrs. exec. officer, later comdr., Sawang, San Marcelino, Zambales, 3 yrs.; became comdg. officer Zambales Mil. Dist., Jan. 1945; this force supported 38th Div., U.S. Army, at Battle of ZigZag Pass and in operations in mountains, 1945; apptd. by U.S. Army, mil. gov. Zambales, and promoted maj., 1945; disch. from service, 1946; rep. Zambales to Congress of the Philippines, 1946-50; chmn. Vets. Mission to Washington, 1948; one-man mission to U.S. to secure mil. aid, 1950; sec. nat. def., Sept. 1950-Mar. 1953 (resigned); pres. Rep. of Philippines since Nov. 1953. Reorganized and retrained army (which absorbed Philippine Constabulary) to fight against Huks (Peoples Liberation Army), 1951; initiated program to subdue Moro outlaws, 1952. Formerly chmn. bd. and gen. mgr. Manila R.R. Recipient Philippine Legion of Honor, Philippine Merit Medal; Bronze Star Medal, Legion of Merit, Presdl. Citation (U.S.); also numerous other awards. Clubs: Manila Polo, Baguio Country, Army and Navy, Casino Español, Manila Yacht, Manila (honl life), Rotary, Kions. Home: Castillejos, Zambales; also Malacañang, Manila, P.I. Died Mar., 1957.

MAGUIRE, HAMILTON EWING, army officer; b. Detroit, Mich., Nov. 24, 1891; s. James Herbert and Ann (Ewing) M.; student U. of Michigan, 1910-12; B.S., U.S. Mil. Acad., 1916; grad. F.A. Sch., 1924, Command and Gen. Staff Sch., 1930, Army War Coll., 1938; m. Anne Droop, June 21, 1924; children—Nancy Ewing, Anne Droop, Mary Ewing, Hamilton Ewing, Edward Frederick Droop. Commd. 2d lt., U.S. Army, 1916, and advanced through the grades to brig. gen., 1944; served War Dept. Gen. Staff, 1938-42; chief of staff, XIX Corps, 1944-48. Decorated Distinguished Service Medal, Legion of Merit, Bronze Star, 5 campaign stars (Normandy, Northern France, Rhineland, Ardennes, Germany) (U.S.), Legion of Honor, Croix de Guerre (France). Mem. Delta Kappa Epsilon. Clubs: Chevy Chase, Army and Navy (Washington). Home: Washington DC Died Feb. 20, 1971; buried Arlington Nat. Cemetery, Arlington VA

MAHAN, ALFRED THAYER rear admiral U.S.N.; b. West Point, N.Y., Sept. 27, 1840; s. Prof. Dennis Hart and Mary Helena (Okill) M.; grad. U.S. Naval Acad., 1859; D.C.L., Oxford, Eng., 1894; LL.D., Cambridge, Eng., 1894, Harvard U., 1895, Yale U., 1897, McGill U., 1900, Columbia U.; 1900; m. Ellen Lyle Evans, June 11, 1872. Promoted to midshipman, June 9, 1859; lt., Aug. 31, 1861; lt. comdr., June 7, 1865; comdr., Nov. 20, 1872; capt., Sept. 23, 1885; retired at own request after 40 yrs.' service, Nov. 17, 1896; advanced to rank of rear admiral retired, June 29, 1906. Served on Congress, 1859-61; Pocahontas,S. Atlantic Blockading Squadron, 1861-62; Naval Acad., 1862-63; Seminole, W. Gulf Blockading Squadron, 1863-64; James Adger, S. Atlantic Squadron, 1864-65; Muscoota, Gulf squadron, 1865-66; ordnance duty, Navy Yard, Washington, 1866; Iroquois, Asiatic Squadron, 1867-69; comd. Aroostook, Asiatic Squadron, 1869; Navy Yard, New York, 1870-71; Worcester, 1871; spl. duty Navy Yard, New York, 1871; receiving-ship at New York, 1872; comd. Wasp, 1873-74; Navy Yard, Boston, 1875-76; Naval Acad., 1877-80; Navy Yard, New York, 1880-83; comd. Wachusett, 1883-85; Naval War Coll., 1885; pres. Naval War Coll., 1886-89; pres. commn. to select site for navy yard on northwest coast, 1889; spl. duty, Bur. of Navigation, 1889-92; pres. Naval War Coll., 1892-93; comd. Chicago, 1893-95; spl. duty in connection with Naval War Coll., 1895-1896; mem. Naval War Bd., during war with Spain, 1898; spl. duty, 1906. Del. to Hague Peace Conf., 1899. Pres. Am. Hist. Assn., 1902-03. Author: The Gulf and Inland Waters, 1883; Influence of Sea Power Upon History, 1890; Influence of Sea Power Upon French Revolution and Empire, 1892; Life of Admiral Farragut, 1892; Life of Nelson, 2 Vols., 1897; The Interest of the United States in Sea Power, 1897; Lessons of Spanish War, 1899; The Problem of Asia, 1900; The South African War, 1900; Types of Naval Officers, 1901; Retrospect and Prospect, 1902; Sea Power in Its Relations to the War of 1812, 1905; From Sail to Steam, 1907; Some Neglected Aspects of War, 1907; Naval Administration and Warfare, 1908; The Harvest Within, 1909; Interest of America in International Conditons, 1910; Armaments and Arbitration, 1912; Major Operations of the Navies inthe War of American Independence, 1913. Address: Quogue, N.Y. Died Dec. 1, 1914.

MAHAN, DENNIS HART commodore U.S.N.; b. West Point, N.Y., Mar. 28, 1849; s. Prof. Dennis Hart and Mary Helena (Okill) M.; student Burlington Coll., N.J.; grad. U.S. Naval Acad., 1869; m. Jeannette Katherine Murat Brodie, Nov. 24, 1875. Promoted ensign, 1876; master, 1873; lt., 1877; lt. comdr. 1898; comdr., 1901; capt., July 1, 1905; retired as commodore, July 1, 1909. Served in Philippine campaign, 1899-1900 on U.S.S. Brooklyn; at Kingston, Jamaica, during earthquake rescue, comdg. U.S.S. Indiana. Episcopalian. Returned to active duty, Apr. 1917, and assigned in charge censorship at Honolulu, T.H.; remanded to retired list, June 1, 1919. Home: Warrenton, Va. Died May 29, 1925.

MAHIN, FRANK CADLE army officer; b. Clinton, Ia., May 27, 1887; s. Frank Webster and Abbie Anna (Cadle) M.; student Nottingham (Eng.) High Sch., 1902-05, Harvard, 1905-07; m. Margaret Mauree Pickering, Sept. 25, 1913; children-Margaret Celeste (Mrs. L. E. Laurion), Anna Yeteve (Mrs. E. D. Jessup), Elizabeth Mauree (Mrs. W. A. Hamilton, Jr.), Frank Cadle. Began as stock clerk W. M. Meyer & Co., N.Y. City, 1907, later with John Wanamaker; enlisted in U.S. Army, 1910; commd. 2d lt., 1912, and advanced through the grades to brig. gen., 1941. Awarded Purple Heart. Mason. Republican. Episcopalian. Clubs: Army and Navy (Washington, D.C.); Service (Indianapolis). Address: War Dept., Washington. Died July 24, 1942; buried in Arlington National Cemetery.

MAHONE, WILLIAM army officer, senator, state polit. leader; b. Southampton County, Va., Dec. 1, 1826; s. Fielding Jordan and Martha (Drew) M.; grad. Va. Mil. Inst., 1847; m. Ortelia Butler, Feb. 1865, 3 children. Operated mail route from Jerusalem (now Courtland) to Hill's Ford (now Empiria), Va.; tchr. Rappahannock Mil. Acad., 2 years; civil engr., constructor Norfolk & Petersburg R.R., pres., chief engr., supt., 1861; served as q.m. gen., lt. col. and col. 6th Va. Regt., Confederate States Army, during Civil War; commanded Norfolk (Va.) Dist. until evacuation, 1862, sent to Drewry's Bluff defenses of James River; promoted brig. gen., maj. gen., 1864; mem. N.C. Senate, 1863-65; pres. Atlantic, Miss. & Ohio R.R., 1867-73; organizer, took command "Readjustors" (advocated reducing Va.'s debt, also popular, social and econ. legislation), 1879; mem. U.S. Senate (Republican from Va., 1881-87; "Anti-Bourbon," defended Negroes rights; boss of Va. Rep. Party until 1882 (temporarily broke "Solid South");

monument to him erected by Daus. of Confederacy, Petersburg, Va. Died Washington, D.C., Oct. 8, 1895; buried Blandford Cemetery, Petersburg.

MAHONEY, GEORGE WILLIAM oculist; born Lawton, Mich., Dec. 31, 1860; s. Michael and Honoria Marie (Davis) M.; student U. Mich., 1885-87; M.D., Bellevue Hosp. Med. Coll.-N.Y.U., 1888; m. Julia Garvy, Oct. 21, 1908; children-Mrs. Miriam M. McDevitt, George J. Began practice at Decatur, Mich., 1888; moved to Chgo., 1893; prof. ophthalmology and dir. Loyola U. Sch. Medicine; cons. oculist St. Vincent Asylum, House of the Good Shepherd; oculist Mercy, Henrotin, U.S. Marine and St. Mary of Nazareth hosps. Commd. by Gov. Atgeld, 1896, capt. and asst. surgeon 7th Regt., Ill. N.G., 1896-1904, resigned; mustered into vol. service of U.S. in spring of 1898; served through Spanish-Am. War; held rank of capt. and asst. surgeon; detached from 7th Regt. during summer of 1898 and placed in charge of hosps. corps of 2d Army Corps. Fellow A.C.S.; mem. A.M.A., Ill. Chgo. med. socs., Chgo. Ophthal. Soc., Am. Bd. of Ophthalmology. Democrat. Catholic. Home: 605 Central Av., Wilmette, Ill. Office: 30 N. Michigan Blvd., Chgo. Deceased.

MAIN, HERSCHEL chief engr., U.S.N., retired; b. in Ill., July 6, 1845; s. Prof. James Main; ed. Washington, 1851-57; Phillips Exeter Acad., N.H., 1858-61; grad. Naval Acad., 1866; spl. studies marine engring.; m. Charlotte A. Bradbury, June 1, 1875. Third asst. engr. U.S.N., Oct. 10, 1866; chief engr., U.S.N., Nov. 11, 1892; retired Sept. 10, 1895. Address: Washington, D.C. Died 1909.

MAJOR, DUNCAN KENNEDY, JR. army officer; b. New York, N.Y., Apr. 2, 1876; s. Duncan Kennedy and Kate (Olwell) M.; grad. U.S. Mil. Acad., 1899; distinguished grad. Inf.-Cav. Sch., 1906; grad. Army Staff Coll., 1907, Army War Coll., 1912; m. Ruth, daughter of James Edward and Ann (Parker) Barkley. Commd. 2d lt. inf., Feb. 15, 1899; promoted through grades to brig. gen., Nov. 1, 1935. Served in Philippine Insurrection, 1899-1900, Boxer Rebellion in China, 1900, World War, 1918-19, as chief of staff 26th Div. A.E.F.; participated in Champagne-Marne defensive and Eisne-Marne, St. Mihiel and Meuse-Argonne offensive; dept. chief and chief of staff Am. Embarkation Center, Le Mans, France, 1919. Was student officer L'Ecole de L'Intendance, Paris, France, 1912, Staff Sch., Langres, France, 1918, Inf. Sch., 1924; served with Gen. Staff, Dept. of War, 1921-24 and 1932-36; aide-de-camp to Gen. of the Armies of U.S., 1923; chief of staff 4th Corps Area, Atlanta, 1930-32; rep. Dept. of War on advisory council of the dir. of Emergency Conservation Work, 1933-36; comd. 21st Inf. Brigade, 1936-38; San Francisco Port of Embarkation, 1938; now retired. Awarded D.S.M., 1919, Purple Heart, 1937. Catholic. Club: Army and Navy. Address: Seminary Rd., Route 2, Alexandria. Va. Died May 26, 1947; buried in Arlington National Cemetery.

MALCOLM, RUSSELL LAING, surgeon; b. Ann Arbor, Mich., Oct. 8, 1906; s. John Karl and Clara (Laing) M.; A.B., U. Mich., 1928, M.D., 1931, M.S. in Surgery, 1935; m. Bernice Frances Staebler, Sept. 1, 1928; children—Russell Laing, Marshall Day, Miller Day (twins). Instr. surgery U. Mich., 1934-37; pvt. practice surgery, Richmond, Ind.; sr. surgeon Reid Meml. Hosp. Trustee Earlham Coll., 1962-67. Served from capt. to col., M.C., AUS, 1942-45. Decorated Bronze Star medal; Bronze Plaque award Am. Cancer Soc. Fellow A.C.S.; mem. A.M.A., Wayne County Med. Soc., Central Surg. Assn., F.A. Coller Surg. Soc., Norman Miller Gynecol. Soc., Ind. Cancer Soc. (past pres.). Rotarian (pres. 1947-48). Home: Richmond IN Died Dec. 21, 1967; interred Earlham Cemetery, Richmond IN

MALLET, JOHN WILLIAM chemist; b. Dublin, Ireland, Oct. 10, 1832; s. Robert and Cordelia (Watson) M.; A.B., Trinity Coll., Dublin, 1853; Ph.D., U. of Gottingen, 1852; M.D., U. of La., 1868; LL.D., Coll. of William and Mary, 1872, U. of Miss., 1872, Princeton, 1896, Johns Hopkins, 1902, U. of Pa., 1906; came to U.S., 1853, but is a British subject; m. Mary E., d. Judge John J. Ormond, of Ala., 1857; m. 2d, Mrs. Josephine Burthe,of La., 1888. Asst. prof. analytical chemistry, Amherst, 1854; chemist to geol. survey, Ala., 1855-56; prof. chemistry, U. of Ala., 1855-60; officer on staff Gen. Rodes, C.S.A., 1861; transferred to arty., 1862, and placed in general charge of ordnance laboratories of Confed.-States; paroled as lt. col. arty., 1865; prof. chemistry, med. dept., U. of La., 1865-68; prof. analytical, industrial and agrol. chemistry, 1868-72, gen. and industrial chemistry, 1872-83 and 1885-1908, emeritus prof. chemistry, 1908, U. of Va. Lecturer, Johns Hopkins, 1877-78; prof. chemistry and physics and chmn. faculty, U. of Tex., 1883-84; prof. chemistry, Jefferson Med. Coll., Phila., 1884-85; mem. U.S. Assay Commn. 3 times. Mem. Am. Chem. Soc. (Pres. 1882). Address: University, Va. Died Nov. 6, 1912.

MALLORY, TRACY BURR pathologist; b. Boston, 1896; s. Frank Burr and Persis (Tracy) M.; M.D., Harvard, 1921; m. Edith Brandt, June 6, 1925; children-Kenneth Brandt, Jean Roberts (Mrs. William J. Childs). Moseley Traveling fellow Harvard, 1925-26, inst. bacteriology med. sch., 1923-26, instr. pathology, 1926-

35, asso., 1935-37, asst. prof., 1937-48, prof. pathology since 1948; chief lab. pathology and bacteriology, Mass. Gen. Hosp., Boston since 1926; cons. pathology Regional Area I, Vets. Adminstrn. Served with Med. Corps., U.S. Army, as maj. to lt. col. 1943-45. Decorated Legion of Merit. Mem. Am. Assn. Pathologists and Bacteriologists (pres., 1950-51), A.M.A., Am. Soc. Exptl. Pathologists, Am. Cancer Soc. Author articles sci. jours. Asst. editor of Am. Jour. Pathology, 1941-43, mem. editorial bd. since 1943; editor case histories of Mass. Gen. Hosp. New Eng. Jour. Pathology since 1926. Contbr. to Medical History of U.S. Army in World War II. Home: 178 South St., Needham 92. Office: Mass. General Hospital, Boston. Died Nov. 11, 1951.

MALONE, GEORGE WILSON consulting engineer; b. Fredonia, Kans., Aug. 7, 1890; s. J. W. and Vienna (McPherson) M.; civil engring., Univ. of Nevada, class of 1917; m. Ruth Moslander, Mar. 20, 1921; 1 dau., Molly. Cons. engr., malone Engrs.; state engr. Nev., 1927-35, serving as mem. Pub. Service Commn., Colorado River Commn., during passage legislation Hoover Dam, advisor Sec. Interior on generation power, completed, 1934, resigned 1935; gen. cons. engring. practice including Central Valley project, Shasta and San Joaquin dams, Cal. 1935, Los Angeles Flood Control project, 1936; mng. dir., editor Indsl. West Found. until Indsl. Ency. pub. 1944; spl. cons. to Sec. War on strategic and critical minerals and materials; cons. U.S. Senate Mil. Affairs Com. on strategic and critical minerals and materials, and on exam. mil. establishments including Pacific, Alaska and the South Seas, 1942-45; U.S. senator from Nev., 1946-58, mem. interior and insular affairs com., finance com. Inspected European Marshall Plan nations and Middle East countries, 1947, Asiatic countries, Malayan states and Indo China, 1948, S. American areas, 1949, Central Am. countries and Mexico, 1950. Served as pvt. and sgt., 40th Div. F.A., World War I, with A.E.F. in France; lt. line officer and Regtl. Intelligence, 1918. Former chmn. Nev. State Bd. Registered Profl. Engrs. Mem. Am. Soc. C.E., Am. Inst. of Mining & Metall. Engineers, Assn. Western State Engrs. (organizer and ex-pres.), Am. Legion past dept. comdr.; nat. vice comdr. 1929, Vets. Fng. Wars, Sigma Alpha Epsilon. Republican. Mason (32ff, K.T., Shriner), Elk, Eagle. Clubs: Army-Navy, National Press (Washington); San Francisco Press. Contbr. engring. and tech. jours. Winner amateur middleweight boxing championship of Pacific Coast (rep. U. of Nev.), 1920. Address: 29 E. First St., Reno. Died May 19, 1961; buried Arlington Nat. Cemetery.

MALONE, KEMP, philologist; b. Minter, Miss., Mar. 14, 1889; s. John W. and Lilliam (Kemp) M.; A.B., Emory U., 1907, Litt.D., 1936; Ph.D., U. Chgo., 1919, L.H.D., 1953; Litt.D., Yale, 1951; Litt. D., University North Carolina, 1964; L.H.D. Johns Hopkins, 1965; LL.D., Kenyon Coll., 1966; grad. study U. Copenhagen, 1915-16, U. Iceland, 1919-20, Princeton, 1920-21; m. Inez Rene, dau. J. Henry Chatain of Richmond, Va., Apr. 28, 1927. High sch. tchr., 1907-11; exchange tchr. to Prussia, 1911-13; instr. Cornell U., 1916-17; asst. prof. English, U. Minn., 1921-24; with Johns Hopkins, 1924-71, prof., 1926-56, prof. emeritus, 1956-71; vis. prof. English and linguistics Georgetown U., 1956-58, also dir. Georgetown English lang. program, sponsored by Internat. Coop. Adminstrn., Ankara, Turkey, 1956-58; Berg vis. prof., English at N.Y.U., 1961-62; vis. prof. English So. Ill. U., Carbondale, 1963-64; vis. prof. English, Catholic Univ. of Am., 1966-67; vis. prof., lectr. numerous Am. and fgn. univs. Co-founder of American Speech, mng. editor, 1925-32; co-editor of Anglia, 1950-64, Acta Philol. Scand., 1952—; asso. editor Early English MSS in Facsimile, 1951-71. Rep. U.S. govt. 4th Internat. Congress Linguistics, 1936, 5th Congress, 1939. Served from 1st lt. to capt. U.S. Army, 1917-19. Decorated King Christian X Freedom Medal, Knight of Dannebrog (Denmark), Knight of Falcon (Iceland). Jubilee vol., Philologica, the Malone Anniversary Studies, 1949; recipient of Guggenheim fellowship, 1958-59. Fellow Mediaeval Acad. Am., Soc. Am. Historians; mem. Am. Philos. Soc., Royal Danish Academy, Islenzkt Bokmentafjelag, Linguistic Society of American (past pres.), Am. Dialect Soc. (past pres.), Am. Name Soc. (past pres.), Modern Humanities Research Assn. (president 1958), Modern Lang. Assn. of Am. (president 1962), numerous other Am. and fgn. learned socs. Episcopalian. Clubs: Maryland, Johns Hopkins, Tudor and Stuart; Army and Navy (Washington). Author and editor various works, 1923-45. Author: Chapters on Chaucer, 1951; Studies in Heroic Legend, published, 1959. Co-author: Literary History of England, 1948; Literary Masterpieces of the Western World, 1953. Editor: Thorkelin Transcripts of Beowulf, 1951; Deor, rev. edit., 1966; Widsith, rev. edit. 1962; Nowell codex in facsimile, 1963. Co-editor: Modern Lang. Notes, 1925-56; etymol. editor Am. Coll. Dictionary, 1947; Random House Dictionary English Lang., 1966. Contbr. verse and articles to lit. and philol. jours. Home: Baltimore MD Died Oct. 13, 1971; buried Hollywood Cemetery, Richmond VA

MALONE, PAUL BERNARD army officer; b. Middleton, N.Y., May 8, 1872; s. John and Anna M.; apptd. from N.Y., and grad. U.S. Mil. Acad., 1894; m. Gertrude E. Kerwin, June 12, 1895. Apptd. 2d lt. 13th Inf., June 12, 1894; promoted through grades to brig.

gen., N.A., Oct. 1, 1918; col., July 1, 1920; brig. gen. regular army, Apr. 27, 1922; maj. gen., June 27, 1928. Served in Santiago campaign, 1898; against Aguinaldo in Luzon, P.I., 1899-1901; instr. chemistry U.S. Mil. Acad., 1901-05; honor grad. Army Sch. of Line, 1909; grad. Army Staff Coll., 1910; gen. staff, Mar. 28, 1911-Sept. 1, 1912. Chief of staff Eagle Pass Dist., July 1916-Jan. 1917; in charge Citizen's Tng. Camps, Hdqrs. Central Dept. to July 1917; operations sect. Gen. Staff, GEn. Hdqrs., France, to Aug. 7, 1917; chief tng. sect. Gen. Staff (G-5), Gen. Hdqrs., France, to Feb. 12, 1918; comdg. 23d Inf. (3d Brig., 2d Div.) in Sommedieu sector, Aisne defensive, Château-Thierry operations, and Aisne-Marne offensive, to Aug. 24, 1918; comdg. 10th Brig., 5th Div., in St. Mihiel and Meuse-Argonne offensives and to Mar. 2, 1919; comdg. 1st Replacement Depot, to June 21, 1919; comdg. 3d Brig., 2d Div., to July 1, 1919; asst. comdt. Inf. Sch., 1919-22, F.A. Sch., Nov. 1922-Feb. 1, 1923; comdg. 2d F.A. Brigade, 1923-28, 2d Div., 1925-26, 12th Inf. Brigade, Mar.-June, 1928, 6th Corps Area, 1928-29; comdg. Philippine Div., Ft. William McKinley, P.I., 1929-31, 3d Corps Area, 1931-35; became comdr. 9th Corps Area and 4th Field Army, 1935; now ret. Decorations: D.S.M., D.S.C., S.S.C.; Officer Legion of Honor and Croix de Guerre with two palms and one star (France); Comdr. Crown of Italy. Author: Winning His Way to West Point, 1905, a Plebe at West Point, 1906; A West Point Yearling, 1907; A West Point Cadet, 1908; A West Point Lieutenant, 1911. Address: 221 Arguella Blvd., San Francisco. Died Oct. 1960.

MALONY, HARRY JAMES, army officer; b. Lakemont, N.Y., Aug. 24, 1889; s. Dr. John Montgomery and Josephine (Huson) M.; student Yale, 1907-08; B.S., U.S. Mil. Acad., 1912; grad. Field Arty. Sch., Ft. Sill, 1922, Command and Gen. Staff Sch., 1926, Army War Coll., 1936; m. Fanny Hunter Lockett, July 21, 1913; 1 son, James Lockett; m. 2d, Dorothy Brentnall Fitch, Nov. 30, 1928; step-children—Dorothy Anne Thurman, Barbara Fitch Thurman, Alice Merritt Thurman. Commd. 2d lt. inf., U.S. Army, 1912; transferred to field arty., 1916, and advanced through the grades to maj. gen., August 1942. Served with 10th Inf., Panama Canal Zone, 1912-16; instr. Machine Gun Sch., Tex., and duty in Exptl. Dept., Springfield Armory, 1916-17, armament officer, Air Service, with A.E.F., France, 1917-19; sec. F.A. Sch., Ft. Sill, 1921-24; 7th F.A., 1926; Gen. Staff Corps, Atlanta, Ga., 1927; instr. mil. science U. of Okla., 1931-35; mem. F.A. Bd., 1936; instr. Army War Coll., 1937-40; mem. Army-Navy Bd. for selection of air-naval bases in Brit. transatlantic possessions, 1940; mem. President's Commn. for negotiating lease of air and naval bases, 1941; War Plans Div., War Dept. Gen. Staff, 1941; dep. chief of staff, G.H.Q., 1941-42; Munitions Assignment Bd. Combined Chiefs of Staff; comdg. gen., 94th Inf. Div. 1942-45; U.S. Exec. London Munitions Assignment Bd. 1945; mem. of Presdl. Mission to Observe Greek Elections with rank of U.S. Minister, 1946; chief Hist. Div., War Dept., 1947-48, ret. 1949; retained by United Nations as deputy dir., Khashmir Plebescite, 1949; consultant Department of Defense, Southeast Asia policies, 1950-51; tech. cons. U.S. Ordnance Co., Washington. Decorated D.S.M. with oak leaf cluster, Silver Star, Bronze Star; Officer Legion d'Honneur, Croix de Guerre, Ordre d'Etoile Noire (France). Mem. Arlington Ridge Rd. Divic Assn. (past v.p.), Sigma Chi. Presbyn. Club: Army and Navy (Washington). Author: Machine Guns (with J.S. Hatcher and G.P. Wilhelm), 1916. Home: Arlington VA Died Mar. 23, 1971; buried Arlington Cemetery, Arlington VA

MANDERSON, CHARLES FREDERICK senator; b. Phila., Pa., Feb. 9, 1837; s. John and Katharine M.; ed. Phila. High Sch. Removed, 1856, to Canton, O.; admitted to bar, 1859; city atty., Canton, 1860-61; in Union Armh, 1861-65; enlisting as pvt., filled all grades, including brig. gen., resigning, Apr. 1865, after participating in all the battles of Middle West, because of severe wounds received in charge at Lovejoy's Station, Ga.; m. Rebekah S. Brown, Apr. 11, 1865. Resumed law practice in Stark County, O.; twice elected pros. atty. of Stark Co.; removed to Omaha, Neb., 1869, Mem. Neb., Constl. convs., 1871, 74; city atty. Omaha over 6 yrs.; U.S. senator, 1883-95; pres. pro tem of Senate in 51st and 52d Congresses. Gen. solicitor Burlington system, West of Missouri River, 1895-. Author: The Twin Seven Shooters, 1902; also many speeches and addresses on polit., legal and war topics. Pres.Am. Bar Assn., 1900-01. Address: Omaha, Neb. Died 1911.

MANDEVILLE, WILLIAM HUBERT lawyer; b. Elmira, N.Y., Apr. 16, 1893; s. Hubert C. and Mary F. (Stoops) M.; B.E., Union Coll., 1915; student Columbia Univ. Law Sch., 1915-17; m. Ruth C. Buck, Oct. 6, 1917; 1 son, David C. Admitted to N.Y. State bar, 1920, since practiced in Elmira; mem. firm of Mandeville Buck Teeter & Harpending and predecessor firms; chmn. exec. com., vice pres. and dir. Thatcher Glass Mfg. Co., Inc. since 1943; dir. Hardinge Bros., Inc., Chemung Canal Trust Co., LeValley McLeod, Inc., Elmira Floral Products Inc. Trustee Elmira Savings Bank. Served as capt., U.S. F.A., A.E.F., 1917-20. Mem. bd. edn., Elmira, 1924-32, pres., 1930-32. Life trustee Union Coll.; trustee Elmira Coll. Mem. Am., N.Y. State and Chemung County (pres., 1949) bar assns., Assn. of Bar of City of New York, Psi Upsilon. Republican. Episcopalian. Clubs: University (New York City); City, Golf. Home: 670 Hoffman St. Office: Robinson Bldg., Elmira, N.Y. Died Mar. 21, 1954.

MANGUM, JOSIAH THOMAS, clergyman; b. Greenville, Ala., Apr. 13, 1876; s. Theophilus Fields and Julia Frances (Perkins) M.; student Southern U., Greensboro, Ala., 1888-89; Ala. Poly. Inst., Auburn, Ala., 1892-96; studied theology, Vanderbilt U., 1909-10; m. Edith Hooper, of Selma, Ala., Apr. 2, 1901; 1 dau., Edith Hooper. Ordained ministry M.E. Ch., S., 1901; pastor Greenville, 1901, Eufaula, 1902, Jackson, 1903, Montgomery, 1904-05, Tallassee, 1906-09, Waynesville, N.C., since 1922. Accompanied Bishop Walter R. Lambuth, as sec., to The Congo, Belge, Africa, 1913-14, and assisted in establishment of the first mission of M.E. Ch., S., in that country. Capt., chaplain 2d Regt., Ala. N.G., 1905-09; gen. sec. Army Y.M.C.A., Camp Greene, N.C., 1918. Trustee Ala. Woman's Coll., 1906-14; trustee Rutherford (N.C.) Coll., Children's Home, Junalusk Summer Sch. Mem. Sigma Nu. Democrat. Mason (K.T., Shriner); Past Grand Prelate Grand Comdry. of Ala., K.T. Home: Waynesville NC

MANIGAULT, ARTHUR MIDDLETON army officer; b. Charleston, S.C., Oct. 26, 1824; s. Joseph and Charlotte (Drayton) M.; m. Mary Huger, Apr. 18, 1851, 5 children. Became sgt. maj. of local company S.C. Militia; served as 1st lt. company E. Palmetto Regt.; fought in Mexican War; elected capt. North Santee Mounted Rifles, 1860; became a.d.c. (volunteer) on staff Gen. Beauregard, 1861; commd. lt. col.; assigned to do duty as adjutant and insp. gen. on Beauregard's staff; elected col. 10th S.C. Volunteers 1861; became comdr. 1st mil. dist. of S.C.; later ordered to Corinth (Miss.); promoted brig. gen., 1863; became adjutant and insp. gen. S.C., 1880. Died South Island, Georgetown County, S.C., Aug. 16, 1886.

MANIGAULT, GABRIEL EDWARD prof. natural history and geology, Coll. of Charleston; b. Charleston, S.C., Jan. 6, 1833; grad. Coll. of Charleston, S.C., 1852; Med. Coll. of S.C., 1854; did not practice medicine, but fitted himself, while completing his medical studies at Paris, 1854-56, for curatorship of Museum of Natural History, Coll. of Charleston, Which position he has held, 1873-; conducted rice plantation on Cooper River, S.C., 1857-73; in Confederate army, 1861-65. Address: Charleston, S.C. Died 1809.

MANLY, JOHN MATTHEWS univ. prof.; b. Sumter County, Ala. Sept. 2, 1865; s. Charles and Mary (Matthew) M.; A.M. Furman U., 1883; A.M., Harvard 1889, Ph.D., 1890; LL.D., Furman, 1912; L.H.D. Brown U., 1914, U. of N.C., 1924; Litt.D., U. of Wis., 1923, Yale, 1925; unmarried. Engaged in teaching, 1884—; asso. prof. and prof. English, Brown U., 1891-98; prof. English, 1898-1929, Sewall L. Avery distinguished service prof. English, 1929-33; also head of dept. of English, 1898-1933, U. of Chicago, prof. emeritus; engaged in making critical text of Chaucer's Canterbury Tales, 1926—; Chicago exchange prof. of Gottingen, 1909; lecturer at Lowell Inst., 1924, at British Acad. (Wharton lecture on poetry), 1926, at Royal Soc. of Lit., 1927. Granted leave of absence for duration of the war; enlisted in U.S.A. for 5 yrs.; commd. capt., Oct. 27, 1917; assigned to Military Intelligence Div., General Staff; chief sect. 8, same, Aug. 1918-May 1919; discharged and commd. maj. O.R.C., July 1919. Mem. Modern Lang. Assn. America (pres. 1922-23); follow Medieval Acad. America (pres. 1929-30); v.p. English Assn. Great Britain. Contbr. to Cambridge History of English Literature, Encyclopedia Britannica (11th edition), the Shakespeare Memorial Volume (1916), and to various periodicals. Editor: Macbeth, 1896; Specimens of the Pre-Shakespearean Drama, 1897; English Poetry, 1907; English Prose, 1909; English Prose and Poetry, 1916. 26; Chaucer (Canterbury Tales), 1928. Author: A Manual for Writers (with J. A. Powell), 1914; The Writing of English (with E. Rickert), 1919, 23, 29; The Writer's Index (with same), 1923; Contemporary British Literature (with Edith Rickert), 1921, 29, 35; Contemporary Am. Literature (with same), 1922, 29, 34; Some New Light on Chaucer, 1926; Chaucer and the Rhetoricians, 1926; The Text of the Canterbury Tales, 8 vols. (with Edith Rickert and others), 1940. Awarded Sir Israel Gollanca biennial prize by British Acad. for The Text of the Canterbury Tales, 1939. Home: Tucson, Ariz. Died Apr. 2, 1940.

MANN, HENRY soldier, author, editor; b. Glasgow, Scotland, Mar. 25, 1848; s. Alexander and Amelia (Carney) M.; ed. Eng. and Scotland, until 15 yrs. of age; came to U.S.; served, 1864-65, in 82d and 59th N.Y. Vols. in Civil War; in 13th and 31st U.S. Inf. against Indians in Northwest; m. Ellen J. Angell, Nov. 14, 1870; m. 2d, Emma C. Lindstrom, Jan. 8, 1887. Reported many famous trials for New York Sun; has been editorial writer New York Sun, Providence Journal, New York Press, New York Times, and editor-in-chief Providence Telegram; Key West corr. Christian Herald and Brooklyn Eagle in Spanish-American War. Was justice of the peace, 6th Jud. Dist., R.I., also mem. town council and Court of Probate, N. Providence, 1886-87. Editor Home and Country, mag., 1895-96; asst. editor Success, mag., 1898-99; with lit. bur. Rep. Nat. Com., 1908-12, and with municipal. Fusion Com., 1913; editor-in-chief Columbian Mag., 1909-11. V.p. 82d Regimental Assn., 1911, pres. 1912-14; a.d.c. to N.Y. department commander G.A.R., 1911. Compiled Trust Problems for Nat. Civic Federation, 1911-12; mem. com. of citizens of New York, apptd. by Mayor Gaynor, on celebration of One Hundredth Anniversary of Peace Among English Speaking Peoples. Author: Ancient and Mediaeval Republics, 1879; Features of Society in Old and New England, 1885; English Free Trade, 1888 (Rep. State Com., R.I.); Handbook for American Citizens, 1895; The Land We Live In, 1896; Turning Points in History, 1895; Story of the Declaration of Independence, 1901; Adam Clarke-A Story of the Toilers, 1905. Editor Crown Encyclopedia, 1903; on editorial staff Encyclopedia Americana, 1904. Am. editor Sir Alfred Harmsworth's Self-Educator. Home: New York, N.Y. Died Nov. 16, 1915.

MANN, LESTER BRADWELL lawyer; b. Long Pond, Ga., Sept. 30, 1886; s. Zachary Taylor and Ida Clementine (McGregor) M.; student S.Ga. Coll.; B.S., Ga. Sch. Tech., 1907; M.P.L., Georgetown U., 1915; m. Helen Moore, Nov. 10, 1920; children-John McGregor, Helen Louise (Mrs. John Masters), Douglas, Donald. Admitted to D.C. bar, 1915, Ill. bar, 1939; asst. commr. patents, Washington, 1920-21; pvt. practice, Chgo., 1921—; sr. mem. Mann, Brown & Hansmann, and predecessors, 1938—, specializing in patent law. Counselor Boy Scouts Am. Trustee Hinsdale (Ill.) Pub. Library. Served as capt., U.S. Army, World War I. Mem. Am., Ill. State, Chgo. bar assns., Am. (bd. mgrs.), Chgo. (pres. 1943) patent law assns., Western Soc. Engrs. Mason (K.T., Shriner). Clubs: Union League, Engrs. (Chicago); Hinsdale (Ill.) Golf; Three Lakes (Wis.) Rod and Gun. Home: 344 N. Radcliffe Way, Hinsdale, Ill. Office: 53 Jackson Blvd., Chgo. 4. Died Mar. 27, 1954; buried Hinsdale.

MANN, WILLIAM ABRAM army officer; b. in Pa., July 31, 1854; grad. U.S. Mil. Acad., 1875; Army War Coll., 1905; married. Commd. 2d lt., 175h Inf., June 16, 1875; promoted through grades to brig. gen., Jan. 20, 1915; retired, July 31, 1918; promoted maj. gen. retired, June 21, 1930. Died Oct. 8, 1934.

MANN, WILLIAM D'ALTON editor; b. Sandusky, O., Sept. 27, 1839; s. William R. and Eliza (Ford) M.; ed. as civ. engr.; m. Sophie Hartog, 1902. Entered United Army at oubreak of Civil War; commd. capt. 1st Mich. Cav.; organized 1st Mounted Rifles, afterwards 5th Mich. Ca., and Daniels' Horse Batters, 1862; organized 7th Mich. Cav. and Gunther's Horse Battery (these troops composing Mich. Cav. Brigade); commd. col., 1862; devised improvements in accoutrements of troops, used in U.S. Army, and Austrian Army. Settled in Mobile, Ala., after the war; pioneer mfr. cotton-seed oil; several yrs. propr. Mobile Register; 1st Dem. candidate for Congress, under Reconstruction, from Mobile Dist. (elected to 41st Congress but not seated); invented and patented the boudoir car, 1871, and introduced it throughout Europe; founded the Compagnie Internationale des Wagons-Lits; organized Mann Boudoir Car Co., New York, 1883 (later bought out by Pullman Co.); pres. and editor Town Topics, 1891—; founder and mgr. The Smart Set. Author: The Raiders, 1876. Home: New York, N.Y. Died May 17, 1920.

MANNEY, HENRY NEWMAN rear adm. U.S.N.; b. La Porte, Ind., Jan. 22, 1844; apptd. to U.S. Naval Acad., from Minn., 1861, grad. 1866. Promoted ensign, Mar. 12, 1868; master, Mar. 26, 1869; lt., Mar. 21, 1870; lt. comdr., Oct. 7, 1886; comdr., May 10, 1895; capt., Mar. 3, 1901; retired as rear adm. of senior adm. of senior grade, Jan. 22, 1906. On board Macedonian, in the summer of 1864, in pursuit of the Confederate steamers Florida and Tallahassee; served on Resaca, 1866-69; Swatara, 1870-72; Michigan, 1872-73; receiving ship Independence, 1873; Tuscarora, 1873-74; Kearsarge, 1875; Yantic, 1876; Alaska, 1878-81; Naval Acad., 1881-84; Powhatan, 1884; Lancaster, 1884-87; Hydrographic Office, 1888; Naval Home, Phila., 1889-91, 1892-95, 1898-99; exec. officer Newark, 1891-92; comd. Alliance, 1895-97; Navy Yard, New York, 1889-1901; comd. Massachusetts, 1901-03; spl. duty with General Bd. of the Navy, 1903-04; chief Bur. of Equipment, with the rank of rear adm., 1904-06; spl. duty Nlavy Dept., 1906-07; spl. duty on Pacific Coast in connection with constrn. of coal depot at California City Point, Calif., 1907-08; rep. Bur. of Equipment, Navy Dept., and charged with the disposition of all chartered colliers, providing the fleet, 1908-09; assumed charge naval coaling sta., being consutrcted at San Diego, Calif., Feb. 10, 1909; retired from active duty, Nov. 20, 1909. Del. Internat. Conf. on Wireless Telegraphy, Berlin, 1906. Address: Point Loma, Calif. Died Oct. 25, 1915.

MANNING, CHARLES HENRY engineer; b. Baltimore, Md., June 9, 1844; s. Joseph Cogswell and Rebecca Parkman Jarvis (Livermore) M.; B.S., Lawrence Scientific Sch. (Harvard), 1862; m. Fanny Bartlett, Jan. 17, 1871. Apptd. engr. U.S. Navy, Feb. 19, 1863; served through Civil War; instr. U.S. Naval Acad., 1870-75, 1878-81; mem. 1st advisory bd. to build new navy, 1881-82; advanced to chief engr., 1906, retired, June 14, 1884; chief engr. Key West Naval Sta. during Spanish-Am. War. Gen. supt. Amoskeag Mfg. Co.,

1883-1913. Designer of Manning boiler, in gen. use in textile mills. Address: Manchester, N.H. Died Apr. 1, 1919.

MANNING, GEORGE CHARLES naval architect; b. Washington, D.C., July 28, 1892; s. Joseph S. and Barbara C. (Miller) M.; B.S., U.S. Naval Acad., 1914; S.M., Mass. Institute Technology, 1920; D.Sc., Villanova College, 1951; married Blanche M. Larue, Feb. 9, 1918; children-George Charles, Ferdinand L., Joseph M. Commd. ensign, United States Navy, 1914; served as lt. (j.g.) to lt. comdr., Constrn. Corps, 1917-39; adminstr. for George C. Sharp, naval architect, 1939-40; mem. faculty, U.S. Navy Post Grad. Sch., 1940-41; lecturer in naval architecture, Mass. Inst. Tech., Cambridge, 1936-39, asso. prof. naval architecture, 1938-44, professor, 1944-58, professor emeritus, 1958-, head of department, 1950-52; professor naval architect Escola Politencica University de Sao Paulo 1957-59, professor emeritus, 1959-. Recipient Medalha Naval de Servicos Distintos, Brazil. Member of Society of Naval Architects and Marine Engineers, American Society Naval Engrs., Instn. Naval Architects. Naval Order of U.S., U.S. Naval Inst., N.E. Coast Inst. of Engrs. and Shipbuilders. rep. Club: Propeller. Author: Manual of Naval Architecture, 1929; Manual of Ship Construction, 1942; Basic Design of Ships, 1945; The Theory and Technique of Ship Design, 1956; Fundamentals of Theoretical Naval Architecture, 1958; co-author: Principles of Warship Construction, 1923; Damage Control, 1944; Principles of Naval Architecture, 1939; also articles on naval architecture and shipbldg. Address: 22 Eel River Rd., Osterville, Mass. Died Sept. 19, 1964; buried Mosswood Cemetery, Cotuit, Mass.

MANNING, JOHN JOSEPH naval officer; s. John G. and Maria (Geer) M.; C.E., Rensselaer Poly Inst., 1915, D.Eng., 1945; m. Catherine Marie Riordan, Apr. 4, 1919; children-Anne Marie, John Joseph, Gerald Riordan. Apptd. lt. (j.g.) C.E., USN, 1917 and advanced through grades to rear adm. Chief Bur. Yards and Docks and chief C.E. USN, head Seabees, since 1945. Decorated D.S.M., Legion of Merit, Bronze Star medal (U.S.); Croix de Guerre with Silver Star (France). Trustee Rensselaer Poly. Inst. Mem. Am. Soc. C.E., Am. Concrete Inst., Rensselaer Poly. Inst. Alumni Assn. (pres.), Newcomen Soc., Am. Soc. Mil. Engrs., (pres.), Am. Inst. Cons. Engrs., Sigma Xi, Tau Beta Pi. Clubs: Army and Navy,Army-Navy Country (Washington). Home: 3113 Woodley Rd., Washington 8, D.C. and Troy, N.Y. Office: Chief of Bur. of Yards and Docks, Navy Dept., Washington 25. Died Sept. 1962.

MANSFIELD, HENRY BUCKINGHAM rear admiral U.S.N.; b. Brooklyn, N.Y., Mar. 5, 1846; s. Capt. Charles and Eliza Maria (Buckingham) M.; ed. pub. sch., Sheffield, Mass., Hudson River Inst.; grad. U.S. Naval Acad., 1867; m. Harriet Sheldon, Oct. 23, 1872. Promoted ensign, 1868; master, 1870; lieut., 1871; lieut. comdr. 1890; comdr., May 1807; captain, 1962; rear admiral and retired, June 15, 1905. While midshipman served in Marion, Macedonian, Winnepec, and Minnesota; spl. service, 1867-68; served on Mohongo and Mohican, Pacific fleet, 1869-70; eclipse expdn. to Siberia, 1869; comd. 2d launch from Mohican, in expdn. which cut out and burned piratical steamer Forward in Tecupan River, Mex.; on various duties, chiefly coast survey and hydrographic work and comdg. coast survey steamers, 1871-93; receiving-ship Vermont, 1893-97; comd. Fern, 1897-98; lighthouse insp., Apr.-May 1898; comd. U.S.S. Celtic N. Atlantic Squadron, May-Sept. 1898; at Navy Yard, N.Y., Sept.-Dec. 1898; light house insp. to Dec. 1899; comdg. U.S.S. Lancaster, Dec. 1899-1901; in charge recruiting rendezvous, New York, Nov. 1901-03, Naval War Coll., Apr.-Oct. 1903; naval examining and retiring bd. to Nov. 1903; comdg. battleship Iowa to Jan. 1905; on duty at New York Navy Yard,1905. Home: Brooklyn, N.Y. Died July 17, 1918.

MANSFIELD, IRA FRANKLIN coal operator; b. Poland, O., June 27, 1842; s. Isaac Kirtland and Lois (Morse) M.; grad. Poland Coll., 1861; m. Lucy E. Mygatt, Dec. 11, 1872. Enlisted 1862, 105th Ohio Vols., serving to close of war; promoted orderly sergt., 2d lt., 1st lt., and promoted capt. and a.-q.-m. 14th Army Corps at Atlanta, Ga.; took part in Sherman's march to the sea and in Grand Review in Washington, 1865. Bought, 1865, and has since operated cannel coal mines at Cannelton, Beaver Co., .; pres. Shenango and Beaver Valley Rys., Rochester Nat. Bank, Greensburg Acad., 25 yrs., 5 terms; 10 yrs. mem. Pa. Legislature. Mem. Am. Philos. Soc., A.A.A.S. Author: Early History of Ohio Valley and Beaver County, 1890; Text List of Native Plants and Orchids of Beaver County, 1900; Fossil Plants and Insects of Beaver County, 1900; also contributions to The Beaver · (Beaver Coll. monthly). Address: Beaver, Pa.

MANSFIELD, JOSEPH KING FENNO army officer; b. New Haven, Conn., Dec. 22, 1803; s. Henry and Mary (Fenno) M.; grad. U.S. Mil. Acad., 1822; m. Louise Mather, Sept. 25, 1838, 4 children. Commd. 2d lt. Corps Engrs., U.S. Army, 1822, 1st lt., 1832, capt. 1838; served in Mexican War, 1846-48; chief engr., brevetted maj., then lt. col., col.; capt. in constrn. coast defenses until 1853; col., insp. gen., 1853; commd. brig. gen. U.S. Army, assigned to command Dept. Washington (D.C.), including capitol and surrounding territory, 1861; commd. maj. gen. U.S. Volunteers, 1862. Died Battle of Antietam (Va.), Sept. 18, 1862.

MANSFIELD, SAMUEL MATHER brig. gen. U.S.A.; b. Middletown, Conn., Sept. 23, 1839; s. Maj. Gen. Joseph King Fenno and Louisa (Mather) M.; grad. U.S. Mil. Acad., 1862; m. Mrs. Anna Baldwin Wright, Apr. 16, 1874 (dec.). Promoted 2d lt., corps engrs., June 17, 1862; promoted through grades to brig. gen. U.S.A., Feb. 20, 1903. In Civil War, col. 24th Conn. Inf., Nov. 18, 1862-Sept. 30, 1863. Bvtd. capt., June 14, 1863, "for gallantry at Port Hudson, La."; maj. and lt. col., Mar. 13, 1865, "for gallant and meritorious services during the war." Has been in charge of constrn. of many fortifications; engr., 9th, 10th and 11th light house dists., and many other works; pres. commn. to run and mark the boundary lines between portion of Ind. Ty. and Texas, 1885-87; pres. Calif. debris commn. to regulate hydraulic mining, 1898-99; pres. Yosemite Nat. Park Commn., 1899; div. engr., Pacific div., Nov. 7, 1898, Northwestern div., May 3, 1901, Eastern div., July 4, 1901; retired at own request, over 40 yrs. service, Feb. 21, 1903. Mass. harbor and land commr., July 23, 1906-July 17, 1912. Address: Boston, Mass. Died Feb. 18, 1928.

MARCH, PEYTON CONWAY ret. gen. U.S. Army; b. Easton, Pa., Dec. 27, 1864; s. Francis Andrew and Mildred Stone (Conway) M.; A.B., Lafayette Coll., 1884, A.M., 1887, LL.D., 1918; LL.D., Union Coll., 1918 and Amherst Coll., 1919; Dr. of Mil. Science, Pa. Mil. Coll., 1934; B.S., U.S. Mil. Acad., 1888; grad. Arty. Sch., Ft. Monroe, 1898; m. Mrs. Josephine (Smith) Cuningham, July 4, 1891 (died Nov. 18, 1904); children-Mrs. Mildred Millikin, Mrs. Josephine Swing, Peyton Conway (dec.), Mrs. Vivian Frank (dec.), Lewis Alden (dec.); m. 2d, Cora V. McEntee, Aug. 25, 1923. Add. 2d lt. 3d Arty., June 11, 1888; 2d lt., Nov. 30, 1888; 1st lt., Oct. 25, 1894; maj. 33d Vol. Inf., July 5, 1889; lt. col., June 9, 1900; hon. discharged vols., June 30, 1901; capt. Arty. Corps, U.S. Army, Feb. 2, 1901; capt. Arty. Corps, U.S. Army, Feb. 2, 1901;maj., Jan. 15, 1907; assigned to 6th F.A., Aug. 26, 1916; brig. gen., June 17, 1917; maj. gen., Nat. Army, Aug. 5, 1917; maj. gen. U. S. Army, Sept. 23, 1917; gen. May 20, 1918. Comd. Astor Battery, 1898 (mountain battery presented to government by Col. John Jacob Astor); comd. Am. forces in action at Tilad Pass, Luzon, P.I., Dec. 2, 1899, in which Gen Gregorio del Pilar was killed; during same expdn. Gen. Vanancio Concepcion, chief of staff to Aguinaldo, surrendered to Maj. March; in charge mil. and civil govt. in district Lepanto-Bontoc and Mocus half Ilocus Sur. Feb.-June 1900; Province of Abra, to Feb. 1901; commissary-gen. of prisoners, P.I., to June 30, 1901; mem. Gen. Staff, 1903-07; mil. attaché to observe Japanese Army in Russo-Japanese War, 1904; army arty. comdr. A.E.F. in France, 1917; apptd. actg. chief of staff U.S. Army, Mar. 4, 1918; gen. and chief of staff, May 20, 1918; retired, 1921. Nominated for bvt. Mar. 20, 1902, "for distinguished gallantry in action," capt. U.S. Army (for action nr. Manila, Luzon, Aug. 13, 1898), lt. col. U.S.V. (for actions nr. Porac, Sept. 28, and at San Jacinto, Luzon, Nov. 11, 1899), col. U.S.V. (for actions at Tilar Pass, Dec. 2 and Cayan, Luzon, Dec. 5, 1899). Recipient Thanks of Congress by resolution, 1953; decorated Silver Star medal (4 oak-leaf clusters) for participation in these engagements; D.S.C. "for distinguished gallantry in action"; D.S.M., 1918, for "exceptionally meritorious and distinguished services"; Grand Cross Order of St. Michael and St. George (Eng.); Grand Officer Legion of Honor (France); Grand Cross Order of George the First (Greece); Grand Cordon Order of Crown (Belgium); Grand Cross Order Crown (Roumania); War Cross (Czechoslovakia); Grand Cordon of the Chia Ho (China); Grand Cordon of the Polonia Restituta (1st class); Grand Cross Order of St. Maurice and St. Lazarus (Italy); Grand Cross Order of the Rising Sun (Japan). Mem. Soc. of the Cincinnati (Va.) Descendants of Signers of Declaration of Independence, Army and Navy Union, Phi Beta Kappa, Delta Kappa Epsilon. Clubs: Army and Navy (Washington, D.C.); Union League (New York). Author: The Nation at War, 1932; also various newspaper articles. Home: 1870 Wyoming Av. N.W., Washington. Died Apr. 13, 1955; buried Arlington Nat. Cemetery.

MARCHAND, JOHN BONNETT naval officer; b. Greensburg, Pa., Aug. 27, 1808; s. David and Catherine (Bonnett) M.; m. Margaret Thorton, 1856/57. Commd. midshipman U.S. Navy 1828; student Norfolk Naval Sch.; passed midshipman, 1834; served in ship Potomac, then the John Adams, Mediterranean Squadron, 1834-37; commd. lt., 1840; served in war against Seminole Indians while in command ship Van Buren, 1841; promoted to comdr. 1855, capt. 1862; assigned to blockade duty in Gulf of Mexico during Civil War; commanded Phila. Navy Yard; commd. commodore, 1866, ret., 1870. Died Carlisle, Pa., Apr. 13, 1875.

MARCHANT, TRELAWNEY E. ret. army officer; b. Lexington County, S.C., May 11, 1887; son of Julian M. and Addie (Senn) M.; grad. Draughons Bus. Coll. (Columbia, S.C.), 1911; Command and Gen. Staff Sch., 1939-40; Inf. Sch., 1940; m. Lila Cave, 1919; children-Trelawney E., Julian M., Nancy C. Engaged in banking 1911-40 less time in active Army service. Service N.G. of U.S., 1905-43; active service Mexican Border 1916-17, World War I 1917-19, World War II 1940-43; ret. 1943 disability incurred in line of duty, rank Brig. Gen., Infantry. Home: 2329 Blossom St., Columbia, S.C. Died June 2, 1950; buried Mt. Hebron Meth. Ch., Lexington County, S.C.

MARCO, HERBERT FRANCIS, state ofcl.; b. Auburn, N.Y., Mar. 27, 1907; s. Dominick A. and Rose Mary (Giannino) M.; B.S., Cornell U., 1929; M.S., Syracuse U., 1932; Ph.D. (Charles Boughton research fellow) Yale, 1935; m. Jane Christine Dry, Oct. 26, 1946; children—Teig, Lynn, Gaird. Engineer in charge r.r. constrn. Cady Corp., 1929; mem. Northeastern Forest Expt. Sta., 1935; mem. Conn. Geodetic Survey, 1938-42; dir. project for computation mil. grid coordinates for U.S., Greenland, Iceland, 1941-42; pres. faculty, mem. team for orgn. Air Force Inst. Tech., 1946-56; participant Gatlinburg Conf. Atomic Energy, 1956; dean engring., dir. research and engring. Expt. Sta., S.D. State Coll., 1956-58; tech. specialist Aerojet-Gen. Corp., 1958-65; pres. Guilford Technical Institute, Jamestown, N.C., 1965-68; with Division of State Planning and Community Affairs, Richmond, Va., 1968-69; division mgr., cons. to chmn. bd. Dayco Corporation also cons. to industry at large. Director Rosemont Home Assn. Served maj. AUS, World War II. Decorated Purple Heart, Air medal with cluster. Mem. of the American Society of Engineering Education (nat. chmn. mechanics div., mem. exec. com.), Am. Inst. Aeros. and Astronautics, Sigma Xi, Tau Beta Pi, Gamma Delta, Pi Epsilon Gamma. Mason, Rotarian. Home: Richmond VA Died Oct. 28, 1969; buried Glendale Nat. Cemetery, Richmond VA

MARCOSSON, ISAAC FREDERICK journalist; b. Louisville, Ky., Sept. 13, 1877; s. Louis and Helene M.; ed. public schs.; m. 2d, Frances Barberey, June 8, 1931 (now deceased); m. 3d, Ellen Petts, Sept. 1, 1942. Mem. staff and later city editor Louisville Times, 1894-1903; asso. editor World's Work, New York, 1903-07; mem. staff and financial editor Saturday Evening Post, 1907-10; asso. editor Munsey's Magazine, N.Y., 1910-13; staff contbr. to Saturday Evening Post, 1913-36. Mem. advisory council New York City Cancer Com.; member board trustees Memorial Hospital for Treatment of Cancer and Allied Diseases. Lt. comdr. U.S.N.R. (retired). Clubs: Players (New York); American (London); Union Interalliée (Paris). Author: How to Invest Your Savings, 1908; The Autobiography of a Clown, 1910; The War After The War, 1916; Leonard Wood, Prophet of Preparedness, 1917; The Rebirth of Russia, 1917; The Business of War, 1917; S.O.S. America's Miracle in France, 1919; Peace and Business, 1919; Adventures in Interviewing, 1919; An African Adventure, 1921; The Black Golconda, 1924; Caravans of Commerce, 1927; David Graham Phillips and His Times, 1932; Turbulent Years, 1938; Wherever Men Trade, The Romance of the Cash Register, 1945; Colonel Deeds, Industrial Builder, 1947; Metal Magic, The Story of the American Smelting and Refining Company, 1949; Marse Henry, the Biography of Henry Watterson, 1951; Industrial Main Street, 1953; Copper Heritage, 1955; Anaconda, 1957; Before I Forget, A Pilgrimage to the Past, pub. 1959. Co-author: Charles Frohman, Manager and Man, 1917. Address: 7 Gracie Sq., N.Y.C. 29; also Windwood, St. James, L.I., N.Y. Died Mar. 1961.

MARCY, HENRY ORLANDO surgeon; b. Otis, Mass., June 23, 1837; s. Smith and Fanny (Gibbs) M.; ed. Wilbraham Acad. and Amherst Coll.; M.D., Harvard, 1863; hon. A.M., Amherst, 1870; LL.D., Wesleyan, 1887; m. Sarah E. Wendell, Oct. 14, 1863. Asst. surgeon 43d Mass. Vols., Apr. 1863; surgeon 35th U.S.C.T., Nov. 1863; med. dir. of Fla., 1864; med. dir. on Sherman' staff, Carolina campaign; made sanitary renovation of Charleston, S.S.; practiced Cambridge, Mass., 1865-69; studied at U. of Berlin, and in London and Edinburgh, 1869-70; was 1st Am. pupil of Dr. Lister, Edinburgh, and later introduced Lister's methods to America. Returned to U.S. and devoted his attention to laboratory and practical study of antiseptic methods of wound treatment; has conducted pvt. hosp. in Cambridge for treatment surgical diseases, 1880-. Was asst. to Dr. Henry J. Bowditch, Boston, and after his death chief dir. in renovation Charles River Basin; built Harvard Bridge, completed cambridge Esplanada Parkway, and placed M.I.T. on Cambridge front, the site of which he chiefly owned; a leader in development of the Parkway reservation. President A.M.A., 1892, Am. Acad. Medicine, 1884. Author: The Reproductive Process (transl. from G. B. Ercolani's work, 2 vols.), 1884; The Anatomy and Surgical Treatment of Hernia; The Radical Cure of Hernia, 1889; The Perineum, Its Anatomy and Surgical Treatment, 1889. Active in surg. service during entire period of the World War. Home: Boston, Mass. Died Jan. 2, 1924.

MARCY, RANDOLPH BARNES army officer; b. Greenwich, Mass., Apr. 9, 1812; s. Laban and Fanny (Howe) M.; grad. U.S. Mil. Acad., 1832; m. Mary Mann, 1833. Brevetted 2d lt., 5th Inf., U.S. Army 1832, commd. 2d lt., 1835, 1st lt., 1837, capt., 1846; acting insp. gen. Dept. of Utah, 1856; commd. maj., apptd. paymaster, 1859, served in N.W. until 1861, then chief-of-staff to Gen. George B. McClellan (his son-in-law); commd. col., insp. gen., 1861; temporary brig. gen., 1861-63, served with Army of Potomac in Md.

campaign, 1862-63; participated in cavalry charge at Brandy Stations in Pa. campaign, 1863; distinguished himself at Battle of Gettysburg, in central Va. operations and actions at Rapidan, Auburn and New Hope Ch.; insp. in various depts., 1863-78; in charge 2d cavalry div. Army of Potomac in Richmond campaign, 1864-65; apptd. insp. gen. with rank brig. gen. U.S. Army, 1878. Died West Orange, N.J., Nov. 22, 1887.

MARDEN, GEORGE AUGUSTUS asst. treasurer U.S. at Boston, 1899-; b. Mt. Vernon, N.H., Aug. 9, 1839; s. Benjamin F. and Betsey (Buss) M.; grad. Dartmouth, 1861; m. Mary P. Fiske, Dec. 10, 1867; entered army, Dec., 1861, in 2d regt. Berdan's Sharpshooters, serving as q.m. and as acting asst. adj. gen. 3d brigade, 3d div., 3d army corps; mustered out, Sept., 1864; studied law; became connected with Concord Monitor, Boston Daily Advertiser; editor and a propr. of Lowell Daily Courier, 1867-; also Lowell Morning Citizen; mem. Mass. legislature, 1873; clerk same, 1874-82. Speaker, same, 1883-84; mem. Mass. senate, 1885; treas. and receiver gen. of Mass., 1889-93. Home: Lowell, Mass. Died 1906.

MARES, LUMIR MARTIN, physician; b. Wilber, Neb., Nov. 11, 1901; s. M.D., Northwestern U., 1927; married, May 30, 1931 (wife dec. 1965); children—Sam, Robert. Intern St. Lukes Hosp., Chgo., 1927-29; attending physician Deaconess Hosp., Wenatchee, Wash., St. Anthonys-Chelan County Hosp., Wenatchee. Served to lt. col. M.C., AUS, 1942-45. Named Wenatchee Pioneer of Year, 1964. Diplomate Am. Bd. Internal Medicine. Mem. A.M.A. Home: Wenatchee WA Died May 30, 1967; buried Wenatchee WA

MARGET, ARTHUR WILLIAM economist; born Chelsea, Mass., Oct. 17, 1899; s. Morris and Celia (Frankel) M.; A.B., Harvard, 1920, A.M., 1921, Ph.D., 1927; student Univs. ofLondon, Cambridge and Berlin, 1920-21; m. Edith F. Pavlo, Mar. 31, 1931; 1 son, Jonathan Pavlo. Asst. and instr. in economics, Harvard, 1923-27; asso. prof. economics, U. of Minn., 1927-30, prof., 1930-48; visiting prof. economics, U. of Calif., summer 1936. Served in U.S. Army, 1918, commd. maj., 1943, lt. col., 1945; Chief, finance div., U.S. Element Allied Commn. for Austria, 1945-48; chief, econ. div. 1947-48; econ. advisor, Council Fgn. Ministers, London and Moscow, 1947; cons. U.S. Treasury, 1948; chief finance div., Office Spl. Rep., E.C.A., 1948-49; director of division of international finance, board of governors, Federal Reserve System, 1950-61; U.S. econ. adviser to C.Am. econ. integration, 1961-62. Awarded Legion of Merit, 1946. Member Am. Econ. Assn., Royal Econ. Soc., Phi Beta Kappa. Jewish. Author: The Theory of Prices, vol. 1, 1938, vol. 2, 1941. Contbr. econ. jours. Home: 3700 Mass. Av. N.W., Washington 16. Address: U.S. AID, care Am. Embassy, Guatemala, C.Am. Died Sept. 5, 1962; buried Guatemala.

MARION, FRANCIS army officer; b. Berkeley County, S.C., 1732; s. Gabriel and Esther (Cordes) M.; m. Mary Videau, 1786. Owner plantation, nr. Eautaw Springs, S.C., 1759-95; served as lt. Royal Scots Regt. in campaigns against Cherokee Indians, 1761; mem. S.C. Provincial Congress from St. John's Parish, 1775; commd. capt. 2d S.C. Regt., served at occupation of Ft. Johnson, 1775; commd. lt. col. Continental Army, 1776, brig. gen. S.C. Militia, 1780; commanded only Revolutionary forces in S.C., 1780-81; continually disrupted Brit. communication and prevented orgn. of Loyalist forces by guerilla warfare tactics; nicknamed "Swamp Fox" by Brit. Gen. Tariton because of tactics, hid in swamps between attacks; served at Battle of Eutaw Springs, 1781; mem. S.C. Senate, 1781, 82, 84; attended S. C. Constl. Conv., 1790; elected to fill unexpired term in S.C. Senate, 1791. Died St. John's Parish, S.C., Feb. 27, 1795; buried Belle Isle, St. Stephen's Parish, Berkeley County.

MARIX, ADOLPH rear admiral U.S.N.; b. Dresden, Saxony, May 10, 1848; s. Henry and Frederica (Meyer) M.; grad. U.S. Naval Acad., 1868; m. Grace Filkins, May 31, 1896. Commd. midshipman, June 1, 1868; promoted through various grades to capt., Mar. 21, 1903; rear admiral, July 4, 1908. Served on European and Asiatic stas.; was judge advocate of Maine court of inquiry; capt. of port of Manila, 1901-03; comd. U.S.S. Scorpion during Spanish-Am. War, and was promoted for conspicuous bravery; chmn. Lighthouse Board, 1907-10; retired, May 10, 1910. Address: New York, N.Y. Died July 12, 1919.

MARK, KENNETH LAMARTINE educator; b. of Am. parents, Leipzig, Germany, Aug. 27, 1874; s. Edward Laurens and Lucy Thorp (King) M.; A.B., Harvard, 1898, A.M., 1900, Ph.D., 1903; m. Florence Louise Wetherbee, June 19, 1907. Asst. in chemistry Harvard, 1900-03; instr. chemistry Simmons Coll., 1903-07, asst. prof., 1907-13, asso. prof., 1913-15, prof., 1915-41 (emeritus), dir. Sch. Science, 1915-41. Fellow Am. Acad. Arts and Sciences; mem. Am. Chem. Soc., Delta Upsilon. Republican. Author: Laboratory Exercises in General Chemistry, 1916; Laboratory Exercises in Inorganic Chemistry, 1922; Delayed by Fire, being the Early History of Simmons College, 1945. Capt. Sanitary Corps. U.S. Army, 1918. Home: 200 Riverway, Boston 15. Died Jan. 12, 1958.

MARKHAM, EDWARD M. ret. army officer; b. Troy, N.Y., July 6, 1877; s. Cornelius and Margaret (Carney) M.; M.A., C.E., U.S. Mil. Acad., 1899, hon. B.S., Rensselaer Polytechnic Inst., 1934; m. Grace S. Markham, Jan. 27, 1904; children-Edward M., Harrison S., Grace K. (Mrs. W. J. Natteson). Commd. 2d lt., Engrs., 1899, advanced through grades to maj. gen., chief of engrs., 1933; retired as maj. gen., 1938; commr. of public works, N.Y.C., 1938; pres. Great Lakes Dredge & Dock Co., Chicago, 1938-45; ret. 1945. Clubs: Army-Navy (Washington); Chicago Athlatic Assn. (Chgo.); Home: 59 Manning Blvd., Albany, N.Y. Died Sept. 14, 1950.

MARKHAM, HENRY HARRISON governor; b. Wilmington, N.Y., Nov. 16, 1840; s. Nathan B. and Susan (McLeod) M.; ed. pub. and pvt. schs.; worked on farm until 1861; removed to Wis.; served in Union Army; was with Sherman on march to the sea; severely wounded at battle of Whippy Swamp, Feb. 3, 1865; studied law; admitted to practice Wis. and U.S. courts; m. Mary A. Dana, May 17, 1876. Practiced at Milwaukee, 1867-78; removed to Pasadena, Calif., 1878; engaged in gold and silver mining; mem. 49th Congress (1885-87); gov. of Calif., 1891-95; mem. bd. mgrs. Nat. Home for Disabled Vol. Soldiers. Republican. Address: Redondo Beach, Calif. Died Oct. 9, 1923.

MARKHAM, JOHN RAYMOND, prof. engring.; b. Cambridge, Mass., July 23, 1895; s. John Henry and Mary (Williams) M.; M.E., Mass. Inst. Tech., 1918; m. Genevieve Triquera, June 5, 1921; 1 son, James Paul (killed in action, Mar. 8, 1945). Began as research asso. aeronaut. engring. dept., Mass. Inst. Tech., 1922, prof. aeronaut. engring. from 1946, dir. supersonic lab. from 1947; dir. Wright Bros. Wind Tunnel, Mass. Inst. Tech., cons. engr. Argentine and Brazillian govts. in design of wind tunnels and equipment, also U.S. A.A.F., Boeing Aircraft, United Aircraft Corp. and Gen. Motors Corp.; mem. sci. adv. bd. to U.S.A.A.F., from 1945; chmn. industry and ednl. adv. bd. U.S.A.F. science com. and sub-com. Nat. Adv. Council for Aeros. Chairman bd. Mithras, Inc. (Cambridge, Mass.). Served as capt. AEF, U.S. Army, 1917-19. Recipient USAF medal, 1955. Fellow Inst. Aero. Sci.; mem. Sigma Xi. Contbr. articles to engring. and sci. publs. Home: Belmont MA Died Dec. 12, 1971; buried Belmont Cemetery, Belmont MA

MARKLEY, ALFRED COLLINS brig. gen. U.S.A.: b. Doylestown, Pa., Apr. 18, 1843; s. John Sorver and Eliza (Collins) M.; ed. pvtly. to 1854, Penn Grammar Sch., 1854-56, and Central High Sch., Phila., 1856-58; m. Rebecca Conrad Morgan, Apr. 23, 1868; 1 son, Edward Browning (dec.). With Browning & Bros., mfrs. Phila., 1861-63; pvt. 25th Pa. Inf., 1862; corporal 52d Pa. Inf. (State Militia), 1863, both in active service in Pa. and Md., sergt. 197th Pa. Vols., 1864, 2d lit. 127th U.S. Colored Inf., Sept. 1864; 1st lt. and adj., Mar. 1865; mustered out, Oct. 1865; apptd. 2d lt., 41st U.S. Inf. (regular army), July 28, 1866; promoted through grades to brig. gen. U.S.A., Mar. 2, 1907. Served in Antietam and Gettysburg campaigns, also in operations before Richmond, Va., 1864-65; siege and capture of Petersburg, Va., Mar. 1865; pursuit of Lee's army to surrender at Appomattox, April 1865; with "Army of Observation" on Rio Grand (to drive French Army out of Mexico), under Gen. Sheridan, May-Oct. 1895; frontier service against Indians, 1867-80; campaign in Cuba, June-Aug. 1898, battle of San Juan Hill, comdg. 24th Inf., after wounding of lt. col., July 1; participated in capture and occupation of Ft. San Juan, which comd. until July 9, 1898 (cited with silver star for gallantry at Santiago, July 1898, 1924); comdg. officer 24th Inf., July 1-Aug. 26, that volunteered, at Santiago, to go to yellow fever camp at Siboney to nurse the sick and bury the dead and do other hosp. service requiring great courage and self-sacrifice, ultimately resulting in death to about one-fourth of the officers and men of the regt.; comd. regt. and other troops, 4,000 men, and depot of supply for army at Siboney, Cuba; comd. Fort D. A. Russell, Wyo., and Vancouver Barracks, Wash., to Dec. 1899, when ordered to Philippines; comd. dist.of 13 towns and system of supply to troops in Caraballo Mountains; returned to U.S. July 1902; comd. Ft. McDowell, 1902-05; went to P.I., Oct. 5, 1905, comd. Fort Wm. McKinley. Manila; retired by operation of law, Apr. 18, 1907; returned to U.S., June 9, 1907. Home: Alton, Ill. Died Aug. 24, 1926.

MARKS, LAURENCE MANDEVILLE partner Laurence M. Marks & Co.; b. Brooklyn, N.Y., Mar. 4, 1892; s. Alexander Drummond and Caroline (Mandeville) M.; grad. Hotchkiss Sch. (Conn.), 1910; A.B., Yale U., 1914; married Mrs. Marjorie G. Martin, Sept. 30, 1946. Started career with Lee, Higginson & Co., investment bankers in N.Y.C. After World War I returned to the company. Resigned in July, 1932, and organized investment banking firm of Laurence M. Marks & Co. in N.Y.C. with branch office in Albany, N.Y. Dir. Air Products, Inc., N.Y., Divco Corp., Detroit, Mich., Nat. City Lines, Inc., Chicago, Ill. Shamrock Oil & Gas Corp., Amarillo, Tex. Gov. Assn. of Stock Exchange Firms, 1945-48. Trustee Brooklyn (N.Y.) Sav. Banks. Served in Mexican Border Campaign with Squadron A, N.Y. Nat. Guard, 1916-17. At Outbreak of World War I joined U.S. Army and was assigned to First Reserve Officers Training Camp at Plattsburg Barracks, N.Y. Was commd. 2d lt., Field Artillery, First Div., served with 5th F.A., A.E.F., from Dec. 1917-May 1919. Promoted to 1st lt., Sept. 1918 and made capt. in Mar. 1919. Was awarded Croix de Guerre and received various citations for bravery while in action. Mem. Governing Com. N.Y. Stock Exchange (1934-38). Gov. Investment Bankers Assn. of Am., 1939-40 (pres. 1951), Nat. Assn. Securities Dealers, 1940-43. Treas. N.Y. State Rep. Com., 1936-37. Chmn. Citizens Family Welfare Com., 1936. Dir. Brooklyn and Queens Y.M.C.A.; Brooklyn Bureau of Charities; Brooklyn Hospital; Travelers Aid Soc. Mem. Phi Beta Kappa, Alpha Delta Phi, Wolf's Head (Yale). Clubs: Union (gov. 1942-46); Yale; Links; Heights Casino (gov., 1938—); Wall St. (gov. 1940-43); Bond of New York, (pres. 1932-33, gov. 1930-34); Piping Rock. Home: 775 Park Av. Office: 49 Wall St., N.Y.C. Died Aug. 25, 1958.

MARKS, SOLON physician and surgeon; b. Stockbridge, Vt., July 14, 1827; ed. pub. schs. Stockbridge, Randolph and Bethel, and at Royalton Acad.; M.D., Rush Med. Coll., Chicago 1853; widower, Surgeon 10th Wis. Inf., Sept. 27, 1861; detached on staff Gen. Sill, as brigade surgeon, until capture of Huntsville, Ala., Apr. 11, 1862; in charge mil. hosps., Huntsville, Ala., until Oct. 1862; accompanied Gen. Sill's brigade until Oct. 8, 1862; then chief surgeon Gen. Rosseau's div. until the organization of the Army of the Cumberland; then chief surgeon of the 1st Div. 14th Army Corps until term of service expired. Is prof. mil. surgery, fractures and dislocations, Wis. Coll. Phys. and Surg.; chief surgeon C.,M.&St.P. R.R. Co., 1870-1902; chief surgeon St. Mary's Hosp., 1866-; mem. from orgn. and many yrs. pres. Wis. State Bd. Health. Home: Milwaukee, Wis. Died Sept. 29, 1914.

MARLEY, JAMES ret. army officer, educator; b. nr. Slayden, Tex., Nov. 20, 1882; s. Thomas Jefferson and Mary Eudora (Powell) M.; student U. Tex., 1901-02; B.S., U.S. Mil. Acad., 1907; hon. grad. Gen. Service Schs., 1923; grad. Army War Coll., 1928, Naval War Coll., 1929; m. Anne Augusta Bonner, June 10, 1909. Commd. 2d lt. F.A., U.S. Army, 1907, promoted through grades to brig. gen., major gen. (temp.), 1941; served various army stations at posts in the U.S., P.I., and Panama Canal Zone; comd. 8th Motorized Div., U.S. Disciplinary Barracks; retired; now head math. dept. Columbian Prep. Sch. Decorated Mexican Border medal, Victory medal, Am. Campaign Medal, World War II Medal. Mason (K.T., Shriner). Club: Army Navy Country (Arlington, Va.). Home: 3514 Quebec St., N.Y. Washington. Died Nov. 27, 1952; buried Arlington Nat. Cemetery.

MARMADUKE, JOHN SAPPINGTON army officer, gov. Mo.; b. nr. Arrow Rock, Mo., Mar. 14, 1833; s. Meredith Miles and Lavinia (Sappington) M.; grad. U.S. Mil. Acad., 1857. Commd. 2d lt. U.S. Army, 1857, assigned to 7th Inf. Regt.; served in Mormon War, 1858-60; became col. Mo. Militia, Confederate Army; commd. 1st lt. Confederate Army, 1861, then lt. col., fought at Battle of Shiloh; commd. brig. gen., 1863 (as of 1862), in command cavalry in Ark. and Mo.; promoted maj. gen., 1864; editor St. Louis Journal of Agr., 1871-74; mem. Mo. Ry. Commn., 1880-85; gov. Mo., 1884-87. Died Jefferson City, Mo., Dec. 28, 1887.

MARMER, MILTON JACOB, physician; b. N.Y.C., Mar. 6, 1913; s. Harry and Lina (Kaplan) M.; A.B., U. Mich., 1934, M.D., 1937; M. Med. Sci. in Anesthesiology, N.Y. Med. Coll., 1951; m. Rose Braver, Sept. 15, 1940; children—Stephen Seth, Betty Elisabeth, Richard Franklin. Intern, Bronx (N.Y.) N.Y., 1938-40; instr. anesthesiology N.Y. Med. Coll., 1948-52, Stanford U. Med. Sch., 1952-53; asso. prof. surgery Med. Sch., U. Cal. Los Angeles, 1954-70; chief anesthesiology Cedars of Lebanon Hosp., Los Angeles, 1954-70. Served to 1st lt. M.C. AUS, 1942-44. Diplomate Am. Bd. Anesthesiology. Fellow Am. Soc. Anesthesiologists, Am. Coll. Chest Physicians, Internat. Soc. Anesthesia Research, A.A.A.S., Soc. Clin. and Exptl. Hypnosis. Author: Hypnosis in Anesthesiology, 1959; also articles in profl. jours. Home: Beverly Hills CA Died May 5, 1970.

MARMION, ROBERT AUGUSTINE med. dir. U.S.N.; b. Harper's Ferry, Va., Sept. 6, 1844; s. Nicholas and Lydia Ingraham (Hall) M.; ed. pvt. schs. of native place, until 13 yrs. old, Mt. St. Mary's Coll., Emmitsburg, Md., A.B., 1861, A.M., 1863, Univ. of Pa., M.D., 1868; m. Beatrice Paul, Oct. 7, 1885. Apptd. from W.Va. asst. surgeon, U.S.N., Mar. 26, 1868; promoted past asst. surgeon Mar. 26, 1871, surgeon, June 3, 1879; med. insp., June 15, 1895, med. dir., Oct. 1899. Served in various depts. of sea and shore service, at hosps., navy yards, etc., trip with Juniata around the world, Jan. 1886-Mar. 1889; on spl. duty Smithsonian Instn., 1894; fleet surgeon S. Atlantic Sta., July 1894-June 1806; etc. Naval del. to Am. Med. Assn., 1900, 02, 03, 04; comdg. U.S. Naval Mus. of Hygiene and Med. Sch., Sept. 1902-. Mem. Anatomical Bd., D.C. Catholic. Home: Washington, D.C. Died 1907.

MARMON, HOWARD C. motor car designer and exec.; b. Richmond, Ind., May 24, 1876; s. Daniel W. and Elizabeth (Carpenter) M.; student Earlham Coll., 1892-94; received degree in mech. engring., U. of Calif., Berkeley, Calif.; m. Florence Myers, 1901; 1 dau., Carol Carpenter (wife of Prince Nicolas Tchkotoua); m. 2d,

Martha Foster, 1911. Began as associate with father in flour mill machinery business which was absorbed by automobile industry; became vice pres. in charge engring., Marmon Motor Car Co., 1902; invented the Marmon automobile and was a pioneer in designing and producing racing cars; designed the Marmon Wasp, which won first 500-mile internat. sweepstakes on Indianapolis Speedway, May 30, 1911 (average speed of 74.61 miles per hour for the course); invented duplex downdraft manifold, widely used in building straight eights; reduced weight of 16 cylinder engine by use of aluminum parts, thus making the engine practical commercially; was a developer developer of Liberty airplane motor during World War I. Served as lieut. col., Army Air Corps during World War I; builder and first comdg. officer, McCook Field, Dayton, O. Mem. U.S. Commn. to Europe for selection of airplane equipment, and examination of prodn at Isotta-Fraschini Motor Car Co., Italy, 1917. Pres. Am. Soc. Automotive Engrs., 1913 and 1914 (awarded medal by Met. sect., 1931, for year's outstanding automotive design, the Marmon Sixteen). Selected as only Am. hon. mem. English Soc. Automotive Engrs., 1913. Mem. Second Presbyn. Ch., Indianapolis, Ind. Clubs: Engineers (N.Y. City); Columbia, Athletic, University (Indianapolis, Ind.). Home: Pineola, Avery County, N.C.; also Columbia Club, Indianapolis, Ind. Died Apr. 4, 1943.

MARQUART, EDWARD JOHN naval officer (ret.); b. Valparaiso, Ind., Mar. 11, 1880; s. Peter Anton and Anna Catherine (Miller) M.; B.S., U.S. Naval Acad., 1902; m. Marie T. Scannell, June 3, 1916 (dec. Mar. 1937); m. 2d Helen Holbert, Apr. 19, 1938. Commd. ensign U.S. Navy, 1904, and advanced through grades to rear adm., 1936; served in U.S.S. Ore., Asiatic sta., 1902-03, U.S.S. Frolic, Philippine insurrection, 1903-06, U.S.S. Illinois, Cuba, 1906-07; U.S.S. New York (later U.S.S. Rochester), 1909-10; comdr., U.S.S. Cuttlefish, 1907-09; ordnance asst. to mgr., N.Y. Navy Yard, 1910-12; engr. officer, U.S.S. Arkansas, Mexican service, 1914-15; with Naval Gun Factory, Washington Navy Yard, 1915-19; comdr. submarine div. and submarine base, Canal Zone, 1919-20; exec. officer, U.S.S. Wyoming, 1921-22; sr. asst. aide for Navy Yards, U.S. Navy Dept., 1922-24; comdr., Submarine div., Asiatic fleet, 1925-27; with Office of Naval Operations, Navy Dept., 1927-30; tech. adviser to Sec. of Navy, 1930-31; comdr., U.S.S. Louisville, Pacific, 1931-32; dir. of fleet maintenance, Office of Naval Operations, 1932-35; comdt., 16th Naval Dist. and Navy Yard, Cavite, P.I., 1935-37; comdr., Yangtze patrol, 1937-38; comdr. mine craft, battle force, 1939-42; comdt., Navy Yard, N.Y., 1941-43, 3d Naval Dist., 1942-44; ret. from active service, Apr. 1, 1944. Mem. of Hepburn Bd. apptd. by Sec. of Navy to investigate and report upon need for nat. defense, 1938-39; mem. Naval Examining Bd., 1939. Awarded letter of commendation, U.S. Navy Dept., World War I; Legion of Merit, World War II; Spanish campaign medal, Philippine campaign medal, Cuban pacification medal, Mexican service medal, Victory medals (both World Wars), Yangtze service medal, Am. Defense service medal, fleet clasp; Officer of Legion of Honor (France); hon. comdr., Order of Brit. Empire. Protestant. Home: 755 South El Molina Av., Pasadena 5, Cal. Died Nov. 4, 1954; buried National Cemetery, Arlington, Va.

MARQUAT, WILLIAM FREDERIC ret. army officer; b. St. Louis, Mo., Mar. 17, 1894; s. William and Sarah (Layden) M.; ed. high and private schs., Seattle, Wash.; grad. Coast Arty. Sch.,1926, Command and Gen.Staff Sch., 1933; m. Eula Dudley, May 4, 1921. Reporter, 1913-17; lt. and capt. Coast Arty., World War I; automobile editor Seattle Times, 1919-20; commd. capt. U.S. Army, 1920, and advanced through grades to maj. gen.; staff officer for Gen. MacArthur, Manila-Bataan campaign and through E. Indies, Papuan, New Guinea, Bismarck Archipelego, So. P.I., Luzon campaigns; Comdr. 14th anti-aircraft command, 1942 to end World War II. Decorated D.S.C. (Bataan campaign); D.S.M. with two oak leaf clusters, Air Medal; Silver Star (New Guinea); Army Citation Ribbon, Distinguished Service Star of Philippines; Officer of the Legion of Honor (France); Ulchi D.S.M. with gold star (Korea); Officer Order Orange Nassau with sword (Netherlands). Organized and opened Allied Council for Japan as U.S. mem. and chmn.; chief Econ. and Sci. Sect., Gen. Hdqrs., SCAP, Tokyo, 1945-52; chief Office of Civil Affairs and Mil. Govt., Dept. of Army, 1952-55; ret. from service with army, 1955. Cons. U.S. Operations Mission, ICA (Iran), 1956-57. Republican. Episcopalian. Mason (Shriner). Home: 1870 Wyoming Av., Washington 9. Died May 29, 1960; buried Arlington Nat. Cemetery.

MARQUIS, GEORGE PAULL M.D.; b. Allegheny, Pa., Sept. 12, 1868; s. Rev. David C. and Anna (Kennedy) M.; A.B., Washington and Jefferson Coll., 1889, A.M., 1892; M.D., Northwestern U. Med. Sch., 1892; post-grad. work Berlin and Vienna; m. Emily Chamberlain, 1899 (died 1919); 1 dau., Anna (Mrs. Arthur Dixon, III). Practiced at Chicago, 1892-; attdg. laryngologist and otologist, St. Luke's Hosp.; formerly attdg. laryngologist and otolo- gist Cook Co., St. Joseph's and Columbus hosps., also asst. prof. laryngology and rhinology Northwestern U. Med. Sch. and asso. prof. otology, Chicago Polyclinic. Chief surgeon 2d Ill. Vols., Spanish-Am. War; served in Cuba. Fellow Am. Coll. Surgeons. Republican. Presbyn. Home: Chicago, Ill. Died Dec. 22, 1933.

MARRON, ADRIAN RAPHAEL naval officer; b. Denver, Dec. 30, 1892; s. John Joseph and Mary Ann (Crowley) M.; B.S., U.S. Naval Acad., 1914; M.S., Mass. Inst. Tech.; m. Katharine M. Ficken, Sept. 22, 1919; children-Mary Louisa (Mrs. Alexander K. Ball), Adrienne (Mrs.John E. Winters), John Ficken. Duty afloat, 1915-16; sta. Charleston Navy Yard, 1917-19, Navy Yards at N.Y., Puget Sound, Cavite, Norfolk and Mare Is., 1920-38; sta. Bur. Ships and Navy Yards, Boston, 1938-46; sr. mem. Settlement Rev. Bd., Bur. of Ships; ret. as commodore USN, 1947. Awarded Mexican Service medal, World War I Victory medal, Am. Def. Service medal, Am. Theatre Campaign medal, World War II Victory medal, Legion of Merit with gold star. Roman Catholic Clubs: Army-Navy (Washington); Charleston, Carolina Yacht (Charleston, S.C.). Address: 6-B Elliott St., Charleston, S.C. Died June 3, 1964; buried Arlington Nat. Cemetery.

MARSCHALL, NICOLA artist; b. Germany, Mar. 10, 1829; studied art, Munich, Germany, and Italy, 1857-59. Came to Am., 1849, settled in Mobile, Ala.; taught painting, music and modern langs. Marion (Ala.) Sem.; designed Confederate flag and uniform for Confederate Army, 1861; served in Confederate Army; moved to Louisville, Ky., 1873. Died Louisville, Feb. 24, 1917.

MARSH, JOHN BIGELOW lawyer; b. Lawrence, Kan., Mar. 4, 1887; s. Arthur Richmond and Marie (Bigelow) M.; A.B., Harvard, 1908, LL.B., 1910; m. Isabel (Mrs. William G. Mundy), Judith (Mrs. Milton L. D. Lange), John Bigelow. Admitted to N.Y. bar, 1911, since practiced in N.Y.C.; partner firm of Turk, Marsh, Kelly & Hoare, and predecessors, 1920-. Pres., St. Barnabas Hosp. Chronic Diseases, N.Y.C., 1953-, Braker Meml. Home, N.Y.C., 1953-; chmn. fund Harvard Law Sch., 1948-50. Bd. dirs. N.Y. chpt. A.R.C., 1940, 45-54, Locust Valley (N.Y.) Cemetery Assn., 1940-; trustee Vassar Coll., 1942, Chapin Sch., N.Y.C., 1938-42. Served to maj. U.S. Army, 1917-19; AEF in France; served to col. AUS, 1942-45; ETO. Decorated Legion of Merit. Mem. Am., N.Y. State bar assns., Bar Assn. City N.Y. (v.p., chmn. coms. grievances, fed. legislation, bankruptcy, municipal cts. and admissions), Assn. ICC Practitioners, Am. Judicature Soc., Am. Law Inst. Harvard Law Sch. Assn. (pres.), 77th Div. Assn. pres.), Am. Legion (comdr. N.Y. County), English Speaking Union, Pilgrims, New Eng. Soc. Clubs: Contemporary (p.p.), University (sec., dir.), Harvard, Century (N.Y.C.); Piping Rock (L.I.); Ekwanok (Manchester, Vt.). Home: Oyster Bay, L.I., N.Y. Office: 666 Fifth Av., N.Y.C. 10019. Died Mar. 1967.

MARSH, ROBERT MCCURDY lawyer; b. Paterson, N.J., Jan. 8, 1878; s. Elias Joseph and Sarah Lord (McCurdy) M.; A.B., Harvard, 1899, A.M., 1900; LL.B., Columbia, 1903; m. Charlotte Delafield, June 1, 1921; 1 dau., Charlotte Prime (Mrs. Donald Eldredge). Admitted to N.Y. State bar, 1903; asso. Guthrie, Cravath & Henderson, 1903-06, Sullivan & Cromwell, 1909-15; practiced alone, 1915-17; mem. Marsh, Emgree & Pfeiffer, and successor Marsh & Pfieffer, 1919-29; partner Delafield, Thorne, Burleigh & Marsh, N.Y.C., and successors Delafield, Thorne & Marsh, Delafield, Marsh, Porter & Hope, now Delafield, Marsh & Hope, 1929—. Served as capt., F.A., U.S. Army, World War I; maj. and lt. col., F.A., U.S. Army Res. Corps, 1919-33. Mem. N.Y. Legislature, 1916-17. Mem. War Dept. Claims Bd., Spl. adviser to sec. of war, 1919-20, Justice Supreme Ct. of N.Y. (by appt. of gov.), 1922. Pres. N.Y. Sch. for the Deaf 1937-47. Fellow American Bar Found. Member of the New York County Lawyers Association (pres. 1940-42), Am. Bar Assn. (mem. ho. of dels. 1942-46); N.Y. State Bar Assn., Assn. Bar of City of N.Y., War Com. of Bar of City of N.Y., 1942-46. Compliance commr., WPB, for N.Y. State and Northern New Jersey, 1942-44, mem. appeals bd. of Motion Picture Arbitration Tribunals, 1943-49. Mem. Board of Health, City of N.Y., 1945-54; pres. Church Club of N.Y., 1945-48; v.p. Protestant Council of N.Y., 1944-56; del. gen. assembly, 1952—, mem. gen. bd. Nat. Council Chs., 1954—. Republican. Episcopalian. Clubs: Union, University, Nat. Republican, Downtown (N.Y.C.); Long Island Country (Eastport, L.I.). Contbr. profl. journals. Home: 570 Park Av., N.Y.C. 21; (country) Old Lyme, Conn. Office: 15 William St., N.Y.C. 5. Died Sept. 9, 1958.

MARSHALL, ALBERT WARE, naval officer; b. Greenville, Tex., Apr. 6, 1874; s. Andrew Soule and Mary Jane (Martin) M.; grad. U.S. Naval Acad., Annapolis, 1896, Naval War Coll., Newport, R.I., 1920; designated naval aviator, Naval Air Sta., Pensacola, Fla., 1926; m. Mabel Flinn, Nov. 14, 1899; 1 son, Ware. Commd. asst. engr., U.S. Navy, 1898; advanced through grades to comdr., 1915, capt., 1920, rear admiral, June 1928. Comd. U.S.S. Baltimore, World War, engaged in mine planting operations off north coast of Ireland, later in North Sea Mine Barrage; comdr. of destroyer squadron, chief of staff to comdr. destroyer squadrons, 1921-22; comdr. aircraft squadrons, Battle Fleet, 1922; in Office of Naval Operations, 1924-27; comdg. U.S.S. Lexington (aircraft carrier), 1927-28; comdr. aircraft squadrons, Scouting Fleet, Sept. 1928-May 1929; comdr. Naval Air Sta., Pensacola, May 1929-July 1931; comdr. Train Squadron 1, Fleet Base Force, 1931-33; sr. mem. Pacific Coast Sect., Bd. of Inspection and Survey, 1933-35; comdr. 15th Naval Dist., Canal Zone, 1935-37; Navy Dept., 1937-38; retired 1938. Mem. Royal Arcanum. Clubs: Army and Navy, Army and Navy Country (Washington); Chevy Chase (Md.); New York Yacht; Army and Navy (Manila, P.I.). Address: Box 342, Pasadena CA*

MARSHALL, ARTHUR LAWRENCE army officer; b. St. Louis, Apr. 9, 1900; s. Jacob Magruder and Lula May (Moore) M.; student Drake Bus. Coll., Jersey City, 1915-16; m. Maude Eloise Adams, Aug. 23, 1937 (div. 1954). Cotton broker M. F. Jones, Lawton, Okla., 1920-30; ice mfr. Anderson Ice Co., Oklahoma City, 1930-36; commd. 2d lt., ORC, 1924, advanced through grades to maj., 1941; commd. lt. col., AUS, 1941, advanced through grades to maj. gen., 1954, brig. gen., U.S. Army, 1955; camp comdr., dist. comdr. Dist. Q.M., Civilian Conservation Corps, 1937-40; utilities officer, post engr. Ft. Sam Houston, Tex., 1940-42; chief of repairs, utilities, dep. to div. engr. N.E. div. Corps Engrs., Boston, 1942-43; exec. to chief engr., asst. chief of staff, G-4, Caribbean Def. Command, 1944-46; spl. asst. to budget officer War Dept. Army Gen. Staff, Washington, 1946; budget officer, chief fiscal div. O.Q.M.G., Washington, 1946-51; comptroller, dep. for adminstrn., 1951-53; comdg. gen., Q.M. Depot, Jeffersonville, Ind., 1953-54; comdg. gen. hdqrs. Q.M. Market Center System, Chgo., 1954—. Decorated Legion of Merit. Mem. Q.M. Assn. Mason. Clubs: Union League, Illinois Athletic (Chgo.). Home: 1645 E. 50th St., Chgo. Office: 226 W. Jackson Blvd., Chgo. 6. Died Oct., 1956.

MARSHALL, CHARLES lawyer; b. Warrenton, Va., Oct. 3, 1830; grad. Univ. Va., 1849; prof. mathematics, Univ. of Ind., 1849-52; practiced law Baltimore. Served in C.S.A. as asst. adj. gen. and inspector-gen. on staff of Gen. Robert E. Lee; afterwar resumed law practice in Baltimore, Md. Died 1902.

MARSHALL, ELDER WATSON, lawyer; b. Dayton, Pa., Sept. 28, 1883; s. Curtis S. and Tirzah (Elder) M.; B.S., Washington and Jefferson Coll., 1904, LL.D., 1934; LL.B., U. Pitts., 1907, LL.M., 1918; m. Bessie Irvine, Apr. 29, 1909; children—Janice (Mrs. August H. Frye), Betty (Mrs. Gardner A. Mundy), Joseph I., Houston B. Admitted to Pa. bar, 1907, since practiced in Pitts.; judge Ct. Common Pleas, Allegheny County, Pa., 1928-38; from instr. to prof. law U. Pitts., 1904-42; mem. firm Reed, Smith, Shaw & McClay, 1938-68. Pres. Peoples Bank of Unity, Plum, Pa., 1948-68, also dir. Coordinator SSS appeals bd., Allegheny County, 1942-50. Candidate for Pa. Supreme Ct., 1935; del. Republican Nat. Conv., 1948. Pres., life trustee Washington and Jefferson Coll.; corporator Homewood Cemetery, Pitts. Served to capt. U.S. Army, 1918-19. Mem. Am., Pa., Allegheny County (pres. 1951) bar assns., Scotch-Irish Society of the United States of Am. (past pres.), Am. Legion (past post comdr.), Phi Beta Kappa, Alpha Tau Omega, Delta Theta Phi. Presbyn. Clubs: Amen Corner (past pres.), Duquesne, University (Pitts.). Author: Notes on Real Estate in Western Pennsylvania, 1935. Home: Pittsburgh PA Died Jan. 19, 1968; buried Homewood Cemetery, Pittsburgh PA

MARSHALL, E(LI) KENNERLY, JR. pharmacologist, physiologist; b. Charleston, S.C., May 2, 1889; s. Eli Kennerly and Julia Irene (Brown) M.; B.S., Coll. Charleston, 1908, LL.D., 1941; Ph.D., in Chemistry, Johns Hopkins, 1911, M.D., 1917; studied Halle, Germany, summer 1912; m. Alice Berry Carroll, Sept. 17, 1917; children-Katherine Berry (dec.), Julia Brown (Mrs. William Manchester), Richard Kennerly. Asst., asso. physiol. chemistry, Johns Hopkins, 1911-14, asso. and asso. prof. pharmacology, 1914-19; prof. pharmacology and exptl. therapeutics, 1932-55, emeritus prof., 1955-. Editor Jour. Pharmacology and Exptl. Therapeutics, 1932-37. Capt., M.C., U.S. Army, 1918. Fellow A.A.A.S.; mem. Am. Physiol Soc., Am. Soc. Biol. Chemists, Am. Soc. Pharmand Exptl. Therapeutics, Assn. Am. Physicians, Nat. Acad. Sci., Am. Philos. Soc., Gamma Alpha, Phi Beta Pi. Conducts research work on urea determination; kidney function; urinary secretion; heart and circulation; respiratory stimulants; bacterial chemotherapy; malarial chemotherapy, alcohol metabolism. Home: Severns Apts., 701 Cathedral St., Balt. 1. Died Jan. 10, 1966.

MARSHALL, FRANCIS CUTLER army officer; b. Galena, Ill., Mar. 26, 1867; s. George A. and Miriam (Cutler) M.; grad. U.S. Mil. Acad., 1890; (M.A., Trinity Coll., 1916); m. Sophie, d. Gen. J. H. Page, U.S.A., Sept. 5, 1894. Commd. 2d lt. 8th Cav.,June 12, 1890; 1st lt. 6th Cav., Jan. 5, 1897; capt. 15th Cav., Feb. 2, 1901; maj. 2d Cav., Sept. 3, 1912; assigned to 11th Cav., Nov. 1, 1914; trans. to 15th CAv., Aug. 15, 1915; lt. col., July 1, 1916; col., June 22, 1917; brig. gen. N.A., Dec. 17, 1917. Comd. 165th F.A. Brig., 90th Div., to Oct. 20, 1918, 2d Brig., 1st Div., to May 28, 1919, 8th Brig., 4th Div., to Aug. 1, 1919. In 1st Army, San Mihiel and Meuse-Argonne operations; in 3d Am. Army, occupation of Germany, Nov. 20, 1918-July 3, 1919. Croix de Guerre, with palm, 1919. Mem. S.R., Order of the Dragon. Episcopalian. Home: Darlington, Wis.

MARSHALL, GEORGE CATLETT army officer; b. Uniontown, Pa., Dec. 31, 1880; s. George Catlett and Laura (Bradford) M.; student Va. Mil. Inst., 1897-1901; hon. grad., U.S. Inf.-Cav. Sch., 1907; grad. Army Staff Coll., 1908; D.Sc., Washington and Jefferson Coll., 1939; Dr. Mil. Science, Pa. Mil. Coll., 1940, Norwich U., 1942; LL.D., William and Mary Coll., 1941, Trinity Coll., 1941, Columbia U., 1947, Princeton, 1947, Harvard, 1947, Amherst Coll., 1947, Brown U., 1947, McGill Univ. (Can.), 1947, Lafayette Coll., 1947, U. of Calif., 1948; Dr. Civil Law, Oxford U., 1947; married Elizabeth Carter Coles, February 11, 1902 (died 1927); m. 2d, Katherine Boyce Tupper Brown (October 15, 1930); stepchildren-Molly B. Winn, Clifton Stevenson (dec.), Lt. Allen Tupper (killed in action Italy, May 29, 1944). Commd. 2d lt. inf., Feb. 2, 1901; promoted through grades to maj. gen., 1939; served in the Philippines, 1902-03, 1913-16 instr. Army Staff Coll., 1908-10; with A.E.F., 1917-19, Gen. Staff 1st Div., chief of operations 1st Army, chief of staff 8th Army Corps; participated in Battle of Cantigny, Aisne-Marne, St. Mihiel and Meuse-Argonne operations; a.d.c. to Gen. John J. Pershing, 1919-24; served in China, 1924-27; instr. Army War Coll., 1927; asst. comdt. Inf. Sch., 1927-32; comdr. 8th Inf., 1933; sr. instr. to Ill. Nat Guard, 1933-36; comdg. general 5th Brig., U.S. Army, 1936-38; chief war plans div. Gen Staff, July-Oct. 1938; deputy chief of staff U.S. Army, Oct. 1938-July 1, 1939; acting chief of staff, July 1-Sept. 1939; chief of staff with rank of general, Sept. 1939-Nov. 1945; General of the Army, Dec. 1944. Chief mil. mission to Brazil, May-June 1939. Apptd. spl. rep. of the Pres. to China with personal rank of Ambassador, Nov. 1945. Council of Fgn. Ministers, Moscow and London, U.N. Gen. Assembly, N.Y., 1947. Appointed secretary of state, Jan. 1947, resigned Jan. 1949; restored to active army list at own request, 1949; secretary defense, September 1950-51; pres. A.R.C., 1949-50. Chmn. U.S. delegation Coronation Queen Elizabeth, 1953. Awarded thanks of Congress with Gold Medal, D.S.M. with oak leaf cluster Silver Star, Victory Medal with 5 bars (U.S.); Croix de Guerre with Palm, Silver Medal of Valor (Montenegro); Grand Croix Legion of Honor (Fr.). Officer Order of Saints Maurice and Lazarus, and Officer Order of the Crown (Italy); Order of La Soledaridad (Panama); Grand Comdr. Order of Merit (Brazil); Star of Aldon Calderon (Ecuador); Gran Oficial del Sol del Peru (Peru); Grand Cross of Ouissam Alaouite (Morocco); Military Order of Merit, 1st Class (Cuba); Order del Merito (Chile); Knight Grand Cross, Order of the Bath (Brit.); Order of Suvarov, 1st Degree (USSR). Received the Theodore Roosevelt Distinguished Service Medal of Honor for 1945; Varieties clubs Humanitarian Award, 1947, Freedom House Award, 1947, Nat. Planning Assn. Gold Medal, 1949, Nat. Civic Service Award, Order Eagles, 1949; N.Y. Bd. Trade Award for distinguished service and contribution to American Way, 1949; U.S. Conf. of Mayors Award for Distinguished Pub. Service, 1949; Disabled Am. Veterans, N.Y. Chpt. Citizenship Award, 1950; Distinguished Service Medal, American Legion, 1951; Four Freedoms Foundation Award, 1952; recipient of the Nobel peace prize, 1953. Member Society of the Cincinnati, Kappa Alpha. Episcopalian. Clubs: Army and Navy, Alibi (Washington); Army and Navy Country; Army and Navy (San Francisco); Metropolitan (N.Y.). Home: Leesburg, Va.; Liscombe Lodge, Pinehurst, N.C. Office: The Pentagon, Washington. Died Oct. 16, 1959; buried Arlington Nat. Cemetery.

MARSHALL, JOHN PATTON musician, educator; b. Rockport, Mass., Jan. 9, 1877; s. John White and Mary Louise (Knowlton) M.; pub. sch. edn.; studied music in Boston with Edward Alexander Macdowell, Benjamin Johnson Lang. George Whitfield Chadwick and Homer Albert Norris, 1895-1900; hon. Mus. Doc., Holy Cross College in 1927; hon. fellow Trinity Coll. of Music, London, 1933; m. Emily Geiger, Nov. 24, 1903; 1 son, John Geiger; m. 2d, Miriam Brooke Smith, July 25, 1930. Organist St. John's Church, Boston, 1896-1903; Boston Symphony Orchestra, 1909-18, First Ch., 1909-26; prof. music Boston U., 1902—; dir. music, Middlesex Sch., Concord, Mass., 1902-12; lecturer on music Harvard Summer Sch., 1908-11, Univ. Extension, 1911—. Capt. U.S.A., 1919; development specialist in music, Gen. Staff, U.S.A., 1920-22; lecturer on music Holy Cross Coll., 1925-29; dean Coll. of Music, Boston U., 1928—. Dean N.E. Chapter Am. Am. Guild Organists, 1925-29; master of music, American section, Anglo-Am. Music Conference, Lausanne, Switzerland, 1931. Republican. Author: Syllabus of History of Music, 1906; Syllabus of Music Appreciation, 1911; Musical Instruction for Army Bandsmen (U.S. War Dept.). Home: Boston, Mass. Died Jan. 17, 1941.

MARSHALL, RICHARD COKE, JR. army officer; b. Portsmouth, Va., Mar. 13, 1879; s. Richard Coke and Kate (Wilson) M.; B.S., Va. Mil. Inst., 1898; hon. grad. Arty. Sch., 1904; m. M. Louise Booker, Oct. 28, 1903. Commd. capt. 4th U.S. Inf., Vols., June 29, 1898; hon. mustered out, June 8, 1899; asst. prof. math., comdt. cadets, Va. Mil. Inst., 1899-1902; commd. 2d lt. Arty. Corps, U.S.A., Feb. 3, 1902; promoted through grades in regular army to capt., 1908; resigned June 1920; served in N.A. as maj., lt. col., col. and brig. gen.; gen. mgr. Asso. Gen. Contractors Am., 1920-28; pres. Sumner Sollitt Co., Chgo., since Apr. 1928. Assigned as officer in charge of cantonment div., later constrn. div., Feb. 18, 1918; was responsible for all bldg. constrn. by War Dept. in U.S. and insular possessions, involving an expenditure of more than $80,000,000 and employing over 400,000 men. Awarded D.S.M., Feb. 13, 1919, "for exceptionally meritorious and conspicuous service" in constrn. div. of army. Mem. Am. Soc. C.E., Am. Soc. M.E., Am. Inst. E.E., Kappa Alpha. Episcopalian. Clubs: Army and Navy, Metropolitan (Washington); Engineers (N.Y.C.); Union League, Engineers (Chgo.). Home: 3200 Sheridan Rd. Office: 307 N. Michigan Av., Chgo. Died Mar. 1961.

MARSHALL, THOMAS ALFRED, JR., mech. engr., assn. exec.; b. Savannah, Ga., Jan. 14, 1911; s. Thomas Alfred and Winefred Turner (Miller) M.; B.S. in Aero. Engring., Ga. Inst. Tech., 1932; m. Mary Lucile Bush, May 27, 1933; children—Thomas Alfred III, Susan Marie, Kathryn Penelope (Mrs. T.M. Staph), John Francis. Stationary engr., air conditioning engr.; office mgmt.; sr. analyst mgmt. engring. Met. Life Ins. Co., N.Y.C., 1932-51; exec. sec. Engring. Manpower Commn., Engrs. Joint Council, 1951-54; sec. Engrs. Joint Council, 1953-54; asst. sec. Am. Soc. M.E., 1954-57, sr. asst. sec., 1958-60, exec. sec. Am. Soc. Testing Materials, Phila., 1960-70. Mgr. Nuclear Congress, 1957-59; U.S. rep. com. on English Mgmt. terminology Comite International de l'Orgn. Sci. Served to comdr. USNR, 1940-45. Fellow A.A.A.S., Am. Soc. M.E.; mem. American Soc. Metals, Engring. Inst. Can, Am. Soc. Engring. Edn., U.S. Naval Inst., Soc. Automotive Engrs., Am. Soc. Testing Materials, Am. Water Works Assn., Standard Engrs. Soc., Instn. Mech. Engrs. (Gt. Britain), Tau Beta Pi, Phi Eta Sigma. Clubs: Army and Navy (Washington); Engineers (Phila.). Author articles on mgmt. indsl. engring. and manpower, standards, also profl. devel. engrs. Home: Radnor PA Died Apr. 9, 1970.

MARSHALL, WALDO H. banker; b. June 7, 1864; ed. pub. schs. Asst. supt. motive power, C.&N.W. Ry., May 1897-June 1899; supt. motive power, 1899-1902, gen. supt., Feb. 1902-July 1, 1903, gen. mgr., 1903-06, L.S.&M.S. Ry.; pres. Am. Locomotive Co., New York, 1906-17. Was also pres. Richmond Locomotive Works; dir. Am. Brake Shoe & Foundry Co., Bucyrus Co., Chatham & Phoenix Nat. Bank of N.Y.; with J. P. Morgan & Co., bankers, New York, 1917. Apptd. chief of Production Div. of Ordnance Dept. U.S.A., Jan. 1918. Formerly mem. Naval Consulting Board. Home: New York, N.Y. Died Aug. 22, 1923.

MARSHALL, WILLIAM ALEXANDER naval officer; b. Lancaster, Pa., Oct. 17, 1849; grad. U.S. Naval Acad., 1871; married. Promoted ensign, July 14, 1872; advanced through grades to rear admiral, Mar. 17, 1910. Assisted in fitting out Mosquito Fleet during Spanish-Am. War; served Navy Yard, Boston, 1901-02; insp., 15th Light House Dist., 1902-03; comdr. Vicksburg, 1903-04; comdr. Raleigh, 1904-05; insp. 2d Light House Dist., 1905-06; Navy Yard, Boston, 1906-08; comd. North Carolina, 1908-09; comdt., Navy Yard, Norfolk, 1909-11; retired on account of age, Oct. 7, 1911. Home: Washington, D.C. Died July 10, 1926.

MARSHALL, WILLIAM LOUIS brig. gen.; b. Washington, Ky., June 11, 1846; s.Col. Charles A. and Phoebe A. (Paxton) M.; ed. Kenyon Coll., Ohio, 1859-61; pvt. Co. A, 10th Ky. Cav., Aug. 16, 1862-Sept. 17, 1863; grad. U.S. Mil. Acad., 1868; m. Elizabeth Hill Colquitt, d. late A. H. Colquitt, U.S. senator from Ga., June 2, 1886. Bvtd. 2d lt. engrs., June 15, 1868; promoted through grades to brig. gen. chief of engrs. U.S.A., July 2, 1908. Acting asst. prof. natural and exptl. philosophy, U.S. Mil. Acad., 1870-71; in charge Colo. sect. "Explorations West of 100th Meridian," 1872-76; discovered "Marshall Pass" across Rocky Mountains, 1873, also gold placers of Marshall Basin, San Miguel River, Colo., 1875; in charge constrn. of levees in Miss., La., and Ark., and improvements of Mississippi River in 3d dist., 1881-84; of harbors on Lake Michigan, 1884-1900, and also of improvement of Calumet, Chicago, Illinois and Rock rivers, Ill., and Fox and Wisconsin rivers, Wis.; in charge of construction Hennepin Canal, 1890-1900; mem. Missouri River Commn., 1898-1902; engr. in charge construction of fortifications at eastern and southern entrances to New York harbor and improvements of main channels of New York harbor, 1900-08; constructed new 40-ft. channel (Ambrose) entrance to New York harbor; in command of the Corps of Engrs. U.S.A. and in charge of river and harbor and fortification works of the U.S. from July 2, 1908; retired, June 11, 1910. Consulting engr. to sec. of the interior, July 2, 1910-. Mem. bds. of engrs. on dam for storage reservoir in Sacramento River, Calif., at Red Bluff, for irrigation and power; on development of hydro-electric power at the Dalles, Columbia River, 1913; engr. in charge protection Imperial Valley, Calif., against overflow of Colorado River, 1914-15; mem. central bd. of review of reclamation project costs, 1919-16. Inventor automatic movable dams, lock gates and valves. Home: Washington, D.C. Died July 2, 1920.

MARSTON, ANSON civil engr.; b. Seward, Ill., May 31, 1864; s. George W. and Sarah (Scott) M.; grad. West Rockford (Ill.) High Sch., 1883 studied Berea Coll., 1884; C.E., Cornell, 1889; Eng.D., U. Neb., 1925, Mich. State Coll., 1927; m. Alice Day, Dec. 14, 1892; children-Morrill Watson, Anson Day. Engr. Mo.P. Ry. on location and constrn., 1889-92; in charge constrn. Ouachita River Bridge, 1891-92; prof. civil engring. Ia. State Coll., 1892-1920, dean and dir. engring. div., 1904-32, senior dean, 1932-37, dean emeritus, 1937—. Mem. Ia. Hwy. Commn., 1904-27, chmn. 1913-15. Commd. maj. C.E., 1917, lt. col., 1918; comd. 97th Engrs. till demobilization, 1918; col. Reserves to 1944. Mem. Engring. Bd. of Review, Sanitary Dist. Chgo., 1924, 25; cons. engr. Miami, Fla., sewerage, 1925-27; mem. (Fla.) Everglades Engring. Bd. of Rev., 1927; mem. Interoceanic Canal Bd., to advise on Nicaragua Canal and enlargement Panama Canal, 1929-32; mem. Mississippi River Engring. Board Review, 1932, 33; chmn. Iowa Merit System Council, 1939—. Mem. NRC (rep. Am. Soc. C.E.), 1919. Recipient Chanute medal Western Soc. Engrs., 1903; Fuertes medal Cornell U., 1904; Lamme medal Soc. for Promotion of Engring. Edn., 1941. Mem. Am. Soc. C.E. (dir. 1920-22, v.p. 1923-24, pres. 1929), Am. Soc. for Testing Materials, Ia. Engring. Soc. (pres. 1900), Soc. Promotion Engring. Edn. (treas. 1906-07, pres. 1914-15), Land Grant Coll. Engring. Assn. (pres. 1913-14-, Am. Assn. of Land Grant Colls. and Univ. (pres. 1929), S.A.R. Mason (32ff, K.T.). Club: Cosmos (Washington). Author: Sewers and Drains, 1907; Engineering Valuation (with T. R. Agg), 1936. Contbr. engring. jours. and trans. Home: Ames, Ia. Died Oct. 21, 1949; buried Ia. State Coll. Cemetery, Ames.

MARTI-IBANEZ, FELIX, physician, editor; b. Cartagena, Spain; M.D., U. Madrid. Apptd. gen. dir. pub. health and social service, Catalonia, 1937, later undersec. pub. health and social service Spain; dir. wartime health edn., Catalonia, 1937-38; with med. dept. Hoffmann-LaRoche Internat. Co., 1941; med. dir. Winthrop Products, Inc., N.Y.C., 1942-46; med. dir. E. R. Squibb & Sons, Internat. and Inter-Am. Cos., N.Y.C., 1946-50; founder MD Publs., Inc., 1950; formerly prof., dir. dept. history of medicine N.Y. Med. Coll.-Flower Fifth Av. Hosps., N.Y.C. Served as maj. M.C., Spanish Air Force. Recipient Order of Carlos J. Finley, Nat. Acad. Scis. Cuba, 1955. Mem. Turkish Soc. for History of Medicine (hon.), Fgn. Press Assn., Overseas Press Club. Author: Centaur: Essays on the History of Medical Ideas, 1958; Men, Molds, and History, 1958; A Prelude to Medical History, 1961; Ariel: Essays on the Arts and The History and Philosophy of Medicine, 1962; All the Wonders We Seek: Thirteen Tales of Surprise and Prodigy, 1963; The Crystal Arrow: Essays on Literature, Travel, Art, Love and The History of Medicine, 1964; Journey Around Myself, 1964; Waltz and Other Stories, 1965; The Ship in the Bottle, 1968. Editor: Medical Writing, 1955; Health and Travel, 1956; Medicine and Writing, 1956; History of American Medicine, 1958; The Pageant of Medicine, 1960; Henry E. Sigerist on the History of Medicine, 1960; The Epic of Medicine, 1962; Tales of Philosophy, 1967; The Patient's Progress, 1967. Contbr. articles and short stories to popular mags. Home: New York City NY Died June 24, 1972.

MARTIN, BRADLEY capitalist; b. N.Y.C., July 6, 1873; s. Bradley and Cornelia (Sherman), M.; B.A., Christ Church, Oxford, Eng., 1894, M.A., 1897; 2, 1904; children-Henry Bradley, Howard Townsend Bradley, Esmond Bradley, Alastair Bradley. Mgr. family estates, 1900-20; ex-chmn. bd. City and Suburban Homes Co.; v.p. and dir. Bessemer Trust Co.; dir. Hudson Trust Co. of N.J. Pres. and dir. Tb Preventorium for Children; v.p., dir. and chmn. exec. com. Phipps House; dir., mem. exec. com., 1st v.p. Nassau Hosp.; pres., dir. Nat. Kindergarten Assn. Commd. maj. Inf., R.C., 1917; adj. 154th Inf. Brigade. Mem. Am. Embassy Assn. Patron Met. Mus. Art. Republican. Episcopalian. Contbr. to Nineteenth Century Mag. Home: Westbury, L.I. Office: 465 E. 57th St., N.Y.C. Died June 1963.

MARTIN, CHARLES FLETCHER author, army officer; b. Indian Bay, Ark., Oct. 25, 1876; s. Micajab David and Sarah (Radman) M.; B.S., U.S. Mil. Acad., 1900, Ecole Supérieure de Guerre, Paris, France, 1921; grad. advanced course Cav. Sch., 1922; spl., advanced courses Field Arty. Sch., 1923; distinguished grad. Command. Gen. Staff Sch., 1924; grad. of Army War Coll., 1929; m. Mabel G. Wood, Aug. 28, 1903; 1 dau., Kelsey Loftus (wife of Col. John W. Mott, U.S. Army). Commd. 2d lt. cav., 1900; advanced through grades to col., 1929; col. (temp.), World War I. Served in Philippines, 1901-03, 14-16, 30-33; asso. prof. modern langs. U.S. Mil. Acad., 1917-18; duty with 5th sect. Gen. Staff, AEF, in France, 1918-19; on Gen. Staff, 1924-28, chief of staff, Philippine Div., 1930-33; comdg. 7th U.S. Cav., 1929-30, 13th U.S. Cav., 1933-36; assigned to Office of Insp. Gen., Washington, 1936; exec. Office of Insp. Gen., 1937-40; ret., 1940; recalled to active status and on duty at Army War Coll., Washington, 1942-46. Additional duty as mem. The Army Ret. Bd., Washington, 1943—. Clubs: Army and Navy (Manila, P.I., West Point, N.Y.C., Washington); Army-Navy Country (Arlington, Va.). Author: The French Verb, Conjugation and Idiomatic Use; Essentials of French Pronunciation; At West Point, French Composition (with George M. Russell); Winning and Wearing Shoulder Straps; Your Boy and the Other One in Universal Training (with Col. P.S. Bond); Medical Service in Modern War (with Col. P. S. Bond); also short stories, spl. articles. Address: care Riggs' Nat. Bank, Washington. Died May 16, 1949; buried Arlington Nat. Cemetery.

MARTIN, CHARLES HENRY ex-gov.; b. Carmi, White County, Ill., Oct. 1, 1863; s. Judge Samuel H. and Mary Jane (Hughes) M.; Ewing (Ill.) Coll., 1881-82; grad. U.S. Military Academy, 1887; LL.D., Portland (Oregon) University, 1935, Oregon State College, Corvallis, 1937; m. Louise J. Hughes, Apr. 15, 1897; children-Ellis H., Samuel H., Jane L. Commd. 2d lt. 14th Inf., May 5, 1894; capt. a.-q.-m. vols., Oct. 17, 1898; capt. U.S. Army, Mar. 2, 1899; hon. discharged from vols., June 13, 1899; q.-m. by detail, Dec. 15, 1903; assigned to 2d Inf., Dec. 15, 1907; trans. to 1st Inf., Dec. 28, 1907, to 23d Inf., Jan. 28, 1910; maj. 1st Inf., Feb. 28, 1910; assigned to 18th Inf., Feb. 1, 1915; lt. col., June 3, 1916; col., May 15, 1917; brig. gen. Nat. Army, Aug. 5, 1917; major gen. N.A., Apr. 12, 1918; brig. gen. Regular Army, Oct. 10, 1921; maj. gen., Jan. 16, 1925. Served under Gen. Merritt in Philippines, 1898-1901; organized and in charge street and sanitary dept. at Manila during mil. occupation; participated in expdn. to Peking, China; mem. Gen. Staff, Washington, 1911-13; comd. 3d Inf. Regt. Ore. Nat. Guard, 1913-15; on Mexican border, 1915-17; chief instr. 1st R.O.T.C., Leon Springs, Tex., 1917; comdg. 172d Brigade, at Camp Grant, Rockford, Ill., Aug. 25, 1917; comd. 86th (Blackhawk) Div., May 1-Nov. 16, 1918, 92d Div., Nov. 19-Dec. 26, 1918, and 90th Div. (Tex., Okla. Troops.), in Army of Occupation (Germany), Dec. 30, 1918-May 28, 1919; asst. chief of staff, Sept. 11, 1922-Sept. 15, 1924. Comd. Panama Canal Div. and Dept., 1925-27; retired, Oct. 1, 1927. Awarded D.S.M. for "exceptionally meritorious and distinguished service in the war." Mem. 72d and 73d Congresses (1931-35), 3d Ore. Dist; governor of Oregon, 1935-39. Democrat. Clubs: Army and Navy (Washington); Arlington, University (Portland, Ore.). Home: 2325 21st Av., Died Sep. 22, 1946.

MARTIN, CHARLES IRVING soldier, lawyer; b. Ogle County, Ill., Jan. 25, 1871; s. William H. and Mary (Nettleton) M.; grad. Ft. Scott (Kan.) Normal Sch., 1892; LL.B., U. of Kan., 1907; m. Lou Ida Ward, Nov. 28, 1894; 1 dau., Mrs. Lillia Mae Markley. Clerk Dist. Court, Bourbon County, Kan., 1901-05; mem. Kan. Senate, 1905-09; admitted to Kan. bar, 1907, and practiced in Ft. Scott, Topeka and Wichita, Kansas; admitted to bar of Supreme Court, U.S., 1923. Enlisted as private Co. F. 1st Inf. K.N.G., Aug. 26, 1890; 2d lt. 1st Inf., Apr. 6, 1893; capt., Aug. 1894; capt. 20th U.S. Vols., Apr. 30, 1898; maj. 20th Kan. Vol. Inf., July 22, 1899; participated in 27 engagements in P.I., col. insp. gen., K.N.G., Mar. 4, 1907; brig. gen., Apr. 29, 1909; adj. gen. of Kan., 1909-17, 1919-23. Brig. gen. U.S. Army, Aug. 5, 1917; comdg. 70th Inf. Brig., 35th Div., A.E.F.; observer with British troops in front line trenches, May 1918; comd. sector in front line trenches, July 20-Sept. 1, 1918; participated in St. Mihiel Offensive; hon. discharged, Dec. 1, 1918; brig. gen. Kan. Nat. Guard, comdg. 69th Inf. Brig., 1921-32, major general commanding 35th Division, National Guard troops, Kansas, Missouri, and Neb., 1932-35; retired; mgr. Veteran Administration Facility, Wadsworth, Kansas, 1927-41; now assistant adjutant general of Kansas. President Adjutants General Association of U.S., 1912-23; former pres. Nat. Guard Assn. U.S.; mem. Philippine Vets., Spanish War Vets, Am. Legion, Forty and eight, Sojourners, Mil. Order of the World War, etc. Republican. Methodist. Mason, etc. Club: Rotary. Address: 3416 Moore Av., Cheyenne, Wyo. Died May 8, 1953; buried Wadsworth Nat. Cemetery.

MARTIN, DANIEL J., tool company exec.; b. Lowell, Mass., Sept. 30, 1902; s. David Patrick and Julia Gertrude (Halloran) M.; B.S., U.S. Naval Acad., 1924; Met.E., Stanford, 1931; Sc.D., Harvard, 1934; m. Gertrude Donald, Nov. 27, 1924; children—Joanne (Mrs. James Early), Julia (Mrs. Sam A. Luce). Vice president in charge of engineering Hughes Tool Company, Houston, 1948-62, v.p. research, from 1962, also dir.; dir. Hughes Gun Co., Hughes Tool Co., Ltd. Mem. bd. dirs. Cath. Family and Children Services, Galveston-Houston Diocese; trustee St. Anthony Geriatrics Center. Mem. Senate St. Thomas U. Served with Ord. Dept., USA, 1924-46; ret. as col. Decorated Legion of Merit, Army Commendation ribbon with oak leaf cluster, Def. Service medal; Star of Abdon Calderon (Republic of Ecuador); Cross of Eloy Alfaro Internat. Found. (Republic of Panama); Knight Comdr. with Star, Equestrian Order of Holy Sepulchre of Jerusalem. Mem. Am. Assn. for Advancement of Sci., Am. Ordnance Assn. (bd. dirs.), Am. Inst. Mining and Metall. Engrs., Sigma Xi. Clubs: Houston, Houston Country (Houston). Home: Houston TX Died July 27, 1970.

MARTIN, EDWARD surgeon; b. Phila., 1859; s. J. Willis and M. (Register) M.; A.B., Swarthmore Coll., 1878, A.M., 1882; M.D., U. of Pa., 1883, LL.D., 1919; Sc.D., Swarthmore Coll., 1020; LL.D., Temple U., 1935; m. Anna Withers, 1887. Clin. prof. surgery, Woman's Med. College of Pa., 1902-; prof. clin. surgery, 1903-10. John Rhea Barton prof. surgery, 1910-18, U. of Pa.; surgeon to University and Howard hosps.; consulting surgeon, Bryn Mawr Hosp., Norristown State Hosp. for Insane and Wernersville State Hosp. for Insane, Welada General Hospital; dir. Public Health and Charities, Phila., 1903-05; mem. Bd. of Education, 1911- (v.p.); commr. of health, State of Pa. Consulting surgeon 5th Army Corps, Spanish-Am. War; lt. col. World War; col. 364th Med. Regt. O.R.C. Now prof. surg. physiology, U. of Pa. Mem. bd. mgrs. Swarthmore Coll., 1895-. Fellow Am. Coll. Surgeons. Home: Media, Pa. Died Mar. 17, 1938.

MARTIN, EDWARD U.S. Senator; b. Ten Mile, Wash. Twp., Greene County, Pa., Sept. 18, 1879; s. Joseph T. and Hannah M. (Bristor) M.; A.B., Waynesburg Coll., 1901; LL.D., Washington and Jefferson Coll., 1938; Dr.Mil. Sci., Waynesburg Coll., 1940; LL.D., U. Pitts., 1941, Temple U., 1943, Pa. Mil. Coll., 1943, U.Pa., 1943, Villanova Coll., 1943, Drexel Inst. Tech., 1943, Lebanor Valley Coll., 1945, Westminster Coll., 1945, Lafayette Coll., 1945, Ursinus Coll., 1945, Beaver Coll., 1946, St. Vincent Coll., 1946, Geneva Coll., 1947; L.H.D., Hahnamann Med. Coll. and Hosp. Phila., 1945; m. Charity Scott, Dec. 1, 1908; children-Lt. Col. Edward S., Mary C. (Mrs. James B.W. Murphy). Admitted to Pa. bar, 1905 and began practice at Waynesburg; dir. Washington County Ins. Co.; pres., dir. Dunn-Mar Oil & Gas Co. (Washington, Pa.); auditor gen. of Pa., 1925-29, state treas., 1929-33; adj. gen. of Pa., 1939-43; gov. of Pa., 1943-47, U.S. senator, 1947-58. Chmn. Republican State Com., 1928-34. Served in Pa. N.G. continuously from 1898; with 10th Pa. Vol. Inf., Philippine Campaign (Spanish-Am. War), 1898-99; Mexican Border Campaign, June-Oct. 1916; with 109th and 110th inf. regts., A.E.F. in France, 1917-19; placed on Gen. Staff eligibility list, 1920; made brig. gen., Aug. 17, 1922; maj. gen., June 26, 1939; assigned command 28th Div. Pa. N.G., 1939; inducted into Fed. service as comdg. gen. 28th Div., U.S. Army, Feb. 3, 1941; relieved of comd. (over age in grade), Jan. 27, 1942; assigned to Hdqrs. 5th Corps Area; placed on inactive list Apr. 1, 1942. Awarded D.S.C. with oak leaf cluster, Purple Heart with oak leaf cluster, Pa. Reilly Medal, 1937, Am. Legion Distinguished Service Medal, Pa. Distinguished Service Medal, Distinguished Service Medal N.G. Assn. U.S. Chmn. exec. com. Govs. Confs., 1945-46; pres. Council of State Govts., 1946. Trustee Waynesburg Coll., Washington and Jefferson Coll. Member V.F.W., Am. Legion, Legion of Valor, Mil. Order of Carabao, Spanish-American War Vets. Republican. Presbyn. (elder). Mason and editor, History of 28th Division. Home: 174 Le Moyne Av. Office: 27 S. College St., Washington, Pa. Died Mar. 19, 1967; buried Waynesburg, Pa.

MARTIN, ERNEST GALE physiologist; b. Minneapolis, Minn., Nov. 16, 1876; s. John Wesley and Mary Esther (Bullard) M.; Ph.B., Hamline U., 1897; Ph.D., Johns Hopkins Univ., 1904; m. Ruby A. Ticknor, Aug. 31, 1904; 1 daughter, Lois Ticknor. Fellow and assistant in physiology, Johns Hopkins, 1902-04; instr. physiology. Purdue U., 1904-06; instr. physiology, 1906-10, asst. prof., 1910-16. Harvard, also lecturer Sargent Sch. for Physical Edn., 1906-14; asst. prof. physiology, Radcliffe Coll., 1914-16, and physiologist, Vt. State Bd. of Health, 1915-16; prof. physiology, Stanford U., 1916-. Scientific asst. (physiologist) U.S. Pub. Health Service; mem. sub-com. on industrial fatigue, Advisory Commn. to Council Nat. Defense, 1917-18; mem. com. on physiology of Nat. Research Council, 1917-18. Capt. Sanitary Corps, U.S.A., Sept. 10, 1918-Jan. 22, 1919; div. nutrition officer 10th Div., Nov. 7, 1918-Jan. 22, 1919. Fellow Am. Acad. Arts and Sciences, A.A.A.S. (v.p. Pacific Div., 1927-31). Conglist. Author: The Measurement of Induction Shocks, 1912. Revised 9th, 10th and 11th edits. of The Human Body (by Henry N. Martin), 1910; vol. on physiology (Collier's Popular Science Library), 1921. Joint author of General Biology (with Burlingame, Health, and Peirce); Elements of Physiology (with Weymouth), 1928. Died Oct. 17, 1934.

MARTIN, FRANKLIN H. surgeon; b. Ixonia, Wis., July 13,1857; s. Edmond and Josephine (Carlin) M.; ed. pub. schs. and acads. of Wis.; M.D., Chicago Med. Coll. (now medical dept. of Northwestern U.), 1880; LL.D., Queen's Univ., Belfast, Ireland, U. of Wales and U. of Pittsburgh; D.P.H., Detroit Coll. of Medicine and Surgery; D.Sc., Northwestern Univ.; m. Isabelle, d. John H. Hollister, M.D., of Chicago, 1886. Prof. gynecology, Polyclinic, Chicago, 1886-88; organized with Dr. W. F. Coleman, Post-Grad. Med. Sch., Chicago, 1888; gynecologist, Woman's Hosp. many yrs.; organized Charity Hosp.; founded Surgery, Gynecology and Obstetrics (med. Jour.), 1905, editor in chief same, and added Internat. Abstract of Surgery, 1913; organized clin. Congress Surgeons of N. America (now Clin. Congress of Am. Coll. Surg.), 1910, dir. gen. same; organized Am. Coll. Surg., 1913, dir. gen. and mem. bd. regents, same pres., 1928-29; asso. editor Am. Jour. Obstetrics and Gynecology. Chmn. bd. Gorgas Memorial Inst. Tropical and Preventive Medicine. Mem. Advisory Commn. of Council National Defense, 1916-21, chmn. Gen. Med. Bd., 1917-19; col. M.C., U.S.A., 1917-19; hon. adviser U.S. Army Industrial Coll., 1925-. Was trustee Northwestern U. Decorated D.S.M. (U.S.); Companion Order of St. Michael and St. George (British); Commander of theOrder of the Crown of Italy. Author: Treatment of Fibroid Tumors of the Uterus, 1897; Treatise on Gynecology, 1903; South America from a Surgeon's Point of View, 1923; (monograph) Australia and New Zealand, 1924; The Joy of Living-An Autobiography, 1933. Home: Chicago, Ill. Died Mar. 7, 1935.

MARTIN, FREDERICK LEROY ret. army officer; b. Liberty, Ind., Nov. 26, 1882; s. John Charles and Nancy Jane (Abbernathy) M.; B.S. in Mech. Engring., Purdue U., 1908; grad. Air Corps Tactical Sch., 1925, Command and Gen. Staff Sch., 1926; Army War Coll., 1935; m. Grace Margaret Griffiths, June 26, 1912; 1 son, John Robert. Commd. 2d lt. CAC, U.S. Army, 1908; transferred to Air Service, 1920; advanced through the grades to temp. rank brig. gen., 1937; wing comdr. 3d Wing, G.H.Q., Air Force, 1937; temp. rank major gen., 1940; comdg. gen., Hawaiian Air Force, 1940-41; comdg. gen., 2d Air Force, U.S. Army, 1942; comdg. gen. 2d Dist., Army Air Forces, Central Tech. Tng. Command, 1942-44, ret. 1944. Awarded D.S.M. and Legion of Merit. Mason. Club: Adventurers (Chgo.). Home: 641 Lorna Lane, Los Angeles. Address: War Dept., Washington. Died. Feb. 24, 1954.

MARTIN, GEORGE WHITNEY lawyer; b. Rochester, N.Y., Dec. 17, 1887; s. Edward Sandford and Julia (Whitney) M.; student Groton Sch., 1900-06; A.B., Harvard, 1910; m. Agnes Wharton Hutchinson, Jan. 29, 1916; children-Amy Pemberton (Mrs. Robt. W. Chapin), Julia Whitney (Mrs. F. Sargent Cheever), Agnes Wharton (Mrs. Ridley Whitaker), George Whitney, Fanny Alice (Mrs. Thomas M. Connelly). Admitted to N.Y. bar, 1913, practiced with Byrne & Cutcheon, N.Y.C., 1912-13; mem. Emmet, Marvin & Martin, N.Y.C., 1923—. Pres. Brearley Sch., 1923-45. Served as 1st lt. U.S.F.A., 1917-19; col. 104th N.Y. Inf., comdg. officer; brig. gen. 5th N.Y. Arty. Brigade, World War II. Decorated Silver Star. Democrat. Episcopalian (vestryman). Clubs: Century, Harvard, Down Town, Somerset (Boston). Contbr. popular mags. Home: Wilton, Conn. Office: 48 Wall St., N.Y.C. 5. Died Jan. 5, 1959.

MARTIN, HAROLD MONTGOMERY, naval officer; b. Bay Mills, Mich., Jan. 18, 1896; s. David A. and Jeanne (Montgomery) M.; student U. of Ill., 1913-14; B.S., U.S. Naval Acad., 1918; m. Elizabeth Risque Bronson, Sept. 26, 1922; 1 son, David Bronson. Commd. ensign, U.S. Navy, 1918, and advanced through the grades to vice adm., 1951; served in U.S.S. Winslow, 1918-19, U.S.S. Nevada, 1919-21; naval aviator, U.S.S. Langley and U.S.S. Saratoga, 1921-38; force aviator, Scouting Force, 1938-40; serving at Naval Air Base, Kaneohe, Oahu, T.H., 1941; comdt. Naval Air Base, Midway, 1942-43; comdg. officer U.S.S. San Jacinto, 1943-44; chief of staff, comdr. air force, Atlantic Fleet, 1944-45; chief Naval Air Tech. Training, Memphis, Tenn; comdr. 1st and 7th Fleets; comdr. Air Force Pacific Fleet; ret., 1956. Decorated D.S.M., Gold Star, Bronze Star, Silver Star, Legion of Merit and star, Presidential citation, Unit Citation. Club: Racquet (Phila.). Address: Memphis TN Died Dec. 3, 1972.

MARTIN, HUGH, architect; b. Paducah, Ky., May 11, 1874; s. John and Frances (Dallam) M.; student U. of Tex., 1890-91; B.S. in Arch., Cornell U., 1894; m. Ellie Gordon Robinson, Nov. 11, 1913; children—Hugh, Gordon Dallam, Ellen Lenoir. Mem. firm Miller & Martin, architects, Birmingham, Ala., 1900-35, Miller, Martin & Lewis, architects and engrs., 1935-52; with Hugh Martin, architect, since 1952. Works include: Birmingham Central Library, Birmingham Trust National Bank, 8 buildings for Birmingham Southern College, 40 bldgs. for U. of Alabama, Central City Housing project for 916 families at Birmingham. Served as capt. Air Service, U.S. Army, 1917-18, in France and England, 1918. Fellow A.I.A.; member Alabama Society of Architects; Alpha Tau Omega (past pres.). Democrat. Presbyterian. Clubs: Birmingham Rotary (dir.); Birmingham Country. Address: 1919 S. 15th Av., Birmingham AL

MARTIN, JAMES GREEN army officer; b. Elizabeth City, N.C., Feb. 14, 1819; s. William and Sophia (Dauge) M.; grad. U.S. Mil. Acad., 1840; m. Marian Read, July 12, 1844; m. 2d Hetty King, Feb. 8, 1858; at least 4 children. Fought in battles of Monterey, Vera Cruz, Churubusco and Contreras during Mexican War; commd. 1st lt. U.S. Army, 1847, capt., 1847; brevetted maj., 1847; adjutant gen. 10 regts. of N.C. Militia, 1861; commd. maj. gen. in command all state supr. entire defense of state, 1861; commd. brig. gen. Confederate States Army, 1862; in command N.C. dist. 1862; command West dist. N.C., 1864-65. Died Asheville, N.C., Oct. 4, 1878.

MARTIN, JOHN ANDREW congressman; b. Cincinnati, O., Apr. 10, 1868; ed. pub. schs.; studied law, 1895-96. Farming and railroad worker, 1884-94; editor La Junta Times, 1895-96; admitted to Colo. bar, 1896; in practice at Pueblo; mem. Colo. Gen. Assembly, 1901-02; city atty., Pueblo, 1905-07, 1915-17; mem. 61st and 62d Congresses (1909-13). 2d Colo. Dist., and 73d to 75th Congresses (1933-39). 3d Colo. Dist. Recruited a vol. batt., World War, enlisted as pvt., later commd. major. Democrat. Home: Pueblo, Colo. Died Dec. 23, 1939.

MARTIN, JOSEPH I. ret. army officer; b. Chicago, Feb. 1, 1894; S. George William and Justine (David) M.; M.D., Chicago Hosp. Coll. of Medicine, 1918; grad. Army Med. Sch., 1925, (hon.) Med. Field Service Sch., 1926, Inf. Sch., advanced course, 1928, Command and Gen. Staff Sch., 1934, Army War Coll., 1940; m. Margaret Anna Schander, Apr. 17, 1914; children-

Justine Estelle (Mrs. Paul R. Smith), George William, Dolores Amanda (wife of Lt. Col. Orville Tackett), Joseph Ignatius, Robert Edward. Physician and surgeon, 1918—; commd. 1st lt., U.S. Army, 1918, advancing through the grades to maj. gen., 1949; served as med. officer at Ft. Riley, Kan.; Camp Grant, Ill.; Sternberg Gen. Hosp., Manila, P.I.; Ft. Sam Houston, Tex.; Army Med. Center, Washington, D.C.; Carlisle Barracks, Pa.; Ft. Snelling, Minn.; Ft. Des Moines, Ia.; Ft. Benning, Ga.; Ft. Leavenworth, Kan.; Ft. Sherman, also Quarry Heights, Canal Zone; Army War Coll., Washington, D.C.; 6th Corps Area, Chicago; with 5th Army overseas; Service World War II; (est. med. dept. Replacement Training Center, Camp Grant, Ill., 1940; chief surgeon, 5th Army in Africa and Italy, 1943-45, Western Pacific, 1945, Gen Hdqrs., Pacific, 1946; commandant Med. Field Service Sch., Ft. Sam Houston, Tex. 1947-53; chief surgeon U.S. Army, Europe, 1953-55, ret. Decorated Victory Medals, World War I, II, Am. Legion of Merit, Pre-Pearl Harbor, Am. Defense, European-North African, Pacific, Japanese Occupation, Typhus Commn., Distinguished Service Medal; Comdr. (British Empire); Croix de Guerre (France); Italian Silver Star, Royal Order of the Crown (Italy); Brazilian Medal of War; Polish Order Crossed Swords; Czechoslovakian Order Mil. Cross. Mem. A.M.A., Assn. Mil. Surgeons U.S. (pres.). Moose, K.C. Home: 2244 Juliet Dr., Santa Rosa, Cal. Died Apr. 13, 1957; buried Arlington, Va.

MARTIN, PAUL ALEXANDER retired editor and pub.; b. Atchison, Kan., May 8, 1886; son John Alexander and Ida (Challis) M.; student Ottawa Univ., 1907-09. D.Litt.; Robert Crisher Martin (adopted son). Learned printing trade; reporter Ottawa (Kan.) Herald, 1909-11; joined staff of Enquirer and News Battle Creek, Mich., 1911, successively telegraph editor, city editor and mng. editor until 1928; editor, pub., gen. mgr. Lansing (Mich.) State Jour., 1928-62; dir., sec., treas., Federated Publications, Incorporated. Served as lt. U.S. Army, 1917-19. Mem. National Committee of Am. Legion, 1919-23, Mich. Comdr. Am. Legion, 1921-22; mem. adv. com. Lansing Symphony Assn.; pres. Mich. State Tb. Sanitorium Commn.; pres. Lansing United Hosp. Expansion Fund, Inc.; pres. Chief Okemes area, Boy Scouts, 1930-39; mem. nat. council Boy Scouts Am. Past pres. Mich. State Asso. Press Assn.; pres. United Community Chest of Ingham Co.; chmn. Lansing War Meml. com.; chmn. Little Arlington Meml. Monument com.; mem. Lansing Centennial Corporation. Member Am. Newspaper Pubs. Assn., Am. Society of Newspaper Editors, Lansing C. of C. (pres.), Sigma Delta Chi. Past pres. Mich. Republican Servicemen's League; chmn. bd. trustees Edward W. Sparrow Hosp.; Lansing Postwar Planning Com. Republican. Baptist. Mason (32ff), Elk. Rotarian. Died Jan. 13, 1965.

MARTIN, THOMAS ELLSWORTH, ex-U.S. senator; b. Melrose, Ia., Jan. 18, 1893; s. David J. and Sara A. (Brandon) M.; A.B., State U. of Ia., 1916, J.D., 1927; LL.M., Columbia, 1928; LL.D., Parsons College, Fairfield, Iowa, 1957; m. Dorris Jeanette Brownlee, June 5, 1920;children—Richard Coupland, Dorris Brownlee Reiser. Sales analyst, accountant, Goodyear Tire & Rubber Co., Akron, O. and Dallas Tex., 1916-17, Oklahoma City, Okla. and St. Louis, 1919, 1921. Served as 1st lt. with 35th Inf., U.S. Army, 1917-19, capt., with U.S. Army retired, R.O.T.C. duty State U. of Iowa, 1921-23; accountant Iowa City, Ia., 1923-27; admitted to Ia. bar 1927, U.S. Supreme Court bar, 1939; began practice in Iowa City; city atty., 1933-35; mayor, Iowa City, 1935-37; mem. 76th to 83d Congresses, from 1st Ia. Dist., mem. com. mil. affairs 1939-47, com. on ways and means, 1947-54; United States senator, 1955-61, ret., mem. coms. govt. operations, post office and civil service, 1955-59, interior, pub. works, aero. and space scis., 1959-61. Chmn. Ia. City Community Chest, 1933, 37. Awarded Columbia U. fellowship, 1927-28. Mem. Am. Bar Assn., Ia. Bar Assn., Am. Legion,. Forty and Eight, Phi Delta Phi, Alpha Tau Omega, Order of Coif, Triangle Club, Disabled Am. Vets., Vets. of Fgn. Wars, Omicron Delta Kappa. Republican. Congregationalist. Mason, Elk, Moose, K.P., Rotarian. Home: Seattle WA Died June 27, 1971; buried National Cemetery, Williamette OR

MARTIN, WALTER BRAMBLETTE physician; b. Pulaski, Va., Jan. 16, 1888; s. David Hall and Louisa Rachel (Sutton) M.; B.S., Va. Poly. Inst., 1909; M.D., Johns Hopkins, 1916; D.Sc. (hon.), Med. Coll. Va., 1956; m. Lucretia Reid de Jarnette, Sept. 18, 1917; children-Lucretia de Jarnette, Nancy Patton, Walter Bramblette. Resident house officer Johns Hopkins Hosp., 1916-17; practice medicine specializing in internal medicine, Norfolk, Va., 1919-; chief med. cons. for St. Vincents Hosp.; attending specialist internal medicine USPHS Hosp. (all of Norfolk); served as capt. M.C. U.S. Army, June 13, 1917-Sept. 1943; med. cons. Fifth Service Command, July 1944; med. cons. 10th Army; hon. cons. Surg. Gen. Navy. Pres. A.M.A. med. task force of Hoover Commn. Mem. bd. visitors U. Va. Diplomate Am. Bd. Internal Med. Fellow A.C.P. (master), Am. Clin. and Climatol. Assn., Am. Soc. Clin. Pathologists; mem. A.M.A. (pres. 1954-55), Seaboard Med. Assn. (past pres.), Assn. for Study Allergy, Am. Assn. for Study Rheumatism, Med. Soc. Va. (pres. 1941), Norfolk County Med. Soc. (past pres.), Phi Beta Kappa, Alpha Omega Alpha. Democrat. Presbyn. Contbr. to med. lit. Home: 7420 Muirfield Rd., Norfolk, Va. 23505. Died Apr. 1966.

MARTIN, WILLIAM FRANKLIN army officer; b. Ripley, O., July 19, 1863; s. Robert F. and Mary E. (Lilley) M.; grad. U.S. Mil. Acad., 1885, Engr. m. Josephine Edgerton, July 20, 1892. Commd. 2d lt. 25th Inf., June 14, 1885; 1st lt. 5th Inf., June 3, 1892; capt., Mar. 2, 1899; maj. 18th Inf., June 30, 1908; trans. to 5th Inf., Mar. 20, 1909; lt. col. of inf., June 5, 1914; col. of inf., July 1, 1916; brig. gen. N.A., Aug. 5, 1917. Served in various capacities in Cuba, 1899-1900, in Philippines, 1900-03, again in Cuba, 1906-08; duty Gen. Staff, 1914-17; apptd. comdr. 174th Inf. Brigade, Camp Pike, Little Rock, Ark., Sept. 1917. Presbyterian. Club: Army and Navy (Washington). Home: Xenia, Ohio. Died Apr. 15, 1942.

MARTIN, WILLIAM JOSEPH, physician; b. Freehold, N.J., Mar. 19, 1918; s. William Redmond and Julia (Conway) M.; M.D., Georgetown U., 1943; M.Sc. in Medicine, U. Minn., 1952; m. Mary Gertrude Adams, Apr. 22, 1944; children—Mary Jo, Julia (Mrs. Thomas Vitullo), William Joseph II. Intern, Georgetown U. Hosp., Washington, 1944; fellow in medicine Georgetown U., 1944-46; postgrad. in medicine U. Minn.-Mayo Found., Rochester, 1949-53; chmn. div. internal medicine (infectious disease) Mayo Clinic, Rochester; cons. in medicine St. Mary's Hosp., Rochester, Methodist Hosp., Rochester; prof. medicine U. Minn., Mpls. Served to maj., M.C., AUS, 1943-48. Diplomate Am. Bd. Internal Medicine. Fellow A.C.P.; mem. A.M.A., Alpha Omega Alpha. Home: Rochester MN Died May 19, 1970; buried Rochester MN

MARTIN, WILLIAM LOGAN lawyer; b. Scottsboro, Ala., Feb. 20, 1883; s. William Logan and Margaret (Ledbetter) M.; B.S., U.S. Mil. Acad., 1907; LL.B., U. of Ala., 1908; married Thelma C. Sloss, June 24, 1954. Commissioned second lieutenant U.S. Army, June 14, 1907; resigned Aug. 15, same yr.; admitted to Ala. bar, 1908, and practiced in Montgomery; asso. in practice with brother, Thomas Montgomery; asso. in practice with brother Thomas W. Asst. pros. atty., Montgomery County, 1909-10; asst. atty. gen. of Ala., 1911-15, atty. gen. term 1915-19 (resigned); apptd. judge 15th (Montgomery) Jud. Circuit, Feb. 3, 1919; settled at Birmingham upon expiration of term, Nov. 18, 1920; mem. firm Martin & Blakey; dir., gen. atty. Ala. Power Co. Commd. maj. aviation sect., Signal Corps, U.S. Army, 1917, trans. to F.A., 1918; hon. disch., Army, 1917, trans. to F.A., 1918; hon. disch., 1919. Mem. Am. (state del. 1937-, gov. 1943-46, chmn. com. employment and socia. security 1946-49, chmn. com. jurisprudence and law reform 1955-57, chmn. spl. com. on submission of amendment to limit income tax. 1951-, vice president association endowment 1953-), Alabama State (president 1946-47), Birmingham bar assns., Assn. Bar City N.Y., Assn. Grads. U.S. Mil. Acad. (trustee 1954-), S.A.R., Soc. Colonial Wars (governor Ala., 1957-59), Phi Delta Theta, Theta Nu Epsilon, Phi Belta Phi. Presbyterian. Clubs: Mountain Brook, Army and Navy (Washington). Author publs. including : Political Parties: The Amending Power, several other articles. Home: 2500 Lanark Rd. Office: 600 N. 18th St., Birmingham 3, Ala. Died Feb. 25, 1959.

MARTIN, WILLIAM THOMPSON lawyer; b. Glasgow, Ky., Mar. 25, 1823; s. John Henderson and Emily Monroe (Kerr) M.; grad. Centre Coll., Ky., 1840; m. Margaret Dunlop Conner, Jan. 5, 1854. Studied law in father's office, Vicksburg, Miss.; admitted to bar, 1844; dist atty., 1st Jud. dist., Miss., 1845-49. Whig in politics prior to Civil war. Served from capt. to maj. gen. Confederate States Army, 1861-63; in siege of Yorktown, battle of Williamsburg (wounded), Seven Pines, 7 days' battles nr. Richmond, Antietam; ordered west after Md. campaign, was in battles at Spring Hill, Tenn., Shelbyville, Chickamauga, Clinch River, Maryville, siege of Knoxville, Fair Garden and Mossy Creek; with Gens. Johnston and Hood from Dalton to the fall of Atlanta; surrendered with Gen. Dick Taylor's command, May, 1865. Del. to State Constitutional Conv., 1865; elected to Congress from 1st Miss. dist., 1868, but was denied the seat; del. Dem. Nat. convs., 1868-1880; mem. State senate, 1882-94. Trustee State U., 1876-88; v.p. for Miss. So. Hist. soc.; pres. bd. trustee Jefferson Coll. (Miss.), 1880-88; mem. State Constitutional Conv., 1890. Completed in 1884, as sole pres. of the co., the N.J.&C. R.R. from Natchez to Jackson. Home: Monteigne, Natchez, Miss. Died Mar. 9, 1910; buried Natchez.

MARTINDALE, EARL HENRY elec. engr.; b. Greenwich, O., Jan. 22, 1885; s. Rev. Henry Cyrus and Mary Elizabeth (Broadwell) M.; spl. studies Ohio, No. U., Ada, 1902-03; B.S., Case Sch. Applied Sci., 1908, E.E., 1912; m. Elsie L. Marty, June 28, 1911; children-George Earl, Robert Henry. Sales engr. Nat. Carbon Co., 1909-19, except while in army; chmn. bd. Martindale Electric Co., Cleve. Capt. engrs. U.S. Army, Aug. 12, 1917-Jan. 28, 1919; served with AEF in France 1 yr., last 5 mos. as engr. officer in charge constrn. of 15,000 volt, 35-mile transmission line. Mem. Am. Inst. E.E. (former chmn. indsl. and domestic power com.; chmn. membership com., mgr. and v.p.), Assn. Iron and Steel Elec. Engrs., Elec. League, Lakewood C. of C., Council on World Affairs, Am. Legion, Smaller Businesses Am. (past dir.), Cleve. Engring. Soc., Ohio Mfrs. Assn., Tau Beta Pi. Unitarian. Contbr. tech. mags. and lectr. colls. and univs. Author: Who Really Owns My Business. Home: 1055 Erie Cliff Dr., Lakewood 7. Address: Martindale Electric Co., Cleve. Died July 1964.

MARTINDALE, JOHN HENRY lawyer, army officer; b. Hudson Falls, N.Y., Mar. 20, 1815; s. Henry C. Martindale; grad. U.S. Mil. Acad., 1835; m. Emeline Holden, June 16, 1840, 5 children. Admitted to N.Y. bar, 1838; organizer volunteer regts. in Civil War; commd. gen. U.S. Volunteers, 1861, served at battles of Yorktown, Mechanicsville, Gaine's Mill, Malvern Hill, Cold Harbor, Bermuda Hundred; mil. gov. D.C.; brevetted maj. gen. volunteers, 1865; atty. gen. N.Y., 1866-68; v.p. bd. mgrs. Nat. Asylum of Disabled Volunteer Soldiers, 1868-79. Died Nice France, Dec. 13, 1881.

MARTINEK, FRANK V(ICTOR), b. Chicago, Ill., June 15, 1895; s. Frank and Mary (Koder) M.; ed. pub. schs., business coll. and Acad. of Fine Arts, Chicago; m. Clara Gault Powell, Aug. 14, 1934. Copy boy and cub reporter Chicago Record Herald, 1910-13; identification insp. Chicago Civil Service Commn., 1913-17; spl. agt. U.S. Dept. of Justice, 1921-25; with Standard Oil Co. of Ind. since 1925, asst. v.p., from 1928; created "Don Winslow of the Navy," and "Bos'n Hal—Sea Scout," newspaper adventure strips, 1934 ("Don Winslow of the Navy" also a radio and motion picture feature). Enlisted in United States Navy as seaman, 1917, served as intelligence officer; honorably discharged with rank of lieutenant, 1921; lt. comdr. U.S. Naval Reserve, 1930-41. Decorated with Order of M. R. Stefanik with star (Czechoslovakian); Order of St. Stanislaus (Russia); 5th Class Civil Tiger Decoration (China); Victory medal with Asiatic clasp (United States). Chairman Central and Illinois Gasoline Tax Evasion committees. Member Chicago Association of Commerce, Am. Legion, Am. Petroleum Inst. Mason (32 deg. Shriner). Author: Don Winslow in Ceylon, 1934; Know Your Man, 1936; Don Winslow Series, 1940. Contbr. articles on crime, sabotage, espionage and personnel to mags. Home: Chicago IL Died Feb. 1971.

MARTS, ARNAUD CARTWRIGHT, financial counsellor, univ. pres.; b. Reeds Corners, N.Y., Oct. 9, 1888; s. Rev. William G. and Irene A. (Cartwright) M.; A.B., Oberlin Coll., 1910, LL.D., 1940 LL.D., Hillsdale Coll., 1936; L.H.D., Bucknell, 1946, College of Hobart and William Smith, 1958; m. Ethel A. Dagett, Oct. 16, 1920 (dec. 1953); m. 2d. Anne McCartney, November, 1958. Formerly identified with boys' work, Pittsburgh; became connected Standard Life Ins. Co., Pittsburgh, 1914, elected v.p. and dir., 1917; served as asso. nat. dir. 18,000,000 campaign for War Camp Community Serv., World War, also as mem. Nat. Com. of 35 in charge United War Work Campaign for 175,000,000; after close of the war continued work of raising funds for philanthropic purposes; an organizer, hon. chmn. bd. Marts & Lundy, Inc., financial counsellors for philanthropic insts., N.Y.; firm has raised over 2,500,-000,000 for colleges, chs., hosps. and other instns.; pres. Bucknell U., 1935-45; apptd. by Governor James exec. dir. of Pa. State Council of Defense, 1941; re-appointed by Gov. Martin, 1943; resigned Feb. 1, 1943, to go to Washington to organize Vol. Port Security Force, U.S. Coast Guard, with rank as capt., U.S. Coast Guard Reserve; named chief of temporary Reserve Div., 1943. Trustee Oberlin Coll.; a founder and trustee Wilkes Coll. Recipient Pa. and Navy Commendation Ribbon. Mem. The Authors Guild, Authors League, S.A.R., American Legion, Phi Beta Kappa, Kappa Delta Omicron. Club: University (N.Y.). Author: Philanthropy's Role in Civilization, 1953; Man's Concern for His Fellow Man, 1961; The Generosity of Americans, 1966; George Lundy of Iowa, 1967. His biography, Arnaud Cartwright Marts-A Winner in the American Tradition, pub. 1970; The Light of Inward Vision: Selected Addresses and Essays of Arnaud C. Marts, 1973. Contbr. mags. Home: New York City NY Died July 11, 1970; buried Oakwood Cemetery, East Aurora NY

MARTZ, HYMAN SCHER, dentist; b. N.Y.C., Oct. 28, 1909; s. Abraham and Sarah (Scher) M.; B.S., N.Y.U., 1929, D.D.S., 1934; M.A., Columbia, 1930; m. Evelyn Pildos, Nov. 16, 1941; 1 dau., Joan. Gen. practice dentistry, N.Y.C., 1934-69, children's dentistry, 1953-69. Participating dentist Dental Health Ins. Plan N.Y.; mem. oral hygiene com. Greater N.Y.; attending dentist N.Y.C. Health Dept., Murray & Leonie Guggenheim Clinic for Children. Served to capt. Dental Corps, AUS, 1942-46. Mem. New York Academy of Science, First District Dental Society, New York Society for Study Orthodontics, Am. Soc. Dentistry Children, International Assn. Orthodontists, N.Y. State Academy General Dentistry. Democrat. Jewish religion. K.P.; mem. B'nai B'rith. Pioneer in use of Andresen activator therapy. Norwegian system functional orthodontics. Address: Bronx NY Died June 5, 1969.

MARVEL, JOSIAH ex-ambassador, lawyer; b. Wilminton, Del., Nov. 26, 1904; s. Josiah and Mary (Jackson) M.; A.B., Yale, 1927, LL.B., Harvard, 1931; m. Gwladys Hopkins Whitney, Feb. 22, 1943; children-Josiah, Jr., Jonathan Hopkins. Partner, firm, Marvel &

Morford, Wilmington, 1932-49, Logan, Marvel & Boggs, Wilmington, 1950—; McNutt, Marvel & Dudley, Washington, 1950; sec. of State, Del., 1938-41; apptd. E.E. and M.P. to Denmark, 1946; apptd. A.E. and P. to Denmark, 1947; chmn., Internat. Claims Commn., Dept. of State, 1950-53. Enlisted as pvt. in Army and advanced through ranks to capt., Southwest Pacific, 1945. Clubs: Wilmington (Del.); Harvard (N.Y.C.); Metropolitan (Washington). Editor: Marvel on Delaware Corporation, 1932. Home: Greenville, Del. Office: Continental American Bldg., Wilmington, Del.; also Barr Bldg., Washington. Died Dec. 29, 1955; buried Centreville, Del.

MARVELL, GEORGE RALPH naval officer; b. Fall River, Mass., Sept. 25, 1869; s. Edward Tracy and Anna Congdon (Wilbur) M.; B.S., U.S. Naval Acad., 1889; m. Anna Nippes Wynkoop, Dec. 15, 1892; 1 son, George. Commd. lt., U.S. Navy, Mar. 3, 1899, and advanced through the grades to rear adm., June 3, 1922; vice adm. (temp.), Nov. 21, 1930; rear adm., Dec. 16, 1931; retired, Oct. 1, 1933. Mem. exlipse expdn. to Africa, 1889-90; patrol duty, Bering Sea, 1894; on Vicksburg, Spanish-Am. War, 1898; survey of Santiago, Cuba, 1899; in charge survey, Cuba and Haiti, 1906, 07, 08; head, dept. of navigation U.S. Naval Acad., 1909-12; on Helena, sr. officer Yangtse Valley, China, 1912-13; Bureau of Ordnance, Navy Dept., 1915; dir. naval dists., 1916-17; comdg. Louisiana, 1917-19, with Atlantic Fleet engaged convoying troops, 1918, and bringing back troops, 1919; insp. ordnance, Naval Ordnance Plant, S. Charleston, W.Va., 1919-21; comdg. Arizona, 1921-22; comdt. 16th Naval Dist., 1922-24; comdr. Fleet Base Force, 1924-25, at Naval War Coll., 1926-27; comdt. 14th Naval Dist. and Naval Sta., Pearl Harbor, Hawaii, 1927-30; comdg. Cruisers Scouting Force, 1930-31; mem. and chmn. General Bd., 1932-33. Mem. S.R., Sojourners. Conglist. Mason. Clubs: Army and Navy (Washington); Army and Navy (Manila). Died Nov. 12, 1941.

MARVIN, WALTER S(ANDS), banker, broker; b. Brooklyn, N.Y., June 24, 1889; s. Charles A. and Mabel S. (Metcalf) M.; student Williams Coll., 1913; m. Jean Murray, May 26, 1917; children—Murray Sands, John Howland, Matthew. Reporter New York Sun, 1911-15; stock salesman Am. Philippine Co., 1915-16; bond salesman Hemphill, Noyes & Co., 1916-22, partner, 1922-29; pres. Curtiss-Wright Airports Corp., 1928-29; partner Foster, McConnell & Co., 1931, Foster, Marvin & Company, 1932-42, financial advisor from 1942; director Edward MacDowell Association Incorporated. Served as 1st lt. Gen. Staff, U.S. Army, Washington, D.C., 1917-19. Trustee Montclair Art Museum; mem. budget com. Montclair Community Chest. Mem. Pilgrims Soc., S.A.R., Chi Psi. Republican. Conglist. Clubs: Williams, Borad Street (New York); Montclair Golf; Aviation Country. Home: Montclair NJ Died Apr. 24, 1971; buried Quoque NY

MARVIN, WILLIAM GLENN lawyer; b. Aberdeen, O., Nov. 16, 1892; s. Gwynne Leabon and Elizabeth Field (Taylor Leggett) M.; grad. Steele High Sch., Dayton, O., 1909; Litt.B., University of California, 1913; LL.B., Hastings College of Law, San Francisco, 1916; m. Charlotte Linden (M.D., Stanford U., 1916), July 3, 1916; children-Dorothy Christine, Wm. Glenn, Elizabeth Anne, Barbara June. Worked way through high school and college; prof. public speaking Wash. State Coll., 1 yr.; practiced law in San Francisco, 1916-17; served as gen. counsel Federal Land Bank, Berkeley, Calif.; with Nat. City Bank, New York, 1919-21, advancing to head of legal dept.; mem. Rosenberg, Ball & Marvin, 1921-22; organizer and head of Marvin & Bergh, internat. lawyers, 1922; gen. counsel Am. Mfrs.' Export Assn.; gen. counsel and mng. dir. Am. Mfrs.' Foreign Credit Exchange; chmn. legal adv. com. Div. of Commercial Laws of U.S. Dept. Commerce; gen. counsel Am. Chamber Commerce, London; Am. counsel Am. Chamber Commerce in Germany and Cuba; pres. Am.-Russian Chamber Commerce; etc.; chmn. Aviation Advisory Com. City of San Francisco; chmn. bd. Ellery A. Baker & Co., New York; president Realty Finance Corporation. Enlisted as private Air Service, U.S.A., and served as lt. until close of World War, retiring as chief of tech. staff, Wilbur Wright Field, Dayton, O. Mem. Rep. State Com. Calif. Baptist. Author: The Defensive Side of Banking, 1926. Home: Los Altos, Calif. Died Jan. 5, 1932.

MARX, ROBERT S. lawyer; b. Cincinnati, O., Jan. 28, 1889; s. William S. and Rose (Lowenstein) M.; LL.B., U. Cin., 1909; L.H.D., Marietta Coll., 1954. Admitted to bars of Ohio, 1910, Ill., 1928, Mich., 1933; practice, Cin., Detroit, adjoining states; judge Superior Ct. of Cincinnati, 1920-26; practiced in Chicago, 1927-28; mem. Nichols, Wood, Marx & Ginter, Cincinnati, since 1928, also Marx, Levi, Thrill & Wiseman, Detroit; counsel for receiver Nat. Bank of Ky. (Louisvl.), 1930-45, First Nat. Bank (Detroit) 1933-48; counsel for numerous nat. retail chains in tax cases; pres. Cin. Oil & Mining Co. since 1945; prof. law (part time) U. Cin. Coll. Law, 1952-56; general counsel Schenley Industries, Ind., 1955-; dir. Model Laundry Co., Portsmouth Steel Corp. Dir. The Dorothy and Lewis Rosenstiel Foundation. Served as capt., operations officer 357th Inf., 90th Div., World War; wounded in action near Baalon, Fr., Nov. 10, 1918; maj. judge adv. gen., 1925-30, U.S. Army Reserve. Awarded D.S.C., Verdun medal, Order of Purple Heart, three battle clasps. Fellow Am. Bar Found., Internat. Acad. Trial Lawyers; mem. Nat. Com. to Study Automobile Accident Compensation, Association of the Bar of New York, American, Ohio, Mich., Detroit, Cin. bar associations, Disabled Am. Vets. of World War (founder, first nat. comdr.), Am. Legion, Legion of Valor, Disabled Emergency Officers Assn. Y.M.C.A. Democrat. Del. to Dem. Nat. Convs., 1932, 1936 from 1st Ohio Dist. Hebrew. Clubs: Cincinnati, Losantiville Country; Detroit Yacht, Great Lakes Cruising; Cincinnati Athletic; Farmers, Cuvier Press; The Tryon (North Carolina) Country, Tryon Riding and Hunt; Clifton Meadows; Harbor Island. Author: Round the World with Stella; articles on compulsory automobile and compensation ins. and taxation. Contbr. Jour.Legal Edn. Founder Robert S. Marx Charitable Found. and Trust. Died Sept. 6, 1960.

MARZO, EDUARDO musician; b. Naples, Italy, Nov. 29, 1852; s. Carlo and Angiola (Bertoleé-Viale) M.; ed. Naples, Italy; m. Clara L. Philbin, 1882; children-Albert Stephen, Mrs. Maria Josephine Flanagan, Clarence Philibin, Rita E. Came to U.S. in boyhood; returned to Naples long enough to finish his studies in composition under Pappalardo; returned to New York as musical dir. with Gazzaniga, Roneoni, Patti, di Murska, Titjens, etc.; for past 40 yrs. teacher of vocal music, organist and composer; specially distinguished for sacred compositions. Mem. Royal Acad. of St. Cecilia, Rome, 1892; Knight of the Crowd of Italy, 1884; Knight Order of San Sylvester by Pope Benedict XV, 1914. Composed 15 masses, 4 vespers and many songs for the Catholic Ch.; also several Te Deums, anthems and songs for Protestant chs.; orchestral preludes, piano pieces, secular songs and duets; operettas and cantatas for children's voices, etc. Editor: Songs of Italy, 1905; The Art of Vocalization; 3 books, Carols of all Nations. Died June 7, 1929.

MASLAND, JOHN W(ESLEY), JR., educator; b. Phila., May 15, 1912; s. John Wesley and Elizabeth (Stager) M.; B.S., Haverford Coll., 1933; M.A., Princeton, 1937, Ph.D., 1938; M.A. (hon.), Dartmouth Coll., 1946; m. Harriet Mary Gilbert, July 22, 1939 (dec.); m. 2d, Mary Sawyer Norton, June 19, 1950; children—Joann Ellis, James Wesley, Thomas Norton, Andrew Tyson; instr., asst. prof., asso. prof. polit. sci. Stanford, 1938-46; prof. govt. Dartmouth Coll., 1946-68, chmn. dept. govt., 1955-59, provost, 1959-67; adviser for edn. for India, Ford Found., 1967-68; divisional assistant Dept. of State, 1942-43; staff Internat. Secretariat, UN Conf., San Francisco, 1945; staff mem., govt. sect. Supreme Comdr. Allied Powers, Tokyo, 1946; dir. studies Nat. War Coll., 1950, 51, mem. board consultants, 1960-63; staff dir. African Study Com., Edn. and World Affairs, 1964-65. Mem. Hanover Sch. Bd., 1957-60; bd. directors U.S. Educational in India; trustee Williston Acad., 1953-58, 63-67, Am. Univs. Field Staff, 1959-66, Inst. Coll. and U. Adminstrs., 1960-66, African Scholarship Program of Am. Univs., 1965-67. Mem. Am. Polit. Sci. Assn., Council Fgn. Relations. Phi Beta Kappa. Club: Cosmos (Washington). Co-author: The Governments of Foreign Powers (Philip W. Buck), 1947, 50; Soldiers and Scholars, Military Education and National Policy (with Laurence I. Radway), 1957; (with Gene M. Lyons) ROTC: Education and Military Leadership, 1959. Home: Hanover NH Died Aug. 3, 1968; buried Hanover NH

MASON, EDWARD WILSON ry. official; b. Moberly, Mo., Mar. 23, 1877; s. John Quincy and Virginia Murdoch (Wilson) M.; ed. high sch., Tacoma, Wash.; m. Elizabeth Burroughs Pratt, Jan. 23, 1906; children-Robert Pratt, Elizabeth Anne. Began as call boy N.P. Ry., June 1893, and continued consecutively as operator, dispatcher, night chief dispatcher, chief dispatcher and trainmaster; wifh Western Pacific R.R. as supt. telegraph and car accountant, div. supt. and gen. supt., 1909-18; federal mgr., same rd., 1919-20, gen. mgr., Mar.-Nov. 1921, v.p. and gen. mgr. since Nov. 1921; v.p. Denver & Salt Lake R.R.; dir. of Western Pacific R.R., Denver & Salt Lake Ry., Alameda Belt Line, Central Calif. Traction Co. (mem. operating com.), Tidewater Southern Ry. Commd. maj. engrs., U.S. Army, May 1918; served with 31st Engrs. and Transportation Corps in France, June 1918-Aug. 1919; lt. col., Feb. 1919; assigned to railroad operations as div. supt. at St. Nazaire, and gen. supt. Nantes, 14th Grand Div., Transportation Corps; hon. discharged, Aug. 13, 1919. Meritorious service citation from U.S. and French govts.; Officer d'Academie (France). Republican. Protestant. Mason (32ff). Club: Lake Merced Golf and Country. Home: 2321 Van Ness Av. Office: Mills Bldg., San Francisco, Calif. Died Mar. 26, 1947.

MASON, FRANK HOLCOMB consul gen.; b. Niles, O., Apr. 24, 18 s. Dean E. and Bertha M. (Holcomb) M.; ed. at pub. schs., Niles, and at Hiram Coll.; was not grad.; served as pvt. 42d Ohio Inf. from July 1861; promoted capt. and a.d.c. July 1863, at Vicksburg; mustered out as capt. 12th Cav., Nov. 25, 1865; m. Jennie V. Birchard, Sept. 26, 1866. Successively reporter, editorial writer and mng. editor Cleveland Leader until 1880; Am. consul at Basie, Switzerland, 1880-84, at Marseilles, 1884-89; consul gen. at Frankfort-on-the-Main, 1889-99, at Berlin, 1899-1905, at Paris, lMar. 6, 1905-Jan. 24, 1914. Chmn. Am. Ambulance Hosp., Paris, Jan. 1914. Died June 21, 1916.

MASON, G(EORGE) GRANT, JR., financier; b. Mason City, Ia., Jan. 2, 1904; s. George and Marion (Peak) M.; student at Browning Sch., New York City, 1912-16, Saint Paul's School, Concord, New Hampshire, 1916-22; A.B., Yale U., 1926; student Guggenheim Sch. of Aviation, N.Y.U., 1926-27; m. Jane Kendall, June 1927 (divorced 1940); children—Anthony, Philip; married 2d, Martha Ashley McMakin, May 1946 (div. Nov. 1968); children—George Grant III, Martha Peak; stepchildren—Richard A., Leigh A. Became district manager new business dept. Corn Exchange Bank, N.Y. City, 1925; one of founders, then rep. of Pan. Am. Airways, Inc., before 21 govts. in Carribbean area, with hdqrs. in Havana, Cuba, 1927-38; pres. and gen. mgr. Compania Nacional Cubana de Aviacion, Havana, 1933-38; mem. Civil Aeronautics Authority, 1938-40, Civil Aeronautics Bd. after reorganization, 1940-42. One of founders, dir. Alloy Products, Inc., Baton Rouge; chmn. bd. Versfelt, Mason & Donegan, Inc., financial services. Pres. Inter-Am. Comml. Arbitration Commn. Apptd. by Pres. Roosevelt, chmn. Am. Del. to 4th Internat. Conf. Pvt. Air Law, Brussels, Belgium, 1938. Administrative asst. in charge South Am. activities, Am. Republics Div., Defense Supplies Corp., Reconstrn. Finance Corp., Jan.-July 1942. Trustee, Skowhegan Sch. Painting and Sculpture. Maj., Air Transport Commands, U.S. Army Air Forces, July 3, 1942; lt. col., A.C., Nov. 6, 1942; asst. chief of staff plans, Air Transport Command, Mar. 6, 1943; lt. col., Gen. Staff Corps, May 11, 1943, col., July 27, 1943; chief Civil Aviation Br., Air Staff Plans, Hdqrs. A.A.F., Sept. 26, 1944. Relieved from active duty, apptd. col., Res. Corps, July 27, 1946. War Dept. rep., world-circling mission with Wendell Wilkie, 1942. Mem. U.S. com. Inter-Am. Arbitration Commn., 1958. Mem. U.S. del. "Quadrant" Conf., Quebec, Aug. 1943; "Sextant" conf., Cairo, Nov. 1943. Mil. adviser to US-UK Conf. on Civil Aviation, Bermuda, Jan.-Feb. 1946. Various other temporary assignments in all theaters of war in connection with official duties of ATC and subsequently with problems relating to postwar transition from mil. to civil aviation; spl. asst. to Asst. Sec. Air Force, 1948-49, cons. Sec. Air Force, 1949-50; vice chmn. bd. dirs., chmn. exec. com., Vision, Inc., pub. Latin Am. news mags. and U.S. industrial and ednl. services. Decorations and Citations: Legion of Merit; Army Commendation Ribbon; American Asiatic Pacific, European-African-Middle Eastern Campaign Medals, World War II Victory Medal. Mem. Am. Arbitration Assn. (dir. 1956, exec. com. 1957, chmn. membership com. 1958-60, pres. 1960-62, chmn. 1962-65, vice chmn. 1965). Christian Scientist. Clubs: Metropolitan, Yale, F Street, National Aviation (Washington, District of Columbia); Yale, University (New York City); Yeamans Hall (Charleston, S.C.); Mid Ocean (Bermuda); Edgartown Yacht (Martha's Vineyard, Mass). Home: New York City NY Died Oct. 16, 1970.

MASON, HAROLD WHITNEY b. Worcester, Mass., Apr. 21, 1895; s. William Lysander and Margaret Etta (Matthews) M.; B.S., Dartmouth, 1917; m. Evelyn Dunham, Mar. 17, 1918 (died Dec. 1930); 1 son, George Dunham. Vice pres. and treas. Dunham Bros. Co., Brattleboro, Vt., since 1927; dir. Dunham Brothers Co., Conn. River Power Co., New England Power Assn., Bellows Falls Hydroelectric Co., Union Mutual Fire Insurance Co. of Vt. Estey Organ Corp., Central Vt. Ry., Nat. Life Ins. Co., C. E. Bradley corporation; secretary Post-War Policy Council at Mackinac Island, Sept. 1943. Lieutenant Air Service U.S. Army, World War I; lt. colonel Army of U.S., May 1942; inactive duty because of health since Oct. 1942, Del. Rep. Nat. Conv. and presdl. elector for Vt., 1932; mem. Rep. Nat. Com. since 1936; mem. of exec. com. and sec. of Rep. Nat. Com. since 1937; sec. Rep. Nat. Conv. at Phila., 1940, Dir. New England Council. Mem. Dartmouth Alumni Council, 1942. Trustee Vermont Acad., Kurn Hattin Homes at Saxtons River, Vt.; dir. Brattleboro Memorial Hosp. Mem. Vt. Soc. Colonial wars, Vt. Soc. Sons. Am. Revolution, Am. Legion, Mil. Order Fgn. Wars, Sigma Nu. Republican. Congregationalist. Clubs: Union League, Dartmouth, Links, National Republican (New York); Union, University, St. Botolph (Boston); Metropolitan, Army-Navy Country (Washington, D.C.); Tobique Salmon (New Brunswick). Home: Brattleboro, Vt. Died Nov. 3, 1944.

MASON, MAX educator; b. Madison, Wis., Oct. 26, 1877; s. Edwin Cole and Josephine (Vroman) M.; B.Litt., U. Wis., 1898, LL.D., 1926; Ph.D., U. Göttingen, 1903; D.Sc., Columbia, 1926; LL.D., Yale, 1926, Dartmouth, 1927, Pomona Coll., 1937; m. Mary Louise Freeman, June 16, 1904 (died 1928); children-William Vroman, Maxwell, Molly; m. 2d, Helen Schermerborn Young, Aug. 5, 1939 (died 1944); m. 3d, Daphine Crane Martin, Nov. 6, 1945. Instr. math. Mass. Inst. Tech., 1903-04, asst. prof. math. Yale, 1904-08; prof. math. physics. U. Wis., 1908-25; pres. U. hgo., 1925-28; dir. natural scis. Rockefeller Found., N.Y.C., 1928-29, pres., 1929-36; chmn. Obs. council and mem. exec. council Cal. Inst. Tech. since 1936. Asso. editor Trans. Am. Math. Soc., 1911-17; lectr. math. physics 2d semester, Harvard, 1911-12. Fellow A.A.A.S.; mem. Nat. Acad. Scis., Am. Math. Soc. (delivered colloquium lectrs. 1906), Am. Phys. Soc., Deutsche Mathematiker Vereinigung, Psi Upsilon, Sigma Xi, Gamma Alpha, Phi Beta Kappa, Phi Kappa Phi. Mem. staff Naval Exptl. Sta., New London, Conn.; mem. submarine com. NRC, 1917-19. Inventor submarine detection devices. Clubs: Commercial, Chicago; Annandale; Vally Hunt (Pasadena). Author: The New Haven Mathematical Colloquium, 1910. Co-author; the Electromagnetic Field. Contbr. papers on math. research to sci. jours. Home: 1035 Harvard Av., Claremont, Cal. Ret., 1949. Died Mar. 1961.

MASON, MICHAEL L(IVINGOOD) surgeon; b. Rossville, Ill., Apr. 23, 1895; s. Francis Marion and Katherine Elizabeth (Livingood) M.; B.S., Northwestern U., 1916, A.M., 1917, M.D., 1924, Ph.D., 1931; m. Alice Frances Kolb, Dec. 28, 1921. Intern, Cook Co. Hosp., Chicago, 1924-25; attending surgeon Wesley Memorial Hosp., Chicago, 1926-29, Passavant Memorial Hosp. since 1929; pvt. practice surgery, Chicago, since 1926; mem. faculty Northwestern U. since 1914, asst., later fellow in zoology, 1914-17, asst. and asso. in anatomy, 1919-27, clin. asst. in surgery, 1925-28, instr., 1929-30, asso. in surgery, 1930-32, asst. prof. surgery, 1932-36, asso. prof. 1936-52, prof. of surgery, 1952-. Mem. med. advisory com. Rehabilitation Ins., Chgo.; sub-chmn., disaster com. Chgo. chpt. A.R.C. President board directions Summer School of Painting, Saugatuck, Michigan Exhibitor: Pennsylvania Academy Fine Arts, 1938-40, Golden Gate Exhbn., 1939, Art Inst. Chicago, 1936, 38, 40, 43, Ill. Soc. Fine Arts, 1937, 38, Soc. Am. Etchers, 1949, Internat. Bienneal Color Litho. Exhibit, 1950-52, 54, 56; Soc. Am. Graphic Arts, 1952, 56; 12th ann. exhibit Am. Color Print Soc, 1951; Print Club Phila., 1953, 56, 57; also exhibited at Brooklyn Museum, 1958. Served as sgt., A.U.S., France, 1917-19; col. Med. Corps, chief of surg., later comdg. officer 12th Gen. Hosp., M.T.O., 1942-46, col. Med. Corps, O.R.C. since 1941. Decorated Legion of Merit (U. S.); Order Nacional Do Cruzcero do Sol (Brazil). Diplomate Am. Bd. Surgery, Am. Bd. Plastic Surgery. Fellow American College of Surgeons (1st vice president 1958-59); mem. Am. Soc. for Surgery Trauma, Am. Soc. Surgery Hand (pres. 1952), Assn. Military Surgeons, A.M.A., Am. Assn. Ry. Surgeons, Am. Western (pres. 1955), Central surg. assns., Sigma Xi, Alpha Omega Alpha, Wranglers. Clubs: Literary, Cliff Dwellers, University, Surgeons (Chicago). Contbr. to Sajours-Cyclopedia of Medicine and Christopher's Text Book of Surgery; also articles in profl. jours. Asso. editor Surgery, Gynecology and Obstetrics since 1929, Quarterly Bull. of Northwestern U. Med. Sch. since 1940; editorial bd. Jour. Bone and Joint Surgery; also editor manual. Home: 443 Grove Av., Wood Dale, Ill. Office: 154 Erie St., Chgo, 11. Died Mar. 30, 1963; buried Mt. Emblem, Elmhurst, Ill.

MASON, NEWTON ELIPHALET rear-admiral U.S. Navy; b. Monroeton, Bradford County, Pa., Oct. 14, 1850; s. Gordon Fowler and Mary Ann M.; ed. Susquehanna Collegiate Inst., Towanda, Pa., until 1865; grad. U.S. Naval Acad., 1869; m. Dora E. Hancock, Apr. 4, 1894. After graduation served on U.S.S. Sabine, special cruise, 1869-70; promoted ensign, 1870; torpedo instrn., 1871; U.S.S. Wabash, European Sta., 1871-72; promoted master, 1872; on monitor Manhattan, 1873; U.S.S. Kansas, 1874-75; commd. lt., 1874; monitor Catskill, 1875-76; U.S.S. Ossipee, 1876-77; receivingship St. Louis, 1878-80; Irish Famine relief ship Constellation, 1889; U.S.S. Monocacy, Asiatic Sta., 1889-83; U.S.S. Pensacola, 1883-84; on ordnance duty, Navy Yard, Washington, 1884-85; Bur. of Ordnance, Navy Dept., 1885-89; U.S.S. Petrel and monitor Miantonomah, N. Atlantic Sta., 1889-92; Bur. of Ordnance and in charge Naval Proving Grounds, Indian Head, Md., 1892-96; commd. lt.-comdr., 1896; U.S.S.. Brooklyn, 1896-99 (including Spanish War); insp. ordnance League Island Navy Yard, 1899; insp. ordnance in charge Naval Torpedo Sta., Newport, R.I., 1899-1902; promoted comdr., Nov. 1899; comdg. U.S.S. Cincinnati, 1902-04; spl. duty, June-Aug. 3, 1904; chief Bur. of Ordnance, Navy Dept. with rank of rear-admiral, from Aug. 1904 to May 1911; mem. gen. bd., 1911-12; commd. capt., Sept. 30, 1904; rear-admiral, Nov. 12, 1908; retired from active service, Oct. 14, 1912. Chmn. D.C. Chapter Am. Nat. Red Cross, 1914-17; ordered to active duty, June 2, 1917; serving in Bur. of Ordnance, Navy Dept., and as mem. priorities com. War Industries Bd. of Council Nat. Defense until Jan. 1919; pres. spl. bd. on naval ordnance, Bur. of Ordnance, till Nov. 1, 1919; returned to inactive list. Was awarded Santiago medal, 1898. Mem. Pa. Commandery Mil. Order Foreign Wars, D.C. Soc. S.A.R. Address: Box 313, Coronado, Calif. Died Jan. 23, 1945.

MASON, RICHARD BARNES army officer; b. Fairfax County, Va., Jan. 16, 1797; s. George and Eleanor (Patton) M. Commd. 2d lt. 8th Inf., U.S. Army, 1817, capt. 1st Inf., 1819; served in Black Hawk War, 1832; commd. maj. 1st Dragoons (later became 1st Regt. U.S. Cavalry), 1833, lt. col., 1836, col., 1846; served with Gen. Kearny in Mexican War, occupied Los Angeles, 1847, became mil. comdr. of region, authorized to establish temporary civil govt. in Cal., served as acting gov., 1847-49; brevetted brig. gen., 1848. Died St. Louis, July 25, 1850; buried Jefferson Barracks, Mo.

MASON, RUFUS OSGOOD physician, author; b. Sullivan, N.H., Jan. 22, 1830; s. Rufus and Prudence (Woods) M.; grad. Dartmouth, 1854 (A.M.); Coll. Physicians & Surgeons, N.Y., 1859; m. Marian Isabel Goodwin, July 3, 1871; m. 2d, Charlotte Van Der Veer Quick, Apr. 27, 1886. Acting asst. surgeon U.S. Navy, 1861-64. Author: Sketches and Impressions, Musical, Theatrical and Social, Including a Sketch of the Philharmonic Society of New York, 1887; Telepathy and the Subliminal Self, 1897; Hypnotism and Suggestion in Therapeutics, 1901. Home: New York, N.Y. Died 1903.

MASSEE, EDWARD KINGSLEY lawyer, retired army officer; b. Alma Center, Wis., July 26, 1871; s. Rev. William and Laura Lane (Davenport) M.; student Hamline U., 1889-91; honor grad. Inf.-Cav. Sch., 1904; grad. Army Staff Coll., 1905; LL.B., U. of Minn., 1908; m. Therese Lyons, Aug. 27, 1902. Served as pvt., corpl., sergt., arty., 1892-95; sergt., later 1st lt. and bn. adj. 3d Wis. Inf., 1898-99; pvt., later regtl. sergt. maj. U.S. Vols., 1899-1901; 2d lt. U.S. Inf., 1901, advancing through grades to maj., judge adv., June 12, 1917; retired with rank lt. col., July 1, 1920. Decorations: Legion of Merit, 1944. Campaign ribbons: Spanish-American War, Puerto Rican Occupation, Philippine Campaign (1900-01), Mexican Border, World War I (France, 3 stars). Judge, 1st Circuit Court, Territory of Hawaii, Mar. 1926-Feb. 1929; judge, U.S. Dist. Court, Hawaii, 1929-35. Engaged in voluntary war work, Dec. 8, 1941-44. Mem. Am. Bar Assn., Bar Assn. Hawaii, C. of C., Am. Legion, Mil. Order World Wars. Home: 1919 N.E. 21st Av., Portland 12, Ore. Died Feb. 15, 1960.

MASSIE, ROBERT KINLOCH JR. educator; b. of Am. parents, Shanghai, China, May 21, 1892; s. Robert Kinloch and Harriet Ross (Milton) M.; brought to U.S., 1895; grad. Episcopal High Sch., Alexandria, Va., 1911; B.A., U. of Va., 1914, M.A., 1916; unmarried. Founder Massie Sch., Lexington, Ky., 1919; school incorporated, 1923, and moved to Versailles; pres. and headmaster same since organization. Grad. Ft. Sill (Okla.) Sch. of Arms, as asst. div. instr., 1918; served as 2d lt., 1st lt., and capt. Inf.U.S.A., 1917-18; maj. O.R.C., 1925. Mem. Southern Assn. Colls. and Secondary Sch., Lexington Y.M.C.A. Democrat. Episcopalian. Home: Versailles, Ky. Died Apr. 7, 1930.

MASSON, ROBERT LOUIS, educator; b. Washington, Ia., Aug. 31, 1891; s. Daniel John and Matilda Mason (Scofield) M.; A.B., State U. Ia., 1912, A.M., 1915; A.M., Harvard, 1922; m. Henrietta H. Worrell June 18, 1923; children—Helen Elaine (Mrs. Carl H. Engel), Jane Cora (Mrs. Roger S. Jackson), Robert Henry. Supt. schs., Winfield, Ia., 1912-13; prin. Washington (Ia.) High Sch., 1913-14; asst. econs., State U. Ia., 1914-16; asst. econs. Harvard, 1916-17, 1919-20, instr., 1920-22, instr. and tutor, 1922-23; asst. prof. econs., U. Mich., 1923-24, asst. prof. finance, 1924-25, asso. prof. finance, 1925-29; vis. prof. U. Wash., summer, 1928; asso. prof. finance Harvard Grad. Sch. Bus. Adminstrn., 1929-39 prof. finance, 1939-58, emeritus, 1958-70, prof. finance Advanced Mgmt. Program, Honolulu, summers 1958-59, Harvard-Radcliffe Program in Mgmt. Tng., 1958-60, 61-63, Advanced Mgmt. Program in Far East, Baguio, Philippines, summer 1967; prof. finance Institut European d'Adminstrn. des Affairs, Fontainebleau, France, 1960-61; vis. prof. finance Northwestern U., 1964, Morris Harvey Coll., Charleston, W.Va., 1968-69. Mem. bd. dirs. Reliance Coop. Bank. Cons. Indian Inst. Mgmt., Ahmedabad, India, 1964-65, prof. program mgmt. devel., Agra, India, 1966. Member of second O.T.C., Ft. Snelling, Minn., 1st lt. inf., U.S. Res., 1917-18; capt. 1918-19. Recipient Fulbright Act award, lectr. in France, 1960-61. Mem. Am. Econ. Assn., Delta Sigma Rho. Author: Problems in Corporation Finance (with S. S. Stratton), 1935; Financial Instruments and Institutions—A Case Book (with same), 1938; A Case Study of Balloting Regulation: The Boston and Maine Recapitalizes, 1948-53, 1956; New Shares for Old: The Boston and Maine Stock Modification, 1958; (with P. Hunt and R. N. Anthony) Cases in Financial Management, 1960. Home: Centerville MA Died Mar. 14, 1970; buried Beechwood Cemetery, Centerville, Cape Cod MA

MATAS, RUDOLPH surgeon; b. Bonnet Carre, nr. New Orleans, La., Sept. 12, 1860; s. Dr. N. Hereu and Teresa (Jorda) M.; ed. Paris, Barcelona, Brownsville (Tex.), Soule's Coll. (New Orleans); grad. Lit. Inst. of St. John, Matamoros, Mexico, 1876; M.D., Tulane, 1880; LL.D., Washington U., 1915, U. of Ala., 1926, Tulane, 1928; Sc.D., U. of Pa., 1925, Princeton, 1928; M.D., honoris causa, Nat. U. of Guatemala, 1934; widower. Began practice at New Orleans, 1880, specializing in surgery since 1895; prof. surgery, Tulane Med. Dept., 1895-1927, emeritus since 1928; sr. surgeon Charity Hosp., 1894-1928, consultant since 1928; chief sr. surgeon Touro Infirmary, 1905-35, hon. chief surgeon, 1935—; cons. surgeon Eye, Ear, Nose and Throat Hosp.; etc. Mem. La. Council Nat. Defense, 1915-18; organizer and dir. Base Hosp. 24 (Tulane Unit) for service in France, 1916-17; maj., dir. New Orleans Sch. for Intensive Surg. War Training, M.O.R.C., 1917-18. Fellow Am. Coll. Surgeons (v.p. 1913, 20; pres. 1924-25), A.A.A.S., Havana Acad. Medical Sciences; mem. A.M.A. (chmn. sect. surg. 1908; v.p. 1920, 32-33), Am. Surg. Assn. (pres. 1909), So. Surg. Assn. (pres. 1911; hon. fellow 1927), Am. Assn. Thoracic Surgeons (pres. 1920), La. State Med. Soc. (pres. 1894-95), New Orleans Med. and Surg. Assn. (pres. 1886), Am. Soc. Clin. Surgery (v.p. 1908-10), Orleans Parish Med. Soc., Am. Assn. Cancer Research, Am. Soc. Control Cancer, Am. Assn. Exptl. Medicine, Am. Assn. Anatomists, Nat. Assn. Study and Prevention Tb, Am. Assn. Endocrinology, Assn. Mil. Surgeons U.S. Army, Nat. Inst. Social Sciences, Am. Assn. Friends of Med. Progress, Nat. Econ. League, Am. Museum Natural History, La. Hist. Soc., So. Art League, Art Assn. New Orleans, New Orleans Zoology, Soc., La. League of Civil Service Reform; hon. fellow Royal Coll. of Surgeons, Eng., 1927; pres. internat. Soc. of Surgery, 1936-38; hon. mem. New Orleans Acad. Scis., La. State Pharm. Assn., Ill. Central and Miss. Valley R.R. Surgeons, Am. Assn. Traumatic Surgery, Acad. Medicine (N.Y.), Am. Soc. Regional Anesthesia, Boston Surg. Soc., Am. Soc. History of Medicine, Phila. Acad. Surgery, Hon. pres. Pan-Am. Med. Congress, Washington, 1895, v.p. for La., 1896; mem. and rapporteur arterial surgery (surg. sect.) Internat. Med. Congress, London, 1913; mem. Assn. Francaise de Chirugie (rapporteur by invitation, and hon. pres. 1922); mem. Soc. Internat. de Chirugie (rapporteur by invitation); hon. pres. Internat. Surgical Congress, Warsaw, 1929; hon. mem. Royal Acad. Medicine (Rome), Assn. Polish Surgeons, Soc. Ital. Physicians in America; corr. mem. Peruvian Surg. Soc., Cuban Surgical Society, Société Nationale de Chirurgie (Paris), Med. Soc. Copenhagen (Denmark), Surg. Soc. Madrid; corr. fellow Royal Acad. Medicine (Madrid); hon. fellow Royal Acad. Medicine, and Catalonian Acad. Med. Sci. (Barcelona), Royal Acad. Medicine (Belgium); hon. pres. Surgical Society (Barcelona); mem. Soc. Internat. pour l'Histoire de la Med. (Paris); hon. surgeon Eye, Ear, Nose and Throat Hosp., New Orleans; asso. mem. French Nat. Acad. Medicine; hon. mem. 12th Congress Internat. Soc. Surgery, London, 1947; hon. fellow Am. Soc. Anesthesiologists, Royal Belgian Acad. Sci.; hon. mem. Belgian Surg. Soc., Greek Nat. Soc., Surg. Soc. Lyons, La. State Acad. Sci., Am. Soc. Univ. Surgeons, American Soc. Vascular Surgeons, La. Surg. Society; hon. mem. 50 yr. Club La. State Med. Soc., Miss. State Med. Soc.; hon. pres. emeritus past pres. adv. council La. Med. Soc. Ofcl. del. from City of New Orleans to Nat. Finlay Celebration, Havana, 1941. Honor guest, City of Havana, Municipal medal, 1941; Finlay medal Cuban Med. Fedn., 1941; Officer Order Public Instruction (Venezuela), 1925; Knight Civil Order of Alfonso XII of Spain, 1929; Chevalier Legion of Honor (France), 1932; Knight Order of Isabella the Catholic (Spanish), 1934; comdr. Nat. Cuban Order of Carlos Finlay, 1936; officer Order of Leopold, Belgium, 1939. Recipient first distinguished service medal A.M.A., 1938. Mem. Italian-Am. Soc., Stars and Bars of Tulane (pres. 1922), Nu Sigma Nu (president hon. council, 1936; merit medal, 1942), Alpha Omega Alpha, Kappa Delta Phi, hon. fellow Alpha Zeta Circle, Omicron Delta Kappa. Clubs: Boston, Round Table, Young Men's Business (honorary), Lions (hon.). Editor New Orleans Med. and Surg. Jour., 1883-85. Henry Bigelow medalist of Boston Surg. Soc., 1926; Times-Picayune award for community service, 1940. Chmn. Violet Hart Com. Award Matas Medal Vascular Surgery. Hon. 1934. Author of many treatises and monographs on surg. subjects, specially vascular surgery, and frequent contbr. to med. jours. and text books. Home: 2255 St. Charles Av., New Orleans. Died Sept., 1957.

MATHER, FRED author, fish-culturist; b. Greenbush, N.Y., Aug. 2, 1833; ed. at acad. in Albany, N.Y., 1854-57; hunter and trapper in Wis., 1857-59; was in the Kan. war, 1862; private 113th N.Y. vols.; then sergt. to capt. 7th N.Y. arty. until discharged, May 1865; lt. col. Albany Rangers, 1898; fish-culturist, 1868; asst. U.S. Fish Commn., 1873; supt. N.Y. Fish Commn., 1883-95; invented hatching cone for shad and other apparatus; had charge Am. exhibit, Fisheries Exhbn., Berlin, 1880; m. Elizabeth McDonald (died 1861), 1854; m. 2d, Adelaide Fairchild, 1877. Author: Men I Have Fished With; Fish-culture; Icthyology of the Adirondacks. Lecturer. Home: Brooklyn, N.Y. Died 1900.

MATHEWS, ALBERT PRESCOTT physiol. chemist; b. Chicago, Ill., Nov. 26, 1871; s. William Smith Babcock and Flora E. (Swain) M.; S.B., Mass. Inst. Tech., 1892; studied biology, Cambridge, Eng., Naples, Italy, and Marburg, Germany, 1895-97; Ph.D., Columbia, 1898; hon. D.Sc. Institutum Divi Thomae, 1940; m. Jessie Glyde Macrum, Feb. 7, 1895; 1 dau., Mrs. Noreen Macrum Koller. Asst. in biology, Mass. Inst. Tech., 1892-93; fellow, 1893-95, hon. fellow, 1897-98, Columbia; asst. prof. physiology, Tufts Coll. Med. Sch., 1899-1900; instr. physiology, Harvard Med. Sch., 1900-01; asst. prof. physiol. chemistry, 1901-04, asso. prof., 1904-05, prof., 1905-18, and chmn. dept. of physiology, 1909-16, U. of Chicago; prof. biochemistry, U. of Cincinnati, 1918—, prof. emeritus, 1940—. Known for original investigations in parthenogenesis, upon the nature of nerve impulse, in pharmacology and chem. biology; trustee Marine Biol. Lab., Woods Hole, Mass. Fellow A.A.A.S.; mem. Am. Chem. Soc., Am. Physiol. Soc., Biochem. Soc., Soc. de chimie biologique, Biochemical Soc. (British), Soc. Exptl. Biology Great Britain; foreign mem. Academia Nationale dei Lincei, Rome. Commd. capt., Quartermasters Corps, Feb. 1917, and on active duty, Aug. 1917-Nov. 1918, at

Hdqrs. Central Dept. Author: Text Book of Physiological Chemistry (6th Edit.); The Nature of Matter, Gravitation and Light; Gravitation, Space-Time and Matter, 1934; of Biochemistry. Contbr. to scientific jours. Home: 1237 Glenwood Blvd., Schenectady 8. Died Sept. 21, 1957; buried Allegheny Cemetery, Pitts.

MATHEWS, FRANK A. JR. congressman; b. Phila., Aug. 3, 1890; s. Frank A. and Mary Isabel (Coad) M.; LL.B., Temple U., 1920; m. Carol Judd Becker, Aug. 20, 1919; children-John Barry, William George, Pauline Mary, Frank C. and Carol Ann. Admitted to New Jersey bar as attorney and solicitor in chancery, 1919, became counsellor and master, 1922; admitted to U.S. Dist. Ct. (N.J.), 1919, U.S. Supreme Ct.; partner in firm Waddington & Mathews, Riverton, N.J., 1921-40; practicing individually since 1940; judge Dist. Ct., 1st Jud. Dist. Burlington County, 1929-33; asst. counsel State Hwy. Dept. N.J., 1934-40; became dep. atty. gen. of N.J., 1944; mem. 79th and 80th Congresses (1945-49), 4th N.J. Dist. Legal adviser and counsel Vets. Commn. N.J. Legislature. Served with ordnance U.S. Army, World WarI; overseas, 19 mos.; 1st lt. Judge Adv. Gen.'s Dept., O.R.C., 1923-26; 1st lt., inf. N.J. N.G., 1926-32, maj. Judge Adv. Gen.'s Dept. 1932-37, lt. col., div. judges adv., 44th Div. Staff, 1937-40; in Fed. service, 1940, and since 1944, as lt. col. Judge Adv. Gen.'s Dept.; now on inactive service. Mem. Burlington County Bar Assn., Artisans Order Mut. Protection, Patriotic Order Sons of Am., Am. legion (40 and 8, past dep. comdr., past nat. exec. committeeman from N.J.). Republican. Episcopalian. Clubs: Union League, Philadelphia Art Alliance, Play and Players (Phila.). Home: 203 Bank Av., Riverton, N.J. Died Feb. 5, 1964.

MATHEWS, JAMES THOMAS naval officer; b. Marion, S.C., Nov. 6, 1891; s. James Thomas and Martha Ellen (Williams) M.; B.S., U.S. Naval Acad., 1913; C.E., Rensselaer Poly. Inst., Troy, N.Y., 1918; m. Isabelle Jane Bradham, July 22, 1914; children-James Thomas (officer U.S. Navy), Laurens Bradham (officer U.S. Navy). Commd. ensign, U.S. Navy, 1913, and advanced through the grades to rear adm., 1942; served as pub. works officer, Naval Air Station, Miami, Fla., Oct. 1918-Aug. 1919; Treaty Engr., Republic of Haiti, Oct. 1919-Sept. 1920; Officer in Charge Constrn. Naval Ordnance Plant, So. Charleston W.Va., July-Nov. 1922; Pub. Works Officer, Submarine Base, New London, Conn., Mar. 1926-Sept. 1928; Navy Yard, Charleston, S.C. and 6th and 7th Naval Dists. Aug. 1930-July 1934; Bur. of Yards and Docks and Bur. of Aeronautics Sept. 1934-Sept. 1937, Naval Operating Base and 11th Naval Dist., San Diego, Calif., Sept. 1937-Jan. 1942, Navy Yard, Portsmouth, N.H., Feb.-Apr. 1942; superintending civil engr., Area IV, since Apr. 1942. Decorations: Legion of Merit, Mexican, Victory, Navy Expeditionary, Haitian, Defense Legion of Merit and Am. Area service medals (U.S.), Order of Honor and Merit (Haiti). Mem. American Society Civil Engineers, Society American Mil. Engrs. Home: Florence, S.C. Address: care Bureau of Naval Personnel, Navy Dept., Washington, D.C. Died Dec. 14, 1947.

MATHEWS, JOSEPH HOWARD, chemist; b. Auroraville, Wis., Oct. 15, 1881; s. Joseph and Lydia Tibbets (Cate) M.; B.S., U. of Wis., 1903, A.M., 1905; A.M., Harvard, 1906, Ph.D., 1908; m. Ella Barbara Gilfillan, June 26, 1909; children—Marion Zoe, Jean Barbara. Assistant in chemistry, U. of Wis., 1905; instr. chemistry, Case Sch. of Applied Science, Cleveland, O., 1906-07; asst. prof. chemistry, U. of Wis., 1911, asso. prof., 1917, prof., 1919-52, also chmn. of dept. and dir. course in chemistry. Commd. capt. Ordnance Dept., U.S. Army, July 10, 1917; maj., Jan. 15, 1918; hon. disch., Dec. 16, 1918; went to France as spl. investigator of problems connected with gas warfare, Sept. 1917; returned to U.S., Jan. 1918, and placed in charge offensive gas and research br. of trench warfare sect. Engring. Div. of Ordnance Dept. Criminal identification expert. Fellow A.A.A.S.; mem. Am. Chem. Soc., Sigma Xi, Alpha Chi Sigma, Phi Lambda Upsilon, Phi Kappa Phi. Presbyterian. Clubs: University, Rotary, Professional, Scabbard and Blade (Madison); Black Hawk Country. Co-author: Experimental Physical Chemistry, 1929; author: Firearms Identification, 2 vols., 1962, reprint, with 3 vols., 1973. over 60 papers on scientific subjects. Home: Madison WI Died Apr. 15, 1970; buried Madison WI

MATHEWS, WILLIAM RANKIN, editor, publisher; b. Lexington, Ky., Oct. 15, 1893; s. Robert Trot and Clara (Murry) M.; A.B., U. of Ill., 1917; LL.D., Butler University, 1957, U. Ariz., 1963; m. Betty Boyers, Apr. 12, 1919; children—Elizabeth Bovers (dec.), William Rankin, Charles Dawes and Ann Caro. Advertising salesman for San Francisco Chronicle, 1919-20; business mgr., Santa Barbara Morning Press, 1920-24; general mgr. Arizona Daily Star, Tucson, 1924-30, editor and publisher, 1930-69; dir. El Paso br. Fed. Res. Bank Dallas, 1958-64. Served as 2d lt. USMC, May 1917-July 1918, capt., July 1918-July 1919; wounded at Blanc Mont, France, Oct. 4, 1918; awarded Croix de Guerre with Palm and cited for capture of enemy machine guns and trench mortars and 75 prisoners nr. Vierzy, France, July 18, 1918. Received honorable mention for distinguished editorial writing by Pulitzer prize com., 1934. Mem. adv. com. Columbia Sch. of Journalism (Pulitzer Prize com.), 1944-56. Democratic presidential elector, 1932. Spl. adviser to Sec. of Defense, 1948; mem. bd. of regents U. of Ariz. and State Colls., 1950-61. Dir. Am. Soc. Newspaper Editors, 1950-52. Mason. Clubs: Old Pueblo, Tucson Country (Tucson). Editor: Europe Will Recover, 1947; The White Man's Future in the Orient, 1949; The Marshall Plan Pays Off, 1951; Are We Being Shouted into an Unwanted War?, 1951; Ten Days Behind the Iron Curtain, 1954. Home: Tucson AZ Died Oct. 27, 1969; buried Frankfort Cemetery, Frankfort KY

MATILE, LEON ALBERT brig. gen. U.S.A.; b. Neuchatel, Switzerland, Sept. 28, 1844; s. George A. and Marie Eugenia (Schaffter) M.; ed. pvt. schs., Princeton, N.J., and Phila.; m. Katherine Agnes Fletcher, Apr. 10, 1875. Entered mil. service in U.S.A., Dec. 3, 1863, and continuously in same until retired, Aug. 17, 1903; wounded in battle of Atlanta, Aug. 1864; participated in campaigns against Comanche, Kiowa, Cheyenne and Sioux Indians; served in Alaska and the Philippines; recommended for brevet in battle against insurcents, Manila, Feb. 4, 5, 1899; in command of 14th U.S. Inf. at battle of Zapota River, June 13,1899; promoted brig. gen. and retired, Aug. 17, 1919. Died Apr. 10, 1938.

MATSON, COURTLAND CUSHING congressman; b. Brookville, Ind., Apr. 25, 1841; s. John Allen and Margaretta Melvina (Woelpper) M.; A.B., Asbury (now DePauw) U., 1862 (enlisted in Union Army, Apr. 14, 1861; at close of jr. yr., and in 1870 by vote of trustees was graduated as of class of 1862); m. Mary Nelson Farrow, Dec. 12, 1871 (died 1893). Pvt. to lt. Co. K, 16th Ind. Vols., Apr. 1861-June 1862; apptd. post adj. Camp Dick Thompson, Terre Haute, Ind., and helped to organize 3 regts.; apptd. lt. col. 71st Ind. Vols. (later 6th Ind. Cav.), Dec. 1862, after all the field officers of the regt. had been killed at battle of Richmond, Ky., and served in that position until near close of war, when was promoted col. 5th and 6th Ind. Cav., consolidated. Pros. atty. various courts in Ind., 1868, 70, 72; mem. 47th to 50th Congresses (1881-89); Dem. candidate for gov. of Ind., 1888; mem. State Bd. of Tax Commrs. of Ind., 1909-13. Methodist. Home: Greencastle, Ind. Died Sept. 4, 1915.

MATSON, DONALD DARROW, neurosurgeon; b. Ft. Hamilton, N.Y., Nov. 28, 1913; s. Joseph and Kathleen (Connor) M.; A.B., Cornell U., 1935; M.D., Harvard, 1939; m. Dorothy Jean Everett, Sept. 11, 1943;children—Martha Jo, Donald Everett, James Edward, Barbara Baker. Intern Children's Med. Center, Peter Bent Brigham Hosp., Boston, 1939-43, neurosurgeon, 1948-69; resident Duke U. Hosp., 1947-48; pvt. practice, Boston, 1948-69; clin. prof. surgery Harvard Med. Sch., 1961-69; cons. neurosurgery VA Hosp., West Roxbury, Mass., Mass. Hosp. Sch.; mem. spl. med. adv. bd. VA, 1963-69. Served from lt. to maj. M.C., AUS, 1943-46. Decorated Bronze Star medal. Diplomate Am. Bd. Neurol. Surgery (chmn. 1965). Fellow A.C.S.; mem. Nat. Inst. Neurol. Diseases and Blindness (neurology postgrad. tng. com.), A.M.A., Soc. Neurol. Surgeons, Harvey Cushing Soc., Acad. Neurosurgery, Soc. U. Surgeons, Halstead Soc., A.A.A.S., Am. Neurol. Soc., New Eng., Boston surg. socs., Scandinavian Neurosurg. Soc., Am. Surg. Assn. Author: Treatment of Acute Cranio Cerebral Injuries Due to Missiles, 1948; Treatment of Acute Spinal Injuries Due to Missiles, 1948; (with Franc D. Ingraham) Neurosurgery in Infancy and Childhood, 1953; also numerous articles in med. publs. Adv. bd. Medical Specialties. Home: Chestnut Hill MA Died May 1969.

MATSON, RALPH CHARLES physican, surgeon; b. Brookville, Pa., Jan. 21, 1880; s. John and Minerva (Brady) M.; M.D., U. of Ore., 1902; grad. student, St. Mary's Hosp., London, Cambridge, U., 1906, U. of Vienna, 1910, 23, 25, Acad. of Medicine, Dusseldorf, Germany, U. of Berlin, 1912, U. of Paris, 1924; m. Adeline Ferrari, Aug. 5, 1907 (divorced Oct. 1922); 1 adopted, dau., Daphne; m. 2d, Chiara De Bona, Nov. 25, 1923. Physician and surgeon, Portland, Ore., since 1902; mem. firm Drs. Matson & Bisaillon; asso. clin., prof. of surgery and medicine, U. of Ore. Med. Sch., since 1935, mem. exec. faculty since 1940, chief surgeon, Univ. State Tuberculosis Hosp., Portland, Ore.; dir. dept. of thoracic surgery, Portland Open Air Sanatorium, Milwaukie, Ore.; mem. visiting staff Good Samaritan Hosp.; chest consultant Multnomah County Hosp., and U.S. Pub. Health Service; attending specialist chest surg. center, Vets. Adminstrn. Hosp.; co-dir. tuberculosis clinic, med. dept., U. of Ore.; consulting thoracic surgeon Doernbecher Memorial Hosp. for Children; med. and surg. dir. Portland Open Air Sanatorium (all Portland); mem. med. advisory bd. Nat. Jewish Hosp., Denver, 1941; hon. 1st lt. Harvard U. Surg. Unit with B.E.F., 1916; served as capt. Royal Army Med. Corps, 1917; maj. Med. Corps, U.S. Army, chief med. examiner and tuberculosis specialist, Camp Lewis, 1917-19, chief of med. staff Gen. Hosp. No. 21, Denver, 1919-20; now lt. col. Med. Res. Corps. Del. to Internat. Union Against Tuberculosis, Washington, D.C., 1908, Rome, 1912, Lausanne, Switzerland, 1923; vice chmn. thoracic sect., 7th cruise congress, Pan-American Surg. Assn., 1938. Diplomate Am. Bd. Internal de Chirurgiens (Geneva), Am. Coll. Chest Physicians (pres. 1939); mem. Am. Assn. Thoracic Surgeons, Am. Med. Assn. of Vienna (life mem.) and Berlin, Am. Climatol. and Clin. Assn., Am. Trudeau Society, National Tuberculosis Association (former v.p.), Pan-Pacific Surg. Assn. (former v.p.), A.M.A., Portland City and County Med. Soc., Pacific Interurban Clin. Club, Pacific Coast Surg. Soc., Internat. Artificial Pneumothorax Assn. (exec. com.), Ore. State Tuberculosis Assn., Alpha Kappa Kappa, Alpha Omega Alpha; hon. mem. Minneapolis Surg. Soc.; hon. mem. staff Lymanhurst Sch. for Tuberculosis Children, Minneapolis. Hollywood (Calif.) Academy Medicine, Sociedad Mexicano de Estudios Sobre Tuberculosis, Mex. Clubs: Arlington (Portland); Highlands Racquet (Oswego, Ore.). Contbr. of sects of chapters to books: "Surgical Treatment of Pulmonary Tuberculosis" in Cyclopedia of Medicine, 1934; "Extrapleural Pneumolysis" in Surgical Diseases of the Chest by Graham, Ballon and Singer, 1935; "Artificial Pneumothorax" in Pulmonary Tuberculosis by Goldberg, 1935; "Operative Collapse ú Therapy in Treatment of Pulmonary Tuberculosis" in Internat. Clinics, Vol. II, 1934; etc. contbr. of numerous articles on the med. and surg. aspects of tuberculosis, in English, French, Spanish and German. Editor in chief Diseases of the Chest; mem. editorial bd. Western Jour. Surgery, Obstetrics and Gynecology, Jour. Internat. Coll. Surgeons. Home: 2960 N.W. Cumberland Rd. Office: Stevens Bldg., Portland, Ore. Died Oct. 26, 1945.

MATTHEWS, BURROWS newspaper editor; b. Buffalo, N.Y., Jan. 27, 1893; s. George Edward and Mary Elizabeth (Burrows) M.; grad. St. Lukes Sch., Wayne, Pa., 1911; m. Edith Peter, June 1, 1916 (died Mar. 6, 1947); one son, James Newson; married 2d, Anne M. McIlhenney. Reporter for the Buffalo Express, 1911, legislative corr. at Albany, N.Y., 1914-15, city editor, 1916-17, Sunday editor, 1919-23, mng. editor, 1923-26, pres. and gen. mgr., 1926; pres. and editor Buffalo Courier-Express, merger of Express and Courier, 1926-30, v.p. and editor, 1930—. Served as 1st lt., later capt. inf., U.S. Army, 1917-18; entered the service Aug. 1943 as major; promoted lt. col., 1944; attached Pub. Relations Div. of SHAEF; spl. adv. Gen. Ridgway, Far East Command, 1952, later at SHAPE. Awarded Bronze Star. Pres. N.Y. State Publs. Assn., 1939; mem. Am. Soc. Newspaper Editors, Sigma Delta Chi, dir. Buffalo Soc. of Natural Scis., Republican. Presbyn. Clubs: Saturn, Country, Pack, Pytonga Fish and Game. Home: 224 Summer St. Address: 787 Main St., Buffalo, N.Y. Died Dec. 30, 1954; buried Forest Lawn Cemetery, Eden, N.Y.

MATTHEWS, EDMUND ORVILLE rear adm. U.S.N.; b. Baltimore, Oct. 24, 1836; s. John and Mary Righter (Levering) M.; apptd. to U.S. Naval Acad. from Mo., 1851, grad. 1855; m. Hattie R. Hammond, of Newport, R.I., May 20, 1878. Promoted passed midshipman, Apr. 15, 1858; advanced through grades to rear adm., June 19, 1897. Served on Potomac and Saratoga, Home Squadron, 1855-58; Macedonian, Mediterranean Squadron, 1858-60; Naval Acad., 1860-61; Wabash, May-Nov. 1861; capture of forts at Hatteras Inlet; Naval Acad., 1861-64; S. Atlantic Blockading Squadron, 1864-65; comd. naval light arty. at Honey Hill. S.C., Nov. 30, 1864; participated in battle at Fullifinny Cross Roads, Dec. 1864; on staff of Admiral Dahlgren, Jan.-July 1865; como. Savannah, Aug.-Nov. 1865; Naval Acad., 1865-69; head of torpedo corps, 1869-73; como. Ashuelot, 1874-77; insp. ordnance, Navy Yard, New York, 1878-81; comd. Powhatan, 1881-83, training-ship New Hampshire, 1883-84; mem. of Gun Foundry Bd., 1883-85; comd. Brooklyn, 1885-87; capt. of yard, Navy Yard, Boston, 1887-90; comd. receiving-ship W 1891-94; chief Bur. of Yards and Docks, 1894-98; pres. Examining and Retiring Bds., 1898-99; retired, Oct. 24, 1898. Home: Cambridge, Mass. Died 1911.

MATTHEWS, FRANCIS PATRICK govt. ofcl.; b. Albion, Neb., Mar. 15, 1887; s. Patrick Henry and Mary Ann (Sullivan) M.; A.B., Creighton U., 1910, A.M., 1911, LL.B., 1913; LL.D., Marquette U., 1940, John Marshal Coll., Jersey City, N.J., 1943; LL.D., Villanova Coll., Phila., 1950, Loyola U., 1950, Holy Cross Coll., Creighton U., U. Notre Dame, 1951; m. Mary Claire Hughes, Nov. 24, 1914; children-Mary Claire (Mrs. John E. Dwyer), Kathleen (Mrs. J. R. O'Connell), Francis P. Jr., Patricia (Mrs. William Rosser), Marian (Mrs. D. Howard), Marguerite (Mrs. Robert G. Schneider). Admitted to Nebraska bar, 1913; consul Reconstruction Finance Corp. Nebraska and Wyo., 1933-49; chmn. bd. and dir. Securities Acceptance Corp.; pres. 1st Fed. Savings and Loan Association of Omaha; director radio station WOW, Inc.; director and member executive committee Northwestern Bell Telephone Co. Chmn. Douglas Co., Neb., Dem. Central Com., 1932-36; dir. for Dept. of Finance, U.S. Chamber of Commerce, 1941-51, chmn. com. on Socialism and Communism; mem. bd. dirs. Omaha Chamber of Commerce, 1937-41; pres., 1938-39; mem. citizens com. Community Chests of America; mem. bd. govs. Omaha Community Chest, 1930-40, pres. 1938-39, chmn. 1936 campaign; mem. bd. dirs. Father Flanagan's Boys Home, Boys Town, Neb., mem. bd. regents Creighton U.; dir. Duchesne Coll. and Convent of the Sacred Heart; past chmn. Met. Utilities Dist. Omaha, Omaha Public Library Board.; vice president National War Fund (mem. bd. and exec. com.); mem. exec. com., Nat. Conf. of Catholic Charities, 1931-34; v. chmn. United Defense Fund; v.p. U.S.O. (mem. bd., exec. com.

and incorporator); chmn. exec. com., Nat. Catholic Community Service; member board American Overseas Aid, Sept. 1948; member board, sec., War Prisoners Aid; mem. Persident's Com. on Civil Rights, 1947; secretary of Navy, May 1949-July 1951; served as U.S. ambassador to Ireland, 1951-53. Awarded Medal for Merit, 1946. Decorated Knight, Order of St. Gregory, 1924. Knight Comdr., 1938, Knight Comdr. with Grand Cross, 1942; Knight Comdr. with Grand Cross of Knights of Holy Sepulchre, 1944; designed Secret Papal Chamberlain with Cape and Sword by Pope Pius XII, 1944; awarded Catholic Action Medal, St. Bonaventure's Coll., N.Y., 1943. Spl rep. of Cath. Adminstr. Bd. of Bishops to visit England, Ireland and Scotland, 1943, various countries in Europe and Middle East, 1944, in connection with welfare services for U.S. armed forces and relief for peoples of liberated areas. Member Am., Neb., Omaha and Fed. Commns. bar assns., Irish-Am. Hist. Soc. of N.Y. Nebraska State Historical Soc. Democrat. Roman Catholic. K.C. (Neb. state dep. 1923-24; supreme board directors, 1924-33; supreme Knight 1939-45). Clubs: Rotary, Omaha Athletic; Metropolitan of N.Y. National Press, hon. Army-Navy (Washington). Home: 3920 Dewey Av. Office: Omaha Nat. Bank Bldg., Omaha, Neb. Died Oct. 18, 1952; buried Calvary Cemetery, Omaha, Neb.

MATTHEWS, HUGH officer U.S. Marine Corps; b. Loudon County, Tenn., June 18, 1876; s. Madison Lafayette and Mary (McConnell) M.; ed. Maryville (Tenn.) Coll.; m. Mary O'Connor Higgins, Sept. 10, 1919. Commd. 2d lt. U.S. Marine Corps, Mar. 3, 1900; promoted through grades to brig. gen., Dec. 26, 1920; major general April 1942, by Congressional enactment. Served in China, Philippine Islands, Panama, Cuba, Santo Domingo; overseas with 2d Div., World War. Head of quartermaster's dept., U.S. Marine Corps, 1929-37; retired. Awarded D.S.M., Army; Navy Cross; Chevalier Legion of Honor; Croix de Guerre. Mem. Mil. Order Carabao, Mil. Order World War, Am. Legion, Nat. Sojourners Mason. Club: Army and Navy. Home: Loudon, Tenn. Died Apr. 9, 1943.

MATTHEWS, WASHINGTON physician, maj. U.S.A., retired, Sept. 25, 1895; b. Killiney, nr. Dublin, Ireland, July 17, 1843; s. Dr. Nicholas Blaney and Anna (Burke) M.; came to U.S. in infancy; lived in Wis., later in Iowa; ed. in common schools; grad. Univ. of Iowa (med. dept.), 1864 (LL.D., 1888). Acting asst. surgeon U.S.A., 1864-65; re-entered mil. service, 1865; asst. surgeon, U.S.A., 1P68; capt. and asst. surgeon, 1871; maj. and surgeon, 1889; retired from active service on account of disability contracted in line of duty. Was on duty at Army Med. Museum, 1884-99. Has made notable investigations in ethnology and philology of the Navajo Indians and other native American races. Author: Navajo Silversmiths, 1883; Navajo Weavers, 1884; The Mountain Chant, a Navajo Ceremony, 1887; Navajo Lebends, 1897; The Night Chant, a Navajo Ceremony, 1902. Home: Washington, D.C. Died 1905.

MATTHIAS, EDWARD SHILOH judge; b. Gilboa, O., Apr. 6, 1873; s. Albert C. and Eleanor P. (Harris) M.; A.B., Ohio Northern Univ., 1893, hon. LL.D., 1925; LL.D., Miami University, 1952; married Mary F. Crouch, April 23, 1898; children-Edward D., John Marshall, Mrs. Mary Ellen Dawson, Mrs. Alice Helen Jacoby, Mrs. Florence Howe Merkel. Admitted to Ohio bar, and began practice in Van Wert, O., 1895; city solicitor, Van Wert, 1896-1900; judge Court of Common Pleas 3d Judiciary Dist. of Ohio, 1904-14; judge Supreme Court of Ohio since Jan. 1, 1915. Served as capt. Co. D, 2d Ohio Vol. Inf., Spanish-Am. War, Apr. 23, 1898-Feb. 10, 1899. Dept. comdr., Dept. of Ohio, United Spanish War Vets., 1927-28, comdr. in chief, 1930-31. Mem. bd. of trustees Ohio Northern U. Mem. Am. and Ohio bar assns., Delta Theta Phi. Clubs: University, Optimist. Republican. Presbyterian. Mason (32ff). Home: 2135 Iuka Av., Columbus, O. Died Nov. 2, 1953.

MATTILL, HENRY ALBRIGHT biochemist; b. Glasgow, Mo., Nov. 28, 1883; s. Henry and Emma (Fryhofer) M.; A.B., Adelbert Coll. (Western Reserve U.), 1906; A.M., 1907; Ph.D., U. of Ill., 1910; S.Dc. (honorary), Western Reserve Univ., 1952; m. Helen Isham, Dec. 31, 1912; 1 son, John Isham. Asst. in chemistry, U. of Ill., 1906-08, fellow in biochem., 1908-10; assistant professor physiol. and physiol. chemistry, U. of Utah, 1910-11, asso. prof., 1911-12, prof., 1912-15; asst. prof. nutrition, U. of Calif., 1915-18; prof. biochemistry, U. of Rochester, 1919-27; prof. of biochemistry and head of department, University of Iowa, since 1927. Captain and maj. Sanitary Corps, Div. of Food and Nutrition, Army U.S. and A.E.F., 1918-19. Recipient Iowa medal Am. Chemical Society, 1950. Fellow A.A.A.S.; mem. Am. Soc. of Biol. Chemists (sec., 1933-38; council 1938-44; edit. com., 1944—; v.p. 1951, pres. 1952), Am. Physiological Soc. (edit. bd. Physiol. Rev. since 1948), Soc. Exptl. Biology and Medicine, Am. Chem. Soc., Am. Inst. of Nutrition, A.A.U.P., Iowa Acad. Sci., Phi Beta Kappa, Sigma Xi, Gamma Alpha, Phi Lambda Upsilon, Alpha Chi Sigma, Alpha Omega Alpha. Unitarian. Home: 358 Lexington Av., Iowa City, Ia. Died Mar. 30, 1953.

MATTOCKS, CHARLES PORTER soldier; b. Danville, Vt.,Oct. 11, 1840; s. Henry and Martha (Porter) M.; A.B., Bowdoin, 1862; A.M., 1865; served in 17th Me. Inf. as lt., Aug. 2,1862; capt., Dec. 4, 1862; maj., Dec. 22, 1863; col., May 15, 1865; comd. 1st U.S. Sharpshooters in winter and spring o 186 vices during campaign ending with surrender of Gen. R. E. Lee; brig. gen. vols., Mar. 13, 1865, "for faithful and meritorious services"; awarded Congressional Medal of Honor, May 29, 1899, "for extraordinary gallantry at Little Sailor's Creek, Va." Apr. 6, 1865, LL.B., Harvard, 1867, and from then in practice at Portland; m. June 27, 1871. County atty. Cumberland Co., Me., 1869-72; mem. Me. Ho. of Rep., 1880-84; mem. exec. commn. for Me., Chicago Expn., 1893; probate judge 1900-07. Republican. Brig. gen. vols., June 8-Oct. 31, 1898. Spanish-Am. War. Home: Portland, Me. Died 1910.

MATZ, PHILIP BENJANIN pathologist; b. Baltimore, Md., Aug. 25, 1885; s. Oscar and Freda (Kaplan) M.; Litt.B., Mather Coll., Kansas City, Kan., 1911; M.D., Coll. of Medicine, L.I. Coll. Hosp., 1908; m. Eleanor Crampton, Nov. 20, 1913. Has specialized in pathology and clin. investigation; served as chief of lab. service, Base Hosp., Camp Travis, Tex., World War; commissioned as surgeon (Res.) U.S.P.H.S., 1920, and served as chief lab. service various hosps. of the U.S. Pub. Health Service; chief of Med. Research Subdivision. Veterans' Administrn., 1925-. Fellow Am. Soc. Clin. Pathologists, Am. Coll. Physicians. Home: Washington, D.C. Died June 25, 1938.

MAUBORGNE, JOSEPH OSWALD, army officer; b. New York, N.Y., Feb. 26, 1881; s. Eugene Charles and Catherine Elizabeth (McLaughlin) M.; A.B., Coll. of St. Francis Xavier, N.Y. City, 1901; art student Art Students League, N.Y. City, 1901-03, Chicago Art Inst., 1922-23, Corcoran Art Gallery, Washington, D.C., 1923-26; student Army Signal Sch., 1909-10, Army War Coll., 1931-32; m. Katharine Hale Poore, Dec. 3, 1907; children—Joseph Oswald, Benjamin Poore. Commd. 2d lt. inf., U.S. Army, 1903, and advanced through the grades to maj. gen., 1937; with Signal Corps from 1916, chief signal officer, 1937-41, retired; in P.I., France and Panama. Radio pioneer; inventor of numerous radio devices; tech. adviser to U.S. delegations at Inter-Allied Radio Conf., 1919, Internat. Conf. on Elec. Communications, Paris, 1921, Pan-American Com. Conf., Mexico City, 1924, International Telegraphic Conference, Paris, 1925, Washington Radio Conference, 1927; member of the Defense Communications Board, Sept. 1940-Sept. 1941. Portrait painter and etcher, exhibited at Washington, D.C., San Francisco, Dayton, O.; portraits in collections at U.S. Mil. Acad. and in pvt. collections of Mrs. Calvin Coolidge and others. Sci. violin builder; two prizes violin making Internat. Competition, Hague, Holland, 1949. Member Institute Radio Engineers, 1914-25. Awarded D.S.M. (U.S.); Marconi Memorial medal of service by Vet. Wireless Oprs. Assn., 1941. Catholic. Club: Army and Navy (D.C.). Author: Practical Uses of the Wavemeter in Wireless Telegraphy, 1914. Contbr. articles on radio to tech. mags.; author of brochures (U.S. Army) on Cryptanalysis. Home: Little Silver NJ Died June 5, 1971.

MAULDIN, FRANK GRATIN army officer; b. in Pickens County, S.C., Aug. 16, 1864; s. Joab and Deborah Reed (Hollingsworth) M.; grad. U.S. Military Acad., 1890; LL.B., Columbian (now George Washington) U., 1893; grad. Sch. of Submarine Defense, Ft. Totten, N.Y.,1904; unmarried. Commd. additional 2d lt. 3d Arty., June 12, 1890; promoted through grades to brig. gen. N.A., Aug. 5, 1917. Instr. law and history, U.S. Mil. Acad., 4 yrs.; served under Gen. Shafter in Cuba, 1898; comdr. of one of U.S.A. mine planters 4 yrs.; with Insp. General's Dept., 1910-13; later comdr. the Presidio, Calif., and Recruit Depot, Ft. Slocum, N.Y.; assigned as comdr. 59th Field Arty. Brigade, Camp Cody, N.M., Sept. 1917. Died Jan. 25, 1940.

MAURY, DABNEY HERNDON author, soldier; b. Fredericksburg, Va., May 21, 1822; grad. Univ. of Va.; and at West Point, 1846; entered Mounted Rifles, June 1846; served in Mexico; marched from Point Isabel to Monterey, thence to Vera Cruz; seriously wounded and bvtd. for gallantry at Cerro Gordo; became instr. in belles lettres at West Point; later regimental adjutant and supt. calvary instruction, Carlisle Barracks; in 1861 was capt. and adj. gen., Dept. of New Mexico, but resigned upon secession of Va. Was col. Confederate army; promoted to brig. gen. for conduct in Elkhorn campaign; held Grant in check at Grenada during Van Dorn's raid, 1864. With Stephenson and Stephen D. Lee defeated Sherman's army before Vicksburg, Dec. 28, 1864. later in command of Dept. of Tenn., then of Dept. of Gulf until May 24, when he was paroled prisoner of war with his forces. U.S. minister to United States of Colombia, 1885-89. Author: System of Tactics in Single Rank (published 1859 and now universally used); Recollections of a Virginian; History of Virginia. Home: Richmond, Va. Died 1900.

MAUS, L(OUIS) MERVIN army officer; b. Burnt Mills, Montgomery Co., Md., May 8, 1851; s. Isaac Rhodes and Mary Malvina (Greer) M.; St. John's College Annapolis, Md.; post graduate, Pasteur Inst., Paris, and medical clinics in Europe, 1890-91; M.D., U. of Maryland, 1874; m. Anna Page Russell, Jan. 5, 1876; children-Mary Thruston (wife of E. A. Fry, U.S.A.), Anna Louise (wife of L. Halstead, U.S.A.). Commd. 1st lt. asst. surgeon U.S.A., Nov. 10, 1874; advanced through grades to col. asst. surgeon gen., May 10, 1907. Served in South, 1874-77; on the plains, 1877-93; participated in several Indian campaigns and was recommended for medal of honor for exceptional bravery, Nov. 5, 1877; chief surgeon 7th Army Corps in Cuba during Spanish-Am. War; 1st commr. pub. health of P.I. under William H. Taft, then gov.; made changes in sanitary conditons reducing mortality of native population from 88 per 1000 to 32 per 1000; eradicated bubonic plague from Manila in 1902; in charge Asiatic cholera epidemic and by vaccination practically eliminated smallpox among the natives; chief surgeon, Central Division, 1911; department surgeon, Department of the East, 1912-15; retired from active service, May 8, 1915; Secretary Kentucky Tuburculosis Commn., Sept. 8, 1915-Jan. 1, 1917; placed on active duty, June 18, 1917, and assigned to the Council of Nat. Defense; dept. surgeon, Western Dept., San Francisco, Calif., 1917-19. Awarded D.S.M. Mason: Author: Army Officer on Leave in Japan, 1911; Glengyle Manor, 1937. Died Aug. 3, 1939.

MAUS, MARION PERRY brig. gen.; b. Burnt Mills, Montgomery Co., Md., Aug. 25, 1850; grad. U.S. Mil. Acad., 1874; m. Lindsay Poor, June 1899. Second lt. 1st Inf., June 17, 1874; promoted through grades to col. 20th Inf., Jan. 24, 1904; brig. gen. U.S.A., June 17, 1909. Had many yrs. service in campaigns against the Sioux, Apache, Cheyenne, Nez Perces, and other Indians; in action with Sioux Indians in the Black Hills, Dak., with the Nez Perces at Bear Paw Mountains, Mont..; with Apaches in Ariz., and Old Mexico, in the Sierra Madre Mountains; in the campaign at Pien Ridge against the Sioux, 1890, awarded Congressional Medal of Honor, Nov. 27, 1894, "for most distinguished gallantry in action against hostile Apache Indians in Sierra Madre Mountains, N.M., Jan. 11, 1886." Went with Gen. Miles to observe the Graeco-Turkish War, to represent the govt. at the Queen's Jubilee in England, 1897; and also to witness the maneuvers of Russia, Germany and France; served throughout Spanish-Am. War as insp. gen.; present during last days of siege and during negotiations for surrender of Santiago, Cuba; accompanied expdn. to Puerto Rico, remaining there until signing of protocol for peace; later on duty as insp. gen. Dept. of Calif. and the Columbia; a.d.c. on staff lt. gen. comdg. the army July 1, 1901-03; served in P.I., 1903-06; on duty at San Francisco during earthquake, Apr. 1906; comd. Presidio of Monterey, Pacific Div., Dept. of Calif., etc., 1906-09; comdg. Dept. of the Columbia, 1909; retired. Died Feb. 9, 1930.

MAXCY, KENNETH FULLER M.D., educator; b. Saco, Me., July 27, 1889; s. Frederick Edward and Estelle Abbey (Gilpatric) M.; A.B., George Washington U., 1911; M.D., Johns Hopkins, 1915, D.P.H., 1921; m. Gertrud Helene McClellan, June 22, 1918; children-Kenneth Fuller, Frederic Reynolds, Selina Gilpatric. Resident house officer Johns Hopkins Hosp., 1915-16, asst. resident pediatrician, 1916-17; asst. in medicine Henry Ford Hosp., Detroit, 1917; fellow Johns Hopkins Sch. Hygiene Detroit, 1917; fellow Johns Hopkins Sch. Hygiene and Pub. Health, 1919-21; asst. surgeon, passed asst. surgeon and surgeon USPHS, 1921-29; prof. bateriology and preventive medicine U. Va., 1929-36; prof. pub. health and preventive medicine U. Minn., 1936-37; prof. bacteriology Sch. Hygiene and Pub. Health, Johns Hopkins, 1937-38, prof. epidemiology 1938-54, emeritus, 1954; cons. internat. Health Div., Rockefeller Found., 1937-40, 42-45, 48-52; cons. sec. of war Army Epidemiological Bd., 1941-49; mem. Nat. Adv. Health Council, 1942-46; cons. Research and Devel. Bd. Nat. Mil. Establishment since 1946; mem. exec. com. Adv. Bd. on Health Services, A.R.C., 1945-48; mem. Med. Adv. Com., Nat. Found. for Infantile Paralysis 1940-48; trustee Internat. Polio Congress; chmn. com. on research and standards Am. Pub. Health Assn., 1939-46. Served as lt. M.C., U.S. Army, 1917, capt., 1918. Fellow Am. Pub. Health Assn. (Sedgwick Meml. medalist 1952); mem. Nat. Acad. Scis., Am. Soc. Epidomiologists, Assn. Am. Physicians, Pithotomy Club, Raven Soc., Phi Beta Kappa, Sigma Xi, Alpha Omega Alpha, Delta Omega, Theta Delta Chi, Phi Beta Pi. Epis-Rosenaus' Preventive Medicine and Hygiene, 8th warded U.S.A. Typhus Commn. medal, 1946. Editor; Papers of Wade Hampton Frost. 1941; Rosenaus' Preventive Medicine and Hygiene, 8th edit., 1956. Home: Park-Lynn Apts. 4 Upland Rd., Balt. 21210. Died Dec. 12, 1966; buried Arlington Nat. Cemetery.

MAXEY, SAMUEL BELL senator, army officer; b. Tompkinsville, Ky., Mar. 30, 1825; s. Rice and Mrs. (Bell) M., grad. U.S. Mil. Acad., 1846; m. Marilda Cassa Denton, July 19, 1853. Commd. 2d lt. 7th Inf., U.S. Army, 1846; brevetted 1st lt. after serving at battles of Contreras and Churubusco; served in capture of Mexico City, resigned, 1849; admitted to Ky. bar, 1850; clk. of county and circuit cts., also master chancery for Ky., 1852-56; moved to Paris, Tex., 1857; dist. atty. Lamar County, Tex., 1858-59; served as col., raised 9th Regt., Tex. Inf., Confederate Army; commd. brig. gen., 1862, maj. gen., 1864; commander Indian Territory Mil. Dist., also supt. Indian affairs, 1863-65; served until surrender of Trans-Miss. Dept., May 1865; declined appointment as judge 8th Dist. Tex., 1873; mem. U.S. Senate from Tex., 1875-1887. Died Eureka Springs, Ark., Aug. 16, 1895; buried Evergreen Cemetery, Paris, Tex.

MAXWELL, RUSSELL LAMONTE, army officer (retired), executive American Machine & Foundry Co.; b. Oakdale, Ill., Dec. 28, 1890; s. Thomas Samuel and Margaret Alzette (Hildebrand) M.; B.S., U.S. Mil. Acad., 1912; grad. Command and Gen. Staff Sch., 1924; Army Indsl. Coll., 1925, Army War Coll., 1934; Coast Arty. Sch.; m. Katherine Winans, Nov. 3, 1914; children—William Ragland, Robert Edwin, James Winans. Commd. 2d lt. F.A., 1912; served overseas in Army of Occupation, Germany, World War I; comd. ordnance depot near Coblenz, 1918; transferred to Ordnance Dept., Washington, D.C., July 1, 1920; detailed to G.H.Q. Air Force as ordnance officer, 1935; returned to Washington, 1939, to serve on staff of asst. sec. of war; apptd. by President Roosevelt lt. col., adminstr. of export control, July 2, 1940; promoted brig. gen. (temp.), Feb. 1941, major gen., Feb. 1942; in charge of U.S. Mil. Mission in Cairo, 1941; comdr. U.S. forces in Middle East, 1942; assistant chief of staff, G-4, September 1943-46; retired from Army. Elected v.p. Am. Machine & Foundry Co., Aug. 1946, v.p. in charge of personnel and public relations, dir., 1946-56. Episcopalian. Mason. Clubs: University (New York); Army and Navy, Army and Navy Country (Washington); Chevy Chase (Md.). Editor Army Ordnance (mag.), 1925-26. Home: Washington DC Died Nov. 24, 1968; buried U.S. Mil. Acad., West Point NY

MAXWELL, WILLIAM JOHN, naval officer; b. Washington, D.C., Apr. 3, 1859; s. Med. Dir. Charles D., U.S.N., and Miriam Kay (Clement) M.; grad. U.S. Naval Acad., 1880. Ensign jr. grade, 1882; ensign, June 26, 1884; lt. jr. grade, July 4, 1893; lt., Apr. 6, 1897; lt. comdr., Dec. 2, 1902; comdr., July 1, 1907; capt., Mar. 4, 1911. Served on Columbia, Spanish-Am. War, 1898; Philippine campaign, 1900-01-02; on Isle de Cuba and Solace, 1903; insp. engring. material Eastern N.Y., and N.J. districts, 1903-05; engr. officer Maryland, 1905-06; insp. ordnance Watervliet Arsenal, 1906-07; comd. Marietta, 1907-09; equipment officer Navy Yard, N.Y., 1909; duty Gen. Bd., Navy Dept., 1909-11; comd. Mississippi, 1911-12, Wisconsin, 1912, Florida, 1912-13; at Naval War Coll., 1913-14; gov. Island of Guam and comdr. naval sta. at that place, 1914-16; at Naval War Coll., 1916-17; retired by reason of physical disability, Aug. 9, 1917. Spl. duty 5th, 9th and 10th Naval dists., 1918. Mem. Am. Soc. Internat. Law, Am. Soc. Naval Engrs., Soc. Carabao, Soc. Foreign Wars, Aztec Club, Am. Legion. Clubs: Metropolitan, Army and Navy, Chevy Chase, University (Washington); Catholic, New York Yacht, Seawanhaka Yacht, St. Nicholas, Army and Navy of America (New York). Address: Care Hamilton Trust Co., 189 Montague St., Brooklyn, N.Y.

MAY, EDWARD naval officer; b. Leicester, Mass., Jan. 20, 1838; s. Samuel and Sarah (Russell) M.; ed. pvt. schs. and Leicester Acad.; m. Mary Mignot Blodgett, Oct. 4, 1871 (died 1901). Apptd. asst. pay master, U.S.N., Sept. 6, 1861; promoted p.m., Apr. 14, 1862; pay insp. Sept. 25, 1875; pay dir., Dec. 24, 1883; retired Jan. 20, 1900, with rank of rear admiral for services during Civil War. Home: Jamaica Plain, Mass. Died Feb. 5, 1917.

MAY, GEOFFREY ex-govt. ofcl.; b. Mpls., Apr. 26, 1900; s. Jacob Lewis and Miriam (Jacobs) M.; A.B., Harvard, 1921, LL.B., 1924; LL.D., U. London (London Sch. of Econ.), 1933; Barrister-at-Law (Eng.), 1935; m. Elizabeth Stoffregen, Sept. 22, 1931. Expert in legal research U.S. Dept. Labor, 1924; mem. staff Russell Sage Found., 1925-27; asso. Harvard Law Sch. Survey of Crime and Criminal Justice, 1927-28; fellow London Sch. Econs., 1928-30; asst. prof. Inst. of Law, Johns Hopkins, 1930-33; gen. sec. Family Service Soc. of Richmond, 1933-36; legal cons. Russell Sage Found. since 1935; successively chief Div. of Plans and Grants, asst. exec. dir. and asso. dir. (Pub. Assistance), Social Security Bd., 1936-41; asst. coordinator health, Welfare and related def. activities, 1941; dep. dir. Def. Health and Welfare Services (Fed. Security Agt), 1941-42; spl. lectr. U. Pa., 1938-41; lectr. U. Chgo., 1941; mem. War Dept. commn. to study civil def. in Great Britain, 1941; mem. various other fgn. missions; lt. comdr. USNR, since 1942; asst. chief (estimates) Bur. of Budget, Exec. Office of Pres., 1944-47; spl. asst. to chief Am. Mission for Aid to Greece, 1947-48; ret. to writing and teaching, 1948. Mem. Assn. of Bar of City N.Y., Inner Temple (London), English Bar; former mem. profl. socs. in fields econs., sociology, social work. Clubs: Harvard (Boston); Devonshire (London). Author: Marriage Laws and Decisions in the United States, 1929; Social Control of Sex Expression, 1931; The Divorce Court (with Leon C. Marshall), vol. I, 1932, Vol. II, 1933; Small Loan Legislation (with D. J. Gallert and W. S. Hilborn), 1932; Money Lending in Great Britain (with D. J. Orchard), 1933. Contbr. articles to legal and sociol. publs. Address: West Bare Hill Rd., Harvard, Mass. 01451. Died Feb. 6, 1964.

MAY, JULIA HARRIS teacher, author; b. Strong, Me., Apr. 27, 1833; d. Rev. William and Della Maria (Johnson) M.; grad. Mt. Holyoke Coll., 1856 (hon. M.A., 1906); unmarried. Taught in various schs., 1848-92; teacher of classes in art and lit. from 1897, in Auburn and Lewiston, Me. Conglist. Lecturer before women's clubs. Author: Songs from the Woods of Maine (poems), 1894; Looking for the Stars (poems), 1903; Pictures Framed in Song, 1907. Home: Auburn, Me. Died May 6, 1912.

MAY, WILLIAM ANDREW officer corps.; b. Hollidaysburg, Pa., Dec. 3, 1850; s. Lewis and Louisa (Haines) M.; A.B., Williamsport Dickinson Sem., 1873; C.E., Lafayette Coll., 1876, A.M., 1879; m. Emma L. Richards,June 5, 1878. Began as roadman on engring. corps, and advanced to chief engr. several coal companies; became supt. Hillside Coal & Iron Co., 1883; with many coal companies in charge of operations, etc.; pres. Pa. Coal Co., Feb. 1913-; pres. Hillside Coal & Iron Co., New York, Susquehanna & Western Coal Co., Northwestern Mining & Exchange Co., Blossburg Coal Co.; pres. Scranton Board of Trade Bldg. Co. Pvt. Co. D. 13th Regt. N.G. Pa., 1878; resigned as capt. 1888. Mem. Select Council, City of Scranton, 2 terms; mem. Bd. Control, Scranton City Schs., 1898-1902. Pres. Scranton Bd. Trade, 1893-97. Dir. Williamsport Dickinson Sem.; trustee Lafayette Colo. Republican. Methodist. Mason. Home: Scranton, Pa. Died June 1, 1923.

MAYER, ERNEST DE W(AEL), fgn. service officer; b. N.Y. City, Mar. 1, 1903; s. Albert E. and Valentine (De Wael) M.; student Lycee d'Anvers, Stanton Mil. Acad.; pvt. tutors Holland and Eng.; m. Jean Heffernan, Apr. 9, 1928; children—Gerald S., Janet. Newspaper work, N.Y. City, 1921-24, comml. work, 1924-30; apptd. fgn. service officer, v. consul career, sec. Diplomatic Service, 1931; various consular and diplomatic capacities, Havre, France, 1932-35, Southampton, Eng., 1935, Paris, 1935-40, Casablanca and Rabat, Morocco, 1940-44, London, Eng., 1944, Brussels, Belgium, 1944-46, Baden Baden, Germany, 1946-49, Montréal, Que., Can., 1949-51; Am. consul, Quebec City, Can., 1951-53; counselor of embassy, Can., 1953; officer in charge No. European Affairs, Dept. State, 1956-59; dep. chief mission, Accra, Ghana, 1959; consul gen., Tangier, Morocco, from 1960. Decorated Medal of Freedom, 1947. Home: Washington DC Died Dec. 1968.

MAYER, RICHARD business exec.; b. Chgo., Dec. 8, 1898; s. David and Florence (Blum) M.; student Phillips Andover Acad., 1913-15; Ph.B., Yale, 1918; J. D., U. Chgo., 1921; m. Elisabeth Goodman, June 23, 1928; children-Margaret and Judith (twins), Elizabeth. Admitted to Ill. Bar, 1921; partner Mayer, Meyer, Austrian and Platt, Chgo., 1931-45; chmn. bd. Reliance Mfg. Co., Chgo., 1945-. Served to 1st lt. F.A., U.S. Army, 1918-19; with A.A.F.; to maj., 1940-44. Mem. Am., Ill., Chgo. bar assns. Jewish religion. Club: Law. Home: 411 Lakeside Terrace, Glencoe, Ill. Office: 212 W. Monroe St., Chgo. Died Arp. 9, 1967.*

MAYFIELD, IRVING HALL naval officer; b. Ruston, La., Aug. 1, 1885; student La. Poly. Inst.; grad. U.S. Naval Acad., 1907; m. Juliet Rhodes Borden. Entered USN, 1907; commd. ensign, 1909, advanced through the grades to rear adm., 1945; dist. naval intelligence officer 14th Naval Dist., Pearl Harbor, T.H., 1941-43; assigned duty with South Pacific Force, 1943; became chief of staff to dep. comdr. South Pacific Force, and chief of staff and aide to comdr. South Pacific Force and Area, 1944; later served as chief of U.S. Naval Mission to Chile; retired, Nov. 1946. Decorated Legion of Merit with 2 gold stars, Am. Def. Service medal with fleet, clasp, Victor, Yangtze Service and Asiatic-Pacific Area Campaign medals; Nichin Iftichkar (Bey of Tunis); Hon. comdr. Order Brit. Empire; Grand Comdr. Order of Merit (Chile). Died Oct. 1963.

MAYNARD, JOHN BLACKWELL army officer; b. Portsmouth, Va., Aug. 12, 1887; s. Harry Lee and Mary Eleanor (Brooks) M.; B.S. in C.E., Va. Poly. Inst., 1907; student Colo. Sch. of Mines, 1907-08, Coast Arty. Sch., 1912, Coast Arty. Sch. (Advanced), 1928, Field Arty. Sch., 1917, 18, Chem. Warfare Sch., 1924, Command and Gen. Staff Sch., 1923-24, Army War Coll., 1928-29; m. Lucy Talbott Dorsey, Oct. 19, 1911; children-John Blackwell, Mary Eleanor (Mrs. Charles Murray Henley), Charles Dorsey, Harry Lee. Commd. 2d lt., Coast Arty. Corps, Sept. 25, 1908; promoted through grades to brig. gen., U.S. Army, Apr. 5, 1941. Mem. Mil. Order World War, Sigma Nu, Omicron Delta Kappa. Mason. Home: Denbigh, Va. Died Feb. 2, 1945; buried in Arlington National Cemetery.

MAYNARD, LESTER, consul gen.; b. San Francisco, Apr. 5, 1877; ed. Polytechnic High Sch.; studied accounting; m. in Paris, France, April 15, 1930. Served as bank clerk 3 yrs., newspaper reporter, war correspondent, publisher and editor; apptd., after examination, consul at Sandakan, June 26, 1906, at Vladivostok, 1908, Harbin, 1911, Amoy, 1912; consul of class 4 by act approved Feb. 5, 1915; detailed to the Dept. of State, Mar. 1, 1916; assigned to Chefoo, 1916, to Alexandria, 1919; promoted class 3, 1920; assigned to Havre, 1923; foreign service officer of class 4, 1924; assigned to Stuttgart, 1929; promoted to class 3 (foreign service), 1929; consul gen. and assigned to Singapore, 1930, to Athens, 1932, to Copenhagen Aug. 23, 1933. Address: Am. Counsulate General, Copenhagen Denmark

MAYNARD, WALTER, investment banker; b. N.Y. City, Apr. 19, 1906; s. Walter Effingham and Eunice (Ives) M.; student Groton (Mass.) Sch., 1919-24; A.B., Harvard, 1928; student Trinity Coll., 1928-29; m. Eileen Burden, Feb. 9, 1932; children—Walter, Sheila, John; m. 2d, Augusta P. Billings, December 26, 1957. Entered securities bus., 1929, partner Shearson, Hammill & Co., 1941, 46-64; sr. v.p. Shearson, Hammill & Co., Inc., 1964-69, vice chairman and executive vice pres., from 1969; dir. Spartan Industries, Inc., from 1959; trustee Austen Riggs Center, from 1952; governor of Greenwich House, from 1947. Governor New York Stock Exchange, 1956-62. Served from 1st lt. to lt. colonel U.S.A.A.F., 1942-46. Decorated Legion of Merit, Order Brit. Empire (hon. officer); mentioned in dispatches. Mem. Assn. Stock Exchange Firms (gov. 1948-51, pres. 1951), N.Y. Soc. Security Analysts, Investment Bankers Assn. (gov. 1953-56). Home: New York City NY Died Nov. 27, 1971.

MAYNARD, WASHBURN rear admiral U.S.N.; b. Knoxville, Tenn., Dec. 5, 1844; s. Horace and Laura Ann (Washburn) M.; bro. of James M.; grad. U.S. Naval Acad., 1866; widower. Promoted to ensign, Apr. 1868; master Mar. 26, 1869; lt., lMar. 21, 1870; lt. comdr., Sept. 27, 1884; comdr., Sept. 27, 1893; capt., Mar. 9, 1900; rear admiral and retired, Nov. 1, 1902. Has from 1866 served consecutively on naval vessels: Susquehanna, Franklin, Frolic, Seminole, California, Saranac, Richmond, Wyandotte, Coast Survey, Tennessee, Brooklyn and Pinta, and comd. Nashville during Spanish-Am. War, Apr.-Aug. 1898; light house insp., 1899-1900; Naval Examining Bd., Oct. 1900-Mar. 1901; naval sec. Lighthouse Bd., Mar, 1901-Nov. 1902. Died Oct. 24, 1913.

MAYO, CHARLES HORACE surgeon; b. Rochester, Minn., July 19, 1865; s. William Worrall (M.D.) and Louise Abigail (Wright) M.; prep. edn., Rochester High Sch., Niles Acad.; M.D., Northwestern U., 188, M.A., 1904; post-grad. study, N.Y. Polyclinic, N.Y. Post-Grad. Med. Sch.; LL.D., U. of Md., 1909, Kenyon Coll., 1916, Northwestern, 1921, U. of Edinburgh, 1925, Queen's U. (Belfast), 1925, U. of Manchester, 1929. Hamline U., 1930, Carleton Coll., 1932, U. of Minnesota, 1935, U. of Notre Dame, 1936, Villanova Coll., 1937; D.Sc., Princeton, 1917, U. of Pa., 1925, U. of Leeds, 1929; M.Ch., U. of Dublin, 1925; D.P.H., Detroit Coll. Medicine and Surgery, 1927; M.D., U. of Havana, 1930; B.S., Yankton Coll., 1937; F.A.C.S., 1913; F.R.C.S., England, 1920; F.R.C.S., Ireland, 1921; F.R.S.M., London, 1926; m. Edith Graham, 1893; children-Margaret (dec.), Dorothy, Charles William, Edith (Mrs. Fred W. Rankin), Joseph Graham (dec.), Louise (lMrs. George T. Trenholm), Rachel (dec.), Esther (Mrs. John B. Hartzell). Practiced surgery at Rochester, 1888-; with brother, W. J., donated $2,800,-000 to establish Mayo Foundation for Med. Edn. and Research at Rochester, in affiliation with U. of Minn; with brother in 1919, Founded the Mayo Properties Assn., to hold all the properties, endowments and funds of the Mayo Clinic and to insure permanency of the instn. for public service; now surgeon and associate chief of staff Mayo Clinic; surgeon to St. Mary's, Colonial and Worrall hosps.; professor surgery Med. Sch., U. of Minn., 1919-36, and prof. surgery Grad. Sch., U. of Minn. (Mayo Foundation), 19195-36, emeritus. Member State Bd. of Health and Vital Statistics, Minn., 1900-02; health officer, Rochester, 1912-37; v.p. Rochester School Bd., 1915-23. Apptd. 1st lt. Med. R.C., Army of U.S., 1913; served as maj., later col., 1917-19; chief consultant (alternating with brother William J.) for all surg. services, Office of Surgeon Gen., 1917-19; rec'd hon. discharge from army, Feb. 28, 1919; apptd. brig. gen. Med. O.R.C., Army of U.S., 1921; brig. gen. Med. Dept., Army of U.S., 1926, and brig. gen. Auxiliary Army of U.S., 1931. Awarded certificate Council of Nat. Defense, 1919; D.S.M. (U.S.). 1920; Officier l'Ordre Nat. de la Legion d'Honneur (France), 1925; Officer l'Instruction Publique et des Beaux Arts (France), 1925; Cross Comdr. Royal Order Crown of Italy, 1932; letter of commendation, Minn. State Med. Assn. 1934; and from Northwestern U. Alumni Assn., in recognition of worthy achievement, 1934; citation for distinguished service given by nat. orgn. Am. Legion; commemorative plaque presented by Pres. of United States in person, 1934; certificate in recognition of service to U. of Minn. and to State as prof. of surgery, 1936; bronze medal presented by Interstate Post Grad. Med. Assn. of North America for contributions to scientific medicine, 1936. Fellow or mem. numerous scientific and non-scientific organizations in U.S. and fgn. countries. Services to scientific and non-scientific periodicals-Anales de Cirugia la Habana, Cuba (fgn. collaborator), Archives of Clin. Cancer Research (editorial bd. 1924-32), Gaceta Medica Espanola (del. in U.S. 1926-30; internat. patron in U.S., 1931-), Internat. Clinics (collaborating editor 1907-33), Narkose Und Anaesthesie (contbr. 1928), Nosokomien (editorial bd.), The Ency. Britannica (mem. advisory bd.). Trustee Carleton Coll., Northwestern U. Ind. Democrat. Mason. Home: Rochester, Minn. Died May 26, 1939.

MAYO, HENRY THOMAS rear adm.; b. Burlington, Vt., Dec. 8, 1856; s. Henry and Elizabeth (Elrie M. Wing,) Mar. 1881; children-Chester G., George. Advanced through various grades and promoted rear adm., June 15, 9 June 15, 1913; advanced to admiral on retired list, June 1930. Served on various vessels of U.S. Navy, also on both naval and coast survey; was comdt. Mare Island Navy Yard; aid for personnel at Navy Dept., Washington; comdr. 4th Div., Atlantic Fleet, Dec. 18, 1913; comdg. battleship squadrons of Atlantic Fleet with rank of vice admiral, June 10, 1915; promoted admiral, 1916, and apptd. comdr.-in-chief Atlantic Fleet, on Pennsylvania. Demanded apology from Mexican comdr. and firing of nat. salute of 21 guns to U.S. flag, to make amends for arrest of paymaster and crew of dispatch boat Dolphin, at wharf in Tampico, Mex., while loading gasoline into whaleboat, Apr. 9, 1914. Comdr.-in-chief Atlantic Fleet during entire period of war, the command including all vessels in the Atlantic and European waters; represented U.S. at naval conf. of allied nations, London, Sept. 1917; made inspection trip to all U.S. naval activities in Great Britain, France and Italy, 1918; command designated as U.S. Fleet, Jan. 1919; hauled down flag as comdr.-in-chief U.S. Fleet, June 30, 1919, whereupon the fleet was divided into the Atlantic and Pacific fleets; reverted to permanent rank of rear adm. and assigned to duty on Navy Gen. Bd.; retired for age, Dec. 1920; gov. U.S. Naval Home, Phila. 1924-28. Home: Burlington, Vt. Died Feb. 23, 1937.

MAYO, WILLIAM JAMES surgeon; b. Le Sueur, Minn., June 29, 1861; s. William Worrall (M.D.) and Louise Abigail (Wright) M.; prep. edn. Rochester High Sch. and Niles Acad.; M.D., U. of Mich., 1883, hon. A.M., 1890; Certificated N.Y. Post Grad. Med. Sch., 1884; M.D., N.Y. Polyclinic, 1885; F.R.C.S., Edinburgh, 1905, Eng., 1913, Ireland, 1921; F.R.S.M., Eng., 1926; LL.D., U. of Toronto, 1906, U. of Md., 1907, U. ofPa., 1912, McGill U., 1923, U. of Pittsburgh, 1924, Carleton Coll., 1928, U. of Manchester, 1929, Temple U., 1930, U. of Aberdeen, Scotland, 1933, U. of Minn., 1935, U. of Notre Dame, 1936, Villanova Coll., Pa., 1937; D.Sc., U. of Mich., 1908, Columbia, 1910, U. of Leeds, 1923, Harvard, 1924, Marquette and Northwestern, 1929, Yankton Coll., S.D., 1937; M.D. in Surgery, U. of Dublin and Trinity College, 1923, U. of Havana, 1929; m. Hattie M. Damon, Nov. 20, 1884; children-Carrie L. (wife of Dr. D. C. Balfour), Phoebe G. (wife of Dr. H. Waltman Walters). Engaged in practice of surgery, Rochester, Minn., 1883-; surgeon Mayo Clinic (St. Mary's Hosp.), 1889-, and asso. chief of staff. With brother donated $2,800,000 to establish Mayo Foundation for Med. Edn. and Research, at Rochester, in affiliation with U. of Minn. First lt. Med. R.C., 1912, maj. Med. O.R.C., 1917; col. M.C. U.S.A., and chief consultant for surg. service, 1917-19; col. M.R.C., 1919, brig. gen. M.O.R.C., 1921; brig. general Auxiliary Res., 1926-31. Awarded gold medal Nat. Inst. Social Sciences, 1918; D.S.M. (U.S.), 1919; certificate Council Nat. Defense, 1919; Henry Jacob Bigelow gold medal of Boston Surg. Soc., 1921; Comdr. Royal Order of Northern Star (Sweden), 1927; Finlay Congressional D.S.M. (Republic of Cuba), 1929; gold medal A.M.A., 1930; Cross of Royal Order of Knight Commander of the Crown of Italy, 1932; special award for distinguished service to science, Sigma Xi (chapter U. of Minn.), 1933; letter of commendation, Minn. State Med. Assn., 1934; citation for distinguished service presented by Nat. Comdr. Am. Legion; commemorative plaque presented by President of U.S. in person, 1934; Scroll of Distinguished Service, Gen. Alumni Assn. U. of Minn., 1935. Regent U. of Minn., 1907—; elector, Hall of Fame, 1920—. Mem. numerous Am. and foreign scientific societies. Home: Rochester, Minn. Died July 28, 1939.

MAYO, WILLIAM KENNON commodore U.S.N.; b. Drummondtown, Va., May 29, 1829; was apptd. from Braden, June 14, 1888. Superintendent schs., Carrolldredge) M.; grad. U.S. Naval Acad., 1876; m. Carla; a midshipman in the navy, Oct. 18, 1841; served in various stations, then through the Mexican war, taking part in blockade of Tampico and Vera Cruz, etc. Went to Naval Acad.; passed midshipman, Aug. 1847; master, Sept. 14, 1855; lt., Sept. 15, 1855; instr. seamanship and naval tactics, Naval Acad., 1854-57; asst. prof. ethics, same, 1859-60; lt. commander, July 16, 1862; comdr., July 25, 1866; capt., Dec. 12, 1873; commodore, July 1882; retired, 1886, on own application, after 40 years' service. Because of adherence to Union, was by vote of Va. Convention, July 1861, declared an alien enemy and forever banished from the State. During Civil war executive officer steamsloop "Housatonic," blockade off Charleston, S.C.; then comdr. "Kanawha" in Western Gulf squadron, having engagements with riflemen and field batteries, Mobile Point, and a fight with Fort Morgan, Oct. 1863. Later engaged in blockade of Charleston, S.C. in command of a monitor; after war on duty at several stations, comdg. Naval Station, Norfolk, Va., 1882-85. Died 1900.

MAZET, ROBERT lawyer; b. Pittsburgh, Pa., May 15, 1857; s. William and Malcena M.; ed. Pittsburgh High Sch.; LL.B., Columbia, 1879; m. Elsie Sawyer Mo. e, Nov. 11, 1899 (dec.); children-Robert Mazet, Horace S.; m. 2d, Frances Cullen, Mar. 25, 1916. Law practice since 1880; dep. atty. gen. State of N.Y., 1898. Mem. of N.Y. Assembly, 1897-99, mem. Com. of N.Y. Legislature, 1897, to investigate trusts; chmn. Mazet Com., 1899, to investigate govt. of N.Y. City; chmn. Bd. of Transfer Tax Appraisers, 1901-05. Republican. Commd. maj. 7th Regt., Nat. Guard N.Y.; maj. 107th Inf., U.S. Army, Aug. 5, 1917; lt. col., 1918; comd. 107th Inf., 27th Div., A.E.F., in Flanders, July-Aug. 1918; hon. discharged, Oct. 31, 1918. Mem. Pa. Soc. Mil. Order of Foreign Wars (judge advocate N.Y. Commandery), Soc. of World War, Pa. Soc. of New York (sec., treas.), Soc. of War Veterans of 7th Regiment (pres.), Chi Phi. Address: 270 Broadway, New York, N.Y. Died Dec. 25, 1945.

MCADAMS JOHN POPE army officer (ret); b. Hawesville, Ky., June 29, 1872; s. Eugene P. and Mary Elizabeth (Pope) McA.; student Army Sch. of the Line, 1913-14, Army Staff Coll., 1914-15, Army War Coll., 1919-20; m. Frances Hennen, Oct. 2, 1906; children-Martha Hennen (Mrs. Howard H. Ruppart), Alfred H., Eugene P. Served as pvt. and sgt., inf., Ky., 1898-1899; pvt. and cpl. Co. C. 13th Inf., U.S. Army, 1899-1901; commd. 2d lt. U.S. Army, July 1, 1901, advanced through grades to brig. gen., June 13, 1940; chief of staff lines of communication AEF, 1917; dep. chief staff Service of Supply AEF, 1918; mem. gen. staff War Dept., 1920-24; chmn. Fed. Liquidation Bd., 1921-22. Awarded Distinguished Service award, World War I. Legion of Honor (France). Republican. Roman Catholic. Clubs: Army and Navy (Washington); Pendennis, Filson (Louisville), Indian Lake Country (Hawesville). Home: Hawesville, Ky. Died Mar. 11, 1960.

MCADOO, HENRY MOLSEED pres. U.S. Leather Co.; b. Phila., June 7, 1880; s. William and Margaret Anne (Campbell) McA.; grad. Friends Central Sch., Phila., 1898; m. Margaret Gaulbert Nice, Apr. 16, 1911; children-William Nice, Henry Molseed, Richard Budd. Began as clerk, McAdd & Allen, leather, Phila., 1898; pres. U.S. Leather Co., 1935—; dir. C.C. Collings & Co., Nice Ball Bearing Co., Empire Electric Brake Co. Mem. war materials div. Council Nat. Def., 1940-41. Served as capt. Q.M. Dept., U.S. Army, World War I. Republican. Episcopalian. Clubs: Union League, Phila. Cricket, Bachelors' Barge (Phila.). Home: Skippack Pike, Fort Washington, Pa. Office: 27 Spruce St., N.Y.C. 8. Died June 4, 1951.

MCAFEE, WILLIAM A(RCHIBALD), lawyer; b. Clavevack, N.Y., Mar. 13, 1890; s. William and Flora (Ackley) McA.; A.B., Yale, 1911; LL.B., Harvard, 1915; LL.D., Lake Erie College, Painesville, Ohio, 1960; m. Sarah Edwards McLoud, Oct. 9, 1920; 1 son, Alexander. Admitted to bar, practiced in Cleve.; partner Squire, Sanders & Dempsey. Trustee Lake Erie Coll., Cleve. Symphony Orch., Inst. of Music. Served capt. to maj., F.A., U.S. Army, 1917-19. Mem. Am., Ohio, Cleve. bar assns., Am. Petroleum Inst. Republican. Clubs: Union, Tavern, University (Cleve.); Kirtland Country (Willoughby, O.); Yale of N.Y.; Edgertown Yacht. Home: Cleveland OH Died Sept. 2, 1971.

MCALESTER, ANDREW WALKER, JR. ophthalmologist; b. Columbia, Mo., Feb. 19, 1876; s. Andrew Walker and Sallie (McConathy) M.; christian Coll., Columbia, Mo.; B.Litt., U. of Mo., 1897, A.B., 1903, M.D., 1905; certificate, Royal London Ophthalmic Hosp., London, 1905; m. Tillie Hall Bedford, Oct. 21, 1899; 1 son, Andrew Walker. Prin. Mo. Sch. for Blind, 1898-1900; practice of ophthalmology, Kansas City Mo., since 1906; attending oculist Menorah, St. Luke's, Research Hosp.; chief of eye service, Kansas City General Hosp.; prof. ophthalmology, Med. Sch. U. of Kan., 1908-12. Oculist for Chicago, Burlington and Qunicy Railroad, K.-K.-T. R.R., Milwaukee R.R., U.S. Compensation Com. Democrat. Fellow Am. Coll. Surgeons; mem. A.M.A. (House of Dels., 1909-15), Mo. State Med. Assn. (sec. 1907-09, pres. 1944), Jackson County Med. Soc., Am. Acad. Ophthalmology and Oto-laryngology, Beta Theta Pi, Phi Beta Pi. Was maj., Med. Corps, U.S. Army, attached to Air Service, A.E.F., in France. Clubs: University, Mission Hills Country. Home: 5509 Mission Drive, Kansas City. Office: Bryant Bldg., Kansas City, Mo. Died Aug. 17, 1954.

MCALEXANDER, ULYSSES GRANT army officer; b. Dundas, Minn., Aug. 30, 1864; s. C. P. and Margaret McAlexander; grad. U.S. Mil. Acad., 1887, Army War Coll., 1907, Gen. Staff Coll., 1920; LL.D., Oregon State Coll., 1930; widower (Aug. 20, 1935). Commissioned second lt. 25th Inf., June 12, 1887; promoted through grades to brig. gen. (temp.), Aug. 16, 1918; brig. gen. (perm.), Mar. 5, 1921, maj. gen., July 21, 1924; retired on account of physical disability, July 22, 1924. Prof. mil. science and tactics, Ia. Wesleyan U., Mt. Pleasant, Ia., 1891-95; in the field, Santiago Campaign, Cuba, Apr.-Aug. 1898; recommended for promotion "for gallantry under fire" in battles in front of Santiago; in charge office Chief Q.-M., Dept. of the East, Nov. 14, 1898-Feb. 17, 1899; with regt. in Philippines, 1900-02; a.d.c. to Maj. Gen. Weston, in Philippines, 1906; mem. Gen. Staff Corps, 1906-07; prof. mil. science and tactics, Oregon Agrl. Coll., 1907-11, 1915-16; with regt. in Philippines, 1912-15; insp.-instr. Ore. N.G., 1916-17; arrived in France, June 26, 1917; comd. 18th Inf., July-Dec. 1917; insp. gen. Base No. 1, Jan.-May 1918; comd. 38th U.S. Inf. in 2d Battle of the Marne, July 15, 1918; at Jaulgonne, July 22, on the Vesle, Aug. 2-10, 1918; comd. 180th Inf. Brigade (Tex. Brigade), Aug. 1918-June 1919; participated, 1918, campaigns, Aisne, Champagne-Marne, Marne defensive, Aisne-Marne, St. Mihiel and Meuse-Argonne; broke last great German offensive on Marne, July 15, 1918; known as "The Rock of the Marne"; wounded, July 16 and July 23, 1918. 1918. Life size portrait presented to State of Texas by Texas Brigade. Comdg. 6th brig., 3d Div., Oct. 1921; as Ft. Douglas, Utah, June 7, 1922-July 21, 1924. Awarded D.S.M., D.S.C., and cited "for distinguished valor" (U.S.); Officer Légion d'Honneur and Croix de Guerre (twice) with palm (French); Croce di Guerra (Italian). Hon. life pres. "Rock of the Marne Post" No. 138, Vets. Foreign Wars, N.Y. City, also of Salt Lake Post, V.F.W.; life mem. Soc. Santiago de Cuba. Author: History of the Thirteenth Regiment, 1905. Lecturers on Second Battle ofthe Marne, and on Leadership. Home: Portland, Ore. Died Sept. 18, 1936.

MCALISTER, HEBER LOWREY educator and military leader; b. Pontotoc Co., Miss., Sept. 18, 1882; s. William Monroe and Annie (Garrett) McA.; B.S., Miss. Coll., 1906, M.A., 1916; LL.D., Quachita Coll., 1932; m. LaNora O'Baugh, May 18, 1909. Asst. in mathematics, Miss. Coll., 1906, prof. mathematics and dean of Quachita Coll., Arkadelphia, Ark., 1907-16; dean of Bryan (Tex.) Acad., 1916-17; dir. extension, Ark. State Teachers Coll., 1919-30; pres., 1930-41; commr. Athletics Ark. Inter-Collegiate Conf. since 1948. Maj., inf., U.S. Army 1917-19; lt. col., inf., Nat. Guard, 1921, col., 1922, brig. gen., Adj. Gen.'s Dept., 1924-26; col. inf., 1928; col. U.S. Army, 1940-43; brig. gen. Adj. Gen.'s Dept. 1945-51, ret. 1951. Democrat. Baptist. Rotarian. Home: Conway, Ark. Died Dec. 22, 1956; buried Conway, Ark.

MCALLISTER, CHARLES ALBERT engineer; b. Dorchester, N.J., May 29, 1867; s. William and Abagail Ann (Shute) M.; M.E., Cornell U., 1887; m. Adelaide Kenyon, Mar. 6, 1907; 1 dau., Clara A. Apptd. 2d asst. engineer, U.S.R.C.S., June 30, 1892; commd. 1st asst. engineer, June 6, 1895, chief engr., Apr. 1st asst. engineer, June 6, 1895, chief engr., Apr. 13, 1902, engineer-in-chief, Mar. 9, 1916, U.S. Coast Guard; retired, July 12, 1919. V.p. Am. Bur. of Shipping, 1919-26, president, 1926-. Passed assistant engr. U.S.N., on board U.S. Flagship Philadelphia, in Spanish-Am. War. Mem. jury awards, machinery, San Francisco Expn., 1915. Episcopalian. Author: The Professor on Shipboard, 1902; McAndrew's Floating School, 1913. Delegate to Internat. Conf. on Safety at Sea, London, 1929. Home: New York, N.Y. Died Jan. 6, 1932.

MCALPINE, KENNETH naval officer; b. Portsmouth, Va., Aug. 16, 1860; grad. U.S. Naval Acad., 1881. Promoted asst. engr., July 1, 1883; passed asst. engr., Sept. 12, 1893; transferred to the line as lt., Mar. 3, 1899; lt. comdr., Mar. 21, 1905; comdr., June 24, 1909; capt., Mar. 4, 1911. Served on Texas, Spanish-Am. War, 1898, Monadnock, 1905-06, at Naval Sta., Cavite, P.I., 1906, on Ohio, 1906; duty at Navy Yard, Norfolk, Va., 1906-08; fleet engr., Atlantic Fleet, 1908; at Navy Yard, Norfolk, 1908-09; apptd. insp. machinery, Newport News, Va., Nov. 16, 1909. Home: Portsmouth, Va.

MCANDREW, JAMES WILLIAM army officer; b. in Pa., June 29, 1862; grad. U.S. Mil. Acad., 1888; honor grad. Army Sch. of the Line, 1910; grad. Army Staff Coll., 1911; Army War Coll., 1913. Commd. 2d lt. 21st Inf., June 11, 1888; promoted through grades to brig. gen. N.A., Aug. 5, 1917; maj. gen. N.A., Apr. 16, 1918; brig. gen. U.S.A., Nov. 8, 1918; maj. gen., Mar. 5, 1921. Was in Sioux Indian Campaign, 1890-91; in Battle of El Caney, Cuba, July 1, 1898, and in investment of Santiago, until its surrender, July 16, 1898; duty in Philippines, 1899-1902; with regt. in Alaska, 1905-06; mem. Gen. Staff Corps, 1916, 17; service in France, June 26, 1917-June 6, 1919; chief of staff, A.E.F., May 6, 1918-May 26, 1919; now comdt. Gen. Staff Coll., Washington. Awarded D.S.M., 1918; Legion of Honor and Croix de Guerre with two palms (French); K.C.M.G. (British); Grand Officer Order of Crown (Belgian); Order of Santi Maurizio and E. Lazzaro (Italian): Montenegran docorations, Panama La Solidaredad. Died Apr. 30, 1922.

MCARTHUR, JOHN mfr.; b. parish of Erskine, Scotland, Nov. 17, 1826; ed. there; learned blacksmith's trade; m. Christina Cuthbertson, of his native parish, 1848. Settled in Chicago, 1849; became boiler mfr.; entered Civil War as col. 12th Ill. vols.; brig. gen., March 21, 1862, and bvt. maj. gen. Had command 2d div., 17th army corps, in operations against Vicksburg; distinguished himself in several battles. Was commr. Public Works of Chicago and pres. of bd. during Chicago fire, 1871; postmaster, Chicago, 1873-77. Home: Chicago, Ill. Died 1906.

MCBEE, EARL THURSTON, chemist; b. Braymer, Mo., July 6, 1906; s. William and Lydia (Post) McB.; A.B., William Jewell Coll., 1929; M.S., Purdue U., 1931, Ph.D., 1936; m. 2d, Viola Renolds, Feb. 15, 1962; children—Beverly Ann, Robert Earl. Prof., Purdue U., 1943, alumni research counselor, 1944-73, head dept. of chemistry, 1949, Shreve prof. indsl. chemistry, 1967-73, ofcl. investigator Nat. Def. Research Com., 1942-43; research cons. U.S. Engr. Office, Madison Square Area, 1943-45; chmn. adv. bd. U.S. Naval Propellant Plant, 1953-73; chmn. bd., pres., chief exec. officer Great Lakes Chem. Corp.; pres. Ark. Chems., Inc., Bromet Co. Received Modern Pioneer award Nat. Assn. Mfrs., 1940; Certificate of Effective Service in Prodn. of Atomic Bomb, 1945; Certificate of Effective Service in

Prosecution of 2d World War, 1945; Ann. Sigma Xi Research award, 1946. Fellow Ind. Acad. Sci., N.Y. Acad. Sci.; mem. Am. Chem. Soc. (chmn. Purdue sect. 1942-43, councilor 1944-45), Mfg. Chemists Assn. (dir.), Am. Inst. Chemists (dir.), Ind. Chem. Soc., A.A.A.S., Sigma Xi, Phi Lambda Upsilon, Alpha Kappa Lambda, Alpha Chi Sigma. Mason (32 deg.), Elk. Clubs: Chemists, Rotary Internat. Contbr. articles to profl. jours. and periodicals, also to publs. Manhattan Project Tech. Series. Home: West Lafayette IN Died Jan. 1973; buried West Lafayette IN

MCBRIDE, ALLAN CLAY army officer; b. Frederick, Md., June 30, 1885; grad. St. John's Coll., Md., 1908; commd. 2d lt., F.A., Sept. 1908, and advanced through the grades to brig. gen., Dec. 1941; became comdr. 12th F.A., Ft. Sam Houston, Tex., 1939; inspector gen. hdqrs. Third Army, San Antonio, Tex., 1940; assigned to hdqrs. Philippine Dept., Manila, P.I., as plans and training officer, Feb. 1941; in Philippine Islands, when hostilities broke out and is now belived prisoner of war in hands of Japanese. Awarded Distinguished Service Medal, Nov. 1942. Died May 9, 1944.

MCBRIDE, ANDREW JAY soldier; b. at Fayetteville, Ga., Sept. 29, 1836; schooling alternated with farm work and teaching; m. 1864, Mary Frances Johnson. Admitted to Ga. bar and practiced in Atlanta circuit until 1861; served in C.S.A., 1861-65, capt. and col.; served under Longstreet and was severely wounded at Cold Harbor. After war, mcht. and importer several yrs.; real estate agt.; one of organizers Confederate Veterans' Assn., Atlanta Chamber of Commerce, and Young Men's Library; mem. Bapt. Ch., Knights Templar, and many other organizations; pres. Ga. State Scotch-Irish Soc. Residence: 188 Cooper St. Office: 318 Empire Bldg., Atlanta, Ga.

MCBRIDE, ROBERT W. lawyer; b. Richland Co., O., Jan. 25, 1842; s. Augustus and Martha Ann (Barnes) M.; pub. schs., Ohio and Ia. and Kirkville (Ia.) Acad., m. Ida S. Chamberlain, Sept. 27, 1868. Admitted to bar, Apr. 1867; practiced at Waterloo, 1867-90 (except when on bench), at Indianapolis from 1893. Judge Circuit Ct., 35th Jud. Circuit, 1882-88; justice Supreme Ct. of Ind., Dec. 17, 1890-Jan. 2, 1893. Republican. Dir. counsel loan dept. State Life Ins. Co. Mem. Union Light Guard of Ohio (Abraham Lincoln's body guard); capt., lt. col. and col. 3d Regt. Ind. N.G. Mason. Author: History of the Union Light Guard Cavalry of Ohio; Abraham Lincoln's Body Guard, Personal Recollections of Abraham Lincoln. Adj. gen. G.A.R., 1917. Home: Indianapolis, Ind. Died May 15, 1926.

MCBRYDE, WARREN HORTON, engr., industrialist; Mobile, Ala., Jan. 20, 1876; s. Thomas Calvin and Julia Pierce (Horton) McB.; B.S. in Engring., Ala. Poly. Inst., 1897; LL.D., U. of Santa Clara, 1948; m. Abbie Ford White, Feb. 15, 1905; children—Lucile, Janet (Mrs. James A. Orser), Warren H., Jr. (dec.). Began with Electric Lighting Co., Mobile, Ala., 1897-98; asst. resident engr., Northern Calif., Yuba Elec. Power Co., asst. supt. Peyton Chem. Co., San Francisco and Martinez, asst. to chief engr. Calif. Gas & Elec. Co. (now Pacific Gas & Elec. Co.), 1899-1903; resident engr. E. I. duPont de Nemours & Co., Rapauno plant, Gibbstown, N.J., 1903-05, placed in charge all engring. and constrn. in Calif., 1905, asst. supt. Hercules plant (dynamite and TNT) throughout World War I; asst. to gen. mgr., sec. of the co., and handler engring. problems Calif. and Hawaiian Sugar Refining Co., 1919-27; cons. engr., San Francisco, since 1927. Served with U.S. Lighthouse Dept. and Corps of Engrs., Ft. Morgan, Ala., also chief electrician U.S. Army Transport Sheridan, Spanish-Am. War, 1898-99; served with War Dept., Washington, redesigning mech. equipment Army constrn. program, later standardizing designs and approving plans Army Ordnance and Chem. Warfare Service projects, also chief cons. mech. engr. and chief consultant munitions plants, 1941-42; chief of engring, div. U.S. Army Transportation Corps, 1942-44; subsequently cons. Transportation Corps, U.S. Army, and cons. Army-Navy Explosives Safety Bd., also mem. adv. council Indsl. Coll. Armed Forces. Mem. adv. bd. Richmond (Calif.) branch of Am. Trust Co. Mem. permanent com. Sacramento-San Joaquin Rivers Problems Conf. since 1924; mem. bldg. com. Grade Cathedral, Episcopal, San Francisco; pres. Contra Costa County C. of C.; mem. San Francisco Area Council Boy Scouts America; mem. adv. bd. Salvation Army. Trustee Mech. Inst. Library (San Francisco); mem. adv. bd. Coll. of Engring., U. of Santa Clara. Fellow Am. Soc. M.E. (pres. 1939-40); mem. Newcomen Soc. (vice chmn. Pacific Coast com.). Kappa Alpha, Tau Beta Pi. Republican. Mason. Clubs: Bohemian, Rotary, Commonwealth, Corinthian Yacht (San Francisco). Made 3 circumnavigations of globe, vis. all continents, some 80 countries, 1929-39. Office: 405 Montgomery St., San Francisco CA

MCCABE, CHARLES CARDWELL M.E. bishop, 1896-; b. Athens, O., Oct. 11, 1836; s. Robert and Sarah (Robinson) M. C.; ed. Ohio Wesleyan Univ., Delaware, O.; entered Ohio Conf., M.E. Ch., 1860. Became, in autumn of 1862, chaplain 122d Ohio inf.; captured at battle of Winchester; was in Libby Prison 4 months; rejoined his regt., but soon after went into service of the Christian Commn., for which he raised large sums; after war became pastor at Portsmouth, O., and financial agt. Ohio Wesleyan Univ.; in 1868 agt., and later asst. corr. sec. Bd. of Ch. Extension, M.E. Ch.; 1884 sec. Missionary Soc. M.E. Ch. His work as sec. added half a million dollars to the annual income of that society. Elected chancellor Am. Univ., Washington, Dec. 10, 1902. Died 1906.

MCCABE, EDWARD RAYNSFORD WARNER, army officer; b. Petersburg, Va., July 12, 1876; s. William Gordon and Jane Pleasants Harrison (Osborne) McC.; student Univ. Sch., Petersburg, Va., 1889-96, U. of Va., 1900; grad. Inf., Cav. Sch., Ft. Leavenworth, 1906, Mounted Service Sch., Ft. Riley, Kan., 1907, F.A. Sch., advanced course Ft. Sill, Okla., 1924, Army War Coll., Washington, D.C., 1931; m. Mary Forsyth, Nov. 12, 1908; children—Virginia Harrison Osborne (dec.), Edward Raynsford Warner, Jr. Commd. 2d lt., 1900, advanced through grades to brig. gen., 1944; served in Philippine Islands, 1900-03, 1907-10; in Mexico with Pershing Expedition, 1916; staff and line duty, France and Germany, 1917-19; mil. attache, Am. Legation, Prague, Czechoslovakia, 1920-22, and Am. Embassy, Rome, Italy, 1924-26; prof. mil. science and tactics, Standford U., Calif., 1927-30; mil. attache, Am. Embassy, Rome, Italy, 1931-33; chief of staff, 6th Corps Area, Chicago, 1936-37; chief Mil. Intelligence Div., Gen. Staff, U.S. Army, 1937-40; retired, July 1940; recalled to active service with Army, May 1943; comdt. The Sch. of Mil. Govt., Charlottesville, Va. Jan. 1944-Mar. 1945. Reverted to retired status June 30, 1946. Officer Legion of Honor and Croix de Guerre with Palm (French); Commander Order of Crown (Italian); Military Cross and Commander Order of the White Lion (Czechoslovakia); Commander Polonia Restituta (Poland); Legion of Merit. Mem. Beta Theta Pi, Scabbard and Blade, Soc. of The Cincinnati. Clubs: Colonnade, Farmington Country (Charlottesville, Va.); Chevy Chase, Army and Navy (Washington, D.C.), Saints and Sinners. Home: 1515 Gordon Av., Charlottesville VA

MCCABE, W(ILLIAM) GORDON educator; b. Richmond, Va., Aug. 4, 1841; s. Rev. John Collins (poet and antiquarian) and Sophia Gordon (Taylor) M.; (g.g.d. George Taylor, Signer of Declaration of Independence); gold medalist twice Hampton (Va.) Acad., 1858; grad. U. of Va., 1861; (hon. A.M., William and Mary, 1868, LL.D., 1906; A.M., Williams, 1885; Litt.D., Yale, 1897); served pvt. to capt. arty., 3d corps, in Army of Northern Va., 1862-65; m. Jenny Pleasants Harrison Osborne, Apr. 1861-65; m. Jenny Pleasants Harrison Osborne, Apr. 9, 1867 (died 1912); m. 2d, Gillie Armistead Cary, Mar. 16, 1915. Established and conducted, 1865-1901, University Sch., Petersburg and Richmond. Visitor, 1888-92, vice-rector, 1892-96, Univ. of Va. Commr. and dir. Jamestown Expn., 1905-07. Pres. Va. Hist. Soc.; pres. S.R. in Va., 1907-09; historian-gen. Gen. Soc. S.R., 1908-11; pres. Soc. Descendants of the Signers; pres. Soc. of Cincinnati, in Va.; col. of the Signers; pres. Soc. of Cincinnati in Va.; col. comdg. A. P. Hill Camp U.C.V., 1880, 1890-95; mem. Va. Gettysburg Mounument Commn.; president Pegram Battalion Assn. Vets. Author: A Grammar of the Latin Language, 1884; Latin Reader, 1886; Caesar's Gallic War, 1886; Virginia Schools Before and After the Revolution, 1890; Memoir of Joseph Bryan, 1909; The First Uniersity in America, 1619-1622, 1911. Home: Richmond, Va. Deceased.

MCCAIN, HENRY PINCKNEY army officer; b. in Carroll Co., Miss., Jan. 23, 1861; s. W. A. McC.; grad. U.S. Mil. Acad., 1885; m. Emeline De Moss, Nov. 14, 1888. Commd. 2d lt. 3d Inf., June 14, 1885; promoted through grades to col., Apr. 23, 1904; brig. gen. the adj. gen., Aug. 27, 1914; maj. gen. the adj. gen., Oct. 6, 1917; maj. gen. Nat. Army, Aug. 27, 1918; maj. gen. regular army, retired, July 22, 1921. Served in Montana and Minn. until 1889; prof. mil. science and tactics, La. State U., 1889-91; acting asst. adj. gen. in Alaska, and in divisions of 8th Army Corps in Philippines, 1898; actg. chief commissary and actg. judge advocate, Dept. of the Columbia, 1899-1900; mem. Gen. Staff Corps and chief of staff, Dept. of Mindanao and of Southwestern Div., Mar. and Apr. 1904; adj. gen. Philippine Div., 1912-14; adj. gen. U.S.A., 1914-18; comdg. 12th Div., Camp Devens, Mass., Aug. 1918. Awarded D.S.M., 1919. Died July 25, 1941.

MCCAIN, JOHN SIDNEY naval officer; b. Carroll County, Miss., Aug. 9, 1884; s. John Sidney and Elizabeth Ann (Young) McC.; student U. of Miss., 1901-02; grad. U.S. Naval Acad., 1906, Naval War Coll., 1929; flight instrn. (naval aviator), Naval Air Station, Pensacola, Fla., 1935-36; m. Katherine Vaulx, Aug. 9, 1909; children-John Sidney, James Gordon, Katherine Vaulx. Commd. ensign, U.S. Navy, 1906; promoted through grades to rear adm., 1941, vice admiral, July 1943; chief Bureau of Aeronautics, Sept. 1942-July 1943; dep. chief naval operations for air, July 1943; comdr. Carrier Task Force 38. Witnessed the Japanese surrender on board U.S.S. Missouri, Sept. 2, 1945. Mem. Phi Delta Theta. Mason. Clubs: Army and Navy, Army and Navy Country (Washington); Jonahtan (Los Angeles). Home: Carrollton, Miss. Died Sept. 6, 1945.

MCCALL, EDWARD RUTLEDGE naval officer; b. Beaufort, S.C., Aug. 6, 1790; S. Hext and Elizabeth (Pickering) McC.; m. Harriett McKnights. Apptd. midshipman U.S. Navy, 1808; acting lt. on Enterprise, 1812, in command of ship when it defeated Brit. ship Boxer, off Me.; promoted lt., 1813; recipient gold medal from Congress, 1814; served in Mediterranean Squadron, 1815-17, various shore duty posts, 1817-25; promoted to master comdt., 1825; in command of the Peacock in West Indian Squadron, 1830-31; promoted capt., 1835. Died Bordentown, N.J., July 31, 1853.

MCCALLA, BOWMAN HENRY rear admiral U.S.N.; b. Camden, N.J., June 19, 1844; s. Auley and Mary Duffield (Hendry) M.; apptd. from N.J. and grad. U.S. Naval Acad., 1864; m. Elizabeth Hazard Sargent, Mar. 3, 1875. Promoted ensign, Nov. 1, 1866; advanced through grades to rear adm., Oct. 11, 1903. Summer of 1864 on board the yacht America, in pursuit of Confederate steamers Florida and Tallahassee; served on Susquehanna, 1865-66; Brooklyn, 1866-67; Sabine, 1867-68; Tuscarora, 1868-71; Wabash, 1871-74; Wachusett, 1874-Naval Acad., 1874-78; exec. officer Powhatan, 1878-81; asst. to Bur. of Navigation, 1882-87; comd. Enterprise, 1887-90; Navy Yard, Mare Island, 1893-97; Naval War Coll., 1897; comd. Marblehead, N. Atlantic Sta., 1897-98, during the war with Spain; "for eminent and conspicuous gallantry in battle during the Spanish War," was advanced 6 numbers in rank; on duty Navy Yard, Norfolk, 1898-99; comd. Newark, Asiatic Sta., 1899-1901; during the Boxer uprising in China, in June, 1900, comd. the landing party from U.S. Asiatic Fleet which formed a part of the column under Vice Admiral Seymour of the British Navy, in an attempt to relieve the legations in Peking. For this service was advanced 3 numbers in rank "for eminent and conspicuous gallantry in battle," comd. Kearsarge, 1901-02; commandant, Naval Training Sta., San Francisco, 1902-03. Navy Yard, Mare Island, Calif., 1903-06; retired, June 19, 1906. Recipient of 2 Congressional medals for battle of Cienfuegos and at Guantanamo; and 1 Congressional Medal for "specially meritorious service other than in battle," during Spanish War. Decorated with Order of the Red Eagle, by Emperor of Germany; China War Medal, by the King of England, in recognition of service during Boxer uprising in China in 1900. Home: Santa Barbara, Calif. Died 1910.

MCCALLAM, JAMES ALEXANDER, army officer; born Phila., May 13, 1894; s. Thomas and Ellen Jane (Halligan) McC.; V.M.D., U. of Pa., 1917; post grad. Army Veterinary Sch., 1925; grad. Med. Field Service Sch., 1925; m. Lillian Galley, July 24, 1917; children—James A. (killed in action, Italy, June 1944); Doris M. (Mrs. Jack T. Walden). Entered the Veterinary Corps of the United States Army, as 2d lt., July 1917, and advanced through grades to brig. gen., Jan. 24, 1948; army vet., hdqrs. 6th Army, Feb. 1943-Dec. 1945; exec. officer, med. sect. advanced echelon, Hdqrs. 6th Army, Aug. 1943-Feb. 1944; med. insp. med. sect., Apr.-Oct. 1944; exec. officer med. sect. Oct. 1944-Dec. 1945; member mil. commn., Hdqrs. Southwest Pacific Area, Mar.-Sept. 1945; New Guinea (Brit. and Dutch), Leyte and Luzon, P.I., Japan (all in S.W. Pacific Theater Operations). Army vet., hdqrs. 6th Army, Southwest Pacific area, 1943-45; chief, vet. div., Office of Surg. Gen., 1946-53; chief Army Vet. Service, 1946-53. Awarded Legion of Merit medal, Bronze star medal, American Vet. Medical Assn. award, 1958, award of merit, Univ. of Pa. Gen. Alumni Society, 1959. Member U.S. com., XIVth Internat. Vets. Congress, 1948-49; mem. Am. Vet. Medical Assn. (1st. v.p., 1949, pres., 1953, Washington representative), American Public Health Association, Dist. Columbia Vet. Medical Assn. (pres. 1949-50), Pa. State Vet. Medical Association, Association of Military Surgeons, United States Livestock Sanitary Assn., Alpha Psi, Phi Zeta. Mason. Club: Army and Navy. Home: Washington DC Died July 15, 1969; buried Arlington Nat. Cemetery, Washington

MCCAMIC, CHARLES lawyer; b. Wellsburg, W.Va.; s. Nathan Stanton and Frances (Dowden) McC.; LL.B., Yale, 1899; LL.D., West Virginia Wesleyan University, 1926; m. Anna F. Smith, Apr. 9, 1902 (deceased); 1 dau., Frances Smith (Mrs. W. R. Tinker, Jr.); m. 2d, Elizabeth McCoach Taylor, Mar. 15, 1943; step son, John Taylor. Admitted Conn. and W.Va. bars, 1899, and to Supreme Court of U.S., 1911; practiced Moundsville, W.Va., 8 years, Wheeling, 1907—; member McCamic & Clark. Pres. Interstate Bridge Co., Bellaire, O.; dir. Sehon-Stevenson Co.; dir. and past pres. American Bridge, Tunnel and Turnpike Assn. Member W.Va. House of Representatives, 1905. Served as captain, World War, 1917-18; ret. lieut. col. J.A.G., Res. member American Bar Assn., W.Va. Bar Assn. (sec. 10 yrs.; Am. Gas Assn. chmn. war effort com.), Am. Law Inst., Internat. Law Assn., W.Va. Hist. Soc. (past pres.), Newcomen Soc., Va. S.A.R., Res. Officers Assn., Am. Legion (1st adj. state orgn.), Johnson Soc., Lichfield, England; Soc. Am. Legion Founders, Military Order Foreign Wars United States 27th Division Association, Kappa Alpha, Phi Alpha Delta, Phi Beta Kappa, Scabbard and Blade, Order of Coif, Phi Beta Kappa (asso.). Director in associates of Phi Beta Kappa. Episcopalian (mem. vestry). Mason. Clubs: Grolier, Yale (New York); Ft. Henry, Wheeling Country, Metropolitan (Washington); Rowfant (Cleve.); Virginia Seniors Golf Assn. Author; Doctor Samuel Johnson and the American Colonies, 1925. Home: Hawthorne Court, Wheeling. Office: Wheeling, W.Va. Died Jan. 13, 1957.

MCCAMPBELL, EUGENE FRANKLIN physician; b. Marysville O., Apr. 15, 1880; s. of James and Flora Jeanette (Ryan) McC.; Ohio State U., 1899-1902; S.B., U. of Chicago, 1906, Ph.D., 1910; M.D., Rush Medical Coll., 1912; m. Katharine Scott, June 14, 1906; children-Jean Katharine, Barbara. Instr. bacteriology, Ohio Med. U., 1903-04; asst. in bacteriology, U. of Wis., 1905-06; asst. in pathology, U. of Chicago, summers, 1908-11; asst. prof. of bacteriology, 1906-10, prof., 1910-12, prof. of preventive medicine, 1912-27, Ohio State U. Pathologist, Columbus State Hosp., 1909-11; sec. and exec. officer Ohio State Bd. of Health, 1912-16; dean Coll. of Medicine, Ohio State U., 1916-27. Lt. col. M.C., U.S.A., 1917-19; col. M.O.R.C., 1922. Fellow Am. Coll. Physicians. Methodist. Mason. Author: General Bacteriology (with Frost), 1910; Laboratory Methods for Study of Immunity, 1910. Home: Columbus, O. Died May 8, 1937.

MCCANDLESS, BRUCE, naval officer; b. Washington, Aug. 12, 1911; s. Byron and Velma May (Kitson) McC.; B.S., U.S. Naval Acad., 1932; student U.S. Naval Postgrad. Sch., 1938-39; M.A. Long Beach State College, 1953; married Sue Worthington Bradley, February 15, 1936; children—Bruce, Sue Worthington, Rosemary, Douglas Montrose. Commd. ensign, U.S.N., 1932, advanced through grades to capt., ret. and advanced to rear adm., 1952; engring., communications, navigation, gunnery, staff and command positions, 1932-52; participated operations Pacific Area, World War II, including battles of Cape Esperance, Guadalcanal, Gilbert Islands, Marshall Islands, Aleutians, Solomon Islands, Iwo Jima, Okinawa; staff Navy Dept., 1946-49; faculty Naval Acad., 1950-52; bd. control, sec.-treas. U.S. Naval Institute 1951-52, editor Proc. 1951-52. Decorated Congl. Medal Honor, Silver Star medal, Purple Heart, Presdl. Unit Citation. Mem. Naval Historical Found., Congl. Medal of Honor Soc., Order of Lafayette, Vets. of Foreign Wars, Naval Inst. Co-author: Naval Leadership, 1959; Service Etiquette. Home: Claremont CA Died Jan. 24, 1968.

MCCANN, WILLIAM PENN commodore U.S.N., retired May 1892; b. Paris, Ky., May 4, 1820; apptd. to U.S.N., Nov. 1848; grad. U.S. Naval Acad., June 15, 1854—passed midshipman; lt., Sept. 16, 1855; lt. comdr., July 16, 1862; comdr., July 25, 1866; capt., Sept. 21, 1876; commodore, Jan. 26, 1887. In blockading and other active duty during Civil war; drove off Confederate battery attacking Franklin's corps, May 2, 1862, at West Point, Va.; captured, July 4, 1862, Confederate gunboat Teaser, with plans of batteries, torpedoes and defenses of Richmond; later in numerous engagements with batteries; captured several blockade runners; took part in battle of Mobile Bay, etc. After war served on many stas.; acting rear admiral comdg. S. Pacific Sta., 1891. With 5 cruisers at Iquique, Chile, June 4, 1891, enforced the surrender of steamer Itata, with arms and ammunition smuggled out of San Diego, Calif., and transferred to the Itata at Santa Catalina Island. Sent the ship and arms back to San Diego and received thanks and commendation of Navy Dept., Mem. bd. for exam. and promotion of officers, 1891-92; during war with Spain, 1898, served as pres. on courts of inquiry, and courts martial, and as prize commr. Southern dist. of N.Y. Home: New Rochelle, N.Y. Died 1906.

MCCANN, WILLIAM SHARP, physician; b. Cadiz, O., July 6, 1889; s. Dr. Charles Fremont and Carolyn (Sharp) McC.; A.B., Ohio State U., 1911, D.Sc., 1934; M.D., Cornell U., 1915; grad. Army Med. Sch., Washington, 1971; LL.D., Hobart and William Smith Colleges, 1954; m. Gertrude Guild Fisher, M.D., Dec. 29, 1916 (deceased); children—Dorothy Elizabeth, William Peter; married 2d, Ella M. Russ, 1957. Surgical house officer, Peter Bent Brigham Hosp., Boston, 1915-16; Arthur Tracy Cabot fellow in surgery, Harvard, 1916-17; instr. in medicine, Cornell U., 1919-21; research fellow, Russell Sage Inst. of Pathology, 1919-21; adj. asst. visiting physician Bellevue Hosp., 1919-21; asso. prof. of medicine, Johns Hopkins, 1921-24; asso. physician Johns Hopkins Hosp., 1921-24; Charles A. Dewey prof. of medicine, University of Rochester, 1924-57, professor emeritus, 1957-71; vis. prof. adminstrv. medicine Sloan Institute of Hospital Administration, Cornell U., Ithaca, N.Y., 1957-59; physician in chief Strong Memorial and Rochester Municipal hosps., 1924-57. Mem. tuberculosis adv. com., N.Y. State Dept. Health; mem. med. adv. com., Masonic Found. for Health and Human Welfare. Served as lt. M.C., U.S. Army, A.E.F., 1917-19; served from comdr. to capt. MC-USNR, 1942-44. Mem. Naval Research Adv. Com., from 1946; dep. chmn. com. on med. scis. Research and Development Board, Dept. of Defense; consultant in Medicine, Veterans Administration, Branch 2, from 1946. Chmn. American Board Internal Medicine, 1947-48; trustee Asso. Universities, Inc., Brookhaven Nat. Lab., 1950. Fellow A.C.P. (regent; master), N.Y. Acad. Medicine; member Assn. Am. Physicians (pres.), A.A.A.S. (v.p., chmn. section N 1952); Soc. for Clin. Investigation, Harvey Society, Society Exptl. Biology and Medicine, A.M.A., Rochester Acad. Medicine, Am. Inst. of Nutrition, American Society Biological Chemists, American Rheumatism Association, Sigma Xi, Alpha Omega Alpha, Phi Beta Kappa; associate member United States Naval Institute United Presbyterian. Mason. Clubs: Oak Hill Country, Cornell, Fortnightly, University (Rochester). Author: Calorimetry in Medicine, 1924. Contbr. many articles to med. jours. Home: Rochester NY Died June 10, 1971; buried Cadiz OH

MCCARTHY, DANIEL EDWARD army officer; b. Albany, N.Y., Apr. 14, 1859; grad. U.S. Mil. Acad., 1881, Inf. and Cav. Sch., Ft. Leavenworth, Kan., 1887, Army War Coll., Washington, 1917; m. Laura Fendrich, Oct. 13, 1892. Commd. 2d lt. 12th Inf., June 11, 1881; 1st lt., Jan. 2, 1888; capt. a.-q.-m., Oct. 14, 1896; maj. q.-m. vols., Dec. 3, 1900; hon. disch. from vols., May 1, 1901; maj. q.-m. U.S. Army, Oct. 2, 1902; lt. col. dep. q.-m. gen., Apr. 13, 1910; col. Q.-M. Corps, Mar. 5, 1913. Served in Indian campaigns in Ariz. and N. and S.D.; in Cuba during Spanish-Am. War, later in Philippines; apptd. chief q.-m. on staff of Gen. Pershing and served with him in France until invalided home, Sept. 1917. Catholic. Elk. Author: Manual for Quartermasters Serving in the Field (Govt. Printing Office), 1900. Home: Chicago, Ill. Died 1922.

MCCARTHY, JOSEPH R(AYMOND) U.S. senator; b. Grand Chute, Outagamie County, Wis., Nov. 14, 1908; s. Timothy Thomas and Bridget (Tierney) McC.; LL.B., Marquette U., 1935; m. Jean Kerr, Sept. 29, 1953. Farm worker and grocery store employee during early years until 1929; practiced law, Waupaca, Wis., 1935-36; mem. firm Everlein & McCarthy, Shawano, Wis., 1936-39; elected circuit judge, 1939, 1945; U.S. senator from Wis., 1946— (vice chmn. Joint Com. on Housing, also mem. Banking and Currency Com., 1947-48; mem. Com. on Expenditures in Exec. Depts. 1947-52, Spl. Com. to Investigate Nat. Def. Program 1949-51, Appropriations Com. 1951—, Rules and Adminstrn. Com. 1952—, Com. on Govt. Operation (chmn), (also chmn Permanent Investigations sub-com. 1953-54) 1953—, Joint Com. on Library (chmn. 1953—). Served from pvt. to capt. USMC, 1942-45; assigned to marine aviation as ground officer; tail gunner (17 missions in S. Pacific). Recipient D.F.C., Air Medal with four gold stars; citation for extraordinary achievement as marine intelligence officer. Mem. Vets. Fgn. Wars, Am. Legion, Amvets, Republican. K.C., Lion, Elk, Eagle. Author: America's Retreat from Victory, The Story of George Catlett Marshall, 1951; McCarthyism, The Fight for America, 1952. Home: 514 Story St., Appleton, Wis. Office: Senate Office Bldg., Washington. Died May 2, 1957.

MCCARTNEY, ALBERT JOSEPH clergyman, lectr.; b. Northwood, O.; s. John Longfellow and Catherine (Robertson) M.C.; student Univs. of Denver, Wis., Princeton, Oxford and Glasgow; D.D., U. Pitts., 1910, Geneva Coll.; LL.D., Beaver Coll., 1937; H.H.D., Rollins Coll., Winter Park, Fla.; m. Mary Hamilton Graham, June 29, 195; children-Lt. Benjamin Conkling, D.F.C., USAAF (lost in action over Italy, Oct. 1, 1944), Albert Noble. Ordained Presbyn. ministry, 1903; pastor successively Westfield, Pa., Sharon, Pa., Kenwood Ch., Chgo., 1st Ch., Santa Monica, Cal.; now emeritus minister Covenant 1st Presbyn. Ch. (now Nat. Presbyn. Ch.), Washington; v.p. com. on Religious Life in Nation's Capital; religious cons. Internat. Information Adminstrn.; chmn. procurement com. gen. commn. Army and Navy Chaplains; liason officer State Dept. with chief of chaplains bd. Dept. Def. Trustee Princeton Theol. Sem. Mem. Chgo. Assn. Commerce and Ill. com. Chgo. Council on Fgn. Relations, Chgo. Crime Commn. Comdr. USNR, Ch. Corps, World War II. Chaplain Rep. Nat. Convs., 1936, 40. Mem. Washington Lit. Soc. Trustee Am. Peace Soc. Dir. Chgo. Sunday Evening Club 1946-50. Republican. Clubs: Chevy Chase, Cosmos, Princeton (Washington). Address: 1302 18th St. N.W., Washington. Died Aug. 15, 1965; buried Arlington Nat. Cemetery.

MCCARTY, DAN governor; b. Ft. Pierce, Fla. Jan. 18, 1912; s. Daniel Thomas and Frances (Moore) McC.; B.S.A., U. Fla., 1934; m. Olie Brown, Sept. 21, 1940; children-Daniel T., III, Michael Samuel, Frances Lela. Citrus grower, packer, rancher; rep. St. Lucie Co., Fla. State Legislature, 1937-43, house speaker, 1941; governor of Fla. since 1953. Chmn. adv. com. on edn. St. Lucie Co., 1946-47, 50-51; chmn. fund drive, community library; state campaign chmn. Am. Cancer Soc., 1949-50; mem. citizens tax com., 1947. Served as battery comdr. Battery B., 172d F.A., U.S. Army, 1941-45, advanced to col. U.S. VII Army. Decorated Legion of Merit, Bronze Star, Purple Heart (U.S.); Croix de Guerre (France). Mem. Jr. C. of C. (past pres.), Sr. C. of C. (past pres.), Presidents' Round Table, Ft. Pierce Vol. Firemen's Assn. (chmn.), Am. Legion, Vets. Fgn., Wars, Blue Key, Sigma Phi Epsilon. Episcopalian (sr. warden). Mason (Shriner), Odd Fellow, Elk (lodge trustee). Woodman of the World, Moose. Club: Ft. Pierce Rotary (past pres.). Home: Fort Pierce, Fla. Office: Governor's Office, Tallahassee. Died Sept. 28, 1953; buried Fort Pierce, Fla.

MCCASKEY, WILLIAM SPENCER major gen. U.S.A.; b. Lancaster Co., Pa., Oct. 2, 1843; s. William and Margaret Eckert (Piersol) M.; bro. of John Piersol M.; ed. pub. schs., Lancaster, Pa., until 1858; m. Eleanor Forsyth Garrison, Nov. 20, 1867. Was one of first 75,-000 men enrolled as vols. in Civil War; pvt. Co. F, 1st Pa. Inf., Apr.20-July 26, 1861; 1st sergt. Co. B, 79th Pa. Inf., Sept. 5, 1861-Oct. 8, 1862; promoted through grades to maj. gen., Apr. 15, 1907. Engaged in all battles of Army of the Cumberland; was on Sherman's marches to the Sea and through the Carolinas to Washington; in Grand Review, Washington, May, 1865; comd. 20th Inf., Cuban campaign, 1898, in battle of El Caney and Santiago; in Philippines, Mar. 1899-Feb. 1902; at Ft. Sheridan, Ill., Mar. 23, 1902-Nov. 20, 1903; comd. 1st brigade and post of Manila, P.I.; later comd. depts. of the Colo., Tex., and Dak.; retired Oct. 2, 1907. Home: Pacific Grove, Calif. Died Aug. 10, 1914.

MCCAULEY, CHARLES ADAM HOKE army officer; b. Middletown, Md., July 13, 1847; grad. U.S. Mil. Acad., 1870. Comm'd. 2d lt. 3d Arty., June 15, 1870; transferred to 3d Cav., Oct. 7, 1878; 1st lt., May 5, 1879; capt. asst. q.-m., Feb. 18, 1881; maj. q.-m., Aug. 8, 1894; lt. col. deputy q.-m.-gen., July 13, 1899; col. asst. q.-m.-gen., Feb. 24, 1903. Served with Red River expdn. into Indian Ty. and Texas as ornithologist, 1876; asst. to chief engr., Dept. of the Mo., 1877-79; q.-m. Dept. of the Platte, 1883-87. Invented system of signaling by means of mirrors, 1871. Author: Ornithology of the Red River Region of Texas, 1877; The San Juan Reconnaissance in Colorado and New Mexico, 1877; Reports on the White River Indian Agency, Colorado, and the Uintah Indian Agency, 1879; Pagosa Springs, Colorado, Its Geology and Botany, 1879. Address: War Dept., Washington.

MCCAULEY, CHARLES STEWART naval officer; b. Phila., Feb. 3, 1793; s. John and Sarah (Stewart) McC.; m. Leila Dickens, Oct. 25, 1831. Apptd. midshipman U.S. Navy, 1809, acting lt., 1813, lt., 1814, master comdr., 1831; commanded ship St. Louis of West India Squadron, 1834; promoted capt., 1839; comdt. Washington (D.C.) Navy Yard, 1846-49; comdr.-in-chief Pacific Squadron, 1850-53; capt., in command of South Atlantic Squadron, 1855, sent by Pres. Pierce to protect Am. interests at Cuba; comdt. Norfolk (Va.) Navy Yard, 1860-61, destroyed guns and ships there to prevent their capture by Confederate forces, 1861; ret. as capt., 1862, promoted to commodore on ret. list, 1867. Died Washington, Mar. 21, 1869.

MCCAULEY, EDWARD YORKE naval officer; b. Phila., Nov. 2, 1827; s. Daniel Smith andSarah (Yorke) McC.; L.L.D. (hon.), Hobart Coll., 1892; m. Josephine Berkeley, Jan. 28, 1858, 1 son, Carter Nelson Berkeley. Commd. midshipman U.S. Navy, 1841, served in ship Constitution, 1846-48, passed midshipman, 1847; lt. in ship Niagara, assisted in laying Atlantic Cable, 1858, then stationed U.S. Naval Observatory; resigned, 1858, became businessman, St. Paul, Minn.; volunteered for service at outbreak Civil War; commd. lt. comdr. U.S. Navy 1862; promoted comdr., 1866, fleet capt. N. Atlantic Squadron at Portsmouth and Boston navy yards, 1867-68; head French dept. U.S. Naval Acad., Annapolis, Md.; comdr. ship Lackawanna in Pacific; supt. Naval Asylum, Phila.; commd. capt., 1872, commodore, 1881, rear adm., 1885, ret., 1887; elected to Am. Philos. Soc., Phila., 1881. Author: A Manual for the Use of Students of Egyptology, 1883. Died Canonicut Island, Narragansett Bay, R.I., Sept. 14, 1894.

MCCAULEY, JAMES WAYNE army officer; b. Jedsonia, Ark., Sept. 24, 1902; s. James Allen and Rose Mae (Best) McC.; student U. Ark., 1921-22; A.B., Ouachita Coll., 1925; grad. Brooks Field AAF Pre-Flight Sch., 1928, Kelly Field AAF Basic Flying Sch., 1929, Maxwell Field AC Tech. Sch. 1929; m. Ruth Friar, Feb. 12, 1934; children-James Wayne, John Milton. Commd. 2d lt. inf. U.S. Army, 1923, trans. AC, advanced through grades to brig. gen., 1944; comdg. officer Seattle Air Def. Wing, fighter group in command air defenses of N.W., 1942; comdr. Fighter Wing, Eng., 6 mos., as comdr. of wing participated in Normandy offensive, June 6, 1944, and established Am. Air Force Hdqrs. on continent, June 7, 1944; also participated fighter bomber operations during campaigns in France and Belgium; comdg. gen. Hdqrs. 70th Fighter Wing, USAAF, Germany; now vice comdr. eastern air def. force, Stewart Air Force Base. Decorated Air Medal, Legion of Merit (U.S.); Legion of Honor (France). Mem. Phi Delta Kappa. Home: 135 E. Merrick St., Shreveport, La. Died Mar. 9, 1958.

MCCAW, WALTER DREW army officer; b. Richmond, Va., Feb. 10, 1863; s. James Brown and Delia (Patterson) McC.; ed. pvt. shcs., Richmond; M.D., Med. Coll. of Va., 1882; M.D., Coll. Phys. and Surg. (Columbia), 1884, D.Sc., 1932; unmarried. Commd. asst. surgeon U.S.A., 1884; capt. asst. surgeon, 1889; maj. surgeon, Feb. 2, 1901; lt. col. Med. Corps, Jan. 1, 1909; col., May 9, 1913; brig. gen. asst. surgeon general U.S.A., Mar. 5, 1919, retired, Feb. 10, 1927. In volunteer service as major brig. surgeon, June 4, 1898; major surgeon, 42d U.S. Vol. Inf., Aug. 17, 1899. Was in campaign of Santiago de Cuba, 1898; in P.I., 1900-01, during insurrection; has served in Depts. of Mo., the Platte, East Tex. and Calif.; on duty in Washington, 1902-13; librari div.; prof. mil. hygiene, 1902-05, prof. mil. and tropical medicine, 1904-13, Army Med. Sch., Washington; chief surgeon Div. of the Philippines, 1914; comdg. Div. Hosp., Manila, 1915; dept. surgeon, Southern Dept., Ft. Sam Houston, Tex., 1916-17; on duty chief surgeon's office, A.E.F., Mar.-Oct. 1918; chief surgeon A.E.F., Oct. 1918-July 15, 1919. D.S.M. (U.S.). also awarded Silver Star medal by U.S. 1932; Comdr. Legion of Honor (French); Companion of the Bath (C.B.) (British); Officer Order of Saints Maurice and Lazarus (Italian). Fellow Am. Coll. of Surgeons; asso. fellow Coll. Physicians Phila.; hon. mem. Royal Soc. Medicine, Va. Soc. of the Cincinnati. Home: Woodstock, N.Y. Died July, 7, 1939,

MCCAWLEY, CHARLES GRYMES marine officer; b. Phila., Jan. 29, 1837; s. Capt. James and Mary (Holt) McC.; m. Elizabeth Colegate, Mar. 1863; m. 2d, Elise Hender, 1870; 2 children. Served at Battle of Chapultupec and capture of Mexico City in Mexican War; apptd. 2d lt. Marine Corps, 1847; brevetted 1st lt., 1847, promoted 1st lt., 1855, capt., 1861, brevetted maj., 1863; present at Morris Island (S.C.) during bombardment and destruction of Ft. Sumter and capture of Fts. Wagner and Gregg, 1863; promoted maj., 1864, lt. col., 1867; ordered to command Marine Barracks, Washington, D.C., also to superintend recruiting, 1871; col.-comdt. Marine Corps, 1876. Died Phila., Oct. 13, 1891; buried Abington, Pa.

MCCAWLEY, CHARLES LAURIE officer U.S. Marines; b. Boston, Mass., Aug. 24, 1865; s. Charles Grymes and Elizabeth Mary (Colegate) M.; ed. pvt. schs.; LL.B., Columbian (now George Washington) U., 1893; m. Sarah Helen Frelinghuysen Davis, July 24, 1906. Apptd. capt. a.-q.-m., U.S. Marine Corps, June 27, 1897; bvtd. maj., June 11, 1898, for "distinguished conduct in the presence of the enemy"; promoted lt. col., May 13, 1908; col. q.-m. , June 2, 1913; brig. gen. q.-m. Marine Corps, Aug. 29, 1916. At hdqrs. Marine Corps, Washington, until April. 1898; at Key West, Fla., and Guantanamo, Cuba, until Aug. 1898; participated in engagements in defense of Camp McCalla, Guantanamo, and in attack on Manzanillo, 1898; with 1st Batt. of Marines, Cavite, P.I., 1899; in charge depot of supplies, Phila. Pa., 1900-02; at headquarters Marine Corps, and on duty with the President, 1902-10; in charge Quartermaster's Department, Marine Corps, 1910-13; appointed q.-m. Marine Corps, June 2, 1913; retired Aug. 24, 1929. Holds West India campaign medal of Spanish-Am. War, Spanish War and Philippine campaign badges, D.S.M., and Brevet medal (Navy), and Victory medal. Died Apr. 29, 1935.

MCCLARAN, JOHN WALTER naval officer; b. Wooster, O., Oct. 1, 1887; s. John Cook and Elisabeth (Deer) McC.; student Wooster Acad., 1901-04, Wooster U., 1905-06, U.S. Naval Acad., 1907-11; m. Stephana Prager, Nov. 25, 1925; Stephen, Ann, Patricia. Commd. ensign USN, 1911; promoted through grades to rear adm., 1941; served in P.R., uprising, 1912, Mexican occupation, 1914, World War, 1917-18; asst. naval attaché Tokyo, 1920-22; staff comdr., Yangtze Patrol, 1922-24; established bases for 1st round-the-world flight in Kurile Islands and Japan, 1924; staff comdr. Battle Force, 1928-30; comdr. Mine Div., 1933-35; comd. Flagship Mine Force, 1937-39; laid first submarine nets in Puget Sound and San Francisco Bay, 1937; assisted in establishing advance base, Midway Islands, 1938-39; ret. because phys. disability, 1941. Awarded D.S.C., Mexican Campiagn medal, Victory medal, etc. Mem. Phi Gamma Delta. Clubs: Chevy Chase (Md.); Army and Navy Country (Washington); Goofy Gooney (Midway Island). Home: 1138 Mission Ridge Rd., Santa Barbara, Cal. Died Mar. 28, 1948.

MCCLATCHY, CARLOS KELLY newspaper editor; b. Sacramento, Calif., Mar. 2, 1891; s. Charles Kenny and Ella (Kelly) McC.; B.S., Columbia, 1911; m. Phebe Briggs, Jan. 17, 1918; children-James Briggs, William Ellery, Charles Kenny. Began as reporter Sacramento Bee, 1911; editor Fresno Bee, 1922—; gen. mgr. Sacramento Bee and Modesto (Calif.) News Herald; v.p. McClatchy newspapers. Served as capt. Inf., U.S.A., World War. Home: Fresno, Calif. Died Jan. 17, 1933.

MCCLAUGHRY, ROBERT WILSON warden; b. Fountain Green, Ill., July 22, 1839; s. Matthew and Mary M.; A.B., Monmouth Coll., 1860 (LL.D., 1906); m. Elizabeth C. Madden, June 17, 1862 (died 1914); m. 2d, Emma F. Madden, Apr. 8, 1915. Private 118th Illinois Inf., Aug. 15, 1862; capt., Nov. 7, 1862; maj., Dec. 8, 1862; served in Army of the Tenn. until May 1864; transferred to pay dept., as maj. and additional p.-m. vols.; mustered out, Oct. 13, 1865. Co. clerk Hancock Co., Ill., 1865-69; warden Ill. State Penitentiary, 1874-88; gen. sutp. Pa. Industrial Reformatory, 1888-91; chief of police, Chicago, 1891-93; gen. supt. Ill. State Reformatory, 1893-97; warden Ill. State Penitentiary, 1897-99, U.S. Penitentiary, Leavenworth, Kan., July 1, 1899-July 1, 1913. Home: Joliet, Ill. Died Nov. 9, 1920.

MCCLEARY, ROBERT ALTWIG, educator; b. Dayton, O., Jan. 9, 1923; s. Harold and Mae (Altwig) McC.; B.A., Harvard, 1944; M.D., Johns Hopkins, 1947, Ph.D. in Psychology, 1951; m. Nan Sarah Brown, Feb. 3, 1945; children—Robert Edward, Beverly Nan, Susan Elaine. Intern internal medicine Barnes Hosp., St. Louis, 1947-48; from asst. prof. to asso. prof. psychology U. Mich., 1953-61; prof. psychology and physiology U. Chgo., 1961-73; cons. Aerospace Med. Center, Brooks AFB, 1961-73, Nat. Insts. Mental Health, 1961-73. Served to capt. USAF, 1951-53. USPHS fellow, 1953-55; Carnegie Sr. Research fellow U. Oslo (Norway), 1957-58. Fellow Am. Psychol. Assn.; mem. Psychonomics Soc., Soc. Exptl. Psychologists. Spl. research exptl. analysis brain-mechanisms of behavior. Home: Chicago IL Died Mar. 20, 1973.

MCCLEAVE, ROBERT, army officer; b. Ft. Union, N.M., Sept. 9, 1874; s. William and Mary (Crooke) McC.; grad. high sch., Berkeley, Calif.; student Merrill Bus. Coll., San Francisco, Calif.; student U. of Calif.; m. Etta Bartlett, 1898; children—Phyllis (dec.), Robert B., Mildred (wife of Newell E. Watts, U.S. Army). Enlisted as pvt., inf., 1894, advanced through grades to col., July 1, 1920; brig. gen., Dec. 13, 1929; now retired. Served in Spanish-Am. War (silver star citation for distinguished service at Battle of Santiago), Philippine Campaign, 1902-03; asst. chief of staff, 1st Am. Army, World War; observation duty, Brit. and French armies, 1917; as chief of operations sect. directed planning and operations of battles of St. Mihiel and Meuse-Argonne. Awarded D.S.M. for World War services. Presbyn. Mason. Club: San Diego (Calif.) Athletic. Address: 5555 Hollywood Blvd., Hollywood CA*

MCCLELLAN, GEORGE BRINTON army officer, gov. N.J.; b. Phila., Dec. 3, 1828; s. Dr. George and Elizabeth (Brinton) McC.; attended U. Pa., 1840-42; grad. U.S. Mil. Acad., 1846; m. Ellen Marcy, 1860, 2 children. Commd. 2d lt. Corps Engrs., U.S. Army, 1846, brevetted 1st lt., 1847; promoted capt., 1847, served in Mexican War; asst. instr. in practical mil. engring. U.S. Ilil. Acad., 1848-51; asst. engr. for constrn. of Ft. Delaware, 1851; chief engr. on staff Gen. Persifor F. Smith, 1852; apptd. capt. U.S. Cavalry, 1855; resigned to become chief engr. I.C. R.R., 1857, v.p. in charge operations in Ill., 1858-60; became pres. Ohio & Miss. R.R., 1860; apptd. maj. gen. Ohio Militia, 1861; apptd. maj. gen. U.S. Army, May 1861, placed in command of Dept. of Ohio (including Ohio, Ind., Ill.); comdr. Division of Potomac, July 1861; became comdr.-in-chief U.S. Army, Nov. 1861; reorganized and retrained Army of Potomac, finally (after prodding from Pres. Lincoln) took offense in Peninsular Campaign, Mar.-Aug. 1862; advanced very slowly, fighting at Yorktown, Seven Pines, Fair Oaks; was stopped at Gaines' Mill, June, 1862; pushed back in Seven Days' Battle; stopped Lee's invasion of North at Battle of Antietam, but did not pursue Lee; replaced by Gen. Burnside, Nov. 7, 1862; Democratic candidate for Pres. U.S., 1864, defeated by Lincoln; chief engr. Dept. of Docks, N.Y.C., 1870-72; gov. N.J., 1878-81. Author: McClellan's Own Story, 1887. Died Orange, N.J., Oct. 29, 1885.

MCCLELLAN, GEORGE BRINTON publicist; b. Dresden, Saxony (where his parents were on a visit), Nov. 23, 1865; 65; s. Gen. George Brinton (U.S.A.) and Ellen M. (March) M.; A.B., Princeton, 1886, A.M., 1889, LL.D., 1905; LL.D., Fordham, 1905, Union U., 1906; m. Georgianna L. Heckscher, Oct. 30, 1889. Was reporter and on staffs of New York dailies; treas. New York & Brooklyn Bridge, 1889-92; admitted to bar, 1892; pres. bd. of aldermen, New York, 1893-94; mem. 54th to 58th Congresses (1895-1903); member Com. on Ways and Means; mayor New York, 1903-09. Hon. chancellor, Union U., 1906; Stafford Little lecturer on pub. affairs, Princeton U., 1908-10, university lecturer public affairs, 1911-12, prof. econ. history, 1921-31, prof. emeritus, 1931-; also lecturer at Cornell, Rutgers, Washington and Jefferson, Washington and Lee, U. of N.C., etc. An incorporator, trustee and vice-pres. Am. Acad. in rome; chmn. exec. com. Smithsonian Gallery of Art Commn. Maj., Ordnance Dept., U.S.R., Apr. 16, 1917; lt. col., U.S.A., Jan. 13, 1918; served in U.S. and overseas, Meuse-Argonne Battle Clasp; hon. disch., Apr. 18, 1919; now col. inactive, U.S. Army. Hon. mem. Am. Inst. of Architects; awarded medal of Beaux Arts Soc. of Architects, 1909; patron Am. Mus. of Natural History; fellow in perpetuity Met. Mus. of Art. Grand officer Order Crown of Italy. Democrat. Episcopalian (sr. warden St. John's Ch., Washington); trustee of Church Charities and Diocesan Church Funds, Diocese of Washington). Author: The Oligarchy of Venice, 1904; The Heel of War, 1915; Venice and Bonaparte, 1931; Modern Italy, 1933. Home: Washington, D.C. Died Nov. 30, 1940.

MCCLELLAN, HENRY BRAINERD prin. of Sayre Female Inst., 1870-; b. Phila., Oct. 17, 1840; s. Samuel McC. (M.D.); grad. Williams Coll., 1858 (A.M.); m. Katherine M. Matthews. Taught school in Va., 1858-61; served 4 yrs. in C.S.A. in Northern Va., and was, 1863-65, maj. and asst. adjt. gen. and chief of staff of the cav. corps, successively, under Gens. J. E. B. Stuart and Wade Hampton. Author: The Life and Campaigns of Major General J. E. B. Stuart, 1886. Home: Lexington, Ky. Died 1904.

MCCLELLAN, JOHN army officer; b. Chicago, Ill., Apr. 11, 1847; s. Col. John and Jane Josephine (Walker) M.; ed. pvt. schs., St. Paul, Detroit, and in Germany; grad. U.S. Mil. Acad., 1867; grad. Arty. Sch., 1888; m. Miss A. R. L. Wüppermann, Of Hamburg, Germany, 1885; children-Frederic W., Rose Lee (wife of Charles W. Exton, U.S.A.), Josephine F. J.; m. 2d, Miss E. A. Halstead, of Honolulu, T.H., Jan. 3, 1905; 1 son, John Halstead. Apptd. 2d lt. 5th U.S. Arty., June 17, 1867; 1st lt., Jan. 5, 1870; capt., Oct. 25, 1894; maj. chief ordnance officer, vols., July 18, 1898; hon. discharged from vol. service, May 12, 1899; maj., U.S. Arty. Corps, Feb. 28, 1901; lt. col., Aug. 11, 1903; col., Mar. 16, 1906; brig. gen., June 1, 1906; retired at own request, over 40 yrs.' service, June 9, 1906. Served as officer of weather bur. of War Dept. for "valuable services," 1883; in charge ordnance depots 7th Army Corps, at Jacksonville Fla., Savannah, Ga., and Havana, Cuba, 1898-99; on staff of Gen. Fitzhugh Lee, Aug. 1898-Jan. 1899; on staff of Gen. Brooke at Havana, Jan.-Apr. 1899. Home: San Diego, Calif. Died Nov. 24, 1928.

MCCLELLAND, HAROLD MARK army officer; b. Tiffin, Ia., Nov. 4, 1893; s. John Mark and Mary Elizabeth (Corbet) McC.; B.S., Kan. State N., 1916; grad. Army Flying Sch., 1918; student Columbia, 1925-26; grad. AC Tactical Sch., 1936, Chem. Warfare Sch., 1936; Command and Gen. Staff Sch., 1937; m. Doris Cruger Mellersh, May 11, 1921; 1 son, Alan John. Commd. 2d lt. Inf., 1917; promoted through grades to brig. gen., 1942, permanent maj. gen., 1944; apptd. asst. chief of staff for operations and tng. G-3, of Spl. Army Observer Group, London, May 1941; air communications officer Army Air Forces, July 1942-Apr. 1946; CG Airways and Air Communications Service (AACS), 1946; now dep. comdr. services, Mil. Air Transport Service. Decorations: D.S.M. Legion of Merit; Comdr. Order of Brit. Empire. Died Nov. 1965.

MCCLERNAND, EDWARD JOHN army officer; b. Jacksonville, Ill., Dec. 29, 1848; s. Maj. Gen. John Alexander (comdr. 13th Army Corps in Civil War) and Sarah (Dunlap) M.; ed. Jacksonville and Springfield, Ill., 1856-66; grad. U.S. Mil. Acad., 1870; m. Sarah Pomp, Nov. 14, 1888. Apptd. 2d lt. 2d Cav., June 15, 1870; promoted through grades to brig. gen. Aug. 27, 1912. Breveted first lieut., Feb. 27, 1890, "for gallantry in pursuit of Indians and in actions against them at Bear Paw Mountains, Mont., Sept. 30, 1877"; awarded Congressional Medal of Honor, Nov. 27, 1894, "for most distinguished gallantry in action against Nez Percé Indians." Served in Santiago Campaign, Spanish-Am. War, later in Philippines; retired from active service, Dec. 29, 1912. Home: Easton, Pa. Died Feb. 9, 1926.

MCCLERNAND, JOHN A. lawyer, veteran general; b. Breckenridge Co., Ky., May 30, 1812; on his father's death, 1816, his mother removed to Shawneetown, Ill.; brought up on farm; admitted to bar, 1832; served in war against Sacs and Foxes, 1832; mem. Ill. legislature, 1836-42; edited Shawneetown Democrat, and practiced law. Mem. Congress, 1843-51 and 1859-61; resigned to enter army; raised McClernand Brigade and served as brig. gen. and maj. gen. vols.; commanded the right of the line at Fort Donelson; a division at Shiloh; relieved Gen. Sherman in Vicksburg expedition, Jan. 1863; led at capture of Arkansas Post; clmd. 13th army corps until relieved, July 1863; resigned from army, Nov. 30, 1864; resumed practice at Springfield, Ill. Home: Springfield, Ill. Died 1900.

MCCLINTOCK, HARRY WINFRED, supt. schs.; b. Johnston City, Ill., May 22, 1907; s. Moses E. and Flora B. (Mosley) McC.; Ph.B., Shurtleff Coll., 1929; M.A. in Edn., U. Ky., 1941; postgrad. Dartmouth, 1943, Ill. State U., 1963; m. Harriet K. Christoe, June 10, 1931; 1 dau., Katheryn Anne. Tchr., Frankfort Community High Sch., West Frankfort, Ill. 1929-43; pub. relations Tomlinson Motors, West Frankfort, 1947-54; co-owner Mack's Super Market, West Frankfort, 1954-55; asst. dir. Ill. Dept. Pub. Welfare, Springfield, 1955-61; tchr. high sch., Springfield, 1961; supt. schs., Gridley, Ill., 1961-69. Mem. Bd. Spl. Edn., McLean County, Ill., 1965-69. Mem. Ill. Ho. of Reps., 1947-55, chmn. mil. affairs com., sec. sch. problems com., 1951-55. Served to lt. comdr. USNR, 1943-46. Mem. Am. Assn. Sch. Adminstrs., N.E.A., Ill. Edn. Assn., Am. Legion. Republican. Mem. United Ch. of Christ. Kiwanian. Club: Community (West Frankfort). Home: Gridley IL Died May 8, 1969.

MCCLINTOCK, JAMES HARVEY writer; b. Sacramento, Calif., Feb. 23, 1864; s. John and Sarah Ann (Brittingham) M.; m. Dorothy Goodson Bacon, June 15, 1900. Formerly teacher pub. schs. and editor in Ariz.; postmaster, Phoenix, 1902-14, 1928-33; state historian Ariz., 1919-23; Rep. candidate for U.S. Senator, 1922. Captain 1st U.S. Vol. Cav. (Rough Riders), Spanish-Am. War; severely wounded in Cuba; col. 1st Regt. Inf., N.G. Ariz., 1902-10; actg. adj. gen., 1908. Mem. Ariz. Folk Lore Soc. (pres.), Ariz. Archaeol. Soc. (pres.), Rough Riders' Assn. (pres.), United Spanish War Vets. (former dept. comdr.); former treas. State Rep. Com.; former chmn., treas., Maricopa County Rep. Com. Unitarian. Author: McClintock's History of Arizona, 1916; Mormon Settlement in Arizona, 1921. Home: Phoenix, Ariz. Died May 10, 1934.

MCCLINTOCK, JOHN CALVIN, thyroid surgeon; b. Iowa City, Mar. 2, 1906; s. John T. and Beulah (George) McC.; B.S., State U. Ia., 1927, M.D., 1929; m. Martha Mumma, July 11, 1930; children—Gail (Mrs. David Pike), Beulah Janes (Mrs. Russell Weidman), John T. II. Intern Montreal Gen. Hosp., 1929-30; fellow surgery Cleve. Clinic Found., 1930-32; clin. asst. surgery Northwestern U., 1933-34; mem. faculty Albany (N.Y.) Med. Coll., 1942-69, asso. clin. prof. surgery, 1956-69; mem. staff Albany Med. Center Hosp., 1937-69, attending surgeon, 1957-69. Served to maj., M.C., AUS, World War II. Fellow A.C.S. (past bd. govs.); mem. Albany County Med. Soc. (pres. 1955-56), Med. Soc.

State N.Y. (exec. council 1955-65), A.M.A. (ho. of dels. 1957-69), Excelsior Surg. Soc., Am. Thyroid Assn. (pres. 1962-63; Distinguished Service award 1965), Pan-Pacific Surg. Assn., Sigma Xi, Alpha Omega Alpha. Presbyn. (trustee). Contbr. med. jours. Home: Slingerlands NY Died Feb. 3, 1969; buried Graceland Cemetery, Delmar NY

MCCLOSKEY, MANUS, army officer, hosp. supt.; b. Pittsburgh, Pa., Apr. 24,21874; s. James E. and Catherine McC.; B.S., U.S. Mil. Acad., 1898; honor grad. Army Sch. of the Line, 1909; grad. Army Staff Coll., 1910; grad. General Staff Coll., Washington, D.C., 1920; m. Sara Monro, Aug. 14, 1901; children—Monro, Sally. Commd. 2d lt. 5th Arty., Apr. 26, 1898; promoted through various grades to col., May 15, 1917; brig. gen. (temp.), Aug. 8, 1918; brig. gen. (permanent), Sept. 1, 1930. At Santiago, Cuba, Aug. 10-19, 1898; comdr. platoon of light battery at Mil. Athletic Tournament, Madison Sq. Garden, N.Y. City, Mar. 20-25, 1899; in Philippines and China, 1899-1901; wounded in action, Oct. 3, 1899; participated in march to Peking and rescue of Legation, Aug. 1900; again in Philippines, 1907; comdg. West Point Battery at U.S. Mil. Acad., 1911-12, 1st Batn., 3d Field Arty., Tex., 1913-14; instr. Nat. Guard F.A., at Tobyhanna, Pa., 1915; comdg. regt. of Va. and N.H. F.A., in Tex., Sept. 1916-May 1917; organized 12th Regt. F.A., U.S. Army, June 1917; took regt. to France, Jan. 1918, and comd. it in action at Verdun, Chateau Thierry, Belleau Wood and Soissons, Mar.-Aug. 1918; wounded in action at Soissons, July 19, 1918; comd. 152d Brigade F.A., 77th Div., in action on the Vesle and through the Argonne-Meuse operations until armistice, and until Feb. 1919; comdg. 2d Brigade F.A., 2d Div., in Germany, until July 1919; comdg. Camp Knox, Ky., Aug. 1920; on Gen. Staff hdqrs., 6th Corps Area, Chicago, Ill., Jan. 1921-June 30, 1924; on organized reserve duty as chief of Staff, 6th Corps, July 1, 1924-Dec. 29, 1925; comdg. 11th Field Arty., Hawaii, 1926-28; organized reserve duty, N.Y. City, Jan.-Apr. 1929; chief of staff Arty. Group, Chicago, Apr. 1929-Aug. 31, 1930; comd. Ft. Sheridan, Ill., to May 23, 1931, Ft. Bragg, N.C., June 3, 1931-Apr. 30, 1938; now retired. Organized, 1933, and administered Civilian Conservation Corps in N.C., 1933-36; supt. Cook County Hosp., Chicago, 1938-47. D.S.M., Silver Star with oak-leaf cluster, Purple Heart with oak-leaf cluster (U.S.); Legion of Honor, Croix de Guerre (French); Crown of Italy (Italian). Mem. Am. Coll. Hosp. Adminstrs. Club: Army and Navy (Washington). Home: 181 Sheridan Rd., Winnetka IL

MCCLUNG, REID LAGE coll. dean; b. Louisa, Ky., Nov. 12, 1885; s. Samuel Floyd and Lorena (Rupert) McC.; B.Pd., Morris Harvey Coll., Barboursville, W.Va., 1902, A.B., 1904, LL.D., 1940; grad. study, Vanderbilt 2 yrs., U. of Chicago, 1 yr.; Ph.D., New York University, 1920, Doctor of Commercial Science, 1950; married Helen Odell, Nov. 21, 1921; children-Mary Eleanor, John Reid. Instr. in Latin, Willia Halsel Coll., Vinita, Indian Ty. (now Okla.), 1904-05; instr. in economics, N.M. Mil. Inst., Roswell, 1907-09; v.p. and prof. economics, Morris Harvey Coll., 1905-15; instr. in economics, Cornell U., 1915-17; instr., advancing to prof. economics, and chmn. department, New York University, 1919-27; dean College of Commerce and Business Administration, U. So. Cal., 1927-51, emeritus since 1951; special Fulbright lectr. U. Alexandria, Egypt., 1952-53; achievement and service awards, Morris Harvey College, 1954. Served as 2d lt. & maj. Machine Gun Corps, U.S. Army, 1917-18; chief personnel statistician, Gen. Staff, Washington, D.C., 1918-19, pres. Southern Calif. Management Council, 1944-45. mem. Am. Econ. Assn., Beta Gamma Sigma, Blue Key, Phi Kappa Sigma, Phi Kappa Phi, Pi Gamma Mu, Alpha Kappa Psi, Phi Delta Kappa, Skull and Dagger; prs. Pacific Coast Economic Assn., 1935. Grand pres. Beta Gamma Sigma. Coll., of Commerce Nat. Scholarship Fraternity since 1946. Southern Methodist. Club: University. Author; Earning and Spending, 1927. Editor; Hull's Industrial Depressions (revised edit.), 1928. Author many articles in scientific and professional publs. Home: 951 Victoria Av., Los Angeles. Died Aug. 18, 1961; buried Forest Lawn Meml. Park, Glendale, Cal.

MCCLURE, GEORGE army officer; b. Londonderry, Ireland, 1770; s. Finla McClure; m. Eleanor Boie, Aug. 20, 1795; m. 2d, Sarah Welles, 1808. Mcht., Bath, Steuben County, N.Y., 1793-1812; served as brig. gen. N.Y. Militia; in command detachment at Ft. George, Can. on Niagara River, 1813; abandoned fort in face of superior enemy forces, burned Newark (once capital of Upper Can.); British burned Buffalo and Black Rock (N.Y.) in retaliation; sheriff Steuben County, 1815; mem. N.Y. Legislature from Steuben County, 3 terms. Died Elgin, Ill., Aug. 16, 1851.

MCCLURE, NATHANIEL FISH retired army officer; b. Crittenden, Ky., July 21, 1865; s. Ezra K. and Nannie (Dickerson) McC.; B.S., U.S. Mil. Acad., 1887; distinguished grad. Army Sch. of the Line, 1909; grad. Army Staff Coll., 1910, Army War Coll., 1917; m. Mamie Chapin, July 14, 1890. Commd. 2d lt. cav. U.S. Army, June 12, 1887, and advanced through grades to brig. gen. Nat. Army, Dec. 17, 1917-Nov. 11, 1918; brig. gen. U.S. Army, retired, June 21, 1930. In Porto Rico, 1899-1900; in Philippines, 1901-03; instr. Army Service Schs., 1913-16; campaign, Northern Mexico, 1916; comdg. Camp No. 1, St. Nazaire, France, 1917-18, Base Sect. No. 5, S.O.S., Brest, France, Feb. 3-May 13, 1918; commanded 69th Inf., Brig. for 2 mos. and 35th Div. for 5 weeks; in line of battle with Div. and Brig. for 3 mos.; duty Office Chief of Staff, Washington, D.C., 1918-19; asst. comdt. U.S. Disciplinary Barracks, Fort Leavenworth, Kan., 1920-22; with Signal Corps, 1923-26; retired as coll, July 21, 1929. Mem. Mil. Order Carabao, Assn. Grads. U.S. Mil. Acad., U.S. Cav. Assn., Am. Legion, United Vets. Foreign Wars, Mil. Order World War. Democrat. Presbyterian. Clubs: Army and Navy (Washington); Sierra (San Francisco); Union League (Chicago). Author: Class of '87; United States Military Academy, 1939. Address: 2660 Woodley Road, Wardman Park Hotel, Washington, D.C. Died June 26, 1942.

MCCLURE, ROBERT A. ret. army officer; b. Mattoon, Ill., Mar. 4, 1897; s. George and Harriet Julia McC.; student Ky. Mil. Inst., London, 1912-15; Inf. Sch., 1923-24; Cav. Sch., 1925-36; Command and Gen. Staff Sch., 1930-32; Army War Coll., 1935; m. Marjory Leitch, Nov. 11, 1918; children-Robert Dugald, Richard Alexis. Commd. 2d lt., 1916; promoted through the grades to maj. gen., 1955; served in P.I., China, Japan, N. Africa, Eng., France; instr. Inf. Sch., 1926-30, Army War Coll., 1935-40; mil. attaché, Am. Embassy, London, 1941-42; chief Intelligence, European Theatre, 1942; Allied Force Hdqrs., 1942-43; chief psychological warfare Div., S.H.A.E.F., 1944-45; director, Information Control Div. of Military Govt., Germany, 1945-47; chief Psychol. Warfare Div., 1950-53; chief U.S. Mil. Mission with Iranian Armed Forces 1953-56, ret. Address: Shalimar, Fla. Died Jan. 1, 1957.

MCCLURE, ROY DONALDSON surgeon; b. Bellebrook, O., Jan. 17, 1882; s. James Albert (M.D.) and Ina Hester (Donaldson) McC.; B.A., Ohio State U., 1904, hon. D.Sc., 1936; M.D., Johns Hopkins, 1908; hon. D.Sc., Washington and Jefferson Coll., 1944; studied U. of Prague, Bohemia, 1906; m. Helen Keene Troxell, March 4, 1916; children-Mary Keene Stearns, Roy Donaldson, M.D., Douglas Templeton. Assistant to Dr. Alexis Carrel, Rockefeller Inst., 1907-08; house surgeon New York Hosp., 1909-11; resident surgeon Johns Hopkins Hosp., 1912-16, also instr. in surgery, Johns Hopkins Univ.; an organizer and surgeon in chief Henry Ford Hosp., Detroit, since 1916; dir. med. dept. Ford Rubber Plantation, Brazil, 1928-46; chief surgeon D.T.&I. R.R.; extramural lecturer in post-grad. medicine, U. of Mich.; Guest Speaker Congres Francais de Chirugie, Paris, 1937. Trustee Henry Ford Hospital since 1938. Mem. sub-com. on surg. infections, sub-com. on burns, 1940-45; committee on prosthetic devices, 1945-46, committee on artificial limbs since 1946, of National Research Council. Regional rep. coms. on admission, Johns Hopkins and Duke University Med. Schools. Chmn. Mich. Med. Advisory Bd. No. 3, World War I, 1917, same, World War II; mem. Detroit committee on Foreign Relations. Member blood procurement com., Detroit, Am. Red Cross. Maj. Med. Corps, U.S. Army, 1918-19; served as comdg. officer Evacuation Hospital No. 33, A.E.F. Member of the board of trustees of the Michigan Foundation for Medical and Health Edn. since 1946. Fellow Am. College Surgeons (gov.), Am. Surg. Assn.; member Southern Surg. Assn., Am. Med. Assn., Société Internationale de Chirurgie, Am. Coll. Surgeons (bd. govs., 1935-38), Ohio State Univ. Assn. (pres. 1925-27), Central Surg. Assn. (founder and first pres. 1940-41), Detroit Acad. of Surgery (pres. 1929), Detroit Acad. Medicine (pres. 1945-46), Johns Hopkins Med. and Surg. Assn. (act. pres. 1946), Phi Beta Kappa (Ohio State; pres. Detroit Assn. 1939-42), Sigma Xi, Delta Upsilon, Nu Sigma Nu. Republican. Presbyterian. Clubs: Detroit, Economic (bd. dirs.) Newcomen Soc., Grosse Pointe Country. Author of numerous papers giving results of studies and experiments, alone and with others. Mem. adv. bd., Annals of Surgery, also editorial bd., Am. Jour. Surgery. Home: 1490 Iroquois Av. Address: Henry Ford Hospital, Detroit 2. Died March 31, 1951.

MCCLURE, WILLIAM L. surgeon; b. Goldendale, Wash., Dec. 24, 1880; s. Edward P. and Mary L. (Davis) McC.; Wash. State Normal Sch.; M.D., Northwestern U., 1909; m. Joy L. Massey, July 11, 1911; 1 dau., Nancy Joy. Began practice at Yakima, Wash., now retired; former mem. staff St. Elizabeth's Hosp.; mem. Sch. Bd., Yakima, 1915-28. Served in M.C., U.S. Army, 1917-19, advancing to lt. col. Fellow A.C.S.; mem. Am., Wash. med. assns., Yakima County Med. Soc., Phi Beta Pi, Alpha Omega Alpha. Republican. Mason (32ff). Clubs: Lions, Elks (Yakima); University (Seattle). Home: 301 N. 41st Av. and Avalanche, Yakima, Wash. Died Oct. 7, 1949; buried Terrace Heights Cemetery.

MCCLURG, ALEXANDER CALDWELL bookseller and publisher; b. Philadelphia, Pa., about 1834; grad. Miami Univ., 1853 (A.M., Yale, 1893). Went to Chicago and entered as clerk the bookselling house of S. C. Griggs & Co. Enlisted, Aug. 15, 1862, as private; later became capt. 88th Ill. vols. and afterward promoted lt. col. in adj. gen.'s dept. Later chief of staff 14th army corps, and bvtd. col. and brig. gen.; participated in battles and campaigns of Perryville, Stone River, Chickamauga, Missionary Ridge, Atlanta and the March to the Sea. After war became a partner in the firm of S.C. Griggs & Co., afterward Jansen, McClurg & Co., succeeded later by A. C. McClurg & Co., booksellers and publishers, of which he became the head. on Feb. 12, 1899, this establishment, with all its rare and valuable contents, was destroyed by fire. The temptation to retire to a life of ease and literary leisure was strong, but the demand in Chicago and the West that the old bookstore should be reestablished on the old lines, and the interests of many competent and faithful assistants, finally induced General McClurg to join in the reorganization of the old concern as a stock company (pres. new company). Home: Chicago, Ill. Died 1901.

MCCLURG, WALTER AUDUBON naval officer; b. Landenberg, Pa., Feb. 4, 1852; s. John Russell (M.D., U.S.V.) and Ruth Ann (Higgins) McC.; ed. Cleveland (O.) Mil. Acad., 1862-64; Kennett Sq. (Pa.) Acad., 1865-68; Millersville (Pa.) State Normal Sch., 1869; M.D., Jefferson Med. Coll., Phila., 1872; m. Edmonia Phelps Mason, d. Rear Admiral T. S. Phelps, Oct. 10, 1906. Commd. asst. surgeon U.S.N., Feb. 8, 1874; promoted passed asst. surgeon, Nov. 2, 1877; surgeon, Jan. 25, 1889; med. insp., Nov. 18, 1900; med. dir., June 16, 1907; voluntarily retired after 34 years' active service, Sept. 1, 1908. Served on fifteen ships, 17 yrs.; duty Bur. Medicine and Surgery, Navy Dept., 1889-93; fleet surgeon N. Atlantic Fleet, 1902-03. Republican. Presbyterian. Deceased.

MCCOACH, DAVID, JR. army officer; b. Phila., Jan. 27, 1887; s. David and Clara (Kelly) McC.; student U.S. Mil. Acad., 1906-10. Engr. Sch., 1911-12, Sch. of the Line, 1921-22. Command and Gen. Staff Sch., 1922-23, Army War Coll., 1927-28; m. Anna C. Black, June 26, 1911; 1 son, David, III. Commd. 2d lt. Engring. Corps, U.S. Army, 1910, advanced through grades to major gen., 1943; engr. commr., D.C., 1938-41; Office of Chief of Engrs., Washington, 1941; in charge Montgomery Ward, Chgo., 1944-45. Mem. Am. Soc. C.E., Am. Soc. Mil. Engrs. Presbyn. Mason (32ff). Clubs: Army-Navy, Army and Navy Country, Chevy Chase Country (Washington). Home: Wardman Park Hotel, Washington. Died Dec. 15, 1951; buried Arlington Nat. Cemetery.

MCCOLLOCH, FRANK CLEVELAND, lawyer; b. Portland, Ore., Aug. 25, 1892; s. Charles Henry and Mary (Wooddy) McC.; LL.B., Stanford, 1917; m. Elizabeth Susanne Meyer, Aug. 15, 1917; 1 son, Charles Koerner. Admitted to Ore. bar, 1919; practiced in Baker, 1919-35; pub. utilities commnr. Ore., 1935-37; partner firm McColloch, Dezendorf & Spears, and predecessors, Portland, 1937-68. Chmn. Ore. Bd. Geology and Mineral Industries, 1961-68; adv. bd. Am. Petroleum Inst., 1961-68; mem. Ore. Interim Com. Water Resources, 1953-55. Served as maj., inf., U.S. Army, 1917-19; AEF in France and Belgium. Decorated Purple Heart; Croix de Guerre with palm (France). Mem. Am., Ore. bar assns., Am. Judicature Soc., Portland C. of C., Phi Delta Phi. Democrat. Mason (32 deg.). Author Ore. ground water act, 1955; co-author Ore. water resources act, 1955. Home: Portland OR Deceased.

MCCOMB, WILLIAM farmer; b. Mercer Co., Pa., Nov. 21, 1828; s. Malcom and Jane McC.; ed. Westminster Coll., New Wilmington, Pa.; spl. studies in engring.and machine work; went to Tenn., 1854; was engaged in developing the mfg. interest in Southern Ky. and Middle Tenn., until 1861; m. Louisa Co., Va., Oct. 6, 1868, Nannie H. Quarles. Served in C.S.A. in 145h Tenn. regt., beginning as pvt.; promoted adj. Aug., 1861; maj., March, 1862; lt.-col., Aug., 1862; col., Sept., 1862; was wounded at Sharpsburg (Antietam), Md., Sept. 17, 1862; and at Chancellorsville, Va., May 3, 1863; promoted brig.-gen., Dec., 1864; Democrat. Address: Cordonsville, Va.

MCCONNEL, MERVIN GILBERT ret. army officer; b. Parma, Ida., Dec. 29, 1882; student U. Ida.; commd. 2d lt. Ida. N.G., 1909, 1st lt. F.A., Officers Res. Corps, 1917; maj. Cav., Ida. N.G., 1924, advanced to brig. gen. of the line, 1936; assigned to command 58th Cav. Brigade; inducted into Fed. Service as brig. gen., Adj. Gen. Dept. assigned as dir. Ida. SSS; ret., brig. gen., 1946. Address: 4614 Fairview Av., Boise, Ida. Died 1948.

MCCONNEL, ROGER HARMON, mining geologist; b. Caldwell, Ida., Dec. 8, 1908; s. Fred Homer and Ellen (Harmon) McC.; student Coll. of Ida., 1927-30; B.S. in Geology, U. Ida., 1932, M.S., 1936; m. Harriet Idell Smith, Nov. 3, 1934; children—Stephen S., Mary Alice. Jr. topographic engr. U.S. Geol. Survey, summers, 1934-35, field asst., 1936-37; geologist Bunker Hill Co., Kellog, Ida., 1938-40, chief geologist, 1940-42, 46-66, chief exploration geologist, 1967, geology cons., 1967-71. Served as capt. AUS, 1942-46; ETO. Fellow Geol. Soc. Am.; mem. Am. Inst. Mining, Metall. and Petroleum Engrs. (Engr. of Year Columbia sect. 1968); N.W. Mining Assn. (life); Mining and Metall. Soc. Am., Soc. Econ. Geologists (pres 1971); Societe de Geologique Appliquee Aux. Gites Minereaux. Contbr. articles to tech. jours. Home: Kellogg ID Died June 19, 1971; buried Greenwood Cemetery, Kellogg ID

MCCONNELL, ROBERT PERCHE, ret. naval officer b. Oakland, Cal., July 8, 1895; s. James Joseph and Augusta (Lehnig) McC.; student U. Cal., 1915-16; m.

Mildred Schafer, Apr. 17, 1920 (dec. 1946); children—Doreen (Mrs. Edward Beverly Johnson), Mildred (Mrs. Albert Kyle Earnest), Josephine (Mrs. Edward Crozer Rutherfurd); m. 2d, Melinda Alexander, 1946. Entered Navy as seaman 2d class, U.S.N.R.F., 1917; commd. ensign Naval Res., 1918, advancing through grades to rear adm., U.S.N., 1946 continuous duty in naval aviation; at sea in observation and scouting squadrons, U.S.S. Arizona, Omaha, Lexington and Saratoga, 1925-36; gen. insp. naval aircraft, central dist., Dayton, O., 1932-34; comd. U.S.N.R. Aviation Base, Miami, Fla., 1937-40, U.S.S. Langley (vessel sunk as result of engagement with Japanese bombers in Indian Ocean south of Java, Feb. 27, 1942), U.S.S. Cowpens, 1943-44; on duty with joint chief of staff, Washington, 1944-46; comdr. Carrier Div. 15, 1947; comdr. Fleet Air Wing One 1947-49; mem. Gen. Bd. of Navy, 1949-50; pres. Bd. of Review, Discharges and Dismissals, 1950-53; pres. Naval Retiring Review Bd., 1951-53, sr. mem. Naval Clemency Bd., 1951-53; retired as vice adm., June 1953. Decorated Silver Star Medal, Navy Unit Commendation Ribbon (Navy). Home: AshevilleNC Died Feb. 10, 1973.

MCCOOK, ALEXANDER MCDOWELL soldier; b. Columbiana Co., O., Apr. 22, 1831; s. Daniel McC.; early edn. in public school, Carrollton, O.; grad. West Point, July 1, 1852; m. Kate Phillips; Jan. 23, 1863; m. 2d, Annie M. Colt, Oct. 8, 1885. Apptd. bvt. 2d lt. 3d Inf., June 30, 1852; promoted through grades to maj. gen. U.S.A., Nov. 9, 1894; retired from active service under the law, April 22, 1895. Bvtd. in regular service for gallant and meritorious services during Civil war as maj., July 21, 1861 (Bull Run); lt. col., March 3, 1862 (capture of Nashville, Tenn.); col., April 7, 1862 (Shiloh); brig. gen., March 13, 1865 (Perryville, Ky.); maj. gen., March 13, 1865, for gallant and meritorious services in field during the war. Represented U.S. at coronation of Czar of Russia, Moscow, May 1-24, 1896; mem. commn. apptd. by President to investigate War Dept., during war with Spain, Sept. 23, 1898 to Feb. 10, 1899; Presbyterian. Died 1903.

MCCOOK, ANSON GEORGE soldier; b. Steubenville, O., Oct. 10, 1835; s. Dr. John and Catharine Julia (Sheldon) M.; bro. of Edward Moody, Henry Christopher and John James M.; pub. sch. edn.; crossed plains to Calif., 1854, returning, 1860; admitted to bar, 1861; capt. 2d Ohio Inf., Apr. 17, 1861; maj., Aug. 6, 1861; lt. col., Jan. 1, 1863; col., Jan. 20, 1863; bvtd. brig. gen. vols., Mar. 13, 1865 "for meritorious services"; hon. discharged, Oct. 21, 1865; served in Army of the Cumberland and with Sherman in Atlanta campaign; m. Hettie B. McCook, June, 1886. U.S. Assessor internal revenue, Steubenville, O., 1866-72; removed to New York, 1873; mem. 45th to 47th Congresses (1877-83), 8th N.Y. Dist.; sec. U.S. Senate, 1884-93; city chamberlain, New York, 1895-97. Republican. Home: New York, N.Y. Died Dec. 30, 1917.

MCCOOK, EDWARD MOODY solider, gov.; b. Steubenville, O., June 15, 1833; s. Dr. John and Catharine Julia (Sheldon) M.; pub. sch. edn.; m. Mary Thompson; m. 2d, Mary McKenna. Removed to Pike's Peak, 1859; mem. Kan. legislature, 1860; U.S. Govt. vol. secret agt. previous to Civil War; entered Union Army, 2d lt. 1st U.S. Cav., May 8, 1861; 1st lt., July 17, 1862; in vol. service was maj., lt. col. and col. 2d Ind. Vol. Cav.; brig. gen. vols.; Apr. 27, 1864; hon. mustered out of vol. service, Jan. 15, 1866. Bvtd. 1st lt., Apr. 7, 1862, for battle of Shiloh; capt., Oct. 8, 1862, for battle of Perryville, Ky.; maj., Sept. 20, 1863, for battle of Chickamauga; lt. col., Jan. 27, 1864, for cav. operations in E. Tenn.; col., Mar. 13, 1865, for capture of Selma, Ala.; brig. gen., Mar. 13, 1865, for gallant and meritorious services in the field during the war; maj. gen. vols., Mar. 13, 1865, for gallant and meritorious services during the war; resigned from regular army, May 9, 1866. U.S. minister to Hawaii, 1866-69; gov. Colo. Ty., 1869-75. Home: Riverside, Conn. Died 1909.

MCCOOK, JOHN JAMES lawyer; b. Carrollton, O., May 25, 1845; s. Daniel and Martha (Latimer) M.; youngest of Ohio family known as "the fighting McCooks"—consisting of father and his nine sons, who, with five cousins, were all officers in the Civil War; enlisted in 52d Ohio Inf.; commd. 1st lt. 6th Ohio Cav., and capt. and a.-d.-c. U.S. Vols., June 18, 1863-Oct. 13, 1864; served in campaigns of Perryville, Stone River Tullahoma, Chattanooga and Chickamauga with Western armies, and in Gen. Grant's campaign with Army of Potomac; severely wounded, Shady Grove, Va., May, 1864; mustered out, bvt. lt. col. vols.; A.B., Kenyon Coll., 1866, A.M., 1869; LL.B., Harvard, 1869; (hon. A.M., Princeton, 1873; LL.D., U. of Kan., 1890, Lafayette, 1893); m. Janetta Alexander, Feb. 17, 1876. Practiced at New York 1871—; sr. mem. Alexander & Green (one of the oldest legal firms in U.S.). Was invited to place in President McKinley's 1st cabinet; chmn. Army and Navy Christian Commn. of the Y.M.C.A. during war with Spain, 1898. Trustee Kenyon Coll.; dir. Princeton Theol. Seminary. Home: New York, N.Y. Died 1911.

MCCORD, MYRON HAWLEY gov. Ariz.; b. Ceres, Pa., Nov. 26, 1844; s. Myron and Anna Eliza M.; ed. Richburgh (N.Y.) Acad.; removed to Wis., 1864; mem. Wis. legislature 1873-74, 1880-82; mem. Congress, 1889-91; removed to Phoenix, Ariz., 1893; mem. territorial Bd. of Control, Ariz., 1895-96; gov. Ariz., 1897-98; resigned to become col. of 1st Territorial Regt. U.S. Vol. Inf., Aug. 1, 1898 and continued in command of regt. until it was mustered out, Feb. 15, 1899; U.S. marshal for Ariz., 1901-05, then collector of customs for dist. of Ariz. Republican. Home: Nogales, Ariz. Deceased.

MCCORMACK, ALFRED lawyer; b. Brooklyn, N.Y., Jan. 13, 1901; s. Lawrence and Susan (Toal) McC.; A.B., Princeton, 1921; LL.B., Columbia, 1925; m. Winifred Byron Smith, May 31, 1930; children-Alfred, Walter B. S. (dec.), Robert C., Winthrop L. Teacher Thacher Sch., Ojai, Calif., 1921-22; law clerk to Mr. Justice Harlan F. Stone, Supreme Court of U.S., 1925-26; asso. law firm Cravath, de Gersdorf, Swaine and Wood, New York City, 1926-35, partner, 1935-42; partner Cravath, Swaine & Moore, N.Y. City, since 1947; spl. asst. to sec. of war, 1942; spl. asst. to sec. of state, 1945-46. Served 3 yr. enlistment, 101st Cav., N.Y. N.G., 1927-30; commd. col., Army of U.S., 1942; dep. chief spl. br. Mil. Intelligence Div., War Dept. Gen. Staff, 1942-44; dir. intelligence Mil. Intelligence Service, 1944-45. Decorated Distinguished Service Medal (U.S.), Hon. Comdr. Order of British Empire. Chmn. bd. visitors Columbia Law Sch.; trustee Mannes Music School, Practicing Law Institute (both of N.Y. City), Brunswick School, Greenwich, Conn. Member American and N.Y. State bar assns., Assn. Bar of City N.Y., N.Y. Co. Lawyers Assn., Am. Geog. Soc., Am. Econ. Assn., Acad. Polit. Sci., Assn. of Ex-mems. of Squad A. (N.Y.), Phi Beta Kappa, Psi Upsilon. Clubs: Univ., Broad Street, Young Republican (N.Y.); Metropolitan (Washington); Casino (Chicago); Indian Harbor Yacht (Greenwich, Conn). Contributor of articles to law and other periodicals. Home: 618 Lake Av., Greenwich, Conn. Office: 15 Broad St., N.Y.C. Died July 11, 1956; buried Putnam Cemetery, Greenwich, Conn.

MCCORMICK, ALBERT M(ONTGOMERY) D(UPUY) naval officer; b. Berryville, Va., Mar. 27, 1866; s. Edward and Ellen Lane Jett (Virginia) M.; prep. edn. Potomac Acad., Alexandria, Va.; M.D., U. of Md., 1888; m. Edith Lynde Abbot, Oct. 25, 1894; children-Lynde Dupuy, Mrs. Edith Berdall, Mrs. Cora Clark, Ellen Jett. Apptd. asst. surgeon, rank ensign, July 23, 1888; promoted through grades to rear adm. (temp.), July 1, 1918; perm. rank of rear adm., Jan. 1, 1921. Served on Panther and ashore at Guantanamo, Spanish-Am. War, 1898; fleet surgeon, Atlantic Fleet, 1910; duty at U.S. Naval Acad., 1910-19; insp. med. dept. activities, U.S.N., Pacific Coast, July 1, 1919; comdr. Med. Supply Depot, Mare Island; became pres. Bd. of Med. Examiners and pres. Naval Retiring Bd. and Naval Examining Bd., 1923, retired, Mar. 27, 1930. Awarded Sampson medal, Spanish camapign medal, Victory medal with silver star for meritorious conduct during World War; Order of the Busto del Libertado conferred by the Gov. of Venezuela. Fellow Am. Coll. Surgeons. Episcopalian. Home: Berryville, Va. Died Apr. 20, 1932.

MCCORMICK, ALEXANDER HUGH rear admiral U.S.N.; b. in D.C., May 9, 1842; s. Alexander and Eliza (Van Horn) M.; apptd. to U.S. Naval Acad. from Tex., 1859; resigned May 22, 1861; reinstated June 3, 1861; m. Isabella Howard, Feb. 9, 1864. Promoted ensign, Dec. 22, 1862; lt., Feb. 22, 1864; lt. comdr., July 25, 1866; comdr., Sept. 30, 1876; capt., Apr. 3, 1892; rear admiral, Sept. 9, 1899. Served on Quaker City, 1861; Norwich, S. Atlantic Blockading Squadron, 1862-63; participated in bombardment of Ft. Pulaski and fort on Winyaw Bay, S.C., 1862; served on Iroquois, spl. service, 1864-65; Chattanooga, 1866; Naval Acad., 1866-69; Lancaster, 1869-72; Naval Acad., 1872-75; exec. officer Pensacola, 1875-76; spl. ordnance duty, 1877-81; comd. Essex, 1881-85; Navy Yard, Washington, 1885-88; Bur. of Ordnance, 1888-89; insp. of ordnance, New York, 1889-92; comd. Lancaster, 1892-94; Navy Yard, Norfolk, 1894-97; mem. armor and personnel bds., 1897-98; comd. Oregon, 1898; comdt., Navy Yard, Washington, 1898-1900; retired, Mar. 26, 1900. Home: Annapolis, Md. Died Aug. 21, 1915.

MCCORMICK, BRADLEY THOMAS mech. engr.; b. Marietta, O., May 28, 1880; s. Frank Ross and Maria Elizabeth (Thomas) M.; M.E., Cornell U., 1903. Apprentice in shops and later in charge induction motor design Bullock Electric Mgf. Co., Cin., 1903-05; chief elec. engr. charge elec. design Allis-Chalmers-Bullock, Ltd., Montreal, 1905-13; mem. firm Forbes & McCormick, cons. engrs., Montreal, 1913-25; chief engr. Miss. Valley Metal Products Co., St. Louis, 1915-17; apptd. engr. charge small motors Wagner Electric Mfg. Co., St. Louis, 1919; now engr. with Wagner Electric Corp. Civilian, later capt. and maj. U.S. Ordnance Dept., 1917-19, serving as chief of projectile and cartridge case br. of arty. ammunition and trench warfare div. Fellow Am. Inst. E.E. Home: 847 Belt Av. Address: Wagner Electric Corp., St. Louis. Died Mar. 14, 1945.

MCCORMICK, CHAUNCEY business exec.; b. Chicago, Ill., Dec. 7, 1884; s. William Grigsby and Eleanor (Brooks) McC.; A.B., Yale, 1907; L.H.D., Northwestern U., 1934; Dr. Social Sci. (hon.), Cath. U. of America, 1952; m. Marion Deering, July 6, 1914; children-C. Deering, Brooks, Roger. Mfg. bus., 1907-22; v.p. Miami Corp., Chicago; dir. Internat. Harvester Co. since 1926. Served as lieut. to capt., in France and Poland with A.E.F., 1917-19; apptd. to Am. Relief Commn. by Herbert Hoover; in charge Eastern Poland, later in Roumania, 1918-19. Capt., 106th Cav. Ill. Nat. Guard, comdg. Chicago Black Horse Troop, 1930-31. Awarded Purple Heart, Victory medal; citation from General Pershing; officer of the Legion of Honor, Croix de Guerre with bronze star (French); The King's Medal (British); Officer Etoil Moire de Benin, Merite Agricole; Officer Am. Field Service French, Order of Orange Nassau (The Netherlands); Commander Polonia Restituta, White Eagle of Llow, Officer Polish Red Cross (Polish). Apptd. by gov., mem. Child Welfare Commn. of Ill.; chmn. Citizens' Com. of United Home Finding Service; mem. Nat. Commn. on Children and Youth; chmn. bd. Ill. Children's Home and Aid Soc.; nat. pres. Commn. for Polish Relief, 1939; vice chmn. British War Relief Soc. of Ill.; Chairman Illinois Committee on Displaced Persons. Pres. Art Inst. of Chicago; founder, trustee and chmn. art exhibit, Chicago Century of Progress, 1933-34; trustee, Am. Foundation for the Blind, Chicago Foundlings' Home. Chmn. Alexander Hamilton Memorial Fund; dir. McCormick Theol. Seminary; dir. Chicago Council Social Agencies, Community Fund, Chicago; Ill. Soc. for Prevention of Blindness; adv. dir. Chicago Lighthouse for the Blind. Former pres. Northern Ill. Guernsey Breeders' Assn.; del. to Republican Nat. Convention, 1936. Mem. Nat. Inst. of Social Scis. (life), Soc. of the Cincinnati (N.C.), Alpha Delta Phi, Kappa Sigma. Clubs: Chicago, Casino, Racquet, Arts, Executives (Chicago); Chicago Golf (Wheaton); Bath (Miami Beach); Pot and Kettle (Bar Harbor, Me.); Harbor (president) (Seal Harbor, Me.). Republican. Presbyterian (elder). Address: 410 N. Michigan Av., Chgo. 11. Died Sept. 8, 1954.

MCCORMICK, CYRUS, b. Chicago, Sept. 22, 1890; s. Cyrus Hall and Harriett (Hammond) M.; grad. Hotchkiss Sch., 1908; A.B., Princeton, 1912; grad. student Oxford U. (Eng.), 1912-14; m. Dorothy C. Linn, Feb. 13, 1915; m. 2d, Florence Sittenham Davey, Mar. 14, 1931; 1 stepson, William Davey. Salesman for Internat. Harvester Co., 1914-16, br. mgr., 1916-17, works mgr., 1919-22, v.p. mfg., 1922-31, retired, 1931; owner El Nuevo Mexicano; dir. Internat. Harvester Co.; chief automobile and truck price sect. OPA, 1941-42. Rep. Nat. committeeman for State of N.M., 1936-42. Served as lt. Air Service, U.S. Army, 1918-19; major, Ordnance, U.S. Army, serving in Eng., 1942-43. Trustee Industrial Relations Counselors, Inc. Presbyn. Elk. Clubs: University (N.Y.C.); Chicago, Tavern (Chgo.). Author: The Century of the Reaper, 1931. Home: Santa Fe3NM Died Apr. 1970.

MCCORMICK, LYNDE DUPUY naval officer; b. Annapolis, Md., Aug. 12, 1895; s. Albert Montgomery Dupuy and Edith Lynde (Abbot) McC.; B.S., U.S. Naval Acad., 1915; m. Lillian Addison Sprigg, Oct. 2, 1920; children-Montrose Graham (dec.), Lynde Dupuy, James Jett II. Commissioned ensign, U.S. Navy, 1915. Advanced through the grades to admiral. Comdr. in chief Atlantic Fleet, 1951; apptd. NATO Supreme allied comdr. Atlantic, January, 1952; appointed president Naval War College, May 1954. Decorated Legion of Merit. Mem. U.S. Naval Inst. Clubs: Chevy Chase, Army and Navy, Army-Navy Country (Washington). Home: "Clermont," Berryville, Va. Office: Naval War Coll., Newport, R.I. Died Aug. 16, 1956; buried U.S. Naval Acad., Annapolis, Md.

MCCORMICK, ROBERT RUTHERFORD editor, lawyer; b. Chicago, Ill., July 30, 1880; s. Robert Sanderson and Katherine Van Etta (Medill) M.; B.A., Yale, 1903; student Northwestern U. Law Sch.; LL.D., The Citadel, Charleston, S.C., 1932; married Amy Irwin Adams, Mar. 10, 1915 (died 1939); m. 2d, Mrs. Maryland Mathison Hooper, Dec. 21, 1944. lMem. Chicago City Council, 1904-06; mem. Chicago Charter Conv., 1907; pres. Sanitary Dist. of Chicago, 1905-10; mem. Chicago Plan Commn.; admitted to Ill. bar, 1908; mem. law firm McCormick, Kirkland, Patterson & Fleming, 1908-20; editor and publisher The Chicago Tribune. Maj. 1st Ill. Cav., on duty on Mexican border, 1916-17; attached to General Pershing's staff, A.E.F., in France, 1917, later assigned as major 5th Arty. Brig.; lt. col. 122d F.A., U.S.N.G.; col. 61st F.A., U.S. Army; served as commandant Ft. Sheridan, Ill. Awarded D.S.M. Republican. Presbyn. Mem. Chicago Bar Assn. Clubs: Racquet and Tennis (New York); Chicago. Author: With the Russian Army, 1915; The Army of 1918, 1920; Ulysses S. Grant, the Great Soldier of America, 1934; Freedom of the Press, 1936; How We Acquired Our National Territory, 1942; The American Revolution and Its Effect on World Civilization, 1945; The War Without Grant, 1950; also shorter works on hist. mil, sci., legal and polit. subjects. Home: Du Page County, Ill. Office: Tribune Sq., Chgo. Died Apr. 1, 1955; buried Wheaton, Ill.

MCCOWN, ALBERT physician; b. Lexington, Va., Aug. 11, 1890; s. James LaRue and Anna Calhoun (Smith) McC.; A.B., Washington and Lee U., 1910; M.D., Johns Hopkins, 1918, D.P.H., 1940. In pvt. practice of pediatrics, Tacoma, 1920-24, Seattle, 1924-34; dir. child health, Wash. Health Dept., Seattle, 1934-35; dir. Div. Maternal and Child Health, U.S. Children's

Bur., 1935-37; dep. commr. health, Mich. Health Dept., 1939; chief research and tng. unit, N.Y.C. Health Dept., 1940; dir. med. and health service A.R.C., 1941-43; dir. Bur. Communicable Disease Control, Va. Health Dept. Served at Base Hosp. No. 18, AEF, 1917-19; lt. col. to col., 1943-46; U.S. Army M.C., SHAEF, Mission to France. Mem. Am. Pub. Health Assn., A.M.A., Phi Beta Kappa, Nu Sigma Nu, Delta Omega. Democrat. Presbyn. Contbr. med. and pub. health jours. Home: 400 W. Franklin St. Office: State Office Bldg., Richmond, Va. Died Aug. 1953.

MCCRADY, EDWARD lawyer, author; b. Charleston, S.C., Apr. 8, 1833; s. Edward McC., lawyer and theologian; grad. Charleston Coll.; admitted to S.C. bar, May 1855; m. Mary F. Davie, Feb. 24, 1863. Took part as capt. vol. co., State service, in the taking of Castle Pinckney, Charleston harbor, Dec. 27, 1860; was present at battle of Ft. Sumter, Apr. 12-13; entered C.S.A. as capt. of 1st co. raised in S.C. for the whole war, June 27, 1861; maj. and lt. col. 1st S.C. vols.; severely wounded at Manassas, Aug. 30, 1862; seriously injured in camp by falling tree Jan. 27, 1863; disabled for field service and transferred to command of camp of instruction, Madison, Fla., Mar. 1864; surrendered May 5, 1865, subsequently maj. gen. State volunteer troops; mem. Ho. of Reps., State legislature, 1880-90; pres. Hist. Soc. of S.C., trustee Charleston Library Soc., trustee Med. Coll. of S.C. Author of Electio and Registration Laws of S.C., known as the eight box law; chmn. vestry of St. Philip's Ch., Charleston. Democrat. Author: The History of South Carolina under the Proprietary Government, 1670-1719, 1897; The History of South Carolina Under the Royal Government, 1719-1776, 1899; The History of South Carolina in the Revolution, 1775-1780, 1901; The History of South Carolina in the Revolution 1780-83, 1902. Home: Charleston, S.C. Died 1903.

MCCRAW, WILLIAM judge, b. Arlington, Tex., Aug. 15, 1896; s. John and Mollie (Clay) McC.; ed. pub. schs. and by pvt. study; m. Louise Carden Britton, July 22, 1931. Admitted to Tex. bar, 1915, at age of 19, and began practice at Dallas; criminal dist. atty. Dallas County 3 terms, 1926-32; atty. gen. of Tex., 1934-38; head consultant War Prodn. Bd., Sept., 1941-Feb., 1942; judge, Spl. Criminal Dist. Ct., Dallas Co., 1954—. Served as lt. U.S. Army, with A.E.F., World War I; capt. Air Corps Res.; in active service as capt. A.C., comdg. 85th Service Group, Air Service Command, Feb. 28-Nov. 2, 1942; promoted major; inspector gen. Mobile Air Depot Control Area Command, 1942-43; promoted lt. col., 1943; comdg. officer 2d Aircraft Repair Unit (floating), 1944-46; participated Saipan and IwoJima campaigns; promoted col., 1945. Mem. Tex. Bar Assn. Comdr. Am. Legion, dept. of Tex., 1948-49; exec. dir. Variety Clubs of Am. since 1946. Democrat. Baptist. Mason. Candidate for Dem. nomination for gov. 1938. Author: Professional Politicians. Home: 978 Hines Blvd. Office: Courthouse, Dallas. Died Nov. 8, 1955.

MCCREA, TULLY brig. gen.; b. Natchez, Miss., July 23, 1839; s. John and Mary McC.; apptd. from Ohio, and grad. U.S. Mil. Acad., 1862; m. Harriet Hale Camp, May 20, 1868. Second lt. 1st Arty., June 17, 1862; promoted through grades to col. 6th Arty., July 15, 1900; brig. gen. U.S.A., Feb. 21, 1903. Served in Civil War in Army of Potomac, taking part in battles of Antietam, Fredericksburg, Chancellorsville, Gettysburg, etc.; later in dept. of South; wounded severely at battle of Olustee, Feb. 20, 1864. Bvtd.: first lt., Sept. 17, 1862, for Antietam; capt., July 3, 1863, for Gettysburg; maj., Feb. 20, 1864, for Olustee. Retired at own request after 40 yrs.' service, Feb. 22, 1903. Died Sept. 5, 1918.

MCCREERY, FENTON REUBEN diplomat; b. Flint, Mich., Apr. 21, 1866; s. Col. William Barker and Ada Birdsall (Fenton) M.; ed. Mich. Mil. Acad. and U. of Mich., class of 1888; unmarried. Clerk in U.S. Consulate, Valparaiso, Chile, 1890-91; sec. legation Santiago, Chile, 1891-93 (chargé d'affaires about 4 mos.); sec. legation and embassy, Mexico City, 1897-1906 (chargé d'affaires, 1905-06); apptd. minister resident and consul gen. to Dominican Republic, Jan. 10, 1907; E.E. and M.P. to Honduras, 1909-11; associated in advisory capacity with subcommittee U.S. Senate Com. on Foreign Relations investigating Mexican affairs, Aug. 3, 1912-Feb. 10, 1913; traveled in Egypt, Palestine, Greece, Feb.-Aug. 1913; lectured on Mexico and ancient races of America, 1915-16; capt. Am. Red Cross, attached to office of commr. for Europe (Paris), Jan.-May 1918; speaker in Ohio and Mich. in 2d Red Cross drive, May 1918; commd. maj., N.A., June 24, 1918; detailed as mil. attaché to Am. Embassy, Rio de Janeiro, Brazil; served on Gen. Staff, mil. intelligence div., Washington, Sept. 3-Oct. 29, 1919, hon. discharged. Traveled in Baltic States and Russia, 1929. Hon. vice chmn. at large Am. Peace Centenary Com., 1914-15; del. to Fourth Pan-Am. Conf., Washington, 1931. Mem. exec. council Am. Soc. Internat. Law, 1923-26; mem. Mich. State Com. Y.M.C.A., 1925; nat. counsellor Flint Chamber of Commerce. Elk. Vestryman P.E. Church; lay dep. from Diocese of Mich to 48th Triennial Conv. P.E. Ch., 1925. Given vote of thanks by Peace Conf., Honduras, 1911, "for opportune and efficient services." Home: Flint, Mich. Died Oct. 6, 1940.

MCCROSSIN, EDWARD FRANCIS consulting engr.; b. Phila., Jan. 8, 1887; s. Judge William P. and Helen Theresa (Delaney) McC.; student O. State University, 1906-09; married Florence Niles Rogers, Feb. 28, 1922; Florence Marion (Mrs. Spottswood D. Bowers), Helen Minna (Mrs. J. W. Tudisco), Edward Francis, Mining Engring. and iron ore exploration work in U.S. and Mexico, 1910-17; organized McCrossin & Co. cons. engrs., New York, 1917, since served as pres.; constructed pig iron blast furnace and chem. plant for U.S. Govt. Defense Plant Corp., McCrossin Sta., Tex., 1944; cons. engr. for numerous U.S. and fgn. indsl. and ins. cos. since 1925; lecturer U.S.Army Indsl. Coll., Wash., 1937, Polytech. Inst., Brooklyn, 1936-37, N.Y. and Conn. Ins. Socs.; dir. Seaboard F. & M. Ins. Co., Cherokee Royalty Co., Yorkshire Insurance Co., N.Y. City, Uba Consolidated Industries; consulting engineer War Department. Served as capt. U.S. Army and asst. dir. of operations U.S. Nitrate Plants, Muscle Shoals, 1917-20, cons. engr. British Joint Insp. Bd., U.K., and Can. on ordnance matters, 1940-43; lt. col. U.S. Army Ordnance Res. Chmn. Leonia Defense Council, vice chmn. northern Valley, N.J. Defense Council, World War II; dist. chief N.Y. ordnance dist. Army Ordnance Corps, 1953-. Licensed mining engr., W.Va., civil engr., N.J., professional engineer, New York and Pennsylvania. Recipient Citation and Certificate, Sec. Army, 1959. Mem. Am. Inst. Mining and Metall. Engrs., Am. Petroleum Inst., Newcomen Soc. of Eng., Beta Theta Pi. Clubs: Mining, Army and Navy, Downtown Association (N.Y.C.); Knickerbocker Country. Home: 100 E. Palisade Av., Englewood, N.J. Office: 120 Wall St., N.Y.C. Died Sept. 10, 1962; buried Elmwood Cemetery, Birmingham, Ala.

MCCROSSIN, WILLIAM PATRICK, JR. surgeon; b. Birmingham, Alabama, February 14, 1890; son of Judge William Patrick and Helen Theresa (Delang) McC; B.S., Univ. Alabama, 1912; M.D., Tulane U., 1916; m. Leonora Marie Hassinger, Apr. 26, 1922; 1 dau., Leonora Virginia. Interne Hillman Hosp., Birmingham, and Post Grad. Hosp., N.Y.C.; resident surgeon Woman's Hosp., N.Y.C.; served as attending surgeon Hillman Hosp., attending gynecologist St. Vincent's Hosp., and asso. surgeon Children's Hosp. (all Birmingham); moved to Colorado Springs, Colo.; now attending surgeon Glockner Penrose Hosp., Meml. Hosp., St. Francis Hosp., Cragmor Sanatorium; mem. staff Penrose Tumor Clinic (all Colorado Springs). Served as 1st lt., later capt., Med. Corps, U.S. Army, in charge operating room, Evacuation Hosp. No. 15, Verdun, France, 1917-19. Mem. Research Found. for Tuberculosis. Fellow A.M.A., A.C.S.; mem. El Paso County (Colo.) Med. Soc., Alpha Tau Omega, Phi Chi. Alpha Omega Alpha, Stars and Bars. Clubs: El Paso, Cheyenne Mountain Country, Cooking; Military and Naval (N.Y.C.); Birmingham (Ala.) Country; Boston (New Orleans). Address: 206 W. Del Norte Rd., Colorado Springs, Colo. Died July 7, 1960; buried Elmwood Cemetery, Brimingham.

MCCULLOCH, BEN army officer; b. Ruthford County, Tenn., Nov. 11, 1811; s. Maj. Alexander and Frances (LeNoir) McC. Mem. Tex. Congress, 1834; organizer company of mounted mem. known as McCulloch's Tex. Rangers, 1846; commd. maj., 1848; marshal for coast dist. of Tex., 1853-59; a commr. to conciliate Mormons in Utah, 1858; col. in command of Tex. troop that received surrender of Gen. Twiggs at San Antonio, 1861; commd. brig. gen. Confederate Army, in command of troops in Ark. Died in Battle of Elkhorn Tavern, nr. Elkhorn, W. Va., Mar. 7, 1862.

MCCULLOCH, CHAMPE CARTER, JR. medical officer U.S.A.; b. Waco, Tex., Sept. 10, 1869; s. Champe Carter (mayor of Waco) and Emma Maria (Basset) M.; A.B., Baylor U., Tex., 1885; C.E., Agrl. and Mech. Coll. of Tex., 1890; M.D., U. of Va., 1891; M.D., Columbia, 1892, A.M., 1904; m. Mary Azalete, d. Davis Gurley, of McLennan Co., Tex., Oct. 23, 1889; children—Mary (wife of Dr. William James), Champe Carter (dec.), Louisa Earle (dec.), Roderick Roy, Sarah Champe (Mrs. Alfred Powis). Apptd. asst. surgeon U.S.N., Mar. 26, 1892; asst. surgeon U.S. Army, May 5, 1892; promoted through grades to col., May 15, 1917, retired Nov. 30, 1922. Dept. state health officer Western Maryland (Cumberland). Died Oct. 14, 1928.

MCCULLOCH, ROBERT farmer; b. Albemarle Co., Va., Nov. 23, 1820; s. Robert and Patsey (Mills) McC.; moved with family to Cooper Co., Mo., 1835; m. Louisa Weight, Jan. 27, 1852. Served in C.S.A., 1861-65; comd. brigade of cav. under Gen. Nathan Bedford Forrest; resumed farming after war; collector Cooper Co., Mo., 1872-78; sheriff, 1878-80; State register of lands, 1880-92. Democrat. Home: Clark's Fork, Cooper Co., Mo. Died 1905.

MCCULLOCH, WILLIAM ALEXANDER army officer; b. Clinton Heights, N.Y., Feb. 10, 1889; s. Aiken and Lottie Lyon (Ham) McC.; B.S., U.S. Mil. Acad., 1913; Inf. Sch., 1922-23; Command and Gen. Staff Sch., 1927-28; m. Florence Alexander Sumner, June 18, 1921; children-Florence Turner, William Alexander. Commd. 2d lt., 1913; promoted through the grades to brig. gen. (temp.), Mar. 1943. Decorated Purple Heart (2 oak leaf clusters), Victory Medal (4 battle clasps), Croix de Guerre (with bronze star), Chevalier (Black Star Order) Legion of Honor, Service medals for Army of Occupation, Defense, Asiatic-Pacific campaign; hon. Citizen of Bourges (France); Gen. Hdqrs. citation (1918), Div. citation (1918); Legion of Merit "for meritorious conduct in the closing phases of the Guadalcanal Campaign," 1943. Home: 5504 Chevy Chase Parkway, Chevy Chase, Md. Died Dec. 2, 1959.*

MCCULLOUGH, ERNEST civil engr.; b. Staten Island, N.Y., May 22, 1867; s. James and Caroline (McBlain) M.; grad. high sch., Wyandotte (now Kansas City), Kan., 1883; Inst. of Technology, Chicago, 1884-85; degree of C.E. from Van der Naillen Sch. of Engineering, San Francisco, 1887; m. Elizabeth Townsend Seymour, 1891 (died 1918); children—George Seymour, Caroline McBain (wife of Col. Paul C. Galleher), Elizabeth Howland (dec.), James David; m. 2d, Therese Claquin, of Tours, France, 1919. In engring. practice, San Francisco, 1887-98, Lewiston, Ida., 1898-1903, Chicago, 1903-17, Syracuse,N.Y., 1920-21, N.Y. City, 1921—. Registered architect, Illinois; registered engineer, New York and New Jersey. Editor Engineer and Contractor, San Francisco, 1893-96; asso. editor Engineering-Contracting, Chicago, 1909, Railway Age Gazette, Chicago, 1910, Am. Architect, New York, 1921-22; editor Building Age and National Builder, New York, 1925-28. Served in Ida. N.G. as capt. inf., in Ill. N.G. as lt. engrs, and lt. F.A. in World War, maj. Engrs. O.R.C., promoted lt. col. Chem. Warfare Service; wounded near Cambrai, Nov. 1917; chief engr. Am. Red Cross, France; chief gas officer, 1st Corps; also chief gas officer, Army Arty., 1st Army; asst. chief and later chief, arty. sect. Chem. Warfare Service; constrn. engr., R.R. and C. Service, June 1917-Aug. 1919 in France; asst. comdt. Lakehurst Proving Ground, N.J., and dir. C.W.S. Officers' Sch., Aug. 1919-July 1920; lt. col. C.W.S., O.R.C., July 1920-Jan. 1926. Mason. Republican. Episcopalian. Author: Reinforced Concrete, 1908; Engineering as a Vocation, 1911; Practical Surveying, 1915, 22; Practical Structural Design, 1917, 3d edit., 1926; Everybody's Money, 1923; La Vie Chére et les Crises Monétires, 1926; Class Warfare, 1927. Home: Long Island City, N.Y. Died Oct. 1, 1931.

MCCULLOUGH, RICHARD PHILIP naval officer; b Bound Brook, N.J., Feb. 14, 1881; s. Richard Henry and Anna (Elder) McC.; B.S., U.S. Naval Acad., 1904; grad. U.S. Naval War Coll., 1916; student Stanford Law Sch., 1933-34; m. Kathleen Gilbert, Oct. 5, 1927. Commd. ensign USN, Feb. 2, 1906, advanced through grades to rear adm., Feb. 23, 1942, ret., Jan. 1, 1932; recalled to active duty, Dec. 1, 1939; comdr. convoy escort vessels based on Gibraltar, 1917-18; chief of Naval Intelligence, 12th Naval Dist., San Francisco, 1939-43; mem. planning bd. and intelligence panel Overseas br. OWI, Feb. 1, 1943-June 1945. Decorated Navy D.S.M.; Brit. Distinguished Service Order. Mem. U.S. Naval Inst., Am. Soc. Naval Engrs. Clubs: Metropolitan, Chevy Chase (Washington); San Francisco Golf, Bohemian (San Francisco); New York Yacht. Home: P.O. Box 485, Los Gatos, Cal. Died Apr. 1966.

MCCUTCHEON, KEITH BARR, marine corps officer; b. E. Liverpool, O., Aug. 10, 1915; s. Merle D. and Louise Alberta (Sturtevant) McC.; B.S. in Mgmt. Engring., Carnegie Inst. Tech., 1937; M.S. in Aero Engring., Mass. Inst. Tech., 1944; grad. Nat. War Coll., 1960; m. Marion Postles Thompson, Nov. 1, 1947; children—Marion Louise, Keith Barr. Commd. 2d lt. USMC, 1937, advanced through grades to lt. gen., 1970; assigned U.S.S. Yorktown, 1938-39. flight tng., 1940; served PTO, World War II; assigned Bur. Aero., 1946-49; designated helicopter pilot, 1950; assigned Korea, 1951-52, staff CINCEUR, 1952-54, Marine Corps Equipment Bd., 1954-57; comdr. helicopter group, 1957-59; dir. Marine Corps Aviation, 1961; comdg. gen. 1st Marine Brigade, Hawaii, 1962; asst. chief staff operations, staff CINCPAC, 1963-65; comdg. gen. 1st Marine Aircraft Wing, also dep. comdr. III MAF, Vietnam, 1965-66; dep. chief staff (air) Hdqrs. USMC, 1966-70; comdg. gen. III Marine Air Force, Vietnam, 1970; ret., 1971. Bd. dirs. Naval Mut. Aid, 1968-71. Decorated D.S.M., Silver Star, Legion of Merit, D.F.C., Air medal. Mem. Am. Helicopter Soc. (bd. dirs.), Marine Corps Assn. (bd. govs.), Beta Theta Pi, Tau Beta Pi, Pi Delta Epsilon. Presbyn. Author articles. Home: Alexandria VA Died July 13, 1971; buried Arlington Nat. Cemetery, Arlington VA

MCDANIEL, ARTHUR BEE army officer; b. San Antonio, Tex., Aug. 31, 1895; s. Arthur Shaw and Leila Grayson (Ervin) McD.; LL.B., U. of Tex., 1917; grad. Command and Gen. Staff Sch., 1936, Army War Coll., 1939; m. Leah Glenn Burpee, Dec. 26, 1933. Commd. 2d lt., U.S. Army, Aug. 15, 1917, Inf., and advanced through the grades to brig. gen., March 27, 1942; trans. to Air Corps, 1922; mem. Pan Am. Goodwill Flight through Central and S.A., 1926-27; now comdg. gen. III Reconnaissance Command, Army Air Forces. Decorated Distinguished Flying Cross (U.S.); Order of the Sun (Peru); Order of the Liberator (Venezuela); Order of Merit (Chile); Order of the Condor (Bolivia). Mem. Sigma Alpha Epsilon. Club: Birmingham Country. Home: 811 N. Alamo St., San Antonio, Tex. Died Dec. 26, 1943.

MCDANIEL, EDWARD DAVIES M.D.; b. Chester Co., S.C., July 7, 1822; grad. Erskine Coll., S.C., 1844 (A.M., LL.D., Univ. ofAla.); grad. Med. Coll. of the State of S.C., 1857; taught high schools in S.C. and Ala., 1844-57; established medical practice, Camden, Ala., 1857; prof. materia medica, therapeutics and clinical medicine, med. dept., Univ. of Ala., 1887-95. During Civil war was on post and hospital duty for the Confederacy as surgeon; and for a time after the war as acting asst. surgeon for the Federal troops. Member Am. Med. Assn. and other medical societies, etc. Retired from practice, 1895, because of failing health. Address: Coy, Ala.

MCDANIEL, HENRY DICKERSON governor; b. Monroe, Ga., Sept. 4, 1836; s. Ira Oliver and Rebecca J. (Walker) M.; A.B., Mercer U., 1856, A.M., 1859; LL.D., U. of Ga., 1907. Admitted to bar, 1857; mem. Ga. Secession Conv., 1861; 1st lt., capt. and maj. 11th Ga., C.S.A., 1861-65; m. Hester, d. Stephen Felker, Dec. 20, 1865. Mem. Ga. Constl. Conv., 1865; disability to hold office removed by U.S. Congress, July 1872; mem. Ga. Ho. of Rep., 1873-74, Senate, 1874-83; gov. of Ga., 1883-86. Democrat. Home: Monroe, Ga. Died July 25, 1926.

MCDERMOTT JACK CHIPMAN journalist; b. Tucson, Jan. 19, 1905; s. Henning and Kate (McDermott) Redford; student Howard Payne Coll., 1923-24, U. Tex., 1924-25, U. Kan., 1925-26; A. B. George Washington U., 1950; m. Evelyn Kennedy, Feb. 15, 1930 (div. 1946); children-Madelaine, Jacqueline, Marsha; m. 2d, Ann Day Jarvis, Jan. 12, 1946. Dist. traffic rep. Nat. Air Transport, Dallas, 1927-29; asst. traffic mgr. Pan-Am. Airways, San Antonio, Mexico City, 1929-31; mgr. C. of C. Lufkin, Tex., 1932-33; editor, pub. Lufkin Daily News, 1933-43; asso. chief Internat. Press and Publs. div., Dept. State, 1946-47, chief, 1947-. Press attaché U.S. Embassy, London, 1950; dep. dir. USIS, HICOG, Conn, Germany, 1954; chief operations adv. service, USIA Washington, 1956; counsellor pub. affairs Am. Embassy, Mexico, 1957; mil. liaison officer USIA, Washington, 1962-64; pub. affairs officer, El Salvador, 1964. Joined U.S. M.C., 1943, intelligence and photog. officer Saipan, Iwo Jima, Okinawa, 1944-45; lt. col. Res., inactive, 1946-. Mem. Marine Corps. Res. Officers Assn. (nat. exec. council), Sigma Phi Epsilon, Sigma Delta Chi, Pi Kappa Delta. Clubs: Rotary; Nat. Press (Washington). Office: USIA, Dept. State, Washington 25. Died Feb. 27, 1966; buried Arlington Nat. Cemetery.

MCDERMOTT, ARTHUR VINCENT lawyer; b. Brooklyn, N.Y., Aug. 27, 1888; s. Michael F. and Mary (Campbell) McD.; student Columbia Coll., 1906-08; LL.B., New York Law Sch., 1912; m. Genevieve Markey, June 4, 1919. Admitted to bar, 1913; engaged in general practice of law, N.Y. City, since 1913; member of firm of Burke & Burke, 72 Wall St., 1st dep. comptroller, City of N.Y., 1938-40; dir. Selective Service System, New York City, 1940-47. Judge advocate gen., N.Y. Nat. Guard, 1919-40; brig. gen. 1947; captain regimental operations officer, 106th Inf., A.E.F., World War I; recalled to active service with U.S. Army Sept. 1940. Awarded Medal of Merit, Columbia University, 1941; annual medal St. Nicholas Society of New York, 1943. Decorated Distinguished Serv. Med. (U.S.), Military Cross (Brit.), Silver Star, Purple Heart, 2 citations for gallantry (U.S.) N.Y. State Conspicuous Service Cross. Trustee Andrew Freeman Home for Aged. Mem. Brooklyn and N.Y. State bar assns., Judge Advocates Assn., Am. Legion, Mil. Order World War, N.Y. Soc. Mil. and Naval Officers, Theta Delta Chi. Republican. Clubs: Montauk, Municipal (Brooklyn); Columbia University (New York); Ship Lore and Model (Brooklyn). Home: 995 Fifth Ave. Office: 72 Wall St., New York, N.Y. Died Dec. 18, 1949.

MCDILL, JOHN RICH surgeon; b. Plover, Wis., July 20, 1860; s. Alexander Stuart (M.D.) and Eliza Jane (Rich) M.; M.D., Rush Med. Coll., Chicago, 1885; interne Cook Co. Hosp., 1885-87; studied univs. Berlin and Munich, 1890-92; m. Josephine Neale, Jan. 27, 1903; children—Alexander Stuart, John Harcourt, Jane Rich. Practiced, Milwaukee, 1887-98 (except when abroad); capt. and surgeon, Wis. N.G., 1893-98; maj. and surgeon vols., Spanish-Am. War, 1898, and until 1903, serving as brigade surgeon and chief operating surgeon in the field in Cuba for 7th Army Corps and as chief operating surgeon in Manila, 1900-03; oragnized and became chief surgeon Woman's Hosp., Manila, 1902, and of St. Paul's Hosp., 1905-10; prof. surgery and head of dept., U. of Philippines, 1906-12; chief surgeon Philippine Gen. Hosp., 1910-12; resumed practice at Milwaukee, Sept. 1912. Asso. prof. surgery, Rush Med. Coll. (U. of Chicago). In med. and surg. relief work in Germany, 10 mos., 1916-17; maj., Med. Corps, U.S.A., 1917; surg. chief Base Hosp., 40th Div., Camp Kearny, Calif., Sept. 1917-July 1918; consultant in reconstruction, Surgeon Gen.'s Office, Aug. 1918-Mar. 1919; chief med. officer, Federal Bd. for Rehabilitation of Disabled Soldiers, with rank of asst. surg. gen. (R.) U.S. Pub. Health Service, 1919-21; chief med. consultant U.S. Veterans' Bur., 1922-23; med. officer in charge U.S. Vets'. Hosp., Waukesha, Wis., 1925, 1932. Surgeon gen. and life mem. Vet. Army of Philippines; lt. col. Med. Aux., U.S.A. Fellow Am. Coll. Surgeons (founder), A.M.A. Mason. Author: Tropical Surgery; Lessons from the Enemy; How Germany Cares for Her War-Disabled, 1918. Home: Cornwall-on-Hudson, N.Y. Died Sept. 15, 1934.

MCDONALD, CHARLES HENRY, lawyer, retired army officer; b. Manchester, Wisconsin, October 16, 1872; s. Daniel and Anne (McLaughlin) M.; preparatory education at the State Normal School, Oshkosh. Wis.; LL.B., Chicago (Ill.) Law Sch., 1897; m. Ella Meisner, Aug. 12, 1902; children—Isabel Anne, Mildred Meisner, John Charles. Practiced at Wittenberg and Oshkosh, Wis., 1897-1913; atty. for Bur. of Corps., Dept. of Commerce, 1913-15; chmn. of Law and Joint Boards of Review of Federal Trade Commn., Washington, D.C., 1915-18. Counsel in charge of administration of Trading with the Enemy Act by the Federal Trade Commn., 1917-18; legal advisor to Am. Forces in Germany on civil affairs, 1919-20. Commd. maj., Judge Advocate's Dept., U.S. Army, 1918, lt. col., 1932; judge advocate 6th Corps Area, 1932-35; ordered to active duty, 6th Service Command, March 1, 1943; law mem. Permanent General Court Martial, World War II. Mem. K.C., Mil. Order of World War, Am. Legion, Am. Bar Assn. Clubs: Union League, Chicago Athletic, South Shore Country (Chicago). Home: 1857 N. Prospect Av., Milwaukee WI

MCDONALD, EUGENE F. JR. pres. Zenith Radio Corp.; b. Syracuse, N.Y., Mar. 11, 1890; s. Eugene F. and Mary McD.; ed. Syracuse U.; m. Inez Riddle, July 16, 1931; children-Jean Marianne, Eugene F. III. Southern rep Franklin Automobile Co., Syracuse, N.Y.; in automobile comml. paper bus., Chicago, 1910-17; in radio business, 1920—; now pres. Zenith Radio Corp.; pres. Seneca Securities Corp.; pres. and dir. Wincharger Corp. (Sioux City, Ia.); dir. Hospital Service Corp. Served as lt. commdr., U.S. Navy, 1917-18; lt. comdr., U.S.N.R. Mem. MacMillan Arctic Expdn., 1923; 2d in command, MacMillan Nat. Geog. Expdn. to Arctic, comdr. S.S. Peary, 1925; comdr. Isle Royale Archaeol. Expdn., 1928, Cocos-Galapagos Islands Archaeol. Expdn., 1929, Georgian Bay Archaeol. Expdn., 1930, expdn. to find LaSalle's lost ship Griffin, 1937. Organizer, 1923, and 1st pres. Nat. Assn. of Broadcasters. Trustee Henrotin Hosp. Fellow Royal Geog. Soc.; mem. Outboard Motor Assn. (Am. nat. commodore). Clubs: Racquet, Chicago Athletic, Tavern, Macinac Island Yacht, Columbia Yacht (Chicago); McGregor Bay Yacht; Royal Canadian Yacht; Explorers (N.Y.C.). Author: Youth Must Fly, 1941; Television Will Cost Big Money, 1946. Home: 2430 Lake View Av. Office: 6001 Dickens Av., Chgo. Died May 15, 1958.

MCDONALD, FLORIN LEE educator; b. Chamberlain, S.D., Dec. 8, 1906; s. Lorne Angus and Ida (May) McD.; A.B., U. S.D., 1928, A.M., 1929; M.S., Northwestern U., 1930; Ph.D., U. Mo., 1937; m. Evelyn Margaret Olson, June 11, 1929; children-Colleen Ann, Sally Jane. Held various newspaper positions, 1926-29; instr. journalism Eleventh Minn. Jr. Coll., 1931-33; prin. Biwabik (Minn.) High Sch., 1933-35; dir. dept. journalism Tex. State Coll. for Women, 1935-52; pres. Lamar State College Tech., 1952-. Served as col. AUS, 1941-46; PTO. Decorated Legion of Merit, Silver Star, Bronze Star, Purple Heart; recipient Distinguished Alumnus award U. S.D., 1965. Mem. Tex. Council State Supported Council (pres.), Am. Soc. Journalism Sch. Adminstrs. (sec.-pres. 1948-50), Am. Assn. Techrs. Journalism, Am. Coll. Pub. Relations Assn., Council Tex. State Coll. and U. Presidents (pres.) Phi Kappa Phi, Phi Tau Theta (nat. v.p. 1928) Sigma Delta Chi, Alpha Tau Omega. Methodist. Club: Kiwanis (gov. Tex.-Okla. dist. 1949). Contbr. numerous articles to edn. publs. and journalism mags. Home: 102 Redbird Lane, Beaumont, Tex. Died Mar. 1967.

MCDONALD, JOHN BACON army officer; b. in Ala., Feb. 8, 1859; grad. U.S. Mil. Acad., 1881; Army War Coll., 1913. Commd. 2d lt. 5th Inf., June 11, 1881; promoted through grades to brig. gen. N.A., Dec. 17, 1917. Commandant cadets, Agril. and Mech. Coll., Auburn, Ala., Sept. 1888-91; prof. mil. science and tactics and comdt. cadets, S.C. Mil. Acad., 1897-98; mustering officer, State of Ala., Sept.-Nov. 1898; in Philippine Islands, 1900-01; wounded in battle at Borongabong, Apr. 27, 1901; comdr. Ft. Ethan Allen, Vt., 1907-08; duty Insp. Gen.'s Dept., 1914-17; brig. gen., in comd. 181st Inf. Brig., 91st Div., in France and Belgium, 1918-19; participated in St. Mihiel, Meuse-Argonne and Ypres-Lys offensives; comd. Presidio, San Francisco, 1919; comd. U.S. Disciplinary Barracks, Alcatraz, Calif., 1920-21. Awarded D.S.M. and D.S.C.; Officer Legion of Honor, Croix de Guerre with Palm (French); Belgian Croix de Guerre and Italian War Cross. Died Mar. 15, 1926.

MCDONALD, JOHN DANIEL ret. naval officer; b. Machias, Me., Nov. 1, 1863; grad. U.S. Naval Acad., 1884. Commd. ensign, 1886, promoted through grades to vice adm., 1930. Served on Monterey, Spanish-American War, 1898; at Naval Torpedo Station, Newport, R.I., 1904; navigator Ohio, 1904-07; in charge 1st Light House Dist., 1907-08, Chattanooga, 1909-10, Hancock, 1911, Virginia, 1911-13; at Naval War Coll., 1913-15; chief of staff Atlantic Fleet, 1915-16; comdr. Arizona, 1916-18; apptd. comdt. Navy Yard, N.Y.C., 1918; became vice-adm., comdt. 14th Naval Dist., retired 1924. Address: Oakland Hotel Oakland, Cal. Died Sept. 2, 1952.*

MCDONNELL, EDWARD ORRICK investment banking; b. Baltimore, Md., Nov. 13, 1891; s. Eugene and Ann (Chilton) McD.; grad. U.S. Naval Acad., 1912; m. Helen Fisher, November 14, 1915; children-Mrs. D. M. Kendall, Mrs. A. R. Barry, Edward Orrick. Commissioned ensign U.S. Navy 1912, and promoted to lieut. comdr. 1918; resigned 1919. Secretary-treasurer. Mexican Internat. Corp., 1920-22; v.p. and gen. mgr. Kelly Springfield Motor Truck Co., 1922-23; v.p. R. J. Caldwell Co., 1923-24; mem. firm Smith & McDonnell, 1924-25; mem. firm and partner G. M. P. Murphy & Co., investment bankers, since 1942; dir. Pan. Am. Airways Corp.; gen. partner Hornblower & Weeks; also the director of The Hertz Corporation. Served World War II, 1940-46, final rank vice admiral. Awarded Congl. Medal of Honor, Navy Cross; Air Medal, 2 Bronze Star Medals; Distinguished Service Cross (Italy). Catholic. Clubs: Brook, Yale (N.Y.C.); Piping Rock, India House, Racquet and Tennis. Home: Mill Neck, N.Y. Office: 40 Wall St. N.Y.C. Died Jan. 6, 1960; buried Arlington Nat. Cemetery.

MCDOUGAL, DOUGLAS CASSEL marine corps officer; b. San Francisco, 23, 1876; s. Comdr. (U.S. Navy) Charles John and Kate (Coffee) McD.; student Bates Prep. Sch., San Rafael, Calif., 1890-93, U.S. Naval Acad., 1893; m. Sabina Wood Watts, Apr. 24, 1909; children-Douglas Cassel, David Slockton, Commd. 2d lt., USMC, 1900, advanced through the grades to maj. gen., 1939; served in Spanish-Am. war as ensign, UN, 1898; cadet U.S. Revenue Cutter Service, 1898-99; comdr. Gendarmerie d' Haiti, 1921-25, Guardia Nacional of Nicaragua, 1929-31. Decorated with D.C.M. (USN) and 15 campaign medals, including Haitien and Nicaraguan Govt. medals. Address: Coronado, Cal. Died Jan. 1964.

MCDOUGALL, ALEXANDER Continental congressman, army officer; b. Islay, Inner Hebrides, Scotland, July/Aug. 1732; s. Ronald and Elizabeth McDougall; m. Hannah Bostwick, 1767, 3 children including Elizabeth. Came to Am., 1783; commanded privateers Tyger and Barrington, 1756-83; author of written attack addressed "to the Betrayed Inhabitants of the City and Colony of New York," signed "A Son of Liberty," 1769; arrested and imprisoned, 1770-71; mem. N.Y. Com. of 51, 177 comm. brig. gen. Continental Army, 1776, maj. gen., 1777, served in battles of Chatterton's Hill, Germantown and White Plains; commanding officer highlands of the Hudson; took command of West Point after discovery of Arnold's treason, 1780; arrested and courtmartialed for insubordination, 1782; mem. Continental Congress from N.Y., 1781-82, 84-85; mem. N.Y. Senate, 1783-86; an organizer, 1st pres. Bank of N.Y.; pres. N.Y. Soc. of Cincinnati. Died N.Y.C., June 9, 1786; buried family vault 1st Presbyn. Ch., N.Y.C.

MCDOWELL, ALFRED HENDERSON, JR. utility exec.; b. Richmond, Va., July 21, 1907; s. Alfred Henderson and Inez (Brown) McD.; B.S. in Civil Engring., Va. Mil. Inst., 1928; m. Katherine Elizabeth White, July 22, 1936; children-Katherine Higgins, Dorothy Henderson. Engring. dept. Va. Electric & Power Co., Richmond, 1928-32, Williamsburg, 1932-35, supt. distbn., 1935-41, asst. to gen. mgr. elec. dept., Richmond, 1941-43, exec. asst. to pres., 1946-53, dist. mgr., div. mgr., 1953-56, system operating mgr., 1956-58, pres., dir., 1958-, chief exec. officer, 1964-; dir., mem. finance com. 1st and Mchts. Nat. Bank, Richmond. Trustee Keep Va. Beautiful, Richmond Found. Ind. Colls.; bd. dirs. Central Va. Ednl. TV Corp., Richmond Symphony Orch., Va. Indsl. Devel. Corp., Richmond Meml. Hosp.; mem. steering com. Pub. Utilities Information Program. Served as lt. comdr. USNR, 1943-46. Mem. Carolinas-Va. Nuclear Power Assos. (v.p. dir.), Southeastern Electric Exchange (v.p., dir.), Edison Elec. Inst. (dir.), Pub. Utilities Assn. Va. (exec. com.), Nat. Assn. Elec. Cos. (dir.), Elec. Heating Assn. Inc. (dir.), Va., Richmond chambers commerce, Va. Industrialization Group, Newcomen Soc., Soc. Va. Creepers, Navy League U.S. Episcopalian. Clubs: Rotary, Commonwealth, Forum, Downtown (Richmond); VMI Sportman's (Lexington, Va.); Country of Va., Farmington Country (Charlottesville, Va.). Home: 310 St. David's Lane, Richmond 21. Office: 7th and Franklin Sts., Richmond 19, Va. Died Mar. 1967.

MCDOWELL, CHARLES army officer; b. Winchester, Va., 1743; s. Joseph and Margaret (O'Neal or O'Neil) McD.; m. Grace or Grizel (Greenlee) Bowman, circa 1780. Served as capt. of a militia regt. in backwater region of South, commd. lt. col., 1776, comdr. a rear guard of Continental Army; helped to bring about 1st Continental victory in the South after Gate's defeat; served as brig. gen. in command expdn. against Cherokee Indians, 1782; mem. N.C. Senate, 1778, 82-88; commr. for settling boundary between Tenn. and N.C., 1797. Died Burke County, N.C., Mar. 31, 1815.

MCDOWELL, IRVIN army officer; b. Columbus, O., Oct. 15, 1818; s. Abram Irvin and Eliza Shelden (Lord) McD.; grad. College de Troyes (France) U.S. Mil.

Acad., 1838; m. Helen Burden, 1849, 4 children. Commd. 1st lt. U.S. Army, 1842; aide-decamp to Gen. Wool during Mexican War, also in Army of Occupation, 18 adj. gen.; brevetted capt., 1847; commd. maj., 1856; brig. gen. in command Army of Potomac, also Dept. of Northeastern Va., 1861, commanded 1st Battle of Bull Run; commd. maj. gen. U.S. Volunteers in command I Corps, Army of Potomac, 1862; commanded troops Army of Rappahannock, territorial dept. of Rappahannock, relieved of command after 2d Battle of Bull Run (where he lost again), held territorial command San Francisco, 1864; commanded Dept. of East, 1868, Dept. of South, 1872; commd. maj. gen. U.S. Army, 1872; ret., 1882; park commr. San Francisco, circa 1882-85; planned park improvements of Presido reservation, laid out roads overlooking Golden Gate Bridge. Died San Francisco, May 4, 1885; buried in San Francisco.

MCDOWELL, JOSEPH congressman, army officer; b. Winchester, Va., Feb. 15, 1756; s. Joseph and Margaret (O'Neal or O'Neil) McD.; m. Margaret Moffett, 8 children including Joseph Jefferson. Served with Charles McDowell (His brother) Regt., N.C. Militia during Revolutionary War, took part in Rutherford expdn. against Cherokee Indians, 1776, also numerous battles against Loyalists in N.C., including Ramsour's Mill, 1780; promoted maj. McDowell Regt., in command at Battle of King's Mountain, 1780; commanded detachment of riflemen from Burke County, N.C. in Battle of Cowpens, 1781; attacked Cherokee Indians, 1781; commanded McDowell Regt. during brother's expdn. against Cherokees, 1782; mem. N.C. Ho. of Commons, 1785-88, N.C. Senate, 1791-95; mem. N.C. convs. to ratify U.S. Constrn., 1788, 89, mem. U.S. Ho. of Reps. from N.C., 5th Congress, 1797-99. Died Feb. 5, 1801; buried "Quaker Meadows," nr. Morgantown, N.C.

MCDOWELL, RALPH WALKER surgeon, capt. Med. Corps U.S.N.; b. Altoona, Pa., Feb. 4, 1883; s. Robert and Ida May (Kolley) McD.; M.D., Jefferson Med. Coll., Phila., Pa., 1905; grad. U.S. Naval Med. Sch., 1909; post-grad. study, U. of Pa., New York Post-grad. Med. Sch.; resident phys. Phila. Gen. Hosp.; m. Ruth, d. Theodore W. Noyes, Feb. 17, 1913; children-Mary, Dean, Theodore Noyes. Commd. med. officer, U.S.N., 1908, and promoted through grades to capt. Med. Corps, 1931. Served as med. officer afloat and ashore, 1908-17; regt. surgeon with U.S. Marines, A.E.F., France, 1918-19; chief of surg. service, U.S. Naval Hosp., San Diego, Calif., 1919-22; surgeon U.S.S. Relief, hospital ship with U.S. Battle Fleet, 1923-25; chief surgeon, U.S. Naval Hosp., Philadelphia, 1926-29; exec. officer and surgeon, U. S. Naval Hosp., Pearl Harbor, T.H., 1929-31; chief surgeon, U.S. Naval Hosp., Washington, D.C., 1931—; instr. in surgery, U.S. Naval Med. Sch., Washington, D.C. Fellow Am. Coll. Surgeons; D.S.M. (U.S.); Legion of Honor (France). Republican. Presbyn. Mason. Home: Washington, D.C. Died Feb. 22, 1935.

MCDUFFIE, WILLIAM C. oil producer; b. Jefferson, Ia., Nov. 7, 1886; s. Marshall B. and Sophie (Warner) McD.; student Stanford; M. Mary Skaife, Oct. 4, 1910; children-William . (dec.), Malcolm. Began as roustabout to well driller, Caribou Oil Co., 1907; production foreman, advancing to mgr. North Am. Oil Consol., 1909-14; supt., later v.p. and dir. in charge production Shell Oil Co. of Calif., 1914-25; gen. mgr. of production Royal Dutch Shell Group, 1925-28; pres. Pacific-Western Oil Co., 1928-31; receiver Richfield Oil Co., Pan-Am. Oil Co.,Calif., 1931-37; chmn. exec. com. Richfield Oil Corp., 1937; now independent oil operator; chmn. bd. Wilmington Gasoline Co.; chmn. bd., director Northrop Aircraft, Inc.; chmn. bd. Mohawk Petroleum Corp. since Aug. 1945. Colonel, dir. 9th Service Comd., S.O.S. (A.S.C.); civilian aide, Sec. of Army, 1952. Member Cal. Inst. Assos.; mem. bd. trustees, exec. council, v.p. Cal. Inst. Tech. Republican. Clubs: Cal. (Los Angeles); Bohemian, Press, Union League, Pacific Union (San Francisco); Valley (Montecito). Home: 665 Picacho Lane, Montecito, Santa Barbara, Cal. Office: 1100 Statler Center, Los Angeles 17. Died Apr. 10, 1963.

MCELDUFF, JOHN VINCENT ret. naval officer; b. N.Y.C., Apr. 5, 1898; s. Patrick Edward and Sarah Ellen (Meenan) McE.; B.S., U.S. Naval Acad., 1919; grad. Army Chem. Warfare Sch., 1930, Naval War Coll., 1932; m. Mary Catherine Boyle, Jan. 26, 1921; children-Edward William, Mary Patricia. Commd. ensign, U.S. Navy, 1919, advanced through grades to rear adm., 1947; on combat duty, World Wars I and II; continuous naval service, 1916-47, ret. Mem. bd. dirs. Apollo Records, Inc. Dir. Civil Def., Delaware County, Pa. Awarded Combat Legion of Merit, 15 area campaign ribbons. Mem. Songwriters Protective Assn. Roman Catholic. Composer and lyricist; Eyes of the Fleet, 1938; The Navy Sweetheart Song, 1943; Men of Victory, The Airforce Song, 1948. Specialist in classical and popular mus. composition. Author: ABCs of Atomic Survival. Home: 152 Academy Lane, Highland Park, Upper Darby, Pa. Office: Court House, Media, Pa. Died Jan. 21, 1959; buried St. Peter and Paul Cemetery, Broomall, Pa.

MCELMELL, JACKSON naval officer; b. Phila., June 4, 1834. Apptd. 3d asst. engr. U.S.N., Aug. 2, 1855; 2d asst. engr., July 21, 1858; 1st asst. engr., Mar. 25, 1861; chief engr., Feb. 2, 1862; retired June 4, 1896; chief engr., Feb. 2, 1862; retired June 4, 1896; advanced to rank of rear admiral retired, June 29, 1906, for services during Civil War. Served on various vessels during Civil War; pres. Naval Examining Bd. at Phila., 1888-96. Home: Philadelphia, Pa. Died 1908.

MCELROY, GEORGE WIGHTMAN naval officer; b. Henry, Ill., Mar. 19, 1858; s. George B. and Mary (Good) M.; grad. U.S. Naval Acad., 1878; unmarried. Asst. engr. June 20, 1880; promoted through grades to rear adm., Aug. 29, 1916. Served on Gloucester, Spanish-Am. War, 1898; in charge engring. dept., Wisconsin, 1901-04; insp. machinery and engring. material, Thurlow, Pa., 1904; in charge dept. steam engring. Naval Sta., Cavité, P.I., 1905-06; insp. machinery, Bath Iron Works, 1906. Babcock & Wilcox Co., Bayonne, N.J., 1906-09; insp. engring. material, Eastern N.Y. and N.J. dists., 1909-11, New York Shipbuilding Co., Camden, N.J., 1911-13; insp. engring. material, Pittsburgh Dist., 1913-15; apptd. insp. machinery and ordnance, Fore River Shipbuilding Co., Quincy, Mass., Mar. 19, 1915; later insp. engring. material, Brooklyn Dist.; retired Mar. 19, 1922. Advanced 3 numbers in rank "for eminent and conspicuous conduct in battle during Spanish-Am. War." Home: Adrian, Mich. Died Jan. 6, 1931.

MCELVENNY, ROBERT TALBOT orthopaedic surgeon; b. Tacoma, Dec. 5, 1904; s. Robert Fay and Alice (Talbot) McE.; student Stanford, 1924-26; M.D., U. Colo., 1932; m. Florence Getsford, Apr. 12, 1933; children-Cita, Alice Fay. Intern, W. Suburban Hosp., Oak Park, Ill., 1932-34; surg. resident N.Y. Orthopaedic Hosp., 1934-36; Annie C. Kane fellow, 1936-38; sr. resident Boston City Hosp., 1938-40; pvt. practice, Chgo., 1941-; sr. surgeon Wesley Meml. Hosp.; asso. prof. Northwestern U., 1945-. Maj., wing comd. C.A.P., Ill., 1954-. Diplomate Am. Bd. Orthopedic Surgery. Fellow A.C.S.; mem. Am. Acad. Orthopedic Surgery, Clin. Orthopedic Soc., Russell A. Hibbs Soc., Assn. Bone and Joint Surgeons, Chi Psi, Nu Sigma Nu. Episcopalian. Asso. editor, Clin. Orthopaedics, 1953. Home: 210 E. Pearson St. Office: 720 N. Michigan Av., Chgo. Died Mar. 1965.

MCELWAIN, EDWIN lawyer; b. Springfield, Mass., Dec. 17, 1908; s. Charles C. and Greta (Parks) McE.: A.B., Yale, 1931; LL.B. cum laude, Harvard, 1934; m. Margaret Banks, Greene, Nov. 12, 1948; children-Charles, James, William. Admitted N.Y. bar, 1935, practiced with Hughes, Schurman & Dwight and successor firms, N.Y.C., 1934-38; law clk. to Chief Justice Hughes, U.S. Supreme Ct., 1938-41 with div. controls, Dept. State 1941, Washington counsel Brit. Purchasing Commn., 1941; navigator Pan Am. Air Ferries, 1942; law practice, Covington, Burling, Rublee, Acheson & Shorb, Washington 1946-50; dep. gen. counsel Dept. Air Force, 1951; law practice, Covington & Burling since 1951. Served in U.S. Army, 1942-46, navigator and intelligence officer, Japanese air specialist M.I. Service, War Dept. General Staff; discharged rank maj. Decorated Legion of Merit. Club: Metropolitan. Home: 4702 Jamestown Rd., Washington 16. Office: 701 Union Trust Bldg., Washington 5. Died Mar. 15, 1960; buried Springfield, Mass.

MCFADYEN, BERNICE MUSGROVE army officer; born Portsmouth, Va., Oct. 21, 1896; s. Oscar Lee and Katherine R. (Musgrove) McF.; m. Courtenay Walthall Ross, Oct. 21, 1920; children-Courteney Walthall (Mrs. Leet), Ross M. Commd., U.S. Army; served with Old Hickory Div., World War I; wartime chief staff Yankee Div., World War II; dep. asst. chief staff, G-1, Dept. Army; presently comdg. gen. U.S. Troops, Free Territory, Trieste. Decorated Legion of Merit, Silver Star, Bronze Star Medal with oak leaf cluster, Army Commendation Ribbon with cluster. Protestant. Home: 6810 Wilson Lane, Bethesda, Md. Office: Dept. of the Army, Pentagon, Washington 25. Died July 23, 1954.

MCFARLAND, EARL, army officer; b. Topeka, Kan., July 7, 1883; s. James Davis and Mathilda (Steele) McF.; B.S., U.S. Mil. Acad., 1906; grad. Ordnance Sch. Tech., 1911, Ordnance Sch. of Application, 1912; M.E., Worcester Poly. Inst., 1923, Command and Gen. Staff Sch., 1931, Army Industrial Coll., 1933, Army War Coll., 1934; m. Mary Edith Cole, June 30, 1911; children—Mary Ann (Mrs. Hamilton Austin Twitchell), Cole, Earl. Commd. 2d lt., arty., 1906, and advanced through grades to brig. gen., 1938; prof. ordnances and gunnery and head dept. U.S. Mil. Acad., 1924-29; asst. Chief of Ordnance, U.S. Army, 1938-42; became comdg. officer Springfield (Mass.) Armory, June 1942; retired from active service, 1943. Elected supt. Staunton (Va.) Mil. Acad. Awarded D.S.M., Legion of Merit, Army Citation. Clubs: Army and Navy, War College (Washington); Colony (Springfield) Author of a U.S. Mil. Acad. textbook. Address: Staunton VA Died Jan. 1, 1972.

MCGAHAN, PAUL JAMES, newspaperman; b. Phila., Pa., Dec. 2, 1888; s. John Paul and Katherine Cecelia (Burke) McG.; ed. pub. schs.; unmarried. Began as office boy Phila. Press, 1904, reporter, 1905-09; news editor Coatesville (Pa.) Record, 1909-10; asst. city editor Phila. Press, 1910-12; with Phila. Inquirer, 1912-62, author weekly agrl. column, Sunday edition, 1954-62; with Washington Bureau since 1920, chief of bureau, 1930-37. Served as pvt. and 1st lt., inf., U.S. Army, 1917-18; commd. in O.R.S., 1919; mem. War Dept. Gen. Staff, May-Sept. 1925; in active service, major, inf., March 1942; assigned as dep. pub. relations officer Hdqrs. 3d Service Command, Baltimore, Md.; promoted lt. col., Sept. 1942, col., Oct. 1946; public relations officer 3d Serv. Command and Hdqrs. 2 Army; disch. Dec. 1946; ret. as Col. A.U.S., 1949 after 31 years service. Dept. commander District of Columbia American Legion, 1923-24; member national executive committee American Legion, 1924-30 and 1936-42; national historian Forty and Eight, 1920-37; state comdr. D.C. Mil. Order of World War, 1929; comdr. D.C. Comdry. Mil. Order Foreign Wars, 1932. Mem. President Hoover's Inaugural Com. 1929; accompanied President Hoover on trip to Virgin Islands and Puerto Rico, 1931; mem. (sec. 1935-36) Standing Com. of Corrs. controlling Press Galleries of 74th to 76th Congresses, 1935-41; mem. President Roosevelt's Inaugural Committees, 1937, 1941. In charge of assignment of press seats and arrangements at Rep. and Dem. nat. convs., 1936, 40. Mem. bd. management, Temp. Home ex-Union Soldiers, Sailors and Marines (G.A.R.), since 1924. Awarded Army Commendation Ribbon with three oakleaf clusters. Hon. mem. United Spanish War Vets., Vets. of Foreign War; member Phi Upsilon Rho Fraternity, Sigma Delta Chi Fraternity. Republican. Roman Catholic. Clubs: Army and Navy, Overseas Writers, Nat. Press (Washington); Pen and Pencil (Philadelphia). Home: Philadelphia PA Died Sept. 7, 1972.

MCGEE, ANITA NEWCOMB writer, M.D.; b. Washington, Nov. 4, 1864; d. Simon and Mary Caroline (Hassler) Newcomb; ed. pvt. schs., Washington, followed by spl. courses abroad , 3 yrs. being spent in Europe; M.D., Columbian (now George Washington) U., 1892; spl. post-grad. course in gynecology, Johns Hopkins Hosp.; m. W. J. McGee, geologist, anthropologist, 1888 (died Sept. 4, 1912); children-Klotho (Mrs. Willis), Donald (dec.), Eric Newcomb (dec.). In practice at Washington, 1892-96. Dir. D.A.R. Hosp. Corps, Apr.-Sept., 1898, which selected trained nurses for army and navy service; apptd. Aug. 29, 1898, acting asst. surgeon U.S.A., being the only woman to hold such a position; assigned to duty in the surgeon-gen.'s office as superintendent army nurse corps, which she organized. When U.S. Congress approved this work by making the nurse corps of trained women a permanent part of the army, the pioneer stage was passed, and she resigned Dec. 31, 1900. In 1904, acting as pres. Soc. Spanish-Am. War Nurses and as representative of Phila. Red Cross Soc., and by agreement with Japanese Govt., took a party of trained nurses formerly in U.S. Army to Japan, for 6 mos., gratuitous service during Russo-Japanese War. Awarded Spanish war medal by U.S. Govt.; decorated Japanese Imperial Order of the Sacred Crown, spl. Japanese Red Cross decoration, also two Russo-Japanese war medals. Member United Spanish War Veterans (dept. surgeon, past camp comdr.). Lecturer in hygiene, U. of Calif., 1911; has lectured throughout the U.S. and written for various mags. Was surgeon-gen., librarian-gen., v.p.-gen. and historian-gen. Nat. Soc. D.A.R. Hon. pres. Spanish-Am. War Nurses Soc. Address: 725 15th St., Washington, D.C.

MCGEHEE, MICIJAH C., JR. president McGehee Oil Company; b. Meadville, Miss., Oct. 1, 1903; s. Micijah C. and Ella (Lumpkin) McG.; A.B., Miss. Coll., Clinton, Miss., 1926; LL.B., U. of Texas, 1929; unmarried. Admitted to Tex. bar, 1929; in legal dept. Shell Petroleum Corp., Houston, Tex., 1929-21; counsel Nat. Hunter Producing Co., Tyler, Tex., Houston, Tex., 1931-33; v.p. Tex. Gulf Producing Co., 1936-37, pres., 1937-41; pres. McGehee Oil Co. since 1941. Served as lt. col. U.S. Army, overseas, 1942-44. Democrat. Baptist. Club: Houston. Office: Esperson Bldg., Houston, Tex. Died Aug. 16, 1960.

MCGILLYCUDDY, VALENTINE TRANT O'CONNELL M.D., surgeon; b. Racine, Wis., Feb. 14, 1894; s. Daniel and Johanna (Trant) McG.; student U. of Mich., 1866-67; M.D., Detroit (Mich.) Coll. of Medicine, 1869; m. Fanny E. Hoyt, of Ionia, Mich., Dec. 19, 1875 (died Oct. 10, 1896); m. 2d, Julie E. Blanchard, of Fayetteville, Ark.; 1 dau., Valentine Trant. Began practice, Detroit, 1869; lecturer Detroit Coll. Medicine and asst. surgeon hosp., 1869-71; asst. engr. and acting physician U.S. Survey of Great Lakes, 1871-74, transferred to Brit.-Am. Boundary Line Survey, 1874; chief engr. U.S. survey and exploration, Black Hills, S.D., 1875-76, transferred to Med. Dept., U.S.A., during Indian outbreak, surgeon U.S. Cav., 1876-79; U.S. Indian agt. in charge Pine Ridge Agency, S.D., 1879-1886; organized mounted police of 50 full-blood Indians, established local Indian courts and restored order in the reservation; surgeon gen. of S.D., 1887-89; asst. adj. gen. of S.D., 1889-98; prs. S.D. State Sch. of Mines, 1893-98; supervising med. insp. for Pacific Coast and Mountain div., Mutual Life Ins. Co. of New York, 1898-1912; moved to Berkeley, Cal., 1912; in charge mountain dist. Cal., Nevada and Utah, for U.S. Pub. Health Service during influenza epidemic, 1918-19; in charge relief expedition in U.S.S. Marblehead, sent to Alaska and Allutian Islands, same epidemic. Pres. Los Verjels Land and Water Co. of Cal. Mem. S.D. State Constl. Conv., 1888. Mem. Assn. Mil. Surgeons of U.S., U.S. Vol. Med. Service Corps, Am.

Inst. Mining Engrs., Assn. Vets. of Indian Wars, Mich. U. Alumni Club of Cal. Republican. Episcopalian. Mason. Address: Hotel Claremont, Berkeley, Cal.

MCGINNESS, JOHN RANDOLPH brig. gen. U.S.A.; b. nr. Dublin, Ireland, Sept. 17, 1840; s. Francis and Anne (Hartford) M.; grad. U.S. Mil. Acad., 1863; unmarried. Apptd. 1st lt. ordnance, June 11, 1863; took part in Civil War, becoming chief ordnance officer Dept. of the South, Apr. 1864, and afterward on various duties; bvtd. capt. and maj. for gallant and metitorious services before Charleston; promoted capt., Feb. 10, 1869; maj., June 1, 1881; lt. col., July 7, 1898; col., June 14, 1902; chief ordnance officer P.I., Dec. 31, 1898-Apr. 1, 1901, Dept. Calif., 1901-02, Dept. Lakes, 1902-04; brig. gen. and retired, Sept. 17, 1904. Died Dec. 17, 1918.

MCGLACHLIN, EDWARD FENTON army officer; b. Fond du Lac, Wis., June 9, 1868; s. Edward Fenton and Mary Eliza (Lawrence) McG.; grad. U.S. Mil. Acad., 1889; course in submarine mining Engr. Sch. of Application, 1893; Arty. Sch., 1896; Sch. of Fire for Field Arty., 1912; Field Officers' Course, Army Service Schs., 1916; Army War Coll., 1917, 22; m. Louisa Harrison Chew, Nov. 26, 1892; children-Fenton Harrison (dec.), Helen Olcott (wife of John E. Hatch, U.S. Army), Elizabeth (wife of Joseph C. Odell, U.S. Army). Additional 2d lt. 3d Arty., June 12, 1889; promoted through grades to col., July 1, 1916, 8th and 10th Field Arty.; brig. gen. N.A., Aug. 5, 1917; maj. gen., Apr. 12, 1918; permanent brig. gen., Jan. 13, 1920; maj. gen., Apr. 1, 1922. Spl. mention for gallantry, Battle of Bud Dajo, Jolo, P.I., 1906; comdr. Recruit Depot, Ft. McDowell, Calif., 1909-11; commandant Sch. of Fire for Field Arty., 1914-16; comdr. 165th F.A. Brig. (90th Div.), Aug.-Dec. 1917, 57th F.A. Brig. (32d Div.), Dec. 1917-Mar. 1918, 66th F.A. Brig. and chief of arty., 1st Army Corps, Mar.-May 1918; comdr. army arty. and chief of arty., 1st Army, May-Nov. 1918; comdr. 1st Div., Nov. 19, 1918-Sept. 30, 1919, 7th Div., Sept. 30, 1919-June 30, 1921; comdr. Army War Coll., July 13, 1921-June 30, 1923; retired Nov. 2, 1923. Awarded D.S.M., silver star. Comdr. Legion of Honor; Croix de Guerre, Club: Army and Navy (Washington). Address: Army and Navy Club, Washington, D.C. Died Nov. 9, 1946.

MCGOVERN, FRANCIS EDWARD ex-governor; b. near Elkhart, Wis., Jan. 21, 1866; s. Lawrence and Ellne (Wren) M.; B.L., U. of Wis., 1890; unmarried. Prin. and supt. schs., Brodhead, Wis., 1890-92; prin. High Sch., Appleton, Wis., 1893-97; admitted to bar, 1897, and practiced at Milwaukee. First asst. dist. atty., Milwaukee County, 1901-05; dist. atty., 1905-09; governor of Wis., 2 terms 1911-13, 1913-15. Commd. maj. U.S.A., Aug. 12, 1918; judge adv. 18th Div., then at Camp Travis, Tex., and Camp Grant, Ill.; promoted to rank of lt. col., June 12, 1919; discharged, Feb. 2, 1920, to accept apptmt. as gen. counsel U.S. Shipping Bd. and Emergency Fleet Corp., Washington; resigned, June 15, 1920, to resume practice of law, Mem. Wis. bar assn., Milwaukee Bar Assn. (pres. 1923), Phi Beta Kappa. Former trustee and dir. Milwaukee Art Inst.; pres. Milwaukee Seven Arts Soc.; dir. Wis. Conf. Social Work of Wis. Assn. for Disabled, County Chapter Am. Red Cross; dist. comdr. Am. Legion (Wis. Dept.); mem. Mil. Order Foreign Wars. Mason (32ff). Clubs: City, Milwaukee Athletic, Kiwanis (hon.). Home: 2333 North 56th St. Office: 108 West Wells Street, Milwaukee, Wis. Died May 16, 1946.

MCGOWAN, JOHN rear admiral U.S.N.; b. Port Penn., Del., Aug. 4, 1843; s. John and Catherine (Caldwell) M.; ed. Phila. pub. schs., 1848-53; pvt. schs., Elizabeth, N.J., 1853-59; m. Evelyn Manderson, Oct. 1871. Acting master's mate U.S.N., Mar. 8, 1862; acting master, May 8, 1862; master (regular service), Mar. 1868; lt., Dec. 1868; lt. comdr., May 1870; comdr., Jan. 1887; capt., Feb. 1899; rear admiral, retired, Apr. 1901. Home: Washington, D.C. Died Aug. 13, 1915.

MCGOWAN, SAMUEL naval officer; b. Laurens, S.C., Sept. 1, 1870; s. Homer L. and Julia Ann (Farrow) M.; B.A., U. of S.C., 1889, LL.B., 1891 (LL.D., 1918); unmarried. Apptd. asst. p.m. U.S.N., Mar. 15, 1894; passed asst. p.m., Mar. 30, 1895; p.m., May 5, 1899; pay insp., May 11, 1906; p.m. gen. of the Navy and chief Bur. Supplies and Accounts with rank of rear admiral, July 1, 1914; promoted to permanent rank of rear admiral, Aug. 29, 1916. Paymaster general of the navy and chief supply officer throughout the World War; voluntarily retired, Dec. 31, 1920. Awarded Navy D.S.M. (U.S.); Comdr. Legion of Honor (France); Royal Order of the Redeemer (Greece). Presbyn. Mason. Home: Laurens, S.C. Died Nov. 11, 1934.

MCGRATH, BENJAMIN R(OBERT) surgeon; b. Jo Daviess County, Ill., May 17, 1873; s. Robert and Esterh (Weir) M.G.; grad. high sch., Savanna, Ill., 1890; student Mation Sims Coll., St. Louis, 2 yrs.; MD., U. of Ill. Coll. of Medicine, 1902; m. Susan E. Williamson, May 30, 1905; children—William M., Esther L., Benjamin R., James R.; m. 2d, Dessie P. Shaffer, May 31, 1928; 1 son, Harvey C. Began practice at Grant, Neb., 1902; moved to Grand Island, 1904; pres. Bd. of Edn., Grand Island, 1908-17. Served as capt. Med. Corps, U.S.A., Aug. 1917-Feb. 1919; surgeon in charge of Operating Team No. 35, A.E.F. Fellow Am. Coll. Surgeons. Republican. Mason. Home: Grand Island, Neb. Died Nov. 18, 1940.

MCGREGOR, THOMAS brig. gen. U.S.A.; b. Paisley, Scotland, June 26, 1837; s. Thomas and Agnes M.; ed. Paisley and Edinburgh; m. Jennie M. S. Woodburne, June 8, 1864. Served as pvt., corporal, sergt., and 1st sergt., Co. A. 1st Dragoons, Apr. 8, 1858-Oct. 1, 1862; apptd. 2d lt. 1st Cav., July 17, 1862; promoted through grades to col. 9th Cav., July 15, 1898; retired by operation of law, June 26, 1901; advanced to rank of brig. gen. retired, by act of Apr. 23, 1904. Bvt. capt., May 6, 1864, for battle of Todd's Tavern, Va.; maj., Feb. 27, 1890, for action against Indians at Santa Maria Mountains, Ariz., May 6, 1873. Home: Benicia, Calif. Died Feb. 4, 1921.

MCGRIGOR, SIR RHODERICK naval officer; b. York, Eng., Apr. 12, 1893; s. Maj. Gen. C.R.R. McGrigor and Ada (Bower) McG.; student Royal Naval Colls. Osborne, Dartmouth, 1906-09; LL.D., St. Andrews U., 1953, Aberdeen U., 1955; m. Gwendoline Glyn Greville, 1931; children-John Andrew. Served European war, 1914-18; participated Dardanelles Campaign, Battle of Jutland; capt. 4th Destroyer Flotilla, 1936-38; chief staff, Comdr. in Chief China, 1939; comdr. His Majesty's Ship Renown, Malta convoys, Operations Mediterranean and Atlantic, 1941; Lord Commr. Admiralty, asst. chief naval staff, 1941-43; comdr. naval forces at capture Pantellaria, Invasion of Sicily, flag officer Sicily, Taranto, Adriatic, 1943; comdr. 1st Cruiser Sqdn. Home Fleet Aircraft Carriers, Norwegian Coast and Russian convoys, 1944-45; Lord Commr. Admiralty, vice chief naval staff, 1945-47; comdr. in chief Home Fleet, 1948-50, Plymouth, 1950-51; Lord Comdr. Admiralty, First Sea Lord and Chief of Naval Staff, 1951-55; now Admiral of the Fleet; lord rector Aberdeen U., 1954-57. Decorated Knight Grand Cross of the Bath, Distinguished Service Order, Home: Hopewell Lodge, Tarland, Aberdeenshire, Scotland. Died Dec. 4, 1959.

MCGUGIN, HAROLD ex-congressman; b. Liberty, Kan., Nov. 22, 1893; s. William and Caroline (Bickell) McG.; student Washburn Law Sch., Topeka, Kan., 1912-14; grad. study, Inns of Court, London, Eng., 1919; m. Nell Bird, Feb. 27, 1921. In practice of law at Coffeyville, Kan., since 1914. Served as 2d lt., Adj. General's Office, U.S. Army, in France, February 1917-June 1919; now lt. col. A. C., Military Government France. Mem. Kansas House of Rep., 1927 (author of bill repealing Kan. anticigarette law); mem. 72d and 73d Congresses (1931-35), 3d Kan. Dist. Mem. Am. Legion. Republican. Mason. Odd Fellow. Home: Coffeyville, Kan. Died Mar. 7, 1946.

MCGUIRE, STUART surgeon; b. Staunton, Va., Sept. 16, 1867; s. Hunter Holmes (M.D., LL.D.) and Mary (Stuart) McG.; Richmond Coll.; M.D., U. of Va., 1891; LL.D., Richmond Coll., 1916; m. Ruth I. Robertson, Aug. 1919. Ex-pres. Med. Coll. of Va.; surgeon in charge, St. Luke's Hosp.; cons. surgeon Med. Coll. Hospital. Lt. col., M.C., U.S. Army, comdg. officer Base Hosp. 45, A.E.F.; retired as colonel, World War I. Ex-president Richmond Acad. Medicine, Medical Soc. of Virginia, Tri-State Med. Assn., Southern Surg. and Gynecol. Assn., Southern Med. Association; mem. Phi Beta Kappa. Phi. Kappa Sigma, Alpha Omega Alpha. Awarded D.S.M. (U.S.); Medal of Honor (France). Clubs: Westmoreland, Commonwealth. Author: Principles of Surgery, 1908; The Profit and Loss Account of Modern Medicine, 1915. Address: 2304 Monument Av., Richmond, Va. Died Oct. 27, 1948.

MCGUNNEGLE, GEORGE KENNEDY army officer; b. Annapolis, Md., June 23, 1854; s. Wilson (U.S.N.) and Isabella Steele (Ray) M.; student St. John's Coll., Annapolis, Md.; m. Caroline S. Hart, of El Paso, Tex., Aug. 17, 1880 (now deceased). Commd. 2d lt. 15th Inf., Oct. 1, 1873; 1st lt., Aug. 23, 1877; capt., June 15, 1891; maj. 3d Inf., Dec. 18, 1899; transferred to 17th Inf., Feb. 7, 1903, to 26th Inf., July 23, 1903; lt. col. 17th Inf., July 30, 1903; col. 1st Inf., July 3, 1906. Duty at Ft. McDowell, Cal., 1917. Episcopalian. Mason. Clubs: Army and Navy (New York and Washington, D.C.); Bohemian (San Francisco). Home: Fort McDowell, Cal.

MCHENRY, JAMES U.S. sec. of war; b. Ballymena, County Antrim, Ireland, Nov. 16, 1753; s. Daniel and Agnes McHenry; m. Margaret Allison Caldwell, Jan. 8, 1784, at least 3 children including John. Came to Phila., 1771; became surgeon Col. Robert Magaw's 5th Pa. Battalion, 1776, sr. surgeon Flying Hosp., Valley Forge, 1778; sec. to George Washington, 1778-80; mem. staff Gen. Jean Lafayette, 1780; commd. maj., 1781; mem. Md. Senate, 1781-86, 91-96; mem. Continental Congress 1783-86; del. from Md. to U.S. Constl. Conv., 1787; U.S. sec. of war, 1796-1800; pres. 1st Bible soc. founded in Balt., 1813; published a Balt. directory, 1807; Ft. McHenry (Md.) named for him. Author: A Letter to the Honourable Speaker of the House of Representatives of the United States (speech in defense of actions as sec. of war) 1803. Died Balt., May 3, 1816; buried Westminster Churchyard, Balt.

MCILHENNY, JOHN AVERY U.S. civ. service commr.; b. Avery's Island, Iberia Parish, La., Oct. 29, 1867; s. Edmund and Mary Eliza (Avery) M.; ed. Tulane U., 1 yr., Phillips Acad., Andover, Mass., 2 yrs.; m. Anita Vincent, d. Col. W. R. Stauffer, of New Orleans, Nov. 30, 1907. Pvt. in La. State Militia, 5 yrs.; trooper 1st U.S.Vol. Cav. ("Roosevelt's Rough riders"), 1898; promoted 2d lt. for gallantry in action at San Juan Hill. Has Been mem. Va. Ho. of Rep., and Senate; mem. U.S. Civ. Service Commn., Nov. 30, 1906-, and pres. same, 1913-. Democrat. First v.p. E. McIlhenny's Son (pepper growers). Clubs: Metropolitan, Alibi, Chevy Chase (Washington). Home: 2030 16th St., N.W., Washington.

MCILVAINE, CHARLES ("TOBE HODGE") author; b. Springton Farm (Penn Manor of Springton), Chester Co., Pa., May 31, 1840; s. Hon Abraham Robinson McI. (congressman 7th Pa., 1842-46); ed. country schools Chester Co., Pa. until 1851; Northwest Grammar School, Phila., 1851-53; studied engring.; civ. engr. div. engr., East Brandywine & Waynesburg R.R., 1859-61; m. Sarah G. McIvain, Oct. 20, 1864. Raised co. of vols. under war dept., which he attached to 97th regt., Pa. vols.; mustered in as capt., Oct. 1861; apptd. capt. 19th inf., U.S.A., Nov. 1861; judge advocate, dept. South, 1862; chief of ordnance, staff Maj. Gen. Alfred H. Terry, Maj. Gen. Joseph R. Hawley; apptd. maj. 1st S.C. cav. (col.), 1863; declined; held important positions upon the staffs of several of our noted generals; resigned on account of ill health, 1863; traveled in Europe, 1873-74; chief engr. Jamesville & Washington R.R., 1888-89; inventor of copyable printing ink. Republican. Pres. Phila. Mycol. Center; prin. School of Mycology, N.Y. Chautauqua. Author: A Legend of Polecai Hollow, 1884; 1,000 American Fungi. 4 to, 705 pp. (fully illustrated by the author), 1900, 02; Outdoors, Indoors and Up the Chimney, 1906. Home: Cambridge, Md. Died 1909.

MCILVAINE, JOHN WILSON dist. judge; b. Washington, Pa., June 22, 1907; s. W.A.H. and Annie G. (Wilson) McI.; grad. Washington and Jefferson Coll., 1928; B.S. U. Pitts. Law Sch., 1932; m. Emsie McKennan Smith, Jan. 30, 1930; children-John Wilson, Emsie Ann. Instr. Washington and Jefferson Coll., 1931-32; admitted to Pa. bar, 1933, since practiced in Washington, Pa.; 1st asst. dist. atty., Washington Co., 1952-53; U.S. atty. Western Dist. Pa., 1953-55; U.S. dist. judge Western District Pa., 1955-. Pres. bd. trustees Washington and Jefferson Coll., 1959-. Served as lt. colonel USAAF, World War II, 7th Bomber Command. Decorated Bronze Star Medal, Purple Heart. Mem. Phi Delta Theta. Phi Delta Phi. Clubs: Basett (Washington, Pa.), University, Duquesne (Pitts.). Home: 150 Wilmont Av., Washington, Pa. Office: New Federal Bldg., Pitts. 19. Died July 1, 1963; buried Washington (Pa.) Cemetery.

MCINERNEY, FRANCIS XAVIER naval officer; born Cheyenne, Wyo., Mar. 28, 1899; s. Thomas and Phyllis (O'Neill) McI.; student U. of Colo., 1916-17; B.S., U.S. Naval Acad., 1920; LL.B., George Washington U., 1935; m. Katharine Hammann, May 20, 1924; children-Joan, Robert. Commd. ensign, U.S. Navy, 1920; and advanced through grades to rear adm., 1947; comd. destroyer Smith, 1941, destroyer div. and squadron, 1942-43; comd. destroyers in Battle of Kula Gulf, 1943; Kalombangoro and Solomons campaign, 1943; comd. battleship Washington, 1945-46, cruiser div., 1947-48. Admitted to bar U.S. Supreme Ct., D.C., 1935. Decorated Navy Cross, Silver Star Medal, Bronze Star Medal, Presidential Unit citation, Commendation ribbon with star, World War I and II medals, also various area ribbons and medals. Mem. Bar U.S. Supreme Ct. D.C., Delta Tau Delta. Clubs: Army-Navy Country (Arlington, Va.); Bohemian (San Francisco). Home: 306 E. 18th St., Cheyenne, Wyo. Died June 24, 1956; buried Ft. Rosecrans Cemetery, Point Loma, Cal.

MCINTIRE, ROSS T. former surgeon gen., U.S.N.; b. Salem, Ore., Aug. 11, 1889; s. Charles Thaddeus and Ada (Thompson) McI.; M.D., Willamette U., Salem, Ore., 1912; student U. Ore., 1907-12; post grad. student Washington U., St. Louis, 1921, U. Pa., 1928; m. Pauline Palmer, Jan. 18, 1923. Began practice of medicine, Oregon, 1912; commd. lt. (j.g.), lMed. Corps, U.S. Navy, 1917, comdr., 1934, vice admiral, 1944; surgeon gen. of the Navy and chief Bureau Medicine and Surgery, 1938-46; specialist in ophthalmology and otolaryngology; inst. Naval Hosp., Washington, 1931-38; White House physician, 1933-45; chmn. president's com. Employment of Physically Handicapped, 1947-54; exec. dir. Internat. Coll. of Surgeons, 1955—. Fellow A.C.S.; mem. Am. Surg. Assn., A.M.A., Assn. Mil. Surgeons. Methodist. Mason (Shriner). Clubs: Army and Navy, Burning Tree (Washington). Home: 825 Adella Av., Coronado, Cal. Office: 1516 Lake Shore Dr., Chgo. Died Dec. 1959.

MCINTOSH, JOHN BAILLE army officer; b. Tampa Bay, Fla., June 6, 1829; s. Col. James Simmons and Eliza (Matthews) Shumate McI.; m. Amelia Stout, 1850. Commd. 2d lt. cavalry U.S. Army, 1861, served in Peninsular Campaign; in temporary command 95th Pa. Regt., 1862; brevetted maj., 1862; col. 3d Pa. Cavalry, commanded a brigade at battles of Chancellorsville and Gettysburg, 1862; distinguished in Wilderness campaign, battles of Osequan, White Oak Swamp, Ashland, and Winchester, 1861-65; received brevets from maj. to maj. gen.; commd. lt. col. U.S. Army, 1865; comd. 42d Inf., 1866-67; dep. gov., then gov. Soldiers' Home, Washington, D.C., 1867-68; supt. Indian affairs in Cal., 1869-70; ret. with rank of brig. gen., 1870. Died New Brunswick. N.J., June 29, 1888.

MCINTOSH, JOSEPH WALLACE ex-comptroller of currency; b. Macomb, Ill., Dec. 23, 1873; s. Joseph Wallace and Frances Boone (Woodyard) McI.; m. Natalie Elise Jordan, July 10, 1907. Began with Farmers State Bank, Eustis, Neb., then with Citizens Bank, Macomb, Ill.; mgr. of dept. Armour & Co., Chgo., 1897-1905; receiver, later v.p. and treas. Western Stoneware Co., Monmouth, Ill., 1907-17; dir. finance U.S. Shipping Bd. Emergency Fleet Corp., 1920-24; comptroller of the currency, 1924-28; became partner W. J. Wollman & Co., stock brokers, New York, 1928; dir. Pure Oil Co. (Chgo), 1st Nat. Bank (Miami, Fla.). Served from maj. to col. U.S. Army, 1917-20; chief of subsistence U.S. Army, 1st 6 mos. of 1918; served in France, Italy and the Balkans. Decorated Croix Merito di Guerra (Italian); Polonia Restituta (Polish); Order of Merit (Serbian); War Cross (Czechoslovakian). Republican. Episcopalian. Clubs: Monmouth Country; The Bath, Committee of 100 (Miami Beach, Fla.); Fauquire (Warrenton, Va.); Serpent and Committee of 100 Miami Beach; Rolling Rock (Laughlintown, Pa.). Home: (summer) Overlook Farm, The Plains, Va.; (winter) 6404 Allison Island, Miami Beach, Fla. Died Sept. 26, 1952.

MCINTOSH, LACHLAN army officer, Continental congressman; b. Raits in Badenoch, Scotland, Mar. 17, 1725; s. John Mohr and Marjory (Fraser) McI.; ; m. Sarah Threadcraft. Came to Am., 1736; mem. Provincial Congress of Ga., from Parish of St. Andrew 1775; col. of a bn. Ga. Militia, 1776; commanded Western Dept., 1778; commanded 1st, 5th S.C. regts. in attack on Savannah, Ga., 1779; brevetted maj. gen., 1783; charter mem. Ga. br. Soc. of Cincinnati, 1784; del. Continental Congress, 1784, never attended sessions; twice commr. to adjust boundary dispute between Ga. and S.C.; commr. of Congress to deal with So. Indians, 1785-86. Died Savannah, Feb. 20, 1806; buried Colonial Cemetery, Savannah.

MCINTOSH, WILLIAM Indian chief, army officer; b. Carroll County, Ga., 1775; s. William McIntosh; several Indian wives. Leader of Lower Creek Indians, friendly to Americans in War of 1812; commd. brig. gen. U.S. Army, served with Gen. Andrew Jackson in campaigns against Seminoles, 1817-18; influenced treaties between Lower Creeks and Ga.; expelled from Cherokee country as a renegade, 1824; signer treaty of cession of Indian lands to State of Ga., 1825, killed by Upper Creek Indians who opposed treaty. Died Ga., May 1, 1825.

MCINTYRE, FRANK army officer; b. Montgomery, Ala., Jan. 5, 1865; s. Denis and Mary (Gaughan) McI.; student U. of Ala., 1880-82; grad. U.S. Mil. Acad., 1886; U.S. Inf. and Cav. Sch., 1887-89; m. Marie Dennett, July 12, 1892; children-James Dennett, Frank (dec.), Edward, Marie Dufilho, Margaret Dennett (dec.), Nora. Commd. 2d lt., July 1, 1886; promoted through grades to brig. general, chief Bur. of Insular Affairs, Aug. 24, 1912; maj. gen. (temp.), Oct. 6, 1917. Served on Rio Grande River and various stations in Texas; instr. mathematics, West Point, 1890-94; at Ft. Wayne, Mich., 1894-98; comd. co. in Porto Rican expdn., 1898; in P.R. on staff of Gen. Guy V. Henry until 1899; in P.I., 1899-1902; mem. gen. staff, 1903-05; with Bur. Insular Affairs since 1905, chief, Aug. 24, 1912-July 10, 1918; asst. chief of staff, July 10, 1918-Dec. 31, 1919; again chief Bur. Insular Affairs, Jan. 1, 1920-Jan. 5, 1929; maj. gen. regular army, Aug. 17, 1928, with rank from Oct. 6, 1917; retired Jan. 5, 1929. Awarded D.S.M., Feb. 13, 1919, "for exceptionally meritorious and conspicuous service to U.S. Government"; Comdr. Legion of Honor, France, 1919; Knight Commander of the Bath, Great Britain, 1919; Czecho-Slovak war cross, 1919; Grand Cordon of the Striped Tiger, China, 1919. Catholic. Clubs: Army and Navy (Washington and New York). Home 1615 S. Hull St., Montgomery, Ala. Died Feb. 16, 1944.

MCINTYRE, ROBSON DUNCAN, univ. prof.; b. Wilmington, Ill., Mar. 11, 1899; s. Daniel J. and Mary R. (Robson) McI.; B.S., U. of Ill., 1921, M.S., 1923; grad. work U. of Ill., 1921-23, Northwestern, 1927, N.Y. Univ., 1937-38. Instr. in commerce, U. of Ill., 1921-23; salesman Marshall Field & Co., Chicago, 1923-25; prof. marketing, Coll. of Commerce, U. of Ky., since 1925. Served as pvt., Inf., U.S. Army, 1918-19; major, A.A.F., 1942-46; chief of information and edn. sect., Santa Ana Army Air Base. Recipient Army Commendation ribbon, 1946. Mem. Am. Marketing Assn., Am. Assn. Univ. Profs., Community Concert Assn. of Central Ky. (pres. 1934-71), Omicron Delta Kappa (nat. treas.), Beta Gamma Sigma, Delta Sigma Pi, Alpha Delta Sigma. Republican. Presbyterian. Club: Optimist. Home: Lexington KY Died Feb. 26, 1971; buried Lexington Cemetery, Lexington KY

MCIVER, GEORGE WILLCOX ret. army officer; b. Carthage, N.C., Dec. 22, 1858; s. Alexander and Mary (Willcox) M.; grad. U.S. Mil. Acad., 1882; m. Helen Howard Smedberg, June 28, 1893. Commd. 2d lt. 7th Inf., 1882; advanced through grades to brig. gen. Nat. Army, 1917; duty with El Caney, Cuba, July 1, 1898, and throughout campaign in Cuba; Alaska, 1900-01, Philippines, 1903-04, 12-14; duty with refugees after San Francisco disaster, 1906; comdt. Sch. Musketry, 1907-11; duty with Militia Bur. War Dept., Washington, 1915-17; apptd. comdr. 161st Inf. Brigade, Camp Jackson, Columbia, S.C., Sept. 1917. Mem. Soc. Army of Santiago de Cuba. Presbyn. Club: Army and Navy (Washington). Address: War Dept., Washington. Died May 9, 1947.

MCKAY, DOUGLAS ex-sec. of interior, ex-governor of Oregon; b. at Portland, Ore., June 24, 1893; s. E.D. and Minnie A. (Musgrove) McK.; B.S. agr., Oregon State College, 1917; LL.D., Willamette U., Dickinson Coll., U. Me., Ore. State Coll.; m. Mabel Hill, Mar. 31, 1917; children-Douglas (dec.), Shirley (Mrs. Wayne Hadley), Mary Lou (Mrs. Lester D. Green). Paper carrier, office boy, Union Pacific Railroad, 1909-13; automobile salesman, and sales mgr. Portland, 1920-27; established automobile business, dealer for Chevrolet and Cadillac, Salem (Ore.) 1927. Mayor of Salem, 1933-34; state senator, 1935-37; 39-41, 43-45, 47-49; gov. of Oregon, 1949-53; sec. of interior, 1953-56; mem. Internat. Joint Commn. representing U.S. and Can., 1957—. Served as 1st lt. Infantry, 91st Div. World War I; capt. and major, Service Command Unit, World War I; capt. and major, Service Command Unit, World War II. Mem. State Automobile Dealers Association (past president), Salem C. of C. (past pres.), Oregon State Coll. Alumni Assn. (past pres.), American Legion (past comdr.), Vets. of Fgn. Wars, S.A.R., Disabled Am. Vets. Phi Delta Theta. Decorated: Purple Heart. Republican. Presbyn. Mason (32ff, K.T., Shriner), Elk. Home: 395 Jerris Av., Salem, Ore. Died July 22, 1959.

MCKAY, NEAL H. army officer; b. Troupe, Tex., June 10, 1896; s. Coleman and Gertrude (Henry) McK.; grad. Taylor (Tex.) High Sch., 1914, Quartermaster Sch., 1939, Army Indsl. Coll., 1940; m. Dorothy Day, June 3, 1930; 1 dau., Eleanor Stuart. Commd. 2d lt., Q.M. Corps, U.S. Army, 1920 and advanced through the grades to brig. gen. Died June 11, 1951.

MCKEAN, JOSIAH SLUTTS vice adm. USN, ret.; b. Mt. Hope, O., May 30, 1864; s. William and Rachel (Slutts) McKean; grad. U.S. Naval Acad., 1884; LL.B., U. Mich., 1888; m. Julie Hawxhurst, 1901. Promoted asst. engr., June 28, 1889; passed asst. engr., Nov. 5, 1895; transferred to line as lt., Mar. 3, 1899; lt. comdr., Feb. 12, 1905; comdr., June 18, 1909; capt., July 1, 1913; rear adm. (temp.), July 1, 1918; rear adm. (perm.), Apr. 14, 1920. Served on Charleston, Spanosh-Am. War, 1898; on Ohio, 1904-07; ordnance officer, Navy Yard, League Island, Pa., 1907-09; exec. officer Conn., 1909-10; comd. Panther, 1910-11; at Naval War Coll., Newport, R.I., 1911-13; with Naval Dept., 1915-19; comd. Ariz., Feb.-Sept. 1918; asst. chief operations, Jan. 5, 1919, and actg. chief, Jan. 5-July 15, and Sept. 25-Nov. 1, 1919; comdg. Div. Six, Pacific Fleet, Flagship Wyoming, 1919-21; comdt. Navy Yard, Mare Island, Cal., 1921-24; vice-adm., comdr. Scouting Fleet, Dec. 22, 1924-Sept. 5, 1926; comdt. 11th Naval Dist. and Naval Operating Base, San Diego, Cal., Sept. 15, 1926-May 30, 1928. ret. Home: Homeport, Carmel Highland, Cal. Died Aug. 1951.

MCKEAN, WILLIAM WISTER naval officer; b. Phila., Sept. 19, 1800; s. Judge Joseph Borden and Hannah (Miles) McK.; m. Davis Rosa Clark, Aug. 25, 1824, 12 children. Commd. midshipman U.S. Navy, 1814, lt., 1825, comdr., 1841, capt., 1855, commodore, 1862; in charge of Naval Asylum, Phila., 1843-4 bd. which recommended locating regular naval sch. at Annapolis (Md.); commanded ship Niagara, carried Japanese embassy staff home to Japan, 1860; in charge of the Gulf Blockading Squadron, occupied Head of the Passes of the Mississippi River, 1861. Died "The Moorings," Binghamton, N.Y., Apr. 22, 1865; buried Spring Forest Cemetery. Binghampton.

MCKEE, OLIVER, JR. newspaperman; born in East Orange, N.J., Dec. 2, 1893; s. Oliver and Julia L. (Wilbur) McK., Taft Sch., Watertown, Conn., 1908-11; B.A., Yale, 1915; grad. 5th class, Sch. Military Government, Charlottesville, Va.; m. Virginia Wilkins, Jan. 7, 1922; 1 son, Oliver II III. Reporter Hartford Times, 1915, Washington staff New York World, 1916-17; editorial staff Boston Evening Transcript, 1919-24, Washington corr., 1924-40; with Washington Evening Star, 1940-43; spl. asst. to asst. sec. of state for pub. affairs since 1946. Served at Platsburg O.T.C., 1915; pvt. Troop B, 5th Conn. Cav., Mexican border, 1916; 2d lt. Cav. Res., 1917; 1st lt. 115th F.A. (formerly 1st Tenn. Inf.), 30th Div.; overseas with 310th F.A., 79th Div.; capt. and major F.A. Res., U.S. Army, 1919-40; commd. maj., specialist, Res. U.S. Army, July 10, 1943; Civil Affairs Div., Chief of Staff, Supreme Allied Comd., London, Nov. 1944; with hdqr. 1st Army Jan. 1944-May 1945; after V-E day transferred to Supreme Hdqrs. Allied Expeditionary Forces, G-5 div.; promoted to lt. col.; inactive duty, 1946. Former member Yale Alumni Advisory Bd. Mem. Am. Legion, Zeta Psi, Chi Delta Theta. Republican. Episcopalian. Clubs: National Press, Yale (pres. 1935-37), Overseas Writers (Washington); Elizabethan (New Haven). Contbr. to mags.; also to Encyclopedia Britannica and Dictionary of American Biography. Home: 1613 30th St. Address: Department of State. Washington, D.C. Died June 2, 1948.

MCKEE, WILLIAM JAMES merchant, soldier; b. Madison, Ind., Dec. 12, 1853; s. Robert S. and Celine L. M.; Sheffield Scientific Sch., Yale; m. Fannie B. McKinney, Feb. 20, 1878. Engaged in commercial pursuits; identified with N.G. of Ind., in which he became brig. gen. comdg. in Mar., 1893, and maj. gen., Apr. 1905; apptd. brig. gen. U.S.V., May 27, 1898; served until Mar. 15, 1899; comdg. 2d Div., 1st Army Corps; 2d Brigade, 2d Div., 1st Corps; 3d Brigade, 1st Div., 1st Corps, and 2d Separate Brigade, 2d Army Corps. Home: Indianapolis, Ind. Died Dec. 24, 1925.

MCKEEHAN, CHARLES LOUIS judge; b. Phila., Pa., Mar. 29, 1876; s. Charles Watson and Mary Anna (Givin) McK.; A.B., U. of Pa., 1897, LL.B., 1900; unmarried. Practiced at Phila., 1900-23; judge U.S. Dist Court, Eastern Dist. of Pa., Feb. 19, 1923-. Commd. maj. Ordnance Corps, U.S.A., Nov. 9, 1917; lt. col., Jan. 12, 1918; with A.E.F., July 1918-Mar. 1919. Republican. Episcopalian. Home: Philadelphia, Pa. Died Mar. 23, 1925.

MCKEEVER, CHAUNCEY col. U.S.A.; retired Aug. 31, 1893; b. in Md., 1828; grad. West Point, 1849; assigned to arty.; 1st lt., Dec. 24, 1853; capt. of staff and asst. adj. gen., Aug. 3, 1861. Took part in Bull Run and other battles in Civil War; reached bvt. rank of brig. gen. After war promoted through grades to colonel. Died 1901.

MCKELVY, FRANCIS GRAHAM pres. Alpha Portland Cement Co.; b. Pittsburgh, Pa., Aug. 9, 1883; s. William M. and Frances (Graham) McK.; student Shady Side Acad., Pittsburgh, 1894-99, Lawrenceville (N.J.) Acad., 1899-1900; A.B., Princeton U., 1904; m. Louise Corwin, Nov. 9, 1910; children-Louise Makepeace, William Graham. Clerk Alpha Portland Cement Co., Easton, Pa., 1906-07, asst. sec., 1907-08, purchasing agent, 1908-11, sec., 1911-14, 2d v.p., 1914-17, 1st v.p., 1917-34, exec. v.p., 1934-35, pres. 1935-49, and chairman of the board since 1949. Served as captain of Ordnance Department, Army, 1917. Trustee Lafayette College, Easton, Pennsylvania. Chmn. bd. dirs. Portland Cement Assn., Chicago, 1943. Mem. Am. Soc. Mech. Engrs., Am. Soc. for Testing Materials. Republican. Presbyterian. Clubs: Country of Northampton County (Easton); University, Princeton (New York, N.Y.); Nassau (Princeton, N.J.); Pine Valley Golf. Home: Oakhurst, High St. Office: 15 S. Third St., Easton, Pa. Died May 7, 1952; buried Hillside Cemetery, Middletown, N.Y.

MCKENZIE, JOHN CUMMINGS lawyer; b. Chgo., July 15, 1913; s. Prentiss and Bertha (Cummings) McK.; student U. Ill., 1932-33; LL.B., Loyola U., 1939; m. Mary Jane Manny, July 12, 1941; children-Prentiss Ann, John Fielding. Admitted to Ill. bar, 1939; claims atty. Yellow and Checker Taxi cos., 1941-42, 45-49; founding partner Baker, McKenzie & Hightower, Chgo., 1949-, specializing pvt. internat. law. Trustee Henry George Sch. Social Sci. Served to lt. comdr. USCGR, 1942-45. Mem. Am., Ill., Chgo. bar assns., Soc. Trial Lawyers (dir.), Blue Key. Clubs: Union League, Columbia Yacht (Chgo.). Contbr. articles profl. jours. Home: 231 Prospect Av., Lake Bluff, Ill. Office: 1 N. LaSalle St., Chgo. 2. Died Sept. 28, 1962.

MCKIBBIN, CHAMBERS brig. gen. U.S.A.; b. Pittsburgh, Nov. 2, 1841; s. Chambers and Jane (Bell) M.; ed. at Andover, Mass.; m. Mary Gaines Sibley, Nov. 3, 1869. Enlisted as pvt., gen. service, U.S.A., Sept. 22, 1862; disch. Sept. 24, 1862; commd. 2d lt. 14th Inf., Sept. 22, 1862; promoted through grades to brig. gen. vols., July 8, 1898; col. 12th Inf., U.S.A., Apr. 1, 1899; hon. disch. from vol. service, May 12, 1899; transferred to 24th Inf., Aug. 12, 1901; brig. gen., Oct. 2, 1902; retired, at own request, after 40 yrs'. service, Oct. 3, 1902. Bvtd. capt., Aug. 18, 1864, for battle of North Anna River, Va., and operations on Weldon R.R. Participated in battle of Santiago, and was mil. gov. Santiago de Cuba; comd. 2d Brigade, 2d Div., 5th Army Corps; comd. 1st Brigade, 1st Div., 2d Army Corps, Sept. 22, 1898-Apr. 1, 1899; comd. Dept. of Tex., 1899. Home: Washington, D.C. Died May 1919.

MCKINLEY, JAMES F. army officer; b. San Francisco, Calif., Feb. 22, 1880; s. James and Eliza Howe (Fuller) McK.; grad. high sch., Canton, O., 1898, Army Sch. of the Line, 1911; m. Margaret Disosway, Sept. 18, 1912; children—Margaret, William, Janes. Served as pvt. 8th Vol. Ohio Inf., Spanish-Am. War, June-Nov. 1898; commd. 2d lt. Cav., U.S. Army, Feb. 3, 1899; advanced through grades to col., May 9, 1921; apptd. asst. to the adj. gen., rank of brig. gen., 1929; maj. gen., the adjutant general, June 1933, term of 4 hrs.; retired with rank of maj. gen., Oct. 31, 1935; now pres. Nat. Bank of Ft. Sam Houston, San Antonio. Awarded 2 silver star citations for gallantry in action; holder of campaign badges for Spanish-Am. War, Cuban Pacification, Cuban Occupation, Philippine Insurrection, Mexican border and World War victory; on Gen. Staff eligible list. Methodist. Died Jan. 17, 1941.

MCKINLEY, WILLIAM President of the United States; b. Niles, O., Jan. 29, 1843; s. Willian and Nancy Campbell (Allison) McK.; ed. at public schools. Poland Acad. and Allegheny Coll. Taught in public schools; enlisted, pvt., 23d Ohio vol. inf., 1861; commissary sergt., 1862; 2d lt., 1862; 1st lt., 1863; capt., 1864; served on staffs of Gens. R.B. Hayes, George Crook and Winfield S. Hancock; bvtd. maj. U.S. vols. by President Lincoln for gallantry in battle, March 13, 1865; detailed as acting asst. adjt. gen., 1st div., 1st army corps, until mustered out, July 26, 1865; m. Ida, d. James A. Saxton, 1871. Studied law in Mahoning Co., O.; took a course at Albany (N.Y.) Law School, 1867; admitted to Ohio bar, 1867, and settled at Canton, O., which has since been his home. Pros. att'y Stark Co., O., 1869; mem. Congress, 1876-91, and as chmn. Com. on Ways and Means reported the tariff bill of 1890, known as the "McKinley Bill"; especially known in Congress as advocate of high protective tariff. His dist., having been changed by Dem. legislature, he was defeated for Congress at Nov. election, 1890. Elected gov. Ohio 1891; re-elected, 1893. Delegate at large to Rep. Nat. Conv., and mem. Com. on Resolutions, 1884, and supported James G. Blaine; to that of 1888 (supporting John Sherman), and was chmn. Com. on Resolutions; delegate at large to conv., 1892, and was made its chmn.; received 182 votes for President, but refused to allow his name to be considered, supporting renomination of Benjamin Harrison. Nominated for President at Rep. Nat. Conv., St. Louis, June 18, 1896, receiving 661 out of a total of 905 votes; elected in Nov., 1896, by popular plurality of 600,000 votes, and received 271 electoral votes as against 176 for William J. Bryan. On June 21, 1900, unanimously renominated by Nov., the leading opposing candidate again being William J. Bryan. Popular plurality, 849,000 votes; received 292 electoral votes against 155 for Mr. Bryan. Died 1901.

MCKINSTRY, CHARLES HEDGES army officer; b. in Cal., Dec. 19, 1866; grad. U.S. Mil. Acad., 1888, Engr. Sch. of Application, 1891. Commd. add. 2d lt. engrs., June 11, 1888; 2d lt., July 22, 1888; 1st lt., Oct. 11, 1892; capt., July 5, 1898; maj., Jan. 1, 1906; lt. col., Feb. 27, 1912; brig. gen. N.A., Aug. 5, 1917. In charge works for defense of Key West, Fla., and improvements of harbor at Key West, 1898-1900; instr. civ. engring., Engr. Sch. of Application, 1901-03; instr. practical astronomy, same, 1902-03; in charge of fortification and river and harbor works of southern Cal., 1903-06; apptd. mem. Cal. Debris Commn., 1905; assigned as comdr. 158th Field Arty., Camp Sherman, Chillicothe, O., Sept. 1917. Address: War Dept., Washington, D.C.

MCKNIGHT, HENRY TURNEY, b. Mpls., April 2, 1913; s. Sumner Thomas and Henriette Denny (Turney) McK.; grad. St. Paul's Sch., Concord, N.H., 1928-32; A.B., Yale, 1936; m. June Hanes, Apr. 11, 1942;children—Henry T., Sumner T. II, Christina Agnes; m. 2d, Grace Carter Lindley, Feb. 1, 1958; children—Clarkson and Kristine Lindley. Began as advertising salesman N.Y. Herald Tribune, 1936-39; account exec. Batten, Barton, Durstine & Osborn, 1939-41; publisher's asst. LOOK mag., 1946-47; owner and operator McKnight Angus Farm, Victoria, Minn.; chmn. bd. Impro Sales, Inc.; pres. Bright Futures, Inc., Carver Co., Ace Development Corp.; vice president S. T. McKnight Co., Mpls. Mem. Minn. Senate, from 1962. Apptd. sec. Nat. Agrl. Adv. Com., 1952; v.p. Keep Minn. Green, Inc.; chmn. Minn. Natural Resources. Served from ensign to lt. comdr., USNR, 1941-45. Decorated Bronze Star. Mem. Mpls. Soc. Fine Arts (trustee), Am. Forestry Assn. (mem. executive com.), C. of C. Clubs: Chicago; Metropolitan (Washington); Links (N.Y.C.); Minneapolis (Mpls.); Wayzata Country, Woodhill Country (Wayzata, Minn.). Home: Wayzata MN Died Dec. 30, 1972.

MCKOWEN, JOHN CLAY physician; b. Jackson, La., Mar. 1842; grad. Dartmouth Coll., A.B., A.M., 1866; Univ. of Munich, Bavaria, M.D.; served in Confederate cav. to lt.-col.; while capt., June 3, 1863, entered lines of Gen. Banks' army, 30,000 strong, with 5 scouts, and captured Gen. Neal Dow and guard (Gen. Dow was exchanged for Gen. Fitzhugh Lee). Has residences at New Orleans and Capri, Italy; at latter has noted collection of arms, curios, pictures, books, antique statues, marbles and inscriptions. Discovered new diseases and remedy and published discovery under title "Aromatic Toxins." Not married. Author: Capri (historical, archaeological and ethnological study); also mag. articles. Lived in New Orleans and abroad.

MCLAIN, RAYMOND S. army officer; b. Washington County, Ky., Apr. 4, 1890; s. Thomas A. and Lucetta (Stallings) McL.; student Hills Bus. Coll., Oklahoma City, 1909; grad. Sch. of Musketry, 1917, Command and Gen. Staff Sch., 1938; m. Norma Leeman, 1910; children-Raymond S., Dorothy V. (Mrs. Norman Rogers), Betty June, Norma Lee; m. 2d, Bertha Cunningham, Aug. 12, 1933; 1 son, Robert Duncan. Clerk in real estate office, 1907-11; abstractor, 1912-15; asst. county treas., 1916; pres. Central Title & Investment Co., 1919-23; v.p. Am. Nat. Co., 1923-28, Am.-First Trust Co., Oklahoma City, 1933-53; pres. Am. Mortgage & Investment Co., 1953—, chmn. bd. Am. First Title & Trust Co., 1953—. Pvt. Nat. Guard, 1912, 2d lt. to 1st lt., serving on Mexican Border and in World War I, 1914-19; capt. O.R.C., 1920-21; capt. to brig. gen., Okla. Nat. Guard, 1921-37; brig. gen., U.S. Army, 1940, comdg. arty. of 45th Inf. Div., Sicily and Italy; transferred to England, Apr. 1944; comdg. general 30th Infantry Division Field Artillery, France, June 9, 1944 (D-3); comdg. 90th Inf. Div., July 1944, corps comdr. XIX corps, Oct. 1944-45; lt. gen., June 6, 1945; in battle of France, Roer, Rhine, Elbe and Germany; permanent grade of brig. gen., U.S. Army, 1945; maj. gen. U.S. Army, 1948, ret. as lt. gen., 1952; asst. chief of information, War Department, 1946-47; appointed chief of Information, Department of the Army, 1948; comptroller U.S. Army, 1949-53. Now member bd. commissioners Nat. Security Tng. Commn. Awarded Distinguished Service Cross with Oak leaf cluster, Distinguished Service Medal with oak leaf cluster, Silver Star, Bronze Star with oak leaf cluster, Legion of Honor, Croix de Guerre with Palm (French); Order of Orange Nassau (Netherlands); medal by Belgian Patriots (not govt. honor); Order of Leopold (Belgian); Croix de Guerre (Belgian). Clubs: Oklahoma City Golf and Country; Kions, Men's Dinner (Oklahoma City); Chevy Chase, Army-Navy (Washington). Home: 1709 Pennington Way. Office: First Nat. Bank Bldg., Okla. City; also 811 Vermont St., N.W., Washington. Died Dec. 14, 1954; buried Oklahoma City.

MCLANAHAN, AUSTIN banker; b. Chambersburg, Pa., Oct. 31, 1871; s. Johnston and Rebecca Anne (Austin) McL.; A.B., Princeton, 1892, LL.B., U. of Md., 1897; m. Romaine Le Moyne, Nov. 8, 1902; children-Jean Romaine (Mrs. Francis C. Taliaferro), Anne Austin (Mrs. John A. Leutkemeyer). With Alex Brown & Sons, 1894-1922, mem. firm, 1902-22; pres. Savings Bank of Baltimore since 1922; dir. First Nat. Bank. Pres. Export and Import Bd. of Trade, Baltimore, 1920-22. Served as maj. A.R.C., France, World War. Trustee Sheppard & Enoch Pratt Hosp. Presybterian. Club: Maryland (Baltimore). Home: 4801 Green Spring Av. Office: Savings Bank of Baltimore, Baltimore, Md. Died Apr. 3, 1946.

MCLANE, PATRICK, congressman; b. County Mayo, Ireland, Mar. 14, 1875; came with parents to Scranton, Pa., 1882; ed. pub. schs. 3 yrs. Worked in coal mines 10 yrs.; entered ry. service and advanced to locomotive engr.; mem. 66th Congress (1919-21), 10th Pa. Dist. Served as pvt. Co. E, 11th U.S. Inf., Spanish-Am. War, 1898-9. Mem. Sch. Bd., Scranton, 8 yrs. Democrat. Roman Catholic. Home: 535 Broadway, Scranton PA

MCLAREN, DONALD rear admiral U.S.N.; b. Caledonia, N.Y., Mar. 7, 1834; s. Rev. Donald Campbell and Jane (Stevenson) M.; A.B., Union Coll., 1853; grad. Princeton Theol. Sem., 1857; (D.D., U. of Wooster, 1882); m. Elizabeth Stockton Green, July 14, 1858. Ordained Presbyn. ministry, 1857; paster Tennent Ch., Monmouth, N.J., 1857-62. Commd. by Pres. Lincoln chaplain U.S.N., Mar. 10, 1863; retired, 1896; promoted, for creditable record during Civil War, rear admiral retired, Jan. 1907. Agt. Am. Bible Soc. in P.R., 1902-04; for W.I. (hdqrs. Havana), 1905-06; for Va., 1906-07; establishing Pacific agency of the Am. Bible Soc., 1907-08, at San Francisco. Republican. Died May 27, 1920.

MCLAUGHLIN, CHESTER BOND lawyer; b. Port Henry, N.Y., Dec. 11, 1895; s. Chester Bentine and Lucy (Warner) McL.; A.B., Harvard, 1915, LL.B., 1919; m. Margaret F. Williston, June 1, 1918; children-Chester Bond, Margaret Fairlie (Mrs. Standrod Carmichael), Elizabeth Annesley. Admitted to N.Y. bar, 1919; lawyer Shearman & Sterling, N.Y. City, 1919-22; in charge uptown office Rounds, Hatch, Dillingham & Debeviose, 1922-24; former McLaughlin & Royce, 1924; mem. McLaughlin, Knollenberg, Royce & Leisure, 1927-29, McLaughlin & Stickles, 1929-50, McLaughlin, Stickles & Hayden since 1950; asst. prof. law N.J. Law Sch., 1927-32; dir. Franco-Am. Aviation Corp., Rinehart & Co., Inc., Wainwright Realty Corp., A. S. Barnes & Co., Inc. Justice of Peace, Town of Eastchester, 1928-32, mem. town bd., 1928-47; acting police judge Village of Bronxville, 1928-32. Dir. Hermitage Found., Westchester Cancer com. Am. Cancer Soc., Inc. Served as 2d lt. to capt., Judge Adv. Gen. Dept., Selective Service Bur. Q.M.C., 1917-19. Mem. Am., N.Y. State, Westchester and City of N.Y. bar assns., Am. Legion (comdr. 1925-26). S.R. Presbyn. Mason (32ff). Clubs: Harvard, University, New York Yacht, Bronxville Field, St. Andrews Golf. Author articles in legal jours. Home: 39 Forest Lane, Bronxville, N.Y. Office: 36 W. 44th St., N.Y.C. 18. Died Jan. 21, 1952; buried Bronxville, N.Y.

MCLAWS, LAFAYETTE army officer; b. Augusta, Ga., Jan. 15, 1821; s. James and Elizabeth (Huquenin) McL.; grad. U.S. Mil. Acad., 1842; m. Emily Taylor, circa 1842. Served as 1st l5. in Scott's Army during Mexican War; acting asst. adj. gen. Dept. of N.M.; mem. Utah expdn. of 1858; participated in campaign against Navajo Indians, 1859-60; commd. maj. Confederate Army, 1861; commd. col. 10th Ga. Regt., brig. gen., 1861, maj. gen., 1862; teamed with Stonewall Jackson in capture of Harpers Ferry, 1862; in command Dist. of Ga., also defenses of Savannah (Ga.); fought in battles of Antietam, Fredericksburg, Gettysburg, Chickamauga; collector of internal revenue, postmaster of Savannah, 1875-76. Died Savannah, July 24, 1897.

MCLEAN, FRANKLIN CHAMBERS, univ. prof.; b. Maroa, Ill., Feb. 29, 1888; s. William Thomas and Margaret Philbrook (Crocker) McL.; B.S., U. of Chicago, 1907, Ph.D., 1915; M.D., Rush Med. Coll., 1910; M.D. (hon.), University of Lund, Sweden, 1957; m. Helen Vincent, June 11, 1923; 1 son, Franklin Vincent (died May 31, 1948). Interne Cook County Hospital, 1910-11; professor pharmacology, University of Oregon, 1911-14; member staff Hosp. of Rockefeller Inst. for Med. Research, New York, 1914-16; dir. Peiping (China) Union Med. Coll., 1916-20, prof. medicine, 1916-23; prof. medicine U. Chgo., 1923-32, prof. pathol. physiology, 1933-53, emeritus, 1953-65, dir. univ. clinics, 1928-32, dir. toxicity lab., 1941-43, dir. spl. AEC project, 1948-51, dir. special project for USAF, 1951-54; visiting professor, department of histology, University of Illinois College Dentistry, 1966-68. Cons. to Santa Fe Operations office, AEC, Los Alamos, N.M., 1947-49; mem. spl. panel AEC, Washington, 1948-50; dep. chmn. Joint Panel on Med. Aspects of Atomic Warfare, 1949-53; mem. tech. adv. panel on biol. and chem. Warfare Office Asst. Sec. of Def., 1955-60; member subcommittee on Skeletal system NRC, 1952-58. Served as 1st lt. to maj. M.C., U.S. Army, World War; sr. consultant in gen. medicine, A.E.F., 1918. Served as civilian in connection with chem. warfare preparedness, Office Sci. Research and Development, 1941-43; lt. col. and col., Med. Corps A.U.S., assigned to Chem. Warfare Service, 1943-45. Mem. Research Council of Chem. Corps Adv. Bd., 1947-49. Awarded Legion of Merit, 1945, Army Commendation Ribbon, 1947; War and Navy Depts. certificate Appreciation, 1947. Trustee Easter Seal Research Found., 1960-68, past chmn.; dir., sec.-treas. Nat. Med. Fellowship, Inc., Chicago; trustee Fisk U. (chmn. bd. 1951-55). Mem. Assn. Am. Physicians, Harvey Soc., Institute of Medicine (pres. 1959) (Chgo.), Chicago Soc. Internal Medicine, American Physiol. Soc.; Am. Acad. Orthopaedic Surgeons (hon.), Assn. Bone and Joint Surgs. (hon.). Clubs: Tavern, Quadrangle (Chgo.); Cosmos (Washington). Author: (with Marshall R. Urist) Bone: An Introduction to the Physiology of Skeletal Tissue, 1955; (with Ann M. Budy) Radiation, Isotopes, and Bone, 1964). Co-editor: Radioisotopes and Bone, 1962. Home: Chicago IL Died Sept. 10, 1968.

MCLEAN, HEBER HAMPTON, ret. naval officer; b. Llano, Tex., Dec. 9, 1899; s. John Hiram and Minnie (Button) McL.; B.S., U.S. Naval Acad.; m. Evelyn Winston Lane, Dec. 11, 1923; 1 dau., Evelyn Lane Ghormley; m. 2d, Ellen Burkhardt Knox, Feb. 25, 1953; 1 dau., Mary Ann. Commd. ensign USN, 1920, and advanced through various grades to rear admiral; ret. 1954 with rank of v. admiral. Awarded Legion of Merit, awarded Gold star in lieu of 2d and 3d awards, Grand Cruz di Aviz (Portugal), Order of St. Charles (Monaco), Order of Military Merit (Korea). Methodist. Mason. Club: Army and Navy Country. Home: San Antonio TX Died Sept. 9, 1971.

MCLEAN, MILTON ROBBINS nat. guard officer; b. Clinton, Ill., Dec. 9, 1874; s. James Oldham and Emma Day (Robbins) McL.; ed. pvt. and pub. schs., Clinton, Ill., and high sch., Havana, Ill.; pvt. instrn. spl. course in elec. subjects, Northwestern U., 1893; grad. U.S. Army Signal Sch., Langre, France, 1918; m. Mary Dougherty Share, Oct. 19, 1898; 1 dau., Mildred Share. Cashier, dir. Farmers State, Wellington, Kan., 1894-1917. Commd. maj. 110th Field Signal Bn., 35th Div., AEF, 1917; promoted lt. col. Signal Corps, U.S. Army; assigned div. signal officer; served in Vosges (Alsace and Lorraine), St. Mihiel, Argonne, Sommedieu and Verdun; brig. gen., Adj. Gen. Dept., Kan. Nat. Guard, 1925—; adj. gen. Kan., 1925—; state dir. selective service for Kan., 1940-47. Dir. Kan. Safety Council. Mem. Mil. Order World Wars (past comdr. Topeka chpt.), Navy League Am., Am. Legion, Vets. Fgn. Wars. Adjutants Gen. Assn. U.S. (sec.-treas.), (pres., dir.). Mason (32ff, K.T., Shriner), Nat. Sojourner (comdr.). Office: State House, Topeka, Kan. Died Apr. 17, 1951.

MCLEAN, RIDLEY naval officer; b. Pulaski, Tenn., Nov. 10, 1872; s. Thornton and Sallie (Ridley) M.; student, U. of Tenn., 1888-90; grad. U.S. Naval Acad., 1894; m. Elive Gale, Nov. 8, 1916; step-children (adopted)—Olive Beatrice, Gale. Commd. ensign, July 1, 1896; promoted lt. (jr. grade), July 1, 1899; lt., Aug. 7, 1901; lt. comdr., July 1, 1907; comdr., July 1, 1913; judge adv. gen. with rank of capt., Nov. 5, 1913; capt., Aug. 31, 1917. Served on bd. protected cruiser San Francisco, 1894-95, later on battleships Indiana, Oregon, and other vessels; on gunboat Marietta during Reyes Rebellion in Nicaragua, 1898; served on ammunition ship Armeria, during Spanish-Am. War; on staff of Rear Admiral Kempff during Boxer rebellion in China, 1900; and Philippine insurrection, 1901-02; specialized in gunnery work, being asst. insp. target practice, 1903-06, and fleet gunnery officer on staff of commander-in-chief, Atlantic Fleet, 1906-09; Gen. Bd., Navy Dept., 1909-11; navigator, 1st lt., and exec. officer Battleships Florida, 1911-13; judge adv. gen. U.S.N., Nov. 5, 1913-Dec. 2, 1916; comd. U.S.S. Columbia, Dec. 1916-Aug. 1917; chief of staff Battleship Force One, Aug. 1917-Oct. 1918; comd. Battleship New Hampshire, Oct. 1918-Nov. 1919, engaged as escort for convoys until armistice and afterward on transport duty return of expeditionary force to the U.S.; comd. Battleship Arkansas, 1922-24; apptd. dir. naval communications, 1924; promoted to rear admiral June 2, 1927; comdr. Submarine Division, Battle Fleet, 1927-29; budget officer Navy Dept., 1929—. Unitarian. Author: Bluejacket's Manual, 1902. Died Nov. 12, 1933.

MCLEAN, THOMAS CHALMERS rear admiral U.S.N.; b. New Hartford, N.Y., Oct. 25, 1847. Apptd. from N.Y., and grad. U.S. Naval Acad., 1868; ensign, Apr. 19, 1869; promoted through grades to rear admiral, July 19, 1908. Served on S. Pacific Squadron in the Tuscarora, 1868-69; Benicia, 1869-71; torpedo duty, 1872-73; exptl. battery, 1873-75; Tennessee, 1875-76; torpedo duty, 1876-77; Navy Yard, Washington, 1878-79; Constellation, 1879-81; spl. duty abroad, 1881-82; Vienna Expn., 1883; Dolphin, 1884-88; torpedo sta., Newport, 1889-92; exec. officer of Detroit, 1893-96; Bur. of Navigation, Navy Dept., 1896-97; torpedo Sta., NewPort, 1897-99; comd. Don Juan de Austria, 1899-1901, Castine, 1901, Cincinnati, 1901-02; in charge recruiting sta., Baltimore, 1902-03; capt. of yard, Navy Yard, League Island, 1903-05; comd. Pennsylvania, 1905-07; on duty at Naval War College pres. Bd. Inspection and Survey, 1907-09; retired by operation of law, Oct. 25, 1909. Home: Utica, N.Y. Died Aug. 29, 1919.

MCLEAN, WALTER rear admiral; b. Elizabeth, N.J., July 30, 1855; s. George Washington and Rebecca J. (McCormick) M.; grad. U.S. Naval Acad., 1876; short course, Naval War Coll., full course Army War Coll.; m. Emma Bowne Jarvis, Dec. 8, 1887. Apptd. at large by Pres. U.S. Grant, to U.S. Naval Acad., 1872; grad., 1876; ensign U.S.N., Feb. 26, 1878; promoted through grades to rear admiral, Mar. 10, 1914. Served on Asiatic Station, 1878-82; made trip across Siberia and Russia from Nagasaki, Japan, to Moscow, June-Sept. 1882; sr. aid on staff of Commodore George Dewey, 1898, in comd. dispatch vessel Zafiro until return to U.S., 1899; commanding 4th Div. Atlantic Fleet, 1914-15; comdt. Navy Yard and Sta., Norfolk, Va., and 5th Naval Dist., 1915; retired. Has taken active part in development of modern ordnance, especially in development of armor from wrought iron to Krupp armor; was mem. bd. to determine cost of armor plate and armor plant, 1905. Republican. Episcopalian. Part author of Observations upon the Korean Coast, Japanese-Korean Ports and Siberia (U.S. Govt. publ.), 1883. Home: Lutherville, Md. Died Mar. 20, 1930.

MCLEARY, JAMES HARVEY judge; b. Smith Co., Tenn., July 27, 1845; s. Samuel D. and Sarah A. (Weller) M.; served in C.S.A., 1861-65; A.B., Washington and Lee U., 1868, LL.B., 1869; m. Miss King, July 11, 1906. Asst. prof. English, Washington Coll., 1868-69; practiced law at San Antonio, Tex., 1869-98; mem. Tex. Legislature, House and Senate, 1874-77; atty. gen. of Tex., 1881-82; justice Supreme Ct. of Mont., 1886-88; maj. and insp. gen. U.S.V., in war with Spain, in Cuba, 1898; alcaide Santiago de Cuba, 1898; asst. sec. of Puerto Rico, 1901; asso. justice Supreme Ct. of P.R., Oct. 8, 1901—. Mason. Home: San Jauan, P.R. Died Jan. 5, 1914.

MCLEMORE, ALBERT SYDNEY, officer U.S.M.C.; b. Franklin, Tenn., May 23, 1869; grad. U.S. Naval Acad., 1891. Apptd. 2d lt. U.S.M.C., July 1, 1893; promoted 1st lt., June 14, 1896; capt., Mar. 3, 1899; asst. adj. and insp. with rank of maj., Dec. 15, 1904; same, with rank of lt. col., Aug. 29, 1916; same, with rank of col., Aug. 29, 1916. Bvtd. capt. for distinguished conduct and pub. service at Guantanamo, Cuba; brigade adj. and insp., 1st Brigade of Marines, Manila, P.I., 1908-09; in charge S. Atlantic Insp. Dist., Norfolk, Va., 1910-11; assigned duty office of adj. and insp. Marine Corps Hdqrs., Navy Dept., May 23, 1911; asst. adj. and insp., San Francisco, Aug, 1919—. Home: Murfreesboro TN

MCLENDON, LENNOX POLK, lawyer; b. Wadesboro, N.C., Feb. 12, 1890; s. Walter Jones and Sarah J. (Polk) McL.; B.S., N.C. State Coll., 1910, H.H.D., 1962; LL.B., U. of N.C., 1912, LL.D., 1955; Dr. of Laws (hon.), University N.C. at Greensboro, 1964; m. Mary Lilly Aycock, June 27, 1917; children—Mary Louise (Mrs. E. K. Atkinson), Lennox Polk, Charles Aycock, William Woodard, John Aycock. Admitted to N.C. bar, 1913; mayor of Chapel Hill, N.C., May-Dec. 1913; practiced law, alone, Durham, N.C., 1914-16; sr. mem. McLendon & Hedrick, Durham, 1919-33; partner McLendon, Brim, Brooks, Pierce & Daniels, Greensboro, 1933-68; solicitor 10th Judicial Dist., 1921-24. Mem. N.C. Gen. Assembly, 1917; chmn. State Bd. of Elections, 1932-36; chmn. Commn. on State Dept. of Justice for N.C., 1937-38; mem. N.C. Probation Commn., 1939-54; declined appointment to the N.C. Supreme Court, 1936. Gen. counsel U.S. Senate Com. Rules and Adminstrn., Baker Investigation, 1963-65. Served as 1st lieutenant N.C. Nat. Guard, Mexican border, 1916; capt. field arty., U.S. Army, 1917, and recruited Battery C, 113th F.A.; sent to France with Advanced Sch. Detachment, 30th Div., May 1918, rejoining 113th F.A., Aug. 1918; participated Battle of St. Mihiel and Argonne Forest Offensive; with Army of Occupation; disch. maj., Mar. 1919. Trustee Cone Meml. Hosp., Greensboro, N.C. Fellow Am. Bar Assn. Found. Mem. N.C. State Bar (pres. 1940-41), Am., N.C. bar assns., N.C. State Bd. Higher Edn. (vice chmn. 1955-60, chmn. 1960-63), Kappa Sigma. Democrat. Baptist. Club: Greensboro Country. Home: Greensboro NC Died Aug. 7, 1968.

MCLEOD, CLARENCE JOHN ex-congressman; b. Detroit, July 3, 1895; s. Malcolm J. and Christina (Darvoux) M.; student U. Detroit; LL.B., Detroit Coll. Law, 1918; m. Marie C. Posselius (died Oct. 9, 1956), May 19, 1920; children-Clarence John, Rosemary, Malcolm, Eugenie; m. 2d, Mary Louise DeMarco, Feb. 9, 1959; Pvt. Aviation Sect., Ground Sch., Cornell U., 1918; trans. to Intelligence Div., U.S. Army; commd. 2d lt. U.S.R., 1919; capt., 1923, maj., 1928, lt. col., 1936. Began practice at Detroit, 1919; mem. law firm Clarence J. McLeod. Mem. 66th and 74th, also 76th Congresses, 13th Mich. Dist. Republican. Catholic. Mem. Am., Mich., Detroit bar assns., Am. Judicature Soc., Delta Theta Phi, K.C. (4ff). Clubs: University, Detroit Golf, Detroit Athletic, Army and Navy. Address: 1440 Lincolnshire Rd., Detroit 3. Died May 15, 1959; buried Mt. Olivet Cemetery, Detroit.

MCLESTER, JAMES SOMERVILLE physician; b. Tuscaloosa, Ala., Jan. 25, 1877; s. Joseph and Nannie (Somerville) M.; A.B., U. Ala., 1896, LL.D.; M.D., U. Va., 1899; post-grad. Gottingen, Freiburg, 1901-02, Berlin and Munich, 1907-08; m. Ada Bowron, 1903; children-Anna, James B., Jane. Prof. medicine U. Ala., 1919-50. Maj. Chief of Med., Base Hosp., Camp Sheridan, 1917; lt. col. AEF, comdg. officer Evacuation Hosp. 20, 1918; cons. AEF, 1918. Research and scientific articles dealing chiefly with diseases of nutrition and metabolism; chmn. subcommittee on med. nutrition NRC. Fellow A.C.P.; mem. A.M.A. (chmn. sect. on practice of medicine, 1920; pres. 1935-36; chmn. council on foods and nutrition), Assn. Am. physicians, Am. Soc. Clin. Investigation, Am. Climatological and Clin. Assn., So., Ala. Med. Assn., (pres. 1920) med. assns. Democrat. Presbyn. Club: Mountain Brook. Author: (textbooks) Nutrition and Diet in Health and Disease; The Diagnosis and Treatment of Disorder of Metabolism. Home: 3224 Country Club Rd. Office: 930 S. 20th St., Birmingham, Ala. Died Feb. 8, 1954.

MCMAHON, ALPHONSE, physician; b. St. Louis, Mo., Aug. 4, 1895; s. John Francis and Margaret Elizabeth (Murphy) McM.; A.B., St. Louis University, 1915, M.D., 1919, M.A., 1935; married Mary Celeste Dolan, December 31, 1954. Intern St. Luke's Hosp., St. Louis, Mo., 1919; St. Vincent's Hosp., Los Angeles, Calif., 1920; asst. resident, Pottenger Sanitorium, Monrovia, Calif., 1920-21; practice of internal medicine, St. Louis, Mo., 1921-42; mem. faculty of sch. of medicine St. Louis Univ.; 1922-46, associate professor medicine, from 1946; chief of staff of St. John's Hospital, 1951. Cons. internal medicine to Surgeon Gen. U.S. Navy. Served as member M.C., U.S.N.R., from 1935; called to active duty, 1942; promoted to rank of commodore, 1945; comdg. officer Naval Res. Med. Co. 9-1; rear adm., 1953. Mem. St. Louis Smoke committee, 1939; mem. bd. St. Louis Opera Guild, 1939. Received Letter of Commendation for Naval Med. Service at base hosp. in South Pacific; awarded Distinguished Service Medal of Miss. Valley Med. Assn., 1944. Diplomate Am. Bd. Internal Medicine. Fellow A.C.P., Assn. Mil. Surgeons, Soc. Med. Cons. to Armed Forces; mem. St. Louis Med. Soc. (pres. 1939), A.M.A. (v.p. 1940, chmn. council on sci. assembly), Soc. Internal Medicine, Am. Therapeutic Soc. (pres. 1938), Nat. Tb Assn., Am. Heart Assn., So. Med. Assn. (councilor 1936-41, pres. 1953-54), Alpha Omega Alpha, Sigma Psi, Alpha Kappa Kappa. Roman Catholic. Knight of Malta, K.C. Club: University (St. Louis). Author med. articles. Home: St Louis MO Deceased.

MCMAHON, HENRY GEORGE, educator, lawyer; b. New Iberia, La., Dec. 27, 1900; s. Richard Supple and Mathilde (Dansereau) McM.; A.B., La. State U., 1923, LL.B., 1925, A.M., 1937; LL.D., Loyola U. of South, 1962; research asso. Raymond Found., Northwestern U., 1940-41; m. Neenah Webster, Dec. 27, 1927; children—Henry George, Philip, Dan, Nancy (Mrs. Charles M. Pecot, Jr.), John. Admitted to La. bar, 1925; practiced in New Orleans, 1926-36; with Normann, McMahon & Breckwoldt, later Normann & McMahon, 1929-36; mem. law faculty Loyola U. of South, 1929-37; prof. law Louisiana State University, 1937-62, Boyd professor, 1962-66, acting dean, 1942, 47-48, dean, 1949-52. Res. counsel The California Co., New Orleans, 1945-46; city-parish atty., Baton Rouge, Parish of East Baton Rouge, 1949; coordinator, reporter La. Code Civil Procedure. Served to lt. comdr. USNR, 1942-45. Recipient Hatton W. Summers award for outstanding services in improvement adminstrn. justice Southwestern Legal Found. Mem. Am., La. (gov. 1941-42, 48-49, 54-55, 58-59, 64-65) bar assns., La. Law Inst. (council 1938-66), Am. Judicature Soc., Phi Kappa Phi, Kappa Sigma, Phi Delta Phi. Democrat. Roman Catholic. Club: Boston (New Orleans). Author: McMahon on Louisiana Practice, rev. edit., 1949; (with Rubin) Anno. La. Pleadings, 1963. Contbr. articles law jours. and reviews. Home: Baton Rouge LA Died Oct. 30, 1966; buried Roselawn Cemetery, Baton Rouge LA

MCMAHON, JOHN EUGENE army officer; b. Buffalo, N.Y., Dec. 8, 1860; s. Col. John E. and Esther (Bryan) M.; A.B., Fordham U., 1880; grad. U.S. Mil. Acad., 1886, Arty. Sch., 1898; m. Caroline Bache, May 12, 1888. Commd. 2d lt. 4th Arty., July 1, 1886; promoted through grades to maj. gen. N.A., Dec. 17, 1917. Instr. modern langs., U.S. Mil. Acad., 1890-91; a.d.c. to Maj. Gen. A. McD. McCook, 1891-95; adj. gen. 2d Brigade Provisional Div., 5th Army Corps, June-July, 1898; adj. gen. 2d Brigade, 2d Div., 4th Army Corps, Oct.-Nov. 1898; adj. gen. U.S. forces, Puerto Principe, Jan.-May 1899; in Philippines, 1901; pres. Field Arty. Brigade, Camp Custer, Battle Creek, Mich., Sept. 1917, 5th Div. U.S.A., Dec. 28, 1917. Home: Utica, N.Y. Died Jan. 30, 1920.

MCMAHON, MARTIN THOMAS judge Court of General Sessions of the Peach, New York Co., for term Jan. 1, 1896, to Dec. 31, 1909; b. La Prairie, Canada, March 21, 1838; grad. St. John's Coll., Fortham, N.Y., 1855 (A.M., 1857; LL.D., 1866); established in law practice; m. Louise Claire Hargous, Apr. 1872 (died 1872). Served through Civil war; was chief of staff 6th army corps; participated in all great battles of Army of Potomac; bvtd. to rank of maj. gen.; recieved from Congress medal of honor for distinguished bravery at Battle of White Oak Swamp; resigned from army, 1866. Corporation atty. New York, 1866-88; U.S. minister to Paraguay, 1869. Receiver of taxes for city of New York, 1873-85; U.S. marshal, 1855-89; mem. of assembly, 1890; State senator, 1891-95. Democrat. Mgr. Nat. Home for Disabled Vol. Soldiers, elected by Congress, 1880, 1886, 1892, 1898, sec. bd. of mgrs., 1880-1898; now pres. same. Home: New York, N.Y. Died 1906.

MCMANES, KENMORE MATHEW, naval officer; born Galion, O., May 22, 1900; s. Albert Flynn and Emma (Olson) McM.; B.S., U.S. Naval Acad., 1922; J.D., George Washington U., 1937; m. Virginia Reed, Oct. 15, 1930; children—Kenmore Reed, Albert Spencer. Commd. ensign, U.S. Navy, 1922, advanced through grades to rear adm., 1950; duty in battleships, submarines, light cruisers, 1922-34; command USS Monoghan, 1939-40; asst. naval attache Am. Embassy, London, 1941-43; comdr. Destroyer Squadron 24, Pacific Fleet, 1943-45, U.S. Naval Group, France, 1945; duty Office Judge Advocate Gen., Navy Dept., 1946; comdr. USS Houston, 1947; with Gen. Planning Group, Office Chief Naval Operations, Navy Dept., 1948-50; comdr. Destroyer Flotilla One, Pacific Fleet, 1950-51; comdr. fleet activities Japan-Korea, 1951-52; asst. chief of naval operations, Naval Reserve, 1953-58; deputy chief of naval operations, 1958-59; comdt. 6th Naval Dist., Charleston (S.C.) Naval Base, 1959-62; ret., 1962; exec. dir. Easter Seal Med. Center, Rockville, Md., 1962-71. Decorated Navy Cross, Legion of Merit (combat), Order Brit. Empire (hon. comdr.), 1943. Episcopalian. Mason. Clubs: Army and Navy (Wash.); Kenwood (Bethesda, Md.). Home: Bethesda MD Died Jan. 20, 1973; buried Annapolis MD

MCMANUS, GEORGE HENRY, army officer (ret.); b. Hudson, Ia., Dec. 23, 1867; s. Thomas Pierson and Sarah (Rupp) McM.; B. Didactics, Ia. State Teachers Coll., 1887; B.S., U.S. Mil. Acad., 1893; m. Emilie Gertrude Kessler, Jan. 7, 1897; children—Sarah Catharine (Mrs. H.W. McCurdy), George Henry Jr., Thomas Kessler, Mary Alice. Commd. 2d lt., U.S. Army, June 12, 1893, and advanced through grades to brig. gen., Oct. 1, 1918; assigned to Coast Arty., 1893, and served on Atlantic and Pacific coasts, in Alaska, China, Philippines and Canal Zone; served as troop movement officer. Port of Embarkation, Hoboken, N.J., Nov. 1917; ret. Dec. 31, 1931. Awarded D.S.M., Navy Cross. Club: Army, Navy and Marine Corps Country (Washington). Home: 7 Newport Rd., Cambridge 40 MA

MCMILLAN, JAMES WINNING mem. bd. of review U.S. Pension Office; b. Clark Co., Ky., 1825; s. Robert McMillan, a son of Col. James McMillan, staff of Gen. George Washington; ed. in country schools of Ky. and Ill.; family lived neighbors with the Lincoln family for many yrs.; m. Minerva Foote, 1860. Commissioned col. by Pres. Lincoln, 1861; served through war; bvtd. maj. gen., March, 1864; comd. 1st and 2d brigade, 19th army corps; served with butler in Gulf campaign; captured blockade runner "Fox," one of the richest prizes captured during the Civil war; wounded 5 times; is also a veteran of the Mexican war. Died 1903.

MCMILLAN, WILLIAM LINN planter; b. Hillsboro, O., Oct. 18, 1829; ed. there; grad. Starling Med. Coll., 1852; practiced medicine in Ohio until July 1862; m. Mrs. Elizabeth I. King, d. William Neil, Columbus, O., April 18, 1861. Surgeon Russian army in Crimean war; surgeon 1st Ohio vols., 1861; surgeon gen. MOved to La., 1866, and engaged in planting cotton. Mem. Constl. Conv., 1868; State senator, 1870-72; chosen, 1872 and 1873, U.S. senator from La. by the McEnery legislature, but was not admitted to a seat; postmaster New Orleans under Hayes; surveyor of port under Harrison. Republican. Home: New Orleans, La. Died 1902.

MCMILLEN, FRED EWING naval officer; b. Springfield, Wis., Apr. 11, 1882; s. Frederick Alonzo and Mary (Ewing) McM.; ed. Whitewater (Wis.) State Teachers Coll.; B.S., U.S. Naval Academy, 1904; m. Ruth Burns, Dec. 4, 1907; children-Mary Thomas (Mrs. Robt. J. Schneider), Jean (Mrs. Hugh R. Jones), Alan Bourne. Instr., U.S. Naval Acad., 1904-07; commd. ensign (SC) Navy, 1907, advancing through the grades to rear adm., 1942. Home: 111 Paris Rd., New Hartford, N.Y. Died Sept. 17, 1959; buried Middleville, N.Y.

MCMORRIS, CHARLES H(ORATIO) naval officer; b. Wetumpka, Ala., Aug. 31, 1890; s. Spencer James and Annie Amanda (Robinson) McM.; B.S., U.S. Naval Acad., 1912; grad. Naval War Coll., 1938; married, Dec.

27, 1916; 1 son, David Spencer. Entered USN, 1908, advanced through grades to vice adm., 1943; head war plans div., staff Comdr. in Chief, Pacific Area, 1941-42; comd. U.S.S. San Francisco during battle Lunga Point, 1942. Task Force in Aleutians during battle of Kormandorskis, 1943; chief of staff Pacific Fleet and Pacific Ocean Areas, 1943-45. Fourth Fleet, 1946. Chmn. Gen. Bd., 1947-48; comdt. 14th Naval Dist. and Hawaiian Sea Frontier, 1948. Decorated Navy Cross. D.S.M. (twice), Legion of Merit, Presdl. Unit Citation, Mexican Border, World War I, Second Nicaraguan, Pearl Harbor, Victory and Asiatic-Pacific ribbons. Home: Honolulu, Hawaii. Office: 14 Naval Dist., Pearl Harbor, Hawaii. Died Feb. 11, 1954; buried Arlington Nat. Cemetery.

MCMORROW, FRANCIS JOSEPH army officer; b. N.Y.C., Aug. 27, 1910; s. Patrick Francis and Sarah Ann (McMorrow) McM.; B.S., U.S. Mil. Acad., 1933; M.S. in Mech. Engring., Mass. Inst. Tech., 1938; grad. Ordnance Sch., 1939, Nat. War Coll., 1955; m. Catherine Fox, Aug. 3, 1933; children-Margaret Mary (Mrs. Richard C. Anglin), Thomas Francis, Mary Fox (Mrs. Paul G. Rund). Commd. 2d lt. U.S. Army, 1933, advanced through grades to maj. gen., 1961; various assignments as anti-aircraft comdr., U.S. and Philippines, 1933-37; me. Material Command, Wright Patterson AFB, O., 1939-44; ordnance officer 7th Air Force, 1944-46; mem. State Dept. Fgn. Liquidation Commn., 1945-46; chief research and devel., charge all mfg. operations Springfield (Mass.) Armory, 1946-51; exec. officer to chief indsl. div., later exec. officer, Office Chief Ordnance, 1951-54; assigned G-4 Hdqrs., U.S. Army Europe, 1955-56; comdg. officer Ordnance Tng. Command, Aberdeen (Md.) Proving Ground, 1956-57; asst. chief ordnance, chief indsl. div. Office Chief Ordnance, 1957-59; dir. procurement Office Dep. Chief Staff Logistics, 1959-61; vice comdg. gen. Army Missile Command, 1961-62, comdg. gen., 1962-. Decorated Legion of Merit, Bronze Star. Mem. Assn. U.S. Army, Armed Forces Communications and Electronics Assn. Club: Army-Navy (Arlington, Va.). Home: 150 Oxford St., Hartford, Conn. Office: Hdqrs. U.S. Army Missile Command, Redstone Arsenal, Ala. 35809. Died Aug. 24, 1963.

MCMULLEN, CLEMENTS ret. army ofcr., b. Largo, Fla., Feb. 5, 1892; s. William and Rose (Ramage) McM.; ed. Washington and Lee U., 1907-11; m. Adelaide Lewis; children-Edward L., Frank M., William C., Thomas H. Civil Engr., 1911-17; entered USAAF, 1917, commd. 2d lt., 1918, promoted through grades to maj. gen., 1942, record flight to Buenos Aires from N.Y. in 5 days, Feb. 1930; chief Air Force Engring. Development Sect., 1931-33; operations officer, Gen. Hdqrs., 1936-37; comdg. officer 3d Air Force Area Service Command, Atlanta, 1942; assigned to Hdqrs. AS Command. Washington, chief mantenance div., 1942; comd. Far East AS Command, 1944-45; chief staff Pacific Air Command, 1946; dep. comdr. strat. air command; commd. San Antonio Air Materiel Area, 1949-54; ret.; chmn. indsl. com. San Antonio C. of C., 1955—. Vice pres. Community Chest; dir. United Fund, 1954-58; nat. comdr. Order of Daedalians, 1952-56. Rated command pilot, combat and tech. observer. Decorated Air Medal, D.S.M. with two oak-leaf clusters. Fellow Inst. Aero. Scis.; mem. Air Force Assn. (v.p. S.W. Region, 1955-57). Address: San Antonio. Died Jan. 1959.

MCNAGNY, PHIL MCCLELLAN, lawyer; b. Columbia City, Ind., Feb. 27, 1886; s. William Forgy and Effie Jane (Wunderlich) McN.; student Culver Mil. Acad., 1901-04; A.B., U. Va. (scholarship), 1907; m. Lucy Cole, Apr. 7, 1920; children—William Forgy, Phil McClellan, Bayard Cole, Lucy McIntosh. Admitted to Ind. bar, 1910; instr. English, French and Latin, Culver Mil. Acad., 2 yrs.; practicing lawyer, Whitley Co., 1910-24, Ft. Wayne, from 1924; mem. Barrett, Barrett & McNagny, specializing in trial law. Mem. Ind. State Legislature, 1917. Served as maj., 46th Inf., U.S. Army, 1917-19. Fellow Am. Coll. Trial Lawyers; mem. American Judicature Soc., Bar Assn. of the Seventh Federal Circuit, Am., Ind. State and Allen Co. bar assns., Am. Legion, Nat. Assn. R.R. Trial Counsel. Episcopalian. Mason. Home: Ft Wayne IN Died Aug. 3, 1969; buried Green Lawn Meml. Cemetery, Fort Wayne IN

MCNAIR, FREDERICK VALLETTE rear admiral U.S.N.; b. Pa., Jan. 13, 1839; entered navy, acting midshipman. Sept. 21, 1853; grad. midshipman U.S. Naval Acad., June 10, 1857; passed midshipman, June 25, 1860; master, Oct. 24, 1860; lt., Apr. 18, 1861; lt. comdr., Apr. 20, 1864; commander, Jan. 29, 1872; capt., Oct. 30, 1883; commodore, May 10, 1895; reear admiral 1898. During Civil war participated in much active war service, including engagements and passage of Forts Jackson and St. Philip. Chalmette batteries and capture of New Orleans, and in the opening up of the Mississippi River and passage of the Vicksburg batteries, etc., engagements and surrender of Fort Fisher. After war served on many stations and assignments; commanded U.S. naval force on Asiatic Station, Dec. 1895, to Jan. 1898. From July 1898, supt. U.S. Naval Academy. HOme: Annapolis, Md. Died 1900.

MCNAIR, LESLEY JAMES army officer; b. Verndale, Minn., May 25, 1883; s. ames and Clara (Manz) McN.; B.S., United States Military Academy, 1904; LL.D., Purdue University, 1941; m. Clare Huster, June 15, 1905; 1 son, Douglas Crevier (died in Guam, Aug. 1944). Commd. 2d lt., June 15, 1904, advanced through grades to maj. gen., 1940, lt. gen., June 1941; apptd. comdr. Ground Forces, U.S. Army, Mar. 1942; wounded in action N. Africa, Apr. 1943; with Funston Expdn. to Vera Cruz, Mexico, 1914. Pershing Expdn. in Northern Mexico, 1916-17; with A.E.F. in France, 1917-19. Awarded D.S.M., 1918; officer Legion of Honro (France). Killed in action on Normandy front July 27, 1944.

MCNAIR, WILLIAM SHARP army officer; b. Tecumseh, Mich., Sept. 18, 1868; s. David and Lucinda M. (Sharp) McN.; grad. U.S. Mil. Acad., 1890. Arty. Sch., 1896, Army War Coll., 1914; m. Louise Bestor Potts. Dec. 26, 1894; children—Mary Louise (Mrs. Edward Arthur Sterling, Jr.). Dorothy. William Douglas, Norma Bestor. Commd. add. 2d lt. arty., U.S.A., June 12, 1890, and advanced through grades to col., July 1, 1916; brig. gen., Dec. 14, 1930. Brig. gen. N.G.N.Y., 1916-17; comdr. F.A. of 1st Div., A.E.F., later 151st Arty. Brig.; participated in Argonne Meuse offensive and advance to Sedan; chief of Arty., 1st Army, 1918-19; comd. 4th Coast Arty. Dist.; retired. Sept. 30, 1932. Awarded D.S.M. (U.S.), silver star citation. Presbyn. Home: San Antonio, Tex. Died Apr. 6, 1936.

MCNARNEY, JOSEHH T., corp. exec.; b. Emporium, Pa., Aug. 28, 1893; s. James Pollard and Helen (Taggert) McN.; B.S., U.S. Mil. Acad., 1915; grad. Air Corps Tactical School, 1921, Command and Gen. Staff School (honor grad.), 1926, Army War Coll., 1930; m. Helen Wahrenberger, June 30, 1917; 1 dau., Betty Joe. Commd. 2d lt., U.S. Army, 1915, and advanced through the grades to major general (permanent), 1943, to general permanent), 1952; with aviation section, Signal Corps, 1916; comdg. corps observation groups, overseas, 1917-19; instr. Air Corps Tactical School, 1921-25; mem. gen. staff, War Dept., 1926-29; comdg. March Field, Calif., 1930-31, 7th Bombardment Group, 1932-33; instr. Army War Coll., 1933-35; staff G.H.Q. Air Force, 1935-38; comdg. 7th Bomber Group, 1939; gen. staff, War Dept., 1939-41; apptd. chmn. War Dept. Reorganization Committee, Jan. 1942; apptd. deputy chief of staff, U.S. Army, Mar. 1942; mil. observer, London, 1941; appointed member bd. of experts to investigate Hawaiian surprise attack, December 7, 1941. Appointed Deputy Supreme Commander-in-Chief Mediterranean and commanding gen. U.S. Mediterranean Theater of Operations, Oct. 23, 1944; acting Allied supreme comdr. in Mediterranean area, October 1, 1945; comdr. U.S. Forces in Europe, Nov. 1945. Apptd. Army Air Force rep., Mil. Staff Com., United Nations, 1947, comdg. gen. materiel command, Wright Field, Dayton, Ohio, 1947, retired, 1952; president Conviar division General Dynamics Corp., senior v.p. General Dynamics Corp., 1952-58, past dir. Appointed mem. U.S.-Canadian Permanent Joint Bd. of Defense, August 1940. Named chairman Nat. Def. Management Com., 1949. Member Order of Daedalliens. Clubs: Army and Navy, Army, Navy and Marine Corps Country (Washington). Home: Alhambra CA Died Feb. 1, 1972.

MCNAUGHTON, ANDREW GEORGE LATTA cons. engr.; b. Moosomin, Saskatchewan, Feb. 25, 1887; s. Robert D. and Christina, Mary Ann (Armour) McN.; B.Sc., McGill U., 1910, M.Sc., 1912, LL.D., 1920; D.C.L., Bishop Univ., 1937; LL.D., Queen's Univ., 1941. U. of Birmingham, 1942, University of Ottawa, 1943. U. Saskatchewan, 1944, Michigan State U., 1955. U. Toronto, 1961; Dr. Mil. Science, Royal Mil. College of Can., 1963; graduate Royal Staff Coll., Camberley, Eng., and Imperial Defense Coll., London, Eng.; m. Mabel Clara Stuart Weir, Sept. 17, 1914; children-Christina Pauline Stuart (Mrs. T.K. McDougall), Andrew Robert Leslie, Edward Murray Delzell, Ian George Armour (killed in action 1941), Leslie Anita (Mrs. H. Calvin Sykes, Jr.). Commd. lt., Canadian Army, 1910, advancing to gen., 1944, ret.; mem. com. for reorganizing Canadian Militia, 1919; dep. chief of gen. staff Nat. Defense Hdqrs., Ottawa, 1923-26, chief, 1929-35; general officer commanding First Canadian Div., 1939, comdr. VII Corps. 1940; general officer commanding-in-chief First Canadian Army Overseas, 1942-44; mem. Privy Council of Can., minister of nat. defence, Nov. 1944-Aug. 21, 1944; pres. Canadian Atomic Energy Control Bd. to Jan. 1948; delegate of Canada to UN, 1948-50, rep. of Canada, AEC, UN, 1946-50; chmn. Internat. Joint Commn., 1950-62; chmn. Canadian sect. Can.-U.S. Joint Bd. on Def., 1945-59. Decorated Commander of Order of Bath, Comdr. Order of St. Michael and St. George D.S.O., Companion of Honor; Order of Leopold (Belgium), 1946; also numerous medals and awards assns. Mem. Anglican Ch. Clubs: Rideau (Ottawa); University, Royal St. Lawrence Yacht (Montreal). Joint inventor cathode ray direction finder, 1926. Home: Fernbank, Rockcliffe Pk., Ottawa, Can. Died July 11, 1966.

MCNAUGHTON, JOHN THEODORE govt. ofcl., lawyer, columnist; b. Bicknell, Ind., Nov. 21, 1921; s. Foye Fisk and Cecille Gertrude (McMillan) McN.; A.B., DePauw U. 1942, LL.D., 1963; LL.B., Harvard, 1948; B.Litt. (Rhodes scholar), Oxford U., 1951; m. Sarah Elizabeth Fulkman, Dec. 15, 1945 (dec. July 1967); children-Alexander, Theodore (dec. July 1967). Admitted to Ill. bar, 1948, Mass. bar, 1956; atty. office Spl. Rep., ECA, Paris, 1949-51; columnist Pekin, (Ill.) Daily Times, 1949-62, editor, 1951-53; legal counsel McNaughton Newspapers, 1951-62; asst. prof. law Harvard, 1953-56, prof., 1956-62; dep. asst. sec. def. internat. security affairs, 1961-62, gen. counsel Dept. Def., 1962-64, asst. sec. def. internat. security affairs, 1964-; sec. of navy designate, 1967; asst. dist. atty. for Middlesex County, Mass., 1959-61. Candidate for Congress from Ill., 1952. Bd. dirs. Avon Home. Served as lt. USNR, 1942-46. Mem. Am. Bar Assn., Inst. Strategic Studies, Council on Fgn. Relations, Phi Kappa Psi, Phi Beta Kappa. Author: (with W. Barton Leach) Handbook of Massachusetts Evidence, 1956; 2 Wigmore, Evidence, rev. 1961; several books exptl. law-teaching materials. Home: 23 Berkeley St., Cambridge 38, Mass.; also 5031 Lowell St. N.W., Washington. Office: Pentagon, Washington. Died July 19, 1967; buried Arlington Nat. Cemetery.

MCNEELY, ROBERT WHITEHEAD, naval officer; b. Salisbury, N.C., Aug. 11, 1873; s. William Gaither and Mildred Ann (Hunt) M.; grad. U.S. Naval Acad., 1894; m. Marie Calhoun Butler, of Edgefield, S.C., Feb. 15, 1900. Promoted through various grades to capt.; served at sea 14 yrs., on shore 12 yrs. Has specialized in naval ordnance; introduced improved method of obtaining velocity at high angles of gun fire; improved methods of placing rotating bands on large caliber projectiles; improvements in naval primers. Episcopalian. Clubs: Army and Navy (Washington), Chevy Chase (Md.). Address: Navy Dept., Washington DC

MCNEIL, EDWIN COLYER army officer; b. Alexandria, Minn., Nov. 13, 1882; s. Robert John and Alice Elizabeth (Hill) NcN.; student U. Minn., 1900-01; B.S., U.S. Mil. Acad., 1907; LL.B., Columbia U., 1916; grad. Gen. Staff Sch., Langras, France, 1918, Army War Coll., 1923; m. Mary Kingsbury MacKay, Oct. 16, 1915; 1 dau., Mary Watts (Mrs. W.D. Sloan, Jr.). Commd. 2d lt., U.S. Army, 1907, advanced through grades to brig. gen., 1942; instr. in law, U.S. Mil. Acad., 1910-13; dist. judge adv., El Paso, Tex., and judge adv. 90th Div., Camp Travis, Tex., 1916-18; asst. judge adv. gen.. G.H.Q., AEF, Chaumont and Paris, France, 1917-19, Washington, 1919-20; in Judge Adv. Gen.'s Office, 1920-22, chmn. bd. rev., 1929-33, 36-42, asst. to judge adv. gen., 1936-42; prof. law, U.S. Mil. Acad., 1923-29, with temp. rank of lt. col.; judge adv. 1st Div., Governor's Island, N.Y., 1933-36; asst. judge adv. gen. in charge of br. office, European Theater, 1943-46; later liaison officer, War Dept. Adv. Com. on Mil. Justice; spl. asst. to Sec. of Army, 1950-. Decorated D.S.M., Legion of Honor (Frances); Officer d'Academic with Silver Palms. Mem. Am. Legion, Phi Delta Theta. Clubs: Chevy Chase Country, Army and Navy (Washington). Home: 2728 34th St. N.W., Washington. Died Oct. 1, 1965; buried West Point, N.Y.

MCNEILL, DANIEL naval officer, privateer; b. Charlestown, Mass., Apr. 5, 1748; s. William and Catherine (Morrison) McN.; m. Mary Cuthbertson, Feb. 10, 1770; m. 2d, Abigail Harvey, circa 1771; 10 children including Daniel. Served as commdr. privateers during Am. Revolution, comdr. ship Hancock, 1776, also ships America, Eagle, Ulysses, Wasp and General Mifflin; commd. capt. U.S. Navy, 1798; commanded ship Portsmouth; commanded frigate Boston, 1801; served in undeclared naval war against France, also against Barbary States. Died 1833.

MCNEW, JOHN THOMAS LAMAR civil engr., educator; b. Belcherville, Tex., Jan. 20, 1895; s. Edgar Ogletree and Sarah Elizabeth (Taylor) McN.; B.S., A. and M. Coll of Tex., 1920, M.S., 1926; C.E., Ia State Coll., 1925; m. Edna Ethel Murphy, May 27, 1920; children-Edna Elizabeth (Mrs. Don Dale Little), John Thomas Lamar. Instr., asst. prof., asso. prof. civil engring. A. & M. Coll. of Tex., 1920-25; engaged in municipal and highway engring. with various cities and counties, 1920-28; prof. highway engring., A. & M. Coll. of Tex., 1925-40, head dept. civil engring., 1940-43, vice pres. for engring. since 1944, dir. engring. extension service since 1945. Served in U.S. Army, France and Germany, as 2d lt. Corps of Engrs., 1918-19; lt. col. Corps of Engrs. as airport engr. China-Burma-India Theatre, World War II; lt. col. engrs., O.R.C. U.S. Army, Vice chmn. A. & M. Coll. of Texas. Development Fund Bd. Mem. Am. Soc. C.E. (sec.-treas. Tex. sect. 1928-37, pres. 1938, ant. dir. dist. 15 (La., Tex., Mex. and N.M.), 1942-45, vice pres. zone 4, 1946-48, chmn. com on engring, edn., 1946, Am. Soc. Engring. Edn., Am. Soc. M.E., Texas Soc. of Professional Engrs. (past dir.). Democrat. Baptist. Club: Kiwanis, Contbr. miscellaneous professional papers and discussions to pubs. of Am. Soc. C.E., Home: 100 Hereford St., College Station, Tex. Died Dec. 21, 1946.

MCNULTA, JOHN lawyer; b. New York, Nov. 9, 1837; went West, 1852; settled in Attica, Ind.; traveling salesman, 1856, partner, 1858. Dick & Co., wholesale tobacco dealers; settled in Bloomington, Ill., March 1859; capt. Co. A, 1st Ill. cav., May 3, 1861; lt. col. 94th Ill. Inf., Aug. 20, 1862; took command of regt. a few days after it was mustered in; promoted col. and bvtd.

brig. gen. for gallant and meritorious services in battle; mustered out, Aug. 9, 1865; m. Laura Pelton, Jan. 15, 1862. Admitted to Ill. bar, 1866, to Supreme Court U.S., 1873; elected State senator, 1868; member Congress, 1873-75; renominated but defeated for succeeding Congress; master in chancery, 1881-85. Receiver of what is now the Toledo, St. Louis & Kansas City Ry., June 1885; receiver Wabash Ry., April 1887, of the Whisky Trust, Feb. 1895, of the Calumet Electric Street Ry. Co., Jan. 3, 1898, of the Nat. Bank of Illinois, Jan. 4, 1898; moved to Chicago, Jan. 1895. Died 1900.

MCNUTT, PAUL VORIES lawyer, diplomat; born Franklin, Indiana, July 19, 1891; son of John Crittenden and Ruth (Neely) McN.; A.B.- Ind. U., 1913; LL.B., Harvard, 1916; LL.D., U. of Notre Dame and Ind. Univ., 1933, Bethany Coll., 1936; Univ. of the Philippines, 1939; University of Maryland, American University, 1941, D. of Humanity, Florida Southern Coll., 1939; D.C.L., Boston U., 1942; m. Kathleen Timolat, Apr. 20, 1918; 1 dau., Louise. Admitted to Ind. bar, 1914, and began practice as mem. McNutt & McNutt, Martinsville; asst. prof. law, Ind. U., 1917, became prof. 1919, dean Ind. U. Sch. Law, 1925-33; gov. State of Ind., 1933-37; U.S. High commr. to P.I., 1937-39 and 1945-46; A.E. and P. to the Philippines, 1946-47; chmn. bd. Philippine-American Life Ins. Co. since 1948; gen. counsel dir. U.S. Life Ins. Co., Am. Internat. Underwriters Corp., Am. Internat. Marine Agy. Fed. secur. adminstr., 1939-45; partner McNutt & Nash, N.Y.C., McNutt, Dudley & Easterwood, Washington; dir. Globe & Rutgers Fire Ins. Co., Am. Home Assurance Co., Am. Life Ins. Co., Am. Internat. Assurance Co. Member exec. com. Govs. Conf., 1933-36 (chmn. 1934-36); mem. nat. advisory bd. Works Progress Adminstrn.; pres. Council of State Govts., 1936-37; dir. Def., Health and Welfare Services 1941-43; chmn. War Manpower Commn., 1942-45; mem. WPB, Econ. Stblzn. Bd. Commd., capt. F.A. Res. 1917; Bd. 1917; major F.A., U.S. Army 1918; lt. col. F.A. Reserve, 1919, col., 1923; instr. O.T.C., Camp Stanley, and comdg. officer 326th F.A., 1924-27; mem. 5th Corps Area Abv. Bd., 1927-34; civilian aide to sec. of War for Ind., 1927-28. Chmn. sub-com. on survey and codification, Ind. Corp. Survey Commn., Chmn. faculty bd. editors Ind. Law Jour., 1926-33; pres. Harvard Legal Aid Bureau, 1915-16; mem. Alumni Council, Ind. U., 1924-30. Mem. Am. Bar Assn., Am. Law Inst., Ind. Bar Assn. (chmn. com. on legal edn. 1927), Assn. Am. Law Schs. (chmn. comml. law sect. 1927), Am. Assn. U. Profs., Reserve Officers Assn. U.S., Am. Peace Soc., Order of Coif, Phi Beta Kappa, Sigma Delta Chi, Beta Theta Pi, Phi Delta Phi, Acacia, Tau Kappa Alpha. Nat. Comdr. Am. Legion, 1928-29, mem. nat. exec. com., 1927-28; comdr. Dept. Ind., 1927; comdr. Burton Woolery Post, 1925-26; dir. Am. Legion Pub. Corp., 1928-31; pres., 1928-29. Decorated Medal for Merit (U.S.); Distinguished Service Star (P.I.), Comdr. Polonia Restituta (Poland); Comdr. Legion d'Honneur (France), Grand Cordon Order of Cambodia (Indo-China); Comdr. Legion of Honor (Philippines). Democrat. Methodist. Mason (32ff), Elk. Clubs: University, Rotary, Kiwanis, Indianapolis Athletic (Indpls.); Army and Navy, Metropolitan, Burning Tree, Chevy Chase (Washington); Wall Street (N.Y.C.). Editor: Indiana General Corp. Act Annotated (with F. E. Schortmeier). Also author articles in law journals. Home: 1155 Fifth Av., N.Y.C. 28. Office: 84 William St., N.Y.C. 38; also Barr Bldg., Washington 6. Died Mar. 24, 1955.

MCPHERREN, CHARLES ELMO, lawyer; b. Pleasant Grove, Miss., June 16, 1875; s. Andrew M. and Fanny E. (Boxley) McP.; student Franklin Coll., Pilot Point, Tex., 1889-93; LL.B., U. of Miss., 1896; m. 2d, Maude A. Moore; children—(by first marriage)—Charles J. (lt. 7th Cavalry, U.S. Army), Margaret Jane, John Martin (sgt. U.S. Army), David A. Admitted to Tex. bar, 1896, practicing at Pilot Point; practiced at Caddo and Durant, Okla., 1897-1924, at Oklahoma City since 1924; mem. firm McPherren & Mauer. Sergt. U.S. Vol. Cav. (Roosevelt-Rough Riders), 1898; now major general, retired, U.S. Army; grad. Army War Coll., Command and Gen. Staff Sch. at Ft. Leavenworth (Kan.); former comdg. gen. 45th Div., U.S. Army. Mem. Okla. State Senate, 1921-25. Mem. Am. Bar Assn., Okla. State Bar Assn., Alpha Sigma Phi. Democrat. Methodist. Clubs: Oklahoma, Army and Navy Club. Home: 1220 W. 20th St. Office: Suite 708-709, Perrine Building, Oklahoma City OK*

MCPHERSON, JAMES BIRDSEYE army officer; b. Green Creek Twp., O., Nov. 14, 1828; s. William and Cynthia (Russell) McP.; grad. U.S. Mil. Acad., 1853, Served as engr. U.S. Army, 1853-58, commd. 1st lt., 1858, capt., 1861, lt. col., later col., camp to Maj. Gen. Halleck; asst. engr. Dept. of Mo.; chief engr. to Gen. Grant, 1862; promoted brig. gen. U.S. Volunteers, 1862; apptd. mil. supt. rys. Dist. of Western Tenn.; commd. maj. gen. U.S. Volunteers, 1862, commanded right wing of Grant's army at Battle of Vicksburg; commanded 2d div. Dept. of Tenn.; received command XVII Army Corps, 1863; commd. brig. gen. U.S. Army, 1863; took command Sherman's Army of Tenn., Huntsville, Ala., 1864. Killed at Atlanta, Ga., July 22, 1864.

MCQUAID, WILLIAM RAVENEL banker; b. Jacksonville, Fla., Jan. 13, 1881; s. Patrick and Kate (Freeland) McQ.; ed. pub. and high schs., Jacksonville, St. Louis; m. Henrietta Murray, July 26, 1923; children-William Ravenel, Charles Murray. Began with Barnett Nat. Bank, Jacksonville, 1897; pres. 1925-52, chmn. bd., 1952-58, chmn. exec. com., dir., 1958-; pres. Barnett Nat. Securities Corp., chmn. bd., dir. St. Augustine (Fla.) Nat. Bank. Capt., Battery A. 8th Div. F.A., U.S. Army, 1918-19; maj., instr. in gunnery, Sch. Fire, Ft. Sill, Okla., World War I. Mem. Fla. Bankers Assn. (pres.), Jacksonville C. of C. (v.p.), Newcomen Soc. Catholic. Clubs: Fla. Yacht, Timuquana Country. Home: 4205 Venetia Rd., Jacksonville 10. Address: Barnett Nat. Bank, Jacksonville, Fla. Died Jan. 31, 1965.

MCQUIGG, JOHN REA lawyer, banker; b. nr. Dalton, O., Dec. 5, 1865; s. Samuel and Jane (McKinney) McQ.; A.B., U. of Wooster (now Wooster Coll.), 1888; student Cornell Law Sch., Ithaca, N.Y., 1888-89; LL.B., Nat. Law Sch., Washington, D.C., 1890; m. Gertrude W. Imgard, Feb. 16, 1892; children—Pauline, Donald. Admitted to Ohio bar, 1890, to U.S. courts, 1893; mem. Riley & McQuigg, 1890—; mayor of East Cleveland 3 terms, 1907-13; pres. and gen. counsel Windermere Savings & Loan Co.; v.p. Am. Realty Co.; dir. Derbyshire Realty Co. Cadet captain at Wooster University; served as 1st lieut. infantry Ohio National Guard, 1890-91; mem. Cleveland Grays, 1892-98; captain 10th Ohio Vol. Inf., Spanish-Am. War, 1898-99; capt., maj., lt. col. engrs., Ohio N.G., 1899-1916; served on Mexican border, 1916; col. engrs., Ohio N.G., July 11, 1917; col. engrs., U.S.A., Aug. 5, 1917; assigned as comdr. 112th U.S. Engrs., 37th Div.; mobilized regt. at Camp Sheridan, Ala.; went overseas, June 1918; served with regiment in Baccarat sector and in Argonne; hon. disch., Jan. 17, 1919; recommissioned col. engrs., Apr. 28, 1920; apptd. brig. gen. Ohio N.G. and federally recognized, May 10, 1921; dept. comdr. Am. Legion of Ohio, 1920-21; elected nat. comdr. Am. Legion, 1925; v.p. Am. Legion Endowment Fund Corp. Chmn. bd. trustees First U.P. Ch. Republican. Mason. Home: East Cleveland, Ohio. Died Oct. 26, 1928.

MCRAE, JAMES HENRY army officer; b. Lumber City, Ga., Dec. 24, 1862; s. Daniel F. and Marion (McRae) M.; grad. c.S. Mil. Acad., 1886, Army War Coll., 1911; m. Florence, d. Lt. Col. Geo. W. H. Stouch, U.S.A., Dec. 14, 1887; children—Donald Marion, Dorothy (wife of Lewis C. Beebe, U.S.A.), Mildred (wife of Archibald M. Mixson, U.S.A.); m. 2d, Mrs. Helen Burgar Stouch, Feb. 24, 1926. Commd. 2d lt. 3d Inf., July 1, 1886; promoted through grades to col., July 1, 1916; brig. gen. N.A., Aug. 5, 1917; maj. gen. N.A., Apr. 12, 1918; brig. gen. regular army, Jan. 1, 1920; maj. gen. regular army. May 10, 1922. Participated in Santiago campaign and Battle of El Caney, Spanish-American War; in Philippine Insurrection, various campaigns and engagements; recommended for bvt. of captain, July 1, 1898, "for gallantry in Battle of Santiago"; to be maj., "for distinguished gallantry in action on Mt. Dumandan, Jan. 17, 1900." Mem. Gen. Staff, 1905-08; adj. gen., 1913-17; apptd. comdr. 158th Depot Brigade, Camp Sherman, Chillicothe, O., Sept. 1917; comd. 9th Brig. 5th Div., U.S.A., Dec. 1917, 78th Div., Apr. 18, 1918-June 1919; asst. chief of staff, 1921-22; comdg. 5th Corps Area, 1922-24; comdg. Filipino Div., Mar.-Nov. 1924; comdg. Philippine Dept., 1924-26; comdg. 9th Corps Area, Feb.-Nov. 1926; comdg. 2d Corps Area, 1926-27; retired Dec. 24, 1927. Participated in St. Mihiel and Meuse-Argonne operations. Awarded D.S.M. and Silver Star (oak-leaf cluster), U.S.; Companion Order of Bath (British); Comdr. Legion of Honor, also Croix de Guerre with palm (French). Home: Berkeley, Calif. Died May 1, 1949.

MCRAE, JAMES WILSON elec. engineer; b. Vancouver, B.C., Oct. 25, 1910; s. James Hector and Isabel C. (Jamieson) McR.; B.S., U. B.C., 1933; M-S., Cal. Inst. Tech., 1934, Ph.D., 1937; D.Sc., (hon), Hobart College, 1958; m. Marian Frances Wooldridge, July 20, 1937; children-Mary Caroline, Marion Elizabeth, James Dean, John Robert. Came to U.S., 1936, naturalized, 1940. Research transoceanic radio transmitters, microwave research Bell Telephone Labs., 1937-42, dir. radio projects, TV research, 1947, electronic, TV research, 1947-49, apparatus development, 1949-51, v.p. charge the systems orgn., 1951-53; v.p. Western Electric Co., 1953-58; pres. Sandia Corp., 1953-58; vice pres. Am. Tel. & Tel. Company 1958—. Served as col. signal corps, U.S. Army, 1942-45. Awarded Legion of Merit. Fellow Inst. Radio Engrs. (pres. 1953; dir.); mem. Am. Inst. E.E., Phi Beta Kappa. Home: 10 West Lane, Madison, N.J. Office: 195 Broadway, N.Y.C. Died Feb. 1960.

MCREYNOLDS, JOHN OLVIER M.D.; b. Elkton, Ky., July 23, 1865; s. Richard Bell and Victoria Campbell (Boone) McR.; B.S., Ky. (now Transylvania) U., 1890, M.S., 1900, LL.D., 1904; student Bellevue Hosp. Med. Coll. (New York U.); M.D. (highest honors in class of 116), Coll. of Physicians and Surgeons (now U. of Med.), Baltimore, 1891; Sc.D., Transylvania U., 1934; 1st asst. resident physician Baltimore City Hosp., 1891-92; attended eye and ear clinics, Chicago, New York, London, Paris, Berlin and Vienna, making many trips to Europe; m. Katherine, d. Judge George E. Seay, Nov. 27, 1895. Prof. mathematics and natural science, Burritt Coll., Tenn., 1886; teacher mathematics and astronomy, Dallas High Sch., 1887-88; began practice at Dallas, 1892; pres. McReynolds Clinic (mem. board govs.); holds certificate of American Board of Ophthalmic Examinations and Am. Bd. of Oto-Laryngology, Maj. Med. Corps, U.S. Army (A.S. Div.) and surgeon 18th Corps Area; colonel M.R.C. Decorated Comdr. Order of Carlos Finlay, Cuba, 1934; also decorated by the government of Venezuela. Past pres. 45h Pan-American Medical Congress and pres. of Pan-Am. Med. Assn.; fellow Am. Coll. Surg. (bd. of govs.; representative to 3d Pan-Am. Med. Congress, Mexico City, 1931), Am. Acad. Ophthalmology and Oto-Laryngology (1st v.p.; chmn. sect. on ophthalmology; life mem.), Am. Laryngol., Rhinol. and Otol. Soc. (v.p.; chmn. western sect.), A.M.A. (v.p.; chmn. sect. ophthalmology); mem. Tex. State Med. Assn. (pres.), Dallas County Med. Soc. (pres.), Med. Vets of World War (pres.), Air Service Med. Assn. of U.S. (pres.), Flight Surgeons Assn. of U.S. (pres.), Assn. Mil. Surgeons of U.S., Zeta Chapter Phi Chi of U. of Tex. (hon.), Oxford Ophthal. Congress; hon. mem. Ophthal. Soc. of Mexico, Nationa. Acadmey of Medicine of Mexico. Episcoplaian. Clubs: Dallas Country; Authors' (London). Author of papers and monographs on med. subjects. Home: Dallas Country Club. Office: Texas Bank Bldg., Dallas, Tex. Died July 7, 1942.

MCSWAIN, JOHN JACKSON congressman; b. Cross Hill, S.C., May 1, 1875; s. Eldredge T. (M.D.) and Janie (McGowan) M.; A.B., and L.L., summa cum laude, S.C. Coll., 1897; LL.D., S.C. Mil. Coll., Charleston, 1935; LL.D., John Randolph Neal Coll. of Law, Knoxville, Tenn., 1936; m. Sarah C. McCullough, Apr. 26, 1905. Admitted to S.C. bar, 1899, and began practice at Greenville, 1901. Referee in bankruptcy, 1912-17; trustee city schs. many yrs.; mem. 67th to 74th Congresses (1921-37), 4th S.C. Dist. Enlisted 1st O.T.C., May 1917; commd. capt. Co. A, 154th Inf.; sailed for France, 1954 Inf., Aug. 4, 1918; overseas service about 6 mos.; hon. disch., Mar. 6, 1919. Democrat. Methodist. Mason, Odd Fellow, K. of P., Elk. Home: Greenville, S.C. Died Aug. 6, 1936.

MCSWEENEY, JOHN, congressman, university trustee; b. Wooster, O., Dec. 19,21890; s. John and Ada Jane (Mullins) McS.; Ph.B., Wooster Coll., 1912, LL.D., 1931; student law Inns of Court, London, Eng., 1918-19, also Trinity Coll., Dublin; m. Abby Schaefer, July 9, 1924. Mem. engring. corps Pa. R.R., 1912-13; tchr. Wooster High Sch., 1913-17, 19-22; admitted to Ohio bar, 1925; practice in Wooster, 1925-31; dir. pub. welfare Ohio, 1931-35; fgn. rep. Am. Relief for Italy, 1946-47. Commr. Am. Legion council Boy Scouts Am. Mem. Wooster Sch. Bd. Mem. 68-70th Congresses, also 81st Congress, 16th Ohio Dist., mem. 75th Congress, Ohio-at-large; candidate U.S. Senate from Ohio, 1940, candidate for gov., 1942; mem. Wooster City Council. Member board trustees Kent (Ohio) State University. Served to capt., inf., U.S. Army, 1917-19, to lt. col. AUS, 1943-47. Decorated Purple Heart with cluster, Legion of Merit, Croix de Guerre (France); commandatore Crown Italy, Italian Red Cross medal; commandatore Order Malta, Order St. George, Order St. Hubert, medal Pope Pius XII. Mem. Am. Legion Disabled Am. Vets. Am. Forestry Assn. (past (v.p.), Ohio Soc. Washington (pres. 1950), Phi Gamma Delta. Democrat. Episcopalian. Clubs: Lamplighters (hon.) (Wooster); University (Cleve.). Home: Wooster OH Died Dec. 14, 1969.

MCVAY, CHARLES BUTLER, JR. naval officer; b. Edgeworth, Pa., Sept. 19, 1868; s. Charles Butler and Annie Huntington (Jones) McV.; grad. U.S. Naval Acad., 1890. Ensign, July 1, 1892; promoted through grades to rear admiral, Jan. 6, 1923. Served on Amphitrite, Spanish-Am. War, 1898; navigator Hartford, 1905; at U.S. Naval Acad., 1905-07; naviagor Alabama, 1907-08; comd. Yankton, 1908-10; at U.S. Naval Acad., 1910-12; chief of staff, Asiatic Fleet, 1912-14; asst. to ur. of Ordnance, Navy Dept., 1914-16; at Naval War Coll., Newport, R.I., 1917; commanded Saratoga, 1917; apptd. comdr., New Jersey, Aug. 1917, Oklahoma (war zone), 1918; chief of Ordnance, 1920-23; comdr. Yangtze Patrol, 1923-25; mem. Gen. Bd. and budget officer, Navy Dept., 1925-29; became comdr.-in-chief Asiatic Fleet, with rank of admiral, Sept. 9, 1929; then mem. Gen. Board; retired, Oct. 1, 1932; commd. admiral by act of Congress, June 1942. Address: 2131 Bancroft Place N.W., Washington. Died Oct. 28, 1949; buried in Arlington Nat. Cemetery.

MCWHORTER, ERNEST D. naval officer; b. in Miss., Sept. 23, 1884. Entered U.S. Navy, May 3, 1911; promoted through grades to rear adm., Dec. 1940; comdr. Naval Air Force in U.S. Occupation of N. Africa, Nov. 1942. Died Jan. 31, 1950.

MCWHORTER, HENRY CLAY lawyer; b. Marion Co., O., Feb. 20, 1836; s. Fields and Margaret (Kester) M.; enlisted in Union Army, as pvt., Sept. 16, 1861; mustered Sept. 30, as 2d lt.; promoted capt., Mar. 2, 1862; resigned on account of wound, Sept. 17, 1863; in provost marshal's enrollment office, chief clerk, 1863-65; m. Mary Hardmann, Dec. 16, 1857 (died 1878); m. 2d, Eliza F. McWhorter, May 8, 1879 (died 1881); m. 3d, Lucy M. Clark, Jan. 8, 1885 (died 1900); m. 4th, Mrs. Caroline M. Gates, May 18, 1904. Admitted to bar, 1866; mem. W.Va. Ho. of Delegates, 4 terms 1865-68 (chmn. jud. com.) and 1885, 1887 (speaker 1868);

pros. atty., 1869-73; postmaster Charleston, W.Va., 1891-93; judge Supreme Ct. Appeals of W.Va., 1897-1908 (president judge 3 yrs.). Mem. Gen. Conf. M.E. Ch., 1880, 1908. Elector for Hall of Fame, Syracuse U., 1905; pres. bd. trustees W.Va. Wesleyan Coll., June 1897—. Mason. Home: Charleston-Kanawha, W.Va. Died Apr. 15, 1913.

MCWILLIAM, CLARENCE A. surgeon; b. Brooklyn, N.Y., Jan. 29, 1870; s. Daniel Wilkin and Helen (Marquand) McW.; grad. Poly. Inst. Brooklyn, 1888; A.B., Princeton, 1892, A.M., 1895; M.D., Coll. Phys. and Surg. (Columbia), 1895; ummarried. Practiced at N.Y. City; attending surgeon New York Skin and Cancer Hosp.; asso. surgeon Fifth Av. Hosp.; prof. clin. surgery New York Polyclinic Hosp., N.Y. City. Served as lt. M.C., Spanish-Am. War; maj. M.C., with A.E.F., in France 2 yrs. World War. Fellow Am. Coll. Surgeons. Decorated Officer de l'Instruction Publique (France). Republican. Presbyn. Died Jan. 20, 1927.

MEAD, ARTHUR EMETT ednl. adminstr.; b. Corydon, Ia. July 8, 1902; s. George and Cora (Perkins) M.; B.A., U. S.D., 1925, M.A., 1930; LL.D., U. Ryukyus, 1951; student U. Ia., U. Minn., University Chgo.; LL.D., Jamestown College, 1959; married to Gwen Thomas, July 31, 1925; children-Dr. Thomas E., John R. Supt. schs., Mission Hill, Brentford and Flandreau, S.D., 1926-37; dir. extension U. S.D., 1937-41, dir. spl. services, 1952-55; dir. information and edn., Ryukyus, 1948-52; exec. dir. S.D. Bd. Regents, 1955-57; commr. higher edn., N.D., 1958-. Founder (with others) U. Ryukyus, Chmn. N.D. Commn. on Alcoholism. Served as lt. col. USMCR. Mem. Am. Municipal Assn. (dir. 1940-41); S.D. Edn. Assn. (pres. 1940), Nat. Assn. Exec. Officers Statewide Bds. Higher Edn. and Bds. Regents (pres.), Alpha Tau Omega, Phi Delta Phi, Theta Alpha Phi. Mason. Club: Lions (dist. gov.). Home: 1303 3d St. N. Office: State Capitol, Bismarck, N.D. Died Nov. 25, 1963; buried Rosehill Cemetery, Spearfish, S.D.

MEAD, WILLIAM WHITMAN naval officer; b. Burlington Ky., Feb. 8, 1845; s. Sackett and Anna A.M.; grad. U.S. Naval Acad., 1865; m. Julia B. Watts, of Ky. Promoted ensign, Dec. 1, 1866; advanced through grades to rear adm., July 1, 1905. Was lt. in command of a steam launch, in 1st day's fight with Corean forts; when expdn. landed for capture and destruction of the forts comd. light arty. from flagship; comd. U.S.S. Machias during latter part of war with Spain; comd. U.S.S. Brooklyn in spring 1899, U.S.S. Phila., Feb. 20, 1900-Jan. 1902; mem. Bd. of Inspection, Mar.-Aug. 1902; comdt. Naval Training Sta., Newport, R.I., Sept. 1902-July 1904, Navy Yard Portsmouth, N.H., 1904-07; retired by operation of law, Feb. 8, 1907. Home: Wayne, Pa. Died Mar. 13, 1930.

MEADE, GEORGE GORDON army officer; b. Cadiz, Spain, Dec. 31, 1815; s. Richard Warsam and Margaret (Butler) Mf.; grad. U.S. Mil. Acad., 1835; m. Margaretta Sergeant, 1840, 6 children. Commd. 2d lt. 3d Arty., U.S. Army, resigned, 1836; became asst. engr. Ala., Fla. & Ga. R.R.; prin. asst. engr. on survey mouths of Mississippi River, 1839; an asst. to joint commn. to establish boundaries between U.S. and Tex., 1840; apptd. 2d lt. Topog. Engrs., U.S. Army, 1842; served in Mexican War at battles of Palo Alto, Monterey, Vera Cruz, brevetted 1st lt., 1846; 1st lt. Topog. Engrs., 1851, capt., 1856, in charge No. Lake Surveys, 1857-61; commd. brig. gen. U.S. Volunteers, 1861, aided in defense of Washington, (D.C.), served in battles of Mechanicsville, Gaine's Mill and New Market Cross Rd., wounded at Glendale; maj. Topog. Engrs., 1862, served at 2d Battle of Bull Run; comdr. Pa. Reserves at battles of South Mountain, Fredricksburg; maj. gen. volunteers, 1862; in command 5th Corps at Battle of Chancellorsville, May 24, 1863; in command Army of Potomac, 1863; promoted brig. gen. U.S. Army, 1863, repulsed Confederate Army under Gen. Lee at Battle of Gettysburg, 1863; commd. maj. gen., serving under Grant, 1864; in command Dept. of East, 1867, 3d Mil. Dist. of South (Ga., Ala., Fla.), 1868, Mil. Div. of Atlantic, 1869-72. Died Pa., Nov. 6, 1872.

MEADE, JAMES J. ret. Marine corps officer; b. Charlestown, Mass., Mar. !4, 1882; s. P.J. and Catherine (Doran) M.; LL.B., Georgetown U., 1917; student Army War Coll., 1928, Naval War Coll., 1938; m. Helen Parmelee, Aug. 27, 1908. Entered U.S. Marine Corps with rank of 2d lt., 1903, and advanced through grades to brig. gen., 1936; served various times in Nicaragua, P.I., Mexico, Cuba, Haiti, France; ret. from active service, 1939. Awarded various decorations and commendations including Navy Cross, 1927. Mem. Ancient and Honorable Artillery Company of Boston. Clubs: Rotary of Long Beach, Chevy Chase (Md.), Army-Navy of Washington, Pacific Coast. Home: 252 Ximeno Av., Long Beach 3, Cal. Died Dec. 26, 1949.

MEADE, ROBERT LEAMY officer U.S. Marine Corps; b. Washington, Dec. 26, 1841; s. Capt. Richard W. (U.S.N.) and Clara Forsyth (Meigs) M.; ed. Mt. St. Mary's Coll., Emmitsburg, Md., and U.S. Naval Acad.; m. Mary, 2d Admiral H. Paulding, U.S.N., Feb. 6, 1865. Apptd. acting midshipman, U.S.N., Sept. 30, 1856; resigned, Dec. 2, 1858; watch officer U.S. coast survey steamer Bibb, 1858-61; commd. 2d lt. U.S. Marine Corps, 1862; promoted through grades to col., Mar. 3, 1899; brig. gen. and retired, Jan. 29, 1906. Bvt. brig. gen. for battle of Tientsin, China; received W. I. campaign medal (congressional), Comd. co. of marines during draft riots in New York, July, 1863; captured, Aug. 8, 1863, and held prisoner of war for 15 mos.; on cruise in U.S.S. Shenandoah, in India, China, Japan and Korea, 1865-69; fleet marine officer of Admiral Sampson's Fleet during Spanish-Am. War; participated in Chinese expdn., 1900. Home: Lexington, Mass. Died 1910.

MEANS, JAMES HOWARD physician; b. Dorchester, Mass., June 24, 1885; s. James and Helen Goodell (Farnsworth) M.; prep. edn., Noble and Greenough's Sch., Boston; spl. student in biology and chemistry, Mass. Inst. Tech., 1902-03; A.B., Harvard, 1907, M.D., 1911, H.P. Walcott fellow 1913-16; m. Marian Jeffries, Jan. 11, 1915 (died Feb. 1950); 1 son, James; m. 2d Carol Lord Butler, Feb. 17, 1951. Interne, Mass. Gen. Hosp., 1911-13; teaching fellow med. Harvard Med. Sch., 1916-18, instr. in medicine, 1919-21, asst. prof. medicine, 1921-24, Jackson prof. clin. medicine, 1924-51. Jackson prof. clin-medicine emeritus since 1951, asso. in medicine. Mass. Gen. Hosp., 1917-24, chief of med. services, 1924-51; physician Mass. Inst. Tech., 1951-57; cons. social medicine Monifiore Hosp., N.Y.C. Mem. nat. adv. health council U.S. Pub. Health Service, 1952-56; hon. mem. faculty U. Cuyo (Argentina); hon. physician Mass. Gen. Hosp.; hon. perpetual student Med. Coll. St. Bartholomew's Hosp., London. Served with Medical corps, U.S. Army, advancing to major, 1917-19. Recipient Sidney Hillman Award, 1951, Squibb award, Endocrine Soc., 1952; George M. Kober medal Assn. Am. Physicians, 1964. Fellow Royal Soc. Medicine (London) (hon.), Am. Coll. Physicians (pres. 1937-38); fellow Am. Acad. Arts and Sciences, Mass. Med. Soc., A.A.A.S., Med. Soc. of Finland (hon.), Am. Soc. for Clin. Investigation, Assn. Am. Physicians (pres. 1942), Am. Assn. for the Study of Goiter (pres. 1947-48), Alpha Omega Alpha; hon. mem. Argentine Assn. for Endocrinology and Nutrition; corr. mem. Nat. Acad. Medicine of Buenos Aires, Gcrgas Meml. Inst., Tropical and Preventive Med. Clubs: Harvard, Somerset (Boston); also Harvard (New York). Author: Dyspncea, 1924; The Diagnosis and Treatment of Diseases of the Thyroid Gland (with E.P. Richardson, M.D.), 1929; The Thyroid and Its Diseases, 1937, 2d ed. 1948; Doctors, People and Government, 1953; Lectures on Thyroid, 1954; War 4, 1958; The Association of American Physicians; Its First Seventy-Five Years, 1961; James Means and His Problem of Manflight, 1964. Contbr. papers to jours. Home: 60 Mount Vernon St., Boston 8. Died Sept. 8, 1967; buried Boston.

MEANS, RICE WILLIAM b. St. Joseph, Mo., Nov. 16, 1877; s. George W. and Sarah D. (McDonald); M.; student Sacred Heart Coll., Denver, Colo.; LL.B., U. of Mich., 1901; m. C. Frances Dickinson, Apr. 23, 1902. Began practice at Denver, 1901; county judge, Adams County, Colo., 1902-04; mgr. of safety and excise, City and County of Denver, 1923 (resigned); atty. City and County of Denver, 1923-24; mem. U.S. Senate from Colorado, 1924-27. Enlisted in Colo. Nat. Guard, 1895, 2d and 1st lt. Colo. Inf., 1898-99; comd. co. of scouts, Philippine campaign, 1899; recommended for Medal of Honor and promotion by Maj. Gens. Greene and Bell; capt. Colo. Nat. Guard, 1903; commd. lt. col. inf., U.S. Army, June 22, 1917; grad. Field Officers Sch., Langres, France; comd. 4th U.S. Inf. in Meuse-Argonne campaign, later comd. 157th Inf.; hon. disch. May 15, 1919. Awarded D.S.C., 1925, for acts of bravery in the Philippine Campaign prior to and during capture of City of Manila. Mem. Soc. Army of the Philippines (comdr. in chief 1913). Vets. Foreign Wars of U.S. (comdr. in chief 1914-15), United Spanish War Vets. (comdr. in cheif 1926). Republican. Methodist. Home: 2081 Fairfax St., Denver, Colo. Died Jan. 30, 1949.

MEARNS, EDGAR ALEXANDER lt. colonel U.S.A.; b. Highland Falls, N.Y., Sept. 11, 1856; s. Alexander and Nancy R. (Carswell) M.; M.D., Coll. Phys. and Surg. (Columbia), 1881; m. Ella Wittich, 1881. Apptd. 1st lt. asst. surgeon, Dec. 3, 1883; capt. asst. surgeon, Dec. 3, 1888; maj. brigade surgeon vols., June 4, 1898; maj. chief surgeon, Jan. 7, 1899; hon. discharged from vol. service, Mar. 22, 1899; maj. surgeon, Feb. 2, 1901; lt. col. retired, Jan. 1, 1909. In charge of the naturalists of the Smithsonian African Expdn. sent out under the director of Col. Theodore Roosevelt, 1909; field naturalist of Childs-Frick African expdan, 1911-12; asso. in zoölogy, U.S. Nat. Museum, Washington. Patron Am. Mus. Natural History, New York. Author: Mammals of the Mexican Boundary of the United States, 1907. Died Nov. 1, 1916.

MEARNS, HUGHES educator, author; b. Phila., Sept. 28, 1875; s. William Hughes and Lelia Cora (Evans) M.; grad. Sch. of Pedagogy, 1894; A.B., Harvard, 1902; postgrad. U. Pa. Grad. Sch., 1902-08; m. Mabel Fagley, Dec. 22, 1904; 1 dau., Petra Cabot. Instr. English Phila. Sch. Pedagogy, 1902-05, prof., 1905-20; mem. staff Lincoln Sch. of Teachers Coll., Columbia, 1920-25; asso. prof. edn. N.Y. U., 1925-26, prof., also chmn. dept. creative edn., 1926-46, prof. emeritus, 1946-. Psychologist med. dept. U.S. Army, World War I.; maj. O.R.C. Mem. Phi Beta Kappa, Phi Delta Kappa, Authors' League Am., Authors' Guild. Episcopalian. Club: Franklin Inn (Phila.). Author: Richard Richard, 1916; The Vinegar Saint, 1919; I Ride in My Coach, 1923; Creative Youth, 1925; Lions in the Way, 1927; Creative Power, 1929; The Creative Adult, 1940; The Little Man Who Wasn't There, Contbr. verse to nat. mags. Home: Bearsville, Ulster County, N.Y. Died Mar. 3, 1965.

MEARS, FREDERICK engineer; b. Ft. Omaha, Neb., May 25, 1878; s. Frederick and Elizabeth (McFarland) M.; prep. edn. Shattuck Sch., Faribault, Minn.; distinguished grad. U.S. Inf. and Cav. Sch., 1904; U.S. Staff Coll., 1905; m. Jennie, d. late Maj. J. P. Wainwright, U.S.A., Apr. 6, 1907. With G.N. Ry., advancing to resident engr., 1897-99; enlisted U.S.A. as pvt., Oct. 1, 1899; commd. 2d lt., 5th Cav., July 1, 1901; 1st lt., 11th Cav., Sept. 20, 1906; capt., July 1, 1916; col., Jan. 1918; lt. colonel engineer corps, Oct. 18, 1920. Served in Philippine Islands until July 1903; duty, Isthmain Canal Commn., 1906-14; surveyed location for new high level ry., 1906-07; res. engr. and engr. constrn. New Panama R.R., 1907-09; chief engr., same rd., 1909-14, also gen. supt., 1913-14; mem. Alsakan Engring. Commn., 1914-17; col. 31st Engrs., Jan. 16, 1918; sailed for France, June 6, 1918; asst. gen. mgr. (Aug. and Sept.) and gen. mgr. Sept. 1918-May 1919, R.R. Dept., S.O.S., France; returned to U.S., May 21, 1919; chmn. and chief engr. Alaskan Engring. Commn., 1919-23; retired as col., July 19, 1923; chief cengr. St. Paul Union Depot Co., St. Paul, Minn., 1923-25; asst. chief engr., G.N. Ry., May 1925—. Awarded D.S.M. (U.S.); Officer Legion of Honor (French), 1919. Episcopalian. Home: Seattle, Wash. Died Jan. 11, 1939.

MEARS, J(AMES) EWING surgeon; b. Indianapolis, Oct. 17, 1838; s. Geoge Washington (M.D.) and Caroline Sidney (Ewing) M.; A.B., B.S., Trinity Coll., Conn., 1858, A.M., 1861 (LL.D., 1908); M.D., Jefferson Med. Coll., Phila., 1865; unmarried. Was lecturer on practical surgery, later clin. lecturer gynecology, Jefferson Med. Coll.; prof. anatomy and surgery, Pa. Coll. Dental Surgery, 1870-98; formerly surgeon various hosps. and surgeon-in-chief Pa. N.G. Served as capt. and q.-m. Ind. vols., med. cadet and acting exec. officer, mil. hosp., during Civil War. Trustee Hort. Hall, Phila. Episcopalian. Fellow Am. Surg. Assn. (editor Trans., 1883-92, pres., 1893). Phila. Acad. Surgery (pres., 1898, Coll. Physicians Phila. (editor Trans., 1872-88), A.A.A.S.; hon. mem. Lehigh Co. (Pa.) Med. Soc., Ga. Med. Soc., Ga. Med. Assn., Mass. Hort. Soc.; life mem. Pa. Hort. Soc., Forestry Assn. Pa., City Parks Assn., Phila., etc. One of editors Universal Medical Sciences. Author: Practical Surgery; contbr. Internat. Text-Book of Surgery; also many articles on surg. and other subjects. Address: Land Title Bldg., Philadelphia.

MEHORNAY, ROBERT LEE merchant; b. Kansas City, Mo., Feb. 25, 1888; s. Charles William and Nancy Eleanor (Crooks) M.; grad. high sch., Kansas City, 1907; student engring. U. of Mich., 1907-09; m. Mabelle Hanawalt, Oct. 17, 1911; children-Robert Lee, John William, Elizabeth. With Mehornay Furniture Co., retail home furnishers, since 1909, successively sec., treas., pres., chmn. board; deputy chmn. bd. Fed. Res. Bank, Kansas City, Mo.; formerly dir. First Nat. Bank Kansas City, Mo.; bureau chief, Office of Production Management, Washington, 1941; director Kansas City Power and Light Company. Member exec. com. bus. adv. council for Dept. of Commerce, Washington, D.C.; 1st chmn. Board of Govs. Midwest Research Institute, Kansas City, Mo. Served as captain A.S., U.S. Army, 1917-19, World War. Mem. advisory council for expenditure of city bond money, Kansas City, 1925; gen. chmn. Allied Charities, Kansas City, 1922; v.p. C. of C., 1924; pres. 1944; member Municipal Art Commn., 1926; pres. Kansas City Merchants Assn., 1937; trustee Liberty Memorial Assn. since 1926 (mem. bd. govs. since 1934); trustee U. of Kansas City; mem. Kansas City Sch. Dist., 1930-36, pres. 1935-36; mem. Nat. Retail Code Authority, 1933; director of American Heart Association since 1947. Mem. Nat. Retail Furniture Assn. (pres. 1926), Am. Legion (City central chmn. 1926), 40 and 8. Sigma Alpha Epsilon. Gen Pershing's citation for meritorious cnd conspicuous service, Colomby les Belle, France, Apr. 19, 1919; Order Purple Heart (U.S. Army), 1932; honor award, Jackson County (Mo.) Medical Society. Democrat. Mem. Disciples of Christ Ch. Mason. Clubs: Cooperative (pres. 1915), Mission Hills Country; Furniture Club of America (Chicago). Home: 5049 Wornall Rd., Kansas City 2. Office: 1101 McGee St., K.C. 6, Mo. Died Nov. 19, 1951.

MEIGHEN, ARTHUR lawyer; b. Anderson, Ont., Can., June 16, 1874; student Collegiate Inst., St. Mary's Ont.; B.A. with honors in math., U. Toronto, 1896; m. Isabel Cox; children-Theodore R. O., Maxwell C. G., Lillian M. L. (Mrs. Donald Wright). Tchr. Collegiate Inst., 1897-98; in mfg. bus. and teaching, Winnipeg. until 1900; studied law 3 yrs., began practice, Portage la Prairie, 1903; elected to Ho. of Commons at gen. elections , 1908, reelected, 1911, 13, 17; solicitor gen. of Can., 1913, sec. of state and minister of mines, 1917, minister of interior and supt. gen. of Indian affairs, 1917; mem. Imperial War Cabinet, 1918; prime minister and sec. for external affairs, Can., 1920-21; mem. Imperial Privy Council, 1920; attended Prime Ministers' Conf. in Loncon, 1921; defeated for Commons, 1921; reelected for Grenville, Man., 1922, and for Portage la Prairie, 1925, again defeated, 1926; served as prime minister in emergency, July-Sept., 1926; apptd. minister without portfolio in Bennett cabinet, 1932-35; served as govt. leader in Senate, 1932-35; resigned from Senate, 1942. Choosen leader of Conservative Party (opposition), 1941; resigned, 1942. Author: The Greatest Englishman of History. Home: 57 Castle Frank Cres. Office: 360 Bay St., Toronto, Can. Died Aug. 5, 1960; buried St. Mary's, Ont.

MEIGS, ARTHUR INGERSOLL (MEGS) architect; b. Phila., June 29, 1882; s. Arthur Vincent and Mary Roberts (Browning) M.; grad. William-Penn Charter Sch., Phila., 1899; A.B., Princeton, 1903; m. Harriet Geyelin, Sept. 13, 1935. Began practice Phila., 1906; mem. archtl. firm Mellor & Meigs, 1906-17, Mellor, Meigs & Howe, 1917-28, Mellor & Meigs, 1928-40; ret. from active practice, 1940. Works: Goodhart Hall, Bryn Mawr Coll.; Sci. Lab. Haverford Coll.; Princeton Charter Club; Phi Gamma Delta fraternity houses, Phila., State College, Pa., and Seattle; Gymnasium Bldg., Pa. Inst. for Deaf; aviary, Phila. Zool. Soc.; residences nr. Phila. for Arthur E. Newbold, Jr., F. S. McIlhenry. Robert T. McCracken, Caspar W. Morris, Melville G. Curtis, Morris E. Leeds, Christopher L. Ward, Col. Henry duPont, and Campbell Weir; residence for Radcliffe Cheston at Georgetown, S.C. Firm awarded gold medal by Archl. League N.Y. for residence of Arthur E. Newbold, Jr., 1925, and ann. medal in architecture, by Phila. Chpt. A.I.A., 1922, for residence of Robert T. McCracken, Fellow A.I.A. Served as capt. F.A., comdg. Co. B. Mil. Police, 4th Div., U.S. Army, 1917-19; in engagements at Aisne-Marne, St. Mihiel and Argonne, Episcopalian, Clubs: Philadelphia Club. Whitemarsh Valley Hunt, Historical Society, Author: A Monograph of the Work of Melior, Meigs & Howe, 1923; An American Country House, 1924. Home: Radnor, Pa. Died June 9, 1956.

MEIGS, MONTGOMERY CUNNINGHAM army officer, engr.; b. Augusta, Ga., May 3, 1816; s. Dr. Charles Delucena and Mary (Montgomery) M.; grad. U.S. Mil. Acad., 1836; m. Louisa Rodgers, 1841, 7 children. Engaged in fed. engring. surveying projects, 1836; commd. capt. U.S. Army, 1853, col. 11th Inf., 1861, planner, organizer expdn. which saved Ft. Pickens and won harbor Pensacola for U.S., 1861; brig. gen., 1861; q.m. Army throughout Civil War; served at battles of Bull Run and Chattanooga; brevetted maj. gen., 1864; supr. plans for new War Dept. Bldg., 1866-67, Nat. Mus., 1876, Washington Aqueduct extension, 1876, Hall of Records, 1878; regent Smithsonian Instn.; mem. Am. Philos. Soc.; an early mem. Nat. Acad. Scis. Died Washington, D.C., Jan. 2, 1892; buried Arlington (Va.) Nat. Cemetery.

MEIKLE, GEORGE STANLEY research dir.; b. Milton Mills, N.H., May 30, 1886; s. George Douglas and Emma Etta (Fox) M.; B. Engring. and Master Civil Engring., Union Coll., Schenectady, N.Y., 1913; m. Louise Juliet Zimmerman (M.D.), Sept. 6, 1910. Chief safety engr., asst. dist. mech. engr. U.S. Steel Corp., 1909-11; scientific research Gen. Electric Co. Labs., Schenectady, 1912-17; pres. G. S. Meikle Co., cons. scientists and engrs., N.Y. City, 1919-24; research and engring. exec., 1924-28; mem. administrative staff, 1928 - , dir. research relations with industry, 1928-, Purdue U.; mem. bd. dirs. and research dir. (officer) Purdue Research Foundation, 1930-; v.p. Better Homes in America, Inc.; v.p. Purdue Aeronautics Corp., Research, education and defense; W.O.C., United States Department of Commerce Coordination and Administration of Univi. and Federal War Research, World War II. Research consultant U.S. Navy, tech. dir. and officer in charge gas mask for U.S. Army (as civilian), World War I; capt. Chem. Warfare Service O.R.C. Fellow Am. Assn. for Advancement of Science, Internat. Anesthesia Research Soc.; mem. Tippecanoe County Med. Assn. (hon.), Sigma Xi, Tau Beta Pi. Scacbbard and Blade. Republican. Mason (Scottish Rite). Rotarian. Research in physical chemistry, discovering hot cathode gas filled rectifers, "Tungar," and allied devices; research in heat transfer resulting in new formula and discovery of methods and devices for heating houses with liquid and gaseous fuels. Home: 606 Terry Lane, W. Lafayette, Ind. Died Mar. 30, 1960.

MEIN, JOHN GORDON, fgn. service officer; b. Cadiz, Ky., Sept. 10, 1913; s. John and Elizabeth M. (Fehsenfeld) M.; A.B., Georgetown Coll., 1936; LL.B., George Washington U., 1939; m. Elizabeth Ann Clay, June 15, 1946; children—David Gordon, Marilyn Elizabeth, Eric Alan. With Dept. Agr., 1936-41, Dept. of State, 1941-42, and 1944-47; assigned Am. Embassy, Rio de Janeiro, 1942-44; fgn. service officer, consul career, sec. Diplomatic Service since 1947, 1st as 2d sec. Am. Embassy, Rome, Italy, later 1st sec. Am. Embassy, Oslo, Norway; student Nat. War Coll., 1953-54; 1st sec. Am. embassy, Djakarta, Indonesia, 1954, counselor, 1955-56; dep. dir., office of Southwest Pacific Affairs, Dept. of State, Washington, 1956-57, dir., 1957-60; minister counselor Am. embassy, Manila, 1960-63, Am. embassy, Rio, 1963-65; ambassador to Guatemala, 1965-68. Mem. Bar Assn. D.C. Baptist. Office: Guatemala City Guatemala First Am. ambassador to be assassinated. Died Aug. 28, 1968; buried Washington DC

MEISSNER, EDWIN BENJAMIN mfg. exec.; b. Milw., Dec. 5, 1884; s. Abraham and Fredericka (Katz) M.; student pub. schs.; m. Edna Rice, June 26, 1911. Messenger, Milw. Electric Ry. & Light Co., 1899, accounting dept., 1900-05, chief clk. to pres., 1905-11, v.p., 1915-22, pres., gen. mgr., 1931922—; pres., treas. St. Louis Mining and Milling Corp., Joplin, 1941—; dir. Nat. Stock Yards, Ill., Nat. Bank of National City, St. Louis Malleable Casting Co., Wagner Electric Co., Consol. Retail Stores. Pres. St. Louis Crime Commn. Pres. Central Inst. for Deaf, St. Louis; pres., dir. New Mt. Sinai Cemetery Assn.; hon. pres., dir. Congregation Shaare Emeth, St. Louis; trustee Nat. Security Indsl. Assn. Served as lt. col. Ordnance Corps, U.S. Army, World War I. Mem. Mexico C. of C. in U.S., St. Louis Electric Bd. of Trade, Am. Inst. E.E., Mo. C. of C. (dir.). Mason (Shriner). Clubs: Mo. Athletic Assn., Westwood Country, Engineers (St. Louis). Home: 6244 Forsythe St., St. Louis. Office: 8000 N. Broadway, St. Louis 15. Died Sept. 10, 1956.

MELINE, JAMES FLORANT asst. treasurer U.S.; b. in Ohio, June 3, 1841; s. Florant M. and Ellen M. (Reilly) M.; entered army as pvt. 6th Ohio Vol. Inf., April 19, 1861; served until June 23, 1864, becoming 1st lt.; wounded at Stone's River, Jan. 2, 1863; 3 mos. clerk in Treasury Dept.; returned to army as capt. 2d regt., U.S. Veteran Inf., Hancock's corps; left army March 26, 1866. Bvt. maj. of vols., June 13, 1865. Again clerk Treas. Dept. Advanced to asst. treasurer of U.S., 1893-1907. Died 1908.

MELLINGER, AUBREY HUGO telephone ofcl.; b. Arcanum, O., Sept. 27, 1881; s. James Monroe and Louise (Ritter) M.; M.E. in Electric Engring., Ohio State U., 1905; m. Carolyn Bunting, Sept. 28, 1910; 1 dau., Carolyn Louise (Mrs. Franklin B. Snyder, Jr.). Engring.and exec. positions N.Y. Telephone Co., 1905-28; gen. mgr. Chicago area Ill. Bell Telephone Co., 1928-30, v.p. and dir., 1930-38, pres., 1938-46; dir. Ill. Bell Telephone Co., A., T. & S.F. Ry., Harris Trust & Savs. Bank. Mem. Community and War Fund, met. Chgo. (pres. 1943); mem. exec. com. Chgo. Community Fund, exec. com. Nat. War Fund; apptd. dir. Civil Defense Planning, Office of Sec. of Defense, Washington, 1948. Bd. dirs. Mus. Sci. and Industry, Chgo. Assn. Commerce; trustee Northwestern Univ. Mem. Delta Tau Delta. Clubs: Commercial of Chicago, Ohio Soc. of Chicago (Chicago). Home: Hendersonville, N.C. Died Aug. 1960.

MELLON, RICHARD KING, banker; b. Pittsburgh, Pa., June 19, 1899; s. Richard Beatty and Jennie Taylor (King) M.; student Princeton Univ.; hon. LL.D., Waynesburg Coll., 1946, Washington and Jefferson Coll., 1947; hon. S.P.D., St. Vincent Coll., Latrobe, Pa., 1946; LL.D. (honorary), University of Pitts., 1948; Pa. Mil. Coll., 1954; D.C.S. (honorary) N.Y. U. Sch. Commerce, 1950; E.D. (hon.), Duquesne U., 1953; Sc.D., Carnegie Institute Technology, 1956; m. Constance Prosser, April 1936; children—Richard, Cassandra, Constance, Seward. Began as messenger Mellon Nat. Bank, 1920, assistant cashier, 1924-28, vice pres. 1928-34, pres. 1934-46; chmn. bd. Mellon Nat. Bank & Trust Co., 1946-66, honorary chairman of the bd., 1967-70; governor and pres., T. Mellon & Sons; director Aluminum Co. of Am., Gen. Motors Corporation, also director Gulf Oil Corporation. Served as student pilot, A.C., 1918; commd. maj. AUS, 1942, promoted lt. col., Oct. 2, 1942; col., April 3, 1943; served as dir. Selective Service, State of Pa.; asst. chief of staff, Internat. Div. War Dept., Washington, D.C.; disch. as col., 1945; brig. gen., 1948, lt. gen. res., 1961. Decorated D.S.M.; recipient Andrew Heiskell Award for civic statesmanship, Action, Inc., 1963; annual citation Midwest Research Inst., 1964. Member bd. trustees Carnigie Inst. Republican. Presbyn. Home: Ligonier PA Died June 3, 1970.

MELVILLE, GEORGE WALLACE rear admiral U.S.N.; b. New York, Jan 10, 1841; s. Alexander and Sarah M.; ed. common schs. and Brooklyn Poly. Inst.; (hon. D. Eng., Stevens Inst. Tech., 1898, Georgetown U., 1899; M.S., Columbia, 1899; LL.D., Georgetown, 1899); twice married; m. 2d, Estella Smith Polis, Oct. 1907 (died 1910). Apptd. to navy as asst. engr., July 29, 1861; served through Civil War; later on various stas. and at navy yards; sailed, 1879, with DeLong in the Jeannette, from San Francisco; comd. the boat's crew which escaped from the wastes f the Lena Delta; later headed the expdns. which recovered the records of the Jeannette expdn. and recovered the remains of DeLong and his companions; made 3 Arctic voyages altogether; gold medallist and advanced 15 numbers by spl. act of Congress, Sept. 1890, for bravery in Arctic; apptd., Aug. 1887, and reapptd., Jan. 1892, and Jan. 1896, engr. in chief of navy; rear admiral from Mar. 4, 1899. During his term designs have been gotten out for 120 ships and 700,000 horsepower. Greatest professional success, probably the triple-screw flyers Columbia and Minneapolis; retired, Jan. 10, 1903. Inventor of many mech. appliances. Decorated with Order of St. Stanislaus, Mil. Order of the First Class (Russia). Home: Philadelphia, Pa. Died Mar. 17, 1912.

MELVILLE, HENRY lawyer; b. Nelson, N.H., Aug. 25, 1858; s. Josiah Henry and Nancy Rebecca (Nesmith) M.; A.B., Dartmouth, 1879; A.M., and LL.B., cum laude, Harvard, 1884. Admitted to bar, 1885, and since in practice at New York; associated with Senator Roscoe Conkling, 1885-88. Capt. Co. A, 8th N.Y. Vols., Spanish-Am. War, 1898. Pres. State Bd. Mgrs. Elmira Reformatory. Author: Ancestry of John Whitney, 1896, etc. Home: New York, N.Y. Died Oct. 21, 1930.

MELVIN, FRANK WORTHINGTON lawyer; b. Phila., Pa., Aug. 7, 1884; s. Bascom Worthington and Amanda Louisa (Merritt) M.; B.S. Econs., U. Pa., 1908; LL.B., Temple U., 1916; m. Bertha Priscilla Haines, June 24, 1911; 1 dau., Ruth Bartram (Mrs. Delp Waldo Johnson). Teacher, Phila. Pub. Schs., 1908-16; admitted to Pa. bar, 1916, and since practiced in Phila.; duty attorney general, 1937-39; standing master, 1942-44, official examiner for orphans court, 1944-. Served as 1st lt., 26th Inf. (under Colonel Theodore Roosevelt), 1st Div. and in 2d Div. with A.E.F.; major, Judge Advocate General's Res. Corps, 79th Div., Col. Staff. Chairman Pa. Hist. Commn., 1936-40, Pa. Hist. and Mus. Commn., 1956-; commr. Valley Forge Park and trustee its funds, 1936-39; vice chmn. commn. Brandywine Battlefield Park, 1952-; chmn. Pa. 300th Anniversary Commn., 1938; president Pa. Fedn. of Hist. Socs., 1934-36. Mem. Bd. of Censors Phila. Bar, chmn. 1932-35. Decorated Comdr., Royal Order of Vasa (Sweden); Comdr., Order of White Rose (Finland). Mem. Am. Bar Assn., Pa. Bar Assn., Phila. Bar Association (board of governors 1935-38), Military Order Foreign Wars (judge advocate 1935-40), Military Order of World War, Am. Legion (founder and 1st commander Post No. 70; member County Council), Swedish Colonial Soc. (gov. 1936-46, hon. gov. for life, 1946), Pa. Soc. Mayflower Descendants (gov. 1937-39), New Eng. Soc. Pa. (pres. 1947-54). Colonial Soc. Pa. (gov. 1951-53), Geneal. Soc. of Pa. (hon. v.p. for life, 1952), Hist. Soc. of Pa., S.R., Soc. of War of 1812 (v.p. 1952), Soc. Colonial Wars, Friendly Sons of St. Patrick (pres. 1934-36, pres. emeritus 1958). Clubs: Lawyers, Caveat (Phila.), Army & Navy, Wash., D.C. Home: 3211 W. Penn St., Phila. 29. Office: Commercial Trust Bldg., Phila. 2. Died Jan. 1962.

MENDELL, CLARENCE WHITTLESEY, educator; b. Norwood, Mass., June 3, 1883; s. Ellis and Clara Eliza (Whittlesey) M.; B.A., Yale, 1904, M.A., 1905, Ph.D., 1910; m. Katharine DeFord Webb, April 14, 1914 (died Jan. 21, 1919); m. 2d, Elizabeth Bailey Lawrence, July 10, 1930. Instr. Latin, 1907-11, asst. prof. Greek and Latin, 1911-19, Yale; apptd. Dunham prof. Latin lang. and lit., same, 1919; dean Yale Coll., 1926-37; chmn. Bd. of Athletic Control, Yale, 1919-25; master Branford Coll., 1932-43, Sterling prof., Yale, from 1947, public orator from 1947. Annual prof. Am. Acad., Rome, 1932-33. With Am. Mil. Intelligence, Paris, 1918; asst. to territorial experts of Am. Commn. to Negotiate Peace, Paris, 1918-19. Served as lt. comdr., U.S.N.R., June 1942; comdr. U.S.N.R., Nov. 1944. Awarded Legion of Merit, Dec. 1945. Chmn. bd. trustees, Salisbury School; trustee Am. Acad. in Rome. Mem. Am. Philological Association, Classical Association Great Britain, Beta Theta Pi, Phi Beta Kappa. Republican. Episcopalian. Clubs: Graduate, Elizabethan, Lawn (New Haven); Yale, Century (N.Y.). Author: Sentence Connection in Tacitus, 1911; Latin Sentence Connection, 1917; Prometheus, 1926; Jeanne d'Arc, 1931; Our Seneca, 1941; Tacitus, The Man and His Work, 1960; Latin Poetry, The New Poets and the Augustans, 1965; Latin Poetry, The Age of Rhetoric and Satire, 1967; Lanx Satura, 1969. Contbr. on classical subjects. Home: Bethany CT Died Dec. 14, 1970.

MENDELSOHN CHARLES JASTROW philologist; b. Wilmington, N.C., Dec. 8, 1880; s. Rev. Dr. Samuel and Esther (Jastrow) M.; grad. Episcopal Acad., Phila., Pa., 1896; A.B., U. of Pa., 1900, Ph.D., 1904. Began as tutor in Greek, Coll. City of New York, 1905, instr., 1907, in history dept., 1920—. Granted leave of absence during World War; engaged in foreign language work, postal and newspaper censorship, 1917-18; commd. capt. Mil. Intelligence Div. of Gen. Staff, U.S.A., July 17, 1918; in charge decipherment of German codes; hon. disch., Aug. 1. 1919; continued research in codes and prepared studies in diplomatic code for U.S. Govt. Harrison Scholar in Classics, 1900-01, fellow, 1901-03, research fellow, 1904-05, U. of Pa. Author: Studies in the Word-Play in Plautus, 1907; Universal Trade Code (with H. O. Yardley), 1921. Home: New York, N.Y. Died Sept. 27, 1939.

MENNINGER, WILLIAM CLAIRE psychiatrist, foundation exec.; b. Topeka, Oct. 15, 1899; s. Charles Frederick and Flora (Knisely) M.; A.B., Washburn Coll. (now Washburn Municipal U.). 1919, D.Sc., 1949; M.A., Columbia, 1922; M.D., Cornell U. Med. Sch., 1924; D.Litt., Mo. Valley Coll., 1951, St. Benedict's Coll., 1963; Sc.D., Woman's Med. Coll. Pa., 1955; LL.D., Adelphi Coll., Kan. State U., 1962; m. Catharine Wright, Dec. 11, 1925; children-Roy Wright, Philip Bratton, William Walter. Intern in med. and surg. Bellevue Hosp., N.Y.C., 1924-26; post-grad. training in psychiatry, St. Elizabeth's Hosp., Wash., 1927; with Menninger Clinic, Topeka, 1925-, psychiatrist, 1927-; pres. Menninger Found.; prof. psychiatry Menninger Sch. of Psychiatry; mem. courtesy staff Stormont-Vail Hosps., 1926-. Mem. nat. exec. bd. Boy Scouts Am., 1935-; mem. Group for Advancement of Psychiatry; mem. expert adv. panel WHO, 1949-50; counselor Nat.

Soc. Crippled Children and Adults; adv. bd. Am. Child Guidance Found.; also mem. or chmn. of panels and coms. of various sci. orgns. many years Bd. dirs. Nat. Com. on Alcholism, Nat. Recreation Assn. Served as 2d lt. U.S. Army, 1918; commd. lt. col. M.C., 1942; neuropsychiat. cons. 4th Service Command, Atlanta, 1943; apptd dir. neuropsychiatry cons. div. Surgeon Gen.'s Office, 1943, promoted col., 1944, brig. gen. M.C., 1945, separted, 1946; apptd. brig. gen. ORC, AUS, 1947; cons. in neuropsychiatry to surgeon gen. U.S. Army, 1946-. Recipient D.S.M., Army Commendation ribbon; chevalier Legion of Honor (France); Lasker award Nat. Com. Mental Health Hygiene; Great Living Americans award U.S. C. of C., 1957. Diplomate psychiatry Am. Bd. Psychiatry and Neurology. Fellow A.C.P. (regent 1958-64, 1st v.p. 1964-65), A.M.A., Am. Psychiat. Assn. (chmn. coordination com. on community aspects of psychiatry 1951-58, past pres.), Am. Orthopsychiat. Assn., Am. Psychopathic Assn., Am. Psychoanalytic Assn. -past pres.), Central Neuropsychiatric Assn. (past pres.), Central Neuropsychiatric Hosp. Assn. (past pres.), Assn. Mil. Surgeons, Assn. for Advancement Research in Nervous and Mental Disease, Am. Philatelic Soc., Alpha Omega Alpha, and other orgns. Presbyn. Mason. Clubs: University (Chgo.); Country (Topeka). Author: Juvenile Paresis (monograph), 1936; Skipper's Handbook (Official Handbook for Leaders of Sea Scouting), 1934; Psychiatry in a Troubled World, 1948; You and Psychiatry, 1948; Psychiatry; Its Evolution and Present Status, 1948; also numerous sci. papers. Mem. editorial bd. Bull. of Menninger Clinic, Nat. Parent-Teacher, Parents Mag., and others. Home: 1724 Collins Av., Topeka 66604. Office: Box 829, Topeka 66601. Died Sept. 6, 1966.

MENOCAL, ANICETO G. civil engr. U.S.N., 1872—; b. Island of Cuba, Sept. 1, 1836; ed. in schools at Havana; C.E. Rensselaer Poly. Inst., 1862; sub-chief engr. Havana water works, 1863-69; engr. dept. public works, New York, 1870-72. Has been chief engr. of all U.S. Govt. surveys for establishing practicability of a ship canal from the Atlantic to the Pacific at Nicaragua and Panama, and of the Maritime Canal Co. of Nicaragua; has made final plans and estimates of cost for a ship canal through Nicaragua. Apptd. delegate to Paris Canal Congress, 1879; decorated by President Grevy, Chevalier Legion of Honor. Has published several official reports on Nicaragua Canal, etc. Mem. commn. to select site for prin. naval station in Philippine Islands, 1900-01; mem. bd. to prepare plans and estimates of cost for naval sta. at Olongapo, Subig Bay, P.I., 1901-02; in 1902 directed by Navy Dept. to select site for coaling sta. on caost of Liberia, Africa; engaged in important drainage work in Cuba, 1906-07. Home: New York, N.Y. Died 1908.

MENOHER, CHARLES THOMAS army officer; b. in Pa., Mar. 20, 1862; grad. U.S. Mil. Acad., 1886, Arty. Sch., 1894; Army War Coll., 1907; m. Nannie Pearson; children—Charles C. (dec.), Pearson, Darrow, William; m. 2d, Elizabeth Painter. Commd. 2d lt. 1st Arty., July 1, 1886; promoted through grades to col., July 1, 1916; brig. gen., N.A., Aug. 5, 1917; maj. gen. N.A., Nov. 28, 1917; brig. gen., U.S.A., Nov. 7, 1918, maj. gen., Mar. 8, 1921. A.D.C. to Brigadier General E. B. Williston, U.S. Vols., 1898; with Light Arty. Brigade, 2d Corps, Chickamauga Park, Ga., July-Dec. 1898; at Havana, Cuba, 1898-99; adj. gen. to provost marshal gen., and of Separate Brigade, Provost Guard, Manila, P.I., 1899-1901; comd. 28th Battery, Field Arty. (mountain), 1901-03; duty Gen. Staff, 1903-07; provost marshal and asst. to chief of staff, Army of Cuban Pacifiication, 1907. Comd. 5th F.A., Sept. 1916-Aug. 26, 1917, and provisional brig. F.A., E. Paso, Tex., Sept.-Nov. 1916; comd. Sch. of Instrn., Saumur, France, Sept. 5-Dec. 14, 1917; comd. 42d (Rainbow) Div., Dec. 19, 1917-Nov. 10, 1918; comd. 6th Corps, Nov. 10-Dec. 17, 1918; dir. Air Service, 1919-21; comdg. Hawaiian Div., 1922-24, Hawaiian Dept., 1924-25, 9th Corps Area, 1925; retired Mar. 20, 1926. Participated in operations in Luneville and Baccarat sectors, Feb. 17-June 21, 1918, Champagne-Marne defensive, July 15-18, attack above Chateau Thierry, July 24-Aug. 2, attack on St. Mihiel salient, Sept. 12-14, and in occupation of the sector to Oct. 1, 1918; attack in Argonne, Oct. 12-Nov. 8, 1918. Awarded SD.S.M., 1919; decorated by the French, Belgian and Italian Govts. Home: Washington, D.C. Died Aug. 11, 1930.

MENOHER, PEARSON ret. army officer; b. Va., Nov. 14, 1892; B.S., U.S. Mil. Acad., 1915; grad. Cav. Sch., advanced course, 1927. Command and Gen. Staff Sch., 1928. Commd. 2d lt., U.S. Army, 1915, advanced through the grades to brig. gen., 1945, ret. 1952. Address: War Dept., Washington 25. Died Feb. 13, 1958; buried Arlington Nat. Cemetery.

MENTZ, GEORGE FRANCIS MILLEN naval officer; b. N.Y. City, Apr. 20, 1896; s. George William and Florence Livingstone (Millen) M.; student St. Luke's Sch., Wayne, Pa., 1905-08; Coll. Scientifique, Lausanne, Switzerland, 1912; B.S., U.S. Naval Acad., 1918; M. Erica Miller Pochon, Oct. 6, 1928; children-Susan Beverley, George F.M. Commd. ensign, U.S. Navy, June 6, 1918, and advanced through grades to capt., 1918, and ret. (physical disability, wounded in action 1945) rank of rear admiral, 1947; served U.S.S. Cassin, 1918; commd. squadron sub-chasers, North Sea, 1918-19, U.S.S. Foote, 1921, U.S.S. Avocet, Asiatic Fleet, 1929-31, 1st lt. and aide, U.S. High Commr. to Turkey, 1924-26; instr., U.S. Naval Acad., 1927-29; charge press relations Navy Dept., 1932-34; Gunnery officer, U.S.S. Richmond, and charge light cruiser gunnery sch., 1935-37; sr. staff officer, U.S. Mediterranean Squadron, 1938-40; exec. officer, Reserve Officers Training Sch., Fort Schuyler, N.Y., 1941-42; comdr. task group of heavy mine layers at Casablanca and invasions of Sicily, 1943; command Mine Force Atlantic Fleet, 1944. Diversionary Attack Group connection, invasion Linguayan Gulf, Philippine Islands, 1944; ret. active service 1947; with Internat. Refugee Orgn., June 1947—, as chief of Mission in Italy. Decorations: Navy Cross, Legion of Merit (combat), Bronze Star, Purple Heart; Star of Solidarity, Knight Comdr. Order St. Gregory the Great, Mil. Class (Pope Pius XII), by Coronna d'Italia. Order of St. Mauritius and Lazarus (Italian). Catholic. Clubs: Army-Navy Country, Washington; Caccia, Rome. Home: Mountain View, Front Royal Va. Office: Palazzo Ruspoli, Rome, Italy. Died Nov. 29, 1957; buried U.S. Naval Acad. Cemetery, Annapolis, Md.

MERAS, ALBERT AMÉDÉE author, educator; b. N.Y. City, May 15, 1880; s. Baptiste and Lousie (Laffont) M.; B.A., Coll. City of New York, 1900; M.A., New York U., 1904, Ph.D., 1908; unmarried. Successively teacher pub. schs., N.Y. City; lecturer French lang. and lit., New York U.; asst. prof. Romance langs., Teachers Coll. (Columbia), and asso. prof. French, same; visting prof. U. of Paris, 1922-24. Served as maj. inf. U.S.A., with A.E.F. Democrat. Mason. Author: Petit Vocabulaire, 1913; Le Premier Livre, 1914; Le Second Livre, 1915; Petits Contes de France, 1915; El Pequeno Vocabulario, 1916; Ein Wartschortz, 1917; La France Esternelle, 1920. Died Mar. 1, 1926.

MERCER, HUGH army officer; b. Aberdeenshire, Scotland, circa, 1721; s. Rev. William and Anna (Munro) M.; ed. Aberdeen U.; m. Isabella Gordon, 4 sons, 1 dau. Asst. surgeon Prince Charles Edward's Army at Battle of Culloden, 1745; rved as capt. in French and Indian War, 1755-56; participated in Battle of Monongahela, 1755; commd. maj., later lt. col., 1758; col. 3d Battalion, 5th Pa. Regt., 1759; apptd. comdt. Ft. Pitt; elected col. of Va. Minutemen for Caroline, Stafford, King George, Spotsylvania counties, 1775; organized, elected col. 3d Va. Regt., 1776, brig. gen., 1776; served in battles of Trenton, 1776, Princeton, 1777. Died Jan. 12, 1777; buried Christ Churchyard, Phila., reinterred Laurel Hill Cemetery, Phila., 1840.

MERCIER, CHARLES ALFRED author; b. nr. New Orleans, June 3, 1816; s. Jean andEloise (Le Duc) M.; attended College Louis-le-Grand, France, circa 1833; studied medicine, Paris, 1855; m. Virginie Vezian, May 10, 1849, at least 3 children. Returned to La., 1838, went to Boston, then to Paris, circa 1840; toured Europe, circa 1843; practiced medicine, New Orleans, 1855-59, also after circa 1866; visited Paris, 1859; founder Athénée Louisianais (orgn. to promote French lang. in La.), 1876; awarded Palmes academiques, 1885. Author: La Rose de Smyrne; L'Ermite du Niagara; Erato Labitte (1840); Biographie de Pierre Soulé (1848); Du Pan-Latinisme-Necessité d'une Alliance entre la France et la Confederation du Sud; La Fille du Pretre (1877); Reditus et Ascalaphos (1890); Johnelle (1891). Died La., May 12, 1894; buried Metairie Cemetery, New Orleans.

MEREDITH, EDWIN THOMAS, JR. publisher; b. Des Moines, Feb. 10, 1906; s. Edwin Thomas and Edna (Elliott) M.; student Culver Mil. Acad., 1921-22, Deerfield Acad., 1923-26, U. Va., 1926, m. Anna Kauffman, June 29, 1929; 1 son, Edwin Thomas III. With Meredith Pub. Co., Des Moines, 1928-, v.p., 1935-; pres. Meredith Syracuse TV Corp., Meredith WOW-TV; v.p. Meredith Broadcasting Co., Meredith Printing, Inc.; dir. Bankers Trust Co., Des Moines, Ia. Power & Light Co., Des Moines, Mut. of Omaha, Omaha. Bd. dirs. Ia. Methodist Hosp. Served as lt. comdr. USNR, 1942-45. Mem. Sigma Chi. Mason (32ff). Home: 3700 John Lynde Rd., Des Moines 50312. Office: 1716 Locust St., Des Moines 50303. Died June 5, 1966.

MEREDITH, WILLIAM MORTON printer, govt. official; b. Centerville, Wayne Co., Ind., Apr. 11, 1835; s. Samuel C. and Margaret (Ballard) M.; ed. pub. schs. and 2 yrs. Whitewater Coll., Centerville; left before graduation, at 18; served apprenticeship to printing business; in Indianapolis, Apr. 23, 1867, Terressa A. Richey. Enlisted pvt. 11th Ind., Apr., 1861; detailed for 1 yr. as asst. commissary-gen. Ind.; commissioned 2d Lt.; raised Co. E, 17th Ind. vols. (Col. Benjamin Harrison); became its capt. and after 2 yrs. service honorably mustered out for disability contracted in service. Resumed printing and became foreman Indianapolis Journal, 1867-72, St. Louis Democrat, 1872-75; supt. plate printing Western Bank Note Co., 1875-89 and 1893-1901; dir. U.S. Bureau of Engraving and Printing, 1889-93, and again since Nov., 1901. Republican. Methodist. Mem. Mil. Order Loyal Legion, G.A.R., Union Veterans' Legion. Residence: 1219 Princeton St., N.W., Washington.

MERLE-SMITH, VAN SANTVOORD banker; b. Seabright, N.J., June 22, 1889; s. Wilton and Zaidee (Van Santvoord) M.; A.B., Princeton, 1911; LL.B., Harvard, 1914; m. Kate Grosvenor Fowler, June 20, 1916; children-Van Santvoord, Nancy, Fowler, Margaret. Began law practice, New York, 1914; mem. Dick & Merle-Smith, investment bankers; member advisory committee New York Trust Co. Fortieth St. office; director Hudson River Day Line, Lincoln Warehouse and Safe Deposit Co., Mississippi Land Co. On secretariat of Peace Conf., Paris, 1919; 3d asst. sec. of state of U.S., 1920-21. Enlisted in Troop C, Squadron A, N.Y. Cav., 1914; promoted through grades to maj., 165th Inf., U.S. Army, 1919; service on Mexican border, June 1916-Mar. 1917; sailed for France, Nov. 4, 1917; participated in battles at Luneville, Baccarat, Espérance-Souain, Champagne-Marne defensive, Aisne-Marne offensive, St. Mihiel offensive, Essey-Pannes, Meuse-Argonne offensive; with Army of Occupation; wounded at Lunevilla and at Villers-sur-Fére; hon. disch., May 7, 1919. Awarded D.S.C. Trustee Hill Sch., Bd. of Nat. Missions, Presbyn. Ch. in U.S.A.; trustee and treas. Church Extension Com. of Presbytery of New York. Republican. Presbyterian. Clubs: Metropolitan (Washington); Knickerbocker, University, Princeton, New York Yacht, Seawanhaka. Home: Oyster Bay, L.I., .Y. Office: 30 Pine St., New York, N.Y., Died Nov. 9, 1943.

MERRELL, JOHN PORTER naval officer; b. Auburn, N.Y., Sept. 7, 1846; s. John Camp and Jane A. (Allen) M.; grad. U.S. Naval Acad., 1867; m. Sarah Frances Tyler, Jan. 22, 1872. Promoted ensign, Dec., 1868; advanced through grades to rear adm., Mar. 19, 1907. Served with European Fleet, 1867-70; signal duty, Washington and Darien Surveying expdn., 1870-71; Torpedo sta., Newport, R.I., 1872-75; Swatara, N. Atlantic Fleet, 1875-77; in charge naval ordnance proving grounds, 1877-79; "Marion," N. Atlantic, and S. Atlantic fleets, 1879-81, "Shenandoah," S. Atlantic Fleet, 1881-82; instr. mathematics, mechanics, physics, chemistry, U.S. Naval Acad., 1882-87; flagships Pensacola, Quinnebaug and Lancaster (on staff comdr.-in-chief) European sta., 1887-89; Naval Acad. (head dept. applied mathematics last 3 yrs.), 1889-93; Baltimore, Asiatic sta., 1893-95; mem. State Dept. Commn. to investigate anti-foreign riots in the province of Szechuen, China, 1895-96; insp. 13th light house dist., 1896-98; on staff Naval War Coll., Jan.-May, 1898; Scipio and Glacier, N. Atlantic Fleet, May-Oct., 1898; equipment officer Navy Yard, Norfolk, Va., 1900-01; comdt., naval station, New Orleans, 1901-03, Naval War Coll., June-Oct., 1903; comdt. New Orleans, 1903-04, U.S.S. Oregon, Asiatic Fleet, 1904; pres. U.S. Naval War Coll., and mem. Gen. Bd., May 24, 1906-Oct. 9, 1909; mem. Joint Army and Navy Bd., 1909; retired by operation of law, Sept. 7, 1908. Home: Washington, D.C. Died Dec. 8, 1916.

MERRIAM, HENRY CLAY major gen. U.S.A.; b. Houlton, Me., Nov. 13, 1837; s. Lewis and Mary (Foss) M.; A.B., A.M., Colby Coll., 1867 (LL.D., 1908); read law; m. McPherson McNeil, June 4, 1876. Capt. 20th Me. Inf., Aug. 29, 1862; resigned Jan. 7, 1863; capt., 80th U.S.C.T., Mar. 11, 1863; lt. col. 85th U.S.C.T., May 21, 1864; transferred to 73d U.S.C.T., June 3, 1864; hon. mustered out. Oct. 24, 1865; maj. 38th U.S. Inf., July 28, 1866; lt. col. 2d Inf., June 10, 1876; col. 7th Inf., July 10, 1885; brig. gen. U.S.A., June 30, 1897; maj. gen. vols., May 4, 1898-Feb. 24, 1899; retired, Nov. 13, 1901; advanced to rank of maj. gen. retired, Feb. 19, 1903. Bvtd. col. vols., Mar. 26, 1865, "for faithful and meritorious services during campaign against Mobile"; lt. col., Mar. 2, 1867, for same at Antietam; awarded Congressional Medal of Honor, June 28, 1894, "for conspicuous gallantry at Ft. Blakely, Apr. 9, 1865." Served in numerous expdns. against defense of Am. citizens on both sides of Rio Grande during revolutionary uprisings, 1873-76; comd. depts. Columbia and Cal., and organized, equipped and forwarded troops for Philippine expdn., 1898; comd. Dept. of the Colo., 1900-01. Inventor of the Merriam infantry pack. Died Nov. 18, 1912.

MERRILL, AARON STANTON naval officer; b. nr. Natchez, Miss., Mar. 26, 1890; s. Dunbar Surget and Charlotte Brandon Stanton Merrill; grad. Natchez Inst., 1906; B.S., U.S. Naval Acad., 1912; grad. Army Chem. Warfare Sch., 1934, Naval War Coll., 1939; m. Louise Gantier Witherbee, Jan. 28, 1922. Commd. ensign USN, 1912, and advanced through the grades to vice adm., 1947; ret. Decorated Navy Cross, D.S.M., Legion of Nerit with gold star, World War I Victory, Yangtze Patrol, Navy Expeditionary (2), World War II Atlantic, Pacific and Nat. Emergency medals (U.S.), Unit Citation, Victory Medal (destroyer clasp); comdr. Order of Crown of Belgium, grand ofcr. Order of Merit (Chile). Mem. Naval Inst., Nat. Geog. Soc., Soc. Cincinnati. Clubs: Army Navy, Chevy Chase (Washington) Army-Navy Country (Arlington); New York Yacht; Boston of New Orleans. Home: Natchez, Miss. Died Feb. 28, 1961; buried Natchez City Cemetery.

MERRILL, ABNER HOPKINS brig. gen. U.S.A.; b. in N.Y., Jan. 19, 1843; grad. U.S. Mil. Acad., 1866. Commd. 2d lt. 1st Arty., June 18, 1866; 1st lt., May 1, 1870; grad. Arty. Sch., 1878; capt., Aug. 14, 1887; maj. 3d Arty., Feb. 23, 1899; lt. col. corps, Aug. 1, 1901; col.,

Apr. 14, 1903; brig. gen. and retired at own request over 40 yrs.' service, Mar. 16, 1906. Home: Poughkeepsie, N.Y. Died Feb. 25, 1923.

MERRILL, CHARLES WHITE, mining engr.; b. La Crescenta, Cal., July 22, 1900; s. Samuel and Emilie (Scherb) M.; A.B. in Geology, Stanford, 1922, E.M., 1924; m. Lillian M. Dobbel, Aug. 15, 1925; children—Lillian D. (Mrs. Archibald C. Coolidge, Jr.), Charles White, Celine W. (Mrs. Francis B. Birkner), Henry D. With various mining cos. in U.S. and Mexico, 1924-28; with U.S. Bur. Mines, San Francisco and Washington, 1928-70, chief div. of minerals, Washington, 1955-70; asso. Behre Dolbear & Co., N.Y., 1970-72. Mem. U.S. delegations Tin Study Group Meetings, 1947-53, U.S. Tin Mission to Malaya, 1951; head U.S. delegation subcom. mineral resources Econ. Commn. Asia and Far East, Tokyo (UN), 1960. Served as pfc., Tank Corps, U.S. Army, 1918-19; capt. specialist res., 1931-42. Mem. Am. Inst. Mining Engrs. (dir. 1955-56, chmn. mineral econs. div. 1955-56; Mineral Economics award 1967), Mining and Metall. Soc. Am. Club: Cosmos (Washington). Author articles mining engring., mineral econs., strategic minerals in govt., profl. and tech. publs., jours. Home: Washington DC Died May 1, 1972.

MERRILL, DANA TRUE ret. army officer; b. East Auburn, Me.; Oct. 15, 1876; s. Daniel C. and Mary (Noyes) M.; B.S., U. Me., 1898; distinguished grad. Army Sch. of the Line, 1908, Army Staff Coll., 1909; student Army War Coll., 1919-20; m. Edith Ferry, Oct. 21, 1903; children-Harwood Ferry, Dana Noyes, Virginia True. Commd. 2d lt. U.S. Army, 1989, promoted through grades to brig. gen., 1934; served in Spanish-Am. War, and Philippine Insurrection, 1898-1902; regt. duty, 1902-24; apptd. mem. Gen. Staff, 1917; chief of staff, 37th Div., AEF, 1917-18; gen. staff, 1920-24; insp. gens. dept., 1927-32; col. 10th inf., 1924-27, 33-34; comdg. 12th Brig. at Ft. Sheridan, Ill., 1935-37, Washington Provisional Brig., 1937-38, 10th Inf. Brig., Ft. Benjamin Harrison, 1938-40; retired. Decorated D.S.M. (U.S.); Officer Legion of Honor (France); Officer Order of Leopold also Croix de Guerre (Belgium). Mem. Sigma Alpha Epsilon. Clubs: Army and Navy; Highland Golf (Ft. Thomas, Ky.). Address: 27 Tower Pl., Ft. Thomas, Ky. Died Aug. 3, 1957; buried Mt. Auburn Cemetery, Auburn, Me.

MERRILL, FRANK D. army officer; b. Woodville, Mass., Dec. 4, 1903; s. Charles W. and Katherine (Donovan) M.; B.S., U.S. Mil. Acad., 1929; B.S. in M.E., Mass. Inst. of Tech., 1932; m. Lucy Kelsall Wright, Nov. 4, 1930; children-Frank D. Jr., Thomas G. W. Commd. 2d lt. Cav., U.S. Army, 1929, and advanced through the grades to brig. gen., Nov. 1943, maj. gen. 1944; served as asst. mil. attaché to Japan, 1938-41; mem. Gen. Stilwell's staff 1943; dep. comdr. U.S. Forces in India-Burma theater, June-Dec. 1944; chief of staff 10th U.S. Army to Oct. 1945; chief of staff 6th U.S. Army, 1946-47, ret. 1947 for disability incurred World War II; commnr. pub. works and hwys. for N.H., 1948—. Awarded Purple Heart, Distinguished Service Medal, Legion of Merit, Bronze Star, Cloud Banner (China); Companion, Order of Indian Empire (Great Britain); Comdr. Legion of Honor (Philippines). Home: Dimond Hill, Concord, N.H. Office: Dept. of Highways, State Capitol, Concord, N.H. Died Dec. 11, 1955; buried West Point, N.Y.

MERRILL, JAMES CUSHING surgeon U.S.A., June 26, 1875—; b. Cambridge, Mass., Mar. 26, 1853; s. James C. M.; grad. Univ. of Pa., M.D., 1874; m. Mary P. Chase, Nov. 16, 1892. Now on duty at Army Med. Museum. Contributor of ornithology to different journals. Home: Washington, D.C. Died 1902.

MERRILL, JOSEPH L., investment banker; b. Boston, Sept. 27, 1899; s. John L. Merrill; A.B., Harvard, 1910; m. Kathleen Cushman, June 10, 1920; children—Arthur Cushman, Robert Gordon. With W. H. McElwain & Co., Boston, 1910-20; partner Merrill Lynch & Co., 1920-40; pres. and dir. Sterling Holding Corp., Wilmington, Del., 1940-70; vice pres. in charge finance and dir. Melville Shoe Corp., N.Y.C., 1940-70; dir. J. F. McElwain Co. Past dir. A. S. Beck Shoe Co., Diamond Shoe Corp., G. R. Kinney Co., Feltman & Curme Shoe Stores, Central Shoe Co., Waldorf System, Inc., Lane Bryant, Inc., Adams-Hills Corp., Struthers Wells, Inc., Beechvale Investments, Ltd., Bird Grocery Stores, Daniel Reeves, Inc., Nat. Tea. Co., Safeway Stores, Inc. Served as capt., U.S. Army, World War I. Owner of "Feather," winner championship Yacht Racing Assn. of L.I. Sound, 1940, 41, 46, 47; and Royal Bermuda Yacht trophy. Clubs: New York Yacht, American Yacht, Southhampton Yacht; Meadow (Southhampton); Harvard (New York); Piping Rock, National Golf Links of America. Home: Locust Valley NY Died May 7, 1970.

MERRILL, SAMUEL publisher; b. Indianapolis, May 30, 1831; s. Samuel and Lydia Jane (Anderson) M.; A.B., Wabash Coll., Ind., 1851, A.M., 1854; m. Emily White, July 19, 1859. Began as pub. and bookseller in Indianapolis, 1852. Served as 2d lt., capt., maj. lt. col., bvt. col., comdg. 70th Ind. Vol. Inf., Civil War. Consul-gen. at Calcutta, India, 1889-93; Whig and Republican. Presbyn. Quartermaster-gen. Dept. of Indiana, G.A.R., 1866; comdr. Dept. of Calif. and Nev., 1908, 09. Retired. Author: The Seventieth Indiana Volunteer Infantry in the War of the Rebellion, 1900. Home: Long Beach, Calif. Died Sept. 3, 1924.

MERRILL, THOMAS EMERY army officer; b. Cincinnati, O., June 1, 1875; s. William Emery and Margaret Ellen (Spencer) M.; student Washington and Lee U., 1891-94; grad. U.S. Mil. Acad., 1898; m. Mary Ryan Malone, Sept. 2, 1930; children-Marian, Jean. Commissioned 2d lt. artillery, 1898; promoted through the grades to brig. gen., 1933; served through Spanish-Am. War, Philippine Insurrection, Pershing Expdn. into Mexico and World War; retired from active service, June 30, 1939. Mem. Am. Theosophical Soc. Home: 651 Spazier St., Pacific Grove, Calif. Address: War Dept., Washington, D.C., Died Aug. 18, 1943.

MERRILL, WILLIAM EMERY army officer; b. Ft. Howard, Wis., Oct. 11, 1837; s. Capt. Moses E. and Virginia (slaughter) M.; grad. U.S. Mil. Acad., 1859; m. Margaret Spencer, Jan. 1873, at least 2 sons. Commd. lt. Corps Engrs., U.S. Army, 1859; captured during W.Va. campaign, 1861, held prisoner until Feb. 1862; brevetted capt. after being wounded, Yorktown, Va., 1862; promoted capt., 1863; brevetted maj., lt. col., col. for services in battles of Chickamauga, Lookout Mountain, Missionary Ridge; chief engr. Army of Cumberland, 1864-65; chief engr. Div. of Mo., under Gen. Sherman, 1867-70; originator, chief engr. of carnalization of Ohio River from Pitts. to its mouth, 1879-85; U.S. del. Congress of Engrs., Paris, France, 1889. Author: Iron Truss Bridges for Railroads, 1870. Died Dec. 14, 1891.

MERRIMAN, HARRY MORTON former textile mfg. exec.; b. Waterbury, Conn., Apr. 16, 1874; s. Henry and Mary A. (Heminway) M.; ed. Sedgwick Inst., Great Barrington, Mass., and Mt. Pleasant Mil. Acad., Ossining, N.Y.; m. Maude A. Jackson, Jan. 9, 1900; children-Harry Morton, John A. Pres. Heminway Silk Co., 1912-27; chmn. bd. dirs. Belding-Heminway Co., 1927-33; dir. belding Heminway Co., Ambassador Hotel Co., 115 East 53rd St. Corp., Campobello Island Co., Yachting Pub. Co. Comdr. submarine patrol USN, World War I. Mem. bd. mgrs. Meml. Hosp., N.Y. Mem. Pilgrim Soc., Mil. Order Fgn. Wars. Formerly pres. Marine Mus. of City of N.Y.; formerly mem. Boy Scout Council of N.Y. Clubs: Century, Explorers, Army and Navy (Washington); Maryland (Balt.); Chesapeake Bay Yacht; Annapolis Yacht Tred Avon Yacht, Royal Kennebacasis Yacht (Can). Home: 204 S. Hanson St., Easton, Md. Died Dec. 30, 1954; buried Arlington Nat. Cemetery.

MERRITT, EDWIN ATKINS b. Sudbury, Vt., Feb. 26, 1828 ; removed to St. Lawrence Co., N. Y., 1841; became surveyor-engr.; held successively several local offices - elected to legislature, 1859; reelected, 1860; at beginning of war was q.m. of 60th N. Y. Regt.; served with Army of Potomac and Sherman's Ga. campaign; appt. capt. and commissary of subsistnece, U. S. vols.; q.m.-gen. of N. Y., 1865-69; also supt. Soldiers' Home in N. Y. City; established free agencies for collections of bounties, pay and pensions that were due N. Y. soldiers; del. Constl. convs., 1867, 1868; naval officer, port of New York, 1869-70; unsuccessful candidate state treasurer, 1875; surveyor port of New York, 1877; collector, same, 1878-82; U.S. consul-gen. London, 1881-85. Pres bd. trustees St. Lawrence U., local bd. Potsdam State Normal and Training Sch.; mem. bd. trustees Thomas I. Clarkson Memorial Sch. Home: Potsdam, N. Y. Died Dec. 26, 1916.

MERRITT, WESLEY army officer; b. New York, June 16, 1836; s. John W. and Julia Anne M.; grad U. S. Mil. Acad., assigned to dragoons; promoted to lst lt., May 13, 1861; capt., Apr. 5, 1862; promoted for bravery to bvt. maj. gen. U. S. A., Mar. 13, 1865, and rank of lt. col., July 28, 1866; commd. brig. gen. vols., June 29, 1863; maj. gen. vols. Apr. 1, 1865. Since war regularly promoted from lt. col. to maj. gen. U. S. A. Served in Army of the Potomac until June 1864; participated in all its battles and earned 6 successive bvt. promotions for gallantry at Gettysburg, Yellow Tavern, Hawes' shop, Five , etc. Afterward accompanied Gen. Sheridan on cavalry raid toward Charlottesville, and engaged in battle of Trevilian's Sta.; comd. cav. div. in Shenandoah campaign, Aug. 1864 to Mar. 1865; was engaged in battles of Winchester, Fisher's Hill, etc.; comd. corps of cav. in Appomattox campaign; one of three comdrs. from Nat. Army to arrange with Confederate comdrs. for surrender of Army of Northern Va. After war served in various depts., participated in several Indian campaigns; supt. U. S. Mil. Acad., 1882-87; comd. Dept. of the Atlantic until assigned May, 1898, to command of U. S. forces in the P. I. continuing there until summoned to the aid of the Am. Peace Commrs. in session in Paris, Dec. 1898; returned to U. S.; on duty in command of Dept. to East, Governor's Island, until retirement, June 16, - 1900. Died 1910.

MERRY, JOHN FAIRFIELD rear admiral U.S.N.; b. Edgecome, Me., Mar. 5, 1840; s. John and Sarah A. M.; ed. pub. schs., Edgecomb; M. Nancy J. Winslow, Aug. 11, 1862. Entered navy, Oct. 15, 1862, and served through the Civil War; served also in the Spanish-Am. War; has served in all the foreign and home stas., in the grades of ensign, lt., lt. comdr., comdr., capt. and rear admiral; last duty comdt. U. S. Naval Sta., Honolulu, H. I.; retired at age limit, Mar. 5, 1902. Chmn. Mass. Nautical Sch. Bd., 1911-13. Home: Somerville, Mass. Died May 30, 1916.

MERSHON, RALPH DAVENPORT elec. engr. inventor; b. Zanesville, O., July 14, 1868; s. Ralph Smith and Mary J. (Jones) M.; M.E., Ohio State U., 1890; asst. in electrical engineering, same, 1890-91; D.Sc., Tufts College, 1918; Dr. of Engring., Ohio State U., 1936. With Westinghouse Electric & Mfg. Co. at Pittsburgh and New York, 1891-1900; represented same at World's Industrial Expn., 1893; consulting practice since 1900. Designed transformers for which the Westinghouse Co. received an award at Chicago Expn., 1893; in charge investigations of phenomena which occur between conductors at high voltages for Telluride (Colo.) Power Transmission, and Westinghouse cos., 1896-97; chief engr. Colo. Electric Power Co., 1897-98; reconstructed the generating, transmitting and receiving equipment of Montreal & St. Lawrence Light & Power Co.; designed various plants in U.S., S. Africa and Japan; was chief engr. during design and constrn. of Niagara, Lockport and Ontario Power Co. Invented: 6-phase rotary converter; compounded rotary converter; system of lightning protection for elec. apparatus; compensating voltmeter (awarded John Scott medal by Franklin Inst.); etc. Mem. joint nat. com. on Reserve Corps of Engrs.; maj., Engr. O.R.C., 1917; maj. and lt. col., Engrs., U.S. Army; in active service, 1917-19, detailed to Naval Consulting Bd. Fellow A.A.A.S., Am. Inst. E.E. (pres. 1912-13); mem. Am. Soc. C.E., Am. Soc. Mech. Engrs., Franklin Inst., Inventors' Guild (ex-pres.), Engineering Inst. of Can., Instn. Elec. Engrs., Eng.; hon. life mem. Res. Officers Assn. of United States. Clubs: University, Engineers' (New York); Cosmos (Washington). Awarded Lamme engring. medal, by Ohio State U., 1932. For work in drafting legislation for R.O.T.C., and getting it included in Nat. Defense Act of 1916 was awarded citation by Ohio State U., 1942. Home: 2000 Tiger Tail Av., Miami, Fla. Died Feb. 14, 1952; buried Zaneville, O.

MERVINE, WILLIAM naval officer; b. Phila., Mar. 1 1815. Apptd. midshipman U.S. Navy, 1809, served on Gt. Lakes during War 1812; became acting lt., 1813, lt., 1815; master comdt., 1834, commanded ship Natchez, 1836-37; capt. 1841, on sea service in command ship Cyane, 1845-46, ship Savannah, 1846-47; mil. comdt. Monterey (Cal.); apptd to command Gulf Blockading Squadron, 1861; promoted commodore, 1862, rear adm., 1866. Died Utica, N.Y., Sept. 15, 1868.

MERWIN, LORING CHASE, publisher; b. Bloomington, Ill., Mar. 26, 1906; s. Louis Buckley and Jessie Fell (Davis) M.; ed. Choate Sch., 1921-24; B.S., Harvard, 1928; Dr. Pub. Service, Ill. Wesleyan U., 1968; m. Marjorie Sward, Jan. 5, 1935; children—Amanda Fell, Susan, Miles. Chmn. bd. Daily Pantagraph, Bloomington; pres. Bloomington Broadcasting Corp. (operating radio sta. WJBC, Bloomington, and sta. WROK, Rockford, Ill.). Trustee Ill. Wesleyan U.; mem. adv. council Ill. State Normal U.; mem. adv. bd. Ill. Dept. Conservation; pres. Bloomington Unlimited, 1969; v.p. Park Lands Found. Served to lt. USNR, 1942-45. Mem. Bloomington Assn. Commerce (dir. 1950-58, chmn. 1956-63), Living Desert Assn. (bd. govs.), Harvard Alumni Assn. (dir.), Inland Daily Press Assn. (pres. 1960-61), Sigma Delta Chi. Unitarian. Clubs: Press, Harvard, Racquet (Chgo.); Iroquois (Harvard Coll.); Bloomington Country; Overseas Press (N.Y.C.); Old Elm (Lake Forest Ill.), Thunderbird (Palm Springs, Cal.); Country of Fla. (Delray Beach). Home: Bloomington IL Died Sept. 6, 1972.

MESSINGER, EDWIN JOHN army officer; b. Kingston, N.Y., Mar. 1, 1907; B.S., U.S. Mil. Acad., 1931; grad. Inf. Sch., Ft. Benning, Ga., 1936; grad. Command and Gen. Staff Sch., Ft. Leavenworth, Kan., 1943; student Latin Am. studies U. Mich., 1945; grad. Armed Forces Staff Coll., Norfolk, Va., 1950; grad. Nat. War Coll., Washington, 1952; Commd. 2d lt. Inf., U.S. Army, 1931, advanced through grades to maj. gen., 1956; assigned 28th Inf., 1931-35, 15th Inf. Am. Barracks, Tientsin, China, 1935-38, Ft. Lewis, Wash., 1938-39; instr. gymnastics and phys. tng. U.S. Mil. Acad., 1939-40, asst. master , 1940-42, comdt. of cadets, 1954-56; asst. chief staff for operations 17th Airborne Div., Camp Mackall, N.C., 1943-44, asst. chief of staff for operations, 1944-45, arty. comdr., 1945; chief U.S. Mil. Mission, San Jose, Costa Rica, 1946-49; comdr. 2d Battalion 23d Inf. Regt., 2d Inf. Div., Ft. Lewis, Wash., 1949, exec. officer 23d Inf. Regt., 1949-50, comdr., 1950, exec. officer, Korea, 1950; comdr. 9th Inf. Regt., Korea, 1950-51; field service liaison officer Office Mil. Assistance, Office Sec. Def., 1952-53; asst. comdr. 24th Inf. Div., Japan, 1953-54; comdg. gen. 25th Div., U.S. Army Pacific, 1956-. Decorated Legion of Merit with clusters. Silver Star with clusters, Bronze Star Medal with clusters, D.S.C. with cluster. Address: Commanding General 25th Infantry Division, U.S. Army Pacific, care The Pentagon, Washington 25. Died Jan. 1965.

MESSLER, EUGENE LAWRENCE, engr.; b. Pittsburgh, Pa., Apr. 6, 1873; s. Thomas D. and Maria R. (Varick) M.; B.Ph., Sheffield Scientific School (Yale), 1894; m. Elizabeth V. Long, Dec. 31, 1898; children—Thomas D., E. Lawrence. Began as pattern maker and moulder, Edgar Thompson Works of Carnegie Steel

Co.; successively civ. engr., gen. supt. labor and transportation and asst. blast furnace supt., Duquesne Works, Carnegie Steel Co., Pa., 1895-99; supt. and gen. supt. Eliza Furnaces, Coke Works, Jones &Laughlin Steel Co., 1899-1911; asst. to pres. Riter-Conley Mfg. Co., 1912-15; v.p. and gen. mgr. Witherow Steel Co., 1916-18; also pres. Eureka Fire Brick Works; dir. Pittsburgh, Fisher Scientific Co. Commd. capt. engrs., May 20, 1918; comdg. Co. G., 21st Engrs., 1st Army A.E.F., Sept. 1918-May 1919; participated in St. Mihiel, defensive sector and Meuse-Argonne offensives; lt. col. Engr. Reserves, to 1938, now inactive due to age limit. Member American Iron and Steel Inst., Am. Inst. M.E., Am. Refractories Inst., Am. Soc. Mil. Engrs., Vets. of Foreign Wars, Engring. Soc. Western Pa., British Iron and Steel Inst., S.A.R., Am. Legion, Reserve Officers Assn. Clubs: Yale (New York); Harvard-Yale-Princeton, Cloister, Pittsburgh Golf, Rolling Rock. Home: 5423 Forbes St. Office: B. F. Jones Bldg., Pittsburgh PA

MESTERN, H. EDWARD, patent agt.; b. Berlin, Germany, Dec. 31, 1909; s. Armand E. and Gertrud (Wurceldorf) M.; M.A., U. Berlin, 1933; Ph.D. cum laude, U. Munster (Germany), 1936; m. Elsa Catherine Sapp, Jan. 24, 1956; 1 son by previous marriage, Douglas Kemp. Came to U.S., 1936, naturalized, 1943. Consultant to U.S. Air Force, 1953, 1956-68. Served to lt. colonel in USAF Res., 1951-53. Mem. Chemists Club, Am. Chem. Soc., Res. Officers Assn. U.S. (pres. Westchester 1959, dist. v.p. 1960-62). Home: Yonkers NY Died Feb. 29, 1968.

METCALF, VICTOR HOWARD secretary of the navy; b. Utica, N. Y., Oct. 10, 1853; s. William and Sarah P. M.; grad. Utica Free Acad., 1871, Russell's Mil. Acad., New Haven, Conn., 1872; entered Yale, academic, 1872; L.L.B., Yale, 1876; m. Emily Corinne Nicholson, Apr. 11, 1882. Admitted to Conn. bar, 1876. N.Y. bar, 1877; practiced at Utica, N. Y. 1877-79, Oakland, Calif., 1879-1904; mem. 56th to 58th Congresses (1899-1904), 3d Calif. Dist.; resigned from 58th Congress, July 1, 1904; sec. Dept. Commerce and Labor, July 1, 1904-Dec. 16, 1906; sec. of the navy, Dec. 17, 1906-Dec. 1, 1908, in cabinets of President Roosevelt. Republican. Home: Oakland, Calif. Died Feb. 20, 1936.

METCALFE, HENRY captain U.S.A.; b. New York, Oct. 29, 1847; s. Dr. John T. and Harriet (Colles) M.; grad. U.S. Mil. Acad., 1868; m. Harriet P. Nichols, of Washington, Apr. 20, 1870. Served U.S. Ordnance Dept.; insp. of contracts with Turkish govt. for arms and ammunition, 1873-75; in charge Govt. exhibit Centennial Expn., 1876; instr. of ordnance U.S. Mil. Acad., 1886-91; retired on account of impaired eyesight, Oct., 1893. Received Order of Osmanie, 2d class, from Turkish govt., 1875. Author: Cost of Manufactures, 1885; A Course in Ordnance and Gunnery, U.S.M.A., 1891, etc. Club: Century. Home: Cold Spring, N.Y. Office: 147 4th Av., New York.

METTS, JOHN VAN BOKKELEN, adjutant general of N.C.; b. Wilmington, N.C., Dec. 17,21876; s. James Isaac and Cornelia (Frothingham) M.; student Tilston Normal Sch., Cape Fear Acad., and Morrell Sch., Wilmington, N.C.; m. Josephine Budd, Nov. 20, 1906 (dec.); children—Josephine (Mrs. Spotswood Hatherway Huntt), John Van Bokkelen. Owner and operator of fire insurance agency, Wilmington, N.C., 1902-17. Enlisted N.C. Nat. Guard, 1894; commd. 2d lt., 1899, and advanced through grades to maj. gen., 1949; selective service on Mexican Border, 1916-17; comdr. 119th Inf., 30th Div., U.S.A., A.E.F.; adjutant gen. of N.C., since 1920; dir. N.C. Selective Service, 1940-50. Awarded Distinguished Service Medal. Mason. Home: 730 N. Blount. Office: Justice Bldg., Raleigh NC

MEYER, GEORGE VON LENGERKE Sec. of the navy; b. Boston, June 24, 1858; s. George A. and Grace Helen (Parker) M.; A.B., Harvard, 1879 (LL.D., 1911); m. Alice Appleton, June 25, 1885. In business as merchant and trustee, 1879-99. Mem. Boston Common Council, 1889-90, Bd. of Aldermen, 1891; mem. Mass. Ho. of Rep., 1892-97 (speaker, 1894-97); chmn. Mass. Paris Expn. mgrs., 1898; mem. Rep. Nat. Com., 1898-1904; ambassador extraordinary and plenipotentiary to Italy, 1900-05, to Russia, 1905-07; Postmaster gen. in cabinet of President Roosevelt, March 4, 1907-Mar. 6, 1909; sec. of the navy in cabinet of President Taft, Mar. 6, 1909-Mar., 1913. Overseer of Harvard U., 1911-. Home: Hamilton, Mass. Died Mar. 9, 1918.

MEYER, HERBERT ALTON ex-congressman; b. Chillicothe, O., Aug. 30, 1886; s. John T. and Louise (Griesham) M.; student Stanton (Va.) Mil. Acad., 1900-04; LL.B., George Washington U. and Nat. U., 1909; m. Mary Davis Watts, Dec. 16, 1909; 1 son, Herbert A. Admitted to D.C. bar, 1909; asst. to sec. of Interior in charge of affairs Alaska R.R. and ty. affairs Alaska and Hawaii, asst. to v.p. Prairie Oil & Gas Co., Independence, Kan., 1919-32; v.p. Sinclair Prairie Oil Marketing Co., Tulsa, 1932-37; mng. dir. Kan. Independent Oil & Gas Assn., Wichita, Kan., 1938-40; pub. Independence (Kan.) Daily Reporter, 1940; mem. 80th, 81st Congresses, 3d dist. Kan. Served as capt. U.S. AAC, World War I. Mem. Kan. Press Assn. (past pres.), Am. Legion, Sigma Chi, Sigma Delta Chi. Republican. Presbyn. Elk. Clubs: Rotary, National Press. Home: 201 S. 6th St. Office: Reporter Bldg., Independence, Kan. Died Oct. 2, 1950

MEYERDING, HENRY WILLIAM, surgeon; b. St. Paul, Minn., Sept. 5, 1884; s. Henry John and Adelgunda (Rosenkranz) M.; B.Sc., U. of Minn., 1907, M.D., 1909, M.Sc. in orthopedic surgery, 1918; m. Lura Abbie Stinchfield, Feb. 12, 1912 (dec. Apr. 1960); children—Augustus (dec.), Edward Henry, Anne (dec.). House surgeon Mayo Clinic, 1911-12, attending physician, 1912-14, asst. orthopedist, 1914-15, asso. orthopedic surgeon, 1915, surgeon from 1915; orthopedic surgeon St. Mary's and Colonial hosps., 1915; instr. orthopedic surgery Mayo Foundation, U. Minn. Grad. Sch., 1918-20, asst. prof., 1920-22, associate professor, 1922-37, prof. 1937-49, emeritus, 1949-69. Served in Minn. Nat. Guard, 1st lt. M.C., 1909, col. 1938. Recipient Gold medals, Am. Med. Assn., 1939; gold medal, Am. Cong. Phys. Therapy, 1939. First award, Chgo. Med. Soc., 1947; medal of honor, from the University of Bordeaux, 1952; Certificate of Merit, U. Minn., 1952. Diplomate Am. Bd. Orthopedic Surgery. Fellow A.C.S. (gov. 1946-53), Internat. Coll. Surgeons (pres. U.S. sect. 1950-51, internat. president 1958), Acad. Surgery, Spain (hon.); mem. Am. Fracture Assn. (pres. 1952-56), Internat. Soc. Orthopaedic Surgery and Traumatology (nat. chmn. U.S. sect., pres. 6th congress 1948; chmn. U.S. delegations 1946-55), hon. mem., corr. mem. fgn., internat. and nat. profl. and scientific orgns. and assns. Italian, Brazilian, Argentine and including hon. memberships in: French Socs. Orthopedic Surgery and Traumatology, Internat. Surg. Soc., World Med. Assn., Netherlands Orthopaedic Soc., Belgian, Czechoslovak, Bordeaux, Madrid, Internat. surg. socs., Brazilian Acad. Medicine, Philippine Coll. Surgeons, Turkish Assn. Surgeons. Conglist. Mason (32 deg., Shriner). Club: University. Home: Rochester MN Died Aug. 1969.

MEYERS, GEORGE JULIAN naval officer; b. Council Bluffs, Ia., April 10, 1881; s. Ferdinand and Emma (Fuss) M; grad. U.S. Naval Acad., 1902, U.S. Naval War Coll., 1922, U.S. Army War Coll., 1923; completed course mech. engring. U.S. Naval p c. 4, 1904; 1 son, George Julian. Entered U.S. Navy, May 23, 1898; advancing through grades to capt., Nov. 22, 1924, rear adm., Dec. 1935; spent 20 years in sea service; now comdt. 16th Naval Dist., P.I. Mem. U.S. Naval Institute. Awarded Navy Cross for service in World War. Mason. Author: Steam Turbines, 1917; Strategy, 1928. Home: Council Bluffs, Ia. Died Dec. 7, 1939.

MEYERS, JOSEPH HUGH, consultant; b. Balt., July 1, 1904; s. J. Herman and Catherine M. (King) M.; student U. Mich., 1923-26; LL.B., Cath. U. Am., 1933, LL.M., 1940; M. Hollis V. Carder, Aug. 21, 1934(dec. June 1966); children—Judith, Thomas, John, Mary; m. 2d, Mary M. Morrison, July 11, 1970. Admitted to D.C. bar, 1934; atty. Dept. Health, Edn. and Welfare, and predecessors, 1936-60, dept. commr. Social Security, 1960-63; dept. commr. welfare Dept. Health, Edn. and Welfare, 1963-67, acting commr. welfare, 1967, dep. adminster, social and rehab. service, 1967-70; cons. pub. welfare, 1970-72; lectr. Barry Coll. Sch. Social Welfare, Miami Shores, Fla., 1970-72. Trustee William J. Kerby Found. Served to maj. AUS, World War II. Mem. Am. Pub. Welfare Assn. (2d v. p. 1969-71), Fed. Bar Assn., Fla. Health and Welfare Council (mem. bd.). Home: Miami Beach FL Died Dec. 29, 1972; buried Arlington Nat. Cemetery.

MICHELSON, ARNOLD, regulator exec.; b. Bismark N.D., July 7, 1893; s. Herman L. and Justyni (Maska) M.; A.B., U. Minn., 1916; m. Esther E. Erickson, Oct. 30, 1920; children—James, Virginia. Sales dept. Northwestern Fuel Co., Duluth, St. Paul Minn., 1918-19, joined Minneapolis Honeywell Regulator Co., 1920, v.p., 1928-64, regional mgr. eastern operations 1934-54, regional v.p., 1954-64. Capt. U.S. Army, 1917-18. Mem. Oil Heat Inst. N.Y. Oil Trades Assn., N.Y., N.J. fuel assns. Beta Theta Pi. Mason. Clubs: Sales Executives (N.Y. City); Lake Placid. Home: New York City NY Died Aug. 1969.

MICHIE, PETER SMITH prof. natural and experimental philosophy, U.S. Mil. Acad., Feb. 14, 1871-; b. Brechin, Scotland, Mar. 24, 1839; went to Cincinnati in boyhood; grad. West Point, 1863; (Ph.D., Princeton, 1871; A.M., Dartmouth, 1873; LL.D., Union Col. 1893); m. Maria L. Roberts, June 21, 1863. Commissioned 1st lt. engrs., June 11, 1863; capt., Nov. 23, 1865; reached bvt. rank brig. gen. vols.; participated in siege of Charleston, and in Fla. and Va. campaigns, becoming chief engr., army of the James. Author: Elements of Wave Motion Relating to Sound and Light; Life and Letters of Maj. Gen Emory Upton; Personnel of Sea Coast Defense; Elements of Analytical Mechanics; Elements of Hydro-Mechanics; Practical Astronomy. Member bd. overseers. Thayer School Civil Engineering,-Coll., mem. Military Commn. to Europe, 1870. Died 1901.

MICHIE, ROBERT EDWARD LEE army officer; b. "Bel Air" Albemarle Co., Va., June 1, 1864; s. Dr. J. Augustus and Susan R. (Jackson) M.; grad. U.S. Mil. Acad., 1885, Army War Coll., 1905; m. Gray Beachy, Jan. 19, 1887. Commd. 2d lt. 2d Cav., June 14, 1885; promoted through grades to col. cav., U.S.A., July 1, 1916; brig. gen. N.A., Aug. 5, 1917. Duty at mil. posts in Ida., Ariz., N.M. and Kan. until 1897; adj. gen. Dept. of Province of Havana and Pinar Del Rio, Cuba, 1899-1900; adj. gen. Dept. of Mo., 1900-01; in Philippines, 1903-04, 1910-11; duty Gen. Staff, Washington, 1905-07; witnessed German Army maneuvers, 1908; duty on Mexican border, various periods, 1912-14; mem. Gen. Staff, 1914-17; with U.S. Commn. to Russia, 1917; apptd. comdr. 53d Inf. Brigade, Camp Wadsworth, Spartanburg, S. C., Sept. 1917. Died June 5, 1918.

MICHIE, THOMAS JOHNSON, U.S. district judge; b. Northport, N.Y., June 7, 1896; s. Thomas Johnson and Emily (Hewson) M.; A.B., U. Va., 1917, A.M., 1920, LL.B., 1921; m. Marcella Guidotti, Jan. 7, 1947; children—Cordelia Ruffin (Mrs. Walter C. Plunkett, Jr.), Thomas Johnson, Emily (Mrs. John Gennari), Virginia. Admitted Va. bar, 1921, partner Allen, Walsh & Michie, Charlottesville, 1921-26; legal dept. Koppers Co., Pitts., 1926-42, chief counsel, 1937-42; partner Michie, Taylor, Camblos & Deets and predecessor firms, 1946-61; U.S. dist. judge Western Dist. of Va., 1961-67. Lectr. U. Va. Law Sch., 1946-61. Mayor of Charlottesville, 1958-60. Dir. Thomas Jefferson Meml. Found. Served as 2d lt. A.C., U.S. Army, 1917-19, lt. col. U.S.A.A.F., 1942-46. Decorated Legion of Merit, Bronze Star, Order Brit. Empire, Order Crown of Italy, Croix de Guerre (France). Home: Charlottesville VA Died Apr. 9, 1973.

MICHLER, FRANCIS, capt. U.S.A.-lt.-col. and asst. adj-gen. U.S. vols.; b. in N.Y.; apptd., 1866; grad. West Point, 1870; 2d lt., June 15, 1870; 1st lt., Nov. 12, 1876; capt., May 22, 1888; apptd. lt-col., U.S. vols., 1898; aide-de-camp, on staff Gen. Miles; took part in campaigns against Apaches in Arizona, 1872-3. Residence: Metropolitan Club, Washington DC

MICHLER, NATHANIEL army officer; b. Easton, Pa., Sept. 13, 1827; s. Peter S. and Miss (Hart) M.; attended Lafayette Coll., 1841-44; grad. U.S. Mil. Acad., 1848; m. Fannie Kirkland; m. 2d, Sallie Hollingsworth, Feb. 12, 1861. Brevetted 2d lt., Topog. Engrs., U.S. Army, made surveys and reconnaissances in Tex., N.M., 1848-51; commd. 2d lt., 1854, 1st lt., 1856; chief topog. engr. in charge of surveys for a canal extending from Gulf of Darien to Pacific Ocean, 1857-60; in charge of running boundary line between Md. and Va., 1858-61; became capt. with armies of Ohio and Cumberland, 1861-63; then on survey of Harpers Ferberland, 1861-63; then on survey of Harpers Ferry; attached to Army of the Potomac, 1863-65, in charge of topog. dept., engaged in making various reconnaissances and bldg. of defensive works connected with battles of Wilderness, Spotsylvania, Cold Harbor, Petersburg; commd. maj. Corps. Engr., 1864, brevetted lt. col., 1864, brevetted col. for services at Battle of Petersburg, brig. gen for services during Civil War, 1865; engaged in selecting site for presdl. mansion and public park, preparing plans for new War Dept. bldg., 1866-67; supt. public bldgs. and grounds, 1867-71, had charge of survey of Potomac River and repairing Fort Foote, Md.; lighthouse engr. on Pacific Coast, 1871-76; proposed canal connecting Coquille River with Coos Bay (Ore.); superintended river and harbor improvements on Lake Erie, 1876-78; mil. attache of U.S. legation, Vienna, Austria, 1879; engaged in river and harbor work for N.Y. and N.J., 1880-81. Died Saratoga Springs, N.Y., July 17, 1881; buried Easton.

MICKELSEN, STANLEY R(AYMOND), army officer; b. St. Paul, Oct. 8, 1895; s. Ole and Anna (Lysne) M.; student Hamlin U., 1913-15; student U. Minn., 1915-17, M.S. (hon.), 1953; grad. Army War Coll., 1938; m. Ruth Klemer, Apr. 5, 1917; children-Ruth (Mrs. C. P. Rountree), Patricia (Mrs. Robert L. Kays), Helen (Mrs. John Q. Henion). Entered U.S. Army, 1917, advanced through grades to lt. gen., 1954; served in Iceland, 1942-43, SHAEF, Europe, 1944-47; dep. for guided missiles and atomic energy Gen. Staff, U.S. Army, also mem. mil. liaison com. A.E.C., 1950-52; comdg. gen. Ft. Bliss, Tex., 1952-54; comdg. gen. Army Antiaircraft command, 1954-57; tech. adviser Hughes Aircraft Co., Fullerton, Cal., 1957-. Decorated D.S.M., Legion of Merit. Mem. Kappa Sigma. Home: 818 S. Lee St., Alexandria, Va. Office: Hughes Aircraft Co., 1612 K St. N.W., Washington. Died Mar. 28, 1966; buried Arlington Nat. Cemetery.

MIFFLIN, THOMAS army officer, gov. Pa.; b. Phila., Jan. 21, 1745; s. John and Elizabeth (Bagnell) M.; grad. Coll. of Phila. (now U. Pa.), 1760; m. Sarahllorris, Mar. 4, 1767. In Europe, 1764-65; mcht. in partnership with brother George, 1765; mem. Am. Philos. Soc., 1765-99; mem. Pa. Provincial Assembly, 1772-76, 78-79, 82-84, pres., 1783-84, opposed Stamp Act; mem. Continental Congress from Pa., 1774-76; commd. maj. Continental Army, 1775, chief a.d.c. to George Washington, 1775, q.m. gen., 1775-77, promoted brig. gen., 1776, served as maj. gen., 1777-79; mem. U.S. Bd. War, 1777-78; involved in cabal to oust Washington as comdr.-in-chief, 1777; trustee Coll. of Phila., 1778-91; mem. spl. bd. of Continental Congress to seek ways of reducing expenses, 1780; mem. U.S. Constl. Conv., 1787; pres. Pa. Supreme Exec. Council, 1788-90; pres. Pa. Constl. Conv., 1789-90; gov. Pa., 1790-99, favored war with

Eng. and alliance with France, 1793, helped suppress Whiskey Rebellion, 1794. Died Lancaster, Pa., Jan. 20, 1800; buried Lutheran Graveyard, Lancaster.

MILEN, FREDERICK BLUMENTHAL civ. and mech. engr.; b. Baltimore, Aug. 7, 1835; s. William and Sarah (Mickle) M.; ed. pvt. French sch., Baltimore, 1841-48; studied navigation, 1851; Md. Inst., 1852-56, Univ. of Glasgow, 1857-58; m. Mar., 1867, Gertrude Woodworth (died 1893). Asst. engr. Brooklyn Water-Works, 1856-59, Baltimore Water-Works, Apr.-Dec., 1859; asst. engr., 1860-63, chief engr., 1863-66, Havana (Cuba) R.R.; studied architecture, 1866-67; designer Bement & Dougherty, Phila., 1867-69, Ferris & Miles, 1869-79, alone, 1879-85, Bement, Miles & Co., 1885-1900; dir. (ex-v.p.) Niles-Bement-Pond Co., since 1900. Invented, 1870, steam hammer now in gen. use; has received 35 patents on machinery; went abroad, 1887, to study most approved foreign machinery for making armor plate, heavy steel cannon and ship-building; on return was engaged by Navy Dept. to design heavy gun lathes and other tools now in several navy yards and arsenals. Mem. Am. Soc. for Extension of Univ. Teaching (pres. since 1903). Residence: 40 W. 9th St. Office: 111 Broadway, New York.

MILES, EVAN army officer; b. McVeytown, Pa., Mar. 28, 1838; s. Richard and Hannah (Van Cleve) M.; m. Martha A. Stitzel, Dec. 17, 1874. Apptd. from Pa., 1st lt. 12th U.S. Inf., Aug. 5, 1861; capt., Jan. 20, 1865; transferred to 21st Inf., Sept. 21, 1866; maj. 25th Inf. Nov. 4, 1895; col. May 4, 1897; brig. gen. vols., Oct. 6, 1898; disch. from vol. service, Jan. 10, 1899; retired on account of disability in line of duty, Apr. 19, 1899; advanced to rank of brig. gen. retired, by act of Apr. 23, 1904. Bvtd. capt., Aug. 18, 1864, for gallantry during operations on Weldon R.R., Va.; maj. Feb. 27, 1890 for gallantry in actions against Indians in Idaho and Oregon.

MILES, MILTON EDWARD naval officer; b. Jerome, Ariz., Apr. 6, 1900; s. George Albert and Mae Belle (Cook) M.; grad. U.S. Naval Acad., 1922, postgrad., 1927-28; M.S., Columbia, 1929; m. Wilma Sinton Jerman, Sept. 4, 1925; children-William (dec.), Murray Edward, Charles Hammond. Apprentice seaman USN, 1917; commd. ensign, 1922, and advanced through grades to rear adm., 1945; comdr. U.S. Naval Group, China, World War II; comdt. 3d Naval District, N.Y.C.; vice adm., ret. 1958. Milton E. Miles Chair Internat. Relations established by Naval War Coll. Awarded D.S.M., Purple Heart (3), Legion of Merit (3); Order of Cloud and Banner Medal by Chinese Govt. (1st, 2d, 4th classes), various other fgn. decorations. Fellow Royal Canadian Geog. Soc.; mem. Am. Soc. Naval Engrs. Author: A Different Kind of War, pub. 1967. Home: 6404 Shadow Road, Kenwood, Chevy Chase, Md. 20015. Died Mar. 25, 1961; buried Arlington Nat. Cemetery.

MILES, NELSON APPLETON lt. gen. U.S.A.; b. Westminster, Mass., Aug. 8, 1839; s. Daniel and Mary (Curtis) M.; academic education; (LL.D., Harvard U., 1896, Brown U., 1901, Colgate U. 1910); m. Mary Hoyt Sherman, June 30, 1868. First lt. 22d Mass. Inf., Sept. 9, 1861; promoted through grades to brig. gen. U.S.A., Dec. 15, 1880; maj. gen., Apr. 5, 1890; lt. gen. U.S.A., June 6, 1900. Bvtd.; maj. gen. vols., Aug. 25, 1864, "for highly meritorious and distinguished conduct throughout campaign and particularly for gallantry and valuable services at battle of Reams Sta., Va." Brig. gen., Mar. 2, 1867, for same at Spottsylvania ; awarded Congressional Medal of Honor, July 23, 1892, "for distinguished gallantry at Chancellorsville (severely wounded)." Comd. an army corps of 26,000 men at twenty-five years of age; conducted several campaigns against hostile Indians on Western frontier, notably that against Sitting Bull, Crazy Horse, Chief Joseph, Geronimo and Natches; commanded United States troops at Chicago, during railroad strike troubles, 1894; represented U.S.A. at seat of Turco-Grecian War, and also at Queen Victoria's Diamond Jubilee, 1897; sr. officer, comdg. U.S.A., 1895-1903, comdg. U.S. Army during Spanis h-Am. War. Retired Aug. 8, 1903. President Jefferson Memorial Assn. Commanded Mass. Militia, 1905. Author: Personal Recollections, or From New England to the Golden Gate, 1896; Military Europe, 1898; Observations Abroad, or Report of Maj. Gen. Nelson A. Miles, Commanding U.S. Army, of His Tour of Observation in Europe, 1899; Serving the Republic, 1911. Home: Washington, D.C. Died May 15, 1925.

MILES, PERRY LESTER, army officer; b. Westerville, O., Oct. 15, 1873; s. James A. and Mary (Longwell) M.; grad. U.S. Mil. Acad., 1895, Army Sch. of the Line, 1916, Gen. Staff Sch., 1920, Army War Coll., 1921; m. Mary Latta Stott, Dec. 28, 1921. Commd. 2d lt. inf., U.S. Army, June 12, 1895, and advanced through grades to col., July 1, 1920; brig. gen., Feb. 1, 1932. Comd. 1st, 2d, 16th Brigs. and 1st Div.; served in Spanish-Am. War, Philippine Insurrection, Mexican border, World War; retired Oct. 31, 1937. Awarded D.S.C., D.S.M., Spanish-Am. War, Philippine Insurrection, Mexican Border and Victory medals (U.S.); officer Legion of Honor, Croix de Guerre with Palm (France). Protestant. Chmn. Shenandoah Valley Regional Defense Council, 1941; chmn. Staunton and Augusta County War Finance Com., 1943-45; chmn. Staunton Salvage Com., 1942-45. Clubs: Army and Navy (Washington); University (Winter Park, Fla.). Author: The Infantry Soldier: Notes for the Private and Corporal. Co-Author: Vol. 4 of Tactical Principles and Decisions, 1923; contbr. articles on military subjects. Home: 501 E. Beverly St., Staunton VA

MILLAR, EDWARD ALEXANDER army officer; b. in Ky., June 25, 1860; grad. U.S. Mil. Acad., 1833; grad. Arty. Sch., 1886; Army War Coll., 1909. Commd. 2d lt. 3d Arty., June 13, 1882; promoted through grades to col. 2d Field Arty. Dec. 1, 1911; trans. to 6th Field Arty., June 13, 1913, to 2d Field Arty., Jan. 27, 1914, to 3d Field Arty., 1916. Asst. instr. engring. and arty., Arty. Sch., Ft. Monroe, Va., 1891-96; a.d.c. to Gen. Edward B. Williston, 1898-99; with regt. in Philippine Islands, 1899; duty on Mexican border, comdr. 6th Brigade F.A., 6th Div., 5th Army Corps, A.E.F. in France, July 1918. Died Jan. 31, 1934.

MILLAR, ROBERT WYNESS lawyer, educator; b. Falkirk, Scotland, Apr. 10, 1876; s. Walter Robert and Dolina (Wyness) M.; came to U.S., 1886; LL.B., Northwestern U., 1897; M.A., 1916; m. Anne Everett George, June 10, 1919. Admitted to Ill. bar, 1897; practiced with Johnson & Morrill, 1897-1901; in partnership with William Herbert Johnson, 1901-09; practiced independently, 1910-15; inst. John Marshall Law Sch., 1903-10; resident prof., 1915-42, prof. emeritus, 1942—. Commd. maj. judge advocate, U.S. Army, Mar. 18, 1918; lt. col., Oct. 29, 1918; col., July 10, 1919; on duty Office of Judge Advocate Gen., Washington, Mar. 18, 1918-Sept. 3, 1919. Cons. to Jud. Adv. Council of Cook County, Ill., 1929-47; sec. for U.S., Stair Soc., (Scotland). Spl. asst. to under-sec. also to asst. sec. of navy, May 1942-Sept. 1945. Received Distinguished Civilian Service Award, Navy Dept., 1945. Mem. Am., Ill. State, Chgo. bar assns., Chgo. Law Inst., Am. Judicature Soc., Delta Theta Phi (hon.); fgn. mem. Acad. Nazionale dei Lincei (Italy), 1947; hon. mem. Instituto Espanol de Derecho Procesal; corr. mem. Associazione Italiana fra gli Studiosi del Processo Civile. Republican. Presbyn. Clubs: University (Chgo. and Evanston), Arts (Chgo.). Author: Common Law Pleading in Library of American Law and Practice, 1912; Formative Principles of Civil Procedure, 1923 (Spanish version, 1945); Civil Procedures of the Trial Court in Historical Perspective, 1952. Translator: Garofalo's Criminology (Modern Criminal Science Series), 1912; portion of History of Continental Criminal Law (Continental Legal History Series), 1916. Translator and editor: History of Continental Civil Procedure by Engelmann and others (in Continental Legal History Series), 1927. Contbr. essays and articles to legal publs. Home: 357 E. Chicago Av., Chgo. 11. Died Feb. 1959.

MILLARD, EARL, corp. exec.; b. Rushville, Ind., Mar. 6, 1905; s. John Akard and Pearl (Faught) M.; D.D.S., Washington U., 1929; m. Dorothy Nester, Oct. 28, 1933 children—Joseph Nester, Earl, Jr. Practiced dentistry, East St. Louis, Ill., 1929-48; exec. v.p. Obear Nester Glass Co., East St. Louis, State Savs. & Loan Assn., East St. Louis; director U.S. Partition & Packaging Corp., Milw., 1st Nat. Bank, E. St. Louis, Ill. Served as lt. comdr., USN, 1942-45; Mem. United States Brewers Association (bd. dirs.), Jr. C. of C. (past pres.), Beta Theta Pi. Clubs: Noonday, Old Warson, University (St. Louis); St. Clair Country (Belleville, Ill.), Racquet (St. Louis). Home: Belleville IL Died Jan. 1970.

MILLER, ALEXANDER MACOMB lt. col. corps of engr., U.S.A.; b. Washington; s. Gen Morris S.M., g.s. Gen. Alexander Macomb; apptd., March 2, 1861; grad. West Point, June 23, 1865, as 1st lt. engrs.; capt., Feb. 22, 1869; maj., April 16, 1883; lt. col., 1898; has been engaged in many engring works; now in charge office of Washington aqueduct. Home: Washington, D.C. Died 1904.

MILLER, CARL A(UGUST) banker; born East Millstone, N.J., July 31, 1891; s. August Christian and Caroline Augusta (Porgess) M.; grad. Peekskill Mil. Acad., 1902-07; B.S. in Civil Engring., New York U., 1911; C.E., 1912; m. Charlotte Sanford Baker, Nov. 3, 1915; children-Carolinn Ten Eyck (Mrs. Joseph H. Holmes, Jr.), William Sanford, Jean Stewart (Mrs. Henry C. Williams). Instr. civil engring. New York U., 1913; with Am. Telephone and Telegraph Co., Commercial Engring. Dept., 1914-20 (except for service World War I); asst. commercial engr. Irving Trust Co. (then Irving Nat. Bank), N.Y. City, 1920-26, asst. sec., 1926-28, asst. v.p., 1928, v.p. 1929-50, senior vice president since 1950; dir. Arkell & Smiths, Three States Realty Corp., Hudson House, Inc. Pilot, aviation section, Signal Corps, U.S. Army, 1917-19; disch. with rank of maj., Air Corps Res., 1919; commd. lt. col., U.S. Army, 1943; disch., 1945; with Mil. Govt. in North Africa, Sicily and So. Italy. Dir. and mem. exec. com. Tarrytown (N.Y.) Hosp., 1934-51; mem. vis. com. N.Y.U. Coll. Engring., 1948-51. Mem. Am. Inst. Banking, Pilgrims of U.S., Mil. Order World Wars, Vets. Fgn. Wars, Delta Phi, Ind. Rep. Episcopalian. Clubs: University, Racquet and Tennis (New York); Ardsley Country (Ardsley on Hudson, N.Y.); Blind Brook Golf (Port Chester, N.Y.); Adirondack League (Old Forge, N.Y.); U.S. Seniors Golf Assn. Home: Ardsley-on-Hudson, N.Y. Office: 1 Wall St., N.Y.C. Died Aug. 23, 1953.

MILLER, CHARLES merchant, soldier; b. Oberhoffen Alsace, France, June 15, 1843; common sch. edn (A.M. Bucknell U.); came to U.S., 1854. Entered oil bus., 1869, and was pres. Galena-Signal Oil Co. many yrs., now chmn. bd. Chmn. bd. Am. Steel Foundry Co., Am. Locomotive Co., and dir. about 40 other corps.; pres. Lake Erie, Franklin & Clarion R.R. Co. Mayor of Franklin, Pa., 2 terms; mem. Pa. State Board of Charities 6 years; maj.-gen. Pa. N.G. 5 years. Supt. 1st Baptist S.S. of Franklin from 1872 and conducts Bible class of more than 600 pupils; has maintained at own expense, at Franklin, the Miller Night Sch., 1890-. Decorated by French Govt. as Chevalier of Legion of Honor for eminent services to industry and commerce. Home: Franklin, Pa. Died Dec. 20, 1927.

MILLER, CROSBY PARKE Brig. gen.; b. Ponfret, Vt., Oct. 20, 1843; s. Crosby and Orpha (Hewitt) M; ed. pub. schs. and West Point; m. Frances Laura Haskin, May 28, 1874. Enlisted as corporal Co. G, 16th Vt. Vol. Inf., Sept. 4, 1862; disch. Mar. 12, 1863; apptd. U.S Mil. Acad., July 1, 1863; commd. 2d lt. 4th U.S. Arty., June 17, 1867; promoted through grades to col. q.m. vols., July 12, 1898-Mar. 2, 1899; lt. col. deputy q.m. gen. U.S.A., Oct. 2, 1902; brig. gen., Mar. 30, 1906; retired at own request, over 40 yrs.' service, Mar. 31, 1906. Home: Burlington, Vt. Died Mar. 20, 1927.

MILLER, EDWARD TYLOR congressman; b. Woodside, Md., Feb. 1, 1895; s. Guion and Annie E. (Tylor) M.; grad. Sidwell's Friends Sch., Washington, D.C., 1912; A.B., Yale, 1916; student George Washington U. Law Sch., 1917; m. Jospehine W. Ford, Nov. 14, 1942; 1 step-son, Theodore G. Miller. Admitted to Md. bar, 1920; in gen. practice of law, Easton, Md., 1920-41 and since May 1946; referee in bankruptcy, Easton, Md., 1924-42; police and juvenile court justice, Talbot County, Md., 1935-39; atty. for town of Easton, 1929-42; mem. 80th-85th Congresses, 1st Md. Dist. Commd. 2d lt. inf. O.R.C., 1917; served as inf. capt. A.E.F., 1918-19; grad. Army Sch. of the Line, Langres, France; commd. col. inf. res., 1937; active duty as col. inf. in maneuvers, 1940-41; served in North Africa, India, China, 1942-46. Awarded Collar Order of Yun Hui (China). Mem. Md. State Bar Assn., Yale Football "Y" Assn., Am. legion (past comdr.), V.F.W., Am. Bar Assn., Phi Beta Kappa, Psi Upsilon, Omicron Delta Kappa. Republican. Mem. Soc. of Friends. Mason (Shriner). Clubs: Chesapeake Bay Yacht (commodore 1941), Miles River Yacht, Talbot Country, 14 W. Hamilton St., (Balt.); The Grange, Lions, Elks. Home: The Pines, Easton. Office: 121 N. Washington St., Easton, Md. Died Jan. 20, 1968.

MILLER, ERNEST B. state ofcl.; b. Gloversville, N.Y., Sept. 15, 1898; s. George J. and Adelaide Rose (Brumaghim) M.; grad. Inf. Sch., Ft. Benning, Ga.; m. Anna Marie Hauber, Oct. 17, 1921; children-Marilynn Ann (Mrs. Paul A. Bender), Patricia Faith, James B. (died on Anzio beachhead 1944) Thomas H., Richard J. Civil engr., land surveyor, 1923—, Park Rapids, Minn., 1923-30; chief engr. Camp Ripley Mil. Reservation, 1930-40; asst. commr. charge airport engring. Minn. Dept. Aeros., 1947-49; mem. state com. for topographic mapping state Minn., 1948-50, dir. Civil Def., 1950-55. Served as enlisted man 1st inf., Minn. N.G., Mexican Border campaign, 1916-17; with 135th inf. 34th Div., also 9th inf. 2d Div., U.S. Army, 1917-19; col., comdr. 194th tank bn., Bataan, 1941-47 (Japanese prisoner 3 yrs., 5 mos). Mem. Internat. War Vets. Alliance (between U.S. and Can.), 2d v.p., 1950-51, 1st v.p., 1951-52, pres., 1952-53, mem. bd. dirs., 1953-55. Decorated 3 Presdl. Unit Citations. Medal of Valor, Silver Star, Purple Heart. Mem. Nat. Assn. State Civil Def. Dirs. U.S. (v.p.), Am. Legion (Past adj., vice comdr., post comdr., dist. comdr., 1931-32, state dept. comdr. 1946-47, chmn. dept. nat. def. com.), 40 and 8, Minn. Soc. Profl. Engrs. (chmn. com. for study efficient procurement, assignment profl. engrs., allied professions for nat. emergency), Nat. Soc. Profl. Engrs. Author: Bataan Uncensored, 1949. Home: 124 Banning Av., White Bear Lake, St. Paul 10. Died Feb. 20, 1959; buried Ft. Snelling Nat. Cemetery, Mpls.

MILLER, FRED W. army officer; b. Manchester, Ia., May 10, 1891; commd. 1st lt. inf., July 1920, and advanced through the grades to brig. gen., June 1942; maj. gen., Oct. 1942; became operations and training officer, G-3, Seventh Corps Area. Omaha, Neb., Aug. 1940; operations and training officer, G-3, VIII Army Corps, hdqrs. Brownwood, Tex., July 1941, later assigned to Inf. Div.; assumed command, 93d Inf. Div., Oct. 1942; retired as major gen., June 1944. Deceased

MILLER, JAMES brig. gen.; b. in Mass., Feb. 11, 1844. Served pvt. Co. B. 50th Mass. Inf., Sept. 11, 1862-Aug. 24, 1863; 2nd lt. 4th Mass. Cav., Jan 2, 1864; lst lt. Feb. 8, 1864; hon. mustered out, Nov. 14, 1865; 2d lt. U.S. Inf., Feb. 23, 1866; 1st lt. July 28, 1866; transferred to 2d Inf., Apr. 17, 1869; capt. June 7, 1879; maj. 20th Inf., Apr. 26, 1898; transferred to 22d Inf., Sept. 10, 1903; retired at own request, over 40 yrs.' service, Aug. 12, 1903. Home: Temple, N.H. Died Dec. 11, 1916.

MILLER, JESSE, lawyer; b. Lexington, Ky., July 12, 1891; s. Lsidor Jacob and Jennie (Faller) M.; A.B., U. of Ky., 1912, M.A., 1913, LL.B., 1914; m. Florence B. Glaser, July 15, 1923; children-Jesse I., Jane Elsie.

Admitted to Ky. bar, 1913; practiced law at Lexington, 1913-17, Washington, D.C., 1920-33, 1934-41 and since 1946; asst. solicitor Bur. Internal Revenue, 1919-20; spl. rep. U.S. Govt. for Nicaraguan presdl. elections, 1920; exec. dir. National Labor Bd., 1933-34; civilian advisory representative on War-Justice Dept. to plan for treatment of enemy aliens. Served as pvt. and sergt. Hdqrs., 38th Div., 1917-18; lt. and capt. U.S. Army, 1918-19; aide-de-camp, Maj. Gen. E. H. Crowder, provost marshal gen., 1918-19; maj. judge adv., 1919-20. Col. U.S. Army, 1942-46; asso. dir. Sch. Mil. Govt., dir. Mil. Govt., div. Provost Marshall Gen's. Office. Awarded Legion of Merit (declined). Mem. Am. Bar Assn., Delta Chi. Democrat. Jewish religion. Clubs: Woodmont Country (Bethesda, Md.): Loudoun Golf and Country (Purcellville, Va.); Army and Navy (Washington). Author: Spirit of Selective Service (with Maj. Gen. E. H. Crowder), 1919; also articles on federal taxation and labor relations. Home: 14 Oxford St., Chevy Chase, Md. Office: Woodward Bldg., Washington, D.C. Died Nov. 9, 1949.

MILLER, JOSEPH NELSON naval officer; b. Springfield, O., Nov. 22, 1836; apptd. acting midshipman, U.S. Naval Acad., from Ohio 1851, grad. 1856; m. Nov. 22, 1866; 2d Nov. 13, 1877. Promoted passed misdhipman, Nov. 22, 1856; advanced through grades to rear admiral U.S.N., Mar. 21, 1897. Served on Independence, 1854-56; instr. Naval Acad., 1857-58; on Preble, 1858-60; comd. Perry and served on Cambridge, at aval Acad., on Pocahontas and Passale, Sacramento and Sangamon, 1860-63; was present at attacks on Forts McAllister and Sumter; on Monadnock, 1864-67; took part in both attacks on Ft. Fisher; Powhatan, 1867-69; chief of staff Southern Squadron, Pacific Fleet, 1870-72; Hydrographic Office, 1873, 1874-75; comd. Ajax, 1873-74, Tuscarora, 1875-76; Bureau Yards and Docks and lighthouse duty, 1876-80; spl. duty at Washington, 1880-81, comd. receiving-ship Wabash, 1881, Tennessee, 1882; Spl. duty and comdg. Tennessee, 1883-84; comd. receiving-ship Wabash, 1885-88; 1888-91; comd. Chicago, 1891-92, receiving-ship 1892-94; com - Vermont dt. Navy Yard, Boston, 1894-97; naval representative at Queen Victoria's jubil ee, 1897, with Brooklyn as flagship; comdr.-in-chief Pacific Fleet, 1897-98; retired Nov. 22, 1898. Died 1909.

MILLER, KNOX EMERSON, U.S. Pub. Health Service; b. Norton, Kan., Nov. 26, 1886; s. Joseph Medford and Martha Washington (Whiteman) M.; A.B., William Jewell Coll., Liberty, Mo., 1908; M.D., Johns Hopkins, 1912; m. Noxie Bliss Miller, Oct. 29, 1915; children—Martha Vincent (Mrs. Pope A. Laurence), Betty Bow (Mrs. Richard O. Madson). Knox Emerson. Staff mem. Va. State Health Dept., 1912-14; commd. asst. surgeon U.S.P.H.S., 1914, passed asst. surgeon, 1918, surgeon, 1922, senior surgeon, 1934, medical director, 1940; research in rural health adminstrn., 1917-19; spl. consultant and dir. rural health adminstrn. N.C. State Dept. of Health, 1919-23; same La. State Dept. of Health, 1923-27; exec. officer Marine Hosp., N.Y., 1927-28; med. officer in charge Marine Hosp., Evansville, Ind., 1928-31; dir. rural health, Tex. State Dept. of Health, 1931-34; health consultant to states of Gulf region and Pacific Southwest, 1934-35, to states of Great Lakes region, 1935-36; asst. to asst. surgeon gen. in charge Domestic Quarantine Div., 1936-38; dir. Med. Research and Advisory Div., Federal Trade Commn., 1938-40; liason officer, 8th Service Command Headquarters, U.S. Army, Dallas, 1940-46; dist. dir. 9th Dist., U.S.P.H.S., Dallas, 1941-49, ret.; asst. state health officer of Fla. from 1949; dir. Chicago-Cook County Health Survey. Member mission to study strategic bombing in Japan. Diplomate, Am. Bd. Preventive Medicine and Pub. Health. Fellow A.M.A., Am. Pub. Health Assn.; mem. Assn. Mil. Surgeons (life), A.A.A.S., Asociacion Nacional de Venereolgia (Mexico), Tex. Acad. Sci., Sci. Soc., San Antonio, U.S.-Mexico Border Pub. Health Assn., Alpha Omega Alpha, Phi Chi, Lambda Chi Alpha, Pi Gamma Mu, Celsus Soc., Ho Din of Southwestern Medical Foundation. Clubs: Cosmos (Washington, D.C.). Contbr. professional articles to med. and pub. health mags. Home: Jacksonville FL Died May 1969.

MILLER, LAWRENCE WILLIAM educator, psychologist; b. Niles, Mich., June 26, 1897; s. Edward F. and Anna C. (Wesselhoft) M.; B.S., Mich. State Coll., 1919; A.M., U. Chgo., 1921; Ph.D., State U. Ia., 1929; m. Ruth Ank Miles, June 24, 1922; children-Jacob Hall, Rebecca Ann, Lawrence William. Food and drug chemist Mich. State Food and Drug Commn., 1919-20; asst. prof. edn. Kent State U., 1922-26, registrar, 1926-27; asst. prof. psychology State U. Ia., 1928-30; prof., chmn. dept. psychology U. Denver since 1930, chmn. div. edn. and psychology, acting dir., sch. edn. 1952; cons. psychologist for nursing schs. since 1938; psychol. examiner Colo. State Civil Service and Merit System intermittently since 1940; civilian psychologist A.U.S., 1942; psychol. cons. VA, 1946-; dir. 2 large research projects USAF, 1954-56; dir. research in exptl. hypnosis under grant from Gesshickter Fund for Medical Research, 1953-56. Trustee Variety Club Found., 1951. Diplomate Am. Bd. Examiners in Profl. Psychology. Fellow Am. Psychol. Assn. (pres. Rocky Mountain br. 1939-40, 44-45), A.A.A.S.; mem. Colo.-Wyo. Acad. Sci. (dir. 1940-45), Midwest, Colo. psychol. assns., Nat. Soc. Study Edn., Soc. Advancement Edn., Am. Assn. U.Profs., N.E.A., COlo. Edn. Assn., Sigma Xi, Phi Delta Kappa, Psi Chi. Clubs: Colorado Schoolmasters; Buchtel. Author articles, monographs and coll. placement exams. Home: 1120 S. Gilpin St., Denver 80210. Died Feb. 16, 1961.

MILLER, LUTHER DECK, army officer; b. Pennsylvania, June 14, 1890; B.D., Chicago Theol. Sem., 1917; grad. Chaplains Sch., 1922. Commd. 1st lt., chaplain, U.S. Army, 1918, and advanced through the grades to maj. gen., 1945; chief of chaplains, U.S. Army. Elected canon and mem. Presbytery of Washington Cathedral. Home: Washington DC Died Apr. 27, 1972.

MILLER, MARCUS P. brig. gen. U.S.A., Feb. 15, 1899; b. in Mass.; entered Mil. Acad., Sept. 1, 1854; bvt. 2d lt. 4th arty., July 1, 1858; commd. 2d lt., Sept. 26, 1859; lst lt., May 14, 1861; capt., May 11, 1864; lt. col. 1st arty., Oct. 10, 1894; col. Apr. 39 8, brig. gen. U.S. vols.; comd. brigade in Manila, 1898-99. Bvtd. capt., July 1, 1862, for gallantry at Malvern Hill; maj., Mar. 13, 1865, for gallantry in cav. campaign from Winchester to Richmond, Va.; lt. col., Mar. 31, 1865, for gallantry at Dinwiddie Court House, Va., col., Feb. 27, 1890 for gallantry and ability in Indian campaigns in Lava Beds, Calif., Apr. 17, 1873, and at Clearwater, Ida., July 1877. Retired Mar. 27, 1899. Died 1906.

MILLER, MERRILL rear admiral U.S.N.; b. Bellefontaine, O., Sept. 13, 1842; s. Henry and Mary M.; apptd. from Ohio, and grad U.S. Naval Acad., 1862; m. Sarah Katharine Lynch, July 11, 1865. Promoted ensign Oct. 13, 1862; lt., Feb. 22, 1864; lt. comdr., July 25, 1866; comdr., Nov. 25, 1877; capt., Feb. 25, 1893; rear admiral, July 1, 1900. Served on Potomac, Atlantic and Gulf coast and Santee, 1861-62; Miss. Squadron, 1862-63; participated in battles of Arkansas Post, 1862, and Haines' Bluff, 1863; in charge of mortar boats... at siege of Vicksburg, 1863; served N. Atlantic Blockading Squadron, 1863-65; expdn. up James River, 1864; both attacks on Ft. Fisher; Monadnock, 1865-66; Naval Acad., 1874-79; Lancaster, 1869-72; receiving-ship Sabine, 1872-73; exec. officer Worcester, 1873-74; Naval Acad. 1874-79; comd. Yantic, 1880-81; light house insp. 6th dist., 1881-85; comd. Marion, 1885-87; Navy Yard, Portsmouth 1888-89; Naval Home, Phila., 1800-92; light house insp. 1st dist., 1892-93; comd. receiving-ship Franklin, 1893-94, Raleigh, 1894-97, receiving-ship Vermont, 1897-1900; commandant, Navy Yard, Mare Island, 1900-03, Pacific naval dist., 1903-04; retired by operation of law, Sept. 13, 1904. Home: Berkeley, Calif. Died Aug. 5, 1914.

MILLER, OTTO investment banker; b. Cleve., July 3, 1874; s. James Hawkins and Sophie (Maxmillian) M.; prep. edn. University Sch., Cleve.; Ph.B., Yale, 1896; m. Elisabeth Clark Tyler, Dec. 4, 1901; children-Otto, Washington Samuel Tyler; m. 2d, Barbara Woolworth. Began in investment banking business with Lamprecht Bros. & Co., Cleve., 1899; founded (with Warren S. Hayden) firm Hayden, Miller & Co., 1903; dir. of many corps. Mem. Ohio N.G., 13 yrs.; 2 mos., advancing to maj. Cav.; served as a.d.c. to Govs. Herrick, Pattison and Harmon; q.m. sgt. Ohio Cav., Span.-Am. War, 1898; commd. maj. 37th Div., U.S. Army, 1917, later asst. chief of staff and lt. col.; in active service at Baccarat, Avocourt and Pannes sectors, also Meuse-Argonne and Ypres-Lys offensives. Mem. S.A.R., Spanish War Vets., Loyal Legion, Am. Legion, Mil. Order Fgn. Wars. Decorated Croix de Guerre (Belgian and French). Republican. Clubs: Union, Mid-Day, Country (Cleve.). Home: 2700 Easton Rd., Shaker Heights, O. Office: 1840 Union Commerce Bldg., Cleve. 14. Died June 13, 1950; buried Lakeview Cemetery, Cleve.

MILLER, RICHARD HENRY surgeon; b. Fitchburg, Mass., Oct. 11, 1884; s. Ernest Parker and Myra Bolles (Richardson) M.; A.B., Harvard, 1905, M.D., 1910; m. Georgina Mary Jardine, Sept. 23, 1922; 1 son, Richard H., Jr. Began practice at Boston, 1910; mem. bd. consultation Massachusetts General Hsop.; cons. surgeon Boston Lying-in Hosp., Heywood, Leominster Hospital; consultant at Pawtucket Hospital, Pawtucket, R.I. Served as maj. Medical Corps, United States Army, regimental surg., 101st F.A., World War I. Awarded Purple Heart with oak-leaf cluster; Silver Star. Fellow American College Surgeons; mem. American Surgical Assn., Internat. Surg. Soc., N.E. Surg. Soc., Surg. Research Soc. Republican. Mason. Club: Harvard (Boston). Author: Tuberculosis of the Lymphatic System, 1934. Contbr. to med. and surg. jours. Home: 64 Myrtle St. (14). Office: 264 Beacon St., Boston 16,. Died June 3, 1953.

MILLER, ROBERT ROWLAND, aircraft mfr.; b. Santa Monica, Cal., July 29, 1903; s. Robert M. and Nettie R. (Rowland) M.; A.B., U. Cal. at Berkeley, 1926; m. Mary Mattison, Mar. 21, 1934. Salesman Wm. Cavalier & Co., Los Angeles, 1926-28; customers man Sutro & Co., mem. N.Y. Stock Exchange, Los Angeles, 1928-35, resident partner, 1935-40; exec. v.p. Menasco Mfg. Co., Burbank, 1940-47; asst. to pres. Republic Aviation Corp., N.Y.C., 1948-50; with Northrop Corp., from 1950, assistant to president 1954, adminstrv. v.p., 1955, v.p., gen. mgr., dir. 1955-58, sr. v.p., dir. from 1958; pres. Alexander Hotel Co., Long Beach, from 1945. Mem. Conquistadores Del Cielo. Clubs: Burning Tree; Los Angeles Country, California. Home: Los Angeles CA Died Dec. 19, 1971; buried Woodlawn Cemetery, West Los Angeles CA

MILLER, SAMUEL WARREN army officer; b. in Pa., Feb. 10, 1857; grad. U.S. Mil. Acad., 1879. Commd. 2d lt. 5th Inf., June 13, 1879; 1st lt., Mar. 7, 1885; capt., Jan. 26, 1898; maj. 46th U.S. Inf., Aug. 17, 1899; hon. mustered out vols., May 31, 1901; maj. 19th Inf. July 30, 1902; insp. gen., May 25, 1906; lt. col. 25th Inf., Apr. 2, 1910; col. of inf., Nov. 2, 1912; assigned to 10th Inf., Apr. 25, 1914; col., Nov. 12, 1912; brig. gen. N.A., Aug. 5, 1917. Prof. mil. science and tactics, Purdue U., Lafayette, Ind., 1894-98; at Tampa, Fla., during Spanish-Am. War; chief mustering officer, State of Pa., 1899; organized 46th Inf., U.S. Vols., and served with regt. in Philippine Islands, 1899-1900; acting and insp. gen. 1st and 2d brigades, Dept. Southern Luzon, 1901; again in P.I., as insp. gen. and asst. insp. gen., 1906-08; apptd. comdr. 160th Depot brigade, Camp Custer, Battle Creek, Mich., Sept. 1917. Died Apr. 22, 1940.

MILLER, TROUP army officer (ret.); b. Percy, Ga., Feb. 10, 1879; s. Alexander Lawton and Katharine Elvira Flewellyn (Hurt) M.; B.S., U.S. Mil. Acad., 1902; grad. Mounted Service Sch., 1911, Army Staff Coll., Lengres, France, 1918, Sch. of the Line, 1921, Army War Coll., 1925; m. Rosa Coffin, Nov. 4, 1903; children-Troup Jr. (Maj. Gen. USAF), Rosa Coffin (wife of Col. Frederic Wood Barnes, Air Force). Commissioned 2d lt., Cav., United States Army, June 12, 1902, and advanced through the grades to brig. gen., Feb. 2, 1943; served on Gen. Staff, 82d Div. I Army Corps, First Army, and Intermediate Sect., Services of Supply World War I; inspector gen. Eastern Defense Command, Governors Island, N.Y., World War II; retired 1946. Decorated D.S.M., Legion of Merit, Army Commendation ribbon, Mem. Mil. Order World Wars, Assn. of Grads. U.S. Mil. Acad., Author: Supply Principles, 1920. Home: 2332 Dellwood Dr., N.W.; Atlanta. Died Jan. 26, 1957; buried Arlington Nat. Cemetery.

MILLER, WARNER senator; b. Hannibal, N.Y., Aug. 12, 1838; reared on farm; A.B. Union Coll., 1860 (LL.D.; LL.D., Syracuse U., 1891); prof. Greek and Latin, Ft. Edward Collegiate Inst., 1860-61; pvt., sergt. maj. and lt. colonel 5th N.Y. Cav., Civil War; m. Caroline Churchill, 1864. Established as paper mfr. in Herkimer, N.Y. Mem. N.Y. Assembly, 1874-76; elected to 46th and 47th Congresses (1879-81); elected U.S. senator for term 1881-87, and resigned from 47th Congress. Has been prominent in Nicaragua Canal project. Home: Herkimer, N.Y. Died Mar. 21, 1918.

MILLER, WARREN HASTINGS author, editor; b. Honesdale, Pa., Aug. 21, 1876; s. Everard Patterson and Sophie Degen (Hastings) M.; M.E., Stevens Inst. Tech., 1898; m. Susan Barse, Nov. 15, 1899; children- Warren Hastings, Peter Cravath. Constrn. engr. Erie Electric Co., Fairbanks-Morse Co., C.C.C. & St.L. Ry., Standard Oil Co., 1900-08; writer in Paris, France, 1909-10; editor Field and Stream, N.Y., also v.p. Field & Stream Pub. Co., 1910-18. Served as able seaman N.J. Naval Reserve, 1896-98; ensign USN, 1898-99, lt. (j.g.) to lt., 1918-19; Fleet Res.; comdr. U.S. W.V., William McKinley Camp, No. 26; past pres. Council No. 7. Episcopalian. Author: Camp Craft, 1915; Boy's Book of Hunting and Fishing, 1916; Airedale Setter and Hound, 1916; Outdoorsman's Handbook, 1917; Canoeing, Sailing and Motor Boating, 1917; Rifles and Shotgun, 1917; Camping Out, 1918; The American Hunting Dog, 1919; Ring-Necked Grizzly, 1920; Sea Fighters, 1920; The Sportsman's Workshop, 1921; The Black Panther of the Navaho, 1921; In Darkest New Guinea, 1921; The Castaways of Banda Sea, 1921; Across Borneo, 1922; Red Mesa, 1923; The Ape-Man of Sumatra, 1923; Medicine Gold, 1924; On Tiger Trails in Burma, 1925; White Buffalo, 1926; Pirate Archipelago, 1926; All Around the Mediterranean, 1926; Sahara Sands, 1927; Ensign Wally Radnor, U.S. Navy, 1928; Under the Admiral's Stars, 1929; Tiger Bridge; 1937; Boys of '17, 1939; Lone Woodsman, 1943; The Home Builders, 1946. Home: 230 3d Av., Indialantic, Fla. Died July 14, 1960; buried East Gloucester, Mass.

MILLER, WATSON B. govt. official; b. Rensselaer Ind., 1878; s. Daniel Bahan and Martha (Kirk) M.; LL.D., Dickinson Coll.; m. Inez Hale Hemphill; 1 son, Watson B. Dir. Am. Legion Rehab. Com., Washington, 1923-41; asst. adminstr. FSA, 1941-45; adminstr. Fed. Security, 1945-47; commr. U.S. Immigration and Naturalization Service, Washington, 1947-50; mem. Subversive Activities Control Bd., Washington. Served as capt. Motor Transport Corps, World War I, Bd. dirs. A.R.C., Washington. Awarded Medal for Merit; Order of Crown of Italy; Medal of Liberation (France). Mem. Menninger Found., Am. Acad. Social and Polit. Sci. Am. Legion (40 and 8), Am. Pub. Health Assn., Am. Social Hygiene Assn., Mil. Order World Wars. Clubs: Army-Navy, Washington Golf and Country, Nat. Press. Post Mortem (Washington). Home: 4704 Yuma St. N.W., Washington. Died Feb. 11, 1961; buried Arlington Nat. Cemetery.

MILLER, WILLIAM DAVIS trustee; b. Providence, Nov. 5, 1887; s. Augustus Samuel and Elizabeth LeMoine (Davis) M.; A.B., Brown U., 1909; postgrad. Harvard, 1910-12; m. Mary Heard Chew Bell, Oct. 11,

1919. Mem. bd. investment Peoples Savs. Bank. Trustee, pres. Providence Pub. Library; trustee Brown U., R.I. Hosp.; v.p. Hosp. Service Corp. of R.I.; mem. bd. mgmt. John Carter Brown Library. Served as comdr. USNR, World War II. Member R.I. Library Assn. (ex-pres.), R.I., (sec., ex-pres.), Mass. (corr.) hist. socs., Am. Antiquarian Soc., Am. Oxford bibliog. socs., Navy Records Soc., Naval Hist. Found., U.S. Naval Inst. (asso.), S.C.W. Walpole Soc. Nautical Research (Eng.). Episcopalian. Clubs: Hope, Art, Agawam Hunt (Providence); Odd Volumes, Union (Boston); Century, Grolier (New York); Metropolitan, Army and Navy (Washington, D.C.); Laurentian (Canada). Author several hist. brochures. Contbr. hist. articles. Home: 118 Woodruff Av., Wakefield, R.I. 02880. Died July 7, 1959.

MILLIGAN, JACOB L. ex-congressman; b. Richmond, Mo., Mar. 9, 1889; s. Wm. M. and Mary (Rothrock) M.; U. Mo., 1910-14; married; 1 stepson, William Finley. Admitted to Mo. bar, 1913, and practiced at Richmond, as mem. Roberts, Milligan & Milligan, now Milligan, J.L. "Tuck" Kansas City, Missouri District February 1920; succeeding Joshua Alexander, term ending 1921; reelected 68th to 72nd Congresses (1933-35), Mo. at large. Capt., 6th Mo. Inf., June 2-Oct. 30, 1917; capt. 140th Inf., U.S. Army, Oct. 30, 1917-May 14, 1919; twice cited for bravery in Meuse-Argonne offensive. Decorated Silver Star, Purple Heart. Democrat. Mason. Home: 501 Knickerbocker Pl. Office: Nat. Fidelity Life Bldg., Kansas City, Mo. Died Mar. 9, 1951; buried, Liberty, Mo.

MILLIGAN, ROBERT WILEY naval officer; b. Phila., Apr. 8, 1843; s. James and Mary (thornton) M; ed. pub. and high schs., Phila.; m. Sarah Ann DuBois, Feb. 17, 1870. Entered U.S.N., as 3d asst. engr., Aug. 3, 1863; 2d asst. engr., July 25, 1866; passed asst. engr., Mar. 25, 1874; chief engr., Feb. 20, 1892; comdr., Mar. 3, 1899; capt. Nov. 7, 1902; advanced to rank of rear adm. and retired, Apr, 8, 1905. Served on U.S.S. Mackinaw in N. Atlantic Blockading Squadron during Civil War, participating in both battles of Ft. Fisher, fall of N.C., and fall of Petersburg and Richmond, Va.; on duty later in N. and S. Atlantic and Pacific Squadrons and as instr. U.S. Naval Acad.; chief engr. battleship Oregon on her run from Pacific to Atlantic coast and engr. same vessel in battle of Santiago; fleet engr. N. Atlantic Fleet, on flagship New York, for 1 yr.; chief engr. Norfolk Navy Yard, 1899-1905. Episcopalian. Republican. Home: Norfolk, Va. Died 1909.

MILLIKAN, GEORGE LEE govt., internat. affairs specialist, educator; b. Murphysboro, Ill., June 10, 1912; s. Elzie Clifton and Edith Leota (Rolens) M.; A.A. cum laude, Compton Jr. Coll., 1932; A.B. magna cum laude, U. So. Cal., 1934, grad. study, 1934-35, M.A., Yale (Cowles fellow govt.), 1938, Ph.D., 1942; grad. Naval Sch. Mil. Govt. and Adminstrn., Columbia, 1943; m. Gertrude Louise Mann, Aug. 23, 1941; children-Louise Cane, James Rolens. Inst. govt. Yale, 1938-39, polit. sci. U. Vt., 1939-45, asst. to dep. sec. U.S. Joint Chiefs Staff, 1942-46; asst. prof. govt. La. State U., 1946-47; mem. Internat. Studies Group, Brookings Inst., Washington, 1947-49; staff cons., com. fgn. affairs U.S. Ho. Reps., 1949—. Served from lt. (j.g.) to lt. comdr. USNR., mem. staff. comdr. 12th Fleet and Naval Forces, Europe, 1943-44, aide, flag sec. to comdr. U.S. Naval Ports and Bases, France, 1944-45. Decorated Sec. Navy's Commendation medal and ribbon, E.T.O. Mem. Am., So. polit. sci. assns., Am. Soc. Internat. Law, Phi Beta Kappa, Phi Kappa Phi, Phi Theta Kappa, Phi Kappa Tau. Conglist. Author staff reports, com. fgn. affairs U.S.Ho. Reps. Editor, contbr. Major Problems of U.S. Fgn. Policy, 1947-48, 1948-49. Contbr. ednl. jours. Home: 2924 Cortland Pl. N.W. Office: Committee on Foreign Affairs, U.S. House of Representatives, Washington Deceased.

MILLIKAN, ROBERT ANDREWS physicist; b. Morrison, Ill., Mar. 22, 1868; s. Rev. Silas Franklin and Mary Jane (Andrews) M.; A.B., Oberlin, 1891, A.M., 1893; Ph.D., Columbia, 1895; univs. of Berlin and Gottingen, 1895-96; Sc.D., Oberlin, 1911, Northwestern, 1913, U. of Pa., 1915, Columbia, 1917, Amherst, 1917, U. of Dublin, 1924, Yale, 1925, Leeds U., 1927, Princeton, 1928, New York U., 1929, Harvard, 1932, U. of Rochester, 1934, U. of Melbourne, 1939; LL.D., U. of Calif., 1924, U. of Colo., 1927, Univ. of Mich., 1929, U. of Southern Calif., 1931, Mills. Coll., 1935, Loyola University, 1938, University of Chicago, 1941, William Jewell College, Liberty, Missouri, 1944; hon. Ph.D., King John Casimer University, Poland, 1926, U. of Ghent, 1927; Docteur Honoris Causa University of Liege, 1930; U. of Paris, 1939; LL.D., Bradley University, 1952. married Greta Irvin Blanchard, April 10, 1902; children-Clark Blanchard, Glenn Allan (dec.), Max Franklin. Tutor physics, Oberlin, 1891-93; member physics staff U. of Chicago, 1896-1921; director Norman Bridge Lab. of Physics, and chmn. exec. council Calif. Inst. Tech., Pasadena, 1921-45; prof. emeritus, v.p. bd. trustees, since 1945. Served as lt. col. Signal Corps, U.S. Army, 1918, and chief of science and research div. of Signal Corps, Am. mem. Com. on Intellectual Cooperation of League of Nations, 1923. Fellow in Germany of Oberlaender Trust, 1931. Trustee Huntington Library. Awarded Comstock prize, National Academy of Sciences, 1913; Edison medalist Am. Inst. E.E., 1922; Hughes medalist Royal Soc. of Great Britain, 1923; Nobel prize in physics, 1923; Faraday medalist London Chem. Soc., 1924; Matteucci medalist Societa Italiana della Scienze, 1925; gold medalist Am. Soc. Mech. Engrs., 1926; Messel medalist Soc. of Chem. Industry (British), 1928; gold medal Holland Soc., 1928, Soc. Arts and Sciences, 1929, Radiol Soc. of North America, 1930; gold medal from Roosevelt Memorial Assn., 1932; gold medal of Franklin Inst., 1937; Joy Kissen Mookerjee gold medal of the Indian Assn. for Cultivation Sci., 1939; Oersted medal of Am. Assn. of Physics Teachers, 1940. Decorated Chevalier de l'Ordre National de la Légion d'Honneur, 1931, comdr., 1936; Order of the Jade (China), 1940; Official of Order Al Merito (Chile), 1944; Medal for Merit (United States), 1947. Fellow of the American Academy Arts and Sciences, A.A.A.S. (pres. 1929); mem. Nat. Acad. Sciences, American Philosophical Society, Am. Physical Soc. (pres. 1916-18), and hon. member 21 foreign scientific societies; member Sigma Xi, Phi Beta Kappa; asso. Royal Acad. Belgium, 1935; hon. fellow Indian Acad. Sciences, Stanford U., 1941. Clubs: University Club (New York); Sunset (Los Angeles). Author: (or co-author) A Course of College Experiments in Physics, 1898; Theory of Optics (translated from the German), 1900; Mechanics, Molecular Physics and Heat, 1901; A First Course in Physics, 1906; A Laboratory Course in Physics for Secondary Schools, 1906; Electricity, Sound and Life, 1923; Elements of Physics, 1917; Evolution of Science and Religion, 1927; Science and the New Civilization, 1930; Time, Matter and Values, 1932; Electrons (and -), Protons, Photons, Neutrons, and Cosmic Rays, 1935, rev. edit., 1947; New Elementary Physics, 1936; Mechancis, Molecular Physics, Heat and Sound, 1937; Cosmic Rays, 1939; Autobiography, 1950. Contbr. to tech. jours. Home: 1640 Oak Grove Av., San Marino, Cal. Died Dec. 19, 1953; buried Forest Lawn Meml. Park, Glendale, Cal.

MILLIKIN, EUGENE DONALD ex-U.S. Senator; b. Hamilton, O., Feb. 12, 1891; s. Dr. Samuel Hunter and Mary (Shelly) M.; LL.B., U. Colo., 1913; m. Delia Alsena Schuyler, Jan. 30, 1935. Admitted to Colo. bar, 1913, and began practice of law. Apptd. mem. U.S. Senate to fill unexpired term of Alva B. Adams, reelected in 1950 for six year term. Served as pvt. U.S. Army, capt. and maj. Inf. and lt.-col. Engrs., World War. Awarded Pershing citation for meritorious services. Mem. Am., Colo., Denver bar assns. Republican. Home: 800 Washington St., Denver 3. Office: 818 17th St., Denver 2. Died July 27, 1958; buried Fairmount Mausoleum, Denver.

MILLING, ROBERT EDWARD, JR. lawyer; b. Boyce, La., Sept. 20, 1898; s. Robert Edward and Ida (Roberts) M.; student Tulane U., 1915-17; A.B., Washington and Lee U., 1919; LL.B., Harvard, 1922; m. Claudia Tucker Pipes, Apr. 17, 1934; children-Robert Edward III, Roswell King, David Pipes. Admitted to La. bar, 1923; partner Milling, Seaal, Saunders, Benson & Woodward, New Orleans, 1923-. Dir. Williams, Inc., Jahncke Service, Inc., Joseph Rathbone Land & Lumber Co., Inc. Served to lt. col. USAAF, 1942-45. Mem. Am., La. New Orleans bar assns. Clubs: Boston, Louisiana, New Orleans Country (New Orleans). Home: 1739 Arabella St., New Orleans 15. Office: Whitney Bldg., New Orleans 12. Died Aug. 5, 1960.

MILLIS, JOHN engineer, officer U.S. Army; b. Wheatland, Mich., Dec. 31, 1858; s. Walter and Jane Clark (Carlow) M.; B.S., U.S. Mil. Acad., West Point, N.Y., 1881 (No. 1 graduate Class of 1881); m. Mary Raoul, Nov. 22, 1893; children-Ralph (dec.), Walter, Janet. Commd. 2d lt. engrs., June 11, 1881; 1st lt., 1882; capt., Sept. 20, 1892; major, Apr. 2, 1900; lt. col., June 7, 1907; col., June 13, 1910. Served Willets Point, N.Y., 1881-83; on lighthouse duty, 1883-90; devised and superintended the installation of electric light plant for illuminating the Statue of Liberty, New York Harbor, October 1886; in charge improvements New Orleans harbor and levees Miss. River, 1890-94; chief engineer U.S. Lighthouse Bd., Washington, 1894-98; on duty with engr. batt., Willets Point, N.Y., and in Cuba, 1898-1900; U.S. del. Internat. Congress of Navigation, Internat. Congress of Electricity and Internat. Congress of Physics, Paris Expn., 1900; inspected and reported upon the canal and reservoir system of the Nile-particularly the great reservior dam at Assourn, nr. 1st cataract, Sept.-Oct. 1900; in charge of constructing fortifications on Puget Sound, of river and harbor improvement in Wash., Ida., Mont., of first road survey and constrn. in Mt. Rainier Nat. Park of surveys and harbor improvements in Alaska, 1900-05, of all fortification constuction, P.I., 1905-07, including defensive works on Corregidor Island; on leave of absence, returning from P.I., visiting works, etc. in China, Burma, India, Egypt and Europe; in charge harbor and river improvement works, Lake Erie and in Ohio and Ind., and mem. spl. bds. on harbor works, etc., 1908-12, in charge of river and harbor improvement works and of sea coast defense works, Mass. and R.I.; sr. mem. spl. bd. on Lake Erie, Lake Mich. inland waterway, spl. duty under Bur. of Lighthouses for N.E. coast, 1912-16; div. engr. Southeast Div. for coast defenses, harbor improvements and inland waterways, in S.C., Ga., Fla., western portion of N.C. and eastern portion of Ala., 1916-18; chief engr. Southeastern Dept., Savannah, Ga., 1917; dept. engr. Central Dept., Chicago, Ill., 1918-22; retired 1922. Mem. Am. Soc. C.E. (mem. spl. com. to investigate Japanese earthquake), Am. Inst. E.E., A.A.A.S., Am. Astron. Soc. Clubs: University, Century (New York); Cosmos (Washington). Author: Safety of Navigation on Great American Lakes (for 12th Internat. Congress Navigation, Phila., 1912); Commercial Waterways of the United States (for Atlantic Deeper Waterways Assn.); The Constructional History of the Solar System and of our Earth (The Dualistic Theory), 1925; Unrealities of the Visible Skies, 1931; Evidences of a Planetoid Fall in East Central Africa, 1933; The Mystery of the Star-Chains, Endogenesis of the Earth, 1940; also author of numerous papers on relativity, gravitation, glacial theory, cause of drumlins, cosmogony, navigation, etc. Originated, 1918, method of observing and photographing solar eclipses from aircraft, used by U.S. Naval Observatory for total eclipse of Jan. 1925. Devised plan for emergency flood relief of Lower Mississippi which saved city of New Orleans in flood of 1927. Devised polyhedral framing system for naval and merchant vessels, airships; earthquake and wind storm resisting buildings, bridges and other shore structures. Home: Fern Hall Hotel, 3250 Euclid Av., Cleve.Died Mar. 20, 1952; buried Wheatland, Mich.

MILLS, ALBERT LEOPOLD army officer; b. New York, May 7, 1854; s. Abiel Buckman and Anne (Warford) M.; grad. U.S. Mil. Acad., 1879; m. Alada Thurston, d. Rt. Rev. John Adams Paddock, of Brooklyn, Nov. 15, 1883. Commd. 2d lt. 1st Cav., June 13, 1879; 1st lt., Jan. 23, 1889; capt. asst. adj. gen. vols., May 12, 1898; hon. disch. from vol. service, Sept. 24, 1898; transferred to 1st Cav., Aug. 9, 1899, to 10th Cav., Feb. 1, 1904; brig. gen. U.S.A., May 7, 1904. Awarded Congressional Medal of Honor, July 28, 1902, "for distinguished gallantry in action nr. Santiago de Cuba, July 1, 1898, in encouraging those nr. him by his bravery and coolness after being shot through the head and entirely without sight." Supt. U.S. Mil. Acad., with rank of col., 1898-1906; comdg. Dept. of the Visayas, Jan. 16, 1907-Mar. 1, 1908, Dept. of Luzon, P.I., Mar. 3, 1908-Apr. 6, 1909, Dept. of the Gulf, Atlanta, Ga., May 28, 1909-Jan., 1912; pres. Army War Coll., Jan.-Sept. 1912; chief, Div. of Militia Affairs, Gen. Staff, Sept., 1912-. Home: Washington, D.C. Died Sept. 8, 1916.

MILLS, ANSON brig. gen.; b. on farm in Boone Co., Ind., Aug. 31, 1834; s. James P. and Sarah (Kenworthy) M.; cadet at West Point, 1855-57; m. Hannah Cassel, Oct. 13, 1868. Engaged in engring. and land surveying in Tex.; laid out first plan of the city of El Paso and in 1859 was surveyor to boundary commn. establishing boundary between N.M., Ind. Ty. and Tex.; left Tex., Mar. 1861; became 1st lt. 18th U.S. Inf., May 14, 1861; capt., Apr. 27, 1863; transferred to 3d Cav., Jan. 1, 1871; maj. 10th Cav., Apr. 4, 1878; lt. col. 4th Cav., Mar. 25, 1890; col. 3d Cav., Aug. 16, 1892; brig. gen. U.S.A., June 16, 1897; retired at his own request, June 22, 1897. During Civil War was never absent, either on leave or from sickness, but was present in all engagements of his regt., participating in most of the Indian wars since, and comdg. U.S. troops at the battle of Slim Buttes, Dak., Sept. 9, 1876; mem. bd. of visitors U.S. Mil. Acad., 1866; mil. attache to the Paris Expn., 1878. Invented the woven cartridge belt (and loom for its manufacture), now exclusively used in U.S. Army and Navy and by the British army. Mem. Mexican Boundary Commn., Oct. 26, 1893-. Died Nov. 5, 1924.

MILLS, AUGUSTUS K(ING), III business exec.; b. Boonville, Mo., Apr. 12, 1902; s. Augustus K. and Martha (Gibson) M.; student Central Coll., 1919-21, U. Mo., 1921-23; m. Louise Iselin, Feb. 11, 1942; children-Pauline Iselin, Peter Augustus. Publicity dir. Amelia Earhart flight, Europe, 1928, Byrd Antarctic Expdn., 1928-30; publicity dept. Batton, Barton & Durstine, 1931-34; dir. pub. relations March of Time, Inc., 1934-36; European rep. Life Mag., London, Eng., 1936-38; asso., later partner Earl Newsom & Co., 1938-49; dir. pub. and employee relations Ford Internat., 1949-50; dir. Ford Motor Co. Archives, exec. dir. Henry Ford Mus. and Greenfield Village, 1950—; dir. Wayside Inn, South Sudbury, Mass., Dearborn (Mich) Inn, Manhattan Storage Co., N.Y.C., Adlon Corp., N.Y.C. Served with Intelligence, A.A.C., Africa, Corsica, No. Italy, 1942-45, advancing from capt. to lt. col. Mem. Am. Assn. Museums, Sigma Nu. Clubs: Racquet and Tennis (N.Y.C.); Grosse Pointe (Mich.); Terratine Yacht (Dark Harbor, Me.). Home: 294 Lincoln Rd., Grosse Pointe. Office: 3000 Schaefer Rd., Dearborn, Mich. Died Sept. 12, 1954; buried Gate of Heaven, N.Y.C.

MILLS, EARLE WATKINS, corp. exec.; born Little Rock, Ark., June 24, 1896; s. Elisha Wright and Angie Irwin (Stansberry) M.; ed. U. of Ark., 1913-14; B.S., U.S. Naval Acad., 1917; post grad. 1922-23; M.S., Columbia U., 1924; D.Eng. (honorary), Univ. of Louisville, 1944; m. Carolyn Hayes Park, July 6, 1918; 1 dau., Shirley Marian. Ensign, 1917; advanced through grades to vice adm., 1945; splty. naval engring.; dep. chief Bur. Ships, 1942-46, chief, 1946-49; ret. as vice adm., 1949. Mem. Research and Development Board, Nat. Mil. Establishment, 1948; later chmn., dir. Foster Wheeler Corp., N.Y.C.; chmn. Nuclear Engring. Co., Walnut Creek, Cal., 1966-68; dir. Liberty Mut. Ins. Co.,

Boston. Decorated D.S.M., Victory, Am. Def., Pacific, European and Am. Theatre medals; Comdr. Order British Empire. Member Newcomen Soc. Am. Soc. Naval Engrs., Soc., Naval Architects and Marine Engrs. (David W. Taylor medal for achievement in marine engring., 1948), Am. Soc. M.E. Clubs: Army and Navy Country (Washington); Bankers, India House, University (N.Y.C.); Baltusrol Golf (Springfield, N.J.). Home: Walnut Creek CA Died Aug. 1968.

MILLS, EDWARD KIRKPATRICK, JR., lawyer; born in Morristown, N.J., March 19, 1906; s. Edward Kirkpatrick and Laura (Slade) M.; grad. Phillips Exeter Acad., 1924; A.B., Princeton, 1928; LL.B., Yale, 1931; m. Shirley R. Burks, Sept. 23, 1944; children-Shirley Neel, Katina Slade. Admitted to N.J. bar, 1931; asso. Pitney, Hardin & Skinner, Newark, 1931-38; sec. bondholders protective coms. for financial reorgn. Central of Ga. Ry., No. Ohio R.R., 1933-38; chief opinion sect. gen. counsel's office Civil Aero. Bd., Washington, 1939-40; partner Mills, Jeffers & Mountain, Morristown, N.J., 1940-56; mem. bd., pres. Morristown Airport Corp., 1946-49; dir. Morristown Trust Co., 1938-56; v.p., dir. Boniface Printing Co. (now L. P. Thebault Co.), Morristown, 1954-56; dep. adminstr. Gen. Services Adminstrn. Washington, 1956-60, also acting commr. transportation and utilities service, 1957, acting commr. of public buildings service, 1959; member Federal Trade Commission, 1960-61; secretariat Joint Chiefs of Staff coms., Army-Navy Air Transport and Atlantic Communications. Mem. bd. aldermen, Morristown, N.J., 1936-39, mayor, 1949-50; chmn. Morris County Citizens for Eisenhower, 1951-52; dir. United Givers Fund, Washington, 1958-60; trustee-at-large Community Chest and Council of Morris County. Served as pilot anti-submarine patrol Civil Air Patrol, flight instr. Air Corps REs., 1942-43; 1st lt. to maj. A.C., AUS, 1943-45. Decorated Air Medal. Recipient Gen. Services Adminstrn.'s Distinguished Service award, 1959. Mem. Morris Co., Fed., Am. bar assns., Am. Legion, N.J. Hist. Soc., Washington Assn. of N.J., Phi Delta Phi. Republican. Episcopalian. Clubs: Metropolitan (Washington), Princeton (New York City); Colonial (Princeton, N.J.); Morristown (past gov.), Morristown Field, Nantucket Yacht. Patentee. Home: Cherry Lane, Mendham, N.J. Died Aug. 8, 1964; buried Mendham.

MILLS, JAMES EDWARD chemist; b. Winnsboro, S.C., Apr. 30, 1876; s. William Wilson and Sarah Edith Ann (Smith) M.; A.B., Davidson (N.C.) Coll., 1896, A.M., 1900; Ph.D., U. N.C., 1901; D.Sc., U.S.C., 1935; studied U. Berlin, 1904-05; m. Mary Gregory Hume, Oct. 15, 1921. Asst. in chem. N.C., 1900-01, instr., 1901-13, asso. prof., 1904-10; lectr. chemistry, 1911-13, prof., 1913-21, U.S.C.; tech. dir. research and development work; Chemical Warfare Serv., Edgewood Arsenal, 1921-24; chief chem. div., same, 1924-29; chmn. div. chemistry and chem. tech., Nat. Research Council, 1929-30; prof. chemistry U.S.C., 1930-34; chief chemist Sonoco Products Co., 1934-47, dir. chem. research, 1947-50. Recipient Herty Award, 1944. Commd. Capt., Engr. O.R.C., Sept. 4, 1917; capt. Chem. Warfare Service; maj., Oct. 16, 1918; served as engr. officer, 1st Gas Regt. (30th Engrs.), A.E.F.; lt. col. C.W. Res., Mar. 14, 1925; ret. Apr. 1940. Fellow N.Y. Acad. Sci., A.A.A.S.; mem. Am. Inst. Chemists, S.C. Acad. Sci., Am. Chem. Soc., Am. Electrochem. Soc., Kappa Sigma, Phi Beta Kappa, Sigma Xi. Presbyn. Contbr. sci. jours. Address: 1212 Home Av., Hartsville, S.C. Died Aug. 12, 1950; buried Camden, S.C.

MILLS, OGDEN LIVINGSTON secretary of treasury, lawyer; b. Newport, R.I., Aug. 23, 1884; s. Ogden and Ruth T. (Livingston) M.; A.B., Harvard, 1904, LL.B., 1907; m. 2d, Dorothy Randolph Fell, Sept. 2, 1924. Admitted to N.Y. bar, 1908, and practiced in New York City; treas. Rep. Co. Com., New York Co., 1911-26; Rep. candidate for Congress, 1912 (defeated), for governor of N.Y., 1916; elected mem. of State Senate, 1914 and 1916. Trustee Provident Loan Soc., Am. Mus. Natural History, Metropolitan Mus. Art; pres. Home for Incurables. Commd. capt. U.S.A., July 1917; with A.E.F. in France, Jan. 1918-Mar. 1919. Mem. 67th to 69th Congresses (1921-27), 17th N.Y. District; under secretary of treasury, 1927-32; secretary of the treasury, Feb. 1932-Mar. 4, 1933. Episcopalian. Home: New York, N.Y. Died Oct. 11, 1937.

MILLS, ROGER QUARLES senator; b. Todd Co., Ky., Mar. 30, 1832; s. Charles H. and Tabitha B. M.; moved to Tex., 1849; m. Caroline R. Jones, Jan. 7, 1858. Admitted to bar (by act of legislature) at 20, and began practice at Corsicana, Tex. Mem. Tex. Ho. of Rep., 1859; was at battle of Wilson's Creek (Oak Hill), Aug. 10, 1861; later col. 10th Tex. Inf., C.S.A., which comd. in battles of Arkansas Post, Jan. 11, 1862, Chickamauga, Sept. 19-20, 1863, until fall of Gen. James Deshler, when he took command of the brigade; comd. regt. at battles of Missionary Ridge, Nov. 24-25, 1863 (wounded), New Hope Ch., May 27, 1864, and Atlanta, July 22, 1864 (twice wounded). Mem. 43d to 52d Congresses (1873-93); resigned from 52d Congress, Mar. 29, 1892, having been elected U.S. senator for unexpired term (1892-93) of Horace Chilton; reelected for term, 1893-97. Democrat. Home: Corsicana, Texas. Died 1911.

MILLS, SAMUEL MYERS officer U.S.A.; b. Pottsville, Pa., Dec. 15, 1843; entered Mil. Acad. from Pa., Graduating 1865; grad. Arty Sch., Ft. Monroe, Va., 1882. Commd. 2d lt. 19th Inf., June 23, 1865; promoted through grades to col. Apr. 14, 1903; brig. gen. and chief of arts., 1905. Served on reconstruction of Southern States; honorably mentioned and congratulated in orders for successful arrest and delivery to U.S. marshal of certain desperadoes, 1866; was in signal service, 1882-85, becoming 2d ranking officer in that service and frequently acting as chief signal officer; inst. at Arty. Sch., Ft. Monore, Va., 1885; and filled many varied duties. Died 1907.

MILLS, STEPHEN CROSBY officer U.S.A.; b. New Hartford, N.Y., May 8, 1854; s. Henry Abiran and Julia (Crosby) M.; ed. pub. schs., Mt. Carroll, Ill., Syracuse, N.Y., Ann Arbor, Mich.; grad. U.S. Mil. Acad., 1877; m. Lillian Lee, Apr. 10, 1894. Apptd. 2d lt. 17th Inf., June 15, 1877; 2d lt. 12th Inf., June 30, 1877; 1st lt., May 28, 1884; capt., Dec. 16, 1894; vaj. insp. gen. vols., May 12, 1898; hon. disch. from vols., July 28, 1898; maj. insp. gen., U.S.A., July 25, 1898; lt. col. insp. gen., Feb. 2, 1901; col. insp. gen., Apr. 12, 1903. Bvtd. 1st lt., Feb. 27, 1890, "for gallant services in action against Indians in the San Andreas Mountains, N.M., Apr. 7, 1880, and in the Las Animas Mountains, N.M., Apr. 28, 1882." Served on plains, 1877-82; abroad collecting information, 1890-91; recorder of commn. apptd. to investigate conduct of War Dept. in Spanish-Am. War; chief of staff, Div. of the Philippines, 1907-09, Dept. of the Lakes, 1909-10; chief of staff, Dept. of the East, 1910-11; insp. gen., Eastern Div., Aug. 15, 1911—. Died Aug. 3, 1914.

MILROY, ROBERT HUSTON army officer, Indian agt.; b. Washington County, Ind., June 11, 1816; s. Samuel and Martha (Huston) M.; B.A., Master of Mil. Science, Norwich U. Vt., 1843; LL.B., Ind. U., 1850; m. Mary Armitage, May 17, 1849, 7 children. Served in Mexican War; admitted to Ind. bar, 1850; elected del. to 2d Ind. Constnl. Conv., 1850; organized volunteer company in Rennselaer, Ind., made capt.; commd. col. 9th Regt. Ind. Volunteers, 1861; promoted brig. gen. U.S. Volunteers, 1861, maj. gen., 1862; served under Gens. McClellan and Rosecrans in Western Va., under Gen. Fremont in Shenandoah Valley, as maj. gen. commanded 2d div. VIII Army Corps; a trustee Wabash and Erie Canal; became supt. Indian affairs for Wash., 1872; Indian agt. with hdqrs. at Olympia, Wash., 1875-85. Died Olympia, Mar. 29, 1890.

MILTON, JOHN BROWN naval officer; b. Lexington, Ky., Oct. 20, 1848; s. Bushrod T. and Mary A. M.; grad. U.S. Naval Acad., 1870; m. Harriet B. Steele, Oct. 20, 1880. Promoted ensign, July 13, 1871; master (lt., jr. grade), Nov. 19, 1874; lt., Sept. 14, 1881; lt. comdr., Mar. 3, 1899; comdr., Sept. 26, 1900; capt., June 6, 1906; rear admiral, Jan. 9, 1910. Served on various vessels during Spanish-Am. War; insp. 12th Light House Dist., 1901-04; comd. Monterey, 1904; at Naval Sta., Cavite, 1904-05; Naval War Coll., Newport, 1906-07; comd. West Virginia, 1907; capt. of yard, Navy Yard, Mare Island, 1907-08; comd. Independence, 1908-10; Naval Training Sta., San Francisco, 1910; retired on account of age, Oct. 20, 1910. On duty at U.S. Naval Sta., New Orleans, La., 1917. Home: Annapolis, Md. Died Jan. 7, 1931.

MIMS, LIVINGSTON underwriter; b. Edgefield, S.C., 1833; s. Henry and Susan (Burr) M.; ed. in Miss.; studied law; m. Sue Harper, 1866. Admitted to Miss. bar before 20 yrs. of age; clerk Superior Court Chancery of Miss.; senator from Jackson and Hinds Co.; presdl. elector on Breckinridge and Lane ticket, 1860; joined first co. of Miss. troops enlisted for the war, 1861; assigned to duty staff of Gen. William Barksdale; apptd. by President Davis chief q.m. dept. Miss. and E.La., with rank of maj.; served on staffs of Gens. Pemberton and Joseph E. Johnston. After war in partnership with Gen. Joseph E. Johnston in ins. business; now mgr. for South, N.Y. Life Ins. Co. Mayor Atlanta, 1901-02; many yrs. pres. Southeastern Tariff Assn. Democrat. Home: Atlanta, Ga. Died 1906.

MINAHAN, VICTOR IVAN newspaper editor; b. Chilton, Wis., June 2, 1881; s. William Burke and Mary (Shaughnessey) M.; student Central Coll., Stevens Point, Wis., 1895-98; LL.B., University of Wisconsin, 1901, married to Bertha Bush Torinus, April 23, 1918 (died April 1959); children-John B. Torinus (stepson), Mary (Mrs. John M. Walter), Victor Ivan. Admitted to Wis. bar, 1901, and practiced in Green Bay, 1901-30; editor Green Bay Press-Gazette and Appleton (Wis.) Post-Crescent since 1930; pres. Green Bay Newspaper Co.; treas. Post Pub. Co.; dir. Kellogg-Citizens Nat. Bank. Capt. U.S. Army, 1917-19. Clubs: Tavern (Chicago); Elks (Green Bay). Home: 823 N. Broadway, De Pere, Wis. Office: Press-Gazette, Green Bay, Wis. Died Aug. 5, 1954; buried Greenwood Cemetery, DePere, Wis.

MINER, ASHER miller; b. Wilkes-Barre, Pa., Nov. 14, 1860; s. Charles Abbott and Eliza Ross (Atherton) M.; ed. Williston Sem., Mass., and grad. Wilkes-Barre (Pa.) Acad., 1879; m. Hettie McNair Lonsdale, Nov. 6, 1889. Pres. Miner-Hillard Milling Co., Pa. Millers' Mutual Fire Insurance Co. Enlisted in Co. D. 9th Regt., N.G.P., 1884; promoted through various grades and apptd. gen. insp. rifle practice with rank of col., 1895; on staff of Gov. Hastings, 1895-98; col. 7th Regt., N.G. Pa., 1898-99; col., 9th Inf., N.G. Pa., 1907-12; apptd. col. Field Arty., N.G. Pa., and assigned to 3d Pa. Field Arty., Aug. 16, 1916; Mexican border service, Aug. 17, 1916-Mar. 29, 1917; commd. in federal service, Aug. 5, 1917; col. 109th Field Arty. with A.E.F. in France, May-Dec. 1918; participated in Fismes-Vesle and Meuse-Argonne offensives; wounded in face and leg necessitating amputation of left leg. Aprement, France, Oct. 4; apptd. brig. gen. Pa. N.H. Comdg. 53d F.A. Brig.; retired with rank of maj. gen., 1923; awarded D.S.C. and D.S.M. Republican. Presbyn. Home: Wilkes-Barre, Pa. Died Sept. 2, 1924.

MINER, CHARLES WRIGHT brigadier-gen. U.S.A.; b. Cincinnati, Nov. 21, 1840; s. John L. and Mary (Wright) M.; ed. Cincinnati pub. schs.; m. Isabella L. Cooley, of Longmeadow, Mass., June 15, 1870. Enlisted as pvt. Co. D, 2d Ohio Inf., Apr. 17, 1861; discharged, Aug. 9, 1861; commd. capt. 22d Ohio Inf., May 1, 1862; hon. mustered out, Aug. 28, 1865; apptd. from Ohio, 2d lt. 119th U.S. Inf., Mar. 31, 1866; transferred to 28th Inf., Sept. 21, 1866; 1st lt., Jan. 1, 1867; capt. 22d Inf., Mar. 7, 1867; maj. 6th Inf., Dec. 29, 1894; lt.-col., July 1, 1898; col., Dec. 15, 1899; brig.-gen. U.S.A., July 29, 1903; retired at own request after 40 yrs.' service, July 30, 1903. Bvtd. maj., Feb. 27, 1890, for action against Indians at Spring Creek, Mont., Oct. 15, and 16, 1876. Home: 70 Lexington Av., Columbus, O.

MINER, ROBERT BRADFORD, educator; b. Conneaut, O., June 1, 1916; s. Charles Warren and Cora Ruth (Carr) M.; student Allegheny Colo. 1934-36; B.S.C., Ohio U., 1938, M.S., 1940; Ph.D., Ohio State U., 1948; m. Margaret Louisa Earnhart, June 5, 1942; children—Richard Lee, Allan Bradford. Asst. price specialist OPA, 1942-43; mem. faculty Ohio State U., 1946-—, prof. bus., 1958-—, chmn. dept. bus. orgn., 1957-68; vis. lectr. U. Wis., summer 1950. Served to 1st lt. AUS, 1943-46. Mem. Am. Marketing Assn. Co-author: Introduction to Business Management, 1951; Distribution Costs, 1953. Contbg. editor Accountants Handbook, 1956, 70; Marketing Handbook, 1965. Home: Columbus OH Died Feb. 6, 1971.

MINGOS, HOWARD L. writer, artist; b. Athens, Pa., Apr. 24, 1891; s. George William and Littie Ellen (Lynch) M.; grad. high sch., Athens, 1910; student Pa. Mus. Sch. Industrial Art, 1911-14; m. Kate Maujorie Hetrick, Aug. 7, 1923. Mem. staff Phila. Telegraph, 1914, Scranton Republican, 1915, New York Evening World, 1916, Evening Sun, 1919; spl. rep. Aeronautical Chamber Commerce of America, 1920-22; spl. writer, New York Times, 1922-30; contbr. about 1,000 articles to mags. and newspapers. Served as vol. Air Service, U.S. Army, July 1917-Dec. 1918, last 5 mos. in England. Republican. Protestant. Mason. Author: The Zeppelins (with E. A. Lehmann), 1927; The Birth of an Industry, 1929; The Air Is Our Concern (with others), 1935; American Heroes of the War in the Air, 1943. Editor of Aircraft Year Book, 1934-47. Editor, The American Swedish Monthly. Home: 299 W. 12th St., N.Y.C. 14. Office: 8 E. 69th St. N.Y.C. 21. Died Dec. 29, 1955; buried Tioga Point Cemetery, Athens, Pa.

MINNEGERODE, MEADE author; b. of Am. parents in London, Eng., June 19, 1887; s. Meade and Eleanor (Coxe) M.; Harrow Sch. (Eng.); B.A., Yale, 1910; m. Mildred Bright Mailliard, Aug. 30, 1932. With Charles E. Merrill Co., pubs., N.Y., 1910-13, Munson S.S. Line, 1913-16; with R.W. Cramer Co., Centerbrook, Conn., 1945. Rep. in France of U.S. Shipping Bd., 1917-18; 1st lt. Am. Red. Cross, with A.E.F., 1918-19; chief observer, Essex Post, U.S. A.A.F., Ground Observer Corps, 1941-44. Member Defense Council; mem. Town Salvage Com. Awarded French Commemorative Medal for service with French troops, French Victory Medal, Army Air Forces Aircraft Warning Service Medal. Mem. Delta Kappa Epsilon, Elihu (Yale). Pi Gamma Mu, Harrow Assn. (England). Republican. Episcopalian. Clubs: Essex Yacht, Rotary Club of Saybrook. Author: Laughing House, 1920; The Big Year, 1921; Oh, Susanna, 1922; Some Personal Letters of Herman Melville, and a Bibliography, 1922; The Queen of Sheba, 1922; The Seven Hills, 1923; The Fabulous Forties, 1924; Lives and Times, 1925; Aaron Burr (with S. H. Wandell), 1925; Some American Ladies, 1926; Cordelia Chantrell, 1926; Cockades, 1927; Certain Rich Men, 1927: Presidential Years, 1928; Jefferson, Friend of France, 1928; Some Mariners of France, 1930; The Magnificent Comedy, 1931; The Son of Marie Antoinette, 1934; Marie Antoinette's Henchman, 1936; Black Forest, 1937; The Terror of Peru, 1940. Contbr. to mags. Home: 9 Little Point St., Essex, Conn. Died Oct. 27, 1967.

MITCHAM, ORIN BURLINGAME army officer; b. in Va., July 25, 1853; grad. U.S. Mil. Acad., 1874. army officer; b. in Va., July 25, 1853; grad. U.S. Mil. Acad., 1874. Commd. 2d lt. 4th Arty., June 17, 1874; promoted through grades to col. Commd. 2d lt. 4th Arty., June 17, 1874; promoted through grades to col. ordnance, Jan. 21, 1909. Asst. Rock Island (Ill.) Arsenal, 1894; ordnance, Jan. 21, 1909. Asst. Rock Island (Ill.) Arsenal, 1894; inspector of powder and in charge mfr. smokeless powder, 1899-1902; inspector of powder and in charge mfr. smokeless powder, 1899-1902; comdg. U.S. Powder Depot, Dover N.J., and insp. powder and high comdg. U.S. Powder Depot, Dover, N.J., and insp. powder and high explosives, 1902-07; apptd. comd. New York Arsenal, Governors Island, explosives, 1902-07; apptd. comd. New York Arsenal, Governors Island, also armament officer and insp. ordnance, 1907. Died Aug. 20, 1934. also armament officer and insp. ordnance, 1907. Died Aug. 20, 1934.

MITCHELL, ALBERT GRAEME M.D., prof. pediatrics; b. Salem, Mass., Feb. 22, 1889; s. Fred Albert and Marie (Graham) M.; grad. Central High Sch., Philadephia; M.D., U. of Pa., 1910; m. Adele Wentz, Oct. 2, 1920; children-Marie Graham, Kathryn Wentz. Began practice at Philadelphia, 1912; asst. pediatrician, Children's Hosp., Phila., 1912; inst. in pediatrics, U. of Pa., 1919-21, asso. in pediatrics, 1921-24; prof. pediatrics, U. of Cincinnati (O.), 1924—; dir. pediatrics and contagious diseases, Cincinnati Gen. Hosp.; chief of staff and med. dir. Children's Hosp., Cincinnati; dir. Children's Hospital Research Foundation. Served as lt., later capt. Med. Corps, U.S.A., med. dir. Am. Hosp. for Civilians, Neufachteau, France, later with 149th Machine Gun Bn., World War. Med. dir. Babies Milk Fund Assn. of Cincinnati; mem. White House Conf. on Child Care; mem. White House Conf. on Children in a Democracy. Chmn. Sect. on Pediatrics of Am. Med. Assn., 1935; v.p. Pan-Am. Assn. Sect. on Pediatrics, 7th Cruise Congress, Jan. 1938. Republican. Presbyn. Co-author: (with J.P.C. Griffith) Diseases of Infants and Children (2 vols.), 1927, (1 vol.), 1933, 2d edit. in one vol., 1937; Pediatrics and Pediatric Nursing (with Echo Upham and Elgie Wallinger), 1939. Pediatric editor The Cyclopedia of Medicine; asso. editor Am. Jour. of Diseases of Children. Home: Cincinnati, O. Died June 1, 1941.

MITCHELL, JAMES FARNANDIS surgeon; b. Balt., July 1, 1871; s. Richard H. and Elizabeth (Farnandis) M.; A.B., Johns Hopkins, 1891, M.D., 1897; m. Eliza Hutchinson Webb, Apr. 20, 1904; m. 2d, Madge Richey, Oct. 25, 1945. Resident surgeon, instr. surgery Johns Hopkins Hosp., 1900-03; clin. prof. surgery George Washington U., 1919-; chief surgeon Emergency Hosp., Washington. Served as lt. col. U.S.Army, World War I; U.S., France. Fellow A.C.S.; mem. Am. Surg. Assn., Soc. Clin. Surgery, Am. Thoracic Surg. Soc., So. Surg. and Gynecol. Assn., Internat. Surg. Soc., A.M.A., Phi Kappa Psi. Episcopalian. Clubs: Metropolitan, Nat. Press, Alibi, Chevy Chase, Bar Harbor, Kebo Valley Golf, Pot and Kettle. Address: 1344 19th St., Washington 20006. Died May 1961.

MITCHELL, JAMES P(AUL) ex-sec. of labor; b. Elizabeth, N.J., Nov. 12, 1900; s. Peter J. and Anna C. (Driscoll) M.; LL.D., Fordham U., 1954, Mich. State Coll., 1955, Temple U., 1957, Lehigh U., 1957, Notre Dame U. 1958, Fairleigh Dickinson U., 1958, Rutgers U., 1959, Catholic U., 1959, Seton Hall U. 1960, Boston U., 1960, Villanova U., 1960; m. Isabelle Nulton, Jan. 22, 1923; 1 dau., Elizabeth Natchez. Dir. indsl. personnel div. Hdqrs. Army Service Forces, Washington, 1942-45; dir. personnel and indsl. relations R.H. Macy & Co., N.Y.C., 1945-47; v.p. Federated Dept. Stores, N.Y.C., 1947; asst. sec. ARmy for manpower and res. forces, 1953; sec. of labor, 1953-61; v.p., dir. Corwn Zellebach Corp., San Francisco, 1961-. Mem. Joint Army-Navy Personnel Bd., 1943-45; mem. personnel adv. bd. Hoover Commn., 1948; mem. Bldg. Trades Stblzn. Bd., 1941-45. Mem. exec. com. Nat. Cath. Conf. Inter-racial Justice; pres. Nat. Council Agrl. Life and Labor. Bd. dirs. Fund for Internat. Social and Econ. Edn., Inst. for Human Progress, Nat. Civil Service League; bd. dirs., nat. brotherhood chmn. Nat. Conf. Christians and Jews, 1963; trustee 20th Century Fund. Recipient Rerum Novarum award St. Peter's Coll., 1955, Am.'s Democratic Legacy silver medallion Anti-Defamation Legacy of B'nai B'rith, 1956, Equal Opportunity Day award Nat. Urban League, 1957, Vincentian award Coll. of St. Elizabeth, 1959, Horatio Alger award Am. Schs. and Colls. Assn., 1959, Bellarmine medal Bellarmine Coll., 1960. Mem. Am. Arbitration Assn. (dir.). Clubs: Stock Exchange, Commonwealth (San Francisco). Home: 5 Laureldale Rd., Hillsborough, Cal. Office: 1 Bush St., San Francisco 19. Died Oct. 19, 1964; buried St. Gertrudes Cemetery, Rahway, N.J.

MITCHELL, JOHN MCKENNEY, physician; ednl. dir.; b. Centreville, Md., Sept. 23, 1895; s. James Archibald and Eleanor Lux (McKenney) M.; A.B., Trinity Coll., 1920, Sc.D. (hon.), 1949; M.D. cum laude, Yale, 1924; LL.D. (hon.), Temple U., 1951; Sc.D., Dickinson Coll., 1953, Union U., 1958; m. Eleanor A. Janeway, Sept. 12, 1925; children—James Andrew. Eleanor Janeway (Mrs. Robert A. Huggins); m. 2d, Harriet Taylor Mauck, September 16, 1961. Intern-Resident New Haven Hosp., 1924-27; practice, specializing in pediatrics, Phila., 1927-42; faculty, sch. medicine U. Pa., 1927-62, prof. pediatrics, 1952-69, dean sch. medicine, 1948-62; dir. med. edn. Bryn Mawr Hosp., Pa., 1962-66; dir. study pediatric edn. Am. Acad. Pediatric Education, Commonwealth Fund, 1949. Served as 1st lt. Inf., U.S. Army, World War I; col. M.C., A.U.S., China-Burma-India Theatre, 1942-45; col. Medical Corps. Ret. Decorated Silver Star; recipient Abraham Jacobi award Am. Med. Assn., 1964. Exec. sec. Am. Bd. of Pediatrics since 1948. Fellow A.M.A., Am. Acad. Pediatrics (recipient Clifford Grulee award 1966); mem. Am. Pediatric Soc., Soc. for Pediatric Research, Assn. Am. Med. Colls. (pres. 1958-59), adv. bd. Med. Spltys. (pres. 1956-58), Assn. Hospital Directors of Medical Education, Sigma Xi, Alpha Omega Alpha, Delta Psi, Nu Sigma Nu. Author articles med. jours. Home: Rosemont PA Died Sept. 18, 1969.

MITCHELL, ORMSBY MACKNIGHT astronomer, army officer; b. Morganfield, Ky., July 28, 1809; s. John and Elizabeth (MacAlister) M.; grad. U.S. Mil. Acad., 1829; LL.D. (hon.), Harvard, 1851, Washington Coll., 1853, Hamilton Coll., 1856; m. Louisa (Clark) Trask, 1831. Asst. prof. mathematics U.S. Mil. Acad., 1829; chief engr. Rittle Miami R.R., 1836-37; prof. mathematics, philosophy, astronomy Cincinnati Coll., 1836-46; published mag. Sidereal Messenger, 1846-1848; adj. gen. Ohio, 1848; Inventor chronography, 1848; chief engr. Ohio & Miss. R.R., 1848-53; dir., largely responsible for erection Cincinnati Observatory; largely responsible for erecting 2d largest telescope, and largest on Western continent under auspices of Cincinnati Astron. Soc., 1845; made approximately 50,-000 observations of faint stars between 1854-59; discovered the duplicity of stars (e.g. Antares); dir. Dudley Observatory, Albany, N.Y., 1859; apptd. brig. gen. U.S. Volunteers, 1861; assigned to command Dept. of Ohio; brevetted maj. gen. volunteers, 1862; surprised and captured Huntsville, Ala. without firing a gun, thus obtained control of Memphis & Charleston R.R.; promoted maj. gen. volunteers; transferred to command Dept. of South and X Army Corps, Sept. 17, 1862. Author: Planetary and Stellar Worlds, 1848; Popular Astronomy, 1860. Died Beaufort, S.C., Oct. 30, 1862.

MITCHELL, SIDNEY ALEXANDER banker; b. Portland, Ore., Oct. 9, 1895; s. Sidney Zollicoffer and Alice Pennoyer (Bell) M.; student Hotchkiss Sch., 1911-14; A.B., Yale, 1919; LL.D., University of Alabama, 1956; married Mary Addison, Apr. 19, 1922; children-Mary Alice (Mrs. Dodderidge), Ann Jordan (Mrs. Payne), Joan (Mrs. Ault), Sidney Alexander. With Internat. Gen. Electric Co., Schenectady, N.Y., and Paris, France, 1919-24; with Bonbright & Co., Inc., N.Y., 1924-44, former pres., dir. since 1933; dir. Am. Electric Power Co., 36 E. 72nd Street Corporation. With Navy Dept., 1942-44, State Dept., 1944-45; exec. dir. Commn. Orgn. Exec. Br. Govt., 1947-49, member, 1953-55; treasurer Belgian Am. Edn. Found. Mem. Food Adminstrn. Commn. for Relief in Belgium; spl. attaché, Am. Embassy, London, rep. War Trade Bd.; mem. council on foreign relations. Vice pres. Inst. for Crippled and Disabled; trustee Inst. for Advanced Study, Herbert Hoover Birthplace Found., French Institute in the United States, Thomas Alva Edison Foundation; president. Federation of French Institute in the United States, Thomas Alva Edison Foundation; president. Federation of French Alliances. Decorated chevalier Legion of Honor (France); Order of the Crown (Belgium); recipient of the U.S. Navy Distinguished Civilian Service award. Mem. Adv. Bd., Hoover Inst. and Library on War, Revolution, and Peace. Republican. Episcopalian. Clubs: University, Union, New York Yacht (New York); Metropolitan (Washington, S.C.); Seawanhaka Corinthian Yacht (Oyster Bay, New York); also Piping Rock (Locust Valley); Porcupine, Royal Nassau Sailing (Nassau, Bahamas); Union Interaliée (Paris.) Author: A Family Lawsuit, 1958; S. Z. Mitchell and the Electrical Industry, 1960. Home: Locust Valley, N.Y.; 36 East 72d St., N.Y.C. 10021. Died Nov. 28, 1966.

MITCHELL, WILLIAM army officer, stock raiser, farmer; b. of Am. parents temporarily sojourning abroad, Nice, France, Dec. 29, 1879; s. U.S. Senator John Lendrum and Harriet Danforth (Becker) M.; attended Racine (Wis.) Coll.; A.B., George Washington U., 1899; distinguished grad. Army Staff Coll., 1909; m. Elizabeth Trumbull Miller, Oct. 11, 1923; children-Lucy Trumbull, William. Enlisted as pvt., Co. M, 1st Wis. Inf., May 14, 1898; advanced through all grades, including brig. gen.; served in Spanish-Am. War, Philippine Insurrection, during construction of telegraph lines in Alaska, Army of Cuban Pacification, on Mexican Border and in World War. Inst. Army Staff Coll., and on Gen. Staff. Comdr. Air Forces, A.E.F., during entire campaign, and later dir. of Military Aviation, U.S.Army; participated in 14 major engagements in World War. Resigned commn. in U.S. Army, Feb. 1, 1926. Awarded grade of Mil. Aviator for service against enemy, also D.S.C. and D.S.M. (U.S.); Corix de Guerre with 5 palms and Comdr. Legion of Honor (French); Companion Order of St. Michael and St. George (British). Commendatore S.S. Maurizio e Labbaro, Medal for Merit in War and Grand Officer Crown of Italy (Italian). Episcopalian. Author: Our Air Force, 1921; Winged Defense, 1925; Skyways, 1930. Home: Middleburg, Va. Died Feb. 19, 1936.

MITCHELL, WILLIAM DEWITT lawyer; b. Winona, Minn., Sept. 9, 1874; William and Frances (Merritt) M.; father justice Supreme Court of Minn., 20 yrs.; prep. edn. Lawrenceville (N.J.) Sch.; student elec. engring., Sheffield Scientific Sch. (Yale) 2 yrs.; A.B., Univ. of Minn., 1895, LL.B., 1896; LL.D., Yale, 1929, Williams Coll., 1930, U. of Mich., 1931; m. Gertrude Bancroft, June 27, 1901; children-William Bancroft. Admitted to Minn. bar, 1896, and began practice at St. Paul; sec. 1st Charter Commn., St. Paul, 1900; regional counsel U.S.R.R. Adminstrn., 1919; chmn. Citizens Charter Com., St. Paul, 1922; was mem. firm Mitchell, Doherty, Rumble, Bunn & Butler, St. Paul; solicitor gen. of U.S. by apptmt. of President Coolidge, 1925-29; atty. gen. of U.S., Mar. 4, 1929-Mar. 4, 1933; chairman Supreme Court of U.S. adv. com. on Fed. Rules of Civil Procedure since 1935; mem. law firm Mitchell, Capron, Marsh, Angulo and Cooney, N.Y. City, Since Apr. 1, 1933; chief counsel, joint Congressional committee investigating Pearl Harbor disaster. Served as 2d lt. 15th Minnesota Volunteer Infantry, 1898-99, and as acting judge advocate 2d Army Corps, 1898; brigadier engr. officer, 3d Brig., 1st Div., 2d Corps, 1899; capt. and adj. 4th Regt., Nat. Guard Minn., 1899-1901; col. 6th Regt. (now 206th) Inf. Nat. Guard Minn., 1918; entered F.A., O.T.S., Camp Taylor, Ky., 1918. Mem. Central Com., also counselor Am. Red Cross, 1925-29. Mem. Am. Bar Assn., Assn. Bar of City of N.Y. (pres. 1941-43), Spanish War Vets., Am. Legion. Democrat. Presbyterian. Clubs: Somerset, University (hon.), White Bear Yacht (St. Paul); Metropolitan, Burning Tree (hon. life) (Washington); Garden City Golf, Century (N.Y.). Home: Syosset, Long Island, N.Y. Office: 20 Exchange Pl., N.Y.C. Died Aug. 24, 1955.

MITSCHER, MARC ANDREW naval officer; b. Hillsboro, Wis., Jan. 26, 1887; grad. U.S. Naval Acad., 1910; commd. ensign U.S. Navy, 1910, and advanced through the grades to rear admiral, 1941, vice admiral, 1944; connected wtih naval aviation since Oct. 1915; served as pilot on first Navy trans-Atlantic flight, 1919; in command Naval Air Station, Anacostia, D.C., 1922-25; exec. officer, U.S.S. Langley, 1929-30; with Bureau of Aeronautics, Navy Dept., 1930-33; chief of staff to comdr. Aircraft, Base Force, U.S.S. Wright, flagship; served as exec. officer Saratoga and 2 yr. tour of duty in Bur. of Aeronautics, then returned to the Wright as comdg. officer; asst. chief Bur. of Aeronautics, 1939-41; comdg. officer, U.S.S. Hornet, 1941-42 (the Hornet was the Shangri-La from which the American planes, under command of Maj. Gen. James Doolittle, took off on Apr. 18, 1942, to bomb mil. objectives in Tokyo and 4 other Japanese cities); in command of carrier Midway during battle of Midway, June 1942; comdr. air, Solomon Islands, Apr.-July 1943; comdr. Task Force 58 Pacific Fleet, 1944 (during operations against the Marshall Islands, Truk and Tinian-Saipan); chief of naval operations for air, 1945; Awarded Navy Cross, Distinguished Service Medal, and The Gold Star in lieu of the second Distinguished Service medal, Victory Medal, Escort Clasp; American Defense Service Medal, Fleet Clasp; The Asiatic-Pacific Area Campaign medal; NC-4 Medal; Order of Tower and Sword with grade of official by Portugal (connection with NC-4 flight, May 6, 1919) cited for third Distinguished Service Medal, 1944. Home: 229 East Park Place. Oklahoma City, Okla. Died Feb. 3, 1947; buried in Arlington National Cemetery.

MITTY, JOHN JOSEPH archbishop; b. New York, N.Y., Jan. 20, 1884; s. John and Mary (Murphy) M.; prep. edn., De La Salle Inst., New York; A.B., Manhattan Coll., 1901; student St. Joseph's Sem., Yonkers, N.Y., 1901-06; S.T.B., Catholic U., Washington, D.C., 1907; D.D., Major Pontifical Sem., Rome, 1908; LL.D., Catholic U. of America, 1939. Ordained priest R.C. Ch., 1906; curate St. Veronica's Ch., N.Y., 1909; prof. dogmatic theology St. Joseph's Sem., 1909-17; pastor Sacred Heart Ch., Highland Falls, N.Y., 1919-22, also chaplain Catholic Chapel, West Point, same period; pastor St. Luke's Ch., New York, 1922-26; consecrated bishop Diocese of Salt Lake, Sept. 8, 1926; appointed co-adjutor archbishop of San Francisco, Jan. 29, 1932, and succeeded as archibishop of San Francisco, Jan. 29, 1932, and succeeded as archbishop, Mar. 5, 1935. Chaplain U.S. Army, Aug. 1917-May 1919; served with 49th Regt. and 101st Regt., U.S. Inf., at Camp Merritt, N.J., Leman Area, France, Meuse-Argonne Offensive. Decorated Officer of the Legion of Honor (France), 1937; Grand Officer of the Military Order of Christ (Portugal). 1939. Office: 445 Church St., San Francisco 94114. Died Oct. 15, 1961.

MIX, CHARLES LOUIS M.D.; b. Byron, Ill., Dec. 3, 1869; s. Ernest and Louise (Misick) M.; A.B., Harvard, 1890, A.M., 1891, M.D., 1894, U. of Vienna, 1896-97; U. of Berlin, 1897; LL.D., Loyola U., Chicago, 1921; m. Jeannette Elise Caldwell, Dec. 27, 1894. Began practice, 1897; specialist in nervous diseases and internal medicine; prof. anatomy, Northwestern U., Woman's Med. Sch., 1899, prof. Dental Sch. of same, 1901; asst. prof. anatomy, 1900-03, prof. physical diagnosis, Sept. 1903-14, clin. prof. medicine, 1914-20, Northwestern U. Med. Sch., Chicago, prof. medicine and head Dept. of Medicine, Loyola U. Med. Sch., 1920-29 (prof. emeritus); cons. internist I.C. R.R. until 1929; senior attending physician, Mercy Hosp., Chicago, until 1929. Commd. maj., Med. R.C., 1917; med. chief Base Hosp., Camp Mills, N.Y., Apr. 1918-June 1918; lt. col. Med. R.C., 1910-29. Retired from active practice 1929. Republican. Baptist. Editor-in-chief Practical Medical Series. Died Nov. 21, 1935.

MIZNER, HENRY RUTGERAS brig. gen.; b. Geneva, N.Y., Aug. 1, 1827. Apptd. from Mich., capt. 18th Inf. U.S.A., May 14, 1861; col. 14th Mich. Inf., Dec. 22, 1862; hon. mustered out of vol. service, July 18, 1865; transferred to 36th Inf., Sept. 21, 1866; maj. 20th Inf., Feb. 22, 1869; transferred to 12th Inf., Mar.

15, 1869, to 8th Inf., May 14, 1877; lt. col. 10th Inf., Dec. 15, 1880; col. 17th Inf., Jan. 2, 1888; retired by operation of law, Aug. 1, 1891; advanced to rank of brig. gen. retired by act of Apr. 23, 1904. Bvtd.; maj., Dec. 31, 1862, for battle of Murfreesboro, Tenn.; lt. col., Sept. 1, 1864, for Atlanta campaign and battle of Jonesboro, Ga.; brig. gen. vols., Mar. 13, 1865, for services during the war. Home: Detroit, Mich. Died Jan. 4, 1915.

MOALE, EDWARD bridadier gen. U.S.A.; b. in Md., Jan. 29, 1840. Apptd. from Md., 1st lt. 19th Inf., May 14, 1861; capt., Sept. 13, 1864; lt. col. a.-a.-g. vols., Mar. 21, 1865; transferred to 37th U.S. Inf., Sept. 21, 1866, to 2d Inf., Aug. 11, 1869; maj. 1st Inf., Feb. 1, 1887; lt. col. 3d Inf., Dec. 4, 1891; col. 15th Inf., Feb. 4, 1897; retired at own request after 40 yrs. service, Jan. 31, 1902; advanced to rank of brig. gen. retired, by act of Apr. 23, 1904. Bvtd.; maj., Dec. 2, 1864, for battle of Spottsylvania and campaign before Richmond; lt. col., Apr. 2, 1865, for service in front of Petersburg, Va.; col. vols., Mar. 13, 1865, for services during the war. Died Sept. 27, 1913.

MOFFETT, DONOVAN CLIFFORD coll. pres.; b. Brockton, Ill., Oct. 31, 1900; s. Charles M. and Cora L. (Dunseth) M.; A.B., DePauw U., 1922; M.A., Columbia, 1930; Ph.D., State U. Ia., 1942; m. Jennie Doyne Davis, June 27, 1928; children-Susan (Mrs. James B. Aitchison), Donovan Davis. Tchr., athletic coach Bainbridge (Ind.) High Sch., 1920-21, Brazil (Ind.) High Sch., 1922-26, Lima (O.) Central High Sch., 1926-27; tchr. phys. edn., athletic coach, dir. athletics, chmn. phys. edn. dept. DePauw U., 1927-46, prof. phys. edn., 1946-52, dir. edn., 1952-54, dean of coll., 1954-59, acting pres., 1959-60; pres. Coll. Edn. at Cortland, N.Y., 1960-. Mem. bd. directors First National Bank of Cortland (N.Y.), Dime Savs. & Loan Assn., Cortland, N.Y. Served from capt. to lt. col., USAAF, 1942-45. Mem. Am., N.Y. State assns. health phys. edn. and recreation, Coll. Phys. Edn. Assn., N.E.A., N.Y. State Tchrs. Assn., Faculties Assn. State U. N.Y. Colls. Edn., Delta Upsilon, Phi Delta Kappa, Phi Epsilon Kappa. Presbyn. (elder, trustee). Home: 44 Graham Av., Cortland, N.Y. Died Apr. 16, 1963.

MOFFETT, WILLIAM ADGER naval officer; b. Charleston, S.C., Oct. 31, 1869; s. George Hall and Elizabeth (Simonton) M.; grad. U.S. Naval. Acad., 1890; m. Jeannette Beverly Whitton, July 26, 1902; children-Janet Whitton, George Hall, William Adger, Elizabeth Simonton, Charles Simonton, Anna Promoted through grades to rear adm., July 25, 1923. Served under Admiral Dewey, on board Charleston, capture of Manila, 1898; comd. Chester at Vera Cruz, and at Tampico, Mex., when demand was made for salute of Am. flag by Admiral Mayo, 1914; comdt. Chester at taking of Vera Cruz, Apr. 22, 1914; comdt. U.S. Naval Training Sta., Great Lakes, Ill., 1914-18; comdt. 9th, 10th, 11th naval dists.; chief Bur. of Aeronautics, rank of rear adm., Sept. 1921; tech. adviser Washington Limitation of Armaments Conf., 1921-22; reappointed chief Bur. of Aeronautics, Mar. 1925; again apptd. Mar., 1929; tech. adviser Limitation of Armaments Conf., at London, 1930. Awarded Congressional Medal of Honor for eminent and conspicuous conduct in battle (capture of Vera Cruz); D.S.M. "for exceptionally meritorious service in a position of great responsibility in the World War." Home: Washington, D.C. Died Apr. 4, 1933.

MOHLER, HENRY KELLER M.D., med. dean; b. Ephrata, Pa., Apr. 2, 1887; s. William K. and Amanda K. Mohler; Pharm.D., Phil. Coll. of Pharmacy, 1907; M.D., Jefferson Med. Coll., 1912; hon. D.Sc., LaSalle Coll., 1939; m. Nellie Whiteley, Feb. 21, 1918; 1 dau., Alicia Whiteley. Interne, Jefferson Hosp., 1912-13; asso. with Jefferson Med. Coll., 1913—, in charge lab. of clin. medicine, 1913-14, instr. in medicine, 1913-22, demonstrator of medicine 1922-25, asso., 1925-29, asst. prof., 1929-32, asso. prof., 1932-38, clin. prof. of therapeutics, 1936-38, dean and Sutherland M. Provost prof. of therapeutics, 1938—; med. dir. Jefferson Med. Coll. Hosp., 1914-38, asst. physician, 1932-38, attending physician, 1938—; also physician in charge dept. of electrocardiology; private practice, Phila., 1915-41. Served as capt. Med. Corps, U.S. Army, World War; asst. and chief med. service Gen. Hosp. 38, Nantes, France; lt. col. Med. O.R.C., resigned 1938. Mem. bd. dirs. Children's Heart Hosp. Fellow Am. Coll. Hosp Adminstrs. (charter mem.). Am. Coll. Physicians, Phila. Coll. Physicians. Co-author Cyclopedia of Medicine. Home: Merion, Pa. Died May 16, 1941.

MOISE, EDWIN WARREN lawyer; b. Montgomery, Ala., Dec. 29, 1889; s. Theodore Sidney and Mary (Gaston) M.; student Phillips Exeter Acad., 1906-07; A.B., U. Ga., 1911; Rhodes scholar Oxford U., B.A., 1913, M.A., B.C.L., 1919; m. Marion Gerdine, Aug. 18, 1917 (dec.) 1 dau., Marion Gerdine (Mrs. John C. Bierwirth); m. 2d, Dorothy Todd, Dec. 6, 1951. Admitted to Ga. bar, 1915; partner Moise, Post & Gardner, Atlanta, 1942-; honorary director First Nat. Bank of Atlanta; director, mem. exec. com. Atlanta Gas light Co.; dir. Retail Credit Co., Am. Cast Iron Pipe Co., Thomaston Mills, Draper-Owens Co., Campbell Coal Co. Chmn. bd. trustees John Bulow Campbell Found., 1940-60; trustee The Berry Schs., 1938-60. Served as maj. inf. U.S. Army, World War I. Mem. Am., Ga., Atlanta bar assns., Am. Law Inst., Phi Beta Kappa, Chi Phi. Club: Piedmont Driving (Atlanta). Home: 101 Brighton Rd. Office: First Nat. Bank Bldg., Atlanta. Died Nov. 9, 1961; buried Westview Abbey.

MOLINEUX, EDWARD LESLIE manufacturer, soldier; b. London, Eng., Oct. 12, 1833; came to U.S. in boyhood; ed. Mechanics Soc. Sch., New York. When Civil War began was lt. col. 23d N.Y.N.G., in war as col. 159th N.Y. Vols.; comd. brigade, 19th Army Corps, in campaigns against Port Hudson, Red River and Petersburg, and in the Shenandoah Valley; bvtd. brig. gen. and maj. gen. vols.; apptd. 1880, brig. gen. 11th Brigade, N.G.S.N.Y., and 1885, maj. gen. 2d div. of same. Comdr. Mil. Order Loyal Legion, 1886. Dir. F.W. Devoe & T.C. Raynolds Co., paint mfrs. Died June 10, 1915.

MOLITOR, FREDERIC ALBERT civil engr.; b. Detroit, Apr. 1868; s. Albert and Lucille I. (Goodell) ed. Trinity Sch., New York, 1881-83, Cornell U. to 1886; m. Katherine Jefferies, 1896. Served in minor capacities on various Eastern R.R. engring. depts., 1886-89; prin. asst. engr. Ky. Central R.R., 1889; engr. maintenance of way, C.&O. R.R., 1890; asst. engr. Phila. & Reading R.R. and engr. Phila. Belt Line R.R., 1891-94; engr.-in-charge of constrn. L.I. R.R., 1895; chief engr. Choctaw, Okalhoma & Gulf R.R., and of allied cos. in charge of constrn. of 900 miles of new road, 1896-1903; gen. mgr., chief engr., and dir. Midland Valley R.R., 1903-06; also chief engr. Cherokee Constrn. Co., 1904-06; supervising ry. expert for the govt. in P.I., 1906-08; pvt. practice, New York, 1908-33, retired. Mem. Spl. Panama Canal Commn., 1921; chmn. Bd. of Economics and Engring., Nat. Assn. Owners of R.R. Securities, 1922; study of terminal and post facilities of New York; rept. for receiver Brazil Ry. Co.; investigation proposed low grade line, N.Y., Pittsburg & Chicago R.R.; mem. Arbitration Bd. St. Paul Union Depot; confidential rept. New York Rapid Transit situation; chmn. and mem. Commn. on Valuation of Damages Nat. Rys. of Mexico; cons. railroad engr. Bd. of Hudson River Regulating Dist., etc. Col. engrs. U.S.A., 1917-19; in charge of all engring. supplies at time of signing Armistice. Episcopalian. Republican. Author: amnual for Constructing Engineers, 1902. Home: New York, N.Y. Died 1938.

MOLLISON, JAMES ALEXANDER, army officer; b. Smith Center, Kan., July 9, 1897; commd. 2d lt. Air Service, July 1920, and advanced through the grades to brigadier general, Nov. 1942; married Betty Bulkeley, March, 4, 1924; children—Lt. Col. Douglas Alexander, Armored Force, United States Army, Molly Bulkeley Kalish, Betsey Barrington Volkert; assigned 2d Air Service Area Command. Ft. Worth, Tex. July 1942. comdg. gen., 1942; became chief, Personnel Training Div., Air Service Command, Patterson Field, O., Dec. 1942. Became comdg. gen., Mobile Air Service Command, Feb. 1943-Sept. 1944; comdg. gen. XV Air Force Service Command, September 1944-May 1945; comdg. gen. XV Air Force, May 1945-July 1945; comdg. gen. Mediterranean Air Force, July 1945-Aug. 1945; joint chief of Staff, Wash., D.C., Sept. 1945-Dec. 1945; chief of Air Installations in Office of comdg. gen. Army Air Forces, Dec. 1945-Jan. 1946. Loaned by War Dept. to War Assets Adminstrn. as dep. adminstr. for aircraft disposal, Jan. 1946-Nov. 1946; vice administr. for Staff Operations, War Assets Adminstrn., 1946-48; retired from U.S. Air Force, June 1948. Dir. McClanahan Oil Co.; exec. v.p. and dir., Great Lakes Chem. Corp.; v.p. Ewin Engring. Corp., D.G. Volkert & Assos. Mem. Washington Bd. Trade. Rated command pilot and combat observer. Home: Washington DC Died Feb. 4, 1970; buried Arlington Nat. Cemetery, Arlington VA

MOLLOY, THOMAS MARCUS coast guard officer; b. Worcester, Mass., June 4, 1874; s. John and Mary (Carey) M.; B.S., Worcester Poly. Inst., 1897; m. Caroline Emily Ainslie, June 24, 1909; children-Marian Ainslie (wife of Dr. Gaudens Megaro), Eleanor Virginia (wife of Dr. Julius S. Prince), Robert Thomas. Cadet, U.S. Revenue Cutter Service (now U.S. Coast Guard), 1897; commd. 3d lt., 1899, and advanced through the grades to rear adm.; served in northern coast patrol, 1917; overseas duty, Oct. 1917-Jan. 1919; retired, 1938, recalled to active duty, 1941, assigned on staff of comdt., U.S. Coast Guard Hdqrs., Washington, D.C. Decorated Navy Cross. Pres. Coast Guard Welfare Assn. Mem. Worcester Poly. Inst. and Coast Guard Acad. alumni assns., U.S. Naval Inst., Am. Soc. Naval Engrs., Mil. Order World Wars, Am. Legion. Home: North Colebrook, Conn.; also 2015 Belmont Road N.W., Washington. Office: U.S. Coast Guard Hdqrs., 1300 E St. N.W., Washington 25. Died Oct. 11, 1945; buried in Arlington National Cemetery.

MOLONEY, HERBERT WILLIAM advt. rep.; b. Rockville Center, L.I., N.Y., Sept. 5, 1895; s. Patrick Henry and Katherine (Keon) M.; student St. Francis Xavier Coll.; m. Elizabeth Rudden, June 12, 1920; children-Herbert W., Philip J. With Moloney, Regan and Schmitt, newspaper gen. advt. reps., and predecessors co. Paul Block & Assos., N.Y.C. (also Chgo, Boston, Detroit, Phila., San Francisco, Los Angeles, Seattle), 1908-, progressed to sales mgr. and exec. v.p., pres., now chmn. bd. Served as pvt., 7th Regt., N.Y. N.G. on Mexican Border, 1916; 2d lt., 369th Inf., U.S. Army, France, 1917, disch. as capt., 1919, a.d.c. to comdg. gen. 35th Div. Decorated Purple Heart, 7th Regt., Cross of Honor, World War I. Fgn. Service medal with 3 battle bars. Mem. Am. Assn. Newspaper Reps., Am. Newspaper Pubs. Assn. (past mem. governing bd. bur. advt.). Mem. Cardinal Spellman's Com. of the Laity. Club: Westchester Country; New York Athletic, Advertising, Union League (N.Y.C.). Home: Ten Gracie Sq., N.Y.C. 28. Office: 777 3d Av., N.Y.C. Died Sept. 28, 1967; buried Gate of Heaven Cemetery, Valhalla, N.Y.

MOLONEY, WILLIAM CURRY, physician, educator; b. Boston, Dec. 19, 1907; s. Francis and Elizabeth (Curry) M.; M.D., Tufts U., 1932; m. Josephine O'Brien, Nov. 1933; children—Patricia, William Curry, Elizabeth, Thomas. Prof. medicine Harvard Med. Sch.; also physician Peter Bent Brigham Hosp. Dep. dir. Atomic Bomb Casualty Commn., Hiroshima, Japan, 1952-54. Served as maj., M.C., AUS, World War II. Diplomate Am. Bd. Internal Medicine. Fellow A.C.P., Internat. Soc. Hematology, Am. Assn. Cancer Research, Mass. Med. Soc.; mem. A.M.A., Asso. Am. Physicians, Alpha Omega Alpha. Office: Boston MA Died Feb. 21, 1972.

MOMSEN, CHARLES B(OWERS) navy ofcr.; b. Flushing, L.I., N.Y.; s. Hart and Susie (Bowers) M.; grad. U.S. Naval Acad.; m. Anne Lyles Offutt, June 7, 1919 (dec.); children-Charles B., Evelyn C.; m. 2d, Mrs. Irvine Schmidt, Dec. 18, 1953. Commd. midshipman U.S. Navy, 1920; grad. U.S. Naval Acad.; rear adm., 1945; asst. chief Naval Operations, Undersea Warfare, Washington; comdr. Submarine Force U.S. Pacific Fleet; later comdr. Joint Task Force Seven; ret. as vice adm., 1955; now cons. Gen. Dynamics Corp. Awarded Navy Cross, D.S.M. (Navy and Army), Legion of Merit (2 gold stars). Home: 719 N. Overlook Dr., Alexandria, Va. Died May 1967.

MONAHAN, ARTHUR COLEMAN, educational expert; b. Framingham, Mass., Mar. 24, 1877; s. Michael and Johannah (Coleman) M.; B.S., Mass. Agrl. Coll., 1900; m. Mary Ellen Cody, June 30, 1904. Instr. Mass. Agrl. Coll. and asst. at Expt. Sta., 1900-01; teacher and prin. pub. high schs., 1901-10; specialist in rural and agrl. edn., U.S. Bureau of Edn., Washington, July 1, 1910-Jan. 8, 1918; maj., U.S. Army, Jan. 8, 1918-Jan. 1, 1921; attached to surgeon general's office in ednl. service, div. of reconstruction, 1918-19; lt. col. U.S. Army Reserves (med. dept.), S.C.; chief of ednl. service, Walter Reed Gen. Hosp., 1919-20; dir. bureau edn., Nat. Catholic Welfare Council, 1921-22, editor and ednl. adviser, 1923-32; asst. to commr. in charge of property, U.S. Office of Indian Affairs, since 1932. Mem. N.E.A. Lecturer on sch. administration and edn.; author various bulletins and contbr. on ednl. topics. Address: 3700 13th St. N.W., Washington DC

MONCKTON, ROBERT army officer, colonial gov.; b. England, June 24, 1726; s. John and Lady Elizabeth (Manners) M.; 4 children. Served with English Army at Flanders and Germany, 1742-43; commd. capt., 1744; served in campaign of 1745; commd. maj., 1747, served in 3d Foot Guard; lt. col. 47th Foot Guard, 1751; mem. Parliament from Pontefract, 1751-52, 71; apptd. provincial councillor for N.S., 1753; lt. gov. Annapolis Royal, 1754; commanded capture of Beausejour and other French ports, 1755; lt. gov. N.S., 1756; apptd. col. comdt. 2d Battalion 60th Royal Am. Regt., 1757; gov. N.S., 1758; 2d in command Quebec expdn. with temporary rank brig. gen., 1759; col. 17th Regt., 1759; commanded So. dist., 1760; maj. gen. and comdr.-in-chief expdn. against Martinque, 1761, effected surrender of Island by Feb. 5, 1761; gov. Province of N.Y., 1761-63; gov. Berwick-on-Tweed and Holy Island, 1765; commd. lt. gen., 1770; gov. Portsmouth (Eng.), 1779, 82. Died Eng., May 21, 1782.

MONELL, AMBROSE commd. col. Aviation Sect., Signal Corps, 1917; resigned as pres. Internat. Nickel Co., 1917, to enter army; was dir. Am. Internat. Corp., Midvale Steel & Ordnance Co., Internat. Motor Co., Liberty Nat. Bank of N.Y., Am. Bank Note Co., Haskell & Barker Car Co., etc. V.p. Soc. for Relief of French War Orphans. Mem. Am. Inst. M.E., Inventors Guild. Home: New York, N.Y. Died May 2, 1921.

MONFORT, ELIAS RIGGS postmaster; b. Greensburg, Ind., Mar. 2, 1842; s. Joseph Glass (D.D.) and Hannah Congar (Riggs) M.; A.B., Hanover (Ind.) Coll., 1865, A.M., 1874, LL.D., 1884; LL.B., Cincinnati Law Sch., 1867; m. Emma A. Taylor, Sept. 4, 1867. Pvt. Co. A. (Guthrie Grays), Ohio Inf., June-Oct. 5, 1861; 2d lt. to capt., 75th Ohio Inf., Oct. 5, 1861-Jan. 3, 1864; in battles of Philippi, Bealington, Laurel Hill, Carrick's Ford, McDowell, Shaw's Ridge, Shenandoah Mountain, Franklin, Cross Keys, Cedar Mountain, Straussburg, Feeeman's Ford, Sulphur Springs, Waterloo Bridge, Warrenton, 2d battle of Bull Run, Fredericksburg, Chancellorsville, and Gettysburg; discharged, Jan. 2, 1864, on account of wounds received at Gettysburg, July 2, 1863, began practice of law at Greensburg, 1867; removed to Cincinnati, 1875; sr. mem. firm of Monfort & Co., pubs. Herald and Presbyter 1874—; editorial writer for many yrs.; pres. Mamolith Carbon Paint Co. Mem. Cincinnati Sch. Bd., 1890-99 (pres. last 3 yrs.); county clerk Hamilton Co., O., 1896, 1897; postmaster of Cincinnati, 1899-1915. Pres. Bd. of Trustees, Hamilton Co. (O.) Soldiers' and Sailors' Memorial

Assn. (built $250,000 memorial bldg.); pres. trustees, Presbytery of Cincinnati, v.p. and trustee Lane Theol. Sem., Cincinnati, 1879—; trustee Hanover Coll., 1878—. Comdr. G.A.P. Dept of Ohio, 1900; comdr. Ohio Commandery Loyal Legion, 1907; comdr.-in-chief G.A.R. 1915-16. Died July 29, 1920.

MONROE, JAMES 5th Pres. U.S.; b. Westmoreland County, Va., Apr. 28, 1758; s. Spence and Elizabeth (Jones) M.; attended Coll. William and Mary, 1774-76; studied law under Thomas Jefferson, 1780-83; m. Eliza Kortright, Feb. 1786, 2 children, Eliza, Maria, Commd. lt. 3d Va. Regt., Continental Army, 1776; served at battles of Harlem, White Plains and Trenton; promoted maj., 1777; side to Earl of Stirling, 1777-78; served at battles of Brandywine, Germantown and Monmouth; as mil. commr. for Va. with rank of lt. col. visited Southern army, 1780; mem. Va. Assembly, 1782, 86, 1810-11; mem. Continental Congress from Va., 1783-86; admitted to Va. bar, 1786; attended Annapolis Conv., 1786; mem. Va. Conv. to ratify U.S. Constn., 1788; mem. U.S. Senate from Va., Nov. 9, 1790-May 27, 1794, mem. senatorial com. to investigate Alexander Hamilton's handling of public funds, 1792; U.S. minister plenipotentiary to France, 1794-96, unable to establish friendly Franco-Am. relations due to French anger over Jay Treaty of 1794; gov. Va., 1799-1802, 11; U.S. minister to France to arrange terms for La. Purchase, 1803; U.S. minister to Eng., 1803-07; U.S. envoy to Spain, 1804; U.S. sec. of state under Pres. James Madison, 1811-17, gave tacit approval to Gen. George Mathews' plans to invade Fla., 1811, withdrew support, 1812; U.S. sec. of war, 1814-15; Pres. of U.S. (Democrat), 1817-25; signed treaty with Spain by which U.S. received Fla., 1819, signed Mo. Compromise Bill, 1820; with Sec. of State John Quincy Adams drew up Monroe Doctrine, 1823, declaring that new world was no longer open to European colonization; mem. bd. visitors U. Va., 1828-31; pres. Va. Constl. Conv., 1829. Died N.Y.C., July 4, 1831; buried Marble Cemetery, N.Y.C.; reinterred Hollywood Cemetery, Richmond, Va., 1885.

MONROE, J(ULES) RABURN lawyer; b. New Orleans, Jan. 6, 1909; s. Jules Blanc and May (Logan) M.; A.B., Princeton, 1929; LL.B., Harvard, 1932; m. Rose Routh Milling, Apr. 24, 1935; children-Marcia Milling, Linda Logan, Alice Blanc. Admitted to La. bar, 1934; atty. RFC, 1932-33; spl. asst. to undersec. Dept. Treasury, 1933; Washington counsel TVA, 1933; asso. Monroe & Lemann, New Orleans, 1934-40, partner, 1940-; gen. counsel La. Power & Light Co., Miss. River Bridge Authority as New Orleans, New Orleans Hotel Assn., New Orleans Terminal Co.; gen. solicitor New Orleans & N.E. Ry. Co., La. So. Ry. Co.; div. counsel So. Ry. Dir. Vicksburg, Shreveport & Pacific Ry., 1946-56; voting trustee St. Charles Hotel, 1946-58; director of Equitable Life Assurance Society; executive council to gov. of La., 1940. Pres. Children's Bur., 1936-37, Orleans Neighborhood Center, 1938-39, Louis S. McGehee Sch., 1952-54; chmn. Gaudet Episcopal High Sch., 1952-54; mem. Citizens Planning Com. Pub. Edn., New Orleans, 1938; dir. Crippled Children's Hosp., 1950-, Council Social Agencies, 1938, Community Chest, 1939, New Orleans Civic Symphony, 1948-54, La. chpt. Am. Heart Assn. La. del-at-large Dem. Nat. Conv., 1940; dir. Crescent City Dem. Assn. Served from lt. (j.g.) to lt. comdr., USCGR, 1942-45; dist. legal officer 8th Naval Dist., 1942. Mem. New Orleans C. of C., Am., La., New Orleans bar assns., Nat. Municipal Assn. (regional v.p.), Am. Ch. Inst. for Negroes (trustee 1948-56), Soc. Colonial Wars (Chancellor 1950-52). Clubs: New Orleans Country, Boston, Yacht, Lawn Tennis (New Orleans). Home: 1424 Louisiana Av., New Orleans 15. Office: Whitney Bldg., New Orleans 12. Died Aug. 17, 1961; buried Metairie Cemetery, New Orleans.

MONROE, THOMAS transportation exec.; b. Washington, July 19, 1899; s. Franklin and Margaret (Melton) M.; student Catholic U., 1919-20, C.F.S., Georgetown U., 1923; m. Helen Rosemary Schladt, July 26, 1923; children-Thomas Melton, Nancy Sue (Mrs. R. P. Briggs). With U.S. Lines, 1923—, v.p., European gen. mgr.; v.p., dir., European gen. mgr., U.S. Lines Operations, Inc.; v.p. Roosevelt S.S. Co., Inc.; chmn. bd., dir. Atlantic Transport Co., Ltd. U.S. del. to and U.S. mem. standing com. Internat. Chamber of Shipping; mem. European com. Nat. Fedn. Am. Shipping. Pres. Service Consignation Atlantique, Paris, Societe Maritime Anversoise, Antwerp, Rossquai, G.m.b.H., Hamburg. Served as shipping advisor on Harriman Mission to Gt. Britain, 1941-42; dir. for United Kingdom and Continent, U.S. War Shipping Adminstrn. Served overseas, U.S. Navy, 1917-19; col. U.S. Army, asst. chief transportation, E.T.O., 1942-46. Decorated U.S. Legion of Merit, French Ordre Du Merite Maritime. Clubs: University, Army and Navy (U.S.); Verbersee (Hamburg); Royal Thames Yacht, Transportation, American (London). Home: 21 Dalecarlia Dr., Westmoreland Hills 16, Md.; also Highfields Farm, Frederick Co., Md.; also Dorset House, Gloucester Pl., London. Office: One Broadway, N.Y.C. 4; also 50 Pall Mall, London, Eng. Died Dec. 9, 1959.

MONTAGUE, FAIRFAX EUBANK, physician; b. Raleigh, N.C., Mar. 7, 1925; s. Edgar Burwell and Mary (Read) M.; M.D., Emory U., 1952; m. Barbara Lucile Wilson, June 4, 1949; children—Sally Paige, David Fairfax, Tyler Clark, Lisa Ashlyn. Intern, Duke Hosp., Durham, N.C., 1952-53; asst. resident in surgery Emory U. Hosp., Atlanta, 1953-54, sr. resident in surgery and neoplastic disease Winship Clinic, 1956-57; asst. resident in surgery Atlanta VA Hosp., 1954-56, sr. resident in surgery and neoplastic disease, 1956-57; mem. staff Putnam Hosp., Palatka, Fla., until 1971, chief staff, 1970. Med. dir. Putnam County Blood Bank, 1957-71. Chmn. Citizens Adv. Com. for Schs., 1967; pres. Putnam County Taxpayers League, 1968. Served with AUS, World War II; ETO. Decorated Bronze Star. Diplomate Am. Bd. Surgery. Fellow A.C.S.; mem. A.M.A., So., Fla. (chmn. com. on blood banks 1965-68), Putnam County (pres. 1967) med. assns., Southeastern Surg. Congress, Putnam C. of C. (dir. 1968-70), Phi Beta Kappa, Alpha Omega Alpha, Sigma Chi. Presbyn. (deacon 1955-57, elder 1958-71). Home: Palatka FL Died July 15, 1971; buried Palatka Meml. Gardens, Palatka FL

MONTAGUE, ROBERT LATANE, marine corps officer (ret.); b. Danville, Va., Apr. 2, 1897; s. Andrew Jackson and Elizabeth Lyne (Hoskins) M.; B.S., Univ. of Va., 1920; student, Univ. of Grenoble, France, 1919; grad. Army Inf. Sch., 1926, Ecole Superieure de Guerre, Paris, 1935, U.S. Naval War Coll., 1941; m. Frances Breckinridge Wilson, June 30, 1932; children—Robert Latane III, Francis Breckinridge. Commd. 2d lt. U.S.M.C., 1917, and advanced through grades to brig. gen., 1946; served in command and staff assignments, World Wars I and II; ret. from active duty, 1946. Awarded Army D.S.C., Navy Cross, Legion of Merit, 2 Presidential unit citations, Cloud and Banner (China). Democrat. Episcopalian. Clubs: St. Anthony, Army Navy (Washington), Country (Texarkana). Home: Urbanna VA Died May 1972.

MONTAGUE, ROBERT MILLER army officer; b. Portland, Ore., Aug. 7, 1899; s. Charles David, and Effie (Miller) M.; student U. of Ore., 1916-17; B.S., U.S. Mil. Acad., 1919; grad. F.A. Basic Sch., 1920, F.A. Sch., Advanced Course, 1933, Command and Gen. Staff Sch., 1938; m. Mary Louise Moran, June 21, 1921; 1 son, Robert Miller. Commd. 2d lt., F.A., U.S. Army, Nov. 1, 1918, and advanced through the grades to lieutenant general, 1955; Operations and Training Div., G-3, July 1941; Artillery Comdr. 83d Inf. Div., June 1942-Mar. 1946; dir. of Antiaircraft and Guided Missiles Br. of the Artillery Sch., 1946-47; comdg. gen., Sandia Base, Albuquerque, N.M., July 1947-Feb. 1951; dir. OPOT Division, Hdqrs. EUCOM, 1951-52; dep. chief army Field Forces, 1952—; comdg. gen., I Corps, 1955-56; comdr. chief, Carribean Command, 1957—. Mem. Delta Tau Delta. Club: Army and Navy Country (Arlington, Va.). Home: 2120 Walnut Pl., Louisville 5. Address: Caribbean Command, Quarry Heights, Canal Zone. Died Feb. 20, 1958.

MONTGOMERY, ALFRED E(UGENE) naval officer; b. Omaha, June 12, 1891; s. Eugene and Julia (Smith) M.; B.S., U.S. Naval Acad., 1912; m. Alice Claire Smith, Mar. 4, 1919; children-Brooke (dec.), Anne. Commd. ensign USN, 1912, advanced through grades to vice adm. Awarded Navy Cross, D.S.M. with 2 Gold Stars, Legion of Merit with 1 gold star; medals Expeditionary, Mexican, Victory, Def. European-African -Middle Eastern, Am. Asiatic-Pacific, medal of Philippine Liberation. Clubs: Army and Navy Country, Chevy Chase Country (Washington). Now retired. Address: The Highlands, Seattle 98177. Died Dec. 15, 1961.

MONTGOMERY, BENJAMIN F., army officer; b. Petersburg, Va., s. Joseph R. and Anne E. (Griffin) M.; ed. pub. and high schs., Petersburg, Va., and Va. Acad.; m. Petersburg, Va., Dec. 27, 1877, Ella Franklin. Electrician; practical telegrapher; early life associated with Western Union and other co's; entered U.S. signal service, 1875; served at hdqrs. chief signal officer of the Army, 1875-7; on detached duty with Presidents Hayes, Garfield and Arthur, 1877-82, at exec. mansion; on exec. staffs Presidents Arthur and Cleveland, 1882-9; exec. clerk and actg. asst. sec. to Presidents Harrison and Cleveland, 1889-97; apptd. by President McKinley, May, 1893, capt. signal corps, U.S.A. Upon declaration of war assigned to duty as chief Telegraph and Cipher Bureau in office of the President, commissioned, Aug. 1, 1898, lieut. col. and chief signal officer 6th army corps. Upon reorganization of the army, Feb. 2, 1901, reassigned to duty, charge of Telegraph and Cipher Bureau, Exec. Office. In Mar., 1903, apptd. by President Roosevelt Chief of Telegraph and Cipher Bureau of the Executive Office and commissioned maj. U.S. A. Residence: 2209 Washington Circle, Washington DC

MONTGOMERY, JAMES EGLINTON retired b. Dutchess County, N.Y., Sept. 20, 18—; s. John Crathorne and Elizabeth (Philips) M.; grad. Princeton, 1845; twice married; m. 2d, Florence Miller, Nov. 15, 1904. Studied law; civ. engr. Pa. R.R., 1847-51. Served as asst. adj. gen. 6th, 13th, 22d corps U.S.A., 1861-66; wounded thrice; sec. to Admiral Farragut on visit to European govts., 1867-68; consul at Geneva, 1877-79, at Leipzig, 1879-82, at Brussels, 1882, at Trieste, 1882; resigned on account of ill health. Republican. Episcopalian. Author: Our Admiral's Flag Abroad, 1870. Home: Pasadena, Calif. Died 1909.

MONTGOMERY, JOHN BERRIEN naval officer; b. Allentown, N.J., Nov. 17, 1794; s. Dr. Thomas West and Mary (Berrien) M.; m. Mary Henry, Aug. 1820, 9 children. Apptd. midshipman U.S. Navy, 1812, lt., 1818; served on African Coast, 1818-20; exec. officer frigate Constitution, 1835; promoted comdr., 1839; in command ship Portsmouth in Sloat's Squadron on West Coast during Mexican War; raised Am. flag at San Francisco and near-by settlements, 1846; commd. capt., 1853; commanded Pacific Squadron, 1861; promoted to commodore (ret.), 1862; commanded Charlestown (Mass.) Navy Yard, 1862-63, Washington Navy Yard, 1863-65; commd. rear adm. (ret.), 1866. Died Carlisle, Pa., Mar. 25, 1873; buried Oak Hill Cemetery, Washington, D.C.

MONTGOMERY, MORRIS CARPENTER, judge; b. Hustonville, Ky., Apr. 1, 1907; s. Charles Francis and Mary Allene (Carpenter) M.; A.B., Transylvania Coll., 1928; student U. Ky., 1927; LL.B., Washington and Lee U., 1930; m. Phoebe Frances Wash., Aug. 22, 1936 (dec. Sept. 1969); 1 dau., Lydia Morris. Admitted to Ky. bar, 1930; practice of law, 1930-54; police judge, 1935-36; city atty., Liberty, Ky., 1938-51, 52-53; commonwealth atty. Commonwealth Ky., 1951-52; judge Ct. Appeals Ky., 1954-69, chief justice, 1959-60. Mem. Ky. Senate, 1954; mem. exec. council Nat. Conf. Chief Justices, 1959-60. Served USAAF, 1942-46; lt. col. Res. Mem. Inst. Judicial Adminstrn; Am. Judicature Soc., Am. Law Inst., Ky. Jud. Council (chmn.), Phi Delta Phi, Kappa Alpha. Mem. Christian Ch. Home: Lawrenceburg KY Died Sept. 3, 1969; buried Lawrenceburg KY

MONTGOMERY, ROBERT HIESTER lawyer, accountant; b. Mahanoy City, Pa., Sept. 21, 1872; s. Thomas and Annie (Kline) M.; ed. pub. and night schs.; LL.D., Dickinson Coll.; m. Elizabeth Adams Shaw, Nov. 5, 1904; children-Robert Shaw (dec.), Arthur, Elizabeth; m. 2d, Lois Cate Gibb, Jan. 6, 1928; m. 3d, Eleanor Foster, July 26, 1934. Partner in firm of Heins, Whelen, Lybrand & Co., accountants, 1896-97, Lybrand, Ross Bros. & Montgomery, 1898—; admitted to bar, Phila., 1900, New York, 1904; instr. economics, Sch. of Business, Columbia, 1912-14; asst. prof. accounting, 1914-19, prof. and mem. administrative bd. 1919-31. Served as pvt. Light Battery A, Phila. Light Arty., Pa. Vols., Spanish-Am. War, including Porto Rican campaign, 1898; mem. N.G. Pa., 1898-1902; commd. lt. col. N.A., Mar. 1918; chief of sect. on organization and methods, Office of Dir. of Purchases, Gen. Staff Washington, Jan.-Apr. 1918; organizer and mem. War Dept. Bd. of Appraisers, Apr. 1918-Apr. 1919; War Dept. rep. on price fixing com., of War Industries Bd., May 1918-Feb. 1919; chief price fixing sect. of Purchase, Storage and Traffic Div. of Gen. Staff, Sept. 1918-Jan. 1919; hon. discharged Apr. 1919. Served as dir. research and planning under NRA. Founder and dir. Fairchild Tropical Garden, Coconut Grove, Fla. Mem. Assn. Bar City of New York, N.Y. State Bar Assn., Am. Bar Assn., Nat. Tax Assn., Am. Inst. Accountants (pres. 1935-37); pres. Am. Assn. Pub. Accountants, 1912-14, N.Y. State Soc. of CPA's (pres. 1922-24); exec. sec. War Policies Commn., Washington, 1931. Republican. Methodist. Mason. Clubs: Union League, Uptown, Round Hill, Greenwich Country. Author: Income Tax Procedure, 1917-27, 29; Federal Tax Practice, 1929, 39; Federal Tax Handbook, 1932-41; Excess Profits Tax Procedure, 1920-21; N.Y. State Income Tax Procedure, 1921; Auditing Theory and Practice, 1912-27, 1934, 1940; Auditing Principles, 1923; Financial Handbook, 1925; 1933; Federal Tax Handbook Supplement, 1941-42; Federal Taxes on Estates, Trusts and Gifts, 1941-51; Excess Profits and Other Federal Taxes on Corporations, 1941-42; Federal Taxes on Corporations, 1942-45; Federal Taxes-Corporations and Partnerships, 1946-52. Home: Coconut Grove, Fla. Office: 2 Broadway, N.Y.C. Died May 2, 1953.

MOOD, ORLANDO CLARENDON army officer; b. South Carolina, Dec. 1, 1899; B.S., The Citadel, 1921; grad. Inf. Sch., company officers course, 1931, Tank Sch., 1932, Command and Gen. Staff Sch., 1937, Army Indsl. Coll., 1940. Commd. 2d lt., U.S. Army, 1921, and advanced through the grades to brig. gen., October 20, 1950; now chief of staff Second Army. Decorations: D.S.M., Legion of Merit with 2 Oak Leaf Clusters. Army Commendation Ribbon; Legion of Honor, Croix de Guerre with Palm (France); Order of Leopold II, Croix de Guerre with Palm (Belgium); Couronne de Chien, Croix de Guerre (Luxembourg). Address: Care Adjutant General, Dept. of the Army, Washington. Died May 2, 1953.

MOODY, GIDEON CURTIS U.S. Senator, lawyer; b. Cortland, N.Y., Oct. 16, 1832; s. Stephen and Charlotte M.; academic edn.; studied law in Syracuse; removed to Indiana and admitted to bar, 1852; pros. atty. Floyd County, 1854; served in Civil War; lt. 9th Ind. vol. inf., April 1861; rose to col., Nov. 15, 1862; mustered out of vols., May 1861; apptd. capt. 19th U.S. inf., and served until 1864. Located in Dak., 1864; mem. and speaker, territorial ho. of reps.; asso. justice Supreme Court of territory 5 yrs.; del. Nat. Rep. Conv., 1868, 1888, 1892; mem. constitutional convs., S.D., 1833, 1885; chmn. of com. to draft and present memorial to Congress asking for admission as a State; elected U.S.

senator for S.D. by legislature under constitution of 1885; reelected Oct. 16, 1889, serving until 1891. Home: Deadwood, S.D. Died 1904.

MOODY, WILLIAM HENRY jurist; b. Newbury, Mass., Dec. 23, 1853; s. Henry L. and Melissa Augusta (Emerson) M.; grad. Phillips Acad., Andover, Mass., 1872; A.B., Harvard, 1876; studied law in office of Richard H. Dana, Boston; LL.D., Amherst and Tufts colls., 1904; unmarried. Admitted to bar, 1878, and began practice at Haverhill, Mass. City solicitor, 1888-90; dist. atty. for Eastern Dist. of Mass., 1890-95; elected 54th Congress, 1895, for unexpired term (1895-97) of Gen. William Cogswell, deceased; reëlected 55th to 57th Congresses (1897-1903); resigned from 57th Congress, Apr. 30, 1902; Sec. of the Navy, May 1, 1902-July 1, 1904; Atty. Gen. of U.S., July 1, 1904-Dec. 16, 1906, in cabinets of President Roosevelt; asso. justice Supreme Court of U.S., Dec. 17, 1906-Nov. 20, 1910, when retired on account of ill health. Republican. Home: Haverhill, Mass. Died July 2, 1917.

MOON, DON P. naval officer; b. Kokomo, Ind., Apr. 18, 1894; s. Barnabas C. and Ellen Pearl (Bennett) M.; B.S., U.S. Naval Acad., 1916; student U.S. Naval Acad. Post Grad. Sch., 1920-21; S.M., U. of Chicago, 1922; student U.S. Naval War Coll., jr. course, Newport, R.I., 1932-33, sr. course, 1937-38; m. Sibyl Peaslee Hall, Sept. 28, 1920; children-Meredith Whittier, Don Pardee, David Peaslee, Peter Clayton. Commd. ensign, U.S.N., 1916, advancing through the grades to rear adm., 1944; served in U.S.S. Arizona, 1916-20, U.S.S. Colorado, 1923-25, U.S.S. Nevada, 1926, U.S.S. John Ford (destroyer), 1934-37; in design sect., in charge patent sect., Bureau of Ordnance, 1927; officer in charge drafting room Naval Gun Factory, 1928-29; destroyer squadron gunnery officer, Pacific, 1929-32; comdr. destroyer div., Pacific and Atlantic Fleets, 1940-41; comdr. destroyer squadron, Atlantic Fleets, 1940-41; comdr. destroyer squadron, Atlantic Fleet, operating in connection with N. African invasion, part of time in British Home Fleet and in support of Russian Convoys, 1941-42; in planning sect. of comdr. in chief, U.S. Fleet, 1943; commd. rear adm. and assigned sea duty, 1944. Decorated World War Victory medal with bronze star, Am. Defense medal with numeral A, Am. Theater medal, European Theater medal with numeral 2 and 2 bronze stars, Commendation Ribbon, Order of Alexandrov (Russia). Mem. Naval Acad. Alumni Assn., Naval Inst. (since 1916). Home: 818 W. Sycamore St., Kokomo, Ind. Died Aug. 5, 1944.

MOONEY, EUGENE FRANCIS, tobacco co. exec.; b. Pawtucket, R.I., Mar. 18, 1907; s. Lawrence Sylvester and Katherine (Radigan) M.; student Providence Coll., 1930; m. Virginia Randall, Dec. 29, 1941. With Am. Tobacco Co., 1933-71, dir. sales, 1963-66, vice president sales, 1966-71, also dir. Served to comdr. USNR, 1942-45. comdr. Res. Catholic. Club: Greenwich Country. Home: Greenwich CT Died Oct. 1971.

MOONEY, JAMES DAVID b. Cleve., Feb. 18, 1884; s. Hon. James David and Mary Elizabeth (Burns) M.; B.S., N.Y.U.; B.S. in Mining Engring., M.E., Dr. Engring., Case Inst. Tech.; m. Leonora Jane Watson, 1914; children-Martha Jane, James David, Patricia Avice; m. 2d, Ida May MacDonald, 1929; children-Michael MacDonald, John Burns, Alan Patrick. Formerly exec. v.p., dir. Gen. Motors Corp.; prin. J.D. Mooney Assos., indsl. cons., N.Y.C.; pres., dir. F. L. Jacobs Co., Detroit, 1943—. Served as capt., 309 Ammunition Reg., U.S. Army in France, World War I. Capt. U.S.N. (Res.) active duty, Bur. Aeros., Advanced Base Div., 11th Amphibious Force in Europe. Staff of Chief of Naval Operations, World War II. Mem. council N.Y.U.; gen. chmn. United Hosp. Fund Campaign, 1952. Mem. Vets. Fgn. Wars. Am. Legion, Am. Soc. Mech. Engrs., Am. Inst. Mining and Metall. Engrs., Soc. Automotive Engrs., Soc. Am. Mil. Engrs., Soc. Am. Mil. Engrs., Sigma Chi, Theta Nu Epsilon, Beta Gamma Sigma, Alpha Delta Sigma. Clubs: Univ., Union League (N.Y.); Creek Piping Rock (Locust Valley, L.I.); Seawanhaka Yacht (Oyster Bay, N.Y.); Army and Navy (Washington). Author: Principles of Orgn. Home: Centre Island, Oyster Bay, N.Y. Died Sept., 1957.

MOONLIGHT, THOMAS governor Wyo.; b. Forfarshire, Scotland, Nov. 10, 1833; emigrated to U.S., 1856; was farmer and later worked in glass factory; served brig. gen. through Civil war; later sec. of State of Kan.; member Kan. senate 1873-74; adj. gen. Kan., 1883-84; nominated for gov., 1886, but defeated gov. Wyo., 1888-90; U.S. minister to Bolivia, 1894-97; Democrat. Died 1899.

MOORE, BRYANT EDWARD army officer; b. Ellsworth, Me., June 6, 1894; grad. U.S. Mil. Acad.; commd. 2d lt. Inf., Aug. 1917, and advanced through grades to maj. gen., 1945; G-2 of expdn. to Caledonia, 1942; C.O. 164th Inf. on Guadalcanal, 1942; assigned 104th Inf.Div., Camp Adair, Ore., 1943; fought in Holland and Germ. with 104th div.; assigned Div. Comdr. 8th Inf. Div., 1945; assigned Div. Comdr. 88th Inf., Div., 1945. Awarded Distinguished Service Medal with 2 oak leaf clusters; Silver Star with cluster; Legion of Merit with cluster; Bronze Star with cluster; Distinguished Service Order (British); Legion of Honor, Croix de Guerre (French); Order of St. Lazarus (Italian). Address: care of The Adjutant General, War Dept., Washington 25. Died Feb. 24, 1951.

MOORE, CHARLES ARTHUR corp. exec.; b. Lynn, Mass., June 23, 1880; s. Charles Arthur and Mary (Campbell) M.; student St. Paul's School, 1893-98; A.B., Yale, 1903; m. Annette Sperry, 1907; m. 2d, Elizabeth Hyde, June 5, 1920. Vice pres. Manning, Maxwell & Moore, Inc., until 1927, pres., 1927-31, chmn. bd., 1931—. Mem. Peary Expdn., 1897. Served with Montenegro Army, Balkan War; served as maj. 56th Arty. A.E.F., World War I. Life mem. Am. Mus. Natural History, N.Y. Zool. Soc. Clubs: Racquet and Tennis, Yale. Home: Round Hill, Greenwich, Conn. Office: Chrysler Bldg., N.Y.C. Died Aug. 23, 1949.

MOORE, CHARLES BRAINARD TAYLOR officer U.S.N.; b. Paris, Ill., July 29, 1853. Apptd. from Ill., and grad. U.S. Naval Acad., 1873; midshipman, May 31, 1873; ensign, July 16, 1874; promoted through grades to rear admiral, June 14, 1911. Served on Alaska and Shenandoah, 1873-74, Pensacola, 1874-75, Pasaic, 1876, Alliance, Monogahela and Wyoming, 1877, Essex, 1877-79, Franklin, 1880-81, Onward, 1881-83, Galena, 1883-85; Navy Yard, Boston, 1885-86; Alert, 1887-90; Naval Acad., 1890-93; Newark, 1893-96; Naval Acad., 1896-97; naval sta., Port Royal, 1897-98; comd. Nantucket, 1898; exec. officer Alexander, 1898, Bennington, 1898-1900, Monterey, 1900-01; comd. Brutus, 1901; Navy Yard, Mare Island, 1901-04; naval gov. of Tutuila, Samoa, commandant of naval sta., and comdg. station ship, 1904-08; Navy Yard, Phila., 1908; comdg. Colorado, 1909; Naval War Coll., and Examining and Retiring bds., 1910; comdt. Naval Training Stas., San Francisco, 1911. Olongapo and Cavite, P.I., 1912, Hawaii, 1913; retired, July 29, 1915. Mem. exec. com. State Council Defense, for Macon Co., Ill., 1917-18; chmn. "Four-Minute Men," Decatur, Ill., Also mem. exec. council "Four Minute Men" of Ill., 1917-18. Del. Ill. Constl. Conv., 1920—. Home: Decatur, Ill. Died Apr. 4, 1923.

MOORE, DAVID HASTINGS bishop; b. Athens, O., Sept. 4, 1838; s. Hon. Eliakim Hastings and Amy (Barker) M.; A.B., Ohio U., 1860, A.M., 1863; D.D., Ohio Wesleyan, 1875; LL.D., Mt. Union Coll., 1896, U. of Denver, 1899; m. Julia Sophia Carpenter, June 21, 1860; son, Eliakim Hastings. Ordained M.E. ministry, 1860. Served in Civil War; pvt. and capt. Co. A, 87th Ohio Inf., and maj. lt. col., 1925th Ohio Inf. in Civil War. Pastor at Columbis, Cincinnati, etc.; pres. Cincinnati, Wesleyan Coll., 1875-80; pres. Colo. Sem., and chancellor U. of Denver, 1880-89; prof. polit. economy, U. of Colo., 1889; editor Western Christian Advocate, 1889-1900; elected bishop, 1900. Stationed at Shanghai, China, with spl. jurisdiction over M.E. missions in China, Japan and Korea, 1900-04; stationed at Portland, Ore., 1904-08, at Cincinnati, 1908-12, retired 1912. Home: Indianapolis, Ind. Died Nov. 23, 1915.

MOORE, E(DWIN), E(ARL) steel exec.; b. Indpls., Jan. 20, 1894; s. Joseph Austin and Anna Eliza (Snyder) M.; student Ind. U., 1913-16; m. Lillian G. Seaney, Aug. 7, 1919; children-Anna Jane (Mrs. Nicholas), Thomas Joseph. Joined U.S. Steel Corp. as constrn. machinist Gary (Ind.) mills Am. Sheet & Tin Plate Co., 1919, foreman machine shop, 1920, gen. engring. staff Pitts. Office, spl. work in connection with mechanization of tinning practices, 1923, acting mgr. roll and machine works, Canton, O., 1924-25, asst. mgr. Shenango works, New Castle, Pa., 1925-27, Gary works, 1927-32; asst. to operating v.p. Ill. Steel Co., 1932 (in 1935 Ill. Steel and Carnegie Steel merged as Carneigie-Ill. Steel Corp.), gen. supt. South steel works, Chgo., 1935, Gary steel works, 1937-40, v.p. indsl. relations, Pitts., 1940-50, v.p. indsl. relations adminstrn. U.S. Steel Co., 1950-53, v.p., asst. to pres., 1953-59 Vice pres. Civic Light Opera Assn. Pitts.; hon. chmn. Jr. Achievement SW. Pa. Bd. dirs. W. Pa. Hosp., Pitts. chpt ARC. Served as q.m. sgt. inf. U.S. Army, Mexican border, 1916; capt., 150th FA. (unit of Rainbow Div.), AEF, overseas, 1917-19; civil ct. judge, civil adminstr. Army of Occupation, Neuenahr, Germany, 1918-19. Mem. Pa. Soc., W. Pa. Hist. Soc. (trustee), Engrs. Soc. Western Pa., Am. Iron and Steel Inst., Assn. Iron and Steel Engrs., Newcomen Soc., Pitts. C. of C., N.A.M. (dir., regional v.p.) Home: 909 Amberson Av., Pitts. 32. Office: 525 William Penn Pl., Pitts. Died Apr. 17, 1965; buried Allegheny Cemetery, Pitts.

MOORE, EDWIN KING rear admiral U.S.N.; b. Georgetown, O., July 24, 1847; s. Joseph Austin and Nancy Jane (King) M.; grad. U.S. Naval Acad., 1868; m. Eva, d. Gen. James H. Carleton, U.S.A., of San Francisco, Oct. 2, 1877 (died 1921). Promoted ensign, 1869; master, 1870; lt., 1873; lt. comdr., 1894; comdr., 1899; capt., Oct. 11, 1903; rear admiral, Sept. 7, 1908. Has served in many capacities; comd. steamer, Patterson, in Alaska, 1 1895-97; U.S. Naval Acad., 1898; comd. Helena, Philippines, 1899-1901; Navy Yard. Boston, 1902-04; comd. flagship Chicago, Pacific Sta., 1905; mem. Naval Examining and Retiring Bds., 1906-07; comdt. Navy Yard, Portsmouth, N.H., 1908-09; retired by operation of law, July 24, 1909. Died Sept. 1, 1931.

MOORE, EDWIN WARD naval officer; b. Alexandria, Va., June 1810; m. Emma (Stockton) Cox, 1849. Commd. midshipman U.S. Navy, 1825, lt., 1835, resigned 1839; accepted command Navy of Republic of Tex., 1839; commd. post capt., commanding with courtesy title commodore, 1842; destroyed Mexican commerce from the Gulf of Mexico, entered into de facto alliance with Yucatan rebels, and captured town of Tabasco, 1841; surveyed, charted Tex. coast, saved federalist Yucatecans from hasty peace with Centralist Santa Anna, continuing an alliance with Texas; agreed with Yucatan authorities, in consideration of a money payment sufficient to finish refitting the fleet, to attack the Mexican Squadron blockading the Yucatan Coast; received a proclamation from Houston declaring him guilty of "disobedience, contumacy, and mutiny", and suspended from command; tried by ct. martial, found not guilty on 18 counts, guilty on 4. Author: To The People of Texas (best collection of source materials on Texan Navy), 1843. Died N.Y.C., Oct. 5, 1865.

MOORE, ERNEST CARROLL, JR., lawyer; b. Youngstown, O., Sept. 6, 1913; s. Roy John and Margaret (Brownlee) M.; B.A., U. Cal. at Los Angeles, 1935; LL.B., Harvard, 1939; m. Frances Marian Miller, Oct. 4, 1943; children—Ernest Carroll III, Meredith Brownleigh. Admitted to Hawaii bar, 1941; with Dillingham Corp., Honolulu, 1940-42; practiced in Honolulu, 1946; partner firm Moore, Torkildson & Schulze, 1967-72. Pres. Duraast, Inc., 1969-72. Bd. govs. Am. Nat. Red Cross 1967-72. bd. dirs., exec. com. Aloha United Fund, 1966; trustee Hawaii Sch. Girls, 1967-72. Served to lt. col. AUS, 1942-46. Decorated Bronze Star. Mem. Am. Bar Assn. (co-chmn. subcom. state labor legislation 1966-67, antitrust devel. 1968-69), Honolulu Wine and Food Soc., U.S. C. of C., C. of C. Hawaii (dir. 1969-72), Phi Beta Kappa. Club: Pacific (bd. govs. 1952-61, pres. 1958-59) (Honolulu). Home: Honolulu HI Died Nov. 4, 1972.

MOORE, FRANCIS brigadier gen. U.S.A.; b. in Scotland, Apr. 6, 1841. Pvt. and sergt. Co. M, 1st Colo. Cav., 1861-63; capt., 65th U.S.C.T., Dec. 29, 1863; lt. col., Feb. 18, 1865; bvtd. lt. col., Mar. 13, 1865, "for faithful and meritorious services during the war"; hon. mustered out, June 21, 1865; maj. 65th U.S.C.T., June 21, 1865; hon. mustered out, Jan. 8, 1867; 2d lt. 9th U.S. Cav., July 28, 1866; 1st lt., July 12, 1867; capt., Aug. 24, 1872; maj. 5th Cav., July 28, 1892; lt. col. 10th Cav., May 6, 1899; col. 11th Cav., Feb. 2, 1901; brig. gen., Feb. 25, 1901; retired by operation of law, Apr. 6, 1905. Died May 2, 1928.

MOORE, FREDERICK FERDINAND, editor, author; b. Concord, N.H., Dec. 24, 1877; s. James Bell and Nell (Collins) M.; ed. Boston Coll.; m. Florence Frisbee, San Francisco, Aug. 25, 1906; 1 dau., Marjorie. m. 2d, Eleanor Gates, dramatist and author, Oct. 18, 1914. Ran away to sea when a boy and served as a sailor, soldier, civilian scout, and war corr. in various parts of world; served in 2d U.S. Cav. in Philippines, but discharged own application, to resume newspaper work during Russo-Japanese War. Arrived San Francisco from Far East, 1905; editorial staff San Francisco Examiner, 1905-13; editor The Argosy, New York, Jan. 1913-15; established Book Dealers Weekly, 1925. Capt. Intelligence Div., Gen. Staff U.S.A., 1918-19, in Siberia (Amur region, and Chita, Trans-Baikalia with Cossack Ataman Semenoff and Lt. Gen. Oba, Japanese forces). Decoration, Order Rising Sun, Japan; Victory medal, Siberian clasp. Contbr. short stories and critical articles on mil. and naval topics. Author: The Devil's Admiral, 1913; Siberia To-Day, 1919; Sailor Girl, 1920; Isle o' Dreams, 1920; The Samovar Girl, 1921. Home: 66 Fifth Av. Office: 730 Fifth Av., New York NY

MOORE, GEORGE CURTIS, fgn. service officer; b. Toledo, Sept. 7, 1925 s. Paul H. and Lucille (Munn) M.; B.A., U. So. Cal., 1949, M.A., 1951; m. Sarah Anne Stewart, June 21, 1950; children—Lucy Anne, Catherine Jane. Joined U.S. Fgn. Service, 1950; assigned Kaufbeuren and Wuerzburg, Germany, 1950-53; vice consul, Cairo, Egypt, 1953-55; detailed Arabic lang. and area specialization, Beirut, Lebanon, 1956-57; consul, Asmara, Eritrea, 1958-59; polit. officer, Benghazi and Tripoli, Libya, 1959-63; officer in charge Arabian peninsula affairs State Dept., Washington, 1964-67, personnel chief Bur. Near East and South Asia, 1967-68, assigned to Nat. War Coll., 1968-69; charge d'affairs Am. embassy, Khartoum, Sudan, 1969-73. Served with AUS, 1944-46; ETO. Mem. Phi Beta Kappa, Chi Phi, Delta Phi Epsilon. Rotarian. Club: Blue Nile Sailing. Home: Washington DC Died Mar. 2, 1973; buried Arlington Nat. Cemetery, Washington DC

MOORE, GEORGE F. army officer; b. July 31, 1887; B.S., Agrl. and Mech. Coll. of Tex., 1908. Commd. 2d lt., Coast Arty. Corps, Sept. 25, 1909; promoted through grades to col., Oct. 1, 1938; temp. rank of maj. gen. since Dec. 1941; fought in Bataan Campaign, P.I., 1941-42; prisoner of war of Japanese Govt.; with Gen. Wainwright, released, Aug. 1945. Awarded D.S.M., Nov. 1942. Address: Care War Deparment, Washington 25, D.C. Died Dec. 2, 1949.

MOORE, HUGH BENTON, ry. official; b. Huntland, Tenn., Jan. 11, 1874; s. Horatio R. and Annie (Hunt) M.; ed. common schs.; m. Helen Edmunds, of Kansas City, Mo., Sept. 5, 1905. Began as messenger T. & P.

Ry. Co., Dallas, Tex., 1890; pres. and gen. mgr. Tex. City Terminal Ry. Co. since 1917. Commd. capt. O.R.C., 1917; apptd. transportation officer on staff of Gen. Pershing, May 1917; arrived in France, June 10, 1917; supt. Army Transport Service at St. Nazaire, later gen. supt. at principal ports of France; promoted to newly created position of dir. Army Transport Service of all ports and steamship operations of A.E.F. in Europe, Jan. 1918; promoted col.; hon. discharged Feb. 1919. Awarded D.S.M. (U.S.); Legion of Honor (French). Mem. Christian (Disciples) Ch. Mason (K.T., 32 deg., Shriner). Home: Texas City TX

MOORE, JAMES MILES soldier; b. Phila., Oct. 26, 1837; s. John W. and Catherine (Miles) M.; ed. grammar schs., Phila., and acad., Pottstown, Pa.; m. Annie L. Werthelm, May 29, 1877. Entered Union Army, Apr. 18, 1861, pvt. Co. G, 19th Pa. Inf.; discharged Aug. 8, 1861; apptd. 2d lt. 90th Pa. Vols. Inf., Feb. 21, 1862; 1st lt., Mar. 10, 1862; capt. a.p.m. March 11, 1863; transferred to regular army with same rank, July 2, 1864; maj. q.m., June 13, 1867; lt. col. and deputy q.m. gen., July 2,1883; col. and asst. q.m. gen., Jan. 14, 1895; retired for age, Oct. 26, 1901; apptd. to the rank of brig. gen., Apr., 1904. Died 1905.

MOORE, JOHN surgeon, brig. gen., U.S.A., retired, 1890; b. Ind., Aug. 16, 1826; entered U.S.A., asst. surgeon, June 1853; served in Fla.; in Utah Expdn., 1857; in Cincinnati Marine Hosp., 1861-62. Promoted surgeon, June, 1862; med. dir. Central Grand Div., Army of Potomac, 1826-63; med. dir. dept. and army of the Tenn., 1863; was with Sherman at Atlanta and March to the Sea; bvtd. lt. col. and col.; asst. med. purveyor with rank of lt. col., 1883-86; surgeon gen. of army with rank of brig. gen., 1886-90. Died 1907.

MOORE, JOHN WALKER educator; b. McConnellsville, S.C., Jan. 29, 1884; s. James Oscar and Hattie (Walker) M.; B.S., Davidson (N.C.) Coll., 1906, hon. D.Sc., 1940; med. student Univ. of N.C., 1908-10; M.D., U. of Pa., 1912; m. Anna Stockett Kent, Aug. 19, 1920; children-Marjorie Kent, William Kent, John Walker. Interne Episcopal Hosp., Philadelphia, Pa., 1913-15; inst. in pathology and bacteriology, U. of Louisville, 1915-17, inst. in medicine, 1923-49, dean of Sch. of Medicine, 1929-49, Alben W. Barkley prof. of medicine, since 1949; director division medicine and staff exec. Louisville City Hosp., 1923-49. Served as capt., Med. Corps, U.S. Army, later maj., lab. officer to hosp. center, Nantes, France, 1917-19. Received faculty award of merit, University of Louisville, 1936. Technical supervisor, American Red Cross Blood Donor Service, since 1942; consultant for Army Specialized Training Program, Member Association American Physicians, American Coll. Physicians, A.M.A., Central Soc. Clin. Research (pres. 1942-43), Am. Clin. and Clinatol. Assn. Southern Med. Assn. (chmn. sect. on med. edn. 1933), Assn. Am. Med. Colleges (v.p. 1942-43, pres. 1945-46), Alpha Omega Alpha, Kappa Sigma, Phi Chi, Phi Beta Kappa, Phi Kappa Phi, Gorgon's Head (U. of N.C.). Democrat. Presbyterian. Clubs: Pendennis, Pierian. Home: 623 Cochran Hill Rd. Office: Louisville General Hosp., Louisville. Died Nov. 10, 1952.

MOORE, JOHN WHITE chief engr. U.S.N.; b. Plattsburg, N.Y., May 24, 1832; s. Amasa C. and Charlotte E. (Moores) M.; ed. Plattsburg Acad. and Williston Sem. and pvt. instrn., New York; m. Emily, d. Capt. Horace B. Sawyer, U.S.N., Nov. 19, 1863. Apptd. 3d asst. engr. U.S.N., May 21, 1853; promoted 2d asst. engr., June 27, 1855; 1st asst. engr., July 21, 1858; chief engr., Aug. 5, 1861; retired with rank of commodore, May 24, 1894; advanced to rank of rear admiral retired, June 29, 1906, for services during Civil War. Served in Navy Dept., 1853; on Saranac, Mediterranean Sta., 1853-56; Niagra, first Atlantic cable expdn., 1857-58, flagships Colorado and Roanoke, Home Squadron, 1858-60; flagship Richmond, Mediterranean Squadron, 1860-61; Richmond in West Indies, West Gulf Blockading Squadron and Lower Miss. River, 1861-63; engagements with rebel batteries and ram Manassas at head of passes and with rebel defenses at Pensacola, 1861; passage and capture of Fts. Jackson and St. Philip; capture of New Orleans; passage of Vicksburg batteries; Vicksburg batteries and ram Arkansas, 1862; batteries at Port Hudson; capture of Port Hudson, 1863; originator of chain cable protection on sides of wooden ships; also of "War paint" for making ships less visible in action and at night, and of fighting-tops, later universally used in war vessels; supt. of ironclads at New York and Boston, 1863-67; fleet engr. on staff of Admiral Farragut, European Squadron, 1867-68; Navy Yard, Portsmouth, N.H., 1868-72; fleet engr. of Asiatic sta., 1872-75; Navy Yard, Washington, 1876-79; Bd. of Inspection, 1879-82; fleet engr. Pacific sta., 1882-84; Navy Yard, New York, 1886-88; Navy Yard, Mare Island, 1888-93; insp. machinery at Union Iron Works, San Francisco, 1893-94; Navy Yard, New York, during the Spanish War, 1898. Home: Brooklyn, N.Y. Died Mar. 30, 1913.

MOORE, MERRILL psychiatrist; b. Columbia, Tenn., Sept. 11, 1903; s. John Trotwood and Mary Brown (Daniel) M.; student Montgomery Bell Acad., Nashville, 1916-20; B.A., Vanderbilt U., Nashville, 1924; M.D., Vanderbilt Med. Sch., 1928; married Ann Leslie Nichol, Aug. 14, 1930; children-Adam G. N. Moore, John Trotwood, Leslie and Hester. Interne, St. Thomas Hospital, Nashville, Tenn., 1928-29; teaching fellow neurology, Harvard Med. Sch., 1930-31, asst. in neuropathology, 1931-32, research fellow psychiatry, 1936-42; neurological house officer, Boston City Hosp., 1930-31, res. neurological physician, 1930-31; asst. physician, Boston Psychopathic Hosp., 1932-35; grad. asst., Psychiatric Clinic, Mass. General Hospital, 1933-34. Military service, S.W. Pacific, 1942-45; col. M.C., A.U.S.; surgeon, Nanking Hdqrs. Command, 1946. Vis. psychiat., Boston City Hosp.; clin. asso. psychiatry, Harvard Med. Sch.; research asso., Boston Psychopathic Hosp. Awarded Bronze Star (Bougainville), 1944; Army Commendation Ribbon (China), 1946. Fellow American Psychiat. Assn., Am. Neurol. Assn., Mass. Med. Soc., Am. Psychopathol. Assn., A.A.A.S., mem. Am. Med. Assn., Sigma Chi, Phi Beta Kappa (hon. 1941). Author: The Noise That Time Makes, 1929; Six Sides to a Man, 1935; M:one thousand autobiog. sonnets; Clinical Sonnets, 1949; Illegitimate Sonnets, 1950; Case Record From A Sonnetorium, 1952; More Clinical Sonnets, 1952; A Doctor's Book of Hours, 1954; Dance of Death, 1957; The Phoenix & The Bees (poems), 1958; also other vols. of poetry, prose essays; contbr. articles on alcoholism, syphillis, suicide, psychiatry and conchology. Home: 10 Crabtree Rd., Squantum, Qunicy 71, Mass. Died Sept. 20, 1957.

MOORE, RICHARD CURTIS army officer; b. California, Mo., Nov. 24, 1880; s. John Wadsworth and Charlotte Whitney (Curtis) M.; student Westminster Coll. (Fulton, Mo.), 1896-99; B.S., U.S. Mil. Acad., 1903; m. Winifred Davis, Dec. 7, 1910; m. 2d, Mercedes Puterbaugh Miller, Nov. 15, 1921; children-Richard Curtis (dec.), Milton S. (adopted). Commd. 2d lt., U.S. Army, 1903, advanced through grades to maj. gen., 1941; comdr. 318th Engrs., 1917-18; asst. engr. 2d Army, 1918; dep. chief staff, 1940-42; maj. gen. on Joint Chiefs of Staff, Washington, 1943-45; ret. 1945. Mem. Soc. Am. Engrs., Beta Theta Pi. Presbyn. Mason. Clubs: Army and Navy (Washington). Home: Del Monte, Cal. Died Aug. 1966.

MOORE, ROBERT MARTIN physician; b. Somerville, Ind., Nov. 18, 1884; s. Robert (M.D.) and Laura (Martin) M.; A.B., Ind. U., 1911, M.D., 1913; post grad work, Harvard Med. Sch., summers 1920-21, 22; m. Eva Belle Van Dyke. Began practice, 1913; prof. clin. cardiology, Indiana University Sch. of Medicine, since 1931, and member of the board of councilors; chief of Cardiac Clinic, Indianapolis City Hospital; past pres. Ind. Heart Found.; chmn. bd. trustees, Ind. Heart Foundn.; member staff Indiana University Hosp.; mem. visiting staff St. Vincent's Hosp., mem. staff and mem. adv. bd. Methodist Hosp. Capt. Med. Corps, U.S. Army with A.E.F., World War I. Certified by American Board Internal Medicine and Cardiovascular Disease Fellow American Coll. Physicians (Ind. gov. 16 yrs.); mem. Am., Ind. State and Marion County med. assns., Indianapolis Med. Soc. (pres. 1938), Am. Heart Assn. (councilor), Indianapolis Acad. of Medicine and Surgery, Central Soc. for Clinical Research, Am. Assn. for Study of Goitre, Delta Tau Delta, Nu Sigma Nu, Sigma Xi. Republican. Presbyterian. Mason. Contbr. to med. jours. Home: 5617 N. Meridian St. Office: Home Mansur Bldg., Indpls. Died June 23, 1952; buried Crown Hill Cemetery, Indpls.

MOORE, SAMUEL PRESTON surgeon gen. Confederate Army; b. Charleston, S.C., 1813; s. Stephen West and Eleanor Screven (Gilbert) M.; grad. Med. Coll. S.C., 1834; m. Mary Augusta Brown, 1845. Commd. ast. surgeon U.S. Army, 1835, surgeon with rank of maj., 1849-61; surgeon gen. Confederate Army; established examining bds. to weed out unfit, introduced orgn. and methods of med. dept. U.S. Army into Confederate Army; organizer, pres. Assn. Army and Navy Surgeons of Confederate States; mem. Richmond (Va.) Sch. Bd., 1877-89, also Va. Agrl. Soc. Died May 31, 1889.

MOORE, SHERWOOD physician; b. Lynchburg, Va., Oct. 28, 1880; s. Israel Sneed and Nellie Hayward (Wise) M.; student U. of Va., 1900-01; M.D., Washington U., St. Louis, Mo., 1905; m. Veronica Mollison, September 1, 1917; children-Andrew, Peter. Interne, St. Louis (Mo.) City Hosp., 1905-06; sr. resident in obstetrics, Washington U. Hosp., 1906-07; surgeon in pvt. practice, 1907-12; asst. in surgery, St. Louis Children's Hosp., 1910-13; resident radiologist, Mass. Gen. Hosp., 1916-17; asst. in surgery and radiology, Washington U. Sch. of Medicine, 1917-20, asso. in surgery, 1920-27, prof. radiology, 1927-49, emeritus; dir. Edward Mallinckrodt Inst. of Radiology since 1930; roentgenologist, Barnes Hosp., St. Louis Children's Hosp., St. Louis Maternity Hosp., Shriner's Hosp. and McMillan Hosp. Recipient (with Dr. Evarts A. Graham, Dr. Warren H. Cole and Glover H. Copher) of gold medal St. Louis Med. Soc., 1927; hon. mention A.M.A. and Canadian Med. Assn., 1935; Silver medal Am. Acad. Orthopedic Surgeons, 1936; hon. mention Southern Med. Assn., 1937; hon. mention 5th Internat. Congress of Radiology, 1937; bronze medal Miss. Valley Med. So., 1938; 1st award Radiol. Soc. of N.A., 1939; certificate of merit Am. Roentgen Ray Soc., 1936, Am. Med. Assn., 1936 and 1939. Served as lt., M.C., U.S.N.R.F., 1917-22; major and lt. col., M.C., Army of U.S., 1922-42. Diplomate Am. Bd. of Radiology, 1935. Director-at-large, American Cancer Society, 1947. Fellow A.M.A., Am. Coll. of Radiology; mem. Am. Roentgen Ray Soc. (past pres.; chmn. exec. council, 1935-36), Nat. Advisory Cancer Council, Radiol. Soc. of N.A., Southern and Mo. State med. assns., St. Louis Med. Soc.; former corr. mem. Deutsche Röntgen Gesellschaft. Author or co-author of books relating to field; recipient many awards for sci. and med. exhibits. Home: 425 Hazelgreen Dr., St. Louis 19. Died July 9, 1963; buried Lynchburg, Va.

MOORE, THOMAS VERNER, clergyman, educator; b. Louisville, Ky., Oct. 22, 1877; s. John Neuton and Charlotte (McIlvain) M.; Ph.D., Catholic U. of America, 1903, student of philosophy, U. of Leipzig, 1904-05; studied medicine Georgetown U., 1911-13, Munich, Germany, 1913-14; M.D., Johns Hopkins, 1915. Ordained priest R.C. Ch., 1901; fellow in psychology, Catholic U. of America, 1903; lecturer Inst. of Pedagogy, same univ., New York, 1903-04; fellow in pyschology, U. of Calif., 1909; prof. philosophy, St. Thomas Coll., Washington, D.C., 1909-11; instr. psychology, Catholic U. of America, 1910-16, asso. prof., 1916-22, prof., 1922-47, head dept. psychology and psychiatry, 1939-47. Benedictine Monk from 1923; joined Carthusian Order, Burgos, Spain, 1947, spent last 20 years in contemplative life there. Served as capt. and maj. M.C., U.S. Army, France, World War, 1918-19. A founder, first pres., Benedictine Foundation, Washington, D.C.; dir. clinic for mental and nervous diseases, Providence Hosp., Washington, D.C., 1916-39. Founded St. Gertrude's Sch. of Arts and Crafts, 1926, a training sch. for girls of borderline intelligence, and acted as dir. Spl. lecturer on psychology, U. of Madrid, Spain, 1947. Author: A Historical Introduction to Ethics, 1915; Dynamic Psychology, 1924; Prayer, 1931; The Essential Psychoses, 1933; Principles of Ethics, 1935; Consciousness and the Nervous System, 1938; Cognitive Psychology, 1939; The Nature and Treatment of Mental Disorders, 1943; Personal Mental Hygiene, 1944; The Driving Forces of Human Nature and Their Adjustments, 1948; Home and its Inner Spiritual Life, 1952; The Life of Man with God, 1956; Heroic Sanctity and Insanity, 1959. Home: Burgos Spain Died June 5, 1969; buried Miraflores, Burgos, Spain

MOORE, WARREN G(IBBS), SR. lawyer; b. nr. Fairfield, Tex., Nov. 26, 1906; s. William Franklin and Edna (Cockerell) M.; A.B., Trinity U., San Antonio, 1930; law student, Nat. Univ., also U. Tex., 1933-36; grad. Naval Intelligence Sch., New Orleans, 1942, Advanced Naval Intelligence Sch., N.Y.C., 1944, Gunnery Sch., Norfolk, Va., 1944; m. Lillian Cochran, Jan. 14, 1943; children-Warren Gibbs, Karen Cochran. Admitted to Tex. bar, 1937, U.S. Supreme Ct., 1941; adminstrv. asst. Gen. Hugh S. Johnson, Washington, 1933-34; chief investigator Fed. Petroleum Bd., Kilgore, Tex., 1936-37, chief atty., 1937-39; asst. U.S. atty., Eastern Dist. of Tex., 1939-41, 1946-47, referee in bankruptcy, 1947-49, U.S. atty., 1949-53. Mem. State Democratic Exec. Com., 1962-64. Served with U.S. Navy, 1941-45; comd. Naval Intelligence Tex. and La. costal area; staff comdt. 8th Naval Dist.; gunnery officer in various ships Atlantic and Pacific fleets; inactive duty with rank of lt. comdr., 1945-. Mem. Am., Tex. and Smith County bar assns., Nat. Assn. Referees in Bankruptcy, Smith County Legal Inst. (chmn.; 1st v.p. 1950), Blue Key, Am. Legion (post comdr., life mem., state judge advocate 1955-56, state comdr. 1957-58, dir. state bd. trustees 1958-64, vice chmn. nat. Americanism commn. 1963-64). Tyler (Tex.) C. of C. Methodist (ofcl. bd.). Mason (32ff, Shriner), Elk Clubs: Rotary; Tyler Petrea; Willow Brook Country. Home: 1614 S. College St. Office: Fair Foundation Bldg., Tyler, Tex. Died Feb. 8, 1964; buried Rose Hill Cemetery, Tyler.

MOORE, WILLIAM STURTEVANT commodore U.S.N.; b. Duxbury, Mass., Feb. 23, 1846; s. Josiah and Maria Foster (Doane) M.; B.S., Lawrence Scientific Sch. (Harvard), 1867; grad. U.S. Naval Acad., 1868; m. Caro Garland Burwell, Feb. 6, 1901. Apptd. from Mass., acting 3d asst. engr. vol. navy, Oct. 10, 1866; 3d asst. engr. in regular service, June 2, 1868; promoted 2d asst. engr. June 2, 1869; passed asst. engr., June 11, 1876; chief engr., Aug. 10, 1893; comdr., Mar. 3, 1899; capt., Mar. 21, 1903; retired as commodore, June 30, 1906. At U.S. Naval Acad., 1866-67; Navy Yard, Boston, 1867; Naval Acad., 1867-68; on board Yantic, 1868-69; Bur. of Steam Engring., 1870-72; Frolic, 1872-73; Navy Yard, Washington, 1873; Bur. Steam Engring., 1873; Brooklyn, 1873-74; Bur. Steam Engring., 1875-76; coast survey steamer Blake, 1876-78; Minnesota, 1878-79; Bur. Steam Engring., 1879-82; Tallapoosa, 1882-84; Ossipee, 1884-87; Bureau of Steam Engineering, 1887-91; Vesuvius, 1891-94; Naval Examining Board, Phila., 1894-95; Dolphin, 1895-96; Texas, 1896-97; Columbia, 1897-98; receiving-ship Vermont, 1898-99; insp. machinery for the navy at Cramps' shipyard, 1899-1903; insp. of machinery for Mass. dist., 1903-05; Navy Yard, Boston, 1905-06. Mem. Mass. Ho. of Rep., 1909, 1910. Died July 12, 1914.

MOORHEAD, DUDLEY THOMAS, coll. dean; b. San Jose, Cal., Mar. 12, 1913; s. Thomas James, Jr., and Hazel Caroline (Green) M.; B.A., San Jose State Coll., 1934; M.A., Stanford, 1938, Ph.D., 1942; m. Lucille Evelyn Meyer, Dec. 19, 1936; 1 son, Dudley Thomas II. High sch. tchr., Salinas, Cal., 1936-38; head social sci., city secondary schs., San Luis Obispo, Cal., 1938-

42; from instr. to prof. dept. history San Jose State Coll., 1946-57, head dept. history, econs. and geography, 1954-57, dean instrn. div. humanities and art, 1957-66, acting acad. v.p., 1966-67, dean Sch. Humanities and Arts, 1967-72, 1st chmn. faculty council, 1953-54. Served from pvt. to capt., USAAF, 1942-45; hist. officer XIII Bomber Command, 13th Air Force, 1944-45. Mem. Cal. Employees Assn. (chpt. pres. 1952), Am. Assn. U. Profs. (chmn. San Jose chpt. 1952-53), Am. Hist. Assn., Phi Alpha Theta, Alpha Kappa Delta, Iota Delta Phi, Tau Delta Phi. Club: Commonwealth of Cal. Contbr. to Ency. Britannica, other publs. Home: San Jose CA Died June 30, 1972.

MOORHEAD, ROBERT LOWRY, publisher; b. Indianapolis, Ind., Sept. 15, 1875; s. Thomas W. and Alice (Griffith) M.; ed. high sch., Indianapolis, and Butler Univ.; m. Roxanna Sanders, Dec. 1, 1916. With The Bobbs-Merrill Co., book pubs., Indianapolis, since 1894, v.p., 1922-29, sec.-treas., 1929, treas., since 1948. Mem. Indpls. Light Inf., 1892; mem. Ind. N.G., 1892-1917, sergt. maj., Ind. Vol. Inf., Spanish-Am. War; served as col., F.A., U.S.A., with A.E.F. in France, 1917-19; col., F.A. Res. Mem. Ind. State Sen., 1921-32, (chmn. budget com. 1924-26). Mem. Warren Township Adv. Bd. since 1938. Mem. Ind. State Armory Bd., 1919-33, and 1945-49. Mem. S.A.R. (p. pres. Ind. Soc.), Ind. Society of War of 1812 (pres. 1947-53), Soc. Ind. Pioneers, Military Order Foreign Wars (past commander Ind. Commandery), Reserve Officers Association of U.S. (president Ind. Dept. 1933-35, 1946; pres. 5th Corps Area 1938-39), Am. Legion (mem. nat. exec. com.), 40 and 8 (Grand Chef de Gare, Indiana Passe), Soc. Am. Legion Founders, Army, Navy and Air Force Vets. of Can., Indpls. C. of C., Phi Delta Theta, Scabbard and Blade (hon.). Republican. Methodist. Mason. Clubs: Century (ex-pres.), Columbia, Rotary. Author: The Story of the 139th F.A., 1921. Home: "Wildwood," Brookville Rd. Office: 724 N. Meridian St., Indianapolis IN

MOORMAN, CHARLES HARWOOD judge; b. Big Spring, Ky., Apr. 24, 1876; s. William James and Margaret (Bush) M.; m. Lily Belknap, Nov. 28, 1914; children—Morris Belknap. Charles H. Admitted to bar 1900; judge Court of Appeals of Ky., 1921-23; judge U.S. Dist. Court, Western Dist. of Ky., 1924-25; judge U.S. Circuit Court of Appeals, 6th Circuit, Jan. 1925—. Served with Am. Red. Cross in France, Nov. 1917-May 1918; commd. capt. J. A. Gen.'s Dept., U.S.A., May 1918; maj., Nov. 1918. Republican. Mason. Home: Louisville, Ky. Died Jan. 26, 1938.

MORAN, RICHARD BARTHOLOMEW, army officer; b. Florence, Colo., Nov. 26, 1895; s. William George and Mary Jane (Coyle) M.; student Colo. State Coll., 1914-17; m. Thelma Thickins, July 15, 1917 (divorced); m. 2d, Blanche Ruth Bird, Feb. 21, 1949. Commd. 1st lt., U.S. Army, May 6, 1917, and advanced through grades to brig. gen., 1942; served World War I; overseas assignment with 5th Army and 15th Army Group in Italy; in Africa and Austria with (General Mark W. Clark; signal officer, 4th Army, Fort Sam Houston, 1947-50; gen. mgr. Imperial Bd. Telecommunications of Ethiopia, 1951-52; now adminstr. civil def. Kerr County, Tex. Decorated D.S.M., Legion of Merit (United States), Comdr. Brit. Empire (Gt. Britain), Croix de Guerre (France), Grand Officer, Crown of Italy, Military Medal (Italy), War Medal (Brazil). Mem. Am. Legion, Sigma Chi. K.C. Retired. Home: Kerrville TX Died Feb. 13, 1972; buried Ft. Sam Houston Nat. Cemetery.

MORAN, ROBERT shipbuilder, mech. engr.; b. N.Y. City, Jan. 26, 1857; s. Edward and Jean Dear (Boyack) M.; ed. pub. schs.; m. Miss M. E. Paul, of Victoria, B.C., 1882; children-John M., Frank G., Malcolm E., Nellie M., Mary R. (Wood). Went to Seattle at 18, and became steamboat fireman, later engr.; established Moran Bros., steamboat and sawmill machy., 1889; organized Moran Bors. Co., Ship & Engine Bldg. Co., 1890; built in 4 mos., fleet of 12 steamers and 10 barges, delivered on the Yukon River to carry food to the miners, 1898; built many large steel and wood vessels, including the 15,000 ton U.S. Battleship Nebraska; sold out business, 1905, and retired, at Rosario, on Orcas Island, Wash. Mayor of Seattle 2 terms, 1888-90; state director Public Service Reserve during the World War. Donated 4,000 acres to the State of Wash., now Moran State Park. Mem. Soc. Naval Architects and Marine Engrs., Soc. of U.S. Mil. Engrs., Am. Shipmasters' Assn., Marine Engrs. Assn., Franklin Inst., Inst. Naval Architects (London), Washington Pioneers' Assn. Clubs: Rainer, Seattle Yacht, Seattle Athletic, Home: Orcas, San Juan Co., Wash.

MORDECAI, ALFRED army officer, engr.; b. Warrenton, N.C., Jan. 3, 1804; s. Jacob and Rebecca (Myers) M.; grad. U.S. Mil. Acad., 1823; m. Sara Hays, 6 children including Alfred. Commd. 2d lt. Corps Engrs., U.S. Army, 1823; asst. prof. engring. U.S. Mil. Acad., 1823-25; asst. engr. in charge of constructing Ft. Monroe, Va., 1825-28; commd. capt. Ordnance Dept., U.S. Army, 1832; commanded 1st Washington (D.C.) Arsenal, then Frankford (Pa.) Arsenal, 1833-38; asst. to chief of ordnance, 1838-42; commanded Washington Arsenal during Mexican War, brevetted maj.; commd. maj. Ordnance Dept., 1854; mem. U.S. Mil. Commn. to Crimea War, 1855-57; resigned from Army at Outbreak of Civil War; tchr. mathematics, Phila., 1861-63; asst. engr. Mexico & Pacific R.R., 1863-66; sec., tras. Pa. R.R., 1867-87. Author: A Digest of Laws Relating to the Miiitary Establishment of the United States, 1833; Artillery for the United States Land Service, 1849. Died Phila. Oct. 23, 1887.

MORDECAI, ALFRED brig. gen. U.S.A.; b. Phila., Pa., June 30, 1840; s. Maj. Alfred (U.S.A.) and Sara Ann (Hays) M.; grad. U.S. Mil. Acad., 1861; m. Sally S. Maynadier, Nov. 1, 1866; m. 2d, Dora Varney, Sept. 6, 1892. Bvtd. 2d lt. topog. engrs., June 24, 1861; promoted through grades to col., ordnance, Jan. 31, 1891; brig. gen. U.S.A., Jan. 19, 1904. Bvtd. maj., Sept. 7, 1863, "for gallant and meritorious services in siege of Ft. Wagner, S.C."; lt. col., Mar. 13, 1865, "for distinguished services in the field and faithful and meritorious services in ordnance dept. during the war." Served as ordnance officer, 1861-65; engaged in operations against Charleston, S.C., 1863-4; chief of ordnance, Army of the James, May-Sept. 1864, later in Army of Tenn. and Army of the Cumberland till July 4, 1865. Instr. ordnance and gunnery, U.S. Mil. Acad., 1865-69 and 1874-81; comd. Leavenworth Arsenal, Kan., 1870-74, Watervliet Arsenal, 1881-86 and 1898-99, New York Arsenal, 1887-92, Springfield Armory, 1892-98, Benecia Arsenal, Calif., 1899-1902; on duty, officer chief of ordnance, U.S.A., 1902-04; retired at own request over 40 yrs'. service, Jan. 20, 1904. Died Jan. 20, 1920.

MORDEN, WILLIAM J(AMES) explorer and field collector; b. Chicago, Jan. 3, 1886; s. William J. and Laura (Houston) M.; Ph.B., Sheffield Sci. School, Yale, 1908; m. Florence H. Rose, Apr. 24, 1920 (died Apr. 9, 1939); m. 2d, Irene Hambright, Apr. 27, 1940. Engr. and mfr., 1908-22; explorer and field collector, 1922—; dir. Union Bag & Paper Corp., mem. sci. staff Am. Museum of Natural History (field asso. dept. mammals), 1926-40, leader Morden-Clark Asiatic Expdn. of Am. Mus. Natural History, 1926-27, also various expdns. for mus., 1930-40; leader Morden-Graves North Asiatic Expdn., 1929-30, Morden African Expn., 1947. Served as 1st lt., Engrs., O.R.C., A.E.F., 1918-19, capt., 1919-20, 1924-36; major, 1936-40; major (inactive) A.U.S., 1940-42; major, Air Corps, A.U.S., 1942-44, lt. col., 1944-47; lt. col. hon. res., O.R.C., 1947-49, lt. colonel U.S. Air Force, retired; rated service pilot, 1943. Life fellow Royal Geog. Soc. (Eng.); hon. fellow Am. Museum Natural History; hon. mem. East African Professional Hunters Assn. Mason. Clubs: American Yacht, Union League, Yale, Explorers (past dir. and v.p.), Campfire, Wings (New York); Bohemian (San Francisco); Himalayan (India) (life mem.); Quiet Birdmen. Author: Across Asia's Snows and Deserts, 1927; articles in various mags. Home: Camp Fire Rd., Chappaqua, N.Y. Died Jan. 23, 1958.

MORE, CHARLES CHURCH engr., educator; b. Rock Island, Ill., Jan. 21, 1875; s. David Fellows and Sara Jane (Hubbell) M.; C.E., Lafayette Coll., 1898, M.S., 1901; M.C.E., Cornell, 1899; m. Myra Hadlock Ober, Aug. 24, 1904; began with Pencoyd Iron Works, Phila, 1899; acting prof. civ. engring., U. Wash., 1900, asst. prof., 1904, asso. prof., 1907, prof., 1912, prof. and head dept., 1917-25, prof. structural engring., 1925-47, emeritus, 1947—; with Am. Bridge Co. (Phila.), D. H. Burnham & Co. (Chgo.), U.S. Engr. Dept. (Ft. Worden, Wash.), 1901-04; with C.M.&St.P. Ry. Co., Seattle, 1906-07, Turner Constrn. Co., N.Y.C., 1911-12. Commd. capt. Engr. R.C., June 19, 1917; in training at Engr. O.T.C., Vancouver Barracks, Wash., Sept.-Oct. 1917; capt. O.R.C., Oct. 18, 1917; maj. ordnance, U.S. Army, July 25, 1918. On duty at Ordnance Office, Washington, Nov. 1917-Nov. 1918; inst. at Engr. Sch., Camp Humphreys, Va., Dec. 1918-Sept. 1919; hon. discharged Oct. 1, 1919. Mem. Soc. for Promotion Engring. Edn. (council, 1919-22), Am. Assn. Univ. Prof., Am. Soc. C.E., Am. Legion, Phi Beta Kappa, Sigma Xi, Tau Beta Pi, Phi Kappa Psi. Sec. John More Assn., 1900-25, asso. sec., 1925—. Conglist. Compiler: Genealogy of Descendants of John More. 1893. Home: 4545 Fifth Av. N.E., Seattle, Wash. Died Nov. 19, 1949.

MOREHEAD, JOHN MOTLEY ambassador; b. Spray, N.C., Nov. 3, 1870; s. James Turner and Mary Elizabeth (Connally) M.; direct desc., Charles Morehead who settled on Kent Island in Chesapeake Bay, 1630; prep. edn., Bingham Mil. Sch., Mebane, N.C.; B.S. U. of N.C., 1891, LL.D., 1926; grad. expert course, Westinghouse Elec. & Mfg. Co., 1895; spl. course in oxy-acetylene welding, Cologne, Germany; D.Engring., Wake Forest Coll., Wake Forest, N.C., 1944; D.Sc., Upsala U., 1944; LL.D., Davidson College, 1956; married Genevieve Margaret Birkhoff, July 3, 1915 (died April 16, 1945); m. 2d, Mrs. Leila Duckworth Houghton, May 11, 1948 (dec.). Engr., Union Carbide & Carbon Corp. and predecessors and subsidiaries, 1891-1930, 1933-54; chief chemist and engr. of tests. Peoples Gas, Light & Coke Co., 1897-1918; chmn. bd. Leaksville Woolen Mills, Charlotte, N.C. E.E. and M.P. to Sweden, Jan. 22, 1930-Apr. 15, 1933. Served as maj., Gen. Staff, Washington, D.C., chief of industrial gases and gas products sect., sec. explosives div. and mem. ammonia com. of War Industries Bd., World War; lt. col., Ordnance Dept., O.R.C. Mayor of Rye, N.Y., 1925-30. Mem. Internat. July of Awards, St. Louis Expn., 1904, San Francisco Expn., 1915. Fellow Am. Inst. E.E.; mem. Internat. Acetylene Assn. (ex-pres.), Am. Electro-chem. Soc., Am. Gas Assn. (ex-v.p.), Am. Welding Soc. (1st v.p.), Soc. Colonial Wars, Soc. of the Cincinnati, Am. Legion. Phi Beta Kappa. Sigma Alpha Epsilon. Awarded gold medal, Kungl. Svenska Vetenskopsakademien (only foreigner ever so honored), 1930. Republican. Baptist. Clubs: Chemist, Uptown (N.Y.C.); Apawamis, American Yacht, Shenorock (Rye); Clove Valley Rod and Gun (N.Y.); University (Niagara Falls); Fishers Island (N.Y.). Author: The Analysis of Industrial Gases, 1900; The Morehead Family of North Carolina and Virginia. 1924. Donor Morehead Planetarium, Morehead Building and Memorial Gallery to University of North Carolina, Chapel Hill, 1949, John Motley Morehead Foundation at University North Carolina, Morehead Athletic Field and Stadium at John Motley Morehead High Sch., Draper, N.C. Home: Rye, N.Y. Office: 270 Park Av., N.Y.C. 17. Retired. Died Jan. 7, 1965.

MOREHOUSE, ALBERT KELLOGG naval officer; b. Brooklyn, Apr. 29, 1900; s. Melvin Wilson and Alice (McHugh) M.; B.S., U.S. Naval Acad., 1922; student U.S.N. Flight Sch., Pensacola, Fla., 1924-25; m. Mrs. Sally B. Lanius, Sept. 8, 1925; children-Sue Gaylord, Sally (Mrs. John D. Price). Enlisted 1st N.Y. Cav., 1917 (later designated 105 MG bn. 27th Div.); commd. ensign U.S. Navy, 1922; and advanced through grades to rear adm., 1949; commanded U.S.N.R. Air Base, Miami, 1934-37; observer with Royal Navy and R.A.F. in Mediterranean, 1941; chief of staff to comdr. A.F., Atlantic Fleet, 1948-50, to comdr. Naval Force Far East, 1950-51; chief Naval Air Advanced Tng., Corpus Christi, Tex., 1951-54; comdr. naval forces of Continental air def. command, 1954—. Decorated Navy Cross, Legion of Merit with gold star, Bronze Star, Silver Life Saving medal, Presdl. Unit citation. Mem. U.S. Naval Inst. Address: Colorado Springs, Colo. Died Dec. 18, 1955.

MOREHOUSE, GEORGE PIERSON lawyer, writer; b. Decatur, Ill. July 28, 1859; s. Horace and Lavinia F. (Strong) M.; Albion High Sch.; U. State of N.Y., 1884; m. Mrs. Louise (Thorne) Hull, of Topeka, Kan., formerly Morgantown, W.Va., Apr. 23, 1906 (she died Aug. 4, 1931). Went to Kan., 1872; mgr. cattle ranch, Diamond Springs, Kan., 1876-81; admitted to Kan. bar, 1889, and practiced at Council Grove; city atty., 1891-95, co. atty., Morris Co., 1894-97; local atty., A.T. &S.F. Ry., 1894-1915; mem. Kan. Senate, 1901-05; removed to Topeka, 1906. Mem. Internat. Soc. Archaeologists; life mem. and dir. Kan. State Hist. Soc. (pres. 1917-18); ex-president Kan. Authors' Club; sec. and genealogist Morehouse Family Association; member Kansas State Bar Association, S.A.R. Lt. Kan. N.G., 1903; active in organizing Kan. State Guard to take the place of Nat. Guard during World War; completed inf. training course, Camp Steever, Lake Geneva, Wis., 1918; commd. capt. Co. B, 9th Bath. Kan. State Guard, 1918-20, and helped train over 300 men who went into World War service; founder, May 5, 1920, comdr. in chief, 1923-25, of Am. Guard, a nat. orgn. of ex-soldiers in state militia forces during World War. Republican. Presbyn. Drafted 1st automobile laws in West, and law making the sunflower the floral emblem of Kan.; originated movement to mark Santa Fe Trail; an authority on history, lang. and legends of Kansa or Kaw Indians, and is official historian of the tribe and keeper of their ancient charts and relics. Author: Kansa, or Kaw Indians and Their History, 1908; An Historic Trail, 1909; History of Kansas Authors' Club, 1913; Padilla, the Priest of the Plains, 1915; Pre-historic Man in Kansas, 1917; Archaeology of Kansas, 1918; The Golden Sunflower, 1927; Along the Neosho and other Verse, 1928. Contbr. to historic publs. upon famous highways, Spanish explorations, archaeology, Indian language and folklore. Home: 216 W. 8th St., Topeka, Kan.

MORELAND, EDWARD LEYBURN cons. engr.; b. Lexington, Va., July 1, 1885; s. Sidney T. and Sally Preston (Leyburn) M.; A.B., Johns Hopkins U., 1905; M.S. Mass. Inst. Tech., 1908; m. Francina H. Campbell, Sept. 18, 1913. Asst. engr. D.C. and William B. Jackson, engrs., Boston, 1908-12; mgr. Boston office, 1912-16, mem. firm, 1916-18; mem. firm Jackson & Moreland, 1919—; head dept. elec. engring., Mass. Inst. Tech., 1935-38, dean engring., 1938-46, exec. v.p. 1946—. Regional adviser to the U.S. Office Edn. of Engring. Defense Training in Region I, 1940-42; mem. adv. com. for Coordinating Available Facilities for Def. Prodn., OPM, in Region I, 1941-42; also member Labor Supply Committee 1941-42; executive officer Nat. Def. Research Com., 1942-45; expert cons. to Sec. War, assigned G.H.Q.-Armed Forces in Pacific; chief, scientific survey in Japan, 1945. Served capt. and maj., E.C., U.S. Army Tech. Board and War Damage Bd., A.E.F., 1918-19. Fellow Am. Inst. E.E.; mem. Am. Soc. M.E., Am. Soc. C.E., Phi Gamma Delta. Republican. Conglist. Clubs: Engineers (N.Y.C.); Engineers, Merchants, St. Botolph (Boston); Algonquin, Cosmos (Washington); Wellesley Country. Home: 4 Berkeley Court, Wellesley Hills 82, Mass. Office: Mass. Institute of Technology, Cambridge, Mass. Died June 17, 1951, buried Druid Ridge Cemetery, Pikesville, Balt.

MORGAN, CASEY BRUCE naval officer; b. Augusta, Ga., Oct. 29, 1867; grad. U.S. Naval Acad., 1888. Promoted ensign, July 1, 1890; lt. jr. grade, Feb. 16, 1898; lt., Mar. 3, 1899; lt. comdr., July 1, 1905; comdr., Sept. 15, 1909; capt., July 1, 1914. Served on Raleigh, Spanish-Am. War, 1898; insp. equipment, San Francisco, Calif., 1905-06; exec. officer, Milwaukee, 1906-08; insp. in charge 11th Light House Dist., Detroit, Mich., 1908-10; comd. Dubuque, 1910-11, Nashville, 1911-12, Missouri, 1912-13; at Naval War Coll., Newport, R.I., 1913; in charge Navy Publicity Bur. and Navy Recruiting Sta., New York, 1913-14; comd. Minnesota, 1914-16; at Naval War College, Newport, R.I., 1917; comd. Squadron Six Patrol Force Atlantic Fleet, 1917; comdr. Agamemnon, Aug. 21, 1917-18; force transport officer, staff comdr. C. and T. Force, 1918-19; comdr. Imperator, May-Aug. 1919; promoted rear admiral, Oct. 1919; comdg. Transport Force, 1919; comdt. Naval Station, Cavite, P.I., 1919-20; comdr. Special Service Squadron, 1921—. Pres. G.C.M. New York, 1922-23; retired on own request, 1923. Died Aug. 17, 1933.

MORGAN, CHARLES HENRY congressman; b. Allegany Co., N.Y., July 5, 1843; ed. pub. and high schs., Wis.; pvt. to capt., 1st and 21st Wis. Inf., 1861-65; LL.B., Albany Law Sch., 1866. Pros. atty. Barton Co., Mo., 4 yrs.; mem. Mo. Ho. of Rep., 1872-74; mem. 44th, 45th, 48th, 53d and 61st Congresses (1875-79, 1883-85, 1893-95, 1909-11). Presdl. elector-at-large, 1882. Lt. col. 5th Mo. Inf. in Spanish-Am. War, 1898. Home: Joplin, Mo. Died 1912.

MORGAN, CLIFFORD VERYL army medical officer; b. Elmwood, Neb., Dec. 18, 1901; s. Butler Garibaldi and Margaret Elizabeth (Murray) M.; A.B., Neb. Wesleyan U., 1922; B.S., U. Neb., 1925, M.D., 1927; grad. Army Med. Sch., 1929, Army Indsl. Coll., 1940. Command and Gen. Staff Sch., 1943, Indsl. Coll. Armed Forces and Nat. War Coll., 1946; m. Anna Marie Herrmann, July 20, 1927; children-Monte Herrmann, Marvin Leon, Walter Albert. Commd. 1st lt. M.C., U.S. Army, 1927, advanced through grades to col., 1942; intern Walter Reed Gen. Hosp., Washington, 1927-28; internist William Beaumont Gen. Hosp., El Paso, Tex., 1929-30, Tripler Gen. Hosp., Honolulu, T.H., 1930-33, U.S. Army Hosp., Ft. Sill, Okla., 1933-36; specialist med. supply and adminstrn. N.Y. Gen Depot and S.G.O., War Dept., 1936-39; army chief, commodities div. Army-Navy munitions Bd., 2940-43; chief, commodities div., planning br. Office Under Sec. War, 1940-42; chief, raw materials br., resources div., Army Service Forces, 1942-43; dep. chief for material, supply div. S.G.O., 1943; dep. gen. purchasing agt., E.T.O., 1943-45; exec. officer Crile Gen. Hosp., 1945-46; dept. post comdr. Walter Reed Army Med. Center, Washington, 1946-48; dep. chief surgeon Hdqrs., European Command, 1948-52; insp. gen. Office Surgeon Gen., Washington, 1952-54; chairman Army Physical Review Council, 1954—. Decorated Legion of Merit with Oak Leaf cluster, Bronze Star Medal, Army Commendation with oak leaf cluster; Croix de Guerre with palm (France); Officer, Order of Oaken Wreath (Luxembourg). Fellow A.M.A., Assn. Mil. Surgeons, A.A.A.S.; mem. Am. Coll. Hosp. Adminstrs., Phi Kappa Tau, Phi Kappa Phi, Phi Chi, Alpha Omega Alpha. Editor of EUCOM Medical Bull., 1948-52. Home: 2945 Macomb St. N.W., Washington 8. Office: Army Physical Review Council, Pentagon Bldg., Washington 25. Died Oct. 3, 1954; buried Arlington Nat. Cemetery.

MORGAN, DANIEL congressman, army officer; lt. Hunterdon County, N.J. or Bucks County, Pa., 1736; s. James and Eleanora Morgan; m. Abigail Bailey, children-Nancy, Betty. Worked in Bucks County (where his father was ironmaster Durham Iron Works); quarrelled with father, moved to Shenandoah Valley, Va., transported supplies to frontier points of Va.; served as lt. in Pontiac's War, 1774, accompanied Lord Dunmore's expdn. to Western Pa.; commd. capt. co. of riflemen from Va., 1775, accompanied Benedict Arnold in assault of Quebec, was captured, 1775; commd. col. 11th Va. Regt., 1776; commd. brig. gen. Continental Army, 1780, joined Gen. Nathaniel Gates; defeated British at Battle of Cowpens (N.C.), 1781, awarded Gold medal by Continental Congress; retired to estate in Va. after Revolutionary War; commanded Va.Militia ordered by Pres. Washington to suppress Whiskey Rebellion in Pa., 1794; mem. U.S. Ho. of Reps. from Va., 5th Congress, 1797-99. Died Winchester, Va., July 6, 1802; buried Mt. Hebron Cemetery, Winchester.

MORGAN, EDWIN FRANKLIN ABELL lawyer; b. Washington, Sept. 28, 1892; s. Dr. James Dudley and Mary (Abell) M.; S.B., Harvard, 1915, LL.B., 1920. Admitted to Md. bar, 1921, since practiced in Balt.; asso. Marbury, Gosnel & Williams, 1921-23; partner Coleman, Fell, Mongan & Brune, 1923-26, Semmes, Bowen & Semmes, 1928-; counsel Fed. Alcohol Control Adminstrn., Washington, 1933-34; dir. A. S. Abell Co., Merc. Safe Deposit & Trust Co. Balt., J. S. Young Co., Balt. Mem. bd. correction State Md., 1947-49. Gov. Happy Hills Convalescent Home for Children. Served from 2d lt. to capt. U.S. Army, 1916-19; with 313th F.A., A.E.F., 1918-19, maj. to lt. col. F.A., O.R.C., 1919-28, staff liaison officer, Md., 1942-45. Mem. Am., Med. State, Baltimore County, Balt. City bar assns., Harvard Law Sch. Assn. Md. (pres. 1957). Clubs: Maryland, Green Spring Valley Hunt, Green Spring Hounds, Elkridge (Balt.); Chevy Chase (Washington); Owl, Choate (Cambridge, Mass.); Harvard of Md. (v.p.). Asso. editor Am. Maritime Cases, 1923-33. Home: Warburton Farm, Glyndon, Md. Office: 10 Light St., Balt. 2. Died Dec. 22, 1965.

MORGAN, GEORGE HORACE army officer; b. St. Catharines, Ont., Jan. 1, 1855; s. George Nelson and Delia Elizabeth (Warner) M.; brought to U.S., 1856; grad. U.S. Mil. Acad., 1880; LL.B., U. of Minn., 1894; grad. Army War Coll., Washington, 1914; m. Mollie Brownson, of Omaha, Neb., Nov. 1, 1882. Commd. 2d lt. 3d Cav., June 12, 1880; 1st lt., Nov. 26, 1884; capt., Mar. 15, 1896; maj. 28th U.S. Vol. Inf., July 5, 1899; hon. mustered out vols., May 1, 1901; maj. 9th U.S. Cav., Apr. 27, 1903; mil. sec., Dec. 8, 1906; assigned to 3d Cav., Dec. 8, 1910; lt. col. 11th Cav., Mar. 3, 1911; col. 15th Cav., Apr. 26, 1914. Served in campaigns against the Indians, Santiago campaign, and in Philippines, 1899-1901. Bvt. 1st lt. "for gallantry in action," July 17, 1882; awarded Medal of Honor "for gallantry in action against Indians," July 17, 1882. Assigned chief of staff 13th Militia Div., Dec. 14, 1915; comdg. provisional cav., 10th Div., El Paso dist., Sept. 26, 1916-Mar. 23, 1917; pres. bd. for selection of site for cantonment in dist., May 15, 1917 (selected Camp Dodge, Ia.); mustering officer for Minn. and Mo., 1917; assigned to 17th Cav., Sept. 28, 1917; retired, Jan. 2, 1919; assigned to active duty with R.O.T.C., Dec 8, 1919. Mem. Sons of Vets., Loyal Legion. Universalist. Mason. Clubs: Army and Navy (Washington and Manila), Minneapolis (Minnaapolis), Minnesota (St. Paul), Travis (San Antonio, Tex.). Address: War Department, Washington, D.C.

MORGAN, HUGH JACKSON physician; b. Nashville, Jan. 25, 1893; s. Joseph Bedinger and Jean (Gibson) M.; B.S., Vanderbilt U., 1914; M.D., Johns Hopkins, 1918; D.Sc., U. N.C., 1946, U. So. Cal., 1953; m. Robert Ray Porter, July 22, 1924; children-Caroline Lee (Mrs. Saxon Graham), Hugh Jackson, Jean (Mrs. J. Alexander Cortner), Robert Porter. Resident house officer Johns Hopkins Hosp., 1919-20, asst. resident physician, 1920-21; instr. medicine Johns Hopkins, 1920-21; asst.and resident physician Rockefeller Inst. for Med. Research, 1922-24, traveling fellow (Europe), 1924-25; asso. prof. medicine Vanderbilt U., 1924-28, prof. clin. medicine, 1928-35. prof. medicine also physician-in-chief Vanderbilt U. Hosp., 1935-58, prof. emeritus, 1958-, trustee Vanderbilt U., 1958-, Hugh Jackson Morgan visiting professorships in medicine established in his honor, 1958. Served as pvt. and 1st lt. M.C., U.S. Army, AEF, 1917-18; lt. col. Med. Res. Corps, U.S. Army, 1940; active duty since 1942, as col., 1942, brig. gen., 1943; chief cons. in medicine, Office of Surgeon Gen, Washington, 1942-46; chmn. com. on medicine N.R.C., 1946-48; mem. med. adv. com. to sec. of war, 1946-48; sci. dir. Internat. Health Div. Rockefeller Found., 1946-48, sci. cons., 1950, Div. of Medicine and Pub. Health, 1952; mem. Nat. Adv. Arthritis and Metabolic Diseases Council, 1954-56; cons., mem. adv. com. Howard Hughes Med. Inst., 1955-; mem. Nat. Adv. Heart Council 1950-52; mem. adv. health council USPHS, 1948-50; Fed. Med. Service Com. Commn. Orgn. of Exec. Br. of Govt. Trustee Meharry Med. Coll., 1946-, chmn. of bd., 1955-57. Decorated D.S.M., 1945, Master A.c.P. (regent 1936-, pres. 1947, Alfred Stengel Meml. award, 1959); mem. A.M.A. (cons Council Nat. Emergency Med. Services, 1948-, Vets. Adminstrn. cons. to Central adv. com. on radioisotopes to dept. medicine and surgery, 1947-58), Am. Bd. Internal Medicine (vice chmn., 1947, chmn., 1948,) Assn. Am. Physicians (pres. 1950), Assn. Hon. Consultants to Army Med. Library, Soc. U.S. Med. Consultants in World War II, Johns Hopkins Med. and Surg. Assn. (pres. 1948). Am. Soc. for Clin. Investigation, Am. Clin. and Climatol. Assn. (pres. 1953), Am. Heart Assn., A.A.A.S., Theta. Sigma Xi. Methodist. Club: Belle Meade Country (Nashville). Contbr. med. articles to profl. jours. Home: 15 White Bridge Rd., Nashville 5. Died Dec. 24, 1961.

MORGAN, JAMES DADA army officer, businessman; b. Boston, Aug. 1, 1810; s. James and Martha (Patch) M.; m. Jane Strachan (dec. 1855); m. 2d, Harriet Evans, June 14, 1869; at least 2 children. Helped organize the Quincy (Ill.) Grays, later the Quincy Riflemen; entered Mexican War as capt. 1st Ill. Volunteer Inf., 1846, promoted maj. at Battle of Buena Vista; brig. gen. U.S. Volunteers, 1862, brevetted maj. gen. 1865; treas. Ill. Soldiers and Sailors Home, 1887; v.p. Soc. of Army of Cumberland; mcht. and banker. Died Quincy, Sept. 12, 1896.

MORGAN, JAMES NORRIS soldier; b. Alton, Ill., Nov. 2, 1839; s. James Madison and Elizabeth (McCrellish) M.; ed. McKendree Coll., Ill., 1854-57; m. Ella Dora Dimmick, May 4, 1875 (died 1909). Traveled across the plains on foot, Leavenworth to Denver, 1859; spent 15 mos. in the gold mines and returned to Alton, Ill.; enrolled in vol. service, Apr. 26, 1861; mustered into Ill., provisional regt., May 11, 1861, and into U.S. Vols., June 25, 1861; 2d lt., Co. B, 22d Ill. Vols., June 25, 1861; 1st lt., Mar. 1, 1862; capt., June 13, 1862; hon. mustered out, July 7, 1864; enlisted as pvt. 144th Ill. Inf., Sept. 10, 1864; commd. capt., Sept. 10, 1864; maj., Sept. 26, 1864; lt. col., Mar. 18, 1865; mustered out, July 4, 1865; commd. 2d lt. 38th U.S. Inf., July 28, 1866; 1st lt., June 12, 1867; capt., June 20, 1873; retired from active service with rank of maj., Apr. 17, 1897; advanced to rank of lt. col. retired, Apr. 23, 1904. Participated in many battles in depts. of Miss. and the South; while serving as capt. at battle of Stone River, Tenn., after serveral color bearers of the regt. had been wounded or killed, took the colors and rallied the regt. (about to disintegrate) and marched the regt. to Gen. Jefferson C. Davis; in action at Adairsville, Ga., May 1864, captured complete complement, as to officers and men of his co.; served in Southwest after the war; with co. built telegraph line, Separ, N.M., to Mex. boundary, 35 miles, in 24 working hours. Bvtd. 1st lt. and capt. "for gallant and meritorious service on the field at New Hope Ch., Ga." Republican. Mason. Home: Alton, Ill. Died Aug. 5, 1925.

MORGAN, JOHN HEATH, foreign service officer; b. Lynn, Mass., Dec. 6, 1901; s. Edward and Martha Ambler (Heath) M.; S.B., Harvard, 1924; m. Katherine Louise Whelchel, June 18, 1926; children—Louise Longstreet, John Heath. Foreign service officer since 1925; vice consul, Budapest, 1926-30, consul, 1930; consul, Berlin, 1931-33; with western European div. Dept. of State, 1933-37; 2d sec., Vienna, 1937-39, Madrid, 1939-42, Bogota, Colombia, 1942-44; asst. chief, Div. of Northern European affairs, Dept. of State, 1944-47, chief, 1947-71; adviser Am. delegation West Indian Conference, St. Thomas, Virgin Islands, Feb. 1946; 1st sec., Rekjavik, Iceland, June-July 1946; became asso. chief Northern European Div., Nov. 1946; Counselor of Embassy, Ottawa, 1951-71; counselor of Embassy, Helsinki, 1953-56; Dept. of State adviser Army War Coll., 1956-58; examiner Bd. Examiners Fgn. Service, Dept. State, 1958-60, spl. asst. to dir., Hist. Office, 1960-71. Home: Chevy Chase MD Died May 1971.

MORGAN, JOHN HUNT army officer; b. Huntsville, Ala., June 1, 1825; s. Calvin Cogswell and Henrietta (Hunt) M.; m. Rebecca Bruce, circa 1848; m. 2d, Miss Ready, Dec. 14, 1862. Served as enlisted man during Mexican War; organized Lexington Rifles,1857; scout Confederate Army, 1861, commd. capt., 1862; began raids in Ky., Ohio, Ind., harassed Federals; commd. col., 1862, headed brigade which raided extensively in Ky.; captured Fed. force, Hartsville, Tenn., took over 1,700 prisoners, 1862, for which action he was commd. brig. gen. in command cavalry div.; a raid of Ky. and Ohio resulted in his surrender, 1863, however he saved E. Tenn. for the Confederacy for several months; escaped, 1863; commanded Dept. of S.W. Va., 1864. Killed in action, Greenville, Tenn., Sept. 4, 1864; buried Lexington, Ky.

MORGAN, JOHN TYLER U.S. senator from Ala., 1877-1907; b. Athens, Tenn., June 20, 1824; emigrated to Ala., when 9 yrs. old; academic edn.; admitted to bar, 1845; practiced until elected to the senate. Presidential elector, 1860; delegate to Ala. Secession Conv., 1861; joined C.S.A., May 1861, as private promoted through all grades to col. 51st Ala. regt., which he raised; was brig. gen., 1863-65. After war resumed practice at Selma, Ala.; presdl. elector, 1876. Democrat. Apptd. by President Harrison as arbitrator on Bering Sea fisheries, 1892; apptd. by President McKinley, July 1898, one of commrs. to organize govt. m. Hawaii, after passage of annexation bill. Home: Selma, Ala. Died 1907.

MORGAN, MICHAEL RYAN brig. gen.; b. Nova Scotia, Jan. 18, 1833; ed. in New Orleans, up to 1850; grad. U.S. Mil. Acad., 1854; m. Judith Porter, d. Edward and Harriet Howard Adams, of Charlestown, Mass., May 30, 1860; m. 2d, Antoinette Mary, d. John S. and Emma S. Prince, of St. Paul, Jan. 9, 1879. Second lt. 3d Arty., July 1, 1854; promoted through grades to lt. col. asst. commissary gen., U.S.A., Aug. 28, 1888; col., July 14, 1890; brig. gen. commissary subsistence U.S.A., Oct. 8, 1894. Bvtd. maj., lt. col. and col., July 6, 1864, "for distinguished services"; brig. gen., Apr. 9, 1865, "for gallant and meritorious services." Served at various frontier posts until 1859; was on Harper's Ferry expdn. to suppress John Brown's raid, 1859; chief commissary of subsistence, Dept. of the South; on staff Gen. U.S. Grant, 1864; took part in siege of Petersburg, Va., June to Sept. 1864, and the engagements in that section, and up to the surrender of Lee; commissary of subsistence U.S.A., 1894-97; retired by operation of law, Jan. 18, 1897. Now v.p. Security Trust Co., St. Paul, Minn. Died 1911.

MORGAN, MINOT CANFIELD, clergyman; b. Princeton, N.J., Sept. 17, 1876; s. Rev. Minot Spaulding and Anna Corilla (Green) M.; A.B., Princeton, 1896, A.M., 1900; grad. Princeton Theol. Sem., 1900; D.D., Lafayette Coll., 1917, Southwestern, 1917; m. Margaretta Webb Holden (A.B., Vassar), May 11, 1911; children—Minot Canfield, Edward Holden, Henry Green. Ordained Presbyn. ministry, 1900; asst. to pastor Tenth Ch., Phila., 1900-01; pastor successively First Ch., Far Rockaway, N.Y., Central Ch., Summit, N.J., Fort Street, Ch., Detroit, Mich., until 1926; co-pastor Fifth Av. Ch., New York, 1926-33; pastor First Ch., Greenwich, Connecticut, 1933-50; moderator of New York Presbytery, 1931-33. Camp religious work dir. Y.M.C.A., 1918; capt. reserve chaplain, U.S. Army, 1925-35. Rec. sec. Presbyn. Bd. of Christian Edn., 1923-45. Trustee Princeton Theol. Sem., since 1911. Mem.

S.A.R. Republican. Traveled around the world visiting mission fields, 1908, 09. Home: 47 Hawthorne Av.,2Princeton NJ

MORGAN, THOMAS ALFRED b. Vance County, N.C., Sept. 27, 1887; s. James T. and Virginia (Wilson) M.; student Littleton (N.C.) High Sch., 1905-08; ScD., Elon Coll., 1939, Duke U., 1943; D.Eng., N.C. State Coll., U. N.C., 1943; m. Celeste Walker Page, Dec. 23, 1941; children (by former marriage), Thomas Alfred, Mary (Mrs. A. R. Hamilton). With Sperry Gyroscope Co., 1912-16, successively sales mgr., gen. mgr. and pres., 1916-32, chmn. bd., 1932-47, also dir.; pres. The Sperry Corp., 1933-46, 49-52, chmn. bd., 1946-52, ret.; chmn. Gen. Aniline & Film Corp., 1961, dir., 1961-65; dir. Bulova Watch Co., Inc., Lehman Corp., Western Union Telegraph Co.; dir., mem. exec. com. U.S. Industries, Inc.; hon. dir. of SFC Financial Corp.; dir. emeritus Shell Oil Co.; trustee Atlantic Mutual Ins. Co.; former dir., now mem. adv. com. Bankers Trust Co. Mem. adv. com. Engring. Sch., N.C. State Coll.; ex-chmn. United Negro Coll. Fund, Inc. Dir. Water Research Found. for Delaware River Basin, N.Y.C. Cancer Com. Mem. N.Y. World's Fair 1964 Corp. Served in USN, 1908-12; maj. U.S. Army Ordnance Res., 1926-33, maj. specialist Res., USAAF, 1933-37. Decorated French Legion of Honor. Mem. Am. Ordnance Assn., Inst. Aerospace Scis., Nat. Aeros. Assn., Japan Soc., Am. Soc. French Legion of Honor, United States Naval Institution. Clubs: Brook (N.Y.C.); Madison Square Garden. Home: 30 Sutton Pl., N.Y.C. 22. Office: 250 Park Av., N.Y.C. 17. Died Oct. 29, 1967.

MORGAN, THOMAS J. Baptist minister, corr. sec. Am. Baptist Home Mission Soc., 1893—; b. Franklin, Ind., Aug. 17, 1839; s. Rev. Lewis M.; ed. Franklin Coll., leaving in senior yr. to enlist in 7th Ind. vol. inf., 1861; served 3 months and then took charge of public schools, Atlanta, Ill.; 1st lt., 70th Ind. vol. inf., 1862; served until 1865, rising to rank bvt. brig. gen.; prominent in enlistment of colored troops. Entered Rochester Theol. Sem., 1865; grad. same, 1868 (LL.D., Franklin Coll., 1894; D.D., Univ. of Chicago, 1874); m. 1870 Caroline Starr. Prof. homiletics and church history, Baptist Theol. Sem., Chicago 7 yrs.; prin. normal schools, Providence, R.I., and elsewhere. Commr. Indian affairs, 1889-93. Editor: Home Mission Monthly. Author: Educational Mossaics, 1887; Students' Hymnal, 1888; Studies in Pedagogy, 1888; Patriotic Citizenship, 1895; Praise Hymnal, 1897; Negro in America, 1900. Home: Yonkers, N.Y. Died 1902.

MORGAN, WILLIAM GERRY physician; b. Newport, N.H., May 2, 1868; s. Gerry and Mary (Strong) M.; A.B., Dartmouth, 1890; M.D., U. of Pa., 1893, postgrad. work, New York; m. Cora Boyd, Nov. 27, 1895. Began practice at Southport, Conn., 1894; settled at Washington, D.C., 1899; prof. diseases of digestive tract, Georgetown U., since 1940, dean of Sch. of Medicine, 1931-35; also regent of univ.; an asso. editor Tice System of Practice of Medicine; asso. editor Lippincott's Am. System of Medicine and Principles and Practice of Physical Therapy. Chmn. D.C. Advisory Draft Bd., also lt. (j.g.) Navy R.C., World War, retired, 1922; maj. M.R.C., U.S. Army from 1922, retired, 1932. Pres. Am. Congress of Internal Medicine, 1922. Fellow and master American College Physicians (regent 1918-30, gov. 1930-33, sec. gen. 1933-37, v.p. 1937); mem. A.M.A. (Ho. of Delegates 1920-25; pres. 1930-31), Am. Gastroenterol, Assn. (pres. 1913), Am. Therapeutic Assn., Clinico-Pathol. Soc. (pres. 1919), D.C. Med. Soc. (pres. 1919), N.Y. Acad. Medicine, Washington Acad. Sciences (v.p. 1919), Southern Med. Soc. (councillor), Va. Med. Soc., Wash. Hist. Soc., Am. Archeol. Assn., Assn., Mil. Surgeons, Med. Vets. of World War, Internat. Med. Club (pres. 1930; mem. U.S. Annual Assay Commn., 1922, 1924), Internat. Gastroentrology Soc. (U.S. del. to Brussels 1935), Psi Upsilon. Republican. Author of Functional Diseases of the Alimentary Tract, The History of the American College of Physicians. Clubs: Metropolitan, Cosmos, Congressional. Home: 3737 Fessenden St. N.W. Office: 1801 Eye St., N.W. Washington. Died July 7, 1949; buried Rock Creek Cemetery, Washington.

MORRILL, EDMUND N. banker, gov.; b. Westbrook, Me., Feb. 12, 1834; s. Rufus and Mary (Webb) M.: Ed. Westbrook Acad.; supt. schools, Westbrook, 1856; removed to Kan., 1857; elected, Oct. 1857, to first Free State legislature; reelected to legislature, Jan. 1858, under the Lecompton constitution; served, pvt. to sergt., 7th Kan. cav., 1861-62; apptd. capt. for commissary of subsistence, Aug. 1862; bvt. maj. for meritorious service; m. Caroline J. Nash, Dec. 25, 1869. Co. clerk, Brown Co., Kan., 1866, 1868 and 1870; clerk dist. court, 1867 and 1869; State senator, 1872 and 1876; pres. pro tem., senate, 1877; mem. Congress, 1883-91; gov. Kan., 1894-96; elected by Congress, 1890, mgr. of the homes for disabled vol. soldiers; opened 1st bank in Brown Co., Kan., 1871; still conducts it; was 7 yrs. pres. 1st Nat. Bank, Leavenworth. Home: Hiawatha, Kan. Died 1909.

MORRILL, WARREN PEARL hosp. consultant; b. Benton Harbor, Mich., Jan. 20, 1877; s. Roland and Ellen (Pearl) M.; Ph.B., U. of Mich., 1898; M.D., Johns Hopkins, 1908; m. Helen Wallace, Oct. 18, 1899; children-Ellen (Mrs. Reid R. Bronson, D.D.S.), Joanna (Mrs. Edward Timke), Helen (Mrs. Arthur E. Olvier, dec.). Superintendent Sydenham Hospital, Baltimore, Md., 1909-12, Winnipeg General Hospital, 1912-13; general practice of medicine, Benton Harbor, Mich., 1913-17; superintendent University Hospital, Augusta, Georgia, 1919-20, Shreveport (La.) Charity Hosp., 1920-24, Columbia Hosp. for Women, Washington, D.C., 1925-29, Me. Gen. Hosp., Portland, 1929-30; field rep. Am. College Surgeons, 1931, survey of state instns., Tex. and Conn., 1932-33. Served as pvt., inf., Spanish-Am. War; 1st lt., Med. R.C., 1911-17; capt. Med. Corps., Dec. 1916 to Dec. 1917, maj., Jan.-Nov. 1918; lt. col. Med. Corps, U.S. Army, A.E.F., Nov. 1918-Aug. 1919; col. Med. Res. U.S. Army (inactive). Mem. A.M.A., Am. Hosp. Assn., Heroes of '76, S.A.R. Mason (K.T.), K.P. Clubs: Army, Navy and Marine Corps Country (Ft. Meyers, Va.); Sojourner. Author: The Hospital Manual of Operation. Editor: Hospital Abstract Service; Medical Abstract Service. Dir. of research Am. Hosp. Assn. Address: 18 E. Division St., Chicago 10, Ill. Died Sept. 27, 1947.

MORRIS, CHARLES naval officer; b. Woodstock, Conn., July 26, 1784; s. Charles and Miriam (Nichols) M.; m. Harriet Bowen, Feb. 1, 1815; 10 children, including Charles, George. Apptd. midshipman U.S. Navy, 1799; on board the Constitution during war with Tripoli, 1803-05; lt. during Mediterranean cruise on ship Hornet, 1807; 1st lt. under Isaac Hull in Constitution at outbreak of War of 1812; promoted to capt. over grade of muster commandant, 1812; on ship Congress, comdg. forces in Carribean while on diplomatic missions to Haiti and Venezuela, 1814-17; mem. Bd. Navy Commrs., 1823-24, 27; commanded ship Brandywine in which Lafayette returned to France, 1825-26; commanded Boston Navy Yard, 1827-32; commanded Brazil and Mediterranean squadrons, 1841-44; head Bur. Constrn., later Bur. Ordnance until 1856. Died Washington, D.C., Jan. 27, 1856.

MORRIS, CHARLES brig. gen.; b. Charlestown, Mass., May 3, 1844; s. Charles W. (U.S.N.) and Caroline (Devens) M.; ed. pub. schs., Charlestown, Mass.; grad. U.S. Mil. Acad., 1865, Arty. Sch., 1878; m. Gertrude Missroon, 1867. Commd. 2d and 1st lt. 19th Inf., June 23, 1865; transferred to 37th Inf., Sept. 21, 1866, to 5th Inf., May 19, 1869, to 5th Arty., Dec. 15, 1870; capt., Mar. 6, 1882; maj. 7th Arty., Mar. 8, 1898; lt. col. Arty. Corps, Feb. 2, 1901; col., Feb. 21, 1902; brig. gen. U.S.A., May 2, 1908; retired by operation of law, May 3, 1908. Home: Portland, Me. Died Oct. 27, 1912.

MORRIS, NEWBOLD b. N.Y. City, Jan. 12, 1868; s. Augustus Newbold and Eleanor Colford (Jones) M.; LL.B., Columbia, 1891; spl. student Columbia U., Sch. Polit. Science 2 yrs.; Ècole des Sciences Politique, Paris, 1 semester; grad. U.S. Command and Gen. Staff Sch., 1924; m. Helen Schermerhorn Kingsland, Apr. 9, 1896; children-Augustus Newbold, George Lovett Kingsland, Stephanus Van Corlandt. Admitted to N.Y. bar, 1892; retired 1913. Capt. 12th Inf. N.Y. Vols., Spanish-Am. War, 1898; lt. col. and chief of Subsection on Enemy Resrouces, Gen. Staff, G.H.Q., A.E.F., World War; col. 432d F.A., O.R.C. Commr. State Training Sch., N.Y. 1908-11. Trustee Columbia U., Teachers Coll. (Columbia), Vanderbilt Clinic; v.p. Home of Incurables. Citation from Gen. Pershing "for exceptionally meritorious and conspicuous services"; Conspicuous Service Cross, N.Y. State; Spanish-Am. War Medal; Victory medal with 2 battle clasps. Trustee Diocese of Mass. P.E. Ch.; mem. Ho. of Deputies, P.E. Ch., 1922, 25; vestryman Trinity Ch., Lenox, Mass. Republican. Home: New York, N.Y., and Lenox, Mass. Died Dec. 20, 1928.

MORRIS, ROGER SYLVESTER M.D.; b. Ann Arbor, Mich., Sept. 24, 1877; s. George Sylvester and Victoria (Celle) M.; A.B., U. of Mich., 1900, M.D., 1902; m. Mary Bledsoe Carter, Sept. 10, 1907; 1 son, Roger Sylvester. Inst. medicine, U. of Mich., 1903-06; asst. res. phys. Johns Hopkins Hosp., and asso. in medicine, Johns Hopkins U., 1906-11; asso. prof. medicine, Washington U. Med. Sch., St. Louis, 1911-13; prof. medicine, U. of Cincinnati, 1915—; dir. med. clinic, Cincinnati Gen. Hosp., 1915—. Commd. maj., MED. O.R.C., 1917; lt. col., M.C. U.S.A., 1918, with A.E.F. Author: Clinical Laboratory Methods, 1913; Clinical Laboratory Diagnosis, 1923. Home: East Cincinnati, O. Died Mar. 2, 1934.

MORRIS, THOMAS ARMSTRONG pres. Indianapolis Water Co., 1888—; b. Nicholas Co., Ky., Dec. 26, 1811; s. Morris and Rachel (Morris) M.; learning printers' trade, 1923-26, at private school, 1926-30; grad. West Point, 1834; m. Elizabeth Rachel, d. John Irwin, 1940. Breveted 2d lt. 1st artillery, U.S.A., 1834; assigned, 1835, to asst. Maj. Ogden, of engineer corps, in constructing National raod in Ind. and Ill., having charge of division between Richmond and Indianapolis; resigned from U.S. service; was resident engr. Ind. State service; had charge construction Central Canal, was chief engr. Madison & Indianapolis R.R., superintended building it from Vernon to Indianapolis, 1841-47; chief engr. Terre Haute & Richmond R.R. and of Indianapolis & Belelfontaine R.R., 1847-52; chief engr. Indianapolis & Cincinnati R.R., 1852-54; pres. same, 1854-57; pres. Indianapolis & Bellefontaine R.R., 1857-59; chief engr. Indianapolis & Cincinnati R.R., 1859-61; planned and superintended construction of Union depot, Indianapolis, 1853. Apptd. q.m. gen. of Ind. by Gov. Morton, 1861; had charge of one of 1st regts. of Ind. vols.; gen. 1st brigade of troops that went from Ind.; served in W.Va. campaign; comd. at and won battles of Philippi, Laurel Hill and Carrick's Ford; mustered out July 27, 1861; chief engr. Indianapolis & Cincinnati R.R., 1862-66; pres. and chief engr. Indianapolis & St. Louis R.R., 1865-69; receiver Indianapolis, Cincinnati & Lafayette R.R., 1869-72; one of commrs. to select plans and superintend constuction new State Capitol, 1877. Life trustee Consumers' Gas Trust Co. Home: Indianapolis, Ind. Died 1904.

MORRIS, WILLIAM HENRY HARRISON, army officer; born Ocean Grove, N.J., March 22, 1890; son Howard F. and Mary (Van Dyke) M.; B.S., U.S. Mil. Acad., 1911; grad. Command and Gen. Staff Sch., 1925, Army War Coll., 1930; m. Marguerite Downing, Dec. 14, 1915. Commd. 2d lt., U.S. Army, June 11, 1911, and advanced through the grades to maj. gen., May, 1942; served as lt. col., 90th Div., World War I; mem. War Dept. Gen. Staff, 1938-40; comdg. gen. 6th Armored Div., Jan. 20, 1942-May 14, 1943; comdg. gen. II Armored Corps, May-Sept. 1943, XVIII Corps, Oct. 1943-July 1944, 10th Armored Div., July 1944-May 1945, VI Corps, May-Sept. 1945; Office of Secretary of War, 1945-47; became senior mem. Joint Brazil-United States Mil. Commn., June 1947; comdr. in chief, with rank of lt. gen., Caribbean command, 1949-52. Commanded 10th Armored Division in capture of Metz, Battle of Bulge (including defense of Bastogne), capture of Trier, breakthrough to the Rhine, capture of Heidelberg and Ulm, crossing Danube River, drive through Alps to Garmisch-Partenkirchen. Decorated D.S.C., D.S.M., Purple Heart, Silver Star, Legion of Merit, Bronze Star Medal (U.S.), Legion of Honor, Croix de Guerre with palm (France), Croix de Guerre (Belgium), Order Mil. Merit grade comdr. (Brazil); Order Vasco Nunez de Balboa (Panama); Order Abdon Calderon (Ecuador). Clubs: Army and Navy, Army-Navy Country (Washington). Home: Washington DC Died Mar. 31, 1971.

MORRIS, WILLIAM HOPKINS army officer; b. N.Y.C., Apr. 22, 1827; s. George and Mary (Hopkins) M.; grad. U.S. Mil. Acad., 1851; m. Catharine (Hoffman) Hyatt, 1870. Commd. 2d lt. 2d Inf., U.S. Army, 1851, resigned commn., 1854; invented repeating carbine with Charles Brown, 1859, patented, 1860; reenlisted as capt. U.S. Volunteers, 1861, promoted brig. gen., 1862; fought at battles of Fair Oaks, Bristol, Wilderness; commd. maj. gen., U.S. Volunteers, 1865; commd. col. N.Y. Nat. Guard, 1866, brig. gen., 1869; mem. N.Y. Constl. Conv., 1867. Author: Field Tactics for Infantry, 1864. Died Long Branch, N.J., Aug. 26, 1900.

MORRISON, DELESSEPS S(TORY) U.S. ambassador; b. New Roads, La., Jan. 18, 1912; s. Jacob H. and Anita (Oliver) M.; A.B., La. State U., man, October 3, 1942 (dec. Feb. 1959); children-deLesseps S., Corinne Ann, John Randolph. Atty. N.R.A., New Orleans, 1934-35; law practice, partner Morrison, Morrison & Boggs, 1935-42; mem. State Legislature La., 1940-46; mayor of New Orleans, 1946-61; U.S. ambassador Orgn. American States, 1961-. Served from 2d lt. O.R.C., to col. and div. chief of staff, 1941-45, now maj. general United States Army Reserve. Decorated B.S.M., Legion of Merit (U.S.); Order of Leopold (Belgium); Chevalier Legion of Honor (France). Recipient LaGuardia award for outstanding municipal adminstrn., 1953. Mem. Am. (past pres.), Inter-Am. (bd.) municipal assns., La. Bar Assn., Sigma Nu. Office: Dept. of State, Washington. Died May 22, 1964; buried Metairie Cemetery, New Orleans.

MORRISON, JASPER NEWTON maj. U.S.A.; b. Wayne Co., Mo., March 17, 1849; ed. in public school and at acad. in Fruitland, Mo.; m. Jane M. Pettit, July 17, 1884. Taught school, 1871; supt. schools, Wayne Co., Mo., 1872; admitted to bar, 1875; pros. atty. Wayne Co., Mo., 1876-82; practiced until 1888; chief clerk Bureau Military Justice, War Dept., 1888-96; apptd. maj. and judge advocate U.S.A., 1896. Died 1902.

MORRISON, JOHN F., army officer; b. Charlottesville, N.Y., Dec. 20, 1857; s. John and Hannah (Lamont) M.; grad. U.S. Mil. Acad., 1881; m. Kate McCleery, Aug. 16, 1887. Commd. 2d. lt., 20th Inf., June 11, 1881; promoted through grades to brig. gen., Nov. 20, 1915; maj. gen., May 15, 1917; retired, Dec. 20, 1921. Served in Cuba with 20th Inf., 1988, in Philippines, 1899-1902; mil. attaché, with Japanese Army, Russo-Japanese War, 1904; sr. instr. Army Staff Coll., 1907-12; later served in Manila, P.I.; apptd. comdr. Camp Sevier, Greenville, S.C., 1917; Europe, Sept.-Dec. 1917; dir. of training, U.S.A., Dec. 1917-Mar. 1918; comd. 8th Div., Mar. 3-June 1918; comd. Western Dept. to Aug. 17, 1919. Awarded D.S.M., 1919. Died Oct. 22, 1932.

MORRISON, OCIE BUTLER, JR., naval officer; b. Petersburg, Va., Nov. 20, 1896; s. Ocie Butler and Mary Young (Barner) M.; M.D., U. Va., 1925; postgrad. U.S. Naval Med. Sch., 1935-36. U.S.M.C. Staff and Command Sch., 1944; m. Stella Holcombe Moodey, August 6, 1919 (dec. Mar. 1966); children—Robert Holcombe, Mary Barner (wife William W. South,

U.S.N.); m. 2d, Mary June Clark, Oct. 8, 1966. Commd. lt. (j.g.), M.C. U.S.N., 1925, advanced through grades to vice adm., 1958; intern, staff Naval Hosp., Norfolk, Va., 1925-27; various assignments, 1927-34; staff U.S. Naval Academy, 1936-40; senior medical officer of U.S.S. Chicago, Pearl Harbor, T.H., 1940-42; profl. asst. comdg. med. officer Naval Hosp., Seattle, 1942; comdg. med. officer Armed Guard Tng. Center, Gulfport, Miss., 1942, sr. med. officer Armed Guard Sch., Advance Base Depot, Receiving Barracks, 1943; corps surgeon 1st Marine Amphibious Corps (later designated Third Amphibious Corps), 1944-45; chief surgery, later exec. officer Naval Hosp., Santa Margarita Ranch, Oceanside, Cal., 1945-48; exec. officer Naval Hosp., Portsmouth, Va., 1948-49; dir. personnel div., bur. medicine and surgery Navy Dept., Washington, 1949-50; comdg. officer Naval Hosp., San Diego, 1950-52; med. officer staff Comdr. Naval Forces Far East, 1952-53; dist. med. officer 1st Naval Dist. Hdqrs., Boston, 1953; dir. for planning and liaison, office or Asst. Sec. Defense, 1953-54; comdg. officer U.S. Naval Hosp., Portsmouth, Va., 1955-57; dist. med. officer Fifth Naval Dist., Hdqrs., Naval Base, Norfolk, 1957-58; dist. med. officer 11th Naval Dist., San Diego, Cal., from 1958. Decorated Legion Merit with gold star and oak leaf cluster, Bronze Star Medal with gold star. Presdl. Unit Citation, Navy Unit Commendation, Breast Order on Yun Hui (China); Danish Red Cross medal; Nat. Def., Korean, UN service medals. Fellow A.C.S.; mem. Assn. Mil. Surgeons, A.M.A. Mason (32 degree). Rotarian. Home: San Diego CA Died Sept. 21, 1969.

MORRISON, WILLIAM RALLS lawyer; b. Monroe Co., Ill., Sept. 14, 1825; s. John and Anne (Ralls) M.; ed. McKendree Coll.; pvt. in Mexican War and in battle of Buena Vista; went to Calif., 1849, returned to Ill., 1851; admitted to Ill. bar. Clerk Circuit Ct., Monroe Co., 1852-54; mem. Ill. legislature, 1854-60, 1871-72 (speaker, 1859-60). Organized and was col. 49th Ill. Vols., 1861-Dec., 1863; mem. Congress, 1863-65, 1873-87; chmn. Com. on Ways and Means, 1875-77, 1883-87; introduced, besides several others, the tariff bill; defeated for reelection, 1886; defeated for U.S. Senate in Ill. legislature, 1885, by John A. Logan; interstate commerce commr., 1887-97, and chmn. of the commn., 1891-97. Democrat. Home: Waterloo, Ill. Died 1909.

MORROW, JAMES E. prin. Allegheny High School; b. Brooke Co., Va., now Hancock Co., W.Va., March 28, 1837; s. Alexander M.; ed. Fairview, Va., Acad., 1850-53; grad. Jefferson Coll., Pa., 1856, A.M., 1875; Ph.D., 1889; m. Clara J. Johnson, Sept. 19, 1867. Engaged in teaching, 1856-58; admitted to bar, 1859; served in Union army, 1861-64, as pvt. and intermediate grades to capt. Co. F., 1st Va. inf. vols. Honorably disch., Dec. 10, 1864, by reason of expiration of term of service. Resumed teaching after war. Republican. Presbyn. Home: Allegheny, Pa. Died 1904.

MORROW, JAY JOHNSON army officer; b. Fairview, W.Va., Feb. 20, 1870; grad. U.S. Mil. Acad., 1891, Engr. Sch. of Application, 1894; m. Harriet M. Butler, Oct. 15, 1895. Commd. add. 2d lt. engrs., June 12, 1891; promoted through grades to lt. col., Mar. 11, 1915; col. (temp.), Aug. 5, 1917; brig. gen. N.A., June 26, 1918; returned to rank of col., May 20, 1919; retired at own request, Aug. 5, 1922, Instr. dept. practical mil. engring., U.S. Mil. Acad., 1895-96, 1898-1901; in Philippines, 1901-03; mil. gov. Province of Zamboanga, 1901-02; engr. Commr. Dist. of Columbia, 1907-09; engr. of maintenance and at times acting gov. Panama Canal, 1916-17; arrived in France, May 12, 1918; chief engr. 1st Army, and dep. chief engr. A.E.F., 1918; assigned to comd. Camp A.A. Humphreys, Va., Dec. 30, 1918; again engr. of maintenance, Panama Canal, June 1919-Mar. 1921; gov. same, Mar. 1921-Oct. 1924; mem. and chmn. Spl. Commn. on Boundaries, Tacna-Arica Arbitration, Mar. 1925-June 1929. Decorated Officer Legion of Honor (France), 1918. Presbyn. Home: Englewood, N.J. Died Apr. 16, 1937.

MORSE, ALEXANDER PORTER lawyer; b. St. Martinsville, La., Oct. 19, 1842; s. Isaac Edward and Margaretta Smith (Wederstrandt) M.; student Mt. St. Mary's Coll., Emmittsburgh, Md.; A.B., Princeton, 1862 (hon. Ph.D., 1885); LL.B., Georgetown U., 1972; ed. in English, French and Spanish; m. Ellen Clarke, Apr. 18, 1883. Pvt. Scott's 1st La. Cav., 1861-62; capt., adj. and instp. gen., Major's div., Green's cav. corps, C.S.A., 1863-64. Admitted to bar, Washington, 1872; practiced before all courts of D.C., exec. depts., and Supreme Ct. of U.S.; has been counsel for citizens of U.S. before several mixed (internat.) commns. of claims sitting in Washington, 1880—; specialty-internat. and constl. law. Was of counsel before Electoral Commn. (Tilden and Hayes), 1878; also for State of La. in several leading cases on constl. law in Supreme Ct. of U.S., and in "Insolar Cases" before same court. Asso. counsel for French Republic before French-Am. Claims Commn., 1881-84; agt. and counsel of U.S. before commn. to arbitrate claims of Venezuela Steam Transportation Co. against Venezuela, 1894; asst. atty. of U.S. before Spanish Treaty Claims Commn., 1901-02; arbitrator under protocol between Hayti and U.S. in Van Bokkelen claim, May 24, 1888. Author: Citizenship by Birth and Naturalization, 1881. Home: Washington, D.C. Died July 2, 1921.

MORSE, BENJAMIN CLARKE army officer; b. Macon, Mo., Oct. 15, 1859; s. Benjamin Clarke and Martha Ellsworth (Blunt) M.; grad. U.S. Mil. Acad., 1884; m. Jessie Cable (grad. Wellesley, 1889), Mar. 6, 1890. Commd. 2d lt. 23d Inf., June 15, 1884; promoted through grades to col. 13th Inf., July 1, 1916; trans. to 44th Inf., June 22, 1917; brig. gen. N.A., Aug. 5, 1917. Prof. mil. science and tactics and comdt. cadets, Agrl. and Mech. Coll. of Tex., 1890-94; participated in Spanish-Am. War, 1898, Philippine insurrection, 1899; personal aide to Mar. Gen. William R. Shafter, 1900-01; asst. adj. gen., 1901, actg. adj. gen., 1902, Dept. of Cal.; participated in Moro campaigns, P.I., 1903-04; 2d occupation of Cuba, 1906-09; prof. mil. science and tactics, and comdt. cadets, U. of Ill., 1910-13; occupation of Vera Cruz, Mexico, 1914; apptd. comdr. 169th Brigade N.A., Camp Custer, Battle Creek, Mich., Aug. 25, 1917; hon. disch. as brig. gen. N.A., Apr. 1, 1918; col. 33d. Inf., Canal Zone, Oct. 1918. Presbyn. Home: Marquette, Mich. Died Apr. 16, 1933.

MORSE, CHARLES WYMAN speculator; b. Bath, Me., Oct. 21, 1856; s. Benjamin and Anna (Rodbird) M.; grad. Bowdoin Coll., 1877; m. Hattie Hussey, Apr. 14, 1884, 4 children; m. 2d, Clemence (Cowles) Dodge, 1901. Engaged in shipping bus. while in coll., 1873-77; formed C. W. Morse & Co., ice and lumber shipping firm; moved to Wall St., N.Y.C., 1897, organized Consol. Ice Co., merged with other cos. to form Am. Ice Co., 1899; manipulated stock trhough Ice Securities Corp. (holding co.), made over $12,000,000 before irregularities and corruption ended his co.'s control of ice market; formed Consol. S.S. Co., 1905, had near monopoly of shipping along Atlantic coast by 1907, came to be called "Adm. of the Atlantic Coast", gained partial control (with F.A. Heinze and E. R. Thomas) of 12 N.Y. banks including Bank of N.Am., Merc. Nat. Bank; investigated and indicted (with assos.) as result of panic of 1907, imprisoned Atlanta (Ga.) Penitentiary, 1910-12; retained H. M. Daughtery (later atty. gen. under Harding) for fee of $5,000 to help secure his release from prison; pardoned by Pres. Taft on report that he was dying (actually had drunk mixture of chemicals and soapsuds calculated to produce grave symptoms); his Hudson Navigation Co. was sued for unfair competition, 1915; proposed orgn. of a trans-oceanic shipping co., 1916; contracted by Shipping Bd. to build 36 ships during World War I, borrowed capital to build ships from Emergency Fleet Corp.; indicated for conspiracy to defraud govt. when an investigation after the war revealed that he had used much of borrowed money to build shipyards instead of ships; also indicated for using mails to defraud prospective U.S. steamship investors; U.S. Govt. was awarded $11,500,-000 for his Va. Shipbuilding Co., 1925; placed under guardianship of probate ct. of Bath, 1926. Died Bath, Jan. 12, 1933.

MORSE, JEROME EDWARD naval officer; b. Leominster, Mass., Feb. 23, 1846; s. Gen. Augustus and Caroline A. (Willard) M.; apptd. by President Lincoln, 1862, and grad. 1866, U. S. Naval Acad.; m. Ella Packard, of Brooklyn, Feb. 15, 1872. Promoted ensign, June 1868; master, 1870; lt., 1872; retired for disability incurred in line of 1872; retired for disability incurred in line of duty, July 22, 1874; served as midshipman during Civil War; comd. Naval Training Sta., Erie, Pa., during Spanish-Am. War, 1898; promoted lt.-comdr., retired, June 29, 1906. V.p. and treas. Hecla Powder Co., 1881-95. Founder and 1st pres. Morse Soc. of America, and pres. of The Morse Co., pubs., 1895-1904. Trustee Adelphi Coll., Brooklyn, 12 yrs. Past Grand Treas. Grand Lodge, F. and A.M. of N.Y. Clubs: Montauk, Aldine, Aurora Grata. Home: 129 St. James Pl., Brooklyn.

MORSE, ROBERT HOSMER machinery mfg. co.; b. Chgo., Dec. 6, 1878; s. Charles Hosmer and Martha Janet (Owens) M.; ed. Manual Tng. Sch., Chgo., to 1890; Shattuck Sch., Faribault, Minn., and Hill Sch., Pottstown, Pa., to 1895; m. Bernice James, 1897 (dec. 1903); children-Charles Hosmer (dec. 1949), Robert Hosmer; m. 2d, Rosalie Dorathea Douglas, July 17, 1904 (dec. 1948); children-Barbara Jean, John Morse (dec. 1941). With Fairbanks, Morse Mfg. Co., Beloit, Wis., 1895-97; with Patterson, Goldfield & Hunter, N.Y.C., 1897-1900, dept. mgr., 1898-1900; asst. mgr. Fairbanks, Morse & Co., Cleve., 1901-03, began with Chgo. office, 1903, 1st vice-pres. 1924-27, vice chmn., 1927-31, pres., gen. mgr., 1931-50, chmn., gen. mgr., 1950-59, pres., chmn. emeritus, 1959-, also dir.; sales mgr., later pres. Fairbanks, Morse Elec. Co., Indpls.; chmn., dir. Canadian Fairbanks-Morse Co. Ltd., Municipal Acceptance Corp.; Trustee St. Johnsbury (Vt.) Acad. Served as lt. col. Signal Corps, U.S. Army, World War. Mem. Chgo. Hist. Soc., Chgo. Loop Post Am. Legion. Episcopalian. Mason (32ff, K.T.), Elk. Clubs: Chicago, Chicago Athletic, South Shore Country, Germania (Chgo.); Knollwood (Lake Forest, Ill.); Bath and Tennis, Everglades, Old Guard, Sailfish, Com. of 100 (Palm Beach, Fla.). Home: 1242 Lake Shore Dr., Chgo. (Summer) 1299 Knollwood Circle, Lake Forest, Ill.; (winter) 210 Dunbar Rd., Palm Beach Fla. Died Apr. 11, 1964; buried Oak Woods Cemetery, Chgo.

MORTON, CHARLES brig. gen.; b. Chagrin Falls, O., Mar. 18, 1846; s. Charles Eldridge and Huldah Atwater (Noah) M.; m. Elizabeth Lloyd, d. Maj. Gen. Landgon C. Easton, U.S.A., Apr. 8, 1873; m. 2d, Mrs. Sabina (page) Pemberton, Sept. 25, 1904. Served as pvt. Co. I, 13th and 25th Mo. Inf., and Co. H, 1st Mo. Engrs., July 29, 1861-Sept. 14, 1864; apptd. U.S. Mil. Acad., July 1, 1865, grad. 1869; apptd. 2d lt. 3d U.S. Cav., June 15, 1869; promoted through grades to brig. gen. U.S.A., Apr. 19, 1907; retired by operation of law, Mar. 18, 1910. Bvtd. 1st lt., Feb. 27, 1890, for action against Indians in Tonto country, Ariz., June 5, 1871. Died Dec. 20, 1914.

MORTON, CHARLES ADAMS farmer; b. at Willoughby, O., May 28, 1839; ed. Des Peres Inst., St. Louis Co., Mo.; clerk, 1855, and partner, 1858, in wholesale grocery and commn. business in St. Louis; served, 1861-65, in U.S.A., becoming col. and commissary of subsistence. Settled in St. Paul, Minn., as mcht.; was mem. Minn. senate, 1877-80; Dakota farmer since 1880; has 10,000 acres in cultivation, with output of about 150,000 bushels of wheat, besides other crops, annually; had other large interests. Address: Fargo, N. Dak.

MORTON, HOWARD MCILVAIN oculist, aurist; b. Chester, Pa., May 23, 1868; s. Charles J. and Annie E. (Coates) M.; B.S., Lafayette Coll., 1888, M.S., 1891; M.D., U. of Pa., 1891; post-grad. work Royal Ophthalmic Hosp., London, and Charite Hosp., Berlin; m. Lucretia Jarvis, Dec. 9, 1891. Interne, St. Luke's Hosp., Bethlehem, Pa., 1891; practiced at Minneapolis, Minn., since 1891; prof. diseases of eye and ear, Hamline U., 1893-95; formerly oculist and aurist, Minneapolis City and Swedish hosps.; chief dept. eye surgery, Minneapolis. Gen. Hosp.; chief eye and ear surgeon, Wells Memorial Clinic and St. Barnabas and Fairview hosps.; now retired. Mem. Internat. Congress Ophthalmologists. Mem. A.M.A., Minn. State Med. Assn., Hennepin County Med. Soc., Am. Acad. Ophthalmology and Oto-Laryngology, Minn. Acad. Ophthalmology and Oto-Laryngology (1st pres.), Assn. Mil. Surgeons of U.S., Internat. Soc. for Prevention of Blindness, Am. Legion; fellow Am. Coll. Surgeons; dep. gov. gen. Nat. Soc. Sons and Daughters of the Pilgrims. Republican. Episcopalian. Maj. Med. Corps, U.S.A., during World War; lecturer Army Sch. of Ophthalmology, Ft. Oglethorpe, Ga. Clubs: Minneapolis, Skylight (Minneapolis); University (St. Paul). Author: Visual Neurology (text book); also Permetry (monograph in Am. Ency. of Ophthalmology); also over 100 articles in tech. jours. Inventor of Morton perimeter and other instruments. Address: Vincentown, N.J. Died July 19, 1939.

MORTON, JAMES PROCTOR, naval officer; b. Rockford, Tenn., Feb. 8, 1874; s. Henry Thomas and Mary Arvilla (Proctor) M.; student U. of Mo., 1890-1; grad. U.S. Naval Acad., 1895; m. Grace L. Howard, of Washington, D.C., Mar. 21, 1911. Promoted ensign, June 1897; advanced through various grades to capt., Oct. 15, 1917. Served on Marblehead and Vixen, Spanish-Am. War, 1898; promoted for spl. service on blockade of Santiago de Cuba; on Monadnock and Bennington, in Philippine Island, 1898-1901, assisting to land the army; head of Post-Grad. Sch. for Officers of Navy, at Annapolis, Md., 1912-15; organized sch. for advanced work in engring., electricity and ordnance, 1912. Naval attache to Turkey, 1915-17, comd. transport President Grant, landing troops in France, Aug. 1917-Feb. 1918; apptd. comdr. battleship Kentucky, Feb. 18, 1918. Mem. Am. Soc. Naval Engrs., Sigma Alpha Epsilon. Medals Spanish-Am. War, West Indies Campaign, Philippine Insurrection. Presbyn. Clubs: Army and Navy, Chevy Chase (Washington, D.C.); Racquet (Philadelphia); New York Yacht. Home: 3009 DeGraff Way,2Kansas City MO

MORTON, JAMES ST.CLAIR army officer, engr., author; b. Phila., Sept. 24, 1829; s. Dr. Samuel George and Rebecca Grellet (Pearsall) M.; grad. U.S. Mil. Acad., 1851. Asst. engr. in constrn. defenses of Charleston harbor, S.C., 1851-52; commd. 2d lt., 1854, asst. prof. engring. U.S. Mil. Acad.; promoted 1st lt., 1856; charge potomac Water Works, 1859-60; engr. in charge Chiriqui Expdn. to C.Am. of Washington Aqueduct, 1860-61; capt. engrs., 1861; chief engr. Army of the Ohio, 1862; brig. gen. U.S. Volunteers, 1862; chief engr. Army of the Cumberland, 1862-63; brevetted lt. col. engrs. in regular army, 1863; maj. Corps Engrs., 1863; brevetted col., 1863; supt. defenses of Nashville, Murfreesboro, Clarksville, Ft. Donelson, 1863-64; asst. to chief engr., Washington, D.C., 1864; brevetted brig. gen., 1864. Author: Memoir on the Dangers and Defences of New York City, 1858; Memoir on American Fortification, 1859. Died Petersburg, Va., June 17, 1864; buried Laurel Hill Cemetery, Phila.

MORTON, PAUL Sec. of the navy; b. Detroit, May 22, 1857; s. J. Sterling (Sec. of Agr., 1893-97) and Caroline (Joy) M.; bro. of Joy M.; m. Charlotte Goodridge, Oct. 13, 1880. With Burlington system Dec., 1872, to Feb. 1, 1890, beginning as clerk in land officer of B.&M. R.R. at Burlington, 1872, serving as asst. gen. freight agt. and gen. pass. agt. and ending as gen. freight agt. of the C.B.&Q. R.R.; v.p. Colo. Fuel & Iron Co.; pres. Whitebreast Fuel Col, 1890-96; 3d v.p. A.,T.&S.F. Ry., 1896-98, 2d v.p. same, 1898-1904; sec. of the navy, July 1, 1904-July 1, 1905, in cabinet of President Roosevelt;

pres. Equitable Life Assurance Soc. of U.S., 1905—. V.p. Pan.-Am. R.R., Mar. 15, 1910—. Home: New York, N.Y. Died 1911.

MOSBY, JOHN SINGLETON lawyer, soldier; b. Powhatan Co., Va., Dec. 6, 1833; s. Alfred D. and Virginia I. (McLaurine) M.; grad. U. of Va., 1852; m. Pauline Clarke, Dec. 30, 1856. Admitted to bar, 1855; practiced at Bristol, Va., 1855-61. Pvt. and later adj. in 1st Va. Cav., C.S.A., 1861-62; was col., 1862-65, of Mosby's Partisan Rangers, as independent cav. command, which did much damage by cutting communications and destroying supply trains in the rear of U.S.A., capturing cav. outposts, etc. Practiced law in Va. after war. Became Republican; supported Grant, 1872; U.S. counsul at Hongkong, 1878-85; then lawyer in San Francisco and as counsel for S.P. R.R. Co.; spl. agt. Gen. Land Office for Colo., 1901; asst. atty. in Dept. of Justice, Washington, May 1904-July 1, 1910. Author: Mosby's War Reminiscences and Stuart's Cavalry Campaign, 1887; Stuart Cavalry in the Gettysburg Campaign, 1908. Home: Warrenton, Va. Died May 30, 1916.

MOSELEY, EDWARD BUCKLAND brig. gen U.S.A.; b. Phila., Oct. 1, 1846; s. Nathaniel B. and Maria (Worthington) M.; acad. edn., Phila.; grad. Auxilliary Faculty of Medicine, U. of Pa., 1866, M.D., 1868; resident phys., Phila. Hosp., 1868-69; m. Florence C. David, Dec. 9, 1875. Sergt. Pa. Militia Arty., 1862, participating in Antietam campaign; 1st lt. asst. surgeon, U.S.A., Nov. 10, 1874; capt. asst. surgeon, Nov. 10, 1879; maj. surgeon, Jan. 9, 1892; lt. col. deputy surgeon gen., Feb. 14, 1902; col. asst. surgeon gen., Mar. 17, 1906; brig. gen. and retired for physical disability incurred in line of duty, May 10, 1907. Served in campaigns against Sioux, Cheyenne, and Ute Indians in Wyo., Neb. and Colo., in P.I., 1899-1900; organized and in charge Santa Monica Mil. Hosp., Manila; in charge 2d Reserve hosp. and chief surgeon Dept. Southern Luzon; later chief surgeon Dept. Colo. until retired. Home: Hollywood, Calif. Died Aug. 3, 1923.

MOSELEY, GEORGE VAN HORN army officer; b. Evanston, Ill., Sept. 28, 1874; s. George Dallas and Alice Kent (Willett) M.; grad. U.S. Mil. Acad., 1899; honor grad. Army Sch. of the Line, 1908; grad. Army Staff Coll., 1909; Army War Coll., 1911; m. Alice A. Dodds, July 20, 1903 (divorced 1924); children-George Van Horn, Francis Loring; m. 2d, Mrs. Florence Du Bois, June 23, 1930; 1 son, James Willett. Second lt. 9th Cavalry, Feb. 15, 1899; promoted through grades maj. gen., 1930; various field assignments U.S., P.I., A.E.F., 1899-1910; camp and Washington assignments, 1920-29; exec. for asst. sec. of war, 1929-30; dep. chief of staff of Army, 1930-33; comdg. 5th Corps Area. 1933-34, 4th Corps Area, 1934-38, 3d Army, 1936-38; retired, 1938. Awards: D.S.M. (with oak leaf cluster). Oak Leaf cluster, Comdr. Order of the Crown (Belgian); Companion Order of the Bath (British); Comdr. Legion of Honor, and Croix de Guerre with Palm (French); Comdr. Order of the Crown (Italian). Pres., Texas Ednl. Assn. Address: Atlanta Biltmore Hotel, Atlanta. Died Nov. 7, 1960.

MOSER, JEFFERSON FRANKLIN naval officer; b. Allentown, Pa., May 3, 1848; s. John B. and Henrietta (Beidelman) M.; grad. U.S. Naval Acad., 1868; m. Nancy C. McDowell, Oct. 20, 1874; children-Robert McD (dec.), Samuel B. (dec.), Jefferson F. (dec.), Helen C. Commd. midshipman, June 2, 1868; promoted through grades to rank of rear adm. and retired after 40 yrs. service, Sept. 20, 1904. Mem. expdns., 1869-70, 72, 73, 75, exploring and surveying ship canal routes across Nicaragua and Panama; coast survey service, 1875-80, 1884-90, 1893-96; comd. U.S. Steamer Albatross in exploring salmon streams of Alaska and on Agassiz expdn. to South Seas, etc.; comd. gunboats Albatross and Bennington during Spanish-Am. War; gen. supt. and v.p. Alaska Packers Assn., San Francisco, 1904-18. Ordered to active service in U.S.N., Apr. 6, 1917, on special duty 12th Naval Dist. until June 15, 1919. Author: Alaska Salmon and Salmon Fisheries, 1899; Alaska Salmon Investigations, 1902. Home: Alameda, Calif. Died. Oct. 11, 1934.

MOSES, ANDREW army officer; b. Burnet County, Tex., June 6, 1874; s. Norton and Lucy Ann (Lewis) M.; student U. of Tex.; B.S., U.S. Mil. Acad., 1897, Sch. of Submarine Defense, 1906, Army War Coll., 1921; m. Jessie Fisher, Sept. 24, 1897; 1 dau., Kathleen (wife of Frank Fenton Reed, U.S. Army). Commd. add. 2d lt., inf., U.S. Army, June 11, 1897, 2d lt. arty., Mar. 8, 1898, and advanced through grades to col., July 1, 1920; brig. gen., Sept. 19, 1929; major general, December 1, 1935, Member General Staff, Nov. 14, 1914-Aug. 16, 1917; brig. gen. (temp.), June 26, 1918-Mar. 15, 1920; comdg. 156th Brigade F.A. (81st Div.) in U.S. and France; chmn. joint bd. for redelivery of troop transports, 1919-20; comdt. cadets, Agrl. and Mech. Coll., Tex., 1907-11, also Nat. Guard and organized reserves duty in various states; dir. Army War Coll., 1921-23, 1928-29; comdg. Coast and Antiaircraft Arty. Defenses, Panama Canal, 1930-31; asst. chief of Staff, War Dept., Oct. 8, 1931-Oct. 7, 1935; on duty Army Group, Washington, D.C., Oct. 8, 1935-Feb. 6, 1936; comdg. Hawaiian Div. and Schofield Barracks, Mar. 11, 1936-July 30, 1937; comdg. Hawaiian Dept., 1937-38; retired June 30, 1938. Awarded D.S.M. Mem. Am. Legion, Mil. Order World War. Mason. Club: Army and Navy (Washington). Address: 5830 Chevy Chase Parkway, Washington. Died Dec. 22, 1946; buried in Arlington National Cemetery.

MOSS, JAMES ALFRED author, army officer; b. Lafayette, La., May 12, 1872; grad. U.S. Mil. Acad., 1894. Commd. 2d lt. 25th Inf., June 12, 1894, promoted through grades to lt. col., Nov. 2, 1918; col. N.A., Aug. 5, 1917-Aug. 31, 1919; col. regular army, Dec. 15, 1920; retired. Oct. 31, 1922. Served in Cuba with 24th Inf., Spanish-Am. War; recommended for two brevets "for gallant and meritorious conduct" at Battle of El Caney, July 1, 1898; in Philippine Insurrection, July 1899-July 1902; awraded silver star "for gallantry in action," in the Cuban campaign; with American Expeditionary Force in France, June 19, 1918-Aug. 31, 1919; oraganized and commanded 367th Infantry, "The Buffaloes," comdt. 1st Corps Schools, chief of staff Provost Marshal Generals Department, deputy provost marshal general, A.E.F.; a.d.c. to Maj. Gen. Henry C. Corbin, 3 years; inst. School of the Line and Army Staff Coll., Ft. Leavenworth, Kan., 4 yrs.; spl. duty Office of Chief of Staff, U.S.A. (Gen. Leonard Wood), 1911-12, in connection with reduction and simplified muster and pay rolls and various other forms. Founder and pres. gen. U.S. Flag Assn. Author: Manual of Military Training, 1914; Questions on Manual of Military Training, 1917; Questions on Infantry Drill Regulations, 1917; Spanish for Soldiers (collaborator), 1916; Junior Military Manual (collaborator), 1917; Manual for Medical Officers (collaborator), 1917; Army Orders, 1914; Trench Warfare, 1917; Our Flag and Its Message (collaborator), 1917; Military Students' Textbook, Vols. I, II, III and IV (collaborator), 1919; Practical Topography (collaborator), 1919; America in Battle (collaborator), 1920; Chateau-Thierry-An American Shrine (collaborator), 1920; The Flag of the United States and the Story of "The Star Spangled Banner," 1923; The American Flag-Its Glory and Grandeur, 1929; The Flag of the United States-Its History and Symbolism, 1930; The Spirit of the American Flag, 1933; Your Rights Under the Constitution, 1935; The Constitution of the United States (People's Edition), 1935; The Fellow-American Service (a patriotic industrial service), 1937; Our Country's Flag, 1937; Your Flag and Mine-Its Message, 1938; Patriotic Revival Manual, 1939. Editor: The Quartermaster Review and sec. The Quartermaster Assn., 1921-23. Originator of Flag Week, June 8 to 14 of each year. Died Apr. 23, 1941.

MOTT, GERSHOM army officer; b. Lamberton, N.J., Apr. 7, 1822; s. Gershom and Phoebe (Scudder) M.; m. Elizabeth Smith, Aug. 8, 1849, 1 child. Enlisted for service in war with Mexico, 1846; commd. 2d lt. 10th U.S. Inf.; worked for Bordentown (N.J.) Bank, 1855-61; lt. 5th Regt., N.J. Volunteers, 1861, col. 6th Regt., 1862; served in 2d battle of Bull Run; brevetted maj. gen. U.S. Volunteers, 1864; commd. maj. gen. of volunteers, 1865; paymaster Camden & Amboy R.R., 1866; maj. gen. N.J. Militia, 1873; treas. of N.J., 1875; keeper N.J. State Prison, 1876-81; mem. Riparian Com. of N.J., 1882-84; mem. firm Thompson & Mott, iron foundry, 1873-76; dir. Bordentown Banking Co.; maj. gen. N.J. Nat. Guard, 1873-84. Died N.Y.C., Nov. 29, 1884.

MOTT, T(HOMAS) BENTLEY army officer; b. Leesbough, Va., May 16, 1865; s. Armistead Randolph and Virginia (Bentley) M.; grad. U.S. Mil. Acad., 1886; m. Georgette Saint Paul, May 1923. Commd. and promoted through grades to lt.-col., 1911; retired, 1914; recalled to active service, 1917; col. Nat. Army, 1918; col. U.S. Army, 1918. Instr. in tactics U.S. Mil. Acad., 1890-94; a.d.c. to Maj.-Gen. Merritt, 1896-98, 1899-1900; commended in orders for gallantry and services in Manila campaign; mil. attaché Am. Embassy, Paris, 1900-05, 09-13; in banking business in Paris, France. With Root Mission to Russia, mission to Italy, 1917; attached to Gen Pershing's staff, in France, 1918, Marshal Foch's staff as rep. of Gen. Pershing. mil. attaché to Am. Embassy, Paris, 1919-30. Decorated Silver Star, D.S.M., Legion of Merit (U.S.); comdr. Legion of Honor (French); Officer de l'Ordre de Leopold (Belgian); Companion of St. Michael and St. George (British); Officer Order of St. Stanislas (Russian). Episcopalian. Clubs: Union (N.Y.C.); Metropolitan (Washington); Union (Paris). Author: Biography of Myron T. Herrick; Twenty Years as Military Attaché; also numerous articles on mil. service and travel; prize medal essayist, Mil. Service Instn. Address: American Battle Monuments Commission, 2 Av. Gabriel, Paris, France. Died Dec. 1952.

MOULTON, FOREST RAY astronomer; b. Le Roy, Mich., Apr. 29, 1872; s. Belah G. and Mary C. (Smith) M.; A.B., Albion Coll., 1894; Ph.D. summa cum laude, U. Chgo., 1899; Sc.D., Albion (Mich) Coll., 1922; LL.D., Drake U., 1939; Sc.D., Case Sch. Applied Sci., 1940; m. Estelle Gillette, Mar. 25, 1897; 2 sons, 2 daus. Asso. in astronomy U. Chgo., 1898-1900; instr., 1900-03, asst. prof., 1903-08, asso. prof., 1908-12, prof., 1912-26; asso. editor Transactions Am. Math. Soc., 1907-12; adminstrv. sec. A.A.A.S., 1937-48. Research asso. Carnegie Instn., 1908-23; dir. Utilities Power & Light Corporation, 1920-38. Maj., Ordnance Dept. U.S. Army, in charge of ballistics of Am. arty., 1918-19; lt. col. Ordnance U.S.R. Fellow Royal Astron. Soc., A.A.A.S., Am. Philos. Soc., Am. Acad. Arts and Sciences; mem. Nat. Acad. Sciences, Am. Math. Soc., Am. Astron. Soc.; hon. fgn. asso. Brit. Assn., Adv. Science. Author: Celestial Mechanics, 1902, 14; Introduction to Astronomy, 1905, 16; Descriptive Astronomy, 1911; Periodic Orbits, 1920; New Methods in Exterior Ballistics, 1926; Differential Equations, 1929; Astronomy, 1931; Consider the Heavens, 1935; Autobiography of Science (with J. J. Schifferes), 1945. Contbr. and editor of the World and Man, 1937. Editor of 25 A.A.A.S. sci. symposium vols. Contbr. to math. and astron. jours. Trustee and dir. of Concessions World's Fair, Chicago, 1933. Home: 1637 Orrington St., Evanston, Ill. Died Dec. 8, 1952.

MOULTON, HAROLD GLEN economist; b. Le Roy, Mich., Nov. 7, 1883; s. Belah G. and Mary C. (Smith) M.; student Albion (Mich.) Coll., 1903-05; Ph.B., U. of Chicago, 1907, Ph.D., 1914; LL.D., Washington Univ., New York Univ., U. of Pittsburgh, George Washington Univ., Syracuse Univ., Oberlin College Northeastern U., U. Chgo. m. Frances C. Rawlins, June 17, 1912 (died 1960); children-John Rawlins, Barbara. Instr. Evanston Acad., 1908-09; fellow in polit. economy, 1909-10, traveling fellow, 1910, asst. in polit. economy, 1910-11, instr., 1911-14, asst. prof., 1914-18, asso. prof., 1918-22, professor, 1922. University of Chicago; pres. The Brookings Instn. (Washington) 1922-52, pres. emeritus since 1952. Member finance com. Variable Insurance Co. Am. Chmn. com. on care of dependents Dept. Def., 1954; chmn. White House task force on budgetary and financial civil control of disarmament, 1955. Fellow Am. Assn. Advancement Sci. (vice president 1936); corr. mem. Institut de France. Club: University. Author: Waterways vs. Railways, 1912 and 25; Principles of Money and Banking, 1916; Commercial Banking and Capital Formation, 1918; Financial Organization of Society, 1921, 3d edit., 1930; The Reparation Plan, 1924; Japan, An Economic and Financial Appraisal, 1931; The American Transportation Problem, 1933; The Formation of Capital, 1935; Income and Economic Progress, 1935; Financial Organization and the Economic System, 1938; Fundamental Economic Issues in National Defense, 1941; The New Philosophy of Public Debt, 1943. Joint author of the following works: Readings in the Economics of War, 1918; America and the Balance Sheet of Europe, 1921; Germany's Capacity to Pay, 1923; Russian Debts and Russian Reconstruction, 1924; The French Debt Problem, 1925; World War Debt Settlements, 1926; The St. Lawrence Navigation and Power Project, 1929; War Debts and World Prosperity, 1932; America's Capacity to Consume, 1934; The Recovery Problem in the United States, 1937; Capital Expansion, Employment and Economic Stability, 1940; The Control of Germany and Japan, 1944; The Regulation of the Securities Market, 1946; Controlling Factors in Economic Development, 1949; The Dynamic Economy, 1950; Can Inflation be Controlled, 1958. Home: Charles Town, W.Va. Died Dec. 1966.

MOWER, JOSEPH ANTHONY army officer; b. Woodstock, Vt., Aug. 22, 1827; s. Nathaniel and Sophia (Holmes) M.; attended Norwich (Vt.) U., 1843-45; m. Betsey Bailey, June 6, 1851. Served as enlisted man in Mexican War; commd. 2d lt., U.S. Army, 1855, 1st lt., 1857; commd. capt. U.S. Volunteers, 1861, maj., 1862, lt. col., 1862, col. 1863, distinguished himself at Battle of Vicksburg; with Gen. Sherman in march from Atlanta to sea; commd. brig. gen. U.S. Volunteers, 1865, maj. gen., 1865; col. U.S. Army; in command Dept. La. received many commendations from superiors during Civil War. Died New Orleans, Jan. 6, 1870.

MOYER, JOSEPH KEARNEY, lawyer; b. Pottsville, Pa., Dec. 22, 1890; s. Morgan G. and Fannie C. (Smith); B.C.S., cum laude, New York U., 1917; LL.B., Southeastern U., Washington, D.C., 1926; spl. course, Cornell, 1912; LL.D. (honorary), Southeastern University, 1947; married Alta C. Turner, Oct. 14, 1922. Bank clerk, 1908; asst. nat. bank examiner, 1912; teacher, 1911-17; U.S. treas., Bur. Internal Revenue, 1919-34; private law practice from 1934; dean, Southeastern U. Served to 2d lt., Chem. Warfare Service, 1918-19; 1st lt., capt. Army Reserves, 1919-34. Mem. Am. Bar Assn., Am. Inst. Accountants, Beta Gamma Sigma. Republican. Lutheran. Mason (Shriner), Rotarian. Author articles on fed. taxation. Home: Washington DC Died Aug. 1969; buried Genoa, OH

MOYLAN, STEPHEN army officer; b. Cork, Ireland, 1734; s. John Moylan; m. Mary Van Horn, Sept. 12, 1778. Came to Phila., 1768; organizer Friendly Sons of St. Patrick, 1771, pres., 1771, 96; became army muster-master gen., 1775. q.m. gen., 1776; recruiter 1st Pa. Regt. of Cavalry, 1776 commd. col.; served at Valley Forge, 1777-78; brevetted brig. gen., 1783; U.S. commr. loans, Phila., 1793. Died Phila., Apr. 13, 1811.

MUDD, SEELEY WINTERSMITH mining engr.; b. Kirkwood, Mo., Aug. 16, 1861; s. Henry Thomas and Sarah Eliz. (Hodgen) M.; E.M., Washington U., St. Louis, 1883; m. Della Mulock, Feb. 24, 1887; children-Harvey S., Elizabeth (dec.), Seeley G., Henry T. (dec.). Assayer and supt. copper dept., St. Louis Smelting & Refining Co., 1883-85; went to Leadville, Colo., 1885; mgr. Small Hopes Consolidated Mining Co. and Borel Mining Co., 1887-1912; mgr. Ibex Mining Co. (Little Johnnie Mine), 1899-1902; consulting engr. in the West for N.J. Zinc Co., 1902-04; moved to Los Angeles,

Calif., 1903; consulting engr. on Pacific Coast for Guggenheim Exploration Co. and Am. Smelting & Refining Co., 1904-05; pres. and mgr. Queen Esther Mining and Milling Co., Kern Co., Calif., 1904-09; pres. Cyprus Mines Corp., Coeur d'Alene Syndicate Mining Co. Commd. maj., Engr., O.R.C., Feb. 12, 1917; active dutyk Jan. 14, 1918; asst. dir. U.S. explosives plants, Washington; promoted col. U.S.A., May 24, 1918; hon. disch., Jan. 20, 1919. V.p. Y.M.C.A., Los Angeles; trustee Pomona Coll., Southwest Museum. Republican. Conglist. Home: Los Angeles, Calif. Died May 24, 1926.

MUDGE, VERNE DONALD army officer; b. Bangor, S.D., Sept. 5, 1898; ed. U. of Florida; B.S., U.S. Mil. Acad., 1920; grad. Cav. Sch., 1921, Command and Gen. Staff Sch., 1935, Army War Coll., 1940. Commd. 2d lt., U.S. Army, 1920, and advanced through the grades to maj. gen., 1944; on duty in personnel division, War Dept. Gen. Staff, Washington, D.C., 1940-42; chief of staff, 1st Cav. Div., 1942; comd. 5th Cav. Brigade, Fort Clark, Tex., 1942-43, 2d Cav. Brigade, Fort Bliss, Tex., Australia, New Guinea and Admiraltys., 1943-44; became commanding general, first Cav. Division, Southwest Pacific Area, Aug. 1944, and led the division to invasion of Leyte, Samar and Luzon, P.I. Wounded in action, Feb. 28, 1945. Apptd. to professional staff, Senate Com. on Armed Services 1947-55. Awarded D.S.C., D.S.M., Legion of Merit, Silver Star, Bronze Star, Air Medal, Purple Heart. Address: 2674 Rosecrans St., San Diego 6, Cal. Died Jan. 29, 1957; buried Ft. Rosecrans Nat. Cemetery. San Diego.

MUELLER, JOHN VICTOR investment exec.; b. Visalia, Cal., Sept. 26, 1893; s. John and Anna (Siddall) M.; student U. Nev., 1917; m. Margaret MacMasters, May 25, 1921; 1 dau., Margaret (Mrs. Richard Hartshorne). Asst. state engr., Nev., 1919-23; pres., dir. Holiday, Inc., 1954-, Nev. Properties Corp., 1953-; treas., dir. Pacific Engring. and Prodn. Co. Nev., 1958-. Master in chancery Carson River Adjudication, 1940—; mem. Colo. River Commn., 1946-48. Served to capt. U.S. Army, 1917-19, to col. AUS, 1941-45. Decorated Silver Star, Bronze Star with cluster; named Distinguished Nevadan, U. Neva., 1962. Mem. Nev. Mining Assn., Reno C. of C., Am. Legion, Retired Officers Assn. Republican. Episcopalian. Clubs: Prospectors, Hidden Valley Country (Reno); Family (San Francisco). Home: 761 Marsh Av. Office: 103 Mill St., Reno. Died Aug. 1, 1963; buried Golden Gate Nat. Cemetery, San Bruno, Cal.

MUELLER, PAUL JOHN army officer; b. Union, Mo., Nov. 16, 1892; B.S., U.S. Mil. Acad., 1915; distinguished grad. Command and Gen. Staff Sch., 1923; grad. Army War Coll., 1928; m. Margaret Martin Brown, June 20, 1923; children-Margaret Elizabeth, Paul John. Commd. 2d lt. U.S. Army, 1915, advanced through grades to maj. gen., Sept. 1942. Served as inf. bn. comdr. AEF, France, 1918; became chief of staff 2d Army, Oct. 1941; comdr. 81st Div., 1942, in U.S. and in combat operations in Western Carolines and Philippines, and in occupation of Japan, 1944-45; comdr. 86th Div., 1946; chief of staff G.H.Q., Tokyo, 1946-49; dep. comdg. gen. 3d Army, 1949-50; chief Career Mgmt. Div., Dept. Army, 1950-53; ret., 1953. Decorations World War I, Silver Star Medal; World War II, Army D.S.M. with oak leaf cluster, Navy D.S.M., Silver Star medal with oak leaf cluster, Officer, Legion of Honor (France); Comdr. Legion of Honor (Republic of Philippines). Mason (32ff, Shriner). Address: 5058 Lowell St., Washington 16. Died Sept. 25, 1964; buried Arlington Nat. Cemetery.

MUIR, CHARLES HENRY army officer; b. Erie, Mich., July 18, 1860; s. James H. and Lydia (Gould) M.; grad. U.S. Mil. Acad., 1885, Inf. and Cav. Sch., Ft. Leavenworth, Kan., 1895 (head of class); m. May, d. Col. C.E. Bennett, Oct. 14, 1887. Commd. 2d lt., 17th Inf., June 14, 1885; promoted through grades to brig. gen. N.A., Aug. 5, 1917—; maj. gen., N.A., Nov. 28, 1917; brig. gen. U.S.A., Jan. 27, 1919; maj. gen. U.S.A., Mar. 8, 1921; retired July 18, 1924. Gained first place in Army Rifle Team, 1890; with 10 companions attacked Roasrio, P.I., Jan. 1900, drove out Gen. Malvar's hdqrs., captured $25,000 from his treasury and released 300 Spanish prisoners; mem. Ga. Staff, Washington, 1903-07; comd. Camp Hancock, Ga., Jan. 1918; 4th Corps, Oct. 13, 1919. Campaign badges Indian Wars, Spanish-Am. War, Cuban Occupation, Philippine Insurrection, China Relief Expdn.; Victory badge with 6 stars; Croix de Guerre with palms; Knight Comdr. Order St. Michael and St. George; Comdr. Légion d'Honneur; D.S.C. and D.S.M.; rifle medals 2d Class Dept., 1st and 2d Class Div., 1st Class Army. Died Dec. 8, 1933.

MUIR, JAMES IRVIN army officer; b. Ft. D. A. Russell, Wyo., Aug. 28, 1888; s. Charles Henry and May (Bennett) M.; B.S., U.S. Mil. Acad., 1910; grad. Field Officers Course, Inf. Sch., 1924; honor grad. Command and Gen. Staff Sch., 1925; grad. Army War Coll., 1930; m. Caroline Hall Lewis, July 2, 1910; children-Edith May (dec.), James Irvin, Thomas Farley (dec.). Commd. 2d lt. Inf., June 15, 1910; promoted through grades to maj. gen., U.S. Army, Feb. 15, 1942. Mem. Phi Kappa Tau, Scabbard and Blade; hon. mem. Pershing Rifles. Club: Chesapeake Bay Yacht, Episcopalian. S.A.R., Mason (32ff). Home: Muirland, Easton, Md. Died May 8, 1964; buried Arlington Nat. Cemetery.

MULLALLY, THORNWELL lawyer; b. Columbia, S.C.; s. Francis P. and Elizabeth Keith (Adger) M.; student Adger Coll., S.C., U. of S.C.; grad. Hopkins Grammar Sch., New Haven, Conn., 1888; A.B. with honors, Yale, 1892, awarded Thomas Glasby Waterman scholarship prize jr. and sr. yrs.; law study U. of Va.; LL.B., New York Law Sch., 1894; unmarried. With law firm Betts, Atterbury, Hyde & Betts, N.Y. City, 1893-93; admitted to N.Y. bar, 1894; with Alexander & Green, N.Y. City, 1893-94; mem. firm Atterbury & Mullally, 1894-1906; asst. to pres. Market St. Rys. (st. ry., San Francisco, Calif.), 1906-17, in charge during San Francisco earthquake and fire, 1906, safeguarding company's property and maintaining valuable service to stricken city, rapidly restored street car transportation (mem. Committee of 50 and Transportation Committee of provisional govt.); chairman committee for removal all debris; specializing in corp. and business law since 1919. Mem. Squadron A, Cav., N.G.N.Y., 1894-99; organizer and comdr. San Francisco Cav. Troop, 1915-17; organizer 2d Calif. F.A. and commd. lt. col. of regt., Aug. 3, 1917, mustered into federal service as 144th F.A., U.S. Army, of which served as col. Oct. 13, 1917-Jan. 3, 1919; also comdr. 65th F.A. Brig. for a time in France; commd. col. F.A., O.R.C., 1919; commd. brig. gen. O.R.C., Dec. 23, 1921, brig. gen. Aux. Res., Dec. 23, 1926; comdr. 188th Arty. Brig., 1923-26; recommd. brig. gen. Aux. U.S. Army, 1926, 1936; brig. gen. Inactive Service since 1936; awarded D.S.M. for services with 144th F.A. Mem. bd. dirs. Panama-Pacific Internat. Expn., 1915, chmn. spl. events com., mem. concessions com., and in charge opening day ceremonies; mem. Advisory Commn., for San Francisco, and mem. State Participation Comm., Golden Gate Internat. Expn., 1939; organizer and grand marshal "Preparedness Day Parade," San Francisco, 1916. Mem. Assn. Bar City of New York, Assn. Army of U.S. (an organizer; 1st nat. comdr.), Assn. Ex-mems. Squadron A, Am. Legion, Vets. of Foreign Wars; hon. mem. Spanish War Vets. Presbyn. Clubs: Bohemian, Army and Navy (hon.), Pres. (San Francisco); Burlingame Country; Monterey Peninsula Country; University (New York). Was editor Yale Lit. Mag. and mem. Scroll and Key (Yale). Home: 1175 Greenwich Terrace. Office: Crocker First Nat. Bank Bldg., San Francisco, Calif. Died Mar. 16, 1943.

MULLANY, JAMES ROBERT MADISON naval officer; b. N.Y.C., Oct. 26, 1818; s. Col. James R. and Maria (Burger) M.; m. twice. Apptd. mdishipman U.S. Navy, 1832, lt., 1844; attached to Coast Survey, 18 Mexican War, participated in attack and capture of Tabasco, 1846; commanded ships Wyandotte and Supply, Pensacola, Fla., 1861; became comdr., 1861; in command ship Bienville in North Atlantic and West Gulf squadrons- 1862-65; capt., 1866; commanded ship Richmond, 1868-70; commd. commodore, 1870, served with Mediterranean Squadron 1870-71; rear adm., 1874 in North Atlantic Squadron, 1874-76; gov. Naval Asylum, Phila., 1876-79; ret., 1879. Died Bryn Mawr, Pa., Sept. 17, 1887.

MULLER, WALTER J. army officer; b. Wyoming, Sept.29, 1895; B.S., U.S. Mil. Acad., 1918; grad. Inf. Sch., company officers course, 1928, tank course, 1937, Command and Gen. Staff Sch., 1938. Commd. 2d lt., U.S. Army, 1918, and advanced through the grades to maj. gen., 1953. Decorated Distinguished Service Medal, Legion of Merit, Bronze Star with oak leaf cluster (U.S.), Russian Order of Fatherland (1st Class), Chevalier Legion of Honor, Croix de Guerre with palm (France), Luxembourg Ordre de la Couronne de Chene Commandeur), Croix de Guerre (Belgium). Address: care Adjutant General, War Dept., Washington 25. Died Nov. 1967.

MULLIGAN, RICHARD THOMAS naval officer; b. N.Y. City, May 14, 1856; grad. U.S. Naval Acad., 1876. Ensign, Jan. 2, 1880; lt., jr. grade, May 23, 1886; lt., Dec. 16, 1891; lt. comdr., Oct. 10, 1899; comdr., June 28, 1905; capt., Mar. 11, 1909. Served on New York during Spanish-Am. war; Office of Naval Intelligence, Navy Dept., 1904-05; comd. Marblehead, 1905-06, Yorktown, 1906-07; with Bur. of Navigation, Navy Dept., 1907-10; comd. North Dakota, 1910; transferred to retired list, upon own application, with rank of commodore, June 30, 1910. Home: lizabeth, N.J. Died Feb. 23, 1917.

MULLINNIX, HENRY MASTON naval officer; b. July 4, 1892; entered U.S. Navy, July 3, 1912; advanced through the grades to capt., July 1941, rear admiral, Aug. 1943; served as engr. on destroyer, World War I; comd. U.S.S. Albermarle, 1941; comdr. Atlantic Patrol Wing in anti-submarine and convoy escort work, 1942; command of aircraft carrier Mar. 1943. Home: Stockton, Calif. Reported missing in action. Nov. 1943.

MUMMA, HARLAN L., army officer; b. Findlay, O., Dec. 6, 1894; s. Eber Leslie Edward and Sarah Amanda (Waltz) M.; student Ohio Northern University, Ada, O., 1910-11; B.S., U.S. Military Academy, 1916; m. Juliette Rathbone; children—Juliette Cherie (wife of Lt. Comdr. J. H. Redington, U.S.N.R.), John Rathbone, Harlan L. Commd. 2d lt., U.S. Army, 1916, and advanced through the grades to brig. gen., 1944. Decorations: Legion of Merit, oak leaf cluster; commendation ribbon, oak leaf cluster. Mem. Scabbard and Blade, Torch and Serpent, The Mountain (W.Va. Univ.). Home: Clearwater Beach FL Died Apr. 1972.

MUMMA, MORTON CLAIRE, JR., naval office (ret.); b. Manila, P.I., Aug. 24, 1904; s. Morton Claire and Gail Cass (Zugschwert) M.; B.S., U.S. Naval Acad., 1925; grad. U.S. Submarine Sch., 1928; m. Virginia Page Elder, Oct. 7, 1925; children—Morton Claire, Ann (Mrs. Ralph Meade Dorsey). Commd. ensign U.S. Navy, 1925, and advanced through grades to rear adm., 1946; served at sea in battleships, destroyers, submarines, 1925-42; coach U.S. Navy rifle team, 1927, 28; comdr. U.S.S. S-43, 1935-38, U.S.S. Sailfish, 1940-41; staff mem., submarines of Asiatic fleet, naval liaison with 5th air force, comdr. motor torpedo boat squadrons, 7th Fleet, 1943-44; naval aide to Under-Sec. of Navy, Forrestal, 1944; planning div., Bur. of Naval Personnel, 1944-46; ret. Aug. 1, 1946, advancing to grade of rear adm.; sec.-treas., Jefferson Pub. Co., Inc. and mng. editor, Spirit of Jefferson-Advocate (newspaper), Charles Town, W.Va., from 1946. Dir. and mem. exec. com., Winchester Memorial Hospital. Awarded Navy Cross, Legion of Merit and Gold Star, Army Distinguished unit badge, Sec. of Navy. unit citation, distinguished marksman and pistol expert medals, campaign, service and area medals; decorated with Order of Brit. Empire. Mem. exec. com. and life mem., Nat. Rifle Assn. of Am.; nat. dir. and v.p., Va. div. Izaak Walton League of Am. Episcopalian. Mason. Club: Army Navy (Washington). Ofcl. referee, Nat. Rifle Assn. registered tournaments. Home: Tucson AZ Died Aug. 1968.

MUNN, JAMES BUELL educator; b. Irvington, N.Y., Sept. 24, 1890; s. John Pixley and Martha Buell (Plum) M.; A.B., Harvard, 1912, A.M., 1915, Ph.D., 1917; student Am. Sch. Archeology, Athens, Greece, 1912-13; Litt.D. (hon.), N.Y. U., 1945; m. Ruth Crosby Hanford, Aug. 31, 1932. Instr. English, N.Y. U., 1920-22, asst. prof., 1922-25, asso. prof., 1925-26, prof., 1926-32, asst. dean Washington Sq. Coll., 1925-28, dean, 1928-32; prof. English, Harvard, 1932-57, prof. English emeritus, 1957-. Commd. 2d lt., 301st Inf., U.S. Army, 1917; capt., 301st Inf., 76th Div., 1919; maj., asst. to chief of staff Dist. of Paris, Mar.-Aug. 1919. Decorated Officier Legion of Honor (France), Order of Danilo, 3d class (Montenegro). Council Tchrs. English, Delta Upsilon, Phi Beta Kappa. Club: Harvard (N.Y.). Editor: (with Homer Andrew Watt) Ideas and Forms in English and American Literature, 1925. Home: 58 Garden St., Cambridge, Mass. 02128. Died Feb. 13, 1967.

MUNROE, WILLIAM ROBERT naval officer; b. Waco, Tex., Apr. 8, 1886; s. Richard Irby and Mary Lelia (Davidson) M.; student Baylor U., 1902-03; B.S., U.S. Naval Acad., 1908; grad. Naval War Coll., 1928; LL.D., (hon.), Baylor U., 1943; m. Katherine Barnwell Johnson, Apr. 8, 1915; 1 son, William Robert. Commd. ensign, USN, 1910, and advanced through the grades to rear admr., Jan. 1941; comdr. submarines during World War; comdr. U.S.S. Paul Hamilton, 1925-27; war plans, Navy Dept., Washington, 1928-30; comdg. Sub. Div. 11, U.S. Fleet, 1930-32; naval intelligence Navy Dept., 1932-34; comdg. Destroyer Div. 60 and Squadron 20, Battle Force, 1935-37; comdg. officer U.S.S. Mississippi, 1939-41; comdr. Battleship Div. 3, Pacific Fleet, Jan. 1941-Mar. 1943; comdr. Gulf Sea Frontier, Mar. 1943-44; promoted to vice adm., assigned command U.S. 4th Fleet, 1944, ret., Oct. 1947. Decorated World War medal; Cuban pacification medal. Def. medal; Asiatic medal; Atlantic medal; D.S.M., 2 Legion of Merit medals, Army Commendatory Medal; Cruzerio del Sol (Brazil); Brazilian Legion of Merit; Creek and Paraguayan Legion of Merit medals. Presbyn. Clubs: Army and Navy (Washington); N.Y. Yacht; Chevy Chase (Md.) Country. Address, California Club, Los Angeles. Died Feb. 1966.

MUNSON, EDWARD LYMAN medical officer U.S. Army; b. New Haven, Conn., Dec. 27, 1868; s. Lyman E. (U.S. judge) and Lucy A. (Sanford) M.; A.B., Yale, 1890, M.D., 1892, A.M., 1893; m. Martha Schneeloch, May 29, 1893; children-Katharine, Edward L. Was asst. surgeon U.S. Navy (resigned); capt. asst. surgeon U.S. Army, May 12, 1898; maj. surgeon, July 11, 1906; lt. col. surgeon, May 9, 1915; col., May 15, 1917; apptd. brig. gen., Oct. 3, 1918. Was prof. hygiene, Army Med. Sch., Washington. Was on Gen. Shafter's staff in expdn. against Santiago; asst to surgeon-gen. U.S. Army, 1898-99, 1901-02, 1915-17 and since June 1, 1931, with rank of brig. general; asst. to chief surgeon, P.I., 1902-03; acting commr. pub. health, P.I., 1903-04; adviser to Philippine govt. in hygiene and sanitation, 1914-15, and 1922-24; prof. mil. hygiene, Army Service Schools, 1908-12; asst. to Surgeon Gen. in charge all training of med. dept. personnel U.S. Army, 1917-18; chief of morale br., Gen. Staff, 1918; retired 1932. Served as prof. preventive medicine, George Washington U. Appointed prof. dept. of preventive medicine, U. of California, 1932, retired as prof. emeritus, 1939. In charge medical service U.S. Relief Mission, earthquake area of Japan, 1923. Inventor of several articles of equipment adopted and now in use in U.S. Army. Awarded D.S.M., 1919. "for exceptionally meritorious and conspicuous service," in connection with med. dept.

and General Staff U.S. Army; Companion Order of the Bath (British), 1919; Order of Red Cross (Japanese), 1923. Fellow Am. Coll. Surgeons; mem. A.M.A., Assn. Mil. Surgeons of U.S. Army. Clubs: Army and Navy (Washington and Manila); Zeta Psi (New York); Elihu (New Haven); Bohemian (San Francisco). Author: Theory and Practice of Military Hygiene, 1902; A Study in Troop Leading and Sanitary Service in War, 1910; Sanitary Tactics, 1911; vol. on hospitals, in Photographic History of Civil War, 1911; The Soldier's Foot and the Military Shoe, 1912; The Management of Men, 1921. Contbr. to current literature on gen. and mil. hygiene. Editor: Military Surgeon, 1915-18. Home: 24 Huntington St., New Haven, Conn. Died July 7, 1947; buried in Arlington National Cemetery.

MURDOCK, JOSEPH BALLARD naval officer; b. Hartford, Conn., Feb. 13, 1851; s. Rev. John Nelson and Martha (Ballard) M.; grad. U.S. Naval Acad., 1870; m. Anne Dillingham, June 26, 1879. On N. and S. Atlantic stas., 1870-74; coast survey duty, 1875-79; instr. in physics, Naval Acad., 1880-83; elec. duty, Phila., 1884; torpedo sta., 1886-88; Asiatic sta., 1888-91; elec. duty, Navy Yard, New York, 1891-94; home and European stas., 1894-97; Naval War Coll., 1897-99; exec. officer U.S.S. Panther during Spanish-Am. War; exec. officer New York, 1899-1901; War Coll., Nov. 1900; comdr., June 16, 1901; capt., Jan. 22, 1906; rear admiral, Nov. 20, 1909. Comd. Alliance, Jan.-Oct. 1903, Denver, May 1904-Oct. 1905; duty at Navy Dept., 1906; comd. Rhode Island in cruise of fleet around the world, 1907-09; comdt. Navy Yard, New York, May 15, 1909-10; comdr. 2d Div. Atlantic Fleet, 1910-11; comdr.-in-chief U.S. Asiatic Fleet, 1911-12; retired on attaining age limit, Feb. 13, 1913. Ordered to duty at Navy Yard, Portsmouth, N.H., 1918, 19. Mem. N.H. Ho. of Rep., 1921, 23. Author: Notes on Electricity and Magnetism, 1884. Home: Hill, N.H. Died Mar. 23, 1931.

MURFIN, ORIN GOULD admiral; born at Ohio Furnace, O., Apr. 13, 1876; s. Henry C. and Margaret (Reilly) M.; prep. edn., pub. schs., Jackson, O., grad. U.S. Naval Acad. Annapolis, Md., 1897, Naval War Coll., Newport, R.I., 1926; m. Anna Williams, Jan. 1, 1903; 1 dau., Winifred Anne. Commd. ensign, U.S. Navy, July 1, 1899; advanced through grades to comdr., Aug. 29, 1916; capt., Feb. 1, 1918; rear admiral, Jan. 7, 1930. Organizer and comdr. mine bases north of Scotland, World War I; served as judge advocate general of the Navy, comdr. in chief Asiatic Fleet and comdt. Pearl Harbor Naval Station, Hawaii; retired from active service May 1, 1940. Recalled to active duty World War II to serve as pres., Pearl Harbor Naval Court of Inquiry. Awarded D.S.M. (U.S.); Companion Order of St. Michael and St. George (British). Presbyterian. Clubs: Army and Navy, Army Navy Country (Washington). Address: 825 Margarita Av., Coronado, Cal. Died Oct. 22, 1956; buried Rosecrans Nat. Cemetery, San Diego, Cal.

MURPHY, ARTHUR ALBAN ry. exec.; b. Portland, Ore., Feb. 8, 1886; s. Daniel R. and Caroline (Kennedy) M.; A.B., Stanford, 1908; m. Saidee Lu Knapp, Nov. 5, 1913 (died Oct. 1, 1939); m. 2d, Mrs. Jeannette Tighe Kemp, Apr. 22, 1941. Admitted to Ore bar, 1908, began practice at Portland; mem. Eastham and Murphy, 1910-13; dep. dist. atty. Multnomah County, 1913-17; atty. and gen. atty. O.-W. R.R. & N. Co., Portland, 1919-25, asst. gen. solicitor, 1925-26; asst. to pres. U.P. R.R., at Seattle, 1926-37, at Los Angeles, 1937-40, at Seattle, 1940—. Served as 1st lt. and capt. Co. C, 362 Inf., U.S. Army, 1917-19; in action Meuse-Argonne (France) and Lys-Scheldt (Belgium) offensives. Commander Dept. of Ore. Am. Legion, 1926-27; pres. Seattle C. of C., 1929-30, now trustee; pres. Wash. Athletic Club of Seattle, 1936-37. Mem. Am. Legion, Phi Delta Phi, Phi Beta Kappa, K.C. (4ff). Clubs: Rainier, Seattle Golf, Washington Athletic (Seattle); Arlington (Portland); Bohemian (San Francisco); Tacoma (Tacoma). Home: The Gainsborough, 1017 Minor. Office: Union Station, Seattle. Deceased.

MURPHY, CHARLES JOSEPH public official; b. Stockport, Eng., June 3, 1832; s. of John and Margaret Ingoldsby (O'Bierne) M.; brought to America in infancy; public school edn.; m. Catherine Tone, of Rochester, N.Y., July 15, 1855 (died 1902). Enlisted at 15 in Mexican War (youngest survivor); engaged in gold mining in Cal., 1849-52; established branch house in Shanghai, 1852, for shipping Chinese agrl. products to Cal.; introduced the naval orange into Cal. from Brazil, 1854. Officer in Civil War; taken prisoner at Bull Run while caring for the wounded; mentioned in official report; also mentioned for making remarkable escape from prison; one of only 3 staff officers of his rank who were awarded Congressional Medal of Honor. Began corn propaganda in Europe, 1887; was the first to introduce Cal. wines and fruit into northern Europe, spending 3 yrs. of this work at own expense; apptd. spl. commr. U.S. Dept. Agr., 1890; spent 20 yrs. in propaganda work in Europe. Organized Am. relief movement at time of Russian famine, 1891, which sent 5 steamer loads of corn and provisions to Russia; at request of Czar was sent by Am. Govt. to Russia to show various uses of Indian corn and to receive the first steamer of the relief fleet. Commr. State of Ia. since 1895. Democrat. Catholic. Mem. St. Vincent DePaul Soc., St. Ignatius' Sodality, 3d Order of Dominicans, G.A.R., Loyal Legion, Soc. Army of Potomac. Decorated Knight of the Order of St. Stanislaus, Russia; Order of Gen. Bolivar; Order of Misericordia, War Medal City of New York and Brooklyn, Blue Ribbon Medal of Honor 7th Regt., New York. Address: 103 W. 93d St., New York.

MURPHY, EDMOND GEORGE, banker; b. Bklyn., May 18, 1910; s. John A. and Irene (Swift) M.; B.S., N.Y.U., 1941; m. Joanna J. Wirska, Apr. 14, 1942; children—Joan, Barbara, Edmond, Thomas. With Chase Nat. Bank, N.Y.C., 1925-27; asst. mgr. Mfrs. Trust Co., N.Y.C., 1927-39; examiner N.Y. State Banking Dept., 1939-49; with Lincoln Savs. Bank, Bklyn., 1949-73, pres., chief exec. officer, 1970-73, also trustee; dir. Savs. Bank Trust Co. Trustee St. Francis Coll., Bklyn. Served to comdr. USNR, 1942-46. Mem. Am. Inst. C.P.A.'s, N.Y. Soc. C.P.A.'s. Clubs: Brooklyn; Union League (N.Y.C.); Cherry Valley (Garden City). Home: Garden City NY Died 1973.

MURPHY, GRAYSON M(ALLET)-P(REVOST); b. Phila., Pa., Dec. 19, 1878; s. Howard and Anita (Mallet-Prevost) M.; student Haverford (Pa.) Coll., 1896-98; grad. U.S. Mil. Acad., 1903; m. Maud Donaldson, Apr. 19, 1906; children—Grayson Robert Donaldson. Second lt. 17th Inf., U.S.A., 1903-07; mem. G.M.P. Murphy & Co.; pres. Fifth Av. Bus. Securities Company; dir. various companies. Mem. War Council and commr. for Europe of Am. Red Cross in France, 1917. Served in Spanish-Am. War as pvt. 1st Pa. Inf., and capt. Provisional N.G. of Pa.; World War as maj. and lt. col. Gen. Staff, 42d Div. in charge of operations; aviation officer A.E.F. in Great Britain, Nov. 1918-Feb. 1919. D.S.M.; Officer Legion of Honor (France); Commendator Order of Crown of Italy; Comdr. Order of Leopold II. Home: New York, N.Y. Died Oct. 18, 1937.

MURPHY, JOHN VERNON ret. naval officer; b. Brownwood, Tex., June 12, 1893; s. John and Alice (Vernon) M.; A.B., U.S. Naval Acad., 1917, grad. student in elec. engring, 1920-22; M.S. Yale, 1924; m. Elizabeth Pearce, Nov. 1, 1928; children-John Vernon, Anne Pearce. Commd. ensign USN, 1917, advanced through grades to commodore, 1945; in charge research and design sect., radio div. Bur. of Engring., 1932-34; comdr. U.S.S. King, 1934-36; navigation officer U.S.S. Qunicy, 1936-37; in charge radio and communication group, Post Grad. Sch., Naval Acad., 1937-40; exec. officer U.S.S. Honolulu, 1940-41; comdr. destroyer div. 10, U.S.S. Cushing, 1941-42; signal communication liaison officer War Dept. Gen. Staff, 1943; Joint Radio Bd., 1942; coordinator Joint Communications Bd. and Combined Communications Bd., Navy Dept., 1943; dep. dir. of Naval communications, 1943-46; alternate mem. War Communications Bd. and combined Communications Bd., 1943-46; ret. from active service, 1946. Mem. Acacia. Presbyn. Mason. Home: 3420 N. Lorcom Lane, Arlington, Va. Died July 31, 1949; buried Arlington Nat. Cemetery.

MURPHY, JOSEPH NATHANIEL naval officer; b. Washington, June 8, 1905; s. Joseph A. and Julia (Reisinger) M.; B.S., U.S. Naval Acad., 1927; student U.S. Naval Post Grad. Sch., 1934-36; M.S., Cal. Inst. Tech., 1937; m. Cecelia Quirk, Jan. 2, 1931. Commd. ensign USN, 1927, advanced through grades to rear adm., 1954; naval aviator, 1929; design desk officer dive bomber aircaft Bur. Aeros., 1940-43; exec. officer U.S.S. Princeton, 1943-44; dir. armament div. Bur. Aeros., 1945-46, dir. piloted aircraft div., 1946-49; mgr. Naval Aircraft Factory, Phila., 1949-50; asst. chief staff logistics Comdr. Fleet Air Japan, 1950; comdr. Naval Air Missile Test Cener, Point Nugu, Cal., 1950-52; exec. dir. research and devel. Bur. Aeros., 1953-54; staff Comdr. Air Force Atlantic Fleet, 1954-55; asst. chief procurement Bur. Aeros., 1956-57; gen. rep. Bur. Aeros. to central dist., Wright-Patterson AFB, 1957-58; comdr. Naval Air Devel. and Material Center, Johnsville, Pa., 1958-59, comdr. Naval Air Research and Devel. Activities Command, 1959-. Decorated Navy Cross, Purple Heart, various campaign, def., service, other medals. Asso. fellow Inst. Aero. Scis.; mem. Am. Ordnance Assn. Club: Army and Navy (Washington). Address: care Navy Dept., Washington 25. Died Mar. 1966.

MURRAY, ALEXANDER naval officer; b. Chestertown, Md., July 12, 1754; s. Dr. William and Ann (Smith) M.; m. Mary Miller, June 18, 1782, 1 son, Alexander M. commd. Lt. Continental Army during Revolutionary War, capt., 1776-77, participated in battles of White Plains and Flatbush; Am. privateer for a time; commd. lt. U.S. Navy, 1781, capt., 1798; comdr. ships Insurgent and Constellation during naval war with France, 1798; commanded Constellation against Barbary pirates in Mediterranean Sea, 1803; commanded ship Adams, 1805; commanding naval officer, Phila., 1808-21, had been ranking Am. Naval Officer since 1811. Died Phila., Oct. 6, 1821.

MURRAY, ARTHUR major general U.S.A.; b. Bowling Green, Mo., Apr. 29, 1851; s. Samuel Fenton and Mary Frances M.; grad. U.S. Mil. Acad. (No. 2 in class), 1874; admitted to bar, U.S. Circuit Ct., St. Louis, 1895; honor grad. No. 1, Arty. Sch., Ft. Monroe, Va., 1880; m. Sara Wetmore De Russy, Apr. 29, 1880. Apptd. 2d lt. 1st U.S. Arty., June 15, 1874; instr. philosophy, U.S. Mil. Acad., 1881-86; acting judge advocate, Dept. of the Mo., 1887-91; acting adj. gen., Dept. of Dakota, 1891; apptd. capt. and q.m., 1896 (declined); prof. mil. science and tactics, Yale, 1896-98; capt. 1st Arty., 1898; acting judge advocate 1st Army Corps, and of depts. of Matanzas and Santa Clara, Jan.-May 1899; on duty in judge advocate gen.'s office, June-Aug. 1899; apptd. col. 43d U.S. Vol. Inf., Aug. 1899; comdg. sub-dist. Samar and Leyte, P.I., 1900; dist. comdr., 1st dist., Dept. of the Visayas, 1900-01; apptd. maj. and judge advocate, 1901 (declined); maj. artillery corps, Aug. 1, 1901; lt. col., Apr. 14, 1905; col., Oct. 1, 1906; brig. gen. chief of arty, U.S.A., Oct. 1, 1906; maj. gen., Mar. 14, 1911; retired, Dec. 4, 1915. Comdt. Sch. of Submarine Defense, 1901; comdr. Western Dept. and 3d Div., San Francisco, 1915; returned to active service as comdr. Western Department, 1917-18. Awarded Distinguished Service Medal. V. chmn. Am. Red Cross, 1915-16. Hon. mem. Berzelius Soc., Yale U. Author: A Manual for Courts-Martial, 1893; Mathematics for Artillery Gunners, 1893; Manual of Arms, Adapted to the Springfield Rifle (Caliber 45), 1898. Home: Washington, D.C. Died May 12, 1925.

MURRAY, GEORGE DOMINIC adm. USN, ret.; b. Boston, July 6, 1889; s. Michael Joseph and Mary Elizabeth (Sullivan) M.; grad. U.S. Naval Acad., 1911; Dr. Naval Sci., Boston Coll.; LL.D., Marquette U.; m. Corinne Montague Mustin, Oct. 10, 1925; children-Lloyd Montague Mustin, Henry Ashmead Mustin, Gordon Sinclair Mustin. Midshipman U.S. Naval Acad., 1907-11; 1st comdg. officer Naval Air Sta., Anacostia, 1918; squadron comdr. 1st aviation unit ordered to Philippines, 1923-25; exec. officer, U.S.S. Wright, 1929; asst. naval attaché in London, Paris, Berlin, The Hague, 1930-33; air officer U.S.S. Saratoga, 1933-39; comdg. officer U.S.S. Langley, 1938-39; Bur. Aeronautics, 1939-41; comdg. officer U.S.S. Enterprise, 1941-42; task force comdr. U.S.S. Hornet, Flagship, 1942; chief of Naval Air Intermediate Tng. and comdt. Naval Air Tng. Center, Pensacola, Fla., 1942-43; chief of Naval Air Tng. Comd., 1944; comdr. Air Force, Pacific Fleet, 1944-45; comdr. Mariannas, 1945-46; comdt. 9th Naval Dist., 1946-47; comdr. 1st Task Fleet, 1947-48; comdr. Western Sea Frontier and Pacific Res. Fleet, 1948-51, ret. Dir. Pacific Tel. & Tel. Co. Dir. Guide Dogs for Blind, Inc. Accepted formal capitulation of Japanese on Truk Atoll, Sept. 2, 1945. Decorated Navy Cross, D.S.M., Presdl. Unit Citation (U.S.S. Enterprise), Asiatic-Pacific Ribbon with stars, World War Victory medal, Vera Cruz Campaign medal (U.S.); Order of British Empire; 1915 qualified Naval Aviator No. 22. Clubs: English Speaking Chase, Army and Navy (WASH). Home: San Francisco. Died June 18, 1956: Buried Arlington Nat Cemetery.

MURRAY, MAXWELL army officer; b. West Point, N.Y., June 19, 1885; s. Gen. Arthur and Sarah Wetmore (de Russy) M.; B.S., U.S. Mil. Acad., 1907; student Mass. Inst. of Tehc., 1919-20, Coast Arty. Sch., 1911-12, Field Arty. Sch., 1924-25, Command and Gen. Staff Sch., 1925-26, Army War Coll., 1928-29; m. Phyllis Muriel Howard, Nov. 18, 1911; children-Arthur Maxwell, Anne Howard (Mrs. Robert W. Van de Velde). Commd. 2d lt., U.S. Army, June 15, 1907; promoted through grades to brig. gen., Dec. 1, 1938; advanced to maj. gen., 1941; capt., maj., lt. col. 5th F.A., 1st Div., A.E.F., 1917-18; comdr. Camp Bragg (N.C.), 1918-19; asst. to chief field arty., 1920-24; asst. and aide to Dwight F. Davis, gov. gen. P.I., 1929-32; mem. Field Arty. Bd., 1932-36; comdr. 5th F.A. and Madison Barracks (N.Y.), 1936-38; asst. comdr. Field Arty. Sch. (Fort Sills, Okla.), 1938. Awarded D.S.M., Silver Star, U.S. Treasury Life Saving Medal (U.S.) Croix de Guerre (France). Club: Army and Navy (Washington, D.C.). Home: 2710 36th St., Washington, D.C. Died Aug. 4, 1948.

MURRAY, PETER army officer; b. in Calif., Apr. 21, 1867; grad. U.S. Mil. Acad., 1890. Commd. 2d lt. 3d Inf., June 12, 1890; 1st lt. 5th Inf., Mar. 18, 1897; trans. to 21st Inf., July 21, 1897; capt. 18th Inf., Nov. 26, 1899; q.m., Aug. 24, 1907; maj. 22d Inf., May 10, 1911; assigned to 3d Inf., Sept. 1, 1914; trans. to 29th Inf., Mar. 1, 1915; lt. col., July 1, 1916; col of inf. (temporary), Aug. 5, 1917; brig. gen. N.A., Feb. 8, 1918; col. of inf., Apr. 2, 1918. With 21st Inf., 5th Army Corps, Santiago, Cuba, 1898; with 21st and 18th Inf. in Philippine Insurrection, 1899-1901; with A.E.F., France, Dec. 1, 1917-May 12, 1918; comd. 3d Brig., 2d Div., Feb. 15-Mar. 15, 1918, in training area; on erdun-St. Mihiel front, Mar. 15-May 8, 1918, when returned to U.S. on account of physical disability; col., Insp. Gen.'s Dept., May 25-June 12, 1918; col., Gen. Staff Corps, June 12, 1918—. Address: War Dept., Washington, D.C. Died Dec. 26, 1941.

MURRAY, ROBERT brigadier gen. U.S.A.; b. Elk Ridge, Anne Arundel Co., Md., Aug. 6, 1822; s. Daniel and Mary (Dorsey) M.; ed. by tutors at home, pub. sch. in Howard Co., Md., and U. of Pa.; m. at Benecia, Calif., Adelaide S. Atwood, of Me., Jan. 10, 1861. Apptd. from Md., asst. surgeon U.S.A., June 29, 1846; capt. asst. surgeon, June 29, 1851; maj. surgeon, June 23, 1860; lt. col. asst. med. purveyor, July 28, 1866; col. surgeon, June 26, 1876; col. asst. surgeon gen., Dec. 14, 1882; brig. gen. surgeron gen. U.S.A., Nov. 23, 1883; retired by operation of law, Aug. 6, 1886. Bvtd. lt. col. and col., Mar. 13, 1865, for services during the war. Home: Elk Ridge, Howard Co., Md. Died Jan. 1, 1913.

MURRAY, ROBERT B(LAINE), JR., airline exec.; b. Hampstead, Md., Jan. 31, 1911; s. R. Blaine and Mabel Fairfax (Abbott) M.; student Mercersburg Acad., 1927-30; A.B., Harvard, 1934; m. Elinor Levering Lindley, Dec. 9, 1939. Investment banker C. T. Williams & Co., Balt., 1934-35, Tucker Anthony & Co., N.Y.C. (mem. N.Y. Stock Exchange), 1935-40, N.Y. Trust Co., 1940-41; pres. Pa. Economy League, Inc., Harrisburg, 1946-53; undersec. commerce for transportation, 1953-55; v.p., dir. and asst. to pres. Baldwin-Lima-Hamilton Corp., Phila., 1955-56; became v.p. Pam American World Airways, Inc., 1956; dir. Andrade & Co., Ltd., Honolulu. Mem. board directors San Francisco chpt. Am. Nat. Red Cross, Internat. Hospitality Center; trustee World Affairs Council No. Cal., from 1959; gov. San Francisco Bay Area Council chmn. San Francisco Pacific Festival, 1958, 59, hon. chmn., 1960; chmn. exec. com. Invest-in-Am. Week, 1959, general chairman, 1960; v.p. Governmental Research Council; pres. San Francisco Airport Sound Abatement Committee. Secretary United Republican Finance Committee, Met. N.Y., 1938-40, chmn. 1941; exec. com. Eisenhower Nat. Finance Com., 1952; mem. Rep. Nat. Finance Com., 1952. Chmn. air coordinating com., chmn. transportation and storage com. O.D.M.; mem. bd. N.A.C.A.; chmn. Am. Delegation to Internat. Civil Aviation Orgn. Conf., Brighton, Eng., 1953; mem. Air Naviagation Development Bd., 1953-56; vice chmn. White House Conf. on Hwy. Safety, 1955; mem. Pres.' Adv. Com. on Weather Control, 1954-56. Trustee United Seaman's Service. Bd. assos. Sch. World Bus. and Internat. Development at the San Francisco State Coll., California. Served as a colonel USAAF, 1942-46. Decorated Legion of Merit, Army Commendation Medal with 3 oak leaf clusters. Mem. Soc. Naval Architects and Marine Engrs., Govtl. Research Assn., Am.-Australian Assn. Cal. (v.p. 1958, pres. 1959), San Francisco C. of C. (dir.), Mercersburg Acad. Alumni Council, American Acad. Polit. Sci., Nat. Tax Assn., Nat. Def. Transportation Assn. Republican. Clubs: Racquet (Phila.), Midday (Phila.); Pilgrims, Pinnacle (New York City); Burlingame (Cal.) Country; 1925 F St., Chevy Chase (Washington); San Francisco Golf. Home: Hillsborough CA Died June 1969.

MURRAY, ROBERT DRAKE senior surgeon U.S. Marine Hosp. Service; b. Ohlton, O., Apr. 21, 1845; s. Joseph Arbor and Nancy (Drake) M.; ed. common schools, Bluffton, O.; grad. Cleveland Med. Coll., 1868; Jefferson Med. Coll., Phila., 1871; m. Lillie, d. Rev. C. A. Fulwood, D.D., Key West, Apr. 18, 1875 (died 1887). Was 1st vol. from Niles, O., in Civil war; served in 7th Ohio vol. inf. and 12th Ohio Vol. cav. Was wounded 4 times and war prisoner. Prominent in quarantine and epidemic service; comd. 1st epidemic cordon in U.S., 1882, at Brownsville, Tex.; served during yellow fever epidemic at Key West, 1875; Fernandina, 1877; New Orleans, 1878. Florida, 1888; runswick, 1983; Mississippi, 1897, 1898; New Orleans and Key West, 1899. Mem. Am. Med. Assn., Am. Public Health Assn., Fla. Med. Assn., Tenn. State Med. Cos., Am. Pomol. Soc., N.Y. Medico-Legal Soc., Am. Assn. Polit. and Social Science, Am. Hist. Assn., A.A.A.S., S.A.R. Writer of yellow fever and quarantine articles published in Treasury Dept. and Reports and med. jours. Address: U.S. Marine Hosp., Key West, Fla. Died 1903.

MURRAY, WALLACE former ambassador to Iran; b. Bardstown, Ky., Mar. 10, 1887; s. John P. and Maude (Cook) M.; A.B., Wittenberg Coll., Springfield, O. O., 1909; A.M., Harvard, 1913; LL.D., Carthage Coll., 1926, Wittenberg, 1949; m. Frances Rabbitts Wilde, Nov. 5, 1924. Master, U. Sch., Cleve., 1913-17; sec. Am. Legation, Budapest, Hungary, 1920-22; sec. and chargé d'affaires, Teheran, Persia, 1922-25; asst. chief Div. Nr. Eastern Affairs, Dept. State, 1925-29, chief, Nov. 1929-Mar. 1942, adviser on polit. relations, 1942; dir. Office Nr. Eastern African Affairs, Jan. 1944; apptd. ambassador to Iran, Jan. 1945-June 1946; mission Nr. East, Sept.-Oct. 1929; on spl. mission to Iran, and other Nr. Eastern countries, Sept.-Nov. 1938; on mission to London with under sec. state, Apr., 1944, to discuss Middle Eastern questions. Served as 1st lt. U.S. Army, 1917-19; participated in Champagne defensive and Marne-Aisne, St. Mihiel and Meuse-Argonne offensives; served as adj. to mil. gov. Aherwiler, Germany, with Army of Occupation. Fellow Am. Geog. Soc. Episcopalian. Clubs: Army and Navy, Cosmos (Washington, D.C.). Died Apr. 28, 1965.

MUSE, WILLIAM SULIVANE brig. gen. U.S. Marine Corps; b. Dorchester Co., Med., Apr. 8, 1842; s. William H. (M.D.) and Elizabeth Richardson (Sulivane) M.; ed. pvt. sch. and Cambridge Acad.; unmarried. Entered U.S. vol. navy, May 11, 1862; commd. 2d lt. U.S. Marine Corps, Mar. 18, 1864; 1st lt., Apr. 24, 1867; capt., Dec. 18, 1880; maj., June 2, 1898; lt. col., Mar. 3, 1899; col., Jan. 31, 1900. Episcopalian. Republican. Home: Cambridge, Md. Died 1911.

MUSGRAVE, GEORGE CLARKE soldier, author; b. Folkstone, Eng., May 1, 1873; s. Rev. J. J. M.; A.B., City of London Coll.; Royal Arty. Coll., Woolwich, Eng. Exploration in Farica; capt. Cuban Army, 1896; attaché intelligence dept. U.S. Army, Santiago Campaign, 1898; scout Boer War, S. Africa, 1899-1900; spl. medal "for valor in the field." Author: The Cuban Insurrection, 1898; Under Three Flags in Cuba, 1899; In South Africa with Buller, 1900; Under Four Flags for France, 1918. Home: New York, N.Y. Deceased.

MUSMANNO, MICHAEL ANGELO, judge; b. nr. Pitts., Apr. 7, 1897; s. Antonio and Maddelena (Castellucci) M.; graduate of George Washington, Georgetown, American and National Univs., U. Rome. Admitted to Pa. bar, 1923; trial lawyer Phila. and Pitts., 1923-31; judge Co. Ct., 1932-34, Ct. Common Pleas, 1935-51; judge Pa. Supreme Ct., 1952-68. Mem. Pa. State Legislature, 1929-31. Mem. Commn. on Internat. Rules of Jud. Procedure; mem. National Citizens Com. on Civil Rights Act. Served as capt. USNR, World War II; aide to Gen. Mark W. Clark; pres. U.S. Bd. Forcible Repatriation, Austria; judge Internat. War Crimes, Tribunal II. Nuremberg. Mem. Am. Legion, Nat. Confedn. Am. Ethnic Groups (president), Vets. Fgn. Wars, Disabled Am. Vets., Mil. Order Purple Heart. Author: Proposed Amendments Constitution, 1929; Black Fury, 1935; After Twelve Years, 1939; The Soldier and the Man, 1946; Listen to the River, 1947; War in Italy, 1948; Ten Days to Die, 1950; Across the Street from the Courthouse, 1954; Justice Musmanno Dissents, 1955; Verdict!, 1958; The Eichmann Kommandos, 1961; The Story of the Italians, 1965; An American Replies, 1966; That's My Opinion, 1966; Columbus Was First, 1966; The Glory and the Dream, 1967. Contributor articles mags.; authored bill in Pa. Legislature which outlawed Communist Party, 1951; co-author Federal Communist Control Act, 1954. Home: McKees Rock PA Died Oct. 12, 1968; buried Arlington Nat. Cemetery, Arlington VA

MUSSER, JOHN HERR physician, educator; b. Phila., Pa., June 9, 1883; s. John Herr and Agnes Gardiner (Harper) M.; B.S. U. of Pa., 1905, M.D., 1908; m. Marguerite Hopkinson, Jan. 7, 1911; children-Frances Avegno, John Herr, III. Asst. editor Am. Jour. Med. Sciences, 1911-20, editor, 1920-24; asso. in medicine, U. of Pa. Med. Sch., 1914-20, asst. prof., 1920-24; was physician Phila. Gen. Hosp., Howard Hosp., and asso. phys. Presbyn. Hosp.; prof. medicine, Tulane U. of La., since Jan. 1, 1925; physician Charity Hosp.; pres. Louisiana State Board of Health. 1940-42. Major Med. Corps, U.S. Army, World War, in U.S. one year, France one year; colonel Med. Reserve Corps since 1938. Member American Medical Assn. (v.p. 1933-34), Assn. Am. Physicians, Coll. of Physicians Phila., Am. Climatol. and Clin. Assn., Am. Soc. for Clin. Investigation, Am. Coll. Physicians (pres. 1929-30), Psi Upsilon, Democrat. Presbyterian. Clubs: Boston, Round Table, Metairie golf. Editor: Internal Medicine, 1932, 4th edit., 1945. Editor New Orleans Med. and Surg. Jour. Home: 1427 2d St. Office: 1430 Tulane Av., New Orleans 13, La. Died Sept. 5, 1947.

MYER, ALBERT JAMES army officer; b. Newburgh, N.Y., Sept. 20, 1829; s. Henry Beckman and Eleanor Pope (McLannan) M.; A.B., Hobart Coll., 1847; M.D., Buffalo lMed. Coll., 1851; m. Catherine Walden, 6 children. Saw the possibilities of visual signals while serving in Tex.; became signal officer, 1860; organized, commanded Signal Corps, U.S. Army, 1861; furnished plans for naval signaling; promoted lt. col., 1862, col., 1862; col. and chief signal officer, 1863-64; signal officer Div. of West Miss., 1864 to end of Civil War; brevetted brig. gen., 1865; commd. col., chief signal officer U.S. Army, 1866; established, supervised U.S. Weather Bur., 1870. U.S. rep. at meteorol. congresses in Vienna, 1873, Rome, 1879; promoted brig. gen., 1880; army camp Ft. Myer (Va.) named for him. Died Buffalo, N.Y., Aug. 24, 1880.

MYER, ALBERT LEE brig. gen. U.S.A.; b. Troy, N.Y., Nov. 14, 1846; s. Col. Aaron B. and Julia A. M.; ed. pub. schs. of Troy; m. Minnie B. Henderson, June 15, 1870. Served as pvt. Co. F, 3d Battalion, 11th U.S. Inf., and sergt. and q.-m.-sergt. Co. F, 29th Inf., Oct. 26, 1865-June 11, 1868; apptd. from army, 2d lt. 29th Inf., Dec. 6, 1867; transferred to 11th Inf., Apr. 25, 1869; 1st lt., June 28, 1878; capt., Dec. 8, 1886; maj., Mar. 2, 1899; lt. col. 27th Inf., Apr. 22, 1901; transferred to 11th Inf., Aug. 1, 1901; col. 17th Inf., Feb. 23, 1903; transferred to 11th Inf., Mar. 24, 1903; brig. gen. U.S.A., Mar. 23, 1907; retired. Mason. Died July 16, 1914.

MYER, JOHN WALDEN, museum dir.; b. London, Eng., Sept. 18, 1901 (parents U.S. citizens); s. Albert James and Gertrude (Sharp) M.; B.S., Harvard, 1923, grad. study archtl. sch., 1924-27, grad. sch., 1927-28; m. Martha Rosalie Humphrey, Sept. 8, 1934; children—Theodore Humphrey, Martha Elizabeth. Asst. to dir. Mus. City of N.Y., 1929-34, v. dir., 1934-51, dir., 1951-58. Fellow The Pierpont Morgan Library. Served as maj., USAAF, 1942-45. Mem. Nat. trust for Hist. Preservation. Mem. Mus. Council N.Y.C., Soc. for Preservation of L.I. Antiquities (pres. 1961-64), Am. Assn. Museums, Archives Am. Art, Soc. Archtl. Historians, Municipal Art Soc. N.Y.C. (member of the historic buildings committee), Holland Society N.Y., Colonial Lords of Manors in America. Clubs: Century Assn. (N.Y.C.); Piping Rock (Locust Valley, N.Y.). Contbr. profl. publs. Home: Wiscasset ME Died Mar. 14, 1972.

MYERS, ALONZO FRANKLIN, educator; b. Grover Hill, O., Apr. 6, 1895; s. Louis and Emma (Evans) M.; A.B., Tri-State Coll., Ind., 1915; A.M., Columbia, 1924, Ph.D., 1927; Litt.D., Newark State Coll., 1962; LL.D., Tri-State Coll., 1959; D.H.L., Pa. Mil. College, 1960; married to Rose M. Chilcote, Sept. 21, 1917; children—John, Alice, Martha, Rose Anne; m. 2d, Louise M. Kifer, 1938. Supt. of schools, Hudson, Ind., 1915-16; prin. high school, Edgerton, O., 1916-17; supt. schs., Edgerton, 1919-20, Port Clinton, O., 1920-22; prof. edn. and dir. teacher training, Ohio, U., 1922-28; dir. teacher preparation Conn. State Bd. of Edn., and dir. summer Normal Sch., 1928-30; prof. edn., New York U. since 1930; chmn. dept. of higher edn., 1941-60; director retirement counseling center, 1955-60; distinguished vis. prof. higher edn. So. Ill. U., from 1960; lectr. sch. administrn., Yale, 1935-36 and 1936-37. Delivered annual Sir John Adams Lecture at U. of Calif. in Los Angeles, 1941. Capt. inf., U.S. Army, 1917-19. Recipient Great Teacher award for outstanding teaching by the New York Univ. Alumni Fedn., 1959. Mem. Accrediting Com. Am. Assn. of Tchrs. Coll., 1936-41, chmn., 1940-41; chairman National Education Assn. Commn. on Defense of Democracy Through Education, 1941-47; mem. exec. com., 1944-46, vice pres., 1946-47; president Department of Higher Education, Nat. Edn. Assn., 1947-48. Mem. Eastern States Assn. Professional Schools for Teachers (pres. 1933-36), National Assn. Supervisors of Student Teaching (pres. 1935-36), New York Adult Education Council (dir. from 1946), Phi Delta Kappa, Kappa Delta Pi. Author or co-author of publications relating to field. Home: Venice FL Died May 24, 1970; buried Ashland KY

MYERS, CURTIS CLARK mech. engr.; b. South Livonia, N.Y., July 9, 1879; s. James E. and Jennie (Eaton) M.; M.E., Cornell U., 1903; lM.M.E., 1905; m. Florence MacClelland, July 22, 1908; 1 son; Curtis MacClelland (dec.). Instr. Cornell U., 1903; constrn. engr. Lackawanna Steel Co., 1906-07; mech. engr. Diamond Chain Co., Indpls., 1907-09; asst. prof. in charge coop. engring. courses, U. Cin., 1909-13, prof. indsl. engring., 1913-18; mech. engr. Aluminum Co. of America, 1919; chief mech. engr. Pitts., 1919-24; supt. Aluminum Co. of Can., Toronto, 1924-29; in charge fgn. bldg. program Aluminum, Ltd., Montreal, Can., 1929-32; chief prodn. engr. Ford Instrument Co., Long Island City, N.Y., 1934-35, factory mgr., 1935-37; N.Y. sales rep. Doyle Machine Tool Co., 1937-39, factory mgr., Syracuse, N.Y., 1939-40; asst. mgr. W.P.B., Syracuse, N.Y., 1940-41, spl. research engr., aluminum and magnesium br. Washington, 1941-43; resident dir. Daniel Guggenheim Airship Inst., Akron, O., 1943-49, ret. Served as capt. ordnance, U.S. Army, 1918-19. Life mem. Am. Soc. M.E. Clubs: Torch, Rotary (Akron); Engineers (N.Y.C.). Home: 211 Aurora St., Hudson, O. Died Dec. 3, 1954.

MYERS, DILLER S. army officer; b. Ill., Nov. 21, 1887; commd. 2d lt. Inf., Ill. Nat. Guard, July 1912; 1st lt. Fed. service, June 1914, and advanced to lt. col. Sept. 1918; col. Officers Reserve Corps, 1919; col. Calif. Nat. Guard, 1924, made brig. gen. of the line, Aug. 1938; entered Fed. service, Mar. 1941; now in command of 65th Inf. Brigade, 33d Div., in training, Camp Forrest, Tenn. Awarded Silver Star, World War I. Address: War Dept., Washington, D.C. Died may 12, 1947.

MYERS, JOHN LLEWELLYN, physician; b. Livingston County, Mo., Mar. 29, 1872; s. Simeon and Susan Leaton (Alexander) M.; A.B., Park Coll., Parkville, Mo., 1901; M.D., Physicians and Surgeons Med. Coll. (now med. dept. U. of Kan.), 1904; studied in London, Eng. and N.Y. City, 1914-15; m. Florence Alverda Young, Apr. 8, 1904. Practiced at Ketchikan, Alaska, 1904-14; specializing in eye, ear, nose and throat work, Seattle, Wash., 1915-16; with Dr. J. E. Sawtell, Kansas City, Mo., 1916-18; together with his brothers, Dr. B. L. Myers and Dr. W. A. Myers, organized and conducted Myers' Clinic since 1919, University of Kansas Medical School, since 1926, now associate professor emeritus. Captain M.R.C., U.S. Army, 1918. President board med. examiners, Alaska, 1912-14; pres. Kansas City Eye, Ear, Nose and Throat Soc., 1921-22, Kansas City-Southwest Clin. Soc., 1931-32; sec. ear, nose and throat sect. Am. Acad. Ophthalmology and Otolaryngology, 1926-42. Fellow Am. Coll. Surgeons, A.M.A., Am. Congress Physical Therapy; mem. A.A.A.S., Am. Laryngol. Assn. Republican. Presbyn. Mason; mem. I.O.O.F., Eastern Star, Redmen. Home: 5401 W. 67th St., Mission P.O., Kan. Office: Shukert Bldg., Kansas City MO

MYERS, JOHN SHERMAN, univ. dean; b. Bklyn., Apr. 7, 1897; s. John A. and Sarah Ann (Sherman) M.; B.S., Harvard, 1919, LL.B. cum laude, 1925; m. Alvina Reckman, Dec. 22, 1928. Admitted to Mass. bar, 1925, N.Y. bar, 1926; with firm Hughes, Schurman & Dwight, N.Y.C., 1925-31; v.p., gen. counsel, then pres. and chmn. Distributors Group, N.Y.C., 1931-37; v.p., gen. counsel, co-owner Lord, Abbott & Co., N.Y.C., 1937-41; prof. law U. Colo., 1941-42; prof. law Washington Coll. Law, Am. U., 1947-69, dean, 1956-67, dean emeritus, research prof. law, 1967-69. Served to colonel U.S. Army and AUS, 1918, 42-47. Decorated Legion of Merit. Mem. Am., D.C. bar assns., Assn. Bar City N.Y., Am. Law Inst., Assn. Am. Law Schs. Mason. Clubs: Cosmos, Congressional, Nat. Lawyers (Washington); Augusta (Me.) Country. Contbr. articles profl. publs. Home: Washington DC Died Jan. 24, 1969; buried Gettysburg Nat. Cemetery, Gettysburg PA

MYERS, JOHN TWIGGS, lt. gen.; b. of Am. parents at Wiesbaden, Germany, Jan. 29,21871; s. Abraham Charles and Marion Ysabelle (Twiggs) M.; grad. U.S. Naval Acad., Annapolis, Md., 1892; Naval War Coll., 1896, 1905; grad. Army War Coll., 1912; m. Alice G. Cutts, Apr. 30, 1898. Commd. 2d lt., U.S. Marine Corps, Mar. 7, 1895, and advanced through grades to lt. gen., May 1942. Served in Spanish American War, Philippine Insurrection, Boxer uprising, China (pvt. maj. while comdr. Legation Guard, Siege of Pekin, 1900), Punitive Expdn., Mexico, World War I. Served as fleet marine officer, European, Asiatic, Pacific and Atlantic fleets; comdr. posts Parris Island, San Diego, Quantico; retired (for age) Feb. 1, 1935. Mem. Aztec Society, Military Order Dragon, Military Order Carabao, Naval and Mil. Order Spanish-Am. War, Spanish War Vets., Am. Legion. Episcopalian. Clubs: Army and Navy, Army Navy Country (Washington). Address: 3919 Braganza Av., Coconut Grove FL!5

MYGATT, GERALD author, editor; born New York, N.Y.; s. Lemuel Carrington and Sophia Hartt (Weidemeyer) M.; ed. Collegiate Sch., N.Y.; A.B., Williams Coll.; m. Gertrude Hitz; children-Donald (lt. Army Air Corps), Judith, Antoinette, Peter. Successively reporter New York Sun; circulation mgr., The Outlook; sales-promotion mgr. Good Housekeeping Mag.; mng. editor and editor Cosmopolitan Mag.; mng. editor The Week Mag.; editor Our Navy Mag.; editor Liberty Mag.; copy chief, adv. dept., Columbia Broadcasting System. Mem. Alpha Delta Phi. Clubs: Williams (N.Y.); Dutch Treat (N.Y.). Author: Nightmare, a novel, 1928; Soldiers' and Sailors' Prayer Book, 1944. Contbr. short stories and serials to Sat. Eve. Post and other mags. Served as pvt., cpl., sgt., 1st sgt., 2d lt., 1st lt., F.A.; capt. 75th F.A., U.S. Army, 1917-19. Major, F.A., AUS, 1924-34. Address: Hotel Carteret, 208 W. 23d St., N.Y.C. 11. Died June 3, 1955; buried Rosedale Cemetery, Orange, N.J.

MYRICK, JOHN RENCKLIN soldier b. Westfield, N.J., Nov. 9, 1841; s. James and Rebecca Aiken (Miller) M.; ed. village schs., Westfield and Cranford, N.J., to 1854; pub. sch., Brooklyn, at Apr. 1855; clerk in stores, 1855-61; m. Harriet Augusta Moore, Jan. 22, 1867. Pvt. Co. B, 13th N.Y. State Militia, Apr. 23-Aug. 6, 1861; 2d lt. and 1st lt. 3d U.S. Arty., Nov. 18, 1861; capt. 38th U.S.Inf. (declined), July 28, 1866; capt. 3d U.S. Arty., Dec. 1, 1872; maj., Feb. 12, 1895; lt. col. 2d U.S. Arty., Oct. 16, 1899; col. Arty. Corps, U.S.A., Aug. 1, 1901; brig. gen. U.S.A., Apr. 17, 1903, retired Apr. 18, 1903. Bvtd. capt. Feb. 20, 1864, maj., Oct. 7, 1864, for gallantry in action. Republican. Died 1909.

NABORS, EUGENE AUGUSTUS prof. of law; b. Naborton, La., Apr. 3, 1905; s. Eugene Augustus and Sallie M. (Cooper) N.; A.B., Washington and Lee U., 1926; LL.B., Yale, 1928, J.S.D., 1932; unmarried. Admitted to La. bar, 1930; asst. prof. of law, Tulane U., 1928-30, asso. prof., 1930-33, prof. since 1933; on leave of absence to serve as Sterling Fellow, Yale U. Law Sch., 1931-32; on leave of absence, Sept. 1942-Jan. 1946, active duty; serving as lt., U.S.N.R., 1942-45; promoted lt. comdr. July 1945, to comdr., 1951. Mem. Motion Picture Panel of Arbitrators, 1941-42; mem. council and exec. com., La. State Law Inst., 1941-42, council 1946-55, 1957-59. Mem. Am., La. (bd. govds. 1941-42, 48-49, 50-51, 54-55, 56-57), New Orleans bar assns., Charter Com. City New Orleans (1950-52), Charter Adv. Com. (1955-59), La. Civil Service League (legal com. and bd. govs., 1952-), Phi Beta Kappa, Phi Delta Phi, Order of the Coif. Clubs: Round Table, Stratford, Country (New Orleans); Boston. Faculty adv. Tulane Law Review, 1941-42, 46-54, bd. adv. editors, 1955-. Died Dec. 23, 1959.

NACHE, ALEXANDER DALLAS physicist, coll. pres.; b., Phila., U. Pa., 1828-41; 1st pres. Girard Coll., Phila., 1836-circa 1848; supt. U.S. Coast Survey, 1843-67; a founder A.A.A.S.; an incorporator, regent Smithsonian Instn., 1846; a founder, 1st pres. Nat. Acad. Scis.; pres. Am. Philos. Soc., 1855; adviser to the Pres. U.S., also v.p. Sanitary Commn. during Civil War; Hon. mem. Royal Soc. London, Royal Acad. Turin, Imperial Geog. Soc. Vienna, Inst. of France. Author: Observations at the Observatory of Girard College, 3 vols, 1840-45. Died Providence, R.I., Feb. 17, 1867.

NAFFZIGER, HOWARD CHRISTIAN surgeon; b. Nevada City, Cal., May 6, 1884; s. Christian Jacob and Lizzie (Scott) N.; B.S., U. of Calif., 1907; M.S., 1908, M.D., 1909; m. Louise McNear, 1919; children-Marion, Jean Louise, Elizabeth. Began practice at San Francisco, 1912; prof. surgery, chmn. dept. U. of Calif., 1929-47, prof. neurological surgery, chmn. dept. 1947-51, prof. emeritus U. of Cal., 1951-61; regent U. of Cal., 1952-61. Served at lt. col. M.C., United States Army, in United States and with A.E.F., 2 years; colonel Medical Reserve; commanding officer U.S. Gen. Hosp. No. 30. Spl. consultant Office Scientific Research and Development; hon. consultant surgeon generals' library; chmn. UNRRA Med. Mission to Poland, 1946, WHO Med. Mission to P.I., 1948; cons. Far Eastern Comd., Korea and Japan, 1951. Fellow Phillipine Coll. Surgeons (hon.); fellow Am. Coll. Surgeons (regent; pres. 1939); fellow Royal Coll. Surgeons (hon.) Eng., 1943; founder, chmn. Am. Bd. Neurol. Surgery, 1939-49; founder, mem. American Bd. of Surgery; mem. A.M.A., Soc. Neurol. Surgeons (pres. 1929), Internat. Neurol. Assn., Internat. Surg. Assn., German Neurosurg. Soc. (hon.), Am. Neurol. Assn., Am. Surg. Assn. (pres. 1953-54), Assn. Research Nervous and Mental Diseases, Pacific Coast Surg. Assn., San Francisco County Med. Soc. (pres.) San Francisco County Neurol. Soc. (pres.), Western Surg. Assn., Cal. Acad. Medicine (pres.), mem. com. on surgery and chmn. subcommittee on neurol. surgery Nat. Research Council, 1940-46; mem. Royal Socl of Medicine (hon.) England, Phila. Academy of Surgery, Southern Surgical Assn., Australasian Society of Neurological Surgeons, Howard C. Naffziger Surg. Soc. (hon.); mem. Psi Upsilon, Alpha Omega Alpha, Nu Sigma Nu. Republican. Episcopalian. Clubs: University, Pacific Union, San Francisco Golf and Country. Conrbr. on surgery and the nervous system and exptl. research in anatomy and surgery of same; mem. editorial bd. Western Jour. of Surgery, Am. Jour. of Surgery, Annals of Surgery, Jour. Neurol Surg. Home: 2565 Larkin St., San Francisco 94109. Died Mar. 21, 1961.

NAGLE, CHARLES FRANCIS naval officer; b. in Ireland, Sept. 4, 1841; s. William and Ellen (Cotter) N.; arrived in America, Dec. 4, 1850; ed. pub. schs. Alice W., d. William Holt, Aug. 11, 1880. Apptd. 3d asst. engr. U.S.N., rank of midshipman, Aug. 3, 1863; promoted master, July 26, 1866; lt., Apr. 15, 1874; chief engr. with rank of lt. comdr., June 29, 1906; retired July 26, 1892, account of physical disability due to exposure on Arctic expdn. With Admiral Farragut in West Gulf Blockading Squadron, 1863 to close of Civ. War; saved U.S. steamer Chicopee from sinking, Jan. 1867, received thanks of admiral comdg. the station. Total sea service 16 yrs., 2 mos., including cruises in N. Atlantic and S. Pacific, Asiatic and European stas., and shore duty at Boston, New York and Portsmouth, N.H., navy yards, Mem. gen. court-martial at Brooklyn Navy Yard 3 yrs. after retirement. Medal for creditable service in Civ. War; medal from King of Siam, Bangkok, 1874, permitted to accept by spl. act of Congress; medal Mil. Order of Loyal Legion of U.S. Home: Brooklyn, N.Y. Died May 26, 1914.

NAIDEN, EARL L. army air corps officer; b. Woodward, Ia., Feb. 2, 1894; s. Henry Richard and Carra (Sanks) N.; ed. Swarely's Prep. Sch., Washington, D.C., 1910-11; B.S., U.S. Mil. Acad., 1915; grad. Command and Gen. Staff Sch., 1920, Army War Coll., 1927, Ecole Supérieure de Guerre, Paris, 1929. Commd. 2d lt., Cav., U.S. Army, 1915, entered aviation 1916, and advanced through the grades to brig. gen., 1942; served in France, Italy, and Eng., World War I. Decorated Black Star; Purple Heart; World War and Mexican Border medals. Deceased.

NAIR, JOHN HENRY, JR., cons. indsl. chemist; b. Chgo., Feb. 20, 1893; s. John H. and Isabel Bratton (Painter) N.; B.S. cum laude, Beloit Coll., 1915; D.Sc., 1958; student Syracuse U. 1916-17; m. Claire Louise Cook, Mar. 22, 1920; children—John, Janet Cook (Mrs. Clarence L. Adams). Chemistry instr. Wausau (Wis.) High Sch., 1915-16, Syracuse U., 1916-17; research chemist Merrell-Soule Co., Syracuse, N.Y., 1919-28; asst. dir. research Borden Co., Syracuse, 1928-38; tech. sales Borden Co., N.Y.C., 1938-42; asst. dir. research T. J. Lipton, Inc., Hoboken, N.J., 1942-57; v.p., dir. L & N Corp., Raleigh, N.C.; secretary-treas. Elmenair Corporation, Raleigh, N.C. Member advisory board Jour. Agrl. and Food Chemists, 1953-57; dir. Avi Pub. Co.; vis. prof. N.C. State Coll., U.N.C., 1963-64. Trustee Beloit Coll., 1961-64. Served as capt. Signal Corps C.W.S., AEF, 1917-19. Mem. Am. Chem. Soc. (nat. councillor, 1929-35, 1945-63, dir. 1964-71), Inst. Food Technologists (chmn. N.Y. sect. 1946-47, nat. council 1947, 51-53, 57-59, pres. elect 1965-66), Am. Inst. Chemists (nat. councilor 1957-61, pres. 1956-57, hon. mem. 1962-71), N.A.M. (research com.), Assn. Research Dirs. (pres. 1956-57), American Dairy Science Assn., Sci. Research Soc. of Am., Society Chimie Industrielle, also Sigma Xi, Phi Tau Sigma, Delta Sigma Rho, Alpha Chi Sigma, Tau Kappa Epsilon. Mason. Clubs: Chemists (N.Y.C.); Raleigh (N.C.) Country; North Carolina State Faculty. Contributing author: Handbook of Food and Agriculture, 1955; Food Dehydration, volume 2, 1964. Contributing editor Food Engring. Author numerous articles on chem. research. Home: Raleigh NC Died July 25, 1971.

NAMM, BENJAMIN HARRISON, business exec.; b. Brooklyn, N.Y., Nov. 29, 1888; s. Adolph Isaac and Cecilia (Meyer) N.; grad. Peekskill (N.Y.) Mill. Acad., 1905; student Brooklyn Polytech. Inst., Brooklyn, 1906-07; m. Margaret Alice Wolf, May 15, 1922; children—Andrew Irving, Peggotty Hanks. Salesman, The Namm-Loeser Store, Bklyn., 1910-16, pres. 1916-46, former chairman of board; chmn. bd. Arebec Corp.; dir. Avco Mfg. Corp., Equitable Fed. Savs. & Loan Assn. Chmn. retail advisory committee U.S. Treasury, 1941; spl. asst. to dir. U.S. Office of Civilian Defense, 1942; exec. dir. U.S. Purchasing Commn. for Brazil, 1943; consultant to State Dept. at U.N. Conf. on Internat. Orgn., San Francisco, 1945; observer to U.N. Conf., Lake Success, New York. Served overseas as chief gas officer of 5th div. World War I; served overseas as civilian cons. U.S. Army, World War II. Decorated Officer French Legion of Honor, Brazilian Southern Cross, Luxemborg Order of Duchy, Italian Legion of Honor, Swedish Royal Order of Vasa. Former chmn. bd. trustees N.Y. City Community Coll.; hon. chmn. Lafayette Fellowship Found.; past chmn. Conf. of National Orgns.; ex-gov. Am. Stock Exchange. Dir. Bklyn. chpt. ARC. Mem. Nat. Retail Merchants Assn. (pres. bd. dirs., winner gold medal award in 1941, chmn. internat. com.), Downtown Bklyn. Assn. (gold medal award), N.Y. U. Sch. of Retailing (mem. adv. com.), U.S. C. of C. (domestic distbrn. com.), Bklyn. C. of C. (dir.). Author: Advertising the Retail Store (forward by Arthur Brisbane), 1924; Would You Enter A Door Marked Socialism. Home: New York City NY Died Aug. 1969; buried Salem Fields Cemetery, Brooklyn NY

NANCRÉDE, C(HARLES) B(EYLARD) GUÉRARD DE, surgeon; b. Phila., Dec. 30, 1847; s. Thomas Dixie and Mary Elizabeth (Bull) N.; student U. of Pa., 1864-66, M.D., 1869, hon. A.B., 1893, as of class of 1868, hon. A.M., 1895; M.D., Jefferson Med. Coll., 1883; LL.D., 1898, hon. A.M., Univ. of Michigan, 1893; m. Alice Dunnington, June 3, 1872. Practiced Phila. and held various surg. chairs and hosp. appointments there; prof. surgery and clin. surgery, and surgeon Univ. Hosp., U. of Mich., 1889-—, Dartmouth Med. Coll., 1900-13; emeritus, 1913. Maj. and chief surgeon, U.S. Volunteers, 1898; chief surgeon 3d Div., 2d Army Corps; served with 5th Army Corps, Cuba, in Santiago campaign. Pres. Am. Surg. Assn., 1908-09. Author: Principles of Surgery, 1899. Contbr. to med. encys. and text books. Address: Ann Arbor, Mich. Died Apr. 13, 1921.

NASH, ABNER gov. N.C., Continental congressman; b. Templeton Manor, Prince Edward County, Va., Aug. 8, 1740; s. John and Ann (Owen) N.; m. Justina (Davis) Dobbs; m. 2d, Mary Whiting Jones, 1774. Mem. Va. Ho. of Burgesses, 1761, 62; mem. N.C. Ho. of Commons, 1764, 65, 70-71, 78, 82, 84, 85, speaker 1777; brigade maj. N.C. Militia, 1768; del. to 5 N.C. provincial congresses, 1774-76; mem. N.C. Provincial Council, 1775, 76, agt. of council, 1776; speaker N.C. Senate, 1779-80; gov. N.C., 1780-81; mem. Continental Congress from N.C., 1782, 83, 84, 85, 86; elected to Annapolis Conv., 1786, did not attend. Died N.Y.C., Dec. 2, 1786; buried "Pembroke" nr. New Bern, N.C.

NASH, FRANCIS army officer; b. Templeton Manor, Prince Edward County, Va., 1742; s. John and Ann (Owen) N.; m. Sarah Moore; at least 2 children. Justice of peace, clk. N.C. Ct. Pleas and Quarter Sessions, 1763; mem. N.C. Ho. of Commons, 1764, 65, 71, 73-75; served as capt. Brit. Army, participated in battle of Alamanance against the Regulators, 1771; mem. N.C. Provincial Congress, 1775; col. N.C. Militia; lt. col., then col. 1st N.C. Regt., Continental Army, 1775, brig. gen., 1777, led a brigade at Germantown, Pa., wounded, 1777. Nash County, N.C., Nashville, Tenn. named in his honor. Died Kulpsville, Pa., Oct. 7, 1777.

NASH, WILLIAM HOLT brig. gen. U.S.A.; b. Gallipolis, O., June 22, 1834; s. Hon. Simeon N.; ed. Gallia Acad., Gallipolis, O., and Marietta Coll., 1849-51; was in large wholesale and retail house in Cincinnati, 1853-56; in business for self, 1857-60; m. 2d, Mrs. Mary Maxon Wilson, Feb. 22, 1892. Entered mil. service as telegraph operator, June 1, 1861, dept. W.Va.; apptd. capt. commissary subsistence vols., Nov. 26, 1862; transferred to same corps, regular army, Nov. 17, 1865; promoted maj. commissary subsistence, July 14, 1890; lt. col. asst. commissary-gen., June 10, 1896; col. asst. commissary-gen., Feb. 4, 1898; apptd. commissary-gen. subsistence, U.S.A., with rank of brig. gen.. April 21, 1898; retired from active service, May 2, 1898. Address: Columbus, O. Died 1902.

NASON, LEONARD HASTINGS (STEAMER), author; b. Somerville, Mass., Sept. 28, 1895; s. Frank Leonard and Jennie Rand (Allen) N.; grad. Newton Tech. High Sch., B.Sc., Norwich U., 1920; m. Lucia Millet, Aug, 12, 1920; children—Jane, Priscilla, Leonard H. In Mexican border service, with 1st Vt. Inf., 1916; sergt. Battery A, 76th F.A., A.E.F.; wounded Mont St. Pere, July 1918, and Montfaucon, Oct. 1918; cited "for gallantry in action" by Gens. Pershing and Howze (2 citations); active duty with U.S. Army, 1941-45; lt. col., cav. (Armored Force), Army U.S., 1942; made initial landing with U.S. forces, Morocco, 1942; mil. gov. of Rabat Dist., 1942; in Tunisian campaign, 1943; campaign of France, and the liberation of Paris, 1944. Sgt.-maj. of honor, Moroccan Regt. of Colonial Inf. (R.I.C.M.), 1943; col. Cavalry, U.S. Army Reserve. Decorated Bronze Star (combat), Purple Heart and Silver Star (U.S.); Ouissam Alaouite (Morocco). Mem. Ancient and Hon. Arty. Co. of Boston, Am. Legion, Soc. Third Division, Sigma Phi Epsilon, S.A.R. Conglist. Clubs: Norwich, Algonoquin (Boston); Cercle Internallie (Paris); Chiberta Country (Biarritz). Author: Chevrons, 1926; Three Lights from a Match, 1927; Sergeant Eadie, 1928; The Top Kick, 1928; The Man in the White Slicker, 1929; Incomplete Mariner, 1929; Livingstone Brothers, 1930; A Corporal Once, 1930; Defenders of the Bridge, 1932; Among the Trumpets, 1932; (screen play) Rodney, 1933; (screen play) Red Night, 1935; Eagles Eastward, 1936; I Spy Strangers, 1940; Approach to Battle, 1941; Contact Mercury, 1946; The Barbary Voyage, 1949. Contbr. stories to Adventure, Saturday Evening Post, Am. Legion Mag., also verse in the "Line o'Type," Chicago Tribune, under pen name of "Steamer." Home: New York City NY Died July 25, 1970; buried Arlington Nat. Cemetery, Arlington VA

NASON, THOMAS WILLOUGHBY, artist, engraver; b. Dracut, Mass., Jan. 7, 1889; s. William Walton and Kate Julia (Hooker) N.; educated in public schools; A.M. (hon.), Tufts College; married Margaret Warren, May 10, 1919. Represented in permanent collections of notable galleries and museums in U.S. and abroad, also private collections. Recipient of numerous prizes and awards. Served with 26th Div., A.E.F., U.S. Army, 1917-19. Fellow Am. Acad. Arts and Sciences; Nat. Acad., Nat. Inst. of Arts and Letters, Lyme Art Assn. Home: Lyme CT Died 1971; buried Cove Cemetery, Lyme CT

NAVARRO, JOSÉ ANTONIO army officer; b. San Antonio, Tex., 1795. Advocate of Tex. independence from Mexico (despite Mexican background); land title commr. Bexar Dist., Tex., 1834-35; a signer Tex. Declaration of Independence, 1836; served in Republic of Tex. Congress, various times; imprisoned by Mexicans in Santa Fe, N.M., 1841-43; mem. Tex. State Constl. Conv., 1845; Navarro County (Tex.) named for him. Died 1870.

NAVE, ORVILLE JAMES army chaplain; b. at Galion, O., Apr. 30, 1841; s. Solomon P. and Jane Ann (Johnson) N.; pvt. Co. A, 111th Ill. Inf., Aug. 14, 1862-June 6, 1865; A.B., Ohio Wesleyan U., 1870, A.M., 1873, hon. D.D., 1895; LL.D., Neb. Wesleyan, 1897; m. Anna Eliza Semans, Sept. 6, 1870; 1 son, Frederick Solomon N. Entered Ohio Conf. M.E. Ch., 1870; post chaplain U.S.A., July 27, 1882; chaplain 3d Inf., 1901-05; chaplain maj. and retired, Apr. 30, 1905; pres. Nave's Topical Bible Home Sch., 1904—. Corr. sec. for Corps of Army Chaplains, 1888-94. Republican. Author: Nave's Topical Bible, 1897; Student's Bible, 1907; also various text-books for use in connection with his Bible sch. Pres. Meth. Hosp. Assn., Los Angeles, 1908-13; pres. and field sec. Assn. of Chaplains of Mil. and Naval forces U.S., 1912-13; pres. Juvenile Protective League of Los Angeles and Los Angeles Co. Chaplain-in-chief G.A.R., 1914-15; chaplain city and county jails; pres. Prisoner's Friend Soc. of City and County of Los Angeles. Address: Los Angeles, Calif. Died June 24, 1917.

NAYLOR, CHARLES congressman; b. Philadelphia County, Pa., Oct. 6, 1806; studied law. Admitted to Pa. bar, 1828, began practice in Phila.; mem. U.S. Ho. of Reps. (Whig) from Pa., June 29, 1837-41; organized a volunteer co. known as Phila. Rangers, during Mexican War, served as capt.; settled in Pitts. after Mexican War, practiced law; returned to Phila. Died Phila., Dec. 24, 1872; buried South Laurel Hill Cemetery, Phila.

NAYLOR, WILLIAM KEITH author, army officer; b. Bloomington, Ill., Nov. 24, 1874; s. William Alexander and Genevieve Charlotte (Hay) N.; grad. Mich. Mil. Acad., 1894; LL.B., U. of Minn., 1898; admitted to Minn. bar; distinguished grad. Inf. and Cav. Sch., Ft. Leavenworth, Kan., 1904; grad. Staff Coll., Ft. Leavenworth, 1905, 21, Army War Coll., Washington, 1910, 23; m. Margaret Wagner, dau. Col. A. L. Wagner, U.S. Army, Dec. 27, 1904; children—Margaret (wife of 1st lt. Dwight L. Adams, U.S. Army), William K., Alexander Hay. Vol. 14th Minn. Inf., May 8, 1898, and commd. 2d lt.; hon. discharged, vol. service, July 24, 1898; commd. 2d lt. regular army, July 9, 1898; promoted through grades to col., July 1, 1920; served in World War as col. N.A., and brig. gen. U.S. Army. With 9th Inf. in Philippines, 1898-99; China Relief Expdn., 1900; later instr. strategy and mil. history, service schs., about 5 yrs.; chief of staff 33d Div. that participated in Somme offensive; in Meuse-Argonne with 3d Corps; promoted, and assigned as chief of staff of corps; after return to U.S., again apptd. instr. strategy and mil. history, Service Schs., later dir. Staff Sch. and dir. War Plans Div. of Army War Coll.; asst. chief of staff and dir. mil. intelligence, gen. staff, 1922-24; commander 15th Infantry in China, 1924-26; appointed commander Infantry Post, Boston Harbor, and 13th Inf., Oct. 16, 1926; apptd. chief of staff 2d Corps Area, Governor's Island, N.Y., May 27, 1929; completed tour as chief of staff, May 26, 1933, and detailed in charge of Corps Area; apptd. prof. mil. science and tactics, U. of Ill., July 1, 1933; promoted brig. gen. regular army, Dec. 1, 1933; apptd., in command Ft. Benjamin Harrison, Ind., Dec. 8, 1933; retired November 30, 1938. Decorated Silver Star with oak leaf cluster, "for gallantry in action" at Tientsin, China, July 13, 1900, and in Meuse-Argonne Offen- sive, Sept. and Oct. 1918; Distinguished Service Medal (U.S.). Comdr. Order of St. Michael and St. George (British); Comdr. Crown of Italy; Officer Legion of Honor and Croix de Guerre (French). Mem. Mil. Order of the Dragon, Delta Chi. Republican. Mason (32 deg.). Club: Army and Navy (Washington). Author: Principles of Strategy, 1922 (adopted as official textbook by Japan); Marne Miracle, 1924; The Principles of War, 1923. Address: War Dept., Washington, D.C. Died Aug. 3, 1942.

NEAL, JOHN RANDOLPH congressman; b. nr. Clinton, Tenn., Nov. 26, 1836; attended Hiwassee Coll., Tenn.; grad. Emory and Henry Coll., 1858; studied law. Admitted to Tenn. bar, 1859, began practice in Athens; served as capt. Tenn. Cavalry Confederate Army, during Civil War, later promoted lt. col.; taught sch.; settled in Rhea Springs, Tenn., practiced law; mem. Tenn. Ho. of Reps., 1874; mem. Tenn. Senate, 1878-79, presiding officer, 1879; Democratic presdl. elector, 1880; mem. U.S. Ho. of Reps. (Dem.) from Tennessee 49th-50th congresses, 1885-59. Died Rhea Springs, Mar. 26, 1889; buried W. F. Brown family cemetery, Post Oak Springs, Tenn.

NEAL, MILLS FERRELL, mfr.; b. Richmond, Va., Aug. 29, 1893; s. Thomas David and Fannie (Mills) N.; ed. pub. schs., Richmond; student bus. adminstrn., 1909-12, Army War Coll., 1934. With Neal & Binford (tobacconists supplies), 1912-27; organized firm M. F. Neal & Co., Inc., 1927, pres., 1927-70; pres. Tuckahoe Warehouse Corp.; dir. Bank of Va. Bd. visitors Va. Mil. Inst. Served to lt. col. Va. N.G., 1911-17, 20-40, in Fed. service on Mex. border 1917; served from 2nd lt. to 1st lt. U.S. Army, 1917-19; to col. AUS, 1940-46; dir. Selective Service for Va., with Supreme Hdqrs. Allied Expeditionary Forces; ETO. Decorated D.S.M. Clubs: Commonwealth, Country Club of Virginia (Richmond). Author of Selective Service Plan for State of Virginia. Home: Richmond VA Died Sept. 1972.

NEALE, M(ERVIN) GORDON educator; b. Moody, Mo., Mar. 25, 1887; s. Andrew and Mamie Eliz. (Dawson) N.; B.S. in Edn., U. Mo., 1911; A.M., Tchrs. Coll. (Columbia), 1917, Ph.D., 1920; m. Margaret Kennedy Mumford, Mar. 21, 1922; children—Julia Anne, Margaret Mumford (dec.), Jane Ellen, Mervin Gordon, Daniel Christopher. Tchr. rural schs., later supt. schools, Platte City and Malden, Mo., until 1913; dir. edn. Maryville (Mo.) State Tchrs. Coll., 1914-15; tchr.-tng. high sch. insp. Mo. Dept. Edn., 1915-16; asso. in ednl. adminstrn. Tchrs. Coll. (Columbia), 1919-20; prof. sch. adminstrn. U. Mo., 1920-21, U. Minn., 1921-23; dean Sch. Edn., U. Mo., 1923-30; pres. U. Ida., 1930-37; prof. ednl. adminstrn. U. Minn., 1937-55, dir. of field studies and surveys, 1948-55; cons. coll. and univ. improvement programs for numerous instns. in St. Paul, other Minn. cities. Student Plattsburg (N.Y.) O.T.C., May-Aug. 1917; went to France with 42d (Rainbow) Div., U.S.A., as 2d lt. inf., Oct. 1917; 1st lt., May 1918; capt., Sept. 1918; served also with 80th Div.; participated in battles at St. Mihiel and Meuse-Argonne; wounded in action, May 1918; hon. discharged, June 19, 1919. Alumni trustee Tchrs. Coll. (Columbia), 1928-30. Coll. examiner for N. Central Assn. Colls. and Secondary Schs. Mem. Assn. Heads of Depts. in Edn. of State Univs. (pres. 1924-25), N.E.A., Nat. Council Edn., Mo. State Tchrs. Assn. (mem. exec. com. 1926-29, pres. 1929-30). Inland Empire Edn. Assn. (pres. 1934-35), Phi Delta Kappa. Author: (brochures) School Reports, 1920; Duluth School Bldg. Survey, 1922; A School Bldg. Program for Winona, Minn., 1922; Studies of Instruction in Public Schools of Austin, Minn., 1923; School Building Program for Columbia, Mo., 1924, for Joplin, Mo., 1925, for Mexico, Mo., 1925, for Sedalia, Mo., 1927, Springfield, Mo., 1928, Moberly, Mo., 1929, Duluth, Minn., 1945, St. Paul, 1951. Home: 1101 E. River Rd., Mpls. 14. Died June 25, 1963.

NEEDHAM, DANIEL, lawyer; b. Groton, Mass., Feb. 5, 1891; s. Daniel and Ellen Mary (Brigham) N.; ed. Groton pub. schs., Phillips (Andover) Acad.; A.B., Harvard, 1913, LL.B., 1916; m. Frances Sarah Topping, Apr. 27, 1921; children—Daniel, Jr., Nathalie. Admitted to Mass. Bar, 1917; since engaged in gen. practice at Boston; mem. firm Sherburne, Powers & Needham, 1919-71; vice president, dir. Nat. Fireworks Ordnance Corp., Clark-Babbitt Foods, Inc., Babbitt Pipe Co., Inc., Nat. Coating, Inc., Babbitt Missile Co.; dir., clk. Waterfront Service Company, Incorporated; trustee Nat. Assos. Commr. pub. safety Mass., 1933-34; mem. Mass. Bd. Probation, 1938-41, Mass. Crime Commission, 1956-58, Electoral Coll., 1956, Assay Commn., 1960; chmn. gov.'s adv. com. civil def. Dir. Boston Met. chpt. A.R.C., chmn., 1956-58; dir. United Fund Greater Boston, Blood Research Institute. Pres. board trustees Lawrence Acad. Lt. and capt., 26th Div., U.S. Army, World War I, maj. gen. comdg. 26th Div. Mass. N.G., 1934-39; honored by 2 citations (U.S.). Decorated Silver Star. Mem. Am., Mass., Middlesex, Boston bar assns., Pi Eta. Republican. Mason. Clubs: Union, YD, Harvard (Boston); Brae Burn Country, Curtis, Middlesex. Home: West Newton MA Died June 1971.

NEEDLES, ENOCH RAY, cons. engr.; b. Brookfield, Mo., Oct. 29, 1888; s. Sim Gesmer and Elma (Bray) N.; B.S., Mo. Sch. Mines, 1914, C.E., 1920, D.Eng. (hon.), 1937; m. Ethel Schuman, Sept. 12, 1916; children—Elma (Mrs. J.W. Wight), Margaret (Mrs. H.P. Williams), Mary (Mrs. H.P. McJunkin), Thomas E., Carolyn (Mrs. C.E. Homer), Sally Jane (Mrs. H.J. Toffey). Various engring. positions, 1914-28; partner Howard, Needles, Tammen & Bergendoff, cons. engrs., N.Y.C., also Kansas City, Mo., from 1928; prin. projects include: Del. Meml. Bridge, Pulaski Skyway, Harlem River Lift Bridge, Me. Turnpike, N.J. Turnpike, W.Va. Turnpike, Ohio Turnpike, 5 other state turnpikes, numerous other state and fed. projects, various Miss. River bridges. Served as col., Corps. Engrs., AUS, 1942-45. Decorated Legion of Merit; recipient UMR Silver Centennial medal honor, 1971. Mem. Am. Road Builders Assn. (pres. 1949-50), Am. Soc. C.E. (pres. 1955-56), Am. Inst. Cons. Engrs. (pres. 1946), Soc. Am. Mil. Engrs., Nat. Soc. Profl. Engrs., Am. Association for Advancement of Science, Engineers Joint Council (president 1958-59), Newcomen Soc., Tau Beta Pi, Phi Kappa Phi, Chi Epsilon, Pi Kappa Alpha. Clubs: Bankers, Engineers (N.Y.C.); Canoe Brook (N.J.) Country; Morris County (N.J.) Golf. Webhannet (Me.) Golf; Army and Navy (Washington). Home: New Vernon NJ Died Jan. 5, 1972; buried New Vernon NJ

NEELANDS, THOMAS D., JR., financial cons.; b. Chicago, July 31, 1902; s. Thomas D. and Catherine E. (Metaxas) N.; ed. Phillips Acad., Andover, Mass., Sheffield Scientific Sch., Yale, 1923; Princeton, 1924; m. Katherine M. O'Connor, July 28, 1934; two children. Asso. with Jackson & Curtis, investment bankers, N.Y. City, 1923-32; pres. and chmn. bd. dirs. N.R. Airways, Inc., N.Y. City, 1927-30; financial cons. Travel Air Airplane Co., Wichita, Kan., 1926-29; Boettcher Newton & Co., investment bankers, N.Y. City, 1932-34; sr. partner Neelands Platte (changed to T.D. Neelands, Jr., & Co.), investment bankers, 1934-42; pres. and chmn. bd. dirs. Kathlands Development Corp., N.Y. City, since 1936; financial consultant Beech Aircraft Corp., Wichita, Kansas, 1941-42, 45-53; chmn. finance com. Robinson Aviation, 1958-72; chmn. bd. dirs. Silex Co., Hartford, Conn.; chmn. bd., mem. exec. com. Capital Airlines, Inc., Wash., 1960-72; chmn. finance com., mem. exec. com., dir. Proctor-Silev Corp., Philadelphia. Served as major, United States Army, Office of Fiscal Dir., Chief of Loan Sect., 1942-45. Mem. N.Y. C. of C. Clubs: Book and Snake (Yale) N. Hempstead (L.I.) Country, Midday, Wall Street, Candian (N.Y.C.); Sands Point Golf. Home: Oyster Bay LI NY Died Jan. 1972.

NEELY, JOHN MARSHALL, III, physician; b. Elmwood, Neb., 1904; s. John Marshall and Edna (Perry) N: M.D., U. Neb., 1930; m. Mary Foulon Barlow, July 9, 1929; children—Mary Jean, Hugh Williams. Intern, U. Neb. Hosp., Omaha, 1930; intern Ancker Hosp., St. Paul, 1930-31, resident in pathology, 1931-32, resident in roentgenology, 1933; postgrad. course U. Minn., 1931-32; resident in radiology Lincoln (Neb.) Gen. Hosp., 1936-37, pathologist and radiologist, until 1969; radiologist Neb. Orthopaedic Hosp.; attending radiologist VA Hosp., St. Elizabeths Hosp, Neb. State Orthopaedic Hosp. (all Lincoln), Lutheran Hosp., Beatrice, Neb.; sr. instr. radiology U. Mich., 1938-39; asst. prof. radiology Creighton U., until 1969. Chmn., Neb. Bd. Med. Examiners, 1949-59. Pres., Lincoln Symphony. Served to capt., M.C., USNR, 1942-45. Diplomate Am. Bd. Radiology. Fellow Am. Soc. Clin. Pathology, A.C.P., Am. Coll. Radiology; mem. A.M.A., Radiol. Soc. N.Am., Am. Radium Soc., Lancaster County Med. Soc. (pres.), Alpha Sigma Phi, Nu Sigma Nu. Elk. Home: Lincoln NE Died May 9, 1969.

NEFF, HAROLD HOPKINS, lawyer; b. Harrisonburg, Va., Oct. 8, 1891; s. Dr. John H. and Brownie (Morrison) N.; B.S., M.A., LL.B., U. of Va., 1917; student U. of Berlin, U. of Marburg, Germany, U. of Caen, France, 1912-13; m. Henriette Thomas, Dec. 16, 1918 (div. Feb. 1950); children—Philippe, Jacqueline (Mrs. Wright). Yvonne (Mrs. Calomeris); m. 2d, Irene F. Getz, Oct. 28, 1950; 1 stepson, Harry D. Getz. Admitted to N.Y. bar, 1917; practiced law in N.Y. City, 1921-24; prof. internat. law, U. of Va., 1924-26; practiced law in Paris, France, 1927-31; represented Am. interests in Europe during liquidation of Kreuger Cos., 1932; spl. adviser to State Dept., 1933; dir. Export-Import Bank, 1933-35; asst. chief securities div. FTC, 1933-34; asst. gen. counsel SEC, 1934-35, dir. forms and regulations div., 1936-38, European rep. in London, Eng., 1939, foreign expert, 1940; spl. asst. to under sec. of war 1941-47; spl. asst. to sec. of army, 1947-48; Am. del. to Internat. Trade Conf., Geneva, Switzerland, 1947; War Dept. rep. on policy com. Bd. Econ. Warfare, Exec. Com. Econ. Fgn. Policy, Trade Agreements Com., Com. for Reciprocity Information, Nat. Munitions Control Bd.; ret. Served as 2d lt., U.S. Army Tank Corps, A.E.F., 1917-19. Recipient Exceptional Civilian Service award, 1946. Mem. Am. Bar Assn., Am. Soc. of Internat. Law, Raven Soc., Phi Beta Kappa, Sigma Chi. Clubs: Army and Navy Country, University (Washington, D.C.). Contbr. articles to law jours. Home: Washington DC Died Apr. 15, 1971; buried Culpeper (Va.) Nat. Cemetery.

NEGLEY, JAMES SCOTT soldier, financier; b. E. Liberty, Pa. (now East End of Pittsburgh), Dec. 22, 1826; ed. public schools and Western U. of Pa.; enlisted in Duquesne Grays at 17, when it became part of 1st Pa. regt., and served through Mexican war; after war engaged in mfg.; elected brig. gen. 18th div. Pa. militia; offered his div. to State authorities in Dec. 1860; in 10 days in April 1861, organized, clothed and equipped brigade for 3 months' service; re-commissioned brig. gen.; served through war, taking part in many battles; took a leading part in battle of Stone River, Dec. 31, 1862, and was promoted maj. gen. of vols.; led forward movement upon Tallahoma and took prominent part at Chickamauga; m. Kate De Losey (died); m. 2d, Grace Ashton. Mem. Congress, 1869-73, 1875-77, 1885-87; actively engaged in promotion and construction of rys.; acted as pres. and v.p. of several ry. cos.; 15 yrs. one of mgrs. Nat. Home for Volunteers; pres. Nat. Union League of America; mem. G.A.R. and other mil. orgns. Home: Plainfield, N.J. Died 1901.

NEILL, THOMAS HEWSON army officer; b. Phila., Apr. 9, 1826; s. Dr. Henry and Martha (Duffield) N.; grad. U.S. Mil. Acad., 1847; m. Eva Looney, Nov. 20,

1873, 3 children. Commd. 2d lt. 5th Inf., U.S. Army, 1847; asst. prof. of drawing U.S. Mil. Acad., 1853-57; served as capt. in Utah expdn. and in N.M., 1857-61; commd. col. 23d Pa. Volunteers, 1862, served at siege of Yorktown; brevetted maj., 1862, promoted brig. gen. U.S. Volunteers, 1862, brevetted lt. col., then col., 1863; brevetted brig. gen. U.S. Army, 1865, maj. gen. U.S. Volunteers; insp. gen. U.S. Army, 1867-69 with hdqrs. at New Orleans; commd. lt. col., 1869; comdt. of cadets U.S. Mil. Acad., 1875-79; known as Beau Neill. Died Phila., Mar. 12, 1885.

NEILSON, JOHN army officer, Continental congressman; b. Raritan Landing, N.J., Mar. 11, 1745; s. Dr. John and Joanna (Coejeman) N.; attended U. Pa.; m. Catherine Voorhees, Dec. 31, 1768, 11 children including James. Commd capt. during Revolutionary War; made col. by Pa. Provincial Congress, 1775; commd. col. 2d Regt., Middlesex Militia, 1776; commd. brig. gen. N.J. Militia, 1777; mem. Continental Congress from N.J., 1778-79; in command N.J. Militia at Elizabethtown and Newark, 1779; dep. q.m. gen. for N.J., 1780-83; mem. N.J. Conv. which ratified U.S. Constn., 1790; judge N.J. Ct. of Common Pleas, 1795-98; mem. N.J. Assembly, 1800-01; register-recorder New Brunswick (N.J.), 1796-1821; elder, trustee 1st Presbyn. Ch. of New Brunswick; trustee Rutgers Coll., 1782-1833; presented with a sword by Lafayette, 1824. Died New Brunswick, Mar. 3, 1833; buried Van Liew Cemetery, New Brunswick.

NELLES, PERCY W. Canadian naval officer; b. Brantford, Ont., Jan. 7, 1892; s. Brig. Gen. C. M. and Ida Maude Mary (Walker) N.; grad. Lakefield Prep. Sch.; student Trinity Coll., Port Hope, Ont.; Royal Naval Staff Coll., Eng., 1924, Imperial Defence Coll., Eng., 1933; m. Helen Schuyler Allen, May 17, 1915; children—Charles Macklem, William Allen. Commd. as cadet (2d to join) Royal Canadian Navy, 1908, advanced to vice admiral, 1941, chief naval staff, 1934-44. sr. flag officer (overseas) head Canadian Naval Mission, Eng., since 1944. Awarded war medals, 1914-18, Star, British War, Victory, King George V Coronation, King George V Jubilee, King George VI Coronation medals. Decorated Companion of the Bath, 1943. Home: Vine Lynne, 7 Rideau Gate. Office: Naval Service Hdqrs., Ottawa, Ont., Can. Died June 13, 1951.

NELSON, CHARLES PEMBROKE congressman; b. Waterville, Me., July 2, 1907; s. John E. and Margaret (Crosby) N.; B.A., Colby Coll., 1928; LL.B., Harvard, 1931; m. Elisabeth Gross, Sept. 18, 1931 (dec.); 1 dau., Elisabeth Ann; m. 2d, Arlene S. Emry, 1954. Admitted to Me. bar, 1931; sec. to Congressman John E. Nelson, 1931-32; in gen. law practice, 1932-42 and 1946-48; city solicitor of Augusta, 1934-42; chief state arson div., 1941-42; mem. Me. State Bd. Bar Examiners, 1946-49; mayor, City of Augusta, 1947-48; mem. 81st to 84th Congresses, 2d Me. Dist.; tchr. U. Fla., Gainesville, 1957; practice law, Bath, Me., 1958. Apptd. dir. Urban Renewal, Bath; chief trial counsel Me. Hwy. Commn. 1958-61. Served with U.S. Army, 1942-46; lt. col. N.G., Res. Home: 5 Prospect St., Augusta, Me. Died June 8, 1962.

NELSON, JOSEPH E. adj. gen. Minn.; b. Crookston, Minn., Jan. 9, 1897; ed. pub. schs. in Crookston; grad. Inf. Sch., Army War Coll. Apptd. asst. adj. gen., Minn., 1927, adj. gen., 1949-—. Enlisted as pvt., Co. I, 3d Minn. Inf., 1915, and advanced through grades to maj. gen.; in Fed. service, Mex. Border, World War I, II; state dir. Selective Service, Minn., World War II. Address: 1389 Grantham St., St. Paul 55108. Died Dec. 30, 1960; buried Ft. Snelling Nat. Cemetery.

NELSON, PERRY ALBERT, communications exec.; b. Rockland, Ida., Dec. 21, 1916; s. Bert Albert and Polly May (Perry) N.; student Ida. State Coll., 1935-36, 40; m. Helen Eleanor Lindsay, Dec. 21, 1941; children—James P., Richard D., Steven B., Connie Jean. Ida. safety dir., 1941; exec. sec. Ida. traffic adv. com. to War Dept., 1942; clk. irrigation and reclamation com. U.S. Ho. of Reps., 1942-43; field rep. Ida. Planning Bd., 1946-47; dist mgr. No. Life Ins. Co., 1947-49; owner Western Real Estate & Ins. Co., Pocatello, Ida., 1949-68; member board of directors Idaho Radio Corporation, Mountain States Tel. & Tel. Co., Denver, also mem. Ida. adv. bd. Power County rep. Ida. Senate, 1941; candidate U.S. Congress, 2d Dist. Ida., 1946. Past pres. Pocatello Real Estate Bd.; member of Idaho Nuclear Commission; vice president Bannock County Centennial Commn. Spl. agt. U.S. Mil. Intelligence, World War II. Decorated Legion of Merit; Man of Year award Jr. C. of C.; Pocatello Chief award for outstanding community service; Ida. Realtor of Year, 1968. Member of Idaho (president 1963-64, dir., member executive committee), Pocatello (past pres.) chambers commerce, Pocatello Property Owners Assn., Ida. Real Estate Assn. (past pres.), Inst. Real Estate Mgmt., Internat. Real Estate Fedn., National Institute of Real Estate Brokers, National Association of Real Estate Bds. (director). Elk (past exalted ruler), Rotarian (past pres. Pocatello). Home: Pocatello ID Died Sept. 28, 1968; buried Rockland ID

NELSON, RALPH THOMAS, army officer; b. Lebanon, Ind., June 19, 1902; s. Lloyd T. and Florence E. (Alexander) N.; student Purdue U., 1920-23; B.S., U.S. Mil. Acad., 1928; grad. Indsl. Coll. of Armed Forces, 1953; m. Christine Clarke, Oct. 10, 1929; children—Thomas C. (U.S. Army), Alexa N. Plantz. Commd. 2d lt. U.S. Army, 1928, advanced through grades to maj. gen., 1958; inf. assignments, U.S. and Hawaii, 1928-42; signal officer, 4th Div., 1942; signal officer 9th div. XV Corps, also dep. signal officer 15th Army and U.S. Forces, Austria, 1943-46; various assignments U.S., 1947-53; signal officer X Corps and 8th Army, Korea, 1953-54; comdg. gen. Signal Tng. Center, Ft. Gordon, also comdg. gen. Electronic Proving Ground, Ft. Huachuca, Ariz., 1955-58; dep. chief signal officer U.S. Army, 1958-59, chief signal officer, 1959-62. Decorated D.S.M., Legion of Merit, Bronze Star, Purple Heart; Ulchi medal (Korea). Mem. Armed Forces Communications and Electronics Assn. (3d v.p.). Home: Arlington VA Died Oct. 1, 1968; buried Arlington Nat. Cemetery, Arlington VA

NELSON, ROBERT FRANKLIN paper mfr.; b. Moultrie, Ga., 1897; s. G.S. and Eugenia Roberta (Greene) N.; B.S., U.S. Naval Acad., 1918; m. Sylvia Hope Anthony, Feb. 19, 1921; children—Robert Franklin, Joan (Mrs. Paul G. Lee). With Rinelander Paper Co., 1947-55, v.p. and sales mgr. exec. v.p., 1948-55, dir., 1950-55; with Shellmar-Betner div. Continental Can Co., Inc., 1955-59; chairman of board, exec. v.p. Electronics Equipment Engineers, Inc., Dallas, 1958-—. Served as midshipman USN, 1915, ensign 1918, lt. (j.g.) 1918-22, comdr. 1944-45. Mem. Kappa Sigma. Republican. Club: Army and Navy (Washington). Address: 1121 Avocado Isle, Ft. Lauderdale, Fla. Died June 1963.

NELSON, ROGER army officer, congressman; b. Frederick County, Md., 1759; s. Dr. Arthur and Lucy (Waters) N.; attended Coll. William and Mary; m. Mary Brooke Sim, 1787; m. 2d, Eliza Harrison, Feb. 2, 1797; 8 children. Commd. lt. Md. Militia, 1780, advanced to brig. gen.; admitted to Md. bar, 1785; mem. Md. Ho. of Dels., 1795, 1801, 02; mem. U.S. Ho. of Reps. from Md., 8th-11th congresses, Nov. 6, 1804-May 14, 1810; asso. judge 6th Jud. Circuit of Md., 1810-15. Died Frederick, Md., June 7, 1815; buried Mt. Olivet Cemetery, Frederick.

NELSON, THOMAS gov. Va., Continental congressman; b. Yorktown, Va., Dec. 26, 1738; s. William and Elizabeth (Burwell) N.; grad. Trinity Coll., Cambridge (Eng.) U., 1761; m. Lucy Grymes, July 29, 1762, 11 children including Hugh. Mem. His Majesty's Council of Va., 1764; mem. Va. Ho. of Burgesses, 1774; del. 1st Va. Provincial Conv., Williamsburg, 1774; del. from Va. to Continental Congress, 1775-77, attended 3d Va. Conv., Richmond, 1776 (where Va. Resolutions were drawn which evolved into Declaration of Independence); signer of Declaration of Independence; brig. gen., comdr.-in-chief Va. Militia, 1778; mem. Continental Congress from Va.; financier, gov., comdr. Va. Militia; mem. Va. Assembly 1779, 80; gov. Va., 1781; took part in Yorktown campaign as head of Va. Militia, 1781; statue of him located in Capital Park, Richmond. Died Hanover County, Va., Jan. 4, 1789; buried Old Churchyard, Yorktown.

NELSON, THOMAS comdr. U.S.N., retired; b. at sea, Dec. 5, 1834; ed. private schools; m. Baltimore, June 14, 1865, Annie J. Ames. Entered merchant marine, 1849; so employed until Jan., 1862; joined navy as vol. with rank of master's mate; served through Civil war and rose to rank of acting master; transferred, 1868, to regular navy, and commissioned master; served successively in West Indies, European, Asiatic and Pacific squadrons; employed during intervals between sea duty on hydrographic equipment and ordnance duty until retired, Dec. 5, 1896, and rank of comdr. During Spanish-Am. war on duty with 2d Light House Dist. and 2d div. of the Coast Defense; insp. 16th lighthouse dist., 1902-03. Mem. Loyal Legion. Clubs: Army and Navy (Washington); Cosmos (San Francisco); Naval Academy (Annapolis). Address: Annapolis, Md.

NELSON, THOMAS MADUIT congressman; b. Oak Hill, Va., Sept 27, 1782; attended common schs. Commd. capt. 10th Inf. Regt., later maj. 30th and 18th inf. regts., during War of 1812; reduced to capt. after war, resigned commn., 1815; mem. U.S. Ho. of Reps. (Democrat) from Va., 14th-15th congresses, Dec. 4, 1816-19. Died nr. Columbus, Ga., Nov. 10, 1853; buried Linwood Cemetery, Columbus.

NELSON, WILLIAM naval officer, army officer; b. Maysville, Ky., 1825; s. Dr. Thomas W. and Frances (Doniphan) N.; Commd. midshipman U.S. Navy, 1840, passed midshipman, 1846; served in Mexican War; commd. master, 1854, lt., 1855; Union supporter, sent by Pres. Lincoln to help organize Loyalist, 1861; established Camp Dick Robinson; commd. brig. gen. U.S. Army, 1861, commanded 4th div. Dept. of Ohio; commd maj. gen. U.S. Volunteers, 1862; commanded Louisville, Ky. Shot in altercation with Brig. Gen. Jeff C. Davis, Louisville, Sept. 29, 1862.

NELSON, WILLIAM, mgmt. exec., ret. naval officer; b. Minn., May 23, 1893; s. C. and M. (Christen) N.; B.S., U.S. Naval Acad., 1915; M.S., Mass. Inst. Tech., 1920; m. Faye Callison, Mar. 6, 1918; children—William Ross, Naida (Mrs. John Salberg) (dec.). Commd. ensign USN, 1915, advanced through grades to capt., 1941; engaged in naval constrn., World War I; gen. insp. naval aircraft Eastern U.S., 1930-34; naval observer, 1937; chief engr. Naval Aircraft Factory, 1938-40; gen. rep. Bur. Aero., 1944-45; ret., 1945; asst. to pres. Gar Wood Industries, 1947-49; with ACF Brill Motors Co., Phila., 1950-55, pres., 1954-55; div. mgr. Hall-Scott, Inc., 1950, pres., 1957-60; pres. J. G. Brill Co., 1956-57; chmn. bd. Teleregister Corp., Stamford, Conn., 1960-61; vice chmn. bd. DuBois Chems., Inc., Cin., 1960-63, dir., 1960-64; cons. W. R. Grace & Co., 1964-67; dir. Nelson Knitting Works, 1950-62; dir. Altamil Corp., Indpls., 1958-69, chmn. bd,. 1961-63; dir. Alson Industries, Inc., 1970-71. Mem. U.S. Naval Inst., U.S. Navy Acad. Alumni Assn. Author: Sea Plane Design, 1936; Airplane Lofting, 1941. Home: Portola Valley CA Died Dec. 8, 1971.

NESLEN, CLARENCE CANNON, lawyer; b. Salt Lake City, Jan. 14, 1907; s. Charles Clarence and Grace (Cannon) N.; A.B., U. Utah, 1933; J.D., George Washington U., 1937; M. Leone Rockwood, Apr. 7, 1937; children—Clarence Cannon, Richard R., Roger H., Elizabeth. Admitted to D.C. bar, 1936, Utah bar, 1937, U.S. Supreme Ct., 1955, U.S. Ct. Mil. Appeals, 1955; review atty. Social Security Bd., 1936-39; area adminstr. Railroad Retirement Bd., Utah, Ida., Nev., 1939-40; counsel Utah Tax Commn., 1946-47; mem. firm Neslen & Mock, Salt Lake City, 1958-70. Dir. Lone Star Mining & Devel. Corp., Monte Cristo Corp. Chairman, Utah Merit Council. Served to lt. col. AUS, 1940-46. col. Judge Adv. Gen. Corps Res.; civilian aide for Utah to Secretary of Army. Decorated Bronze Star medal. Mem. Am. Legion (state comdr. 1949-50), Beta Theta Pi. Mem. Ch. Jesus Christ of Latter-day Saints. Club: Lions (pres. 1953-54). Home: Salt Lake City UT Died May 2, 1970; buried Salt Lake City Cemetery.

NESMITH, JAMES WILLIS army officer, senator; b. New Brunswick, Can., July 23, 1820; s. William Morrison and Harriet (Willis) N.; m. Pauline Goff, 1846. Went to Ohio, 1838; among 1st settlers to Ore., 1843; judge Provisional Govt. of Ore. Territory, 1845; commd. capt. Volunteers in Cayuse War, 1848; U.S. marshal for Ore., 1853-55; in Yakima War of 1855-56; supt. Indian affairs for Ore. Territory, 1857-59; mem. U.S. Senate from Ore., 1861-67; mem. bd. visitors U.S. Mil. Acad., 1866; road supr. Polk County (Ore.), 1868; mem. U.S. Ho. of Reps. from Ore., 43d Congress, Dec. 1, 1873-1875. Died Rickreall, Ore., June 17, 1885.

NETHERWOOD, DOUGLAS B(LAKESHAW) army officer; b. Birmingham, Eng., Feb. 4, 1885; s. Tom and Ann (Wood) N.; brought to U.S., 1887, naturalized, 1910; B.S. in Mech. Engring., Agr. and Mech. Coll. of Tex., 1908; M.B.A., Harvard Grad. Sch. of Business Adminstrn., 1927; grad. Army Industrial Coll., 1925, Air Corps Tactical Sch., 1932, Army War Coll., 1936; m. Harriet V. C. Browne, April 30, 1919; children—Douglas Blakeshaw, Francis Bowne, William Draper, Elisabeth Grant. Enlisted in U.S. Army, 1908; commd. 2d lt. Coast Arty. Corps, 1911, and advanced through the grades to brig. gen. (temp.), Oct. 1940; detailed to Signal Corps for flying training, Dec. 1913; made first solo flight, San Diego, Calif., Feb. 7, 1914; comd. Aviation Repair Dept., Dallas, Texas, Nov. 1917-Mar. 1921; comd. Borinquen Field, Puerto Rico. Awarded Victory medal. Mem. Early Birds. Clubs: Army and Navy (Manila, P.I.). Home: 4936 Rodman St. N.W., Washington, D.C.* Deceased.

NETTLETON, ALVRED BAYARD soldier, journalist, writer; b. Berlin, Delaware Co., O., Nov. 14, 1838; s. Hiram and Lavinia (Janes) N.; reared on farm; A.B., Oberlin Coll., 1863, A.M., 1866; m. Melissa Tenney, Jan. 8, 1863; 1 dau., Caroline Nettleton Thurber. Enlisted in U.S. vols. while at Oberlin Coll., 1861; served in the field through the Civ. War; promoted 1st lt. 2d Ohio Cav., Oct. 8, 1861; capt., Mar. 10, 1862; maj., July 18, 1863; lt. col. comdg. regt., Nov. 5, 1864; col., Apr. 22, 1865; bvtd. brig. gen. vols., Mar. 13, 1865, "for gallant and meritorious service"; resigned after close of war, June 13, 1865; fought in 72 battles and minor engagements, including capture of Knoxville, Grant's campaign of the Wilderness, Sheridan's campaigns of the Shenandoah Valley, the siege of Richmond and service against Confed. Indians in Ind. Ter.; had 3 horses shot in action; after war studied law; editor and part propr. Sandusky (O.) Daily Register, 1867-68; del. Rep. Nat. Conv., 1868; pub. Chicago Advance, 1868-69; associated with Jay Cooke in projection and constrn. of N.P. R.R., 1870-75; mng. editor Philadelphia Inquirer, 1875-76; in mining and mfg., 1877-80; founder, editor and propr. Minneapolis Daily Tribune, 1880-85; mem. Anti-Saloon Rep. Nat. Com., 1884-89; asst. sec. U.S. Treasury, 1890-93, acting sec. several months after death of Sec. Windom. Mem. World's Columbian Commn., 1890-93; trustee of Oberlin Coll., 22 yrs. Retired from business to do lit. work, 1909. Republican. Congregationalist. Author: Trusts or Competition, 1900. Address: Chicago, Ill. Died 1911.

NEUBERGER, RICHARD LEWIS U.S. senator, author; b. Portland, Ore., Dec. 26, 1912; s. Isaac and Ruth (Lewis) N.; student U. Ore., 1930-35; m. Maurine Brown, Dec. 20, 1945. Newspaperman, writer, 1928-—; N.W. corr. N.Y. Times, 1939-54. Ore. state senator, 13th Dist., 1948-54; U.S. senator from Ore., 1955-—. Served from 2d lt. to capt. AUS, 1942-45. Mem. Am. Polar Soc. (dir.), Soc. Mil. Engrs., Vets. Fgn. Wars, Ore.

State Grange, Pi Tau Pi. Democrat. Jewish religion. Clubs: City, Tualatin Country (Portland). Author: An Army of the Aged (with Kelley Loe), 1936; Integrity—The Life of George W. Norris (with Stephen B. Kahn), 1937; Our Promised Land, 1938; The Lewis and Clark Expedition, 1951; Royal Canadian Mounted Police, 1953; Adventures in Politics—We go to the Legislature, 1954. Home: 1910 S.W. Clifton St., N.W., Portland, Ore. Died Mar. 9, 1960.

NEUMANN, ERNEST K(ARL) lawyer; b. Delavan, Ill., Dec. 15, 1898; s. Ernest W. and Lina (Baessler) N.; LL.B., U. Kan., 1923; m. Elizabeth Ellen Hogue, Dec. 2, 1931. Admitted to N.M. bar, 1923, practiced at Carlsbad, until 1931; police judge, Carlsbad, 1924-25; city atty. of Carlsbad, 1926-31; atty. gen. of N.M., 1931-35; mem. N.M. Ho. of Reps. (Dem. floor leader), 1927; interstate river commr. of N.M., 1931-35; chmn. bd. supervisors N.M. Motor Patrol, 1934-35; mem. State Bd. Liquor Control, 1933-35; asst. gen. counsel in charge of litigation and asso. gen. counsel in charge legal dept. H.O.L.C., Washington; later asso. gen. counsel Fed. Home Loan Bank Bd.; gen. counsel, mem. bd. trustees Group Health Assn., Washington, 1935-42. Served with USN, 1917-19; commd. officer N.M. N.G., 1923, capt. cav., 1931-35; lt. comdr. USNR, 1935-41; to active duty USAF, 1942-47, assigned to mil. govt., 1943, separated as lt. col. and assigned exec. officer Mil. Govt. Hesse in civilian capacity; upon assumption of occupational duties by State Dept. assigned pub. affairs officer for Hesse-HICOG, resigned 1951; pvt. practice law Carlsbad, N.M., 1951; now mem. law firm Neal, Neuman & Neal. Mem. Am., N.M. bar assns., Am. Legion, Res. Officers Assn. U.S. (pres. Wiesbaden, Germany, chpt. 3d term; nat. v.p. for ETO), Phi Alpha Delta. Quaker. Mason (32 deg.). Home: 712 Riverside. Office: 601 N. Canal St., Carlsbad, N.M. Died Apr. 3, 1959; buried Carlsbad Cemetery.

NEVILLE, JOHN army officer; b. Occoquan River, Va., July 26, 1731; s. George and Ann (Burroughs) N.; m. Winifred Oldham, Aug. 24, 1754; a son, Col. Presley Neville. Served under Washington in Gen. Braddock's expdn. against Ft. Duquesne, 1755; sheriff Winchester (Va.); comdr. Ft. Pitt; commd. lt. col. Continental Army, 1776, col., 1777; served in battles of Trenton, Germantown, Princeton, Monmouth; brevetted brig. gen., 1783; mem. Supreme Exec. Council of Pa.; mem. Pa. Conv. to ratify U.S. Constn.; mem. Pa. Constl. Conv., 1789-90; insp. survey for collection of whiskey tax in Western Pa., 1792-95, participated in Whiskey Rebellion, 1794; fed. agt. for sale pub. lands N.W. of Ohio, 1796. Died Montour's Island, Pa., July 29, 1803.

NEVILLE, ROBERT, fgn. corr.; b. Vinita, Okla., May 12, 1905; s. Oliver and Alice (McClure) N.; student U. Cal.; Litt.B., Columbia, 1928, M.S., 1929; m. Mary Sentinelli, 1947. Typesetter Campbell Co. Record, Gillette, Wyo., 1919; reporter N.Y. Post, N.Y. Times, 1929; reporter N.Y. Herald Tribune, 1929-36, fgn. corr., 1936-37; fgn. news writer Time, 1937, fgn. news editor, 1938-40; fgn. news editor PM, 1940-41; head news bur. Time-Life, New Delhi, India, 1946-48, Buenos Aires, 1948-50. Far East corr., Hong Kong, 1950-53, head news bur., Rome, 1953-56, head news bur., Istanbul, Turkey, 1956-59; contbr. Look, Harper's, Encounter on Vatican affairs, 1959-70. Served as lt. col., AUS, 1942-46; editor, publs. officer Stars and Stripes, Mediterranean. Decorated, Legion of Merit. Club: Overseas Press (N.Y.C.). Author: The World of the Vatican, 1962. Died Feb. 1970.

NEVILLE, WENDELL CUSHING officer U.S.M.C.; b. Portsmouth, Va., May 12, 1870; s. Willis H. and Mary Elizabeth (Cushing) N.; ed. Galt's Acad. (Norfolk, Va.), U.S. Naval Acad.; m. Frances Adelphia Howell, Jan. 4, 1898; 1 dau., Frances Howell (Mrs. J. P. W. Vest). Apptd. naval cadet, Sept. 13, 1886; commd. 2d lt. U.S. Marine Corps, July 1, 1892; promoted through grades to maj. gen., Dec. 9, 1920. With 1st Batt. at taking of Guantanamo Bay, Spanish-Am. War, 1898; comdr. co. in Boxer Campaign, China; participated in capture of Peking; in Philippine Campaign; mil. gov. Province of Basilan, 1901-02; comdr. marines at taking of Havana, 1906; comd. 2d Regt. Marines at taking of Vera Cruz, Mexico, Apr. 1914; comdr. Am. Legation Guard, Peking, 1915-17; comd. 5th Regt., 4th Brigade Marines, 2d Div., A.E.F., Jan.-July 1918, participating in occupation Toulon sector and in Aisne-Marne offensive (Bois de Belleau); comd. 4th Brigade, July 1918-Aug. 1919, participating in battles of Soissons, St. Mihiel, Blanc Mont, Meuse-Argonne, march to the Rhine, occupation of Coblentz bridgehead, etc. Bvtd. capt., Aug. 10, 1898, "for conspicuous conduct" in Battle of Guantanamo Bay, Cuba; awarded Congressional Medal of Honor, "for distinguished conduct" during engagement at Vera Cruz, Apr. 21 and 22, 1914; D.S.M., "for exceptionally meritorious and distinguished services," in World War; D.S.M. (Navy); Croix de Guerre with palm (French) "for gallantry in action," also Croix de Guerre with palm "for Battle of Blanc Mont," and 3 other croix de guerre, 2 bronze stars and 2 palms (all French); Officer Legion of Honor (French). Episcopalian. Apptd. comdt. Marine Corps, Mar. 5, 1929. Address: Washington, D.C. Died July 8, 1930.

NEVIN, ROBERT JENKINS clergyman; b. Allegheny, Pa., Nov. 24, 1839; s. Rev. Dr. John W. N.; grad. Franklin and Marshall Coll., Lancaster, Pa., 1859, hon. D.D., Union; LL.D., Hobart; unmarried. Served in Civil war as lt. 122d Pa. vols., 1862; later capt., Battery I, Pa. vol. arty., and bvt. maj. U.S. vols. Grad. Gen. Theol. Sem., New York, 1867; rector Ch. of the Nativity, Bethlehem, Pa., 1868; rector St. Paul's Ch., Rome, Italy, 1869-—; pres. conv., and of standing com., Am. Chs. in Europe; del. Am. Chs. in Europe to Gen. Conv. P.E. Ch. in U.S., 1889-—. Built St. Paul's Am. Ch., Rome, 1870-76. Author: St. Paul's Within the Walls, 1878; Reunion Conf. at Bonn, 1875. Address: Rome, Italy. Died 1906.

NEVIUS, HENRY M. lawyer; b. Monmouth Co., N.J., Jan. 30, 1841; s. James S. and Hannah (Bowe) N.; descendant of Joanus Nefus, Newburgh, N.Y., 1636; acad. and high sch. edn., Freehold, N.J., and Grand Rapids, Mich.; m. Matilda H. Herbert, Dec. 27, 1871. Pvt. Co. K, 1st N.Y. Lincoln Cav., Aug. 12, 1861 (co. recruited in Grand Rapids and joined N.Y. regt. in field); discharged as regimental q.m. sergt., Dec. 31, 1862, to become 2d lt. Co. D, 7th Mich. Cav.; later joined 25th N.Y. Cav.; while serving as 1st lt. in comd. of co. in front of Washington, lost left arm, July 11, 1864; hon. discharged, July 1865. Engaged in ins. business; apptd. U.S. assessor internal revenue, Monmouth County, N.J., 1866; admitted to practice as atty., 1873, counsellor, 1876; practiced at Freehold, 1873-75, then at Red Bank, N.J.; mem. N.J. Senate, 1888, 1889, 1890 (pres. 1890); judge Circuit Ct., Hudson County Dist., 1896-1903; pros. atty. Monmouth County, 1904-08, resigned. Republican. Comdr. Dept. of N.J. G.A.R., 1884-86; comdr.-in-chief G.A.R., 1908-09. Address: Red Bank, N.J. Died 1911.

NEW, ANTHONY congressman; b. Gloucester County, Va., 1747; studied law. Admitted to Va. bar, practiced law; served as col. Continental Army during Revolutionary War; mem. U.S. Ho. of Reps. (Democrat) from Va., 3d-8th congresses, 1793-1805; moved to Elkton, Ky.; mem. U.S. Ho. of Reps. (Dem.) from Ky., 12th, 15th, 17th congresses, 1811-13, 17-19, 21-23; engaged in farming. Died "Dunheath" nr. Elkton, Mar. 2, 1833; buried "Dunheath."

NEW, HARRY STEWART postmaster gen.; b. Indianapolis, Ind., Dec. 31, 1858; s. John C. and Melissa B. N.; ed. Indianapolis pub. schs. and Butler University; hon. LL.D. from Butler University, 1927. With Indianapolis Journal for twenty-five years, as reporter, editor, and pub., 1878-1903; later pres. Bedford Stone and Construction Co. Mem. Ind. State Senate, 1896-1900; mem. Rep. Nat. Com., 1900-12 (chmn. 1907-08); U.S. Senator, 1917-23; postmaster general, Mar. 5, 1923-Mar. 5, 1929; capt. and a.a.g. 3d Brigade, 2d Div., 7th Army Corps, Spanish-Am. War, 1898. U.S. Commr. Century of Progress Expn., Chicago, 1933-34. Home: Indianapolis, Ind. Died May 9, 1937.

NEWBERRY, TRUMAN HANDY ex-secretary of navy, ex-senator; b. Detroit, Mich., Nov. 5, 1864; s. John S. and Helen Parmelee (Handy) N.; Ph.B., Yale, 1885, hon. A.M., 1910; m. Harriet Josephine Barnes, February 7, 1888 (died Jan. 18, 1943); children—Mrs. Carol Lord, Barnes, Phelps. Superintendent of construction, p.m. and general freight and passenger agent, Detroit, Bay City & Alpena Ry., 1885-87; pres. and treas. Detroit Steel & Spring Co., 1887-1901; dir. Packard Motor Car Co. since 1903; chmn. bd. dirs. Detroit Steel Casting Co. since 1937; director Detroit Trust Co., Cleveland-Cliffs Iron Co., Grace Hosp. Asst. sec. of navy, 1905-08, sec. of navy, in cabinet of President Roosevelt, Dec. 1, 1908-Mar. 6, 1900; mem. U.S. Senate from Mich., term 1919-25, resigned 1922. One of organizersch. State Naval Brigade, serving as landsman, 1895, lt. and navigator, 1897-98; commd. U.S. Navy as lt. (jr. grade), May, 1898, and served on U.S.S. Yosemite through Spanish-Am. War; col. and a.d.c. to the govt., Mich. Nat. Guard, 1899. Lt. comdr. U.S. Naval Fleet Reserve, June 6, 1917, and asst. to comdt. 3d Naval Dist., N.Y. Republican. Presbyterian. Clubs: Union, University, New York Yacht, St. Anthony (New York); Chicago, Yondotega, Detroit, Country Club, Detroit Boat, Bloomfield Country (Detroit); Grosse Pointe, Grosse Pointe Hunt (Grosse Pointe). Author: Log of the U.S.S. Yosemite, 1899. Home: 123 Lake Shore Road, Grosse Pointe Farms, Mich. Office: Buhl Bldg., Detroit, Mich. Died Oct. 3, 1945.

NEWBERRY, WALTER CASS capitalist; b. Waterville, N.Y., Dec. 23, 1835; s. Col. Amasa S. N. (U.S. loan commr. under President Polk); acad. edn.; entered commercial house of uncle, Oliver Newberry, Detroit, 1858; was one of executors of his estate. Enlisted in Civil War, pvt. 81st N.Y. Inf.; lt., 1861; capt., 1862; maj. (promoted in 24th N.Y. Cav.), 1863; col., 1864; bvt. brig. gen., Mar. 31, 1865, for services at Dinwiddie C.H., where he was severely wounded. Settled in Petersburg, Va., Sept. 1865; mayor, 1869; supt. pub. property, Va., 4 yrs.; built reservoir water works, Richmond. Removed to Chicago, 1876; engaged in mercantile business and as executor and trustee estates of his family; postmaster, 1888-89; mem. 52d Congress, 1891-93. Home: Chicago, Ill. Died July 20, 1912.

NEWBILL, WILLARD DOUGLAS ret. army officer; b. Tappahannock, Va., Aug. 28, 1874; s. William Jeffries and Annie Eliza (Cauthorn) N.; grad. U.S. Mil. Acad., 1897, Sch. Submarine Defense, 1905. Commd. add. 2d lt. 5th Inf., 1897, trans. to 7th Arty., 1898; capt. 34th Vol. Inf., 1899; hon. mustered out vols., Apr. 17, 1901; 1st lt. 6th Arty., Apr. 8, 1900; capt. Arty. Corps, Aug. 22, 1901; assigned to 3d Field Arty., Jan. 28, 1910; maj. 2d Field Arty., Dec. 27, 1912; trans. to 4th Field Arty., June 16, 1913; maj. q.m., Jan. 2, 1914; lt. col., July 26, 1916; col., May 15, 1917. Served in Spanish-Am. War in P.R., 1898-99, in P.I. 1899-1901; with Gen. Lawton in Northern Luzon campaign; served on Mexican border, 1911-13, 16-17; staff duty, 1906-10, 14-17; in charge reunion of Blue and Gray, Vicksburg Nat. Mil. Park, 1917; comd. 3d F.A., AEF, France, 1918-19; participated in last Meuse-Argonne offensive. Mem. S.A.R. Clubs: Army and Navy (Washington), University (Buffalo). Home: Irvington, Va. Deceased.

NEWCOMER, HENRY CLAY army officer; b. Upton, Pa., Apr. 3, 1861; s. David and Mary Shelley (Funk) N.; grad. U.S. Mil. Acad., 1886, Engr. Sch. of Application, 1889; m. Rebecca E. Kosier, of Byron, Ill., Dec. 29, 1886 (died Mar. 31, 1913); m. 2d, Mrs. Lily A. Foster, of Washington, D.C., May 18, 1915. Commd. 2d lt. engrs., July 1, 1886; 1st lt., July 23, 1888; capt., July 31, 1897; maj., Apr. 23, 1904; lt. col., Feb. 9, 1910; col., May 2, 1915; brigadier general, Aug. 8, 1918-Feb. 5, 1919. Asst. to Col. Mendell, San Francisco, Cal., on fortification work, 1889-92; instr. and asst. prof. engring., U.S. Mil. Acad., 1892-96; in charge river improvements, 3d Dist., improvement Miss. River, 1896-1900, and Little Rock (Ark.) Dist., 1898-1900; asst. to engr. commr. of D.C., 1900-03; comd. Co. E, 3d Batln. Engrs., Washington Barracks, D.C., 1903-04; mem. Bd. Engrs. for Rivers and Harbors, 1904, 1908-09, and 1910-19; div. engr. Central Div., 1910-14; asst. to chief of engrs. in charge River and Harbor Sect., 1916-18; asst. dir. Chem. Warfare Service, Aug. 6, 1918-Jan. 6, 1919; in charge harbor improvements, Honolulu (Hawaii) Dist., dept. engr. Hawaiian Dept., and comdg. 3d Engrs., 1919-20. Unitarian. Clubs: Army and Navy (Washington), Oahu Country (Hawaii). Address: U.S. Engineer Office, Honolulu, T.H.

NEWELL, CICERO soldier; b. Ypsilanti, Mich., Aug. 12, 1840; s. Josiah and Priscilla (Chamberlain) N.; ed. dist. sch.; m. Nellie Lerch, Apr. 2, 1863. Enlisted Co. H, 1st Mich. Vol. Inf., Apr. 16, 1861, 3 mos. service; reënlisted and elected 1st lt. Troop D, 3d Mich. Cav., Aug. 1861; capt., Troop K. Mar. 31, 1862; maj. 10th Mich. Cav., Aug. 19, 1863; hon. discharged, 1865; participated in more than 30 battles and many skirmishes; had command of 10th Mich. Cav. at Battle of Greenville, Tenn., when Gen. John A. Morgan was killed. U.S. Indian agt. for the Brule Sioux, of Dak., 1879-80. Founder Parental Sch., Seattle, Wash., 1891. Republican. Mason. Author: Indian Stories, 1912. Home: Portland, Ore. Deceased.

NEWELL, QUITMAN UNDERWOOD physician; b. Whistler, Ala., June 14, 1886; s. William Henry and Minerva Amita (Thompson) N.; prep. edn. Barton Acad., Mobile, Ala., 1902-04; M.D., U. of Ala., 1911; m. Katie Lou Kelley, June 30, 1920 (died 1924); children—Quitman Underwood, Doris Louise. Interne Washington U. Hosp., 1911-12, resident obstetrics and gynecology, 1912-14; asst. in clin. obstetrics and gynecology, Washington U. Med. Sch., 1914-21, instr., 1921-25, asst. prof., 1925-33, asso. prof., 1933-36, prof., 1936; mem. staff of Barnes, St. Louis Children's, St. Louis Maternity, St. Lukes, Mo. Baptist, Mo. Pacific hosps. Served as capt. Evacuation Hosp., 18, U.S. Army, 1917-19. Diplomate Am. Bd. Obstetrics and Gynecology; fellow Am. Coll. Surgeons. Democrat. Baptist. Mason. Author of numerous med. articles and of monograph, "Human Tubal Ova," 1930. Home: St. Louis, Mo. Died Nov. 5, 1940.

NEWGARDEN, PAUL W. army officer; b. Phila., Pa., Feb. 24, 1892; s. George Joseph and Margaret (Woolever) N.; B.S., U.S. Military Acad., 1913, distinguished grad. Command and Gen. Staff Sch., 1926, Army War Coll., 1932; m. Priscilla Quinby, Dec. 28, 1927. Commd. 2d lt., Inf., 1913 and advanced through the grades to maj. gen. (temp.), 1942; Instr. of tactics, U.S. Mil. Acad., 1917-21; with Inspector General's Dept., 1925; comdr. bat., 20th Inf., 27th Inf., 18th Inf.; exec. officer, 18th Inf., 1936, gen. staff, G-3, 6th C.A., 1936-40; comdr. 41st Armored Inf., 1941; combat comdr. A., 2nd Armored Div., 1942; comdr. 10th Armored Div., since 1942; organized and trained 41st Armored Inf., 1941-42, 10th Armored Div., 1942-43. Distinguished pistol shot; nat. junior saber champion, 1919. Clubs: Army-Navy, Country (Washington, D.C.). Died July 14, 1944.

NEWHALL, THOMAS born in Philadelphia, Pennsylvania, Oct. 17, 1876; s. Daniel Smith and Eleanor (Mercer) N.; student Haverford (Pa.) Sch., 1884-93; m. Honora Guest Blackwell, May 28, 1898; children—Blackwell, Campbell, Charles Mercer. Began with Chester (Pa.) Pipe & Tube Co., 1893; with John Wanamaker, Phila., 1898; pres. Newhall & Co., Baltimore, 1900-07; partner E. B. Smith & Co., Phila., 1910-20; pres. Phila. & Western Ry., 1910-22; partner Drexel & Co., Phila., 1922-36, J. P. Morgan & Co. (N.Y. City), Morgan, Grenfell & Co. (London), and Morgan

& Cie (Paris), 1929-36; financial v.p. Penn Mutual Life Ins. Co., 1937-43; dir. The Pa. R.R. Co.; dir. Pa. Co., 1938-45. Trustee Estate of H. H. Houston, Phila. Lieut. comdr. U.S.N.R.F., World War I; with mining squadron, A.E.F. Republican. Episcopalian. Clubs: Philadelphia, Union League; Metropolitan (Washington). Home: Green Hill Farms, Overbrook, Pa. Died May 9, 1947.

NEWMAN, JAMES JOSEPH, corp. exec.; b. Brooklyn, N.Y., March 11, 1889; s. Dr. Charles F. and Margaret F. (McNally) N.; B.C.S., New York U., 1912; m. Marie Louise Kevin, April 14, 1920; children—Patricia (Rummage), James Kevin. Pub. accountant 1908-19; treas., v.p., Loft, Inc., 1919-27; treas. Stanley Co. Am., 1927-29; pres. Pick, Barth Holding Co., 1929-31; v.p. The B.F. Goodrich Co., 1931-53; special cons. U.S. Treasury Dept., from 1953. Served as capt. and maj. Signal Corps, U.S. Army, A.E.F., 1917-19. Dir. and trustee several civic organizations, C.P.A., N.Y. Clubs: Paradise Valley Country (Scottsdale, Ariz.); Metropolitan (N.Y.C.); Portage Country (Akron, O.); Union (Cleve.). Home: Scottsdale AZ Died July 27, 1971; buried St. Francis Cemetery, Phoenix AZ

NEWMAN, OLIVER PECK, b. Lincoln, Neb., Apr. 20, 1877; s. George Clyde and Sallie Nicholson (Shivers) N.; ed. Des Moines Coll., Highland Park Coll., Des Moines, Ia.; U.S. Mil. Acad., 1897-98; m. Mrs. Jennie E. Bixby, of Beaumont, Tex., Sept. 19, 1904. Began as reporter Des Moines Leader, 1898; civilian officer, U.S. Tuberculosis Sanitarium, Ft. Stanton, N.M., 1902-04; reporter Washington Post and Washington Times, 1901-02, Beaumont (Tex.) Enterprise, 1904, San Antonio Express, 1905; polit. editor Des Moines News, 1906; editor Sioux City News, 1907-09; St. Joseph (Mo.) Star, 1909; mng. editor Lincoln Star, 1910; chief editorial writer Washington (D.C.) Times, 1911-12; commr. D.C. by apptmt. of President Wilson, term 3 yrs., and elected pres. of bd.; reapptd. 1916 (resigned 1917). Student 1st Mil. Training Camp, Ft. Myer, Va., 1917; commd. maj. and assigned 313th F.A., 80th Div., Camp Lee, Va.; grad. Sch. of Fire for F.A., Ft. Sill, Okla., 1918; sailed with 80th Div., May, 1918; served in France with 80th Div. and as counter battery officer Arty. Information Service, 1st Am. Army, on staff of comdr. of arty. in Meuse offensive; journalist since 1919; v.p. Thomas R. Shipp, Inc., advertising and publicity counsellors, Washington, 1926. Democrat. Club: Cosmos. Contbr. mag. articles on Nat. politics and govt. Home: Mayflower Hotel,2Washington DC

NEWMAN, WILLIAM TRUSLOW judge; b. Knoxville, Tenn., June 23, 1843; s. Henry B. and Martha A. N.; m. Fanny Alexander, Sept. 1871. Entered 2d Tenn. Va., C.S.A., in the ranks, when 17 yrs. of age; promoted lt., 1862; wounded and captured in Ky., 1863; exchanged Aug. 1863; wounded, losing right arm, nr. Jonesboro, Ga., July, 1864. Located at Atlanta, Ga., at close of war and studied law; admitted to bar, 1866; city atty., Atlanta, 1871-83; U.S. dist. judge, Northern Dist. of Ga., 1886-—. Address: Atlanta, Ga. Died Feb. 14, 1920.

NEWNAN, DANIEL congressman; b. Salisbury, N.C., circa 1780; attended U. N.C., 1796-97. Commd. ensign and 2d lt. 4th inf., U.S. Army, 1799, promoted to 1st lt., 1799, resigned commn., 1801; engaged in planting; comdr. Ga. Volunteers during Creek War, 1812-14; commd. maj. gen. 3d div. Ga. Militia, 1817; supt. Ga. State Penitentiary, 1823-25; sec. of state Ga., 1825-27; City of Newnan (Ga.) named for him, 1828; mem. U.S. Ho. of Reps. (State Rights Democrat) from Ga., 22d Congress, 1831-33. Died nr. Rossville, Ga., Jan. 16, 1851; buried Newnan Springs (Ga.) Churchyard.

NEWSOM, WILLIAM MONYPENY stock broker; b. Columbus, O., July 7, 1887; s. Logan Conway and Sally (Monypeny) N.; grad. Hill Sch., Pottstown, Pa., 1906; Ph.B., Yale, 1909; m. Frances Billings, May 15, 1915; 1 dau., Sally. Mgr. N.E. div. Breakwater Co., builders of govt. breakwaters, 1909-13; with Parkinson & Burr, stock brokers, New York, 1913-14; asst. to mgr. military and promotion depts. Remington Arms Co., 1915; sec. and treas. Sundstrand Adding Machine Sales Co., 1916-25; with Watson & White, brokers, 1927; mem. Berg, Eyre & Kerr, 1928-38, Hubbard Bros. & Co., 1938-39, Lawrence Turnure & Co., members N.Y. Stock Exchange, 1939-—. Served as 1st lt. Mil. Intelligence Div., U.S. Army, 1917-18. Protestant. Author: White-tailed Deer, 1926. Contbr. to Forest and Stream, Outdoor Life, Field and Stream. Home: New York, N.Y. Died Feb. 1, 1942.

NEWTON, JOHN army officer, engr.; b. Norfolk, Va., Aug. 24, 1823; s. Thomas and Margaret (Jordan) Pool N.; grad. U.S. Mil. Acad., 1842; LL.D., St. Francis Xavier Coll., 1886; m. Anna M. Starr, 1848, 6 children. Commd. 2d lt. Corps Engrs., 1842; asst. to Bd. of Engrs.; asst. prof. engring. U.S. Mil. Acad.; 1st lt., 1852, capt., 1856; chief engr. Utah Expdn., 1858; chief engr. Dept. of Pa. and Dept. of Shenandoah; commd. brig. gen. U.S. Volunteers, 1861; constructed Ft. Lyon; commanded brigade at West Point, Va., also at battles of Gaines' Mill, Glendale, South Mountain, and Antietam, 1862; maj. gen.; brevetted lt. col., col., brig. gen., maj. gen. of volunteers, 1863-64; maj. gen. U.S. Army; lt. col. engrs., 1865, col., 1879, brig. gen. and chief engrs., 1884; commr. public works of N.Y.C., 1886; pres. Panama R.R. Co., 1888-95; mem. Nat. Acad. Scis.; hon. mem. Am. Soc. C.E. Died N.Y.C., May 1, 1895; buried Post Cemetery, N.Y.

NEWTON, JOHN HENRY naval officer; b. Pittston, Pa., Dec. 13, 1881; s. John Henry and Elizabeth (Moon) N.; A.B., U.S. Naval Acad., 1905; m. Elise Barr Curry, Apr. 28, 1915; 1 son, John Henry. Commissioned ensign U.S. Navy, 1907, and advanced through the grades to vice adm., 1943; comdr. S. Pacific Force, S. Pacific area. Decorated Navy Cross and Legion of Merit. Presbyterian. Home: Carbondale, Pa. Died May 2, 1948.

NEWTON, MAURICE, investment banker; b. Elberon, N.J., July 2, 1892; s. Sigmund and Agnes Richard N.; A.B., Princeton, 1913; m. Marguerite Storm, Oct. 4, 1924; children—Joan, Diane; m. 2d, Lucienne Legarcon, Sept. 11, 1937. Began as statistician, 1914; in statistical dept., Hallgarten & Co., 1914-17; mem. N.Y. Stock Exchange, 1919-21; partner Hallgarten & Co., investment banking, from 1921; member of the executive committee, and of the bd. mgrs. Adams Express Co.; dir. Frederick H. Cone and Co.; dir. Hotel Waldorf-Astoria Corp.; dir., mem. exec. com. Am. Internat. Corp.; dir., mem. exec. com., Austin, Nichols & Co.; dir. The Anaconda Company. Served as major, Quartermaster Corps, U.S. Army, World War I. Clubs: Princeton, Leash, Recess, Madison Square Garden, Turf and Field (N.Y.C.); Saint James (London, Eng.); Saint Cloud Country (Paris); Deepdale Gold (Manhasset, N.Y.); The Travellers (Paris); Meadow Brook (Westbury, L.I.). Home: Old Brookville LI NY Died Apr. 25, 1968.

NEYLAND, ROBERT REESE, JR., football coach, army officer; b. Greenville, Tex., Feb. 17, 1892; s. Robert Reese and Pauline (Lewis) N.; student Burleson Coll., Greenville, 1909-10, Tex. A. and M. Coll., 1910-11; grad. U.S. Mil. Acad., 1916; B.S. in Civil Engring., Mass. Inst. Tech., 1921; m. Ada Fitch, July 16, 1923; children—Robert Reese, Lewis Fitch. Commd. 2d lt. C.E., U.S. Army, June 13, 1916; advanced through grades to brig. gen. Nov. 11, 1944; prof. mil. sci., tactics U. Tenn., 1926-31; also head football coach, 1926-34 (only 7 games lost by teams in this period), became head coach U. Tenn. Feb. 1936; detailed by War Dept. as dist. engr. on river and harbor work, Nashville Dist., Tennessee and Cumberland rivers and their tributaries. Served as capt. and adj. 1st Bn., 1st Engrs., later instr. 1st C.E. Sch., Gondrecourt, France; in charge pioneer sect. 1st Army Sch., Langres, France, Dec. 1917-Aug. 1918; comdg. 8th Engrs., Mounted, El Paso, Tex., Oct. 1918-May 1920, 1st Bn., 11th Engrs., 1935-36; ret. as maj. U.S. Army, voluntarily, Feb. 29, 1936, after 24 yrs. service. Recalled to active duty U.S. Engrs., assigned as dist. engr. Norfolk (Va.) Dist., May 1941; assigned as div. engr. Southwestern Div., Dallas, Oct. 1942; served overseas; comdg. Advance Sect. 1, S.O.S., C.B.I., June-Nov. 1944; comdg. gen. Base Sect., I.B. Theater Nov. 1944; ret. brig. gen. 1946. Awarded Legion of Merit with oak leaf cluster, D.S.M. (U.S.), Order of Brit. Empire; Chinese Order of Cloud and Banner. Mem. Am. Mil. Engrs. Episcopalian. Club: Army and Navy. Address: U. Tenn., Knoxville, Tenn. Died Mar. 28, 1962; buried Nat. Cemetery, Knoxville.

NIBLACK, ALBERT PARKER naval officer; b. Vincennes, Ind., July 25, 1859; s. Hon. William E. and Eliza (Sherman) N.; grad. U.S. Naval Acad., 1880; grad. Naval War Coll., 1916; m. Mary A. Harrington, Nov. 24, 1903. Promoted through grades to rear adm., Aug. 1917; retired July 25, 1923. Served on Pacific Sta., 1880-82; survey and exploration, Alaska, 1884-88; Squadron of Evolution, 1889-92; flag lt. N. Atlantic Squadron, 1893-94; insp. naval militia, 1895-96; writer and lecturer, Naval War Coll., on signaling and naval tactics, 1893-96; prize essayist, Naval Inst., 1890 and 1896; naval attaché at Berlin, Rome and Vienna, till breakin out of war with Spain, in which he served on blockade of Cuban ports, participating in battle of Nipe Bay; transferred to Flagship Olympia at Manila, Nov. 1898; participated in suppression of the Filipinio insurrection, Feb. 1899-July 1, 1901; in campaigns about Manila, Ilo Ilo, Subig Bay and Lyngayen Gulf; China, Feb.-Oct. 1900, during "Boxer" campaign; sec. naval commn. in P.I., 1901; insp. target practice, 1902; Naval Station, Hawaii, 1903; comdg. U.S.S. Iroquois, 1904-06; Pacific Squadron, 1906-07; comdg. ships at Naval Acad., 1907-09; comdg. U.S.S. Tacoma, June 1909-May 1910; naval attaché, Am. Legation, Buenos Aires, June 1, 1910-Nov. 1911; naval attaché, Am. Embassy, Berlin, Dec. 30, 1911-July 1913; Atlantic Fleet, 1913-16, comdg. U.S.S. Michigan; comd. 3d seaman regt. in occupation of Vera Cruz, Mex., Apr. 1914; mem. Gen. Bd.; on outbreak of war ordered to command Div. 1 and later Squadron 1, battleship force, Atlantic Fleet; comdg. Squadron 2, patrol force and of U.S. naval forces based on Gibraltar, Nov. 1917; comd. of U.S. naval forces in Western Mediterranean until after armistice; in Eastern Mediterranean, in Adriatic, Jan.-Mar. 1919; dir. Naval Intelligence, Navy Dept., Apr. 1, 1919-Sept. 15, 1920; naval attaché Am. Embassy, London, Oct. 1, 1920-Jan. 1921; vice admiral comdg. U.S. Naval Forces in European waters, Jan. 15, 1921. Elected dir. Internat. Hydrographic Bur. of Monaco, Feb. 1924, and elected pres. Mar. 1, 1927, for term of 5 yrs.; v.p. Soc. Naval Architects and Marine Engrs. 12 yrs., later hon. v.p. for life. Commended for rescue of crew of Am. ship, ,'Ocean King," which foundered in May 1887. Awarded D.S.M. (U.S.) for services in World War; Comdr. Royal Victorian Order, Companion St. Michael and St. George, and Kt. Comdr. St. Michael and St. George (Gt. Britain); Comdr. Legion of Honor (France); Grand Officer Avis (Portugal); Comdr. St. Maurice and St. Lazarus (Italy); White Eagle, 2d Class (military) and White Eagle, 1st Class (civil) by Serbia; Order of the Sacred Treasure (Japan); Grand Officer Ouissam Alonite, by the Sultan of Morocco; Grand Officer of Niftar Ichitar, by the Bey of Tunis; Grand Officer St. Charles of Monaco; Grand Officer of Striped Tiger (China). Author: The Coast Indians of Alaska and Northern British Columbia, 1889. Address: Washington, D.C. Died Aug. 20, 1929.

NIBLO, URBAN (nib'lo), army officer; b. Galveston, Tex., Nov. 20, 1897; s. Henry Grady and Anna (Fahner) N., B.S., U.S. Mil. Acad., 1919; grad. F.A. Sch., basic course, 1920. Ordnance Sch., 1928; B.S. in Mech. Engring. and M.S., Mass. Inst. Tech., 1928; m. Katharine Louise Earle, June 8, 1921; children—Virginia Fahner (Mrs. Jewel Richard Browder), Katharine Elizabeth (Mrs. Kyle Watson Bowie). Commissioned second lt., Field Arty., U.S. Army, 1919, advanced through the grades to brig. gen., 1944; served with Army of Occupation in Germany, 1919; post ordnance officer, Scofield Barracks, Hawaii, 1923-26; chief, experimental and research div., Springfield (Mass.) Armory, 1928-30, armory inspector, 1930-32; exec. officer, chief small arms div., Office Chief of Ordnance, 1932-35; exec. officer to ordnance officer, 8th Corps Area, Fort Sam Houston, Tex., 1936-39; chief of ordnance publications, Supt. Gen. Supply and Ammunition, Raritan (N.J.) Arsenal, 1939-41; ordnance officer, II Corps, 1942-43; participated in initial landing North Africa and advanced into Tunisia, 1942; army ordnance comdr., Fifth Army, 1943-45; participated in landing at Salerno, Italy, 1943, and then advanced northward in Italy; chief ordnance officer Mediterranean Theater, VE to VJ Day; ordnance officer, 4th Army, 1945-46; chief ordnance officer Far East Command, Tokyo, 1946-51; chief ordnance officer United Nations Command, 1950-51; ordnance officer Army Field Forces, 1952-54; dep. commandant Indsl. Coll. of Armed Forces, 1954-—. Decorated D.S.M. With oak leaf cluster, Legion of Merit, W.W.I. Service Medal, Army of Occupation and Pre-Pearl Harbor ribbons, N. African Theater with 7 stars and arrowhead, World War II Service Medal; Silver Star (Korean Conflict, 1950); also decorated by Italy, France, England, Mexico, and Brazil and Korea. Mem. Am. Soc. M.E., Army Ordnance Assn., Heroes of '76. Mason, Sojourner. Address: 5016 Loughboro Rd., Washington 16. Died Aug. 12, 1957; buried Arlington Nat. Cemetery.

NICHOL, EDWARD STERLING, physician; b. Granville, O., Oct. 14, 1894; s. Edward Apollis and Lydia (Greene) N.; student Ohio State U., 1913-15, 1919-20, University of Illinois, 1916-17, (A.B.), Northwestern University, 1920-23 (M.D.); married Dorothy M. Evans, June 21, 1924 (div. 1955); children—Nancy Evans (Mrs. James W. McLamore) Dorothy Patricia (Mrs. Richard Barnes); m. 2d Polly Edgeworth Davidson, July 19, 1956; stepchildren-—Carolyn (Mrs. Ferdinand Kuehn), Richard Davidson. Interne, Children's Meml. Hosp., Chgo., 1923, Cook Co. Hosp., Chgo., 1924-25; practicing physician, specializing in heart diseases, Miami, Fla., 1925-70; asso. clin. prof. Med. U. of Miami Sch. of Medicine; Founder Miami Heart Institute, director of professional services, 1960-70. Fellow International College of Angiology, A.C.P., American College Chest Physicians; mem. Am., Fla. (pres. 1949, dir.), Miami (pres. 1939, dir.) heart assns., Am., So. (chmn. med. sect. 1949), Fla. Med. assns., Dade County Medical Society, Am. Geriatrics Society, Am. Coll. Cardiology (vice president 1961), American Therapeutic Society (president 1945, chairman council 1956), Phi Kappa Psi, Alpha Kappa Kappa. Served as 1st lt. comdg. Sect. 534, U.S. Army Ambulance Service (France), 1917-19. Awarded Croix de Guerre with silver and gold stars (France). Republican. Presbyn. Clubs: Bath, La Gorce Country, Committee of 100 (Miami Beach); University (Chgo.). Home: Miami Beach FL Died June 24, 1970.

NICHOL, FREDERICK WILLIAM business exec.; b. Ottawa, Can., Mar. 8, 1892; s. William Robert and Jemima (Davis) N.; ed. pub. and comml. schs., Ottawa; LL.D., Hartwick Coll., Oneonta, N.Y., 1944; m. 2d, Adair Stoughton Thayer, June 11, 1953. Came to U.S., 1907, naturalized, 1919. Began as clk. N.Y. & Ottawa Ry. Co., Ottawa, 1906, later sec. gen. passenger agt.; became successively stenographer tariff bur. N.Y. Central R.R., N.Y.C., later Nat. Rys. of Mexico; stenographer, corr., N.Y., and asst. sec. to gen. sales mgr. and sec. dist. mgr. Nat. Cash Register Co., Toronto, Can.; sec. sales mgr. Arbuckle Brothers, N.Y.C.; sec. pres. Internat. Bus. Machines Corp., 1914, later exec. sec., N.Y.C.; v.p., sales mgr. Turbine Air Tool Co., Cleve.; sales mgr. Internat. Bus. Machines Co., Ltd., Toronto, later asst. gen. mgr.: mgr. bus. service dept. Internat. Bus. Machines Corp., N.Y.C.; pres., dir. Dayton Scale Co. (subsidiary Internat. Bus. Machines Corp.); asst. to v.p. charge sales Internat. Bus. Machines Corp., asst. to pres., and in charge operations in fgn. countries; v.p.; v.p., gen. mgr., mem. bd. dirs., mem.

exec. and finance com., directing head dept. of logistics; v.p., dir. Electromatic Typewriter Co., Rochester, N.Y., IBM of Del.; dir. IBM of Can., Maquinas, Commerciales Watson de México, S.A., Jugoslovensko Watson, A.D., Watson Belge, S.A. Dir. Holland House Corp. of The Netherlands, Maple Leaf Found., Inc.; governing mem., mem. bd. dirs. Nat. Fgn. Trade Council; asso. mem. staff faculty Babson Inst. Bus. Adminstrn., Boston; mem. bd. advisers Vocational Adv. Service for Jrs., Vocational Adv. Service; mem. governing council and exec. com. N.Y.U. (chmn. adv. com. Grad. Sch. Bus. Adminstrn. and Sch. Commerce, Accounts and Finance; mem. com. membership and honors; mem. exec. bd. soc. for libraries); dir., mem. exec. com. Inter-Am. Comml. Arbitration Commn. Served from pvt. to maj., U.S. Army, World War I; adminstrv. officer Ordnance Dept.; on spl. duty with sec. of war for 1 yr. after armistice; apptd. spl. adviser to sec. state on adminstrn., 1944. Mem. U.S. C. of C. (councilor representing Office Equipment Mfrs. Inst.), C. of C. State of N.Y., Internat. C. of C. (exec. com. U.S. Assos., Argentine-Am. Venezuelan and Mex. chambers commerce, Com. Internat. Econ. Reconstrn., Com. Internat. Econ. Policy (dir.), Nat. Fedn. Sales Execs. (chmn. adv. com.; mem. exec. com.; com. on coöp. schs. and colls.; com. ednl. coöp.; subcom. vocational guidance), Commerce and Industry Assn. N.Y. (mem. program com. of members council; spl. com. on priorities), N.A.M. (com. coöp. schs. and colls; com. ednl. coöp.; subcom. vocational guidance; exec. com. of nat. information com.; com. world trade policy), Internat. Affiliation Sales and Advt. Clubs (life mem. at large), Am. Soc. Sales Execs. (chmn. exec. com.), Advt. Fdn. Am., Nat. Indsl. Advertisers Assn., Am. Arbitration Assn., Ry. Bus. Assn., Am. Marketing Soc. (charter mem.), N.Y. Bd. Trade (bd. dirs.), Maritime Assn. Port of N.Y., Travelers Aid Soc. N.Y., Pilgrims of U.S., Pan Am. Soc. (dir.), Canadian Soc. N.Y., Grand Central Art Galleries N.Y.; hon. mem. Beta Gamma Sigma. Presbyn. Clubs: Sales Executives (v.p., dir.), Advertising, Rotary, Export Managers, Metropolitan, India House, Bankers (N.Y.C.); Dallas Sales Managers; (hon. life mem.); Metropolitan, Army and Navy, University (Washington); Gulf Stream Golf (Delray Beach, Fla.); Rawdon (Que.) Golf and Country; Sewanee Harbor (Hewlett Harbor, (L.I.). Home: 167 E. 62d St., N.Y.C. 21. Office: Gallatin House, 6 Washington Sq. N., N.Y.C. 3. Died Oct. 27, 1955; buried Woodlawn Cemetery, N.Y.C.

NICHOLAS, GEORGE state ofcl.; b. Williamsburg, Va., 1755; s. Robert Carter and Anne (Cary) N.; grad. Coll. William and Mary, 1772; m. Mary Smith, circa 1778; Served as maj. 2d Va. Regt., 1777, later col.; mem. Va. Ho. of Dels., 1787; mem. Va. Conv. which ratified U.S. Constn., 1788; mem. 1st.Ky. Constl. Conv., 1792; 1st atty. gen. Ky.; helped to frame, advocate Thomas Jefferson's Ky. Resolutions of 1798 in response to Alien and Sedition Acts of 1798. Died June 1799.

NICHOLAS, RICHARD ULYSSES army officer; b. York, Pa., Nov. 16, 1890; s. Byrd Calvin and Annie Susan (Heiland) N.; B.S., U.S. Mil. Acad., 1913; grad. Engr. Sch., 1916, Command and Gen. Staff Sch., 1936, Army War Coll., 1940; m. Ethel R. Ballinger 1945. Commd. 2d lt. U.S. Army, 1913, and advanced through the grades to brig. gen., 1945; platoon comdr. 1st Engr. Regt., 1913-14, 16-17; served with 2d, 26th and 214th Engr. regts. and as instr. O.T.C., 1917-19; dist. engr. Chgo. U.S. Engr. Dist., 1940; engr. IX Corps, 1940-41; engr., 4th Army, 1941-43, 9th Army, 1943-—. Decorated Legion of Merit, Bronze Star Medal (U.S.); Legion of Honor, Croix de Guerre with palm (France); Order of Wars for Fatherland, class 1 (U.S.S.R.). Mem. Soc. Am. Mil. Engrs. Home: 224 Primera Dr., San Antonio. Address: War Dept., Washington 25. Died May 7, 1953; buried Arlington Nat. Cemetery.

NICHOLLS, FRANCIS TILLON judge; b. Donaldsonville, Ascension Parish, La., Aug. 20, 1834; grad. U.S. Mil. Acad., 1855; assigned to 3d Arty.; served against Seminole Indians; was on frontier duty, 1856; resigned, Oct. 1, 1856; practiced law, Napoleonville, La., 1857-61; in C.S.A., 1861-65; capt. and lt. col. 8th La., 1861-62; col. 15th La. and brig. gen., 1862; lost an arm at battle of Winchester, Va., and a foot at Chancellorsville; supt. conscript bur., trans-Miss. dept., 1864-65; practiced law in Ascension Parish, La., 1865-76, and in New Orleans, 1880-88; gov. of La., 1877-80 and 1888-92; chief justice Supreme Ct. of La., 1893-1904, asso. justice, 1904-—. Democrat. Address: New Orleans, La. Died 1912.

NICHOLLS, JOHN CALHOUN congressman; b. Clinton, Ga., Apr. 25, 1834; grad. Coll. William and Mary, 1855; studied law. Admitted to Ga. bar, 1855, practiced in Clinch and Ware counties; engaged in planting; served as capt. Co. I, 4th Regt., Ga. Cavalry, Confederate Army during Civil War; mem. Ga. Constl. Conv., 1865; del. Democratic nat. convs., Cincinnati, 1866, St. Louis, 1876; Dem. presdl. elector, 1868; mem. Ga. Senate, 1870-75; mem. U.S. Ho. of Reps. (Dem.) from Ga., 46th, 48th congresses, 1879-81, 83-85; resumed law practice, Blackshear, Ga. Died Blackshear, Dec. 25, 1893; buried Blackshear Cemetery.

NICHOLS, EDWARD HALL surgeon; b. Reading. Mass., Jan. 6, 1864; s. Edward Childs and Abbie Susan (Hall) N.; A.B., Harvard, 1886, A.M., 1892, M.D., 1892; m. Edith Walker Judd, Oct. 3, 1894. Exec. asst. and asst. supt., Boston City Hosp., 1892-94; asst. pathologist, 1896-99, demonstrator surg. pathology, 1897-1901, instr., 1901-04, asst. prof. in surg. pathology and surgery, 1904-13, asso. prof., 1914-16, clin. prof. surgery, 1916-—, Harvard Med. Sch. Dir. Cancer Lab., Research Croft Fund, Boston, 1899-1905; in med. charge of Harvard football team, 1904-—; surgeon-in-chief to 1st Harvard surg. unit with B Am. Coll. Surgeons. Author of numerous articles pertaining to surgery. Address: Boston, Mass. Died June 12, 1922.

NICHOLS, EDWARD WEST educator; b. Petersburg. Va., June 27, 1858; s. James Nathaniel and Anne (Wynn) N.; ed. McCabe's U. Sch., Va. Mil. Inst., U. of Va. (summer courses); m. Evelyn Junkin Rust, Nov. 14, 1905. Prof. engring., 1882-90, mathematics, 1890-1907, supt. with rank of maj. gen. of engrs., Va. Mil. Inst. Chmn. Va. Council of Defense, 1917-18; maj. engrs., U.S.A., 1918-19. Engaged for several yrs. in collaboration with Dr. P. H. Dudley in scientific work connected with rys., especially in matter of correlation of rolling stock and permanent way. Democrat. Episcopalian. Author: Nichols's Analytic Geometry, 1891; Nichols's Differential and Integral Calculus, 1901. Home: Lexington, Va. Died July 1, 1927.

NICHOLS, GEORGE WARD army officer, coll. pres.; b. Mt. Desert, Me., June 21, 1831; s. John and Esther (Ward) N.; m. Maria Longworth, May 6, 1868. Art editor and critic N.Y. Evening Post, 1859; commd. capt. U.S. Army, 1862, aide-de-camp on Gen. Sherman's staff, 1864, resigned as brevet lt. col. U.S. Volunteers; a founder Sch. of Design of U. Cincinnati; pres. Harmonic Soc. Cincinnati; head May Festival Assn. of Cincinnati, 1872-80; founder, also a financial backer Coll. Music of Cincinnati, 1879, became 1st pres. Author: The Story of the Great March; 1865; Art Education Applied to Industry, 1877. Died Cincinnati, Sept. 15, 1885.

NICHOLS, NEIL ERNEST naval officer; b. Mich., Sept. 16, 1879; entered U.S. Navy, May 1898; advanced to rear admiral, Feb. 1942; retired June 30, 1937; recalled to active duty. Deceased.

NICHOLS, SPENCER VAN BOKKELEN publicist; b. N.Y. City, July 30, 1882; s. Allan and Elizabeth Morris (Van Bokkelen) N.; law, University of N.C.; spl. courses in internat. law, Columbia and Yale; m. Virginia Center Ward, July 30, 1918; children—Spencer Van Bokkelen, Virginia Center. Apptd. asst. sec. of State by President Wilson, 1913; associated with Schermerhorn Estate; v.p. Hamilton & Wade, ins. advisors; trustee of estates. Long active as layman P.E. Ch. and in boys' work, prison reform, rescue missions, forwarding Boy Scout and Big Brother movements; former traveling sec. Delta Kappa Epsilon. Served as officer U.S. Navy, 1917-20, duty U.S. Naval Acad.; aide to Rear Adm. H. F. Bryan; mem. staff of Adm. Caperton; mem. mission to S. Am. Republics, 1918. Trustee, dir., member or hon. mem. numerous socs., among them, League of Nations Assn. (chmn. of board and chmn. of exec. com.), Woodrow Wilson Foundation, Nat. Peace Conference, Am. Colony Charities Assn. of Jerusalem (sec.), Naval Hist. Soc. (sec.), N.Y. Hist. Soc., Am. Geog. Soc., Naval Inst., Am. Bookplate Soc., Am. Merchant Marine Library Assn., Soc. for Nautical Research (London), Naval Records Soc. (London), Delta Kappa Epsilon, etc. Democrat. Warden and vestryman Grace Episcopal Ch., Norwalk, Conn., Trinity Church, N.Y. City; treas. Church Army in U.S.A.; mem. Permanent Com. on Archives, Diocese of Conn.; N.Y. chmn. St. Luke's Internat. Hosp., Tokio. Clubs: Century, D.K.E., Grolier (gov.), Church (N.Y.); Samuel Pepys and First Edition clubs (Londdon). Author of various works, including, Volcanic Action, 1910; Fiona Macleod, William Sharp, 1913; Toby Jugs, 18th Century, 1913; John Rogers, Sculptor, 1913; John Dryden, Master, 1914; Samuel Pepys, the Man, 1913; A Pepysian Admiral, 1914; Disraeli, Political Novelist, 1915; The Significance of Anthony Trollope, 1925; Nelson (play), 1929. Also wrote Woodrow Wilson, Internationalist, Has the League Failed?, The Machinery of Peace, Moral Disarmament, Tariffs-Intergovernmental Debts, The Psychology of the American People Toward the Administration's Foreign Policy, The Non-Political Aspects of the League of Nations. Contbr. on lit. subjects, also verse, short stories and editorials. Book collector. Public speaker on League of Nations, World Court and internat. subjects. Home: 192 E. 75th St. Office: 52 William St., New York, N.Y. Died June 30, 1946.

NICHOLSON, DONALD W. congressman; b. Wareham, Mass., Aug. 11, 1888; s. Angus and Annie (McLeod) N.; ed. pub. schs. of Wareham; m. Ethel Patten, Oct. 17, 1921; children-Malcolm McLeod, Mary Patten. Owner fish market, Wareham, 1908-09; engaged in polit. work, 1920-; selectman, assessor, pub. welfare, Wareham, 1921-26; rep. from Plymouth, Dist., Mass. Legislature, 1925-26, senator, 1927-47, pres. senate, 1947; mem. 80th to 85th Congresses, 9th Mass. Dist. Served as sgt., 302d Inf., U.S. Army, 1917-20; prisoner of war escort, Co. 236, France. Mem. Am. Legion, Vets. Fgn. Wars. Elk, Odd Fellow; mem. Grange. Home: 12 Highland St., Wareham, Mass. Address: House Office Bldg., Washington, 25. Died Feb. 18, 1968.

NICHOLSON, FRANCIS colonial gov.; b. Downhame Parke, Eng., Nov. 12, 1655; probable son of Francis Nicholson. Began career in English Army, 1679; mem. Council for Dominion of New Eng., 1686; commd. lt. gov. N.Y., 1688; lt. gov. Va., 1890-92; a founder Coll. William and Mary; gov. Md., 1694-98, largely responsible for moving Md. capital to Annapolis, Md.; a founder King William's Sch. (now St. John's Coll.), Annapolis; gov. Va., 1698-1705, largely responsible for moving Va. capitol to Williamsburg; elected fellow Royal Soc., 1706; commd. brig. gen., comdr. in chief expdn. to reduce Port Royal, N.S., Can., 1710; commd. lt. gen. in Am., 1711; gov. N.S., 1713-17; gov. S.C., 1721-25. Author: Journal of an Expedition . . . For the Reduction of Port Royal, 1711. Died London, Eng., Mar. 5, 1728.

NICHOLSON, JAMES naval officer; b. Chestertown, Md., 1737; s. Joseph and Hannah (Smith) Scott; m. Frances Wilter, Apr. 30, 1763, 8 children including Hannah (Mrs. Albert Gallatin). In command of ship Defence, 1775; apptd. by Congress as capt. Continental Navy, 1776; comdr. ship Virginia, 1777; sr. officer Continental Navy, 1777; comdr. frigate Trumbull, 1779; commanded fleet including ship Nesbit, 1781; an active Republican in N.Y.C.; commr. of loans for N.Y., 1801. Died N.Y.C., Sept. 2, 1804.

NICHOLSON, JAMES THOMAS, executive vice president American National Red Cross; born Leominster, Mass., Oct. 31, 1893; s. Joseph and Elizabeth (Ayers) N.; B.S., Massachusetts State College, 1916, LL.D., 1946; married Marguerite Elaine Dobson, Nov. 9, 1918; children—Elizabeth, James T. Dir. Junior Red Cross, Atlantic Div., New York City, 1919-22, asst. nat. dir., Washington, D.C., 1922-24, asst. mgr. eastern area, Am. Nat. Red Cross, Washington, D.C., 1924-30, mgr. Chicago Chapter, Chicago, Ill., 1930-39; nat. dir. Am. Junior Red Cross, Washington, D.C., 1939-42; vice chmn., Am. Nat. Red Cross, Washington, D.C., from 1942, exec. v.p., Am. Red cross, until 1969; delegate, Internat. Conf. of Social Work, Paris, 1928, London, 1936 (chmn.); mem. Am. Red Cross delegation to the XIV Internat. Red Cross Conf., Tokyo, 1934, XV Conf., London, 1938; XVII Conf., Stockholm, 1948; XVIII Conf., Toronto, Canada, 1952; XIX Conference New Delhi, 1957; member of the Standing Commn. Internat. Red Cross Conf.; vice chmn. League Red Cross Socs., Toronto, 1952; del. to Germany for Poland, Am. Red Cross War Mission to Europe, 1939-40; mem. A.R.C. delegation to IV Pan-Am. Red Cross Congress, Chile, 1940, V Cong., Venezuela, 1948, VI Conf., Mexico City, 1951; Am. Red Cross del. to the U.S.S.R., accompanying the Am. and British Special Missions, 1941. Served as 2d lt., 41st Machine Gun Batt., 14th Div., U.S. Army, World War I. Chmn. Chicago Chapter, Am. Assn. of Social Workers, 1937-39, mem. bd. dirs., Council of Social Agencies, Chicago, 1931-39; Traveller's Aid Soc., Chicago, 1937-39, Chicago Community Fund, 1934-39; mem. adv. bd. Cook County Bur. of Public Welfare, 1932-39; mem. bd. dirs. Cook County Training Sch. for Nurses, 1937-39. Mem. Am. Assn. of Social Workers, Belgian, Cuban, Danish, French, Chilean and Bulgarian Red Cross socs., (hon.) Brazilian Red Cross, Sigma Phi Epsilon. Episcopalian. Contbr. articles to Red Cross periodicals and pamphlets. Completed negotiations with German Govt. whereby relief for Poland was effected after occupation in 1939 and 1940, and distributed without diversion on basis of need and without regard to race, religion or politics. Recipient annual award from Parents' Mag. for outstanding service to children, 1943; Officer's Cross of Polona Restituta (Poland); Grand Cross, Order of Honor and Merit (Cuba); Officer French Legion of Honor; Comdr. Royal Order of Dannebrog (Denmark); Associate Commander Order of St. John of Jerusalem; Royal Gold Medal, Swedish Red Cross; Finnish, Greek, German (Fed.), South Korean, Mexican, Netherlands, Norwegian, Polish Red Cross honors and medals; Grand Silver medal (Austria). Home: Washington DC Died Apr. 15, 1969.

NICHOLSON, JAMES WILLIAM educator; b. Tuskegee, Ala., June 18, 1844; s. Washington Biddle and Martha William (Wafer) N.; removed to La. with parents in infancy; A.M., Homer Coll., 1870; LL.D., Poly. Inst. of Ala., 1893, Tulane U., 1904; m. Sallie D. Baker, July 30, 1876. Entered C.S.A. in 17th yrs., 1861; served throughout the war in 12th La. Inf.; 2d sergt. for 3 yrs.; twice promoted to lieutenancy but declined. At close of war began teaching; prof. mathematics, Homer Coll., 1870-72; founded and conducted seminary in Claiborne Parish, La., 1868-77; prof. mathematics, 1877-—, pres. 1882-84, 1887-96 (resigned both times), La. State U. Twice elected state lecturer of Patrons of Husbandry, and led in movement which resulted in establishment of the state Bur. of Agr. and Immigration, 1879; one of the founders, 1883, pres. 1892 and for many yrs. chmn. exec. com., La. Ednl. Assn.; pres. Southern Ednl. Assn., 1903. Author of a series of arithmetics, an elementary algebra, a trigonometry, a differential and integral calculus; also many monographs on math. subjects. Address: Baton Rouge, La. Deceased.

NICHOLSON, JAMES WILLIAM AUGUSTUS naval officer; b. Dedham, Mass., Mar. 10, 1821; s. Nathaniel Dowse and Hannah (Gray) N.; m. Mary

Heap, at least 1 child. Apptd. midshipman U.S. Navy, 1838, 1st active service on Levant of West Indies Squadron; passed midshipman, 1844, ordered to vessel Princeton; promoted lt., 1852; served on Vandalia, 1853; received 1st command Isaac Smith, 1861; participated in Battle of Mobile Bay in ship Manhattan, 1862; commanded Mohongo, 1865-66; promoted capt., 1866, commodore, 1873; comdt. N.Y.C. Navy Yard, 1876-80; commanded European station as acting rear adm., 1881, commended by several countries for aid and other duties rendered during Brit. bombardment of Alexandria, Egypt, 1881; ret. as rear adm., 1883. Died N.Y.C., Oct. 28, 1887.

NICHOLSON, JOHN PAGE soldier, editor; b. Phila., July 4, 1842; s. James B. and Adelaide B. N.; hon. A.M., Marietta College, 1882; Litt.D., Pennsylvania Coll., 1888; married. Enlisted 28th Pennsylvania Infantry, July 23, 1861; regimental commissary sergt., Aug. 2, 1861; 1st lt., July 21, 1862; 1st lt. q.-m., Sept. 10, 1862; hon. mustered out, Oct. 10, 1865; bvts. for meritorious services and gallantry; capt., maj. and lt. col., Mar. 13, 1865; served in and with Army of Western Va., Banks' corps; Armies of Va., the Potomac, the Cumberland and Ga., in many battles from Bolivar, Va., Sherman's march to the sea and through the Carolinas, to the final surrender of the Confederate forces. Recorder-in-chief Mil. Order Loyal Legion, 1885—; chmn. U.S. Gettysburg Nat. Park Commn.; mem. G.A.R., Mil. Service Instn. U.S., and other mil. socs.; v.p., trustee Soldiers' and Sailors' Home, Erie, Pa. Translator and Editor: The History of the Civil War in America (Comte de Paris). Editor and Compiler: Pennsylvania at Gettysburg, 2 vols. Home: Philadelphia, Pa. Died Mar. 8, 1922.

NICHOLSON, RALPH, newspaper publisher and exec.; b. Greens Fork, Ind., Feb. 12, 1899; s. F.C. and Fannie (Davis) N.; A.B., Earlham Coll., 1920; student Harvard Grad. Sch. Arts and Scis., 1921-22; M.A., 1941; LL.D., Earlham College, 1962; m. to Jane E.B. Harvey, April 5, 1926; children—Martha Jane, Anne Blayney. President of Interstate Oratorical Assn., 1918-20; began as carrier boy, 1912-16; part time reporter, 1916-20, Richmond (Ind.) Item; European correspondent Philadelphia Public Ledger, 1920-21; vice president and treasurer Editorial Research Association (New York), 1923-25; production manager New York Evening Post, 1925-27; gen. mgr. Japan Advertiser and Trans-Pacific Advertising Agency (Tokyo), 1927-28; production mgr. New York Telegram, 1928-29; asst. business mgr. Pittsburgh Press, 1929-30; mgr. dept. pub. relations Gen. Motors Corp., 1930-31; gen. mgr. McFadden Newspapers, 1932; asst. pub. New York Daily Mirror, 1932-33; gen. mgr., treas. Tampa Times Co. (Tampa Daily Times, Radio Station WDAE), 1933-41, v.p., dir., 1933-51; pres., pub. New Orleans Item, 1941-49; spl. cons. Sec. Army, 1949; dir. office Pub. Affairs, U.S. High Commn., Germany, 1949-50; pres. and pub. St. Petersburg (Fla.) Ind., 1950-52, The Charlotte Observer, 1951-53; owner, pres., pub. Dothan (Ala.) Eagle, 1955-66, The Troy (Ala.), Messenger, 1960-66, The Brundidge (Ala.) Banner, 1961-66, Chronicle, Pascogoula-Moss Point, Miss., 1963-66; director Pullman Co., 1947-50, Tallahassee Bank & Trust Company, 1959-64; sr. adviser to Freedom Newspapers for Acquisitions in Southeastern States, from 1968; adviser to pres., pub. Gate City daily newspaper, Keokuk, Ia. Mem. Judicial Council, Fa., 1955-60, vice-chmn., 1957-60; member National Defense Executive Reserve, from 1959. Served as student pilot Flying Corps, U.S.N.R., 1918-19. Trustee Earlham Coll., 1948-51. Mem. Associated Dailies of Fla., 1934-41 (v.pres. 1936-37, president 1937-38); Chmn. Business Affairs Com. of Southern Newspaper Pub. Assn., 1936-37, chmn. Pub. Relations Com., 1941-44, dir., 1937-39, treas., 1947-49; chmn. New Orleans Red Cross Fund, 1944; La. chmn. Ducks Unlimited, 1944-49. War corr. European Theater of Operations, 1944. Mem. Newcomen Soc., Soc. Friends, So. (chmn. postal com.) Am. newspapers pub. assns., Sigma Delta Chi. Episcopalian. Mason. Clubs: Metropolitan, Nat. Press (Washington); Boston; New Orleans; Harvard (N.Y.C.). Home: Tallahassee FL Died July 10, 1972; buried Episcopal Cemetery, Tallahassee FL

NICHOLSON, REGINALD FAIRFAX naval officer; b. Washington, D.C., Dec. 15, 1852; grad. U.S. Naval Acad., 1873; served during Civil War as captain's clk., U.S.S. State of Georgia, Aug. 1 to 31, 1864; promoted ensign, July 16, 1874; lt., jr. grade, Jan. 22, 1880; lt., Jan. 17, 1886; lt. comdr., Mar. 3, 1899; comdr., Sept. 17, 1902; capt., July 1, 1907; rear admiral, May 19, 1911. Served on Oregon during Spanish-Am. War; Bur. of Navigation, Navy Dept., 1901-04; comd. Tacoma, 1904-05; Bur. of Equipment, Navy Dept., 1906; Bur. of Navigation, 1906-07; comd. Nebraska, 1907-09; Bd. of Inspn. and Survey, Navy Dept., 1909; chief Bur. of Navigation, 1909-12; comd. Asiatic Fleet, 1912-14; mem. Gen. Bd., Navy Dept., 1914; retired on account of age, Dec. 15, 1914; recalled to active duty, Sept. 1917, as naval attaché, Chile, Peru and Ecuador. Address: Washington, D.C. Died Dec. 19, 1939.

NICHOLSON, ROBERT HARVEY, utility exec.; b. Anderson, Cal., Nov. 25, 1889; s. William Drake and Abigail (Cochrane) N.; student pub. schs., Cal.; m. Leona Browne, Aug. 1912; 1 dau., Nadine R. (Mrs. Merideth E. Moseley); m. 2d, Helene Strauss, Sept. 21, 1929; children—Nancy H. (Mrs. Cunningham), Robert Harvey. Engr. Santa Fe Ry., Oakland, Cal., and Cal. R.R. Commn., 1913-22; cons. engr., Los Angeles, 1923-26; pres. So. Cal. Utilities, Inc., 1926-28; pres. San Gabriel Valley Water Co., El Monte, Cal., 1936-59, chmn. bd., 1959-69. Served as capt. Engrs., U.S. Army, AEF, 1917-20, col., C.E., 1941-45; ETO. Clubs: California (Los Angeles); Annandale Golf (Pasadena); Newport Harbor Yacht, Irvine Coast Country (Newport Beach, Cal.). Home: Pasadena CA Died May 8, 1969.

NICHOLSON, SAMUEL naval officer; b. Chestertown, Md., 1743; s. Joseph and Hannah Smith (Scott) N.; m. Mary Dowse, Feb. 9, 1780, at least 4 children. Commd. capt. Continental Navy, 1776, secured English cutter Dolphin for U.S.; commanded frigate Deane, 1778; commd. capt. U.S. Navy, 1794; supt. bldg. of frigate Constitution; 1st supt. Charlestown (Mass.) Navy Yard, 1801; torpedoship Nicholson named for him, 1901. Died Charleston, Dec. 29, 1811.

NICHOLSON, SOMERVILLE commodore U.S.N.; b. New York, Jan. 1, 1822; s. Maj. A. A. and Helen Bache (Lispinard) N.; apptd. midshipman, June 21, 1839; passed midshipman, July 2, 1845; master, Sept. 9, 1853; lt., May 5, 1854; lt. comdr., July 16, 1862; comdr., Jan. 2, 1863; capt., June 1870; commodore, Jan. 1880; retired, Apr. 1881. During Civil War comd. steam gunboat "Marblehead" and steamer "State of Georgia" in blockading service. Address: Washington, D.C. Died 1905.

NICHOLSON, SOTERIOS (name adopted), lawyer; b. Kalliani, Corinth, Greece, April 7, 1885; s. Nicolaos J. and Evdokia (Kerasiotis) Papasoteriou; came to U.S., 1903, naturalized, 1910; ed. pub. and pvt. schs. Athens and Tripolis; student Emerson Inst., Washington, D.C., 1906-08; LL.B., George Washington Univ., 1911; m. Anna Bresnahan, Sept. 21, 1916 (died 1918); m. 2d, Edith H. Tharp, Aug. 16, 1920 (died 1947); married 3d, Dora Papara, December 19, 1953. Washington correspondent Atlantis, Greek Daily, N.Y. since 1912. Admitted to bars: District of Columbia, 1911, Ct. of Claims, 1915, U.S. Supreme Court, 1917, District Court of U.S. for the District of Maryland, 1917, Supreme Court of Appeals, Va., 1926, Court of Appeals of Md., 1928, Dist. Court of U.S. for 6th Circuit and Eastern Dist. of Mich., 1928; assisted in purchase by Greece from U.S. Govt. of U.S. ships Idaho and Mississippi, 1914, counsel for the Greek Embassy; asst. counsel, N.R.A. of U.S., Dec. 11, 1933-Nov. 5, 1934, asst. dep. adminstr., Nov. 6, 1934-June 16, 1935, tech. adviser June 17, 1935 to Oct. 15, 1935. Pres. and director Nicholson and Company, Incorporated Real Estate, Capital Features Syndicate. Campaign speaker for Rep. Nat. Com. 1916, 1920, 1924, for Dem. Nat. Com., 1936. Commd. capt. ordnance finance, U.S. Army, Dec. 11, 1917; served as disbursing office, summary Court officer, Motor Transport Corps Officer, Liberty Loan Officer, hon. disch. July 31, 1919. Decorated: Knight of the Royal Order of the Redeemer, Greece, 1922; Knight of the Order of the Holy Sepulcher, 1924, Greek Patriachate Jerusalem, comdr. same order, 1929; U.S.A. Service, 1920; selective service medal, 1946; gold cross of the Order of Phoenix Greece, 1949; gold cross of veterans of National Union of American and Greek W.W. Vets., 1950; gold cross of George A (Greece) 1953; Croix de Lorraine (France) 1954. Mem. D.C., Am., Fed. bar assns., Am. Soc. Internat. Law, Assn. Oldest Inhabitants of D.C., past comdr. Nat. Press Club No. 20 Am. Legion, Mid-City Citizens Association (president), Federation Citizens Assn. (del., interfederation council), Central Bus. Assn. (ex.-pres.), Fedn. Bus. Men's Assn. (general counsel), Washington Bd. of Trade. Member Greek Orthodox Church. Member Order of Ahepa. Club: National Press. Pub. Nation's Capital Mag., 1930-31. Author: War or A United World, 1916; A World City of Civilization (brochure), 1913. Home: Burlington Hotel, Washington 5. Office: 1120 Vermont Av. N.W., Washington. Deceased.

NICHOLSON, WILLIAM JONES army officer; b. Washington, D.C., Jan. 16, 1856; s. Commodore Somerville (U.S.N.) and Hannah (Jones) N.; grad. Inf. and Cav. Sch., 1883; LL.D., Georgetown U., 1919; m. Harriette Fenlon, Feb. 6, 1833; children—William Fenlon, Mrs. Helen Lispenard Crean. Commd. 2d lt. cav., U.S.A., Aug. 15, 1876; advanced through grades to col., Aug. 24, 1912; brig. gen. N.A., Aug. 5, 1917. Served in Spanish-Am. War, Mexican Punitive Expdn., and as comdr. Camp Meade, 1917, Camp Upton, 1918; in France, 1918, participating in Avocourt sector, Meuse-Argonne offensive, Bois Belleu-Côte 360 sector, Nov. 8-11, 1918; retired Jan. 16, 1920. Awarded D.S.M., 1919, "for exceptionally meritorious and distinguished services"; D.S.C. for "distinguished and exceptional gallantry at Bois de Bouge on Sept. 29, 1918"; officer, Legion of Honor (France); promoted brig. gen. regular army, Feb. 28, 1927, by spl. act of Congress. Catholic. Home: Washington, D.C. Died Dec. 20, 1931.

NICKELS, JOHN AUGUSTINE HEARD commodore U.S.N.; b. Boston, Jan. 12, 1849; s. Capt. Edward C. and Sarah (Colburn) N.; grad. U.S. Naval Acad., 1869; m. Cornelia A. Parker, Nov. 13, 1879. Promoted ensign, July 12, 1870; master, Nov. 20, 1872; lt., June 10, 1876; lt. comdr., Feb. 1, 1898; comdr., Nov. 29, 1900; capt., June 28, 1905; commodore and retired, June 30, 1906. Served on Sabine and Richmond, 1869-71; Iroquois and Lackawanna, Asiatic station, 1872-75; Navy Yard, Boston, 1875; Montauk, 1875-76; Adams, 1876-79, Navy Yard, Boston, 1879-80; coast survey duty, 1880-81; Navy Yard, Norfolk, 1881-82; Hartford, 1882-85; Navy Yard, New York, 1885-87; Chicago, 1887-91; Navy Yard, New York, 1891-94; Newark, Chicago and San Francisco, 1894-95; Navy Yard, New York, 1896-97; exec. officer of Marblehead, 1897-99; Navy Yard, New York, 1899-1901; comd. Topeka, 1901-03; insp. 7th light house dist., 1903-05; commandant naval stas. Charleston and Port Royal, S.C., 1905-06. Address: Washington, D.C. Died 1910.

NICKELS, MERVYN MILLARD, physician; b. New Brighton, Pa., Aug. 4, 1898; s. John Hobbs and Viola May (McFarland) N.; M.D., Loyola U., Chgo., 1927; m. Loretta Nickels; children—Nedra (Mrs. Fitch Williams III), Rita (Mrs. John Selden), Michael David and Daniel Arthur (twins). Intern, Grace Hosp., Detroit, 1927-28; asst. physician Traverse City (Mich.) State Hosp., 1936-39, clin. dir., 1942-46, asst. supt., 1946-70, acting supt., 1955-56. Served to comdr., M.C., USNR, 1943-46. Diplomate Am. Bd. Psychiatry and Neurology. Mem. Am. Psychiat. Assn. Home: Traverse City MI Died Apr. 16, 1971; buried Oakwood Cemetery.

NICKERSON, FRANK STILLMAN lawyer; b. Swanville, Me., Aug. 27, 1826; grad. East Corinth, Me., Coll., 1841; admitted to bar at 21, and engaged in practice; was connected with U.S. customs for nearly 16 yrs. Entered Union army as pvt. at Lincoln's 1st call; elected capt., maj., lt.-col. and apptd. col. and brig.-gen.; served with distinction in Army of Potomac under Gens. McDowell and McClellan, and in Dept. of the Gulf under Gens. Butler, Banks and Canby to close of war; was mentioned in general orders for distinguished service by Gens. Halleck, Butler and Howard. Since 1874 has practiced law in Boston; m. Dec. 31, 1849, Augusta A. Pitcher, d. William Pitcher, Belfast, Me. Address: 257 Washington St., Boston.

NICKERSON, HOFFMAN author; b. Paterson, N.J., Dec. 6, 1888; s. Thomas White, Jr., and Mary Louisa (Hoffman) N.; B.A., Harvard, 1911, M.A., 1913; m. Ruth Constance Comstock, July 11, 1916; children—Schuyler Hoffman (dec.), Eugene Hoffman, Adams Hoffman; m. 2d, Jane Soames, Mar. 5, 1938; children—William Hoffman, Martinus Hoffman. Pres., Estate of E. A. Hoffman, Inc. Mem. Republican County Com., N.Y. County, 1913-26; mem. N.Y. State Assembly, 1916. Commd. 1st lt. 71st Inf., N.Y. N.G., 1916; capt. ordnance dept. U.S. Army, 1917; duty with 2d sect. Gen. Staff, AEF, 1918; mem. U.S. sect. Interallied Armistice Commn., Spa Belgium, 1918, 19; commd. capt. AUS, 1942, ret. as maj., 1944. Mem. N.Y. Hist. Soc., N.Y. Zool. Soc., Am. Hist. Soc., M.I. Res. Soc., Medieval Acad. Am., St. Nicholas Soc., Colonial Lords of Manors, S.R., Army Ordnance Assn. Episcopalian. Clubs: Union, University, Harvard, Piping Rock Country, Sewanhaka Yacht, Crusing Club of Am.; Tennis and Racquet (Boston). Author: The New Slavery, 1947; The Loss of Unity, 1961; others. Home: Yellow Cote House, Oyster Bay, N.Y. 11771. Died Mar. 1965.

NICOLA, LEWIS patriot; b. France, 1717. Came to Phila. from Dublin, Ireland, circa 1766; editor American Magazine or Gen. Repository; wholesale mcht.; propr. circulating library, Phila.; elected mem. one of Phila.'s 2 scientific socs., 1768, negotiated merger by which Am. Philos. Soc. was formed, often served as curator; a justice Northampton County (Pa.), 1774; published 3 mil. manuals during Revolutionary War; apptd. barrack master Phila., 1776; town maj., commanding Home Guards, 1776-82; col. Invalid Regt., 1777, commandant, 1788; brevetted brig. gen., 1783; a proponent of crowning George Washington "King of America." Author: A Treatise of Military Exercise, 1776. Died Alexandria, Va., Aug. 9, 1807.

NIEHAUS, FREDRICH WILHELM, physician; b. Treynor, Ia., Feb. 11, 1889, s. Friedrick Karl and Rosetta (Huelle) N.; M.D., U. Neb. 1916; postgrad. U. Vienna (Austria), 1929-30; m. E. Effie Ruth Kelley, Aug. 5, 1918; children—Virginia (Mrs. Robert Auracher), Karl Friedrich. Intern Bishop Clarkson Meml. Hosp., 1916-17, later chief staff; staff Bellevue Hosp., N.Y.C., also St. Vincent's Hosp., N.Y.C., 1917-18; later U. Neb. Hosp. Prof. medicine U. Neb., from 1935, prof. emeritus, 1954-69, also sr. cons. Served to capt. M.C., U.S. Army, World War I. Diplomate Am. Bd. Internal Medicine. Fellow Am. Heart Assn., A.C.P., Am. Coll. Chest Physicians; mem. A.M.A., Neb., Omaha-Douglas County med. socs., Midwest Clin. Soc. (founder, pres.), Alpha Omega Alpha, Phi Rho Sigma. Contbr. papers to profl. publs. Home: Omaha NE Died Oct. 6, 1969; buried Fairview Cemetery, Treynor IA

NIELDS, JOHN P. judge; b. Wilmington, Delaware, August 7, 1868; s. Benjamin and Gertrude (Fulton) N.; prep. edn., Haverford Coll., Pa.; A.B., Harvard, 1889; Harvard Law Sch., 1890, 92; m. Mary Blanchard Craven, Jan. 23, 1907; 1 dau., Ann. In practice at Wilmington since 1892; apptd. U.S. atty. for Dist. of Del. by President Roosevelt, 1903, reapptd. 1907, and by President Taft, 1912; U.S. dist. judge, Dist. of Delaware, since 1930. Attended Plattsburg Training Camp, 1915; capt. U.S. Army, 1918. Pres. Wilmington Pub. Library; hon. pres. Wilmington Boys' Club. Mem. Am. and Delaware bar assns.; chancellor and chmn. membership com. Soc. of Colonial Wars; chmn. membership com. Del. Hist. Society; mem. Loyal Legion; hon. mem. Soc. of The Cincinnati. Republican. Episcopalian. Clubs: Wilmington, Wilmington Country; Harvard. Editor Harvard Law Review and Phi Delta Phi Law School. Home: Aston, R.D. 1, Wilmington, Del. Died Aug. 26, 1943.

NILES, ALVA JOSEPH brig. gen.; b. Whitehall, Ill., Apr. 5, 1882; s. Albert George and Sarah Ruth (Pruett) N.; student Winfield Coll., 1899-1901; m. Ethel M. McNeal, Jan. 3, 1906; children—Joe Allen, Mary Louise. Treas. sch. land funds, Okla. Ty., 1903-05; adj. gen. Okla. Ty., 1906-07; pres. Farmers & Merchants Bank, Mountain View, Okla., 1908-09, 1st Nat. Bank, Sentinel, 1911-12, Citizens State Bank, Okemah, 1912-14; oil producer, Tulsa, Okla., 1915; organizer, 1919, pres., 1919-23, Security (now Tulsa) Nat. Bank; oil production and investment business since 1923; pres. Trevino Oil Corp. of Texas. Served as pvt. U.S. Vols., Spanish-Am. War (enlisted at age of 16); in State-Federal Nat. Guard Service, 1900-17, advanced from capt. to brig. gen. and adj. gen., 1906; brig. gen. and judge adv. Okla. Nat. Guard, and ex-officio U.S. disbursing officer, 1908-12; company and bn. comdr., Mexican border service, 1916-17; maj. and insp. gen. U.S. Army, France, World War; participated in Meuse-Argonne engagements and defensive operations Toul sector; col. O.R.C., 1921-23; apptd. brig. gen., 1923; organized and commanded 70th F.A. Brig., Federal Nat. Guard, Okla., Colo., N.M. and Ariz., 1923-26. Chmn. and mgr. Rep. Campaign Com., Okla., 1910; treasurer of Rep. Nat. Com. for Oklahoma, 1920. Mem. board advisers Castle Heights Mil. Acad.; formerly mem. bd. regents U. of Tulsa, Okla. Mil. Acad. (Claremore); mem. Am. advisory council, Yenching U., Peiping, China. Awarded Distinguished Service medal. Member national advisory com. Am. Legion Marksmanship; mem. exec. com. Nat. Guard Assn. America, 1907-10; dir. and life mem. Nat. Rifle Assn. America, 1906-10; past president Tulsa (Oklahoma) Chamber of Commerce. Mem. Am. Bankers Assn., Okla. Bankers Assn., United Spanish War Vets. (an organizer; Okla. state comdr. 1905-08), Am. Legion (del. to St. Louis meeting, May 1919, when Am. Legion was organized, and mem. com. on preamble), Joe Carson Post Am. Legion No. 1 of Tulsa (an organizer and past post comdr.), Mil. Order World War, Mil. Order Foreign Wars (vice comdr. Okla. Dept.). Republican. Presbyterian. Mason 33 deg., Shriner), Elk. Clubs: City, Scottish Rite (Tulsa); Tulsa (Okla.) Country; Virginia Country (Long Beach, Calif.); La Grulla Gun, Baja California (Mexico); Casa Blanca Country (Laredo, Tex.); Casino Mexicano (Nuevo Laredo, Mexico). Home: 1500 S. Frisco St., Tulsa 5, Okla. Died Jan. 19, 1950.

NILES, KOSSUTH rear admiral U.S.N.; b. Belleville, Ill., June 14, 1849; s. Nathaniel and Maria Louisa (Thoma) N.; served in Civil War, 142 Ill. Vols., 1864; grad. U.S. Naval Acad., 1869; m. Elizabeth Challenor, Dec. 31, 1873. Promoted through the various grades and retired by statutory age limit, June 14, 1911, in the grade of rear admiral. Light-house insp., 8th dist., 1901-03; comdg. Bennington, Pacific sta., 1903-04, Boston, Pacific sta., 1904-05; gen. insp. ordnance, New York, 1905-08; comdg. Battleship Louisiana on cruise around the world, 1908-09; mem. Lighthouse Bd., 1909-10; mem. and pres. Naval Exam. and Retiring Bds., Washington, 1910-11. Mem. Mil. Order Loyal Legion, U.S. Naval Inst. Home: Winsted, Conn. Died Dec. 6, 1913.

NILES, NATHAN ERIE rear admiral U.S.N.; b. Wellsboro, Pa., Dec. 27, 1847; s. Alanson E. and Angeline N.; apptd. from Pa. and grad. U.S. Naval Acad., 1868; m. Blanche Rousseau, Oct. 12, 1876. Promoted ensign, Apr. 19, 1869; master, July 12, 1870; lt., July 7, 1874; lt. comdr., Jan. 5, 1896; comdr., Mar. 25, 1899; capt., Sept. 13, 1904; rear admiral, Nov. 12, 1908. Served in Nipsic, N. Atlantic sta. and Darien surveying expdn., 1868-70; in Saranac, Resaca, and St. Marys, Pacific Fleet, 1870-73; Manhattan, and Ossipee, N. Atlantic sta., 1873-75; Marion, European sta., 1875-78; Navy Yard, Portsmouth, 1879-82; Iroquois, 1882-85; Hydrographic Office, 1885-88; Atlanta, 1888-91; Navy Yard, Norfolk, Va., 1891-95; Lancaster, 1895-97; Bureau of Equipment, 1898; comd. Piscataqua during Spanish-Am. War, 1898; Navy Yard, Norfolk, Va., 1898-1900; comd. Nashville, 1900-03; Naval Home, Phila., 1903-05; comd. Maine, 1905-07; comdg. receiving-ship Hancock, July 1907-Dec. 1908; gov. Naval Home, Phila., 1908-09; retired by operation of law, Dec. 27, 1909. Address: Washington, D.C. Died Nov. 28, 1930.

NIMITZ, CHESTER WILLIAM naval officer; b. Fredericksburg, Tex., Feb. 24, 1885; s. Chester Bernhard and Anna (Henke) N.; B.S., U.S. Naval Acad. 1905; student U.S. Naval War Coll., 1922-23; LL.D. (hon.), Columbia, 1947; m. Catherine Vance Freeman, Apr. 9, 1913; children—Catherine Vance (Mrs. Jas. T. Lay), Chester William, Anna Elizabeth, Mary Manson. Commd. ensign USN, 1907, advanced through grades to fleet adm., 1944; chief of staff, comdr. Submarine Force, Atlantic Fleet, 1918; exec. officer U.S.S. South Carolina, 1919; attached to U. Cal. Naval Res. Unit, 1926-29; comd. U.S.S. Augusta, 1933-35; asst. chief Bur. Nav., Navy Dept., 1935-38; comdr. Battleship Div. 1, Battle Force, 1938-39; chief Bur. Nav. June 1939-Dec. 1941; comdr.-in-chief Pacific Fleet Dec. 1941-Nov. 1945; made fleet adm. Navy, Dec. 1944; chief Naval Operations, 1945-47, spl. asst. to sec. Navy since 1947; apptd. chmn. Presdl. Commn. on Internal Security and Individual Rights. Regent U. Cal. Decorations: D.S.M., D.S.M. by Congress and gold star, Army D.S.M., Silver Life Sav. Medal, Victory Medal of World War I with one silver and one bronze star, Am. Def. Service Medal, Asiatic-Pacific Campaign Medal, World War II Victor Medal; Knight, Grand Cross of Bath (Gt. Britain); Philippine Medal of Valor; Grand Cross of Order of George I (Greece); Order of Grand Cordon of Pao-Ting (China); La Cruz de Merito Militarde Primara Clase (Guatemala); Pacific Star (Gt. Britain); Knight Grand Cross of Order of Orange-Nassau (Netherlands); Grand Officer in Nat. Order of Legion of Honor (France); Order of Liberator (Argentina); Grand Cross of Order of Carlos Manuel de Cespedes (Cuba); Grand Cross of Order of Crown with Palm and Croix de Guerre (Belgium); Star of Abdon Caldron (Ecuador); Knight of Grand Cross of Mil. Order of Italy. Has received hon. degrees from many univs. and colls. Address: U.S. Naval Sta., Treasure Island, San Francisco 30. Died Feb. 1966.

NISLEY, HAROLD A. army officer; b. on farm nr. Washington Court House, O., Jan. 16, 1892; s. Albert C. and Ellen (Sollars) N.; student Ohio State U., 1910-11; B.S., U.S. Mil. Acad., 1917; M.S. in Mech. Engring., Mass. Inst. Tech., 1923; grad. Army Indsl. Coll., 1931, Army War Coll., 1936; m. Margaret Warren, Jan. 4, 1933; 1 son, Albert Warren. Commd. 2d lt., U.S. Army, 1917, advanced through grades to brig. gen., 1945; served with F.A. during World War I; transferred to Ordnance Dept., 1920; ordnance officer Hdqrs. Armored Force, Fort Knox, Ky., 1940-42; chief, automotive maintenance sect. field service Office Chief of Ordnance, 1942-43; dep. to chief ordnance officer E.T.O., Oct. 1943-Mar. 1944; ordnance officer Hdqrs. 12th Army Group 1944-45; ordnance officer Hdqrs. Ground Forces, 1945-48; ret. 1948 because of phys. disability. Chmn. bd. Warren Paint & Color Co., Nashville since 1948. Decorated D.S.M., Legion of Merit; Legion of Honor, Croix de Guerre with palm (France); Comdr. Order Brit. Empire; Couronne de Chene (Luxembourg); Order Orange-Nassau (Netherlands); Order of Leopold, Croix de Guerre (Belgium); War Cross (Czech.); numerous others. Service mem. Soc. Automotive Engrs.; mem. Army Ordnance Assn., numerous others. Mason. Address: Lynwood Blvd. and Westview Av., Belle Meade, Nashville 5. Died Dec. 23, 1965; buried Arlington Nat. Cemetery.

NIXON, JOHN army officer; b. Framingham, Mass., Mar. 1, 1727; s. Christopher and Mary (Seaver) N.; m. Thankful Berry, Feb. 7, 174; m. 2d, Hannah (Drury) Gleason, Feb. 5, 1778; 5 sons, 5 daus. Served in expdn. against Louisbourg, 1745; commd. lt. Continental Army, 1755, capt., 1775; capt. of a co. Col. Ruggles' Regt., Half Moon, N.Y., 1758; commanded a co. of minute-men, Lexington and Concord (Mass.) Apr. 19, 1775; col. 4th Inf., Continental Army, 1776, elected brig.-gen., 1776, resigned, 1780. Died Middlebury, Vt., Mar. 24, 1815.

NIXON, JOHN army officer, financier; b. Phila., 1733; s. Richard and Sarah (Bowles) N.; m. Elizabeth Davis, Oct. 1765, 4 daus., 1 son. Lt., Dock Ward Co. (home guard orgn.), 1756; apptd. warden Delaware River Port, 1766; a signer Pa. paper money, 1767; mem. 1st Com. of Correspondence, 1774; dep. to Gen. Conf. Province of Pa., 1774; del. Pa. Provincial Conv., 1775; an organizer, lt. col. 3d Battalion of Assos., 1775; mem. Pa. Com. of Safety, 1775, pres. pro tem; comdr. defenses Delaware River at Ft. Island, 1776, Phila. City Guard, 1776; mem. Continental Navy Bd.; leader Phila. Guard in defense of Perth Amboy (N.Y.) and Battle of Princeton, 1777; mem. com. to settle and adjust accounts of Pa. Com. and Council of Safety, 1778; an organizer, dir. Bank of Pa., formed to aid in supplying Continental Army, 1780; dir. Bank of N.Am., 1784, pres., 1792; alderman Phila., 1789-96; bd. mgrs. Pa. Hosp., 1768-72; trustee Coll. Phila., 1789-91. Died Phila., Dec. 31, 1808; buried St. Peter's Church Yard, Phila.

NIXON, LEWIS shipbuilder; b. Leesburg, Va., Apr. 7, 1861; s. Joel Lewis and Mary Jane (Turner) N.; early edn. Leesburg; grad. U.S. Naval Acad., 1882, at head of class, and sent to Royal Naval Coll., Greenwich, Eng., by Navy Department; m. Sally Lewis Wood, Jan. 29, 1891 (died 1937); 1 son, Stanhope Wood; m. 2d, Mary Doran Martin, June 28, 1938. Transferred to construction corps of navy, 1884; in 1890 designed battleships Oregon, Indiana and Massachusetts, and then resigned from Navy to become superintending constructor of Cramp Shipyard, Phila.; resigned, 1895, and started Crescent Shipyard, Elizabeth, N.J., on own account, where he built 100 vessels in 6 yrs., among others the submarine topedo-boat Holland and seven other submarines, the monitor Florida, torpedo-boat O'Brien and cruiser Chattanooga; organized Standard Motor Constrn. Co.; propr. Lewis Nixon's Shipyard; started, 1895, and president until 1904, International Smokeless Powder Company; pres. Nixon Nitration Works, Raritan River Sand Co. Apptd. by Mayor Van Wyck, pres. East River Bridge Commn., 1898; trustee and pres. Webb Inst. of Naval Architecture. Democrat; succeeded Richard Croker as leader of Tammany Hall, Nov. 1901-May 1902; chmn. finance com. Dem. Congressional Campaign Com., 1902. Mem. N.Y. State Commn. to St. Louis Expn. Commr. pub. wks. Borough of Richmond, 1914-15; supt. pub. works of State of N.Y., 1919; pub. service commr. State of N.Y., 1919-20. Mem. bd. of visitors to U.S. Naval Acad., 1902, by appmt. of President Roosevelt. Received in spl. audiences by the King of England, Popes Pius X and XI, Emperor Nicholas of Russia, King of Belgians, Premier Mussolini and presidents of Argentine, Chile, Colombia, Panama, Costa Rica and Guatemala. Del. Dem. Nat. convs., 1900, 04, 08, 12, 20, 24, 32; chmn. Dem. State Conv., Buffalo, 1906; apptd. by President Taft, del. 4th Pan-Am. Conf., Buenos Aires, 1910, and E.E. and M.P. on special mission to represent U.S. at Chilean Centenary, 1910. Home: New York, N.Y. Died Sept. 23. 1940.

NIXON, OLIVER WOODSON literary editor The Inter Ocean; b. Guilford County, N.C., Oct. 25, 1825; s. Samuel N. His father was first man in State to free his slaves, removing to Ind., 1830. B.S., Farmers' Coll., O., 1848; Jefferson Med. Coll., Phila., 1854; LL.D., Whitman Coll., Wash., 1897; m. Louise Elstun, Batavia, O., 1855. Went to Calif., overland, 1850; raised 39th O. vols., 1861; was med. dir. Army of Mo.; on Gen. Pope's staff; served 2 terms treas. Hamilton Co., O., at Cincinnati. Established Evening Chronicle, Cincinnati, 1870, and with brother, William Penn N., consolidated it with Cincinnati Times; joined him, 1878, in purchase of The Inter Ocean, later disposing of it. Author: How Marcus Whitman Saved Oregon for the Union, 1895; Memories of a Forty-Niner, 1903. Residence: Chicago, Ill. Died 1905.

NOAILLES, LOUIS MARIE (Vicomte de Noailles), army officer; b. Paris, France, Apr. 17, 1756; son of Philippe, duc de Mouchy; m. Louise de Noailles (cousin), Sept. 19, 1773, at least 2 children. Served with French Army during Am. Revolution; col. Royal-Soissonais Regt. at battles of Savannah and Yorktown; rep. French Army at surrender negotiations; mem. French Estates-General, leader in nobles' renunciation of ancient privileges, 1789; fled France, 1792; became partner Bingham & Co., banking firm, Phila., 1793; speculated in Pa. lands; served as mil. officer in French West Indies during Napoleonic Wars. Died of wounds received in naval battle off Havana, Cuba, Jan. 5, 1804.

NOBLE, CHARLES HENRY brigadier gen. U.S.A.; b. Dayton, O., May 10, 1843; s. Danile Wintrhrop and Harriet Maria (Blood) N.; ed. at Indianapolis; m. Mary E. Palmer, Aug. 21, 1890. Served pvt. and corporal, Co. K, 1st Ind. Cav., June 20, 1861-June 19, 1864; capt., Aug. 1864-Feb. 1866; 2d lt. 16th U.S. Inf., Feb. 23, 1866; transferred to 34th Inf., Sept. 21, 1866; 1st lt., Feb. 10, 1867; transferred to 16th Inf., Apr. 14, 1869; capt., Nov. 26, 1884; maj. 25th Inf., Oct. 4, 1898; lt. col. 16th Inf., Feb. 2, 1901; col. 10th Inf., June 9, 1902; brig. gen. U.S.A. and retired, Oct. 20, 1906. In Civil War served in W.Va. under Gens. Reynolds and Milroy; escort to Gens. Fremont, Sigel and Howard in Va. campaigns; taken prisoner at 2d Bull Run; after exchange joined Army of Potomac, and attached to hdqrs. Army and engaged in Richmond campaign; after appmt. in regular service was with regt. in South and at frontier and other posts; in Spanish-Am. War, 1898, comd. battalion, 16th Inf., in Cuba, and regt. at battle of San Juan Hill; maj. 25th Inf., lt. col. 16th Inf., and col. 10th Inf., in P.I. Home: Indianapolis, Ind. Died Mar. 4, 1916.

NOBLE, EDWARD JOHN b. Gouverneur, N.Y., Aug. 8, 1882; s. Harvey H. and Edna L. (Wood) N.; A.B., Yale, 1905; LL.D., St. Lawrence U., 1939; m. Ethel Louise Tinkham, Nov. 6, 1920; children—June, Sally. Chairman of the Civil Aeronautics Authority, Aug. 1938-May 1939; under-secretary of Commerce, June 1939-Aug. 1940; mem. Indsl. Advisory Com. of Fed. Res. Bank of N.Y.; was chmn. bd. Life Savers Corp., chmn. exec. com., 1955—; pres., dir. Heart Island Operating Co., Inc., Heart Island Transportation Corp., Inc.; mem. adv. com. Bankers Trust Co. of New York; chmn. bd. and dir., American Broadcasting Company, Inc., purchased controlling interest, Oct. 1943. Maj., Ordnance Dept., U.S.A., 1917-19. Founder and trustee Edward John Noble Foundation (a charitable orgn.). Pres. bd. trustees St. Lawrence Univ.; chmn. bd. trustees North Country Hosps. Gouverneur, N.Y. Mem. Beta Theta Pi. Rep. Unitarian. Clubs: Round Hill, Field, Greenwich Riding (Conn.); Chevy Chase (Md.); Cloud, Yale, Racquet and Tennis (New York); Thousand Islands Club, Inc. (pres. and dir.). Home: Round Hill Rd., Greenwich, Conn. Died Dec. 28, 1958; buried Greenwich, Conn.

NOBLE, GEORGE BERNARD, former govt. cons.; b. Leesburg, Fla., July 11, 1892; s. Charles Samuel and Eva Susanna (Hall) N.; ed. U. Wash., 1910-13; B.A., Oxford U. (Rhodes scholar, 1913-16), Eng., 1915, M.A., 1923; U. of Wis., 1916-17; Columbia 1919-20, 1925-26, Ph.D., 1935; LL.D. Reed Coll, 1962; m. Matilda

Thomas, Dec. 24, 1917. Reporting on French opinion U.S. commn. to Negotiate Peace, 1918-19; asst. prof. polit. sci. U. of Neb., 1920-22; asst. prof. polit. sci., Reed Coll., Portland Ore., 1922-28, prof., 1928-43; vis. lecturer polit. sci., Barnard Coll., 1926-27; chmn. 12th Regional W.L.B., 1943-45; asst. chief div. research and publ., Dept. of State, Mar.-Sept. 1946, chief div. hist. policy research, 1946-53, chief hist. div., 1953-59, director historical office, 1959-62; cons. to Dept. State Pub. Affairs Bur., 1962-65. Member Oregon State Senate, 1941-42; chmn. Oregon State Adjustment Bd. (N.R.A.), 1934-35. Served as 1st lt., 168th inf., World War I. Decorated Distinguished Service Cross, 1918. Mem. Am. Polit. Sci., Am. Soc. Internat. Law, Am. Hist. Assn., Alpha Delta Phi, Phi Beta Kappa, Unitarian. Club: Cosmos (Washington). Author: Policies and Opinions at Paris, 1919, 1935; Christian A. Herter, 1970; various articles. Home: Falls Church VA Died Nov. 28, 1972.

NOBLE, HAROLD JOYCE historian; b. Pyeng Yang, Korea (of Am. parents), Jan. 19, 1903; s. William Arthur and Mattie (Wilcox) N.; A.B., Ohio Wesleyan U., 1924; M.A., Ohio State U., 1925; Ph.D., U. of Calif., 1931; m. Myrtle Bell Rinehart, June 25, 1941; 1 dau., Joyce. Instr. Ewha Coll., Seoul, Korea, 1926-28; teaching fellow, U. of Calif., 1929-31; asst. prof. history, U. of Ore., 1931-34, asso. prof., 1934-45, prof. since 1945; prof., Third Coll., Kyoto, Japan, 1939-40; fgn. corr. Saturday Evening Post, Japan, Korea, China, Australia, 1946; Rockefeller fellow Chinese and Japanese studies, U.S., Japan and China, 1936-38, in humanities since 1946, chif publs. branch Civil Intelligence Sect., GHQ, Far East Command, Tokyo, Japan, 1947-48; chief of polit. liaison office, Hdqrs., Seoul, Korea, 1948; mem. U.S. delegation to U.N. Gen. Assembly, 1949-51; 1st sec. Am. Embassy, Korea, 1951-53; exec. with Com. for Free Asia, San Francisco. Served in U.S.N.G., 1920-23; USMC, 1942-44, maj., 1943, seeing service in New Zealand, New Caledonia, Solomon Islands, as combat intelligence and Japanese langs. officer and co-comdr.; now mem. USMC Res. Decorated Navy Commendation Ribbon (Bougainville campaign). Mem. Vets. Fgn. Wars, Marine Corps Res. Officers Assn. Author: What It Takes to Rule Japan, 1946; also articles in Am. Jour. Internat. Law, Pacific Hist. Rev., Far Eastern Quarterly, Nankai (Tientsin) Soc. and Econ. Quarterly, Transactions of Korea Branch of Royal Asiatic Soc., Ore. Law Rev., Amerasia, Saturday Evening Post, Current History. Mem. bd. editors, Pacific Hist. Rev.; contbg. editor, Far Eastern Quarterly. Specializes in history and current affairs of Japan, Korea, and China. Home: 5 El Patil, Orinda, Cal. Died Dec. 22, 1953.

NOBLE, JAMES senator; b. Clarke County, Va., Dec. 16, 1783; s. Thomas and Elizabeth Claire (Sedgwick) N.; studied law under Richard Southgate, Newport, Ky.; m. Mary Lindsey, Apr. 7, 1803. Moved to Ky., circa 1800, to Ind., circa 1809; admitted to Ind. bar, began practice law, Lawrenceburg; pros. atty. Franklin County (Ind.), 1810; commd. lt. col. Ind. Militia, 1811; operated ferry across Ohio River from Switzerland County, Ind., 1815; apptd. to Ind. 3d Dist. Ct. by Gov. Thomas Posey, 1815; mem. Ind. Constl. Conv. from Franklin County, 1816, mem. coms. on legislative dept., elections, banks and militia; mem. 1st Ind. Ho. of Reps., 1816; mem. U.S. Senate from Ind., Dec. 11, 1816-Feb. 26, 1831, worked for internal improvements and devel. of West. Died Washington, D.C., Feb. 26, 1831; buried Congressional Cemetery, Washington.

NOBLE, JOHN WILLOCK Sec. of the Interior; b. Lancaster, O., Oct. 26, 1831; s. Col. John and Catherine (McDill) N.; A.B., Yale, 1851; LL.B., Cincinnati Law Sch., 1852; LL.D., Miami U., 1890, Yale, 1892; m. Lizabeth Halsted, Feb. 8, 1864 (died 1894). Admitted to bar, Columbus, O., 1853, St. Louis, 1855, Keokuk, Ia., 1856; city atty., Keokuk, 1859-60; enlisted in Union Army, serving through war in 3d Ia. Cav. as lt., adj., maj., lt. col. and col.; bvtd. brig. gen. by act of Congress for service in the field, Mar. 13, 1865. After war returned to St. Louis and engaged in practice there; U.S. dist. atty., 1867-70, prosecuting whisky and tobacco frauds of that period; was offered portfolio of solicitor-gen. by Gen. Grant, but declined. Sec. of the Interior, in cabinet of President Harrison, 1889-93. Republican. Mem. G.A.R., Mo. Commandery Loyal Legion, Sons of Veterans. Home: St. Louis, Mo. Died Mar. 22, 1912.

NOBLE, ROBERT ERNEST army surgeon; b. Rome, Ga., Nov. 5, 1870; s. George and Lucy (Wadsworth) N.; M.S., Ala. Poly. Inst., 1891; M.D., Columbia, 1899; honor grad. Army Med. Sch., 1901; m. Ella L. Lupton, Nov. 23, 1905. Apptd. asst. surgeon, June 29, 1901; capt. asst. surgeon and capt. M.C., June 29, 1906; maj., Jan. 1, 1910; lt. col., May 15, 1917; col. N.A., Jan. 26, 1918; brig. gen. Med. Corps, N.A., May 9, 1918; maj. gen. (temp.) asst. surgeon gen. AEF, Oct. 30, 1918; brig. gen. asst. surg. gen. U.S. Army, Mar. 5, 1919. In Philippines, 1900-03; with dept. of sanitation, Isthmus Canal Commn., 1907-14; in charge anti-mosquito campaign, P.R., 8 mos., 1911-12; mem. san. commn. to Guayaquil, Ecuador, to study yellow fever, 1912-13; mem. commn. to Rand mines, Transvaal, South Africa, to study cause of pneumonia, 1913-14; at Vera Cruz, Mexico, May-Sept. 1914; duty War Dept., Washington, 1914-18; arrived in France, Oct. 25, 1918; returned to U.S., Aug. 3, 1919; retired as maj. gen., Feb. 8, 1925; mem. and later dir. Rockefeller Found. Yellow Fever Commn. to the West Coast of Africa, May 4-Dec. 3, 1920. Decorated D.S.M. (U.S.); Comdr. Legion of Honor (France). Mem. A.M.A., A.C.S., Soc. Colonial Wars. Soc. of the Cincinnati, Newcomen Soc. of England American (Ala.) Branch, Phi Delta Theta. Episcopalian. Club: Army and Navy (Washington). Address: Crowan Cottage, 1401 Woodstock Av., Anniston, Ala. Died Sept. 18, 1956; buried Anniston.

NOBLE, ROBERT HOUSTON army officer; b. Federalsburg, Md., Nov. 3, 1861; s. Dr. William D. and Mary A. (Houston) N.; grad. U.S. Mil. Acad., 1884; LL.B., U. of Md., 1892; A.M., St. John's Coll., Md., 1894; admitted to bar, Md., 1892, Calif., 1910; graduate of The Army War College, 1912; m. Mrs. Ethel E. Sherwood, May 14, 1921. Commd. 2d lt. 1st Inf., June 15, 1884; 1st lt. 15th Inf., June 15, 1891; trans. to 1st Inf., July 20, 1891; maj. a.-a.-g. vols., June 20, 1898; hon. discharged vols., Mar. 19, 1889; maj. a.-a.-g. vols., Sept. 5, 1899; hon. discharged vols., June 30, 1901; capt. inf., U.S.A., Oct. 12, 1898; assigned to 3d Inf., Jan. 1, 1899; maj. 9th Inf., Oct. 4, 1907; trans. to 1st Inf., Nov. 11, 1907, to 12th Inf., May 8, 1911; lt. col. inf., Feb. 1, 1913; assigned to 22d Infantry, July 22, 1914; colonel, July 1, 1916; brigadier general N.A., April 16-Nov. 12, 1918. Participated in Geronimo campaign, 1885-86; a.-d.-c. to Gen. Shafter, 1897-99; Santiago campaign; Philippine Insurrection; adj. gen. to Gens. Grant, Hughes, Snyder and Baldwin, and adj. gen. Dept. Visayas, 1900-02; a.-d.-c. to Govs. Gen. Taft, Wright, Ide and Smith, P.I., 1902-08; in charge militia affairs, Western Dept., 1913-14; comdg. 22d Inf., Mexican border, Sept. 1914-Sept. 1916; punitive expdn. in Mex., Nov. 1916-Feb. 1917; at El Paso, Tex., and Chickamauga Park, Ga., to Apr. 6, 1918, and in 5th Div. A.E.F., France, to May 2, 1918; attached to 30th and 77th divs. A.E.F. to Aug. 11, 1918; comd. 158th Brig. and attached to 79th Div., Aug. 14-Oct. 11, 1918; returned to U.S., Mar. 24, 1919; in charge nat. guard affairs, Western Dept., Apr. 21, 1919—. Recommended for bvt. lt. col., Spanish-Am. War. Address: Washington, D.C. Died Oct. 26, 1939.

NOBLE, THOMAS SATTERWHITE artist; b. Lexington, Ky., May 29, 1835; studied in Paris, France. Served as capt. Confederate Army during Civil War; opened studio, N.Y.C., after Civil War, became known as hist. painter; prin. and prof. art Sch. of Design, McMicken U., Cincinnati, 1869-1904; elected asst., N.A.D., 1867. Died N.Y.C., Apr. 27, 1907.

NOE, JAMES THOMAS COTTON prof. education; b. Washington Co., Ky., May 2, 1864; s. John Washington and Margaret Anne (Trowbridge) N.; A.B., Franklin (Ind.) Coll., 1887, A.M., 1890, D.Litt., 1919; studied Cornell U., 1891-92, U. of Chicago, 1899; m. Sidney Stanfill, of Williamsburg, Ky., May 2, 1894. Teacher secondary schs., Ky. and Ind., 1887-92, Williamsburg (Ky.) Inst., 1893; practiced law, 1894-98; prin. Hartsville (Tenn.) Masonic Inst., 1898-1901, Theodore Harris Inst., 1901-04; instr. Lincoln Memorial U., 1904-06; same, State Coll. Normal Sch., Ky., 1906-08; asst. prof. edn., 1908, asso. prof., 1911, prof. and head dept., 1912-34, University of Ky.; now prof. emeritus. Editor Ky. High Sch. Quarterly. Mem. Bd. of Edn., Lexington, Ky. Mem. Nat. Edn. Assn., College Teachers of Education, American Assn. Univ. Profs., Southern Edn. Conf., Kentucky Folk-Lore Soc., Louisville Arts Club, Phi Delta Theta. Republican. Baptist. Mason. Clubs: Scribblers, Louisville Arts (non-res.). Authors: The Loom of Life, 1912, 17; The Blood of Rachel, 1917; Lincoln and Twenty Other Poems, 1922; Tip Sams of Kentucky, 1926; The Legend of the Silver Band, 1932; The Valleys of Parnassus, 1934; Anthology of Kentucky Poetry, 1935. Chautauqua lecturer. Poet-laureate of Kentucky by joint resolution of General Assembly of Ky., 1926. Home: 231 E. Maxwell St., Lexington, Ky.

NOEL, EDMUND FAVOR governor; b. nr. Lexington, Miss., Mar. 4, 1856; s. Leland and Margaret A. (Sanders) N.; ed. Louisville (Ky.) High Sch., 3 yrs.; read law under uncle, Maj. D. W. Sanders, Louisville, 1875-76; m. Loula Hoskins, June 4, 1890 (died 1891) m. 2d, Mrs. Alice Tye Neilson, Sept. 12, 1905. Admitted to bar, 1877, in practice at Lexington, 1877—; mem. law firm Noel & Neilson. Mem. Miss. Ho. of Rep., 1881-82; dist. atty., 1887-91; mem. Senate, 1895-1903 and 1920-28; capt. Co. K, 2d Miss. Inf., Spanish-Am. War; gov. of Miss., 1908-12. Democrat. First chmn. of 1st Conf. of Govs. held in U.S., at Washington, May 1908. Bapt. Mason. Home: Lexington, Miss. Died July 30, 1927.

NOELL, THOMAS ESTES congressman; b. Perryville, Mo., Apr. 3, 1839; s. John William Noell; attended pub. schs.; studied law. Admitted to Mo. bar, 1858, began practice in Perryville; apptd. mil. commr. during Civil War, 1861; served as maj. Mo. Militia, 1861-62; capt. Co. C, 19th Inf., U.S. Army, 1862-65; mem. U.S. Ho. of Reps. (Radical) from Mo., 39th-40th congresses, 1865-67. Died St. Louis, Oct. 3, 1867; buried St. Mary's Cemetery, Perryville.

NOLAN, DENNIS EDWARD army officer; b. Akron, N.Y., Apr. 22, 1872; s. Martin N.; grad. U.S. Mil. Acad., 1896; m. Julia Grant Sharp, Aug. 21, 1901; children—Dennis Edward (dec.), Ellen Honora. Commd. add, 2d lt. 3d Inf., June 12, 1896; 2d lt. 1st Inf., Aug. 27, 1896; 1st lt. of inf., Dec. 14, 1898; assigned to 1st Inf., Jan. 1, 1899; trans. 13th Inf., Mar. 14, 1890; maj. 11th U.S. Cav., Aug. 10, 1899; hon. discharged vols., Mar. 13, 1901; capt. 30th inf., July 6, 1901; maj., July 1, 1916; lt. col. (temp.), Aug. 5, 1917; col. (temp.), Aug. 5, 1917; brig. gen. (temp.), Aug. 8, 1919; brig. gen. regular army, Mar. 6, 1921; maj. gen., Jan. 18, 1925. In Cuba, Spanish-Am. War; participated Battle of El Caney, July 1, 1898; a.-d.-c. to Brig. Gen. Chambers McKibbin, at Santiago, Cuba, and Montauk Pt., N.Y.; duty at Camp Meade, Md., and Camp McKenzie, Ga.; in Philippines, 1901-02, 1906-11, in Alaska, 1912-13; duty Gen. Staff, 1903-06, 1915-19; arrived in France, June 9, 1917; with Gen. Staff Corps, AEF, 1917-19, chief of Intelligence Service, AEF, until demobilization; comd. 55th Brigade, 28th Div., in Argonne-Meuse offensive. Dep. Chief of Staff, U.S. Army, Sept. 14, 1924; chief of Army rep. with Prep. Commn. on Reduction and Limitation of Armaments, Geneva, 1926-27; comdr. 5th Corps Area, 1927-31, 2d Corps Area, 1931-36; retired. Dir. states participation N.Y. World's Fair, 1936-40; chmn. bd. trustees Citizens Budget Commn., N.Y.C., 1940-51. Recommended for bvts. of 1st lt. and capt., U.S. Army, for services in Spanish-Am. War; D.S.M., 1918, "for organizing and administering the Intelligence Service": D.S.C., "for conduct in action" at Apremont; Croix de Guerre with Palm and Comdr. Legion of Honor (France); Comdr. of the Bath (Gt. Britain) Comdr. of the Crown (Italy); Comdr. of the Crown (Belgium); Medal of La Solidaridad (Panama). Roman Catholic. Clubs: Army and Navy (Washington); Chevy Chase (Md.). Home: 50 E. 58th St., N.Y.C. Died Feb. 24, 1953; buried Arlington Nat. Cemetery.

NOLAN, EDWARD JAMES oil operator; b. Rochester, N.Y., May 10, 1888; s. Peter and Margaret (Purcell) N.; LL.B., U. So. Cal., 1911; m. Grace Morse, July 12, 1928. Admitted to Cal. bar, 1911, and practiced at Los Angeles until 1924; v.p. Merchants Nat. Bank of Los Angeles, 1924-26; pres. Merchants Nat. Trust & Savings Bank, 1926-28; pres. Bank of America of Cal., 1928-30; chmn. Bank of America Nat. Trust & Savings Ass., 1930-39. Commd. as maj., A.C., 1942, promoted to lt. col., 1942, col., 1944; served on staff comdg. gen. 9th Air Force; later asst. to comdg. gen. 1st Allied Airborn Army; disch. Jan. 1946. Dec. Legion of Merit, Bronze Star, Purple Heart. Home: Houston. Died Feb. 4, 1957.

NOLAN, VAL lawyer; b. Evansville, Ind., Feb. 21, 1892; s. John J. and Valentine F. (Fitz-William) N.; student Ind. U., 1912-15, U. of Chicago, 1917; m. Jeannette Covert, Oct. 4, 1917; children—Val, Alan Tucker, Kathleen Covert. Admitted to Indiana bar, 1915; dep. pros. atty. 1st Jud. Circuit, Ind., 1916-17; in practice at Evansville, 1919-30; city atty., Evansville, 1930-33; U.S. dist. atty. Southern Dist. of Ind., 1933—. V.p. and cons. counsel Hearthstone Life Insurance Co., Indianapolis, 1938. Declined position of chief counsel to U.S. High Commr. to Philippines, 1937. Pvt. U.S.A., 1917; 1st lt. F.A., 1918; lt. F.A., U.S.R., 1919. Mem. Social Service Commn., Venezuela, 1939. Trustee Evansville Coll., Ind. U., James Whitcomb Riley Hosp. for Crippled Children, Indianapolis. Mem. Evansville Bar Assn. (pres. 1930). Democrat. Catholic. Home: Evansville, Ind. Died Oct. 11, 1940.

NOLAND, LLOYD surgeon; b. Gordonsville, Va., July 25, 1880; s. Cuthbert Powell and Rosalie (Haxall) N.; grad. Central High Sch., Washington, 1898; M.D., Baltimore Med. Coll., 1903; m. Margaret Gillick, Nov. 7, 1907. Began practice, Baltimore, 1903; exec. officer to chief sanitary officer, Isthmian Canal Commn., 1904-05; chief of surg. clinic, Isthmian Canal Hosp., Colon, 1906-13; commd. asst. surgeon Med. Reserve Corps, U.S. Navy, 1913-21; supt. dept. of health, and chief surgeon, Tenn. Coal, Iron & R.R. Co., since 1913. Democrat. Episcopalian. Mem. A.M.A. (chmn. sect. on surgery, 1941; mem. Judicial council since 1942), Am. Pub. Health Asso., Canal Zone Med. Asso., Medical Assn. State of Ala. (past pres.), Southern Med. Assn.; fellow Am. Coll. Surgeons, Southern Surg. Assn. (past pres.). Clubs: Mountain Brook Country, Army and Navy. Home: 3240 Sterling Road, Birmingham, Ala. Died Nov. 27, 1949.

NOLL, EDWARD ANGUS AUGUST file co. exec.; b. Cumberland, Md., May 19, 1867; s. Henry and Elizabeth (Sheermeeser) N.; student pub. schs.; m. Lulu Miller, Mar. 1893; 1 son, Edward Leonard. Pres., gen. mgr. The Nat. Tool Co., 1905-25; pres. The Nolvex Tile Co.; dir. The Lang Body Co. Joined Euclid Light Inf., 1888, Ohio N.G., 1889; promoted through grades to maj. Fifth Regt., 1900; capt. Ohio Vol. Inf., Spanish-Am. War. Mem. U.S., Cleve. C.'s of C., Nat. Aero. Assn. Mem. K.P. Clubs: Nat. Town and Country, Cleveland Aviation, Cleveland Athletic. Home: 570 Morewood Pkwy., Rocky River 16, O. Office: 10329 Detroit Av., Cleve. Died Oct. 29, 1939; buried Elmhurst Park, Avon, O.

NORBECK, KERMIT GEORGE, judge; b. Redfield, S.D., June 18, 1909; s. George and Jane M. (Olson) N.; student S.D. State Coll., 1926-27, U. S.D., 1930-32, LL.B., 1937; m. Winfree Virginia Farmer, Aug. 7, 1935; children—George Philip, Winfree Judith, Mary Virginia. Admitted to S.D. bar, 1937; spl. counsel S.D. Supt. Banks, Pierre, 1937-38; practiced in Redfield, 1939-56; states atty. Spink County, S.D., 1941-44, 51-52; judge 9th Jud. Circuit Ct., Redfield, 1956-70. Served with inf., AUS, 1944-46, as capt. Judge Adv. Gen's Corps., 1952-54. Mem. Am., S.D. bar assns., National Coll. State Trial Judges (faculty 1964). Republican. Lutheran. Mason (Shriner), Elk. Home: Redfield SD Died Dec. 19, 1970.

NORCROSS, FRANK HERBERT, judge; b. Reno, Nev., May 11, 1869; s. Thomas W. and Caroline B. (Sherman) N.; A.B., U. of Nev., 1891, LL.D., 1911; LL.B., Georgetown U., D.C., 1894; m. Adeline L. Morton, July 10, 1895; 1 dau., Adele Cutts (Mrs. Edwin S. Bender). County surveyor, Washoe County, Nev., 1891-92; clerk U.S. Census Office, Washington, 1892-94; admitted to Nev. bar, 1894, Calif. bar, 1903, bar of Supreme Court of U.S., 1922. Dist. atty. Washoe County, 1895-97; mem. Nev. Assembly, 1897-99; justice Supreme Ct. of Nev., 1904-16 (chief justice, 1909-11, 1915-16); resumed practice at Reno, Nev., 1917; U.S. dist. judge, District of Nevada, 1928-45. Served pvt. to capt. Co. C, Nev. Nat. Guard; U. of Nev. R.O.T.C., Co. A, 1886-91; commd. hon. col., 1941. Mem. Nat. Civic Fedn., Am. Bar Assn., Nev. Bar Assn. (pres. 1920), Am. Inst. Criminal Law and Criminology (v.p. 1913-15). Elector, New York U. Hall of Fame. Chmn. Nev. delegation Rep. Nat. Conv., 1920; mem. council Nat. Econ. League; mem. Phi Kappa Phi. Kiwanian. Grand Master of Masons, Nev., 1909-10; 33 deg.; A.A.S.R. Author: Christianity and Divorce. Contbr. to legal mags., etc. Asso. editor Jour. Am. Inst. Criminal Law and Criminology, 1909-15. Home: Reno NV

NORD, JAMES GARESCHÉ army officer; b. Fort Lewis, Colo., Oct. 18, 1886; s. Maj. Edward Otho Cresap Ord II, U.S. Army, and Mary Frances (Norton) O.; B.S., U.S. Mil. Acad., West Point, 1909; student Sch. of Musketry, Monterey, Calif., 1910, Inf. Sch., Fort Benning, Ga., 1921-22, Command and Gen. Staff Sch., 1923-24, Army War Coll., 1928-29; m. Irene H. Walsh, Apr. 19, 1927; children—James Garesché, Jr., Marian Eleanor, Edward Otho Cresap. Commd. 2d lt., U.S. Army, 1909, advanced through ranks to maj. gen., 1944; on Mexican border, central Alaska, 1909-17; instr. 1st Plattsburg Camp, 1916; at Culver Mil. Acad., and O.T.C., at Fort Des Moines, Iowa, 1917; with A.E.F., France, 1917-19, participated in Aisne-Marne, St. Mihiel, Argonne campaigns, occupation of Rhineland; operations staff officer, 1st Army Corps and 3d Army; on staff, 9th Corps Area, San Francisco, 1919-21; War Plans Div., War Dept. Gen. Staff, Washington, D.C., 1930-34; instr. Command and Gen. Staff Sch., 1924-28; maj., 30th Inf., 1929-30; comdg. Ft. Washington, Md., 1934-36; dir., Inf. Bd., Ft. Benning, Ga., 1936-38; comdg. 57th Inf., P.I., 1938-40; sr. instr., Pa. Nat. Guard, June to Oct., 1940; brig. gen., 1st Div., comdg. Army contingents of Spl. Task Force, specializing with Atlantic Fleet in landing operations, 1940-42; comdg. 28th Inf. Div., 1942. Chairman, Joint Brazil-U.S. Defense Commission, June 1942-—; U.S. Army delegate on the Inter-American Defense Board, Feb. 1943-—. Died Apr. 15, 1960.

NORMAN, EDWARD A(LBERT) financier; b. Chgo., Mar. 9, 1900; s. Aaron Edward and Charlotte (Rosenfield) N.; A.B., Harvard, 1923; M.A., Columbia, 1944; m. Dorothy Stecker, June 10, 1925; children—Nancy, Andrew Edward; m. 2d, Elizabeth Blair, Nov. 8, 1953. Dir. Palestine Economic Corp., Trade Bank & Trust Co., N.Y.C. Dir. Health Ins. Plan of Greater N.Y., Play Schs. Assn. N.Y., Am. Friends of Hebrew U.; trustee Mt. Sinai Hosp.; gov. Hebrew U. in Jerusalem. Served from lt. to lt. comdr., USN, 1942-45. Mem. Group Farming Research Inst.(pres.), Am. Fund for Israel Instns. Clubs: Adirondack Mountain, Amateur Ski, Harvard, Goldens Bridge Hounds (N.Y.C.); Quissett Yacht (Falmouth, Mass.); Woods Hole (Mass.) Yacht; American (London, Eng.). Home: Pound Ridge, N.Y. Office: 654 Madison Av., N.Y.C. 21. Died June 20, 1954; buried Hickory Hill, Katonah, N.Y.

NORRIS, CHARLES GILMAN author; b. Chicago, Ill., Apr. 23, 1881; s. Benjamin Franklin and Gertrude G. (Doggett) N.; Ph.B., U. of Calif., 1903; m. Kathleen Thompson (now the well known author), Apr. 30, 1909; children—Frank, Josephine (dec.), Gertrude (dec.). Asst. editor Country Life in America, 1903, Sunset Mag., 1905; asst. editor Am. Mag., 1908-13. Entered R.O.T.C. at Madison Barracks, N.Y., Apr. 1917; grad. capt. inf.; assigned to 153d Depot Brigade, Camp Dix, N.J.; maj. inf., Aug. 1918; resigned, Dec. 1918. Mem. Phi Gamma Delta. Clubs: Players, Dutch Treat (New York); Bohemian (San Francisco); Menio Country (Menio, Calif.). Republican. Episcopalian. Author: The Amateur, 1915; Salt, or the Education of Griffith Adams, 1917; Brass, 1921; The Rout of the Philistines (poetic drama—"grove play" of Bohemian Club), 1922; Bread, 1923; Pig Iron, 1925; Zelda Marsh, 1927; A Gest of Robin Hood ("grove play" of Bohemian Club), 1929; Seed, 1930; Zest, 1933; Hands, 1935; Ivanhoe ("grove play" of Bohemian Club), 1936; Bricks without Straw, 1938; Flint, 1944; also numerous short stories in mags. Home: 1247 Cowper St., Palo Alto, Calif. Died July 25, 1945.

NORRIS, EARLE BERTRAM, dean emeritus; born Jamestown, N.Y., Sept. 17, 1882; s. Harry E. and Belle (Barker) N.; B.S. in M.E., Pa. State Coll., 1904, M.E., 1908; M. Faye Hurd, 1905. Designer of spl. machinery, E. Bement's Sons, Lansing, Mich., 1904, cost clk., 1905; asst. supt. Central Implement Co., Standish, Mich., 1905; instr. in mech. engring., Pa. State Coll., 1906-08; asst. prof. mech. engring., U. of Wis., 1908-12, asso. prof., 1912-16; industrial commr. St. Paul (Minn.) Assn. of Commerce, 1916-17; dean of engring, U. of Mont., 1919-28; dean of engring., Va. Poly. Inst., Blacksburg, 1928-52, dean emeritus, 1952, also dir. Engring. Expt. Sta., 1931-52; pres. Va. Poly. Inst. Research Foundation, 1935-53; consulting mechanical engineer. Capt. and maj. Ordnance Dept. U.S. Army, 1917-19; chief engr. Rock Island Arsenal, 1919; lt. col. Ordance Reserve, 1925-40. Cited by General Pershing for eminently meritorious and conspicious services in the A.E.F., 1919; awarded Purple Heart medal. Profl. mech. engr. Va. Mem. So. Assn. Sci. and Industry (trustee), A.S.M.E., Virginia Acad. Science (pres. 1939), Am. Soc. Engring. Education (v.p. 1946-47), Newcomen Soc., Phi Gamma Delta, Tau Beta Pi, Phi Kappa Phi, Sigma Xi, Pi Tau Sigma, Omicron Delta Kappa, Alpha Pi Mu, Scabbard and Blade. Mason. (32 degree). Co-author: Shop Arthmetic (with K.G. Smith), 1912; Advanced Shop Mathematics (with R.T. Craigo), 1913; Gas Engine Ignition (with W.C. Weaver and R.K. Winning), 1916; Heat Power (with Eric Therkelsen), 1931; The Plastic Flow of Metals, 1936; Applied Thermodynamies (with C.E. Trent), 1955. Home: Blacksburg VA Died Oct. 15, 1966.

NORRIS, ERNEST EDEN ry. official; b. Hoopeston, Ill., Jan. 21, 1882; s. Luther Calvin and Amanda (Lightner) N.; ed. pub. schs., Hoopeston; D.Sc., U. Tenn., 1951; LL.D., Davidson Coll., 1951; m. Kathryn Augusta Callan, Aug. 10, 1905; children—Frank Callan, Eden. Messenger boy Western Union, Hoopeston, 1892-95, mgr. Watseka (Ill.) office, 1895-96; asst. baggage master, telegrapher C. & N.W. R.R., Arlington Heights, Ill., 1896-97, clerk., telegrapher, Reedsburg, Wis., 1897-98, dispatcher at Chgo., 1898-99, trainmaster at Chgo., 1899-1901; became car service agent for the Southern Ry., at Washington, D.C., 1902; continued with same rd., trainmaster, Norfolk, Va., asst. supt., and supt. Knoxville, Tenn., supt., Atlanta, gen. supt., Knoxville, and asst. to pres., Washington, D.C., 1918-19; v.p. Mobile & Ohio R.R. Co., 1919-32, receiver, 1932-33; v.p. Southern Ry. System, 1933-37, pres., 1937-52, chmn. bd., 1952, dir., 1953-—; dir. Riggs Nat. Bank, Washington, Met. Life Ins. Co. Comm. & col. transportation corps, U.S.Army, 1943, ordered to duty as regional dir. Southeastern Region 1943-44, 48, 50 during fed. seizures of railroads. Nat. asso. Boys Clubs Am. Mem. Nat. Geog. Soc. (life trustee), So. Research Inst. (adv. council), So. States Indsl. Council (dir.), Transportation Assn. Am. (dir.). Mason (Shriner). Clubs: Manhattan (N.Y.); Met. (Wash.). Voted one of America's 50 foremost bus. leaders, Forbes Mag. poll, 1947. Home: 2204 Wyoming Av. N.W. Office: Southern Ry. Bldg., McPherson Sq., Washington. Died Apr. 23, 1958; buried Hoopeston, Ill.

NORRIS, GEORGE WILLIAM physician; b. Phila., Jan. 1, 1875; s. William Fisher (M.D.) and Rosa Clara (Buchmann) N.; B.A., U. of Pa., 1895, M.D., 1899; unmarried. Practiced, Phila., 1899-1932, was prof. clin. medicine, U. of Pa.; chief of medical service "A," Pennsylvania Hospital. Colonel Med. Corps, U.S. Army, World War, later col. Med. O.R.C. Trustee of Mutual Assurance Co. of Phila. Fellow Coll. Physicians of Phila.; mem. Am. Philos. Soc., Assn. Am. Physicians, A.M.A., Phila. Pathol. Soc., Acad. Natural Sciences, Phi Kappa Sigma Fraternity. Club: Philadelphia. Author: Studies in Cardiac Pathology; Blood Pressure, Its Clinical Applications also articles on "Pneumonia," in Osler's Modern Medicine, and numerous contbns. in med. jours. Co-author of Norris & Landis Diseases of the Chest and the Principles of Phys. Diagnosis. Address: Dimock, Pa. Died Apr. 7, 1948.

NORRIS, JAMES FLACK chemist; b. Baltimore, Jan. 20, 1871; s. Rev. Richard and Sarah Amanda (Baker) N.; A.B., Johns Hopkins, 1892, fellow in chemistry, 1894-95, Ph.D., 1895; honorary Sc.D., Bowdoin Coll., 1929; m. Anne Bent Chamberlin, Feb. 4, 1902. Asst., 1895-96, instr., 1896-1900, asst. prof. organic chemistry, 1900-04, Mass. Inst. Tech.; prof. chemistry, Simmons Coll., Boston, 1904-15, Vanderbilt U., 1915-16; prof. organic chemistry, in charge grad. students in chemistry, dir. research lab. organic chemistry, Mass. Inst. Tech., 1916-—. In charge offense chem. research, war gas investigations, U.S. Bur. Mines, 1917-18; asso. mem. Naval Consulting Bd., 1916; lt. col., U.S.A., in charge U.S. Chem. Warfare Service, Eng., 1918; in charge investigation mfr. war gases in German chem. plants, 1919. Chmn. div. chemistry and chem. tech. Nat. Research Council, 1924-25, mem. exec. bd., 1925-33. Lecturer on organic chemistry, Harvard, 1912-14, Clark U., 1913-14, Bowdoin, 1929. Medalist American Institute of Chemists, 1937; Secretary Soc. of Arts of Boston, Mass., 1902-04; president Am. Chem. Soc., 1925-26 (pres. Northeastern sect., 1905-06); pres. Chem. Teachers' Assn. of N.E., 1906-08, Technology Club, 1906-09; v.p. Internat. Union of Pure and Aplied Chemistry, 1925-28. Fellow Am. Acad. Arts and Sciences (v.p., 1934-—), A.A.A.S. (chmn. Sect. C, 1930). Author: The Principles of Organic Chemistry; Experimental Organic Chemistry; Text-book of Inorganic Chemistry for Colleges (with R. C. Young); Laboratory Exercises in Inorganic Chemistry (with K. L. Mark). Home: Boston, Mass. Died Aug. 4, 1940.

NORTH, ARTHUR A(LEXANDER) coll. dean; b. Nyack, N.Y., Oct. 6, 1907; s. John T. and Anna R. (Kelly) N.; student St. Francis Xavier, N.Y.C., 1919-27; A.B., Fordham U., 1931, Ph.D., 1951; A.M., Boston Coll., 1933; Ph.D., Weston Coll., Boston, 1934, S.T.L., 1938. Entered Order of Jesuits 1927; ordained priest, Roman Catholic Ch., 1937; prof. history Loyola Coll., Balt., 1939-41; prof. philosophy, Scranton (Pa.) U., 1945-48, dean coll., 1948; dean Loyola Coll. Evening Sch. and Grad. Div., Balt., 1949-52; vice chmn. dept. polit. philosophy and social scis., prof. gov. and polit. sci. Fordham U., dean Grad. Sch., Fordham U., 1953-64, also asso. prof. dept. polit. philosophy. Served as maj. chaplain corps U.S. Army, 1941-44; overseas in S.W. Pacific; disch. to Reserves as lt. col. Mem. N.E.A., Nat. Cath. Edn. Assn., Balt. Edn. Assn., Am. Polit. Sci. Assn. Author: The Supreme Court: Judicial Process and Judicial Politics, 1966. Address: Fordham U., N.Y.C. 58. Died Jan. 1966.

NORTH, FRANK JOSHUA scout, plainsman; b. Ludlowville, N.Y., Mar. 10, 1840; s. Thomas Jefferson and Jane (Townley) N.; m. Mary Smith, Dec. 25, 1865, 1 dau. Moved with family to Neb. Territory, 1856; clk.-interpreter at Pawnee reservation on Loup River, Neb., 1861; commd. capt. of scouts, 1864, took part in Powder River Indian Expdn., other expdns.; commd. maj. of 4 Pawnee battalions for protection of U.P. R.R. during constrn., 1867; guide-interpreter at Ft. D.A. Russell (Wyo.) and Sidney Barracks (Neb.); leader Pawnee scouts in expdn. against the Cheyennes, 1876; elected to Neb. Legislature, 1882; mem. William F. Cody's Wild West Show; known as leading plainsman of his time; good pistol shot, beat James Butler ("Wild Bill") Hickok in competition, 1873. Died Columbus, Neb., Mar. 14, 1885.

NORTH, WILLIAM senator, army officer; b. Ft. Frederic, Pemaquid, Me., 1755; s. John and Elizabeth (Pitson) N.; m. Mary Duane, Oct. 14, 1787, 6 children. Moved to Boston after father's death, 1763; became 2d lt. in Col. Thomas Craft's train of arty., 1776; apptd. aide-de-camp to Baron von Steuben, 1779 (mil. relationship grew into close friendship), wrote biog. sketch of Von Steuben; served as insp. of army with rank of maj., after war; mem. commn. to strengthen defenses of N.Y. State, 1794; speaker N.Y. Assembly, 1795, 96, 1810; mem. U.S. Senate (Federalist) from N.Y., May 5, 1798-Aug. 17, 1798, voted for Alien and Sedition Acts; commd. brig. gen., served as adjutant gen. of provisional army, 1798-1800; mem. commn. to report on possibility of canal between lakes Erie and Ontario and Hudson River, 1810. Died Duanesburg, N.Y., Jan. 3, 1836; buried Christ Episcopal Ch., Duanesburg.

NORTHINGTON, JAMES MONTGOMERY editor med. jours.; b. Mecklenburg County, Va., Oct. 11, 1885; s. Oscar Fitzallen and Nannie Page (Perkinson) N.; M.D. (scholarship), Med. Coll. Va., 1905; student N.Y. Postgrad. Med. Sch., 1911, 14; m. Mary Elizabeth Clark, Apr. 11, 1931; children—Nancy (Mrs. Hubert V. Davis, Jr.), Betty, Sarah (Mrs. Tom E. Terrill). Intern Meml. Hosp., Richmond, Va., 1905-07, also instr. physiology Med. Coll. Va.; gen. practice of medicine, 1908-15; instr. medicine U. Minn. Med. Sch., 1915-17; practice internal medicine, Mpls., 1915-17; Charlotte, N.C., 1920-60; staff St. Peters, Mercy, Presbyn., Meml., Good Samaritan hosps., Charlotte, N.C.; editor med. jours., 1924-—; editor So. Medicine and Surgery, 1924-50, So. Gen. Practice, 1950-53, Clinical Medicine, 1953, Medical Digest, 1954, EENT Digest, 1957-—. Served to maj. M.C., U.S. Army, 1917-20; AEF in France; chief medical service Base Hosp. No. 65 and Hosp. Center, Kerhuon, France. Mem. Am. Med. Writers Assn. N.Y. Acad. Scis., A.A.A.S., N.C. Lit. and Hist. Assn., Med. Coll. Va. Alumni Soc. (past pres.), Tri-State (past sec.-treas.), Mecklenburg County (past pres.) med. socs., Med. Soc. State N.C., A.M.A. Address: 2148 Malvern Rd., Charlotte, N.C. 28207. Died Jan. 15, 1964; buried Evergreen Cemetery, Charlotte.

NORTHROP, LUCIUS BELLINGER army officer; b. Charleston, S.C., Sept. 8, 1811; s. Amos Bird and Claudia (Bellinger) N.; grad. U.S. Mil. Acad., 1831; m. Maria de Bernabeu, 1841. Brevetted 2d lt. inf., U.S. Army, 1831; transferred to 1st Dragoons, 1833; commd. 1st lt., 1834, capt., 1839; col. and commissary gen. Confederate Army, 1861; responsible for feeding of Confederate troops and Northern war prisoners; unpopular among many Confederate gens., some of whom (Lee, Johnston, Beauregard) pressed for his removal. Died Pikesville, Md., Feb. 9, 1894.

NORTON, A(RTHUR) WARREN, business exec.; born Meriden, Conn., Dec. 4, 1896; s. Frank Hall and Caroline (Carter) N.; student Browne and Nichols Prep. Sch., Mass., 1915-16; Rose Polytech. Inst., Terre Haute, Ind., 1916-17; S.B., Mass. Inst. Technol., 1921; M. Helen Westfall, 1923; children—Edward Westfall, Warren Stevens. Asst. to works Mgr., Continental Motors Corp., 1921-22; salesman Brooklyn Daily Eagle, 1922-23; partner O'Mara and Ormsbee, Inc., 1923-39; mgr. Christian Sci. Publishing Soc. (and mem. editorial council), 1939-44; chmn. bd., pres., wireless communications system, Press Wireless, Inc., 1944-47; chmn. bd., pres. wireless communications equipment, Press Wireless Mfg. Corp., 1945-48; asst. to Arthur Hays Sulzberger, pub. N.Y. Times. Served in World

War I, Naval Aviation. Mem. industry adv. com. and radiocommunications com., Bd. War Communications, World War II; spl. recognition from War Dept. for outstanding civilian service. Mem. Corp. Mass. Inst. Tech. (mem. vis. com. for dept. physics, elec. engring., English and history, food tech.). Trustee World-wide Boradcasting Found. Mem. N.E. Council (dir. aviation com., financial policy com., 1940-44). Asso. press Am. Newspaper Pub. Assn., Boston Com. Econ. Development, New Eng. Shippers (mem. adv. bd. 1942-44). Mass. Inst. Tech. Alumni Assn. (pres. 1945-46), Execs. Club of Boston (mem. 1940-44), Phi Beta Epsilon, Pi Delta Epsilon. Christian Scientist. Mason. Clubs: Union League, M.I.T. (mem. bd. 1945-47) (New York); Westchester Country. Home: White Plains NY Died May 20, 1970; buried Kensico Cemetery, Valhalla NY

NORTON, CHARLES LEDYARD author; b. Farmington, Conn., June 11, 1837; s. John Treadwell and Elizabeth (Cogswell) N.; grad. Yale, 1859; studied in Yale Scientific Sch. until outbreak of Civil war; private 7th N.Y.N.G., 1861-62; capt. 25th Conn. vols., 1862-63; col. 78th U.S. colored troops, 1863-66; served mainly in Dept. of Gulf; mustered out, Jan. 1866; m. E. Mélanie Richards, Sept. 1, 1863 (died 1900); m. 2d, A. E. Phillips, 1904. Editor Christian Union, 1868-78; editor Domestic Monthly, American Canoeist, Outing, etc. Author: Canoeing in Kanuckia (with John Habberton); A Handbook of Florida; Political Americanisms; Jack Benson's Log; A Medal of Honor Man; Midshipman Jack; A Soldier of the Legion; The Queen's Rangers. Home: Sandwich, Mass. Died 1909.

NORTON, CHARLES STUART rear adm. U.S.N.; b. Albany, N.Y., Aug. 10, 1836; grad. U.S. Naval Acad., 1855; m. Mary E. Pentz, Mar. 29, 1872; m. 2d, Elisabeth Killough, July 25, 1906. Passed midshipman, 1858; master, 1858; lt., 1860; lt. comdr., 1862; comdr., 1870; capt., 1881; commodore, 1894; rear adm., Feb. 1, 1898. Served during Civil War on Charleston, S.C., blockade, Potomac Flotilla and at Hampton Roads, Va., 1861-62, participating in several engagements; at battle of Port Royal, S.] C.; in N. Atlantic Blockading Squadron, 1862-64; W. Gulf Blockading Squadron, 1864-65; after war comd. several vessels and served on Bd. of Inspection and Survey; rear adm. comdg. S. Atlantic Sta., 1894-96; comd. Washington Navy Yard and Sta., 1896-98; retired by operation of law, Aug. 10, 1898. Home: Westfield, N.J. Died 1911.

NORTON, HAROLD PERCIVAL naval officer; b. New York, N.Y., Nov. 4, 1855; s. Charles E., and Emily A. (Norton) N.; grad. U.S. Naval Acad., 1879; m. Mrs. D. P. McCartney, née Mary V. Barbour, Dec. 27, 1911. Promoted asst. engr., June 10, 1881; passed asst. engr., Oct. 12, 1891; chief engr., Feb. 10, 1899; transferred to the line as lt., Mar. 3, 1899; lt. commander, Oct. 26, 1901; commander, Oct. 10, 1906; captain, Sept. 16, 1910; rear admiral, July 1, 1918. Served at Elswick, England, as insp. machinery for the Albany, 1898-1900; on Albany, 1900-04; at Navy Yard, N.Y. City, 1904-06; with Bur. Steam Engring., Navy Dept., 1906-10; insp. engring., Navy Dept., 1910-11; with Bur. Steam Engring., 1911-12; mem. Bd. Inspection Shore Stations, Navy Dept., 1912-13; apptd. mem. Naval Examining Bd., Washington, D.C., July 28, 1913. Episcopalian. Home: Washington, D.C. Died Feb. 11, 1933.

NORTON, LAURENCE HARPER mining & shipping exec.; b. Cleve., May 8, 1888; s. David Z. and Mary H. D. (Castle) N.; grad. Univ. Sch., Cleve., 1906; A.B., Yale, 1910; A.M., Harvard, 1912; LL.D., Kenyon Coll., 1944. Attache, Am. Embassy, Paris, 1912-14, 3d sec., 1921-24; with Citizens Savs. & Trust Co., 1915-16; dir. of Oglebay, Norton Co., Cleve., 1928-—, treas., 1957-—; trustee Soc. for Savs. Bank, 1929-—. Mem. port and harbor commn., Cleve. Mem. Ohio Gen. Assembly, 1925-31, Senate, 1931-32; mem. Cleve. Bd. Edn., 1933-37, pres., 1934; exec. com. Republican Finance Com. Trustee Cleve. Mus. Art, Cleve. Sch. Art, Kenyon Coll., Univ. Sch., Cleve. Community Fund, Cleve. Play House (pres. 1934-38), Citizens League, Playhouse Found., Hinman Hurlburt Art Found. John Huntington Found., Horace Kelley Found. Served as capt. U.S. Army, 1917-19; AEF, Mem. Ohio Archaeol. and Hist. Soc. (trustee), Western Res. Hist. Soc. (pres. 1934-—), Early Settlers Assn. (v.p.), Sons Colonial Wars, S.A.R., Newcomen Soc., Phi Beta Kappa, Elihu, Psi Upsilon. Republican. Episcopalian (trustee Diocese Ohio, mem. nat. council 1949-55; del. Episcopal Gen. Conv. 1943, 46, 49, 52, 55). Clubs: Union (pres. 1936), Tavern, City Kirtland Country, Rowfant, Fifty (Cleve); Yale (N.Y.C.); Union Interallie, Travellers (Paris). Home: 2215 Overlook Rd., Cleveland Heights 6. Office: Hanna Bldg., Cleve. 15. Died June 11, 1960; buried Lake View Cemetery, Cleve.

NORTON, ROBERT CASTLE mining, shipping exec.; b. Cleve., Dec. 28, 1879; s. David Z. and Mary H. (Castle) N.; A.B., Yale, 1902. Chmn. bd. and dir. Oglebay, Norton & Co.; pres., dir. Fortune Lake Mining Co., D. Z. Norton, Inc., David Z. Norton Co.; vice president, director Lakeside & Marblehead R.R. Co.; director of the American Shipbuilding Co., Troop A. Armory Co., Union Commerce Bank. Trustee Church Home, Lakeview Cemetery Assn., Playhouse Found. Cleveland. Served from capt. to maj. U.S. Army, World War I. Mem. Am. Legion, S.A.R., Soc. Sons Colonial Wars, Western Res. Hist. Soc. (trustee), Yale Alumni Assn. (Cleveland past pres.), Cavalry Veterans Assn. (pres.), Alpha Delta Phi, Scroll and Key. Rep. Episcopalian. Clubs: Union, Tavern, Rowfant, Kirtland, Winous Point Shooting, Chagrin Valley Hunt (Cleve.); Yale (N.Y.C.). Home: 2215 Overlook Rd., Cleveland Heights 6, O.; also Woodnorton, Mentor, 9. Office: Hanna Bldg., Cleveland 15. Died Nov. 22, 1959.

NORWOOD, GEORGE banking; b. Greenville, S.C., Sept. 9, 1892; s. John Wilkins and Lidie Cleveland (Goodlett) N.; Litt.B., Princeton U., 1916; student, Princeton Grad. Sch., 1916-17; m. Aimee Sloan, Feb. 14, 1923; children—Wilkins, Lillian Sloan. Cashier Norwood Nat. Bank, Greenville, S.C., 1920-25, pres., 1925-26; v.p. S.C. Nat. Bank, 1925-31; pvt. banker since 1931; pres. and treas., Convenience, Inc., Greenville. Staff officer with Adm. Dun, World War I, attached to Am. Peace Mission, Paris, 1919-20; lt. U.S.N.R.F., 1920-30; major, U.S. Army, 1942-45; served with B.E.F., Eritrea, Egypt, Tripolitania, with Am. Mil. Govt., Algeria; mgr. Allied Financial Agency, Sicily; with S.H.A.E.F., Eng., France, Germany; dsch., 1945. Member S.C. Rep. Nat. Com. since 1940. Mem. Acad. of Polit. Science, Nat. Geographic Soc. Republican. Unitarian. Elks. Clubs: Poinsett (Greenville); Princeton, National Republican (New York). Home: 201 East Park Av. Office: 200-A W. McBee Av., Greenville, S.C. Died July 6, 1949; buried Springwood Cemetery, Greenville.

NOTT, CHARLES COOPER judge; b. Schenectady, N.Y., Sept. 16, 1827; s. Joel Benedict and Margaret Tayler (Cooper) N.; A.B., Union College, 1848; LL.D., Williams, 1874; m. Alice Effingham Hopkins, Oct. 22, 1867. Practiced law at New York until outbreak of Civil War; served as captain 5th Iowa Cavalry and colonel 176th New York Volunteers; captured at fall of Brashear, La., June 1863; prisoner in Tex. for 13 months. Apptd. by President Lincoln, Feb. 22, 1865, jugde of Court of Claims; apptd. chief justice same, Nov. 23, 1896, by President Cleveland; retired, Dec. 31, 1905. Author: Mechanics' Lien Laws; Sketches of the War; Sketches of Prison Camps; The Seven Great Hymns of the Mediaeval Church; Court of Claims Reports (48 vols.); The Mystery of the Pinckney Draught, New York, 1909. Home: Princeton, New Jersey. Died Mar. 6, 1916.

NOURSE, HENRY STEDMAN civil engr.; b. Lancaster, Mass., April 9, 1831; s. Stedman N.; grad. Harvard, 1853, A.M.; m. Mary B. Thurston, Sept. 12, 1870. Prof. ancient languages, Phillips Exeter Acad., 1853-55; adj. and capt. 55th Ill. vol. inf. and commissary of musters, 17th army corps, 1861-65; constructional engr. and supt. Bessemer Steel Works, Steelton, Pa., 1866-74; mem. Mass. Ho. of Reps., 1883; mem. Massachusetts senate, 1885-86; trustee Worcester Insane Hosp., 1888-98; mem. Mass. Free Public Library Commn., 1890-1903, Mass. Bd. Charity, 1898-1903. Republican. Author: Early Records of Lancaster, 1643-1725, 1884; The Story of the 55th Regiment of Illinois Infantry, 1887; The Military Annals of Lancaster, 1740-1865, 1889; The Birth, Marriage and Death Register, etc., of Lancaster, Mass., 1643-1850, 1890; History of the Town of Harvard, Mass., 1891; The Ninth Report of the Free Public Library Commission, 1899; Narrative of the Captivity and Restoration of Mrs. Mary Rowlandson, 1903. Address: South Lancaster, Mass. Died 1903.

NOVER, BARNET, newspaper corr., columnist, editor, author; b. Feb. 11,21899; s. Louis and Beulah (Wilk) Nover; B.A., Cornell U., 1919, M.A., 1920; m. Naomi A. Goll, June 28, 1934. Reporter, asso. editor, columnist Buffalo Eve. News, 1920-36; professorial lectr. history and internat. relations U. Buffalo, 1923-36; asso. editor, columnist fgn. affairs Washington Post, 1936-47; chief Washington bur. Denver Post, 1947-72; editor Nover News Service, 1972-73; recorded nat. radio program Washington Views and Interviews, 1944-47; writer weekly article OWI, for shortwave broadcast enemy and neutral countries, also translated 35 langs. for 600 publ. world newspapers World War II; cons. Pres.'s air policy commn., 1947. Mem. standing com. corrs. Congl. Press Galleries, 1964-73, sec.-treas., 1965, chmn., 1965-66. Served with S.A.T.C., U.S. Army, 1917-18. Recipient award of distinction as outstanding former resident of Buffalo, 1955. Mem. Am. Hist. Assn., Council Fgn. Relations, White House Corr. Assn., Phi Beta Kappa, Sigma Delta Chi. Clubs: Nat. Press, Overseas Writers (pres. 1940-43) (Washington). Home: Washington DC Died Apr. 15, 1973.

NOYES, C(HARLES) REINOLD economist; b. St. Paul, Minn., May 2, 1884; s. Charles Phelps and Emily Hoffman (Gilman) N.; student Barnard Sch., now St. Paul Acad., 1894-1901; A.B., Yale, 1905; spl. student Johns Hopkins, 1930-33; m. Dorothy Quincy Grinnell, Oct. 3, 1908 (divorced, 1931); children—Charlotte Irving (Mrs. William Raymond Driver, Jr.), Charles Phelps, Dorothy Quincy; m. 2d, Henriette Denney Turney McKnight, Jan. 14, 1933. Asso. Noyes Bros & Cutler, Inc., St. Paul, Minn., 1905-29, vice pres., 1914-20, pres., 1920-29; economist, 1930-—; dir. Nat. Bur. Econ. Research, New York, N.Y., 1940-—, v.p. 1942-44, pres., 1946-48, chmn. 1948-50. Served as 1st lt., then capt., Chem. Warfare Service, A.E.F., 1918-19. Dir. Merchants, now 1st Nat. Bank, St. Paul, 1921-30, Empire Nat. Bank, St. Paul, 1926-30. Dir., trustee or officer numerous bus., civic, ednl. and charitable orgns., St. Paul, 1905-30. Fellow A.A.A.S.; mem. Am. Econ. Assn., Royal Econ. Soc., Am. Statis. Assn., Econometric Soc., Econ. Hist. Assn., Am. Polit. Sci. Assn., Acad. Polit. Sci., Council of Fgn. Relations. Clubs: Century (New York). Author: America's Destiny, 1935; The Institution of Property, 1936; Economic Man, 1948. Contbr. articles on economics to scientific jours., 1948-—. Home: 12 Library Pl., Princeton, N.J. Died July 5, 1954; buried St. Paul.

NOYES, CHARLES RUTHERFORD army officer; b. Springfield, Mass., Apr. 16, 1858; s. Horatio S. and Abbie S. (Woodman) N.; grad. U.S. Mil. Acad., 1879; Army War Coll., 1914; m. Gertrude H. Noyes, of Kenwood, N.Y., Mar. 26, 1898. Commd. 2d lt. 9th Inf., June 13, 1879; 1st lt., Aug. 28, 1887; capt. Apr. 26, 1898; maj., Aug. 12, 1903; a.a.g., Apr. 7, 1904; assigned to 9th Inf., Apr. 7, 1908; lt. col. 21st Inf., Mar. 3, 1911; col. of inf., Mar. 8, 1913; assigned to 30th Inf., Nov. 29, 1913, to 22d Inf., Apr. 25, 1914, to 17th Inf., Mar. 8, 1916. Instr. mathmatics, U.S. Mil. Acad., 1888-92; served in Ute campaign, 1879-80; in campaign against Santiago de Cuba, 1898; in Philippine Islands with regt., 1899-1900, and 1901-02; participated in China Relief Expdn., 1900; wounded at Battle of Tien Tsin, July 13, 1900; duty hdqrs. Dept. of Mo., 1903-08; hdqrs. Central Dept., 1912-13; hdqrs. Eastern Dept., 1914-16; duty in Mexico, Aug. 1916-Feb. 1917. Address: War Dept., Washington, D.C.

NOYES, EDWARD ALLEN army officer; b. Ore., Oct. 11, 1891; M.D., U. Ore., 1913; grad. Army Med. Sch., 1916. Commd. 1st lt. M.C., U.S. Army, 1916, advanced through the grades to maj. gen., 1948. Address: Hdqrs. Brooke Army Med. Center, Fort Sam Houston, Tex. Died July 1963.

NOYES, EDWARD FOLLANSBEE gov. Ohio, diplomat; b. Haverhill, Mass., Oct. 3, 1832; s. Theodore and Hannah (Stevens) N.; grad. Dartmouth, 1857; grad. Law Sch., Cincinnati Coll., 1858; m. Margaret Proctor, Feb. 15, 1863, 1 son. Served as maj. 39th Ohio Inf., U.S. Army, 1861; became col.; commanded Camp Dennison, O.; brevetted brig. gen.; resigned, 1865; city solicitor in Hamilton County, O., 1865; probate judge Hamilton County; gov. Ohio, 1872-74; chmn. Ohio delegation Republican Nat. Conv., 1876; U.S. minister to France, 1877-81; elected judge Superior Ct. at Cincinnati, 1889. Died Sept. 4, 1890.

NOYES, HENRY ERASTUS brigadier gen. U.S.A.; b. Belfast, Me., Aug. 23, 1839; s. Henry and Rebecca (Tyler) N.; grad. U.S. Mil. Acad., 1861; m. Louise W. Walker, July 2, 1864. Apptd. 2d lt. 2d Dragoons, June 24, 1861; assigned to duty with Light Battery E, 3d Arty.; participated in battles of Bull Run, on defenses of Washington and expdn. to Port Royal, S.C.; 1st lt, 2d Cav., Feb. 15, 1862; served in battles of South Mountain, Antietam, Fredericksburg, Beverly Ford, Brandy Sta. (bvtd. capt., Aug. 1, 1863, "for gallant and meritorious services"), later in Shenandoah Valley campaign, battles of Winchester, Opequan, and Nashville; capt. 2d Cav., Jan. 25, 1865; bvtd. maj., Apr. 2, 1865 "for gallant and meritorious services at capture of Selma, Ala." After Civil War participated in Indian campaigns against the Sioux in Wyo., etc.; maj. 4th Cav., June 14, 1879; served in campaign against Warm Spring Apaches, 1880; lt. col. 5th Cav., July 1, 1891; transferred to 2d Cav., Aug. 1892; col. 2d Cav., May 31, 1898; served at Chickamauga, Mobile and Tampa, in Aug. 1898, and afterward in Cuba; retired, Nov. 16, 1901; advanced to rank of brig. gen. retired, by act of Apr. 23, 1904. Author: Noyes' Genealogy. Address: Berkeley, Calif. Died July 10, 1919.

NOYES, JOHN RUTHERFORD army officer; b. Oneida, N.Y., Apr. 5, 1902; s. Charles Rutherford and Gertrude Hayes (Noyes) N.; B.S., U.S. Mil. Acad., 1923; C.E., Cornell, 1926; grad. Army Indsl. Coll., 1939; m. Eunice Gertrude Zimmerman, Mar. 6, 1928 (dec. 1952); children—John Zabriskie, Daniel Hayes; m. 2d, Lily Florence Ericson, Mar. 4, 1955; 1 son, Eric Rutherford. Commd. 2d lt., U.S. Army, 1923, advanced to col., 1942; served in C.E., 1923-50, in Alaska, 1926-28, 1931-32, 1948-51; asst. district engineer Juneau, 1926-28, Seattle, 1932-34, Conchas, 1935-37, Mobile Engr. Dist., 1939-42; instr. engrs., N.M.N.G., 1934-38; served as transportation officer, Services of Supply and Transportation Officer, Sixth Army Group, No h Africa, Italy, France, and Germany, World War II; asst. to dir. gen. railways in Germany, 1945; transferred to Transportation Corps, 1950; commr. roads for Alaska, hdqrs. Juneau, 1948-51; transferred Corps Engineers, 1952, management officer, The Engr. Sch. U.S. Army, 1952, ret. 1953, brig. gen., N.G. U.S., adj. gen. Alaska, 1953. Lectr. hist. 1947, 48, 49. Awarded Bronze Star medal with Oak Leaf Cluster, Legion of Honor (French), Croix de Guerre (French). Fellow Am. Geog. Soc., Royal Geog. Soc. (British); mem. Am. Soc. C.E., Soc. Am. Mil. Engrs., Nat. Defense Transportation Assn., Permanent Internat. Assn. Navigation Congresses, A.A.A.S., N.G. Assn. U.S., Arctic Institute N. America (asso.), West Point Soc. N.Y. Elk. Author: Transportation in Alaska; the Influence of Geographical Environment Thereon (with Gen. James G. Steese), 1934; Transportation in Undeveloped Regions (with Gen. James G. Steese), 1938; Transportation in Alaska,

1952. Club: Army and Navy (Washington). Geographer-historian. Address: Kenwood Station, Oneida, N.Y. Died Jan. 30, 1956; buried Oneida.

NOYES, ROBERT GALE (noice), educator; b. Norwich, Conn., Sept. 1, 1898; s. George Frederic and Lotta Orline (Champlin) N.; A.B., Brown U., 1921, M.A., 1921; A.M., Harvard, 1923, Ph.D., 1929; m. Barbara Reed Brayton, Aug. 4, 1945. Instr. English, Brown U., 1921-22, Harvard, 1924-36, asst. prof., 1936-37, head tutor Dunster House, 1930-34; asso. prof. Brown U., 1937-51, prof. 1951—. Served as 2d lt. Coast Arty. O.R.C., 1919-24; capt. AUS, 1942-45. Mem. Phi Beta Kappa, Delta Phi. Author: Ben Jonson on the English Stage, 1935; The Thespian Mirror: Shakespeare in the Eighteenth-Century Novel, 1953; The Neglected Muse: Restoration and Eighteenth-Century Tragedy in the Novel (1740-1780), 1958. Home: 68 Barney St., Rumford 16, R.I. Office: Brown U., Providence 12. Died Mar. 25, 1961; buried Norwich, Conn.

NUESSLE, FRANCIS E., naval officer; b. Washburn, N. Dak., Jan. 23, 1911; s. William L. and Emma N.; B.S., U.S. Naval Acad. 1932, Air War Coll. 1950, Nat. War Coll., 1955; m. Elizabeth Virginia Hoover, Nov. 4, 1939; children—Warren G., William P., Francis E., Jr., Virginia D. Commd. ensign USN, 1932, advanced through grades to rear adm., 1961; naval aviator, 1935; squadron and ship's officer U.S.S. Saratoga, U.S.S. Lexington, U.S.S. Ranger, U.S.S. Princeton; comdg. officer U.S.S. Gannet until 1942; comdr. bombing Squadron 105 and ASW Group II, 1943; staff, comdr. Naval Task Force for Normandy invasion 1944; successively assigned staffs Chief of Naval Operations, Operational Devel. Force, Naval Striking and Support Force, Southern Europe; commdg. officer U.S.S. Midway, 1957; comdr. Carrier Div. FOURTEEN, 1961-62; comdr. in chief Pacific rep. Joint Strategic Target Planning Staff, 1962-64; chief of staff Naval War College, 1964-66; commander of Fleet Air Norfolk, 1966-67; office of chairman Joint Chiefs of Staff, 1967-70. Clubs: Metropolitan (Washington); N.Y. Yacht, Chevy Chase. Home: Chevy Chase MD Died Nov. 1970.

NULSEN, CHARLES KILBOURNE ret. army officer; b. Kilbourne, La., July 9, 1886; s. Augustus John and Minnie (Kilbourne) N.; student Georgetown (Ky.) Coll., 1901-02, Nat. Prep. Acad., Highland Falls, N.Y., 1903-04; B.S., U.S. Mil. Acad., 1908; grad. Inf. Sch. Advanced Course, 1926, Command and Gen. Staff Sch., 1927, Army War Coll., 1932, Chem. Warfare Sch., 1936; m. Marion Long, Sept. 15, 1914; children—Marion (Mrs. Jesse Duncan Elliott, Jr., dec.), Charles Kilbourne. Commd. 2d lt. Inf., U.S. Army, 1908, advanced through grades to brig. gen., 1943; served as capt. and maj., 15th and 13th Inf., 1917-18; with Army of Occupation of Germany, 1920-22; in command 23rd Inf., 1940-41; comdr. Ft. Sam Houston, 41-47; became comdg. gen. Ft. Sheridan, 1947; retired with permanent rank of brig. gen., 1947. Decorated Mexican Border, World War I, Army Occupation of Germany, and War Dept. Gen. Staff medals, World War II, Legion of Merit. Home: 332 Arcadia Place, San Antonio. Died Mar. 13, 1959.

NULTON, LOUIS MCCOY naval officer; b. Winchester, Va., Aug. 8, 1869; s. Joseph A. and Annie Virginia (Clark) N.; grad. U.S. Naval Acad., 1889; m. Minnie Clark Evans, Sept. 5, 1895; children—Virginia Adams, Dorothy Evans. Promoted asst. engr., July 1, 1891; passed asst. engr., July 4, 1896; transferred to the line as lt., Mar. 3, 1899; lt. comdr., July 1, 1905; comdr., July 1, 1910; capt., Nov. 26, 1915; rear admiral, Aug. 12, 1921; vice admiral, June 21, 1928; admiral, May 26, 1929. Served on Minneapolis, 1898; Texas, 1902-05; at U.S. Naval Acad., 1905-07; exec. officer Olympia, 1907; exec. officer and navigator Panther, 1907-08; ordnance officer Ohio, 1908; exec. officer Wisconsin, 1909-10; at U.S. Naval Acad., 1910-13, Naval War Coll., Newport, R.I., 1913; comd. Nashville, 1913, Montana, 1914-15; comdt. of midshipmen, U.S. Naval Acad., 1915-18; comdg. Pennsylvania, flagship of Atlantic Fleet, 1918-20; comdt. Phila. Naval Dist. until June 1923; comdg. Battleship Div. Three until Jan. 1925; supt. U.S. Naval Acad., 1925-28; vice admiral, in command battle divs., Battle Fleet, 1928-29; admiral, comdr. in chief U.S. Battle Fleet, 1929-30; apptd. comdt. 1st Naval Dist., Boston, May 1930; retired on account of age limit, Sept. 1, 1933. Participated in Cuban, Philippine and Boxer (China) campaigns, and in World War; was at Vera Cruz, 1914. Mem. U.S. Naval Inst., Mil. Order of the Dragon. Commendatory letters from Dept. of State for work done in diplomatic-naval service in Haiti and San Domingo; Grand Officer Order of the Crown of Rumania; awarded Navy Cross for services in World War I. Clubs: Army and Navy (Washington); New York Yacht. Home: 321 N. Loudoun St., Winchester, Va. Died Nov. 10, 1954; buried U.S. Naval Acad., Annapolis.

NUTT, CLIFFORD CAMERON army officer; b. Kansas City, Mo., July 25, 1896; s. Alva V. and Blanche C. (Jett) N.; grad. Army Indsl. Coll., Washington, D.C., 1939, Air Corps Tactical Sch., 1938; m. Edna G. Morgan, Feb. 22, 1931. Commd. 2d lt., Jan. 1918, and advanced through ranks to brig. gen., U.S. Army, Oct. 25, 1945; rated command pilot, combat observer; served as dept. comdr. Fairfield Air Service Command, Patterson Field, Dayton, O., Feb. 1942-Mar. 1944; comdg. gen. Hawaiian Air Depot, Apr. 1944-July 1946; comdg. gen. Atlantic Overseas Air Materiel Dist., Port of Newark (N.J.) Aug. 1946-Apr. 1947; dep. comdr. 1st AF, Ft. Slocum, N.Y. since Apr. 1947. Decorated: Distinguished Flying Cross, Mackay Trophy award, 1920, Bronze Star medal, Commendation ribbon. Address: Hdqrs. First Air Force, Fort Slocum, N.Y. Deceased.*

NUTTER, DONALD GRANT gov. of Mont.; b. Lambert, Mont., Nov. 28, 1915; s. C. E. and Anne Grant (Wood) N.; student N.D. State Sch. Sci., Wahpeton, 1933-35; LL.B., Mont. State U., 1954; m. Maxine Trotter, Apr. 16, 1938; 1 son, John Grant. Dep. clk. Richland County (Mont.) Ct., 1937-38; undersheriff Richland County, 1938-39; with Tractor and Equipment Co., Sidney, Mont., 1938-42, 45-57; propr. implement bus., Sidney, 1947-50; admitted to Mont. bar, 1954, since practiced in Sidney; mem. Mont. Senate from Richland County, 1951-58, chmn. labor and compensation com., 1955; gov. of Mont., 1961—. Chmn. Mont. Republican Central Com., 1958-60. Mem. Mont. N.G., 1933-35; served to capt., pilot, USAAF, 1942-45; CBI. Decorated Air medal with clusters, D.F.C. with clusters; Recipient Good Govt. award Sidney Jr. C. of C., 1958. Mem. Am. Legion, Vets. Fgn. Wars, DeMolay Legion of Honor. Mason (Shriner), Kiwanian, Moose, Elk. Home: 2 Carson St. Office: State Capitol Bldg., Helena, Mont. Died Jan. 25, 1962; buried Sidney, Mont.

NUTTMAN, LOUIS MEREDITH, army officer; born Newark, N.J., Jan. 28, 1874; s. George and Louise (Mentz) N.; grad. U.S. Mil. Acad., 1895; m. Mrs. Alice Long Mitchell, Mar. 9, 1909. Commd. 2d lt. inf., U.S. Army, June 12, 1895, and advanced through grades to col., July 1, 1920, brig. gen., May 1, 1932; retired Jan. 31, 1938. Served in Spanish-Am. War, Philippine Insurrection, Boxer Campaign, Mexican Punitive Expdn., World War. Awarded D.S.M., Silver Star Medal (U.S.); Croix de Guerre (France). Club: Army and Navy (Washington). Address: War Dept., Washington DC

NYE, FRANK E. soldier; b. in Maine; grad. U.S. Mil. Acad., 1869. Apptd. 2d lt. 2d Cav., June 15, 1869, serving principally on frontier until Apr. 10, 1873, when resigned. Engaged in ins. business, Augusta, Me., 1873-84. Reëntered army as capt. commissary of subsistence, Nov. 20, 1884, and continued in commissary dept.; promoted maj., June 1, 1896, lt. col. commissary gen., Sept. 9, 1898, col. asst. commissary gen., Apr. 1, 1901—. Lt. col., July 1898, and col., Oct. to Dec. 1898, in commissary service, U.S.V. Deceased.

OAKES, JAMES soldier; b. nr. Limestoneville, Pa., Apr. 4, 1826; s. Samuel and Sarah (Montgomery) O.; grad. U.S. Mil. Acad., 1846; m. Anna Maria de Beelen, Nov. 11, 1854. Served in Mexican War; bvtd. 1st lt. and capt. for gallantry; afterward on frontier service; wounded by Indians, Aug. 12, 1850; 1st lt., June 30, 1851; capt. 2d Cav., Mar. 3, 1855; maj. 5th Cav., Apr. 6, 1861; lt. col. 4th Cav., Nov. 12, 1861; col. 6th Cav., July 31, 1866. Declined commn. of brig. gen. vols., May 17, 1861; led regt. in Tenn. and Miss. campaign, 1862; in mustering and recruiting service, 1863; comd. dist. of Ill., 1863-66; bvtd. brig. gen. U.S.A., Mar. 30, 1865. In charge, Freedman's Bur. and comd. dist. of Austin, Tex., 1867-69; afterward on northern frontier of Tex. and in Kan. and Ariz.; retired at own request, over 30 yrs.' service, Apr. 29, 1879. Home: Washington, D.C. Died 1910.

OAKES, THOMAS FLETCHER ins. exec.; b. Tacoma May 24, 1900; s. Walter and Mary Beekman (Taylor) O.; grad. Pomfret Sch., 1919; A.B., Harvard, 1923; m. Jeanne Stanley, May 31, 1935; m. 2d, Elinor Righter, Aug. 9, 1946; children—Leslie Taylor, Elinor Foster. With Standard Fire Ins. Co. of Hartford, Conn., 1924-31; with Allen, Russell & Allen, Hartford, 1931—, partner, 1936-65, inc., 1965, pres., dir. 1965—; v.p., dir. Alexander Sexton & Carr; dir. Phoenix Ins. Co., Conn. Printers, Inc., Inst. Living (all Hartford); sr. v.p., dir. Allen, Russell & Allen, Inc. of N.Y. Trustee, treas. Pomfret Sch.; trustee Newington Hosp. Served from pvt. to maj. AUS, World War II. Clubs: Harvard (Conn.); Hartford; Fishers Island (N.Y.); Farmington (Conn.) Country. Home: Cider Brook Rd., Avon, Conn. Office: 31 Lewis St., Hartford 4, Conn. Died Feb. 6, 1966.

OAKLEY, FRANCIS CLARK extract mfg. exec.; b. Galliapolis, O., Aug. 26, 1907; s. Davis Samuel and Winifred (Clark) O.; A.B., Oberlin Coll., 1930; H.M. (hon.), Springfield Coll., 1951; m. Mabel Adelle Waters, Mar. 1, 1931; children—Gary William, Elizabeth Adelle. Teacher Deerfield (Mass.) Acad., 1930-31; asso. dir. of admissions, Oberlin Coll., 1931-33; sec.-treas. Oakley Co., Bristol, Tenn., 1933-34; asst. sec.-treas., American Seating Co., Grand Rapids, Mich., 1934-36; dir. of public relations, Babson Inst., Wellesley, Mass., 1936-41; v.p. Springfield (Mass.) Coll., 1945-51, trustee and corporators, 1951; treas., dir. Baker Extract Co., 1952-56, pres., dir., 1956—; corporator 5 Cent Savs. Bank. Corporator Springfield Hosp.; adv. bd. Community Center Springfield; chmn. adv. bd., state sec., Salvation Army; mem. bd. YMCA, Springfield Home Aged Men; sec. Springfield Coll. Served as 1st lt., later lt. col., U.S. Army Air Force, 1941-45; lt. col., U.S. Army Air Force Res. Mem. Eastern Assn. of Coll. and Univ. Bus. Officers, Oberlin Coll. Alumni Pres. Council (past pres.), Western Mass. Oberlin Alumni Assn. (past pres.); C. of C. (chmn. com. on TV., dir.), Homer P.T.A. (co-pres.). Conglist. (deacon). Club: Kiwanis (pres., Springfield). Named Neighbor of Month, Springfield, July 1948. Home: 108 Tatham Hill Rd., W. Springfield, Mass. Office: 1 Extract Pl., Springfield, Mass. Died Sept. 4, 1967.

OATES, WILLIAM CALVIN governor; b. in Pike (now Bullock) Co., Ala., Dec. 1, 1835; s. William O. and Sarah (Sellers) O.; ed. at Lawrenceville Acad., Ala.; m. Sallie Toney, Mar. 1882. Served capt. to col., C.S.A.; was in 27 battles; wounded 6 times and lost his right arm. Practiced law after war; mem. Ala. Ho. of Rep., 1870-72; mem. Constl. convs., 1875, 1901; elected 47th to 53d Congresses (1881-95); resigned from 53d Congress, 1894; gov. of Ala., 1895, 1896. Democrat. Defeated for U.S. senator because not an advocate of free coinage of silver at the 16 to 1 ratio. Brig. gen. vols., May 28, 1898-Mar. 10, 1899. Author: The War Between the Union and the Confederacy and Its Lost Opportunities. Home: Montgomery, Ala. Died 1910.

OBEAR, HUGH HARRIS, lawyer; b. Winnsboro, S.C., Dec. 20, 1882; s. Henry Norwood and Eunice (Harris) O.; B.L., U. of Va., 1906; student U. of Paris (spl. course for officers of U.S. Army), 1919; m. Mildred Fleenor. Admitted to D.C. bar, 1907, practice Wash., 1907-71; sr. partner Douglas, Obear & Campbell, 1939-71. Served as maj. comdg. 1st Batt., 319th Inf., 80th Div., World War I; grad. Army Gen. Staff Coll., Langres, France, 1919. Awarded silver star with oak leaf cluster. Officer Order of Carlos Manuel de Cespedes (Cuba). Former dir. Children's Hosp., Washington; former trustee The Louise Home. Mem. Am., D.C. (pres. 1945) bar assns., Newcomen Soc. N. Am., Thomas Jefferson Soc. Alumni U. Va. (life), Phi Delta Phi. Clubs: Metropolitan (past gov. and v.p.), Army and Navy, Lawyers' (past pres.) (Washington); Chevy Chase (Md.). Home: Washington DC Died Mar. 16, 1971.

O'BRIEN, EDWARD FRANCIS editor, pub.; b. Adams, Mass., Apr. 25, 1876; s. William and Louise Ruth (Stark) O'B.; desc. John and Priscilla Alden, and 3 other Mayflower passengers; ed. high sch. and self instructed; m. Elsa de Lila, 1904 (died 1904); m. 2d, Mildred Josephine Correard, 1907. Newspaper work in various cities, until 1898; mem. 14th N.Y. Inf., Spanish-Am. War; in Philippines as mem. 22d U.S. Inf., 1898-1901; War Dept. clerk, Manila, 1901-02; editor Manila Daily Freedom, 1902-03; pub. Manila Sun, 1903-05; prosecuted for polit. writings and pardoned after serving 4 mos. of 6 mos. sentence, telegraph editor N.Y. Tribune, 1906-11; editor Havana Daily Post, 1911-12; founder, 1913, and editor Times of Cuba (monthly); founder Habana, 1928; merged as Pan-Am. Review (P.A.R.), 1933. Member Soc. Mayflower Descendants, S.A.R., Descendants of Robert Bartlett of Plymouth, Mass., United Spanish War Vets. Mason (33 deg., K.T., Shriner, Jester), Elk. Clubs: American, Country, British, Propeller (Havana); Circumnavigators, Philippine (New York). Address: P.O. Box 329, Havana, Cuba. Died Jan. 18, 1945; buried at Adams, Mass.

O'BRIEN, FRANK CORNELIUS, lawyer; b. Jersey City, N.J., May 15, 1915; s. George J. and Kathryn (Driscoll) O'B.; J.D., John Marshall Coll., Jersey City, 1938; m. Bernice Hoos, Aug. 4, 1945; children—Roger, Frank Cornelius, Edward, Bernice, Dora Jean. Admitted to N.J. bar, 1938, since practiced in Newark; partner firm Pitney, Hardin & Kipp, 1948-70. Served to capt. AUS, 1942-45. Decorated Bronze Star. Mem. Am., N.J., Essex County bar assns. Home: Glen Ridge NJ Died Mar. 1, 1970.

O'BRIEN, HENRY RUST, physician; b. Oberlin, O., July 14, 1891; s. James Putnam and Lizzie (Coffin) O'B.; M.D., U. Mich., 1919; M.P.H., Johns Hopkins U., 1931; m. Mary L. Phillips Carr, Mar. 24, 1926; children—Martha Jane (Mrs. Giles C. Fenn), Susan (Mrs. Susan Bowman), James Putnam.. Intern, Bklyn. Hosp., 1919, U.S. Marine Hosp., Ellis Island, N.Y., 1919-20, Manhattan Maternity Hosp. and Dispensary, 1920; staff mem. Bur. Mines, USPHS, 1920-21; mem. internat. health bd. Rockefeller Found., Thailand, 1921-25; asst. resident in surgery Cin. Gen. Hosp., 1925-26; asso. physician McCormick Hosp., Chiengmai, Thailand, 1926-31; commr. health Lorain County, O., 1931-34, Chattaraugus County, N.Y., 1935-41; asst. dist. state health officer N.Y. State Dept. Health, 1934-35; dir. local health adminstrn. Conn. Dept. Health, 1941-43; commd. lt. col. USPHS, 1943, advanced through grades to col.; assigned to Cairo, Sydney, Manila, Shanghai, Washington, Addis Ababa, 1943-55; dir. profl. edn. Pa. Dept. Health, 1955-64. Guest lectr. Western Res. U., Cornell U., U. Minn. Diplomate Am. Bd. Preventive Medicine. Fellow Am. Pub. Health Assn., A.C.S., Royal Soc. Tropical Medicine and Health, Am. Coll. Preventive Medicine; mem. A.M.A., Am. Soc. Tropical Medicine and Health, Sigma Xi, Alpha Omega Alpha. Home: Camp Hill PA Died Aug. 16, 1970; buried Camp Hill PA

O'BRIEN, JEREMIAH naval officer; b. Kittery, Me., 1744; s. Morris and Mary (Hutchins) O.; m. Elizabeth Fitzpatrick, no children. Led group of volunteers in seizure of Brit. sloops Unity and Margaretta (1st naval engagement of Am. Revolution), 1775, commd. capt. Unity (renamed Machias Liberty) and Diligent (1st ships of Mass. Navy), 1775-76; privateer, 1777-80; captured by British, 1780, escaped, 1781; commanded privateers Hibernia and Tiger, 1781; U.S. collector customs for Machias dist. of Me., 1811-18. Died Sept. 5, 1818.

O'BRIEN, JUSTIN MCCORTNEY, educator; b. Chicago, Nov. 26, 1906; s. Quin and Ellen (McCortney) O'B.; student Phillips Exeter Acad., 1921-24; Ph.B., U. Chicago, 1927; A.M., Harvard, 1928, Ph.D., 1936; Doctor of Letters, Wesleyan University, 1966; m. Isabel Ireland, Jan. 24, 1931. Instr. French, Harvard, 1930-31, Columbia, 1931-37, asst. prof., 1937-45, asso. prof., 1945-48, prof. French, 1948-68, Blanche Knopf prof. French, 1968, chairman of the department of French, 1958-63. Board trustees, 2d v.p. French Institute. Served as chief of French sect. with O.S.S., Washington, London, Paris, Washington, Feb. 1943-Oct. 1945; capt. to lt. col., U.S. Army, 1943-45. Decorated Legion of Merit, Croix de Guerre with palm, Chevalier Legion of Honor (France), Order of the British Empire (Great Britain). Awarded Denyse Clairouin prize, 1947; Medalle d'Or du Rayonnement Francais, French Acad., 1965. Fellow John Guggenheim Found., 1943. Mem. Modern Lang. Assn. (exec. council, 1952-55), Societe des Amis d' Andre Gide (v.p. 1968), Phi Beta Kappa, Council on Fgn. Relations. Club: University (N.Y.). Author: The Novel of Adolescence in France, 1937; Portrait of Andre Gide, 1953; Index detaille des Oeuvres completes d' Andre Gide, 1953; French Literary Horizon, 1967. Editor, translator, The Journals of Andre Gide, 4 vols., 1947-51, The Maxims of Marcel Proust, 1948, Madeleine (by Andre Gide), 1952; The Myth of Sisyphus (by Albert Camus), 1955; The Fall (by Albert Camus), 1957; Exile and the Kingdom (by Albert Camus), 1958; From the N.R.F., 1958; So Be It (by Andre Gide), 1959; Pretexts (by Andre Gide), 1959; The Possessed, Caligula (both books by Albert Camus), 1960; Resistance, Rebellion and Death (by Albert Camus), 1961; Altona (by Jean-Paul Sartre), 1961; contributor to the Columbia Dictionary of Modern European Lit., 1947; mem. editorial bd. The Romanic Review (sec. 1937-41; gen. editor, 1954-61, mem. editorial bd.); contbr. articles to various periodicals. Home: New York City NY Died Dec. 7, 1968.

O'BRIEN, KENNETH judge; b. N.Y.C., Mar. 15, 1895; s. Morgan J. and Rose (Crimmins) O'B.; student Newman School, Lakewood, N.J.; A.B., Yale, 1917; LL.B., Fordham U., 1922; m. Katherine Mackay, Sept. 21, 1922; children—Marie Louise, Katherine, Morgan J. Entered practice in New York, 1922; became mem. firm O'Brien, Boardman, Conboy, Memhard & Early, 1926; apptd. justice Supreme Court, N.Y., Feb. 1, 1934, elected, 1934, reelected for 14 yr. term, 1948. Del. Dem. Nat. Conv., 1928, 32. Served as capt. 306th F.A., 77th Div., AEF, 1917-19. Mem. Am., N.Y. State bar assns., Bar Assn. City N.Y., N.Y. County Lawyers Assn. Roman Catholic. Clubs: Yale, Catholic Club, Lawyers, Manhattan. Home: 28 E. 70th St. Address: 60 Centre St., N.Y.C. Died Jan., 1954.

OCHS, ARTHUR JR., finance co. exec.; b. N.Y.C., Nov. 9, 1919; s. Arthur and Sue (Bloch) O.; B.S. in Econs., U. Pa., 1939. With United Factors Corp., 1939, v.p., 1954-69; former pres. Fiber Producers Credit Assn.; v.p. United Mchts. & Mfrs., Inc., 1967-69. Former mem. Scarsdale Bd. Edn. Vice chmn. bd. dirs. Surprise Lake Camp. Served with mil. intelligence, AUS, 1942-46. Mem. Tau Epsilon Phi (chmn. bd. trustees). Home: Scarsdale NY Died Apr. 5, 1969.

OCHS, MILTON BARLOW (ox), b. Cin., Jan. 29, 1864; s. Julius and Bertha (Levy) O.; student Chickering Inst., Cin., U. Tenn.; m. Fannie Van Dyke, Apr. 26, 1893; children—William Van Dyke, Adolph Shelby, Margaret E. (Mrs. Theodore DeCue Palmer). Newsboy in Knoxville, Tenn., 1876; removed to Chattanooga, 1878, and entered service of elder brother (Adolph S.), then pub. Chattanooga Times, of which became v.p., mng. editor; gen. tourist agent passenger dept. Colo. Midland Ry., 1890, 91; again mng. editor Chattanooga Times, 1892-99, 1913-22; Sunday editor, later gen. mgr. Phila. Public Ledger, 1912-13; now v.p. Times Printing Co. Former exec. pub., controlling owner Nashville American, 1909-11; v.p. and chmn. exec. com. Chattanooga-Lookout Mountain Park (given to U.S. Govt. 1935); dir. Dixie Highway; former pres. Taft Meml. Hwy.; former pres. Lookout Mountain Scenic Hwy.; former chmn. Selective Service Bd. No. 3, Hamilton County, Tenn.; pres. Robert Burns Soc. of Chattanooga, Capt. 5th Tenn. Inf., Jan. 19, 1918; lt. col., Feb. 15, 1918; col. 4th Tenn. Inf., Nov. 23, 1918; resigned following Armistice. Elk. Comdr. N.B. Forest Camp Confederate Vets. (asso. mem.). Clubs: Mountain City Fairyland, Chattanooga, Half-Century (pres.); hon. mem. Kiwanis and Civitan. Home: Northcrest, Missionary Ridge. Office: Dome Bldg., Chattanooga, Tenn. Deceased.

O'CONNELL, DESMOND HENRY, mgmt. cons.; b. N.Y.C., Apr. 20, 1906; s. Charles D. and Mary (Grout) O'C.; B.S., U.S. Mil. Acad. 1928; m. Rosemary McGough, May 25, 1935; children—Desmond Henry, Gerald Francis, Timothy Edward. Engr., credit man Gen. Motors Corp., 1929-33; asst. code administr., examiner NRA, NLRB, 1934-38; supr. employee relations S. H. Kress & Co., 1938-47; cons. labor relations, 1947-50; dir. indsl. relations Am. Bakeries Co., Chgo., 1950-56, v.p., 1956-61, dir., 1957-69, exec. v.p., 1961, pres., 1961-68, chmn. bd., chief exec. officer, 1963-68, cons., 1969-73; dir. Upper Av. Nat. Bank, Chgo. Served form 1st lt. to maj., USAAF, 1942-45. Mem. Am. Bakers Assn. (gov.), Mil. Order Loyal Legion, Newcomen Soc., Roman Catholic. Clubs: Westmoreland Country; Chicago Athletic Assn. Home: Hollywood FL Died Feb. 12, 1973.

O'CONNELL, JAMES TIMOTHY business exec.; b. N.Y.C., May 27, 1906; d. Timothy J. and Anna (Huber) O'C.; B.A., Columbia, 1928, B.S., 1929, C.E., 1930; m. Adele Quilgan, Sept. 12, 1936; children—James Timothy, Katherine, Anne, Dorothy, Mary G. Constrn. engr., supt. various firms, govt. agys., 1930-40; asst. regional expeditor Nat. Housing Authority, N.Y.C., 1946; v.p. Publix Shirt Corp., N.Y.C., 1946-57, dir., 1952-57; cons. Dept. Army, 1953-54, sec. labor, 1954-57; mem. sec. army's adv. com. civilian personnel mgmt., 1955-57; under sec. labor, 1957-61; dir. indsl. relations Hudson Pulp & Paper Corp., N.Y.C., 1961-62, v.p. adminstrn., 1962-—. Industry trustee Amalgamated Cotton Garment and Allied Industries Retirement and Ins. Funds, 1947-57. Served from capt. to col. AUS. 1940-46. Decorated Legion of Merit; recipient Exceptional Civilian Service award Dept. Army, 1957; Dean's award Columbia, 1957, Pupin medal, 1959; Distinguished Service award Dept. Labor, 1963. Mem. Columbia Alumni Assn., Holy Name Soc. (past local pres.). Club: Serra (past 1st v.p. Montclair, N.J.). Home: Little Silver Point Rd., Little Silver, N.J. Office: 477 Madison Av., N.Y.C. 22. Died Oct. 12, 1966.

O'CONNELL, JOHN JOSEPH army officer; b. Co. Kerry, Ireland, Dec. 16, 1840; s. John and Nan (Cahill) O'C.; came to U.S. in youth; acad. edn. in Can.; m. Margaret Le Boutillier, 1870. Prof. mathematics and literature, Seton Hall Coll., N.J., at outbreak of Civil War; served as Private Co. A, U.S. engrs., Feb. 3, 1865-Nov. 11, 1867; 2d lt. 1st Inf., Oct. 28, 1867; promoted through grades in regular army to col. 30th Inf., Apr. 20, 1903; brig. gen. and retired by operation of law, Dec. 16, 1904. Served in Black Hills campaign, against Sioux Indians, 1875; in Geronimo campaign against Apaches, 1882; in Pine Ridge (Dak.) Indian campaign, 1894; was the first Am. officer in command of troops to land in Cuba after declaration of war, 1898, swam ashore from boat; also served in P.I. Catholic. Home: Washington, D.C. Died Jan. 4, 1927.

O'CONNELL, JOHN MATTHEW congressman; b. Westerly, R.I., Aug. 10, 1872; s. Michael Berkeley and Ellen (Hurley) O'C.; D.D.S., Phila. Dental Coll., Temple U., 1905; m. Marie Galli, Nov. 28, 1907; 1 son, John Matthew. Began as dentist, Westerly, 1905; mem. R.I. Ho. of Reps., 1928-31; member 73d to 75th Congresses (1933-39), 2d R.I. Dist. Served as 1st lt. Headquarters San. Train, U.S.A., 16 mos., World War; now maj. Dental Reserve. Democrat. K.C., Elk. Home: Westerly, R.I. Died Dec. 6, 1941.

O'CONNOR, DENIS S., physician; b. Biddeford, Me., July 31, 1893; s. Maurice L. and Hanorah M. (Murphy) O'C.; M.D., Bowdoin Coll., 1919; m. Lillian K. Hodson, Oct. 29, 1930. Orthopaedic house officer Mass. Gen. Hosp., Boston, 1924-25; grad. course in orthopaedic surgery Harvard, 1924-26; intern Children's Hosp., Boston, 1925; attending orthopaedic surgeon Yale-New Haven Hosp.; cons. orthopaedic surgeon Griffin Hosp., Derby, Conn., Meriden (Conn.) Hosp., Stamford (Conn.) Hosp., Waterbury (Conn.) Hosp., St. Charles Children's Hosp., Grace-New Haven Community Hosp., New Haven Area Rehab., Inc., Hosp of St. Raphael, New Haven; clin. prof. orthopaedic surgery Yale Med. Sch. Served to capt. M.C., U.S. Navy. Diplomate Am. Bd. Orthopaedic Surgery. Fellow A.C.S.; mem. A.M.A., Am. Acad. Orthopaedic Surgeons, Ar. Rheumatism Assn., Nat. Rehab. Assn. Home: New Haven CT Died May 29, 1971; buried New St. Joseph's Cemetery, Waterbury CT

O'CONNOR, JEREMIAH J(EROME) fgn. service officer; b. Washington, Feb. 2, 1913; s. Jeremiah Jerome and Deborah (Stack) O'C.; A.B., Georgetown U., 1934, LL.B., 1937, LL.M., 1938; student U. Vienna, 1949-51. Admitted to D.C. bar, 1937; practiced law, 1937-39; atty. SEC, 1939-41; dep. dir., then dir. legal div. Office U.S. High Commr. for Austria, 1948-55; fgn. service officer, 1955-—; 1st sec., consul, Vienna, 1955; consul, Salzburg, 1955; dep. operations coordinator Office Under Sec. of State, 1957, operations coordinator, 1958-62, senior foreign service inspector, 1962-—; consul gen., 1959. Served from 1st lt. to col., AUS, 1941-47. Decorated Legion of Merit, Bronze Star (U.S.); Spl. Breast Order of Yun Hui (China). Mem. Am. Fgn. Service Assn., Coronelli-Weltbund der Globusfreunde. Home: 1513 35th St., Washington 20007. Office: Dept. of State, Washington 25. Died Jan. 27, 1964; buried Mt. Olivet Cemetery, Washington.

OCONOSTOTA Indian chief; at least 1 child, Tuksi. Chief, Cherokee Indians; sided with British during French and Indian War; made repeated attacks on frontier settlement when some of his warriors were killed by Americans after they had helped them in attack on Ft. Duquesne, 1759; massacred inhabitants of Ft. Loudoun after they had surrendered to him, 1760; went to England, 1762; signed peace treaty with Iroquois, 1768; fought against Americans during Revolutionary War; resigned chieftainship after signing peace treaties with Am. states, 1782. Died 1785.

O'DONNELL, EMMETT, JR., ret. air force officer; b. Bklyn., Sept. 15, 1906; s. Emmett and Veronica (Tobin) O'D.; B.S., U.S. Mil. Acad., 1928; grad. Air Corps Primary Flying Sch., 1929, Advanced Flying Sch., pursuit course, 1930; Tactical Sch., 1939; m. Lorraine Muller, Dec. 29, 1930; children—Dale Tobin, Patrick Emmett, Terrence. Commd. 2d lt., U.S. Army, 1928, advancing through the grades to general, 1959; dir. of information U.S. Air Forces, 1946-Sept. 29, 1947; dep. dir. pub. relations, Office Sec. Air Force, Sept. 30, 1947-Jan. 1948; steering and coordinating mil. mem. Permanent Joint Bd. on Defense, Can.-U.S. Defense Com., Jan. 1948-Sept. 1948; Air Force mem. Joint Brazil-U.S. Defense Com., Mex.-U.S. Defense Com.; comdg. gen. 15th Air Force, March Air Force Base, 1948-53; also Comdg. Gen. Far East Air Force Bomber Command. Korean Conflict, 1950-51; dep. chief of staff of personnel Hdqrs. USAF, Washington, 1953-59; comdr. in chief Pacific Air Forces, 1959-63, ret.; pres. USO, from 1964; asso. Marx Co. N.Y. Marriott Corp., Washington, Bunker Ramo Corp., Martin Marietta Corp. Member of the board of visitors U.S. Air Force Academy. Decorated D.S.M., D.S.C., Distinguished Flying Cross with 3 oak leaf clusters, Air Medal with oak leaf cluster, Legion of Merit, Presdl. Citation with oak leaf cluster, Silver Star, Korean Service and U.N. medals, Companion of the Bath (Eng.), Asiatic Theatre Ribbon with 4 campaign stars. Clubs: Burning Tree, Army-Navy (Washington), Sky (N.Y.C.). Home: McLean VA Died Dec. 26, 1971; buried U.S. Air Force Acad. Cemetery, Colorado Springs CO

O'DWYER, WILLIAM lawyer; b. Bohola, County Mayo, Ireland, July 11, 1890; student U. Salamanca (Spain); LL.B., Fordham U.; m. Sloan Simpson, Dec. 1949. Served as dist. atty. Kings County, N.Y.; judge County Ct., Kings County, N.Y., 1937-40; commd. maj. U.S. Army, 1942, advanced through grades to brig. gen., 1944; asst. corps area provost marshal Hdqrs. II Corps Area, Governors Island, N.Y., 1942, later with dist. plans protection sect. AC Materiel Command, Eastern Procurement Dist., N.Y.C. until Oct. 1942; spl. air insp. hdqrs., Materiel Command, Washington, Oct. 1942-Mar. 1943; spl. adviser Office of Asst. Chief of Air Staff, Materiel, Maintenance and Distbn. Hdqrs. Army AF, Washington, 1943-44; chief Investigations div., Office of Legislative Service, Hdqrs. Army AF, Washington, Jan.-June 1944; assigned as rep. Fgn. Econ. Adminstrn. in Italy, June 1944; elected mayor N.Y.C., Nov. 1945, reelected Nov. 1949; apptd. U.S. ambassador to Mexico, 1950-52; now practicing lawyer, firm O'Dwyer, Bernstein & Correa, Mexico City. Recipient Pan-Am. Collar, Golden Palms of Ams., Pan-Am. Legion. Address: 1 Paseo de la Reforma, Mexico City, D.F. Died Nov. 1964.

OEMLER, ARMINUS agriculturist; b. Savannah, Ga., Sept. 12, 1827; s. Augustus Gottlieb and Mary Ann (Shad) O.; grad. with honors Dresden Technische Bildungsanstalt, 1848; M.D., U. City N.Y., 1856; m. Elizabeth P. Heyward, Apr. 10, 1856, 6 children. Joined Confederate Army, commd. capt. 2d Company, deKalb Riflemen; made 1st map of Chatham County (Ga.); founder 1st comml. oyster packing plant in South, Wilmington Island, Ga.; discoverer presence of nitrogen-fixing bacteria in nodules of leguminous plants, 1886, discouraged from further research by U.S. Dept. of agr. (actual discovery made in Germany 2 years later). Died Savannah, Aug. 8, 1897; buried Wilmington Island.

O'FALLON, JAMES army officer; b. Ireland, Mar. 11, 1749; s. William and Anne (Eagan) O'F.; attended U. Edinburgh (Scotland); m. Frances Clark, Feb. 1791; children—John, Benjamin. Came to Am., 1774; served as surgeon U.S. Army during Am. Revolution; mem. Charleston (S.C.) Marine Anti-Britannic Soc., 1785; gen. agt. S.C. Yazoo Co., 1790; intrigued with Spain and France in role of mil. leader; Pres. Washington issued public proclamation against Am. support for his plans, 1791; served as officer under George Rogers Clark, 1791. Died circa 1794.

O'FALLON, JOHN philanthropist; b. Louisville, Ky., Nov. 17, 1791; s. Dr. James and Frances Eleanor (Clark) O'F.; m. Harriet Stokes, 1821; m. 2d, Ruth Caroline Sheets, Mar. 15, 1827; 5 children. Served from 2d lt. to capt. in War of 1812, acting dep. adj. gen. at Ft. Meigs; pres. St. Louis br. U.S. Bank, Miss. & Ohio R.R., N. Mo. R.R.; liberal contbr. to O'Fallon Poly. Inst., St. Louis U., Washington U. Died St. Louis, Dec. 17, 1865.

O'FARRELL, PATRICK lawyer; b. Ireland, 1832; s. James O'F.; ed. in Ireland; came to U.S., 1862, to enlist in Union army; served in 69th N.Y. (Corcoran's Irish Legion), pvt. to capt., ending at Appomattox; wounded 5 times in battle; bvtd. capt. "for gallant and distinguished conduct at battle of Reams' Station, nr. Petersburg, Va.," Aug. 25, 1864; grad. Nat. Univ., Washington (LL.B., LL.M.); admitted to bar, Supreme Court, D.C., Juen 1885, Supreme Court, U.S., April 1889. Active Republican until campaign of 1900;

changed to Democrat on issue of imperialism. Wrote: O'Farrell's Financial Dialogue, 1896 (in favor of gold standard). Home: Washington, D.C. Died 1902.

OFFLEY, CLELAND NELSON naval officer; b. Georgetown, D.C., June 8, 1869; s. Holmes E. and Mary (Nelson) O.; grad. U.S. Naval Acad., 1889; m. Margaret A. Greenlees, July 14, 1891. Promoted asst. engr., July 1, 1891; passed asst. engr., Dec. 14, 1896; transferred to the line as lt., Mar. 3, 1899; lt. comdr., July 1, 1905; comdr., July 1, 1910; capt., Aug. 10, 1916. Served on Oregon, Spanish-Am. War, 1898, Solace, 1903-05; engr. officer Colorado, 1905-06; with Bur. Steam Engring., Navy Dept., 1906-08; fleet engr. Pacific Fleet, 1908-09; at U.S. Naval Acad., 1909-10; engr. officer Navy Yard, Puget Sound, 1910-13; exec. officer New Hampshire, 1913-14; comdr. Prometheus, 1914-15; engr. officer Navy Yard, Mare Island, Calif., 1915-19; insp. engring. material, Pittsburgh, 1919-21; insp. engineering material, Hartford, Conn., 1921—. Advanced 4 numbers in rank "for eminent and conspicuous conduct in battle" during Spanish-Am. War. Home: Hamilton, Va. Died 1935.

O'FLAHERTY, HAL, newspaper corr.; b. What Cheer, Ia., July 8, 1890; s. Peter M. and Lavina (Flathers) O'F.; ed. Des Moines (Ia.) schs.; grad. U.S. School of Military Aeronautics, U. of Ill., 1918; m. Sabine Siebel Smith, May 8, 1919; children—Barry, Sheila. Began as reporter, Des Moines Capital, 1909; bureau mgr. United Press, Omaha, 1912-13; legislative corr., Albany, N.Y., 1915; corr. on Mexican border, 1916; foreign corr. United Press, 1916; London corr. New York Sun, 1917, 19; corr. Chicago Daily News in Scandinavia and the Baltic states, Dec. 1919-22, London corr., 1922, European mgr., 1924, fgn. editor of same, 1926, asst. mng. editor, 1932, managing editor, 1936, then dir. fgn. news service, ret., 1972. War correspondent in Pacific theaters, 1943. Covered Salamaua campaign; Kwajalein, Eniwetok, Emirau landings. Director Foreign Service, 1945. Enlisted in U.S. Air Service, December 1917; trained as pilot at Eberts Field, Lonoke, Ark., and commd. 2d lt.; lt. comdr. U.S.N.R., 1941. Home: Carmell Valley CA Died Dec. 24, 1972.

OFSTIE, RALPH ANDREW naval officer; b. Eau Claire, Wis., Nov. 16, 1897; grad. U.S. Naval Acad., 1918; m. Joy Bright Hancock, USN (ret.), former dir. of WAVES, Aug. 16, 1954. Commd. ensign, United States Navy, and advanced through the grades to vice admiral, 1952; served in U.S. ships Chattanooga and Whipple during World War I; asst. naval attaché, Am. Embassy, Tokyo, Japan, 1935-37; operations officer, staff of Adm. William F. Halsey, Jr. (on flagships Saratoga and Yorktown), 1939-41; naval attaché for air and asst. naval attaché, Am. Embassy, London, 1941-42; on staff comdr. in chief U.S. Fleet, 1942; aviation officer, staff of Adm. Chester W. Nimitz (Pacific Fleet), 1942-43; comd. U.S.S. Essex, 1943-44, participating in aerial attacks on Rabaul, invasion of Gilbert Islands, raid on Kwajalein (all 1943), operations against Truk, attacks on Tinian, Saipan and Guam, invasion of Marshall Islands, and First Battle of Philippine Sea (all 1944); comdr. carrier division, 1944-45, participating as comdr. carrier task group in amphibious assault on Anguar and Peleliu (Palau Group), and as 2d in command, under Rear Adm. C.A.F. Sprague, of escort force in Battle for Leyte Gulf; comdr. of another carrier div., Jan.-Apr. 1945; became chief of staff to Vice Adm. Patrick N. L. Bellinger, comdr. Air Force, Atlantic, Apr. 1945. Senior Naval Member, U.S. Strategic Bombing Survey, Japan, 1945-46. Member, Military Liaison Committee to the Atomic Energy Commission, 1946-50; comdr. carrier div. five, and Task Force 77 (Korea), 1950-51; chief of staff Naval Forces Far East, 1951-52; comdr. First Fleet, 1952-53; deputy chief Naval Operations (Air), 1953-54; became commander of Sixth Fleet, Dec. 1954. Decorated Navy Cross; D.S.M. and Gold Star; Silver Star Medal; Legion of Merit and three Gold Stars with Combat V; Gold Cross of Merit (Poland), White Cross of Naval Merit, 2d class (Spain). Home: 3516 N. Valley St., Arlington 7, Va. Address: Navy Dept., Washington 25. Died Nov. 18, 1956; buried Arlington Nat. Cemetery.

O'GARA, JOHN EDWARD, govt. official; b. Hanover, N.H., July 8, 1895; s. Edward David and Margaret (Hayes) O'G.; B.S., Dartmouth, 1918; M.C.S., 1920; m. Adele Dreger, Sept. 15, 1925; m. 2d, Lucille Vachon. Prodn. planning, Nashua (N.H.) Gummed & Coated Paper Co., 1920-22; asso. with Macy's New York (unit of R. H. Macy & Co., Inc.) since 1922; management methods dept., 1922-26, delivery supt., 1926-29, asst. personnel dir., 1929-32, asst. gen. mgr., 1932-35, gen. mgr. and exec. vice pres., 1935-42, gen. mgr. and vice pres., 1945-50; numerous posts CIA, 1950-61. Dep. asst. sec. of state for econ. affairs, 1948. Dir. Webster Apts., N.Y., N.Y. Served as ensign (T), U.S. Navy, World War I; as col. U.S. Army, Army Service Force, 1942-44; dep. dir. Office of Strategic Services, 1944-45; col. and comdg. officer 176th Staff and Adminstrn. Group, O.R.C., U.S. Army. Mem. Retail Dry Goods Assn. (mem. exec. com.), Stores Mutual Protective Assn. (pres.), Nat. Urban League (chmn. management adv. com.), Phi Kappa Psi. Clubs: Dartmouth College, Union League (New York); North Hempstead Country, Manhasset Bay Yacht (Long Island, N.Y.). Home: Boca Raton FL Died Mar. 1, 1973.

OGDEN, AARON senator, gov. N.J.; b. Elizabeth, N.J., Dec. 3, 1756; s. Robert and Phebe (Hatfield) O.; grad. Coll. of N.J. (now Princeton), 1773; m. Elizabeth Chetwood, Oct. 27, 1787, 7 children. Tchr., Barber's Grammar Sch., Elizabeth, 1773-75; served to brig. maj. 1st Regt., N.J. Militia 1776-83; admitted to N.J. bar, 1784; commanded N.J. 15th Inf., 1797-1800, also lt. col. 11th Inf.; mem. U.S. Senate (Federalist, filled vacancy), from N.J., 1801-03; mem. N.Y.-N.J. Boundary Commn., 1807; built steamer Sea Horse to run between Elizabethtown and N.Y.C., 1811; gov. N.J., 1812-13; applied to N.J. Legislature for monopoly of steamboat navigation between Elizabethtown and N.Y.C., 1815 (monopoly granted); litigant famous U.S. Supreme Ct. case, Gibbons vs. Ogden, 1824 (John Marshall gave ct. decision that there could be no monopolies in interstate commerce); apptd. collector of customs Jersey City (N.J.), 1829. Died Elizabeth, Apr. 19, 1839; buried 1st Presbyn. Ch. Burial Ground, Elizabeth.

OGDEN, HENRY WARREN congressman; b. Abingdon, Va., Oct. 21, 1842; s. Elias and Louisa (Gordon) O.; removed to Warrensburg, Mo., 1851; worked on father's farm summers and attended common schools winters; served in C.S.A., lt., 16th Mo. inf.; later on staff Brig. Gen. Lewis; paroled, Shreveport, June 8, 1865; then engaged in farming in La.; mem. State Constl. Conv., 1879; mem. La. ho. reps., 1880-88, and speaker, 1884-88; elected to 53d Congress to fill vacancy caused by apptmt. of N. C. Blanchard to be U.S. senator; reëlected to 54th and 55th Congresses. Home: Benton, La. Died 1905.

OGLE, ALEXANDER congressman; b. Frederick, Md., Aug. 10, 1766; children include Charles. Moved to Somerset, Pa., 1795; mem. Pa. Ho. of Reps., 1803-04, 07-08, 11, 19-23; served as maj. gen. Pa. Militia; prothonotary, recorder of deeds, clk. of cts., 1812-17; mem. U.S. Ho. of Reps. (Democrat) from Pa., 15th Congress, 1817-19; mem. Pa. Senate, 1827-28. Died Somerset, Oct. 14, 1832; buried Union Cemetery, Somerset.

OGLESBY, RICHARD senator, gov. Ill.; b. Oldham County, Ky., July 25, 1824; s. Jacob and Isabella (Watson) O.; studied law under Silas W. Robbins, Springfield, Ill.; m. Anna White, 1859; m. 2d, Emma Keyes, 1873. Moved to Decatur, Ill., after death of parents, 1833; admitted to Ill. bar, 1845, started practice of law, Sullivan, Ill.; served as 1st lt. 4th Ill. Volunteers in Mexican War, 1846; went to prospect for gold, Cal., 1849-51; mem. Ill. Senate, 1860; served as col. 8th Ill. Volunteers, 1861-64, served under Ulysses S. Grant at forts Henry and Donelson, promoted maj. gen., 1863; gov. Ill., 1865-69, 73, 85-89, supported Lincoln's war policies, later denounced Andrew Johnson and sent formal demand that action be taken against him to Washington, D.C.; mem. U.S. Senate from Ill., 1873-79, chmn. coms. on public lands and Indian affairs. Died Elkart, Ill., Apr. 24, 1899; buried Elkart Cemetery.

O'HALLORAN, CORNELIUS HAWKINS justice Ct. of Appeal, B.C., Can.; b. Pavillion, B.C., Jan. 10, 1890; s. Cornelius and Bridget (Hawkins) O'H.; student U. Ottawa, Can., 1908-11; B.A., U. N.B., Fredericton, 1912, M.A., 1914; m. Ada Schaper, Apr. 4, 1917; children—Aileen, Desmond, Deirdre, Brian. Called to bar, 1915; practiced law with Henry C. Hall and Robert D. Harvey, Victoria, B.C., 1915-38; King's counsel, 1935; counsel for B.C. before Tariff Bd., Ottawa, on inquiries relating to tariff on gasoline and motor cars, 1935-36, also before Transport Bd. concerning rail freight on motor cars, 1937; counsel to Macdonald Commn. investigating costs in prodn., distbn. petroleum products and coal, 1934-37; justice Ct. of Appeal, B.C. since 1938. Hon. consul for Belgium at Victoria, 1933-38; mem. adv. bd. St. Joseph's Hosp. and dir. Victoria Children's Aid Soc. to 1938. Unsuccessfully contested Nanaimo Riding for House of Commons, 1926 and 1930 elections. Served as pvt. Can. Army in France and Belgium, 1917-18, World War I; later capt. Can. Militia with militia staff course certificate. Mem. B.C. Hist. Assn. Club: Union (Victoria, B.C.). Roman Catholic. Contbr. to law periodicals. Home: 999 Beach Dr., Oak Bay. Address: Law Courts, Victoria, B.C., Can. Died Sept. 9, 1963; buried Ross Bay Cemetery, Victoria.

O'HARA, BARRATT, congressman; b. St. Joseph, Mich., Apr. 28, 1882; s. Judge Thomas and Mary (Barratt) O'H.; ed. Benton Harbor (Mich.) High Sch., U. of Mo., Northwestern U. Law Sch.; LL.B., Chicago-Kent Coll. of Law, 1912; LL.D., Shorter Coll.-Jackson Seminary, 1962; m. Florence M. Hoffman, Feb. 28, 1906; children—Barratt, Lorence Hoffman, Howard Mears, Florence Frances Louise (dec.). Mem. newspaper editorial staffs, St. Louis and Chicago, 1901-11; lt. gov., Ill., 1913-17 (chmn. Ill. senate vice and wage com. responsible for passage state minimum wage laws, 1913-15); acting gov. at time of S.S. Eastland disaster (Chicago) and as mem. Fed. Bd. of Investigation drafted legislation to prevent similar disasters on Great Lakes; admitted to practice law Supreme Ct. of Ill. and Supreme Ct. of U.S., 1912; spl. asst. corp. counsel in traction reorgn. and subway constrn., 1939-48; mem. 81st to 90th Congresses, 2d Illinois Dist. U.S. delegate 20th General Assembly UN Nightly commentator A.F. of L. radio station, Chicago, 1933-38. Served as corpl., 33d Mich. Vol. Inf., Spanish-Am. War; officer 80th Div., divisional judge adv., 12th and 15th divs., U.S. Army, 1917-18. Awarded medal distinguished mil. service in White, Cuba. Mem. Vets. Fgn. Wars, Am. Legion, United Spanish War Vets. Chgo. Press Vets, Assn., 80th Div. Vets. Assn., Phi Gamma Delta, Phi Delta Phi. Democrat. Author: From Figg to Johnson, 1908; Report of Ill. Senate Vice Commission, 1915; Legislative Compendium (annually), 1925-29; Inside Secrets of Defaulted Real Estate Bonds 1935; Who Made the Constitution? (with Marie Crowe), 1936. Home: Chicago IL Died Aug. 1969.

O'HARA, JAMES army officer, mfr.; b. Ireland, 1752; s. John O'Hara; ed. Sem. of St. Sulpice, Paris, France; m. Mary Carson, circa 1782, 6 children. Came to Am., settled in Phila., 1772; became govt. agt. among Indians, circa 1774; capt. Revolutionary Army, 1775; became commissary at gen. hosp., stationed Carlisle, Pa., circa 1780; asst. q.m. for Gen. Nathaniel Greene, 1780-83; apptd. q.m. U.S. Army by Pres. Washington, 1792; govt. contractor, 1796-1802; founder (with Maj. Isaac Craig) 1st glassworks in Pitts., (1st plant of its kind to use coal for fuel, 1st successful product was bottles) circa 1800; a pioneer in exporting cotton to Liverpool, Eng., built vessels for the purpose; dir., pres. Pitts. br. Bank of Pa.; partner (with John Henry Hopkins) in iron works, Ligionier, Pa. Died Dec. 16, 1819; buried 1st Presbyn. Ch., Pitts.; reinterred Allegheny Cemetery, Pitts.

O'HARA, THEODORE editor, army officer; b. Danville, Ky., Feb. 11, 1820; s. Kean O'Hara; grad. st. Joseph's Coll., Bardstown, Ky., 1839. Admitted to Ky. bar, 1842; served as capt. and asst. q.m. Ky. Volunteers, Mexican War, 1846-48, brevetted maj., 1847; capt. Ky. Regt. in Narciso Lopez's expdn. to "liberate" Cuba, winter 1849-50; an editor Louisville (Ky.) Times, 1852-55; capt. 2d Cavalry, U.S. Army, 1855-56; editor Mobile (Ala.) Register, 1856-61; seized Ft. Barrancas in Pensacola Harbor, 1861; col. 12th Ala. Inf., circa 1861; became cotton mcht., Columbus, Ga., circa 1865. Author poetry: "The Old Pioneer" (poetic elegy); "The Bivouac of the Dead" (in memory of heroic dead at Battle Buena Vista, 1847). Died nr. Guerryton, Ala., June 6, 1867; reinterred State Mil. Cemetery, Frankfort, Ky., 1874.

OHLINGER, GUSTAVUS, lawyer; b. Foochow, China, July 15, 1877; s. Franklin and Bertha S. O. (Am. missionaries); B.A., U. of Mich., 1899, LL.B., 1902, honorary M.A., 1919; Ph.D. (hon.), U. Toledo, 1961; m. to Helen E. Rinehart, 1914; children—John Franklin, Lucy Jane, Mary Alice. Practiced in Shanghai, China, 1903-05, Toledo, O., 1905-62. Captain U.S. Army, 1918, assigned to Military Intelligence Div., Gen. Staff, Washington, D.C. Mem. Toledo Bd. of Edn., 1926-33. Member Phi Beta Kappa fraternity. Unitarian. Contbr. to Atlantic Monthly, Mich. Law Rev., Ency. Americana, etc. Lectr. summer session, Law Sch. U. Mich., 1931-37. Mem. Am. Assn. for UN (bd. govs. 1950-53). Author: Ohlinger's Federal Practice, 8 vols., 1948-54, rev. edit., 1964. Home: Toledo OH Died June 12, 1972; buried Woodlawn Cemetery, Toledo OH

OHLSON, OTTO FREDERICK, ry. official; b. Sperlingsholm, Halland, Sweden, June 6,21870; s. Otto and Cecelia (Swenson) O.; grad. high sch. in Sweden, 1887; came to America, 1893; m. Marie E. Ricketts, Sept. 1897. Telegraph operator in Sweden, S. America and India, 1887-93; switchman and brakeman Pa. R.R., 1893-1900; with N.P. Ry. as telegraph operator, sta. agent, train dispatcher, chief dispatcher, train master, asst. to gen. supt. and div. supt., 1901-28; gen. mgr. The Alaska R.R. (govt. owned, operated under Dept. of Interior) since 1928. Capt. Engrs., R.C., attending O.T.C., Camp Grant, Ill., 1917; maj. and lt. col. Engr. R.C., A.E.F., Jan. 1918-Dec. 1919; served as terminal supt., div. supt. and gen. supt. in France. Lutheran. Home: Anchorage AK*

O'LAUGHLIN, JOHN CALLAN (o-lok'lin), publisher; born Washington, D.C., January 11, 1873; son John and Mary (Osborne) O'L.; public school education; course in European diplomacy, Columbia U., hon. M.A., LL.D., Villanova Coll.; m. Mabel Hudson, July 15, 1896. With Washington bur. N.Y. Herald, 1893-1902; went to Venezuela, 1902, and reported blockade of that country by Great Britain, Germany and Italy; mem. European staff Associated Press, 1903-04; in Russia during Russo-Japanese War; on staff the Chicago Tribune, 1905-14, Washington corr., 1909-14; Washington corr. of Chicago Herald, 1914-17; v.p. Lord & Thomas, Chicago, 1917; pub. Army and Navy Journal; specializes in national defense and foreign affairs. Secretary of United States Commission to Tokyo Expn., 1908, 11; first asst. sec. of state, Jan. 19-Mar. 5, 1909; declined office of asst. secretaryship of treasury and minister to Argentine; acted as sec. to Theodore Roosevelt in Africa and Europe. During World War I as rep. of Chicago Herald and other papers, took Christmas ship laden with 6,000,000 gifts to war orphans in Europe. Del. Progressive Nat. Conv., 1912; exec. sec. policy com. of Rep. party, 1920; asst. to chmn. Rep. Nat. Com., 1933-34; chmn. Goethals Memorial Com.; vice-chmn. U.S. Goethals Memorial Commn. Chmn.; mem. and later coordinator of Selective Service Board of Appeals, District of Columbia, since 1941. Member board visitors United States Naval Academy, 1932. Commissioned major, Jan. 25, 1918, and assigned as aide to Major General Goethals, acting q.m. general United States Army; subsequently served in France with intelligence sect. General Staff, and later as sec. for the U.S. Inter-Allied Munitions Council; col. O.R.C., 1921-35. Catholic. Clubs: Chevy Chase, Gridiron (Washington). Author: With Roosevelt from the Jungle Through Europe, 1910; Imperiled America, 1916. Address: Army and Navy Journal, Washington. Died March 14, 1949; buried in Arlington National Cemetery.

OLCOTT, CHARLES SUMNER publisher, author; b. Terre Haute, Ind., Feb. 20, 1864; s. John Milton and Merrium (Brown) O.; A.B., DePauw U., 1883, A.M., 1886; m. Allie Gage, June 23, 1886; children—Gage (dec.), Charles Milton, Lyman Howard. Gen. mgr. private library dept. of Houghton, Mifflin Co., publishers, 1891-1933. Mem. Prudential Com. Am. Bd. Commrs. Foreign Missions and chairman finance committee of same. Republican. Conglist. Author: George Eliot—Scenes and People in Her Novels, 1910; The Country of Sir Walter Scott, 1913; The Lure of the Camera, 1914; The Life of William McKinley, 1916. Home: Cambridge, Mass. Died May 3, 1935.

OLD, FRANCIS PAXTON retired naval officer, savings and loan executive; born Norfolk, Virginia, December 19, 1897; s. Johnathan Whitehead and Claudia (Paxton) O.; B.S., U.S. Naval Acad., 1919; M.S. (engring.), Columbia, 1927; m. Florine Graff, Sept. 28, 1920; children—Beverley Benbury (Mrs. William Baker), Claudia Paxton (Mrs. Malcolm Chandler). Commissioned ensign United States Navy, June 7, 1919, and advanced through grades to vice adm.; served U.S.S. Nebraska, World War I; comd. U.S.S. Prairie, North Atlantic Patrol, 1942-43; served in assault and occupation Sicily, Salerno, chief of staff to attack force comdr. at Anzio and Southern France, 1943-45; comd. U.S.S. Indiana in Okinawa campaign and at Japanese surrender, 1945; comdr. mine force U.S. Atlantic Fleet, U.S.S. Terror (flagship), 1946; U.S. naval advisor to Republic of China, 1948-49; comdr. U.S. Naval Forces, Philippines, 1949-51; comdr. 9th Naval Dist., 1951-54, ret.; exec. dir. Illinois Toll Road Commn., 1954-55; with Sumner-Sollitt Co., construction, 1955-—; vice chmn. bd. Mid-Am. Appraisal Corp., Ralston Steel Corp. Decorated Legion of Merit (Salerno, Anzio), D.S.M. United States; Legion of Honor, Croix de Guerre with palm (France); D.S.O. (Eng.); Mil. Order of World Wars; Philippine Legion of Honor (comdr.). Episcopalian. Clubs: Chicago, Onwentsia Country. Home: 451 N. Green Bay St., Lake Forest. Office: 307 N. Michigan Av., Chgo. Died Sept. 23, 1963; buried Arlington Nat. Cemetery.

OLD, WILLIAM D(ONALD) army officer; b. Uvalde, Tex., Nov. 21, 1901; s. William Archer and Nancy Elizabeth (Spencer) O.; B.S. (elec. engring.), Tex. Agrl. and Mech. Coll., 1924; AC Flying Sch., 1924-25; AC Tactical Sch., 1935-36; Command and Gen. Staff Sch., 1936-37; rated command pilot, combat observer; m. Conquiesee A. Green, Sept. 20, 1925; children—William Donald, Sally Conquiesee. Commd. 2d lt., AS, 1924, and promoted through grades to maj. gen., July 1946; overseas assignment, 1941. Decorated D.S.M., Air medal, Silver Star, Southern Cross of Brazil. Address: War Dept., Washington. Died June 28, 1965.

OLDFIELD, WILLIAM ALLAN congressman; b. Franklin, Ark., Feb. 4, 1874; s. Milton T. and Anne (Matheny) O.; A.B., Ark. Coll., 1896; m. Fannie Pearl Peden, June 1, 1901. Sergt. and 1st lt. Co. M, 2d Ark. Vols., Spanish-Am. War, 1898. Admitted to bar, 1899; pros. atty. 3d Jud. Circuit of Ark., 1902-06; mem. 61st to 70th Congresses (1909-29), 2d Ark. Dist. Democrat. Methodist. Home: Batesville, Ark. Died Nov. 19, 1928.

OLDHAM, LEMUEL E., lawyer; b. Kosciusko, Attala Co., Miss., Feb. 8, 1870; s. Emmett Charles and Malvina Murphy (Doty) O.; ed. U. of Miss. and Eastman Coll. Poughkeepsie, N.Y.; studied law in office of U.S. Dist. Judge H. C. Niles, 1903-06; m. Lida Corinne Allen, of Kosciusko, Miss., June 27, 1895; children—Estelle (wife of Judge C. S. Franklin), Victoria (dec., wife of Paul F. Allen, U.S.A.), Dorothy Zollecoffer, Edward de Graffenried (dec.). Clk. U.S. Circuit Court, Northern Dist. of Miss., 1903-12, and of U.S. Dist. Court, same dist., 1905-18; U.S. commr., 1906-17; U.S. atty., Northern Dist. of Miss., by appmt. of President Harding, since June 23, 1921; mem. law firm of Stone, Oldham, Stone & Stone. Maj. a.d.c. Governor's Staff, Miss. N.G., 1912-16; del. Rep. Nat. Conv., 1920; mem. Rep. Nat. Advisory Com., 1920; mem. Miss. State Rep. Com. Mem. Am., Miss State and Lafayette County bar assns., Miss. Hist. Soc., Sigma Alpha Epsilon. Presbyn. Home: Oxford MS

OLDS, ROBERT army officer; b. Woodside, Md., June 15, 1896; s. Henry W. and May Clendening (Meigs) O.; ed. Central High Sch., Washington, D.C., and private tutors; grad. Air Corps Tactical Sch., 1928. Command and Gen. Staff Sch., 1935; m. Eloise Wichman, Oct. 22, 1921 (died 1926); children—Robin, Stevan Meigs; m. 2d, Marjorie Marvin, 1928 (divorced); m. 3d, Helen Post Sterling, 1933 (divorced); children—Sterling Meigs, Frederick Sterling. Joined Aviation Sect. of Signal Corps, Jan. 1917; rated Reserve mil. aviator, May 1917; commd. 1st lt. Signal Officers Reserve Corps, June 1917; comd. 17th Air Squadron, San Antonio, Tex., 1917; instr. Scott Field, Belleville, Ill., Ellington Field, Houston, Tex., later officer in charge of flying; arrived in France with A.E.F., Sept. 1918, assigned officer in charge of training at Clermont Ferrand instrn. center; then on staff 2d Army Air Service comdr. at Toul; with Hawaiian Dept., 1919-22, War Plans Div. Office of Chief of Air Corps, Washington, D.C., 1922-26; promoted to major, 1935; rated command pilot, mil. airplane pilot, combat observer; asst. to chief inspector, later chief of inspection sect., G.H.Q., Air Force, 1935-37; as comdg. officer 2d Bombardment Group, Langley Field, Va., piloted Flying Fortress No. 10, on non-stop transcontinental flights; comd. 6 Flying Fortresses on group flight to Buenos Aires and return Feb. 1938; flight leader on flight of 7 Flying Fortresses to Rio de Janeiro, Nov. 1939; promoted to col., Oct. 1940; command of Air Corps Ferrying Command, delivering bombers to Eng., since June 1941. Awarded bronze trophy of Internat. League of Aviators, 1941; also Victory medal, Mackay trophy, Harmon trophy. Decorated Distinguished Flying Cross (U.S.); Officer of Southern Cross (Brazil). Episcopalian. Mem. Order of Daedalians. Clubs: Columbia Country, Army and Navy (Washington, D.C.). Contbr. on flying to jours. Address: War Dept., Washington, D.C. Died Apr. 28, 1943.

OLIN, GIDEON congressman; b. East Greenwich, R.I., Nov. 2, 1743; children include Abram Baldwin. Engaged in farming; moved to Shaftsbury, Vt., 1776; del. Windsor Conv., 1777; mem. Vt. Ho. of Reps., 1778, 80-93, 99, speaker, 1788-93; served as maj. during Revolutionary War; asst. judge Bennington County (Vt.) Ct., 1781-98, chief judge, 1807-11; del. Vt. Constl. Conv., 1791; mem. Vt. Gov.'s Council, 1793-98; mem. U.S. Ho. of Reps. (Democrat) from Vt., 8th-9th congresses, 1803-07; resumed farming. Died Shaftsbury, Jan. 21, 1823; buried Shaftsbury Center.

OLIN, HUBERT LEONARD chem. engring.; b. Marcus, Ia., May 10, 1880; s. Frank William and Christine (Johnson) O.; B.A., U. of Ia., 1908; student U. of Chicago, 1910; M.S., U. of Ill., 1911, Ph.D., 1914; studied Columbia, 1914-15; m. Helen Leigh Hanes, June 2, 1917; 1 dau., Ida Helen. Instr. in chemistry, Vassar, 1913-14, U. of Ill., 1914-16; asst. prof. chemistry, Ohio State U., 1916-18; research chemist Barrett Co., 1919; asso. prof. chem. engring. U. of Ia., 1919-29, prof., 1929-50, emeritus 1950-—; chairman of Iowa State Mining Board, 1962-—; tech. adviser to Mexican govt., 1949. Made numerous researches in utilization of coal and its by-products, colloidal clays and activated carbons. Served as capt. 3d Chem. Batt., Edgewood Arsenal, 1918. Mem. Governor's Coal Com. Dir. Ia. Coal Institute; tech. adviser Iowa State Planning Bd. Fellow Royal Soc. Arts; mem. Society of Chemical Industry, American Institute Chemical Engineers, American Chem. Soc. Am. Gas Assn.; mem. Am. Water Works Assn., Soc. for Promotion of Engring. Edn., Am. Legion, Tau Beta Pi, Gamma Alpha, Phi Lambda Upsilon, Sigma Xi. Republican. Presbyterian. Clubs: Triangle, Research, Kiwanis, Engineers (Iowa City); Executives (Cedar Rapids). Writer numerous papers on tech. and scientific subjects in field of chem. engring. and fuel technology. Home: 321 Blackhawk St., Iowa City, Ia. Died Mar. 6, 1964; buried Oakland Cemetery.

OLIN, STEPHEN HENRY lawyer; b. Middletown, Conn., Apr. 22, 1847; s. Stephen (D.D., LL.D.) and Julia (Lynch) O.; A.B., Wesleyan U., 1866, A.M., 1869, LL.D., 1894; Litt.D., Columbia U., 1923; m. Alice, d. S. L. M. Barlow, Oct. 23, 1879 (died 1882); m. 2d, Emeline Dodge, d. Oliver Harriman, Mar. 21, 1903. Acting pres. Wesleyan U., 1922-23. Trustee Astor Library, 1888-95, New York Pub. Library, 1895-—, and Wesleyan U., 1880-—; v.p. N.Y. Bar Assn., 1898-99; pres. Univ Settlement Soc., 1902-06. Maj. and judge advocate 1st and 2d brigades, N.G.S.N.Y., 1882-89; lt. col. and a.-a.-g. 1st Brigade, 1889-98; col. and chief of staff N.G.S.N.Y., 1898-1903. Mem. exec. com. Internat. Conciliation. Homes: Rhinebeck, N.Y., and New York, N.Y. Died Aug. 6, 1925.

OLIPHANT, CHARLES LAWRENCE, physician; b. Kinsley, Kan., July 30, 1889; s. Hugh Bartus and Alice Mae (Blair) O.; B.S., Valparaiso U., 1913; M.D., St. Louis U., 1917; postgrad. Harvard, 1918, U. Pa., 1929-30; m. Mary Goss Romig, Nov. 29, 1916; children—Charles Romig, M.D., Mary Goss (wife of Robert Fadem, M.D.). Commd. lt. (j.g.), Med. Corps, USN, 1917, promoted through grades to comdr., 1935, retired, 1943, asst. dir. service de-hygiene, Haiti, 1930-34; instr. tropical medicine Women's Med Sch., Phila., 1930-34; instr. hygiene Harvard Med. Sch., 1941; pvt. practice internal medicine, San Diego, Cal., 1943-70; staff Mercy Hosp., Doctor's Hosp., Sharp Meml. Hosp. Fellow Am. Coll. Cardiology; mem. A.M.A., Cal., San Diego County medical societies, Sons Am. Revolution, Nat. Sojourner, Phi Delta, Alpha Epsilon. Republican. Methodist. Mason (32 deg., K.T., Shriner). Charter mem. Army and Navy Country (Washington). Home: San Diego CA Died Aug. 8, 1970.

OLIVER, ARTHUR L. lawyer; b. Leemon, Mo., Jan. 5, 1879; s. Henry Clay and Mary Louise (Alexander) O.; ed. State Normal Sch., Cape Girardeau, Mo.; LL.B., U. of Tex., 1900; m. Mary Esther Roberts, Nov. 27, 1907; children—John Roberts, James Arthur. Began practice at Caruthersville, 1900; served as mem. Mo. Ho. of Rep. and Mo. Senate; U.S. atty., Eastern Dist. of Mo., Aug. 4, 1914-—. Elected 1st lt. N.G. Mo., Dec. 1901, later capt.; maj. 6th Unattached Batt., 1904; organized 6th Regt. N.G. Mo., 1908, and elected col. Democrat. Presbyn. Mason, K.P., Elk. Home: St. Louis, Mo. Died July 3, 1928.

OLIVER, EDWARD ALLEN dermatologist; b. Crestline, O., Apr. 15, 1883; s. Ernest Allen and Carrie (Miller) O.; A.B., Kenyon Coll., Gambier, O., 1905; M.D., Rush Med. Coll., 1909; m. Bertha Montgomery, Dec. 30, 1911; children—Mrs. James B. Handy, Richard M. Began practice at Chicago, 1910; professor emeritus dept. of dermatology and Syphilology, Northwestern U. Med. Sch.; sr. dermatologist emeritus St. Luke's Hosp.; cons. dermatologist to Passavant, Vets., Wesley, Swedish Covenant and St. Francis Hosps.; cons. dermatologist U.S. Vets, Hines Hosp., Chicago; American Academy Dermatology and Syphilology (pres. 1946-47), Society for Investigative Dermatology; American Medical Assn., Chicago Medical Soc. Served as capt. Med. Corps, U.S. Army, 1918-19. Mem. Am. Dermatol. Assn. (pres. 1951-52), Chgo. Dermatol. Soc. pres., 1923-24, 1939-40. Inst. Medicine, Psi Upsilon, Nu Sigma Nu. Episcopalian. Club: University. Author numerous articles on dermatology. Home: 1161 Spruce St., Winnetka, Ill. Office: 55 E. Washington St., Chgo. Died Nov. 5, 1957.

OLIVER, HENRY KEMBLE educator, state ofcl., musician; b. Beverly, Mass., Nov. 24, 1800; s. Rev. Daniel and Elizabeth (Kemble) O.; grad. Dartmouth, 1818, Mus. D. (hon.), 1883; A.B., A.M. (as of 1818), Harvard, 1862; m. Sarah Cook, Aug. 30, 1825, 7 children. Became 1st master Salem (Mass.) High Sch., 1827; founded and conducted acad. for boys, Salem, 1830-35; entered Salem Light Inf., 1821; lt. col. 6th Mass. Inf., 1832; adj. gen. Mass. Militia, 1844-48; capt. Ancient and Hon. Arty. of Boston, by 1846; supt. Atlantic Cotton Mills, 1848-58; treas. State of Mass., 1860-65; organist various chs., Salem, 1823-59; founder Salem Oratorio Soc.; attended Peace Jubilee, Boston, 1872; organizer, developer Mass. Bur. Statistics of Labor (1st of its kind in U.S.), 1870, 1st chief, 1870-73; mayor Salem, 1877-80. Author: Original Hymn Tunes, 1875. Died Salem, Aug. 12, 1885.

OLIVER, JAMES HARRISON naval officer; b. Houston Co., Ga., Jan. 15, 1857; s. Thaddeus and Sarah Penelope (Lawson) O.; Washington and Lee U., 1872; grad. U.S. Naval Acad., 1877; m. Marion Carter Oliver, Dec. 7, 1893. Ensign, 1881; promoted through grades to rear adm., Jan. 5, 1917. Made 9 cruises at sea, averaging a little over 2 1/2 yrs. each; station duty at Ft. Monroe, Providence, Newport, R.I., Cincinnati; dir. Naval Intelligence Office, Jan. 20, 1914; gov. Virgin Islands and comdt. Naval Sta., 1917-19; duty Navy Dept., Apr. 1919-Jan. 1921 (retired.). Home: Shirley, Va. Died Apr. 6, 1928.

OLIVER, PAUL AMBROSE manufacturer; b. at sea, July 18, 1831, on his father's ship, "Louisiana," flying the U.S. flag; s. of Capt. Paul A. and Mary (Van Dusen) O.; ed. at Hamburg and Altona, Germany; unmarried. Second lt. 12th N.Y. Inf., Oct. 29, 1861; 1st lt., May 17, 1862; capt., Apr. 22, 1864; transferred to 5th N.Y. Inf., June 1, 1864; bvtd. brig. gen. vols., Mar. 8, 1865; awarded Congressional Medal of Honor, Oct. 12, 1892, "for while being in charge of a brigade assisted in preventing Union troops firing into each other at Resaca, Ga., May 15, 1864." Powder mfr., Luzerne County, Pa., 1870-—. Died May 18, 1912.

OLIVER, ROBERT SHAW assistant sec. of war; b. Boston, Sept. 13, 1847; ed. at Milton, Mass., Concord, N.H., and Churchill's Mil. Sch., Sing Sing, N.Y.; married; children—John Rathbone, Mrs. Elizabeth Stevens, Mrs. Cora Choate, Marion L. Apptd. 2dt lt. 5th Mass. Cav., Spet. 27, 1864 (at 17 yrs. of age); a.-d.-c., Cav. Brigade, 3d Div., 25th Army Corps, Feb. 3, 1865; asst. adj.-gen. 3d Div., 25th Army Corps, Sept. 3, 1865; entered regular army as 2d lt. 17th Inf., Feb. 25, 1866; 1st lt. 8th Cav., Mar. 7, 1867; resigned, Oct. 31, 1869; with Rathbone, Sard & Co., stove mfrs., Albany, N.Y., 1871-1903; asst. sec. of war, Sept. 1, 1903-Apr. 30, 1913. Served in N.Y.N.G. as col. 10th Inf., Aug. 25, 1873; lt. col. and asst. adj. gen. 9th Brigade, July 11, 1878; brig. gen., insp. gen. State of N.Y., Jan. 1, 1880; brig. gen. 5th Brigade, Jan. 10, 1883, 3d Brigade, Dec. 30, 1890; hon. retired at own request, Aug. 30, 1903. Civ. service commr. of Albany, May 28, 1894-Jan. 1, 1895; police commr., Jan. 1, 1895-June 1898. Home: Washington, D.C. Died Mar. 16, 1935.

OLMSTED, GIDEON naval officer; b. East Hartford, Conn., Feb. 12, 1749; s. Jonathan and Hannah (Meakins) O.; m. Mabel Roberts, 1777. Master sloop Seaflower, 1776-78; capt. French ship Polly, captured as privateer, taken prisoner, 1778; captured sloop Active with support of other Am. prisoners, sailed to America; served as privateer around N.Y. harbor, 1779-82; served as French privateer, 1793-95; mcht., East Hartford. Died East Hartford, Feb. 8, 1845.

OLNEY, WARREN lawyer; b. Davis Co., Ia., March 11, 1841; s. William and Eliza Ann (Green) O.; student Central U. of Ia., U. of Mich., 1 year; LL.B., Univ. of Mich., 1868; m. Mary Jane Craven, Sept. 11, 1865; father of Warren O., Jr. Pvt. to capt. in Civil War, May 21, 1861-Aug. 15, 1865; served in West and Southwest; admitted to bar, San Francisco, 1869; nominated as mayor of Oakland, Calif., by both Rep. and Dem.

convs., 1903; elected. Dir. Calif. Title Ins. & Trust Co.; pres. S. San Francisco Dock Co. Trustee Mills College. Home: Oakland, Calif. Died June 2, 1921.

O'LOUGHLIN, JOHN M(ARTIN), librarian; b. Malden, Mass., Oct. 27, 1895; s. Michael and Alice (O'Connor) O'L.; A.B., Boston Coll., 1918; m. Anna G. O'Connor, Oct. 12, 1927 (dec.); children—Mary Alice, Anne, John S. High sch., librarian Boston Coll. 1925-29, coll. librarian from 1929; trustee Medford Savs. Bank. Mem. spl. commn. to write secret history 1st Naval Dist., World War I; mem. Medford War Price and Rationing Bd., 1942-45. Mem. corp. Lawrence Meml. Hosp.; trustee Medford Pub. Library. Served as chief yeoman, asst. recorder, 1st Naval Dist., World War I. Named Boston Coll. Alumnus of Year, 1961. Mem. Cath. (pres. 1951-53), Am. library associations, Massachusetts Library Trustees Assn. and Spl. Library Assn., Am. Legion, Roman Catholic. K.C. (Past Grand Knight). Editor: Catholic Library World, 1931-37, Reading Lists for Catholics, 1940-41. Home: Medford MA Died June 30, 1964; buried Malden MA

OLSEN, CLARENCE EDWARD, naval officer; b. Aloha, Mich., Oct. 7, 1899; s. Hjalmer Eugene and Anna Gustava (Amundson) O.; B.S., U.S. Naval Acad., 1920; grad. Naval Line Post Grad. Sch., 1928, Naval War Coll., 1929; m. Elisabeth Warren, May 24, 1929 (dec. Dec. 1972); children—Betsey Jane, Charles Frank (adopted). Commd. ensign U.S. Navy, June 1920, and advanced through grades to rear admiral, August 1947; command U.S.S. Arctic, 1941-42, U.S.S. Baltimore, Japanese occupation, 1945-46; comdr. Cruiser Div. Two, since 1950; plans div. of comdr.-in-chief U.S. Fleet, 1942-43; sr. Naval officer in Mil. Mission to Russia, 1943-45; asst. dir. Central Intelligence, 1946-48; comdr. Naval Base, Norfolk, Va., 1948-50; later chief military assistance advisory group, Norway; ret., 1959. Awarded Legion of Merit, Bronze star, Occupation area ribbons. Conglist. Home: Bethesda MD Died Nov. 11, 1971; buried U.S. Naval Acad. Cemetery, Annapolis MD

OLSON, RALPH J., adjutant gen. Wis.; b. Marinette, Wis., Mar. 3, 1904; s. A.B., Ripon (Wis.) Coll., 1926; attended Res. Officers Sch., Command and Gen. Staff Schs.; married Ruth. Comml. survey supvr., later mgr. Milwaukee pub. office, Wis. Telephone Co., Milwaukee; founded glass company, 1937; apptd. state dir. civil defense, State Wis., Sept. 1950, also The Adjutant General (rank brig. gen., then major gen.), from Oct. 1950; dir. Anchor Savings and Loan Assn. Chmn. Wis. Vets. Bd.; director Rotary Found.; state chairman and member national council U.S.O. Commissioned 2d lt., and entered U.S. Army as capt.; served as regimental adjutant Tank Bn. Comdr.; asst. chief of staff G-1, 11th Armored Div. (part of 3rd Army), E.T.O.; separated as col., 1945; col. Wis. N.G., 1950. Decorated Order of the Fatherland, Order of Valor (Russia); Bronze star. Mem. Am. Legion, Nat. Guard Assn. Mason (Shriner). Elk. Clubs: Rotary, Madison, Maple Bluff Country, Hole-in-One (Golf). Home: Madison WI Died Jan. 29, 1969; buried Forest Hill Cemetery, Madison WI

OLSON, RAYMOND FERDINAND army officer; b. Oregon City, Ore., Oct. 26, 1891; s. Otto Ferdinand and Anna B. (Peterson) O.; student Ore. Inst. Tech., Portland, 1909-10; 1st Corps Sch., U.S. Army, Gondrecourt, France, 1918; Command and Gen. Staff Sch. U.S. Army, Fort Leavenworth, Kan., 1930; Army Finance Sch., Duke, 1943-44; m. Doris Marjorie Taylor, Mar. 25, 1933; children—Thomas Raymond, Marjorie Lee. Pvt., 1st lt. Ore. N.G., May-July 1917; Fed. service with 116th engrs., 41st div.; 1st engrs., 1st div.; dir. gen. transp. A.E.F., France, Nov. 1917-Sept. 1919; 1st lt., 116th engrs., Ore. N.G., Nov. 1921-June 1923; capt. 186th inf., Ore. N.G., June 1923-Mar. 1927, maj. 82d inf. brig., Mar. 1927-July 1931, lt. col. 41st inf. div., July 1931-Nov. 1939, lt. col. U.S.P. and D.O., Nov. 1939-Sept. 1940, lt. col., finance officer, 41st inf. div., Sept. 1940; service in Southwest Pacific, Mar. 1942-Feb. 1943; fiscal dir. Fort Bragg, N.C., Feb.-June 1944; brig. gen., acting adj. gen. of Ore., 1944-47, now asst. adj. gen. Mem. Adj. Gen. Assn., N.G. Assn. of U.S. (life), Am. Legion, V.F.W. Republican. Methodist. Mason (Shriner). Clubs: Army and Navy, Multnomah Athletic (life mem.). Home: 1590 N. 19th St., Salem 97303. Office: State Office Bdlg., Salem, Ore. Died Jan. 15, 1965; buried Portland Meml. Cemetery.

OLYPHANT, ROBERT b. N.Y. City, Aug. 26, 1853; s. Robert Morrison and M. Sophia (Vernon) O.; ed. pvt. schs. and 1 yr. in Paris; m. Caroline Wetmore Muller, May 1880 (died 1910); children—Mrs. Amy Gordon Anderson, Robert Morrison, Sophie Vernon (dec.), Donald; m. 2d, Marie Viele, Aug. 1912. Began with Union Car Spring Co., 1872; mem. Ward, Talbot & Olyphant, coal mchts., N.Y. City, 1874-1910. Enlisted in 7th Regt., N.G.N.Y., 1871; successively a.d.c. staff of Gov. Robinson, acting gen. insp. and gen. insp. rifle practice, insp. 1st Brigade, asst. adj. gen. 1st Brigade, bvt. brig. gen. (retired 1914). Hon. pres. U.S. Hosp. Fund of N.Y. Fellow Nat. Acad. Design. Republican. Presbyn. Home: New York, N.Y. Died Nov. 30, 1928.

O'MAHONY, JOHN revolutionist; b. Mitchelstown, Ireland, 1816; son of Daniel O'Mahony; attended Trinity Coll., Dublin, Ireland. Mem. Young Ireland nat. revolutionary movement; took part in abortive insurrection, 1848, escaped to France; came to N.Y., 1853; an organizer Emmet Monument Assn. to turn Britain's difficulties in Crimean War into advantages for Ireland, 1854; founder and head of Fenians (Am. br. of Irish Revolutionary Brotherhood), 1858; raised and served as col. 99th Regt., N.Y. Nat. Guard, 1854; became pres. Fenian Brotherhood at Fenian Congress (which also adopted constn. for group), Phila., 1865; forced to resign after consenting to an abortive demonstration against Campobello Island, 1866; again leader of Fenians, 1872-77. Died Feb. 6, 1877; buried Glasnevin Cemetery, Dublin.

OMAN, CHARLES MALDEN (o'man), naval officer; b. Columbia County, Pa., Oct. 23, 1878; s. Henry Freas and Mary Jane (Shannon) O.; M.D., U. of Pa., 1901; m. Heloise Graham Brinckerhoff, Jan. 3, 1916. Commissioned lt. (j.g.), Med. Corps, U.S. Navy, 1902, and advanced through all grades to rear adm., 1936; served at Asiatic Station (Philippines, U.S.S. Monadnock and Frolic), 1902-05; Naval Hosp., Norfolk, Va., 1905-07; U.S.S. Ohio, 1906-07; U.S.S. Illinois, 1907-09; assisted at rescue work Messina earthquake, 1909; Naval Hosp., N.Y. City, 1909-12, 1915-18; on flagship Wyoming, 1912-15; commanded hosp. ship Comfort and later Navy Base Hosp., Brest, France, during World War; fleet surgeon on staff Adm. Henry B. Wilson, Atlantic Fleet, 1919-20; comd. Naval Med. Sch., Washington, 1920-21; Naval Hosp., Washington, 1921-24; med. officer, American Legation, Peking, China, 1924-27; pres. Bd. of Med. Examiners, Washington, 1927-28; comd. Naval Dispensary, Washington, 1928-31; Naval Hosp., Annapolis, 1931-35; Naval Hosp., N.Y. City, 1935-37; dist. med. officer 3d Naval Dist., 1937-39; inspector Med. Dept. Activities of Atlantic Coast, 1939-41; comdg. Nat. Naval Med. Center, Bethesda, Md., 1941-42; comdg. U.S. Naval Convalescent Hospital, Harriman, N.Y., since 1942. Awarded Navy Cross with citation for distinguished service in line of profession as Officer in Command of Navy Base Hosp. at Brest, France, 1918; Philippine Campaign medal, 1902; Cuban Pacification medal, 1907; Vera Cruz medal, 1914; Great War medal with overseas clasp; Marine Expeditionary Force medal, Peking, China, 1925; Italian Red Cross medal (for work in Messina earthquake), 1909; Defense Medal, World War II Medal. Served as delegate of American Red Cross at the international congress of experts to consider the revision of the Hague Conv. of 1907, Geneva Switzerland, 1937; mem. Nat. Bd. of Med. Examiners since 1921. Mem. Am. Coll. of Surgeons (mem. bd. of govs.); fellow A.M.A.; Sigma Xi. Republican. Episcopalian. Mason (32 deg.). Clubs: Chevy Chase, Army and Navy (Washington); N.Y. Yacht (N.Y. City). Author: Minor Surgery, Doctors Aweigh. Address: Beacon, N.Y. Died Nov. 1, 1948.

OMAN, JOSEPH WALLACE naval officer; b. Columbia County, Penn., Aug. 15, 1864; s. Henry Freas and Mary Jane O.; grad. U.S. Naval Acad., 1886; m. Virginia Center Morse, Nov. 22, 1907; children—Joseph Wallace, William Morse, Virginia Morse. Ensign, July 1, 1888; lt. jr. grade, Oct. 11, 1896; lt., Mar. 3, 1899; lt. comdr., Jan. 1, 1905; comdr., Mar. 2, 1909; capt., Feb. 13, 1912; promoted rear admiral, July 1, 1918. Served on Helena, Spanish-Am. War, 1898; comdg. Mariveles, in Philippine insurrection, 1899; at Naval War Coll., Newport, R.I., 1905; exec. officer, Lancaster, 1905-06; navigator, Rhode Island, 1906; exec. officer same, 1906-09; at Naval War Coll., 1909; insp. equipment, Navy Yard, N.Y. City, 1909-11; comd. Tacoma, 1911, Des Moines, 1911, Maine, 1911-12; capt. of yard, Navy Yard, Boston, 1912-14; comd. North Carolina, 1914-15. Georgia, 1915-16; supervisor New York Harbor, 1916-17; comdr. Squadron Five, Patrol Force, Atlantic Fleet, 1917; comdr. Leviathan, July 1917-Mar. 1918; comdt. 2d Naval Dist., Mar. 1918-Mar. 1919; gov. Virgin Islands (U.S.), 1919-21; retired. Address: New York, N.Y. Died July 1, 1941.

O'NEAL, CHARLES THOMAS ry. exec.; b. Brandywine Springs, Del., Dec. 29, 1873; student pub. schs., Wilmington, Del., and Goldey Coll. Began as trainmaster's clerk Phila. & Reading Ry. (now Reading Co.), 1890; with Lehigh Valley R.R., in various capacities, 1891-1918, advancing to gen. supt.; furloughed to U.S. R.R. Adminstrn., 1919-20, and commd. maj. U.S. Army; v.p. Ft. Smith & Western Ry., 1921-29, Buffalo, Rochester & Pittsburgh Ry. Co., 1929-30; pres. Chicago & Eastern Ill. R.R. Co. 1931-44, chmn. bd. dirs. since 1944. Clubs: Chicago, Calumet Country, Old Elm. Home: 255 Genesee St., Avon, N.Y. Office: 332 S. Michigan Av., Chgo. Died Apr. 15, 1950; buried Allentown, Pa.

O'NEAL, EDWARD ASHBURY gov. Ala., Confederate soldier; b. Madison County, Ala., Sept. 21, 1818; s. Edward and Rebecca (Wheat) O'N.; grad. La Grange Coll., 1836; m. Olivia Moore, Apr. 12, 1838; Admitted to Ala. bar, 1840; solicitor 4th dist. Ala., 1841-45; one of leaders of secession in Northern Ala.; commd. maj. 9th Ala. Inf., Confederate Army, 1861, lt. col., 1861; promoted to col., assigned to 26th Ala. Inf., 1862; fought in battles of Chancellorsville and Gettysburg; acted as brig.-gen., 1864-65; leader Democratic party in N. Ala. during reconstruction period; mem. Ala. Constl. Conv., 1875; gov. Ala., 1882-86, responsible for ednl. and prison reform, establishing normal schs., bd. convict insps. Died Nov. 7, 1890; Florence, Ala.

O'NEIL, CHARLES rear admiral U.S.N.; b. Manchester, Eng., Mar. 15, 1842; s. John and Mary Anne (Francis) O.; m. Mary C. Frothingham, Apr. 6, 1869. Entered U.S.N. as master's mate, July 1861, on sloop "Cumberland," and with it at capture of Forts Hatteras and Clarke, Aug. 1861, and in engagement with Confederate iron-clad "Merrimac," Mar. 8, 1862; rescued Lt. Morris from drowning; was favorably mentioned in dispatches and promoted acting master, May 1, 1862; was in both attacks on Fort Fisher; promoted acting vol. lt., May 30, 1865. Commd. lt., Mar. 11, 1868; lt. comdr., Dec. 18, 1868; comdr., July 1884; capt., July 21, 1897; rear admiral, Apr. 22, 1901. Chief Naval Bur. of Ordnance, 1897-1904; retired, Mar. 15, 1904; detailed for spl. ordnance duty abroad for 1 yr., Mar. 27, 1904. Address: Washington, D.C. Died Feb. 28, 1927.

O'NEIL, RALPH THOMAS lawyer; b. Osage City, Kan., Aug. 8, 1888; s. Thomas J. and Margaret (Hughes) O'N.; grad. high sch., Osage City, 1905, Baker U., Baldwin, Kan., 1909; LL.B., Harvard, 1913; m. Margaret Heizer, Aug. 15, 1919; children—Robert Heizer, Ralph Thomas. Admitted to Kan. bar, 1913, and began practice at Osage City; moved to Topeka, Kan., 1919; mem. firm O'Neil & Hamilton, 1924—; dir. and gen. counsel Victory Life Ins. Co.; gen. counsel Preferred Risk Fire Ins. Company; pres., O'Neil Hardware Company, Osage City, Kan.; dir. Citizens State Bank, Pyramid Life Ins. Co. Nat. comdr. American Legion, 1930-31 (dept. comdr. of Kan. 1925; nat. vice comdr., 1927; chmn. nat. citizens mil. training camps com., 1929; mem. nat. defense com., 1930). County atty., Osage County, Kan., 1914-17; city atty., Topeka, 1921-27. Mem. Kan. State Bd. of Regents, 1932-40, chmn., 1938-39. Served with 11th U.S. Inf., advancing to capt., 1917-19; divisional citation. Decorated silver star, Order of Comdr. of the Crown of Italy. Mem. Kan. State Bar Assn. (pres.). Democrat. Presbyn. Mason, Elk. Home: Topeka, Kan. Died May 25, 1940.

O'NEILL, JOHN army officer; b. Drumgallon, parish of Contibret, County Monaghan, Ireland, Mar. 8, 1834; m. Mary Crow, 1864. Came to Am., 1848; served with 2d U.S. Dragoons in Mormon War, 1857; served with 1st Cav. in Cal., became agt. by 1861; commd. 2d lt. 5th Ind. Cav., U.S. Army, 1862, 1st lt., 1863, resigned, 1864, apptd. capt. 17th U.S. Colored Inf.; a Fenian organizer in his dist., led detachment from Nashville to attack Can., 1866, led raid from Buffalo into Can., occupied Canadian village Ft. Erie, 1866; apptd. insp. gen. Irish Republican Army in U.S., late 1866; attempted another raid on Can., 1870, arrested and jailed, made another attack on Can., 1871, seized Hudson's Bay post, Pembina; agt. for land speculators desiring Irish settlers for tract of land in Holt County, Neb., in 1870's. Died Omaha, Neb., Jan. 7, 1878.

OPIE, EUGENE LINDSAY, pathologist; b. Staunton, Va., July 5, 1873; s. Thomas and Sallie (Harman) O.; A.B., Johns Hopkins, 1893, M.D., 1897, LL.D., 1947; Sc.D., Yale, 1930; LL.D., Washington U., 1940; D.Sc. (hon.), Rockefeller University, 1966; m. Gertrude Lovat Simpson, Aug. 6, 1902; children—Thomas Lindsay, Anne Lovat, Helen Lovat, Gertrude Eugenie; m. 2d, Margaret Lovat Simpson, Sept. 16, 1916. Medical house officer Johns Hopkins Hosp., 1897-98; asst. instr., asso. in pathology Johns Hopkins, 1898-1904; mem. Rockefeller Inst. for Med. Research, 1904-10. bd. sci. dirs., 1928-32; vis. pathologist Presbyn. Hosp., N.Y.C., 1907-10; prof. pathology Washington U., St. Louis, 1910-23. dean med. sch., 1912-15; prof. pathology, dir. dept. U. Pa., dir. labs. Henry Phipps Inst., 1923-32, acting dir., 1942-46; prof. pathology Cornell Med. Coll. and pathologist to N.Y. Hosp., 1932-41; sci. dir. Internat. Health Div., Rockefeller Found., 1935-38; vis. prof. Peiping Union Med. Coll., 1939; research Rockefeller Inst. Med. Research, 1941-70. President Nat. Tb. Assn., 1929; research Council Pub. Health Research Inst., N.Y.C. Served from capt. to col. Med. R.C., A.E.F., 1917-19. Awarded Gerhard, Trudeau medals, 1929; medal. Soc. Puertorriquena de Tisologos. 1938; Weber-Parkes Medal and Award of Royal Coll. of Physicians. 1945: Banting Medal, 1946; Jessie Stevenson Kovalenko medal Nat. Acad. Scis., 1959; medal of New York Academy of Medicine, 1960; T. Duckett Jones Memorial award Helen Hays Whitney Found., 1965. Fellow Am. Assn. Advancement Sci.; mem. Nat. Acad. Scis., Assn. Am. Physicians, Am. Assn. of Pathologists and Bacteriologists (pres. 1917). American Association Immunologists (president 1929) Harvey Society (president 1936-38). A.M.A. Episcopalian. Author: Diseases of the Pancreas, 1902; Epidemic Respiratory Disease, 1921. Co-editor of The Jour. Exptl. Medicine, 1904-10. Home: New York City NY Died Mar. 12, 1971; buried Baltimore MD

OPPENHEIMER, FRITZ ERNEST, internat. lawyer; b. Berlin, Germany, Mar. 10, 1898; s. Ernst and Amalie (Friedlander) O.; ed. College Royal Francais, Berlin, 1908-15, Berlin U., 1919-20. Freiburg U., 1920-21; LL.D., Breslau U., 1922; Paris U., 1924-25; London U., 1925; m. Elizabeth Kaulla, Oct. 23, 1927; children—Ellen (Mrs. Paul Handler), Ernest. Mem. Soc. Inner

Temple, London, 1938; English barrister-at-law, 1946. Practiced law as mem. German bar, also Paris (France), The Hague (Holland); asso. with solicitors, London, Eng., 1925-35; counselor in chambers of atty. gen. for Eng. and to Brit. Treasury, 1936-40; with law firm Cadwalader, Wickersham & Taft, New York, 1940-43; chief analyst Bd. Econ. Warfare, Washington, 1943; spl. asst. U.S. Mil. Govt. for Germany, Berlin, 1946; spl. asst. for German-Austrian affairs, office of legal adviser, Dept. of State, 1946-48, legal adviser to sec. of State at confs., Council of Fgn. Ministers, Moscow, 1947, London, England, 1947; also Paris, France, 1949; United States deputy fgn. minister on treaty for Austria, 1947; legal adviser to U.S. ambassador at 6-Power Conf. on Germany, London, 1948; pvt. practice, New York, from 1948. Served with the German Army, 1915-18; enlisted as pvt., U.S. army, 1943, advanced through grades to lt. col., 1945; legal staff officer, AUS S.H.A.E.F., London, Versailles, Rheims, Frankfurt, in charge reform of German law and court system, 1944-45; contbd. to preparation of documents and plans in connection with Germany's mil. surrender at Rheims, France, and Berlin, Germany, 1945; participated in drafting mil. govt. and control council legislation for Germany. Mem. Officers Reserve Corps since 1946. Decorated Legion of Merit, Bronze Star Medal. Mem. N.Y. City Bar Assn., Am. Soc. International Law, International Law Association, Council Fgn. Relations. Author various publs. on internat., corporate and tax law in English, French and German. Home: Palo Alto CA Died Feb. 4, 1968.

ORAHOOD, HARPER M. lawyer; b. Columbus, O., June 3, 1841; s. William J. and Ann (Messenger) O.; pub. and high sch. edn.; m. Mary Esther Hurlbut, Oct. 1, 1863. Joined emigrant train for Colo. in 1860; spent 10 yrs. in mercantile pursuits at Black Hawk and Central City; admitted to bar, 1873; practiced for many yrs. in partnership with Henry M. Teller and his bro., Willard; mem. firm of Orahood & Orahood; pres. Riverside Cemetery Assn., Fairmount Cemetery Assn. Was 1st lt. and commissary of subsistence, and later capt., Co. D, 3d Regt. Colo. Vol. Cav., Civil War; col. on staff of Gov. McIntire, 1895; served as city atty., Blackhawk, Central City and Denver; postmaster Blackhawk, 1862-71; county clerk Gilpin Co., Colo., 1866, 1867; dist. atty. 1st Jud. Dist., Colo., 1877-80; mem. sch. bd. Dist. No. 1, Denver, 7 yrs. (pres. 1 yr.). Republican. Presbyn. Mason (33 deg.); Past Grand Master of Masons of Colo.; Past Grand Comdr. K.T. Comdr. Dept. of Colo. and Wyo., G.A.R., 1901. Home: Denver, Colo. Died Sept. 15, 1914.

ORBISON, THOMAS JAMES M.D., neuro-psychiatrist; b. India (parents U.S. citizens), Nov. 13, 1866; s. James and Nancy Dunlop (Harris) O.; student Haverford Coll., 1884-88; M.D., U. of Pa., 1898, also Doctor of Medical Jurisprudence; m. 2d, Paula Poedder, Nov. 6, 1923; children—(by former marriage) Virginia Thomas, Joan Winsor. Began practice, Phila., 1899; served as asst. instr. mental and nervous diseases, U. of Pa., also on faculty Polyclinic Hosp. and Orthopedic Hosp.; removed to Los Angeles, Calif., 1907; practice limited to mental and nervous diseases; served on faculty Los Angeles County Gen. Hosp., Whittier State Sch., Children's Hosp., Santa Rita Clinic, etc. Mem. N.G. Pa., 1885-86; served in Spanish-Am. War, 1898; mem. 1st Troop, Phila. City Cav., 1899-1907; capt. Med. Corps, World War, with A.E.F., 1917-19; chief of Latvian Sect., Baltic Mission. Mem. Los Angeles Soc. Mental and Nervous Diseases (pres.), Southern Calif. Acad. Criminology (pres.). Awarded Baltic Cross; Latvian Jubilee medal; Order of St. Vladimir, 4th Class. Republican. Presbyn. Mason. Author: Children, Inc. Home: Los Angeles, Calif. Died Mar. 26, 1938.

ORD, EDWARD OTHO CRESAP army officer; b. Cumberland, Md., Oct. 18, 1818; s. James Ord; grad. U.S. Mil. Acad., 1839; m. Mary Mercer Thompson, Oct. 14, 1854, 3 children. Commd. 1st lt. U.S. Army, circa 1840, served in Seminole War; sent in ship Lexington from N.Y., around Cape Horn to Cal., 1847; capt., 1850; served in expdn. suppressing John Brown's raid at Harper's Ferry, 1859; promoted brig. gen. U.S. Volunteers, 1861, commanded brigade defending Washington, D.C., 1861-62; leader attack against Confederate Army under Gen. J.E.B. Stuart, Dranesville, Va., 1861; brevetted lt. col. U.S. Army; maj. gen. U.S. Volunteers, 1862; commanded left wing Army of Tenn., Aug.-Sept., 1862, brevetted col. U.S. Army, 1862; commanded 13th Corps, Army of Tenn. in Vicksburg campaign, June-Oct. 1863; served in capture of Jackson, Miss., 1863; served with Gen. George Crook, 1864, directed campaign against Staunton, Va.; in command 8th Army Corps, 1864, later of 18th Army Corps, in operations before Richmond; assumed command Army of the James and Dept. N.C., 1865; brevetted maj. gen. U.S. Army, 1865; maj. gen. on ret. list, 1881. Died Havana, Cuba, July 22, 1883; buried Arlington (Va.) Nat. Cemetery.

ORDWAY, SAMUEL HANSON, lawyer, assn. exec.; b. N.Y.C., Jan. 20, 1900; s. Samuel Hanson and Frances Hunt (Throop) O.; A.B., Harvard, 1921, LL.B., 1924; m. Anna Wheatland, June 24, 1924; children—Ellen, Samuel Hanson, Stephen Wheatland (dec.). Admitted to N.Y. bar, 1925; asso. firm Burlingham, Veeder, Master & Fearey, 1924-26; asso. Spencer, Ordway & Wierum, 1926-28, mem. firm, 1928-37, counsel, 1940-58; lectr. Am. U., 1938, Inst. Govt., U. So. Cal., 1939, N.Y.U., 1946; Pres. Nat. Civil Service Reform League, 1940-41; mem. U.S. Council Personnel Adminstrn., 1938-41; cons. Nat. Roster Sci. and Profl. Personnel, 1940-41; mem. U.S. Civil Service Commn., 1937-39, Civil Service Commn. City N.Y., 1934-36; chmn. exec. com. N.Y. Civil Service Reform Assn., 1936; mem. Art Commn. City N.Y., 1937, 41; chmn. N.Y.C. Conf. on Charter Revision, 1934; mem. examining bd. to certify 1st personnel dir. for states R.I., 1939, La., 1944. Vis. com. Littauer Sch. Pub. Adminstrn., Harvard, 1945-57; mem. adv. com. N.Y.U. Div. Tng. for Pub. Service; v.p. Conservation Found., 1948-61, pres., 1961-65, trustee, 1961, chmn. bd., 1969; trustee Am. Constn. Assn. Served from lt. comdr. to capt., USNR, 1941-43. Mem. Assn. Bar City N.Y., Soc. Personnel Adminstrn. (v.p. 1939), Natural Resources Council Am. (chmn. 1954). Republican. Episcopalian. Clubs: Century, University, City, Harvard, Fencers (N.Y.C.); Cosmos (Washington). Author of several books, 1929, including: Resources and American Dream, 1953; Prosperity Beyond Tomorrow, 1956. Home: Yorktown Heights NY Died Nov. 18, 1971.

O'REILLY, ALEXANDER army officer; b. Baltrasna, County Meath, Ireland, 1722; s. Thomas Reilly; m. Rosa de las Casas, at least 2 children. Became cadet Hibernia regt. Spanish Army, 1732; leader in Spanish Army reform; maj. gen., 1763, lt. gen., 1767, sent to take formal possession province of La., punish rebels and assimilate govt. to that of other Spanish dominions in Am., 1768-69; insp. gen., inf., 1770, in charge sch. for officers; given title Count, 1771; mil. gov. Madrid (Spain), circa 1773; leader unsuccessful expdn. against Algiers, 1775; participant in intrigues against Jose conde de Floridablanca, which later led to banishment to Province of Galicia; recalled to take command army in Catalonia, 1794. Died Bonete, nr. Chincilla, Murcia, Spain, Mar. 23, 1794.

O'REILLY, ROBERT MAITLAND surgeon gen. U.S.A.; b. Phila., Jan. 14, 1845; s. John and Ellen (Maitland) O.; M.D., U. of Pa., 1866; m. Miss Pardee, Aug. 16, 1877. Apptd. from Pa., med. cadet, U.S.A., Jan. 7, 1864; apptd. asst. surgeon, May 14, 1867; capt. asst. surgeon, May 14, 1870; maj. surgeon, Nov. 1, 1886; lt. col. deputy surgeon gen., Feb. 21, 1900; col. asst. surgeon gen., Feb. 14, 1902; brig. gen. surgeon gen. U.S.A., Sept. 7, 1902; retired with rank of major gen., Jan. 14, 1909. During Spanish-Am. War was in vol. service May 9, 1898, to May 12, 1899, as lt. col. chief surgeon. Address: Washington, D.C. Died Nov. 3, 1912.

ORMSBEE, EBENEZER JOLLS governor; b. Shoreham, Vt., June 8, 1834; s. of John Mason and Polly (Willson) O.; ed. pub. schs., Vt. Scientific and Lit. Instn. (Brandon) and Green Mountain Acad., Woodstock, Vt.; hon. A.M., Middlebury, 1875, Dartmouth, 1884; LL.D., Norwich U., 1893; m. Jennie L. Briggs, Aug. 27, 1862; m. 2d, Mrs. Frances (Wadhams) Davenport, Sept. 26, 1867. Admitted to bar, 1861; 2d lt. Co. G, 1st Vt. Inf., and capt. Co. G, 12th Vt. Inf., 1861-63. Asst. U.S. internal revenue collector, Dist. of Vt., 1868-72; state's atty., Rutland Co., Vt., 1870-74; mem. Gen. Assembly, 1872, Senate, 1878; trustee Vt. Reform Sch., 1880-84; lt. gov. of Vt., 1884-88; gov., 1886-88; commr. to Pi-Ute Indians, 1891; U.S. land commr. of Samoa, 1891-93. Republican. Episcopalian. Pres. Brandon Nat. Bank. Trustee Vt. Soldiers' Home. Address: Brandon, Vt. Died Apr. 3, 1924.

ORMSBY, STEPHEN congressman; b. County Sligo, Ireland, 1759; studied law. Came to U.S., settled in Phila.; admitted to the bar, 1786; began practice of law, Danville, Ky.; dep. atty. gen. Jefferson County (Ky.), 1787; served in Indian wars as brig. gen. under Gen. Josiah Harmar in campaign of 1790; judge Jefferson County Dist. Ct., 1791; presdl. elector, 1796; judge circuit ct., 1802-10; mem. U.S. Ho. of Reps. (Democrat) from Ky., 12th, 13th-14th congresses, 1811-13, Apr. 20, 1813-17; 1st pres. Louisville (Ky.) br. U.S. Bank, 1817. Died nr. Louisville, 1844; buried Ormsby Burial Ground, Lyndon, Ky.

ORNDOFF, BENJAMIN HARRY, physician; b. Graysville, Pa., Feb. 3, 1881; s. John and Minerva (Roseberry) O.; Ph.G., Valparaiso U., 1905, M.A., 1916; M.D., Loyola U., 1906; Dr. Med. Radiology and Electrology, Cambridge U., Eng., 1926; m. Bernice Harvey, June 29, 1907; children—John Roseberry, Ruth, Jane, Sarah, Harvey Hawkins. Intern Frances Willard Hosp., Chicago, 15 months, 1906-07; pathologist and roentgenologist, same, 1907-21; prof. pathology and roentgenology, Chicago Coll. of Medicine and Surgery, 1910-16; surgeon div. of electrosurgery, Grant Hosp.; med. staff Swedish Covenant Hosp.; sr. staff mem. dept. radiology, Luth. Gen. Hosp., Park Ridge, Ill. prof. and chmn. dept. of radiology, Loyola U. School of Medicine, Chgo. U.S. Navy, 1937-39 (lt. comdr. MC-V), USNR (ret.). Awarded Silver Medal, Western Roentgen Soc., 1916; Gold Medal Radiol. Soc. of N.A., 1927; Gold Medal Am. Coll. of Radiology, 1954; Silver Medal, Swedish delegation, 5th Internat. Congress of Radiology, 1937; Gold Medal, English delegation, 5th Internat. Congress of Radiology, 1950; Citation and Scroll, Radiol. Soc. of N.A., 1954; Stritch gold medal Stritch Sch., Loyola U., 1960; gold medal Centre Antoine Beclere, Paris, 1965. Fellow Am. Coll. of Surgeons, Am. Med. Assn., Am. Coll. of Radiology (treas. 1925-31, exec. sec., 1931-36), Inter Am. Coll. of Radiology, A.C.P.; hon. mem. Italian Soc. of Radiol. Medicine, Columbian Soc. of Radiology, Argentina Assn. of Radiology, Argentina Radiol. Soc., Soc. of Radiology and Physiotherapy of Cuba, Cuban Radiol. Soc.; mem. Radiol. Soc. of N.A. (pres. 1917-18), Am. Roentgen Ray Soc. Soc., Ill. State and Chgo. Med. Socs., British Inst. of Radiology, Rocky Mountain Radiological Soc., (hon. member), Inst. of Medicine of Chgo., Am. Phys. Soc., Am. and Chgo. Heart Assn., Am. Geriatrics Soc., Egon Fischman Meml., S.A.R., Chgo. Art Inst., Chgo. Museum Nat. History, Century of Progress Assn., Chgo. Roentgen Soc. (pres. 1921-23, sec. 1919-21), Physics Club of Chgo., Ill. Acad. of Sci., Chgo. Hist. Soc., A.A.A.S., Sigma Xi, Lambda Rho, Theta Kappa Psi. Del. Internat. Congress of Radiology, Stockholm, 1928, Paris, 1931, pres. of delegates, 4th Congress, Zurich, Switzerland, 1934; del. 2d Inter Am. Congress Radiology, Havana, 1946; chmn. exec. council First Am. Congress of Radiology, 1933; gen. sec. 5th Internat. Congress of Radiology, Chicago, 1937; mem. internat. executive committee 6th International Congress of Radiology, London, 1950; mem. 6th International Congress on Cancer, Paris, 1950. Mason (32 deg., K.T., Shriner). Engaged in research in radiology and electrosurgery. Author of articles in exptl. research and clin. medicine. Address: Park Ridge IL Died Mar. 6, 1971; buried Rogersville PA

ORNDUFF, WILLIAM WILMER, pediatrician; b. Cathage, Mo., Sept. 19, 1910; M.D., U. Ore., 1937. Rotating intern Touro Infirmary, New Orleans, 1937-38; asst. resident pediatrics Bobs Roberts Meml. Hosp., Chgo., 1938-40; resident contagious disease Municipal Contagious Disease Hosp., Chgo.; practice medicine specializing in pediatrics, Portland, Ore. Instr. pediatrics U. Ore., 1959-62, asst. prof., 1962-63. Served to capt. M.C., AUS, 1942-46. Diplomate Am. Bd. Pediatrics. Fellow Am. Acad. Pediatrics; mem. North Pacific, Portland pediatric socs. Research in pediatric neurology. Home: Portland OR Died Oct 5, 1964.

ORNITZ, SAMUEL author; b. N.Y.C., Nov. 15, 1890; s. Morris and Deborah (Badisch) O.; student Coll. City of New York 2 yrs.; evening courses, N.Y. U., 1 yr.; m. Sadie Florence Lesser, Dec. 22, 1914; children—Arthur Jaques, Donald Ray. Asst. supt. Brooklyn Soc. for Prevention of Cruelty to Children, 1914-20; engaged in penol. research, probation and parole work, for Prison Assn. of N.Y. City, 1909-14; auly Pub. Co., 1925, 27, 28; photoplay Originator Paramount Studios 1928-29; with Metro-Goldwyn-editor Macfadden Publs., 1924-25; edit. dir. Mac-Mayer Studio, 1929-31, RKO Studios, 1932-33, Universal Studios, 1934-35. Mem. Nat. Com. for Def. of Polit. Prisoners, Internat. Labor Defense Com., Hollywood Anti-Nazi League, Motion Picture Artists Com. Atheist. Clubs: Friday Luncheon, Bachman Loyal. Author: The Sock, 1919; Haunch, Paunch and Jowl, 1923; Round The World with Jocko The Great, 1925; A Yankee Passional, 1927; (motion picture plays) The Case of Lena Smity) Chinatown Nights; The Man Who Reclaimed His Head; Three Kids and a Queen; Portia on Trial; (also plays) One Year to Pay, In New Kentucky, Back to the Baboons, Mythical Kingdom. Known as a "freak fancier"; rescued many deformed young people who were being exploited by showmen. Home: 1632 N. Martel Av., Los Angeles. Died Mar. 1957.

ORR, GEORGE consular service; b. Phila., Pa., Sept. 29, 1886; s. William and Annie (Millikin) O.; grad. Northeast High Sch., Phila., 1903; student Temple Coll., 1906-07; m. Clara H. Rose, Aug. 11, 1920. Ry. and municipal engr. until 1920; consul at Panama, 1920-25, at Paris, 1925-29, Stavanger, Norway, 1929-32, Caracas, Venezuela, 1932-—. Served as 1st lt. and capt. 32d Engrs., U.S.A., 1917-19. Home: Atlantic City, N.J. Died Apr. 3, 1937.

ORR, H(IRAM) WINNETT surgeon; b. West Newton, Pa., Mar. 17, 1877; s. Andrew Wilson and Frances J. (Winnett) O.; U. of Neb., 1892-95; M.D., U. of Mich., 1899; m. Grace Douglass, Sept. 7, 1904; children—Douglass, Willard, Josephine, Dorothy, Gwenith. In practice at Lincoln, Neb., since 1899. Editor Western Medical Review, 1899-1906; lecturer on history of medicine, Coll. of Medicine, U. of Neb., since 1903; chief med. insp., Lincoln pub. schs., 1908; supt. Neb. Orthopedic Hosp., 1911-17, chief surgeon, 1919-47, cons. surgeon since 1947; cons. surgeon dept. orthopedic surgery Lincoln Gen. Hosp. Editor Jour. Orthopedic Surgery, 1919-21. Commd. capt., Med. R.C., May 18, 1917; on duty Welsh Met. War Hosp., Witchurch, Cardiff, Wales, June 1917-Aug. 1918; with A.E.F., France, Aug. 1, 1918-Feb. 24, 1919; maj. M.C., Oct. 1, 1918; lt. col., Feb. 17, 1919; relieved, June 1, 1919; was col. M.C., U.S. Army Reserve, with spl. assignment as consultant orthopedic surgery. Librarian, Neb. State Med. Assn., 1900-12, sec., 1907, pres., 1919-20; sec. Am. Orthopedic Assn., 1915-17, editor, 1919-21, pres., 1936; sec. Central States Orthopedic Club, 1913-17. Recipient Distinguished Service award (posthumously) from the American College of Surgeons. Member A.M.A. (chmn. orthopedic sect., 1921-22), Miss. Valley and Mo. Valley med. assns., Elkhorn Valley Med. Soc., Lancaster County Med. Soc., Soc. Internat. de Chirurg Orthopedique (U.S.), Am. Med. Library Assn. (hon. mem.); Assoc. Bone and

Joint Surgeons (hon.); member Chi Phi, Phi Rho Sigma, Sigma Xi, Alpha Omega Alpha (Nebraska). Clubs: Commercial, Country, Lincoln University; University (Chgo.). Author numerous books, 1903-—; latest publ. Selected Pages from the History of Medicine in Nebraska, 1952; contbr. to Sajous Cyclo., 1931; speaker on osteomyelitis Brit. Med. Assn., Dublin, 1933, on surgery Ill. State Med. Soc., 1939, on compound fractures So. Med. Assn., 1940; lectr. Am. Acad. Orthopedic Surgeons, 1952. Home: 1601 Smith St., Lincoln 2. Office: 2300 S. 13th St., Lincoln, Neb. Died Oct. 11, 1956; buried Arlington Nat. Cemetery.

ORR, ROBERT JR. congressman; b. nr. Hannastown, Pa., Mar. 5, 1786; s. Robert Orr. Attended pub. schs. Dept. sheriff Armstrong County (Pa.), 1805; apptd. dep. dist. surveyor; served to col. during War of 1812; mem. Pa. Ho. of Reps., 1817-20, Pa. Senate, 1821-26; mem. U.S. Ho. of Reps. (Democrat) from Pa., 18th-20th congresses, Oct. 11, 1825-29; rose to rank of gen.; became holder of extensive lands. Died Kittanning, Pa., May 22, 1876; buried Kittanning Cemetery.

ORR, THOMAS GROVER surgeon; b. Carrollton, Mo., May 9, 1884; s. Thomas Albert and Mildred Jane (Cook) O.; grad. high sch., Carrollton, 1903; A.B., U. of Mo., 1907; M.D., Johns Hopkins, 1910; m. Irene Helen Harris, Dec. 22, 1913; 1 son. Dr. Thomas Grover. Instr. in surgery, U. of Kan., 1914-17, asso. prof. surgery, 1917-24, prof. surgery and head of dept., U. of Kan., and surgeon in chief to U. of Kan. Hosp., 1924-49; prof. of surgery and chief second surg. service University Kansas Med. Center, 1949-54, emeritus prof., 1954-—; cons. surg. VA Hosp., Kansas City, U.S. Army Hosp., Leavenworth, Kan.; in spl. research in intestinal obstruction, 1922-31. Served as maj. Med. Corps, U.S. Army, 1918-19. Fellow American College Surgeons (gov.); mem. A.M.A., American Surg. Assn. (former pres.), Southwestern Surg. Congress (former pres.), American Society of the History of Medicine, Southeastern Surgical Congress, Chicago Surgical Society (hon.), Western Surgical Association (former pres.), Soc. Univ. Surgeons, Soc. Internationale de Chirurgie, Central Surg. Assn., Am. Board Surgery (foundation mem.), Sigma Xi, Alpha Omega Alpha, Nu Sigma Nu, Beta Theta Pi. Republican. Episcopalian. Author: Modern Methods of Amputation, 1926; Operations of General Surgery, 1944, 49. Editor Am. Surgeon; Survey Surg. Technique; editorial board Surgery and Quarterly Rev. of Surgery. Contbr. articles to surg. publs. Home: 5930 Mission Dr., Kansas City, Mo. Office: University of Kansas Med. Center, Kansas City, Kan. Died Nov. 19, 1955.

ORTON, EDWARD JR. engineer, mfr.; b. Chester, N.Y., Oct. 8, 1863; s. Dr. Edward and Mary (Jennings) O.; E.M., Ohio State U., 1884; D.Sc. from Rutgers Coll., N.J., 1922; m. Mary Princess Anderson, Oct. 30, 1888 (died 1927); m. 2d, Mina Althea Orton, Oct. 6, 1928. Chemist and supt. blast furnaces, 1884-88; 1st to regularly mfr. "ferro-silicon," or high silicon alloy of iron in U.S., Bessie Furnace New Straitsville, O., 1887-88; entered clay industries, 1888; managed several plants, 1888-93. Began agitation, 1893, which resulted in establishing, 1894, of 1st school in U.S. for instr. in tech. of clay, glass and cement industries, of which was dir. until 1916; dean Coll. Engring. Ohio State U., 1902-06 and 1910-16; retired from univ. work, 1917. State geologist of Ohio, 1899-1906. Commd. maj., O.R.C., Jan. 5, 1917; called into active service in motors div. Q.M. Corps, May 9, 1917; lt. col. Motor Transport Corps, Sept. 6, 1918. Awarded D.S.M., June 2, 1919. Col. Q.M., O.R.C., Spet. 25, 1919; brig. gen. Q.M., O.R.C., Sept. 27, 1923. Pres. Reserve Officers' Assn. of Ohio, 1922-23. Began manufacture, 1896, of pyrometric cones, for regulating firing process of ceramic products and other wares burned in kilns; developed lab. and testing sta. for study of clay and ceramic products, 1900. Wrote: Clays of Ohio and the Industries Established Upon Them, Rep. Ohio Geol. Survey, Vol. V, 1884; The Clay-Working Industries of Ohio, Vol. VII, same, 1893. Also numerous tech. articles and reports. Home: Columbus, O. Died Feb. 10, 1932.

ORVILLE, HOWARD T(HOMAS) naval officer retired, meteorological consultant, corp. executive; born Saratoga, Wyo., June 16, 1901; s. William and Lucy D. (Wiant) O.; student Army and Navy Prep. Sch., 1918-19; B.S., U.S. Naval Acad., Annapolis, 1925; student Navy Post Grad. Sch., 1928-29; S.M. in meteorology, Mass. Inst. Tech., 1930; m. Lillian L. Duvall, June 5, 1926; children—Howard Thomas, Harold Duvall, Richard Edmonds. Bank clk. Stockgrowers State Bank, Saratoga, Wyo., 1917-18, Rawlins Nat. Ban, 1919-21; commd. ensign U.S. Navy, 1925, and advanced through grades to capt., 1944, ret. 1950; assigned to battleships and destroyers, 1925-28; officer in charge aerographer's sch. Naval Air Sta., Lakehurst, N.J., 1930-31, 1934-35; co-pilot nat. and internat. free balloon races, 1934-35; aerolog. officer U.S.S. Langley, 1931-32; force aerolog. officer on staff comdr. battleships, Battle Force, 1932; fleet aerologist on staff comdr. in chief, U.S. Fleet, 1936-38; lighter-than-air pilot, head aerolog. dept. and sch., Lakehurst, N.J., 1938-40; head naval aerology, flight div. Bur. Aeronautics, 1940-43, transferred to dept. chief Naval Operations (Air), 1943-50; during these yrs. served on numerous commns. and coms. working in meteorol. field; served as del. or mem. delegations several internat. confs.; ordered to North Atlantic Treaty Orgn., 1950; mem. vis. com. Blue Hill Obs., Harvard; cons. to gen. mgr. Friez Instrument Div., Bendix Aviation Corporation, 1950-58; vice president of Beckman & Whitley, Incorporated, 1958-—. Awarded the Legion of Merit; Commendation Ribbon; Officer Military Order of British Empire; Cravate Blue of Yun Hwei (cloud and banner) (China). Mem. several profl. and scientific orgns. and assns. Kiwanian (dir.). Author instrn. manuals and numerous articles on meteorology. Home: Long Green, Md. Office: care Beckman & Whitley, Inc., Long Green, Md. Died May 24, 1960; buried Arlington Nat. Cemetery.

O'RYAN, JOHN F. lawyer; b. N.Y.C., Aug. 21, 1874; s. Francis and Anna (Barry) O'R.; LL.B., N.Y. U., 1898, LL.D., 1919; grad. Army War Coll., 1914; m. Janet Holmes, Apr. 9, 1902. Admitted to N.Y. bar, 1898; mem. firm Loucks, O'Ryan & Cullen; N.Y. state transit commr., 1921-26; apptd. police commr. N.Y.C., Jan. 1, 1934. N.Y. State Dir. Divilian Def., 1941. Enlisted as pvt. Co. G, 7th Inf., N.Y.N.G., 1897; capt. 1st Battery, 1907; maj. F.A., 1911, maj. gen. comdg. N.G.N.Y., 1912; comd. N.Y. Div. on Mex. border, 1916; apptd. maj. gen., N.A.; comdr. 27th Div. U.S. Army, 1917; with AEF in Belgium and France, 1917-19. Awarded D.S.M. (U.S.); Knight Comdr. Order St. Michael and St. George, Comdr. Victorian Order (Eng.); Comdr. Legion of Honor, Croix de Guerre with palm (France); Comdr. Order of Leopold, Croix de Guerre with palm (Belgium); Comdr. Order St. Maurice and St. Lazarus (Italy). Chmn. Econ. Commn. to Japan, Manchuria, North China, 1940. Mem. Delta Upsilon. Clubs: Lawyers (N.Y.C.); Metropolitan (Washington). Home: Purdy's, Westchester County, N.Y. Office: 230 Park Av., N.Y.C. Died Jan. 1961.

OSBON, BRADLEY SILLICK naval officer; b. Rye, Westchester County, N.Y., Aug. 16, 1828; s. Rev. Abiathar Mann and Elizabeth E. (Sillick) O.; ed. common schools, New York, and Conn., until went to sea at 10 yrs. of age; self-taught; m. Eliza Balfour, Feb. 14, 1868. Served in Chinese Navy (as comdr.), Argentine Navy (as comdr.), U.S. Navy (signal officer) and Mexican Navy (admiral). During Civil War served under Du Pont, Farragut and Worden (specially mentioned by Farragut); during Spanish-Am. War was vol. naval scout and was 1st to discover Cervera's fleet off Island of Curaçoa, May 14, 1898, and reported to State Dept.; received letter of thanks for service; twice in Artic Ocean and once in Antarctic Ocean. One term capt., one commodore, and two rear adm., Nat. Assn. Naval Veterans, U.S. of A.; was flag officer comdg. U.S. Veteran Navy, with rank of commodore. Decorated by Venezuelan Govt. with Order of "Busto del Liberatador." Founder and editor The Nautical Gazette, 1871, 1st maritime newspaper published in the U.S. Author: Osbon's Hand Book United States Navy, 1863; United States Veteran Navy List, 1900; A Sailor of Fortune, 1906. Lecturer on travels and adventures; asso. editor of the American Shipbuilder, and of Tourist Magazine, 1910. Address: New York. N.Y. Died May 6, 1912.

OSBORN, ALEXANDER PERRY lawyer; b. Garrison-on-Hudson, N.Y., June 6, 1884; s. Henry Fairfield and Lucretia (Perry) O.; A.B., Princeton, 1905; LL.B., Harvard, 1909; student Trinity Coll., Cambridge Eng., 1905-06; m. Marie Cantrell, Aug. 22, 1933; children by previous marriage—Lucretia (Mrs. William H. McKleroy), Alexander Perry, Mary (Mrs. Duncan L. Marshall) and Anne (Mrs. Ezra P. Prentice, Jr.) (twins); adopted children—Lou Belew, Clyde Belew. Admitted to bar, 1909; with Winthop & Stimson, 1909-11, Spooner & Cotton, 1911-15; partner in firm Beekman, Menken & Griscon, 1915-21, Redmond & Co., 1921-34; practicing alone since 1934. Dir. Western Pacific R.R. Corp., Denver & Rio Grande Western R.R. Co. Served as lt. col., U.S. Army, 1917-18. Decorated Chevalier of Legion of Honor (France). Commended by undersecretary of war for exceptional services in connection with reorgn. of gen. staff, 1918. Acting pres., 1st vice-pres. and trustee Am. Museum Natural History. Trustee Five Points House, Theodore Roosevelt Meml. Assn. Mgr. Hosp. of Special Surgery. Dir. Belgian War Relief Soc. Republican. Clubs: Ivy (Princeton); Down Town Assn., Racquet and Tennis, Century (N.Y.C.). Home: 990 Fifth Av., N.Y.C. 28. Office: 20 Exchange Pl., N.Y.C. 5. Died Mar. 6, 1951; buried Garrison, N.Y.

OSBORN, THOMAS OGDEN soldier, lawyer, diplomat; b. Jersey, O., 1832; s. Samuel and Hannah (Meeker) O.; ed. Delaware Coll., O.; grad. Ohio State U., 1854; unmarried. Read law with Gen. Lewis Wallace, began practice Chicago, 1859. Recruited 39th regt., Ill. inf., at beginning of Civil war, serving as col. (regt. selected to represent Ill. in the Army of the Potomac), and fought in Shenandoah Valley. Apptd. to command 39th Ill., 13th Ind., 62d and 67th Ohio regts., which were actively engaged in siege and capture of Fort Sumter and Forty Drury; received commn. of maj. gen. "for promptly and efficiently placing his command in position and attacking and driving off the enemy." After war resumed practice; elected treas. Cook County, Ill. Apptd. one of mgrs. Nat. Soldiers Home. Mem. Internat. Commn. to settle disputed claims between U.S. and Mexico; apptd. minister to Argentine Republic, 1873, served until 1885. Address: Chicago, Ill. Died 1904.

OSBORNE, EDWIN SYLVANUS soldier, lawyer; b. Bethany, Pa., Aug. 7, 1839; grad. U. of Northern Pa. and Nat. Law School, Poughkeepsie, N.Y.; admitted to Pa. bar, Feb. 26, 1861; served, private to maj., U.S. vols., 1861-65; led notable charge at the battle of the Wilderness, May 6, 1864; took part in many battles; apptd. judge advocate in regular army, with rank of maj., 1865, but resigned and practised law at Wilkesbarre; maj. gen. 3d div. Pa. Nat. Guard, 1870-80; dept. commander G.A.R., Pa., 1883; member Congress, 1885-91. Address: Wilkesbarre, Pa. Died 1900.

OSBORNE, JAMES VAN WYCK lawyer; b. New York, N.Y., May 28, 1897; s. James W. and Leila Grey (van Wyck) O.; student Hackley Sch., Tarrytown, N.Y., 1912-15, Yale, 1915-17; A.B., Columbia, 1921, LL.B., 1922; m. Calvert Cabell, Sept. 25, 1917. Reporter N.Y. Times, 1917-18; admitted to N.Y. bar, 1923; partner Osborne and Shrewsbury, N.Y. City, 1923-35; later practiced in own name as of counsel with Cabell and Cabell. Served with United States Naval Reserve, in active service in Office of Naval Intelligence, 1918-19. Independent Democrat. Episcopalian. Author: The Greatest Norman Conquest, 1937. Home: New York, N.Y. Died July 23, 1940.

OSBORNE, REGINALD STANLEY, elec. exec.; b. nr. Foxton, N.Z., Feb. 2, 1892; s. Edmund John and Harriet (Nye) B.; student Tech. Coll., Palmerston North, N.Z., 1910; extension courses Columbia, N.Y., William and Mary, Va. univs.; m. Olga Wood, Mar. 25, 1923; children—Jacquelyn Wood (Mrs. William Ross), Geraldyn Frances (Mrs. Robert K. Molloy). Came to the United States, 1912, naturalized, 1924. Gen. superintendent, consulting engineer Acme Bldg. Corp., N.Y. City, 1914-18; orgn. Virginia-Carolina Elec. Works, Inc., Norfolk, Va., 1918, served as pres., 1922-45, director, from 1918, chairman of the board, from 1956; president of Virginia-Carolina Electric Sales, Inc., from 1945, Petroleum Shipping Company, Incorporated, from 1946, Stanart Corporation, from 1954, Electrical Suppliers, Inc., 1936-44, Virginia-Caroline Engineering, Inc., 1930-42. Orgn. received Certificate of Achievement (Navy) for services rendered during World War II. Mem. Am. Orchid Soc., Norfolk Portsmouth Real Estate Board, Y.M.C.A. (director), Society Naval Architects and Marine Engrs., Maritime Assn., Isaac Walton League, C. of C., Nat. Defense Transportation Association (1st v.p.). Presbyn. (deacon). Clubs: Cedar Island Gunning (pres.); Lions; Propeller of U.S. (nat. v.p., mem. bd. govs., Port of Norfolk, com. sponsoring sea scout activities, Norfolk); The Cavalier Yacht and Country, Norfolk Yacht and Country, Virginia (Norfolk). The Osborne Family portrait hangs in the Nat. Archives Gallery, Wellington, N.Z., in recognition of family contribution toward World War I effort. Home: Virginia Beach VA Died Feb. 8, 1967; buried Forest Lawn, Norfolk VA

OSBORNE, THOMAS MOTT penologist; b. Auburn, N.Y., Sept. 23, 1859; s. David Munson and Eliza (Wright) O.; A.B., Harvard, 1884; L.H.D., Hobart, 1905; m. Agnes Devens, Oct. 27, 1886 (died 1896); children—David Munson, Charles Devens, Lithgow, Robert Klipfel. Pres. Auburn Pub. Co. (Auburn Citizen); connected other mfg. cos. Mem. Auburn Bd. Edn., 1885-91, 1893-95; candidate for lt. gov. of N.Y. on Independent ticket, 1898; mayor of Auburn, 1903-05; mem. Pub. Service Commn., 2d Dist., N.Y., 1907-09; forest, fish and game commr., N.Y., Jan.-May 1911 (resigned). Del. Dem. Nat. Conv., 1896, Nat. (gold standard) Conv., 1896, Monetary Convs., 1897, 98, Trust Conf., Chicago, 1899, Dem. State Convs., 1904, 06, 12, Dem. Nat. Com., 1924. Chmn. N.Y. Commn. on Prison Reform, 1913. Spent a week in Auburn, New York, Prison under conditions of convict, 1913, to study prison conditions; apptd. warden Sing Sing Prison and assumed charge Dec. 1, 1914; indicted by Westchester County Grand Jury for alleged "perjury and neglect of duty," 1915; upon trial case was dismissed by judge without hearing defendant's testimony; reinstated as warden, July 1916; resigned Oct. 1916; lt. comdr. naval reserve, Aug. 1, 1917; comd. naval prison, Portsmouth, N.H., Aug. 1, 1917-Mar. 17, 1920, relieved at own request. Chmn. Nat. Soc. Penal Information. Traveled extensively, 1872-78, 1894-1901. Author: Within Prison Walls, 1914; Society and Prisons, 1916; Prisons and Common Sense, 1924. Home: Auburn, N.Y. Died Oct. 20, 1926.

OSCEOLA (KNOWN AS POWELL) Indian chief; b. nr. Tallapoosa River, Ga., circa 1800. Fought against Andrew Jackson in War of 1812, also in 1818; opponent of Treaty of 1832 at Payne's Landing, rejected Treaty of 1833 at Ft. Gibson, again rejected Payne's Landing treaty at meeting of chiefs called by Wiley Thompson, 1835; arrested and imprisoned, 1835; gathered opposition forces, murdered Wiley Thompson and Charley Emalthia, precipitating 2d Seminole War; led warriors to harass U.S. army after hiding women and children in swamps; seized on order of Gen. Thomas S. Jesup when he came for interview, 1837, taken to Ft. Marion at St. Augustine, Fla., later removed to Ft. Moultrie, Charleston, S.C. Died Ft. Moultrie, Jan. 30, 1838.

OSGOOD, HENRY BROWN army officer; b. in Me., Oct. 13, 1843. Apptd. 2d lt. 27th Me. Inf., Sept. 30, 1862; 1st lt., Dec. 15, 1862; hon. mustered out of vols.,

July 17, 1863; apptd. U.S. Mil. Acad. from Me., 1863, grad. 1867; apptd. 2d lt. 3d Arty., June 17, 1867; 1st lt., Apr. 20, 1870; capt. commissary of subsistence, Oct. 5, 1889; maj. same, Jan. 26, 1897; lt. col. commissary of subsistence vols., Aug. 5-Oct. 24, 1898, and Dec. 20, 1898-Mar. 2, 1899; lt. col. deputy commissary gen., Feb. 2, 1901; col. asst. commissary gen., Jan. 19, 1905; brig. gen. and retired, Oct. 13, 1907. Awarded medal of honor, Jan. 24, 1865, for voluntarily remaining in the service during the invasion of Pa., July 1863, his term of service having expired. Address: Washington, D.C. Died 1909.

OSGOOD, SAMUEL Continental congressman; b. Andover, Mass., Feb. 3, 1748; s. Capt. Peter and Sarah (Johnson) O.; grad. Harvard, 1770; m. Martha Brandon, Jan. 4, 1775; m. 2d, Maria Bowne Franklin, May 26, 1786. Mem. Essex Conv. (opposed to more radical element of Am. Revolution), 1774; served as maj., later col. as aide-de-camp to Gen. Artemas Ward, Continental Army, 1775; became mem. Mass. Provincial Congress, 1775; del. Mass. Constl. Conv., 1779, del. to conv. for the limitation of prices, Phila., 1780; mem. Continental Congress, 1780-84; apptd. a dir. Bank of N. Am., 1781; largely responsible for commissioning of U.S. Treasury, 1784, 1st commr. U.S. Treasury, 1785-89; postmaster-gen. U.S. under Pres. Washington, 1789-91; speaker N.Y. Assembly, 1800; supt. internal revenue for Dist. of N.Y., 1801-02; naval officer Port of N.Y., 1803-13; organizer and incorporator Soc. for Establishment of Free School for Edn. of Poor Children; a founder Am. Acad. Fine Arts. Died N.Y.C., Aug. 12, 1813; buried Brick Presbyn. Ch., N.Y.C.

OSLAND, BIRGER ret.; b. Stavanger, Norway, Mar. 1, 1870; s. Torger O. and Helene (Meling) O.; B.A., Royal Frederick U., Norway, 1888; student Bryant & Stratton Bus. Coll., Chgo., 1888-89; LL.D., St. Olaf Coll., Northfield, Minn., 1935; m. Therese Korsvik, Mar. 15, 1890; children—Alice Rosalie, Helene (dec.), Therese Mildred (Mrs. Omer B. Dahm). Came to U.S. 1888, naturalized, 1893. Began active career as office boy with John Anderson Pub. Co., Chgo., 1888; with C. Jevne & Co., Chgo., 1891-93; officer in various enterprises Charles H. Wacker, 1893-1911; founder, 1911, and since pres. Birger Osland & Co., investments, Chgo.; sec.-treas. Lake Otis Groves, Inc. Organized Am. financial participation in Norwegian-Am. S.S. Line, 1911-12, and served many yrs. as mem. of its bd. of reps.; dir. Scandinavian Trust Co. of N.Y. until its merger with N.Y. Trust Co. Served as maj. inf. U.S. Army (mil. attaché), World War; was mem. Am. Food Adminstrn. for No. Europe, Copenhagen, Denmark. Trustee Century of Progress Expn., 1933, 34; pres. Norwegian Am. Hosp., Inc.; dir. Norwegian Am. Hist. Assn. Mem. Am. Legion, Sons of Norway. Decorated Knight of Royal Order of St. Olav, U.S. Presdl. Citation. Republican. Clubs: Norwegian, Park Ridge Country (Chgo.); Dairymen's Country (Boulder Junction, Wis.). Author: A Long Pull From Stavanger. Home: 1602 Chase Av., Chgo. Died Aug. 1, 1963.

OSMUN, RUSSELL A. (os'mún) ret. army officer; b. Detroit, May 19, 1887; s. Gilbert R. and Caroline (Conger) O.; grad. Central High Sch., Detroit, 1901-05; A.B., U.S. Naval Acad., 1910; student L'Ecole de l'Intendence, Paris, 1923-25; Comd. and Gen. Staff Sch., Ft. Leavenworth, 1928-30; Army Indsl. Coll., Washington, 1932-33; Army War Coll., Washington, 1933-34; m. Edith Moss, Dec. 30, 1914; children—William Gilbert, Helen Edith (Mrs. Pierce E. Parker). Commd. ensign USN, 1910, resigned because of physical disability, 1911; after 2 1/2 yrs. convalescence on Colo. ranch was commd. in U.S. Army, CAC, 1914; asst. in organizing Plattsburg Tng. Camps, served as aide to Gen. Leonard Wood; served in various capacities in U.S. and Hawaii; observer in England at outbreak of World War II, later in India; with M.I. in Turkey, Syria, Palestine, Egypt and Persia; chief M.I. Service in U.S., 1943-44; brig. gen. comdg. Kansas City Q.M. Depot, ret. 1946. Decorated Legion of Merit (U.S.); Order of White Eagle of Yugoslavia; Comdr. Order of Brit. Empire. Mason (32 deg.). Clubs: Army-Navy (Washington); Kansas City (Mo.). Home: 5305 Albemarle St., Washington 16. Died Aug. 9, 1954; buried Arlington Nat. Cemetery.

OSTER, HENRY RICHARD naval officer; b. Utica, N.Y., May 23, 1895; s. Henry and Carrie (Metzler) O.; B.S., U.S. Naval Acad., 1917; M.S., Mass. Inst. Tech., 1921; naval aviator, Flight Training, Naval Air Sta., Pensacola, Fla., 1932; m. Elda Kay, Dec. 25, 1934. Commd. ensign, U.S. Navy, 1917, advanced through the grades to rear adm., 1946. Specialist in aeronautical engring. since 1922; chief engr. and prodn. supt. Naval Aircraft Factory, Phila., Pa.; dir. design div., Bur. Aeronautics, Navy Dept., asst. chief, 1946-48; gen. rep. Western Dist., Bur. Aeronautics, since 1948; material officer on Adm. Halsey's staff, 1940-43; Bureau of Aeronautics, Western Dist., Los Angeles. Decorated Legion of Merit; Commendation ribbon; Campaign medals: World Wars I and II, Asiatic-Pacific Area, American Area. Home: 858 Devon Av., Los Angeles. Office: 1206 Santee St., Los Angeles 15. Died Aug. 9, 1949; buried in Arlington Nat. Cemetery.

OSTERHAUS, HUGO rear admiral; b. Belleville, Ill., June 15, 1851; apptd. from Mo., and grad. U.S. Naval Acad., 1870; promoted ensign, July 13, 1871; master, Feb. 12, 1874; lt., Mar. 13, 1880; lt. comdr., Mar. 3, 1899; comdr., July 2, 1901; capt., Feb. 19, 1906; rear admiral, 1909. Served on Plymouth, 1870-73; N. Atlantic Sta., 1873-76; Powhatan, 1876-77; Hydrographic Office, 1877-78; Navy Yard, Norfolk, 1878-79; coast duty, 1879-82; Enterprise, 1882-86; Navy Yard, Norfolk, 1886-89; Enterprise, 1889-90; Franklin and Pensacola, 1890; Baltimore, 1890-91; Atlanta, 1891-92; Naval Acad., 1892-95; staff N. Atlantic Fleet, 1895-97; Naval Acad., 1897-99; Monongahela, 1899-1900; exec. officer Kentucky, 1900-01; comd. Culgoa, 1901; Naval Acad., 1901-03; comd. Monterey, 1903-04; Cincinnati, 1904-05; mem. Bd. Inspection and Survey, Washington, 1905-07; comd. Connecticut, 1907; comdr. 2d div. Atlantic Fleet, 1910; comdr.-in-chief Atlantic Fleet, 1911; retired June 15, 1913. Address: Washington, D.C. Died June 11, 1927.

OSTERHAUS, HUGO WILSON, naval officer (ret.); b. Norfolk, Va., Nov. 12, 1878; s. Hugo and Mary Willoughby (Wilson) O.; grad. U.S. Naval Acad., 1900; m. Helen Huntington Downing, Dec. 4, 1913; 1 son, Hugo Wilson. Served with U.S. Navy, 1896-1935, progressing through various grades to rear adm., 1935; served actively in Cuban waters, 1898, Cuban Pacification, 1906, Philippine Insurrection, 1900-04, in European waters during World War; retired, 1935; recalled to active duty as commander Patrol Forces, 12th Naval District, June 1941. Episcopalian. Republican. Clubs: Army and Navy Club, Army and Navy Country Club (Washington); Chevy Chase (Md.) Country; N.Y. Yacht (N.Y. City); Racquet, University (Phila.); Presidio Golf, Bohemian (San Francisco). Address: Saratoga CA Died Sept. 17, 1972; buried Arlington Nat. Cemetery, Arlington VA

OSTERHAUS, PETER JOSEPH brigadier gen. U.S.A.; b. Coblentz, Germany, Jan. 4, 1823; came to U.S., 1849; LL.D., Northwestern, 1904. Commd. maj. 2d Mo. Rifle Battalion, Apr. 27, 1861; hon. mustered out, Aug. 27, 1861; col. 12th Mo. Inf., Dec. 19, 1861; brig. gen. vols., June 9, 1862; maj. gen. vols., July 23, 1864; hon. mustered out, Jan. 15, 1866; apptd. brig. gen. U.S.A., by spl. act of Congress, Mar. 3, 1905, and retired, Mar. 17, 1905. Comd. a div. under Gen. Curtis, at Pea Ridge, Ark., March 6-8, 1862, and a div. Army of the Southwest, May 1862; comd. 9th Div., 13th Army Corps during Vicksburg campaign, May-July 1863; comd. 1st Div., 15th Army Corps, under Gen. Grant, at Chattanooga, Nov. 23-25, 1863; comd. same div. during Atlanta campaign, May-Sept. 1863; comd. 15th Army Corps, Army of the Tenn., Sept. 1864-Jan. 1865; chief of staff to Gen. Canby during Mobile campaign; later comd. mil. dist. of Miss. until Jan. 15, 1866. U.S. consul at Lyons, France, 1866-77. Died Jan. 2, 1917.

O'SULLIVAN, CURTIS D(ION) estate trustee; b. London, Eng., Oct. 29, 1894; s. Denis and Elisabeth (Curtis) O'S.; A.B., U. Cal., 1915, A.M., 1916; m. Helen Hooper, Dec. 29, 1917; children—Cornelius Dion, Curtis Hooper. Brought to U.S., 1895, citizen by birth. With Mills Estate, Inc., San Francisco, 1919-42, pres., 1926-42. Served as capt. inf., U.S. Army, 1917-19; maj. 362d inf. O.R.C., 1923-29, lt. col. asst. chief of staff G-2, 40th div. Cal. N.G., 1929-39, col., chief of staff, 40th div., 1939-40, col. 184th inf., 1941-45; adj. gen. of Cal., 1946-51, rank brig. gen., 1946-47, comdg. gen. 49th inf. div., 1950, maj. gen., 1947-—. Decorated Bronze Star, Inf. Combat badge, Legion Merit. Mem. Bldg. Owners and Mgrs. of San Francisco (pres. 3 terms), San Francisco Real Estate Bd. (dir. 1927-42), San Francisco Employers Council (treas. 1937-42). Chmn., Mayor's Com. on Traffic and Transp., 1936-37. Trustee Phelan Estate. Mem. N.G. Assn. (exec. council), Am. Legion, Mil. Order of World Wars, Phi Delta Theta, Phi Delta Phi, Phi Beta Kappa. Republican. Home: 2750 Soda Canyon Rd., Napa, Cal. Died June 27, 1967; buried Holy Cross, Colma, Cal.

OTEY, PETER JOHNSTON congressman, 6th Va. dist., 1895-1903; b. Lynchburg, Va., Dec. 22, 1840; grad. Va. Mil. Inst., July 1, 1860; participated as cadet in defense of Va. in John Brown raid; engr. on Va. & Ky. R.R., 1860-61; joined C.S. Army, Apr. 1861; took part in Western campaign culminating at Donelson and Shiloh; in inf. Army Northern Va. until close of war; wounded at battle of New Market; after 4 months returned; comd. brigade under Early, for some months as senior field officer. In railroad, banking and ins. business in Va., 1860-—. Democrat. Address: Lynchburg, Va. Died 1902.

OTIS, ELWELL STEPHEN army officer; b. Frederick City, Md., Mar. 25, 1838; s. William and Mary A. C. (Late) O.; grad. U. of Rochester, 1858; LL.B., Harvard Law Sch., 1861. Commd. capt. 140th N.Y. Inf., Sept. 13, 1862; lt. col., Dec. 23, 1863, later promoted to col.; hon. mustered out, Jan. 14, 1865, because incapacitated by wound; bvtd. brig. gen., Mar. 13, 1865; apptd. from N.Y., lt. col. 22d U.S. Inf., Mar. 2, 1869; col. 20th Inf., Feb. 8, 1880; brig. gen., Nov. 28, 1893; maj. gen. vols., May 4, 1898; maj. gen. U.S.A., June 16, 1900; retired by operation of law, Mar. 25, 1902. Bvtd. col., Mar. 2, 1867, for battle of Spottsylvania, Va.; maj. gen., Feb. 4, 1899, for mil. skill and most distinguished service in P.I. Assigned to duty in San Francisco, May 19, 1898, mobilizing and shipping troops to P.I.; departed for Philippines, July 15, 1898, and relieved Maj. Gen. Merritt as comdg. gen. U.S. Philippine forces and gov. of islands, Aug. 29, 1898; conducted operations against insurgents and performed duties of mil. gov. until May 5, 1900. Mem. of U.S. Philippine Commn., 1899. Assigned to command Dept. of the Lakes, headquarters Chicago, on Oct. 29, 1900. Residence: Rochester, N.Y. Died 1909.

OTIS, GEORGE ALEXANDER mil. surgeon; b. Va., Nov. 12, 1830; s. George Alexander and Anna Marie (Hickman) O.; grad. Princeton, 1849, A.M., 1851; grad. U. Pa. Sch. Medicine, 1851; m. Pauline Clark Baury, 2 children. Practiced gen. surgery, Paris, France, 1851-52; founded Va. Med. and Surg. Jour., 1852; gen. practice medicine, Springfield, Mass., 1854-61; apptd. surgeon 27th Mass. Volunteers, 1861, served in Md., Va., S.C.; asst. surgeon U.S. Volunteers, 1864, surgeon, 1864-81; asst. surgeon U.S. Army, 1866; invalid due to stroke, 1877-81. Author: Report of Surgical Case Treated in the Army of the United States from 1865-1871, 1871; A Report on a Plan for Transporting Soldiers by Railway in Time of War, 1875. Died Feb. 23, 1881.

OTIS, HARRISON GRAY journalist, soldier; b. nr. Marietta, O., Feb. 10, 1837; s. Stephen and Sarah (Dyar) O.; (paternal grandfather a Revolutionary soldier); m. Eliza A. Wetherby, Sept. 11, 1859 (died 1904). Enlisted as pvt. 12th Ohio Inf., June 25, 1861; 2d lt., Nov. 12, 1862; 1st lt., May 20, 1863; transferred to 23d Ohio Inf., July 1, 1864; capt., July 15, 1864; bvtd. maj. and lt. col. vols., Mar. 13. 1865, 'for gallant and meritorious services during the war"; hon. mustered out, July 26, 1865; twice wounded. Official Reporter Ohio Ho. of Rep., 1866-67; foreman Govt. Printing Office, 1868-69; chief of div. U.S. Patent Office, 1870-76; spl. agt. U.S. Treasury in charge of Seal Islands of Alaska, 1879-81. In Calif. journalism, 1876-—; editor and gen. mgr. Los Angeles Times. Apptd. brig. gen. U.S.V., May 27, 1898; comd. 1st Brigade, 2d Div., 8th Army Corps in the P.I.; led brigade at capture of Caloocan, Feb. 10, 1899; bvtd. maj. gen. vols., Mar. 25, 1899, "for meritorious conduct at battle of Caloocan"; hon. discharged, July 2, 1899. U.S. commr. to Centennial of Mexican Independence, 1910. Address: Los Angeles, Calif. Died July 30, 1917.

OTTOFY, LOUIS, dental lexicographer, educator; b. Budapest, Oct. 22, 1860; s. Leopold and Louise (Lauffer) O.; came to U.S., 1874; D.D.S., Western Coll. Dental Surgeons, St. Louis, Mo., 1879; hon. M.D., St. Louis Coll. Phys. and Surgs., 1915; LL.D., McKendree Coll., Lebanon, Ill., 1928; m. Nellie Freeman, Dec. 27, 1887; children—Gloria Columbia (dec.), Frederic Freeman. Practiced at Chicago, Yokohama and Manila; prof. physiology, 1890-93, prof. clin. dental therapeutics, 1896-98, Chicago Coll. Dental Surgery; dean and prof. dental pathology, Am. Coll. Dental Surgery, Chicago, 1893-96; resided Japan, 1898-99 and 1920-21, Manila, 1899-1920; dir. Sch. of Dentistry, U. of Philippines, 1915-19; maj. and supervising dental surgeon, Dental Corps, U.S. Army, 1918; ednl. dir. McCarrie Schs. of Mechanical Dentistry, 1926-28, ednl. counselor same since 1928; dean and prof. dental technology, Institute of Dental Science, Oakland, Calif., 1929-30. Made first survey and tabulation of condition of human teeth in the history of dentistry of a group of children in pub. sch., Lebanon, Ill., 1882; made similar surveys in Japan and Philippines, of Chinese, Igorots, Negritos, lepers, etc. Mem. Am. and Ill. (life) dental socs., Chicago Dental Soc. (pres. 1896), Am. Soc. Stomatologists (pres. 1927), Alameda County (Calif.) Dist. Dental Soc., Assn. Mil. Dental Surgeons of U.S.; Mil. Order World War, Delta Sigma Delta, Pi Gamma Mu; founder, fellow and registrar Internat. Coll. of Dentists, 1928; sec. Bd. of Dental Examiners of Philippine Islands, 1914-15. Mason (K.T., Shriner). Club: University (Manila). Author: Outlines of Dental Pathology, 1895; Plantation of Teeth (in Am. Textbook of Operative Dentistry), 1897-1911; All About Your Teeth, Gums and Dentist, 1938; compiler and editor Standard Dental Dictionary, 1923; editor Polk's Dental Register of U.S. and Can., 1925-27 and 1928-30, Internat. Dental Review since 1931. Contbr. over 200 articles on dentistry to jours. Hon. mention and cash prize for essay on "Rootfilling and Focal Infection," Internat. Bur. for Protection of Animals, Geneva, 1933. Address: 175 Vernon Terrace, Oakland CA*

OUGHTERSON, ASHLEY W. surgeon; b. Geneva, N.Y., Sept. 28, 1895; s. Nathan and Mary Ann (Hatch) O.; student Syracuse U., 1918-20; M.D., Harvard Med. Sch., 1924; m. Dr. Marion Howard, March 21, 1942. Intern Peter Bent Brigham Hosp., Boston, Mass., 1924-25, New York Hosp., 1925-27, Bellevue Hosp., 1927-28, Peter Bent Brigham Hosp., 1928-29, William Harvey Cushing fellow in surgery, Yale Sch. of Medicine, 1929-30; postgrad. study, Europe, 1930. Surgeon, New Haven, Conn., 1930; asst. prof. surgery, Yale, 1930-34, asso. prof., 1934-42, now clinical prof. surgery. Served as cons. surgeon, Pacific Ocean areas; col. Med. Corps, World War II, 1942-46. Awarded Legion of Merit with oak leaf cluster. Chmn. Joint Commn. for Investigating Med. Effects of Atomic Bomb in Japan. Exec. v.p., med. and scientific dir. Am. Cancer Soc., Inc.; mem. Am. Med. Assn. A.C.S. (gov.),

Am. Surg. Assn., Am. Cancer Soc., Am. Assn. Cancer Research, Am. Heart Assn., N.E. Surg. Soc. (pres.), New England Cancer Soc., Am. Radium Soc., Soc. Exptl. Biology and Medicine, Sigma Xi. Clubs: Lawn, Grad. (New Haven); Yale (New York). Contbr. numerous papers on Surgery and Cancer. Address: Rockefeller Found., 49 W. 49th St., N.Y.C. Died Nov. 17, 1956; buried Bellona Cemetery, Yates County, N.Y.

OURAY Indian chief; b. Colo., circa 1833; m. Chepeta, 1859. Became chief Uncompahgre Utes, 1860; apptd. interpreter Los Pinos Agy., So. Colo., 1862; visited Washington, D.C., on behalf of tribe, 1862; signer, as head chief of Western Utes, treaty at Conejos, 1863; served with Kit Carson in suppressing uprising of Ute Sub-chief Kaniatse, 1867; a negotiator Treaty of 1868, Washington; accepted compromise relinquishing certain Ute lands to fed. govt., 1873; became Methodist, 1878. Died Los Pinos Agy., Aug. 24, 1880.

OURY, GRANVILLE HENDERSON congressman; b. Abingdon, Va., Mar. 12, 1825; studied law, Bowling Green, Mo. Admitted to Mo. bar, 1848; moved to San Antonio, Tex., 1848, to Marysville, Cal., 1849; engaged in mining; went to Tucson, Ariz., 1856, began practice of law; chosen capt. of a party sent from Tucson to relief of Crabbe Expdn. besieged at Caborca, Sonora, Mexico, 1857; presiding judge Dist. Ct. for Ariz. and N.M., Misilla, N.M.; del. from Ariz. to Confederate Congress, 1862; served as capt. Herbert's Bn., Ariz. Cavalry, Confederate Army, 1862; col. on staff of Gen. Sibley in Tex. and La., 1862-64; resumed practice of law, Tucson; mem. Ariz. Territorial Ho. of Reps., 1866, 73, 75, speaker, 1866; apptd. atty. gen. Ariz. Territory, 1869; moved to Phoenix, Ariz., 1870; dist. atty. Maricopa County (Ariz.), 1871-73; dist. atty. Pinal County (Ariz.), 1879, 89-90; del. U.S. Congress from Ariz. Territory, 1881-85; del. Dem. Nat. Conv., 1884; resumed law practice, Florence, Ariz., 1885. Died Tucson, Jan. 11, 1891; buried Masonic Cemetery, Florence.

OUTACITY (known as Ostenaco, Mankiller, also other names), Indian chief; probably born in Tenn., flourished 1756-77. Cherokee Indian, took active part in uprising led by Oconostota, 1757; visited Eng. under guidance of Henry Timberlake, 1762, had an audience with King George III (in order to increase Timberlake's reputation of influence over Indians); fought on side of Gt. Britain during Am. Revolution. Died circa 1777.

OVENSHINE, ALEXANDER THOMPSON, army officer; b. Ft. Leavenworth, Kan., June 25, 1873; s. Samuel and Sallie Yeatman (Thompson) O.; student Infantry and Cavalry Sch., 1907, Army Signal Sch., 1908; m. Mary Louise Powell, Dec. 24, 1898; children—Richard Powell, Eugene Samuel, Mary Louise. Enlisted in pvt. 21st Inf., U.S. Army, 1894; commd. 2d lt., 1897; advanced through grades to brig. gen., 1933; retired, June 30, 1937. Awarded D.S.M. and Silver Star (U.S.). Episcopalian. Club: Army and Navy Country (Arlington, Va.). Address: 304 Geneseo Road., San Antonio 9 TX

OVENSHINE, SAMUEL brigadier gen. U.S.A.; b. in Pa., Apr. 2, 1843. Apptd. from Md., 2d lt. 5th U.S. Inf., Aug. 5, 1861; 1st lt., Sept. 25, 1861; capt., March 30, 1864; maj. 23d Inf., July 10, 1885; lt. col. 15th Inf., Jan. 31, 1891; col. 23d Inf., April 26, 1895; brig. gen. U.S.A., Oct. 19, 1899; retired at own request, over 30 yrs.' service, Oct. 20, 1899; brig. gen. U.S.V., Aug. 13, 1898; hon. discharged, Apr. 17, 1899; brig. gen. U.S.V., Apr. 17, 1899; hon. discharged, Oct. 20, 1899. Home: Washington, D.C. Died July 5, 1932.

OVERESCH, HARVEY E., ret. naval officer, ins. exec.; b. Lafayette, Ind., January 20, 1893; s. Henry B. and Anna B. T. (Weil) O.; student Purdue U., 1910; grad. U.S. Naval Acad., 1915; M.S. in Elec. Engring., Columbia, 1922; m. Emily Hodges Forman, Apr. 14, 1917; 1 dau., Emily Hodges (Mrs. James C. Castle). Commd. ensign USN, 1915, advanced through grades to rear adm., 1945; served in U.S.S. South Carolina, World War I; naval attach, Peiping, China, 1937-40; comdr. Destroyer Squadron 5, comdt. Midshipment U.S. Naval Acad.; comdg. officer, Cruiser U.S.S. San Francisco, World War II; ret. as vice adm., 1946; v.p. Hawaiian Pineapple Co., 1946-47; resident v.p., dir. N.Am. Life Ins. Co., Chgo., 1948-67; U.S. Dept. State, attache Am. Embassy, Tokyo, Japan, 1952-55, London, Eng., 1955-57. Clubs: Chevy Chase, Army and Navy (Washington); N.Y. Yacht; Ends of the Earth, St. James (London); Cypress Point (Pebble Beach); Old Capitol (Monterey, Cal.). Home: Pebble Beach CA Died Jan. 19, 1973.

OVERTON, WALTER HAMPDEN congressman; b. nr. Louisa Court House, Va., 1788; attended common schs., Tenn. Commd. 1st lt. 7th Inf. Regt., U.S. Army, 1808, promoted capt., 1810, maj. 3d Rifles, 1814, transferred to Arty. Corps, 1815; brevetted lt. col. for gallant conduct at Battle of New Orleans, 1814, comdr. forts Jackson and St. Phillip; resigned commn., 1815; commd. maj. gen. La. Militia; settled nr. Alexandria, La.; mem. Ct. House Bldg. Commn., 1820-21; mem. Commn. on Navigation of Bayou Rapides, 1824; engaged in planting; mem. U.S. Ho. of Reps. (Democrat) from La., 21st Congress, 1829-31. Died nr. Alexandria, Dec. 24, 1845; buried McNutt Hill Cemetery, nr. Alexandria.

OWEN, ALLISON architect and landscape architect; b. New Orleans, Dec. 29, 1869; s. Gen. William Miller and Caroline Amanda (Zacharie) O.; student Tulane U., 1885-88; Mass. Inst. Tech., 1892-94; course Sch. of Fire, U.S. Army, Ft. Sill, Okla., 1918; War Coll., Washington, 1924; m. Blanche Pothier, Sept. 16, 1896 (dec.); children—William Miller (dec.), Cecile Violet, Allison, Louis Benjamin (dec.). Began practice New Orleans, 1895; architect on $4,000,000 White Slum Clearance project, New Orleans. Prin. works: New Orleans Pub. Library, Municipal Office Bldg., La. Bank Bldg., Met. Bank Bldg. United Fruit Co. Bldg., Notre Dame Sem., Am. Sugar Refining Office, Pythian Temple Office Bldg., Mergenthaler Bldg., New Orleans Athletic Club Bldg., Criminal Court and Jail Bldg. (all New Orleans); Westminster Ch. (Kansas City); St. Joseph's Ch. (Mobile); Presbyn. Ch. (Yazoo City, Miss.); St. Landry Church, Opelousas, La.; and many schs., coll. bldgs., chs., etc. Pres. Judah P. Benjamin Meml. Assn.; past pres. Community Chest of New Orleans; pres. New Orleans Parkways Commn.; mem. City Planning and Zoning Commn.; mem. bd. St. Mary's Orphan Boys Asylum; past pres. Associated Catholic Charities; pres. Met. and Particular Council New Orleans Soc. St. Vincent de Paul. Served as maj. comdg. Washington Arty. (1st La. F.A.), on Mexican Border, 1916; col. comdg. 141st F.A. (Washington Arty.), in France, 1918-19; brig. gen. comdg. 56th F.A. Brigade, 1924-33; maj. gen. retired, 1934. Decorated Chevalier Legion of Honor (France); Knight of St. Gregory the Great. Fellow A.I.A. (ex-pres. La. chpt.); mem. Mil. Order World War, Am. Legion, La. Hist. Assn. (pres.), New Orleans Assn. Commerce (pres. 1927, 32). K.C. (4 deg.; past grand knight, Marquette Council). Democrat. Clubs: Round Table (past pres.), Army and Navy, Boston. Recipient of Annual Loving Cup, Times-Picayune, 1928. Home: 1237 State St. Office: Pere Marquette Bldg., New Orleans. Died Jan. 30, 1951; buried Metairie Cemetery, New Orleans.

OWEN, EDWARD city official, veteran soldier; b. Cincinnati, 1838; s. Allison and Caroline (Miller) O.; went in boyhood to New Orleans; ed. pub. and pvt. schs. When war broke out was partner in J. W. Champlin & Co., cotton factors; served as sergt., 1st lt. and capt., 1st Co. Washington arty. of New Orleans, C.S.A., May, 1861, to May, 1865; promoted 1st lt. for "gallant and meritorius services" at 1st Bull Run; fought at Second Manassas, Seven Pines, Gaines Mills, Frazer's Farm, Malvern Hill, Wilcox Bluff, Rappahannock Station, Sharpsburg, Antietam (wounded in leg), Chancellorsville, Gettysburg, Drewry's Bluff (wounded in head), Chickahominy, siege of Petersburg for entire year; promoted to capt. 1st Co. Washington Arty., Jan., 1864; at surrender of Lee, Appomattox Court House; captured with battery at Chancellorsville, imprisoned in Capitol Prison 2 months until exchanged. In cotton business after war, New Orleans and New York; apptd. in 1885 to position in office of commrs. of accounts, New York; chief clerk same, 1885-93, 1895-98, commr. of accounts, 1893-95, and Jan., 1898-1905; is now a certified public accountant. One of founders, now comdr. Confederate Veteran Camp, New York; sec. Assn. Southern Democrats, New York. Office: 52 Broadway, New York.

OWEN, JOHN PAUL naval officer (ret.); b. Milford, Mo., Jan. 29, 1889; s. Walter Wilson and Mary Belle (Vick Roy) O.; M.D., St. Louis U., 1913; grad., U.S. Naval Med. Sch., 1917; m. Miss Coates, June 1, 1936. Interne, Kansas City (Mo.) General Hosp., 1914-15; commd. lt. j.g., U.S. Navy, 1915, and advanced through grades to rear adm., 1946; fleet surgeon, convoy task force, World War I; fleet surgeon, U.S. Asiatic Fleet, 1939-41; established and comd., U.S. Naval Amputation and Rehabilitation Center, Mare Island, Calif., 1942-44; fleet surgeon, U.S. 7th Fleet, World War II. Awarded Legion of Merit for rehabilitation of amputees; 2d Legion of Merit for work with 7th Fleet. Mem. Radiological Soc. of N. Am., A.M.A. Democrat. Mason. Club: Bohemian (San Francisco). Home: 1880 Pacific Av., San Francisco. Died June 14, 1954; buried Golden Gate Nat. Cemetery, San Francisco.

OWEN, WILLIAM OTWAY army officer; b. Nollichucky River, Tenn., July 6, 1854; s. Robert Latham and Narcissa Clarke (Chisholm) O.; ed. Va. Mil. Inst., 1873-75; M.D., U. of Va., 1878; m. Anna Rives Chalmers, July 14, 1884. Apptd. asst. surgeon, U.S. Army, May 23, 1882; capt. asst. surgeon, May 23, 1887; maj. brigade surgeon, U.S. Vols., June 4, 1898; hon. discharged June 30, 1899; retired on account of disability in line of duty, Nov. 23, 1905; re-commissioned as col. Med. Corps, by act of Congress, May 27, 1916; curator Army and Med. Mus. and Library, Washington, to July 6, 1918, when retired. Prof. anatomy, Georgetown U. Mem. bd. dirs. Garfield Memorial Hosp., Washington. Mason, K.P. Home: Washington, D.C. Died Dec. 25, 1924.

OWENS, MADISON TOWNSEND b. Apollo, Pa., Apr. 13, 1852; s. Samuel and Elizabeth (Townsend) O.; matriculated in State U. of Ia., 1872, LL.B., 1878; unmarried. Admitted to Ia. bar, 1878, and began practice at Waterloo; county atty. Black Hawk Co., Ia., 5 yrs.; moved to Los Angeles, Calif., 1888; police judge, Los Angeles, 1889-99; settled in Whittier, Calif., 1900, and served as city atty.; mem. firm Owens & Wingert; 1st v.p. United Bond & Mortgage Co., Los Angeles. Served as lt. col. staffs of Govs. Sherman and Larabee, Ia.; joined Calif. N.G., 1889; served as maj. and signal officer, col. and judge adv. gen.; retired with rank of brig. gen., Feb. 1916. Mem. bd. trustees Whittier Library, 1906—; chief of Whittier Div., Am. Protective League, World War. Mem. Rep. State Central Com.; presdl. elector, 1924. Mason. Home: Whittier, Calif. Died Jan. 29, 1929.

OWENS, RAY L. army officer; b. Chillicothe, Mo., April 7, 1891; s. David and Mary Margaret (Dryer) O.; student Moore's Normal Sch., Chillicothe, Mo., 1908-10, Northwestern State Normal, Alva, Okla., 1911; grad. Air Service Pilots Schs., 1921, Air Service Observation Sch., 1921, Air Corps Tactical Sch., 1935, Command and Gen. Staff Sch., 1938; rated command pilot, combat observer; m. Ada Louise Belt, Jan. 25, 1919; children—Ada Louise (wife of Capt. Leo Beldo, U.S. Army), Mary Margaret, Carolyn Ray. Teacher in pub. schs., 1912-17; served with U.S. Army, June 10, 1917 to Aug. 23, 1919; commd. 2d lt., Air Service, U.S. Army, Sept. 21, 1920, and advanced through the grades to brig. gen., Dec. 4, 1942. Decorated Victory Medal, Legion of Merit, Battle Honors (North Solomons). Club: Army and Navy (Manila, P.I.). Home: 1344 Ballou Rd., Spokane, Wash. Deceased.

OWENS, ROBERT BOWIE electrical engr.; b. Anne Arundel County, Md., Oct. 29, 1870; s. James and Maria Louise (Bowie) O.; grad. Charlotte Hall Mil. Sch., Md., 1886; Johns Hopkins, 1887-89; E.E., Columbia, 1891, A.M., 1899; B.Sc., ad eundem, McGill U., Montreal, 1900, M.Sc., 1900, D.Sc., 1903; research student Cambridge U., Eng., 1899; unmarried. Supt. Greenwich Gas & Elec. Co., 1889-91; prof. elec. and steam engring., U. of Neb., 1891-98; Tyndall fellow in physics, Columbia, 1898-1901; Macdonald prof. elec. engring., McGill U., 1898-1909; elec. engr. Southern Power Co., 1909-10; sec. Franklin Inst., Phila., 1910-24, also editor Jour. Franklin Inst., and dir. Bartol Research Foundation, 1921-24; pres. Fox Hall Farm, Harwood, Md., 1927—; dir. Md. Acad. Scis., 1930-31, and editor its jour. Commd. capt. Signal Corps, U.S.A., May 1917, and served in office of chief signal officer, Washington, D.C.; liaison officer French and British scientific commns., and with Personnel Div. of Aviation Sect. Signal Corps; capt. and maj. Signal Corps, A.E.F.; chief of Signal Corps Intelligence Div. in charge of organization; chief signal officer A.E.F., H.Q., London; in charge of and operated all telephone and telegraph communications between A.E.F, France and Eng., and all Am. owned cables (Western Union and Commercial) between Eng. and U.S., June-Dec. 1918. Mem. Internat. Elec. Congress and Internat. Jury of Awards, World's Fair, Chicago, 1893; dir. Electricity and Machinery Bldg., Trans-Miss. Expn., 1898 (gold medal); mem. Internat. Elec. Congress and Internat. Jury Awards, La. Purchase Expn., 1904 (commemorative medal). Mem. Am. Inst. E.E. (v.p.), Canadian Soc. of Civil Engineers (pres. elec. sect.). Hon. Companion D.S.O. (British); fellow Royal Soc. Can. Discoverer of the Alpha ray; inventor of radio direction finding, electromagnetic system for guiding ships and aeroplanes, differentiating machine, electric accelerometer. Address: Washington, D.C. Died Nov. 1, 1940.

OWSLEY, ALVIN MANSFIELD lawyer; b. Denton, Tex., June 11, 1888; s. Alvin Clark and Sallie (Blount) O.; grad. Va. Mil. Inst., 1909; studied law, U. Tex., 1911-12, also in Law Courts, London, Eng.; LL.D., Hillsdale Coll., 1941; L.H.D., Lincoln Meml. U., 1941; m. Lucy Ball, May 25, 1925; children—Alvin, Junior, Constance (Mrs. Joseph L. Garrett), David. Admitted to Tex. bar, 1912; mem. Tex. Ho. of Reps., 1912-14; county and dist. atty., Denton County Tex., 1915-17; asst. atty. gen. of Tex., 1919-20; later practicing Dallas; apptd. Am. minister to Rumania, 1933, to Irish Free State, 1935, Denmark, 1937; resigned Diplomatic Service, 1939; dir. Ball Brothers Co., Muncie, Ind., Bus. and Profl. Men's Ins. Co., Dallas; radio and television narrator. State chmn. Citizens Com. for Hoover Report; dir. A.R.C., War Finance Com.; ch-chmn. Savs. Bond Dr. Sponsor, Dallas Symphony Orch.; underwriter Dallas Grand Opera Assn. Trustee S.W. Legal Found. Student 1st O.T.C., Leon Springs, Texas, 1917; sr. instr. 3d O.T.C., Camp Bowie, Ft. Worth, Tex.; commd. maj. inf., later lt. col.; served as adj. 36th Div. AEF; participated in Champagne and Meuse-Argonne offensives. Recipient Freedom award Order of Lafayette. Mem. Am. Legion (nat. comdr., 1922-23; chmn. Americanism Endowment Fund, Mil. Order World Wars, Am., Tex. State bar assns.; mem. Newcomen Soc. Am., Air Force Assn., Dallas Hist. Soc., Assn. U.S. Army, Beta Theta Phi, Delta Sigma Rho. Donor award R.O.T.C. N. Dallas High Sch. Decorated Comdr. Legion of Honor (France), 1923; Order of Polonia Restituta (Poland), 1924; Confederate Service Cross, 1927; hon. mem. Boy Scouts, Tex. and N.Y.; made chief of Chippewa Tribe of Indians. Democrat. Mem. Chistian Church. Clubs: Lions, Reserve Officers, Dallas Country; Hermitage Golf (Dublin); Copenhagen Golf, Rungsted Golf (Copenhagen); Army and Navy (Washington, D.C.);

Rotary (hon.); Dallas Business Executives, City (Dallas). Home: 6801 Turtle Creek Blvd., Dallas 5. Office: Davis Bldg., Dallas 2. Died Apr. 3, 1967.

PABST, CHARLES FREDERICK, physician, dermatologist; b. N.Y.C., Dec. 3, 1887; s. Charles and Margaret (Connorton) P.; M.D., L.I. Coll. Hosp., 1909; intern Brooklyn Hosp., 1910-12; unmarried. Student skin diseases in Puerto Rico and Venezuela; conducted clinic for skin diseases at Brooklyn and Greenpoint hosps., 1914-28; attending dermatologist and chief of clinic for skin diseases at Greenpoint Hosp., 1915-57, consultant dermatologist, 1957-71. Commissioned lieutenant (jr. grade), U.S. Navy R.F., Feb. 20, 1918; lt., grade of passed asst. surgeon, Sept. 18, 1918, in charge treatment of skin diseases at U.S. Naval Hosp., Norfolk, Va., until May 1, 1919. Recipient award from Med. Soc. of State N.Y. Fellow A.M.A., Am. Acad. of Dermatology and Syphilology; mem. N.Y. State Med. Soc., Kings County Med. Soc., Alumnus Club L.I. Hosp., Brooklyn Hosp. Presbyn. Mason (32 deg., K.T.). Contbr. numerous articles on skin diseases and regarded as an authority on the subject. An expert swimmer, and saved several persons from drowning, at different times, on L.I. beaches. Gave U.S. Govt., 1934, nonpatented inexpensive formula for fireprofing ships, clothing and other fabrics; called attention to widespread prevalence of ringworm infection of feet, and started health campaign against bare feet; originated term "athlete's foot"; secured almost universal adoption of distinctive shape and color for bichloride of mercury tablets; pointed out dangers of overexposure to summer sun and gave the term "heliophobe" to individual whose skin will not tan. Address: Brooklyn NY Died Apr. 15, 1971; buried Long Island Cemetery, Farmingdale NY

PACE, LEO L. naval officer (ret.); b. Guide Rock, Neb., Aug. 21, 1898; s. Dr. Ira Albert and Nellie P.; A.B., U. Neb., 1917; B.S., U.S. Naval Acad., 1920; m. Winifred Williams, June 8, 1921; 1 son, Robert Bruce. Commd. ensign USN, 1920, advanced through grades to rear adm., 1946; served at sea and shore stas.; ret. from active duty, Aug. 1, 1946. Awarded combat Legion of Merit (World War II). Mem. Sigma Chi. Protestant. Clubs: Army Navy (Washington), Country (Hendersonville). Home: 1612 Kensington Rd., Hendersonville, N.C. Died Sept. 24, 1963; buried Arlington Nat. Cemetery.

PACKARD, FRANCIS RANDOLPH physician; b. Phila., Mar. 23, 1870; s. John Hooker and Elisabeth (Wood) P.; grad. biol. dept., U. of Pa., 1889; M.D., U. of Pa., 1892, LL.D., hon., 1939; m. 1st, Christine B. Curwen (died 1901); m. 2d, Margaret Horstman, Feb. 10, 1906; children—Margaret, Ann, Elizabeth, Frances Randolph. Resident physician, Pennsylvania Hosp., 1893-95; ex-prof. otology, Post-Grad. Sch., Univ. of Pa.; chief otolaryngologist, Pa. Hosp. Served as 1st lt., asst. surgeon, 2d Pa. Vol. Inf., Spanish-Am. War; commd. 1st lt. M.C., U.S. Army, May 16, 1917; capt., Sept. 1, 1917; maj., Oct. 1, 1918; sailed for France, May 18, 1917; with Base Hosp. 10, chief centre consultant in oto-laryngology, Dist. of Paris, Oct. 1918-Jan. 1919. Pres. Am. Laryngol. Assn., 1930, Am. Otol. Soc., 1936; pres. Coll. of Physicians of Phila., 1931-34; pres. Library Company of Philadelphia, 1936-41; mem. Am. Philos. Soc., Delta Psi. Republican. Episcopalian. Clubs: Philadelphia, University Barge. Author: History of Medicine in the United Sfates, 1901, 2d edit., 1919; Diseases of the Ear, Nose and Throat, 1909; The School of Salerno, 1920; The Life and Times of Ambrose Paré, 1921; Some Account of the Pennsylvania Hospital. Editor: The Gold-Headed Cane, 1915. Editor Annals of Medical History, 1917-42. Home: 304 S. 19th St., Philadelphia 3. Died Apr. 18, 1950.

PACKARD, JOSEPH lawyer; b. Fairfax Co., Va., Apr. 10, 1842; s. Joseph (D.D.) and Rosina (Jones) P.; A.B., Kenyon Coll., Ohio, 1860, A.M., 1867; studied in Law School, U. of Virginia; (hon. D.C.L., U. of the South, 1901; LL.D., Kenyon, 1911); m. Mrs. Laura Dillon, Apr. 13, 1868; m. 2d, Meta Hanewinckel, Dec. 27, 1882. Instr. history and lit., Kenyon Coll.. 1860-61; served as pvt. and corporal of arty., Stonewall Brigade, and lt. of arty. on ordnance duty with reserve train, Army of N.Va., 1861-65; began practice at Leesburg, Va., 1868; removed to Baltimore, 1868; mem. Venable & Packard, 1871-92, since alone. Pres. Baltimore Reform League, 1894-1900, Baltimore Sch. Bd., 1900-08; chmn. Charter Revision Commn. of Baltimore, 1909. Democrat. Episcopalian; deputy Gen. Conv. P.E. Ch., 1886-1919. Home: Baltimore. Died Nov. 24, 1923.

PACKARD, LAURENCE BRADFORD prof. history; b. Brockton, Mass., Jan. 20, 1887; s. William Forest and Mary Florence (Hyslop) P.; A.B., Harvard, 1909, Ph.D., 1921; studied in grad. sch., same univ., 1909-13, and as Rogers traveling fellow, 1911-12; A.M., Amherst (Mass.) Coll., 1934; m. Leonore Healey, May 6, 1927; 1 dau., Ann. Instr. in history, U. of Rochester, 1913-15, asst. prof. history, 1915-20, prof. history and head of dept., 1920-25; prof. history, Amherst Coll., since 1925; lecturer, U. of Mich., 1921, U. of Calif., 1923, Harvard, 1928; visiting prof. history, Yale, 1929-30, Wesleyan U., 1931, 32, New York U., 1933; visiting professor, Smith Coll., 1939, Mt. Holyoke Coll., 1940-43, 1947-48, Harvard Univ., 1942. Capt. Military Intelligence Div., Gen. Staff, U.S. Army, Siberia, 1918-19. Mem. Am. Hist. Assn., Société d'Histoire Moderne (France), Phi Beta Kappa, Delta Upsilon. Author: The Commercial Revolution, 1927; The Age of Louis XIV, 1929; also of monographs for U.S. War Dept. on Czecho-Slovaks in Siberia and on U.S. Expeditionary Force in Siberia. Asso. ed. Berkshire Studies in European History. Contbr. to Am. Hist. Rev. Quarterly Jour. Economics, Political Science Quarterly, Hist. Outlook, Jour. of Modern History, Jour. of Econ. History. Home: Amherst, Mass. Died Jan. 14, 1955; buried Mt. Vernon Cemetery, Abington, Mass.

PACKARD, WINTHROP naturalist; b. Boston, Mass., Mar. 7, 1862; s. Hiram Shepard and Maria (Blake) P.; Mass. Inst. Tech., class of 1885; m. Alice Harrington Petrie, 1905; children—John Winthrop, Theodore, David. Chemist with Henry A. Gould & Co., Boston, 1885; with A. W. Folsom & Co., Boston, 1889; editor Canton (Mass.) Journal, 1894; associated with National Magazine, Boston, 1896; editorial staff, Youth's Companion, 1899; mem. Corwin exploring expdn. to Alaska, Siberia and the Arctic, 1900, as corr. for Boston Transcript, New York Evening Post and St. Paul Dispatch. Then special article writer on Boston Transcript, and in general journalism; editor The New England Magazine, 1905-08. Served 3 yrs. in Mass. Naval Brigade; landsman, ordinary seaman and able seaman U.S. Navy, in Spanish-Am. War, 1898; 1st lit. Co. D, 13th Regt., Mass. State Guard, 1917. Field sec., Nat. Assn. Audubon Socs., 1914-18; field sec., then sec.-treas. and exec. officer Mass. Audubon Soc., 1913-36, an incorporator, 1915, established and financed society's nat. known Moose Hill Bird Sanctuary at Sharon, Mass., and established its ednl. and protective work there. Founder and editor Bull. of Mass. Audubon Soc., 1914-36. Established "Everything for Wild Birds," a nat. service in bird study and protection, 1936. Author: The Young Ice Whalers, 1908; Wild Pastures, 1909; Wildwood Ways, 1909; Woodland Paths, 1910; Wood Wanderings, 1910; Florida Trails, 1910; Literary Pilgrimages of a Naturalist, 1911; White Mountain Trails, 1912; Old Plymouth Trails, 1920; He Dropped Into Poetry, 1940. Home: Canton, Mass. Died Apr. 1, 1943.

PADDOCK, GEORGE ARTHUR ex-congressman; b. Winnetka, Ill., Mar. 24, 1885; s. George Laban and Caroline Matilda (Bolles) P.; B.L., U. Va., 1906; m. Elsie Elizabeth Mauritzon; 1 son, George Arthur. Vice pres. Rogers & Tracy, Inc., Chgo., since 1933; mem. 77th Congress (1941-43), 10th Ill. Dist. (mem. Interstate and Fgn. Commerce Com.). Attended Plattsburg Tng. Camp, 1916; 1st Officers' Tng. Camp, Fort Sheridan, Ill., 1917; served as capt., later maj. 342d Inf., 86th Div., 1917-18. Former bd. of dirs. Chgo. Crime Commn., Legislative Voters' League, Citizens' Assn. Mem. Evanston City Council, 1931-37; Evanston Rep. township committeeman, 1938-42; treas. Cook County Rep. Central Com., 1938-42. Treas. North East Park Dist. of Evanston. Mem. Soldiers' and Sailors' Service Council Ill. Mem. Am. Legion (received Founders' medal, charter mem., past comdr. Evanston Post 42), Loyal Legion, Delta Tau Delta (Distinguished Service chpt.), Delta Chi. Republican. Episcopalian. Mason. Clubs: Arts, Bond, University (Chgo.). Home: Orrington Hotel, Evanston, Ill. Office: 120 S. La Salle St., Chgo. Died Dec. 29, 1965.

PADDOCK, R(ICHARD) B(OLLES) mech. and elec. engr.; b. Ft. McKinney, Buffalo, Wyo., Apr. 16, 1891; s. Capt. Richard Bolles and Grace (Pershing) P.; student U. Neb., 1907-10; B.S., U.S. Mil. Acad., 1914; grad. Army War Coll. (war course), 1918; grad. U.S. F.A. Sch., Ft. Sill, Okla., 1921 and 1925; grad. U.S. Command and Gen. Staff Sch., 1926; m. 2d Kathryn Fowler Wilson, June 4, 1949; children by previous marriage—Richard Bolles, John Pershing. Commd. 2d lt., C.A.C., 1914; mil. instr., N.Y. City Police Dept., 1916; transferred to Signal Corps, 1916; promoted through grades to lt. col., 1918; transferred to Field Arty., 1920; chief engring. and research div., Signal Corps, 1919; instr. Signal Sch., 1919, 1920, Field Arty. Sch., 1921-25; served as maj. Gen. Staff Corps and chief of staff, Philippine Div., 1927-29; dep. adminstr. NRA, 1933-34; exec. dir. Cotton Garment Code Authority, 1934-36; v.p. Wilson-Jones Co., 1937-40; chief tech. service, engr. and gen. sales mgr., Western Plastics, Inc., 1943-45; pres. Bone Engring. Corp., 1945-46; internat. rep. Tech. Oil Tool Corp., 1949-50; mem. engring. staff Gilfillan Bros., Inc. since 1950. Mem., Gen. Pershing's original staff; tech. officer staff of chief signal officer, A.E.F.; signal officer 1st Div., A.E.F., World War I. Awarded Silver Star, Order of the Purple Heart, Oak Leaf Cluster (U.S.), Croix de Guerre (France) Fourragère, Croix de Guerre (France) as personal decoration (2d Field Signal Batn.). Mem. Inst. Radio Engrs., Phi Gamma Delta. Democrat. Episcopalian. Mason (32 deg., K.T., Shriner). Clubs: University (Washington); Baltic Society, University, Army and Navy (Manila); Jefferson Islands (Tilghman, Md.). Home: 156 S. Canyon View Dr., Brentwood, Los Angeles 49. Office: 1815 Venice Bldg., Los Angeles. Deceased.

PADGETT, LEMUEL PHILLIPS, JR., naval officer; b. Columbia, Tenn., June 24, 1897; s. Lemuel Phillips and Ida (Latta) P.; student Vanderbilt U., 1914-16; B.S., U.S. Naval Acad., 1919; m. Frank Sanders, Feb. 2, 1921; children—Lemuel Phillips (died 1936), Mary Geraldine (Mrs. Earl B. Shaw, Jr.). Gen. service in various types of surface ships, specializing in gunnery and other deck duties, 1920-42; command cargo ship in Pacific, 1941-42; participated in 1st landing N. Africa, Nov. 1942; with Army-Navy Petroleum Bd., Washington, 1943-46; loaned to State Dept. as U.S. Petroleum attache in Middle East (Libya, Palestine, Transjordan, Syria, Lebanon, Iran, Iraq, Arabia, Ethiopia), hdqrs. Cairo, Egypt, Mar.-July, 1946; comdt. cadets Columbia Mil. Acad., Tenn., 1946-48; tchr. Evening Coll., U. Chattanooga, since 1948. Decorated Legion of Merit. Mem. Sigma Chi, Alpha Psi. Home: 918 Ridgeway Dr., Signal Mountain, Tenn. 37377. Died Aug. 22, 1957; buried U.S. Naval Acad. Cemetery, Annapolis, Md.

PAGE, CHARLES soldier; b. in Va., 1829. Apptd. asst. surgeon, U.S.A., Dec. 2, 1851; capt. asst. surgeon, Dec. 2, 1856; maj. surgeon, Apr. 16, 1862. Bvtd. lt. col., U.S.A., for faithful and meritorious services during war; promoted lt. col., surgeon, June 30, 1882; col., asst. surgeon-gen., Nov. 17, 1887; retired Dec. 4, 1893; advanced to brig. gen., U.S.A., retired, Apr. 23, 1904. Served during Civil War in various hosps. and with Army of the Potomac, of which was asst. med. dir., 1864-65, and med. dir., 2d corps, Mar.-Aug. 1865. Home: Baltimore, Md. Died 1906.

PAGE, FRANK COPELAND public utilities; b. Brooklyn, N.Y., Mar. 17, 1887; s. Walter Hines and Alice (Wilson) P.; Harvard, 1910; m. Anna Howard Harbison, Sept. 25, 1920; children—Shelby Harbison, Allison Francis, Cecily. Started as bond salesman White Weld & Co., N.Y. City, 1909-12; partner Page Bros., Aberdeen, N.C., 1912-15; edit. staff Doubleday Page & Co., Garden City, L.I., 1915-17; editor Country Life in America, Garden City, L.I., 1919-20; mng. editor Winston-Salem (N.C.) Journal, 1920; sec. Am. Relief Adminstrn., N.Y. City, 1920-23; dept. mgr. U.S. C. of C., Washington, D.C., 1923-28; v.p. Internat. Telephone & Telegraph Corp., N.Y. City, since 1928, former director; dir. Cuban-Am. Telephone & Telegraph Co., Am. Cable & Radio Corp. Served as capt., later maj. A.S., U.S. Army, 1917-18. Dir. Nat. Foreign Trade Council, Beekman-Downtown Hospital. Dir. Am. Children's Fund. Democrat. Episcopalian. Clubs: Metropolitan, Burning Tree (Washington, D.C.); Harvard (N.Y. City). Home: 1406 29th St. N.W., Washington. Office: 67 Broad St., N.Y. City. Died Dec. 18, 1950.

PAGE, JOHN HENRY brig. gen.; b. New Castle, Del., Mar. 26, 1842; s. Capt. John (U.S.A.) and Mary Elizabeth (Blaney) P.; early edn. in Italy and France; returned to U.S., 1857; student at Northwestern U. when war broke out; m. Eliza Tracy Shaw, May 1, 1871. Served pvt. Chicago Light Arty., May-Aug. 1861; apptd. 2d lt. 3d U.S. Inf., Aug. 5, 1861; promoted through grades to col. 3d Inf., May 30, 1895; brig. gen. vols., Sept. 21-Nov. 30, 1898; brig. gen. U.S.A., July 26, 1903. Bvtd. capt., Dec. 13, 1862, "for gallant and meritorious services" in battle of Fredericksburg, Va.; maj., July 2, 1863, for same in battle of Gettysburg. Served with regt. 1st Brigade 2d Div. 5th Corps Army of the Potomac; participated in the sieges of Yorktown, Richmond, battles of Gaines' Mill, White Oak Swamp, Malvern Hill, 2d Bull Run, Antietam, Fredericksburg, Chancellorsville, Gettysburg, Siege of Petersburg, and Appomatox, after war in frontier service in Kan.; had command of inf. column on Sully Expdn. against Indians in Ind. Ty. and established, in 1868, Camp Supply; after that in various camps and stas.; comd. regt. during Coeur d'Alene mining troubles, 1893, and Coxeyite troubles on Northern Pacific; comd. regt. at Battle of El Caney and Siege of Santiago; comd. regt. 3 yrs. in Philippines, returning, 1902; retired at own request after 40 yrs.' service, July 27, 1903. Mem. Loyal Legion, G.A.R., Army and Navy Union, Soc. of Santiago. Died Oct. 9, 1916.

PAGE, RICHARD LUCIAN naval officer; b. Fairfield, Va., Dec. 20, 1807; s. William Byrd and Anne (Lee) P.; ed. Clarke Co. and Alexandria, Va.; m. Alexina, d. Richard and Elizabeth (Calvert) Taylor. Entered U.S.N., 1824; served until outbreak of Civil war; resigned; became brig. gen. C.S.A. Took part in fight at Port Royal; was in command Ft. Morgan in Mobile Bay, when, after gallant defense, it finally fell. At close of war retired to civil life. Vestryman and senior warden Christ P.E. Ch. Home: Norfolk, Va. Died 1901.

PAGE, THOMAS JEFFERSON naval officer; b. Matthews County, Va., Jan. 4, 1808; s. Mann and Elizabeth (Nelson) P.; m. Benjamina Price, 1838, 7 children. Apptd. midshipman U.S. Navy, 1827; participated in coast survey work, 1833-42; promoted lt., 1837; on voyages to Mediterranean and Brazil, 1842-44; attached to U.S. Naval Observatory, 1844-48; commanded brig Dolphin in Far East, 1848-51; commanded steamer Water Witch in exploration of Paarara, Paraguay, La Plata rivers, 1853-55, 59-60; resigned commn., 1861, joined Confederate Navy; in charge of various shore defenses, 1861-63; commanded ironclad Stonewall, 1864-65; never saw action; rancher, shipbuilder, Argentina, 1865-80. Author: La Plata: The Argentine Confederation and Paraguay, 1859. Died Rome, Italy, Oct. 26, 1899.

PAHLOW, EDWIN WILLIAM (pä'lo), college prof.; b. Milwaukee, Wis., Jan. 11, 1878; s. Lewis F. and Anna (Becher) P.; B.L., U. of Wis., 1899; A.M., Harvard, 1901, Ph.D., 1912; m. Gertrude Curtis Brown, June 14, 1905 (she died Jan. 29, 1937); children—Hugh, Gertrude. Instr. in history, U. of Wis., 1905-06; preceptor, Princeton, 1907-10; head of history dept. Lawrenceville (N.J.) Sch., 1912-21, Ethical Culture Sch., New York, 1922-25; prof. teaching of history, Ohio State U., since 1925. Dean U.S. Army Ednl. Corps, Gt. Britain, 1918-19. Mem. Am. Hist. Assn., Phi Delta Kappa, Beta Theta Pi. Episcopalian. Home: 2026 Iuka Av., Columbus, O. Died June 29, 1942.

PAINE, BRYON jurist; b. Painesville, O., Oct. 10, 1827; s. James H. and Marilla (Paine) P.; LL.D. (hon.), U. Wis., 1869; m. Clarissa Wyman, Oct. 7, 1854, 4 sons. Went to Wis. Territory, 1845; admitted to Milw. bar, 1849; counsel for Sherman Booth in famous fugitive slave law case before Wis. Supreme Ct., won writ of habeas corpus with his defense attacking constitutionality of law; became famous among anti-slavery proponents; judge Milw. County Ct., 1856-59; asso. justice Wis. Supreme Ct., 1859-64, 67-71; apptd. lt. col. 43d Wis. Volunteers, 1864. Died Madison, Wis., Jan. 13, 1871.

PAINE, CHARLES JACKSON soldier; b. Boston, Aug. 26, 1833; s. Charles Cushing and Fannie Cabot (Jackson) P.; brother of Robert Treat P.; g.g.s. Robert Treat P. (signer Declaration of Independence); A.B., Harvard, 1853, A.M., 1858; admitted to Mass. bar, 1856; m. Julia, d. John Bryant, of Boston, 1867. Capt. 22d Mass. Inf., Oct. 5, 1861; maj. 30th Mass. Inf., Jan. 16, 1862; col. 2d La. Inf., Oct. 23, 1862; brig. gen. vols., July 4, 1864; bvtd. maj. gen. vols., Jan. 15, 1865, "for meritorious and valuable services"; hon. mustered out, Jan. 15, 1866; comd. brigade during siege of Pt. Hudson, 1863; served under Gen. B. F. Butler, 1864; led div. colored troops in attack on Newmarket, Va., Sept. 29, 1864; after Lee's surrender comd. dist. of Newbern. For many yrs. dir. C.,B.&Q. R.R., A.,T.&S.F. R.R. and Mexican Central R.R. Was one of the three spl. envoys accredited to the govts. of France, Great Britian, and Germany in the interests of internat. bimetallism, 1897. Mem. Corp., Mass. Inst. Tech. Prominent yachtsman; owned Puritan, Mayflower and Volunteer, all successful defenders of America's cup. Home: Weston, Mass., and Boston. Died Aug. 12, 1916.

PAINE, GEORGE H. army officer; b. Scranton, Pa., July 14, 1884; B.S., U.S. Mil. Acad., 1906; grad. Mounted Service Sch., 1911, Staff Sch., 1923, Army War Coll., 1924; distinguished grad. Sch. of the Line, 1922. Commd. 2d lt., Inf., June 12, 1906; advanced through grades to brig. gen., April 1941. Died May 11, 1949.

PAINE, HALBERT ELEAZER lawyer; b. Chardon, O., Feb. 4, 1826; grad. Western Reserve Coll., 1845 (A.M.; LL.D.). Served in Union army through Civil war, becoming brig. gen. and bvt. maj. gen. U.S. vols. Mem. Congress from Milwaukee dist., 1865-71. Practiced law in Milwaukee. Apptd. commr. of patents, 1888, to succeed Ellis Spear. Author: Paine on Elections, 1888. Home: Washington, D.C. Died 1905.

PAINE, ROBERT TREAT congressman; b. Edenton, N.C., Feb. 18, 1812; grad. Washington (now Trinity) Coll., Hartford, Conn.; studied law. Admitted to the bar, practiced law; held local offices; engaged in shipping bus., owner shipyards; mem. N.C. Ho. of Commons, 1838, 40, 44, 46, 48; served as col. of a N.C. regt. during Mexican War; war gov. of Monterey (Mexico), 1846; mem. Mexican Claims Commn.; mem. U.S. Ho. of Reps. (Am. Party rep.) from N.C., 34th Congress, 1855-57; moved to Austin County, Tex., 1860, engaged in farming. Died Galveston, Tex., Feb. 8, 1872; buried Brenham (Tex.) Cemetery.

PAINE, ROGER W(ARDE) naval officer; b. Springfield, O., Sept. 7, 1887; s. Emer Ellsworth and Margaret (Humphreys) P.; A.B., U.S. Naval Acad., 1911, postgrad. 1916-17, 19; M.S. in E.E., Columbia, 1920; m. Corine Malone, Sept. 7, 1916; children—Roger Warde, Margaret Elizabeth (Mrs. W. G. Whyte), Helen (Mrs. G. J. Davis). Commd. ensign USN, 1911, and advanced through grades to rear adm., June 22, 1942; destroyer duty, Mexican campaign, 1913-14; destroyer command during World War I; destroyer command and electric drive battleship engring. afloat, and elec. and marine engring. design duty ashore, 1918-42; designated engring. duty only, 1932; mgr. Navy Yard, Pearl Harbor, T.H., May 1942-Nov. 1944; navy material and products control officer in liaison with WPB, Dec. 1944-Nov. 1945, dep. exec. chmn. (Navy), Army and Navy Munitions Bd., 1945-48; dep. insp. gen. Western Sea Frontier, 1948-49, ret. Awarded Destroyer clasp for service in World War I; Legion of Merit and gold star in lieu of 2d award for service in World War II. Mem. Am. Soc. Naval Engrs. (sec.-treas., 1936-38, council, 1946-47), Nat. Indsl. Conf. Bd., 1946-48. Clubs: Army-Navy, Army and Navy Country. Editor: Jour. Am. Soc. Naval Engrs., 1936-38. Address: 221 Wardour Dr., Annapolis, Md. Died May 1964.

PAINE, WILLIAM WISEHAM congressman; b. Richmond, Va., Oct. 10, 1817; attended sch., Mount Zion, Ga.; studied law, Washington, Ga. Served in Seminole War, 1836; admitted to Ga. bar, 1838; moved to Telfair, Ga., 1840, began practice of law; mem. Ga. Constl. Conv., 1850; pvt. sec. to Gov. Howell Cobb of Ga., 1851-52; mem. Ga. Senate, 1857-60; served as capt. 1st Ga. Regt., Confederate Army, during Civil War; moved to Savannah, Ga., practiced law; mem. U.S. Ho. of Reps. (Democrat) from Ga., 41st Congress, Dec. 22, 1870-71; mem. Ga. Ho. of Reps., 1877-79; curator Ga. Hist. Soc. Died Savannah, Aug. 5, 1882; buried Bonaventure Cemetery, Savannah.

PAINTER, GAMALIEL army officer, legislator; b. New Haven, Conn., May 22, 1743; s. Shubael and Elizabeth (Dunbar) P.; m. Abigail Chipman, Aug. 20, 1767; m. 2d, Victoria Ball, 1795; m. 3d, Mrs. Ursula Bull, 1807; 3 children. Served as lt. in Seth Warner's Additional Continental Regt., 1776; capt. Baldwin's Arty. Artificer Regt.; attended Windsor Conv. which formed Vt. Constn., 1777; bought part of site of future village of Middlebury, Vt., 1787, layed out village streets, sold lots, erected gristmill; asst. judge Addison County, 1785-86, 87-95; mem. lower house Vt. Legislature, various times, 1786-1810; mem. Gov.'s Council sharing exec. power with gov. Vt., 1813-14; a Federalist; a founder Middlebury Coll., 1800, fellow, 1800-19. Died Middlebury, May 22, 1819.

PAINTER, THEOPHILUS SHICKEL, zoologist; b. Salem, Va., Aug. 22, 1889; s. Franklin Verzelius Newton and Laura Trimble (Shickel) P.; B.A., Roanoke Coll., Salem. Va., 1908; M.A., Yale, 1909, Ph.D., 1913, hon. Sc.D., 1936; studied U. of Wurtzburg, 1913-14; LL.D., Roanoke Coll., 1942; m. Anna Mary Thomas, Dec. 29, 1917; children—Elizabeth Tyler (Mrs. S.P.R. Hutchins), Anne Trimble (Mrs. Thornton C. Greer), Theophilus S., Joseph Thomas. Instr. in zoology, Yale, 1914-16; adj. prof. zoology, U. Texas, 1916-21, prof., 1922-44, acting pres., 1944-46, pres., 1946-52, distinguished prof., 1952-66, prof. emeritus, 1966-69, also dir. U. Tex. Radiobiol. Lab. Adviser on research Am. Cancer Soc.; bd. dirs. Oak Ridge Inst. Nuclear Studies. Recipient Daniel Giraud medal for sci. research, 1934; 1st Anderson award M.D. Anderson Hosp. and Tumor Inst., 1969. Mem. 10th F.A., Conn. N.G., 1916; 1st lt. S.C., U.S. Army, later capt. A.S., till 1919. Mem. Am. Soc. Zoologists, Nat. Acad. Sci., English Speaking Union, Sigma Xi, Phi Eta Sigma, Alpha Omega Alpha, Phi Kappa Phi, also numerous other sci. socs. Presbyn. Clubs: University, Town and Gown. Am. editor 10th edit. Vade-Mecum. Contbr. numerous sci. articles on cytology, cytogenetics and exptl. zoology. Home: Austin TX Died Oct. 5, 1969; buried Austin Meml. Park, Austin TX

PALLETTE, EDWARD MARSHALL (pal-let'), physician; b. Wichita, Kansas, January 13, 1874; s. Samuel Drew and Caroline Elizabeth (Cartwright) P.; Ph.B., Northwestern U., 1894, Ph.M., 1895; Oliver Marcy scholar of Northwestern U. at Marine Biol. Lab., Woods Hole, Mass., 1894; M.D., Coll. of Medicine U. of Southern Calif., 1898; grad. ork, New York Polyclinic, 1901, univs. of London, Vienna and Berlin, 1902, 09, 24; m. Mary Elizabeth Brown, Sept. 16, 1903; children—Edward Choate, Warren Sumner, Drew Brown, Elizabeth Delight. Asst. instr. zoölogy, Northwestern U., 1894-95; instr. in biology, Los Angeles High Sch., 1896-98; instr. in histology and embryology, Coll. of Medicine, U. of Southern Calif., 1896-98; practiced at Los Angeles since 1898, giving spl. attention to gynecology; asst. health officer, Los Angeles, 1898-99; mem. Los Angeles City Bd. of Health, 1905-06; prof. physiology, Coll. of Dentistry, Univ. of Southern Calif., 1900-12; lecturer in obstetrics and gynecology, Training Sch. for Nurses, St. Vincent's Hosp.; examiner Calif. State Lunacy Commn., 1905-15; mem. staffs St. Vincent's (ex-pres.), Hollywood, French and Calif. Luth. hosps.; v.p. Los Angeles County Med. Holding Corp.; v.p. California State Board of Pub. Health, 1932-40; mem. Retirement Bd., Los Angeles City Schools, 1938-39; mem. (treas.) bd. dirs. Hosp. Service of Southern Calif. (Blue Cross) since 1938. Capt. Med. Corps, U.S. Army, World War I; served as surgeon Letterman Gen. Hosp., Presidio, San Francisco, and at Camp Crane, Allentown, Pa. Southern Calif. State chmn. procurement and assignment service for physicians War Manpower Commn. since 1942. Ex-pres. Los Angeles County Bd. of Edn. Mem. Med. Sch. Advisory Com. of U. of Southern Calif. Trustee Med. Soc. State of Calif.; fellow Am. Coll. Surgeons, A.M.A. (mem. Ho. of Dels., 1932-42; trustee since 1942); member California State Medical Assn. (pres. 1936-37); Los Angeles County Medical Assn. (ex-pres.), Los Angeles Surgical Society, Los Angeles Obstet. and Gynecol. Soc. (ex-pres.), Los Angeles Academy of Medicine, Southern California Medical Alumni (ex-pres.), S.R. (ex-pres. Calif. State Soc.), Hollywood Acad. of Medicine (hon.), Internat. Med. Club (hon.), Inst. of Am. Genealogy, A.A.A.S., Delta Tau Delta, Theta Nu Epsilon, Nu Sigma Nu (hon. nat. councilor), Psi Omega, Pi Gamma Mu. Republican. Mason (K.T., Shriner). Home: 5224 W. 2d St. Office: 1930 Wilshire Blvd., Los Angeles 5, Calif. Died Nov. 16, 1944.

PALMER, ALBERT KENNY CRAVEN (päm'er), retired army officer; b. Washington, D.C., June 5, 1887; s. Aulick and Alice (Craven) P.; ed. pub. and pvt. schs. of U.S. and Europe; grad. U.S. Mounted Service Sch., 1914, Field Arty. Sch., 1916; m. Josephine Hodges Lee, Sept. 25, 1917 (died 1935); children—Alice Craven, Joan, Kenny Craven; m. 2d, Ethel M. de Ortiz, Sept. 1935. Commd. 2d lt. Field Arty., U.S. Army, 1908, and advanced to lt. col. Nat. Army, June 18, 1918; maj. Q.M.C., 1920; retired, Nov. 13, 1920; lt. col. U.S. Army, June 21, 1930; mem. commn. in charge sale of U.S. Govt. horses in France, 1919. Engaged in investment banking, Denver, Colo., 1922-26, ins. business, N.Y. City, 1927-30; dir. Chile-Am. Assn. since 1930; foreign corr. of "El Mercurio," Santiago, Chile. Decorated Order of Al Merito (Chile), Grade Oficial, 1933, Grade Gran Oficial, 1935. Mem. Assn. of Foreign Corrs. in U.S., S.A.R., Mil. Order World War. Republican. Episcopalian. Clubs: Knickerbocker (New York); Army and Navy (Washington). Author: Chiam News Service. Home: 55 E. 86th St. Office: 31 Nassau St., New York, N.Y. Died Aug. 28, 1942.

PALMER, ARTHUR physician; b. Oswego, N.Y., Aug. 30, 1889; s. William H. and Jennie (Roberts) P.; A.B., Brown U., 1911; M.D., Cornell U., 1915; student. U. of Pa., 1924-25, U. of Cincinnati, 1925, U. of Vienna, 1929; m. Lillis Oliver, Apr. 13, 1921; children—Arthur, Lillis Oliver; married 2d, Inga Wolford, January 1, 1950. Interne, Bellevue Hosp., New York City, 1916-17; consultant in laryngology and otology, Southside Hosp.; consultant laryngology, N.Y. Infirmary for Women and Children; consultant otolaryngology, Mather Memorial and State Reconstruction; prof. clin. surgery (otolaryngology), New York Hospital-Cornell Med. Assn.; attending surgeon, New York Hospital. Served as first lieutenant, Medical Corps Reserve, United States Army, 1917, captain, 1919, major, 1924-29. Certified by Am. Bd. Otolaryngology and Am. Bd. Plastic Surgery. Mem. Soc. Plastic and Reconstructive Surgery (pres. 1939-42), Am. Laryngol., Rhinol. and Otol. Soc., Am. Acad. Ophthalmology and Otolaryngology, N.Y. Acad. Medicine, Assn. Mil. Surgeons, Harvey Society, A.A.A.S., Nu Sigma Nu, Lambda Chi Alpha. Clubs: Carmel Country, North Hills Country. Contbr. med. articles to various publs. Home: 31 Greenway Terrace, Forest Hills, N.Y. Office: 667 Madison Av., N.Y.C. 21. Died Feb. 18, 1954; buried Spencerport, N.Y.

PALMER, C. WILLIAM architect; b. Milford, Mich., June 30, 1886; s. William C. and Anna (Wallace) P.; student architecture Harvard, 1911-13; year's study abroad, 1913-14; m. Nina Estabrook Nation, June 26, 1920. Archtl. draftsman Albert Kahn, Detroit, 1903-11, archtl. designer, 1914-15; pvt. practice architecture, 1915-17, 24-43, 46—; mem. firm Malcomson, Higginbotham & Palmer, 1919-24. Mem. Detroit Housing and Planning Council. Served as capt., A.S., U.S. Army, 1917-19; comdr. USNR, 1943-46. Registered mem. Nat. Council Architects Registration Bd., 1948. Fellow A.I.A. (pres. Detroit chpt. 1932-34); mem. Mich. Soc. Architects (pres. 1942-43), Mich. Engr. Soc., Engring. Soc. Detroit, Am. Legion, Sigma Alpha Epsilon. Club: Detroit Athletic. Home: 1039 Seminole Av., Detroit 14. Office: 409 Griswold St., Detroit 26. Died Nov. 4, 1965.

PALMER, DAVID J. soldier; b. Washington, Pa., Nov. 15, 1938; s. Samuel R. and Margaret (Munce) P.; ed. pub. schs.; m. Letitia Helen Young, Oct. 25, 1866. Enlisted as pvt. in Co. C, 8th Ia. Regt., Aug. 10, 1861; attached to Army of the West, later to Army of the Tenn.; severly wounded at Battle of Shiloh; organized Co. A, 25th Ia. Regt.; promoted capt., 1862; lt. col., 1863; participated in siege of Vicksburg, battles of Lookout Mountain and Mission Ridge, expdn. to relieve Knoxville, and Atlanta campaign; mustered out at Washington, 1865. Engaged in farming at Washington, Ia., since close of war; auditor Washington Co., 1876-80; mem. Ia. Senate, 1891-98; railroad commr. of Ia., 1898-1915; frequent del. to Rep. nat. convs.; elected comdr.-in-chief G.A.R., Sept. 1914; mem. Ia. Commandery Loyal Legion. Mem. State Council Def. Presbyn. Clubs: Commercial (Washington, Ia.), Grant (Des Moines). Home: Washington, Ia. Deceased.

PALMER, FREDERICK writer; b. Pleasantville, Pa., Jan. 21, 1873; s. Amos F. and Amy C. Palmer; grad. Allegheny Coll., 1893; LL.D., 1919; Litt.D., Princeton U., 1935; m. Mrs. Talmadge Runkle, Sept. 5, 1924; stepchildren—Helen, Harry. London corr., 1895-97, Greek war, 1897; Klondike and Philippines, 1897-98; returned around the world with Admiral Dewey, 1899; to Philippines and expdn. for relief of Peking, 1900; Central America and the Macedonian insurrection, 1903; with the first Japanese Army in the field for Collier's Weekly and London Times, 1904-05; with the around-the-world cruise of the Am. Battleship Fleet, 1907-08; investigation of Central Am. conditions, 1908-09, the Turkish revolution, 1909; the Balkan War, 1912; only accredited corr. Am. press with British army and fleet, 1914-16. Maj. and lt. col. Signal R.C., 1917-18, serving on staff duty at front with A.E.F. in France and as press censor; later traveled as corr. in Europe and Asia; with British Army in France, 1940, Am. forces Germany and Pacific, 1945. Decorated D.S.M. Mem. Phi Beta Kappa. Clubs: Century (N.Y. City); Cosmos (Washington). Mem. Soc. of Am. Historians. Author: Going to War in Greece, 1897; The Ways of the Service, 1901; The Vagabond (fiction), 1903; With Kuroki in Manchuria, 1904; Central America and Its Problems, 1910; Over the Pass (fiction), 1912; The Last Shot (fiction), 1914; My Year of the War, 1915; My Second Year of the War, 1917; American in France, 1918; Our

Greatest Battle, 1919; The Folly of Nations, 1921; Clark of the Ohio, 1929; Newton D. Baker—America at War, 1931; With My Own Eyes, 1933; Bliss, Peacemaker, 1934; The Man With a Country, 1935; Our Gallant Madness, 1937; It Can Be Done, 1944; Life of John Pershing, 1948. Home: 1810 Edgewood Lane, Charlottesville, Va. Died Sept. 2, 1958; buried Grace Ch. Cemetery, Cismont, Va.

PALMER, GORDON DAVIS bank exec.; b. Joliet, Ill., July 7, 1896; s. Robert F. and Elinore (Davis) P.; B.S., U. Ala., 1920; m. Elizabeth Cade, Oct. 8, 1930; children—Elizabeth, Natalie. Foreman Sloss Sheffield Coke plant, 1920-21; bursar Birmingham So. Coll., 1921-23; exec. sec. U. Ala., 1923-26; asst. to pres. v.p., trust officer City Nat. Bank of Tuscaloosa, 1926-35; exec. v.p. First Nat. Bank of Tuscaloosa, 1935-41, pres., 1941-56, chmn. bd., 1956-—; dir. So. Co., Atlanta, 1950-—; dir. Ala. Gt. So. R.R., First Nat. Bank of Tuscaloosa, Ala. Power Co., Allen & Jemison Co., Birmingham Fire Ins. Co. Trustee, mem. exec. com., U. Ala., David Warner Found.; chmn. bd. trustees Stillman Inst., 1931-47; Synod of Ala., Ala. State Insane Hosp. Served as 2d lt. to capt., with 82d inf. div., U.S. Army, 1917-19, A.E.F. Mem: Tuscaloosa (past pres., dir.), Ala. State (past pres.) C.'s of C., Newcomen Soc., Am. (pres. nat. bank div., 1947-48), Ala. (past pres.) bankers assns., Phi Beta Kappa, Phi Gamma Delta, Omicron Delta Kappa, Beta Gamma Sigma. Presbyn. Kiwanian (past pres. Tuscaloosa br., lt. gov. Ala. Dist. of Internat. group). Home: 11 Druid Ct. Office: First National Bank Bldg., Tuscaloosa, Ala. Died July 11, 1956; buried Memorial Park, Tuscaloosa.

PALMER, HENRY E. insurance; b. Centerville, O., July 31, 1841; s. Levi S. and Elizabeth (Cowles) P.; ed. country schs., Wis., few months; chiefly self ed.; enlisted Union Army, July 31, 1861; 2d lt., Co. A, 11th Kan. Inf., Aug. 20, 1862; 1st lt., Dec. 31, 1862; capt., Feb. 24, 1863; regt. changed to cav., May 1863; acting asst. adj. gen., Dist. of the Plains, chief of staff of Gen. P. E. Connor's command, Powder River Indian expdn., June-Nov. 1865; pioneer in Wis., 1853, Neb., 1860, Colo., 1860, Kan., 1861, Wyo., 1865-66 (1st settler on Big Horn River, 1866), Mont., 1866, Ida., 1867; m. Laura Z. Case, June 25, 1870. Sr. mem. H. E. Palmer, Son & Co., gen. insurance, 1869-—; sec. Sheridan (Wyo.) Land Co.; mem. fire and police commn., Omaha, 1897-98; postmaster, Omaha, 1904-08; pres. Omaha Bd. of Trade; 2d v.p. bd. mgrs. Nat. Home for Disabled Vol. Soldiers, 1903-10. Comdr. Neb. dept. G.A.R., 1884-85; Grand High Pirest R.A.M., Neb., 1884-85. Republican. Episcopalian. Home: Omaha, Neb. Died Apr. 2, 1911.

PALMER, INNIS NEWTON army officer; b. Buffalo, N.Y., Mar. 30, 1824; s. Innis Bromley and Susan (Candee) P.; grad. U.S. Mil. Acad., 1846; m. Catharine Jones, 1853, 4 children. Apptd. brevet 2d lt. U.S. Army, 1846; served at battles of Cerro Gordo, Contreras, Churubusco, Chapultepec and Mexico City during Mexican War; brevetted capt., 1848; served in cavalry in Western U.S., 1848-61; promoted maj., 1861; brevetted lt. col. regular army and promoted brig. gen. U.S. Volunteers, 1861; served at battles of Bull Run, Fair Oaks, Glendale and Malvern Hill during Civil War; brevetted col. 2d Cavalry, promoted maj. gen. U.S. Volunteers, 1865; commanded 2d Cavalry in West, 1865-79; promoted col., 1868, ret., 1879. Died Chevy Chase, Md., Sept. 9, 1900.

PALMER, JAMES CROXALL naval surgeon; b. Balt., June 29, 1811; s. Edward and Catherine (Croxall) P.; grad. Dickinson Coll., 1829, med. course U. Md., 1833; m. Juliet Gittings, May 22, 1837, 2 children. Commd. asst. surgeon U.S. Navy, 1834; served in Wilkes' Antarctic exploring expdn., 1838-42; promoted to surgeon, 1842, in charge hosp. Washington (D.C.) Navy Yard; served on steam frigate Niagara (employed in laying 1st Atlantic cable), 1857; in charge med. service Naval Acad., Newport, R.I., 1861-62; fleet surgeon West Gulf Blockading Squadron under Adm. Farragut, 1863-65; in charge Naval Hosp., Bklyn., 1866-69, med. dir., 1871; surgeon gen. U.S. Navy, 1872-73. Author: The Antarctic Mariner's Song (poem), 1868. Died Washington, D.C., Apr. 24, 1883.

PALMER, JAMES SHEDDEN naval officer; b. N.J., Oct. 13, 1810. Became midshipman U.S. Navy, 1825; lt., 1838; commanded schooner Flirt, during Mexican War; made unsuccessful attempt to capture Confederate raider Sumter, 1861; sent by David Farragut to take possession of Baton Rouge (La.) and Natchez (Miss.), 1862; commanded ship Hartford; succeeded Farragut in command on Mississippi River; commd. commodore, 1863; commanded West Gulf Squadron, 1864; commanded West India Squadron in ship Susquehanna, 1865; commd. rear adm., 1866. Died of yellow fever in W.I., Dec. 7, 1867; buried N.Y.C.

PALMER, JOHN MCAULEY lawyer, senator; b. Eagle Creek, Ky., Sept. 13, 1817; removed to Ill., 1831, settling in Carlinville, 1839; admitted to bar, 1839; delegate to State constl. convention, 1847; State senator, 1852-56; Presdl. elector on Rep. ticket, 1860; del. to Peace Convention, Washington, Feb. 4, 1861. Col. 14th Ill. vols., May 1861; brig. gen. vols., Dec. 20, 1861; with Gen. Pope at capture of New Madrid and Island No. 10; commanded 1st brigade, 1st div., army of the Mississippi; afterward comd. a division; promoted maj. gen. vols., Nov. 29, 1862; participated in battle of Stone River, Chickamauga; led 14th corps in Atlanta campaign. Gov. Ill., 1869-73, as Republican; rejoined Democratic party; U.S. senator, 1891-97; presdl. candidate of National ("gold standard") Democrats, 1896. Home: Springfield, Ill. Died 1900.

PALMER, JOHN MCAULEY army officer; b. Carlinville, Ill., Apr. 23, 1870; s. John Mayo and Ellen (Robertson) P.; B.S., U.S. Mil. Acad., 1892; honor grad. Army Sch. of the Line, 1909; grad. Gen. Staff Coll., 1910; m. Maude Laning, June 14, 1893; children—John McAuley (dec.), Mary Laning (Mrs. George Helm Rockwell). Commd. 2d lt. inf., June 11, 1892; promoted through grades to brig. gen., Dec. 4, 1922; served in Cuba, 1899; Boxer Campaign, China, 1900; instr. chemistry U.S. Mil. Acad., 1901-06; gov. Dist. of Lanao, P.I., 1906-07; Gen. Staff Corps, 1911-12, 16-20; mem. com. apptd. by Sec. of War Stimson, 1912; to report on orgn. of land forces of United States; assistant chief of staff Author: Army of the People, 1916; Statesmanship of AEF, 1917-18; comdr. 58th Inf. Brig., Meuse-Argonne offensive, 1918; duty as mil. adviser to Senate Com. on Mil. Affairs, 1919-20; mem. tech. staff Conf. on Limitation of Armament, 1921-22; a.d.c. to Gen. Pershing, 1921-23; comd. 19th Inf. Brig., Canal Zone, 1923-25; retired, 1926; recalled to active duty, 1941-46. Decorated D.S.M. (U.S.), 1918, oak leaf cluster, 1946; Officer Legion of Honor, Croix de Guerre (French); Order of St. Maurice and St. Lazarus (Italian). Mem. U.S. Inf. Assn., Am. Legion. Episcopalian. Mason. Club: Army and Navy. Author: Army of the People, 1916; Statesmanship of War, 1927; Washington, Lincoln, Wilson—Three War Statesmen, 1930; General von Steuben, 1937; America in Arms, 1941, rev. edit., 1943. Contbr. to mags. Address: Washington. Died Oct. 26, 1955. Buried Arlington National Cemetery.

PALMER, JOSEPH mfr., army officer; b. Higher Abbotsrow, Shaugh Prior, Devonshire, Eng., Mar. 31, 1716; s. John and Joan (Pearse) P.; m. Mary Cranch, 1745, 3 children. Came to Am., 1746; erected (with brother-in-law Richard Cranch) glass manufactory in Germantown (now part of Quincy), Mass., 1752; mem. Mass. Provincial Congress, 1774-75; mem. Cambridge Com. of Safety; commd. col. 5th Suffolk Regt., Mass. Militia, 1776; chosen brig. gen. for Suffolk County, 1776, apptd. brig. gen. to command forces on a secret expdn. to attack enemy at Newport, R.I., 1777, expdn. failed; started salt factory, Boston Neck, Mass., circa 1784. Died Dorchester, Mass., Dec. 25, 1788.

PALMER, LEIGH CARLYLE naval officer; b. St. Louis, Jan. 11, 1873; s. Enrique and Laura (Creighton) P.; grad. U.S. Naval Acad., 1896; LL.D., Wesleyan U., Conn., 1919; m. Bessie Draper McKeldin, June 10, 1911; 1 dau., Laura Creighton. Promoted lt. jr. grade, 1901; lt., 1903; lt. comdr., 1908; comdr., 1908; comdr., 1915; rear admiral, 1916. Participated in Battle of Santiago, 1898; Cuban Naval Campaign; Philippine Naval Campaign; duty in Atlantic, Pacific and Asiatic fleets; U.S. naval representative at wedding of King Alfonso of Spain, 1906; naval aide to Sec. of State Root, on S. Am. trip, 1906; gunnery officer of U.S.S. Vermont, battle efficiency pennant winner, 1908; dir. target practice and engring., 1909-12; naval aide to Pres. Taft, 1909-12; comdg. destroyers Aylwin and McDougal, and Seventh Destroyers Div., 1913-14; exec. officer, battleship New York, 1915-16; chief of staff, Battleship Fleet, 1916; chief Bur. of Navigation, 1916-18; chief of staff Am. Battleship Squadron in the North Sea, 1918-19; comdg. U.S.S. Georgia, 1919; pres. U.S. Shipping bd. Emergency Fleet Corpn., 1924-25. Decorated Order of Naval Merit (Spanish), 1906; D.S.M. (U.S.), 1918; Order of Leopold (Belgian), 1919. Clubs: Chevy Chase, Metropolitan, Army and Navy (Washington); Metropolitan (N.Y.C.). Home: 1709 Massachusetts Av. Address: Navy Dept., Washington. Deceased.

PALMER, RAY consulting engr.; b. Sparta, Wis., Mar. 29, 1878; s. George Hegeman and Mary Delemar (Canfield) P.; B.S., U. of Wis., 1901; m. Daisy Wentworth, Dec. 11, 1901; children—Chester Llewellyn, Delemar Elizabeth, Ray. Began as asst. supt. J. G. White & Co., New York, 1901; with same firm, London, 1901-04; elec. engr., Union Traction Co., Chicago, 1904-05; cons. engr., Chicago and Milwaukee, 1905-12; commr. gas and electricity, Chicago, 1912-15; pres. and gen. mgr. New York & Queens Electric Light & Power Co., 1915-25; cons. engr., New York and Chicago, since 1925. Corpl. Wis. N.G., Porto Rico Campaign, Spanish-Am. War; Queensboro (N.Y. City) war industries commr., World War. Fellow Am. Inst. E.E.; mem. Illuminating Engring. Soc., New York Elec. Soc., Kappa Sigma. Republican. Clubs: Engineers (New York); Wyantenuck Country (Great Barrington, Mass.). Home: Great Barrington, Mass.; and Daytona Beach, Fla.* Died Sep. 10, 1947.

PALMER, STUART author; b. Baraboo, Wis., June 21, 1905; s. Jay Sherman Palmer and Nellie (Secker) P.; student Art Inst., Chgo., 1923-24, U. Wis., 1924-26, U. Cal. at Los Angeles, 1961; m. Melina Racioppi, 1928 (div. 1937); m. 2d, Margaret Greppin, 1939 (div. 1945); children—Philip Stuart, Penelope; m. 3d, Ann Higgins, 1947 (div. 1950); 1 son, Jay Deighton; m. 4th, Winifred Graham, 1952 (div. 1963); m. 5th, Jennifer Elaine Venala, 1966. Screenwriter, 1932-58; TV writer, 1950-—. In charge of liaison between the Office of the Chief of Staff U.S. Army and all Hollywood and newsreel film prodn., 1943-48. Served as maj., AUS, 1942-48. Mem. Mystery Writers Am. (pres. 1954-55), Writers Guild of America. Club: National Press (Washington). Author: The Penguin Pool Murder, 1931; Ace of Jades, 1931; Murder on Wheels, 1932; Murder on the Blackboard, 1932; The Puzzle of the Blue Banderila, 1937; Omit Flowers, 1937; Miss Withers Regrets, 1947; Before It's Too Late, 1947; Riddles of Hildegarde Withers, 1947; Four Lost Ladies, 1949; The Monkey Murders and other stories, 1950; The Green Ace, 1951; Nipped in the Bud, 1951; Cold Poison, 1954; Unhappy Hooligan, 1956; People vs Malone & Withers, 1963; Rook Takes Knight, 1968. Address: 625 North Ranch Ln., Glendora, Cal. Died Feb. 4, 1968.

PALMER, THOMAS WAVERLY, lawyer; b. Tuscaloosa, Ala., Feb. 25, 1891; s. Thomas Waverly and Lulu (Rainer) P.; A.B., U. of Ala., 1910, LL.D. (honorary), 1954; LL.B., Harvard University, 1913; awarded Sheldon traveling fellowship for legal research in Spain, 1913-14; married Marguerite Ellen Meehan, July 2, 1919;children—Thomas Waverly (dec.), Eleanor (dec.), Evelyn (deceased), James, Meehan (killed in action), Richard Rainer, and Marguerite (Mrs. Edward G. Haladey). In practice Birmingham, Ala., 1914-17; atty. Chile Exploration Co. (Chile Copper Co.), and U.S. consular agt., Chuquicamata, Chile, 1919-21; atty. for Standard Oil Co. of N.J., 1921-26; exec. rep. and counsel Tropical Oil Co. (Internat. Petroleum Co., Ltd.) with temporary residence in Colombia, S.A., 1927-29; counsel Standard Oil Co. (N.J.), 1929-50; pres. and dir. Ancon Insurance Co., Balboa-Insurance Co., 1950-56. Dir. The Americas Foundation, Inc., Caribbean Conservation Corps. With Alabama National Guard Mexican border service; capt. 117th F.A., 31st Div., assigned as instr. in reconnaissance, Sch. of Fire for Field Arty., Ft. Sill, Okla.; maj. F.A., Oct. 1918. Counsel Petroleum Supply Committee for Latin American under Petroleum Admn. for War, during World War II. Decorated Officer Nat. Order of the Southern Cross (Brazil); Commander Order of Liberator (Venezuela); Officer Nat. Order Carlos Manuel de Cespedes (Cuba), 1954. President Pan-Am. Soc. U.S. Inc., 1946-49, honorary president (life), 1949-68. Pres. N.Y. So. Society, 1938-39; councilor (director) Am. Geographical Soc.; corr. and hon. member Instituto da Ordem dos Advogados Brasileiros; pres., dir. Venezuelan C. of C. of U.S., Inc. 1942-45. Mem. Am. Bar Assn., S.R., Soc. Colonial Wars, Sigma Alpha Epsilon, Phi Beta Kappa, Pi Gamma Mu. Presbyn. (elder). Mason. Clubs: Southern Cross (past pres.); Pilgrims, Univ., Am. Yacht (Rye, N.Y.); Acacia; Army and Navy (Wash.). Author: Guide to Law and Legal Lit. of Spain, 1915; The Law and Legal Literature of Curacoa (with others), 1934; Gringo Lawyer, 1956. Contbr. to legal jours. Home: Scarsdale NY Died May 28, 1968.

PALMER, WALTER WALKER physician, educator; b. Southfield, Mass., Feb. 27, 1882; s. Henry Wellington and Almira Roxana (Walker) P.; B.S., Amherst, 1905, Sc.D., 1922; M.D., Harvard, 1910; Sc.D., Columbia, 1929; m. Francesca Gilder, Oct. 12, 1922; children—Helena Francesca Gilder, Gilder, Walter de Kay. H. P. Walcott fellow in medicine and instr. in physiol. chemistry Harvard, 1913, asst. in medicine, also resident physician Mass. Gen. Hosp., 1913-15; asst. in medicine Rockefeller Inst., N.Y.C., 1915-17; asso. prof. medicine Columbia, 1917-19, also acting dir. med. service Presbyn. Hosp.; asso. prof. medicine Johns Hopkins Med. Sch., 1919-21, also asso. vis. physician Johns Hopkins Hosp.; Bard prof. medicine Columbia, 1921-47; cons. Presbyn. Hosp., 1947-—; dir. Pub. Health Research Inst. of N.Y., 1947-—. Commd. 1st lt. Med. R.C., U.S. Army, 1917-19, maj., 1926-31. Mem. Nat. Bd. of Med. Examiners, 1921-43. Mem. A.M.A. (council pharmacy and chemistry), Soc. for Clin. Investigation, Assn. Am. Physicians, N.Y. Acad. Medicine, Harvey Society of N.Y.C. (pres. 1926-27), Theta Delta Chi, Phi Beta Kappa, Alpha Omega Alpha. Republican. Club: Century Assn. Specializes in research work in metabolic fields—diabetes, nephritis, etc. Contbr. to profl. jours. Home: 24 Gramercy Park. Address: Foot of E. 15th St., N.Y.C. 9. Died Oct. 28, 1950; buried Tyringham, Mass.

PALMER, WILLIAM JACKSON ry. official; b. Kent Co., Del., Sept. 18, 1836; s. John and Matilda (Jackson) P.; ed. pub. and pvt. schs., Phila.; m. Queen M. Palmer, Oct. 30, 1870. Commissioned capt. 15th Pa. Cav., Sept. 28, 1861; col., Sept. 8, 1862; bvt. brig. gen. vols., Nov. 6, 1864, for valuable services during the war; hon. mustered out, June 21, 1865; awarded congressional medal of honor, Feb. 24, 1894, for having with 150 men attacked and defeated a superior force of the enemy, capturing their field piece and about 100 prisoners, without the loss of a man, at Red Hill, Ala., Jan. 14, 1865. Entered ry. service, 1853, as rodman; employed 4 yrs. Pa. R.R.; treas., dir. surveys and mgr. construction Kan. Pacific Ry., 1861-70; pres. Denver & Rio Grande Ry., 1870-83; pres. Mexican Nat. Ry., 7 yrs.; pres. Rio Grande Western Ry., 1883-1901. Home: Colorado Springs, Colo. Died 1909.

PANNELL, FAYE, nurse educator; b. Red Oak, Tex., July 28, 1912;2d. Frank P. and Lillie (Warren) Pannell; diploma Baylor U. Sch. Nursing, 1932; B.S., Columbia Tchrs. Coll., 1939, M.A., 1951. Engaged in pub. health nursing Tex. Health Dept, 1935-42; dir. pub. health nursing Dallas Health Dept., 1946-47; dir. nursing Parkland Meml. Hosp., Dallas, 1947-54; dean Coll. Nursing, Tex. Woman's U., Denton, 1954-69. Profl. nurse traineeship program Dept. Health, Edn. and Welfare; mem. Gov.'s Adv. Com. on Mental Health and Mental Retardation Planning; participant expert adv. com. White House Conf. on Health, 1965. Served to capt. Army Nurse Corps, 1942-46. Named Dallas Woman of Yr., Women's Civic Clubs, 1954. Mem. Am. Nurses Assn., Nat., States (exec. com. So. regional council 1958-62), Tex. (pres. 1954-58, chmn. workshop com. 1958-63) leagues for nursing., So. Regional Edn. Bd. (nursing project adv. com., council on nursing), Tex. Heart Assn. (chmn. nursing com. 1960-64), Am. Assn. U. Women, Delta Kappa Gamma, Phi Lambda Theta. Democrat. Baptist. Club: Altrusa. Home: Denton TX Died Apr. 10, 1969.

PAPPENHEIMER, ALWIN M(AX) pathologist; b. N.Y.C., Dec. 4, 1878; s. Max and Henrietta (Loewenstein) P.; A.B., Harvard, 1898; M.D., Columbia, 1902; grad. study Vienna, Leipzig, Freiburg; m. Beatrice Leo, Nov. 12, 1907; children—Alwin M., Anne, John Richard. Intern Bellevue Hosp., N.Y.C., 1903-05, pathologist, 1905-11; demonstrator of pathology, Columbia, 1909, asso., 1909-14, asst. prof., 1914-19, asso. prof., 1919-23, prof., 1923-45, prof. emeritus 1945—; vis. pathologist, mem. med. bd. Presbyn. Hosp., N.Y.C. Mem. Com. on Pathology, NRC. Served from capt. to maj. M.C., U.S. Army, pathologist and dir. labs., 1917-18; mem. Trench Fever Commn., 1918. Fellow New York Acad. Sciences, New York Acad. Medicine; mem. Am. Soc. Exptl. Pathology, A.A.A.S., Soc. Exptl. Biology and Medicine, Am. Assn. Pathologists and Bacteriologists. Contbr. to med. jours. Home: 45 Holden St., Cambridge 38, Mass. Died Feb. 21, 1955.

PARDEE, DON ALBERT judge; b. Wadsworth, Medina Co., O., Mar. 29, 1837; s. Aaron and Eveline (Eyles) P.; acting midshipman U.S. Naval Acad., 1854-57; m. Julia E. Hard, Feb. 3, 1861. Admitted to bar, 1859; practiced at Medina, O., 1859-61; maj. 42d Ohio Inf., Oct. 27, 1861; lt. col., Mar. 14, 1862; bvtd. col. vols. and brig. gen. vols., Mar. 13, 1865, "for gallant and meritorious services during the war." Resumed practice at New Orleans, 1865; register in bankruptcy, 1867; judge 2d Jud. Dist. of La., 1868-80; del. La. Constl. Conv., 1879; Rep. candidate for atty.-gen., 1880; U.S. circuit judge, 5th Jud. Circuit, May 1881—. Removed to Atlanta, June 1898. Home: Atlanta, Ga. Died Sept. 26, 1919.

PARDEE, HAROLD ENSIGN BENNETT, physician; b. N.Y. City, Dec. 11, 1886; s. Ensign Bennett and Clara (Burton) P.; A.B., Columbia, 1906; M.D., Coll. Physicians and Surgeons (Columbia), 1909; m. Dorothy Dwight Porter, Apr. 15, 1918; children—Althea, Hobart Porter, Pamela. Interne, New York Hosp., 1909-11; in practice in N.Y. City, specializing on diseases of heart and circulation, since 1911; instr. in physiology, Coll. Physicians and Surgeons, 1912-15; instr. in clin. medicine, Cornell U. Med. Sch., 1916-22, asso. in medicine, 1923-27, asso. prof. clin. medicine since 1927; asso. attending physician New York Hospital; attending phys. (cardiac diseases) Polyclinic Hosp.; cons. physician for cardiac disease, Woman's Hosp., M.E. Hosp., N.Y. City. Served as 1st lt. Med. Corps, U.S. Army, July 1917-Jan. 1918; capt. Jan. 1918-Apr. 1919. Mem. A.M.A., Am. Soc. Clin. Investigation, Assn. Am. Physicians, Am. Heart Assn., N.Y. State Med. Soc., New York County Med. Soc. Republican. Conglist. Clubs: Rockaway Hunting (Lawrence, L.I.); Union Club (N.Y. City). Author: Clinical Aspects of the Electrocardiogram, 1924, 4th edit., 1941; What You Should Know About Heart Disease, 1928. Chmn. com. which wrote Criteria for Diagnosis of Heart Disease, 1928, 4th edit., 1939. Many articles on diagnosis and treatment of heart disease in various medical journals. Home: New York City NY Died Feb. 28, 1972.

PARIS, W(ILLIAM) FRANCKLYN architect-decorator; b. N.Y. City, 1871; s. Auguste Jean-Baptiste and Anne (Mercer) P.; ed. by pvt. tutors, at Art Students' League, N.Y.C. and in London, Paris, Rome; hon. L.H.D., St. John's Coll., 1917; hon. M.A., New York U., 1921; m. Margaret Wynne-Jones, Apr. 14, 1914; children—Francklyn Mercer (dec.), Francklyn Wynne. U.S. dir. of decorative art, Paris Expn., 1900; professional work in N.Y. since 1901; pres. Paris & Wiley Associates; archtl. decorative work in state capitols of Mo., Minn., and W.Va., also U. of Tex., Princeton, Yale, U. of Chicago, Fountain St. Bapt. Ch. (Grand Rapids), A.I.A., Elks Nat. Meml. (Chgo.), Detroit Pub. Library, supreme cts. of U.S., N.J., W.Va., N.Y. Life Ins. Co. new bldg. Exhibited at most of the important arch. exhbns. since 1901. Occasional lecturer on fine arts at Cornell, Vassar, St. John's, U. of Maryland, U. of Penn., U. of Wis., William and Mary Coll., Am. Inst. Architects. Inaugurated 1912 Museum French Art, French Inst. in U.S. (N.Y. City). Permanent expn. archtl. drawings, Columbia U. Sch. Architecture; an organizer of the Municipal Christmas Tree, Madison Square, New York City, 1912; organizer, 1919, and hon. dir. Hall of Am. Artists and Hall of Chancellors, N.Y.U. Mem. Louvain Library Com., Dec. 1921; inaugurated Cardinal Mercier Memorial at New York U., 1921; dir. Schola Cantorum 10 yrs.; chmn., 2d biennial art exhbn. of Americans at Venice, Italy, 1923. First sec., Art Alliance of Am.; hon. life mem. Met. Museum of Art; mem. Archtl. League, 1900-34, Beaux-Arts Inst. of Design, 1926-35; dir. Fountainbleau Sch., mem. National Sculpture Society, 1900-19; mem. Am. Fedn. Arts, Artists Fellowship, Bibliophile Soc. (Boston); corr. mem. Société des Gens de Lettres de France; mem. soc. de l'Histoire de l'Art Francais, Spanish Acad., Acad. of Coimbra (Portugal); hon. mem. Comité Cultural Argentino (Buenos Aires); hon. mem. Inst. de Cultura Am. Republica Argentina (Tolosa); former v.p. and dir. Alliance Français; founded 1922, and v.p. Am. Soc. French Legion of Honor (pres. 1946). Hon. del. for United States at Antwerp Exposition, 1930; mem. orgn. com. 1935, dir., 1935-39, N.Y. World's Fair, 1939; chmn. Ambassador Jusserand Memorial, Rock Creek Park, Wash., D.C., 1936. Served in Naval Militia of N.Y., 1891-95; capt. 108th Regt. N.Y. Vols., May 1898. Volunteered as pvt., U.S. Army, 1917, commd. lt., June 23; 1st lt. acting adj. 102 Trains, 27th Div., U.S. Army, Aug. 5, 1917, capt. 1919. Represented 27th Division U.S. Army at unveiling of battle monument, Brest, France, August 1937. Member Union Fédérale Combattants (Veterans of France). Knight Crown of Belgium for services, World War I; Knight Crown of Italy, 1924; Knight St. John (honorary), Knight St. Michel (honorary); Officer Legion of Honor, for services to Art as "Architecte Décorateur"; Grand Officer Ordre du Nichan-Iftikhar, 1929; mem. d'hon. Ordre du St. Sepulchre, Province de France. Clubs: Century, Authors and Authors, Athenaeum (London); Cercle Interalliée (Paris, France). Author: Decorative Elements in Architecture, 1917; The House That Love Built, 1925; Napoleon's Legion, 1927; Personalities in American Art, 1930; French Arts and Letters and Other Essays, 1937; Personalities, Hall of American Artists, vol. II, 1942, vol. III, 1944, vol. IV, 1945-46, vol. V, 1948-49. Editor, French Legion of Honor mag., since 1930. Frequent contbr. lit. and art mags., U.S. and Europe. Home: Plaza Hotel, N.Y.C. Died June 5, 1954.

PARISH, JOHN CARL prof. history; b. Des Moines, Ia., July 25, 1881; s. Leonard Woods and Emma White (Stuart) P.; M.Di., Ia. State Normal Sch., 1902; Ph.B., State U. of Ia., 1905, A.M., 1906, Ph.D., 1908; m. Ruth Leavitt Davison, Oct. 6, 1908; 1 son, David Stuart. Teacher high sch., Winterset, Ia., 1902-04; asst. editor State Hist. Soc. of Ia., 1907-10; student of archives in France and Spain, 1908-09; engaged in writing, 1910-14; asst. prof. history, 1914-15, prof., 1915-17, Colorado Coll.; asso. editor State Hist. Soc. of Ia., 1919-22; editor of The Palimpsest (hist. monthly), 1920-22. Sec. Conf. of Hist. Socs., 1919-22; lecturer on Ia. history, State U. of Ia., 1920-22; asst. prof. history, 1922-24, asso. prof., 1924-27, prof., 1927—, U. of Calif. at Los Angeles. Commd. 1st lt. Inf., U.S.A., 1917, capt., 1919; served with Intelligence Sect., 1st Am. Army, A.E.F., 1918. Conglist. Author: Robert Lucas (biography), 1907; John Chambers, 1909; George Wallace Jones, 1912; The Man with the Iron Hand, 1913. Editor Robert Lucas Journal of the War of 1812; Autobiography of John Chambers. Mng. editor Pacific Historical Review, 1932-36. Died Jan. 13, 1939.

PARK, EDWARDS ALBERT, pediatrician; b. Gloversville, N.Y., Dec. 30, 1877; s. William Edwards and Sara Billings (Edwards) P.; grad. Phillips Acad., Andover, Mass., 1896; A.B., Yale, 1900, hon. A.M., 1922; M.D., Coll. Physicians and Surgeons (Columbia), N.Y. City, 1905; hon. D.Sc., U. of Rochester, 1936; m. Agnes Bevan, Aug. 2, 1913; children—Sara Bevan, Charles Rawlinson, David Chapman. Interne, Roosevelt Hosp., N.Y. City, 1906-08, New York Foundling Hosp., 1908-09; Proudfit fellow in medicine and instr. in medicine, Coll. Physicians and Surgeons, 1909-12; instr. in pediatrics, Johns Hopkins, 1912-15, asso. prof., 1915-21; Sterling prof. pediatrics, Yale Sch. Medicine, 1921-27; prof. pediatrics, Johns Hopkins Sch. of Medicine and pediatrician Johns Hopkins Hosp., 1927-46; prof. pediatrics emeritus, Johns Hopkins School of Medicine, since 1946. Editor Excerpta Medica, Revue Francaise de Pediatrie. Jahrbuch fur Kinderheilkunde. Major Am. Red Cross, World War. Mem. Assn. of Am. Physicians, Am. Pediatric Soc., Acad. of Pediatrics, Soc. Clin. Investigation, A.A.A.S., Am. Soc. Exptl. Pathology, Soc. Exptl. Biology and Medicine, Interurban Clin. Club, Brit. Pediatric Assn., Alpha Delta Phi. Decorated Order of Leopold (Belgium), 1919; Reconnaissance Francaise (France), 1919. Contbr. on rickets, deformities of the skull, physiology of the thymus gland. Home: Birdwood, Garrison, Md. Office: Johns Hopkins Hosp., Baltimore 5, MD

PARK, ROYAL WHEELER headmaster; b. Kaufman, Tex., June 20, 1897; s. James Walter and Lyda Matilda (Thompson) P.; student Southern Meth. U., 1915-16, Army and Navy Sch., 1916-17; B.S., U.S. Mil. Acad., 1919; grad. Inf. Sch., 1920; M.A., Stanford U., 1931; m. Katherine Alice Blake, May 8, 1925. Commd. 2d lt. U.S.A., Nov. 1, 1918; 1st lt. inf., 1920; comdg. company, and battalion adj., 4th Inf., 1920-22; with 7th Inf., June 30-Sept. 28, 1922 (resigned); comdt. of cadets, Palo Alto Mil. Acad. and Urban Mil. Acad., 1923-25; founder and headmaster of Pacific Coast Mil. Acad., Menlo Park, Calif., 1925-35; founder and headmaster Park Mil. Acad., Menlo Park, Calif., 1935—. Maj. of inf., Calif. N.G., Sept. 1924—. Methodist. Mason. Home: Menlo Park, Calif. Died Mar. 1, 1941.

PARKE, BENJAMIN territorial del. to Congress, jurist; b. N.J., Sept. 22, 1777; m. Eliza Barton, 2 children. Moved to Lexington, Ky., 1797; admitted to Ky. bar, circa 1800; moved to Vincennes, Ind. Territory, 1804-08; elected to 1st Ind. Territorial Legislature, 1805; 1st del. to U.S. Congress from Ind. Territory, Dec. 12, 1805-Mar. 1, 1808; mem. staff Gov. William Henry Harrison; territorial judge, 1808-17; del. Ind. Constl. Conv., 1816, responsible for adoption provisions which became basis of state pub. sch. system, 1816; served with Ind. Militia, 1801-11, raised a dragoon (cavalry) company which saw action at Battle of Tippecanoe, 1811; became maj. of cavalry; served as Indian agt. and U.S. commr. in drawing up land treaties with Indians, especially St. Marys (O.) Treaty deeding central Ind. to White settlement, 1818; judge U.S. Dist. Ct., 1817-35; 1st pres. Ind. Hist. Soc.; chmn. bd. trustees Vincennes U. Died Salem, Ind., July 12, 1835; buried Crown Hill Cemetery, Salem.

PARKE, JOHN army officer, poet; b. Dover, Del., Apr. 7, 1754; s. Thomas Parke; A.B., Coll. of Phila. (now U. Pa.), 1771, A.M., 1775. Apptd. asst. q.m. gen. Continental Army, Cambridge, Mass., 1775; lt. col. artificers, N.Y.C., 1776. Author: The Lyric Works of Horace, Translated into English Verse: to Which Are Added, a Number of Original Poems, by a Native of America, 1786. Died Kent County, Del., Dec. 11, 1789.

PARKE, JOHN GRUBB engineer-soldier; b. Chester Co., Pa., Sept. 22, 1827; grad. West Point, 1849; assigned to topographical engrs.; engaged in boundary surveys for Govt. until 1861. Promoted capt. topographical engrs., Sept. 9, 1861; apptd. brig. gen. vols., Nov. 23, 1861; served in Burnside's expedition to N.C.; bvtd. lt. col. U.S. army; promoted maj. gen. vols.; chief of staff under Burnside; reached bvt. rank maj. gen., U.S. army; commd. maj. engrs., June 17, 1864; lt. col., Mar. 4, 1879; col., Mar. 7, 1884; retired, 1889; supt. Mil. Acad., West Point, 1887-89. Author: Explorations and Surveys for a Railroad Route from the Mississippi River to the Pacific Ocean. Died 1900.

PARKER, ALEXANDER WILSON, lawyer; b. Franklin, Va., June 21, 1898; s. John Crafford and Emily Virginia (Norfleet) P.; A.B., Va. Mil. Inst., 1918; LL.B., U. Va., 1923; m. Mary S. McDaniel, June 28, 1924 (dec. June 1959); children—Douglas (Mrs. John Moncure), Emily (Mrs. Edward T. Lemmon, Jr.), Dorothy (Mrs. Robert E. Hale); m. 2d, Elizabeth Taylor Valentine, July 1, 1960; stepchildren—Elizabeth (Mrs. Thomas Wood), Frederick S. Valentine III. Admitted to Va. bar, 1923; counsel Atlantic Life Ins. Co., Richmond, Va., 1925-29; joined firm Christian, Barton, Parker, Epps & Brent, Richmond, 1929, now partner; spl. counsel of Barbara Powers, wife of U-2 pilot Francis Gary Powers at Moscow trial, 1960. Sec., dir., gen. counsel Thalhimer Bros. Inc., Richmond, 1947-72; dir., gen. counsel Broad-Grace Arcade Corp., Richmond, 1946-72; dir. Miller Hofft, Inc. Pres., dir. Richmond War and Community Fund, 1939; v.p. Va. Tb Assn., 1941, Va. Cancer Soc., 1941. Mem. Va. Democratic Central Com. Served as gunnery sgt., U.S. Marine Flying Corps, World War I; lt. comdr., air combat intelligence officer USNR, 1943-45; P.T.O. Mem. Am., Va. (pres. 1951-52), Richmond (past pres.) bar assns., Am. Judicature Soc., Internat. Assn. Ins. Counsel, Soc. Cincinnati, Am. Law Inst., Assn. Life Ins. Counsel, Am. Life Conv., Inst. Jud. Adminstrn., U. Va. Law Sch. Assn. (pres. 1958-59), Navy League U.S. (past pres. Va. council), Va., Richmond chambers commerce, Res. Officers Assn., Mil. Order Caraboa, Soc. Colonial Wars, Sigma Chi. Democrat. Episcopalian (past vestryman). Clubs: Deep Run Hunt (dir.), Commonwealth (past mem. bd. govs.). Home: Richmond VA Died July 11, 1972.

PARKER, AMASA JUNIUS lawyer; b. Delhi, N.Y., May 6, 1843; s. Judge Amasa Junius and Harriet Langdon (Roberts) P.; A.B., Union Coll., 1863, A.M., 1866, LL.D., 1904; LL.B., Albany Law Sch., 1864; m. Cornelia Kane Strong, 1868 (died 1883). Admitted to bar, and law partner with father, 1865-90; mem. N.Y. Assembly, 1882, Senate, 1886-87, 1892-93, 1894-95. A.-d.-c. and maj. 3d Div., N.G.S. N.Y., 1866; lt.-col., 1875; col. 10th Regt. Inf., 1877; gen. of its 3d Brigade, 1886-91. Chief organizer and pres. Nat. Guard Assn., 1878-80; during service in assembly compiled mil. code of State of N.Y.; drafted, 1894, and secured passage in Senate and Assembly, or a joint resolution calling upon Congress to provide the Nat. Guard of states with modern magazine rifles and ammunition, but the officers in charge of the resolution failed in their duty, and as a result thousands of Nat. Guard troops entered the Spanish-American War in 1898 with old weapons and black powder while Spanish troops were armed with modern weapons and smokeless powder. Rank of major general on retired list conferred by special act of legislature of N.Y., 1933. Trustee Albany Law School, and president board nearly 25 years; alumni trustee Union Coll. and gov. Union U. many yrs.; trustee Albany Med. Coll.; 16 yrs. trustee Union Trust Co. of New York; 16 yrs. mgr. and pres. bd. mgrs. Hudson River State Hosp. for Insane, Poughkeepsie, N.Y. Democrat. Episcopalian. Mem. Kappa Alpha. Clubs: Ft. Orange, University, Country. Home: 143 Washington Av., Albany, N.Y. Died May 2, 1938.

PARKER, BENJAMIN FRANKLIN secretary; b. Conneaughtville, Pa., July 27, 1839; s. Ledyard and Hannah (Thompson) P.; ed. Meadville (Pa.) pub. schs. and Acad.; pvt. to 1st lt. U.S.V., 1861-65, participating in battles of 2d Bull Run, Missionary Ridge, etc.; m. Lucille W. Penniman, Feb. 3, 1868. Served lt. to lt. col. Wis. N.G., 28 yrs.; lt. col. 3d Wis. Inf., Spanish-Am. War, serving in Puerto Rico. Past Grand Master Ancient Order United Workmen of Wis.; Internat. Sec. Internat. Order of Good Templars, 1885-1908. Grand Sec. of Wis., 1873-1900, and from 1909. Home: Milwaukee, Wis. Died Jan. 24, 1912.

PARKER, CHARLES A(MES) assn. exec.; b. Lynnfield Center, Mass., June 10, 1909; s. Bertram Munson and Mina Mary (Hoeffling) P.; diploma Tabor Acad., 1926; B. Indsl. Engring., Northeastern U., 1930; F.C.C. comml. radio lecense, F.C.C. amateur operators license, Gulf Radio Sch., 1931. Sales Curtiss-Wright Flying Service, 1929; treas., dir. Hyannis Airport Corp., 1933-37; v.p., dir. sales Inter-City Aviation, Inc., 1936-41, Eastern Aviation, Inc., 1941-42; with Robinson Aviation, Inc., aircraft distbrs., 1946-48; exec. dir. Nat. Aviation Trades Assn. since 1949. Mem. air coordinating com. Aviation Industry Adv. Panel; air transportation adv. panel Fed. Civil Def. Adminstrn.; civil aviation air def. adv. com. Joint Civil Aeros. Adminstrn.-USAF Air Def. Planning Bd.; industry adv. com. Airport Use Panel of Air Coordinating Com. Served as maj. Air Transport Command, Hdqrs. USAAF, 1942-45. Recipient Certificate of Merit, 3rd Ann. Amvets., 1954. Mem. Nat. Aviation Trades Assn. (v.p., 1947-48), Amvets, National Air Taxi Conference (exec. vice president), Aviation Writers Assn., Am. Radio Relay League, Nat. Aeronautic Assn., Aircraft Owners and Pilots Assn. Editor of NATA-Operators Washington News Letter and the Aerial Applicators Washington Release (monthly) since 1949. Contbr. nat. aviation trade jours. Home: 327 Ocean St., Hyannis, Mass. Office: 1346 Connecticut Av., Washington 6. Died Apr. 21, 1959; buried Beechwood Cemetery, Centerville, Mass.

PARKER, CHARLES MORTON pres. Am. Radiator Co.; b. Charleston, Ill., June 1, 1868; s. George W. and Nellie (Ferguson) P.; C.E. Rensselaer Poly. Inst., 1889. Began in employ of Rio Grande Western R.R., 1890; became connected with Am. Radiator Co. as foundryman, 1899, then sec. to exec. com., European dir., 1901-08, treas., 1908-13, later pres. Served as maj. Air Service, with A.E.F., World War. Home: New York, N.Y. Died Sept. 27, 1934.

PARKER, CHARLES WOLCOTT judge; b. Newark, N.J., Oct. 22, 1862; s. Hon. Cortlandt and Elisabeth Wolcott (Stites) P.; A.B., Princeton, 1882, A.M., 1885, LL.D., 1919; LL.B., Columbia, 1885; m. Emily Fuller, Nov. 22, 1893; children—Charles W. (dec.), Dudley F., Philip M., Elinor M., Robert M. (dec.). Practiced at Newark, 1885-90, later at Bayonne City and Jersey City; judge 2d Dist. Court, Jersey City, 1898-1903; judge New Jersey Circuit Court, 1903-07; justice Supreme Court of N.J., 1907-47; retired since Sept. 15, 1947. Supervising editor New Jersey Digest, 1907. Private, corporal and sergt. Essex Troop, of Newark, 1890-99; 1st lt. and capt. 4th N.J. Regt., 1899-1902; lt. col. and a.-a.-g. of N.J., 1902-07; a.-d.-c. on staff of Gov. Franklin Murphy. Pres. emeritus N.J. Hist. Soc.; ex-gov. Soc. Colonial Wars; mem. S.R., Founders and Patriots, N.J. State Bar Assn. Republican. Episcopalian (chancellor Diocese of Newark). Clubs: University (N.Y. City); Essex (Newark); Morris County Golf. Home: 63 Macculloch Av. Address: 19 South St., Morristown, N.J. Died Jan. 23, 1948.

PARKER, CORTLANDT army officer; b. Fort Apache, Ariz., Dec. 10, 1884; s. Major Gen. James and Charlotte (Condit) P.; student Newark (N.J.) Acad., 1897-1902; B.S., U.S. Mil. Acad., 1906; grad. Army Sch. of the Line, 1922, Army Staff Sch., 1923, Army War Coll., 1924; m. Elizabeth Gray, Nov. 11, 1918; children—Cortlandt, James. Commd. 2d lt., 5th Cav., U.S. Army, 1906, and advanced through the grades to maj. gen., 1942; retired 1946; with 6th F.A., 1907-13; other assignments in U.S. and Philippines, 1913-16; with 6th F.A. went to France with 1st Div., A.E.F., 1917; dir. training artillery, Camp Coëtquidan, 4 mos.; lt. col. and adj. F.A. Brigade, Feb.-Mar. 1918; comd. 6th F.A. Regt., Cantigny and Soissons, Apr.-July 1918; assigned 57th F.A., 19th Div., in U.S.; dir. gunnery dept. F.A. Sch., 1919-21; War Dept. Gen. Staff, 1924-28; mil. attaché Am. embassy, London, 1931-35; Hawaii, 1936-38; comd. 19th F.A., 5th Div., 1939-40; comd. div. arty, to May 1941, 5th Div. to June 1943 (last 15 mos. in Iceland); comdr. Southern Calif. sector, 1943-45. Decorated D.S.M., Silver Star, Legion of Merit. (U.S.), French Fourragère, Officer Legion of Honor (France). Mem. Soc. 1st Div., 5th Div., Cincinnati Club: Army-Navy Country (Washington). Address: Greenvale Farm, Newport, R.I.; also 51 Chestnut St., Boston. Died Jan. 19, 1960.

PARKER, DAINGERFIELD brig. gen.; b. New Rochelle, N.Y., May 23, 1832; s. Foxhall Alexander, Sr. (commodore U.S.N.) and Sara Jay Bogardus P.; of old Va. Parker family; ed. various leading schs. and acads.; m. Amelia Nisbet, 1861. Served as subaltern and capt., 3d U.S. Inf., Apr. 26, 1861-Apr. 14, 1884; maj. 9th Inf. to May 15, 1889; lt. col. 20th and 13th Inf. to Nov. 26, 1894; col. 18th Inf. to May 23, 1896, when retired for age; promoted brig. gen. U.S.A. retired, by act of Apr. 23, 1904. Participated in battles of 1st and 2d Bull Run, Antietam, Fredericksburg, Chancellorsville, Gettysburg (where won bvt.), and comd. Fort Slocum in Early's attack on Washington; comd. 3d Inf., at times, during Civ. War; afterward comd. Mil. Prison, St. Louis. Comd. troops at opening of Cherokee strip. Episcopalian. Home: Washington, D.C. Died Feb. 25, 1925.

PARKER, ELY SAMUEL (Indian name: Do-ne-ho-ga-wa, or Keeper of the Western Door of the Long House of the Iroquois) Indian chief; b. Indian Falls, Pembroke, N.Y., 1828; s. William and Elizabeth Parker (Indian names: Jo-no-es-do-wa and Ga-ont-gwut-turus); attended Rensselaer Poly. Inst.; m. Minnie Sackett, Dec. 25, 1867. Represented his people in prosecuting Indian claims, Washington, D.C.; chief of Seneca Indian tribe, 1852; gave Lewis Morgan important help in preparing 1st sci. study of Indian tribe, published as League of the Ho-de-no-sau-nee Iorquois, 1851; supt. constrn. for govt. works, Galena, Ill., 1857-62; commd. capt. of engrs., 1863; div. engr. 7th Div., 17th Corps, U.S. Army; commd. lt. col. and Grant's mil. sec., 1864; transcribed ofcl. copies of document ending Civil War; commd. brig. gen. U.S. Volunteers, 1865; brevetted capt., maj., lt. col., col., brig. gen., 1867; commr. Indian affairs, commd. by Grant, 1869; tried by U.S. Ho. of Reps. on charges of defrauding govt., acquitted, 1871. Died Fairfield, Conn., Aug. 31, 1895; buried Forest Lawn Cemetery, Buffalo, N.Y.

PARKER, FOXHALL ALEXANDER naval officer; b. N.Y.C., Aug. 5, 1821; s. Foxhall Alexander and Sarah (Bogardus) P.; m. Mary Greene, Feb. 10, 1846; m. 2d, Lydia Mallory, Nov. 2, 1853; m. 3d, Caroline Donaldson, Oct. 20, 1863; 10 children. Apptd. midshipman U.S. Navy, 1839, commd. lt., 1850; exec. officer Washington (D.C.) Navy Yard, 1861; manned Ft. Ellsworth, Alexandria, for defense of Washington, 1861; comdr., 1862; commanded ship Mahaska, sr. officer in operation against Matthews Court House, 1862; commd. capt., 1866; commanded ship Franklin, European Squadron, 1870-71; chief of staff North Atlantic Fleet, 1872, drew up new signal code for steam tactics; commd. commodore, 1872; chief signal officer, 1873-76; in charge of Boston Navy Yard, 1876-78; supt. Naval Acad.; chmn. com. organizing U.S. Naval Inst., 1873, pres., 1878. Author: Squadron Tactics under Steam, 1864; Fleet Tactics under Steam, 1870; The Naval Howitzer Ashore, 1865; Th Naval Howitzer Afloat (latter two used as textbooks), 1866. Died Annapolis, Md., June 10, 1879.

PARKER, FRANCIS LEJAU, army officer; b. Abbeville, S.C., June 24, 1873; s. William H. and Lucia G. P.; grad. U.S. Mil. Acad., 1894; honor grad. Army Sch. of the Line, 1908; grad. Army Staff Coll., 1909, Army War Coll., 1920; unmarried. Commd. 2d lt. 5th Cav., U.S. Army, 1894; advanced through grades to brig. gen., 1933; col. and brig. gen. Nat. Army, 1917-19. Instr., U.S. Mil. Acad., 1897-98, and Gen. Service Schs., 1904-07; duty in Cuba, 1898-99, Puerto Rico, 1899-1900, Philippine Islands, 1901, 1903-04, 1910-12, 1931 and 1934-36, China, 1912, and Colo. coal strike, 1914-15; mem. bd. to revise cav. drill regulations, 1915-16; a.-d.-c. to Brig. Gen. L.H. Carpenter, to Brig Gen. George W. Davis, and to Gov. Gen. W. Cameron Forbes, P.I.; Gen. Staff Corps, 1915-17 and 1920-21; mil. observer with Roumanian armies, 1916-17; mil. attache, Petrograd. and mil. observer with Russian armies, June-Aug. 1917. Comdr. 119th Inf., 30th Div., Jan.-Apr. 1918, 312th Cav., Apr.-May 1918, 171st Inf. Brigade, A.E.F., Aug.-Nov. 1918; with 2d sect. Gen. Staff, Hdqrs. A.E.F., Nov. 1918-June 1919; comdr. 1st Cav., 1920-21; chief of staff 6th Division, Jan.-July, 1921; mil. attache, Mexico, 1921-23; detailed in F.A., 1923-26; comdr. 12th F.A., July-Nov. 1924; with U.S.-Mexico Mixed Claims Commn., Dec. 1924-Dec. 1925; with Tacna-Arica Arbitration Commn., Dec. 1925-June 1926; in Inspr. Gen.'s Dept., Oct. 1926-Dec. 1927; vice-chmn. Nat. Bd. of Elections, Nicaragua, 1928; chief of Bur. Insular Affairs, with rank of brig. gen., Jan. 1929-Jan. 1933, continuing as acting chief to Aug. 1933; comdr. 2d F.A. Brig., Oct. 1933-May 1934; comdr. Ft. Stotsenberg, P.I., 1934-36; comdr. 1st Cav. Div., Sept. 1936; retired from active service, 1936. Clubs: Army and Navy, Army and Navy Country (Washington, D.C.); Army and Navy (Manila); Charleston. Home: 14 Lamboll St., Charleston 2 SC

PARKER, FRANCIS WAYLAND pres. Chicago Inst., 1899—; b. Beford, N.H., Oct. 9, 1837; s. Robert and Mille (Rand) P.; reared on farm; ed. village school and acads.; had charge of schools in N.H. and Ill. until 1861. Served through Civil War, pvt. to col. 4th N.H. vols.; severely wounded at Deep Bottom, James River; mustered out, Aug. 1865. Prin. grammar school, Manchester, N.H., 1865-68; Normal School, Dayton, O., 1868-72; supt. schools, Quincy, Mass., 1875-80; a supervisor of schools, Boston, 1880-83; prin. Cook Co. Normal School (Ill.), 1883-96. Principal Chicago Normal School, 1896-99. Studied psychology, philosophy, history and pedagogy, King William's Univ., Berlin, 1872-75 (A.M., Dartmouth; LL.D., Lawrence Univ.). Author: How to Study Geography, 1889; Uncle Robert's Geographies. Home: Chicago, Ill. Died 1902.

PARKER, FRANK army officer; b. Georgetown County, S.C., Sept. 21, 1872; s. Arthur Middleton and Emma Izard (Middleton) P.; grad. U.S. Mil. Acad., 1894; grad. Cav. Sch., Saumur, France, 1904; LL.D., U. of South Carolina, 1927, Mich. State Coll., Agr. and Applied Science, 1933; m. Katherine Hamilton Lahm, November 20, 1906; children—Katherine Lahm, Ann Middleton. 2d Lieut 5th Cav., U.S. Army, 1894; promoted through grades to major general, 1929; brig. general (temp.) (World War), 1918-19. At Tampa, Fla., during Spanish-Am. War, 1898; in Puerto Rico, 1898-1900; instr. U.S. Mil. Acad., 1900-03; student at French cav. sch., 1903-04; mil. attaché, Caracas, Venezuela, 1904-05, Buenos Aires, Argentina, 1905-06, in Cuba, 1906-08; instr. and organizer of cav., Cuba, 1909-12; at École Supérieure de Guerre, France, 1912; mem. Cav. Bd., 1913-14; again at École Supérieure de Guerre, 1914-15; observer with French armies in field, 1916-17, chief of Am. Mil. Mission at French Gen. Hdqrs., Apr.-Dec. 1917; comdr. 18th Inf. and 1st Inf. Brigade (both of 1st Div.); apptd. comdr. 1st Div., A.E.F., Oct. 17, 1918, and recommended for promotion to maj. gen. by Gen. Pershing, but Armistice stopped all promotions of gen. officers; grad. École Superieure de Guerre, France, 1920; asst. prof. and student in École Supérieure de Guerre and centre des Hautes Études, 1920-21; grad. and instr. Command and Staff Sch., Leavenworth, 1923; grad. and instr. Army War Coll., 1923-24; comd. 2d Brigade, 1st Div., 1925-27; asst. chief of staff U.S. Army, 1927-29; comdr. 6th Corps Area, 1929-32, 2d Army, 1932-33, Philippine Dept., 1933-35, 1st Div., Feb.-Mar. 1936; 8th Corps Area and 3d Army,.Mar.-Sept. 1936; retired, September 30, 1936. Executive director Illinois War Council, 1942-45. Awarded D.S.M.; 2 silver star citations U.S.); Comdr. Legion of Honor (France); Comdr. Order of the Crown (Belgium); War Cross with 3 palms (France); Order of Military Merit (Cuba); Grand Cross Order of Crown (Italy); Comdr. Order of Polonia Restituta; Order of St. Olaf, Norway (first class). Comdr. Dept. of Philippine Islands, Am. Legion, 1934-35; mem. nat. exec. com., Am. Legion, 1939-44; mem. Am. Legion 5 yrs. Commn. on Postwar America, 1943-48. Mem. Nat. exec. com. and Nat. defense com., Am. Legion, 1939-41; mission to Gt. Britain (Am. Legion), 1941. Memorialized by National Convention, American Legion, Sept. 20, 1944. Awarded Certificate for Meritorious Service by U.S. Office Civilian Defense, 1945. Home: Union League Club, 65 W. Jackson Blvd. Office: 188 W. Randolph St., Chicago, Ill. Died Mar. 13, 1947.

PARKER, H. WAYNE, govt. ofcl.; b. Newago County, Mich., Dec. 3, 1904; s. Ernest E. and Ella M. (Stevens) P.; grad. high sch.; m. Marjorie Rice, Mar. 15, 1947; children—Elaine (Mrs. Frank Shaw). John Wayne, James Edward, Thomas Jethro. Asst. paymaster Bissell Carpet Sweeper Co., Grand Rapids, Mich., 1922-46, asst. traffic mgr., 1923-46; life ins. agt. Mut. Benefit Life Ins. Co. of Newark, Grand Rapids, 1946-54; postmaster Grand Rapids Post Office, 1954-67; mem. Gent County Bd. Suprs., Grand Rapids, 1952-54. Pres., Union High Sch. Community Council, Grand Rapids, 1937-38; mem. traffic squad Grand Rapids, 1940-61, capt., 1948-49; mem. Grand Rapids Pub. Recreation Bd., 1938-48; chmn. Individual Gifts div. Grand Rapids Community Chest, 1935-40; chmn. individual gifts A.R.C., 1946; team capt. U.S.O. fund drive, 1940-41; team capt., joint YWCA-YMCA drive, 1951; co-chmn. individual 1941; chmn. membership campaign Grand Rapids Civic Theater, 1940, 46, 65; Kent County chmn. Mich. Week, 1965, 66; mem. exec. bd. Kent County Tb Soc. Campaign chmn. Harry Kelly for Gov., Kent County, 1950, Fred Alger for Gov., Kent County, 1952; campaign exec. Republican campaign for Eisenhower, 1952. Bd. dirs. Grand Rapids Community Concert Assn., pres., 1952-53; adv. bd. Grand Rapids Citizens for Decent Literature; mem. adv. com. Aquinas Coll. Served from specialist 1st class to chief specialist, USNR, 1942-45. Recipient Distinguished Service award Grand Rapids Jr. C. of C., 1940. Mem. Nat. Assn. Postmasters (past pres., past sec.-treas.), Am. Bus. Club (past pres., dist. gov. Grand Rapids chpt.), Am. Legion, Grand Rapids Assn. Life Underwriters (past treas., past sec., past v.p. past pres.), Grand Rapids Jr. C. of C. (past 2d v.p., past 1st v.p., past chmn. "Cheers for Victory" program). Conglist. (past deacon, past pres. men's club). Mason (Shriner, Scottish Rite). Clubs: Rotarian (past v.p., past program chmn. Grand Rapids), Grand Rapids Breakfast (sec.). Home: Grand Rapids MI Died June 4, 1967.

PARKER, HILON ADELBERT engineer; b. Plessis, N.Y., Dec. 30, 1841; s. Alpheus and Lucinda P., of Revolutionary stock; acad. edn.; m. Mary E. Cunningham, May 25, 1871 (dec.); 2d, Grace Rowley, Nov. 1894. Served pvt. to 1st lt., 1861-65; fought at Cold Harbor, Petersburg, Shenandoah Valley, Richmond, etc. Entered ry. service, 1866; held various positions, 1866-85; v.p. and chief engr. Chicago, Kansas & Neb. Ry., 1885-89, also gen. mgr., 1888; asst. to the pres. C.,R.I.&P. Ry., 1889-90, and 1893-98, 3d v.p. 1890-93, 2d v.p. 1898-99, 1st v.p. and gen. mgr. Mar. 1899-Apr. 1903; resigned; cons. engr. Grand Trunk Pacific Ry., 1909. Home: Chicago, Ill. Died 1911.

PARKER, HOMER CLING ins. commr.; b. Baxley, Ga., Sept. 25, 1885; s. William Cling and Sarah Belle (Mattox) P.; B.L., Mercer U., 1908; m. Annie Laurie Mallary, Nov. 9, 1910 (died Nov. 15, 1916); children—

Martha Lewis, Helen Isabel, William Mallary; m. 2d, Lenore L. Leedom, Oct. 15, 1922 (divorced); m. 3d, Wilhelmina Lowe, Jan. 26, 1942. Practiced law Statesboro, 1908-27; solicitor, City Court, Statesboro, 1914-17; mayor of Statesboro, 1924-27; elected mem. 72d Congress, Sept. 1931, to fill vacancy, and reelected to 73d Congress (1933-35), 1st Ga. Dist.; comptroller-general of Ga., June 1936-Jan. 1937; comptroller gen. and insurance commr. State of Ga., term 1941-42, re-elected for term, 1943-46. Cadet Officers Training Camp, Ft. McPherson, Ga., May-Aug. 1917; served as capt. inf., maj., judge advocate A.U.S., 1917-20; capt. regular army, 1920-22; maj., judge advocate Reserve Corps, 1922-28; adj. gen. Ga. Nat. Guard, 1927-31 (retired). Mem. Phi Delta Theta. Democrat. Baptist. Mason, Eagle, Elk. W.O.W. Home: 1097 Briarcliff Pl., N.E. Office: State Capitol, Atlanta, Ga. Died June 22, 1946.

PARKER, JAMES officer U.S.A.; b. Newark, N.J., Feb. 20, 1854; s. Hon. Cortlandt and Elisabeth Wolcott (Stites) P.; student Phillips Acad., Andover, and Rutgers Coll.; grad. U.S. Mil. Acad., 1876; A.M., Rutgers, 1878; m. Charlotte M. Condit, 1879. Second lt. 4th Cav., June 15, 1876; promoted through grades to brig. gen., Mar. 3, 1913; maj. gen. N.A., Aug. 5, 1917. Served in Indian Ty., 1876-77, Mexican border disturbances (Tex.), 1878-79, Ute campaign, Colo., 1879-81, Geronimo Apache campaign, Ariz., 1885-86; instr. cav., West Point, 1894-98; served in Spanish-Am. War and Philippine insurrection, 1898-1901; a.-a.-g., Washington, 1901-03; adj. gen. Northern Div. U.S.A., 1904-05; dir. Cav. Sch., Ft. Riley, Kan., 1905-06; with Cuban army of pacification, 1906-09; comdg. 11th Cav., Ft. Oglethorpe, Ga., 1909-12; in Europe on cav. reorganization bd., Sept. to Dec. 1912; assigned as comdr. 1st Cav. Brigade, San Antonio, Tex., Mar. 25, 1913; comd. mobilization troops, Brownsville Dist., Tex., 1916; comdr. 1st Provisional Inf. Div.. Camp Wilson, Tex., 1917; comd. and trained all troops in Dept. of Tex., May-Aug. 1917; comd. 32d Div. (Mich. and Wis. troops) to Dec. 1917, 85th Div. (Mich. and Wis. troops), to Feb. 20, 1918; on observation duty in France, Oct., Nov. 1917; in action nr. Armentiéres, nr. St. Quentin and at Chemin des Dames, Oct. 1917; retired by operation of law, Feb. 20, 1918. Pres. bd. charged with revision small arms firing regulations, 1904; bd. which revised cav. drill regulations, 1902; in charge Militia Div., War Dept., 1903-04; recommended for bvts. for gallantry in action at San Mateo, Manaoag, and Vigan, P.I., 1899; awarded Congressional Medal of Honor "for distinguished gallantry" at Vigan, P.I., Dec. 4, 1899, and silver stars for gallantry in 3 actions; D.S.M. for services in World War. Author: The Mounted Rifleman, 1916; The Old Army, Memories, 1929. Home: Newport, R.I. Died June 2, 1934.

PARKER, JAMES EDMUND army officer; b. Anniston, Ala., Aug. 9, 1896; s. William Edmund and Margaret (Dothard) P.; student Ala. Presbyn. Coll., 1912-15, Ala. Poly. Inst., 1915-16, Marion Mil. Inst., 1916-17; B.S., U.S. Mil. Acad., 1919; grad. F.A. Sch., 1920, Air Corps Training Sch., 1921, Air Corps Engring. Sch., 1933, Air Corps Tactical Sch., 1936; m. Florence Olsen, Dec. 11, 1920; children—Shirley, James Edmund. Commd. 2d lt., Nov. 1918, 2d lt., F.A., June 12, 1919, and advanced through the grades to maj. gen., Nov. 7, 1944; now comdg. gen. 4th Air Force, San Francisco, Calif. Mason. Clubs: Olympic, Bohemian, Presidio Golf. Address: 341 Infantry Terrace, Presidio of S.F., San Francisco, Calif. Died Mar. 19, 1946.

PARKER, JOEL gov. N.J., jurist; b. Freehold, N.J., Nov. 24, 1816; s. Charles and Sarah (Coward) P.; grad. Coll. of N.J. (now Princeton), 1839; LL.D. (hon.), Rutgers Coll., 1872; m. Maria Gummere, 1843, at least 3 children. Admitted to N.J. bar, 1842; mem. N.J. Legislature (Democrat) from Monmouth County, 1847-51; pros. atty., 1852-57; brig. gen. N.J. Militia, 1857; Dem. presdl. elector, 1860; gov. N.J., 1863-66, opposed move in Congress to secure use of roadway of Raritan & Delaware Bay R.R. for War Dept., helped supply troops for Civil War, sponsored establishment of sinking fund for redemption of war loans; gov. N.J., 1872-75; atty. gen. N.J., Jan.-Apr. 1875; judge N.J. Supreme Ct., 1880-88. Died Phila., Jan. 2, 1888.

PARKER, JOHN army officer; b. Lexington, Mass., July 13, 1729; s. Josiah and Anna (Stone) P.; m. Lydia Moore, May 25, 1755; 7 children. Engaged in farming; served at battles of Louisburg and Quebec during French and Indian War; capt. co. of Mass. Minutemen at outbreak of Revolutionary War; assembled group of 130 men to defend the house in which John Hancock and Samuel Adams were staying, Lexington (8 Americans were killed, 10 wounded when British attacked), Apr. 1775; led force in pursuit of British as far as Concord, Mass.; became too ill to serve in Battle of Bunker Hill. Died the following autumn, Sept. 17, 1775.

PARKER, JOHN HENRY army officer; b. nr. Tipton, Mo., Sept. 19, 1866; s. Thomas H. and Nancy (Maxey) P.; grad. U.S. Mil. Acad., 1892; admitted to Mo. bar, 1896; m. Ida Burr, Sept. 22, 1892; children—Mrs. Naidene Calvert, Henry Burr; m. 2d, Bertha E. (Blair) Bortell, July 13, 1935. Second lt. 13th Inf., U.S. Army, 1892; promoted through grades to col., July 1, 1920; retired Feb. 28, 1924; promoted to brig. gen. (retired), 1941. Comd. Gatling Gun Battery, Santiago, Cuba, 1898; hon. mem. Roosevelt's Rough Riders' Assn., 1898; in Philippines, 1899-1901, and was asst. to chief judge advocate; devised in 1903, and organized at Ft. Leavenworth, Kan., the first Model Machine Gun Detachment, U.S. Army, made permanent by Gen. Order 16, War Dept., Jan. 22, 1904. Adviser to gov. of Matanzas Province, Cuba, during second Cuban intervention, and in charge of municipal improvements of province; 1908 on spl. duty organizing first Model of Unit of Machine Guns (a company) for duty with a regt. of inf., and writing necessary texts for future development of machine gun service for infantry; judge advocate, punitive expdn. to Mex., 1916; went to France as machine gun expert on Gen. Pershing's Staff, May 1917; mem. gen. staff com. on orgn. A.E.F.; organized 1st Div. and 1st Corps automatic weapons schools at Gondrecourt, army automatic weapons schools at Langres; col. 102d Inf. (Charter Oak Regt.) at Chavignon, at Chemin des Dames, at Seicheprey, at Bois de Jury, and at Château-Thierry; col. 362d Inf. (Pine Tree Regt.) at Bois de Cheppy, at Epinonville, at Gesnes; organized and comd. Am. garrison in Paris, Jan.-June 1919. Put over vocational training with aid of Red Cross, Y.M.C.A., K. of C., and Salvation Army, for the first time in Am. Army. Thrice wounded in France. Gold medallist, Mil. Service Instn., 1911; awarded D.S.M.; citations in orders of 26th (Yankee) Div. for "gallantry in action" in 12 combats; Croix de Guerre with palm; Officer Legion of Honor; Distinguished Service Cross with two oak leaves; third oak leaf awarded, 1923; Commandeur Ordre de l'Étoile Noire; recommended for brig. gen. for services in battle. Author: Gatlings at Santiago, 1898; Tactical Uses and Organization of Machine Guns in the Field, 1898; Trained Citizen Soldiery, 1915. Also author of slogan "The Army Trains Young Men for Peace," 1920. Judge advocate Dept. of Com., Disabled Vets. of World War, 1936-37. Home: Garde Hotel, New Haven, Conn. Died Oct. 13, 1942.

PARKER, JOSEPH BENSON rear admiral U.S.N.; b. Carlisle, Pa., June 20, 1841; s. Rev. Joseph and Mary (Sheerer) P.; A.B., Dickinson Coll., 1860, A.M., 1863; M.D., Bellevue Hosp. Med. Coll., 1862; m. Margaret J. Yorke, Oct. 1868. Appt. asst. surgeon U.S.N., Mar., 1863; advanced through various grades to med. dir., and retired, June 20, 1903, with rank of rear-admiral. Served on Asiatic Pacific, West India stas. and at various navy yards and hosps. Home: Philadelphia, Pa. Died Oct. 21, 1915.

PARKER, LEONARD FLETCHER college prof.; b. Arcade, N.Y., Aug. 3, 1825; s. Elias and Dorothy F. (Fletcher) P.; A.B., Oberlin, 1851, A.M., 1860 (D.D., 1895); Oberlin Theol. Sem., 1851-53; m. Sarah C. Pearse, Aug. 21, 1853; m. 2d, Mrs. Nellie Greene Clarke, Aug. 19, 1903. Supt. schs., Brownsville, Pa., 1853-56, Grinnell, Ia., 1856-60; ordained Congl. ministry, 1862; prof. Greek, Iowa (now Grinnell) Coll., 1860-70; prof. history, State U. of Ia., 1870-87; Parker prof. history, 1888-98 (emeritus), Iowa Coll. First lt. Co. B, 46th Ia. Inf., May-Sept. 1864; mem. Ia. Ho. of Rep., 1868-70. Republican. Author: History of Education of Iowa, No. 17 of state monographs for U.S. Bur. of Edn., 1890; History of Poweshiek County, Iowa, 1911. Home: Grinnell, Ia. Died 19—.

PARKER, SEVERN EYRE congressman; b. nr. Eastville, Va., July 19, 1787; attended common schs.; studied law. Admitted to the bar, practiced law; held local offices; mem. Va. Ho. of Dels., 1809-12, 28-29, 34-36; dep. clk. Northampton County (Va.), 1813; served as capt. of a rifle co., 1814; mem. Va. Senate, 1817-20; mem. U.S. Ho. of Reps. from Va., 16th Congress, 1819-21. Died Northampton County, Oct. 21, 1836; buried nr. Eastville.

PARKER, STANLEY V., officer U.S. Coast Guard; b. Cincinnati, O., Oct. 26, 1885; s. Samuel Boardman and Elizabeth Helen (Chappell) P.; student Tech. Sch. of Cincinnati, 1901-04; grad. Coast Guard Acad., 1906; m. Doris Devereux, Aug. 24, 1916; children—Stanley Devereux, Robert Devereux. Commd. 3d lt. (now ensign), U.S. Coast Guard, Oct. 1906, and advanced through the grades to rear adm., 1942; served as comdr. Naval Air Stations, Key West, Fla., and Rockaway, N.Y., 1917-19; admitted to Calif. bar, 1934. Capt. of Port, N.Y. City, 1942-45; Comdr. Western Area, U.S. Coast Guard, 1946-47; ret. 1947. Decorated Victory and Defense medals, Legion of Merit. Mason. Author: Coast Guard Boarding Manual, Maual for U.S. Commissioners in Alaska, 1937. Home: Oakland CA Died Jan. 1968.

PARKER, THEODORE BISSELL civil engr.; b. Roxbury, Mass., Aug. 20, 1889; s. Franklin Wells and Sarah (Bissell) P.; B.S. in C.E., Mass. Inst. Tech., 1911, grad. study, 1912; grad. U.S. Army Engr. Sch., 1922, U.S. Command and Gen. Staff Sch., 1933; m. Estelle Peabody, May 10, 1913; children—Franklin Peabody, Nancy. Asst. instr. in civil engring., Mass. Inst. Tech., 1911-12; engr. with H. C. Keith, N.Y. City, 1912; engr. Utah Power & Light Co., Salt Lake City, 1912-17; with Elec. Bond & Share Co., N.Y. City, 1919-20; engr. with Stone & Webster, Inc., 1922-33; state engr. and acting state dir. Pub. Works Administrn. for Mass., 1933-35; chief constrn. engr. Tenn. Valley Authority, 1935-38, chief engr., 1938-43; prof. civil engring., Mass. Inst. Tech. and head dept. civil and sanitary engring. since 1943. Served as 1st lt. and capt. U.S. Army Engrs., 1917-19; capt. Corps of Engrs., 1920-22. Mem: American Soc. Civil Engrs., Soc. Am. Mil. Engrs., Boston Soc. Civil Engrs., Sigma Chi. Home: 115 Woodlawn Av., Wellesley Hills, Mass. Office: Mass. Institute of Technology, Cambridge, Mass. Died Apr. 27, 1944.

PARKER, WALTER HUNTINGTON, mining co. exec.; b. Stillwater, Minn., Aug. 1 1884; s. Reuben S. and Jennie Annette (Huntington) P.; E.M., U. of Minn., 1907; hon. grad. Sch. of Fire, Field Arty., Fort Sill, 1917; m. Veola Fourrell, Aug. 16, 1921. With Pa. Mining Co., Argentine, Colo., 1905, Bingham, Utah, 1906; mgr. Fairview Mining Co., Berlin, Wash., 1907; chief engr. Internat. Coal Co. and Mont. Coal & Iron Co., 1908-12; cons. city engr. Bearcreek, Mont., 1909; cons. structural and mining engr., Vancouver, B.C., Can., 1913-14, Mont., Colo., Minn., and Alberta, 1914-17; asso. prof. mining and head of dept. Sch. of Mines and Metallurgy, U. of Minn., 1919-23; prof. mining and head of dept., 1923-49, prof. of mining emeritus from 1949; cons. mining engr.; president San Juan Mining and Exploration Company. Mem. Minn. Nat. Guard, 1903-07; captain C.A.C., U.S. Army, World War; mem. Gen. Court Martial, 1917; mem. staff Sch. of Fire, Fort Sill, 1917; overseas, 12 mos., as bn. comdr. 69th Arty., C.A.C., and camp adjt. Romagne, France. Fellow A.A.A.S.; mem. Am. Inst. Mining and Metall. Engrs., Soc. for Promotion Engring. Edn. Am. Soc. Civil Engrs., Gen. Alumni Assn. U. of Minn. (dir.). Veterans of Foreign Wars, American Legion, Order of Founders and Patriots of America, Soc. of Colonial Wars, Engineers Club of Minneapolis, Soc. Westcott Descendants, Huntington Family Assn., Minn. Fed. Engr. Soc., New England Hist.-Geneal. Soc. Minn. Hist. Soc., Inst. of Mining and Metallurgy (England), Mining and Metall. Soc. Am., Am. Forestry Assn., Am. Mus. Natural Hist., Forty and Eight, Theta Tau. Republican. Episcopalian, Scottish Rite Mason. (K.T., Shriner). Clubs: Lions, Campus. Editor: Bluebooks. Sch. of Mines, 1922-50. Home: Phoenix AZ Died Jan. 25, 1968.

PARKER, WALTER ROBERT physician; b. Marine City, Mich., Oct. 10, 1865; s. Leonard Brooks and Jane (Sparrow) P.; prep. edn. Mich. Mil. Acad.; B.S., U. Mich., 1888; M.D., U. Pa., 1891, Sc.D., 1927; Sc.D., U. Mich., 1934; m. Margaret W. Watson, Dec. 28, 1907. Practiced in Detroit 1894-—; prof. ophthalmology, U. Mich., 1905-33 (emeritus); cons. ophthalmic surgeon Harper Hosp., Woman's Hosp. Served as ensign U.S. Navy, Spanish-Am. War; col. Med. Corps, U.S. Army, World War. Fellow Am. Coll. Surgeons; mem. A.M.A., Am. Acad. Ophthalmology and Oto-Laryngology, Am. Ophthal. Soc., Ophthal. Soc. of United Kingdom, Internat. Ophthal. Soc. (council). Republican. Presbyterian. Clubs: University, Detroit City, Detroit Country, Yondotega. Home: 1 Woodland Pl., Grosse Pointe, Mich. Office: David Whitney Bldg., Detroit, Mich. Died Apr. 1, 1955.

PARKER, WILLIAM EDWARD civil engr.; b. Newton, Mass., Mar. 21, 1876; s. William Chipman and Emily A. (Goodwin) P.; B.S. in C.E., Mass. Inst. of Tech., 1899; m. Annie Marie Knowles, June 5, 1905; 1 dau., Emily Louise. With Boston & Albany R.R., 1899; asst. engr. Newport News (Va.) Shipbuilding & Dry Dock Co., 1900-01; successively aid, asst. hydrographic and geodetic engr., U.S. Coast and Geodetic Survey, since 1901; transferred to Naval R.F., Sept. 24, 1917, with rank of lt. comdr. for duration of war; in charge compass office, Naval Obs., to Mar. 1919; chief of div. of hydrography and topography, U.S. Coast and Geod. Survey, 1919-31; retired from active duty with relative rank of capt., U.S.N., Nov. 1934. Mem. Am. Soc. C.E., Am. Geophys. Union, Washington Acad. Sciences, Assn. Mil. Engrs., Am. Legion. Club: Federal (Washington). Home: Fort Lauderdale, Fla. Died Sept. 30, 1942.

PARKER, WILLIAM HARWAR naval officer; b. N.Y.C., Oct. 8, 1826; s. Foxhall Alexander and Sara (Bogardus) P.; grad. (1st in class) U.S. Naval Acad., 1848; m. Margaret Griffin, Dec. 14, 1853. Served from midshipman to lt. U.S. Navy, 1841-61; served in Mexican War; instr. U.S. Naval Acad., Annapolis, Md., 1853-57, 60-61; translated Tactique Navale from French; joined Confederate Navy, took command gunboat Beaufort Roanoke Island, 1862; exec. officer in ironclad Palmetto State at Charleston, winter 1862-63; promoted capt. 1863; organizer, supt. Confederate Naval Acad., 1863-65 (on evacuation of Richmond, Va. he and his cadets were given charge of govt. archives and treasure); capt. Pacific mail steamer between Panama and San Francisco, 1865-74; pres. Md. Agrl. Coll., 1875-83; U.S. minister to Korea in Cleveland's adminstrn., 1886. Author: Instructions for Light Naval Artillery, 1862; Elements of Seamanship, 1864; Remarks on the Navigation of the Coasts between San Francisco and Panama, 1871; Recollections of a Naval Officer 1841-65, published 1883. Died Washington, D.C., Dec. 30, 1896; buried Norfolk, Va.

PARKER, WILLIAM HENRY, law enforcement officer; b. Lead, S.D., June 21, 1902; s. William H. and Mary (Moore) P.; LL.B., Los Angeles Coll. Law, 1930; postgrad. Northwestern U., 1940-41; m. Amelia H.

Schultz, May 6, 1928. With Los Angeles Police Dept., from 1927, chief police, from 1950. Chmn. Gov's. Law Enforcement Adv. Com., 1957-58, Los Angeles Civil Def. Disaster Bd., 1962-63. Pres. Los Angeles Area council Boy Scouts Am., 1962; mem. adv. bd. Bd. Deliquency Control Inst. U. So. Cal. Served to capt. AUS, 1943-45; ETO. Decorated Purple Heart; Croix de Guerre; Star of Solidarity; named Hon. Chief Nat. Police, Korea, 1952, Citizen of Year, Los Angeles C. of C., 1953; recipient B'nai B'rith Merit award, 1953, Sylvania award, 1954, James Madison award Los Angeles Freedom Club, 1959, Freedom award Immaculate Heart Coll., 1960, Service Mankind award Los Angeles Sertoma Club: Catholic Big Brothers (Dir.). Mem. Peace Officer's Assn. Cal., Internat. Assn. Chiefs Police, Am. Legion, Sigma Delta Kappa. Club: Catholic Big Brothers (dir.). Home: Los Angeles CA Died July 16, 1966.

PARKES, CHARLES HERBERT, surgeon; b. Chicago, Ill., Oct. 15, 1872; s. Charles Theodore and Isabella Jane (Gonterman) P.; grad. Lake View High Sch., Chicago; student Northwestern U.; M.D., Rush Med. Coll., 1897; m. Edna Bigelow, of Toronto, Can., Sept. 21, 1916. Practiced at Chicago since 1897; attending surgeon Illinois Masonic Hospital. Mem. Ill. National Guard, 1899-1910; member M.C., U.S.A., July 1917-Aug. 1919; served with A.E.F. in France; hon. discharged as maj. Fellow Am. Coll. Surgeons, A.M.A., Chicago Med. Soc. (sec. 1913-14). Republican. Mason. Home: 1910 Lincoln Av., Chicago IL*

PARKHILL, CHARLES BRECKINRIDGE lawyer; b. Leon Co., Fla., June 23, 1859; s. George W. and Elizabeth (Bellamy) P.; student Randolph-Macon Coll., Va., 1876-78, U. of Va., 1880-82; m. Genevieve Perry, 1884 (died 1885); 1 dau., Genevieve (Mrs. J. M. Lykes); m. 2d, Helen Wall, Nov. 30, 1891; children—Barbara (Mrs. Beman Beckwith), Elizabeth (Mrs. S. L. Lowry, Jr.), Joseph F., Charles B., Richard C. (dec.), Helen (Mrs. C. A. Rudisill), Emala (Mrs. A. Pickens Coles), John. Admitted to Florida bar, 1882; member Florida Senate, 1888-90; solicitor of Criminal Court of Record of Escambia County, Fla., 1897-1904; judge Circuit Court, 1st Judicial Circuit, Florida, 1904-05; asso. justice Supreme Court of Fla., 1905-12 (resigned); in law practice at Tampa, 1912-—; city atty. of Tampa, 1913-16. Commd. maj., judge advocate U.S.A., Nov. 15, 1917; served with A.E.F.; state's atty. 13th Jud. Circuit, Fla., 1920-—, present term ending 1933. Democrat. Methodist. Past Grand Chancellor K.P.; Elk. Home: Tampa, Fla. Died May 13, 1933.

PARKHURST, JOHN GIBSON lawyer; b. Oneida Castle, N.Y., Apr. 17, 1824; s. Stephen and Sally (Gibson) P.; grad. Oneida Acad., 1843. Read law in office of Graves & Dodge, 1843-47; admitted to N.Y. bar, 1847; practiced Oneida Co., N.Y., 1847-49; practiced in Mich., 1849-61; m. Amelia C. Noyes, Nov. 10, 1852 (died 1861); 2d, Josy B. Reeves, Aug. 10, 1863 (died 1870); 3d, Frances J. Fiske, Apr. 23, 1874 (died 1900). Sec. Nat. Dem. Conv., Charleston, 1860; enlisted Union army, Sept. 10, 1861; served lt. col. and col. 9th Mich. inf.; provost marshal 14th Army corps, provost marshal-gen. Dept. of the Cumberland; provost marshal-gen. Mil. Div. of the Tenn.; brig. gen. vols. on staff Gen. George H. Thomas, 1862-65; U.S. marshal, dist. of Mich., 1866-69, resumed practice; E.E. and M.P. of U.S. to Belgium, 1888-89. Democrat. Home: Coldwater, Mich. Died 1906.

PARKINSON, DONALD BERTHOLD architect; b. Los Angeles, Calif., Aug. 10, 1895; s. John and Meta (Breckenfeld) P.; B.S., Mass. Inst. of Tech., 1920; special student Am. Acad. at Rome (Italy), 1921; m. Frances Grace Wells, Sept. 12, 1921; 1 son, Donald Wells. Began as an architect, 1920; now mem. John Parkinson & Donald B. Parkinson, architects, designed war plants for Lockheed Aircraft Corp., Vega Aircraft Corp. and Lockheed Navy Service Center; dir. Bowlus Sailplanes, Inc.; sec. and dir. Paul Mantz Air Services Ltd. Served in air service, U.S. Army, 1917-18; major, corps of engineers, U.S. Army, 1942-43, major, air corps, Nov. 1943-Dec. 1944, retired. Member Los Angeles Earthquake Advisory Commission 1933; mem. Los Angeles Municipal Art Commission 2 years. Received 5 honor awards of Am. Inst. of Architects, 2 certificates of merit; hon. mention in 5th Pan-Am. Congress of Architects, Montevideo, 1940; highest award Architectural Forum jury, 1940. Mem. Delta Kappa Epsilon. Democrat. Episcopalian. Clubs: Kennebunk (Me.) Beach Chowder and Marching; California; Los Angeles Country; Santa Monica (Calif.) Beach. Home: 1605 San Vicente Blvd., Santa Monica, Calif. Died 1946.

PARKINSON, WILLIAM NIMON, surgeon; b. Philadelphia, Pa., Sept. 17, 1886; s. Walter and Sarah (Nimon) P.; B.S., Villanova (Pa.) Coll., 1907, LL.D., 1932; M.D., Temple U., 1911; M.S., U. of Pa., 1925; D.Sc., Pa. Mil. Coll., 1949, Ed.D. (honorary), Dickinson College, 1951, L.H.D. Hahnemann Medical College, 1955; LL.D., Jefferson Medical College, Phila., 1957; Dr. Med. Sci., Woman's Medical College, Phila., 1959. Assistant surgeon Joseph Price Hosp., Phila., 1912-17; surg. Montgomery Hosp., Norristown, Pa., 1922-25; chief surg. Fla. East Coast Hosp., St. Augustine, Fla., 1926-28; prof. clin. surgery, Temple U., 1928-71, dean sch. medicine, 1929-59, dean emeritus, 1961-71; v.p. in charge med. center, 1953-61, med. director Temple U. Hosps., 1929-61. Trustee Magee Hosp. for Convalescents, Skin and Cancer Hosp., Philadelphia. Served as captain M.C., U.S. Army, World War I, Fellow Am. Coll. Surgeons; mem. A.M.A., Pa. State Medical Society, Philadelphia Medical Society, Phi Chi, Alpha Omega Alpha. Republican. Baptist. Clubs: Medical, Philadelphia Country, Union League, Rotary. Address: Philadelphia PA Died Apr. 19, 1971.

PARKMAN, HENRY govt. ofcl.; born Boston, Apr. 26, 1894; s. Henry and Mary Frances (Parker) P.; A.B., Harvard U., 1915, A.M., 1916; student Harvard Law Sch., 1915-17, Northeastern U. Law Sch., 1922-23; grad. School of Military Government, Charlottesville, Va., 1943; m. Doris Montague Leamy, June 26, 1936. Admitted to Mass. bar, 1924, and since in practice at Boston; now partner Parkman, Robbins & Russell, Boston. Member City Council of Boston, 1926-29, Mass. Senate, 1929-36; corporation counsel, Boston, 1938-40; Rep. candidate for U.S. senator (Mass.), 1940. Mass. dir. Office Price Adminstrn., May, 1942-Jan., 1943; Govt. affairs advisor, U.S. Mil. Govt., Germany, 1946-47; U.S. rep. Internat. Authority for Ruhr, Duesseldorf, 1949-50; chief E.C.A. Spl. Mission to France, 1950-51; assistant U.S. High Commr. Germany, 1953-55; dep. commr. Savs. Bank Life Ins. Co., Mass., 1956-—. Capt., 320th Inf., U.S. Army, with A.E.F., 1918-19. Commd. lt. col., A.U.S., Jan. 13, 1943; col. Aug., 1944; brig. gen., Oct. 1945; served overseas as staff officer, Allied Hdqrs., and as A.C.S., G-5, Hdqrs. 6th Army Group; asst. U.S. High Commissioner for Germany, 1954. Awarded D.S.M., Legion of Merit; Comdrs. Cross Republic Germany, 1958; Commandeur French Legion of Honor, 1958. Former president American Legislators Assn.; pres. Rep. Club of Mass., 1928-30; v.p. Council of State Govts., 1936-38. Mem. Am. Bar Assn., Mass. Bar Assn., and Boston Bar Assn., Phi Beta Kappa. Republican. Unitarian. Mason. Clubs: Union Boat, Tavern (Boston). Home: 30 W. Cedar St., Boston. Office: 30 State St., Boston. Died May 27, 1958.

PARKS, CHARLES WELLMAN naval officer; b. Woburn, Mass., Mar. 22, 1863; s. Granville and Elizabeth A. P.; C.E., Rensselaer Poly. Inst., 1884; LL.B., Columbia Law Sch., 1899; LL.D., George Washington U., 1921; m. Miss M. B. Frear, Apr. 14, 1887. Served as chief engr. Denver, Memphis & Atlantic Ry., and elec. engr. Elec. Mfg. Co., Troy, N.Y.; head dept. of physics, Rensselaer Poly. Inst., 9 yrs. Commd. civ. engr. U.S.N., rank of ensign, July 19, 1897; promoted through grades to rear adm., Jan. 11, 1918; retired Dec. 1, 1921. Served with Bur. Yards and Docks, Navy Dept., Spanish-Am. War, 1898; pub. works officer, Navy Yard, Phila., 1912-14, Naval Sta., Hawaii, 1908-09 and 1915-17; apptd. chief Bur. Yards and Docks, Navy Dept., Jan. 11, 1918. Supt. liberal arts, Paris Expn., 1889; special agent Bur. of Education, at Chicago Expn., 1893, exhibiting model town library of 5,000 vols.; visited and reported on expns. at Antwerp, Lyon and Zürich; reported on forestry systems of Europe. Officier de l'Instruction Publique (France), 1889; D.S.M. (U.S.), 1919, for distinguished services in World War; Comdr. Legion of Honor (France), 1920. Home: Woburn, Mass. Died June 25, 1930.

PARKS, EDD WINFIELD, writer, univ. prof.; born Newbern, Tenn., Feb. 25, 1906; s. Edward Winfield and Emma (Wallis) P.; student U. of Tenn., 1922-23, Occidental Coll., 1923-24; A.B., Harvard, 1927; A.M., Vanderbilt University, 1929, Ph.D., 1933; married Aileen, Wells, November 3d, 1933. Fellow and instr. English, Vanderbilt U., 1928-33; prof. English, Cumberland U., 1933-35; asst. prof. advancing to prof. English, U. of Ga., 1935-64, Alumni Found. Distinguished prof. English, 1964-68; vis. prof. Duke U., summers 1936, 38, 39, U. N.C., 1953; Fulbright lectr. Am. Literature, U. Copenhagen, 1955; vis. prof. Am. Lit., U. Brazil, 1949, Fulbright prof., 1958; Carnegie fellow, 1948, 52. Served as 2d lt., later capt., Mil. Intelligence, U.S.A., 1943-46; spl. mission to England, spring, 1945. Awarded Army Commendation Ribbon. Mem. Am. (executive council), Southeastern (pres. 1961-62) studies assns., So. Humanities Conf. (chairman 1962-63), Modern Lang. Assn. (chmn. So. lit. discussion group 1960) and South Atlantic Modern Lang. Assn. (pres. 1958-59). Author, co-author or editor books, 1933-—, including: Safe on Second, 1953; Backwater, 1957; William Gilmore Simms as a Literary Critic, 1960; Ante-Bellum Southern Literary Critics, 1962; Nashoba, pub. 1963; Henry Timrod, 1963; Edgar Allan Poe as Literary Critic, 1964; Sidney Lanier, The Man, the Poet, the Critic, 1968; Hints to the Gentle Reader, 1969; (with Aileen Wells Parks) The Collected Poems of Henry Timrod, 1966. Thomas MacDonagh The Man-The Patriot-The Writer. 1967. Mem. editorial bd. Am. Quar., 1957-58, Miss., Quar. Contbr. articles to symposia, anthologies and mags. Address: Athens GA Died May 7, 1968.

PARKS, FLOYD LAVINIUS army ofcr. ret.; b. Louisville, Feb. 9, 1896; s. Lyman L. and Lizzie Pratt (Manly) P.; student Cumberland Coll., Prep. Dept., 1912-13, Frazer Fitting Sch., Anderson, S.C., 1913-14; B.S., Clemson Coll., 1917, Doctor of Military Science, 1954; B.S. in Mech. Engring., Yale, 1924; grad. Tank Sch., 1924, Inf. Sch., 1933, Command and Gen. Staff Sch., 1935, Army War Coll., 1940; m. Mary M. Trowbridge, Nov. 26, 1924 (div. 1927); m. 2d, Harriet Marie Applebye-Robinson, Sept. 24, 1931; children—Edwyna Anne, William Robinson, Floyd Lavinius, Basil Manly. Private, 2d lt., 1st lt., and capt., Tank Corps, 1918; commd. 1st lt., regular army of U.S., July 1, 1920, and advanced through the grades to lieutenant general, 1953; became deputy chief of staff, Army Ground Forces, March 9, 1942, chief of staff, June 1942 to Feb. 1943; asst. div. comdr., 69th Inf. Div., Feb. 1943-July 1944; chief of staff, First Allied Airborne Army, Aug. 1944-May 26, 1945; comdg. First Airborne Army, U.S., May-Oct. 1945; comdg. U.S. sector and mil. govt., Berlin, from entry U.S. troops, July-Oct. 1945; chief, Pub. Information Division, Dept. of Army, 1945-48; deputy comdg. general U.S. Army, Pacific, 1948-49; chief of information Department of Army, 1949-53; comdg. gen. 2d Army, 1953-56, retired from active duty; exec. dir. Nat. Rifle Assn. Am., 1956-—. Member exec. com. region 3, exec. bd. nat. capital area council, mem.-at-large nat. council Boy Scouts Am. Decorated D.S.M. with oak leaf cluster, Bronze Star Medal, Air Medal, Legion of Merit, Commendation Ribbon, Victory Medal (World War I); Nat. Defense Medal, Am. Theater Campaign Ribbon, European-African-Middle East Campaign Ribbon with 3 battle stars, Victory Medal (World War II), Occupation Medal (Germany); Abdon Calderon, 3d Class (Ecuador); Companion of Bath (Gt. Britain); Order Kutuzov, 1st Class (Russia); Polonia Restituta, Commander's Cross (Poland); Comdr. 1st Class, Order of Dannebrog (Denmark); Officer Legion of Honor (France); Grand Officer, Order Orange-Nassau (Netherlands); Croix de Guerre with Palm (Belgium). Mem. Washington Bd. Trade, Am. Legion, Vets. Fgn. Wars, Assn. U.S. Army, West Point Soc., Am. Ordnance Assn., Nat. Security Indsl. Assn. (hon. life), Nat. Rifle Assn. (endowment mem.), U.S., Am., So. srs. golf assns., Middle Atlantic Golf Assn. (v.p.), S.C. Soc. Washington, Nantucket Hist. Soc., Tau Beta Pi. Clubs: Chevy Chase, Columbia Country (Chevy Chase, Md.); Army-Navy Country, Army-Navy, University, Nat. Press (Washington). Home: 3650 Upton St., Washington 8. Office: 1600 Rhode Island Av., Washington 6. Died Mar. 10, 1959; buried Arlington Nat. Cemetery.

PARKS, RUFUS rear admiral U.S.N.; b. Bangor, Me., Apr. 9, 1837. Apptd. asst. p.m. U.S.N., Sept. 12, 1861; p.m., Apr. 14, 1862; pay insp., Feb. 23, 1877; pay dir., Aug. 10, 1886; retired, Apr. 9, 1899, with rank of rear admiral for services during Civil War. Home: Norfolk, Va. Died Aug. 9, 1913.

PARKS, WYTHE MARCHANT naval officer; b. Norfolk, Va., Sept. 8, 1856; s. of John W. and Victoria P.; ed. at Norwood, Va., and at Norfolk Academy; m. Lilian Baird, Aug. 17, 1882; children—Lilian Baird, Victoria Marchant, Marshall. Appointed assistant engineer U.S. Navy, May 8, 1877; promoted through grades to rear admiral, Feb. 13, 1913. Made Arctic cruise on U.S.S. Alliance, 1881, search of the Jeannette; served in Miantonomoh during Spanish-Am. War; was fleet engr. Pacific Squadron on Flagship Iowa; Bur. of Steam Engring., Navy Dept., 1901-08; head Dept. of Steam Engring., Navy Yard, New York, 1908-10; mem. Naval Examining Bd., Washington, 1910-13; gen. insp. of machinery for Navy, July 11, 1913-Sept. 8, 1920; retired Sept. 8, 1920. Home: Philadelphia, Pa. Died Sept. 17, 1938.

PARROTT, ENOCH GREENLEAFE naval officer; b. Portsmouth, N.H., Nov. 17, 1815; s. Enoch Greenleafe and Susan (Parker) P. Commd. lt. U.S. Navy, 1841; in frigate Congress accompanied Fremont's expdn. from Monterey to Los Angeles, 1846-48; promoted comdr., 1861; commanded ship Perry, captured the Savannah (1st privateer captured), June 1861; sr. officer in steamer Augusta, off Charleston; 1862; commanded Monadnock in 2 attacks on Ft. Fisher, 1864-65, and in blockade of Charleston; commd. capt., 1866, commodore, 1870, rear adm., 1873; comdr. of receiving ship, Boston, 1865-68, Portsmouth Navy Yard, 1869; comdt. Mare Island Yard, 1871-72; commanded Asiatic Squadron, 1872-74. Died N.Y.C., May 10, 1879; buried St. John's Episcopal Ch., Portsmouth, N.H.

PARROTT, ROBERT PARKER ordnance inventor, manufacturer; b. Lee, N.H., Oct. 5, 1804; s. John Fabyan and Hannah (Parker) P.; grad. U.S. Mil. Acad., 1824; m. Mary Kemble, 1839, 1 adopted son. Asst. prof. natural and experimental philosophy U.S. Mil. Acad., 1824-29; commd. 1st lt., 1831; promoted capt. of ordnance, 1836, went to Washington (D.C.) as asst. to bur. of ordnance; resigned from army to become supt. West Point Foundry, Cold Spring, N.Y., 1836, became lessee of foundry, 1839, directed bus. until 1877; bought 7,000 acre tract of land, built Greenwood Iron Furnace (ran with his brother), 1839-77; patented design for strengthening cast-iron cannon with a wrought-iron hoop shrunken on the breech, also an improved expanding projectile for rifled ordnance, 1861; received large orders for guns and projectiles in Civil War; began (with brother) 1st comml. prodn. of slag wool in U.S., 1875; 1st judge Ct. of Common Pleas for Putnam County, N.Y., 1844-47. Died Cold Spring, Dec. 24, 1877.

PARRY, SIDNEY LOREN, stock broker; b. Worthington, Minn., Aug. 4 1902; s. William John and Katherine (Prideaux) P.; student Yankton (S.D.) Coll.,

1922-24; B.S., Northwestern, 1926; m. Elizabeth Beckwith, Sept. 1, 1928; 1 dau. Elizabeth Jane (Mrs. Duane Miller). Private secretary to the Public Service Company of Northern Illinois, Chicago, Ill., 1926-28; asst. to pres. Chicago Stock Exchange, 1928-39, vice pres., 1939-45; exec. vice pres. Assn. Stock Exchange Firms, 1945-50; director public relations and advertising, Charles W. Scranton & Co., New Haven, 1951-53; partner DeCoppet and Doremus, from 1956, members N.Y. Stock Exchange. Chmn. bd. trustees Yankton Coll. Served in USNR, 1942-45; active duty as lt. comdr. Mem. Sigma Chi, Delta Sigma Pi. Republican. Presbyn. Clubs: Union League, New York Stock Exchange Luncheon, City Midday (N.Y.C.); Wee Burn Country (Darien, Conn.). Home: Westport CT Died Nov. 10, 1968; buried Evergreen Cemetery, Westport CT

PARSONS, ARCHIBALD LIVINGSTONE retired rear admiral; b. Derry, N.H., Sept. 20, 1875; s. Benjamin Franklin and Mary Ann (Nesmith) P.; B.S., Mass. Inst. of Tech. 1897; m. Laura Reeves, July 1913. Commd. lieut. (j.g.) Navy Corps, Civil Eng., 1903; served as asst. and in charge of shore construction at various Navy yards and stations, 1903-12; Bureau of Yards and Docks, Washington, D.C., 1912-18, asst. chief of Bureau, 1916-18; Phila. Navy Yard 1919; engr. in chief, Republic of Haiti, 1920-24; Navy Yard, New York and Boston, 1924-29; chief of Bureau of Yards and Docks, Washington, D.C., 1929-33; New York Yard and District, 1934-38; retired own application, 1938; now cons. engr. with Frederic R. Harris, Inc., New York. Life mem. Am. Soc. of Civil Engrs. Awarded Navy Cross, World War. Clubs: Chevy Chase, Army and Navy (Washington, D.C.). Home: 160 Columbia Heights, Brooklyn, N.Y. Office: 27 William St., New York, N.Y. Died Sept. 24, 1953; buried Arlington Nat. Cemetery.

PARSONS, CHARLES BALDWIN ship broker; b. Middletown, N.J., July 3, 1835; s. Walter Chamberlain and Mary (Morford) P.; acad. edn.; m. Elizabeth M. Bergen, Jan. 20, 1868. Served in Civil War, 1861-65; rank, capt. engrs., and bvt. maj.; was chief engr., 25th Army Corps; sea capt., 1865-90. Treas. Shrewsbury Twp., 1890-99; trustee Am. Seaman's Friend Soc., 1904—; sec. N.J. Bd. Pilot Commrs.; chmn. bldg. com. Seaman's Home and Inst., 1907-09. Pres. New York Maritime Exchange, 1902-06, N.J. S.S. Assn., 1898-1901, Mission Yacht Assn., 1904—. Comdr. Arrowsmith Post G.A.R., 1892-93 and 1902-05; mem. N.Y. Commandery Loyal Legion; high priest, Hiram Chapter, R.A.M. Author: Genealogical Record of Morford Family of Middletown, 1910. Home: Red Bank, N.J. Deceased.

PARSONS, FREDERICK WILLIAMS physician; b. Buffalo, Nov. 13, 1875; s. Frederick John and Ann (Williams) P.; M.D., U. of Buffalo, 1901; unmarried. Began practice at Buffalo, 1901; in state hosp. service Hudson River State Hosp., Poughkeepsie, N.Y., advancing to 1st asst., 1902-19; supt. Buffalo State Hosp., 1919-26; med. commr. N.Y. State Hosp. Commn., 1926-27; commr. dept. mental hygiene, 1927-37. Mental hygiene cons. to USPHS. Mem. med. bd. U.S. Vets. Bur. Served from capt. to lt. col. M.C., U.S. Army, 1917-19; comdg. officer Base Hosp. 117, AEF. Diplomate Am. Bd. Psychiatry and Neurology. Mem. Am. Psychiatric Soc., Assn. Research Nervous and Mental Diseases, Buffalo Acad. Medicine, N.Y. State, Albany County med. socs., New York Psychiatric Soc., N.Y. Soc. for Clinical Psychiatry. Clubs: University (Albany); Amrita (Poughkeepsie). Home: 10 Park Av., Albany, N.Y. Died July 1957.

PARSONS, HERBERT congressman; b. New York, Oct. 28, 1869; s. John Edward (q.v.) and Mary Dumesnil (McIlvaine) P.; A.B., Yale, 1890; U. of Berlin, 1890-91, Harvard Law Sch., 1891-93, Metropolis Law Sch., 1893-94; m. Elsie Worthington Clews, Sept. 1, 1900. Admitted to bar, 1895; sr. mem. Parsons, Closson & McIlvaine. Alderman of New York, 1900-03; candidate for Congress, 1900, 12th N.Y. Dist.; mem. 59th to 61st Congresses (1905-11), 13th N.Y. Dist. Chmn. Rep. Co. Com., 1905-10; mem. Rep. Nat. Com. and of exec. com., 1916-20; del.-at-large N.Y. State Constl. Conv., 1915. Vet. 7th Regt., Co. K, and formerly maj. and judge advocate on staff of 1st Brigade N.G.N.Y.; commd. maj., Aviation Sect. Signal O.R.C., July 1917, and detailed to Mil. Intelligence; lt. col. on Gen. Staff A.E.F., Sept. 1918; served during last half 1918 as asst. chief of staff, G2, 5th Div.; asst. to mil. attaché, Berne, Switzerland, Jan., Feb. 1919. Pres. Greenwich House Settlement, Memorial Hosp. for Treatment of Cancer and Allied Diseases; pres. trustees Canton Christian College. Presbyn. Home: Rye, N.Y. Died Sept. 16, 1925.

PARSONS, JAMES KELLY, army officer (ret.); b. Rockford, Ala., Feb. 11, 1877; s. Lewis E. and Catherine (Kelly) P.; prep. edn., pub. and pvt. schs., Birmingham, Ala.; grad. Inf. and Cav. Sch., Fort Leavenworth, Kan., 1904, Command and Staff Sch., Fort Leavenworth, 1923, Army War Coll., Washington, 1924, Navy War Coll., Newport, R.I., 1925; m. Volinda Henderson, July 23, 1904. Commd. 1st lt., 3d Ala. Vol. Inf., 1898; commd. 2d lt., inf., U.S. Army, 1899, and advanced through grades to maj. gen. 1936; served in Spanish-Am. War; with inf. and Castner's Native Scouts, Philippine Insurrection, 1899-1901; co. comdr. and bn. adj., 20th Inf., 1904-09, post q.m., Monterey, Calif., 1909, regtl. q.m., 1909-11; insp. instr. N.Y.N.G., 1916-17; served on Gen. Staff, Tours, France, World War I; participated St. Mihiel and Meuse-Argonne offensives; comdr. Embarkation Camp, St. Nazaire, 1918-19, gassed, 1919; duty with N.Y.N.G., 1919-20; officer in charge Nat. Guard affairs, 5th Corps Area, 1920-22; with Office of Chief of Inf., 1925-26, War Dept. Gen. Staff, 1926-29; comdt. Tank Sch. and comdg. officer Ft. George G. Meade, 1929-30; comd. 9th C.A. Dist., 1931, 23d Inf. Brigade, 1931-33, 5th Brigade and Vancouver (Wash.) Barracks, 1933-36, 2d Div. and Ft. Sam Houston, Tex., 1936-38, 3d Corps Area, Baltimore, 1938-40, ret. 1941. Decorated D.S.C., D.S.M., Purple Heart. Club: Army-Navy (Washington). Home: 1661 Crescent Pl., Washington 9

PARSONS, LEWIS BALDWIN soldier, lawyer; b. Genesse Co., N.Y., April 5, 1818; s. Lewis Baldwin and Lucina (Hoar) P.; grad. Yale, 1840, A.M., in course, 1843, LL.B., Harvard Univ. Law School, 1844; city atty., Alton, Ill., 1846-49; atty., treas., pres. Ohio & Mississippi R.R., 1854-78; capt. vols., Oct. 31, 1861; col., April 4, 1862; brig. gen., May 11, 1865, on autographic order of Pres. Lincoln for spl. services; was chief of rail and river transportation of the armies of U.S. during the Civil war; bvt. maj. gen. for meritorious services and mustered out April 30, 1866; m. Sarah Green Edwards, Sept. 21, 1847 (died 1850); m. 2d, Julia Maria Edwards, July 5, 1852 (died 1857); m. 3d, Elizabeth Darrah, Dec. 28, 1869 (died 1887). Dem. candidate for lt. gov. Ill., 1880, with U.S. Senator Lyman Trumbull, candidate for gov.; pres. Ill. Soldiers' and Sailors' Home, 1895-98. Retired. Home: Flora, Ill. Died 1907.

PARSONS, SAMUEL HOLDEN Revolutionary patriot; b. Lynne, Conn., May 14, 1737; s. Jonathan and Phebe (Griswold) P.; grad. Harvard, 1756, Master's Degree, 1759; m. Mehetable Mather, Sept. 1761, 8 children. Admitted to Conn. bar, 1759; mem. Conn. Gen. Assembly, 1762-74; active Conn. Com. of Correspondence; commd. col. 6th Regt., Conn. Militia, 1775, served in taking of Ft. Ticonderoga; commd. brig. gen. Continental Army, 1776, was depended upon for defense of Conn.; in charge of important secret service post; promoted comdr. Conn. div., 1779, maj. gen., 1780; on Sept. 22, 1785 Congress named him commr. to deal with Indian claims to territory N.W. of Ohio River; became a promoter, dir. Ohio Co., 1787; apptd. 1st judge of Northwest Territory, 1787. Author: (essay) Antiquities of the Western States. Drowned in Big Beaver River, O., Nov. 17, 1789.

PARSONS, WILLARD H., surgeon; b. Brookhaven, Miss., May 3, 1898; s. William F. and Ophelia (Herring) P.; student Tulane U., 1914-17; M.D. Jefferson Med., Edna Earl Sparks, Oct. 23, 1922; children—Edna Earl (Mrs. H. Thurston Whitaker), Ruth Lee (Mrs. Emmett C. Neil). Practice of medicine, Vicksburg, Miss., 1922; chief staff and dir. surgery Vicksburg Clinic, 1929-62; dir. surgery Vicksburg Hosp., Inc., 1929-62; civilian cons. surgery to surgeon-General Army U.S. Far Eastern Theatre, 1962-63, to Surgeon Gen. of U.S.A., Dept. of Defense, 1964-69; emeritus cons. surgery to surgeon gen. of Army, 1967-69; former cons. thoracis surgery U.S. Vets Hosp., Jackson; prof. clinical surgery emeritus U. of Miss. Medical Sch.; past dir. grad. tng. in surgery Vicksburg Hosp. and Vicksburg Clinic. Diplomate Am. Bd. Surgery Founders Group. Fellow A.C.S. (chmn. bd. govs. 1953-56, regent 1956-65, vice chmn. bd. regents 1963-65, 1st v.p. 1965-66), Internat. Cardiovascular Soc.; mem. Soc. Surgery Alimentary Tract, Am. Cancer Soc. (Miss. Cancer pres. 1955-57, nat. dir.), Southeastern Surg. Congress (pres. 1960-61), Pan-Pacific Surgical Soc., Royal Soc. Medicine (affiliate), Southern Soc., Clin. Surgeons (pres. 1950-51), So. (v.p. 1950-51), Western, Am. surg. assns., New Orleans Surg. Soc., Societe Internationale de Chirurgie, Issaquena-Sharkey-Warren Counties Med. Soc. (past pres.), Miss. State Med. Assn. (past chmn. surgery sect.). Sigma Alpha Epsilon, Alpha Omega Alpha, Alpha Kappa Kappa. Presbyn. Club: Vicksburg Country. Author: Cancer of Breast, 1960; also surg. publs. Adv. editorial bd. Cancer. Contbr. books and numerous clin. papers. Home: Vicksburg MS Died Mar. 9, 1969.

PARSONS, WILLIAM BARCLAY civil engr.; b. N.Y. City, Apr. 15, 1859; s. William Barclay and Eliza Glass (Livingston) P.; A.B., Columbia, 1879, C.E., 1882; LL.D., St. John's, Md., 1909; Sc.D., Princeton, 1920, Trinity, 1921; D.Eng., Stevens, 1921; m. Anna DeWitt Reed, May 20, 1884; children—Mrs. Sylvia Weld, Wm. Barclay. Consulting engr., N.Y. City, 1885; dep. chief engr., 1891-94, chief engr., Rapid Transit Commn. New York, 1894-1904; survey Chinese railways, 1898-99; mem. Isthmian Canal Commn., 1904; bd. of consulting engrs., Panama Canal, 1905; advisory engr. Royal Commn. London Traffic, 1904; chief engr. Cape Cod Canal, 1905-14; chmn. Chicago Transit Com., 1916; also many other engring. wks. Lecturer Cambridge U., 1929. Chief of engrs. (brig. gen. N.G.N.Y.), Spanish-Am. War; maj., lt. col., col. 11th U.S. Engrs., World War; now brig. gen. engr. R.C., U.S.A. Awarded D.S.M. (U.S.), also citation for conspicuous distinguished service and victory medal and 5 clasps; D.S.O. (British); Officer Legion of Honor (French); Order of Crown (Belgian). Fellow Am. Acad. Arts and Sciences; etc. Trustee Columbia U., 1897-— (chmn. bd. from 1917), N.Y. Pub. Library, Carnegie Instn. (Washington). Vestryman Trinity Ch., New York. Author: Turnouts, 1883; Track, 1885; Rapid Transit in Foreign Cities, 1895; American Engineer in China, 1900; The American Engineers in France, 1920; Robert Fulton and the Submarine, 1923; etc. Home: New York, N.Y. Died May 9, 1932.

PARSONS, WILLIAM BARCLAY, surgeon; born N.Y. City, May 22, 1888; s. William Barclay and Anna DeWitt (Reed) P.; grad. St. Mark's Sch., 1906; A.B., Harvard, 1910; M.D., Coll. Physicians and Surgs., Columbia U., 1914; m. Rose Saltonstall Peabody, Mar. 22, 1919; children—William Barclay, Jr., Rose Peabody (Mrs. Russell Vincent Lynch), Anne Barclay (now Mrs. Harold A. Priest, Jr.). Member of the faculty of medicine, Coll. Phys. and Surgs, Columbia U., 1935-39, and 1945-53, attending surg. Presbyn. Hosp., Vanderbilt Clinic, 1939-52, mem. med. bd., from 1945; prof. clin. surgery, Coll. of Phys. and Surg., 1949-53, professor emeritus clinical surgery, 1953-73; director of surgery, first surg. div. Welfare Hosp.; cons. in surg., N.Y. Orthopedic Hosp., from 1946. Served as lt., later capt., Am. Ambulance Field Service, France, 1916. Presbyn. Hosp. Unit, France, Mobile Hosp., Champagne, Aisne-Marne, St. Mihiel, Meuse Argonne offensives, Army Occupation, 1916-19; served as lt. col. to col., chief surg. service and unit dir. 2d Gen. Hosp., chief surg. cons. Southwest Pacific area; chief surg. cons., 6th Service Command. Awarded Legion of Merit, 1945. Trustee N.Y. Inst. for Edn. of the Blind, and St. Mark's School. Fellow Am. Coll. Surgeons; fellow Sect. Surgery, N.Y. Acad. Medicine; mem. Am. Surg. Assn. Am. Bd. Surg. (founders' group), Soc. clin. Surg. (sec. 1934-35), Med. and Surg. Soc., New York Surg. Soc., New York Acad. Med. (chmn. com. on professional standards, 1932-42, com. on med. information, pres. 1951-52), A.M.A. (vice-chmn. sect. on surg., gen. and abdominal, 1940), Soc. Clin. Research, Harvey Society, Nat. Bd. Med. Examiners (2d term of 6 yrs. 1947), Soc. Med. Consultant to the Armed Forces (councilor, 1946), Societe Internationale de Chirurgie (sec. Am. br. 1947-49), Century Assn., Soc. of The Cincinnati, New Hampshire Br. Chmn. coms. on radioactive research and blood bank, Presbyn. Hosp. Republican. Episcopalian. Clubs: Harvard (New York and Boston). Author: Sections in Surgical Clinics of North America, vol. 16, 1936, vol. 19, 1939, 1947; sect. in Operative Surgery, 1941; sect. in Surgical Treatment, 1947; also numerous papers on surg. Home: Darien CT Died Jan. 2, 1973; buried Wilton CT

PARSONS, WILLIAM STERLING naval officer; b. Chicago, Ill., Nov. 26, 1901; s. Harry Robert and Clara Sterling (Doolittle) P.; B.S., U.S. Naval Acad., 1922; m. Martha Cluverius, Nov. 23, 1929; children—Hannah (deceased), Margaret Sampson, Clara Doolittle. Commd. ensign, U.S.N., 1922, and since advanced through grades to rear adm., 1946; assigned to exptl. ordnance development, Naval Proving Ground, Dahlgren, Va., 1939-42; special asst. to dir., O.S.R.D., for development of radio proximity fuse, 1942-43; ordnance div. leader, and later asso. dir., atomic bomb project, Los Alamos, N.M., 1943-45; flew with first atomic bomb to Hiroshima, Japan, Aug. 6, 1945; asst. chief Naval Operations (spl. weapons), 1945-46; dep. for tech. direction to Comdr. Joint Task Force One (Operation Crossroads, Bikini tests of atomic bomb), 1946; dir. Atomic Defense, Office Chief of Naval Operations; mem. Mil. Liaison Com. to the Atomic Energy Commn., 1946-49; dep. comdr. Joint Task Force 7 (atomic tests at Eniwetok Atoll), 1948; with Weapons Systems Evaluations Group of Joint Chiefs of Staff and Research and Development Bd., 1949-51; comdr. cruiser div. six Atlantic Fleet, 1951; dep. chief Bur. of Ordnance, Navy Dept., since 1952. Awarded Silver Star, Distinguished Service Medal. Mem. U.S. Naval Inst. Clubs: Army and Navy (Washington); Army and Navy Country (Arlington, Va.); Cosmos; Chevy Chase (Md.). Home: 6125 33d St. N.W., Washington. Office: Bur. of Ordnance, Navy Dept., Washington. Died Dec. 5, 1953; buried Arlington Nat. Cemetery.

PARTIPILO, ANTHONY VICTOR, surgeon; b. Bari, Italy, Sept. 1900; s. Victor and Claudia (Mazzone) P.; student Northwestern U., 1918-19, DePaul U., 1919-20; M.D., Loyola U., Chgo., 1924; m. Marion Webber Killeen, Apr. 24, 1926 (dec.); 1 dau., Marion (Mrs. Stuart A. Helffrich). Naturalized, 1927. Intern St. Mary's of Nazareth Hosp., Chgo., 1924-26; sr. attending surgeon St. Mary's Hosp., 1925-46; pvt. practice of medicine, 1925-66; house surgeon Lakeview Hosp., 1925-26; asso. anatomy Stritch Sch. Medicine, Loyola U., 1925-28, instr. surgery, 1928-31, clin. asso. surgery, 1931-33, asst. prof., 1933-38, asso. prof. surgery, 1938-57, clin. prof. surgery, 1957-66; attending surgeon Mercy Hosp., 1928-46; dir. Chgo. Postgrad. Sch. Surgery, 1936-42; sr. attending surgeon Columbus Hosp., 1946-66; chief surg. staff Mother Cabrini Hosp., 1950-66; cons. surgeon Ill. Pub. Welfare Dept., Cuneo Meml. Hosp. Served as lt. col. AUS, 1942-46. Decorated Cavallieri Ufficiale (Republic Italy), 1959. Fellow A.M.A., A.C.S., Internat. Coll. Surgs.; mem. Ill., Chgo. med. socs., Phi Beta Phi. Roman Catholic. Club: Lake Shore (Chgo.). Author: Surgical Technique and

Principles of Operative Surgery, 6th edit., 1957. Contbr. to Treatment of Cancer and Allied Diseases (Pack and Ariel), 1958. Died Jan. 6, 1966.

PATCH, ALEXANDER MCCARRELL JR. army officer; b. Fort Huachucua, Ariz., Nov. 23, 1889; s. Alexander McCarrell and Annie (Moore) P.; student Lehigh U., 1908-09; grad. West Point Mil. Acad., 1913; student British G.H.Q. Machine Gun Sch., Sept.-Dec. 1917, Gen. Staff Coll., 1924-25, War Coll., 1930-31; m. Julia A. Littell, Nov. 20, 1916; children—Alexander McCarrell, III, (killed, France, October 22, 1944), Julia Ann. Commissioned 2d lieutenant, U.S. Army, 1913; promoted through grades to lt. col., 1935; temporary rank of brig. gen., 1941; major gen., Mar. 1942; became comdr. U.S. Forces on Guadalcanal, Dec. 1943; returned to U.S. comdg. Desert Training Center; then comdr. IV Army Corps, Calif.; comdr. 7th Army, Allied invasion ground forces, Southern France, Aug. 1944. Comdr. 7th Army, Mar. 1, 1944, lt. gen. Aug. 7, 1944; brig. gen. (permanent), Oct. 1945. Mem. Psi Upsilon. Club: Army-Navy Country (Washington). Address: care War Dept., Washington, D.C. Died Nov. 21, 1945.

PATCH, NATHANIEL JORDAN KNIGHT commodore U.S.N.; b. Otisfield, Me.; s. Benjamin and Harriet E. F. P.; apptd. to U.S. Naval Acad. from Mass., Sept. 20, 1865, grad. 1869; unmarried. Served in sea service 22 yrs. and shore or other duty 14 yrs.; retired with rank of commodore, June 30, 1905. Home: Buffalo, N.Y. Died Jan. 12, 1913.

PATCH, RALPH REGINALD mfr.; b. Stoneham, Mass., May 9, 1882; s. Edgar Leonard and Matilda Smith (Ferguson) P.; S.B., Mass. Inst. of Tech., 1906; m. Christine Vaughn Johonnot, Sept. 4, 1907; children—Charlotte (Mrs. Earle L. Sims), Edgar Leonard, Alma Ferguson. Joined E. L. Patch Co., pharm. mfrs., 1906, gen. mgr., 1916-24, pres., treas., 1924-48, now chmn. bd. Served in Sanitary Corps Res., 1923-42; lieut. col., Sanitary Corps, U.S. Army, 1942-45. Vice pres., mem. exec. com. Am. Drug Mfrs. Assn.; pres., v.p., sec., treas., Am. Pharm. Mfrs. Assn.; trustee, Mass. Col. of Pharmacy, Charlestown Five Cents Savs. Bank, Student Loan Fund; dir., Stoneham Home for Aged; town moderator; mem. bd. of pub. works, planning bd. sch. com., organ com., town of Stoneham, Mass. Home: 28 Lincoln St., Stoneham, Mass. Office: 38 Montvale Av., Stoneham, Mass. Died Sept. 18, 1957.

PATE, RANDOLPH MCCALL ret. marine corps ofcr.; b. Port Royal, S.C., Feb. 11, 1898; s. McCall and Annie (Cornick) P.; A.B., Va. Mil. Inst., 1921; m. Mary Elizabeth Bunting, July 2, 1926. Commd. 2d lt., U.S.M.C., 1921, and advanced through grades to gen., 1956; duty Santo Domingo, Haiti, Hawaiian Islands, China, 1927-29; with 1st Marine Div., participating battle of Guadalcanal, 1942; comdt. 1959. USMC, ret. gen., 1960. Vice pres. Ph. Wechsler & Co., N.Y.C., 1960—. Decorated Legion of Merit (2), D.S.M., Korean Order of Taiguk, Navy D.S.M., Purple Heart; Brazilian Order of Naval Merit; Belgian Order of Leopold. Mem. S.A.R., Kappa Alpha. Episcopalian. Club: Army and Navy (Washington). Home: Spanish Point, Beaufort, S.C. Office: 110 E. 138th St., N.Y.C. Died July 31, 1961; buried Arlington Nat. Cemetery.

PATERSON, DONALD GILDERSLEEVE psychologist; b. Columbus, O., Jan. 18, 1892; s. Robert and Rosa (Gildersleeve) P.; student Olivet Coll., 1910-12; A.B., Ohio State U., 1914, A.M., 1916, LL.D., 1952; m. Margaret Young, June 22, 1920; children—Philip, Margaret Louise. Asst. in psychology, Ohio State U., 1914-16; instr., U. of Kan., 1916-17; cons. psychologist The Scott Co., Phila., Pa., 1919-21; asso. prof. psychology, U. Minn., 1921-23, prof., 1923-60, now emeritus; asst. exec. sec. Minn. Civil Liberties Union, 1960—; vis. prof. summers, U. Chicago, 1931, U. So. Cal., 1936-38, 47; chmn. tech. committee Nat. Occupational Conf., 1933-38; member advisory com. Occupational Research Program, U.S. Employment Service, U.S. Dept. of Labor, 1934-40; chmn. com. individual diagnosis and tng. Employment Stablzn. Research Inst., U. Minn., 1931-45; mem. indsl. relations staff U. Minn., 1945—; cons. training program for vocational counselor VA; Walter V. Bingham lectr. Ohio State University, 1956. Served on various coms. of Am. Council of Edn. Social Science Research Council, Nat. Research Council, White House Conf. on Child Health and Protection (Vocational Guidance), 1927-30. Capt. and chief psychol. examiner, Sanitary Corps, U.S. Army, World War I, Diplomate in Industrial Psychology, 1949. Fellow A.A.A.S., Am. Psychol. Assn. (sec. 1931-37; rep. on Nat. Research Council 1935-38); member American Assn. Applied Psychol. (pres. 1938-39), Vocational Guidance Assn., Am. Assn. Univ. Prof., Sigma Xi, Chi Phi. Club: Campus (Minneapolis). Author or co-author books relating to field since 1916; latest publ.: Studies in Individual Differences: The Search for Intelligence (with others), published in 1961; editor of Journal of Applied Psychology, 1942-54; associate editor Mental Measurement Monographs, 1925—; member editorial board, Journal of Psychology since 1936. Jour. of Consulting Psychology, 1937-38; Public Personnel Quarterly, 1939-41; Rev. Minn. Occupational Rating Scales (with others), 1954. Contbr. tech. jours. Home: 134 Arthur Av. S.E., Mpls. 14. Died Oct. 4, 1961; buried Hallsville, O.

PATERSON, JOHN army officer, congressman, landowner; b. Newington Parish, Wethersfield, Conn., 1744; s. John and Ruth (Bird) P.; grad. Yale, 1762; m. Elizabeth Lee, June 2, 1766. Practiced law in Conn.; moved to Lenox, Mass., 1774; elected mem. Berkshire County Conv. which adopted "Solemn League and Covenant" (boycotting Englishmade products), 1774; rep. from Lenox to 1st, 2d Mass. provincial congresses, 1774, 75; raised a regt. Mass. Militia, 1775, commd. col., 1775; commd. col. 15th Inf., Continental Army, 1776; served in rear position at Battle of Bunker Hill; ordered to relief of Am. troops in Can., on retreat through Crown Point and Ticonderoga, served in battles of Trenton and Princeton; commd. brig. gen., 1777; participated in capture of Gen. Burgoyne at Battle of Saratoga; wintered at Valley Forge, 1777-78; served in Battle of Monmouth; mem. court martial which tried Maj. Andre; brevetted maj. gen., 1783; comdr. Mass. Militia in suppression of Shays' Rebellion, 1787; moved to Lisle (now Whitneys Point), Broome County, N.Y., 1790, an owner land co. with extensive holdings in N.Y. State; mem. N.Y. State Assembly, 1792-93; mem. N.Y. Constl. Conv. from Broome County, 1801; mem. U.S. Ho. of Reps. from N.Y., 8th Congress, 1803-05; apptd. judge Broome and Tioga counties (N.Y.), 1798, 1807; an organizer Soc. of Cincinnati, Ohio Co. Died Lisle, July 19, 1808; buried Lenox Cemetery.

PATRICK, EDWARD army officer, Indian fighter, pioneer; b. County Kerry, Ireland, Mar. 17, 1820; m. Johanna Connor, Aug. 1854. Commd. 1st lt. Tex. Volunteers, 1846, capt. under Albert Signey Johnston, 1847; commd. col. 3d Cal. Inf. during Civil War, commanded mil. dist. of Utah (including Nev.); brevetted maj. gen. U.S. Volunteers, 1865; organized 16,000 non-Mormons, founded community Camp Douglass, nr. Salt Lake City, Utah, 1866; located 1st silver mine in Utah Territory; wrote 1st mining law, placed 1st steamboat on Gt. Salt Lake, built 1st silver smelting works; founded Town of Stockton (Utah); established paper Union Vidette (Utah's 1st daily newspaper). Died Salt Lake City, Dec. 17, 1891.

PATRICK, EDWIN DAVIESS army officer; b. Tell City, Ind., Jan. 11, 1894; s. John Thomas and Anna Elizabeth (Menninger) P.; student Ind. U., 1912-15; U. of Mich., 1915-16; m. Nellie May Bowen, May 15, 1925; children—Edwin Daviess, Thomas Bowen, (stepson) Ulric Boquet. Commd. 2d lt., U.S. Army, Mar. 1917, and advanced through the grades to brig. gen., May 1943. Served on Mexican border, 1917-18; A.E.F., World War I, 1918-19, Luxemburg Army of Occupation, after Dec. 1918; China, 1926-29; served on staff, commdr. S. Pacific, Dec. 1942-June 1943; chief of staff, 6th Army, South Pacific Area and southwest Pacific area, since Dec. 1943. Mem. Phi Delta Theta. Mason. Home: Tell City, Ind. Address: A.P.O. 442, care Postmaster, San Francisco, Calif. Died Mar. 15, 1945.

PATRICK, MARSENA RUDOLPH army officer, agriculturist; b. Jefferson County, N.Y., Mar. 11, 1811; s. John and Miriam (White) P.; grad. U.S. mil. Acad., 1835; m. Mary McGulpin, 1836. Served in Seminole War and Gen. Wool's Mexican expdn.; served as capt. in Mexican War, 1846-48; brevetted maj., by 1850, resigned; pres. N.Y. State Agrl. Coll., 1859; insp. gen. N.Y. Volunteers, 1861; commd. brig. gen. U.S. Volunteers, 1862; appted. provost marshal-gen. Army of Potomac, 1862; designed by Grant as provost marshal-gen. all armies operating against Richmond, 1864; brevetted maj. gen. U.S. Volunteers, 1865; commanded dist. of Henrico (including Richmond), 1865; pres. N.Y. State Agrl. Soc., 1867-68; pioneered for conservation and reforestation; gov. central br. Nat. Home for Disabled Volunteer Soldiers, Dayton, O., 1880-88. Died Dayton, July 27, 1888.

PATRICK, MASON MATHEWS army officer; b. Lewisburg, W.Va., Dec. 13, 1863; s. Alfred Spicer (M.D.) and Virginia (Matthews) P.; B.S., U.S. Mil. Acad., 1886; grad. Engring. Sch. of Application, 1889; m. Grace W. Cooley, Nov. 11, 1902; 1 son, Bream Cooley. Commd. add. 2d lt. engrs., U.S. Army, 1886; promoted through grades to col., 1916; brig. gen. N.A., 1917, and maj. gen. Nat. Army, 1918; maj. gen. U.S. Army, 1921. Asst. instr., practical mil. engring., U.S. Mil. Acad., 1892-95; in charge 1st and 2d dists., improvement Miss. River, 1897-98; sec. Miss. River Commn., St. Louis, Mo., 1898-1901; duty Office, Chief of Engrs., Washington, D.C., 1901-03; instr. U.S. Mil. Acad., 1903-06; comdg. U.S. Mil. Acad. detachment of engrs., 1904-06; chief engr. Army Cuban Pacification, 1907-09; river and harbor work, Norfolk, Va., 1909-12; mem. bd. raising U.S.S. Maine, 1910-12; improvement Great Lakes, Detroit, Mich., 1912-16; comdg. 1st Regt. Engrs., 1916-17; comdt. Engr. Sch., Washington Barracks, D.C., 1916-17; chief engr. lines of communication, and dir. constrn. and forestry operations, A.E.F. in France, Sept. 1917-May 1918; chief of Air Service, A.E.F., May 1918-July, 1919; div. engr., Gulf Div., New Orleans, La., 1919-20; asst. chief of engrs., 1920-21; comdt. Engr. Sch., Camp Humphreys, Va., July-Oct. 1921; apptd. chief of Air Service, Oct. 1921, reapptd. Oct. 1925; retired Dec. 13, 1927; apptd. Pub. Utilities Commr. of D.C., June 1929, resigned as chmn. Sept. 1933. Awarded D.S.M.; Comdr. Legion of Honor, Order Sts. Maurice and Lazarus; Knight Comdr. Order of the British Empire; Comdr. Crown of Belgium; Grand Officer Crown of Italy. Died Jan. 29, 1942.

PATTEN, JOHN congressman; b. Kent County, Del., Apr. 26, 1746; attended common schs. Engaged in farming; served from lt. to maj. Continental Army, participated in all battles from Long Island to Camden during Revolutionary War; mem. Continental Congress from Del., 1785-86; mem. U.S. Ho. of Reps. from Del., 3d, 4th congresses, 1793-Feb. 14, 1794, 95-97; engaged in farming. Died "Tynhead Court" nr. Dover, Del., Dec. 26, 1800; buried Presbyn. Churchyard, Dover.

PATTERSON, ALEXANDER EVANS life ins.; b. Washington, D.C., June 23, 1887; s. William Hart and Georgie Anna (Evans) P.; ed. pub. school in Middle West; LL.D., Coe Coll., 1938; married Eleanor Morgan, Oct. 5, 1920; children—Alexander Evans, Jr., Portia. Salesman, later mgr. Equitable Life Assurance Soc., Pittsburgh, New York, Chicago, 1908-28; genl. agent, later v.p., Penn Mutual Life Ins. Co., Chicago, Phila., 1928-41; v.p., later exec. v.p., Mutual Life Ins. Co. of N.Y., 1941, pres. until Sept., 1948. Served 27 months in U.S. Army, World War I, final rank, maj. F.A. Pres. Nat. Assn. Life Underwriters, 1936; chmn. Life Agency Officers' Assn., 1939-40. Trustee Mutual Life Ins. Co. of N.Y., Roosevelt Hosp., Sigma Alpha Epsilon. Dir. N.Y. chapter Am. Red Cross. Republican. Episcopalian. Clubs: Links, River (New York); Chicago Club (Chicago). Home: 455 E. 57th St., New York; also Pineville, Pa. Office: 34 Nassau St., New York, N.Y. Died Sept. 10, 1948; buried at Mifflintown, Pa.

PATTERSON, DANIEL TODD naval officer; b. L.I., N.Y., Mar. 6, 1786; s. John and Catherine (Livingston) P.; m. George Ann Pollock, 1807, 5 children including Carlile Pollock, George Ann (Mrs. David D. Porter), Thomas Harman. Commd. midshipman U.S. Navy, 1800, lt., 1808; semi independent command 12 gunboats, La., 1810-11; promoted master comdt., 1813; commanded New Orleans (La.) station, 1813; captured 6 schooners and other small vessels of pirate Jean Lafite, 1814; caused enemy delay by gunboat action on Lake Borgne, aiding Gen. Andrew Jackson's final victory, 1815; commd. capt., 1815; fleet capt., comdr. flagship Constitution, Mediterranean Squadron, 1824-28; mem. Bd. of Navy Commrs., 1828; commanded Mediterranean Squadron, 1832-36; comdt. Washington (D.C.) Navy Yard, 1836-39. Died Washington Navy Yard, Aug. 25, 1839; buried Congressional Cemetery, Washington, D.C.

PATTERSON, FREDERICK BECK, b. Dayton, O., June 22, 1892; s. John Henry and Katherine Dudley (Beck) Patterson; educated in public and private schools, Dayton, O.; preparatory sch., Chatham House, Ramsgate, England, 2 years; m. 2d, Armenal W. Gorman, Oct. 25, 1928. Began as helper in foundry of Cash Register Co. (founded by father) and advanced through various depts. to sec. and 3d v.p., pres. 1921-35, vice-pres. and dir., 1935-36, dir., 1937-41. Volunteered as private, World War; served as lt. commanding 15th Photographic A.S., in France. Called a meeting of citizens, 1923, and in 2 days raised §0,000 to purchase 5,000 acres of land required for U.S. Air Service at Dayton, presenting same to Govt. Mem. Nat. Aeronautic Assn., Ohio Soc. of N.Y. Chevalier Legion of Honor (France). Republican. Episcopalian. Mason. Clubs: Dayton Country, Miami Valley Hunt. Made a five months' hunting expedition through British East Africa in 1927, and brought back many specimens to Dayton Museum of Natural History, also 8,000 feet of motion picture film. Home: Delray Beach FL Died June 1, 1971.

PATTERSON, JOHN HENRY brig. gen.; b. New York, Feb. 10, 1843; s. Edward and Martena G. (Talmage) P.; brother of Edward P.; ed. pub. schs. and acad., Brooklyn; m. Mary E. Forbes, Dec. 27, 1871. m. 2d, Grace L. Learned, Jan. 3, 1900. Apptd. from N.Y., 1st lt. 11th Inf., May 14, 1861; transferred to 20th Inf., Sept. 21, 1866; capt., July 28, 1866; maj. 3d Inf., May 19, 1891; lt. col. 1st Inf., Jan. 21, 1895; transferred to 22d Inf., Nov. 4, 1895; col. 20th Inf., Sept. 28, 1898; brig. gen. vols., Sept. 21-Nov. 30, 1898; brig. gen. U.S.A., Jan. 18, 1899; retired Feb. 6, 1899, on account of wounds received July 1, 1898, El Caney, Cuba. Bvtd. capt., Oct. 1, 1864, "for gallant services at Chapel House, Va."; Congressional Medal of Honor, July 23, 1897, "for most distinguished gallantry in action at the Wilderness, May 5, 1864." Home: Albany, N.Y. Died Oct. 5, 1920.

PATTERSON, JOSEPH M(EDILL) journalist; b. Chicago, Jan. 6, 1879; s. Robert Wilson and Elinor (Medill) P.; student Groton School, 1890-96; B.A., Yale U., 1901; m. Alice Higinbotham, Nov. 19, 1902 (divorced); children—Elinor Medill, Alicia, Josephine Medill, James; m. 2d, Mary King, July 1938. With Chicago Tribune, 1901-05; with R. R. McCormick, co-editor and pub. same; 1914-25; founded Daily News, New York, 1919, editor and publisher, 1914-46. Member Illinois Ho. of Rep., 1903; commr. of public works, Chicago, 1905-06. War corr. in China, 1900, Germany and Belgium, 1914; in France, 1915. Noncommd. officer Ill. F.A. in Tex., 1916; capt. Battery B, 149th F.A., 42d (Rainbow) Div., in actions, Lorraine sector 3 months, defense of Champagne under

Gouraud, 2d battle of Marne, St. Mihiel, Argonne. Author: A Little Brother of the Rich; Dope; The Fourth Estate (with J. Keeley and Harriet Ford); By-Products; Rebellion. Clubs: Yale, The Cloud (New York): Tavern, University (Chicago). Office: 220 E. 42d St., New York. Died May 26, 1946; buried in Arlington National Cemetery.

PATTERSON, PAUL lawyer; b. West Newton, Pa., Aug. 25, 1888; s. John Gilfillan and Harriet (McCune) P.; A.B., Yale, 1911; LL.B., Harvard, 1914; unmarried. Admitted to Ohio bar, 1914, since practiced in Cleveland; mem. firm Baker, Hostetler & Patterson; controller and gen. counsel Scripps-Howard concern, 1936-50. Mem. Troop A. of Cleveland, and served on Mexican Border, 1916; entered First Officers Tng. Camp, 1917; served overseas with 42d Div., later detached as a balloon observer; comdg., officer, 4th Corps Balloon Group, 1918; mem. Third Army, Germany, 1918; disch. rank of capt. F.A. Mem. Am., Ohio, Cleve. bar assns., Psi Upsilon, Nisi Prius. Clubs: Union, Mid-Day, University, Kirtland Country, Pepper Pike Country (Cleve.); Yale (New York); Valley (Santa Barbara, Cal.); Duquesne (Pitts.). Home: University Club, Cleveland 15. Office: Union Commerce Bldg., Cleve. 14. Died Nov. 11, 1954.

PATTERSON, ROBERT army officer, industrialist; b. County Tyrone, Ireland, Jan. 12, 1792; s. Francis and Ann (Graham) P.; m. Sarah Engle, 1817, 11 children including Francis Engle. Came to Am., 1799; served as capt., lt. col., col. Pa. Militia in War of 1812; commd. lt. 22d U.S. Inf., then capt. and dep q.m. 32d Inf., mustered out as capt., 1815; mem. Pa. Democratic-Republican Conv., Harrisburg, 1824; commr. internal improvements Pa., 1827; presdl. elector twice; commd. maj. gen. Volunteers, 1847, took Jalapa, Mexico; prominent in sugar industry in La.; owned 30 cotton mills in Pa.; commanded div. Pa. Militia, 1833-67; an original trustee Lafayette Coll., 1825-35, 74-81, pres. bd., 1876-81; commd. maj. gen. Volunteers in command of mil. dept. of Pa., Del., Md., D.C., 1861; failed to give battle to Joseph E. Johnston and to cooperate with McDowell at Bull Run (claimed Gen. Scott did not send him orders to attack.) Author: A Narrative of the Campaign in the Valley of the Shenandoah in 1861, 1865. Died Phila., Aug. 7, 1881; buried Laurel Hill Cemetery, Pa.

PATTERSON, ROBERT FRANKLIN consular official; b. Belfast, Me., Mar. 9, 1836; s. John T. and Mary F. P.; academic edn., Belfast, Me.; m. Marion B. Hudson, Aug. 3, 1878. Enlisted June 1861, 2d lt. and regimental q. m. 5th Iowa inf.; in Mo. campaign under Gn. Fremont; took part in capture New Madrid and Island No. 10; siege and capture Corinth, Miss., battle of Iuka (wounded), battle of Corinth; promoted lt. col. 29th Iowa inf., took part in siege of Vicksburg, battle of Helena, Ark., capture Little Rock, siege Spanish Fort, Ala., capture Mobile; promoted bvt. col. and brig. gen. "for gallant and meritorious service at Spanish Fort and Mobile." Settled at Memphis, Tenn., after war; 13 yrs. collector internal revenue at Memphis; postmaster Memphis, 1889-93; consul gen. at Calcutta, India, May, 1897-—. Republican. Deceased.

PATTERSON, ROBERT PORTER former secretary war; b. Glens Falls, N.Y., Feb. 12, 1891; s. Charles R. and Lodice E. (Porter) P.; A.B., Union College, 1912; LL.B., Harvard, 1915; m. Margaret T. Winchester, Jan. 3, 1920; children—Robert P., Aileen W. (Mrs. Timothy Seldes), Susan Hand (Mrs. Stephen R. Petschek), Virginia D. (Mrs. Robert L. Montgomery, II). Admitted to the N.Y. bar, 1915, and practiced at N.Y. City; apptd. judge U.S. Dist. Court, Southern N.Y. Dist., 1930; apptd. judge U.S. Circuit Court of Appeals, 1939; resigned, July 1940, to become asst. sec. of war; apptd. undersec. of war, Dec. 1940; apptd. sec. of war, U.S. War Dept., Sept. 1945; resigned, July 1947. Dir. Federal Reserve Bank of New York; pres. Practicing Law Inst. Trustee Union Coll., pres. Harvard Law Sch. Assn. 1937-49. Pvt. 7th Regiment Nat. Guard N.Y., Mex. Border, 1916; capt., maj. 306th Inf., U.S. Army, World War I. Pres. Freedom House. Mem. Am. Bar Assn. (chmn. commn. on organized Crime), N.Y. State Bar Assn., Association Bar City of New York (president), American Acad. Arts and Scis., Am. Legion, N.Y. Soc. Mil. and lNaval Officers World Wars (pres.), Phi Beta Kappa, Phi Delta Theta. Awarded D.S.C. for "extraordinary heroism in action on Aug. 14, 1918." Awarded Silver Star and Purple Heart in World War I; awarded D.S.M. for service in World War II. Clubs: Harvard, Lawyers, Century Assn. Home: Cold Spring, N.Y., also 1 E. 84th St., N.Y.C. 23. Office: 1 Wall St., N.Y.C. Died at Elizabeth, N.J., Jan. 22, 1952; buried Arlington Cemetery, Arlingtin, Va.

PATTERSON, ROBERT URIE physician, ret. army officer; b. Montreal, June 16, 1877 (parents Am. citizens); s. William James Ballantyne and Eleanor Haight (Lay) P.; prep. edn. San Antonio (Tex.) Acad., Bishop's College Sch., Lennoxville, Que., Berthier Grammar Sch., Berthier-en-haute, Que., Montreal Collegiate Inst., 1892-94; M.D. and C.M., McGill U. Montreal, 1898, LL.D., 1932; honor grad. Army Med. Sch., 1902; grad. Med. Field Service School, Fort Leavenworth, Kan., 1912, Army War Coll., 1921; m. Eda Beryl Lorraine Day, Mar. 28, 1905 (dec. Apr. 1918); children—Eleanor Lyman, Janet; m. 2d, Eleanor Reeve, Aug. 14, 1920; children—Margaret Baden, Robert Urie. House surgeon Montreal Gen. Hosp., 1898-99; resident accoucher Montreal Maternity Hosp., 1899-1900; in practice at Belt, Mont., 1900-01; commd. 1st lt. and asst. surgeon U.S. Army, June 29, 1901, and advanced through grades to col. M.C., 1927; served as temp. col. N.A., World War; surgeon gen. U.S. Army, rank of major gen., 1931-35; retired, Nov. 30, 1935; dean Med. Sch., U. Okla., 1935-42; dean Sch. of Medicine, U. Md., 1942-—. Service in P.I., Cuba, Hawaii, Italy, France. Decorated D.S.M., 2 silver star citations for "gallantry in action," Philippine Campaign, Cuban Pacification and Victory medals (United States; British war Medal; mentioned in despatches by the British Commander-in-chief for gallantry on Western front, Dec. 1917; Fatiche di Guerra, Medale de Independencia, Officer Crown of Italy (Italy); Officer Order of White Lion (Czechoslovakia); Serbian Red Cross. Fellow A.C.S., A.C.P.; mem. A.M.A., Assn. Mil. Surgeons of U.S., Second Div. Vets Assn., Mil. Order of Carabao, Alpha Delta Phi, Phi Beta Kapp, Phi Beta Pi, Alpha Omega Alpha. Episcopalian. Mason (32 deg., K.T.). Clubs: Army Navy, Alfalfa (Washington); Army and Navy (Oklahoma City); Army and Navy (San Francisco); Chevy Chase (Md.); Hot Springs (Ark.) Golf and Country, Oklahoma City Golf and Country. Home: 5801 Roland Av., Balt. 10. Died Dec. 5, 1950.

PATTERSON, THOMAS EDWARD soldier; b. W. Chester Co., N.Y., June 2, 1867; s. John and Elizabeth P. Served as co. comdr. and paymaster, State troops, Jan., 1892-Oct., 1893, during mining trouble in Tenn.; lt.-col. 2d Tenn. vol. inf. Spanish-Am. war; provost marshal gen. 2d army corps on staff of Gen. Graham and later S.B.M. Young; jr. v.-comdr. in chief Spanish-Am. War Veterans, 1901-02. Treas. Hamilton Co., Tenn., since 1902. Address: Chattanooga, Tenn.

PATTERSON, THOMAS HARMAN naval officer; b. New Orleans, May 10, 1820; s. Daniel Todd and George Ann (Pollock) P.; m. Maria Wainwright, Jan. 5, 1847, 5 children. Commd. midshipman U.S. Navy, 1836, lt., 1849; commanded ship Chocura in naval force which cooperated with McClellan during Peninsular Campaign, 1862; promoted comdr., 1862; sr. officer in York and Pamunkey rivers, 1862, offshore blockade, Charleston, S.C., 1864-65; commd. capt., 1866, commodore, 1871; rear adm., 1877; commanded flagship Brooklyn, Brazil Squadron, 1865-67; comdt. Washington (D.C.) Navy Yard, 1873-76; commanded Asiatic Squadron, 1878-80. Died Washington, Apr. 9, 1889.

PATTESON, SEARGENT SMITH PRENTISS lawyer; b. Amherst Co., Va., Dec. 15, 1856; s. Dr. David and Elizabeth (Camm) P.; ed. pvt. sch. and pvt. teachers and Randolph-Macon Coll., 1872-73; unmarried. Admitted to Va. bar, 1877; served pvt., non-commd. and commd. officer in Va. vols. in Richmond 7 yrs.; chmn. City Dem. Com., 1892; mem. Va. Legislature, 1899-1901; practicing at Richmond; elected member Virginia legislature, Nov. 1927. Episcopalian. Democrat. Home: Richmond, Va. Died Jan. 26, 1931.

PATTISON, EVERETT WILSON lawyer; b. Waterville, Me., Feb. 22, 1839; s. Robert Everett (D.D.) and Frances (Wilson) P.; brother of James William P. (q.v.); A.B., Waterville (now Colby) Coll., 1858 (LL.D., 1906); A.M., Shurtleff Coll., Ill., 1867; m. Marcia Scott Whitehouse, June 15, 1861 (died 1884); m. 2d, Alice M. Gould, Sept. 24, 1892. Prin. West Gardiner (Me.) Acad., 1859; prof. Oread Inst., Worcester, Mass., 1859-61; entered U.S. Vols. at Boston, May 28, 1861, as pvt. Co. I, 2d Mass. Inf.; became 1st sergt., 2d lt., 1st lt. and capt. Co. F, same regt. Practicing law, St. Louis, 1865-—; was atty. St. Louis Sch. Bd. 2 terms. Author: Digest of Missouri Reports (9 vols.); a work on Missouri Code Pleading; and one on Criminal Instructions. Home: St. Louis, Mo. Died Nov. 14, 1919.

PATTISON, THOMAS naval officer; b. Troy, N.Y., Feb. 8, 1822; s. Elias and Olivia (Gardiner) P.; m. Serafina Catalina Webster, July 1, 1850, 1 dau., Maria Webster. Apptd. midshipman U.S. Navy, 1839; served in Mexican War; sailing master on ship Portsmouth, China Sta., circa 1852, promoted to lt. while on cruise; escorted 1st Am. minister to Japan from Simoda to Tokyo, 1858 (became 1st Am. naval officer to enter Tokyo); exec. of sloop Perry which captured privateer Savannah (1st privateer taken), off Charleston, N.C., 1861; in command steamer Sumter on S.E. coast blockade, 1861; sr. officer at Fernandina, Fla., summer and autumn 1862; comdt. naval. sta. established at former Confederate base, Memphis, Tenn., 1863-65; commd. lt. comdr., 1862, comdr., 1865, capt., 1870, commodore, 1877, rear adm.; 1883; commanded naval sta. Port Royal, S.C., 1878-80, Washington Navy Yard, 1880-83. Died New Brighton, S.I., N.Y., Dec. 17, 1891.

PATTON, GEORGE SMITH, JR., army officer; b. San Gabriel, Calif., Nov. 11, 1885; s. George Smith and Ruth (Wilson) P.; student Classical Sch. for Boys, Pasadena, Calif., 1897-1903, Va. Mil. Inst., 1903-04; B.S., U.S. Mil. Acad., 1909; grad. Cavalry Sch., 1913; grad. Advanced Equitation Class, Cav. Sch., 1914; honor grad. Command and Gen. Staff Sch., 1923; grad. War Coll., 1932; m. Beatrice Ayer, May 26, 1910; children—Beatrice (wife of Col. John K. Waters, U.S. Army), Ruth-Ellen (wife of Lt. Col. James W. Totten, U.S. Army), George, IV. Began as 2d lt., 15th Cav., U.S. Army, 1909, and advanced through the grades to general, 1945; instr. in weapons, Cav. Sch., 1914-16; aide-de-camp to Gen. Pershing, Mexico, 1916-17; sailed to England as same, May 1917; first man detailed in Tank Corps, U.S. Army, Nov. 1917; organized and comd. Tank Sch. and 1st (later 304th) Brig., 1917-19; wounded, Sept. 1918; comd. 304th Tank Brig., Camp Meade, Md., 1919-21; comd. 1st Squadron, 3d Cav., Ft. Meyer, Va., 1921-22; on gen. staff, 1923-27; in Office Chief of Cav., 1928-31; exec. officer 3d Cav., 1932-35; on Gen. Staff, 1935-37; comd. 9th Cav., 1938, 5th Cav., 1938, 3d Cav., 1938-40, 2d Armored Brig., July-Nov. 1940; became comdg. officer 2d Armored Div., Fort Benning, Ga., Nov. 1940; comd. U.S. Forces on West Coast, Morocco, N. Africa, Nov. 1942; Comdr. Central Sector, Am. Forces in Tunisia, Mar. 1943; comd. 7th Army in Sicily, July 1943 ; organized and comd. desert training center, March 1944; comdr. 3d Army, in France, Belgium, Luxembourg, Germany, Aug. 1944; comdr. 15th Army, France, Oct. 1945. Decorated with D.S.C., Distinguished Service medal, Silver Star, Purple Heart; Congressional Medal of Honor for Life Saving (2d class), Mexican Service medal, World War medal with 4 battle clasps, D.S.C. (with Oak Leaf Cluster), D.S.M. (2 Oak Leaf Clusters), Silver Star (Oak Leaf Cluster), Legion of Merit, Bronze Star, Life Saving Medal, Companion of the Bath, Knight Commander of British Empire, French Legion of Honor (Grand Officier), Croix de Guerre (with palm), Medal of Verdun, Grand Cross of Ouissam Alaouite. Clubs: Army and Navy, Capital Yacht (Washington, D.C.); Eastern Yacht (Marblehead, Mass.); Manchester (Mass.) Yacht; Cruising of America. Died Dec. 21, 1945.

PATTON, HENRY WILLIAM editor; b. Palmyra, Mo.; July 14, 1856; s. Alfred and Priscilla (Thomas) P.; ed. pub. schs.; law student, U. of Mo., 1879-80; m. Mrs. Sarah S. McMillan, Oct. 1, 1914. Reporter and city editor, Los Angeles Times and Herald, 1884-87; editor and owner successively Los Angeles Capital, Everett (Wash.) Independent, Aberdeen (Wash.) Bulletin, Eureka (Calif.) Standard, and mgr. American-Reveille, Bellingham, Wash. Discoverer and first explorer Salton Sea, 1891 (trip made for San Francisco Examiner); exploration trip to Tiburon Island, Gulf of Calif., 1896. Maj. and ordnance officer, N.G. Calif., 1888. Register U.S. Land Office, Los Angeles, 1886-91; spl. agt. Interior Dept. Indian Service, 1893-98; chmn. Exemption Bd., Hoquiam, 1917; sec. to congressional party visiting battle front in France, 1917. Made cruise of 7 months to South Sea Islands, 1918; sailed to west coast of South and Central America and Mexico, 1919, New Zealand and The Fiji Islands, 1921. Now special writer for Seattle, Portland and Los Angeles papers. Mason, Elk. Home: Hoquiam, Wash. Deceased.

PATTON, JAMES MCDOWELL M.D., ophthalmologist; b. Mercersburg, Pa., Sept. 24, 1876; s. John Samuel and Mary Holmes (McDowell) P.; B.S., Bellevue (Neb.) Coll., 1901, A.M., 1904; M.D., U. of Neb., 1904; m. Agnes Deborah Hatfield, Aug. 16, 1904; 1 son, John Hatfield. Began practice at Omaha, 1904; mem. firm Gifford, Patton, Callfas, Potts, Cassidy and Fairchild, oculists and aurists; prof. ophthalmology, Coll. of Medicine, U. of Neb., 1925-—; ophthalmologist M.E. Hosp., Clarkson Memorial Hosp., University Hosp. Served as maj. Med. Corps, U.S.A., overseas, 1918-19. Fellow Am. Coll. Surgeons. Republican. Presbyn. Home: Omaha, Neb. Died June 20, 1930.

PATTON, RAYMOND STANTON hydrographic engr.; b. Degraff, O., Dec. 29, 1882; s. Oliver and Ida M. (Cloninger) P.; Ph.B., Western Reserve U., 1904; m. Virginia Mitchell, Nov. 7, 1912; children—Raymond Stanton, Virginia Mitchell, Helen Mitchell. With Coast and Geodetic Survey, 1904-—; engaged in field surveys, Atlantic and Pacific coasts of U.S., Alaska and Philippine Islands, and was made chief of party and comdg. officer survey vessels, in charge surveys in Western Alaska, among them, of approaches to Kuskokwin River, 1912-13, 1914-15; chief of Coast Pilot Sect., 1915-17; lt. and lt. comdr. U.S. Navy, 1917-19; in charge chart production and correction to 1929; dir. Coast and Geodetic Survey, Apr. 29, 1929-—. Life trustee Nat. Geog. Soc. Mem. engineering advisory com. on coast erosion, N.J. State Bd. of Commerce and Navigation; mem. National Research Council. Dir. Am. Shore and Beach Preservation Assn.; trustee Woods Hole Oceanographic Institute. Author: U.S. Coast Pilot, Alaska—Yakutat Bay to Arctic Ocean (Govt. Printing Office), 1916; U.S. Coast Pilot, Pacific Coast—California, Oregon and Washington (same), 1917; Report of Engring. Advisory Com. of N.J. Bd. of Commerce and Navigation on Coast Erosion, 1922-24. Died Nov. 25, 1937.

PATTY, WILLARD WALTER ret. u. prof.; b. Redfield, Ia., Mar. 9, 1892; s. David Sylvester and Elmina Jane (Hastings) P.; A.B., Ia. State Tchrs. Coll., 1914; student Ia. State Coll., summer 1915; A.M., U. Cal., 1920, Ph.D., 1925; student Columbia, 1932; m. Ferol Irene McKinney, Aug. 29, 1914; children—Betty Jane (Mrs. Thomas Gerard McManus), Robert Hastings. Tchr. sci., coach, and prin. Iowa Falls (Ia.) High Sch., 1914-15; tchr., coach and supt. schs., Adair, Ia., 1915-17; dir. vocational and part-time edn., Berkeley, Cal., 1920-23; asso. in edn. (half-time), U. Cal., 1923-25; asst. prof.

edn. Ind. U., 1925-26; prof. edn. Ohio State U., 1926-27; prof. edn. Ind. U., 1927-46, dir. phys. welfare tng., dept., 1931-46, dir. Normal Coll., Am. Gymnastic Union, Ind. U., 1941-46; dean Sch. Health, Phys. Edn. and Recreation, Ind. U., 1946-57, ret. 1958; tchr. u. summer session since 1927 (except 1931); tchr. summer session U. Cal., 1921-24, U. Cal. at Los Angeles, 1925, U. Mich., 1931; extension teaching Ia. State Tchrs. Coll., 1916-17, U. Cal., 1920, Ind. U. 1925-58. Served as capt., inf. U.S. Army, 1917-19. Fellow Am. Acad. Phys. Edn.; mem. A.A.H.P.E.R. (honor fellow), Am. Pub. Health Assn., N.E.A., Phi Delta Kappa (past pres.), Am. Legion, Kiwanian (past pres.). Author: Legal Basis of Public School Secondary Program, 1926; Teaching Health and Safety in Elementary Grades, 1940; also author 16 monographs. Contbr. articles to mags. Home: Nashville, Ind. Died Mar. 26, 1962; buried Val Hallah Cemetery, Bloomington, Ind.

PAUL, JOHN judge; b. Harrisonburg, Va., Dec. 9, 1883; s. John and Katherine (Green) P.; grad. Va. Mil. Inst., Lexington, 1903; LL.B., U. Va., 1906; m. Frances Dannehower, Oct. 14, 1914 (died 1919); m. 2d, Alice Kelly Taylor, June 24, 1939. Admitted to Va. bar, 1906, practiced at Harrisonburg; mem. Va. State Senate, 1912-16, 1919-22; mem. 67th Congress (1921-23), 7th Va. Dist.; spl. asst. to U.S. atty. gen., 1924-25; U.S. dist. atty. Western Va. Dist., 1929-31, U.S. dist. judge since Jan. 1932. Served as capt. F.A., U.S. Army, 1917-19; with AEF, May 1918-May 1919. Mem. Raven Soc. (U. of Va.), Kappa Alpha, Phi Delta Phi, Phi Beta Kappa. Republican. Episcopalian. Home: R.F.D., Dayton, Va. 22821. Address: Federal Bldg., Harrisonburg, Va. Died Feb. 13, 1964; buried Woodlawn Cemetery, Harrisonburg.

PAUL, WILLARD STEWART army officer, coll. pres.; b. Worcester, Mass., Feb. 28, 1894; s. Warrington Irving and Etta M. (Fish) P.; student Clark U., Dartmouth; B.S., Johns Hopkins, 1924; M.A., Am. U., 1942, LL.D., 1958; LL.D., Roanoke (Va.) Coll., 1959; m. Ruth Sieurin, Apr. 14, 1919 (dec. 1953); 1 son, Richard; m. 2d, Louella Musselman Arnold, Aug. 12, 1958. Enlisted Colo. F.A., 1916; became lt. U.S. Army, 1917; advanced through grades to lt. gen., 1948; grad. Inf. Sch., officers course, 1921, advanced course, 1930. Command and Gen. Staff Sch., 1935, Army War Coll., 1937; instr. Inf. Sch., 1930-33; detailed to Adj. Gen.'s Dept., 1937-41, in charge classification all mil. personnel; Gen. Staff Corps as G-4, Gen. Hdqrs. and Army Ground Forces; World War II, comdr. 26th Inf. Div.; G-I, S.H.A.E.F.; dep. chief of staff U.S.F.E.T., asst. chief of staff G-I, dir. Personnel W.D.G.S.; cons. Asst. Sec. Def. for Manpower; asst. dir. ODM; pres. Gettysburg Coll., 1956—. Dir. Internat. Christian Leadership. Mem. Ret. Officers Assn. (pres.), Sigma Nu. Republican. Mason (32 deg.). Presbyn. Clubs: Cosmos (Washington); Army and Navy. Address: Gettysburg College, Gettysburg, Pa. Died Mar. 21, 1966.

PAULDING, HIRAM naval officer; b. Westchester County, N.Y., Dec. 11, 1797; s. John and Esther (Ward) P.; grad. Capt. Alden Partridges Mil. Acad., Norwich, Vt., 1823; m. Ann Kellogg, 1828, 6 children. Apptd. midshipman U.S. Navy, 1811; served as acting lt. in Ticonderoga in Battle of Lake Champlain, 1813, commended by U.S. Congress; commd. lt., 1816; 1st lt. in Dolphin, 1825, pursued mutineers from whaleship Globe during cruise in South seas; capt., in ship on China cruise, Vincennes 1844-47; in command of frigate St. Lawrence (1st Am. warship to reach Bremen, Germany), 1848; in charge of Washington (D.C.) Navy Yard, 1849-53; command of Home Squadron, seized Gen. William Walker and about 150 filibusterers who had landed in defiance of U.S. sloop Saratoga at Grey Town, Nicaragua, 1855-58; Apptd. head Bur. of Detail, 1861; led expdn. which evacuated Norfolk Navy Yard, 1861; head N.Y. Navy Yard, 1861-65; retired as rear adm., 1861; gov. U.S. Naval Asylum, Phila., 1866-69; port admiral of Boston, 1869-70, Author: Journal of a Cruise of the United States Schooner Dolphin, 1831. Died L.I., N.Y., Oct. 20, 1878.

PAULDING, JAMES KIRKE author, sec. of navy; b. Putnam County, N.Y., Aug. 22, 1778; s. William and Catharine (Ogden) P.; m. Gertrude Kemble, Nov. 15, 1818, several children including William. Mem. Calliopean Soc. (one of earliest literary socs. in N.Y.); collaborated with Washington Irving in periodical Salmagundi, 1807-08; wrote against Brit. criticism in his work, The United States and England, 1814; sec. Bd. Navy Commrs., 1815-23; navy agt. for N.Y., 1823-38; U.S. sec. of navy under Van Buren, 1838-41, sent South Sea Exploring Expdn. on its 4 year cruise to Ore. coast and Antarctic. Author: The Diverting History of John Bull and Jonathan Brother, 1812; (poem) The Lay of the Scottish Fiddle; A Tale of Havre de Grace, 1813; Letters from the South, by a Northern Man, 1817; (chief poetical work) "The Backwards Man," 1818; (second series) Salmagundi, 1819; (1st novel) Koningsmark, or The Long Finne, 1823; (contbrns. to so-called literary war between Eng. and Am.) A Sketch of Old England, 1822, John Bull in America, 1825; New Mirror for Travelers, 1828; The Dumb Girl, 1830; (best novel) The Dutchman's Fireside, 1831; Westward Ho!, 1832; A Life of Washington, 1835; (lesser known works) The Merry Tales of the Three Wise Men of Gotham, 1826; Tales of the Good Woman, 1829; The Lion of the West, 1831; The Book of St. Nicholas, 1837; A Gift from Fairy Land, 1838; American Comedies, 1847. Died Apr. 6, 1860; buried Greenwood Cemetery, Bklyn.

PAULDING, WILLIAM JR. congressman, mayor N.Y.C.; b. Phillipsburgh (now Tarrytown), N.Y., Mar. 7, 1770; s. William Paulding; studied law. Admitted to N.Y. bar, began practice in N.Y.C.; mem. U.S. Ho. of Reps. (Democrat) from N.Y., 12th Congress, 1811-13; served as brig. gen. N.Y. Militia during War of 1812; del. N.Y. Constl. Conv., 1821; adj. gen. State of N.Y.; mayor N.Y.C., 1824-26. Died Tarrytown, Feb. 11, 1854; buried Old Dutch Burying Ground at Sleepy Hollow, Tarrytown.

PAULLIN, CHARLES OSCAR author; b. Jamestown, O.; s. Enos and Malinda (Moorman) P.; student Antioch College, 1890-93; grad. student Johns Hopkins University, 1894-95, 1901 (fellow); B.S.S., Catholic U. of America, 1897; Ph.D., U. of Chicago, 1904; unmarried. Instr. mathematics, Kee Mar Coll., Hagerstown, Md., 1893-94; nautical expert U.S. Hydrog. Office, Navy Dept., Washington, 1896-1900; research asst. of Carnegie Instn., Washington, in London, 1910-11; lecturer on diplomatic history, Johns Hopkins, 1911, on naval history, George Washington U., 1911-13; research staff Carnegie Instn. Washington, 1912-36. Mem. Am. Hist. Assn., Am. Polit. Science Assn., Naval History Soc., U.S. Naval Inst., Va. Hist. Soc., N.Y. Hist. Soc., Naval Hist. Foundation (trustee and treas.), Columbia Hist. Soc. (mgr.), Wilderness Soc. Club: Cosmos. Author: The Navy of the American Revolution, 1906; Commodore John Rodgers, 1773-1838, 1910; Diplomatic Negotiations of American Naval Officers, 1912; Guide to Materials for United States History since 1783, in London Archives (with F. L. Paxson), 1914; Atlas of the Historical Geography of the United States, 1932; (monographs) American Naval Administration, 1775-1911, 1905-14; Voyages of American Naval Vessels to the Orient, 1800-1910, 1910-12. Editor: Out-Letters of the Continental Marine Committee and Board of Admiralty, Aug. 1776-Sept. 1780, 2 vols., 1914-15; Documents Relating to the Battle of Lake Erie, 1918; European Treaties Bearing on the History of the United States and Its Dependencies, 1716-1815. Awarded (with John K. Wright) Loubat prize, Columbia Univ., 1933. Staff contbr. Dictionary of American Biography s- ince 1941. Address: Cosmos Club, Washington, D.C. Died Sep. 1, 1944.

PAXSON, EDGAR SAMUEL artist; b. E. Hamburg, N.Y., Apr. 25, 1852; s. William Hambleton and Christian (Hambleton) P.; ed. log sch. house and 1 yr. at Friends' Inst., E. Hamburg, N.Y.; m. Laura Milicent Johnson, June 5, 1874. Began art work as a scenic painter at Deed Lodge, Mont., 1878, with splty. in painting of the Am. Indian and hist. incidents connected with him and the Am. pioneer. Took part in Nez Percé War, 1877-78; served 10 yrs. pvt. to 2d lt., 1st Regt. Nat. Guard, Mont.; 1st lt. 1st Mont. Inf., U.S.V., for Spanish-Am. War; served 8 mos. in Philippines but resigned because of failing health; award silver medal as Mont. soldier. Engrossed memorial of appreciation by Mont. Legislature, 1905, for work and display at La. Purchase Expn.; exhibited at Portland Expn., 1905. Represented in collections in U.S., London, Paris, etc. Prin. works: Custer's Last Fight; 6 hist. murals in Mont. Capitol; 8 murals in new County Court House, Missoula, Mont.; Reception and bronze tablet "Sacaye-wea," and "From the High Places They Watched the Tide of Emigration," etc. Republican. Home: Missoula, Mont. Died Nov. 9, 1919.

PAXSON, FREDERIC LOGAN historian; b. Phila., Pa., Feb. 23, 1877; s. Joseph A. (M.D.) and Ada (Fell) P.; B.S., U. of Pa., 1898, Harrison scholar, 1898-99, Harrison fellow, 1902-03, Ph.D., 1903; A.M., Harvard U., 1902; Litt.D., Lawrence Coll., 1932, U. of Wis., 1935, U. of Pa., 1940; LL.D., Mills College, Calif., 1933; m. Helen Hale, d. Joseph T. Jackson, Dec. 26, 1906; children—Jane T., Emma F., Patricia. Instr. history in secondary schs., 1899-1901; asst. prof., 1903-04, prof. history, 1904-06, of Colo.; asst. prof. Am. history, 1906-07, jr. prof., 1907-10, U. of Mich.; prof. Am. history, U. of Wis., 1910-32; Margaret Byrne prof. history, U. of Calif., since 1932. Prof. Am. history, (summers), U. of Chicago, 1909, U. of Calif., 1913, U. of Mich., 1915, U. of Pa., 1917, U. of Calif. (Los Angeles), 1929, U. of Wis., 1935-47, Columbia, 1941, Harvard, 1948; research asso. Carnegie Instn., in British archives, summer 1910; mem. Com. on Management Dictionary of Am. Biography, 1924-36; mem. bd. editors Pacific Hist. Review, 1933-39; mem. advisory com. Franklin D. Roosevelt Library, 1939. Major United States Army in charge economic mobilization section of historical branch war plans division General Staff, 1918-19. Member American Hist. Assn. (councillor 1921-25; 2d v.p. 1937; pres. 1938), State Hist. Soc. Wis. (curator 1911-32, v.p. 1919-32), Mass. Hist. Soc. (corr.), Miss. Valley Hist. Assn. (pres. 1917), Pacific Coast Br., Am. Hist. Assn. (pres. 1942-43); Phi Beta Kappa. Mem. Soc. of Friends (Quakers). Author: The Independence of the South American Republics, 1903, 1916; The Last American Frontier, 1910; The Civil War, 1911; The New Nation, 1915; Guide to Materials for United States History since 1783, in London Archives (with C. O. Paullin), 1914; Recent History of the United States, 1921, revised edit., 1928 and 1937; History of the American Frontier, 1924 (awarded Pulitzer prize for 1924); The United States in Recent Times, 1926; When the West Is Gone (Colver Lectures, Brown U.), 1929; American Democracy and the World War: Pre-War Years, 1913-1917, 1936; America at War, 1917-1918, 1939; The Great Demobilization and Other Essays, 1941. Editor Com. Pub. Information Handbook, War Cyclopedia, 1917; also (War Dept. monographs) Economic Mobilization for the War of 1917, 1918; Handbook of Economic Agencies of the War of 1917, 1919. Address: 30 Wheeler Hall, Berkeley 4, Calif. Died Oct. 24, 1948.

PAXTON, JOHN RANDOLPH clergyman; b. Canonsburg, Pa., Sept. 18, 1843; s. John and Elizabeth Dill (Wilson) P.; A.B., Jefferson Coll., Pa., 1866; grad. Western Theol. Seminary, Allegheny, Pa., 1869; (D.D., Union Coll., 1883). Served pvt. and 2d lt., 140th Pa. Regt., Union Army, 1862 until end of Civil War; then reëntered coll.; ordained Presbyn. ministry, 1871; pastor Churchville, Md., 1871-74, Pine St. Ch., Harrisburg, Pa., 1874-78, New York Av. Sch., Washington, D.C., 1878-82, West Ch., New York, 1882-93, New York Ch., New York, 1897-98; retired. Home: New York, N.Y. Died Apr. 11, 1923.

PAYEN DE NOYLAN, GILLES-AUGUSTIN army officer; b. France, 1697; s. Pierre and Catherine Jeanne (Le Moyne) P. de N.; m. Jeanne Faucon Du Manoir, May 1, 1735, at least 2 children including Jean Baptiste. Came to La. as lt. in French Army, 1717-18; engaged in capture of Pensacola (Fla.) from Spanish, 1719; in command of New Orleans and an inf. co., 1720; dismissed from army, 1726; adjutant of Mobile (Ala.), 1732, New Orleans, 1733; acted as diplomatic agt. to Choctaw Indians and commanded several raids against them; wounded, 1736; sent on unsuccessful expdn. up Mississippi River to prepare sites for battle against Chickasaw Indians by a combined French and Indian army, 1739; made lieutenant du roi, 1741; mem. La. Supreme Council; acting gov. La., 1748. Died Feb. 26, 1751.

PAYNE, EUGENE BEAUHARNAIS lawyer, govt. official; b. Seneca Falls, N.Y., Apr. 15, 1835; s. Thomas H. and Susannah N. S. P.; (nephew late U.S. Senator Henry B. Payne); ed. Waukegan, Ill., Acad.; grad. law dept. Northwestern Univ., 1860; admitted to bar, 1860; m. Adelia T. Wright, Jan. 26, 1862. Organized 1st co. of Union troops at Waukegan, Ill., Apr. 16, 1861; served through Civil war as 2d lt., capt., maj. and lt. col., 37th Ill. vols.; bvtd. brig. gen. U.S. vols. Mem. Ill. legislature, 1866-69; practiced law, 1869-87; from 1887 officer of Pension Bureau. Author: Payne's Annotated Digest of the Decisions of Dept. of Interior in Pension Claims, 1897 to 1905. Home: Washington, D.C. Died 1910.

PAYNE, FREDERICK HUFF ex-asst. sec. war; b. Greenfield, Mass., Nov. 10, 1876; s. Samuel Brewer and Eva Caroline (Huff) P.; ed. pub. schs., Greenfield; m. Mary Blake, Nov. 8, 1900; children—Frederick Blake, Groverman Blake, Carolyn Huff (Mrs. Bernard Barnes). Bank examiner State of Massachusetts, 1906-09; pres. Mechanics Trust Co., Boston, 1910; v.p. Federal Trust Co., 1911; successively treasurer, v.p., pres. and chmn. bd. Greenfield Tap & Die Corp., 1912-40; assistant chief Springfield Ordnance District, Springfield, Mass., Sept. 1940-Jan. 1946; partner Tucker, Anthony & Co., investment bankers, New York and Boston, 1919-24; dir. Am. Mutual Liability Insurance Co., Boston. Trustee Franklin Savings Institution (v.p.). Asst. sec. of war, 1930-1933. Maj. ordnance U.S. Army and dist. procurement officer, 1918; mem. Bridgeport Dist. Claims Bd., 1919; asst. dist. chief Bridgeport Dist. Ordnance Dept., 1919-30 and 1933—; now colonel O.R.C. Rep. Unitarian. Clubs: Metropolitan (N.Y.); University (Boston); Colony (Springfield); Greenfield. Address: Colony Club, Springfield 5, Mass. Died Mar. 24, 1960.

PAYNE, LEON MATHER, lawyer; b. Pitts., June 3, 1915; s. Leon Frank and Sarah Brownson (Mather) P.; A.B. cum laude, Brown U., 1936; LL.B., U. Tex., 1939; m. Carolyn Lelia Wilson, 1951; children—Leon Mather, Miriam Wilson. Lawyer, Andrews, Kurth, Campbell and Jones, Houston, 1939, partner, 1947-72; gen. counsel. sec., dir. Fla. Gas Transmission Co., Fla. Gas Co.; dir. El Paso Natural Gas Co., El Paso Products Co., Wilson Industries, Inc. Adv. dir. Mus. of Fine Arts; trustee emeritus Brown U. Served as maj. USAAF, 1942-45. Decorated D.F.C. (2), Air Medal (6). Mem. Am., Fed. Power, Houston bar assns., State Bar Tex., Am. Judicature Soc., Phi Beta Kappa, Phi Delta Phi. Presbyn. Bd. student editors Tex. Law Review. Home: Houston TX Died May 24, 1972.

PAYNE, OLIVER HAZARD capitalist; b. Cleveland; s. U.S. Senator Henry B. and Mary (Perry) P.; grad. Yale, 1863, A.B., 1878, as of class of 1863. First lt., capt., maj., and lt. col. 124th Ohio Inf., Sept. 11, 1862; col., Jan. 1, 1863; bvtd. brig. gen. vols., Mar. 13, 1865, "for faithful and meritorious services." Iron mfr. and oil refiner, Cleveland, 1866-84, New York, 1884—. Dir. Coal Creek Mining and Mfg. Co., Va. & Southeastern Ry. Co. Gave $500,000 to aid in establishing and maintaining Cornell U. Med. Coll., New York. Home: New York, N.Y. Died June 27, 1917.

PAYNE, WILLIAM HENRY lawyer, soldier; b. Clifton, Va., June 15, 1830; ed. Univ. of Mo., Va. Mil. Inst. and Univ. of Va. Organized and was 1st capt. Black Horse cav., comdg. it at Bull Run; promoted maj. 2 weeks after that battle; lt. col. 4th Va. cav., June 1862, col. Sept., 1863, brig. gen., C.S.A., Nov. 1864, comdg. brigade in Gen. Fitzhugh Lee's div.; 3 times seriously wounded in battle. Practiced law in Washington, D.C., after war, becoming counsel for the Southern R.R. Died 1904.

PEABODY, FRANCIS WELD M.D.; b. Cambridge, Mass., Nov. 24, 1881; s. Francis Greenwood and Cora (Weld) P.; A.B., Harvard, 1903, M.D., 1907; m. Virginia Grigsby Chandler, 1919; 1 son, Francis Weld. Assistant resident phys., Johns Hopkins Hosp., 1908-09; fellow in pathology, Johns Hopkins U., 1909-10; asst. resident phys., Rockefeller Hosp., 1911-12; resident phys., 1912-15, phys., 1915-21, Peter Bent Brigham Hosp., Boston; visiting phys. and dir. Thorndike Memorial Lab., Boston City Hosp.; prof. medicine, Harvard Med. Sch., 1921. Mem. bd. trustee China Med. Bd. of Rockefeller Foundation. Commd. 1st lt. Med. R.C., maj. M.C. U.S.A., 1918; mem. Red Cross Commn. to Roumania, 1917. Home: Boston, Mass. Died Oct. 13, 1927.

PEABODY, NATHANIEL Continental congressman, army officer, physician; b. Topsfield, Mass., Mar. 12, 1742; s. Jacob and Susanna (Rogers) P.; studied medicine privately with father; m. Abigail Little, Mar. 1, 1763. Began practice of medicine, N.H., 1761; justice of peace Rockingham County N.H.), 1771; commd. lt. col. Brit. Army, resigned to enter Continental Army, 1774; a leader at capture Ft. William and Mary, New Castle, N.H., (one of 1st open acts of Am. Revolution), 1774; mem., later chmn. N.H. Com. of Safety, 1776; mem. N.H. Ho. of Reps., 1776-79, 81-85, 87-90, 93-96, speaker, 1793; adjutant gen. N.H. Militia, 1777, participated in R.I. expdn., 1778; del. from N.H. to Continental Congress, 1779-80; mem. N.H. constl. convs., 1781-83, 91-92, chmn. com. to draft N.H. Constn., 1782-83; mem. N.H. Senate, 1785, 86, 90-93, chosen to serve as councilor (mem. Gov.'s Council) from N.H. Ho. of Reps., 1784, from N.H. Senate, 1785; an organizer N.H. Med. Soc., 1791; maj. gen. N.H. Militia, 1793-98; spent last 20 years of life in debtor's prison. Died Exeter, N.H., June 27, 1823; buried Old Cemetery, Exeter.

PEABODY, STUYVESANT coal; b. Chicago, Ill., Aug. 7, 1888; s. Francis Stuyvesant and May (Henderson) P.; Yale, 1907-11; m. Anita Healy, Feb. 21, 1914; children—Stuyvesant, Patrick Healy. Pres. Peabody Coal Company; president Black Mountain Coal Corp., Crerar Clinch Coal Co., Cook County Coal & Ice Co., Am. Eagle Colliery, Bellwood Coal Co.; dir. Lyon & Healy, Inc., Chicago, and Eastern Air Lines, Inc., N.Y. City; v.p. and dir. Am. Turf Assn. Served in World War as 1st lt. Sanitary Corps, later capt. Chem. Warfare Service. Trustee Ill. Inst. Tech. Mem. Delta Kappa Epsilon. Catholic. Mem. K.C. (past grand knight; past dist. deputy). Pres. and dir. Lincoln Fields Jockey Club. Fellow Photographic Society of America; fellow Royal Photographic Society. Clubs: Chicago, University, Racquet (Chicago); Grolier (N.Y. City); Pendennis (Louisville, Ky.). Home: 1525 N. State Parkway. Office: 231 S. LaSalle St., Chicago, Ill. Died June 7, 1946.

PEACH, ROBERT ENGLISH, airlines exec.; b. Syracuse, N.Y., Mar. 9, 1920; s. John Clayton and Emily (Kelley) P.; B.A., Hamilton Coll., 1941; student U. Chgo., 1941, Cornell U., 1945-47; m. Martha Minge Clarke. Aug. 8, 1944 (div.); children—Robert English John Minge, Timothy English, David, Martha; m. 2d, Ann C. Tarbania, June 6, 1960; 1 son, Ryan English. Asst. to pres. Hamilton Coll., 1941; flight capt. Robinson Airlines (now Mohawk Airlines, Inc.), 1946, traffic mgr., 1947, gen. mgr., exec. v.p., 1948-54, pres., dir., 1954-68, chmn. bd., 1968-71; dir. Homestead Sav. & Loan Assn., Hayes Nat. Bank First Trust & Depository Co., Syracuse, Lab. for Electronics, Waltham, Mass., Oneida County Indsl. Devel. Corp. Trustee Hamilton Coll., N.Y. State Regional Hosp. Rev. and Planning Council; pres. bd. mgrs. Faxton Hosp. Served as lt. comdr. USNR, 1942-45. Mem. Empire State (chmn. bd.), Utica chambers commerce, Nat. Alliance Businessmen (past chmn.). Clubs: Kiwanis, Yahnundasis Golf, Fort Schuyler (Utica); Wings (N.Y.C.); Sadaquada (New Hartford, N.Y.); Nat. Aviation (Wash.); Century (Syracuse, N.Y.). Home: Clinton NY Died Apr. 20, 1971; buried Hamilton College Cemetery.

PEARCE, CHARLES EDWARD lawyer, congressman; b. Whitesboro, N.Y., May 29, 1842; grad. Union Coll., 1863; served in U.S.V., 1863-65 as capt. and maj. 16th N.Y. H. Arty.; participated in battles before Petersburg and Richmond, and in capture of Ft. Fisher and Wilmington, N.C.; later served on staff Maj. Gen. A. H. Terry, and as provost marshal gen., E. Dist., N.C.; received thanks of legislature of N.Y. for meritorious conduct at siege of Ft. Fisher. Settled in St. Louis, 1866; admitted to bar, 1867; comd. St. Louis Nat. Guard, 1875; organized 1st regt., 1877, and was its 1st col.; chmn. Sioux Treaty Commn., 1891; went to India, China and Japan, 1895, to investigate industries of the Orient. Mem. Congress, 12th Mo. dist., 1897-1901. Republican. Home: St. Louis, Mo. Died 1902.

PEARCE, RICHARD MILLS JR. pathologist; b. Montreal, Can., Mar. 3, 1874; s. Richard Mills and Sarah (Smith) P.; ed. Boston Latin Sch.; M.D., Harvard, 1897; spl. study at U. of Leipzig, Germany, 1902, D.Sc., Lafayette Coll., Pa., 1915; m. May Harper Musser, Nov. 6, 1902; children—Agnes M., John M. Resident pathologist, Boston City Hosp., 1896-99; instr. pathology, Harvard, 1899-1900; demonstrator and later asst. prof. pathology, U. of Pa., 1900-03; dir. Bender Hygienic Lab., Albany, N.Y., 1903-08; prof. pathology and bacteriology, Albany Med. Sch., 1903-08; dir. Bur. of Pathology and Bacteriology, N.Y. State Dept. of Health, 1903-08; prof. pathology, Univ. and Bellevue Hosp. Med. Coll. (New York U.), 1908-10; prof. pathology, 1910-11, prof. research medicine, 1910-20, U. of Pa.; gen. dir. Div. of Med. Edn., Rockefeller Foundation, 1920-;. Chmn. med. div. Nat. Research Council, 1918; maj., M.C. U.S.A., 1918. Author: Medical Research and Education, 1913; The Spleen and Anemia, 1917. Home: New York, N.Y. Died Feb. 16, 1930.

PEARSON, ALFRED L. lawyer; b. Pittsburgh, Pa., Dec. 28, 1838; s. Joseph and May P.; ed. Jefferson Coll., Pa. Entered Union army, Aug. 1862 as capt. Co. A 155th Pa. vols.; promoted to maj., lt. col., and col.; bvtd. brig. gen. and maj. gen. of vols.; received congressional medal of honor for gallant conduct. Maj. gen. Nat. Guard of Pa. for 7 yrs. Admitted to bar, 1861; dist. atty. Allegheny Co., Pa., 3 yrs.; has served in select councils, Pittsburgh; now in third term as mem. bd. of mgrs., Nat. Home for Disabled Soldiers. Home: Shields, Pa. Died 1903.

PEARSON, THOMAS b. Asheville, N.C., June 24, 1893; s. Richmond and Gabrielle (Thomas) P.; prep. edn. St. Paul's Sch., Concord, N.H., 1911; A.B., Princeton U., 1915; unmarried. With Am. Internat. Corp., New York, 1916 and 1919-20; fgn. trade editor New York Evening Post, 1920-21; mem. Am. Commn. invited by the Persian Govt. to reorganize and administer the finances of Persia and dir. Civil Service Adminstrn., Persian Ministry of Finance, 1922-27; with Am. sect. Internat. Chamber of Commerce, Washington, D.C., 1929-31, Am. Commr. Internat. Chamber of Commerce in France, 1931-36; apptd. deputy gen. receiver of Dominican customs by President Roosevelt, 1937, acting gen. receiver, 1939-41. Member board directors and vice-president in charge fiscal department National Bank of Haiti, 1941-47; dir. dept. econ. research, Central Bank of the Dominican Republic, 1948-51; pres., acting dir. Instituto Cultural Dominico-Americano, 1951. Commissioned by Pres of Haiti as Capitaine de Vaisseau in charge of Haitian Ports, 1942. Served as lieutenant, later as captain, U.S. Army, with A.E.F. in France, 1917-19. Trustee Am. Library, Paris, 1933-36. Decorated Legion of Honor (France); Order of Crown and Croix de Guerre (Belgium); Order of Prince Danilo I (Montenegro); Officer Honneur et Mérite (Haiti). Mem. Mayflower Soc. (Mass.). Home: 45 Richmond Hill Rd., Asheville, N.C. Died Apr. 16, 1963; buried Riverside Cemetery, Asheville.

PEARY, ROBERT EDWIN arctic explorer, discoverer of North Pole; rear admiral U.S.N. (retired); b. Cresson, Pa., May 6, 1856; s. Charles N. and Mary (Wiley) P.; C.E., Bowdoin Coll., 1877 (Sc.D., 1894, LL.D.; LL.D., Edinburgh and Tufts); m. Josephine Diebitsch, 1888. Entered U.S. Navy as civil engr., Oct. 26, 1881; asst. engr. Nicaragua Ship Canal under Govt. orders, 1884-85; engr. in charge of Nicaragua Canal Surveys, 1887-88; invented rolling-lock gates for canal. Made reconnaissance, 1886, of the Greenland inland ice-cap, east of Disco Bay, 70 deg. N. lat.; chief of Arctic expdn. of Acad. National Sciences of Phila., June 1891-Sept. 1892, to N.E. angle of Greenland (Independence Bay, 81 deg. 37' N. lat.); discovered and named Melville Land and Heilprin Land, lying beyond Greenland; determined insularity of Greenland, for which he received the Cullom medal of Am. Geog. Soc., Patron's medal of Royal Geog. Soc., London, and medal of Royal Scottish Geog. Soc., Edinburgh. Made another arctic voyage, 1893-95; made thorough study of little tribe of Arctic Highlanders; discovered, 1894, famous Iron Mountain (first heard of by Ross, 1818), which proved to be meteorites, one of them weighing 90 tons (the largest known to exist); made summer voyages, 1896-1897, bringing the Cape York meteorites to U.S.; comdr. Arctic expdn. under auspices of Peary Actic Club of New York, 1898-1902; rounded northern extremity of Greenland Archipelago, the last of the great Arctic land groups; named the northern cape, the most northerly land in the world (83 deg. 39' N. lat.), Cape Morris K. Jesup; attained highest north in Western Hemisphere (84 deg. 17' N. lat.). Sailed north again, July 1905, in S.S. Roosevelt, specially built by Peary Arctic Club; returned Oct. 1906, having reached "highest north" (87 deg. 6' N. lat.). Started on 8th Arctic expdn., July 1908, on the Roosevelt, proceeding northward to Kane Basin, through Robeson channel, establishing winter base at Cape Sheridan, Sept. 5, 1908; left Cape Sheridan for Cape Columbia, Feb. 15, 1909, in 5 detachments; the detachments were sent back one after another, the 4th, in command of Capt. Bartlett, leaving Peary nr. the 88th parallel; from here, with 1 member of his crew and 4 Eskimos, made final dash of 130 miles to the pole in 5 days, which they reached Apr. 6, 1909; spent 30 hours at and beyond the pole; the journey from Cape Columbia to the pole was made in 27 marches, the return trip to Cape Columbia was made in 16 marches. Promoted to rank of rear admiral, and given thanks of Congress by special act of Congress, Mar. 3, 1911. Spl. gold medals of Nat. Geog. Soc. (Washington); Royal Geog. Soc. (London); Phila. Geog. Soc., Peary Arctic Club and Explorers Club; awarded the Hubbard gold medal by the Nat. Geog. Society, Culver gold medal, Chicago Geog. Soc.; Kane gold medal, Phila. Geog. Soc.; Daly and Cullom gold medals, Am. Geog. Soc.; gold medal of Imperial German, Austrian, and Hungarian socs.; Royal, Royal Scottish, Italian, and Belgian socs.; Swiss, Paris, Marseilles, Normandy, and City of Paris. Pres. Am. Geog. Soc., 1903; pres. 8th Internat. Geog. Congress, Washington, 1904; hon. v.p. 9th Internat. Geog. Congress, Geneva, 1908, and 10th, at Rome, 1913; pres. Explorers Club, and Aerial League America. U.S. Govt. del. Internat. Polar Commn., Rome, 1913; sec. Internat. Polar Commn.; chmn. Nat. Aerial Coast Patrol Commn. Made Grand Officier d'Honneur, France, 1913; hon. mem. Philadelphia Geog. Soc., Am. Alpine Club, Nat. Geog. Soc., Am. Mus. Natural Hist., N.Y. Chamber of Commerce, and all prin. home and foreign geog. socs. Author: Northward Over the Great Ice, 1898; Nearest the Pole, 1907; The North Pole, 1910; Secrets of Polar Travel, 1917. Died Feb. 20, 1920.

PEASE, THEODORE CALVIN teacher, editor; b. Cassopolis, Mich., Nov. 25, 1887; s. Thomas Huntington and Caroline Phipps (Anderson) P.; grad. Lewis Inst., Chicago, 1904; Ph.B., U. of Chicago, 1907, Ph.D., 1914; m. Marguerite Edith Jenison, Aug. 15, 1927. Asso. in history, U. of Ill., 1914-17, 1919-20, asst. prof., 1920-23, associate prof., 1923-26, professor since 1926, head department of history since 1942. Agent of com. for ednl. survey of U. of Ill., 1926-27. Editor Ill. Hist. Collections of Ill. State Hist. Library, 1920-39; dir. Ill. Hist. Survey since 1939. Corr. mem. Chicago Hist. Soc.; chairman hist. manuscripts commn., Am. Hist. Assn., 1925-31. Second lt. inf. U.S.R., Nov. 27, 1917; 1st lt. 126th Inf., Sept. 5, 1918; served with A.E.F., Jan. 8, 1918-May 16, 1919; participated in battles with 32d Div., Alsace Marne-Aisne, Oise-Aisne, Meuse-Argonne offensives, and in Army of Occupation, Germany; hon. discharged, May 24, 1919. Mem. Ill. State Hist. Soc. (pres., 1946-47); founder mem. Soc. of Am. Archivists since 1936 (editor, 1937-46). Conglist. Clubs: University (Urbana, Ill.); Army and Navy (Chicago). Author: (or compiler) County Archives of Illinois, 1915; The Leveller Movement, 1917; Centennial History of Illinois, Vol II, 1918; Illinois Election Returns, 1818-1848, 1923; Laws of the Northwest Territory, 1925; The Story of Illinois, 1925, revised edition, 1949; The United States, 1927; Diary of O. H. Browning I (with J. G. Randall), 1927; Selected Readings in American History (with A. S. Roberts), 1928; George Rogers Clark and the Revolution in Illinois, 1929; The French Foundations (with R. C. Werner), 1934; Anglo-French Boundary Disputes in the West, 1749-1763, 1936; Illinois on the Eve of the Seven Years' War, 1747-1755 (with Ernestine Jenison), 1939; also various articles in reviews. Editor The American Archivist since 1938. Home: 708 Indiana Av., Urbana, Ill. Died Aug. 11, 1948.

PEASLEE, AMOS JENKINS, retired ambassador, born at Clarksboro, New Jersey on March 24, 1887; son of Gideon and Emma (Waddington) P.; A.B., Swarthmore (Pennsylvania) Coll., 1907; studied Birmingham U., Eng.; LL.B., Columbia, 1911; LL.D., Swarthmore College, Earlham College and State University N.J.; married Dorothy K. Quimby, Feb. 12, 1920; children—Dorothy Waddington, Amos Jenkins, Lucy Raynes, Richard Cutts. International lawyer; U.S. ambassador to Australia, 1953-56; dep. spl. asst. to President, 1956-59. Dep. chmn. U.S. delegation UN Disarmament Conf., London, 1957. Director Am. Courier Serv., World War I, with rank of major attached to General Pershing's headquarters, France; chairman New York-European Election Commission which held election in Army and Navy in Europe, 1917; judge advocate of Gen. Court Martial in France, 1918; represented U.S. at Liabach conference, 1919, Penal Law Soc. conf. at Geneva, 1947, German dept. settlement conf. at London, 1952; rep. U.S. as adviser U.S. delegation UN General Assembly, 1957, UN Disarmament Commn., 1957; attached to American Commission to Negotiate Peace, Paris, France, 1919; chmn. Appeals Board Washington, D.C., 1933-34; commander U.S. Coast Guard, World War II. National commander U.S. Coast Guard League, 1947. Mem. U.S. Council of Def., 1947. Rep. Am. Soc. Internat. Law at San Francisco Conference, 1945. Hon. president bd. trustees Friends Central Sch., Phila.; trustee Underwood Hosp., Bryn Mawr Coll. Decorated D.S.M., Panama. President Swarthmore Coll. Alumni Association, 1941. Member American Bar Assn., Inter-Am. Bar Assn. (del. Rio and Mexican confs.), Assn. Bar of City of N.Y., Am. Soc. Internat. Law, Internat. Law Assn. (pres. Am. br. 1928-29); Internat. Bar Assn. (sec. gen. 1947-53), Am. Council Learned Socs., Delta Upsilon, Phi Beta Kappa, Delta Sigma Rho. Republican. Quaker. Clubs: Metropolitan, Army and Navy also the Capitol Hill (Washington); University, Columbia University (N.Y.C.); Union League (Phila.); Mantoloking, Bay Head Yacht. Author: Proposed Amendments to Judiciary Articles of the Covenant of the League of Nations, 1918; a Permanent U.N., 1942;

Three Wars with Germany, 1944; U.N. Govt., 1945; Constitutions of Nations, 3 vols., 1950, 56, 65; Constitutional Documents of International Governmental Organizations, 2 vols.; also internat. law, world order, and other legal topics. Home: Clarksboro NJ Died Aug. 29, 1969.

PEASLEE, HORACE WHITTIER cons. architect; b. Malden Bridge, N.Y., Nov. 9, 1884; s. John Nolan and Sarah (Rider) P.; B. Arch., Cornell U., 1910, Fellow, 1910-11; m. Frances Monroe Hopkins, Dec. 31, 1928; 1 son, John Rider. Public service and private practice (D.C.) since 1911. Lecturer, U. of Ill., 1912-13; served as capt. Engrs. Corps, U.S. Army, 1917-19. Architect, Office of Public Bldgs. and Grounds, 1911-22; sec. Allied Archts. of Washington, 1923-33, vice-pres., 1945; PWA Housing and USHA, 1933-38; consultant, Corps of Engrs., 1937-38; cons. archt., Pub. Bldgs, Adminstrn., 1938-42; sec. Central Housing Com. (U.S. agencies), 1935-42; sec. OCD Tech. Bd., 1942-44. Executed works include: Meridian Hill and other parks, gardens and cemeteries: resdntl. developments, motor courts, embassies of Peru and Korea, Cosmos Club, Marine Corps War Meml. setting; restorations, Belle Grave, Dumbarton, two Latrobe Churches; and private residences. Organized Architects Adv. Council; Dicesan Commn. on Architecture; A.I.A. com. on Nat. Capital (chmn., 1924-34); Joint Com. on Nat. Capital; com. of 100 on Federal City. Fellow A.I.A.; Am. Planning and Civic Assn. Clubs: Cosmos, Cornell. Misc. writing on park architecture, controlled developments, national capital compilations. Home: 1234 19th St. N.W. Office: 1228 Connecticut Av. N.W., Washington. Died May 18, 1959; buried Prospect Hill Cemetery, Valatie, N.Y.

PECK, ALLEN STEELE forestry; b. West Barre, N.Y., Apr. 17, 1880; s. Charles Bickford and Alice (Steele) P.; Ph.B., Union Coll., 1903, hon. M.S., 1933; B.S. in forestry, U. of Mich., 1905; m. Jessie Douglas Pearson, Nov. 11, 1908; children—Allen Steele, Alice Steele (wife of Rev. Arthur A. Vall-Spinosa), Kate Stott (Mrs. Arthur T. S. Kent). Student asst. Bur. of Forestry, Dept. of Agr., 1902; with U.S. Forest Service, 1905-— (except for mil. service), regional forester in charge Rocky Mt. Region, including nat. forests fo Colo., Eastern Wyo., S.D. and Neb., 1920-43, retired, 1944. Past pres. Colorado Engineering Council; member Denver Regional and National Councils Boy Scouts of America (ex-pres. Denver Council). Served as maj. and lt. col. Engrs. Corps, U.S. Army (1917-20), with A.E.F., 22 mos., asst. to dir. of contrn. and forestry G.H.Q., Chaumont. Decorated D.S.M. (U.S.), Chevalier Legion of Honor (France). Fellow Soc. American Foresters, member Am. Forestry Assn., Colo. Forestry and Hort. Assn. (dir.), Soc. Am. Mil. Engrs., S.A.R., Am. Soc. French Legion of Honor, Am. Legion, Sigma Phi, Episcopalian. Clubs: Army and Navy (Washington, D.C.); University (Denver); Colorado Mountain; Mile High. Contbr. to jours. Home: 18 So. Ogden, Denver 9. Died Feb. 4, 1951.

PECK, CHARLES HOWARD surgeon; b. Newtown, Conn., June 18, 1870; s. Albert W. and Louise W. (Booth) P.; prep. edn., Newtown Acad.; M.D., Coll. Phys. and Surg. (Columbia), 1892; LL.D., Fordham U., 1924; m. Betsy F. Chaffee, of Montreal, Can., Sept. 2, 1896; children—Charles Howard (dec.), Nelson Chaffee, Dexter Belknap. Surg. practice in N.Y. City, 1895-—; asst. instr. operative surgery, 1900, instr. surgery, 1904, asso. in clin. surgery, 1908, asst. prof., 1909, prof., 1910-—. Coll. Phys. and Surg.; surgeon to Roosevelt Hosp.; cons. surgeon to French, Memorial, Rupture and Crippled, Stamford (Conn.), White Plains (N.Y.), Greenwich (Conn.), and Vassar Brothers (Poughkeepsie, N.Y.) hosps. Commd. maj. Med. O.R.C., May 9, 1917; lt. col. Med. Corps, N.A., June 6, 1918; col. M.C., Aug. 24, 1918; col. Med. O.R.C., May 9, 1919. Served as mem. Gen. Med. Bd. Council Nat. Defense and as chmn. N.Y. State Nat. Defense Assn.; organizer and dir. Base Hosp. No. 15, U.S.A., at Chaumont as a 3,000 bed hosp.; apptd. sr. consultant in gen. surgery, A.E.F., Apr. 1918; served in France until July 7, 1918; chief Dept. of Gen. Surgery (in rotation with Drs. W. J. and C. H. Mayo), Surgeon Gen.'s Office, Washington, D.C., Aug. 1, 1918-Feb. 4, 1919. Awarded D.S.M., Mar. 26, 1919; made hon. mem. 68th Batt., Alpine Chasseurs, "for services rendered to French Army" during Battle of Chemin des Dames, Oct. 1917; Officier de l'Instruction Publique (French). Home: New York, N.Y. Died Mar. 28, 1927.

PECK, GEORGE BACHELER M.D.; b. Providence, R.I., Aug. 12, 1843; s. George Bacheler and Ann Power (Smith) P.; A.B., Brown, 1864 (also same yr., diploma for course in civ. engring.), A.M., 1867; Hahnemann Med. Coll., Phila., 1869-70; M.D., Yale, 1871; post-grad. Scheffield Scientific Sch. (Yale), 1871-72; unmarried. Practiced medicine, Providence, 1875-1928; admitting phys. R.I. Homoe. Hosp., 1886-1901, also trustee. Mem. Providence Sch. Com., 1881-96; mem. bd. mgrs. R.I. Bapt. State Conv., 1876-1910; clk. Narragansett Bapt. Assn., 1877-87, 1892-1915 (moderator 1889). Major Providence Marine Corps of Arty., 1869-71; lt. 2d Regt., R.I. Vols., Dec. 13, 1864-July 5, 1865; wounded at Sailor's Creek, Apr. 6, 1865; surgeon Battalion Light Arty. Div. R.I. Militia, 1876-79; lt. comdg. Battery A, R.I. Militia, during the Spanish-Am. War. Asst. chemist U.S. Naval Torpedo Sta., 1872-74; in charge chem. dept. U. of Vt., fall of 1874. Republican. Hon. pres. Am. Inst. Homoeopathy, 1912 (and chmn. of International Bur., 1902-18); pres. R.I. Homoe. Med. Soc., 1885, 86, R.I. Soldiers and Sailors Hist. Soc., 1892-96. Mason. Editor (largely author): Seventh Regiment R.I. Vols. in Civil War, 1862-65, 1903. Home: Woodville, R.I. Died Nov. 20, 1934.

PECK, GEORGE RECORD lawyer; b. Steuben Co., N.Y., May 15, 1843; s. Joel M. and Amanda (Purdy) P.; ed. common schs.; (LL.D., U. of Kan., 1887, Union Coll., N.Y., 1896, and Bethany Coll., W.Va.; A.M., Milton Coll., 1902); m. Arabella Burdick, Oct. 24, 1866 (died 1896). Pvt. to capt. 1st Wis. Heavy Arty. and 31st Wis. Inf., 1861-65; admitted to bar, 1866; practiced at Independence, Kan., 1871-74, Topeka, Kan., 1874-93, Chicago, 1893-—; sr. mem. Peck, Miller (John S.) & Starr (Merritt), 1894-1912. Gen. solicitor A.,T.&S.F. R.R. Co., 1881-95; gen. counsel C.,M.&St.P. Ry., Sept. 15, 1895-Jan. 1910, from then consulting counsel. U.S. atty. Dist. of Kan., 1874-79; declined appmt. to U.S. Senate for unexpired term, from Kan., 1892. Republican. Home: Oconomowoc, Wis. Died Feb. 22, 1923.

PECK, JOHN JAMES army officer; b. Manlius, N.Y., Jan. 4, 1821; s. John Wells and Phoebe (Raynor) P.; grad. U.S. Mil. Acad. 1843; m. Robie Loomis, Nov. 20, 1850, 6 children. Served with U.S. Army in battles of Palo Alto, Resaco de la Palma, Contreras, Churubusco, Maleria del Rey, during Mexican War; resigned from U.S. Army, 1853; treas. N.Y., Newburgh & Syracuse R.R. Co.; pres. Syracuse (N.Y.) Bd. Edn., 1859-61; v.p. Franklin Inst., Syracuse; del. Democratic Nat. Conv., 1856, 60; twice nominated for U.S. Congress; commd. brig. gen. U.S. Volunteers, 1861, maj. gen., 1862; served in defenses of Washington, D.C., 1861-62; given command on Canadian frontier, 1864; organizer N.Y. State Life Ins. Co., 1867, pres. Died Syracuse, Apr. 21, 1878.

PECK, THEODORE SAFFORD soldier; b. Burlington, Vt., Mar. 22, 1843; s. Theodore Augustus and Delia Horton (Safford) P.; prepared for coll. and then enlisted in Civil War; (hon. A.M., Norwich U., Vt., 1896); m. Agnes Louisa Leslie, Oct. 29, 1879; father of Theodora Agnes P. Served in 1st Vt. Cav. and 9th Vt. Inf., pvt. to capt. and on staff in Army of the Potomac almost 4 yrs.; awarded Congressional Medal of Honor "for distinguished gallantry in action at Newport Barracks, N.C., Feb. 2, 1864"; later comd. 1st Brigade Vt. N.G. and adj. gen. of Vt., 1881-1900. In ins. business, 1868-—. Mem. Bd. of Visitors U.S. Mil. Acad., 1891. Republican. Conglist. Past. comdr. Vt. Commandery Loyal Legion, Medal of Honor Legion of the U.S., Dept. Vt. G.A.R.; 1st gov. Vt. Soc. Colonial Wars; deputy gov. gen. for Vt. of Gen. Soc. of Colonial Wars; S.A.R. Mason (grand marshal Grand Lodge of Vt., 10 yrs.). Home: Burlington, Vt. Died Mar. 15, 1918.

PECKHAM, HOWARD LOUIS, army officer; b. Norwich, Conn., May 29, 1897; s. Frank E. and Frances E. (Beckwith) P.; B.S., U.S. Mil. Acad., 1918; grad. Inf. Sch., 1926, Command and Gen. Staff Sch., 1940; m. Marion Davis Shaw, June 16, 1925; children—Howard Louis, Jean Anne. Commd. 2d lt., Corps of Engrs., Nov. 1, 1918, and advanced through the grades to maj. gen., U.S. Army, April 1952; chief of staff, 8th Armored Div., Ft. Knox, Ky., April-July 1942; combat comdr., 12th Armored Div., Aug. 1942-Oct. 1943; dir. fuels and lubricants div., Office Q.M. Gen., Oct. 1943-March 1946; dir. procurement div., Office Q.M. Gen., Jan.-June 1946; air Q.M., Hq. Army Air Forces, June 1946-Apr. 1947; comdg. gen., Am. Graves Registration Comd., European Area, Paris, 1947-49; comdg. gen. N.Y. Q.M. Procurement Agency, 1950-51; acting dep. Q.M. gen., 1951-52; comdg. gen. Ft. Lee, Va., 1952-54; chief Army & Air Force Exchange Service, 1954-72. Decorated D.S.M., U.S. Army. Club: Army and Navy Washington. Died Oct. 1972.

PEELE, STANTON JUDKINS judge; b. Wayne Co., Ind., Feb. 11, 1843; s. John Cox and Ruth (Smith) P.; ed. pub. schs., and sem. in Ind.; LL.D., Valparaiso and Howard univs.; corporal, later 2d lt. Ind. Vols., in Civil War; m. Lou R. Perkins, July 16, 1866 (died 1873); m. 2d, Arabella, d. Judge Milton C. Canfield, Oct. 16, 1878 (died 1915); m. 3d, Bertha (Barnitz) Byrne, d. Col. Albert Barnitz, U.S.A., Apr. 16, 1918. Admitted to bar, 1866; practiced at Winchester, Ind., 1866-68, Indianapolis, 1869-92. Mem. Indiana House of Representatives, 1877-79; mem. 47th Congress (1881-83); judge 1892-1905; chief justice, 1906-13, U.S. Court of Claims; retired. Mem. bd. of control, Ind. Reform Sch. for Boys, 1891-92; prof. law of partnership and bailment, George Washington U., 1901-11. Pres. trustees Washington Coll. of Law, Presbyterian Home for the Aged, and Garfield Hospital, 1910-24; pres. West Nottingham (Synodical) Academy, Cecil Co., Md., 1914-25; pres. Sch. Bd., Montgomery Co., Md., 1914-18; pres. Chevy Chase com. governing village, 1914-18; advisory mem. bd. of mgr. Y.M.C.A., Washington; vice-moderator Washington Presbytery, 1916. Vice moderator Synod of Balitmore, 1920-21. Home: Washington, D.C. Died Sept. 4, 1928.

PEEPLES, THOMAS H. (pe'p'lz), lawyer; b. Beaufort, S.C., Aug. 4, 1882; s. Benjamin Franklin and Leila (Hay) P.; student U. of S.C.; m. Halie Armstrong, Jan. 8, 1921. Began practice in Blackville, S.C., 1908; mem. S.C. Ho. of Rep. from Barnwell County, 1911-12, from Richland County, 1925-26; mem. judiciary com. of House and chmn. spl. com. on investigation and consolidation of state offices; atty. general of S.C. 3 terms, 1913-18 inclusive. Commd. lt. col. governor's staff, 1913; maj. judge advocate U.S. Army, 1919, and assigned as chief counsel War Dept. Bd. of Appraisers; then maj. judge advocate; later lt. col. J.A.G. (Res.) Commd. by Gov., Apr. 17, 1944, as mem. Com. to Revise Code of Civic Procedure of S.C. Commissioner State and County Elections, 1948. President Nat. Assn. Attys. Gen., 1917. Hon. mem. Vets. Foreign Wars. Democrat. Presbyterian. Mason. Odd Fellow, Elk. Home: Blackville, S.C., Office: 1410 Main St., Columbia, S.C. Died July 31, 1954; buried Blackville (S.C.) Cemetery.

PEERY, WILLIAM Continental congressman; studied law. Engaged in farming; organizer, commd. capt. of an independent co. during Revolutionary War, 1777; mem. Del. Ho. of Reps., 1782, 84, 87, 93, 94; admitted to the bar, 1785; began practice of law, Sussex County, Del.; mem. Continental Congress from Del., 1785-86; treas. Sussex County, 1785-96; apptd. mem. commn. to purchase land and build a ct. house and prison for Sussex County, 1791. Died Cool Spring, Del., Dec. 17, 1800; buried Cool Spring Presbyn. Churchyard.

PEFFER, WILLIAM ALFRED senator; b. Cumberland Co., Pa., Sept. 10, 1831; s. John and Elizabeth (Souder) P.; m. Sarah Jane Barber, Dec. 28, 1852. Began teaching at 15, working on his father's farm summers; removed to Ind., 1853, to Mo., 1859, thence to Illinois; engaged in farming. Enlisted as pvt. 83d Ill. Inf., 1862, mustered out, June 1865-— rank of lt.; acted as adj. and judge-advocate and q.m. Began law practice, Clarksville, Tenn., Aug. 1865; removed to Kan.; established Fredonia Journal, and Coffeyville Journal; mem. Kan. Senate, 1874; Rep. presdl. elector, 1880; editor Kansas Farmer, 1881; U.S. senator. 1891-97, elected by People's Party; Prohibition candidate for gov., 1898. Now engaged in lit. work. Author: Peffer's Tariff Manual, 1888; The Way Out; The Farmer's Side, 1891; Americanism and the Philippines, 1900; Rise and Fall of Populism in the United States, 1900. Home: Topeka, Kan. Died Oct. 7, 1912.

PEGRAM, JOHN congressman; b. "Bonneville," Danville County, Va., Nov. 16, 1773; attended common schs. Held local offices; mem. Va. Ho. of Dels., 1797-1801, 13-15, Va. Senate, 1804-08; served as maj. gen. Va. Militia during War of 1812; mem. U.S. Ho. of Reps. from Va., 15th Congress, Apr. 21, 1818-19; apptd. U.S. marshal for Eastern Va., 1821. Died in a burning boat on the Ohio River, Apr. 8, 1831.

PEGRAM, JOHN COMBE lawyer; b. Owensborough, Ky., Aug. 26, 1842; s. William B. and Charlotte Amelie (Combe) P.; grad. U.S. Naval Acad., 1863; m. Isabel Homer, Nov. 3, 1864 (died 1892). Served with S. Atlantic Blockading Fleet off Charleston on various vessels and on staff comdr.-in-chief; resigned from navy, 1866; grad. Harvard Law Sch., 1868; admitted to R.I. bar, 1868; sr. mem. Pegram & Cooke, 1885-—; mem. R.I. Ho. of Reps., 1869-70; mem. Providence City Council, 1873-75; U.S. register in bankruptcy, 1875-89; acting judge Municipal Ct., Providence, 1889 and 1901; master in chancery, 1900-—. Trustee R.I. Hosp., R.I. State Sanitorium. Pres. R.I. br. Am. Red Cross. Home: Providence, R.I. Died 1909.

PEIRCE, WILLIAM S. army officer; b. Burlington, Vt., May 16, 1864; s. Albert Gallatin and Delia Juliet (Benjamin) P.; student U. of Vt., 1881-84 (hon. A.M., 1908); grad. U.S. Mil. Acad., 1888; m. Harriet Roberts, Apr. 19, 1911. Additional lt., 1st Arty., June 11, 1888; 2d lt. 2d Arty., Sept. 3, 1888; 1st lt. Ordnance Dept., Jan. 15, 1892; capt., July 7, 1898; maj., June 25, 1906; lt. col., Feb. 12, 1910; colonel, Apr. 6, 1915; brig. gen., Feb. 18, 1918. Served as assistant officer, Watervliet Arsenal, Sandy Hook Proving Ground, Rock Island Arsenal and Springfield Armory; as inspector of ordnance Midvale and Bethlehem Steel companies; as asst. in Office of Chief of Ordnance; comdr. Springfield Armory; served overseas and as asst. chief of ordnance, Washington, 1917-—. Specialist in matters pertaining to mfr. of small arms. Episcopalian. Died July 10, 1923.

PEIXOTTO, ERNEST CLIFFORD artist, writer; b. San Francisco, Oct. 15, 1869; s. Raphael and Myrtilla J. (Davis) P.; ed. San Francisco; art at Acad. Julian, Paris, under Benjamin-Constant and Jules Lefebvre; m. Mary G. Hutchinson, Jan. 28, 1897. Exhibited Paris Salons many times and in leading Am. exhbns.; hon. mention at Salon for picture, "A Woman of Rijsoord," also awards at other exhibitions; has illustrated for Scribner's Magazine, besides many books, including Theodore Roosevelt's "Life of Cromwell" and Henry Cabot Lodge's "Story of the Revolution." Lived many years in Europe, writing and illustrating papers for Scribner's and other leading Am. periodicals. Painted large murals "Le Morte d'Arthur" for library, Cleveland, 1911, and since in many rooms in Paris, New York and Calif.; murals in Seamen's Bank for Savings, New York, 1927, Bank of New York, also Embassy Club of New York, 1928. Went to France, Mar. 1918, as official artist attached to A.E.F., with rank of captain, following entire American campaign (drawings now in

New National Museum, Washington); dir. painting studios, A.E.F. Art Training Center, Bellevue, France, 1919; dir. dept. of mural painting, Beaux-Arts Inst. of Design, New York, 1919-26; consultant on murals N.Y. World's Fair, 1939; chmn. Am. com. Fontainebleau Sch. Fine Arts. A.N.A., 1909. Decorated Chevalier Legion of Honor, 1921, Officier, 1924. Pres. School Art League, 1936. Mem. National Society Mural Painters (pres.), Architectural League (vice-pres.); painter mem. Art Commn. of City of New York; corr. mem. Hispanic Soc. America (rep. in permanent collection by three paintings and many drawings); hon. mem. of Am. Institute of Architects. Author: By Italian Seas, 1906; Through the French Provinces, 1910; Romantic California, 1911; Pacific Shores from Panama, 1913; Our Hispanic Southwest, 1916; A Revolutionary Pilgrimage, 1917; The American Front, 1919; Through Spain and Portugal, 1922; A Bacchic Pilgrimage, 1932. Died Dec. 6, 1940.

PELHAM, JOHN army officer; b. Benton (now Calhoun) County, Ala., Sept. 14, 1838; s. Atkinson and Martha (McGehee) P.; attended U.S. Mil. Acad., 1856-61; never married. Commd. lt. Confederate States Army, 1861; promoted capt. in charge of Stuart Horse Arty. under Gen. J. E. B. Stuart, 1861, unit became famous for its mobility, effectiveness and recklessness; promoted maj., 1862; active in battles of Seven Days, 2d Manassas, Antietam, Stuart's raid on Loudoun County, battles of Port Royal and Fredericksburg. Killed in action at Battle of Kelly's Ford (Va.), Mar. 17, 1863.

PELL, PHILIP Continental congressman; b. Pelham Manor, N.Y., July 7, 1753; grad. King's Coll. (now Columbia), 1770; studied law. Admitted to N.Y. bar, practiced in N.Y.C. and Westchester County; served as lt. N.Y. Volunteers, 1776; dep. judge adv. Continental Army, 1777; mem. N.Y. State Assembly, 1779-81, 84-86; judge adv. gen. U.S. Army, 1781-83; mem. staff of Gen. Washington at evacuation of N.Y.C., 1783; regent Univ. State N.Y., 1784-87; surrogate Westchester County, 1787-1800; mem. Continental Congress from N.Y., 1788-89. Died Pelham Manor, N.Y., May 1, 1811; buried St. Paul's Churchyard, Eastchester (now Bronx), N.Y.

PELLEW, CHARLES ERNEST (seventh viscount of Exmouth since February 1923), chemist; b. London, Eng., Mar. 11, 1863; s. Henry Edward and Eliza (Jay) P.; E.M., Columbia, 1884; m. Margaret W. Chandler, of New York, Apr. 29, 1886; 2d, Mabel Gray, of New York, May 12, 1923. Demonstrator chemistry and physics, 1892-97, adj. prof. chemistry, 1897-1911, Columbia. Chemist, Hygeia Distilled Water Co., 1890-1908; chemist, Maxim Munitions Corp., 1915-17, Alaska Products Co., 1917, 18. Capt. signal corps U.S.V., during Spanish-Am War; 1st lt. Depot Bn., 12th N.Y. Inf., 1916, 17. Mem. Am. Chem. Soc., Soc. Chem. Industry, Am. Federation of Arts, Boston Soc. Arts and Crafts, N.Y. Soc. of Craftsmen (pres. 1920-23), N.Y. Micros. Society; fellow N.Y. Acad. Sciences. Clubs: Century, Columbia University, Chemists', Squadron A (New York); Arts, Cosmos (Washington, D.C.). Author: Manual of Practical Medical and Physiological Chemistry, 1893; Laboratory Textbook of General Chemistry, 1903; Dyes and Dyeing, 1912, 1918. Address: 65 E. 56th St., New York, N.Y.

PELOUZE, WILLIAM NELSON (pe-looz'), mfr.; b. Washington, D.C., Sept. 12, 1865; s. Gen. L. H. (U.S. Army) and Ellen L. (Doolittle) P.; grad. Mich. Mil. Acad., 1882; m. Helen G. Thompson, Feb. 1, 1888; 1 dau., Medora. Came to Chicago, 1882; with Walter A. Wood, reaping machines, 1882-84; with the Tobey Furniture Co., 1884-92; pres. Pelouze Scale & Mfg. Co. (now the Pelouze Mfg. Co.) since 1884. Commd. capt. and adj. 2d Inf., Ill. Nat. Guard, 1883; capt. Co. H, 1885; maj. 2d Inf., 1890; asst. adj. gen., 1st Brigade Ill. Nat. Guard, 1894; col. 1st Inf. Ill. Reserves. Past chmn. Ill. Deep Waterway Commn.; mem. exec. com. Gt. Lakes-St. Lawrence Tidewater Assn.; pres. Assn. of Arts and Industries; ex-pres. Ill. Mfrs. Assn. Mem. Mil. Order Loyal Legion. Clubs: Chicago, Chicago Athletic, Lake Geneva Yacht (past commodore), Lake Geneva Country. Home: 2150 N. Lincoln Park W. Office: 232 E. Ohio St., Chicago, Ill. Died June 19, 1943.

PEMBERTON, JOHN CLIFFORD army officer; b. Phila., Aug. 10, 1814; s. John and Rebecca (Clifford) P.; grad. U.S. Mil. Acad., 1837; m. Martha Thompson, Jan. 18, 1848, 5 children. Served as 2d lt. arty. in Seminole War, 1837-39; commd. 1st lt., 1842; brevetted capt., 1846, maj., 1847, for services in Mexican War; commd. capt., 1850; served in operations against Mormons in Utah, 1858; commd. lt. col. Confederate Army, 1861, then col., brig. gen., 1861, maj. gen. and lt. gen., 1862; surrendered to Grant at Vicksburg; somewhat suspect throughout South because of No. birth. Died "Penllyn," Pa., July 13, 1881; buried Laurel Hill Cemetery, Phila.

PENBERTHY, GROVER CLEVELAND surgeon; b. Houghton, Mich., Mar. 1, 1886; s. Edward Rawlings and Ellen Martha (McKernan) P.; M.D., U. Mich., 1910, M.S. (hon.), 1942; U. Pa., 1918 (Army assignment); m. Elizabeth Wardner, July 16, 1921 (div. 1939); children—Philip Edward, Grover Wardner, John McKernan. House officer, N.Y.C. Hosp., 1910-12, dep. med. supt., 1912-13; began genl. practice, Detroit, 1913; instr. anatomy, Detroit Coll. Medicine (now Med. Coll., Wayne U.), 1913-14; asst. to Harry N. Torrey, surgeon, 1915-17; in gen. practice of surgery, 1919-42; in military service, 1942-46; surgeon, out-patient clinic, Harper Hosp., Detroit, 1915, junior surgeon Harper Hospital, 1919, surgeon, 1934-48, chief, general surgery, 1948-49, and sr. surgeon, cons. staff since 1950; asso. surgeon Childrens Hospital of Mich., 1919, dir. dept. of surgery, 1920, cons., 1953; asso. surgeon Herman Kiefer Hosp., 1926, also chief of staff; non-resident lecturer, dept. surgery U. Mich., 1920-55, prof. emeritus, 1955-—, prof. clin. surgery, Wayne U., 1935; now clin. surgeon at Wayne State U.; extramural lecturer, Post Graduate School, U. Mich. cons. surgeon, Detroit Receiving Hospital, Jennings Memorial Hospital, Detroit Orthopedic Clinic, Sinai Hosp., Detroit Meml. Hosp. and Blain Hospital, surg. dir., Mich. Mutual Liability Co., 1946, Cons. Surgeon, Herman Kiefer Hospital, 1946; cons. surgeon Vets. Adminstrn. Hosp., 1946. Mem. adv. bd. to Surgeon Gen. AUS, 1951-52. Member Detroit City Plan commn., 1957-—. Served as seaman Michigan Naval Brigade, 1908, hospital steward, 1909; lieut., Med. Corps, U.S. Army, 1917, advancing through grades to maj. 1918; lt. colonel, Med. Reserve Corps, 1919, col., 1925; called to active duty as col., Med. Corps, U.S. Army, 1942; serving as surg. cons., 7th S.C. Hdqrs., Omaha, Neb., discharged as col. June 1946. Hon. Reserve Med. Corps, U.S. Army, 1948. Dir. Cranbrook Sch., 1950-55, chmn. bd. dirs., 1954-55. Legion of Merit, Res., 1946. Diplomate Am. Bd. of Surgery, 1928. Fellow A.C.S. (gov., regent); mem. Soc. Med. Consultants to Armed Forces (pres. 1951-52), Wayne Co. Med. Soc., Mich. State (pres. 1935-36), Medical Society, Detroit Academy Surgery (past pres.), Detroit Academy of Medicine (past pres.) Mich. Soc. Mental Hygiene (past pres.), Detroit Med. Club (hon.), Flint (Michigan) Academy Surgery (hon.), Terre Haute (Ind.) Acad. Med. (hon.), A.M.A. (rep. surg. sect., sci. exhibit 1938-44; del. sect. abdominal and gen. surgery 1942-45), Royal Soc. Medicine (London), Am., So., Western surg. assns., Am. Assn. Surgery Trauma (pres. 1944-45), Central Surg. Assn. (pres. 1941-42), Am., Mich. (past pres.) indsl. med. assns., Detroit Bd. Commerce, Assn. Mil. Surgeons, Société Internationale de Chirurgie, Detroit Bd. of Commerce, A.A.A.S., Phi Rho Sigma, Alpha Omega Alpha. Republican. Episcopalian. Mason (Shriner). Clubs: Detroit, University, Athletic, University Mich. (gov. 1957), Economic, Torch (Detroit). Home: 1130 Parker Av. Office: 1553 Woodward Av., Detroit 26. Died Sept. 2, 1959.

PENCE, ARTHUR W(ILLIAM) army officer; b. Ft. Monroe, Va., July 18, 1898; s. William Perry and Alice (Dunbar) P.; grad. Poly. Prep. Sch., Bklyn., 1915, Columbia Prep. Sch., Washington, 1916; B.S., U.S. Mil. Acad., 1918; m. Elizabeth E. Fuller, Sept. 5, 1923; children—Arthur William, William Fuller, Betty Sue. Commd. 2d lt., U.S. Army, 1918, advanced through grades to maj. gen., 1948, jr. officer U.S., P.I., 1918-28; in charge R.O.T.C. unit U. Ala., 1928-32; assigned U.S. area engr., Greenville, Miss., 1932-33; in charge tunnel constrn. Ft. Peck Dam, Mont., 1933-37; grad. Command and Gen. Staff Sch., Ft. Leavenworth, Kan., 1937-38; instr. Engr. Sch., Ft. Belvoir, Va., 1938-41; exec. officer constrn. Atlantic bases, N.Y., 1941-42; dep. engr. S.O.S., E.T.O., 1942; engr. Mediterranean Base sect., 1942; comdg. gen. Eastern Base sect., Tunisia, 1943, Peninsular Base sect., Italy, 1943-44; comdt. Sch. Logistics, Ft. Leavenworth, 1944-48; chief of staff Engr. Center, Ft. Belvoir, 1948-49; U.S. dist. engr., Nashville, 1949-50; U.S. div. engr., Cin., 1950-51; asst. chief C.E., Washington, 1951-53; comdg. gen. 6th Armored Div., Ft. Leonard Wood, 1953-54, comdg. gen. Engr. Center, Ft. Belvoir, Va., 1954-—. Decorated D.S.M., Legion of Merit with oak leaf cluster, Bronze Star medal, Typhus Commn. medal. Mem. Soc. Am. Mil. Engrs. Office: Hdqrs. TEC, Ft. Belvoir, Va. Deceased.

PENDER, WILLIAM DORSEY army officer; b. Edgecombe County, N.C., Feb. 6, 1834; s. James and Sarah (Routh) P.; grad. U.S. Mil. Acad., 1854; m. Mary Shepperd, Mar. 3, 1859; children—Turner, William D., Stephen Lee. Brevetted 2d lt., 2d Arty. U.S. Army, 1854, promoted 1st lt., 1858; apptd. adjutant 1st Dragoons, 1860-61; commd. capt. arty. Confederate Army, placed in charge of recruiting, Balt.; elected col. 3d N.C. Volunteers, then transferred to command 6th N.C. Regt., 1861; served in Battle of Fair Oaks, 1862; promoted to brig. gen., served with Jackson at battles of Cedar Run, Fredericksburg, Chancellorsville; commd. maj. gen., 1863. Died as a result of wounds received at Battle of Gettysburg, Staunton, Va., July 18, 1863.

PENDLETON, EDMUND author; b. Cincinnati, 1845; s. Col. Nathaniel Greene and Anne (James) P.; ed. by pvt. tutors; m. Cornelia Marcy; m. 2d, Margaret Rivière Hetzel. Served in Civil War as 2d lt., 4th N.Y. Heavy Arty., 1863-64; pres. Cincinnati Expn. Arts and Industries, 1875-79; pres. Cincinnati Musical Festivals, 1880-82. Author: A Conventional Bohemian, 1886; A Virginia Inheritance, 1888; One Woman's Way, 1890; A Complication in Hearts, 1902. Address: Laurel, Md. Died 1910.

PENDLETON, EDWIN CONWAY rear admiral U.S.N.; b. Richmond, Va., May 27, 1847; s. A. G. and Selina C. P.; apptd to U.S. Naval Acad. by the President, at-large, Oct. 10, 1863, grad. 1867; m. Mary R. Saxton, Apr. 2, 1872. Promoted ensign, Dec. 18, 1868; master, Mar. 21, 1870; lt., Mar. 21, 1871; lt. comdr., Aug. 4, 1889; comdr., Mar. 21, 1897; capt., Jan. 21, 1902; rear admiral, Aug. 28, 1907. Summer of 1864 was in active service on Marion in pursuit of Confederate steamers Florida and Tallahassee; served on Minnesota and Onward, 1867-70; Portsmouth and Wasp, 1871; Supply, 1872-73; on duty Navy Yard, Washington, 1872, 1874, 1876-78, 1888-92; on bd. Congress, 1874-76; Swatara, 1879-82; on duty Naval Obs., 1883-86; on bd. Atlanta, 1886-88; exec. officer Monterey, 1893-95; on duty Bur. of Ordnance, Navy Dept., 1895-97; supt. naval gun factory, Washington, 1897-1900, 1902-05; comd. Atlanta, 1900-02; commandant, Navy Yard, Washington, 1905; comd. Missouri, 1905-07; commandant Navy Yard, League Island, Pa., 1907-09; retired, May 27, 1909. Address: Washington, D.C. Died Sept. 27, 1919.

PENDLETON, JOSEPH HENRY officer U.S.M.C.; b. Rochester, Pa., June 2, 1860; s. Joseph Rhodes and Martha J. (Cross) P.; grad. U.S. Naval Acad., 1882; m. Mary Helen Fay, Aug. 20, 1884; children—Helen Fay (Mrs. Albert Rockwell) Edgar Bache. Apptd. 2d lt. U.S.M.C., July 1, 1884; promoted through grades to brig. gen., Aug. 29, 1916; maj. gen., Dec. 9, 1923. Comdr. marine barracks, Sitka, 1892-94, 1899-1904; on Yankee, Spanish-Am. War, 1898; comd. 1st Regt., 1st Brig. of Marines, 1904-06; comd. Marine Barracks, Guam, 1906; same, Puget Sound, Wash., 1906-09; comd. 1st Brig. of Marines, P.I., 1909-10; post comdr. and comdg. officer 2d Regt., Olongapo, P.I., 1910-12; comd. Marine Barracks, Portsmouth, N.H., 1912; comd. 1st Provisional Regt., Nicaragua, 1912; comd. forces at Masaya, Nicaragua, at bombardment of fortifications of Coyotepe and Barranca, Oct. 3, 1912; led assault and capture of those places, Oct. 4; comd. 2d Regt., 2d Provisional Brig., at Guantanamo Bay, Cuba, 1913; comd. Marine Barracks, Puget Sound, Wash., 1913-14; comd. 4th Regt., San Diego, Calif., and two expdns. to waters of Pacific coast of Mexico, 1914-16; comd. 4th Regt. U.S. Marines and U.S. forces on shore in Santo Domingo, from June 19, 1916; comd. column U.S. Marines on advance into Santo Domingo from Monte Cristo to Santiago; received surrender of City of Santiago, D.R., July 6, 1916; apptd. comdr. 2d Provisional Brig., Santo Domingo, Dec. 31, 1916; administered depts. of War and Navy and of Interior and Police, Nov. 1916-Oct. 1918, and for 6 months of 1917-18 was, also actg. mil. gov. of Dominican Republic; comd. Marine Barracks, Paris Island, S.C., Nov. 11, 1918-Sept. 26, 1919; comdg. 2d Advanced Base Force, U.S. Marine Corps, San Diego, Calif., Oct. 1, 1919-Oct. 4, 1921; comdg. 5th Brig. Marines, San Diego, Oct. 4, 1921-Mar. 1924; comdg. Marine Corps Base, San Diego, Mar. 1924-June 2, 1924 (retired). Mayor of Coronado, Calif., 1928-30; mem. Coronado Sch. Bd. 14 yrs. Past pres. San Diego Chapter S.A.R. Dir. Calif.-San Diego Centennial Expn., 1934-35. Episcopalian. An adopted mem. Thlingket tribe of Alaskan Indians. Home: Coronado, Calif. Died Feb. 4, 1942.

PENDLETON, WILLIAM NELSON clergyman, army officer; b. Richmond, Va., Dec. 26, 1809; s. Edmund and Lucy (Nelson) P.; grad. U.S. Mil. Acad., 1830; m. Anzolette Elizabeth Page, July 15, 1831, several children including Alexander, Susan (Pendleton) Lee. Apptd. 2d lt. 4th Arty. Regt., U.S. Army, 1830, resigned, 1833; prof. mathematics Bristol Coll., Pa., 1833-37, Del. Coll., Newark, 1837-39; ordained deacon Protestant Episcopal Ch., 1837, priest, 1838; prin. Episcopal High Sch. of Va., Alexandria, 1839-44; taught pvt. sch., pastor 2 chs., Balt., 1844-47; rector All Saints Ch., Frederick, Md., 1847-53, Grace Ch., Lexington, Va., 1853-61, 65-83; dep. to Gen. Conv. Protestant Episcopal Ch., 1856; commd. capt. Rockbridge Arty., Confederate States Army, 1861, promoted col., 1861, brig. gen., 1862; chief of arty. Army of Northern Va., 1863-65. Died Lexington, Va., Jan. 15, 1883.

PENICK, JOHN NEWTON lawyer; b. Jackson, Tenn., Oct. 3, 1895; s. Isaac Newton and Martha Josephine (Shankle) P.; B.S., Hall-Moody Coll., Martin, Tenn., 1912; A.B., 1913; LL.B., Harvard, 1921; m. Mabel Helen Anderson, Aug. 30, 1932 (dec. Aug. 1953). Admitted to Mass. bar, 1922, N.Y. bar, 1931; practice in N.Y.C., 1931-—; sr. partner firm Penick, Gass & Mitchell, and predecessors, 1940-—. Officer, dir. numerous corps. Served to capt., A.C., U.S. Army, 1917-19. Mason (Shriner). Clubs: Harvard, Bankers, Metropolitan (bd. govs.), Metropolitan Opera (N.Y.C.); Saratoga Reading Room (Saratoga Springs, N.Y.). Home: 1140 Fifth Av., N.Y.C. 10028. Office: 37 Wall St., N.Y.C. 10005. Died June 29, 1967.

PENN, ALBERT MILLER naval officer; b. Laredo, Tex., Sept. 11, 1885; s. James Saunders and Virginia Josephine (Miller) P.; B.S., U.S. Naval Acad., 1908; m. Helen Huffington Smith, June 29, 1910; children—Helen Smith (Mrs. Robert W. Page), Emily Virginia (Mrs. Harry H. Howard). Commd. ensign USN, 1908, advanced through grades to rear adm., 1942; dir. indsl. survey div. Office Sec. Navy, Washington, since Feb.

1945. Decorated Mexican, Victory and Def. medals. Mem. Am. Soc. Naval Engrs., U.S. Naval Inst. Clubs: Army and Navy (Washington); New York Yacht. Home: 4531 Nebraska Av. N.W. Office: Office Sec. Navy, Navy Dept., Washington 25. Died July 1962.

PENN, JULIUS AUGUSTUS army officer; b. Mattoon, Ill., Feb. 19, 1865; s. Julius Augustus and Mary (Brock) P.; grad. U.S. Mil. Acad., 1886; Inf. and Cav. Sch., Ft. Leavenworth, Kan., 1891 (valedictorian); Army War Coll., 1907; unmarried. Commd. 2d lt. 13th Inf., July 1, 1886; promoted through grades to rank of col., July 5, 1916. Transferred to 49th Inf., June 1917; brig. gen. N.A., Aug. 5, 1917; served with A.E.F., 1918-19; adj. gen., Mar. 10, 1919, in charge war prison sec. and gen. prisoners sec. Methodist. Mason. Home: Batavia, Clermont County, O. Died May 13, 1934.

PENNEY, CHARLES GEORGE brig. gen. U.S.A.; b. Newark, O., July 14, 1844; s. George W. and Ermina G. (Smith) P.; ed. Kenyon Coll., Ohio; m. Ida Walker. Enlisted pvt. Co. C, 76th Ohio Inf., Aug. 16, 1862; discharged, July 10, 1863; 2d lt. U.S..CT., July 10, 1863; 1st lt., Jan. 8, 1864; capt., Mar. 20, 1864; hon. mustered out, June 16, 1866; apptd. 2d lt. 38th U.S. Inf., July 28, 1866; 1st lt., Nov. 4, 1867; assigned to 6th Inf., Dec. 15, 1870; capt., June 26, 1883; maj. chief q.-m. vols., May 12, 1898; lt. col. chief q.m. vols., Aug. 11, 1898; hon. discharged from vols., Mar. 15, 1899; maj. 8th U.S. Inf., Aug. 15, 1898; transferred to 22d Inf., Oct. 24, 1898; lt. col. 23d Inf., Feb. 2, 1901; col. 29th Inf., May 9, 1902; brig. gen., Aug. 13, 1903; retired at own request after 40 yrs.' service, Aug. 14, 1903. Bvtd. 1st lt., Mar. 2, 1867, for Vicksburg; capt., Mar. 2, 1867, for Ft. Blakely, Ala. Home: Nordhoff, Calif. Died Dec. 13, 1926.

PENNINGTON, ALEXANDER CUMMINGS MCWHORTER brig. gen. U.S.A.; b. Newark, N.J., Jan. 8, 1838; s. Alexander C. M. and Ann Johnston (Kennedy) P.; ed. pvt. schs. and acad., 1844-55; grad. U.S. Mil. Acad., 1860; A.M., Princeton, 1864; m. Clara Miller French, Feb. 5, 1863. Bvt. 2d lt. 2d Arty., July 1, 1860; commd. 2d lt., Feb. 1, 1861; 1st lt., May 14, 1861; capt., Mar. 30, 1864; col. 3d N.J. Cav., Oct. 1, 1864; hon. mustered out of vol. service, Aug. 1, 1865; maj. 4th Arty., Nov. 8, 1882; lt. col., Nov. 28, 1892; col. 2d Arty., Oct. 29, 1896; brig. gen. vols., May 4, 1898; hon. discharged from vols., Apr. 12, 1899; brig. gen. U.S.A., Oct. 16, 1899; retired at own request after 40 yrs.' service, Oct. 17, 1899. Bvtd.: capt., June 9, 1863, for Beverly Ford, Va.; maj., July 3, 1863, for Gettysburg campaign; lt. col., Oct. 19, 1864, for Cedar Creek, Va.; col., Mar. 13, 1865. for services during the war; brig. gen. vols., July 15, 1865, "for faithful and meritorious services during the war." Served throughout Civil War in the field, at Fort Pickens, Fla., and Army of the Potomac; comd. 1st Brigade, 3d Cav. Div., Army of the Potomac; comd. Camp Black, Hempstead, L.I., May-July 1898; comd. Dept. of the Gulf, July 1898-Mar. 1899. Address: New York, N.Y. Died Nov. 30, 1917.

PENNOCK, ALEXANDER MOSLEY naval officer; b. Norfolk, Va., Oct. 1, 1814; s. William Pennock; m. Margaret Loyall. Apptd. midshipman U.S. Navy, 1828, passed midshipman, 1834; commd. lt., 1840, served ship Decatur, Brazil Squadron, 1843-46, store-ship Supply during Mexican War; served 1st extended shore duty as lighthouse insp., 1853-56; commanded steamer Southern Star in Paraguay Expdn.; became fleet capt. in charge of flotilla equipment, 1862; commanded naval base, Cairo, Ill., 1862-64; promoted capt., 1863, commodore, 1868; commanded European Squadron, 1868-69; commandant Portsmouth Navy Yard, 1870-72; rear adm., 1872, in command of Pacific Squadron, 1874-75. Died Portsmouth, N.H., Sept. 20, 1876; buried Norfolk, Va.

PENNOYER, ALBERT SHELDON (pen-noi'er), artist; b. Oakland, Calif., Apr. 5, 1888; s. Albert Adams and Virginia (Edmands) P.; prep. edn., Chateau de Lancy, Geneva, Switzerland, and Lawrenceville (N.J.) Sch.; student U. of Calif., 1908-09; art edn., École des Beaux Arts, in architecture, 1912, in painting at Acad. de la Grande Chaumiére, 1913 (both of Paris), Pa. Acad. Fine Arts. Phila.,; pupil of Casciaro, Naples, of Los, Rome, of Harold Speed, London. Represented Met. Mus. Art, N.Y.C., deYoung Mus. and Cal. Palace Legion of Honor, San Francisco. Served as sergeant Camouflage C.E., United States Army, 1917-20; 2d lt. O.R.C., 1922-28. Capt. U.S. Air Forces (camouflage), 1942; capt. Corps of Engrs. (camouflage), 1943. Member American Water Color Club: Monuments, Fine Arts and Archives Subcommission, Italy, 1944-45; Psi Upsilon. Republican. Episcopalian. Clubs: Century Association (New York); Sanctum (Litchfield, Conn.) Studio: 8 E. 62d St., N.Y.C. 21. Died Aug. 17, 1957; buried Britsih Cemetery, Madrid, Spain.

PENNOYER, FREDERICK WILLIAM, JR., naval officer; b. East Orange, N.J.; s. Frederick William and Huldah (Palmer) P.; student Stevens Inst. Tech., 1910-11; B.S., U.S. Naval Acad., 1915; M.S., Mass. Inst. Tech., 1920; naval aviator, Flight Training Naval Air Station, Pensacola, Fla., 1923; m. Margarette W. Bispham, Apr. 6, 1918; 1 son, Frederick William III (capt. USN ret.). Commd. ensign, U.S. Navy, 1915, and advanced through the grades to vice adm., 1950; specialized in aeronautical engineering since 1921; Bureau of Aeronautics general representative, Wright Field, Dayton, Ohio; ret. comdr. Naval Air Material Center, U.S. Naval Base, Phila. Decorated Legion of Merit (Gold Star), Air Medal, Commendation ribbon. Fellow Inst. Aeronautical Sciences. Address: Coronado CA Died Jan. 21, 1971; buried Mt. Rosecrans Cemetery, San Diego CA

PENNOYER, PAUL GEDDES, lawyer; b. Oakland, Cal., Oct. 30, 1890; s. Albert Adams and Virginia (Edmands) P.; student U. Cal. at Berkeley, 1907-08; A.B., Harvard, 1914, LL.B., 1917; m. Frances Tracy Morgan, June 16, 1917; children—Virginia (Mrs. Norman B. Livermore, Jr.), Paul G., F. Tracy (Mrs. August H. Schilling), Robert M., Katherine (Mrs. Eugene E. O'Donnell), Jessie (Mrs. Frank V. Snyder). Admitted to N.Y. bar, 1919; asso. White & Case, N.Y.C., 1920, partner, 1928-71; partner A. Iselin & Co., 1929-33. Rep. State Dept. UN, San Francisco Conf. on Internat. Orgn., 1945; secretariat State-War-Navy Coordinating Com., 1945. Mem. United Republican Finance Com. N.Y. Hon. gov. N.Y. Hosp.; chmn. Riverside Found.; dir., trustee N.Y. Philharmonic, N.Y.C.; trustee, and former secretary of the Pierpont Morgan Library, N.Y.C. Served as capt., F.A., AEF, U.S. Army, World War I, as col. GSC, World War II. Decorated Legion of Merit; chevalier Legion d'Honneur. Mem. Police Relief Assn. Nassau County (trustee), Locust Valley Cemetery Assn. (dir.), Assn. Bar N.Y.C., Am., N.Y., Internat. bar assns., N.Y. County Lawyers Assn., Bar Assn. Nassau County, Soc. Mayflower Descendents, France Am. Soc., Inc. (dir., mem. exec. com.), Fedn. des Alliances Francaises aux Etats-Unis (trustee). Episcopalian. Clubs: Down Town Association, Recess Board Room, Harvard, Links, Brook, Century (N.Y.C.), Travellers (Paris), Bohemian (San Francisco), Piping Rock, Creek (bd. govs.) (Locust Valley). Home: Locust Valley NY Died June 30, 1971; buried Locust Valley (N.Y.) Cemetery.

PENNYPACKER, GALUSHA brig. gen., bvt. maj. gen. U.S.A., retired; b. Chester County, Pa., June 1, 1844; s. Joseph J. and Tamson Amelia (Workizer) P.; ed. Phoenixville, Pa., Classical Inst.; unmarried. Entered Union Army, Apr. 1861, as non-commd. staff officer 9th Pa. Vols. for 3 months; served in the Shenandoah Valley, Va.; entered for the war, Aug. 22, 1861, as capt. Co. A, 97th Pa. Vols.; promoted maj., Oct. 7, 1861; served in 10th corps in Dept. of the South, 1862-63, including the engagements at Fts. Wagner and Gregg, James Island, siege of Charleston, capture Ft. Pulaski, and taking of Fernandina and Jacksonville, Fla.; joined Army of the James in Va., Apr. 1864; promoted lt. col., Apr. 3, 1864; col., June 23, 1864; comd. at Swift Creek, May 9, Drury's Bluff, May 16, Chester Station, May 18, and Green Plains, May 20, 1864; assigned to command 2d Brigade, 2d Div., 10th corps, Sept. 1864; was in successful assault on Ft. Fisher, N.C., Jan. 15, 1865; awarded Congressional Medal of Honor "for distinguished bravery in battle"; brig. gen. vols., Feb. 18, 1865; bvt. brig. gen. vols., Jan. 15, 1865; bvt. maj. gen. vols., Mar. 13, 1865; apptd. col. 34th (later changed to 16th) Inf., U.S.A., July 28, 1866; bvt. brig. gen. U.S.A., Mar. 2, 1867, bvt. maj. gen. U.S.A., Mar. 2, 1867; brig. gen. U.S.A., retired, Apr. 23, 1904; several times severely wounded, and was youngest general officer in War of the Rebellion; after war served as regimental and post comdr. and comd. departments at various times; placed on retired list on account of wounds, 1883. Home: Philadelphia, Pa. Died Oct. 1, 1916.

PENROSE, CLEMENT ANDARIESE physician; b. St. Louis, Mo., Jan. 2, 1874; s. Col. Charles Bingham (U.S.A.) and Clara (Andariese) P.; B.A., Johns Hopkins, 1893, M.D., 1897; m. Helen Stowe, Dec. 14, 1905. Served on staffs of Drs. Osler. Halsted and Kelly, and later practiced alone in Baltimore; licensed also to practice in Mass., Pa. and D.C.; specialist in dietetics, general efficiency and functional disorders; surgeon in chief and v. dir. Bahama Expdn., 1903; chmn. Food Economy Commn., Baltimore, 1917; capt. Med. O.R.C., Apr. 9, 1917; maj., Sept. 4, 1917; with British and Am. armies in Europe, studying sanitation in camps and army fronts; report filed with surgeon gen. U.S.A. Mem. exec. com. Ch. Home and Infirmary. Republican. Presbyn. Author of med. part "Bahama Islands," 1905. Home: Baltimore, Md. Died July 4, 1919.

PENROSE, GEORGE HOFFMAN army officer; b. Whitehall, N.Y., June 4, 1861; s. Gen. William Henry (U.S.A.) and Harriet Elizabeth (Adams) P.; prep. edn. high sch., Phila.; M.D., U. of Buffalo, 1886; m. Katherine Oden Hughart, of Grand Rapids, Mich., Oct. 22, 1901. Apptd. actg. asst. surgeon U.S.A., 1887; maj. brigade surgeon vols., June 16, 1898; capt. q.-m. dept., U.S.A., Feb. 2, 1901; hon. discharged vols., Apr. 19, 1901; maj. q.-m., Feb. 6, 1909; lt. col., Nov. 1, 1915. Served as chief surgeon, 1st Div., 8th Army Corps, 1899; comdg. officer Gen. Depot Q.-M. Corps, U.S.A., Phila., 1914-17; assigned duty, Office Q.-M. Gen., U.S.A., June 1917. Episcopalian. Club: Army and Navy (Washington). Address: War Dept. Washington.

PENROSE, WILLIAM HENRY col. U.S.A., retired Mar. 10, 1896; b. Madison Barracks. Sackett's Harbor, N.Y., Mar. 10, 1832; s. Capt. James W. P.; U.S.A.; ed. Dickinson Coll.; became civ. and mech. engr.; m. Harriet E. Adams, g.d. Maj. Gen. Brown, U.S.A. Apptd., Apr. 1861, 2d lt. 3d U.S. inf., and in May, 1st lt.; served through Civil War in Army of Potomac; col. 15th N.J. vols., Apr. 1863; brig. gen. vols., 1865; won bvts. through all grades in regular army to brig. gen.; after war promoted through regular grades to col., 1893, and was in command 16th inf. when retired. Residence: Salt Lake City, Utah. Died 1903.

PEOPLES, CHRISTIAN JOY naval officer; b. in Iowa, Oct. 17, 1876; s. Robert A. and Lydia (Love) P.; St. Ignatius Coll., Sacred Heart Coll., Vallejo High Sch.; spl. course U. of Calif.; m. Leila Warren, Mar. 18, 1901; children—Leila, Pamela. Appointed to the Supply Corps of the Navy, with rank of ensign, Mar. 27, 1900; promoted through the grades to rear adm., July 1, 1917. Supply officer of U.S.S. Wilmington, Asiatic Sta., 190104; Navy Dept., 1904-11; supply officer battleship Utah, Atlantic Fleet, 1910-14; apptd. gen. insp. Supply Corps and asst. to chief of bur. of supplies and accounts, Navy Dept., 1914-20. Developed purchase system of the navy; standardized the steaming coal and fuel oil system; navy rep. of exports control com. during World War; also of clearance div. War Industries Bd., etc.; actg. paymaster gen. of the Navy, Jan.-May 1921; gen. insp. Supply Corps for Pacific Coast, 1921-30; in charge of Naval Supply Depot, Brooklyn, N.Y., 1930-33; paymaster gen. of Navy and Chief of Bur. Supplies and Accounts, Navy Dept., 1933-35; dir. Procurement Div. of Treasury, 1933-39; gen. inspector Supply Corps for Pacific Coast, 1939-—. Home: Washington, D.C. Died Feb. 3, 1941.

PEPPER, O(LIVER) H(AZARD) PERRY physician; b. Phila., Apr. 28, 1884; s. William and Frances S. (Perry) P.; B.S., U. Pa., 1905, M.D., 1908; Sc.D., Lafayette Coll., 1938; m. Eulalie Wilcox, Dec. 2, 1916; children—Eulalie, Oliver H.P. Interne U. Hosp., Phila., 1908-10, asst. physician, 1913-37, physician since 1937; asst. instr. U. Pa., 1911-12, asso. in medicine, 1912-19, asso. in research medicine, 1913-19, asst. prof. medicine, 1922-28, prof. clin. medicine, 1928-34, prof. medicine, 1934-51, Com. on Fed. Med. Services, Hoover Commn. on Orgn. Exec. Br. of Govt. Served as lt. col. M.C., U.S. Army; chief med. service Base Hosp. 69, Savenay, France, World War. Mem. A.M.A., Assn., Am. Physicians (past pres.), Am. Soc. for Clin. Investigation, Am. Climatol. and Clin. Assn., A.C.P., Coll. Physicians of Phila. (ex-pres.), Am. Philos. Soc.; Com. on Vets Med. Problems, N.R.C. (chmn.). Republican, Episcopalian, Club: Philadelphia. Author: (with Dr. David L. Farley) Practical Hematological Diagnosis, 1933; Medical Etymology, 1949. Contbr. to med. jours. Home: Ithan, Pa. Office: 36th and Spruce St., Phila. Died Jan. 28, 1962.

PEPPER, WILLIAM physician, educator; b. Philadelphia, Pa., May 14, 1874; s. William and Frances Sergeant (Perry) P.; A.B., U. of Pa., 1894, M.D., 1897, Sc.D., 1932; LL.D., Temple University, 1942; m. Mary Godfrey, Dec. 31, 1904 (died Oct. 2, 1918); m. 2d, Phoebe S. (Voorhees) Drayton, Apr. 3, 1922 (dec.). With med. dept., U. of Pa., 1899; dean Sch. of Medicine, 1912-45. Lieut. Col., M.C., U.S. Army, World War; comdg. officer Base Hospital 74. Fellow College Physicians of Phila., Assn. Am. Med. Colleges (pres. 1920-21); mem. A.M.A., Am. Philos. Soc., trustee Univ. of Pa., trustee Philadelphia Free Library. Zeta Psi. Republican. Episcopalian. Home: Ithan, Delaware Co., Pa. Died Dec. 3, 1947.

PEPPERRELL, SIR WILLIAM army officer; b. Kittery Point, Me., June 27, 1696; s. William and Margery (Bray) P.; m. Mary Hirst, Mar. 16, 1723; 4 children including Elizabeth, Andrew. Col. in command all militia in Province of Me., 1726; mem. Mass. Gen. Ct. from Kittery, 1726; became mem. Council, 1727, pres., 18 years; apptd. chief justice 1730; col., 1745; created baronet, 1746; mem. Council, Boston, 1746; a commr. to negotiate treaty with Me. Indians, 1753; maj. gen., 1755; de facto gov. Mass.; apptd. comdr. in-chief Castle William and all mil. forces Me. Colony, strategy led to tremendous Am. victory at French ft. at Louisburg, N.S., Can.; commd. lt. gen. Brit. Army, 1759. Died Kittery, July 6, 1759.

PERCIVAL, JOHN naval officer; b. West Barnstable, Mass., Apr. 5, 1779; s. John and Mary (Snow) P.; m. Maria Pinkerton, 1823, no children. Sailed on ships in Atlantic trade, 1793-97; impressed into Brit. Navy, 1797, escaped, 1799; warranted midshipman U.S. Navy, 1800, discharged, 1801; mate and master in mcht. trade, 1801-09; known as "Mad Jack" or "Roaring Jack"; sailing master U.S. Navy, 1809; captured Brit. tender Eagle, 1813; promoted lt., 1814; served against pirates in West Indies; commanded schooner Dolphin (1st Am. warship to visit H.I.) in pursuit of mutineers aboard Globe in Pacific, 1825-26; courtmartialed for violating Hawaiian anti-prostitution ordinances, acquitted because he had helped to quell riot his libertine action had instigated; promoted comdr., 1831, capt., 1841; commanded Cyane in Mediterranean, 1838-39, Constitution on voyage around world, 1844-46; put on reserve list, 1855. Died Sept. 17, 1862.

PERCY, JAMES FULTON surgeon; b. Bloomfield, N.J., Mar. 26, 1864; s. James and Sarah Ann (Fulton) P.; M.D., Bellevue Hosp. Med. Coll. (now Med. Dept. New York U.), 1886; postgrad. student on experimental problems in abdominal surgery, Chicago Vet. Coll., 1895; postgrad. student pathology and surgery, in

Germany, Switzerland, Belgium, 1897-98; visited clinics, in England, France, Germany, Austria, 1914; hon. A.M., Knox Coll., Galesburg, Ill., 1914; m. Mrs. Edna B. Post, 1925. Med. practice, Mazeppa, Minn., 1886-88, Galesburg, Ill., 1888-1917; developed surgical instruments, 1904, known as Percy actual cauteries for treatment of accessible cancers; practice limited treatment of cancer since 1917; surgical practice, San Diego, Calif., 1920-22, in Los Angeles, since 1922; attending sr. surgeon, cancer service, and founder member (1922) Malignancy Board and Tumor Clinic, Los Angeles County Hospital (vice chairman and chairman 8 years); clinical professor of surgery (neoplasms), College of Medical Evangelists Medical School (emeritus); attending surgeon French Hospital, 12 years; consulting surgeon, Orthopedic Hospital and School for Crippled Children (all in Los Angeles). Member 1st draft board, Knox County, Ill., 1916; student training courses for officers, Fort Riley, Kan., 1917; chief of surgical staff, U.S. Army Base Hosp., Camp Kearny, Calif., 1917-19; retired with rank of major; apptd. lt. col., Med. Reserves, U.S. Army, 1925, reapptd. for term, 1940-45, called first meeting, Galesburg, Ill., out of which grew Galesburg Cottage Hosp., 1888. Was honor guest at Clinical Congress of Surgeons, North America, at meeting held in London, 1914. Fellow Am. Coll. Surgeons (founder mem.); mem. A.M.A., Calif. Med. Assn., Los Angeles Med. Assn. (v.p. 1931), Los Angeles Surg. Soc. (pres. 1929), Los Angeles Cancer Soc. (pres. 1939), American Board of Surgery (founder member), Western Surgical Association (president 1918), Illinois State Medical Soc. (pres. 1907; sec. Jud. Council 17 years), Southern Calif. Med. Assn. (hon. 1914), Am. Soc. for Control of Cancer, Am. Assn. Obstet., Gynecol. and Abdominal Surgeons, Hollywood Acad. of Med. (hon. 1926), Reserve Officers Assn., U.S. Army, U.S. Mil. Surgeons Assn. Mason (32 deg.). Bahai religion. Contbr. about 40 articles to med. jours., principally on actual cautery in treatment of cancer. Home: 1030 S. Alvarado St., Los Angeles 6. Died Apr. 26, 1946; buried in Forest Lawn Memorial Park, Glendale, Calif.

PERCY, NELSON MORTIMER surgeon; b. Dexter, Ia., Nov. 7, 1875; s. Mortimer and Mary F. (Amidon) P.; prep. edn. Dexter Normal Sch.; M.D., Rush Med. Coll., Chgo., 1899; m. Alfie Hokland, Feb. 5, 1927. Practiced in Chgo., 1901-—; surgeon in chief Augustana Hospital, 1925-35, chief of staff, 1935-57, emeritus chief of staff, 1957-—; senior attending surgeon St. Mary's of Nazareth Hospital; professor emeritus clinical surgery University Illinois. Served as lt. col. U.S. Army in France, 1918-19, organized Base Hosp. 11. Founder mem. Am. Bd. Surgery. Fellow Am. Surg. Assn., A.C.S.; mem. Chgo. Surg. Soc., A.M.A., Ill. State, Chgo. med. socs., Am. Assn. for Study of Goiter, Mil. Order World Wars, Assn. Commerce and Industry, Art, Inst., Chgo. Natural Mus., Phi Rho Sigma. Republican. Methodist. Clubs: University, Lake Shore. Author (with Albert J. Ochsner) Clinical Surgery, 1912. Contbr.; Ochsner's Surgical Diagnosis and Treatment, 1920. Home: 2130 Lincoln Park W. Office: 2051 Sedgwick St., Chgo. Died Oct. 10, 1958; buried Meml. Park, Evanston, Ill.

PERCY, WILLIAM ALEXANDER lawyer, author; b. Greenville, Miss., May 14, 1885; s. U.S. Senator LeRoy and Camille (Bourges) P.; A.B., U. of the South, 1904, Litt.D., 1939; LL.B., Harvard, 1908; unmarried. Began practice at Greenville, 1908; retired. With Commn. for Relief in Belgium, 1916; 1st lt. infantry, 2d Officers' Training School, Leon Springs, Tex., Aug.-Oct. 1917; served with 37th Div., A.E.F., in France; hon. discharged as capt., 1919. Author: (verse) Sappho in Levkas, 1915; In April Once, 1920; Enzio's Kingdom, 1924; Selected Poems, 1930; Lanterns on the Levee (autobiography), 1941. Home: Greenville, Miss. Died Jan. 21, 1942.

PERKINS, ALBERT THOMPSON ry. official and consulting engineer; b. at Brunswick, Me., Oct. 2, 1865; s. Charles S. and Mary S. (Murray) Perkins; A.B. magna cum laude, Harvard, 1887, hon. A.M., 1919; m. Eva Spotswood Lemoine, Feb. 16, 1898; 1 dau., Katherine Lemoine (Mrs. Lloyd C. Stark). With C.,B.&Q. Ry. at Chicago, 1887, supt. terminals, St. Louis, 1897-1902, supt. St. Joseph div., 1902-06; consulting engr. and r.r. adviser to Municipal Bridge and Terminals Commn., St. Louis, 1906-08; same to St. Louis Union Trust Co., 1908-—; served as exec. officer, engr. or pres. various rys., including St. Louis, Brownsville & Mexico, New Iberia & Northern, Chicago, Milwaukee & Gary and Apalachicola Northern, and as adviser on terminal matters to several cities; pres. Peoples Motorbus Co. (St. Louis); director numerous corps., including Laclede Steel Co., St. Louis Pub. Service Co., St. Louis Refrigerating & Cold Storage Company. Mil. training, Plattsburg Camp, and St. Louis; maj. Engr. R.C., June 28, 1917; lt col. N.A., July 6, 1917; col. U.S.A., Aug. 13, 1918, and assigned to 14th Engineers. Sailed for France, July 1917; with British 3d Army and 2d Army; successively dep. mgr., mgr. and dir. Light (Combat) Rys., A.E.F.; participated at Paaschendaele Ridge, Cambrai, 1917, Marne-Aise, Somme, St. Mihiel, Meuse-Argonne offensives; hon. discharged, Mar. 11, 1919; col. U.S., comdg. 327th (Combat) Engrs. to 1930; now col. Aux. Res. Decorated D.S.M. (U.S.); Order St. Michael and St. George (British). Mem. Bd. of Overseers, Harvard, 1925-31, pres. bd., 1930-31. Trustee Mo. Bot. Garden, Ranken Sch. of Mech. Trades; mem. nat. exec. com. Mil. Training Camps Assn.; pres. Community Fund of St. Louis; dir. St. Louis Chamber of Commerce. Mem. Nat. Aeronautic Assn. (pres. St. Louis Chapter), Soc. Am. Mil. Engrs. (pres.). Republican. Home: Clayton, Mo. Died Nov. 22, 1936.

PERKINS, BISHOP WALDEN senator, congressman; b. Rochester, O., Oct. 18, 1841; attended Knox Coll., Galesburg, Ill.; studied law. Prospector, Cal. and N.M., 1860-62; served as sgt. 83d Regt., Ill. Volunteer Inf., later adj. and capt. 16th Regt., U.S. Colored Inf., Union Army, during Civil War; admitted to the bar, 1867, began practice in Princeton, Ind.; moved to Oswego, Kan., practiced law; county atty. Mo., Kan. & Tex. R.R., 2 years; pros. atty. Labette County (Kan.), 1869; judge Labette County Probate Ct., 1870-82; editor Oswego Register, 1873; mem. U.S. Ho. of Reps. (Republican) from Kan., 48th-51st congresses, 1883-91; mem. U.S. Senate from Kan., Jan. 1, 1892-93; resumed law practice, Washington, D.C. Died Washington, June 20, 1894; buried Rock Creek Cemetery, Washington.

PERKINS, CHARLES PLUMMER commodore U.S.N.; b. Great Falls, N.H., Feb. 18, 1848; s. Moses P. and Elizabeth (Nute) P.; early edn. schs. of Dover, N.H., Haverhill and Salem, Mass.; grad. U.S. Naval Acad., 1869; m. Kate Stevens, Aug. 19, 1885; m. 2d, Ellen O., d. Judge J. J. Graves, Oct. 8, 1904. Promoted ensign, 1871; master, 1872; lt., 1874; lt. comdr., 1896; comdr., 1899; captain, 1904; retired as commodore, June 30, 1908. Served on many duties and stas.; was on Amazon survey, 1878, "Jeannette" search expdn., 1881, Tampico River expdn., 1883; comdg. coast survey steamer Eagre, Hydrographic Survey, Hell Gate, 1886; supt. compasses, Navy Dept., 1892-95; Spanish-Am. War Service on board monitor Monadnock, Manila; later comd. U.S.S. Michigan, Adams, Alert, Philadelphia, Boston, Concord, and Pensacola; in Panama campaign, 1903-04; commandant Naval Training Sta., San Francisco, 190-07; later asst. to commandant Pacific Naval Dist.; pres. Statutory Bd. Survey, and commandant Pacific Naval Dist., 1908-09. Author of monograph on cruise of "Alliance" in search of "Jeannette," and collaborator textbook for U.S. Naval Acad., in "Marine Surveying." Address: Berkeley, Calif. Died Oct. 5, 1913.

PERKINS, FREDERICK army officer; b. in Me., Aug. 21, 1857; grad. U.S. Mil. Acad., 1883. Commd. 2d lt. 5th Inf., June 13, 1883; 1st lt. 16th Inf., Feb. 24, 1891; trans. to 8th Inf., July 20, 1891; capt. inf., July 26, 1898; assigned to 8th Inf., Jan. 1, 1899; maj. 13th Inf., Aug. 7, 1906; adj. gen., Apr. 7, 1908; lt. col. 20th Inf., Mar. 2, 1912; col., Feb. 21, 1916; brig. gen. N.A., Aug. 5, 1917; hon. discharged as brig. gen. N.A., Mar. 1918. Comd. Provost Guard at Mil. Prison, Ft. Leavenworth, Kan., 1891-94, adj. of Mil. Prison, 1894-95; in Cuba, Spanish-Am. War, to July 15, 1898; apptd. comdr. 166th Inf. Brigade, Camp Sherman, Chillicothe, O., Sept. 1917. Address: Washington, D.C. Died Apr. 25, 1940.

PERKINS, GEORGE HAMILTON naval officer; b. Hopkinton, N.H., Oct. 20, 1836; s. Hamilton Eliot and Clara (George) P.; grad. U.S. Naval Acad., 1855; m. Anna Minot Weld, July 25, 1870, 1 dau. Isabel (Perkins) Anderson. Apptd. midshipman U.S. Navy, 1855; acting master ship Sumter in suppression of African slave trade, 1859-61; promoted lt., 1861; served in West Gulf Blockading Squadron, 1861-65; with Capt. Theodorus Bailey entered city of New Orleans, walked unarmed through hostile mob, accepted surrender of city, 1862; commanded ships Sciota in blockade of Tex. coast and Chickasaw on lower Mississippi River; promoted comdr., 1871, commanded ships Ashuelot, Asiatic Station, 1877-79, Hartford off South America, 1884-85; promoted capt., 1882; ret., 1891; promoted commodore ret., 1896. Died Boston, Oct. 28, 1899.

PERKINS, GEORGE WALBRIDGE exec., adminster.; b. Riverdale-on-Hudson, N.Y., May 2, 1895; s. George Walbridge and Eveline (Ball) P.; student Hill Sch., 1910-13; Litt.B., Princeton U., 1917, LL.D., 1957; M.A., Columbia, 1921; m. Katharine Trowbridge, June 19, 1917 (died 1918); m. 2d, Linn Merck, Dec. 17, 1921; children—Penelope, George Walbridge, Jr., Linn Marie-Anne. Sec. Princeton Endowment Fund Com., 1919-20; executor George Walbridge Perkins Estate since 1920; exec. sec. to Postmaster Gen. Hays, Washington, 1921-22; asst. treas. Rep. State Com., 1922; exec. vice-pres., dir. Merck & Co., Inc., 1927-48, treas., 1927-June 1947, now mem. bd. of directors; chief industries div. E.C.A., Paris, July 1948-Aug. 1919; asst. sec. of state for European affairs, 1949-53; U.S. permanent rep. N. Atlantic Council and Orgn. European Econ. Cooperation, rank of ambassador, 1955-57; dir. various corps. Dir. of American Council on NATO, 1957. Served as pvt., regimental supply sergeant, 2d lt., F.A., 1st Div., U.S. Army, A.E.F., Army of Occupation, 1917-19. Col., Chem. Warfare Service, U.S. Army, 1942-45; service in European, Pacific Theatres, and Washington. Awarded Legion of Merit. Mem. Palisades Interstate Park Commn., 1922-—, pres., 1945-—; pres. bd. edn. Cold-Spring-on-Hudson, N.Y., 1933-42; dir., treas. N.Y.C. YMCA, 1935-40; trustee Hill School, Pottstown, Pa., pres., 1946-48, 53-54; trustee of Robert College, Istanbul, pres., 1954; alumni trustee Princeton, 1935-39; adv. bd. Inst. Nutrition Scis., Columbia. Republican. Presbyterian. Clubs: University, Union League, Princeton, City, National Republican, Down Town Assn., Century Assn., Knickerbocker (N.Y.C.); Chevy Chase, Metropolitan (Washington). Home: Glynwood Farm, Cold Spring-on-Hudson, N.Y. Office: 342 Madison Av., N.Y.C. Died Jan. 1960.

PERKINS, JAMES HANDASYD banker; b. Milton, Mass., Jan. 11, 1876; s. Edward Cranch and Jane Sedgwick (Watson) P.; A.B., Harvard, 1898; m. Katrine Parkman Coolidge, Nov. 22, 1906; children—Eleanor H. (Mrs. Franklin E. Parker, Jr.), Richard S., Elizabeth Joan. With Walter Baker & Company, Ltd., 1898-1905; v.p. Am. Trust Co., Boston, 1905-08; v.p. Nat. Commercial Bank, Albany, N.Y., 1908-12, pres. 1912-14; v.p. Nat. City Bank, New York, 1914-19, exec. mgr., 1916-19; mem. banking firm Montgomery & Co., 1919; pres. Farmers Loan & Trust Co., 1921-29; chmn. City Bank Farmers Trust Co.; chmn. bd. Nat. City Bank of N.Y., 1933-—; chmn. bd. Internat. Banking Corp.; dir. Anaconda Copper Mining Co., Am. & Foreign Ins. Co., Eagle Indemnity Co., Federal Union Ins. Co., Globe Indemnity Co., Liverpool & London & Globe Ins. Co., Ltd., Newark Fire Ins. Co., Queen Ins. Co. of America, Royal Indemnity Co., Star Ins. Co. of America, Consol. Edison Co. of N.Y., New York Edison Co., Sperry Realty Co., Union Pacific System, 150 William St. Corporation, and many other insurance companies. Pres. New York Clearing House, 1937-—. Trustee Miriam Osborn Memorial Home Assn. Mem. 1st comm. to France, American Red Cross; commissioner to France and Europe, Am. Red Cross, June 1917-Sept. 1918; resigned to enter A.E.F.; duty at G.H.Q., asst. chief of staff 2d Army, later of 3d Army; lt. col. Q.M.C., Nov. 7, 1918; asst. chief of staff, 3d Army (Army of Occupation), Nov. 1918-Jan. 1919. D.S.M. (U.S.); Officer Legion of Honor (France); Comdr. Order of the Crown (Belgium). Treas. New York Co. Chapter Am. Red Cross, Jan. 1920-July 1921. Mem. Am. Bankers' Assn. (exec. council, finance com., 1915-18), N.Y. State Bankers' Assn. (pres. 1913-14). Home: Greenwich, Conn. Died July 12, 1940.

PERKINS, RALPH corp. exec.; b. Cleve., Nov. 29, 1886; s. Jacob B. and Sallie (Wilshire) P.; Ph.B. lit., Williams Coll., 1909; m. Margaret Keyes, Apr. 29, 1911 (dec.); children—Elizabeth (Mrs. George C. Miller), Jacob B., Ralph; m. 2d, Katharine Haskell, Oct. 12, 1926; children—Leigh H., Gertrude (Mrs. George Oliva, Jr.), Sallie (Mrs. Barry Sullivan). With Hill Acme Co., Cleve., 1911-—, pres., 1920-36, now chmn.; dir. M. A. Hanna Co., Cleve., 1950-—. Dir. pub. welfare, Cleve., 1921-24. Served as capt. 37th Div., U.S. Army, World War I, AEF; lt. col. cav. AUS, World War II. Mem. Alpha Delta Phi. Home: West Hill Dr., Gates Mills, O. Office: 401 Euclid Av., Cleve. 14. Died Nov. 20, 1964.

PERKINS, THOMAS HANDASYD mcht., philanthropist; b. Boston, Dec. 15, 1764; s. James and Elizabeth (Peck) P.; m. Sarah Elliot, Mar. 25, 1788, 7 children. Partner with brothers in merc. firm trading between U.S. and Santo Domingo, 1785-92; partner with brother James in firm J. & T. H. Perkins, Boston, 1792-1822, traded with China, chief partner, 1822-38; mem. Mass. Senate, 8 terms, Mass. Ho. of Reps., 3 terms; presdl. elector from Mass., 1816, 32; diplomatic courier to France for U.S. ministry at London, Eng., 1811-12; col. Mass. Militia; pres. Boston br. of U.S. Bank; contbd. to Mass. Gen. Hosp., Boston Athenaeum, Bunker Hill and Nat. Monument assns., New Eng. (later Perkins) Asylum for Blind. Died Boston, Jan. 11, 1854.

PERKINS, WILLIAM HARVEY med. educator; b. Germantown, Philadelphia, Pa., Oct. 21, 1894; s. Penrose Robinson and Marion (Harvey) P.; M.D., Jefferson Med. College, 1917; Sc.D., Franklin and Marshall College, Lancaster, Pa.; LL.D., Dickinson College, Carlisle, Pa.; m. Barbara Isabelle Bond, June 25, 1918; children—Barbara Jeanne (Mrs. Walter J. Binnings), Harriet June. Interne Jefferson Med. Coll. Hosp., 1917; 1st lt. Med. Corps., U.S. Army, detachment comdr. with Base Hosp. No. 120, Tours, France, 1918-19; med. missionary Presbyn. Bd. of Fgn. Missions to Siam, 1919-23; fellowship in med. edn., Rockefeller Found., 1924-26; prof. medicine and dir. clinics, Chulalangkarana U., Siam, 1926-30; instr. in medicine, Tulane U., 1930-31, prof. preventive medicine, since 1931; dean preventive medicine, Jefferson Med. Coll., 1941-50. Awarded Order of White Elephant, Siam, 1930. Fellow Am. Coll. Phys., 1942, Coll. of Phys. of Phila., Phila. County Med. Soc., Phila. Council of Social Agencies, Mem. A.M.A., Am. Soc. Tropical Medicine, Am. Public Health Assn., Phila. Tuberculosis and Health Assn. (bd. dirs.), Med. Club of Phila., Theta Kappa Psi, Alpha Omege Alpha. Presbyterian. Author: Cause and Prevention of Disease, 1938; Obstetric Medicine, 1934; also many med. articles. Home: 1025 Walnut St., Phila. 7. Died Oct. 1967.

PERRIN, HERBERT TOWLE (pâr'in), army officer; b. Platville, Wis., Sept. 8, 1893; s. John William and Harriet Naylor (Towle) P.; student Western Reserve U., 1912-15; Ph.B., Kenyon Coll. (O.), 1916, LL.D., 1946; A.M. Princeton, 1917; grad. Inf. Sch., 1923, Comd. and Gen. Staff Sch., 1933; m. Anne Wilby, Oct. 1, 1921; children—Susanne Wilby, Herbert Towle. Commd. 2d lt., U.S. Army, Oct. 26, 1917, and advanced through the grades to brig. gen., April 2, 1943; served as 2d and 1st lt., World War I. Asst. chief of staff G-3, Hdqrs. Phil. Dept. 1938-40; War Dept Gen. Staff 1940-42; chief of staff, 76th Inf. Div., 1942; comdg. gen. 106th Inf. Div. Dec. 22, 1944. Decorations: Distinguished Service Cross, Legion of Merit; French Legion of Honor, Croix de Guerre with Palms. Mem. Delta Kappa Epsilon. Home: P.O. Box 294, Gambier, O. Died June 9, 1962; buried Arlington Nat. Cemetery.

PERRINE, HENRY PRATT (per rin'), army officer; b. Trenton, N.J., July 22, 1891; s. Henry Pratt and Louisa (Scudder) P.; B.S., U.S. Mil. Acad., 1913; M.B.A., Harvard, 1931; m. Anita Allen, Nov. 4, 1917; m. 2d, Florence Bradley, June 18, 1924; children—Henry Pratt, David Perry. Commd. 2d lt., Inf., U.S. Army, June 12, 1913, and advanced through the grades to brig. gen., 1943; became exec. officer Inf. Sch., Ft. Benning, Ga., 1941; comdg. Inf. Sch., Ft. Benning, Ga., 1943, comdg. IRTC., Camp Jos. T. Robinson, Ark., Feb. 1945. Died Dec. 30, 1954.

PERRY, ALEXANDER JAMES brigadier gen. U.S.A.; b. New London, Conn., Dec. 11, 1828. Grad. U.S. Mil. Acad., 1851; bvt. 2d lt. 2d Arty., July 1, 1851; 2d lt., July 1, 1852; 1st lt., Sept. 27, 1854; capt. asst. q.m., May 17, 1861; lt. col. q.m. vols., Aug. 20, 1862-Jan. 15, 1863; col. q.m., Aug. 2, 1864-Jan. 1, 1867; maj. q.m. U.S.A., July 29, 1866; lt. col. deputy q.m. gen., Mar. 3, 1875; col. asst. q.m. gen., Aug. 31, 1883; retired by operation of law, Dec. 11, 1892; advanced to rank of brig. gen. retired, by act of Apr. 23, 1904. Bvtd. maj., lt. col., and col., Mar. 13, 1865, for services during the war; brig. gen., Mar. 13, 1865, for service in q.m. dept. during the war. Home: Washington, D.C. Died Mar. 26, 1913.

PERRY, ANDRE JAMES banker; b. Fond du Lac, Wis., Aug. 20, 1909; s. Ernest James and Jeannette Isabelle (Andrae) P.; Ph.B., Brown U., 1932; grad. sch. banking Am. Bankers Assn. and Rutgers U., 1947-49; m. Helen Barkhausen, Aug. 1, 1936; children—Andre James, Catherine Campbell, Susan Hopkins. Liquidator Wis. State Banking Dept., 1933-36; joined First Fond du Lac Nat. Bank, 1936, pres. 1948-63; v.p., dir. First Wis. Bankshares Corp.; dir. Gen. Telephone Co. Wis. Trustee Ripon Coll., Nashotah House Sem. Served as lt. col. U.S. Army Ordnance Dept., 1942-45. Recipient Legion of Merit. Mem. Robert Morris Assos., Financial Pub. Relations Assn., Wis. C. of C. (pres.), Young President's Orgn., Alpha Delta Phi. Mem. Diocese of Fond du Lac (treas.). Home: 355 Rose Av., Fond du Lac 54935. Office: 55 S. Main St., Fond du Lac, Wis. Died May 6, 1963.

PERRY, CHRISTOPHER RAYMOND naval officer; b. South Kingstown, R.I., Dec. 4, 1761; s. Freeman and Mercy (Hazard) P.; m. Sarah Wallace Alexander, Aug. 1784, 8 children including Oliver Hazard, Matthew Calbraith, Ann Maria. Served in several Continental privateers during Am. Revolution; present at siege of Charleston (S.C.); served in Trumbull during Trumbull-Watt battle; captured by British, 4 times; capt. in mcht. service, 1784-98; commd. capt. U.S. Navy, 1798; commanded ship General Greene in suppression of pirates of Cuba and escorting mcht. vessels to U.S. during naval war with France; re., 1801; comdt. Charlestown (Mass.) Naval Yard, 1812. Died Newport, R.I., June 1, 1818.

PERRY, CLARENCE ARTHUR b. Truxton, Cortland County, N.Y., Mar. 4, 1872; s. Duane Oliver and Hattie E. (Hart) P.; student Stanford 2 yrs.; B.S., Cornell U., 1899; studied Teachers Coll. (Columbia), summer, 1904; m. Julia St. John Wygant (M.D.), Apr. 27, 1901; 1 dau., Sara Janet. Prin. high sch., Ponce, Porto Rico, 1904-05; spl. agt. U.S. Immigration Commn., 1908-09; lecturer, New York U., summer, 1912; became connected with Russell Sage Foundation, 1909, asso. dir. dept. of recreation, 1913; retired, 1937. Student Business Men's Mil. Training Camp, Plattsburg, Aug. 1915, 16; commd. capt. Q.-M. R.C., U.S. Army, Aug. 9, 1917; maj. Q.-M.C., Oct. 26, 1918; in France with 77th Div., Apr. 1918-Apr. 1919; apptd. div. q.-m., Apr. 15, 1919; hon. disch. Oct. 14, 1919; commd. maj. Finance, O.R.C., Dec. 16, 1919; lt. col., Dec. 8, 1924. Mem. Sigma Alpha Epsilon, Sigma Xi. Conglist. Author: Wider Use of the School Plant, 1910; Educational Extension, 1916; Community Center Activities, 1916; Attitude of High School Students Toward Motion Pictures, 1923; The Work of the Little Theatres, 1933; The Rebuilding of Blighted Areas, 1933; Housing for the Machine Age, 1939; also pamphlets and bulletins on ednl. topics. Co-author: Neighborhood and Community Planning, 1929. Contbr. to Cyclo. of Edn., The Modern High Sch., Educational Hygiene, Principles of Secondary Education. Home: 80 Beechknoll Rd., Forest Hills, L.I., N.Y. Died Sep. 5, 1944.

PERRY, DAVID army officer; b. Ridgefield, Conn., June 11, 1841; s. Samuel and Sophia P.; ed. Rev. D. H. Short's prep. sch.; m. S. Louise Hoyt, Jan. 28, 1885. Apptd. from N.J., 2d lt. 1st Cav., U.S.A., Mar. 24, 1862; 1st lt., July 27, 1862; capt., Nov. 12, 1864; maj. 6th Cav., Apr. 29, 1879; lt. col. 10th Cav., Apr. 20, 1891; col. 9th Cav., Dec. 11, 1896; retired on account of disability in line of duty, July 5, 1898; advanced to rank of brig. gen. retired, by act of Apr. 23, 1904. Bvtd. maj., Apr. 1, 1865, for faithful and meritorious services during the war; lt. col., Dec. 26, 1866, for engagement with Indians on Owyhee river, Ida., Dec. 26, 1866; col., Apr. 5, 1868, for engagement with Indians on Malheur river, Ore., Apr. 5, 1868. Home: Washington, D.C. Died 1908.

PERRY, EDWARD AYLESWORTH gov. Fla.; b. Richmond, Mass., Mar. 15, 1831; s. Asa and Philura (Aylesworth) P.; attended Yale, 1850-51; m. Wathen Taylor, Feb. 1, 1859, 5 children. Practiced law, Pensacola, Fla., 1857-61, 65-84; commd. capt. 2d Fla. Inf., Confederate Army, 1861, promoted col., brig. gen., 1862; served at battles of Frayser's Farm, Chancellorsville and Wilderness; gov. Fla., 1885-87. Died Kerrville, Tex., Oct. 15, 1889; buried Pensacola.

PERRY, JOHN, naval officer; b. Enoree, S.C., July 29, 1897; s. William Gregory and Frederica (Mc Kenzie) P.; student, Clemson (S.C.) Coll., 1914-16; B.S., U.S. Naval Acad., 1919; m. Madeline Gleason, July 15, 1921; children—John (dec.), Madeline. Commd. ensign U.S. Navy, 1919, and advanced through grades to vice adm.; served in U.S.S. New York and Dorsey, 1919-23; flight training, Pensacola Naval Air Sta., 1923, received wings, June 1923; served in various Pacific aircraft squadrons, 1923-26, piloted plane in 1st squadron west coast to Hawaii flight, 1934; commd. and comdr. Naval Base, Kodiak, 1941-42; chief of staff, Fleet Air, West Coast, 1942-43; comdr. U.S.S. Belleau Wood, participating in Hollandia, Mariannas and Philippine campaigns, 1944; comdr. Fleet Air Wing 1, Okinawa, 1945-46; chief of staff, Air Force Atlantic, div. comdr. Essex type carriers, Atlantic, 1946-48; comdr. Fleet Air Wing 4, operating in N.W. and Alaska, and comdr. Fleet Air, Seattle, Wash., 1948-50; comdr. NAAT, Corpus Christi, Tex., 1950-51, cardivs. land 5, 1951-52, Alaskan Sea Frontier, also COM 17, 1952-54, Com FAIR, Jacksonville, Fla., 1954-55, Com FAIR, Whidbey, Wash., 1955-59, ret., 1959. Decorated Distinguished Service medal, Silver Star, Combat Legion of Merit, Presidential unit citation (2); various campaign, area and fgn. medals. Episcopalian. Home: Greenville SC Died Aug. 7, 1972; buried Washelli Cemetery, Seattle WA

PERRY, JOHN RICHARD naval officer; b. May 24, 1899. Commd. Civil Engrs. Corps USN, 1923, advanced through grades to rear adm., 1953; now chief of Civil Engrs., USN. Address: 4220 43d St. N.W., Washington. Died Sept. 25, 1955.*

PERRY, LEWIS EBENEZER univ. dean and v.p.; b. Alma, N.Y., July 24, 1899; s. Ebenezer Lee and Ida Belle (Eastabrook) P.; A.B., Bethany (W.Va.) Coll., 1920; A.M., Columbia Tchrs. Coll., 1925; Ph.D., U. Pitts., 1939; m. Lillian Lorraine Ash, Dec. 25, 1920; children—Alice Virginia (Mrs. Thomas F. Lewin), William E. Tchr. sci. and athletics, Manlius (Ill.) High Sch., 1920-22, prin. high Sch., 1922-26; prin. Pitcairn (Pa.) High Sch., 1926-28; prin. Mt. Lebanon (Pa.) High Sch., 1928-41, supt. schs., 1945-46; resident dean U. Md. br., Munich, Germany, 1955-57; dean Norwich U., Northfield, Vt., 1957—, v.p., 1961—. Served to col. AUS, 1941-45, 46-54; comdt. Strategic Intelligence Sch., 1952-53; exec. officer G-2, Dept. of Army, 1953-54. Decorated Legion of Merit, Bronze Star; Legion of Honor, Croix de Guerre (France). Mem. Vt. Hist. Soc., Nat. Geog. Soc., Am. Soc. Engring. Edn., Sigma Nu, Phi Delta Kappa. Mason. Home: 82 S. Main St., Northfield, Vt. Died June 7, 1963; buried Arlington Nat. Cemetery.

PERRY, MATTHEW CALBRAITH naval officer; b. Newport, R.I., Apr. 10, 1794; s. Christopher Raymond and Sarah (Alexander) P.; m. Jane Slidell, Dec. 24, 1814, 10 children including Carline Slidell. Commd. midshipman U.S. Navy, 1809, lt., 1813; held 1st command in ship Shark, 1821; exec. officer in ship North Carolina, 1825-26; master comdt., 1826; comdr. ship Brandywine, 1832; 2d officer N.Y. Navy Yard, 1833; mem. bd. examiners preparing 1st course of instrn. for U.S. Naval Acad., Annapolis, Md., 1845; leader in organizing U.S. Naval Lyceum to promote diffusion of knowledge among naval officers, 1833, 1st curator, v.p., 1836, later pres.; commd. capt., 1837, in command ship Fulton; comdt. N.Y. Navy Yard, 1841; in command African Squadron, 1843; 1st comdr. ship Mississippi; 2d officer in command of squadron operating on East coast of Mexico, later comdr.-in-chief; selected to negotiate treaty with Japan (at that time sealed against intercourse with Western countries), 1852, treaty of peace, amity and commerce signed between U.S. and Japan, Mar. 31, 1854. Author: Narrative of the Expedition of an American Squadron to the China Seas and Japan, published by U.S. Govt., 1856. Died N.Y.C., Mar. 4, 1858.

PERRY, OLIVER HAZARD naval officer; b. South Kingstown, R.I., Aug. 20, 1785; s. Christopher Raymond and Sarah (Alexander) P.; m. Elizabeth Mason, May 5, 1811; 5 children. Apptd. midshipman U.S. Navy, 1799; promoted acting lt., 1803, lt., 1807; commanded schooner Revenge, 1809; master commandant, 1812; in charge Am. fleet on Lake Erie, defeated British in battle, Sept. 9, 1813 (enabled Americans to make a strong claim to N.W. at peace negotiations in Ghent, Belgium); after this battle sent message "we have met the enemy and they are ours"; commended by U.S. Congress, received gold medal; commd. capt., 1813; aide-de-camp to comdr.-in-chief in Battle of Thames; took command ship Java, 1814. Died Angostura, Venezuela, Aug. 23, 1819; buried Port of Spain, Trinidad; reinterred Newport, R.I., 1826.

PERRY, OSCAR BUTLER mining engr.; b. Bloomington, Ind., Sept. 1876; s. Maj. H. F. P.; A.B., Ind. U., 1897, LL.D., 1931; E.M., Columbia U., 1900; m. Anlo Marquee Cramer, Apr. 1923; children—Anlo Louise, Yvonne Chauvigny. Manager Ind. Gold Dredging Co., 1900-02, Western Engring. & Construction Co., San Francisco, 1902-04; engr., 1904-06, gen. mgr. placer mining properties since 1906, Guggenheim Exploration Co.; gen. mgr. Yukon Gold Co., operating gold mines in U.S. and Yukon Territory, and tin mines in Malay, 1920-26; mng. dir. Bolivian Internat. Mining Corp. since 1930. Entered U.S. Army, May 1917; discharged, Apr. 1919, with rank of col. of engrs.; comd. 27th Engrs., A.E.F.; asst. engr. light rys. and roads, and engr. in charge of bridge sect., 1st Army. Mem. Beta Theta Pi, Tau Beta Pi. Clubs: Family (San Francisco); Engineers', Columbia University, Bankers (New York). Author of Gold Dredging in the Yukon and other professional papers. Home: 444 El Arroyo Rd., Hillsborough, Calif. Address: 315 Montgomery St., San Francisco 4, Calif. Died July 24, 1945.

PERRY, RALPH BARTON univ. prof.; b. Poultney, Vt., July 3, 1876; s. George Adelbert and Susannah Chase (Barton) P.; A.B., Princeton Univ., 1896; A.M., Harvard Univ., 1897; Ph.D., 1899; Litt.D., Princeton, 1936; Doctor of Humane Letters, Clark Univ., 1939; LL.D., Colby College, Waterville, Me., 1942; LL.D., U. of Penn. 1944; Litt.D., Harvard Univ. 1944; m. Rachel Berenson, Aug. 15, 1905 (died Oct. 23, 1933); children—Ralph Barton, Bernard Berenson. Instr. philosophy, Williams Coll., 1899-1900, Smith Coll., 1900-02; instr. philosophy, Harvard Univ., 1902-05, asst. prof., 1905-13, prof., 1913-46, prof. emeritus, 1946—. Gifford lecturer at the University, Glasgow, Scotland, 1946-47, 1947-48. Maj. U.S. Army and secretary War Dept. Com. on Education and Spl. Training, 1918-19; Hyde lecturer in French univs., 1921-22. Chmn. Am. Defense-Harvard Group, 1940-45; chmn. Univs. Com. on Postwar Internat. Problems, 1942-45. Decorated Chevalier Legion of Honor (France), 1936. Mem. of National Institute of Arts and Letters. Mem. Am. Philos. Soc. Author: The Approach to Philosophy, 1905; The Moral Economy, 1909; Present Philosophical Tendencies, 1912; The New Realism, 1912; The Free Man and the Soldier, 1916; The Present Conflict of Ideals, 1918; Annotated Bibliography of the Writings of William James, 1920; The Plattsburg Movement, 1921. Editor: William James's Essays in Radical Empiricism, 1912; William James's Collected Essays and Reviews, 1920; Revision of Weber's History of Philosophy, 1925; Philosophy of the Recent Past, 1926; General Theory of Value, 1926; A Defense of Philosophy, 1931; The Thought and Character of William James (Pulitzer prize biography), 1935 (briefer edit. 1948); In the Spirit of William James, 1938; (with others) The Meaning of the Humanities, 1938; Shall Not Perish from the Earth, 1940; On All Fronts, 1941; Plea for an Age Movement, 1942; Our Side Is Right, 1942. Puritanism and Democracy, 1944; Hope for Immortality, 1945; One World in the Making, 1945; Characteristically American, 1949; General Theory of Value, 1950; The Citizen Decides, 1951; Realms of Value, 1953; The Humanity of Man, 1956. Home: 985 Memorial Dr., Cambridge 38, Mass. Died Jan. 22, 1957.

PERRY, THOMAS rear admiral U.S.N.; b. Elmira, N.Y., May 26, 1844; s. Guy Maxwell and Elizabeth Asia (Taylor) P. Grad. U.S. Naval Acad., 1865; promoted through successive grades until commissioned capt. During Spanish-Am. War comd. flagship Lancaster at base of supplies, Key West, Fla.; naval sec. Lighthouse Bd., 1899-1901; comd. U.S. battleship Iowa; attached to Pacific and N. Atlantic sta., 1901-03; capt. New York Navy Yard, May 1903-May 1904; commandant Pensacola Navy Yard, May 1904-May 1905; pres. Naval Examining Bd., May 1905-May 26, 1906; rear admiral, Sept. 8, 1905; retired, May 26, 1906. Address: Port Deposit, Md. Died Mar. 7, 1918.

PERRY, WILLIAM FLAKE prof. English and philosophy Ogden Coll., 1883—; b. Jackson County, Ga., Mar. 12, 1823; s. Hiram and Nancy (Flake) P.; grad. Brownwood Acad., 1846; A.M., Howard Coll., Marion, Ala.; m. Ellen Douglas Brown, Jan. 1, 1851. Engaged in teaching in 1848; elected, Feb. 1854, to organize public ednl. system in Ala.; held the office 3 terms; entered C.S.A., May 1862, as maj. 44th Ala. regt.; became col. and brig. gen. Comd. regt. at Antietam, Fredericksburg, Gettysburg; comd. brigade at Chickamauga, in Longstreet's E. Tenn. campaign, battle Wilderness, Spottsylvania, Cold Harbor, seige of Petersburg, Appomattox. Address: Bowling Green, Ky. Died 1901.

PERSHING, JOHN JOSEPH general of Armies of U.S.; b. Linn Co., Mo., Sept. 13, 1860; s. John F. and Ann E. (Thompson) P.; student Kirksville (Mo.) Normal Sch., 1880; grad. U.S. Mil. Acad., 1886; LL.B., U. of Neb., 1893; LL.D., U. of Neb., 1917, U. of St. Andrews, Scotland, 1919, U. of Cambridge, Eng., 1919, Yale, 1920; D.C.L., U. of Oxford, Eng., 1919; Dr. Mil.

Science, Pa. Mil. Acad., 1921; etc.; m. Washington, Helen F., d. Senator Francis E. Warren, of Cheyenne, Wyo., Jan. 26, 1905; 4 children (wife and 3 daughters lost their lives in the burning of the Presidio, Aug. 27, 1915). Commd. 2d lt. 6th U.S. Cav., July 1, 1886; 1st lt. 10th Cav., Oct. 20, 1892; maj. chief ordnance officer vols., Aug. 18, 1898; hon. disch. from vols., May 12, 1899; maj. a.-a.-g., vols., June 6, 1899; capt. 1st U.S. Cav., Feb. 2, 1901; hon. disch. from vols., June 30, 1901; transferred to 15th U.S. Cav., Aug. 20, 1901; brig. gen., Sept. 20, 1906; maj. gen., Sept. 25, 1916; gen. U.S. Army (emergency), Oct. 6, 1917; confirmed by U.S. Senate "General of Armies of United States," Sept. 3, 1919; retired Sept. 13, 1924. Served in Apache Indian campaign, N.M. and Ariz., 1886, and in Sioux campaign, Dak., 1890-91; comd. Sioux Indian scouts until Aug. 1891; mil. instr. U. of Neb., 1891-95; instr. in tactics, U.S. Mil. Acad., 1897-98; served with 10th Cav. in Santiago campaign, Cuba, 1898; organized the Bur. of Insular Affairs and was its chief until Aug. 16, 1899; served in P.I., Nov. 1899-June 1903; first as adj.-gen. Dept. of Mindanao till August 8, 1901; in charge Moro affairs and comd. military operations in Central Mindanao against Moros, April 1902-June 1903; military attaché Tokio, Japan, 1905-06, and was with Kuroki's army in Manchuria, Mar.-Sept. 1905; served on Gen. Staff, 1903-06; duty P.I., 1906-08, 1909-14; was comdr. Dept. of Mindanao, and gov. Moro Province; comd. successful mil. operation against hostile Moros terminating with their defeat at the battle of Bagsak, June 12, 1913; comd. 8th Brig., Presidio, Calif.; temporarily in command of El Paso patrol dist., on Mexican border; in command of U.S. troops sent into Mexico in pursuit of Villa, Mar. 1916. Comdr.-in-chief A.E.F. in World War, 1917-19; apptd. Chief of Staff, U.S. Army, July 1, 1921. Awarded D.S.M. (U.S.); Grand Cross Order of the Bath (British); Grand Cross Legion of Honor (French) Croix de Guerre and Médaille Militare (French); Grand Cordon Order of the Paulawnia (Japanese); Grand Cordon Order of Leopold and Croix de Guerre (Belgian); Great Cross Order of White Lion and Croix de Guerre (Tcheco-slovaque); Order Saint Savoir (Greek); Grand Cross Order of St. Maurizio e Lazzaro, and Military Order of Savoy (Italian); Grand Cordon of Prince Danilo I, and Obilitch Medal (Montenegrin); Medal of La Solaridad (Panama); Virtuti Militari and Polonia Restituta (Polish); Grand Cordon Order of the Precious Light of Chia Ho (Chinese); Grand Cordon Order of the Star of Kara-Georges (Serbian); Order of Mihai Bravul (Rumanian); and others. Chmn. Am. Battle Monuments Commn.; chmn. Goethals Memorial Commn. Mason (33 deg.). Clubs: Metropolitan, Army and Navy (Washington). Author: My Experiences in the World War, 1931. Address: War Dept., Washington, D.C. Died July 15, 1948; interred at Arlington National Cemetery, Arlington, Va.

PERSON, HARLOW STAFFORD economist; b. Republican City, Neb., Feb. 16, 1875; s. Rollin Harlow and Ida M. (Madden) P.; Ph.B., U. Mich., 1899, A.M., 1901, Ph.D., 1902; m. Mary Trowbridge Carson, Oct. 29, 1902; children—Eleanor Madden, Harlow Stafford (dec.), Miriam Frances. Instr. in commerce and industry Amos Tuck Sch. of Adminstrn. and Finance, Dartmouth, 1902-04, sec. and asst. prof., 1904-08, dir. and prof. of business orgn. and mgmt., 1908-22; mng. dir. Taylor Society, N.Y., 1919-33; cons. bus. orgn. and mgmt., 1933-—; mem. Miss. Valley Com., 1934; acting chmn. water planning com., acting dir. water resources sect. Nat. Resources Bd. and Nat. Resources Com., 1934-35; econ. cons. Nat. Resources Com., 1935, Rural Electrification Adminstrn., 1935-—; mem. President's Great Plains Com. 1936; cons. economist and chief of staff, U.S.-Mexico Oil Commn., 1942. Major Ordnance R.C. and maj., Insp., Gen's Dept., 1918. Mem. Am. Econ. Assn., Taylor Soc., Am. Statis. Assn., Am. Soc. for Pub. Adminstrn., Am. Assn. U. Profs., Nat. Planning Assn., Masaryk Acad. (Prague, hon.), Phi Beta Kappa, Artus. Recipient Taylor Key of Soc. for Advancement Mgmt.; gold medal Comite Internat. de L'Orgn. Sci., 1947. Decorated Knight Order of White Lion (Czechoslovakia). Clubs: Faculty (Columbia U.), City. Author: Industrial Education, 1907; Little Waters, 1935; Mexican Oil, 1942; also articles on indsl. and comml. edn., sci. mgmt. Editor and part author of Scientific Management in American Industry, 1929; many govt. reports. Home: 94 Southlawn Av., Dobbs Ferry, N.Y. Office: 420 Lexington Av., N.Y.C. Died Nov. 7, 1955; buried Lansing, Mich.

PERSON, JOHN L., assn. exec.; b. Attleboro, Mass., Dec. 16, 1907; s. Axel and Grace (Woodbury) P.; B.S., U.S. Mil. Acad., 1929; B.S. in Civil Engring., Mass. Inst. Tech., 1932; postgrad. Berlin Tech. Inst., 1938-39, Nat. War Coll., 1947-48; m. Beth Christian, Aug. 26, 1932; 1 son, John L. Commd. 2d lt. U.S. Army, 1929, advanced through grades to brig. gen.; comdg. officer Mil. Pipeline Service, dep. chief engr. ETO, 1944-45; mem. Miss River Commn., 1954-56; mem. bd. engring. for rivers and harbors, 1954-56; dir. civil works Office Chief Engrs., 1956-59; ret., 1959; exec. cons., 1959-65; exec. v.p. Nat. Rivers and Harbors Congress, Washington, 1965-69. Decorated D.S.M., Legion of Merit with oak leaf cluster, Medailee de Reconnaissance. Fellow Am. Soc. C.E.; mem. Permanent Internat. Assn. Navigation Congresses (past chmn. Am. sect.), Soc. Am. Mil. Engrs. Club: Army Navy (Washington). Home: Kensington MD Died Oct. 3, 1969; buried Arlington Nat. Cemetery, Arlington VA

PERSONS, JOHN WILLIAMS, air force officer; b. Montgomery, Ala., Sept. 19, 1899; s. Frank Stanford and Kate Minnis (Abrams) P.; grad. Gulf Coast Mil. Acad., Gulfport, Miss., 1915; student Ala. Poly. Inst.; grad. AC Tactical Sch., Maxwell Field, Ala., 1939; m. Juliette Florence McLendon, Mar. 19, 1927; 1 dau., Juliette (Mrs. Charles S. Doster, Jr.). Served as 2d lt. Royal Flying Corps, Can., 1917-19; commd. 2d lt. AC, U.S. Army, 1929, advanced through grades to maj. gen. USAAF, 1953; flying instr. AC Advanced Flying Sch., Kelly Field, Tex., 1939; comdr. 54th Bomb Squadron, Maxwell Field, 1939; chief test Eglin AFB, Fla., 1941; dir. tng. AC Advanced Flying Sch., Moody Field, Ga., 1942; comdr. Marianna Army Air Field, Fla., 1942; comdr. Atsugi Army Air Field, Japan, 1945-46; chief USAF Flying Safety Service, Langley Field, Va., 1946, insp. gen. 1st Region, Langley AFB, 1948-50; comdr. Alaska AF Depot, 1953; dep. comdr. Alaskan Air Command, 1953; dep. dir. personnel procurement and tng., Hdqrs. AF, Washington, 1953-54; comdr. 3510th Flying Tng. Wing, Randolph AFB, Tex., 1954-57; comdr. 14th Air Force, Robins AFB, Ga., 1957-72. Decorated Legion of Merit with cluster. Mem. Phi Delta Theta. Address: Robins AFB GA Died Jan. 1972.

PETER, GEORGE congressman; b. Georgetown, Md. (now D.C.), Sept. 28, 1779; grad. Georgetown Coll. Entered army as 2d lt. 9th Inf., 1799, later transferred to Arty.; organized and commanded 1st light battery of arty in country, 1808; engaged in agriculture, after 1809; served as maj. Volunteers in War of 1812; mem. U.S. Ho. of Reps. (Democrat, filled vacancy) from Md., 14th-15th, 19th congresses, Oct. 7, 1816-19, 25-27; mem. Md. Ho. of Dels., 1819-23; commr. public works of Md., 1855. Died nr. Darnestown, Montgomery County, Md., June 22, 1861; buried Oak Hill Cemetery, Georgetown.

PETERMAN, MYNIE GUSTAV, pediatrist; b. Merrill, Wis., Mar. 5, 1896; s. Albert Frederick and Ida (Braatz) P.; Sc.B., U. of Wis., 1918; A.M., Washington U., St. Louis, 1920; M.D., Washington U. Sch. of Medicine, 1921 (fellowship, scholarship, 1920-21); m. Mildred Mackenzie, Sept. 29, 1924; children—Albert Frederick, Mary Jean. Practiced as physician in Milwaukee since 1925; introduced new treatment for epilepsy in childhood, 1924, new test for syphilis, 1927, classification for convulsions, 1933; chief resident physician City and County Hosp., St. Paul, 1921-22; fellow, 1st asst. and asso. in pediatrics, Mayo Foundation and Clinic, 1922-25; dir. laboratories and research, Milwaukee Children's Hosp., 1925-33; former chief staff Milwaukee County Hospital; med. dir. Nat. Children's Rehab. Center, 1967-68; cons. USPHS Bur. Indian Affairs; cons. Bur. Medicine, FDA, med. staff drug surveillance br., 1964-67; cons. staff Columbia Hosp., Milw. In Chem. Warfare Div. U. Wis., 1917-18; 1st sgt. S.A.T.C., 1918, World War; 1st lt. Med. R.C., 1924, col., 1950. Diplomate Am. Bd. Pediatrics. Fellow Am. Acad. Neurology; mem. A.M.A., Internat. Congress Pediatrics, Am. Academy of Pediatrics, Central Soc. Clin. Research, American Association for research Nervous and Mental Diseases, Wis. State and Milwaukee Co. med. soc., Am. Epilepsy Soc., Milw. Pediatric Soc., Osler Soc., Madrid Pediatric Society, Sigma Xi, Phi Sigma. Clubs: Army and Navy, Torch (Washington). Author chpts. in med. works and research articles in med. publs. Editor English transl. Diseases of Children (5 vols.), 1935. Home: Milwaukee WI Died Oct. 14, 1971.

PETERS, GEORGE HENRY commodore U.S.N.; b. Chester County, Pa., Sept. 22, 1854; s. John and Lavinia Urner (Price) P.; grad. U.S. Naval Acad., 1874, at head of class and with highest cadet mil. rank; m. Louisa Beardsley McCarty, June 17, 1878. Promoted ensign, 1875; master, 1881; lt., 1886; lt. comdr., 1899; comdr., 1903; capt., 1907; commodore, and retired at own request, June 30, 1908. Routine and spl. naval service to 1885; had charge of Atlantic coast pilot work, Coast Survey, and instituted gen. plan still followed by the Survey in this work, 1886-88; served in Squadron of Evolution (1st "white squadron"), 1888-91; at office of Naval Intelligence and on bd. Minneapolis, 1891-97; comd. Sylvia on blockade duty N. Coast of Cuba. 1898, War with Spain; exec. officer Iowa, 1900; comd. force landed at Panama to maintain free transit of the Isthmus, during a revolution, 1901, specially commended in despatches; supt. compasses, Navy Dept., 1903, mem. bd. on wireless telegraphy (then being introduced into the service); Asiatic Sta., 1905-07, comd. Cincinnati, Raleigh, and commandant Cavite and Olongapo (P.I.). Mem. U.S. Naval Inst. Home: Washington, D.C. Died June 15, 1916.

PETERS, HEBER WALLACE, executive; born at New Bedford, Massachusetts, December 13,21892; s. Heber Cushing and Agnes Winonah (Thurber) P.; A.B., Cornell U., 1914; m. Elsie Frieda Germain, Sept. 1, 1922; children—Wallace Cushing, Joy Germain. Sec., Cornell U., 1914-16; asst. to pres. Packard Motor Co., Detroit, Mich., 1916-18, office mgr., 1919-21, gen. mgr. Detroit Br., 1921-24, Packard Motor Co. of Chicago, 1924-28; v.p. of distribution Packard Motor Co., 1928-32; asst. gen. sales mgr. Cadillac Motor Car Co., 1934-36; investment counselor, Detroit, 1936-38; provost, Cornell U., 1938-43; executive Edward G. Budd Mfg. Co., 1943-45; vice president, John Price Jones Corp., 1946-51, G.A. Brakeley & Co., 1962-65. Devel. cons. Bowdoin Coll., 1958-61. Woods Hole Oceanographic Instn., 1959-64. Trustee Air Force Museum Foundation. Chairman of the Tompkins County chapter, Am. Red Cross, 1941-43. Served as pursuit pilot, 1st lt. Air Service, U.S. Army, and officer in charge of flying, Field No. 9, 3d Aviation Instrn. Center, Issoudun, France, 1918-19; cited for exceptionally meritorious service. Mem. Foreign Policy Assn., Phi Delta Theta. Republican. Clubs: Cornell of Mich., Cornell, University (N.Y.C.). Home: Summit NJ Died Dec. 27, 1971.

PETERS, JOHN DWIGHT wholesale mcht.; b. Sanford, Fla., Nov. 13, 1911; s. Walter Henry and Alice May (Smith) P.; B.B.A., U. Fla., 1933; m. Eleanor May McKay, Feb. 15, 1939; children—Eleanor Ann, John Charles. House salesman Bentley-Gray Dry Goods Co., Tampa, Fla., 1937-40, v.p., sales mgr., 1940-47, v.p., gen. mgr., 1947-50, pres., 1950-—, dir., 1940-—; pres. Boca Grande Dept. Store, Inc. (Fla.), 1950-—, Maas Realty Co., Tampa, 1950-—; dir. Exchange Nat. Bank of Tampa, Tampa Ship Repair & Drydock Co. Adv. com. OPA, 1951-52; dir. Community Chest of Tampa, 1951-52. Mem. Hillsborough County Crime Commn., 1951-56; dir. personnel Hillsborough County Civilian Def., 1951-56. Served from lt. to col. USAAF, 1942-46. Decorated Legion of Merit, Bronze Star, Croix de Guerre with palm. Mem. Nat. Wholesale Dry Goods Assn. (pres. 1955-56), Wholesale Dry Goods Inst. (dir. 1941, 46-52, v.p., exec. com. 1949-52), Mchts. Assn. Tampa (dir.), Hillsborough County Taxpayers Assn. (dir. 1948-56), Tampa Assn. Credit Men (dir.), YMCA (dir. 1948-56), Ye Mystic Krewe of Gasparilla (dir.; chmn. exec. com. 1952), C. of C. (gov. 1946-52, chmn. taxation com. 1950, pres. 1953), Fla. State Fair and Gasparilla Assn. (dir. 1950-—), Am. Legion, Pi Kappa Alpha. Episcopalian. Clubs: University, Tampa Yacht and Country, Palma Ceia Golf and Country, Tampa Touchdown.

PETERS, JOHN RUSSELL, physician, educator; b. Cin., Oct. 4, 1896; s. Ezra and Lillian (Hodge) P.; B.S., M.D., Ohio State U., 1928; m. Gertrude Elvina Mann, Dec. 24, 1918; 1 dau., Gwendolyn Carol (Mrs. Robert A. Jasperson). Intern St. Francis Hosp., Columbus, O., 1928; mem. staff VA Hosp., Chillicothe, O., 1929-34; asst. to asst. prof. psychiatry, U. Louisville, 1934-50; asst. supt. Dayton (O.) State Hosp., 1950-51; asso. prof., then prof. psychiatry, now emeritus Loma Linda U.; sr. attending psychiatrist Los Angeles County Gen. Hosp., 1951-68; dir. Glendale (Cal.) Mental Health Service, 1956-59, Los Angeles County Assn. Mental Health, 1956-58; dir. out-patient dept. White Meml. Hosp., Los Angeles, 1952-60; sr. cons. Armed Forces Examining St., Los Angeles, 1952-68. Mem. bd. dirs. Asheville Rural Sch. and Sanitarium, 1953-68. Served from lt. comdr. to capt., USNR, 1940-47. Diplomate Am. Bd. Psychiatry and Neurology. Fellow Am. Psychiat. Assn., A.A.A.S., A.M.A.; mem. Cal., Los Angeles County med. socs., Los Angeles Assn. Neurology and Psychiatry. Address: Glendale CA Died Feb. 20, 1968.

PETERS, RICHARD Continental congressman, jurist, agriculturist; b. Phila., June 22, 1743; s. William and Mary (Breintnall) P.; grad. Coll. of Phila. (now U. Pa.), 1761; studied law; m. Sarah Robinson, Aug. 1776, 6 children. Admitted to bar, 1763; commr. Indian Conf., Ft. Stanwix, 1768; register of admiralty, Phila., 1771-76; commd. capt. Pa. Militia, 1775; sec. bd. war Continental Congress, 1776-81, mem. from Pa., 1782-83; mem. Pa. Assembly, 1787-90, speaker, 1788-90; trustee U. Pa., 1788-91; speaker Pa. Senate, 1791-92; judge U.S. Dist. Ct. for Pa., 1792-1828; 1st pres. Phila. Soc. for Promotion of Agr.; published several volumes and more than 100 papers on agr.; specialist in maritime law; published Admiralty Decisions in the District Court of the United States for the Pennsylvania District, 1780-1807; Died Phila., Aug. 22, 1828; buried St. Peter's Churchyard, Phila.

PETERS, WILLIAM E. prof. Latin, Univ. of Va., 1866-1902; b. Bedford Co., Va., Aug. 18, 1829; s. Elisha P.; prep. edn. New London Acad., Bedford Co., Va.; grad. Emory and Henry Coll., Va., and Univ. of Va.; studied 2 yrs. in Univ. of Berlin (A.M., LL.D.); m. Marion, Smythe Co., Va., July 14, 1873, Mary Sheffey. Prof. Latin and Greek, Emory and Henry Coll., 1852; entered C.S.A., April 17, 1861, as pvt.; elected 1st lt. cav., later capt.; lt.-col. inf., col. cav. (21st regt.); surrendered at Appomattox, 1865. Author: Work on Latin Case Relations; Syntax of Latin Verb. Address: Charlottesville, Va.

PETERSEN, CARL EDWARD naval architect, marine engr.; b. Brooklyn, N.Y., Jan. 21, 1897; s. Christian Edward (Thinggaard) and Magdalene (Hoy) P.; ed. Pratt Inst., Tri-State Coll. of Engring., Brooklyn Poly. Inst.; grad. U.S. Navy Steam Engring. Sch., Stevens Inst. Tech., 1918; m. 2d, Ann Suber, Oct. 28, 1937; children—Carl Thinggaard (by 1st marriage), Dianne Mary. With Morse Dry Dock & Repair Co., 1910-18, successively as marine machinist, draftsman, estimator and outside superintendent; engr. officer, transport duty, U.S. Navy, 1918; supt. engr. U.S. Army Transport Service, during period of conversion of merchant vessels to troop ships, 1919; estimator in charge cost of ship repairs at Port of New York, U.S. Shipping Bd., 1919-20; naval architect U.S. Mail Steamship Co., 1920; naval architect U.S. Lines in charge reconditioning the George Washington, America, President Harding, President Roosevelt, etc., 1921-27; asst. to v.p. Newport News Shipbuilding Dry Dock Co., 1928-37; asst. mgr. const. and repair dept. Matson Navigation Co., 1938-41; had charge gen. design steamships President Hoover and President Coolidge. Lt. comdr. U.S. Naval Res. Called to active duty as comdr. Vol. Naval Res., engr. spl. service duties, Dec. 17, 1941; coordinator ship repairs and asst. material officer, Honolulu, T.H., on spl. orders from sec. of navy, Dec. 21, 1941-Apr. 1942; exec. and repair officer, U.S. Naval Sect. Base, New Orleans (Algiers), La., to July 1943; stationed Tampa, Fla., sr. asst. supervisor of shipbuilding U.S.N., 1943-44. Mem. Am. Soc. Mech. Engrs., Am. Bur. of Shipping (also Pacific Coast Com.); life mem., hon. corr. mem. Institution of Naval Architects, London; life mem. N. E. Coast Institution of Engrs. and Shipbuilders (Newcastle-on-Tyne, Eng.); life mem., v.p. Inst. Marine Engrs. (London), life mem. Soc. Naval Architects and Marine Engrs. (council mem.); naval mem. Am. Soc. Naval Engrs.; tech. mem. Tech. Com. of Engring. Am. Bur. Shipping. Fellow Am. Geographic Soc. Licensed engr. State of N.Y., chief engr. ocean steam vessels (any tonnage). Address: care Supervisor of Shipbuilding, U.S. Navy, Tampa, Fla. Died in active service, July 23, 1944.

PETERSON, ALFRED WALTER univ. adminstr.; b. Waupaca, Wis., May 12, 1900; s. Lars H. and Ida (Olstad) P.; B.A. cum laude, U. Wis., 1924; m. Irene L. Hull, June 28, 1924; 1 son, Thomas Hull. Student financial advisor U. Wis., 1923-24, asst. accountant, 1924-27, asst. to bus. mgr., 1937-34, comptroller, 1934-46, lectr. accounting, 1935-38, sec. regents, 1946-49, dir. bus. and finance, 1946-48, v.p. bus. and finance, 1948-62, trust officer, 1949-62, v.p. and trust officer, 1962-—; pres. Wis. U. Bldg. Corp.; pres., dir. Univ.-Park Corp.; dir., treas. Starks Farms, Inc., dir., adminstrv. v.p., Wis. State Agys. Bldg. Corp. Served as sgt. maj. U.S. Army, 1918-19; cons. USAF, World War II. Mem. Central Assn. Coll. and U. Bus. Officers (pres. 1945-46), Wis. Edn. Assn., Midwestern Univs. Research Assn., Am. Legion, U. Wis. Alumni Assn., Delta Sigma Pi. Lutheran. Club: University. Author articles profl. jours. Home: 1509 Wood Lane, Madison, Wis. 53705. Died Oct. 23, 1965; buried Forest Hill Cemetery.

PETERSON, JOHN VALDEMAR, retired naval officer; b. Harlan, Ia., Dec. 22, 1898; s. Paul and Emma (Jorgensen) P.; B.S., U.S. Naval Acad., 1923; m. Elizabeth Greene, Feb. 28, 1931; 1 dau., Marcia St. John. Commd. ensign, U.S.N., 1923, served in fleet, 1923-25, naval aviator, on U.S. Saratoga and U.S.S. Ranger, 1926-52, retired as rear adm., 1952; prof. naval sic. U. Kan., 1946-48, U. Cal. at Berkeley, 1951-53. Decorated Distinguished Flying Cross, Legion of Merit, Presidential Unit Citation, Netherlands Distinguished Service Medal. Mem. Delta Upsilon. Club: San Diego Country (Chula Vista, Cal.). Home: Coronado CA Died May 1968.

PETERSON, MELL ANDREW, orgn. exec.; born Algona, Ia., Sept. 7, 1908; s. Albert Leroy and Viva Beatrice (Norton) P.; B.S., U.S. Naval Acad., 1930; student ordnance engring., Naval Postgrad Sch., 1936-39; m. Ann M. Murtagh, Sept. 17, 1931; children—Mell, Charles A., Elizabeth Ann. Commd. ensign, USN, 1930, advanced through grades to rear adm., 1959; indsl. control and mfg. officer Naval Weapons Plant, Washington, 1951-52; comdg. officer Naval Ordnance Plant, Indpls., 1952-54; asst. chief Bur. Ordnance, Navy Dept., 1957-58; comdr. Naval Ordnance Lab., White Oaks, Silver Spring, Md., 1958-59, ret.; exec. v.p., dir. Bulova Research & Development Labs., Inc., Woodside, N.Y., 1959-61; corporate devel. planning, Northrop Corp., Beverly Hills, Cal., 1962-63; Western rep., exec. dir. Los Angeles Post Am. Ordnance Assn., 1963-—. Profl. engr., D.C. Decorated Silver Star, Bronze Star. Mason. Clubs: Kiwanis (Indpls.); N.Y. Yacht. Home: Los Angeles CA Died Dec. 1970.

PETERSON, REUBEN obstetrician, gynecologist; b. Boston, Mass., June 29, 1862; s. Reuben and Julia Turner (Beale) P.; desc. George Soule and John Alden of the Mayflower; A.B., Harvard U., 1885, M.D., 1889; hon. Sc.D., Univ. of Mich., 1936; m. Josephine Davis, Mar. 6, 1890; children—Reuben, Marion, Ward Davis, Julia. In gen. practice at Grand Rapids, Mich., 1890-98; prof. gynecology, Post-Grad. Med. School of Chicago, 1898-1901; asst. prof. obstetrics and gynecology, Rush Med. Coll., 1898-1901; prof. obstetrics and gynecology, U. of Mich. Med. Sch., 1901-31; eneritus professor 1931-—; med. dir. U. of Mich. Hosp., 1911-18; retired from practice, 1933. Maj. M.C., U.S. Army, and med. adviser to governor of Mich., 1917-19. Fellow American Coll. Surgeons (a founder), Am. Gynecol. Soc. (hon. 1931-—; pres. 1911); member Massachusetts Medical Society, hon. fellow American Medical Assn., Michigan State Med. Society (pres. 1915), Edinburgh Obstet. Society, Michigan Obstet. and Gynecol. Society, Washtenaw County Med. Society (pres. 1902). Democrat. Unitarian. Author: Demonstration Course in Obstetrics, 1930, 2d edit., 1937. Editor: Peterson's Obstetrics, 1907. Contbr. many articles on medical topics to professional publications. Home: Powder Point, Duxbury, Mass. Died Nov. 25, 1942.

PETERSON, VIRGIL LEE ret. army officer; b. Campbellsville, Ky., Sept. 22, 1882; B.S., Centre Coll. (K.), 1902, U.S. Mil. Acad., 1908; grad. Engring. Sch., 1910, Army War Coll., 1933; hon. grad. Command and Gen. Staff Corps Sch., 1925. Commd. 2d lt., 1908, advanced through grades to maj. gen., 1939; insp. gen. War Dept., 1940-46, ret. Decorated D.S.M. Address: Office of Inspector General. War Dept., Washington. Died Feb. 15, 1956; buried Arlington Nat. Cemetery.*

PETTENGILL, GEORGE (TILFORD) naval officer (ret.); b. Boise, Ida., Oct. 25, 1877; s. George and Anne (Worden) P.; grad. U.S. Naval Acad., 1898; m. Leila Marion Price, Jan. 16, 1909; children—George Tilford, III (lost on U.S.S. Liscome Bay, 1943), William Van Horne. Commd. ensign U.S. Navy, 1898, and advanced through grades to rear adm., 1930; served on U.S.S. New York and U.S.S. Puritan, Spanish-Am. War, participating in Battle of Mantanzas; served in Samoan trouble, 1899, and Boxer Rebellion in China; with British Grand Fleet, 1917-19, U.S.S. Wyoming; insp. Midvale Steel Co., Phila., 1919-22, comd. U.S.S. Destroyers, Asiatic Fleet, 1922-24, with Bur. Navigation, 1924-25; naval attaché Peking, China, 1925-28; capt. U.S.S. Tenn., 1928-29; student War Coll., 1929-30; comd. submarine force, Battle Fleet, 1930-31, mine force, U.S. Fleet, 1931-32, submarine base, New London, Conn., 1932-34, base force, U.S.S. Fleet, 1934-35, Battleship Div. 2, battle force, 1935-1936; comdt. Washington Navy Yard and supt. Naval Gun Factory, 1936-42; comdt. Potomac River Naval Command, 1941-42; comd. U.S. Naval Ordnance Plant, Charleston, W.Va., 1942-45; ret., 1946. Awarded Sampson Medal (Spanish-Am. War), Navy Cross, Legion of Merit, Order of Striped Tiger (Chinese), 1928. Mem. Mil. Order of Caraboa, Mil. Order of Dragon. Clubs: Chevy Chase (MD.); Old Lyme Beach (Conn.), Old Lyme Country. Home: Old Lyme, Conn. Died Jan. 11, 1959; buried at sea from U.S.S. Tringa.

PETTIBONE, AUGUSTUS HERMAN lawyer; b. Bedford, O., Jan. 21, 1835; s. Augustus Norman and Nancy Leonard (Hathaway) P.; A.B., U. of Mich., 1859; read law at Milwaukee; m. Mary Clarinda Speck, July 16, 1868; m. 2d, Seraphine Deery, Nov. 22, 1899. Enlisted as pvt., 19th Wis. Inf., 1861; 2d lt. and capt. Co. A, 20th Wis. Inf., 1862; promoted maj. during siege of Vicksburg; served to end of war. Practiced law Greenville, Tenn., 1865-75, Knoxville, 1875-85; presdl. elector, 1868; atty. gen. 1st Jud. Circuit, Tenn., 4 yrs.; mem. 47th to 49th Congresses (1881-87), 1st Tenn. Dist.; asst. U.S. atty., Dist. Tenn., 6 yrs.; mem. Tenn. Ho. of Rep., 1896-98; spl. agt U.S. Land Office, 1898-1904; apptd. agt. U.S. Dept. Agr., 1904. Republican (voted for Lincoln). Presbyterian. Comdr. Dept. Tenn., G.A.R., 1888-89. Mason. Address: Nashville, Tenn. Died Nov. 26, 1918.

PETTIGREW, JAMES JOHNSTON lawyer, army officer; b. "Bonarva," Tyrell County, N.C., July 4, 1828; s. Ebenezer and Ann (Shepard) P.; grad. U. N.C., 1847. Asst. prof. U.S. Naval Observatory, Washington, D.C., 1847-49; practiced law, Charleston, South Carolina, 1850-61; mem. S.C. Gen. Assembly, 1856; col. 1st Regt. of Charleston Rifles; commd. col. 12th Regt., Hamptons Legion, Confederate Army, 1861, promoted brig. gen., 1861; served in Peninsular Campaign, battles at Blount's Creek and Gettysburg. Mortally wounded during retreat from Gettysburg, died Raleigh, N.C., July 17, 1863; buried Raleigh, reinterred "Bonarva," 1866.

PETTIT, CHARLES Continental congressman, businessman; b. nr. Amwell, Hunterdon County, N.J., 1736; s. John Pettit; pvt. classical edn.; m. Sarah Reed, Apr. 5, 1758, 4 children including Elizabeth, Theodosia. Apptd. a N.J. provincial surrogate, 1767; surrogate, keeper and register of records Province of N.J., 1769-78; clk. N.J. Gov.'s Council, also clk. N.J. Supreme Ct., 1769-71; admitted to N.J. bar as atty., 1770, as counselor, 1778; dep. sec. Province of N.J.; lt. col. N.J. Militia, aide to Gov. William Franklin, 1771; 1st sec. of state N.J., 1776-78; col., aide to Gov. William Livingston, 1776; asst. q.m. gen. (under Gen. Nathanael Greene) Continental Army, 1778-81; became importer in Phila.; mem. Pa. Assembly, 1783-84; chmn. com. of mchts. to promote nat. commerce, 1784; mem. Continental Congress, 1785-87; recognized fiscal expert, established Pa.'s funding system; delegated to present Pa.'s Revolutionary War claims against fed. govt. to Congress, 1790-91; original dir. Ins. Co. of N.Am., pres., 1796-98, 99-1806; trustee U. Pa., 1791-1802; mem. Am. Philos. Soc. Died Phila., Sept. 4, 1806.

PETTUS, EDMUND WINSTON U.S. senator from Ala., 1897-1909; b. Limestone County, Ala., July 6, 1821; ed. common schools, Ala., and Clinton Coll., Tenn.; admitted to bar, 1842; began practice at Gainesville, Ala.; m. Mary S. Chapman, June 27, 1844. Elected, 1844, solicitor for 7th circuit; served as lt. in Mexican war. Went on horseback, with party of neighbors, to Calif., 1849; returned, 1851; judge 7th circuit, 1855-58; resigned and moved to Selma, practicing law there; in C.S.A., maj. to brig. gen., 1861-65. Democrat. Residence: Selma, Ala. Died 1907.

PETTY, ORLANDO HENDERSON M.D.; b. Cadiz, O., Feb. 20, 1874; s. Asbury F. and Sarah (Kyle) P.; B.S., Franklin Coll., New Athens, O., 1890, A.M., 1900; M.D., Jefferson Med. Coll., 1904; m. Marcia P. Mellersh, Apr. 8, 1908; children—Clara M., Orville A. II. Began practice at Phila., 1904; prof. metabolic diseases, U. of Pa. Grad. Sch. of Medicine; chief dept. of diseases of metabolism, Phila. Gen. Hosp. and Hosp. U. of Pa. Grad. Sch. of Medicine; consultant in diseases of metabolism and malnutrition, Shriners' Hosp. for Crippled Children; consultant in metabolic disorders, Rush Hosp. for Consumptives. Served as lt. Med. Corps U.S.N., with 5th U.S.M. in France, World War. Dir. pub. health, city of Philadelphia. Mem. Phila. County Med. Soc. (pres.), Med. Club of Phila. (pres.), Army and Navy Legion of Valor (past nat. comdr.). Decorated Congressional Medal of Honor and D.S.C. (both U.S.); Croix de Guerre with Palm (France); War Cross (Italy). Republican. Episcopalian. Mason. Author: Diabetes—Its Treatment by Insulin and Diet, 1924. Address: Philadelphia, Pa. Deceased.

PETTY, ORVILLE ANDERSON clergyman; b. Cadiz, O., Feb. 20, 1874; s. Asbury F. and Sarah (Kyle) P.; A.B., Muskingum Coll., 1898; Pittsburgh Theol. Sem., 1901; A.M., Colorado Coll., 1905; grad. student U. of Chicago, 1907-10; Ph.D. in Philosophy and Edn., Yale, 1915, D.D., Yale, 1919; m. Evelyn Hammond, July 17, 1902; 1 dau., Mabel Kyle. Ordained 1901; pastor Greeley, Colo., 1901-06, First Ch., Aurora, Ill., 1906-11, Plymouth Ch., New Haven, 1911-29; pres. Arnold Coll., 1929-30; mem. India staff of Laymen's Foreign Missions Inquiry, 1930-31, adviser of Appraisal Commn., same, 1931-32, and editor of research materials, same, 1932-33; dir. research A Movement for World Christianity (formerly The Modern Missions Movement) since 1934. Lecturer, Dept. Race Relation, Grad. Sch., Yale, 1938-41. Chaplain 2d Conn. Inf., Mexican border, 1916; served overseas as chaplain 102d Inf., and sr. chaplain and morale officer, 1917-19; served as maj., chaplain 169th Inf., 1921-23; lt. col. same regt., 1923-29, and col. same regt., 1929-38; retired brig. gen. Cited in General Orders, and by General Pershing; decorated Croix de Guerre and Chevalier de L'Ordre de l'Etoile Noire (French); Chevalier Ordre de la Couronne (Belgian). Served as pres. Grace Hosp., City Mission, Conn. Council Religious Edn., New Haven Council Chs.; trustee Arnold Coll.; trustee Organized Charities, New Haven. Mem. S.A.R., Mil. Order Foreign Wars (chaplain gen.). Republican. Mason. Club: Graduate. Author: Did the Term "The Gospel" Originate with Paul?, 1925; Kindling the Christmas Fire (verse), 1929; Common Sense and God, 1935. Editor of Supplementary Series to Re-Thinking Missions (7 vols.). Home: 275 W. Rock Av., New Haven, Conn. Died Aug. 12, 1942.

PEYTON, BERNARD ROBERTSON (pa'tun), army officer; b. Raymond, Miss., Sept. 24, 1886; s. John William and Lucretia (Moseley) P.; B.S., U.S. Naval Acad., 1910; grad. Mounted Service Sch., 1914, Field Arty. Sch., 1923, Command and Gen. Staff Sch., 1925, Army War Coll., 1933; m. Evelyn Haile, June 20, 1917; 1 dau., Evelyn Haile (wife of Capt. Richard Watson, U.S.A.). Commd. 2d lt., F.A., U.S. Army, 1910; advanced through the grades to col. 1939. Served as capt. with 6th F.A., 1st Div., France, 1917-19; prof. mil. sci. and tactics, Stanford, 1936-39; mil. attaché Berlin, Germany, Sept. 1939-July 1941. Democrat. Episcopalian. Club: Rotary (pres. 1939), Palo Alto, Calif. Died Mar. 2, 1959.

PEYTON, EPHRAIM GOEFFREY army officer; b. Gallatin, Miss., Jan. 19, 1876; s. Judge Ephriam Geoffrey and Annie (Coleman) P.; B.S., U.S. Mil. Acad., 1899; m. Bertha Augusta Moore, Oct. 15, 1919; 2 step-daus., Helen Van Rensselaer Stillman (wife of Gen. George Honnen, U.S. Army), Charlotte Aleta Crawford Stillman (wife of Col. Norman A. Matthias, U.S. Army). Commd. 2d lt. U.S. Army, 1899, advanced through grades to brig. gen., 1938; assigned to 6th U.S. Inf. and participated in The Philippines Insurrection, Spanish-Am. War, 1899-1901, with 18th U.S. Inf., 1901-10, with Philippine Scouts, 1910-12; served under Gen. Pershing in his Moro disarmament campaigns, 1910, 11, 12; with 18th Inf., Mexican Border, 1913-15; tactical officer, U.S. M.A., 1915-17; trained emergency officers, Fort Meyer, Va., 1917; with 320th inf., 80th div., Camp Lee, Va. and in France, 1917-19, served on British front, July-Sept. 1918; comd. 320th Inf., 80th Div. in St. Mihiel offensive, and in Meuse Argonne offensive, 1918; assigned to command of Mil. Personnel assisting Am. Commn. to negotiate peace in Paris, 1919; ret. for disability in line of duty, 1940; organized Atlanta Ga. Civilian Defense Corps, 1941, and served as comdr., 1941-42. Decorated D.S.M., Purple Heart, Silver Star citation. Presbyn. Mason (Shriner). Elk. Home: 147 17th St. N.E., Atlanta 5. Died Jan. 1, 1950; buried Arlington Nat. Cemetery.

PEYTON, GARLAND, geologist; b. Mt. Airy, Ga., Oct. 2, 1892; s. John Thomas and Emma Jane (Ayers) P.; B.S., E.M., Sch. Mines N. Ga. Agrl. Coll., 1914; student, Ohio State U., 1926, U. Minn., 1930; m. Martha Gara Griswold, Aug. 28, 1918; children—Garland, Martha Ann, Barbara Jane. Mining engr. U.S. Smelting, Refining & Mining Co., 1914-17; dir. Sch. Mines N. Ga. Agrl. Coll., 1919-29; research engr. Tenn. Copper Co., 1929-31; state mining engr. Ga. Dept.

Mines and Geology, 1937-38; dir., state geologist Ga. Dept. Mines, Mining and Geology, from 1938. Served as 1st lt., inf., U.S. Army, 1917-19, as capt., 1933-37. Mem. Geol. Soc. Am., Am. Assn. Petroleum Geologist, Am. Inst. Mining and Metall. Engrs., Soc. Econ. Geologists, Assn. Am. State Geologist (pres. 1948), Pi Kappa Alpha, Sigma Gamma Epsilon. Democrat. Baptist. Mason, Elk. Home: Decatur GA Died Oct. 18, 1964.

PFAHLER, WILLIAM H. mfr.; b. Columbia, Pa., Mar. 27, 1844; s. Henry and Mary P.; ed. in schs. of Columbia, Pa., Millersville (Pa.) State Normal Sch.; left to enter Union Army as pvt., Mar. 1862, and served 3 yrs. in 45th Pa. Vols.; discharged at end of war as 1st lt. and regimental q.m.; regt. served during entire war with Burnside, 9th Army Corps, and participated in battles of Antietam, South Mountain, Vicksburg, Knoxville, Tenn., and last of Grant's campaign from the Wilderness to the close of war; m. Anna Bilderback, 1874. Associated with Abram Cox Stove Co., 1885, of which was treas.; pres. Model Heating Co. Organized and later pres. Nat. Founders' Assn.; assisted in organizing Nat. Metal Trades Assn.; hon. mem. administrative council of two bodies. One of original com. of 7 which organized Com. of 70 which brought about overthrow of polit. ring which had ruled Phila. With Senator Marcus A. Hanna was associated in organizing Civi Federation (mem. exec. council). Republican. Mem. Loyal Legion. Home: Philadelphia, Pa. Died 1908.

PFEIFFENBERGER, JAMES MATHER surgeon; b. Alton, Ill., June 18, 1879; s. Lucas and Elizabeth Campbell Millen (Mather) P.; M.D., Washington U., St. Louis, 1902; postgrad., Berlin and Vienna, 1913; m. Ethel Hortense Rodgers, Jan. 20, 1915; children—Ella Elizabeth Anschuetz, Mary Josephine, Mather, Jr., Jane Hortense Luer, Lucas Edward, Andrew Rodgers, Franklin Hewit. Extern St. Luke's Hosp., 1899-1901; intern St. Louis City Hosp., 1902-03; asst. supt. St. Louis Female Hosp., 1904; asso. with a surgeon in St. Louis, 1905; practiced in Alton, since 1907; past chief of staff St. Joseph Hosp. and Alton Meml. Hosp.; pres. Piasa Bldg. & Loan Assn. since 1918. Served as capt. M.C., U.S. Army, World War I. Awarded World War medal. Speaker of Assembly of Interstate Postgrad. Med. Assn. N.A. since 1935. Mem. founders group Am. Bd. Surgery. Fellow A.C.S.; mem. Alton C. of C. (past pres.), Am. Legion (past comdr.), Ill. State Med. Assn. (past pres.), Madison County Med. Soc. (past pres.), Alton, St. Louis med. socs. Democrat. Mason (K.T.). Contbr. med. jours. Home: 463 Bluff St. Office: 300 Piasa St., Alton, Ill. 62002. Died Jan. 22, 1963.

PFEIFFER, TIMOTHY NEWELL, lawyer; b. Camden, N.J., Nov. 3, 1886; s. George and Adaline (Adams) P.; grad. William Penn Charter Sch., Phila., Pa., 1904; A.B., Princeton, 1908; LL.B., Harvard, 1912; m. Eleanor Knox Wheeler, June 10, 1914; children—Egbert Wheeler, Timothy Adams, Katharine Bradford, Eleanor Knox. Admitted to N.Y. bar, 1912, practicing at N.Y. City; dep. asst. dist. atty. N.Y. County, 1913-15; counsel Am. Social Hygiene Association, 1915-17, former treas.; spl. dep. atty. gen. N.Y., in prosecutions under Anti-Trust Act, 1921-22, in Nassau County Investigations, 1923; mem. Milbank, Tweed, Hadley & McCloy. Chief counsel N.Y. State Temp. Commn. Courts, 1956-57; vice chmn. N.Y. State Temp. Commn. on Revision Penal Law, 1961-71. Trustee Teachers Coll. Columbia University, Woodrow Wilson Found. (v.p.). Served as capt. Sanitary Corps, U.S. Army; War Dept. Commn. on Training Camp Activities, later transferred to F.A. Camp Taylor, World War. Organizer, 1917, Voluntary Defenders Com. for Criminal Courts. Mem. Am. Bar Assn., Am. Law Inst. (mem. council, adv. drafting code of criminal procedure), N.Y. State, N.Y. City (v.p.) bar assns., Legal Aid Society N.Y. (pres., 1950-55, dir.), Nat. Health Council (treas., 1937-48), Nat. Probation and Parole Assn. (pres., 1937-41); The Youth House (v.p. and dir. 1944-55), N.Y. City Mission Society (director). Presbyn. Clubs: Century, University. Home: New York City NY Died Feb. 12, 1971.

PFEIL, JOHN SIMON, corp. exec.; born Wertheim, Baden, Germany, Aug. 24, 1889; s. Simon and Elizabeth (von Oberndorff) vonP.; ed. schs. of Heidelberg, Germany; grad. Harvard, 1913; m. Marie deCoen, Oct. 31, 1922; children—Theodor, John S. New England mgr. Frigidaire Div., Gen. Motors Corp., Boston, 1913-41; v.p. Stone & Webster, Inc., N.Y.C., 1946-56, ret.; v.p. Am. Ordnance Assn.; treas. and director of Associated Industries of Massachusetts. Commissioner Massachusetts Port Authority. Served as col., ordnance dist. chief, Boston Ordnance Dist., U.S. Army, 1941-46. Decorated Legion of Merit. Received Gold Medal of Am. Ordnance Assn., 1954. Mem. Benjamin Franklin Found., Franklin Inst. (v.p.). Republican. Clubs: Down Town, Harvard. Home: Wellesley Hills MA Died June 1967; buried Newton MA

PFLUEGER, JOHN SEIBERLING mfg. exec.; b. Akron, O., Nov. 24, 1898; s. E. A. and Ruth (Seiberling) P.; grad. Culver (Ind.) Mil. Acad., 1916; A.B., Cornell U., 1920; m. Ruth Robinson, Sept. 7, 1925; children—Ruth (Mrs. R. V. Thomas), John Seiberling. With Enterprise Mfg. Co., Akron, 1925, beginning in accounting dept., successively treas., exec. v.p. and dir., pres. 1950-—, chmn. bd., 1953-—; pres., dir. 2d, Nat. Bldg. Co. Dir. Akron Gen. Hosp.; nat. asso. Boys' Club Am. Served as 2d lt. AS, World War I; capt. Troop E, 107th Cav. Regt., 1921-27. Mem. U.S. Akron C.'s of C., Am. Ordnance Assn., N.A.M., Izaa 912 Merriman Rd. Office: 110 N. Union St., Akron, O. Died June 19, 1967; buried Rose Hill Burial Park, Akron.

PHALEN, JAMES MATTHEW (fa'len), editor; b. Harvard, Ill., Nov. 26, 1872; s. John Dennis and Anastasia (Lawless) P.; Ph.G., Northwestern U., 1892; M.D., Univ. of Ill., 1900; hon. grad. Army Medical Sch., 1902, London Sch. Tropical Medicine, 1907; distinguished grad., Army Sch. of the Line, 1920; grad. Gen. Staff Sch., 1921, Army War Coll., 1922; m. Gertrude Sibley, Apr. 14, 1904. Interne Cook County Hosp., Chicago, 1900-01; commd. 1st. lt. Med. Corps, U.S. Army, 1901, and advanced to col. 1927; pres. Army Bd. for Investigation of Tropical Diseases, Manila, 1907-10; lecturer on tropical medicine, N.Y. Post-Grad. Med. Sch., 1911-13; chief hosp. div., Surgeon Gen. Office, 1922-24; librarian, Army Med. Library, 1924-27; surgeon, Panama Dept., 1927-30; editor, The Military Surgeon, since 1940. Served as div. surgeon, 86th (Blackhawk) Div., Med. inspector First Army A.E.F.; surgeon, Port of Bordeau; surgeon 6th Div., in Army of Occupation in Germany, World War I. Sec. Asso. Military Surgeons. Fellow Am. Coll. of Surgeons; mem. Am. Med. Assn., Am. Legion, Mil. Order Carabao. Awarded Hoff medal, 1902. Clubs: Army and Navy, Army and Navy Country. Author: Chiefs of Med. Dept. U.S. Army, 1940; Sinnissippi, 1942; I Follow Thackeray, 1945; In the Path of Stones, 1950; also 150 jour. articles on military and medical history and biography. Contributed to Dictionary of American Biography. Home: 3000 Tilden St. N.W. Office: Armed Forces Inst. of Pathology, Washington. Died Oct. 5, 1954; buried Arlington Nat. Cemetery.

PHELPS, CHARLES EDWARD soldier, jurist, author; b. Guilford, Vt., May 1, 1833; s. John and Almira Hart (Lincoln) P.; lived in Md. from 1841; A.B., Princeton, 1852; A.M., 1855, LL.D., 1906; studied law at Harvard, 1852-53; after some time spent in foreign travel began practice in Baltimore; m. Martha Woodward, 1868. Mem. city council, Baltimore, on Reform ticket, 1860 (popular revolt against local misrule of "Know Nothing" party); capt. and maj., 1859-61, Md. Guard; in Union Army as lt. col. and col. 7th Md. Vol. Inf., 1862-64; horse killed under him, was wounded and taken prisoner, May 8, 1864, while leading charge on works at Spottsylvania, having assumed command while charge was in progress, after fall of two successive commanders; recaptured by Sheridan's cav.; promoted bvt. brig. gen. U.S.V. and awarded Congressional medal of honor for "most distinguished gallantry." Elected to Congress on Union ticket, 1864; re-elected on Conservative ticket, 1866; as mem. Naval Committee was instrumental in securing retention of U.S. Naval Acad. at Annapolis; supported 14th amendment to Constitution, but opposed the radical measures and policy of reconstruction, and particularly the 15th amendment; declined exec. apptmt. as judge Md. Court of Appeals; pres. Baltimore sch. bd., 1876; served during strike riots, 1877, as col. 8th Md. regt. Elected judge, Surpeme bench, Baltimore, 1882 (Independent ticket), for 15-yr. term; re-elected for like term, 1897; term unanimously extended by Md. legislature of 1902. Prof. law, Univ. of Md., 1884-1906. Author: Juridical Equity, 1894; Falstaff and Equity, 1901; One of the Missing, 1905. Home: Baltimore, Md. Died 1908.

PHELPS, DARWIN congressman; b. East Granby, Conn., Apr. 17, 1807; attended Western U., Pitts.; studied law, Pitts. Admitted to bar, began practice of law, Kittanning, Pa., 1835; mem. bd. trustees Kittanning Acad.; member town council, 1841, 48, burgess, 1844-45, 49, 52, 55, 58-59, 61; Whig presdl. elector, 1852; del. Republican Nat. Conv., Chgo., 1860; commd. maj. 22d Regt., Pa. Volunteer Militia, 1862; mem. Pa. Ho. of Reps., 1865; mem. U.S. Ho. of Reps. (Rep.) from Pa., 41st Congress, 1869-71. Died Kittanning, Dec. 14, 1879; buried Kittanning Cemetery.

PHELPS, HARRY officer U.S.N.; b. Jersey City, N.J., Feb. 10, 1861; s. Henry E. and Julia A. (Truesdale) P.; grad. U.S. Naval Acad., 1880; m. Mary E. Thompson, Apr. 1, 1883. Served on European Sta., 1880-82; apptd. midshipman, June 22, 1882; ensign (jr.), Mar. 3, 1883; ensign, June 26, 1884; lt. (jr.), June 19, 1892; lt., May 10, 1896; lt. comdr., June 8, 1902; comdr., July 1, 1907; capt., Mar. 4, 1911; commodore, retired, June 30, 1911. Served on Coast Survey, 1882-84; on N. Pacific Survey, 1884-88; on board U.S.S. Texas, blockade and battles off Santiago, Cuba, May-July 1898; on active duty at Navy Yard, Norfolk, Va., Apr. 1918-—. Author: Practical Marine Surveying, 1890. Home: Southport, N.C. Deceased.

PHELPS, JOHN SMITH gov. Mo., congressman, army officer; b. Simsbury, Conn., Dec. 22, 1814; s. Elisha and Lucy (Smith) P.; A.B., Washington (now Trinity Coll.), Hartford, Conn., 1859; m. Mary Whitney, Apr. 30, 1837, 5 children. Admitted to Mo. bar, 1835; mem. Mo. Ho. of Reps., 1837, 40; mem. U.S. Ho. of Reps. (Democrat) from Mo., 29th-37th congresses, 1845-63; enlisted as pvt. Capt. Coleman's Mo. Inf., later organized Phelps Regt., during Civil War; promoted lt. col., 1861, col., 1861; apptd. mil. gov. Ark. by Pres. Lincoln; 1862; resumed law practice after Civil War; gov. Mo., 1877-81; again resumed law practice. Died St. Louis, Nov. 20, 1886; buried Hazelwood Cemetery, Springfield, Mo.

PHELPS, THOMAS STOWELL rear admiral U.S.N., retired Nov. 2, 1884; b. Buckfield, Me., Nov. 2, 1822; apptd. to U.S. Navy Jan. 17, 1840; grad. U.S. Naval Acad.; passed midshipman, 1846; promoted through grades to rear admiral, Mar. 1, 1882. Served in Mexican war; Indian war on the Northwest coast, 1855-56; Paraguay expedition, 1858-59; also throughout Civil war. Before the war saw extensive service in U.S. Coast Survey; commander-in-chief S. Atlantic station, 1883-84. Author: Sailing Directions for the Straits of Magellan; Reminiscences of Seattle; also many historical articles. Died 1901.

PHELPS, THOMAS STOWGLL JR. rear admiral U.S.N.; b. Portsmouth, Va., Nov. 7, 1848; s. Rear Admiral Thomas Stowell and Margaret Riché (Levy) P.; grad. U.S. Naval Acad., 1869; m. Elwena Dewees Martin, Oct. 18, 1877. Promoted through the various grades to rear admiral, July 24, 1909. Served at all the stations and on various vessels; on board U.S.S. Raleigh, at Manila, in Spanish-Am. War; commandant Mare Island Navy Yard and Sta., 1907-Mar. 25, 1910; retired, Nov. 7, 1910. Republican. Episcopalian. Home: Oakland, Calif. Died Nov. 3, 1915.

PHELPS, WILLIAM WOODWARD naval officer; b. Baltimore, Md., Nov. 26, 1869; grad. U.S. Naval Acad., 1889; married; children—Constance (dec.), Woodward (dec.), Southwick. Commissioned ensign, U.S. Navy, July 1, 1891, and promoted through grades to rear admiral, Dec. 31, 1921. Served on Bancroft, Spanish-Am. War, 1898; exec. officer Mayflower, 1905-06; navigator and exec. Kentucky, 1906-07; on Constellation, and at Naval Sta., Newport, R.I., 1907-10; exec. officer Delaware, 1910-12; comdr. Iowa, 1912, Baltimore, 1912-13, Iowa, 1913, Reina Mercedes, 1913-15; at Naval War Coll., Newport, R.I., 1915-16; comd. Louisiana, 1916-17; actg. hydrographer, 1917; comdr. transport Great Northern, Nov. 1917-Sept. 1918; comdr. Leviathan, Sept. 1918-Apr. 1919; staff Naval War Coll., Apr. 1919-May 1920; comdg. Arizona, June 1920-June 1921; chief of staff, Naval War Coll., Aug. 1921-June 1922; comdr. Yangtze Patrol, U.S. Asiatic Fleet, July 1922-Nov. 1923; mem. Gen. Bd. of the Navy, 1924-26; comdr. Fleet Base Force, U.S. Fleet, 1926-28; comdt. Navy Yard, Portsmouth, N.H., 1928-31, N.Y. Naval Dist. and Navy Yard, Brooklyn, 1931-33; retired, July 1, 1933. Awarded Navy Cross and letter of commendation from sec. of War for services in World War. Episcopalian. Died May 11, 1938.

PHILIP, JOHN W. commodore U.S.N.; b. New York, N.Y., Aug. 26, 1840; apptd. to Naval Acad., 1856; midshipman, Jan. 1, 1861; promoted through grades to commodore, 1898; blockading service in Civil war and while executive officer of the Pawnee was wounded in the leg in the Stone River fight; on detatched service in command of Woodruff Scientific Expedition Around the World, 1877; afterward on various duties and stations; in command of battleship Texas, Oct. 18, 1897; served in Cuban waters in the Spanish war, and was in the engagement with Cervera's fleet in July 1898. Commanding North Atlantic squadron, flagship Texas. Died 1900.

PHILIPS, CARLIN, physician; b. Kenton, O., Dec. 17, 1871; s. William Hunter (M.D.) and Harriet (Carlin) P.; B.S. U. of Mich., 1894. M.D., 1897; m. Emma English of Birmingham, Ala. Feb. 19, 1905. Practiced New York, 1897-—; instr. nervous and mental diseases, also in pathology of nervous system, New York Post Grad. Med. Sch., 1899-1903; asso. pathologist, Bellevue Hosp., 1897-1903; visiting phys. prison, alcoholic and psycopathic wards, and asst. visiting phys. med. wards, same; 1st lt. Med. Reserve Corps, 1917; later maj. M.C. U.S.A. and in service 25 months. Democrat. Episcopalian. Mem. A.M.A., N.Y. State and New York County med. socs., New York Path. Soc., Phi Kappa Psi. Home: 2025 Broadway, New York

PHILIPS, JOHN F. judge; b. Thralls Prairie, Mo., Dec. 31, 1834; s. John G. P.; student U. of Mo., 1851-53; A.B., Centre Coll., Ky., 1855; LL.D., Centre Coll., Ky., Central Coll., Mo., Univ. of Missouri, 1890, and Missouri Valley College. Admitted to bar, 1857; practiced at Georgetown, Mo.; del. Missouri Constl. Conv., 1861; col. 7th Mo. Cav. U.S.V., 1861-65; practiced law, Sedalia, Mo., 1865-82; del. Dem. Nat. Conv., 1868; elected to 44th Congress (1875-77); reëlected to 46th Congress, Jan. 10, 1880, for unexpired term (1880-81) of A. M. Lay, deceased; removed to Kansas City, 1882; Supreme Ct. commr., 1883-85; presiding judge Kansas City Court of Appeals, 1885-88; U.S. dist. judge, Western Dist. Mo., 1888-1910; retired. Del. Pan-Presbyn. Conv., Edinburgh, 1877. Home: Kansas City, Mo. Died Mar. 13, 1919.

PHILLIPS, CHARLES LEONARD army officer; b. in Ill., Oct. 16, 1856; grad. U.S. Mil. Acad., 1881, Arty. Sch., 1890. Commd. add. 2d lt. 4th Arty., June 11, 1881; 2d lt., July 1, 1881; 1st lt., Dec. 31, 1887; capt., Mar. 2, 1899; maj. Arty. Corps, June 8, 1905; lt. col. Coast Arty. Corps, July 10, 1908; col., Mar. 13, 1911; brig. gen. N.G., Aug. 5, 1917. Instr. mil. science and tactics,

Cornell Coll., Mt. Vernon, Ia., 1892-96; adj. Ft. Monroe, Va., and sec. U.S. Arty. Sch., 1896-99; comd. Ft. Dade, Fla., Key West Barracks, Ft. McKinley, Me., etc.; apptd. comdr. 52d Field Arty., Camp Wadsworth, Spartanburg, S.C., Sept. 17, 1917. Address: War Dept., Washington, D.C.

PHILLIPS, GEORGE FELTER, lawyer; b. Davenport, Ia., Mar. 5, 1892; s. Charles J. and Emma (Felter) P.; A.B., Princeton, 1914; LL.B., Columbia, 1917; m. Mary Weston, June 2, 1921 (dec. Aug. 1958); children—Lydia (Mrs. David J. Laub), Charles Weston, George Felter; m. 2d, Gwen Irwin Wheeler, Sept. 24, 1959. Admitted to N.Y. State bar, 1917, since practiced in Buffalo; partner Phillips, Lytle, Hitchcock, Blaine & Huber, and predecessors, 1928-1971. Dir. emeritus Marine Midland Banks, Inc., Marine Midland Trust Co. Western N.Y.; dir. Dunlop Tire & Rubber Corp., cpl., Spl. asst. Office Chief Ordnance, U.S. Army, 1942-45. Bd. dirs., past pres. Children's Aid Soc. Buffalo; dir. Buffalo Mus. Natural Sci. Served as maj., F.A., U.S. Army, 1917-18. Mem. Buffalo and Erie County Hist. Soc. (dir., past pres.). Clubs: Buffalo, Saturn (Buffalo); The Brook (N.Y.C.); Cottage, Nassau (Princeton). Home: Buffalo NY Died Feb. 14, 1971.

PHILLIPS, JAMES FREDERICK, ret. USAF officer; b. Cambridge, Ida., Feb. 25, 1900; s. Nelson George and Laura (Bender) P.; B.S., U. Ia., 1922; grad. Engr. Sch., 1924, Army Flying Sch., 1928, Chem. Warfare Sch., 1935, Army Air Forces Tactical Sch., 1939; m. Marcella Lindeman, June 27, 1927; children—Laura Marley, Frederica Lindeman. Commd. 2d lt. U.S. Army, 1923 and advanced through the grades to maj. gen., 1950; exptl. devel. work in aerial photography and mapping, Wright Field, Ohio, 1929-35; staff work on aero. research, devel. and prodn. aircraft, 1940-45; chief materiel div. Office Asst. Chief of Staff, Materiel and Services; Cambridge Research Center, 1951-52, Hdqrs. AAF, 1944-45; fgn. service, 1945-46; A.F. sec. Research and Devel. Bd., 1947-50; staff asst. Aircraft Industries Assn.; dir. Guided Missile Council Aerospace Industries Assn.; cons. missiles and space vehicles. Distinguished marksman, and mem. 3 Internat. Rifle Teams, 1923, 24, 25. Mem. Tau Beta Pi, Sigma Xi, Theta Tau. Clubs: Cosmos, Army and Navy (Washington). Home: Mount Vernon VA Died Feb. 5, 1973.

PHILLIPS, JESSE J. justice supreme court of Ill., 1893-—; b. Montgomery County, Ill., 1837; grad. Hillsboro (Ill.) Acad., 1857; admitted to bar, 1861; served, capt., maj. and lt. col. 9th Ill. regt.; bvt. col. and brig. gen.; twice nominated for State treasurer, but defeated; practiced law at Hillsboro until elected judge 5th circuit, Ill., 1879-93. Democrat. Died 1901.

PHILLIPS, JOHN CHARLES naturalist; b. Boston, Mass., Nov. 5, 1876; s. John Charles and Anna (Tucker) P.; S.B., Lawrence Scientific Sch. (Harvard), 1899; M.D., Harvard, 1904; grad. Boston City Hosp., 1906; m. Eleanor Hyde, Jan. 11, 1908; children—John C., Jr., Madelyn, Eleanor, Arthur. Not in practice. Trustee Peabody Mus., Cambridge; pres. bd. trustees Peabody Mus., Salem. Joined second Harvard Surgical Unit, November 1915, and assigned to British Gen. Hosp. No. 22, in France; served with Med. Corps, Sept. 20, 1917-July 22, 1919; maj. in comd. Field Hosp. No. 33, 4th Div. regular army. Asso. curator of birds, Mus. Comparative Zoölogy, Harvard. Trustee Boston Soc. Natural History; chmn. Mass. Conservation Council. Author of papers on birds, genetics, experimental animal breeding, sport, travel and conservation. Home: Wenham, Mass. Died Nov. 14, 1938.

PHILLIPS, THOMAS RAPHAEL army officer ret.; b. Black River Falls, Wis., Jan. 27, 1892; s. Thomas and Eugenia (Strang) P.; attended lectures U. Wash.; grad. AC Tactical Sch., 1928. Coast Arty. Sch., 1929, Command and Gen. Staff Sch., 1936; m. Grace Crim, Sept. 5, 1923; 1 dau., Jane. Apptd. 2d lt. CAC, U.S. Army, 1917, advanced to brig. gen., 1943; served as chief of staff Antilles Dept.; G-1, Service Forces, E.T.O.; dep. chmn. Joint Export-Import Agy., U.S.-U.K., Office Mil. Govt. in Germany, 1941-47, ret. 1950; sr. staff mem. Brookings Instn., 1950-51; mil. analyst St. Louis Post-Dispatch, 1951-—. Decorated D.S.M., Legion of Merit; recipient citation of honor Air Force Assn., 1955. Author: Combat Orders (with others), 1936; Tactical Employment of Anti-air-craft Artillery, 1937; Chancellorsville Source Book (with others), 1937 (textbooks at Command and Gen. Staff Sch.); Roots of Strategy, 1940; Major Problems of U.S. Foreign Policy (with others), 1950-51, volume two 1951-52. Editor: The Art of War by Sun Tzu, 1944; The Military Instructions of the Romans, by Vegetius, 1944; Editor and Translator: My Reveries on the Art of War, by Marshal de Saxe, 1944; The Instruction of Frederick the Great for his Generals, 1944. Contbr. to mil. periodicals since 1923; also to Ency. Brit., U.S. and fgn. periodicals. Home: 5900 Connecticut Av., Chevy Chase 15, Md. Office: 1028 Connecticut Av., Washington 6. Died July 28, 1965.

PHILLIPS, ULRICH BONNELL univ. prof.; b. LaGrange, Ga., Nov. 4, 1877; s. Alonzo Rabun and Jessie Elizabeth (Young) P.; A.B., U. of Georgia, 1897, A.M., 1899; Ph.D., Columbia U., 1902, hon. Litt.D., 1929; hon. A.M., Yale, 1929; m. Lucie Mayo-Smith, Feb. 22, 1911; children—Ulric Bonnell, Richmond Mayo (dec.), Mabel Elizabeth, Worthington Webster. Fellow and tutor in history, U. of Georgia, 1897-1900; fellow Columbia, 1900-02; instr. history, 1902-07, asst. prof., 1907-08, U. of Wis.; prof. history and polit. science, Tulane U., 1908-11; prof. Am. history, U. of Mich., 1911-29; same, Yale, 1929-—. Albert Kahn fellow, tour around world and to central Africa, 1929-30. Lecturer in Am. history, U. of Calif., 1924. Ednl. dir. Y.M.C.A., Camp Gordon, Ga., 1917-18; capt. U.S.A., Mil. Intelligence, 1918-19. Author: Georgia and State Rights (awarded Justin Winsor prize, Am. Hist. Assn. 1901), 1902; History of Transportation in the Eastern Cotton Belt, 1908; Life of Robert Toombs, 1913; American Negro Slavery, 1918; Life and Labor in the Old South (awarded Little, Brown & Co. prize for best unpublished work on Am. history), 1929. Editor: Plantation and Frontier Documents, 1909; The Correspondence of Robert Toombs, Alexander H. Stephens and Howell Cobb, 1913; Florida Plantation Records (with James David Glunt), 1927. Home: New Haven, Conn. Died Jan. 21, 1934.

PHILLIPS, WILLIAM ADDISON journalist, congressman; b. Paisley, Scotland, Jan. 14, 1824; s. John Phillips; studied law; m. Carrie Spillman, 1859; m. 2d, Anna Stapler, 1885; 4 children. Newspaper correspondent, 1845-62, corr. N.Y. Tribune, 1855, famous anti-slavery journalist; admitted to Ill. bar, 1852; moved to Lawrence, Kan., 1855, began practice of law; a founder Town of Salina (Kan.), 1858; 1st justice Kan. Supreme Ct. under Leavenworth Constn., 1857; raised some of 1st troops in Kan. during Civil War, served as officer U.S. Army, prominent as comdr. Cherokee Indian Regt. in Indian Territory and Ark., left army as col. 3d Indian Regt., 1865; pros. atty. Cherokee County (Kan.), 1865; mem. Kan. Legislature, 1865; mem. U.S. Ho. of Reps. from Kan., 43d-45th congresses, 1873-79, chiefly interested in land legislation; pres. Kan. Hist. Soc. Author: The Conquest of Kansas by Missouri and her Allies (an anti-slavery polit. tract supporting Fremont), 1856; Labor, Land and Law, A Search for the Missing Wealth of the Working People, 1888. Died Ft. Gibson, Muskogee County, Ind., Nov. 30, 1893; buried Gypsum Hill Cemetery, Salina.

PHILLIPS, WILLIAM ERIC mfr.; b. Toronto, Can., Jan. 3, 1893; s. William Charles and Ella Louise (MacMillan) P.; student Upper Can. Coll.; B.A. Sc., U. Toronto, 1914, LL.D., 1947; children—Derek M., Diana (Mrs. Philip Jackson), Michael M., Cecil (Mrs. Walter Pady). Chairman board, chief exec. officer Massey-Ferguson, Ltd.; chmn. bd. Argus Corp., Ltd., Canadian Pitts. Industries, Ltd.; served as chmn. of Duplate Canada, Limited. World War II; president of Research Enterprises, Ltd., producers optical glass, instruments, 1940-45; dir. Hollinger Consol. Gold Mines, Ltd., Brazilian Traction, Light & Power Co., Ltd., Dominion Tar & Chem. Co., Ltd., Stone & Webster, Can., Ltd., Pitts. Plate Glass Co., Royal Bank of Can., Remington Rand, Ltd. Chmn. bd. govs. U. Toronto. Served as lt. col., Royal Warwickshire Regt., British Army, 1914-20, 43. Decorated Companion Distinguished Service Order, Mil. Cross, Comdr. Order Brit. Empire. Fellow Soc. Glass Tech. (Eng.), Chem. Inst. Can.; mem. Engring. Inst. Can. Mem. Church of Eng. Clubs: Toronto, Toronto Hunt, University, York (Toronto); Mount Royal (Montreal). Home: 174 Teddington Park, Toronto 12. Office: 50 St. Clair Av. W., Toronto 7, Can. Died Dec. 26, 1964; buried St. John's Anglican Ch. Cemetery, York Mills, Toronto.

PHILLIPSON, IRVING JOSEPH ret. army ofcr.; b. Dowagiac, Mich., Apr. 3, 1882; s. Emanuel and Barbara (Guggenheim) P.; B.S., U.S. Mil. Acad., 1904; attended Sch. of the Line, 1921-22, Gen. Staff Sch., 1922-23, Army War Coll., 1923-24; m. Florence Morrison, Sept. 1, 1909 (dec.); m. Elsie Salvadori, April 27, 1954. Commd. 2d lt. Inf., U.S. Army, 1904, advanced through ranks to maj. gen., 1941; chief, Budget and Legislative Planning Branch, War Dept. Gen. Staff, 1930-35; comd. 30th Inf., Presidio, San Francisco, 1935-38, 2d Brigade, 1st Div., 2d Corps Area, 1938-40; chief of staff, Governor's Island, N.Y., 1940, comdg. gen., 2d Corps Area, Governor's Island, 1940-42; exec. dir. Army Emergency Relief, 1942-44; member War Department Dependency Bd., Jan. 11, 1944 to Dec. 31, 1944; retired as maj. general, U.S. Army, Dec. 31, 1944; dir. of indsl. relations, Botany Mills, Inc., Passaic, N.J., 1944-52. Chmn. Civil Defense Council, Passaic, N.J. 1950-53. Trustee Disabled Am. Vets. Service Found. and chmn. budget and finance com. Comd. bn. regt. and brigade, 142d and 143d Inf., 36th Div., in Meuse-Argonne, France, 1918. Awarded Distinguished Service medal, Victory medal (2 bronze stars), Croix de Guerre (Gold Star). Mem. Scabbard and Blade, Newcomen Soc. of Eng., New York Society, Military and Naval Officers, World Wars; New York Chapter, M.O.W.W. (comdr., 1945-46), Honorary vice pres. Am. Hygiene Soc. Clubs: Army and Navy (Washington) Address: 240 Central Park South, N.Y.C. Died April 4, 1955.

PHILSON, ROBERT congressman; b. County Tyrone, Ireland, 1759. Came to U.S., settled in Berlin, Pa., 1785; engaged in agriculture; held various local offices; asso. judge Somerset County, 20 years; commd. brig. gen. 2d Brigade, 10th Div., Pa. Militia, 1800; served as brig. gen. 2d Brigade, 12th Div., Pa. Volunteers, during War of 1812; mem. U.S. Ho. of Reps. from Pa., 16th Congress, 1819-21. Died Berlin, June 25, 1831; buried Reformed Church Cemetery.

PHIPPS, FRANK HUNTINGTON brigadier gen. U.S.A.; b. Northampton, Mass., Aug. 9, 1843; s. George W. and Sophia Ann (Lyman) P.; ed. in various pub. and pvt. schs.; entered U.S. Mil. Acad., 1859, grad., 1863; m. Louisa De Hart Patterson, June 11, 1867 (died 1881); m. 2d, Anna Lally, Nov. 13, 1894. Commd. 1st lt. ordnance, June 11, 1863; capt., June 23, 1874; maj., Dec. 4, 1882; lt. col., July 7, 1898; col., Feb. 17, 1903; retired by operation of law, Aug. 9, 1907; advanced to rank of brig. gen. retired, Aug. 9, 1907. Bvtd. capt., Mar. 13, 1865, "for faithful and meritorious services in ordnance dept." In ordnance dept., served at various arsenals and dept. headqrs.; mem. Bd. Ordnance and Fortification, 1894-99; comd. Springfield Armory, Mass., until 1907. Home: Washington, D.C. Died Mar. 28, 1925.

PHIPPS, JOHN SHAFFER corp. ofcl.; b. Allegheny, Pa., Aug. 11, 1874; Ph.B., Sheffield Scientific Sch. (Yale), 1896; LL.B., Harvard, 1899; m. Margarita Celia Grace, of Sussex, Eng., Nov. 4, 1903; children—John Henry, Hubert Beaumont, Margaret Helen, Michael Grace. Former dir. U.S. Steel Corp., Internat. Paper Co., Grace (Steamship) Line, Guaranty Trust Co. Commd. maj. U.S.A., and served as liaison officer at aviation hdqrs., Ft. Worth, Tex., World War. Clubs: Links, Orange County Hunt, Meadow Brook, Racquet and Tennis. Home: Palm Beach, Fla. Office: 800 2d Av., N.Y.C. 17. Died Apr. 27, 1958.

PHIPPS, MICHAEL GRACE, business exec.; b. Little Daly, Eng., Jan. 10, 1910; s. John Shaffer and Margarita (Grace) P.; grad. St. Paul's Sch., Concord, N.H., 1928; B.A., Yale, 1932; m. Muriel Pillans Lane, Apr. 10, 1936; children—Elaine Lane, Susan Grace. Pres. Bessemer Properties, Inc., Palm Beach, Fla.; dir. W. R. Grace & Co., N.Y.C. Served as lt. col. USAAF, 1942-45. Decorated Air Medal. Home: Palm Beach FL Died Mar. 13, 1973.

PHOENIX, LLOYD yachtsman; b. N.Y. City, Oct. 7, 1841; s. J. Phillips and Mary (Whitney) P.; grad. U.S. Naval Acad., 1861; unmarried. Served as midshipman, master and lt. through the Civil War; resigned commn., 1865; prominent as yachtsman after leaving the navy. Episcopalian. Mem. Loyal Legion. Home: New York, N.Y. Died Mar. 31, 1926.

PHYTHIAN, ROBERT LEES commodore U.S.N.; b. Johnstown, Pa., July 31, 1835. Grad. U.S. Naval Acad., 1856; served in navy during Civil War, 1861-65, as exec. officer of large ships, and in command of a small vessel; was supt. N.Y. Nautical School; 3 times supt. U.S. Naval Obs.; served in U.S. Naval Acad. 5 yrs. as head Dept. of Navigation, and 4 yrs. supt.; retired, July 29, 1897. Home: Annapolis, Md. Died Jan. 20, 1917.

PIASECKI, PETER F., postmaster; b. Milwaukee, Wis., May 30, 1876; s. Theophil and Catharine (Inda) P.; ed. pub. schs.; m. Emily Sonnenberg, of Milwaukee, Oct. 25, 1899; 1 son, Peter F. Postmaster of Milwaukee since 1923. Served as lt. 1st Wis. Vols., U.S. Vols., Spanish-Am. War; lt. col. 1st Wis. Inf., on Mexican border, 1916; col. inf., U.S.A., World War; with 32d Div., A.E.F., occupation sector in Alsace, Aisne Marne, Oise Aisne and Meuse Argonne offensives, march to the Rhine, and with Army of Occupation; col. O.R.C. Mem. Nat. Aeronautic Assn., Izaak Walton League, Spanish War Vets., Mil. Order Foreign Wars, Mexican Border Vets. Assn., Am. Legion, Milwaukee Assn. Commerce (air service com.), Rotary Internat., Milwaukee Advertising Club. Elk. Club: Milwaukee Yacht. Home: 3046 S. Superior St. Office: Main Post Office, Milwaukee WI

PIATT, DONN journalist; b. Cincinnati, June 29, 1819; s. Judge Benjamin and Elizabeth (Barnett) P.; ed. St. Xavier Coll., Cincinnati; m. Louise Kirby, 1847; m. 2d, Ella Kirby, 1866. Began to publish Democratic Club, West Liberty, O., 1840; judge Ct. Common Pleas, Hamilton County, O., 1852-53; sec. to Am. legation, France, 1853-55; commd. capt. 13th Ohio Inf. during Civil War, 1861, maj., 1862, lt. col., 1863; elected to Ohio Legislature, 1865; Washington corr. Cincinnati Comml., 1868; editor Club Room column of Galaxy, 1871; co-editor, founder weekly Capital, 1871-80; printed editorial The Beginning of the End (interpreted as a threat to assassinate Pres. Hayes), Feb. 18, 1877; indicted on charge of inciting rebellion, insurrection and riot, prosecution dropped; introduced term "twisting the British lion's tail". Author: Memories of the Men Who Saved the Union, 1887; The Lone Grave of the Shenandoah and Other Tales, 1888; Rev. Melanchthon Poundex, 1889. Died West Liberty, Nov. 12, 1891.

PIAZZA, FERDINAND, hosp. adminstr.; b. Burgio, Italy, Nov. 15, 1902; s. Joseph and Antionette (Serra) P.; came to U.S., 1909, naturalized, 1925; B.S., City Coll. N.Y., 1925; M.D., George Washington U., 1929; m. Connie Lavoti, Sept. 6, 1936; 1 son, Frederick; m. 2d, Marjorie Ruggieri, Nov. 27, 1966; adopted son, Frank Daniel. Intern Met. Hosp., N.Y.C., 1929-30, admitting physician, 1930-31, resident surgery, 1931-32, vis. surgeon, 1933-38; pvt. practice, 1933-38; exec. physician Harlem Hosp., N.Y.C., 1938-40; dep. med.

supt. Fordham Hosp., N.Y.C., 1940-42; gen. med. supt. Met. Hosp., N.Y.C., 1954-57, med. supt., 1948-54, 57-67; med. supt. Sydenham Hosp., N.Y.C., 1946-48; asst. clin. prof. preventive medicine N.Y. Med. Coll., 1958-67. Served to lt. col., M.C., AUS, 1942-46. Decorated Order Merit (Republic Italy), 1965. Fellow Am. Coll. Hosp. Administrs.; mem. Am. Hosp. Assn. Home: Great Neck NY Died Apr. 21, 1968.

PIBUL SONGGRAM, LUANG field marshall, prime minister Thailand; b. Bangkhen, Bangkok, Siam (now Thailand), July 14, 1897; s. Keet and Sam Ang Kittasangka; ed. mil. acad., Arty. Sch. Poitiers, 1924-25, Ecole d'application d'Artillerie at Fontainebleau, 1926-27; m. Madame La-iad; 3 sons, 3 daus. Returned to Thailand and became capt., 1927, maj., 1930; took leading part in Bloodless Coup d'Etat to set up Constl. Monarchy in Thailand, 1932; minister def. since 1934; prime minister, 1938-44, since 48. Decorated Dushdi Mala medal, Knight Grand Cordon of Most Noble Order Crown of Thailand, Royal Cypher medal of King Ananda, Knight Grand Cordon of Most Exalted Order of White Elephant, Chai Samoraphum medal, Knight of Ancient and Auspicious Order of Nine Gems, Knight Grand Cordon of Most Illustrious Order Chula Chom Klao, Ratna Varabhorn Order of Merit, Dushdi Mala medal, Medal of Bravery (all Thailand); Ehrenzeichen des Deutschen Roten Kreuzes, Gran Croce, Corona d'Italia, Gran Corce, SS. Maurizio e Lazzaro, Grand Croix de la Legion d'Honneur, Kyokujitsu, (first and spl. classes), Knight Grand Cross of Most Distinguished Order St. Michael and St. George, Der Verdienstorden vom Deutschen Adler (Grosskreuz), Royal Cypher Medal of King Phumipol Aduldej. Home: Chitlom, Ploenchitr Rd., Bangkok. Office: Government House, Bangkok, Thailand. Died June 11, 1964.

PICK, LEWIS ANDREW army officer; b. Brookneal, Va., Nov. 18, 1890; s. George and Annie (Crouch) P.; B.S. Va. Poly. Inst., Blacksburg, Va., 1914; grad. Engrs. Sch. Ft. Belvoir, Va., 1924, Command and Gen. Staff Sch., Ft. Leavenworth, Kan., 1934, Army War Coll., Ft. Humphries, D.C., 1939; m. Alice Cary, Dec. 15, 1925; 1 son, Lewis Andrew, Jr. Civil engr. with Southern Ry., 1914-16; commd. 1st lt., Corps of Engrs., U.S. Army, 1917, advancing to lt. gen., 1951; comd. Co. E, 23d Engrs., A.E.F., France, 1917; on duty in Philippines, 1920-23; U.S. dist. engr., New Orleans, La., 1925-28; instr. Command and Gen. Staff Sch., Ft. Leavenworth, Kan., 1934-38; exec. officer to div. engr., Ohio River Div., Cincinnati, Ohio, 1939-41; division engineer, Missouri River Division, Omaha, Nebraska, 1942-Sept. 1943; comd. Advance Sect. 3, China-Burma-India, in charge constrn. Ledo Rd., 1943-45; assigned Missouri River Div. engrs., 1945; comdr. 5th army emergency relief in midwest, Operation Snowbound, Feb. 1949; chief of engrs., Dept. of Army, March 1949. Vice chmn. Georgia-Pacific Plywood Co., 1953—. Decorated Distinguished Service Medal with Oak Leaf Cluster; Cloud and Banner (China); Royal Order of Bath (Britain). Mem. Am. Society C.E., Soc. Am. Mil. Engrs., Theta Chi, Chi Epsilon. Author of the Pick Plan for development of Mo. River Basin. Address: 360 N. College St., Auburn, Ala. Died Dec. 2, 1956; buried Old Cemetery, Auburn.

PICKARD, WARD WILSON lawyer, oil operator; b. Wilson, N.Y., Mar. 24, 1878; s. Ward Beecher and Myra (Gibbs) P.; A.B., Wesleyan U., Conn., 1899; LL.B., New York Law Sch., 1902; m. Alice Rossington, Sept. 14, 1910; children—William Rossington, Nicholas, Mary Linn. Admitted to N.Y. bar, 1902; in practice, 1902-15, and since 1925; pres. Eagle Saving & Loan Co., Brooklyn, N.Y., 1915-17; treas. Seabrook Co., Bridgeton, N.J., 1919-25; pres. Plains Oil Co., Wichita, Kan., since 1925; dep. administrator paper div. NRA, 1933-34; coördinator paper industries, 1935-36, mgr. eastern container group since 1936. Corpl. 1st Conn. Vol. Inf., Spanish-Am. War, 1898; chief of contract div. and chmn. claims bd. Q.M.C., 1917-19. Mem. Alpha Delta Phi. Clubs: Yountakah Country (Nutley, N.J.); Country (Pine Orchard, Conn.). Home: 131 Satterthwaite Av., Nutley, N.J. Office: 295 Madison Av., New York, N.Y. Died Aug. 23, 1943.

PICKENS, ANDREW army officer; b. Paxton, Pa., Sept. 19, 1739; s. Andrew and Nancy Pickens; m. Rebecca Calhoun, Mar. 19, 1765, at least 4 children. fought against Cherokee Indians, 1761; served as capt. S.C. Militia in 1st fight at Ninetysix fort, 1775; commd. col., circa 1777, brigadier, circa 1780; mem. S.C. Ho. of Reps., 1781-94, 1800-12; mem. S.C. Constl. Conv., 1790; mem. U.S. Ho. of Reps. from S.C., 3d Congress, 1793-95; maj. gen. S.C. Militia, circa 1795; served in War of 1812. Died Pendleton Dist., S.C., Aug. 11, 1817; buried Old Stone Ch., nr. Pendleton Dist.

PICKENS, ANDREW CALHOUN naval officer; b. Mobile, Ala.; s. Andrew Calhoun and Ella (Pollard) P.; grad. U.S. Naval Acad.; m. Harriette Fowle Taylor, Sept. 25, 1915. Comd. transport U.S. Navy, in first expdn. to France, World War, and then served with Brit. Grand Fleet in North Sea; commd. rear admiral U.S. Navy, 1937, now comdg. Cruisers, Atlantic Fleet. Democrat. Presbyterian. Clubs: Chevy Chase, Army and Navy (Washington, D.C.); New York Yacht; University, Racquet (Phila.). Address: Navy Dept., Washington, D.C. Died Nov. 29, 1944.

PICKERING, ABNER army officer; b. Wabash Co., Ind., July 11, 1854; s. Hiram and Margaret (Jackson) P.; grad. U.S. Mil. Acad., 1878; m. Celeste Florence Kuykendall, of Santa Rosa, Cal., May 13, 1879. Commd. 2d lt. 2d Inf., June 14, 1878; 1st lt., Feb. 17, 1887; capt., Aug. 8, 1897; maj. 22d Inf., June 9, 1902; transferred to 1st Inf., Sept. 30, 1909; lt. col. 22d Inf., Feb. 23, 1910; trans. to 9th Inf., Mar. 12, 1910; col., Mar. 30, 1912; assigned to 11th Inf., May 12, 1913. Served in the Northwest until 1898; participated in Santiago Campaign, Cuba, and with Army of Occupation, 1899; in Philippine Islands, 1900-02, 03-05, 10-12; on Mexican border, 1913-17; comdg. Regular Army troops at Chickamauga Park, Ga., to Dec. 28, 1917. Republican. Methodist. Mason. Author: As a Soldier Would (novel), 1912. Address: War Dept., Washington, D.C.

PICKERING, LORING editor; b. San Francisco, Aug. 31, 1888; s. Loring and Rose (Crothers) P.; student Stanford, Oxford U., Sorbonne, U. Chgo. Law Sch.; m. Harriett Alexander, June 17, 1916 (div. 1938); children—Loring, Alexander; m. 2d, Chouteau Scott Walker, 1940. Organizer, 1922, and since gen. mgr. N. Am. Newspaper Alliance, N.Y.; asso. editor The Bulletin, San Francisco. Commd. capt. Air Service, U.S. Army, 1917; maj. (pilot) 1918; comdr. A.S., Panama Canal Zone, 1918-19. Lt. col. A.C., U.S.A., 1942-43, col. Air Staff, 1943-45; organized Army Courier Service. Organizer of Capt. Wilkins Expedition to North Pole. Charter mem. Am. Soc. of Newspaper Editors, Am. Soc. Colonial Wars, NE. Historic-Geneal. Soc.; fellow Am. Geog. Soc., Royal Geog. Soc.; mem. gen. com. Pan-Am. Congress of Journalists, Washington, 1926. Clubs: Players, Dutch Treat (N.Y.C.); Army and Navy (Washington); Burlingame (Burlingame, Cal.); Pacific-Union (San Francisco); Savile (London); Travellers (Paris); Peking (Peiping, China). Address: Todos Bancos, Woodside, via Redwood City, Cal. Died Mar. 11, 1959.

PICKERING, TIMOTHY senator, cabinet officer; b. Salem, Mass., July 17, 1745; s. Timothy and Mary (Wingate) P.; grad. Harvard, 1763; studied law; m. Rebecca White, Apr. 5, 1776, 10 children including John, Timothy. Clk., Office of Register of Deeds for Essex County, Salem, 1763; admitted to Mass. bar, 1768; selectman, town clk., assessor, Salem, 1772-77; rep. Mass. Gen. Ct.; register of deeds Salem, 1775; judge Maritime Ct. of Province of Mass., 1775-76, Essex County Ct. of Common Pleas, 1775; commd. lt. Essex County Militia, 1776; elected to Mass. Legislature, 1776; commd. col. Continental Army, 1776, apptd. adj. gen. by Gen. Washington, 1777; elected to Bd. of War by Continental Congress, 1777; q.m. gen. Continental Army, 1780-83; moved to Phila., then to Wyoming County (Pa.), 1787, organized Luzerne County, 1787; rep. from Luzerne County to Pa. Conv. which ratified U.S. Constn., 1789; mem. Pa. Constl. Conv., 1789-90; went on mission to Seneca Indians to prevent an Indian war, 1790; postmaster gen. U.S. (apptd. by Pres. Washington), 1791-95, sec. of war, 1795; U.S. sec. of state, 1795-1800, actins in preparing for war with France ("Quasi-War"), 1797-98, support of Britain, and intrigues against John Adams resulted in his removal from office; re-entered local politics, Mass.; mem. U.S. Senate from Mass., 1803-11; mem. U.S. Ho. of Reps. (Federalist) from Mass., 13th-14th congresses, 1813-17; bitterly opposed War of 1812; a scientific farmer in Mass.; Author of a widely used drill manual, also numerous articles and letters on politics and farming. Died Salem, Jan. 29, 1829; buried Broad Street Cemetery, Salem.

PICKETT, GEORGE EDWARD army officer; b. Richmond, Va., Jan. 25, 1825; s. Col. Robert and Mary (Johnston) P.; grad. U.S. Mil. Acad., 1846; m. Sally Minge, Jan. 1851; m. 2d, La Salle Corbell, Sept. 15, 1863; 2 children. Served in Mexican War; commd. 2d lt. 2d Inf., U.S. Army, 1847, brevetted 1st lt., 1847; served frontier duty in Tex., commd. capt., 1855; served on Indian duty in Northwest, 1856-61; seized control of San Juan Island in Puget Sound under orders (during Brit.-Am. controversy over control); resigned commn., 1861; commd. col. Confederate Army, 1861, brig. gen., 1862; served in battles of Williamsburg, Gaines Mills, Seven Pines; commd. maj. gen., 1862; served in Battle of Fredericksburg; most famous as leader Pickett's charge during Battle of Gettysburg, 1863; commanded Dept. of Va. and N.C., 1864; saw action at Battle of Petersburg; after war refused offer of Khedive of Egypt of commn. in Egyptian Army; in charge Va. agency Washington Life Ins. Co. Died Norfolk, Va., July 30, 1875; buried Hollywood Cemetery, Richmond.

PICKING, HENRY F. commodore U.S.N.; b. Somerset Co., Pa., Jan. 1840; apptd. to navy, Sept. 28, 1857; Naval Acad., 1857-61; apptd. acting master, June 4, 1861; lt., July 1862; lt. comdr., July 25, 1866; comdr., Jan. 25, 1875; capt., Aug. 4, 1889; commodore, Nov. 22, 1898; rear admiral, Mar. 3, 1899; m. Laura Sherwood, May 2, 1879. In Civil war on blockading service, at sinking of privateer Petrel, engagement with Confederate ram Merrimac, and Sewell's Point batteries (monitor engagement), 1862; in several skirmishes with batteries on Sullivan's Island, etc. Since Civil war on various duties and stations. Ordered to command navy-yard at Boston, Mar. 25, 1899. Died 1899.

PIER, GARRETT CHATFIELD author, archaeologist; b. London, Eng., Oct. 30, 1875; s. Garrett Ryckman and Eleanor (Blackman) P.; student Columbia, 1896-98; studied in museums of Europe 2 yrs., in Egyptian and Arabic museums 2 years, Egyptology and Assyriology, U. of Chicago, 1906; m. Adelaide Wilson, June 25, 1902 (died Feb. 22, 1926); m. 2d, Riva Greenwood, Nov. 10, 1927. Asst. curator decorative arts, Met. Mus., New York, 1907-10; traveled in Japan, China and Orient, buying antiques for Met. Mus., 1911-14. Served as lt. Old Guard Vol. Regt., N.Y., Spanish-Am. War; commd. 1st lt. inf., 2d Plattsburg Camp, 1917; commd. capt. inf., Aug. 1918; in France, Oct. 1918-Apr. 1919; attached to Dept. of State, and with Peace Commn.; mem. state founders com. Woodrow Wilson Foundn., 1921. Mem. Alpha Delta Phi. Republican. Episcopalian. Clubs: Field, Greenwich Country (Greenwich, Conn.); Cliff Dwellers (Chicago); Salmagundi, Columbia, Coffee House (New York); Indian Harbor Yacht (Conn.). Author: Egyptian Antiquities in the Pier Collection, 1906; Inscriptions of the Nile Monuments, 1908; Pottery of the Near East, 1909; Catalogue of Pottery, Porcelain and Faience, 1911; Temple Treasures of Japan, 1914; Catalogue of the Draper Collection of Antique Gems, 1914; Hanit, the Enchantress, 1921; Hidden Valley, 1925; Jeweled Tree (play), 1927; Kimon's Model, 1932. Died Dec. 30, 1943.

PIERCE, BENJAMIN gov. N.H.; b. Chelmford, Mass., Dec. 25, 1757; s. Benjamin and Elizabeth (Merrill) P.; m. Elizabeth Andrews, May 24, 1787; m. 2d, Anna Kendrick, Feb. 1, 1790; 9 children including Franklin (14th pres. U.S.). Served as pvt. in Mass. Militia, then became lt. in command of a co.; brigade-major, apptd. to organize Hillsborough County (N.H.) Militia, 1786-1807, became brig. gen., 1805; mem. N.H. Ho. of Reps., 1789-1802; mem. N.H. Constl. Conv., 1791; mem. N.H. Gov.'s Council, 1803-09, 14; apptd. sheriff Hillsborough County, 1809-12, 18-27; elected gov. N.H., 1827, 29; Democratic elector in 1832. Died Hillsborough, N.H., Apr. 1, 1839.

PIERCE, BYRON ROOT soldier; b. E. Bloomfield, N.Y., Sept. 30, 1829; s. Silas and Mary (Root) P.; acad. edn. Rochester, N.Y.; began business life in his father's wollen factory; later became dentist, removed to Grand Rapids, Mich., 1856; also had branch office at Joliet, Ill.; m. Abbie L. Evans, Oct. 12, 1881. Entered Union Army as capt. Co. K, 3d Mich. Regt., May 13, 1861; rapidly promoted for bravery and meritorious conduct; maj. 3d Mich. Inf., Oct. 21, 1861; lt. col., July 25, 1862; col., Jan. 1, 1863; brig. gen. vols., June 7, 1864; bvtd. maj. gen., Apr. 5, 1865, "for gallant service at battle of Salor's Creek." Commandant Mich. Soldiers' Home from its opening, 1887, until 1891. Employed in P.O. Dept. Home: Grand Rapids, Mich. Died July 13, 1924.

PIERCE, CARLETON CUSTER, former dir. select. serv. W.Va.; b. Rowlesburg, W.Va., Oct. 19, 1877; s. John Franklin and Amanda Elizabeth (Moore) P.; student Franklin Coll., New Athens, O., 1896-97; diploma in law, West Virginia U., Morgantown, W.Va., 1901; m. Mary May Buckner, Nov. 28, 1902; children—Carleton Custer (officer U.S.N.R.), Oscar Buckner (U.S. Army). Began as school teacher, 1895; engaged in various businesses, including fruit growing, coal mining and public utilities, and holding official positions in corporations, which relinqushed when apptd. dir. selective service for West Virginia, 1941; now dir. office selective service records. Served as 1st lt., U.S. Vols., during Spanish-Am. War; mem. W.Va. Nat. Guard, advancing through the grades to brig. gen., 1929; called to Federal duty, 1940, retired for age, 1941, continuing to serve as acting adj. and dir. of selective service; brig. gen. hon. ret. list. A.U.S. Presdl. Medal for Merit; decorated Spanish-Am. War and Good Conduct medals. Former mem. legislature, W.Va., past pres. bd. of edn., and pros. atty., Preston County, W.Va. Mem. Sigma Chi. Mason, K.P. Club: Preston Country (Kingwood, W.Va.) Home: 112 Morgantown St., Kingwood, W.Va. Office: 513 1/2 Capitol Street, Charleston WV

PIERCE, CLAUDE CONNOR sanitarian; b. Chattanooga, Tenn., June 15, 1878; s. David James and Annie (Flora) P.; Chattanooga High School, 1895; M.D., Chattanooga Med. Coll., 1898; m. Miss Reeves, May 17, 1905; children—John Reeves (killed in naval action Jan. 1943), George Ellis (U.S. Navy), Claude Connor, Jr. (U.S. Army). Served in Spanish-American War; appointed assistant surgeon U.S. P.H.S. June 20, 1900; passed assistant surgeon, July 26, 1905; surgeon, December 1912; senior surgeon, Act of Congress, March 4, 1915; assistant surgeon general, July 13, 1918. Quarantine officer, Panama, 1904-12; superintendent Colon Hospital, 1913; established disinfection plants along Texas-Mexico border to prevent introduction of typhus fever, 1916; in charge of extra cantonment sanitation, Little Rock, Ark., 1917; in charge div. of venereal diseases, U.S.P.H.S., Washington, 1918-22; director of District 3, Chicago, 1922-26; med. dir. in supervisory charge of U.S.P.H.S. activities in Europe, 1934-37; dir. Dist. 1, U.S.P.H.S., 1937-42; retired July 1942; now med. dir. Planned Parenthood Fedn. Member American Med. Assn., tel, Brooklyn, N.Y. Office: 501 Madison Av., New York, N.Y. Died Mar. 19, 1944.

PIERCE, FRANKLIN 14th Pres. U.S.; b. Hillsborough, N.H., Nov. 23, 1804; s. Benjamin and Anna (Kendrick) P.; grad. Bowdoin Coll., 1824; studied law under Levi Woodbury, Portsmouth, N.H.; m. Jane Means Appleton, Nov. 18, 1834, 3 children. Admitted to Hillsborough County (N.H.) bar, 1827, practiced law, Hillsborough; mem. N.H. Ho. of Reps., 1829-33, speaker, 1832-33; mem. U.S. Ho. of Reps. (Democrat) from N.H., 23d-24th, congresses, 1833-37; mem. U.S. Senate from N.H., 1837-42; resumed practice law, Concord, N.H., 1842; leader Dem. Party politics in N.H., 1842-47; declined appointment as U.S. atty. gen., 1845; commd. col. 9th Regt., N.H. Inf., 1846; apptd. brig. gen. U.S. Volunteers, 1847, served in battles of Contreras and Churubusco, resigned from service, 1847; pres. N.H. Constl. Conv., 1850; nominated for Pres. U.S. as compromise candidate on 49th ballot at Dem. Nat. Conv., Balt., 1852; Pres. U.S., 1853-57; sent James Gadsden to Mexico to purchase land for Southern railroad to Pacific, 1853; believed continued existence of slavery guaranteed by U.S. Constn.; approved Kan.-Neb. Bill, 1854; sought to restore order under legal, pro-slavery govt. when civil war broke out in Kan.; attempted to purchase Cuba, 1854; toured Europe, 1857-60; resumed practice law, Concord. Died Concord, Oct. 8, 1869; buried Minat Inclosure Cemetery, Concord.

PIERCE, JASON NOBLE clergyman; b. Pittsburgh, Pa., Aug. 28, 1880; s. Albert Francis (D.D.) and Rebecca (Noble) P.; B.A., Amherst, 1902, D.D., 1922; B.D., Yale Div. Sch., 1906; m. Mary Gertrude Fairchild, March 9, 1904; children—Margaret Williams, Edward Fairchild. Ordained Congl. ministry, 1906; pastor Davenport Ch., New Haven, Conn., 1906-08, Puritan Ch., Brooklyn, 1908-10, 2d Ch., Oberlin, O., 1910-14, 2d Ch., Dorchester, Boston, Mass., 1914-20, First Ch., Washington, D.C., 1920-30, Collegeside Ch., Nashville, Tenn.; prof. practical theology, Atlanta Sem. Foundation and head dept. practical theology, Vanderbilt U. Sch. of Religion, 1930-32; pastor Christian Temple, Norfolk, Va., 1932-33, First Congregational Ch., San Francisco, since June 1, 1933. On staff of preachers at several colls. Sr. chaplain 2d Div. A.E.F., in France, Belgium and Germany, 1918-19; lt. col., chaplain O.R.C.; pres. Nat. Assn. Chaplains, U.S. Army, O.R.C. and N.G., 1926-28; pres. 2d Div. Assn., D.C., 1927-28. Trustee Amherst Coll., 1922-27; trustee Piedmont Coll., Ga.; pres. bd. trustees Country Life Acad., N.C.; pres. Congl. Home, D.C.; chmn. gen. com. Army and Navy Chaplains; dir. Boston City Missionary Soc., Mass. Home Missionary Soc., Congl. Ednl. and Pub. Soc.; trustee Uplands Sanatorium; ex-pres. Washington Federation Chs.; mem. exec. com. Nat. Council Congl. Chs.; trustee N. Calif. Congl. Conf., pres. San Francisco Fed. of Chs., 1936-37; pres. and moderator Bay Assn. Congl. Chs.; pres. bd. dirs. and mem. exec. com. Northern Calif. Congl. Conf., 1936-37; moderator State Conf. Congl. Churches; bd. of dirs. Prison Assn. of Calif.; vice-pres. and dir. Veterans Christian Service Commission since 1945; vice-pres. Chaplains Assn. San Quentin Prison since 1944; vice pres. and dir. N. Calif. and W. Nevada State Council of Churches since 1945; Christian Council on Palestine since 1945. Member Theta Sigma, Chi Phi, Delta Sigma Rho, Pi Gamma Mu, Am. Legion (post chaplain). Mason. Clubs: Monday (Boston); National Sojourners, Cosmos, Congregational, Torch (Washington, D.C.); Commonwealth, Presidio (San Francisco); Rotary (hon.). Author: The Masculine Power of Christ, 1912; The Mystery of His Own Person, 1913; Together in the Heavenly Home, 1916. Contbr. to Boston Monday Club Sermons since 1915. Address: 432 Mason St., San Francisco, Calif. Died March 16, 1948; buried in Golden Gate National Cemetery.

PIERCE, JOSIAH JR. engr., maj. and engr. officer, U.S.V.; b. Alexandrofsky, Russia, Jan. 30, 1861; ed. in Russia, England and U.S.; asso. King's Coll., London, 1879; grad. Emmanuel Coll., Cambridge, Eng., B.A., 1882 (M.A., 1886); student Mass. Inst. Tech., 1883; later at Johns Hopkins, Baltimore. Lecturer and prof. Columbian Univ.; instrn. and asst. prof. Catholic Univ., Washington; asso. mem. (Telford medal and premium) Instn. Civil Engrs., London; topographer and engr., Northern Transcontinental Survey, 1883; U.S. Coast and Geodetic Survey, 1885; U.S. Geol. Survey, 1886; Ordnance Survey of Great Britain, 1888; U.S. Irrigation Surveys, 1888-91; Sinipuxent Beach Co., 1893; C.,B.&Q. R.R. and B.&O. R.R. Prin. asst. engr., topog. survey, city of Baltimore, 1893; chief engr., Va. Electric Co., 1897; chief engr., 1st div., 2d army corps, Camp Alger, 1898; chief engr., San Juan dist., Puerto Rico, 1898-99. Consulting engr. Great Falls Power Co., Washington, D.C. Home: Boonsboro, Md. Died 1902.

PIERCE, NORVAL HARVEY oto-laryngologist; b. Washington, May 13, 1863; s. Harvey Lindsley (M.D.) and Katherine Elizabeth (Purington) P.; M.D., Coll. P. and S., Chicago, 1885; post-grad. work, Royal U., Würzburg, Bavaria, and Imperial U., Vienna; m. Drucilla Wahl, 1895. Appointed prof. and head dept. laryngology, rhinology and otology, U. of Ill. Coll. of Medicine, 1915, now emeritus and head of dept.; formerly surgeon ear, nose and throat, Ill. Eye and Ear Infirmary and St. Luke's Hosp. Surgeon Ill. Naval Reserve, 1896-1900; passed asst. surgeon, rank of lt., sr. grade, U.S. Navy, Spanish-Am. War, 1898; apptd. 1st lt. Med. R.C., Feb. 1911; capt., Apr. 9, 1917; maj., M.C., Aug. 11. 1917; served as chief Camp Grant, and chief surg. diseases of oto-laryngology, Base Hosp. No. 115, Vichy, France. Fellow Am. Coll. Surgeons, Chicago Acad., Medicine, Inst. of Medicine (Chicago); mem. A.M.A., Ill. State and Chicago med. socs., Am. Laryngol., Rhinol. and Otol. Soc. (pres., 1903-04), Am. Laryngol. Assn. (pres., 1919), Am. Otol. Soc., (pres., 1917-18; chmn. research com. on oto-sclerosis), Chicago Medico-Legal Soc., Chicago Laryngol. and Otol. Soc. (pres. 1900), Nat. Inst. of Social Sciences, Chicago Hist. Soc., Chicago Soc. Med. Hist. Republican. Clubs: University, City, Army and Navy. Author numerous essays in otolaryngology. Address: Del Mar, Calif.* Died Oct. 26, 1946.

PIERCE, PALMER EDDY army officer; b. Savanna, Ill., Oct. 23, 1865; s. Henry Clay and Laura (Shepherd) P.; student Grinnell (Ia.) Coll.; grad. U.S. Mil. Acad., 1891; honor grad. Army Srvice Sch., 1910; Army Staff Coll., 1911; m. Agnes Young, Dec. 3, 1891. Commd. 2d lt., June 12, 1891; 1st lt. 13th Inf., Mar. 23, 1898; capt. 8th Inf., Oct. 9, 1900; maj. 15th Inf., Mar. 28, 1912; lt. col., May 15, 1917; col. (temp.), Aug. 5, 1917; brig. gen. N.A., Dec. 17, 1917. Instr. chemistry, U.S. Mil. Acad., 1895-99; served in Puerto Rico, Spanish-Am. War, 1898; in Philippine Islands, 1899-1901; instr. and asst. prof. philosophy, U.S. Mil. Acad., 1901-07; instr. Army Service and Staff Sch., 1911-12; in China, 1912-14, Philippine Islands, 1914-15; apptd. mem. Gen. Staff, Feb. 16, 1916; was mem. Gen. Munitions Bd., War Industries Bd., Training Camps Athletic Commn., The War Council; arrived in France as comdr. 54th Inf. Brigade, May 1918; participated Ypres-Lys defense, Ypres-Lys offensive, Somme offensive, battles of Hindenburg line, La Selle River; returned to U.S., Mar. 1919; comdr. 151st Depot Brigade, Camp Devens, Mass., Apr.-June 1919. Awarded D.S.M. "for exceptionally meritorious and distinguished service"; Companion of the Bath (British). Conglist. Home: New York, N.Y. Died Jan. 17, 1940.

PIERCE, WILLIAM LEIGH army officer, Continental congressman; b. Ga., 1740; m. Charlotte Fenwick, circa 1783, 2 sons including William Leigh. Served as aide-de-camp to Gen. Nathanael Greene during Revolutionary War; presented with sword by Continental Congress for conduct at Battle of Eutaw Springs; left army as brevet maj., 1783; became head mcht. house William Pierce and Co.; mem. Continental Congress, 1787, concurrently mem. U.S. Constl. Conv. of 1787, wrote notes on proceedings; original mem., v.p. Soc. of Cincinnati; trustee Chatham County Acad. Died Savannah, Ga., Dec. 10, 1789.

PIERSON, J(OHN) FRED soldier; b. N.Y. City, Feb. 25, 1839; s. Henry L. and Helen Maria P.; seventh in descent from Abraham Pierson, 1st pres. of Yale; acad. edn.; m. S. Augusta Rhodes, Dec. 16, 1869. Enlisted, 1857, pvt. Co. K, 7th Regt. N.Y.N.G.; attached to staff Brig. Gen. William Hall; promoted through grades 1st N.Y. Vol. Inf. to col., Oct. 9, 1862; bvtd. brig. gen., Mar. 13, 1865, "for gallant and meritorious services"; was attached to Army of Potomac; fought in most battles of that army; wounded and horse killed at Glendale; shot through chest at Chancellorsville; taken prisoner at Bristol Sta.; confined in Libby Prison. Was pres. Ramapo Foundry & Wheel Works, Ramapo Mfg. Co., New York Stamping Co., Pierson & Co., Inc. Republican. Home: New York, N.Y. Died Dec. 20, 1932.

PIGGOTT, JAMES pioneer ofcl. in Ill.; b. Conn., circa 1739; married twice; m. 2d, Francies James; 8 children. Commd. capt. from Westmoreland County in Pa. Militia, served under Gen. Arthur St. Clair, 1776-77; had command of Ft. Jefferson, nr. mouth Ohio River, during seige of Chickasaw Indians, 1780; a leader against French in area, 1787, signed contract appointing Bartholomew Tardiveau as agt. to U.S. Congress; apptd. capt. Ill. Territorial Militia, also justice of peace at Cahokia, Ill., circa 1790; judge of common pleas Cahokia, 1795, judge of quarter sessions, 1796; proclaimed opening of Orphans' Ct.; started ferry service and bldgs. (nucleus of present-day East St. Louis), Ill. Died Kaskaskia, Ill., Feb. 20, 1799.

PIGMAN, GEORGE WOOD rear admiral U.S.N.; b. Delphi, Ind., Dec. 19, 1843; s. George W. and Caroline (Swarmstead) P.; apptd. to U.S.N., Sept. 28, 1861, Naval Acad., 1861-64; m. Lillie C. Howard, Nov. 7, 1871. Served on steam sloop Brooklyn, flagship Brazil Squadron, 1866-67; promoted master, Dec. 1, 1866; lt., Mar. 12, 1868; lt. comdr., Oct. 28, 1869; comdr., Oct. 12, 1886; capt., Mar. 3, 1899; rear admiral, Oct. 4, 1904. Served on various duties; comd. Alliance, 1888-89, Bennington, 1895-97, Wabash, 1901-04; retired, Jan. 11, 1905. Home: Takoma Park, Md. Died June 30, 1920.

PIKE, ALBERT lawyer; b. Boston, Dec. 29, 1809; s. Benjamin and Sarah (Andrews) P.; A.M. (hon.), Harvard, 1859; m. Mary Ann Hamilton, Oct. 10, 1834, 6 children. Tchr. various schs. in East; went to St. Louis, 1831; became fur trader; owner, editor Ark. Advocate, 1835; licensed to practice law, 1837; asst. clk. Ark. Territorial Legislature; 1st reporter Ark. Supreme Ct., work appears in 1st 5 vols. of Reports, 1840-45; admitted to practice before Ark. Supreme Ct., 1842; served in Mexican War; commr. to negotiate treaties with Indian tribes west of Ark., 1861; commd. brig. gen. Confederate Army with orders to recruit Indians, had troubles with his superiors, once arrested as being hostile to Confederate cause; Mason (sovereign grand comdr. Supreme Grand Council, So. Jurisdiction of U.S., 1859). Author: Morals and Dogma of the Ancient and Accepted Scottish Rite of Freemasonry (several edits.); Prose Sketches and Poems Written in the Western County, 1839. Died Washington, D.C., Apr. 2, 1891; buried Oak Hill Cemetery, Washington.

PIKE, CHARLES BURRALL capitalist; b. Chicago, Ill., June 29, 1871; s. Eugene S. and Mary (Rockwell) P.; A.B., Harvard, 1893, LL.B., 1896; m. Frances Alger, May 18, 1898. Admitted to Ill. bar, 1898, and began practice at Chicago; mem. firm Pike & Gade, 1899-1902; v.p. Western State Bank, 1901-02; pres. Hamilton Nat. Bank, Merchants Safe Deposit Co., 1903-10; mng. trustee Eugene S. Pike Estate Land Trust since 1917. Chief civilian aide to sec. of war, 1922-38; pres. Mil. Training Camps Assn., U.S. Army, 1922-38; mem. Chicago Hist. Soc. (1st v.p., 1924; pres. since 1927). Republican. Presbyterian. Clubs: Racquet (pres. 1924-29 and 1933-39), Chicago, Saddle Cycle, Old Elm, Shoreacres, Onwentsia. Home: 1100 Lake Shore Drive, Chicago; Lake Forest, Ill., and Bar Harbor, Me. Office: 6 N. Michigan Blvd., Chicago, Ill. Died Apr. 26, 1941.

PIKE, CLAYTON WARREN consulting elec. engr.; b. Fryeburg, Me., July 11, 1866; s. Cassius W. and Abbie J. (Barker) P.; ed. Fryeburg Acad.; Mass. Inst. Tech., 1886-89; m. Margaret E. Rattoo, June 30, 1909; children—Helen Margaret, John Clayton (dec.). Elec. engr., Merrimack Mfg. Co., Lowell, Mass., 1889-90; instr. elec. engring., U. of Pa., 1890-92; elec. engr., Queen Co., Inc., Phila., 1893-94, Falkenau Engring. Co., 1894-900; v.p. and gen. mgr. Keller-Pike Co., Phila., 1900-11; chief of Elec. Bur., Phila., 1912—; cons. engr. City of Pittsburgh, 1919, Pub. Improvement Commn., Baltimore, 1922, Phila. Rapid Transit Co., 1923—, Ambassador Bridge (Detroit to Can.), 1929, Public Service Commission of New Hampshire, 1930, State Tax Commn. of N.H., 1931, Power Authority State of N.Y., 1931. Mem. Park Commn., Fryeburg, Me., 1933. Trustee Fryeburg Acad. Republican. Author: Roper's Engineers' Handbook (joint author), 1899; Questions and Answers for Engineers, 1901. Commd. maj. Ordnance Dept. U.S.A., 1918; chief statis. sect., 1919. Home: Fryeburg, Me. Died Dec. 30, 1938.

PIKE, JAMES congressman, clergyman; b. Salisbury, Essex County, Mass., No. 10, 1818; studied theology Wesleyan U., Conn., 1837-39. A minister, 1841-54; moved to Pembroke, N.H., 1854; mem. U.S. Ho. of Reps. (Am. Party) from N.H., 34th-35th congresses, 1855-59; served as col. 16th Regt., N.H. Volunteer Inf., 1862-63; unsuccessful candidate for gov. N.H., 1871; became presiding elder Dover dist.; ret. from preaching, 1886. Died Newfields, N.H., July 26, 1895; buried Locust Cemetery.

PIKE, ROBERT colonial ofcl.; b. Whiteparish, Wiltshire, Eng., 1616; s. John and Dorothy (Daye) P.; m. Sarah Sanders, Apr. 3, 1641; m. 2d, Martha (Moyce) Goldwyer, Oct. 30, 1684; 8 children including John. Arrived in Boston, 1635; was part of colony which founded Salisbury (Mass.); took oath as freeman, 1637; elected to Gen. Ct. of Mass., 1648, reelected; served as maj. during Indian Wars; elected a magistrate, 1688-89; mem. Mass. Gov.'s Council, 1689-96; mem. group which bought Island of Nantucket from Thomas Mayhew, 1659; a leader in fight for civil and religious liberties. Died Dec. 12, 1708.

PIKE, ZEBULON MONTGOMERY explorer, army officer; b. Lamberton (now part of Trenton), N.J., Feb. 5, 1779; s. Zebulon and Isabella (Brown) P.; m. Clarissa Brown, Mar. 1801, several children. Commd. 1st lt., 1st Regt., U.S. Inf., 1799; led exploring party to mouth of Mississippi River; at head of company of 20 set out for St. Louis, Aug. 9, 1805; explored headwaters of Arkansas and Red Rivers, 1806, discovered Pike's Peak (named for him) in Colo.; commd. capt., 1806; explored South Park and head of Arkansas River; commd. maj., 1808, col. of inf., 1810; promoted brig. gen., 1813; killed in War of 1812. Died York (now Toronto), Can., Apr. 27, 1813.

PILCHER, JAMES EVELYN surgeon; b. Adrian, Mich., Mar. 18, 1857; s. Elijah Holmes (D.D., LL.D.) and Phebe Maria (Fisk) P.; A.B., U. of Mich., 1879; M.D., L.I. Coll. Hosp., 1880; A.M., Ph.D., Ill. Wesleyan U., 1887; L.H.D., Allegheny Coll., 1902; m. Mina Adela Parker, June 5, 1883. Asst. surgeon U.S.A., Dec. 3, 1883; capt. asst. surgeon, Dec. 3, 1888; maj. brigade surgeon U.S.V., June 4, 1898; retired, Oct. 31, 1900. Prof. mil. surgery, Ohio Med. U., 1896-98; lecturer on mil. hygiene, Starling Med. Coll., 1896; prof. mil. surgery, Creighton U., 1898-99; prof. anatomy and embryology, 1899-1900, sociology and economics, 1900-03, Dickinson Coll.; prof. med. jurisprudence, Dickinson Sch. of Law, 1899-1909. Mng. editor Annals Anatomy and Surgery, 1881-83, office editor Annals of Surgery, 1887-89; editor health dept. New York Christian Advocate, 1887-95; asso. editor Columbus Medical Journal, 1896-99; editor publs. Assn. Mil. Surgeons U.S., 1897-99 and 1901—. Enno Sander prize essayist, 1906; editor The Military Surgeon, 1901-09. Hon. mem. Am. Med. Editors' Assn. (pres. 1906);

fellow Am. Acad. Medicine. Author: First Aid in Illness and Injury, 1892; Life and Labors of Elijah Holmes Pilcher, 1893; Columbus Book of the Military Surgeons, 1897; The Arms and Seals of the State of Pennsylvania (State Doc.), 1902; The Surgeon Generals of the Army, 1905. Died 1911.

PILCHER, JAMES TAFT (pil'cher), surgeon; b. Brooklyn, N.Y., Mar. 31, 1880; s. Lewis Stephen and Martha S. (Phillips) P.; student New York U., 1898-1900; A.B., U. of Mich., 1902; M.D., Coll. Physicians and Surgeons, Columbia, 1904; studied univs. of Göttingen, Berlin and Vienna, 1907-08; m. Effie D. Curtis, June 30, 1909; children—Edith Mayo, Ruth Adelaide (dec.). Practiced in Brooklyn since 1904; founder and surgeon Pilcher Hosp.; cons. surgeon Eastern L.I. Hosp.; attending surgeon State Hosp. Commn. N.Y. Unity Hospital; visiting surgeon Peck Memorial; director urology, Downtown Hospital. Commd. maj. Med. Corps, 1st Cav., N.G.N.Y.; maj. comdg. Field Hosp. 108, World War, awarded D.S.O. and conspicuous service cross of N.Y. State, Am. Bd. of Surgery. Fellow Am. Coll. of Surgeons; mem. A.M.A., Med. Soc. State of N.Y., Kings County Med. Soc., Assn. Physicians L.I., Am. Gastro-Enterol. Assn., Mayo Clin. Soc., New York Surg. Soc., Brooklyn Surg. Soc., Pan-Am. Assn., Zeta Psi, Nu Sigma Nu. Theta Nu Epsilon. Republican. Episcopalian. Clubs: University, Brooklyn Cavalry, North Fork Country. Editor, Annals of Surgery. Home: 121 Gates Av., Brooklyn, N.Y. Died Apr. 4, 1947.

PILE, WILLIAM ANDERSON congressman, gov. N.M.; b. nr. Indpls., Feb. 11, 1829; studied theology. Ordained to ministry Methodist Episcopal Ch., became mem. Mo. Conf.; commd. chaplain 1st Regt., Mo. Light Arty., U.S. Army, 1861; promoted lt. col. 33d Regt., Mo. Inf., 1862, then col., 1862; commd. brig. gen. Volunteers, 1863; brevetted maj. gen., 1865; mem. U.S. Ho. of Reps. (Republican) from Mo., 40th Congress, 1867-69; gov. N.M., 1869-70; minister resident to Venezuela, 1871-74. Died Monrovia, Cal., July 7, 1889; buried Live Oak Cemetery.

PILLOW, GIDEON JOHNSON army officer; b. Williamson County, Tenn., June 8, 1806; s. Gideon and Anne (Payne) P.; grad. U. Nashville, 1827; m. Mary Martin, 10 children. Admitted to Tenn. bar; practiced in partnership with James K. Polk in Columbia, Tenn.; apptd. brig. gen. U.S. Volunteers, 1846, promoted maj. gen. due to friendship of Pres. Polk, 1846; served at battles of Vera Cruz, Cerro Gordo, Contreras and Chapultpec; mem. So. Conv., Nashville, 1850; apptd. sr. maj. gen. Provisional Army of Tenn., later brig. gen. Confederate Army, 1861; served at Battle of Belmont (Mo.), 1861; practiced law in partnership with Isham G. Harris, Memphis, Tenn., after 1865. Died Helena, Ark., Oct. 8, 1878.

PILLSBURY, GEORGE BIGELOW, army engr.; b. Lowell, Mass., Dec. 19, 1876; s. George Harlin and Mary Augusta (Boyden) P.; student Mass. Inst. Tech., 1894-96; grad. U.S. Mil. Acad., 1900; m. Bertha Eldredge Smith, June 22, 1909; children—George Harlin, Elizabeth Eldredge (Mrs. William B. Pringle, Jr.), Philip Lansdale, Thomas Sidney. Commd. 2d lt. Engr. Corps, U.S. Army, June 13, 1900, and advanced through grades to col., Nov. 30, 1928; engr. Alaska Rd. Commn., 1904-08; asso. prof. mathematics, U.S. Mil. Acad., 1908-12; dist. engr., New London (Conn.) Dist., 1912-16, Los Angeles (Calif.) Dist., 1916-17; comdr. 115th Engrs., 1917-18, 102d Engrs., 1918; corps engr., 2d Corps, A.E.F., 1918-19; mem. joint bd. of engrs., St. Lawrence Waterway, 1923-26; dist. engr., Phila. Dist., 1928-30; asst. to chief of engrs. U.S. Army, with rank of brig. gen., June 27, 1930, to Dec. 31, 1937; retired from active service, on own request. Awarded Distinguished Service Medal (U.S.). Clubs: Rittenhouse (Philadelphia); Bohemian (San Francisco). Home: Ross CA

PILLSBURY, HENRY CHURCH ret. army officer; b. Lowell, Mass., May 27, 1881; s. George Harlan and Mary (Boyden) P.; A.B., Dartmouth, 1902; M.D., Harvard, 1906; attended Army Med. Sch., 1906-07; m. Janet Wood, June 5, 1912 (dec.). Commd. 1st lt. M.C., U.S. Army, 1907, advanced through grades to brig. gen., 1941; div. surgeon, 11th Div., 1918-19; prof. roentgenology Army Med. Sch., 1919-25; chief health officer Panama Canal, 1936-39; surgeon 3d Corp Area, 1940; comdg. officer Lovell Gen. Hosp., Ft. Devens, Mass., 1941; comdg. officer Thayer Gen. Hosp., Nashville, 1943-45, retired. Fellow A.C.S., A.C.P.; mem. A.M.A., Soc. Tropical Medicine Episcopalian. Mason. Club: Army and Navy (Washington, D.C.). Author: U.S. Army X-Ray Manual, 1933. Home: Ross, Cal. Died July 18, 1955.

PILLSBURY, JOHN ELLIOTT rear admiral U.S.N.; b. Lowell, Mass., Dec. 15, 1846; s. John Gilman and Elizabeth (Wimble) P.; grad. U.S. Naval Acad., 1867; m. Florence Greenwood Aitchison, 1873. Promoted through grades to rear admiral, July 4, 1908. Served on various duties and stas., including 1 yr. in Hydrographic Office and 10 yrs. in coast survey service; comd. Coast Survey Steamer Blake, 1884-91, investigating Gulf Stream currents by anchoring the Blake in the Stream and observing the current (by means of an instrument of his invention) at various depths below surface; established position of axis of the stream in Straits of Florida and off Cape Hatteras and determined many of the laws by which its flow is governed; comd. dynamite cruiser Vesuvius off Santiago during Spanish-Am. War; afterward stationed at Boston Navy Yard, in charge of the equipment dept.; comd. U.S.S. Prairie, 1901-02; afterward on duty in Washington as mem. Gen. Bd. and asst. to chief of Bur. of Navigation, and in 1905 chief of staff North Atlantic Fleet; chief Bur. Navigation, 1908-09; retired, Dec. 15, 1898; relieved from active duty, July 1909. Died Dec. 30, 1919.

PINCKNEY, CHARLES COTESWORTH diplomat, army officer; b. Charlestown (now Charleston), S.C., Feb. 25, 1746; s. Charles and Elizabeth (Lucas) P.; matriculated at Christ Ch. Coll., 1764; m. Sarah Middleton, Sept. 28, 1773; m. 2d, Mary Stead, June 23, 1786; 3 children. Admitted to Middle Temple, 1764, English bar, 1769, S.C. bar, 1770; mem. S.C. Provincial Assembly, 1769, 75; acting atty. gen. for Camden, Georgetown and the Cherows, 1773; mem. lower house S.C. Legislature, 1778, 82; pres. S.C. Senate, 1779; ranking capt. 1st Regt., S.C. Militia, 1775, apptd. col., 1776; aide to George Washington, served at battles of Germantown and Brandywine, 1777; commanded his regt. at seige of Savannah, commanded Ft. Moultrie at attacks on Charlestown; taken prisoner by British when Charlestown fell, exchanged, 1782; apptd. brig. gen. Continental Army, 1783; del. U.S. Constl. Conv., 1787; mem. S.C. Conv. to ratify U.S. Constn., 1788; mem. S.C. Constl. Conv., 1790; apptd. U.S. minister to France, 1796 (French Directory refused to recognize his status due to reaction over Jay Treaty), left Paris for Amsterdam (Holland); apptd. rep. of Am. (with John Marshall, Elbridge Gerry) to France to negotiate situation (series of letters between Talleyrand's ministers and the 3 Americans precipitated the XYZ affair); left Paris, 1798, apptd. (by Washington) comdr. all forces and posts South of Md.; Federalist candidate for U.S. Pres., 1800, 04; 1st pres. Charleston Bible Soc., 1810. Died Charleston, Aug. 16, 1825.

PINCKNEY, THOMAS gov. S.C., diplomat; b. Charleston, S.C., Oct. 23, 1750; s. Charles and Elizabeth (Lucas) P.; grad. Oxford (Eng.) U.; studied Middle Temple, London, Eng., 1768; m. Elizabeth Motte, July 22, 1779; m. 2d, Frances Motte, Oct. 19, 1797; 4 children. Admitted to English bar, 1774, S.C. bar, 1774; served as capt. 1st Regt., S.C. Militia, 1775, promoted maj., 1778; mil. aide to Count d'Estaing at Savannah, Ga.; served under marquis de Lafayette at Yorktown; gov. S.C., 1787-88; pres. S.C. Conv. to ratify U.S. Constn., 1788; mem. lower house S.C. Legislature, 1791; U.S. minister to Eng., 1791-95; spl. commr. to Spain, 1795, determined So. boundary of U.S. and navigational arrangements for Mississippi River in Treaty of San Lorenzo el Real (Pinckney Treaty), 1795; unsuccessful Federalist Party candidate for vice pres. U.S., 1796; mem. U.S. Ho. of Reps. from S.C., 5th-6th congresses, 1797-1801; maj. gen. U.S. Volunteers in command of dist. extending from N.C. to Mississippi River, 1812; negotiated Treaty of Ft. Jackson with Creek Indian Nation ending the Creek War, 1814. Died Charleston, Nov. 2, 1828; buried St. Philip's Churchyard, Charleston.

PINE, DAVID ANDREW, judge; b. Washington, D.C., Sept. 22, 1891; s. David Emory and Charlotte (McCormick) P.; LL.B., Georgetown University, 1913; honorary Doctor of Laws, 1954; graduate work at Georgetown U., 1913-14; m. Elizabeth Bradshaw, Aug. 23, 1916 (dec.); 1 dau., Elizabeth Pine Dayton; m. 2d, Elenore E. Townsend, July 8, 1959. Admitted to D.C. bar, 1913; with Dept. of Justice as confidential clerk to United States attorney general, 1914-16, law clerk, 1916-17, asst. attorney, 1919; special assistant to United States atty. gen. in Western States, 1919-21; private practive of law, Washington, D.C., 1921-34; mem. of firm of Easby-Smith, Pine & Hill, 1925-29; chief asst. U.S. atty., Dist. of Columbia, 1934-37; U.S. atty. for D.C., 1938-40; judge U.S. Dist. Ct. for D.C., 1940-70, chief judge, 1959-61, sr. judge, 1965. Served as 1st lt., later capt. inf., assigned to Provost Marshal Gen., World War I. Mem. Am. Bar Assn., Bar Assn. D.C. Democrat. Episcopalian. Clubs: Lawyers (past pres.), Barristers (past pres.); Metropolitan (Washington); Chevy Chase (Md.). Home: Washington DC Died June 11, 1970.

PINE, JAMES ret. Coast Guard officer; b. Cin., O., Oct. 19, 1885; s. James Arthur Washington and Mary (Hattersley) P.; grad. U.S. Coast Guard Acad., Dr. Eng. (hon.), Rensselaer P.I., 1946; m. Ysabel Cooper, 1911; children—Barbara Alice (wife of Comdr. Lawson P. Ramage, U.S.N.), James Francis (dec.), Robert Beekman, Joan. Commd. ensign, 1908; advanced through grades; retired as vice adm. 1947, after 41 years service on Atlantic, Pacific, Great Lakes and Arctic ocean; in command U.S.S. May and U.S.S. Zeelandia during first World War; in command Div. III, destroyer force, and as force gunnery officer; chief ordnance and gunnery section, Hdqrs., member general board and special asst. to The Commandant, Coast Guard; supt. Academy, 1940-47. Decorated: Victory medal (patrol clasp), Congressional gold life saving medal of honor, Legion of Merit, Danish Order of Danneborg, 1st cl., American Defense (sea clasp), American Theatre, Victory, World War II. Mem. Naval Inst., Newcomen Soc. of England. Clubs: University (New York) (hon.); Ariston (New London). Author: The Place of the Coast Guard in the Government; Procurement and Education of Coast Guard Officers, The Sea and Its Lore; and service pamphlets. Home: South Harwich, Mass. Address: care U.S. Coast Guard Hdqrs., Washington. Died Feb. 21, 1953; buried Arlington Nat. Cemetery.

PINGREE, SAMUEL EVERETT governor; b. Salisbury, N.H., Aug. 2, 1832; s. Stephen and Judith (True) P.; A.B., Dartmouth Coll., 1857, A.M., 1867 (LL.D., Norwich University); m. Lydia M. Steele, of Stanstead, Que., Sept. 15, 1869. Pvt. Co. F, 3d Vt. Vols., 1861; 1st lt., 1861; capt., Aug. 1861; maj., Sept. 27, 1862; lt. col., Jan. 15, 1863; awarded Congressional Medal of Honor, "for gallantry at Lee's Mills, Va." (wounded). Admitted to bar, 1859, and began practice at Hartford, Vt. State's atty. Windsor Co., 1868-69; lt. gov. of Vt., 1882-84, gov., 1884-86; chmn. State Ry. Commn., 1886-94. Home: Hartford, Vt. Died June 1, 1922.

PINKERTON, ALLAN detective; b. Glasgow, Scotland, Aug. 25, 1819; son of William Pinkerton; m. Joan Carfrae, 1842, at least 2 children. Apprenticed to cooper, Glasgow, 1831-39; came to U.S., 1842; cooper, Dundee, Ill., 1842-50; dep. sheriff Kane County, Ill., 1846; operated sta. of Underground R.R. at his home; 1st detective Chgo. police force, 1850-51; established Pinkerton Detective Agy., Chgo. (one of 1st pvt. detective agys. in U.S.), 1850; established Pinkerton's Preventive Watch (one of 1st corps of night-watchmen in U.S.), 1860; discovered and squelched plan to assassinate Pres. Lincoln, 1861; organized 1st secret service div. of U.S. Army, 1861; toured Tenn., Ga., Miss. as a spy, 1861; 1st chief U.S. Secret Service, 1861-62; head secret service Dept. of Gulf, 1862-65; worked under name Maj. E. J. Allen during Civil War; important cases solved include $40,000 robbery of Bank of Carbondale, Pa., 1866, $700,000 train robbery of Adams Express Co., 1866, $300,000 robbery of express car on Hudson River R.R. Author: 15 books narrating his experiences including: The Molly Maguires and the Detectives, 1877; Criminal Reminiscences, 1878; The Spy of the Rebellion, 1883; Thirty Years a Detective, 1884. Died July 1, 1884.

PINKERTON, WILLIAM ALLAN principal of Pinkerton's Nat. Detective Agency; b. Dundee, Ill., Apr. 7, 1846; s. Allan P. (noted detective) and Joan (Carfrae) P.; ed. pub. and pvt. schs., and Notre Dame Coll.; entered secret service div. U.S. Army, 1861; m. Margaret S. Ashling, Dec. 14, 1866 (died 1895). Served through Civil War, chiefly in Army of Potomac; became clerk in his father's office; later with his brother, chief asst. in the agency, succeeding to the business on death of Allan Pinkerton, July 1, 1884; operations extended to all parts of the world. Home: Chicago, Ill. Died Dec. 11, 1923.

PINKNEY, NINIAN naval surgeon; b. Annapolis, Md., June 7, 1811; s. Ninian Hobbs and Amelia (Grason) P.; grad. St. John's Coll., Annapolis, 1830, LL.D. (hon.), 1873; M.D., Jefferson Med. Coll., 1833; m. Mary Sherwood Hambleton, 1 dau., Amelia. Commd. asst. surgeon U.S. Navy, 1834; served in S.Am. and Mediterranean; stationed Phila. Naval Hosp., 1838-39; promoted surgeon, 1841; served at Callao, Peru, 1841-44; on blockade duty during Mexican War; apptd. instr. U.S. Naval Acad., 1852; fleet surgeon Miss. Squadron, 1863-65; established naval hosp., Memphis, Tenn., 1863 (named Pinkney Hosp. in his honor); apptd. med. dir. with rank of commodore, 1871; retired 1873. Died Easton, Md., Dec. 15, 1877.

PINTO, ALVA SHERMAN (pin'to), surgeon; b. Chillicothe, O., May 29, 1872; s. Augustus Miles and Margaret (Reed) P.; grad. Omaha Commercial Coll., 1893; M.D., Creighton U., 1898; m. Mabel B. Spalding, Dec. 10, 1903; children—Sherman Spalding, Harvey Elmore. Enlisted as pvt. U.S. Vols., 1898, serving in Cuba and the Philippines, resigned as capt. Med. Dept., Feb. 1903; returned to Army as maj. Med. Dept., Aug. 7, 1918; served in France till July 1919; promoted lt. col.; comdg. officer Camp Hosp. No. 48, at Recey sur Orce; hon. discharged July 23, 1919; apptd. col. Med. Reserve Corps, U.S. Army, 1931. Health commr. of Omaha since 1921. Volunteered as one of first 3 to be bitten by infected mosquito, at Havana, Cuba, July 1900, proving the manner of infection of yellow fever. Mem. Am., Neb. State and Douglas County med. socs. Republican. Methodist. Mason. Elk. Clubs: Athletic, Prettiest Mile Country. Home: 6532 Florence Blvd. Office: First National Bank, Omaha, Neb.* Died Dec. 7, 1944.

PIPER, ALEXANDER ROSS railroad exec.; b. Fort Wadsworth, S.I., N.Y., Mar. 1, 1865; s. Capt. James Wilson and Sarah Van Dyke (Ross) P.; B.S., U.S. Mil. Acad., 1889; m. Marie Susan Cozzens, June 24, 1890 (dec.); children—Marie Adelaide (Mrs. Frank Richardson Oates), Alexander Stanley (dec.), Marjorie Wheaton (widow of Herman Siefke), Anne Alexandra (wife of Rev. Hollis Samuel Smith) (dec.), Emily Cozzens (Mrs. Philip Keep Reynolds), Alexander; m. 2d, Ruth Evelyn Fitch. Began as 2d lt., inf., U.S. Army, 1889; participated in Sioux campaign, 1890-91 capt. C.S. of V. in Porto Rican expedition, 1898, ret. as capt., 1899; recalled to active service, 1917; lt. col., later col., Q.M.C.N.A.; depot Q.M., N.Y.C. and port supply officer N.Y.C. and Newport News, Va.; utilities officer,

Port of Embarkation, N.Y., 1918-19, World War; relieved active duty, 1919; col. Q.M. Res. 1922, now ret. Dep. police commr. N.Y., 1902-03, established Block Control System of Traffic; gen. supt. Am. Ry. Traffic Co., 1904-08; gen. freight agt. S. Bklyn. Ry. Co., 1908-16, pres., 1916-40, ret., 1940; asst. gen. mgr. Bklyn. Rapid Transit Co., 1919-24; in charge Med. and Welfare Bur., Bklyn.-Manhattan Transit Corp., 1923-40, ret. 1940; dir. Technicolor, Inc., 1932-34. Pres. Assn. of Grads. U.S. Mil. Acad., 1934-36; trustee Eno Foundation. Awarded Silver Star Citation (U.S.), 1898. Mem. West Point Soc. of N.Y., Order of Indian Wars, S.R., Soc. of Colonial Wars. Republican. Episcopalian. Clubs: University (New York), Farmington Country (Va.). Home: South Salem, N.Y. Died Nov. 22, 1952; buried West Point (N.Y.). Cemetery.

PIPER, HORACE L. asst. general supt. U.S. Life Saving Service since June, 1890; b. Limerick, Me., 1842; entered Bowdoin, 1860; was not graduated; entered U.S. army; served to 1865; was bvt. maj. U.S. vols., and received a medal of honor from Congress. Grad. Columbian Law School, Washington, 1868; sent to Europe as U.S. commr. of immigration, 1873; later, clerk U.S. Treasury Dept.; m. Oct. 18, 1862, Tryphena S. Gove. Residence: 1505 L St. N.W., Washington.

PIPER, WILLIAM congressman; b. Bloody Run (now Everett), Bedford County, Pa., Jan. 1, 1774. Commanded a regt. during War of 1812; adj. gen. Pa., after the war; mem. U.S. Ho. of Reps. from Pa., 12th-14th congresses, 1811-17. Died nr. Everett, 1852; buried Piper Cemetery on his farm nr. Everett.

PIPER, WILLIAM THOMAS, airplane manufacturer; b. Knapps Creek, N.Y., Jan. 8, 1881; s. Thomas and Sarah (Maltby) P.; B.S., Harvard Univ., 1903; m. Marie Vandewater, July 30, 1910 (dec.); children—William Thomas, Jr., Mary Vandewater (Mrs. John Savage Bolles), Thomas Francis, Howard, Elizabeth Maltby (Mrs. Thomas Hartford); m. 2d, Clara S. Taber, Dec. 22, 1943. Employed as construction supt., 1903-14; oil producer, Bradford, Pa., since 1914; pres. and dir. Piper Aircraft Corp., mfg. airplanes, 1929-70; mem. firm Dallas Oil Company. Served as private Pennsylvania Volunteer Inf., 1898; capt., engrs., U.S. Army, 1918-19. Mem. Pa. C. of C. (dir.). Republican. Rotarian. Home: Lock Haven PA Died Jan. 1970.

PIRCE, WILLIAM ALMY congressman; b. Hope, Providence County, R.I., Feb. 29, 1824; attended Smithville Sem. (now Lapham Inst.). Became a school tchr.; mgr. of store and counting room of his father's cotton mill, Simmons Upper Village, R.I., 10 years; mfr. of cotton goods, 1854-63; mem. R.I. Senate, 1855, 82; mem. R.I. Ho. of Reps., 1858, 62, 79-81; assessor internal revenue for 2d Dist. R.I., 1862-73; apptd. paymaster with rank of maj. R.I. Militia, 1863; chmn. R.I. delegation to Republican Nat. Conv., Chgo., 1880; mem. Rep. Nat. Com., 1880, 84; mem. U.S. Ho. of Reps. (Rep.) from R.I., 49th Congress, 1885-Jan. 25, 1887; justice of peace, assessor of taxes, Johnston, R.I. Died Johnston, Mar. 5, 1891; buried Swan Point Cemetery, Providence, R.I.

PITCAIRN, JOHN army officer; b. Dysart, Scotland, 1722; s. David and Katherine (Hamilton) P.; m. Elizabeth Dalrymple, several children including Robert, David. Commd. capt. Royal Marines, 1756, promoted maj., 1771; came to Am., 1774; stationed at Boston; with detachment ordered to destroy rebel stores, Concord, Mass., 1775; in command of advance forces which fought battle with minutemen on Lexington Common, 1775; insisted that Americans fired first; mortally wounded in Battle of Bunker Hill. Died Boston, June 1775; buried Christ Ch., Boston; reinterred Ch. of St. Bartholomew the Less, London, Eng.

PITKIN, FRANCIS ALEXANDER, planning cons.; former state ofcl., b. Akron, O., June 2,21899; s. Stephen Henderson and Bessie Hamilton (Alexander) P.; B.S. in M.E., Case Inst. Tech., 1922; m. Ruth Elizabeth Mason, Mar. 17, 1928; 1 son, Stephen Henderson. Asso. with several engring. cos., Pitts. and Phila., 1923-30; chief engr. and constrn. supt. water supply and sewage system devel., 1930-34; mem. staff Nat. Resources Com., loaned to Pa. to assist in establishment state planning activities, 1934-35; asst. dir. Pa. State Planning Bd., 1934, exec. dir., 1936-55, 59-64; dir. community devel. Pa. Dept. Commerce, 1955-59; adminstr. Pa. Housing and Redevel. Program, 1949-59; chmn. Interstate Commn. on Delaware River, 1948-62; mem. exec. com. Gt. Lakes Commn., 1956-69, chmn. Pa. delegation, 1961-69; 1st chmn. Interstate Conf. on Water Problems, 1958-60; sec.-treas. Pa. Planning Assn.; mem. various tech. coms. Interstate Commn. on Potomac River Basin, Interstate Com. Postwar Reconstrn. and Devel. Council State Govts., 1943-44; mem. bd. Pa. Roadside Council, Pa. Forestry Assn. (past v.p., dir.); chmn. Pa. Pub. Service Inst. Bd., 1951-61, sec. Pa. Recreation Council, 1952-55; past v.p., bd. Harrisburg Symphony Soc.; nat. dir. Nat. Rivers and Harbors Congress, 1949-69, mem. exec. com., 1961-69; mem. adv. bd. Harrisburg Hosp.; trustee Harrisburg Pub. Library, pres. bd., 1948-62. Served in heavy arty. Officers Tng. Sch., Ft. Monroe, Va., World War I; served in USCGR, World War II. Recipient silver medal meritorious award Am. Soc. Planning Ofcls., 1961; Breidenthal Distinguished Service medal Nat. Rivers and Harbors Congress, 1964; Distinguished Service award Am. Inst. Planners, 1964. Mem. Am. Soc. Planning Ofcls. (pres. 1953-54), Nat. Assn. State Planning and Devel. Agys. (past pres.), Am. Inst. Planners, Am. Planning and Civic Assn., Pa. Soc. of N.Y., Engrs. Soc. Pa., Phi Delta Theta. Methodist (chmn. ch. bldg. com., past pres. bd. trustees, past pres. ofcl. bd.). Clubs: Eclectic, Torch (past pres.). Author articles in field. Contbg. editor Planning and Civic Comment. Lectr., cons. state, regional and community planning. Address: Camp Hill PA Died May 27, 1969.

PITKIN, WILLIAM colonial gov., jurist; b. Hartford, Conn., Apr. 30, 1694; s. William and Elizabeth (Stanley) P.; m. Mary Woodbridge, May 7, 1724. Rate collector Hartford, 1715; capt. train band, 1730; del. Conn. Assembly, 1732-34; commr. to treat with Indians; judge Hartford County Ct., 1735-52; served as maj., then col. 1st Conn. Regt., 1739; judge Conn. Superior Ct., 1741, chief judge, 1742-54; dep. gov. Conn., 1754-66, gov., 1766-69. Died Conn., Oct. 1, 1769.

PITKIN, WILLIAM jurist, mfr.; b. Hartford, Conn., 1725; s. William and Mary (Woodbridge) P.; m. Abigail Church. Owner various power sites and mills; commd. capt. 3d Militia Co. of Hartford, 1756; became maj.-comdr. 1st Regt. Conn. Militia, 1758, lt. col., 1762; asst. to Conn. Gov.'s Council, 1766-85; mem. Council of Safety during Am. Revolution; elected to U.S. Congress, 1784, but did not serve; del. from East Hartford to Conn. Conv. to ratify U.S. Constn.; judge Superior Ct., 1769-89, chief justice, 1788-89. Died Hartford, Dec. 12, 1789.

PITMAN, JOHN brig. gen. U.S.A.; b. Providence, R.I., Nov. 12, 1842; s. John T. and Caroline (Richmond) P.; grad. U.S. Mil. Acad., 1867; m. Miss L. E. Plympton, Sept. 15, 1868; m. 2d, Anne C. de Mille, Aug. 14, 1903. Enlisted as pvt. Co. G, 1st R.I. Inf., July 18, 1861; discharged, Aug. 2, 1861; pvt. Co. D, 10th R.I. Inf., May 26, 1862; disch. Aug. 30, 1862; sergt. maj. 11th R.I. Inf., Sept. 22, 1862; discharged and commd. 2d lt. 11th R.I. Inf., Apr. 14, 1863; hon. mustered out, July 13, 1863; apptd. U.S. Mil. Acad., Sept. 29, 1863; commd. 2d lt. ordnance, June 17, 1867; 1st lt., June 23, 1874; capt., May 27, 1878; maj., Sept. 2, 1894; lt. col., Feb. 17, 1903; col., Jan. 21, 1904; retired and advanced to rank of brig. gen., Nov. 12, 1906, under act of Apr. 23, 1904. Served at various arsenals, ordnance depots, foundry duty, Cold Spring, N.Y., and instr. chemistry, U.S. Mil. Acad. Home: Orange, N.J. Died Aug. 29, 1933.

PITNEY, SHELTON lawyer; b. Morristown, N.J., Mar. 29, 1893; s. Mahlon and Florence T. (Shelton) P.; grad. Hill School, Pottstown, Pa., 1910; A.B., Princeton, 1914; LL.B., Harvard, 1917; m. Etta Carrington Brown, May 14, 1918; children—Shelton, Mary Foster, James Carrington. Admitted to N.Y. bar, 1920, N.J. bar, as atty., 1921, as counsellor, 1924; in practice since Mar. 1, 1919; mem. Pitney, Hardin & Ward since 1922; trustee Central R.R. Co. of N.J. since 1939; director Morristown Trust Co., director of New York, Long Branch R.R. Co. Served in U.S. Army, 1917-19; capt. 313th F.A., 80th Div., Sept. 1917-Feb. 1919; with A.E.F. in St. Mihiel and Argonne, wounded Oct. 2, 1918. Mem. Am. Bar Assn., N.J. Bar Assn., Essex County Bar Assn., Morris County Bar Assn. Republican. Presbyterian. Clubs: Essex, Down Town (Newark); Morris County Golf, Morristown (Morristown, N.J.); Edgartown Yacht (Edgartown, Mass.); Cap and Gown (Princeton). Railroad, Machinery Club (New York City). Home: Morristown, N.J. Office: 744 Broad St., Newark, N.J. Died Jan. 13, 1946.

PITTS, LLEWELLYN WILLIAM, architect; b. Uniontown, Ala., Sept. 10, 1906; s. William Llewellyn and Mattie (Harwood) P.; B.S., Ga. Inst. Tech., 1927; m. Garnette Northcott, June 5, 1935; 1 dau., Sally (Mrs. James M. Stokes). With Robert & Company and Felch & Southwell, architects, Atlanta, Georgia, 1927-30; member of firm Stone & Pitts, architects and engrs., Beaumont, Tex., 1930-57; sr. partner Pitts, Mebane & Phelps, architects and engrs., Beaumont, 1957-64, Pitts, Mebane, Phelps and White, 1964-67; principal works include 19 Coca-Cola bottling plants (first honor award indsl. architecture Houston plant, A.I.A. 1951), 1940-60, master plan and 35 bldgs. Lamar State Coll. Tech., Beaumont (medal of honor S.E. Tex. chpt. A.I.A. 1955), numerous bldgs. for Gulf Oil Co., Port Arthur, Tex., 1952-60, Socony Mobil Oil Co. bldgs., Beaumont, 1952, Shell Oil Lab., New Orleans, 1958, library bldg. Tex. Tech. Coll., Lubbock, 1960, Texaco Research Center, Port Arthur, 1960, also university buildings, schools and hosps. in Texas; co-designer State Office Bldg., 1957, Tex. Employment Commn. Bldg. (both Austin), 1958, U.S. Embassy Office Building, Mexico City, 1959, Labor Dept. Building, Washington; consultant Beaumont Planning Commn., 1953; chmn. archtl. adv. com. Tex. Bldg. Commission, 1958-61. Member of board of directors First Security National Bank (Beaumont, Texas). A.I.A. del. to Union Internat. Architects, 1963. Gen. chmn. Beaumont United Appeals fund campaign, 1954. Served to lt. comdr. USNR, 1942-45. Fellow A.I.A. (nominating committee 1961; member nat. bd. dirs. 1963-66, chmn. com. on future of the profession 1966-67); member of the Texas Soc. Architects (pres. 1961), Sociedad de Arquitectos Mexicanos (hon.), Alpha Tau Omega, Phi Kappa Phi, Tau Beta Pi, Pi Delta Epsilon. Episcopalian. Clubs: Beaumont Country (pres. 1953), Rotary (pres. 1956), Round Table (pres. 1952), Beaumont Downtown (Beaumont); The Citadel, Headliners (Austin, Tex.). Home: Beaumont TX Died June 23, 1967; buried Magnolia Cemetery, Beaumont TX

PIXLEY, HENRY DAVID ins. co. exec.; b. Utica, N.Y., Apr. 2, 1892; s. George W. and Elizabeth (Mase) P.; grad. Hotchkiss Prep. Sch., 1912; B.S., Yale, 1915; m. Angele Jova, Nov. 20, 1924; children—George W., Francois V., Marie Vatable, David Mase. With Commercial Travelers Mut. Accident Assn., Utica, N.Y., 1936-—, dir., 1936-52, pres., 1952-—. Exec. com. Utica chpt. A.R.C., 1920-45. Served as lt. Gen. Staff, 27th Div., U.S. Army, 1918; maj. 6th Regt., N.Y. N.G., 1945. Mem. Mil. Order World Wars (past chpt. comdr.), Oneida Hist. Soc. (counsellor). Clubs: Sadaquade Golf (Whitesboro, N.Y.); Yale of Central N.Y. (past sec.-treas.). Home: 131 Paris Rd., New Hartford, N.Y. Office: 70 Genesee St., Utica, N.Y. Died Dec. 12, 1960.

PLAISTED, HARRIS MERRILL gov. Me., congressman; b. Jefferson, N.H., Nov. 2, 1828; s. William and Nancy (Merrill) P.; grad. Waterville (now Colby) Coll., 1853, Albany (N.Y.) Law Sch., 1855; m. Sarah Mason, Sept. 21, 1858; m. 2d, Mabel Hill, Sept. 27, 1881; 4 children. Supt. schs., Waterville, Me., 1850-53; admitted to Me. bar, 1856; apptd. by Gov. Washburn to raise mil. co. in Bangor for U.S. Army; became lt. col. 11th Me. Regt., 1861, promoted col., 1862; brevetted brig. gen. Me. Volunteers, 1865, maj. gen., 1865; mem. Me. Legislature, 1867-68; del. at large Republican Nat. Conv., 1868; elected atty. gen. Me., 1873; mem. U.S. Ho. of Reps. (Rep.) from Me., 44th Congress, 1875-76; gov. Me., 1880-82; editor The New Age, 1883-98; supporter of William Jennings Bryan. Died Bangor, Me., Jan. 31, 1898; buried Mt. Hope Cemetery, Bangor.

PLATER, THOMAS congressman, lawyer; b. Annapolis, Md., May 9, 1769; son of George Plater; attended Coll. William and Mary, Williamsburg, Va.; studied law. Admitted to bar, practiced law; served as lt. col. Md. Militia during Whisky Insurrection, 1794; held several local offices; mem. U.S. Ho. of Reps. from Md., 7th-8th congresses, 1801-05. Died Poolesville, Montgomery County, Md., May 1, 1830.

PLATT, JOHN engineer; b. Gloucester, Eng., June 1, 1864; s. James and Elizabeth (Waddington) P.; engring. student Univ. Coll., London, 1886-87; m. Mary Bourne Bartlett, 1891; children—Hilda (Mrs. Wilfred H. Wolfs), John, Robert, Hugh. Came to U.S., 1888; introduced marine steam turbine into U.S. Navy and Merchant Marine. Mem. Am. Soc. M.E., Soc. Naval Architects and Marine Engrs., Instn. Civ. Engrs. (Eng.). Clubs: Engineers (New York); Army and Navy (Washington, D.C.); St. Stephen's (London). Collector early Chinese and Korean pottery. Home: 532 Woodland Av., Westfield, N.J. Died Apr. 27, 1942.

PLATT, ROBERT SWANTON geographer; b. Columbus, O., Dec. 4, 1891; s. Rutherford H. and Maryette A. (Smith) P.; student St. George's Sch., Newport, R.I., 1906-09, Hotchkiss Sch., Lakeville, Conn., 1909-10; A.B., Yale, 1914; Ph.D., U. Chgo., 1920; m. Harriet Shanks, Dec. 30, 1922; children—Robert Swanton, Nancy Field (Mrs. R. C. Rayfield). Instr., Yale-in-China, 1914-15; instr. geog. U. Chgo., 1919-22, asst. prof., 1922-28, asso. prof. 1928-39, prof. since 1939, chmn. dept. geography since 1949; adviser Office of Geographer, U.S. Dept. State, 1943. Chief, Div. of Maps, Library Congress, 1944-45. Adviser, Conselho Nacional de Geographia, 1947. Served as capt. 82d Inf., U.S. Army, W.W. I. Mem. NRC, 1936-39; mem. Assn. Am. Geographers (treas. 1929-34, v.p. 1943, pres. 1945), Sigma Xi, Phi Beta Kappa, Gamma Alpha, Zeta Psi. Episcopalian. Clubs: University (Chgo.); Explorers (N.Y.C.); Cosmos (Washington). Author: Latin America, Countrysides and United Regions, 1942. Home: 10820 Drew St., Chgo. 60643. Died Mar. 1964.

PLEADWELL, FRANK LESTER (pleed-'wel), medical officer U.S. Navy, ret.; b. Taunton, Mass., Aug. 9, 1872; s. Wm. Henry and Kate Sophia (Bradley) P. M.D., cum laude, Harvard, 1896; grad. Naval War Coll., 1920; m. 2d, Laura Mell Stith, 1931; 1 dau., Theodora Hunt (by first marriage). Asst. surgeon U.S. Navy, 1896; promoted through grades to capt., Feb. 1, 1918. Served on "Nashville," Spanish-Am. War; spl. observer, British services, 1916-17; asst. naval attaché Am. Embassy, London, and aide on staff comdr. in chief U.S. Naval Forces in European waters; fleet surgeon and aide on staff of comdr. in chief Atlantic Fleet, 1920-21; asst. Bureau Medicine and Surgery, Washington, D.C., 1921-24; comdg. naval hosp., Pearl Harbor, Hawaii, 1925-28; comdg. naval hospital, Boston, 1928-29 (retired). Awarded bronze medal for services at Cienfuegos, Spanish-Am. War; recommended by Adm. Sims for Navy Cross, World War; received certificate of commendation; Comdr. British Empire. Del. of U.S. Navy at internat. congresses on Nomenclature of Diseases, Paris, and Alcoholism, London, 1909; tech. adviser to Am. delegation at Geneva, July 1929; del. of U.S. Govt. and chmn., Am. delegation, XI Internat.

Congress, History of Medicine at Zagreb, Belgrade, Sarajevo and Dubrovnik, Yugoslavia, 1938. Fellow Am. Coll. Surgeons, Am. Coll. Physicians, A.M.A.; Assn. of Mil. Surgeons (pres. 1921-22). Clubs: New York Yacht; Authors' (London); Pacific (Honolulu). Editor: (with Prof. T. O. Mabbott) Life and Works of Edward Coote Pinkney, 1925; Life and Works of Joseph Rodman Drake, 1935. Contbr. professional and biog. articles to Mil. Surgeon, Navy Med. Bull. and Annals of Med. History. Address: 1522-C Alewa Drive, Honolulu 17, Hawaii. Died Jan. 30, 1957 buried Arlington Nat. Cemetery.

PLEASANT, RUFFIN GOLSON governor; b. Shiloh, La., June 2, 1871; s. Benjamin Franklin and Martha Washington (Duty) P.; Ruston Coll., 1885; Mt. Lebanon Coll., La., 1887-88 and 1888-89; La. State U., 1890-94; studied law Harvard and Yale; m. Anne Ector, Feb. 14, 1906. Lt. col. 1st La. Regt. Inf., U.S. Vols., Spanish-Am. War, 1898; began practice, Shreveport, La., 1899; city atty., Shreveport, 1902-08; asst. atty. gen., La., 1911-12; atty. gen., June 1, 1912-16; gov. of La., term 1916-20. Democrat. Baptist. Home: Shreveport, La. Died Sept. 12, 1937.

PLEASANTS, HENRY, JR., (plez'ants), physician, author; b. Radnor, Pa., May 23, 1884; s. Henry and Agnes (Spencer) P.; ed. Haverford Sch., 1895-1901; A.B., Haverford Coll., 1906; M.D., U. of Pa. Med. Sch., 1910; m. Elizabeth W. Smith, June 9, 1909 (divorced); children—Henry 3d, William Wilkins, Richard Rundle, Howard S. (dec.), Constantia Elizabeth (Mrs. Nathaniel Bowditch), Dallas (dec.); m. 2d, Vera M. Kilhefner, Jan. 28, 1932; 1 child, Ann Franklin. Engaged in gen. practice of medicine at West Chester, Pa., 1911-49; emeritus member staff Chester County Hosp., chief diabetes clinic, 1934-38, med. dir. State Teachers Coll., W. Chester, 1940-43; engaged in writing since 1919. Sec. Bd. Health West Chester, 1942-45. Chmn. med. adv. com. Chester Co. Council Defense, 1941-46; dist. med. dir. Dept. of Health of Pa., 1949-57; cons. in medicine Chester County Hosp. since 1949; retired from gen. practice of medicine, 1949. Served in Med. Corps Reserve, United States Army, 1917-19, major, 1919, AEF; lieutenant colonel AUS, retired 1954. Awarded Victory Medal and 2 stars, Order Purple Heart; and other assn. awards. Fellow Am. Coll. Phys., Phila. Coll. Phys.; mem. nat., state, and local med., profl. and social assns. and orgns., Am. Soc. Sanitary Engrs. (mem. bd. dirs. E. Pa. chpt.). Republican. Epis. Clubs: St. Elmo (Phila.), Nat. Geneal. Soc., St. Andrews Soc. Asso. ed. Med. World, Phila., 1934-36. Author several works, mainly hist. in nature; also articles popular mags. Home: 18 W. Chestnut St., West Chester, Pa. 19380. Died Feb. 7, 1963; buried Oaklands Cemetery, West Chester.

PLEASONTON, ALFRED army officer; b. Washington, D.C., June 7, 1824; s. Stephen and Mary (Hopkins) P.; grad. U.S. Mil. Acad., 1844. Commd. 2d lt. 2d Dragoons, U.S. Army, 1845; brevetted 1st lt. for bravery in Mexican War, 1846; promoted 1st lt., 1849, capt., 1855; led march of 2d Cavalry from Utah to Washington, D.C., Sept.-Oct. 1861; commd. maj. 2d Cavalry, 1862; served in Peninsular campaign, promoted brig. gen. U.S. Volunteers, 1862; commanded cavalry div. of Army of Potomac which pursued Lee's forces into Md., Sept.-Nov. 1862; served in battles of S. Mountain, Antietam, Fredericksburg; brevetted lt. col., 1862; helped check advance of Stonewall Jackson's forces against Hooker at Chancellorsville, 1863; promoted maj. gen. U.S. Volunteers, 1863; commanded cavalry at Gettysburg, brevetted col. U.S. Army; transferred to Mo., 1864, campaigned against Gen. Sterling Price; defended Jefferson City, 1864, routed Price nr. Marais des Cygnes River, Kan.; brevetted brig. gen., also maj. gen., Mar. 13, 1865, resigned commn., 1868; collector internal revenue 4th Dist. N.Y., 1869-70, 32d Dist., 1870; commr. internal revenue, 1870-71; pres. Cincinnati & Terre Haute R.R., 1872-74; commd. maj. on retired list, 1888. Author: The Successes and Failures of Chancellorsville, published in Battles and Leaders of the Civil War, Volume 3, 1888. Died Feb. 17, 1897; buried Congressional Cemetery, Washington.

PLEASONTON, AUGUSTUS JAMES lawyer, army officer; b. Washington, D.C., Aug. 18, 1808; s. Stephen Pleasonton; grad. U.S. Mil. Acad., 1826. Served at arty. sch., Fortress Monroe, Va., 1826-30; resigned from U.S. Army, 1830; admitted to bar, began practice of law, Phila., 1832; commd. maj. Pa. Militia, 1833, col., 1835, brig. gen. in charge of organizing defense of Phila., 1861-65; pres. Harrisburg, Portsmouth, Mountjoy & Lancaster R.R., 1839-40; originated "Blue-glass" theory of beneficial effects of sun's rays. Author: Influence of the Blue Ray of the Sunlight . . . in Developing Animal and Vegetable Life, 1876. Died Phila., July 26, 1894.

PLUMB, PRESTON B. senator, editor; b. Berkshire, O., Oct. 12, 1837; s. David and Hannah (Bierce) P.; m. Caroline (Carrie) A. Southwick, Mar. , 1867, 6 children. Co-founder Xenia (O.) News, 1854, editor, 1854-56; became mcht., transported arms and munitions to Kan. Territory, 1856; founder Kan. News (vigorous advocate of free-state cause), Emporia; 1857; sec. Kan. Free-State Conv., 1857; mem. Leavenworth Constl. Conv., 1859; admitted to Ohio bar, 1861; 1st reporter Kan. Supreme Ct., 1861; mem. Kan. Ho. of Reps., 1862, 67-68, speaker, 1867; commd. maj. 11th Kan. Cavalry, U.S. Army, 1862, apptd. chief-of-staff and provost marshal, 1863, partially cleared Dist. of the Border of guerrilla fighters, promoted lt. col., 1864; founder Emporia Nat. Bank (Kan.), 1865, pres., 1873; mem. U.S. Senate (Republican), 1877-91, made greatest contbn. in Land Law of 1891, repealing timber-culture and preemption acts and inaugurating reclamation and conservation projects. Died Washington, D.C., Dec. 20, 1891; buried Maplewood Cemetery, Emporia.

PLUME, JOSEPH WILLIAMS financier, soldier; b. Troy, N.Y., Aug. 23, 1839; pvt. sch. edn.; engaged in banking business; rose to be pres.; served in Civil War as adj. 2d N.J.; a.d.c. to Brig. Gen. French; acting adj. gen. 3d Brigade, Sumner's division; acting adj. gen. 3d Div. 2d Corps; 42 yrs.' continuous service in N.J.N.G., holding every rank from pvt. to maj. gen. During Spanish-Am. War was made brig. gen. of vols. and served with 2d Corps under Gen. Graham; mustered out, Sept. 1898. Pres. Mfrs.' Nat. Bank, Now treas.-in-chief Commandery-in-Chief Loyal Legion. Died Jan. 12, 1918.

PLUME, STEPHEN KELLOGG (plu-me'), brass mfr.; b. Waterbury, Conn., May 16, 1881; s. Frank Cameron and Sarah Andrews (Kellogg) P.; ed. Taft Sch. and Holbrooks Mil. Acad.; m. Pauline Brooke Parke, Oct. 20, 1917; 1 son, Stephen Kellogg (U.S. Army). Began in brass mfg. bus. with Plume & Atwood Mfg. Co., Waterbury, now chmn. bd. dirs.; dir. Thomaston Nat. Bank. Served as capt., U.S. Army, World War I; lt. col., U.S.R.C.; served as exec. officer, Aberdeen (Md.) Proving Ground, with grade of col., U.S. Army, World War II; ret. Republican. Episcopalian. Mason. Clubs: Waterbury, Watertown Golf; Army and Navy (Washington); American Legion, Thomaston Rod and Gun. Address: Watertown, Conn. Died May 6, 1950.

PLUMMER, EDWARD HINKLEY army officer; b. Esperanza, Elkridge, Md., Sept. 24, 1855; s. William Walker and Harriet Leoj (French) P.; grad. U.S. Mil. Acad., 1877; m. Georgia Alice Moody, Oct. 13, 1880; children—Bessie Moody, Edward Hinkley (dec.), Harriet French (dec.), Dwight Kelton (dec.), Thorington Preston, Georgia Moody. Commd. 2d lt. 10th Inf., June 15, 1877; promoted through grades to col. 35th Vol. Inf., Dec. 16, 1899 (organized the regt. and commanded it during its entire service); col. regular army, Mar. 11, 1911; brig. gen., July 1, 1916; maj. gen. N.A., Aug. 5, 1917. Q.m. in field, and regimental q.m., 1885-91; agt. Navajo and Moqui Indians, 1893-94; a.-q.m. hdqrs. 5th Army Corps, Santiago, Cuba, in charge all land transportation, wagon and pack trains, July 3-Aug. 17, 1898; aide to Maj. Gen. W. R. Shafter, Aug. 18, 1898-July 4, 1899, and May-July 1901; comdr. Ft. Egbert, Eagle, Alaska, 1904-06; at Zamboanga, P.I., 1909-10; comdg. 28th Inf. Maneuver Div., San Antonio, Tex., 1911; provost marshal gen. and acting mayor of Vera Cruz, Mexico, Apr.-Nov. 1914; comdg. regt. at Dallas State Fair, and mil. tournament, Oct. 1915; various commands in Tex. and on Mexican border; organized Dept. of Panama Canal, first comdr. of new dept., conprising canal and appurtenances, and troops, Apr.-Aug. 1917; organized and comd. 88th Div., Camp Dodge, Ia., Aug.-Nov. 1917; visited battle fronts in France, Dec. 1917-Feb. 1918, with 46th British Div., Woevre trench sector, 62d French Div., La Fere sector, 1st U.S. Div., Mars la tour; comdg. 88th Div., Feb.-Mar. 1918; discharged as maj. gen. N.A., March 14, 1918; comd. Ft. Sill, Okla., Mar.-Oct. 1918, Camp Grant, Ill., Oct.-Dec. 1918; retired as brig. gen., Nov. 30, 1918. Episcopalian. Home: Pacific Grove, Calif. Died Feb. 11, 1927.

PLUMMER, RALPH WALTER, physician; b. Chicago, Ill., Oct. 18, 1874; s. George Washington and Emily Elvira (McClintock) P.; student Allegheny Coll., 1890-94; M.D., U. of Chicago, 1897; student Naval War Coll., 1921-22; H.M.D., Hahnemann Med. Coll., 1935; m. Lillian Cecile Butts, Oct. 19, 1899. Began as physician, U.S. Navy, 1897; served with U.S. Navy Med. Corps, 1899-1929, retiring with rank of capt.; med. dir. Hahnemann Hosp., Phila., since 1930. Awarded citations in Philippine Insurrection and World War. Fellow Am. Coll. of Surgeons, A.M.A.; mem. Phi Kappa Psi. Republican. Methodist. Mason (32 deg., Shriner). Club: Union League (Phila.). Home: 4224 Pine St. Office: Hahnemann Hospital, Philadelphia PA*

PLUMMER, SAMUEL C., retired surgeon; b. Rock Island, Ill., Apr. 27, 1865; s. Samuel C. and Julia (Hayes) P.; desc. Francis Plummer, Newburyport, Mass., 1633; A.B., Augustana Coll., 1883, A.M., 1886, Ph.D., 1900; M.D., Chicago Medical College, 1886; Sc.D., Northwestern U., 1940; m. Mary Louise Middleton, March 18, 1903; children—Susan M., William M. (dec.), Samuel C, III. Practiced surgery, Chicago, 1891-1936; successively prof. anatomy, operative surgery and clin. surgery Northwestern U. Med. Sch., 1891-1908; hon. staff surgeon to St. Luke's Hosp.; chief surgeon, C., R.I.&P. Ry., 1902-36; retired, 1936. Apptd. 1st lt. Med. Reserve Corps, U.S. Army, 1911; served 16 mos. in World War (8 mos. in France) as maj. Med. Corps, U.S. Army. Fellow Am. Coll. Surgeons; mem. Am. and Western surg. assns., Chicago Surg. Soc., A.M.A., Ill. State and Chicago med. socs., Inst. of Medicine Chicago. Home: 914 Thirteenth St., Boulder CO

PLUNKETT, CHARLES PESHALL naval officer; b. Washington, D.C., Feb. 15, 1864; grad. U.S. Naval Acad., 1884. Promoted ensign, July 1, 1886; lt. jr. grade, Nov. 5, 1895; lt., Nov. 15, 1898; lt. comdr., June 1, 1904; comdr., July 1, 1908; captain, Apr. 27, 1912; rear admiral (temporary), July 1, 1918, permanent rank, Apr. 7, 1919. In office of Naval Intelligence, Navy Department, 1904-05; executive officer Texas, 1905-06, Georgia, 1906-07; duty at Navy Yard, Boston, 1907-08; insp. euipment, Fore River Shipbuilding Co., Quincy, Mass., 1908-10; exec. officer North Dakota, 1910; comd. Missiouri, 1910-11, Culgoa, 1911, Wabash, 1911-12; in charge navy recruiting sta., Boston, Mass., 1912, comd. South Dakota, 1913, North Dakota, 1913-15; at Naval War Coll., Newport, R.I., 1915-16; dir. gunnery training and engring., also comdg. 14-inch Naval Ry. Batteries, Jan. 3, 1916-July 7, 1918; comdg. 14-inch Naval Ry. Batteries operating with French and Am. armies in France, July 7, 1918-Jan. 1919; comdg. destroyer force U.S. Fleet, Jan.-July 1919; in charge all operations Navy transatlantic flight, May-June 1919; comdg. destroyer squadrons Atlantic Fleet, July 1, 1919-Nov. 30, 1920; chief of staff, Naval War Coll., Dec. 1, 1920-Aug. 1, 1921; pres. Bd. Insp. and Survey, Aug. 1, 1921-Dec. 1, 1922; comdt. 3d Naval Dist. and Navy Yard, New York, 1922-28, retired. Navy D.S.M. and Army D.S.M. (U.S.); Comdr. Legion of Honor (France); Portuguese Decoration, Tower and Sword. Died Mar. 24, 1931.

POE, ORLANDO METCALFE army officer; b. Navarre, O., Mar. 7, 1832; s. Charles and Susanna (Warner) P. grad. U.S. Mil. Acad., 1856; m. Eleanor Brent, Mar. 17, 1861, 4 children. Asst. topog. engr. on survey northern lakes, 1856-61; commd. 1st lt. U.S. Army, 1860; assisted in organizing Ohio Volunteers, 1861; col. 2d Mich. Volunteers, 1861; brig. gen. Volunteers, 1862; chief engr. 23d Army Corps in march on Knoxville, Tenn., 1863; chief engr. Army of Ohio; brevetted maj., 1864; asst. engr. Mil. Div. of Mississippi, 1863; chief engr. to Gen. Sherman, 1864; brevetted lt. col., then col., 1864; brevetted brig. gen. U.S. Army, 1865; engr. sec. Lighthouse Bd., 1865-70; maj. Corps Engrs., 1867; engr. Upper Lakes Lighthouse Dist., also supt. river and harbor work in Lake region, 1870; built Spectacle Reef Light, Lake Huron; col., aide-de-camp to Gen. Sherman, 1873-84; lt. col. Corps Engrs., 1882, col., 1888; superintending engr. of improvement rivers and harbors on lakes Superior and Huron, also St. Mary's Falls, Can., 1883. Died Detroit, Oct. 2, 1895; buried Arlington (Va.) Nat. Cemetery.

POINDEXTER, MILES lawyer; b. Memphis, Tenn., Apr. 22, 1868; s. William B. and Josephine Alexander (Anderson) P.; ed. Fancy Hill Acad., Va., and Washington and Lee U.; LL.B., Washington and Lee, 1891; LL.D., George Washington U., 1919; moved to Walla Walla, Wash., 1891; m. Elizabeth Gale Page, June 16, 1892 (died Dec. 20, 1929); 1 son, Gale Aylett, comdr. U.S. Navy, retired. Elected pros. atty. Walla Walla County, 1892; moved to Spokane, Wash., 1897; asst. pros. atty., Spokane County, 1898-1904; judge Superior Court, 1904-08; mem. 61st Congress (1909-11), 3d Wash. Dist.; U.S. senator from Wash., 2 terms, 1911-23; acting chmn. Senate Com. on Naval Affairs, 1919-23; chmn. Rep. Senatorial Campaign Com., 1920-21; received 19 votes in Rep. Conv., 1920, for President of U.S.; A.E. and P. to Peru, 1923-28. Hon. mem. Geog. Soc. Lima, Am. Ethnol. Soc., A.A.A.S.; fellow Am. Geog. Soc., Royal Geog. Soc.; mem. Phi Beta Kappa. Mem. Order El Sol de'el Peru. Received special gold medal from City of Lima in recognition of travel in interior of Peru, 1923, 24. Author: Ayar-Incas, Peruvian Pharoahs; also articles in mags. and in Congressional Reports. Correspondence and papers deposited in Alderman Library, Univ. of Va. Home: Spokane, Wash. Address: Greenlee, Va. Died Sep. 21, 1946.

POINSETT, JOEL ROBERTS sec. of war, diplomat; b. Charlestown (now Charleston), S.C., Mar. 2, 1779; s. Dr. Elisha and Ann (Roberts) P.; attended med. sch. of St. Paul's Sch., Edinburgh, Scotland, 1796-1800; LL.D. (hon.), Columbia, 1825; m. Mary (Izard) Pringle, Oct. 24, 1833. U.S. spl. agt. in Rio de la Plata and Chile, 1810-14; mem. S.C. Ho. of Reps., 1816-20; chmn. S.C. Bd. Pub. Works, 1818-20; mem. U.S. Ho. of Reps. from S.C., 17th-18th congresses, 1821-25; made spl. mission to Mexico, 1822-23; 1st Am. minister to Mexico, 1825-30; unsuccessful leader Unionist party in S.C., 1830-33; largely responsible for raising S.C. Militia to defend Unionist cause; U.S. sec. of war, 1837-41, improved status of U.S. Army, proposed plan for universal mil. tng. and frontier def., organized gen. staff, improved arty., strengthened U.S. Mil. Acad., removed more than 40,000 Indians to territory West of Mississippi River, directed war against Seminole Indians in Fla.; a founder Nat. Inst. for Promotion of Sci. and Useful Arts, 1840; developed poinsettia from a Mexican flower. Author: Notes on Mexico, 1824. Died Statesburg, S.C., Dec. 12, 1851; buried Ch. of Holy Cross, Statesburg.

POLING, DANIEL ALFRED, clergyman, editor, author; b. Portland, Ore., Nov. 30, 1884; s. Charles C. and Savilla (Kring) P.; A.B., Dallas (Ore.) Coll., 1904, A.M., 1906; student Lafayette (Ore.) Sem.; grad work, Ohio State U., 1907-09; LL.D., Albright Coll., 1916; Litt.D., Defiance Coll., 1921, Norwich University, 1952; D.D., Hope College, 1925; S.T.D., Syracuse U., 1927; D.D., U. of Vt., 1934; LL.D., Temple U., 1937;

D.D., Phillips U., 1939; L.H.D., Bucknell U., 1946, Bates Coll., 1952, Clarkson Coll.; H.H.D., Huntington Coll.; D.D., William Jewell Coll., 1960; m. Susan Vandersall, Sept. 25, 1906 (died July 1918); m. 2d, Lillian Diebold Heingartner, Aug. 11, 1919; 8 children. Prohibition candidate for governor of Ohio, 1912. Pastor of the Marble Collegiate-Dutch Reformed Ch., N.Y., 1922-30, Bapt. Temple, Phila., 1936-48. Chaplain, Chapel of Four Chaplains, 1948 (Inter-faith Shrine). Honorary life pres. World's Christian Endeavor Union; chmn. bd., editorial cons. Christain Herald; corporator Presbyn. Ministers Life Insurance Fund. Trustee Bucknell U.; mem. General War-Time Commission of the Churches; maj. Chaplain Officers' Reserve. Received Silver Buffalo award, Boy Scouts of America; humanitarian award, Welcome Chapter, Pa. Eastern Star, 1940; War Dept. award for conspicuous service as accredited war corr. overseas theater of combat, 1946; Medal of Merit, United States Government, 1947; Benjamin Franklin award 1961; Order of Lafayette, 1961; Clergyman of the Year, Religious Heritage Assn., 1963; Ten Commandments award Order of Eagles, 1964; citation from the Government of Israel, 1965. President of the Greater New York Federation of Chs., 1926-27. Gen. Synod Reformed Ch. Am., 1929-30. Mem. Am. Legion, Military Order Fgn. Wars, Newcomen Soc. Mason (33 deg.). Clubs: Nat. Press (Washington); Explorers (New York City); Overseas Press (New York City); Union League (N.Y.C.). Author: Mothers of Men, 1914; Huts in Hell, 1918; Learn to Live, 1923; What Men Need Most, 1923; An Adventure in Evangelism, 1925; The Furnace (novel), 1925; John of Oregon (novel), 1926; Radio Talks to Young People, 1926; Dr. Poling's Radio Talks, 1927; The Heretic (novel), 1928; Youth and Life, 1929; Between Two Worlds (novel), 1930; John Barleycorn–His Life and Letters (novel), 1933; Youth Marches, 1937; Fifty-two Story Sermons for Children, 1940; Opportunity Is Yours, 1946; A Treasury of Best-Loved Hymns, 1942; A Preacher Looks at War, 1943; Your Daddy Did Not Die, 1944; A Treasury of Great Sermons, 1944 Faith is Power for You, 1950; Prayers for the Armed Forces, 1950; The Glory and Wonder of the Bibel (with Dr. Henry Thomas); Your Questions Answered with Conforting Counsel; Mine Eyes Have Seen, 1959; Jesus Says To You, 1961; He Came from Galilee, 1965. Home: Philadelphia PA Died Feb. 7, 1968.

POLK, FRANK LYON lawyer; b. New York City, Sept. 13, 1871; s. Dr. William M. and Ida A. (Lyon) P.; g.s. Leonidas P., "the fighting bishop"; grad. Groton Sch., 1890; B.A., Yale, 1894, hon. M.A., 1918; LL.B., Columbia, 1897; hon. D.C.L., U. of the South, Sewanee, 1928; LL.D., Rollins, 1930; LL.D., N.Y. U., 1935; m. Elizabeth Sturgis Potter, 1908; children—John M., Elizabeth S. (Mrs. Raymond Guest), Frank L., James P., Alice P. (Mrs. Winthrop Rutherfurd Jr. Began practice in N.Y. City, 1897; pres. Civil Service Commn. of N.Y., 1908-09; corp. counsel, 1914-15; counselor for Dept. of State, 1915-19; under sec. of State, 1919-20; acting sec. of State, Dec. 4, 1918-July 18, 1919; apptd. commr. plenipotentiary of the U.S. to negotiate peace, July 17, 1919; head of Am. delegation to Peace Conf. at Paris, July 28-Dec. 9, 1919. Dir. N.P. Ry. Co.; trustee Bowery Savings Bank, U.S. Trust Co., Mutual Life Ins. Co. of N.Y. Pres. and trustee Pub. Library; trustee Cathedral of St. John. Mem. Troop A, N.Y. Nat. Guard, Spanish-Am. War; served as capt. and asst. q.m. staff of Gen. Ernst, and in Porto Rico. Mem. N.Y. State and N.Y. County bar assns., Bar Assn. City of New York, Pilgrims Soc., New York Southern Soc., S.R. Episcopalian. Clubs: Knickerbocker, Racquet and Tennis, Down Town, Broad Street, Piping Rock, Century, Deepdale (New York); Metropolitan, University (Washington, D.C.). Office: 15 Broad St., New York, N.Y. Died Feb. 7, 1943.

POLK, JAMES KNOX 11th Pres. U.S.; b. Mecklenburg County, N.C., Nov. 2, 1795; s. Samuel and Jane (Knox) P.; grad. U. N.C., 1818; read law under Felix Grundy; m. Sarah Childress, Jan. 1, 1824. Admitted to Tenn. bar, 1820; chief clk. Tenn. Senate, 1821-23; mem. Tenn. Ho. of Reps., 1823-25; mem. U.S. Ho. of Reps. (Jacksonian Democrat) from Tenn., 19th-25th congresses, 1825-39, mem. ways and means com. (placed there to lead fight against U.S. Bank), 1832, chmn., 1833, speaker of house, 1835-39; gov. Tenn., 1838-41; nominated for U.S. Pres. by Dem. Party largely through support of Andrew Jackson and because of his stand on so-called reannexation of Tex. and Ore., 1844, elected under slogan "Fifty-four forty or fight;" inaugurated Pres. U.S., Mar. 4, 1845; success of his programs caused further conflict between North and South and directly influenced Civil War; reduced tariff by Walker Tariff Law, 1846, angered North; signed Independent Treasury Bill of 1846, antagonized supporters of nat. bank; compromised on annexation of Ore. in treaty with Gt. Britain, 1846; made unsuccessful attempt to buy Cal. from Mexico, used skirmish on Tex.-Mexican border as grounds for war; declared war on Mexico, 1846; received Cal. and N.M. in treaty with Mexico, 1848; opposed Wilmot Proviso (attempt to exclude slavery from territory acquired in war), 1848; did not receive nomination for reelection, left office, 1849. Died Nashville, Tenn., June 15, 1849; buried Tenn. Capitol Grounds, Nashville.

POLK, LEONIDAS clergyman, army officer; b. Raleigh, N.C., Apr. 10, 1806; s. Col. William and Sarah (Hawkins) P.; grad. U.S. Mil. Acad., 1827; ed. Va. Theol. Sem.; m. Frances Ann Devereux, May 1830, 8 children. Ordained deacon Protestant Episcopal Ch., 1830, priest, 1831; missionary bishop of S.W., 1838; bishop of La., 1841; chiefly responsible for founding U. of South, 1860; commd. maj. gen. Confederate Army, 1861; in charge of defending Mississippi River, 1861-62; his troops 1st to violate neutrality of Ky. at Columbus, 1861; defeated Grant at Belmont, Mo., 1861; commd. lt. gen., 1862; fought at battles of Shiloh, Murfreesboro, Chickamauga. Died Pine Mountain nr. Marietta, Ga., June 14, 1864.

POLK, LUCIUS EUGENE army officer; b. Salisbury, N.C., July 10, 1833; s. Dr. William Julius and Mary Rebecca (Long) P.; attended U. Va., 1850-51; m. Sallie Moore Polk, Aug. 19, 1863, 5 children including Rufus. Commd. col., then brig. gen. Confederate Army, 1862, commanded Cleburne's brigade; fought at battles of Shiloh, Murfreesboro, Chickamanga, Kenesaw Mountain; del. to Democratic Conv., Chgo., 1884; mem. Tenn. Senate, 1887. Died Maury County, Tenn., Dec. 1, 1892.

POLK, RUFUS KING congressman, steel mfr.; b. Columbia, Tenn., Aug. 23, 1866; s. Gen. L. E. (C.S.A.) and Sally (Moore) P.; grad. Lehigh Univ., B.S., 1887 (E.M.); m. Isabella Grier. Mem. Congress, 17th Pa. dist., 1899-1903. Democrat. In Spanish-Am. war, 1st lt. Co. F 12th regt., Pa. vols. Home: Danville, Pa. Died 1902.

POLK, THOMAS army officer, Continental congressman; b. Cumberland County, Pa., circa 1732; s. William and Margaret (Taylor) P.; m. Susan Spratt, 1755, 9 children including William. Led in War of Sugar Creek, 1760; commr. and 1st treas. Charlotte (N.C.), 1768; mem. N.C. Ho. of Commons, 1766-71, 73-74; served as capt. N.C. militia, 1758-71, fought against Regulators; surveyor in running N.C.-S.C. boundary line, 1772; mem. Mecklenburg Com., 1775; mem. N.C. Provincial Congress, 1775; col. N.C. Militia, 1775; commd. col. 4th N.C. Continental Regt., 1776; served in battles of Brandywine and Valley Forge; commissary gen. of provisions N.C., 1780; commissary of purchases Continental Army; commd. col. comdt., 1781; councilor of N.C., 1783-84; del. to Continental Congress, 1786; promoter, trustee Queen's Coll., Charlotte, 1771, Liberty Acad., 1777, Salisbury Acad., 1784. Died Charlotte, Jan. 26, 1794.

POLK, TRUSTEN senator, gov. Mo.; b. Sussex County, Del., May 29, 1811; s. William Nutter and Lavenia (Causey) P.; grad. Yale, 1831, postgrad. in law 1832-34; m. Elizabeth Skinner, Dec. 26, 1837, 5 children. Admitted to bar, 1835; counselor of St. Louis, 1843; St. Louis del. to conv. to revise Mo. constn., 1845; gov. Mo., 1857, resigned to become mem. U.S. Senate from Mo., 1857-62; commd. col. Confederate Army, 1861; presiding mil. judge Dept. of Miss., 1864, 65. Died St. Louis, Apr. 16, 1876; buried Bellefontaine Cemetery.

POLK, WILLIAM army officer; b. Charlotte, N.C., July 9, 1758; s. Thomas and Susan (Spratt) P.; studied Queen's Coll.; m. Grizelda Gilchrist, Oct. 15, 1789; m. 2d, Sarah Hawkins, Jan. 1, 1801; 14 children. Maj. 9th Regt. of N.C. Militia, 1776; served in battles of Brandywine and Germantown (1776), Camden, Guilford Ct. House; lt. col. comdt. 4th S.C. Cavalry, circa 1782; surveyor gen. N.C. Land Office, 1783; mem. N.C. Ho. Commons, 1785-86, 87, 90; supr. internal revenue for N.C., 1791-1808; pres. N.C. State Bank, 1811-19; pres. Neuse River Navigation Co.; trustee U. N.C., 1790-1834, pres. bd. trustees, 1802-05; grand master Masons for N.C. and Tenn., 1799-1802; managed Jackson's campaign in N.C., 1824, 28. Counties in Tenn., N.C. named after him. Died Raleigh, N.C., Jan. 14, 1834.

POLK, WILLIAM HAWKINS congressman, lawyer; b. Maury County, Tenn., May 24, 1815; attended U. N.C. at Chapel Hill, 1832-33; grad. U. Tenn. Knoxville; studied law. Admitted to bar, 1839, began practice of law, Columbia, Tenn.; mem. Tenn. Ho. of Reps., 1842-45; minister to Kingdom of Naples, 1845-47; served as maj. 3d Dragoons in Mexican War, 1847-48; mem. U.S. Ho. of Reps. (Democrat) from Tenn., 32d Congress, 1851-53. Died Nashville, Tenn., Dec. 16, 1862; buried Greenwood Cemetery, Columbia.

POLLARD, JOHN WILLIAM HOBBS, N.D.; b. Brentwood, N.H., Feb. 22, 1872; s. Francis Dow and Mary Jane (Gray) P.; B.L., Dartmouth, 1895; M.D., with honors, U. of Vt., 1901; student in physical culture, Harvard, summer semesters, 1896, 1902; post-grad. work in medicine, Harvard, 1905-06; student in biology, Harvard, summer semesters, 1910, 11; m. Kate Marion Blunt, of Haverhill, Mass., Dec. 28, 1898. Physical director and instr. physiology, Union Coll., Schenectady, N.Y., 1897-1900, phys. dir. Lehigh U., 1901-02, dir. dept. physical edn., U. of Rochester, 1902-05, prof. physical edn. and lecturer on hygiene, U. of Ala., 1906-10; prof. physical edn. and asso. prof. biology, Washington and Lee U., 1910-15; prof. hygiene and physical edn., same, 1915-21, health commissioner, Quincy (Illinois) Public Health District, 1921-24. In practice of medicine 1924, dist. health supt. of Ill. State Dept. Pub. Health, 1925; commr. of health, Evanston, Illinois, since 1926. President S. Atlantic Intercollegiate Athletic Assn., 1913-—, Va. State Public Health Assn., 1914-—; mem. Am. Pub. Health Assn., International Soc. of Medical Health Officers, American Micros. Soc., Am. Assn. Advancement Physical Edn., Soc. Coll. Gymnasium Dirs., Theta Delta Chi, Alpha Kappa Kappa. Mason (32 deg., K.T.). Mem. Soc. of the Genessee (Rochester, N.Y.), N.H. Hist. Soc. Commd. 1st lt. Med. R.C., May 19, 1917; post surgeon, Coast Defenses of New Bedford, July 4, 1917-July 26, 1918; capt. Med. R.C., Dec. 31, 1917; maj., Med. Corps U.S.A., July 27, 1918; attending surgeon for the army, Phila., July 26, 1918-May 31, 1919; hon. discharged, May 31, 1919; commd. lt. col. Med. R.C., June 4, 1919, col., 1924; recommissioned col. Med. Res., 1929; now comdg. officer 119th Gen. Hosp. Home: 919 Washington St., Evanston IL

POLLOCK, EDWIN TAYLOR naval officer; b. Mt. Gilead, O., Oct. 25, 1870; s. Joseph Harper and Olive Orlinda (Taylor) P.; 2 ancestors in the Mayflower and 7 in Am. Revolution; grad. credit U.S.N. Acad., 1891; hon. D.Sc., Wittenberg Coll., Springfield, O., 1926; m. Beatrice Law Hale, Dec. 5, 1893; 1 dau., Beatrice Hale (wife of Robert S. Chew, U.S.N.). Promoted ensign, U.S. Navy, July 1, 1893; lt. jr. grade, Mar. 3, 1899; lt., Sept. 9, 1899; lt. comdr., Sept. 30, 1905; comdr., Mar. 4, 1911; capt., Jan. 1, 1917. Served on New York, Spanish-Am. War, 1898; at Naval Sta., Cavite, P.I., 1905-06; aide to comdr.-in-chief Asiatic Fleet, 1906; navigator Alabama, 1906-07; instr. U.S. Naval Academy; exec. officer Massachusetts, 1910, Virginia, 1910-12; comd. Kearsarge, 1912-13; at Naval Obs., 1913-16; comd. Alabama, 1916, Hancock, 1916-17. Designated by President Wilson to represent U.S. in taking over the Danish West Indies, and acting gov. of Virgin Islands of the U.S., Mar. 31-Apr. 9, 1917; comd. 4th convoy group of first expdn. to France, June 1917, and comd. George Washington, 1917-18, carrying over 40,000 men to France, and comd. 8 convoy groups of over 140,000 men; mem. Naval Examining and Retiring Bds., 1918-20; Naval War Coll., 1920-21; comdg. Oklahoma and Battleship Div. 6, Pacific Fleet, 1921-22; gov. Am. Samoa, 1922-23; supt. U.S. Naval Obs., 1923-27; retired June 30, 1926, and placed on inactive list, Oct. 1, 1927. Campaign badges for West Indian, Spanish and Philippine campaigns, Cuban pacification, Mexican expdn., Dominican Occupation Victory (World War). Navy Cross; medal for expert rifleman; Order of El Sol, on Centenary of Peru, 1921. Mem. Order of Cincinnati of Mass., Soc. Colonial Wars, S.R., S.A.R. Republican. Presbyterian. Club: Army and Navy (Washington, D.C.). Head of depts. of mathematics and astronomy, Cranbrook School, Bloomfield Hills, Mich., 1928-30. Home: Jamestown, R.I. Address: 1661 Crescent Place N.W., Washington, D.C. Died June 4, 1943; buried in Arlington National Cemetery.

POMEROY, JOHN LARRABEE M.D.; b. Louisville, Ky., Dec. 19, 1883; s. Danforth Wetherby and Martha Buchanan (Norris) P.; A.B., Louisville Male High Sch., 1899; M.D., Hosp. Coll. Medicine, Louisville, 1903, Bellevue Med. Coll., N.Y. City, 1909; m. Alice Lillian Brennan, Feb. 10, 1907; 1 son, Stanley Norris; m. 2d, Lecile Jones, July 6, 1930; 1 dau., Joan Lee. Interne City Hosp., N.Y. City, 1903-05; resident phys. Ward's Island Hosp., N.Y., 1905-07; asst. surgeon, U.S.A., 1907-09; asst. supt. North Brother Island Hosp., 1909-10; asst. supt. Pottenger Sanatorium, Monrovia, Calif., 1910-11; in pvt. practice at Monrovia, 1911-15; health officer Los Angeles County (comprising 36 cities, 600 employes), 1915-—; prof. of public health, Coll. Medical Evangelists Medical School, Los Angeles, 1935. Served as captain Medical Corps, U.S.A., 1917-19. Dir. Los Angeles Co. Tuberculosis Assn. Fellow Am. Pub. Health Assn. (pres. Western branch). Republican. Mason. Author: Manual of Food Laws, 1928; Information for Physicians Concerning County 1928; Public Health Report, 1928-29; Los Angeles County Health News (2 vols.), 1929, 30. Home: Los Angeles, Calif. Died Mar. 24, 1941.

POMEROY, SETH army officer; b. Northampton, Mass., May 20, 1706; s. Ebenezer and Sarah (King) P.; m. Mary Hunt, Dec. 14, 1732; 9 children. Commd. capt. Mass. Militia, 1744; served as maj. 4th Mass. Regt. in expdn. against French fortress at Louisbourg, 1745; an organizer opposition to pastor of Northampton Ch. (Jonathan Edwards), 1750; commd. lt. col. Continental Army, fought at Battle of Lake George, 1775; head West Mass. dist. Mass. Militia, in command forts along Mass. frontier, late 1775; mem. Northampton Com. of Safety, 1774; rep. 1st, 2d Mass. provincial congresses; mil. commander Province of Mass.; raised and drilled troops in West Mass., 1775-76; 1st brig. gen. Continental Army, 1775; fought at Battle of Bunker Hill; gunsmith in spare time. Died Peekskill, N.Y., Feb. 19, 1777.

POND, CHARLES FREMONT naval officer; b. Brooklyn, Conn., Oct. 26, 1856; s. Enoch and Sarah Ann (Utley) P.; grad. U.S. Naval Acad., 1876; m. Emma McHenry, Aug. 10, 1880; children—Charles McHenry, John Enoch, Elizabeth Keith. Ensign U.S.N., July 26, 1878; lt. (jr. grade), Oct. 2, 1885; lt., May 19, 1891; lt. comdr., July 1, 1899; comdr. Mar. 31, 1905; capt., Nov. 12, 1908; rear admiral, Feb. 13, 1914. Served at sea 24 yrs., 2 mos., on shore duty 17 yrs., 11 mos.; U.S.S. Pensacola, Lackawanna, Tuscarora and Jamestown, 1877-78; U.S. Coast and Geodetic Survey Office, Wash., 1879; engaged in survey, Pacific coast, U.S. Coast and Geodetic Survey Ship Hassler, 1879-83, 1886, U.S.S. Ranger, 1887-90, inaugurating coast and geodetic survey in Alaskan waters, 1881-83; Hydrographic Office, Wash., 1883-84, br. Hydrographic Office, S.F., 1884; U.S.S. Hartford and Wachusett, 1884-85; Naval Obs., Mare Island, Calif., 1885-87; in charge same 1890-94; U.S.S. Alert, 1894-97; asst. insp. ordnance, Navy Yard, N.Y., 1897-98; U.S.S. Panther, Spanish-Am. War, 1898; comd. U.S.S. Iroquois, 1898-1902, and comd. Naval Sta., Hawaii, during absence of commandant, 1900-01; surveyed Midway Islands, 1900; selected site for Naval Sta., Pearl Harbor, Hawaii, and inaugurated condemnation proceedings in U.S. Courts, 1901; Naval Training Sta., San Francisco, 1902-04; superintended landing Trans-Pacific cable, Midway Islands, 1903; comd. U.S.S. Supply, Guam, 1904-05; ins. ord., comd. Naval Magazine, Mare Island, 1905-07; comd. U.S.S. Lawton, 1906, Buffalo, 1907-08; insp. 13th lighthouse dist., 1908-09; comd. Pennsylvania, 1909-11, U.S.S. Oregon and Pacific Reserve Squadron, 1911-12; comd. 12th Naval Dist., 1912-15; comdr.-in-chief Pacific Reserve Fleet, Apr.-Oct. 1915; comdr. Train, Atlantic Fleet, Dec. 1915-July 1916; comdr. Cruiser Force, Atlantic Fleet, July-Nov. 1916; retired Dec. 30, 1918. Home: Berkeley, Calif. Died Aug. 4, 1929.

POND, JAMES BURTON lecture mgr.; b. Cuba, N.Y., June 11, 1838; s. Willard Elmer and Clarissa (Woodford) P.; went to Ill., 1844; to Wis., 1847; brought up on farm; learned printing trade; m. Ann Frances Lynch, Jan. 21, 1859 (died 1871); m. 2d, Martha Marion Glass, March 10, 1888. Published Markesan, Wis., Jouranl, 1860-61. Lt. to maj. in 3d Wis. cav., 1861-65; one of 17 survivors of band of 118 in Baxter Springs massacre by guerrila chief Quantrell, Oct. 1863; engaged in mercantile business in West, 1865-74; bought Lyceum Lecture Bureau, Boston, 1874; removed office to New York, 1879. Author: Eccentricities of Genius, 1900; D1; A Summer in England with Henry Ward Beecher, etc. Home: Jersey City, N.J. Died 1903.

POOK, SAMUEL HARTT naval constructor U.S.N., retired Jan. 17, 1889; b. Brooklyn, N.Y., Jan. 17, 1827; s. Samuel Moore and Martha Crum (Dickinson) P.; grad. Portsmouth Acad., N.H., 1843; apprenticed as shipwright with his father, serving 7 yrs.; m. Ellen M., d. James K. Frothingham, Charlestown, Mass., 1850. Established as naval architect Boston, designed many merchant vessels, including the clippers Red Jacket, Ocean Telegraph, Northern Light, and others, several iron ships, war frigates for Spanish govt., etc. Entered Govt. service at beginning of war, superintended construction of iron-clad Galena; placed in charge of shipyard at New Haven where 16 steamships were built during war. At close of war entered navy, asst. naval constructor Portsmouth, Boston; promoted naval constructor, 1871, served at Mare Island (San Francisco), Boston, Washington and New York until retired. Home: Washington, D.C. Died 1901.

POOL, DAVID DE SOLA, rabbi; b. London, Eng., May 16, 1885; s. Eleazar Solomon and Abigail (Davis) P.; B.A., 1st class honors, U. of London, 1903; studied univs. of Berlin and Heidelberg; Ph.D., summa cum laude, Heidelberg; Rabbinerseminar, Berlin; hon. degrees Columbia, N.Y. U., Jewish Theol. Sem. Am., Hebrew Theol. Coll., Chgo., Chgo. Coll. Jewish Studies; m. Tamar Hirschenson, February 6, 1917; children—Prof. Ithiel de Sola, Dr. Naomi de Sola. Minister Spanish and Portuguese Synagogue, Shearith Israel, N.Y.C., 1907-70. One of the three Jewish representatives appointed to serve on Herbert Hoover's food conservation staff, 1917; co-founder, v.p. Jewish Welfare Board; field organizer of army welfare work, 1917-18, and chairman Committee Army and Navy Religious Activities of J.W.B. 1940-47; appointed one of three Am. representatives on Zionist Commission to Palestine, 1919; regional dir. for Palestine and Syria of Am. Joint Distribution Com. War Relief and Reconstrn., 1920, 21. A founder Palestine Lighthouse, Am.-Israel Cultural Found., Am. Friends of Alliance Israelite Universelle, U.S.O., Conf. Christians and Jews. Dir. Jewish Edn. Assn., N.Y.; president Young Judea of America, 1915-19, 24, 25; pres. N.Y. Bd. Jewish Mins., 1916-17; founder, pres. Union Sephardic Congregarions, 1928-67, hon. pres., 1967-70; co-founder, pres. Synagogue Council Am., 1938-40; mem. Pres.'s Advisory Com. National Youth Adminstrn.; rep. of Jewish Army and Navy chaplains to Chief of Chaplains. U.S. del. NATO Parliamentary Congress, London, 1959; lectr. Jewish music; organizer Am. Jewish Tercentenary. Author: The Kaddish, 1909; Hebrew Learning Among the Puritans of New England, 1911; Capital Punishment in Jewish Literature, 1916; Portraits Etched in Stone, published in 1952; (with Tamar de Sola Pool) An Old Faith in the New World, 1955; Why I Am a Jew, 1957; (with Tamar de Sola Pool) Is There An Answer? An Inquiry Into Some Human Dilemmas, 1966. Editor, translator numerous volumes Hebrew liturgy, Spanish, Jewry, pamphlets; reviews. Home: New York City NY Died Dec. 1, 1970; buried Congregation Shearith Israel Cemetery, Cypress Hills.

POOLE, SIDMAN PARMELEE geographer; b. Syracuse, N.Y., Oct. 19, 1893; s. Theodore Lewis and Carrie (Law) P.; B.S., Syracuse Univ., 1921, M.S., 1925; Ph.D., Univ. of Chicago, 1932; student Cambridge (Eng.) Univ., 1925; m. Rachel Sumner, August 31, 1922. Instr. Syracuse Univ., 1921-25, asst. prof. of geography, 1925-32, asso. prof., 1932-39, prof., 1939-40; summer lecturer Cornell Univ., 1932; prof. and chmn. Dept. of Geography, Univ. of Va., since Sept., 1946; dir. Virginia Geographical Institute since 1947. Geographer to Syracuse Andean Expdn., 1930-31, Syracuse Gaspe Expdn., 1933, dir. and geographer to Syracuse Yucatan Expdn., 1937-38; detailed field work in New York State, Vermont (with Vt. geol. survey), upper Great Lakes region, Chicago area, England, Brittany, Venezuela, Gaspe and Yucatan. Geographic advisor Air Command and Staff Sch., Air Univ., Maxwell Field, Ala. since Oct. 1946. Served as 1st lt., F.A., A.E.F., World War I; capt. and maj. F.A., O.R.C., 1920-40; col. chief topographic br., War Dept., Washington, D.C., U.K., N. Africa, 1940-46. Decorated Hon. Comdr. Order British Empire, Am. Legion of Merit. Mem. U.S. Bd. on Geog. Names, 1943-46. Fellow Am. Geog. Soc., Royal Geog. Soc.; mem. Nat. Council Geography Teachers (contbg. mem. and chmn. com. on geographic edn. for world understanding), Assn. Am. Geographers (mem. com. on Atlas of U.S., inter-soc. com. on sci. foundation legislation), Am. Soc. for Profl. Geographers (v.p. 1947), Am. Unitarian Assn. (nat. dir.), Phi Beta Kappa, Sigma Xi, Phi Gamma Delta. Clubs: Cosmos (Washington); Farmington Country (Charlottesville, Va.); Colonnade; Rotary International; Explorers (New York). Author: Manual for College Geography, 1933; chapter on Georgraphy of Central New York (An Inland Empire by W. Freeman Galpin), 1941; chapter on Geography in America's Life (Twentieth Century America), 1947-51; History of Virginia (junior author). Contbg. editor: Econ. Geography. Contbr. articles to geog. pubs., mags. and newspapers. Consultant editor Bobbs-Merrill Co. series of geog. texts and readers 1945—. Home: Rio Rd., Box 83, R. 5, Charlottesville, Va. Died Oct. 28, 1955; buried U. Va. Cemetery, Charlottesville.

POOR, CHARLES HENRY naval officer; b. Cambridge, Mass., June 9, 1808; s. Moses and Charlotte (White) P.; m. Mattie Stark, May 13, 1835, 8 children. Commd. lt. U.S. Navy, 1835, comdr., 1855; commanded ship St. Louis of the Home Squadron, 1860-61; commanded landing party of soldiers, marines, sailors sent ashore to reinforce garrison of Ft. Pickens, Fla. 1861; ordnance officer North Atlantic Blockading Squadron stationed at Ft. Monroe, 1862; commd. capt., 1862, commodore, 1863; commanded naval sta. Mound City, Ill., 1865-68; commd. rear adm., 1868; head Washington (D.C.) Navy Yard, 1869; commanded North Atlantic Squadron, 1869-70. Died Washington, D.C., Nov. 5, 1882; buried Oak Hill Cemetery, Washington.

POOR, ENOCH army officer; b. Andover, Mass., June 21, 1736; s. Thomas and Mary (Adams) P.; m. Martha Osgood, 1760. Fought in French and Indian War in Nova Scotia, 1755; twice mem. N.H. Provincial Congress; commd. col. 2d N.H. Regt. of foot soldiers, 1775; took part in battles of Trenton, Princeton, Saratoga, Monmouth; commd. brig. gen. Continental Army, 1777; accompanied Gen. John Sullivan in expdn. against Six Nations, 1779. Died Paramus, N.J., Sept. 8, 1780.

POORE, BENJAMIN ANDREW army officer; b. Centre, Ala., June 22, 1863; s. Andrew and Keziah (Brooks) P.; grad. United States Military Academy, 1886. Infantry and Cavalry Sch., 1893; Army War Coll., 1909; m. Miss Carleton, June 20, 1888 (died 1929); children—Katharine Hale, Priscilla Carleton, Adelaide Carleton; m. 2d, Mrs. Flora B. Bullock, Oct. 22, 1930. Commd. 2d lt. 12th Infantry, July 1, 1886; promoted through grades to col. 8th Inf., July 1, 1916; brig. gen., N.A., Aug. 5, 1917; brig. general regular army, Dec. 21, 1921; maj. gen., Oct. 11, 1925. Instructor, U.S. Mil. Acad., 1893-95; engaged at Guanica, P.R., July 25, 1898, and at Hormigueros, Aug. 10, 1898; q.m. of regt. and regimental adj., 1899-1903; in Philippines, 1899-1902; comd. detachment of 6th Inf. in fight at Guin-Tabuan, Negros, Oct. 1, 1899, also various expdns.; served in field in Samar, 1905; in Alaska, 1909-10; duty Gen. Staff, Washington, D.C., 1912-14, 1914-16; dir. Army War Coll., 1912-16; in Philippine Islands and China, 1916; comdr. 162d Depot Brigade, Camp Pike, Little Rock, Ark., Sept.-Dec. 1917; comdr. 14th Inf. Brig., El Paso, Tex., Dec. 1917; comd. 7th Inf. Brig., 4th Div., Apr. 3, 1918-Aug. 1, 1919; arrived in France, May 23, 1918; engaged in Aisne-Marne offensive and defensive, St. Mihiel offensive, Meuse-Argonne offensive, July 18-Nov. 11, 1918, in Army of Occupation, Germany, Dec. 1918-July 1919; returned to U.S., Aug. 1919, and assigned to comd. Ft. D. A. Russell, Wyo.; comd. Camp Lewis and Vancouver barracks, Wash., Feb.-Sept. 1920; comd. 1st Inf. and 4th Inf. Brig. 2d Div., Ft. Sam Houston, Tex., Oct. 1920-Nov. 1924; comd. Ft. Sheridan, Ill., and 12th Inf. Brig., Nov. 1924-Oct. 1925; comd. 7th Corps Area, Omaha, Neb., 1925-27; retired June 22, 1927. Awarded D.S.M. and D.S.C. and 2 War Dept. citations (U.S.); Officer Legion of Honor and Croix de Guerre with Palm (French); Croce di Guerra al Merito (Italian). Unitarian. Home: Fitchburg, Mass. Died Aug. 27, 1940.

POORE, CHARLES GRAYDON, writer; b. Monterrey, Mexico, Aug. 20, 1902; s. Charles Graydon and Anne Elizabeth (Lynch) P.; Ph.B., Yale, 1926; m. Mary Elizabeth Carter, Jan. 11, 1930; children—Charles Graydon (dec.), Susan C. (Mrs. Thaddeus Brys). Writer various depts. N.Y. Times, 1929-71, asst. editor N.Y. Times Book Review, 1934-41, co-editor and daily book critic, 1945-71; panelist Invitation to Learning, CBS. Served from capt. to maj., Gen. Staff Corps, AUS, 1942-45. Decorated Croix de Guerre (France). Mem. N.Y. Newspaper Guild (mem. rep. assembly), Yale Library Assos., Authors League. Clubs: Elizabethan (New Haven, Connecticut); Century Association (N.Y.C.). Author: Goya, A Biography, 1938. Editor The Hemingway Reader, 1953. Home: New York City NY Died July 26, 1971.

POORMAN, ALFRED PETER prof. engring. mechanics; b. Altamont, Ill., Feb. 13, 1877; s. George Warner and Eliza Jane (Watson) P.; B.S. in C.E., U. of Ill., 1907; A.B. and C.E., U. of Colo., 1909; m. Sarah Elizabeth Ellmaker, June 22, 1910 (died Jan. 30, 1935); children—Mary Esther, George Ellmaker; married 2d, Genevieve Louise Lippoldt, June 29, 1936. Engineer, Weber Concrete Chimney Company, June-Aug. 1907; instructor in civil engineering, Univ. of Colo., 1907-09; hydrographer, Wind River Indian Reservation, July-Nov. 1909; asst. prof. applied mechanics, Purdue, 1909-17, 1919-20, asso. prof., 1920-22, prof. since 1922, head dept. applied mechanics, 1942-44, professor emeritus, 1947. Capt. Engr. Corps U.S. Army, 1917-18; supply officer, Gen. Hdqrs., A.E.F., June 1918-June 1919. Mem. Am. Soc. Civil Engrs., Am. Soc. for Testing Materials, American Soc. of Engring. Edn., Am. Concrete Inst., A.A.A.S., Am. Assn. Univ. Profs., Tau Beta Pi, Sigma Xi, Chi Epsilon, Scabbard and Blade. Methodist. Club: University. Author: Applied Mechanics, 1917 (5 edits.); Strength of Materials, 1925 (4 edits.); Sect. on theoretical mechanics O'Rourke's Engineering Handbook, 1940. Home: 329 Russell St., West Lafayette, Ind. Died Feb. 12, 1952; buried Grand View Cemetery, West Lafayette.

POPE, ALBERT AUGUSTUS mfr. bicycles and automobiles; b. Boston, Mass., May 20, 1843; pub. sch. edn., Brookline, Mass.: because of family reverses left sch.; was clerk in shoe findings store in Boston at $4 a week; capt. in Home Guards, 1861-62; Aug. 1862, lt. 35th Mass. inf.; served until end of war, becoming lt. col.; bvtd. for gallant conduct battles of Fredericksburg and Knoxville, Poplar Springs Church, and Petersburg; m. Abby, d. George and Matilda Linder, Newton, Mass., Sept. 20, 1871. In wholesale shoe findings business, 1865-76. Established, 1877, the Pope Mfg. Co. to manufacture and sell small patented articles; same yr. began selling imported bicycles; in 1878 introduced the bicycle mfg. industry in U.S.; became a leading manufacturer. Founded The Wheelman (absorbed in Outing) in the interests of cycling; leader in good-roads movement; has large interests in banks and other corps. Home: Boston, Mass. Died 1909.

POPE, ALLAN MELVILL investment banker; b. Boston, Mass., Nov. 24, 1879; s. William Carroll and Mabel Richmond (Downer) P.; grad. Boston Latin Sch., 1898; B.Sc., U.S. Mil. Acad., 1903; m. Elvira Dickson, Nov. 23, 1910 (dec.); children—Elvira Dickson, Allan Melvill (dec.), Thomas Melvill. Became connected with First Nat. Corp., Boston, 1920. v.p. in charge New York office, same corp., 1921-25, exec. v.p. and dir., 1925-28, pres., 1928-29; on separation of The First of Boston from parent instn., First Nat. Bank of Boston, in 1934, became pres., dir., mem. exec. com. The First Boston Corp., now dir., retired as pres., 1947; mem. board of directors Black Starr Gorham, Incorporated, Insuranshares Certificates, Inc., Knapp Bros. Shoe Mfg. Corporation. Commissioned second lieutenant, cav., U.S. Army, 1903, and advanced through the grades to lt. col., 1919; served in Philippines; mem. Gen. Staff, France, 1918; participated with 53d French Div. in attack on Montdidier-Moyon front; with 30th Am. Div. on various sectors from Ypres to Amiens and in Meuse-Argonne; instr. Gen. Staff Coll., also staff officer G.H.Q., Chaumont; sec. Gen. Staff, Washington; resigned from service. Trustee Silver Hill Foundation. Vice pres. council N.Y.U., 1938-51; Commerce and Industry Assn. of N.Y. (pres. 1945-48); pres. Welfare Council N.Y.C., 1943-46. Mem. Assn. Grads. U.S. Mil. Acad. (hon. mem., trustee endowment fund), Investment Bankers Assn. (pres. 1931-32), Am. Acceptance Council (pres. 1933-35), Nat. Inst. Social Scis. (v.p.), West Point Soc. of N.Y. (pres. 1936-38), Beta Gamma Sigma (hon.), Pilgrims of U.S. Rep. Episcopalian. Clubs: West Point University (N.Y.C.); Army and Navy (Washington). Home: Mt. Holly Rd., Katonah, N.Y. Office: 15 Broad St., N.Y.C. 5. Died Mar. 29, 1963; buried St. Matthew's Ch., Bedford, N.Y.

POPE, FRANCIS HORTON, army officer; b. Fort Leavenworth, Kan., May 7, 1876; s. John (maj. gen., U.S. Army) and Clara Pomeroy (Horton) P.; grad. U.S. Mil. Acad., 1897; grad. Ecole de l'Intendance, Paris, 1914, Army War Coll., 1924; m. Harriet Ankeny, Oct. 20, 1908; 1 dau., Mary Ankeny; m. 2d, Blanche Wilson Hampson, Sept. 27, 1924. Commd. 2d lt. Cav., U.S. Army, 1897; promoted through grades to col., July 1, 1920; apptd. asst. q.m. gen., Jan. 24, 1927, with rank of brig. gen., term of 4 yrs.; served in Cuba, Spanish-Am. War; with Army of Cuban Occupation, 1899; instr.

mathematics, U.S. Mil. Acad., 1899-1903; Philippine campaigns, 1903-05; Mexican Punitive Expdn., 1916; lt. col. and col. (temp.), in France, World War, 1917-19; dir. Motor Transport Service, A.E.F., Feb.-Aug. 1918; dep. dir. Motor Transport Corps, Aug. 1918-Aug. 1919; retired from active service by operation of law, May 31, 1940, brig. gen. U.S. Army (retired); on active duty to December 31, 1943. Mem. Mil. Order World War, Soc. Army of Santiago de Cuba, Soc. Moro Campaigns, Mil. Order Loyal Legion, Am. Legion. Decorated D.S.M. (U.S.); Officer Legion of Honor (Franch). Episcopalian. Clubs: Army and Navy, Chevy Chase. Home: Washington DC Died June 1971.

POPE, FREDERICK, corp. official; b. Boston, Mass., Nov. 20, 1877; s. Eugene Alexander and Ella M. (Brown) P.; S.B., Lawrence Scientific Sch. (Harvard), 1901; m. Mary Stockton McLaughlin, Apr. 8, 1912; children—Frederick, Richard Stockton. Cons. engr., 1912; organized the Standard Aniline Products Co. and built the first dye plant to start in U.S. after beginning of World War; cons. engr. Newport Chem. Works, 1915-17; refinanced New York Steam Corp., 1920, 1st v.p. in charge operations, 1920-23; dir. Fiduciary Trust Co., Salvage Process Corp. (N.Y.), Rio Grande Gateway Bridge Corp. (Brownsville, Tex.). Served as major and assistant chief of Chemical Warfare Service in A.E.F., 1917-19; reorganized Chem. Warfare Service for A.E.F. Consultant to War Dept. since 1942, to Office War Mobilization since 1943. At request of Gen. Lucius Clay went to Germany for Survey of German chem. plants, chem. industry, 1948; at request of Gen. MacArthur went to Japan for survey of Japanese chem. plants, chem. industry, 1949. Trustee Lingnan U.; member Overseer's Com. to Visit Grad. School Engrng. and Physics Dept., Harvard. Mem. Council of Fgn. Relations. Decorated Officier d'Academie (French). Republican. Episcopalian. Clubs: Century, Union, Harvard, New York Yacht, Traveller's (Paris). Home: 969 Fifth Avenue, New York, N.Y.; and "Little River Farm," Wilton, Conn. Office: 30 Rockefeller Plaza, New York NY

POPE, JAMES WORDEN army officer; b. Louisville, Ky., June 6, 1846; s. Edmund Pendleton and Nancy (Johnson) P.; student Indiana U., Bloomington, Ind., 2 yrs.; grad. U.S. Mil. Acad., 1868; m. Mary E. Lynch, Oct. 27, 1880. Commd. 2d lt. 5th Inf., June 15, 1868; 1st lt., Mar. 20, 1879; capt. asst. q.m., Feb. 20, 1885; maj. q.m., June 11, 1897; lt. col. chief q.m. U.S. Vols., May 9, 1898; hon. disch. from vol. service, Sept. 2, 1899; lt. col. dep. q.m. gen., July 5, 1902; col. asst. q.m. gen., Feb. 16, 1907; retired, by operation of law, June 6, 1910; brig. gen. retired, Aug. 29, 1916. Participated in numerous campaigns against Indians during first 10 yrs. of service, including expdn. under Gen. Eugene A. Carr, 1868-69, campaign of Gen. Miles in I.Ty., 1874-75, operations following the Custer Massacre, 1876-77, Bannock War, 1878, etc.; in comd. U.S. Mil. Prison, 1887-95; in charge improvements in Yellowstone Park, 1897; chief q.m. Philippine Expdn., under Gen. Merritt, 1898-99; later chief q.m. depts. of Colo. and the Gulf, under Gens. Merriam, MacArthur, Funston, Baldwin, Duvall, Davis and Thomas. Recommended for bvt. of capt. "for distinguished and valuable service" in campaign against Kiowa and other Indian tribes, 1874-75. Home: Denver, Colo. Died Aug. 23, 1919.

POPE, JOHN army officer; b. Louisville, Ky., Mar. 16, 1822; s. Nathaniel and Lucretia (Backus) P.; grad. U.S. Mil. Acad., 1842; m. Clara Pomeroy Horton, Sept. 15, 1859, 4 children. Brevetted 1st lt. U.S. Army, 1846, served under Gen. Taylor in Mexican War; commd. capt., 1847; chief topog. engr. Dept. of N.M., 1851-53; commd. 1st lt., 1853, capt., 1856; mustering officer at Chgo., 1861; promoted brig. gen. U.S. Volunteers, 1861; commanded Army of the Mississippi for opening of river 1862; maj. gen. U.S. Volunteers, 1862; organized and concentrated all separate forces in region of Rappahannock and Shenadoah into Army of Va.; commd. brig. gen. U.S. Army, 1862; defeated in 2d Battle of Manassas, relieved of command, 1862; brevetted maj.-gen. U.S. Army, 1865; commanded 3d Mil. Dist. (Ga., Ala., Fla.), 1867, Dept. of the Lakes, 1868-70, Dept. of Miss., 1870-83, Dept. of Cal. and Div. of Pacific, 1883-86; commd. maj. gen., 1882. Died Sandusky, O., Sept. 23, 1892.

POPE, PERCIVAL CLARENCE officer U.S.M.C.; b. Charlestown, Mass. Feb. 28, 1841; s. Commodore John and Sarah W. P.; ed. pub. schs.; m. Sarah W. Hartwell. Apptd. captain's clk., July 9, 1861; and served on Richmond until Nov. 4, 1861 (resigned); commd. 2d and 1st lt., U.S. Marine Corps, Nov. 25, 1861; promoted through the grades to rank of brig. gen. U.S.M.C., and retired Feb. 28, 1905. Bvtd. capt., Sept. 8, 1863, "for gallant and meritorious service in night attack upon Ft. Sumter"; also received medal for distinguished services in civil war. Home: Milton, Mass. Died Jan. 23, 1922.

POPE, RALPH ELTON ret. naval officer; b. Waupaca, Wis., Jan. 28, 1875; s. George Freeborn and Jennie Maria (Fisher) P.; M.A., U.S. Naval Acad., 1899; student Naval War Coll., 1926-27, Georgetown U., 1931; m. Nellie Belle Drum, June 4, 1904; 1 son, Earl Hallet. Commd. ensign U.S. Navy, 1901, and advanced through grades to rear adm., 1934; ret., 1934; served in West Indies Campaign, 1898, and on U.S.S. Texas; served in Cuban Pacification, 1908, in Mexico, 1911-17, Nicaraguan Pacification, 1912, with U.S. Naval escort, 1918, in Europe, 1918-19. Awarded Santiago Medal, 1898; U.S. Navy Cross (for disablement of German submarine off coast of Africa), 1918; Merito di Guerra, Italy (for rescue of Italian Seaplane and compilation of war instructions for Italy), 1918. Mem. Ancient and Hon. Sons of Gunboats (Philippine order, 1899-1905), Hi-Hatters (Cal.). Republican. Clubs: Coronado (Cal.) Country, Coronado Beach. Author articles for U.S. Naval Inst. Home: 475 A Av., Coronado, Cal. Died May 13, 1959.

PORTER, ANDREW army officer, surveyor; b. Montgomery County, Pa., Sept. 24, 1743; s. Robert Porter; m. Elizabeth McDowell, Mar. 10, 1767; m. 2d, Elizabeth Parker, May 20, 1777; 13 children. In charge of an English and math. sch. Phila., 1767-76; commd. capt. of Marines, 1776; fought at Trenton, Princeton, Brandywine, Germantown; joined Sullivan's expdn. against Indians of Central N.Y., 1779; supervised manufacture ammunition at Phila. for siege of Yorktown, 1781; lt. col., also col. 4th (Pa.) Arty., 1782; commisssary for commn. which surveyed southwestern boundary of Pa., 1784, assisted in determining Western termination of Mason-Dixon line; commr. to run Western and No. boundaries of Pa., 1785-87; commd. brig. gen. Pa. Militia, 1800, later maj. gen.; surveyor gen. Pa., 1809-13. Died Harrisburg, Pa., Nov. 16, 1813.

PORTER, CHARLES VERNON lawyer; b. Natchitoches, La., Apr. 29, 1885; s. Charles Vernon and Violet (Lachs) P.; grad. La. State Normal Coll., 1903; LL.B., Yale, 1910; m. Jayne Lobdell, June 18, 1914; 1 dau., Jane (Mrs. Frank W. Middleton, Jr.). Admitted to La. bar, 1910, since practiced in Baton Rouge; mem. Taylor, Porter, Brooks, Fuller & Phillips, 1912—; dir. La. Nat. Bank of Baton Rouge, Gulf States Utilities Co., California Co., Baton Rouge Water Works Co. Mem. La. State Civil Service Commn., 1941-44. Served as lt. col. Judge Adv. Gen. Dept., U.S. Army, World War I; div. judge adv. 79th Div. Mem. Am., La. (past pres.) bar assns., Newcomen Soc. N.A., Phi Delta Phi, Sigma Nu. Episcopalian (sr. warden, vestryman 1919—). Clubs: Boston (New Orleans, La.); Baton Rouge Country; City (Baton Rouge, La.). Member of the board of editors of Yale Law Jour., 1909-18; Compiler (with H. P. Breazeale) Revenue Law of Louisiana, 1911. Home: 2230 Oleander St. Office: La. Nat. Bank Bldg., Baton Rouge. Died July 4, 1962.

PORTER, DAVID naval officer, diplomat; b. Boston, Feb. 1, 1780; s. David and Rebecca (Gay) P.; m. Evelina Anderson, Mar. 10, 1808, 10 children including David Dixon, William D., 1 adopted son, David Glasgow Farragut. Commd. lt., 1799; comdr. ship Enterprise during Tripolian War, captured with ship Philadelphia, imprisoned; commd. master comdt., 1806; commanded New Orleans Naval Sta., 1809-11; comdr. Essex raiding English commerce during War of 1812, 1811, took Essex to Pacific (1st U.S. naval vessel in that ocean); commd. capt., 1812; renamed one of Marquesas islands Madison Island, 1813, took possession on behalf of U.S., erected Ft. Madison and Village of Madison; commr. Navy Bd., 1815-23; comdr.-in-chief West India Squadron, 1823-25; recalled by sec. of navy and ct. martialled for retaliatory action against Spanish authorities in P.R., 1825; resigned from Navy, 1826; comdr.-in-chief Mexican Navy with rank of gen. of marine, 1826-29; U.S. consul gen. to Algiers, 1830-36; chargé d'affaires to Turkey, 1836-43, minister, 1839. Author: Journal of a Cruise Made to the Pacific Ocean, 1815; Guide-Book to Constantinople, circa 1842. Died Pera, Constantinople, Mar. 3, 1843; buried Woodlands Cemetery, Phila.

PORTER, DAVID DIXON naval officer; b. Chester, Pa., June 8, 1813; s. David and Evelina (Anderson) P.; m. George Ann Patterson, Mar. 10, 1839, 10 children. Commd. lt. U.S. Navy, 1841; commanded landing party of 70 seamen, captured fort, Tabasco, Mexico, 1847; commanded mcht. steamer Panama, 1849, made voyage through Straits of Magellan to Pacific; commanded privately owned mail steamer Georgia, 1850-52, made regular trips between N.Y.C., Havana, Chagres; capt. ship Golden Age between Melbourne and Sydney for Australian S.S. Co., 1852-circa 1855; 1st lt. Portsmouth (Va.) Navy Yard, 1857-60, took prominent part in preliminary planning of New Orleans expdn.; in command mortar flotilla under Adm. Farragut, New Orleans and on Mississippi River, 1862; commanded fleets below fts. St. Philip and Jackson, demanded and accepted their surrender (on favorable terms), 1862; served as acting rear adm., comdr. Mississippi Squadron, 1862, aided U.S. Army in capture of Ark. Post, cooperated with Grant in assault on Vicksburg, 1863; commd. rear adm., 1863, took charge of lower Mississippi River as far down as New Orleans; commanded naval force cooperating with army in Red River expdn., 1864; commanded naval forces attacking Ft. Fisher, 1864-65; with Gen. Terry captured defenses of Wilmington, N.C.; commanded N. Atlantic Blockading Squadron, 1864; supt. U.S. Naval Acad., 1865-69, improved curriculum and instrn. methods; conducted unsuccessful diplomatic mission to Santo Domingo to secure cession or lease of Samana Bay, 1866-67; apptd. adviser to Sec. of Navy Adolph Borie by Pres. Grant, 1869-70, instituted reform policy, organized bds. to inspect fleets and navy yards, began to repair many vessels; promoted adm., 1870; chosen to command fleet assembled at Key West, 1873; head Bd. of Inspection, 1877-91. Author: Memoir of Commodore David Porter, 1875. Died Washington, D.C., Feb. 13, 1891; buried Arlington (Va.) Nat. Cemetery.

PORTER, DAVID DIXON officer U.S. Marine Corps; b. Washington, D.C., 1878: s. Col. Carlile Patterson Porter; g.s. famous admiral of same name; m. Winifred Metcalf Mattingly, June 24, 1908; 1 dau., Carlile Patterson. Commissioned officer U.S. Marine Corps, 1899, and advanced through the grades to maj. gen.; served through Spanish-Am. War, Boxer war in China and in Philippines; adj. and insp. U.S. Marine Corps, Washington, D.C., from 1929; now retired. Awarded Medal of Honor, 1933. Home: 2023 De Lancey Place, Philadelphia, Pa. Died Feb. 25, 1944.

PORTER, FITZ-JOHN maj. gen. vols. and col. U.S.A.; b. Portsmouth, N.H., Aug. 31, 1822; son of Capt. John Porter, U.S.N.; grad. West Point, 1845; instr. West Point, 1849-55; m. Harriet Pierson, dau. John Cooke, New York. Served in Mexican war, 1846-48, in principal battles; wounded at Belen Gate, City of Mexico; bvtd. capt. and maj. for gallantry; asst. adjt. gen. at Ft. Leavenworth during Kansas troubles; later asst. adjt. gen. and chief of staff on Utah expedition, when he detected and defeated scheme of Mormon authorities to make and pass $2,000,000 in counterfeit checks on U.S. Treasury, and secured conviction of the engraver. On special duty in Gulf of Mexico, Feb., 1861, saved companies of art. and inf. from surrender to Texas. Commissioned col., May 14, 1861; brig. gen. vols., May 17, 1861; maj. gen. vols., July 4, 1862; and commanded 5th army corps; bvtd. brig. gen. U.S.A. for gallant conduct battle of Chickahominy, Va. Participated in the battles of the Peninsula campaign until cashiered, Jan. 21, 1863, and "forever disqualified from holding any office of profit or trust under the Govt. of the U.S." for alleged violation of Articles of War. Charges were re-examined and new testimony (inaccessible during trial) taken by bd. apptd. by Pres. Hayes, and he was found not guilty. It was also found that he had saved the army of Northern Va. from disaster. He was reinstated as col., 1886, and retired at his own request. Was supt. mining operations in Colo., 1864-65; merchant, New York, 1865-71; supt. in erection of N.J. State Asylum for the Insane, Morristown, 1872-75; commr. public works, New York, 1875-76; asst. receiver Central R.R. of N.J., 1877-82; police commr. New York, 1884-88; fire commr., 1888-89; merchant, 1889-93; cashier postoffice, New York, 1893-97. Home: Morristown, N.J. Died 1901.

PORTER, GEORGE FRENCH b. Chicago, Ill., July 26, 1881; s. Henry Holmes and Eliza French P.; B.A., Yale, 1903; married. Dir. Chicago Daily News, Chicago Transfer & Clearing Co., Nevada Land Co. Trustee, Art Inst. Chicago. Western treas. Prog. Nat. Com., 1912; chmn. conv. com. Prog. Nat. Com., 1916; asst. to chmn. Rep. Nat. Conv., 1920. Asst. to dir. and chief State Councils Sect. of Council Nat. Defense, Washington, Apr. 1917-Mar. 1918; capt. C.W.S.; hon. discharged, Dec. 1918. Home: Chicago, Ill. Died Feb. 23, 1927.

PORTER, HAROLD EVERETT ("HOLWORTHY HALL"), author; b. Boston, Sept. 19, 1887; s. Albert de Lance and Louella (Root) P.; A.B., cum laude, Harvard, 1909; Litt.D., Wake Forest Coll., 1921; m. Marian, d. John L. Heffron, M.D., Sc.D., of Syracuse, N.Y., Oct. 25, 1911; children—Jean, John Heffron, Richard Montgomery Sears. With A. D. Porter Co., pubs., New York, 1910-16, pres., 1915-16. Commd. 1st lt., A.S., Sig. R. C., Feb. 27, 1918; capt. Air Service, U.S.A., July 20, 1918; maj. Air Service, O.R.C., Apr. 9, 1920. Author: Pepper, 1915; Paprika, 1915; What He Least Expected, 1917; Dormie One, 1917; The Man Nobody Knew, 1919; The Six Best Cellars (with Hugh M. Kahler), 1919; Egan, 1920; Aerial Observation, 1921; Rope, 1921; (with Robert Middlemass) The Valiant (1-act play), 1921; Colossus, 1930. Died June 20, 1936.

PORTER, HORACE diplomatist, soldier; b. Huntingdon, Pa., Apr. 15, 1837; s. late David Rittenhouse P. (gov. Pa.) and Josephine (McDermett) P.; ed. Lawrence Scientific Sch. (Harvard); grad. U.S. Mil. Acad., 1860; (LL.D., Union Univ., 1894, Princeton Univ., 1906, Williams Coll., 1907, Harvard niv., 1910); m. Sophie K. McHarg, Dec. 23, 1863 (died 1903). Second lt. U.S.A., Apr. 22, 1861; 1st lt., June 7, 1861; capt., Mar. 3, 1863; lt. col. and a.-d.-c. to Gen. Grant, Apr. 4, 1864; col. of staff and a.-d.-c. to the gen.-in-chief U.S.A., July 25, 1866; bvtd. capt., Apr. 11, 1862, for seige of Pulaski; Congressional Medal of Honor for Chickamauga, Sept. 20, 1863; bvtd. maj., May 6, 1864, for Wilderness; lt. col., Aug. 16, 1864, for New- market Heights, Va.; col. U.S.V., Feb. 24, 1865; col. U.S.A., Mar. 13, 1865, for services during war, and brig. gen., Mar. 13, 1865, "for gallant services in the field." Asst. sec. of war, 1866; exec. sec. to President Grant, 1869-73. Became v.p. Pullman Palace Car Co., 1873; was pres. N.Y., West Shore & Buffalo R.R., St.L.&S.F. Ry. Co. U.S. ambassador to France, 1897-1905. Orator at inauguration of Washington Arch, New York, May 4, 1895, and dedication of Grant's Tomb, New York, Apr. 27, 1897 (for the building of which he collected the necessary funds by private subscription); at inauguration Rochambeau Statue, Washington, May 24, 1902; at Centennial of foundation of West Point Mil. Acad., June 11, 1902; interment of Paul Jones' body at

Annapolis, Apr. 23, 1906, etc. Decorated with Grand Cross of Legion of Honor by French Govt., 1904; gold medal for patriotism by Sultan of Turkey, 1901. Recovered body of Paul Jones at personal expense in Paris, Apr. 7, 1905. Received by unanimous vote the thanks of Congress and privilege of the floor of both houses for life. Author: West Point Life, 1860; Campaigning with Grant, 1897. Home: New York, N.Y. Died May 29, 1921.

PORTER, JAMES DAVIS governor; b. Paris, Tenn., Dec. 7, 1828; A.B., U. of Nashville, 1846, A.M., 1849 (LL.D., 1884); law student Cumberland U., Tenn.; m. Susanna, d. Gen. John H. Dunlop, 1851. Began practice, 1850; mem. Tenn. Legislature, 1859-61; adj. gen. on staff Maj. Gen. Cheatham, C.S.A.; del. Tenn. Constl. Conv., 1870; judge 12th Jud. Circuit, 1870-74; gov. of Tenn., 1874-78; pres. Nashville & Chattanooga R.R. Co., 1879-83; asst. sec. of state, U.S., 1885-89; E.E. and M.P. to Chile, 1893-97. Chancellor U. of Nashville, 1901-—; trustee Peabody Edn. Fund from 1883. Pres. Tenn. Hist. Soc. Author: Confederate Military History of Tennessee. Home: Nashville, Tenn. Died May 18, 1912.

PORTER, JAMES MADISON sec. of war, railroad pres.; b. nr. Norristown, Pa., Jan. 6, 1793; s. Gen. Andrew and Elizabeth (Parker) P.; m. Eliza Michler, Sept. 18, 1821. Raised volunteer company, Phila., 1813, commd. 2d lt. (co. served as garrison until relieved by Pa. Militia); continued mil. service in Pa. Militia, reached rank of col.; admitted to Pa. bar, 1813; a founder Lafayette Coll. (chartered 1826), Easton, Pa., pres. bd. trustees, 1826-52, prof. jurisprudence and polit. econ., 1837-52; mem. Pa. Constl. Conv., 1838; pres. judge 12th Jud. Dist., 1839-40; U.S. Sec. of War ad interim, 1843-44 (Senate refused to ratify his nomination); elected to Pa. Legislature, 1849; pres. judge 22d Jud. Dist., 1853-55; 1st pres. Delaware, Lehigh, Schuylkill & Susquehanna R.R. (chartered 1847), name changed to L V. R.R., 1853, pres., 1853-56; pres. Belvidere Delaware R.R.; Mason. Died Easton, Nov. 11, 1862.

PORTER, JAMES PERTICE psychologist; b. Hillsboro, Ind., Sept. 23, 1873; s. Alfred and Elizabeth (Marksbury) P.; student Normal Sch., Terre Haute, 1890-91, 1892-93; A.B., Ind. U., 1898, A.M., 1901; hon. fellow Clark U., 1903-07, Ph.D., 1906; Sc.D., Waynesburg Coll., 1917; m. Myrta Wayne Brown, Dec. 24, 1895; children—Ernest C. (dec.), Helen, Marjorie. Instr. psychology Ind. U., 1900-03; asst. prof. psychology Clark Coll., 1907-12, prof. psychology, 1912-22, dean of faculty, 1909-22; prof. psychology Ohio U., 1922-43, prof. emeritus, 1943; instr. psychol. U. Ill. Extension, Danville, Ill., 1948. With Adj. Gen.'s Office, N.Y. 1944. Has made spl. studies of the English sparrow, of spiders, and of intelligence and imitation in birds, human intelligence and personality. Lecturer ednl., psychology, Columbia, 1913-14. Capt., Sanitary Corps U.S. Army, 1918; maj. R.C. Mem. Am., Midwestern (pres. 1941-42) psychol. assns., N.E.A., Internat. Congress of Zoology, Am. Assn. Applied Psychologists, Sigma Chi, Phi Beta Kappa. Editor Journal of Applied Psychology, 1920-43. Mem. Internat. Congress of Psychology and Psycho-technique, Paris, 1927. Home: 1124 Grant St., Danville, Ill. Died Sept. 1956.

PORTER, JAMES W(INTERS) judge; b. Humeston, Ia., June 16, 1887; s. Harvey and Nevada (Ulm) P.; LL.B., Drake U., 1910; m. Birdie Gwinn, Sept. 25, 1910; 1 son, Gwinn Ulm. Admitted to Ida. bar, 1910, practiced in Twin Falls, 1910-37; dist. judge 11th Jud. Dist., 1937-48; justice Supreme Court of Ida., 1949-—, chief justice, 1953-54, 54-59, 59-—. Served with the Mexican Border Service, 1916-17; capt. F.A., U.S. Army, A.E.F., France and Germany, 1917-19. Decorated Campaign medal with five stars. Mem. Am. Legion (past post comdr.), Ida. State Bar Assn. Democrat (past co. chmn., state committeeman). Elk. Clubs: Kiwanis, Nat. "D." Home: 1603 E. Jefferson. Office: Statehouse, Boise. Died Dec. 9, 1959.

PORTER, JOHN LINCOLN surgeon; b. Alstead, N.H., July 2, 1864; s. Samuel H. and Harriet (Emerson) P.; M.D., Northwestern U., 1894; m. Ethel, d. David Quigg, of Chicago, Feb. 9, 1899. Interne, St. Luke's Hosp., 1894-95; prof. orthopedic surgery, U. of Ill. Med. Sch., 1900-17; prof. same, Northwestern U. Med. Sch., 1917-—; attending orthopedic surgeon, St. Luke's Hosp. Apptd. mem. Advisory Bd. on Orthopedics, U.S.A., Aug. 1917. Maj. M.C., U.S.A., 1918-19. Republican. Home: Evanston, Ill. Died Aug. 11, 1938.

PORTER, JOSEPH YATES physician; b. Key West, Fla., Oct. 21, 1847; s. Joseph Yates and Mary (Randolph) P.; ed. in N.J.; M.D., Jefferson Med. Coll., Phila., 1870; m. Louisa Curry, 1870. Entered army, July 1870, as acting asst. surgeon; asst. surgeon U.S.A., June 26, 1875; capt. asst. surgeon, June 26, 1880; apptd. deputy surgeon-gen. with rank of lt. col., and placed on retired list, Mar. 8, 1907, by Act. of Congress, Mar. 2, 1907. Went through yellow fever epidemic at Dry Tortugas, 1873, Key West and Tampa, Fla., 1887, Key West, 1899, Miami, 1899, Pensacola, 1905; in charge govt. relief measures at Jacksonville, Fla., during epidemic in 1888; made 1st demonstrations of mosquito law of yellow fever transmission in U.S. in Tampa, 1905, in an imported case of yellow fever from New Orleans. State health officer of Fla., 1889-1917; recalled to active duty as lt. col., Med. Corps U.S.A., June 6, 1917; camp surgeon, Camp Joseph E. Johnston, Jacksonville, Fla., Oct. 1, 1917-Jan. 31, 1919; now quarantine insp. U.S. Pub. Health Service. Home: Jacksonville, Fla. Died Mar. 16, 1927.

PORTER, PETER BUELL congressman, sec. of war; b. Salisbury, Conn., Aug. 14, 1773; s. Joshua and Abigail (Buell) P.; grad. Yale, 1791; attended Litchfield (Conn.) Law Sch.; m. Letitia Breckenridge, 1818. Admitted to bar; began practice law, Canandaigua, N.Y., 1795; clk. Ontario County (N.Y.), 1797-1804; mem. N.Y. State Legislature, 1801-02; mem. firm Porter, Barton & Co. (which acquired monopoly of transp. bus. on portage between Lewiston and Schlosser); mem. U.S. Ho. of Reps. from N.Y., 11th-12th, 14th congresses, 1809-13, 1815-Jan. 23, 1816, leader "War Hawks"; mem. N.Y. Canal Commn., 1810; q.m. gen. N.Y. Militia, 1812; authorized by War Dept. to raise, command brigade of volunteers militia, 1813, instructed to incorporate them with "corps" from Six Nations Indians, commanded both, 1813; 14; commd. maj. gen. N.Y. Militia, 1814; voted gold medal by Congress, 1814; sec. state N.Y., 1815, 16, U.S. commr. to determine internat. boundary from St. Lawrence to Lake of Woods, 1816-22; regent U. State N.Y., 1824-30; U.S. sec. of war, 1828-29; Whig presdl. elector, 1840. Died Niagara Falls, N.Y., Mar. 20, 1844; buried Oakwood Cemetery, Niagara Falls.

PORTER, THEODORIC commodore; b. in D.C., Dec. 14, 1849; s. late Admiral David D. P. (U.S.N.); g.s. Commodore David P.; descendant of fighting stock on both sides; grad. U.S. Naval Acad., 1869; m. Bettie, d. Judge J. Thompson Mason, of Annapolis, Md., Feb. 12, 1873 (died 1909); m. 2d, Henrietta McCulloch Cheston, d. late Michael McCulloch, of Montreal, 1910. Promoted through the various grades to capt., June 19, 1905; commodore, June 30, 1908, and retired at own request. Served 43 yrs. in U.S. Navy, 20 yrs. at sea and 23 yrs. on shore or other duty; last comd. U.S. cruiser Washington. Home: Annapolis, Md. Died June 18, 1920.

PORTER, WHITNEY CLAIR, physician; b. Indpls., Aug. 19, 1897; s. Harry Alfred and Daisy (White) P.; M.D., U. Colo., 1926; m. Sarah Jane Hunter, Aug. 27, 1928; children—Whitney Allen, Catherine (Mrs. William Stevens Cole). Intern, Denver Gen. Hosp., 1926-27, cons. ophthalmologist, until 1970; postgrad. in phys. ophthalmology U. Pa. Grad. Sch. Medicine, 1929-30; resident in ophthalmology U. Ia., 1931-33, asst. in ophthalmology, 1932; hon. staff Mercy, Childrens hosps.; cons. staff St. Lukes Hosp.; ophthlmology staff Colo. Gen. Hosp.; asso. clin. prof. ophthlmology U. Colo. Sch. Medicine, Denver. Served to lt. col., M.C., AUS. Diplomate Am. Bd. Opthalmology. Mem. A.M.A., Am. Acad. Ophthalmology and Otolaryngology. Home: Denver CO Died Aug. 25, 1970; buried Denver CO

PORTER, WILLIAM N(ICHOLS), ret. army officer, business exec.; b. Lima, O., Mar. 15,21886; s. William Harley and Ilva (Nichols) P.; B.S., U.S. Naval Acad., 1909; grad. Army Indsl. Coll., Washington, 1926, Command and Gen. Staff Sch., Ft. Leavenworth, Kan., 1927, Chem. Warfare Sch., Edgewood, Md., 1931, Air Corps Tactical Sch., Maxwell Field, Ala., 1937, Army War Coll., Washington, 1938; m. Gladys Baxter, July 20, 1910; children—William Baxter (U.S.N.), John Harley (dec.), Margaret Baxter (wife L.M. Stevens, Jr., U.S.N.). Commd. ensign, U.S.N., 1909, resigned, 1910; commd. 2d lt., U.S. Army, 1910, advanced through grades to maj. gen., 1941; comd. 30th Arty. C.A.C., 1918-19; transferred to C.W.S., 1920, chief, 1941-45; ret. 1945; pres. Chem. Constrn. Corp., 1947-53; chmn. bd. 1953-54; chemical consultant American Cyanamid Company; cons. Byrne Assos., N.Y., profl. engr. N.Y., O. Awarded Distinguished Service Medal, Comdr. Order Brit. Empire, Order of Leopold (Belgium). Past mem. Nat. Research Council. Mem. Am.-Arab Assn. for Commerce and Industry (pres.). Epis. Clubs: Army and Navy, Army-Navy Country (Washington). Home: Key West FL Died Feb. 1973.

PORTERFIELD, LEWIS BROUGHTON naval officer; b. Greenville, Ala., Oct. 30, 1879; s. James Richard and Flora McFayden (Cowart) P.; B.S., U.S. Naval Acad., 1902; student U.S. Naval War Coll., 1924-25; m. Maud Paxton Starke, Aug. 5, 1908; children—Paul Lee, Alice Starke, James Temple Starke. Commd. ensign U.S. Navy, May 5, 1902, and advanced through grades to capt., Feb. 16, 1925; nom. rear adm., Dec. 12, 1935. Mem. Soc. of Cincinnati. Awarded D.S.M. (U.S.); Italian War Cross. Protestant. Clubs: Army and Navy (Washington, D.C.); Bohemian (San Francisco). Address: Navy Department, Washington, D.C. Died Apr. 5, 1942.

POSEY, CHESTER ALFRED, advt. exec.; b. Peekskill, N.Y., Jan. 14, 1896; s. Alfred and Christine Eliza (Cooke) P.; A.B., Yale, 1917; m. Olive Clarke Lewis, Sept. 14, 1921; children—Chester Lewis, Priscilla. Copy editor J. Walter Thompson Co., N.Y.C., 1919-25; established firm Olmstead, Perrin & Leffingwell, advt., N.Y.C., 1925, merged with H.K. McCann Co., 1929; v.p., dir. McCann-Erickson, Inc., 1929-58, sr. v.p. Captain, 30th F.A., U.S. Army, World War I. Home: Scarsdale Manor S., Scarsdale, NY; also Candlewood Lake Club, Brookfield, CT Home: Pompano Beach FL Died Feb. 11, 1971.

POSEY, THOMAS army officer, senator; b. Fairfax County, Va., July 9, 1750; m. Martha Matthews; m. 2d, Mary (Alexander) Thornton; 1 dau., Mary. Served with Va. militia against Indian tribes on Western frontier, 1774; mem. Va. Com. of Correspondence; commd. maj. 7th Va. Regt. during Revolutionary War; promoted lt. col., 1782, brig. gen., 1793; moved to Ky., 1794; mem. Ky. Senate, presiding officer, 1805, 06; lt. gov. Ky., 1805-09; commd. maj. gen. U.S. Volunteers, 1809; moved to Attakapas, La.; mem. U.S. Senate from La., Oct. 1812-Feb. 1813; gov. Ind. Territory, 1813-16; Indian agt. Ill. Territory, 1816-18. Died Shawneetown, Ill.; buried Westwood Cemetery, Shawneetown.

POST, CHANDLER RATHFON prof. fine arts; b. Detroit, Mich., Dec. 14, 1881; s. William R. and Anne M. (Rathfon) P.; A.B., Harvard, 1904, A.M., 1905, Ph.D., 1909; student American School at Athens, 1904-05; L.H.D. (honorary), University of Michigan, 1953. With Harvard, 1905-—, various positions, including asst. in English, 1905-06, instr. in English, French, Italian, Greek, Romance langs., fine arts, until 1912, asst. prof. Greek and fine arts, 1912-20, asso. prof., 1920-23, prof., 1922-34, Boardman prof. fine arts, 1934-50. Capt. inf., World War, serving as asst. to mil. attaché, Rome, 1917-18. Chevalier Order of St. Maurice and St. Lazarus (Italy), 1918; Real Academia de Bellas Artes De San Jorge (Barcelona), 1957; Real Academie de la Historia, 1958; Commendador Encomienda De Isabel La Catolica (Spain), 1959. Mem. Am. Acad. Arts and Scis., Coll. Art Assn. Hispanic Soc. of Am., Am. Philos. Soc., Academia de San Luis (Saragossa, Spain), Acad. de Bellas Artes de Santa Isabel de Hungrid (Seville). Phi Beta Kappa. Democrat. Episcopalian. Club: Faculty (Cambridge). Author: Mediaeval Spain, Allegory, 1915; A History of European and American Sculpture, 1921; A History of Sculpture (with George H. Chase), 1924; A History of Spanish Painting (12 vols.), 1930-47. Contbr. to periodicals. Home: 11 Hilliard St., Cambridge, Mass. Died Nov. 2, 1959; buried Foxboro Cemetery, Foxboro, Mass.

POST, ELWYN DONALD army officer; b. Shelby, O., Nov. 30, 1899; s. Oliver Clyde and Mary Ann (Cumberworth) P.; student Coe Coll., 1917-19; B.S., U.S. Mil. Acad., 1923; grad. Inf. Sch., 1933, Command and Gen. Staff Coll., 1938; m. Virginia Rodney Ewalt, Sept. 14, 1925; children—Patricia Ann (wife H. F. G. Boswgll, Brit. Army), Elwyn Donald. Command. 2d lt., inf., U.S. Army, 1923, advanced through grades to maj gen., 1950; instr. tactics, asst. comdt. U.S. Mil. Acad., 1933-37; chief staff Lt. Gen. S. B. Buckner, Alaska, 10th Army on Okinawa, 1940-45; chief staff Command and Gen. Staff Coll., 1946-50; asst. div. comdr. 1st Cav. Div., Korea, 1951-52; G-3, Army Field Forces, Ft. Monroe, Va., 1952-54; dep. chief of staff U.S. Army, Europe, 1954; now chief U.S. Army Mil. Dist. Ga., Atlanta. Decorated D.S.M., Silver Star, Legion of Merit, Commendation medal; Order of King of Thailand. Home: 12920 Fairhill Rd., Shaker Heights, O. Office: care Adjutant General, Department of Army, Washington. Died 1961.

POST, GEORGE BROWNE architect; b. New York, Dec. 15, 1837; s. Joel B. and Abby M. P.; C.E., New York U., 1858 (LL.D., Columbia, 1908); studied architecture with Richard M. Hunt; m. Alice M., d. William W. Stone, of New York, Oct. 14, 1863. Capt., maj., lt. col., and col. 22d N.Y. Vols. in Civil War. Engaged as architect at New York since the war; now head of Geo. B. Post & Sons, architects. Mem. expert com. to appoint a sculptor and select design for the LaFayette Monument erected in the Louvre, Paris; apptd. collaborator U.S. Forest Service, 1906; mem. Nat. Advisory Bd. on Fuels and Structural Materials, 1906-—; mem. Bur. Fine Arts, 1909-—; mem. bd. commrs. to St. Louis Expn., 1904; dir. Municipal Art Soc., 1906-—; mem. council Nat. Sculpture Soc.; pres. Fine Arts Fedn. of New York, 1898. Chevalier de la Legion d'Honneur, France, 1901; A.N.A., 1907, N.A., 1908; hon. corr. mem. Royal Inst. Brit. Architects, 1907; pres. Am. Inst. Architects, 1896-99, N.Y. Chapter same, 1904, Architectural League of New York, 1893-97. Home: Bernardsville. N.J. Died Nov. 28, 1913.

POST, WILEY aviator; b. Grand Plain, Tex., 1900; s. William Frank and May P.; m. May Lane, 1927. Farmer in Tex., later oil driller in Okla.; lost one eye in an accident, and was awarded $2,000; invested the award in a 2d hand airplane and began as flyer, 1924; made nearly 100 parachute jumps; winner of Chicago-Los Angeles Air Derby, in 9 hrs., 9 minutes and 4 seconds, 1930; made trip around the world with Harold Gatty, in 8 days, 15 hrs. and 51 minutes, in 1931; 2d round-the-world trip alone (the 1st to fly alone around the world), in 7 days, 18 hrs. and 49 minutes, in 1933. Served as aerial navigation instr. and adviser, U.S. Army. Home: Oklahoma City, Okla. Died Aug. 15, 1935.

POSTNIKOV, FEDOR ALEXIS (F. A. POST), engineer, aeronaut; b. Kovno, Russia, Feb. 29, 1872; s. Alexis Semen and Mary Fedor (Radchenko) P.; grad. 1st Imperial Mil. Sch. (Petrograd), 1891, with rank 2d lt. of Ussuri Cossack Army; Officers' Aeronautical Sch., St. Petersburg, 1897; grad. as mil. engr., St. Petersburg,

1899; capt., mil. engr., 1901; lt. col. Russian Admiralty (Navy Dept.), 1905; M.S. in C.E., U. of Calif., 1907; m. Mary Nicolas Smirnov, of St. Petersburg, Aug. 9, 1895. Cossacks scout comdr., 1892-4; sr. engr. Yards and Docks Dept., under Russian Govt., 1899-1906; officer-aeronaut in Russian Army, 1898; as head Navy Aero Detachment took part in defense of Vladivostok, and in raids with cruisers during Russo-Japanese War, in capacity as organizer and comdr. Navy Aero Detachment, 1904-5; commd. 1st lt. Aviation Sect. Signal Corps, U.S.A., Mar. 27, 1917; capt. jr. mil. aviator, July 24, 1917, at Ft. Omaha, Neb.; asst. aero engr., experimental work and designing dirigibles, with Good year Co., Akron, O., Jan.-May 1918; designing engr., with dock and terminal sect. Constrn. Corps, U.S. Army, Washington, D.C., until June 1919. Has designed and built numerous buildings, dams, harbors, etc. Internat. balloon pilot certificate No. 77. Mem. Russian Tech. Soc. (life), Aero Club of America, Internat. Esperanto Assn., etc. Author: Siberian Cossack Cousin, 1916. Writer on tech. subjects in English, Russian and Esperanto langs. Home: 1633 Dwight Way, Berkeley CA

POTT, WILLIAM SUMNER APPLETON govt. ofcl.; b. N.Y.C., Dec. 24, 1892; s. Francis Lister Hawks and Susan (Wong) P.; grad. Episcopal High Sch., Alexandria, Va., 1909; A.B., U. of Va., 1912, A.M., 1913, Ph.D., 1922; post grad. study Columbia, 1917; LL.D. (hon.), Union Coll., 1945; honorary L.H.D., Elmira Coll., Elmira, N.Y., 1949; m. Eleanor Welsh, December 30, 1931. Instructor in philosophy, St. John's U., Shanghai, China, 1913-16, prof., 1919-22; adjunct prof., U. of Va., 1916-17, asso. prof., 1922-27; chmn. dept. Oriental Langs. and Lit., U. of Calif., 1927-28; gen. mgr. staff Gen. Motors Export Co., 1928-30; pub. relations staff Gen. Motors Corp., 1930-35; pres. Elmira (N.Y.) Coll. 1935-49; cultural attaché, U.S. Embassy, Thailand since 1950. Mem. bd. of dirs. Elmira (N.Y.) Savings Bank. Served in O.T.C., Plattsburg, N.Y., Aug.-Dec. 1917; commd. 1st lt. 312th Inf., 78th Div., A.E.F., Dec. 1917; capt. and adj. 312th Inf., Dec. 1918. Sec. priorities div., Office Prodn. Management, Jan.-Apr. 1941. Trustee Elmira Coll., mem. bd. dirs. Arnot Art Gallery, 1945-46 Pres. Assn. Colls. and Univs., State of N.Y. Mem. Am. Philos Assn., N.Y. State Hist. Assn., Sigma Chi, Phi Beta Kappa, Pi Gamma Mu. Episcopalian. Clubs: City, Torch (Elmira, N.Y.); Century (New York). Author: Chinese Political Theory, 1925. Collaborator (with A.G.A. Balz) The Basis of Social Theory, 1924. Address: care of Elmira Bank & Trust Co., Elmira, N.Y.; also American Embassy, Bangkok, Thailand. Died Nov. 1967.

POTTER, CHARLES LEWIS army engr.; b. Lisbon Falls, Me., Jan. 24, 1864; s. Benjamin R. and Susan E. (Smullen) P.; grad. U.S. Mil. Acad., 1886; grad. Engr. Sch. of Application, 1889; m. Mrs. Sophie H. Nichols, Feb. 15, 1905. Commd. 2d lt. 5th Cav., July 1, 1886; transferred to engrs., Feb. 2, 1887; promoted through grades to col., Nov. 27, 1916. Spanish War and Philippine Insurrection, 1898-1900; with river and harbor works, Memphis, 1900-03, Duluth, 1903-06, Puerto Rico, 1907-10, St. Louis, 1910-12, St. Paul, 1912-15, Portland, Ore., 1915-16, Boston, 1916-17; dir. gas service, Washington, 1917-18; in charge 2d San Francisco Engr. Dist., 1918-20; pres. Miss. River Commn., Mar. 19, 1920-—. Mason. Died Aug. 6, 1928.

POTTER, DAVID, naval officer; b. Bridgeton, N.J., 1874; s. William Elmer and Alice (Eddy) P.; B.A., Princeton, 1896; admitted to N.J. bar, 1897; m. Jane, d. late Vice Chancellor Martin Philip Grey, 1904. Entered U.S. Navy 1898; served at sea during war with Spain and Philippine campaign; fiscal officer of customs, Vera Cruz, Mexico, during Am. occupation, 1914; mem. Navy Compensation Board, 1917-19; fleet paymaster Atlantic Fleet, 1919-21; paymaster gen. of Navy and chief Bur. of Supplies and Accounts, with rank of rear adm., 1921-25; mem. bd. for settlement of claims arising from treaty limiting naval armament, 1923; mem. Naval War Claims Bd., 1926-30; gen. insp., Supply Corps, West Coast, 1930-34; in charge Naval Finance and Supply Sch., 1934-38; promoted rear adm. Supply Corps, Nov. 14, 1927; retired Jan. 1, 1939. Author: (novels) The Lost Goddess, 1908; The Eleventh Hour, 1910; The Lady of the Spur, 1910; I Fasten a Bracelet, 1911; An Accidental Honeymoon, 1911; The Unspeakable Turke, 1912; The Streak, 1913; Diane of Star Hollow, 1918; The Marshes, 1919; (memoirs) Sailing The Sulu Sea, 1940, also monographs on financial and business affairs of the Navy, and has lectured on such subjects. Address: 2999 Pacific Av., San Francisco CA

POTTER, DELBERT MAXWELL, mining man; b. Canton, O.; s. Hiram B. and Arminda E. (Carter) P.; ed. grammar and high schs., Canton; m. Lizzie S. Dorsey, of Paola, Kan., Oct. 31, 1882. Began mining in New Mexico, 1882; was one of discovers of the Telegraph and Bald Mountain mining districts in N.M.; operated mines extensively in Colo., Cal., Ariz. and Mexico; now sec. and gen. mgr. of the Home Stake Gold Mining and Milling Company; pres. Ariz. Power & Water Co.; v.p. Ariz. Gold Mining & Milling Co.; builder and dir. Clifton Northern R.R.; prin. owner Morenci Inspiration Copper Co.; largely interested in irrigation projects and cattle ranching. Served as guide and scout in expdns. against Apache Indians and in Geronimo campaign; dep. U.S. marshal for Southern N.M. under Marshal Romero; chief dep. sheriff in Grant Co., N.M., under Sheriff Whitehill; p.m. gen. with rank of col., Ariz. N.G., on staff of Gov. R.E. Sloan. Originator, 1906, of movement to unite the states in behalf of good roads; pres. Southern Nat. Highways Assn. since 1912; v.p. Robert E. Lee Nat. Highways Assn. Pres. and gen. mgr. Morenci-Inspiration Copper Mining Co. Republican.

POTTER, EDWARD EELS commodore U.S.N., retired, May 9, 1895; b. Medina, N.Y., May 9, 1833; ed. Rockford, Ill., public schs.; apptd. to navy from Ill., Feb. 5, 1850; grad. U. S. Naval Acad., 1856; lt., July 9, 1858; convoyed 1st Japanese embassy to their home with steam-frigate Niagara, 1860; arrived home, Apr. 1861; ordered to Wissahickon and in war passed forts Jackson, St. Philip, etc. After war served on various duties and on many stas.; promoted capt., July 11, 1880; commodore, Jan. 1893; gov. U.S. Naval Home, Phila., 1893-95. Home: Washington, D.C. Died 1902.

POTTER, JAMES army officer, farmer; b. County Tyrone, Ireland, 1729; s. John Potter; m. Elizabeth Cathcart; m. 2d, Mary (Patterson) Chambers; 7 children. Came to Am., 1741; served as capt. under Gen. Armstrong in victorious Kittanning campaign, 1755; served as maj., then lt. col. fighting French and Indians, 1763-64; commr. to induce settlers in western Pa. to withdraw from Indian lands under Treaty of 1768; col., battalion of associators, 1776; mem. Constl. Conv., Phila., 1776; commd. brig. gen., 1777, fought at Trenton, Princeton, Brandywine, Germantown; mem. Supreme Exec. Council Pa. (Constitutionalist), 1780-81, v.p., 1781; commd. maj. gen. Pa. Militia, 1782; mem. Council of Censors, 1784; dep. surveyor for Pa. in Northumberland County, also supt. devel. of land schemes in Penn's Valley for land speculation co., 1785-89; a commr. rivers and streams, 1785. Died Centre Point, Pa., Nov. 1789.

POTTER, ROBERT congressman; b. Granville County, N.C., circa 1800; m. Miss Pelham; m. 2d, Mrs. Harriet A. Page. Became a lawyer, Halifax, N.C.; mem. N.C. Ho. of Commons, 1826-28, 34-35, introduced bill to organize state instn. to train poor boys for public service, expelled for fighting, 1835; mem. U.S. Ho. of Reps. (Democrat), from N.C. (21st-22d congresses, 1829-Nov. 1831), offered bill to destroy banks, also bill to sell public lands and divide the proceeds among the states, resigned from Ho. of Reps. to serve jail term for his part in a riot; went to Tex., became del. to Tex. Conv., 1835-36, signed Tex. Declaration of Independence, 1836; sec. of navy Tex.; mem. Tex. Senate, 1842. Died in polit. feud (shot while trying to escape from another senator), Lake Caddo, Tex., Mar. 2, 1842.

POTTER, ROBERT BROWN lawyer, army officer; b. Schenectady, N.Y., July 16, 1829; s. Bishop Alonzo and Sarah Maria (Nott) P.; attended Union Coll.; m. Frances Paine Tileston, Apr. 14, 1857; m. 2d, Abby Austin Stevens, Sept. 29, 1865; at least one child. Admitted to N.Y. bar; commd. maj. Scott Rifles, 1861; commd. lt. col. 51st Regt. N.Y. Volunteers, 1861, col., 1862, fought in Battle at Antietam; commanded 51st Regt. at Battle of Fredericksburg, 1862; brig. gen. U.S. Volunteers, 1863; commanded 2d Div. participating in capture of Vicksburg, 1863; maj. gen. U.S. Volunteers, 1864-65; receiver for Atlantic and Gt. Western R.R., 1866-69. Died Newport, R.I., Feb. 19, 1887.

POTTER, WILLIAM HENRY dentist; b. Boston, June 20, 1856; s. Silas and Caroline Daniels (Allen) P.; grad. Roxbury Latin Sch., 1874; A.B., Harvard, 1878; D.M.D., Harvard Dental Sch., 1885; hon. M.A., Harvard, 1927; m. Mary Louise Allen, June 21, 1893; children—Allen, Caroline, Mary, William, Roger. Practiced, Boston, 1885-—; lecturer on operative dentistry, 1890-96, asst. prof., 1900-04, prof. 1904-27. Harvard Dental Sch. (emeritus). Fellow Am. Coll. Dentists. Dental surgeon, Am. Ambulance Hosp., Neuilly, France, 3 mos., 1914-15; commd. 1st lt. Dental Corps, U.S.A., May 7, 1917; sailed for France, May 11, 1917; mem. U.S.A. Base Hosp. No. 5; served in British hosps., later as instr. Army Sanitary Sch., Langres, France, returned to U.S., Apr. 1919; promoted maj. and lt. col. Decorated Chevalier Legion of Honor (France), 1927. Republican. Conglist. Home: Boston, Mass. Died July 27, 1928.

POTTER, WILLIAM PARKER rear admiral U.S.N.; b. Whitehall, N.Y., May 10, 1850. Apptd. from N.Y., and grad. U.S. Naval Acad., 1869; promoted ensign, July 12, 1870; master, July 12, 1871; lt., Aug. 9, 1874; lt. comdr., June 12, 1896; comdr., Sept. 9, 1899; capt., Sept. 13, 1904; rear admiral, Oct. 30, 1908. Served successively on the Sabine, Franklin, Constellation, Hartford, Iroquois, 1869-74; Naval Acad., 1874-78; flag secretary N. Atlantic Fleet on board Powhatan, Marion, and Tennessee, 1878-81; Naval Acad., 1881-84; Lancaster, 1884-87; flag sec. European Squadron, 1885-86; Naval Acad., 1887-91; Baltimore, 1892; flag sec. European Squadron on board Philadelphia and Chicago, 1893-94; Naval Acad., 1895-97; exec. officer New York, 1897-99; took part in destruction of Cervera's squadron off Santiago, Cuba, July 3, 1898, and was advanced five numbers for "eminent and conspicuous conduct" in that battle; Navy Yard League Island, 1899-1901; comd. Ranger, 1901-03; Navy Dept., 1903-05; asst. to Bur. of Navigation, Navy Dept., 1905-07; comdg. Vermont, 1907; later comd. 4th div. Atlantic Fleet; chief Bur. Navigation, 1909; aid for personnel, Navy Dept. 1910-11; retired May 10, 1912. Died June 21, 1917.

POTTER, WILLIAM WARREN physician, editor; b. Strykersville, N.Y., Dec. 31, 1838; s. Dr. Lindorf and Mary G. P.; ed. Arcade (N.Y.) Sem. and Genesee Sem. and Coll., Lima, N.Y.; M.D., Buffalo U., 1859; m. Emily A. Bostwick, Mar. 23, 1859 (dec.). Practised medicine, Cowlesville, N.Y., 1859-61; commd., 1861, asst. surgeon 49th N.Y. Vols., served with Army of Potomac; in Libby prison 3 weeks, June 1862, but exchanged; promoted surgeon, Dec. 1862, and served with 57th N.Y. Vols. during Chancellorsville and Gettysburg campaigns; in charge 1st Div. Hosp., 2d Army Corps, 1863-65; bvtd. lt. col. N.Y. Vols. and lt. col. U.S. Vols. "for faithful and meritorious services." In practice at Buffalo, 1866-—; editor Buffalo Med. Jour., July 1888-—; also edits annual volume of Transactions of Am. Assn. Obstetricians and Gynecologists. Examiner obstetrics and gynecology and pres. N.Y. State Med. Examining and Licensing Bd., 1895-1909. Chmn. Sect. Obstetrics and Diseases of Women of A.M.A., 1890. Home: Buffalo, N.Y. Died 1911.

POTTS, BENJAMIN FRANKLIN army officer, territorial gov.; b. Carroll County, O., Jan. 29, 1836; s. James and Jane (Maple) P.; ed. Westminster Coll., 1854-55; m. Angeline Jackson, May 28, 1861. Admitted to Ohio bar, 1859, and began practice law; del. Balt. Democratic Conv., 1860; commd. capt. Co. F, 32d Ohio Volunteers, U.S. Army, 1861, lt. col., then col., 1862, fought at Memphis, Vicksburg, Atlanta, Savannah, brig. gen., 1865, ret., 1866; mem. Ohio Senate (Republican), 1868; territorial gov. Montana, 1870-83, wrote Report of the Governor of Montana . . . to the Secretary of the Interior . . . 1878-79; under his adminstrn., territorial debt almost paid off, legislation passed to modernize civil and criminal laws and procedures; mem. Mont. Territorial Legislature, 1884. Died Helena, Mont., June 17, 1887.

POTTS, ROBERT officer U.S.N.; b. Dublin, Ireland, May 8, 1835; s. Robert and Mary (Thompson) P.; ed. pub. schs. of New York; m. Fannie Griffiss, Jan. 25, 1876 (died 1909). Apptd. 3d asst. engr. U.S.N., Feb. 17, 1860; 2d asst. engr., June 27, 1862; 1st asst. engr., Mar. 1, 1864; chief engr., Jan. 22, 1873; retired May 8, 1897; advanced to rank of rear admiral retired, June 29, 1906, for services during Civil War. Home: Baltimore, Md. Died June 24, 1913.

POTTS, TEMPLIN MORRIS captain U.S.N.; b. Washington, Nov. 1, 1855; s. John and Louisa (Rose) P.; ed. Emerson Inst., Washington, and pvt. sch.; grad. U.S. Naval Acad., 1876; m. Marie Alden-Brown, May 10, 1902. Promoted midshipman, June 20, 1876; ensign, Nov. 25, 1877; lt. jr. grade, Feb. 9, 1884; lt., Feb. 28, 1890; lt. comdr., Mar. 3, 1899; comdr., Nov. 8, 1904; capt., July 19, 1908. Served on Plymouth, 1876-77; Powhatan, 1877; Constitution, and Portsmouth, 1878; Powhatan, 1879; Swatara, 1880-82; spl. duty Navy Dept., 1883-85; on Pensacola, 1885-87; Naval Acad., 1888-90; on San Francisco, 1890-93; Navy Yard, Washington, 1894-96; on Massachusetts, 1896-99; Navy Yard, New York, 1900, League Island, 1900; in charge branch Hydrographic Office, Phil., 1900-01; exec. officer Richmond, 1901-02; naval attaché, Berlin, Vienna, and Rome, 1902-04; exec. officer Brooklyn, 1904; mem. Bd. Inspection and Survey, 1904-05; naval gov. of Guam, P.I., 1905; Navy Yard at Washington, 1908-09; comdg. Georgia, 1909; chief intelligence officer, Navy Dept., 1910; also mem. Gen. Bd. and Joint Bd.; retired June 30, 1913. Died Mar. 22, 1927.

POTTS, WILLIS JOHN, surgeon; b. Sheboygan, Wis., Mar. 22, 1895; s. Horace and Hannah (Boeyink) P.; A.B., Hope Coll., Holland, Mich., 1918; S.B., U. of Chicago, 1920; M.D., Rush Med. Coll., 1924; interne Presbyn. Hosp., Chicago; Logan fellowship in surg. Rush Med. Coll., 1925-26; post grad. work, Frankfort, Germany, 1930-31; m. Henrietta Neerken, July 7, 1922; children—Willis John, Edward Eugene, Judith Eleanor. Began gen. practice, Oak Park, Ill., 1925; specialized in surgery, 1931-65, ret.; author syndicated newspaper column, 1965-68; professor of emeritus surgery Northwestern U. Med. sch., 1960-68; cons. surgery, Children's Memorial Hospital, Chicago. Sergt. Chem. Warfare Service, 1917-18; 1 year in U.S. and 1 year in France; lt. col. &colonel A.U.S., serving in Southwest Pacific with 25th Evacuation Hosp., 1942-45. Fellow Am. Coll. Surgeons; certified by Am. Bd. of Surgery; mem. Am. Med. Assn., Ill. and Chicago Med. Socs., Chicago Surg. Soc., Western Surg. Soc., Inst. Med. of Chicago, Am. Assn. Thoracic Surgery, Am. Surg. Assn., Central Surg. Assn. Am. Heart Assn. (pres. Chgo. 1960-61). Unitarian. Author: The Surgeon and The Child, 1959; Your Wonderful Baby, 1966. Contbr. to med. jours. Home: Sarasota FL Died May 5, 1968.

POUND, THOMAS cartographer, naval officer; b. Eng., circa 1650; m. Elizabeth. Apptd. pilot on ship Rose by gov. Mass., 1687; pirate along Atlantic Coast of Am., captured and condemned to hang, 1689, reprieved, 1690; capt. frigate Sally Rose of Royal Navy, 1691; produced 1st engraved map of Boston Harbor,

1691-92; served as capt. Brit. Navy, in Europe, 1692-95, off Ireland, 1698-97, off Am., 1697-98. Died Middlesex, Eng., 1703.

POWEL, HARFORD writer, editor; born Phila., Aug. 20, 1887; s. Harford W. Hare and Marion C. (Howard) P.; St. George's Sch., Newport, R.I.; A.B., Harvard, 1909 (pres. Lampoon, 1909); m. Harriet S. Motley, February 17, 1952; 1 son, Harford, by previous marriage. With the Vogue Company of New York, 1909-14, also International Mag. Co., 1914-17; editor Harper's Bazaar, 1917; editor Collier's, 1919-22, The Youth's Companion, 1925-28; v.p. Kimball, Hubbard & Powel, Inc., 1932-38; exec. and vice-pres. Inst. of Pub. Relations, 1938-41; information dir. Defense and War Bonds, Treasury Dept., 1941-42. Publicity dir. Selective Service, N.Y. City, 1948. Capt. Air Service, 1918. Publicity director, Block-Aid Campaign, N.Y. City, 1931; lt. col., Air Corps, 1945. Club: Harvard. Author: Walter Camp, 1926; What About Advertising? (with Kenneth M. Goode), 1927; The Virgin Queene, 1928; Married Money, 1929; The Invincible Jew, 1930; Oh Glory! 1931; Widow's Mite, 1935; Good Jobs for Good Girls, 1949. Editor (with Grantland Rice): Omnibus of Sport, 1933. Address: 65 Main St., Concord, Mass. Died Aug. 17, 1956; buried Newport, R.I.

POWEL, JOHN HARE legislator, agriculturist; b. Phila., Apr. 22, 1786; s. Robert and Margaret (Willing) Hare; ed. Coll. of Phila., 1800-03; m. Julia DeVeaux, Oct. 20, 1817, 9 children. Sec. U.S. legation under William Pinkney, London, Eng., 1809-11; commd. brig. maj. U.S. Volunteers, 1812; commd. insp. gen. with rank of col., 1814; livestock breeder, introduced improved Durham Short Horn cattle from Eng., also Southdown breed of sheep; a organizer Pa., Agr. Soc., sec., 1823; mem. Pa. Senate, 1827-30. Contbr. to agrl. periodicals including Am. Farmer, Memoirs of Pa. Agrl. Soc. Author: Hints for American Husbandmen, 1827. Died Newport, R.I., June 14, 1856.

POWELL, CARROLL A. army officer; b. Ohio, Sept. 3, 1892; E.E., U. of Cincinnati, 1917; M.S., Yale, 1922; grad. Signal Sch., 1923, Army Indsl. Coll., 1935. Commd. 2d lt., U.S. Army, 1917, and advanced through the grades to brig. gen., 1944. Address: War Dept., Washington 25, D.C. Died June 20, 1948; buried in Arlington National Cemetery.

POWELL, CHARLES FRANCIS officer of engr. corps, U.S.A.; b. Jacksonville, Ill., Aug. 13, 1843; ed. pub. high schs., Milwaukee; m. Margaret, d. James H. Foster, Albany, Ore., May 17, 1883. Served pvt. to sergt. maj. 5th Wis. vols., May 1861, to Sept. 1863; apptd. cadet at West Point by President Lincoln for gallantry on the field of battle; grad., 1867, as 2d lt., corps engrs.; promoted successively, 1st lt., capt., maj., lt. col. Has served with U.S. battalion of engrs.; on geodetic and topographic surveys, etc.; engr. in charge Cascades Canal, Ore., and at commencement of great jetty, mouth of Columbia River; sec. Mississippi River Commn.; engr. in charge Missouri River survey and improvement; engr. commr. D.C.; engr. Monongahela River Slack-Water System; engr. defenses and certain harbors, Long Island Sound. Home: New London, Conn. Died 1907.

POWELL, DAVID clergyman; b. Harrison Co. (now Taylor Co.), W.Va., July 18, 1831; s. Elijah and Sarah (Cather) Pa.; ed. common schs. in W.Va.; studied divinity partly under Rev. Benj. Bailey, but mainly by self culture; ordained to Free Bapt. ministry; m. Ellen E. Hughes, Apr. 20, 1858. Entered Union army, serving 3 yrs. 7 mos.; was on staff Gen. D. Hunter, and became 1st lt. Co. H, 12th W.Va. vols.; was in 13 regular battles and about 40 days' fighting. Supt. pub. schs., 1868-69; mem. W.Va. legislature, 1882-86. Republican. In active ministry, 1886-98; retired because of failing health. Home: Flemington, W.Va. Deceased.

POWELL, JOHN BENJAMIN newspaperman; b. Marion County, Mo., Apr. 18, 1886; s. Robert and Flora B. P.; grad. Gem City Business Coll., Quincy, Ill., also a student of the high school, same city; grad. School of Journalism, Univ. of Mo., 1910; m. Martha Hinton; children—Martha Bates, John William. Adv. mgr. Courier Post, Hannibal, Mo., 1910-13; instr. U. of Mo., 1913-17; mng. editor China Weekly Review, Shanghai, China, since 1917; editor China Press, Shanghai, 1923-25; spl. corr. Chicago Tribune, 1918-38; corr. Manchester Guardian, 1925-36; corr. at Conf. on Limitation of Armament and Pacific Problems, Washington, 1921-22; spl. rep. Am. commerical interests in China at Washington, 1920-22, and obtained Congressional enactment, China Trade Act. Reported Nationalist revolution, Central and South China, 1926-27, Sino-Russian conflict, North Manchuria, 1929, Sino-Japanese conflict, Manchuria, 1931-32; traveled in Soviet Union and Japan; wrote series for Chicago Tribune dealing with Russo-Japanese crisis and war preparation in Far East, 1934-35; corr. Daily Herald, London, 1937-41; mng. dir. China Press; covered outbreak Sino-Japanese War, Marco Polo bridge, Peiping and Shanghai, 1937, later, in Nanking, Central and South China until outbreak of World War II; interned by Japanese, Shanghai, Dec. 20, 1941-May 23, 1942; released in serious physical condition; returned to U.S. on S.S. Gripsholm, Aug. 25, 1942; receiving med. treatment, Presbyn. Med. Center, N.Y. City, since 1942. Clubs: Overseas Press (New York); American, Columbia (Shanghai); Nat. Press (Washington). Author: Building Circulation for Country Newspapers; Who's Who in China, 1926; Efficiency in the Newspaper Plant; My Twenty-Five Years in China, 1945. Address: Grosvenor Hotel, New York, N.Y. Died Feb. 28, 1947.

POWELL, JOHN WESLEY naturalist; b. Mt. Morris, N.Y., Mar. 24, 1834; s. of Methodist minister; attended schools in Ohio, Wis., and Ill., 2 yrs. each at Oberlin and Wheaton (Ill.) colls.; grad. Ill. Wesleyan, A.M., Ph.D. (LL.D., Columbian, 1882, Harvard, 1886, Ill. Coll., 1889; Ph.D., Heidelberg, 1886); m. Emma Dean, 1861. Served through Civil war in 2d Ill. arty., reaching rank of maj., losing right arm at Shiloh. Explored Grand Cañon of the Colorado River, 1869. Apptd. dir. U.S. Bureau of Ethnology, 1879, and of U.S. Geol. Survey, 1880; resigned latter, 1894, retaining former. Author: Explorations of the Colorado River; Report on Geology of the Uinta Mountains; Report on Arid Regions of United States; Introduction to the Study of Indian Languages; Studies in Sociology; Cañons of the Colorado; etc. Home: Washington, D.C. Died 1902.

POWELL, LEVIN congressman; b. nr. Manassas, Prince William County, Va., 1737; attended pvt. schs.; at least 1 son, Cuthbert. Dep. sheriff Prince William County; moved to Loudoun County, 1763, engaged in merc. activities; served as maj. Continental Army in Revolutionary War, 1775, lt. col. 16th Regt., 1777-78; mem. Va. Ho. of Dels., 1779, 87-88, 91-92; del. Va. Conv. which ratified U.S. Constn., 1788; presdl. elector, 1796; mem. U.S. Ho. of Reps. (Federalist) from Va., 6th Congress, 1799-1801; a builder of turnpike from Alexandria, Va. to upper country. Died Bedford, Pa., Aug. 23, 1810; buried Old Presbyn. Graveyard.

POWELL, PAULUS PRINCE naval officer; b. Brunswick Co., Va., Apr. 25, 1892; s. Robert Simmons and Ellen Virginia (Huff) P.; student Randolph Macon Coll., 1907-08; B.S., U.S. Naval Acad., 1913; grad. U.S. Naval War Coll., 1937; m. Francis Evelyn Paton, Feb. 1, 1934. Sr. Naval Aide, White House, 1932-34; promoted capt., 1940, organized, operated fast convoys in Pacific, World War II; chief of staff 3d Amphibious Force, service in Pacific Theater; promoted commodore, 1944; upon retirement, 1946, promoted rear adm. for heroic action in combat Battle of Leyte; rep. Pan Am. World Airways in S.A., since 1946. Decorated Legion of Merit with gold star, El Sol del Peru; specially commended by sec. navy for rapid, skillful and efficient evacuation of wounded. Mem. Soc. Cin. (Va.). Clubs: N.Y. Yacht, University (N.Y.C.); Army and Navy (Washington); Chevy Chase (Md.); Half Way House (Rio de Janeiro). Home: 37 W. 44th St., N.Y.C. Died July 31, 1963; buried Arlington Nat. Cemetery.

POWELL, TALCOTT WILLIAMS author and newspaperman; b. Lansdowne, Pa., Apr. 27, 1900; s. Dr. Lyman Pierson and Gertrude (Wilson) P.; student Wesleyan U., Middletown, Conn., 1918-20; m. Ysabel Allen Loney, Sept. 15, 1923 (divorced 1928); 1 son, David Talcott; m. 2d, Helen Ann Ranney, Aug. 4, 1928; 1 dau., Edes Lawrence. Began as reporter Paper Trade Jour., New York, 1920; with New York Sun, 1921-22; reporter and asst. city editor New York Tribune and New York Herald-Tribune, 1922-25; gen. mgr. and treas. Orange County Independent Corp., pub. Middletown (N.Y.) Times-Herald, 1925-27; reporter N.Y. Telegram, 1927-31; asst. exec. editor N.Y. World-Telegram, 1931-32; editor Indianapolis Times, 1933-35; exploration and writing for Cosmopolitan Mag. and Harcourt, Brace and Co. in Venezuela and West Indies, 1936; discovered and excavated site of town of Caparra, established in Puerto Rico by Ponce de Leon in 1510 and abandoned in 1521. Pulitzer Prize Committee cited articles on veteran relief in awarding N.Y. World-Telegram, 1932 gold medal, for "most meritorious public service." Served as pvt. of infantry, U.S.A., 1918, now 1st lt. Mil. Intelligence Reserve, U.S.A. Episcopalian. Author: Tattered Banners, 1933. Home: Mountain Lakes, N.J. Died Apr. 4, 1937.

POWELL, WILLIAM DAN army officer; b. Kansas City, Mo., Nov. 11, 1873; s. Dan and Mary Idela (Porterfield) P.; B.S., U. of Mo., 1916; Inf. Sch., 1924-25, advanced course, Inf. Sch., 1931-32, Command and Gen. Staff School, 1939; m. Blanche Marvin Sullivan, Feb. 12, 1923; children—Rosemary, Elizabeth Ann, William David. Commd. 2d. lt. inf., Reg. Army, 1917 and advanced through the grades to brig. gen.; served in France and Germany, 1917-22; prof. military science and tactics, U. of S.D., 1925-31; Philippine Islands, 1932-35; Gen. Staff duty, 3d Army Corps, 1940-41; foreign service since 1941. Decorated Liberty medal, Army of Occupation (Germany) medal, Emergency medal. Mem. Sigma Nu. Home: 7th and Casanova St., Carmel, Calif. Died Oct. 6, 1943.

POWELL, WILLIAM HENRY iron mfr.; b. Monmouthshire, S. Wales, May 10, 1825; in U.S., Mar. 30, 1830; settled in Nashville, Tenn., 1833; removed to Wheeling, Va., Mar. 1843; m. Sarah Gilchrist, Dec. 24, 1847; 2d, Mrs. E. P. (West) Weaver, Apr. 29, 1879. Removed, remodeled and erected Va. Iron and Nail Works, Benwood, 1852-53; organizer and mgr. Star Nail Co., Ironton, O., 1853; gen. mgr. Lawrence Iron Works, Ironton, 1857-61. Entered Union service Aug. 1, 1861, recruited co. mustered in Petersburg, Va.; capt. Co. B, 2d regt. Va. cav. vols., Oct. 1861; served through all intermediate grades to brig. gen., and bvt. maj. gen. U.S.V., under Gens. Crook, Averill and Phil. Sheridan; comd. 2d cav. div., Sheridan's cav. corps, Shenandoah Valley Campaign, 1864-65; was seriously wounded while leading charge, Wytheville, Va., July 16, 1863; left on battlefield and captured; exchanged for Gen. R. H. Lee, March 1864. Mgr. Ironton, O., Rolling Mill Co., 1865-67; gen. mgr. Clifton Nail Works, Mason Co., W.Va., 1867-76; Rep. presdl. elector 3d Va. dist., 1868; offered and declined nominations to Congress in Ohio, 1866, W.Va., 1868; gen. mgr. Belleville (Ill.) Nail Co., 1876-82; organized 1882, becoming pres. and gen. mgr. Western Nail Co.; dept. comdr. Ill. G.A.R., 1895; internal revenue collector 13th revenue dist., Ill., Mar. 1898-—. Home: Belleville, Ill. Died 1904.

POWERS, CHARLES ANDREW surgeon; b. Lawrence, Mass., Feb. 2, 1858; s. George Eliot and Jennie (Stone) P.; 9th in descent from Walter Powers, Concord, Mass., 1642; M.D., Coll. Phys. and Surg. (Columbia), 1883; attending surgeon New York Cancer and St. Luke's hosps., 1892; (hon. A.M., U. of Denver, 1901). Settled at Denver, 1894; emeritus prof. surgery, U. of Colorado; surgeon to various hosps.; 1st lt. Med. R.C., 1908-17; attending surgeon Am. Ambulance Hosp. of Paris (for French wounded), May 5, 1916-July 22, 1917; maj., M.C. U.S.A., assigned duty Am. Mil. Hosp. No. 1, Neuilly, sur Seine, July 22, 1917; discharged, Dec. 5, 1918; commd. lt. col. Med. R.C., July 1919. Pres. Am. Surg. Assn., 1912; fellow Am. Coll. Surgeons. Received letter of thanks (Apr. 21, 1919) and citation (Mar. 15, 1920) from Gen. John J. Pershing; officer of Order of Leopold II (Belgian). Médaille de la Reconnaissance Française, Chevalier Legion of Honor (French). Home: Denver, Colo. Died Dec. 23, 1922.

POWERS, RIDGELY CEYLON governor; b. Mecca, O., Dec. 24, 1846; s. Milo and Lucy Ann (Dickinson) P.; student, U. of Mich., 1859-62 (A.B., 1910) A.B., Union Coll., N.Y., 1862, A.M., 1865; m. Louisa Born, May 5, 1875 (died 1882); 2d, Mary J. Wilson, Oct. 27, 1892. Enlisted as pvt., Co. C, 125th Ohio Vol. Inf., 1862; promoted 2d lt., 1st lt., capt., maj.; bvtd. lt. col. "for gallant conduct in Atlanta campaign"; served in 2d Div., 4th Army Corps, Army of the Cumberland; participated in battles of Murfreesboro, Chattanooga, Chickamauga, Missionary Ridge, Dandridge, Knoxville, Franklin, Nashville, etc.; was a.-a.-g. 1st Brigade and a.-a.-g. 2d Div., 4th Army Corps; mustered out, New Orleans, 1865. Bought 2,000 acre plantation in Noxubee Co., Miss., 1865, and engaged in cotton raising. Sheriff, Noxubee Co., 1868-69; elected lt. gov., Miss., 1869, becoming gov. for unexpired term (Nov. 30, 1871-Jan. 4, 1874) of Gov. J. L. Alcorn elected to U.S. Senate. Practiced civ. engring. in Ariz., 1879-1905; retired. Home: Los Angeles, Calif. Died Nov. 11, 1912.

POWERS, ROBERT DAVIS, JR., naval officer; b. Gloucester County, Va., Mar. 21, 1908; s. Robert Davis and Hattye Ruth (Lewis) P.; LL.B., Washington and Lee U., 1929, LL.D., 1962; m. Mary Kathryn Carney, Oct. 15, 1937; children—Robert Carney, David Lewis, Mary Kathryn. Admitted to Va. bar, 1929; practice in Norfolk and Portsmouth, 1929-41; asst. city atty., Portsmouth, 1941; commd. lt. (j.g.) USNR, 1937, advanced through grades to rear adm., USN, 1961; counsel Judge Advocate Navy Ct. Inquiry Japanese Attack on Pearl Harbor, 1944; fleet legal officer Atlantic Fleet, 1947-50; asst. judge adv. gen. internat. and adminstrv. law U.S. Navy, 1956-58; dir. W. Coast Office Judge Advocate Gen., 1958-60; dep. judge advocate gen. U.S. Navy, 1960-64; practice law, Portsmouth, Va., 1964-71; asso. judge Portsmouth Juvenile and Domestic Relations Ct., 1971; lectr. internat. law. Mem. Am., Fed., Va. bar assns., Judge Advocates Assn., Am. Soc. Internat. Law, Pi Kappa Phi, Omicron Delta Kappa, Phi Alpha Delta. Methodist. Home: Portsmouth VA Died Dec. 1971.

POWERS, SIDNEY geologist; b. Troy, N.Y., Sept. 10, 1890; s. Albert W. and Tillie (Page) P.; A.B., Williams Coll., 1911; M.S., Mass. Inst. Tech., 1913; Sheldon traveling fellow to Hawaiian Island, Harvard, 1915, A.M., Ph.D., 1915, research fellow, 1915-16; m. Dorothy Edwards Powers, Sept. 8, 1917; children—Deborah, Eleanor. Div. geologist Tex. Co., 1916-17; asst. geologist U.S. Geol. Survey 1917-18; geol. officer, A.E.F., U.S.A., 1918-19; chief geologist Amerada Petroleum Corp., 1919-26, consulting geologist, 1926-—. Fellow Geol. Soc. America (councilor 1931-33). Home: Tulsa, Okla. Died 1932.

POWERS, THOMAS JEFFERSON, author; b. at Phila., Sept. 2, 1875; s. Thomas Joseph and Jennie (Ross) P.; cadet U.S. Mil. Acad., July 5-Dec. 31, 1892; m. Jane Masten Ewell, of San Francisco, Dec. 27, 1910. Actor, with Girard Ave. Stock Co., Forepaugh Stock Co., Phila., and Murry Hill Stock Co., New York, and in vaudeville, 1893-8. Commd. 2d lt. 25th U.S. Inf. July 9, 1898; 1st lt. 20th Inf., Sept. 8, 1899; capt. 13th Inf., July 28, 1905. Author: The Garden of the Sun, 1911. Address: War Dept., Washington

POWHATAN (personal name Wa-hun-sen-a-cawh or Wa-hun-son-a-cock), Indian chief; father of Pocahontas. Chief or emperor of Powhatan federation which extended over Tidewater Va., conquered other tribes, increased empire inherited from his father; crowned under orders from Christopher Newport, agent of Va. Co., 1609; harassed English with ambushes, murders and cruelties; concluded a peace when daughter married Englishman, John Rolfe. Died Powhatta, Va., Apr. 1618.

POYNTZ, JAMES M. physician; b. Scott Co., Ky., Mar. 22, 1838; s. John P.; grad. Forest Acad., 1858, med. dept. Univ. of Louisville, 1873; m. Clara Lilly, Nov. 15, 1870; 2d, Mrs. Bettie Gatewood, Feb. 9, 1886. Served in C.S.A., 1861-65; at close maj. and surgeon. Mem. State Med. Soc. of Ky., 1876—; mem. State bd. health of Ky., 9 yrs.; maj. gen. Ky. div. United Confederate Vets, 1899—. Democrat. Home: Richmond, Ky. Died 1904.

PRAHL, AUGUSTUS JOHN, educator; b. Lingenau, Germany, Oct. 18 1901; s. Anton and Maria Barbara (Saalmann) P.; student U. Koenigsberg, Germany, 1923-25; M.A., Washington U., St. Louis, 1928; Ph.D., John Hopkins, 1933; m. Hermine Eleanor Rickl, Mar. 13, 1939. Came to U.S., 1925, naturalized, 1932. Instr. German, Ind. U., 1928-30, Johns Hopkins, 1933-36; asst. prof. U. Md., 1936-39, asso. prof., 1939-45, prof. fgn. langs. since 1945, resident dean grad. year abroad, Zurich, Switzerland, 1949-50, asso. dir. overseas program, 1952-53, dir., 1953-54, dir. Far East Program, 1956-57, asso. dean grad. sch., 1957-66. In charge of naval document section U.S.N., Bremen, Germany, 1947-48; mem. bd. ednl. advisors U.S. Army in Europe, 1952. Mem. Modern Lang. Assn. Am., American Association of University Professors, Goethe Soc. Md. and D.C., Delta Sigma Phi, Phi Kappa Phi. Author: Gerstaecker und die Probleme seiner Zeit, 1938. The Forty-Eighters (with A.E. Zucker) 1950. Home: College Park MD Died Oct. 29, 1970; buried Cedar Hill Cemetery, Suitland MD

PRATHER, PERRY FRANKLIN (pra'ther), physician; b. Clear Springs, Md., Nov. 4, 1894; s. George Carlisle, Pa., 1916, A.M., 1925; M.D., U. of Pennsylvania, 1924; m. Jessie Williams, Sept. 5, 1923; children—Elizabeth Ann, Frances Jean, Charles Williams. Engaged in general practice of medicine, 1925-47; spl. cons. to U.S.P.H.S. since 1947; dir. Washington County Veneral Disease Clinic, 1943-59; vis. cons. Veneral Disease clinics of Western Maryland; acting dep. state health officer, Washington County; dep. state health officer, Hagerstown, 1947-52; dep. dir. Md. State Department Health, 1952-56, dir., 1956-61, also chmn. state bd. health, 1956-61, commr., 1961—; lectr., sch. hygiene and pub. health Johns Hopkins. Mem. of Nat. Adv. Com. to Selective Service. Served as pvt. 1st class, U.S. Army, 1917-19; major, Med. Corps., Maryland State Guard, 1942-46. Recipient Silver Beaver Award from Boy Scouts of America. Diplomate American Bd. of Preventive Medicine and Pub. Health. Fellow American Public Health Association, American Coll. Physicians; mem. Am. Med. Assn., State and Territorial Health Officers Assn., State Med. Soc. Md., Washington County Med. Soc. (past pres.), Baltimore City Med. Soc. Club: Johns Hopkins. Co-author: Studies on Pneumococcus; numerous articles on pub. health. Home: 5203 Falls Rd., Balt. 10. Office: 301 W. Preston St., Balt. 1. Died Dec. 22, 1967.

PRATT, DON FORRESTER army officer; b. Brookfield, Mo., July 12, 1892; student U. of Wis.; comd. 2d lt. Inf., Aug. 1917, and advanced through the grades to brig. gen., Aug. 1942; served as adjutant of the U.S. Army Troops, 15th Inf., Tientsin, China, 1932-36; returned to U.S., Aug. 1936; instr. Inf. Sch., Ft. Benning, Ga., 1937-41; chief of staff, 43rd Inf. Div., Camp Blanding, Fla., 1941-42; assigned to 101st Airborne Div., Aug. 1942. Died June 6, 1944.

PRATT, EDWARD BARTON brigadier-gen. U.S.A.; b. Fortress Monroe, Va., May 7, 1853; s. Henry Clay and Mary C. (Clitz) P.; common sch. edn.; m. Kate E. C. Copeland, of Omaha, Neb., Oct. 25, 1876. Commd. 2d lt. 23d Inf., Dec. 12, 1872; 1st lt., June 25, 1878; capt., Jan. 15, 1891; maj., July 19, 1899; lt.-col. 15th Inf., Oct. 7, 1902; col. 30th Inf., Dec. 16, 1904; brig.-gen. U.S.A., Nov. 27, and retired, Nov. 30, 1909. Served in Philippines, 1898-1901 and 1907-09. Mem. Soc. Army of the Philippines, Moro Campaigns. Home: 1869 Wyoming Av., Washington.

PRATT, GEORGE COLLINS, lawyer; b. Flandreau, S.D., Nov. 20, 1882; s. Collins and Sarah (Daley) P.; student U. of S.D., 1900-03; LL.B., Chicago Kent Coll. Law, 1905; married Alice Chambers, 1916 (died 1945); m. 2d, Marcella Morin, 1946. Admitted to Ill. bar, 1905, N.Y. bar, 1909, Calif. bar, 1931; began practice at Chicago; sec. Western Electric Co., 1908-25, gen. atty., 1919-27, v.p. and gen. counsel, 1927-30; dir. and gen. counsel Graybar Electric Co., 1925-28, Elec. Research Products, Inc., 1926-30, (v.p., 1930-39), Los Angeles counsel, Western Electric Co. Mem. Squadron A Cav., N.G.N.Y., 1913-16, serving on Mexican Border, 1916; served as capt. Signal Corps, U.S. Army, 1917-19, with 319th Field Signal Batt., A.E.F., later radio officer 1st Army. Mem. Am. and Los Angeles bar assns., Assn. Bar City New York, State Bar of Calif., S.R. Republican. Clubs: Jonathan, Shadow Mountain. Address: Palm Desert CA Died Mar. 23, 1968.

PRATT, GEORGE K. psychiatrist; b. Detroit, Mich., Dec. 17, 1891; s. George Oscar (M.D.) and Alice Elizabeth (Beedzler) P.; M.D., Detroit Coll. Medicine and Surgery, 1915; grad. study, State Psychopathic Hosp., U. of Mich., 1917; m. Neva Emma MacArthur, Dec. 30, 1916; children—Shirley Jane (Mrs. Carleton W. Clark), Rodney George, Douglas MacArthur. Asst. physician Oak Grove Hosp., Flint, Mich., 1915-20; capt. U.S. Army Medical Corps, Neuro-Psychiatric Div., 1917-19; in private practice and asst. health officer, Flint, 1920-21; med. dir. Mass. Soc. for Mental Hygiene, 1921-25; also in out-patient dept. Boston Psychopathic Hosp., 1921-25; lecturer in mental hygiene, Smith Coll., 1923-25; asst. med. dir. Nat. Com. for Mental Hygiene, New York, 1925-33; med. dir. Mental Hygiene Com. N.Y., State Charities Aid Assn., 1930-35, and Conn. Society for Mental Hygiene, 1936-42; consultant mental hygiene, U. of Vt., 1925-29; grad. study psychoanalytic therapy, Europe, 1926; mem. faculty New Sch. for Social Research, N.Y. City, 1930-33, and Brooklyn Inst. Arts and Sciences; consultant in psychiatry, St. Christopher's School, Dobbs Ferry, N.Y., 1932-36 and since 1942; assistant clinical professor of psychiatry and mental hygiene, School of Medicine, Yale, 1936-43; psychiatric director Stamford Child Guidance Service, also Bridgeport Mental Hygiene Clinic, 1936-1947; instr. Mental Hygiene, New Haven State Teachers Coll., 1939-42. Nat. chmn. mental hygiene, Congress of Parents and Teachers, 1926-34; chmn. tech. advisory com. Emergency Work Bur., N.Y. City, 1933. Consultant in psychiatry Med. Adv. Bd. No. 5, Fairfield County, Selective Service System; psychiatric examiner, Induction Center, New Haven, 1943-46; associate neuro-psychiatrist, Bridgeport Hospital; medical director Hall-Brooke Sanitarium, 1948-54. Diplomate Am. Board of Psychiatry and Neurology. Fellow American Psychiatric Association, also Royal Medico-Psychological Assn. Great Britain, Connecticut State and Fairfield County med. socs. Nu Sigma Nu. Author: Your Mind and You, 1924; Why Men Fail (with others), 1928; Our Neurotic Age (with others), 1932; Morale; the Mental Hygiene of Unemployment, 1933; Three Family Narratives, 1935; Soldier to Civilian, 1944. Contbr. tech. articles. Home: Woods Grove, Westport, Conn. Office: 881 Lafayette St., Bridgeport 4, Conn. Died Dec. 11, 1957; buried Westport, Conn.

PRATT, HENRY CONGER army officer (ret.); b. Fort Stanton, N.M., Sept. 2, 1882; s. Henry Clitz and Elizabeth VanVleck (Conger) P.; grad. U.S. Mil. Acad., 1904, AC Bombardment Sch., 1921, Army Sch. of Line, 1922, Army Gen. Staff Sch., 1923, Army War Coll., 1924; m. Sadie DeRussy Murray, Feb. 11, 1914. Commd. 2d lt., cav. U.S. Army, June 1904; advanced through grades to maj. gen., Mar. 1941; transferred to AS, Aug. 6, 1920; brig. gen. and asst. chief AC, July 17, 1930-July 16, 1934, in command Materiel Div., Wright Field, Dayton, O.; brig. gen. AC in command 2d Wing Gen. Hdqrs. Air Force and Langley Field, Va., Mar. 1935-Mar. 1937; brig. gen. U.S. Army, Jan. 1, 1937; comdt. AC Tactical Sch., 1936-38; comdg. 23d Brig., Nov. 1938-Nov. 40, comdg. II Army Corps, Dec. 1940-Aug. 1941; maj. gen. U.S. Army, Mar. 1, 1941; comdg. 3d Corps Area, Aug. 1941-Jan. 1942; comdg. Trinidad Sector, Jan. 1941-Mar. 1943; comdg. Antilles Dept., June 1943-Nov. 1943; comdg. So. Def. Command, Jan. 1944-Dec. 1944; comdg. Western Def. Command, Dec. 1944-45; ret. Sept. 1946. Mem. Am. Legion. Episcopalian. Clubs: Army and Navy (Washington); Chevy Chase (Md.). Home: 3133 Conn Av., Washington 8. Died Apr. 1966.

PRATT, JAMES TIMOTHY congressman; b. Cromwell, Conn., Dec. 14, 1802; attended common schs. Engaged in business and agriculture, Hartford, Conn.; joined "Horse Guard," 1820; maj. 1st Regt. of Cavalry, 1834, col., 1836, brig. gen., 1837-39, maj. gen., 1839-46, adj. gen., 1846; ret. from business, settled in Rocky Hill, Conn.; mem. Conn. Ho. of Reps., 1847-48, 50, 57, 62, 70-71; mem. Conn. Senate, 1852; mem. U.S. Ho. of Reps. (Democrat) from Conn., 33d Congress, 1853-55; unsuccessful candidate for gov. Conn., 1858, 59; mem. Washington (D.C.) Peace Conv., 1861; engaged in farming. Died Wethersfield, Conn., Apr. 11, 1887; buried Indian Hill Cemetery, Middletown, Conn.

PRATT, JOSEPH HERSEY M.D.; b. Middleboro, Mass., Dec. 5, 1872; s. Martin Van Buren and Rebecca Adams (Dyer) P.; Ph.B., Yale, 1894; M.D., Johns Hopkins, 1898; A.M., Harvard, 1901; med. research work, univs. of Tübingen, 1902, Heidelberg, 1908; Sc.D., Colby Coll., 1941; m. Rosamond Means Thomson, Oct. 23, 1909; children—Sylvia Mayo (Mrs. John M. Kemper), Thomas Dennie, Rosamond (Mrs. Robert Walcott, Jr.), Joan. Asst. resident pathologist, 1898-99, then resident pathologist, 1899-1900, asst. visiting pathologist, 1900-02, Boston City Hosp.; asst. pathologist, Children's, and Carney hosps., and pathologist to Floating Hosp., 1900-02; instr. pathology, 1900-02, asst. in medicine, 1902-09, instr. medicine, 1909-17, Harvard Med. Sch.; prof. clinical medicine, Tufts Med. School, since 1929; fellow Rockefeller Inst., 1903-05; visiting physician to out-patient dept., Mass. Gen. Hosp., 1903-13, asst. visiting physician, 1913-17; physician in chief of Boston Dispensary, 1927-31, New England Medical Center since 1931, Joseph H. Pratt Diagnostic Hosp., Boston; cons. physician Brockton Hosp., Sharon (Conn.) Hosp., Eastern Maine Gen. Hosp. (Bangor). Mem. Assn. of Am. Physicians, Mass. Med. Soc., Am. Climatol. Clin. Assn. (pres. 1927-28), Soc. Exptl. Biology and Medicine, Soc. Advancement of Clinical research (pres. 1910-11), Am. Physiol. Soc., Am. Pharm. Assn., Am. Soc. for Exptl. Pathology, Am. Assn. of Pathologists and Bacteriologists, Am. Acad. Arts and Sciences, Am. Coll. Physicians, Nat. Tuberculosis Assn. (dir. 1926-28). Mem. Alumni Council, Johns Hopkins U., 1908-16; advisory council, Phipps Inst., University of Pennsylvania; vice-pres. Bingham Associates Fund for Advancement of Rural Medicine. Author of numerous med. papers. Republican. Episcopalian. Clubs: Harvard, Boston. Author: (with Col. George E. Bushnell) The Physical Diagnosis of Diseases of the Chest, 1925. Commd. maj., Med. R.C., Sept. 20, 1917; chief med. service Base Hosp., and pres. tuberculosis board, Camp Devens, Mass., 1917. Home: 94 Upland Rd., Brookline, Mass. Office: 30 Bennet St., Boston, Mass. Died June 2, 1942.

PRATT, JOSEPH HYDE geologist, engr.; b.Hartford, Conn., Feb. 3, 1870; s. James C. and Jennie A. (Peck) P.; Ph.B., Sheffield Scientific Sch. (Yale), 1893, Ph.D., 1896; hon. M.A., 1923; m. Mary Dicus Bayley, Apr. 5, 1899; 1 son, Joseph Hyde; m. 2d, Harriet White Peters, Aug. 29, 1930. Instr. mineralogy, Yale, 1895-97; summer, Harvard, 1895; lecturer mineralogy, U. of N.C., 1898-1901; state mineralogist of N.C., 1897-1906; state geologist, 1906-24; asst. field geologist, U.S. Geol. Survey, from 1899; prof. econ. geology, U. of N.C., 1904-25; chief Dept. Mines and Metallurgy, Jamestown Exposition, 1907. Member Internat. Jury of Awards, St. Louis Expn., 1904; spl. expert 12th U.S. Census on asbestos, etc.; dir. briquetting expts., U.S. Geol. Coal Testing Plant, St. Louis, 1904-05. Awarded diploma and gold medal, Pan-Am. Expn., 1901, for exhibit N.C. gems and gem minerals, etc.; diplomas, gold medal and silver medals for same, Charleston Expn., 1902. Lt.-col. N.C. N.G. (engr. dept.). Pres. Am. Peat Soc., 1907-09, Southern Appalachian Good Roads Assn., 1909-15; sec. N.C. Drainage Assn., 1908-11 and 1912-23 (pres. 1911); sec. N.C. Fisheries Assn., 1911-19, N.C. Good Roads Assn., 1908-20, N.C. State Highway Commn., 1915-19, N.C. Lit. and Hist. Soc., N.C. Forestry Assn. (pres. 1925-27; chmn. exec. com., 1927-40), Am. Assn. State Highway Officials, 1914-20; pres. Nat. Assn. Shell Fish Commrs., 1912-13; dir. Am. Assn. Highway Improvement, Nat. Drainage Cong.; fellow Geol. Soc. America, Am. Chem. Soc., A.A.A.S., Nat. Geog. Soc., Mineralogical Soc. of America, Am. Geog. Soc.; mem. Am. Soc. Civil Engrs., Am. Inst. Mining Engrs., Mining and Metall. Soc. America, Sigma Xi, N.Y. Acad. Sciences, N.C. Acad. Science, Am. Forestry Assn. (dir. 1922-29 and since 1934), Nat. Parks Assn. (dir. since 1936), Wilderness Soc., Am. Road Builders Assn., Am. Fisheries Soc., Mil. Engineers Soc. (dir. since 1926); v.p. N.C. Agrl. Soc., 1921-28; pres. Western North Carolina, Inc., 1924-25; pres. Southern Forestry Congress, 1916-19 (chmn. exec. com., 1919-25; exec. sec., 1928-40); pres. Southern Appalachian Power Conf., 1922 (chmn. exec. com., 1923-40); pres. N.C. Conf. for Social Service, 1924, dir. since 1925; pres. N.C. Soc. for Preservation of Antiquities since 1940; hon. mem. Appalachian Engring. Soc.; apptd. by sec. of agr. mem. Appalachian Forest Research Council (chmn. exec. com. since 1925); chmn. Chapel Hill Chapter Am. Red Cross; pres. N.C. Symphony Soc. since 1932; pres. Battle Park Assn.; mem. advisory com. President Hoover's Timber Conservation Board; chmn. Central Welfare Com., Orange County; chmn. Chapel Hill Health and Welfare Com. since 1940; pres. Chapel Hill Pub. Recreation Commn. since 1940; chmn. Chapel Hill Negro Community Center Assn. since 1940; mem. Chapel Hill City Planning Board since 1941. Received annual award as Chapel Hill's most valuable citizen, 1940. Clubs: Cosmos (Washington, D.C.); Washington Philatelic Soc., Chapel Hill (North Carolina) Country. Contbr. many articles to scientific mags., domestic and foreign, on mineral., geol. and chem. subjects, since 1895. Publisher War Diary of Col. Joseph Hyde Pratt, 1928. Member State Council Defense. Major, Engr. R.C., 1917, and assigned to 105th Regt. Engrs.; lt. col., Nov. 11, 1917; col., Oct. 9. 1918; with regt. at Camp Sevier, Greenville, S.C.; ordered to France, May 1918; comdr. of regt. and div. engr., 30th Div., A.E.F., July 1918-May 1919; served 6 mos. at the front in Ypres sector, Flanders and Belgium, and in Somme offensive in breaking the Hindenburg line; former col. Engr. R.C., U.S. Army. Awarded D.S.M. State engr. C.W.A. for N.C., Nov. 1933-Feb. 1934; senior regional engr. C.W.A. and F.E.R.A., 1934-35; senior regional engr. Resettlement Adminstrn., 1935; research engr. Works Progress Adminstrn., 1936, 37; engr. consultant, U.S. Geol. Survey, 1938, senior engr., consultant, 1939, 40. Home: Chapel Hill, N.C. Died June 2, 1942.

PRATT, RICHARD HENRY brig. gen. U.S.A.; b. Rushford, N.Y., Dec. 6, 1840; s. Richard S. and Mary (Herrick) P.; ed. Logansport, Ind.; (LL.D., Dickinson, 1898); m. Anna L. Mason, Apr. 12, 1864. Corporal Co. A, 9th Ind. Inf., sergt. Co. A, 2d Ind. Cav., and 1st lt. and capt. 11th Ind. Cav., 1861-65; 2d lt. 10th U.S. Cav., Mar. 7, 1867; promoted through grades to col. 13th Cav., Jan. 24, 1903; retired, Feb. 17, 1903; advanced to rank of brig. gen. retired, by act of Apr. 23, 1904. Was provost marshal, Dist. of N. Ala., summer and fall 1864, and insp. and judge advocate 5th Div. Cav. Mil. Div. of Miss., Dec. 1864 to close of vol. service. Suggested and organized the Industrial Sch. for Indians at Carlisle, Pa., in 1879, and was its only supt. to July 1, 1904. Home: Rochester, N.Y. Died Mar. 15, 1924.

PRATT, SEDGWICK brig. gen. U.S.A.; b. Georgetown, D.C., May 20, 1845; s. Henry C. and Mary Clarissa (Clitz) P.; grad. U.S. Mil. Acad., 1867; m. Martha W. Keith, Nov. 19, 1869. Served as 2d lt., 4th N.Y. Arty. and as a.-d.-c. to Brig. Gen. G. A. De Russy, U.S.V., May 26-Sept. 9, 1863; commd. 2d lt. 3d U.S. Arty., June 17, 1867; promoted through grades to col. Arty Corps, Feb. 9, 1906; brig. gen. and retired, June 22, 1906, at own request, over 40 yrs.' service. Served as arty. insp. Dept. of Calif., chief mustering officer for State of Calif., 1898; mem. Bd. of Engrs. U.S.A., 1901-03, Bd. of Ordnance and Fortifications, 1902-03; detailed to gen. staff, May 1903, and on spl. duty at hdqrs. Dept. of the Columbia, 1903-04; insp. gen. and arty. insp. Div. of the Pacific, 1904-06; in command arty. dist. of the Potomac, June 1906. Home: Washington, D.C. Died Mar. 25, 1920.

PRATT, STEWART CAMDEN banker; b. Washington, D.C., Sept. 30, 1885; s. James Calcott and Margaret Stewart (Johnston) P.; student Trinity Coll., 1904; LL.B., U. of Pa., 1907; m. Geraldine Fleshman Graham, June 20, 1936; 1 dau., Ann Leigh Graham. Admitted to N.Y. Bar, 1908; asso. with law firm, Winthrop & Stimson, New York, N.Y., 1907-09; asst. gen. counsel, Lehigh Valley R.R. Co., 1910-17; partner, Cobe & Pratt, investments, 1920-24; asst. to pres., Farmers Loan & Trust Co., 1925-29; v.p., The Nat. City Bank of N.Y. and City Bank Farmers Trust Co., N.Y. City, 1929-50. Chmn., rep. N.Y. banks to negotiate with German govt. settlement of payments due on German dollar bonds outstanding in U.S., exclusive of Young and Dawes loans, 1935-39. Served as maj., U.S. Army, on duty with storage officer for Port of New York, 1918-19. Mem. Delta Kappa Epsilon, Phi Delta Phi. Clubs: Union (N.Y. City). Home: Bleak Hill Farm, Culpepper, Va. Died June 14, 1951.

PRATT, WILLIAM VEAZIE naval officer; b. Belfast, Me., Feb. 28, 1869; s. Nichols and Abigail Jane (Veazie) P.; grad. U.S. Naval Acad., 1889; m. Louise Johnson, Apr. 15, 1902; 1 son, William Veazie. Ensign, July 1, 1891; promoted through grades to rear adm., June 3, 1921; served on Atlanta and Chicago in White Squadron, 1889-91; on U.S.S. Petrel, 1891-95; at U.S. Naval Acad., 1895-97; on Mayflower, Spanish-Am. War 1898; on U.S.S. Newark, Bennington, Monterey, 1898-1900; at Naval Acad., 1900-02; navigator Kearsarge, flagship Atlantic Fleet, 1902-05; at U.S. Naval Acad., 1905-06, 1906-08; navigator Newark, 1906; exec. officer St. Louis, 1908-10, California, 1910; at Naval War Coll., Newport, R.I., 1911-13; on staff of comdr. Torpedo Flotilla, Atlantic Fleet, and comdg. U.S.S. Birmingham, 1913-15; duty Panama, Canal Zone, 1915-16; at Army War Coll., Washington, D.C., 1916-17; duty Office Chief of Naval Operations, Navy Dept., May 1917; asst. chief of naval operations, Aug. 1917-Jan. 1919; accompanied President Wilson on trip to France, Dec. 1918; comdg. U.S.S. New York, 1919-20; commanding destroyer force, Pacific Fleet, 1920-21; duty with General Board U.S. Navy, 1921-23; naval expert asst. to Am. Commn. at Washington Conf. on Limitation of Armaments, 1921-22; comdg. Battleship Div. 4, Battle Fleet, 1923-25; spl. duty with Gen. Bd. U.S. Navy, June-Sept. 1925; pres. Naval War Coll., 1925-27; apptd. comdr. Battleship Divisions, Battle Fleet, with rank of vice admiral, Sept. 1927; comdr. in chief Battle Fleet, 1928-29; comdr. in chief U.S. Fleet, 1929-30, with rank of admiral; naval advisor to Am. delegation at London Conf., 1930; chief of naval operations, Sept. 17, 1930-July 1, 1933; became adm. on retired list Aug. 14, 1938; recalled to active duty, Jan. 6, 1941, and returned to inactive status July 1941. Associate editor Newsweek, 1940. Decorations: service medals of Spanish-Am. War, Philippine Insurrection, Boxer Insurrection; D.S.M. (Navy and Army); Grand Officer Legion of Honor (France); Order of El Merito (Chile). Home: Belfast, Me. Died Nov. 25, 1957; buried Family Mausoleum, Grove Cemetery, Belfast.

PREBLE, EDWARD naval officer; b. Falmouth, Me., Aug. 15, 1761; s. Gen. Jedidiah and Mehitable (Bangs) Roberts P.; m. Mary Deering, Mar. 17, 1801. Served in ship Winthrop (a captured, armed English brig of superior force), until 1783; lt. in command brig Pickering, West Indies, 1798; capt. frigate Essex, 1799, (1st Am. warship to sail flag beyond Cape of Good Hope, 1800-02); protected Am. trade from French privateers in East Indies; commd. commodore, in command 3d squadron sent to Mediterranean, 1803; made 1st assault on Tripoli, 1804, made 4 subsequent attacks, failed to capture Tripoli; built gunboats for navy, circa 1805-07. Died Portland, Me., Aug. 25, 1807.

PREBLE, GEORGE HENRY naval officer, author; b. Portland, Me., Feb. 25, 1816; s. Enoch and Sally (Cross) P.; m. Susan Cox, Nov. 18, 1845, 4 children. Served as midshipman U.S. Navy, 1835-41; commanded 1st Am. armed landing force in China, Canton, 1844; blockade service in Mexican War on schooner Petrel and siege of Veracruz, 1846-47; accompanied Perry's mission to Japan in ship Macedonian, 1853-56; prepared surveys and sailing directions for Wu-Song River leading to Shanghai, 1855; exec. officer Narragansett in Pacific, 1858-61; in command of gunboat Katahdin during Civil War, 1861; fought at battles of New Orleans, Vicksburg; promoted comdr., 1862; allowed Confederate cruiser Oreto to break through blockade of Mobile Bay, dismissed from service; restored to previous rank, 1863; comdr. fleet brigade of Southeastern Am. coast, 1864; commanded ship State of Ga., protected comml. interests at Panama, 1865; commd. capt., 1867, comdr., 1871; chief of staff in Pacific, circa 1868-74; promoted rear adm., 1876, commanded South Pacific Squadron, 1876. Author: Our Flag: Origin and Progress of the Flag of the United States of America..., 1872, other books and articles. Died Boston, Mar. 1, 1885.

PREBLE, ROBERT BRUCE physician; b. Chicago, Ill., Mar. 14, 1866; s. Eber C. and Mary Kate (Barnes) P.; A.B., U. of Mich., 1889, M.A., 1914; M.D., Northwestern U., 1891, D.Sc., 1931; interne Cook County Hosp., 1891-93; U. of Vienna, 1893-94; m. Alice M. Hosmer, June 12, 1889; children—Norman Hosmer, Barbara, Marcia. Prof. medicine, Northwestern U., since 1895; attending physician St. Luke's and Wesley hosps. Commd. maj. Med. R.C., Apr. 1917; med. chief hosp. center, Mars sur Alliers, France; discharged Jan. 31, 1919, with rank of lt. col. M.C., U.S. Army. Am. Citation and French Legion of Honor. Mem. Assn. Am. Physicians, A.M.A., Ill. State Med. Soc., Chicago Med. Soc. (pres. 1903-04), Phi Beta Kappa. Clubs: University, Racquet, Glenview Golf. Author: Pneumonia and Pneumococcus Infections, 1905. Home: 900 N. Michigan. Office: 30 N. Michigan, Chicago, Ill.* Died July 5, 1948.

PRENTICE, WILLIAM PACKER lawyer; b. Albany, N.Y., August 26, 1834; s. Ezra P. and Philena C. P.; A.B., Williams Coll., 1855 (LL.D., 1905); A.M., Ph.D., U. of Göttingen, 1858; m. Florence Kelly, Jan. 29, 1863. Commissioned capt. a.a.g. vols., Nov. 26, 1861; maj., Sept. 2, 1862; lt. col. adj. gen. 10th Army Corps and chief of staff of Maj. Gen. O. M. Mitchel, Oct. 1862; resigned, Dec. 23, 1862; LL.B., Albany Law Sch., 1861; practiced in New York City, 1863-1913. Counsel, Health Bd. New York, 1873-92, State Bd. Health, 1875. Author: Police Powers, 1894. Home: New York, N.Y. Died Dec. 22, 1915.

PRENTISS, BENJAMIN MAYBURY soldier; m. Bellville, Va. (now W.Va.), Nov. 23, 1819; ed. dist. schools Mo.; left home, 1841, settling at Quincy, Ill.; learned trade of rope-making, afterward engaged in the commn. business; 1st lt. in a co. formed to march against Mormons, 1844-45; capt. co. vols., Mexican war; gained distinction at Buena Vista and fought in prin. battles of war. Organized and offered co. to govt., 1861; apptd. col. 7th Ill. regt.; brig. gen., May 17, 1861; placed in command of Cairo; directed attack on large Confederate force Mt. Zion, Dec. 28, 1861, completely routing the enemy. Joined Gen. Grant at Pittsburgh Landing and arrived 3 days before battle of Shiloh; comd. new div. (6th), which had but 2 regular brigades; compelled to surrender 1st day of battle, April 6, 1862; released Oct. 1862. Apptd. maj. gen. vols., Nov. 29, 1862; served on court martial convened to try case of Fitz John Porter, Nov. 27, 1862; in command post at Helena, Ark., 1863, and on July 3, 1863, was attacked by Gens. Holmes and Price, whom he defeated. Resigned command in army, Oct. 28, 1863, and engaged in civil pursuits. Home: Quincy, Ill. Died 1901.

PRESCOTT, FRANK CLARKE lawyer; b. Ottawa, Ill., Nov. 15, 1859; s. Fernando Cortes and Juliette Estelle (Clarke) P.; ed. pub. and pvt. schs. and under pvt. tutors in law, English, Spanish and French; m. Maria de los Reyes Tebbetts, Jan. 1879; 1 son, Frank C. (dec.); m. 2d, Henrietta May Pierce Barrett, Mar. 1898 (died 1929). Was telegrapher, 1876-88; then practiced law in Los Angeles, Calif., 1888-91, Redlands, 1891-1903, San Bernardino, 1903-06, Los Angeles, 1906-—; sr. mem. Prescott & Prescott. City atty., Redlands, 1899; mem. Calif. Assembly, 1903-06 (speaker 1905); regent Univ. of Calif., 1905; register U.S. Land Office, Los Angeles, 1906-10. Enlisted as pvt. Oakland Light Cav., N.G.C., 1880; retired as brig. gen., 1903; served as maj., 1st Battalion, 7th Inf., U.S. Vols., Spanish-Am. War; capt. 43d Inf., Philippine Insurrection; provost judge, Island Samar, 1900; brigade staff, Iloilo, 1900-01; recommended for bvt. maj. vols., "for meritorious conduct." Republican. Episcopalian. Mason. Home: Los Angeles, Calif. Died Jan. 6, 1934.

PRESCOTT, OLIVER physician; b. Groton, Mass., Apr. 27, 1731; s. Benjamin and Abigail (Oliver) P.; grad. Harvard, 1750, M.D. (hon.), 1791; studied medicine under Dr. Ebenezer Robie; m. Lydia Baldwin, Feb. 19, 1756. Commd. brig. gen. Middlesex County (Mass.) Militia, 1775, maj. gen. Mass. Militia, 1778; mem. Mass. Com. of Correspondence, mem. supreme exec. council, 1777-80; judge of probate Middlesex, 1799-1804; trustee, 1st pres. bd. Groton Acad.; an original incorporator Mass. Med. Soc.; mem. N.H. Med. Soc.; pres. Middlesex Med. Soc., also Western Soc. of Middlesex Husbandmen; fellow Am. Acad. Arts and Scis., 1780. Died Groton, Nov. 17, 1804.

PRESCOTT, SAMUEL physician, patriot; b. Concord, Mass., Aug. 19, 1751; s. Dr. Abel and Abigail (Brigham) P.; Successfully completed the midnight ride of warning after Paul Revere was captured, Apr. 18, 1775, reached Concord where his warning enabled Minute Men to assemble and to hide most of mil. stores before British arrived; in service at Fort Ticonderoga, 1776; captured by British, 1777. Died Halifax, Nova Scotia, circa 1777.

PRESCOTT, WILLIAM army officer; b. Groton, Mass., Feb. 20, 1726; s. Benjamin and Abigail (Oliver) P.; m. Abigail Hale, Apr. 13, 1758, at least 1 child, William. Served as lt. in French and Indian War, 1758; col. of regt. of Minute Men, 1775; mem. Council of War, Cambridge, Mass.; in direct charge of fortifying Breed's Hill, 1775, co-comdr. at Battle of Bunker (Breed's) Hill, 1775; served in Long Island Campaign and at surrender of Burgoyne, 1777. Died Pepperell, Mass., Oct. 13, 1795.

PRESTON, GUY HENRY army officer; b. in Mass., May 29, 1864; grad. U.S. Mil. Acad., 1888. Commd. add. 2d lt. 1st Cav., June 11, 1888; 2d lt. 9th Cav., July 16, 1888; 1st lt. 4th Cav., Feb. 25, 1896; trans. to 9th Cav., Mar. 14, 1896; maj. 41st Vol. Inf., Aut. 17, 1899; hon. mustered out vols., June 30, 1901; capt. U.S.A., Feb. 2, 1901; trans. to 13th Cav., Aug. 28, 1901; to 8th Cav., Dec. 27, 1911; maj. 4th Cav., Feb. 29, 1912; later trans. to 2d Cav.; lt. col., July 1, 1916; col., May 15 1917; brig. gen. N.A., Apr. 16, 1918. Organized 4th F.A. Brigade, Camp Greene, N.C., comd. 160th F.A. Brig., Camp Custer, Mich.; sailed with brigade July 31, 1918, to training center, Coetquidan, Brittany; with brigade at front, operations 2d Army, 6th Corps, as corps arty., Oct. 30-Nov. 11, 1918; attached to Provost Marshal Gen.'s Office, Advance G.H.Q., Treves, Germany, Mar. 9-June 12, 1919; hon. discharged as brig. gen., July 15, 1919; col. comdg. 1st Cav., Douglas, Ariz., 1919-20; now comdg. Gen. Intermediate Depot, San Francisco. Address: War Dept., Washington, D.C. Died Dec. 12, 1952.

PRESTON, JOHN FISHER, army officer; b. Baltimore, Md., Nov. 5, 1872; s. John Fisher and Eliza (Thomas) P.; A.B., Baltimore City Coll., 1890; B.S., U.S. Mil. Acad., 1894; distinguished grad. Sch. of the Line, 1920; grad. Gen. Staff Sch., 1921. Army War Coll., 1923; mem. General Staff Corps eligible list; m. Meeta Campbell Graham, Dec. 23, 1896. Commd. 2d lt. 16th U.S Inf., 1894; promoted through grades to col., July 1, 1920. Served in Santiago Campaign, Spanish-Am. War, 1898; participated in 5 engagements, Philippine Insurrection; apptd. col. 303d Inf., 76th Div., 1917; served in France, 1918, 19; col. 63d Inf., Madison Barracks, N.Y., July 1919; chief of staff, 8th Corps Area, U.S., 1923-26; col. 1st U.S. Inf., 1926-28; assigned to Command 4th Brig., 2d Div., June 20, 1927; detailed to Insp. Gen.'s Dept., 1928; apptd. insp. gen., rank of maj. gen. for 4 years. from Dec. 1, 1931; retired Nov. 30, 1936 with rank of maj. gen. U.S. Army. Awarded Silver Star and cited "for gallantry in action"; nominated for brevet capt., Santiago, 1898. Dir. Nat. Bank of Fort Sam Houston, San Antonio, Tex. Episcopalian. Clubs: Army and Navy (Washington); Army-Navy Country (Arlington, Va.). Home: Baltimore, Md. Address: 149 Davis Court, San Antonio TX

PRESTON, JOHN SMITH army officer; b. Abingdon, Va., Apr. 20, 1809; s. Francis Smith and Sarah Buchanan (Campbell) P.; attended Hampden-Sydney Coll., 1823-25, U. Va., 1825-27; studied law at Harvard; m. Caroline Hampton, Apr. 28, 1830. Admitted to Va. bar, circa 1827; owned large sugar plantation "The Homus" in La., circa 1840-50; mem. S.C. Senate, 1848-56; chmn. S.C. delegation Democratic Nat. Conv., Charleston, S.C., 1860; commr. to visit Va. and urge secession, 1861; commd. asst. adjutant with rank lt. col., 1861; participated in 1st battle of Bull Run, 1861; command prison camp at Columbia, Ga., 1862; supt. Bur. of Conscription, Confederate Govt., 1863-65; commd. col. Confederate Army, 1863, given control of conscription in West, 1863, promoted brig. gen., 1864; spent rest of life defending Confederacy and principles of state's rights. Died Columbia, S.C., May 1, 1881.

PRESTON, ORD business exec.; b. St. Helena, Cal., Aug. 15, 1874; s. Albert Wm. (col. U.S. Army) and Mary Elizabeth (Ord) P.; grad. Phillips Andover Acad., 1894; A.B., Yale, 1899; m. Frances Jane Converse, June 7, 1902 (died 1911); children—Mary Ord, Eleanor Converse; m. 2d, Carolyn Merritt Murray, Dec. 4, 1912 (died Apr. 30, 1941); children—Arthur Murray, Ord; m. 3d, Margaret Helen Coe, Oct. 14, 1946. Clk. with W. H. Goadby & Co., brokers, N.Y.C., 1900-02; with Neale & Thorne, coal operators, Minerville, Pa., 1903-05; mem. N.Y. Stock Exchange and mem. C. E. Welles & Co., 1905-12; elected dir. Washington Gas Light Co., 1910, pres., 1923-30; dir. Union Trust Co., 1912-—, pres., 1932-45, chmn. bd. dirs., 1945-46. Served as maj. AS, U.S. Army, World War I. Republican. Episcopalian. Clubs: Metropolitan, Chevy Chase (Washington); University (N.Y.C.); Tennis and Beach (La Jolla). Home: 7910 Prospect Pl., La Jolla, Cal. Died Feb. 4, 1949.

PRESTON, PRINCE HULON congressman; born Monroe, Ga., July 5, 1908; s. Prince Hulon, Sr. and Mary Elizabeth (Lane) P.; LL.B., Univ. of Ga., 1930; m. Myrtice Alice Robinson, Sept. 22, 1934; children—Anne Christian, Owen Kay. Admitted to the bar of Ga., June 1930; pvt. practice of law, Statesboro, Ga., 1930-46; mem. Ga. Gen. Assembly, 1935-38; elected judge of City Court of Statesboro (Ga.), Mar. 1946, resigned; mem. 80th to 86th Congresses, 1st Dist. Ga. Served as pvt. U.S. Army; overseas 20 months; disch. as capt., 1945. Mem. Ga. Bar Assn., Jr. Order of Am. Mechanics (Statesboro council). Democrat. Baptist. Mem. Am. Legion, Vets. of Fgn. Wars, Pi Kappa Phi. Mason. Eagle. Home: 218 College BlVd., Statesboro, Ga. Office: House Office Bldg., Washington, D.C. Died Feb. 8, 1961; buried Statesboro.

PRESTON, WILLIAM diplomat, congressman; b. Louisville, Ky., Oct. 16, 1816; s. William and Caroline (Hancock) P.; attended Yale, 1835; LL.B., Harvard, 1838; m. Margaret Wickliffe, 1840, 6 children. Admitted to Louisville bar, circa 1838; served as lt. col. 4th Ky. Inf., Mexican War, 1846-48; del. from Louisville to Ky. Constl. Conv., 1849 mem. Ky. Ho. of Reps., 1850, 68-69; mem. U.S. Ho. of Reps. (Whig) from Ky., 32d-33d congresses, 1852-55; U.S. minister to Spain, 1858-61; commd. col. Confederate Army, 1861, brig. gen., 1862, maj. gen., 1864; apptd. Confederate minister to Maximilian, Emperor of Mexico, 1864. Died Louisville, Sept. 21, 1887; buried Cave Hill Cemetery, Louisville.

PRESTON, WILLIAM BALLARD congressman, sec. of navy; b. "Smithfield," Montgomery County, Va., Nov. 25, 1805; s. James Patton and Ann (Taylor) P.; grad. Coll. William and Mary, 1823; postgrad. U. Va., 1825; m. Lucinda Redd, Nov. 21, 1839. Admitted to Va. bar, 1826; mem. Va. Ho. of Dels., 1830-32, 44, 45, Va. Senate, 1840-44; mem. U.S. Ho. of Reps. (Whig) from Va., 30th Congress, 1847-49; U.S. sec. of navy, 1849-50; went on unsuccessful mission to France to negotiate establishment of steamship line from Norfolk, Va. to LeHavre, France, 1858; mem. Va. Secession Conv., 1861; met Lincoln informally, 1861, heard him read statement of policy and reported it to conv.; mem. Confederate Senate, 1861-62. Died Nov. 16, 1862; buried "Smithfield."

PRETTYMAN, E(LIJAH) BARRETT, judge; b. Lexington, Va., Aug. 23, 1891; s. Forrest Johnston and Elizabeth Rebecca (Stonestreet) P.; A.B., Randolph-Macon Coll., 1910, A.M., 1911, LL.D., 1961; LL.B., Georgetown U., 1915, LL.D., 1946; LL.D., Wm. Mitchell Coll. Law, 1961; m. Lucy C. Hill, Sept. 15, 1917; children—Elizabeth Courtney, Elijah Barrett. Admitted to Va. bar, 1915; mem. Potter, Prettyman & Fisher, Hopewell, Va., 1915-17; spl. atty. Internal Revenue Dept., Washington, D.C., and N.Y. City, 1919-20; asso. and mem. firm Butler, Lamb, Foster and Pope, Chicago, and Washington, D.C., 1920-33; gen. counsel Bur. Internal Revenue, Washington, 1933-34; corporation counsel of D.C., 1934-36; mem. Hewes, Prettyman and Awalt, Washington, D.C., and Hartford, Conn., 1936-45; professor of taxation, Georgetown University Law Sch.; judge United States Court of Appeals for D.C., from 1945, chief judge, 1958-60, later senior circuit judge. Chairman of the President's Conference on Adminstrv. Procedure, 1953-54; chmn. Adminstrv. Conf. of U.S., 1961-62; chmn. Pres.'s Adv. Commn. Narcotics and Drug Abuse, Jud. Conf. U.S. Adv. Com. Appellate Rules. Served U.S. Army, 1917-19, advancing to capt. inf. Trustee Randolph-Macon Coll., Am. U. Mem. Am., Fed. D.C. (past pres.) bar associations, Washington Board of Trade (past president), Phi Beta Kappa, Order of Coif, Sigma Upsilon, Kappa Sigma, Gamma Eta Gamma, Omicron Delta Kappa. Democrat. Methodist. Clubs: Civitan Internat., Burning Tree, Metropolitan. Chevy Chase, Lawyers. Author articles on taxation and administrative practice of law. Home: Washington DC Died Aug. 4, 1971.

PRICE, ABEL FITZWATER naval officer; b. Lawrenceville, Pa., Dec. 13, 1847; s. William Harley and Hannah (Detwiler) P.; ed. high sch., Phila.; M.D., U. of Pa., 1868; m. Clara L. Wollaston, Dec. 27, 1883. Commd. asst. surgeon U.S.N., Nov. 10, 1868; passed asst. surgeon, Nov. 10, 1871; surgeon, Aug. 14, 1878; rank of capt., Apr. 9, 1899. Served on U.S. Flag Ship Olympia as fleet surgeon to Admiral Dewey's fleet in Philippine campaign, 1898, 1899; pres. Naval Examining Bd., 1904-09; retired, Dec. 13, 1909. Episcopalian. Home: Sandwich, Mass. Died Mar. 22, 1919.

PRICE, BUTLER DELAPLAINE brig. gen. U.S.A.; b. Phila., May 27, 1845; s. Richard Butler and Elizabeth Senter (Huntt) P.; ed. Short's Acad., Phila.; m. Clara Agnes Gilmore, Oct. 10, 1866. Apptd. 2d lt. 2d Pa. Cav., Dec. 6, 1861; 1st lt., Feb. 2, 1863; capt., Feb. 23, 1864; hon. mustered out of vol. service, Jan. 5, 1865; commissioned 2d lt. 4th U.S. Inf., May 11, 1866; promoted through grades to col. 16th Inf., Oct. 18, 1902; brig. gen. and retired at own request, after 42 yrs.' service, Dec. 26, 1905. Participated in campaigns of Army of the Potomac (except Wilderness), 1862-65; served on plains, 1867-82 and 1886-96, participating in Indian Campaigns, 1867-79; served in Cuban campaign of 1898 and in Philippines, 1899-1901 and 1905. Episcopalian. Home: Washington, D.C. Died Aug. 29, 1919.

PRICE, HARRISON JACKSON army officer; b. Belington, W.Va., Apr. 3, 1868; s. Albert and Sofia (Bonner) P.; A.B., Ohio Northern U., 1891; grad. Inf. and Cav. Sch., 1897, Sch. of the Line, 1920, Gen. Staff Sch., 1921; m. Lucille Longuemare, June 18, 1895; children—Helen (Mrs. W. F. Sutter), Hardin Bonner, Lucille (Mrs. P. S. Jessup). Commd. 2d lt. 24th Inf., Oct. 7, 1891; promoted through grades to lt. col., May 15, 1917; col. N.A., Aug. 5, 1917; brig. gen. (temp.), Oct. 1, 1918-June 30, 1919; col. regular army Apr. 2, 1920. In Cuba, June-Sept. 1898, and July-Oct. 1899; three tours to Philippines, 1900-03, 1906-07, 1915-17; comd. 350th Inf., 88th Div., Oct. 1917-Oct. 1918; comd. 154th Inf. Brigade, 77th Div., Oct. 1918-May 1919; participated in Alsace-Lorraine Sector, and in Meuse-Argonne offensive, Oct. 28, to close of war; in drive from Grande Pré to Meuse River, east of Sedan, capturing 8 towns whose inhabitants had been cut off from the world for 4 yrs. Gen. staff corps and asst. chief of staff G-3, 2d Corps Area, Governors Island, N.Y., 1922-26; in charge Nat. Guard Affairs, 2d Corps Area, 1926-28; chief of staff, 80th Div., Richmond, Va., Sept. 1, 1928-Apr. 30, 1932; retired as brig. gen. Apr. 30, 1932. Decorated Purple Heart. Citation, "for exceptionally meritorious and conspicuous services," as comdr. 154th Inf. Brigade, A.E.F., in France. Mem. S.A.R. (pres. Va. Soc. 1941), Vets. of Foreign Wars, Soc. of Santiago de Cuba, Soc. of the Philippines. Clubs: Army and Navy (Manila); Army and Navy (Washington, D.C.). Home: 3605 Brook Rd., Richmond, Va. Died Sep. 16, 1945.

PRICE, HOWARD CAMPBELL army officer (ret.); b. Chester, Pa., Apr. 15, 1872; s.William Gray and Jane Eliza (Campbell) P.; student pub. and pvt. schs., Pa.; grad. Army Sch. of the Line, 1921, Command and Gen. Staff Sch., 1924, Army War Coll., 1928; m. Alice Blakeley Gilroy, June 16, 1908; children—Howard Campbell, Jane Blakeley (wife of Capt. Walter Coulter Winn). Commd. 2d lt. U.S. Army, 1899, advanced through grades to brig. gen. (ret.), 1940; served in Spanish-Am. War; with Army of Cuban Occupation, 1899-1900, Philippine Insurrection, 1900-03; comd. 360 Inf., 90th Div., France and Germany, 1917-18, 38th Inf., Fort Douglas, Utah, 1928-31, 57th Inf. (Philippine Scouts), P.I., 1931-34; ret., 1936. Decorated D.S.M., 3 Silver Star citations (U.S.); Croix de Guerre (France). Mem. Mil. Order World Wars, Pa. S.R. Republican. Episcopalian. Mason. Club: Army and Navy (Manila, P.I.). Home: 1218 Prospect St., La Jolla, Cal. Died Feb. 1, 1950.

PRICE, JOHN D. ret. naval officer; b. Augusta, Ark., May 18, 1892; s. David Flournoy and Anna Frances (Corley) P.; B.S., U.S. Naval Acad., 1916; grad. Naval Aviation Sch., Pensacola, Fla., 1920; m. Miriam Johnston, May 17, 1924; children—Dale (Mrs. A. B. Conner), John. Commd. ensign, 1916, and advanced through the grades to adm.; gunnery and mining officer U.S.S. Quinnebang, World War I; commended by sec. of navy for experimental flying on aircraft carriers; comd. U.S.S. Jason, U.S.S. Pocomoke (aircraft tenders), 1931, 1939, Naval Air Sta., Seattle, 1928-30, Anacostia, D.C., 1937-39, Jacksonville, Fla., 1942-43, Patrol Wings 3 and 8; comdr. A. F. Pacific; nominated chief Naval Air Operations, Washington; ret. 1954. Awarded W.W. I medal, Mexican, Yangtse medals; Navy Cross, Distinguished Flying Cross, Legion of Merit. Club: Army-Navy Country (Washington). Home: 1801 S. Taylor St., Little Rock, Ark. Address: care Naval Operations (Air), Navy Dept., Washington 25. Died Dec. 19, 1957.*

PRICE, JOSEPH LINDON, physician; b. Davenport, Okla., Mar. 22, 1911; s. Thomas E. and Florence (Elliott) P.; M.D., U. Ia., 1937; m. Edna Henrie, June 1, 1940, (div.); children—Michael, Patrick, Sally. Intern, Salt Lake County Gen. Hosp., Salt Lake City, 1937-39; asst. to Dr. E.R. Dumke, Ogden, Utah, 1940-41; gen. practice medicine and surgery, Redding, Cal., 1946-68; mem. staff Meml. Hosp., Redding, 1946-68, bd. dirs., 1963-68, pres. bd., 1963-68. Cattle rancher, 1951-68; almond rancher, 1953-68. Mem. Shasta County, Cal. Republican Central Com., 1951-59, chmn., 1957-59; mem. Cal. Rep. Central Com. Served to capt., M.C., AUS, 1941-46. Mem. Am., Cal. med. assns., Shasta County Med. Soc., Am. Hereford Assn. Republican. Elk. Developer almond tree; inventor vet. instrument. Home: Cottonwood CA Died Sept. 17, 1968.

PRICE, RICHARD NYE clergyman; b. Elk Garden, Va., July 30, 1830; s. John Wesley and Mary (Miller) P.; A.B., Emory and Henry Coll., Va., 1854, later A.M.; (D.D., Weaverville Coll., Trinity Coll., and Emory and Henry, 1913); m. Ann, sister of U.S. Senator Z. B. Vance, of N. Carolina, May 8, 1855. Ordained ministry M.E. Ch., S., 1852; served in various pastorates, on circuits, in schs. and colls. and as editor ch. publs.; prof. mathematics and ancient langs., Holston Conf. Female Coll., 3 yrs.; pres. People's Coll., Pikesville, Tenn., 4 yrs.; prof. mathematics, Emory and Henry Coll., 4 yrs., Harriman U., 3 yrs. Served as pvt. Rough and Ready Guards, May-Oct., 1861; chaplain 26th N.C. Vols., 1861-62; chaplain 4th Tenn. Vols. Spanish-Am. War, Dec. 1898-Apr. 1899. Democrat. Author: Cofractions, 1898; Holston Methodism (5 vols.), 1903. Home: Morristown, Tenn. Deceased.

PRICE, SAMUEL WOODSON artist; b. Nicholasville, Ky., Aug. 5, 1828. Painted portraits in Ky. and Tenn. until 1861; served as col. Union Army during Civil War, wounded at Battle of Kennesaw Mountain, brevetted brig. gen., 1865; painted portraits, Washington, D.C., after Civil War; postmaster of Lexington (Ky.), 1869-76; painted portraits and figure paintings until he went blind, 1881. Author: Old Masters of the Bluegrass (biographical accounts of Ky. painters dictated after he went blind), 1902. Died St. Louis, Jan. 22, 1918.

PRICE, STERLING gov. Mo., army officer; b. Prince Edward County, Va., Sept. 20, 1809; s. Pugh Williamson and Elizabeth (Williamson) P.; attended Hampden-Sydney Coll., 1826-27; m. Martha Head, May 14, 1833. Moved to Mo., 1831; mem. Mo. Ho. of Reps., 1836-38, 40-45, speaker, 1840-44; mem. U.S. Ho. of Reps. from Mo., 29th Congress, 1845-Aug. 12, 1846; served as col. 2d Mo. Inf., Mexican War, 1846-48, promoted brig. gen., mil. gov. Chihuahua; gov. Mo., 1853-57, reorganized public sch. system; bank commr. Mo., 1857-61; pres. Mo. Democratic Conv., 1860; in command Mo. Militia, circa 1860; collected and trained approximately 5,000 troops, united forces with smaller Confederate army of Gen. Ben McCulloch; defeated U.S. Army in Battle of Wilson's Creek, 1861, captured 3,000 fed. troops, Lexington, Ky., 1861; officially joined Confederate Army, Ark., 1862; retreated to Tex. plains, 1864-65; resided in Mexico until fall of Maximilian's Empire, 1866. Died St. Louis, Sept. 29, 1867; buried Bellefontaine Cemetery, St. Louis.

PRICE, THOMAS LAWSON congressman, mayor; b. Danville, Va., Jan. 19, 1809; s. Maj. and Mrs. (Lawson) Price; m. Lydia Bolton, 1828; m. 2d, Caroline V. Long, Apr. 20, 1854; at least 2 children. Organized merc. and trading bus., Jefferson City, Mo., 1831; established 1st stage-line between St. Louis and Jefferson City, 1838, controlled all stage-line bus. in Mo.; 1st mayor Jefferson City, 1839-42; organized Capitol City Bank, Jefferson City; brevetted maj. ge. 6th Div., Mo. Militia, 1847; lt. gov. (Democrat) Mo., 1849-52; mem. Mo. Ho. of Reps., 1860-62; served as brig. gen. in charge Mo. Militia, U.S. Army, 1861; mem. U.S. Ho. of Reps. (War Democrat) from Mo., 37th Congress, Jan. 21, 1862-63, instrumental in defeat of compensated emancipation for Mo. slaves by fed. appropriation; a reorganizer Democratic Party in Mo., circa 1865. Died Jefferson City, July 15, 1870; buried Riverview Cemetery, Jefferson City.

PRICE, WILLIAM CECIL proslavery leader; b. Russell County, Va., Apr. 1, 1818; s. Crabtree and Linny (Cecil) P.; m. Sarah J. Kimbrough, June 1842; 7 children; m. 2d, Lydia C. Dow, Aug. 1860, 3 children. Admitted to Mo. bar, 1838; judge Green County (Mo.), 1842-45; worked for repeal of Mo. Compromise, advocated proslavery policy for state; led campaign against Thomas H. Benton's antislavery convictions, 1844-50; mem. Mo. Senate, 1854-57; treas. U.S., 1860-61; served with Confederate Army, 1861, taken prisoner, held in Alton, Ill., until Sept. 1862; lived in Springfield, Mo., 1870-1907, loaned money to Easterners. Died Chgo., Aug. 6, 1907.

PRICE, WILLIAM GRAY, JR., maj. gen., retired; b. Chester, Pa., Mar. 23, 1869; s. Wm. Gray and Jane Elizabeth (Campbell) P.; ed. pub. and private schs.; hon. Doctor Mil. Sci., Pa. Mil. Coll.; m. Sallie Pennell Eyre, June 1, 1893. Entered Nat. Guard of Pa., April 1886; promoted through grades to brig. gen. N.G. Pa., 1910; brig. gen. N.A., Aug. 5, 1917; maj. gen. Pa. N.G., May 16, 1919; maj. gen. U.S.R.C., Apr. 9, 1921. Served as lt. col. 3d Pa. Vols., Spanish-Am. War; apptd. comdr. 53d Arty. Brig., Camp Hancock, Ga., Aug. 5, 1917, and comdr. same throughout its service in Europe; participated in Marne, Vesle, Argonne, Leys-Scheldt operations, Fr. and Belgium; apptd. comdg. gen. Pa. N.G. on return from France, May 15, 1919; retired Mar. 23, 1933. Awarded D.S.M. (U.S.); Croix de Guerre (Belgium and France); Comdr. Legion of Honor (France). Republican. Episcopalian. Clubs: Union League, Corinthian Yacht (Phila.); Chester (Chester); Army and Navy (Washington). Home: 24 W. Sellers Av., Ridley Park PA

PRICE, WILLIAM PIERCE congressman; b. Dahlonega, Ga., Jan. 29, 1835; s. William P. P.; ed. county schools; learned printing trade; foreman printing office, 1850-54; editor, 1854, at Greenville, S.C.; studied law; admitted to S.C. bar, 1856; m. Martha Ann Martin, 1856. Practiced law, Greenville, S.C.; entered Kershaw's 2d S.C. regt.; took part in battles of Bull Run and Manassas; severely wounded at Lewinsville, Va., Sept. 11, 1861; discharged from service; mem. S.C. legislature, 1864-66; resigned and returned to Dahlonega; mem. and speaker pro tem Ga. legislature during reconstruction period; twice arrested as ineligible and tried by mil. courts, which acquitted him; mem. Congress, 1871-74; pres. bd. trustees North Ga. Agrl. Coll., 34 yrs.; mayor of Dahlonega for 6 yrs. (1901). Home: Dahlonega, Ga. Died 1908.

PRICHARD, VERNON E. army officer; b. Smithland, Ia., Jan. 25, 1892; s. Jacob A. and Emma Grace (Jones) P.; student Morningside Coll., Sioux City, Ia., 1908-11; B.S., U.S. Mil. Acad., 1915; m. Charlotte Gibbs Blesse, Sept. 6, 1916; 1 dau., Carlotta. Commd. 2d. lt., U.S. Army, 1915, and advanced through grades to maj. gen. (temp.), 1942; now with Gen. Staff, Dept. of the Army. Recipient Mex. Punitive Expdn. medal, D.S.M., Purple Heart (U.S.), Companion Order of Bath (Gt. Britain),

Legion of Honor (France), Order of St. Maurice and St. Lazarus (Italy), War Cross (Brazil), War Cross (Czechoslovakia). Mason (32 deg.). Home: Fort Myer, Va. Office: Pentagon Bldg., Washington 25. Died July 10, 1949.

PRIME, EBENEZER SCUDDER rear admiral U.S.N.; b. New York, Jan. 16, 1847; s. Edward Youngs and Emma (Cotrel) P.; apptd. to U.S. Naval Acad. from N.Y., Sept. 21, 1863; m. Eva Prime, Nov. 21, 1883. Promoted through the various grades to rear admiral, June 25, 1905, and retired on own request. Home: Huntington, N.Y. Died Apr. 27, 1912.

PRIME, FREDERICK EDWARD maj. U.S.A.; retired, Sept. 5, 1871; b. Florence, Italy, Sept. 24, 1829 (son of Rufus Prime, New York merchant); grad. West Point, 1850; employed on fortifications; taken prisoner at Pensacola, Fla., 1861; later, as capt. engrs., served in Manassas campaign; successively chief engr. depts. Ky., the Cumberland and the Ohio; wounded and again prisoner; then chief engr. in Grant's Mississippi campaign, 1862-63; maj., June 1, 1863; took part in siege of Vicksburg; bvtd. col.; retired through disability from wounds received in line of duty. Home: Litchfield, Conn. Died 1900.

PRIME, RALPH EARL lawyer; b. Matteawan, N.Y., Mar. 29, 1840; s. Alanson Jermain (M.D.) and Ruth Havens (Higbie) P.; ed. schs. and acad. White Plains, N.Y., and pvt. tutors; studied medicine with father; studied law in offices at White Plains, admitted to bar, 1861; (D.C.L., Bellevue Coll.; LL.D., U. of Wooster, 1897); enlisted pvt. 5th N.Y. Inf., Apr. 21, 1861; held four regimental commissions, participated in 13 battles, severely wounded at battle of Gaines' Mill; twice promoted "for signal bravery on field of battle," as promulgated in general orders of Army Corps Headquarters; nominated, Mar. 4, 1863, by President Lincoln to be brig. gen.; m. Annie Richards-Wolcott, Aug. 9, 1866. Began law practice late in 1863; has been city atty. of Yonkers and deputy atty. gen. N.Y.; has crossed ocean 36 times, traveled in Europe, Asia and Africa. For over 30 yrs. Presbyn. elder and represented Presbyterian Ch. in the U.S.A. at Pan-Presbyn. councils, Belfast, 1884, London, 1886, Glasgow, 1894, Washington, 1899, Liverpool, 1904, New York, 1909, Aberdeen, 1913; moderator, Presbytery of Westchester, 1894, Synod of N.Y., 1896; permanent clerk Presbytery of Westchester, 1895-1917. Chmn. Western Sect. Pan-Presbyn. Alliance. Mason. Democrat. Author: Descendants of James Prime. Home: Yonkers, N.Y. Died Sept. 27, 1920.

PRINDLE, FRANKLIN COGSWELL officer U.S.N.; b. Sandgate, Vt., July 8, 1841; s. Hawley and Olive (Andrew) P.; ed. pub. schs. and Rensselaer Poly. Inst., Troy, N.Y.; thrice married; m. 3d, Mrs. Fidelia E. (White) Mead, Apr. 8, 1896. Apptd. 3d asst. engr., Aug. 3, 1861; 2d asst. engr., Apr. 21, 1863; civ. engr. U.S.N., Apr. 17, 1869; retired with rank of rear adm., Feb. 27, 1901, on account of disability incurred in line of duty. Served in S. Atlantic Blockading Squadron and participated in many engagements under Commodores Dupont and Dahlgren during Civil War; served as civ. engr. of navy yards and stations, and in constrn. of naval training sta., Yerba Buena Island, San Francisco Bay, 1898-1900. Engr. and sec. Am. Dredging Co., Phila., 1876-77; engr. and supt., also sec. and treas., Carolina Oil & Cresote Co., Wilmington, N.C., 1888-90; dir., v.p., pres. Aztec Oil Co., Bakersfield, Calif., 1900-04. Republican. Baptist. Mason. Author: The Prindle Genealogy, 1906. Home: Washington, D.C. Died Mar. 7, 1923.

PRING, MARTIN explorer, naval officer; b. Eng., circa 1580; s. John Pring; m. Elizabeth, 6 children. Sent on expdn. to No. Va., 1603; in command of ships Speedwell and Discoverer, sighted land at Penobscot Bay, drifted westward into Cape Cod Bay, landed at Plymouth Harbor (naming it Whitson Bay); built a barricade; sent on expdn. to join Challons on coast of Va.; explored the coast, made chart and report; employed to survey Bristol Channel, 1610; master in service of East India Co., 1613, comdr. naval forces of co., 1619; launched policy of friendship with Dutch in order to secure monopoly against the Spanish and Portuguese; became mem. Mcht. Venturers Soc. of Bristol, 1623, a warden of soc., 1625; took command of 300-ton privateer, Charles, 1626. Died 1626; buried St. Stephen's Ch., Bristol, Eng.

PRINGLE, JOEL ROBERTS POINSETT rear adm.; b. Georgetown, S.C., Feb. 4, 1873; s. Dominick Lynch and Caroline (Lowndes) P.; grad. U.S. Naval Acad., 1892; m. Cordelia Phythian, Jan. 25, 1899; 1 dau., Cordelia Phythian (wife of Lieut. J. D. H. Kane, U.S.N.). Commd. ensign U.S.N., July 1, 1894; advanced through grades to rear adm., Dec. 6, 1926. Became pres. Naval War Coll., Newport, R.I., 1927; now comdr. Battleship Div. 3. Died Sept. 25, 1932.

PRITCHARD, ARTHUR JOHN officer U.S.N.; b. Dorchester Co., Md., Feb. 12, 1836; s. Nicholas B. and Elizabeth A. P.; pub. sch. edn.; m. Sarah E. Harrington, Oct. 19, 1871. Entered U.S.N. as asst. p.-m., Oct. 7, 1861; promoted p.-m., 1864; pay insp., Dec. 24, 1883; pay dir., 1895; retired, Feb. 12, 1898; advanced to rank of rear adm. retired, June 29, 1906. Served in Itaska, in Rear Admiral Farragut's Squadron, 1861-63, participating in engagements on Miss. River; wounded, 1862, and incapacitated 7 months; served in Wyalusing, 1863-64; Ticonderoga, European Sta., 1864-69; Benicia, 1869-71; sick leave, 1871-72; in Saranac, N. Pacific Squadron, 1872-75; Powhatan, 1875-77; trainingship Minnesota, 1878-81; served at navy pay office, Baltimore, 1882-85, 1888-92, 1896-98, 1902-05; in Pensacola, 1885-88; served navy pay office, Norfolk, Va., 1893-96. Mason. Republican. Home: Baltimore, Md. Died Sept. 5, 1916.

PRITCHARD, ARTHUR THOMAS M.D., surgeon; b. Marshall, N.C., Jan. 28, 1882; s. Judge Jeter C. and Augusta Lilian (Ray) P.; ed. Horner Mil. Sch., Oxford, N.C., and U. of N.C.; M.D., Jefferson Med. Coll., Phila., 1905; m. Robin Gertrude Kennett, June 6, 1910; 1 son, Arthur Thomas. Practiced at Asheville, 1906—; a founder and pres. French Brood Hosp. Commd. capt., later maj., Med. Corps, U.S.A., World War; served at Base Hosp. No. 65, Evacuation Hosp. No. 11; duty at Argonne; hon. disch., Apr. 6, 1919. Fellow Am. Coll. Surgeons. Republican. Baptist. Mason. Home: Asheville, N.C. Died May 26, 1927.

PRITCHETT, CLIFTON AUGUSTINE army officer; b. Baltimore, Dec. 6, 1888; s. Capt. Thomas A. and Cora Elizabeth (Marlatt) P.; attended U. of Md., 1907-10; grad. Inf. Sch. Co. Officers, 1922, Field Officers, 1927, Command and Gen. Staff Coll., 1930; Field Officers Chemical Warfare School, 1930; m. Elsie May Freedenburg; children—Jacqueline Anne (Mrs. Vernon L. Smith), Patricia Eileen, Clifton Augustine. Commd. 2d lieut., 1st lt. (1950) Md. N.G., 1912-17; capt., U.S. Army, 1918, advancing through grades to col., 1941; assigned Gen. Pershing's Staff, GHQ, A.E.F., 1918-19; chief of staff, G.S.C. Mil. Dist. of Washington, 1942-47; v.p. U.S. Inf. Jour., Inc., 1946-50. Awarded Legion of Merit, Army Commendation Ribbon, Mexican Border, Victory Ribbon (with 3 stars), Occupation of Ger. Ribbon, Am. Defense Ribbon (with 1 star), North American Theatre Ribbon, Victory Ribbon World War II, French Croix de Guerre (World War I), French Commemorative Ribbon, Verdun Medal. Dir. U.S. Inf. Assn., 1941-50; mem. Mil. Order World Wars, Am. Legion, 40 et 8. Episcopalian. Mason (32 deg., K.T., Shriner). Clubs: Army and Navy, U.S. Naval Gun Factory, Carabao, Officers (Washington); Officers (Ft. Meyer, Va.); Army and Navy (Manila), Mil. and Naval, Camp Fire of Am. (N.Y. City). Home: "Stack Arms," 2316 N. Stafford St., Lee Heights, Arlington 7. Office: 2173 N. Glebe Rd., Arlington 7, Va. Deceased.

PROBASCO, SCOTT LIVINGSTON banker; b. Chattanooga, Sept. 6, 1890; s. Harry Scott and Alice Gray (Moore) P.; grad. Baylor Sch., Chattanooga, 1906, Hotchkiss Sch., Conn., 1910; m. Margaret Williams, June 26, 1926; children—Alice Moore (Mrs. John T. Lupton), Scott Livingston, Margaret Williams (Mrs. Robert C. Jones, III). Chmn. bd. dirs. Am. Nat. Bank & Trust Co.; pres. Benwood Found., Inc.; dir. Davenport Hosiery Mills, La. Furs Corp., Provident Life & Accident Ins. Co., Combustion Engring., Inc. (mem. exec. com.). Maj., U.S. Army, World War I; now col. USAAF. Trustee U. Chattanooga, Baylor Sch. Rep. Presbyn. Clubs: Mountain City, Chattanooga Golf and Country (Chattanooga). Home: 1616 Edgewood Lane, Riverview, Chattanooga. Office: care Am. Nat. Bank & Trust Co., Chattanooga 1. Died June 25, 1962; buried Forest Hills Cemetery, Chattanooga.

PROBST, NATHAN, lawyer; b. New York, N.Y., June 21, 1897; s. Nathan and Clara (Roth) P.; A.B., Columbia, 1918, LL.B., 1920. Admitted to N.Y. bar, 1920; asso. with Curtis, Mallet-Prevost & Colt, New York, 1920-21; asst. U.S. atty. Southern Dist. N.Y., 1921-22; spl. asst. U.S. atty. gen. 1922-24; engaged in the private practice of law, 1924-66; professor at St. Johns University Law Sch., Brooklyn, 1925-50; co-adjutor in preparation of constitution for Virgin Islands. Major, A.U.S.; in mil. service, 1942-46. Jewish religion. Address: Brooklyn Heights NY Died Dec. 30, 1966.

PROCTOR, JAMES MCPHERSON judge; b. Washington, D.C., Sept. 4, 1882; s. Alexander M. and Annie Elizabeth (Ashford) P.; LL.B., George Washington U., 1904, LL.D.; married Mary S. Harrington, September 20, 1902 (died September 1946); children—Edward A., James M.; m. 2d, Elizabeth Barry Coleman, Sept. 30, 1947. Admitted to District of Columbia bar, 1903; asst. U.S. atty. for D.C., 1905-09, chief asst., 1909-13; private practice until 1931; spl. asst. atty. gen., 1929-31, in charge suits of U.S. to clear titles to river front properties in D.C.; asso. justice Dist. Court of U.S. for the Dist. of Columbia, 1931-48; circuit judge, U.S. Court of Appeals, since Mar. 9, 1948. Served as capt. inf., A.E.F., World War. Mem. American Bar Association, Gen. Alumni Assn. George Washington University (past pres.). Mason. Clubs: Chevy Chase, Civitan (ex-pres.), Lawyers. Home: Kennedy-Warren Apts. Address: U.S. Court of Appeals, Washington 1. Died Sept. 17, 1953; buried Arlington Nat. Cemetery.

PROCTOR, REDFIELD U.S. senator; b. Proctorsville, Vt., June 1, 1831; s. Jabez and Betsey (Parker) P.; A.B., 1851; A.M., 1854, Dartmouth Coll.; LL.B., Albany Law Sch., 1860; m. Emily J. Dutton, May 26, 1858. Practiced law, Boston, 1860-61; enlisted as q.m. 3d Vt. regt., 1861; promoted maj. 5th Vt. regt., Sept. 1861, col. 15th Vt. vols., 1862; served as brigade and div. q.m. on staff Gen. William F. Smith; mustered out, 1863. Long head of largest mable producing co. in the world; retired. Mem. Vt. legislature, 1867, 1868, 1888; mem. and pres. pro tem. Vt. Senate, 1874-75; lt. gov. Vt., 1876-78; gov., 1878-80; sec. of war, U.S., 1889-91; U.S. senator, Vt., 1891-1911. Republican. Visited Cuba, Mar. 1898, and his speech on Cuban reconcentrados in senate after his return attracted wide attention. Home: Proctor, Vt. Died 1908.

PROCTOR, REDFIELD ex-gov. Vt., marble co. exec.; b. Proctor, Vt., Apr. 13, 1879; s. Redfield and Emily J. (Dutton) P.; Mass. Inst. Tech., 1902; M.S., U. Vt., 1916, LL.D., 1924; LL.D., Middlebury Coll., 1923; m. Mary Sherwood Hedrick, Oct. 24, 1905; children—Margaret (Mrs. Jos. P. Kelly), Robert Dutton, Katharine (Mrs. Rowland Douglas). Began practice as mech. engr., 1902; chmn. bd. dirs. Vt. Marble Co., Yule Colo. Marble Co. Mem. Vt. Ho. of Rep., 1912, 15, Senate, 1917-19; del. Rep. Nat. Conv., 1920; gov. of Vt., 1923-25; pres. N.E. Council, 1929-31. Trustee Middlebury Coll.; mem. corp. Mass. Inst. Tech. Served as capt. Engr. Corps, 1917-19. Mem. bd. dirs. U.S. C. of C., 1932-38; mem. N.A.M. (dir. 1942-47), Am. Soc. M.E., Vt. Soc. Engrs., S.A.R., Loyal Legion, Mil. Order World War, Am. Legion, Newcomen Soc., Delta Upsilon. Republican. Clubs: University (N.Y.C.); Union (Boston). Home: Proctor, Vt. Died Feb. 5, 1957; buried Proctor.

PROCTOR, ROBERT, lawyer; b. Newton Centre, Mass., Dec. 1, 1898; s. Thomas W. and Anne Louise (White) P.; student Country Day Sch., Newton, Mass., 1909-15; A.B., Dartmouth, 1919; LL.B., Harvard, 1924; m. Nathalie H. Bishop, May 20, 1939. Admitted to Mass. bar, 1924, practiced as asso. firm of Choate, Hall & Stewart, Boston, 1924-27, mem. firm, 1927-42 and from 1946; admitted to D.C. bar, 1946, also mem. firm Douglas Proctor, MacIntyre & Gates, Washington, 1946-48; asst. to pres. Lockheed Aircraft Corp., Burbank, Calif., 1942-43; dir., mem. exec. com. State Street Bank and Trust Co.; trustee Am. Optical Co.; dir. OK Tool Company, Lockheed Aircraft Corporation. Member of Procurement Task Force, Second Hoover Commn., 1953-55. Served as 2d lieutenant, infantry, U.S. Army, 1918; spl. cons. to sec. of War, Aug.-Dec. 1940; commd. lt. col., A.A.F., Aug 1943, and advanced to col., Sept. 1944; served as exec. asst. and exec. to comdg. gen., A.A.F., Aug. 1943-Feb. 1946, Washington. Awarded Legion of Merit. Mem. Air Force Assn. (director 1947-51), American Massachusetts, Essex County, Salem, Boston (member of the council, 1929-35, mem. grievance com., 1929-35) bar assns., Phi Beta Kappa, Alpha Delta Phi. Clubs: Somerset Tavern (Boston); Myopia Hunt (Hamilton). Home: Manchester MA Died Sept. 25, 1967; buried Newton Cemetery, Newton MA

PROFFITT, EDWARD J(OSEPH) W(ALTER) finance; b. Providence; S. Nahum J. and Winifred (O'Brien) P.; grad. Bryant Coll.; grad. G-4, U.S. Army Wa. Coll., Washington; D.Sc., Bryant Coll., 1948; m. Florence B. Fletcher, Oct. 8, 1908; children—Edward R. (USAF), Raymond F. Advt. mgr. The Shepard Co., Providence, 1906; pres. Proffitt-Larchar Advertising Corp., Providence, 1910-18; pub., editor R.I. Advertiser, 1910-18; nat. councillor U.S. C. of C., 1916-18; pub. relations counsel Union Trust Co., Providence, 1910-18; treas. Trading Co. of N.A., 1916-31, now exec. partner; treas., gen. mgr. U.S. Stores Co. of Ind., 1920-21; dir. U.S. Stores Corp. (Del.) 1920-21; asst. to pres. U.S. Shipping Bd. Fleet Corp., 1923-24; pres. Investing Co. of N.Y., 1934-36; pres. Investing Corp. of N.Y., 1925-30, v.p. 1930-34; v.p. Dorrance, Sullivan & Co., advt., N.Y.C., 1930; v.p., dir. Greenway Mortgage Corp. (Balt.), 1923-24; dir. Nat. Refinance Corp., Washington, 1934-36; resident dir. Internat. Bank, Washington, 1932-52; asst. to pres. Brooklyn Eagle (N.Y.), charge met. adv., 1934-35; investment counsel Fenner & Beane, 1930-37; U.S. Govt. bond counsel Nat. City Bank, N.Y.C., 1935-36; mgr. U.S. Govt. bond dept. Delafield & Delafield, 1937-38; spl. counsel U.S. Govt. securities Lazard Freres, N.Y.C. and Paris, France, 1938-41; Mfrs. & Traders Trust Co., Buffalo, 1938-52, Franklin Nat. Bank, Franklin Sq., N.Y., 1953-54; asst. to pres. Duffy Constrn. Corp., N.Y. Chmn. com. on cooperation Nat. Monetary Affairs, N.Y. Bd. of Trade, 1946. Mil. aide-de-camp, rank of maj., R.I. N.G., 1917-18; col. inf., U.S. Army, mem. Gen. Staff, 1918-19; asst. chief staff, 84th Div., U.S. Army, 1923-24; col. F.A. Res., U.S. Army, 1926-45; comdr. 571st F.A., 1927-28, 580th F.A., 1929-32, 570th F.A., 1932-41, 152d F.A. Brig., 1933; ofcl. observer, field maneuvers, First Field Army, U.S. Army, Pine Camp, N.Y., 1935; dir. Liaison Officer, 3d Corps, First Army maneuvers at Canton N.Y., 1940; observer, test of 1st Armored Div., Ft. Knox, Ky., 1941; exec. officer purchase br. Purchase, Storage and Traffic Div., Gen. Staff, U.S. Army, 1918; chmn. steering com., mem. War Dept. Claims Bd., 1918-19; asst. to dir. budget U.S. Treasury, 1921-22, legal aide to chief coordinator Bur. Budget, 1922; asst. counsel U.S. Shipping Bd., 1922. Mem. Officers Hon. Retired list, U.S. Army, 1946; commd. col. reserve, AUS, 1953. Mem. nat. laymen's com. Boy Scouts Am. Nat. treas. Nat. Rep. League, 1933; dir. Civic Research Inst., 1939-41. Mem. C. of C. State N.Y., Am. Inst. Banking, Foreign Policy Assn. Republican. Clubs: Metropolitan (N.Y.C.); Army Athletic Assn. (West

Point); Army and Navy (Washington); Army, Navy and Marine Corps Country; Admirals (La Guardia Field, N.Y.); Pemex Travel (Mexico City, Mex.). Contbr. to newspapers and trade papers. Home: "Overlook," Hilltop Drive, Great Neck Estates, L.I., N.Y.; Army and Navy Club, Washington. Office: 726 Jackson Pl., Washington; also 61 Broadway, N.Y.C. Died Jan. 10, 1963; buried Arlington Nat. Cemetery.

PROSSER, PAUL PITTMAN lawyer; b. Fayette, Mo., Nov. 7, 1880; s. Lewis Smith and Mary Catherine (Dines) P.; A.B., Central Coll., Fayette, Mo., 1900; LL.B., Washington U., 1903; unmarried. In practice of law, St. Louis, Mo., 1903-07, Fayette, Mo., 1907-20; pros. atty., Howard Co., Mo., 1909-12, 1916-19; removed to Denver, Colo., 1920; atty. gen. of Colo., terms 1933-37. Maj., judge adv., U.S.A., Washington, D.C., 1918-19. Mem. advisory bd. Bur. of Charities, Denver and Denver County, 1928-—; chmn. Colo. George Washington Bicentennial Commn., 1931-32. Democrat. Methodist. Home: Denver, Colo. Died June 26, 1936.

PROUDFIT, DAVID LAW author; b. Newburgh-on-the-Hudson, N.Y., Oct. 27, 1842; m. Frances Marian Dodge, July 8, 1868, 3 children. Served from pvt. to maj. 1st N.Y. Mounted Rifles, 1861-65, served at Richmond and Petersburg. Author: Love among the Gamins, 1877; From the Chapparal to eet; or a Man from the West, 1891. Died N.Y.C., 1897.

PRYOR, JAMES CHAMBERS rear adm.; b. Winchester, Tenn., Mar. 13, 1871; s. James Jones and Nannie Buchanan (Brazelton) P.; A.B., U. of Nashville; M.D., Vanderbilt, 1895; spl. med. courses in clinics, Vienna, Paris and London; M.A., Johns Hopkins, 1913; grad. U.S. Army War Coll., 1928; m. Georgia Leontine Mackay, June 16, 1906 (died 1914); 1 son, James Chambers; m. 2d, Frances Pierpont Siviter, June 9, 1917; 1 dau., Frances Pierpont. Entered U.S. Navy as asst. surgeon with rank of ensign, 1897; advanced through grades to rear admiral, Oct. 1, 1934; retired April 1, 1935. Served on U.S.S. Albatross during Spanish-Am. War.; med. officer Agassiz Expdn. to South Pacific Ocean on same ship, 1898-99; served as med. attendant to Theodore Roosevelt at White House and Oyster Bay; brigade surgeon Naval forces ashore at Vera Cruz, Mexico, 1914; head dept. hygiene, U.S. Naval Med. Sch., Washington, D.C., 1917-20; prof. preventive medicine, George Washington U., 1917-19; lecturer on naval hygiene, Johns Hopkins, 1919; commanded U.S. Naval Hosps., Yokohama, Japan, Pensacola, Fla., Hampton Roads, Va., U.S. Naval Med. Sch., 1925-28; med. officer and head of dept. hygiene U.S. Naval Acad., 1928-31; comdg. Naval Med. Supply Depot, Brooklyn, N.Y. Spl. commendation of sec. of Navy "for extraordinary devotion in line of duty," at Battle of Ciudar Bolivar, Venezuela, 1903; service medals, Spanish-Am. War, Occupation of Vera Cruz, Mexico, and World War. Fellow Am. Coll. Surgeons; mem. A.M.A., Assn. of Mil. Surgeons of U.S. (ex-pres.), Med. Soc. of D.C.; sec. Sect. on Mil. Medicine 14th Internat. Congress on Hygiene and Demography; chmn. delegation sent by U.S. to 6th Internat. Congress on Mil. Medicine and Pharmacy, at The Hague, 1931, and delegate to 8th Congress, Brussels, 1935. Democrat. Methodist. Mason. Clubs: N.Y. Yacht, Quill (New York); Rembrandt (Brooklyn); Sherwood Forest (Md.); Army and Navy, Chevy Chase (Washington). Author: Naval Hygiene, 1918. Contbr. to Ency. Britannica, 14th edit., and to Johns Hopkins and U.S. Naval med. bulls. Home: 184 Columbia Heights, Brooklyn; (summer) Sherwood Forest, Md. Address: 184 Columbia Heights, Brooklyn, N.Y. Died Sept. 8, 1947; buried in Arlington National Cemetery.

PRYOR, NATHANIEL army officer; b. Amherst County, Va. (probably), circa 1775; m. an Osage Indian, circa 1820. Enlisted with Lewis and Clark expdn., Louisville, Ky., 1803; apptd. sgt., 1804; ensign 1st Inf., U.S. Army, 1807; resigned from army, 1810; reentered army as 1st lt., 1813; promoted capt., 1814; fought with distinction in Battle of New Orleans; honorably discharged, 1815; apptd. sub-agt. Osage Indians, 1831. Died June 10, 1831.

PRYOR, ROGER ATKINSON judge; b. Dinwiddle Co., Va., July 19, 1828; s. Rev. Theodorick Bland and Lucy (Atkinson) P.; grad. Hampden-Sidney Coll., 1845 (LL.D.), U. of Va., 1848; m. Sara Agnes Rice, Nov. 8, 1848. Admitted to bar, 1849; editor South Side Democrat, Petersburg, Va., Enquirer and The South, Richmond, several yrs.; U.S. spl. minister to Greece, 1855; elected mem. 36th Congress (1859-61), reëlected to 37th Congress, but did not serve; del. to provisional Confederate Congress and mem. 1st Confederate States Congress, 1862; entered C.S.A. as col., 1861; brig. gen., Apr. 16, 1862; resigned commn. and reëntered service as pvt.; prisoner at Ft. Lafayette, N.Y., 1864-65. Admitted to N.Y. bar, 1866; practiced N.Y., 1866-90; judge Ct. of Common Pleas, 1890-94; justice Supreme Ct., 1894-99; resumed law practice. Home: New York, N.Y. Died Mar. 14, 1919.

PUCKETT, CHARLES ALEXANDER, educator; b. Gainesville, Texas, Oct. 24, 1889; s. John William and Stella Viola (Meachum) P.; A.B., U. of Tex., 1911; M.A., Harvard, 1916; m. Fidelia Miller, Oct. 6, 1920. Prin., Huntsville and Waco, Tex., 1911-20; supt. pub. schs., Gainesville, 1920-23, Mexia, Texas, 1923-26; dean arts and scis. Tex. Western Coll., 1927-34, from 1935, acting pres., 1934-35. Served as capt., inf. U.S. Army, 1917-19. Mem. Tex. State Teachers Assn., Kappa Delta Pi, Phi Delta Kappa. Home: El Paso TX Died Feb. 1, 1970.

PULASKI, CASIMIR army officer; b. Podolia, Poland, Mar. 4, 1748; s. Count Joseph Pulaski. Joined in active rebellion to combat fgn. domination of Poland through Stanislaus II, 1768; fled to Turkey, 1772, tried to incite Turkey to attack Russia, 1772-75; arrived in Boston, 1776; served as volunteer in battles of Brandywine and Germantown; commanded cavalry at Trenton, winter 1777, later at Flemington; commd. by Congress to organize independent cavalry corps, 1778; ordered to support of Gen. Lincoln in S.C., 1779. Died of wounds suffered at Battle of Charleston (S.C.), on board the Wasp, off Charleston, Oct. 11, 1779.

PURNELL, WILLIAM C(HILDS), lawyer; b. Elkton, Md., Sept. 14, 1903; s. William Greenbury and Matilda (Childs) P.; B.S., St. John's Coll., Annapolis, Md., 1923; LL.B., Harvard, 1927; m. Charlotte M. Thilo, Feb. 4, 1928; children—George W.T., Charlotte E. Admitted to Md. bar, 1926, since practiced in Baltimore; asst. U.S. atty., Md., 1928-30; asst. gen. atty. Western Md. Ry. Co., 1931-34, gen. atty., 1934-48, gen. counsel, 1948, v.p., gen. counsel, 1948-71, also dir.; director Union Trust Company of Maryland. Chairman Baltimore chapter of A.R.C., 1962-65, mem. nat. bd. govs., 1965-68. Mem. bd. election supervisors, Balt., 1938-39, bd. zoning appeals, 1939-41, Civil Service Commn., 1947-66; chmn. Balt. City Hosps. Commn., 1966-68. Bd. visitors and govs. St. John's Coll., Annapolis, 1947-59; dir. S. Balt. Gen. Hosp. Commd. capt., U.S. Army, 1941; served as maj., lt. col. and col. 175th Inf. Regt., 29th Inf. Div., E.T.O., 1944-46; brig. gen., 29th Inf. Div., Md. N.G., 1947-57, major general, 1957-62. Member of American Bar Assn., Maryland, Baltimore (v.p. 1950) bar assns., Gamma Eta Gamma, Phi Sigma Kappa. Republican. Episcopalian. Clubs: Merchants (pres. 1959-62), University (pres. 1960-65), Green Spring Valley Hunt, Center, Maryland. Home: Towson MD Died Jan. 1971.

PURNELL, WILLIAM REYNOLDS naval officer; b. Sept. 6, 1886; entered U.S. Navy, 1904, and advanced through the grades to rear adm., 1941; serving as member munitions assignment board of U.S. and Great Britain. Address: 31 Tevis Pl., Palo Alto, Cal. Died Mar. 5, 1955; buried Golden Gate Nat. Cemetery.

PURVES, EDMUND RANDOLPH (pûr'ves), architect; b. Philadelphia, Pa., June 20, 1897; s. Austin Montgomery and Betsey Preston (Coleman) P.; B.S. in Architecture, U. of Pa., 1920; student Atelier Gromort, Paris, 1920-21; m. Mary Carroll Spencer, Dec. 11, 1926; children—Edmund Spencer, Alan Carroll. Began as draughtsman, 1921; became practicing architect, 1927, with Purves & Day, 1927-32, as Edmund R. Purves, 1932-37; mem. Purves, Cope & Stewart since 1937; director of public and professional relations American Institute of Architects, Washington, 1941-49, exec. dir., 1949-61, consulting dir., 1961-62. Adv. bd. contract appeals AEC 1952-58; industry adv. com. FHA, 1954-55; adv. com. urban renewal House and Homes Finance Agy., 1955-—. Served with American Field Service, 1917; with A.E.F., 1917-19; serving as major, 7th Air Force, U.S. Army, 1942-46; overseas 2 years. Decorated Victory Medal with 4 clasps, Pacific-Asia Ribbon with bronze star, Croix de Guerre with silver star, Verdun Medal, Medaille Commemorative; recipient Kemper award A.I.A., 1958, citation, 1961. Mem. state bd. examiners of architects Commonwealth of Pa., 1938-51. Delegate to International Technical Congress Paris, Sept. 1946 (delivered report of U.S. housing). Fellow A.I.A.; mem. Delta Psi; hon. corr. mem. Royal Archtl. Inst. Can., Royal Institute of British Architects. Clubs: University Barge (Phila.); Cosmos (Washington); Century (N.Y.C.). Home: 1524 30th St. N.W., Washington 7. Office: 1735 New York Av., Washington 6. Died Apr. 7, 1964.

PUSEY, EDWIN DAVIS, educator; b. Princess Anne, Md., Jan. 6, 1870; s. Edwin and Katharine Ellen (Davis) P.; A.B., St. John's (Md.) Coll., 1889, LL.D., 1919; A.M., Columbia, 1924; m. Anita Mary Southgate, Jan. 31, 1894 (dec.); 1 dau., Frances Southgate (Mrs. Herbert Ruhrman); m. 2d, Bessie H. Payne, Aug. 26, 1926. Instr. Yates Inst., Lancaster, Pa., 1889-90; same, St. John's Coll., 1892-94, asst. prof. Latin, 1894-1902; prin. high sch., Roberdel, N.C., 1907-09; supt. schs., Laurinburg, N.C., 1909-12, Goldsboro, N.C., 1912-14, Durham, N.C., 1914-23; prof. edn., Winthrop Coll., Rock Hill, S.C., 1924-25; prof. edn., U. of Ga. 1925-44, dean Coll. of Edn. 1941-44; retired Jan. 1945. Captain infantry, U.S. Volunteers, 1898-99. Author: Per Pupil Costs in Georgia Schools, 1931. Editor: Proceedings of Assn. Colls. and Secondary Schs. of Southern States, 1922, 23; editor of High School Quarterly, 1933-36, School and College, 1936-37. Home: 387 Milledge Av., Athens GA

PUSHMATAHAW (The Eagle), Indian chief; b. Noxubee County, Miss., circa 1765. Elected chief of Choctaw Indians 1805; signer Treaty of Mt. Dexter, providing for cession large tract of land in Ala. and Miss., 1805; opposed efforts of Tecumseh to form Indian Confederacy against westward thrust of white settlement; leader (with John Pitchlynn) in persuading Choctaws to join U.S.; leader band of some 500 warriors in Andrew Jackson's forces in War of 1812; signed treaties of cession, 1816, 20. Died Washington, D.C., Dec. 24, 1824; buried Congressional Cemetery, Washington.

PUTNAM, ALBERT WILLIAM lawyer, corp. exec.; b. Spuyten Duyvil, N.Y., Sept. 22, 1877; s. Albert Edward and Margaret Elizabeth (Morrison) P.; A.B., Columbia, 1897, LL.B., 1900; grad. Gen. Staff Coll., U.S. Army, 1918; m. Grace Witherbee Tucker, May 23, 1908; children—Mary Elizabeth (Mrs. Jonathan Fairchild Butler), Betty Waters (Mrs. Challen R. Parker, Jr.), Nancy Tucker (Mrs. Walter K. Howard), Grace Mitchell (Mrs. Augustus B. Wadsworth, Jr.). Engaged in practice of law, N.Y.C., 1900-—; with Winthrop & Stimson, 1904-08, mem. firm, 1908-—, now Winthrop, Stimson, Putnam & Roberts; dir. Rye Trust Co., Tingue Brown & Co. Mem. Troop B, Squadron A, N.Y. Cav., 1898-1917; capt. of troop, Mexican Border, 1916; capt. Machine Gun Bn., later major cav. and maj. F.A., U.S. Army, 1918. Trustee Columbia U., United Hosp., Port Chester, N.Y.; pres. N.Y. Law Inst. Mem. Phi Beta Kappa, Alpha Delta Phi, Phi Delta Phi. Republican. Clubs: Century, University, Down Town, Columbia University (N.Y.C.); Ekwanok Country (Manchester, Vt.); Manursing Island, Apawamis. Home: Highland Rd. Rye, N.Y. Office: 40 Wall St., N.Y.C. 5. Died Mar. 31, 1955.

PUTNAM, EBEN b. Salem, Mass., 1868; s. Prof. Frederic Ward and Adelaide Martha (Edmands) P.; ed. Cambridge (Mass.) schools; m. Florence Tucker, 1890; children—Eben Fiske-Appleton, Frederic Lawrence, Margaret Adelaide. Clerk in banker's office, Boston, 1885-90; mgr. Salem Press, 1890-94, pub., 1894-1906; mng. editor Internat. Monthly, 1899-1902; dir. and treas. F. L. Putnam & Co., Inc., investments, of Boston, also of F. L. Putnam Securities Co., until 1931. Capt. Q.M. Corps, June 25, 1917-Aug. 22, 1919; served in France; lt. col. Q.M. R.C. Official historian of Mass., World War, 1923-—; dept. historian, Mass. Dept. Am. Legion, 1919-20, nat. historian, 1920-—. Has carried on extensive geneal. and hist. research, America and abroad. Unitarian. Mason. Author: History of Putnam Family in England and America; Putnam Lineage; Military and Naval Annals of Danvers; Gold Star Record of Mass.; History of Massachusetts in World War; Holden Genealogy; Lt. Joshua Hewes, a New England Pioneer; and other family histories. Part-author and editor of Osgood Genealogy, Converse and Allied Families, Bixby Genealogy. Editor Genealogical Magazine, 1890-1917, Genealogical Bulletin, Vt. Antiquarian, 1900-1903. Home: Wellesley Farms, Mass. Died Jan. 22, 1933.

PUTNAM, EDWIN officer U.S.N.; b. Bath, Me., Sept. 28, 1840; s. Israel and Sarah Emory (Frost) P.; m. Annie M. Salter, Dec. 1870. Entered U.S.N., Sept. 1862. as asst. p.m.; served during Civil War, on Monitor Nahant in naval attacks on Charleston, S.C., and capture of the Confederate ironclad Atlanta, in Wassaw Sound, Georgia, and during latter part of war on U.S.S. Portsmouth, Adm. Farragut's W. Gulf Fleet; in charge of U.S. naval depot, St. Paul da Loanda, Africa, 1868-69; on duty on various ships and at various stas., as pay officer and gen. storekeeper, 1870-1902; advanced to rank of rear admiral and retired for age limit, Sept. 28, 1902. Home: Portsmouth, N.H. Died Dec. 31, 1925.

PUTNAM, GEORGE HAVEN publisher; b. London, Eng., Apr. 2, 1844; s. George Palmer and Victorine (Haven) P.; ed. Columbia Grammar Sch., New York, The Sorbonne, Paris, and U. of Göttingen; hon. A.M., Bowdoin, 1894; Litt.D., U. of Pittsburgh, 1899, Columbia, 1912; served as pvt. advancing to maj. 176th N.Y. Vols., 1862-65; prisoner at Libby and Danville, Va., winter of 1864-65; m. Rebecca Kettell Shepard, July 7, 1869 (died 1895); m. 2d, Emily James Smith, Apr. 27, 1899. Pres. G. P. Putnam's Sons, publishers, New York; dir. Knickerbocker Press. Led in organizing, 1887, The Am. Copyright League, originally organized by late G. P. Putnam, 1851; became its sec. during contest for internat. copyright, resulting in copyright bill of Mar. 1891. Decorated with Cross of the Legion of Honor, France, 1891. Founder of English-Speaking Union in U.S. Author: Authors and Publishers, 1883; Question of Copyright, 1891; Authors and Their Public in Ancient Times, 1893; The Artificial Mother, 1894; Books and Their Makers in the Middle Ages, 1896; The Censorship of the Church of Rome and Its Influence upon the Production and the Distribution of Literature (2 vols.), 1907; Abraham Lincoln—the People's Leader in the Struggle for National Existence, 1909; George Palmer Putnam, 1912; Memories of My Youth, 1914; Memories of a Publisher, 1915; Some Memories of the Civil War, 1924. Pres. Am. Rights League, 1915-16, Free Trade League, 1916. Died Feb. 27, 1930.

PUTNAM, GEORGE PALMER publisher, author; b. Rye, N.Y., Sept. 7, 1887; s. John Bishop and Frances (Faulkner) P.; educated Harvard and U. of Calif.; m. Dorothy Binney, Oct. 26, 1911 (divorced 1928); children—David Binney, George Palmer III; m. 2d, Amelia Earhart, Feb. 7, 1931 (lost on Pacific flight, July 1937); m. 3d, Jean Consiguey, May 21, 1939; (div. Feb. 15, 1944); m. 4th, Margaret Haviland, 1945. With ednl.

dept. G. P. Putnam's Sons, pubs., New York, 1909; in newspaper and publicity work, Oregon, 1910; publisher and editor Bend (Oregon) Bulletin; mayor of Bend, Oregon, 2 terms, 1912-13; sec. to gov. of Ore., 1914-17. Lieut., F.A.R.C., U.S. Army, 1918. Pres. bd. of pubs. The American Legion Weekly, 1919; pres. The Knickerbocker Press, and treas. G. P. Putnam's Sons, New York, 1919-30; v.p. Brewer, Warren & Putnam, 1930-32; chmn. editorial board Paramount Productions, 1932-35. Director American Museum Natural History Greenland Expn., 1926. Putnam Baffin Island Expedition, 1927. Major, Army Air Forces, 1942-45; overseas service, India and China; intelligence officer, B-29 units. Member Psi Upsilon fraternity. Clubs: Coffee House, Explorers (New York). Author: The Southland of North America, 1913; In the Oregon Country; The Smiting of the Rock, 1918; Andree—The Record of a Tragic Adventure, 1930; Last Flight (with Amelia Earhart), 1938; Soaring Wings, 1939; Wide Margins, 1941; Duration, 1943; Death Valley, 1946; Mariner of the North, a Biography of Cap'n Rob Bartlett, 1947; Handbook of Death Valley, 1947; Hickory Shirt: A Tale of Death Valley in 1850. Home: Lone Pine, Calif. Died Jan. 4, 1950.

PUTNAM, ISRAEL army officer; b. Salem Village (now Danvers), Mass., Jan. 7, 1718; s. Joseph and Elizabeth (Porter) P.; m. Hannah Pope, July 19, 1739; m. 2d, Deborah (Lothrop) Gardiner, June 3, 1767; 10 children. Commd. 2d lt. Conn. Militia, 1754, capt., 1755, maj., 1758; lt. col., 1759; served in French and Indian Wars; maj., then lt. col. Conn. Militia, 1764, served in Pontiac's War; an organizer Sons of Liberty, del. to warn Gov. Fitch of Conn. that he could not enforce Stamp Act; mem. exploration expdn. to discover possible values of West Fla., cruised through W.I., Gulf of Mexico, up to Mississippi River 1773; lt. col. 11th Regt., Conn. Militia, brig. gen., 1775; maj. gen. Continental Army, 1775; a leader in planning for Battle of Bunker Hill; chief in command of N.Y. before Washington arrived, 1776; in charge of removal of all troops and stores from N.Y.C. after retreat, 1776, then had command of Phila.; command in the Highlands (upper N.Y. State), delayed twice in obeying orders from Gen. Washington, acquitted of charges of refusing to obey orders by ct. of inquiry; in charge recruiting service in Conn., 1778-79. Author: Two Putnams—in the Havana Expedition 1762 and in the Mississippi River Exploration 1772-73, published 1931. Died Brooklyn, Conn., May 29, 1790.

PUTNAM, RUFUS army officer, pioneer; b. Sutton, Mass., Apr. 9, 1738; s. Elisha and Susanna (Fuller) P.; m. Elizabeth Ayres, Apr. 6, 1761; m. 2d, Persis Rice, Jan. 10, 1765; 10 children. served as ensign during French and Indian Wars, 1757-60; mem. com. to explore and survey lands on Mississippi River which were claimed as bounties for veterans of French and Indian Wars, 1773; commd. lt. col. Continental Army, 1775; took charge defensive works around Boston and N.Y.C., 1775-76; chief engr. with rank of col., 1776; served under Gates in campaign against Burgoyne; rebuilt fortifications at West Point, 1779; commd. brig. gen., 1783; chmn. of an officers' orgn., framed Newburgh Petition (on behalf of land bounties for revolutionary vets.), 1783; undertook survey and sale of lands in Me. belonging to Mass.; surveyor of Western lands, 1785; an organizer of Ohio Co., purpose to colonize on North bank of Ohio River, led colony to Marietta, O., 1788, laid out town, 1st organized territory of N.W.; judge of N.W. Territory, 1790-96; commd. brig. gen. U.S. Army, 1792; made treaty at Vincennes with lower Wabash Indian tribes, 1792; took charge important surveys in neighborhood of Marietta, circa 1794; surveyor gen. U.S., 1796-1803; del. to Ohio Constl. Conv., 1802. Died Marietta, O., May 4, 1824.

PUTNAM, RUSSELL BENJAMIN Marine Corps officer; b. Abbeville Vermillion Parish, La., Jan. 7, 1878; s. James Henry and Mary Pauline (Johnson) P.; B.S., Centenary Coll., Jackson (now at Shreveport), La., 1894; M.E., Cornell U., 1901; m. Mabel Henry Triplett, Apr. 5, 1909; children—Edwina Triplett (wife of William Vincent Deutermann, U.S. Navy), Mary Russell (Mrs. Charles M. Bounds), Russell Henry. With Buffalo (New York) Forge Company, 1901-02, Am. Blower Company, New York, 1902-04; commd. 2d lt. U.S. Marine Corps, 1904, and advanced through the grades to brig. gen., Marine Corps May 1, 1938; served in the Philippines, 1909-12, Nicaraguan campaign, Sept.-Dec. 1912, occupation of Vera Cruz, 1914, Haitian campaign, 1915-16, Dominican campaign, 1916-17, Hdqrs. U.S. Marine Corps, 1917-19, duty in Haiti, 1919-21, Hdqrs. and stations of Paymaster Dept., 1921-38; retired, Feb. 1942. Wounded in action Guayacannes, San Domingo, July 3, 1916; awarded Purple Heart, Legion of Merit; also medals of Nicaraguan Campaign, 1912, Vera Cruz Campaign (with star), 1915, Dominican Campaign, 1916, Victory medal, 1919 (U.S.); Medaille Militaire (Haiti), 1921. Mem. Kappa Sigma. Mason, Sojourner, Heroes of '76. Clubs: Army and Navy, Army and Navy Country (Washington, D.C.); Huntington Valley Country (Ridal, Pa.). Home: 801 Russel Rd., Alexandria, Va. Office: Hdqrs., U.S. Marine Corps, Washington, D.C. Died May 29, 1959.

PYLE, ERNES TAYLOR (pil), newspaperman; b. Dana, Ind., Aug. 3, 1900; s. William Clyde and Maria (Taylor) P.; ed. grade and high sch.; student Indiana U., 1919-28; m. Geraldine Siebolds, July 7, 1925. Cub reporter LaPorte (Ind.) Herald, Jan.-May 1923; reporter, later desk man, Washington (D.C.) Daily News, 1923-26; desk man New York Evening World and New York Evening Post, 1926-27; aviation editor Scripps-Howard Newspapers, 1928-32; mng. editor Washington (D.C.) Daily News, 1932-35; roving columnist since 1935; war corr., 1942-45; daily column appears from all over world for Scripps-Howard Newspapers and others (about 200). Mem. Sigma Alpha Epsilon, Sigma Delta Chi. Author: Ernie Pyle in England, 1941; Here Is Your War, 1943; Brave Men, 1944; collection pre-war columns, Home Country (publ. posthumously), 1947. Received Pulitzer Prize for distinguished correspondence, 1944. Office: 1013 13th St. N.W., Washington. Killed by Japanese machine-gun fire, Ie Shima, Apr. 18, 1945; buried in Punchbowl Memorial Cemetery, Hawaii.

PYNE, FREDERICK GLOVER naval officer; b. Central Falls, R.I., June 5, 1879; s. Charles March and Eliza (Glover) P.; ed. pvt. schs.; m. Ellen Roosevelt Jones, Sept. 23, 1901; children—Frederick Cruger, Schuyler Neilson, Charles Crosby. Commd. asst. paymaster (ensign), 1901, advanced through grades to rear adm., 1941; U.S.S. Chesapeake, 1901; Island of Guam, 1901-03; U.S.S. Monterey, 1903-04; Navy Yards, N.Y., and Pensacola, Fla., 1905-08; U.S.S. Georgia, 1908-10; Navy Dept., purchasing officer, 1910-14; U.S.S. Michigan, 1914-17, U.S.S. George Washington, Navy Yard, N.Y., 1917-21; fleet paymaster, Asiatic Fleet, 1921-23; coordinator traffic, Bur. Budget, 1923-25; asst. to paymaster gen. Navy, 1927-32; supply officer Navy Yard, Phila., 1932-35; Navy purchasing officer, N.Y., 1935-38; officer-in-charge Naval Finance and Supply Sch., 1937-41; gen. insp., Supply Corps., 1941-44. Awarded World War medal (Transport clasp). Ret. from active duty Dec. 15, 1944. Mem. Newcomen Soc. Eng., Loyal Legion, Society Colonial Wars, S.R. Mason. Clubs: Army-Navy, Chevy Chase (Washington, D.C.); N.Y. Yacht; University (Phila.); Cazenovia. Home: "Dunharrow," Cazenovia, N.Y. Died Apr. 1962; buried Arlington Nat. Cemetery.

PYRON, WALTER BRAXTON army officer; b. Matthews, N.C., April 10, 1882; married Gertrude Magdalena Drach, May 19, 1946. Commd. 1st, lt. Cav. Tex. N.G., 1921, advanced to brig. gen. of the line, 1938; on active duty with 56th Cav. Brigade, Ft. McIntosh, Tex., 1940-41; in office of under sec. of war, Washington, 1941-42; became liaison officer, for petroleum in the resources div. at hdqrs. Services of Supply (Production Div., Army Service Forces), 1942-43; on duty in the Office Q.M.G., Washington, 1943; duty with Army-Navy Petroleum Bd.; mem. Joint Chiefs of Staff; lived in Europe, 1946-50. Home: 4909 Fairview Dr., Austin 3, Tex. Died Jan. 8, 1951.

QUACKENBUSH, STEPHEN PLATT naval officer; b. Albany, N.Y., Jan. 23, 1823; s. John N. and Nancy (Smith) Q.; m. Cynthia Herrick Wright, Jan. 18, 1849, 3 children. Commd. midshipman U.S. Navy, 1840, passed midshipman, 1846; served in Mexican War, then in various squadrons and posts throughout world; commd. lt., 1855, at Phila. Naval Yard, 1857-58, commanded gunboat Delaware, 1861; commd. lt. comdr., 1862, engaged in blockade duty and coastal operations against Confederate forts, lost right leg in patrol action on James River, Va., 1864; on duty with Atlantic Squadron, 1866-72; commanded ship New Hampshire, 1873-75; commanded Pensacola (Fla.) Naval Sta., 1880-82; commd. comdr., 1866, commodore, 1880, rear adm., 1884, ret., 1885. Died Washington, D.C., Feb. 4, 1890; buried Oak Hill Cemetery, Washington.

QUADE, OMAR H. army officer; b. St. Charles, Mo., Aug. 18, 1886; s. Charles George and Julia Anna (Barklage) Q.; M.D., Washington U., St. Louis, 1909; hon. grad. Army Med. Sch., Washington, 1912; m. Julia Louise Ortmann, Dec. 30, 1911; 1 son, Omar Henry. Interne St. Louis City Hosp., 1909-10; commd. 1st lt. Med. Res. Corps, 1911; 1st lt. M.C., Regular Army, 1912, advanced through grades to brig. gen., 1942; served with 1st Div. AEF in France and Germany, 1917-19; ret. army, 1948; dep. dir. civil def., Denver. Awarded Legion of Merit, Mil. Order Purple Heart. Address: 655 Dahlia St., Denver 80220. Died May 9, 1965; buried Ft. Logan Nat. Cemetery, Denver.

QUAIN, ERIC P., surgeon; b. Sorsjon, Dalecarlia, Sweden, Aug. 22, 1870; s. Per H. and Margaret (Ericson) Q.; M.D., U. of Minn., 1898; m. Fannie A. Dunn, 1903; children—Marion Margaret, Buell Halvor (dec.); m. 2d, Hilda Gustafson, 1940. Came to United States, 1888, became a naturalized citizen, 1895. Began practice at Bismarck, N.Dak., 1899; organized the Quain & Ramstad Clinic (20 members), 1910, and served as chief of staff until 1939; now retired except as surgical consultant; former coroner and health officer, Bismarck; served as lt. col. M.C., U.S. Army, with A.E.F., World War I; organized med. unit known as Base Hosp. No. 60, A.E.F.; now col. med., inactive. Fellow Am. Coll. Surgeons; mem. Founders Group, Am. Bd. of Surgery; mem. A.M.A., N.D. State Med. Assn. (ex-pres.), Western Surg. Assn., Soo Line Ry. Surgeons' Assn. (ex-pres.), Alpha Kappa Kappa, Pi Gamma Mu. Republican. Mason. Retired. Author numerous med. and surgical articles; travelogues from fgn. lands. Home: 2075 Raynor St., Salem OR

QUALTROUGH, EDWARD FRANCIS naval officer; b. Rochester, N.Y., Oct. 30, 1850; s. Joseph and Elizabeth (Gibson) Q.; apptd. from N.Y., and grad. U.S. Naval Acad., 1871; m. Leila Ray, Nov. 6, 1879. Promoted ensign, 1874; master, 1876; lt., 1883; lt. comdr., 1899; comdr., 1902; capt., July 1, 1906; commodore, 1909. Served in various capacities on board Macedonian, Savannah, Wabash, Wauchusett, Despatch, Marion, Trenton, Gettysburgh, Hartford, Charleston, Mohican, Terror, Chicago, 1871-1902; comd. Atlanta, 1904-05, Yankee, 1905-06, Cleveland, 1906-07, Georgia, 1908-09; retired, July 1, 1909. Active mem. expdn. sent by U.S. to Caroline Islands, Pacific Ocean, to observe total solar eclipse, May 1883. Republican. Episcopalian. Author: Sailor's Handy Book, 1881; Boat Sailor's Manual, 1885. Home: Rochester, N.Y. Died Nov. 18, 1913.

QUANAH Indian chief; b. No. Tex.; s. Peta Nocone and Cynthia Ann Parker (a White captive), married 3 wives, including Too-nicey. Organized band of Comanche Indians, 1866, became chief, 1867; refused to accept Medicine Lodge Treaty of 1867 which required Comanches, Kiowas, Kiowa Apaches, So. Cheyennes and Arapahos to settle on reservation in Indian Territory; led series of raids terrorizing frontier; in continual warfare with white settlers, 1867-75; defeated by Ranald S. Mackenzie and Nelson A. Miles, 1875; after defeat took up ways of white man, initiated bldg. projects, agrl. improvements; grew wealthy as result of leasing surplus lands to stockmen; rode with Geronimo in Pres. Theodore Roosevelt's inaugural procession. Died Indian Territory, Feb. 23, 1911.

QUANTRILL, WILLIAM CLARKE outlaw; b. Canal Dover, O., July 31, 1837; s. Thomas Henry and Caroline (Clark) Q. Settled in Kan., 1857; travelled to Utah with an army provision train, 1858; gambled under name Charley Hart, Salt Lake City, Utah; taught sch., Kan., 1859-60; fled when accused of murder and horse theft; betrayed plot of 5 abolitionists to seize and free slaves, 3 were killed; connected with Confederate Army during Civil War; chief of a band of guerrillas which plundered Unionist communities in Mo. and Kan.; part of Confederate force which captured Independence (Mo.), 1862; commd. capt. Confederate Army; pillaged Lawrence (Kan.) with a force of 450 men, killed about 150 people, 1863; defeated a body of Union cavalry, killed 17 musicians and non-combatants; fatally wounded, Taylorsville, Ky., May 10, 1865. Died Louisville, Ky., June 6, 1865.

QUARLES, DONALD A(UBREY) dep. sec. of def.; b. Van Buren, Ark., July 30, 1894; s. Robert W. and Minnie (Hynes) Q.; B.A., Yale, 1916; grad. study Columbia, 1920-24; D.E., U. Ark., 1953, N.Y.U., 1956; D.Sc., Grinell Coll., Stevens Inst., 1956; LL.D., Yale, 1957; m. Rosina Cotton, Oct. 27, 1939; children (by former marriage)—Carolyn Anne, Donald Aubrey, Elizabeth Whittemore (Mrs. Stanley C. Lewis). Engineer with the Bell Telephone Labs. (formerly engineering department Western Electric Co.), 1919-53, v.p., 1948-52; v.p. Western Electric Co., pres. Sandia Corp., 1952-53; asst. secretary of defense, (research and development), Washington, 1953-55, sec. Air Force 1955-57; dep. sec. of defense, 1957-—. Former mayor of Englewood N.J. Recipient award of merit American Inst. Cons. Engrs., Exceptional Service award, Dept. Air Force, 1957; Cruz Peruana Al Merito Aeronautico, 1956; Brazilian Ordem Do Merito Aeronautic 1957; Capo dell Ordine Al Merito della Republica Italiana; Spanish Grand Cross, Order of Mil. Merit (posthumous), Medal of Freedom United States (posthumous). Served as captain, FA, U.S. Army, 1917-19. Fellow Am. Inst. E.E. (pres. 1952-53), Am. Phys. Soc., Am. Inst. Radio Engrs.; mem. A.A.A.S., Yale Engineering Society, Telephone Pioneers of America, Sigma Xi., Phi Beta Kappa, also Eta Kappa Nu (honorary). Republican. Clubs: Englewood; Knickerbocker Country (Tenafly, N.J.); Cosmos (Washington); Engineers (N.Y.C.). Address: 3041 Porter St., Washington 8. Office: The Pentagon, Washington. Died May 8, 1959; buried Arlington Nat. Cemetery.

QUAY, MATTHEW STANLEY U.S. senator; b. Dillsburg, Pa., Sept. 30, 1833; grad. Jefferson Coll., 1850; admitted to bar, 1854; elected prothonotary Beaver Co., 1856 and 1859; in mil. service, 1861-65, as lt. 10th Pa. reserves, col. 134th Pa. vols.; received congressional medal of honor; lt. col. and asst. commissary gen. State mil. agt. at Washington; private sec. to gov. of Pa. Mem. legislature, 1865-67; sec. of commonwealth, 1872-78 and 1879-82; recorder of Phila., 1878-79; State treas., 1885; mem. of Rep. Nat. Com., 1885-—, and its chmn. during successful presdl. campaign of 1888; mem. exec. com., 1896; U.S. senator from Pa., 1887-99; tried for misappropriation of public funds and acquitted, April 21, 1899; same day apptd. U.S. senator, ad interim, by Gov. Stone; reëlected U.S. senator Jan. 1901, to fill vacancy caused by failure of legislature to elect in Jan. 1899; term expiring 1905. Home: Beaver, Pa. Died 1904.

QUAYLE, JOHN HARRISON surgeon; b. Madison, O., June 25, 1874; s. Henry and Mary E. (Bower) Q.; grad. New Lyme Inst., 1892; M.D., Cleveland U. of Medicine and Surgery, 1895, New York Post-Grad. Coll., 1901, Cleveland Coll. Physicians and Surgeons, 1904; post-grad. work, Berlin, Vienna, London; m. Grace Dayton, Oct. 3, 1896; children—Mrs. Alice Lynnette Osborne, John H., Wm. Henry. Practiced at Cleveland since 1896. Devised plan for reclamation of men rejected for mil. service, which was adopted by Surgeon Gen. Gorgas, 1917, and which increased the accepted men from 17% to 90%. Mem. A.M.A., Ohio State Med. Assn., Cleveland Acad. Medicine, Cleveland Med. Library, Cleveland Chamber of Commerce (life). Clubs: Big Ten University (life), Cleveland Athletic, Cleveland Automobile, Shaker Heights Country, Willowick Country; Seaview Golf (Absecon, N.J.); Mentor Harbor Yacht (Mentor-on-the-Lake, O.); Surf, Committee of One Hundred, University. Miami Quarterback (Miami, Fla.); Century (Coral Gables, Fla.). Home: Garden Lane Apts., 1100 Brickell Av., Miami, Fla.; (summer) Lake Shore Blvd., Willoughby, O. Office: Murray Hill Hotel, New York, N.Y. Died Apr. 25, 1945.

QUEEN, WALTER naval officer; b. Washington, D.C., Oct. 6, 1824; s. John W. and Mary (Wells) Q.; m. Christiana Crosby. Commd. midshipman U.S. Navy, 1841; served in West India Squadron, 1841-43, East India Squadron, 1843-45; fought in battles of Palo Alto, Tampico and Vera Cruz during Mexican War; promoted lt., 1855; participated in bombardment of Ft. Jackson, Ft. St. Phillip, Vicksburg, capture of New Orleans, during Civil War; promoted lt. comdr., 1862; ordnance insp. Scott Foundry, Reading, Pa., 1865-67; promoted comdr., 1866, capt., 1874, commodore, 1884, rear adm., 1886; ret., 1886. Died Washington, Oct. 24, 1893; buried Arlington (Va.) Nat. Cemetery.

QUESNAY, ALEXANDRE-MARIE army officer; b. Saint-Germain-en-Viry, France, Nov. 23, 1755; s. Blaise and Catherine (Deguilon) Q.; m. Catherine Cadier, 1 son. Arrived in Va., 1777; served as capt. Continental Army, 1777-78; conducted a sch., Phila., 1780-84; produced 1st French play in Am. (Beaumarchais's Eugenie); returned to France, 1786; proposed an Acad. of U.S.A., including an extensive system of schs. and univs. and a learned soc. for advancement of art and science at Richmond (Va.), plan rejected by Pres. Jefferson who felt that the U.S. was too poor to support such a program. Died St. Maurice, France, Feb. 8, 1820.

QUESTA, EDWARD J. banker; b. Reno, Apr. 30, 1898; s. Fred and Camelia (Prosole) Q.; student pub. schs., Reno; hon. degree dr. banking and finance, U. of Nev. With Stockgrowers & Ranchers Bank, Reno, 1917-20, asst. cashier, 1918-20; staff Bank of Am. Nat. Trust & Savs. Assn., 1920, mgr. Sunset, also Ocean-Faxon brs., San Francisco, 1920-34, v.p., Far Eastern rep., 1948-52; asst. cashier First Nat. Bank of Nev. (formerly First Nat. Bank in Reno), 1934-42, v.p., 1942, v.p. charge adminstrn., 1946-48, pres., 1952—. Mem. Atomic Energy Utilization Com.; Italian vice consul for Nev.; mem. Pres.'s Com. for Traffic Safety. Chmn. Nev. Olympic Commn.; dir. Nat. Jr. Achievement. Trustee Washoe Med. Center; mem. Citizen's Adv. Com. for Coll. Bus. Adminstrn., U. Nev. Organizer, wing comdr. Nev. wing Civil Air Patrol; served as comdr. USN, World War II, chief staff, div. transports Okinawa landing. Mem. Reno C. of C., VIII Olympic Winter Games Com. (dir.), Navy League, Cal. Grays. Clubs: Hidden Valley Country; Prospectors; Reno Golf. Home: 142 Greenridge Dr. Office: 206 N. Virginia St., Reno. Died Feb. 10, 1962; buried Reno.

QUEZON, Y MOLINA MANUEL LUIS (MANUEL QUEZON) (ka'son-e-mo-le'nä), president of Philippines; born Baler, Province Tayabas, P.I., Aug. 19, 1878; s. Lucio and Maria (Molina) Q.; B.A., Coll. of San Juan de Letran, Manila, 1893; studied law, U. of St. Thomas, Manila; m. Aurora Aragon, 1918; children—Maria Aurora, Maria Zeneida, Manuel L., Jr. Maj. in Philippine army, 1898-1900, serving on staffs of Gens. Aguinaldo and Mascardo. Admitted to bar, 1903; pros. atty., provinces of Mindoro and Tayabas, 1903-04; provincial gov. Tayabas, 1905-06; mem. Philippine Assembly, 1906-09; resident commr. to U.S., 1909-16, and campaigned for Philippine independence; sen. 5th Philippine Senatorial Dist. and first and only pres. Philippine Senate, 1916-35; pres. of Philippines since Sept. 17, 1935. Decorated Officer French Legion of Honor; mem. Order of Jade (China); Grand Cavalier of the Republic (Spain); Grand Cross of Order of Crown of Belgium. Founded Collectivist party, 1922, serving as pres. until 1928; head consolidated Nationalist party, 1928-33; pres. Nationalist Dem. party, 1934-35; pres. coalition of 2 major parties, 1935. Address: Shoreham Hotel, Washington, D.C. Died Aug. 1, 1944.

QUIGLEY, WILLIAM MIDDLETON ret. naval officer; b. Bklyn., July 9, 1890; grad. U.S. Naval Acad., 1911; m. Jeannette Orr; children—Stephen M., Jane Orr. Commd. ensign USN, 1912, advanced through grades to commodore, 1943; served in U.S. ships Michigan, Monterey, Wilmington, Mohican, 1911-15; comd. submarine A-7, 1915-16, U.S.S. F-3, 1917-18, O-16, 1918-19, U.S.S. Delaware, 1919, S-2, 1920-21; chief of U.S. Naval Mission to Peru, 1940-42; on duty with amphibious force, Atlantic Fleet, 1942, assigned landing craft group, Dec. 1942; comdr. naval bases, Solomon Islands, naval bases, Forward Area, and comdr. South Solomons, sub. area, 1943-44; comd. Forward Area, Central Pacific, 1944-45; became comdr. Naval Base, Port Heune, Calif., 1945, retired with rank of commodore, 1946. Decorated Legion of Merit, Victory Medal with submarine clasp, Am. Def. Service Medal with fleet clasp, Am. Area Campaign and Asiatic-Pacific Area Campaign medals; Legion of Merit; Comdr. Order British Empire; Comdr. Order of Sun (Peru). Home: 9 E. 96th St., N.Y.C. 28. Address: Navy Dept., Washington 25. Died Apr. 1957.*

QUILICI, GEORGE L., Judge; b. Chicago, Ill.; s. Henry and Anna (Martinelli) Q.; LL.B., De Paul U.; graduate work, Northwestern U.; J.D., John Marshall Law Sch.; m. Virginia Iralson (artist). Admitted to Ill. bar; elected judge of the Municipal Court, Chicago, 1940; reelected, 1942, 1948, 54, 60; Judge Circuit Court, State of Illinois, 1962-69; apptd. spl. prosecutor of election fraud cases in County Court of Cook County (Ill.), on recommendation of Citizens Assn., 1935-38; apptd. com. on character and fitness of Supreme Court of State of Ill., reappointed 1938, 39. Served with signal corps in France, formerly major, United States Army (Res.) Mem. nat. panel Am. Arbitration Assn.; past chmn. bd. Nat. Pub. Housing Conf., past pres. Pub. Housing Assn. Chicago; treas. Citizens Com. for Better Music; chmn. com. on Awards of Chicago Commn. on Human Relations, 1946-55. Recipient 1950 community services award, Chgo. Indsl. Union Council; Star of Solidarity (Italy); Commendatore Al Merito (Republic of Italy); Citation of Merit, Am. Legion. Mem. Am., Ill., Chgo. bar assns., Am. Legion, Am. Contract Bridge Assn., Am. Civil Liberties Union, Res. Officers Assn., Vets. Fgn. Wars, Chgo. Contract Bridge Assn. (pres. 1956-58), Phi Alpha Delta. Clubs: City (bd. govs.), Chicago Literary (v.p.). Home: Chicago IL Died May 6, 1969; buried Rose Hill Cemetery, Chicago IL

QUINBY, ISAAC FERDINAND army officer, educator; b. Morris County, N.J., Jan. 29, 1821; s. Isaac and Sarah (De Hart) Q.; grad. U.S. Mil. Acad., 1843; m. Elizabeth Gardner, Oct. 6, 1848, 13 children. Instr. mathematics U.S. Mil. Acad., 1845, asst. prof. natural philosophy, 1845-47; prof. mathematics, natural and exptl. philosophy U. Rochester (N.Y.), 1851-61, 1861-62, 69-77; raised 13th N.Y. Volunteer Regt., 1861, 1st U.S. force to enter Balt. after attack on 6th Mass. Regt., reestablished order in Balt.; led regt. in Battle of Bull Run, 1861; brig. gen. U.S. Volunteers, 1862, command Dist. of the Miss., later 7th Div., Army of Tenn.; commanded Yazoo Pass expdn., 1863; provost marshal 28th Congl. Dist. in N.Y., 1864-65; U.S. marshal for No. Dist. of N.Y., 1869; surveyor City of Rochester, 1885-89; trustee Soldiers Home, Bath, N.Y., v.p., 1879-86. Died Rochester, Sept. 18, 1891.

QUINN, JAMES BAIRD colonel U.S.A.; b. Cincinnati, June 9, 1843; s. David and Jane (Baird) Q.; grad. U.S. Mil. Acad., 1866; m. 3d, Estelle C. LeBlanc, June 11, 1907. Apptd. 2d lt. U.S. Engrs., June 18, 1866; 1st lt., Mar. 7, 1867; capt., Mar. 4, 1879; maj., July 22, 1888; lt. col., Jan. 29, 1903; col., May 5, 1906; retired by operation of law, June 9, 1907. Served on improvement rivers and harbors, Atlantic and Gulf coasts, and harbors of lakes Superior and Mich., construction of fortifications Atlantic and Gulf, etc. Home: New York, N.Y. Died Feb. 23, 1915.

QUINTON, WILLIAM brigadier gen. U.S.A.; b. Dublin, Ireland, Oct. 9, 1838; s. Arthur and Letitia (Maclean) Q.; grad. Chicago (Ill.) High Sch., 1860. Enlisted as 1st sergt. Co. C, 19th Ill. Inf., June 17, 1861; disch. Nov. 2, 1861; commd. 2d lt., 19th Ill. Inf., Nov. 2, 1861; 1st lt., Mar. 1, 1863; hon. mustered out, Sept. 10, 1864; 2d lt. signal corps, Mar. 3, 1863; hon. mustered out. May 1, 1866; apptd. from Ill. 1st lt. 33d Inf., June 12, 1867; assigned to 7th Inf., May 3, 1870; capt., Apr. 18, 1884; transferred to 25th Inf., Sept. 16, 1898; maj. 14th Inf., Sept. 10, 1898; lt. col. 27th Inf., Feb. 2, 1901; transferred to 14th Inf., Apr. 22, 1901; col. 1st Inf., May 28, 1902; brig. gen., Oct. 6, 1902; retired at own request after 40 yrs.' service, Oct. 9, 1902. Home: Buffalo, N.Y. Died Sept. 16, 1916.

QUITMAN, JOHN ANTHONY gov. Miss., congressman; b. Rhinebeck, N.Y., Sept. 1, 1798; s. Rev. Frederick Henry and Anna (Hueck) Q.; grad. Hartwick Sem., 1816; m. Eliza Turner, Dec. 24, 1824, 4 children. Instr., Mt. Airy Coll., Pa., 1818; admitted to bar, 1821, moved to Natchez, Miss.; mem. Miss. Ho. of Reps., 1826-27; grand master Miss. Masons, 1826-38, 40, 45; chancellor Miss., 1828-35; supporter of nullification, 1834; mem. Miss. Senate, 1835-36, became pres., Dec. 1835; acting gov. Miss., 1835-36; served as brig. gen. Volunteers, participated in Battle of Monterey, promoted maj. gen. U.S. Army, 1847; gov. Miss., 1850-51; mem. U.S. Ho. of Reps. from Miss., 34th-35th congresses, 1855-58. Died "Monmouth," nr. Natchez, July 17, 1858; buried Natchez City Cemetery.

QUYNN, ALLEN GEORGE, naval officer; b. Baltimore, Md., June 16, 1894; s. Daniel Hauer and Mary (Whiting) Q.; grad. U.S. Naval Acad., 1915; m. Rachel Motter, Sept. 14, 1918; children—Allen George, Serene Kunkel, Margaret Motter. Commd. ensign, U.S. Navy, 1915, and advanced through the grades to commodore, 1944; served in ocean escort duty, World War I; placed U.S.S. Tennessee in commn.; comd. U.S.S. Mindanao and U.S.S. Asheville, China Station, 1936-38; present during Japanese attack, Pearl Harbor, 1941; dep. comdr. and chief of staff Service Force, Pacific Fleet, 1943-49; ret. as rear adm., 1949. Rep. of U.S. Navy in logistic matters, Trident Quebec Conf., 1943. Decorated D.S.M., Legion of Merit; recipient letters of commendation from Comdr. in Chief Asiatic Fleet, U.S. State Dept. and Foreign Missionary Soc. Mason. Home: Frederick MD Died June 17, 1971; buried Mt. Olivet Cemetery, Frederick MD

RAAB, WILHELM, physician and univ. prof.; b. Vienna, Austria, Jan. 14,21895; s. Dr. Richard and Rosa (Gerenyi) R.; grad. cum laude, Schotten-Gymnasium, Vienna, 1913; M.D., Med. Faculty, U. of Vienna, 1920; 'M.d., German U. of Prague (Czechoslovakia), 1926; research fellow, Harvard Med. Sch., 1920-30; m. Olga Elizabeth Palmborg, June 17, 1930; children—Karl-Herbert, Fredrik-Holger; m. 2d, Helen Hubaczek, May 26, 1970; came to U.S. to reside, 1939. Began as med. house officer, Vienna, 1920; first asst. to Clin. Prof. Biedl, German U., Prague, 1921-26, privat-dozent in pathol. physiology, 1926-35; asst. and first asst., First Med. Clinic, U. of Vienna, 1926-36, privat-dozent in internal medicine, 1935-39; ofcl. examiner in internal medicine, U. of Vienna, 1936; physician in chief, Krankenhaus d. Kaufmannschaft, Vienna, 1936-39; asst. prof. clin. medicine, U. of Vt., 1939-45; prof. experimental medicine, since 1945; cons. specialist Mary Fletcher Hosp., Placid Meml. Hosp.; attending physician and head cardiovascular research unit, DeGoesbriand Meml. Hops., Burlington, Vt.; founder Preventive Heart Reconditioning Found., 1963. Cons. High Commrs. Office, Germany, 1950; Fulbright research prof. U. of Innsbruck, Austria, 1957-58. Mem. Pres.' Citizens' Com. on Fitness of Am. Youth, 1959. Served as lt. Med. Corps., Austro-Hungarian Army and German Army, 1916-18, 1938. Awarded 2 Austrian war medals for bravery (silver 1st class and bronze), other Austrian and Hungarian war decorations. Diplomate Am. Bd. Internal Medicine. Fellow Am. Coll. Physicians, Am. Coll. Cardiology, Am. Coll. Chest Physicians, Am. Coll. Sports Medicine, Life mem. Austro-Am. Inst. of Edn.; mem. A.M.A., New York Acad. Sciences, Soc. Exptl. Biology and Medicine, Vt. State Med. Soc., Chittenden Co. Med. Soc., Am. Physiol. Soc., Endocrine Soc., Soc. Internal Medicine, American Heart Association, Society of Gerontology, Society Study Arteriosclerosis, N.E. Cardiovascular Soc.; corr. mem. Gesellschaft d. Aerzte, Vienna; mem. Sigma Xi. Unitarian. Clubs: Research, Faculty, Layman's League. Author: Hormone und Stoffwechsel, 1926; Innersekretorische Storungen und Organotherapie, 1932; Hormonal and Neurogenic Cardiovascular Disorders, 1952; (with Hans Kraus) Hypokinetic Disease, 1961; Preventive Myocardiology, 1970; also numerous sci. articles and monographs. Editor: Prevention of Ischemic Heart Disease, 1966. Home: Burlington VT Died Sept. 21, 1970.

RABY, JAMES JOSEPH naval officer; b. Bay City, Mich., Sept. 17, 1874; s. Cyril and Mary (Billiard) R.; grad. U.S. Naval Acad., 1895; grad. U.S. Naval Air Sta., 1926; grad. Naval War Coll., 1930; m. Jane Callaghan, Oct. 12, 1897; children—Jane McCombe (wife of Lt. Lawrence Varsy Castner, U.S.A.), John (U.S.N.), Marie Louise. Commd. ensign U.S.N., 1897; advanced through grades to capt., 1919; rear admiral, Nov. 1, 1927. Served successively on U.S.S. Constellation, Bancroft, Monongahela, Philadelphia, Oregon, Farragut, Marietta and Nero, 1895-1905; also as gun officer Monadnock, navigator of Iris, chief engr. of S. Dakota, exec. officer Maryland and in command of Ohio, and U.S.S. Supply; comdr. successively, Albany, Missouri and Georgia, World War; later comdr. Destroyer Squadron 1921, Rochester, 1922-23; comdt. Naval Air Sta.. Pensacola, 1923-26; then comdr. Aircraft Squadrons of Scouting Fleet, Land service at Naval Tr. Sta., San Francisco, 1905-06; insp. machinery, Union Iron Works, San Francisco, 1907-08; later various periods at U.S. Naval Acad., as instr. in depts. of English, Marine Engring. and Seamanship, and as head of depts. of English and Seamanship; dir. personnel div. Bur. of Navigation and dir. ship movements Naval Operations Office, Navy Dept., Washington, 1918-19; capt. of Navy Yard, Washington, and asst. supt. Gun Factory, 1920-21, later comdt. 6th Naval Dist., Charleston, S.C. Took deepest known sounding nr. Guam—5269 fathoms; took out first merchant convoy under Am. escort in World War I; escorted largest number of ships to Europe; brought home first returning soldiers to be transported in battleship (U.S.S. Georgia); became naval aviator at age of 51—only admiral qualified as aviator up to 1928. Home: San Francisco. Calif. Died Jan. 15, 1934.

RACKEMANN, FRANCIS MINOT, physician; b. Milton, Mass., June 4, 1887; s. Felix and Julia (Minot) R.; A.B., Harvard, 1909, M.D., 1912; m. Dorothy Mandell, Apr. 28, 1917; children—Dorothy, Francis M., Elizabeth, William M. Research fellow in medicine, Presbyterian Hosp., 1914-16; resident in medicine, Mass. Gen. Hosp., 1916-17; asst. in medicine, Harvard Med. Sch., 1916-25, instr., 1925-35, lecturer in medicine, 1935-73; physician Mass. Gen. Hosp., 1918-48, consultant. First lt., Med. Corps, U.S. Army, 1918-19; dist. Med. Officer for Civilian Defense, 1942-45; civ. expert consultant to the Surgeon Gen., 1946-73. Chmn.

bd. trustees Boston State Hosp.; sec. Harvard Med. Sch. Dormitory Fund, 1923-27. Mem. Am. and Mass. med. assns., Assn. American physicians, Am. Society Clinic Investigation, American Assn. Study of Allergy (pres. 1925), American Academy Allergy, American Academy Arts and Sciences, Harvey Society, American Society Study of Asthma and Allied Conditions (pres. 1917), Am. Clin. and Climatol. Assn. (sec. 1933-41, pres. 1948), Harvard Med. Sch. Alumni Assn. (sec. and treas. 1923-27, pres. 1929). Clubs: Harvard, Union Boat (Boston); Country (Brookline); Harvard (New York). Author: Clinical Allergy; Asthma and Hay Fever, 1931. Home: Boston MA Died Mar. 1973.

RACKLEY, JOHN RALPH, educator; b. Lambert, Okla., Aug. 29, 1907; s. John William and Mertie (Hammer) R.; A.B., U. of Okla., 1931, A.M., 1935; grad. wcrk, Yale, Vanderbilt U.; Ph.D., George Peabody Coll., 1940; m. Virginia Douthit Mills, Feb. 4, 1937; 1 son, Gordon Mills. High sch. teacher of social science, Oklahoma City, Okla., 1930-39; (leaves of absence for grad. study, 1933-34, 1937-38); mem. faculty, Teachers Coll. of Com., 1939-49, prof. of social science and dean of college, 1946-49; prof. of edn. and dean, Coll. of Edn., U. of Okla., 1949-55; deputy United States commissioner of education, 1955-56; prof. edn. and dean coll. edn. Pa. State U., 1956-62, v.p. resident instrn., professor of education, 1962-65, provost of the university, 1967-69; supt. pub. instrn. Commonwealth, Pa., 1965-67. Chmn. of Gov's Adv. Com. Pub. Edn. Pa., 1957-58. Mem. Nat. Council Accreditation of Tchr. Edn., 1957-60; mem. Middle States Assn. Commn. on Instns. Higher Edn., 1962-65; Chmn. Cornell U. Adv. Council for Edn., 1962-67; mem. adv. com. on education in armed forces Dept. Def., 1957-60; member adv. com. on edn. of deaf Dept. Health, Edn. and Welfare, 1964-65. Served with Signal Corps, U.S. Army, 1943-46, now lt. col. Res. ret. Pres. Am. Assn. Colls. for Tchr. Edn., 1961-62. Mem. Alpha Tau Omega. Home: State College PA Died Dec. 24, 1969; buried Centre County Memorial Park, State College PA

RADCLIFFE, HARRY SOUTHWELL trade assn. exec.; b. Cornwall-on-Hudson, N.Y., Nov. 30, 1894; s. Harry Richardson and Mary Anna (Ehlers) R.; student Phila. Optical Coll., 1915-16, N.Y. U., 1936-37; m. Sarah E. Randall, July 2, 1917; children—Byron Mason, Margaret Jane (Mrs. Stephen Henry Jacobus). Stock clerk, M. N. Trafford Co., importers, 1912-13, salesman, 1913-15, partner, 1919-30; pres. Harry S. Radcliffe, Inc., 1928-32; registrar, N.Y. Coll. Chiropractic, 1932-34; asst. dir. Book Mfrs. Inst., 1935-36; exec. sec. Nat. Council Am. Importers, Inc., Lace and Embroidery Assn. Am., Inc., 1936-50; sec. Linen Trade Assn., Inc., since 1936; exec. v.p. Nat. Council Am. Importers Inc. and exec. dir. Lace and Embroidery Assn. since 1950; mem. nat. panel, Am. Arbitration Assn. since 1928; bus. adv. com. Inter Am. Comml. Arbitration Commn. since 1941; import cons., O.P.A., 1942-46; mem. of import advisory com. of Department of Commerce; member advisory com. (Depts. State and Commerce) on comml. activities of the Fgn. Service, 1946-50. Member fgn. trade com. Com. Econ. Development, 1945; com. on formalities in int. trade U.S. Council Internat. C. of C., 1948-—; fgn. commerce dept. com. U.S. C. of C., 1952-59; lectr. transportation and fgn. trade, Columbia, 1945; marketing and fgn. trade, N.Y. U., 1947-56. Decorated Officer l'Order du Mérite Commercial (France), 1948; Chevalier l'Ordre de la Couronne (Belgium), 1957; Hon. Officer Order of British Empire (U.K.), 1958; Officer Order of Orange-Nassau (Netherlands), 1958; Office Order of Merit (Italy), 1959; recipient World Trade Writers Assn. Award, 1953; Medal of Honor, Am. C. of C. in France, 1954. Served as pvt., later 1st lt. U.S.M.C., 1917-19; yeoman, 1916-17, capt., M.C. Br., Naval Militia, New York, 1922-24. Methodist. Club: Madison Golf. Author: The American Tariff on Alcoholic Beverages, 1933. Editor: The American Importer, 1936-40. Contbr. articles on import trade in export trade publs., N.Y. Jour. of Commerce, N.Y. Times, etc. Home: 25 Wilmer St., Madison, N.J. 07940. Office: 111 Fifth Av., N.Y.C. 10003. Died Jan. 2, 1968.

RADFORD, CYRUS S(UGG) retired brig. gen.; b. Hopkinsville, Ky., June 3, 1868; s. William Tandy and Mary Elizabeth (Sugg) R.; student U. of the South, Sewanee, Tenn., 1884-85; grad. U.S. Naval Acad., 1890; m. Catherine Thomas Manson, June 12, 1907; children—Francis Manson, Margaret Lewis, Catherine Manson, Cyrus S. Commd. 2d lt. USMC, 1892, advanced through grades to q.m. gen. 1929; retired with rank of brig. gen., 1929; v.p. Bankers Trust Co., Phila., until 1930. Served in U.S.S. Texas, Battle of Santiago, Spanish-Am. War; with USMC, Guantanamo expdn. to Cuba and Panama; in Philippines, 1901-03; built, equipped and developed USMC mfg. and supply base, Phila., 1903-29; tech. adviser on mil. supplies and equipment for Cuba, Haiti, San Domingo and Nicaragua. Assisted in developing Adm. Farragut Acad., Pine Beach, N.J., 1933-—, now pres. bd. trustees. Democrat. Episcopalian. Clubs: University, Corinthian Yacht (Phila.). Home: 501 Main St., Toms River, N.J. Died Jan. 19, 1951; buried Arlington Nat. Cemetery.

RADFORD, WILLIAM naval officer; b. Fincastle, Va., Sept. 9, 1809; s. John and Harriet (Kennerly) R.; m. Mary Elizabeth Lovell, Nov. 21, 1848, 6 children. Apptd. midshipman U.S. Navy, 1825, commd. lt., 1837, comdr. 1855, commodore, 1863, rear adm. 1866; served in various capacities in West Indies, Mediterranean and Pacific; participated in Mexican War; lighthouse insp. at N.Y., 1858-59, 61-62; comdr. steam sloop Dacotah, (1st Am. naval expdn. up Yangtse River to Hankow), 1860; comdr. Cumberland at Hampton Roads, 1862; exec. N.Y. Navy Yard, 1862-64; comdr. New Ironsides (leader ironclads in attacks on Ft. Fisher), 1864, 1865; comdr. Atlantic Squadron, 1865, Washington (D.C.) Navy Yard and European Squadron, 1869-70. Died Washington, D.C., Jan. 8, 1890.

RADO, SANDOR, psychiatrist; b. Hungary, Jan. 8, 1890; s. Adolph and Cornelia (Rado) R.; grad. Humanistic Gymnasium, 1907; Dr. Polit. Sci., U. Budapest, 1911, M.D., 1915; m. Emmy Krissler, Dec. 1, 1926 (dec.); children—George, Peter. Came to U.S., 1931, naturalized, 1937. Intern Zeitschrisft fur Psychoanalyse, Imago, 1925-34; dozent Berlin (Germany) Psychoanalytic Inst., 1923-31; dir. N.Y. Psychoanalytic Inst., 1931-41; clin. prof. psychiatry, dir. Psychoanalytic clinic Columbia, 1944-55; prof. psychiatry and dir. Grad. Sch. Psychiatry State U. N.Y. College of Medicine N.Y.C., 1956-58; pres., prof. at New York School of Psychiatry, 1958-67, dean emeritus, 1968-72; attending psychiatrist N.Y. State Psychiatric Inst. and Hosp., Army Med. Center, Walter Reed Hosp., 1946-52; cons. Manhattan State Hosp. Cons. Army Induction Center, 1942-45; examiner S.S.S., 1943-47; mem. N.Y. State Mental Hygiene Council, 1956-68. Recipient Samuel W. Hamilton award, Am. Psychopathological Assn., 1956. Fellow N.Y. Acad. Medicine, Am. Psychiatric Assn., A.A.A.S., mem. Internat. Psychoanalytic Assn., Am. Orthopsychiatric Assn., Am. Psychopathological Association, Society for Human Genetics, American Medical Assn., N.Y. Acad. Sciences, Assn. for Psychoanalytic Medicine, Am. Psychoanalytic Association, Assn. for Research Nervous and Mental Diseases. Author Psychoanalysis of Behavior, Collected Papers, Vol. I, 1956, Vol. II, 1962. Editor: Changing Concepts of Psychoanalytic Medicine, 1956. Author articles sci. publs. U.S. and Germany, and others. Home: New York City NY Died May 14, 1972.

RADO, TIBOR educator; b. Budapest, Hungary, June 2, 1895; s. Alexander and Gizella (Knappe) R.; student Poly. Inst., Budapest, 1913-15; Ph.D., U. Szeged, Hungary, 1923; D.Sc. (hon.), Kenyon Coll., 1960; m. Ida Barabas de Albis, Oct. 30, 1924; children—Judith Viola (Mrs. W. Santasiere), Theodore Alexander. Came to U.S., 1929, naturalized, 1935. Privat-docent U. Szeged, 1927; Internat. Research fellow Rockefeller Found., Germany, 1928, 29; vis. lectr. Harvard, Rice Inst., 1929-30; prof. math. Ohio State U., 1930-48, chmn. dept., 1946-48, research prof. math., 1949-—; vis. prof. math. U. Chgo., 1942, U. P.R., 1947; cons. Battelle Meml. Inst., Columbus, O., 1961-—. Served as 1st lt. Royal Hungarian Army, World War I; sci. cons. to USAAF, ETO, World War II. Mem. Am. Math. Soc. (Colloquim lectr. 1945), Assn. for Computing Machinery, Math. Assn. Am. (Hedrick Meml. lectr. 1952), A.A.A.S. (v.p. 1953). Presbyn. Mason. Author: On the Problem of Plateau, 1933; Subharmonic Functions, 1937; Length and Area, 1948; Continuous Transformations in Analysis (with P.V. Reichelderfer), 1955; also research papers. Home: 2299 Tremont Rd., Columbus 21, O. Died Dec. 29, 1965; buried Bellview Meml. Park, Daytona Beach, Fla.

RAE, CHARLES WHITESIDE naval engr.; b. Hartford, Conn., June 30, 1847; s. Rev. Luzern and Martha (Whiteside) R.; prep. edn. Champlain (N.Y.) Acad.; C.E., Rensselaer Poly. Inst., 1866; grad. U.S. Naval Acad., 1868; D.Sc., U. of Pa., 1906; m. Rebecca Gilman Dodge, Jan. 9, 1890. Promoted through grades, becoming capt., Jan. 3, 1903; served at bombardment of San Juan, P.R., also in several minor actions on S. coast of Cuba and at naval battle of Santiago, July 3, 1898; advanced "for eminent and conspicuous conduct in battle" (medal). Apptd. engr.-in-chief U.S.N., with rank of rear admiral, and chief bureau of steam engring., Navy Dept., Aug. 9, 1903. Residence: Washington, D.C. Died 1908.

RAFFERTY, WILLIAM CARROLL army officer; b. in Ind., Apr. 11, 1859; grad. U.S. Mil. Acad., 1880, Arty. Sch., 1884; m. Julia, d. Gen. Judson Kilpatrick, 1894. Commd. 2d lt. 1st Arty., June 12, 1880; 1st lt., Aug. 11, 1887; capt., Mar. 2, 1899; maj. Arty. Corps, Apr. 14, 1905; lt. col. Coast Arty. Corps, Jan. 20, 1908; col., Mar. 3, 1911; brig. gen. N.A., Aug. 5, 1917. Mem. Bd. on Regulation of Coast Arty. Fire, 1894-97; prof. mil. science, Seton Hall Coll., South Orange, N.J., 1897-98; comd. defenses at Galveston, Tex., 1900 at time of great cyclone and tidal wave; apptd. comd. Arty. Dist. of Baltimore, 1908; apptd. comdr. 54th Field Arty. Brigade, Camp McClellan, Anniston, Ala., Sept. 1917; comd. 29th Div., Oct.-Dec. 1917; relieved as brig. gen., May 1918; retired Dec. 31, 1919. Address: Washington, D.C. Died May 22, 1941.

RAGSDALE, JAMES W. consul-gen.; b. Monroe Co., Ind., Feb. 12, 1848; s. Daniel S. and Louisa (Lindsay) R.; student Cornell Coll., Ia., 3 yrs.; pvt. Co. C, 13th Ia. Inf., with Sherman in Ga., and March to Sea; m. Effie L. Hines, of Chariton, Ia., Feb. 3, 1870. Was in newspaper work in Ia. and Cal., 20 yrs.; mem. Cal. Assembly, 1888, Senate, 1890; consul, 1897-1903, consul-gen., 1903-08, at Tientsin, China; consul-gen., Mar.-June, 1908, consul, 1908-09, at St. Petersburg, Russia; consul-gen. at Halifax, N.S., since Sept. 11, 1909. Was among the besieged at Tientsin during the "Boxer" uprising in 1900. Home: Santa Rosa, Cal. Address: Am. Consulate, Halifax, N.S., Can.

RAGSDALE, VAN HUBERT naval officer; b. Aug. 9, 1892; entered U.S. Navy, 1912, and advanced through the grades to rear adm., 1942. Decorated Navy Cross. Address: Navy Dept., Washington 25, D.C. Deceased.*

RAINES, GEORGE NEELY psychiatrist, neurologist; b. Jackson, Miss., Apr. 2, 1908; s. William Giles and Bessie Whitworth (Hoskins) R.; B.S., U. of Miss., 1928; M.D., Northwestern U., 1930; m. Kate Oliver St. Clair, July 12, 1932; children—Mary Anne, George Neely. Intern U.S. Naval Hosp., Mare Island, Calif., 1930-31, U.S. Naval Med. Sch., Washington, 1934-35, St. Elizabeths Hospital, 1935-36 Washington-Baltimore Psychoanalytic Institute, 1946-53; entered M.C., U.S. Navy, 1930, commd. June, 1930, advanced through grades to capt., 1945; served aboard U.S.S. Idaho and in spl. service squadron, 1931-34, U.S.S. Saratoga and U.S.S. Lexington, 1938-40; med. officer in psychiatry and neurol. U.S. Naval Hosp., Washington, 1934, 1941-42, U.S. Naval Hosp., Phila., 1935-38, 1940-41, Bethesda, Md., 1942-43, chief neuropsychiatry U.S. Naval Hosp., Portsmouth, Va., 1943-45, U.S. Naval Hosp., Nat. Naval Med. Center, Bethesda, 1945-50; med. officer charge Naval med. unit, St. Elizabeths Hosp., head dept. neurology and psychiatry Naval Med. Sch., 1945-50; head, neuropsychiatry br., Bur. Medicine and Surgery, Navy Dept., 1950-53, 1955-58, retired; exec. officer U.S. Naval Hosp., Portsmouth, Va., 1953-55. Prof., dir. dept. psychiatry, Georgetown U. Med. Center since 1948; asso. Wash. Sch. Psych., since 1950; instr. clin. neurol. Temple U. Sch. Med., 1937-41; clin. prof. psychiatry, Georgetown U. Sch. Med., 1947-48. Cons. neurol., psychiatry to profl. div., Bur. Med. and Surgery Navy Dept., 1949-50; cons. Naval Dispensary, 1949-50; spl. cons. to Nat. Inst. Mental Health, U.S. Pub. Health Service, Bethesda, since 1949. Diplomate Am. Bd. Psychiatry and Neurol. (dir.); fellow A.M.A., Am. Psychiatric Assn. (chmn. committee on nomenclature and statistics 1948-54; councillor, 1954-57), A.C.P.; mem. Am. Neurol. Association, Washington Psychoanalytic Society, Assn. Research Nervous and Mental Diseases, Am. Psychopathol. Assn., Wash. Psychiatric Soc. (councillor 1950-51), Sigma Chi, Phi Chi. Contbr. to profl., med. jours. Office: 3800 Reservoir Rd., N.W., Washington 7. Died Sept. 16, 1959.

RAINES, JOHN MARLIN, educator; b. Tarkio, Mo., Sept. 8, 1907; s. E.N. and Anna Grace (Marlin) R.; A.B., Mus. B., Tarkio Coll., 1928; A.M., Cornell U., 1929, Ph.D., 1935; m. Ann Herrick, Dec. 26, 1935; 1 dau., Margaret. Instr. English, Muskingum Coll., New Concord, O., 1929-31; prof. English, Mo. Valley Coll., Marshall, 1935-39; instr. English, Woodrow Wilson Jr. Coll., Chgo., 1939-43, Cornell U., 1945-46; asst. prof. U. Okla., 1946-50, prof. English, 1950, 1951-71, David R. Boyd prof., chmn. dept., 1951-53; vis. asso. prof. English, U. Cal., Davis, 1957. Served from lt. (j.g.) to lt. USNR, 1943-45, lt. comdr. Res. Mem. Modern Lang. Assn., Am. Assn. U. Profs., Phi Kappa Phi. Episcopalian. Contbr. articles profl. jours. Home: Norman OK Died July 24, 1971.

RAINS, GABRIEL JAMES army officer; b. Craven County, N.C., June 4, 1803; s. Gabriel M. and Hester (Ambrose) R.; grad. U.S. Mil. Acad., 1827; m. Mary Jane McClellan, 6 children. Commd. capt. U.S. Army, 1839; took part in Seminole War, 1839-42; brevetted maj., 1842; served in Mexican War; took part in 2d Seminole War, 1849-50; promoted lt. col., 1860; commd. brig. gen. Confederate States Army, 1861; in command at Yorktown, mined nearby waters, 1861-62; withdrew from Yorktown, 1862, left shells with percussion fuses in the road; employed early land mines at Battle of Williamsburg; in charge of Bur. of Conscription, Richmon., 1863; given series of defense missions, 1863. let to assignment as supt. Torpedo Bur., Confederacy, 1864-65; arranged demolitions, mines and torpedo protection for Richmond, Mobile, Charleston, the James River; two of his operations blew up two U.S. barges and an ammunition warehouse, City Point, Va., 1864; clk. U.S. Quartermaster Dept., Charleston, S.C., 1877-80. Died Aiken, S.C., Aug. 6, 1881.

RAINS, GEORGE WASHINGTON army officer, educator; b. Craven County, N.C., 1817; s. Gabriel M. and Hester (Ambrose) R.; grad. (1st in science studies), U.S. Mil. Acad., 1842; M.D. (hon.), Med. Coll. Va., 1867; m. Frances Josephine Ramsdell, Apr. 23, 1856. With Corps. Engrs. U.S. Army, 1842, 4th Arty., 1843; asst. prof. chemistry, geology, mineralogy U.S. Mil. Acad., 1844-46; 1st lt. Mexican War; brevetted capt., 1847, maj., 1848; resigned 1856; pres. Washington Iron Works and Highland Iron Works, Newburgh, N.Y., 1856-61; commd. maj. Corps Arty., Confederate Army, 1861; lt. col., 1862, col., 1863; initiated wholesale collection of nitre from limestone caves in Tenn., Ala., Ga., N.C.; improvement in gunpowder plant efficiency patented in Confederate States Patent Office, 1864; in charge all munitions operations in Augusta, 1862, commanding officer troops at Augusta, 1864; prof. chemistry Med. Coll. Ga., 1866-94; dean, circa 1868-

83, prof. emeritus, 1894-98; regent Acad. of Richmond County, 1867. Author: pamphlet Notes on Making Saltpetre from the Earth of the Caves,irca 1862; History of the Confederate Powder Works, 1882. Died nr. Newburgh, N.Y., Mar. 21, 1898.

RALSTON, BYRON BROWN, lawyer; b. Fostoria, O., Sept. 26, 1890; s. William McCamus and Wealtha Jane (Brown) R.; B.S., U.S. Naval Acad., 1914; M.S., Columbia, 1921; J.D., N.Y.U., 1931; m. Lucy Virginia Gordon, June 4, 1919; 1 dau., Lucy Virginia. Commd. ensign U.S.N., 1914, advanced through grades to lt. comdr., 1921, ret. 1928; trust dept. Chem. Bank & Trust Co., N.Y.C., 1928, legal staff trust dept., 1933-71, co. merged with Corn Exchange Bank Trust Co., to form Chem. Corn Exchange Bank, 1954; admitted to New York bar, 1932; dir. Internat. Minerals & Chem. Corp. Dir. John Jay and Eliza J. Watson Found. Served with U.S.N.; 1940-45. Profl. engr., N.Y.; licensed ship engr. Protestant Episcopal. Mason. Clubs: Pelham Country; Lawyers, Yacht (N.Y.C.); Army and Navy (Washington). Home: Pelham NY Died Apr. 9, 1971.

RALSTON, HON. JAMES LAYTON K.C. former minister national defence for Canada; b. Amherst, N.S., Sept. 27, 1881; s. Burnett William and Bessie (Layton) R.; ed. Amherst Acad. and Dalhousie Law Sch.; D.C.L. (hon.) Acadia U. (Wolfville, N.S.); LL.D. (hon.) U. of Dalhousie (Halifax, N.S.), Union Coll. (Schenectady, N.Y.), U. of Toronto (Toronto, Can.); married Nettie Winnifred McLeod, 1907; 1 son, Stuart Bowman Ralston. Read law in offices of Logan & Jenks, 1898-1903; admitted to Nova Scotia bar, 1903; partner Logan, Jenks & Ralston, 1903-09, Logan & Ralston, 1909-11, Ralston, Hanway & Ralston, Amherst, 1911-12, Maclean, Burchell & Ralston, Halifax, and later Burchell & Ralston, 1912-26; minister of National Defense, Ottawa, 1926-30; partner Mitchell, Ralston, Kearney & Duquet, Montreal, 1930-35, Ralston, Kearney & Duquet, 1935-39; Ralston, Kearney, Duquet & Mackay, since 1945. Dir. Eastern Tr. Co., Gillette Safety Razor Company of Canada, Ltd., Canadian Vickers, Limited, Montreal Dry Docks, Ltd., Montreal Locomotive Works, Ltd., Elected to Nova Scotia Legislature, Cumberland, 1911 and 1916; apptd. chmn. Royal Commission on Pensions and re-establishment by Federal Government, July 1922; accepted portfolio of National Defense, Mackenzie King Cabinet, October 8, 1926; elected to House of Commons, Shelburne-Yarmouth, 1926 and 1930; Canadian delegate to London Naval Conference, 1930; accepted portfolio of Finance in Mackenzie King Cabinet, September 6, 1939; elected to House of Commons (Prince, P.E.I.) by acclamation, January 2, 1940, re-elected March 1940; appointed minister nat. defence, July 5, 1940; resigned Nov. 1944. Commd. major, Can. Inf., Oct. 1916; commd. 85th Can. Inf. Batn., France, Apr. 1918-June 1919; gazetted lt. col., Aug. 21, 1918, col. Apr. 28, 1924. Decorated D.S.O., 1917, Bar to D.S.O., 1918, C.M.G. 1918; mentioned twice in dispatches. Gov. Acadia U. and McMaster U. Baptist. Clubs: Mount Royal, St. James; Forest and Stream, Montreal, Montreal Reform, Canadian Rotary (Montreal); Rideau (Ottawa); Halifax (Halifax, N.S.); Yarmouth Golf and Country; Summerside Rotary (Summerside, P.E.I.). Home: Gleneagles Apts. Office: 360 St. James St. West, Montreal 1, Que. Died May 22, 1948.

RAMSAY, FRANCIS MUNROE rear admiral U.S.N.; b. Washington, April 5, 1835; s. Bvt. Maj. Gen. George Douglas and Frances Whetcroft (Munroe) R.; m. Anna McMahon, 1869. Apptd. midshipman from Pa., Oct. 5, 1850; served in Pacific Squadron, 1851-55; at Naval Acad., 1855-56, grad., 1856; passed midshipman, 1856; master, and lt., 1858; lt. comdr., 1862; comdr., 1866; capt.. 1877; commodore, 1889-94; rear admiral, 1894-97, retired on reaching age limit, Apr. 5, 1897. Comd. U.S.S. Choctaw, and 3d div. of Mississippi Squadron, 1863-64; in engagements at Haines' Bluff, Yazoo River, Milliken's Bend, Mississippi River; commanded battery of 3 heavy guns, mounted on scows, before Vicksburg; later comd. gunboat Unadilla, N. Atlantic Squadron, 1864-65; was in engagements with Forts Fisher, Anderson, etc. After war in various services. Supt. Naval Acad., 1881-86; chief Bur. of Navigation, Navy Dept., 1889-97. Home: Washington, D.C. Died July 19, 1914.

RAMSAY, GEORGE DOUGLAS army officer; b. Dumfries, Va., Feb. 21, 1802; s. Andrew and Catherine (Graham) R.; grad. U.S. Mil. Acad., 1820; m. Frances Whetcroft Munroe, Sept. 23, 1830; m. 2d, Eliza Hennen Gales, June 28, 1838; 6 children including Francis Monroe. Commd. 1st lt., 1st Arty., 1826, adjutant to regt., 1833; commd. capt. of ordnance, 1835-61, commanded arsenals in Washington, D.C., N.Y., Pa., N.J., Ga., 1835-45; brevetted maj. for distinguished service at Battle of Monterey, 1847; chief of ordnance, 1847-48; maj. 1861, lt. col., 1861, col. ordnance, 1863, brig. gen. and chief of ordnance U.S. Army, 1864; insp. of arsenals, 1864-66; brevetted maj. gen., 1865 Died May 23, 1882.

RAMSAY, NATHANIEL army officer, Continental congressman; b. Lancaster County, Pa., May 1, 1741; s. James and Jane (Montgomery) R.; grad. Coll. of N.J. (now Princeton), 1767; m. Mary Jane Peale, 1771; m. 2d, Charlotte Hall, 1792; 3 children. Del to Md. Conv., 1775, signer Md. Declaration of Freemen; mem. Continental Congress from Md., 1775, 85-87; capt. Smallwood's Md. Regt., 1776; commd. lt. col. 3d Md. Regt., Continental Army, 1776-81; served at Battle of Monmouth, 1778, helped check retreat begun by Gen. Charles Lee; U.S. marhsal. Dist. of Md., 1790-98; naval officer Port of Balt., 1794-1817. Died Balt., Oct. 24, 1817; buried 1st Presbyn. Ch., Balt.

RAMSDELL, EDWIN GEORGE surgeon; b. New York, N.Y. May 14, 1886; s. Edwin Benjamin and Sarah Eloise (Finlayson) R.; A.B., Columbia, 1905, M.D., 1908; m. Bessie Alan Sadler, Dec. 16, 1911; children—Edwin Alan, John Alan. Practicing physician and instr. in surgery, Columbia U. Coll. of Physicians and Surgeons, 1910-17; asst. Surgeon White Plains (N.Y.) Hosp., 1910-19, attending surgeon, 1919-33, surg. dir., 1933-—; cons. surgeon Mt. Vernon (N.Y.) Hosp., 1931-—, New York Hosp. Westchester Br., 1936-—, v.p. and dir. White Plains Med. Center, 1928-—, pres. bd., 1942-—; gov. White Plains Hosp., chief of staff, 1941-—; mem. Westchester County Board of Health, 1931-—, pres., 1934-—. Mem. bd. Man. Westchester County Dept. of Labs., dir. County Trust Co. Dep. dir. and chief med. officer Civil Defense; dir. Civic and Businessmen's Assn., White Plains. Served in Am. Hosp., Juilly, France, 1915; capt., later maj. A.U.S. Med. Corps, 1917-19; participated in St. Mihiel-Argonne offensive; col. U.S. Med. Res. Corps. Chevalier, Legion of Honor; Croix de Guerre with Palm. Diplomate, Am. Bd. Surgery. Fellow Am. Coll. of Surgeons, N.Y. Acad. of Medicine. Mem. Am. Med. Assn., American Goitre Society. Westchester Surgical Soc., Westchester Cancer Com. (dir.), Med. Editors and Authors Assn., International Surgical Society, Society Older Graduates of Columbia, S.A.R., Alpha Omega Alpha, Phi Gamma Delta. Republican. Methodist. Clubs: University, Columbia (New York); University Rotary (White Plains); Bayhead Yacht (N.J.); Scarsdale Golf; Union Interalliee (Paris). Contbr. of med. articles to profl. jour. Home: 14 Winslow Rd. Office: Medical Centre Bldg., White Plains, N.Y. Died Apr. 12, 1960.

RAMSEUR, STEPHEN DODSON army officer; b. Lincolnton, N.C., May 31, 1837; s. Jacob A. and Lucy M. (Wilfong) R.; grad. U.S. Mil. Acad., 1860; m. Ellen E. Richmond, Oct. 22, 1863, 1 child. Served from lt. arty. to capt. N.C. battery in Confederate Army, 1861; commd. col. 49th N.C. Inf., 1863; commd. brig. gen.; served in battles of Gettysburg, Wilderness, Spotsylvania; promoted maj. gen., 1864. Died of wound received at Cedar Creek, Va., Oct. 20, 1864.

RAMSEY, DEWITT CLINTON naval officer; b. Whipple Barracks, Ariz., Oct. 2, 1888; s. Frank DeWitt and Lillian Carlotta (Zulick) R.; B.S., U.S. Naval Acad., 1912; student Flight Tng. Sch., Pensacola, Fla., 1915-17; Naval War Coll., Newport, R.I., 1936-37; m. Juanita Gabrielle, July 25, 1926 (dec.). Advanced through grades to adm., Jan. 1946; service afloat, 1912-15; naval aviator No. 45; duty in France, Eng., World War I in naval aviation; four tours duty as fleet aviation officer on staff of comdrs. in chief of fleet; supt. flight tng. Pensacola, 1924; navigator U.S.S. Langley, 1926-28; exec., U.S.S. Wright, 1932-34, U.S.S. Saratoga, 1938; asst. chief Bur. Aeros., 1941-42; war time comdr. aircraft carrier and task force comdr.; staff comdr. Fifth Fleet; dep. comdr. in chief, Pacific Fleet, Nov. 1945; vice chief naval operations, Navy Dept., Jan. 1946; comdr. in chief, Pacific and U.S. Pacific fleet, Jan. 1948; U.S. High Commr. Trust Ty. of Pacific Islands, Apr. 1948; ret. as adm. May 1, 1949; pres., gen. mgr. Aircraft Industries Assn. Am., Inc., 1949-57, vice chmn. bd. govs., 1957-—. Awarded Navy Cross, World War medal, Mexican War medal Def. medal, Order of Couronne de Chene (Luxembourg), D.S.M., with one star, Campaign medals Am. and Pacific Areas (World War II); Hon. Comdr. Mil. Div., Order Brit. Empire. Awarded Legion of Merit, June 1945. Mem. U.S. Naval Inst. Home: 3661 Upton St. N.W., Washington. Office: Shoreham Bldg., Washington 5. Died Sept. 7, 1961; buried U.S. Naval Acad. Cemetery, Annapolis, Md.

RAMSEY, NORMAN FOSTER army officer; b. Oakdale, Ill., July 9, 1882; s. James Arthur and Harriet Louisa (McClurkin) R.; student Washburn Coll., Topeka, 1900-01; B.S., U.S. Mil. Acad., 1905; LL.D., St. Ambrose Coll., 1942; attended Army War Coll., 1920-21, Command and Gen. Staff Sch., 1926-27; m. Minna B. Bauer, Oct. 12, 1910; children—John George (dec.), Norman Foster. Served successively as pvt. Co. E, 20th Kan. Vol. Inf., U.S. Army, 1898-99, 2d lt., 9th Inf., Manila, P.I., 1905-07, 1st lt., Ordnance Dept., Sandy Hook Proving Ground, N.J., 1907-09, same, Watertown (Mass.) Arsenal, 1909-11, capt., Ordnance Dept., Office of Chief of Ordnance, Washington, 1912-16, maj., Ordnance, Rock Island (Ill.) Arsenal, 1916-18, col. (temp.), Ordnance, A.E.F., France, 1918-20, maj. Ordnance, Picatinny Arsenal, N.J., 1922-26, lt. col. Ordnance, Fort Leavenworth, Kan., 1926-31, Hdqrs. 2d Corps Area, Governors Island, N.Y., 1931-33, col. Office of Chief of Ordnance, Washington, 1933-37, Rock Island Arsenal, 1937-44, brig. gen., Ordnance Dept., U.S. Army, Rock Island Arsenal, since 1940, Springfield Armory 1944-45; ret. Dec. 1945. Awarded Soldiers medal, 1930, Purple Heart, 1932, Knight of Legion of Honor (France), 1921; Officer of the Black Star (France), 1919; Officer Order of the Crown (Roumania), 1921. Mem. Army Ordnance Assn. Presbyn. Clubs: Army and Navy (Washington). Died Apr. 1963.

RAMUS, CARL, surgeon U.S.P.H.S.; b. Chicago, Ill., Oct. 1, 1872; s. Christian Emil and Sybla (Faulds) R.; student under mother and tutors; M.D., Rush Med. Coll., 1897 (De Laskee Miller prize for best essay on obstetrics and gynecology); m. Anna Tucker, of Sacramento, Calif., and Honolulu, Sept. 27, 1912; children—Michael, Francesca. Commd. asst. surg. U.S.P.H.S., Mar. 9, 1899; passed asst. surgeon, Mar. 20, 1904; surgeon Mar. 3, 1913. Quarantine duty, Havana, 1899-1900; asst. med. officer, Ft. Stanton (N.M.) Sanatorium, 1900-02; chief quarantine officer, Hawaiian Islands, 1909-12; med. examiner, Ellis Island, N.Y., 1912-16; med. attache Am. Consulate, Naples, 1916-20; in charge First Aid Sta., Naples, during World War; apptd. surgeon in charge U.S. Marine Hosp., Evansville, Ind., 1920. Del. Office Internationale d'Hygiene Publique, Paris, 1919; Internat. Conf. on Care of Wounded Soldiers, Rome, 1920. Student of Oriental philosophy. Mem. A.M.A., Astron. Soc. of Pacific, Am. Legion, Vets. of Foreign Wars. Decorated for war service by Italian Govt. Author: Marriage and Efficiency, 1922; Outwitting Middle Age, 1926; Behind the Scenes with Ourselves, 1931; also articles in jours. Address: U.S. Public Health Service, Washington DC*

RAND, FREDERICK HENRY fruit grower; b. Boston, July 19, 1846; s. Edward S. and Elizabeth A. (Arnold) R.; Norwich U., Vt., 1861-63, B.S., 1911, as of 1864; m. Julia Frances Hasbrouck, of Boston, Feb. 10, 1874. Engaged in mining in Cal.; in mercantile business, Boston, 1869-76; orange grower, Fla., 1876; incorporator South Fla. R.R., 1879, sec., gen. passenger and freight agent, 1879-86; pres. Sanford Water Works, 1886-1906; pres. Sanford Light & Fuel Co., 1886-1900; agent, atty. in fact and mgr. Fla. Land & Colonization Co., 1886-1916; pres. 1st Nat. Bank, Sanford, Fla. Commd. 1st lt. 1st Independent Battalion, 1st Mass. Cav., July 2, 1863; capt. 4th Mass. Cav., Jan. 19, 1864; hon. discharged Aug. 1864; 2d lt. 1st Battalion Cav., frontier service, Dec. 27, 1864; capt., Dec. 30, 1864; discharged Aug. 30, 1865. Trustee U. of the South, Sewanee, Tenn.; trustee Ch. Home and Hosp., Orlando, Fla. Mem. Loyal Legion, Theta Chi. Republican. Episcopalian (has served 4 times as deputy in Gen. Conv. P.E. Ch.). Mason (32 deg.). Home: Sanford, Florida. Died July 12, 1933.

RAND, STEPHEN naval officer; b. at Norwich, Vt., May 11, 1844. Apptd. acting 3d asst. engr. U.S.N., Dec. 17, 1864; hon. discharged, Aug. 8, 1869; apptd. asst. p.-m. Aug. 12, 1869; passed asst. p.-m., Apr. 30, 1874; p.-m., Jan. 19, 1885; pay insp., Sept. 1, 1899; pay dir., July 1, 1902; advanced to rank of rear adm. retired, May 11, 1906, for services during Civil War. Address: Washington, D.C. Died July 12, 1915.

RANDALL, ALBERT BORLAND master mariner, naval officer; b. Brookhaven, L.I., N.Y., Sept. 11, 1879; s. William Frederick and Sarah Elizabeth (Smith) R.; student Vermont Acad., Saxton's River, Vt., 1896-97; m. Dorothy Clara Boyer, June 6, 1908; children—Sylvia Elizabeth (wife of Dr. Harold S. Hain), Albert Borland, Jr., Dorothy Virginia (wife of Eugene Francis Mooney). Began as seaman in sailing vessels; promoted through grades and ranks, receiving his masters license, 1905, and receiving 1st command, January 17, 1907; commander various ships including the Republic, George Washington, Leviathan and Manhattan; commodore United States Lines, Jan. 1931-Oct. 1939; retired because of age limit, Oct. 2, 1939; apptd. rear adm., U.S. Naval Reserve, Jan. 17, 1942; recalled to active duty; assigned to War Shipping Administration Training Organization as comdt. stationed Washington, D.C., March 29, 1943. Member various Naval Reserve Organizations since May 12, 1902. Decorated Chevalier Legion of Honor (French); awarded Certificate of Appreciation, U.S. Navy Dept.; letter of commendation from President F. D. Roosevelt for outstanding service in Merchant Marine and Navy, upon retirement from Merchant Service. Mem. Marine Soc. of City of New York, S.A.R.; hon. mem. Propeller Club. Democrat. Mason (K.T.). Home: Whitestone, L.I., N.Y. Died Dec. 1, 1945.

RANDALL, ALEXANDER urologist; b. Annapolis, Md., Apr. 18, 1883; s. John Wirt and Hannah Parker (Parrott) R.; B.A., St. Johns Coll., Annapolis, 1902, M.A., 1907; studied Johns Hopkins, 1902-03, Johns Hopkins Med. Sch., 1903-07, M.D., 1907; m. Edith T. Kneedler, June 2, 1915; children—Alexander, Peter, Virginia. Resident German Hosp., Phila., 1907-09; pvt. asst. to Dr. H.H. Young, Balt., 1910; resident urologist Johns Hopkins Hosp., 1911; asst. prof. surgery U. Pa., 1923-26, asso. prof., 1926-29, prof. urology, 1929-46; retired. Served from lt. to maj. M.C., U.S. Army, 1917-19; with AEF, 1918-19. Fellow A.C.S.; mem. A.M.A., Phila. Acad. Surgery, Coll. Physicians Phila., Am. Surg. Assn., Am. Urol Assn (pres. 1932), Am. Assn. Genito-Urinary Surgeons (pres. 1938), Société Internationale d'Urologie. Republican. Episcopalian. Clubs: Rittenhouse, Corinthian Yacht (Phila.). Author: Surgical Pathology of Prostatic Obstructions, 1931; also articles giving results of med. research. Home: 20

Laughlin Lane, Phila. Office: Medical Arts Bldg., Phila. Died Nov. 18, 1951; buried St. Thomas Cemetery, White Marsh, Pa.

RANDALL, CLARENCE BELDEN steel co. ofcl.; b. Newark Valley, N.Y., Mar. 5, 1891; s. Oscar Smith and Esther Clara (Belden) R.; student Wyo. Sem., Kingston, Pa., 1906-08; A.B., Harvard, 1912; LL.B., 1915; D.Eng. (hon.), Mich. Coll. Mining and Tech., 1947; LL.D., Northeastern U., 1948; D.E., Rose Polytechnic Inst., 1952; Dr. Bus. Adm. instrn., Denison U., 1953; LL.D., U. Mich., 1953, Brown U., Dartmouth, Harvard, Kenyon Coll., 1954, Northwestern U., 1955, Colby Coll., 1956, Amherst Coll., 1957, Lake Forest Coll., 1957, Knox Coll., 1963, Beloit Coll., 1964; L.H.D., Nat. Col. Edn., 1960; J.S.D., Suffolk U., 1964; m. Emily Fitch Phelps, Aug. 18, 1917; children—Mary Fitch (Mrs. J. Gordon Gilkey, Jr.), Miranda Belden (Mrs. Lemuel B. Hunter). Admitted to Mich. bar, July 1915, and practiced Ishpeming, 1915-25; with Inland Steel Co., Chgo., 1925-—, asst. v.p. in charge of raw materials 1925-30, v.p., 1930-48, asst. to pres., 1948, pres., 1949-53, dir., 1935-—, chmn. bd., 1953-56; Charles R. Walgreen Found. lectr. U. Chgo., 1954. Served as capt., inf., U.S. Army, 1917-19. Pres. Bd. of Edn., Winnetka, Ill., 1930-36. Trustee U. Chgo., 1936-61, Wellesley Coll., 1946-49; gen. chmn. Chgo. Community and War Fund Campaign, 1944; dir. of Nat. War Fund, 1944-45; trustee Chicago Natural History Museum, 1946-61; vice chmn. bd. dirs. Chgo. Heart Assn. Mem. Harvard Bd. Overseers 1947-53. Mem. Indsl. Conf. Bd., 1946-56. Steel cons., E.C.A., Paris, summer, 1946; mem. bus. adv. council U.S. Dept. Commerce, 1951-57; chief Spl. U.S. Econ. Mission to Turkey, 1953; chmn. Commn. on Fgn. Ecno. Policy, 1953-54; spl. cons. to Pres. Eisenhower on fgn. econ. policy, 1954-56; spl. asst. to Pres. Eisenhower on matters fgn. econ. policy, 1956-61; chmn. Council on Foreign Economic Policy, 1956-61, Special Mission to Turkey, 1956; spl., emissary Pres. Kennedy to Ghana in connection Volta River Project, 1961; chmn. Presidential Panel to Review Fed. Pay Schedules, 1962-63; hon. chmn. Ill. Com. on Export Expansion, 1962-63; chmn. adv. com. on internat. bus. problems Dept. State, 1963; Godkin lectr., Harvard, 1938; Fund for Adult Edn. lectr., Harvard, 1956. Recipient medal Am. Iron and Steel Inst., 1933, hon. citation, 1952; Man of the Year, N.A.M., 1952; Business Statesman of the Year, Nat. Sales Execs., 1954; Capt. Robert Dollar Meml. award, Nat. Fgn. Trade Council, 1954; other honors and awards for pub. service, Presidential medal of Freedom, 1963. Pres. Asso. Harvard Clubs, 1937-38. Fellow Am. Acad. Arts and Scis.; mem. Am. Ornithologists Union (asso.), Am. Philos. Soc., Harvard Alumni Assn. (pres. 1949), Phi Beta Kappa Assos., Phi Beta Kappa, Delta Upsilon. Republican. Episcopalian. Clubs: Metropolitan (Washington); Commercial, Chicago, University, Mid-day (Chgo.); Indian Hill Country (Winnetka); Union Interalliee (Paris). Author: Civil Liberties and Industrial Conflict (with Roger N. Baldwin), 1938; A Creed for Free Enterprise, 1952 (Colonial Dames of America award 1953); Freedom's Faith, 1953 (Freedoms Found. Honor medal 1953, Colonial Dames of Am. award 1954); A Foreign Economic Policy for the United States, 1954; Over My Shoulder, 1956; The Communist Challenge to American Business, 1958; The Folklore of Management, 1961; Sixty-Five Plus, 1963; Making Good in Management, 1964; also mag. articles. Home: 700 Blackthorn Rd., Winnetka, Ill. Office: 30 W. Monroe St., Chgo. Died Aug. 4, 1967.

RANDALL, GEORGE MORTON major gen. U.S.A.; b. in Ohio, Oct. 8, 1841. Pvt. Co. A, 4th Pa. Inf., Apr. 20, 1861; discharged, July 25, 1861; apptd. from Pa., 2d lt. 4th Inf. U.S.A., Oct. 24, 1861; 1st lt., Nov. 6, 1862; maj. 14th N.Y. Arty., Aug. 16, 1864; lt. col., June 1, 1865; hon. mustered out of vol. service, Aug. 26, 1865; capt., Sept. 23, 1865; assigned to 23d Inf., Jan. 1, 1871; maj. 4th Inf., Jan. 15, 1891; lt. col. 8th Inf., Mar. 1, 1894; brig. gen. vols., May 4, 1898; col. 17th U.S. Inf., Aug. 8, 1898; transferred to 8th Inf., Sept. 16, 1898; hon. discharged from vols., Apr. 12, 1899; brig. gen. vols., Jan. 20, 1900; brig. gen. U.S.A., Feb. 6, 1901; maj. gen., June 19, 1905; retired by operation of law, Oct. 8, 1905. Bvtd. capt., Sept. 17, 1862, "for gallant and meritorious services at battle of Antietam, Md."; maj., Apr. 2, 1865, for same, Petersburg, Va.; lt. col. and col. vols., Mar. 26, 1865, "for gallantry in attack on Ft. Stedman, Va."; lt. col., Feb. 27, 1890, "for gallant service in action" against Indians at Turret Mountain, Ariz., Mar. 27, 1873, and at Diamond Butte, Ariz., Apr. 22, 1873; col., Feb. 27, 1890, "for gallant service in action" against Indians nr. Pinal. Ariz., Mar. 8, 1874, and "distinguished service" during campaign against Indians in Ariz., 1874. Home: Denver, Colo. Died June 14, 1918.

RANDALL, SAMUEL JACKSON congressman, state polit. leader; b. Phila., Oct. 10, 1828; s. Josiah and Ann (Worrell) R.; attended Univ. Acad., Phila.; m. Fannie Agnes Ward, June 24, 1851, 3 children. Mem. Phila. Common Council, 1852-55; mem. Pa. Senate, 1858-59; served with 1st Troop of Phila., U.S. Army, 1861, promoted capt., 1863; served as provost marshall, Battle of Gettysburg; mem. U.S. Ho. of Reps. from Pa. (Democrat), 38th-51st congresses, 1863-90, speaker, 1875-81, conducted filibusters against Civil Rights and Force bills, 1875, helped institute investigations of Credit Mobilier, Sanborn contracts and Pacific Mail subsidy, chmn. com. on appropriations, reduced total appropriations by $30,000,000, 1876, codified rules of Ho. of Reps:, 1880, strengthened speaker's power; del. to Nat. Dem. Conv., 1884, responsible for non-committal tariff plank; lost control of Dem. orgn. in Pa., 1887. Died Washington, D.C., Apr. 13, 1890; buried Phila.

RANDLE, THURMAN small arms expert; b. Glen Rose, Tex., Oct. 24, 1890; s. George D. and Emma (Thurman) R.; grad. Carlisle Mil. Acad., U. Tex.; m. Betty Polvozt, Dec. 25, 1927. Dir. Nat. Rifle Assn., 1928-—, mem. exec. com., 1931-—, pres. 1944-45; officer-in-charge Navy Small Arms Program, 1942-45; pres. Texas State Rifle Assn., 1933-36; coach, Pershing trophy U.S. Internat. Team, Bisley, Eng., 1937; rifle championships, Texas, 1927-31-36-42, Oklahoma, 1931-33-37-39, California, 1933, nat. midwinter, 1933-34, eastern small bore, 1934, eastern all around, 1942; partner, gen. mgr. Thurman Randle & Co., 1934-—; commd. to organize, standardize and put into operation entire small arms tng. program USN, 1942. Dir. Small Arms Firing Sch. Nat. Matches, Camp Perry, O., 1941. Commd. lt. comdr. USN, 1942, comdr., 1944. Recipient Distinguished Marksman Medal, 1937. Mem. U.S. Dewar Internat. Rifle Team, 1926-34, capt. 1931 and 1939; R.W.S. Internat. Rifle Team, 1933; F.I.D.A.C., U.S. Internat. Rifle Team, 1929-30-31-32-34, capt., 1933; U.S. Internat. Rifle Team to British Nat. Matches, 1931, 37; mem. Am. Legion. Home: 6930 Lakewood Blvd. Office: 208 N. Akard St., Dallas. Died Feb. 1957.

RANDOLPH, GEORGE WYTHE Confederate sec. of war, army officer; b. "Monticello," Va., Mar. 10, 1815; s. Gov. Thomas Mann and Martha (Jefferson) R.; attended U. Va., 1837-39; m. Mary E. (Adams) Pope, circa 1852. Practiced law in Richmond, Va., 1849-61; organized Richmond Howitzers (arty. co.), 1861; peace commr. from Va. to U.S. Govt., 1861; secessionist to Va. Conf. of 1861; commd. col., 1861, promoted to chief of arty. under Magruder; promoted brig. general, 1862; sec. of war Confederate States Am., Mar. 22-Nov. 15, 1862. Died "Edgehill," Va., Apr. 3, 1867.

RANDOLPH, ROBERT ISHAM cons. engr.; b. Chicago, Ill., Apr. 14, 1883; s. Isham and Mary Henry (Taylor) R.; student Cornell U., 1903-04; m. Martha A. Maclean, Oct. 17, 1912. Asst. engr. Sanitary Dist. of Chicago, 1904-07, sec. Internal Improvement Commn. of Ill., 1908-11, Rivers and Lakes Commn. of Ill., 1911-13; sec. Isham Randolph & Co., 1913-21, Randolph-Perkins Co. since 1921; dir. of operations, Century of Progress Exposition, Chicago, 1932-34; chief engr. Construction Div., Office of Quartermaster General, Zone 6, Chicago, 1941. Served on Mexican border with Battery C, 1st Ill. F.A., 1916; maj. comdg. 535th Engrs., A.E.F., 1918; lt. col. comdg. 381st Engrs., O.R.C., 1923-24; colonel Gen. Staff Corps, Asst. Chief of Staff, G-4, Seattle Port of Embarkation, 1942-43. Deputy chief Chicago ordnance district, 1943-46; associate director War Assets Adminstrn., Chicago, 1946-47. Mem. Am. Soc. C.E., Western Soc. Engrs., Psi Upsilon, Citizens' Assn. (dir.), Mississippi Valley Assn. (pres., 1932-35), Chicago Assn. Commerce (pres. 1930-31). Republican. Episcopalian. Clubs: University, Engineers', Home: 1731 Santa Barbara St., Santa Barbara, Cal. Died Oct. 18, 1951.

RANDOLPH, THOMAS JEFFERSON banker, legislator; b. "Monticello," Albemarle County, Va., Sept. 11, 1792; s. Thomas Mann and Martha (Jefferson) R.; m. Jane Nicholas, 1815. Mgr., Thomas Jefferson's financial affairs, 1816-26; chief executor Jefferson's estate, 1826; mem. bd. visitors U. Va., 1829-60, rector, 7 years; mem. Va. Ho. of Dels., 1831; mem. Va. Constl. Conv., 1850-51; Secession Conv., Montgomery, Ala., 1861; commd. col. Confederate Army; chmn. Nat. Democratic Conv., 1872; mem. Albemarle Agrl. Soc.; pres. Farmers' Bank of Charlottesville (Va.). Author: Memoir, Correspondence, and Miscellanies from the Papers of Thomas Jefferson, 4 vols., 1829; Sixty Years' Reminiscences of the Currency of the United States. Died "Edgehill," Albemarle County, Oct. 7, 1875; buried "Monticello."

RANDOLPH, THOMAS MANN gov. Va., congressman; b. Tuckahoe, Va., Oct. 1, 1768; s. Thomas Mann and Anne (Cary) R.; attended Coll. William and Mary, U: Edinburgh (Scotland), 1785-88; m. Martha Jefferson (dau. Thomas Jefferson), Feb. 23, 1790, 10 children including Thomas Jefferson, George Wythe. Claimed to have originated practice of transverse rather than horizontal plowing on hillsides; mem. Va. Senate, 1793-94; mem. U.S. Ho. of Reps. from Va., 7th-9th congresses, 1803-07; col. 1st light corps of 20th U.S. Inf., 1812; mem. Va. Ho. of Dels., 1819, 20, 23-25; gov. Va., 1819-22; noted botanist. Died "Monticello," Albemarle County, Va., June 20, 1828; buried family burial ground.

RANDOLPH, WALLACE F. brig. gen. U.S.A.; b. in Pa., June 11, 1841. Pvt. Co. F, 17th Pa. Inf., Apr. 18-June 28, 1861; apptd. 2d lt. 5th U.S. Arty., May 14, 1861; 1st lt., Mar. 1862; capt., July 1866; maj. 3d Arty., Apr. 1888; lt. col., Mar. 1898; col. 1st Arty., Oct. 19, 1899; chief of arty. U.S.A., Apr. 9, 1901; chief of arty. with rank of brig. gen., Feb. 27, 1903; maj. gen., Jan. 22, 1904; retired, Jan. 23, 1904. Served in many battles of Civil War; bvtd. capt., June 1863, "for gallantry in defense of Winchester, Va.," and maj., Mar. 1865, "for good conduct and meritorious service during the war"; commd. brig. gen. U.S.V., May 1898; mustered out of vol. service, Nov. 1898. Home: Washington, D.C. Died 1910.

RANDOLPH, WILLIAM MANN M.D.; b. Albemarle County, Va., Jan. 14, 1870; s. William L. and Agnes (Dillon) R.; M.D., U. of Va., 1890; grad. study N.Y. Post Grad. Hosp., 1890-92, Vanderbilt Clinic, New York, 1890; m. Mary Walker, Oct. 20, 1894; children—Carolina R., Sarah Nicholas, Agnes Dillon, Thomas J., Mary Walker, Hollins N., Francis M. Practiced Charlottesville, Va., 1892-1913, and since 1930; prof. gynecology and surgery, U. of Va., 1905; surgeon Phelps-Dodge Corp., Douglas, Ariz., 1913-18, Central Copper Co., Mascot, Ariz., 1924-28; clinician and specialist in tuberculosis, Va. State Dept. of Health, since 1930, holding "traveling clinics" to reach effectively country dists. Capt. Troop K, Albemarle Light Horse, 1892-97; maj. Med. Service, 17th Inf., Va. Vols., 1898-1904, commd. capt. M.C., 1917; chief of med. service and comdg. officer hospital, Camp Harry J. Jones, Douglas, Ariz., 1918; maj. M.C., 1918, surgeon Ariz. dist. Mem. bd. visitors U. of Va., 1912; mem. sch. bd., Tombstone, Ariz., 1918, Dem. County Com., 1924. Democrat. Episcopalian. Address: State Dept. of Health, Richmond, Va.* Died Jan. 25, 1944.

RANEY, WILLIAM EUGENE editor; b. Chgo., Jan. 9, 1916; s. Joseph Ira and Mabel (Knaggs) R.; student pub. schs. Exec. editor Rinehart & Co., 1946-50; exec. editor Henry Holt & Co., 1950-52, editor-in-chief, 1952-54; sr. editor E.P. Dutton & Co., Inc., N.Y.C. 1954-56; editor McGraw-Hill Book Co., Inc., 1956; exec. editor Rinehart & Co., 1957-60; editor-in-chief McDowell-Obolensky, 1960, v.p., dir., 1961; editor-in-chief Bobbs-Merrill Co., Inc., 1962-64; faculty Bread Loan (Vt.) Writer's Conf., 1949, 50, 56, 57. Served in U.S. Army, 1941-45, staff sgt. Home: 6 W. 9th St., N.Y.C. Died Oct. 1, 1964.

RANGER, RICHARD H(OWLAND) electronic mfr.; b. Indianapolis, Ind., June 13, 1889; s. Rev. John Hilliard and Emily Anthen (Gillet) R.; B.S., Mass. Inst. Tech., 1911; post war course Ecole Superievre de l'Electricite, Paris, 1919; m. Laura Anne Lewis, Nov. 27, 1923; children—Mary Wheatley (Mrs. John L. Scripp). Prop. Ranger Co., printers, Boston, 1911-17; design engr. Radio Corp. of Am., New York, N.Y., 1920-30; pres. Rangertone, Inc., Newark, N.J., since 1930. Served as 2d lt., F.A., U.S. Army, World War I; as capt. signal corps in France, 1918-19, in charge signal corps labs., Fort Monmouth, 1919-20; in signal corps in charge radar and communication field lab. for Air Corps, Orlando, Fla., 1942, tech. exec. signal corps Standards Agency, Red Bank, 1943; on tech. intelligence missions to Europe, 1944-46; disch. as col. Fellow Inst. Radio Engrs., Royal Soc. (London), Am. Institute Elec. Engrs., Audio Engring. Soc., Soc. Motion Picture Engineers; mem. Am. Guild of Organists, Acoustical Society, Optical Society, Franklin Institute, Phi Beta Epsilon. Republican. Episcopalian. Clubs: M.I.T., Downtown, Sapphire (New York); M.I.T. of Northern New Jersey, Downtown, Forest Hill Literary (Newark). Inventor: transoceanic radio facsimile, 1924; electronic organ, 1932; electronic chimes, 1933; radar developments, 1938-44; airbourne radio relay, 1942; magnetic recording, 1947; synchronized tape and motion pictures (received Oscar award, 1956, Samuel L. Warner award, 1957, in recognition of this invention), stereo-dimensional sound for legitimate theatres, 1958. Author: Artillery Lines of Information, 1918; Radio Pathfinder, 1922; Fighter Control Communications, 1943. Established transoceanic radio pictures transmission, 1924. Home: 574 Parker St., Newark 4. Office: 73 Winthrop St., Newark 4. Died Jan. 10, 1962.

RANKIN, FRED WHARTON surgeon; b. Mooresville, N.C., Dec. 20, 1886; s. Watson Wharton and Margaret (Houston) R.; A.B., Davidson Coll., 1905; M.D., U. of Md., 1909; A.M., St. John's Coll., 1913; hon. Sc.D., Davidson Coll., 1937, U. of Md., 1939, U. of Ky., 1942; LL.D., Temple U., 1943, Northwestern U., 1943; Sc.D., U. of Louisville, 1947; m. Edith Mayo, June 12, 1923; children—Fred Wharton, Edith Graham, Charles Mayo, Thomas Alexander. Resident surgeon Univ. Hosp., Baltimore, 1909-12; asst. demonstrator anatomy and asso. in surgery, Univ. of Md. Med. Sch., 1913-16; asst. surgeon St. Mary's Hosp., Mayo Clinic, Rochester, 1916-22; prof. surgery, U. of Louisville, 1922-23; served as asso. prof. surgery, U. of Minn. Med. Sch., Mayo Foundation; surgeon to Mayo Clinic, 1926-33; surgeon to St. Joseph Hospital, Lexington, Ky., since Jan. 1, 1934; clinical prof. of surg., U. of Louisville, since 1941. Pres. Interstate Postgrad. Assembly, 1943. Served as maj. Medical Corps, U.S. Army, 17 mos., World War; attached to 1st A.C., 4th and 26th divisions, in France; commanding officer Base Hospital No. 26; col. Med. Reserve, U.S. Army; chief cons. surg. U.S. Army, rank brig. gen. Awarded Victory Ribbon, World War I; Distinguished Service Medal, Victory Ribbon, E.T.O. Ribbon, Asiatic-Pacific Ribbon, Am. Defense and Am. Theatre Ribbons; Cross, Chevalier Legion of Honor, World War II. Fellow Am. Coll. Surgeons, Am. Surg. Assn. (pres. 1948-49), A.M.A. (pres. 1942), Am. Proctologic Soc. (hon.), Southern Surg. Assn. (past pres.); fellow Internat.

Société Chirurgie; mem. Eastern Surg. Assn., Western Surg. Assn., Southern Med. Assn., Southeastern Surg. Congress (past pres.), Minn. and Ky. medical societies, Southern Minnesota Medical Society, Society of Clinical Surgery, Visiting Surgeons Club, Beta Theta Pi, Phi Chi, Phi Beta Kappa, Sigma Xi, Alpha Omega Alpha; founder mem. Am. Bd. Surgery. Democrat. Episcopalian. Clubs: Army-Navy, Idle Hour Country, Filson. Author: (monograph) Surgery of the Colon. Co-Author: (with J.A. Bargen and L.A. Buie) The Colon, Rectum and Anus, 1932; (with A.S. Graham) Cancer of the Colon and Rectum, 1939. Contbr. chapter in Lewis' Surgery entitled "Malformations of the Colon"; chapter Sajous Med. Cyclo. "Surgery of the Colon"; chapters "Carcinoma of the Rectum," "Carcinoma of the Colon" in Christopher's A Textbook of Surgery; also numerous papers on operative and clin. surgery. Home: Cave Hill Farm. Office: Security Trust Bldg., Lexington, Ky. Died May 22, 1954.

RANKIN, JOSEPH congressman; b. Passaic, N.J., Sept. 25, 1833; had academic course. Moved to Mishicott, Manitowoc County, Wis., 1854, became mcht.; mem. Manitowoc County Bd., 1859; mem. Wis. Assembly, 1860, 71-74; enlisted in Union Army in Civil War, 1862, chosen capt. Company D, 26th Regt., Wis. Volunteer Infantry; settled in Manitowoc, Wis., after war; clk. City of Manitowoc, 1866-71; mem. Wis. Senate, 1877-82; mem. U.S. Ho. of Reps. (Democrat) from Wis., 48th-49th congresses, 1883-86. Died Washington, D.C., Jan. 24, 1886; buried Evergreen Cemetery, Manitowoc.

RANNO, FREDERICK SEBASTIAN hosp. adminstr., physician; b. N.Y.C., June 5, 1910; s. Sebastian and Frances (Pedivillano) R.; student L.I.U., 1931; M.D., U. Naples (Italy), 1936; m. Rose Altieri, Nov. 26, 1937; children—Joy (Mrs. George Robert Dion), Arlene (Mrs. Dennis R. Nolan). Intern Columbus Hosp., N.Y.C.; resident N.Y. Colony Hosp., Staten Island; with VA, 1940-—; adminstr. VA Hosp., Marion, Ind., 1961-65, VA Hosp., Pitts., 1965-—. Served to maj., M.C., AUS, World War II. Mem. Am. Coll. Chest Physicians, Mil. Surgeons U.S., Nat. Tb Assn., N.Y. State, Ontario County med. socs., Am. Trudeau Soc., A.M.A., Am. Psychiat. Assn., N.Y. State, Finger Lake neuropsychiat. assns. Kiwanian. Address: Veterans Administration Hosp., Pitts. Died July 21, 1965.

RANSOM, GEORGE BRINKERHOFF rear admiral U.S.N.; b. Chazy, N.Y., June 28, 1851; s. Harry Sawyer and Martha (Bosworth) R.; Oswego (N.Y.) Normal and Training Sch., 1869; grad. U.S. Naval Acad., 1874 (2d in class); B.C.E., U. of Wis., 1891; LL.B., Suffolk Law Sch., Boston, 1917; m. Sarah Upham, Sept. 15, 1880 (died 1912); m. 2d, Ruth Barber, Sept. 4, 1917. Commd. asst. engr. U.S.N., 1875; passed asst. engr., 1880; chief engr., 1895; comdr., 1904; capt., 1907; rear admiral, 1911; retired June 28, 1913. Chief engr. U.S.S. Concord, May 1, 1898, participating in battle of Manila Bay. Instr. in steam engring. Naval Acad., 3 yrs., and at U. of Wis., 3 yrs. Home: Plattsburg, Clinton County, N.Y. Died Feb. 25. 1924.

RANSOM, MATHEW WHITAKER U.S. senator; b. Warren County, N.C., Oct. 8, 1826; atty. gen. N.C., 1852; mem. N.C. legislature, 1858-60; peace commr. from N.C. to Congress of Southern States, Montgomery, Ala., 1861; served lt. col. to maj. gen. C.S.A., 1861-65; U.S. senator, 1872-95; U.S. minister to Mexico, 1895-97. Address: Weldon, N.C. Died 1904.

RANSOM, RONALD vice chairman board of governors Federal Reserve System; b. Columbia, S.C., Jan. 21, 1882; s. Luther A. and Elizabeth Chaffin (Cocke) R.; LL.B., U. of Georgia, 1903; married Mary Brent, d. of Hon. Hoke Smith, of Atlanta, Dec. 19, 1908; 1 dau., Barbara (Mrs. Keith Jopson). Admitted to Ga. bar, 1903, and practiced at Atlanta until 1922; v.p. Fulton Nat. Bank of Atlanta, 1922-33, exec. v.p., 1933-36; mem. Bd. of Governors of Federal Reserve System since Feb. 1, 1936, vice chmn. since Aug. 6, 1936. Dir. in charge bur. of personnel for foreign service, southern div. Am. Red Cross, 1918; served as 1st lt. Chem. Warfare Service, U.S. Army, 1918. Pres. Atlanta Clearing House Assn., 1929; mem. Special Relief Com., Atlanta, 1932-33; chmn. Ga. Relief Commn., 1933. Mem. Am. Bankers Assn. (chmn. bank management commn., 1932-34, chmn. bankers NRA com., 1933-34, chmn. com. on federal legislation 1934-35, mem. com. on banking studies, mem. spl. com. on the Banking Act of 1935), Ga. Bankers Assn. (pres. 1931-32), Sigma Alpha Epsilon, Beta Gamma Sigma. Democrat. Episcopalian. Home: 2311 Connecticut Av. N.W., Washington 8. Office: Federal Reserve Bldg., Washington 25. Died Dec. 2, 1947.

RANSOM, THOMAS EDWARD GREENFIELD army officer; b. Norwich, Vt., Nov. 29, 1834; s. Truman Bishop and Margaret Morrison (Greenfield) Ransome; completed civil engring. course Norwich U., 1851. Raised a company which was incorporated into 11th Ill. Inf., 1861; maj., then lt. col. in command of a regt.; volunteer aide in surprise of Confederate Army at Charleston, 1861; col., serving at Newbern, Beaufort, Goldsboro, Kingston (all N.C.), 1861-62; brig. gen. in command of a brigade in Vicksburg campaign, 1863; in charge expdn. against Natchez, Miss., 1863; joined Tex. expdn., 1863; conducted successful operations along the Gulf Coast; commanded XIII Corps, U.S. Army, 1864; assigned to command XVI Corps, 1864, participated in siege of Atlanta (Ga.); brevetted maj. gen. U.S. Volunteers, 1864, assigned to command XVII Corps; fought at Ft. Donelson, Shiloh, Corinth. Died nr. Rome, Ga., Oct. 29, 1864; buried Rosehill Cemetery, Chgo.

RAPPORT, DAVID, physiologist; b. Pitts., Aug. 29, 1891; s. John and Fannie (Binder) R.; A.B., Harvard, 1912, M.D., 1916; m. Jean DeWilde Simpson, June 18, 1931; children—Elizabeth, Nancy. Austin teaching fellow in physiology, Harvard, 1919, instr., 1920-21; research fellow, Cornell Med. Sch., 1921-24; instr. and sr. instr., Western Res. Med. Sch., 1925-29; prof. physiology, Tufts U. Med. Sch., 1929-70. Served as 1st lt. med. corps, A.E.F., 1917-19. Fellow Am. Acad. Arts and Sciences, A.A.A.S.; mem. Am. Physiol. Soc., Soc. Exptl. Biology and Medicine, Radiation Research Soc., Alpha Omega Alpha, Sigma Xi. Clubs: Harvard (Boston), Faculty (Cambridge). Contbr. articles on circulation, metabolism, endocrines, cellular respiration. Home: Cambridge MA Died Oct. 1970.

RASMUSSEN, OTHO MILLS educator; b. Irving, Kan., May 3, 1913; s. Ernest Otho and Hazel Susan (Mills) R.; B.S., A.B., Kan. State Tchrs. Coll., 1938, M.S., 1940; Ph.D., U. Kan., 1952; m. Charlotte Louise Emmingham, June 25, 1939; children—Sandra Ann, Laura Louise. Tchr. rural schs. Marshall County, Kan., 1931-35; research asst. bur. ednl. measurements Kan. State Tchrs. Coll., 1938-41; prin. Hoyt (Kan.) High Sch., 1941-42; instr. mathematics U. Kan., 1945-52; asst. prof. mathematics U. Denver, 1952-—, chmn. dept., 1953-—; asso. Denver Research Inst., 1955-—. Chmn. bd. Meth. Student Found., Denver, 1955-—. Lt. comdr. USNR. Mem. Am. Math. Soc., Math. Assn. Am., Nat., Colo. councils tchrs. mathematics, Am. Assn. U. Profs., Kan. Assn. Tchrs. Mathematics, Kappa Mu Epsilon, Pi Mu Epsilon, Phi Delta Kappa, Lambda Delta Lambda. Author ednl. and mathematics tests. Home: 2476 S. Madison St., Denver 10. Died June 20, 1958.

RASSIEUR, LEO judge; b. Wadern, Russia, Apr. 19, 1844; s. Theodore and Margaret (Klauck) R.; came to U.S. in early childhood; grad. St. Louis Central High Sch., 1860; LL.D., McKendree Coll.; m. Mary C. Kammerer, July 9, 1872; children—Mrs. Estelle Kelsey, Leo, Mrs. Cora Parsons. Served pvt. to maj. in Mo. vols., Union Army, 1861-65; taught in pub. schs., St. Louis, 1866-67; admitted to bar, Apr. 1, 1867, at St. Louis; atty. sch. bd. by election, 1880-90; judge Probate Court, St. Louis, 1895-99, declining renomination; resumed law practice. Comdr.-in-chief G.A.R., 1900-01; pres. Mo. Vicksburg. Nat. Mil. Park Commn., 1911-17. Republican. Home: St. Louis, Mo. Died June 1, 1929.

RATHBONE, JARED LAWRENCE capitalist, soldier; b. Albany, N.Y., Sept. 28, 1844; s. Jared Lewis and Pauline N. (Pinney) R.; stepson of U.S. Senator Ira Harris; prep. edn. Phillips Acad., Andover, Mass., and Rensselaer Poly. Inst.; grad. West Point, 1865; entered 12th inf. and was transferred 1st U.S. arty.; a.d.c. to Lt. Gen. Schofield, 1866-73; resigned from army, 1873; m. Miss M. A. Atherton, Feb. 20, 1871. Developed the noted Palo Alto ranch, on which Leland Stanford Jr. U. is now located; apptd. consul gen. of the U.S. to Paris, France, 1887-91; served in war with Spain as spl. aide at hdqrs. div. of the Pacific, on staffs Gen. Merriam, Wesley, Merritt and Otis. Decorated by French govt. as Officer Legion of Honor, for spl. and brilliant services rendered to France. Address: New York, N.Y. Died 1907.

RATHBONE, JOHN FINLEY mfr.; b. Albany, N.Y., Oct. 12, 1819; ed. Albany Acad. and Collegiate Inst., Brockport, N.Y.; built, 1845, at Albany, a stove foundry which was later the largest in the world; brig. gen. comdg. 9th brigade N.Y. Nat. Guard, 1861-67; at beginning of war was commandant Albany depot of vols.; sent 34 regts. to front; adj. gen. with rank of maj. gen. under Gov. Dix's administration; one of founders Albany Orphan Asylum; gave $40,000 to build Rathbone Library, U. of Rochester. Pres. Dudley Observatory, Mutual Fire Ins. Co. of Albany. and Albany Orphans' Asylum. Address: Albany, N.Y. Deceased.

RATHBORNE, J(OSEPH) CORNELIUS business exec.; b. Harvey, La., June 17, 1909; s. Joseph Cornelius and Georgie (Winship) R.; student Aiken (S.C.) Prep. Sch., 1919-23; St. Pauls Sch., Concord, N.H., 1923-27; A.B., Yale, 1931; m. Nancy Nelson Huidekoper, Nov. 23, 1935 (dec. 1953); children—Joseph Cornelius, Prescott Huidekoper, Nancy Ernestine; m. 2d, Beatrice Trostel Weicker, Feb. 20, 1954. Head expdn. on Yale U. Peabody Mus. to Kenya, East Africa, 1931; clerk in credits and security analysis, N.Y. Trust Co., 1933-37; asst. to partners in pvt. banking firm of H.E. Talbott & Co., 1937-40; pres. Joseph Rathborne Land Co., Harvey, La., 1938-—; dir. Nat. Bank of Commerce in New Orleans, Oil Royalties Asso., Times Picayune Pub. Co. Dir. Fair Ground Corp., New Orleans, 1947, C. of C. New Orleans Area, 1951, New Orleans Community Chest, 1951, La. Forestry Association, 1952-53. Served as 1st lt. to maj., A.A.F., 1942-45; overseas E.T.O., with 8th Fighter Comd. Hdqrs. 16 mos. Awarded Bronze star medal. Mem. squad U.S. Polo Team vs. England, 1930, Internat. games vs. Argentina, 1932. Mem. Nat. Small Bus. Mens Assn., Yale Alumni Assn. of La. (vice pres.; regional mem. for La. and Ark. Yale Univ. development com.), Delta Kappa Epsilon. Roman Catholic. Clubs: Boston (New Orleans); Links, Racquet and Tennis, Yale, Meadowbrook (New York). Home: Harvey, Jefferson Parish, La. Died July 21, 1954.

RATHJE, FRANK C. banker; b. Bloomingdale, Ill., Aug. 20, 1882; s. William and Louise (Ehlers) R.; ed. St. John's Mil. Acad., Delafield, Wis.; Armour Inst., Chgo.; LL.D., Northwestern U., 1907, D.Bus. Administrn., 1946; LL.D., Monmouth (Ill.) Coll., 1946; m. Josephine Logan, Oct. 16, 1915; children—Theron L., Josephine, Frank C. Shirley. Admitted to bar, 1907; mem. firm Rathje, Kulp, Sabel & Sullivan; pres. Mut. Nat. Bank of Chgo., 1918-54, chmn. bd., 1954-—; pres. Chgo. City Bank & Trust Co., 1926-—. Chmn. Navy Renegotiation Bd. for 9th Naval Dist., Chgo. office, 1942-43; v. chmn. Chgo. Plan Commn. Mem. Chgo. Assn. Commerce, Ill. State C. of C. (bd. dirs.), Transp. Assn. Am. (pres. 1950-52), Chgo. Financial Writer's Assn., Am. (pres. 1946), Ill. (pres. 1936-37) bankers assns., Am. Inst. Banking, Assn. Res. City Bankers. Clubs: Union League (pres. 1947-49), Chicago, Lake Shore, South Shore Country, Executives, Camp Fire (Chgo.); Elmhurst Country; Brookwood Country; Saddle and Sirloin. Home: 860 Lake Shore Dr., Chgo. 11. Office: 815 W. 63d St., Chgo. 21. Died Feb. 1967.

RATTELMAN, WILLIAM ADAM ins. exec.; b. Pitts., Sept. 17, 1893; s. William Henry and Mathilda (Weidman) R.; student Columbia (nights), U. Pitts. (nights); m. Ann O'Brien, Oct. 20, 1919; 1 dau., Caroline (Mrs. David H. Esperson); m. 2d Rita Kastner, Oct. 20, 1939. Pres. Nat. Union Fire Ins. Co. since 1951, dir. since 1949; pres. Birmingham Insurance Company, 1951-—, National Union Indemnity Company, 1951-—. Served with the infantry, A.E.F., France, Army of Occupation, Germany, Mexican Border, 1916-19; disch. as maj. Clubs: Duquesne, Oakmont Country, Athletic Assn. (Pitts.). Home: 724 S. Negley Av. Office: 139 University Pl., Pitts. Died July 3, 1956.

RAUCH, RUDOLPH STEWART, business exec.; born N.Y. City, Feb. 21, 1892; s. William and Susan Spring (Paton) R.; student St. Pauls Sch., Concord, N.H., 1903-09; Litt.B., Princeton, 1913; m. Mary Banks French, Oct. 11, 1913; children—Rudolph Stewart, Mary Paton (Mrs. Henry B. Roberts), Thomas Morton. Pres. Winchester Simmons Co., Phila., 1922-24; vice pres. Phila. Rubber Works Co., 1924-29; dir. B. F. Goodrich Co. from 1932, mem. exec. com., 1935-60; pres. North Bros. Mfg. Co., 1939-46. Trustee St. Pauls Sch., 1933-36; mem. indsl. adv. bd., Nat. Recovery Adminstrn., 1934-35; member of board of trustees Trudeau Sanatorium; 1947-52; and manager of the Overbrook School for the Blind. Served as capt., U.S. Army, 1917-19. Mem. Soc. of the Cincinnati, Vets. Foreign Wars. Episcopalian. Clubs: Philadelphia; Racquet and Tennis (N.Y. City). Home: Villa Nova PA Died Oct. 13, 1971.

RAUDENBUSH, GEORGE KING (rou'den-bush), conductor and composer; b. Jersey Shore, Pa., Mar. 13, 1899; s. Henry William and Creacie Cordelia (Bower) R.; student Detroit Conservatory of Music, 1908-09, New Eng. Conservatory of Music, 1912-13, Am. Inst. of Applied Music, N.Y.C., 1914-17; studied violin with Arnold Volpe, Henry Schradedick, Theodore Spiering, Eugene Ysaye; studied composition with R. Huntingdon Woodman, Mortimer Wilson, etc.; fellow in composition MacDowell Colony, 1934; m. Marguerite Wernimont (stage name, Marion Wells). Began as concert violinist at age 11, N.Y.C., 1910; asst. tchr. violin to Henry Schraedick, Am. Inst. Applied Music, 1915-17, to Theodore Spiering, 1919-21; concert tour, West Coast, 1921; made debut recital Aeolian Hall, N.Y.C., 1922; on concert tour and studying, Germany, 1922-23; mem. City Symphony Orchestra, N.Y.C., 1923; asst. concertmaster, German Opera, N.Y.C., 1923; 1st violinist N.Y. Symphony, 1923-29; asst. music dir. with Elliott Schenck, Theatre Guild, and Walter Hampden Repertoire Co., N.Y.C., 1922-29; asst. condr. Fairbanks-Pickford Studios, Special Features, N.Y.C. and Boston, 1928-29; asst. concertmaster NBC Orchestra with Walter Damrosch on Gen. Motors Hour, Packard Hour, Music Appreciation Hour, 1929-34; concertmaster Barrere Little Symphony, 1929-31, Chatauqua (N.Y.) Opera Co., 1930-31, Worcester Festival, Spartenburg Festival, Harrisburg Mozart Festival and others, 1928-31, founder, 1929, and condr., 1929-50 of Harrisburg (Pa.) Symphony Orchestra; founder York (Pa.) Symphony Orchestra, 1933-34; founder and musical dir. Harrisburg Symphony Choir, 1938; founder, 1939, and conductor, 1939-43 of Toledo Symphony Orchestra; condr. N.Y. Philharmonic Symphony Orchestra, Lewisohn Stadium, N.Y.C., 1937, guest condr. Phila. Orchestra, 1938, 39, 44; musical dir. Piedmont Music Festival, Winston Salem, N.C., 1943-47; musical dir. Music Festival Assn. of Central Pa., 1945-47; guest condr. Nat. Symphony Orchestra, Washington, 1946; engaged in research and musical composition, 1950-53. Served as regtl. sgt. maj. 16th, 57th and 80th Inf., U.S. Army, 1917-19. Mem. MacDowell Colony Assn., Am. Fedn. of Musicians, Am. League of Composers and Conductors. Composer many unpub. orchestral, choral and chamber music works. Died May 26, 1956.

RAUM, GREEN BERRY lawyer; b. Golconda, Ill., Dec. 3, 1829; s. John and Juliet C. R.; ed. common schs.; m. Maria Field, Oct. 16, 1851. Admitted Ill. bar, 1853; later Supreme Court U.S.; mem. Nat. Dem. Conv., and supported Douglas for President, 1860. After fall of Ft. Sumter made 1st war speech in Southern Ill.; entered Union army, 1861, as maj. 56th Ill. vols.; promoted through successive grades to brig. gen.; ordered and led a successful bayonet charge at Corinth, Oct. 4, 1862; served under Grant and Sherman; severely wounded at Missionary Ridge; in Atlanta campaign held line of R.R. in rear of Sherman's army; discovered and defeated Gen. Wheeler's raid; reinforced Resaca at night and held it against Gen. Hood. In March to the Sea; had command under Gen. Hancock in Shenandoah Valley at close of war. Congressman, 1867-69; U.S. commr. internal revenue, 1876-83; commr. of pensions, 1889-93. Republican. Author: The Existing Conflict, 1884; History of Illinois Republicanism, 1900; also 7 official reports as commr. internal revenue: 1877-82, inclusive, and 4 as commr. pensions, 1889-92. Address: Chicago, Ill. Died 1909.

RAVDIN, ISIDOR SCHWANER, phys. and surg.; b. Evansville, Ind., Oct. 10, 1894; s. Marcus and Wilhelmina (Jacobson) R.; B.S., Ind. U., 1916; M.D., U. Pa., 1918; L.H.D. (hon.); LL.D., Sc.D.; m. Elizabeth Glenn, June 2, 1921; children—Robert Glenn (dec. 1972), Elizabeth, William Dickie. Intern U. Pa. Hosp., 1918-19, chief resident phys., 1919-20; instr. surgery U. Pa., 1920, asso. in surgery, 1922-27, asst. prof. surg. research, 1927, prof., 1928-35, Harrison prof. surgery, 1935-45, John Rhea Barton prof. surgery, 1944-59, dir. Harrison Dept. Surg. Research, 1944-59, prof. surgery, v.p. for med. affairs University Pennsylvania, 1959-65, vice chmn. medical devel., from 1965; surgeon in chief U. Pa. Hosp., 1945-59. Dir. Mead Johnson & Co., 1962-68. Pres. American Cancer Society, 1962-63; mem. Nat. Adv. Health Council; alternate mem. Civilian Advisory Council to Sec. of Def.; sr. civilian cons. surgeon Surgeon Gen. of the Army. Chmn. clin. studies panel Cancer Chemotherapy Nat. Service Center, Nat. Insts. Health. Member board of trustees Phila. Mus. Art, Rosenbach Mus. Phila. Served as brig. gen. M.C., AUS, 1942-45; maj. gen. ret. Decorated Legion of Merit with oak leaf cluster; Olaf of Acrel medal (Sweden); recipient Phila. award. Diplomate of American Board of Surgery. Hon. fellow England, Scotland, Canada royal colls. surgeons; mem. Internat. Fedn. Surg. Colleges and Societies (vice president), Am. Surgical Association (pres. 1958-59), A.C.S. (pres. 1960), International Blood Transfusion Soc. (past president), Pan-Pacific Surg. Assn. (ex-pres.), Phila. Acad. Surgery (ex-pres.), Am. Assn. Surgery Trauma, A.M.A., Am. Soc. Exptl. Pathology, Societe Internat. de Chirurgie, Internat. Soc. Surgery, Am. Physiol. Soc. Editor: Kirschner Surgery (3 vols.), 1932-36. Home: Philadelphia PA Died Aug. 27, 1972; buried West Laurel Hill Cemetery

RAVEL, VINCENT MARVIN, physician; b. El Paso, Tex., Jan. 22, 1914; s. Joseph B. and Theresa (Hurwitz) R.; M.D., Baylor U., 1937; postgrad. U. Pa., 1945-46; m. Annette Kluger, Mar. 30, 1941; children—Rita L., Jerrold M., Benita, Elsie F. Intern, R. E. Thomason Gen. Hosp., El Paso; resident Albert Einstein Hosps.; dir. dept. radiology Providence Meml. Hosp., El Paso, R.E. Thomas Gen. Hosp., 1952-69; sr. El Paso Radiol. Group, 1960-69. Vice pres. El Paso Symphony Orch. Assn.; vice chmn. Liberty Hall and Coliseum Bd., 1962; pres. Jewish Community Council. Served to comdr. USNR, 1940-46. Diplomate Am. Bd. Radiology. Fellow Am. Coll. Angiology, A.A.A.S., Am. Coll. Radiology, Acad. Internat. Medicine, Am., Tex. med. assns., Radiol. Soc. N.Am., Soc. Nuclear Medicine. Mem. B'nai B'rith. Clubs: Coronado Country, El Paso. Contbr. articles profl. jours. Home: El Paso TX Died Feb. 13, 1969.

RAWLES, JACOB BEEKMAN brig. gen. U.S.A.; b. Romeo, Mich., Aug. 4, 1839; s. Aaron B. and Elizabeth (Beekman) R.; grad. U.S. Mil. Acad., 1861; m. Phoebe A. Garretson, Mar. 20, 1862. Second lt. 3d Arty., May 6, 1861; 1st lt. 5th Arty., May 14, 1861; capt., July 28, 1866; maj. 4th Arty., Aug. 10, 1877; lt. col. 1st Arty., Apr. 30, 1897; col. 3d Arty., Feb. 23, 1899; brig. gen. U.S.A., Apr. 14, 1903; retired, Apr. 15, 1903. Served first on recruiting service, then in Dept. of Gulf and on Red River Campaign from Dec. 1862, to Aug. 1864, after that in 5th Arty., Army of the Potomac, to end of war; took part in first attack on Port Hudson, La. (bvtd. capt.), and in final siege on same, in battle of Sabine Cross Roads, in operations around Mobile Bay and siege of Ft. Morgan, and in operations and battles of the 5th Corps in Va., after Aug. 1864; bvtd. maj. Apr. 9, 1865. In command Angel Island, Calif., 1899-1900, comd. Presidio of San Francisco, 1900-03. Address: San Francisco, Calif. Died July 1, 1919.

RAWLINGS, NORBORNE L., naval officer, corp. exec.; born Lawrenceville, Va., June 18, 1894; s. James and Jane Gee (Meredith) R.; B.S., U.S. Naval Acad., 1917; M.S., Mass. Inst. Tech., 1921; m. Lucy Dabney Hix, June 8, 1921; children—Dabney Hix (Mrs. J. L. Holloway III), Norborne. Commd. ensign U.S.N., 1917 and advanced through grades to rear admiral, Feb. 22, 1943; naval architect, June 1921; served on U.S. Destroyer based on Queenstown, Ireland, World War I; head of shipbuilding div. Bur. of Ships, Navy Dept., Washington, D.C., 1939-42; in command of U.S. Naval Drydocks, in charge of constrn. and expansion of ship repair yard and operations, Hunters Point, San Francisco, 1943-45; work in navy related to designing, constrn., and maintenance of naval vessels and operation of naval shipyards; vice chief, material div. office asst. sec. of Navy, Navy Department, Washington, until retirement, 1947; spl. rep. Newport News Shipbuilding and Dry Dock Co., 1947-49, asst. gen. mgr., 1949-50, gen. mgr., from 1950, v.p., 1952-53, exec. v.p., 1953-60, v.p. nuclear power activities, 1960, ret., then dir., chmn. exec. com. Recipient 2 Legion of Merit awards. Mem. U.S. Naval Inst., Soc. Naval Architects, Marine Engrs., Soc. Naval Engrs. Clubs: James River Country; India House, University (N.Y.C.). Presbyn. Home: Newport News VA Died May 2, 1972; buried Arlington Nat. Cemetery, Arlington VA

RAWLINS, GEORGE HERNDON lawyer; b. Solomonville, Ariz., Mar. 4, 1901; s. Charles L. and Jennie V. (Kelly) R.; student Va. Mil. Inst., 1918-19, Northwestern U., 1919-20; A.B., Leland Stanford U., 1923; m. Louise Lansden, Dec. 23, 1923 (dec.); children—Harriet V. (Mrs. Navor Proctor), Alice Louise (Mrs. Arthur N. Talbot); m. 2d, Thelma Rabb Collier, June 1, 1937. Admitted to Ariz. bar, 1924, Cal. bar, 1928; practice of law, Globe, Ariz., 1924-32, Phoenix, 1932-—, sr. mem. Rawlins, Davis, Ellis, Burrus & Kiewit. Adv. bd. Colorado River Tribes. Dir. Producers Cotton Oil Agrl. Found. Served as maj. USAAF, 1942-45. Mem. Am. Bar Assn. Home: Phoenix Towers, 2201 N. Central Av. Office: Security Bldg., Phoenix. Died Feb. 26, 1963; buried Greenwood Meml. Park.

RAWLINS, JOHN AARON army officer, U.S. sec. of war; b. Galena, Ill., Feb. 13, 1831; s. James Dawson and Lovisa (Collier) R.; attended Rock River Sem., Mt. Morris, Ill.; m. Emily Smith, June 5, 1856; m. 2d, Mary Hurlburt, Dec. 23, 1863; 3 children. Admitted to Ill. bar, 1854; city atty., Galena, 1857; participated in orgn. 45th Ill. Inf., became maj., 1861; aide de camp to Gen. Grant; lt., Aug. 1861; capt., asst. adj. gen. U.S. Volunteers as mem. Grant's staff, Aug. 30, 1861; verified, edited, finalized Grant's papers; promoted maj., then lt. col., 1862, brig. gen. U.S. Volunteers, 1863; brig. gen., chief of staff Army, 1865; promoted maj. gen. U.S. Army, 1865; U.S. sec. of war, 1869. Died Washington, D.C., Sept. 6, 1869.

RAWSON, EDWARD KIRK professor U.S.N.; b. Albany, N.Y., Feb. 21, 1846; s. Rev. Thomas R. and Louise W. (Dawes) R.; A.B., Yale, 1868; grad. Andover Theol. Sem., 1872; ordained Congregational ministry, 1872; m., Phila., Eleanor Wade, Apr. 10, 1888 (now deceased). Chaplain U.S.N., 1871-90, U.S. Naval Acad., 1886-90; head dept. ethics and English studies at Naval Acad., 1888-90; supt. Naval War Records, 1897-1902; head dept. English and law, U.S. Naval Acad., 1902-07; retired on account of age, Feb. 21, 1908. Author: Twenty Famous Naval Battles, Salamsi to Santiago, 1899. Contbr. to reviews and mags. Home: 2137 LeRoy Pl. N.W., Washington, D.C.

RAY, ARTHUR BENNING chemist; b. Leaksville, N.C., Sept. 12, 1889; s. Bryant Wesley and Helen (Betts) R.; A.B., Wake Forest (N.C.) Coll., 1910, M.A., 1911; Ph.D., Cornell U., 1916; m. Deolice Hickman, June 21, 1919; children—Margaret Benning, Joan Rutledge. Asso. prof. Industrial Chemistry, Texas A. & M. Coll., 1916-17; chemist, Nat. Carbon Co., Inc., New York, N.Y., 1919-34; sales engr. and exec., Carbide and Carbon Chem. Corp., New York, N.Y., since 1934. Capt., C.W.S., U.S. Army, 1917-19; member National Technol. Advisory Com. Mem. Am. Chem. Soc., Am. Inst. Chem. Engrs. Club: Chemists. Author technol. monographs. Home: 104 Summit Rd., Port Washington, N.Y. Office: 30 E. 42d St., N.Y.C. Died Dec. 24, 1951.

RAY, DAVID HEYDORN engr.; b. N.Y.C., July 14, 1878; s. Martin Hasset and Caroline (Heydorn) R.; A.B., Coll. City N.Y., 1897; B.S., Columbia, 1901, A.M., 1902; C.E., N.Y. U., 1902, Sc.D., 1908; studied abroad, 1898, 1905, 1908; m. Sara Beecher, June 25, 1908 (did Apr. 17, 1940); 1 son, S. David Tryon; m. 2d, Florence A. Grasmuk, Aug. 20, 1941. Engr., N.Y. Instn. Blind and N.Y. Rapid Transit Subway, 1902; examining engr. Municipal Civil Service Commission N.Y. City 1902-04; instr. physics and engring., Coll. City N.Y., 1905-10; chief engr. Bur. Bldgs., N.Y.C., 1910-12; U.S. appraisal officer N.Y. Dist., 1918-19; prof. mechanics Cal. Inst. Tech., 1919-20; structural engr. Bur. Bldgs., Los Angeles, 1923-27; examining engr. Civil Service Commn., Los Angeles, 1927, also spl. examiner in engring. Civil Serv. Commn. Los Angeles, 1933; asst. mech. engr. Bur. Power and Light, Los Angeles, 1936; sr. structural engr. State Dept. Pub. Works, 1933. Dir. lab. U.S. Signal Corps Sch., N.Y., 1917-18; capt. insp. gen. Res.; served in N.Y.N.G. 7 yrs. capt. engr. corps. Sec. Planning Commn., High Sch. Bd. (both Arcadia, Cal.). Mem. Dist. Sch. Bd., Queens and Manhattan, N.Y.C. Fellow A.A.A.S., Am. Geog. Soc.; mem. Am. Soc. M.E. Author: Articles on engring. topics Home: 214 Harwood Av., Philipse Manor, N. Tarrytown, N.Y. Died Apr. 2, 1960; buried Woodlawn Cemetery, Bronx, N.Y.

RAY, HERBERT JAMES, naval officer; b. Feb. 1, 1893; entered U.S. Navy, 1910, and advanced through the grades to commodore, 1945. Decorated Silver Star, Distinguished Flying Cross (both Army). Address: Washington DC Died Dec. 1970.

RAY, MILTON S. industrialist, ornithologist, poet; b. San Francisco, Feb. 26, 1881; s. William S. Ray (mfr., shipowner) and Julia Henrietta (Ruth) R.; ed. Crocker High Sch.; Univ. of Calif.; m. Rose Carolyn Etzel, Oct. 7, 1915; children—Cecily, Virginia, Rosalyn. Secretary, treas. and dir. W.S. Ray Mfg. Co., San Francisco, 1907, elected v.p., 1915; sec., treas. Ray Burner Co. of Calif., 1929, Ray Burner Co. of Delaware, 1930; pres., treas., dir. Ray Burner Co. of Del., San Francisco, and New York, 1933, and same, Ray Oil Burner Co. and subsidiaries since 1935; curator and director Pacific Museum of Ornithology since 1904; has made exploration trips to over 35 countries, obtaining specimens for the Museum. Owner, Ray Park Subdivision, Burlingame, Calif., and Raycliff Terrace Subdivision, San Francisco. Member San Francisco Contract Bd., War Dept., San Francisco Dist. Ordnance Office since 1934. Received Honor Flag from U.S. Government as dir. of an auxiliary War Plant, 1918. Academician Acad. of Coimbra, Portugal. Fellow Am. Geog. Soc.; asso. Am. Ornithologists Union; research asso. in ornithology, Calif. Acad. Sciences; mem. P.E.N., Am Ornithologists Union, Cooper Ornithol. Club, Nat. Geog. Soc. Brit. Oologists Club. Republican. Protestant. Club: Burlingame Country. Awarded prize for poem, "San Francisco," used for Sesquicentennial Celebration in San Francisco, 1926. Author: The Farallones, The Painted World and Other Poems (2 vols.), 1934; Poems (1 vol.), 1936; The Poet and The Messenger; Dune-Glade and Other Poems, 1945, also over 100 mag. articles. Home: 2901 Broadway; (summer) Snow Line Villa (Vade P.O.), Lake Tahoe, Calif. Office: 401-499 Bernal Av., San Francisco 12, Calif. Died May 5, 1946.

RAY, P(ATRICK) HENRY brig. gen. U.S.A.; b. Waukesha County, Wis., May 8, 1842; s. Adam E. and Eliza (Breasted) R.; com. sch. edn.; m. Adah Blackman. Apr. 22, 1889. Served as pvt., corpl., sergt., and 1st sergt. cos. K and A, 2d Wis. Inf., and 1st Wis. Heavy Arty., May 7, 1861-July 12, 1863; commd. 2d lt. 1st Wis. Heavy Arty., July 13, 1863; capt., Sept. 13, 1864; hon. mustered out, June 26, 1865; capt. 6th U.S. Vet. Inf., Aug. 9, 1865; hon. mustered out, Apr. 12, 1866; apptd. from Wis. 2d lt. 33d U.S. Inf., Mar. 7, 1867; transferred to 8th Inf., May 3, 1869; 1st lt., Dec. 31, 1875; capt., May 27, 1889; col. 3d U.S. Vol. Inf., May 20, 1898; maj. 8th Inf., Mar. 2. 1899; hon. mustered out of vol. service, May 2, 1899; lt. col. 7th U.S. Inf., Dec. 8, 1901; transferred to 8th Inf., May 15, 1902; col. 4th Inf., Aug. 12, 1903; brig. gen. U.S.A., and retired by operation of law, May 8, 1906. Served through Civil War in Army of the Potomac; served in Sioux and Apache Indian campaigns, 1872-76; comd. Internat. Polar expdn. to Point Barrow, Alaska, June 1881-Oct. 1883, during which traveled over 1,000 miles with dogs and sled, over unexplored region, discovered and partly explored Meade River, picked up Lieut. Schwatka and party at Ft. St. Michael and brought him to U.S.; on duty with Signal Corps, Washington, 1883-85; U.S. del. Internat. Polar Congress, Vienna, May-July, 1884; sent by President McKinley, as spl. commr. to mining dists. of Northern Alaska and British N.A., Aug. 1897; wrecked by ice nr. Ft. Yukon; seized in name of U.S. caches of food belonging to trading cos. to prevent looting by mob, and fed starving and destitute fleeing from Dawson; left Ft. Yukon, Feb. 22, 1898, and traveled by dog team up the Yukon over 1,100 miles via Chilcoot Pass to Dyea, arriving there Apr. 7, 1898. Comd. dist. of Guantanamo, Cuba, Aug. 1898-Apr. 1899; took possession of Manzanillo, Cuba, Oct. 1898, upon evacuation by Spanish Army, first occupation by U.S. of Spanish Ty. under treaty of Paris, and rules there made were precedents for all other occupations in the war; assigned by President to comd. dist. of North Alaska (all ty. N. of lat. 60 deg. N.) and established and built the first mil. posts at Nome, Ft. Gibbon and Ft. Egbert; served in Philippines, Mar. 1902-Apr. 1903, and Sept. 1903-June 1905; comd. 3d Brigade, Dept. of Luzon, Jan.-Mar. 1904. Author of Report of International Polar Expedition, 1884. Home: Youngstown, N.Y. Died 1911.

RAY, PHILIP ALEXANDER, lawyer, author; born in the city of Salt Lake City, Utah, on May 27, 1911; son of William W. and Leda (Rawlins) R.; student U. Utah; B.A. (cum laude), Stanford, 1932, LL.B., 1935; m. Denece Sanford, Sept. 12, 1935. Admitted to Cal. bar, 1935; asso. partner McCutchen, Olney, Mannon & Greene, and successor firms, San Francisco, 1935-54, 46-54, 57-58; gen. counsel Dept. of Commerce, 1954-56, under-sec., 1959-61. Vice pres., dir. J. H. Pomeroy & Co., Incorporated, San Francisco, 1958-59; senior research asso. Hoover Inst., Stanford; partner law firm Kelso, Cotton, Seligman & Ray, San Francisco, Cal., 1967-70. Trustee, San Francisco Symphony, also trustee Am. Enterprise Inst. for Pub. Policy Research. Served as combat intelligence officer USNR, World War II, lt. comdr. Decorated Bronze Star. Mem. Am., Cal. bar assns., Am. Law Inst., World Affairs Council No. Cal. (trustee). Clubs: Burlingame Country; Cypress

Point (Cal.); Pacific Union (San Francisco). Author: South Wind Red, 1962. Home: Hillsborough CA Died July 16, 1970.

RAYMOND, ALEXANDER GILLESPIE cartoonist-illustrator; b. New Rochelle, N.Y., Oct. 2, 1909; s. Alexander Gillespie and Beatrice Wallaz (Crossley) R.; student Iona Prep. Sch., New Rochelle, 1925-28, Grand Central Sch. of Art, 1928-29; m. Helen Frances Williams, Dec. 31, 1930; children—Alexander Gillespie III, Lynne Clark (wife of Doctor William Arthur Ryan), Duncan Laurens, Judith, Helen Frances. Began as clerk Chisholm & Chapman, stock brokers, N.Y. City, 1928-29; solicitor James Boyd, mortgage broker, 1929-30; artist's apprentice King Features Syndicate, 1930-32; originated cartoon strips, Flash Gordon and Jungle Jim, 1934, co-creator with Dashiell Hammett, cartoon strip, Secret Agent X-9, 1935; creator newspaper feature, Rip Kirby, since 1946; spare-time illustrator nat. mags. since 1935. Commd. capt., U.S.M.C. Reserve, 1944; served as art dir., publicity bur., U.S.M.C., Phila., June-Nov. 1944; combat duty as pub. information officer and combat artist with U.S. Navy, aboard aircraft carrier U.S.S. Gilbert Islands, off Okinawa, Balikpapan, Borneo, Southern Japan; permanent rank major, U.S.M.C.R., 1946; inactive since 1946. Recipient DeBeck award outstanding cartoonist of year, 1949. Mem. Soc. Illustrators, Nat. Cartoonists Soc. (pres. 1950-52), Artists & Writers, The Lambs, Banshees, Marine Public Relations Assn., Marine Corps League, Marine Corps Reserve Officers Assn., Seventh Co. Vets. Assn. (Co. G. 7th Regt., N.Y.N.G.), Arts for Youth Council, Gamma Eta Kappa. Republican. Roman Catholic. Clubs: Kiwanis Internat., Woodway Country (Stamford, Conn.). Home: Mayapple Rd., Stamford, Conn. Office: King Features Syndicate, N.Y. City 17. Studio: 55 Ridgeway Professional Bldg., Stamford, Conn. Died Sept. 6, 1956.

RAYMOND, CHARLES WALKER brig. gen. U.S.A.; b. Hartford, Conn., Jan. 14, 1842; s. Prof. Robert R. R.; grad. Brooklyn Poly. Inst., 1861; Ph.D., Lafayette Coll., 1875; grad. U.S. Mil. Acad., 1865; spl. studies civ. and mil. engring.; M. Clara Wise, Nov. 8, 1866. Apptd. 1st lt. engrs., June 23, 1865; capt., Mar. 21, 1867; maj., Feb. 20, 1883; lt. col., May 18, 1898; col., Jan. 23, 1904; brig. gen. and retired at own request after 40 yrs.' service, June 11, 1904. Engaged on exploration of Yukon River, Alaska, 1869; prin. asst. prof. natural and experimental philosophy, U.S. Mil. Acad., 1872-74; comd. U.S. expdn. to Northern Tasmania to observe transit of Venus, 1874; instr. mil. engring., mil. signaling and telegraphing, U.S. Mil. Acad., 1878; engr. commr., D.C., 1888-89; on engr. duty at New York and Phila.; chmn. bd. engrs. in charge of constrn. of tunnels at New York for Pa. R.R. Address: Philadelphia, Pa. Died May 3, 1913.

RAYMOND, JOHN BALDWIN congressman; b. Lockport, Niagara County, N.Y., Dec. 5, 1844; attended public schs., Poughkeepsie (N.Y.) Bus. Coll., 1865-66. Enlisted as pvt. 31st Regt., Ill. Infantry in Civil War, 1861, promoted capt. Company E after siege of Vicksburg, 1863, served through war; settled in Miss.; publisher Miss. Pilot (Jackson) during reconstruction of Miss., until 1877; asst. treas. Miss., 1873-75; apptd. U.S. marshal of Dakota Territory, headquarters at Yankton, later Fargo, 1877-82; mem. U.S. Congress (Republican) from Dakota Territory, 48th Congress, 1883-85; became wheat grower. Died Fargo, Dak. (now N.D.), Jan. 3, 1886; buried public vault in Rock Creek Cemetery, Washington, D.C.

RAYMOND, ROSSITER WORTHINGTON mining engr.; b. Cincinnati, Apr. 27, 1840; s. Prof. Robert R. and Mary Ann (Pratt) R.; grad. Brooklyn Poly. Inst., 1858; studied univs. Munich and Heidelberg and Mining Acad., Freiberg; hon. Ph.D., Lafayette, 1869; LL.D., Lehigh U., 1906, and U. of Pittsburgh, 1915; m. Sarah M. Dwight, 1863. Capt. a.d.c. in Union Army, 1861-64; consulting engr., New York, 1864-68; U.S. commr. of mining statistics, 1868-76; lecturer on econ. geology, Lafayette Coll., 1870-82; editor Am. Jour. of Mining, 1867-68; an editor and spl. contbr. Engineering and Mining Journal, 1868-—. U.S. commr. to Vienna Expn., 1873; N.Y. State commr. of electric subways for Brooklyn, 1885-88; lecturer on mining law, Columbia, 1903. One of original mes., v.p., 1871, 1876-77, pres., 1872-74, sec., 1884-1911, sec. emeritus, 1911-—, Am. Inst. Mining Engrs.; Japanese Imperial Order of Rising Sun, 4th class, 1911. Author: Die Leibgarde (German), 1863; Mineral Resources of the United States in and West of the Rocky Mountains (8 vols.), 1868-75; Brave Hearts, 1873; The Man in the Moon, 1874; The Book of Job, 1878; Camp and Cabin, 1879; Glossary of Mining and Metallurgical Terms, 1881; Two Ghosts, 1879; Life of Alex L. Holley, 1883; Life of Peter Cooper, 1901; also tech. works and papers, especially on mining law. Home: Brooklyn. Died Dec. 3, 1918.

RAYNOR, HAYDEN govt. ofcl.; b. Bklyn., Aug. 28, 1906; s. Clarence E. and Lulu B. (Hayden) R.; A.B., U. Ala., 1927; M.B.A., Harvard, 1929; m. Jane C. Geer, Oct. 8, 1932; children—George Hayden, Jane Calhoun. Irving Trust Co., N.Y.C., 1929-30, Guaranty Trust Co., 1931-37; in office of chmn. U.S. Steel Corp., N.Y.C., 1937-39; mem. staff War Resources Bd., Washington, 1939; asst. to commr. in charge indsl. materials Adv. Commn. to Council of Nat. Def., 1940; asst. to dir. priorities Office Prodn. Mgmt., 1941; spl. asst. to adminstr. Lend-Lease Adminstrn., 1941-43; spl. asst. to under-sec. state, 1943-44, spl. asst. to sec. state, 1944-45; became spl. asst. to dir. Office European Affairs, 1951; dir. Office Brit. Commonwealth and No. European Affairs, 1951-55; counselor of embassy, Oslo, 1955-58; became consul gen., Vancouver, 1958, then with Dept. consul gen., Vancouver, 1958, then with Dept. State, Washington. Mem. Delta Chi. Office: Dept. of State, Washington 25. Died Oct. 7, 1963.

REA, JOHN congressman; b. Rea's Mansion, nr. Chambersburg, Pa., Jan. 27, 1755; completed prep. studies. Served as lt. and capt. with Cumberland County (Pa.) Militia, during Revolutionary War; commd. 1st coroner Franklin County, Pa., 1784; mem. Pa. Ho. of Reps., 1785, 86, 89-90, 92-93, 1801-02; county auditor, 1793, 94; mem. U.S. Ho. of Reps. (Democrat, filled vacancy) from Pa., 8th-11th, 13th congresses, 1803-11, May 11, 1813-15; served as maj. gen. 11th Div. of Militia during War of 1812; mem. Pa. Senate, 183-24. Died Chambersburg, Feb. 26, 1829; buried Rocky Spring Churchyard, nr. Chambersburg.

REA, JOHN PATTERSON commander-in-chief G.A.R.; b. Lower Oxford, Chester County, Pa., Oct. 13, 1840; ed. in public schools; removed to Miami County, O., 1861; enlisted in spring of 1861 as private 11th Ohio ing.; joined 1st Ohio cav., Aug. 1861; became 2d and 1st lt., capt. and bvt. maj., serving in Loring's cav. brigade, Army of the Cumberland. Grad. Ohio Wesleyan U., 1867, admitted to Pa. bar, 1868; assessor internal revenue, Pa., 1869-73; moved to Minn.; editor Minneapolis Tribune, 1874-77; esta- blished law practice, 1877; judge of probate, 1878-80; judge 4th Minn. dist., 1880-92; quartermaster gen., Minn., 1883-86, with rank of brig. gen.; commander-in-chief G.A.R., 1887. Address: Minneapolis, Minn. Died 1900.

READ, ALBERT CUSHING naval officer; b. Lyme, N.H., Mar. 29, 1887; s. Joseph Brown and Mary Elizabeth (Barker) R.; grad. U.S. Naval Acad., 1906 (in class of 1907); m. Bess Anderson Burdine, Jan. 30, 1918; children—Albert Cushing, Elizabeth Burdine. Commd. ensign, 1908, and advanced through the grades to rear adm., 1942, detailed to naval aviation, 1915; detailed for flight across the Atlantic in charge of NC-4 seaplane, in trip from Rockaway, N.Y., to Plymouth, Eng., via Azores, Portugal and Spain (57 hrs. 16 min. flying time; first flight in aircraft across the Atlantic Ocean), May 1919. Decorated: D.S.M., Legion of Merit, NC-4 Medal, Comenda de Torre d'Espada (Portugal), British Royal Air Force Cross, Mil. Order of Brit. Empire. Mem. Naval History Soc. Baptist. Clubs: Army-Navy (Washington), New York Yacht, Seawanhaka Yacht, Chevy Chase (Md.). Address: care Burdine's, Miami, Fla. Died Oct. 1967.

READ, CHARLES jurist, iron mfr.; b. Phila., Feb. 1, 1715; s. Charles and Anne (Bond) R.; m. Alice Thibou, at least 2 children, Jacob, Charles. Clk. Burlington (N.J.), 1739; collector Port of Burlington, circa 1739; surrogate, Burlington; apptd. clk. N.J. Circuit Cts., 1739, sec. Province of N.J., 1744; mem. Burlington City Assembly, 1757-60, speaker, 1751-54; mem. N.J. Gov.'s Council, 1758-74; Indian commr., 1755, 58, instrumental in setting aside Indian reservation in So. Burlington County; apptd. asso. justice N.J. Supreme Ct., 1749, chief justice, 1764; admitted to bar, 1753; land speculator on large scale; experimented to improve farm practices; began mfg. iron from bog ore, 1765, established iron furnaces at Taunton, Etna, Atsion, Batsto, (all N.J.), circa 1765-68; served as col. Burlington County Militia in French and Indian Wars. Author: Charles Read's Notes on Colonial Agriculture most fruitful known source of information on agr. in Am. colonies, edited by C.R. Woodward, now in Rutgers U. Library). Died Martinburg, N.C., Dec. 27, 1774.

READ, CHARLES WILLIAM naval officer; b. Yazoo County, Miss., May 12, 1840; grad. U.S. Naval Acad., 1860. Served as midshipman U.S. Navy aboard Pawnee and Powhatan, 1860-61, resigned, 1861; apptd. midshipman Confederate States Navy, 1861, promoted lt. Confederate Provisional Navy, 1862; in action at Ship Island, Head of the Passes, and Island No. 10, 1862; promoted 2d lt. Regular Navy, 1863; given command of brig. Clarence with orders to raid U.S. coast, 1863; captured 21 prizes, 1863; captured in attack on revenue cutter Caleb Cushing in harbor of Portland (Me.), 1863; promoted 1st lt. Provisional Navy, 1864; exchanged, 1864; commanded torpedo boat div. on James River, 1865; captured again in attempt to run blockade on Mississippi River, Apr. 1865, released, July, 1865; became mcht., New Orleans, after Civil War; later harbor master Port of New Orleans. Died Meridian, Miss., Jan. 25, 1890.

READ, GEORGE CAMPBELL naval officer; b. Ireland, 1787; s. Benjamin Read. Entered U.S. Navy as midshipman from Pa., 1804, commd. lt., 1810; served in battle between ships Constitution and Guerriere in War of 1812, participated in her escape from Sir Philip Broke's squadron, July 1812, won victory over Guerriere, Aug. 1812; on ship United States in action with Macedonian, Oct. 1812; commanded ship Chippewa in William Bainbridge's squadron against Algiers, 1815; on ship Hornet in West Indies, 1818-21, then on 2 voyages to Spain during treaty negotiations, 1819; commd. comdr., 1816, capt., 1825; commanded Constitution, 1826, Constellation, 1832-34; received much publicity due to difficulties with refractory officers, requested court martial, Balt., 1835, sentenced to year's suspension; best known service on flagship Columbia and John Adams; sailed for Orient on expdn. to punish Sumatrans and obtain restitution for capture of schooner Eclipse, 1838, bombarded Quallah Battoo, Sumatra, landed 350 men at town of Muckie, 1839, razed villages and secured pledge of restitution and friendship for local rajah; acting pres. of midshipmen's examining bd., 1845; commanded African Squadron, 1846-49; served at Phila. Navy Yard until 1853; on reserved list, 1855; gov. Phila. Naval Asylum, 1861-62; ret. with rank of rear adm. 1862. Died Phila., Aug. 22, 1862; buried Phila. Naval Asylum.

READ, GEORGE WINDLE army officer; b. Indianola, Ia., Nov. 19, 1860; s. James Crisfield and Elizabeth Snell (Windle) R.; grad. U.S. Mil. Acad., 1883; grad. Army War Coll., 1914; m. Burton, d. Lt. Gen. S. B. M. Young, U.S.A., Sept. 2, 1886; children—Burton Young, Margaret Elizabeth, George W. Commd. 2d lt., 16th Inf., June 13, 1883; promoted through grades to maj. gen., March 8, 1921. Served on frontier, 1883-89; prof. mil. science, and tactics, U. of Ia., 1889-93; service in Tex., 1893-97; with Evacuation Commn., Cuba, 1898-99; in Philippine Islands, 1901-02; in Calif., Hawaii, and confidential mission abroad, 1902-04; with Gen. Staff, 1905-09; with Mil. Govt., Cuba, 1906-08; pres. Claims Commn.; gov. Province Pinar del Rio, Apr.-Oct. 1908; chief umpire, Ft. Riley, Kan., 1910; in Philippine Islands, 1910-12; insp. gen., Dept. of Mindanao; border service, Ariz., 1912-14; adj. gen., 1914-17; adj. 2d Div., Texas City, Tex., 1914-15; duty at War Dept., 1915-17; apptd. comdr. brigade, Camp Upton, L.I., N.Y., Aug. 5, 1917; apptd. comdr. cav. div., El Paso, Tex., Dec. 1917, 30th Div., Apr. 27, 1918; comdg. 2d Army Corps, June 13, 1918, until demobilization, Feb. 1, 1919; comd. Am. Embarkation Center, Le Mans, France, Feb. 1-— Apr. 8, 1919; comdg. Camp Jackson, S.C., May 1, 1919-Aug. 31, 1920; comdg. 5th Corps Area, Sept. 1, 1920-Aug. 31, 1922; comdg. Philippine Dept., Oct. 4, 1922-Nov. 19, 1924; retired Nov. 19, 1924. Overseas service, May 6, 1918-Apr. 25, 1919. Gold medal Mil. Srvice Instn., 1889; D.S.M. (U.S.); Knight Comdr. Order Bath (British); Comdr. Legion of Honor, Croix de Guerre with palm (French). Episcopalian. Home: Washington, D.C. Died Nov. 6, 1934.

READ, JACOB army officer, Continental congressman, senator; b. Christ Church Parish, S.C., 1752; s. James and Rebecca (Bond) R.; m. Catherine Van Horne, Oct. 13, 1785, 4 children. Admitted to Ga. bar, 1773; admitted to Gray's Inn, Eng., 1773; a signer of petition of Americans in London protesting against Mass. Govt. Acts, 1774; capt. S.C. Militia, 1776; speaker S.C. Ho. of Reps., 1781, 82, 89-94; Charleston rep. to Jacksonborough Assembly of 1782; mem. S.C. Privy Council, 1783; mem. S.C. Legislative Council, 1783, 84, also justice of quorum; del. Continental Congress from S.C., 1783-86; charter mem. co. to build canal from Ashley to Edisto rivers, S.C., 1787; mem. S.C. conv. to ratify U.S. Constn., 1788; admitted to S.C. bar, 1799; mem. U.S. Senate (Federalist) from S.C., 1795-1801; comdg. officer 7th brigade S.C. Militia, 1808-16, brig. gen., 1808-16. Died Charleston, July 16, 1816; buried Family Cemetery, Hobcaw, S.C.

READ, JOHN JOSEPH rear admiral U.S.N.; b. Mt. Holly, N.J., June 17, 1842; s. Joseph S. and Mary (Black) R.; apptd. to U.S. Naval Acad. from N.J., 1858. Ordered into active service on Frigate Potomac, acting midshipman, 1861; promoted ensign, Nov. 25, 1862; lt., Feb. 22, 1864; lt. comdr., July 25, 1866; comdr., Dec. 11, 1877; capt., Apr. 27, 1893; rear admiral, Nov. 29, 1900. Served on Atlantic and Gulf coasts, 1861; div. officer Hartford flagship W. Gulf Blockading Squadron, 1862-63; participated in attack on Port Hudson, La., Grand Gulf, Miss., and batteries at Warrington, below Vicksburg, Miss., S. Atlantic Squadron, 1863-64; exec. officer Cuyler, participated in attack and capture of Ft. Fisher, N. Atlantic Blockading Squadron, 1864-66; De Soto, 1865-66; Rhode Island, 1866-67; exec. officer Susquehanna, 1867, Michigan, 1868-70; on Guerriere, 1870-72; exec. officer receiving-ship Vermont, and Kearsarge, 1863; exec. officer and comd. flagship Richmond, 1874-77; duty Bur. of Yards and Docks, 1878-79; light house insp., 15th dist., 1879-83, 4th dist., 1887-90, 11th dist., 1892-93; comd. Michigan, 1883-87, Iroquois, 1891-92, receiving-ship Independence, 1894-95, flagship Olympia, 1895-97, receiving-ship Richmond, 1898-1900; commandant Portsmouth Navy Yard, 1901-03, chmn. Lighthouse Bd., 1903-04; retired by reason of age, June 17, 1904. Home: Mt. Holly, N.J. Died 1910.

READ, JOHN MEREDITH diplomat; b. Phila., Feb. 21, 1837; s. John Meredith and Priscilla (Marshall) R.; grad. Brown U., 1858, Albany Law Sch., 1859; m. Delphine Pumpelly, Apr. 7, 1859, at least 4 children. Admitted to Phila. bar, 1859; served as adj. gen. with rank brig. gen. N.Y. Volunteers, 1860-61, directed mil. efforts of N.Y. State in opening months of Civil War; consul gen. at Paris, France, 1869; consul gen. to Germany during Franco-Prussian War, 1870-72; minister resident in Greece, 1873; secured revocation of order against sale of translations of Bible and other religious works circulated by Brit. and Am. bible societies; for purposes of economy U.S. Congress reduced his rank to chargé d'affaires, 1876, cut off all appropriations for the legation, 1878; he served at post without compensation until Sept. 1879; received highest Greek decoration. Author: A Historical Inquiry Concerning Henry Hudson, 1866; Historic Studies in Vaud, Berne, and Savoy: From Roman Times to Voltaire, Rousseau, and Gibbon, 1897. Died Paris, Dec. 27, 1896.

READ, OLIVER MIDDLETON, naval officer; b. Hobonny Plantation, S.C., Jan. 12, 1889; s. Oliver Middleton and Mary Louise (Gregory) R.; student Virginia Mil. Inst., 1905-06; B.S., U.S. Naval Acad., Annapolis, Md., 1911; m. Constance Sears, Dec. 18, 1918;children—Mary Louise, Oliver Middleton, III. Commd. ensign. U.S. Navy, 1911, promoted through grades to rear adm.; served in various types of ships, U.S. Navy, at Vera Cruz, Mexico, 1914, submarine service, World War, 1917-18, in Chinese waters and at Shanghai, 1932; became first U.S. naval attache and U.S. naval attache for air, U.S. Legation, Ottawa, Can., Aug., 1940; on duty as staff comdr. in chief, U.S. Fleet until Mar. 1942, on sea duty, 1942-46; deputy commander of the Atlantic Reserve Fleet, 1946-51; promoted rear adm., Oct. 1942. Awarded Navy Cross for submarine service during World War; Mexican Service medal, Victory medal (with one star), Yangtze Service medal, Legion of Merit, gold star in lieu of second Legion of Merit, Combat Distinguishing Device (for actual combat with the enemy for which first Legion of Merit was awarded), Am. Defense Service Medal, Asiatic-Pacific Area Campaign Medal, Am. Area Campaign Medal, European-African-Middle Eastern Area Campaign Medal, Victory Medal (World War II), Cruzeiro do Sul (Order of the Southern Cross—Brazil), War Service Medal, Diploma, and Citation (Brazil), Comdr. of British Empire. Mem. Soc. of Cincinnati in State of S.C., Hero of Washington chapter of Heroes of 76. Mason (K.T.), Sojourners. Episcopalian. Club: Soc of the Cincinnati in State of S.C. Home: MA Died Mar. 1972.

READ, THOMAS naval officer; b. New Castle County, Del., 1740; s. John and Mary (Howell) R.; m. Mary Peele, circa 1782. Served as commodore Delaware River defense flotilla in Am. Revolution; became 2d in rank, Pa. State Navy, 1775 with command of brig Montgomery; resigned for captaincy in Continental Navy; ordered to protect Chesapeake Bay, Feb. 1779; apptd. to frigate Bowbon, Sept., 1779; made voyage on frigate Alliance to China by new route east of Dutch Indies and through Solomon Islands, discovered 2 islands which were thought to be Ponape and another of the Carolines, renamed islands Morris and Alliance. Died Fieldsboro, N.J., Oct. 26, 1788.

READE, PHILIP brig. gen. U.S.A.; b. Lowell, Mass., Oct. 13, 1844; s. Henry and Rowena (Hildreth) R.; cadet, U.S. Mil. Acad., July 1, 1864-Jan. 14, 1865, and June 20, 1865-Jan. 21, 1867; m. Jessie Eaton, Oct. 30, 1878. Commd. 2d lt. 3d Inf., May 13, 1867; 1st lt., Dec. 8, 1878; capt., Nov. 13, 1889; maj. insp. gen. vols., May 12, 1898; lt. col. insp. gen. vols., Jan. 18, 1899; hon. discharged from vol. service, June 30, 1901; maj. 8th U.S. Inf., Mar. 31, 1899; transferred to 5th Inf., Oct. 28, 1899; lt. col. 25th Inf., Mar. 12, 1902; transferred to 23d Inf., Apr. 6, 1903; col., Aug. 13, 1903; brig. gen. U.S.A., May 4, 1911; retired by operation of law, Oct. 13, 1908. In military service of U.S. 44 yrs., in Indian campaigns, Civil War, Spanish-Am. War in Cuba and P.I., Aguinaldo insurrection and Moro campaigns. Gov. and historian Mass., Wis. and Ill. socs. Colonial Wars; register gen. Army of Santiago-de-Cuba; founder and 1st v.p. Mil. Order Moro Campaigns; patriarch of Mass. Corral Mil. Order of the Carabao; historian Mass. Soc. S.A.R. Mason. Address: Boston, Mass. Deceased.

READER, FRANCIS SMITH editor; b. Coal Centre, Pa., Nov. 17, 1842; s. Francis and Eleanor B. (Smith) R.; ed. common schs. and Mt. Union Coll., O.; m. Merran F. Darling, Dec. 24, 1867. Served, July 10, 1861-July 28, 1864, in 2d Va. Inf., changed in 1863 to 5th W.Va. Cav., U. S.V. In U.S. civ. service 10 yrs.; editor Beaver Valley News. Mem. G.A.R., S.A.R., Nat. Geog. Soc. Republican. Author: Life of Moody and Sankey, 1876; History Fifth West Virginia Cavalry, 1890; History of New Brighton, Pa., 1899; Some Pioneers of Washington County, Pa., 1902; History of the Newspapers of Beaver County, Pa., 1905; History of Schools, New Brighton, Pa., 1910; also various monographs on local and family history. Address: New Brighton, Pa.

READY, JOSEPH LOUIS army officer; b. Brighton, Mass., Nov. 17, 1895; s. Patrick and Annie Elizabeth (Keenan) R.; grad. Inf. Sch., 1923, Command and Gen. Staff Sch., 1936, Army War Coll., 1939; m. Inez Eliza Stevens, Aug. 2, 1927; children—Joseph Leo, Helen Elizabeth, Barbara. Promoted through grades to brig. gen., 1942; asst. div. comdr. 7th Inf. Div.; comdr. forward echelon inf. attack on Marshall Islands, Feb. 1944; asst. comdr. 7th Div. in Leyte campaign and battle of Okinawa; 1st mil. occupational comdr. Seoul, Korea, 1944-45; sr. comdr. N.G. Me., 1946-49; ret. Camp Keyes, Augusta, Me., 1949; asst. civil defense dir. Me., 1951-52. Awarded Silver Star, Bronze Star, Legion of Merit (Oak-Leaf Cluster), American Defense Service Medal, American Campaign Medal, Victory Medal, Army of Occupation Medal (Japan clasp), Asiatic Pacific Campaign Medal (four Bronze Service Stars), Philippine Liberation Ribbon (two Bronze Stars). Address: 641 49th St. N., St. Petersburg, Fla. Died Feb. 14, 1955; buried Arlington Nat. Cemetery.

REAGAN, JOHN HENNINGER U.S. senator; b. Sevier County, Tenn., Oct. 8, 1818; youth on farm; ed. in country school and a yr. in coll., Maryville, Tenn.; married; went to Republic of Texas; served in Texan war against Indians; deputy surveyor public lands, 1839-44; capt. militia; capt. in active service; col. of militia; justice of the peace; began law practice, 1846; probate judge; mem. Tex. legislature, 1847, judge 9th jud. dist., Tex., 1852-57; congressman, 1857-61; mem. Tex. Secession Conv., 1861; mem. provisional Confederate Congress, 1861; postmaster-gen. Confederate States, 1861-65, sec.-treas., 1865; prisoner of war, May to October, 1865; practiced law in Palestine, Tex.; member Congress, 1875-87; author "Reagan Inter-State Commerce Bill," afterward modified by amendments of Senator Cullom into the law now in force; U.S. senator, 1887-91; chmn. Tex. State R.R. Commn. Address: Palestine, Tex. Died 1905.

REANEY, GEORGE HUMES (ran'e), ins. exec.; b. New York, N.Y., Jan. 27, 1887; s. George Upton and Emma (Humes) R.; A.B., Columbia U., 1907; m. Gertrude C. Slattery, Oct. 23, 1912. In ins. brokerage, 1908-14; mgr., Aetna Life Ins. Co., Hartford, Conn., 1914-25; v.p. U.S. Guarantee Co., N.Y. City, 1925-29, pres. and dir. since 1929; dir. Guarantee Co. of N. Am. Capt. C.A.C., U.S. Army, 1917-19. Mem. Assn. of Casualty and Surety Execs. (exec. com.), Theta Delta Chi. Republican. Roman Catholic. Clubs: Columbia, Drug and Chemical, Down Town Assn. (New York, N.Y.); Siwanoy Country, Bronxville (N.Y.). Home: 25 Hillside Rd., Bronxville, N.Y. Office: 90 John St., New York. Died July 12, 1947.

REBER, SAMUEL, foreign service officer; b. Easthampton, N.Y., July 15, 1903; s. Samuel and Cecilia Sherman (Miles) R.; student Groton Sch., Groton, Mass., 1916-21; A.B., Harvard U., 1925; unmarried. Foreign service officer since Oct. 1, 1926; vice consul, Callao, Lima, Peru, 1927-29; charge d'affaires, U.S. legation, Monrovia, Liberia, 1930-31; U.S. mem. League of Nations Com. on Libera, 1931-32; sec. U.S. delegation, Gen. Disarmament Conf., Geneva, 1932-35; tech. adviser, U.S. delegation, London Naval Conf., 1935-36; sec. of Embassy, Rome, 1936-39; assigned to Dept. of State, 1939-42; spl. mission to Martinique, 1942; asst. to President's special rep. in N. Africa, 1943; mem. of Allied Mil. Mission to Italy, 1943; dep. vice-pres., Allied Control Commn., Italy; Political Officer, S.H.A.E.F., 1944-45; polit. adviser U.S. delegation Council of Fgn. Ministers Conf., Paris, 1946; dep. dir. Office European Affairs, State Dept., 1947; U.S. dep., Council Fgn. Minsters for Austria, 1948; political adviser U.S. High Commission for Germany; now deputy U.S. High Commissioner for Germany. Clubs: Metropolitan, Chevy Chase (Washington, D.C.). Home: Washington DC Died Dec. 25, 1971.

REBER, SAMUEL army officer; b. St. Louis, Oct. 16, 1864; s. Samuel and Margaret Messier (Reese) R.; grad. U.S. Mil. Acad., 1886; grad. course in electricity, Johns Hopkins, 1894; grad. Army War Coll., 1905; m. Cecelia Sherman Miles, Jan. 10, 1900; children—Miles, Samuel. Commd. 2d lt. 4th Cav., July 1, 1886; 1st lt. 9th Cav., July 28, 1892; 1st lt. signal corps, Jan. 27, 1894; maj. U.S.V., May 12, 1898; maj. signal officer, May 20, 1898; lt. col. chief signal officer, July 18, 1898; hon. discharged Apr. 17, 1899; capt. U.S.A., July 1, 1900; maj., Mar. 2, 1903; lt. col., Mar. 5, 1913; col. S.C., July 1, 1916; retired Nov. 30, 1919; now gen. foreign rep. Radio Corp. America. Service against hostile Indians in Arizona; in Puerto Rico campaigns; recommended for brevet capt. in action at Guanica. Served as chief signal officer of depts., divs. and army corps; extensive experience in ballooning and aviation; supervised nearly all internat. meets held in U.S.; in charge aviation sect. Signal Corps; with 28th and 88th divs. and with Hdqrs. 2d Army, A.E.F. in France. Sec. sect. B Internat. Elec. Congress, 1893. Mem. elec. jury Chicago and St. Louis expns.; War Dept. del. Internat. Elec. Congress, 1904; del. Internat. Telegraph Conf. Paris, 1925, Internat. Radio-telegraph Conference, Washington, 1927, World Engring. Congress on Radio (v.p.), Liege, 1930, 2d Conf. Internat. Tech. Cons. Com. on Radio, Copenhagen, 1931. Author various tech. books and papers. Home: New York, N.Y. Died Apr. 16, 1933.

RECK, FRANKLIN MERING author; b. Chgo., Nov. 29, 1896; s. Samuel Henry and Anna (Nelson) R.; student U. Pa., 1916-17; B.S., Ia. State Coll., 1925; m. Anna Claire Yungelas, Jan. 27, 1926; children—Linda Mering, Sarah Dickson. Asst. to pres. Ia. State Coll., 1925-26; asst. editor Am. Boy Mag., 1926-27, became asst. mng. editor, 1927, mng. editor, 1936-41; mng. editor Lincoln-Mercury Times, 1948-57. Editor Quill, 1927. Pvt., U.S. Army, 1917, promoted to 2d lt., 1918. Mem. Delta Tau Delta, Sigma Delta Chi (pres. 1931), Alpha Zeta, Phi Kappa Phi, Gamma Sigma Delta. Conglist. Club: The Players. Author: Sergeant Pinky, 1931; Automobiles from Start to Finish, 1935; The Romance of American Transportation, 1938, rev. 1962; One Man Against the North, 1940; Power from Start to Finish, 1941; Varsity Letter, 1942; Radio from Start to Finish, 1942; Tomorrow We Fly (with William B. Stout), 1943; Beyond the Call of Duty, 1944; On Time, The History of Electro-Motive Division of General Motors, 1948; American Boy Anthology, 1951; several others. Contbr. articles and fiction mags. Address: 665 W. Main St., Manchester, Mich. 48158. Died Oct. 14, 1965; buried Oak Grove Cemetery. Manchester.

RED CLOUD Indian chief; b. Blue Creek, Neb., 1822; s. Lone Mann and Walks As She Thinks. Born into Oglala Tribe of Teton Sioux Indians; became known as great warrior; head of an Indian band; chief Oglala tribe, main spokesman of allied Sioux and Cheyenne Indians, 1866; walked out of Ft. Laramie council talks because of Whites' attitude, 1866; leader Sioux and Cheyenne warfare which succeeded in temporarily closing Bozeman trail to settlers; advocated peace with U.S. Govt., after 1868; visited Washington (D.C.) and N.Y.C., 1870; constant critic of corrupt Indian agts.; opposed Sioux's desire for war, 1876; sent letter to Pres. Garfield demanding removal of Indian agt. V.T. McGillycuddy, 1881, deposed as tribal chief by McGillycuddy. Died Pine Ridge Indian Agy., S.D., Dec. 10, 1909.

REDDING, JOHN MAC LEAN govt. ofcl., writer; b. Chgo., Dec. 25, 1908; s. Ray M. and Elizabeth (MacLean) R.; A.B., Brown U., 1931; m. Virginia Anne Seeds, Oct. 17, 1936; children—Marian Elizabeth, Alexander MacLean, Russel Michael, Sean Heather. Newspaperman Chgo. Herald Am., 1935-41; asst. adminstr. Surplus Property Adminstrn., Washington, 1945-47; publicity dir. Democratic Nat. Com., Apr. 1947-50; asst. postmaster gen., 1950-53; pub. relations cons., 1953-65. Dir. Nat. Council for Indsl. Peace, 1957-65. Treas., Dem. Congl. Campaign Commn., 1953-65. Served as lt. col., pub. relations USAAF, 1942-45; E.T.O., 1942-45. Author: Skyways to Berlin, 1943; Wake of Glory, 1945; Inside the Democratic Party, 1958; Inside the New Frontier, 1963; How to Succeed in Politics, 1964. Contbr. articles to nat. mags. Home: R.F.D. 2, Rockville, Md. Died Apr. 1, 1965; buried Arlington Cemetery.

REDDING, ROBERT JORDAN editor, lecturer; b. Monroe County, Ga., Dec. 28, 1836; s. Anderson Westmoreland and Susan Randall (Jackson) R.; ed. in pvt. schs., and Dahlonega (Ga.) Acad. and Brownwood Inst., La Grange, Ga.; m. Mary E. Bivins, May 19, 1858; m. 2d, Sarah E. Worrill, Apr. 10, 1877; m. 3d, Sarah Elizabeth Redding, Oct. 12, 1887. Reared on farm; practiced law, 1857-59; judge inferior ct., Schley Co., Ga., 1860-61; engaged in farming, 1859-76; served capt. 46th Ga. Inf., C.S.A., 1862-65, wounded at Kenesaw Mountain, 1864. Assistant commr. of agr. of Ga., 1875-89; dir. Ga. Agrl. Expt. Sta., 1889-1906. Gen. supt. Ga. Bldg. and exhibits, Jamestown Expn., 1907. Democrat and Single Taxer. Mem. M.E. Ch., S. Author of many expt. sta. and state dept. bulls. Editor Southern World, 2 yrs., Southern Cultivator, 6 yrs.; for 20 yrs. of farm dept., Atlanta Constitution. Address: Griffin, Ga. Died June 4, 1914.

REDMAN, JOSEPH REASOR, naval officer; b. Grass Valley, Calif., Apr. 17, 1891; s. Joseph Reasor and Katherine (Dwight) R.; B.S., U.S. Naval Acad., 1914; M.S., Columbia, 1921; m. Marion Smith, 1932. Commd. ensign, U.S. Navy, 1914, and advanced through the grades to rear adm., 1943; comd. U.S.S. C-5 on submarine duty during World War I; radio duty fleet, 1921-24; bureau engring., 1924-27, fleet 1927-30; chief of frequencies sect., naval communications, 1930-33, 1937-39; tech. adviser to U.S. delegation Internat. Radio Telegraphy Conf., Madrid, 1932, Cairo, 1938; comd. U.S.S. Canopus, 1934-36, Henderson, 1939-41, Phoenix, 1942-43; dep. dir. naval communications, 1942, dir. since 1943; mem. Bd. of War Communications, Joint Communications Bd. and Combined Communications Bd., State Dept. special com. on communications. Home: Bethesda MD2Died Sept. 1968.

REECE, B(RAZILLA) CARROLL (res), congressman; b. at Butler, Tennessee, December 22, 1889; son of John Isaac and Sarah E. (Maples) R.; Carson and Newman Coll., 1910-14, N.Y.U., 1915-16, U. of London 1919; LL.D., Cumberland, 1928, Tusculum College; H.H.D., Lincoln Memorial Univ. 1946; m. Louise Despard Goff, Oct. 30, 1923; 1 dau., Louise Goff (wife of George W. Marthens, II, Col., USAF). Asst. sec. and instr. economics, New York U., 1916-17; dir. Sch. of Commerce, Accounts and Finance, New York U., instr. economics (day div.), 1919-20; chairman board Carter Co. Bank, First Peoples Bank of Johnson City, Kingsport National Bank; Farmers Bank of Blountville; pub. Bristol Herald Courier. Mem. 67th-71st, 73d-79th, 82-86th Congresses, 1st Tenn. Dist.; mem. spl. House Committee on Post-war Economic Policy and Planning; chmn. spl. Com. to Investigate Tax Exempt Foundations. Republican National committeeman and state chairman for Tenn.; chmn. Republican National Com., Apr. 1946-July 1949. Regent, Smithsonian Inst. Pres. Robert A. Taft Meml. Found.; vice pres. Am. Good Govt. Soc., Inst. Polit. and Fiscal Affairs. Enlisted in U.S. Army, May 1917; commd. lt. inf., Aug. 1917; served with 26th Div., A.E.F., Oct. 1917-July 1919; commd. 3d Batt., 102d

Inf. Decorated D.S.C., D.S.M. and Purple Heart (U.S.); Croix de Guerre with palm (French); cited for bravery by Marshal Petain and Gens. Edwards, Hale and Lewis. Mem. Am. Econ. Assn., Am. Statis. Assn., Am. Acad. Polit. Science, American, Tennessee and D.C. bar associations. Republican. Baptist. Mason (32 deg., Shriner). Clubs: Metropolitan, Capitol Hill (president), Chevy Chase, Burning Tree (Washington); Lotos (N.Y.C.); Johnson City (Tenn.) Country. Author: Courageous Commoner; Peace Through Law; also addresses and articles on life of Andrew Johnson. Home: Johnson City, Tenn. Office: House of Representatives, Washington 6. Died Mar. 19, 1961; buried Monte Vista Cemetery, Johnson City.

REED, ALLEN VISSCHER rear admiral U.S.N.; b. Oak Hill, N.Y., July 12, 1838; s. James Warren and Adaline (Allen) R.; ed. pub. and pvt. schs.; grad. Naval Acad., 1858, No. 1 of class; m. Jane Augusta Valentine, Mar. 28, 1871. Master, Feb. 23, 1861; lt., Apr. 18, 1861; lt. comdr., Mar. 3, 1865; comdr., Apr. 1, 1872; capt., July 28, 1884; retired at own request after over 40 yrs. service, June 11, 1896; advanced to rank of rear admiral retired, June 29, 1906. Performed blockading duty in Gulf of Mexico during first 3 yrs. of Civil War, on the Water Witch, Potomac, Lackawanna and flag-ship Colorado; in N. Atlantic Blockading Squadron later, on Tuscarora and Pawtuxet, participating in both attacks on Ft. Fisher and in operations in Cape Fear and James rivers; comdg. Kansas, 1872-74; engaged in Nicaragua Canal survey; asst. hydrographer, U.S. Hydrographic Office, 1875-80; comdg. U.S.S. Alliance, 1882-84; comdg. training-ship Minnesota, 1884-86; comdg. flag-ship Richmond, S. Atlantic Sta., 1888-90; comdg. Pensacola Navy Yard, 1890-93, Navy Yard, Portsmouth, N.H., 1894-96; in June 1873, while comdg. U.S.S. Kansas at Colon, U.S. of C., convoyed the steamer Virginius out from under the guns of the Spanish steamer Bazan after the latter had officially declared the intention to strenuously oppose the Virginius from continuing her career of running arms and men into Cuba. Republican. Home: Washington, D.C. Died Jan. 14, 1917.

REED, BOARDMAN physician; b. Scottsville, Monroe County, N.Y., Apr. 30, 1842; s. William N. and Hylinda Lydia (Harmon) R.; ed. Beaver Dam (Wis.) Coll., 1859, Beloit (Wis.) Coll., 1865-66, arts dept. U. of Pa., 1867-68, med. dept. same, 1876-78, M.D., 1878; post-grad. courses at hosp. U. of Pa., 1880, U. of Vienna, 1885, New York Post-Grad. Med. Sch., and New York Polyclinic at various times, 1889-91, at Chicago Post-Grad. Med. Sch., 1894, Berlin, 1895; m. Gertrude Redfield Phelps, June 22, 1871. Served pvt. Co. C, 2d Wis. Inf., May 1861-Jan. 1863; capt. Co. I, 50th Wis. Inf., Apr. 1865-June 1866. In med. practice, Mar. 8, 1878-—; pres. Atlantic City (N.J.) Bd. of Health, 1882-85; prof. diseases of the gastro-intestinal tract, hygiene and climatology, dept. of medicine, Temple U., Phila., from shortly after dept. was instituted to 1906; attending phys. Samaritan Hosp. and Am. Oneologic Hosp., Phila., 1905-06. Editor Internat. Med. Magazine, 1898-1904. Author: Lectures to General Practitioners on Diseases of the Stomach and Intestines, 1904. Edited Am. edit. of Prof. Von Noorden's series of monographs on Diseases of Metabolism and Nutrition. Home: Alhambra, Calif. Died Oct. 31, 1917.

REED, CHARLES MANNING congressman, mcht.; b. Erie, Pa., Apr. 3, 1803; grad. Washington (Pa.) Coll.; studied law. Admitted to Phila. bar, 1824, did not practice; in business with his father (owner vessels on Great Lakes), Erie; apptd. col. of militia, 1831, brig. gen. at end of his commn.; mem. Pa. Ho. of Reps., 1837, 38; mem. U.S. Ho. of Reps. (Whig) from Pa., 28th Congress, 1843-45; engaged in banking, mcht. activities, railroad business, shipping on Great Lakes, 1846-49. Died Erie, Dec. 16, 1871; buried Erie Cemetery.

REED, DAVID AIKEN lawyer; b. Pittsburgh, Pa., Dec. 21, 1880; s. James H. and Kate J. (Aiken) R.; grad. Shadyside Acad., Pittsburgh, 1896; B.A., Princeton, 1900, LL.D., 1925; LL.B., U. of Pittsburgh, 1903; m. Adele Wilcox, November 12, 1902; children—David Aiken, Rosamond; married 2d, Edna French, December 15, 1948. Began practice of law at Pittsburgh, 1903; apptd. mem. U.S. Senate, by gov. of Pa., Aug. 8, 1922, to succeed William E. Crow, deceased, and elected to same office following Nov., term 1923-29; reelected, term 1929-35; now mem. Reed, Smith, Shaw & McClay, Pittsburgh. Del. to London Naval Conf., 1930. Major 311th F.A., A.E.F., World War. Trustee of Princeton University. Member American Battle Monuments Commission, 1923-47. Awarded D.S.M. (U.S.); Chevalier Legion of Honor (French). Republican. Protestant. Home: 5611 Aylesboro Av. Office: 747 Union Trust Bldg., Pitts. Died Feb. 10, 1953; buried Arlington Nat. Cemetery.

REED, GEORGE LETCHWORTH, housing cons.; b. Olean, N.Y., Oct. 14, 1900; s. Newton Luther and Ella Letchworth (Smith) R.; B.S. in Civil Engring., U. Wis., 1924; m. Reese Louise Cofer, Aug. 31, 1927; children—Charlotte Hampton (Mrs. Keith E. Hall), George Letchworth, structural engr.; Boston, Fla. and Atlanta, 1925-35; with U.S. Pub. Housing Authority, Washington, 1935-38, planner in P.R., 1938-42; engaged in war workers housing, Hampton Roads, Va., 1942-43; housing attache embassy, London, Eng., 1946; housing adviser FOA mission to Greece, 1947-51, Burma, 1953-55; pvt. cons. practice, 1956-62; cons. Dominican Republic, 1955-57, P.R. Urban Renewal and Housing Corp., 1958-61, World Bank, Govt. Chile, Interam. Bank on Housing and Urban Growth, 1961-62; housing cons. Alliance for Progress, 1962-63; housing finance cons. UN, 1963-64; tech. adviser W. Africa Operations Office, AID, 1964-67. Bd. directors St. Johns Sch., San Juan, P.R., 1939, Anglo-Am. Sch., Athens, Greece, 1948; bd. govs. Rangoon (Burma) Sailing Club, 1951. Served with U.S. Navy, 1918-19; to lt. col. AUS, 1943-45; ETO. Decorated Royal Order St. George (Greece), 1951. Registered profl. engr., Fla., 1928, P.R. Coll. Engrs., 1961. Life mem. Chilean Soc. Planning and Devel.; mem. Am. Soc. C.E. (pres. Ga. 1930), Interam. Planning Soc. (founder mem. 1946), Am. Fgn. Service Assn., Am. Soc. Pub. Adminstrn., Internat. Fedn. Housing and Planning, Nat. Assn. Housing and Redevel. Ofcls., Res. Officers Assn., Pro-Arte (Santo Domingo), Acacia, Theta Tau. Presbyn. Clubs: Royal Hellenic Yacht (Athens); West River Sailing (Galesville, Md.). Home: Kensington MD Died Aug. 11, 1970.

REED, HARRY E. govt. ofcl.; b. Atchison, Kan., Aug. 31, 1892; s. Fred M. and Alice K. (Glaze) R.; B.S., U. Mo., 1914; M.S., Kan. State Agrl. Coll., 1928; m. Florence Evans, Dec. 29, 1921; children—(twins) Susan King, Sarah Ann. Mgr., Mo. livestock farm, 1914-17, 19-21; asst. prof. animal husbandry U. Ark., 1921-23; prof. animal husbandry Kan. State Agrl. Coll., 1923-31; U.S. Dept. Agr., Bur. of Agrl. Econs., fgn. agrl. service, London, Eng., Berlin, Germany, 1931-39; asst. chief Agrl. Marketing Service, U.S. Dept. Agr., Washington, 1939-42, dir. livestock div. U.S. Dept. Agr., Washington, since 1942. Served as capt. U.S. Army, World War I. Mem. Farm House, Gamma Sigma Delta, Phi Kappa Phi. Home: 5420 Connecticut Av. N.W., Washington 20015. Office: U.S. Dept. Agr., Washington 25. Died Mar. 7, 1961.

REED, HENRY ALBERT brig. gen. U.S.A.; b. Plattsburg, N.Y., June 23, 1844; s. Paul Adam and Charlotte Helena (Luther) R.; grad. U.S. Mil. Acad., 1870; m. Gertrudis Asenjo y del Valle, July 10, 1899; children—Henry Frederick, Paul Adam (dec.). Served pvt. to 1st lt. in command of Co. I, 24th Wis. Inf., in Civil War, 1862-65; cadet U.S. Mil. Acad., Sept. 1, 1866; apptd. 2d lt. U.S. Arty., June 15, 1870; promoted through grades to brig. gen., Feb. 17, 1906; retired, Feb. 19, 1906. Asst. prof. U.S. Mil. Acad., 1876-80, 1883-88; grad. Arty. Sch., 1874, Signal Service Sch., 1876; served in Mil. Information Div., War Dept., 1897-98; in Spanish-Am. War, Puerto Rico, Aug. 3, 1898, to close; comdg. arty. Dist. of San Juan, P.R., 1902-04; Ft. Caswell, N.C., 1904-05; comdg. arty. Dist. of Columbia, Ore., 1905. Gold medalist, Mil. Service Inst., 1891. Mason. Author: Topographical Drawing and Sketching, 1886; Photography Applied to Surveying, 1886; Spanish Legends and Traditions, 1913. Address: San Juan, P.R. Died Nov. 21, 1930.

REED, JAMES army officer; b. Woburn, Mass., Jan. 8, 1724; s. Thomas and Sarah (Sawyer) R.; m. Abigail Hinds, 1745; m. 2d, Mary Farrar, 1791; 2 children. Served as capt. during French and Indian War; went with expdn. of 1775 to Crown Point; served under Gen. Abercromby, 1758; raised troops after Battle of Lexington; commd. col. 3d N.H. Regt., 1775; served at Battle of Bunker Hill; commd. col. 2d Regt., Continental Army, 1776, while in Canada promoted to brig. gen. by Act of Congress, Aug. 1776; retired, Sept. 1776. Died Fitchburg, Mass., Feb. 13, 1807.

REED, JOHN ALTON physician; b. Altoona, Pa., July 19, 1898; s. George and Bessie (Lee) R.; M.D., George Washington U., 1922, A.B., 1928. Dir. dispensary Washington U. Hosp., 1924-49; physician Esso Standard Oil Co., 1934-48; cons. diabetes Doctors Hosp., Washington; attending physician Brit. Embassy Clinic, 1944-46. Chief med. officer Emergency Med. Service, Civilian Def., met. area of Washington; cons. diabetes U.S. Civil Service Commn., U.S. Veterans' Administration Clinic, Washington, mem., sec. Bd. Police and Fire Surgeons, 1929-40, chmn. bd., 1940-—; trustee Health Service Agy., 1943, pres., 1948-50; chmn. Emergency Ambulance Service Com. of Washington, 1944-57. Served with USMC, 1918; adv. bd. SSS, 1941-46. Diplomate Am. Bd. Internal Medicine. Fellow Am. Coll. Physicians; mem. A.M.A., Galen-Hippocrates Med. Soc. (past pres.), Washington Acad. Medicine, A.A.A.S., Am. Diabetes Assn. (mem. council, sec. 1949-—, past pres.), Diabetes Assn. D.C., D.C. Med. Soc. Mason. Clubs: Congressional Country, Cosmos, Nat. Press (Washington). Address: 1720 Connecticut Av., Washington 9. Died June 7, 1962; buried Arlington Nat. Cemetery.

REED, JOHN CALVIN lawyer; b. Appling, Ga., Feb. 24, 1836; s. Rev. John W. and Sophia Amanda (Morgan) R.; A.B., Princeton, 1854, A.M., 1857; studied law pvtly.; admitted to bar, 1857; m. Sarah Platt, June 2, 1880 (died 1901). Served 2d and 1st lt. and capt. Co. I, 8th Ga. Vols., C.S.A., 1861-65, participating in battles of Manassas, Gettysburg, Wilderness, etc.; twice wounded. Solicitor Oglethorpe County (Ga.) Ct., 1866-67; Grand Giant, Province of Oglethorpe County, in Ku Klux Klan, 1868-71; mem. Atlanta city council, 1901-02; retired from bar, 1907, and settled at Montgomery, Ala. Author: Georgia Criminal Law, 1873; Conduct of Law Suits, 1875, 1885; American Law Studies, 1882; The Brothers' War, 1905. Home: Montgomery, Ala. Died 1910.

REED, JOSEPH Continental congressman; b. Trenton, N.J., Aug. 27, 1741; s. Andrew and Theodosia (Bowes) R.; B.A., Coll. of N.J. (now Princeton), 1757; studied Middle Temple, London, Eng. 2 years; m. Ester de Berdt, May 22, 1770; Admitted to N.J. bar, 1763; apptd. dep. sec. Colony of N.J., 1767; apptd. mem. Com. of Correspondence for Phila., 1774; pres. 2d N.J. Provincial Congress, 1775; apptd. lt. col. Pa. Asso. Militia, 1775, became mil. sec. to Gen. Washington; mem. Pa. Com. of Safety, 1775; mem. Continental Congress from Pa., 1775, 77-78; adj. gen. Continental Army with rank of col., 1775, participated in L.I. campaign, promoted brig. gen., 1777; served at battles of Brandywine, Germantown, Monmouth, Portsmouth; pres. Supreme Exec. Council Pa., 1778-81; responsible for abolition of slavery in Pa.; prosecuted Benedict Arnold, a founder U. Pa., trustee, 1782-85. Died Phila., Mar. 5, 1785; buried Arch St. Presbyn. Ch. Cemetery, Phila.

REED, JOSEPH REA judge; b. Ashland County, O., Mar. 12, 1835; s. William and Rosannah (Lyle) R.; ed. Vermillion Inst., Haysville, O., 1854-57; m. Jennette E. Dinsmore, 1865; m. 2d, Edith M. Evans, Feb. 8, 1893. Admitted to bar, 1859; settled at Adel, Dallas Co., Ia., 1857; practiced law there till July 1, 1861, when became 1st lt. 2d Ia. Battery; mustered as capt. same battery, Oct. 1, 1864; mustered out, June 10, 1865. Resumed practice of law at Adel; removed to Council Bluffs, 1869; mem. Ia. Senate, 1866-68; apptd. judge Dist. Ct., Sept. 1, 1872, elected to same in same yr. and reëlected, 1876, 1880; judge Supreme Ct., Ia., 1883-89; mem. 51st Congress (1889-91); apptd. chief justice U.S. Ct. of Pvt. Land Claims, June 1, 1891, and served until that ct. terminated by limitation, June 30, 1904. Republican. Presbyn. Address: Council Bluffs, Ia. Died Apr. 2, 1925.

REED, PHILIP senator, congressman; b. nr. Chestertown, Kent County, Md., 1760; completed prep. studies. Served in Revolutionary Army, attained rank capt. of Infantry; mem. Md. Ho. of Dels., 1787; sheriff Kent County, 1791-94; mem. Exec. Council, 1805, 06, resigned. Mem. U.S. Senate (filled vacancy) from Md., Nov. 25, 1806-13; lt. col. 21st Regt., Md. Militia in War of 1812, lt. col. commandant of 1st Regt., 1814, defeated British in Battle of Caulk's Field, made brig. gen. Md. Militia in recognition of his service; mem. U.S. Ho. of Reps. (contested election) from Md., 15th, 17th congresses, 1817-19, Mar. 19, 1822-23. Died Huntingtown, Kent County, Nov. 2, 1829; buried cemetery of Christ Ch., nr. Chestertown.

REED, PHILIP LORING business exec.; b. Beverly, Mass., July 29, 1883; s. Edwin and Emily P. (Fellows) R.; student Phillips Acad., Andover, Mass., 1902; m. Sarah Shattuck, Oct. 14, 1916 (dec. Apr. 1964); children—Philip L., Samuel M., Sarah S., Wm. M., Howard S., Nathaniel. With Winslow Bros. & Smith Co., leather and wool, Boston, 1903; treas., 1911-23, vice chmn. bd., 1935-50, ret. 1950; 1st v.p. and treas. Armour & Co., Chgo., 1923-35; dir. Newport Gas Light Co.; Photon, Inc., Cambridge, Mass., Baystate Corp., Ritz-Carlton Hotel. Trustee Boston Mus. Sci., Faulkner Hosp., Phillips-Andover Acad. Served as maj. Chem. Warfare Service, U.S. Army, 1917-19. Mem. nat. bd. Boy Scouts Am. Episcopalian. Clubs: Tennis and Racquet, Union, Algonquin, Country (Boston); Racquet (Chgo.); Links (N.Y.C.). Home: 69 Common St., Dedham, Mass. Died July 26, 1964.

REED, WALTER physician; b. Belroi, Gloucester County, Va., Sept. 13, 1851; s. Lemuel Sutton and Pharaba (White) R.; M.D., U. Va., 1869, Bellevue Hosp. Med. Coll., N.Y.C., 1870; A.M. (Hon.), Harvard, 1902; LL.D. (hon.), U. Mich., 1902; m. Amelia Laurence, 1876, 2 children. Commd. asst. surgeon with rank of lt., M.C., U.S. Army, 1875; stationed at Ft. Lowell, Ariz., 1876-87; attending surgeon and examiner of recruits, Balt., 1890-93; promoted maj., 1893; curator Army Med. Museum, prof. bacteriolo in. microscopy Army Med. Sch., Washington, D.C., 1893-1902; made extensive studies of bacteriology of erysipelas and diptheria; apptd. chmn. com. to study typhoid fever among U.S. soliders in Cuba, 1898, proved that disease transmitted by dust and flies; head commn. to study yellow fever, Cuba, 1900, discovered disease transmitted by mosquito Aëdesoegypti; prof. pathology and bacteriology Columbian U., Washington, 1901-02; died of appendicitis, 1902. Author: The Contagiousness of Erysipelas, 1892. Died Washington, Nov. 22, 1902; buried Arlington Nat. Cemetery.

REED, WALTER LAWRENCE army officer; b. Ft. Apache, Ariz., Dec. 4, 1877; s. Maj. Walter and Emily Blackwell (Lawrence) R.; ed. in high schs. and Randolph-Macon Acad., Bedford City, Va.; grad. Army Sch. of Line, 1921, Army Gen. Staff Coll., 1922, Army War Coll., 1923, Navy War Coll., 1924; m. Lucy Landon Carter Blackford, Oct. 28, 1901; children—Mary Berkeley (Mrs. Charles H. Royce), Landon Carter (wife Dr. John K. Monro). Enlisted in 2d U.S. Arty., June 1898, and served in Cuba, 1898-1901; commd. 2d lt. 10th Inf., 1900, and advanced through grades to maj. gen., 1935; was insp.-gen. of the army, Washington;

served in Philippines, 1902-03, in Panama, 1911-14, in France, as div. insp., asst. army insp., later insp.-gen. of Am. forces in France, 1918-20; ret., 1940. Awarded D.S.M. for service in France. Home: 2810 36th Pl., N.W., Washington. Died May 1, 1956; buried Arlington Nat. Cemetery.

REEDER, EDWIN THORLEY architect; b. Laurium, Mich., Dec. 14, 1908; s. Edwin Colville and Algenore (Roehm) R.; B.Arch., U. Ill., 1931; m. Ruth Elizabeth Searle, June 15, 1943; 1 son, Edwin Searle. Archtl. adviser Design Derby, Miami, Fla., 1958—; prin. works include Miami Beach Fed. Savs. & Loan Assn., 1955, Indsl. Nat. Bank, Miami, 1957, Central Nat. Bank, Jacksonville, Fla., 1958, South Fla. Psychiat. Hosp., Hollywood, Fla., 1958, Dade Fed. Savs. & Loan Assn., Miami, 1959, Dade County Jail and Criminal cts., Miami, 1959. Chmn. planning adv. bd. Met. Dade County, 1959-61, Dade County Contractors Exam. Bd., 1948-58; mem. tech. com. South Fla. Bldg. Code, 1957-58. Bd. dirs. Cancer Inst., Miami, 1954-58. Served to capt., C.E., USNR, 1941-45. Recipient award of honor Fla. Assn. Architects, 1958; Hosp. of Month award Modern Hosp. Pub. Co., 1958. Fellow A.I.A. (past pres. S. Fla.); mem. Am. Inst. Decorators, Designers and Decorators Guild, Kiwanian. Home: 525 N.E. 93d St., Miami 38. Office: 1114 duPont Plaza Center, Miami 32, Fla. Died Feb. 21, 1963.

REEDER, FRANK lawyer; b. Easton, Pa., May 22, 1845; s. Andrew H. R. (1st gov. of Kan.) and Amelia H. R.; A.B., and A.M., Princeton, 1863; LL.B., Albany Law Sch., 1868; m. Grace E. Thompson, Oct. 21, 1868. Served in Union Army, Sept., 1862-June 1866, as adj. 174th Pa. Inf., and, capt. to col., 19th Pa. Cav.; collector internal revenue, 11th Dist. Pa., 1873; brig. gen. Pa. N.G., 1874; sec. of state of Pa., 1895; commr. of banking, Pa., 1900. Home: Easton, Pa. Died Dec. 7, 1912.

REEDER, WILLIAM HERRON rear admiral U.S.N.; b. Muscatine, Ia., Aug. 24, 1848; s. Dr. George and A.L. (Olds) R.; apptd. from Ia., and grad. U.S. Naval Acad., 1867; m. Ellinor Wells, Nov. 29, 1873. Ensign, Dec. 18, 1868; master, Mar. 21, 1870; lt., Jan. 31, 1872; lt. comdr., Dec. 4, 1892; comdr., Aug. 10, 1898; capt., Dec. 2, 1902; retired as rear admiral June 30, 1907. In active service during Civil War, in summer of 1863, on board the Marion, in pursuit of the Confederate steamer Tacony; served on the Piscataqua and Delaware, 1867-70; Wabash and Shenandoah, 1871-74; Navy Yard, Philadelphia, 1874-75; Alliance, 1875-77; Powhatan, 1877-80; Navy Yard, Portsmouth, 1881-83; Despatch, 1883-84; aid on expedition to Isthmus of Panama during insurrection there; Navy Department, 1885-86; Galena, 1886-89; Bureau of Equipment, Navy Department, 1889-90; Naval Acad., 1890-93; exec. officer of Charleston, 1893; comd. Naval Brigade in railroad strike, 1894, at Oakland, Calif., and opened up Southern Pacific R.R.; exec. officer Charleston in Luzon and Japan during Chinese-Japanese War; Navy Yard, Washington, 1896-97; comd. St. Mary's, 1897-98, Marcellus, 1898, St. Mary's, 1898-1901, Hartford, 1901-03; Naval War Coll., 1904; comd. Alabama, 1904-05; Navy Yard, New York, 1906-07; comd. Hancock until June 30, 1907. Address: New York, N.Y. Died 1911.

REES, CORWIN POTTENGER rear admiral U.S.N.; b. Reily, O., Sept. 4, 1848; s. Thomas and Elizabeth S. (Griffin) R.; enlisted as musician, 54th O.V.I., Mar. 1864; participated in battles of Resaca, Kenesaw Mountain, Dallas, Atlanta and in march to the sea; hon. discharged, Aug. 1865; apptd. midshipman U.S.N., July 1866; grad. U.S. Naval Acad., 1870; m. Louise Merrill, Oct. 28, 1886. Promoted through various grades to rear admiral, 1909; served at all prin. ports and stas.; exec. officer U.S.S. Olympia at Battle of Manila Bay; subsequently at Torpedo Sta. 3 yrs.; comdg. U.S.S. Monongahela 2 yrs.; light house insp. 1st dist., 2 yrs.; at Navy Yard, Portsmouth, N.H., 2 yrs.; comdt. U.S. Naval Sta., Honolulu, H.I., 1908-10; retired, Sept. 4, 1910. Advanced 6 numbers "for eminent and conspicuous conduct in battle," at Manila. Republican. Home: Erie, Pennsylvania. Died Sept. 12, 1924.

REES, ROBERT IRWIN army officer; b. Houghton, Mich., Nov. 9, 1871; s. Seth and Eugenie Malinda (Livermore) R.; B.S. and E.M., Mich. Coll. of Mines; student Harvard 1 yr., New York Law Sch., 1 yr.; distinguished grad., Army Sch. of the Line, 1913; grad. Army Staff Coll., 1914; m. Sara Isabel Gannett, Apr. 24, 1904. Corpl. Co. B, batt. engrs., May 7, 1897-Nov. 24, 1899; commd. 2d lt. 3d Inf., Oct. 1, 1899; 1st lt., Apr. 9, 1901; capt., Mar. 11, 1911; maj., Sept. 18, 1917; lt. col. (temp.), Aug. 5, 1917; col. N.A., July 27, 1918; brig. gen. (temp.), Oct. 1, 1918; col. (temp.), Aug. 6, 1918. Detailed as mem. Gen. Staff Corps, June 4, 1917; mem. war plans div., exec. div., and operations div., Gen. Staff, Washington, D.C., June 1917-Dec. 1918; Chmn. Com. on Edn. and Spl. Training in charge mil. and tech. training of technicians and mechanics for the Army in ednl. institutions; later organized S.A.T.C.; arrived in France, Dec. 1918, and assigned on Gen. Pershing's staff in charge of all ednl. work in A.E.F.; returned to U.S., July 1919, and assigned as chief recreations br. of war plans div., Gen. Staff. Awarded D.S.M., Feb. 13, 1919, "for exceptionally meritorious and conspicuous service" to U.S. Govt.; Officer Legion of Honor (French), Apr. 30, 1919. Republican. Address: Washington, D.C. Died Nov. 23, 1936.

REES, THOMAS HENRY army officer; b. Houghton, Mich., Oct. 18, 1863; s. Seth and Eugenie (Livermore) R.; grad. U.S. Mil. Acad., July 1, 1886, Engring. Sch. of Application, 1889; Army War Coll., 1911; m. Miss Happersett, 1890; m. 2d, Mrs. Blanche (Baxter) Jones, Dec. 28, 1907. Apptd. add. 2d lt. engrs., July 1, 1886; 2d lt., Dec. 31, 1886; 1st lt., Apr. 1, 1890; capt., July 5, 1898; maj., July 11, 1904; lt. col., Feb. 27, 1911; col., July 1, 1916; nom. brig. gen. by Pres. Wilson, Jan. 4, 1918. Instr. civil and mil. engring., U.S. Mil. Acad., 1893-98; with battalion of engrs., 5th Army Corps, Santiago Campaign, 1898, comdg. same, Aug. 1898; comd. Co. C, Battalion of Engrs., Willets Pt., N.Y., 1898-99; in charge fortification work and river and harbor improvements, Fla. Dist., 1899-1901; duty Dept. of Engring., Inf. and Cav. Sch., and Army Staff Coll., Leavenworth, Kan., 1902-05; comdr. 3d Battalion Engrs., 1905-08; duty Army War Coll., 1910-11; dept. engr., and river and harbor works, Chicago, 1908-10, San Francisco, 1911-17; at Manila, P.I., and Honolulu, H.Ty., 1917; apptd. comdr. 152d Field Arty. Brigade, Camp Upton, L.I., N.Y., Feb. 6, 1918. Clubs: Bohemian, Family (San Francisco). Address: War Dept., Washington. Died Sept. 20, 1942.

REEVE, CHARLES MCCORMICK lawyer, soldier; b. Dansville, N.Y., Aug. 7, 1847; s. Gen. I.V.D.R., U.S.A.; prep. edn. Canandaigua Acad.; grad. Yale, 1870 (A.M.); admitted to bar, 1872; m. Minneapolis, June 4, 1873, Christine Lawrence. Elected to State legislature, 1890; famine relief commr. from Minn. and Neb. to Russia, 1892; sec. Minn. World's Fair Commn., 1891-93; col. 13th Minn. vols., May 7, 1898; brig.-gen., Aug. 13, 1898, for gallant and meritorious service in the battle of Manila; deputy provost-marshal and 1st Am. chief of police of Manila; warden Minn. State Prison, Dec. 1, 1899. Author: How We Went and What We Saw, 1890 P2. Address: Minneapolis, Minn.

REEVE, FELIX ALEXANDER asst. solicitor of the Treasury; b. Cocke County, Tenn., Sept. 4, 1836; s. Thomas J. R. and Rebecca Ann (Earnest) R. (descendant of the Oliphants of Scotland); admitted to bar at Knoxville, 1861; authorized by Pres. Lincoln to recruit and command a regt.; col. of the 8th Tenn. Inf.; m. Wilhelmina Donelson, d. of Hon. Horace Maynard. Settled first at Greenville, then at Knoxville, Tenn.; practiced law; asst. solicitor of the Treasury, 1886-93; solicitor of the Treasury, 1893-97; later again asst. solicitor of the Treasury; independent in politics. Home: Washington, D.C. Died Nov. 15, 1920.

REEVES, ALEC HARLEY, scientist; b. Redhill, Eng., Mar. 10, 1902; s. Edward Ayearst and Grace (Harley) R.; B.S. in Engring., Imperial Coll. Sci., London, 1923. Research engr. Internat. Western Electric Co., London, 1923; project leader Paris (Eng. and France) lab. Internat. Tel. & Tel. Co., 1924-40; prin. sci. officer Royal Aircraft Establishment, 1940-45; divisional head Standard Telecommunications Labs., Ltd., Harlow, Eng., 1945-60, senior scientist, 1964-70, sr. prin. research engr.; head Reeves Telecommunications Labs., London, 1970-71. Boy Scout leader, 1918-29, 35-40; vol. probation officer, Surrey and London, 1950-71. Mem. Outward Bound Trust of Eng., 1950-71; bd. govs. Royal Hosp. Incurables, London, 1952-71. Served to wing comdr. RAF, World War II. Decorated officer British Empire, 1965, also Commander Order of British Empire, 1969; recipient Ballantine Gold medal Franklin Inst., Phila., 1965; City of Columbus award Internat. Communications Inst., Genoa, Italy, 1966. Fellow Radar and Electronics Assn., Instn. Elec. Engrs. Club: Ski of Great Britain. Inventor pulse code modulation, 1937; co-inventor, oboe system bombing through overcast, 1941. Home: Harlow Essex England Died Oct. 13, 1971.

REEVES, IRA LOUIS b. Jefferson City, Mo., Mar. 8, 1872; s. Martin Rhodes and Rebecca (Zimmerman) R.; student Purdue U., 1902; C.E., U. of Vt., 1915; Litt.D., Norwich U., 1916; LL.D., Middlebury Coll., 1917; m. Carolyn Louise Smith, Dec. 28, 1898; children—Capt. Louis Paul Denslow, Dorothy Virginia Randolph. Pvt. N.G. Mo., 1891-92; pvt., corpl., sergt., Co. B, 4th U.S. Inf., 1893-97; commd. 2d lt. 17th U.S. Inf., Apr. 19, 1897; 1st lt. 17th, 4th and 16th Inf., 1899-1902; retired with rank of capt., Nov. 11, 1902, account of wounds received in action in Philippine Insurrection; recommended for brevet "for bravery and unexcelled energy," Santiago Campaign, 1898. Comdt. and prof. mil. science, Purdue U., 1902; same Miami (O.) Mil. Inst., 1910; same U. of Vt., 1912-15; pres. Norwich U., Nov. 1, 1915-Oct. 1918. Bn. q.m. Mass. Vol. Militia, 1912-14; capt. and adj., 1st Inf., Vt. N.G., 1914-15; col. same regt., 1915-17; comd. same on Mex. border, July-Sept. 1916; chmn. Vt. Com. Public Safety, 1917. Returned to active list U.S.A., Aug. 5, 1917, with grade of maj.; lt. col., Aug. 23, 1917; col., Dec. 1917. Asst. and exec. officer Militia Bur.; adj. gen. and insp. gen.'s depts., June 1917-Sept. 1918; mem. 7th, 31st and 35th divs. in France; wounded Nov. 11, 1918. Pres., comdg. officer A.E.F. Univ., Beaune, France, Feb. 9-June 15, 1919; mem. War Claims and War Credits Bd., 1919; pres. Ira L. Reeves and Associates, Chicago. Western mgr. "Crusaders," opposed to prohibition, 1931-33. Capt. Vt. Rifle Team, nat. matches, 1915. Chevalier Legion of Honor (France); D.S.M. and Purple Heart (U.S.). Republican. Methodist. Mason. Author: Bamboo Tales, 1901; Manual for Aspirants for Commissions in the United States Army, 1902; Manual for Aspirants for Commissions in the United States Military Service, 1910; ABC of Rifle, Revolver and Pistol Shooting; Military Education in United States; Ol' Rum River, 1931; Is All Well On The Potomac?. Address: Eldon, Mo. Died Oct. 23, 1939.

REEVES, ISAAC STOCKTON KEITH commodore U.S.N.; b. Fortress Monroe, Va., Nov. 26, 1850; s. Capt. I. S. K. (U.S.A.) and Annie Dorsey (Read) R.; Lehigh U., Pa., 1872-74; Cornell U., 1874, spl. course in mech. engring.; m. Henrietta M. Young, Apr. 16, 1879. Apptd. asst. engr. U.S.N., June 30, 1875; promoted through the various grades to rank of commodore and retired, at own request, June 30, 1909. Twice consulting engr. U.S. Fish Commission; mem. Bd. Inspection and Survey, 6 yrs.; on U.S.S. Montgomery during Spanish-Am. War, and on New York in Philippine waters, 1900-03; mem. Bd. Construction, 1908-09. Home: Washington, D.C. Died July 16, 1917.

REEVES, JAMES HAYNES, army officer; b. Centre, Ala., Sept. 20, 1870; s. James A. and Mary E. (Haynes) R.; grad. U.S. Mil. Acad., 1892; grad. Inf.-Cav. Sch., 1897, Gen. Staff Sch., 1920, Army War Coll., 1921; m. Katharine V. S. Richardson, 1914; 5 children. Commd. 2d lt., cav., June 11, 1892; advanced through grades to brig. gen., Oct. 2, 1927. Served as aide to Maj. Gen. Joseph Wheeler, May-Oct. 1898, Spanish-Am. War; participated in Santiago campaign and recommended for brevet of 1st lt. for conduct at Battle of Santiago; with China Relief Expdn., 1900; in Phillippines, 1903-06; mil. attache Am. Legation, Pekin, China, 1901-03 and 1907-12; organized 353d Inf., N.A., and served as col. World War I, participating in St. Mihiel and Meuse-Argonne offensives; with Army of Occupation, Germany, 1918-May 1919; comdr. 8th Cav., 1921-23; mem. Gen. Staff, 1923; asst. chief of staff (Mil. Intelligence), 1924-27; comdr. Vancouver Barracks, 1928-Sept. 1929, 21st Inf. Brigade, Schofield Barracks, Hawaii, 1929-31, 9th Coast Arty. Dist., Fort Winfield Scott, Calif., 1931-32, 4th Coast Arty, Dist., Fort McPherson, Ga., 1932-34; retired, Sept. 30, 1934. Awarded D.S.C. (U.S.) for exceptional heroism in action near St. Mihiel, Sept. 12-13 1918; D.S.M. for exceptionally meritorious and distinguished services; 2 Silver Star citations; Croix de Guerre and Officer de l'Ordre de l'Etoile Noire (France); Order of Double Dragon (China). Chmn. Atlanta chapter Am. Red Cross, 1934-37, exec. dir., 1938-46. Club: Army and Navy (Washington). Home: 307 2d Av. S.E., Atlanta GA

REEVES, JOHN WALTER, JR., naval officer; b. Haddonfield, N.J., Apr. 25, 1888; s. George Washington and Annie (Everman) R.; ed. Penn Charter Sch., Phila., 1899-1906; B.S., U.S. Naval Acad., 1911; m. Dorothy Hutchinson, June 2, 1923; children—Margaret Elizabeth (Mrs. Adrian N. Balstra), Lt. John W., III (lt. U.S. Navy; killed in crash of tng. plane, Oct. 30, 1941). Promoted through grades to vice adm., 1949; comdr. Alaskan Sector, 1942-43, carrier div., 1943-44, Eastern Carolinas, 1944-45, Naval Air Transport Service, 1944-48; chief Naval Air Training Command, 1948-50; ret. with rank of adm., 1950; now gen. mgr. Dept. of Airports, City of Los Angeles. Decorated D.S.M. (twice); Legion of Merit (thrice); Companion Distinguished Service Order (Brit.). Home: 200 H Av., Coronado, Cal. Office: 5800 Avion Dr., Los Angeles 45. Died July 1967.

REEVES, JOSEPH MASON admiral; b. in Illinois, Nov. 20, 1872; grad. U.S. Naval Acad., 1890; diploma Naval War Coll. Rear adm., June 2, 1927. Comdr. in chief U.S. Fleet, June 15, 1934-Dec. 1, 1936, retired, 1937; recalled to active duty, May 1940; U.S. rep. on Munitions Assignment Bd.; adm., June 16, 1942. Advanced "for eminent and conspicuous conduct" in battle, Spanish-Am. War; served as naval aviation observer. Awarded Navy Cross. Home: The Brighton Hotel, 2123 California St., Washington, D.C. Died Mar. 25, 1948.

REEVES, OWEN THORNTON university dean; b. Ross Co., O., Dec. 18, 1829; s. William and Mary (M'Lain) R.; A.B., Ohio Wesleyan U., 1850, A.M., 1853; (LL.D., Monmouth, 1878); m. Mary E. Hawks, of Bloomington, Ill., Oct. 30, 1862. Admitted to bar, 1854; practiced at Bloomington, Ill., 1854-77; judge Circuit Ct., Mar., 1877-June 16, 1891, last 3 yrs. judge of Appellate Ct., 4th Dist.; dean Law Dept., Ill. Wesleyan U., since 1891. Col. 70th Regt. Ill. Inf. in Civil War. Address: Bloomington, Ill.

REGAN, LOUIS JOHN physician, lawyer; b. East Bloomfield, N.Y., Feb. 20, 1892; s. John and Anna Mary (Brown) R.; M.C., George Washington U., 1913; grad. Army Med. Sch., 1917; LL.B., LaSalle Extension U., 1938; grad. med. courses Am. and European univs.; m. Isabelle Williamson Price, Apr. 13, 1914; children—Jean (Mrs. Eugene Robert Purpus), Louis John. Intern, asst. phys. George Washington U. Hosp., Utica State Hosp., 1913-16; specialist in legal medicine, Los Angeles, 1939—; cons. staff Hollywood Presbyn. Hosp., Meth. Hosp. So. Cal., Phys. and Surg. Hosp.,

Glendale, Cal., prof. legal medicine Coll. Med. Evangelists, 1942—, sch. medicine U. So. Cal., 1952—; instr. extension div. U. Cal. at Los Angeles, 1950, 52. Served with M.C., U.S. Army, ret. as maj. Fellow Am. Pub. Health Assn.; mem. Am. Acad. Forensic Scis. (dir., pres.-elect), A.M.A., Cal. State, Los Angeles bar assns., Hollywood Acad. Medicine (past pres.), Cal. (former councillor), Los Angeles Co. (legal counsel, past pres.) med assns., Cancer Prevention Soc. Cal. (dir.), Los Angeles Co. Med. Assn. Research Found. (dir., past pres.), Phi Chi. Author: Medical Malpractice, 1943; Doctor and Patient and the Law, 949; also articles legal medicine. Home: 122 N. Carmelina Av., L.A. 49. Office: 1925 Wilshire Blvd., Los Angeles 5. Died Dec. 3, 1955; buried Forest Lawn Meml. Park, Glendale 5, Cal.

REGISTER, HENRY BARTOL architect; s. Dr. Henry Carney and Terasita (Bartol) R.; grad. William Penn Charter Sch., 1905; student Sch. of Architecture, 1909-12; married; children—Henry Bartol (dec.), Philippe deM. Employed in various offices, 1912-14; with Tilden & Register, 1914-20, Tilden, Register & Pepper, 1920-36; asso. Davis & Dunlap, 1936—. Served 1st lt. to capt., World War I, 1917-19; A.E.F. Fellow A.I.A.; mem. Art Alliance of Phila., Sigma Xi, Psi Upsilon. Clubs: University (Phila.); Merion Cricket (Haverford, Pa.). Office: 1717 Sansom St., Phila. Died Dec. 10, 1956.

REICHARD, JOHN DAVIS pub. health officer (ret.); b. Fairplay, Md., Feb. 19, 1889; s. Valentine Milton and Fanny (Line) R.; grad. St. James Sch., 1907; A.B., Trinity Coll., 1910; M.D., Johns Hopkins, 1914; m. Pansy Guyther Mitchell, Nov. 2, 1916 (dec.); married second, Mrs. Bernice C. Hires, 1955. Commd. asst. surgeon USPHS, 1916, passed asst. surgeon, 1920, surgeon, 1924, sr. surgeon, 1936, med. dir., 1941, positions included field duty in pellagra investigations, hosps., quarantines and immigration duty; immigration duty in Germany and Poland, 1926-29; charge neuro-psychiatric service, Ellis Island, 1930-39; med. officer USPHS, Hosp., Lexington, Ky., 1939-46; retired; spl. cons. Diplomate Am. Bd. Psychiatry and Neurology. Fellow Am. Psychiatric Assn., A.M.A.; mem. Soc. Biol. Psychiatry, A.A.A.S., N.Y. Acad. Scis., N.Y. Neurol. Soc., Assn. Mil. Surgeons, Phi Chi. Author bulls, USPHS, also articles profl. jours. Produced med. motion pictures: An Introduction to Clinical Neurology; The Nature and Treatment of Narcotic Drug Addiction; Disturbances in Human Behavior. Clubs: Army & Navy (Coral Gables); Propeller (Port of Miami). Home: 1541 Palancia Av., Coral Gables 34, Fla. Died Aug. 18, 1961; buried Arlington Nat. Cemetery.

REICHELDERFER, LUTHER (HALSEY) ex-pres. Commrs. D.C.; b. Hallsville, O., Feb. 4, 1874; s. Alben and Sophia (Halsey) R.; grad. high sch., Washington, 1892; M.D., Columbian (now George Washington) U., 1899, LL.D., 1932; m. Mary Macauley, Nov. 18, 1903. Mem. faculty Business High Sch., Washington, 1895-99; supt. and chief resident physician Garfield Hosp., 1900-07; med. dir. George Washington U. Hosp., 1907-08; mem. faculty med. dept. George Washington U., 1900-24; mem. surg. staff Garfield, Children's and Tuberculosis hosps., until 1924; retired from med. practice, 1924; mem. cons. staff Garfield and Children's hosps.; pres. Bd. of Commrs., D.C., 1930-33; trustee George Washington U. since 1932. Served as 1st lt. and inspector rifle practice, advancing to lt. col. inf. and chief surgeon D.C. Nat. Guard, lt. col. Med. Corps, U.S. Army in France, World War; col. Med. B.C. Fellow Am. Coll. Surgeons; mem. A.M.A., Hippocrates-Galen Med. Soc., Clinico-Pathol. Soc., Anthropol. Soc. Washington, D.C., Med. Soc. (pres. 1923), Assn. Mil. Surgeons of U.S. Club: University. Home: 1661 Crescent Pl., Washington 9, D.C. Died June 19, 1945; buried in Arlington National Cemetery.

REICHMANN, CARL army officer; b. Unterböhringen, Co. Geislingen, Wurttemberg, Dec. 23, 1859; s. Rev. Carl F.P. and Mathilde (Speidel) R.; grad. Gymnasium of Tubingen, Wurttemberg, 1877; student U. of Tubingen, 1877-80, U. of Munich, 1880-81; m. Anna Day Van Derlip, of Dansville, N.Y., Nov. 26, 1890. Pvt., corporal, sergt., 1st sergt. Co. I, 20th Inf. U.S.A., Dec. 6, 1881-Aug. 6, 1884; commd. 2d lt. 24th Inf., Aug. 4, 1884; grad. Inf. and Cav. Sch., 1889; 1st lt. 7th Inf., June 19, 1891; transferred to 9th Inf., July 20, 1891; capt. a.-a.-g. vols., May 12, 1898; capt. of Inf. U.S.A., Dec. 13, 1898; assigned to 17th Inf., Jan. 1, 1899; maj. 24th Inf., Nov. 8, 1907; lt. col. 25th Inf., May 29, 1913; col., July 1, 1916. Served in the West, 1882-93; in P.I., Mar. 1899-Jan. 1900, July 1901-Feb. 1902, July 1903-Apr. 1904; mil. attaché with Boer Army in S.Africa, Feb.-Oct. 1900, with Russian Army in Manchuria, Apr.-Dec. 1904; in Cuba, Oct. 1906-Feb. 1908; mem. Gen. Staff, 1911-13; apptd. dept. intelligence officer, Central Dept., Dec. 1917, also in charge militia affairs and chief mustering officer. Translated into English several German military works. Club: Army and Navy (Washington, D.C.) Address: War Dept., Washington, D.C.

REID, CHARLES SIMPSON judge; b. Blairsville, Ga., Sept. 25, 1897; s. Norville Young and Sarah Elizabeth (Daniel) R.; ed. Blairsville Collegiate Inst., 1910-13, Young Harris (Ga.) Coll., 1915-17, Atlanta (Ga.) Law Sch., 1918; LL.D., Atlanta Law Sch., 1940; m. Agnes Jones Baker, July 31, 1943. Asst. cashier First Nat. Bank, Lavonia, Ga., 1917; teller Lowry Nat. Bank, Atlanta, 1918; v.p. Citizens Bank, Gainesville, Ga., 1919-22; admitted to Ga. bar, 1922; mem. firm Davie & Reid, Gainesville, 1922-26, Jones, Davie & Reid, 1926-27, Jones & Reid, 1927-29, Little, Powell, Smith & Goldstein, 1929, Little, Powell, Reid & Goldstein, 1930-38; special counsel Ga. State Banking Dept., 1926-27; apptd. chief justice Ga. Supreme Court, 1938, resigned Aug. 7, 1943; dir. Fulton Nat. Bank, Atlanta. Chmn. State Dem. Exec. Com., 1937-38. Col., U.S. Army; chief, Property Control Branch, Office Military Govt., Germany; chmn. adv. bd., I. G. Farbenindustrie. Trustee and vice chairman endowment com. Young Harris Coll. Mem. Am., Ga. and Atlanta bar assns., Lawyers Club, Newcomen Soc., Delta Theta Phi. Mason (K.T., Shriner). Clubs. Capital City, Atlanta Atheletic. Home: 4443 Wieuca Road, N.E., Atlanta, Ga. Died Nov. 7, 1947.

REID, GEORGE CROGHAN brig. gen. U.S. Marine Corps; b. Lorain, O., Dec. 15, 1840; s. Conrad and Abigail (Murdock) R.; student Oberlin Coll., 1860-63; LL.B., Columbian Law Coll., Washington, 1873; m. Ada Savage, Feb. 13, 1877. Commd. lt. U.S.M.C., July 2, 1864; served at hdqrs., 1864-66; on steam-sloop Monongahela, West Indies Squadron, 1867; a.-d.-c. to commandant, 1867; 1st lt., 1869; capt., Apr. 2, 1884; adj. and insp. with rank of maj., May 1894; promoted col., 1899; brig. gen. and retired, Dec. 15, 1904. Served in Civil War, Spanish-Am. War, and in various depts. of sea and barracks duty. Address: Washington, D.C. Died Mar. 15, 1914.

REID, MONT ROGERS surgeon; b. Oriskany, Va., Apr. 7, 1889; s. Benjamin Watson and Harriet Pendleton (Lemon) R.; student Daleville (Va.) Normal Sch., 1902-04; A.B., Roanoke Coll., Salem, Va., 1908; M.D., Johns Hopkins, 1912; m. Elizabeth Harmon Cassatt, Jan. 26, 1929; 1 son, Alfred Cassatt. Interne Johns Hopkins Hosp., Baltimore, Md., 1912-13, asst. resident pathologist, 1913-14, asst. resident surgeon, 1914-18, resident surgeon, 1918-21, asso. surgeon, 1921-22; instr. in pathology, Johns Hopkins, 1913-14, instr. in surgery, 1914-18, asso. in surgery, 1918-22; asso. prof. surgery, U. of Cincinnati, 1922-31, prof. since 1931; visiting prof. surgery, Peking (now Pieping, China) Union Med. Coll., 1925-26; dir. surg. service Cincinnati Gen. Hosp., Children's Hosp. Served as 1st lt. Med. Corps, U.S. Army, World War. Recipient of first presentation of Rudolph Matas vascular surgery award, 1934. Fellow Am. Coll. Surgeons; mem. A.M.A., Am. Surg. Assn. (v.p. 1934-35), Southern Surg. Soc., Internat. Surg. Assn., Soc. Clin. Surgery, A.A.A.S., Soc. of U. Surgeons, Central Surg. Assn., Nat. Advisory Cancer Council, Am. Soc. for the Control of Cancer (dir.), Phi Chi, Alpha Omega Alpha, Sigma Chi, Pi Kappa Epsilon; hon. mem. Detroit Acad. Surgery. Republican. Presbyterian. Clubs: Camargo, Optimists, Halsted, Cincinnati Country, Commercial, Commonwealth (Cincinnati); Queen City. Contbr. chapter on surgery of the arteries, Nelson's Loose Leaf System of Surgery, 1928; chapter on surgery of sympathetic nervous system, Dean Lewis' System of Surgery, 1929; also contbr. to Jour. Exptl. Medicine, Bulls. of Johns Hopkins Hosp., Trans. Southern Surg. Assn., Jour. A.M.A., Jour. of Medicine, etc. Home: 1908 Dexter Av. Office: Holmes Hospital, Cincinnati, O. Died May 11, 1943.

REID, THOMAS MAYNE author; b. Ballyroney, County Down, Ireland, Apr. 4, 1818; s. Thomas Mayne and Miss (Rutherford) R.; m. Elizabeth Hyde, 1853; at least 1 child. Came to New Orleans, circa 1838; published early verse in Pitts. Morning Chronicle under penname The Poor Scholar, 1842, also poems in Godey's Lady's Book; wrote 5-act tragedy Love's Martyr produced at Walnut Street Theatre, Oct. 23, 1848; became society corr. for N.Y. Herald at Newport, R.I., summer 1846; wrote for Spirit of the Times, fall 1846; served from 2d lt. to 1st lt., 1st N.Y. Volunteers in Mexican War, 1846-48, served at Veracruz, Battle of Chapultepec; published Little Times (evening daily), London, Eng., 1866; returned to Am., 1867; published mag. Onward, 1869-circa 1870. Author of more than 90 books including books for boys and nearly 70 novels, novels include The Rifle Rangers, 1850, The Quadroon, 1856, The Child Wife, 1868. Died London, Oct. 22, 1883.

REID, WILLIAM CLIFFORD lawyer; b. Etha Green, Ind., Dec. 16, 1868; s. John M. and Mary C. (Iden) R.; student Purdue U., Lafayette, Ind., 1 yr.; married; 1 son, Thomas M. Admitted to Ohio bar, 1894; moved to Roswell, N.M., and then to Albuquerque; asst. U.S. atty., Dist. of N.M., 1901-04; atty. gen. N.M., 1906-07; solicitor for N.M. of A.,T.&S.F. Ry.; mem. law firm of Reid & Iden. Served as capt. Co. F, 1st Territorial U.S. Inf., Spanish-Am. War, 1898. Mem. Am. Bar Assn. Republican. Home: 1010 W. Tijeras Av. Office: First Nat. Bank, Albuquerque, N.M. Died Dec. 1, 1941.

REID, WILLIAM DUNCAN physician; b. Newton, Mass., Dec. 30, 1885; s. Robert Alexander and Carrie (Stickle) R.; A.B., Harvard, 1906, M.D., 1909; studied Berlin, Germany, 1911-12; m. Blanche Adeline McDonald, Sept. 23, 1913; children—William Duncan, Claire McDonald, James Alexander. Interne Boston City Hosp., 1909-11; served as chief of heart clinic, Boston Dispensary, and as jr. asst., phys., in charge of heart lab., Boston City Hosp. (resigned), 1923; asst. prof. in cardiology, Boston U. Sch. of Medicine and cardiologist Mass. Memorial Hosp. and heart consultant, Waltham Hosp. to 1939; retired from practice, 1940. Captain U.S. Army, 1917; with A.E.F. in France 17 months, 1917-18; lt. comdr., Medical Corps, U.S.N.R., Sept. 1944-Jan. 31, 1946; now on inactive duty; mem. U.S.N.R. Mem. A.M.A., Mass. Med. Soc., New Eng. Heart Assn., Am. Heart Assn., New Eng. Med. Soc., Alpha Omega Alpha; fellow Am. Coll. Physicians. Congregationalist. Club: Harvard. Author: The Heart in Modern Practice, 1923, 2d edit., 1928; Diseases of the Heart, 1933; Teaching Methods in Medicine, 1933; Manual of Cardiology, 1939. Home: North Parsonsfield, Me. Died Sep. 29, 1949.

REID, WILLIAM THOMAS educator; b. on a farm nr. Jacksonville, Ill., Nov. 8, 1843; s. George Washington and Martha (Williams) R.; worked on farm until 1859; studied at Ill. Coll., 1859-61; entered Union Army, 1861, as sergt.; A.B., Harvard, 1868, A.M., 1872; m. Julia Reed, of Jacksonville, Ill., Aug. 16, 1870. Head master High Sch., Newport, R.I., 1868-71; head master's asst., Boston Latin Sch., 1871-73; supt. Brookline (Mass.) schs., 1873-75; prin. San Francisco Boys' High Sch., 1875-81; pres. U. of Cal., 1881-85; founder, owner and head master Belmont (Cal.) Sch. for Boys, 1885-1918; retired. LL.D., U. of Cal., 1918. Address: 2727 Dwight Way, Berkeley, Cal.

REIFSNIDER, LAWRENCE FAIRFAX (ref'sni:-der), naval officer; b. Westminster, Md., Nov. 26, 1887; s. John Milton and Eleanor Fisher (Reese) R.; student Western Md. Coll., Westminster; grad. Naval Acad., 1910; grad. Submarine School, New London, Conn., 1917, and qualified to command submarines; grad. senior course Naval War College, Newport, R.I., 1936; m. Louise Munroe, 1912; 1 dau., Mary Louise (wife of Glover T. Ferguson, USN). Commd. ensign 1912, advanced through grades to rear adm., 1943; served in various types of ships and on shore in Navy Dept.; chief 1st USN Mission to Colombia, 1939-41; comd. 8th Naval Dist. and comdr. Gulf Sea Frontier, 1947—. Participated in amphibious operations World War II: in command Transport Group, Guadalcanal, 1942; tactical comd. transports Bougainville landing, 1943; attack group comdr. seizure of Emirau, 1944; comdr. of an attack group during assault and capture of Guam, 1944; comdr. of an attack force during assault on Okinawa, 1945; attack group comdr. for capture of Ie Shima, 1945; attack group comdr. for seizure of Iheya Shima and Aguni Shima, 1945; task group and subsequently task force comdr. for occupation of Southern and Western Japan, 1945. Decorated Navy Cross (submarine service World War I); D.S.M. with two gold stars for services at Bougainville, Guam, and Okinawa Gunto operations; Legion of Merit with combat distinguishing device for Guadalcanal operations; Mexican Service medal; World War I Victory medal with Submarine clasp; Am. Def. Service medal with bronze star; Am. Theatre Service Medal; European-African-Middle Eastern Service Medal; Asiatic-Pacific Area Service Medal with six engagement stars; World War II Victory medal; Navy Occupation Service Medal (Japan). Address: 839 Adella Av., Coronada 18, Cal. Died May 14, 1956; buried Ft. Rosecrans Nat. Cemetery, San Diego, Cal.

REIK, HENRY OTTRIDGE author, medical editor, lecturer; b. Baltimore, Md., May 23, 1868; s. Henry A. and Mary A. (Neilson) R.; Ph.G., Md. Coll. of Pharmacy, 1888; M.D., U. of Md., 1891; post-grad. work, Johns Hopkins, Harvard, London and Glasgow; m. Mary Watson, June 17, 1896 (divorced Mar. 1930); m. 2d, Helen B. Calhoun, June 21, 1930. Practiced surgery (eye, ear, nose and throat), at Baltimore, 1891-1917; asso. in ophthalmology and otology, Johns Hopkins, 1896-1912; lost use of right hand through sepsis, 1916, and abandoned active practice. Exec. sec. New York Assn. for Med. Edn., 1919-20; mng. editor Internat. Med. and Surg. Survey, Mar. 1921-Apr. 1924; editor N.J. State Med. Journal, and exec. officer Med. Soc. of N.J., 1924—. Entered U.S.A. as vol., Aug. 1917; commd. capt. M.R.C., Oct. 1917; maj., Apr. 1918; lt. col., Feb. 1919; served at Camp Sheridan, Ala.; sailed for France, July 8, 1918; apptd. comdg. officer of Base Hospital 67, A.E.F., Oct. 18, 1918; hon. discharged, May 13, 1919; re-commd. lt. col., M.R.C., July 12, 1919; commd. col., June 2, 1924. Author: Surgical Pathology and Treatment of Diseases of the Ear, 1906; Diseases of Ear, Nose and Throat, 1911; Safeguarding the Special Senses, 1912; Tour of America's National Parks, 1920. Lecturer on travels, with illustrations made entirely by true color photography. Address: New York, N.Y. Died June 2, 1938.

REILLY, HENRY JOSEPH army officer, writer; b. Fort Barrancas, Fla., Apr. 29, 1881; s. Capt. Henry Joseph and Frances Mary (Kimball) R.; student U. Kan., Northwestern U., Bklyn. Poly. Inst., each 1 yr. B.S., U.S. Mil. Acad., 1904; 2d lt. cav., 1904; 1st lt., Apr. 13, 1911; instr. history U.S. Mil. Acad., 1911-13; resigned Jan. 8, 1914. Capt. 1st Ill. F.A., Oct. 23, 1915-May 22, 1917, col., (149th U.S. F.A., 42d Div.), May 23, 1917-Oct. 16, 1918, Nov. 1918-May 1919; comd. 83d Inf. Brig., 42d Div., Oct.-Nov. 1918; recommended 4 times for promotion to grade of brig. gen.; col. 7th Inf. Ill. N.G., May 13, 1919; brig. gen. I.N.G., Apr. 1921; brig.

gen. O.R.C., May 1921. Served in Philippines, 1904-06, 1909-11; ambulance service Brit. and French armies, World War, 1914-15; U.S. service Mexican border, 1916; with 42d (Rainbow) Div., from orgn., Aug. 1917; participated in battles Luneville, Baccaret, Esperance-Sonain sectors, Champagne defensive, Aisne-Marne offensive, St. Mihiel. Meuse-Argonne, with Army of Occupation in Germany. On Initial Gen. Staff Eligibility List. Commended by sec. war, 1909; awarded D.S.M. (U.S.); Croix de Guerre with palm (French); Comdr. Legion of Honor; Officier Ordre l'Etoile Noire (French). With Poles Kief Campaign, Apr.-May, 1921. Vistula Campaign, Aug.-Oct. 1921; with General Kuo-Sun-lin Manchurian Campaign, Dec. 1925; war corr. Chicago Triune, Mexico, 1913, Far East, Jan.-Aug. 1914, Europe, 1915-17; pub. and editor Army and Navy Jour., 1921-25; editorial commr. Hearst newspapers in China, 1925-26; writing for Cosmopolitan Mag., 1927-28; corr. Nationalist Army, Spain, 1938; collecting data internat. and mil. affairs, Europe, Near East, N. Africa, 1937-39, 1940-41; lectured in 175 places in 43 States on gen. war situation, and in Inf., Cav., F.A., Command and Gen. Staff Sch., on mil. lessons of war, 1942-43. Mem. Loyal Legion, Rainbow Div. Vets, Am. Legion, Ill. Soc. S.A.R.; past comdr. Res. Officers Assn. U.S. Episcopalian. Clubs: Army and Navy (Washington); Lotos (N.Y.C.); Army and Navy (Manila); Nat. Press, Overseas Workers. Author: Why Preparedness?, 1916; America's Part, 1928; Americans at War; History of the Rainbow Division, 1936. Contbr. to Liberty, Worlds Work, Century, Nations Business, Illustrated London News, American, Fortune, l'Illustracion, Esquire, Cosmopolitan, Am. Legion Monthly, Flying, Banking; also Army jours., newspapers; contbr. to Ency. Brit. and its yearbooks. Author of 6 newsreels. Broadcast from Paris, Sept. 1939. Home: Winnetka, Ill. Died Dec. 1963.

REILLY, JAMES WILLIAM brig. gen. U.S.A.; b. Chambersburg, Pa., Aug. 2, 1839; s. Hon. Wilson and Elizabeth McCullough (Mills) R.; ed. Chambersburg Acad.; grad. U.S. Mil. Acad., 1863; m. Helen Julia Griffin, Nov. 4, 1875. First lt. ordnance, June 11, 1863, capt., June 23, 1874; maj., May 9, 1885; lt. col., Apr. 7, 1899; col., Feb. 18, 1903; brig. gen., Aug. 1, 1903; retired by operation of law, Aug. 2, 1903. Bvtd. capt., Mar. 13, 1865, "for faithful and meritorious services"; on staff of Gen. Schofield, in campaign of Nov.-Dec. 1864, including battles of Franklin and Nashville; also participated in Atlanta campaign on staff of Gen. McPherson; also on staff of Gen. P. H. Sheridan, 1875-80. Episcopalian. Home: Washington, D.C. Died 1910.

REINHARDT, EMIL FRED, army officer; b. Bay City, Mich., Oct. 27, 1888; s. C. H. and Sybilla (Tomhafe) R.; B.S., U.S. Mil. Acad., West Point, N.Y., 1910; grad., Command and Gen. Staff Sch., 1923, Army War Coll., 1931; m. Laura Bishop, Oct. 2, 1919; children—Laura Jane (Mrs. Robert E. Smock), Ann Sybil (Mrs. William G. Stevenson). Commd. 2d lt., U.S. Army, 1910, advanced through ranks to maj. gen., Apr. 1942. Comd. 69th Div. in action (European Theater) which made initial contact with Soviet Army on the Elbe River; ret. Sept. 30, 1946. Home: San Antonio TX Died July 24, 1969; buried Ft. Sam Houston Nat. Cemetery.

REINHARDT, G(EORGE) FREDERICK, inst. adminstr.; b. Berkeley, Cal., Oct. 21, 1911; s. George Frederick and Aurelia Isabel (Henry) R.; A.B., U. of Calif., 1933; A.M., Cornell U., 1935; diploma, Cesare Alfieri Inst., Florence, Italy, 1937; LL.D. honoris causa, Mills College, 1962, University of California, 1963, Gonzaga U., 1964; m. Lillian Larke Tootle, Sept. 10, 1949; children—George Frederick, III, Anna Aurelia, Charles Henry, Catherine Jane. Andrew D. White fellow in political science Cornell University, 1936; with International Boundary Commn., U.S. AND Mexico, 1935-36; fgn. service officer, 1937-68, served in Vienna, Tallinn, Riga, Moscow, Algiers, Naples, Paris, Frankfurt, and duty with Dept. of state, Washington; consul gen., 1947; chief, Div. of Eastern European Affairs, Dept. of State, 1948, dir. Office of Eastern European Affairs, 1950; counselor of Embassy, Paris, 1951-55; U.S. ambassador to Viet Nam, 1955-56; counselor Dept. of State, 1957-60; U.S. ambassador to United Arab Republic, U.S. minister to Kingdom of Yemen, 1960-61; ambassador to Italy, 1961-68; sr. dir. Stanford Research Inst. Internat., 1968-71. Served as ensign, USNR, 1932-37. Mem. Am. Fgn. Service Assn. (pres. 1959-60), Zeta Psi. Clubs: Bohemian (San Francisco); Metropolitan (Washington); Brook (N.Y.C.); Caccia (Rome). Address: Zurich Switzerland Died Feb. 22, 1971; buried Protestant Cemetery, Rome, Italy

REINICKE, FREDERICK GEORGE, naval officer; b. Tripoli, Ia., Apr. 8, 1888; s. Rev. Joseph and Katherine (Forler) R.; grad. U.S. Naval Acad., 1910; m. Nan Chadwick, Aug. 22, 1921; children—Ann Chadwick, Frederick Rogers. Commd. ensign, U.S. Navy, 1912, and advanced through the grades to commodore, 1943; served in U.S.S. Va., 1910-13, U.S.S. Galveston, 1913-16; comd. U.S.S. Aylevin in Eng. Channel and North Sea; gunnery officer U.S.S. Miss., 1921-24; comdr. U.S.S. Osborne and U.S.S. Paulding, 1926-29, U.S.S. Tulsa, 1932-35; exec. officer U.S.S. Tenn., 1937-38; served ashore, instr. U.S.N.A. 1919-21, Training Sta., Newport, 1924-26; grad. mgr. athletics, U.S.N.A., 1929-31; sr. course Naval War Coll., 1931-32; in charge pub. relations, office Naval Operations, Navy Dept., 1935-37; naval director, Port of New York, 1939-45; commissioner, Marine and Aviation City of New York and mem. N.Y. Air Authority, 1946-47; advisor to the government of Thailand, 1950-51. President, Am. Asiatic Assn.; hon. mem. Maritime Assn. Decorated Navy Cross, Second Nicaraguan Campaign, Yangtze Service, Victory and Defense medals, Legion of Merit medal, Commander Order of the British Empire; Order of Orange and Nassau with Swords (Netherlands). Clubs: New York Yacht, Tuxedo, Leash. Home: New York City NY Died Nov. 1969.

REISINGER, HAROLD CARUSI (ri'sing-er), Marine Corps officer; b. Washington, D.C., Oct. 10, 1876; entered Marine Corps, Feb. 1900; advanced through the grades to brig. gen., Mar. 1936; retired May 1938.* Died Jan. 29, 1945.

REITER, GEORGE COOK rear admiral U.S.N.; b. Mt. Pleasant, Pa.; s. W. C. (M.D.) and Eliza Reynolds R. Grad. U.S. Naval Acad., 1865; ensign, Dec. 1, 1866; master, Mar. 12, 1868; lt., Mar. 26, 1869; lt. comdr., Nov. 1880; comdr., July 31, 1890; capt., Mar. 3, 1899; rear admiral, Mar. 31, 1905; retired, July 6, 1907. Home: Canton, O. Died May 9, 1930.

REITH, FRANCIS C. (JACK) automotive exec.; b. Des Moines, Ia., Sept. 4, 1914; s. Frank S. and Emma (Carlson) R.; B.C.S., Drake U., 1936; m. Maxine Wallace, Sept. 20, 1945; children—Donna, Francis C., Charles. With Gen. Electric Credit Corp., Dallas and New Orleans, 1936-41; with Ford Motor Co., Detroit, 1946-57, beginning as mgr. budget dept., successively mgr. product programming Ford div., mgr. product and facility programming, mng. dir. and vice chmn. bd., Ford of France, spl. exec. office exec. v.p. car and truck divs., 1946-55, v.p., gen. mgr. Mercury div., 1955-57; pres. Crosley Div. Avco Mfg. Corp., 1957-—; vice pres. Avco Manufacturing Corp., 1957-—. Served as lt. colonel USAAF, 1943-46. Decorated Legion of Merit, Legion of Honor (France). Mem. Soc. Automotive Engrs., Am. Ordnance Assn., Nat. Assn. Accountants, Sigma Alpha Epsilon. Clubs: Queen City, Hyde Park Country, Detroit Athletic. Home: 1243 W. Rookwood Dr., Cin. 8. Office: 1329 Arlington St., Cin. 25. Died July 3, 1960; buried Gate of Heaven Cemetery; Montgomery, O.

REMEY, GEORGE COLLIER rear admiral; Burlington, Ia., Aug. 10, 1841; s. William Butler and Eliza Smith (Howland) R.; apptd. to U.S. Naval Acad. from Ia., 1855, grad. 1859; m. Mary J., d. Judge Charles Mason, July 8, 1873. Midshipman, June 9, 1859; promoted through grades to rear admiral, Nov. 22, 1898; retired Nov. 10, 1903. Served on Hartford, E. India Squadron, 1859-61; Marblehead, N. and S. Atlantic Blockading squadrons, 1862-63, Canandaigua, 1863; participated in siege of Yorktown, engagement with Confederates at White House, Pamunky River, June 29, 1862; engagements with batteries on Sullivan's Island, S.C.; engagement of Battery Wagner, Aug. 17, 1863; comd. naval battery on Morris Island, Aug. 23-Sept. 8, 1863, bombardments of Fts. Sumter and Gregg; comd. div. of boats in night attack on Ft. Sumter, Sept. 8, 1863, and was taken prisoner; exchanged as a prisoner of war, Nov. 15, 1864; served on Mohongo, 1865-67; Naval Acad., 1867-69; Sabine, 1869-70; Tehauntepec, 1870-71; Naval Obs., 1871-72; Worcester, 1872-73; Bur. of Yards and Docks, 1874-76; comd. Enterprise, 1877-78; torpedo instrn., 1878; Bur. of Yards and Docks, 1879-81; Lancaster, 1881-83; Navy Yard, Washington, 1884-86, Norfolk, 1886-89; comd. Charleston, 1889-92; Navy Yard, Portsmouth, 1892-95; mem. Naval Examining and Retiring Bds., 1895-96; comdt. Navy Yard, Portsmouth, 1896-98, 1898-1900; comdt. naval base, Key West, Fla., 1898, during war with Spain; comdr. in chief, Asiatic Fleet, 1900-02; chmn. Lighthouse Bd., 1902-03. Home: Washington, D.C. Died Feb. 10, 1928.

REMICK, J(OSEPH) GOULD stock broker; b. Melrose, Mass., Sept. 4, 1897; s. Joseph and Anne (Gould) R.; ed. Milton Acad., 1912-17, Noble & Greenough Sch., 1917-18, Harvard, 1918-21; m. Eleanor Francke, Sept. 30, 1922; children—Joan Francke, Eleanor Huntington. Began as clerk with H. Hentz & Co., brokers, New York, July 21, 1921; with Foster & Gibson, New York, 1924-25; partner Edey & Gibson, New York, 1925-30; partner Paige, Smith & Remick, stock brokers, New York, 1930-37; with Stillman, Maynard & Co. (firm name Evans, Stillman & Co. until merged with Maynard, Oakley & Lawrence, 1942), stock brokers, New York, as partner, since 1937. Gov. N.Y. Stock Exchange, 1939-42. Served as 2d lt. inf., U.S. Army, 1918; served as major, U.S. Army, World War II, discharged, 1944. Republican. Episcopalian. Clubs: Rockaway Hunting, Racquet and Tennis (N.Y.C.). Home: 131 E. 69th St., N.Y.C. 21. Office: 61 Broadway, N.Y.C. Died July 20, 1962.

REMINGTON, WILLIAM PROCTER bishop; b. Phila., Mar. 13, 1879; s. Joseph Price and Elizabeth Baily (Collins) R.; prep. edn. DeLancey Sch., Phila.; B.S., U. Pa., 1900; B.D., Theol. Sem. Va., 1905, D.D., 1918; ST.D., U. Pa., 1940; m. Florence Lyman Allen, Burlington, Vt., Sept. 9, 1905. Began as tchr. DeLancey Sch.; was in charge track athletics; mem. team at Olympic games, London and Paris, 1900; deacon, 1905, priest, 1906, P.E. Ch.; curate Holy Trinity Ch., Phila., 1905-07; vicar Meml. Chapel of Holy Communion, Phila., 1907-11; rector St. Paul's Ch., Mpls., 1911-18; consecrated suffragan bishop of S.D., Jan. 10, 1918; elected bishop Eastern Ore., Sept. 20, 1922, and installed Nov. 19, 1923; elected suffragan bishop Pa., June 26, 1945; instituted Nov. 1945, ret. 1951. Apptd. chaplain Base Hosp. 26, organized by Mayo Clinic and U. Minn., 1917; duty in the field. Pres., Province of Pacific, 1944. Trustee Whitman Coll., U. Pa. Mem. Psi Upsilon, Sphinx (sr. soc. U. of Pa.). Phi Beta Kappa. Ret. Home: Box 316, Rancho Santa Fe, Cal. Died Dec. 19, 1963; buried Ch. of Redeemer, Bryn Mawr, Pa.

RENIER, JOSEPH EMILE sculptor; b. Union City, N.J.; s. Jean Joseph and Eleonore (Bailey) R.; studied in N.Y.C., Paris, Brussels and Rome; m. Margaret Carey, Jan. 20, 1934; 1 dau., Margaret Josephine (now Mrs. Carl P. Donner II). Has exhibited widely in United States; works include series of seven metopes, Postal Adminstrn. Bldg., Washington; Great Star of Tex., relief of Tex. history with allegorical figures State of Tex. Bldg., Dallas; heroic equestrian statue, Speed, in lagoon Ct. of Communications, also 2 statues on approach to Empire State Bridge, N.Y. World's Fair; numerous portraits, plaques, statuettes, statues, panels and reliefs; represented in pub., pvt. collections; exec. meml. designs; designer Omar N. Bradley distinguished service award medal, 1951, Medal for Merit award for V.F.W., 1951, Civil War Centennial medal, 1961, also designed several other spl. medals for various orgns. Awarded Prix de Rome, 1915; 2 prizes for sketches, Garden Club of Am.; gold medal for sculpture Am. Artists Profl. League, 1959, Samuel Finley Breese Morse medal N.A.D., 1962; Mark Hopkins medal N.Y.U. Hall of Fame series, 1964; Elizabeth N. Watrous Gold medal Nat. Acad., 1965, Daniel Chester French medal, 1966. Lt. A.R.C. Italy, World War I. Fellow Am. Acad. in Rome; mem. Nat. Sculpture Soc. (rep. on N.Y. State Fine Arts Commn.), Archtl. League of N.Y., Soc. of Medalists. Club: National Arts. National Academician. Studio: 11 West 29th St., N.Y.C. 1. Home: 145 E. 22d St., N.Y.C. 10010. Died Oct. 8, 1966.

RENO, JESSE LEE army officer; b. Wheeling, Va. (now W. Va.), June 20, 1823; s. Louis and Rebecca (Quinby) R.; grad. U.S. Mil. Acad., 1846; m. Mary Cross, Nov. 1, 1853. Brevetted 2d lt. of ordnance U.S. Army, 1846; brevetted for gallant and meritorious conduct at Cerro Gordo in Mexican War; brevetted capt. for actions at Chapultepec; asst. prof. mathematics U.S. Mil. Acad., 1849; sec. bd. on heavy arty. technique, 1849-50; asst. to ordnance bd. Washington (D.C.) Arsenal, 1851-52; on border and coast surveys, 1853-54; in command of arsenal, Mt. Vernon, Ala., 1859-61, Leavenworth, Kan. until fall 1861; commd. 1st lt., 1853, capt., 1860; brig. gen. U.S. Volunteers, 1861, commanded brigade in Gen. Ambrose Burnside's expdn. to N.C.; commanded div. in Dept. of N.C., 1862, took part in movement to Newport News, Va., and the Rappahannock; commd. maj. gen., 1862; commanded IX Corps of Burnside's right wing in August campaign in Va. and took part in Battle of Manassas, Aug. 1862; served at Battle of Chantilly, Sept. 1862; Reno (Nev.) named in his honor. Killed in Battle of South Mountain (Md.), Sept. 14, 1862; buried Trinity Ch., Boston.

RENTSCHLER, FREDERICK B(RANT) (rent'shle—r), aircraft mfr.; b. Hamilton, O., Nov. 8, 1887; s. George Adam and Phoebe (Schwab) R.; B.S., Princeton, 1909; LL.D., Trinity Coll., 1955; m. Faye Belden, July 25, 1921; children—Helen R. Patch, Ann B. Cassady. Associated with family plants, Hamilton, Ohio, 1910-17; served as captain Air Service, U.S. Army, in charge aircraft production, New York District, 1917-18; a founder and pres. Wright Aeronautical Corp., 1919-24; founder, 1925, pres. until 1930, Pratt & Whitney Aircraft Corp.; an organizer, 1928, United Aircraft & Transport Corp., and pres. until 1933; now chmn. United Aircraft Corp.; director Nat. City Bank of N.Y., Hamilton Foundry & Machinery Company; trustee Hartford Nat. Bank & Trust Company. Dir. Hartford Hosp. Officer French Legion of Honor; recipient U.S. Air Force Civilian Service Award; Guggenheim award, 1957; spl. gold medal, State of Conn., 1953. Clubs: Hartford, Hartford Golf; Links (New York City); Everglades Bath and Tennis (Palm Beach, Fla.); Gulf Stream (Delray Beach, Fla.). Home: "Renbrook," W. Hartford, Conn. Office: E. Hartford, Conn. Died Apr. 25, 1956; buried Fairview Cemetery, West Hartford, Conn.

RENTSCHLER, GEORGE ADAM, machinery mfr.; b. Fairfield, O., Nov. 14, 1892; s. George Adam and Phoebe (Schwab) R.; Litt.B., Princeton U., 1915; m. Rita Rend Mitchell, Nov. 11, 1936; children—George A., Charles E. M., Frederick B. II. Began as machinist with Hooven, Owens, Rentschler Co., Hamilton, O., 1915; organized Gen. Machinery Corp. by merging H.O.R. with Niles Tool Works Co., 1928, merged Gen. Machinery Corp. with Lima Locomotive Works to create Lima Hamilton Corp., 1948, merged this with Baldwin Locomotive Works to form Baldwin-Lima Corp., mfrs. heavy machinery, Eddystone, Pa., 1950, chmn. exec. com., 1950-65; organized and controlled def. plants during World War II, including Am. Oerlikon Co., Charleston Shipbldg. & Dry Dock Co., Gen. Machinery Ordnance Co., Southeastern Shipbldg. Co. (built 88 Liberty ships at Savannah); dir. Armour

& Co., Barber Oil Corp., Bendix Aviation, Cin. & Suburban Bell Telephone Co., Cin. Gas & Electric Co., Fifth Third Union Trust Co., Cin., Motor Wheel Corp., Philip Carey Mfg. Co. (chmn.), U.S. Lines, William Powell Mfg. Co., Cin. Served in Air Service, U.S. Army, World War I. Recipient certificate of Commendation for wartime services Sec. Navy, World War II. Clubs: Chicago; Camargo (Cin.); National (Southampton); Brook, Twenty-Nine, Lambs, Links (N.Y.). Address: New York City NY Died May 22, 1972; buried Sacred Heart Cemetery, Southampton NY

REPASS, WILLIAM CARLYLE (re-pas'), mng. editor; b. Lebanon, Va., Jan. 3, 1896; s. Joseph Wharton and Sarah (Barbe) R.; student Bethel Coll., Russellville, Ky., 1914-15, Princeton U., 1915-17; m. Zora Owings, May 20, 1924; children—Marjorie Ann, William Carlyle, Jr. Asst. city editor, San Antonio Light, 1919-21; night editor, Galveston News, 1921-22; state editor, Houston Chronicle, 1922-24; mng. editor, Fort Worth Press, 1924-25; news editor, Houston Chronicle, 1925-34, mng. editor since 1934. First lt., A.C., U.S. Army, 1918-19. Mem. Tex. Inst. of Letters, Sigma Alpha Epsilon. Democrat. Methodist. Club: Princeton Elm. Home: 2045 Brentwood Av. Office: Houston Chronicle Pub. Co., Houston, Tex. Died Mar. 11, 1945.

RETHERS, HARRY FREDERICK army officer; b. San Francisco, Calif., Aug. 7, 1870; A.B., U. of Calif., 1893; m. Maude H. Lee, d. Maj. Gen. J. M. Lee, Oct. 19, 1898. Served as pvt., corpl. and sergt., Co. A, 1st Inf., U.S.A., 1893-96; commd. 2d lt. Apr. 10, 1896; promoted through grades to col., July 1, 1920; apptd. brig. gen., asst. to q.m. gen., Apr. 16, 1926; retired, 1931. Participated in Santiago Campaign, Spanish-Am. War, 1898, Philippine Insurrection, 1899, Boxer Rebellion, China, 1900; col. (temp.), World War I. Awarded D.S.M. (U.S.); Order of St. Michael and St. George (British); Officer Legion of Honor (French). Home: San Francisco, Calif. Died Jan. 17, 1941.

REVERE, JOSEPH WARREN naval officer; b. Boston, May 17, 1812; s. John and Lydia LeBaron (Goodwin) R.; m. Rosanna Duncan, Oct. 4, 1842; 5 children. Became midshipman U.S. Navy, 1828; made Pacific cruise in ship Guerriére, 1828-31, China cruise, 1838-40; promoted lt., 1841; assigned to Cal. coast, 1845, in command of landing party from the Portsmouth; raised flag at Sonoma, 1846; served in conquest of Cal., 1846-48; participated in subsequent naval activities on Mexican west coast; resigned from Navy, 1850; organizer artillery of Mexican army, col., 1851; commd. col. 7th N.J. Volunteers, 1861; fought in Peninsular Campaign, battles of Seven Pines and Antietam in Civil War; promoted brig. gen., 1862, led 2d Brigade, 2d Div., III Corps, at Fredericksburg; led Excelsior Brigade, 2d Div., at Chancellorsville; court martialed and dismissed for withdrawal of orders at Chancellorsville (decision revoked); resigned, Sept. 1864. Author: A Tour of Duty in California, 1849; A Retrospect of Forty Years of Military and Naval Service, 1872. Died Hoboken, N.J., Apr. 20, 1880.

REVILL, MILTON KIRTLEY (revel), banker; b. Covington, Ky., Jan. 8, 1900; s. Rankin R. and Elizabeth (Kirtley) R.; A.B., U. Ky., 1921; student Harvard Sch. Bus. Adminstrn., 1921-22; m. Elizabeth Reeves, Mar. 15, 1934. With Harris Forbes & Co., N.Y.C., 1922-23, Harris Trust & Savs. Bank, Chgo., 1923-27; v.p. Union Planters Nat. Bank, Memphis, 1927-50, bd. dirs. since 1947, exec. v.p. since 1950; dir. Bluff City Abstract Co., Union Planters Title Guaranty Co., Goodman Bldg. Co., Loeb's Laundry. Apprentice seaman to ensign, USN World War I; U.S.N., World War II, chief staff officer Naval advanced bases Italy, So. France, Palermo, comdg. officer bases Toulon, Marseille, chief staff officer operating base Oran, comdg. officer bases Algeria; commodore U.S.N.R., 1946. Decorated Bronze Star medal (2); Comdr. Order of Crown (Italy). Mem. Am. Bankers Assn., Assn. Res. City Bankers, Sigma Alpha Epsilon, Phi Alpha Delta, Tau Kappa Alpha. Democrat. Baptist. Clubs: Memphis Hunt and Polo, Tennessee. Home: 471 Yates Rd., Memphis. Office: Union Planters Nat. Bank, Memphis 1. Died Feb. 8, 1955.

REYBOLD, EUGENE cons. engr.; b. Delaware City, Del., Feb. 13, 1884; s. John Franklin and Lydia Maxwell (Tybout) R.; B.C.E., Del. Coll., 1903; grad. Coast Arty. Sch., Fort Monroe, Va., 1916, Coast Arty. Field Officers Sch., Monroe Va., 1922, Command and Gen. Staff Sch., Fort Leavenworth, Kan., 1923, Army War Coll., Washington, D.C., 1927; hon. D.Eng., U. Del., 1941; D.Sc., U. Ark., 1942, Drexel Inst. Tech., 1943; m. Margaret Eyre Moore, Jan. 6, 1906 (dec.); children—Elizabeth Tybout (Mrs. Paul F. Yount), Franklin Bell; m. 3d, Marie Stanley Elder, Aug. 1, 1949. Engr. with U.S. Engr. Dept., 1903-08; commd. 2d lt. CAC, U.S. Army, 1908, advanced through grades to brig. gen., 1940, lt. gen., Apr. 1945; duty at Fort Mott, N.J., 1908; in P.I., 1910-13; coast defs. Boston Harbor, 1913-15; instr., dir., comdt. Coast Arty. Sch., Fort Monroe, Va., 1916-22; instr. Command and Gen. Staff Sch., Fort Leavenworth, 1923-26; transferred to C.E., 1926; asst. to dist. engr. in Buffalo Engr. Dist., 1927, later dist. engr.; then assigned to Bd. Engrs. for Rivers and Harbors, Washington; dist. engr., Wilmington, N.C., to 1935; dist. engr., Memphis (flood control work on Miss.), 1935-37; div. engr. S.W. Div., Little Rock, 1937-40; asst. chief of Staff for Supply, War Dept. Gen. Staff, Aug. 1940-Sept. 1941; chief engrs., 1941-45; ret. Apptd. exec. v.p. Am. Road Builders Assn. Awarded D.S.M. with oak leaf cluster; hon comdr. Order Brit. Empire; Officer Legion of Honor (French). Mem. Am. Soc. Mil. Engrs., Am. Soc. C.E. Clubs: Army and Navy, Columbia Country (Washington). Address: Washington. Died Nov. 1961.

REYBURN, ROBERT physician; b. Glasgow, Scotland, Aug. 1, 1833; s. James and Jane (Brown) R.; ed. Phila. public schools; grad. Phila. Coll. of Med., 1856; A.M., Howard U.; m. Catharine White, Feb. 5, 1854. Practiced medicine at Phila., 1856-62; entered U.S. army, 1862, as acting asst. surgeon, surgeon and bvt. lt. col. U.S. vols., 1863; asst. surgeon U.S.A., 1867. Continued practice in Washington; in 1881 was one of the surgeons in attendance upon Pres. Garfield; later dean and prof. hygiene and preventive medicine, med. dept. Howard U. Author: Clinical History of the Case of President Garfield. Frequent contbr. to med. jours. Address: Washington, D.C. Died 1909.

REYNAL, EUGENE, publisher; b. New York, N.Y., Mar. 31, 1902; s. Eugene Sugny and Adele (Fitzgerald) R.; student St. George's Sch., Newport, R.I., 1915-20; A.B., Harvard, 1924; M.A., Oxford U., Eng., 1926; m. Elizabeth Young, June 21, 1938; children—Eric Young, Anthony; m. Katherine Beall, June 12, 1947. Began with Harper & Brothers, 1926, advertising mgr. and asst. to pres. until 1930; organized and managed Blue Ribbon Books, Inc., 1930; pres., 1934-39; founded with Curtice N. Hitchcock, Reynal &Hitchcock, Inc., pubs., 1934, chmn. bd., pres. and dir.; joined Harcourt, Brace & Co. with which Reynal & Hitchcock was merged in 1948, v.p., dir. charge trade dept., 1948-55; resigned to reorganize own firm Reynal & Co., pres. 1955-68; mng. dir. U.S. Internat. Book Assn., 1945-46 (on leave of absence from Reynal & Hitchcock, Inc.). Commd. capt., Air Corps, Army of the U.S., Aug. 8, 1942., maj., 1944, inactive duty, 1945. Democrat. Clubs: Century, Coffee House, Dutch Treat. P.E.N. (N.Y.C.). Home: New York City NY Died Mar. 20, 1968.

REYNAL, LOUIS indsl. designer, assn. exec.; b. White Plains, N.Y., Oct. 26, 1905; s. Eugene S. and Adele (FitzGerald) R.; B.A., Harvard, 1928; m. Katherine W. Whelan, Apr. 22, 1935. Propr. Louis Reynal, designer, N.Y.C.; sec., dir. Am. Soc. for Prevention Cruelty to Animals, 1950-—; v.p., dir. Animal Med. Center, 1949-—. Dir. Madison Sq. Boys' Club. Served to lt. comdr., USNR, 1942-46. Clubs: Racquet and Tennis, Westminster Kennel (N.Y.C.). Home: 1112 Park Av., N.Y.C. 28. Died Feb. 20, 1960.

REYNIERS, JAMES A. scientist; b. Mishawaka, Ind., Apr. 16, 1908; s. Leo A. and Alice Ann (Bath) R.; B.S., U. Notre Dame, 1930; M.S. (magna cum laude), 1931; LL.D., St. Thomas University, 1952; m. Carolyn M. Shelton, June 15, 1930; children—James A., Carol Lee, Leon Francis, Jon Philip, Yvonne Ann. Mem. faculty, U. Notre Dame, 1931-59, research prof. bacteriology since 1945, Head Lobund (labs. of bacteriology, U. Notre Dam), 1937, dir. 1937-50, dir. Lobund Inst. for Research in Life Scis. 1950-59; director Germ-free Life Research Center, 1950-—. Recipient faculty prize for Distinguished Service, U. Notre Dame, 1934-35, faculty award, Notre Dame Club of Chgo., 1948; Pasteur award, Soc. Am. Bacteriologists of Ill., 1954; Centennial award, Mich. State Coll., 1955. Mem. sci. adv. bd. Damon Runyon Fund Cancer Research 1949-—. Lt. comdr. USNR, 1950-—. Mem. A.A.A.S., Am. Assn. U. Professors, Am. Pub. Health Assn., Soc. of Bacteriologists, Hist. of Sci. Soc., Philosophy of Sci. Assn., N.E.A., Catholic Round Table of Sci., Catholic Commn. on Intellectual and Cultural Affairs, Am. Assn. for Cancer Research, also Sigma Xi. Roman Catholic. Club: Cosmos (Washington). Holder patents on germ-free apparatus, biological equipment, surgical operating devices, etc. Home: 72 Ladoga Av. Office: One Davis Blvd., Tampa 6. Fla. Died Nov. 1967.

REYNOLDS, ALEXANDER WELCH army officer; b. Clarke Co., Va., Aug. 1817; grad. U.S. Mil. Acad., 1838; 1 son, Frank. Served in Seminole War, 1838-40; commd. 1st lt., 1839; frontier duty in Ia., Wis., Mo., 1841-46; asst. q.m. with staff rank of capt., 1847; went to Mexico, 1848-52; joined Confederacy, commd. col. 50th Va. Inf., 1861; served in W.Va. under Gen. John Floyd, 1861-62; captured in defense of Vicksburg, later exchanged; commd. brig. gen., 1863, served in Atlanta campaign; col. in forces of Ismail Pasha during Abyssinian War, Egypt, 1869. Died Alexandria, Egypt, May 26, 1876.

REYNOLDS, ALFRED naval officer; b. Hampton, Va., Sept. 7, 1853; s. Maj. Gen. Joseph J. (U.S.A.) and Mary E. (Bainbridge) R.; grad. U.S. Naval Acad., 1873; m. Louise S. Norton, April 28, 1880; m. 2d, Sarah Josephine LeCand, Oct. 4, 1921. Ensign, July 16, 1874; promoted through grades to rear adm., July 13, 1911. Served on Swatara, 1888-91, and comd. expdn. to Seoul, Korea, to protect U.S. minister and foreigners; comd. Massasoit during Spanish-Am. War; ordnance officer, Navy Yard, League Island, Pa., 1902-05; comd. Nevada, 1905-07; Naval War Coll., Newport, 1907; comd. receiving ship Franklin, 1907-08; comd. Montana, 1908-09; comd. Franklin, 1909-11; gov. of Naval Home, Phila., 1911-12; comd. Pacific Reserve Fleet, 1912-13; apptd., Aug. 15, 1912, by Pres. of U.S., to accompany Sec. of State as naval representative to funeral of Emperor of Japan; pres. Naval Examining and Retiring bds., Washington, D.C., 1913-15; retired on account of age, Sept. 7, 1915. Placed on active duty, July 20, 1917; establishing training sta., Gulfport, Miss., and in command of naval reservation there. Home: Gulfport, Miss. Died Sept. 9. 1936.

REYNOLDS, CHARLES ALEXANDER guide, scout; b. Stephensburg, Ky., Mar. 20, 1842; s. Joseph Boyer and Phoebe (Buah) R.; never married. Pvt., U.S., Army, 1861-64; became hunter in Dakotas, 1867-73; scout for Yellowstone expdn. under Col. David Stanley, 1873; guide for Black Hills expdn. under Col. George A. Custer, 1874; partly responsible for capture of Chief Rain-in-the-Face, 1876; scout for Big Horn expdn. under Custer, 1876. Killed in Battle of Little Big Horn, nr. junction of Big Horn and Little Big Horn Rivers, Mont., June 25, 1876; buried Custer Field, Mont.

REYNOLDS, CHARLES RANSOM, former surgeon gen., U.S. Army; b. Elmira, N.Y., July 28,21877; s. George Gardiner and Lucy (Pratt) R.; student Elmira (N.Y.) Acad., 1895, U. of Mich., 1895-97; M.D., Univ. of Pa., 1899; Sc.D., Dickinson Coll., Carlisle, Pa.; m. Jane Boyd Hurd, Dec. 26, 1910; children—Charles Ransom, Hebe Louise. Mem. Med. Corps, U.S. Army, 1900-39; surgeon gen. with rank of maj. gen., 1935-39; retired. Served in Philippine Insurrection; surgeon 77th Div., chief surgeon 6th Corps, chief surgeon 2d Army, A.E.F., World War I; comdt. Med. Field Service Sch., Carlisle, Pa., 1923-31. Decorated Legion of Honor (France), 1919; Silver Star "for gallantry while aiding wounded," in Philippines, 1906, also D.S.M., World War (both U.S.). Comdr. Order Public Health, France. President 10th Internat. Çongress of Military Medicine and Pharmacy. Dir. Am. Trudeau Soc. Fellow Am. Coll. Surgeons, Am. Coll. Physicians; mem. A.M.A., Am. Acad. of Medicine, Assn. of Military Surgeons of Am. (past pres.); bd. dirs. Gorgas Memorial Inst., Walter Reed Memorial Assn.; mem. Nu Sigma Nu, Alpha Omega Alpha. Presbyn. Clubs: Army and Navy (Washington, D.C.). Home: Keene Valley NY

REYNOLDS, CUYLER author; b. Albany, N.Y., Aug. 14, 1866; s. Dexter and Catherine M. (Cuyler) R.; ed. boarding sch., Catskill, N.Y., and 10 yrs. Albany Acad.; m. Janet Gray Gould, of Albany, Sept. 24, 1891. Engaged in lit. work, 1889-—; dir. and librarian Albany Inst., 1899-1910, for which has made some noteworthy collections; dir. N.Y. state exhibit at Jamestown Expn., 1907, and author of its Report, 1910. Historian Albany Acad. Alumni Assn.; hon. mem. N.Y. State Hist. Assn., Am. Hist. Assn., Am. Scenic and Historic Preservation Soc.; mem. Nat. Geog. Soc., Am. Copyright League. Trustee Albany Inst. By study of recurrence of letters of alphabet made a standard table which is used on typesetting machines and on typewriters. Author: Janet, a Character Study, 1889; The Rosamond Tales, 1901; The Banquet Book of Classified Familiar Quotations, Toasts, etc., 1902, 1905; Albany Chronicles, 1907. Wrote monographs: Recurrence of Letters, 1894, and Albany Authors, 1902 (Albany Inst.); contbr. to magazines. Editor-in-chief Hudson and Mohawk Valleys Genealogies and Family Memoirs, 4 vols., 1913; New York City Genealogies, 3 vols., 1914; New York History, 1915; Annals of American Families, 3 vols., 1916. Home: 197 Western Av., Albany, N.Y.

REYNOLDS, FRANK JAMES advt.; b. N.Y.C., Feb. 19, 1890; s. James and Vera (Frank) R.; grad. N.Y. Mil. Acad., Cornwall-on-Hudson, N.Y., 1908; m. Lillian Heidelbach, Feb. 19, 1909; children—Marguerite Vera (Mrs. Lawrence T. Rassmussen, now deceased), Vivian Gunther (Mrs. Jon Williams); m. 2d, Margaret G. Madar, Sept. 10, 1927; 1 dau., Hope Valerie. Began as file clerk with advt. agy., 1908; v.p. Albert Frank Co., 1911-17, pres., 1917-32; v.p. Hamilton Press, 1912-17, pres. 1917-50, v.p., 1951; pres. Albert Frank-Guenther Law, Inc., advt., 1932-50, vice chmn. bd., 1951. Served as 1st lt. Air Corps, U.S. Army, 1917-19; now capt. U.S. Air Corps; ret. Trustee N.Y. Mil. Acad., Cornwall-on-Hudson. Roman Catholic. Clubs: Lawyers', Advertising (N.Y.C.); Westchester Country (Rye, N.Y.). Home: 180 E. 79th St. Office: 131 Cedar St., N.Y.C. Died Feb. 1958.

REYNOLDS, GEORGE DELACHAUMETTE judge; b. Gettysburg, Pa., Dec. 16, 1841; s. William M. (D.D.) and Anna (Swan) R.; A.B., Ill. State U., 1861, A.M., 1866; enlisted as pvt. in 2d Ill. Light Arty., 1861; mustered out 1866 as lt. col. 6th U.S.C. Artillery; m. Julia, d. Augustus S. and Maria Vogdes, Oct. 10, 1876. Admitted to bar at Hannibal, Mo., 1867; circuit atty., old 15th Circuit, 1868-71; removed to St. Louis, 1871, to Colo., 1874; practiced at Boulder, Colo., until 1877, when returned to St. Louis; judge St. Louis Ct. of Appeals, 1908-— (later presiding judge). U.S. atty. for Eastern Dist. of Mo., 1889-93. Author of amendment to U.S. Statutes under which the La. Lottery was excluded from use of the mails, and of that part of the section of U.S. laws which excluded from naturalization persons believing in or practicing polygamy. Episcopalian. Mason. Home: St. Louis, Mo. Died Mar. 18, 1921.

REYNOLDS, JOHN FULTON army officer; b. Lancaster, Pa., Sept. 20, 1820; s. John and Lydia (Moore) R.; grad. U.S. Mil. Acad., 1841. Commd. 1st lt. U.S. Army, accompanied Gen. Taylor to Mexico, 1846; fought at battles of Monterey and Buena Vista; brevetted capt. U.S. Army, 1846, maj., 1847, promoted capt., 1855; comdt. of cadets U.S. Mil. Acad., 1860-61, instr. ar., cavalry and inf. tactics; commd. lt. col., 1861; commd. brig. gen. U.S. Volunteers, 1861; mil. gov., Fredericksburg (Va.), 1862; returned to Army of Potomac in command I Army Corps, 1862; commd. maj. gen. U.S. Volunteers, 1862; commd. col. U.S. Army, 1863; fought at Battle of Gettysburg (Pa.), 1863, in command of I, III and XI Corps, Army of Potomac. Killed at Battle of Gettysburg, July 1, 1863; buried Lancaster, Pa.

REYNOLDS, JOHN LACEY, JR., newspaperman; b. Erin, Houston County, Tenn., Feb. 5, 1910; s. John Lacey and Harriett Edwina (Glasgow) R.; B.A., Vanderbilt U., 1932; children—Ann LaMar, John Lacey, III. Reporter Nashville Eve. Tennessean, 1932-34; on staff Washington Herald (now Times-Herald), 1934-35; with Ind. Syndicate, 1935-38; Washington corr. for Nashville Tennessean, Chattanooga News-Free Press, Tulsa World, Fort Worth Star Telegram, Youngstown Vindicator, Oklahoma City Oklahoman, 1938-51; chief Washington bur. Toledo Blade and Pitts. Post Gazette, 1951-53; chief Washington bur. Erie Dispatch; Washington rep. Edward Lamb Enterprises, Inc., WICU-TV and affiliated radio and TV stas. Sr. cons. to House Govt. Information Sucom.; pub. relations Nat. Rivers and Harbors Congress. Served as lt. comdr. USN; asst. naval attache and press attache Am. Embassy, Chungking, World War II. Recipient citation sec. Navy, 1956. Corr., Eng., France, Germany, Austria, Turkey, Greece, Italy, Hong Kong, Thailand, Indonesia, Spain, Japan, Formosa years, 1946, 50, 51, 55, 57. Mem. Phi Kappa Psi, Phi Beta Kappa. Democrat. Club: National Press (Washington). Home: 3210 Wisconsin Av. N.W. Office: Nat. Press Bldg., Washington. Died July 1963.

REYNOLDS, JOSEPH JONES army officer; b. Flemingsburg, Ky., Jan. 4, 1822; s. Edward and Sarah (Longley) R.; grad. U.S. Mil. Acad., 1843; m. Mary Elizabeth Bainbridge, Dec. 3, 1846, 4 children. Brevetted 2d lt. 4th Arty., U.S. Army, 1843, promoted 2d lt., 1846; tchr. U.S. Mil. Acad., 1846-55; resigned from Army, 1857; prof. mechanics and engring. Washington U., St. Louis, 1857-60; partner with brother in grocery business, Lafayette, Ind., 1860-62; apptd. col., then brig. gen. Ind. Volunteers, U.S. Army, 1861; maj. gen. U.S. Volunteers, 1862; commanded Cheat Mountain Dist., 1861-62; commanded division in Army of Cumberland, 1862; served at battles of Hoover's Gap and Chickamauga; chief staff of Army of Cumberland, 1863-64; at battles of Chattanooga and Missionary Ridge; commanded Dept. of Ark., 1864-66; became col. 26th Inf., U.S. Army, 1866; commanded successively Dist. of Tex., 5th Mil. Dist. of U.S. and Dept. of Tex.; brevetted brig. gen. for service at Chickamauga and maj. gen. for service at Missionary Ridge, both 1867; transferred to cavalry, 1872; commanded various posts in Indian Territory, 1872-76; retired, 1877. Died Washington, D.C., Feb. 25, 1899.

REYNOLDS, JOSEPH JONES maj. gen. vols., col. U.S.A., retired June 1877; b. Flemingsburg, Ky., Jan. 4, 1822; grad. West Point, 1843; served in Texas, 1845-46; 1st lt., 1847; asst. prof. natural philosophy West Point, 1849-56; resigned from army; prof. mechanics and engring. Washington U., St. Louis, 1856-60; col. 10th Ind. vols., April, and brig. gen. vols., May 1861; served in Army of Cumberland, 1862-63; maj. gen. vols., Nov. 1862; chief of staff, Army of Cumberland; was at Chickamauga and Mission Ridge; in command Dept. of Ark., Nov. 1864 to April 1866; mustered out volunteer service, Sept. 1866; col., U.S.A., July 1866; bvtd. brig. gen. and maj. gen., 1867; commanded 5th Mil. Dist. (La. and Texas), 1867-72; elected U.S. senator from Texas, 1871, but declined; commanded 3d cav. in the Dept. of the Platte, 1872-76; m. Mary E., dau. William P. Bainbridge, 4th U.S. arty., Dec. 3, 1846. Address: Washington, D.C. Died 1899.

REYNOLDS, JOSEPH SMITH lawyer; b. New Lenox, Ill., Dec. 3, 1839; s. Isaac N. and Rue Ann (Holderman) R.; grad. Chicago High Sch. and Northwestern U., 1866; enlisted Co. F, 64th Ill. Inf. (Yates' Sharpshooters), Oct. 19, 1861; promoted 2d lt., Dec. 31, 1861; 1st lt., Sept. 2, 1862; capt., Aug. 14, 1863; maj., Nov. 1, 1864; lt. col., May 8, 1865; bvt. col. and brig. gen., July 11, 1865; took part in 17 battles and many skirmishes; wounded at Corinth; had sword shot from hand at Resaca; comd. regt. on Sherman's March to the Sea and through the Carolinas; led column that captured Confed. position to the left of Bentonsville, N.C., Mar. 21, 1865; took part in grand review, Washington, June 1865; m. Mattie A. Cary, Jan. 31, 1877 (died 1890). Admitted to bar, 1866; mem. Ill. Ho. of Rep., 1866-70, Senate, 1872-74; one of founders Chicago park system; mem. Chicago Bd. of Edn., 1870-74; commr. from Ill. to Vienna Expn., 1873; commr. to establish State Sch. for Feeble-Minded Children, 1875. Senior vice-comdr.-in-chief G.A.R. of U.S., 1875-76; comdr. Ill. G.A.R., 1877; 1st v.p. Soc. Army of the Tennessee, 1879. Home: Pasadena, Calif. Died 1911.

REYNOLDS, LAWRENCE physician; b. Skipperville, Ala., Feb. 11, 1889; s. Dr. Robert Davis and Mary Frances Reynolds; A.B., U. Ala., 1912, LL.D., 1950; M.D., Johns Hopkins, 1916; Doctor of Laws, Wayne State University, 1956. Interne Johns Hopkins, 1916-17, instr., roentgenology, Johns Hopkins, 1919, roentgenol., Peter Bent Brigham Hosp., Boston, 1919-22; instr. roentgenol., Harvard, 1920-22, private practice, 1922-—; chief dept. radiology, Harper Hosp.; pres. Am. Coll. Radiology; adv. com. Hist. Med. Library, Yale; exec. com. William L. Clements Library, University of Mich.; pres. Detroit Pub. Library Com. Began medical career as vol. with Am. Ambulance Hosp., Neuilly-sur-Seine (France), 1917; 1st lt., in chg. X-Ray dept., Red Cross Mil. Hosp., Neuilly, 1917-19, capt., 1918. Recipient Gold Medal award, Radiological Society N.A., 1956, American College of Radiology, 1960; award from Michigan State Med. Soc. for distinguished service rendered to medicine and teaching, 1959. Editor: Am. Jour. Roentgenol. and Radium Therapy, since 1930; diplomate, Am. Bd. Radiol. Mem. Am. Roentgen Ray Soc., A.M.A., Radiol. Soc. of N.Am., Am. Coll. of Radiology, A.C.P., Detroit Acad. Medicine, Detroit Roentgen Ray and Radium Soc., Mich. State Med. Soc., A.A.A.S., Deutsche Roentgen-Geselschaft, Societas Radiologiae Medicar Italiana, Detroit Med. Club, Harvey Cushing Soc., Sigma Psi, Sigma Alpha Epsilon, Corinthians. Mason (K.T.). Club: Grolier (New York). Home: 2100 Seminole Av. Office: Professional Bldg., Detroit. Died Aug. 17, 1961; buried Ozark, Ala.

REYNOLDS, WILLIAM naval officer; b. Lancaster, Pa., Dec. 18, 1815; s. John and Lydia (Moore) R.; m. Rebecca Krug. Became midshipman U.S. Navy, 1833; sent with Lt. Charles Wilkes on exploring expdn. to South Seas, 1838, discovered a mountain peak in Antarctic; became lt., 1838; retired, 1855; naval storekeeper, Honolulu, Hawaii, 1857-61; commd. comdr. on U.S. Navy reserve list, given command naval depot, Port Royal, S.C., 1862-65; became commodore, 1866, rear admiral, 1873; chief bur. equipment and recruiting, 1870-75, had condensers for distilling fresh water and ovens for baking fresh bread installed for the 1st time on all naval vessels; commanded Asiatic Sta., 1875-77; did much to promote friendly relations between U.S. and Far East; retired, 1877. Died Nov. 5, 1879, Washington, D.C.

REYNOLDS, WILLIAM HOWARD, univ. dean; b. Herrin, Ill., Sept. 8, 1922; s. Herbert Emuel and Ruby (Hood) R.; B.Ed., So. Ill. U., 1943; Ph.D., U. Chgo., 1951; m. Harriet A. Ravnahrib, June 9, 1949; children—Margaret Jean, William George. Prof. polit. sci. Ill. Inst. Tech., 1948-52; regional dir. case analysis Office Salary Stblzn., Chgo., 1952-53; with Ford Motor Co., 1953-63; prof. marketing U. So. Cal., 1963-67, U. Ill., Chgo. Circle, 1967-68; dean, prof. bus. adminstrn. Sch. Bus. Adminstrn., Wayne State U., 1968-72. Dir. Inst. Advanced Advt. Studies, Los Angeles, 1965-67; research dir. Mgmt. Council Merit Employment, Tng. and Research, 1965-67. Served to capt. USMCR, 1943-46. Decorated Purple Heart. Mem. Am. Marketing Assn. (chmn. travel and transp. sect. 1965-67, book and monograph editor 1967-68), Econ. Club Detroit, Beta Gamma Sigma. Author: (with J.H. Myers) Consumer Behavior and Marketing Management, 1967; Products and Markets, 1969. Home: Birmingham MI Died Nov. 12, 1972.

RHIND, ALEXANDER COLDEN naval officer; b. N.Y.C., Oct. 31, 1821; s. Charles and Susan (Fell) R.; attended Naval Sch., Phila., 1844-45. Became midshipman U.S. Navy, 1838; served at capture of Alvarado and Tabasco during Mexican War; promoted lt., 1854; commanded ship Crusader in S. Atlantic Blockading Squadron, 1861; commanded ship Seneca, 1862; commd. lt. comdr., 1862; commanded iron clad Keokuk, 1862-63; comdr. Paul Jones and flagship Wabash, took part in attacks on Ft. Wagner and other Charleston defenses; promoted comdr., 1863; light house insp., 1880-82; commd. rear adm., 1883. Died N.Y.C., Nov. 8, 1897; buried Coldenham, N.Y.

RHOADS, CORNELIUS PACKARD dir. hosp. research; b. Springfield, Mass., June 20, 1898; s. George Holmes and Harriet (Barney) R.; A.B., Bowdoin Coll., 1920, D.Sc. (hon.), 1944; M.D. cum laude, Harvard, 1924; D.Sc. (honorary), Williams College, 1952; married Katherine S. Bolman, Sept. 9, 1936. Interne, dept. of surgery, Peter Bent Brigham Hosp., Boston, 1924-25, Trudeau fellow, Trudeau Sanatorium, N.Y.C., 1925-26; instr. in pathology Harvard Med. Sch., and asst. pathologist Boston City Hosp., 1926-28; asso. Rockefeller Inst. for Med. Research, 1928-33; asso. mem. in charge service for study hemotologic disorders, 1933-39; pathologist Hosp. of Rockefeller Inst. for Med. Research, 1931-39, dir. Memorial Center for Cancer and Allied Diseases, N.Y.C., 1940-52, scientific dir., 1953-—; dir. of The Sloan-Kettering Inst. for Cancer Research, 1945-—, James Ewing Hosp., N.Y.C., 1950-—; prof. pathology, dept. pathology, Cornell U. Med. Coll. 1940-52; prof. pathology, dept. biology and growth, Sloan Kettering Div., Cornell U. Med. Coll., 1952-—, spl. cons. U.S. Public Health Service, Nat. Adv. Cancer Council, 1947-—; cons., med. div., Chem. Corps, Army Chem. Center, Md., 1948-50. Col., M.C., A.U.S.; chief med. div., Chem. Warfare Service, 1943-45. Awarded Legion of Merit. Mem. com. to visit dept. of chemistry, Harvard. Trustee Kettering Foundation. Member National Research Council (member sub. com. on blood substitutes 1940-42; chmn. blood procurement 1941-42; mem. com. for treatment of war gas casualties 1941-43; mem. com. on veterans med. problems 1945-47; chmn. com. on growth 1945-48; mem. com. on atomic bomb casualties, 1946; chmn. exec. com. of com. on growth, 1946-47; mem. adv. com. of chem.-biol. coordinator center 1946-47; mem. at large, div. of med. sciences 1946-49), Office of Sci. Research and Dev. (mem. com. on insect and rodent control 1945-46). Fellow A.C.P., N.Y. Acad. Medicine (mem. com. on public health relations 1942-43; v.p. 1943-45), A.A.A.S. (v.p. 1953, chmn. sect. med. sci. 1953), Am. Geriatrics Soc.; mem. Am. Pub. Health Assn., Am. Soc. Control Cancer, Am. Cancer Soc. (bd. dirs. 1941-46; exec. com. 1944-46; mem. N.Y.C. cancer com. 1943-51) Blood Transfusion Assn. (bd. 1940-51), Harvey Soc., Soc. Exptl. Biology and Medicine, Soc. of Med. Jurisprudence, Am. Assn. Pathologists and Bacteriologists, Am. Assn. for Cancer Research, Am. Indsl. Hygiene Assn., A.M.A., Am. Radium Soc., Am. Soc. for Clin. Investigation, Am. Soc. Exptl. Pathology, Am. Soc. Tropical Med., Armed Forces Chem. Assn., Assn. Am. Physicians, Med. Soc. of State of N.Y., Med. Soc. of County of N.Y. (mem. spl. com. on cancer control, spl. com. on illegal practice of medicine), N.Y. Soc. Tropical Medicine, N.Y. Acad. Scis., N.Y. Zool. Soc., N.Y. City Welfare Council (mem. com. on chronic illness), Harvard Med. Alumni Assn., Interurban Pathol. Club, Interurban Clin. Club, Halsted Club. Clubs: University, Century Assn. (N.Y.C.); Harvard (Boston). Contbr. med. articles in profl. jours. Address: Sloan-Kettering Institute for Cancer Research, 410 E. 68th St., N.Y.C. 21. Died Aug. 13, 1959.

RHODES, CHARLES DUDLEY (rodz), army officer; b. Delaware, O., Feb. 10, 1865; s. Maj. Dudley Woodbridge and Marcia (Parrish) R.; A.B., Columbian (now George Washington) U., 1885; grad. U.S. Mil. Acad., 1889; honor grad. Inf. and Cav. Sch., 1907; grad. Army Staff Coll., 1908; Army War Coll., 1920; m. Mary F. Counselman, Dec. 2, 1890. Apptd. add. 2d lt. 7th Cav., 1889; advanced through grades to brig. gen. N.A., 1918, maj. gen. U.S. Army (temp.), 1918, brig gen. regular army, 1925, maj. gen., 1928; ret. from active service, 1929. In Sioux Indian Campaign, 1890-91; prof. mil. sci. and tactics, Ohio Wesleyan U., 1893-95; in Santiago Campaign as a.d.c. to insp. gen. of Army, and adj. gen. 2d Brigade, 2d Div., 5th Army Corps, 1898; recommended bvt. maj. "for gallant and meritorious services," at Santiago de Cuba, 1898; comd. Troop C, 6th Cav., on China Relief Expdn., 1900, later adj. gen. 1st Brigade in China and adj. gen. combined Anglo-Am. Expdn.; in numerous engagements with insurgents in Philippine Islands, 1900-03; published in Division orders "for distinguished conduct in action," P.I., 1901; received surrender insurgent battalion of Tiradores, at Binan, 1902; participated in Gen. Bell's campaigns in Philippine Islands; twice commended for services; commended for killing Moro outlaw, Jammang, Island of Jolo, 1910; duty Gen. Staff Corps, 1903-06, 1909-12; comdt. Mounted Service Schs., 1914-17 (awarded silver medal, San Francisco Expn., 1915, for excellence of exhibit of Mounted Service Schools); mem. Cav. Equipment Bd., 1915-17; comd. 21st Cav. (79th F.A.), 1917; brig. gen. comdg. 157 F.A. Brig., 1917-18, in Aisne-Marne, St. Mihiel, and Meuse-Argonne offensives, France; maj. gen. 42d and 34th divs., France; chief Am. sect., Permanent Interallied Armistice Commission, Spa, Belgium, 1918-19; maj. gen. comdg. Base Sect. 2 (Bordeaux), 1919. Awarded D.S.M. and D.S.C. (U.S.), also the Distinguished Service Star (U.S.); Knight Comdr. of the Bath (British); Comdr. Legion of Honor (French); Comdr. Order of the Crown (Belgium). Editor Jour. U.S. Cav. Assn., 1899-1900; prize essayist, same, 1898; Seaman prize essayist, Mil. Service Instn., 1901; gold medalist same, 1904. Asso. editor Upton's Military Policy of U.S., 1903. Lectr. before Army War Coll., 1906, Nat. Guard Assn. Pa., 1907, Nat. Guard Cal., 1908, Va. Mil. Inst., 1912. Trustee Assn. Graduates, U.S. Mil. Acad., 1935. Mem. Mil. Order of the Dragon, Mil. Order World War, Vets. Fgn. Wars, Army and Navy Union, Order of Shrine, Soc. of Army of Santiago de Cuba (pres. 1934-35), Phi Kappa Psi. Episcopalian. Clubs: Army and Navy (Washington and Manila). Author: The Cavalry, 1911; Robert E. Lee—The West Pointer, 1932. Address: War Dept., Washington. Died Jan. 24, 1948.*

RHODES, ELISHA HUNT soldier; b. Pawtuxet, Cranston, R.I., Mar. 21, 1842; s. Elisha Hunt and Eliza Ann (Chace) R.; ed. pub. schs. and commercial acad.; m. Caroline Pearce Hunt, of Cranston, R.I., June 12, 1866. Collector U.S. internal revenue, 1875-85; assessor of taxes, Providence, June, 1885-1913, ex-chmn. of board; Republican. Deacon Central Bapt. Ch., Providence; supt. S.S. for many yrs. until retired, 1902. Pres. Home for Aged Men and Aged Couples; dir. Old Colony Cooperative Bank. Pvt. 2d R.I. Vols., June, 1861; corpl. Co. D, June 5, 1861; sergt.-maj., Mar. 1, 1862; 2d lt., July 24, 1862; 1st lt., Mar. 2, 1863; comd. Co. B, May 1-Nov. 7, 1863; adj. 2d R.I. Vols., Nov. 7, 1864; capt., May 5, 1864; comd. regt., June 6-July 28, 1865; bvtd. maj. U.S.V., Dec. 5, 1864, "for gallant conduct at battle of Winchester," Sept. 19, 1864; lt.-col. 2d R.I. Vols., Jan. 31, 1865; bvtd. col. U.S.V., Apr. 2, 1865, "for gallant conduct before Petersburg," Apr. 2, 1865; col. 2d R.I. Vols., July 13, 1865; discharged July

28, 1865; brig.-gen. R.I. Militia, June 25, 1879; retired Mar. 21, 1892. Comdr. Prescott Post No. 1, G.A.R., 1867; comdr. Dept. of R.I., 1873-74; sr. vice-comdr.-in-chief G.A.R., 1877. Mem. Mass. Commandery Loyal Legion; v.p. 6th Army Corps Soc.; v.p. Army of the Potomac Soc.; pres. 2d R.I. Vol. Assn.; ex-pres. Soldiers and Sailors Hist. Soc. of R.I.; etc. Mem. Nat. Com. Gettysburg Celebration, 1913. Past Master and Past Grand Master of Masons of R.I.; Past Grand Dictator Grand Lodge Knights of Honor of R.I. Has made many hist., dedication, religious and Memorial Day addresses. Home: 77 Lloyd Av. Office: Industrial Trust Bldg., Providence, R.I.

RIBBLE, FREDERICK D. G., univ. prof.; b. Culpeper, Va., Jan. 14, 1898; s. Frederick Goodwin and Caroline Stribling (Marshall) R.; A.B., William and Mary Coll., 1916; M.A., U. of Va., 1917, LL.B., 1921; LL.M., Columbia U., 1932; Jur. ScD., Columbia, 1937; LL.D., Washington and Lee U., 1949, William and Mary College, 1952, Northwestern University, 1960; married to Mary Mason Anderson, December 18, 1940; 1 son, Frederick Goodwin. Instructor law U. Va., 1920-21; asst. prof. law, 1921-24, associate prof., 1924-27, prof. since 1927, acting dean, law dept., 1937-39, dean, 1939-63, emeritus, 1963-71; asso. Sands, Williams and Lightfoot, Richmond, Va., 1928. Alternate member board of Appeals in Visa Cases, 1942-44, mem. 1944-45. Served as pvt., F.A., U.S. Army, 1918. Mem. U.S. Nat. Commn. for UNESCO, 1946-51. Pres. Assn. of Am. Law Schs., 1951. Mem. council Am. Law Inst.; mem. Am., Va. (pres. 1955-56) bar assns., Kappa Sigma, Phi Delta Phi, Omicron Delta Kappa, Phi Beta Kappa. Episcopalian. Clubs: Colonnade, Cosmos (Washington). Author: State and National Power Over Commerce, 1937. Editor: Minor on Real Property, 2d edit., 1928. Home: Charlottesville VA Died Dec. 1, 1971.

RICE, DEVEREUX DUNLAP mfr. mica; b. Memphis, Tenn., Feb. 27, 1898; s. John Ewing and Willie McGavock (Dunlap) R.; B.S. (engring. chemistry), Ga. Sch. of Tech., Atlanta, 1921; m. Dorothy Bailey, Apr. 11, 1921; children—Martha, Charles Bailey. Began with La. Oil Refining Co., Shreveport, 1921; apptd. chemist Southern Mica Co., miners and grinders of mica, Franklin, N.C., and Johnson City, Tenn., 1923, continuing successively as sec.-treas., v.p. and gen. mgr.; pres. since 1940. Pres. Dry Ground Mica Assn., 1939-40; Johnson City Community Chest, 1944. Served as 2d lt. inf., U.S. Army, World War, 1918. Chmn. Divisional Code Authority of Mica Industry. Mem. Scabbard and Blade, Pi Kappa Phi (dist. archon, 1936-43, nat. historian, 1943-46, nat. pres. 1946-48). Democrat. Presbyterian. Mason (Shriner). Clubs: Rotary (pres. Franklin, N.C., Rotary, 1928-29; pres. Johnson City Rotary, 1945-46; dist. gov. 186th Dist., Rotary Internat., 1947-48), Johnson City Country (pres. 1941), Hurstleigh. Home: Johnson City, Tenn. Died Aug. 11, 1948.

RICE, EDMUND army officer; b. Cambridge, Mass., 1842; enlisted in Union army at beginning of Civil war; apptd., July 25, 1861, capt. 19th Mass. inf.; mustered out as col., June 30, 1865; received Congressional medal of honor for conspicuous bravery in leading his div. in a countercharge against Pickett's div., he himself falling, severely wounded, within the enemy's lines, in the battle of Gettysburg. Entered regular army, 1st lt. 40th inf., July 28, 1866; bvt. capt., maj. and col., U.S.A.; assigned to 5th inf., Dec. 31, 1870; regimental adj., July 5, 1879, to Mar. 10, 1883; on leave of absence, 1877, at time of Turko-Russian war; temporarily attached to staff of Gen. Skobeleff; promoted capt., Mar. 10, 1883; organized and comd. Columbian Guards at World's Columbian Exposition; later military attaché, Tokio, Japan; appointed col. 6th Mass. regt. by Gov. Wolcott on recommendation of Gen. Miles; apptd. insp. gen. U.S.A., May 1898; served on Gen. Miles' staff; later col. 26th vol. inf.; col. 19th U.S. inf., 1902-03; brig. gen. and retired, 1903. Invented a trowel bayonet, stacking swivel and knife-in-trenching bayonet, used in army. Address: Washington. Died 1906.

RICE, HEBER HOLBROOK lawyer; b. Paintsville, Ky., Dec. 21, 1882; s. Harvey Burns and Mary Louisa (Hurt) R.; B.S. U. Ky., 1904, LL.D., 1956; LL.B., Harvard, 1907; LL.D., Athens Coll., 1944; m. Ruth Straughan, Sept. 6, 1917; children—Heber H., Jr., Craig Shelby. Admitted to Ky. State bar 1907, W. Va., 1908, Tenn., 1919, D.C. 1922, Ct. of Claims, 1923, U.S. Supreme Ct., 1928; practiced law Huntington, W.Va., 1908-16; asst. pros. attorney, Cabell County, 1909-11; counsel for gov. in martial law litigation, 1914-15; atty. Old Hickory Powder Plant, Nashville, 1919-21; atty., later spl. asst. to U.S. Atty. Gen., Washington, D.C., 1921-34; also spl. asst. to U.S. atty., D.C., 1922-23; atty., later head atty. H.O.L.C., Washington, 1934-44, supervising 150,000 land law suits and proceedings in all 48 states; on gen. counsel staff, comptroller gen. Office, Washington, D.C., 1944-52; exec. director Federal Bar Assn., 1952-53; pvt. practice law 1952-—; director various organizations. Served as maj. comdg. bn., U.S. Army, Mex. Border Service, World War I, 1916-18; lt. col., judge advocate gen. Dept. Reserve, War Dept., World War II, 1940-43; asst. chief legal div., Office Chief Chem. Warfare, Washington, D.C., 1942; staff judge advocate and chief of legal div., Huntsville (Ala.) Arsenal, 1942-43; inactive status since Dec. 1943, promoted to col. Inactive Res., 1945. Mem. Am. Bar Assn. (former chmn. com. on pvt. claims, and of com. on comparative land laws, mem. ho. dels., rep. Fed. Bar Assn. 1948), Columbia and Montgomery historical societies, Inter-American Bar Association (delegate to Havana conf., 1941), Fed. Bar Assn. (chmn. of admissions com., member nat. council, pres. 1940-41, former chmn. membership, speakers, keymen, reception Coms., recipient meritorious service award, 1952), Am. Trade Assn. Execs., U.N. League of Lawyers (hon. pres. original sec. gen., 1946, del. to Paris Conf., 1948), U. of Ky. Alumni Assn., W. Va. Soc. of D.C. (pres. 1938-40). Judge Advocates Assn. (chmn. Harvard Law Class Reunion, 1947, 57), Conference of State Societies (pres. 1953-54), Ky. and Md. State Societies, Am. Legion (past comdr.), Mil. Order World Wars, Res. Officers Assn., Sigma Alpha Epsilon. Meth. Mason (Shriner). Clubs: Post Mortem, Sertoma, Harvard. Author: Collected Speeches, 1947; U.S. Land Law Procedural Map; Thirty Years in the Nations Capital, 1957; articles: Behind the Iron Curtain, etc. Contbr. to law jours. Home: 3807 Taylor St., Chevy Chase, Washington 15. Deceased.

RICE, JOHN HODGEN army officer; b. St. Louis, Mo., Jan. 6, 1870; s. Virgil and Aurelia R. R.; grad. U.S. Mil. Acad., 1893; m. Mary L. Angell, Nov. 7, 1903. Commd. 2d lt. 3d Cav., June 12, 1893; 1st lt. ordnance, Nov. 21, 1898; capt., Apr. 5, 1903; maj., Oct. 10, 1907; lt. col., July 1, 1916; col. N.A., Jan. 8, 1918; brig. gen. N.A., Feb. 18, 1918; lt. col. ordnance, Sept. 15, 1919. Served during strikes at Chicago, and at Ft. Sheridan, Ill., July-Oct. 1894; instr. mathematics, U.S. Mil. Acad., 1895-97; with regt. in Fla., Spanish-Am. War, 1898; at Manila, P.I., 1901-03; asst. to chief of ordnance, Washington, D.C., 1906-12; comdg. San Antonio Arsenal, and chief ordnance officer Southern Dept., 1912-14; chief of carriage div., Office Chief of Ordnance, 1915-17; chief of engring. div. Ordnance Dept., Washington, D.C., 1917-18; arrived in France, June 26, 1918; apptd. chief ordnance officer, A.E.F., Oct. 9, 1918; returned to U.S. Aug. 26, 1919; duty as chief of mfr. Ordnance Dept., Oct. 1919-July 1, 1921; retired from active service, July 1, 1921, on own application. Awarded D.S.M.; Comdr. Legion of Honor (French). Address: Washington, D.C. Died Jan. 7, 1940.

RICE, LEWIS FREDERICK architect, civil engr.; b. Boston, Mass., May 17, 1839; s. Lewis and Susan Augusta (Brigham) R.; ed. public schools, 1845-52; West Point, 1853-54; grad. Rensselaer Poly. Inst., C.E., 1858; engr. on construction, Brooklyn water works, 1858-59; div. engr. Troy & Greenfield (Hoosac Tunnel) R.R., 1860-61; in U.S. army as lt., capt. and maj. 31st Mass. vols., 1862-65; gen. practice civ. engr., Boston, 1865-66; asst. engr. Reading & Columbia R.R., Pa., 1867; asst. engr. St. Louis, Mo., water works, 1867-71; in gen. practice architect and civ. engr., Boston, 1872-90; asst. engr. and architect Am. Bell Telephone Co., 1890-—. Home: Brookline, Mass. Died 1909.

RICE, STEPHEN EWING judge; b. Apalachicola, Fla., July 23, 1905; s. Stephen Ewing and Carolyn (Floyd) R.; B.S., U.S. Naval Acad., 1922-26; LL.B., Columbia U., 1931; m. Lida Carolyn Johns, Dec. 26, 1936; children—Stephen Ewing, Jeffrey Bourke. Admitted to N.Y. bar, 1932; asst. legislative counsel United States Senate, 1933-42, legislative counsel 1945-50; judge U.S. Tax Court, Washington, since October 1950. Served as ensign, U.S. Navy, 1926-28; asst. air officer, U.S.S. Lexington, Pacific, wounded in action off Manila, 1944, ret. as capt. USNR. Mem. bar U.S. Supreme Ct. and Dist. of Columbia. Awarded Bronze star, Purple Heart, Presidential Unit Citation with bronze star, Am. Theatre and Asiatic Pacific Campaign medals with 9 combat stars, Philippine Liberation and Victory medals. Club: Army-Navy Country, (Arlington, Va.). Home: Holly Ridge, R.F.D. 1, Oakton, Va. Office: 12th and Constitution Av. N.W., Washington. Died Feb. 1958.

RICH, ARNOLD RICE, pathologist; b. Birmingham, Ala., Mar. 28, 1893; s. Samuel and Hattie (Rice) R.; A.B., U. of Va., 1914, M.A., 1915; M.D., Johns Hopkins University, 1919; M.D. (honorary) University Zurich; married Helen Elizabeth Jones, June 3, 1925; children—Adrienne Cecile, Cynthia Marshall Asst. in pathology, Johns Hopkins U., 1919-20, instr., 1920-21, asso., 1921-23, asso. prof., 1923-44, prof., 1944-47, Baxley prof., dir. dept., 1947-58, Baxley professor emeritus, 1958-68; resident pathologist, Johns Hopkins Hosp., 1920-26, asso. pathologist, 1929-44, pathol.-in-chief, 1947-58, now hon. cons.; expert cons. to the Surg. Gen., U.S. Army; mem. sci. adv. bd. Armed Forces Inst. of Pathology (chmn. 1951); special cons. USPHS; consultant in pathology Veterans Administration; consultant in med. research, Chem. Warfare Service, since 1943; adv. consultant Tuberculosis Control Div., U.S.P.H.S.; Nat. Research Council (com. on pathol., 1947-52). U.S. State Dept. del., 1st Internat. Allergy Congress, 1951; mem. Comite d'Honneur, 50th anniversary celebration of discovery of anaphylaxis, Paris, 1952. Served with U.S. Army, 1917-18; lt. commander USNR, ret. Decorated Chevalier Legion of Honor (France); awarded Charles Mickle hon. fellowship, U. Toronto Faculty of Medicine, 1956; Kober medal, Assn. of Am. Physicians, 1958; Gordon Wilson medal, Am. Clin. and Climatol. Assn., 1960; Trudeau medal, Nat. Tb Assn., 1960; Gairdner Found. (Can.) Internat. award, 1960; honorary Plaque, Japanese Soc. for Tb, 1960; medal A.C.P., 1963; Seaman award Assn. Mil. Surgeons U.S., 1963. Trustee Roland Park Co. Sch., 1944-51. Fellow A.A.A.S., Internat. Assn. Allergists, Royal Soc. Medicine London (hon.); honorary member Pathological Society of Great Britain and Ireland, Am. Clin. and Climatol. Assn., Harvey Soc., Soc. Francaise d'Allergie; fgn. corr. mem. Soc. Med. des Hopitaux de Paris; fgn. mem. Soc. Aregentina de Anat. Norm. y Patol.; corr. mem. Soc. Brasileria de Tuberc., Tb Soc. of Scotland; asso. mem. Soc. Anat. de Paris. Dir. Md. Tb Assn., 1947-51. Mem. Nat. Acad. Scis., Assn. Am. Physicians, Soc. Exptl. Biology and Medicine (editorial bd. Proc. 1943-47), Soc. Exptl. Pathology, Am. Assn. Pathologists and Bacteriologists, Phi Beta Kappa, Sigma Xi, Alpha Omega Alpha. Club: 14 W. Hamilton St. Author: The Pathogenesis of Tuberculosis 1944, rev. 1951, Spanish edit., 1946, Japanese edit., 1954. Mem. editorial bd. Bull. of the Johns Hopkins Hosp., 1925-63, Internat. Archives Allergy and Immunology, Internat. Review Experimental Pathology. Contributor articles in field. Home: Baltimore MD Died Apr. 17, 1968; buried Baltimore Nat. Cemetery, Baltimore MD

RICH, CARL W., congressman; b. Cin., Sept. 12, 1898; s. David William and Rosa (West) R.; A.B., U. Cin., 1922, LL.B., 1924, LL.D., 1959; m. Frances Ivins, Sept. 8, 1926. Admitted to Ohio bar; asst. city solicitor, asst. city pros., Cin.; judge Common Pleas Ct. of Hamilton County; mem. 88th U.S. Congress 1st Ohio Dist. Pres., chmn. bd. Cin. Royals, profl. basketball team; pres. Kennedy Savs. & Loan Co.; v.p. Central Hyde Park Savs. & Loan Co.; dir. First Nat. Bank, Morrow, O., Grand Central Savs. & Loan Co., Home State Savs. & Loan Co., Hamilton Mut. Ins. Co.; legal counsel bldg. and loan cos. Mem. adv. bd. Greater Cin. unit Salvation Army. Mem. city council, Cin., then mayor. Trustee Cin. Zool. Soc. Served with U.S. Army, World War I; served to col., CWS, AUS, World War II. Recipient Nat. Distinguished Alumni award Tau Kappa Alpha; 1961. Mem. Lambda Chi Alpha, Phi Alpha Delta, Omicron Delta Kappa, Tau Kappa Alpha. Republican. Mason (33 degree, Shriner), Moose, Eagle. Club: Cincinnati (past v.p.). Home: Cincinnati OH Died June 26, 1972; interred Spring Grove Mausoleum, Spring Grove Cemetery, Cincinnati OH

RICH, CHARLES SWIFT civil engr.; b. Philadelphia, Pa., July 19, 1864; s. George Inman and Elizabeth Ramsay (Wetherill) R.; grad. Friends' Central Sch., Phila., 1881; grad. U.S. Mil. Acad., 1886; grad. Engr. Sch. of Application, Willet Point, N.Y., 1889; m. Annie Weir, June 6, 1889 (died 1897); children—Swift, Weir (killed in France Dec. 19, 1918). Commd. add. 2d lt. Corps of Engrs., July 1, 1886; promoted through grades to col., July 1, 1916; served as col. 1st U.S. Vol. Inf., May 30, 1898-Oct. 28, 1898; retired Jan. 18, 1921. Engaged extensively in river and harbor work; Great Lakes harbors and connecting channels; U.S. lake survey; upper Miss. River improvement; completion Hennepin Canal, Tex. harbors, Coast Canal, Houston Ship Channel and Texas City Dike; fortifications of New Orleans, Galveston and Panama Canal; consulting engr. on grade raising of City of Galveston, Tex., 1903-04. Mem. Engring. Bd. of Rev., Sanitary Dist. of Chicago, 1924-25. Democrat. Episcopalian. Mason, Elk. Died Mar. 20, 1836.

RICH, GILES WILLARD lawyer; b. Rochester, N.Y., Dec. 13, 1875; s. Willard Giles and Rebecca Cameron (Luitwieler) R.; ed. Purdue U., U. of Rochester, Mass. Inst. Tech.; m. Sarah T. Sutherland; children—Giles S., Eleanor H. (Mrs. H. H. Van Staagen). Admitted to N.Y. bar, 1899; Pa. bar, 1945; District of Columbia bar, 1947; member firm Williams, Rich & Morse, New York, 1928-41; specializes in patent law, trade marks and copyrights; partner in firm Church & Rich, Rochester, N.Y., 1905-19; patent counsel Western Electric Co., 1919-26; spl. asst. to atty. gen., 1934-37; became pres. Richtex Oil Corp., 1939; now mem. firm Munn, Liddy, Glaccum & Rich, Washington, D.C. Attended O.T.C., Plattsburg, New York, 1915; mem. Aircraft Prodn. Bd., equipment sect., during World War; lt. col. Air Corps Res. Head Army Air Corps Sect., Div. Contract Distribution, O.P.M., 1941. Mem. Am. Bar Assn., Assn. Bar City of N.Y., Am. Patent Law Assn., Air Reserve Assn. (exec. com. 2d Corps Area), Nat. Air Defense League (nat. v.p., dir. N.Y. Chapter), Soc. of Genesee (gov.), Mayflower Soc., S.R., Delta Psi. Democrat. Presbyn. Mason (32 deg., K.T., Shriner); past dist. dep. N.Y. State. Clubs: Advertising, Kiwanis (New York); Army and Navy (Washington, D.C.); Seigniory. Home: 1734 P St. N.W. Office: 1319 F St. N.W., Washington, D.C. Died Feb. 6, 1949.

RICH, JOHN LYON educator; born at Hobart, Delaware County, N.Y., Dec. 1, 1884; s. Thomas and Marion Augusta (Lyon) R.; A.B., Cornell U., 1906, A.M., 1907, Ph.D., 1911; m. Genevieve Cynthia Potts, June 28, 1912 (dec.); children—Ralph Albert, Catherine Louise (Mrs. Donald Salisbury Getchell); m. 2d, Nellie Okla Barrett, Apr. 22, 1922. Instr. in geology, Cornell U., 1908-09; instr. and asso. in geography, U. of Ill., 1911-18; petroleum geologist with oil cos., 1919-22; cons. petroleum geologist, 1922-31; successively asst. prof., asso. prof. and prof. of economic geology, U. Cincinnati, from 1931, later research prof. of geology, now emeritus professor; geologic aid, U.S. Geol. Survey, part time, 1907-10, 1917; asst. geologist, Ill. Geol.

Survey, part time, 1914-17, N.Y. Geol. Survey, part time, 1916, 17, 19, technical cons., Petroleum Adminstrn. for War; mem. Am. War Prodn. Mission to China, Apr.-June 1945. Member Ohio Natural Resources Commn., 1952-—. Vice pres., chmn. Sect. E (geol. and geog.), Am. Assn. Advancement Sci., 1946. Editor Bull. of Am. Assn. Petroleum Geologists, 1926-29. Capt. Mil. Intelligence Div., U.S. Army, 1918-19. Mem. Geol. Soc. Am. (mem. publ. com.). Am. Inst. of Mining and Metall. Engrs., Soc. Economic Geologists, Assn. Am. Geographers, Geophys. Union, Am. Geog. Soc., American Association of Petroleum Geologists, Ohio Acad. Sci., Gamma Alpha, Sigma Xi, Sigma Gamma Epsilon. Author: Glacial Geology of the Catskill Mountains, 1935; The Face of South America; an Aerial Traverse, 1942; and numerous papers in scientific jours. Home: 848 Dunore Rd., Cin. 20. Died May 21, 1956; buried Hobart, N.Y.

RICHARD, CHARLES col. Med. Corps, U.S. Army; b. New York, Nov. 10, 1854; s. Jacob and Fredericka (Herbig) R.; B.S., Coll. City of New York, 1874; M.D., New York U., 1876; m. Laura R. Bailey, Nov. 8, 1887. Interne, Charity Hosp., New York, Apr. 1876-Sept. 30, 1877; asst. phys., Randall's Island Hosp., Oct. 1, 1877-Apr. 1, 1878; attending phys., Essex Market Dispensary, New York, 1878-79; lecturer on mil. surgery, and prof. surgery, U. of Colo., 1889-91. Apptd. from N.Y. 1st lt. asst. surgeon U.S.A., June 3, 1879; capt. asst. surgeon, June 3, 1884; maj. surgeon, Nov. 15, 1897; lt. col. Med. Corps, U.S.A., Apr. 10, 1908; col. Med. Corps, Feb. 18, 1910; brig. gen. Med. Corps N.A., Aug. 5, 1917. Dept. surgeon, Hdqrs. Eastern Dept., and asst. to Surgeon Gen. of the Army, War Dept., 1917-18. Retired from active service, Nov. 10, 1918. Address: New York, N.Y. Died Apr. 19, 1940.

RICHARD, MATTHIAS congressman, b. nr. Pottstown, New Hanover Twp., Montgomery County, Pa., Feb. 26, 1758; prep. studies under pvt. tutoring. Served as pvt. in Col. Daniel Udree's 2d battalion, Berks County (Pa.) Militia in Revolutionary War, 1777-78; participated in battles of Brandywine and Germantown; maj. 4th Battalion, Philadelphia County Militia, 1780; apptd. justice of peace, 1788, held office 40 years; judge Berks County Ct., 1791-97; insp. customs, 1801-02; mem. U.S. Ho. of Reps. from Pa., 10th-11th congresses, 1807-11; apptd. collector revenue Pa. 9th Dist., 1813; clk. Berks County Orphans Ct., 1823; asso. judge Berks County Cts.; became mcht., Reading, Pa. Died Reading, Aug. 4, 1830; buried Charles Evans Cemetery.

RICHARDS, ALFRED NEWTON pharmacologist, b. Stamford, N.Y., Mar. 22, 1876; s. Rev. Leonard E. and Mary E. (Burbank) R.; B.A., Yale, 1897, M.A., 1899; Ph.D., Columbia, 1901; hon. Sc.D., U. Pa., 1925, Western Res. U., 1931, Yale, 1933, Harvard, 1940, Columbia, 1942. Williams Coll., 1943, Princeton, 1940. N.Y. U., 1955, Rockefeller Inst., 1960, Oxford U., 1960; hon. M.D., U. Pa., 1932, U. Louvain, 1949; LL.D., U. Edinburgh (Scotland), 1935; Johns Hopkins, 1949; m. Lillian L. Woody, Dec. 26, 1908. Instr., physiol. chemistry Columbia, 1898-1904, pharmacology, 1904-08; prof. pharmacology Northwestern U., 1908-10; prof. pharmacology U. Pa., 1910-46, emeritus prof., 1946-—, v.p. charge med. affairs, 1939-48; Herter lectr. N.Y. U., Bellevue Hosp. Med. Coll., 1926; Beaumont lectr., 1929; Croonian lectr. Royal Soc. London, 1938. Chmn. Com. on Med. Research, Office Sci. Research and Devel., U.S. Govt., 1941-46. Mem. Com. on Fed. Med. services Hoover Commn. on Orgn. Exec. Br. Govt., May-Dec. 1948. Mem. sci. staff Brit. Med. Research Com., London, 1917-18; maj. San. Corps, U.S. Army, attached to Chem. Warfare Service. Chaumont, France, July-Dec. 1918. Mem. Nat. Acad. Scis. (pres. 1947-50), Assn. Am. Physicians, Am. Philos. Soc., (v.p. 1944-47), Am. Physiol. Soc., Wistar Assn., Brit. Physiol. Soc. (hon.), Am. Soc. Biol. Chemists, Am. Pharmacol. Soc., Soc. Exptl. Biology and Medicine, Harvey Soc., Physiol. Soc. Phila., Phila. County Med. Soc. (hon.). Interurban Clin. Club (hon.), Sigma Xi, Alpha Omega Alpha, Phi Beta Kappa (hon.), corr. mem. Gesellsch. der Aertze in Wien; hon. mem. Am. Urol. Soc., Royal Soc. Medicine (London); fgn. mem. Royal Soc., London, Royal Danish, Acad. Sci., Royal Soc. Edinburgh; fellow Am. Acad. Arts and Scis., A.A.A.S., Coll. of Physicians Phila. (hon.); fgn. corr. mem. Brit. Med. Assn. Awarded Gerhard medal, 1932; Kober medal, 1933; Keyes medal, 1933; John Scott medal, 1934; N.Y. Acad. Med. medal, 1936; Phila. award, 1937; Procter medal; Guggenheim Cup Award; Lasker award, 1946; Kovalenko medal Nat. Acad. Sci., 1953; Abraham Flexner award Assn. Am. Med. Colls., 1959, Decorated Medal for Merit, 1946; hon. comdr. Order Brit. Empire, 1948. Trustee Rockefeller Found., 1937-41. Clubs: Century (N.Y.); Rittenhouse, Republican. Presbyn. Author papers on action chloroform, histamine, function of kidneys. Successively asst., assoc. and mng. editor Jour. Biol. Chem., 1905-14. Home: 737 Rugby Rd., Bryn Mawr, Pa. 19010. Died Mar. 24, 1966.

RICHARDS, E(DWARD) F(RANKLIN) educator, b. San Juan, P.R., Aug. 22, 1903; s. Rev. Herbert Franklin and Lillian Ainsley (McDavid) R.; student Balt. City Coll., 1920; A.B., Johns Hopkins, 1924, Ph.D., 1929; studied in Germany, summer 1923, Spain, 1924; m. Katharine Coles Gregory, Nov. 1, 1930; children—Edward Franklin, Katharine Coles. Instr. Latin and Spanish, Shenandoah Valley Acad., Winchester, Va., 1924-26; instr. Spanish, Johns Hopkins U., 1927-29; field asst. U.S. Geol. Survey, summers 1927, 28; asso. geol. Venezuela Gulf Oil Co., exploration work in Venezuela and Colombia, 1929-32; head Spanish sect., modern lang. dept. U. Md., 1933-35; instr. geology and paleontol. U. Ala., 1935; asst. prof., 1937-45, asso. prof., 1945-46, prof. since 1946, head department of geology, since 1954-—. Commd. lt. (j.g.) USNR, 1942; active service, 1942-46; tng. duty at sea (Atlantic) 1944; lt. comdr. since 1946. Fellow Geol. Soc. Am.; mem. Paleontol. Soc., Am. Assn. Petroleum Geologists, Am. Inst. Mining and Metall. Engrs., Ala. Acad. Scis., Phi Beta Kappa, Sigma Xi, Gamma Alpha, Delta Upsilon. Club: University. Author: Part II, of Mesozoic Fossils of the Peruvian Andes, Johns Hopkins Studies in Geology No. 15, 1947. Home: 27 Guild's Woods, Tuscaloosa, Ala. 35401. Died Dec. 1, 1965.

RICHARDS, EMERSON LEWIS b. Atlantic City, July 9, 1884; s. Jacob R. and Martina (Mada) R.; LL.B., U. Pa., 1906; m. Admitted to N.J., bar, 1907, counsellor at law, 1910; mem. Ho. of Assembly, N.J., 3 terms, 1912-14, leader House, 1913-14; mem. Senate N.J., 1917-18, 1922-35; elected pres. Senate, 1933; acting gov., Aug.-Oct. 1933. Apptd. dep. atty. gen. N.J., 1919, assigned as counsel N.J. Interstate Bridge and Tunnel Commn., later as counsel for Del. River Bridge Joint Commn. (resigning Sept. 1923). Now dep. atty. gen. N.J. Served as capt., later maj. U.S. Army, World War. Mem. Mil. Order World War (jr. vice comdr. 1941), Am. Legion (post comdr. 1941). Republican. Episcopalian. Clubs: Penn Athletic, Elks. Home: 1245 Boardwalk, Atlantic City. Died Oct. 21, 1963; buried Atlantic City Cemetery, Pleasantville, N.J.

RICHARDS, GEORGE officer U.S. Marine Corps; b. Ironton, O., Feb. 6, 1872; s. Samuel and Laura Ann (Westlake) R.; grad. U.S. Naval Acad., Academic Course, 1891, full course, 1893; grad. Sch. of Application, U.S. Marine Corps, 1894; m. Lydia Knechtel Putney, Sept. 28, 1936. Commd. 2d lt. U.S. Marine Corps, July 1, 1893; 1st lt., Feb. 11, 1898; maj. asst. paymaster, Mar. 11, 1899; paymaster U.S. Marine Corps with rank of brig. gen., Sept. 8, 1916. Served on Newark and Lancaster, S. Atlantic Sta., 1895-97; Newark, Spanish-Am. War, south coast of Cuba, May-Nov. 1898; participated in bombardment of Santiago de Cuba, July 2, 1898, and Battle of Manzanillo, Aug. 12, 1898; served in Philippine Islands, 1899-1900; in Boxer Rebellion, June-Sept. 1900; took part in Battle of Tientsin, July 14, 1900; participated in march to Peking and relief of the legations at Peking, Aug. 1900; served with Army of Cuban Pacification, Havana, Cuba, 1906-07; retired from service, Mar. 1, 1936. Was nominated bvt. lt. colonel "for distinguished conduct in the presence of the enemy," at the Battle of Tientsin; awarded Sampson medal, 1898; West Indian, Philippine, China and Cuban Pacification, Victory, Expeditionary, Nicaragua, and Brevet medals; D.S.M. for service in World War. Officer Legion of Honor (France); Merito Militar (Republica Dominicana); Order of Merit (Nicaraguan Rep.). Mem. D.C. Soc. S.R. (sec. 1914-16; pres. 1917-26). Episcopalian. Mason. Clubs: Army and Navy (ex-pres.), Chevy Chase. Address: Route 4, Staunton, Va.* Died Jan. 9, 1948.

RICHARDS, GEORGE GILL physician; b. Mendon, Utah, Sept. 5, 1883; s. Dr. Stephen L. and Emma Louise (Stayner) R.; student U. of Utah, 1898-1902, U. of Chgo., 1903-04; M.D., N.Y. U., Bellevue Hosp. Med. Sch., 1906; grad. work, Vienna, 1910-13; engaged in practice as physician, 1906-—; clin. prof. internal medicine U. of Utah, 1942-—. Served as capt. M.C., U.S. Army Reserve, 1918-34. Mem. med. adv. bd. Selective Service 1940-—. Lt. col. USPHS. Mem. Am. Bd. Internal Medicine, 1936-46. Fellow Am. Coll. Physicians (gov. 1924-34; regent 1934-37; v.p. 1937-38); mem. A.M.A. (chmn. med. sect. 1932), Salt Lake County, Utah State med. assns., Salt Lake Clinic, Interurban Club of Pacific Coast. Clubs: Salt Lake Country, Rotary, Alta (Salt Lake City). Home: 360 A St., Salt Lake 3. Office: 115 East South Temple, Salt Lake City. Died Apr. 20, 1950; buried Salt Lake City Cemetery.

RICHARDS, PRESTON govt. ofcl.; b. Chariton Co., Mo., Nov. 23, 1905; s. William D. and Lula Belle (Hampton) R.; B.S. in agr., U. Mo., 1927, A.M., 1929. Livestock economist Bur. Agrl. Economics, U.S. Dept. Agr., 1930-41, livestock br., 1941-42, dep. dir., 1946-50, dir. dairy br. Prodn. Marketing Adminstrn. 1950-53, asst. adminstr. commodity operations, 1953; now dep. adminstr. Commodity Stablzn. Service. Served as maj., Q.M.C., U.S. Army, 1942-45. Home: 3130 Wisconsin Av. N.W., Washington 16. Office: Adminstration Bldg. Agr., Washington 25. Died Aug. 26, 1957.

RICHARDSON, DAVID CROCKETT mayor; b. New Kent Co., Va., June 7, 1845; s. Turner and Margaret Ann (Robertson) R.; removed to Richmond, Va., 1855; ed. pvt. schs.; enlisted at beginning of Civil War in Packer's Battery of Art., C.S.A.; wounded at 2d battle of Manassas, discharged, but reenlisted within a few mos. and served until end of war; LL.B., Richmond Coll. Sch. of Law, 1874; m. Alice A. Fellows; 2d, Florence B. Hechler. Clerk Police Ct., Richmond, 1870-80; justice Police Ct., 1880-88; commonwealth's atty., 1896-1906 (declined reelection); practiced law, 1906-08; mayor of Richmond, 1908-—; Democrat. Recording sec. Va. Hist. Soc., 20 yrs.; mem. Va. State Bar Assn., Richmond Bar Assn., Am. Hist. Soc., R.E. Lee & Camp No. 1, George E. Pickett Camp Confederate Vets., bd. visitors Confederate Soldiers' Home. Clubs: Commonwealth, Business Men's Home: Richmond, Va.

RICHARDSON, EDWARD PEIRSON surgeon; b. Boston, Mass., Apr. 7, 1881; s. Maurice Howe and Margaret White (Peirson) R.; A.B., Harvard, 1902, M.D., 1906; m. Clara Lee Shattuck, May 26, 1917 (died Dec. 6, 1921); children—Edward Peirson, Elliot Lee, George Shattuck. Surg. asst. to father, 1907-12; gen. practice, Boston, 1912-22; on staff Mass. Gen. Hosp., Boston, from 1911, now honorary mem. staff; with Harvard Med. Sch. from 1913, John Homans prof. surgery, now emeritus. Served with 1st Harvard Unit, 22, Gen. Hosp., B.E.F., 1915; capt., later maj. Med. Corps, U.S. Army, in France and Germany, 1918-19. Fellow Am. Coll. Surgeons; mem. A.M.A., Am. Surg. Assn., Southern Surg. Assn., Soc. Clin. Surgery. Republican. Clubs: Harvard, Somerset (Boston); Brookline Country. Co-author: (with J. H. Means) Diseases of the Thyroid, 1929. Contbr. various surg. articles. Home: 617 Boylston St., Brookline, Mass. Died Jan. 26, 1944.

RICHARDSON, GEORGE ADAMS business exec.; b. Auburn, N.Y., Nov. 23, 1887; s. Frank Wood and Charlotte Letchworth (Adams) R.; grad. Groton Sch., 1906; A.B., Yale, 1910; m. Mrs. Anne Thompson Morse, Oct. 19, 1918; stepchildren—Samuel F.B. Morse, Jr., John B. Morse, Mrs. Kenneth S. Walker. Ranch hand, Durango, Mexico, 1911-14; with Armour & Co., Chgo., 1914-21, No. Trust Co., 1921, Estate of Marshall Field, 1921-27, trustee, 1927-43, asst. to Marshall Field, 1943-—; v.p., dir. Field Enterprises, Inc.; owner The Inn at Rancho Santa Fe, Cal. Alderman, Lake Forest, 1923-27. Asst. dir. aviation div. Surplus War Property Adminstrn., 1944-45. Trustee Chgo. Mus. Natural History; pres. Chgo. Council Fgn. Relations, 2 terms. Served as capt. Battery C, 149th F.A.; maj. adj., 171st F.A. Brigade, World War I, subsequently lt col. 865th F.A., O.R.C.; lt. col. Air Transport Command, A.A.F., 1943-44. Mem. Alpha Delta Phi. Republican. Episcopalian. Clubs: Chicago, Attic (Chgo.); Old Elm (Lake Forest, Ill.); Kona Kai (San Diego, Cal.). Home: Rancho Santa Fe, Cal. Office: 135 S. LaSalle St., Chgo. Died Apr. 15, 1958; buried Fort Rosecran Nat. Cemetery, San Diego, Cal.

RICHARDSON, HENRY BROWN mem. U.S. Miss. River Commission; b. Winthrop, Me., Aug. 23, 1837; ed. in public and private schools, Portland, Me.; 1857-59 in civil engring. offices in Portland, Milwaukee, Chicago, Boston and La.; m. Anna Howard Farrar, June 18, 1867; 1861-65, pvt. 6th La. vol. inf., lt. engrs. and capt. engrs., provisional army Confederate States army Northern Va.; prisoner of war, Johnson's Island. Mem. La. Bd. State Engrs., 1877-1904; chief State engr., 1880-1904. Home: New Orleans, La. Died 1909.

RICHARDSON, ISRAEL BUSH army officer; b. Fairfax, Vt., Dec. 26, 1815; s. Israel Putnam and Susan (Holmes) R.; grad. U.S. Mil. Acad., 1841; m. Rita Stevenson, Aug. 3, 1850; m. 2d, Francis A. Traver, May 29, 1861; 1 child. Commd. brevet 2d lt. 3d Inf., U.S. Army, 1841, promoted 2d lt, 1841; in Seminole Indian War in Fla., 1841-42; commd. 1st lt., 1846; at battles of Resaca-de-la-Palma, Monterrey, Cerro Gordo, Palo Alto, Vera Cruz and Mexico City in Mexican War; brevetted capt. and maj., 1848; promoted capt., 1851; resigned from army, 1855; farmer in Mich., 1855-61; apptd. col. 2d Mich. Volunteer Regiment, U.S. Army, 1861; at Battle of Bull Run; promoted brig. gen. of Volunteers, 1861, maj. gen., 1862; mortally wounded in battle of Antietam, 1862. Died Sharpsburg, Md., Nov. 3, 1862.

RICHARDSON, JOHN SMYTHE congressman, lawyer; b. Bloomhill plantation, nr. Sumter, S.C., Feb. 29, 1828; grad. S.C. Coll. (now U. S.C.), 1850; studied law. Admitted to bar, 1852, practiced in Sumter; entered Confederate Army as capt. of Infantry during Civil War, served under Gen. Joseph Brevard Kershaw until after 1st Battle of Manassas where he was wounded; later promoted adjutant 23d Regt., S.C. Infantry, served until 1865; mem. S.C. Ho. of Reps., 1865-67; apptd. agt. State of S.C. to apply for and receive land script donated by S.C. to Congress, 1866; del. Nat. Democratic Conv., St. Louis, 1876; mem. U.S. Ho. of Reps. (Democrat) from S.C., 46th-47th congresses, 1879-83; master in equity for Sumter County, 1884-93. Died at his country home Shadyside, nr. Sumter, Feb. 24, 1894; buried Sumter Cemetery.

RICHARDSON, ROBERT CHARLWOOD, JR., ret. army officer; b. Charleston, S.C., Oct. 27, 1882; s. Robert Charlwood and Julia Anna (Driscoll) R.; student Coll. of Charleston, S.C., 1898-1900; B.S., U.S. Mil. Acad., 1904; student U. of Grenoble, France, 1908; grad. Command and Gen. Staff Sch., 1924, Ecole Superieure de Guerre, Paris, 1926, Army War Coll., 1934; m. Lois Elbertine Farman, Nov. 18, 1916; 1 son, Robert Charlwood, 3d. Commd. 2d lt., U.S. Army, 1904, advanced through grades to general, 1954; served with 14th Cavalry, P.I., 1904-06; asst. instr. of modern langs., U.S. Mil. Acad., 1906-11; with 23d Inf., Tex., 1913-14; asst. prof. of English, Mil. Acad., 1914-16; maj. and lt. col., with A.E.F., as liaison officer, 1918;

with Army of Occupation, Germany, and Peace Commn., Paris; Philippine Dept., Manila, 1921-23; mil. attaché, Am. Embassy, Rome, 1926-28; comdt. of cadets, U.S. Mil. Acad., 1929-33; comd. 5th Cav., Ft. Clark, Tex., 1935-38, Cavalry Sch., Ft. Riley, Kan., 1939-40; comd. 1st Cav. Div., 1940-41; dir. War Dept. Bur. of Pub. Relations, 1941; apptd. comdg. gen. 7th Army Corps, 1941; apptd. comdr. Hawaiian Dept. and mil. gov. of Hawaii, 1943; ret. 1946. Named comdg. gen. U.S. Army Forces in the Central Pacific area, 1943. Became comdg. gen. U.S. Army Forces in the Pacific Ocean Areas, 1944. Decorated D.S.M., Legion of Merit (1944), Allies Victory medal with 3 stars, Purple Heart, Silver Star (U.S.); Navy Distinguished Service Medal, Air Medal; Croix de Guerre with Palm, Officer Legion of Honor (France); Order of Leopold (Belgium); Officer Order of St. Maurizio and St. Lazarus (Italy); Officer La Solidaridad (Panama). Episcopalian. Clubs: Ends of the Earth (N.Y.); Army and Navy (Washington, Manila). Author: West Point—An Intimate Picture of the National Military Academy, 1917. Home: Upper Village, Bath, N.H. Died Mar. 2, 1954; buried West Point, N.Y.

RICHARDSON, WILDS PRESTON army officer; b. in Tex., Mar. 20, 1861; grad. U.S. Mil. Acad., 1884. Commd. 2d lt. 8th Inf., June 15, 1884; 1st lt., Dec. 16, 1889; capt., Apr. 26, 1898; maj. 9th Inf., Apr. 7, 1904; trans. to 13th Inf., Apr. 7, 1908; lt. col. of inf., Mar. 11, 1911; col., Apr. 28, 1914; brig. gen. N.A., Aug. 5, 1917. A.d.c. to Brig. Gen. A. V. Kautz, Dept. of Columbia, 1891-92; instr. tactics, U.S. Mil. Acad., 1892-97; in Alaska, 1897-99; assigned as adj. Dept. of Alaska, 1900; constructing Ft. William H. Seward, 1902-04; mem. Bd. Road Commrs. for Alaska, 1905-—. Died May 20, 1929.

RICHARDSON, WILLIAM ALEXANDER senator, congressman; b. nr. Lexington, Ky., Jan. 16, 1811; attended coll., Walnut Hill, Ky., also Centre Coll., Danville, Ky., Transylvania U., Lexington; studied law. Taught sch.; admitted to bar, 1831, practiced in Shelbyville, Ill.; state's atty., 1834, 35; mem. Ill. Ho. of Reps., 1836-38, 44-46, speaker, 1844; mem. Ill. Senate, 1838-42; Democratic presdl. elector, 1844; enlisted as capt. during Mexican War, promoted maj.; moved to Quincy, Ill., 1849; mem. U.S. Ho. of Reps. (Democrat, filled vacancy) from Ill., 30th-34th, 37th congresses, Dec. 6, 1847-Aug. 25, 1856 (resigned), 61-Jan. 29, 1863 (resigned); mem. U.S. Senate (filled vacancy) from Ill., Jan. 30, 1863-65; del. Nat. Dem. Conv., Charleston, S.C., 1860, N.Y.C., 1868; engaged in newspaper work. Died Quincy, Dec. 27, 1875; buried Woodland Cemetery.

RICHARDSON, WILLIAM LLOYD, AF officer, ret.; b. Saginaw, Mich., Dec. 14, 1901; grad. U.S. Mil. Acad., 1924; m. Georgia Richardson; children—Patricia, Janet. commd. 2d lt. Coast Arty., June 1924, advanced through the grades to maj. gen., July 28, 1950; became comdg. officer, Company of Cadets, and instr., U.S. Mil. Acad., June 1939; on duty in the Operations and Training Div., War. Dept. Gen. Staff, Washington, D.C., 1941-42; assigned to 8th Air Force overseas, July 1942; returned to this country to command the 51st Coast Arty. Brigade (Antiaircraft), Fort Bliss, Tex., Feb. 1943; comdg. IX Air Defense Command Ninth Air Force, Europe, Dec. 1943; chief, guided missiles group, Hdqrs. U.S. Air Forces, 1946-50; comdg. Air Force Missile Test Center, Patrick Air Force Base, Cocoa, Fla., 1950-54, (ret.); asst., Defense Electronic Products Div., Radio Corp., Am. Home: Vienna VA Died Mar. 21, 1973.

RICHART, DUNCAN GRANT army officer; b. Ludys, Ky., Nov. 10, 1887; B.S., U.S. Mil. Acad., 1910; grad. Cav. Sch., advanced course, 1925, Command and Gen. Staff Sch., 1926, Army War Coll., 1938. Commd. 2d lt., U.S. Army, 1910; resigned from army, 1914; in fed. service as 1st lt., Utah Nat. Guard, 1916; commd. 2d lt., U.S. Army, 1916, and advanced through the grades to brig. gen., 1944; on border duty, 1916-18; comd. Fort Oglethorpe, Ga., 1941-43; assumed command Fort Jackson, S.C., 1943. Address: War Dept., Washington 25. Died June 11, 1950.

RICHEY, THOMAS B. engring. cons.; b. Capon Rd., Va., Nov. 24, 1887; s. John Sinnard and Ellen Marshall (Locke) R.; student Augusta Mil. Acad., Ft. Defiance, Va., 1901-05, U.S. Naval Acad., 1905-09; M.S., Mass. Inst. Tech., 1914; m. Katherine M. Fowler, Nov. 6, 1914; children—Thomas Beall, Katherine Elizabeth. Passed midshipman, 1909, and advanced through the ranks to rear adm., 1942; indsl. dept., Boston Navy Yard, 1914-20, Naval Station, New Orleans (indsl. mgr.), 1920-21, San Diego, 1921-23, Norfolk Navy Yard (planning officer), 1923-27; production supt., Phila. Navy Yard, 1927-31, Mare Island Navy Yard, 1931-34, Brooklyn Navy Yard, 1934-41; mgr. Norfolk Navy Yard 1941 to 1943, attached to Joint Chiefs of Staff, Washington, D.C., 1943-45; retired from Navy Nov. 6, 1945. Consultant, Cargoaire Engring. Corp., N.Y. City, since 1945. Awarded Victory medal. Mem. Soc. Naval Architects and Marine Engrs., Soc. Naval Engrs., Naval Inst. Home: 405 W. 118th St., New York 27. Office: 15 Park Row, New York 7. Died March 30, 1949; buried Arlington National Cemetery, Washington.

RICHMAN, ARTHUR playwright; b. New York, N.Y., Apr. 16, 1886; s. William and Jennie (Swan) Reichman; ed. under pvt. tutors; m. Madeleine Marshall, July 18, 1925 (divorced, 1929); 1 son, John Marshall. Served as 2d lt. U.S. Army, 1918. Mem. Soc. Am. Organists and Composers (pres. 1925-27), Authors League America (pres. 1927-29), Screen Writers Guild. Chmn. amusement div. of Am. Com. for Christian German Refugees. Mem. bd. dirs. Am. Theatre Whig War Service, Inc. Author: Not so Long Ago, 1920; Ambush, 1921; The Serpent's Tooth, 1922; The Awful Truth, 1922; The Far Cry, 1924; Isabel (adapted), 1924; All Dressed Up, 1925; Antonia (adapted), 1925; A Proud Woman, 1927; Heavy Traffic, 1928; The Season Changes, 1936. Home: 419 E. 57th St., New York, N.Y. Died Sep. 10, 1944.

RICHMOND, ADAM army officer; b. Council Bluffs, Ia., Sept. 24, 1889; s. William and Anna (Fulton) R.; A.B., U. of Wis., 1912, LL.B., 1914; m. Anna Pagenstecher, Aug. 22, 1917; children—Virginia (Mrs. John Bernard Wagoner, Jr.), Ruth May (Mrs. James Kenneth Chenault), Frances Anna (Mrs. Vitaly Kovalevsky). Practiced law at Milw., 1914-17; Inf. capt. in World War I; commd. capt. Inf., U.S. Army, 1920; transferred to Judge Advocate, General's Dept., 1924, and promoted through grades to brig. gen., Mar. 1943. Went overseas 1942. Served in England, Africa and Italy; retired, Feb. 1947. Awarded Legion of Merit in 1948; Oak Leaf Cluster, 1946; Hon. Comdr. Order Crown of Italy, 1945; Order of British Empire, 1946. Mem. Phi Delta Phi. Home: 7816 Glenbrook Rd. Bethesda Md. Died Dec. 1, 1959. Buried Arlington National Cemetery.

RICHTER, JOHN FREDERICK govt. ofcl.; b. Washington, Dec. 11, 1897; s. John Frederick and Lottie M. (Keefer) R.; LL.B., Georgetown U., 1921, LL.M., 1922; m. Laurette M. Martin, Feb. 18, 1939. Newspaper reporter, mag. writer, pub. relations advisor, Washington, N.Y. Jour. Commerce, Central News London and N.Y.C., 1914-21; admitted to D.C. bar; practiced in Washington; U.S. legal advisor Tacna-Arica Plebiscitary Boundary Commn., Chile-Peru; N.R.A. legal code advisor, 1921-33; sr. atty. Fed. Trade Commn., 1933-40, sr. atty., legal advisor since 1948. Dir. Big Brothers of Washington. Served as col. judge adv. gen. dept., U.S. Army, World War II; staff Judge Adv. U.S. Armed Forces South Atlantic; acting dir. war crimes office Judge Adv. Gen. Office, 1940-46. Mem. Inter-Am., D.C., Fed. (1st v.p.), bar assns., Barristers (gov.) Club: Nat. Press (Washington). Home: 19 W. Underwood St., Chevy Chase 15, Md. Office: Tower Bldg., Washington. Died Jan. 25, 1954; buried Arlington Nat. Cemetery.

RICHTER, PAUL E. airline exec.; b. Denver, Colo., Jan. 20, 1896; s. Paul E. and Margaret (Herpich) R.; student Colo. Agr. Coll.; m. Daisy Cooke, June 23, 1926; children—Paul E., Ruth Alice. V.p., gen. mgr. and dir. Aero Corp. of Calif. 1926-31; supt. Western Region Transcontinental & Western Air, Inc., 1931-34, dir. 1934-47, v.p. charge operations, 1934-38, exec. v.p., 1938-47; pres., chmn. bd. Taca Airways, Mobile, Ala., since 1947; exec. Coca Cola Bottling Co. of Calif., since 1949. Served as capt., U.S. Navy on active duty, 1943-45 Address: 1580 Hawthorne Terrace, Berkeley, Calif. Died May 15, 1949.

RICKARDS, GEORGE COLLINS, first chief Militia Bur.; b. Phila., Pa., Aug. 25, 1860; s. Col. William, Jr. and Eliza A. (Tucker) R.; ed. pub. schs., Franklin, Pa.; m. Amelia Ellen Edinger, Apr. 6, 1882 (died 1927); children—Mrs. Mary E. Johnson, Mrs. Agnes F. Howe. In hardware business, Oil City, Pa., 1882-1915. Joined National Guard of Pa., 1877; promoted through grades to brig. gen., June 19, 1919; lt. col. and col. 16th Inf., U.S.A., Spanish-Am. War, 1898; served in Puerto Rico, on Mexican border, 1916-17, at head of same regt., reorganized as 112th Inf., as comdr. of which went to France and participated in battles, July-Nov., 1918, at Chateau-Thierry, Champaigne - Marne, Aisne - Marne, Fismes. Oise-Aisne, Meuse-Argonne; chief of Mil. Bur., rank of maj. gen., July 2, 1921-June 29, 1925 (retired). Served 40 yrs. in state and 8 yrs. 28 days in federal service. Awarded Long Service Medal of Pa., 1920; D.S.M. (U.S.); recommended for D.S.C. by comdg. gen. 55th Inf. Brig. and cited by Gen. Pershing. Exec. officer Polk State Sch., Polk, Pa., 1 yr. (resigned); elected register of wills, recorder of deeds and clk. of Orphans' Court, of Venango Co., Pa., Nov. 1927, reëlected, Nov. 3, 1931. Dir. ZemZem Temple Hosp. for Crippled Children, Erie, Pa. Republican. Methodist. Mason. One of ten major generals who acted as pall bearers at funeral of President Harding, also at burial of the Unknown Soldier, at Arlington Cemetery. Home: Oil City, Pa. Died Jan. 15, 1933.

RICKENBACKER, EDWARD VERNON ("EDDIE"), aviator; b. Columbus, O., Oct. 8, 1890; s. William and Elizabeth R.; Dr. Aeronautical Sci., Pa. Mil. Coll., 1938, Brown U., Siloam Springs, 1940 U. of Miami, 1941; D.Sc., U. of Tampa (Fla.), 1942; L.H.D., U. Founds. and Am. Theol. Sem., Wilmington, Del., 1943; Sc. D., Westminster Coll., New Wilmington, Pa., 1944; LL.D., Okla. City U., 1944, Capital U., Columbus, O., 1945, Coll. of South Jersey, 1948, Hamilton Coll., 1956, William Jewell Coll., 1962; Dr. Eng., Lehigh U., 1948; Sc.D. (hon.), Lafayette Coll., Easton, Pa., 1952; Sc. D., The Citadel, Charleston, S.C., 1954, Ohio State U., 1957; graduate Internat. Correspondence Sch.; m. Mrs. Adelaide F. Durant, Sept. 16, 1922; children—David E., William F. Became widely known as auto-racer and won championships at nat. and internat. meets; accompanied Gen. Pershing to France as mem. Motor Car Staff, June 1917; trans. to Air Service at own request, Aug. 25, 1917, and assigned as engr. officer to Issoudon Tng. Field; became comdg. officer 94th Aero Pursuit Squadron, the first Am. aero unit to participate actively on the Western front (this unit was credited with 69 victories-the largest number of victories of any Am. unit-Rickenbacker heading the list with 26 victories to his credit); was the first comdg. officer to conduct his own squadron into Coblenz; retired at close of war with rank of capt. World War II activities included; spl. mission for sec. of War to England, So. Pacific, N. Africa, Iran, India, China, Russia, Iceland, Greenland and Aleutians. Awarded Medal of Merit, 1947; awarded D.S.C. with 9 oak leaves, Congressional Medal of Honor (U.S.); Legion of Honor, Croix de Guerre with 4 palms (French). Silver Buffalo Boy Scouts Am., 1944, Big Brother of the Year, 1953. V.p. Am. Airways, Inc., asst. to pres. Aviation Corp., 1932-33; v.O. North Am. Aviation, Inc., 1933-34; gen. mgr. Eastern Air Lines, Inc., 1935; pres., gen. mgr., director, 1938-53, chairman bd., 1954-63; director Wackenhut Corp., Fla. Press. Air Force Aid Soc. Mem. exec. bd. Boy Scouts Am.; dir. Boys' Clubs of Am. Forced down while on a Pacific flight, 1942, rescued after 24 days at sea on a life raft. Author: Fighting the Flying Circus, 1919; Seven Came Through, 1943; Rickenbacker An Autobiography, 1967. Home: New York City NY Died July 23, 1973.

RICKETTS, CLAUDE VERNON naval officer; b. Greene County, Mo., Feb. 23, 1906; s. Gilbert Luther and Sarah Bertha (Smith) R.; B.S., U.S. Naval Acad., 1929; grad. Naval War Coll., 1947; m. Margery Bernice Corn, May 15, 1930; children—Myron V., James B. Commd. ensign USN, 1929, advanced through grades to admiral, 1961; designated naval aviator, 1932; various assignments in ships and aircraft squadrons, 1929-41; assigned U.S.S. West Virginia, Battle of Pearl Harbor, 1941, U.S.S. Maryland, 1941-43; operations officer on staff Comdr. Amphibious Group II and Comdr. Fifth Amphibious Force, 1943-45, participated battles of Tarawa, Eniwetok, Saipan, Tinian, Iwo Jima, Okinawa, Occupation of Japan; assigned Naval War Coll., 1946-49; comdr. U.S.S. Alshain, 1949-50; staff Comdr. Amphibious Force Atlantic, 1950-52, Office Chief Naval Operations, 1952-54; comdr. U.S.S. St. Paul, 1954-55; with strategic plans div. Office Chief Naval Operations, 1955-57, 58-61; comdr. Destroyer Flotilla Four, 1957-58, U.S. Second Fleet also Striking Fleet Atlantic (NATO), 1961; vice chief naval operations, 1961-—. Home: Route 2, Fair Grove, Mo. Office: Vice Chief Naval Operations, Navy Dept., Washington. Died July 6, 1964; buried Arlington Nat. Cemetery.

RICKETTS, JAMES BREWERTON army officer; b. N.Y.C., June 21, 1817; s. George R.A. and Mary (Brewerton) R.; grad. U.S. Mil. Acad., 1839; m. Harriet Josephine Pierce, 1840; m. 2d, Frances Lawrence, 1856; 6 children. Commd. 2d lt. U.S. Army, 1839, 1st lt., 1846; served at battles of Monterey and Buena Vista during Mexican War, in Seminole War in Fla., 1852; promoted capt., 1852; commanded battery U.S. Army under Gen. McDowell, 1861; commd. brig. gen. U.S. Volunteers, 1861; assigned to command div. in Gen. McDowell's Corps, 1862, fought at battles of Cedar Mountain and Manassas, in Joseph Hooker's Corps at Battle of Antietam; court martial duty, 1862-64; joined army under Gen. Philip Sheriden in Shenandoah Valley, at Battle of Cedar Creek, 1864; temporarily in command VI Corps; discharged as brig. gen. volunteers, reverted to rank maj. U.S. Army, 1866; ret. as maj. gen., 1867. Died Washington, D.C., Sept. 23, 1887.

RICKEY, BRANCH ex-baseball exec.; b. Stockdale, O., Dec. 20, 1881; s. Jacob Franklin and Emily (Brown) R.; B.Litt., Ohio Wesleyan U., 1904, A.B., 1906, hon. degree, 1947; Dr. of Jurisprudence, Michigan University, 1911; hon. degrees, McKendree Coll., 1928, U. Rochester, 1946, Allegheny Coll., 1951, Waynesburg College, 1951, Bethune-Cookman Coll., 1952, Howard U., 1953, Morgan State Coll., 1955, Salem College 1958; married to Jane Moulton, June 1, 1906; children—Mary Emily, Branch, Jane Ainsworth, Mabel Alice, Sue Moulton, Elizabeth Ann. Started major league career in baseball with Cin. Reds, as catcher, 1904, with St. Louis Browns 2 yrs., with Yankees, 1907; with St. Louis Browns as sec., mgr., 1913-15, v.p. and bus. mgr., 1916; became pres. St. Louis Cardinals, 1917, mgr., 1919-42; pres. and gen. mgr. Brooklyn Dodgers, 1942-50; v.p. and gen. mgr. Pitts. Baseball Club (Pirates), 1950-55, chmn. bd. and dir., 1955-59; pres. of newly organized Continental League, 1959-62; cons. St. Louis Cardinals, 1963-64. The Cardinals won pennants during management by Rickey, 1926, '28, '30, '31, '34, '42, World Champions four times; Brooklyn Club won two pennants. Vice chmn. Pres.'s Com. on Employment Policy in Fed. Govt., 1957-61; active YMCA; dir. Salvation Army, Pitts. Served to maj. U.S. Army, A.E.F., 1918. Trustee Ohio Wesleyan U., nat. chmn. capital fund raising dr., 1965-66. Mem. Am. Legion, Mil. Order World War, Delta Tau Delta, Omicron Delta Kappa. Mason (32 deg., K.T., Shriner). Clubs:

University, Racquet (St. Louis). Author: The American Diamond, 1965. Home: 3 Warson Lane, Ladue, St. Louis 63124. Died Dec. 9, 1965.

RIDDELL, HERMAN ELLIS lawyer; b. Boston, June 16, 1890; s. Charles Frederick and Clara (Evons) R.; B.A., U. Ga., 1911; LL.B., Harvard, 1914; m. E. Louise Menefee, Jan. 4, 1936 (dec. 1958). Admitted to Ga. bar, 1914, N.Y. bar, 1921; asso. Robert C. and Philip H. Alston, 1914-16; partner Moise & Riddell, 1916-21 (both Atlanta); asso. Forsyth Wickes, Esquire, 1921; partner Wickes & Neilson, 1922, Wickes, Riddell, Bloomer, Jacobi & McGuire, N.Y.C., 1942—. Dir. emeritus Philip Morris, Inc.; dir. Pagel, Horton & Co., Inc. Mem. exec. com. and trustees Nantucket Cottage Hosp. Served as 1st lt. U.S. Army Service Corps, 1918. Mem. Am., N.Y. State bar assns., N.Y. Co. Lawyers Assn., Assn. of Bar City N.Y. Clubs: University, Down Town Assn., Union (N.Y.C.); Yacht, Pacific (Nantucket, Mass.); Piedmont Driving (Atlanta). Home: 150 E. 69th St., N.Y.C. 21. Office: Chase Manhattan Plaza, N.Y.C. 5. Died July 13, 1966.

RIDDER, HERMAN HENRY, publisher; b. New York, N.Y., June 25, 1908 s. Bernard Herman and Hilda (Luyties) R.; student, Blessed Sacrament Acad., All Hallows Inst., student, Columbia; m. Virginia Randolph, Feb. 11, 1938 (divorced); 1 dau., Marsha Randolph; m. 2d, Florence Murphy Pearson, April 18, 1953; one adopted son, Thomas P. LeBosquet. Publisher St. Paul (Minn.) Daily News, 1937; publisher, St. Paul Dispatch and Pioneer Press, 1945-69; v.p. Northwest Publs.; pres. and dir. Ridder Publications publisher of Independent-Press-Telegram, Long Beach, Cal., 1952-69. Served with U.S. Marine Corps, disch. as maj. Group Intelligence Officer, Okinawa, World War II. Awarded Bronze Star. Mem. Reserve Officers of the Naval Services, Marine Corps Reserve Officers Assn., C. of C. Clubs: Long Beach Yacht; Racquet, Thunderbird Country (Palm Springs). Home: Long Beach CA Died Sept. 15, 1969; buried Rye Beach NH

RIDDICK, WALLACE CARL (rid'ik), educator; b. Wake County, N.C., Aug. 5, 1864; s. Wiley Goodman and Anna Ivy (Jones) R.; ancestors among earliest settlers of Va. and N.C.; student Wake Forest Coll., 2 yrs.; A.B., U. of N.C., 1885; C.E., Lehigh U., 1890; LL.D., Wake Forest and Lehigh, 1917; D.Eng., N.C. State Coll., 1939; m. Lillian Daniel, Oct. 18, 1893; children—W. W., Lillian, Narcissa, Anna, Eugenia. Practiced as civ. engr., 1890-91; prof. civ. engring., N.C. Coll. Agrl. and Mech. Arts, 1892-1916, pres. 1916-23, resigned to become dean Sch. of Engring., 1923, dean emeritus and prof. of hydraulics since 1937 (name of coll. changed to N.C. State Coll. of Agr. and Engring. 1917). Had charge reconstruction water works of Raleigh, constrn. water works and sewers of Weldon, N.C., etc.; cons. expert to legal dept. Seaboard Air Line ry. until 1916; cons. hydraulic engr. since 1936; v.p. Neuse Mfg. Co.; mem. State Highway Commn., N.C., 1915-19; mem. State Bd. Vocational Edn., 1917-19; mem. Conservation Commn. N.C., 1918; mem. bd. visitors, U.S. Naval Acad., 1920-21. Lt. col. on staff of Governor Glenn, 1905-09. Mem. N.C. Acad. Science, N.C. Teachers' Assn., N.C. Soc. Engrs. (pres. 1919), Am. Soc. Civ. Engrs., Am. Assn. Engrs., Kappa Alpha, Phi Kappa Phi, Tau Beta Pi. Knight Order of St. Sava (Jugoslavia). Clubs: Capital, Rotary, Raleigh Country. Home: 225 Woodburn Rd., Raleigh, N.C. Died June 9, 1942.

RIDDLE, JOHN WALLACE diplomat; b. Phila., Pa., July 12, 1864; s. John Wallace and Rebecca Blair (McClure) R.; A.B., Harvard, 1887; student Columbia Law Sch., New York, 1888-91; École des Sciences Politiques, Paris, 1891-93; certificate of proficiency in Russian lang. from Collège de France, 1893; m. Theodate Pope, May 6, 1916. Sec. U.S.-Legation to Turkey, 1893-1900; sec. U.S. Embassy to Russia, 1901-03; diplomatic agt. and consul-gen. to Egypt, 1903-05; E.E. and M.P. to Roumania and Servia, 1905-06; ambassador to Russia, 1906-09, to Argentina, 1921-May 28, 1925 (resigned). Served in Mil. Intelligence Div. of Gen. Staff, Army War Coll., Washington, 1917-18. Republican. Episcopalian. Clubs: Century, Union, Knickerbocker (New York); Rittenhouse, Philadelphia (Phila.); Minnesota (St. Paul); Cercle de l'Union (Paris); Brooks' (London). Died Dec. 8, 1941.

RIDENOUR, LOUIS N(ICOT), JR., physicist; b. Montclair, N.J., Nov. 1, 1911; s. Louis Nicot and Clare (Wintersteen) R.; B.S., U. of Chicago, 1932; Ph.D., Calif. Inst. Tech., 1936; m. Gretchen Hinckley Kraemer, June 18, 1934; 2 daus., Eleanor, Nancy Page. With Inst. for Advanced Study, Princeton, N.J., 1935-36; instr. Princeton U., 1936-38; asst. prof., U. of Pa., 1938-41, asso. prof., 1941-46, prof. 1946-47; prof. physics, dean Grad. Coll., U. of Ill., 1947-51, on leave as spl. asst. to Sec. of Air Force, 1950-51; dir. of research for Missile Systems div. Lockheed Aircraft Corp., 1956-59, v.p. in charge electronics and avionics div., 1959—; v.p. Internat. Telemeter Corp. Cons., Sec. of War, 1942-46, radar adviser U.S. Strategic War Forces in Europe, 1944, member radar committee, Combined Chiefs Staff, 1943-45; mem. div. 5, div. 15, Nat. Defense Research Com. Awarded Bronze Star; President's Medal for Merit. Fellow Am. Phys. Soc., A.A.A.S. (councillor), Institute of Radio Engrs.; mem. Phi Beta Kappa, Sigma Xi. Clubs: Cosmos (Washington); University (Chgo.). Contbr. articles on mil. and sci. subjects to various publs. Editor-in-chief Radiation Lab. Series of 27 tech. vols. Editor Radar System Engineering, 1947, Modern Physics for the Engineer, 1954. Home: 1425 University Av., Palo Alto, Cal. Office: Missile Systems div. Lockheed Aircraft Corp., Sunnyvale, Cal. Died May 21, 1959.

RIDGELY, CHARLES GOODWIN naval officer; b. Balt., July 21, 1784; s. Dr. Lyde and Abigail (Levy) G.; m. Cornelia L. Livingston, 1822, 3 children. Commd. lt. U.S. Navy, 1807; comdr., 1813, master-comdt., 1813; commanded brig Jefferson on Lake Ontario, 1814, sloop-of-war Erie, Independence in Bainbridge's squadron during and after Algerian war, circa 1815-17; promoted capt., 1815; commanded naval sta., Balt., 1820; in command flagship sloop-of-war Natchez, West India Squadron, 1827-circa 1829; comdr. N.Y.C. Navy Yard, 1834-39; served in command Brazil Squadron with flagship frigate Potomac, 1840-41; took command naval sta., Balt., 1842-43. Died Balt., Feb. 4, 1848.

RIDGELY, DANIEL BOWLY naval officer; b. nr. Lexington, Ky., Aug. 1, 1813; s. Daniel Bowly and Jane (Price) R.; m. Johanna M. Clemm, Oct. 11, 1837; m. 2d, Elizabeth Dulany Rogers, Feb. 8, 1858; 2 children including Dr. Nicholas. Commd. lt. U.S. Navy, 1840; served as 1st lt. on ship Albany, participated in bombardment and capture of Vera Cruz, taking of Tuspan, Alvarado, Tampico, during Mexican War, 1846-48; became comdr., 1855; held 1st command, steamer Atalanta, dispatched to demand satisfaction from govt. of Paraguay for an insult to U.S. flag and injuries to Am. citizens, 1857-58; commanded steamer Santiago de Cuba, 1861-62, cruised in Gulf of Mexico, West Indian waters, capturing several blockade runners; commd. capt., 1862; commanded steam sloop Shenandoah, N. Atlantic Blockading Squadron, 1863, then cruised independently in West Indian waters, participated in blockade of Wilmington and New Inlet (N.C.); commd. commodore, 1866, mem. Naval Examining Bd. in Phila., 1868. Died Balt., May 5, 1868; buried Greenmount Cemetery, Balt.

RIDGWAY, THOMAS army officer; b. in N.Y., Aug. 18, 1861; grad. U.S. Mil. Acad., 1883; grad. Arty. Sch., 1896. Commd. 2d lt. 5th Arty., June 13, 1883; 1st lt. 4th Arty., Feb. 12, 1891; trans. to 5th Arty., May 23, 1891, to 6th Arty., Mar. 8, 1898, to 5th Arty., Apr. 29, 1898; capt., Mar. 18, 1899; maj. Arty. Corps, June 30, 1906; lt. col. Coast Arty. Corps, July 1, 1910; col., Jan. 17, 1912. Served with light battery at Ft. Riley, Kan., 1896-98; comdr. Battery N, 5th Arty., Jan.-Aug. 1900; in China and Philippine Islands, 1900-01; comd. Ft. Warren, Mass., 1916-17. Address: War Dept., Washington, D.C.

RIDINGS, EUGENE WARE, army officer; b. Grant County, Okla., Jan. 9, 1899; s. Samuel P. and Nettie (Lewis) R.; student Oklahoma U., 1917-18, Marion (Ala.) Mil. Inst., 1918-19; B.S., U.S. Mil. Acad., 1923; grad. Inf. Sch., 1931, Command and Gen. Staff Sch., 1937, Army War Coll., 1940; m. Vera Bernhard, Oct. 3, 1928; 1 son, Eugene Ware. Commd. 2d lt., U.S. Army, 1923, and advanced through the grades to brig. gen., Jan. 1945. Decorated Bronze Star, Silver Star with oak leaf cluster, Legion of Merit with oak leaf cluster. Home: Staunton VA Died 1969.

RIDLEY, CLARENCE SELF, army officer; b. Corydon, Ind., June 22, 1883; s. William and Margaret (Inman) R.; B.S., U.S. Mil. Acad., 1905; m. Bessie Thomson, July 10, 1907; m. Gladys Peard Kay, July 21, 1965. Commd. 2d lt. Corps of Engrs., U.S. Army, 1905, advanced through the grades to col., 1935, brig. gen., 1938, maj. gen., 1941; gov. Panama Canal and pres. and dir. Panama R.R. Co., 1936-40; duty with 3d Div., Fort Lewis, Wash., 1940-41; comdg. gen. 6th Div., Fort Snelling, Jan. 1941; chief military mission to Iran, 1942-46; ret. 1947. Decorated D.S.M., 1946; Order of Hamayoun, 2d Class of Iran, 1947; Officer Order of Leopold by King of Belgium. Address: Carmel CA Died July 26, 1969; buried U.S. Military Academy Cemetery West Point NY

RIDLON, JOHN orthopedic surgeon; b. Clarendon, Vt., Nov. 24, 1852; s. Noel P. and Nancy B. (Hulett) R.; A.B., U. of Chicago, 1875, A.M., 1878; M.D., Coll. Phys. and Surg. (Columbia), 1878; hon. A.M., Tufts College, 1899, Sc.D. from same coll., 1926; m. Emily C. Robinson, June 4, 1879. Prof. orthopedic surgery, Northwestern Univ., 1892-1908, Chicago Post-Grad. Med. Sch., 1892-93, Northwestern Woman's Med. Sch., 1898-1902, Rush Med. Coll., 1909-12; cons. sr. orthopedic surgeon, Mercy, Michael Reese and Evanston hosps., Chicago, for many yrs., and Newport (R.I.) Hosp.; cons. orthopedic surgeon, Home for Destitute Children. Capt. Med. R.C., Apr. 2, 1917; maj., Sept. 10, 1917; disch. Feb. 8, 1919; lt. col. Aux. Reserve, U.S. Army, retired, account of disabilities, 1929. Home: Newport, R.I. Died Apr. 27, 1936.

RIDPATH, ROBERT FERGUSON physician; b. Jenkintown, Pa., Apr. 3, 1876; s. John Waddell and Rachel Ann (Ferguson) R.; M.D., Medico-Chirurg, Coll., 1899; Sc.D., Ursinus Coll., 1935; m. Johanne Ogrodowski, Nov. 22, 1922; 1 son, Robert Ferguson. Asso. prof. of rhino-laryngology, Medic-Chirurg. Coll., Sept. 1913-24; asst. prof. U. of Pa. Post Grad. Sch., 1924-30; prof., Temple U. Sch. of Medicine, 1930—; practicing physician 1900—. Cons. in rhinology at Phila. Skin & Cancer Hosp.; cons. otology and rhinology, Seashore Home (Atlantic City). Served as capt. in Med. Corps, U.S. Army, World War. Fellow A.C.S., Coll. Physicians (Phila.), Am. Laryngol., Rhinol. and Otol. Soc., Am. Laryngol. Soc.; mem. A.M.A. (chmn. rhinolaryngol. sect.), Am. Acad. Ophthalmology, Otology and Laryngol., Phila. Laryngol. Soc., Pa., Montgomery County med. socs. Republican. Mason. Clubs: University. Medical (Phila.). Contbr. to sci. and profl. jours. Home: 1117 New Jersey Av., Cape May, N.J. Office: 1720 Spruce St., Phila. 3. Died Aug. 10, 1950; buried Hillside Cemetery, Jenkintown, Pa.

RIELY, JOHN WILLIAM asso. justice supreme court of appeals of Va.; b. Jefferson Co., Va., Feb. 26, 1839; ed. at Washington and Lee Univ., Lexington, Va.; grad., 1861; was a staff officer in Confederate army with rank of maj.; was atty. for commonwealth, Halifax Co., Va., 1871-94. Home: Richmond, Va. Died 1900.

RIGBY, WILLIAM CATTRON lawyer; b. Waterloo, Ia., May 11, 1871; s. William Titus and Eva (Cattron) R.; A.B., Cornell Coll., Mt. Vernon, Ia., 1892, Ph.B., 1892, A.M., 1897, LL.D., 1942; LL.B., Northwestern U., 1893; m. Grace Gilruth, Oct. 25, 1893 (died May 1, 1940); children—Cecil Collin (Mrs. Frederick L. Nussbaum), Eveyln Cattron (Mrs. Lewis B. Moore), Carol Gilruth (Mrs. Arthur Bronson Rigby); m. 2d, Mrs. Clare B. Hoffman, June 30, 1942. Admitted to bar, Ill., 1899, Calif., 1909, Canal Zone, 1924, Dist. of Columbia, 1927, N.Y., 1930; admitted to practice before U.S. Supreme Ct., 1917; practiced in Chicago, 1893-1918; commd. maj. judge advocate U.S. Army, 1918, advanced to lt. col., 1919; commd. lt. col. U.S. Army, 1920; col., 1931; detailed to examine adminstrn. of mil. law in allied armies and revise Articles of War and Manual for Courts Martial, 1919-20; chief Insular Affairs Sect. Judge Advocate Gen.'s Office, asst., and acting judge advocate general, 1931-34; retired, 1934; reentered private practice; recalled to active duty and detailed to examine and report on adminstrn. of mil. law and kindred matters in England, Oct. 1941-June 1942; counsel for Govt. of Puerto Rico, 1934-43; many cases before U.S. Supreme Court and other courts of appeal; lecturer Am. U. Grad. Sch., 1927-30. Mem. Inter-Am. Bar Assn. (chmn. organizing com. and provisional treas., 1940-41; chmn. exec. com. and treas. since 1941), Am. Bar Assn. (mem. gen. council, 1924-26; v.p. for Canal Zone, 1927; chmn. com. on Latin-Am. Law of Section of International and Comparative Law, 1937-40, of military and naval law, since 1942; member Dist. of Columbia, Chicago, and Federal bar assns., Assn. of the Bar of City of N.Y., Chicago Law Inst., Phi Beta Kappa, Delta Chi. Mason (K.T.). Clubs: University (Chicago); Army and Navy, Cosmos (Washington, D.C.); Lotos (N.Y.); Athenaeum (London, Eng.). Home: East Falls Church, Va. Office: Southern Bldg., Washington 5, D.C. Died Apr. 16, 1945.

RIGBY, WILLIAM TITUS soldier; b. Red Oak Grove, Ia., Nov. 3, 1841; s. Washington Augustus and Lydia (Barr) R.; A.B., Cornell Coll., Ia., 1869, A.M., 1872; m. Eva Cattron, June 18, 1870; children—William Cattron, Charles Longley, Grace Kendrick. Entered service as 2d lt. Co. B, 24th Ia. Inf., Sept. 18, 1862; capt., Oct. 2, 1863, until hon. mustered out, July 17, 1865; engaged in farming after war. Elected sec. Vicksburg Nat. Mil. Park Assn., 1895, and was one of its most active promoters before Congress; apptd. commr. same, by sec. of war, 1899, and from then in charge of work as resident commr. Prominent advocate of "sound money," 1896, 98. Mem. Miss. Hist. Soc. Democrat. Methodist. Home: Vicksburg, Miss. Deceased.

RIGGINS, RUSSELL MYERS oil and gas exec.; born Gainesville, Texas, Nov. 13, 1894; son Reid and Ethel Fay (Mershon) R.; student pub. schs. of Asher, Okla.; m. Jessie Ruth Spires, May 25, 1918. Clk. St.L. & S.F. Ry., Stroud, Okla., 1909-11; chief clk. M.-K.-T. R.R., Oklahoma City, 1911-14, livestock agt., Oklahoma City, 1914-15; asst. traffic mgr. Morris & Co. (now Armour & Co.), Oklahoma City, 1915, exec. accountant, 1916-20; sr. partner Riggins & Beck, C.P.A.'s, Oklahoma City, Okmulgee, Bartlesville, Okla., also Washington, N.Y.C., 1920-22; sec.-treas., dir., exec. com. Independent Oil & Gas Co., Ind. Pipe Line Co., Ind. Natural Gas Co., Manhattan Oil Co., Tulsa, 1922-30; comptroller, treas., operating com. Phillips Petroleum Co., Phillips Pipe Line Co., Standish Pipe Line Co., Western Radio Telegraph Co., Ind. Natural Gas Co., Bartlesville, 1930-44; v.p. Phillips Venezuelan Co., Phillips Columbian Co., 1944; comptroller Parke, Davis & Co., Parke, Davis & Co., Ltd., Parke-Davis Inter-Am. Corp., Parke-Davis Internat. Corp., Detroit, Parke, Davis & Co. of Mexico, Heston Products Co. of Eng., 1945-48; sr. partner Russell M. Riggins & Co. C.P.A.'s, Houston, also Washington, 1948-49; Tex. partner Arthur Young & Co., Dallas, also Houston, 1949-51; pres. Tex. Gas Corp., Tex. Gas Pipe Line Corporation of Houston, Texas, 1951—. Served from 2d lt. to lt. col. Inf., U.S. Army Res., 1918-42; col. Office Chief Ordnance, Washington, 1942-44, chief of army ordnance depots in U.S. Decorated Legion of Merit. Mem. Am. Inst. Accountants, Controllers Inst. of America, Oklahoma, Texas, New Mexico societies C.P.A.'s., Am. Petroleum

Inst., Mid-Continent Oil and Gas Assn., Res. Officers Association of United States. Democrat. Methodist. Mason (32 deg., Shriner). Clubs: Army and Navy (Washington); Bankers (N.Y.C.); Cherokee Yacht (commodore 1942, Tulsa); Houston, Petroleum, River Oaks Country, Internat. (Houston). Home: 3805 Inverness Dr., Houston 19. Office: Tex. Gas Bldg., Houston 5. Died Jan. 9, 1961.

RIGGS, CHARLES EDWARD naval officer (ret.); b. Iowa City, Sept. 15, 1869; s. Joseph Samuel and Cordelia (Robbins) R.; M.D., Ia. State U., 1892; m. Louise Benton Pugh, Dec. 21, 1921; children—Louise Catherine (Mrs. Roman Smoluchowski), Edward Benton. Interne N.Y., 1892; entered Med. Dept. USN, May 11, 1893, rank of ensign, and advanced through grades to rear adm., 1929; apptd. surgeon-gen. USN, Jan. 19, 1929; ret. from active duty, Oct. 1, 1933; dir. 2d Nat. Bank, Washington. Mem. A.A.A.S., Med. Soc. Greater N.Y., Am. Legion, Mil. Order World War. Clubs: Army-Navy, Chevy Chase (Washington); Yacht (New York). Contbr. numerous articles to profl. jours. Home: 3105 36th St. N.W., Washington 16. Died May 31, 1963; buried Arlington Nat. Cemetery.

RIGGS, THEODORE SCOTT, ret. army officer; b. Ft. Leavenworth, Kan., Apr. 1, 1907; s. Kerr Tunis and Mary Virginia (Fosdick) R.; grad. Phillips Acad., Andover, Mass., 1924; B.S., U.S. Mil. Acad., 1928; student Imperial Defence Coll., London, Eng., 1951; m. Phillis Wey Symmonds, Jan. 11, 1930; children—Theodore Scott (U.S. Army), Robert M., Goerge T., David K. Commd. 2d lt., U.S. Army, 1928, advanced through grades to maj. gen., 1953, ret.; instr. U.S. Mil. Acad., 1934-38; chief staff U.S. Army Forces Middle East, 1942; dep. chief of staff Allied Land Forces So. Europe, 1952-53; chief information and edn., U.S. Army, 1955-56; comdg. gen. VI U.S. Army Corps, 1958-59; chief staff Combined Mil. Planning Staff, Central Treaty Orgn., Ankara, Turkey, 1959-60, ret., 1960. Decorated Legion of Merit with cluster; Order Brit. Empire. Mem. Assn. Grads. U.S. Mil. Acad., Andover Alumni Assn. Home: Washington DC Died Aug. 10, 1970; buried Arlington Nat. Cemetery, Arlington VA

RIGSBEE, ALBERT VINSON, life ins. co. exec.; b. Durham, N.C., Mar. 26, 1925; s. Hubert Alexander and Annie (Crabtree) R.; M.D., U. Va., 1949; m. Patricia Moore, Nov. 24, 1949; children—Douglas Craig, Patricia Ann, Mark Allen. Asst. med. dir. Acacia Life Ins. Co., Washington, 1952-61, med. dir., 1961-69; postgrad. tng. Charlotte (N.C.) Meml. Hosp., also Harvard Med. Sch., Cambridge, Mass., 1962. Pres., Heart Assn. No. Va., 1966-67; chmn. Sci. Fair Judges, Va., 1955-65. Served to ensign USNR, World War II; to 1st lt. AUS, 1947-50; to capt. USAF, Korean War. Recipient Welburn award Arlington County Med. Soc., 1959. Mem. Assn. Med. Dirs. Home: Alexandria VA Died May 6, 1969.

RILEA, THOMAS EDWARD (ri-le'ä), adj. gen. Ore.; b. Chicago, Ill., May 5, 1895; s. George Washington and Mary Eve (Minnick) R.; E.E., Ore. Inst. Tech., 1916; m. Helen Coe Webster, 1946. Began as elec. engr., 1916. Served as bugler and corporal of inf. on Mexican Border, 1916; in World War served in U.S. and with A.E.F., France; successively sergt. maj., 2d and 1st lt., capt.; following World War I, became exec. officer Ore. Nat. Guard, and advanced through grades to brig. gen. comdg. 82d Brigade, 1931, maj. gen. 1948; Fed. service, 1940-46; asst. comdr. 41st Div. S.W. Pacific; participated New Guinea, Papuan campaigns; comd. large supply base, Australia. Now adj. gen. of Ore. Decorated D.S.M., Bronze Star Medal, Purple Heart, Commendation Ribbon, Presidential Unit Citation, Mexican Border, World War I, German Occupation, Defense, Am. Theater, Asiatic-Pacific and Victory (World War II) ribbons, Legion of Merit. Cited outstanding service, Ore. legislature, 1931. Mem. Nat. Guard Assn. U.S. (v.p., 1934-35, pres., 1935-36), exec. council 6th Army Area. Mem. Am. Legion, Vets. Fgn. Wars. Mason (32 deg., Shriner). Clubs: Portland Army-Navy, Columbia Athletic. Home: Box 145, Clackamas, Ore. Office: Military Dept., State Office Bldg., Salem, Ore. Died Feb. 3, 1959.

RILEY, BENNET army ofcl., govt. ofcl.; b. Nov. 27, 1787; s. Bennet and Susanna (Drury) R.; m. Arabella, 5 children. Entered U.S. Army as ensign of riflemen, 1813; fought at Sacketts Harbor (N.Y.) in War of 1812; regtl. adj., 1816-17; promoted capt., 1818; served with inf. 1821-46; brevetted maj. for distinguished service in battle with Ark. Indians in Dakota Territory, 1823; fought in Black Hawk War, 1831-32; commd. maj., 1837, lt. col., 1839; fought in Seminole War in Fla., 1839-42; brevetted col.; commanded 2d Inf. during Mexican War; adviser to commander of brigade; brevetted brig. gen. at Battle of Cerro Gordo, brevetted maj. gen. at Battle of Contreras, 1847; served in La. and Mo., until 1848; commanded Dept. of Pacific, became ex officio provisional gov. Cal., circa 1848; convened constituent assembly at Monterey which drew up 1st constn, of Cal. and applied for admission to Union, 1849; promoted to col. 1st Inf., 1850. Died Buffalo, N.Y., June 9, 1853.

RILEY, EARL ex-mayor; b. Portland, Ore., Feb. 18, 1890; s. Lester and Harriett Miranda (Richardson) R.; student Portland Acad., 1907, Ore. State Coll., 1908-10, Holmes Bus. Coll., Portland; m. E. Faye Wade, Mar. 25, 1920; 1 dau., Doris Lee Hoffpauer. Supt. machine shop Columbia Engine Works, 1914-18; partner Edwards Tire Shop, 1919-31; commr. finance, City of Portland, 1931-40; mayor City of Portland, 1941-49; dir. 1st Fed. Savs. & Loan Assn. Exec. dir. Civil Emergency Relief Com., 1930-31; mem. Municipal Civil Service Bd., 1928-30; dir., past pres. Ore. Finance Officers Assn., pres. Portland unit; pres. Portland unit Vols. of Am.; pres. Ore. State Coll. Meml. Union Assn.; chmn. bd. Shriners' Hosp. for Crippled Children; v.p. Am. Municipal Assn.; trustee U.S. Conf. of Mayors; dir., past pres. League Ore. Cities. Apptd. by Brit. Ministry of Information and OWI, Washington, to represent U.S. cities on mission to Eng., Scotland, North Ireland and Wales, 1943. Served as 2d lt. 4th Officers Tng. Sch., 1918-19; O.R.C., Inf., 1919-25. Mem. Ore. State Coll. Alumni, E. Portland Automotive Trades Assn., Grange, Nat. Sojourners, Native Sons and Daus. Ore., Neighbors of Woodcraft, Eagles, Moose, Woodmen of World, K.P., Royal Arcanum, Maccabee, Mason (33 deg., Shriner), Royal Order of Jesters, 40 and 8, Am. Legion, Phi Delta Theta, Phi Theta Pi. Republican. Baptist. Clubs: Portland Golf, East Side Commercial, Optimist, Multnomah Athletic, Rotary. Home: 3410 N.E. Beakey St., Portland, Ore. Died Aug. 17, 1965.

RILEY, HERBERT DOUGLAS, naval officer; b. Balt., Dec. 24, 1904; s. Marion Herbert and Sarah Maud (Mealy) R.; grad. Balt. Polytech. Inst., 1923; B.S., U.S. Naval Acad., 1927; grad. Nat. War Coll., 1950; divorced; 1 dau., Lynne Lovelace. Commd. ensign U.S. Navy, 1927, advanced through grades to vice adm., 1958; designated naval aviator, 1930; served in various aviation squadrons, 1929-41; operations officer patrol wings, Pacific, 1942, dep. comdg. naval officer (air), 1933-44; comdg. officer U.S.S. Makassar Strait, 1944-45; operations officer 1st Carrier Task Force, 1945; dep. airborne comdr. Bikini atomic bomb tests, 1946; strategic planner Office Chief Naval Operations, Navy Dept., 1946-47; naval asst. to sec. def. Forrestal, 1948-49, asst. chief staff plans Atlantic Fleet, 1950-51; dep. chief staff SACLANT, NATO, 1951-52; comdg. officer U.S.S. Coral Sea, 1952-53; chief staff Carrier Div. 2, 1953-54; dir. politico-mil. policy Office Chief Naval Operations, 1955-56; comdr. Carrier Div. 1, also attack carrier task force, 7th Fleet, 1957; chief staff U.S. Pacific Command, 1958-61; dep. chief naval operations, 1961-62; dir. Joint Staff, Joint Chiefs of Staff, 1962-64. Decorated D.F.C., also Bronze Star medal with combat V, Navy and Air Force Commendation medal (3) (U.S.); comdr. Order British Empire; Peruvian Air Cross 1st class. Mem. Md. Hist. Soc., S.A.R. Clubs: Chevy Chase (Md.); Army and Navy (Washington); Queen Anne (Md.). Home: Kent Island MD Died Jan. 17, 1973.

RILEY, JAMES BREINIG judge; b. Wheeling, W.Va., July 26, 1894; s. Thomas Sylvester and Minnie (Breinig) R.; A.B., W.Va. U., 1916; student Georgetown U., 1916-17; LL.B., Columbia, 1921, A.M., 1921; m. Frances Wood, Oct. 25, 1925; children—Frances Wood, James Breinig. Admitted to W.Va. bar, 1921; mem. Riley and Riley, Wheeling, 1921-37; judge W.Va. Supreme Court of Appeals since 1937. Served as 2d lt., 1st lt. and capt. U.S.M.C., 1917-19. Mem. Am., W.Va. State, and Ohio County bar assns., Am. Law Inst. Democrat. Roman Catholic. Elk. Club: Fort Henry (Wheeling). Home: Wheeling, W.Va. Address: Capitol Bldg., Charleston, W.Va. Died June 29, 1958.

RINEHART, ROY JAMES dean; b. nr. Deland, Ill., Oct. 24, 1880; s. Joel and Mary (Miles) R.; student Marion (Ind.) Coll.; D.D.S., Western Dental Coll., Kansas City, Mo., 1902; m. Myrtle Harmision, Sept. 24, 1903. Practiced dentistry, Canton, Ill., 1902-07, Peoria, Ill., 1907-10, Kansas City, 1911; lectr. dentistry Western Dental Coll., 1912-16, sec.-treas. and supr., 1916-17, dean, sec.-treas., trustee and chmn. exec. com. Kansas City-Western Dental Coll., 1919-27, exec. dean, 1922-27, dean, 1927-—. Merged Kansas City-Western Dental Coll. with U. of Kansas City as Sch. of Dentistry, 1941, dean and mem. adv. council of u., interim acting pres., 1953. Examiner of dentists for commns. in U.S. Army, 1918; mem. Med. Adv. Bd., Kansas City, 1917-19; major Dental Corps, U.S. Army, 1925-45; profl. counselor Office of Surgeon Gen., 7th Corps Area; chmn. defense com., State of Mo., 1940-42. Established Lowry Dental Clinic. Del. to Am. Dental Assn., 1916-45. Pres. legislative sect. Internat. Dental Congress, 1926; Mo. del. to Internat. Dental Congress, Vienna, 1936. Mem. Am. Coll. Dentists, Am. Assn. History Medicine, Am. Social Hygiene Assn., Spl. Libraries Assn., A.A.A.S., Central Hist. Com. of Mo., Am. Assn. Dental Editors, Am. Assn. Dental Schs. (pres. 1948), Pan-Am. Odontol. Assn., Mo. State Dental Assn. (pres. 1928), Kansas City Dist. Dental Soc. (pres. 1912), Alumni Assn. Western Dental Coll. (pres. 1915), Kansas City C. of C., Xi Psi Phi, Omicron Kappa Upsilon. Republican. Mason (Shriner). Clubs: University, Professional Men's (Kansas City); Mission Hills Country. Contbr. to profl. jours. Home: 850 W. 55th St., Kansas City, Mo. Died Mar. 22, 1957.

RING, BLANCHE actress, vocalist; b. Boston, Apr. 24, 1877; d. James H. and Mena Frances (Ross) R.; ed. Girls' Latin Sch., Boston. Appeared in Boston and N.Y.C. in "The Defender," 1902; later starred as "Miss Innocence Demure," in "Tommy Rot," New York; made tour with James T. Powers in "The Jewel of Asia" London debut at Savoy Theatre, as "Effie Doublehurst," in "The Love Birds," Feb. 10, 1904; played "Helen," in "About Town," Herald Sq. Theatre, N.Y.C., 1906; starred as "Jessie Gorden," in "The Yankee Girl," 1909, again 1910-11; "Jimmy Green," in "The Wall Street Girl," 1912, and "Claudia Rogers," in "When Claudia Smiles," 1913; starred in "Broadway and Buttermilk," 1 season; in "What Next?" 1917; in vaudeville, 1918-19; Winter Garden, N.Y., 1919-20. Died Jan. 1961.

RING, RICHARD WARNER accountant; b. Savannah, Ga., Sept. 27, 1901; s. John R. and Agnes (Meskel) R.; grad. Eastman Coll., Poughkeepsie, N.Y., 1923; m. Ethel Marshall, Aug. 5, 1930; children—John M., Michael W. Partner firm Ring, Mahony & Arner, C.P.A.'s, Miami, Fla., 1926-—. Mem. Fla. Bd. Accountancy, 1955-—; pres. So. States Accountants Conf., 1955-56. Pres. Dade County Citizens Safety Council, 1955-—; v.p. Dade County Community Chest, 1954-—. Served as comdr. USNR, 1942-45. Mem. Am. Inst. Accountants (v.p. 1956-57; com. on awards, 1954-—; trial bd. 1955-—). Catholic. Clubs: Kiwania (pres. 1957), Miami (Miami); Bath La Gorce country (Miami Beach, Fla.). Home: 672 N.E. 98th St., Miami Shores, Fla. Office: duPont Bldg., Miami 32, Fla. Died June 7, 1958.

RINGER, PAUL HENRY physician; b. New York, N.Y., Nov. 6, 1881; s. Severin and Elisa (Minot) R.; A.B., Columbia, 1901, M.D., 1904; m. Eleanor Varick Morrison, May 1, 1915 (died September 1942); children—Paul Henry, Eleanor Morrison; married 2d, Mary Averell Brown, April 27, 1946. Engaged in practice as physician in Ashville, N.C., 1906-50; mem. Asheville Mission Hosp. staff, 1909-35; cons. physician 1935-50. Pres. N.C. Med. Soc., 1935-36; pres. Southern Tuberculosis Conf., 1937-38, Southern Med. Assn., 1940-41; Pres. Asheville Community Chest, 1936, Asheville Civic Music Assn., 1937-47; dir. Y.M.C.A. Captain Med. Corps, U.S. Army, with A.E.F., 1918-19. Presbyterian. Clubs: Columbia University (New York); Asheville Civitian (pres. 1929), Pen and Plate, Biltmore Forest Country (Asheville). Author: Clinical Medicine for Nurses, 1918. Contbr. to med. jours. Retired. Home: 423 Park Av., N.Y.C. 22. Died May 8, 1952; buried Riverside Cemetery, Asheville, N.C.

RINGGOLD, CADWALADER naval officer; b. Washington County, Md., Aug. 20, 1802; s. Samuel and Maria (Cadwalader) R. Apptd. midshipman U.S. Navy, 1819, commd. lt., 1828, comdr., 1829; commanded schooner Weasel against West Indian pirates; cruised in ship Vandalia in Pacific, 1828-32, in ship Adams in Mediterranean Sea, 1834-35; comdr. Porpoise in Wilkes Antarctic Exploring Expdn., 1838-42, commanded North Pacific surveying and exploring expdn., left Norfolk, June 1853, reached China, Mar. 1854; declared insane, made inactive, 1854, recovered, commd. capt. on active list with promotion to date from Apr. 2, 1856; commanded sail-frigate Sabine during Civil War; commd. commodore, 1862, ret., 1864, commd. rear adm. (ret.), 1866. Author: A Series of Charts, with Sailing Directions ... to the Bay of San Francisco, 1851; Correspondence to Accompany Maps and Charts of California. Died N.Y.C., Apr. 29, 1867; buried Greenmount Cemetery, Balt.

RIPLEY, CLEMENTS writer; b. Tacoma, Aug. 26, 1892; s. Thomas Emerson and Charlotte Howard (Clement) R.; prep. edn., Taft Sch., Watertown, Conn.; A.B., Yale, 1916; m. Katharine Ball, June 7, 1919 (dec. July 1955); 1 son, William Young Warren. Commd. 2d lt. F.A., U.S. Army, 1916, and advanced to capt., leaving service 1920; engaged in peach growing and writing, 1920-28. Episcopalian. Author: Dust and Sun, 1929; Devil Drums, 1931; Black Moon, 1933; Murder Walks Alone, 1935; Gold Is Where You Find It, 1936; Clear for Action, 1940; Mississippi Belle, 1942. Contbr. fiction and articles mags. Short Story, "Cities of Fear," included in World's Best Short Stories of 1929. Author of motion pictures, Jezebel; Love, Honor and Behave; Buffalo Bill; In Old Los Angeles. Home: 1922 S. Bentley Av., Los Angeles 25, (winter) 18 Lamboll St., Charleston, S.C. Died July 22, 1954.

RIPLEY, ELEAZAR WHEELOCK congressman, army officer; b. Hanover, N.H., Apr. 15, 1782; s. Sylvanus and Abigail (Wheelock) R.; grad. Dartmouth, 1800; m. Love Allen, 1811; m. 2d, Mrs. Smith; 2 children. Mem. Mass. Legislature, 1807-11, speaker, 1811; mem. Mass. Senate, 1812; commd. lt. col. to rank, 1812; commanded 21st Infantry or regular army; took part in Gen. William Wilkinson's unsuccessful invasion of Canada, 1813; commd. col. U.S. Army, 1813; in attack on York (now Toronto), Ont., Can., 1813; commd. brig. gen. U.S. Army, 1814, brevetted maj. gen., 1814, commanded brigade; fought at battles of Ft. Erie, Chippewa, Lundy's Lane, 1814; received gold medal from Congress for gallantry and good conduct in battle, 1814; resigned from army, 1820; practiced law, New Orleans; mem. La. Senate, 1832; mem. U.S. Ho. of

Reps. from La., 23d-25th congresses, 1835-39. Died West Feliciana, La., Mar. 2, 1839; buried St. Francisville, La.

RIPLEY, JAMES WOLFE army officer; b. Windham County, Conn., Dec. 10, 1794; s. Ralph and Eunice (Huntington) R.; grad. U.S. Mil. Acad., 1814; m. Sarah Denny, Aug. 11, 1824, 9 children. Commd. 2d lt. arty. U.S. Army, 1814, ordered to duty at Sacketts Harbor, N.Y.; served in garrisons, circa 1814-17; commd. 1st lt. during Seminole War; asst. commr. under James Gadsden to run boundaries of Indian reservations of Fla., 1823-24; commd. capt., stationed in Charleston, S.C. when state threatened secession; assigned to command arsenal, Kennebec, Me., 1833-41; promoted maj., 1838; commanded armory, Springfield, Mass., 1841-54, arsenal, Watertown, Mass., 1824; commd. lt. col., 1854; chief of ordnance Pacific Dept., Cal., 1855-59, insp. arsenals, 1857; spl. duty in Japan, 1860; chief of ordnance with rank of col., 1861; commd. brig. gen., 1861, ret., 1863; insp. armaments, until 1869; brevetted maj. gen., 1865. Died Hartford, Conn., Mar. 15, 1870; buried Springfield Cemetery, Hartford.

RIPLEY, ROSWELL SABINE army officer; b. Worthington, O., Mar. 14, 1823; s. Christopher and Julia (Caulkins) R.; grad. U.S. Mil. Acad., 1843; m. Alicia Burroughs, Dec. 22, 1852. Brevetted 2d lt., assigned to 3d Arty., U.S. Army; served at Ft. McHenry, Md., Ft. Johnston, N.C., Augusta (Ga.) Arsenal, 1843-46; asst. prof. mathematics U.S. Mil. Acad.; served on Coast Survey, 1846; commd. 2d lt. 2d Arty., 1846; served in Mexican War under gens. Taylor and Pillow; commd. 1st lt., then maj., 1847; took part in battles from Monterey to taking of Mexico City; brevetted capt. and maj. for gallantry at battles of Cerro Goredo and Chapultepec; resigned, 1853; officer S.C. Militia, 1853-60, apptd. maj. ordnance, 1860; commd. lt. col. Confederate Army, brig. gen. in command S.C., 1860, maj., 1860; directed firing on Ft. Sumter, 1861; served in defense of Charleston, 1863; served under Gen. Lee to end of war; poem in his honor written by Timrod. Author: History of the War with Mexico, 2 vols., 1849; Correspondence Relating to Fortification of Morris Island (pamphlet), 1878. Died N.Y.C., Mar. 29, 1887.

RISER, WILLIAM HENRY, JR., physician, educator; b. Milltown, Ala., June 25, 1911; s. Dr. William H. and Bertha Mae (Carlson) R.; B.S., Ala Poly. Inst., 1933; student U. Ala., 1933-36; M.D., Emory University, 1938; married Roberta Alice Johnson, October 5, 1940; children—Jeanne, Susan, William H., III, Julie. Intern Grady Memorial Hospital, Atlanta, Georgia, 1938-39; house officer internal medicine Peter Bent Brigham Hosp., Boston, 1939-40; asst. in clin. hematology and clin. pathology, med. sch. Emory U., Ga., 1940-41; asso. prof. clin. hematology Med. Coll. Ala., Birmingham, 1945-46, asso. prof. medicine, 1946-49, acting prof., chmn. dept. medicine, 1949-50, asso. prof., 1950-52, prof. since 1952, dir. sch. med. technologists since 1945, hematology clinic since 1945; clin. labs. Jefferson Hillman Hosp. since 1945, house staff since 1947, med. dir. since 1948; cons. internal medicine V.A. Hosp., Montgomery, Ala., chmn. deans com., ednl. dir. residency tng. program V.A. Hosp., Tuskegee, Ala.; cons. internal medicine, med. div. Oak Ridge Inst. Nuclear Studies. Mem. Regional Blood Bank for No. Ala. Served as lt. col., med. corps, U.S. Army, 1941-45, N. Africa and France. Diplomate Am. Bd. Internal Medicine. Mem. Gorgas Med. Soc., Southeastern Clin. Club, Am. College Physicians, American, Southern and Ala. State med. assns., A.A.A.S., Am. Heart Assn., Jefferson Co. Med. Soc., Sigma Xi, Pi Kappa Alpha, Alpha Omega Alpha, Phi Chi. Baptist. Club: Mountain Brook Country. Author articles in med. jours. Contbr. med. textbooks. Home: 2132 Vestaria Lake Dr., Birmingham, Ala. Died Jan. 11, 1961; buried Lafayette, Ala.

RISNER, HENRY CLAY clergyman, author; b. Magoffin County, Ky., Nov. 11, 1869; s. Archibald and Narcissus (Prater) R.; student Georgetown (Ky.) Coll.; M.Th., Southern Bapt. Sem., Louisville, Ky., 1899; D.D., Women's Coll., Bryan, Tex., 1906; m. Hattie Carson, 1892. Ordained ministry Southern Bapt. Ch., 1887; teacher pub. schs. 3 yrs.; prin. high schs., Dunkirk, Ind., 1891-92; pastorates in Ky., Tex., Tenn., Md., N.J., Mass., Calif., etc., also supply various chs. including 5th Av. Ch., Huntington, W. Va. Mem. World's S.S. Conv., Jerusalem, 1904, and, apptd. mem. of com. to write the "Jerusalem Pilgrim's Book," 1904; known as "The friend of the boys," in Am. Army camps, World War I, France and Germany; assigned to Army of Occupation at Coblentz 1 yr.; traveled extensively in Europe meeting the leaders in the interest of better relations between the U.S. and European countries; preaching tour in England, 1920; made prayer that unlocked the 13-day deadlock in Dem. Nat. Conv., New York, 1924. Author: Pinnacles of Personality, 1930, 32. Lecturer. Address: Huntington, W.Va. Died May 2, 1948.

RITCHIE, WILLIAM (ritchie), lawyer; b. Ravenswood, Ill., July 28, 1886; s. Wiliam and Charlotte (Congdon) R.; LL.B., U. Neb., 1915; m. Eunice Arthur, Apr. 26, 1916. Admitted to Neb. bar, 1915, U.S. Supreme Ct., 1926; engaged in practice of law 1915-53; dir. Kennedy & Parsons Co., C.B. Brown Co., Omaha. Trustee U. Neb. Found. Served as capt. 69th Inf., U.S. Army, 1917-19. Mem. Am., Neb. and Omaha bar assns., Am. Legion (dept. comdr. 1921-22), S.A.R., Beta Theta Pi, Phi Delta Phi. Democrat (state chmn.; nominee for Senate 1952, for gov. 1954). Catholic. Home: 5822 Western Av., Omaha 3, Neb. Died Feb., 1956.

RITER, FRANKLIN corp. exec.; b. Logan, Utah, Sept. 27, 1886; s. Benjamin Franklin and Maria Inez (Corlett) R.; B.S., Utah State U., 1907; Cornell U., 1908; LL.B., Columbia, 1910; m. Lesley Day Woodruff, Nov. 2, 1911. Admitted to N.Y. bar, 1910, Ore., 1911, Cal., 1913, Utah, 1914, Tex., 1919, U.S. Supreme Ct., 1942; mem. Riter, Cowan, Finlinson & Daines, 1914-—; pres., dir. E.D. Woodruff Co., Tracy-Collins Bank & Trust Co. Mem. O.R.C. since World War I; ordered to active duty 1941; contract coordinator Office Judge Adv. Gen., Washington, 1941; col., assigned as chmn. and coordinator Bds. Rev., E.T.O., 1942-46; spl. legal assignment Office; Judge Adv. Gen., 1946-47; brig. gen., O.R.C. Mem. House of Del., Am. Bar Assn., 1952-66. Pres. Utah League for Prohibition Repeal. Past chmn. adv. council and dir. Salt Lake C. of C. Past mem. nat. council Boy Scouts Am., past treas. Gt. Salt Lake council. Decorated Legion of Merit with oak leaf cluster; recipient Silver Beaver award Boy Scouts Am. Fellow Am. Bar Found.; mem. Am. Bar Assn. (gov. 1958-60), Am. Legion (comdr. Dept. Utah 1948), S.A.R. (nat. trustee, nat. soc.), Civic Music Assn. Mason (Shriner, 33 deg.). Clubs: Lawyers' (N.Y.C.); Army and Navy (Washington); Officers (Fort Douglas, Utah); University (Salt Lake City). Home: 839 E. South Temple. Office: Kearns Bldg., Salt Lake City 1. Died May 25, 1966; buried Mt. Olivet Cemetery, Salt Lake City.

RITTER, WILLIAM LEONARD, army officer; b. Hartford City, Ind., Jan. 12, 1898; s. Charles E. and Sara M. (Hess) R.; grad. Inf. Sch., company officers course, 1923, advanced course, 1931; m. Grace E. Moore, Sept. 27, 1924; 1 dau., Anne Slocum. Commd. 2d lt., U.S. Army, 1917, advancing through the grades to brig. gen., 1944; served with 4th Div. during World War I; participated in Tunisian, Sicilian and Italian campaigns during World War II; chief of staff and dep. comdr. U.S. Army Forces in Africa and the Middle East, 1944-46; prof. mil. science and tactics U. of Calif., Berkeley, 1946-50. Decorated Distinguished Service Medal, Bronze Star Medal with Oak Leaf Cluster, Purple Heart with oak leaf cluster; Order British Empire. Home: St Petersburg FL Died July 6, 1971.

RIVERS, G(EORGE) L(AMB) BUIST lawyer; b. Charleston, S.C., May 26, 1896; s. Moultrie Rutledge and Eliza Ingraham (Buist) R.; A.B., Coll. Charleston, 1916, A.M., 1916; ed. Harvard Law Sch., 1916-17, 1919; m. Ethel Pinckney Rutledge, Nov. 20, 1930; children—George Lamb Buist, Thomas Rutledge. Admitted to S.C. bar, 1919; asst. U.S. dist. atty., Eastern Dist. S.C., 1922; mem. Hagood, Rivers & Young since 1920; pres. The Central R.R. of S.C.; chmn., dir. counsel First Fed. Savs. & Loan Assn. of Charleston; dir. and counsel Citizens & So. Nat. Bank, S.C., Carolina Supplies & Cement Co., Am. Mutual Fire Ins. Co.; dir. Planters Fertilizer & Phosphate Co., Colonial Life & Accident Ins. Co.; v.p., counsel of Station WCSC, Inc.; dir., counsel Wm. M. Bird & Co. Govt. appeal agt. Selective Service Bd. No. 15, Charleston, S.C.; mem. County Council of Defense for Charleston County, S.C. Mem. S.C. Ho. of Reps., 1924-28, Senate, 1930. Mem. Charleston NRA Compliance Bd., 1933. First lt. 18th F.A., 3d Div., A.E.F.; in Aisne-Marne, Champaigne-Marne campaigns, 2d battle of Marne; capt. 48th F.A. Decorated D.S.C., "for extraordinary heroism," 1918. Trustee bd. visitors S.C. Mil. Coll., 1930; pres. bd. trustees Coll. of Charleston; pres. Charleston C. of C., 1933; dir. Charleston Y.M.C.A.; mem. nat. com. Civilian Mil. Edn. Fund, Internat. Assn. Ins., Counsel; chmn. Vets. Adv. Counsel for Charleston County. Mem. Am., S.C. State and Charleston County bar assns., St. Georges Soc., St. Andrew's Soc. (past pres.), Footlight Players (past pres.), S.C. Soc., St. Cecilia Soc., Alpha Tau Omega. Democrat. Episcopalian. Mason. Clubs: Carolina Yacht, Old Town Club, Kiwanis. Home: 7 Orange St. Office: 28 Broad St., Charleston, S.C. Died Sept. 12, 1963; buried Magnolia Cemetery, Charleston, S.C.

RIVERS, THOMAS MILTON med. research; b. Jonesboro, Ga., Sept. 3, 1888; s. Alonzo Burrel and Mary Martha (Coleman) R.; A.B., Emory Coll., Oxford, Ga., 1909; M.D., Johns Hopkins, 1915; hon. Sc.D., Emory University, 1936, Rochester University, 1938, University of Chicago, 1941; m. Teresa Jacobina Riefle, August 5, 1922. Intern Johns Hopkins Hospital, 1915-16, assistant resident physician, pediatrics, 1916-17, resident pediatrician and instr. in pediatrics, 1917-18; instr. in bacteriology, Johns Hopkins, 1919-21, asso. in bacteriology, 1921-22; pathologist St. Joseph's Hosp., Baltimore, 1920-22; asso. Rockefeller Inst., N.Y. City, 1922-25, asso. mem., 1925-27, mem. since 1927; dir. of Hosp. of Rockefeller Inst., 1937-55; dir. 1953, member emeritus, 1955; med. dir. Nat. Found. Infantile Paralysis, 1956-58; vice president med. affairs Nat. Found., 1958-—. Served as 1st lt. Med. Corps, U.S. Army, February 1918-Jan. 1919; captain Medical Corps, U.S. Naval Reserve; rear admiral, retired reserves, 1955. Was president of the 3d International Congress for Microbiology, New York, 1939. Mem. A.A.A.S., Am. Soc. Clin. Investigation (pres. 1932), Assn. Am. Physicians, Interurban Clin. Club (pres. 1942-43), American Pediatric Society, American Epidemiological Soc., Am. Soc. Exptl. Pathology, Soc. Am. Bacteriologists (pres. 1936), Soc. Am. Immunologists (pres. 1934), Harvey Society, Am. Assn. Pathologists and Bacteriologists, Am. Clin. and Clinatological Assn., Nat. Acad. Sciences, Am. Philos. Soc., Phi Beta Kappa, Alpha Omega Alpha, Sigma Nu, Pi Mu, Century Assn. Democrat. Contbr. to E.L. Opie's Epidemic Respiratory Disease, 1921; editor and contbr. to Filterable Viruses, 1928, to Viral and Rickettsial Infections of Man, 1948, 52, 58. Discover Bacillus Parainfluenzae, and Virus III infections in rabbits; cultivated vaccine virus for human use. Home: 163 Greenway S., Forest Hills, L.I., N.Y. Address: York Av. and 66th St., N.Y.C. 21; also 800 2d Av., N.Y.C. 17. Died May 12, 1962; buried Arlington Nat. Cemetery.

RIVERS, WILLIAM CANNON army officer; b. Pulaski, Tenn., Jan. 11, 1866; s. William and Julia (Flournoy) R.; grad. U.S. Mil. Acad., 1887; m. Mary Dancey Battle, Oct. 19, 1897; children—James Battle, William Flournoy. Commd. 2d lt. 1st Cav., U.S. Army, June 12, 1887; promoted through grades to col., July 1, 1916; brig. gen. (temp.), Oct. 1, 1918; apptd. by President Coolidge insp. gen. U.S. Army, rank of maj. gen., 1927, retired, Jan. 11, 1930. Served in troubles with Northern Cheyenne and Sioux Indians, 1890-91; in charge White Mountain Apache Indians, 1895-97; adj. U.S. Mil. Acad., 1890-1903; with regt. at Santiago, Cuba, June 25-June 30, 1898; duty Gen. Staff, 1903-04; asst. chief of constabulary, Philippines, rank of col., 1906-13; brig. gen. U.S. Army (temp.) and chief Philippines Constabulary, 1914; organized and trained the 76th Field Arty., 3d Arty. Brigade, 3d Regular Div., and commanded the regt. in Battle of the Marne at Chateau-Thierry, the advance to the North of the Ourcq to Aug. 2, 1918, and in battles of St. Mihiel and Meuse-Argonne; comd. 5th Brigade, F.A., 2d Army, between Pout-à-Mousson and Thiacourt, Oct. 14, until Armistice. Awarded D.S.M. (U.S.); Croix de Guerre (French); colors of 76th F.A. decorated with Croix de Guerre. Mem. Huguenot Soc. America, S.R. Soc. Army of Santiago de Cuba, Am. Acad. Polit. and Social Sciences. Episcopalian. Clubs: Army and Navy, Pilgrims, University (New York). Address: Warrington, N.C.* Died July 10, 1943.

RIVES, ALFRED LANDON engr.; b. Paris, France, March 25, 1830; s. William Cabell R. (then U.S. minister to France); studied at Va. Mil. Inst. and Univ. of Va.; grad. École des Ponts et Chaussées, Paris, 1854; asst. engr. in completing U.S. Capitol Bldg., Washington; later engr. on aqueduct, Washington; then in charge U.S. Survey in improving Potomac River; later col. engrs. Confederate army; after was engr. on Chesapeake & Ohio R.R., chief engr. South & North Ala. R.R. Offered charge of civ. engring. works of Egypt; v.p. and gen. mgr. Mobile & Ohio R.R.; v.p. and gen. mgr. Richmond & Danville R.R.; gen. supt. Panama R.R. Now chief engr. Cape Cod Canal, and gen. consulting engr. Is father of Amélie Rives (Princess Troubetzkoy) authoress. Home: Cobham, Va. Died 1903.

RIVES, EDWIN EARLE (revz), judge; b. Winston Salem, N.C., Nov. 19, 1898; s. Edward Andrew and Florence (Goldston) R.; LL.B., U. N.C., 1922; m. Mary Tankersley, Nov. 15, 1922 (dec.); children—Frances Adele, Edwin Earle, Mary Roselia; married 2d, Margaret Hunter Stout, Aug. 15, 1953. Admitted to N.C. bar, 1922 and practiced in Greensboro, 1922-29; judge Municipal Ct. apptd. by Greensboro City Council, 1929-33; apptd. judge Municipal-Co. Ct. by Gov. of N.C. since 1933; spl. assignment as personal rep. Sec. of Army, Berlin, 1947-48; cons. Sec. Army since 1948, apptd. Civilian Aide, 1952; apptd. dir. Fed. Prison Industries, Inc. by Pres., 1949. Dem. candidate for nomination U.S. Congress, 1946. Served as sgt., A.U.S., World War I; lt. col., Judge Adv. Gen. Dept., World War II. Mem. Am., N.C. (chmn. exec. com., 1937, v.p., 1941), Greensboro (v.p., 1942) bar assns., N.C. Bar, Inc., Gen. Alumni Assn. U. N.C. (pres., 1951-52), Phi Delta Theta, Phi Delta Phi. Club: Kiwanis. Home: 207 N. Ridgeway Dr. Office: Post Office Box 2759, Greensboro, N.C. Died Dec. 12, 1953; buried Greenhill Cemetery, Greensboro, N.C.

RIVKIN, WILLIAM ROBERT ambassador; b. Muscatine, Ia., Apr. 16, 1919; s. Samuel Wulf and Florence (Freyer) R.; B.A., U. Ia., 1941; J.D., Northwestern U., 1948; m. Enid Hammerman, Apr. 5, 1959; children—Laura, Julia, Robert, Charles. Admitted to Ill. bar, 1947, Ia. bar, 1948; asso. Goldberg & Weigle, Chgo., 1948-55; partner Goldberg, Weigle, Mallin & Rivkin, Chgo., 1955-62, 65-66; U.S. ambassador to Luxembourg, 1962-65, Senegal and the Gambia, 1966-—. Consultant Bur. of Intelligence and Research, Dept. of State, 1965-—. Served from pvt. to lt. col., AUS, 1941-46. Decorated Bronze Star; French Ordre Publique; Crown of Oak (Luxembourg). Mem. Am., Ill., Chgo., Fed. Communications bar assns., Am. Soc. Internat. Law, Order of Artists, Omicron Delta Kappa. Clubs: Standard, Arts (Chgo.); Briarwood Country (Deerfield, Ill.); Federal City (Washington).

Home: 2014 Old Briar Rd., Highland Park, Ill. Office: Am. Embassy, Dakar, Senegal. Died Mar. 19, 1967; buried Arlington Nat. Cemetery, Washington.

RIX, CHARLES NORTHRUP banker; b. Kalamazoo, Mich., May 28, 1843; s. George and Olive (Northrup) R.; grad. high sch., Dowagiac, Mich.; m. Lucy Emma Thomas, Dec. 19, 1870 (dec.); children—Fred Northrup (dec.), Lila Thankful (dec.). Served as q.m. sergt. to capt. 1st Ind. Regt. in Civil War; in pay dept. U.S.A., 1865-67; began in banking business as bookkeeper, 1867; cashier, v.p. and pres., in bank, Topeka, to 1879; removed to Ark.; pres. Ark, Nat. Bank, Hot Springs, 27 yrs.; pres., treas. City Ice Co., New Waverly Hotel Co., Hot Springs Obs. Co. Mem. Rep. State Central Com. Episcopalian. Mason; Grand Comdr. K.T. of Ark., 1891; Grand High Priest Grand Chapter Royal Arch Masons, 1890, and Grand Master Grand Council Royal and Select Masters, 1893, 94, 95; Deputy General Grand High Priest of General Grand Chapter R.A. Masons of U.S.A. Home: Hot Springs, Ark. Died Sept. 2, 1927.

RIXEY, PRESLEY MARION surgeon gen. U.S.N.; b. Culpeper, Va., July 14, 1852; s. Presley Morehead and Mary F. (Jones) R.; ed. in schs. at Culpeper and Warrenton, Va.; M.D., U. of Va., 1873; matriculated at Jefferson Med. Coll., Phila., 1873; m. Earlena I. English, Apr. 25, 1877. Asst. surgeon U.S.N., Jan. 28, 1874; passed asst. surgeon, Apr. 18, 1877; surgeon, Nov. 27, 1888; med. insp., Aug. 24, 1900; surgeon gen. with rank of rear admiral, Feb. 10, 1902-Feb. 25, 1910; med. dir. May 7, 1907. Spent 11 1/2 yrs. on sea duty, 25 1/2 yrs. shore duty; on shore attached successively to Naval Hosp., Phila., Navy Yard, Norfolk, and Naval Dispensary, Washington. Was the official physician to President McKinley from 1898 to time of his death, of Mrs. McKinley to time of her death, of President Roosevelt from 1901 to time of his death, and was phys. to White House 10 yrs., to Mar. 4, 1909, in addition to other duties; retired, Feb. 4, 1910; farming, 1910-17. Active service, Apr. 11, 1917, with Bur. Medicine and Surgery, Council Nat. Defense, and as insp. gen. med. activities of Navy in U.S. until Sept. 18, 1918. Decorated by Alphonso XIII, King of Spain, for services rendered officers and men on the Santa Maria following an explosion on that vessel. Home: "Rixey," Arlington Co., Va. Died June 17, 1928.

RIZER, HENRY CLAY chief clerk U.S. Geol. Survey since May, 1891; b. Cumberland, Md., Feb. 1, 1844; s. Jacob R.; ed. Cumberland, Md., leaving school in 1861 to enter U.S.A., in which he served until close of war; mustered out col. of his regt.; widower. Studied law, admitted to bar, 1867; practiced law 15 yrs.; edited weekly newspaper 6 yrs. Mem. Nat. Geog. Soc. Club: Cosmos. Address: U.S. Geol. Survey, Washington.

ROANE, JOHN SELDEN lawyer, army officer, gov. of Alabama; born in Wilson County, Tennessee, Jan. 8, 1817; s. Hugh and Hannah (Calhoun) R.; ed. Cumberland Coll., Princeton, Ky.; m. Mary K. Smith, July 5, 1855, 4 children. Admitted to the bar, 1842; pros. atty. 2d Judicial Dist. 1840; mem. Ark. Legislature, elected speaker; served as lt. col. Archibald Yell's Regt. during Mexican War, took over command at Battle of Buena Vista when Col. Yell was killed; gov. Ala., 1849-52; favored geol. survey, use of land granted by Congress for internal improvements to promote railroad building and edn.; endorsed Memphis as starting point proposed Pacific R.R.; opposed secession, 1861; volunteered, then commd. brig. gen. Confederate Army, 1862; chief in command of Ark. at Battle of Prairie Grove. Died Pine Bluff, Ark., Apr. 8, 1867; buried Oakland Cemetery, Little Rock, Ark.

ROBB, RUSSELL director and trustee; born in Concord, Mass., Nov. 13, 1900; son of Russell and Edith Owen (Morse) R.; A.B., Harvard Coll., 1923; married Katharine Moxley Armstrong, Jan. 3, 1933; children—Gale Armstrong, Russell Jr. With Stone and Webster, Inc. (except for war leave with the Armed Services), 1923-49, v.p. and dir., 1929-41, 1946-49, still dir.; dir. Stone and Webster Engring. Corp., Stone and Webster Service Corp., N.Y., Colonial Fund Inc., Stone and Webster Realty Corp., Boston; trustee, Franklin Savings Bank City of Boston. Joined Army Air Forces, 1941, with rank of capt., released 1946, with rank of col. Awarded Legion of Merit. Trustee Concord (Mass.) Acad., Concord, trustee Museum of Science, Boston. Member Delta Psi. Unitarian. Clubs: Fly (Cambridge); Somerset, Harvard (Boston); Social Circle (Concord); Brook (N.Y.). Home: Concord, Mass. Office: 75 Federal St., Boston 10. Died June 3, 1957.

ROBBINS, CHARLES BURTON lawyer; b. Hastings, Ia., Nov. 6, 1877; s. Lewis and Harriett Elizabeth (Benson) R.; B.A., U. of Neb., 1898; studied Columbia U., College of Law; A.M., Columbia, 1903; m. Helen Larrabee, Sept. 9, 1903 (dec.); children—Anna Marcella (Mrs. Thomas C. Yarnall), Julia Larrabee (Mrs. Alvin W. Allen), Lewis Frederic. Served as pvt., 1st Neb. Inf., U.S.V., Apr. 28, 1898, first sergt. Co. B, May 10, 1898; 2d lt. Co. I, Apr. 27, 1899; served in the Spanish-Am. War at Manila until close of war; Philippine insurrection from outbreak, Feb. 3, 1899-June 1899; wounded in head at battle of Marilao, Mar. 27, 1899; took part in 27 engagements; awarded Silver Star and Purple Heart medals; mem. Co. C, 7th Regt., Nat. Guard, N.Y., 1901-03; capt. Ia. Nat. Guard, 1914-16; maj., adj. gen.'s dept., Ia., Nov. 2, 1916; maj., adj. 67th and later 69th Inf. Brigade., U.S. Army, Aug. 1917-May 1919; with A.E.F., 1918-19; maj. U.S.R., 1921; lt. col., 1923; col. since 1926; comdr. Ia. dept. Am. Legion, 1922-23. Civilian aide to sec. of War for Ia. C.M.T.C., 1924-27; asst. sec. of War, 1928-29. Admitted to Ia. bar, 1904; judge Superior Court, Cedar Rapids, 1909-19. Chmn. bd. Federal Home Loan Bank of Des Moines; dir. Merchants Nat. Bank, Cedar Rapids. Mem. exec. com. Am. Life Conv., 1925-33, pres., 1930-31, mgr. and gen. counsel since 1934. Republican. Universalist. Mem. Am. Bar Assn., Ia. State Bar Assn., Ia. State Hist. Soc., Delta Tau Delta. Mason (32 deg.). Clubs: Cedar Rapids Country; Army and Navy, Nat. Press (Washington); Tavern, Union League (Chicago). Home: 3750 Lake Shore Drive. Office: 230 N. Michigan Av., Chicago, Ill. Died July 5, 1943.

ROBBINS, EDWARD EVERETT congressman; b. Greensburg, Pa., Sept. 27, 1861; s. Joseph and Rachel G. R.; A.B., Washington and Jefferson Coll., 1881; studied law dept. Columbia U.; m. Luella Stauffer Moore, 1886. Admitted to Pa. bar, 1886, and began practice at Greensburg; also in coal and banking business; mem. Pa. Senate, 1888-94; mem. 55th and 65th Congresses (1897-99 and 1915-17), 22d Pa. Dist. Republican. Entered Pa. N.G., 1887; left Congress, and commd. capt. a.q.m. vols. Spanish-Am. War, May 27, 1898; maj. q.m., Aug. 27, 1898; served in Cuba and Puerto Rico; hon. disch. from vol. service, Oct. 14, 1898; apptd. q.m. gen. of Pa., rank of col., staff of Gov. Stone, 1900, and served 4 yrs. Presbyn. Elk. Home: Greensburg, Pa. Died Jan. 25, 1919.

ROBBINS, FRANKLIN G., ry. official; b. La Crosse, Wis., Feb. 15, 1876; s. Edwin G. and Alice N. Stafford R.; ed. pub. schs., Minneapolis, and Shattuck Sch., Faribault, Minn.; m. Alice R. Rexroat, of Concord, Ill., June 2, 1906. Messenger, rodman and telegraph operator M., St.P. and S. Ste. Marie Ry.; with C.,B. & Q. Ry. Co., 1906-13, advancing to div. supt.; supt. Erie R.R., Buffalo, N.Y., 1913-16; gen. supt. Erie R.R. at Chicago 1917; dir. Bur. of Service, Interstate Commerce Commn., Washington, D.C., 1920-22; v.p. Chicago region, Erie R.R., since 1922; dir. C. & W.I. R.R., Belt Line Ry. Co. of Chicago. Entered U.S. Army as maj., Dec. 1917, later lt. col.; served as aide to S. M. Felton, dir. gen. of rys.; asst. gen. mgr. railroads in France; hon. discharged, June 1919. Mem. Old Time Telegraphers' Assn. Republican. Christian Scientist. Mason. Clubs: Union League, Traffic (Chicago); Army and Navy (Washington, D.C.). Home: 4828 Dorchester Av. Office: 1303 Transportation Bldg., Chicago IL

ROBBINS, GEORGE RIDGWAY clergyman; b. Trenton, N.J., Oct. 3, 1850; s. Enoch and Louisa (Flock) R.; State Model Sch., Trenton, N.J.; A.B., Colgate U., 1874; A.M., 1877 (D.D., 1902); studied at Hamilton Theol. Sem.; m. Florence Mix, of Binghamton, N.Y., June 17, 1876. Ordained Bapt. ministry, 1876; pastor 1st Ch., Hoosick Falls, N.Y., 1876-88, Lincoln Park Institutional Ch., Cincinnati, 1888-—. Editor of weekly ch. paper, 1895-—. Chaplain 1st Regt. Ohio N.G. Republican. Contbr. to newspapers. Address: 2085 Harrison Av., Cincinnati.

ROBBINS, HARRY CLARK banker; b. Somerville, Mass., Sept. 11, 1890; s. William H. and Susan M. (Clark) R.; student pub. schs., Somerville; m. Vera M. Mersereau, Oct. 17, 1925; children—Hollis L., Susanne. With Old Colony Trust Co., Boston, 1908-12, F.S. Moseley & Co., Boston, 1912-—, partner, 1927-—; dir. Bigelow Sanford Carpet Co., Sprague Electric Co., Bohn Aluminum & Brass Corporation, Manchester Electric Company, Nantucket Gas & Electric Co., Gas Service Co. of N.H., Keystone Fund of Can. Served as lt. U.S. Army, A.E.F., 1917-18. Clubs: Union, University, Eastern Yacht, Dublin Lake; Tedesco Country (Swampscott). Home: 26 Mostyn St., Swampscott, Mass. Office: 50 Congress St., Boston. Died July 25, 1960; buried Swampscott.

ROBBINS, HARRY PELHAM b. New York, N.Y., May 10, 1874; s. Henry Asher and Elizabeth Pelham (Bend) R.; A.B., Columbia, 1894; m. Emily Welles, Apr. 1908. Began as partner Vassar & Son, building constrn., 1897; was dir. Waltham Watch Co. (father a founder); dir. Empire Trust Co. since 1905. First lt. 12th Inf., N.Y. Nat. Guard, drilling draft recruits, World War; capt. regtl. adj. 369th Inf., 1921-22. Trustee Columbia U., Bard Coll., Am. Foundation Mental Hygiene, St. Andrew's Dune Ch. (Southampton, N.Y.); pres. Memorial Hosp. (N.Y. City). Pres. bd. of visitors Central Islip State Hosp.; mem. administrative com. Nat. Com. for Mental Hygiene. Mem. Am. Legion, S.R. Democrat. Episcopalian. Clubs: Knickerbocker, University, Columbia U. (New York); Meadow (Southampton). Home: 9 E. 79th St. Office: 500 5th Av., New York, N.Y.* Died Mar. 20, 1946.

ROBBINS, HARRY WOLCOTT educator; b. Vershire, Vt., Jan. 31, 1883; s. Henry Clarke and Caroline Abagail (Wolcott) R.; A.B., Brown U., 1908, A.M., 1908; student U. of Chgo., summer 1912, U. of Wis., summer 1914, U. of Grenoble, 1919; Ph.D., U. of Minn., 1923; m. Florence Bliss Lyon, Aug. 30, 1910. Asst. in English, Brown U., 1908-09; instr. in English, Marblehead (Mass.) High Sch., 1909-11, Calumet (Mich.) High Sch., 1911-14, North High Sch., Mpls., 1914-17; instr. in English, U. of Minn., 1919-23; prof. English, Bucknell U., 1923-54, ret. prof. Enlisted in 1st O.T.C., Ft. Snelling, Minn., 1917; commd. 2d lt. and advanced to capt.; served as adj. 804th Pioneer Inf., with A.E.F., 1918-19; capt. Inf. O.R.C., 1920-39; 2d lt. Cav., Pa. Nat. Guard, 1925. Mem. Modern Lang. Assn. Am., Am. Assn. Univ. Profs., Phi Beta Kappa, Sigma Tau Delta, Lambda Chi Alpha. Republican. Baptist. Author: Advanced Exposition (with R. E. Parker), 1933; Developing Ideas for Essays and Speeches (with R. T. Oliver), 1943. Editor: Le Merure de Seinte Eglise, 1925; Western World Literature (with W. H. Coleman), 1938. Translator: Le Roman de la Rose. Contributor to journals. Home: 124 S. George Street, Lewisburg, Pa.; (summer) Colchester, Vt. Died June 19, 1954.

ROBBINS, IRVIN soldier; b. Moscow, Ind., Mar. 30, 1839; s. Richard and Sarah Ann (Wood) R.; A.B., Butler Coll., Indianapolis, 1860, in law, 1860, A.M., 1863; m. Cassandra Cobb, Apr. 10, 1862. Pvt. 7th Ind. Vols., Apr. 24, 1861; adj. 76th Ind. Vols., July 1862; capt. 123d Ind. Vols., Nov. 1863; maj. same, July 1, 1864; insp. gen. and a.a.g., 1st div. 23d Army Corps in N.C., 1865; provost marshal west part N.C., summer 1865. Carriage mfr., 1871-—; supt. of police, 1883. Mason. Adj. gen. of Ind. G.A.R., 1891-93; adj. gen. Nat. Encampment G.A.R., 1896; sr. v.-comdr.-in-chief G.A.R., 1899-1900. Democrat. Home: Indianapolis, Ind. Died 1911.

ROBBINS, MERTON COVEY publisher; b. Brattleboro, Vt., Aug. 18, 1875; s. Marcus R. and Almira L. (Covey) R.; B.S. in C.E., U. of Vt., 1898; m. Florence R. Page, Dec. 27, 1900; children—Marcus Page, Merton C., Mary Elizabeth. Western rep. Engring. News, hdqrs. in Chicago, 1899-1907; v.p. and western mgr. Am. Architect and Municipal Journal, 1907-09; adv. mgr. Class Journal Co., New York, 1909-10; gen. mgr. Iron Age and associated publs., 1910-18; became president and treas. Robbins Pub. Co., also of Robbins Publs., Inc.; pub. of Gas Age-Record, Industrial Gas, Gas Appliance Merchandising, Advertising and Selling, Am. Perfumer, Brown's Dir. of Am. Gas Cos., Gas Engring. and Appliance Catalog. Pres. New York Business Publishers Assn., 1915-16; pres. Associated Business Papers, Inc., 1920-21. Served as maj. comdg. Univ. Batt., U. of Vermont; 2d lt. and batt. adj. 1st Vt. Vols., Spanish-Am. War. Trustee U. of Vermont. Republican. Presbyn. Mason. Home: Pelham, N.Y. Died May 20, 1937.

ROBBINS, MILTON HERBERT, physician; b. N.Y.C., May 23, 1903; s. Abraham Elliot and Rebecca Robbins; M.D., George Washington U., 1928; m. Alice Robbins, Sept. 16, 1933; children—Dolores (Mrs. Donald Jacobsen), Paul. Intern, Hosp for Joint Disease, N.Y.C., 1928-30, adj. in medicine and cardiology, 1934-50, asso. in medicine and cardiology, 1950-71; intern Jewish Maternity Hosp., 1930; asso. physician Fordham Hosp., N.Y.C., 1950, attending physician, 1951; asso. in medicine Bronx (N.Y.) Municipal Hosp. Center, 1955-71; attending physician Lincoln Hosp.; asso. attending Peninsula Gen Hosp., Far Rockaway, N.Y., St. Joseph's Hosp., Far Rockaway; physician, staff in internal medicine Nassau Communities Hosp., Oceanside, N.Y., Franklin Gen. Hosp., Valley Stream, N.Y. Served to capt., M.C., AUS, 1942-46. Diplomate Am. Bd. Internal Medicine. Fellow A.C.P., Am. Coll. Cardiology; mem. A.M.A., Am. Heart Assn., Bronx County, Nassau County med. socs. Home: North Woodmere NY Died Feb. 8, 1971; buried Beth David Cemetery.

ROBBINS, THOMAS HINCKLEY, JR., naval officer; b. Paris, France, of Am. parents, May 11,21900; s. Thomas Hinckley and Alice Bradford (Ames) R.; ed. Gilman Country Sch., Baltimore, Md., 1914; B.S. (distinguished grad.) U.S. Naval Acad., 1919; m. Barbara Little, Nov. 19, 1930; 1 dau., Barbara. Commd. ensign, 1919 and advanced through the grades to rear admiral, 1945; with naval forces Europe, 1920-24; command U.S.S. SC96, 1923; naval aviator since 1927; continued through grades on aviation duties in various squadrons; command U.S.S. Sandpiper, 1934-35; VS Squadron 4, U.S.S. Langley, 1935-36; student Naval War Coll., 1936-37; aviation officer, staff Naval War Coll., Newport, R.I., 1937-39; navigator U.S.S. Lexington, 1939-40; aviation officer, staff Scouting Force, 1941; aviation plans officer, hdqrs. Cominch, Washington, D.C., 1942; chief of staff, Fleet Air Quonset, 1943; staff, Army-Navy Staff Coll., Washington, D.C., 1943-44; command U.S.S. Lexington, 1945; Office of the Sec. of Navy, Washington, D.C., 1946-47; Commander Carrier Div. 17, 1948-49; joint strategic survey com. of Joint Chiefs of Staff, 1949-52; commander carrier division 2 1952-53; Chief of Staff, Naval War Coll., 1953-56, pres., 1944, 56-57; with Office of Sec. of Navy, Washington, 1957-60; commandant Potomac River Naval Command, 1960-62, ret., 1962. Decorated Legion of Merit with comabt surharge, Sec. of War Commendation ribbon, Presidential Unit Citation (2 stars); World War I Victory medal (1 star, Atlantic fleet), Defense ribbon (1 star, Pacific fleet), Am. Theatre medal, Pacific theatre medal (3 campaign stars), World War II Victory medal, Philippine Liberation medal (1 campaign star). Clubs: N.Y. Yacht; Army and Navy (Washington); Exploreres. Home: Stonington3CT Died Dec. 12, 1972.

ROBE, CHARLES FRANKLIN brig. gen.; b. Canastota, N.Y., Nov. 23, 1841; s. Harvey Wayne and Parlyncia (Stevens) R.; ed. "red school houses"; m. Kate Eloise Stevens, Feb. 13, 1867. First lt. and capt., 147th N.Y. Vols. and Veteran Reserve Corps, 1862-66; 1st lt. 29th U.S. Inf., July 28, 1866; assigned to 25th Inf., Jan. 31, 1870; capt., Jan. 25, 1872; maj. 14th Inf., July 5, 1895; lt. col. 17th Inf., Sept. 16, 1898; col. 9th Inf., July 13, 1900; brig. gen. and retired, 1903. Admitted to Tex. bar. Regt. N.Y. Vol. Inf.; life mem. Nat. Rifle Assn. of America. Home: San Diego, Calif. Died 1910.

ROBERDEAU, ISAAC civil and mil. engr.; b. Phila., Sept. 11, 1763; s. Daniel and Mary (Bostwick) R.; studied engring. London, Eng., 1785-87; m. Nov. 7, 1792, 3 children. Employed with U.S. Topog. Engrs. to lay out new City of Washington (D.C.), 1791-92; most important work was canal to connect Schuylkill and Susquehanna rivers; mem. Topog. Engrs. U.S. Army in war with Great Britain, 1813-15, commd. maj. 1813; assigned to duty at Ft. Mifflin; employed on fortification work; charged with survey of No. boundary which he carried westward to Sault St. Marie; reinstated as maj., 1816; stationed at U.S. Mil. Acad., until 1818; became chief Topog. Bur., Washington, 1818; brevetted lt. col., 1823. Author: Observations of the Survey of the Seacoast of the U.S., 1827; Mathematics and Treatise on Canals; An Oration upon the Death of Gen. George Washington (delivered at Trenton, N.J. Feb. 22, 1800), published 1800. Died Georgetown, D.C., Jan. 15, 1829.

ROBERT, HENRY MARTYN brig. gen. U.S.A.; b. Robertville, S.C., May 2, 1837; s. Rev. Joseph Thomas and Adeline (Lawton) R.; brother of Joseph Thomas R.; grad. U.S. Mil. Acad., 1857; m. Helen M. Thresher, Dec. 24, 1860; m. 2d, Isabel Livingstone Hoagland, May 8, 1901. Bvt. 2d lt. engrs., July 1, 1857; 2d lt., Dec. 13, 1858; promoted through grades to brig. gen. chief of engrs. U.S.A., Apr. 30, 1901; retired by operation of law, May 2, 1901. Acting asst. prof., 1856-57, in charge dept. practical mil. engring., 1865-67, U.S. Mil. Acad.; in command of exploration of a mil. route from Vancouver to Puget Sound, 1860; engr. on defenses of Washington, 1861; in charge defenses of Phila., 1861-62, New Bedford, 1862-65; chief engr. Mil. Div. of the Pacific, 1867-71; in charge various light house dists., and river and harbor improvements, 1871-95; engr. commr. D.C. and mem. Rock Creek Nat. Park Commn., 1890-91; supervising engr. 12 U.S. engr. dists., Pittsburgh to Galveston, 1897-1901; pres. U.S. Bd. of Engrs. for Fortifications, 1895-1901, New York Harbor Line Bd., 1895-1901, Phila. Harbor Line Bd., 1894-1901, etc.; mem. commn. to design sea-wall for Galveston, 1901-02 and 1915; cons. engr. to design a causeway and bridge to connect Galveston with mainland, 1907-08, 15; to design improvement of port of Frontera, Mex., 1911. Author: Robert's Rules of Order, 1876, 1893; Robert's Rules of Order Revised, 1915; Analytical and Topical Index to Reports of Chief of Engineers, U.S.A., on River and Harbor Improvements, from 1866-1887, Vol. I, 1881, Vol. II, 1889; Parliamentary Practice, 1921; Parliamentary Law, 1922. Home: Owego, N.Y. Died May 11, 1923.

ROBERT, JAMES MARSHALL univ. dean; b. St. Paul, June 20, 1885; s. Alonzo Beauregard and Alice (Fonseca) R.; B.Engring., Tulane U., 1906; m. Gladys Roberta Kearny, Apr. 21, 1909; children—James Marshall (dec.), Kearny Quinn, William Douglas, Gladys Kearny (dec.). Instr. mech. engring. Tulane U., 1906-12, asst. prof. exptl. engring., 1912-16, asso. prof. machine design, 1916-20, prof., 1920-34, prof. mech. engring., 1934-50, acting dean coll. engring., 1935-36, dean, 1936-50; cons. and testing engr. since 1906; in charge motor mechanics div., Camp Martin, during World War; in charge U.S. Shipping Bd. Marine Engr. Sch., Tulane U., 1917-21. Mem. Bd. Examiners for Operating Engrs., New Orleans, 1934-1940. Mem. Am. Soc. M.E. (chmn. New Orleans sect. 1923-24), La. Engring. Soc. (sec. 11 yrs., v.p. 1923, pres. 1924), Soc. for Promotion Engring. Edn. (vice chmn. S.E. sect. 1937-38, chmn. 1938-39), Newcomen Soc., Sigma Phi Delta, Omicron Delta Kappa, Tau Beta Pi, Pi Kappa Alpha. Clubs: Rotary, Boston (New Orleans). Editor Proc. La. Engrs. Soc., 1931-41. Home: 2141 State St., New Orleans. Died June 8, 1964; buried Metairie Cemetery, New Orleans.

ROBERT, WILLIAM PIERRE naval officer; b. Wilkinson County, Miss., July 23, 1873; s. Joseph Clark and Martha Rebecca (Whitaker) R.; grad. U.S. Naval Acad., 1894, grad. Royal Naval Coll., Eng., 1897; m. Bessie H. Stark, Mar. 19, 1902; children—Robert Pierre, Elizabeth Stark (Mrs. Robert Gilmor). Began as asst. naval constructor USN, 1896, advanced through ranks to rear adm. Constrn. Corps, July 1, 1936; served in Spanish-Am. War and Philippine campaign as asst. naval constructor; in World War as capt. Constrn. Corps; decorated for service all 3 wars. Placed on retired list Aug. 1, 1937; tech. asst. to pres. Bath (Me.) Iron Works Corp. since Aug. 1, 1937. Mem. Soc. Naval Architects and Marine Engrs., Soc. Colonial Wars, Soc. Am. Mil. Engrs., Nat. Aero. Assn., Huguenot Soc. S.C. Episcopalian. Club: Chevy Case (Washington). Home: 1132 Washington St., Bath, Me. Died Sept. 1963.

ROBERTS, BENJAMIN KEARNEY brig. gen. U.S.A.; b. Memphis, Tenn., Nov. 28, 1846; s. Gen. Benjamin Stone and Elizabeth (Sperry) R.; ed. pvt. schs., and Norwich (Vt.) U. to 1863, A.M., 1864; m. Julia A. Roberts, Jan. 25, 1887. Second lt. 7th Ia. Cav., July 25, 1863; hon. mustered out, Dec. 22, 1864; capt. a.a.g., Nov. 12, 1864; on staff of Gen. George H. Thomas, 1865-June 1866; bvtd. maj., Mar. 13, 1865; apptd. from Conn., 2d lt. 5th U.S. Arty., Apr. 18, 1866; hon. mustered out of vol. service, July 1, 1866; 1st lt. 5th Arty., Feb. 7, 1867; capt., Apr. 25, 1888; maj. 2d Arty., Oct. 17, 1899; lt. col. Arty. Corps, Sept. 23, 1901; col., Aug. 3, 1903; brig. gen. chief of arty., June 19, 1905; retired, June 20, 1905, at own requests after 40 yrs.' service. Died July 10, 1921.

ROBERTS, BENJAMIN STONE army officer, engr.; b. Manchester, Vt., Nov. 18, 1810; s. Gen. Martin and Betsey (Stone) R.; grad. U.S. Mil. Acad., 1835; m. Elizabeth Sperry, Sept. 18, 1835, 3 children. Chief engr. Champlain & Ogdensburg R.R., 1839; geologist N.Y. State, 1841; assisted in constrn. of ry. in Russia from St. Petersburg to Moscow, 1842-43; began practice of law, Des Moines, Ia., 1843; lt. col. Ia. Militia, 1844-46; commd. lt. U.S. Army, 1846, capt., 1847; brevetted maj. for gallantry at Battle of Chapultepec, 1847, lt. col. for gallantry nr. Matamoras, 1847; received sword of honor from State of Ia.; maj. 3d Cavalry, 1861, commanded Southern mil. dist. of N.M.; active in battles at Ft. Craig, Albuquerque, Valverde, Peralta; brevetted col., 1862; promoted brig. gen. U.S. Volunteers, 1862, brig. gen., maj. gen., 1865; in command 1st Div., XIX Army Corps in La., 1864; chief cavalry Dept. of Gulf, until 1865; lt. col. 3d Cavalry, 1866; served in N.M., 1867-68; prof. tactics in mil. science Yale, 1868-70; ret. from active service, 1870; practiced law and prosecution of claims before govt., Washington, D.C. Author: Description of Newly Patented Solid Shot and Shells for Use in Rifled Ordnance, 1864; Lt. Gen. U.S. Grant, an address delivered at Yale, 1864. Died Washington, Jan. 29, 1875.

ROBERTS, CHARLES DUVAL army officer; b. Cheyenne Agency, S.D., June 18, 1873; s. Cyrus Swan and Nannie (DuVal) R.; grad. U.S. Mil. Acad., 1897; honor grad. Army Sch. of Line, 1912; grad. Army Staff Coll., 1913, Army War Coll., 1920; m. Eugenia Bradford, Nov. 16, 1898; children—Heyward Bradford, Thomas DuVal, Charles DuVal (dec.), Eugenia Bradford. Commd. 2d lt. inf. U.S. Army, June 11, 1897; advanced through grades to col., July 1, 1920; brig. gen., Feb. 19, 1929; ret. June 18, 1937. Served in Spanish-Am. War, Philippine Insurrection, World War. Mem. S.A.R., loyal Legion of United States, Mil. Order World War, Am. Legion, Am. Mil. Inst., Order of Indian Wars of U.S. Awarded D.S.M., Congl. Medal of Honor (U.S.); Croix de Guerre (France); Officer Order of Leopold (Belgium). Episcopalian. Clubs: Army and Navy (Washington); Army and Navy (Boston). Address: 6510 Maple Av., Chevy Chase, Md. Died Oct. 24, 1966; buried Arlington Nat. Cemetery.

ROBERTS, CYRUS SWAN brig. gen.; b. Sharon, Conn., Aug. 23, 1841; s. Virgil B. and Harriott (Swan) R.; fitted for coll. at Stratford (Conn.) Acad.; m. Nannie R., d. Judge Thomas H. Du Val, of Austin, Tex., Jan. 30, 1870. Enlisted as vol. in 22d N.Y. Militia, Civil War; served at Baltimore and Harper's Ferry, Va., until mustered out of service, Sept. 6, 1862; enlisted, same day, in 150th N.Y. Vols.; sergt. maj. of regt., Oct. 11, 1862; 2d lt., Feb. 13, 1863; 1st lt., Jan. 1, 1865; capt. and a.d.c., June 22, 1865; mustered out of vol. service, Dec. 7, 1865; second lt. 17th U.S. Inf., May 11, 1866; 1st lt., Sept. 18, 1867; capt., June 28, 1878; maj., Apr. 26, 1898; lt. col. 13th U.S. Inf., Aug. 14, 1899; col. 2d Inf., Apr. 13, 1901; brig. gen. U.S.A., Aug. 8, 1903; retired at own request after more than 40 yrs.' service, Aug. 9, 1903. During Civil War, served in campaign in western Va. and the Shenandoah, 1863-64, under Gen. Geo. Crook, to whom was aid; with Sheridan's Cav., 1865, and took part in battles of the army (wounded at Lynchburg). Served in regular army in Tex., 1866-69, in Va., 1870, Dak. and Ariz., 1870-86, Wyo. until 1894, Columbus Barracks, O., until 1899; in Tex. again until 1901; in Philippines until June 1903. Was a.d.c. to Maj. Gen. Griffin in Texas, Maj. Gen. J. J. Reynolds, Brig. Gen. George Crook in Ariz., 1882-86, during the Chiricahua, Indian troubles; adj. gen. vols. with 2d Corps during war with Spain, 1898; adj. gen., dept. Texas, 1899-1901. Home: Lakeville, Conn. Died Mar. 19, 1917.

ROBERTS, ELLSWORTH A(LAN) ins. exec.; b. Houghton, Mich., July 3, 1896; s. Charles and Minnie (Hooper) R.; student U. Minn.; LL.B., Yale, 1922; LL.D., Beaver Coll., 1948; m. Adair Douglas McRae, June 3, 1923 (dec. Jan. 4, 1953); children—Jean Adair, Charles McRae. Admitted to Minn. bar, 1922, practiced in Duluth, 1922-25; law dept. Minn. Mut. Life Ins. Co., 1925-34, v.p., gen. counsel, 1934-43; pres., dir. Fidelity Mut. Life Ins. Co., Phila., 1943—; dir. 1st Pa. Banking & Trust Co., Bell Telephone Co. of Pa., Trenton-Princeton Traction Co., Del. & Bound Brook R.R. Co.; dir., Am. National Fire Insurance Company, One Liberty Street. Corporation, Great American Corporation. Mem. life insurance committee National Fund for Medical Edn., 1954—. Member of board Phila. War Chest, 1943-45, gen. chmn. campaign Community Chest, 1948; pres. Nat. Community Chests and Councils, N.Y.C., 1943-46; dir., mem. exec. com. Nat. War Fund, Inc., 1943-47. Trustee, mem. exec. com. Beaver Coll., 1946—; trustee, sr. v.p. Hahnemann Med. Coll. and Hosp., 1947-56; dir. Phila. Orchestra Pension Found., 1948—. Served 2d lieutenant in the United States Army, World War I. Served with U.S. Army, World War I; maj. inf. Minn. N.G. Mem. Am. Life Conv. (past v.p. Minn.), Newcomen Soc., Internat. Assn. Ins. Counsel, Assn. Life Ins. Counsel (hon.), Am. Bar Assn., Ins. Fedn. Pa., Inc. (pres. 1951-53, dir. 1944—), Community Chest Phila. and Vicinity (v.p. 1948—, dir. 1946—), United Fund Phila. (dir. 1950—), Pa. United Fund (v.p., dir., exec. com. 1952—), United Def. Fund, Inc. (dir., exec. com. 1950—, vice chmn. bd. 1953—), Am. Acad. Music (dir. Phila. 1951—), Phila. Orchestra Assn. (dir. and mem. of the executive com. 1948—), Kappa Sigma, Phi Delta Phi, Corbey Ct. Republican. Methodist. Mason. Clubs: St. Paul Athletic; Union League, Rotary, Phila. Gyro, Anglers, Welsh Soc., Country, Sunday Breakfast (Phila.); University (N.Y.C.). Home: 805 The Kenilworth Apts., Germantown, Phila. 44. Office: Fidelity Mutual Life Insurance Co., Phila. Died June 29, 1960; buried Lakewood Cemetery, Mpls.

ROBERTS, ELZEY radio executive; b. St. Louis, Mo., Mar. 22, 1892; s. John Calvin and Anna (Kiser) R.; ed. Central High Sch., Manual Training Sch., Smith Acad. (all of St. Louis) until 1910; grad. Lawrenceville (N.J.) Sch., 1911; Litt.B., Princeton, 1915; m. Isabella Wells, June 18, 1917; children—Elzey, Isabella. Began, 1915, with St. Louis Star, purchased by father in 1913; became pub. of Star, 1916, pres. and part owner, 1917, acquiring controlling interest, 1925; purchased St. Louis Times and consolidated it with Star as St. Louis Star-Times, 1932; purchased radio station KFRU, Columbia, Mo., and became president KFRU, Inc., June 30, 1936; acquired radio station KXOK, 1938; KXOK-FM, 1947; sold KFRU, Inc. 1948, sold Star Times Pub. Co. name and pub. equipment, 1951; retained radio properties and buildings sold KXOK, 1954; former dir., part owner KWK, Inc., St. Louis; chmn. bd., dir. 800 N. 12th, Inc.; owner Roberts Bldg. Served as first lt. Intelligence Div. General Staff, AUS, Feb. 1-Dec. 18, 1918. Received 1950 Missouri U. award for distinguished service in journalism for The St. Louis Star-Times. Mem. bd. St. Louis Municipal Theatre Assn. Presbyterian. Clubs: St. Louis Country, Indian Creek, The Surf (Miami). Home: 38 Glen Eagles Dr., St. Louis 63124. Office: 800 N. 12th, Inc., Roberts Bldg., St. Louis, Mo. Died May 14, 1962; buried Bellefontaine Cemetery, St. Louis.

ROBERTS, HARRIS LEE army officer; b. in D.C., May 6, 1858; grad. U.S. Mil. Acad., 1880. Commd. 2d lt. 4th Inf., June 12, 1880; trans to 19th Inf., Mar. 22, 1881; 1st lt. 21st Inf., Nov. 14, 1890; trans. to 19th Inf., July 20, 1891; capt., Apr. 26, 1898; trans. to 2d Inf., Nov. 22, 1904; maj. 26th Inf., July 28, 1905; lt. col. 22d Inf., Mar. 11, 1911; col. of Inf., Mar. 13, 1914. Served as regimental q.m., 1891-95; in charge constrn. Ft. Wayne, Mich., 1895-97; in Puerto Rico, 1898-99, Philippine Islands, 1899-1901 and 1907-08; duty Ft. Sam Houston, Tex., 1916-17. Died Dec. 27, 1918.

ROBERTS, JOHN S. ret. naval officer; b. Danville, Ky., Oct. 30, 1892; s. John Summerfield and Susan Eleanor (Gilmore) R.; B.S., U.S. Naval Acad., 1916; m. Margaret Vail Jenkins, July 13, 1918; 1 son, John S. Jr. Commd. ensign U.S. Navy, 1916, and advanced through grades to rear adm., 1945; convoy duty, U.S.S. De Kalb, 1917-19; destroyer duty, Asiatic sta., 1925-28; comdr. destroyer div., later destroyer squadron in cooperation with Brit. fleet, North Atlantic and Iceland waters, 1941-42; comdg. officer U.S.S. Boise, Mediterranean, 1943, S.W. Pacific, 1944; ret. from active duty, 1945. Awarded Navy Cross and Legion of Merit. Home: 728 Glorietta Blvd., Coronado, Cal. Died Apr. 9, 1953; buried Arlington Nat. Cemetery.

ROBERTS, KENNETH (LEWIS) author; b. Kennebunk, Me., Dec. 8, 1885; s. Frank Lewis and Grace Mary (Tibbetts) R.; A.B., Cornell, 1908; Litt.D., Dartmouth, 1934, Colby Coll., 1935, Bowdoin Coll., 1937, Middlebury Coll., 1938, Northeastern U., 1945; m. Anna Selberling Mosser, Feb. 14, 1911. Reporter, columnist Boston Post, 1909-17; staff Life (N.Y.), 1915-18, Puck, 1916-17; European corr. Sat. Eve. Post, 1919-29, Washington corr., 1921-26; retired from journalism, Porto Santo Stefano, 1929-37. Served as capt. Intelligence Sect., Siberian Expeditionary Force, 1918-19. Recipient of a Special Pulitzer Prize, 1957. Mem. Nat. Inst. Arts and Letters, Order of Cincinnati of State of N.J., Phi Beta Kappa, Chi Psi, Kappa Beta Phi, Ends of the Earth Club. Club: Royal Bermuda Yacht. Author: (non-fiction) Trending Into Maine, 1938; March to Quebec, 1939; Good Maine Food (with Marjorie Mosser) 1939; The Kenneth Roberts Reader, 1945; I Wanted to Write, 1949; Don't Say That About Maine, 1950; Henry Gross and His Dowsing Rod (also pub. in Germany), 1951; The Seventh Sense, 1953; Foods of New England (with Marjorie Mosser), 1957; Water Unlimited, 1957; (novels) (also pub. in Braille and Talking Books) Arundel, 1930; The Lively Lady, 1931; Rabble in Arms, 1933; Captain Caution (filmed by Hal Roach), 1934; Northwest Passage (filmed by MGM), 1937; Oliver Wiswell, 1940; Lydia Bailey (filmed by 20th Century-Fox), 1947. Translator: (with Anna M. Roberts) Moreau St. Méry's American Journey, 1793-1798, 1947. With Henry Gross, pioneered in locating fresh water springs, Bermuda, 1949; cooperated in successful drilling of springs at Royal Barracks. Home: Kennebunkport, Me. Died July 21, 1957; buried Arlington Nat. Cemetery.

ROBERTS, MADISON HINES physician; b. Milledgeville, Ga., Sept. 5, 1895; s. Rufus Winston and Mary Marwood (Herty) R.; B.S., U. Ga., 1916, M.D., 1918; m. Delia Page Johnston, Jan. 8, 1927. Interne, St. Christopher's Hosp. for Children, 1919-20, Boston Children's Hosp. and Boston Infant's Hosp., 1921-22; specialist in pediatrics since 1922; asst. in pediatrics Emory U., 1922-27, asso. in pediatrics, 1927-31, asst. prof., 1931-32, asso. prof., 1932-44, chmn. dept. pediatrics, 1932-Oct. 1944, prof. pediatrics, Feb.-Oct. 1944; med. dir. Henrietta Egleston Hosp. for Children since 1928. Served as med. officer USN, 1918-19. Recipient L.C. Fisher award in research, 1925 and 1927, Crawford W. Long award in research, 1927. Past pres. Ga. Pediatric Soc. Mem. A.M.A., So. Med. Assn. (chmn. pediatric sect. 1936), Med. Assn. Ga., Am. Acad. Pediatrics, Am. Bd. Pediatrics (dir.), Kappa Alpha. Clubs: Piedmont Driving, Capital City (Atlanta, Ga.). Home: 393 W. Wesley Rd., N.W. Office: 24 14th St. N.E. Atlanta 5. Died July 29, 1961.

ROBERTS, MARY M(AY) editor, nurse; b. Cheboygan, Mich., Jan. 31, 1877; d. Henry W. and Elizabeth Scott (Elliot) Roberts; R.N., Jewish Hosp. Sch. of Nursing, Cin., 1899; B.S., Tchr. Coll., Columbia, 1921. Supt. of nurses Savannah (Ga.) Hosp. (now Warren A. Chandler Hosp.), 1900-02; asst. supt. Jewish Hosp., Cin., 1902-04; supt. C.R. Holmes Hosp.; Cin., 1908-17; dir. nursing service, Lake div., A.R.C., Cleve., 1917-18, chief nurse and dir. Unit of Army Sch. of Nursing, Camp Sherman, O., 1918-19; editor Am. Jour. of Nursing, N.Y., 1921-48, emeritus. Decorated Bronze medal of Ministry of Social Welfare of France, July 1933. Certificate of Appreciation from Dept. of Army; Florence Nightingale Medal, Internat. Red Cross. Formerly trustee Tchrs. Coll., Columbia. Mem. Am. Nurses Assn., Nat. League for Nursing. Republican. Episcopalian. Club: Cosmopolitan. Author: American Nursing: History & Interpretation, 1954. Contbr. articles ency., publs. Home: 8309 94th St., Woodhaven, L.I., N.Y. Died Jan. 1959.

ROBERTS, PHILL TANDY, JR., business exec.; b. Gracey, Ky., June 19, 1898; s. Phill Tandy, Sr., and Laura (McCarroll) R.; m. Margaret Hazlewood, Nov. 6, 1930; children—Donald T., Linda Ann. With U.S. Tobacco Co. since Mar. 1918, dir. and v.p. since June 1946; dir. Nat. Tobacco Co. of Can.; dir. Planters Bank & Trust Co, Hopkinsville, Ky. Served as 2d lt., Inf., U.S. Army, World War I. Mem. First Baptist Church (Hopkinsville, Ky.). Home: Cox Mill Rd. Office: Box 365, Hopkinsville, Ky. Died Aug. 30, 1960; buried Riverside Cemetery, Hopkinsville.

ROBERTS, ROY ALLISON newspaperman; b. Muscotah, Kan., Nov. 25, 1887; s. Thomas Stone and Nellie (Allison) R.; U. Kan., 1905-08; LL.D., Northwestern U., 1947; Park Coll., 1951; Litt.D., William Jewell Coll., 1955; m. Barbara Schwartz, June 10, 1914; children—Kate Schwartz (Mrs. Theodore S. Valentine); m. 2d, Florence G. Ross, May 25, 1955. Began with Lawrence (Kan.) World, 1905, and became city editor; with Kansas City Star since 1909, corr. Mo. legislature 4 sessions, Washington corr., 1915-28, mng. editor, 1928-45, became pres., gen. mgr., 1947, past chmn. bd.; covered nat. presdl. nominating convs., 1912-—; specialized in politics and econs. Past pres. Am. Soc. Newspaper Editors; mem. adv. com. on censorship and OWI. Capt., Adj. Gen.'s Dept., Camp Sherman, O. and Ft. Benjamin Harrison, Ind., World War. Mem. Alpha Tau Omega. Republican. Episcopalian. Clubs: Nat. Press, Gridiron, Columbia, Overseas Writers (Washington); University, Kansas City Country, River. Home: 5433 Mission Drive. Office: Kansas City Star, Kansas City, Mo. Died Feb. 1967.

ROBERTS, STEWART RALPH prof. clin. med.; b. Oxford, Ga., Oct. 2, 1878; s. James William and Clifford Rebecca (Stewart) R.; A.B., Emory Coll., Oxford, Ga., 1902; M.D., Atlanta Coll. Phys. and Surg. (med. sch. Emory U.), 1900; B.S. and M.S., U. of Chicago, 1904; studied Harvard Medical Sch. Prof. biology, Emory Coll., 1902-06; prof. physiology, Atlanta Sch. of Medicine, 1906-09; prof. physiology, 1909-10, asso. prof. medicine, 1910-13, prof., 1913-15, prof. clin. medicine, 1919-—, Atlanta Med. Coll. (Emory U.); physician to Wesley Memorial Hospital. Lt. col., Med. Corps U.S.A. and comdg. officer Base Hosp., Camp Jackson, S.C., 1918. Fellow Am. Coll. Physicians. Methodist. Author: Pellagra, 1912. Home: Atlanta, Ga. Died Apr. 14, 1941.

ROBERTS, WILLIAM ALLERTON, lawyer; b. Brooklyn, N.Y., July 16, 1900; s. William Allerton and Helen Elizabeth (O'Sullivan) R.; C.E., Tufts Coll., 1918; LL.B., Georgetown U., 1925; m. Caro-Margaret Chenay, December 15, 1923; children—William Allerton, Jr. (killed in action 1944), Helen Emily Shields, John Arthur (dec.), Martha Alice (Mrs. Creath). C.E. various construction companies, 1920-22. Transit Commissioner, Boston, 1922-23, Interstate Commerce Commn., 1923-26; began practice law, 1926; sr. atty. examiner Interstate Commerce Commn., 1927-30; spl. asst. corp. counsel for D.C. and counsel of Pub. Utilities Commission, D.C., 1930-34; people's counsel, Washington, 1934-36; sr. partner Roberts & McInnis, 1936-65; chmn., dir. Nat. Film Studios, Inc.; pres., dir. South Fla. Broadcasting Co.; Roberts Bros. Co., Big Horn Powder River Co.; pres. Fla. Air-Power, Inc. Nat. treas. Kefauver Com. Served as 2d lt. Signal Corps, 1918; 1st lt. Mass. Nat. Guard, 101st F.A., 1923; col. Air Corps, on active duty including South Pacific theatre, 1941-44, on inactive duty since Aug. 1944, USAF Ret. Res. Mem. Inter-Am. (chmn. transportation and communications com.), Am. bar assns., D.C. Bar Assn., Fed. Bar Assn. (ex-pres.; dir. Fed. Bar Bldg. Corp.), Interstate Commerce Practitioners Assn., Fed. Communications Bar Assn., Am. Vets. World War II, Sigma Delta Kappa. Democrat. Catholic. Mem. K.C. Clubs: Cosmos (Washington), Congressional Country, Capitol Yacht; Nat. Lawyers. Author: Valuation of Public Utilities, 1934. Home: Washington DC Died Apr. 8, 1968; buried Arlington Nat. Cemetery, Arlington VA

ROBERTSON, A. WILLIS, former United States senator; born at Martinsburg, West Virginia, May 27, 1887; son of Franklin Pierce and Josephine Ragland (Willis) R.; B.A., Univ. of Richmond, 1907, LL.B., 1908, LL.D., 1945; LL.D., Washington & Lee, U., 1949, Coll. of William and Mary, 1956; m. Gladys C. Willis, October 19, 1920; children—A. Willis, Marion Gordon. Admitted to Va. bar and began practice at Buena Vista, Va., 1908; mem. firm Willis & Robertson, 1908-10; mem. Va. State Senate, 2 terms, 1916-22 (resigned); commonwealth's atty., Rockbridge County, 1922-28; chmn. Va. Com. Game and Inland Fisheries, 1926-32; mem. 73d Congress 1933-35), Va. at large; 74th to 79th Congresses (1935-47), 7th Va. Dist.; elected to U.S. Senate, Nov. 5, 1946, for unexpired term of Carter Glass, dec.; relected U.S. Senate, 1948, 54, 60, chmn. com. banking and currency, also joint com. def. production; consultant International Bank for Reconstruction and Devel., from 1966. Served as first lieutenant, captain, and major, inf., U.S. Army, 1917-19. Mem. Jamestown Soc., S.A.R., Soc. Cin., Sons Confederate Vets., Phi Alpha Delta, Pi Kappa Alpha, Omicron Delta Kappa, Phi Beta Kappa. Democrat. Baptist. Home: Lexington VA Died Nov. 1, 1971.

ROBERTSON, ASHLEY HERMAN naval officer; b. Ashmore, Ill., Dec. 14, 1867; grad. U.S. Naval Acad., 1888. Ensign, July 1, 1890; promoted through grades to rear adm., Sept. 23, 1918. Served on Castine during Spanish-Am. War, 1898; exec. officer Terror, 1905; at U.S. Naval Acad., 1905-06; engr. officer Tennessee, 1906-08; exec. officer same, 1908-09; duty Navy Yard, Puget Sound, 1909-13; comdr. Charleston, 1913, Denver, 1913-14, California, 1914-15, Colorado, 1915, San Diego, 1915-16; at Naval War Coll., Newport, R.I., 1916-17; chief of staff, 1st Naval Dist., 1917; apptd. comdr. Mount Vernon (formerly Kronprinzessin Cecile), troop transport, July 28, 1917; naval transport officer, Feb.-Apr. 1918; comdg. New Mexico (first electric drive battleship), 1918; comdg. destroyer force, Jan.-June 1919; chief of staff, Naval War Coll., 1919; comdt. 11th Naval Dist., 1923-26; vice admiral comdg. Scouting Fleet, 1926-28; apptd. comdt. 11th Naval Dist., 1928. Home: Kansas, Ill. Died July 13, 1930.

ROBERTSON, BEVERLY HOLCOMBE soldier; b. Amelia Co., Va., June 5, 1827; s. Dr. William Henry and Martha Maria (Holcombe) R.; m. Virginia Neville Johnston, Mar, 26, 1855 (died 1869). Apptd. to U.S. Mil. Acad. from Va., 1849; bvtd. 2d lt. 2d Dragoons, July 1, 1849; promoted 2d lt., July 25, 1850; 1st lt., Mar. 3, 1855; capt., Mar. 3, 1861; dismissed Aug. 8, 1861; entered C.S.A., and promoted brig. gen., June 3, 1862. Comd. brigade in Gen. Stuart's cav. div. in 2d Bull Run; participated in battle of Gettysburg; comd. coast line bet. Charleston and Savannah; subsequently took part in many engagements until close of war. Engaged in ins. business, Chicago and Washington, 1873-84; real estate business, 1884-—. Died 1910.

ROBERTSON, DAVID RITCHIE musician, educator; b. Paola, Kan., Dec. 22, 1911; s. Robert Ritchie and Lily Margaret (Peters) R.; Mus. B., Drury Coll., 1932; Fellow. Juilliard Grad Sch., 1932-34; M.A., State U. Ia., 1943; m. Virginia Ragsdale Fewell, June 7, 1936; children—Jean Curry, Gail Peters. Mem. Chautauqua Symphony, 1933-34; concertmaster Greenwich (N.Y.) Sinfonietta, 1933; staff artist N.B.C. and C.B.S., 1934; Juillard Sch. Music extension rep., 1935-42, also music dir. Ark. State Symphony, head music dept. Hendrix Coll.; guest lectr. music State U. Ia., summers 1938-42; concertmaster, asso. condr. Wichita Symphony, 1946-49, also head orchestral dept. U. Wichita; vis. prof. Tufts Coll., summer 1948, U. Ida., summer 1949; dir. Oberlin (O.) Conservatory Music, 1949-—; faculty Akademie für Musik und Darstellende Kunst, Mozarteum, Salzburg, Austria, 1961-—; member of the bd. dirs. Nat. Guild Community Music Schs.; numerous engagements as guest condr. profl. and amateur symphony orchestras. Mem. bd. advisers Moravian Music Found., 1959-—; mem. N.E.A. Commn. Academically Talented Student, 1959-—; mem. music adv. commn. U.S. Information Agency, 1960-—. Served as lt. 7th Fleet Headquarters Staff, USNR, 1942-45. Fellow Internat. Acad. Arts and Letters (life); mem. Nat. Assn. Schs. Music (regional v.p.), Music Teachers National Association, Music Educators National Conference (member of editorial board of journal 1958-—), National Assn. Am. Composers and Condrs., Pi Kappa Lambda. Phi Mu Alpha Sinfonia. Mem. editorial staff Instrumentalist. Died July 12, 1961.

ROBERTSON, DENNIS HOLME economist; b. Lowestoft, Eng., May 23, 1890; s. James and Constance Elizabeth (Wilson) R.; student Eton Coll., 1902-08; B.A., Trinity Coll., Cambridge, 1911, M.A., 1915; Hon. Dr., U. Amsterdam, 1932, Harvard, 1936, Louvain, 1947, Durham, 1951, London, 1952. Lectr., Trinity Coll., 1918-38, prof. polit. economy 1944-57, fellow 1914-38, since 1944; Cassel prof. econs. London U., 1938-44; fellow Eton Coll. since 1948; adviser in H.M. Treasury, 1939-44. Mem. U.K. delegation to Bretton Woods Financial Conf., 1944; mem. Royal Commn. on Equal Pay, 1944. Served as lt. 11th bn. London Regt., Egypt and Palestine, 1914-18. Decorated C.M.G., 1944, Knight Bachelor, 1953. Fellow Brit. Acad.; hon. mem. A.A.A.S., Am. Econ. Assn.; mem. Royal Econ. Soc. (mem. council, ex-pres., Am. Philos. Soc., Cambridge Union Soc. (past pres., trustee). Author: A Study of Industrial Fluctuation, 1915; Money, 1922, rev., 1924, 28, 48; The Control of Industry, 1923; Banking Policy and The Price Level, 1926, rev., 1950; Economic Fragments, 1931; Economic Essays and Addresses (with A.C. Pigou), 1931; Essays in Monetary Theory, 1940; also articles in econ. jours. Home: Trinity College, Cambridge, Eng. Died Apr. 21, 1963.

ROBERTSON, FELIX HUSTON soldier; b. Washington, Tex., Mar. 9, 1839; s. Gen. Jerome B. and Mary E. (Cummins) R.; ed. U.S. Mil. Acad., 1857-61; resigned from West Point, Jan. 1861; spl. studies in engring. and law; m. Sarah Davis, Sept. 11, 1864; 2d, Elizabeth Dwyer, Nov. 10, 1892. Second lt. C.S.A., Mar. 8, 1861; rose successively to capt. of arty., lt. col. of arty. and in 1864, made brig. gen. of cav. and assigned to Gen. Joseph Wheeler's corps; served with him until surrender; admitted to Texas bar, 1876; farmer, 1903-—. Comdr. Texas Div. U.C.V., 1911-—. Home: Crawford, Tex. Died Apr. 20, 1928.

ROBERTSON, GEORGE geographic sculptor; b. Glasgow, Scotland, 1878; s. William and Sarah (Johnston) R.; came to U.S., 1883; ed. Brimmer Sch. and Sch. of Art, Mus. Fine Arts, Boston; grad. in architecture Drexel Inst., Phila., 1908; m. Mary T. Reynolds, Apr. 17, 1915. With art dept. Boston Herald, 1895-98; with George Carrol Curtis, relief map maker, Boston, 1898-1901; mgr. Howell's Natural Sci. Establishment, Washington, 1911. Mem. Battery D, 1st Regt. Mass. Heavy Arty., U.S.V., Spanish-Am. War. Prepared ofcl. relief map of Panama Canal, as a part of govt. exhibit San Francisco (awarded gold medal); also topographic map N.Y. State, largest relief map of any state ever prepared from instrumental survey (30x40 feet, awarded grand prize); prepared large relief model European war zone for Chgo. Daily News, 1917. Div. mineral tech. Nat. Mus. Models showing prodn. and conservation natural gas, sulphur, oil, soda and copper, 1918-19; relief model D.C., showing the permanent system parks and hwys., 1921; archtl. model showing details Wilson Dam, at Muscle Shoals (War Dept.), 1926; model showing successive steps in lock design of Am. Locks at Sault Ste. Marie, Mich. (War Dept.), 1927; large relief of N.Am. Continent, installed in lobby Tribune Tower, Chgo., 1927; relief map Great Smoky Mountain Nat. Park, Tenn. (1st relief map to be prepared from aerotopographic survey), 1930; developed for War Dept. new method of preparing topographic relief-maps by use of unvulcanized rubber. Commd. capt. C.E., O.R.C., spl. topographic engring. duties, Army Map Service, Corps of Engineers, U.S. Army, Washington, D.C. since 1922. Mem. Soc. Am. Mil. Engrs., Washington Soc. Engrs., Sojourners Club. Mason. Odd Fellow. Home: 5925 16th St. North, Arlington, Va. Died Oct. 19, 1960.

ROBERTSON, H(AROLD) E(UGENE) pathologist; b. Waseca, Minn., Oct. 8, 1878; s. James M. and Kate (Deuel) R.; A.B., Carleton Coll., Minn., 1899; M.D., U. of Pa., 1905; studied Columbia, 1900-01, U. of Berlin, 1914, U. of Freiburg, 1915; m. Edith Ellam, July 31, 1907. Instr. pathology, Albany Med. Coll., 1905-06; asst. pathologist Boston City Hosp., 1906-07, instr. pathology, Harvard, 1907 (resigned); instr. in pathology, U. of Minn., 1907, asst. prof. pathology and bacteriology, 1909, asso. prof., 1910, prof. pathology, 1914-21; also dir. dept. pathology, bacteriology and pub. health until 1921; prof. pathology, University of Minnesota Graduate School and head section pathologic anatomy, Mayo Clinic, 1921-43. Consultant, sect. pathologic anatomy, Mayo Clinic, since 1943 (Oct.) Commissioned maj. Med. O.R.C., June 20, 1917; sailed for France, July 26, 1917; served in laboratory div., A.E.F., 18 mos.; hon. discharged Jan. 28, 1919. Member American Association Pathologists and Bacteriologists, A.M.A., Am. Soc. of Clinical Pathologists, Assn. Military Surgeons of the U.S., Phi Beta Kappa, Sigma Xi, Alpha Omega Alpha, Nu Sigma Nu. Republican. Presbyterian. Club: University. Contributor of numerous articles on pathology of tetanus, pathology of poliomyelitis, etc. Col. Med. O.R.C. Home: Rochester, Minn. Died Mar. 8, 1946.

ROBERTSON, HOWARD PERCY scientist; b. Hoquiam, Wash., Jan. 27, 1903; s. George Duncan and Anna (McLeod) R.; B.S., U. of Wash., 1922, M.S., 1923;

Ph.D., Calif. Inst. of Tech., 1925; m. Angela Turinsky, Jan. 27, 1923; children—George Duncan, Mariette. Nat. research fellow, Göttingen, Munich, Princeton U., 1925-28; asst. prof. mathematics, Calif. Inst. Tech., 1927-29; asst. prof. math. physics, Princeton U., 1928-31, asso. prof., 1931-38, prof., 1938-47; prof. math. physics, Calif. Inst. Tech., 1947-—; sci. adviser Supreme Allied Comdr. Europe, 1954-56; dir. Northrop Corp. Chmn. sci. bd. Dept. of Defense; member div. I, sect. B, Nat. Defense Research Com., 1940-43; sci. liaison officer, London Mission, Office Sci. Research and Development, 1943-46; expert cons. Office sec. of War, 1944-47; director of research Weapons Systems Evaluation Group, Office Sec. Def., 1950-52. Trustee Carnegie Endowment International Peace. Awarded Medal for Merit, 1946. Fellow Am. Phys. Soc., Royal Astron. Soc.; mem. Am. Math. Soc., Am. Philos. Soc., Nat. Acad. Scis. (fgn. secretary 1958-—), Am. Astronomical Society Edinburgh Math. Soc., Sigma Xi, Phi Beta Kappa. Clubs: Athenaeum, Cosmos. Author: researches on differential geometry, theory of relativity, quantum theory, cosmology and applied mechanics. Home: 590 Auburn Av., Sierra Madre, Cal. Office: Cal. Inst. Tech., Pasadena, Cal. Died Aug. 29, 1961.

ROBERTSON, JAMES pioneer; b. Brunswick County, Va., June 28, 1742; s. John and Mary (Gower) R.; m. Charlotte Reeves, Oct. 20, 1768, 11 children. Crossed Blue Ridge Mountains with Daniel Boone, 1769; mem. ct. created by Watauga Assn., N.C.; participated in Lord Dunmore's War at Battle Point Pleasant, 1774; agt. to Cherokee Indians for N.C. and Va.; conducted defense of Watauga Ft. against Cherokee, 1777, held rank of capt.; apptd. agt. by N.C. Assembly to reside permanently among Cherokee, 1778, resigned, 1779; explored Cumberland Valley, 1779; led group of settlers to present site of Nashville (Tenn.), 1780, adopted Cumberland Compact as basis of govt.; served as presiding officer of ct.; made alliance with Chickasaw Indians, 1781; col. regional militia; trustee U. Nashville, 1785; county rep. in N.C. Assembly, 1785; led Coldwater Expdn. against Indians, 1787; brig. gen. Territorial Govt. S.W. of Ohio, until 1794; aided Blount in negotiating Holston Treaty, 1791; mem. Tenn. Constl. Conv. from Davidson County, 1796; served in Tenn. Senate, 1798; rep. from Tenn. at 1st treaty of Tellico between U.S. and Cherokee, 1798. Died Chickasaw Bluffs, Tenn., Sept. 1, 1814; buried Old City Cemetery, Nashville.

ROBERTSON, JEROME BONAPARTE physician, army officer; b. Woodford County, Ky., Mar. 14, 1815; s. Cornelius and Clarissa (Hill) R.; grad. in medicine Transylvania U., 1835; m. Mary Elizabeth Cummins, May 4, 1838; m. 2d, Mrs. Harriet Hendly Hook, 1879; at least 3 children. Raised company of volunteers for Tex. Revolution; arrived in Tex., 1836, mustered out, 1837; began practice of medicine, Washington, Tex.; took active part in campaigns against Vasquez and Wohl; held numerous civil offices, including coroner Washington County; mem. Tex. Senate from Washington County; mem. conv. which passed ordinance of secession in 1861; one of 1st in Tex. to raise a company for service in Civil War; served as capt. 5th Tex. Inf., Confederate Army, later brig. gen. Hood's Brigade, 1862, fought in more than 40 battles; supt. Tex. Bur. Immigration, 1874; active promoter railroad bldg. in West Tex., 1881-91. Died Jan. 7, 1891.

ROBERTSON, JOHN BRUNT marine mfg. exec.; b. Chgo., July 21, 1917; s. Hugh and Mabel (Brunt) R.; student Carleton Coll., 1935-36, Northwestern U., 1937-38; m. Marjorie Davidson, Aug. 14, 1943; children—David MacLeod, Laurie. With Outboard Marine Corp., Waukegan, Ill., 1952-—, sales mgr. Gale Products div., 1952-53, sales mgr. Lawn-Boy div., 1953-56, corp. dir. of sales, 1956-59, v.p., 1957-—; dir. Cushman Motors (Lincoln, Neb.), Midland Co. (Milw.). Served as lt. USNR, 1942-45. Decorated Air Medal. Presbyn. Home: 23 S. Negaunee St., Lake Forest, Ill. Office: Outboard Marine Corp., Waukegan, Ill. Died July 20, 1965; buried Lake Forest Cemetery.

ROBERTSON, MARION CLINTON ret. naval officer, b. Calvert, Tex., Sept. 30, 1885; s. Julian and Mary (Taylor) R.; student U. of Tex., 1903-05; B.S., U.S. Naval Acad., 1909. Commd. ensign U.S. Navy, 1911, and advanced through grades to rear adm.; ret. from active service, 1947. Served as sea, World Wars I and II. Awarded Legion of Merit with 2 gold stars, combat insignia. Mem. Mil. Order of Carabao. Sigma Nu. Presbyn. Clubs: Yacht (N.Y.C.); Army-Navy (Washington); Army-Navy Country (Arlington, Va.). Address: Army-Navy Club, Washington.* Died Nov. 19, 1953.

ROBERTSON, OSWALD HOPE physician, educator; b. Woolwich, Eng., June 2, 1886; s. Theodore and Kathleen (Conlan) R.; came to U.S., 1888; B.S., U. Cal., 1910; M.D., Harvard, 1913; m. Ruth Allen, Nov. 30, 1916; children—Alan Morley, Donald Irwin, Robert Conlan. Dalton fellow Mass. Gen. Hosp., Boston, 1914-15; asst. Rockefeller Inst., 1915-17; asso. prof. medicine Peking (China) Union Med. Coll., 1919-23, prof. and head dept., 1923-26; prof. medicine U. Chgo., 1927-51, emeritus prof. U. Chgo. since 1951; lectr. biology Stanford, since 1949. Served as 1st lt., capt. and maj. Med. Res. Corps, U.S. Army, 1917-19. Decorations: Distinguished Service Order, 1918 (Brit.). Mem. Nat. Acad. Scis., Assn. Am. Physicians. Writer numerous papers on investigation of pneumonia disinfection air with glycol vapors and the biology of salomonoid fishes. Home: Star Route, Los Galós, Cal. Died Mar. 1966.

ROBERTSON, REUBEN B., JR., corp. exec.; b. Asheville, N.C., June 27, 1908; s. Reuben B. and Hope (Thomson) R.; Chem.E., Sheffield Scientific Sch., Yale, 1930; married Margaret Watkins, Dec. 17, 1938; children—Reuben B., III, Daniel Huger, Peter T., Margaret, Louise Hope, George. With Champion Paper & Fibre Co., 1934-—, successively asst. mgr. Canton div., prodn. mgr., v.p., 1938, gen. prodn. manager all divisions, 1940, executive vice president, 1946-50, president, director 1950-—; deputy, sec. of defense, 1955-57; director B.F. Goodrich & Company, Cin. & Suburban Bell Telephone Co., Dairypak, Inc. Procter & Gamble Co. Vice chmn. com. bus. orgn. Dept. Def., 1955. Trustee Miami U., 1957-—, Duke, 1957-—, Asheville Sch. Boys, 1952-—, Am. Assembly Columbia U., 1957-—. Served from capt. to lt. col., AUS, 1942-45. Recipient award as man of yr. in paper industry for service to country Paper and Twine, Assn., 1957., Employers Labor Relations Information Com. (pres. 1953-55, dir., v.p. 1957-—), Am. Pulp and Paper Assn. (exec. com., v.p. 1958-—), Nat. Indsl. Conf. Bd., Indsl. Relations Counselors (trustee 1957-—), Cin. Council World Affairs (bd. mem. 1958-—). Episcopalian. Mason. Clubs: Queen City, Commonwealth, Commercial (Cin.); Links (N.Y.C.). Home: 9974 McKelvey Road, Cin. 31. Office: 601 N. B St., Hamilton, O. Died Mar. 13, 1960.

ROBERTSON, ROBERT CRAWFORD, orthopedic surgeon; b. Coulterville, Ill., July 29, 1899; s. John Wylie and Mary Elizabeth (Crawford) R.; A.B., U. Ill., 1921, B.S., 1922, M.S., 1924, M.D., 1925; m. Frankie Marion Condray, Sept. 7, 1925; children—Elizabeth Eugenia (Mrs. Stephen Tripp Smith), Mary Louise (Mrs. Thomas Burke Hodgson). Intern, resident St. Luke's Hosp., Chgo., 1924-26; fellow Willis C. Campbell Clinic, Memphis, 1926-27; practice medicine, specializing in orthopedic surgery, Chattanooga, 1927-69; founder, chief orthopedic services Baroness Erlanger Hosp., T.C. Thompson's Childrens Hosp.; mem. staff Meml. Hosp., Tenn. State Tb. Hosp., past chief of staff Pine Breeze Sanitorium; cons. Hamilton Meml. Hosp., Dalton, Ga., Copper Basin Gen. Hosp., Copper Hill, Tenn., Emerald-Hodgson Hosp., Sewanee, Tenn.; designated orthopedic surgeon U.S. Employees Compensation Commn., Tenn. Crippled Children's Service Bd. dirs. Little Theater, Meml. Hosp., Chattanooga. Served to 2d lt. with inf., U.S. Army, 1918-19, to col. with M.C., AUS, 1942-45, 51-55. Decorated Legion of Merit, Bronze Star medal, Purple Heart; recipient Arrowhead award. Diplomate Am. Bd. Orthopedic Surgery. Fellow A.C.S., Am. Acad. Orthopedic Surgeons, Internat. Acad. Medicine, Am. Geriatric Soc.; mem. A.M.A., So. Tenn. med. assns., Hamilton County (past pres.), Chattanooga med. socs., Chattanooga Acad. Surgery (past pres.), Clin. Orthopedic Soc. (past v.p.), Internat. Soc. Orthopedic Surgery and Traumatology, Soc. Med. Cons. to Armed Forces, Sigma Xi, Alpha Omega Alpha, Zeta Psi, Phi Beta Pi. Rotarian. Clubs: Chattanooga Golf and Country, Lookout Mountain Fairyland. Contbr. articles to profl. jours. Home: Chattanooga TN Died Jan. 15, 1969; buried National Cemetery Chattanooga TN

ROBERTSON, WALTER MELVILLE ret. army officer; b. Nelson Co., Va., June 15, 1888; s. William Walter and Mary Fannie (Pettit) R.; grad. Central State Normal Sch., Okla., 1907; student U. of Okla., 1907; B.S., U.S. Mil. Acad., 1912; grad. Infantry Sch. (advanced course), 1925; hon. grad. Command and Gen. Staff Sch., 1926; grad. Army War Coll., 1930; m. Lorene Powell Crebs, Aug. 10, 1916. Commd. 2d lt., June 12, 1912; promoted through grades to major general, January 24, 1948; served in Hawaii, 1912-15, with A.E.F., May 1918-Feb. 1920, in P.I., 1933-36; inspector Gen. Dept., 1920-24; instr. Command and Gen. Staff Sch., 1926-29, Army War Coll., 1930-33; mem. War Dept. Gen. Staff, 1936-40; comdg. officer, 9th Inf., Nov. 8, 1940-Dec. 15, 1941; asst. div. comdr. 2d Inf. Div., Dec. 15, 1941-May 11, 1942; div. comdr., 2d Inf. Div., May 1942-June 1945; comdg. gen. XV Corps (occupational forces in Austria), June-July 1945; occupation Germany, Aug. 1945-Mar. 1946; head U.S. delegation A.C.C., Bulgaria, Mar. 1946-Sept. 1947; deputy comdr. 6th Army, 1947; Cal. state dir. Civil Defense, Sacramento, Cal., since 1950. Decorated Distinguished Service Cross, Distinguished Service Medal, Legion of Merit, Silver Star, Bronze Star Medal, E.T.O. Service Medal with five campaign stars (U.S.); Companion of the Bath (British); Legion of Honor, Croix de Guerre with Palm (French); Military Cross, Order of White Lion, 3rd Class (Czechoslovakia); Order of Wars of Fatherland (Russian). Mem. Newcomen Soc., Kappa Alpha. Democrat. Methodist. Clubs: Army and Navy, Army and Navy Country (Washington); Columbia Country, Chevy Chase Country (Chevy Chase, Md.). Address: 1960 10th Av., Sacramento, Cal.; also 311 W. Main St., Carmi, Ill. Died Nov. 22, 1954; buried Arlington Nat. Cemetery.

ROBERTSON, WALTER SPENCER, business executive; b. Nottoway Co. Va., Dec. 7, 1893; s. William Henry and Anne M. (Robinson) R.; student Hoge Military Acad., 1907-09, Coll. of William and Mary, 1910-11, Davidson College, 1911-12; LL.D., Davidson Coll., 1955, U. Richmond, 1955, Hampden-Sydney Coll., 1958, Univ. S.C., 1959, Coll. William and Mary, 1960; m. Mary Dade Taylor, Nov. 4, 1925; children—Walter Spencer, Jr., Catherine Taylor (Mrs. Herbert A. Claiborne, Jr.), and Jaquelin Taylor. Partner of Scott & Stringfellow, Richmond, Va., 1925-42, 46-65. Chief United States Lend-Lease Mission to Australia, 1943-44; econ. adviser to U.S. Dept. of State, 1945; minister and counselor econ. affairs U.S. Embassy, Chungking, 1945-46; charge d'affaires, Sept. 1945-July 1946; U.S. Commr., Peiping Exec. Hdqrs. (Marshall Truce Commn.), 1946; mem. pub. adv. com. to E.C.A. China Aid Program, 1948; asst. sec. state for Far East Affairs, 1953-59. Mem. U.S. delegation Geneva Conf., 1954, Manila Pact Conf., Bangkok, 1955, ministerial meeting North Atlantic Council, Paris, France, 1955, SEATO Fgn. Ministers Conf., Karachi, 1956, Canberra, 1957, Manila, 1958; chmn. U.S. delegation Colombo Plan Conf. Wellington, New Zealand, 1956; U.S. delegate 14th United Nations Gen. Assembly. V.p. State and City (now State-Planters) Bank & Trust Co., 1922-25; pres. Richmond Stock Exchange, 1930-33; governor New York Stock Exchange, 1961-64; pres. Robertson Investment Corp.; trustee Geo. C. Marshall Found.; mem. adv. bd. Robert E. Lee Meml. Found., Hoover Instn. War, Revolution and Peace Stanford, Dulles oral history project Princeton. Trustee Va. Hist Soc., Richmond Meml. Hosp.; bd. visitors Coll. William and Mary; pres. Va. Mus. Fine Arts, 1959-67, Richmond Community Council, 1940-43; past mem. bd. govs. Assn. of N.Y. Stock Exchange Firms, Invstmnts. Bankers Assn. Am. Served in U.S. Air Corps (pilot), 2d lt., World War I. Mem. English Speaking Union, Soc. of Cinn., Soc. Colonial Wars, Phi Beta Kappa, also member Omicron Delta Kappa. Decorated: Medal for Merit (1946); Grand Cordon of the Order of Propitious Cloud (Chinese); Knight Grand Cross Most Exalted Order of the White Elephant (Thailand); Republic of Korea Medal; Philippine Legion of Honor (comdr.). Episcopalian. Clubs: Metropolitan, Alibi (Washington); Brook (N.Y.C.); Commonwealth (Richmond). Home: Richmond VA Died Jan. 18, 1970; buried Hollywood Cemetery, Richmond VA

ROBERTSON, WILLIAM BRYAN aviation exec.; b. Nashville, Tenn., Oct. 8, 1893; s. John Joseph and Myrtle (Harmon) R.; ed. pub. schs.; m. Marjorie Livingston, May 3, 1924; 1 son, James Livingston. Pres. Robertson Aircraft Corp., 1919-28; pres. and chmn. bd. Curtiss-Robertson Airplane Mfg. Co., 1928-30; v.p. Curtiss-Wright Airplane Co. and St. Louis Aviation Corp., 1930-33; now pres. Robertson Aircraft Corp. Was maj. Mo. N.G. A.S. and capt. Air Service, U.S. Army. Mem. Soc. Automotive Engrs., Quiet Birdmen of America, Inst. Aeronautical Sciences. Club: Bellerive Country. Was employer and backer of Charles A. Lindbergh. Home: Bridgeton, Mo. Office: Lambert Field, Robertson, Mo. Died Aug. 1, 1943.

ROBERTSON, WILLIAM JOSEPH editor; b. Fincastle, Botetourt County, Va., Sept. 19, 1888; s. William Gordon and Anne Anthony (Breckinridge) R.; ed. high sch. and 1 yr. at Virginia Mil. Inst., Lexington, Va.; m. Susan Radford Preston, of "Greenfield," Nov. 14, 1918; children—Preston Breckinridge, William Joseph, Mason Gordon, Susannah Preston. With engring. dept. Louisville & Nashville Ry. at Louisville, Ky., 1905-09; civ. engr. in mountains of Ky., Tenn., Va. and Ala., 1909-12; began newspaper work with Roanoke (Va.) Times, 1912; later with newspapers and Associated Press in South and dailies in Del. and Phila.; then editor Easton (Pa.) Express; asso. editor, Savannah Morning News, 1944-48, editor since 1948. Commd. capt. inf. U.S. Army, O.T.C., Ft. McPherson, Ga., 1917; later served at Camp Gordon (Ga.), Kelly Field (Tex.) and Camp McClellan, Anniston, Ala.; hon. discharged, Feb. 1919. Mem. Society of Colonial Wars. Democrat. Episcopalian. Clubs: Rotary, Cosmos. Author: The Changing South, 1927; A History of du Pont Company's Relations with the American Government, 1927; contbr. to mags. Office: Savannah News, Savannah, Ga. Died July 19, 1955.

ROBESON, HENRY BELLOWS rear admiral U.S.N.; b. New Haven, Conn., Aug. 5, 1842; s. Dr. Abel Bellows and Susan (Taylor) R.; apptd. to U.S. Naval Acad. from Conn., 1856, grad. 1860; m. Katharine Nichols Bellows, June 11, 1872. Midshipman, June 15, 1860; promoted through grades to rear adm., Mar. 28, 1899. Served on Niagara, Blockading Squadron, 1860-62; engagement at Fort McRea, Nov. 23, 1861; New Ironsides, spl. service, 1863, and S. Atlantic Blockading Squadron, 1864; participated in capture of fortifications, Morris Island, July 10, 1863; bombardments Fts. Wagner, Sumter and Moultrie; served Colorado, N. Atlantic Blockading Squadron, 1864-65; both attacks on Ft. Fisher, and comd. a landing party in attack on Ft. Fisher, Jan. 15, 1865; served Colorado, European Squadron, 1865-67; Piscataqua, Asiatic Squadron, 1867-70; aid to Vice-Admiral Rowan, 1871-73; Dictator, 1873-74; Navy Yard, New York, 1874-76; comd. Vandalia, 1876-77, 1877-79, Despatch, 1877; Naval Acad., 1877-83; Navy Yard, New York, 1883-88; mem. Advisory Bd., 1888-89; comd. Chicago, 1889-91; supervisor of New York Harbor, 1891-92; Naval War Coll., 1895; capt. of yard, Navy Yard, Portsmouth, 1895-98; retired, Mar. 28, 1899. Home: Walpole, N.H. Died July 16, 1914.

ROBEY, WILLIAM HENRY physician; b. Boston, Mass., July 3, 1870; s. William H. and Mary V. (Smith) R.; M.D., Harvard, 1895; m. Isabelle T. Alexander, Apr. 22, 1897; 1 son, Andrew Alexander. House physician Boston City Hosp., 1894-96, Boston Lying-In Hosp., 1896; practiced at Boston since 1897; asst. in bacteriology, Harvard, 1900-04; with med. dept. Harvard since 1904, asst. prof. medicine, 1919-27, now clin. prof. medicine, emeritus; George W. Gay lecturer Harvard Med. Sch., 1930; cons. physician to Boston City, Milton, Marlborough and Norwood hosps. Mem. exec. com. Permanent Charity Fund, Boston. Maj. Med. Corp, U.S. Army and chief of med. service Camp McClellan, 1917-18; lt. col. and consultant in medicine, Advance Sect., A.E.F., World War; col. Med. O.R.C., U.S. Army. Diplomate American Board of Internal Medicine; fellow A.M.A., A.A.A.S., Mass. Med. Soc. (Shattuck lecturer, 1929; pres. 1933-35), Am. Coll. Physicians; mem. Am. Assn. Pathologists and Bacteriologists, 1901-38; mem. Am. Clin. and Climatol. Assn., Am. Heart Assn. (pres. 1929-31, life mem. since 1948, mem. Founders Group for Sci. Research) (Silver Medallion Distinguished Service Award), Suffolk Dist. Med. Soc. (pres.), Northeast Heart Association (pres. 1927-30), Delta Upsilon, Phi Beta Pi (hon.), AEsculapian Club (hon.). Republican. Conglist. Clubs: St. Botolph, Harvard (Boston). Author: Causes of Heart Failure, 1922; Headache, 1930; also of various articles on medicine, especially the heart and circulation. Editor: Health at Fifty, 1939. Office: 202 Commonwealth Av., Boston. Died Feb. 23, 1954; buried Stonington (Conn.) Cemetery.

ROBIE, EDWARD DUNHAM rear admiral U.S.N.; b. Burlington, Vt., Sept. 11, 1831; s. Jacob Carter and Louisa Willes (Dunham) R.; ed. pvt. schs. and Binghamton (N.Y.) Acad.; m. Helen Adams, June 3, 1858. Asst. engr. U.S.N., Feb. 16, 1852; promoted through various grades and retired on account of age, with rank of commodore, Sept. 11, 1893; advanced to rank of rear admiral retired, by Congress for creditable record in Civil War, May 29, 1906. Circumnavigated the globe in U.S. flagship Mississippi, of Commodore M. C. Perry's Japan Expdn., 1852-55; erected and operated the first line of electric telegraph ever seen in Japan and instructed Japanese in building and operating the first steam railroad and in taking the first daguerreotypes ever seen there; on bd. U.S.S. flagship Susquehanna in expdn. to capture filibusters in Nicaragua and in laying the first ocean electric cable, Ireland to America, 1857, when cable broke; on bd. U.S. steam frigate Niagara when that vessel left Charleston, S.C., 1858, with 271 captured slaves and landed 200 of them in Monrovia, Liberia; chief engr. U.S.S. Mohican at capture of fts. at Port Royal, S.C., 1861; mem. bd. which designed the first iron floating dry dock for the U.S.N.; fleet engr. of the combined fleets at Key West, Fla., during the trouble with Spain over the Virginius, 1874, and selected and fitted out many vessels for the auxiliary naval force during Spanish-Am. War, 1898. Sr. engr. mem. of "Goldsborough Bd." to decide condition of naval vessels on Atlantic coast after Civil War; fleet engr. N. Pacific sta., 1866-69, European sta., 1871-74, Pacific Fleet, 1879-81; chief engr. Norfolk Navy Yard, 1874-77 and 1887-91, Boston Navy Yard, 1881-84, New York Navy Yard, 1884-87. Was mem. guard of honor over body of Gen. W. S. Hancock, Norristown, Pa., and body of Abraham Lincoln, City Hall, New York, Apr. 25, 1865. (Of 191 officers serving on Perry's Japan Expdn., 3 were alive Oct. 7, 1909.) Home: Washington, D.C. Died 1911.

ROBIE, FREDERICK governor; b. Gorham, Me., Aug. 12, 1822; s. Hon. Toppan and Sarah T. (Lincoln) R.; desc. of Henry Robie, of Exeter, N.H., 1639, and of Samuel Lincoln, of Hingham, Mass., ancestor of Abraham Lincoln; A.B., Bowdoin. 1841; M.D., Jefferson Med. Coll., Phila., 1844; m. Olivia M. Priest, Nov. 27, 1847; m. 2d, Martha E. Cressey, Jan. 12, 1900. Practiced medicine at Biddeford, Me., 1844-55, Waldoboro, 1855-58, Gorham, 1859-60; apptd. additional p.m. vols., June 1, 1861; bvtd. lt. col. vols., Nov. 24, 1865, "for faithful and meritorious services"; hon. mustered out, July 20, 1866. Pres. First Nat. Bank, Portland, Me., 1891-—; pres. Derigo Fire Ins. Co. of Me. Mem. Me. Ho. of Rep., 8 terms, during the period 1859-89 (speaker 1872, 1876), Senate, 1866-67; spl. agt. U.S. treasury, 1866-67; mem. Gov.'s Exec. Council, under Govs. Washburn, Davis and Plaisted, 1860, 1880, 81, 82; gov. of Me., 1883-87. Master Me. State Grange, 1881-89; commr. to Paris Expn., 1878; comdr. Dept. of Me. G.A.R., 1899; pres. bd. trustees of Insane Hosps. of the State of Me., 1879-99. Home: Gorham, Me. Died 1912.

ROBINEAU, SIMON PIERRE (ro-bi-no), lawyer; b. Versailles, France, Apr. 8, 1882; s. Jean and Helene (Copelin) R.; A.B., Lake Forest Coll., 1908; A.M., U. of South, 1909; post grad. Sorbonne and U. Freiburg, 1908-09; LL.B., Harvard, 1912; m. Frances Oliver, May 19, 1917 (died July 5, 1942); children—Jeanne Jacqueline (Mrs. F.W. Ludington, Jr.), Frances Patricia (Mrs. Robineau Van Devere). Tchr. modern langs. Sewanee Mil. Acad., U. of South, 1908-09; social service worker West Edn. House, Boston, 1910-13; practice of law, Boston, 1912-15, Miami, Fla., since 1915; sr. mem. firm. Robineau, Budd & Levenson; city atty. Miami, 1919-21; v.p. Zonite Products Co., 1924-25; regent and lectr. coml. law U. Miami, 1934-35. Mem. Fla. State Legislature, 1929-37. Served as capt. M.I., A.E.F., 1917-19; col., U.S. A.A.F., 1942-46. Decorated 5 battle stars, Bronze star, Purple Heart, Legion of Merit, Citation by Gen. Pershing, 1918. Mem. Am., Fla. and Dade Co. bar assns., Am. Legion, Mil. Order World Wars, Alpha Tau Omega. Democrat. Episcopalian. Mason (33 deg.). Clubs: Harvard, Bankers, Lawyers (N.Y. City); Army-Navy, National Press (Washington); Surf, Committee of 100 (Miami Beach). Author various mags. and newspaper articles. Home: 454 N.E. 23rd St., Miami 37. Office: Alfred I. DuPont Bldg., Miami 32, Fla. Died Dec. 6, 1952.

ROBINETTE, EDWARD BURTON banker; b. Gilpentown, Md., Dec. 22, 1879; s. Hanson B. and Amanda (Shryock) R.; prep. edn., Chestnut Hill Acad., Phila., Pa.; B.S., U. of Pa., 1909; m. Mrs. S. Crozer Robinson (Meta Craig Biddle). Was asst. to provost, U. of Pa.; began banking with George S. Fox & Sons, becoming partner; partner of Stroud & Co., 1922-24, owner, 1924-—; pres. Federal Bond & Share Co., U.S. Bond & Share Co. Served in U.S. Navy during the World War; attached to Admiral Sims' headquarters, London, later lt. comdr., acting as naval attaché, Stockholm, Sweden. Trustee U. of Pa., Thomas W. Evans Dental Mus. and Inst., Chestnut Hill Acad., Grad. Sch., U. of Pa., Austen Riggs Foundation; dir. Pa. Acad. Fine Arts; mem. bd. mgrs. U. of Pa. Mus., U. of Pa. Grad. Hosp. Decorated D.S. Navy Cross (U.S.); Legion of Honor (France); Order of the Crown, Médaille Commémorative de Comité National (Belgium); Order of the Sword (Sweden); Order of the White Rose (Finland). Republican. Episcopalian. Donor of $1,000,000 to U. of Pa. for establishment of a foundation for study of diseases of heart, and for development of edn. in liberal arts. Home: Philadelphia, Pa. Died Mar. 7, 1936.

ROBINS, AUGUSTINE WARNER army officer; b. Gloucester County, Va., Sept. 18, 1882; s. Col. William Todd and Sally Berkeley (Nelson) R.; grad. U.S. Mil. Acad., 1907, also Mounted Service Sch., A. C. Tactical Sch., Army Industrial Coll., Army War Coll.; m. Dorothy Gretchen Hyde, Jan. 6, 1915; children—Dorothy Gretchen, Elizabeth Warner, Helen Hyde. Served in U.S. Cav., 2d lt. to maj., 1907-17; in Air Corps, maj. to brig. gen., 1917-—; apptd. chief of A. C. Matériel Div., Wright Field, Dayton, O., Apr. 4, 1935. Episcopalian. Mason. Home: Fairfield, O. Died June 16, 1940.

ROBINS, CHARLES RUSSELL surgeon; b. Richmond, Va., Dec. 31, 1868; s. William Broaddus and Bessie (Mebane) R.; M.D., Med. Coll. of Va., 1894; studied Harvard University Medical School, summer 1895; married Evelyn Spotswood Berkeley, October 18, 1899; children—Francis Berkeley, Mrs. Dorothy Randolph Martin, Charles Russell, Jr. (M.D.), Mrs. Evelyn Berkeley Harrison, Mrs. Elizabeth Mebane Dowd, Alexander Spotswood (M.D.). Intern at U.S. Marine Hospital, Boston, 1893-95; assistant to Dr. George Ben Johnston, Richmond, 5 years; formerly member Drs. Robins and Geisinger; professor gynecology, Med. Coll. of Va., 1907-38, emeritus prof. since 1938; formerly chief surgeon of Virginia Hosp.; gynecologist Hosp. Div. Med. Coll. Va.; a founder and formerly mem. exec. com., sec., and treas. Memorial Hosp. Corporation; prin. work done at Stuart Circle Hosp., of which was an organizer and pres. many years; retired from practice, April 1, 1946; former dir. Broad St. Bank, State Planters Bank & Trust Co. Mem. Richmond Sch. Bd. 6 yrs. Served as 1st lt. and surgeon Richmond Light Inf. Blues, Va. State Militia, World War I; mem. Richmond Council of Defense; four-minute man. Chmn. Richmond Com. of Va. Hist. Commn.; mem. Southern Surg. Assn. (ex-v.p.), Tri State Med. Assn. of Va., N.C. and S.C., Founders Group Am. Bd. Surgery, Soc. of Colonial Wars (gov. for Va., 1940), S.R. (ex-pres. Va. Soc.), Society of the Cincinnati, Omega Upsilon Phi. Democrat. Baptist. Clubs: Old Westmoreland (mem. bd.), Commonwealth, Rotary (pres. 1928-29), Country of Virginia. Author: Notes on Obstetrics, 1895. Home: The Prestwould, 612 W. Franklin St., Richmond, Va. Died Oct. 16, 1948; buried Holly Wood Cemetery, Richmond, Va.

ROBINS, RAYMOND social economist, lecturer and writer; b. Staten Island, New York, Sept. 17, 1873; s. Charles Ephraim and Hannah M. (Crow) R.; educated at home and in country schs., Ohio, Ky., and Fla.; LL.B., Columbian (now George Washington) U., 1896; LL.D., Hillsdale College (Mich.), 1923 and U. of Florida, 1941; m. Margaret Dreier, June 21, 1905. Superintendent Chicago Municipal Lodging House, 1902-05; head worker Northwestern Univ. Settlement, 1903-05; mem. Chicago Bd. of Edn., 1906-09; mem. Chicago Charter Conv.; social service expert The Men and Religion Forward Movement campaign, 1911-12, and world tour, 1913; chmn. State Central Com. Prog. Party in Ill.; Prog. party candidate for U.S. senator, 1914; temporary and permanent chmn. Prog. Nat. Conv., 1916. Leader in Nat. Christian Evangelistic Social campaign in Am. univs. and colls., 1915-16, under Internat. Y.M.C.A. and Y.W.C.A. Dep. commr. and maj. U.S. Army, in Am. Red Cross mission to Russia, June 1917; promoted commr. and lt. col. U.S. Army, comdg. Am. Red Cross mission in Russia, Nov. 1917-May 1918. Mem. exec. com. Rep. Nat. Com., campaigns, 1920-24; trustee and charter mem. Roosevelt Memorial Assn.; v.p. William Jennings Bryan Memorial Assn. Advocate of organized labor and land value taxation. Transcontinental and European tour advocating the outlawry of war, 1923; v. chmn. Am. Com. for Outlawry of War, 1925-27; v.p. Citizens Com. of 1000 for Law Observance & Enforcement; campaigned Fla. citrus belt for growers' coöp. control in marketing citrus crop, 1931. Deeded with wife, Apr. 9, 1932, as donation to Federal Dept. of Agr., their Chinsegut Hill Plantation Groves and Forest Winter Home, 2080 acres, now U.S. wild life refuge forest conservation agrl. and hort. expt. station, known as Chinsegut Hill Sanctuary, Hernando County, Fla.; traveled 8,000 miles in April, May and June, 1933, in Soviet Union, studying mass production on farms, in mines and factories, and primary education under Soviet system of social control. Conglist. Clubs: City (Chicago). Home: Chinsegut Hill, Hernando County (P.O.) Brooksville, Fla. Died Sept. 26, 1954; buried Chinsegut Hill.

ROBINSON, ARTHUR GRANVILLE naval officer; b. Bklyn., May 21, 1892; s. Edward Stanley and Laura (Hewitt) R.; ed. U.S. Naval Acad., 1909-13; m. Inez Buck, Nov. 27, 1918 (dec.); m. 2d, Elizabeth C. Clemons, May 27, 1961. Commd. ensign, 1913; promoted through grades to rear adm., 1942; commanded naval vessels, Robinson, Monocacy, Palos, Luzon, Marblehead; comdt. Naval Base, Trinidad, B.W.I., comdr. All Forces, Aruba, Curacoa; comdr. U.S. Naval Ports and Bases, Germany. Pres. mil. commn. on war crimes Pacific area. Decorated Navy Cross, Order of Leopold (Belgium), Order of Orange Nassau (Netherlands), Order Brit. Empire, Naval Medal of War Service (Brazil), Legion of Merit, Commendation Ribbon; French Legion of Honor. Club: Army and Navy, Washington. Home: Los Robles Dr., Carmel Valley, Cal. Died Jan. 31, 1967; buried Arlington Nat. Cemetery, Ft. Myers, Va.

ROBINSON, ARTHUR R. ex-senator; b. Pickerington, O., Mar. 12, 1881; grad. Ohio No. U., 1901; LL.B., Ind. Law Sch., 1910; Ph.B., U. Chgo., 1913; hon. LL.D., Ohio No. U. and Marietta Coll.; m. Freda A. Elfers, Dec. 27, 1901; children—Arthur Raymond, Willard E., Kathryn C. Admitted to Ind. bar, 1910, and practiced as mem. firm Robinson, Symmes & Melson until 1925, mem. Ind. Senate, 1915-18 inclusive, floor leader 4 yrs., pres. pro tem, last 2 yrs.; apptd. judge Marion County Superior Ct. to fill vacancy, 1921; del. Rep. Nat. Conv., 1924, 32; apptd. mem. U.S. Senate, 1925, elected for term ending 1929; reelected for term 1929-35. Enlisted in 1st O.T.C., May 10, 1917; commd. 1st lt. inf., Aug. 1917; assigned to 334th Inf., Camp Zachary Taylor; promoted capt. and maj. Served in A.E.F. and Army of Occupation, on the Rhine. Mem. Am., Ind., Indpls. bar assns., Phi Delta Theta, Delta Theta Phi. Methodist. Mason (33 deg.). Home: 421 Blue Ridge Rd., Indpls. Died Mar. 17, 1961.

ROBINSON, BERNARD BUCKLEY business exec.; b. Butte, Mont., June 29, 1894; s. Dayton Oliver and Maude Lucy (Wood) R.; A.B., Stanford, 1918; m. Laura McLaughlin Bollinger, July 27, 1954. Asst. finance mgr. Weinstock-Lubin & Co., Sacramento, Calif., 1920-21; vice pres. in charge buying Banks-Huntley & Co., investment bankers, Los Angeles, 1922-30; pres. Maximum Safety Airplane Co., 1927-28; fiscal agent Asso. Gas & Electric Co., 1930-38; pres. Kinner Motors, 1938-42; vice pres. Beverly Hills Hotel Corp., 1944-46; pres. B.B. Robinson Enterprises, Berob Corp. of Can., Ltd., 1953-55; v.p. Gen. Am. Oil Co. of Tex., 1953-54; vice president Ambassador Hotel of N.Y., 1955-57. Served as 2d lt., U.S. Army Res. Aviation Sect., 1917-20; lt. comdr., U.S.N.R., 1942-44. Home: 1600 N. Capri Dr., Pacific Palisades, Cal. Office: 10889 Wilshire Blvd., Los Angeles 24. Died June 16, 1963.

ROBINSON, CLARKE journalist; b. Bradford, Pa., Nov. 26, 1894; s. Henry Barsto and Mary (Glass) R.; ed. grade schs., pvt. tutors; studied voice in Italy and France; m. Esther Joa Ford. Made his debut as a singer at 15 yrs., 1909; on vaudeville, light opera and opera stage as leading tenor, throughout Ams., Europe; sales mgr. Royal Typewriter Co., 1921-28, Underwood Co., 1928-35; radio performances over maj. networks, 1925-—; creator TV programs The Screamliner, How Can I Sell It?, Press Car. Officer with Canadian and Brit. army, 1914-17; with Am. Army in France, 1918; lt. col. now Chem. Warfare Service and chief hist. br., 1942-47. Decorated Legion of Merit (U.S.); Croix de Guerre, Fourragere Medaille Militaire (France); Mons Star (Britain); White Eagle (Serbia). Mem. Authors League, Am. Legion. Mason. Clubs: Lambs, Wayfarers. Author: Fate Is a Woman, 1936; Underdusk, 1938; Behold This Woman, 1938; Sing, Sucker, Sing: Biography of Fortune Gallo; Magic Wand of Fortune; (biog. profiles) Arturo Toscanini, Walter Winchell, Damon Runyon, Lily Pons, Gigli, Al Jolson, Joe DiMaggio. Co-author: Play the Races and Win, 1939; Systems Succeed, 1941. Contbr. to mags. Raced own stables of horses over U.S. tracks and is considered an authority on horses in articles on turf. Address: Lambs Club, N.Y.C. Died Jan. 17, 1962; buried Arlington Nat. Cemetery, Arlington, Va.

ROBINSON, CLINTON FREDERICK army officer; b. Danville, O., Aug. 21, 1902; grad. U.S. Mil. Acad.; commd. 2d lt. Corps. of Engrs., June 1924, and advanced through the grades to maj. gen., 1944; became dir. of operations of the Works Progress Adminstrn.,

N.Y.C., July 1938; assigned to duty in Office of Quartermaster Gen., Washington, D.C., Dec. 1940, then to Office of Chief of Staff, Dec. 1941; became dir. of Control Branch at Hdqrs., Services of Supply (now Army Service Forces), Washington, D.C., Mar. 1942; dep. dir. War Assets Adminstrn., 1946; exec. asst. to chmn. Nat. Security Resources Bd., 1947; ret. from army as maj. gen. 1949; became v.p. Frederic R. Harris, Inc., cons. engrs., N.Y., 1949; became pres. Carborundum Co., 1952. Address: 27 William St., New York 5, N.Y., and 2810 44th St. N.W., Washington. Died Apr. 10, 1962; buried Arlington Nat. Cemetery.

ROBINSON, ERNEST FRANKLIN surgeon; b. Lawrence, Kan., Feb. 13, 1872; s. David Hamilton and Henrietta (Beach) R.; B.A., U. of Kan., 1893; M.D., U. of Pa., 1896; m. Mary Kip, Feb. 6, 1904 (died 1923); children—Ernest Kip, Mary Clementine (Mrs. Fred Chase Koch), William Ingraham; m. 2d, Ruby Shellabarger, Apr. 9, 1927. Interne Philadelphia Emergency Hosp. and Boston Emergency Hosp., 1896-98; removed to Kansas City, Mo., 1901; surgeon, C.,B.&Q. R.R. and prof. surgery, Med. Dept. U. of Kan., 1901-09; chief surgeon Kansas City Terminal R.R., 1903-15; surgeon Kansas City Gen. Hosp., 1908-16; mem. and pres. Mo. State Bd. of Health, 1909-14; now surgeon St. Luke's Hosp., Research Hosps.; med. dir. Business Men's Assurance Co. Served in Spanish-Am. War, asst. surgeon U.S. Army, Philippine Islands, 1898-1900; maj. surgeon U.S. Army, World War. Fellow Am. Coll., Surgeons; mem. Mo. State Med. Assn., Jackson County Med. Soc., Acad. of Medicine, William Pepper Med. Soc., Phi Kappa Psi, Phi Alpha Sigma. Republican. Episcopalian. Clubs: University, Kansas City Country. Home: 5021 Sunset Drive. Address: Professional Bldg., Kansas City, Mo. Deceased.

ROBINSON, FRANK UPHAM brig. gen.; b. Geneseo, N.Y., Oct. 7, 1841; s. Horatio Nelson (LL.D.) and Emma Rogers (Tyler) R.; ed. Munroe Collegiate Inst., Elbridge, N.Y.; m. Nina Louise Henderson, Apr. 29, 1890. Commd. 2d lt. 41st U.S.C.T., Oct. 1, 1864; hon. mustered out, Dec. 10, 1865; 2d lt., 125th U.S.C.T., Apr. 26, 1866; hon. mustered out, Dec. 20, 1867; apptd. 2d lt. 19th U.S. Inf., Mar. 13, 1868; assigned to 2d U.S. Cav., July 14, 1869; 1st lt., Mar. 31, 1878; capt., Dec. 28, 1888; maj., Feb. 2, 1901; lt. col. 5th Cav., May 25, 1903; transferred to 13th Cav., Aug. 28, 1903; brig. gen. U.S.A., Apr. 8, 1905; retired, Apr. 9, 1905, at own request, over 62 yrs. of age. Episcopalian. Republican. Died Dec. 18, 1927.

ROBINSON, GEORGE WILSE neuro-psychiatrist; b. St. Clair County, Mo., Aug. 1, 1871; s. George Woodford and Cornelia (Beckwith) R.; grad. Appleton City Acad., 1892, M.D., Beaumont Hosp. Med. Coll., St. Louis, 1896; grad. study in nervous and mental diseases, England, Switzerland and Germany; m. Olive Bradley, Dec. 28, 1898; children—Dr. George Wilse, Jr. (U.S. Navy), Paul Edward (U.S. Army). Began practice at Appleton City, 1896; became professor of physiology, University Medical College, Kansas City, Mo.; supt. State Hospital No. 3, Nevada, Mo., 1907-09, Kansas City Gen. Hosp., 1909-10; supt. Punton Sanitarium, 1910-23, G. Wilse Robinson Sanitarium, 1923-35; med. director The Neurological Hospital of Kansas City. Served as neuro-psychiatrist, Base Hosp. 28, Limoges, France, capt. and maj. Med. Corps, U.S. Army, World War; lt. col. Med. R.C. Fellow A.M.A.; mem. Am. Psychiatric Assn., Central Neuro-Psychiatric Assn., Mo. State Med. Assn. (pres. 1923), Kansas City Acad. Medicine (pres. 1920), Jackson County Med. Soc. (pres. 1917), Kansas City Chamber Commerce, Phi Beta Pi. Democrat. Presbyterian. Clubs: Rotary, Mission Hills Country. Contbr. papers on neurology and psychiatry. Home and Office: 2625 Paseo, Kansas City, Mo. Died Jan. 22, 1958.

ROBINSON, GEROLD TANQUARY, univ. prof.; b. Chase City, Va., June 21, 1892; s. George Benson and Anna May (Hervey) R.; A.B., Stanford U.; A.M., Columbia U., 1922, Ph.D., 1930; m. Clemens Tanquary, Mar. 4, 1921. Mem. editorial bd. The Dial, 1919, The Freeman, 1920-24; teacher of history, Columbia Univ. since 1924, mem. faculty of polit. sci. since 1931, dir. Russian Inst., 1946-51, Seth Low professor history since 1950; research in Russia studying agrarian history of country, 1925-27 and 1937; corr. mem. Sch. Slavonic Studies, U. of London (England) since 1927; mem. adv. com., Russian lang. sect., Harvard U., 1934, Columbia U., 1935, U. of Calif., 1936, 37; chief, USSR Division, Research and Analysis Branch, Office of Strategic Services, U.S. Government, 1941-45; same, Department of State, 1945. Awarded Medal of Freedom by War Department, 1947. Served as 1st lieut., United States Army, 1917-19. Mem. Com. on Slavic Studies of Am. Council of Learned Socs. 1937-48; com. World Area Research, Social Sci. Research Council, 1946-51; joint com. Slavic studies Am. Council Learned Socs. and Social Sci. Research Council, 1948-51; trustee Institute of Current World Affairs, 1939-43; Council on Foreign Relations, American Hist. Association, Am. Philos. Soc. (received Lewis prize, 1956), Sigma Delta Chi, Phi Beta Kappa. Club: Century (N.Y. City). Author: Rural Russia Under the Old Regime, 1932. Contbr. to Persistent Questions in Public Discussion, 1924; Civilization in the United States, 1922; Nationalism and Internationalism, 1950; Foundations of National Power, 1951; also articles on Russian history and other subjects to books and jours.; editorial adviser to Encyclopedia of Social Sciences, Social Science Abstracts; mem. editorial bd. of Jour. of Modern History, 1937-39, Am. Slavic and East European Review. Home: New York City NY Died Apr. 1971.

ROBINSON, GUSTAVUS HILL, lawyer, educator; b. Whitestone, N.Y., Jan. 11, 1881; s. Gustavus Hawes and Margaret (Hill) R.; grad. Mt. Hermon (Mass.) Sch., 1901; A.B. summa cum laude, Harvard U., 1905, LL.B., cum laude, 1909, S.J.D., 1916; m. Sarah Fuller Anderson, Aug. 15, 1916; children—Douglas Hill Robinson, M.D., Margaret Hill Robinson (Mrs. Frederick L. Olmsted). Admitted to Mass. and N.Y. State bar, 1910; asso. firm Burlingham, Montgomery and Beecher, N.Y.C., 1909-12; prof. law. Tulane U., 1912-15, U. Mo., 1916-18, U. Cal., 1919-22, Boston U., 1922-29, Cornell U., Ithaca, N.Y., from 1929, William Nelson Cromwell prof. internat. law, emeritus, until 1972. Lectr. admiralty law U. Cal., 1949; vis. prof. U. Leiden, Netherlands, spring 1959; cons. N.Y. State Law Revision Commn.; admiralty cons. Lend-Lease Adminstrn., Washington; cons. Comml. Code for U.S. Served as capt., San. Corps, AUS, 1918-19. Mem. Phi Beta Kappa, Phi Delta Phi, also various prof. assns. Episcopalian. Clubs: Savage, Cornell (N.Y.). Author: Cases and Authorities in Public Utilities, 1926, 2d edit., 1935; Admiralty Law in the U.S., 1939. (U.S. Maritime Commn. placed a copy on each ship, 1944). Mem. bd. editors, Harvard Law Rev., 1907. Contbr. to law revs. Home: Ithaca NY Died Sept. 11, 1972.

ROBINSON, JACK ROOSEVELT, athlete, business exec.; b. Cairo, Ga., Jan. 31, 1919; s. Jerry and Mallie (McGriff) R.; student U. Cal. at Los Angeles, 1939-41; LL.D., Berthune Cookman Coll., Daytona Beach, Fla., 1951, Howard U., 1957; m. Rachel A. Isum, Feb. 10, 1946;children—Jack Roosevelt (dec.), Sharon A., David R. First negro to enter profl. baseball, 1946; played with Bklyn. Dodgers, 1946-56; retired, 1956; former v.p. Chock Full O'Nuts Co., N.Y.C. Chmn. N.A.A.C.P. Fight for Freedom Fund, 1957. Mem. bd. parole Conn. State Prison; board of directors, aldo cons. A.T.I.; dir. YMCA Greater N.Y.C., board mgrs. Harlem br. Served as 2d lt., cav., AUS, 1941-44. Recipient Spingarn medal, 1956. Mem. N.A.A.C.P., Nat. Conf. Christians and Jews. Home: Stamford CT Died Oct. 24, 1972.

ROBINSON, JAMES SIDNEY congressman; b. nr. Mansfield, Richland County, O., Oct. 14, 1827; attended common schs.; learned printing. Moved to Kenton, O., 1845; editor, publisher Kenton Republican; chief clk. Ohio Ho. of Reps., 1856; enlisted in Co. G, 4th Regt., Ohio Volunteer Infantry in Civil War, 1861, 1st lt., capt., 1861, apptd. maj. 82d Regt., 1861, lt. col.. col., 1862, brevetted brig. gen., 1864, became brig. gen., 1865, brevetted maj. gen., 1865; chmn. Ohio Republican Exec. Com., 1877-79; apptd. commr. railroads and telegraphs in Ohio, 1880; mem. U.S. Ho. of Reps. (Rep.) from Ohio, 47th-48th congresses, 1881-Jan. 12, 1885 (resigned); sec. State of Ohio, 1885-89. Died Kenton, Jan. 14, 1892; buried Grove Cemetery.

ROBINSON, JOHN CLEVELAND army officer; b. Binghamton, N.Y., Apr. 10, 1817; s. Dr. Tracy and Sarah (Cleveland) R.; grad. U.S. Mil. Acad., 1838; m. Sarah Pease, May 15, 1842, 9 children. Commd. 2d lt. 5th Inf., U.S. Army, 1839; served as regtl. and brigade q.m. during Mexican War; fought in battles of Pato Alto, Resaca de la Palma, siege of Monterey; commd. capt., 1850; fought in Seminole War, 1856-57; commd. col., 1861, brig. gen. U.S. Volunteers, 1862; brevetted for actions at battles of Gettysburg, Wilderness; served with Army of Potomac until Battle of Spotsylvania; commanded mil. dist. of N.Y.; brevetted maj., 1864; mil. comdr., commr. Bur. Freedmen, N.C.; comdr. Dept. of South, 67, Dept. of Lakes, 1868; lt. gov. N.Y., 1872-74; comdr.-in-chief G.A.R., 1877-78; pres. Soc. Army of Potomac, 1887; recipient Congressional Medal of Honor for gallantry, Laurel Hill, Va., 1894; statue dedicated to him, Gettysburg, Pa., 1917. Died Binghampton, Feb. 18, 1897.

ROBINSON, JOHN MARSHALL commodore U.S.N.; b. Syracuse, N.Y., Nov. 12, 1851; s. John (maj. gen. U.S.A.) and Sarah Maria (Pease) R.; grad. U.S. Naval Acad., 1873; m. Anne Gertrude Harmonson, Oct. 21, 1891. Ensign, June 1874; master, Jan. 1880; jr. lt., Mar. 1883; lt., Dec. 1886; lt. comdr., Mar 1899; comdr., Jan. 1903; capt., July 1907; retired at own request, June 30, 1908, with rank f commodore. Served on board Pensacola, Saranac, and Omaha, Pacific sta., 1873-75; Passaic, N. Atlantic sta., 1876; Yantic, Palos, and Alert, Asiatic sta.. 1876-79; Michigan, on Great Lakes, 1879-82; Kearsarge, N. Atlantic, and European stas., 1882-85; Minnesota, training-ship, New York, 1886-87; inspector steel for new cruisers, 1887-88; Richmond, flagship S. Atlantic sta., 1888-90; Atlanta, White Squadron, 1890-91; Hydrographic Office, 1891-94; Navy Yard, Washington, and War Coll., 1894; Yorktown, and Monocacy, Asiatic sta., 1894-97; in charge seamen gunners, under instrn. at Navy Yard, Washington, 1897-98. During Spanish-Am. War served as navigating officer of cruiser Minneapolis and later comd. converted yacht Siren on blockade of North coast of Cuba; again in charge of seamen gunners, 1899; exec. officer Wilmington, S. Atlantic, and Asiatic stas., 1899-1902; pres. bd. examination of candidates for warrant officers in Navy and Naval Obs., Washington, and War Coll., Newport, 1902-05; comd. Cincinnati, Asiatic sta., 1905-07, War Coll., Newport, June-Aug. 1907; comd. receiving-ship Independence, 1907-08. Awarded service medals, War with Spain, Philippine Insurrection. Republican. Episcopalian. Died 1910.

ROBINSON, JOSEPH GIBSON lawyer; b. Pitts., May 8, 1909; s. William M. and Eleanor (Gibson) R.; grad. Shady Side Acad., 1927; A.B., Princeton, 1931; LL.B., Harvard, 1934; m. Frances Vincent Keeble, Aug. 3, 1940; children—William M. III, Joseph Gibson, Ann Keeble. Admitted to Pa. bar, 1934, since practiced in Pitts., asso. Reed, Smith, Shaw & McClay, partner, 1940—; dir. Diamond Alkalai Co. (Cleve.), Union R.R. Co. (Pitts.), S.P. Kinney Engrs., Inc. (Carnegie, Pa.), Nat. Union Indemnity Co., Birmingham Fire Ins. Co., Nat. Union Life Insurance Company, also the National Union Fire Ins. Co. Pitts. Trustee Carnegie Inst., Grove City Coll., Western Pa. Sch. for Blind Children. Served as capt. USAAF, 1942-45. Mem. Am., Pa., Allegheny County bar assns., Am. Law Inst., Am. Judicature Soc. Presbyn. Clubs: Law, Duquesne, Fox Chapel Golf and Pittsburgh Golf; Rolling Rock (Ligonier, Pa.). Office: Union Trust Bldg., Pitts. 19. Died Oct. 26, 1963.

ROBINSON, KARL FREDERIC educator; b. Chgo., Mar. 4, 1904; s. Carl Eldred and Emma (Germer) R.; B.S., U. Ill., 1925; M.A., U. Mich., 1935; student U. Wis., summer 1935; Ph.D., Northwestern U., 1940; m. Frances Knight, Dec. 31, 1927; children—Karl Willard, Frances Ann. Tchr. English and speech high schs. in Charleston and Maywood, Ill., Kalamazoo, Battle Creek and Ann Arbor, Mich., 1925-35; instr. speech, dir. forensics Albion Coll., 1935-38; pub. speaking and dir. varsity debate Nat. High Sch. Inst., Sch. Speech Northwestern U., 1938-41, dir., 1944—; asst. prof. speech edn. Northwestern U., 1944-47, asso. prof., chmn. dept., 1947-50, prof., chmn. dept., 1950-65; prof. speech and drama, coordinator grad. studies in speech Cal. State Coll., Hayward, 1965—; asst. prof. speech, chmn. dept. U. High Sch., State U. Ia., 1941-44. Civilian instr. communic, meteorology program USAAF, 1943-44, USN V-12 program, 1945; co-ordinator Functional Speech, USN Orientation Course, 1948—. Mem. Speech Assn. Am. (v.p. 1945, exec. council 1945, chmn. secondary sch. com., 1941-45, chmn. visual aids com. 1952—, adminstrv. council, 1957—), Central States, Ill. (pres. 1945) speech assns., N.E.A., Am. Ednl. Theater Assn., Phi Delta Kappa, Kappa Delta Pi, Sigma Delta Sigma, Scabbard and Blade. Methodist. Author: Teaching Speech in Secondary Schools, 1951, rev. 1954; Practical Speech for Modern Business, 1963; Teaching Speech: Methods and Materials, 1963; (with Charlotte Lee) Speech is Action, 1964; Speech in Action, 1965. Asst. editor Quar. Jour. Speech, 1944-47; asst. editor, Speech Teacher, 1952-58, editor 1958-61. Home: 40 Willow Rd., Menlo Park, Cal. Died June 2, 1967; buried Alta Mesa, Palo Alto, Cal.

ROBINSON, LELAND REX economist, educator, bus. exec.; b. Athens, Pa., June 12, 1893; s. William Oscar and Minnie Wright (Smith) R.; student Hillsdale (Mich.) Coll., 1911-12; A.B., Columbia, 1915, Ph.D., 1923; m. Helen Rogers Ball, Sept. 22, 1924; children—Leland Ball (dec.), Lucius Ashley, Sarah Rogers (Mrs. Maynard L. Harris, Jr.). Lecturer economics of Columbia, lectr. N.Y.C. Bd. of Edn. and Acad. Arts and Scis., 1915-17, 1920-21; mem. Am. Persian Relief Commn., 1918-19, dir. Am. Relief at Teheran, Persia, 1919; asst. dir. U.S. Bur. Fgn. and Domestic Commerce, Washington, 1921-22; Am. financial trade commr., London, 1922-23; exchange, and Westinghouse prof. in Italy, 1923-25; pres. Second Internat. Securities Corp., Internat. Securities Corp. Am., U.S. and Brit. Internat. Co., Ltd., until Nov. 1935 when merged into Am. Gen. Corp. of which was chmn. investment adv. com., 1936-37; adviser Higher Edn. N.Y. State Dept. Edn. (1941-42); moderator radio programs Am. Bar Assn. (1944-45); chmn. Bishop's Service, Inc. Former lectr. Sch. Bus., Columbia, emeritus prof. polit. economy N.Y. U.; adv. council dept. oriental langs. and lit. Princeton. Mem. Dept. Internat. Affairs, Nat. Council Chs.; hon. trustee Inst. Internat. Edn., Am. Bur. Med. Aid to China; mem. exec. com. Am. Council Vol. Agys. Fgn. Service; vice chmn. Keuka Coll.; Economists' Nat. Com. on Monetary Policy; mem. Commn. to Study Orgn. of Peace; mem. Alien Enemy Hearing Bd., 1943-45; former chmn. and v.p. Iarn Found. Recipient Presdl. Citation; Rosette Order Brilliant Star (China); Companion, Royal Order of Homayun (Iran), 1957. Fellow Royal Econ. Soc. (Eng.), A.A.A.S.; mem. Am. Econ. Assn., Acad. Polit. Sci., Council Fgn. Relations, Pilgrims, Phi Beta Kappa Assos., Pi Gamma Mu. Mem. Dutch Reformed Ch. Clubs: University, Quill (N.Y.C.); Siwanoy (Bronxville, N.Y.), Cosmos (Washington); Authors (London). Author: Foreign Credit Facilities in the United Kingdom, 1923; (in Italian) Economic and Spiritual Forces in the Development of the U.S., 1925; Investment Trust Organization and Management, 1926, 29; also contbr. to financial and sci. periodicals. Editor, contbr.: An Introduction to Modern Economics, 1952. Home: Stoneleigh, One, Bronxville, N.Y.; also The Birches, Jefferson, N.H. Office: 76 Beaver St., N.Y.C. Died Nov. 15, 1966.

ROBINSON, LEWIS WOOD capt. U.S.A.; b. Camden Co., N.J., Mar. 7, 1840; s. William and Anna (Wood) R.; grad. Polytechnic Coll. of Pa., civil engring. course, 1861; (master mech. engring., 1864); m. Mary De'A. Rupp, Sept. 5, 1865. Entered U.S. Navy, Sept. 21, 1861, as 3d asst. engr.; served in W. Gulf blockading squadron; took part in capture Forts Jackson and St. Philip and of city of New Orleans, Apr. 1862; attack on Vicksburg by Farragut's fleet, June 28, 1862, and many other engagements, including battle of Mobile Bay, etc.; from close of Civil war on many stations and various engr. duties. Promoted 1st asst. engr., with rank of lt., Oct. 11, 1866 (title changed by law, 1874, to "passed asst. engr."); chief engr., with rank of lt. comdr., Aug. 19, 1883; grade of comdr., Mar. 21, 1895; capt., June 6, 1898. Commissioned a capt. in the line, Mar. 3, 1899. Was gen. supt. bureau of machinery, U.S. Centennial Expn., 1876; chief dept. of machinery, World's Columbian Expn., 1891-94. On duty U.S. Cruiser Atlanta, 1894, flagship Newark, Oct. 23, 1894, as fleet engr., U.S. battleship Indiana, Aug. 13, 1896, Navy Yard, Phila., 1897; inspection and recruiting duty, 1898; on duty as insp. machinery, Feb. 21, 1900. Home: Philadelphia, Pa. Died 1903.

ROBINSON, MOSES senator, gov. Vt.; b. Hardwick, Mass., Mar. 26, 1742; s. Samue (Len m. Mary Fay; m. 2d, Susana Howe; 6 children. Town clk., Bennington, Vt., 1762; admitted to Vt. bar by spl. act of legislature, 1777; col. Vt. Militia during Revolutionary War, head of regt. on Mt. Independence when Ft. Ticonderoga was evacuated by Gen. Edmund St. Clair, 1777; mem. Vt. Council of Safety; mem. conv. which declared independence of Vt., 1777; mem. Vt. Gov.'s Council, 1778-85; 1st chief justice Vt. Supreme Ct., 1778-81, 82-84, 85-89; del. from Vt. to Continental Congress to join articles of union and confederation with U.S., 1779; served on commn. authorized to agree upon terms for admission of Vt. to Union, 1782; Vt. agt. to Continental Congress in adjustment of boundary dispute with N.Y.; mem. 3d Council of Censors (supervised constn., legislative, exec. depts. of Vt.); gov. Vt., 1789, 90; mem. Vt. Conv. which ratified U.S. Constn., 1791; mem. U.S. Senate from Vt., Oct. 17, 1791-Oct. 17, 1796; opposed Jay Treaty, 1794; mem. Vt. Gen. Assembly from Bennington, 1802. Died Bennington, May 26, 1813; buried Old Bennington Cemetery.

ROBINSON, P(AUL) GERVAIS physician; b. at Charleston, S.C., August 22, 1834; s. Stephen Thomas and Mary Margaret (Gervais) R.; A.B., Charleston Coll., 1854; M.D., S.C. Med. Coll., 1856; Ecole de Medicine, Paris, France, 1856-57; (hon. M.D., Mo. Med. Coll.; LL.D., St. Louis U., 1884); m. Elizabeth R. Dickson, of Charleston, S.C., Jan., 1858 (died 1861); 2d, Lina Pratt, of St. Louis, June, 1869 (died 1882). Practiced at Charleston, 1858-60; surgeon 1st S.C. Arty., occupying Ft. Moultrie, abandoned by Maj. Anderson, U.S.A., Dec. 26, 1860; surgeon 1st S.C. Inf. until surrender of Gen. Lee at Appomattox; resumed practice at Charleston, 1865; was adj. prof. and lecturer on practice of medicine, S.C. Med. Coll.; removed to St. Louis, Sept., 1867; prof. practice of medicine, 1868, Mo. Med. Coll., and dean same for more than 20 yrs. until coll. combined with St. Louis Med. Coll. as Med. Dept., Washington U., in which is emeritus prof. Mem. A.M.A., S.A.R., etc. Democrat. Address: 3550 Pine St., St. Louis.

ROBINSON, RICHARD HALLETT MEREDITH naval architect; b. Ravenna, O., Apr. 2, 1875; s. George Foreman and Mary A. (Gillis) R.; grad. U.S. Naval Acad. (first honors), 1896; grad. in naval architecture and engring., U. of Glasgow, 1898; m. Rosalind Wood Smith, Jan. 2, 1899; children—Rosalind (Mrs. Henry L. Chisholm), George Foreman. In service of U.S. as naval constructor at Cramp's Shipyard, Phila., 1898-1902; in charge battleship Connecticut, New York Navy Yard, 1902-05; naval constructor (lt.-comdr.) and asst. to chief constructor, in charge of design and constrn. of all ships, 1905-13; resigned, with rank of naval constructor, Feb. 1913; chmn. bd., Minn. & Ont. Paper Co., dir. subsidiaries; dir. Merchant Sterling Corp. Decorated Commander Order of White Rose of Finland. Member Society Naval Architects and Marine Engineers (honorary vice president), Military Order Fgn. Wars (past comdr. Conn. Commandery), U.S. Naval Inst., Loyal Legion. Republican. Episcopalian. Clubs: University, Tuxedo (New York), Army and Navy (Washington); Chicago (Chicago); Minneapolis Club. Office: Baker Arcade Bldg., Minneapolis. Died Apr. 23, 1951.

ROBINSON, SAMUEL MURRAY, naval officer; b. Eulogy, Tex., Aug. 13, 1882; s. Michael and Susan Sinai (Linebarger) R.; grad. U.S. Naval Acad., 1903; post grad. in elec. engring.; hon. Dr. Science, Union Coll., Schenectady, N.Y.; Dr. of Engring., Stevens Inst., Hoboken, N.J.; m. Emma Mary Burnham, Mar. 1, 1909; children—James Burnham (comdr. U.S.N.), Murray. Served 11 years at sea; manager Puget Sound Navy Yard, 1925; promoted through grades to rear admiral, 1931, and apptd. chief of Bureau of Engring. and engr. in chief of Navy; inspector of machinery, Schenectady, N.Y., 1935; head of Compensation Bd., 1938; chief of Bureau of Engring. and Coordinator of Shipbuilding, 1939; chief of Bureau of Ships and coordinator of shipbuilding, 1940; promoted to vice admiral, 1942, and apptd. chief of Office of Procurement and Material; promoted to admiral 1945; adminstr. Webb Inst. Naval Architecture, 1949-52; ret., 1952. Decorated D.S.M.; Order British Empire; Officer de l'Ordre de la Couroune (Belgium); Order Southern Cross (Brazil). Mem. Am. Soc. Naval Engrs., U.S. Naval Inst.; hon. mem. Soc. of Mech. Engrs. Clubs: University (Washington, D.C.); New York Yacht, Nassau (New York). Author: Electric Ship Propulsion. Home: Houston TX Died Nov. 11, 1972; buried Houston TX

ROBINSON, STEWART MACMASTER clergyman, editor; b. Clinton, N.Y., July 21, 1893; s. Rev. William Courtland and Frances Augusta (Horner) R.; Tusculum Coll., Greenville, Tenn., 1929; m. Anne MacGregor Payne, Sept. 4, 1917; children—Stewart Payne, Anne MacGregor (Mrs. Wm. A. Eddy, Jr.), James, Alexander, Nancy (Mrs. DeLong). Ordained to ministry Presbyn. Ch., 1918; asst. pastor Ch. of Covenant, Cleve., 1919-21, 1st Ch., Lockport, N.Y., 1921-28, 2d Ch., Elizabeth, N.J., 1929-62; editor The Presbyn. 1934-46. Treas. Christian Freedom Found. Trustee Bloomfield Coll. and Sem. Served as divl. chaplain U.S. Army with AEF, 1918-19. Freedom Found. award, 1951, 60. Mem. br. Am. Tract Soc.; dir. Stony Brook Assembly and Sch. Mem. Hist. Soc. Pa., N.Y. Hist. Soc., Acad. Polit. and Social Sci., N.J. Hist. Soc. Phi Beta Kappa. Del. Pan-Presbyn. Alliance, 1941; mem. Interim Com. Internat. Calvinistic Congress; chmn. gen. commn. on chaplains, Washington, 1951-53, mem. exec. com. 1940-58. Republican. Club: Nassau (Princeton, N.J.). Author: The First Continental Congress and the Clergy of the Time; The Young Calvin; We Mutually Pledge, 1964. Editor: Political Thought of Colonial Clergy. Contbr. to jours. Home: Cherry Hill, Delhi, N.Y. Died Sept. 22, 1965.

ROBINSON, THOMAS LINTON banker; b. Ravenna, O., June 28, 1880; s. George Foreman and Mary G. (Gillis) R.; Ph.B., U. of Mich., 1900, LL.B., 1902; m. Ysabel Bonnell, 1907; children—Laura, Henry B. Law practice, banking and mfg., Youngstown, O., 1902-17; dep. commr. for Kingdom of Italy, permanent commissioner Am. Red Cross, 1917-18; maj. U.S.A., service in France and Germany, 1918-19; officer 3d Army, Coblenz, Dec. 1918-Apr. 1919; in Berlin, Mar. 1919, on spl. mission for G.H.Q.; abroad as asst. to member of Dawes Commission, when Dawes plan became effective, 1924. Vice-pres. Am. Exchange Nat. Bank, New York, 1919-26; v.p. Guaranty Trust Co. of N.Y., 1926-29; asso. with W. C. Langley & Co., Mar. 15, 1929-Jan. 1, 1930. Vice chmn. Emergency Unemployment Relief Com., New York, 1931-33, also chmn. of mass canvass for relief, New York; appointed deputy administrator all finance codes under National Recovery Administration, resigned because of illness, Apr. 1934. Decorated Order of the Crown (Italy), Order Crown Belgium. Republican. Episcopalian. Home: E. Williston, L.I., N.Y. Died Feb. 20, 1940.

ROBINSON, WILLIAM MORRISON, JR., historian; b. Augusta, Ga., May 30, 1891; s. William Morrison and Minnie Lee (Allen) R.; student Sacred Heart Coll., Augusta, 1904-07; B.S. in Civil Engring., Ga. Inst. Tech., 1911, C.E., 1924, H.H.D. (hon.), Fla. State U., 1955; m. Sarah Blanchard Watson, July 23, 1928. Licensed profl. engr., Ga.; admitted to practice before ICC; engaged in corporate, pvt. and pub. practice civil engring. Served to 1st lt. Engr. Officers Res. Corps, 1917-19, overseas, France; capt., 1924, advancing to col., 1947; air field constrn., 1941-43, overseas Insp. Gen.'s Dept., Guadalcanal, New Caledonia, New Zealand, Oahu, Okinawa, 1943-45. Mem. Army Disability Rev. Bd., 1945-50; retired, 1950. Recipient Purple Heart. Mem. Soc. Am. Archivists, Ch. History Soc., Soc. Am. Mil. Engrs. (charter mem.), Am. Mil. Inst., Naval Hist. Found., Am. and So. hist. assns., Fla. Hist. Soc., U.S. Naval Inst. (asso.), S.C.V. (past camp comdr.), Phi Alpha Theta. Episcopalian (registrar, historiographer Diocese of Fla.). Clubs: Rotary, Sawano Country. Author: The Alabama-Kearsarge Battle, 1924; The Confederate Privateers, 1928; Justice in Grey, A History of the Judicial System in the Confederate States of America, 1941; First Coming of the Book of Common Prayer to America, 1965. Contbr. publs. relating to field. Home: P.O. Box 996, Quincy, Fla. Died Sept. 24, 1965; buried Eastern Cemetery, Quincy.

ROBINSON, WILLIAM WALLACE JR. brig. gen. U.S.A.; b. in Ohio, Apr. 21, 1846; s. William Wallace R.; pvt. Co. E, 7th Wis., Inf., Mar. 17-June 30, 1865; apptd. from Wis., and grad. U.S. Mil. Acad., 1869. Commd. 2d lt. 3d Cav., June 15, 1869; transferred to 7th Cav., June 26, 1876; 1st lt., Aug. 14, 1876; capt. a.q.m., June 1, 1891; maj. q.m. vols., Aug. 14-Nov. 14, 1900; maj. q.m. U.S.A., Nov. 14, 1900; lt. col. deputy q.m. gen., Jan. 20, 1904; col. a.q.m. gen., Feb. 14, 1910; brig. gen. and retired by operation of law, Apr. 21, 1910. Served for many yrs. at western posts and engaged in many fights with the Indians, including Apaches, Utes, Sioux, etc.; participated in battles at Wounded Knee and Drexel Mission, S.D.; as depot q.m. commenced reconstruction of Jefferson Barracks, St. Louis, 1891; later in charge of construction of Fort Sam Houston, Tex.; had charge of shipments of supplies and troops for Alaska and Philippine Islands, during which time several millions of dollars were disbursed by him; chief q.m. Dept. of Luzon, 1902-04, Dept. of Dak., 1904-05, Dept. of the Lakes, 1905-10. Home: Seattle, Wash. Died Mar. 24, 1917.

ROBINSON, WIRT army officer; b. Buckingham Co., Va., Oct. 16, 1864; s. William Russell and Evelyn (Cabell) R.; student Richmond (Va.) Coll., 1879-82; grad. U.S. Mil. Acad., 1887; m. Alice Phinney, Apr. 7, 1890 (died 1918); children—Alice Evelyn Rose (dec.), Wirt Russell; m. 2d, Nancy Hinman Henderson, April 22, 1920; 1 dau., Evelyn Byrd. Commd. 2d lt. 4th Arty., June 12, 1887; 1st lt., Aug. 1, 1893; capt. asst. q.m., June 20, 1898; trans. to Coast Arty. Corps, Feb. 2, 1901; maj., Jan. 25, 1907; lt. col., Apr. 1, 1911; col. and prof. U.S. Mil. Acad., 1911-—. Instr. French and Spanish, U.S. Mil. Acad., 1891-92; prof. mil. science, Harvard, 1894-98; asst. prof. modern langs., U.S. Mil. Acad., 1899-1903; head Dept. of Chemistry and Explosives, School of Submarine Defense, Fort Totten, N.Y., 1904-06; asst. prof. chemistry. U.S. Mil. Acad., 1906-11, prof. and head of dept., 1911-—. Author: A Flying Trip to the Tropics, 1896; Elements of Electricity, 1914. Exploring and collecting trips to various points in Colombia, Venezuela, Central America and West Indies. Home: West Point, N.Y. Died Jan. 19, 1929.

ROBINSON, WM. HENRY univ. prof., clergyman; b. LaFayette, Ind., July 22, 1897; s. Wm. Henry and Clementine (Gruber) R.; ed. parochial and pub. schs., Ind.; grad. Notre Dame Prep Sch., 1916; A.B., U. of Notre Dame, 1920; Ph.D., Gregorian U., Rome, 1923, S.T.D., 1927. Final vows as Religious of Congregation of Holy Cross, 1924; ordained priest of Roman Cath. Ch., Rome, Italy, Apr. 16, 1927; prof. dogmatic theology, Holy Cross Coll., Catholic U., Washington, 1927-39; Master of Novices, St. Joseph's Novitiate, Rolling Prairie, Ind., 1939-42; prof. philos., Univ. Notre Dame, 1942-43, asst. religious superior, 1946-52, prof. theol. since 1946; pres. St. Edward's U., Austin, Tex., 1943-46. Served as auxiliary chaplain to U.S. Army and Air Corps Camps in central Tex., World War II. Mem. Am. Cath. Philos. Assn. K.C. (4 deg.). Republican. Collector periodical articles on theology, Christian practice, religious life; writer for Cath. periodicals. Home: Univ. Notre Dame, Notre Dame, Ind. Died Jan. 30, 1955; buried Notre Dame, Ind.

ROBISON, SAMUEL SHELBURN (rob-i-sun), ret. naval officer; b. Juanita County, Pa., May 10, 1867; grad. U.S. Naval Acad., 1888; m. Mary Louise Clark, 1893. Commd. ensign, 1890 advanced through the grades to rear admiral, 1918. Served in U.S.S. Boston during Spanish-Am. War, 1898; with Bur. of Equipment, Navy Dept., 1904-06; navigator Tennessee, 1906-08; exec. officer U.S.S. Pennsylvania, 1908-09; with Bur. Equipment, 1909-10, Bur. of Steam Engring., 1910-11; comd. U.S.S. Cincinnati, 1911-13; asst. to Bur. Steam Engring., Navy Dept., 1913-14, 1914-15; comd. in U.S.S. Jupiter, 1914; comd. U.S.S. South Carolina, 1915-17; comdr. Submarine Force, Atlantic Fleet, 1917-18; mem. Naval Armistice Commn., 1918-19; comdt. Navy Yard, Boston, 1919-21; mil. gov. Santo Domingo, 1921-22; mem. Gen. Bd., Navy Dept., 6 mos., 1923; adm. in command Battle Fleet, 1923-25, U.S. Fleet, 1925-26; comdr. 13th Naval Dist., 1926-28; apptd. supt. U.S. Naval Acad., 1928; ret. 1931; now supt. Adm. Farragut Acad., Tom's River, N.J. Author: History of Naval Tactics, 1942. Home: Tom's River, N.J.; (summer) Academia, Juniata County, Pa. Deceased; buried Arlington Nat. Cemetery.

ROCHE, ARTHUR SOMERS author; o. Somerville, Mass., Apr. 27, 1883; s. James Jeffrey and Mary (Halloran) R.; student Holy Cross Coll., Worcester, Mass., 1899-1901; LL.B., Boston U., 1904; m. Ethel Kirby Rowell, Aug. 12, 1910 (died 1915); 1 son, Jeffrey; m. 2d, Ethel Pettit, Sept. 28, 1917; 1 son, Clyde. Practiced law 18 mos.; entered newspaper work, 1906. Commd. capt., Mil. Intelligence Div. U.S.A., Sept. 1918; hon. discharged, Dec. 1918. Author: Loot, 1916; Plunder, 1917; The Sport of Kings, 1917; Ransom, 1918; The Eyes of the Blind, 1919; Uneasy Street, 1920; Find the Woman, 1921; The Day of Faith (Gov. Thomas C. McRae, of Ark., declared Nov. 1, 1921, to be legal holiday in honor of book), 1921; A More Honorable Man, 1922; The Pleasure Buyers, 1925; Devil-May-Care, 1926; Come to My House, 1927; What I Know About You, 1927; The Wise Wife, 1928; The Woman Hunters, 1928; Marriage for Two, 1929; Four Blocks Apart, 1930; Rhapsody in Gold, 1931; The Wrong Wife, 1931; The Great Abduction, 1932; Slander, 1933; Conspiracy, 1934. Co-author: (play) The Scrap of Paper, 1917. Home: Palm Beach, Fla. Died Feb. 17, 1935.

ROCHE, FREDERICK W., lawyer; b. Boston, July 23, 1914; s. David F. and Gertrude (Kelley) R.; A.B., Boston Coll., 1936; LL.B., 1939; m. Nancy N. Coffin, June 28, 1947; children—Frederick C., Thomas N., David W. Admitted to Mass. bar, 1939; law clk. Supreme Jud. Ct., 1939-40; asst. corp. counsel City Boston, 1940-41; legal counsel to gov. of Mass., 1946; mem. firm Roche, Carens & De Giacomo, Boston, 1947-71. Mem. Finance Commn. Boston, 1946-48; chmn. Mass. Housing Bd., 1949-50; judge adv. Mass. N.G., 1948-64. Bd. dirs. Ford Found. Program for Bonding Minority Contractors, Boston; mem. president's council Boston Coll, 1969-71. Served to maj. AUS, 1941-46. Fellow Boston Coll. Law Sch, 1969-71. Mem. Mass., Boston bar assns. Club: Engineers (Boston). Home: Belmont MA Died July 13, 1971; buried Belmont MA

ROCHESTER, WILLIAM BEATTY brig. gen. U.S.A., retired Feb. 15, 1890; b. Angelica, N.Y., Feb. 15, 1826; s. Hon. William B. R.; g.s. Nathaniel R., founder of city of Rochester; academic edn.; m. Anna L. Martin, June 19, 1862. Lived in Calif., 1851-59, entered army as paymaster U.S. vols., June 1861, with rank of maj.; transferred to regular army as paymaster, Jan. 17, 1867; promoted, Feb. 17, 1882, to be paymaster gen. U.S. army, with rank of brig. gen.; retired on reaching age limit. Died 1909.

ROCK, GEORGE HENRY rear admiral; b. Hastings, Mich., Nov. 21, 1868; s. Adam and Sarah Anne (Crawley) R.; grad. U.S. Naval Acad., Annapolis, Md., 1889; B.S. in Naval Architecture, U. of Glasgow, Scotland, 1892; m. Edith Gertrude Neumann, January 5, 1893; children—Albert Neumann, Bertram Neumann. Constrn. officer U.S. Navy Yards, at N.Y. City, 1892-95, Portsmouth, N.H., 1902-06, Boston, 1909-11, New York, 1915-21; mem. Bd. of Inspection and Survey, 1911-15; superintending constructor, Baltimore, Md., 1895-98, Newport News, Va., 1898-1901, Bath, Me., 1901-02, Newport News, 1906-09; mgr. navy yard, Norfolk, Va., 1921-23; asst. chief of Bur. of Constrn. and Repair, 1923-29; promoted to rank of permanent rear admiral, Aug. 1, 1926; chief constructor 1929-32, retired from active service; head of Webb Inst. of Naval Architecture since Sept. 15, 1932. Mem. Soc. Naval Architects and Marine Engrs. (pres. 1934-37), Naval Inst. Awarded Navy Cross for services in World War I. Del. to Internat. Conf. on Safety of Life at Sea, London, 1929. Episcopalian. Clubs: Engineers (New York); Army and Navy (Washington, D.C. and N.Y.); Andiron Club of N.Y. City (dictator), 1937-41). Home: Webb and Sedgwick Av., New York. Died Apr. 20, 1946; buried in Arlington National Cemetery.

ROCKEFELLER, WINTHROP, former gov. Ark.; b. N.Y.C., May 1, 1912; s. John D. Jr. and Abby Greene (Aldrich) R.; ed. Lincoln Sch., N.Y.C., Loomis Sch. Windsor, Conn., 1928-31, Yale, 1931-34; LL.D., U. Ark., Hendrix Coll., Coll. William and Mary, Coll. Ozarks; L.H.D., N.Y.U.; H.H.D., U. San Francis Xavier, Sucre Bolivia; D.C.L., Southwestern at Memphis; m. Barbara Sears, Feb. 14, 1948 (div. 1954); 1 son, Winthrop; m. 2d, Jeannette Edris, June 11, 1956 (div. 1971). With Humble Oil & Refining Co. (Tex.), 1934-37, Chase Nat. Bank, 1937-38; exec. v.p. Greater N.Y. Fund, 1938; fgn. dept. Socony-Vacuum Oil Co., 1939-51; trustee Rockefeller Brothers Fund, dir. Rockefeller Center, Inc. Chmn. bd. Colonial Williamsburg Found. Republican Nat. Committeeman, Ark., 1961-—, gov. Ark., 1967-70. Chmn. Ark. Indsl. Devel. Commn., 1955-64; mem. nat. adv. health manpower council NIH. Trustee Nat. Urban League, 1940-64, Loomis Sch., Nat. 4-H Club Found., Vanderbilt U. Served from pvt. to lt. col. U.S. Army, 1941-46; with 77th Inf., invasion Guam, Leyte, Okinawa. Recipient Bronze Star medal with oak leaf cluster, Purple Heart. Mem. Santa Gertrudis Breeders Internat. Assn. (pres., dir.), Delta Kappa Epsilon, Kappa Delta Pi. (hon.) Baptist. Clubs: Yale, Links (N.Y.C.); Little Rock Country; Pleasant Valley Country. Home: Morrilton AR Died Feb. 1973.

ROCKENBACH, SAMUEL DICKERSON (rok'en-bak), army officer; b. Lynchburg, Va., Jan. 27, 1869; s. Frank J.R. (lt. C.S.A.); C.E., Va. Mil. Inst., 1890; Army War Coll., 1912; m. Emma Baldwin, Oct. 19, 1898. Commd. 2d lt. 10th Cav., 1891; promoted through grades to brig. gen. regular army, 1924. Served as brig. gen. N.A., 1918-20; comdt. Va. Mil. Inst., 1894-95; participated in Santiago Campaign, 1898, Porto Rican Expdn., 1898; engr. officer Dept. of Santiago, Cuba, 1900-02; civ. gov., Cottabato Dist., Mindanao, P.I., 1908; arrived in France, 1917; chief q.-m. Base Sect. No. 1, 1917; chief of Tank Corps, A.E.F., 1917-19; comdr. Base Sect. No. 1, 1919; chief Tank Corps, U.S. Army, 1918-20; ret., 1933. Awarded D.S.M.; Officer Legion of Honor and Croix de Guerre with palm (French); hon. Companion of the Bath (British); campaign badges—Cuba, Porto Rico, Mexican border, Victory Medal with four stars. Mem. D.C. Chpt. Soc. Colonial Wars, Va. Soc. S.A.R., Pa. Soc. War of 1812, Soc. Army Santiago de Cuba. Episcopalian. Clubs: Army and Navy, and Chevy Chase. Home: Brownsville, Tex. Deceased.

ROCKEY, ALPHA EUGENE surgeon; b. Freeport, Ill., July 5, 1857; s. Paul Warren and Katherine (Motter) R.; A.M., Parson's Coll., 1891; M.D.. Rush Med. Coll., Chicago, 1891; m. Phila Jane Watson, Oct. 10, 1880; children—Paul, Eugene Watson. Began practice at Iowa City; moved to Portland, Ore., 1891; associated in practice with sons; surgeon Multnomah Hosp. clinician in surgery U. of Oregon. Formerly lt. M.R.C., U.S.A.; served as capt. and maj. World War; lt. col. and col. M.R.C. Fellow Am. Coll. Surgeons. Republican. Home: Portland, Ore. Died Mar. 28, 1927.

ROCKEY, KELLER E., marine corps officer; b. Columbia City, Ind., Sept. 27,21888; s. Charles Henry and Florence Ida (Emrich) R.; grad. Mercersburg Acad., 1905, B.S., Gettysburg Coll., 1909; student Yale Univ. Forest Sch., 1910-11, Marine Corps Sch., 1924-25, Command and Gen. Staff Sch., 1925-26; Mil. Science Dr. (hon.), Gettysburg College, 1947; m. Frances Maria Masury, June 1, 1916 (dec.); children—Martha Maria, William Keller; married 2d, to Susan McGee, August 4, 1948. Commissioned second lt., Marine Corps, 1913 and advanced through the grades to lt. gen. (temp.); capt. and major 5th Marines, 2d Div., A.E.F.; major, Gendarmerie d'Haiti, 1919-22, battn. comdr. in Nicaragua, 1928-29; instr. Marine Corps Sch., 1926-28; staff, Marine Corps Hdqrs., 1922-24, 1934-37; staff, Comdr. Battle Force, U.S. Fleet, 1937-39; Office, Chief of Naval Operations, 1939-41; chief of staff, 2d Marine Div., 1941-42; dir., Div. of Plans and Policies, Marine Corps Hdqrs., 1942-43; asst. comdt. U.S. Marine Corps, 1943-44; comdg. gen. 5th Marine Div., 1944; comdg. 5th Div. U.S. Marines, at Iwo Jima, 1945; comdg. 3d Amphibious Corps, Northern China, 1945-46. Comdg. F.M.F. Atlantic, 1947-49, ret. 1950. Awarded Navy Cross, with Star (two citations), D.S.C. (Army); Distinguished Service Medal (Navy); Distinguished Service Medal (Army), Expeditionary medal (navy and marine corps), Victory medal, Medale Merite (Nicaragua); Cloud and Banner (China). Mem. Sigma Chi, Theta Nu Epsilon. Clubs: Army-Navy, Army-Navy Country. Address: Washington DC Died June 1970.

ROCKWELL, ALFRED PERKINS mining engr., soldier; b. Norwich, Conn., Oct. 16, 1834; s. John Arnold and Mary Watkinson (Perkins) R.; grad. Yale, 1855; studied mining engring. 2 yrs. in scientific dept., Yale; 1 yr. in Mus. of Practical Geology, London, and 1 yr. at Sch. of Mines, Freiberg, Saxony (Ph.B., 1857, A.M., 1858, Yale); m. Katharine Virginia, d. Samuel E. Foote, New Haven, Conn., June 20, 1865 (died 1902). Pulled an oar in the Atlanta boat, 1852, in 1st regatta ever rowed bet. Yale and Harvard. Served 3 yrs. in army during Civil war, as capt., 1st Conn. Light Battery, Jan. 21, 1862, to June 18, 1864; col. 6th Conn. vol. inf., June 18, 1864, to Feb. 9, 1865; took part in many active engagements; bvtd. brig. gen. U.S.V., 1865, for "gallant and distinguished services in the field during campaign of 1864." On bd. of visitors U.S. Mil. Acad., 1865; prof. mining, Sheffield Scientific Sch., 1865-68, same Mass. Inst. Tech., 1868-73; chmn. bd. fire commrs., Boston, 1873-76; pres. Eastern R.R. Co., 1876-79; treas. Great Falls Mfg. Co., 1879-86; retired from active business, 1886. Represented Yale Univ. at Millenary celebration of King Alfred the Great, Winchester, Eng., Sept. 1901. Author: Roads and Pavements in France, 1896. Died 1903.

ROCKWELL, CHARLES HENRY naval officer; b. Chatham, Mass., Apr. 29, 1840; s. Rev. Charles and Mary (Howes); ed. Sharon, Conn., and Phila.; m. Esther H. Gould, Apr. 7, 1861; m. 2d, Marianna C. Butler. Entered naval service of U.S. as acting master, July 5, 1862; acting vol. lt. Dec. 16, 1863; acting vol. lt. comdr. Mar. 27, 1865; acting master U.S.N. Nov. 19, 1866; master Mar. 12, 1868; lt. Dec. 18, 1868; lt. comdr. Feb. 26, 1878; comdr. Oct. 31, 1888; capt. Mar. 3, 1899; retired as rear admiral Apr. 29, 1902. During Civil war took part in numerous engagements and earned commendation from superiors and several promotions by good service; afterwards followed usual career of naval officer in active service. Home: Chatham, Mass. Died 1908.

ROCKWELL, KIFFIN YATES aviator; b. Newport, Tenn., Sept. 20, 1892; attended Va. Mil. Inst., U.S. Naval Acad., Washington and Lee U. Went to Pacific coast, 1912, ran advt. agy., San Francisco, for a time; enlisted in French Fgn. Legion to aid France in World War I, 1914; transferred to 1st Fgn. Regt., 1915, served in Battle of La Targette, wounded during attack; became pilot in Escadrille Lafayette, 1916, became 1st American to shoot down an enemy plane; fought 70 battles, July-Aug. 1916; decorated Medaille Militaire, Cross of chevalier Legion of Honor. Killed over Thann, Alsace, Sept. 23, 1916.

ROCKWOOD, ROBERT EVERETT educator; b. Worcester, Mass., Mar. 1, 1887; s. John and Harriet Eldora (Butterfield) R.; A.B., Clark U., 1908; A.M., Harvard, 1915, Ph.D., 1924; student Université de Grenoble, 1908, La Sorbonne, France, 1908-09; m. Helen Louise Miller, June 14, 1921; 1 son, Albert Miller. Instr. Romance langs., Harvard, 1915-16, Columbia, 1916-17, Ohio State U., 1911-13, asst. prof., 1919-24, professor, 1924-57, professor emeritus, 1957-—, chairman of the department, 1948-57. Served with U.S.N.R.F., 1917-19; disch. rank lt.; lt. comdr., U.S.N.R., 1942-44, inactive since 1944. Officier d'Academie. Mem. Modern Lang. Assn. Am., Am. Assn. Teachers French, Phi Beta Kappa (hon.). Home: 173 Parkview Av., Bexley 9, O. Office: Derby Hall, Ohio State University, Columbus 10. Died Aug. 3, 1958.

RODDEY, PHILIP DALE army officer, mcht.; b. Moulton, Ala., 1820; m. Margaret McGaughey, 4 children. Formed cavalry troop, elected capt. during Civil War, 1861; became col., 1862; organizer, comdr. 4th Ala. Cavalry, 1862-65; defended banks of Tennessee river; executed successful raid towards Corinth, Miss., 1862; called Swamp Fox of Tennessee Valley; operated in Miss., Tuscumbia, Ala., Columbinn., 1863; comd. brig. gen.; active in Atlanta campaign, Hood's campaign in Tenn.; entered commission bus. in N.Y.C. after Civil War. Died London, Eng., Aug. 1897.

RODDY, GILBERT MORGAN, ins. co. exec.; b. Bellevue, Pa., Oct. 17, 1910; s. Edward Grieves and Alice (Morgan) R.; S.B., Mass. Inst. Tech., 1931, S.M., 1932; m. Frances Kellogg Newbury, Apr. 27, 1942; 1 son, Gilbert Morgan. With Arkwright-Boston Ins. Co., also Mut. Boiler and Machinery Ins. Co., Waltham, Mass., 1934-72, successively security analyst, asst. treas., treas., v.p., exec. v.p., 1934-58, pres., dir., 1958-65, chmn., pres., dir., 1965-72; dir. New Eng. Mchts. Nat. Bank, Am. Mut. Reins. Co., Chgo., W.H. Nichols Co., Waltham, FM Ins. Co. Ltd. (London). Pres. Emerson Hosp., Concord, 1952-57; life mem. corp. Mass. Inst. Tech.; trustee Wheaton Coll., 1951-57, Fenn Sch., Concord, Mass., 1967-70, Boston Mus. Sci. Served to col. AUS, 1941-46. Mem. Mass. Inst. Tech. Alumni Assn. (pres. 1957-58). Home: Concord MA Died Oct. 15, 1972; buried Sleepy Hollow, Concord MA

RODE, ALFRED, ins. exec.; b. Bellingham, Wash., Aug. 11, 1895; s. Charles and Lena (Wahl) R.; LL.B., U. Wash., 1921; m. Cora Louise Gardiner, Nov. 30, 1922; children—Coral Ann (Mrs. Harlan K. Veal), Helen Virginia (Mrs. Halden L. Conrad, Jr.), Alfred Gardiner. Admitted to Wash. bar, 1921; with Shank, Belt & Fairbrook, then Shank, Rode, Cook & Watkins, Seattle, 1921-47; asst. gen. counsel Northwestern Mut. Fire Assn. and Northwest Casualty Co. (later merged as Northwestern Mut. Ins. Co.), Seattle, 1937-45, dir., 1943-69, gen. counsel, vice chmn. bd., 1945-54, chmn., 1954-69. Served as ensign USN, World War I. Mem. Am., Wash. bar assns. Republican. Episcopalian. Clubs: Rainier, Washington Athletic. Home: Seattle WA Died Jan. 7, 1969.

RODEBUSH, WORTH HUFF educator; b. Selden, Kan., May 24, 1887; s. Milton Leander and Rosa Elizabeth (Huff) R.; A.B., U. Kan., 1912, A.M., 1914; Ph.D., in chemistry, U. Cal., 1917, NRC fellow, 1919-21; m. Esther Kittredge, Feb. 5, 1919; children—Harriet Rose, Susan Emily, Annette Linn. Instr. chemistry U. Kan., 1912-15; chemist U.S. Bur. Mines, 1918; research chemist U.S. Indsl. Alcohol Co., Balt., 1919; chemist U.S. Bur. Mines (helium investigation), 1921; asso. prof. phys. chemistry U. Ill., 1921-24, prof., 1924-—, research prof., 1953-55, ret., 1955. Invited contbr. Oxford Meeting of Faraday Soc.; 1934. Mem. adv. bd. U.S. Naval Ordnance Test Sta., China Lake, 1949-54; adviser Ordnance Dept. Army and Navy; cons. cloud Physics Project, U. Chgo., NIH Project on Water Pollution, U. Fla. Recipient Merit certificate U.S. Govt., 1948. Fellow Am. Phys. Soc.; mem. Am. Chem. Soc., Nat. Acad. Scis., Faraday Society, Phi Beta Kappa Associates, Phi Beta Kappa, Sigma Xi, Alpha Chi Sigma. Club: Chaos. Joint Author: Treatise on Physical Chemistry, 1924; (with wife) Introductory Physical Chemistry, 1932. Contbr. to Jour. Am. Chem. Soc., Phys. Rev., other sci. jours. Home: 302 Michigan Av., Urbana, Ill. Died Aug. 16, 1959.

RODENBOUGH, THEOPHILUS FRANCIS brig. gen. U.S.A.; b. Easton, Pa., Nov. 5, 1838; s. Charles and Emily (Cauffman) R.; ed. Lafayette Coll.; m. Elinor Frances Foster, Sept. 1, 1868. Apptd. from Pa., 2d lt. 2d Dragoons, Mar. 27, 1861; 1st lt. 2d Cav., May 14, 1861; capt., July 17, 1862; col. 18th Pa. Cav., Apr. 29, 1865; comd. brigade and Dist. of Clarksburg, W.Va.; hon. mustered out of vol. service, Oct. 31, 1865; maj. 42d U.S. Inf., July 28, 1866; retired with rank of col., Dec. 15, 1870, "loss of right arm from wound in line of duty"; advanced to rank of brig. gen. retired, by act of Apr. 23, 1904. Bvtd. maj., Sept. 19, 1864, for battle of Trevillian Sta. and Opequan, Va.; lt. col., Mar. 13, 1865, for services during war; col., Mar. 13, 1865, for battle of Todd's Tavern, Va.; brig. gen., Mar. 13, 1865, for battle of Cold Harbor, Va.; awarded Congressional Medal of Honor, Sept. 21, 1893, "for distinguished gallantry in action at Trevillian Sta., Va.," June 11, 1864, where he was severely wounded while commanding 2d U.S. Cav. Served in all campaigns of Army of the Potomac; asst. insp. gen., N.Y., 1880-83; chief bur. of elections, City of New York, 1890-1901. Sec. Mil. Service Instn., 1878-—. Editor: The Army of the United States, 1896; Journal Military Service Institution, 1899. Died Dec. 19, 1912.

RODES, ROBERT EMMETT army officer; b. Lynchburg, Va., Mar. 29, 1829; s. David and Martha (Yancey) R.; grad. Va. Mil. Inst., 1848; m. Virginia Woodruff, Sept. 10, 1857, 2 children. Became civil engr., 1851; chief engr. N.E. & S.W. Ala. R.R., 1858; capt. Mobile (Ala.) Cadets, 1861; volunteered, became col. 5th Ala. Inf., 1861; commd. brig. gen. in Manassas campaign, 1861; commanded brigade at Battle of Fair Oaks (Va.); served in Battle of Gaines' Mill; fought at battles of Bloody Lane, Antietam; given command of Daniel Hill's division, 1863; with Stonewall Jackson led van of flank march at Battle of Chancellorsville; apptd. maj. gen., 1863; served in Battle of Gettysburg; stopped Union advance in Battle of Wilderness, 1864; in action at Battle of Spotsylvania; took part in raid Washington, D.C. Killed in action at Winchester, Va., Sept. 19, 1864.

RODGERS, CHRISTOPHER RAYMOND PERRY naval officer, ednl. adminstr.; b. Bklyn., Nov. 14, 1819; s. George Washington and Ann (Perry) R.; m. Jane Slidell, July 7, 1845, 5 children. Commd. midshipman U.S. Navy, 1833; served at N.Y. Navy Yard, 1836-37; on a cruise on ship Fairfield in Brazil Squadron during Seminole War, 1839-42, served on board ships Flirt,

Wave; comdr. ship Phoenix, passed midshipman, 1839, lt., 1844; with ship Saratoga in African Squadron, 1842-43; Cumberland, Mediterranean Squadron, 1843-45, acting master on both ships; served at Veracruz during Mexican War, 1846-48; served with ship Constitution of African Squadron, 1852-53, Wabash, Mediterranean Squadron, 1858-59; comdt. of midshipmen U.S. Naval Acad., 1860-61, played active part in moving acad. to Newport, R.I.; ordered to take command of ship Wabash, 1861, commanded vessel as flagship at Battle of Port Royal; promoted comdr., 1861; fleet capt. South Atlantic Blockading Squadroon, 1862-63; served on ship New Ironsides during Battle of Charleston, 1863; commd. capt., 1866, commodore, 1870; rear adm., 1874; chief Bur. of Yards and Decks, 1871-74; acting chief Bur. of Equipment; supt. U.S. Naval Acad., 1874-78; comdr. in chief Pacific Squadron, 1878-80; pres. U.S. Naval Inst., 1875-78, 82-83; pres. Internat. Meridian Conf., 1884. Contbr. article "DuPont's Attack at Charleston" to Battles and Leaders of the Civil War, 1887-88. Died Washington, D.C., Jan. 8, 1892; buried Annapolis, Md.

RODGERS, FREDERICK rear admiral U.S.N.; b. Havre de Grace, Md., Oct. 3, 1842; s. Robert Smith and Sarah (Berry) R.; bro. of John Augustus R.; apptd. to U.S. Naval Acad. from Md., 1857, grad. 1861; m. Sarah M., d. John C. Fall, of San Francisco, Feb. 2, 1882. Warranted midshipman, June 1, 1861; promoted through grades to rear adm., Mar. 3, 1899. Served on Wabash, 1861; Santee, 1861-62; exec. officer Kineo, 1862-63; participated in engagements at Donaldsonville, Port Hudson, and College Point, La., Feb.-Mar. 1862; served on Grand Gulf, Atlantic and West Gulf blockading squadrons, 1863-65; Chattanooga, 1866; Sacramento, 1866-June 6, 1867, when she was lost in the Bay of Bengal; Michigan, 1868-69; N. Pacific Squadron, 1869-72, serving on the Pensacola, St. Mary's and Saranac; insp. ordnance, Navy Yard, Washington, 1872-73; comd. Despatch, 1873-76; light house insp. 11th dist., 1876-77, 4th dist., 1881-83, 3d dist., 1887-90; comd. Adams, 1877-79, Independence, 1883-87, Philadelphia, 1890-92; supervisor New York Harbor, 1892-93; capt. of yard, Navy Yard, New York, 1893-96; comd. Massachusetts, 1896-97; mem. Naval Retiring Bd., July-Sept. 1897; mem. Bd. of Inspection and Survey, 1897, and pres. of bd., 1897-98; comd. Puritan, June-Oct. 1898, during war with Spain; pres. Bd. of Inspection and Survey, 1898-1901; sr. squadron comdr., Asiatic Fleet, 1901, and commander-in-chief, 1902; comdt., Navy Yard, New York, 1903-04; retired Oct. 3, 1904; spl. bd. duties, 1904-07. Home: St. James, R.I. Died Nov. 3, 1917.

RODGERS, GEORGE WASHINGTON naval officer; b. Cecil County, Md., Feb. 22, 1787; s. John and Elizabeth (Reynolds) R.; m. Ann Perry, July 5, 1815, at least 3 children, including George Washington, Christopher Raymond Perry, Alexander P. Commd. midshipman U.S. Navy, 1804; acting lt., served on ship United States, 1809; commd. lt., 1810; served on ship Wasp during War of 1812; voted silver medal by U.S. Congress for services in engagement with ship Frolic; commanded ship Firefly, 1815; commd. master comdt., 1816; comdr. ship Peacock, Mediterranean Squadron, 1816-19; with N.Y. Navy Yard, 1819-25, comdt. part of this period; commd. capt., 1825; served on Naval Bd. Examiners; commanded Brazil Squadron, 1831-32. Died Buenos Aires, Argentina, May 21, 1832; buried New London, Conn.

RODGERS, GEORGE WASHINGTON naval officer; b. Bklyn., Oct. 20, 1822; s. George Washington and Ann (Perry) R.; m. Kate Lane, Aug. 21, 1842. Commd. midshipman U.S. Navy, 1836, passed midshipman, 1842; served with Col. Herney, then in ship John Adams in the Gulf of Mexico, 1846-48; promoted lt., 1850; commanded ship Constitution, 1860; comdt. midshipman, 1861; commd. comdr., 1862; appointed chief of staff, 1863; commanded Catskill in attack on Charleston (S.C.), 1863. Killed in attack on Charleston., Aug. 17, 1863.

RODGERS, JOHN naval officer; b. Lower Susquehanna Ferry, Md., 1773; s. John and Elizabeth (Reynolds) R.; m. Minerva Denison, Oct. 21, 1806, 11 children including John, Louisa. Apptd. 2d lt. U.S. Navy on board Constellation by Pres. Adams, 1798, exec. officer (capt.), 1799; participated in capture of frigate Insurgenta; at end of war honored by being selected to convey John Dawson (bearer of French-Am. treaty) to France; in mcht. service, 1801; recalled to U.S. Navy, 1802; forced Tripoli to sign treaty to end slavery of Christians, 1805; in command N.Y. flotilla and naval station, 1807; had duty enforcing Embargo in waters between The Delaware and Passamaquddy Bay, 1808; commanded Northern div. of ships for protection of Am. coast with frigate President, 1810; in active service War of 1812; in command of Del. flotilla and ship Guerriere, 1814; chosen by Pres. Madison to head newly created Bd. of Navy Commrs., 1815-24, 27-37; sr. officer in navy, 1821; served as sec. of navy and interim, 1823; commanded Am. Squadron, 1825-27. Died Naval Asylum, Phila., Aug. 1, 1838; buried Congressional Cemetery, Washington, D.C.

RODGERS, JOHN naval officer; b. Sion Hill, Md., Aug. 8, 1812; s. Capt. John and Minerva (Denison) R.; attended U. Va. one year; m. Ann Hodge, Nov. 27, 1857, 3 children. Apptd. midshipman U.S. Navy, 1828, passed midshipman, 1834; comdr. in Wave, then Jefferson in Seminole War; commd. lt., 1840; commanded ship Boxer of Home Squadron, 1842-44; ordered to duty with North Pacific Surveying Expdn., 1852, 2d in rank commanding ship John Hancock; surveyed Liu-Kius, Ladrones and other islands, Hawaiian and Society Islands; promoted comdr., 1855; in charge of office in Washington (D.C.) preparing results of expdn. for publication, 1856; commanded ship Flag, 1861; aide to Rear Adm. Samuel Du Pont at Battle of Point Royal (S.C.); commanded ship Galena, 1862; commd. capt., 1862; served in attack on Ft. Sumter, 1863; promoted to commodore by Congress, 1863; served in ships Dictator, 1864, Monadnock, 1866-67; comdt. Boston Navy Yard, 1866-69; commd. rear adm., 1869; commanded Asiatic Squadron as rear adm., 1870-72; pres. Naval Examining and Retiring bds., 1872-73; comdt. Mare Island (Cal.) Navy , 1873-77; supt. Naval Observatory, 1877-82; chmn. Light House Board, 1878-82; pres. U.S. Naval Inst., Transit of Venus Commn., 1st Naval Adv. Bd., Jeannette Relief Bd.; charter mem. Nat. Acad. Scis. Died Washington, May 5, 1882.

RODGERS, JOHN naval officer; b. Washington, D.C., Jan. 15, 1881; s. John A. and Elizabeth B. (Chambers) R.; prep. edn., Lawrenceville (N.J.) Sch., 1896, 97; grad. U.S. Naval Acad., 1903; unmarried. Ensign U.S.N., Feb. 3, 1905; promoted through grades to comdr., Nov. 4, 1920; served in Spanish-Am. War; 2d naval aviator licensed (1911); in Submarine Service and on North Sea mine barrage, World War; comdr. Naval Air Sta., Pearl Harbor, T.H., 1922-25; apptd. asst. chief Bur. of Aeronautics, Sept. 1925. In charge navy sea plane in attempted non-stop flight, San Francisco to Hawaiian Islands, Sept. 1925. Home: Havre de Grace, Md. Died Aug. 27, 1926.

RODGERS, JOHN AUGUSTUS rear admiral U.S.N.; b. Havre de Grace, Md., July 26, 1848; s. Robert Smith and Sarah (Perry) R.; bro. of Frederick R.; apptd. to the U.S. Naval Acad. by the President, at-large, July 30, 1863, grad. June 2, 1868; m. Elizabeth B. Chambers, Mar. 30, 1880. Promoted ensign, Apr. 19, 1869; advanced through grades to rear adm., Sept. 7, 1908. Was in active service during Civil War, in the summer of 1864, on board the Marion, pursuit of the Confed. steamers Florida and Tallahassee; served successively in the Pacific squadron, on Supply and Nipsic, in the torpedo service, Hartford, Juniata, Monongahela, Trenton and Constellation, 1868-80; Navy Yard, Washington, 1880-83; Ossipee, 1884-87; mem. Steel Bd., 1887-90; Pensacola, 1890-91; Naval War Coll., 1892; Miantonomah, 1892-94; inspection duty, 1895-97; exec. officer Indiana, 1897-99; took part in the destruction of Cervera's squadron off Santiago, Cuba, July 1898, and was advanced five numbers in rank for "eminent and conspicuous conduct" in that battle; in charge 6th light house dist., 1899-1902; comd. Marietta and Albany, 1902-04; Illinois, 1904-06; insp. 3d light house dist., 1906-07; comdt. Navy Yard, Puget Sound, Wash., 1908-10. Retired July 26, 1910. Comdt. naval units, Harvard U., Mass. Inst. Tech., Boston U. and Tufts Coll., 1918. Home: Havre de Grace, Md. Died Mar. 2, 1933.

RODGERS, JOHN GILMOUR ry. official; b. Phila., Pa., Nov. 14, 1863; s. Samuel Maurice and Isabel (Gilmour) R.; ed. Lehigh U. and under private tutors; m. Agnes P. Barney, Feb. 4, 1901. Became connected with Pennsylvania R.R. as asst. engr., 1886, supt., 1900, asst. to gen. mgr., 1909, gen. supt., 1911. asst. to pres. 1917, v.p., Mar. 1920-—. Served as lt. col. engrs., U.S.A., Oct.-Dec. 1918. Republican. Presbyn. Home: Chicago, Ill. Died Apr. 12, 1923.

RODGERS, JOHN ISAAC brig. gen. U.S.A.; b. Fayette Co., Pa., Apr. 18, 1839; s. John and Eliza R.; A.B., Waynesburg Coll., Pa., 1855; grad. U.S. Mil. Acad., 1861; m. Esther F. Rogers, Sept. 25, 1872; children—Mrs. Louisa Hall, Robert Clive. Second lt. 2d Arty., May 6, 1861; promoted through grades to brig. gen. vols., May 4, 1898; brig. gen. U.S.A., Oct. 1902, retired. Served during Civil War; comd. battery at Ft. Pickens, and light battery in La.; was in Gen. Banks' expdns. and battles in Red River campaigns, 1863-64, and siege of Port Hudson. Instr. mathematics, West Point, Oct. 1864 to June 1865; served with regt., 1865-89 (including railroad riot service in Md. and W.Va., 1877, and Mexican border trouble, 1877-81); arty. insp., 1889-98, except part of the 1895-96, comdr. Fort Schuyler, N.Y.; brig. gen. vols., 1898, and chief of arty. of the army, was charged with organization and equipment of a siege train of 96 guns and mortars for service with army in the field. Has prepared Range Tables, Coast Arty. Drill Regulations and other papers on arty. pub. by War Dept. Died Aug. 2, 1931.

RODGERS, RAYMOND PERRY rear admiral U.S.N.; b. Washington, D.C., Dec. 20, 1849; s. Rear Admiral Raymond and Julia (Slidell) R.; grad. U.S. Naval Academy, 1868; m. Gertrude Stuyvesant. Ensign, 1869; promoted through grades to rear admiral, July 4, 1908. Served as naval attaché in France and Russia, 1893-97; exec. officer Iowa, throughout Spanish-Am. War and at Santiago, 1897-99; was advanced 5 numbers in rank for "eminent and conspicuous conduct" in battle which destroyed Cervera's Squadron off Santiago; comd. Nashville, 1899-1901, in W.I., in Philippines, and in China during Boxer troubles; capt. Kearsarge, 1904-06, in Atlantic Fleet; chief intelligence officer, Navy Dept., 1906-09; pres. Naval War Coll. and comdt. Naval Sta. in Narragansett Bay, Oct. 1909; retired by operation of law, Dec. 20, 1911. Died Dec. 28, 1925.

RODGERS, THOMAS SLIDELL naval officer; b. Morristown, N.J., Aug. 18, 1858; s. C. Raymond Perry and Julia (Slidell) R.; grad. U.S. Naval Acad., 1878; unmarried. Ensign, Dec. 1, 1881; promoted through grades to rear admiral, June 13, 1916. Served on Bennington and Monterey, Spanish-Am. War, 1898; exec. officer Maine, 1902-05; in charge 10th Lighthouse Dist., 1905-06; asst. comdt. 4th Naval Dist., 1906; comd. Dubuque, 1906-08; equipment officer, Navy Yard, Phila., 1908-09; comd. New Hampshire, 1909-11; supervisor, New York Harbor, 1911-12; dir. naval intelligence, 1912-13; comd. New York, 1913-15; at Naval War Coll., 1915-16; apptd. comdr. Div. Seven, Battleship Force, Atlantic Fleet, June 19, 1916; retired July 1919. Episcopalian. Died Feb. 28, 1931.

RODGERS, WILLIAM, corp. exec.; b. Pitts., Oct. 22, 1903; s. Joseph H. and Alzona (Finley) R.; grad. Mercersburg Acad., 1922; student Lehigh U.; m. Dorothy Taylor, June 11, 1929. With Rodgers Sand Co., Pitts., 1926-29, (became McCrady-Rodgers Co.), v.p., 1929-48; prin. owner Moore Flesher Hauling Co., Inc., Pitts., 1938-72, chmn. bd., 1953-72; gen. sales mgr. Blaw-Knox Co., Pitts., 1953, v.p., gen. sales mgr., 1953-59, sr. v.p., gen. sales mgr., 1959-64, dir.; dir. Heppenstall Co., Pitts., White Cross Stores, Inc., Monroeville, Pa., Pitts. Brewing Co. Bd. dirs. Boys Club Western Pa., Vocational Rehab. Center Pitts.; bd. mgrs. Western Pa.-Humane Soc. Served from lt. to lt. col., AUS, 1942-45; Italy, Africa. Decorated Legion of Merit. Mem. Pitts. Athletic Assn., Sigma Nu. Republican. Presbyn. Clubs: Rolling Rock (Ligonier, Pa.); Pittsburgh Athletic Assn. Pittsburgh Golf, Duquesne (Pitts.); Internat., Army and Navy (Washington); Pike Run Country (Jones Mills, Pa.). Home: Pittsburgh PA Died June 10, 1972.

RODGERS, WILLIAM LEDYARD naval officer; born Washington, Feb. 4, 1860; s. John and Ann E. (Hodge) R.; grad. U.S. Naval Acad., 1878; unmarried. Ensign U.S.N., 1882; lt., 1894; lt.-comdr., 1901; comdr., 1905; capt., 1909; rear admiral, Aug. 29, 1916. Comdg. U.S.S. Georgia, 1909-11; pres. U.S. Naval War Coll., 1911-13; comdg. U.S.S. Delaware, 1913-15; mem. Gen. Bd. of the Navy, 1915-16; comdg. train, Atlantic Fleet, 1916-18, comdr.-in-chief Asiatic Fleet, 1918-19; mem. Gen. Bd. and chmn. exec. com., 1920-24, retired Feb. 4, 1924. Mem. adv. council, Conf. on Limitation of Armament, Washington, 1921; tech. adviser, Commn. of Jurists on Laws of War, The Hague, 1923. Clubs: Metropolitan (Washington); University, New York Yacht (New York). Author: Greek and Roman Naval Warfare; Naval Warfare Under Oars, 4th to 16th Centuries. Address: 1738 R St. N.W., Washington. Died May 7, 1944.

RODGERS, WILLIAM S(TARLING) S(ULLIVANT) ret. oil co. exec.; b. Columbus, Feb. 19, 1886; s. William S.S. and Florence (Eberly) R.; student Asheville (N.C.) Sch., 1902-04; Ph.B., Sheffield Sci. Sch., Yale, 1907; m. Ana Maria Morales, Feb. 3, 1940. Mining Bus., Colo., Nev., Cal., 1907-11; oil bus., Cal., 1911-15; with refining dept. Tex. Co., 1915-26, asst. to pres., 1926, v.p. and dir., 1928, mem. exec. com., 1929, pres. 1933-44, chmn. bd., 1944-53, ret.; dir. Freeport Sulphur Co., Nat. Dairy Products Corp., Empire Trust Co., Armstrong Cork Co., Great Am. Ins. Co., Jeffrey Co., Tex. Co., Met. Opera Assn. Chmn. bd. trustees Nat. Safety Council. Trustee Asheville (N.C.) Sch. Capt., Ordnance Dept., World War I. Mem. Chi Phi. Clubs: Yale, Cloud, Nat. Golf Links of America, Turf and Field, Madison Square Garden, Links, Twenty Nine, Links Golf, Havana Yacht, Havana Country (Cuba); Meadow Brook. Home: 640 Park Av. Office: 135 E. 42d St., N.Y.C. Died Sept. 1965.

RODMAN, HUGH naval officer; b. Frankfort, Ky., Jan. 6, 1859; s. Hugh and Susan Ann (Barbour) R.; grad. U.S. Naval Acad., 1880; Naval War Coll., 1907; m. Elizabeth Ruffin Sayre, July 3, 1889. Ensign, jr. grade, Mar. 3, 1883; promoted through grades to rear adm., May 23, 1917; admiral, July 1, 1919; retired Jan. 6, 1923. Served on Raleigh, Spanish-Am. War, 1898; exec. officer New Orleans, 1904; on Cincinnati, 1904-05, Wisconsin, 1905; comd. El Cano, 1905-07, West Virginia, 1907; insp. in charge 6th Lighthouse Dist., 1907-08; comd. Cleveland, 1909-10; inspection officer, Navy Yard, Mare Island, Calif., 1910-11; capt. same, 1911; comd. Connecticut, 1912, Delaware, 1912-13; superintendent transportation, Panama Canal and dir. Panama Railroad Co., 1914-15; comd. New York, 1915-16; mem. Gen. Bd., Navy Dept. 1916-17; comd. Div. Three, Atlantic Fleet, 1917; comd. Squadron One, Battleship Force, Atlantic Fleet, 1917; apptd. comdr. Div. Three, Battleship Force One, Atlantic Fleet, Sept. 1917; apptd. comdr. Div. 9, Battleship Force, Nov. 1917, for duty with British Grand Fleet; apptd. comdr. U.S. battleships, Apr. 1918; comd. 6th Battle Squadron in North Sea, with British Grand Fleet, 1 yr.; commd. admiral and commander-in-chief Pacific Fleet, July 1, 1919. Awarded D.S.M. and Dewey medal, Spanish War Medal and World War Medal (U.S.); Knight Comdr.

Order of the Bath (British), 1918; Order of Rising Sun (Japan); Grand Cordon of Leopold II (Belgium); Comdr. Legion of Honor (France); El Sol (Peru); El Merite (Chile). Medals for Battle of Manila Bay and Spanish-Am. War. U.S. del. coronation of King George VI, London, May 1938. Presbyn. Mason. Home: Washington, D.C. Died June 7, 1940.

RODMAN, ISAAC PEACE state legislator, army officer; B. South Kingston, R.I., Aug. 18, 1822; s. Samuel and Mary (Peckham) R.; m. Sally Arnold, June 17, 1847, 7 children. Pres., South Kingston Town Council; dir. Wakefield Bank; mem. both branches R.I. Legislature; commd. capt. 2d R.I. Inf., 1861; served in 1st Battle of Bull Run; commd. lt. col., then col., 1861; at Battle of New Bern, South Mountain, 1862; promoted brig. gen., 1862; fatally wounded in Battle of Antietam. Died Hagerstown, Md., Sept. 30, 1862; buried South Kingston, R.I.

RODMAN, T. CLIFFORD investment banker; b. Los Angeles, Feb. 8, 1895; s. Wiloughby and Arabella (Page) R.; student Phillips-Andover Acad., 1915; Yale, 1919; m. Katherine Field, Jan. 28, 1922. With Dillon, Read & Co., investment bankers, 1919-31; became partner Shields & Co., banking house, Chicago, 1931; partner Rodman & Renshaw, Chgo. mem. of the New York Stock Exchange, since 1951; member board of directors Board of Trade, 1940-43 (chmn. bus. conduct com.); gov. Chicago Stock Exchange, 1936-42. Served as lt. naval aviator, U.S. Navy, 1917-19; served with U.S. Navy, 1942-45, retired with rank of comdr.; combat duty on carriers Saratoga, Bunker Hill, Enterprise and Essex Pacific area, 2 1/2 yrs. Awarded Combat Legion of Merit and Comdr. in Chief Pacific commendation. Clubs: Old Elm (Ft. Sheridan, Ill.); Onwentsia, Shoreacres (Lake Forest); Chicago, Attic (Chicago). Home: 370 Moffett Rd., Lake Bluff, Ill. Office: 209 La Salle St., Chgo. 4. Died Oct. 5, 1966.

RODMAN, THOMAS JACKSON inventor, army officer; b. Salem, Ind., July 30, 1815; s. James and Elizabeth (Burton) R.; grad. U.S. Mil. Acad., 1841; m. Martha Black, 1843, 7 children. Commd. capt. U.S. Army, 1855, lt. col., 1856; had original idea of casting guns upon hollow core, cooling inner surface by flow of waters; did experiments resulting in successful manufacture of so-called mammoth and perforated-cake, or prismatic gun powder; inventions approved and adopted by govt., 1859; methods utilized by Russia, Gt. Britain, Prussia; commanded arsenal at Watertown, Mass.; supervised casting of smooth bores and rifled guns during Civil War; brevetted lt. col., col., brig. gen., 1865; comd. Rock Island (Ill.) Arsenal, 1865. Died Rock Island Arsenal, June 7, 1871.

RODNEY, CAESAR AUGUSTUS senator, diplomat; b. Dover, Del., Jan. 4, 1772; s. Thomas and Elizabeth (Fisher) R.; grad. U. Pa., 1789; studied law with Joseph McKean, Phila.; m. Susan Hunn, 15 children. Admitted to Del. bar, 1793; mem. Del. Ho. of Reps. from New Castle County, 1796-1802; mem. U.S. Ho. of Reps. from Del., 8th Congress, 1803-05, a mgr. to conduct impeachment proceedings against John Pickering (judge U.S. Dist. Ct. for N.H.), 1804, for impeachment proceedings against Justice Samuel Chase, 1804; U.S. atty. gen., 1807-11; active in defense of Del., War of 1812, capt. 2d Arty. Co., 1813, mem. Del. Com. of Safety, 1813, maj. bn. of arty., 1815; mem. Del. Senate, 1815, 16; mem. Pres. Monroe's commn. to determine polit. status of new S. Am. republics, 1817; mem. U.S. Ho. of Reps. from Del., 17th Congress, 1821-22; mem. U.S. Senate from Del., Jan. 24, 1822-Jan. 29, 1823; E.E. and M.P. (apptd. by Pres. Monroe) to Argentine Republic, 1823-24. Died Buenos Aires, Argentina, June 10, 1824; buried English Churchyard, Buenos Aires.

RODNEY, GEORGE BRYDGES brig. gen. U.S.A.; b. New Castle, Del., Oct. 17, 1842; s. Hon. George Brydges and Mary J. (Duval) R.; ed. at Phila.; m. Janet Warren, Jan. 27, 1870. Enlisted as pvt. independent co., Pa. arty., Apr. 24, 1861; disch., Aug. 5, 1861; apptd. from Del., 2d lt. 4th U.S. Arty., Aug. 5, 1861; 1st lt., Aug. 5, 1861; capt., Mar. 4, 1869; grad. Arty. Sch., 1869; maj., Nov. 28, 1892; lt. col., Feb. 13, 1899; col. Arty. Corps, Feb. 2, 1901; brig. gen. U.S.A., Aug. 4, 1903; retired at own request after 40 yrs.' service, Aug. 5, 1903. Bvtd. capt., Dec. 31, 1862, for battle of Stone River, Tenn.; maj., Sept. 20, 1863, for battle of Chickamauga, Ga. Died Sept. 21, 1927.

RODRIQUEZ, ABELARDO Mexican army officer, politician; b. Sonora, Mexico, May 12, 1889; studigd in Sonora; m. Aida S. de Rodriquez. Commd. 2d capt., Revolutionary Army, 1913, later lt. col., gen. of a div.; fought in various mil. expdns.; gov. northern dist. of Lower Cal., 1924-28; sec. of industry, commerce, labor; sec. of war and navy, 1932; pres. of Mexico, 1932-34, distinguished his term with land reform. A right wing influence on President Avila Camacho; placed in command of Mexican patrol and mobilized forces in Gulf of Mexico, July 1942. Died Feb. 13, 1967.*

ROE, CHARLES FRANCIS soldier; b. New York, May 1, 1848; s. Stephen Romer and Josephine Augusta (Foster) R.; grad. U.S. Mil. Academy, 1868; m. Katherine Bissell Bogert, July 29, 1874. Commd. 2d lt. 1st Cav., June 15, 1868; transferred to 2d Cav., Oct. 29, 1870; mustered out of service, Dec. 28, 1870; 2d lt. 2d Cav., Dec. 9, 1871; 1st lt., Dec. 20, 1880; regtl. adj., Nov. 2, 1876-Mar. 31, 1878, and Dec. 20, 1880-May 1, 1886; resigned Jan. 31, 1888; brig. gen. vols., June 10, 1898; hon. disch., Sept. 10, 1898. Served on frontier in Indian campaigns, including the Custer massacre, 21 yrs. Engaged in real estate business. Organized, 1889, Troop A, N.G.N.Y., afterwards Squadron A.; apptd. maj., N.G.N.Y., Feb. 1895; maj. gen. by Gov. Black, Feb. 9, 1898; retired on account of age, May 1, 1912. Republican. Episcopalian. Home: New York, N.Y. Died Dec. 1, 1922.

ROE, FRANCIS ASBURY rear admiral U.S.N., retired Oct. 4, 1885; b. Oct. 4, 1823; ed. Elmira Acad.; grad. U.S. Naval Acad., June 1847; m. Eliza J. Snyder, Sept. 1849. Apptd. acting midshipman U.S.N., Oct. 19, 1841; warranted midshipman, Feb. 3, 1842; promoted through grades to rear adm., Nov. 3, 1884. Served in China, Japan, Polar regions Exploring Expdn., Brazil, E. and W. Africa, West Indies, Mediterranean and Great Lakes. As exec. officer of Porpoise, 1854, had an action with 13 heavily armored pirate junks, at Koulan Bay, China, destroying 6 and dispersing the others; exec. officer of Pensacola, 1861, when it passed down the Potomac through nine miles of Confederate batteries, under constant fire; in Farragut's fleet, 1862-63, and in 6 days' battle below New Orleans and may other fights during war; suppressed 2 insurrections on great lakes during Civil war. Comd. at Vera Cruz when Maximilian was executed by Republican army of Mexico; comd. U.S.S. Saxsacus, May 5, 1864, in action with the rebel ram Albemarle, in the sounds of N.C., and defeated the ram. Author: Naval Duties and Discipline, 1864. Died 1901.

ROE, JAMES A. ex-congressman; b. Flushing, N.Y., July 9, 1896; s. James A. and Elizabeth (McDonnell) R.; ed. public, parochial schs., Flushing High Sch.; m. Margaret Farrell, July 16, 1921; children—Capt. James A., Jr. (U.S. Army, Germany), Patrica E., Frances C., John E. Mem. 79th Congress (1945-47), 5th N.Y. District. Served with U.S. Army Air Corps during World War I; commd. lt. and assigned instr. advanced flying at various U.S. fields; lt. col., Corps of Engrs., U.S. Army, since 1943. Mem. bd. govs. Holy Family Hosp., Brooklyn, N.Y. Mem. North Shore Civic Assn., Y.M.C.A., C. of C. (all Flushing). Chmn. Democratic County Com., Dem. Exec. Com. (both Queens County); gov. Nat. Dem. Club of N.Y.; state committeeman 6th Assembly Dist., N.Y. Mem. Am. Legion, Reserve Officers Assn., Flushing Meml. Assn., Am. Soc. Mil. Engrs., Nat. Rifle Assn., Order Daedalians, Holy Name Soc., St. Vincent DePaul Soc., Am. Red Cross. Roman Catholic. K.C., Elk. Home: 3562 167th St., Flushing, L.I., N.Y. Died Apr. 1967.*

ROE, JOSEPH WICKHAM educator; b. Geneva, N.Y., Oct. 3, 1871; s. Alfred Cox and Emma (Wickham) R.; Ph.B., Yale, 1895, M.E., 1907; D.Sc., Middlebury Coll., 1945; m. Nelly Allen, 1902 (died 1903); m. 2d, Mary Sherwood Lambertson, 1915. Instr. and asst. prof. M.E., Yale, 1906-19; dir. study civil aviation U.S. Dept. Commerce and Am. Engring. Council, 1925. Head indsl. engring. dept. N.Y. U., 1921-37; vis. prof. indsl. mgmt. Yale, 1932-38. Served as maj. AS, U.S. Army, World War I. Cons. engr. WPB, Bur. Ordnance; USN, World War II. Awarded Melville medal, 1929; Gilbreth medal, 1939. Decorated Order of White Lion, Czechoslovakia, 1927. Fellow Am. Soc. M.E.; mem. Torch, Berzelius Soc., Soc. Colonial Wars, Newcomen Soc. (London), Masaryk Acad., Prague (hon.), Tau Beta Pi, Sigma Xi. Republican. Conglist. Clubs: Graduate, Yale (N.Y.C.); Cosmos (Washington); Pequot Yacht. Author: Steam Turbines, 1910; English and American Tool Builders, 1916; Mechanical Equipment, 1918; Materials (joint author), 1921; Management's Handbook (joint author), 1924; Factory Equipment (joint author), 1935; Life of James Hartness, 1937; also numerous sci. papers and articles. Address: Southport, Conn. Died Nov. 9, 1960.

ROEBLING, WASHINGTON AUGUSTUS engineer; b. Saxonburg, Pa., May 26, 1837; s. late John A. and Johanna (Herting) R.; bro. of Ferdinand W. R.; C.E., Rensselaer Poly. Inst., 1857; m. Emily Warren, Jan. 18, 1865. Joined father in constrn. of Pittsburgh suspension bridge across Allegheny River; served in Union Army, pvt. to bvtd. col., 1861-65; resigned Jan. 1865, to assist his father in building Cincinnati and Covington suspension bridge. The Brooklyn bridge was undertaken by his father, but his death, July 22, 1869, before the work had been begun, left the entire construction in his hands, and he directed it to completion. Pres. and dir. John A. Roebling's Sons Co., mfrs. iron and steel wire and wire rope, Trenton, N.J. Author: Military Suspension Bridge; etc. Home: Trenton, N.J. Died July 21, 1926.

ROEDER, BERNARD FRANKLIN, ret. naval officer; b. Cumberland, Md. Feb. 4, 1911; s. William Phillip and Anna (Ritter) R.; B.S., U.S. Naval Acad., 1931; student U.S. Naval War Coll., 1949-50; m. Kathleen Fitch, July 11, 1936; children—Bernard Franklin, Franke (Mrs. Hans G. Haimberger), Anne, Kathleen. Commd. ensign U.S. Navy 1931, advanced through grades to vice adm., 1965; various assignments in cruisers, destroyers, also aircraft carriers, prior to 1941; mem. staff U.S. Naval Forces in Philippines, Java and Australia, 1941-42; assigned Navy Dpet., 1943; at sea, 1945-49; comdr. destroyers off Korea, 1950-51; dir. naval communications U.S. Navy, 1961-65; comdr. amphibious force Pacific Fleet, 1965-66, 1st Fleet, 1966-69; ret., 1969. Bd. dirs. San Diego Opera Guild, San Diego A.R.C. Decorated D.S.M., Legion of Merit with 4 oak leaf clusters, Navy Commendation medal, various campaign and unit ribbons; Philippine Presdl. citation; Korean Presdl. citation. Mem. Vets. Wireless Assn. (hon.), I.E.E.E. (sr.), Armed Forces Communications and Electronics Assn. (dir.), U.S. Srs. Golf Assn. Home: Coronado CA Died Sept. 3, 1971.

ROELKER, CHARLES RAFAEL rear admiral U.S.N.; b. Osnabrück, Hanover, Germany. Apptd. from N.Y., 3d asst. engr. U.S.N., 1862; 2d asst. engineer, 1865; 1st asst. engr., 1868; chief engr., Nov. 1890; comdr., March 3, 1899; capt., March 5, 1902. Served on engring. duties at sea and on shore; mem. Bd. Inspection and Survey; rear admiral, Sept. 22, 1903, retired. Home: Washington, D.C. Died 1910.

ROEMER, JOSEPH ret. coll. dean; b. Sugar Grove, Ky., Sept. 25, 1884; s. Adolph and Sallie Trice (Tuck) R.; student So. Normal Sch., Bowling Green, Ky., 1902-06, Western Ky. State Normal Sch., 1906-07, Bowling Green Bus. U., 1907; A.B., U. Ky., 1914; A.M., Peabody Coll. for Tchrs., 1915, Ph.D., 1919; grad. study Columbia, 1924-25; LL.D., Tampa U., 1938; m. Louise Beasley, June 15, 1911; 1 dau., Mary Jo (Mrs. E.N. Higgins). Prin. Peabody Demonstration School, 1914-16; head of dept. edn. Sam Houston State Tchrs. Coll., Huntsville, Tex., 1916-20; prof. secondary edn. and high sch. visitor U. Fla., 1920-31; prof. secondary edn. and dir. instr. Peabody Jr. Coll. and Demonstration Sch., 1931-36; dean Peabody Jr. Coll., 1936-41, dean of the college, 1941-52; helped organize grad. dept. McMurray Coll., Abilene, Tex., 1952-55; mem. faculty, summer schs. Peabody Coll. for Tchrs. 1920, 26, U. Wyo., 1927, 29, U. Mich., 1928, 29, U. Pa., 1930; chief tchr. tng. br., sect. edn. and cultural relations br. OMGUS, Germany, 1948. Dist. supr. S.A.T.C. personnel, World War; maj. O.R.C. Sec. Com. on Secondary Schools, So. Assn. Colls. and Secondary Schools, 1921-36, (pres. 1932); mem. cons. com. Nat. Survey of Secondary Edn.; pres. Officers of Regional Standardizing Agencies. Pres. Fla. YMCA, 1921-31. Mem. N.E.A., Fla. Edn. Assn. (pres. 1926), Phi Beta Kappa, Phi Delta Kappa, Kappa Delta Pi, Phi Kappa Phi, Tau Kappa Alpha, Alpha Phi Epilon, Kappa Phi Kappa (nat. pres., 1933-36), Kappa Sigma, Blue Key (nat. v.p.). Democrat. Presbyn. Mason (K.T.). Kiwanian. Co-author: Extra Curricular Activities, 1926; Readings in Extra Curricular Activities, 1929; Syllabus of a Course in Extra Curricular Activities, 1929; Secondary School Administration, 1932; Basic Student Activities, 1935; Gentleman Commander, 1936; My Activity Book, 1937; Dean of Boys in High School, 1939; The Administration of the Modern Secondary School, 1941. Contbr. to High Sch. Quarterly, Junior-Senior High Sch. Clearing House, Sch. Review, etc. Home: Leesburg, Fla. Died July 1, 1955.

ROETHKE, WILLIAM A(LBERT) C(ARL) lawyer; b. Saginaw, Mich., Aug. 25, 1907; s. Carl L. and Norna M. (Tausend) R.; A.B., U. Mich., 1929, LL.B., 1932; m. Harriet Richardson Kline, May 11, 1933; children—Johanna Leigh (Mrs. Robert Davis Kroger), Gretchen Elise. Admitted to Cal. bar, 1932, since practiced in Los Angeles, with the firm of Lillick, Geary, McHose & Roethke, and predecessor firms, 1932-—, partner, 1946-—. Dir. Dominguez Estate Co., Carson Estate Co. (Los Angeles); Post Pub. Co. (Appleton, Wis.); Green Bay Newspaper Co. (Wis.). Fellow Pierpont Morgan Library. Bd. dirs. Hosp. Good Samaritan Med. Center, Los Angeles. Served lt. to comdr., USNR, 1942-45. Mem. Am., Cal., Los Angeles (trustee 1955-58) bar assns., Maritime Law Assn. U.S., Navy League (pres. Los Angeles council 1949-51, pres. So. Cal. 1952-53), U. Mich. Alumni Assn. (dir. 1955-—). Phi Delta Phi. Republican. Episcopalian. Clubs: University (dir. 1948-—, pres. 1951), California, Beach (dir. 1949-54, v.p. 1954), Los Angeles Country (dir. 1951-56, sec. 1953-56), Stock Exchange (Los Angeles). Home: 1222 Coldwater Canyon Rd., Beverly Hills, Cal. Office: 600 S. Spring St., Los Angeles 14. Deceased.

ROGERS, ALLEN chem. engineer; b. Hampden, Me., May 22, 1876; s. Franklin G. and Georgianna (Higgins) R.; B.S. in Chemistry, U. of Maine, 1897, M.S., 1900; Ph.D., U. of Pa., 1902; m. Maude F. Couillard, Dec. 25, 1897; 1 son, Allen Ellington. Instr. chemistry, U. of Me., 1897-1900; sr. fellow U. of Pa., 1902-03; instr. organic chemistry, same, 1903-04; research chemist Oakes Mfg. Co., L.I. City, N.Y., 1904-05; in charge industrial chemistry, Pratt Inst., Brooklyn, 1905-—, also supervisor course in industrial chem. engring.; consulting practice. Maj. Chem. Warfare Service, U.S.A., in charge industrial relations, May 1917-Jan. 1918. Awarded Grasselli medal, 1920, for work done in connection with fish skins for leather. Democrat. Universalist. Mason. Author: Manual of Industrial Chemistry, 1912, 15, 20, 25. Laboratory Guide of Industrial Chemistry, 1908, 17; Elements of Industrial Chemistry, 1916, 26 (spl. overseas edition, 1919); Practical Tanning, 1922. Home: Brooklyn, N.Y. Died Nov. 4, 1938.

ROGERS, CHARLES CUSTIS naval officer; b. Smyth Co., Va., May 11, 1856; s. Charles G. and Mary W. (Campbell) R.; grad. U.S. Naval Acad., 1876; m. Alice Ashmore Walker, Jan. 3, 1888. Promoted ensign, Apr. 26, 1878; advanced through grades to capt., Oct. 25, 1908. Exec. officer of Sesolute during Spanish-Am. War; comdt. Naval Sta., Guantanamo, Cuba, 1904-06; hydrographer, Navy Dept., 1906-08; comd. Milwaukee, 1908-09; comd. Washington, 1909-10; Navy Yard, Norfolk, 1910-11; comdt., Navy Yard, Portsmouth, N.H., 1911-14; retired on account of physical disability, with rank of rear admiral, Apr. 27, 1914. Awarded medal for action off Santiago de Cuba; clasp for action off Manzanillo, Cuba; medal for Spanish-Am. War. Home: Winchester, Va. Died Dec. 4, 1917.

ROGERS, DAVID CAMP psychologist; b. New Britain, Conn., May 25, 1878; s. Daniel Owen and Emma Jane (Camp) R.; student Amherst, 1895-97; A.B., Princeton, 1899; student Hartford Theol. Sem., 1899-1901; A.M., Harvard, 1902, Ph.D., 1903; m. Grace Gladys Gage, 1907 (div.); 1 son, David Camp (dec.); m. 2d, Gerda Carlson Fay, 1940. Asst. in philosophy, 1902-03, asst. and instr. social ethics, 1903-09, asst. in applied psychology, 1908-09, Harvard; asst. prof. psychology U. Kan., 1909-14; prof. psychology Smith Coll., 1914-42. Fellow A.A.A.S.; mem. Am. Psychol. Assn. Capt., San. Corps U.S. Army, Sept. 1918-May 1919. Address: 26 Pine St., Middletown, Conn. Died Oct. 13, 1959.

ROGERS, DONALD AQUILLA, judge; b. Evansville, Ind., Feb. 17, 1901; s. Lon D. and Florence (Barnhill) R.; J.D., Ind. U., 1927; m. Marie Woolery, Aug. 20, 1924; children—Barbara (Mrs. John H. Houseworth), Jack, David. Admitted to Ind. bar, 1924; dep. clk. Monroe County, 1923-27; pros. atty. 10th Jud. Circuit Ind., 1928-29; with firm Rogers & Steckley, 1928-30, Blair & Rogers, 1930-33; judge 10th Jud. Circuit Ind., 1933-43; pvt. practice, Bloomington, 1946-55, partner with son, 1955-65; judge Monroe Superior Court, Bloomington, from 1965. Dir. Monroe County State Bank, Bloomington, Workingmens Fed. Savs. and Loan Assn., Bloomington. Chmn. Monroe County UN Com., 1951-52; pres. White River council Boy Scouts Am., 1942-43. Mem. Ind. Ho. of Reps. from Monroe County, 1949-50; chmn. Monroe County Central Democratic Com., 1960-62. Trustee Ind. U., 1963-66; bd. dirs. Ind. Sch. Religion, from 1955. Served to maj. AUS, 1943-46, ETO. Mem. Am. Judicature Soc., Am. Law Inst., Ind. Hist. Soc., Ind. Bar Assn. (bd. mgrs. 1936-38), Phi Delta Phi, Phi Delta Theta, Order of Coif. Mem. Christian Ch. (past chmn. ofcl. bd., elder). Kiwanian (past pres. Bloomington) Mason. Home: Bloomington IN Died Oct. 19, 1969.

ROGERS, EDITH NOURSE congresswoman; b. Saco, Me., 1881; d. Franklin and Edith Francis (Riversmith) Nourse; grad. Rogers Hall Sch. (Lowell, Mass.), Madame Julien's Sch., Paris, France; hon. M.A., Tufts and Bates colls.; LL.D., Washington Coll. of Law, Lowell Techn. Inst.; m. John J. Rogers, 1907 (died Mar. 28, 1925). Red Cross Worker Walter Reed Hosp., 1918-22. Rep. presdl. elector, 1924; elected mem. 69th Congress, 5th Mass. Dist., June 30, 1925, at spl. election, for unfinished term of husband, ending Mar. 3, 1927, reëlected mem. 70th to 86th Congress, from same dist. Apptd. personal rep. of President Harding, in care of disabled soldiers, Apr. 1922, reapptd. by President Coolidge, 1923, and by President Hoover, Mar. 1929. Served overseas, 1917; with Am. Red Cross in care of the disabled, 1918-22. Del. to Inter-Am. Conf., Mexico City. Recipient Am. Legion's D.S.M. President of board of trustees Rogers Hall School, Lowell, Mass. Member Women's Overseas Service League, Am. Legion Auxiliary. Republican. Episcopalian. Clubs: Congressional, Sulgrave (Washington, D.C.). Home: 354 Andover St., Lowell, Mass. Died Sept. 10, 1960; buried Lowell Cemetery.

ROGERS, ERNEST ELIAS b. Waterford, Conn., Dec. 6, 1866; s. Elias Perkins and Lucy Almira (Smith) R.; desc. James Rogers, New London, Conn., born 1615; grad. Bulkeley High Sch., New London, 1884; m. Fanny Gorton, Oct. 28, 1896; 1 son, Ernest Gorton. Began with Brainerd & Armstrong, silk mfrs., 1884; with Arnold Rudd, wholesale flour and grain, 1905, pres. Arnold Rudd Co., Mystic Grain & Oil Co., etc.; pres. Winthrop Trust Co., 1922; mayor of New London, 1915-18; treas. State of Conn., 1925-29; lt. gov. State of Conn., term 1929, 30 inclusive. Mem. Coast Arty., 1902-09, retiring as capt. Mem. Selective Service Bd., 1917-19; mem. present Selective Service Bd. since 1940. Former pres. Conn. State Chamber Commerce; hon. pres. New London County Historical Soc. (pres. 25 yrs.); past pres. Am. Bapt. Home Mission Soc., New York; trustee Eastern Bapt. Theol. Sem., Phila.; mem. Nat. Soc. S.A.R. (former pres. gen.), Conn. Hist. Soc. (v.p.). Republican. Baptist. Mason. Author: Sesquicentennial of the Battle of Groton Heights and the Burning of New London, 1931; Connecticut's Naval Office at New London During the War of the American Revolution, 1933; New London's Participation in Connecticut's Tercentenary, 1935; Cedar Grove Cemetery, Vol. 1, 1941. Home: 605 Pequot Av. Office: Winthrop Trust Co., New London, Conn. Died Jan. 28, 1945.

ROGERS, EUSTACE BARRON paymaster gen. U.S.N.; b. San Francisco, May 29, 1855; s. Robert Clay and Eliza Hamilton (Ritchie) R.; ed. Lehigh (Pa.) U., U. of California; m. Anna N. Alexander, Jan. 17, 1882 (died 1908); m. 2d, Marguerite Bosch, of Spa, Belgium, May 22, 1913. Apptd. from Calif. to U.S.N., Mar. 3, 1879; p.m., May 24, 1894; pay insp., Sept. 21, 1902; pay dir., Mar. 13, 1905; p.m. gen. with rank of rear admiral, Nov. 1, 1906, and chief Bur. of Supplies and Accounts; retired, June 30, 1910. Served on U.S.S. Monterey in Spanish-Am. War; was present at taking of Manila. On duty at Navy Yard, Bremerton, Wash., and with U.S. Shipping Bd., 1917, and gen. insp., Supply Corps, on Pacific Coast, to Jan. 1918. Home: Washington, D.C. Died Mar. 5, 1929.

ROGERS, GEORGE BARTLETT lawyer, banker; b. Chgo., June 10, 1909; s. George Thomas and Belle (Bartlett) R.; student Lake Forest Coll., 1926-28; B.S., Lafayette Coll., 1931; J.D., Northwestern U., 1934; m. Margaret Waller, Aug. 19, 1938; children—Lynn Waller, George Thomas II, Anne Bartlett. Admitted To Ill. bar, 1934; practiced in Chgo., 1934—; mem. firm Tenney, Sherman, Bentley & Guthrie, 1934-55; v.p., asso. gen. counsel First Nat. Bank, Chgo., 1955-63, v.p., gen. counsel, 1963—. Instr. Indsl. Mgmt. Inst., Lake Forest Coll., 1950-55; sect. leader law U. Wis. Summer Sch. Banking, 1960—. Served from lt. (j.g.) to lt. comdr., USNR, 1942-45. Decorated Bronze Star with combat V. Mem. Am., Ill., Chgo. bar assns., Am. Judicature Soc., Lake Forest Coll. Alumni Assn. (pres. 1954-55), Lafayette Coll. Midwest Alumni Assn. (pres. 1950-58). Presbyn. (deacon). Clubs: Law, Legal (pres. 1964-65), Executives, Bankers, Economics, Curling, Arts, Attic (Chgo.); Winter (Lake Forest, Ill.). Home: Mettawa, Ill. Office: 38 S. Dearborn St., Chgo. 60690. Died July, 1967.

ROGERS, GORDON B. army officer; b. Manchester, Tenn., Aug. 22, 1901; s. Jesse Rice and Florence Wilburn (Byrom) R.; student U. Tenn., 1919-20; B.S., U.S. Mil. Acad., 1924; grad. Cav. Sch., troop officers course, 1929, advanced equitation course, 1930, Command and Gen. Staff Sch., 1939; m. Mary Louise Watson, Jan. 20, 1934; children—Gordon Byrom, Susan Louise, Mary Alice. Commd. 2d lt., U.S. Army, 1924, advanced through grades to lt. gen.; served in Australia and New Guinea, 1942-43; asst. chief of staff (G-2), Hdqrs. Army Ground Forces, Washington, 1944-45; chief tng. br. Office of Dir. Intelligence, War Dept. Gen. staff, 1945-46; regt. comdr., 12th, 5th cav. regts., Japan, 1946-49; dir. dept. intelligence Command and Gen. Staff Coll., 1949-50; mem. faculty, acting dep. comdt. Army War Coll., 1950-52; asst. div. comdr. 40th Inf. Div. in Korea, 1952-53; chief Korean Mil. Adv. Group, 1953; comdg. gen. 3d Armored Div., Ft. Knox, Ky., 1953-55; Office Chief of Staff, Dept. of Army, 1955-56; comdg. gen. So. Area Command, A.U.S., Europe, 1956-58; dep. comdg. gen. 7th Army, 1957-58; lt. gen. comdg. VII Corps, 1958-59; dep. comdg. gen. for development USCONARC, 1959—. Decorated D.S.C. (Oak-Leaf Cluster), Silver Star (Oak-Leaf Cluster), Legion of Merit (two Oak-Leaf Clusters), Purple Heart, Bronze Star (Oak-Leaf Cluster); Taeguk Distinguished Mil. Service Medal with silver star (Korea); Commendation Ribbon with Oak Leaf Cluster and Combat Inf. Badge. Home: Morrison, Tenn. Office: Dep. Comdg. Gen. for Development, U.S. Continental Army Command, Fort Monroe, Va. Died July 4, 1967.

ROGERS, HARRY LOVEJOY army officer; b. Washington, D.C., Jan. 29, 1867. Commd. maj. p.m., May 2, 1898; lt. col. dep. p.m. gen., Apr. 15, 1907; col. asst. p.m. gen., Mar. 4, 1909; brig. gen. Q.M. Corps, N.A., Aug. 5, 1917-Mar. 15, 1918; brig. gen. Q.M. Corps, U.S.A., Feb. 26, 1918; q.m. gen. with rank of maj. gen., July 22, 1918, term of 4 yrs. Served under Gen. Funston, in Vera Cruz Expdn., Apr. 1914; in charge later of supply problems of expdn. under Gen. Pershing, punitive expdn., Mexico, 1916; chief q.m. with A.E.F. in France, 1917-July 1918. Died Dec. 12, 1925.

ROGERS, HENRY HUDDLESTON capitalist; b. N.Y. City, Dec. 28, 1879; s. Henry Huddleston and Abbie Palmer (Gifford) R.; prep. edn. Berkeley Sch. and Browning Sch., New York; student Columbia, 1901; grad. Sch. of Fire, Ft. Sill, Okla., 1913; m. Mary Benjamin, Nov. 7, 1900; children—Mary Millicent, Henry Huddleston; m. 2d, Mrs. Basil Miles, 1929; m. 3d, Mrs. Pauline Van Der Voort Dresser, Aug. 28, 1933. Successively vice-pres. and gen. mgr. Atlantic Coast Electric R.R., Staten Island Midland R.R.; pres. Richmond Light & R.R. Co.; v.p. Virginian Ry. Co. Was 2d and 1st lt. and capt. inf., N.Y.N.G., 1904-09; 1st lt. engrs., 1909-11, capt., 1911, advanced to colonel 1st Field Arty., 1913, and directed to reorganize regt.; maj., later lt. col. arty., U.S.A., World War; served on Mexican Border, 1916, later in comd. 3d F.A., O.T. Regt., and in Aisne-Marne offensive, July 1918, and Oise offensive, action at Veste, France. Decorated D.S.M. (U.S.), Croix de Guerre with Palm (France). Home: Southampton, L.I., N.Y. Died July 25, 1935.

ROGERS, HERBERT WESLEY psychologist; b. Kennebunkport, Me., June 16, 1890; s. John Zadock and Hattie Elizabeth (Morey) R.; B.S., Columbia, 1915, A.M., 1916, Ph.D., 1921; certificate U. Paris, 1918-19; m. Margaret E. Cobb, Apr. 8, 1922; children—Charles Morey, Virginia Elizabeth, Evertson, Prudence. Psychologist, Charles William Stores, Bklyn., 1916-17; instr. psychology Yale, 1920-23; research asst. prof. psychology U. Minn., 1923-24; prof. psychology Lafayette Coll., since 1924. Served as 1st lt. coast arty. U.S. Army, 1917-19. Pub. panel mem., arbitrator Regional W.L.B., 1943-45; arbitrator U.S. Conciliation Service, 1943-46, Fed. Mediation and Conciliation service since 1948. Panel arbitrators Am. Arbitration Assn.; Pa. State, N.J. State rosters of arbitrators; mem. Nat. Acad. Arbitrators. Dir. Community Chest 1941; Council Social Agys. (pres. 1946); vice chmn. Housing Authority of Easton, 1946. Registered pub. sch. psychologist Pa. Fellow A.A.A.S., Assn. Applied Psychologists; mem. Am. Psychol. Assn., Eastern Psychol. Assn. (sec. 1936-39), Assn. Cons. Psychologists, Assn. Psychologists to Study Social Issues, Am. Statis. Assn., Assn. Clin. Psychologists, Children's Aid Soc. Northampton County (pres. 1938-41), U.S. Com. for Care European Children (pres.), Easton Peace Action Assn. (sec), 1931-1938, Lehigh Valley Child Guidance Clinic (sec.), 1928-1941, Lehigh Valley Mental Health Conf. (sec.), Rev. Bd., State Employment Relief Bd., Phi Gamma Delta. Author: Some Empirical Tests in Vocational Selection, 1922. Contbr. to psychol. and ednl. publs. Home: R.F.D. 1, Easton, Pa. Died Jan. 1964.

ROGERS, HORATIO jurist; b. Providence, R.I., May 18, 1836; s. Horatio and Susan (Curtis) R.; grad. Brown U., 1855; LL.D., Trinity Coll., 1896; m. Lucia Waterman, January 28, 1861; m. 2d, Emily P. Smith, Oct. 6, 1869. Studied law in office of Hon. Thomas A. Jenckes, Providence, and at Harvard Law School; admitted to R.I. bar, Jan. 1858; served in Civil war, 1st lt. to maj., 3d R.I. heavy arty.; col. 11th R.I. vols.; col. 2d R.I. vols., and bvtd. brig. gen. U.S. vols. Successively justice police court, Providence, mem. and part of time pres. common council, Providence; mem. gen. assembly of R.I., 1864-67 and 1888-89; atty. gen. of R.I.; justice Supreme Court R.I., 1891-1903. Chmn. Record Commn., city of Providence. Author: Private Libraries of Providence, 1878; Mary Dyer of Rhode Island, the Quaker martyr, 1896. Edited Hadden's Journal and Orderly Books, 1884. Address: Providence, R.I. Died 1904.

ROGERS, JOHN WILLIAM journalist, playwright, editor; b. Dallas, Sept. 27, 1894; s. John William and Lena (Wells) R.; student Terrill Prep. School, Dallas, Texas; A.B., Dartmouth, spl. work Columbia. Associated with Daily Times Herald, Dallas, for many years as feature writer, music and dramatic critic, book editor; lit. editor Chgo. Sun, since May 1946; now columnist Daily Times-Herald. Author, Judge Lynch, Saved, Bumble-Puppy and other one-act plays; Roam Though I May! Where The Dear Antelope Play (3 act play); The Lusty Texans of Dallas (Soc. Am. Series), 1951; plays in numerous anthologies. Home: 4600 Lakeside Dr., Dallas 5. Office: Dallas Times Herald, Dallas 1. Died Nov. 1965.

ROGERS, MARVIN CARSON, chem. engr.; b. North St. Paul, Minn., May 13, 1904; s. Charles Wesley and Marie (Rufenacht) R.; B.S., U. Minn., 1926; M.S., U. Mich., 1927, Ph.D. 1929; m. Evelyn Beatrice Zehner, June 11, 1932; children—John William, Marvin Carson. Engr., Whiting-Swenson Co., Ann Arbor, Mich., 1929-32; group leader research Standard Oil Co. (Ind.), Whiting, 1932-37; asst. prof. chem. engring. U. Minn., 1938-40; dir. research R. R. Donnelley &Sons Co., Chgo., 1940-57; exec. dir. Photoengravers Research Inst., Chgo. and Park Forest, Ill., 1957-68; cons., dir. Chgo. Paper Testing Lab., 1957-68; corp. dir. Printing Plate Supply Co., Chgo.; mem. adv. bd. ABC Industries, Inc., Paterson, N.J. Mem. exec. bd. Calumet Council, Boy Scouts of Am., 1952-68, Silver Beaver award, 1954, nat. council rep., Cal. Council, 1959-64. Mem. graphic arts adv. com. Carnegie Inst. Tech., 1959-68. Served to lt. col. Chem. Corps, AUS, 1943-45. Fellow Inst. of Printing; mem. T.A.P.P.I., Am. Chem. Soc. (dir., chmn. 1946-60), A.A.A.S., Am. Inst. Chem. Engrs., Tech. Assn. for Graphic Arts (pres. 1950-51). Mason. Home: Flossmoor IL Died Mar. 13, 1968.

ROGERS, MCLAIN surgeon; b. Clyde, N.C., June 5, 1874; s. James Jackson and Amanda (Stillwell) R.; student Weaverville (N.C.) Coll. 1 yr.; M.D., Atlanta Coll. Physicians and Surgeons, 1902; m. Bessie E. Alexander, Apr. 27, 1907. Practiced at Geary, Okla., 1903-09, Clinton, 1909—. Fellow Am. Coll. Surgeons; mem. A.M.A., Southern Surgical Congress, Clinical Congress of Surgeons of N.A., Okla. State Med. Assn. (pres. 1922-23). Served as capt. M.C., U.S. Army, June 7-Dec. 16, 1918. Democrat. Methodist. Mason (Shriner). Home: Clinton, Okla. Died Jan. 29, 1960.

ROGERS, PHILIP FLETCHER surgeon; b. Milwaukee, Aug. 14, 1870; s. George James and Mary M. (Hanson) R.; A.B., Yale, 1894; M.D., Northwestern U., 1897; interne Mercy Hosp., Chicago, 1897-99; m. Cornelia Meinhardt, Oct. 25, 1900; children—Philip M., Antoinette M., Albert Francis. Practiced, Milwaukee, 1899—. Surgeon to Emergency, Mt. Sinai, and Columbia hosps. of Milwaukee. Conglist. Commd. capt. Med. Dept. U.S.A., July 10, 1917; on surg. staff Base Hosp. No. 22, in France, June 15, 1918-Mar. 19, 1919. Maj. O.R.C., 1922. Home: Milwaukee, Wis. Died June 20, 1928.

ROGERS, ROBERT army officer; b. Methuen, Mass., Nov. 7, 1731; s. James and Mary R.; m. Elizabeth Browne, June 30, 1761, 1 child. Entered N.H. Regt., 1755; capt. William Johnson's Crown Point Expdn.; scouted enemy forces and positions; apptd. capt. of an independent co. of rangers, 1756; served with generals Loudon at Halifax, 1757, Abercombie at Ticonderoga, 1758, Amherst at Crown Point, 1759; destroyed St. Francis Indians in raid, Crown Point; in final campaign about Montreal, 1760; served as capt. of an independent co. against Cherokee Indians in S.C., 1761; supt. So. Indians; capt. of a N.Y. independent co., 1763; aided in defense of Detroit against Pontiac; involved in illicit trading with Indians; sailed for Eng. to solicit preferment, 1765; apptd. to command Ft. Michilimackinac; arrested on charge of treasonable dealings with French, acquitted for lack of evidence; returned to Eng., put in debtors prison, rescued by brother, 1769; returned to Am., 1775; imprisoned as spy by George Washington, 1776; escaped to British; fled to Eng., 1780; kept jour. from Sept. 21, 1766-July 3, 1767 printed by William L. Clements in Proceedings of the Am. Antiquarian Soc., Oct. 1918. Died London, Eng., May 18, 1795; buried St. Mary's, Newington, Eng.

ROGERS, WALTER STOWELL b. Chgo., Oct. 25, 1877; s. Charles A. and Ella (Stowell) R.; Ph.B., U. Chgo., 1901; LL.B., Chgo. Kent Coll. Law, 1905; m. Edith Carey, 1903; children—Lora Elizabeth, Ruth Louise, Jane Cornelia. Asst. to v.p., later asst. to pres. Crane Co., Chgo., 1903-14; pub. Washington Herald, 1919-20. Dir. Div. Fgn. Cable News Service, Com. on Pub. Information, 1917-19; adviser Am. Delegation, Peace Conf., Paris, 1919; del. to Internat. Conf. on Elec. Communications, 1920-22; tech. adviser on elec. communications Am. Delegation to Conf. on Limitation of Armament, 1921-22. Lectr., Army War Coll., 1923, 24, 26, Post Grad. Sch. U.S. Naval Acad., 1926. Dir. Inst. Current World Affairs 1926-59, dir. emeritus, 1959-—. Mem. Delta Tau Delta. Lectured on elec. communications, U. Chgo., summers, 1924-25. Clubs: Cosmos (Washington); University (Chgo.). Home: Shelton Towers Hotel. Office: 366 Madison Av., N.Y.C. 17. Died Oct. 23, 1965; buried Columbia Gardens, Arlington, Va.

ROGERS, WEAVER HENRY corporate financing; b. Pittsburgh, Pa., Nov. 9, 1876; s. Joseph Butcher and Margaret Thompson (Matthews) R.; desc. of Colonial ancestry; grad. U. of Pittsburgh, 1896; m. Analdean Friebertshauser, May 22, 1901; children—Dorothy Analdean (Mrs. Lloyd Hornbostel), Virginia Emily (Mrs. Nathan H. White). Became sec. and treas. of the Pittsburgh and Birmingham Traction Co., 1898; later connected with Mellon pub. utility corps. and with Gulf Refining Co.; an organizer Pittsburgh & Butler Ry. Co., Andrews Steel Co., Weaver H. Rogers & Co., etc.; served as v.p. underlying pub. utility corps. of West Penn Co. Maj. Ordnance Dept., U.S.A., World War; with Gen. staff at Tours, France, 1918; mustered out as lt. col., 1919; served as emergency adminstrn. chief, Watertown (Mass.) Arsenal. Pres. 14th Ward Bd. of Edn. Republican. Episcopalian; trustee and sec. bd. Ch. Home Assn. of W.Pa.; trustee Clergy Life Ins. Assn., Roselia Foundling Asylum and Maternity Hosp.; trustee Diocesan Council of Pittsburgh; pres. Ch. Club of Western Pa.; vestryman Ch. of the Redeemer, Mason. Home: Pittsburgh, Pa. Died Feb. 17, 1936.

ROGERS, WILLIAM LOVELAND, air force officer; b. Larchwood, Ia., Dec. 29, 1911; s. William B. and Olivia B. (Loveland) R.; student U. S.D., 1929-30; B.S., U.S. Mil. Acad., 1934; M.S. in Engring., Cornell U., 1939; m. Dolores Stack, Mar. 15, 1947; children—Jonathan S., Martha O., James B., Genevieve L. Commd. 2d lt. U.S. Army, 1934, advanced through grades to maj. gen. USAF, 1961; comdr. 1141st Engr. Combat Group, 1943-46, 347th Engr. Gen. Service Regt., 1946-47; engr. 10th Air Force, 1947-49; student Air War Coll., 1949-50; chief air installations div., D/Mat. Hdqrs. Mil. Air Transp. Service, 1950-51, dep. dir. materials Hdqrs., 1951-52; dir. air installations Air Research and Devel. Command, 1952-54, asst. dep. comdr., supr. operations, 1954; asst. devel. programming Hdqrs. USAF, 1954-58; vice comdr. Air Force Missile Test Center, Cape Canaveral, Florida, 1958-61; commander Arnold Engring. Devel. Center, Air Force Systems Command, 1961-68. Decorated Silver Star, Legion of Merit with oak leaf cluster, Commendation ribbon with oak leaf cluster. Mem. Am. Rocket Soc., Soc. Am. Mil. Engrs., Beta Theta Pi. Club: N.Y. Athletic Club. Home: Tullahoma TN Died Sept. 1968.

ROGERS, WILLIAM OSCAR educator; b. New York, Apr. 12, 1825; s. Andrew Yelverton and Jane (Phillips) R.; entered New York Univ., 1845, Williams Coll., Mass., 1847 in class of 1849, but did not graduate on account of ill health; went South, 1848; (LL.D. from Univ. of Ohio, 1884); m. 1st, Mary Williams Martin; 2d, Nov., 1858, Isabella Osgood, Norwich, Conn. Teacher of English literature, 1850-56; supt. public school, New Orleans, 1856-61; in C.S.A. as capt., 1861-65; supt. public schools, New Orleans, 1865-84; pres. Sylvester-Larned Inst., 1870-75; dir. public school, 1884-97; one of 15 administrators named by Paul Tulane to establish univ.; sec. and treas. Tulane Univ., 1884-1901; acting pres. from death of Pres. Johnston, July, 1899-Oct. 1, 1900; resigned. Democrat. Deceased.

ROGERS, WILLIAM PENNOCK brig. gen. U.S.A.; b. Harford County, Md., Sept. 16, 1842; s. Elisha Hartshorne and Anna (Pennock) R.; ed. Aldino pub. sch.; m. Dee Browning, 1878. Corporal Co. H, 7th Md. Inf., Aug. 21, 1862; discharged, May 4, 1865; apptd. from Md., 2d lt. 44th U.S. Inf., July 28, 1866; transferred to 17th Inf., May 27, 1869; 1st lt., Oct. 3, 1872; capt., Dec. 23, 1884; maj. 20th Inf., Dec. 15, 1898; lt. col. 29th Inf., Feb. 2, 1901; transferred to 22d Inf., Mar. 21, 1901; col. 30th Inf., June 28, 1902; brig. gen., Apr. 20, 1903; retired at own request, over 30 yrs.' service, Apr. 21, 1903. Served in Army of the Potomac; participated in battle of Spottsylvania C.H., May 8, 1864, where was wounded, losing left arm; served in South, 1866-70, in West, 1870-94; wounded in affair with Sioux Indians, on Heart River, Dak., Oct. 3, 1872. Address: San Antonio, Tex. Died May 12, 1916.

ROHDE, RUTH BRYAN (RUTH BRYAN OWEN; MRS. BORGE ROHDE) (ro'da); b. Jacksonville, Ill., Oct. 2, 1885; d. William Jennings and Mary Elizabeth (Baird) Bryan; student Monticello Sem., Godfrey, Ill., 1899-1901, University of Neb., 1901-03; LL.D., Rollins College, Fla., 1927, Woman's College of Fla., 1935; L.H.D., Russell Sage Coll., 1931, also L.H.D., Temple University; LL.D., Denison University, 1946; married 2d, Reginald Owen (major Royal Engineers, Brit. Army), May 3, 1910 (died Dec. 1927); children—Ruth (Mrs. Jonas Reiner), John, Reginald, Helen (Mrs. Harrison Brown); m. 3d, Capt. Borge Rohde, July 11, 1936 (mem. Danish Royal Guards, also Gentleman-in-waiting to King Christian X of Denmark). Lyceum and Chautauqua lecturer, 1919-28; mem. 71st and 72d Congresses (1929-33), 4th Fla. Dist.; E.E. and M.P. to Denmark, Apr. 1933-36; alternate U.S. rep. to 4th Gen. Assembly of U.N., Oct. 1949. Served as nurse, vol. aid detachment, Brit. Army, Egypt-Palestine campaign, World War. V.p. bd. of regents U. Miami (Fla.), 1925-28, mem. faculty, 1926-28. Member Beta Sigma Phi, Business & Professional Woman's Club, D.A.R., Women's Overseas League, Delta Gamma, Chi Delta Phi. Democrat. Episcopalian. Author: Elements of Public Speaking, 1931; Leaves from a Greenland Diary, 1935; Denmark Caravan, 1936; The Castle in the Silver Wood, 1939; Picture Tales from Scandinavia, 1939; Look Forward Warrior, 1943; Caribbean Caravel, 1949. Home: Wolden Rd., Ossinning, N.Y. Died July 27, 1954; buried St. Albans Ch., Copenhagen, Denmark.

ROHRER, KARL commodore U.S.N.; b. Am Randen-Blumberg, Baden, Germany, Jan. 28, 1848; s. Philip and Anna Maria (Durst) R.; came to U.S., 1857; grad. U.S. Naval Acad., 1869; m. Charlotte Haight Arthur, Apr. 24, 1877. Apptd. midshipman U.S.N., 1869; promoted through various grades to commodore and retired, June 30, 1906. Home: Washington, D.C. Died May 29, 1913.

ROLER, EDWARD OSCAR FITZALAN physician; b. Winchester, Va., Mar. 6, 1835; s. Peter W. and Catherine (Carson) R.; grad. Asbury (now De Pauw) Univ., 1855; Rush Med. Coll., Chicago, 1859; student Univ. of Berlin, 1865-66; m. Berea, O., Aug. 27, 1867, Doretta J. Doering. Enlisted May, 1861, and served as surgeon 55th Ill. vols., becoming med. dir. 15th Army Corps, 1863. Prof. emeritus, med. dept. Northwestern Univ. Mem. Chicago Med. Soc., Chicago Commandery Loyal Legion. Address: 218 E. 60th St., Chicago.

ROLLER, CHARLES S., JR., school adminstr.; b. Fort Defiance, Va., Sept. 8, 1879; s. Charles S. and Rosabelle (Moorman) R.; grad. Augusta Mil. Acad.; B.S., M.S., Va. Mil. Inst., 1901; m. Janet Stephenson, Sept. 8, 1909; children—Charles III (dec.). Football coach, Furman Univ., 1901-02, Va. Mil. Inst., 1907-08, Washington and Lee Univ., 1908; co-prin. Augusta Mil. Acad., Fort Defiance, Va., 1905, now supt., owner. Served with A.E.F., 314th Sanitary Train, 89th division, World War I; colonel Virginia Nat. Guard; captain Co. 8, Virginia Minute Men during World War II; col. Va. res. militia. Mem. Sons of Confederate Veterans, American Legion, Veterans of Foreign Wars, Kappa Alpha, Phi Beta Gamma. Republican. Presbyterian. Club: Kiwanis (lt. gov. internat.). Address: Augusta Military Academy, Fort Defiance, Va. Died Mar. 16, 1963; buried Augusta Stone Presbyn. Ch. Cemetery, Ft. Defiance.

ROLLER, ROBERT DOUGLAS JR. M.D.; b. Richmond, Va., May 24, 1879; s. Robert Douglas and Caroline (Booker) R.; A.B., W.Va. U., 1900; M.D., Univ. Coll. of Medicine (now Med. Coll. of Va.), Richmond, Va., 1905; unmarried. Began practice at Charleston, W.Va., 1920; chief of med. staff, Charleston Gen. Hosp.; med. dir. Hillcrest Sanatorium; consultant U.S. Vets. Bur., Charleston. Served as maj. Med. Corps, U.S.A., 1918-19; later major Medical Corps, W.Va. Nat. Guard. Democrat. Episcopalian. Home: Charleston, W.Va. Died Aug. 10, 1935.

ROMBAUER, RODERICK EMILE lawyer; b. Seleszto, Hungary, May 9, 1833; s. Theodore and Bertha (Rombauer) R.; ed. pvt. instrn., pvt. schs., and Hungarian colls.; LL.B., Dane Law Sch., Cambridge, Mass., 1858; m. Dec. 28, 1865, Belleville, Ill., Augusta Koerner. Vol. student guard in Hungary, 1848; capt. inf. U.S.V., 1861; judge Law Commrs., Ct., St. Louis, 1863-66; judge Circuit Ct., St. Louis Co., 1867-71; presiding judge, St. Louis Ct. Appeals, 1885-97; atty. Bd. of Edn., St. Louis, 1872-79 and 1897-1903; prof. law and equity, Washington Univ., St. Louis, 1871-73, 1894-99, 1904-06. V.p., 1869-70, pres., 1870-73, Law Library Assn. of St. Louis. Contbr. to Cyclo. Law Procedure. Author: The History of a Life, 1903 01. Residence: 4119 Magnolia Av. Office: 611 Roe Bldg., St. Louis.

ROMODA, JOSEPH J. educator; b. Chgo., Nov. 13, 1907; s. Edward and Anna (Kriston) R.; B.S. magna cum laude, St. Lawrence U., 1933, M.S. in Edn., 1937; Ph.D., Syracuse U., 1942; m. Ruth E. Whitnall, Aug. 15, 1941; children—Thomas Halsey, Alan Joseph. Reporter Lorain (O.) Times-Herald, 1925-27; sales and indsl. work, 1927-29; tchr. high sch. sci. and coach, Webster, N.Y., 1933-37; instr. and asst. prof. Sch. Edn., Syracuse U., 1938-43, chmn. admissions Sch. Edn., 1941-43; prof. and head dept. of edn., dir. summer session, dir. extension services St. Lawrence U., 1946-49, dean coll. letters and scis. since 1949; dir. N.Y. State Winter Sports Sch., 1946-49. Dir. First Nat. Bank, Canton, N.Y. Exec. sec. Com. on Adult Civic Edn., N.Y. State Council Supts., 1939; dir. Watertown Collegiate Center; mem. N.Y. State Citizens' Com. of One Hundred for Children and Youth; del. Mid-Century White House Conf. on Children and Youth. Served as comdr. USNR, 1943-46; naval aviation observer (nav.); officer-in-charge operational tng. and instr. tng. officer, 3d Naval Dist.; Iwo Jima and Okinawa campaigns. Mem. St. Laurence Valley Assn. C.'s of C. (dir.), Beta Theta Pi (v.p.), Pi Delta Epsilon, Tau Kappa Alpha, Kixioc, Phi Delta Kappa, Phi Beta Kappa. Universalist. Home: 9 University Av., Canton, N.Y. Died Dec. 19, 1966.

ROMSEY, CHARLES CARY sculptor; b. Buffalo, N.Y., Aug. 29, 1879; s. Laurence Dana and Jennie (Cary) R.; A.B., Harvard, 1902; art student, Paris, 1902-06; m. Mary Harriman, May 26, 1910. Bronze medal, San Francisco Expn., 1916; exhibited "The Pagan," at Met. Mus. of Art, New York, 1921; executed frieze on arch. Manhattan Bridge, N.Y.; soldiers and sailors memorial, Brownsville (Brooklyn); statue of Pizarro, San Francisco Expn., etc. Served as capt. Hdqrs. Troop, 77th Div., and 40th Engrs., World War. Home: Westbury, L.I., N.Y. Died Sept. 21, 1922.

ROOP, JAMES CLAWSON, b. Upland, Pa., Oct. 3, 1888; s. Albert A. and Mary (Clawson) R.; grad. Blight School, Phila., Pa., 1905; B.S. in E.E., U. of Pa., 1909; m. Rebecca Haigh, Mar. 7, 1929. Instr. in elec. engring., U. of Pa., 1909-10; with Phila. and West Chester Traction Co., 1910-15; cons. work under Prof. G. F. Sever, N.Y. City, 1915-16; in charge constrn. and testing work, J. G. White Management Corp., 1916-17, gen. supervision and spl. reporting on pub. utilities, 1919-21; with Bur. of Budget, Washington, D.C., June 1921-June 1922, asst. dir., Jan.-June 1922; with Woods Bros. Constrn. Co., Lincoln, Neb., 1922-25; pres. Monomarks, Inc., May 1925-Oct. 1926; with Dawes Bros., Inc., Chicago, 1926-29; mem. Dominican Econ. Commn., Apr.-July 1929; dir. U.S. budget, Aug. 1929-Mar. 1933; with Pan-Am. Airways, Inc., 1935-49; consultant to chmn. munitions bd., 1949, retired. Vice president and treas. Pan-Am. Airways Corp. and its principal subsidiaries. Served as captain, major and lt. col. Engr. Corps, U.S. Army, World War I; in Engr. Supply Office, Sept.-Dec. 1917, Office of Gen. Purchasing Agt., A.E.F., Dec. 1917-Sept. 1919; mem. staff Mil. Bd. of Allied Supply, July-Nov. 1918; served as col., brig. gen. U.S. Army, 1942; gen. purchasing agt. U.S. Army Forces in Australia and U.S. Mem. of Allied Supply Council in Australia. Decorated D.S.M. (U.S.); Legion of Honor (France); Order Crown of Italy. Republican. Episcopalian. Clubs: Army and Navy (Washington); University (New York). Home: New Canaan3CT Died Jan. 23, 1972; buried New Canaan CT

ROOS, ROBERT ACHILLE corporation official; b. San Francisco, Calif., June 7, 1883; s. Adolphe and Ernestine (Mahler) R.; B.S., Univ. of Calif., 1904; m. Louise Swabaker, Apr. 26, 1915; 1 son, Robert A. With Roos Bros., Inc., since 1904, pres. and gen. mgr. since 1927. Govt. industrial adviser for NRA; asst. coordinator of Nat. Defense Purchases, 1940-41; mem. advisory commn. to Council of Nat. Defense, 1940. Organizer and pres. San Francisco Fair Play League; organizer and chmn. Labor Relations Com., San Francisco-Oakland Met. area; ex-v.p. Nat. Retail Dry Goods Assn., re-elected vice-president, January 1944; (originator of economic committee to prevent unwarranted price increases); mem. Boston Retail Conf. on Distribution; former pres. Civic League of Improvement Clubs of San Francisco; dir. Chamber of Commerce, panel mem. 10th Regional Labor Bd. Chief of Sect., Staff of Comdg. Gen., 9th Corps Area, July 1, 1941-Dec. 29, 1941, Chief of Sect., Staff of Comdg. Gen., Western Defense Command and 4th Army, Dec. 30, 1941-Apr. 14, 1942. Chief of Branch, Staff of Comdg. Gen. 9th Service Command, Apr. 14, 1942-Nov. 16, 1943; retired with rank of col. Inf., Recipient Legion of Merit. Hon. mem. Beta Gamma Sigma. Author of Roos Plan (1940) adopted by many municipalities and industries, to pay full month's wage to men volunteering for Army training and to return them to their jobs without impairment of service; also many pub. addresses, broadcasts, articles, relating to business and to distributive and econ. problems. Home: 615 Brewer Dr., Burlingame. Office: 798 Market St., S.F. Died June 30, 1951.

ROOSEVELT FRANKLIN D(ELANO) thirty-first President; b. Hyde Park, N.Y., Jan. 30, 1882; s. James and Sara (Delano) R.; A.B., Harvard, 1904; Columbia U. Law Sch., 1904-07; LL.D., Rutgers, postgrad., 1933, Washington Coll., 1933, Yale, 1934, William and Mary Coll., 1934, U. of Notre Dame, 1935; Litt.D., Rollins Coll., 1936; Dr. Civil Law, Oxford U., Eng., 1941; m. Anna Eleanor Roosevelt, Mar. 17, 1905; children—Anna Eleanor (Mrs. John Boettiger), James, Elliott, Franklin D., John A. Admitted to New York State bar, 1907; practiced with firm Carter, Ledyard & Milburn, N.Y.C., 1907-10; mem. firm of Roosevelt & O'Connor, 1924-33. Mem. N.Y. Senate, 1910-Mar. 17, 1913 (resigned); asst. sec. of the navy, 1913-20; elected gov. N.Y. State for 2 terms, 1929-33; Dem. nominee for vice-pres. of U.S., 1920. Dem. nominee for Pres. of U.S., 1932, elected for term, 1933-37; Dem. nominee for second term, 1936, re-elected for term 1937-41; Dem. nominee for third term, 1940, re-elected for term 1941-45; Dem. nominee for fourth term, 1944; re-elected for term, 1945-49. Mem. Hudson-Fulton Celebration Commn., 1909, Plattsburgh Centennial, 1913; mem. Nat. Commn. Panama P.I. Expedition, 1915, overseer Harvard U., 1918-24. Pres. American National Red Cross, Ga. Warm Spring Foundation. In charge of inspection U.S. Naval forces in European waters, July-Sept. 1918, and of demobilization in Europe, Jan.-Feb. 1919. Mem. Alpha Delta Phi, Phi Beta Kappa. Mason. Episcopalian (sr. warden St. James Ch., Hyde Park). Author: Whither Bound, 1926; The Happy Warrior, Alfred E. Smith, 1928; Government-Not Politics, 1932; Looking Forward, 1933; On Our Way, 1934. Known for New Deal program for econ. recovery from depression in which fed. govt. exerted strong measures to improve economy; initiated Good Neighbor policy Latin Am.; supporter UN; only U.S. Pres. to serve more than two terms. Home: Hyde Park, Dutchess County, N.Y. Died April 12, 1945.

ROOSEVELT, GEORGE EMLEN investments; born at New York, N.Y., Oct. 13, 1887; s. William Emlen and Christine (Kean) R.; grad. St. Mark's Sch., Southboro, Mass., 1905; A.B., Harvard, 1909; m. Julia M. Addison, Oct. 24, 1914 (dec.); children—Margaret Christine (Mrs. George Philip Kent), Medora Thayer (Mrs. Herbert Whiting) (deceased), George Emlen, Julian Kean; m. 2d, Mrs. Mildred Cobb Rich, Jan. 14, 1939, Mem. Roosevelt & Son since 1908; chmn. bd. dirs. Investors Mgmt. Co.; advisor council Guaranty Trust Co.; dir. Union Pacific R.R., Bank for Savs., and many other cos. Served as col. U.S. Army, chief staff 82d Div., World War I. Chmn. bd. N.Y.U., v.p., treas. Roosevelt Hosp.; past pres. Chapin Sch. Episcopalian. Clubs: New York Yacht (ex-commodore), Union; Seawanakha Corinthian Yacht (ex commodore). Home: 110 E. 57th St., N.Y.C. 22. Office: 48 Wall St., N.Y.C. 5. Died Sept. 3, 1963.

ROOSEVELT, GEORGE WASHINGTON consul; b. Chester, Pa., Feb. 14, 1844; s. James S. (of New York) and Esther (Vicery) R.; ed. pub. schs., Chester, Pa., and by pvt. tutors; clerk in store until enlisted Apr. 16, 1861; served corpl. to 1st sergt., Co. K, 26th Regt., Pa. Vols.; bvtd. capt. for meritorious conduct at Gettysburg, where was severely wounded through hips and lost left leg, July 2, 1863; awarded congressional medal of honor for gallant and meritorious conduct at battles of Bull Run and Gettysburg; raised co. in Phila. upon President Lincoln's 2d call, and was elected capt., but loss of leg prevented service at front again; m. Ida Edmonston, May 1874. Apptd. U.S. consul at Auckland, New Zealand, Mar. 28, 1878; to St. Helena, Apr. 30, 1879; to Matanzas, Cuba, Sept. 1, 1880; to Bordeaux, France, May 23, 1881; consul, 1889-1905, consul-gen., Mar. 6, 1905-—, at Brussels, Belgium. Republican. Presbyn. Died 1907.

ROOSEVELT, HENRY LATROBE asst. sec. of the Navy; b. Morristown, N.J., Oct. 5, 1879; s. Nicholas Latrobe and Eleanor (Dean) R.; student U.S. Naval Acad., class of 1900; m. Eleanor Morrow, Jan. 15, 1902; children—William Morrow, Henry Latrobe, Eleanor Katherine. Commd. 2d lt. U.S.M.C., 1899; promoted through grades to lt. col., 1917; during Spanish-Am. War attached to U.S.S. Mayflower, operating off coast of Cuba; asst. naval attaché, Paris, France, 1914; hdqrs. U.S. Marine Corps, Washington, 1914-16; brig. q.m. Haiti, 1916; col. in Gendarmerie d'Haiti, 1916-17; at Quantico, Va., 1917; resigned, 1920; with Radio Corp. of America, 1923, European mgr., 1925-30; pres. Radio Real Estate Corp., 1930; asst. sec. of the Navy, Mar. 17, 1933-—. Episcopalian. Home: Washington, D.C. Died Feb. 22, 1936.

ROOSEVELT, KERMIT b. Oyster Bay, N.Y., Oct. 10, 1889; s. Theodore (26th President of U.S.) and Edith Kermit (Carow) R.; A.B., Harvard, 1912; m. Belle Wyatt Willard, June 11, 1914. With father on hunting trip in Africa, 1909-10, also exploration trip on "River of Doubt," in Brazil, 1914; engaged in engring. and banking in S. America, 1911-16; pres. Roosevelt Steamship Co.; v.p. U.S. Lines Co. Commd. capt. in British Army, July 1917, and served with Motor Machine Guns, in Mesopotamia; trans. to 7th F.A., 1st Div., U.S. Army, June 1918; hon. discharged, Mar. 1919. Commd. major Middlesex Regt., Brit. Army, Oct. 10, 1939; col. in Finnish Army to raise vols. in England for Fiish campaign, Jan.-Feb. 1940; with Brit. Army in Norwegian campaign, Mar.-June 1940; to Egypt, Aug. 1940; invalided to England, Dec. 1940, to U.S., June 1941. Awarded Military Cross (British); Montenegrin War Cross. Republican. Member Dutch Reformed Church. Clubs: Knickebocker, Racquet, River (founder), India House, Boone and Crocket (former pres.). Author: War in the Garden of Eden, 1919; The Happy Hunting Grounds, 1920; Quentin Roosevelt—A Sketch with Letters; (with brother Theodore) East of the Sun and West of the Moon, 1926; Cleared for Strange Ports, 1927; American Backlogs, 1928; Trailing the Giant Panda (with brother Theodore), 1929. Home: Oyster Bay, N.Y. Office: One Broadway, New York, N.Y. Died on active service in U.S. Army on June 4th, 1943; buried in Military Cemetery, Fort Richardson, Alaska.

ROOSEVELT, PHILIP J(AMES) corp. exec.; b. New York, N.Y., May 15, 1892; s. W(illiam) Emlen and Christine Griffin (Kean) R.; prep. edn., St. Mark's Sch., Southboro, Mass.; A.B., Harvard, 1913; married, May 9, 1925; children—Philippa, Philip James, John Ellis II. Reporter, 1913-15; investment dealer, 1919-33; partner Roosevelt & Son; officer or dir. many other corps. Served as lt., capt. and maj. Air Service, U.S. Army, 1918; awarded Croix de Guerre with palm (France). Trustee Village of Cove Neck, N.Y. Pres. North Am. Yacht Racing Union. Clubs: Cruising Club of America, Knickerbocker, Downtown, Lunch, New York Yacht, Seawanhaka-Corinthian Yacht (commodore), Cold Spring Harbor Beach, Beaver Dam Winter Sports. Died Nov. 8, 1941.

ROOSEVELT,THEODORE twenty-sixth President of the U.S.; b. N.Y.C., Oct. 27, 1858; s. Theodore (1831-78) and Martha (Bulloch) R.; A.B., Harvard, 1880; LL.D., 1902; LL.D., Columbia, 1899, Hope Coll., 1901, Yale, 1901, Northwestern, 1893, U. of Chgo., 1903, U. of Calif., 1903, U. of Pa., 1905, Clark U., 1905, George Washington U., 1909, Cambridge U., 1910; D.C.L., Oxford U., 1910; Ph.D., U. of Berlin, 1910; m. Alice Hathaway, Oct. 27, 1880 (died 1884); m. 2d, Edith Kermit, Dec. 2, 1886; children—Theodore, Kermit, Ethel Carow, Archibald Bulloch, Quentin. Mem. N.Y. Legislature, 1882-84; del. rep. Nat. Conv., 1884; resided on ranch in N.D., 1884-86; candidate for mayor of New York, 1886; U.S. civil service commr., 1889-95; pres. New York Police Bd., 1895-97; asst. sec. of the navy, 1897-98; resigned to organize, with Surgeon (later Maj.-Gen.) Leonard Wood, 1st U.S. Cav. (popularly known as Roosevelt's Rough Riders); was lt. col. of regt., which distinguished itself in Cuba; promoted col. for gallantry at battle of Las Guasimas; mustered out Sept. 1898. Gov. N.Y. state, Jan. 1, 1899 to Dec. 31, 1900; elected Vice Pres. U.S., Nov. 4, 1900, for term, 1901-05; succeeded to the presidency on death of William McKinley, Sept. 14, 1901; elected Pres. of the U.S., Nov. 8, 1904, for term 1905-09, by largest popular majority ever accorded a candidate; Progressive Party candidate for Pres. of U.S., 1912. Recipient Nobel Peace Prize ($40,000),1906. Spl. ambassador of U.S. at funeral of King Edward VII, 110. Offered to raise an army division, after declaration of war, and to go to France with same, 1917, but offer was declined by Pres. Wilson. Hon. fellow Am. Mus. Natural History, 1917. Author: Winning of the West, 1889-96; History of the Naval War of 1812, 1882; Hunting Trips of a Ranchman, 1885; Life of Thomas Hart Benton, 1886; Life of Gouverneur Morris, 1887; Ranch Life and Hunting Trail, 1888; History of New York, 1890; The Wilderness Hunter, 1893; American Ideals and Other Essays, 1897; The Rough Riders, 1899; Life of Oliver Cromwell, 1900; The Strenuous Life, 1900; Works (8 vols.), 1902; The Deer Family, 1902; Outdoor Pastimes of an American Hunter, 1906; American Ideals and other Essays; Good Hunting, 1907; True Americanism; African and European Addresses, 1910; African Game Trails, 1910; The New Nationalism, 1910; Relizable Ideals (The Earl lectures), 1912; Conservation of Womanhood and Childhood, 1912; History as Literature, and Other Essays, 1913; Theodore Roosevelt, an Autobiography, 1913; Life Histories of African Game Animals (2 vols.), 1914; Through the Brazilian Wilderness, 1914; America and the World War, 1915; A Booklover's Holidays in the Open, 1916; Fear God, and Take Your Own Part, 1916; Foes of Our Own Household, 1917; National Strength and International Duty, 1917. Contbg. editor The Outlook, 1909-14. Contbr. to leading mags. and revs. Known as Trust Buster for attempts to limit power of big bus.; promoted regulation of industry to protect public; initiated Roosevelt Corollary to Monroe Doctrine; noted conservationist. Home: Oyster Bay, L.I., N.Y. Died Jan. 6, 1919.

ROOSEVELT, THEODORE, JR., soldier, publisher, author; b. Oyster Bay, New York, September 13, 1887; s. Theodore (26th President of the United States) and Edith Kermit (Carow) Roosevelt; B.A., Harvard University, 1908, hon. M.A., 1919; m. Eleanor Butler Alexander, June 20, 1910; children—Grace Green, Theodore, Cornelius Van Shaack, Quentin. Member New York State Assembly, 1919-20; assistant sec. of the navy, Mar. 4, 1921-Oct. 5, 1924 (resigned); chmn. com. of naval experts at Limitation of Armament Conf., 1922; Rep. candidate for gov. of N.Y., 1924; temp. chmn. N.Y. State Rep. Conv., 1927; leader of James Simpson-Roosevelts-Field Museum Expdn. to Asia, 1925; of Kelley-Roosevelts-Field Museum Expdn., Asia, 1928-29; gov. of Puerto Rico, 1929-32; gov. gen. of Philippine Islands, 1932-33; chmn. bd. American Express Co., 1934-35, vice-president Doubleday Doran & Co. since 1935. Commd. major 26th Inf., U.S. Army, 1917; lt. col., Sept. 2, 1918; arrived in France, June 1917; with 1st Div., 1st Army, A.E.F.; participated in battles at Cantigny, Soissons, Argonne-Meuse offensive, St. Mihiel offensive; twice wounded. Returned to active duty, U.S. Army, as colonel commanding 26th Infantry, 1st Div., Apr. 1941; advanced to brig. gen., Dec. 1941. Decorated D.S.C. and D.S.M., Order of Purple Heart, Silver Star with Oak Leaf Cluster (United States); Legion of Honor and Croix de Guerre with three palms (France); Grand Cordon of Prince Danilo I and War Cross (Montenegro); Grand Croix de la Couronne and Croix de Guerre with palms (Belgium); Grand Blue Cordon of Order of the Jade (China) (World War I); two Oak Leaf Clusters for Silver Star, Legion of Merit, French Croix de Guerre, Legion of Honor (World War II); (posthumously awarded) Medal of Honor (U.S.A.); Croix de Guerre (French). President National Health Council, 1935; national chairman United Council for Civilian Relief in China, 1938-40; chmn. Am. Bur. for Med. Aid to China, 1940. V.p. Boy Scouts of Am. An organizer American Legion, 1919. Member American Geog. Soci; mem. bd. trustees Field Museum Natural History; fellow Royal Geog. Soc. (London). Republican. Clubs: Harvard, River, Nat. Republicans of New York (pres. 1934-36), Explorers. Author: Average Americans, 1919; (with brother Kermit) East of the Sun and West of the Moon, 1926; Rank and File, 1928; All in the Family, 1929; (with brother Kermit) Trailing the Giant Panda, 1929; Taps (with Grantland Rice), 1932; Three Kingdoms of Indo-China (with Harold J. Coolidge, Jr.), 1933; Colonial Policies of the United States, 1937; The Desk Drawer Anthology (with Alice Roosevelt Longworth), 1937. Home: Oyster Bay, L.I., N.Y. Office: 14 W. 49th St., New York, N.Y. Died July 12, 1944; buried in Am. Military Cemetery, St. Laurent, Fr.

ROOT, EDWIN ALVIN army officer; b. in Ind., Dec. 9, 1860; grad. U.S. Mil. Acad., 1883; honor grad. Inf. and Cav. Sch., 1889; Army War Coll., 1906. Commd. 2d lt. 22d Inf., June 13, 1883; 1st lt. 19th Inf., Feb. 20, 1891; capt. of Inf., July 1, 1898; maj. engrs., vols., July 16, 1898; hon. discharged vols., May 12, 1899; assigned to 10th Inf., U.S.A., Jan. 1, 1899; maj. 19th Inf., May 25, 1906; lt. col. of inf., Sept. 6, 1911; assigned to 15th Inf., Oct. 25, 1911, to 16th Inf., Nov. 24, 1914; col. of inf., Feb. 7, 1915; assigned to 30th Inf., July 1, 1915. Asst. instr. engring., Inf. and Cav. Sch., 1890-95; duty Adj. Gen.'s Office, Washington, D.C., 1896; engr. officer Porto Rican Campaign, 1898; participated in Battle of Hormigueros, Aug. 10, 1898; engr. in charge harbor works, San Juan, P.R., 1899; duty Adj. Gen.'s Office, 1899-1901; in Philippine Islands, 1902-03; acting judge advocate, Dept. of Cal., Apr.-July, 1907; comd. Ft. McIntosh, Tex., 1908; duty with Ill. N.G., 1917. Address: War Dept., Washington, D.C.

ROOT, ELIHU sec. of State, senator; b. Clinton, N.Y., Feb. 15, 1845; s. Prof. Oren and Nancy Whitney (Buttrick) R.; A.B., Hamilton Coll., 1864, A.M., 1867; taught at Rome Acad., 1865; LL.B., New York U., 1867; LL.D., Hamilton, 1894, Yale, 1900, Columbia, 1904, New York U., 1904, Williams, 1905, Princeton 1906, U. of Buenos Aires, 1906, Harvard, 1907, Wesleyan, 1909, McGill, 1913, Union Univ., 1914, U. of State of N.Y., 1915, U. of Toronto, 1918, Colgate, 1919, U. of Calif., 1923; Dr. Polit. Science, Univ. Leyden, 1913; D.C.L., Oxford, 1913, New York U., 1929; mem. Faculty of Political and Administrative Sciences, U. of San Marcos, Lima, 1906; Doctor, honoris causa, U. of Paris, 1921; m. Clara Wales, Jan. 8, 1878 (died 1928); children—Edith (wife of U. S. Grant, 3d, U.S.A.), Elihu, Edward Wales. Admitted to bar, 1867, and engaged in practice at New York. U.S. dist. atty., Southern Dist. of N.Y., 1883-85; del.-at-large N.Y. Constl. Conv., 1894 (chmn. judiciary com.); sec. of war in cabinet of President McKinley, Aug. 1, 1899-Feb. 1, 1904; sec. of State in cabinet of President Roosevelt, July 1, 1905-Jan. 27, 1909; U.S. senator from N.Y., 1909-15. Mem. Alaskan Boundary Tribunal, 1903; counsel for U.S. in N. Atlantic Fisheries Arbitration, 1910; mem. Permanent Court of Arbitration at the Hague, 1910-—; mem. Commn. Internat. Jurists, which, on invitation of Council of League of Nations, reported plan of new Permanent Court of Internat. Justice, established 1921. President Carnegie Endowment for International Peace, 1910-25; pres. Hague Tribunal of Arbitration between Great Britain, France, Spain and Portugal, concerning church property, 1913; ambassador extraordinary at head of special diplomatic mission to Russia, during revolution, 1917; commr. plenipotentiary for U.S., Internat. Conf. on Limitation of Armament, which met at Washington, Nov. 12, 1921; mem. League of Nations com. of experts to revise World Court statute on basis of experience at court meeting at Geneva, Mar. 1929. Awarded Nobel Peace Prize for 1912; Roosevelt medal for Administration of Public Office, 1924; Woodrow Wilson Foundation medal and prize, 1926, for championship of Court of Internat. Justice. Dodge lecturer, Yale, 1907; Stafford Little lecturer, Princeton, 1913. Temporary chairman Republican National Convention, 1904, and temporary and permanent chmn., 1912; chmn. N.Y. Rep. State convs., 1908, 10, 13, 14, 16, 20, 22; pres. N.Y. College of Presdl. Electors, 1925; pres. N.Y. Constitutional Conv., 1915; chmn. trustees Carnegie Instn. of Washington, 1913-—, Hamilton Coll., 1912-—; trustee N.Y. Pub. Library, Met. Mus. of Art, Am. Federation of Arts, N.Y. State Charities Aid Assn. Pres. of New England Soc. in New York, 1893-95, Union League Club (New York), 1898-99, and 1915-16, Assn. Bar City of N.Y., 1904-05, Am. Soc. Internat. Law, 1906-—, N.Y. State Bar Assn., 1910, Am. Bar Assn., 1915; pres. N.Y. Law Inst.; mem. Mexican Acad. of Legislation and Jurispru- dence; hon. mem. Inst. of Advocates of Brazil; hon. pres. Pan-Am. Conf., Rio de Janeiro, 1906; hon. pres. Am. Inst. Internat. Law, Nat. Security League, N.Y. Assn. for the Blind, Nat. Soc., for Prevention of Blindness; pres. Century Club, New York, 1918-—; corr. fellow British Acad., 1916-—; hon. mem. Institut de Droit International; hon. mem. A.I.A., New York Chamber of Commerce, Soc. of the Cincinnati; mem. Am. Philos. Soc., Am. Acad. Arts and Letters; corr. fellow Mass. Hist. Soc.; fellow Am. Acad. Arts and Sciences; chmn. U.S. Govt. War Savings Investments Soc., Jan. 1918-—; hon. pres. and mem. council Am. Law Inst. Del. and hon. pres. N.Y. State Convention, 1933, to act on Repeal of 18th Amendment to U.S. Constn. Grand Cordon de l'ordre de la Couronne of Belgium, 1919; grand comdr. Royal Order of George the First (Greece), 1923. Author: The Citizen's Part in Government, 1907; Experiment in Government and the Essentials of the Constitution, 1913; Addresses on International Subjects, 1916; Addresses on Government and Citizenship, 1916; Military and Colonial Policy of the United States, 1916; Latin America and the United States, 1917; Russia and the United States, 1917; Miscellaneous Addresses, 1917; Men and Policies, 1924. Home: New York, N.Y. Died Feb. 7, 1937.

ROOT, ELIHU, JR., lawyer; b. N.Y.C., May 7, 1881; s. Elihu and Clara (Wales) R.; A.B., Hamilton Coll., N.Y., 1903, A.M., 1905, LL.D., 1939; LL.B., Harvard, 1906; m. Alida Stryker, Dec. 7, 1907 (dec.); children—Elizabeth (dec.), Elihu Root III, Woolsey Stryker (dec.); m. 2d, Nancy Root, Oct. 13, 1953. Admitted to N.Y. bar, 1906; mem. Root, Clark & Bird, 1909-53; now counsel to Cleary, Gottlieb & Steen; dir. Mut. Life Ins. Co., N.Y., Ficuciary Trust Co., N.Y. Maj. 304th Infantry, A.E.F., 1917-19. Mem. U.S. Army Air Corps strategic target bd. 1943-44. Medal for Merit. Mem. U.S. Panama Gen. Claims Commn., 1932-33; mem. bd. overseers, Harvard, 1930-36. Trustee Hamilton Coll. (emeritus), Carnegie Inst. Washington, N.Y. Pub. Library (hon.), Met. Mus. Art. Mem. Am., N.Y. State bar assns., Bar Assn. N.Y.C., Am. Law Inst., Phi Beta Kappa, Sigma Phi. Republican. Clubs: Century, Knickerbocker, Seawanhaka-Corinthian, Down Town, Crusing. Home: 25 Sutton Pl. S., N.Y.C. 22. Office: 52 Wall St., N.Y.C. 5. Died Aug. 27, 1967; buried Clinton, N.Y.

ROOT, HOWARD FRANK physician; b. Ottumwa, Ia., Aug. 28, 1890; s. Frank Lane and Clara B. (Squire) R.; A.B., Harvard, 1913, M.D., 1919; H H.D., Suffolk U., 1953; m. Hester King, Oct. 8, 1921 (dec. Feb. 9, 1954); m. 2d, Kathleen Berger. House officer Peter Bent Brigham Hosp., Boston, 1919-20; May fellow Johns Hopkins Med. Center; practice of medicine, Boston, 1921-—; medical director of Joslin Clinic, 1962-—; physician-in-chief New Eng. Deaconess Hosp.; lectr. medicine Harvard Med. Sch. Served as lt. comdr. USNR, surgeon USPHS. Mem. Am. coll. Physicians, Am. Soc. Clin. Investigation, Am. Coll. Chest Physicians, Mass. Med. Soc. (past pres.), Am. Diabetes Assn. (past pres.), Internat. Diabetes Fedn. (pres. 1961-—), Am. Therapeutic Soc., Am. Endocrine Soc., Am. Clin. and Climatol. Assn., Am. Soc. Nutrition, Diabetes Found., Inc. (pres.) Mass. Soc. Internal Medicine (past pres.), Phi Beta Kappa, also Sigma Xi. Author: (with others) Treatment of Diabetes, 1958; (with L.S. McKittrick) Surgery and Diabetes, 1928; (with P. White) Diabetes Mellitus, 1956. Home: 195 St. Paul St., Brookline 46, Mass. Office: 15 Joslin Rd., Boston. Died Nov. 1967.

ROOT, ROBERT KILBURN ex-univ. dean; b. Brooklyn, N.Y., Apr. 7, 1877; s. William Judson and Mary Louisa (Kilburn) R.; A.B., Yale, 1898, Douglas fellow, 1899-1900, Ph.D., 1902, hon. Litt.D., 1937; hon. LL.D., Brown Univ., 1940; unmarried. Tutor in English, Yale, 1900-03, instr., 1903-05; asst. prof. of English, Princeton, 1905-16, prof. 1916-46, dean of faculty 1933-46, dean and prof. emeritus since 1946, Acting prof. Eng., Stanford U., summer 1921. Lecturer on Eng., Harvard U., Feb.-June, 1927; vis. prof. of Eng., Yale U., 1927-28. Mem. Mod. Lang. Assn. Am., Am. Assn. Univ. Profs.; fellow Mediaeval Acad. America, Am. Acad. Arts and Sciences. Episcopalian. Democrat. Clubs: Century, Princeton (New York). Author: Classical Mythology in Shakespeare, 1903; The Poetry of Chaucer, 1906, 22; Manuscripts of Chaucer's Troilus, 1914; The Textual Tradition of Chaucer's Troilus, 1916; The Poetical Career of Alexander Pope, 1938; The Princeton Campus in World War II, pub. 1951. Translator: The Legend of St. Andrew, 1899. Editor: Ruskin's Sesame and Lilies, 1901; Specimen Extracts from the Unprinted Manuscripts of Chaucer's Troilus (with Sir William S. McCormick), 1914; Chaucer's Troilus and Criseyde, 1926; (with P.R. Lieder and R.M. Lovett) British Poetry and Prose (2 vols.), 1928, rev. 50; British Drama (with same), 1929; Letters of Lord Chesterfield to His Son, 1929; Pope's Dunciad Variorum, 1929; (with L.I. Bredvold and G. Sherburn) Eighteenth Century Prose, 1932. Contbr. to philol. journals and various magazines. Commd. capt. Ordnance Dept., U.S. Army, Dec. 15, 1917; aircraft armament officer, 1st Army A.E.F.; maj., Feb. 17, 1919; discharged, Mar. 17, 1919; service in France, Feb. 1918-Mar. 1919; maj. Ordnance Dept. U.S.R., 1919-29. Address: 25 Mercer St., Princeton, N.J. Died Nov. 20, 1950.

ROPER, JOHN WESLEY naval officer; b. nr. Gibson, N.C., May 31, 1898; s. Daniel Calhoun and Lou (McKenzie) R.; student U.S. Naval Acad., 1915-18; m. Hazel Nelson, Sept. 15, 1931; 1 dau., Margaret. Commd. ensign USN, 1918, advanced through grades to vice admiral, 1945; on destroyer Roe, based at Brest, France, 1918; served in U.S.S. Chicago on staff comdr. South Pacific, and as comdg. officer U.S.S. Wisconsin, World War II; later comdr. amphibious group, duty in Bur. Naval Personnel; apptd. chief Bur. of Naval Personnel and chief Naval Personnel in Dept. Navy, for term of 4 yrs., 1949. Comdr. Cruiser, Destroyer Force, Pacific Fleet, 1951; comdt. 11th Naval Dist., 1952; ret. May 1, 1953, vice admiral. Meth. Clubs: Army-Navy, Army and Navy Country. Home: 1520 Ynez Pl., Coronado, Cal. Died Sept. 8, 1963.

RORTY, MALCOLM CHURCHILL engineer; b. Paterson, N.J., May 1, 1875; s. Richard Mackay and Octa (Churchill) R.; grad. Walkill Acad., Middletown, N.Y., 1892; M.E. in E.E., Cornell U., 1896; m. Margaret McNaughten, Mar. 23, 1904; children—Margaret McNaughten, Malcolm McNaughten, James McNaughten (dec.). With J. G. White Co. and New York Telephone Co. until 1899; engr. and traffic engr. with Am. Bell Telephone Co., 1899-1903; gen. supt. traffic, etc., Central Dist. Telephone Co., Pittsburgh, Pa., 1903-10; comml. engr. Am. Telephone & Telegraph Co., 1910-13; asst. v.p. Western Union Telegraph Co., New York, 1913-14; spl. agt. Am. Tel. & Tel. Co., 1914-17, chief statistician, 1919-21; v.p. Bell Telephone Securities Co., 1921-22; asst. v.p. Am. Tel. & Tel. Co., 1922-23; pres. Internat. Telephone Securities Corp., 1923-27; v.p. Internat. Telephone & Telegraph Corp., 1923-30; v.p. American Founders Corp., 1930-31. President Am. Management Assn., 1934-—. Served as lt. col. U.S.A., 1917-18; with Ordnance Dept. and Gen. Staff; attached to Interallied Munitions Council; participated in Meuse-Argonne offensive. Fellow Am. Statistical Assn. (pres. 1930-31); mem. Nat. Bur. Economic Research (pres. 1922-23, chmn. bd. 1924-25); corr. mem. faculty Univ. of Buenos Aires. Republican. Author: Some Problems in Current Economics, 1922; Bolshevism, Fascism, and Capitalism (with others), 1932. Home: Lusby, Md. Died Jan. 18, 1936.

ROSE, ARNOLD M(ARSHALL) sociologist; b. Chgo., July 2, 1918; s. Frank A. and Ruth (Wilansky) R.; A.B., U. Chgo., 1938, M.A., 1940, Ph.D. (Marshall Field fellow 1940-41, Social Sci. Research Council fellow 1945-46), 1946; m. Caroline Baer, Dec. 24, 1942; children—Richard, Ruth, Dorothy. Research asso. Carnegie Corp. of N.Y., 1940-41-43; statistician War Dept., 1943-44; faculty Bennington (Vt.) Coll., 1946-47; asso. prof. sociology and social work Washington U., St. Louis, 1947-49; asso. prof. sociology U. Minn., 1949-52, prof. sociology, 1952-—; Fulbright research scholar, France, 1951-52; Fulbright prof., Italy, 1956-1957; research cons. Human Resources Research Office, Community Studies, Inc. Chmn. Minn. delegation White House Conf. on Aging, 1961. Mem. Minn. House of Reps., 1963-65. Recipient of prize for essays in social theory A.A.A.S., 1953. Mem. Soc. Study Social Problems (pres. 1955-56), Internat. Midwest (pres. 1961-62) American (v.p. 1965-66) sociol. assns., Internat. Gerontological Assn., American Committee Cultural Freedom, Am. Assn. U. Profs., Soc. Psychol. Study Social Issues, Sociol. Research Assn., Phi Beta Kappa. Author: Studies in Reduction of Prejudice, 1947; The Negro in America, 1948; The Negro's Morale, 1949; Union Solidarity, 1952; Theory and Method in the Social Sciences, 1954; Sociology, The Study of Human Relations, 1956, others. Co-author: An American Dilemma, 1944; America Divided, 1948. Editor: Race Prejudice and Discrimination, 1951; Mental Health and Mental Disorder, 1955; Institutions of Advanced Societies, 1958; Human Behavior and Social Processes, 1961; Aging in Minnesota, 1963; Assuring Freedom to the Free, 1964; Minority Problems, 1965. Home: 178 Malcolm Av. S.E., Mpls. 14. Died Jan. 3, 1968.

ROSE, BENJAMIN MORRIS, merchant; b. Warsaw, Poland, May 6, 1898; s. Hyman and Yetta (Bernstein) R.; came to U.S., 1903, naturalized, 1908; C.E., Coll. City N.Y., 1920; m. Bessie O. Ox, Aug. 15, 1920; children—Barbara (Mrs. Lawrence Bensman), Eloise (Mrs. Selwyn Blumberg), Hermina (Mrs. Joseph Shugol), Gilbert E. Exec., Samuel Stores, N.Y.C., 1920-38; mgr. Star Clothing, Detroit, 1938-43; pres. Chelsea Clothes, Wyandotte, Mich., 1943-69. Chmn., Mich. Anti-Defamation League, 1956-69; mem. Mich. Bd. Vocational Edn., Lansing, 1958-63; pres. Jamestown Gen. Hosp., 1934-35; v.p. Wyandotte Gen. Hosp., 1953-57. Gov., Wayne State U., co-chmn. bd. govs., 1969. Served to 2d lt. U.S. Army, 1918. Mem. Am. Arbitration Assn., Zionist Orgn. (dir. Detroit 1967-69). Lion (pres. 1937-38). Home: Allen Park MI Died Apr. 24, 1969.

ROSE, DWIGHT CHAPPELL, investment counsel; b. Waterford, Conn., Sept. 7, 1897; s. Frank Bowen and Nellie Avery (Chappell) R.; grad. Bulkeley Sch., New London, Conn., 1915; student U. of Mich., 1915-16; B.S., Harvard, 1919; student Harvard Law Sch., 1920-21; unmarried. Bond salesman Lee, Higginson & Co., 1919-20; asso. with Scudder, Stevens & Clark, investment counsel, 1922-31, gen. economist and mgr. instns. dept., 1927-31; gen. partner Brundage, Story & Rose, investment counsel, 1931-56, ret., now cons. Served in Officers' Training Corps of the United States Army, Plattsburg, and Camp Lee, Va., Feb.-Nov. 1918. On active duty as lt. comdr. U.S.N.R., May 29, 1942 to October 15, 1945, commander (inactive) since 1945. Mem. Investment Counsel Assn. of Am. (pres. 1937-48), American Econ. Assn., Am. Statis. Assn., Acad. Polit. Sci., Fed. Grand Jury Assn. So. Dist. N.Y. Republican. Unitarian. Club: Harvard, U. Mich. Author: A Scientific Approach to Investment Management, 1928; The Practical Application of Investment Management, 1933; The Policyholders' Interest in Equity Investment, 1939. Home: Waterford CT Died Oct. 2, 1969.

ROSE, FRANK BRAMWELL chaplain U.S.N.; b. Tuckerton, N.J., Apr. 5, 1836; s. Francis Bodine and Sarah (Early) R.; ed. Central High Sch., Phila.; m. Mary Anna King, Apr. 2, 1851. Ordained 1862; chaplain 14th N.J. Inf., Sept. 1, 1862-June 18, 1865; apptd. from N.J., chaplain U.S.N., Feb. 3, 1870; retired Apr. 5, 1898; advanced to rank of rear admiral retired, June 29, 1906, for services during Civil War. Home: Swarthmore, Pa. Died 1910.

ROSE, FRANK WATSON, contracting co. exec.; b. Cohutta, Ga., Sept. 3, 1917; s. Frank Watson and Bonnie (Rollins) R.; B.S. in Civil Engring., Ga. Inst. Tech., 1943; m. Ellen Radcliff Nooe, Mar. 15, 1944; children—Georgann (Mrs. Charles B. Cunningham III), Frank Watson III, Margaret, Richard. With Richards & Assos., Inc., Carrollton, Ga., 1946-69, exec. v.p., 1946-69; dir. Southwire Co., Carrollton. Pres., Carroll Service Council, Carrollton, 1946. Trustee W. Ga. Coll. Found., Carrollton. Served to capt. AUS, 1943-46. Mem. Power and Communication Contractors Assn. (pres. 1961, dir.), V.F.W., Am. Legion, Carrollton C. of C. (v.p. 1965). Episcopalian (sr. warden 1968-69). Mason. Clubs: Lions International, Sunset Hills Country (pres. 1956). Home: Carrollton GA Died Jan. 20, 1969.

ROSE, MAURICE army officer; b. Middletown, Conn., Nov. 26, 1899; s. Samuel and Katherine (Brown) R.; grad. Inf. Sch., Columbus, Ga., 1926, Cavalry Sch., Ft. Riley, Kan., 1931, Command and Gen. Staff Sch., Ft. Leavenworth, Kan., 1937, Army Industrial Coll., Washington, D.C., 1940; m. Virginia Barringer, Sept. 12, 1934; 1 son, Maurice Roderick. Commd. 2d lt. Inf., Aug. 1917, capt. 1920; major Cav., Aug. 1930, and advanced through the grades to brig. gen., June 1943; served with A.E.F., 1918, World War I; on Gen. Staff duty with troops, chief of staff, 2d Armored Div., Jan. 1942-June 1943; overseas assignment since Dec. 1942. Awarded Silver Star with 2 oak leaf clusters, Purple Heart. Home: 20 S. Ogden St., Denver, Colo. Killed in action, Mar. 1945.

ROSE, THOMAS ELLWOOD maj. U.S.A.; b. Bucks County, Pa., Mar. 12, 1830; common school edn.; became private 12th Pa., Apr. 1861; capt. 77th Pa., Oct. 1861; served at Shiloh, Corinth, Murfreesboro; col., Jan. 1863; taken prisoner at Chickamauga; escaped at Weldon, N.C.; recaptured next day; sent to Libby Prison, Oct. 1, 1863. With Maj. Hamilton, of 12th Ky., and working party of 15, cut through the stone wall of cellar and dug a tunnel 50 feet long, completing it in three months; 109 soldiers escaped; 48 were retaken, including Col. Rose; again confined in Libby until exchanged, Apr. 30, 1864; served until close of war; bvtd. brig. gen. vols. and col. U.S.A.; after war capt. and maj. U.S. inf., retired 1894. Address: Baltimore, Md. Died 1907.

ROSECRANS, WILLIAM STARKE army officer, diplomat; b. Kingston Twp., Delaware County, O., Sept. 6, 1819; s. Crandall and Jemima (Hopkins) R.; grad. U.S. Mil. Acad., 1842; m. Ann Eliza Hegeman, Aug. 24, 1843, 8 children. Brevetted 2d lt. of engrs., 1842; served as 2d lt. on the fortifications of Hampton Roads, Va., 1843-47; asst. prof. natural and exptl. philosophy dept. engring. U.S. Mil. Acad.; supt. repairs at Ft. Adams, Mass., also in charge of various govt. surveys and improvements, 1847-53; promoted 1st lt., 1853, resigned commn., 1854; architect and civil engr., Cincinnati; pres. Coal River Navigation Co., Kanawha County, Va. (now W. Va.), 1856; organizer Preston Coal Oil Co., mfrs. kerosene, 1857; became volunteer a.d.c. to Gen. George B. McClellan in Ohio, 1861; made col., chief engr. Dept. of Ohio, U.S. Army, 1861; apptd. col. 23d Ohio Volunteer Inf., 1861; commd. brig. gen. U.S. Army, 1861; commanded brigade, won Battle of Rich Mountain, 1861; succeeded McClellan as comdg. gen. Dept. of Ohio, 1861; chief new dept. of western Va., 1861, expelled Confederates, making formation of W.Va. possible; promoted maj. gen. U.S. Volunteers, 1862; succeeded Gen. John Pope in command Miss.

Army, involved in successful engagements at Iuka and Corinth, 1862; commanded Army of the Cumberland; defeated at Battle of Chickamauga, 1863, relieved of command; commanded Dept. of Mo., 1864; brevetted maj. gen. for services at Murfreesboro, 1865; resigned from U.S. Army, 1867; U.S. minister to Mexico, 1868, 69; engaged in mining operations, Mexico, later Cal.; pres. Safety Powder Co., Los Angeles, Cal., 1875; mem. U.S. Ho. of Reps. from Cal., 47th-48th congresses, 1881-85, chmn. com. on mil. affairs; commd. brig. gen. on ret. list U.S. Army, 1889; register of the treasury, 1885-93. Died Mar. 11, 1898; buried Arlington (Va.) Nat. Cemetery.

ROSEN, VICTOR HUGO, psychoanalyst; b. N.Y.C., Nov. 21, 1911; s. Alexander and Mary (Schwartzman) R.; A.B., Columbia, 1932, M.D., 1936; m. Elizabeth Ruskay, June 7, 1936 (div. June 1965); children—Barbara (Mrs. Norton Garber), Winifred; m. 2d, Elise Snyder, Dec. 15, 1965. Intern pathology Mt. Sinai Hosp., N.Y.C., 1936-37; rotating intern Bklyn. Jewish Hosp., 1937-38; resident neurology Montifiore Hosp., N.Y.C., 1938-39; fellow psychiatry Johns Hopkins Hosp., 1939-41, N.Y. Psychoanalytic Inst. 1946-51, asst. attending psychiatrist, 1950-55; attending psychiatrist Bronx VA Hosp., 1948-52; med. dir. treatment center N.Y. Psychoanalytic Inst., 1955-62, mem. faculty, 1956-66; clin. prof. psychiatry Albert Einstein Coll. Medicine, Yeshiva U., 1967-73; attending psychiatrist Bronx Municipal Hosp., 1967-73; pvt. practice, N.Y.C., 1946-73. Served to maj. M.C., AUS, 1941-45; ETO. Fellow Am. Psychiat. Assn.; mem. Acad. Neurology, Am. Psychoanalytic Assn. (pres. elect 1964-65, pres. 1965-66, mem. editorial bd. jour. 1960-73), A.M.A., A.A.A.S. Editorial bd. Psychoanalysis and Contemporary Science, 1969-73. Contbr. articles to profl. jours. Home: Deep River CT Died Feb. 5, 1973.

ROSENBAUM, EDWARD PHILIP editor; b. New Haven, Apr. 19, 1916; s. Harris and Anne (Cugell) R.; student Harvard, 1932-35; A.B., Yale, 1937; m. Madge Salomon, Oct. 2, 1943; children—Thomas E., Judith E. Tchr., Milford Sch., 1937-40, tchr., adminstr., 1946-52, now dir.; pub. accountant, 1940-42; bd. editors Scientific American, 1952-—, exec. editor, 1960-—. Served to capt. USAAF, 1942-46. Club: Yale (N.Y.C.). Home: 22 Woodbine Av., Larchmont, N.Y. 10538. Office: 415 Madison Av., N.Y.C. 17, N.Y. Died Apr. 25, 1963.

ROSENBAUM, OTHO BANE, army officer; b. Marion, Va., Aug. 26, 1871; s. Thomas Marion and Nannie Victoria (Bane) R.; grad. U.S. Mil. Acad., 1894, Gen. Staff Sch., 1923, Army War Coll., 1924; hon. grad. Sch. of the Line, 1922; m. Katherine Marie Rawolle, Aug. 26, 1895 (now deceased); children—Frederick Buchanan, Elizabeth Carlotta (wife of Col. John Adams Ballard, U.S. Army), Otho Bane (dec.), William Lockridge (dec.). Commd. 2d lt. inf., U.S. Army, June 12, 1894; advanced through grades to brig. gen., Nov. 6, 1927; retired Aug. 31, 1935. Served in Cuban Campaign, Spanish-Am. War, Philippine Insurrection, World War. Given distinguished service citation "for gallantry in action," at Santiago, Cuba, 1898. Lutheran. Clubs: Army and Navy, Army and Navy Country (Washington). Home: 2115 P St. N.W., Washington 7 DC Address: War Dept., Washington 25 DC

ROSENBAUM, SAMUEL RAWLINS, lawyer; b. Phila., Pa., Sept. 28, 1888; s. Morris and Hannah (Rottenburg) R.; B.A., Central High Sch., Phila., 1906; B.S., U. Pa., 1910, LL.B., 1913, LL.M., 1917; LL.D., Wesleyan U., 1962; Mus.D., Phila. Mus. Acad., 1967; student Inns of Ct., London, 1913-16; m. Rosamond May Rawlins, 1913 (dec. 1924); children—Jack Rawlins (dec.), Rosamond Margaret (Mrs. Rosamond Bernier), Hugh Samuel (dec.), Heather May (Mrs. Manuel de Jimenez); m. 2d, Edna Phillips, 1933; children—Joan Davies (Mrs. Mauricio Solaun), David Hugh. Admitted to Pa. bar, 1913, practiced in Phila., 1913-72. Vice pres. Albert M. Greenfield & Co., Bankers Securities Corp., 1926-43; pres. WFIL Broadcasting Co., 1932-43. Impartial trustee, Music Performance Trust Fund of Am. Phonograph Industry, 1949-69; chmn. Independent Radio Network Affiliates, 1937-40. Asst. city solicitor, 1920-24. Vice pres. Phila. Orch. Bd.; pres. Robin Hood Dell Concerts, 1938-41; trustee Phila. Coll. Art; chmn. Phila. Council for Performing Arts, 1964-65; mem. music adv. panel USIA, 1965-72; trustee Phila. Mus. Art, 1962, 66. Legislative draftsman Judge Adv. Gen., U.S. Army, 1917; spl. asst. U.S. atty. East Dist. Pa. 1918-19. Served to col. AUS, World War II; comdg. Officer Radio, Luxembourg. Decorated Legion of Merit (U.S.), Legion of Honor (France), also decorations from Luxembourg, Czechoslovakia, Italy, Poland, Belgium and China: recipient Am. Composers Alliane Laurel Leaf award, 1962; Nat. Assn. Composers and Conductors award, 1962; Distinguished Service award Wayne State U. Mem. Am., Pa., Phila., Phila., FCC bar assns., Order of Coif., Phi Beta Kappa, Sigma Delta Chi. Author: The English County Courts, 1916; Commercial Arbitration in England, 1916; The Rule-Making Authority in the English Supreme Court, 1917; Henry S. Drinker, a biographical memoir. Translator numerous works. Home: Philadelphia PA Died Nov. 9, 1972.

ROSENBERRY, M(ORRIS) CLAUDE dir. music edn.; b. Lower Mt. Bethel Twp., Northampton County, Pa., Jan. 7, 1889; s. Edward Shimer (M.D.) and Gertrude (McDonald) R.; student State Normal Sch., E. Stroudsburg, Pa., 1908-10; Cornell U., summers 1912-15; B.S., N.Y. U., 1926; Mus.D. (hon.), Temple U., 1937; Pd.D. (hon.), Lebanon Valley Coll., 1939; m. Mary E. Hoffman, June 12, 1915; 1 son, Edward Hoffman. Rural sch. tchr., 1906-08; head dept. of English, Westerleigh Collegiate Inst., New Brighton, N.Y., 1910-11; supr. music, East Stroudsburg, Pa., 1911-15, Easton, Pa., 1915-19; dir. music, Girard Coll., Phila., summers 1915-19; dir. music, Reading, Pa., 1919-26; state dir. music edn., Dept. Pub. Instrn., Harrisburg, Pa., 1926-—; mil. leave of absence as capt. A.U.S. (music officer, Army Service Forces), 1943-44. Music Educators Nat. Conf., Eastern Music Educators Conf. (pres. 1929-31), N.E.A., Pa. State Edn. Assn., Pa. Music Educators Assn. (sec.-treas.), Nat. Assn. of State Dirs. Music Edn. (founder; pres. 1950-52), Civic Music Assn. of Harrisburg (hon. pres.), Harrisburg Symphony Soc., Phi Mu Alpha, Sinfonia. Lutheran. Mason (32 deg., Shriner). Clubs: Wednesday Music Club, Torch, West Shore Country. Contbr. to mags. Home: 219 N. 23d St., Camp Hill, Pa. Address: State Dept. of Public Instruction, Harrisburg, Pa. Died Mar. 2, 1957; buried East Stroudsburg, Pa.

ROSENBLATT, SOL A(RIAH), lawyer; b. Omaha, Neb., Dec. 11, 1900; s. Morris M. and Mollie R.; A.B. cum laude, Harvard, 1922 (awarded Harvard scholarships and Coolidge medal), LL.B., 1924; married to Elizabeth Block, 1927 (divorced 1946); children—Robert Alan, Richard Lee; married second, Estrella Carroll Boissevain, August 19, 1946. Admitted to New York bar, 1925; gen. counsel Dem. Nat. Com., 1936-42; apptd. div. administrator under NRA, 1933; appointed national director of compliance and enforcement, NRA, 1934; apptd. impartial chmn. under collective agreements of Coat and Suit Industry, 1935-40, reapptd. 1947-54, 1954-68; mem. N.Y. State commn. Uniform State Laws, 1956-62; adv. bd. High Sch. Fashion Industries, N.Y. Apptd. capt. Specialist Res., U.S. Army, 1934, maj., 1940, on active duty, 1942-45, col., Air Corps. Charter mem. Air Force Association, Incorporated. Member of the American, New York State, N.Y. County bar assns., Assn. Bar City of N.Y., Delta Sigma Rho, Am. Legion. Club: Sands Point, L.I., N.Y. Home: New York City NY Died May 4, 1968.

ROSENFIELD, JOHN newspaperman; b. Dallas, Apr. 5, 1900; s. Max John and Jenny Lind (Kramer) R.; student U. Tex., 1917-19, Columbia, 1919-21; D.Litt. (hon.), Southwestern University, 1965; m. Claire Burger, June 28, 1923; 1 son, John III. Asst. drama editor, asst. drama critic N.Y. Evening Mail, 1920-21; asst. exploitation mgr., editor Paramount Exploiteer, N.Y.C., 1921-23; amusements editor, also dramatic music, motion picture, and art critic Dallas Morning News, 1925-—; asso. editor Southwest Rev., 1953-—. Pres. Southwest Theater Conf., ANTA, Ballet Theater Found.; mem. U. Tex. Fine Arts Found. Council. Recipient motion picture criticism award Screen Dirs. Guild, 1957. Clubs: Variety, Dallas Athletic. Author: (with Jack Patton) Texas History Movies, also 3 Southwest plays. Home: 3536 University Blvd., Dallas 5. Office: Dallas Morning News, Dallas 2. Died Nov. 26, 1966; buried Hillcrest Meml. Park.

ROSENGARTEN, JOSEPH GEORGE lawyer; b. Phila., July 14, 1835; s. George D. and Elizabeth (Bennett) R.; A.B., U. of Pa., 1852, A.M., 1855; admitted to bar, 1856; studied U. of Heidelberg, 1857; (LL.D., U. of Pa., 1906); unmarried. In practice at Phila. since 1856. Was on staff of Gen. John F. Reynolds during Civil War. Author: The German Soldier in the Wars of the United States; The German Allied Troops in the War of Independence; Sources of American History in German Archives; French Colonists and Exiles in the Unitgd States, 1907; etc. Home: 1704 Walnut St. Office: 1318 Real Estate Trust Bldg., Philadelphia.

ROSENSTEIN, DAVID sociologist, toy mfr.; b. N.Y. City, July 18, 1895; s. Jacob M. and Sarah (Fenster) R.; B.S., Coll. City of N.Y., 1916; grad. study philosophy Columbia, 1916-17; m. Emily Michtom, May 8, 1921 (dec. Feb. 1956); children—Paul Michtom, Elinor; m. 2d Frances Dibner, Aug. 3, 1959 (dec. May 1963); m. 3d, Frances D. Fried, Aug. 3, 1963. Research in econs. War Trade Board, 1917; statistician Treasury Dept., Wash. 1919; tng. supervisor Fed. Bd. Vocational Rehabilitation, 1920; pres. Ideal Toy Corp., 1939-62, chairman executive committee, 1962-—; president Ideal Plastics Corp., N.Y.C., since 1940; founder, pres. U.S.-Israel Plastics Corp. Former mem. toy adv. com. W.P.B.; panel mem. Am. Arbitration Assn. N.Y.C. Director Nat. Fedn. Settlements, pres., 1952-54; dir. Am. Orgn. for Rehabilitation Through Tng. Fedn.; dir., v.p. World Orgn. for Rehabilitation Through Tng. Union (Geneva, Switzerland); director of University Settlement (New York City); chairman Conference Jewish Social Studies; dir. United Def. Fund. United Community Def. Services; trustee Nat. Urban League; mem. reconstrn. commn. Joint Distbn. Com.; treas. Jewish Cultural Reconstrn. Served as 2d lt. Gen. Staff, U.S. Army, World War I. Mem. Nat. Assn. Doll Mfrs. (pres.), Am. Jewish Hist. Soc. (exec. council), Emerson Society N.Y. (historian). Jewish religion. Author articles ednl. and profl. journals. Home: 1056 Fifth Av., N.Y.C. 28. Died May 8, 1963.

ROSENTHAL, LOUIS S. banker; b. St. Louis, Mo., Nov. 9, 1890; s. Louis S. and Margaret (Burke) R.; ed. Cornell U. (class of 1912); m. Sara Beauvais, Dec. 14, 1917; children—Sally Ann Beauvais, Louis S. Asst. resident engr., Alaskan Engring. Commn., 1914-16; 1st lt. Coast Arty., U.S. Army, 1917-19; asst. mgr. Mercantile Bank of the Americas, 1919-20; asst. mgr., then gen. mgr., Nat. Bank of Nicaragua, Managua, Nicaragua, also gen. mgr. Cia. Mercantil de Ultramar, Managua; 2d v.p. Chase Nat. Bank of the City of New York, 1931-33, v.p. since 1934. Mem. Republic of Nicaragua Bd. to supervise expenditures from $1,500,000 loan for payment troops, settlement war claims, Nicaragua, 1928; mem. Social Service Commn. to Venezuela apptd. by Pres. Lopez Contreras, Venezuela, 1939; dir. Am. Chamber of Commerce of Cuba since 1931; dir. Haytian Corp. of America, New York. Major U.S. Marine Corps Reserve since 1934. Clubs: India House (New York); Larchmont Shore Club (Larchmont, N.Y.); Havana Country, Jaimanitas Yacht, Havana Yacht, American (Havana). Home: Country Club Park, Marianao, Cuba. Office: Agular 310, Havana, Cuba. Died Jan. 20, 1943.

ROSS, ALBERT officer U.S.N.; b. Clarion, Pa., Jan. 3, 1846; s. Dr. James and Mary A. (Wilson) R.; grad. U.S. Naval Acad., 1867; m. Alice Brewer, Mar. 1870. Midshipman, U.S.S. Minnesota, 1867-78; ensign, 1868; Powhatan, 1868-69; master, 1870; retired, 1871; Wachusett, 1873, Ossipee, 1874; restored to active list, 1874; lt., 1871; Worcester, flagship N. Atlantic sta., 1874-75; spl. duty, Annapolis, 1876; Passaic N. Atlantic sta., 1876-77; comd. Wyandotte, Washington, 1877-88; Portsmouth, apprentice training service, 1878-82; Navy Yard, Washington, 1882-83; Miantonomoh, 1883; torpedo instrn., Newport, R.I., 1883, 1889; U.S. Naval Acad., 1883-86; Alert, Pacific sta., 1887-89; Pensacola, 1889-90; training-ship Jamestown, 1890-92; lt. comdr., 1890; Naval Acad., 1892-98; comdr., Aug. 1897; comdg. Alliance, Jan. 1898-Dec. 1899; light house insp., 5th dist., 1900-02; capt., Apr. 1902; comdg. Buffalo 1902-03; insp. naval colliers, 1904-05; comdt. Naval Training Sta., Great Lakes, Ill., and mem. Lighthouse Bd., July 1, 1905; rear admiral, Oct. 13, 1907; retired Jan. 3, 1908; continued on duty as comdt. Naval Training Sta., Great Lakes, until Nov. 1912. Gen. Insp. of naval training activities for regulars and reserves, Sept. 1917-—. Comdr. Culver Summer Naval Sch., Culver, Ind., 1917-—. Home: Coconut Grove, Fla. Died Jan. 23, 1926.

ROSS, ARTHUR LEONIDAS paper co. exec.; b. Bastrop, La., Apr. 15, 1895; s. J.A. and Nora M. (Polk) R.; B.S. in Chem. Engring., La. State U., 1921; m. Dorothy Taylor, Nov. 17, 1926; children—Nancy T., Arthur W. With Internat. Paper Co., 1925-—, pulp mil. supt. La. and Bastrop mills, 1932-36, gen. supt. La. and Bastrop plants, 1936-38, mgr. Georgetown (S.C.) mill, 1938- 39, gen. prodn. mgr. So. Internat. Paper Co., Mobile, 1939-52, asst. gen. mgr. So. kraft div., v.p. of company, 1952-—. Served to capt., F.A., U.S. Army, World War I; AEF in France. Club: Mobile Country (past pres.). Home: 115 Beverly Ct. Office: P.O. Box 1649, Mobile, Ala. Died May 1963.

ROSS, EDMUND GIBSON senator, journalist; b. Ashland, O., Dec. 7, 1826; s. Sylvester F. and Cynthia (Rice) R.; m. Fanny M. Lathrop, 1848, 5 children. Worked as apprentice, later journeyman printer; joined Republican Party, 1856, led party of free state settlers to Kan., owner, publisher (with his brother) Kan. Tribune, Topeka, 1857-59; owner, publisher Kan. State Record, 1859-62; mem. Free State Wyandotte Constl. Conv., 1859; promoter, dir. Santa Fe R.R.; suggested name Atchison, Topeka and Santa Fe R.R.; served as capt. 11th Kan. Volunteer Regt., 1862, promoted maj., 1864; editor Lawrence (Kan.) Tribune, 1965-66; mem. U.S. Senate (Republican) from Kan., 1866-71, entered Senate as staunch radical, later changed his views, voted against conviction of Pres. Johnson at impeachment trial; left Republican Party, 1872; publisher various newspaper in Kan., 1871-82; unsuccessful Democratic candidate for gov. Kan., 1880; del. Dem. Nat. Conv., St. Louis, 1876; gov. N.M. Territory (apptd. by Pres. Cleveland), 1885-89; admitted to N.M. bar, 1889; sec. Bur. of Immigration, 1894-96. Died Albuquerque, N.M., May 8, 1907; buried Fairview Cemetery, Albuquerque.

ROSS, FRANK ALEXANDER, educator, statistician; b. N.Y. City, Jan. 23, 1888; s. James Alexander and Elizabeth Wordin (Naramore) R.; Ph.B., Yale, 1908, grad. study, 1909-11; M.A., Columbia, 1913, Ph.D., 1924; m. Dorothy Gere Reddy, Nov. 24, 1926; 1 dau., Elizabeth Gere. Civil engr. in Calif., 1908-09; teacher sociology and statistics, Columbia, 1914-17, 1919-26; asst. prof. sociology, 1926-37; prof. sociology and chmn. dept. Syracuse Univ., 1937-41; dir. survey of Near East for Near East Relief and other philanthropies, 1926; dir. research and surveys on Negro since 1926; various connections with Federal Govt. since 1917, Federal Emergency Relief Administrn., 1934-35. Editor Jour. Am. Statis. Assn., 1925-34 and 1941-45 (originator Procs. same 1928); sec.-treas. Social Science Abstracts, 1928-34; editor of History, Economics and Public Law

(Columbia), 1934-37. Mem. bd. of trustees and treas. Thetford Acad., 1942-48. Served as 1st lt., capt., maj. San. Corps, U.S. Army, chief surgeon's office, A.E.F., 1917-19; maj. San. R.C., 1919-33. Fellow Am. Statis. Asso.; mem. Inst. of Mathematical Statistics, Sociol. Research Assn., A.A.A.S., Sigma Xi, Alpha Kappa Delta. Republican. Mason. Author: School Attendance in the U.S., 1920 (census monograph), 1924; Near East and American Philanthropy (with C. L. Fry and E. Sibley), 1927; Bibliography of Negro Migration (with L. V. Kennedy), 1934. Contbr. to sociol. publs. Home: Thetford VT Died Jan. 30, 1968; buried North Thetford (Vt.) Cemetery.

ROSS, LAWRENCE SULLIVAN army officer, gov. Tex.; b. Bentonsport, Ia., Sept. 27, 1838; s. Capt. Shapely P. and Catherine (Fulkerson) R.; grad. Wesleyan U., Florence, Ala., 1859; m. Elizabeth Finsley, 1859, 6 children. Served as capt. of a co. of rangers, assigned to guard border and to defeat Comanche Indians, 1859; aid-de-camp with rank of col., circa 1860; commd. maj. 6th Tex. Cavalry, 1861; promoted col., May 1862; promoted brig. gen., 1864; sheriff McLennan County (Tex.), 1873-75; mem. Tex. Constl. Conv. of 1875; mem. Tex. Senate, 1881-85; gov. Tex., 1887-91, led legislature in passing laws prohibiting dealing in cotton futures, stopped sale of pub. land to corps., increased powers of land commn.; pres. Tex. A. and M. Coll., College Station, 1891-98; apptd. railroad commr., 1895, accepted, then declined. Died Waco, Tex., Jan. 3, 1898.

ROSS, LEONARD FULTON veteran soldier; b. Lewistown, Ill., July 18, 1823; s. Ossian M. R.; ed. common schools, Lewistown, Havana and Canton, Ill., and 1 yr. (1841-42) at Ill. Coll.; read law and was admitted to bar, Dec. 1844, at Springfield, Ill.; m. Catherine M. Sims, Nov. 13, 1845; m. 2d, Mary E. Warren, Jan. 10, 1865; now widower 2d time. Enlisted as pvt. Co. K, 4th regt., Ill. vol. inf., for Mexican war, July 18, 1846; promoted 1st lt., Sept. 1846; comd. co. at Vera Cruz and Cerro Gordo; elected probate justice, Fulton Co., Aug. 1847; co. clerk, same, Nov. 1849; raised co. for Civil war, elected capt.; commd. col. 17th regt., Ill. vols., May 1861; served in Mo., Ky. and Tenn.; promoted to brig. gen. vols., Apr. 1862; engaged in farming and stock-raising at Avon, Ill., Mar. 1866; apptd. collector internal revenue, 1867; unsuccessful candidate for Congress on Rep. ticket, 1868; removed to Iowa City, Ia., 1882, and engaged importing and breeding cattle; visited England to examine the best herds of cattle, 1884; sold farm and stock, 1893, and in 1894 returned to Lewistown, Ill. Assisted in organizing the Lewistown Nat. Bank, served 2 yrs. and v.p. and mgr. of bank. Revisited Mexico, 1898, and visited Havana, Cuba; was in the city when the Maine was destroyed, Feb. 1898. Enlisted men enough in Fulton and adjoining counties for a regt. to serve in the Spanish war, but failed to get into the service. Was delegate to Nat. Dem. Convs., 1852, 1856, and Rep. Nat. Conv., 1872. Republican. Home: Lewistown, Ill. Died 1902.

ROSS, LEWIS T. army officer (ret.); b. D.C., March 16, 1896; B.S., U.S. Mil. Acad., 1918; grad. Engr. Sch., civil engr. course and basic course, 1921; m. Marian E. Kutz, 1920; children—Marian, Tenney K., Katharine R. Commd. 2d lt., U.S. Army, 1918, and advanced through grades to brig. gen., 1944; ret. 1946; civil engr. with Sverdrup & Parcel, St. Louis, 1946. Home: 419 Belleview Av., Webster Groves 19. Office: 1118 Syndicate Trust Co., St. Louis 1. Died Sept. 3, 1958; buried Arlington Nat. Cemetery.

ROSS, MALCOLM author; b. Newark, June 1, 1895; s. William Lawrence and Gertrude Estelle (Ross) R.; grad. Hotchkiss Sch., 1915; A.B., Yale, 1919; m. Camille Miller, Apr. 18, 1936; children—Alexander Clinton, Malcolm, Jr., David. Served as 1st lt. AS, U.S. Army, 1917-18; reporter Dallas News, Louisville Courier-Jour., N.Y. Morning World; with Am. Friends Service Com. in So. coal fields, 1932; dir. information NLRB; writer OWI, 1942; chmn. President's Com. on Fair Employment Practice, 1943-46. U. editor U. Miami, 1947—. Democrat. Author: (novels) Deep Enough, 1926; Penny Dreadful, 1929; Hymn to the Sun, 1931; (novel) The Man Who Lived Backward, 1950; (technical) Sailing the Skies, 1932; (sociol. books) Machine Age in the Hills, 1933; Death of a Yale Man, 1939; All Manner of Men, 1948. Contbr. to mags. Home: 100 Prospect Dr., Coconut Grove, Fla. Died May 23, 1965.

ROSS, OGDEN, army officer; b. Troy, N.Y., Apr. 6, 1893; s. E. Ogden and Jean (Neely) R.; LL.B., Albany Law Sch., Union Univ., 1915; m. Elizabeth W. Cheney, Feb. 17, 1920; children—Ogden Cheney, Cynthia. Enlisted, 105th Inf., N.Y. Nat. Guard, 1910, and advanced through the grades to brig. gen., 1940; served on Mexican Border, 1916; with 27th Div., A.E.F., France and Belgium, World War I; asst. div. comdr. 27th Div., Pacific Area, 1940-44, comdr. Marshall-Gilbert Islands, 1944-45, World War II. City Treasurer, Troy, 1920-25; assistant to v.p. and gen. mgr., D.&H. R.R., 1924-38; N.Y. State senator, 1933-37; mem. N.Y. Constitutional Conv., 1938; N.Y. State tax commr., 1939-45; called into active service, Oct. 1940, on duty in the Pacific Area for four years. Pub. relations dir. Troy (N.Y.) Savings Bank. Awarded Legion of Merit, Silver Star, Purple Heart, Croix de Guerre. Clubs: Troy, Troy Country. Home: Troy NY Died Oct. 27, 1968; buried Oakwood Cemetery, Troy NY

ROSS, WILLIAM HORACE chemist; b. N.S., Can., Dec. 27, 1875; s. Daniel and Mary (Murray) R.; B.Sc., Dalhousie U., Halifax, N.S., 1903, M.Sc., 1904, 1851 sci. research scholar, 1905-07; Johns Hopkins, 1904-05; Ph.D., U. of Chicago, 1907; m. Catherine Allen, June 10, 1908; children—Allen Murray, William Horace. Asst. chemist, Agrl. Expt. Sta., U. of Ariz., 1907-12; scientist Bur. of Soils, 1912-27; sr. chemist, Bur. of Chemistry and Soils, 1927-40; senior chemist Bureau of Plant Industry, 1940-44; principal chemist 1944-45. Capt., C.W.S., United States Army, 1918-19. Abstracter Chemical Abstracts since 1907. Mem. Am. Chem. Soc., A.A.A.S., Am. Soc. Agronomy, Am. Inst. Chemists, Assn. of Official Agricultural Chemists (pres. 1945-46), Sigma Xi. Presbyterian. Co-author: Fixed Nitrogen; Principles and Practice of Agricultural Analysis. Contbr. to chem. and other scientific jours. Home: 2811 Woodley Rd., Washington, D.C. Died May 16, 1947.

ROSS, WORTH GWYNN officer U.S. Coast Guard; b. Cleveland, O., Apr. 19, 1854; s. Gen. Samuel and Phebe (Wierman) R.; ed. Lititz (Pa.) Acad.; grad. Sch. of Instrn. Revenue Cutter Service, 1879; m. Hannah T. Gilbert, Jan. 11, 1882 (died 1888); m. 2d, Abby G. W. Bartlett, Oct. 29, 1895. Third lt., July 2, 1879; 2d lt., Oct. 24, 1884; 1st lt., Apr. 18, 1895; capt., June 3, 1902; capt. commandant, Apr. 25, 1908; chief of Revenue Cutter Service, Apr. 1, 1905-Apr. 30, 1911, when voluntarily retired on account of ill health. Served on Atlantic and Pacific coasts, Puget Sound, Behring Sea, Great Lakes, various foreign cruises, N. Atlantic Squadron during Spanish-Am. War, after which awarded medals by Congress; personally comd. fleet of revenue cutters in Gulf of Mexico, enforcing sanitary regulations, during the yellow fever epidemic of 1905. Home: New Bedford, Mass. Died Mar. 24, 1916.

ROSSELL, WILLIAM TRENT army officer; b. Mt. Vernon, Ala., Oct. 11, 1849; s. Maj. William H. and Lucinda Gayle (Eastin) R.; apptd. from N.J., and grad. U.S. Mil. Acad., 1873; m. Jeanie Ellis, Dec. 27, 1881 (died 1897). Commissioned 2d lt. of engrs., June 13, 1873; promoted through grades to brig. gen. and chief of engrs. U.S.A., Aug. 12, 1913. Served on the Atlantic and Gulf Coast and on the Ohio and Miss. rivers; mem. Miss. River Commn., 1906-13; pres. bd. engrs. for rivers and harbors, 1909-13; pres. examining bd. for promotion engr. officers; sr. mem. Harbor Line Bd., New York harbor, and Bd. of Engrs. Fortification; div. engr. Eastern Div.; retired by operation of law, Oct. 11, 1913. Advisory engr. N.Y. State Highway Commn., 1914; fed. commr. N.Y. Harbor Line Commn., 1915. Called into active duty, Apr. 1917. Mem. Bd. Engrs. for Rivers and Harbors. Home: New Brighton, S.I., N.Y. Died Oct. 11, 1919.

ROSSER, THOMAS LAFAYETTE soldier, civ. engr.; b. Campbell Co., Va., Oct. 15, 1836; s. John and Martha M. (Johnson) R.; family removed to Tex., 1849; entered West Point, 1856, in class of 1861; class being ordered into army when Fort Sumter was fired upon, he resigned; went to Montgomery, Ala.; apptd. 1st lt. arty., C.S.A.; soon after capt. Co. D, Washington arty., New Orleans; severely wounded, Mechanicsville, Va., 1862; promoted lt. col. arty., and a few days later col. 5th Va. cav., in brigade of J. E. B. Stuart; brig. gen. cav. fall of 1863; maj. gen. cav. fall 1864; served in Army of Northern Va.; refused to surrender at Appomattox with Lee, but charged through lines and escaped; while endeavoring to reorganize scattered troops of the army was captured and made prisoner of war; was seriously wounded 4 times in battle; m. Betty B. Winston, 1863. Studied law after the war, but did not enter profession; was one of supts. Nat. Express Co. under Gen. Joe Johnston; later engr. in ry. service, including chief engr. Northern and Canadian Pacific railroads from 1870 until 1886, when he retired to an estate in Va.; apptd. brig. gen. U.S.V., June 10, 1898, and comd. 3d brigade, 2d div., 1st army corps, composed of 14th Minn., 2d Ohio and 1st Pa. regts., vol. inf., in war with Spain. Home: Charlottesville, Va. Died 1910.

ROSSETTER, GEORGE W. (ros-e-te—r), C.P.A.; s. George W., Sr., and Mary A. (Flood) R.; m. Marjorie Aylesworth Mihills; children—George M., William A., Thomas B. Pres. Rossetter Industries, Inc., Peoria, Ill.; chmn. bd. Rossetter Motor Co., Dealers Equipment Co., both Peoria, Ill. Former pres. Chgo. Assn. of Commerce; former mem. price adjustment sect. bd., Chgo. Ordnance District War Dept.; mem. Northwestern U. Associates. Served as machine gun officer, with A.E.F., World War I. Lt. Colonel Illinois Reserves Militia, World War II. Mem. Illinois and Minnesota socs. C.P.A.'s, Am. Instn. Accountants, S.A.R., Am. Legion, Beta Alpha Psi, Beta Gamma Sigma. Republican. Episcopalian. Clubs: Chicago, Economic (ex-pres.), Knollwood (ex-pres.) Forty, Commercial, Mid-way, Chicago Farmers (ex-pres.); Peoria (Ill.) Country; Creve Coeur (Peoria), Illinois Seniors Golf Assn. (past pres.). Home: Wadsworth, Ill. Office: 621 Franklin St., Peoria, Ill. Died Sept. 1959.

ROSSITER, PERCEVAL SHERER, surgeon general U.S. Navy; b. Shepherdstown, W.Va., Nov. 30, 1874; s. Joel Tomkins and Benetta (Sherer) R.; student U. of Md.; m. Isabel P. Jacobi, July 25, 1898; 1 dau., Ernestine Sherer. Capt. asst. surgeon, U.S.V., Spanish-Am. War, 1898; entered Med. Corps of the Navy, 1903; mem. U.S. Naval Mission to Brazil, 1922-26; comdg. officer Brooklyn (N.Y.) Naval Hosp., 1929-32, Washington (D.C.) Naval Hosp., 1932-33; became surgeon gen. U.S. Navy, 1933; retired Dec. 1, 1938; chief of staff Gallinger Municipal Hosp., Washington, D.C. Fellow Am. Coll. Surgeons, Am. Coll. Physicians, A.M.A.; mem. Assn. Mil. Surgeons (pres. 1936-37). Home: 111 N. Alfred St., Alexandria, Va. Office: Gallinger Hospital, Washington DC

ROSZEL, BRANTZ MAYER supt. mil. school; b. Baltimore, Md., Mar. 16, 1869; s. Stephan George and Anna Maria (Mayer) R.; A.B., Johns Hopkins U., 1889, Ph.D., 1896; certificate, Army War Coll., 1923; m. Christine Washington Chew, Feb. 2, 1905. Began as instr. mathematics, Johns Hopkins U., 1895; instr. in science, high schs., Washington, D.C., 1896-1903; headmaster Sewanee Grammar Sch. of U. of the South, 1903-08; supt. Shenandoah Valley Acad., Winchester, Va., 1908—. Commd. Maj. Q.M.O.R.C., U.S.A., 1916; served in U.S. and France, 1917-18; promoted through grades to col. M.I. Res., Oct. 1925; now col. Aux. Res., U.S.A.; dir. R.O. Sch., Winchester, 1933-35. Mem. Constl. Conv. to repeal 18th amendment, 1934. Dir. Winchester Memorial Hosp. Companion Mil. Order of World War. Mil. Order Fgn. Wars of U.S. Democrat. Episcopalian. Mason. Author of the Commander's Tour, 1928. Also Fixing Commn. and Jewish Welfare Bd. for Army and Navy, World War. Pres. Zionist Orgn. America; co-chairman council Jewish Agency for Palestine. Democrat. Died Mar. 16, 1938.

ROTHBERG, SIDNEY, pharmacologist; b. Bklyn., Apr. 17, 1914; s. Harry and Sarah (Horowitz) R.; B.S., Bklyn. Coll., 1939; postgrad N.Y.U., 1947-48, U. Md., 1956-60; m. Dorothy Schaffel, Oct. 15, 1939 (dec. Apr. 1959); children—David Michael, Frances B., Eric Joseph, Cathy Ann. Research asso. Jewish Hosp., Bklyn., 1930-33; biochemist Cumberland Hosp., Bklyn., 1933-43; research pharmacologist, directorate med. research Med. Research Lab., Edgewood Arsenal, Md., 1954-70. Served with AUS, 1943-54, now lt. col. Res. Mem. Armed Forces Chem. Assn., Soc. Exptl. Biology and Medicine, Soc. Am. Microbiologists, Sci. Research Soc. Am., A.A.A.S. Contbr. articles in field to sci. jours. Patentee in field. Home: Edgewood MD Died July 26, 1970.

ROTHROCK, EDWARD STREICHER chem. co. exec.; b. Ellsworth, Kan., Mar. 31, 1896; s. Ellsworth and Addie (Streicher) R.; B.S., Rice Inst., 1917; m. Elizbeth Phillips Stockton, 1921; children—Edward Streicher, Janet Elizabeth (Mrs. Renfroe W. Johnson). With Consolidated Chem. Co. (formerly Texas Chem. Co.), Houston, 1920—, successively chemist, chem. and sales staff, plant supt., Baton Rouge, asst. mgr. So. div., gen. mgr. So. div., v.p., gen. mgr. So. div., 1920-54, exec. v.p., 1954-55, merged with Stauffer Chem. Co., 1955, gen. mgr. Consol. Chem. Industries div., sr. v.p. Stauffer Chem. Co., 1955—. Served from 2d to 1st lt., U.S. Army, 1917-19. Mem. Am. Inst. Chem. Engrs. Club: Houston Rotary. Home: 3257 Ella Lee Lane, Houston 77019. Office: 6910 Fannin St., Houston 77025. Died Jan. 23, 1964.

ROTHSCHILD, MARCUS A. M.D.; b. Woodville, Miss., July 4, 1887; s. Morris H. and Emily Blanche R.; grad. Randolph-Macon Acad., Bedford City, Va., 1901, Horace Mann Sch., N.Y. City, 1904; A.B., Columbia, 1907; M.D., Coll. Phys. and Surg., N.Y. City, 1911; grad. study U. of Freiburg, Germany, 1912-13, Univ. Coll. Hosp., London, 1913-14; m. Edna E. Liebman, June 2, 1910; children—Edna Liebman, Marcus Adolphus. Began practice at N.Y. City, 1911; externe Mt. Sinai Hospital, 1911-12, asso. physician, 1925-30, cardiographer, 1930-33; physician Beth Israel Hospital; cardiologist Broad Street-Pan American Hospital, 1930. Served as major Med. Corps, U.S.A., 1917-19. Director Am. Jewish Physicians Com. Fellow N.Y. Acad. Medicine. Democrat. Hebrew religion. Home: New York, N.Y. Died Feb. 16, 1936.

ROTHSCHILD, WALTER NATHAN chmn. Abraham & Straus; born New York, N.Y., April 28, 1892; son Simon Frank and Lillian (Abraham) R.; student Brooklyn Poly. Prep. Sch., 1905-08; grad. Lawrenceville Sch., 1909; Litt.B., Princeton U., 1913; LL.D., Polytech. Inst. Bklyn., 1955, Long Is. U., 1957; m. Carola Warburg, Jan. 27, 1916; children—Carol W. (Mrs. Amory H. Bradford), Walter Nathan Jr., Phyllis Frederica (Mrs. C. Brooks Peters). Dir. Asso. Merchandising Corp. and Retail Research Assn. (chmn. bd., 1944-46); chmn. exec. com. Federated Dept. Stores, Incorporated; director of Douglas Gibbons & Co., Lt. (j.g.), U.S. Naval Res., World War I. Mem. State N.Y. Temp. Commn. on need for State U.; mem. adv. council Art Mus. Princeton U., 1956-59; member of the Lincoln Sesquicentennial Commission, 1958-59; member of the board of trustees of the Sarah Lawrence Coll., U.S. Trust Co., N.Y. Mem. Council N.Y. State University Colleges of Medicine, 1955-60. Chairman of the Army and Navy committee, National Jewish Welfare Bd., 1942-46; dir. and mem. exec. com. United Service Orgns.; v.p. Nat. War Fund, Inc., 1943-46; trustee Federation of Jewish Philanthropies N.Y. (v.p. 1943-47); mem. bd. trustees, com. econ. development;

mem. exec. com. Am. Jewish Com.; mem. nat. adv. council Girl Scouts; chmn. adv. council dept. economics and social instns. Princeton U., 1951-54, mem. grad. council, 1952-53, 1954-59; mem. Two Hundred and Fifty Associates of Harvard Business Sch.; rep. of United Service Orgns. and Jewish Welfare Bd., Gt. Brit., 1943; pres. N.Y. City Conf. of Charities and Corrections, 1923. Recipient Medal of Freedom from War Dept., 1947. Mem. Mil. Order Fgn. Wars. Republican. Clubs: Princeton, Century Assn. (N.Y.C.); Nassau (Princeton, N.J.); Eastern Yacht (Boston); New Bedford (Mass.) Yacht; Century Country (White Plains); Unity, Brooklyn (Bklyn.). Home: 1 E. 87 St., N.Y.C. 28; and Woodlands, White Plains, N.Y. Office: 422 Fulton St., Bklyn. Died Oct. 8, 1960.

ROULHAC, THOMAS RUFFIN lawyer; b. at Raleigh, N.C., Nov. 8, 1846; s. Joseph B.G. and Katherine (Ruffin) R.; ed. Dr. Alexander Wilson's Sch., Melville, N.C., and Hillsborough (N.C.) Mil. Sch.; m. Greensboro, Ala., Dec. 29, 1870, Julia Erwin Jones. The day after N.C. seceded was apptd. drill master and served as such until early organized N.C. regts. were sent to field; later was mem. Manly's Battery of Arty. until after battle of Gettysburg, then served as 1st lt. 49th N.C. Inf., C.S.A., until captured at battle of Five Forks, Va., Apr. 1, 1865; prisoner on Johnston's Island, in Lake Erie, until June, 1865. Admitted to bar by Supreme Court of N.C. on exams. of 1867 and 1868; engaged in practice of law in Ala. since 1871; mayor of Greensboro, Ala., 1873; State judge 11th jud. circuit of Ala., 1894-98; U.S. atty. for Northern dist. of Ala. since Oct., 1902. Pres. Ala. State Bar Assn.; mem. Am. Bar Assn. Catholic. Sound Money Democrat. Address: Sheffield, Ala.

ROURKE, FRANK W(ILLIAM) r.r. exec.; b. Somerville, Mass., Feb. 7, 1892; s. John and Mary (O'Connell) R.; B.S. in civil engring., Tufts Coll., 1915; m. Leah C. Doiron, June 14, 1916; children—Margaret (Mrs. J.H. Graham), John, James, Janet. Joined B. & M. R.R., 1914, v.p. operations, 1950-—. Served as 1st lt. to capt. Transp. Corps. U.S. Army, World War I. Mem. Am. Legion. Elk. Home: 45 Wentworth Rd., Melrose 76, Mass. Office: 150 Causeway St., Boston 14. Died Aug. 4, 1964.

ROUSE, JOHN DELOS lawyer; b. Miller Tp., Knox Co., O., July 24, 1838; s. Erastus S.S. and Polly (Mills) R.; ed. Sloan's Acad. and pvt. tutor, Mt. Vernon, O.; m. Josephine Julian, Sept. 6, 1866 (now deceased); 2d, Mrs. Blanche Wainwright Shakespeare, of Wilmington, Del., Nov. 26, 1906. Admitted to bar, 1860; capt. 77th Ill. Vols. from Sept. 2, 1862, afterward transferred to 130th Ill. Vols.; mustered out Aug., 1865; bvtd. maj. U.S.V. "for faithful and meritorious services during the campaign against the City of Mobile and its defenses." Chief deputy collector and afterward acting collector of internal revenue at New Orleans, 1866-67; practicing law in New Orleans, 1867-1912; retired and removed to Atlantic City, N.J. Mem. Nat. Geog. Soc., Loyal Legion; chmn. delegation La. Bar Assn. to Universal Congress Lawyers and Jurists, St. Louis, 1904. Republican. Home: Hotel Dennis, Atlantic City, N.J.

ROUSH, GAR A. (roush), mineral economist; b. Harrisburg (now Gas City), Ind., Oct. 21, 1883; s. Isaac N. and Clementine H. (McCarty) R.; A.B., Ind. U., 1905; M.S., U. Wis., 1910; m. Lillian Belle Coleman, July 16, 1911. Asst. prof. metallurgy, 1912-20, asso. prof., 1920-26, Lehigh U.; acting prof. metallurgy, Mont. Sch. Mines, 1926-27; spl. adviser Mus. Peaceful Arts, N.Y., 1927-30; editor, 1913-43, Mineral Industry, ann. devoted to world mineral interests; mineral technologist, U.S. Bur. of Mines, 1943-46; became metals engr., Strategic and Critical Materials Div., bur. Fed. Supply (formerly U.S. Treasury Dept.) 1946, with planning br. procurement div., Gen. Service Adminstrn. until 1955, ret. 1955. Appointed supr. tng. of inspection div. Ordnance Dept., AUS, 1918; commd. capt. Ordnance Dept., 1918, and appointed head of ednl. br., inspection div., and later chief of tests, metall. br.; hon. discharged, 1919, commd. maj., Staff Specialist Reserve, U.S. Army, 1924, and for several years served as spl. lectr. on strategic mineral supplies, Army Industrial Coll.; later assigned to Commodities Div., Planning Branch Office of Asst. Sec. of War; mem. Inactive Reserve, 1941-—. Mem. Electrochem. Soc. (asst. sec. 1912-18), Am. Inst. Mining and Metall. Engrs. (mng. editor 1917), Soc. of Am. Mil. Engrs. (Toulmin medalist, 1939). Presbyn. Contbr. numerous articles on electrochem. and metall. and mineral econs. in the tech. press, various standard encyclos. and other works of reference. Author of the sect. on Mineral Industries in rev. edit. Van Hise's Conservation of Natural Resources; sect. on Electrochemistry and Electrometallurgy in 6th edit. and on Electrochemistry in 7th edit. Standard Handbook for Electrical Engineers; Strategic Mineral Supplies; articles on strategic mineral supplies in foreign countries in Mil. Engr. Home: 4416 Seventeenth St. North, Arlington, Va. Address: Planning Branch, Procurement Div., General Service Administration, Washington 25. Died Aug. 17, 1955.

ROUSSE, THOMAS ANDREW educator; b. Kranidion, Greece, Nov. 15, 1901; s. Andrew Peter and Helen (Pappastaureu) R.; B.B.A., U. Tex., 1928, LL.B., 1927, M.A., 1933; grad. study Columbia, 1941; m. Mary Shackelford, May 17, 1942. Prof. speech U. Tex., 1927-41, since 1945, chmn. dept. speech since 1945; prof. speech Tex. State Coll. for Women, summer sessions, 1937-38, Coll. City N.Y. summer, 1939, 40, 41; dir. U. Tex. Vets. Adv. Service, 1945-47. Served as maj., U.S.A.A.F., 1942-45. Decorated Legion of Merit. Mem. Speech Assn. Am. (council 1941-44, 1952-54, vice president, 1954, president, 1955-—), Texas Speech Association (president, 1941-42, 1946-47), Acad. Polit. Sci., Tex. Bar Assn., Delta Sigma Rho (v.p.), Pi Sigma Alpha. Mason. Club: University Faculty. Author: How to Debate, 1950; Political Ethics and the Voter, 1952; Bicameralism v. Unicarmeralism, 1937. Home: 5202 Shoal Creek Blvd., Austin, Tex. Died Feb. 9, 1961; buried Austin Meml. Park.

ROUSSEAU, HARRY HARWOOD rear adm., U.S.N.; b. Troy, N.Y., Apr. 19, 1870; s. William White and Jeanette (Parker) R.; C.E., Rensselaer Poly. Institute, 1891; m. Gladys Fargo Squiers, 1908. Draftsman and engineer for pvt. cos., 1891-98; apptd., after competitive exam., civ. engr. U.S.N., rank of lt., 1898; engr. Bur. of Yards and Docks, Washington, 1899-1903; engr. pub. improvements, Mare Island Navy Yard, Calif., 1903-07; apptd. chief Bur. of Yards and Docks, with rank of rear adm., Jan. 1907. Mem. Isthmian Canal Commn., 1907-14; engr. terminal constrn., Panama Canal, 1914-16; mem. Commn. on Navy Yards, 1916-—; mgr. shipyard plants div. Emergency Fleet Corp., 1917-19. Given thanks of Congress and promoted to rank rear adm., Civil Engr. Corps, 1915. Dir. Panama R.R. Co.; v. chmn. U.S. Shipping Bd., Port Facilities Commn., 1918-20; dir. Naval Petroleum Reserves, 1927-—; chief co-ordinator of Federal Service, 1928-—. Episcopalian. Died July 25, 1930.

ROUSSEAU, LOVELL HARRISON, congressman; b. nr. Stanford, Lincoln County, Ky., Aug. 4, 1818. Admitted to bar, Bloomfield, Ind., 1841; Whig mem. Ind. Ho. of Reps., 1844-45; commd. capt. 2d Ind. Inf., 1846; capt. 2d. Ind. Regt. Volunteers, Mexican War, received spl. mention for gallantry at Battle of Buena Vista, 1847; mem. Ind. Senate, 1847-49, Ky. Senate, 1860-61; organized 5th Regt., Ky. Militia, 1861; credited with preventing sucession of Ky. from Union; commd. col. 3d Ky. Inf., 1861, brig. gen. U.S. Volunteers, 1861; served in battles of Shiloh and Perryville; promited to maj. gen. Volunteers, 1862; mem. U.S. Ho. of Reps. from Ky., 39th Congress, 1865-67; brig. gen. with brevet rank of maj. gen. U.S. Army, 1867, in charge of Dept. of La., 1868. Died New Orleans, Jan. 7, 1869; buried Arlington (Va.) Nat. Cemetery.

ROUTLEY, THOMAS CLARENCE physician; b. Victoria County, Ont., Mar. 11, 1889; s. Obadiah William and Eliza (Silverwood) R.; M.B., U. Toronto, 1915, M.D., 1930, LL.D., 1955; LL.D., Queen's U., 1931, Dalhousie U., 1953; D.Sc., Laval U., 1956; m. Florence Johnston, July 1, 1916; children—Muriel (Mrs. Wm. Weir), Marianne (Mrs. David Gibson), Patricia (Mrs. Andrew Clarke), Eric. Intern Toronto Gen. Hosp., 1915; practice of medicine, Toronto, 1918-23; med. adviser Canadian delegation to UN on establishment of WHO, 1946, mem. expert adv. panel on profl. and tech. edn. WHO, 1952-—, chmn. com. med. care, 1956-—; chmn. organizing com. to establish World Med. Assn., 1946, chmn. council World Med. Assn., 1947-51, cons. gen., 1951-—. With Royal Army M.C., Canadian Army M.C., World War I; exec. dir. Canadian Med. Procurement and Assignment Bd., World War II. Decorated Comdr. Order Brit. Empire, 1945; awarded Starr medal, Canadian Med. Assn., 1948; Medal of Honour, Canadian Pharm. Mfrs. Assn., 1952. Fellow Royal Coll. Phys. and Surg. of Can.; mem. Brit. (pres. 1955-56), Canadian (gen. sec. 1923-54, pres. 1955-—), Ont. (sec. 1918-38) med. assns., Brit. Commonwealth Med. Conf. (pres. 1956). Home: 17 Heathdale Rd. Office: 150 St. George St., Toronto, Can. Died Mar. 31, 1963.

ROVENSTINE, E(MERY) A(NDREW) physician; b. Atwood, Ind., July 20, 1895; s. Cassius Andrew and Lulu (Massena) R.; A.B., Wabash Coll., Crawfordsville, Ind., 1917, D.Sc., 1948; M.D., Ind. U., 1928; student Grad. Sch., U. of Wis., 1930-34; m. Jewel Sonya Gould, 1939. Asst. prof. of anesthesia, U. of Wis., 1934; asst. prof. surgery, Coll. of Medicine, New York U., 1935-36, prof. of anesthesia since 1937, prof. of anesthesia Coll. of Dentistry since 1938; dir. of div. of anesthesia, Bellevue Hosp. since 1935; guest dir. anesthesia, Oxford (Eng.) U., 1938; guest prof. anesthesia, U. Rosario (Argentina), 1939; mem. med. teaching mission to Czechoslovakia, 1946. Cons. anesthetist—Beth Israel Hosp., Hosp. for Spl. Surgery, Goldwater Meml. Hosp., Knickerbocker Hosp., Horace Harding Hosp., Gouverneur Hospital (N.Y.C.). Sr. cons. in anesthesia Veterans Hosp. (Bronx, N.Y.); director of anesthesia, University Hospital, 1949-—. Served as 1st lt. Engrs., A.U.S., 1917-19. Fel. A.M.A., N.Y. Acad. Med., N.Y. Acad. Science; mem. Am. Bd. Anesthesiology (pres. 1948), Am. Soc. Anesthetists (past pres.), Am. Soc. Regional Anesthesia (past pres.), Nat. Research Council (med. sci. div., 1941-46), Soc. Exptl. Biology and Medicine, Soc. Pharmaceutical and Experimental Therapy, International Anesthesia Research Society, Alpha Omega Alpha, Sigma Xi; honorary member French and Mexican socs. of anesthesia, honorary member South African Society Anesthesia. Recipient Internat. Anesthesia Research Award, 1938. Decorated Order of the White Lion (Czechoslovakia). Asso. editor: Anesthesiology, Geriatrics. Contbr. to numerous med. and dental publs. Conducted original research in cyclopropane anesthesia and spinal anesthesia, devising endotracheal airway and laryngoscope; prepared system for collecting statis. data of anesthesia and surgery. Home: 320 E. 57th St. Office: 550 First Av., New York 16. Died Nov. 9, 1960.

ROWAN, ANDREW SUMMERS (rou'an), army officer, author; b. Gap Mills, Va., Apr. 23, 1857; s. John M. and Virginia Wirt (Summers) R.; grad. U.S. Mil. Acad., 1881; m. Ida Symms, Apr. 12, 1887; m. 2d, Mrs. Josephine Morris de Greayer, 1904. Commd. 2d lt. infantry, U.S. Army, June 11, 1881; promoted through grades to maj. Oct. 11, 1905; served on staff of Gen. Nelson A. Miles, Cuban and Porto Rico campaigns, as lt. col. 6th U.S. Vols.; retired, Dec. 1, 1909. Member Intercontinental Ry. Survey, in charge hypsometric work of Central Am. party; spl. duty information Bureau, in charge map sect., adj.-gen. office; mil. attaché, Chile; sent to communicate with Gen. Garcia after declaration of Spanish-Am. War; landed from open boat near Turquino Peak, Apr. 24, 1898; successfully executed mission, bringing full information as to insurgent army; was 1st U.S. Army officer to enter Cuba after the declaration of war, and for this service was the subject of Elbert Hubbard's essay, "A Message to Garcia," which holds the world's record for circulation and translation into foreign tongues. Awarded D.S.C. "for extraordinary heroism in connection with the operations in Cuba in May 1898, securing secret information relative to existing conditions in that region of such great value that it had an important bearing on the quick ending of the struggle and the complete success of the U.S. Army." On duty Visayas Group, P.I., 1899-1902; prof. mil. science and tactics, Kan. State Agrl. Coll., 1902-03; on duty Fort Riley, Kan., 1902; at West Point, in Kentucky, and at Fort Riley, 1903, and at American Lake, Washington, 1904; on duty Island of Mindanao, 1905-07, in the Lake Lanao region; in command of the Malaig River expdn., 1906. Awarded S.S.C. "for gallantry in action displayed while placing and operating a field gun during the attack on Sudlón Mountain, Cebú, Philippine Islands, Jan. 8, 1900"; mem. Legion of Valor (U.S.); decorated Order Carlos Manuel de Céspedes (Cuba), 1938; awarded Distinguished Service medal by W.Va. Legislature, 1940. Author: The Island of Cuba, 1898; How I Carried the Message to Garcia, 1923. Clubs: Army and Navy (Washington, New York and Manila); Strollers (New York); Commonwealth (San Francisco). Address: 1036 Vallejo St., San Francisco, Calif.; (summer) Mill Valley, Marin Co., Calif. Died Jan. 10, 1943.

ROWAN, STEPHEN CLEGG naval officer; b. nr. Dublin, Ireland, Dec. 25, 1808; s. John Rowan; m. Mary Stark, at least 1 child, Maj. Hamilton Rowan. Came to U.S., 1818; promoted to lt., 1837; served in ship Delaware in Brazil and Mediterranean stations, 1841-44; became exec. officer ship Cyane, Pacific Station, 1845; helped retake Los Angeles during Mexican War; served 2 tours of duty as ordnance insp. N.Y. Navy Yard; commd. comdr., 1855; in command steam sloop Pawnee which supplied chief defense of Washington (D.C.) during Lincoln's inauguration, 1861; directed 1st shot fired from naval vessel in Civil War against batteries at Aquia Creek, 1861; cooperated with Gen. Burnside in capture of Roanoke Island and destruction of Confederate gunboat, 1862; attacked Cable's Point on Pasquotank River, destroyed fort and captured or routed Confederate squadron, 1862; assisted army to capture New Bern, 1862; promoted capt. and commodore, 1862; commanded New Ironsides in Charleston Harbor, 1863; detached to command all naval forces in N.C. Sound, 1864; promoted rear adm., 1866; in command Norfolk (Va.) Navy Yard, 1866-67, Asiatic Squadron, 1867-70, N.Y. Navy Yard, 1872-76; gov. Naval Asylum, Phila., 1881; supt. Naval Observatory, 1882; commd. vice adm., 1870; retired, 1889. Died Washington, D.C., Mar. 31, 1890; buried Oak Hill Cemetery, Washington.

ROWCLIFF, GILBERT (JONATHAN) naval officer (ret); b. Peoria, Ill., July 22, 1881; s. John Wesley and Caroline Matilda (Gilbert) R.; B.S., U.S. Naval Acad., 1902; grad. Naval War Coll., 1920; m. Marion Alice Leutze, Sept. 28, 1918; children—Caroline Gilbert (Mrs. C.R.J. Schaible), Marion McAlpine (Mrs. William A. Howard), Joan Leutzo (Mrs. Richard Lee Brecker). Commd. ensign USN, 1904, advanced through grades to rear adm., Jan. 1, 1936; sea service for 25 years; Asiatic sta., 1902-06; gunnery officer U.S.S. Virginia and U.S.S. New York, 1911-16; staff gunnery officer Battleship Force, 1916-18; gunnery officer, staff comdr. 6th B.S. and exec. officer, U.S.S. New York, with Brit. Grand Fleet, World War I; comdr. destroyer div., scouting fleet, 1922-23; staff material officer and tactical officer to comdr.-in-chief, U.S. Fleet, 1923-25; comdg. U.S.S. Cincinnati, 1928-30; destroyer squadron, 1933-35; cruiser div. and heavy cruiser force, U.S. Fleet, flagship Chicago, 1938-41; shore service included White House aide to Pres. Theodore Roosevelt and W.H. Taft; asst. Office of Fleet Tng.; mem. War Plans Div.; asst. budget officer USN Dept.; head dept. of engring. and aeros. U.S. Naval Acad., 1925-28; comdg. officer Naval Tng. Sta., Newport, R.I., 1930-33;

dir. naval communications, 1935-36; judge adv. gen., U.S. Navy Dept., 1936-38; mem. Gen. Bd., Navy Dept., 1941-45; sr. mem. Bd. Inspection and Survey, West Coast, 1945; ret. from active duty, Dec. 8, 1945; in charge Washington office Fitch Investors Service, since 1945. Trustee Mills Coll. Awarded Navy Cross, Victory medals (both World Wars), Spanish, Mexican, Am. campaign medals, Am. Def. medal. Presbyn. Mason. Clubs: Army Navy, Chevy Chase, Metropolitan (Washington); Yacht (N.Y.). Contbr. several articles to profl. jours. Home: 2100 Mass. Av., Washington 8. Office: Union Trust Bldg., 740 15th St., N.W., Washington 5. Died July 14, 1963; buried Arlington Nat. Cemetery.

ROWELL, JONATHAN HARVEY lawyer; b. Haverhill, N.H., Feb. 10, 1833; s. Jonathan B. and Cynthia (Abbott) R.; grad. Eureka Coll., Ill., 1861, (A.M., in course); law dept. Chicago Univ., 1865; m. Maria S. Woods, Oct. 23, 1866. Served lt. and capt. Co. G, 17th Ill. inf., 1861-64. Admitted to Ill. bar, 1865; State's atty. 8th jud. circuit, Ill., 1868-72; mem. Congress 4th Ill. dist., 1883-91. Home: Bloomington, Ill. Died 1908.

ROWELL, ROSS ERASTUS Marine Corps officer; b. Ruthven, Ia., Sept. 22, 1884; s. Elmore Curtis and Jessie Maria (Rogers) R.; student Ia. State Coll., 1901-03, U. of Ida., 1904-05; grad. naval aviator, Naval Flying Sch., 1923, mil. aviator, Air Corps Advanced Training Sch., 1924, air observer, Air Corps Tech. Sch., 1929; m. Marguerita Isabel Sangren, Mar. 6, 1912. Commd. 2d lt., U.S. Marine Corps, 1906, and advanced through the grades to brig. gen., 1939, maj. gen., 1942; served in Cuba, Haiti, Santo Domingo, Nicaragua, Philippine Islands, Great Britain, the Middle East, France and at sea; qualified as naval aviator, 1923; trained with Army Air Corps, 3 years; naval attaché, Am. Embassy, Havana, 1939-40; commanding general, Marine Aircraft Wings, Pacific Fleet from July 1942-Sept. 1944, chief of United States Naval Aviation to Peru since Nov. 1944. Decorated Navy Distinguished Service medal, Legion of Merit, Distinguished Flying Cross, Nicaraguan Cross of Distinction, Nicaraguan Medal of Merit; Cuban Naval Medal of Merit; 7 campaign medals. Member Phi Delta Theta. Clubs: Army and Navy, Army and Navy Country (Washington, D.C.); Cuyamaca (San Diego). Contbr. prof. articles on aviation to jours. Home: Am. Embassy, Lima, Peru. Died Sept. 6, 1947.

ROWLAND, HENRY COTTRELL author; b. New York, May 12, 1874; s. George and Maria Townsend (Durfee) R.; ed. pvt. schs., New York and Stanford, Conn., 1 yr. Williams Coll.; M.D., Yale Med. Sch., 1898; m. Mary Fulton Parkinson, June 22, 1910; children—Henry C., Peter Morgan (dec.), Diana. Able seaman, U.S. auxiliary cruiser Yankee, Spanish-Am. War; actg. asst. surgeon U.S.A., Philippine campaign, 1899-1900; physician in Vermenton and Accolay, France, 1914-15; dir. local mil. auxiliary hosp., 1916; allied publicity and propaganda work in U.S., 1917; war corr. Collier's Weekly and accredited special agent of the intelligence dept. U.S.N., in France, 1918. Episcopalian. Republican. Author: Across Europe in a Motor Boat, 1908; The Magnet, 1910; Duds, 1919; The Peddler, 1920; Mile High, 1921; Hirondelle, 1922; The Return of Frank Clamart, 1923; Of Clear Intent, 1923; Many Mansions. Home: Washington, D.C. Died June 6, 1933.

ROWLEY, FRANK S. prof. of law; b. Chicago, Ill., Dec. 16, 1896; s. John Arthur and Florence Mary (Smithies) R.; A.B., George Washington Univ., 1923, LL.B., 1923, LL.M., 1924; m. Lorel Bowling, Apr. 2, 1919. Asst. prof. law, Univ. of N.D., 1923-24; asso. prof. of law, Univ. of N.C., 1924-26; prof. of law, Univ. of Cincinnati, since 1926, dean, Coll. of Law since 1946; vis. prof. of law, summer, Univ. of Ia., 1929, Cornell, 1930, Chicago, 1931, Ohio State, 1936, Stanford, 1942. Served in U.S. Navy, 1918-20; U.S. Army, Jan. 1943-Feb. 1946; chief, legal br., hdqrs. A.S.F., War Dept., 1944-46; major, 1943, lt. col., 1944, col., 1945; released from active duty, rank of colonel, Feb. 1946. Awarded Legion of Merit and Army Commendation Ribbon. Pres., League of Ohio State Law Schools, 1948. Mem. bd. dir. Legal Aid Soc., Cincinnati. Mem. Cincinnati Bar Assn., Am. Assn. Univ. Profs., Order of the Coif, Phi Sigma Kappa, Phi Delta Phi, Omicron Delta Kappa. Club: Army and Navy (Washington, D.C.). Republican. Contbr. numerous articles to legal periodicals. Home: Hill Top Lane, Wyoming 15, O. Office: College of Law, Univ. of Cincinnati, Cin. Died July 26, 1952; buried Resthaven Meml. Park, Cin.

ROWLEY, GEORGE educator; b. Snow Hill, Md., Jan. 18, 1892; s. William Aaron and Mary Elizabeth (Conner) R.; A.B., U. Pa., 1913, postgrad., 1914-15, 19-20; M.F.A., Princeton, 1921; m. Ethel Packard, June 14, 1921 (dec.); m. 2d, Marion McGinley Mackie, Jan. 18, 1957. Instr. English, U. Pa., 1915-17; instr. art history Bryn Mawr Coll., 1921-24; dept. art and archaeology Princeton, 1925-—, curator oriental art Art Mus., 1935-—. Served as 2d lt. U.S. Army, 1917-19. Mem. Archaeol. Inst. Am., Coll. Art Assn., Chinese Art Soc., Japan Soc., Phi Beta Kappa, Delta Sigma Rho, Alpha Chi Rho. Republican. Episcopalian. Author: Principles of Chinese Painting, 1947; Ambrogio Lorenzetti, 1955. Home: 91 Edgerstowne Rd., Princeton, N.J. Died Jan. 4, 1962; buried Rocky Hill Cemetery, Princeton.

ROXAS, MANUEL (raw'häsh), pres. of Philippines; b. Capiz, Capiz, The Philippines, Jan. 1, 1892; s. Gerardo and Rosario (Acuna) Roxas; LL.D. (honoris causa), Univ. of Manila, Philippines, 1913; m. Trinidad de Leon, 1921; children—Ruby, Gerardo. Admitted to bar of Philippines with highest rating, 1913; law clerk to Chief Justice Arellano, Manila, 1913-17; municipal councilor, Capiz, Capiz, 1918; provincial gov., Capiz, 1920; rep. 1st dist. of Capiz, 1924-36, speaker of House of Rep., 1924-35; sec. of Finance, 1938-41; elected to senate 1941, pres. 1945; pres. of the Philippines since 1946. Mem. Constitutional Conv., 1934; head of Philippine independence missions in Washington, 1923, 29, 31-33, with others secured the Hare-Hawes Cutting Law; mem. joint preparatory com. on Philippine Affairs, 1935; chmn. Nat. Econ. Council, Tax Commn., Rural Progress Adminstrn., bd. of dirs. of Nat. Development Co., Com. on Ednl. Policy to reorganize the Univ. of Philippines; mem. Nat. Rice and Corn Corp., 1939-41, Mindanao Land Settlement Project, 1939-41, the Nat. Relief Bd., 1939-41, Bd. of Regents of Univ. of Philippines, 1936-41. Entered Philippine Army as colonel Dec. 1941; brig. gen. as aide to Gen. MacArthur, 1942. Mem. Nationalista Liberal Party. Roman Catholic. Club: Wack Wack Golf and Country. Home: Malacanan Palace, Manila, Philippines. Died Apr. 15, 1948; buried in North Cemetery, Manila, P.I.

ROY, SHARAT KUMAR geologist; b. Shamnagar, India, Aug. 27, 1897; s. Nabin Krishma and (Devi) Govinda Mohini R.; student St. Columbus Coll., Hazaribagh, India, and Bangabashi Coll., Calcutta; spl. student, London, 1919; I.Sc., U. of Calcutta, 1915; A.B., U. of Ill., 1922, M.S., 1924, Ph.D., 1941; m. Elsa Barandun. Research in geology and paleontology, U. Chgo., 1925-37. Naturalized Am. citizen. Assistant paleontologist New York State Museum, Albany, 1924-25; asst. curator paleontology Chicago Natural History Museum, 1925-34, asst. curator geology, 1934-37, curator, 1937-42, acting chief curator geology, 1946-47; chief curator geology since 1947; geologist Rawson-MacMillan Arctic Expdn. of Chicago Natural History Museum, 1927-28; leader Capt. Marshall Field Geol. and Paleontol. Expdn. to Newfoundland, 1928; Geol. Expdn. to the Salt Range, Punjab, India, 1945; conducted expdns. in many parts of United States, Mexico and Central America, 1950-—. Nat. Sci. Found. Grant for Europe, India, 1957-58. Private Calcutta U. Inv., 1917-18; capt., U.S. Air Corps, 1942-46, Am., European and Pacific theatres, World War II; maj., O.R.C., mem. A.F.A. Fellow Royal Geog. Soc., Geol. Soc. America, Artic Inst. N. America, Geol. Soc. London; mem. A.A.A.S., Paleontol. Soc., Polar Soc., Mineral Soc., Soc. Research in Meteorites, Royal Soc. Arts, N.Y. Acad. Sci., Sigma Xi, Theta Delta Phi, Theta Epsilon Pi. Clubs: Cosmopolitan, Quadrangle. Author of numerous papers in geology and paleontology, arctic stratigraphy, meteorites, volcanology. Contbr. to Science, Popular Astronomy, Outdoor America, Esquire, Gemological Mag., Delphian. Home: 5523 Everett Av., Chicago, Ill.; Beach Point, Provincetown, Mass. Home: 5523 S. Everett Av., Chgo. 60637. Office: Chicago Natural History Museum, Chicago, Ill. Died Apr. 17, 1962.

ROYAL, FORREST naval officer; b. New York, N.Y., Feb. 10, 1893; s. Forrest Betton and Mary Cornelia (Holmes) R.; B.S., U.S. Naval Acad., 1915; post grad. work in ordnance, Post Grad. Sch., Annapolis, Md., 1921-22; S.M., Mass. Inst. Tech., 1924; grad senior class, Naval War Coll., 1939; m. Katharine Knight, Dec. 28, 1922; children—Elizabeth Harwood (wife of Lt. James Wood Burch, U.S.N.R.), Katharine Knight. Commd. ensign, U.S. Navy, 1915, promoted through grades to rear adm., 1944; mem. U.S. Naval Mission to Brazil, 1939-41; comdg. officer U.S.S. Milwaukee, 1941-42; U.S. sec. Combined Chiefs of Staff, 1942-44; comdr. Amphibious Group Six since June 1944; comd. attack group in amphibious assault on Leyte, P.I., Oct. 1944, on Lingayen, Luzon, P.I., Jan. 1945, Mindanao invasion, March 1945; also Bruni Bay and Borneo. Decorated Cruzeiro do Sul, Medal of Services of War (Brazil); Distinguished Service Medal (star in lieu of second medal presented posthumously); Order Comdr. of British Empire. Mem. Am. Soc. Naval Engrs., Naval Inst., Mil. Order World War, Newcomen Soc. Clubs: Union League (New York); Army and Navy (Washington); Army-Navy Country (Arlington, Va.). Home: 2208 Knoll Road South, Arlington Ridge, Arlington, Va. Address: Navy Dept., Washington 25, D.C. Died June 18, 1945; buried in Arlington National Cemetery.

ROYALL, KENNETH CLAIBORNE, former sec. of war, lawyer; b. Goldsboro, N.C., July 24,21894; s. George and Clara Howard (Jones) R.; A.B., U. of N.C., 1914; LL.B., Harvard, 1917; m. Margaret Best, Aug. 18, 1917; children—Kenneth Claiborne, Jr., Margaret (Mrs. James Evans Davis). Admitted to the North Carolina bar, 1916; private law practice, Goldsboro, North Carolina, 1919-30, Raleigh and Goldsboro, N.C., 1931-42; law practice as Dwight, Royall, Harris, Koegel & Caskey, New York City and Washington, 1949-57; Royall, Koegel, Harris & Caskey, 1958-61, Royall, Koegel and Rogers, 1961-—. State senator of North Carolina in 1927 (author North Carolina Bank Liquidation Statute); Presidential elector (N.C.), 1940. Served as 2d lt. F.A., 1917-18, 1st lt. overseas, 1918-19; col. Army U.S., 1942-43, brigadier general, 1943-45; special assistant to Secretary of War, service overseas, 1944, 45. Counsel in sabateur case before special session of U.S. Supreme Court, 1942, appointed under secretary of war, November 1945; apptd. Sec. of War, July 1947, Sec. of Army, 1947-49. Del.-at-large Democratic Nat. Conv., 1964. Mem. Presidential Racial Com., Birmingham, 1963; nat. chmn. Lawyers Com. for Johnson and Humphrey, 1964. Trustee John Fitzgerald Kennedy Library. Decorated D.S.M. Mem. Gen. Alumni Assn. of Univ. of N.C. (president 1959-60), Am., N.C. (pres. 1929-30), New York bar associations, American Law Institute, Phi Beta Kappa, Delta Kappa Epsilon (hon. nat. pres. 1948). Episcopalian. Clubs: Carolina Country (Raleigh, N.C.); Metropolitan (Washington). Asso. editor of Harvard Law Review, 1915-17. Home: Raleigh NC Died May 27, 1971.

ROYCE, ALEXANDER BURGESS lawyer; b. St. Albans, Vt., Apr. 2, 1894; s. H. Charles and Christiana (Burgess) R.; A.B., Yale, 1915; LL.B., Harvard, 1920; m. Barbara Burgess, Mar. 12, 1921 (div. 1960) children—Martha (Mrs. W.J. Lacey), Robert S.; m. 2d, Virginia Scott Keating, Oct. 24, 1960. Admitted to the New York State bar, 1920; with Root, Clark, Buckner & Howland, 1920-24; mem. firm McLaughlin & Royce, 1924-28; special asst. to attorney general and U.S. atty., enforcing anti-trust laws, N.Y., 1925-26; with Chadbourne, Stanchfield & Levy, later Chadbourne, Wallace, Parke & Whiteside, 1928-42; in South America with Defense Supplies Corps, Reconstruction Finance Corp., de-Germanizing air transport lines, 1941-42; London dir. U.S. Commercial Co., 1943; dir. econ. operations North and West Africa, and co-chmn. of North African Econ. Bd., 1943-44; chmn. airlines com. U.S. Air Policy, Washington and New York, 1944-45; mem. firm Chadbourne, Parke, Whiteside & Wolff, 1945-—. Capt. to maj. 2d Battalion, 320th F.A., 82d Div., A.E.F., 1917-19. Home: 40 Fifth Av. Office: 25 Broadway, N.Y.C. Died Feb. 1968.

ROYSE, SAMUEL DURHAM (rois), lawyer; b. Terre Haute, Ind., Aug. 8, 1878; s. Samuel and Harriett (Durham) R.; student Mich. Mil. Acad., Orchard Lake, Mich., 1894-96; Ind. U., 1896-97; A.B., Amherst Coll., 1900; LL.B., Columbia, 1903; unmarried. Admitted to Ind. bar, 1903, and since practiced in Terre Haute; sr. partner firm of Cooper, Royse, Gambill & Crawford and its predecessors; mem. Ind. State Senate, 1900-13; county atty. Vigo County, 1911-17; v.p. Ind. Gas and Chem. Corp., J.W. Davis Co.; v.p. and chmn. bd. Terre Haute Boiler Works Co.; director Merchants National Bank of Terre Haute. Served as captain infantry, U.S. Army, 1917-18; maj. 39th Machine Gun Batt., 1918-19, World War. Dir. Union Hosp., Terre Haute, Rose Poly. Inst.; trustee Ind. World Memorial since 1920. Mem. Am., Ind. State and Vigo County bar assns., Delta Kappa Epsilon, Phi Delta Phi. Democrat. Methodist. Mason, Elk. Clubs: Terre Haute Country; Indianapolis Athletic; University (Washington, D.C., and Indianapolis); Bankers of America. Home: 431 S. 5th St. Office: Merchants Nat. Bank Bldg., Terre Haute, Ind. Died Apr. 8, 1945.

RUBEL, A(LBERT) C(HATFIELD) business exec.; b. Louisville, Mar. 30, 1895; s. Samuel B. and Nancy L. (White) R.; B.S., U. Ariz., 1917, Sc.D.; m. Henrietta Rockfellow, Mar. 4, 1921; children—Mary Ann (Mrs. T.A. Duddelson), John Pierpont. Petroleum exploration work various cos., Mex. and C.A., 1919-23; joined Union Oil Co. of Cal., Los Angeles, 1923, v.p., dir., 1938-56, became pres., chief exec. officer, chmn., retired as chmn., 1965; dir. Cyprus Mining Co., Northrup Corp. Served to capt., C.E., U.S. Army, 1917-19. Recipient D.S.C. Mem. Am. Inst. Mining and Metall. Engrs., Legion of Valor, Tau Beta Pi, Sigma Nu. Mason (K.T.). Clubs: California (Los Angeles); Bohemian (San Francisco). Home: 11 Packsaddle Rd. E., Rolling Hills, Cal. Office: Box 7600, Los Angeles 54. Died May 31, 1967.

RUBENS, HORATIO SEYMOUR lawyer, corp. official; b. N.Y. City, June 6, 1869; s. Rudolph and Cecelia R.; B.S., Coll. City of New York, 1888; M.S., 1891; LL.B., Columbia, 1891. Studied law in office of Elihu Root and became his managing clerk; was counsel to Salvador and in other Spanish Am. affairs; gen. counsel of Cuban Junta in successful Cuban revolution against Spain, 1895-98; counsel to Am. Insular Commn. to Puerto Rico, 1900; counsel to U.S. Mil. Govt. in Cuba, 1900; mem. commn. for division of codes and laws in Cuba, 1901, also of tax, prison and electoral law commns. in Cuba; chmn. com. on alcohol, Council of Nat. Defense, 1917; pres. Consolidated Railroads of Cuba; pres. and chmn. bd. The Cuba R.R. Co.; chmn. bd. Cuba Northern Rys. Co.; director The Cuba Company. Colonel Auxiliary Res., U.S.A.; colonel Cuban Army of Liberation; Decorated Order Bust of Liberator (Venezuela), 1895; Grand Medal of Merit and Honor, 1922; given spl. vote of thanks by Cuban Revolutionary Congress, 1897; awarded spl. gold medal by Cuba, 1915, for services rendered during Cuban Revolution; was declared "Adopted Son of Havana," 1922; declared "Adopted Son of Camagüey," 1930; accorded, by act of Cuban Congress, title of "The Great Friend of Cuba," with spl. decoration created for this title; Comdr. Grand Cross of Carlos Manuel de Cespedas (Cuba); "Adopted Son of Santa Clara" (Cuba), 1933; made hon. pres. of Cuba Vets. of Independence. Author: Liberty—The Story of Cuba. Home: Garrison, N.Y. Died Apr. 8, 1941.

RUCKER, ALLEN WILLIS business exec.; b. Bristol, Va., July 23, 1897; s. Allen T. and Mary Frances (Plunkett) R.; student pub. schs. Bristol, Tenn.; m. Elise Patricia Murtagh, Oct. 23, 1920; 1 son, Allen Willis (killed in action, Apr. 7, 1945); m. 2d, Dr. Waltrude M. Bruch, 1953; 1 son, Allen W.B. Purchasing agt. City Bristol, Va., 1919-20, credit mgr., 1920-22, sales mgr. 1922-23; ind. bus. adv., 1924-27; mem. U. Staff, Cambridge, Mass., 1927-29; pres. Edy-Rucker Nickels Co., Cambridge, 1929-60; chairman and chief executive officer, 1960-—; now management cons. various industries, U.S., Can. and Europe. Chief observer U.S. Aircraft Warning Service, Lexington, Mass., World War II; controller Mass. Com. Pub. Safety, Area 5-C; co-organizer 1st Town Civilian Def. Unit. Former mem. Mut. Security Agy. adv. group European Productivity. Served as pvt., non-commd. and commd. officer, 117th Inf., A.E.F., World War I. Mem. Tool Owners Union (founder, p. pres.). Rep. Presbyn. Clubs: Algonquin, Beacon Soc. (pres.) (Boston). Author: Share of Production Wage Plan, 1934; Labor's Road to Plenty, 1937; Scientific Price Management, 1941; Scientific Price Management II, 1945; Progress in Productivity and Pay, 1952; German lang. edit., 1954; Wages, Prices and Productivity, 1956; Incentives for Executives, 1958; Gearing Wages to Productivity, 1962; also articles. Office: 4 Brattle St., Cambridge, Mass. Died May 14, 1964.

RUCKER, CASPER BELL army officer; b. Mo., Sept. 9, 1886; student U. of Mo.; commd. 2d lt. Inf., Sept. 1911, and advanced to brig. gen., June 1943; asst. inspector gen., Philippine Dept., Manila, P.I., July 1938-40; chief of staff, 5th Div., Fort Benjamin Harrison, Ind., and Fort Custer, Mich., 1940-41; dep. chief of staff, Eighth Corps Area (now Eighth Service Command), Fort Sam Houston, Tex., 1941-42; chief of staff, Eighth Service Command, Army Service Forces, Dallas, Tex., since Jan. 1942.* Died Mar. 30, 1948.

RUCKER, DANIEL HENRY army officer; b. Belleville, N.J., Apr. 28, 1812; s. John A. and Sarah (Macomb) R.; m. Jane Curtis, 1850. Apptd. from Mich., 2d lt. 1st Dragoons, Oct. 13, 1837; 1st lt., Oct. 8, 1844; capt., Feb. 7, 1847; transferred to capt. asst. q.m., Aug. 23, 1849; maj. q.m. (14 yrs. service), Aug. 3, 1861; col. additional a.d.c. vols., Sept. 28, 1861; brig. gen., May 23, 1863; bvtd. maj. gen., Mar. 13, 1865; col. asst. q.m. gen., U.S.A., July 28, 1866; hon. mustered out of vol. service, Sept. 1, 1866; brig. gen. q.m. gen., Feb. 13, 1882; retired at own request, over 40 yrs.' service, Feb. 23, 1882. Bvtd. maj., Feb. 23, 1847, for battle of Buena Vista, Mex.; lt. col., col. and brig. gen., July 5, 1864, for services during the war; maj. gen. U.S.A., and U.S.V., Mar. 1865, for services during the war. Home: Washington, D.C. Died 1910.

RUCKER, ELBERT MARION prof. law; b. Anderson, S.C., Mar. 15, 1866; s. Elbert Marion and Sarah Frances (Whitner) R.; ed. Adger Coll., Walhalla, S.C.; A.B., U. of S.C., 1885, LL.B., 1887; m. Susan Elizabeth Kinard, 1886 (died 1913); children—Elizabeth (Mrs. George Rainsford Norris), Frances Louise (Mrs. William Webster Moore); m. 2d, Mary Mitchell Martin, Aug. 26, 1915. Admitted to S.C. bar, 1887, and began practice at Anderson; U.S. asst. atty., Washington, D.C., 1893-97; mem. S.C. Ho. of Rep., 1900-10 (chmn. ways and means com., 1908-10); prof. law, U. of S.C., 1910-26; served as lecturer summer schs. U. of Ga., U. of Ky., etc., and exchange prof. at U. of N.C.; was spl. asso. justice Supreme Court of S.C. various times. Democrat. Presbyn. Lived at Columbia, S.C. Died Aug. 16, 1926.

RUCKER, LOUIS H. soldier; b. in Illinois, Jan. 13, 1842. Entered Union Army, Apr. 19, 1861, as pvt., Capt. Barker's Chicago Dragoons, with which served to Aug. 18, 1861; pvt., sergt. and 1st sergt. Co. G, 8th Ill. Vol. Cav., Sept. 14, 1861-Feb. 8, 1864; 2d lt., Feb. 9, 1864, and 1st lt., Nov. 26, 1864, 8th Ill. Cav., serving until Apr. 21, 1865. Apptd. 2d lt. 9th U.S. Cav., July 28, 1866, 1st lt., July 31, 1867, capt., Mar. 20, 1879; maj. 4th Cav., Jan. 13, 1896, 6th Cav., Jan. 2, 1900; lt. col., Feb. 2, 1901; col. 8th Cav., Sept. 17, 1901, until retired as brig. gen. U.S.A., 1903. Died 1906.

RUCKMAN, JOHN WILSON army officer; b. Sydney, Ill., Oct. 10, 1858; s. Thomas and Mary (O'Brien) R.; grad. U.S. Mil. Acad., 1883, Arty. Sch., 1892, Army War Coll., 1915, Naval War Coll., 1916; m. May, d. of late Col. John Hamilton, U.S.A., June 16, 1887. Commd. 2d lt. 5th Arty., June 13, 1883; promoted through grades to col. C.A. Corps, Mar. 7, 1912; brig. gen., July 20, 1916; maj. gen. N.A., Aug. 5, 1917-May 1, 1918. First editor of Journal of U.S. Artillery, 1892-96; served in Havana, Cuba, with Army of Occupation, 1899-1901; instr. Sch. of Submarine Defense, 1901-04; in Philippine Islands, 1911-14, and insp. gen. there, 1911-12. Assigned to command 5th provisional regt. coast arty., Del Rio, Tex. border, July 3, 1916; later also comdg. dist. of El Paso Rio Grande, and dist. of Laredo, to July 1917; comd. S. Atlantic Coast Arty. Dist., Charleston, S.C., July-Aug. 1917, Southern Dept., Aug. 30, 1917-May 1, 1918, Northeastern Dept., Boston, May 23-July 20, 1918, N. Atlantic Coast Arty. Dist., Boston, July 21, 1918-—. Wrote: The Command and Administration of the Fortress of Port Arthur during the Russo-Japanese War. Inventor many devices for use in war. Died June 7, 1921.

RUDDER, JAMES EARL, educational administrator and reserve army officer; born at Eden, Texas, May 6, 1910; son of Dee Forest and Annie (Powell) R.; student John Tarleton Agrl. Coll., Texas, 1927-30; Indsl. Edn. degree, Tex. A. and M. Coll., 1932; grad. study Tex. Chirstian U., 1939; LL.D., Baylor University, Waco, 1960; married to Margaret E. Williamson, June 12, 1937; children—James Earl, Margaret Anne, Linda, Jane, Robert. Tchr., football coach Brady High Sch., 1933-38, John Tarleton Coll., Stephenville, 1938-41; operator Brady Drug Store, 1935-49; rancher, businessman, Brady, Tex., 1946-—; v.p., pub. relations counsellor Brady Aviation Corp., 1953-55; commr. Gen. Land Office State Tex., 1955-58; v.p. Tex. A. & M. U., 1958-59, pres., 1959-70; pres. Texas A. & M. U. System, 1965-70. Member of the executive committee of the Tenneco, Incorporated. Mayor of Brady, 1946-52; mem. State Bd. Pub. Welfare, 1953-55; chmn. Vets. Land Bd., 1955-58; mem. Inf. Adv. Bd.; mem. Tex. Governor's Commission on Education Beyond High School, 1966; member National Advertising Commission on Rural Poverty, 1966-67; state chmn. March of Dimes, 1966. Hon., vice pres. State Fair of Texas; member council and exec. bd. Tex. A. and M. Coll. Trustee Research Analysis Corp., Southwest Research Institute; member of the board of directors Texas United Fund, Sam Houston area council Boy Scouts Am., Nat. Space Hall of Fame Found., 1968; bd. visitors U.S. Mil. Acad. 1st lieutenant to colonel AUS, 1941-46; commanded Provisional Ranger Force at Normandy, 109th Inf. Regt., 28th Div. in Battle of Bulge, and liberation of Colmar; comdg. gen. 90th Inf. Div. Res., 4th Army, Austin, Tex., 1955-65; asst. dep. comdg. gen. for moblzn. Continental Army Command, 1965-67. Decorated D.S.C., Legion of Merit, Silver Star, Bronze Star with oak cluster, Purple Heart with oak-leaf clusters (U.S.); Legion of Honor with Croix de Guerre and palm (France); Order of Leopold with Croix de Guerre and palm (Belgium); recipient gold citizenship award V.F.W., 1965; Army and Navy Legion of Valor, 1965; Outstanding Citizenship award Tex. Dist. Exchange Clubs, 1967; Distinguished Service Medal. Mem. Res. Officers Assn., Am. Legion (post comdr. 1949), Vets. Fgn. Wars (nat. security com.), Land-Grant Assn. (nat. def. com.), Assn. U.S. Army (adv. bd.), Assn. Tex. Colls. and Univs. (commn. ednl. policy), Am. Council Edn. (commn. adminstrv. affairs), Asso. Western Univs., Inc. (exec. com.). Mason (33 deg.). Home: College Station TX Died Mar. 23, 1970; buried College Station City Cemetery, College Station TX

RUDDOCK, JOHN CARROLL physician; b. San Francisco, Calif., Feb. 19, 1891; s. John Carroll and Mary Geraldine (Hildreth) R.; B.S., U. of Calif., 1913; M.S., U. of Calif., 1914, M.D., 1916; m. Agnes Julia Scholl, Sept. 12, 1917; children—John Carroll, Mary Margaret. Began gen. practice of medicine, 1916; in private practice since 1920; mem. staff Los Angeles Gen., St. Vincent's hosps., Los Angeles; asso. clin. prof. medicine U. So. Cal., 1951-53, emeritus; med. dir. Richfield Oil Corp. Served in USN, 1917-19; capt. USNR, ret. 1951; active duty U.S. Navy, 1942-46. Received Alumnus Alpha Theta award for distinguished achievement, 1937, Medallion, Society of Friendly Sons of St. Patrick, 1957. Certified Internist and Cardiologist, Am. Bd. Internal Medicine. Fellow A.C.P., American College of Cardiology; member Royal Society of Medicine London (hon.), So. Cal. Med. Assn. (pres.), Cal. Heart Assn. (pres.), Sigma Xi, Beta Kappa Alpha, Alpha Omega Alpha. Republican. Roman Catholic. Club: University (Los Angeles). Contbr. med. articles to Jour. A.M.A., Western Jour. of Surgery, etc. Home: 450 Scholl Drive, Glendale 6. Cal. Office: 555 S. Flower St., Los Angeles 17. Died May 14, 1964.

RUDDOCK, MALCOLM IRVING lawyer; b. Lynn, Mass., Oct. 10, 1912; s. Ralph E. and Marion A. (Blake) R.; A.B. cum laude, Harvard, 1934, LL.B., 1937; m. Ruth Goodwin Brown, June 25, 1938; children—David Blake, Malcolm Irving, Martha Louise. Admitted to Mass. bar, 1937, N.Y. bar, 1938; staff atty. Cadwalader, Wickersham & Taft, N.Y.C., 1937-48, partner, 1949-—, specializing corporate, financial, anti-trust law. Dir. Macmillan Co. Lectr. Inst. Orgn. Mgmt., Yale, summers 1958, 59. Dir. civil def., Garden City, N.Y.; trustee Sch. Dist. 16, L.I., N.Y., 1946-47. Trustee Garden City Pub. Library, 1955-57. Served to lt., Air Combat Intelligence, USNR, 1943-45. Mem. Eastern Property Owners' Assn. (pres. Garden City, 1957-59), Am. Bar Assn. (chmn. com. on trade assns.), Bar Assn. City N.Y. Clubs: Harvard, Downtown Assn. (N.Y.C.); Cherry Valley (Garden City). Home: 411 Stewart Av., Garden City, N.Y. Office: 14 Wall St., N.Y.C. 5. Died June 18, 1961; buried Nassau Knolls, Port Washington, N.Y.

RUDOLPH, JACOB H. army officer; b. Mar. 25, 1886. Commd. 2d lt. inf., Sept. 25, 1908; promoted through grades to col., Feb. 1, 1938; temporary rank of brig. gen., Oct. 1, 1940; apptd. comdg. gen. Spokane Air Depot Control Area, Jan. 1943; retired July 1944. Address: War Dept., Washington. Died Mar. 19, 1960.*

RUE, LARS (LARRY) newspaperman; b. Fosston, Minn., Mar. 10, 1893; s. Rev. Halvor Eilef and Anna Johanna (Hanson) R.; grad. Fosston (Minn.) High Sch., 1913; student U. of N.D., 1914-15. Reporter, Duluth (Minn.) News Tribune, 1913-14; city editor, Hibbing (Minn.) Daily Tribune, 1914; asst. city editor, Minneapolis (Minn.) Daily News, 1915; war corr. with Mich. Nat. Guard for Detroit Free Press, 1916; asst. state editor, Detroit News, 1917; with Chicago Tribune, 1919-32 and since 1939, as mem. staff fgn. news service, Paris, covered Nationalist riots (Cairo, Egypt), initial Zionist movement (Palestine), enthronement of King Feisal (Damascus), Turkish Nationalist movement (with Gen. Wrangel in Crimea), return of King Constantine (Greece), 1919-20; reported progress of Turkish Nat. movement, (Constantinople), Korfanty putsch (Upper Silesia), traveled through Russia covering Russian famine, also covered Karl putsch (Hungary), 1921; as chief of Berlin bureau, attended Lausanne Conf., later accompanying Ismet Pasha to Ankara, covered death of the Pope (Rome) and Fiume march on Rome, 1922; covered Balkans and the Hitler putsch in Munich, 1923; as roving corr. wrote polit. and econ. articles on Can., West Indies, etc., 1924; attended Disarmament Conf., Geneva, also accompanied French forces in Morocco, later interviewing Abdul Krim in the Riff, 1925; reported Spanish Revolution, 1926; with hdqrs. in Vienna toured Balkans and Near Middle East, 1927-28; interviewed King Ammanullah in Afghanistan, also acted as pilot and navigator of own plane in Mediterranean region, 1929; collaborated with Floyd Gibbons, noted corr., 1930-31; with N.Y. Daily News, 1932-38, but with spl. assignment to Lindbergh kidnapping, 1934; with Chicago Tribune, Luxembourg, Holland, Belgium, 1939-44, chief of Tribune Paris bureau, 1939-40, chief of London bureau, 1940-44; with SHAEF, 1944-45; based Paris-Frankfurt, Germany, 1945-47; based Frankfurt-Berlin, 1948-51, covering Central European and Benelux countries, tour of USSR, 1957, covered Iraqi revolution, tour of East European countries, 1958; European corr. Chgo. Tribune Press Service; covered Pope John's election, coronation, 1961, interview Turkish Premier Inonu, 1963, others. Enlisted in the Aviation Corps, U.S. Army, 1917. commd., 1918. Recipient Edward S. Beck award for coverage Hungarian Revolt, Chgo. Tribune, 1956. Author: I Fly For News, 1932. Contbr. mags. Died July 13, 1965.

RUFF, ROBERT HAMRIC clergyman, educator; b. Chester, Miss., July 27, 1887; s. George Thomas and Mary (Hamric) R.; B.A., M.A., Millsaps Coll., Jackson, Miss., 1910; B.D., Emory U., Atlanta, Ga., 1915; grad. study Vanderbilt, U. of Chicago, Columbia U.; D.D., Kentucky Wesleyan College, 1928; LL.D., Ohio Northern University, 1929, Millsaps College, 1941; m. Annie Mae Gallbreth, July 15, 1925 (died May 6, 1931). Principal high school, Rolling Forks, Miss., 1910-11, Moorhead, Miss., 1911-13; ordained ministry M.E. Ch., S., 1915; pastor Moorhead, Miss., 1915-17; sec. rural work, Bd. Missions, M.E. Ch., S., 1921-26; sec. adult edn., Gen. S.S. Bd., M.E. Ch., S., 1926-27; pres. Morris Harvey Coll., Barboursville, W.Va., 1927-29; pres. Central Coll., Fayette, Mo., since 1930. Served as 1st lt., chaplain, U.S. Army, 1917-19. Mem. Mo. Conf., Meth. Ch.; pres. Ednl. Assn. Meth. Ch. Mem. Kappa Sigma, Sigma Upsilon, Omicron Delta Kappa. Democrat. Mason. Club: Kiwanis. Contbr. to religious and ednl. press. Home: Fayette, Mo. Digd May 5, 1942.

RUFFNER, ERNEST HOWARD colonel U.S.A.; b. Louisville, Ky., June 24, 1845; s. Lewis and Viola (Knapp) R.; ed. pub. and pvt. schs.; grad. 1st in class U.S. Mil. Acad., 1867; A.B. and A.M., Kenyon Coll., Gambier, O., 1877; m. Mary Hungerford Watson, of Detroit, Dec. 7, 1869. Second lt. and 1st lt. engr. corps, June 17, 1867; capt., Oct. 31, 1879; maj., July 2, 1889; lt.-col., Apr. 13, 1903; col., Sept. 9, 1906; retired, June 24, 1909. Engaged on river and harbor work at Detroit, Ft. Leavenworth, Leavenworth, Charleston, W.Va., Willets Point, N.Y. Harbor, Rock Island and Quincy, Ill., Buffalo, Baltimore, Charleston, S.C., New York, Cincinnati, New Orleans. Address: 2038 Auburn Av., Cincinnati.

RUGER, THOMAS HOWARD maj. gen. U.S.A., retired, 1897; b. Lima, N.Y., April 2, 1833; grad. West Point, 1854; assigned to engr. corps; resigned April 1, 1855; practiced law, Janesville, Wis., 1855-61; lt. col. 3d Wis. regt., June 1861; col., Aug. 20, 1862; brig. gen. vols., Nov. 29, 1862; served in Rappahannock campaign; comd. div. at Gettysburg; aided in suppressing draft riots, New York, 1863; served under Sherman and, Nov. 30, 1864 bvtd. maj. gen. for services at battle of Franklin; col. U.S.A., July 28, 1866; bvt. brig. gen. U.S.A., March 2, 1867, for services at battle of Gettysburg; mil. gov. Ga., 1868; supt. U.S. Mil. Acad., 1871-76; comd. dept. South, 1876-78; brig. gen., March 19, 1886; maj. gen., 1895. Home: Stamford, Conn. Died 1907.

RUGG, CHARLES BELCHER lawyer; b. Worcester, Mass., Jan. 20, 1890; s. Hon. Arthur P. (chief justice Supreme Court of Mass., 27 years) and Florence M. (Belcher) R.; A.B., Amherst, 1911, hon. A.M., 1936; LL.B., Harvard, 1914; m. Marjory L. Boynton, June 21, 1917; children—Cynthia, Deborah. Admitted to Mass. bar, 1914, and began practice at Worcester with firm of Sibley, Sibley & Blair; later mem. Mirick, Rugg &

Whitcomb until 1930; mem. Ropes, Gray, Boyden & Perkins, 1933-40, Ropes, Gray, Best, Coolidge & Rugg since 1940; mem. City Council, Worcester, 1915-17; apptd. U.S. commr., 1920; asst. dist. atty. Middle Dist. of Mass., 1921-26, elected dist. atty., 1926; asst. atty. gen. of U.S., Feb. 6, 1930-Jan. 23, 1933, in charge defense of claims against U.S. Govt.; acts as special assistant to attorney general of Mass. and of U.S. occasionally on special cases; member U.S. Commn. for Adjustment of British Claims, London, 1932; mem. Massachusetts Bar Examiners, 1953-—. Delegate Rep. Nat. Conv., 1940, 44. Ensign and lt. j.g., U.S.N.R., World War; lt. comdr. U.S.N.R. since 1933. Mem. bd. trustees Worcester Acad., Amherst and Simmons Colls. Mem. Am., Federal, Mass. and Worcester County bar assns., Am. Law Inst., Bar Assn. City of Boston, Am. Unitarian Assn. (v.p. and dir. 1941), Am. Legion, Chi Phi. Republican. Unitarian. Mason. Club: Union (Boston). Home: 301 Berkeley St. Office: 50 Federal St., Boston. Died Nov. 25, 1962; buried Oak Hill Cemetery, Sterling, Mass.

RUGGLES, ARTHUR HILER (rug'lz), physician; b. Hanover, N.H., Jan. 26, 1881; s. Edward Rush and Charlotte (Blaisdell) R.; A.B., Dartmouth, 1902, A.M., 1910, Sc.D., 1926; M.D., Harvard, 1906; Sc.D., Brown U., 1929; m. Hazel M. Wheeler, Apr. 22, 1914 (died Apr. 29, 1939); children—Arthur Hiler, Ann. Began practice at Providence, R.I., 1906; intern R.I., Hosp., 1907-09; asst. physician Butler Hosp., 1909-22, supt. since 1922; supt. Emma Pendleton Bradley Home, 1931-41, exec. v.p. bd. of trustees, 1941-43, pres. since 1943; consultant in mental hygiene, Dept. of University Health, and lecturer in psychiatry, Yale; mem. advisory council on research in nervous and mental diseases and cons. U.S.P.H.S.; mem. adv. council Dept. of Social Welfare of R.I. chief psychiatrist, 2d Div., U.S. Army, A.E.F. Mem. Am. Psychiat. Assn. (pres. 1942-43); R.I. Med. Soc. (pres. 1947-48), N. England Soc. Psychiatry (ex-pres.), National Com. for Mental Hygiene (pres. since 1948), Am. Psychiatric Assn. (sec.-treas. 1938-41; pres. 1942-43), hon. mem. Phi Beta Kappa (Dartmouth). Republican. Congregationalist (deacon Central Ch.). Clubs: University, Art. Home: 234 Irving Av., Providence 6. Office: Butler Hospital, Providence, R.I. Died Jan. 2, 1961; buried Swan Point Cemetery, Providence.

RUGGLES, COLDEN L'HOMMEDIEU army officer; b. Omaha, Neb., Mar. 18, 1869; s. George D. (brig. gen. U.S.A.) and Alma (L'Hommedieu) R.; grad. U.S. Mil. Acad., 1890; E.E., Lehigh U., 1903; grad. Army War Coll., 1922; m. Mary Appleton, d. Brig. Gen. Marcus P. Miller, U.S.A., Nov. 28, 1894; 1 dau., Colden (Mrs. E. L. Florance). Commd. add. 2d lt. 1st Arty., June 12, 1890; promoted through grades to col., May 15, 1917; brig. gen. (temp.), Aug. 8, 1918-Mar. 10, 1919. Duty Governor's Island, Ft. Monroe, Sandy Hook Proving Ground and Frankford (Pa.) Arsenal until 1900; insp. ordnance, U.S.A., Bethlehem Steel Co., 1900-03; at Watertown (Mass.) Arsenal, 1903-08; prof. ordnance and science of gunnery, U.S. Mill. Acad., 1908-11; comdg. officer Benicia (Calif.) Arsenal and ordnance officer Western Dept., 1911-13; comdg. officer, Manila Ordnance Depot and ordnance officer Philippine Dept., 1913-15; comdg. officer Sandy Hook Proving Ground, 1915-18, also Aberdeen Proving Ground, 1917-18; chief of insp. div. Ordnance Dept., 1918; duty with A.E.F., Oct.-Dec. 1918; chief of tech. staff, Ordnance Dept., 1919-21; on duty as student officer, Army War Coll., Aug. 15, 1921-June 30, 1922; chief of tech. staff. Ord. Dept., Sept. 4, 1922-Aug. 27, 1923; apptd. asst. to the chief ordnance with rank of brig. gen., Mar. 28, 1923; became asst. chief ordnance and chief manufacture, Ord. Dept., 1923; retired. Delegate to Conf. for the Supervision of the International Trade in Arms and Ammunition, and in Implements of War, held in Geneva, Switzerland, May 4-June 17, 1925. Awarded D.S.M. Episcopalian. Died Apr. 2,3.

RUGGLES, GEORGE DAVID brig. gen. U.S.A., retired, Sept. 11, 1897; b. Newburgh, N.Y., Sept. 11, 1833; s. David and Sarah (Colden) R.; m. Alma Hammond L'Hommedieu. Entered West Point, Sept. 1, 1851; grad. July 1, 1855; commd. 2d lt. 2d inf.; became adj. of his regt., Sept. 10, 1857; asst. adj. gen. July 1, 1861. During war served as adj. gen. of brigade in 3-months' campaign; then assigned to duty in charge of the organization of vol. army; later became chief of staff, Army of Va.; later asst. chief of staff, Army of Potomac; then on spl. duty, under Sec. Stanton, in War Dept.; assisted Gen. Fry in organization of the conscription; served in spl. inspection service, and later as adj. gen. Army of the Potomac, under Gen. Meade, to end of war; reached bvtd. rank of brig. gen.; participated in many battles. After war adj. gen. of several divs. and depts. with successive promotions, becoming brig. gen. U.S.A., and adj. gen. of the army, Nov. 6, 1893, until retired. Under assignment of the President, was gov. Soldiers' Home, 1898-1903. Died 1904.

RUHE, PERCY BOTT (roo), newspaper editor; b. Allentown, Pa., May 28, 1881; s. E. Lehman and Sallie (Marsteller) R.; A.B., Muhlenberg Coll., Allentown, 1901, D.Litt., 1948; m. Amy Sieger, Mar. 20, 1912; children—Sara Louise (Mrs. Richard Ruhf), Dr. David S., W.J. (captain U.S.N.), Dr. Joseph S., Edward L., Judith (Mrs. Wm. E. Diehl), Benjamin. Reporter Allentown Call, 1898; editor Allentown Morning Call, 1910-61. Founder of Allentown playground system, 1912; pres. Allentown Municipal Opera Company; mem. Lehigh County Humane Soc. (pres.), trustee Community Chest. Republican. Episcopalian. Clubs: Kiwanis, Lehigh Valley, Torch, Exchange. Home: Emmaus, R. 1. Office: 101 N. 6th St., Allentown, Pa. Died Nov. 28, 1962.

RUMBOLD, FRANK MEEKER physician; b. Lafayette Co., Wis., Jan. 4, 1862; ed. public schools and Washington Univ.; grad. St. Louis Med. Coll., 1884; editor St. Louis Med. and Surgical Journal, 1887-96; editor The Laryngoscope, 1896-99; mem. several nat. and local med. socs.; practice limited to diseases nose, throat and ears. Capt. Light Battery A, Mo. vols., in Spanish-Am. war; capt. and adj. 32d inf. U.S.V., in Philippines, 1899-1901; unmarried. Address: 313 N. 9th St., St. Louis.

RUMPLE, J.N.W. congressman; b. Fostoria, O., March 4, 1841; moved to Iowa, Sept. 1853; attended Ashland Sem., Western Coll. and normal dept., Iowa State Univ.; enlisted in 2d Iowa cav., Aug. 1861; mustered out as capt., Oct. 1865. Commenced study of law in Hon. H. M. Martin's office in Marengo, Ia., Dec. 1865; was admitted to practice Feb. 1867. Elected to State senate in 1873, and served in 14th, 15th, 16th and 17th gen. assemblies. Was Regent of State Univ. for several yrs.; also curator State Hist. Soc., co. atty., alderman, mayor, city solicitor and mem. bd. edn.; mem. Congress, 1901-03, 2d Ia. dist. Republican. Home: Marengo, Ia. Died 1903.

RUMSEY, DEXTER PHELPS banker; b. Buffalo, Aug. 31, 1893; s. Dexter Phelps and Susan Reid (Fiske) R.; student Nichols Sch., Buffalo, and St. Marks', Southborough, Mass.; B.A., Harvard, 1916; student Buffalo Law Sch., 1915-16; m. Margaret Adam Ramsdell, May 30, 1916; children—Dexter Phelps, Rollin Douglas, Donald Scott, Margaret Diane. Partner O'Brian, Potter & Co., investment bankers, Buffalo, 1918-22; pres. Dexter P. Rumsey & Co., 1930-41; mem. Rumsey, Read & Kimberly, Buffalo, 1941-54; pres. Erie Co. Savs. Bank, 1943-60, chmn. bd., 1960, chmn. exec. com., 1961-—; dir. Marine Trust Co., 1926-42, Marine Midland group of banks. Served as captain F.A., U.S. Army, World War I. Republican. Episcopalian. Clubs: Saturn, Buffalo Tennis and Squash, Harvard (N.Y.C.). Home: Faraway Farm, Derby Erie Co., N.Y. Office: 16 Niagara St., Buffalo. Died Dec. 6, 1966; buried Forest Lawn, Buffalo, N.Y.

RUMSEY, ISRAEL PARSONS commission mcht.; b. Stafford, Genesee Co., N.Y., Feb. 9, 1836; s. Joseph Elicot and Lucy (Ransom) R.; ed. common schs., Bethany Acad.; m. Mary Matilda Axtell, of Batavia, N.Y., June 12, 1867. Established as commn. mcht., Chicago, 1859. Helped organize Taylor's Chicago Battery (Co. B, 1st Ill. Arty.), Apr., 1861; served as lt. and capt.; 1st battle was at Belmont, Mo., Nov. 6, 1861; was with Grant, Sherman, Logan, McPherson and Smith in campaigns until Atlanta, 1864. Resumed commn. business in Chicago after war, on Board of Trade. Dir. Chicago Bd. of Trade, 1871-73, 1900-03; several times active in city elections; Republican. For 20 yrs. dir. and pres. Chicago Citizens' League. Mem. Loyal Legion. Thomas Post G.A.R. Club: Union League. Home: Lake Forest, Ill. Office: 97 Board of Trade, Chicago.

RUMSEY, WILLIAM justice of Supreme Court, State of N.Y., 1880-—; b. Bath, N.Y., Oct. 18, 1841; s. David and Jane E. (Brown) R.; grad. Williams Coll., 1861 (LL.D., 1888); m. Ella Moore, Feb. 1, 1872. Served during Civil War, 1861-65, in Peninsula, Shenandoah Valley, and other campaigns, engaging in many actions, severely wounded at Fair Oaks; promoted several times for bravery and distinguished services; retired with rank of lt. col. After war served for 2 yrs. with Robert E. Van Valkenberg, minister to Japan, as private sec. After return practiced law at Bath, N.Y., until elevation to bench; from March, 1895, asso. justice appellate div., Supreme Court, for 1st dept., State of N.Y. Republican. Received Republican nomination, 1888, for asso. judge, Court of Appeals, running ahead of his ticket. Author: Rumsey's Practice, 3 vols., 1887; joint author (with David Dudley Field) of A Codification of the Law of Evidence for the State of N.Y. Home: Bath, N.Y. Died 1903.

RUNKLE, BENJAMIN PIATT soldier; b. West Liberty, O., Sept. 3, 1837; s. Ralph Edwin and Hannah Isabella (Piatt) R.; A.B., Miami U., 1857 (L.H.D., 1899); m. Lalla, d. Andrew McMicken, of Cincinnati, Feb. 10, 1894. Admitted to bar, 1859; practiced at Cincinnati, 1859-61; capt. 13th Ohio Inf., Apr. 22, 1861; maj., Nov. 8, 1861; col. 45th Ohio Inf., Aug. 19, 1862; hon. mustered out, July 21, 1864; lt. col. Vet. Reserve Corps, Aug. 22, 1864; bvtd. col., brig. gen. and maj. gen. vols., Nov. 9, 1865, "for meritorious services"; hon. mustered out, Oct. 5, 1866; maj. 45th U.S. Inf., July 28, 1866; bvtd. lt. col. U.S.A., Mar. 2, 1867, "or gallant and meritorious services at Shiloh" (wounded and left for dead on the field); col. U.S.A., Mar. 2, 1867, for same during the war. Editor Urbana (O.) Union, 1873-75. Ordained deacon P.E. Ch., Oct. 1882; ch. work, 1879-84; resigned diaconate, 1884; prof. mil. science, Kenyon Coll., 1879-81, Miami U., 1899-1901, U. of Me., 1901-02, Peekskill Mil. Acad., 1902-04, N.J. Mil. Acad., 1904-05, Germantown (Ohio) Mil. Inst., 1905-09; assigned to duty with N.G. of Ohio, 1909. A founder (grand consul, 1895-97) of Sigma Chi Fraternity, del. 1st and 22d and orator before 22d Grand Chapters. Home: Hillsboro, Ohio. Died June 28, 1916.

RUOTOLO, ONORIO sculptor; b. Cervinara, Italy, Mar. 3, 1888; s. Pietro and Concetta (Caruso) R.; ed. Reale Academia de Belle Arti, Naples, and under Vincenzo Gemito; m. Lucia Sperling, Vienna, Austria, Apr. 12, 1923; 1 son, Lucio. Came to U.S., 1908, naturalized citizen. Founder and exec. dir. Leonardo da Vinci Art Sch., N.Y.C. Prin. works: Pres. Wilson Meml., U. Va.; bust of Dante, N.Y. U., and City Coll.; symbolic group The Father of a Race; bust of Caruso Met. Opera House lobby; bust of Cardinal Mercier, and "Jesus Wept" (bas relief), in Belgium; winged centaur, presented to U.S. Army AS by Corriere d'America for rescue of Lt. Locatelli and his crew; "Pilgrims of Life," monument in Cath. Cemetery, N.Y.; Paino mausoleum, St. John's Cemetery, Bklyn., granite group of "Pieta" and bronze door of St. Francis d'Assisi; Calderoni mausoleum, Greenfield Cemetery, Hempstead, L.I.; "The Doomed," statue against capital punishment; busts of Edison, Helen Keller, Steinmetz, Theodore Dreiser; bust of Toscanini at High Sch. of Music and Arts N.Y.C. and others; ofcl. commemorative medal of Italo Balbo's transatlantic mass flight; commemorative medal, 1933, for election of Fiorello H. La Guardia, mayor N.Y.C.; bronze plaque, "Beethoven of Victory"; "Four Freedoms" allegoric panel presented to Francis Biddle, Apr. 13, 1943, to Pres. Roosevelt Oct. 19, 1944, to Gen. Mark Clark, Oct. 12, 1945, as award of Italian-Am. Labor Council (rep. 300,000 organized workers); a heroic meml. bust of Giacome Matteotti, prof. Albert Einstein, Sidney Hillman memls. Deborah Sanatorium, N.J., Amalgamated Bank of N.Y., and Sidney Hillman Health Center, N.Y.C. Created a Bas Relief of Don Luigi Sturzo; dir. Union's Cultural Center of A.C.W. of Am. Roman Catholic. Illustrated The Story of the World's Literature, and The Romance of America (both by John Macy). Works reproduced in Ruotolo, Man and Artist with over 100 illustrations of his work and an appreciation by Frances Winwar. Co-editor of "Leonardo" (year book). Wrote (poem), "America, Our Great Mother," "My First Teacher" 1958; Accordi e Dissonanze. Art Criticism. Home: 20 Bank St., N.Y.C. 10014. Studio: 1 Union Sq. W., N.Y.C. Died Dec. 1966.

RUPERTUS, WILLIAM HENRY (roo per'tus), Marine Corps officer; b. Washington, D.C., Nov. 14, 1889; s. Charles and Augustina (Meile) R.; ed. U.S. Coast Guard Acad., 1910-13; Army Command and Gen. Staff Sch., 1925-26; m. Alice Hill, Mar. 4, 1933; 1 son, Patrick Hill. Commd. 2d lt. Marines, 1913; promoted through grades to maj. gen., 1943; commanded operations against Japanese in Tulagi area, Br. Solomon Islands, 1942. Decorated D.S.M. of Haiti. U.S. Navy Cross. Home: 3732 Van Ness St., N.W., Washington, D.C. Died Mar. 25, 1945.

RUPPEL, LOUIS (rupp'el), publisher; b. N.Y.C., N.Y., June 11, 1903; s. Frederick and Lillian (Schultz) R.; m. Margit Gabrielsen, Dec. 5, 1926; children—Philip, Joseph. Reporter, N.Y. Am., 1924-27, N.Y. Jour., 1928-29; polit. writer, N.Y. News, 1929-33; U.S. dep. commr. of narcotics, Washington, 1933-34; mng. editor, Chgo. Times, 1935-38; publicity dir. Columbia Broadcasting System, 1939-41; asst. to pres. Crowell-Collier Pub. Co., 1942; exec. editor Chgo. Herald-Am., 1945, resigned, Sept. 1945; editor of Collier's Weekly, 1949-52; owner, pub. Mill Valley (Cal.) Record, 1953-54; news editor Phila. Daily News, 1954-56; asso. editor Am. Weekly, 1956-—. Served as capt. U.S.M.C., 1943-44; South Pacific Medal with 1 star. Member Mill Valley Post 284 American Legion, Sigma Delta Chi. Clubs: Nat. Press (Washington); Tough (N.Y.C.). Address: 25-29 120th St., College Point, Queens, N.Y.C. Died Jan. 1958.

RUPPENTHAL, JACOB CHRISTIAN lawyer; b. Phila., Jan. 16, 1869; s. Jacob Christian and Anna Barbara (Immendorf) R.; A.B. and LL.B., U. Kans., 1895; m. Sarah Spalding, Jan. 1, 1895 (died 1914); children—Harold Fred, Lloyd Henry, Mary Lois (Mrs. Wallace M. James); m. 2d, Margaret Cameron Eastland, Dec. 26, 1922; 1 son, Philip Lee. Began as pub. sch. tchr., 1888; admitted to Kan. bar, 1895; atty. Russell County, Kan., 1897-98, 1902-03; judge 23d Jud. Dist. Kan., 1907-18 and 1923-31; prof. law U. Kan., 1919-20; mem. and sec. Jud. Council Kan., 1927-41. Mem. Russell Sch. Dist. Bd., 1906-18. Served as maj. judge adv. U.S. Army, 1918-19, and Officers Res. Corps, since 1920. Bd. dirs. Russell Pub. Library since 1901; mem. Kan. State Library Survey Commn., 1949. Lay del. to Gen. Conf. Meth. Ch., 1916 and 24. Mem. Am. Bar Assn., Bar Assn. Kan., Bar Assn. Northwestern Kan. (sec., 1931-—); Internat. Bar Assn. (charter patron, 1947-—), Bar Assn. Russell County (1st pres.), Am. Law Inst., Am. Judicature Soc., Am. Inst. Criminal Law and Criminology, Am. Inst. Genealogy, Nat. Geneal. Soc., Kan. State Hist. Soc. (life), A.L.A. (life), Internat. Phonetic Assn., Kan. Authors Club (life), Alumni Assn. U. Kan. (life), Nat. Municipal League, Proportional Rep. Soc. (Eng.), Am. Dialect Soc., Kan. Commn. for UNESCO; Kan. Library Assn. (hon. life). Democrat. Club: Rotary (Russell). Editor: Wharton's Criminal Law, 12th edit., 1932. Mem. editorial staff Jour. of Bar

Assn. Kan. since 1932. Home: 1208 Lincoln St., Russell, Kan. 67665. Died Mar. 27, 1964; buried Russell City Cemetery.

RUSH, BENJAMIN physician, Continental congressman, humanitarian; b. Phila., Jan. 4, 1746; s. John Harvey and Susanna (Hall) R.; A.B., Coll. of N.J. (now Princeton), 1760; studied medicine under Dr. John Redman, 1761-66; attended 1st lectures of Dr. William Shippen and Dr. John Morgan in Coll. of Phila.; M.D., U. Edinburgh (Scotland), 1768; m. Julia Stockton, Jan. 11, 1776, 13 children including James, Richard. Returned to Phila., 1769, began practice of medicine; prof. chemistry Coll. of Phila., 1769-91, also prof. theory and practice, 1789; published A Syllabus of A Course of Lectures on Chemistry (1st Am. text on chemistry), 1770, reissued 1773; published anonymously Sermons to Gentlemen upon Temperance and Exercise (one of 1st Am. works on personal hygiene) 1772; mem. Am. Philos. Soc.; published An Address to the Inhabitants of the British Settlements in America, upon Slave-Keeping, 1773; an organizer Pa. Soc. for Promoting the Abolition of Slavery, 1774, pres. 1803; elected to Pa. Provincial Conv., 1776; mem. Continental Congress, 1776-77, signer Declaration of Independence; apptd. surgeon gen. Armies of the Middle Dept. Continental Army, 1777; became lectr. U. State of Pa., 1780; mem. staff Pa. Hosp., 1783-1813; established 1st free dispensary in Am., 1786; recognized as the "instaurator" of the Am. temperance movement; persuaded the Presbyns. to found Dickinson Coll., 1783, served as trustee; mem. Pa. Conv. which ratified U.S. Constn. 1787, with James Wilson led successful fight for adoption; with James Wilson inaugurated a campaign which secured a more liberal and effective constn. for Pa., 1789; apptd. treas. U.S. Mint by Pres. John Adams, 1797-1813; became prof. the Institutes Medicine and Clin. Practice, U. Pa., 1792, prof. theory and practice, 1796; a founder Phila. Coll. Physicians, 1787; thought to be pioneer worker in exptl. physiology in U.S.; 1st Am. to write on cholera infantum, 1st to recognize focal infection of the teeth; greatly contributed to the establishment of Phila. as the leading Am. center of med. tng. during 1st half of 19th century. Author: Medical Inquiries and Observations, initial vol., 1789; An Account of the Bilious Remitting Yellow Fever, As It Appeared in the Essays, Literary, Moral and Philosophical, 1798; Medical Inquiries and Observations upon the Diseases of the Mind, 1812. Died Phila., Apr. 19, 1813; buried Christ's Church Graveyard, Phila.

RUSK, THOMAS JEFFERSON senator; b. Pendleton Dist., S.C., Dec. 5, 1803; s. John and Mary (Sterritt) R.; m. Mary F. Cleveland, 1827, 7 children. Admitted to bar; began practice of law, Clarksville, Ga., 1825; became partner of John Cleveland in merc. bus., circa 1828; elected capt. of a co. of rangers, circa 1835, joined Stephen F. Austin, San Antonio, Tex.; apptd. col., authorized to raise men, arms, food in East Tex.; signer Declaration ondepende aided in drafting and adoption of Constn. of Republic of Tex.; elected sec. of war Provisional Govt. of Tex., 1836; took command of Army Republic of Tex. after Battle of San Jacinto, 1836; apptd. sec. of war Republic of Tex. under Houston, 1837; mem. Ho. of Reps. in 2d Congress of Republic of Tex., 1838; elected maj. gen. Militia of Republic of Tex., 1838, cleared East Tex. of hostile Indian tribes, 1838-39, promoted brig. gen., maj. gen., 1843; chief justice Supreme Ct. of Republic of Tex., 1838-42; favored annexation of Tex. to U.S., pres. Tex. Conv. which confirmed annexation and formulated Constn. of 1845; mem. U.S. Senate from Tex., Feb. 21, 1846-July 29, 1857, supported adminstrn. in Mexican War, sponsored final settlement of Tex. debt, 1854, pres. pro tem, 1857. Committed suicide, Nacogdoches, Tex., July 29, 1857; buried Oak Grove Cemetery, Nacogdoches.

RUSLING, JAMES FOWLER lawyer; b. Washington, N.J., Apr. 14, 1834; s. Gershom and Eliza B. (Hankinson) R.; A.B., Dickinson Coll., 1854, A.M., 1857; LL.D., 1889; m. Mary F. Winner, Jan. 1, 1858; 2d, Emily W. Wood, June 30, 1870. Prof. natural science, Dickinson Sem., Pa., 1854-57; admitted to bar, Pa., 1857, N.J., 1859. First lt. 5th N.J. Inf., Aug. 24, 1861; capt. asst. q.-m. vols., June 11, 1862; lt. col., May 27, 1863; col., Apr. 29, 1865; bvtd. maj., lt. col. and col. vols., Mar. 13, 1865, "for faithful and meritorious services during the war"; brig. gen. vols., Feb. 16, 1866, for same; hon. mustered out, Sept. 17, 1867. U.S. pension agt., N.J., 1868-77; mem. Tex. Commn., N.J., 1896. Pres. N.J. Centennial Commn. to Tenn., 1897; trustee Dickinson Coll., 1861-83 and 1904-—, Pennington Sem., 1869-99, and pres. bd. many yrs.; mem. gen. missionary bd. M.E. Ch., 1891; del. Gen. Conf. M.E. Ch., 1896. Pres. Mercer County Soldiers' and Sailors' Monument Assn., 1891-1911. Author: Across America, or the Great West and Pacific Coast, 1874; History of State Street Methodist Episcopal Church, Trenton, N.J., 1886; History of Pennington Seminary, 1890; Men and Things I Saw in Civil War Days, 1899; European Days and Ways, 1902; History of Rusling Family, 1908. Died Apr. 1, 1918.

RUSSEL, EDGAR army officer; b. Pleasant Hill, Mo., Feb. 20, 1862; s. Richard and Elizabeth (Williams) R.; grad. U.S. Military Acad., 1887; m. Florence Kimball, Apr. 18, 1893; Commd. 2d lt. 3d Arty., June 12, 1887; 1st lt. 5th Arty., Nov. 2, 1893; trans. to 6th Arty., Mar. 8, 1898; capt. signal officer vols., June 20, 1898; maj. signal officer, Apr. 12, 1901; hon. discharged vols., June 30, 1901; 1st lt. Signal Corps, U.S.A., Aug. 30, 1900; capt., Feb. 2, 1901; maj., July 6, 1904; lt. col., July 1, 1916; col., Apr. 12, 1917; brig. gen. N.A., Oct. 2, 1917; brig. gen. U.S.A., Oct. 11, 1921; maj. gen., Dec. 5, 1922; retired from active service, Dec. 6, 1922. Instr. chemistry and asst. prof. chemistry, mineralogy and geology, U.S. Mil. Acad., 1893-98; comd. Signal Corps Co., Philippine Islands, 1898-1900; chief signal officer, Dept. Southern Luzon, 1900; duty Office of Chief Signal Officer, Washington, D.C., 1901-03; assisted in laying Wash.-Alaska Cable, 1903, and installing same, 1904; in charge Sitka-Valdez cable, 1904-05; asst. to chief of Signal Office, Washington, D.C., 1906-08; dir. Army Signal Sch., Ft. Leavenworth, Kan., 1908-12; duty Office of Chief Signal Officer, Washington, D.C., 1912-15; chief signal officer, Hawaii, 1916; same, Southern Dept., 1916-17; chief signal officer, A.E.F., with Gen. Pershing, May 29, 1917, until departure for U.S., July 15, 1919; hon. discharged as brig. gen. N.A., Aug. 15, 1919; brig. gen. U.S.A., Oct. 11, 1921; signal officer, Eastern Department, N.Y. City, Sept. 3, 1919-—. Recommended for bvts. by Gen. Lawton and Maj. Gen. MacArthur, "for exceptionally skillful and meritorious services," in P.I. Awarded D.S.M., 1919; Companion of the Bath (British), 1919; Comdr. Legion of Honor (French), 1919. Del. Internat. Radio Conf., London, 1912; mem. Am. Inst. E.E., Inst. Radio Engs. Protestant. Home: New York, N.Y. Died Apr. 27, 1925.

RUSSELL, ALEXANDER WILSON naval officer; b. in Md., Feb. 4, 1824. Apptd. purser U.S.N., Feb. 28, 1861; pay insp., Mar. 3, 1871; pay dir., Feb. 23, 1877; retired Feb. 4, 1886; advanced to rank of rear admiral retired, June 29, 1906, for services during Civil War. Home: Philadelphia, Pa. Died 1908.

RUSSELL, CLINTON WARDEN army officer; b. Hico, Tex., May 6, 1891; s. William E. and Mollie (Anderson) R.; student Tex. A. and M. Coll., 1907-08; B.S., U.S. Mil. Acad., 1913; grad. Command and Gen. Staff Sch., 1925, Army War Coll., 1930, Naval War Coll., 1931; m. Dorothy Kendall, Jan. 11, 1917; children—William Kendall, Peter Talbot, Kendall. Commd. 2d lt., U.S. Army, 1913, and advanced through grades to brig. gen., 1940; served in Inf., U.S. and P.I., 1913-16; took flying training, 1916; served in punitive expdn. to Mexico, 1916; comdr. 7th Aero Squadron, Canal Zone, 1917; served in various capacities at flying fields during World War; instr. R.O.T.C., Tex. A. and M. Coll., 1920-24; instr. Command and Gen. Staff Sch., 1924-29; in War Dept. Gen. Staff, 1931-35; chief of staff, Air Force Combat Command, since 1938. Awarded Victory medal, 1918; Punitive Expdn. medal, 1917; Mil. medal "La Estrella de Abdon Calderon" (Ecuador), 1935. Home: Hico, Tex. Address: care Adjutant General, U.S. Army, Washington, D.C. Died Mar. 24, 1943.

RUSSELL, DANIEL LINDSAY lawyer, gov.; b. Brunswick County, N.C., Aug. 7, 1845; s. Daniel Lindsay and Caroline Elizabeth (Sanders) R.; ed. Univ. of N.C., 1860-61; capt. C.S.A. in Civil War; admitted to bar, 1866; m. Sarah Amanda Sanders, Aug. 16, 1869. Mem. N.C. legislature, 1864-65, 1865-66 and 1876-77; judge 4th jud. circuit, 1868-74; mem. Congress, 1879-81; gov. N.C., 1897-1901. Republican. Died 1908.

RUSSELL, DAVID ALLEN army officer; b. Salem, N.Y., Dec. 10, 1820; s. David Abel and Alida (Lansing) R.; grad. U.S. Mil. Acad., 1845. Served in U.S. Army under Gen. Scott's Army during Mexican War; brevetted 1st lt., 1847; commd. 1st lt., 1848, capt., 1854; col. 7th Mass. Volunteers; commd. brig. gen. U.S. Volunteers, 1862; assigned to command of a brigade in VI Corps, Army of Potomac, 1862, participated in battles of Fredericksburg, 1862, Gettysburg, 1863, Rappahannock Station, Va., 1863; fought in all battles of Grant's campaign of 184 from the Wilderness to Petersburg; brevetted maj. U.S. Army for gallantry at Battle of Williamsburg, brevetted full maj. 8th Inf. at Battle White Oaks, lt. col. for service in Peninsular Campaign, maj. gen., 1864. Killed in battle of Opequan, nr. Winchester, Va., Sept. 19, 1864.

RUSSELL, EDWARD LAFAYETTE lawyer; b. Franklin County, Ala., Aug. 19, 1845; s. George Daniel and Emily (Stovall) R.; ed. by father; worked on farm until Feb. 1862. Served in 41st Miss. Regt., C.S.A., pvt. and ensign; color bearer of regt.; when Confed. lines were broken at Nashville retreated to Franklin and swam Harper's Creek during night to save his colors; cotton planter after war; m. Emma Davis, Jan. 1869. Admitted to bar, 1871; practiced Verona, 1872; gen. counsel, May 1876, 1st v.p. and acting pres., Mar. 1897, Mobile & Ohio R.R.; later v.p. and gen. counsel same, Mobile, Ala. Presdl. elector, 1888, 1892, 1896; del. Ala. State Conv., on gold standard platform, 1896. Democrat. Died 1911.

RUSSELL, FREDERICK FULLER physician; b. Auburn, N.Y., Aug. 17, 1870; s. George Daniel and Anna Cecelia (Fuller) R.; M.D., Coll. Phys. and Surg. (Columbia), 1893; U. Berlin, 1897-98; Sc.D., George Washington U., 1917; m. Mathilde J.W. Busse, Nov. 2, 1899. Commd. 1st lt. asst. surgeon, U.S. Army, Dec. 12, 1898; capt. asst. surgeon, Dec. 1903; maj., Jan. 1909, col., May 1917, resigned July 11, 1920. Brig. gen. M.O.R.C., U.S. Army, Nov. 4, 1921. Curator, Army Med. Mus., Washington, 1907-13; instr. bacteriology and clin. microscopy Army Med. Sch., 1907-13; pathologist Columbia Hosp., 1908-13; prof. pathology and bacteriology George Washington U., 1909-13; lectr. tropical medicine N.Y. Post-Grad. Med. Sch., 1913-14; chief Bd. of Health Lab., Ancon, C.Z., 1915-17; in charge Div. Infectious Diseases and Lab. Service of Surgeon Gen.'s Office, U.S. Army, during World War; dir. Pub. Health Lab. Service of Internat. Health Bd., 1920-23; gen. dir. Internat. Health Bd., div. Rockefeller Found., 1923-35; lectr. preventive medicine and hygiene Harvard Med. Sch., Harvard Sch. Pub. Health, 1935, prof. preventive medicine and epidemiology, 1936-38, prof. emeritus since 1938. Mem. Pub. Health Council, State N.Y., 1924-36. Decorated D.S.M.; recipient Marcellus Hartley medal Nat. Acad. Scis., Washington, 1936; Buchanan medal Royal Soc. London, 1937; Gorgas medal, 1942. Fellow A.S.C., Am. Pub. Health Assn., N.Y. Acad. Medicine; mem. A.M.A., Assn. Am. Physicians, Royal Med. Soc. Budapest, Hungary, Zeta Psi, Theta Chi; corr. mem. Gesellschaft der Aerzte, Vienna, Austria. Club: Harvard (Boston). Address: Rural Route 6, Box 39, Louisville. Died Dec. 1960.

RUSSELL, GEORGE HARVEY insurance; b. Milwaukee, Nov. 3, 1866; s. Harvey and Mary Jane (Guilds) R.; pvt., pub. and high sch. edn., to 18; m. Laura Eustis, Jan. 18, 1893; children—Laura (Mrs. Bradlee Van Brunt), Marion (Mrs. Edgar J. Tapping, Jr.). In ins. business, 1887-—; state agt. Standard Accident Ins. Co. of Detroit, 1892-—; pres. George H. Russell Co.; dir. Standard Accident Ins. Co., Detroit; mgr. ins. dept. C.,M.&St.P. R.R. Co., 1913-—. Republican. An organizer and sec. first young men's Republican club in Wis., 1888. Episcopalian. An organizer Cadet Light Inf., 1884, and advanced to capt.; insp. small arms practice 4th Wis. Inf.; was col. on staff of Gov. W. D. Hoard; apptd. as del. Ann. Conv. Nat. Civic Fedn., Washington, Mar. 1912; chmn. Local Bd., Div. 1, Milwaukee, under Selective Service Act, 1917-18. A.d.c. to Gov. E. L. Phillipp, with rank of col. in Wis. State Guard, 1917; commd. capt., Q.M.R.C., 1918. Mem. numerous underwriters assns. Made many trips abroad and has contbd. extensively on travel and ins. Home: Milwaukee, Wis. Deceased.

RUSSELL, HENRY DOZIER, lawyer; b. McDonnough, Ga., Dec. 28, 1889; s. Henry McDowell and Molly (Kelley) R.; A.B., U. of Ga., 1912, B.L., 1914; m. Carolyn Crawley, Feb. 18, 1921. Admitted to Ga. bar, 1914, practiced in Macon; city atty., Macon, Ga., 1924-25. Mem. Nat. Guard 33 yrs.; active service World War I and II; comdg. gen. 30th Div., 1932-42; comdg. gen. 48th Div., 1946-52. Mem. Phi Beta Kappa. Home: Macon GA Died Dec. 31, 1972; buried Riverside Cemetery, Macon GA

RUSSELL, JOHN HENRY naval officer; b. Frederick, Md., July 4, 1827; s. Robert Grier and Susan Hood (Worthington) R.; grad. U.S. Naval Acad., 1848; m. Cornelia Pierpont Treadway, 1864, 3 children. Commd. midshipman U.S. Navy, 1841; assigned to North Pacific Exploring Expdn. as acting navigator and lt. in sloop Vincennes under Cadwalader Ringgold, 1853; commd. master, 1855, lt., 1855; ordnance duty Washington (D.C.) Navy Yard, 1857-61, 64; sent to Norfolk (Va.) Navy Yard to assist in saving Union Vessels from capture by Confederates, 1861; commanded boat expdn., destroyed privateer Gudah, Presacola, Fla., 1861; given command of steamer Kennebec in Rear Adm. David Farragut's Squadron, 1861, participated in all operations of Farragut's squadron up Mississippi River to Vicksburg, 1861-62; commd. lt. comdr., 1862, commanded Kennebec in blockade of Mobile and Pontiac in South Atlantic Blockading Squadron; commanded ship Cyane, 1865; promoted comdr., 1867, capt., 1874, commodore, 1883, rear adm., 1886; rescued shipwrecked passengers and crew of steamer Continental in Gulf of California, 1869; command Mare Island Navy Yard, 1883-86. Died Washington, D.C., Apr. 1, 1897.

RUSSELL, JOHN HENRY major gen. U.S. Marines; b. Mare Island, Calif., Nov. 14, 1872; s. John Henry and Cornelia Pierrepont (Treadway) R.; grad. U.S. Naval Acad., class of 1892; m. Mabel Howard, June 12, 1901; 1 dau., Roberta Brooke (Mrs. Charles H. Marshall). Served through grades to maj. gen. U.S.M.C., Sept. 13, 1933; mem. staff U.S. War Coll., 1908-10; served in Spanish-Am. War, World War and several Marine Corps expeditionary campaigns; American high commissioner with the rank of ambassador Port-au-Prince, Haiti, by appointment of President Harding, 1922-30; appointed assistant to maj. gen. comdt., Feb. 1933, then comdt. Marine Corps; retired, Dec. 1, 1936; now in newspaper work. Awarded U.S. Navy Cross, D.S.M., Haitian Medaille Militaire and campaign medal, West Indies medal, Spanish Campaign medal, Expeditionary medal with Numeral 4, Mexican Service medal, Victory medal with West Indies clasp. Mem. (be desc.) Calif. Pioneers. Episcopalian. Club: Army and Navy (Washington, D.C.). Home: Coronado, Calif. Died Mar. 6, 1947.

RUSSELL, MARTIN J. pres. Chicago Chronicle Co. and editor Chicago Chronicle, 1895-—; b. Chicago, Dec. 20, 1845. Accompanied his uncle, Col. James A.

Mulligan, with his regt. to Mo., 1861, was present at surrender of Lexington; on reorganization of regt. (23d Ill.) the following winter, enlisted and became 2d lt. in Co. A; later adj. gen. on staff of Col. Mulligan. After death of latter in battle of Winchester the depleted regt. was consolidated into 5 companies and Lt. Russell was mustered out, Sept. 1864. Reporter on Chicago Evening Post, 1870-73; on city staff and later writing editor Chicago Times, 1873-83; editor Chicago Herald, 1883-87; on Chicago Times, 1887-91. Mem. bd. of visitors to West Point, 1887; was South Park commr., Chicago, 14 years; collector of customs, Chicago, 1894-98. Married. Home: Chicago, Ill. Died 1900.

RUSSELL, PAUL SNOWDEN banker; b. Oak Park, Ill., May 10, 1893; s. John Kent and Adelyn Frances (Mayo) R.; A.B., University of Chicago, 1916; married Carroll A. Mason, April 7, 1922; children—Carroll Russell Sherer, Paul Snowden, Jr., Adelyn Mayo, Ann Mason, Harold Swift. With Harris Trust & Savings Bank, Chicago, since 1916, v.p., 1930-46, pres. since 1946, dir. since 1942; dir. Hoover & Mason Phosphate Co. Served as capt. Inf., U.S.A., 5th Div., World War, 1917-1918. Trustee U. of Chicago, Chicago Orphan Asylum; governor of International House. Member advisory committee Chicago Loan Agency of Reconstruction Finance Corp. Mem. adv. bd., Research and Development Br. Office Q.M. Gen., Washington, D.C. Mem. adv. council, Chicago Community Trust; mem. Assn. Reserve City Bankers. Trustee Chicago Memorial Hosp.; v.p. and dir. C. of C. Assn., 1944-45; mem. Assn. of Reserve City Bankers, Newcomen Soc., Delta Kappa Epsilon. Republican. Clubs: University, Chicago, Attic, Economic, Commercial, Glen View (Golf, Ill.); Old Elm (Fort Sheridan, Ill.). Chikaming Country Club (Lakeside, Mich.). Home: 4901 Greenwood Av., Chicago 15. Died Jan. 8, 1950.

RUSSELL, WALTER C(HARLES) biochemist; b. Bellaire, O., Oct. 1, 1892; s. Charles C. and Eliza Jane (Kneff) R.; B.S., Ohio Wesleyan, 1914, Sc.D. (hon.), 1947; student Sorbonne, 1919, Harvard (grad. fellow in biochem.), 1919-20; M.S., Syracuse U., 1923; Ph.D., U. of Chicago (Swift fellow in chem., 1923-25), 1927; m. Mildred Irene Stephens, Aug. 25, 1923; 1 dau., Ruth Elizabeth. Teacher Chillicothe (O.) high sch., 1914-15; instr. chem., Ohio Wesleyan, 1915-17, Syracuse U., 1920-23; asst. prof. agrl. biochem., Rutgers, 1925-29, asso. prof. agrl. biochem., 1929-31; prof. and chmn. dept. agrl. biochem.; research splist. in agrl. biochem., N.J. Agrl. Expt. Sta., Rutgers, since 1925; exec. sec. grad. faculty, Rutgers U., 1935-52, dean of the graduate school since July 1952. Member adv. scientific council Com. on Foods of Am. Vet. Med. Assn. and Am. Animal Hosp. Assn. since 1937; mem. Nat. Research Council since 1943. Served as pvt. to capt., San. Corps, U.S. Army, 1917-19; overseas. Mem. Am. Chem. Soc., Am. Soc. Biol. Chemists, Am. Inst. Nutrition (mem. council 1950-53), Assn. Land-Grant Colls. and Univs. (chairman council on instrn. 1952), A.A.A.S., Society Exptl. Biol. and Medicine, Delta Tau Delta, Sigma Xi, Phi Lambda Upsilon, Alpha Chi Sigma, Phi Kappa Phi, Phi Beta Kappa (hon.). Presbyn. Author: Grass Silage and Dairying (with Ray Ingham, Willis A. King and Carl B. Bender), 1949. Mem. editorial bd. Journal of Nutrition, 1945-49. Contbr. articles on nutrition and biochemistry to various professional jours. Home: 27 Oak Hills Rd., Metuchen. Office: Rutgers Univ., New Brunswick, N.J. Died Mar. 10, 1954.

RUSSUM, B(ENJAMIN) C(ARL) physician; b. Topeka, Kan., Jan. 6, 1892; s. William Benjamin and Louisa May (Gunn) R.; A.B., Creighton U., 1912, M.D., 1916; m. Harriett May Jarrett, Aug. 14, 1922; children—Dorothy May (Mrs. Walter Gerhard Nelson), William John, Paul Eugene. Intern, Kings Co. Hosp., Brooklyn, 1916-17; postgrad. study pathology Rush Med. Coll., Chicago, 1920; resident pathology St. Joseph Hosp., Omaha Neb., 1921-22; mem. faculty Creighton U. Sch. Medicine since 1922, prof. pathology, head dept. since 1947; attending pathologist St. Joseph's, Douglas Co. hosps.; cons. pathologist St. Catherine's Hosp., Veterans Administration Hospital, Omaha; pathologist U.P. Ry. Co. since 1943. Served as 1st lt. to capt. Med. Res. Corps. U.S. Army, France, 1917-19; maj. Med. Res. Corps, 1925-35. Fellow A.M.A., Coll. Am. Pathologists; mem. Internat. Assn. Med. Mus., American Association for Advancement Sci., Am. Soc. Clin. Pathologists, Physicians Health Assn. (pres. dir.). Editor of Jour. Omaha Mid-West Clin. Soc. 1950-53. Home: 2524 N. 55th St., Omaha 4. Office: 306 N. 14th St., Omaha 2, Neb. Died May 25, 1956; buried Hillcrest Meml. Park, Omaha, Neb.

RUTGERS, HENRY army officer, philanthropist; b. N.Y.C., Oct. 7, 1745; s. Hendrick and Catharine (dePeyster) R.; grad. King's Coll. (now Columbia), 1766. Supported Sons of Liberty; served as capt. 1st Regt., N.Y. Militia, Battle of White Plains, 1776, resigned command 1st Regt., 1795; mem. N.Y. Assembly, 1784, 1800; raised fund of $28,000 for constrn. 1st Great Wigwam of Tammany Hall, N.Y.C., 1811; gave land for 2d free sch. established for city's poor; pres. Free Sch. Soc., 1828-30; regent U. State N.Y., 1802-26; trustee Princeton, 1804-17; trustee Queen's Coll., 1816-21, also benefactor, name changed to Rutgers Coll. in his honor, 1825; pres. bd. corp. Dutch Reformed Ch.; gave land to Rutgers Street Presbyn. Ch., opened 1798. Died N.Y.C., Feb. 17, 1830.

RUTH, CARL DOUGLAS newspaper corr.; b. Mazeppa, Minn., July 11, 1884; s. Reuben Eugene and Minnesota (Hyde) R.; B.S., Dak. Wesleyan U., Mitchell, S.D., 1905; spl. studies, Oberlin, 1905-06; m. Cora M. Walker, Mar. 9, 1911; 1 son, Robert Walker. Reporter Cleveland Leader, 1906-09; chief of Columbus bur., Cleveland Leader and Cincinnati Commercial-Tribune, 1909-15; Washington corr. Cleveland Leader, 1915-17, Cleveland News, 1915-29, Toledo Blade, Newark Star-Eagle and Duluth Herald, 1929—. Mem. standing com. of correspondents of Press Galleries of Congress, 1923-25. Capt. Mil. Intelligence Div. of Gen. Staff, U.S. Army, Aug.-Dec. 1918. Republican. Presbyn. Home: Washington, D.C. Died Jan. 25, 1936.

RUTH, HENRY SWARTLEY physician, anesthesiologist; b. Phila., Pa., Aug. 12, 1899; s. Henry Laban Swartley and Carrie Anders (Kindig) R.; student Swarthmore Coll., 1917-18; student Hahnemann Sch. of Science, 1918-19, B.S., 1921; M.D., Hahnemann Med. 1923; m. Lola Althouse Zendt, July 16, 1924; children—Patricia Anne (Mrs. James C. Straus, 3d), Henry Swartley, Jr. Anesthetist Hahnemann Hosp., 1924—, St. Luke's and Children's Hosp., Phila., 1927-41; clin. prof. anesthesia, Hahnemann Med. Coll. and Hosp., 1933-40, prof. and head dept. Anesthesiology since 1942; chief, div. of anesthesia Phila. Gen. Hospital, 1933-40, consulting anesthetist since 1940; chief, anesthetic service, West Jersey Homeo. Hosp., Camden, 1941-42. Civilian cons. U.S. Naval Hospital, Phila., 1948-52. Served in S.A.T.C., 1918. Director courses in anesthesiology, U.S. Army and Navy, World War II. On Am. Bd. of Anesthesiology, 1937-52 (pres. 1943-44). Fellow Internat. College of Surgeons, Am. Med. Writers Assn.; mem. Soc. of Anesthetists, Inc. (pres. 1938); Phila. County Med. Soc. (chmn. anesthesia study commn.), A.M.A., (rep. sect. on anesthesiology in Ho. Dels., 1941-54), Internat. Anesthesia Research Soc., Homeo. Med. Soc. of Pa., Germantown Homeo. Med. Soc. of Phila. (pres. 1936), Am. Inst. Homeop., Montgomery Co. Med. Society, Phila. Soc. Anesthesiol. (pres. 1947-48), Pa. Soc. Anesthesiol. (pres. 1943-49), World Med. Assn. Episcopalian. Mason. Clubs: Union League, Rotary, Penn, Merion Golf, Bachelor's Barge, Merion Cricket (Phila.). Author: Sect. on "Anesthetics," Revision Service Vol. of Cyclopedia of Medicine, 1944; sect. on "Regional Anesthesia," Bancroft's Operative Surgery, 1941. Asso. editor: Anesthesia Subjects in Cyclopedia of Medicine, Surgery and Specialties, 1939-52; articles on anesthesia, scientific and medical subjects in med. jours. Editor: Anesthesiology (organ of Am. Soc. Anesthetists, Inc.) since 1940. Mem. editorial bd., Am. Journal of Surgery. Home: 225 Cheswold Lane, Haverford, Pa. Office: Hahnemann Med. Coll. and Hosp., 230 N. Broad St., Phila. 2. Died 1956.

RUTHERFORD, JOHN broker; b. Warwick, N.Y., June 29, 1895; s. Morris and Sarah (Christie) R.; grad. Hill Sch., Pottstown, Pa., 1913; A.B., Princeton, 1917; m. Clarisse de Rham, May 26, 1923; children—Barbara, Emily Clarisse, Sally Christie, John. With N.J. Zinc Co., 1919-21; asso. with Davies, Thomas & Co., brokers, N.Y.C., 1921, partner, 1923-29 (co. dissolved); now partner John Rutherford & Co., N.Y.C. Entered 2d Plattsburg O.T.C., commd. 2d lt.; served with 308th F.A., 78th Div., U.S. Army, 1918. Trustee and treas. West Side Day Nursery, N.Y.; chmn. and trustee Gratuity Fund, N.Y. Stock Exchange. Mem. Soc. Colonial Wars of N.J. Republican. Mason. Clubs: Racquet and Tennis (N.Y.); Piping Rock, Cold Spring Harbor Beach (L.I.). Home: Laurel Hollow, Syosset, L.I., N.Y. Office: 120 Broadway, N.Y.C. Died May 19, 1965.

RUTLEDGE, BENJAMIN HUGER lawyer; b. Charleston, S.C., Sept. 4, 1861; s. Benjamin Huger and Eleanor Maria (Middleton) R.; grad. Va. Mil. Inst., Lexington, Va., 1880; B.A., Yale, 1882; m. Emma Blake, of Fletcher, N.C., Oct. 5, 1892. Admitted to S.C. bar, 1884. Mem. firm Mordecai & Gadsden & Rutledge. Major of S.C. vols.; clerk judiciary com. of S.C. Legislature 4 yrs.; mem. S.C. Gen. Assembly, 1890; electoral messenger from S.C., for Cleveland's first election. Del.-at-large Universal Congress Lawyers and Jurists, St. Louis, 1904. Mem. St. Cecelia Soc., etc. Episcopalian. Democrat. Club: Charleston. Address: Charleston, S.C.

RUTLEDGE, EDWARD gov. S.C.; b. Charlestown (now Charleston) or Christ Church Parish, S.C., Nov. 23, 1749; s. Dr. John and Sarah (Hext) R.; m. Henrietta Middleton, Mar. 1, 1774; m. 2d, Mary Shubrick Eveleigh, Oct. 28, 1792; 3 children including Henry Middleton. Admitted to Middle Temple, London, Eng., 1767, called to the English bar, 1772; returned to S.C. as a barrister, 1773; mem. Continental Congress, 1774-77, 79 (did not reach Phila. due to ill health, 1779), mem. 1st bd. of war, 1776, voted for resolution of independence, July 2, 1776, signed Declaration of Independence, 1776; member of the 1st, 2d S.C. provincial congresses, 1775-76; capt. S.C. Arty., 1776; fought at Beaufort, 1779, captured at fall of Charleston, imprisoned by British, 1780-81; one of the St. Augustine "exiles", Sept. 1780-July 1781; mem. S.C. Ho. of Reps., 1782, 86, 88-92, drew up bill proposing confiscation of Loyalist properties, 1782, author act abolishing law of primogeniture, 1791; investor in plantations as partner of brother-in-law Charles Cotesworth Pinckney; Federalist presdl. elector, 1788, 92, 96; mem. S.C. Senate from Charleston, 1796, 98; gov. S.C., 1798-1800. Died Charleston, Jan. 23, 1800.

RUTTER, JOSIAH BALDWIN business exec.; b. Waltham, Mass., March 30, 1892; s. Nathaniel and Elizabeth M. (Lang) R.; B.S., Civil Engring., Tufts Coll., Medford, Mass., 1914; student law, N.Y. U., 1915-16; m. Miriam Goss, May 18, 1918; children—Nathaniel P., Miriam G. (Mrs. E.T. Otis, Jr.). Dir. Rutland R.R., 1942-47; chief engr. Merrimac Chem. Co., 1922; dir. engring. Monsanto Chem. Co., 1936, vice president, gen. mgr. Merrimac div., 1947-49; industrial consultant since 1949; director Merritt-Monsanto Corp., Nat. Shawmut Bank, New England Alcohol Co.; pres. and dir. Merrimac Chem. Transportation Corp.; cons. engr. J. R. Worcester, 1914-15; industrial mgr. Russell Co., Boston, 1919-20; trustee New England Alcohol Co. Served as capt. engrs., U.S. Army, World War I. Mem. Am. Soc. C.E. Clubs: Algonquin (Boston); Detroit (Detroit); Tuscarora (Lockport, N.Y.); Metropolitan (N.Y. City); Mo. Athletic (St. Louis). Home: 90 Commonwealth Av., Boston. Office: 90 Commonwealth Av., Boston 16. Died Jan. 28, 1951.

RYAN, CLENDENIN J(AMES) business exec.; b. Suffern, N.Y., July 16, 1905; s. Clendenin James and Caroline (O'Neil) R.; student St. Georges' School, 1918-24; Princeton, 1924-28; m. Jean Harder, Nov. 18, 1837; children—Clendenin James, Caryn, Cyr Annan, Jean. With Guaranty Trust Co. of N.Y., 1929-32; vice pres., 15th Assembly Dist. Republican Club, N.Y., 1932-33; asst. to Mayor La Guardia, 1933-38; asst. commr. dept. of sanitation, N.Y. City, 1938-40; commr. of commerce, N.Y. City, 1940; director Companhia de Diamantes de Angola (Portugal); owner Panther Ledge Farms, New Jersey. Delegate from New Jersey to Republican Nat. Conv., 1948. Served as lt., U.S.N.R., active duty, 1941, flag sec. to comdr. of Carrier Task Force, So. Pacific, 1942-43, and on staff of comdr. air, Solomon Islands, Feb.-March 1943; Guadalcanal; comdr. U.S.N.R., inactive duty, 1945. Received citation and Naval Commendation Ribbon. Fellow Pierpont Morgan Library. Mem. Am. Legion, Reserve Officers Assn., Am. Irish Hist. Soc., Nat. Urban League (dir.). Republican. Roman Catholic. Clubs: Ivy of Princeton, Brook, Racquet and Tennis, Knickerbocker (N.Y.). Home: Allamuchy, N.J. Office: 515 Madison Av., N.Y.C. 22. Died Sept. 1957.

RYAN, CORNELIUS EDWARD, army officer; b. Boston, May 12, 1896; s. Thomas Joseph and Julia Elizabeth (Driscoll) R.; B.S., U. Conn., 1918; student Mass. Inst. Tech., 1924-25; grad. French Tank Sch., Versailles, France, 1928; grad. Command and Gen. Staff Coll., Ft. Leavenworth, Kan., 1939; m. Inez Marie Brown, May 18, 1931; children—Walter Joseph, Edward Francis, Elizabeth Anne. Commd. 2d lt. U.S. Army, 1917, advanced through grades to maj. gen., 1952; with AEF, World War I; assigned European campaigns, World War II; comdr. U.S. garrison, Berlin, Germany, 1946-47; rep. U.S. to Berlin Allied Kommandatura; comdr. Camp Breckinridge, Ky., 1949-51, Pa. Mil. Dist., 1949-50, Ft. Dix, N.J., 1953-55; comdg. gen. 101st Airborne div., 9th Inf. Div., then 69th Inf. Div.; chief Korean Mil. Adv. Group, 1951-53; chief Mil. Assistance Adv. Group to France, 1956, 57; exec. vice chmn. President's Com. on Govt. Contracts, 1957; now dir. multilateral finance div. U.S. Mission to NATO, also U.S. rep. infrastructure com. NATO. Recipient D.S.M. with oak leaf cluster, Legion of Merit, Bronze Star medal (U.S.); Order of Leopold II, Croix de Guerre with palm (Belgium); Mil. Cross (Czechoslovakia); Legion of Honor, Croix de Guerre with palm (France); Ulchi Distinguished Mil. Service medal with gold star, Presidential Unit citation, Taekuk Distinguished Mil. Service medal with silver star (Korea); Order of Merit of Adolphe de Nassau (Luxembourg); Order Orange Nassau (Netherlands); Commemorative Cross (Poland); Comdr. Brit. Empire. Mem. Am. Legion, Mil. Order World Wars, Phi Kappa Tau, Eta Lambda Sigma, Phi Phi. Roman Catholic. Home: Paris France Died 1972.

RYAN, ELMER JAMES ex-congressman; b. Rosemount, Minn., May 26, 1907; s. John Owen and Agnes Teresa (Hyland) R.; LL.B., U. of Minn. Law Sch., 1929; m. Elenore Ann Moravec, June 21, 1932 (died Feb. 1938); children—Elmer James, Jacqueline Marie; m. 2d, Marjorie Fuller, July 31, 1939; children—John Fuller, Geoffrey Fuller, Jeremy de March, Joseph de March. Admitted to Minn. bar, 1929; in practice at South St. Paul, asso. with Harold E. Stassen, atty. of City of South St. Paul, 1933-34; mem. 74th to 76th Congresses (1934-41), 2d Minn. Dist. Ordered to active duty as 1st lt. Officers Res. Corps, U.S. Army 1942, capt., 1942, maj., 1945, discharged 1945. Democrat. Catholic. K.C. Home: 89 Virginia St., St. Paul, Minn. Office: Grand Bldg., South St. Paul, Minn. Died Feb. 1, 1958.

RYAN, FRANKLIN WINTON economist; b. Meadville, Pa.; s. Augustus Eddy and Femma Jane (Marley) R.; M.B.A. cum laude, Harvard, 1921, M.A., 1923; Ph.D., 1925; m. Katherine Ann MacMillan, July 5, 1925; 1 dau., Sara Grace. Teaching asst. U. Chgo., 1920; instr. bank mgmt. Harvard, 1922-25; asst. chief finance div. U.S. Dept. of Commerce, 1925-26; v.p. Gilbert Badger's investment banking enterprises, N.Y.

and N.J., 1927-32; asst. dir. div. research and statistics Fed. Home Loan Bank System, D.C. charge statistics HOLC, 1935-40; research adviser WPB, 1941-42; economist in depts., Army and Navy, 1943-—. Commd. maj. finance dept. res. AUS, 1926; mem. staff Indsl. Coll. Armed Forces, Office Sec. War, 1944-47. Recipient Jesse Isidor Straus prize scholarship, Harvard, 1922, Hart, Schaffner & Marx $1000 prize, 1923, Rockefeller Found. grant for municipal research at Harvard, 1933-35. Mem. Am. Econ. Assn., Pi Gamma Mu. Episcopalian. Club: Harvard. Author: Usury and Usury Laws, 1924; Municipal Control of Retail Trade, (with Miller McClintock), 1935. Home: 2437 N. Taylor St., Arlington 7, Va. Died Mar. 13, 1957; buried Arlington Nat. Cemetery.

RYAN, JAMES AUGUSTINE army officer; b. Danbury, Conn., Oct. 22, 1867; s. James Ryan and Hanna (Doran) R.; grad. U.S. Mil. Acad., 1890; honor grad. Inf. and Cav. Sch., 1906; m. Rosemary Tarleton, Feb. 16, 1911. Commd. 2d lt. 10th Cav., June 12, 1890; 1st lt., Feb. 3, 1897; capt. 15th Cav., Feb. 2, 1901; maj. 5th Cav., Sept. 15, 1912; assigned to 13th Cav., Sept. 1, 1914; lt. col., Oct. 1, 1916; col., July 22, 1917; brig. gen. N.A., Dec. 17, 1917. Apptd. comdr. 1st Cav. Brigade, 15th Cav. Div. Roman Catholic. Clubs: Army and Navy (Washington), Catholic (N.Y.C.). Home: 14 Bellevue Pl., Chgo. Died Jan. 14, 1956.

RYAN, JOHN D. mining man; b. in Mich., 1864; m. Nettie Gardner, 1896; 1 son, John C. Chmn. Anaconda Copper Mining Co., Chile Copper Co.; pres. United Metals Selling Co., Mont. Power Co.; dir. Nat. City Bank of New York, Emigrants Industrial Savings Bank. Apptd. dir. aircraft Aircraft production by President Wilson, Apr. 1918, also chmn. Aircraft Bd.; 2d asst. sec. of war and dir. air service, Aug.-Nov. 1918. Mem. War Council Am. Nat. Red Cross (mem. Central Com.). Home: Butte, Mont. Died Feb. 11, 1933.

RYAN, JOHN WILLIAM, telephone co. exec.; b. Newton, Mass., June 3, 1919; s. George B. and Mary (Dinegan) R.; B.A., U. N.C., 1941; grad. Advanced Mgmt. Program, Harvard, 1961; m. Helen Perot Walker, Feb. 23, 1952; children—Elizabeth Perot, John Walker, Mary Webb, Nancy Morris. With New Eng. Telephone Co., 1946-56, Am. Tel. & Tel. Co., 1956-58; asst. comptroller, then gen. accounting mgr. Bell Telephone Co. Pa., 1958-59; asst. comptroller Am. Tel. & Tel. Co., 1959; with Northwestern Bell Telephone Co., 1959-70, v.p., gen. mgr. Neb. area, 1963-64, v.p. pub. relations, 1964-70. Mem. Central Omaha Study Com., 1962-70; dir. devel. Econ. Devel. Council Omaha, 1965-70; trustee Omaha Indsl. Found., 1963-70; adv. com. econ. edn. Omaha pub. schs., 1963-70. Bd. govs., mem. pub. relations com. Boys Clubs Omaha, 1963-70; adv. bd. Duchesne Coll., 1963-70; devel. bd. Duchesne Acad., 1963-70, also mem. exec. com., chmn. finance and scholarship com.; trustee, mem. exec. and membership coms. Neb. Council Econ. Edn., 1964-70; bd. dirs., v.p. Omaha Civic Music Assn., 1962-70; bd. dirs. Omaha Civic Opera Assn., 1960-70, Omaha United Community Services, 1963-70, Omaha Sister City Assn., 1964-70; adv. council nursing Creighton Meml. St. Joseph's Hosp., Omaha, 1964-70. Served with British Am. Ambulance Corps, 1941; to lt. USNR, 1941-46; ETO, PTO. Mem. Omaha C. of C. (bd. dirs., v.p., mem. exec. com.). Clubs: Omaha, Omaha Country; St. Anthony (N.Y.C.). Home: Omaha NE Died Aug. 18, 1970.

RYAN, THOMAS assistant sec. of the interior; b. Oxford, N.Y., Nov. 25, 1837; reared on farm; ed. Dickinson Sem., Pa. Admitted to bar, 1861; served in Union Army, 1862-64; mustered out, with rank of capt., on account of wounds received in battle of the Wilderness. In practice at Topeka, Kan., from 1865; county atty., 8 yrs.; asst. U.S. atty., 1873-77; elected 45th to 51st Congresses (1877-91); resigned, 1889; U.S. minister to Mexico, 1889-93; apptd. 1st asst. sec. of the interior, Mar. 1897, serving several yrs. Republican. Died Apr. 5, 1914.

RYAN, WILLIAM FITTS, congressman; b. Albion, N.Y., June 28, 1922; s. Bernard and Harriet (Fitts) R.; A.B., Princeton, 1944; LL.B., Columbia, 1949; m. Priscilla Marbury; children—William, Priscilla, Virginia, Catherine. Admitted to N.Y. State bar, 1949; asso. firm Hatch, Wolfe, Nash & Teneyck, N.Y.C., 1949-50; asst. dist. atty. N.Y. County, 1950-57; mem. 87th-92d congresses from 20th Dist. N.Y. Pres., N.Y. Young Democrats Club, 1955-56; founding mem. Riverside Dems., Inc., N.Y. Reform Dem. Movement; Democratic leader 7th Assembly Dist., N.Y. County, 1957-61; Reform Dem. candidate for mayor of N.Y.C., 1965; del. Dem. Nat. Conv., 1968. Served to 1st lt. F.A., AUS, World War II; PTO. Home: New York City NY Died Sept. 17, 1972; buried St. Thomas Ch., Croom MD

RYDER, CHARLES WOLCOTT army officer; b. Topeka, Jan. 16, 1892; s. Lewis Alonzo and Minnie (Wolcott) R.; B.S., U.S. Mil. Acad., 1915; attended Inf. Sch., Ft. Benning, Ga., 1924-25, Command and Gen. Staff Sch., Ft. Leavenworth, 1925-26, Army War Coll., 1933-34; m. Ida Quinby Perrine, Feb. 16, 1916; children—Louise Perrine (Mrs. John F. King), Charles Wolcott. Commd. 2d lt., inf. U.S. Army, 1915, advanced through ranks to col., 1941, brig. gen., 1942, maj. gen., 1942; served as maj., lt. col., 16th and 26th Inf., 1st Div., France and Germany, 1917-19; office asst., chief of staff, G-3, 1st Div., 1920-21; asst. instr., dept. tactics U.S. Mil. Acad., 1921-24; instr. Inf. Sch., Ft. Benning, 1926-30; with 15th Inf., Tientsin, China, 1930-33; assigned 34th Inf., Camp Meade, Md., May-Aug. 1933; G-2 Sect., War Sept. Gen. Staff, 1934-37; comdt. cadets U.S. Mil. Acad., 1937-41; chief of staff 6th Army Corps, 1941-42; with 90th Div. to June 1942; comdg. gen. 34th Div., North Ireland, Capture of Algiers, Tunisian Campaign. Italian Campaign including advance from Salerno beachhead, capture of Benevento, three forced crossings of Volturno River, Mt. Patano, Cassino, Anzio beachhead, advance to Rome, capture of Leghorn. Awarded D.S.C. with oak leaf cluster, D.S.M., Silver Star with Oak Leaf Cluster, Legion of Merit, Purple Heart, Victory Medal with four battle clasps, European-African-Middle Eastern medal with four stars, Asiatic-Pacific Theater Medal (U.S.); Companion of the Most Honorable Order of Bath (Brit.); Officer of Legion of Honor, Croix de Guerre with Palm (French); Silver Star (Italian); Star of Abdon Calderon, 2d Class (Ecuador). Episcopalian. Address: Vineyard Haven, Mass. Died Aug. 17, 1960; buried Arlington Nat. Cemetery.

RYERSON, EDWIN WARNER surgeon; b. N.Y.C., Mar. 14, 1872; s. George Wilson and Sarah Dean (Brown) R.; M.D., Harvard, 1897; house surgeon Boston Children's Hosp., 1897-98; post-grad. study, Berlin and Vienna; m. Adelaide Kendall Hamilton, Dec. 6, 1904. Practiced at Chgo. since 1899; emeritus orthopedic surg. St. Luke's Hosp.; former prof. orthopedic surgery Northwestern U. Med. Sch. Apptd. 1st lt. Med. R.C., Feb. 1911; capt. Apr. 1918; maj. M.C., U.S. Army, Aug. 27, 1918; hon. discharged Aug. 7, 1919. F.A.C.S.; mem. A.M.A., Am. Orthopaedic Assn. (pres. 1925), Am. Acad. Orthopaedic Surgeons (pres. 1933), Am. Bd. Orthopaedic Surgery, Inc. (v.p. 1935-38), Internat. Orthopedic Soc., Inst. Medicine (Chgo.), Chgo. Med. Soc., Chgo. Orthopedic Soc., Chgo. Surg. Soc., Internat. Soc. Orthopaedic Surgery and Traumatology. Republican. Episcopalian. Clubs: University, Casino, Onwentsia. Home: 232 E. Walton St., Chgo. 11; (winter) 316 Royal Plaza, Ft. Lauderdale, Fla. Ret. Died Mar. 6, 1961; buried Chgo.

RYON, HARRISON, lawyer; born New Hampton, Ia., Feb. 14, 1892; s. John A. and Mary Emily (Fitch) R.; student Beloit (Wis.) Coll., 1911-13; A.B., Leland Stanford, Jr., U., 1915; J.D. cum laude, U. of Chicago, 1917; m. Elizabeth Edwards, June 22, 1917 (divorced June 9, 1925); 1 dau., Patricia (Mrs. Eugene F. Foubert); m. 2d, Hazel Cowan, June 24, 1926. Consulting engr. in indsl., personnel and labor relations as associate, later partner, The Scott Co., Phila., 1919-20; mng. indsl. relations, Chicago and South Bend factories, Wilson Bros., Chicago, 1920-22; admitted to Calif. bar, 1922; Nev. bar, 1930; mem. Schauer, Ryon & McIntyre, Santa Barbara, 1922-70; specializes trial practice, trust, probate law. Attended 2d O.T.C., Fort Sheridan, Ill., and commd. 2d lt. Inf., 1917; attached to 86th Div. staff; later with Adj. General's Dept., Newark, N.J.; assigned to standardizing trade tests for Army; capt. Adj. General's Reserve Corps to 1934. Pres. Santa Barbara County Bar Assn., 1934-35; vice chmn. Cal. State Bar Conf. of Bar Assn. Dels., 1936-37, chmn. 1937-38. Fellow Am. Coll. Probate Counsel; mem. Assn. Bar City of N.Y., State Bar of Cal. (mem. legislative com., 1938-39, chmn., 1939-41; member board of governors, 1939-42; vice president, 1940-42); mem. Am. Bar Assn., Am. Law Inst. (Calif. rep., 1940, 42, 45), State Bar of Calif., Nev. State Bar, Sigma Chi. Active in establishment of Pub. Relations Dept., Calif. State Bar; chmn. nat. defense and pub. relations com., same 1941, 42; war service commn. same, 1945; pres. Santa Barbara Museum of Art, 1945-49, first vice president, 1950. Republican. Presbyn. Clubs: Montecito Country, University (Santa Bsrbara.) Home: Santa Barbara CA Died Dec. 22, 1970; buried Santa Barbara Cemetery.

SACHS, PAUL JOSEPH educator; b. N.Y.C., Nov. 24, 1878; s. Samuel and Louisa (Goldman) S.; ed. Sachs Sch., N.Y.; A.B., Harvard, 1900; LL.D.; D.A.; L.H.D., Colby Coll., 1949; hon. degrees, Yale, Princeton, U. Pitts.; m. Meta Pollak, Jan. 14, 1904; children—Elizabeth, Celia, Marjorie. Partner banking house Golldman, Sachs & Co., N.Y., 1904-14; lectr. art Wellesley Coll., 1916-17; asst. prof. fine arts Harvard, 1917-22, asso. prof., 1922-27, prof. fine arts, 1927-48, now emeritus; hon. curator drawings; exchange prof. to France, 1932-33. Mem. food adminstrn., Boston; maj. A.R.C., with A.E.F., in France, 1918. Past chmn. adminstrv. com. Dumbarton Oaks Research Library and Collection, Washington; ex-chmn. bd. syndics Harvard U. Press. Trustee Ella Sachs Plotz Foundn. for Advancement Med. Sci., Mus. Fine Arts, Boston, Mus. Modern Art, N.Y.C. Mem. Am. Assn. Mus., Assn. Mus. Dirs., Am. Fedn. Arts, Am. Acad. Arts and Scis., Archaeol. Inst. Am., Coll. Art Assn. Mem. Am. Commn. for Protection and Salvage of Artistic and Historic Monuments in Europe. Clubs: P.B.K., Harvard, Club of Odd Volumes; St. Botolph (Boston), Faculty (Harvard); Harvard, Grolier, Century (N.Y.C.). Co-author: Drawings in the Fogg Museum, 3 vols., 1940. Author: Great Drawings, 1951; Modern Prints and Drawings, 1954; Tales of an Epoch, 1960. Contbr. on art topics. Home: 987 Memorial Dr., Cambridge 38, Mass. Died Feb. 1965.

SACK, LEO R. pub. relations; b. Tupelo, Miss., July 9, 1889; s. Isaac and Sarah Lee (Romansky) S.; high sch., Greenville, Miss., 1907; student U. Mo., 1907-09 (one of student founders of U. of Mo. Sch. of Journalism, 1st of its kind in U.S.); m. Regina Rogers, Nov. 12, 1913; 1 dau., Sarita (Mrs. Joseph Lester Jones). Began as reporter with Natchez (Miss.) News, 1909, and continued with Springfield (Mo.) Rep., city and night editor Texarkana Four State Press until 1911; with San Antonio Express, 1911-15; Washington corr. San Antonio Light, Ft. Worth Star-Telegram, Houston Chronicle, 1915-17, Scripps-Howard group of newspapers, 1919-33; apptd. E.E. and M.P. to Costa Rica, 1933-37; v.p. in charge pub. relations Schenley Products Co., 1937-39; pub. relations cons. Washington, 1939-—. Negotiated and signed Reciprocal Trade Agreement between Costa Rica and U.S., 1936. Spl. asst. to James A. Farley. Chmn. Dem. Nat. Com. during 1936 Presidential Campaign. Author of newspaper articles which led to investigation of Pa. and Ill. senatorial elections resulting in refusal of Senate to seat William S. Vare and Frank L. Smith; dir. Washington bur. Am. Zionist Emergency Council, Washington, 1943-48. Capt. and maj. Air Service, U.S. Army, A.E.F., 1917-19; maj. Res. Hon. mem. Boy Scouts; benefactor mem. Costa Rica Red Cross; hon. col. on staff gov. of Miss.; lt. col. on staff Gov. of Tex. Independent Democrat. Mason. Clubs: National Press (Washington); Union (San José): Overseas Press (N.Y.C.). Speaker at Latin Am. Seminar, Panama and U. of Mo. Sch. of Journalism, 1935, and Washington Seminar for Better Understanding Between Christians and Jews, 1940. Mem. and former dir. Nat. Assn. of Accredited Publicity Dirs., Inc. Home: 841 South Serrano Av., Los Angeles 5. Office: National Press Club, Washington. Died Apr. 15, 1956; buried Mausoleum, Hollywood (Cal.) Cemetery.

SACKETT, EARL L., naval officer (ret.); b. Bancroft, Neb., Mar. 29, 1897; s. Samuel Lazier and Minnie Estelle (Armstrong) S.; B.S., U.S. Naval Acad., 1919; M.S., U. Cal., 1934; m. Elizabeth Louise Stanford, June 1, 1921; 1 dau., Maidie Mason (wife of Lt. Col. ret. H. R. Barr, U.S.M.C.). Commd. ensign U.S. Navy, 1919, and advanced through grades to rear adm., 1947; submarine or engring. duty, 1924-42; assisted raising U.S.S. Squalus, 1939; comdr. sub-tender, Canopus, 1940-42 (scuttled at Corregidor to avoid capture); mem. staff of Am. Nimitz, 1944-46; ret. from active service, Jan. 1, 1947. Awarded Navy Cross, Army Distinguished unit badge, Bronze Star, Navy commendation ribbon, various area and service medals and ribbons. Republican. Episcopalian. Clubs: Yacht (Coronado), Margate (Md.) Yacht, Annapolis (Md.) Yacht; Army-Navy (Manila, P.I.). Home: Coronado CA Died Oct. 7, 1970; buried Arlington National Cemetery, Arlington VA

SADLAK, ANTONI NICHOLAS, congressman; b. Rockville, Conn., June 13, 1908; ed. St. Joseph's Parochial Sch., George Sykes Manual Training and High Sch.; student Georgetown Coll.; LL.B., Georgetown U.; m. Alfreda Janina Zalewska, May 30, 1939; children—Antoni, Alita. Former asst. sec.-treas. Hartford Prodn. Credit Assn.; spl. inspector, Spl. Inspections Div., U.S. Dept. of Justice, 1941-42; formerly exec. sec. to B. J. Monkiewicz, congressman-at-large, edn. supervisor, Conn. Dept. Edn., 1946; mem. 80th to 85th Congresses, congressman-at-large, Conn.; probate judge, Vernon, until 1969. Commd. lt. U.S.N.R., 1944, assigned to staff Adm. Thomas C. Kincaid; duty in New Guinea, Philippines and China. Home: Rockville CT Died Oct. 18, 1969.

SADLER, E(VERIT) J(AY) oil producer; b. Brockport, N.Y., May 1, 1879; s. Holmes E. and Mary (C.) S.; grad. U.S. Naval Acad., Annapolis, Md., 1899; m. Lorena Bilisoly, Aug. 2, 1902; children—Elizabeth, Isabel. Midshipman and ensign U.S. Navy, 1899, and served in Navy until 1902; roustabout and operator Kan. oil fields, 1902-06; draftsman, civ. engr., Prairie Oil & Gas Co., 1906-09; mng. dir. Romano-Americano, Bucharest, Rumania, 1909-16; served as lt. comdr. U.S.N.R.F., 1917; pres. Transcontinental Oil Co., Mexico, 1918-19; dir. Standard Oil Co. (N.J.), 1920-42, vice-pres., 1930-42. Clubs: University, Army and Navy. Home: Scarsdale, N.Y. Office: 30 Rockefeller Plaza, New York, N.Y. Died Oct. 28, 1947.

SAFANIE, MURRAY D. broker; b. N.Y.C., Sept. 30, 1899; s. Andre and Sara (Manzell) S.; ed. N.Y. U. Sch. of Commerce and extension courses; m. Jean Karr, Aug. 29, 1920. Successively stenographer, sec., bus. exec., 1913-18; auditor Arthur Young & Co., James Barr & Co., 1918-20; accountant and asst. comptroller, A. H. Bull Steamship Co., 1920-22; spl. auditor U.S. Treasury, Washington, 1922; spl. examiner U.S. Steel Corp. taxes for war yrs., 1922-25; security analyst and statistician, Shearson, Hammill & Co., Inc., 1926-—, later head investment dept., partner, 1936-—, mng. partner, 1947-57, directing partner, 1957-—, chmn. exec. com.; appraiser preferred stock of Jones & Laughlin Steel Corp., 1940; chmn. bd. Interstate Dept. Stores, Inc.; dir. Reece Corp. (Boston), Pitts. Steel Corp., Felmont Petroleum Corp., Leslie Fay, Inc., Park Electrochemical Corp., Interstate Dept. Stores, Inc. Served with Q.M. Corps, Washington, 1918; served as asst. chief procurement and material, Navy Dept., asst. to sec. of Navy, 1942-44. C.P.A., State N.C., 1924. Gov. N.Y.

Stock Exchange, 1941, 1946-49. Mem. Am. Numismatic Assn. Clubs: Wall Street, Analyst, Stock Exchange Luncheon, Pinnacle. Awarded Distinguished Civilian Service medal, 1944; Navy Distinguished Public Service Award, 1946. Home: Katonah, N.Y. Office: 14 Wall St., N.Y.C. 5. Died Jan. 12, 1968.

SAFAY, FRED A. (sa-fa), army officer; b. Jacksonville, Fla., June 15, 1898; s. Abraham and Jasmine (Dumont) S.; student Fla. Mil. Acad., Jacksonville, Fla., 1916-17, spl. student, U. of Fla., 1930-38; m. Iva McKendree, Apr. 25, 1921; children—Dorothy Louise (Mrs. Paul E. Hall). Sanitation officer, Fla. Health Dept., 1923-38, dir. sanitation dept., 1938-40; mil. service, 1940-46, sanitation cons. Fla. State Bd. of Health, 1946—. Served with A.E.F., 1917-18, Army of Occupation, 1919; commd. 1st lt., inf., Fla. Nat. Guard, and advanced through the grades to col., comdr., 124th Inf., 1940; inducted into Fed. service, 1940; brig. gen., Sept. 1942; ret. as brig. gen. Mem. Fla. and Am. Pub. Health Assn., Forty and Eight, Am. Legion. Home: 2751 Post St., Jacksonville, Fla. Died Jan. 4, 1952; buried Evergreen, Cemetery, Jacksonville, Fla.

SAGE, CHARLES GURDON adj. gen. N.M.; b. Sparks, Kan., Apr. 10, 1895; s. Charles Franklin and Sophronia Stewart (Jackson) S.; student Occidental Coll., 1913-17; m. Dorothy Louise Haynes, June 1, 1924; children—Dorothy Charline, Mary Louise. Pub. The Deming (N.M.) Headlight (weekly newspaper), 1926-41, 49—, The Deming Graphic, weekly, 1948—, Deming Headlight, Deming Graphic, Lordsburg (N.M.) Liberal, Silver City (N.M.) Enterprise, Hatch (N.M.) Reporter. Dir. N.M. Civilian Det., 1949-50. Served as 2d lt. 326th F.A., World War I; officer N.M. N.G. 1921-41; comdg. officer 200th CA (AA) and Philippine provisional coast arty. brigade, World War II, surrendered to Japanese Apr. 9, 1942, on Bataan, prisoner of war until Aug. 1945; brig. gen. AUS, Jan. 1946; adj. gen. N.M., Santa Fe, 1946, brig. gen. N.G., 1947, lt. gen., 1960. Decorated D.S.M., Bronze Star, Purple Heart. Recipient Distinguished Alumnus award Occidental Coll., 1963; named hon. mem. Jicarilla Apache Tribe, 1965. Democrat. Presbyn. Mason (32 deg., Shriner), Lion. Home: Santa Fe. Office: P.O. Box 4277, Santa Fe. Died Feb. 4, 1967; buried Santa Fe Nat. Cemetery.

SAGE, WILLIAM HAMPDEN army officer; b. in N.Y., Apr. 6, 1859; grad. U.S. Mil. Acad., 1882; Army War Coll., 1907. Commd. 2d lt. 5th Inf., June 13, 1882; promoted through grades to col. 12th Inf., Feb. 7, 1915; temporary maj. gen. N.G., Aug. 5, 1917. Prof. mil. science and tactics, Central U. of Ky., Richmond, Ky., 1892-93; garrison duty in Tex., 1894-98; a.d.c. to Gen. Ovenshine, in Philippine Islands, 1898; served as adj. gen. 1st and 2d brigades, 1st Div., 8th Army Corps; adj. gen. 3d Dist., Minanao and Jolo; duty at Malabang, P.I., 1903; duty at War Coll., Washington, D.C., 1906-07; adj. gen. Dept. of Columbia, 1907; duty on Mexican border, 1916-17; comdr. Camp Shelby, Hattiesburg, Miss., Sept. 1917-Mar. 1918; served with A.E.F. Medal of honor for action at Zapote River, P.I., June 13, 1899. Died June 4, 1922.

SAGENDORPH, KENT (sa'gen-dorf), author, publicist; b. Jackson, Mich., Apr. 23, 1902; s. William Kent and Ethel (Abbott) S.; grad. Jackson High Sch., 1920; student U. of Mich. and U.S. Army Tech. Sch., 1922; m. Ruth D. Howard, Nov. 11, 1933; children—Mary Lou, Wallace Kent. Aerial photographer, U.S. Army Air Service, Clark Field and Nichols Field, Philippine Islands, 1922-24; travel in China, Siberia, Japan, summer and fall, 1924; commercial aerial photographer, Los Angeles, 1925, Mexico, 1926; mem. staff Fairchild Aerial Surveys, preparing tech. manuals and trade magazine summaries to 1929; contbr. editor Aero Digest, 1929-31; author of 800 magazine articles on aviation and current history; lecturing on aviation since 1939. Lt. col., U.S. Air Force Reserve; on active duty May 1942-Nov. 1945. Pres. Veterans' Flying Assn. of America. Grad., Air Command & Staff Sch. USAF, 1950. Club: Aero. (Omaha). Author: Radium Island, 1937; Beyond the Amazon, 1937; Sin Kiang Castle, 1938; Thunder Aloft, 1942; Stevens Thomson Mason, 1947; Michigan, the Story of the University, 1948; Charles Edward Wilson, American Industrialist, 1949; How to Solve a Problem, 1952. Home: 333 W. Mason St., Jackson, Mich. Died Feb. 5, 1958; buried Woodland Cemetery, Jackson, Mich.

ST. ANGE, LOUIS DE BELLERIVE army officer, colonial gov.; b. Montreal, Que., Can., Oct. 3, 1698; s. Robert Groston and Marguerite Crevier (de Bellerive) de St. A. In command of one detachment with Etienne Vinyard on expdn. Westward to make alliance with Padouka Indians, 1724; apptd. to succeed Jean Baptiste Bissot at Ft. Orleans on Wabash River, with rank of capt., 1736-1764 conducted evacuation of Ft. Chartres as successor to Neyon de Villiers, the comdt., 1764, acting gov. Upper La., 1764-65; in command of St. Louis, 1765-70. Died St. Louis, Dec. 27, 1774.

ST. CLAIR, ARTHUR pres. Continental Congress, army officer, territorial gov.; b. Thurso, Aithness County, Scotland, Apr. 3, 1737; s. William and Elizabeth (Balfour) St.C.; m. Phoebe Bayard, May 15, 1760, 7 children. commd. ensign Brit. Army, 1757, served with Gen. Jeffrey Amherst at capture of Louisburg, Can., 1758; resigned as lt., 1762; bought estate in Ligonier Valley, Western Pa., circa 1762, became largest resident property owner in Pa. West of mountains; apptd. colonial agt. in this frontier area by gov. Pa., 1771; justice Westmoreland County (Pa.) Ct., 1773; mem. Westmoreland County Com. Safety; sent as col. to take par in retreat of Contnental Army for Can., 1775; commd. brig. gen., served with Washington in campaign and battles of Trenton, Princeton, 1776-77; as maj. gen. ordered to defense of Fort Ticonderoga, 1777, evacuated post, exonerated by ct. martial, 1778; mem. Pa., Council of Censors, 1783; del. from Pa. to Continental Congress, 1785-87, pres. 1787; 1st gov. Northwest Territory, 1787-1802; maj. gen. comdr. U.S. Army, defeated by Indians nr. Fort Wayne, 1791; ordered to erect chain mil. posts from Fort Washington, nr. mouth of Miami River, to rapids of Maumee River, work very poorly planned and executed; resigned comm., 1792; Federalist; objected to statehood for Northwest Territory as premature, sought to gerrymanader territory into smaller territories so as to postpone statehood indefinitely; denounced the Ohio enabling act of Congress as a nullity at Ohio Constl. Conv. of 1802; Died at home "Hermitage," nr. Ligonier, Pa., Aug. 31, 1818.

SAINT-GAUDENS, HOMER SCHIFF (sant-gaw'denz), dir. fine arts; b. Roxbury, Mass., Sept. 28, 1880; s. Augustus and Augusta F. (Homer) S.; A.B., Harvard, 1903; m. Carlota Dolley, June 3, 1905 (died Oct. 24, 1927); children—Augustus, Carlota; m. 2d, Mary Louise McBride, Feb. 27, 1929. Asst. editor The Critic, N.Y., 1904; mng. editor Met. Mag., 1905; stage dir. for Maude Adams in "Legend of Leonara," "Kiss for Cinderella," etc., 1908-17; dir. production of "Beyond the Horizon," "The Red Robe," etc., 1919-21; asst. dir. Fine Arts, Carnegie Inst., Pitts., 1921, dir., 1922-50, dir. emeritus, 1950—. Capt. Co. A, 40th Engrs. (1st Camouflage Unit), A.E.F. in charge camouflage work on front; completed various temporary duties in Engrs. Res. Corps to Jan. 4, 1941; active service 1941-45; col., Corps of Engrs., Chief of Camouflage Sect., Office of Chief of Engrs., Washington, 1941-43; chief, Camouflage Sect., for Chief Engr., E.T.O., 1943-45; thereafter with Office of Chief of Engrs., Washington. Decorations: Legion of Merit, Bronze Star Medal, Purple Heart, Victory Medal, six stars, Am. Def. Medal, one star, Am. Theatre Medal, European Theatre Medal, five stars; Meritorious Medal, State of Pa.; Officer Legion of Honor, Croix de Guerre with palm (France); Officer Crown of Italy; Chevalier, Order of Leopold (Belgium); Comdr. Hungarian Order of Merit. Hon. corr. mem. Royal Acad., London. Clubs: Century, Harvard (N.Y.C.). Author: Reminiscenses of Augustus Saint-Gaudens, 1909; The American Artist and His Times, 1941; also short stories and spl. articles in mags. Lectr. on art subjects. Home: Box 246, Route 2, Miami, Fla. Died Dec. 8, 1958; buried Cornish, N.H.

ST. JOHN, FRANCIS R., librarian; b. Northampton, Mass., June 16, 1908; s. Edward B. and Mary (Shaughnessy) St. J.; A.B., Amherst Coll., 1931; B.L.S., Columbia Sch. Library Service, 1932; m. Helen McLeod, Dec. 26, 1931. Asst., reference dept., N.Y. Pub. Library, 1931-39; asst. librarian Enoch Pratt Free Library, Baltimore, 1939-41; chief, circulation dept., N.Y. Pub. Library, 1941-47; dir. library service Veterans Adminstrn., 1947-49; acting librarian Army Med. Library, U.S. Army, Washington, 1943-45; chief librarian Brooklyn Pub. Library 1949-63, Franklin Publs.; cons. on library mgmt. and bldgs., 1947—; pres. Francis R. St. John Library Consultants, 1964-67; trustee Flatbush Savs. Bank. Mem. N.Y. Commr. Edn.'s com. on reference and research library resources, 1960-62. Served with U.S. Army, 1943-45; commd. 1st lt., 1944, disch. as capt., 1945. Decorated Legion of Merit. Mem. Am. (exec. bd. 1950-54, chmn. adv. com. library tech. project 1962), N.Y. library assns., Am. Acad. Polit. Sci., Archons of Colophon, Delta Upsilon, Alpha Beta Alpha. Author: Internship in the Library Profession, 1938; also articles profl. publs. Home: New York City NY Died July 19, 1971.

ST. JOHN, ISAAC MUNROE army officer, engr.; b. Augusta, Ga., Nov. 29, 1827; s. Isaac Richards and Abigail Richardson (Munroe) St.J.; grad. Yale, 1845; m. Ella J. Carrington, Feb. 28, 1865, 6 children. Asst. editor Balt. Patriot, circa 1847; mem. engring. staff B. & O. R.R., 1848-55; in charge of constrn. divs. Blue Ridge R.R. in Ga., 1866-60; enlisted for engring. duty in U.S. Army, 1861, transferred to Magruder's Army of Peninsula, became chief engr.; commd. capt. engrs., 1862, promoted to maj. 1862, chief of the nitre and mining bur., Richmond, Va.; lt. col. and col.; apptd. commissary gen. with rank brig. gen. Confederate States Army, 1865, organized an efficient system for collecting and storing supplies and for forwarding them to the armies; chief engr. Louisville, Cincinnati & Lexington R.R., 1866-69; city engr. Louisville (Ky.), 1869-71; made 1st topog. map of Louisville and planned city's 1st complete sewerage system; became cons. engr. C. & O. R.R., 1871; chief engr. Elizabeth, Lexington & Big Sandy R.R., 1873. Died "Greenbrier," White Sulphur Springs, W.Va., Apr. 7, 1880.

ST. JOHN, JOHN PRICE gov. Kan.; b. Brookville, Franklin County, Ind., Feb. 25, 1833; s. Samuel and Sophia (Snell) St. John; m. Mary Jane Brewer, 1852; m. 2d, Susan J. Parker, Mar. 28, 1861; at least 2 children. Admitted to Ill. bar, 1860; served to lt. col. 43d Ill. Regt. during Civil War; practiced law, Independence, Mo., 1866-69; mem. Kan. Senate, 1873-74; gov. Kan. (Prohibitionist), 1878-82, secured adoption of constl. prohibition of liquor in Kan., 1882; unsuccessful Nat. Prohibition Party candidate for Pres. U.S., 1884 (supported by many Republicans, which led to election of 1st Democrat since Civil War). Died Olathe, Kan., Aug. 31, 1916.

ST. LEWIS, ROY, lawyer; b. Sharon, Pa., Sept. 27, 1891; s. John Griffith and Mary Ann (Davis) St. L.; prep. edn., high sch., Sharon, Pa., 1906-10; LL.B., U. of Okla., 1915; m. 2d, Peggy Hammond Taylor, July 29, 1943. Practiced at Holdenville, Okla., 1915-17, 1919-20; assistant attorney for Okla. of Chicago, Rock Island & Pacific Railway Company, with hdqrs. at El Reno, Okla., 1920-22; asst. U.S. atty. Western Dist. of Okla., 1922-24; gen. practice at Oklahoma City, 1925; U.S., atty. Western Dist. of Okla., 1925-28; apptd. spl. asst. to atty. gen. of U.S., 1928, in prosecution of W. K. Hale and John Ramsey for murder of Osage Indians in Okla.; reapptd. U.S. atty., 1929, resigned Aug. 1931; asst. atty. gen. U.S., 1931-33; ex-mem. Long. St. Lewis & Nyce, Washington; president Rocky Mountain Fuel Co., Denver, 1951-69; president, publisher The Diplomate Magazine; apptd. general counsel with rank of col. Civil Air Patrol, auxilliary U.S.A.F., 1952. Served overseas regimental sergeant major, 345th Infantry, 87th Division, U.S. Army, 1917-19. Am. Legion del. to Fidac Congress, Morocco, Africa, Sept. 1933, London, Eng., 1934, Brussels, Belgium, 1935; commander National Press Club Post, 1943. Mem. American Bar Association (v.p. 1930-32), Okla. State and Okla. County, District of Columbia bar assns.; Kappa Sigma, Phi Alpha Delta. Pres. Okla. State Soc. in Washington, D.C., 1938-41. Republican. Baptist. Mason (32 deg., Shriner), Moose. Clubs: Oklahoma City; National Press (Washington, D.C.). Home: Washington DC Died Nov. 1, 1969.

SALISBURY, GEORGE ROBERT officer U.S.N.; b. Canandaigua, N.Y., Mar. 2, 1855; s. Samuel W. and Agnes (Walker) S.; high sch., Kansas City, Mo.; grad. as engr. cadet U.S. Naval Acad., 1879; m. Adele Trowbridge, of Brooklyn, Jan. 19, 1889. Promoted asst. engr., June 30, 1884, p.a. engr., 1892; lt., May 5, 1899; lt. comdr., June 30, 1902; comdr., Mar. 19, 1907; capt. Nov. 14, 1910. Served on U.S.S. Shenandoah, 1879-82; Juanita and Enterprise, in China and Japan, 1882-86; New York Navy Yard, 1886-89; U.S.S. Chicago, 1889-90; U.S.S. Baltimore, 1890-92; Navy Dept., Washington, 1892; U.S. Schoolship Enterprise, 1892-95; Fern and Indiana, 1895-98; on U.S.S. Annapolis during Spanish-Am. War, in engagements at Barracoa AND Nipe Bay; New York Navy Yard, 1899; U.S.S. Texas, New York and Massachusetts, 1899-1902; Montgomery, 1902-04; New York Navy Yard, 1904-05; Olympia, 1905-06; Hancock and Alliance, 1906-09; comdg. Mohican, Monterey and Wilmington, on Asiatic Sta., 1909-10; gov. Guam, Jan. 12, 1911-May 1, 1913; retired with rank of commodore, June 30, 1913; active duty during war period, Apr. 14, 1917-Dec. 31, 1919, as insp. engring. material and machinery, Buffalo, N.Y. Episcopalian. Mem. Am. Soc. Naval Engrs. Home: Independence, Missouri.

SALISBURY, STANTON W. clergyman; b. Decatur, Neb., Jan. 12, 1891; s. Joseph Read and Lydia A. (Bicknell) S.; A.B., U. Omaha, 1913, LL.D., 1949; B.D., Auburn, (N.Y.) Theol. Sem., 1916; m. Adelina Phebe Williams, May 22, 1917. Asso. pastor Trinity Center, San Francisco, 1919-21; chaplain (at sea and ashore) USN, since 1921, asst. dir., chaplain's div., 1943-44, now rear adm. in chaplain corps USN. Served as chaplain 327th Inf., 82d Div., AEF, 1918-19; chaplain U.S.S. Blackhawk, 1921-22, U.S.S. Bridgeport, 1922-24, naval sta., Guam, Marianas Islands, 1924-26, Navy yard, Bklyn., 1926-29, U.S.S. Detroit, 1929-30, U.S.S. Omaha, 1930-32, at Navy Dept., 1932-35, U.S.S. Henderson, 1935-38, Marine Barracks, Quantico, Va., 1938-40, U.S.S. Pennsylvania, 1940-42, Chaplain's Sch., Norfolk, Va., 1942-43, Navy Dept., 1943-44, dist. chaplain, Fifth Naval Dist., 1944-46; fleet chaplain U.S. Atlantic Fleet, 1946-49; asst. dir. Chaplains Div., since 1949, chief chaplains since Sept. 1, 1949. Decorated: Commendation ribbon, World War I Victory medal (3 stars), China medal. Def. medal (1 star), Pacific Area medal (1 star), Am. Area medal, World War II Victory Medal. Mem. VFW. Mason, Sojourer, Heroes of '76. Home: 40 S Marvin Av., Auburn, N.Y. Office: Arlington Annex, Navy Dept., Washington 25. Died Mar. 1966.

SALMON, THOMAS WILLIAM M.D.; b. Lansingburg, N.Y., Jan. 6, 1876; s. Thomas H. (M.D.) and Annie E. (Frost) S.; M.D., Albany Med. Coll., 1899; m. Helen Potter Ashley, Dec. 21, 1899; children—Thomas K., Edwin A., Richard, Russell G., Helen E., Barbara. Pvt. practice and Willard (N.Y.) State Hospital, 1899-1903; commd. asst. surgeon U.S. Marine Hosp. Service (now U.S. Pub. Health Service), Oct. 29, 1903; passed assistant surgeon, 1908, resigned Jan. 1, 1915; chmn. N.Y. State Bd. Alienists, 1911; med. dir. Nat. Com. for Mental Hygiene, 1915-21; staff Rockefeller Foundation, 1915-21; prof. psychiatry, Columbia U., 1921—; cons. psychiatrist, Presbyn. Hosp., 1922—. Maj., lt. col. and col., M.C. U.S.A., 1917-19; brig. gen. M.R.C.; sr. consultant in neuro-psychiatry, A.E.F. Awarded D.S.M. Mem. Permanent

Inter-Allied Com. After-Care Disabled Soldiers; mem. Internat. Jury of Award, Panama-P.I. Expn. Author of chapter on "Immigration," in Modern Treatment of Mental and Nervous Diseases, 1913; chapter on "Mental Hygiene," Am. Year Book, 1917-20, and in Preventive Medicine and Hygiene, 1916-20; etc. Home: Larchmont, N.Y. Died Aug. 13, 1927.

SALM-SALM, PRINCESS (AGNES ELISABETH WINONA LECLERCQ JOY), adventuress; born Vt. or Que., Can., Dec. 25, 1840; d. William and Julia (Willard) Joy; m. Felix Constantin Alexander Johann Nepomuit (Prince Salm-Salm), Aug. 20, 1862; m. 2d, Charles Heneage, 1876. Spent most of childhood in Que.; went to Washington, D.C. at start of Civil War, there met and married Prince Salm-Salm, a German soldier of fortune who was attempting to get commn. in U.S. Army; aided in getting her husband apptd. col. 8th N.Y. Volunteers; accompanied husband in field, became an acquaintance of many notable Union figures; accompanied husband to Mexico when he entered service under Emperor Maximilian, 1866; decorated Grand Cordon of Order of San Carlos by Maximilian; attempted to use bribery to effect release of Maximilian after his capture, also pleaded for mercy for him before Jaurez; later served as nurse, did army relief work for German Army during Franco-Prussian War, 1870; pensioned by Austrian emperor; decorated Prussian Medal of Honor; resided in Germany, visited Am. in effort to get support for Boers in S. Africa during Boer War, 1899-1900 elected mem. N.J. chpt. D.A.R., 1900; subject of an hist. painting by Manuel Ocaranza, 1873, also subject in several novels; a figure in Franz Werfel's play Juarez and Maximilian. Author: Zehn Jahre Aus Meinem Leben, 1875, translated into English as Ten Years of My Life, 2 vols., 1876. Died Karlsruhe, Germany, Dec. 21, 1912.

SALTONSTALL, DUDLEY naval officer; b. New London, Conn., Sept. 8, 1738; s. Gen. Gurdon and Rebecca (Winthrop) S.; m. Frances Babcock, 1765, 7 children. Privateersman in French and Indian Wars; commanded fort at New London, 1775; given command in Alfred, flagship of Commodore Esek Hopkins, 1775; apptd. 4th on list of captains, 1776; commanded expdn. of Bagaduce (now Castine), in Penobscot Bay, arrived in Penobscot Bay, 1779, fled at arrival of Brit. fleet; dismissed from navy because two ships were taken by Brit., 1779; became successful privateer and mcht. Died Mole St. Nicolas, Haiti, 1796.

SALTZMAN, CHARLES MCKINLEY army officer; b. Panora, Ia., Oct. 18, 1871; s. F. J. and Lovina Elizabeth (Lahman) S.; grad. U.S. Mil. Acad., 1896; honor grad. Signal Sch., 1906; grad. Army War Coll., 1921; m. Mary Peyton Eskridge, May 9, 1899; 1 son, Charles Eskridge. Apptd. add. 2d lt. 5th Cav., June 12, 1896; promoted through grades to col., May 15, 1917; brig. gen. N.A., July 24, 1917. A.d.c. to Brig. Gen. H. C. Merriam, 1900-01; engagements at Guasimas and San Juan, Santiago Campaign, 1898, also in Philippine Insurrection and Moro campaigns; signal officer, Eastern Dept., 1913-15; signal officer, U.S. troops, Panama, C.Z., 1915-16; apptd. exec. officer, Office of Chief Signal Officer, Sept. 1, 1916; chief signal officer, rank of maj. gen., Jan. 9, 1924; retired Jan. 8, 1928; apptd. mem. Federal Radio Commn., 1929, chmn., 1930-32 (resigned); appointed vice-pres. U.S. Shipping Board Merchant Fleet Corp., 1933. Delegate from U.S. to Internat. Radio Conf., London, 1912, to Internat. Telegraph Conference, Paris, 1925. Internat. Radio Telegraph Conf., Washington, D.C., 1927; chmn. U.S. delegation to Internat. Radio Tech. Consulting Com., The Hague, 1929. Given two citations "for gallantry in action," Spanish-Am. War; awarded D.S.M., "for exceptionally meritorious and conspicuous services," World War; Silver Star medal with Oak Leaf Cluster, 1934. Address: Burnt Mills Hills. Silver Spring, Md. Died Nov. 25, 1942.

SAMFORD, JOHN A., air force officer; b. Hagerman, N.M., Aug. 29, 1905; s. Charles MacDanial and Adline Williams (Shepperson) S.; student N.M. Normal U., Las Vegas, N.M., 1919-23, Columbia U., 1923-24; B.S., U.S. Mil. Acad., 1928; grad. Air Corps Primary Flying Sch., 1929. Advanced Flying Sch., attack course, 1929, Air Corps Tech. Sch., engr.-armament course, 1935, Air Corps Tactical Sch., 1939; m. Elizabeth Baylor Illg, July 18, 1929; 1 son, John Alexander. Commd. 2d lieut., F.A., 1928, transferred to Air Corps, 1929, advancing through the grades to lt. gen., 1956; dep. chief of staff 8th Air Force, Eng., 1944; comdt. Air Command and Staff Sch., 1949-50, Air War Coll., 1950-51; dir. intelligence USAF, 1952-56; dir. Nat. Security Agy., 1956-69. Home: Washington3DC Died Nov. 20, 1968; buried Arlington Nat. Cemetery Arlington VA

SAMMOND, FREDERIC lawyer; b. Milw., June 15, 1895; s. Charles E. and Jeannie (Stowell) S.; student Galahad Acad., 1908-12; m. Marie Freitag, Sept. 12, 1925; children—John Stowell, Peter Hefty. Mdse. broker, 1915-16; mem. firm Reilly, Penner & Benton, C.P.A.'s, Milw., 1920-28; admitted to Wis. bar, 1927, since practiced in Milw.; mem. firm Floley, Sammond & Lardner, 1928-33, partner, 1933—. Dir., v.p. Clement Constrn. Co.; dir. Mirro Aluminum Co., Menominee Enterprises, Inc., W. H. Bendfelt Co., Dartwell co., Heil Co., Lake Shore, Inc., Arnold Dryer Co., Gen. Charities, Inc., Wis. Broadway Co., Kurth Malting Co., T. A. Chapman Co., Wis. Securities Co. Dela., Marion Finance Co. Mem. Citizens Govt. Research Bur., Gr. Milw. Com.; chmn. bd. appeals, Village of River Hills. Corp. mem. United Community Services; dir., Episcopal Found. Milw.; trustee Lawrence U.; adv. council Marquette U. Law Sch.; mem. Columbia Hosp. Corp. Served as capt. F.A., 32d Div., U.S. Army, 1916-20; ret. as col. Wis. N.G., 1940. Fellow Am. Bar Found.; mem. Am. Law Inst., Am., Wis., Milw. bar assns., Hist. Soc. Wis. (bd. curators), Phi Delta Phi (hon.). Episcopalian. Clubs: Milwaukee, University, Milwaukee Country, Madison, Chippewa. Home: 7275 N. River Rd., Milw. 53217. Office: First Wisconsin Nat. Bank Bldg., Milw. 53202. Died Mar. 1966.

SAMPEY, JOHN RICHARD, JR., educator; b. Louisville, Aug. 5, 1896; s. John Richard and Annie (Renfroe) S.; student U. Louisville, 1919; S.B., U. Chgo., 1920, S.M., 1921, Ph.D., 1923; post doctorate research, Johns Hopkins, 1923-24, 30-31; m. Jewell Cheatham, Sept. 4, 1925; children—John Richard III, Jane Renfroe. Grafflin scholar Johns Hopkins, 1923-24; asso. prof. chemistry Howard Coll., 1924-26, prof., 1926-34; prof. chemistry Furman U., 1934-67. Served from pvt. to 2d lt., inf., U.S. Army, 1918-19; AEF in France; as lt. col., inf., AUS, 1941-45; ETO, PTO. Decorated various service medals. Recipient coll. chemistry teacher award, Manufacturing Chemists Association, 1961. Fellow A.A.A.S.; member American Chemical Society (chmn. Ala. and S.C. sects; Charles H. Herty medal 1954), Ala. (past pres.), S.C. (pres. 1940) acads. scis., So. Assn. Sci. and Industry (trustee). Res. Officers Assn., Am. Legion. Baptist (deacon, Sunday sch. tchr.). Contbr. numerous articles profl. jours. Home: Greenville SC Died 1967.

SAMPLE, JOHN GLEN, exec.; born Lutesville, Mo., July 3, 1891; s. William W. and Mattie (Glen) S.; B.S., Will Mayfield Coll., Marble Hill, Mo., 1909; m. Helen M. Scanlon, Nov. 1, 1921; children—Joseph, Sally (Mrs. Sally S. Aall). Co-founder of Blackett-Sample-Hummert, Inc. (later Dancer-Fitzgerald-Sample, Inc.), 1923, ret. 1948; pres. Port Royal, Inc., Naples, Fla. Capt. Inf., 89th Div., U.S. Army, World War I. Comdr. U.S.N.R., with 7th Amphibious Force, Pacific, World War II. Decorated Bronze Star medal (Navy), Navy Commendation medal, Purple Heart (Army), World Wars I and II medals; also campaign badges and Philippine Liberation ribbon. Presbyterian. Clubs: Chicago, Racquet (Chicago); Onwentsia (Lake Forest, Ill.); Yacht, Hole-in-the-Wall Golf (Naples, Fla.); Delray Beach (Fla.) Yacht. Home: Naples FL Died Nov. 25, 1971.

SAMPLE, WILLIAM DODGE naval officer; b. Buffalo, N.Y., Mar. 9, 1898; s. Brig. Gen. (ret. U.S.A.) William Roderick and Elizabeth (McCullough) S.; grammer sch., Spokane and Seattle, Wash., Chicago, Ill., St. Louis, Mo., Alaska and Philippine Islands, 1904-11; Lowel High Sch., San Francisco, 1912-14; New Mexico Mil. Inst., Roswell, N.M., 1914-15; B.S., U.S. Naval Acad., 1918; m. Mary Lee Lamar, Apr. 18, 1928; 1 dau., Carolyn. Midshipman, U.S. Navy, 1915; comd. ensign, 1918, and advanced through the grades to rear admiral, 1943; naval aviator, 1923; exec. officer, Naval Air Station, Pensacola, 1941-42; comdg. officer, 10th fleet, 1943-44; comdg. officer, U.S.S. Intrepid, 1944; comdg. officer, U.S.S. Hornet, 1944; comdr. carrier div. 27, 1944-45; comdr. carrier div. 22, 1945. Awarded Legion of Merit with two Gold Stars; Commendation Ribbon, Purple Heart. Club: Army and Navy Country (Washington). Address: 204 W. Gonzalez St., Pensacola, Fla. Died Oct. 3, 1946.

SAMPLE, WILLIAM RODERICK army officer; b. Memphis, Tenn., June 29, 1866; s. Rev. W. A. S.; grad. U.S. Mil. Acad., 1888; m. Bettie M. C. Saunders, of Birmingham, Ala., May 27, 1891. Apptd. add. 2d lt. 14th Inf., June 11, 1888; 2d lt., July 1, 1888; 1st lt. 13th Inf., Oct. 1, 1895; capt., a.a.g., vols., May 20, 1898; hon. discharged vols., Apr. 7, 1899; capt. 3d Inf., Apr. 1, 1899; maj., Mar. 11, 1911; adj. gen., Mar. 28, 1912; assigned to 20th Inf., Dec. 6, 1914; lt. col., July 1, 1916; col. May 15, 1917; nom. brig. gen. by Pres. Wilson, Dec. 17, 1917. Duty with Ark. N.G., 1893-95; participated in assault on San Juan Hill, Cuba, July 1, 1898, and recommended for brevet; in Philippine Islands, 1899-1902, and 1909-12, Alaska, 1904-06; comd. base of Mexican Punitive Expdn. at Columbus, N.M., Mar.-June, 1916; apptd. comdr. Officers' Training Camp, Madison Barracks, N.Y., May-Oct., 1917; brig. gen. comdg. advance sect. of S.O.S. of the A.E.F. in France, Nov. 1917-June 1919. Home: Ft. Smith, Ark.

SAMPSON, ARCHIBALD J. lawyer; b. nr. Cadiz, O., June 21, 1839, s. of Francis and Margaret Griffith (Evans) S.; bro. of Francis A. S.; pvt. to capt. in Union Army in Civil War; B.S., Mt. Union Coll., Ohio, 1861, A.M., 1865 (LL.D., 1890); LL.B., Cleveland Law Coll., 1866; m. Kate I. Turner, Sept. 18, 1866 (died 1886); m. 2d, Frances S Wood, Mar. 19, 1891. Admitted to bar, 1865; practiced at Sedalia, Mo., 1865-73, Cañon City, and Denver, Colo., 1873-93, Phoenix, Ariz., from 1893. Nominated for U.S. consul at Palestine, 1873, but declined; atty. gen. Colo., 1876-79; consul at El Paso del Norte, Mex., 1889-93; E.E. and M.P. to Ecuador, 1897-1907, being first person for over 80 yrs. living in a territory to receive a diplomatic appmt. Republican. Past dept. comdr. G.A.R. and now a.-a.-g. G.A.R. Mason. Died Dec. 24, 1921.

SAMPSON, WILLIAM THOMAS rear adm. U.S.N.; b. Palmyra, N.Y., Feb. 9, 1840; s. James and Hannah (Walker) S.; apptd. to navy, Sept. 24, 1857; grad. at head of class, U.S. Naval Acad., 1861 (LL.D., Harvard, 1899); m. Margaret Sexton, Aldrich, 1863; m. 2d, Elizabeth Susan Burling, 1882. Promoted to master, 1861; commd. lt., July 16, 1862; was exec. officer on ironclad "Patapsco" when it was blown up by a mine in Charleston harbor; he was blown into the water, but rescued; commd. lt. comdr., July 25, 1866; comdr., Aug. 9, 1874; capt., March, 1889; supt. Naval Acad., 1886-90. Has been in all branches of naval service; expert on ordnance, torpedoes, etc.; with Lt. Joseph Strauss, devised and perfected the superimposed turrets introduced into the navy, Feb. 1898, pres. bd. of inquiry as to cause of destruction of U.S.S. "Maine" in Havana harbor, Feb. 15, 1898; after declaration of war with Spain comd. N. Atlantic squadron, with rank of acting rear adm.; promoted to commodore, 1898, rear adm., 1899. In Spanish-Am. war his command numbered 125 vessels—the strongest ever organized for hostile purposes; this fleet captured many Spanish merchant vessels and blockade runners and finally defeated Spanish fleet under Admiral Cervera. Apptd., Sept. 1898, one of the 3 commrs. to Cuba; resumed command N. Atlantic fleet, Dec. 1898; commandant Boston Navy Yard, Oct. 14, 1899—. Died 1902.

SAMUEL, SHEPARD congressman, lawyer; b. Exeter, N.H., circa 1783; attended Philips Exeter Adad., 1794; grad. Yale, 1806; studied law. Admitted to bar, practiced in Waterville, Me. (then dist. of Mass.), 1810; served as maj. 21st Inf. in War of 1812, lt. col. 13th Inf., 1813-14; mem. U.S. Ho. of Reps. from Mass., 14th Congress, 1815-17; apptd. surveyor gen. Ohio land dist. 1819. Died Cowington, Ky., Dec. 17, 1820.

SAMUELS, ARTHUR HIRAM editor; b. Hartford, Conn., Apr. 15, 1888; s. Louis L. and Minna (Krotoshiner) S.; A.B., Princeton, 1909; m. Vivian Martin, Feb. 28, 1926. Reporter N.Y. Sun, 1909-13 (spl. corr. with Theodore Roosevelt); mgr. promotion dept. Curtis Pub. Co., 1913-16; partner Barrows, Richardson & Alley, 1920-28; exec. editor The New Yorker, 1928-30; editor Home and Field, 1930-31, Harper's Bazaar, 1931-34, House Beautiful, 1934—. Mng. editor for Food Adminstrn., Washington, D.C., 1916-17; served as capt. in office of surgeon gen., in charge of publicity in behalf of reconstruction of disabled soldiers, 1917-19. Composer musical comedy "Poppy" (with W. C. Fields), 1926. Home: New York, N.Y. Died Mar. 20, 1938.

SANBORN, ALVAN FRANCIS journalist, author; b. Marlboro, Mass., July 8, 1866; s. Alvin P. and Sarah B. (Weeks) S.; A.B., Amherst Coll., 1887, Litt.D., 1917; studied 1 yr. Columbia Sch. of Polit. Science, New York; m. Marie Perrin, of Paris, France, Oct. 5, 1904. Asso. editor with D. Lothrop Co., Boston, 1888-90; asso. editor International Cyclopaedia, 1891; editor Cottage Hearth, 1891-92; resident worker South End House, Boston (univ. settlement), 1892-96; regular Paris corr. Boston Transcript, 1899-1902, Atlantic Monthly, Boston, 1900, 1904-05; on staff of Boston Traveler, 1905-06; New York spl. corr. of Boston Transcript, 1906-07; asso. editor Grafton Press, New York, 1906-07; spl. Paris corr. of Boston Traveler, 1907-08; regular Paris corr. of Boston Transcript, 1907-36 and of New York Times Saturday Review, 1907-14, of Book News rep. New York Independent, 1913-15. Enlisted as Monthly, 1908-15, of The Bellman, 1910-11; Paris foreign vol. in French Army (3d Régt. de Uarche du ler Sstranger, Sept. 1, 1914, and passed the winter-of 1914-15 at the front in the trenches of LaSomme, near Pèronne. Decorated Cross of Legion of Honor (France), 1932. Mem. Inter-Allied Com. for Professional Re-edn. of War Cripples, as rep. Dept. of the Interior, Sept. 1917-23. Spl. Paris corr. New York Tribune, 1919. Member Assn. des Anciens Combattants Engagès Volontaires trangers dans l'Armée Francaise, Paris Post of American Legion, Trench and Air, Syndicat de la Presse trangere (Paris), La Maison des Journalistes, Phi Beta Kappa, Psi Upsilon. Author: Mooody's Lodging House and Other Tenement Sketches, 1895; Meg McIntyre's Raffle, and Other Stories, 1896; Paris and the Social Revolution, 1905; Report on Agricultural Instruction in France (for Mass. Commn. on Industrial Edn.). Editor: Masterpieces of Prose, 1893; Reminiscences of Richard Lathers, 1907; Two Centuries of New Milford, 1908. Contbr. to mags. on lit. and sociol. topics, and especially upon French life and letters. Address: 49 Boul. des Marronniers, Draveil, Seine-et-Oise, France.

SANBORN, JOHN BENJAMIN veteran general; b. Epsom, N.H., Dec. 5, 1826; ed. Dartmouth Coll.; studied law; admitted to N.H. bar. July 1854; removed to St. Paul, Dec. 1854; engaged in practice; m. Catherine Hall, March 17, 1857, Newton, N.J.; m. 2d, Anna Nixon, Nov. 26, 1865; m. 3d, Rachel Rice, April 18, 1880. As adj. gen. and q.m. gen. organized and sent Minn. troops to war, 1861; col. 4th Minn., 1862; served to close of war, becoming brig. gen. and bvt. maj. gen.; participated in battles of Iuka, Corinth, Port Gibson, Raymond, Jackson, Champion's Hill, and in assault and siege of Vicksburg; in Oct. 1864 took command of Dist. of Southwest Mo., and fought the successful engagements of that period and section; fought against Indians of the Southwest in summer and fall of 1865; apptd. by President Johnson to settle difficulties with Indians in following winter; mem. Indian Peace Commn., 1867-68; has served in Minn. house and senate. Home: St. Paul, Minn. Died 1904.

SANBORN, JOSEPH BROWN soldier; b. Chester, N.H., Dec. 8, 1855; s. Josiah and Rachael S.; ed. pub. schs.; m. Julie F. Flanders (died 1922); children—Mrs. Helen F. Kline (dec.), Mrs. Katharine S. Boice; m. 2d, Willa Alice Weck, Sept. 4, 1924. Moved to Chicago, 1877; pres. J. B. Sanborn Co., merc. agency, 1886-1925; mem. State Tax Commn., 1919-21. Identified with Ill. N.G. from 1879; maj. 1st Ill. Inf., Spanish-Am. War, 1898, serving in Santiago Campaign; col. same regt., 1899, and continued as col. same regt. (later 131st U.S. Inf.); arrived in France with regt., May 30, 1918; participated in Somme and Argonne-Meuse offensives, beginning Aug. 8, 1918, and closing Nov. 11, 1918, comprising in all 25 engagements. Decorated D.S.C., "for extraordinary heroism" nr. Gressaire, France, Aug. 9, 1918; D.S.M.; British D.S.O.; Officer Legion of Honor, France, and Croix de Guerre with palm; Officer Belgian Order of Leopold. Maj. gen. Ill. N.G., June 23, 1920; retired, June 20, 1921; lt. gen. retired, Apr. 6, 1931. Mem. Soc. of Santiago, Am. Legion. Mason. Republican. Home: Chicago, Ill. Died Dec. 22, 1934.

SANCHEZ, ALLAN JUAN, corp. exec.; b. Garyville, La., Nov. 30, 1908; s. Anatole J. and Alcidie (Chapron) S.; student Tulane U., 1935-41; m. Gladys Barbara Scott, May 9, 1935; 1 dau., Emily Elizabeth. Accountant, Fed. Land Bank of New Orleans, 1932-38, City of New Orleans, 1938-40; state auditor La. Hwys. Dept., 1940-42; v.p. finance, sec. Lykes Bros. S.S. Co., Inc., New Orleans, 1946; v.p. finance, sec., comptroller Lykes Corp., New Orleans; v.p., controller, sec. Lykes-Youngstown Corp.; sec.-treas. Lykes Financial Corp., 1966-70. Served to maj. AUS, 1942-46; lt. col. Res. ret. Mem. Assn. Waterline Accounting Ofcrs., Data Processing Assn. (past dir.), Mil. Order of World Wars, Res. Officers Assn. Roman Catholic. Club: Propellar. Home: New Orleans LA Died June 5, 1970; buried Lakelawn Mausoleum.

SANDERS, LOUIS PECK lawyer; b. Helena, Mont.; s. Wilbur Fisk and Harriet Peck (Fenn) S.; grad. Phillips Exeter Academy, 1889; A.B., Harvard Univ., 1893; m. Natalie Rood Brown, Sept. 16, 1920; children—Helen, Wilbur Fisk, Louise Merris, Jean Edgerton. Admitted to Montana bar, 1900; mem. Kremer, Sanders & Kremer, Butte, 1907-34, when firm dissolved; now engaged in gen. practice. Served in Spanish-Am. War and Philippine Insurrection, 1898-99; with 1st Mont. Inf., as battalion adj., and capt. Co. B; was a.d.c. staff Brig. Gen. Harrison Gray Otis and staff Maj. Gen. Elwell S. Otis, comdg. 8th Army Corps in Philippines; organized 2d Mont. Inf., N.G., and served as first regt. adj.; civilian aide to sec. of War for Mont. C.M.T.C. Assn. Republican. Pub. first edit. Montana Codes. Home: Butte, Mont. Died July 21, 1940.

SANDERS, ROBERT DAVID textile exec.; b. Tuscaloosa, Ala., Sept. 28, 1898; s. James William and Julia (Lockett) S.; student U. of South, 1915, Mercer U., 1916; A.M., Coll. of Miss., 1917; m. Catherine Williams, Sept. 1940; children—James William, Julia Sheila, June Kelley, Robert David. Began as mill and office employee, Aponaug Mfg. Co., Kosciusko, Miss., 1920; office mgr. and gen. supt. cotton mills operated by father, Kosciusko, Starkville, Natchez, Winona, and Yazoo City, Miss., and Mobile, Ala., 1920-27; purchasing agt. for all mills and asst. to pres., Jackson, Miss., 1927-37; pres. and treas. since 1937 various corps. Sanders Industries including Aponaug Mfg. Co., Kosciusko, J. W. Sanders Cotton Mill, Inc., Starkville, Miss., Magnolia Textiles, Inc., Magnolia, Miss., Delta Chenille Co., Inc., Summit, Winona and Durant, Miss., Kay Ruth Dress Co., Inc., Jackson, Miss., Jackson Opera House Co., The Sanders Co., Jackson, Miss., Sanders Motors, Inc., Jackson, Miss., Deep South Motor Co., Jackson, Miss., Indsl. Suppliers, Inc., Jackson, Miss. Dir. Century Aviation Co., M.-K.-T. R.R. Lt. col., Govs. Staff, State Ga., since 1948; col. Govs. Staff, State Miss. since 1948. Served as capt., Tank Corps, U.S. Army, 1918-20, overseas, 1918-20. Pres. Robert D. Sanders Foundation. Mem. Internat. Trade Mart, Nat. Assn. Mfrs., Am. Cotton Mfrs. Inst., Nat. Cotton Mfrs. Inst., Nat. Cotton Council Am. (del. mem.), Nat. Football Hall of Fame (charter mem.), Miss. Economic Council, Jackson C. of C., Kappa Alpha (life mem. scholarship fund, exec. council), Omega Delta Kappa, Beta Gamma Sigma. Raises pheasants and turkeys and registered cattle, Kaywood Plantations; interested in reforestation. Home: Kaywood Plantations, Hazlehurst, Miss. Office: Century Bldg., Jackson, Miss. Died Sept. 24, 1954; buried Lakewood Meml. Park, Jackson.

SANDERS, WALTER BENJAMIN, educator; b. Ann Arbor, Mich., July 30, 1906; s. Chauncey K. and May B. (Paine) S.; B.S. in Architecture, U. Ill., 1929; M. Architecture, U. Pa., 1930; m. Carroll Thompson, Aug. 25, 1935. Instr. architecture Columbia, 1930-36; asso. editor Am. Architect mag., 1937-38, Archtl. Forum mag., 1938-39; vis. lectr. Pratt Inst., 1939-40, Columbia, 1946-49, U. Mich., 1947-49; prof. architecture U. Mich., 1949-72, chmn. dept., 1954-64; partner Sanders & Breck, Architects, N.Y.C., 1938-42, Sanders & Malsin, N.Y.C., 1946-50; prin. Walter Sanders, Architects, Ann Arbor, 1950-72; design cons. Albert Kahn Asso. Architects & Engrs., Detroit, 1955-72. Cons. community facilities div. FHA, 1952. Served from lt. to lt. col., USAAF, 1942-46. Decorated Bronze Star medal, Legion of Merit; recipient hon. mention Smithsonian Gallery of Art, 1940, spl. commendation N.Y. chpt. A.I.A. House awards, 1940, 2d and 3d prizes Bloomingdale's House Competition, N.Y.C., 1946, gold medal Mich. Soc. Architects, 1964. Fellow A.I.A. (dir. 1968-72); mem. Assn. Collegiate Schs. Architecture (dir. 1963-65, pres. 1965-67), Mich. Soc. Architects (dir. 1968-72), Congresses Internationeaux d'Architecture Moderne, Bldg. Research Inst. (dir. 1959-67), Mich. Acad. Sci., Arts and Letters, Sigma Nu, Phi Kappa Phi, Alpha Rho Chi, Tau Sigma Delta, Scarab. Contbr. articles profl. jours. Home: Ann Arbor MI Died Mar. 19, 1972.

SANDS, BENJAMIN FRANKLIN naval officer; b. Balt., Feb. 11, 1812; s. Benjamin and Rebecca (Hooks) Norris; m. Henrietta Maria French, Nov. 15, 1836, 8 children. Commd. lt. U.S. Navy, served in African Squadron as comdr. ship Porpoise, 1848-50; promoted comdr., chief Bur. of Constrn., 1858-61; sent with expdn. to evacuate Norfolk (Va.) Navy Yard, Apr. 1861, in charge of party which fired ships and ship-houses; commd. capt., 1862, served as sr. officer on Cape Fear River and Wilmington (Del.) blockade until late 1864; claimed to have originated idea of additional outer line of blockaders; participated in both attacks on Ft. Fisher, Dec. 1864, Jan. 1865; commanded 2d div. West Gulf Squadron, until July 1865; surrender of last Confederate troops occurred on his ship, Galveston, Tex., June 2, 1865; promoted commodore, 1866, rear adm., 1871; in charge of Naval Observatory, Washington, D.C., 1867-74. Author: From Reefer to Rear Admiral, 1899. Died Washington, June 30, 1883; buried Mt. Olivet Cemetery, Washington.

SANDS, JAMES HOBAN rear adm. U.S.N.; b. Washington, July 12, 1845; s. Benjamin F. and Henrietta M. (French) S.; apptd. from Md., and grad. U.S. Naval Acad., 1863; m. Mary Elizabeth Meade, Oct. 28, 1869; father of William Franklin S. Promoted ensign, May 28, 1863; advanced through grades to rear adm., Apr. 11, 1902. Served on Tuscarora, N. Atlantic Blockading Squadron, 1863-64; Juniata, May-Aug. 1864; Shenandoah, N. Atlantic Blockading Squadron, 1864-65; participated in evacuation of Charleston, and both attacks on Ft. Fisher; served on Hartford, E. India Squadron, 1865-68; Naval Obs., 1868, 1869-70; Richmond, 1869; Navy Yard, Washington, 1870; California, 1871-73; Hydrographic Office, 1873-75; Minnesota, 1875-76; Navy Yard, New York, 1877-79; spl. duty, Washington, 1880-82; comd. Iroquois, 1882-84; Navy Yard, Washington, 1884-86, 1892-93; comd. Monongahela, 1891-92; Navy Yard, Boston, 1893-95; comd. Columbia, 1895-97; Minneapolis. 1897-98; gov. Naval Home, Phila., 1898-1901; mem. Naval Retiring Bd., 1901, pres., 1902; comdt. Navy Yard, League Island, 1902-03; comd. Coast Squadron, N. Atlantic Fleet, 1903-05; supt. Naval Acad., 1905-07; retired, July 12, 1907. Died 1911.

SANDS, JOSHUA RATOON naval officer; b. Bklyn., May 13, 1795; s. Joshua and Ann (Ayscough) S.; m. Mary Steven, 1826; m. 2d, Henrietta Steven; m. 3d, Ellen Ann Crook, 1830; 4 children. Commd. midshipman U.S. Navy, 1812; served in War of 1812, distinguished in attack upon British ship Royal George, in capture of Toronto and Ft. George; commd. lt., 1818; fought 1st duel with Lt. T.S. Hamersley which led to ct. martial and long confinement, 1823; fought another duel killing opponent Surgeon H. Basset, exonerated, 1830; became comdr., 1841; commanded steamer Vixen participating in operations at Alvarado, Tabasco, Laguna, elsewhere during Mexican War, 1846-48; served as gov. Laguna (Mexico), circa 1846; commanded ship St. Lawrence carrying Am. exhibits to London (Eng.) World's Fair, 1851; promoted capt., 1854; assisted in Atlantic cable-laying operations in ship Susquehanna, 1857; commanded Brazil sta. in ship Congress, 1859-61; commd. commodore (ret.), 1862, rear adm., 1866; lighthouse insp. on lower Gt. Lakes, 1862-66; port adm., Norfolk, Va., 1869-72. Died Balt., Oct. 2, 1883; buried Greenwood Cemetery, Bklyn.

SANDSTROM, (ALFRED) EMIL (FREDRIK) jurist, internat. Red Cross ofcl.; b. Nykôpring, Sweden, Oct. 11, 1886; s. Carl and Hilma (Nordin) S.; student Coll. of Nykoping; LL.B., U. Uppsala, 1908; m. Anna Akerman, Mar. 28, 1915; 1 son, 2 daus. Judge of First Instance, Ct. of Appeals, Gota, 1912-17; judge Mixed Ct. in Egypt, 1918-26; mem. 3d Div., Anglo-German Mixed Arbitration Tribunal, 1926-29; pres. Labor Contract Ct., Stockholm, 1929-31; with Supreme Ct. (becoming chief justice), 1931-33, 1935-43; chmn. com. investigating subversive polit. activities, also mem. bd. to handle complaints on wages of pub. works employees, 1933-35; conducted investigations German property in Sweden, also chief del. to U.S. in negotiations with Allies concerning this property, 1945-46; chmn. alien property custodian bd., Sweden, also rep. Sweden on Internat. Ct. of Arbitration, The Hague, since 1946; chmn. UN Spl. Com. on Palestine, 1947; mem. Internat. Commn. UN, 1948; chmn. Permanent Conciliation Commn., Belgium-Denmark, 1951; Italy-Gt. Britain, Italy-U.S., 1954. Apptd. mem. bd. dirs. Red Cross pub. hosp. and made mem. bd. dirs. Swedish Red Cross, 1939; chmn. Joint Swedish-Swiss Relief Mission in Greece, 1943-45; became 1st v.p. central bd. Swedish Red Cross, 1946, chmn., 1948 (succeeding the late Count Bernadotte); elected chmn. bd. govs. League Red Cross Socs. Monte Carlo, 1950; mem. Internat. Law Commn. UN since 1948, chmn. Belgian-Danish Conciliation Commn., 1952-54. Comdr. Royal Order North Star with Cross. Mem. Internat. Law Assn., Inst. de Droit Internat., Stockholm Jurist Assn., Swedish Overseas Assn., Soc. de Legislation Comparee. Address: Eriksbergsgatan 5, Stockholm, Sweden. Died July 6, 1962.

SANFORD, ARTHUR HAWLEY physician; b. New Albin, Ia., Jan. 12, 1882; s. Alcimore Mead and Amanda Elizabeth (Gilbert) S.; A.B., Northwestern U., 1904, A.M., 1907, M.D., 1907; m. Margaret Loretta Seager, Aug. 23, 1906; children—Hawley Seager, Raymond Arthur, Gertrude Loretta Elizabeth. Asst. prof. physiology, Med. Sch., Marquette U., 1907-08, asso. prof., 1908-09, prof. 1910-11; bacteriologist, Mayo Clinic, 1911; head div. of clin. pathology, 1915; now emeritus; apptd. asso. prof. pathology, 1915, prof. pathology, Mayo Found., U. of Minn., 1921-50; dir. lab. Rochester State Hosp., 1950-—. Served as maj., Med. Corps, U.S. Army, with inactive reserves. Hon. Cons. Army Med. Library. Mem. Rochester (Minn.) Pub. Library Bd., 1914-24; pres. Bd. of Edn., 1924-40. Spl. cons. U.S.P.H.S. Ex-pres. Am. Bd. Pathology. Fellow Am. Coll. Physicians; mem. A.M.A., Am. Soc. Clin. Pathology (pres. 1927-28; recipient Ward Burdick medal, 1933), A.A.A.S., Am. Soc. Immunologists, Soc. Exptl. Biology and Medicine, Sigma Nu, Alpha Kappa Kappa, Phi Beta Kappa, Sigma Xi, Alpha Omega Alpha. Mason (32 deg., K.T.). Author: Clinical Diagnosis by Laboratory Methods (with Dr. J. C. Todd), 11th edit., 1948. Home: 506 10th Av. S.W. Office: 102-110 2d Av. S.W., Rochester, Minn. Died Apr. 28, 1959.

SANFORD, FILLMORE HARGRAVE psychologist; born Chatham, Va., Jan. 26, 1914; s. Thomas Ryland and Margaret (Taylor) S.; student Hargrave Mil. Acad., Chatham, Va., 1929-31; A.B., U. of Richmond, 1935; A.M., Harvard, 1937, Ph.D., 1941; m. Ann Lawrence Snow, June 29, 1940; children—Sarah Ann, Margaret, Thomas, Mary, John, David, Robert. Instructor psychology, Hofstra Coll., Hempstead, N.Y., 1940-41, Harvard, 1941-43; asst. prof. psychology, U. of Md., 1945-48; asso. prof. psychology, Haverford Coll., 1948-50; continuing consultant, Inst. for Research in Human Relations, Phila., 1948-50; cons. to various mil. and govtl. research programs, 1945-50; exec. sec., Am. Psychol. Assn., Washington, 1950-56; associate director Joint Commission on Mental Illness and Health, Cambridge, Massachusetts, 1956-57; professor department of psychology University of Tex., 1957-64, chmn., 1958-60; dean div. Social Scis., prof. psychology New Coll., Sarasota, Fla., 1964-65; prof. psychology Macalester Coll., 1965; professor of psychology University Tex., Austin, 1966-—; editor Contemporary Psychology, 1962-—. Pres. Am. Bd. Examiners in Profl. Psychology, 1956-59. Served as lt. (aviation psychologist), USNR, 1943-45; lt. comdr., M (S), USNR, 1946-—. Fellow Am. Psychol. Assn.; mem. Sigma Xi, Sigma Phi Epsilon, Phi Beta Kappa, Omicron Delta Kappa. Author: Psychology: A Scientific Study of Man, 1961. Contbr. articles in psychol. jours. Home: 1706 Summit View, Austin, Tex. 78703. Died Apr. 5, 1967.

SANFORD, GEORGE BLISS col. U.S.A., retired; b. New Haven, Conn., June 28, 1842; s. Wm. Elihu and Margaret Louisa (Craney) S.; grad. Yale, 1863; m. Gertrude Minturn, Sept. 15, 1874. Entered service Apr. 26, 1861, as 2d lt. 1st U.S. Dragoons; promoted 1st lt., capt., maj., 1st U.S. Cav.; lt. col., 9th U.S. Cav.; col., 6th U.S. Cav.; served throughout the Civil War in cav. corps, Army of Potomac. In campaigns against hostile Indians, 1865-92. Pres. Conn. State soc. Soc. of the Cincinnati. Home: Litchfield, Conn. Died 1908.

SANFORD, JAMES CLARK army officer; b. in New York, Sept. 26, 1859; grad. U.S. Mil. Acad., 1884. Commd. 2d lt. engrs., June 15, 1884; 1st lt., Oct. 12, 1886; capt., Aug. 13, 1895; maj., Jan. 22, 1904; lt. col., July 6, 1908; col., Feb. 27, 1914. Sec. Mo. River Commn., 1890-94; in charge improvement upper Mo. and Yellowstone rivers, 1896-98; constrn. mil. rd., Ft. Washakie to Jackson's Lake, Wyo., 1898-99; in charge Charleston (S.C.) Engr. Dist. and engr. 6th Lighthouse Dist., 1900-03; constrn. seagoing self-propelling suction dredges, 1900-08; in charge Newport (R.I.) Engr. Dist., 1908; duty at New Orleans, La., 1916-17. Official del. of U.S. to Internat. Congress of Navigation, Milan, Italy, Sept. 1905, St. Petersburg, Russia, May-June 1908; mem. Permanent Internat. Com. of Navigation Congresses. Died Dec. 25, 1926.

SANFORD, JOSEPH WILLIAM penologist, warden; b. Washington, D.C., Jan. 14, 1889; s. Andrew Joseph and Annie Margaret (Tupper) S.; prep. edn. pub. schs., Washington, D.C.; student U. of Md., 1903-06; m. Nellie Gertrude Cowsill, Nov. 30, 1907; children—Joseph Nathan, Margaret Tupper, Evelyn. Business, 1906-11; probation officer Juvenile Court, Dist. of

Columbia, 1911-15, chief probation officer, dir. of probation, 1915-27; chief investigator U.S. Bureau of Efficiency, 1927-31; warden U.S. Bureau of Prisons, Dept. of Justice, since 1931, at Federal Reformatory, Chillicothe, O., 1933-38, U.S. Penitentiary, Atlanta, Ga., 1938-48; commr. of corrections, Mich., Feb.-Dec. 1948; U.S. Bureau of Prisons, 1949; penologist Department of the Air Force since 1949. Mem. Council for the Clin. Training of Theol. Students, New York; member advisory bd., The Osborne Assn., New York. Past pres. Am. Prison Assn., Wardens Assn.; mem. Alumni Assn. of U. of Md., Civ. Episcopalian. Home: 4220 Reno Rd. N.W., Washington 8. Office: Pentagon Bldg., Washington. Died Feb. 6, 1952; buried Fort Lincoln Cemetery.

SANFORD, STEADMAN VINCENT educator; b. Covington, Ga., Aug. 24, 1871; s. Charles Vincent and Lizzie (Steadman) S.; A.B., Mercer U., 1890, LL.D., 1932; student U. of Berlin, 1912-13; Oxford U., Eng.. summer, 1913; Litt.D., U. of Ga., 1914; m. Grace McClathey, June 16, 1895; children—Shelton Palmer, Grace Devereaux (dec.), Charles Steadman, Homer Reynolds. Pres. Marietta Male Acad., 1890-92; prin. Marietta High Sch., 1892-97; supt. schs., Marietta, 1897-1903; successively instr., adj. prof. and jr. prof. rhetoric and Eng. lit., 1903-13, prof. English lang. since 1913, head and founder Henry W. Grady School of Journalism since 1921, U. of Ga., dean of the U., 1927-32, pres., 1932-35; chan- cellor University System of Ga. since 1935. Pres. Southern Conf., 1921-30. Capt. Co. F, 3d Regt. Inf., U.S. Vols., Spanish-Am. War, 1898; lt.-col. a.-d.-c. staffs of Govs. Brown, Slaton and Harris. Mem. Assn. of Am. Schs. of Journalism, S.A.R., United Spanish War Veterans (dept. comdr. Ga., 1942-43), Georgia Edn. Assn. (Pres. 1936); mem. Am. Acad. Polit. and Soc. Sci. Kappa Alpha, Phi Kappa Phi, Phi Beta Kappa, Omicron Delta Kappa, Sigma Delta Chi, Blue Key. Democrat. Baptist. Mason, Odd Fellow, Knight of Pythias. Part Author: Literature and Composition, 1914; Composition and Grammar, 1914; English Grammar for High Schools, 1914. Home: Athens, Ga. Address: State Capitol Bldg., Atlanta, Ga. Died Sept. 15, 1945.

SANGER, JOSEPH PRENTICE major gen. U.S.A.; b. Detroit, May 4, 1840; s. Henry Kirkland and Caroline (Prentice) S.; U. of Mich., 1858-60; (hon. A.M., Bowdoin, 1872); m. Frances E. Kent, Dec. 27, 1877. Served 2d lt. 1st Mich. Inf., May 1, 1861; mustered out of vol. service, Aug. 7, 1861; 2d lt. 1st U.S. Arty., Aug. 5, 1861; 1st lt., Oct. 26, 1861; with battery of light arty.; twice bvtd. for gallantry; orderly officer to President Lincoln 1 week, 1862. After war adj. of his regt.; in expdn. against Fenians, 1866; honor grad. Arty. Sch., 1869, and its first adj.; capt. 1st Arty., Feb. 7, 1875; maj. insp. gen., Feb. 12, 1889; comd. battery in Brooklyn "Whisky Riots," 1871; prof. mil. science, tactics and law, Bowdoin, 1872-75; admitted to bar, Portland, Me., Apr. 21, 1874; detailed to accompany Gen. E. Upton on tour of inspection of armies of Japan, China, Persia, India, Turkey, Italy, Russia, Austria, France and Eng., 1875-77; comd. battery, 1877-84, serving in r.r. riots; aide to Maj. Gen. Schofield, 1884-88; aide and acting sec. to President Harrison, 1891; mil. sec. to lt. gen., 1895; insp. S. Atlantic inspection dist. and prin. asst. to insp. gen. of army, 1895-98; lt. col. insp. gen. U.S.V., May 9, 1898; acting insp. gen. of the army; brig. gen. U.S.V., May 27, 1898; in command consecutively of 2d Brigade, 2d Div., 1st Corps, June 19, 1898; 3d Div., 1st Corps, June 29-Nov. 19, 2d Brigade, 2d Div., 1st Corps, to Dec. 12; 2d Div., 1st Corps, Dec. 4-Dec. 23; assigned to command dept. and subsequently Dist. of Matanzas, Cuba, Jan. 11, 1899; hon. disch., June 12, 1899, and assigned to duty with asst. sec. of war, July 3, 1899; apptd. by the president dir. census, Cuba and P.R., Aug. 9, and Sept. 8, 1899, respectively; apptd. mem. of War Coll. Bd., June 21. 1900; col. insp. gen., Feb. 2, 1901; insp. gen. and chief of the staff, Div. of the Philippines, July 4, 1901-Oct. 1, 1902; brig. gen., July 23, 1902; dir. Philippine Census, Oct. 6, 1902; maj. gen., Jan. 20, 1904; retired, Jan. 21, 1904. Mem. Brownsville Ct. of Inquiry, 1908-09. Mem. Medal of Honor Bd., 1916—. Died Mar. 15, 1926.

SANGER, PAUL WELDON, surgeon; b. Minco, Okla., Sept. 17, 1906; s. Paul and Frances (Jones) S.; grad. Webb Sch., Bell Buckle, Tenn., 1924; B.A., U. Okla., 1928; M.D., Vanderbilt U., 1931; m. Mary Ann Carr, Dec. 30, 1936; children—Paul Weldon, Ann, Frances Bailey. Intern Duke Hosp., 1931-32, resident, 1932-37; pvt. practice thoracic and cardiovascular surgery, Charlotte, N.C., 1938-68; dir. Heineman Research Lab., Charlotte Meml. Hosp., 1946-68, dir. Hartford Research Lab., 1959-68. Dir. Consol. Credit Co., Builders Life Ins. Co. Mem. med. adv. com. Duke, 1965-68; mem. Presidents' Commn. Heart Disease, Cancer and Stroke; exec. com. United Med. Research N.C., 1956-68; mem. Nat. Heart Council, NIH, 1963-68. Trustee Charlotte Country Day Sch., Webb-Bell Buckle Sch.; mem. central com. Morehead Scholarship Fund. Served to col., M.C., AUS, 1942-45. Decorated Legion of Merit. Mem. A.C.S., A.M.A., So. Surg. Club, Am. Thoracic Assn. (exam. bd. 1961-67), Am. Assn. Thoracic Surgery, Soc. Vascular Surgeons, N.C. Med. Soc., Excelsior Surg. Soc., Internat. Cardiovascular Soc., Med. Assn. Vanderbilt U. (pres. 1967). Episcopalian. Author articles synthetic fibers for artery replacement, pulmonary vascular and cardiac problems. Home: Charlotte NC Died Sept. 8, 1968; buried Yokon OK

SANGER, WILLIAM CARY assistant sec. of war; b. Brooklyn, May 21, 1853; s. Henry and Mary E. (Requa) S.; grad. Poly. Inst. of Brooklyn, 1869; A.B., Harvard, 1874, A.M., 1875; LL.B., Columbia, 1878; (LL.D., Hamilton, 1902); m. Mary Ethel Cleveland, d. Gen. C. C. Dodge, Feb. 23, 1892. Mem. N.Y. Assembly, 1895-97; lt. col. 203d N.Y. Inf., Spanish-Am. War, 1898; asst. sec. of war, 1901-03. Pres. U.S. delegation to Internat. Conf., Geneva, 1906, to revise the treaty of 1864. Trustee Hamilton College. U.S. del. Internat. Red Cross Conf., London, 1907. Presdl. elector, 1908; mem. war relief bd. Nat. Red Cross; chmn. N.G. Commn. apptd. by Gov. Hughes, 1907; mem. N.Y. State Commn. in Lunacy, 1910-11; pres. State Hosp. Commn., 1911-13; was designated by the President to receive, on behalf of the U.S. Govt. the lighthouse at Crown Point, Lake Champlain, June 19, 1912. Chancellor N.Y. Chapter Colonial Order of Acorn; gov. N.Y. State Soc. of Colonial Wars; gov. gen. Order Founders and Patriots America; pres. Oneida Hist. Soc. Dir. mil. relief Potomac Div. Am. Red Cross, Washington, 1917-18, mgr., 1918-19. Author: The Reserve and Auxiliary Forces of England and the Militia of Switzerland (report to the President and the Secretary of War, prepared 1900), 1903. Home: Sangerfield, N.Y. Died Dec. 6, 1921.

SANNO, JAMES MADISON JOHNSTON army officer; b. New Hampton, N.J., Dec. 10, 1840; s. William P. and Hannah (Zeller) S.; ed. in N.J.; asst. sergt.-at-arms, N.J. senate, 1858; apptd. cadet from N.J., 1859; grad. West Point, 1863; m. Mary Worth, d. Gen. John T. Sprague, U.S.A. (g.d. Gen. W. J. Worth, U.S.A.), June 10, 1868. Commissioned 2d lt. 7th Inf., June 11, 1863; promoted through grades to col. 18th Inf., Dec. 18, 1899; brig. gen. U.S.A. and retired, 1903. Provost marshal, adj. and insp. gen. Dept. Florida, 1865-69; frontier duty, 1869-78, insp. Indian supplies in Mont., 1877-78; in charge Dept. of Law, U.S. Inf. and Cav. Sch., Ft. Leavenworth, 1889-94; engaged June-Aug. 1896, collecting and deporting 537 refugee Canadian Cree Indians; insp. gen. depts. Mo., Dak. and the Lakes, April-Dec. 1898; pres. bd. claims against U.S., Manila, P.I., Jan.-Aug. 1900; organized 27th U.S. inf., 1901; comd. Dept. Colo., Nov.-Dec. 1901; comdg. regt. and Ft. D. A. Russell, Wyo., Jan. 1902—. Mem. various mil. organizations; insp. gen. A.A.S.R. (Masons), Southern Jurisdiction U.S. Died 1907.

SANSBURY, MARVIN ORVILLE clergyman; b. Moberly, Mo., Feb. 6, 1891; s. George Mansfield and Fannie Vernon (Miller) S.; A.B., Drake U., 1914; student Union Theol. Sem., 1917-18; A.M., Columbia, 1922; D.D., Spokane U., 1922, Drake U., 1945; LL.D., Texas Christian University, 1955; m. Mary Hughes, June 2, 1915 (died Feb. 1957). Pastor, Redfield, Ia., Christian Ch., 1911-14, Logan, Ia., Christian Ch., 1914-17, Jennings, La., 1919-21, St. Charles Av. Christian Ch., New Orleans, 1921-27, First Christian Ch., Seattle, 1927-36, Community Ch., Kansas City, Mo., 1936-39, University Christian Ch., Des Moines, Iowa, 1939-52, First Christian Church, Hammond, La., 1952-59, ret.; served Planning, Zoning Commission, Des Moines, Ia., 1940-48. Served as chaplain, A.U.S., World War I. Pres. International Convention Disciples Christ, 1950-52. Member Phi Beta Kappa, Sigma Alpha Epsilon. Mason (33 deg.). Club: University (Des Moines) (past pres.). Exchange preacher to Great Britain, Fed. Council Chs. Christ Am., 1949. Home: 309 W. Dakota, Hammond, La. Died Feb. 22, 1962; buried Neosho, Mo.

SANTE, CHRISTOPHER ALFRED, market research exec.; b. N.Y., Oct. 12, 1919; s. Alfred and Elizabeth M. (Meertens) S.; B.A., N.Y. U.; m. Louise Brown, Sept. 11, 1943; children—Lucinda J., Chandler A. From trainee to research dir. William Esty Co., 1941-52; v.p., dir. research Lennen & Newell, Inc., N.Y.C., 1952-57, sr. v.p. research and market planning, 1957-68; v.p. O'Brien Sherwood Assos., 1968-72. Active Boy Scouts Am. Served from pvt. to 1st lt., AUS, 1942-46. Mem. Am. Marketing Assn., Nat. Campfire Club Am. Am. Mgmt. Assn., Advt. Research Found., A.I.M. Home: Forest Hills NY Died Oct. 9, 1972; buried Princeton ME

SANTELMANN, WILLIAM HENRY musician; born Offensen, Hanover, Ger., Sept. 24, 1863; s. Heinrich W. and Henrietta (Sahnemann) S.; grad. Conservatory of Leipzig, Germany, in practical and theoretical music; Mus.D., George Washington Univ., 1908; m. Washington, Clara Becke, Nov. 10, 1888. Enlisted as mem. U.S. Marine Band, Sept. 24, 1887; resigned and became leader orchestra, Columbia Theatre, Washington, Sept. 4, 1895; apptd. capt. U.S.M.C. by spl. act of Congress, Mar. 3, 1898; leader of band, U.S. Marine Corps, until May 1, 1927 (retired). Home: 44 Grafton St., Chevy Chase, Md. Died Dec. 18, 1932.

SAPIRO, AARON lawyer; b. San Francisco, Calif., Feb. 5, 1884; s. Jacob and Selina (Wascerwitz) S.; grad. Lowell High Sch., San Francisco, 1900; B.A., U. of Cincinnati, 1904, M.A., 1905; studied Hebrew Union Coll., Cincinnati; B.L., Hastings Law Coll. (U. of Calif.), 1911; m. Janet Arndt, of Stockton, Calif., Nov. 17, 1913; children—Jean Louise, Andree, Stanley, Leland. Admitted to Calif. bar, 1911; served as 1st sec. and counsel Calif. Industrial Accident Bd.; moved to Chicago, Ill., 1923, N.Y. City, 1927; specializes in combinations, coöperative transactions and rural credits; with co-author, Standard Coöperative Marketing Act, adopted in whole or in part in 41 states; assisted in organizing the Canadian wheat pools, Burley Tobacco Assn., Tex. and other cotton assns. Enlisted in F.A., U.S.A., 1918; batt. sergt.-maj. 38th F.A.; at F.A. Officers' Training Sch. at Armistice. Mem. Phi Beta Kappa. Republican. Jewish religion. Clubs: Concordia (San Francisco); Covenant, Standard (Chicago). Home: Scarsdale, N.Y. Office: 11 W. 42d St., New York, N.Y. Died Nov. 1959.

SARBACHER, GEORGE W(ILLIAM), JR., former congressman; b. Phila., Pa., Sept. 30, 1919; s. George W. and Martha (Hunter) S.; B.S. in Commerce, Temple U., 1942; m. Florence Wintz Forsyth, Aug. 15, 1942; children—Susan Pence, Sandra Ann, George William III. Enlisted in U.S. Marine Corps, commd 2d lt., June 13, 1942; served 2 1/2 yrs. S.W. Pacific on Guadalcanal, Bougainville, and Guam; received permanent capt. commn. regular U.S. Marine Corps, 1946; mem. 80th U.S. Congress (1947-49), 5th Dist. Pa. (N.E. Phila.); dep. dir. revenue for Pa.; dir. field engring., sec., v.p., pres., chmn. bd. Nat. Sci. Labs., Inc., 1950-69; chmn. mgmt. adv. team U.S. Postal Service, 1970-73. Mem. I.E.E.E., U.S. Navy League. Republican. Methodist. Mason (32 deg.). Club: Army-Navy. Home: Bethesda3MD Died Mar. 4, 1973.

SARGENT, CHARLES WESLEY educator; b. Groveland, Mass., Apr. 12, 1894; s. Charles Dustin and Margaret T. (Lucey) S.; A.B., Dartmouth, 1915, A.M., 1916; student U. Mich., 1916-17; m. Bertha Bortman, July 1, 1924; children—Charles Philip, John Winthrop, Priscilla Ann. Instr. econ. U. Mich., 1916-17; examiner accounts N.Y. Central Lines, N.Y.C., 1919-22; gen. auditor, treas. subsidiary firms Townsend Co., New Brighton, Pa., 1922-28; asst. prof. accounting U. Pitts., 1928-30; asst. prof. accounting Amos Tuck Sch. Bus. Adminstrn., Dartmouth Coll., 1930-34, prof., 1934-54, prof. bus. adminstrn., 1954—. Served as 2d lt. USAAF, 1918. Mem. Am. Accounting Assn., Soc. Advancement Management, Nat. Assn. Cost Accountants, Phi Beta Kappa, Phi Kappa Sigma. Cons. editor: Cost Accountants Handbook, 1944; Fringe Benefits, 1954. Contbr. Handbook Cost Accounting Methods, 1949; Executive Course Profitable Business Management, 1952; Handbook of Business Management, 1955. Home: Brewster, Mass. Died Jan. 28, 1963.

SARGENT, HERBERT HOWLAND officer U.S.A.; b. Carlinville, Ill., Sept. 29, 1858; s. Joseph True and Maria L. (Braley) S.; B.S., Blackburn U., 1878; grad. U.S. Mil. Acad., 1883; m. Alice C. Applegate, Aug. 11, 1886. Second lt. 2d Cav., June 13, 1883; 1st lt., June 19, 1890; capt., Mar. 2, 1899; maj., Jan. 8, 1909. Served on frontier (and prof. mil. science at U. of Ill., 1886-87) till outbreak Spanish-Am. War; served at Washington, May 1898, in organizing vols.; col. 5th U.S. Vol. Inf., May 20, 1898-May 31, 1899; organized regt. at Columbus, Miss.; at Santiago, Cuba., Aug. 12, 1898; comd. dist. of Guantanamo under Gen. Wood, 1899; lt. col. 29th U.S. Vol. Inf., July 5, 1899-May 10, 1901; fought insurgents on island of Luzon; comd. attacking forces Dec. 19, 1899, at battle of San Mateo in which Gen. Lawton was killed; recommended by Gens. Wood and Otis for bvts. for meritorious service in Cuba and Philippines, 1898-99. Prof. mil. science and tactics, Agrl. and Mech. Coll. of Tex., 1903-07; grad. Army War Coll., 1909; retired Nov. 1911. Recalled to active duty, June 27, 1917; asst. to dept. q.m. Western Dept., San Francisco, until Sept. 25, 1917; prof. mil. science and tactics, Princeton U., 1917-18; detailed to war plans div., Gen. Staff, Army War Coll., Washington, Mar. 28, 1918; lt. col. N.A., May 23, 1918; lt. col. U.S.A. retired, July 9, 1918; relieved from active duty and ordered home, Nov. 26, 1918. Recommended for command of a brigade in World War by Pres. Roosevelt and 24 gen. officers of regular army. Author: Napoleon Bonaparte's First Campaign, 1893; The Campaign of Marengo, 1897; The Campaign of Santiago de Cuba, 1907; The Strategy on the Western Front, 1919. Ordered to Washington, Nov. 1907, from S.D., to receive from President Roosevelt in person an especial compliment on his history of the Campaign of Santiago de Cuba. Home: Jacksonville, Ore. Died Sept. 16, 1921.

SARGENT, JAMES CLYDE physician and surgeon; b. Piqua, O., Oct. 3, 1892; s. Charles Roger and Emma G. (Bishop) S.; student Denison U., 1909-10; M.D., Ohio State U., 1915; m. Mary Genevieve Cook, Jan. 3, 1917; children—James Wellington, Mary Genevieve (Mrs. Andrew Galbraith Miller), Suzanne (Mrs. Robert Llewellyn Warnock). Intern, Minneapolis City Hosp., 1915-16; post grad. study James Buchanan Brady Urologic Inst., Johns Hopkins Hosp., 1916-17; pvt. practice medicine limited to urology, Milwaukee, 1917—; mem. faculty Marquette U. Sch. Medicine, 1917—, clin. prof. and dir. dept. urology, 1919—; staff St. Joseph's, Evang. Deaconess, Milwaukee Co. Gen., Milwaukee Co. Emergency and Johnston Emergency hosps.; urology consultant U.S. Naval Hosp., Great Lakes, Ill., 1947—, to Surgeon Gen., U.S. Navy, 1949—; sr. consultant urology U.S. V.A. Hosp., Wood, Wis., 1946—. Served as capt., med. corps U.S.N.R., active duty, 1942-45. Mem. med. adv. com. to med.

services div. Nat. Security Resources Bd., 1949-50, health resources adv. com., 1950, trans. to ODM, 1951—. Presidential apptmnt. to Nat. Adv. Com. on the selection of doctors, dentists and allied specialists advisory to the Selective Service System, 1950—. Recipient Carnegie Hero Bronze medal and award, 1915; Alumni Achievement award, Ohio State U. Coll. Medicine, 1951. Diplomate Am. Bd. Urology. Fellow A.C.S., A.M.A. (Wis. mem. ho. dels. 1938-50; chmn. council Nat. Emergency Med. Service, 1947—), Acad. Internat. of Medicine, Am. Urol. Assn. (pres. N. Central sect. 1947), Assn. Genito-Urinary Surgeons, Wis. State (pres. 1937-38) and Milwaukee Co. (pres. 1933) med. socs., Phi Gama, Delta, Alpha Kappa Kappa, Mason (Shriner). Club: Rotary. Contbr. chpt. on Injuries of the Genital Tract in Urology (edited by Dr. M. F. Campbel), 1952. Home: 2138 E. LaFayette Pl., Milw. 2. Office: 324 Wisconsin Av., Milw. Died Oct. 7, 1954.

SARGENT, NATHAN naval officer; b. New York, Oct. 29, 1849; s. D. H. and Katherine (Sargent) Dustin; assumed name of grandfather, Nathan Sargent, by act of Congress, 1866; prep edn., Emerson Inst. and Gonzaga Coll., Washington; apptd. to U.S. Naval Acad., from Mont.. 1866, grad., 1870; m. Isabel Hill, Apr. 26, 1879. Promoted ensign, July 1871; master, July 1864; lt., Jan. 1881; lt. comdr., Mar. 1899; comdr., Sept. 1901; capt., May 13, 1906. Naval atttaché at Rome, Berlin and Vienna, 1889-93; comdg. U.S.S. Scorpion and Machias, Atlantic Fleet, 1899-1901, U.S.S. Baltimore, Asiatic Fleet, 1904-06; mem. Gen. Bd. Home: Washington, D.C. Died 1907.

SARGENT, WINTHROP territorial gov.; b. Gloucester, Mass., May 1, 1753; s. Winthrop and Judith (Saunders) S.; grad. Harvard, 1771; m. Rowena Tupper, Feb. 9, 1789; m. 2d, Mary (McIntosh) Williams, Oct. 24, 1798; 3 sons. Joined Continental Army, 1775; brevetted maj., 1781; surveyor on Seven Ranges in Ohio, 1786; an original member Ohio Co., 1786, elected sec., 1787; a founder Marietta (O.), 1788; apptd. by Congress as sec. Territory N.W. of River Ohio, 1787-98; adj. gen. to Gen. Arthur St. Clair's expdn. against the Indians; acting gov. Territory N.W. of River Ohio, organized militia to repel anticipated Indian attacks, 1791; 1st gov. Miss. Territory, 1798-1801; mem. Am. Philos. Soc., Soc. of Cincinnati, Am. Acad. Arts and Scis., Mass. Hist. Soc.; published (with Benjamin Smith) Papers Relative to Certain American Antiquities; wrote poem entitled Boston, 1803; name possibly Sargeant. Died nr. New Orleans, June 3, 1820.

SARTORI, LOUIS CONSTANT commodore U.S.N., retired June 3, 1874; b. Bloomsbury, Burlington Co.. N.J., June 3, 1912; entered navy midshipman, Feb. 2, 1829; promoted lt., Sept. 8, 1841; served on bomb-brig "Stromboli" during Mexican war, taking part in capture of Goatzacoalcas and Tabasco; while on Pacific squadron, 1855-56, commanded an expedition and had an engagement with Fijis; comdr., April 7, 1861; in blockading service during Civil war; capt., Sept. 26, 1866; commodore, Dec. 12, 1873. Home: Philadelphia, Pa. Died 1899.

SASSACUS Indian chief; b. nr. what is now Groton, Conn., 1560; s. Wopigwooit. Chief sachem of Pequot Indians, 1633-37; involved in conflict with English settlers, 1633-36, became full scale war, 1636; attempted to persuade Narragansett Indians to ally with him; made frequent raids on Conn. settlements, 1636-37; an English force led by John Mason attacked and killed most of his tribe at camp on Mystic river in Conn., May 1637. Killed by Mohawk Indians while fleeing from English, June 1637.

SASSCER, LANSDALE G. congressman; b. Upper Marlboro, Md., Sept. 30, 1893; s. Frederick and Lucy (Clagett) S.; LL.B., Dickinson Sch. Law, 1914; m. Agnes Coffren, Feb. 15, 1919; children—Agnes Lansdale (Mrs. Hal B. Clagett, Jr.), Lucy Clagett (Mrs. W. Murray Sanders), Lansdale G., Jr. Admitted to Md. bar, 1915, and since practiced in Upper Marlboro; mem. Md. senate, 1922-38, pres., 1934-38; mem. 77th to 82d Congresses (1941-53), 5th Md. Dist.; pub. Enquirer Gazette (with S. A. Wyvill); dir. Md. Nat. Bank, Hyattsville Bldg. Assn., Bank of Brandywine. Served as 1st lt., arty. U.S. Army, AEF. Mem. Am. Legion, VFW. Democrat. Episcopalian. Mason, I.O.O.F., W.OW, Elk. Clubs: Lions (Upper Marlboro). Home: Upper Marlboro, Md. Died Nov. 5, 1964; buried Trinity Cemetery, Upper Marlboro.

SATTERFIELD, JOHN VINES, JR., banker; born Marion, Ark., May 14, 1902; s. John Vines and Mary L. (Marshall) S.; attended Earle High Sch.; m. Thelma Holt, June 26, 1928; children—John Vines III, William Walter, Hammond Holt. Chairman of the board, chief executive officer First National Bank of Little Rock, Arkansas. Mayor, City of Little Rock, 1939-41. Commd. maj., Army Air Forces, Feb. 13, 1942, lt. col., June 1943; col. Dec. 30, 1944. Democrat. Presbyterian. Clubs: Country, Pulaski Heights Lions (past pres.). Home: Little Rock AR Died Mar. 6, 1966.

SATTERLEE, HERBERT LIVINGSTON lawyer; b. New York, N.Y., Oct. 31, 1863; s. George B. and Sarah S.; B.S., Ph.B., Columbia, 1883, A.M., 1884, Ph.D., LL.B., cum laude, 1885; m. Louisa Pierpont, d. J(ohn) Pierpont Morgan, Nov. 15, 1900. Pvt. sec. Senator William M. Evarts, 1885-87; navigator 1st Naval Battalion, N.Y., 1891-95; col. and a.-d.-c. to Gov. L.P. Morton, 1895-96; capt. (naval militia) and a.-d.-c. to Gov. Frank S. Black, 1897-98; lt. U.S. Navy (war with Spain) and chief of staff to Capt. John R. Bartlett, U.S. Navy; counsel M.K.&T. Ry. Co., 1898-1902; asst. sec. of the Navy, Dec. 1, 1908-Mar. 6, 1909; chmn. N.Y. State Commn. for the Blind, 1914-16; now mem. firm of Satterlee, Warfield & Stephens, N.Y. Capt. Naval Militia Reserve List. Trustee Columbia U., 1917-23; pres. Wilmer Foundation, pres. Naval Militia Vet. Assn., 1891-1922; mem. Nat. Inst. Social Sciences, Soc. Colonial Wars, S.R., Soc. War 1812, Soc. Foreign Wars, Vet. Arty. Corps; a founder Navy League U.S.; comdr. gen. Naval Order U.S., 1925-28; mem. Mil. and Naval Order Spanish-Am. War, Am. Bar Assn., N.Y. State Bar Assn., Assn. Bar City N.Y., Am. Mus. Natural History, N.Y. Hist. Soc., Met. Mus. Art, American Geographic Society, St. Nicholas Society (president 1936-38), Medal of Merit, 1946, Seamen's Church Institute of New York City (vice pres.), Life Saving Benevolent Assn. (president 1930-40), State Charities Aid Assn., Grant Monument Assn. (pres.); hon. mem. Naval Acad. Grads. Assn. of New York, Marine Museum City of N.Y. (pres. 1934-44). Clubs: Century, University, Church, Union League (pres. 1938-39), Military and Naval, Columbia University, St. Anthony (New York); Army and Navy (Washington); Bohemian (San Francisco). Home: 1 Beekman Pl. Office: 49 Wall St., New York 5, N.Y. Died July 14, 1947.

SATTERLEE, RICHARD SHERWOOD army surgeon, physician; b. Fairfield, Herkimer County, N.Y., Dec. 6, 1798; s. William and Hannah (Sherwood) S.; attended Fairfield Acad.; m. Mary S. Hunt, June 1827. Licensed to practice medicine, 1818; entered U.S. Army as asst. surgeon, 1822; served with brigade of Col. Zachary Taylor during Seminole War in Fla., 1837; received ofcl. commendation for med. service at Battle of Okeechobee, 1837; with army at Veracruz and Mexico City during Mexican War, sr. surgeon Gen. William Worth's div. of regulars, dir. med. service of div. at battles of Cerro Gordo, Churubusco, Molino del Rey, Chapultepec; apptd. med. dir. on staff Gen. Scott, charged with establishment of gen. hosp. to care for bulk of army casualties; commd. maj., 1832; apptd. med. purveyor, 1853; brevetted lt. col., then brig. gen., 1866; apptd. chief med. purveyor with rank lt. col.; in charge of med. supply depot, N.Y.C., 1866-69. Died N.Y.C., Nov. 10, 1880.

SATTLER, WILLIAM MARTIN, educator; b. Tyndall, S.D., Oct. 31, 1910; s. John Jacob and Paulina (Max) S.; B.A., Yankton Coll., 1932; M.A., U. Mich., 1934; Ph.D., Northwestern U., 1941; m. Dorothy Ogborn Sept. 3, 1939; children—Richard W., Robert J. Tchr. pub. high schs., S.D., 1932-37; teaching fellow Northwestern U., 1937-38; teaching asst. U. Ill., 1938-39; instr. English, U. N.H., 1939-40; asst. prof. speech U. Okla., 1940-43, asso. prof., 1943-48; asst. prof. speech U. Mich., 1948-51, asso. prof., 1951-57, prof., 1957-69, chmn. dept., 1960-69. Served from lt. (j.g.) to lt. (s.g.), USNR, 1944-46. Mem. Speech Assn. Am. (chmn. com. on publs. 1953-57), Central States Speech Assn. (pres. 1950-51, exec. sec. 1947-50), Nat. Soc. Study Communication, Internat. Soc. Study Gen. Semantics. Co-author: Discussion and Conference, 1954, 2d edit., 1968. Contbr. to publs. in field: also articles, profl. papers. Home: Ann Arbor MI Died Apr. 4, 1969.

SAUER, WILLIAM EMIL (sour), physician, univ. prof.; b. Evansville, Ill., Apr. 17, 1875; s. Nicholas and Elizabeth (Gerlach) S.; Shurtleff Coll., Alton, Ill., 1891-93; M.D., Wash. U. Med. Sch., St. Louis, Mo., 1896; m. Mary Irene Borders, Dec. 18, 1901; 1 son, William Nicholas. Otolaryngologist in St. Louis since 1900; instr. diseases of the ear, nose and throat, Wash. U. Med. Sch., 1905-13; prof. and dir. dept. otolaryngology, St. Louis U. Sch. Medicine, 1925-45, Distinguished Service prof. otolaryngology, 1945. Capt. Medical Corps, 1918-19. Member Am. Bd. Otolaryngology. Mem. Am. Laryngol. Soc., Am. Otol. Soc., Am. Laryngol., Rhinol. and Otol. Soc. (vice chmn.), Pan-Am. Med. Soc. (chmn. sect. otolaryngology, 1935), Acad. Ophthalmology and Otolaryngology, Alpha Omega Alpha; hon. mem. Nat. Acad. of Medicine of Brazil. Presbyterian. Republican. Clubs: University, St. Louis Country. Home: 6309 McPherson Av., University City 5, Mo. Office: 3720 Washington Blvd., St. Louis 8. Deceased.

SAUL, CHARLES DUDLEY physician; b. Phila., Pa., Jan. 25, 1880; s. Charles G. and Lidie (Bower) S.; student Temple U., 1897-98; M.D., Hahnemann Med. Coll. and Hosp., Phila., 1901; m. Fay Bruch, June 17, 1915; children—Charles Dudley, Jr., Maurice Biddle. Began as asst. med. dept., Hahnemann Hosp., later demonstrator, asso. prof. medicine, 1931-36, lecturer, medicine, 1928-31; pres. State Homeopathic Hosp. of Pa., 1934-35; chief, dept. of medicine, St. Luke's and Children's Med. Center, 1935-41, med. dir. since 1940. Pres. League for Socialized Med. of Pa. Served as capt., U.S. Army, Base Hosp. 48, A.E.F. Mem. Homeopathic Med. Soc. Episcopalian. Contbr. monographs to med. publs. Home: 1512 Spruce St. Office: 1530 Locust St., Philadelphia, Pa.* Died Jan. 8. 1947.

SAUNDERS, HAROLD EUGENE naval officer; b. Washington, Nov. 29, 1890; s. Fred Henry and Rose Henrietta (Stoll) S.; B.S., U.S. Naval Acad., 1912; M.S., Mass. Inst. Tech., 1916; hon. Sc.D., Stevens Inst. Tech., 1950; m. Grace Eugenia Gibson, May 5, 1920; children—David McKeon, Marion Lovewell, Roger Lane, Margery Gibson. Commd. ensign, U.S. Navy, 1912, advanced through grades to capt., 1939; mem. spl. longitude mission to Paris, France, 1914; supervisor maj. overhauls and conversions ex-German ships and submarines Navy Yard, Mare Island, Cal., 1916-20; in charge submarine design Bur. Constrn. Repair, Washington, 1921-24; bldg. 2,000 and 3,000 ton submarines Navy Yard, Portsmouth, N.H., 1924-29; model tester, full-scale ship trials Exptl. Model Basin, 1929-33; battle force constructor at sea, 1933-35; in charge final design Bur. Constrn. Repair, 1935-36; tech. dir. David Taylor Model Basin, 1937-46, dir., 1946-47; tech. asst., design cons. Bur. Ships, Navy Dept. since 1947; salvage officer U.S. Submarine S-4, 1927-28; chief cartographer 1st and 2d Byrd Antarctic expdns., 1930-37. Chmn. spl. adv. com. Antarctic names U.S. Bd. Geog. Names; mem. Internat. Conf. Ship Tank Supts. and Am. Towing Tank Conf. Decorated: D.S.M., Legion of Merit, Victory Medal (world wars I and II) (all Navy); hon. officer Order of Brit. Empire. Awarded: Joseph H. Linnard prize, David W. Taylor Gold Medal (soc. Naval Architects and Marine Engrs.), Fellow Am. Geog. Soc.; mem. Soc. Naval Architects and Marine Engrs. (honorary life mem.), American Society of Naval Engineers, Académie de Marine, France, U.S. Naval Inst., Nat. Geog. Soc., Nat. One-Design Racing Assn. (honorary commodore, life member), Sigma Xi. Author: Technical Report of Salvage, U.S. Submarine S-4, 1928; Prediction of Speed and Power By Model Testing Methods, 1933; Hydrodynamics in Ship Design, 1957. Home: 7206 Maple Av., Takoma Park 12, Md. Office: Code 106, Bureau of Ships, Navy Dept., Washington 25. Died Nov. 11, 1961.

SAVAGE, EZRA PERIN ex-governor; b. Connorsville, Ind., 1842; s. Benjamin Warren and Hannah (Perin) S.; student Ia. (now Grinnell) Coll.; served under Grant and Sherman in Civil War; m. Anna C. Rich, of Chicago, 1866 (died Aug. 25, 1883); 2d, Elvira Hess, of Lyons, Ia., Apr., 1896 (died Mar. 1, 1899). Admitted to bar; in grain and implement business, Lyons, Ia.; cattle raiser, Crawford Co., Ia., Custer Co., Neb.; in business, S. Omaha, Neb.; now retired. Was first mayor of S. Omaha; mem. Neb. Ho. of Rep.; elected lt.-gov. of Neb., 1900, succeeding as gov. for unexpired term (1901-03) of Charles Henry Dietrich, resigned. Address: Tacoma, Wash.

SAVAGE, JAMES EDWIN, educator; b. Nowata, Okla., Oct. 13, 1903; s. William Currens and Myrtle (Arnold) S.; B.A., Coll. of Emporia, 1928; M.A., U. Ark., 1937; Ph.D., U. Chgo., 1942; m. Mary Kathryn Johnston, Aug. 13, 1935; children—Margaret Louise, Kathryn Mary (dec.). Coach, prin. twp. high sch., Kirkwood, Ill., 1930-39; instr. English, Cornell U., 1942-43, 1945-46; prof. English, U. Miss., 1946-72, chmn. dept., 1953-60. Served from lt. to lt. comdr. USNR, 1943-45. Recipient Henry E. Huntington Library research grant, summer 1954. Mem. Modern Lang. Assn., The Malone Soc., Am. Assn. U. Profs. Presbyn. Author articles in field. Home: Oxford MS Died June 5, 1972.

SAVAGE, JOHN HOUSTON lawyer; b. McMinnville, Tenn., Oct. 9, 1815; s. George and Elizabeth (Kenner) S.; brought up on farm; ed. subscription schs. and Carroll Acad., McMinnville; studied law; admitted to Tenn. bar, Smithville, 1839; unmarried. Served 6 months as vol. in war with Seminole Indians, 1835; maj. 14th U.S. inf. and lt. col. 11th U.S. inf. in Mexican war; was in all the battles around the City of Mexico until wounded by a shell and disabled at Battle of Molino del Rey; later comd. dept. of Toluca until peace was declared. Resumed practice; was atty. gen. Tenn., 1842-47; elector on Polk ticket, 1844; mem. Congress, 1849-53 and 1855-59. Democrat. During Civil war was col. 16th Tenn. inf., C.S.A.; wounded at Perryville and at Murfreesboro; mem. Tenn. legislature, 1877, 1879 and 1887; again practicing in McMinnville. Died Apr. 5, 1904.

SAVAGE, PHILIP HENRY author; b. No. Brookfield, Mass., Feb. 11, 1868; s. Rev. Minot J. Savage; grad. Harvard, 1893 (A.M., 1896). Author: First Poems and Fragments (1895); Poems (1898). Home: Boston, Mass. Died 1899.

SAVAGE, RICHARD HENRY author, maj. U.S. vol. engrs.; b. Utica, N.Y., June 12, 1846; s. Richard and Jane Moorhead (Ewart) S.; apptd. from Calif., 1864, and grad. U.S. Mil. Acad., 1868; served, 2d lt., corps of engr., 3 yrs.; in Egyptian army, 1871-74; engr. on a ry. in South, 1874-84; then lawyer and author in New York; m. Anna Josephine Scheible, of Berlin, Germany, at German embassy, Washington, Jan. 2, 1873. Traveled in Turkey, Asia Minor, Russia, Siberia, Korea, China, Japan, Honduras, 1884-91. Apptd., May 1898, senior maj. 2d U.S. vol. engrs.; served through war with Spain; in Nov. 1898 went with his command to Havana, personally hoisting 1st Am. flag in Havana or Havana province; senior capt. (acting maj), 27th U.S. vol. inf., July 5 to Dec. 1, 1899; brig. gen. and chief engr. Spanish war veterans, Oct. 10, 1900; elected comdr.-in-chief

Nat. Spanish-Am. War Vets., Washington, Oct. 11, 1903. Author: After Many Years; My Official Wife; For Love and Life; A Daughter of Judas; The Anarchist; Delilah of Harlem; The Little Lady of Lagunitas; The Flying Halcyon; Miss Devereaux of the Mariquita; In the Shadow of the Pyramids; The Last Days of Ismail Khedive; In the Swim; The Princess of Alaska, 1895; In the Old Chateau, 1896; His Cuban Sweetheart, 1896; The Hacienda on the Hill, 1900; The Shield of His Honor, 1900; The Midnight Passenger, 1900; Brought to Bay, 1900; Poems, 1900; In the House of His Friends, 1900; In the Esbekieyeh Gardens, 1900; The Mystery of a Shipyard, 1901; Special Orders for Commander Leigh, 1902; For a Young Queen's Bright Eyes, 1902; The Golden Rapids of High Life, 1903. Died 1903.

SAVILLE, THORNDIKE, cons. engr.; b. Malden, Mass., Oct. 3, 1892; s. Caleb Mills and Elizabeth (Thorndike) S.; A.B., Harvard, 1914, M.S., 1917; B.S., Dartmouth, 1914, C.E., 1915; M.S., Mass. Inst. Tech., 1917; E.D. (hon.), Clarkson Coll., 1944, Syracuse University, 1951; D.Sc., New York University, 1957; m. Edith Stedman Wilson, Sept. 10, 1921; 1 son, Thorndike. Sheldon traveling fellow, Harvard, 1919; asso. prof., later prof. hydraulic and sanitary engring., U. of N.C., 1919-32, also chief engr. N.C. Dept. of Conservation and Development, 1920-32; prof. hydraulic and sanitary engring., New York U., 1932-57, emeritus, 1957-69, asso. dean Coll. of Engring., 1935, dean, 1936-57, now emeritus; vis. prof. in hydraulics, U. Cal. at Berkeley, 1956; director Science and Engring. Center Study, University of Florida, 1958-60, consultant, 1960-66; chmn. Cons. Panel on Water Supply, N.Y.C., 1950-51; engr. mem. N.Y. State Pub. Health Council, 1947-58; rep. N.Y. State to Del. River Adv. Com., 1956-58; cons. Water Resources, N.Y. State Commn. Revision Constrn., 1957-58; cons. engr. Rockefeller Found. to govt. of Venezuela on water supply for Caracas, leave of absence, 1926-27. Student O.T.C., Plattsburg and Ft. Monroe, Aug.-Nov. 1917; commd. 2d lt. C.A.C., 8th Co.; transferred to Signal Corps, Dec. 12, 1917; promoted 1st lt. and detailed to Langley Field, Va., as sanitary engr.; mem. Beach Erosion Bd., Office of Chief Engr. U.S. Army, 1930-63, Coastal Engineering Research Board, 1963-69; exec. engr. water resources sect. of Nat. Resources Bd., 1934-35; mem. water resources com. of Nat. Resources Planning Bd., 1935-43, chairman project review com., 1940-43; cons. engr. on water resources and coastal engring. Mem. adv. council USPHS, 1949-52. Recipient jubilee medal Am. Soc. Mech. Engineers. Del. engring. socs. U.S. to Conf. Engring. Edn., London, 1953, Zurich, 1954; chmn. U.S. delegation, Paris, 1957, London, 1962; pres-gen. 5th Internat. Congress Coastal Engring., 5th, 1954, 6th, Fla., 1957. Fellow Am. Pub. Health Assn., A.A.A.S., Am. Soc. C.E. (hon. mem.; pres. met. sect. 1942-43, dir. 1945-48); mem. Water Pollution Control Fedn., Engrs. Joint Council (pres. 1954-55), Engrs. Council for Profl. Devel. (pres. 1955-56), Am. Soc. Engring. Edn. (hon.), Am. Water Works Assn., N.E. Water Works Assn., N.Y. Sewage Works Assn., Boston Soc. C.E., Am. Soc. Engring. Edn. (v.p. 1948-49, pres. 1949-50; Lamme award 1954), Harvard Engring. Soc. (pres. 1948), Mayflower Descs., Am. Inst. Cons. Engrs., Am. Meteorol. Soc., Am. Geophys. Union, Am. Acad. San. Engrs., Nat. Soc. Professional Engineers, International Association Hydraulic Research, Phi Beta Kappa, Sigma Xi, Tau Beta Pi. Clubs: Harvard (New York City). Author reports and articles on hydrology, water power, water supply, sewage and coastal engring. Home: Gainesville FL Died Gainesville FA Died Feb. 21, 1969; buried Chapel Hill NC

SAWDERS, JAMES CALEB chem. engr., lecturer; b. Pitts., Sept. 21, 1894; s. Francis Patrick and Mary (Reddy) S.; B.S., Carnegie Inst. Tech., 1916; m. Eunice Yasinski, June 7, 1932. Began as chem. engr. Goodyear Tire & Rubber Co., 1916; mem. Sawders & Fulton, chemists, Pitts., 1919-23; has made 19 expdns. to various parts of Latin America, visited many sections of Mexico, Central America, the West Indies and S.A. Has lectured on Latin Am. travel and on both N. and S. Am. archaeology. Travels and studies in Italy, 1937, Scandinavian countries, 1938, Hawaii, 1941. Served as maj. O.R.C., 1917-19; from lt. col. to col., asst. chief indsl. div. C.W.S., U.S. Army, 1942-46. Fellow Am. Geog. Soc.; mem. Soc. for Am. Archaeology, Am. Chem. Soc., Alpha Tau Omega. Democrat. Catholic. Clubs: University (Pitts.); Town Hall, Chemists (N.Y.C.); Army-Navy (Washington); Rotary (hon.). Author articles on Latin Am. travel and history, Pre-Columbian history, gen. Am. archaeology, and Latin Am. economics. Address: Briarcliffe Acres, Myrtle Beach, S.C. 29577. Died Aug. 7, 1960; buried Ocean Woods Meml. Park, Myrtle Beach.

SAWTELLE, CHARLES GREENE brig. gen. U.S.A.; b. Norridgewock, Me., May 10, 1834; grad. U.S. Mil. Acad., 1854; m. Alice C. Munroe, 1869. Entered army as bvtd. 2d lt. inf., serving in Sioux expdn.; 2d lt. 6th Inf., Mar. 3, 1855; promoted through grades to col. asst. q.m. gen., Sept. 12, 1894; brig. gen. q.m. gen., Aug. 19. 1896; was q.m. gen. in Washington until retired, Feb. 16, 1897. In Civil War was engaged as chief q.m. in many of the more important operations of the war; remained in that branch of the service until retired at its head. Home: Washington, D.C. Died Jan. 4, 1913.

SAWTELLE, GEORGE oil exec.; b. Wheeling, W. Va., Feb. 27, 1892; s. William D. and Adaline (Emsley) S.; B.S., Lehigh U., 1916; D.Sc. Marietta Coll., 1956; m. Mary Seymour Sawtel, Nov. 1, 1917 (dec. 1962); children—George Flint, Ermina Mae (wife of Maj. Edmund Burke Berry, III). Football coach Northwestern, 1920-21; with Kirby Petroleum Co., Houston, 1922-—, pres., 1934-—, also chmn.; dir. 1st Nat. Bank, Houston, Chmn. Houston Community Chest, 1943. Dist. dir., Facility Security Div., Petroleum Adminstrn. for War, 1942. Served as capt. 79th Field Artillery, U.S. Army, France, 1918; Mexican Border, 1916. Recipient of highest award Lehigh Alumni Assn. Mem. Houston C. of C. (past pres.), Texas Mid-Continent Oil and Gas Assn. (past pres.), Am. Assn. Petroleum Geologists (past v.p.), Independent Petroleum Assn. Am. (dir.), Am. Inst. Mining and Met. Engrs., Houston Geol. Soc. (hon. life mem.), Newcomen Soc., Delta Upsilon. Clubs: Houston, Petroleum, Houston Geophysical, Ramada, Houston Country, Champions Gulf, Dallas Petroleum; Mill Reef (Antiqua, B.W.I.), Editor: Gulf Coast Oil Fields, 1936 (with Donald C. Barton); articles profl. jours. Home: 204 Arborway St. Office: P.O. Box 1745, Houston 1. Died Sept. 3, 1967.

SAWYER, CARL WALKER physician; b. LaRue, O., May 30, 1881; s. Charles E. (M.D.) and May E. (Barron) S.; grad. Morgan Park (Ill.) Acad., 1900; B.S., U. Chgo., 1904; M.D., Rush Med. Coll., 1906; m. Grace Farlin Curtis, Dec. 28, 1905; 1 son, Warren C. Partner, firm of Drs. Charles E. and Carl W. Sawyer, Sawyer Sanatorium, Marion, O., 1906-23, chief of staff since 1923. Mem. Med. Adv. Bd. No. 7, Selective Service, for State of Ohio. Commd. 1st lt. M.C., U.S. Army; mem. Neuro-Psychiat. Bd., World War I. Fellow A.M.A., A.C.P., Am. Psychiat. Assn.; diplomate Am. Bd. Psychiatry and Neurology; mem. Ohio, Northwestern Ohio med. assns., Marion, Cleve. acads. medicine, Assn. for Research in Nervous and Mental Diseases, A.A.A.S., Central Neuro-Psychiatric Assn., Ohio State Archaeol. and Hist. Soc., Ohio Acad. Sci., Am. Therapeutic Soc., Rotary Internat., Marion C. of C. Pres. Harding Meml. Assn. Republican. Methodist. Author: The Psychology of the Sick. Home: White Oaks Farm. Address: Sawyer Sanatorium, Marion, O. Died Feb. 22, 1966.

SAWYER, CHARLES BALDWIN metall. engr.; b. Cleve., July 15, 1894; s. John Pascal and Mary Candee (Baldwin) S.; B.A., Yale, 1915; Ph.D., Mass. Inst. Tech., 1921; m. Caroline Fisher, 1921; children—Baldwin, Margaret Hazard; m. 2d, Katherine Beaumont Hirsh, Aug. 19, 1933; children—Samuel Prentiss, Charles Brush, William Beaumont. Instr. naval aviation inspection and heat treatment of metals Mass. Inst. Tech., 1917-19, mem. vis. com. of corporation, dept. metallurgy, 1954-58; co-founder Brush Laboratories Co., 1921, pres., 1927-36, 52-55, chmn., 1936-52; co-founder Brush Development Co. (now Brush Electronics Co.), 1930, treas., 1930-47, chmn. bd., 1935-38, v.p., 1938-52; founder Brush Beryllium Co., 1931, pres., 1931-46, chmn. bd., 1936-60, dir., chmn. exec. com., 1960-62, vice chmn. bd., 1962-—; founder Sawyer Research Products, Inc., 1956, pres., 1956-—, also dir.; dir. Clevite Corp., United Improvement Co. Mem. U.S. tech. indsl., intelligence com. mission to Germany and Italy, 1945. Mem. A.A.A.S., Am. Chem. Soc., Am. Inst. Mining and Metall. Engrs., Am. Phys. Soc., Am. Soc. Metals, Inst. of Metals (Brit.). Clubs: Kirtland Country, Union (Cleve.); Yale (N.Y.C.); Mentor (O.) Harbor Yacht. Home: 17485 Shelburne Rd., Cleveland Heights 18, O. Office: 35400 Lakeland Blvd., Eastlake, Ohio. Died Mar. 24, 1964.

SAWYER, CHARLES E. physician; b. Nevada, O., Jan. 24, 1860; s. Alonzo N. and Harriet M. (Rogers) S.; ed. pub. schools., Nevada; M.D., Homoe. Hosp. Coll. (now Ohio State Homoe. Med. Coll. of Ohio State U.), 1881; m. May E. Barron, Aug. 11, 1879. Began practice at LaRue, O., 1881; established the Sawyer Sanatorium, 1890; removed to Marion, O., 1893, and established the Dr. C. E. Sawyer Sanatorium, later The Sawyer Sanatorium; gen. mgr. and consulting phys., C. E. & Carl W. Sawyer; v.p. Marion Nat. Bank; dir. Cleveland-Pulte Med. Coll., Masonic Temple Co. (Marion), etc. Commd. brig. gen. M.R.C., U.S.A., Mar. 12, 1921, and called to active duty same day as physician to the President (Harding); apptd. physician to President Coolidge, Aug. 11, 1923. Apptd. chief co-ordinator of Federal Bd. of Hospitalization by executive order; assigned a number of special services under the Veterans' Bureau. Trustee and chmn. exec. com. Harding Memorial Assn. Trustee Am. Inst. Homoepathy (gov.); fellow Am. Coll. Surgeons. Republican. Lutheran. Home: Marion, O. Died Sept. 23, 1924.

SAWYER, HENRY BUCKLAND, b. Lowell, Mass., Apr. 28, 1871; s. Jacob Herbert and Mary Elizabeth (Wentworth) S.; ed. private schs., traveled extensively; m. Georgia W. Pope, Apr. 28, 1906; children—Henry B., Jr., Avery, Elizabeth W. Began with Chicopee Mfg. Co., Chicopee Falls, Mass., 1888; with Stone & Webster, engrs. and mgrs. pub. service cos., 1890, later becoming member of firm and then v.p. of corporation (retired, Apr. 30, 1931; formerly president and dir. New England Transportation Co.; mem. advisory board Mass. Investors Trust; trustee New York, N.H.&H. R.R. Co., Old Colony R.R. Co., Providence, Warren & Bristol R.R. Co., Hartford & Conn. Western R.R. Company, The Boston Terminal Company, Suffolk Savings Bank. Mem. Board of Finance of City of Fall River, 1932-36. Served with Battery A, Field Arty., Mass. Vols., from 1896 until resignation as lt. comdg., 1906. Trustee Boston Symphony Orchestra, Incorporated; trustee New England Conservatory of Music; mem. Franklin Foundation; dir. Home for Aged Men. Life member New England Historic Geneal. Society. Republican. Unitarian. Clubs: Union (Boston); Harvard Travellers; Country (Brookline). Home: 274 Beacon St., Boston 16

SAWYER, J(AMES) ESTCOURT brig. gen. U.S.A.; b. Washington, D.C., July 3, 1846; s. Capt. H.B.S. (U.S.N.); grad. Arty. Sch., 1871; m. Elizabeth Thompson, June 1873. Apptd. from N.J., 2d lt. 5th Arty., Nov. 11. 1867; 1st lt., Nov. 10, 1874; capt. a.q.m., Dec. 1, 1893; maj. q.m. vols., May 12, 1898-Mar. 11, 1901; maj. q.m. U.S.A., Feb. 2, 1901; lt. col. deputy q.m. gen., July 10, 1904; col. a.q.m. gen., Apr. 21, 1910; brig. gen. U.S.A., July 3, 1910; retired by operation of law, July 3, 1910. Home: New York, N.Y. Died May 29, 1914.

SAWYER, PRINCE EDWIN physician; b. Phillips, Me., June 1, 1874; s. Prince A. and Alvira C. (Oakes) S.; student Bates Coll., Lewiston, Me., 1889-1890, U. of Northwest, Sioux City, Ia., 1889-91; M.D., U. of Ia., 1895; m. Cornelia Johnson, Sept. 6, 1899. Physician and surgeon, 1895-1909; gen. surgery, 1909-—. Served as maj. M.C., U.S. Army, A.E.F. Fellow A.C.S.; mem. A.M.A., Ia. (pres. 1936-37), Sioux Valley, Mississippi Valley med. socs., Alpha Omega Alpha. Republican. Mason, Elk. Home: 2020 Nebraska St. Office: Toy Nat. Bank Bldg., Sioux City Ia. Died Jan. 17, 1954.

SAWYER, WESLEY CALEB university prof.; b. Harvard, Mass., Aug. 26, 1839; s. Luke and Mercy Blood (Whitcomb) S.; A.B., Harvard, 1861, A.M., 1864; theol. course, Concord, N.H., 1862-65; studied Berlin, Sorbonne (Paris), and Göttingen, 1866-70; Ph.D., Göttingen, 1870; m. Minnie Edmea Birge, of Appleton, Wis., July 1, 1877. Engaged in recruiting service with Gen. Henry Wilson, Aug.-Oct., 1861; capt. Co. H., 23d Mass. Inf., Oct. 8, 1861; engaged in battle of Roanoke Island, Feb. 8, 1862; on March 14, 1862, had left leg shot away in battle of Newbern, North Carolina, by cannon-ball; appointed, Sept. 1862, by Governor Andrew, to command Camp Stevens, Groton Junction, Mass., and, while there, organized and drilled 53d Mass. Inf.; hon. discharged, Nov. 17, 1862. Teacher Greek, Lasell Sem., 1870-71; instr. German and history, Univ. of Minn., 1871-74; prof. philosophy and German, Lawrence U., Wis., 1875-82; inst. dir. and prof. social science, Oshkosh (Wis.) Normal Sch., 1882-85; prof., v.p., acting pres. and dean, U. of the Pacific, 1888-95; master in French and German, Belmont Sch., 1895-98; lecturer on Teutonic mythology, 1901-03, prof. German and French, 1903-08, prof. emeritus, 1908-—, U. of the Pacific. Methodist. Republican. Author: Practical German Grammar, 1882; Complete German Manual, 1887; Teutonic Legends in the Nibelungen Lied and the Nibelungen Ring, 1904. Address: San Jose, Cal.

SAWYER, WILBUR AUGUSTUS pub. health; b. Appleton, Wis., Aug. 7, 1879; s. Wesley Caleb and Minnie Edmea (Birge) S.; Univ. of California, 1898-99; A.B., Harvard, 1902; M.D., Harvard Medical School, 1906; LL.D., University of California 1945; m. Margaret Henderson, Oct. 14, 1911; children—Margaret (Mrs. J. Wallace Carroll), Gertrude (Mrs. R. W. Howell), Ruth Henderson (Mrs. D. P. Yeuell, Jr.), Wilbur Henderson. Interne Mass. General Hospital, 1906-08; medical examiner, University of California, 1908-11; director Hygienic Laboratory, 1910-15, sec. and exec. officer, 1915-18, Calif. State Bd. of Health; lecturer in hygiene and preventive medicine, 1914-16, clin. prof., 1916-19, U. of Calif. Med. Sch. On active duty as capt. and maj., M.C., U.S. Army, Feb. 6, 1918-May 31, 1919; chief of sec. on combating venereal diseases, Surgeon Gen.'s Office, War Dept., actg. mem. Interdepartmental Social Hygiene Bd., actg. dir. of social hygiene div. of Commn. on Training Camp Activities, and acting gen. sec. Am. Social Hygiene Assn., 1918-19; lt. col. M.R.C., 1919-20. Apptd. state dir. Internat. Health Bd., New York, June 1, 1919; dir. Australian hookworm campaign, 1919-22; adviser in pub. health, Australian Ministry of Health, 1922-24; asst. regional dir. for the East, 1923-24, dir. Public Health Lab. Service, 1924-27, Internat. Health Bd. of Rockefeller Foundation; also asso. dir. Internat. Health Division of Rockefeller Foundation, 1927-35, director, 1935-44; director of health, U.N.R.R.A., 1944-47; secretary general 4th International Congress Tropical Medicine and Malaria, Washington, 1948; member West African Yellow Fever Commission, Rockefeller Foundation, 1926-27, in charge Yellow Fever Lab., 1928-35; mem. Nat. Adv. Health Council of U.S. Pub. Health Service, 1937-40; mem. subcom. on Tropical Diseases, Nat. Research Council, 1940-44 (chmn. 1940); dir. commn. on tropical diseases, Army Epidemiol. Bd., 1942-44; hon. cons. to med. dept., U.S. Navy, 1941-44; mem. Ethnogeog. Bd., 1942-44; dir. Rockefeller Foundation Health Commn., 1940-44; convener Sect. Viruses and Viral Diseases, Third Internat. Congress for Microbiology, 1939; mem. adv. sci. bd., Gorgas Memorial Inst., 1944-46 (dir. 1946-49).

Methodist. Fellow Am. Pub. Health Assn., A.A.A.S., N.Y. Acad. Medicine, Washington (D.C.) Acad. Medicine, Royal Soc. Tropical Medicine and Hygiene (hon.); mem. Am. Found. Tropical Med., Assn. of Am. Physicians, Am. Acad. Tropical Medicine (pres. 1936-37), Am. Soc. Tropical Medicine, (pres. 1943-44), Am. Epidemiol. Soc., Am. Soc. Exptl. Pathology, Sigma Xi, Alpha Omega Alpha; hon. mem. Société Belge de Médicine Tropicale; corr. mem. Société de Biologie (Paris); hon. life mem. Conf. of State and Provincial Health Authorities of N. Am., Tenn. Pub. Hlth. Assn. U.S. del. Pan. Am. San. Conf., Bogota(, 1938. Decorated Knight 1st Class Order of St. Olav (Norway) 1926; Gran Oficial Order of Carlos J. Finlay (Cuba), 1940. Awarded Leon Bernard prize (League of Nations), 1939; Richard P. Strong medal, 1949. Clubs: Cosmos (Washington); Commonwealth (San Francisco); Berkeley, Faculty (Berkeley). Contbr. on yellow fever, internat. health, etc. Home: 2565 Rose St., Berkeley 8, Cal. Died Nov. 12, 1951.

SAWYER, WILLIAM L(INCOLN) coll. dean; b. July 18, 1905; Decatur, Ill.; s. William Ira and Celia Florence (Lincoln) S.; student James Millikin U., 1924-26; B.S., civil engring., U. Ill., 1926-28; M.S.E., U. Fla., 1937; m. Enid Janice Friend, Aug. 26, 1930; children—Janice Rosemary, William Lincoln, Jr. Structural draftsman, Miss. Valley Structural Steel Co., Decatur, 1928-29; successively instr., asst. prof., asso. prof., prof. civil engring., U. of Fla., 1929-49, head prof., dept. engring. mechanics, 1949-64, asst. dean Coll. of Engring., 1964-—. Registered profl. engr., Fla. Served as lt. (j.g.) to capt. USNR; resident officer charge constrn. yards, docks, Jacksonville and Key West, Fla., San Diego. Fellow Am. Soc. Civil Engrs.; mem. Am. Soc. for Engring. Edn., Sigma Tau. Presbyn. Mason, Kiwanian. Home: 411 N.W. 21st St., Gainesville, Fla. Died Nov. 25, 1966.

SAXTON, RUFUS army officer; b. Greenfield, Mass., Oct. 19, 1824; s. Jonathan Ashley and Miranda (Wright) S.; ed. pub. schs. and acad., Deerfield, Mass.; grad. U.S. Mil. Acad., 1849; A.M., Amherst, 1853; m. Matilda Gordon Thompson, Mar. 11, 1863. Bvt. 2d lt. 3d Arty., July 1, 1849; commd. 2d lt. 4th Arty., Sept. 12, 1850; 1st lt., Mar. 2, 1855; capt. asst. q.m., May 13, 1861; brig. gen. vols., Apr. 15, 1862; hon. mustered out of vol. service, Jan. 15, 1866; maj. q.m. U.S.A., July 29, 1866; lt. col. deputy q.m. gen., June 6, 1872; col. asst. q.m. gen., Mar. 10, 1882; retired by operation of law after 43 yrs.' service, Oct. 19, 1888; advanced to rank of brig. gen. by act of Apr. 23, 1904. Bvtd. maj., lt. col. and col., Mar. 13, 1865, and brig. gen., Apr. 9. 1865, and maj. gen. vols., Jan. 12, 1865; awarded medal of honor, Apr. 25, 1893, for distinguished gallantry and good conduct in defense of Harper's Ferry, Va., May 26-30, 1862. Served on coast survey, 1853-61; chief q.m. on staff Gen. Lyon in Mo. campaign, of Gen. McClellan in western Va., and of Gen. Sherman's Port Royal expdn.; comd. forces at Harper's Ferry, 1862; mil. gov. Dept. of the South, 1862-65; comd. div. of 10th Army Corps and forces on Morris' and John's islands in attack on Charleston; commr. Freedmen's Bur. for S.C., Ga. and Fla. until end f war. Republican. Unitarian. Mem. Mil. Order of Medal of Honor Legion of U.S. Residence: Washington, D.C. Died 1908.

SAYERS, REAGAN, lawyer; b. Lufkin, Tex., June 21, 1914; s. Sam R. and Clyde (Philen) S.; student Tex. Christian U., 1930-32; LL.B., U. Tex., 1936; m. Katherine O'Brien. Admitted to Tex. bar, 1936, since practiced in Ft. Worth; partner Rawlings, Sayers & Scurlock, 1936-69. Dir. Tex.-Okla. Express, Inc., Hood Rentals, Inc., C & J Leasing Co., Cherokee Terminal Co., Bonded Safeway Van Lines, Inc., Merchants Fast Motor Lines, Inc., Gem Storage & Terminal Co. Served from pvt. to capt., AUS, 1942-46. Decorated Croix de Guerre avec palme, Medal of Metz (France). Mem. Am., Ft. Worth bar assns., State Bar Tex., Motor Carrier Lawyers Assn. (pres. 1954-55), ICC Practitioners Assn., Phi Kappa Psi. Methodist. Mason. Clubs: Rivercrest Country, Forth Worth (Ft. Worth); Nat. Lawyers (Washington); Austin, Headliners (Austin, Tex.); Imperial (Dallas). Home: Ft Worth TX Died Oct. 27, 1969.

SAYLOR, JOHN HENRY educator; b. Lamar, Me., July 22, 1904; s. James Clyde and Mary (Shackelford) S.; student S.W. Mo. State Coll., 1921-23; A.B., So. Meth. U., 1925; student U. Ill., summer 1926; M.A., Duke, 1928, Ph.D., 1930; m. Lettie McLane, Apr. 3, 1926; children—Letty Lois (Mrs. H. J. Lewis), John Henry. Instr. high sch., Mo., 1925-26; faculty Duke, 1927-—, prof. chemistry, 1946-—, dir. undergrad. studies, 1946-54, exec. officer dept. chemistry, 1948-51, chmn. dept., 1954-65. Mem. civilian nat. def. research com. USN, 1944; sci. adviser Office Ordnance Research, U.S. Army, 1951-61, Army Research Office, Durham, 1961-—. Outstanding Civilian Service medal, Army, 1967. Mem. Am. Chem. Soc., A.A.A.S., Am. Assn. U. Pros., N.C. Acad Sci., Sigma Xi, Phi Lambda Upsilon. Methodist. Author: (with Hill, Vosburgh and Wilson) Elementary Chemistry, 1937; also articles. Home: 2500 Perkins Rd., Durham, N.C. Died June 15, 1966.

SAYRE, FARRAND ret. army officer; b. Lewis County, Mo., June 17, 1861; s. Emilius Kitchell and Elizabeth Stanford (Pierson) S.; B.S., U.S. Mil. Acad., 1884; U.S. Inf. and Cavalry Sch., 1905; hon. grad. Army Staff Coll., 1906; A.M., Johns Hopkins, 1936, Ph.D., 1938; Army War Coll., 1916-17; m. Kate Hamlin Phelps, May 10, 1888; children—Elizabeth Stanford (Mrs. Robert H. Kilbourne). Service in Indian Wars, 1885-86, Spanish-Am. War, 1898-99, World War I, 1917-19; comd. Brownsville Dist. Texas frontier, 1917-20; brig. gen., comdg. 1st Cav. Brigade, 1918-19, ret. from active service, 1925; instr. Army Service Schs., 1906-13; comd. dist. in Panama Canal Zone, 1920-26; in charge Reserves, 1st Corps area, Boston, 1922-25; parole agt. State of Mass., 1925-31. Mem. Assn. of Grad. U.S. Mil. Acad., Assn. Vets. of 8th U.S. Cavalry. Author: Map Maneuvers, 1912; Diogenes of Sinope, 1938; The Greek Cynics, 1948. Home: 325 Padington Rd., Balt. 12. Died Apr. 17, 1952; Buried Lexington, Ky.

SAYRE, ROBERT H(AROLD) mining engr.; b. Denver, Dec. 18, 1885; s. Hal and Elizabeth (Dart) S.; A.B., Harvard, 1908; m. Gertrude Bart Berger, July 9, 1912; children—Robert, Hal, William, Damaris, Phyllis, Constance. Engaged in mining and leasing Colo., 1908-12; cons. engr., mine operator, 1913-16; field engr. Ludlum Steel Co., 1919-21; operating mines nr. Breckenridge, Colo., 1922; cons. engr. Chipman Chem. Co., 1923-24, U.S. Dept. Justice, 1927-28; operating Lake Mine, nr. Idaho Springs, Colo., 1925; cons. engr. Western Exploration Co., 1926; gen. mgr. Quartz Hill Holding Co., 1928-29; cons. mining engr. Ludlum Steel Co., 1929; then in gen. cons. work; mine mgr. Pardners Mines Corp., operating in N.M., 1933-34; pres. and gen. mgr. Veta Mines, Inc., 1935-40; v.p. in charge prodn. Rustless Mining Corp. (subsidiary Rustless Iron & Steel Co. of Baltimore) producing chrome on Pacific Coast, 1941-42; chief Strategic Mineral Mission to Guatemala and other Central Am. countries for Bd. Econ. Warfare, 1942-44. Pres., Compañia Minera de Guatemala, S. A., 1944-46; Cons. engr., Central Am. since 1946. Aviator, U.S. Army advancing to 1st lt., 1917-18. Pres. bd. Colo. Sch. of Mines, 1934-35, trustee 12 yrs.; dir. Colo. Metal Min. Fund, 8 yrs. Mem. Am. Inst. Mining and Metall. Engrs. (chmn. Colo. sect.), Mining and Metall. Soc. Am., Colo. Sci. Soc., Colo. Mining Assn. (formerly a dir.), Denver C. of C. (formerly a dir.). Republican. Episcopalian. Clubs: University, Mile High (Denver); Harvard (N.Y.C.); American (Guatemala). Home: 2400 E. Iliff Av., Denver 80210. Office: Boston Bldg., Denver. Died May 8. 1960.

SCAIFE, ALAN MAGEE (skaf), manufacturer; b. Pittsburgh, Pa., Jan. 10, 1900; s. James Verner and Mary (Magee) S.; prep. edn., Shadyside Acad., Pittsburgh; Ph.B., Sheffield Scientific School (Yale), 1920; LL.D., U. Pitts., 1950; m. Sarah C. Mellon, Nov. 16, 1927; children—Cordelia M. (Mrs. C. Scaife May), Richard Mellon. With Scaife Co., steel tank mfrs., Pittsburgh, since 1920, now chmn.; dir., member executive committee, Gulf Oil Corp.; dir. Consolidated Coal Company, Mellon Nat. Bank and Trust Co., Pullman-Standard Car Mfg. Co., M. W. Kellogg Co., Trailmobile, Inc., Pullman, Inc., Air Reduction Company, also director Washington-Waynesburg Railroad, Bell Telephone Co. of Pa., T. Mellon and Sons. Served in U.S.N.R., World War I; lt. col., United States Army, World War II. Trustee Elizabeth Steel Magee Hospital, Mellon Institute of Indsl. Research, Carnegie Hero Fund Commn. (all of Univ. Pitts. (pres. board). Fellow Yale Corp. Republican. Clubs: Pittsburgh, Pittsburgh Athletic Assn., Pittsburgh Golf, Duquesne, Allegheny Country (Pitts.); Racquet and Tennis, The Lins (N.Y.C.); Rolling Rock (Ligonier, Pa.). Home: Ligonier, Pa. Office: 525 William Penn Pl., Pitts. Died July 24, 1958; buried Allegheny Cemetery, Pitts.

SCALES, A(RCHIBALD) H(ENDERSON) naval officer (ret.); b. Greensboro, N.C., Apr. 14, 1868; s. Junius Irving and Euphemia Hamilton (Henderson) S.; B.S., U.S. Naval Acad., 1887; LL.D., St. John's Coll., 1920; master naval sci., Penn. Mil. Coll., 1924; m. Harriet Pierce Graham, July 11, 1899 (dec. May 8, 1925); children—Harriet Graham (Mrs. A. G. Cook), Aroostine Henderson (Mrs. F. L. Riddle), Effie Irving (Mrs. A. L. Thompson). Commd. ensign USN, 1889, and advanced through grades to rear adm., 1919; retired from active service, 1926. Awarded Sampson medal, Spanish-Am. war, D.S.M., World War I; decorated Comdr. Order of Leopold (Belgium). Episcopalian. Club: Yacht (N.Y.). Address: care Capt. F. L. Riddle, Naval Gun Factory, Washington 25. Died Feb. 16, 1952; buried U. S. Naval Acad. Cemetery, Annapolis, Md.

SCALES, JOSEPH E(DWARD) ret. tobacco exec.; b. Balt., Apr. 13, 1891; s. Joseph Edward and Minnie Elizabeth (Smith) S.; ed. pub. schs., Balt.; m. Edith Morris Caulk, Aug. 26, 1918 (dec. November 1952); children—Dorothy Caulk, Edith Janet (Mrs. John C. Stidman), Marjorie Morris (Mrs. Frank M. Williams, Jr.). Entered tobacco bus., 1912; mem. sales dept., Liggett & Meyers Tobacco Co., Balt., 1916-17, salesman, 1919-20, div. sales mgr., 1920-26, dept. mgr., Richmond, Va., 1926-43, sales supr., N.Y.C., 1943-53, dir., 1944-53, ret. Served as 2d lt., inf. (aide-de-camp), U.S. Army, World War I. Home: Bon Air, Chesterfield County, Va., also Plankatank River, Middlesex County, Va.; 2425 Burroughs St., Richmond, Va. 23235. Died June 1, 1959; buried Hollywood Cemetery, Richmond.

SCAMMELL, ALEXANDER army officer; b. Mendon (now Milford), Mass., Mar. 27, 1747; s. Samuel Leslie and Jane (Libbey) S.; grad. Harvard, 1769. Went to Portsmouth, N.H., 1772, employed in surveying and exploring for lands and for royal navy timber; participated in capture of Ft. Willian and Mary, nr. Portsmouth, 1774; commd. brig. gen., 1775; brigade maj. Gen. John Sullivan's brigade, 1778, served in seige of Boston; participated in L.I. campaign as aide-de-camp to Sullivan; became brigade maj. in div. of Gen. Charles Lee, then col. 3d N.H. Bn., Continental Army, 1776; served with Gen. Arthur St. Clair at Ticonderoga, 1777; adj. gen. Continental Army, 1778-81; arrested his old gen., Charles Lee, after Battle of Monmouth; took charge of execution of Maj. John Andre, 1780; took command 1st N.H. Regt., led a party of continental light horse; captured at Battle of Yorktown, Sept. 30, 1781. Died from brutal handling, Williamsburg, Va., Oct. 6, 1781.

SCANNELL, DAVID D., surgeon; b. Boston, Mass., June 24, 1874; s. Daniel and Joanna (Lyons) S.; grad. Boston Latin Sch., 1893; A.B., Harvard, 1897, M.D., 1900; m. Elizabeth A. Macdonald, Feb. 14, 1912; children—David D., John Gordon. Began practice at Boston, 1900; interne Boston City Hosp., 1900-02, Boston Lying-In Hosp., 1902; instr. in anatomy, Harvard Med. Sch., 1903-08, in surgery, 1908-11; asst. prof. clin. surgery, Tufts Coll. Med. Sch., 1911-12; lecturer on surgery, Grad. Sch. of Medicine, Harvard, 1912-15; cons. surgeon Boston City Hosp. and Quincy City Hosp.; cons. surgeon, U.S.P.H.S.; surgeon-in-chief Whidden Hosp., Everett, Mass.; trustee Home Savings Bank. Del. from Mass. to A.M.A. House of Delegates. Served as 1st lt., advancing to col., Med. Corps, U.S. Army, 18 months, World War. Mem. Boston Sch. Com. 11 yrs., chmn. twice. Member Mass. State Board Education, since 1947. Fellow Am. Coll. Surgeons; mem. A.M.A., Mass. Med. Soc. Democrat. Catholic. Clubs: Harvard. Home: 489 Walnut Av., Jamaica Plain, Boston. Office: 475 Commonwealth Av., Boston MA

SCARBOROUGH, (WILLIAM) BYRON, lawyer; b. Ft. Worth, Oct. 6, 1912; s. L.R. and Neppie (Warren) S.; A.B., Baylor U., 1933, LL.B., 1935; m. Joyce Cole; children—Karen, William Byron. Admitted to Tex. bar, 1935; partner firm Cantey, Hanger, Gooch, Cravens & Scarborough, Ft. Worth. Cons. edn., mem. adv. com. local pub. schs. Served to lt. USNR, World War II; PTO. Mem. Am., Tex., Ft. Worth bar assns. Baptist (deacon). Mason, Lion (past pres.). Clubs: River Crest Country, Shady Oaks Country, Ridglea Country, Fort Worth, Petroleum, Fort Worth Boat. Home: Fort Worth TX Died June 6, 1968; buried Greenwood Cemetery, Fort Worth TX

SCARRITT, NATHAN SPENCER lawyer; b. Belton, Mo., Sept. 29, 1898; s. Charles Wesley and Clara (Spencer) S.; A.B., U. Mo., 1919; LL.B., U. Okla., 1923; m. Rilla Fayette Winn, 1923; m. 2d, Ann Chapek, Feb. 21, 1944; children—Nathan Spencer, Richard Winn, Marilyn Chapek. Admitted to Okla. bar, 1923; atty. Champlin Refining Co., Enid, Okla., 1923-—, exec. v.p., 1943-—, gen. counsel, dir. 1954-—; v.p., gen. atty. Champlin Petroleum Co., 1956-—. Trustee Scarritt Coll. Donor Scarritt award U. Okla., 1936-—. Served as 2d lt., inf. U.S. Army, 1918. Mem. Am., Okla. bar assns., S.A.R., Order of Coif, Phi Beta Kappa, Phi Delta Theta, Phi Delta Phi. Methodist. Home: 1309 Vinita Av. Office: P.O. Box 552, Enid, Okla. Died July 25, 1965; buried Enid Cemetery.

SCHAAF, ROYAL ALBERT surgeon; b. Boone, Ia., Mar. 28, 1892; s. Rudolph Beorge and Susan Maria (Doud) S.; M.D., New York University, 1913; D.Sc., Rutgers University, 1956; LL.D., (hon.), Bloomfield College and Seminary, 1957; married Helen Devore Thomas, Jan. 1, 1917; children—Royal Sommer (M.D.), Kate Coleman (Mrs. Perry J. Culver). Intern, resident Bellevue Hosp., N.Y.C., 1913-15; practice medicine, 1916, specializing surgery, Newark, 1919-—; trustee, chmn. bd. United Hosps. Newark; consulting surgeon St. Barnabas Hospital Women and Children, Newark, St. Mary's Hospital, Orange, N.J.; mem. sr. staff Harrison S. Martland Med. Center, Babies Hosp., Coit Meml., Presbyn. Hosp.; (all Newark); chmn. bd. Medical-Surgical Plan of N.J.; pres. Med. Service Adminstrn. of N.J.; pub. dir. Prudential Ins. Co. Am., 1953-62; mem. of state board of med. examiners N.J., 1940-60. Trustee N.Y. University, Trustee N.J. division American Cancer Soc. Served as capt. M.C., U.S. Army, World War I. Recipient Edward J. Ill. award Acad. Medicine of N.J., 1948, Am. Cancer Soc. award, 1951, also N.J. div. award, 1952. Fellow A.C.S., Acad. Medicine of N.J. (past pres.), Med. Soc. of N.J. (past pres.); mem. Soc. Surgeons of N.J. (past pres.), Essex County Med. Soc. (past pres.), A.M.A., Bellevue Hosp. Alumni Assn. Home: Stillpond, Califon, N.J. 07830. Died Apr. 14, 1964.

SCHAFF, MORRIS author; b. Kirkersville, O., Dec. 28, 1840; s. John and Charlotte (Hartzell) S.; grad. U.S. Mil. Acad., 1862; LL.D., Williams Coll., 1913; Litt.D., Otterbein U., 1914; m. Alice Page, Aug. 8, 1868. Second lt. Ordnance Corps, June 17, 1862; 1st lt., Mar. 3, 1863; capt., Mar. 7, 1867; bvtd. capt., May 6, 1864, "for gallant and meritorious service in battle of the Wilderness"; resigned, Dec. 31, 1871; insp. gen. Mass. Militia, 1882; mem. Board of Visitors to West Point,

1882. President West Point Alumni Assn., 1913. Democrat. Author: Etna and Kirkersville, 1905; Spirit of Old West Point, 1907; Battle of the Wilderness, 1908; Sunset of the Confederacy, 1912; Jefferson Davis, His Life and Personality, 1922. Address: Cambridge, Mass. Died Oct. 19, 1929.

SCHARFF, MAURICE ROOS, cons. engr.; b. Natchez, Miss., Apr. 14, 1888; s. Monroe and Rosa (Roos) S.; prep. edn., Phillips Exeter Acad., Exeter, N.H.; B.S., Mass. Inst. Tech., 1909, M.S., 1911; m. Jeanne Adler, Apr. 30, 1919; 1 son, Samuel Adler. Asst. engr., Morris Knowles, cons. engr., Pittsburgh, Pa., 1911-14, prin. engr., 1914-16, asst. chief engr. and v.p., 1916-21; valuation engr., Phila. Co. and affiliated corps, 1921-25, chief engr., 1925-27; chief engr., Pittsburgh br. Byllesby Engring. and Management Corp., 1927-28; cons. engr., Pittsburgh, 1928-32, N.Y.C., 1932-42, 1946-67; director Duquesne Light Company (Pittsburgh). Consultant to Task Force on Water Resources, Commn. on Orgn. Exec. Branch of Govt., 1954-55; cons. ICA and govts. Viet Nam, Laos, 1956-58. 1st lt. to capt. C.E., U.S. Army, 1918-19. Maj. to col., Corps of Engrs., U.S. Army, 1942-46. Mem. Am. Inst. Cons. Engrs., Am. Soc. C.E.; asso. mem. Am. Inst. E.E., Soc. Am. Military Engrs., Military Order World War. Republican. Clubs: City, Technology (New York); Cosmos (Washington, D.C.). Author: Electrical Utilities (with W. E. Mosher and others), 1929; Depreciation of Public Utility Property, 1940. Home: New York City NY Died Apr. 6, 1967; buried Arlington Nat. Cemetery Arlington VA

SCHAUFFLER, ROBERT HAVEN author, lectr.; b. Brunn, Austria, Aug. 8, 1879, of Am. parents; s. Rev. Henry A. (D.D.) and Clara Eastham (Gray) S. (missionaries); student Northwestern U., 1898-99; B.A., Princeton, 1902; U. Berlin, 1902-03; pupil of cellists, Steindel, Schroeder and Hekking; m. Katharine de Normandie Wilson, Dec. 21, 1904 (died May 4, 1916); Editor, Nassau Lit. Mag., 1901-02; music editor Independent, 1903-04; spl. contbr. Collier's Weekly in Italy and Greece, 1906, of Century and Outlook in Germany, 1907, of Success in the West, 1909, 10, of Atlantic and Metropolitan, 1911, 12, of Century, 1913. Decorated by Queen of Italy, 1906, for winning nat. tennis championship (doubles), Rome; played in Athenian Olympic Games, 1906; winter of Austrian handicap tennis doubles, 1931. With wife, and blind violinist, Edwin Grasse, mem. (1906-09) The Grasse Trio. As an amateur sculptor has exhibited in Nat. Sculpture Soc. exhbns. Commd. 2d lt. Inf., U.S. Army, Nov. 27, 1917; attached 315th Inf., Dec. 15, 1917; instr. Officers Tng. Sch., Camp Meade, Md., Jan. 19-Apr. 1, 1918; regtl. intelligence officer 313th Inf., Apr. 15, 1918; 1st lt., June 8, 1918; landed in France with 79th Div., July 15; severely wounded before Sept. 26, 1918, in Meuse-Argonne offensive; asst. gen. staff officer 3, 79th Div., Jan. 5-Feb. 1, 1919; detached service Adv. Gen. Hdqrs., Germany, Feb. 1-Apr. 10, 1919; disch., May 28, 1919. Decorated Purple Heart. Author: Where Speech Ends, 1906; Romantic Germany, 1909; The Musical Amateur, 1911; Scum o' the Earth and Other Poems, 1912; Romantic America, 1913; The Joyful Heart, 1914; Fiddler's Luck, 1920; The White Comrade, and Other Poems, 1920; Selected Poems (London), 1922; Magic Flame and Other Poems, 1923; Peter Pantheism, 1925; The Science of Practice, 1927; Music as a Social Force in America, 1927; Who's Who in the Orchestra, 1927; Hobnaisl in Eden (Poems of a Maine Vagabond), 1929; Beethoven—the Man Who Freed Music (2 vols), 1929; The Mad Musician—A Shorter Life of Beethoven, 1931; The Unknown Brahms—His Life, Character and Works, Based on New Material, 1933; Enjoy Living (An Invitation to Happiness), 1939; New and Selected Poems, 1942; Fiddler's Folly and Encores, 1942; Brahms, the Master (with Madeleine Goss), 1943; Florestan: Life and Work of Robert Schumann, 1945; Franz Schubert: the Ariel of Music, 1949. Editor: Thanksgiving, 1907; Christmas, 1907; Through Italy with the Poets, 1908; Lincoln's Birthday, 1909; Arbor Day, 1909; Washington's Birthday, 1910; Memorial Day, 1911; Flag Day, 1912; Independence Day, 1912; Mothers' Day, 1915; Easter, 1916; The Poetry Cure (a pocket medicine chest of verse), 1925; Armistice Day, 1927; The Poetry Cure with Music and Pictures, 1927; Plays for Our American Holidays (4 vols.), 1928; Little Plays for Little People, 1929; The Magic of Books (An Anthology for Book Week), 1929, Graduation Day, 1930; A Manthology, 1931; The Junior Poetry Cure, 1931; Roosevelt Day, 1932; Halloween, 1933; The Magic of Music (an anthology for music weeks and days), 1935; The Days We Celebrate (4 vols), 1940; and (with Hilah Paulmier) Columbus Day, 1938; Democracy Days, 1942; Pan America Day, 1943; Peace Days, 1946; Goodwill Days, 1947. Contbr. to mags. Clubs: Colonial (Princeton); The Players (New York). Home: 299 W. 12th St., New York 14, N.Y. Address: care Dodd, Mead & Co., 432 4th Av., N.Y.C. 10016. Died Nov. 24, 1964; buried Arlington Nat. Cemetery.

SCHAUFFLER, WILLIAM GRAY M.D.; b. of Am. missionary parents, Constantinople, Turkey, Oct. 28, 1863; s. Henry Albert (D.D.) and Clara Eastham (Gray) S.; B.A., Amherst, 1886, M.A., 1903; M.D., Coll. Phys. and Surg. (Columbia), 1889; m. Eleanor H. Hawkes, Jan. 14, 1891 (died 1891); 1 son, William Gray; m. 2d, Lilian Miner Boswell, Sept. 5, 1894. Prof. of physiology and diseases of women, med. dept. Am. Univ., Beirût, Syria, 1891-96; practiced, Lakewood, N.J., 1896-1917, Princeton, 1920-—; med. adviser to Princeton Theol. Sem. Mem. N.J. N.G., 1905-—; lt. col. M.C., surgeon gen. N.J., 1911-17; a.d.c. to 3 govs. of N.J.; lt. col., sanitary insp., 39th Div., Camp Beauregard, La., and in France; col. M.C., U.S.A.; information officer Advance G.H.Q., Germany; attached to High Rhineland Commn., Germany. Republican. Presbyn. Mason. Home: Princeton, N.J. Died Apr. 30, 1933.

SCHEALER, SAMUEL RAYMOND educator; b. Reading, Pa., Jan. 11, 1887; s. Samuel Gardner and Adaline Kemp (Wesner) S.; E.E., Lehigh U., 1909, M.S., 1921; m. Evelyn Barlow, July 24, 1915 (died Apr. 30, 1933); 1 son, Robert Barlow; m. 2d, Louise Jenkins Rose, June 15, 1940; 1 stepdau., Louise Rose. Successively instr., asst. prof., asso. prof. elec. engring. Lehigh U., 1909-11, 1912-17, and 1919-27; prof. elec. engring. and head dept. Duke, 1927-35, Vanderbilt U., since 1938; summer employment with Gen. Electric and Westinghouse Elec. & Mfg. Co. Served as lt. USNRF, 1917-19. Registered profl. engr., Tenn. Mem. Am. Inst. E.E., Am. Soc. for Engring. Edn., Phi Beta Kappa, 7au Beta Pi, Eta Kappa Nu. Mason. Republican. Presbyn. Home: 2304 Woodmont Blvd. Address: Vanderbilt U., Nashville. Died Sept. 10, 1964; buried Woodlawn Cemetery, Nashville.

SCHEETZ, FRANCIS HARLEY, lawyer; b. Norristown, Pa., Sept. 30, 1894; s. Remandus and Elizabeth (Harley) S.; B.A., Cornell U., 1915, B.Chem., 1916; LL.B., Harvard, 1921; m. Virginia DeMorat Smith, May 27, 1926. Admitted to Pa. bar, 1922, U.S. Supreme Ct., 1940; asso. Evans, Bayard & Frick, Phila., 1921-28, partner, 1928-54; partner Pepper, Hamilton & Scheetz and predecessor, Phila., 1954-68. Trustee emeritus, presdl. councillor Cornell U.; asso. trustee U. Pa. Am. Field Service, French Army, 1917; served 2d lt. to capt., U.S. Army, 1918; AEF. Mem. Am., Pa., Phila. bar assns., Bar Assn. City N.Y., Juristic Soc., Theta Delta Chi. Clubs: Merion Cricket, Midday, Racquet; Century Assn.; Union League. (N.Y.C.). Home: Villanova PA Died Sept. 25, 1968; buried Riverside Cemetery, Norristown PA

SCHEIBERLING, EDWARD NICHOLAS, lawyer; b. Albany, N.Y., Dec. 2, 1888; s. Martin and Mary (Schneider) S.; LL.B., Union U., 1912; m. Ethel F. Fitzpatrick, Nov. 11, 1939; 1 son, Edward N. (died 1948). Engaged in practice of law, Albany, N.Y., since 1912; sr. mem. firm of Scheiberling & Schneider, later Scheiberling, Rogan & Maney; justice, City Ct., Albany, 1924-29; admitted to practice before U.S. Supreme Ct., 1940. Served with inf., U.S. Army, 1916-19; 2d lt., 312th Inf., 78th (Lightning) Div., 1917; promoted 1st lt., Dec. 1917; with A.E.F., France, 1918; participated in offensives St. Mihiel and Meuse-Argonne; promoted capt., Oct. 1918; hon. disch. June 1919. Awarded Legion d'Honneur by Govt. of France, 1945. National commander American Legion, 1944 (New York department commander, 1935-36; charter member 40 and 8 (Albany); v.p. and dir. Nat. Conv., N.Y. City, 1937, 1947; mem. nat. legislative com., 1939, 1940, 1941, vice chmn. 1943-44). Dir. Albany County Am. Red Cross; chmn. Community Chest Campaign, 1939; gen. chmn. Albany U.S.O. campaign, 1941; mem. nat. council Boy Scouts of Am. (v.p. Ft. Orange Council); official consultant to American delegation, San Francisco Conf., 1945; chmn. N.Y. State World War Memorial Authority, 1935-41. Director Catholic Charities, Albany Diocese. Trustee State University of New York, 1948. Member American Bar Association, N.Y. State Bar Assn., Albany County Bar Assn. (past pres.), 312th U.S. Inf. Assn., 78th Div. Assn., Military Order of the World Wars. Democrat. Roman Catholic. Elks. Clubs: Albany (N.Y.), Manhattan, Military-Naval (N.Y. City). Home: Albany NY Died Sept. 10, 1967; buried Lady Help of Christians Cemetery Glenmont NY

SCHELDRUP, NICOLAY HILMAR, surgeon retired; b. Tovik, Norway, Sept. 1, 1873; s. Andrew Martin and Hannah (Wanvig) S.; came to U.S., 1891; M.D., Rush Med. Coll., 1897; m. Eva Dunsmoor, Aug. 5, 1897; children—Alfred H., Sylvia Louise (wife of Dr. Harold R. Leland), Eugene W., Robert D. Began practice, Granite Falls, Minn., 1897; associated in surgery with Prof. Frederick A. Dunsmoor, Minneapolis, 1906-14; founder, 1925, and pres. Med. and Surg. Clinic; dir. Perfection Mfg. Co.; retired. Served as capt. Med. Corps, U.S. Army, 1918-19. Decorated Knight Order of St. Olaf, first class (Norway). Republican. Lutheran. Home: Miami FL Died 1968.

SCHELLING, ERNEST HENRY pianist, composer and conductor; b. N.J., July 26, 1876; s. of Felix and Rose (White) S.; studied music under Mathias Moszkowski (Paris), Huber (Basel), Paderewski (Switzerland); Doctor of Music, U. of Pa., 1928; m. Lucie How Draper, May 3, 1905. Composer: Légendes Symphoniques, 1904; Symphony Fantastic Suite, piano and orchestra; Impressions, variations for piano and orchestra (Boston Symphony, 1915); Violin Concerto (Kreisler, Boston Symphony, 1916); Victory Ball (after poem by Noyes), first perf. in New York with Phila. Philharmonic Orchestra, Feb. 1923; "Morocco" for orchestra (N.Y. Philharmonic, 1927); divertimento for string quartet and piano (Flonzaley, New York, 1925). Conductor children's and young people's concerts, N.Y. Philharmonic, Boston, Phila., Baltimore, San Francisco, Los Angeles, Hollywood Bowl and Cincinnati orchestras, etc., comdr. Baltimore Symphony Orch., 1936, 37, 38. Commd. capt. of cavalry, Aug. 5, 1917, promoted maj., Nov. 10, 1918; served with army abroad, Oct. 1917-Apr. 1920. Decorated French Legion of Honor, 1919; D.S.M. (U.S.), 1923; Comdr. Alphonso XII (Spain); Officer Polonia Restituta (Poland). Home: New York, N.Y. Died Dec. 8, 1939.

SCHENCK, HUBERT GREGORY geologist; b. Memphis, Sept. 24, 1897; s. William Johnson and Lida (Egbert) S.; A.B., Ore. U., 1922, A.M., 1923; Ph.D., U. Calif., 1926; m. Inga Bergström, Nov. 5, 1924; 1 dau., Ingrid (Mrs. Edward L. Beach). Geologist, div. mines, Bur. Science, Manila, P.I., 1920-21; instr. U. Calif., 1923-24; asst., asso. and prof. geology, Stanford, 1924-43; advance fellow, Belgium-Am. Ednl. Found., 1934, 1935, paleontologist Amiranian Oil Co. (Iran and Afghanistan), 1937-38; cons. geologist at intervals, 1926-—. Served with U.S. Army, 1916-19, maj. to col., 1943-51, col. USAR retired, 1953; chief of Natural Resources Section, General Hdqrs., Supreme Comdr. Allied Powers, Tokyo, 1945-51; chief Mut. Security Mission to China, 1951-54; cons. Fgn. Operations Adminstrn., 1954-55; prof. geol. Stanford U., 1954-—; cons. Pacific Sci. Bd., 1955-—; mem. adv. council. Inst. Marine Resources, U. of Cal., 1956-59; research asso. Hoover Institution, Stanford, 1945-—. Awarded Bronze Star, Bronze Star with oak leaf cluster, Legion of Merit, Distinguished Service Medal, Philippine Legion of Honor medal; Order of Brilliant Star (China). Member Geological Society Am., Am. Assn. Petroleum Geologists, Geol. Society France, Paleontological Society Japan, Geol. Society Belgium (corr. mem.), Malacol. Soc. London, Paleontol. Soc., Soc. Econ. Paleontologists and Mineralogists, Geol. Soc. Philippines, A.A.A.S., Cal. Acad. Sci., Am. Malacological Union, Am. Acad. Polit. Social Sci., Phi Beta Kappa, Sigma Xi, Theta Tau. Mason (32 deg., Shriner). Club: Explorers. Contbr. U.S. and fgn. publs. Home: 585 Washington, Palo Alto, Cal. Office: School of Mineral Sciences Stanford, Cal. Died June 19, 1960.

SCHENCK, JAMES FINDLAY naval officer; b. Franklin, O., June 11, 1807; s. William Cortenus and Elizabeth (Rogers) S.; attended U.S. Mil. Acad., 1822-24; m. Dorothea Ann Smith, July 27, 1829, 4 children. Apptd. midshipman U.S. Navy, 1825; commanded sloop Surprise in action against pirates in W.I., 1828; promoted lt., 1835; assigned to frigate Congress under Commodore Robert F. Stockton, 1845; active in campaign against California, 1846-49, present at capture of Santa Barbara, led landing party that captured San Pedro, participated in capture of Los Angeles, Guaymas, Mazatlan; commanded U.S. mail steamer Ohio, 1849-52; promoted comdr., 1855; in command of ship North Carolina, 1858-60; commanded brig Saginaw at East India station, 1860-62; on blockading duty Gulf of Mexico, 1862-64; promoted commodore, 1864; commanded 3d div. N. Atlantic Blockading Squadron, 1864; commanded naval sta., Mound City, Ill., 1866-68; promoted rear adm., 1868, ret., 1869. Died Dayton, O., Dec. 21, 1882.

SCHENCK, MICHAEL judge; b. Lincolnton, Lincoln County, N.C., Dec. 11, 1876; s. Judge David and Sallie Wilfong (Ramseur) S.; student U. of N.C., 1893-95; student law dept., 1902-03, LL.D., 1936; m. Rose Few, Nov. 15, 1909; children—Michael, Rosemary Ramseur, Emily Floreid. Admitted to N.C. bar, 1903, and began practice at Greensboro; moved to Hendersonville, N.C., 1905; mayor of Hendersonville, 1907-09; solicitor 18th Jud. Dist., N.C., 1913-18 (resigned to enter army); maj. Judge Advocate Gen.'s Dept., U.S.Army, 1918-19; reelected solicitor but did not accept; judge Superior Court, 18th Jud. Dist. of N.C., 1924-34; asso. justice Supreme Court N.C., 1934-48. Mem. N.C. Constitutional Commn. to redraft Constn. of N.C., 1931. Mem. N.C. bar assn. (ex-v.p.), Am. Legion. Democrat. Episcopalian; former mem. Bishop's council Diocese of Western N.C. Mason. Home: Hendersonville, N.C. Address: Raleigh, N.C. Died Nov. 5, 1948.

SCHENCK, PETER LAWRENCE physician; b. Flatbush, L.I., N.Y., Oct. 25, 1843; s. John and Catherine Van Dyck (Ryder) S.; A.B., New York U., 1862, A.M., 1865 (LL.D., 1898); M.D., Coll. Phys. and Surg. (Columbia), 1865; m. Sarah Elizabeth White, of Canajoharie, N.Y., June 10, 1896. Acting asst. surgeon, U.S.A., in charge hosp., Wilmington, N.C., 1865; assistant phys. Cholera Hosp., Brooklyn, N.Y., 1866; med. supt. Kings Co. Hosp., 1872-81; consulting surgeon same, 1882-14; visiting phys. Kings Co. Penitentiary, 1889-05; retired from active practice, 1907. Mem. Am. Acad. Medicine (life), Kings Co. Med. Soc., Zeta Psi. Member Rev. Dutch Ch. Mason. Club: Montauk. Address: 95 6th Av., Brooklyn, N.Y.

SCHERER, WALTER H(ENRY) dental surgeon; b. Newport, Ky., Sept. 15, 1880; s. Henry and Fredericka (Weber) S.; D.D.S., U. of Cincinnati, 1900; unmarried. Prof. oral medicine, Sch. of Dentistry, U. of Texas, 1920-45; in private practice as dental surgeon, Houston, Tex., since 1900. Served as major, Dental Corps, U.S. Army, World War I. Mem. bd. regents, U. of Tex.

Fellow Am. Coll. Dentists; mem. Tex. State Dental Soc. (pres. 1918), Houston Dist. Dental Soc. (pres. 1913), Am. Dental Assn. (pres. 1945-46), Am. Acad. Periodentology (pres. 1936), Ill. State (life) and Chicago dental socs., Internat. Assn. Research, Houston Chamber of Commerce (mem. bd. dirs.), Psi Omega, Omicorn Kappa Epsilon. Mem. Christ Episcopal Ch. Mason (Shriner, K.T.), Rotarian. Clubs: Houston, Houston (Tex.) Country. Author: Dentistry National and International, Present and Postwar, 1945. Contbr. Numerous articles to professional jours. Home: Montrose Blvd. Apartments. Office: Medical Arts Bldg., Houston 22. Deceased.*

SCHERMERHORN, RICHARD, JR., landscape architect and city planner; b. Brooklyn, N.Y., Oct. 17, 1877; s. Richard and Jane Agnes (Fiske) Schermerhorn; educated Brooklyn Poly. Prep. Sch. and Inst., 1888-94, Rensselaer Poly. Inst., 1894-97; m. Margaret Medbury Doane, June 2, 1930; 1 son, Derick Doane. Began as landscape architect, 1900, in pvt. practice since 1909; engaged on over 100 private estates, also parks, cemeteries, country clubs, subdivisions, college campuses; consultant Allegany and Taconic state parks; designed master plans for Great Neck, Huntington, Lawrence, in N.Y., Newark, N.J., etc.; lecturer on landscape architecture, Columbia, 1935-39; landscape architect and site planner, Elizabeth (N.J.) Housing Authority; consultant landscape architect, Hudson River Conservation Society; landscape architect and planner for U.S. Army (Fort Hamilton), 1941. Cons. Architects Def. Housing Projects, Bound Brook, N.J., 1942; cons., planner projects of housing developments since 1942. Served as capt. engring. sect. Sanitary Corps, U.S. Army, 1917-19; with A.E.F. 8 mos., participated St. Mihiel offensive; assignment with Engring. Dept. on Commn. to Negotiate Peace. Fellow Am. Soc. Landscape Architects (former nat. trustee, ex-pres. N.Y. Chapter); mem. Am. Soc. Civil Engrs. (life), Holland Society New York (ex-trustee), N.Y. State Historical Assn., Dutch Settlers Soc. of Albany, N.J. Society Architects (asso.), Chi Phi. Licensed professional engr., N.Y. and N.J. Author: Schermerhorn Genealogy and Family Chronicles, 1914. Contbr. to jours. on landscape architecture, city planning, etc., and genealogy. Home: 173 Orange Road, Montclair NJ Office: 342 Madison Av., New York 17 NY

SCHERR, HARRY, JR., lawyer; b. Cin., Feb. 23, 1915; s. Harry and Rosa Lee (Wall) S.; grad. Woodberry Forest Sch., Va., 1932; A.B., Yale, 1936; LL.B., W.Va. U., 1939; m. Marguerite LeCron Thompson, May 8, 1943; children—Harry 3d, Herbert Thompson, Leslie LeCron. Admitted to W.Va. bar, 1939, practiced in Huntington, 1939-72. Pres., dir. Dacon Constructors; dir. Thomas Co. Mem. Nat. Conf. on Continuing Edn. of the Bar, Arden House, 1958; mem. W.Va. Gov.'s Commn. on Water Resources, 1968-72. Served as comdr. United States Navy, 1941-46, captain USNR. Member of American, W.Va. (exec. council 1953-56, 57-58, pres. 1958-59), Cabell County bar assns., W.Va. State Bar, W.Va. (pres. 1950-51), Huntington Chambers Commerce Beta Theta Pi, Phi Alpha Delta. Republican (vice chmn. Cabel County exec. com. 1939-40). Episcopalian (vestryman 1949-52, chmn. W.Va. Conf. Episcopal Laymen 1951-53). Elk. Clubs: Engineers, City (Huntington); Guyan Golf and Country; Press (Charleston, W.Va.). Home: Huntington WV Died Apr. 19, 1972.

SCHICK, LAWRENCE E. army officer; b. Chgo., Sept. 24, 1897; s. David W. and Mary A. (Thomas) S.; student Pomona Coll., 1916-17; B.S., U.S. Mil. Acad., 1920; grad. Cav. Sch., 1921; m. Frances M. Moore, July 14, 1921; children—Mary Lou (wife of Paul C. Root, Jr., U.S. Army), John Lawrence. Commd. 2d lt., U.S. Army, 1920, advancing through grades to brig. gen., 1945; head dept. mil. topography and graphics U.S. Mil. Acad., West Point, N.Y., 1946-60, head dept. earth, space and graphic scis., 1960-—. Recipient Legion of Merit, D.S.M. Address: U.S. Mil. Acad., West Point, N.Y. Died Oct. 14, 1967.

SCHILLINGER, ARNOLD ARTHUR psychiatrist, hosp. adminstr.; b. Bklyn., 1912; M.D., U. St. Louis, 1937. Intern Braddock (Pa.) Gen. Hosp., 1937-38; clin. tng. VA neuropsychiat. hosps., 1940-41; psychiatrist, neurologist Mayo Found., 1942, Met. State Hosp. Mass., 1945; courtesy staff Roslyn Park (N.Y.) Hosp.; dir. VA Hosp., Northport, N.Y., 1955-—; with Neurol. Inst., Columbia; instr. psychiatry Cornell U. Med. Sch.; clin. asst. prof. psychiatry State U. N.Y., Med. Sch., N.Y.C., 1956-—. Served to lt. col. M.C., AUS, 1941-46; col. Res. Diplomate Am. Bd. Psychiatry and Neurology. Decorated Conspicuous Service Cross, Army Commendation ribbon. Fellow Am. Psychiat. Assn., A.C.P.; mem. Am. Assn. Psychotherapy, Rehab. Therapeutics, A.M.A. Address: VA Hosp., Middleville Rd., Northport, N.Y. 11768. Died July 1965.

SCHINDEL, S(AMUEL) JOHN BAYARD army officer; b. Camden N.J., June 3, 1871; s. J. P. (capt. U.S. Army) and Martha Pintard (Bayard) S.; grad. U.S. Mil. Acad., 1893; Army War Coll., 1908; m. Isa Urquhart Glenn, Nov. 11, 1903. Commd. add. 2d lt. 3d Arty., June 12, 1893; 2d lt., Nov. 2, 1893; trans. to 16th Inf., Feb. 25, 1895, to 6th Inf., Apr. 12, 1895; 1st lt. 3d Inf., Apr. 26, 1898; trans. to 6th Inf., Dec. 19, 1898; capt., Feb. 2, 1901; maj., June 12, 1916; lt. col., June 30, 1917; col. N.A., Aug. 5, 1917; brig. gen. (temp.), Aug. 8, 1918. With regt. at Ft. Thomas, Ky., 1895-98; in Santiago Campaign, 1898, participated in Battle of San Juan Hill and Siege of Santiago; in Philippines, 1899-1902, and 1905-06, participating in engagement at Valdes, July 1899, and Bud Dajo, Mar. 4-9, 1906; attended Swiss autumn maneuvers, 1907; duty Gen. Staff, 1912 to 1916, June-Aug. 1918; assigned to Camp Meade, Md., Aug. 26, 1918; duty Gen. Staff, Mar.-Sept. 1919, later at Ft. Leavenworth. Episcopalian. Home: Allentown, Pa. Died Mar. 11, 1921.

SCHLAIKJER, ERICH MAREN, cons. geologist, engineer; b. Newton, O., Nov. 22, 1905; s. Erich and Clara (Ryser) S.; B.S., Harvard, 1929, M.A., Columbia, 1931, Ph.D., 1935; m. Jospehine Ayres, Apr. 28, 1951; children—Maren, Michael, Patrecia Jo. In charge, 10 geol. and paleontol. expedn., Gt. Plains Area of U.S. for Harvard U., 1925-34, Yukon Terr. Alaska Expdn. for Am. Museum of Nat. History, 1936, with Barnum Brown, Am. Museum-Sinclair Expdn., southwestern Wyo., 1937; Am. Museum-Sweet Expdns., Big Bend Area, Tex., 1939-40, Comml. Petroleum and Mining Geology, Rocky Mountain Area, 1946-49, Tutor of geology, Bklyn. Coll., 1932-34, instr., 1935-39, asst. prof., 1940-47, prof., 1948-50; pres. Lakota Petroleum Corp., 1950-67. Served in U.S. Air Force, 1st lt., 1942, active duty, advanced to lt. col., 1945. Awarded Bronze Star Medal, Army Commendation Ribbon, seven campaign stars to the Asiatic Pacific Theatre Ribbon. Awarded (with Barnum Brown) Cressy Morrison prize, N.Y. Acad. Sci., 1939. University fellow Columbia U. Fellow Geol. Soc. Am., Paleontol. Soc. Am., A.A.A.S.; mem. Am. Assn. Petroleum Geologists, Nat. Soc. Profl. Engrs., Am. Geophys. Union, Soc. for the Study of Evolution, Am. Inst. Profl. Geologists (charter), Sigma Xi. Clubs: Explorer's (dir., 1942-43, sec., 1947-49 and various coms.), Harvard (N.Y.C.); Petroleum, Columbine Country (Denver). Author articles on geology and paleontology profl. jours. Home: Littleton CO Died Nov. 5, 1972; buried Tower of Memories, Denver CO

SCHLEY, JULIAN LARCOMBE army officer; b. Savanah, Ga., Feb. 23, 1880; s. Julian and Eliza Ann (Larcombe) S.; grad. Lawrensville (N.J.) Sch., 1898, U.S. Mil. Acad., 1903, Engr. Sch., U.S. Army, 1908; m. Denise Vary, Oct. 31, 1931. Commd. 2d lt. C.E., 1903; promoted through grades to col., 1934, maj. gen., 1937; instr. U.S. Mil. Acad., 1909-12; asst. to engr. commr. D.C., 1912-13; exec. officer Pub. Utilities Commn. D.C., 1913-16; commdr. 307th Regt. Engrs. and later corps engr., 5th Corps, World War, 1917-18; dir. purchase and mem. War Dept. Claims Bd., 1919-21; asst. comdt. and dir. of dept. Engr. Sch., 1922-24; in charge improvement of rivers 23 in vicinity of New Orleans, 1916-17, Nashville, 1921-22, and Galveston, 1924-28; engr. of maintenance Panama Canal, 1928-32; gov. Panama Canal, 1932-36, dir., 1936-60; dir. Panama R.R. Co. since 1928 (pres. 1932-36); comdr. Engr. Sch., U.S. Army, Fort Belvoir, Va., 1936-37; maj. gen. chief of engrs. U.S. Army, 1937-41, ret.; recalled as dir. transp. Office Coordinator Inter-American Affairs, to 1945; ret.; exec. dir. Baltimore City Aviation Commn., 1946. Awarded D.S.M. Episcopalian. Fellow Am. Soc. C.E.; mem. Soc. of Cin., Soc. Colonial Wars, Soc. Am. Mil. Engrs. (past pres.), Sons of Revolutionary War. Clubs: Chevy Chase, Army and Navy (Washington). Address: 2815 Dumbarton Av., Washington 20007. Died Mar. 29, 1965; buried Arlington Nat. Cemetery.

SCHLEY, WINFIELD SCOTT rear admiral U.S.N.; b. nr. Frederick City, Md., Oct. 9, 1839; s. John Thomas and Georgiana Virginia (McClare) S.; apptd. to U.S. Naval Acad. from Md., 1856, grad. 1860; m. Annie R. Franklin, Sept. 10, 1863. Promoted midshipman, June 15, 1860; master, Aug. 31, 1861; lt., July 16, 1862; lt. comdr., July 25, 1866; comdr., June 10, 1874; capt., Mar. 31, 1888; commodore, Feb. 6, 1898; rear admiral, Mar. 3, 1899. Served on Niagara, 1860-61; Keystone State, 1861; Potomac, storeship, at Ship Island, 1861-62; Winona, W. Gulf Blockading Squadron, 1862-63; participated in engagement with a battery near Port Hudson, Dec. 14, 1862; all engagements which led to capture of Port Hudson, Mar.-July 1863; served on Wateree, Pacific Squadron, 1864-66; on duty Naval Acad., 1866-69, 1872-76; served on Benicia, 1869-72; participated in attack on Salee River forts in Korea, 1871; comd. Essex, 1876-79; light house insp. 2d dist., 1880-83; comd. the Thetis and Greely expdn., 1884, and rescued Lt. Greely and 6 survivors at Cape Sabine, for which was awarded a gold watch and vote of thanks of Md. legislature and gold medal from Mass. Humane Soc.; chief Bur. of Equipment and Repair, 1884-89; comd. Baltimore, 1889-92; mem. Bd. Inspection and Survey, 1896-97; chmn. Lighthouse Bd., 1897-98; during war with Spain comd. Flying Squadron, 1898; was in immediate command in battle of Santiago de Cuba, July 3, 1898, which resulted in the destruction of Admiral Cervera's Fleet; commander-in-chief S. Atlantic Squadron, 1899-1901; retired, Oct. 9, 1901. Presented with gold sword by people of Pa., a silver sword by Royal Arcanum, a gold and jeweled medal, with the thanks of Md. legislature, a silver service, etc., for services at battle of Santiago. Author: The Rescue of Greely, 1885; Forty-Five Years Under the Flag, 1904. Address: Washington, D.C. Died 1911.

SCHLOERB, ROLLAND WALTER (shlûrb), clergyman; b. Oshkosh, Wis., Mar. 1, 1893; s. Albert Peter and Sarah M. (Hammetter) S.; student Marquette U., 1910-11; B.A., North Central Coll., Naperville, Ill., 1915; B.D., Evang. Theol. Sem., 1917; S.T.B., Union Theol. Sem., N.Y., 1920; M.A., Northwestern U., 1921; student U. Chgo., 1928-29; D.D., North Central Coll., Naperville, Ill., 1936; m. Edith Gransden, June 12, 1920; children—Geraldine (Mrs. F. R. Meyer), Robert Gransden. Ordained ministry Evangelical Ch., 1918; pastor Highland Park. (Ill.) Evang. Ch., 1920-21, First Evang. Ch., Naperville, Ill., 1921-28, Hyde Park Bapt. Ch., Chgo., 1928-—. Trustee George Williams Coll., Bapt. Theol. Union. With Y.M.C.A. at outbreak of World War (mem. bd. mgrs.; Chgo.); chaplain U.S. Army, 1918-19. Fellow Nat. Council for Religion in Higher Edn. Author: God in Our Lives, 1938, The Preaching Ministry Today, 1946, The Interpreter's Bible, 1955. Club: Quadrangle (Chgo.). Contbr. articles to religious pubis. Home: 5842 Stony Island Av., Chgo. Died Mar. 15, 1958.

SCHLUETER, ROBERT ERNST (shle'ter), surgeon; b. St. Louis, Mo., June 9, 1872; s. Ernst and Elizabeth (Pullmann) S.; Ph.G., St. Louis Coll. Pharmacy, 1891; M.D., Mo. Med. Coll., 1895; grad. study in Europe, 1909-10; m. Katharyne B. Weber, Sept. 19, 1916. Asst. in physiology, Mo. Med. Coll., 1896-99; lecturer in pharmacy, Mo. Med. Coll., 1897-99; instr. in surgery, Washington U., 1899-1916; asso. prof. of surgery, St. Louis U. Sch. of Medicine, since 1923; asst. surgeon, St. John's Hosp., 1899-1903; surgeon, O'Fallon Dispensary, 1903-12, visiting surgeon, St. Louis City Hosp., 1912-16; surgeon, Luth. Hosp. since 1911, St. Louis Mullanphy Hosp., 1920-30, De Paul Hosp. since 1930, Deaconess Hosp. since 1932, St. Anthony's Hosp. since 1933. Hon. cons. Army Med. Library, Wash., 1944-52. Fellow Am. College Surgeons (life), A.M.A. (Mo. del. 1921, 22, 1940-53); mem. St. Louis Med. Soc. (pres. 1911), Mo. State Med. Assn. (president 1918), American Bd. Surgery (founders group), St. Louis Surg. Soc. (pres. 1941), So. Med. Assn., Hist. of Science Soc., St. Louis Acad. Science, Med. Library Assn. (v.p. 1940-41), A.A.A.S., Société Francaise d'Histoire de la Medicine. Served as maj. Med. Corps, U.S. Army, World War I. Republican. Mason. Club: University. Contbr. numerous articles to med. jours. Home: 245 Union Blvd. Office: 3839 Lindell Blvd., St. Louis 8. Died 1955.

SCHMIDLAPP, CARL JACOB banking; b. Cin., Aug. 10, 1888; s. Jacob G. and Emilie (Balke) S.; A.B., Cornell U., 1908; m. Frances Cooper, Mar. 15, 1920; children—Frances Downing (Mrs. Washington Irving), Jean Cooper., (Mrs. John P. Humes). Vice pres. Chase Nat. Bank, N.Y.C., 1915, former vice chmn. exec. com., now ret.; dir. Austin, Nichols & Co., Continental Ins. Co., Chgo. Pneumatic Tool Co., Punta Alegre Sugar Corp. Served as lt. 51st Inf., U.S. Army, during World War I. Mem. Sigma Chi, Alpha Phi. Clubs: University, Cornell, Recess, Racquet and Tennis, The Links, Links Golf, Turf and Field, Piping Rock, Knickerbocker (N.Y.C.). Home: 834 Fifth Av., N.Y.C. 10021. Died May 13, 1960.

SCHMIDT, ARTHUR ALEXANDER, pub. relations counsel; b. Indpls., May 6, 1901; s. Benjamin F. and Evelyn (Benner) S.; B.S., U.S. Naval Acad., 1922; m. Vella Griffith Brittein, Feb. 1930; 1 dau., Nancy (Mrs. Richard Sherman); m. 2d, Valerie Bettis, 1959. Resigned USN, 1922; advt. and promotion exec. Paramount Theatres, Detroit, 1928-32; advt. mgr. Loew's Theatres and Metro-Goldwyn-Mayer, N.Y.C., 1932-41; asst. to pres. Columbia Pictures, Los Angeles, 1946-48, dir. advt. and publicity, 1948-52; mng. dir. Pub. Relations Mgmt. Corp., 1952-54; now chmn. Arthur Schmidt & Assos., N.Y.C. Served from lt. comdr. to comdr., USNR, 1941-46; dep. dir. Naval Photog. Services, 1943-45. Mem. Pub. Relations Soc. Am. Clubs: Army and Navy (Washington); New York Yacht, Union League (N.Y.C.). Home: New York City NY Died June 7, 1969.

SCHMIDT, EDWARD CHARLES mech. engr.; b. Jersey City, N.J., May 14, 1874; s. John Frederick and Katharine (Bisbord) S.; M.E., Stevens Inst. Tech., Hoboken, N.J., 1895; m. Violet Delille Jayne, June 15, 1904; 1 dau., Katharine. In employ of Kalbfleisch Chem. Co., New York and Buffalo, 1895-96; with C. W. Hunt Co., New York, 6 mos., 1896; in steam dept., as asst. to mech. engr., Edison Electric Illuminating Co., Brooklyn, 1897; with Am. Stoker Co., New York, 6 mos., 1898; instr. in machine design, later instr. and asst. prof. ry. engring. and experimental engring.. U. of Ill., 1898-1903 (made many tests with 2 ry. dynamometer cars owned by U. of Ill., I.C. R.R. and C.,C.,C.&St.L. Ry.); asst. engr. Am. Hoist & Derrick Co., St. Paul, Minn., 1903-04; engr. of tests, Kerr Turbine Co., Wellsville, N.Y., 1904-06; asso. prof. and prof. ry. engring., U. of Ill., July 1, 1906-Apr. 12, 1919. Commd. maj., Ordnance Dept. U.S. Army, Aug. 11, 1917; served in N.Y. Dist. Ordnance Office, and on detached service in U.S. Fuel Adminstrn. and U.S. R.R. Adminstrn.; discharged, July 16, 1919. Mech. engr. North American Co., New York, 1919-21; prof. ry. engring. and head of dept., U. of Ill., 1921-40, prof. ry. engring. emeritus since Sept. 1, 1940. Mem. Am. Soc. M.E., mech. div. of Am. Ry. Assn., Western Ry. Club, Ry. Fuel and Traveling Engrs. Assn., Soc. Promotion Engring. Edn.,

Tau Beta Pi, Sigma Xi, etc. Club: University. Author of numerous articles, reports, etc., in the tech. press and trans. tech. socs. Home: 1 University Pl., Apt. 19C, New York, N.Y. Died Mar. 21, 1942.

SCHMIDT, ERWIN RUDOLPH surgeon; b. Alma, Wis., Dec. 19, 1890; s. George and Lina (Ochsner) S.; A.B., U. of Wis., 1913; M.D., Washington U. Med. Sch., 1916; m. Mary Adelaide Newlove, May 7, 1919; children—Erwin Rudolph, Mary Allison, Margot Ochsner, Courtland Mercer. Intern, Barnes Hosp., St. Louis, Mo., 1916-17; surg. asst. Augustana Hosp., Chicago, 1917 and 1919-21, on surg. staff, 1925-26; exchange asst. Maria Hosp., Stockholm, Sweden, 1921-22, U. of Frankfurt, Germany, 1922-23; in practice at Billings, Mont., 1923-25; prof. of surgery, U. of Wis. Med. Sch. and chief surgeon Wis. U. Hosps., since 1926. Served as capt. Med. Res. Corps, U.S. Army, World War; later maj. M.R.C. Licensed by Am. Bd. of Surgery. Fellow of American College of Surgeons; Fellow in American Br. of Internat. Soc. of Surg.; mem. A.M.A., Am. Surg. Assn., Am. Assn. Traumatic Surgery, Western Surg. Association, Am. Society Univ. Profs., Wis. State and Dane County med. socs., Wis. Acad. of Science, Arts and Letters, Wis. State Hist. Soc., Central Surg. Assn., Minn. (hon.), Wis. Surg. Socs., Swiss-Am. Hist. Soc., Terre Haute Acad. of Medicine (hon.), Chi Phi, Nu Sigma Nu, Sigma Sigma, Alpha Omega Alpha, Sigma Xi, Phi Kappa Phi. Episcopalian. Club: University. Writer of articles on med. subjects. Home: 1937 Arlington Place, Madison 5. Office: 1300 University Av., Madison 6, Wis. Died July 9, 1961; buried Madison.

SCHMIDT, FRANCIS ALBERT football coach; b. Downs, Kan., Dec. 3, 1885; s. Francis Walter and Emma Katherine (Mohrbacher) S.; LL.B., U. of Neb., 1907; m. Evelyn Keesee, June 9, 1926. Admitted to Neb. bar, 1907; practiced in Neb. and Kan., 1907-10; coach of athletic sports in Arkansas City, Kan., to 1915; dir. of athletics and athletics coach, Kendall Coll., 1915-19, U. of Tulsa, 1920-21, U. of Ark., 1922-28; head football and basketball coach, Texas Christian U., 1929-33; head football coach, Ohio State U., 1934-40; head football coach, U. of Idaho, since 1941. Served capt. 347th Inf., 87th Div., U.S. Army, 1917-19; with A.E.F., 12 months; head bayonet instr. for 87th Div.; also capt. 50th Inf. Regular Army. Formerly mem. Nat. Basketball Com. of U.S. and Canada. Mem. Am. Football Coaches Assn., Am. Legion, Sigma Alpha Epsilon, Phi Delta Phi, Theta Nu Epsilon. Mason (K.T., 32 deg., Shriner), Elk. Mem. Rotary Internat. Home: 605 Moore Av., Moscow, Idaho. Died Sept. 19, 1944.

SCHMIDT, HARRY Marine Corps officer; b. Holdrege, Neb., Sept. 25, 1886; s. William Henry and Nettie (Anderson) S.; ed. Neb. State Normal Sch., Kearney, Army and Navy Prep Sch., Washington, D.C., Sch. of Application, U.S. Marine Corps, 1909-10, Field Officers Sch. Quantico, Va., 1922-23, Command and Gen. Staff Sch., Ft. Leavenworth, Kan., 1931-32; m. Doris L. Körner, July 27, 1913; children—Bernice E. (wife of Lt. Col. W. R. Wendt, U.S. M.C.), Richard K. (lt. col. U.S.M.C.). Commd. 2 lt. U.S. M.C., Aug. 17, 1909, and advanced through grades to coll, 1937; placed on eligible list as head of Paymasters Dept. with rank of brig. gen., 1938; selected brig. gen. of line, Oct. 29, 1941; fgn. duty in Guam, China, Philippine Islands and Nicaragua and at sea on various ships; served in cruiser and transport force during World War I; asst. paymaster, 1933-37, and 1938-41; promoted maj. gen., 1942; comd. 4th Marine Div. which captured Roi Namur and assisted in capture of Saipan, 1943; comdr. gen. 1944, 5th Amphibious Corps; comd. 5th Amphibious Corps in occupation of Japan; at capture of Tinian and Iwo Jima; comd. all forces ashore at Tinian and Iwo Jima; promoted lt. gen. Mar. 1, 1946; gen. commanding San Diego Area; ret. with rank of lt. gen., advanced to rank of gen., July 1, 1949. Decorated Navy Cross, D.S.M. (3), Legion of Merit, Bronze Star Medal, Presidential Unit Citation, Navy Unit Commendation, Marine Corps Expeditionary Medal (3), Mexican Service, Yangtse, Service, World War I (with escort clasp), 2d Nicaraguan Campaign, China Service, Am. Theater, Am. Defense, Asiatic Theater, World War II and Occupation (Japan) medals (U.S.), Medal of Merit, D.S.M. (Nicaragua), Mem. Soc. Cruiser and Transport Force. Heroes of 1776, Sojourner. Mason. Clubs: Army and Navy (Washington); San Diego (San Diego). Home: 3105 Elliott St., San Diego, Cal. Died Feb. 10, 1968.

SCHMIDT, HERBERT WILLIAM physician, med. dir.; b. Red Wing, Minn., Feb. 23, 1904; s. Edward William and Inga (Eistensen) S.; B.A., St. Olaf Coll., 1926; M.D., U. Minn., 1932, M.S., 1938; m. Kathleen Campbell, Nov. 27, 1937; children—William Alexander, Jean Elizabeth, Judith Kathleen. Intern Mpls. Gen. Hosp., 1932-33; fellow Mayo Found., 1934-36, instr. to asso. prof., 1939-57, prof. medicine, 1957-64; cons. physician Mayo Clinic, 1936-48, head sect. medicine, 1948-62, sr. cons. internal medicine, 1962-64; med. dir. Minn. Mining and Mfg. Co., 1964-66. Bd. govs. Mayo Clinic, 1959-60; bd. regents St. Olaf Coll., 1960-65. Served from maj. to lt. col. M.C., AUS, 1943-46. Mem. A.M.A., Am., Internat. bronchoesophegol. assns., Am. Gastroscopic Soc., Am. Assn. Thoracic Surgery, Am. Thoracic Soc., Minn. Thoracic Soc. (pres. 1957), Central Soc. Clin. Research, Chest Club, Sigma Xi. Lutheran (bd. trustees). Contbr. articles to med. jours. Home: 713 Park Av., Mahtomedi, Minn. 55115. Office; 2501 Hudson Blvd., St. Paul. Died Apr. 6, 1966.

SCHMIDT, PETER PAUL, physician; b. Phila., Apr. 26, 1912; s. Joseph M. and Anna (Skafarek) S.; B.A., N.Y.U., 1933; M.D., L.I. Coll. Medicine, 1937; m. Mary Ann Campanaro, Oct. 1, 1939; children—Cristina, Lucy, Victoria. Intern at Kings County Hospital, 1937-38; resident pulmonary diseases Riverside Hosp., N.Y.C., 1938-40; resident internal medicine Kennedy Gen. Hosp., 1947-49; with VA, 1941-42, 46-49, cardiologist, clin. dir., chief of medicine, 1946-47, 49-50, part time pulmonary clinic. Served from 1st lt. to maj., M.C., AUS, 1942-46; ETO. Mem. Am., N.Y. State, Nassau County med. assns., Am. Fedn. Clin. Research, Nassau Soc. Internal Medicine. Diplomate Am. Bd. Internal Medicine. Address: Merrick NY Died Sept. 11, 1969; interred Calvary Cemetery Woodside NY

SCHMIDT, WILLIAM RICHARD army officer; b. Verdigre, Neb., Oct. 14, 1889; s. Joseph Karl and Anna (Haman) S.; B.S., U.S. Mil. Acad., 1913, Inf. Sch., 1927, Command and Gen. Staff Sch., 1928; Army War Coll., 1931, Army Indsl. Coll., 1932, Chem. Warfare Sch., 1931; m. Helen Munn Goodier, Apr. 24, 1919; children—Helen Jane, Suzanne. Commd. 2d lt., 1913, advanced through grades to maj. gen., 1942; Mexican Border, 1913-17, 8th Div., 1918; instr. U.S. Mil. Acad., 1921-23; Hawaii, 1923-26, 1938-40; War Dept. Gen. Staff, 1934-38; comd. 39th U.S. Inf., 1940-41; comdg. gen. 76th Inf. Div. from Dec. 13, 1942 to Aug. 2, 1945; comdg. gen. 3d Inf. Div., Aug. 3, 1945 to May 20, 1946; chief of staff, 3d U.S. Army, May 20, 1946 to Feb. 15, 1947; dep. comdg. gen. U.S. Constabulary, Feb. 16-May 30, 1947; mem. Personnel Bd., Sec. of War, June 1947-July 1948; comdg. gen. 101st Airborne Div., July 1948-May 1949. Awarded D.S.M., Silver Star, Legion of Merit and Bronze Star (U.S.); Legion of Honor and Croix de Guerre with Palm (France); Order of Orange-Nassau with Swords (Grand Officer) (Netherlands); War Cross (Czechoslovakia); Croix de Gueere with Palm (Belgium); awarded Estrella de Abdon Calderon (second class) from Republic Ecuador. Club: Army-Navy Country (Washington). Address: care Adj. Gen., War Dept., Washington. Died July 1966.

SCHMITZ, DIETRICH, banker; b. Seattle, Wash., Oct. 25, 1890; s. Ferdinand and Emma (Althof) S.; ed. public schools, Seattle, Wash., student University of Wisconsin, 1913-14; m. Margaret Huteson, October 20, 1920; children—Gloria Gretchen, Alan Frederic, Margaret Ann. With Union Savings & Trust Co., Seattle, 1907-14, William A. Read & Co., Chicago, 1915-16, Union Nat. Bank, Seattle, 1916-24 (v.p. 1921-24); v.p. Nat. Bank of Commerce, Seattle, 1924-28, Pacific Nat. Bank, 1928-34; pres. Pacific Nat. Co., 1928-34; pres. and trustee Wash. Mutual Savings Bank, Seattle, Washington, 1934-57, chairman of the board and trustee, 1958-68, honorary chairman and trustee, 1968-70; exec. com., dir. Pacific Nat. Bank; dir., chmn. finance com. Gen. Ins. Co. Am., 1929-66; trustee No. Life Ins. Co.; treas. Seattle Found. Served as ensign, later lt. (j.g.) U.S. Navy, overseas duty with Atlantic Cruiser and Transport Force, 1917-19. Mem. Seattle Bd. Edn., 1928-61 (pres. 1932, 36, 37, 42, 46, 51, 53, 60); mem. coun. of adminstrn. Nat. Assn. of Mut. Savs. Banks, 1934-56; adv. com. Children's Orthopedic Hosp.; chairman King County War Finance (now Savs. Bonds) coms., 1941-70. Mem. Wash. Bankers Assn. (v.p. 1953-54, pres. 1954-55), Am. Bankers Assn. (state v.p. 1952-53), Phi Gamma Delta. Republican. Clubs: Rainier, University, Washington Athletic, Seattle Yacht. Home: Seattle WA Died Apr. 11, 1970; buried Acacia WA

SCHMON, ARTHUR ALBERT business exec.: b. Newark, May 10, 1895; s. Peter Paul and W. (Schaefer) S.; A.B., Princeton, 1917; m. Eleanor Celeste Reynolds, Aug. 12, 1919 (Dec. Apr. 1963); children—Richard Reynolds (A.U.S., killed in action, France, 1944), Robert McCormick. Plant mgr. Ont. Paper Co., Ltd., Shelter Bay, Que., Can., 1919-23, mgr. woodlands, P.Q., 1923-25, 2d v.p., 1927-30, gen. mgr. since 1930, dir. since 1931, pres., 1933-62, chmn., pres., 1962, chmn., chief exec. officer, 1963-—; pres., dir., gen. mgr. Que. North Shore Paper Co., 1938-62, chmn., pres., 1962, chmn., chief exec. officer, 1963-—; chmn., chief exec. officer Marlhill Mines, Ltd., Que. & Ont. Transportation Co., Ltd., Baie Comeau Co.; pres. Ill. Atlantic Corp.; chmn. bd. Manicouagan Power Co., St. Raymond Paper Ltd.; dir. Royal Bank of Can., vice chmn. bd. Canadian British Aluminum Co., Ltd.; Foster Wheeler, Ltd., Tribune Co. (Chgo.), Indsl. Acceptance Corp., Ltd., News Syndicate Co., Inc., N.Y.; chmn. adv. bd. Can. Trust Co., Huron & Erie Mortgage Corp. (St. Catharines, Ont. and dist.). Dir. Great Lakes Waterways Development Assn.; v.p., dir. Lower St. Lawrence and Gulf Development Assn. Trustee McCormick-Patterson Trust, Robert R. McCormick Charitable Trust, Cantigny Trust; president, director Cantigny 1st Div. Mus. Found. Chmn., bd. govs., chmn. exec. com. St. Catharines Gen. Hospital. Honorary gov. McMaster U., Hamilton, Ont.; gov. Laval U., Quebec, Ridley College, St. Catharines, Ont.; chmn. bd. St. Catharines Riding and Driving Club, Ltd. Served as battery officer, bn. operations officer, adj., later regl. adj., 5th Field Artillery, AEF, 1917-19. Mem. Canadian Pulp and Paper Assn. (exec. bd. and tech. sect.), T.A.P.P.I., Nat. Alumni Assn. Princeton U. (exec. com.), Princeton Alumni Assn. Can. (exec. com.), Canadian Mfrs. Assn. (nat. exec. council). Office: care Ont. Paper Co. Ltd., Thorold, Ont., Can. Died Mar. 18, 1964; buried Victoria Lawn Cemetery, St. Catharines, Ont., Can.

SCHNABEL, TRUMAN GROSS, physician, educator; b. Georgetown, Pa., Feb. 7, 1886; s. Edwin Daniel and Emeline (Woodring) S.; A.B., Lehigh U., 1907; M.D., U. Pa., 1911; m. Hildegard Rohner, Oct. 21, 1916;children—Truman Gross, Elizabeth S. (Mrs. Chamblin). Intern Hosp. U. Pa., 1911-13; practice internal medicine, Phila., since 1913; tchr. med. sch. U. Pa., 1913-51, emeritus prof. medicine, 1951-71; former staff mem. Howard Hosp.; dir. out-patient dept. medicine Hosp. U. Pa.; cons. Phila. Gen., Presbyn., Rush, Kensington and Nazareth hosps. Mem. com. Am. Found. Studies in Govt. since 1934. Recipient of Strittmatter award, Philadelphia County Medical Society, 1960; also Shaffrey award from St. Joseph's College in 1963. Served as major M.C., Army of the U.S., 1917-19. Diplomate Am. Bd. Internal Medicine (chmn. 1949-50). Fellow A.C.P. (v.p. 1956-57), Phila. Coll. Physicians; mem. Am. (chmn. sect. internal medicine 1953), Pa. (speaker 1940-44), Phila. Co. (pres. 1953) med. socs., Am. Gastro Enterological Assn., Am. Clin. and Climatol. Assn., Phila. Pathol. Soc., S.R., Sigma Nu, Alpha Omega Alpha, Phi Alpha Sigma Sigma Xi. Author articles in med. jours. Home: Wynnewood PA Died Aug. 27, 1971.

SCHNEIDER, CARL E(DWARD) computing machine mfg. exec.; b. Palmyra, Mo., Oct. 25, 1903; s. Edward Fred and Adelia (Baker) S.; student pub. schs.; m. Elizabeth V. Rooney, Mar. 5, 1935. Accounting supr. Bklyn. Edison Co., 1925-29; coordinator methods, personnel dir. Nat. Life Ins. Co. of Vt., Montpelier, 1937-42; sales, sales promotion Burroughs Corps., Detroit, 1929-37, dir. indsl. relations, 1947-51, v.p., 1951-57, v.p., gen. mgr., 1957-60; v.p., group exec. Graphic Systems Group; gen. mgr. Todd Co. div. of Burroughs Corp.; dir. Genesee Valley Union Trust Co. Served as lt. col. Ordnance, AUS, 1942-46. Clubs: Oak Hill Country, Rochester (Rochester, N.Y.). Home: 2415 East Av. Office: Burroughs Corp., Todd Div., Rochester, N.Y. Died Nov. 29, 1966.

SCHNEIDER, EDWARD CHRISTIAN biologist; b. Wapello, Ia., Aug. 21, 1874; s. John George and Augusta J. (Bauersfeld) S.; B.S., Tabor Coll., Ia., 1897; Ph.D., Yale, 1901; Sc.D., U. of Denver, 1914; M.P.E., International Y.M.C.A. Coll., 1923; Sc.D., Colorado Coll., 1932; m. Elsie M. Faurote, June 24, 1902; children—Edwin George, Marion Elsie (Mrs. R. E. Joyce). Instr. chemistry, 1897-99, prof. biology and physiol. chemistry, 1901-03, Tabor Coll.; prof. biology, 1903-07, head prof., 1907-19, Colo. Coll.; Daniel Ayres prof. biology, Wesleyan U., Conn., 1919-44, retired June 1944. John Jeffries award for contrbts. to aeromedicine Inst. Aeronautical Sciences, 1942. Member and sec. board control Conn. Agrl. Expt. Station, New Haven, Conn. Physiologist in charge of dept. Med. Research Lab., Air Service, U.S. Army, and later, officer in charge same to Aug. 1918; capt. Sanitary Corps, Dec. 1917, maj., June 1918; mem. Med. Research Bd. No. 1, A.E.F., Aug. 1918-Mar. 1919. Dir. physiology, Sch. of Aviation Medicine, Mitchel Field, L.I., N.Y., 1919-26; lt. col., S.R.C., 1920-30. Fellow A.A.A.S., Am. Phys. Edn. Assn.; mem. Am. Physiol. Soc., Am. Soc. Biol. Chemists, Am. Pub. Health Assn., Soc. Exptl. Biology and Medicine, Soc. Am. Bacteriologists, Sigma Xi, Phi Beta Kappa, Beta Theta Pi. Author: Physiology of Muscular Activity, 1933, revised edition, 1939 revised (with P. K. Karpovick), 1948. Part Author: Report of Pike's Peak Expdn., 1911; Manual of the Med. Research Laboratory, Air Service, publishing chiefly studies of the influence of high altitudes and low oxygen on mankind, aviation physiology, and effects of physical exercise and training. Home: 25 Gordon Pl., Middletown, Conn. Died Oct. 3, 1954.

SCHNEIDER, GEORGE, chemist, textile co. exec.; b. Bklyn., Mar. 28, 1897; s. Peter and Rose (Gelden) S.; grad. U. Buffalo, 1918; m. Gladys Bower, Jan. 1, 1919; 1 dau., Dorothy (Mrs. Henry Staehling); m. 2d, Hazel McIntyre, Sept. 4, 1956. Chemist, Celanese Corp. of Am., 1920-45, v.p., dir., 1945-50, sr. v.p., 1950-59, vice chmn., 1959-71; dir. Canadian Chem. Co., Celanese Mexicana, Celanese Colombiana, Celanese Venezolana. Served as lt., C.W.S., U.S. Army, 1917-18. Fellow Am. Inst. Chemists; mem. Am. Inst. Chem. Engrs., Soc. Chem. Industry. Clubs: Chemists (N.Y.C.); Rock Spring (N.J.). Home: Short Hills NJ Died Nov. 1971.

SCHOBECK, ARTHUR ELLWYN iron mfr.; b. Jamestown, N.Y., Feb. 1, 1893; s. Olof Bernard and Hilma Christina (Erickson) S.; grad. pub. schs. of Jamestown; m. Mildred Vanstrom, Sept. 29, 1928; 1 dau., Ann Elizabeth (Mrs. Arthur P. Darling). With Jamestown Malleable Iron Corp., 1920-—, pres., gen. manager, director, 1930-—; executive vice president, director of The Blackstone Corp., Jamestown; dir. Jamestown Telephone Corp., Jamestown Mutual Ins. Co., Chautauqua Nat. Bank & Trust Co. Served as capt. U.S. Army, 1917-19. Mem. Asso. Industries N.Y. State (dir., mem. exec. com.). Mason. Home: 35 Sunset Av., Lakewood, N.Y. Office: Jamestown Malleable Iron Corp., Jamestown, N.Y. Died May 2, 1962.

SCHODER, ERNEST WILLIAM, educator, hydraulic engr.; b. Dewey, Fidalgo Island, Wash., Aug. 17, 1879; s. Herman and Sophia (Huntemann) S.; B.S. and B.S. in Mining, U. of Washington, 1900; Ph.D., Cornell U., 1903; unmarried. In charge Hydraulic Lab., Cornell U., Sch. of Civil Engring., 1904; asst. prof. exper. hydraulics, Cornell U., 1904-19, prof. 1919-47, emeritus, 1947-68. Was hydraulic expert for U.S., State of N.Y., municipal and corporate interests; consultant for Army Engrs. on river models, 1937-38. Commd. capt. engrs., U.S. Army, Aug. 1917; instr. and engr. officer Camp Lee, Petersburg, Va.; asst. dir. of training, Camp Humphreys, Va.; spl. duty in Office of Chief of Engrs., Washington. Fellow A.A.A.S., Am. Soc. C.E.; mem. Soc. Am. Mil. Engrs., Phi Gamma Delta, Sigma Xi, Phi Beta Kappa. Author: Hydraulics Section, Marks' Mechanical Engrs'. Handbook (1st 4 edits.); Hydraulics (with F. M. Dawson), also author of papers on exptl. studies of pipes and wires in Trans. Am. Soc. C.E. and M.E. since 1902. Home: Seattle WA Died May 16, 1968; buried Lakeview Cemetery, Seattle WA

SCHOELLKOPF, J. FRED IV, corp. exec.; b. Buffalo, Oct. 1, 1910; s. Jacob Frederick Jr. and Olive C. (Abbott) S.; B.A., Cornell U., 1935; m. Patricia Calkins, Aug. 28, 1935; children—J. Fred, V. Marion, Sandra, Phoebe, Patricia. Gen. sales mgr., asst. sec. Bell Aircraft Corp., 1935-42; dir., chmn. exec. com. Crescent Niagara Corp., 1960-68; sr. and ltd. partner Schoellkopf & Co., 1947-50; pres., dir. Niagara Share Corp., Buffalo, 1950-61, chmn. bd., dir., 1961-69; pres., dir. Marine Midland Corp., 1966-68; chmn. bd., dir. Marine Midland Banks, Inc.; v.p., dir. Marine Midland Bldgs. Corp., Marine Midland Properties Corp.; director Gen. Signal Co., Marine Midland Trust Co., Western N.Y., Seventy Niagara Services, Incorporated Ont. Marine, Inc., Carborundum Company, Buffalo Ins. Corp. (Chgo.), Dunlop Tire & Rubber Corp., Umont Mining, Inc., N.Y. Telephone Co., Marine Midland Internat. Corp., Baseball Holding Corp. Dir. mem. finance com. Buffalo Soc. Natural scis.; trustee YMCA Buffalo; bd. trustees, dirs., United Fund Buffalo and Erie County, Dir. Buffalo Fine Arts Acad., Albright-Knox Art Gallery, Greater Buffalo Development Foundation; trustee Berkshire Sch. Served as lt. col. USAAF, 1942-45, inactive Res., 1945-69. Decorated Distinguished Flying Cross, Air Medal with 6 oak leaf clusters. Mem. Buffalo Hist. Soc. (life), Am. Inst. Banking, Navy League (dir. Niagara Frontier council), Newcomen Soc. Clubs: Mid-Day, Buffalo, Bond, Pack, Buffalo Athletic, Thursday, Chairman's (Buffalo); Lunch, Fifth Avenue, Governor's (N.Y.C.); Wanakah Country (Hamburg, N.Y.); Metropolitan (Washington). Home: Lake View NY Died Dec. 7, 1969.

SCHOFIELD, FRANK HERMAN naval officer; b. Jerusalem, N.Y., Jan. 4, 1869; grad. U.S. Naval Acad., 1890; m. Clara Isabel Cox, July 1, 1893; 1 son, Franklin Perry (U.S. Naval Reserve). Commissioned ensign, July 1, 1892; advanced through grades to rear admiral, Feb. 4, 1924. Exec. officer, Hawk, Spanish-Am. War, 1898; duty with Bur. of Ordnance, Navy Dept., 1905-07; comd. Supply, 1907-09, Concord, 1909; exec. officer New Hampshire, 1909-11; at Naval War Coll., 1911-13; exec. officer Arkansas, 1913-14; comd. Isla de Luzon, 1914; exec. officer Delaware, 1914-15; comd. Chester, 1915-16; assigned duty Office Chief of Naval Operations, May 10, 1916; staff of comdr. U.S. Naval forces in Europe, Dec. 1917-Dec. 1918; U.S. naval advisory staff to Peace Commn., Paris, Dec. 1918-May 1919; made comdr. U.S.S. Texas, July 1919; mem. Gen. Bd., Navy Dept., 1921-23; comdr. Destroyer Squadrons, Battle Fleet, 1924-26; head of War Plans Div., Office of Chief of Naval Operations, 1926-29; mem. Naval Advisory Staff, Geneva Conf., 1927; apptd. comdr. Battleship Div., June 1929; comdr. Battle Fleet, 1930; comdr. in chief U.S. Fleet, 1931; retired, Feb. 1, 1933. Address: Navy Dept., Washington, D.C. Died Feb. 20, 1942.

SCHOFIELD, JOHN MCALLISTER lt. gen. U.S.A.; b. Gerry, N.Y., Sept. 29, 1831; s. Rev. James and Caroline (McAllister) S.; ed. there and in Bristol and Freeport, Ill.; entered West Point, 1849; grad. 1853; LL.D., Chicago U. Served in garrison in S.C. and Fla. until 1855; asst. prof. natural philosophy West Point, 1855-60; under leave of absence, prof. physics, Washington U., St. Louis, until April 1861; in Civil War became brig. gen., Nov. 1861, and maj. gen., Nov. 1862, of vols.; comd. a dept. and army in the field; in the Atlanta campaign and later comd. at battle of Franklin, Tenn., for which he was made brig. gen. and bvt. maj. gen. in regular army. After war became div. comdr.; was sec. of war, 1868-69; comd. the Army of the U.S., 1888-95; was made lt. gen., 1895; retired from active service by operation of law, Sept. 29, 1895. Comdr.-in-chief Mil. Order Loyal Legion, 1900; re-elected, 1902. Author: Forty-six Years in the Army, 1897. Address: Bar Harbor, Me. Died 1906.

SCHOLL, JOHN WILLIAM (shul), prof. German; b. near Springfield, O., Aug. 17, 1869; s. Harrison and Catharine (Ryman) S.; A.B., Valparaiso (Ind.) Coll., 1896; A.B., U. of Mich., 1901, A.M., 1902, Ph.D., 1905; m. Clara Harwood, Dec. 20, 1896; children—Evelyn Harwood, Dorothy Mayhew, Catherine Daggett. Prof. modern langs., Chattanooga Normal Sch., 1896-1900; instr. German, 1902-12, U. of Mich., asst. prof., 1912-22, asso. prof., 1922-39, emeritus since 1939. Mem. Modern Lang. Assn. America, Phi Beta Kappa, Modern Lang. Research Assn. of Eng., Mich. Acad. Science, Arts and Letters (v.p. sect. for letters, 1922-24), Michigan Authors' Assn. (exec. council; pres. 1932-34). Detroit Philosophical Soc., Mich. Poetry Soc. Club: Research (Ann Arbor). Republican. Unitarian. Author: The Light-Bearer of Liberty, 1899; Social Tragedies, and Other Verse, 1900; Ode to the Russian People, 1907; Hesper-Phosphor and Other Poems, 1910; Children of the Sun (poems), 1916; Scholl, Sholl, Shull Genealogy, 1930; Edith—A Sonnet Sequence, 1930; The Nymph and the Rose, 1931; In Gaea's Garden, 1932; The Rose Jar, 1936; The Thinker, 1940; On the Road to Joyeuse Garde, 1942; Yellow Dwarf and Haughty Rose, 1942; Strenae, 1943; The Unknown Soldier and Other Poems, 1950. Contributor of notable letters to New York Times, from beginning of the war, 1914, advocating complete identification of German-Americans with Am. interests and ideals. Lecturer on patriotic topics. Home: 917 Forest Av., Ann Arbor, Mich. Died Sept. 2, 1952.

SCHOLLE, HARDINGE, retired cons.; b. St. Paul, Minnesota, Apr. 30, 1896; s. Gustave and Lillian (Jones) S.; ed. La Villa, Switzerland, 1909-12; Coite School, Munich, 1912-14; A.B., Harvard, 1918; m. Elizabeth Klapp, Apr. 10, 1917; children—Margaret Lillian (Mrs. Nicholas Forell), Oliver Coleman; m. 2d, Eleanor Peabody, Apr. 24, 1930. Asst., decorative arts dept., Metropolitan Museum of Art, N.Y. City, 1921-23; asst., curator decorative arts dept., Chicago Art Inst., 1923-26; dir. Museum of the City of N.Y., 1926-51; cons. Nat. Trust for Historic Preservation in U.S., Washington, 1951-63. Corpl. 437th engineer detachment, 2d lt. Mil. Intelligence Div., 1918. Clubs: Harvard, Grolier (New York City). Home: San Mateo CA Died May 1969.

SCHOOLER, LEWIS surgeon; b. Bartholomew Co., Ind., Mar. 17, 1848; s. Benjamin Harrison and Mary (Hughes) S.; ed. in Ind. pub. schs. and coll. (now extinct) at Hartsville, Ind.; grad. Ky. Sch. of Medicine; (LL.D., Drake U.); m. Alice J. Hoskins, of Polk Co., Ia., May 31, 1876. Pvt. Co. A, 145th Ind. Inf. in Civil War; maj. chief surgeon 2d Div., 3d Army Corps, Spanish-Am. War. Mem. A.M.A., Ia. State Med. and Western Surg. and Gynaecol. socs., Nat. Geog. Soc. Republican. Home: 1721 Pleasant St. Office: 203 Citizens' Nat. Bank Bldg., Des Moines, Ia.

SCHOONMAKER, FREDERIC PALEN (shoon'ma-ker), judge; b. Limestone, Cattaraugus County, N.Y., Mar. 11, 1870; s. Elijah R. and Eliza (Palen) S.; student, Alfred U.; A.B., Cornell U., 1891; LL.D., Alfred, 1917; studied law under Judge James Schoonmaker, of St. Paul, Minn., and Col. W. W. Brown, of Bradford, Pa.; m. Jessie L. Brown, June 23, 1892 (died 1921); children—Susie Rae (Mrs. Walter G. Blaisdell), Fay Lillian (Mrs. Laurent Erny), Max Van Palen; m. 2d, Virginia Elliott Taylor, Dec. 23, 1937. Mem. Brown & Schoonmaker, of Bradford, Pa., 1894-1913, then Brown, Schoonmaker & Nash; became judge of U.S. Dist. Court, Western Dist. of Pa., Jan. 2, 1923. Joined Pa. Nat. Guard, 1912; capt. 16th Regt., Mexican Border service, 1916-17; entered U.S. service, 1917, with regt. as 112th Inf., 28th Div., A.E.F., also served as asst. chief of staff G-2, 28th Div. and 92d Div., A.E.F.; detached duty with Army Gen. Staff, Langres, France, also with 2d Can. Div., B.E.F.; hon. discharged Feb. 1919, as lt. col. inf. Mem. Psi Upsilon, Phi Beta Kappa. Mason, Odd Fellow, Elk. Republican. Baptist. Clubs: Bradford, University, Athletic (Pittsburgh, Pa.); Psi Upsilon (New York). Home: Bradford, Pa. Died Sept. 6. 1945.

SCHOULER, JOHN rear admiral U.S.N.; b. Lowell, Mass., Nov. 30, 1846; s. William and Frances (Warren) S.; brother of James S.; apptd. to U.S. Naval Acad. from Mass., 1861, grad. 1864; m. Hope Day. Aug. 31, 1881. Promoted ensign, Nov. 1, 1866; master, Dec. 1, 1866; lt., Mar. 12, 1868; lt. comdr., June 3, 1869; comdr., June 8, 1885; capt., June 5, 1898; retired with rank of rear admiral, Nov. 21, 1899. Summer of 1864, was attached to the Marblehead, in pursuit of the Confederate steamers Florida and Tallahassee; served on Colorado, 1865-67; Frolic, 1867-68; Portsmouth, 1869-70; exec. officer of Terror, 1871-72; in Hydrographic Office, 1872-73; Naval Acad., 1873-76, 1880-84, 1885-88; exec. officer Essex, 1876-79, Lancaster, 1884-85; comd. Portsmouth, 1889-91; Bureau of Navigation, 1891-92; mem. Naval Examining and Retiring Bds., 1893-95; chief of staff, N. Atlantic Fleet, flagship New York, 1895-97; spl. duty Bureau of Navigation, 1897-99. Home: Catskill, N.Y. Died Dec. 26, 1917.

SCHRIVER, EDMUND army officer; b. York, Pa., Sept. 16, 1812; s. Daniel and Rebecca (Zinn) S.; grad. U.S. Mil. Acad., 1833. Brevetted 2d lt. 2d Arty., U.S. Army, 1833, commd. 2d lt., 1834; asst. instr. inf. tactics U.S. Mil. Acad., 1834-35; served in office of adj. gen., 1835-41, asst. adj. gen., 1838-41; commd. 1st lt., 1836; brevetted capt., 1838; promoted capt., 1842; resigned, 1846; treas. Saratoga and Washington R.R., 1847-52, Saratoga, & Schenectady R.R. (both N.Y.C.), 1847-61; treas. Rensselaer & Saratoga R.R., 1847-61; pres. 1851-61; commd. lt. col. 11th U.S. Inf., 1861; chief of staff 1st Corps, Army of Potomac, 1862-63; commd. col., 1862; served at battles of Cedar Mountain, Chantilly and Manassas; insp. Army of Potomac, 1863-65; at battles of Chancellorsville and Gettysburg; active in Richmond campaign of 1865; brevetted brig. gen., 1864, maj. gen., 1865; in charge of inspector's bur., Washington, D.C., 1865-69, 71-76; insp. U.S. Mil. Acad., 1869-71; insp.-gen. Div. of Pacific, 1876-81; retired, 1881. Died Washington, Feb. 10, 1899; buried Oakwood Cemetery, Troy, N.Y.

SCHROEDER, PAUL LOUIS psychiatrist; b. Hoyleton, Ill., July 6, 1894; s. Simon Phillip and Eunice (Rohlander) S.; B.S., U. Ill., 1917, M.D., 1919; m. Julia Anne Nolen, Sept. 17, 1949; children (by former marriage—Ann, Robert Louis, Marjorie Katherine. Intern Michael Reese Hosp., 1919; jr. physician, later sr. physician Peoria State Hosp., 1919-22; neuro-psychiatrist U.S. Vets. Bur., 1921-22; asst. mng. officer and acting mng. officer Lincoln State Sch. and Colony, 1922-24; psychiatrist Div. of Criminology Dept. of Pub. Welfare, Ill., 1924-30; state criminologist and dir. Ill. Inst. for Juvenile Research, 1930-48; prof., head dept. criminology, med. jurisprudence and social hygiene U. Ill., 1930-48; former prof. psychiatry in charge children's psychiat. services Ill. Neuropsychiat. Inst., U. Ill.; former attending physician Cook County Psychopathic Hosp.; chief psychiat. service St. Joseph's Hosp., Chgo.; former asso. in neurol. Michael Rese Hosp.; clin. prof. psychiatry Emory U. Med. Sch., Atlanta, 1949-—; cons. psychiatrist Ga. Dept. Pub. Health, Child Welfare Assn. (all Atlanta); cons. psychiatrist Ga. Citizens Council; cons. Grady Meml. Hosp., Atlanta, 1949-—; pvt. practice, Atlanta. Dir. Atlanta Child Guidance Clinic, 1953-55, cons., 1955-—. Served in World War I as chief cons. neuropsychiatry, 4th Service Command, World War II; col. M.C., A.U.S., ret. 1946; hon. cons. Neuropsychiatric Div., Office Surgeon Gen., U.S. Army; also psychiat. cons. to Internat. Mil. Tribunal at Nurenberg in trials of war criminals. Awarded Legion of Merit. Mem. State Bd. Pardons and Paroles, 1941-42; bd. edn. Oak Park, 1933-38. Diplomate in psychiatry, also child psychiatry Am. Bd. Psychiatry and Neurology. Fellow Am. Psychiat. Assn.; mem. A.M.A., Assn. Army Consultants, Med. Assn. Ga., So., Ga. psychiat. assns., Atlanta Soc. Neurology and Psychiatry (pres. 1957), Ill. Psychiat. Soc. (life mem.), Am. Orthopsychiatric Assn. (pres. 1940), Internat. Assn. Child Psychiatrists, A.A.A.S., Chgo. Inst. Medicine (life mem.), Am. Legion, Alpha Omega Alpha, Sigma Xi. Presbyn. Co-author: Child Guidance Procedures, 1937; Series II Medicolegal Problems, 1948; Some Observations on School Phobias in Children. Mem. editorial bd. Jour. Criminal Psychopathology, 1940-51. Home: 790 Longwood Dr., N.W., Atlanta 30305. Office: 478 Peachtree St., N.E., Atlanta 30308. Died Oct. 1966.

SCHROEDER, RUDOLPH WILLIAM (shro'der), aviation; b. Chgo., Aug. 14, 1886; s. John August and Nora Ann (Reidy) S.; student Crane Tech. High Sch., Chgo. (about), 1906-07. Engaged in airplane exhbns., 1910-16; aviation engr., Underwriters Labs., 1920-25; supt. Ford Airline, 1925-27; Guggenheim Safe Aircraft Competition, 1927-29; mgr., Chgo. Curtiss Flying Service, 1928-30, Skyharbor Airport, 1930-33; chief airline insp. and asst. dir., Bur. of Air Commerce, 1933-37; v.p. in charge safety, United Airlines, Chgo., 1937-42, now retired. Served in U.S. Army Air Corp., 1916-20; rank of maj.; made seven-mile flight into stratosphere, Feb. 1920; awarded Army Air Force Citation; Distinguished Flying Cross, 1945. Mem. Inst. Aeronautical Science. Methodist. Home: 4136 N. Melvina Av., Chgo. 34. Died 1952.

SCHROEDER, SEATON rear admiral U.S.N.; b. Washington, Aug. 17, 1849; s. Francis and Caroline (Seaton) S.; apptd. to U.S. Naval Acad. from S.C., 1864, grad. 1868; m. Maria C. B. Wainwright, Jan. 16, 1879. Promoted ensign, Apr. 19, 1869, master, July 12, 1870; lt. Oct. 29, 1872; lt. comdr., Sept. 27, 1893; comdr. Mar. 3, 1899; capt., Aug. 10, 1903; rear admiral, July 11, 1908. Served on Saginaw, Pensacola and Benicia, 1868-72. Mem. Commodore John Rodgers' expdn. against Korean forts, 1871, being in landing party and taking part in the several engagements; Canandaigua, Pinta, Mayflower and Swatara, 1873-75; Hydrographic Office, 1875-76, 1880-81; Gettysburg, 1876-78; on leave associated with H. H. Gorringe in removing obelisk from Egypt to New York, 1879-80; Despatch, 1881-82; fish commn. steamer Albatross, 1882-85; Bur of Navigation, Navy Dept., 1886-88; spl. duty with building dynamite cruiser Vesuvius, 1888-90; comd. Vesuvius, 1890-93; Navy Yard, Washington, 1893; mem. Bd. of Inspection and Survey, 1894-96; exec. officer Massachusetts, 1897-99; was advanced 3 numbers in rank "for eminent and conspicuous conduct" in the war with Spain, 1898; duty Navy Yard, Washington, 1899-1900; naval gov. Island of Guam and comdg. Yosemite, 1900-03; chief intelligence officer, 1903-06; comdg. Virginia, 1906-08; comdg. a div. of Atlantic Fleet, 1908-09; comdr.-in-chief Atlantic Fleet, Mar. 1909-June 1911; mem. Gen. Bd. to Aug. 17, 1911, when retired for age; continued on spl. duty in Navy Dept. for 3 yrs. after retirement; hydrographer, Oct. 1917-Mar. 1919. Author: Fall of Maximilian's Empire,

1887. Prize essayist U.S. Naval Inst., 1894; writer of other essays and contbr. to mags. Home: Washington, D.C. Died Oct. 19, 1922.

SCHUH, HENRY FREDERICK clergyman; b. Tacoma, May 30, 1890; s. Dr. Lewis and Mary (Loy) S.; grad. Capital U., Capital Sem., 1915, LL.D. (hon.), 1937; A.M., Toledo U., 1922; LL.D., Carthage, 1951, Augustana, 1953; D.D. (hon.), Warburg Coll., 1955; m. Amelia Koerner, July 11, 1916; children—Mary (Mrs. Stauffer), Virginia (Mrs. Leiter), Emily. Ordained to ministry Luth. Ch., 1915; pastor, Ashland O., 1915-16, Toledo, 1916-30; dir. stewardship, finance Am. Luth. Ch., 1930-50, pres. 1951-—, chmn. policy com., 1954-—. Del. Luth. World Fedn., Lund, Sweden, 1947, Hannover, Germany, 1952, Mpls., 1957; mem. com., div. pub. relations, councillor Nat. Luth. Council, v.p. 1954; mem. Luth. World Service Commn. and exec. com. Luth World Fedn.; mem. central com., mem. exec. com. U.S. Conf. World Council Chs. Home: 1114 Euclaire Av., Columbus 9. Office: 57 E. Main St., Columbus 15, O. Died Dec. 1965.

SCHUIRMANN, ROSCOE ERNEST, naval officer; b. Chenoa, Ill., Dec. 17, 1890; grad. U.S. Naval Acad., 1912; m. Hardinia Taylor; 1 dau., Hardy. Entered U.S. Navy, 1908, and advanced through the grades to rear adm., 1942; ret., 1951. Home: Washington DC Died July 1971; buried Arlington Nat. Cemetery.

SCHULGEN, GEORGE FRANCIS army officer; b. Traverse City, Mich., Apr. 23, 1900; B.S. in Mech. Engring., Mich. Agrl. Coll., 1922; m. Lillian Jacob, May 14, 1932. Commd. 2d lt. Air Service, 1924, and advanced through the grades to brig. gen., 1943; became asst. chief Inspection Sect., Air Corps Material Div., Wright Field, Dayton, O., June 1939; with Operations and Tng. Div. G-3, War Dept. Gen. Staff, Washington, 1941-42; became asst. sec. of the Gen. Staff, 1942; named wing comdr. First Air Force, Phila. Air Defense Wing, Phila., July 1943. Rated command pilot, combat observer, aircraft observer. Chief of staff, First Air Force, Oct. 1943; assigned to Southwest Pacific Theater, Jan. 1944, to Southeast Asia Command as dir. Plans Air, Sept. 1944; dep. dir. Civil Affairs Div., War Dept. Special Staff, July 1945; chief Air Intelligence Requirements Div., Hdqrs. A.A.F., asst. chief of air staff—Jan. 2, 1947. Address: Suttons Bay, Mich. Died Feb. 17, 1955; buried Arlington Nat. Cemetery.

SCHULHOFF, HENRY BERNARD, army engr.; b. Keyport, N.J., Oct. 30, 1904; s. Adolph and Amalia (Feuerlicht) S.; B.S., Rutgers U., 1930, M.S., 1936; M. Esther Graham Bell, May 8, 1938; 1 son, Kenneth Bell. San. engr. Hdqrs. 1st U.S. Army Engrs., 1942-55; v.p. Lanning San. Engring. Co., 1955-58; san. engr. Hdqrs. 1st U.S. Army Engrs., 1958-61, Hdqrs. Eastern Transport Air Force, 1961-64; civil engr. (san.) Office of Post Engr., Ft. Dix. N.J., 1964-68. Fellow Am. Inst. Chemists; mem. Soc. Am. Mil. Engrs. Republican. Presbyn. Home: Yardville NJ Died Mar. 20, 1968.

SCHULL, HERMAN WALTER, army officer; b. Liverpool, Eng., May 30, 1875; s. of Ludolph Morris and Anne Jane (Johnson) S.; brought to U.S., 1880; grad. U.S. Mil. Acad., 1899, Army War Coll., 1923; m. Loraine Edson, Jan. 26, 1901; children—Marion (dec.), Herman Walter, Edson. Commd. 2d lt. 6th Arty., Feb. 15, 1899; promoted through grades to brig. gen., June 3, 1934. Served in artillery in Cuba, 1899-1902; detailed in Ordnance Dept., 1902; served Sandy Hook Proving Ground, N.J., 1902-03, Frankford Arsenal Phila., 1903-06; comdg. officer 73d Co., Coast Artillery, Fort Monroe, Va., also mem. Arty. Bd., 1906-07; duty in Office of Chief of Ordnance, Washington, D.C., 1907-09; asst. to comdg. officer Watertown Arsenal, 1909-10; served Manila (P.I.) Ornance Depot, 1910-13; officer in charge of shops, Springfield Armory, 1914-15; comdg. officer Benicia Arsenal. Calif., 1915-17; acting chief inspection div. Ordnance Dept., 1917-19; comdg. officer, Aberdeen Proving Ground, 1919-22; student Army War Coll., 1922-23; mem. tech. staff, Washington, D.C., 1923-24; comdg. officer, Springfield Armory, Mass., 1924-29, Watervliet Arsenal, N.Y., 1929-32, Rock Island Arsenal, Ill., 1932-34; became chief of mfg. service Ordnance Dept., Washington, with rank of brig. gen., 1934; retired May 31, 1938; recalled to active duty Jan. 26, 1942, relieved Nov. 23, 1943. Awarded D.S.M. (U.S.). Episcopalian. Clubs: Army and Navy, Army-Navy Country (Washington); Rotary of Rock Island Ill. (hon.) Address: Box 2097, Carmel CA

SCHULLINGER, RUDOLPH NICHOLAS, surgeon; b. N.Y.C., Mar. 11, 1896; s. Julius and Alexandrina (Sorg) S.; grad. Lawrenceville Sch., 1913; B.S., Princeton, 1917; M.D., Columbia, 1923; m. Audrey Poole Bender, Mar. 8, 1926; children—John Nicholas (M.D.), Joan S. (Mrs. DeLacy H. Seabrook). Intern Roosevelt Hosp., N.Y.C., 1923-26; practice surgery, N.Y.C., 1926-68; professor clin. surgery Columbia, 1958-61, prof. emeritus clin. surgery, 1961-69; consultant in surgery Presbyterian Hosp., N.Y.C. Charter trustee emeritus of Princeton; trustee of the Brook Found. Served as col., M.C., AUS, World War II; surg. dir. Gen. Hosp. No. 2, 1942-45. Decorated Legion of Merit, 1945. Fellow Am. Surg. Assn., N.Y. Surg. Soc., N.Y. Acad. Medicine; mem. N.Y. Acad. Scis., Alumni Assn. Coll. Physicians and Surgeons, Columbia U. (pres. 1959-60), Alpha Omega Alpha. Presbyn. Clubs: Princeton, University, Century Assn. (N.Y.C.). Home: Woodstock VT Died June 27, 1969; buried Woodlawn Cemetery, New York City NY

SCHULMAN, JACK HENRY scientist; b. Sao Paulo, Brazil, Nov. 22, 1904; s. Henry and Lucy Augusta (Heine) S.; student Haileybury Coll., Eng., 1918-21; diploma chem. engring., Swiss Fed. Engring. U., Zurich, 1926; Ph.D., Cambridge U., 1930, Sc.D., 1940; m. Frances Holt Logie, Sept. 9, 1950. Came to U.S., 1957. Asst. dir. research, dept. colloid sci., Cambridge U., 1937-50, fellow Trinity Hall, 1946-57, dir. Ernest Oppenheimer Lab., dept. colloid sci., 1949-57, readership in surface chemistry, 1950-57; Stanley Thompson prof. chem. metallurgy, Columbia, 1957-—. Dir. Imperial Smelting Corp., London, 1951-57. Mgr. Royal Inst. of Gt. Britain, 1951-56; pres. sci. sect. World Meeting of Surface Activity, Paris, 1954, London, 1957. Decorated Officer Order Brit. Empire, 1945. Mem. Faraday Soc. (council 1949-58, v.p. 1954-56). Clubs: St. James; British University Ski (pres. 1940-57), Kandahar Ski (hon.), (London); Cambridge University Ski (pres. 1935-57), Hawk's (Cambridge). Home: 169 E. 69th St., N.Y.C. 10021. Died June 19, 1967.

SCHULTHEISS, CARL MAX (shoolt'his), artist; b. Nuremberg, Bavaria, Aug. 4, 1885; s. Max and Elisabeth (Hafner) S.; student Sch. of Arts and Crafts, Nuremberg, 1900-04, Royal Acad., Munich, 1904-10; m. Alice Trier, Mar. 23, 1914; 1 son, Peter Max. In U.S. since 1940, U.S. citizen. Artist, painter, etcher, engraver, since 1910. Awarded J. Frederick Talcott prize, 1940; second Pennell Purchase Prize, 1943; John Taylor Arms prize, 1943 and 1944; first Pennell Purchase Prize (Library of Congress), 1944; first Pennell Purchase Prize (Library of Congress), 1945. Gold Medal of Honor, Audubon Artists, 1946; Eyre Medal, Pa. Acad., 1947; Nat. Acad. Prize, 1948; Gold Medal of Honor, Audubon Artists, 1952; National Acad. Prize award, 1952; grant in graphic arts Nat. Inst. Arts and Letters, 1953; John T. Arms Meml. prize award Nat. Acad., 1955, Audubon Artists, 1956, Soc. Am. Graphic Artists, 1957; first graphic prize, Springfield, Mass., 1960. Member N.A.D., Society Am. Graphic Artists (pres. 1948-49), Audubon Artists. Home: 84-44 Beverly Rd., Kew Gardens 15, N.Y. Died Nov. 9, 1961.

SCHULZ, EDWARD HUGH (shoolts), army officer; b. Wheeling, W.Va., Jan. 23, 1873; s. Henry John and Gertrude (Niesz) S.; Sc.B., U.S. Mil. Acad., 1895; m. Katherine Julia Muhleman, Oct. 12, 1898; children—Gertrude Adams (Mrs. Wm. A. Hausman), Katherine Louise (Mrs. Albert W. Bruce), Caroline Edward (Mrs. John S. Service). Commd. add. 2d lt. Engrs., June 12, 1895; advanced through grades to col., July 1, 1920. Asst. river, harbor and fortifications, Charleston, S.C., 1895-96, New London, Conn., 1899-1901; submarine defense, Hampton Roads and Charleston, S.C., 1898-99; recorded Bd. of Engrs., New York, 1901-05, in charge New York dist. river and harbor works, 1905-05; forts, Guantanamo, Cuba, 1905-07; river and harbor works, Sioux City, Ia., and Kansas City (Mo.) district, 1907-12; consulting engineer Kaw Valley Drainage District, Kansas City, Kan., 1909-12; New Orleans district, 1912-16, St. Paul and Duluth districts, 1916-17; commander 109th Engrs., Camp Cody, N.M., and 604th Engrs., Vancouver Barracks, Wash., and Camp Leach, D.C., 1917-18; in charge Milwaukee dist., 1919-20, Seattle dist., 1920-23; div. engr., comdr. 3d Engrs., Schofield Barracks, Hawaii, 1923-26; in charge Chicago dist. and corps engr. 6th Corps Area, 1926-28; div. engr., Lakes Div., Cleveland, O., 1928-29; comdg. officer Ft. Humphreys, Va. (now Ft. Belvoir, Va.), also of Engr. Sch., Ft. Humphreys, 1929-33; mem. Bd. Engrs. Rivers and Harbors, 1929-33; engr. 9th Corps Area, San Francisco, and supervising Golden Gate Bridge approaches through Presidio, Fort Scott and Fort Baker, mil. reservations, 1934-37, retired. Engaged in translations for War Dept. and Corps of Engrs., informal, 1940-45. Was member of Mississippi River Commission, Great Lakes Ship Canal Board, Ill., and Bd. on Diversion Channels Mississippi River, 1927-29. Mem. Am. Soc. C.E., Soc. Am. Mil. Engrs. Conglist. Clubs: Army and Navy (Washington); Union League (San Francisco). Author: Use of Search Lights, 1904; Report on Missouri River, 1909; Report on South West Pass, 1916; Diversion Channels of Mississippi River (all publs. U.S. War Dept.); also rept. of Miss. River Commn. on Flood Control, 1927. Contbr. to Engring. News Record, Mil. Engr. Address: 204 El Camino Real, Berkeley 5, Calif. Died Mar. 3, 1951; buried Presidio of San Francisco Nat. Cemetery, San Francisco.

SCHUMANN, EDWARD ARMIN, surgeon; b. Washington, D.C., July 9, 1879; s. Francis and Augusta (Jung) S.; A.B., Central High Sch., Phila., 1897; M.D., U. of Pa., 1901; m. Hazel Prince, June 8, 1910; children—Edward Armin, Francis, Robert. Practiced in Phila., 1901-70, limiting to obstetrics and gynecology; intern Phila. General Hosp., 1901-03; surgeon Gynecean Hosp., 1906-10; dir. obstetrics and gynecology Frankford Hosp., gynecologist and obstetrician Phila. Gen. Hosp., 1916-44; obstetrician Chestnut Hill Hosp., 1919-70; lecturer obstetrics Jefferson Med. Coll., 1916-24; surgeon-in-chief Kensington Hosp. for Women, 1931-44; chief of service, obstetrics and gynecology, Protestant-Episcopal Hosp.; prof. obstetrics, U. of Pa., 1935-39; cons. gynecologist, Jewish, Burlington County, Misericordia and Meml. hosps.; civilian coms. USN Hosp. Phila. Lt. comdr. U.S. Naval R.C., A.E.F. Hon. fellow Am. Assn. Obstetricians, Gynecologists and Abdominal Surgeons; fellow A.C.S.; mem. Am. Bd. Obstetrics and Gynecology (charter mem., v.p.), Am. Gynecol. Soc. (pres. 1945), Coll. of Physicians in Phila., Delta Upsilon, Alpha Mu, Pi Omega, Alpha Omega Alpha. Honorary member Central Association Obstetricians and Gynecologists. Republican. Clubs: Gynecologists, Cricket, Franklin Inn (Phila.). Author: Ectopic Pregnancy, 1921; Gonorrhea in Women, 1928; Text Book of Obstetrics, 1936; also 5 chapters in Curtis' Obstetrics and Gynecology, 1933. Contbr. profl. articles. Home: Lafayette Hill PA Died Oct. 18, 1970.

SCHUMM, HERMAN CHARLES orthopedic surgeon; b. Fort Wadsworth, Staten Island, N.Y., Nov. 23, 1889; s. Herman C. and Anna (Kilshaw) S.; B.S., U. of Pa., 1911, M.D., 1914; m. Sarah Jane Johnson, Apr. 20, 1918; children—Herman Charles, David Kilshaw. Began practice as surgeon, Chicago, 1914; orthopedic surgeon. Lt., later capt. Med. Corps, U.S. Army, 1918-19; specialist in orthopedic surgery, Milwaukee, Wis., 1919-—; asso. prof. orthopedic surgery, U. of Wis., 1926-—, Marquette U., 1930-—, dir. dept. of orthopedics, Marquette U., 1938-—. Licentiate Am. Bd. Orthopedic Surgery. Fellow Am. Coll. surgeons, Am. Acad. Orthopedic Surgeons; mem. Am. Orthopedic Soc., Clinical Orthopedic Soc., Milwaukee Surg. Soc., Milwaukee Acad. Medicine, Alpha Mu Pi Omega, Phi Gamma Delta. Republican. Clubs: University, Milwaukee, Oconomowoc Lake. Contbr. to med. jours. Home: R.D. 5, Oconomowoc, Wis. Office: 1024 E. State St., Milw. Died Dec. 21, 1955.

SCHURZ, CARL publicist; b. Liblar, nr. Cologne, March 2, 1829; s. Christian and Marianne S.; ed. gymnasium, Cologne, Univ. of Bonn; LL.D., Harvard, and of U. of Mo.; LL.D., Columbia, 1899. Published liberal newspaper at Bonn; took part in revolutionary movements in 1848-49, and was compelled to leave Bonn, 1849; joined revolutionary army, but finally had to flee to Switzerland. Newspaper corr., Paris, 1851; teacher in London; m. Margaretta Meyer, July 1852. Came to U.S., 1852; settled in Watertown, Wis.; defeated as Rep. candidate for lt. gov. Wis., 1857; mem. Nat. Rep. Conv., 1860; U.S. minister to Spain, 1861; resigned to enter army; apptd. brig. gen., April 1862; maj. gen., March 14, 1863; comd. div. at Second Bull Run and at Chancellorsville, and a corps of Gettysburg. Washington corr. New York Tribune, 1865-66; founded Detroit Post, 1866; editor St. Louis Westliche Post, 1867; temp chmn. Rep. Nat. Conv., Chicago, 1868; U.S. senator from Mo., 1869-75; one of organizers Liberal party, 1872; presided over conv. at Cincinnati which nominated Greeley for President; supported Hayes, 1876; Sec. of the Interior, 1877-81; editor New York Evening Post, 1881-84. One of leaders Independent movement, 1884; supported Cleveland for President; contbr. to Harper's Weekly, 1892-98; pres. Nat. Civil Service Reform League, 1892-1901. Author: Speeches, 1885; Life of Henry Clay, 1887; Abraham Lincoln, an Essay, 1889; etc. Home: New York, N.Y. Died 1906.

SCHUYLER, MONTGOMERY diplomatic service, retired; b. Stamford, Conn., Sept. 2, 1877; s. Montgomery and Katherine Beeckman (Livingston) S.; A.B., Columbia, 1899, A.M., 1900; univ. scholar in Indo-Iranian langs., Columbia U., 1899-1900, univ. fellow, 1900-02; m. Edith Lawyer, Aug. 22, 1906. Second sec. Am. Embassy at St. Petersburg, Russia, 1902-04; sec. legation and consul-gen. at Bangkok, Siam, 1904; chargé d'affaires, 1905; chargé d'affaires to Roumania and Servia, Sept. 1906-May 1907; 1st sec. and chargé d'affaires Am. Embassy at St. Petersburg, 1907-09; at Tokyo, Japan, 1909-11, at Mexico City, Mex., 1911-13; E.E. and M.P. to Ecuador, March 1913; spl. agt. of U.S. to Russia, 1914-15; apptd. chief of Russian div. Dept. of State, April 1921; E.E. and M.P. to Salvador, 1921-Dec. 1925. Partner Schuyler, Earl & Co., members N.Y. Stock Exchange, 1926-31; pres. Roosevelt & Schuyler Co., Ltd.; pres., chmn. exec. com. Nat. Bank of Yorkville, N.Y. City, 1934-—; v.p. Century Bank; dir. various banks and corps. Trustee Am.-Scenic and Historic Preservation Soc. Commd. capt. U.S. Army, 1918; service in Ordnance Dept., trench warfare, May 1918; duty Intelligence Div., Gen. Staff, July 1918; chief intelligence officer of A.E.F. at Omsk, Siberia, Oct. 1918-May 1919; hon. disch., Aug. 26, 1919; commd. maj. R.C., Dec. 1919. Col., chief of staff, N.Y. City Patrol Corps, 1942-45. Mem. Am. Oriental Soc., Am. Soc. Internat. Law, Siam Soc., Mayflower Soc., Descendants of Colonial Governors (v.p.), Huguenot Soc., Order of Colonial Lords of Manors (pres.), Mil. Order World Wars, Am. Immigration Soc., Grange, Nat. Trust, Bill of Rights Soc. Clubs: Century, India House (New York). Episcopalian. Author: Index Verborum of the Fragments of the Avesta, 1901; Bibliography of the Sanskrit Drama, 1906; also many articles on Oriental and lit. subjects and colonial history in periodicals. Home: 192 E. 75th St., N.Y.C. 21. Died Nov. 1, 1955; buried Greenwood Cemetery, Bklyn.

SCHUYLER, PHILIP JOHN Continental congressman, senator, army officer; b. Albany, N.Y., Nov. 20, 1733; s. Johannes and Cornelia (Van Cortlandt) S.; m. Catherine Van Renselaer, Sept. 17,

1755, 8 children including Elizabeth (wife of Alexander Hamilton). Commd. to raise and command company in Gen. William Johnson's expdn. against Crown Point, 1755; mem. forces under Col. John Bradstreet which carried provisions to Oswego and cleared Oneida portage of French raiders, spring 1756; dep. commissary with rank of maj. in Brit. Army under Lord George Howe, 1758; stationed at Albany in campaigns of 1759-60, collected and forwarded provisions to Amherst's forces; inherited his father's estate, 1763, large land holder in Mohawk Valley and along Hudson River; inherited additional land from uncle and developed waterpower for his sawmills and gristmills, built 1st water-driven flaxmill in N.Y., had fleet of 1 schooner and 3 sloops engaged in trade on Hudson; mem. boundary commn. to settle line between N.Y. and Mass., 1764; mem. N.Y. Assembly, 1768; mem. Continental Congress from N.Y., 1775, 78-81; one of 4 maj. gens. under Washington, 1775, assigned to command Northern Dept.; organized expdn. against Can. 1775-76; supported N.Y.'s claims to N.H. (later Vt.) Grants; reprimanded by Congress and relieved of command, 1777, later reinstated, 1777; superseded by Gen. Horatio Gates (by order of Congress) because of loss of Ft. Ticonderoga, 1777, charged with incompetence, acquitted by court martial, 1778; resigned from service, 1779; remained on Congressional Bd. Commrs. for Indian Affairs; chmn. com. at hdqrs. authorized to assist Washington in reorganizing staff depts. of army, 1780; mem. N.Y. State Senate, 1780-84, 86-90, 92-97; mem. U.S. Senate (Federalist) from N.Y., 1789-91, 97-98; mem. N.Y. Bd. Regents, promoted plan for establishment of Union Coll., Schenectady, N.Y., subscribed 100 pounds to endowment. Died Albany, Nov. 18, 1804; buried Albany Rural Cemetery.

SCHUYLER, WALTER SCRIBNER brig. gen. U.S.A.; b. Ithaca, N.Y., Apr. 26, 1850; s. George Washington and Matilda (Scribner) S.; grad. U.S. Mil. Acad., 1870; m. Mary Miller Gardiner, Dec. 20, 1883 (died 1902); m. 2d. Elizabeth Stanton, Mar. 3, 1921. Commd. 2d lt. 5th Cav., June 15, 1870; promoted through grades to brig. gen. U.S.A., Jan. 5, 1911. Bvtd. capt. U.S.A., Feb. 27, 1890, for services in Indian campaigns in Ariz., Wyo., Mont.. Colo., 1871-79; prof. mil. science, Cornell U., 1883-86, 1896-98; col. 203d N.Y. Inf., July 3, 1898-Mar. 25, 1899; col. 46th U.S. Inf., Aug. 17, 1899-May 31, 1901; served in P.R., P.I., and Cuba, 1899-1902; mil. observer with Russian army in Manchuria, 1904; mem. Gen. Staff U.S.A., 1904-06, 1910; comdr. Mil. Dist. Hawaii, 1909-10, Dept. of the Colo., Feb. 6-Mar. 8, 1911; comd. independent cav. brigade, San Antonio, Tex., Mar. 12-July 15, 1911; comdg. Ft. Riley, Kan., July 1911-June 1912; comdg. Dept. of Calif., June-Dec. 1912; 8th Brigade, Dec. 1912-Apr. 1913; retired Apr. 26, 1913. Home: Carmel, Calif. Died Feb. 17, 1932.

SCHWAB, SIDNEY ISAAC neuro-psychiatrist; b. Memphis, Tenn., Nov. 22, 1871; s. Isaac and Ella (Marks) S.; Harvard, 1890-92; M.D., Harvard Med. Sch., 1896; univs. of Berlin, Paris and Vienna, 1896-99; m. Helen Stix, 1903; children—Robert S., Frances Troy, Mack W. Practiced neurology at St. Louis, Mo., since 1899; became prof. clin. neurology, Washington U., 1917, now prof. emeritus; consulting neurologist Barnes Hospital; neurologist Jewish Hospital, St. Louis Children's and Maternity Hosps.; served as mil. neurologist to Base Hospital 21 and med. dir. Base Hospital 117, A.E.F., June 1917-Jan. 1919, rank of captain, maj. Formerly councillor Med. Council of U.S. Vets. Bureau, Washington, D.C. Mem. Am. Neurol. Assn. (pres. 1920-21), A.M.A., etc. Mem. commn. of Assn. for Research in Nervous and Mental Disease. Clubs: University; Harvard (New York). Author: The Adolescent—His Conflicts and Escapes, 1929; also articles on neurology and psychiatry. Mem. sub-com. war neurosis Nat. Research Council. Home: Old James Town Road, Florissant, Mo. Office: Beaumont Medical Bldg., St. Louis, Mo. Died Nov. 12, 1947.

SCHWAMM, HARVEY banker; b. N.Y.C., Oct. 26, 1904; s. Moritz and Dora (Eckstein) S.; m. Lillian Tverskoi, Mar. 14, 1924; children—Jay Marc, Judith Dawn. Real estate broker, operator, 1919-30; sr. partner H.L. Schwamm & Co., underwriters, distbrs. state and municipal bonds, 1930-42; pres., chmn. bd. Nat. Bronx Bank, N.Y.C., 1944-50; pres. Am. Trust Co., N.Y.C., 1950-54, chairman of the board of directors, 1957-—. Director of Bronx Board Trade. Mem. nat. adv. com. U.S. Senate Banking and Currency Com. Served as maj. U.S. Army, 1942-44. Recipient Knights of Pythias Marc Antony ann. award, 1941. Mem. internat. (U.S. council), U.S., N.Y., U.S.-Mexican (dir., mem. exec. com.) C.'s of C., Nat. Fgn. Trade Council, Bankers Assn. Fgn. Trade, Am. Bankers Assn., Pan Am. Soc. U.S., Consular Law Soc. (hon. fellow; U.S.-Mexico Good Neighbor Policy award 1953), Bronx Soc. Prevention Cruelty to Children (trustee). Republican (exec. com. N.Y. County 1940-42; del. Rep. Conv. State N.Y. 1951; presdl. elector N.Y. 1952, 56). Mason. Clubs: Lotos, National Republican, Manhattan, Economic, Bankers, Saints and Sinners (N.Y.C.). Home: 4650 Fieldston Rd., Riverdale 63, N.Y. Office: 70 Wall St., N.Y.C. 5. Died Aug. 15, 1958.

SCHWAN, THEODORE major general U.S.A.; b. Hanover, Germany, July 9, 1841; s. Rev. H. C. S.; ed. gymnasium in Germany; came to U.S., 1857; m. Elizabeth M. Steele (dec.). Served as pvt., corporal, sergt. and 1st sergt., C. K, and q.m. sergt. 10th U.S. Inf.. June 12, 1857-Nov. 6, 1863; 2d lt. 10th Inf., Oct. 31, 1863; 1st lt.. Apr. 9, 1864; capt., Mar. 14, 1866; assigned to 11th Inf., Dec. 13, 1869; maj. a.-a.-g., July 6, 1886; lt. col. a.-a.-g., Feb. 19, 1895; brig. gen. vols., May 4, 1898; col. a.-a.-g. U.S.A., May 18, 1898; hon. discharged from vol. service, Apr. 14, 1899; brig. gen. vols., Apr. 14, 1899; brig. gen. U.S.A., Feb. 2, 1901; hon. discharged from vol. service, Feb. 21, 1901; retired at own request after 40 yrs.' service, Feb. 21, 1901. Bvtd. captain, Oct. 1, 1864. .'for gallant services" in battle of Chapel House, Va.; maj., Mar. 2, 1867, "for gallant and meritorious services," during the war; awarded medal of honor, Dec. 12, 1898. "for most distinguished gallantry" in action at Peebles Farm, Va., Oct. 1, 1864. Attached to Am. Embassy, Berlin, Germany, 1892-93. Comd. 1st Div., 9th Army Corps, May-July 1898; comd. western column in Puerto Rican campaign; chief of staff, Div. of P.I. and prin. asst. to mil. gov., also in command of Southern Luzon expdns., 1899-1900; promoted maj. gen. U.S.A., Aug. 29, 1916. Author Report on the Organization of the German Army with Supplement showing the orgn. of the German Gen. Staff. Address: Washington, D.C. Died May 27, 1926.

SCHWARTZ, JACK WILLIAM, army officer; b. Ft. Worth, Dec. 12, 1905; s. Abraham Benjamin and Lena (Halpern) S.; student Texas Christian U., 1922-23; B.S., U. Tex., 1926, M.D., 1928; m. Jessie Augusta Wickham, June 1, 1937; children—Jean Anne, William Wickham. Intern, Fitzsimons Gen. Hosp., Denver, 1928-29; commd. 1st lt., M.C., U.S. Army, 1929, advanced through grades to maj. gen., 1959; various assignments Army gen. hosps.; chief surgery Bataan Gen. Hosp., World War II; Japanese prisoner, 1942-45; chmn. urol. Service Letterman Gen. Hosp., 1946-53, Walter Reed Gen. Hosp., 1953-56; comdg. gen. Madigan Gen. Hosp., 1956-58; comdg. gen. Tripler Army Hosp., Hawaii, also chief surgeon U.S. Army Pacific, 1958-60; comdg. gen. Letterman Gen. Hosp., San Francisco, 1960-68. Decorated Legion of Merit with oak leaf cluster. Fellow A.C.S.; mem. A.M.A., Am. Urol. Assn., Pan Pacific Surg. Assn., Alpha Omega Alpha. Mason (32 deg.). Home: San Francisco CA Died May 1968.

SCHWEINITZ, GEORGE EDMUND DE M.D.; b. Phila., Oct. 26, 1858; s. Rt. Rev. Edmund and Lydia de S.; A.B., A.M., Moravian, 1876; M.D., U. of Pa., 1881, LL.D., 1914; L.H.D., Moravian Coll.; D.Sc., U. of Mich., 1922, Harvard, 1927. Prof. ophthalmology, U. of Pa. Grad. Sch. of Medicine, 1902-24, emeritus, 1924-—; cons. ophthalmologist Phila. Hosp. Maj. Med. R.C., 1917; active service, Sept. 29, 1917-Apr. 1, 1919; lt. col. M.C., U.S.A., in France, Oct. 1917-Mar. 1918; on duty in U.S. as officer in charge of and consultant in ophthalmology, Surgeon Gen.'s Office; brig. gen. Aux. Med. Res.; mem. editorial bd. for med. and surg. history of the war. V.p. Pa. Inst. for Instrn. of Blind; trustee U. of Pa. Mem. A.M.A. (pres. 1922-23), Am. Ophthal. Soc. (pres. 1916). Author: Diseases of the Eye, 1924; Diseases of the Eye, Ear, Nose and Throat (with Dr. Randall), 1899; Toxic Amblyopias, 1896 (Alvarenga prize essay). Am. editor Haab's Ophthalmoscopy and External Dases of Eye and Operative Ophthalmology; Pulsating Exophthalmos (with Dr. Holloway); Ophthalmic Year Book (with Dr. Jackson), 1905-09. Contbr. numerous articles and monographs on ophthal. and neurol. subjects. Bowman lecturer, London, 1923. Awarded plaque from Soc. Française U'Ophthalmologie, 1924; Howe prize medal in ophthalmology, 1927; Huguenot Cross, 1928; Leslie Dana medal for prevention of blindness, 1930. Address: Philadelphia, Pa. Died Aug. 22. 1938.

SCHWEITER, LEO HENRY, army officer; b. Wichita, Kan., Apr. 16, 1917; s. Otto T. and Bertha (Schmid) S.; student U. Wichita, 1935-36; B.S., Kan. State Coll., 1939; M.A., U. Mo., 1940; m. Virginia Van Pflaum, July 24, 1954; children—Henry J., Gail A., Mary Jean, Caroline V. Commd. 2d lt., U.S. Army, 1941, advanced through grades to maj. gen., 1968; comdg. officer 5th Spl. Airborne Force Group, 1st Spl. Forces, 1961-62; with Office Spl. Asst. for Counterinsurgency and Spl. Activities, Joint Chief Staff, Washington, 1962-64, with Office Dep. Chief Staff for Operations, 1964-66; assigned to Ft. Campbell, Ky. and Vietnam, 1966-69; dep. comdg. gen. U.S. Army Combat Devel. Command, Ft. Belvoir, Va., 1969-71; chief of staff U.S. Army Vietnam, 1971-72; ret., 1972. Decorated D.S.M., Silver Star with oak leaf cluster, D.F.C., Legion of Merit with oak leaf cluster, Bronze Star with three oak leaf clusters, Air medal with 24 oak leaf clusters, Purple Heart with two oak leaf clusters. Mem. De Molay, Phi Kappa Phi, Alpha Zeta. Home: Carlisle PA2Died Aug. 23, 1972.

SCHWENTKER, FRANCIS FREDERIC prof. pediatrics; b. Schenectady, N.Y., Feb. 13, 1904; s. Frederic Ferdinand and Marie Rose (Bildhauser) S.; B.S., Union Coll., Schenectady, N.Y., 1925, D.Sc.; M.D., Johns Hopkins Medical Sch., Balt., 1929; m. Madalyn Elphic Crockett, July 2, 1932; children—Frederic Noel, Ann Cole, Edwards Park. Interne pediatrics, Johns Hopkins Hosp., 1929-30; asst. resident pediatrician, 1930-31, resident pediatrician, 1934-35, prof. pediatrics, 1946-—, pediatrician-in-chief, 1946-—; asst. Rockefeller Inst. for Med. Research, 1931-34; resident physician Sydenham Hosp., Baltimore, 1935-36, asso. dir.; dir. med. research, Baltimore City Health Dept., 1936-38; staff mem. Internat. Health Div., Rockefeller Found., 1938-46. Mem. Rockefeller Health Commn. to Europe, 1940. Cons. to sec. of War on epidemic diseases, 1940-42; now consultant in pediatrics U.S. Navy. Served as med. officer, U.S. Naval Res., 1942-46. Mem. Am. Bd. of Pediatrics, Am. Acad. of Pediatrics, Soc. for Pediatric Research, Am. Pediatric Soc., Society Am. Bacteriologists, Interurban Clin. Soc., Assn. Am. Physicians, Sigma Xi, Alpha Kappa Kappa. Author about 36 articles in med. literature. Home: 209 Tunbridge Rd., Baltimore 12. Office: Johns Hopkins Hosp., North Broadway, Balt. 5. Died Nov. 8, 1954.

SCOFIELD, WALTER KEELER med. dir. U.S.N.; b. Stamford. Conn., Apr. 28, 1839; s. Alfred and Maria S.; M.D., Coll. Phys. and Surg. (Columbia). 1868; m. Mary Candee, Jan. 14, 1876. Asst. surgeon U.S.N., July 12, 1861; passed asst. surgeon, June 22, 1864; surgeon, Apr. 7, 1866; med. insp., Nov. 21. 1883; med. dir., Feb. 8, 1890; retired with rank of rear admiral, Apr. 28, 1901. Home: Stamford, Conn. Died 1910.

SCOTT, CHARLES gov. Ky.; b. Goochland County, Va., 1739; m. Frances Sweeney, Feb. 25, 1762; m. 2d, Judith Cary (Bell) Gist, July 25, 1807. At beginning of Revolution raised 1st companies of volunteers South of James River; apptd. lt. col. 2d Va. Regt., 1776, later col. 3d Regt., 1776; commd. brig. gen. Continental Army, 1777, captured at Charleston, S.C., 1780; brevetted maj. gen., 1783; an original mem. Soc. of Cincinnati; rep. from Woodford County (Ky.) in Va. Assembly, 1789, 90; comdt. Ky. dist. with rank of brig. gen., 1791; conducted expdn. against Indians on Wabash River, 1791; Scott County (Ky.) named for him, 1792; fought against Indians with Gen. Anthony Wayne at battle of Fallen Timbers, 1794; chosen presdl. elector from Ky., 1793, 1801, 05, 09; gov. Ky., 1808-12. Died "Canewood", Clark County, Ky., Oct. 22, 1813; buried State Cemetery, Frankfort, Ky.

SCOTT, CHARLES HERRINGTON, business man; b. Montgomery, Ala., Dec. 27, 1870; s. Thomas Jefferson and Mary A. (Taylor) S.; ed. Montgomery High Sch., U. of Ala., 1887 (left in jr. year), Howard Coll., 1888 (left in sr. yr.); m. Josephine Bennett, of Jefferson, Ga., Aug. 22, 1900. Since 1890 engaged in mineral and timber land business in firm of T. J. Scott & Son, of which is now sr. mem.; v.-p. and treas. Pacific Co.; dir. Empire Land Co. and Peru cos., Ala. Marble Quarries, Scott Investment Co., Ala. Colony Co. Civ. engr. Capt. 3d Ala. Vol. Inf. Spanish-Am. War, detailed as a.-a.-g., 1st div., 3d Army Corps, Camp Shipp. Apptd. Rep. referee by Pres. Roosevelt, 1903; Ala. mem. Rep. Nat. Com., 1904-—. Progressive Rep. candidate for gov. of Ala., 1910. Baptist. Clubs: Lawyers, Republican, New York Athletic (New York). Home: Sycamore, Ala. Address: Montgomery, AL and 54 W. 40th St., New York NY

SCOTT, CHARLES L. ret. army officer; b. Oct. 22, 1883; B.S., U.S. Mil. Acad., 1905; grad. Mounted Service Sch., 1912, Command and Gen. Staff Sch., 1929, Army War Coll., 1933; married; 1 son, Dean Robert. Commd. 2d lt., June 13, 1905; promoted through grades to maj. gen. (temp.), Oct. 1, 1940; served as lt. col. Quartermaster Corps, 1918-20; mem. Gen. Staff Corps, 1939-40; comdg. 2d Armored Div., July-Nov. 1940, 1st Armored Corps, 1940-42, sr. U.S. mil. observer in Middle East, Mar.-Aug. 1943; comdg. Armored Force Replacement Training Center, 1943-45. Decorated D.S.M. (U.S.); Hon. Comdr., Most Excellent Order Brit. Empire. Address: 4000 Massachusetts Av., Washington. Died Nov. 27, 1954; buried Arlington Nat. Cemetery.

SCOTT, DONNELL EVERETT hosiery mfr.; b. Graham, N.C., Mar. 3, 1887; s. John Levi and Fannie Logan (Brady) S.; B.S., Davidson Coll., 1907; m. Margie Norwood Gray, Oct. 7, 1916; children—Jean Gray, Donnell Everett. Cotton goods mfr., Graham, N.C., 1907-29; hosiery mfr., Graham, N.C., 1929-—; pres. Scott Hosiery Mills, Inc.; dir. Nat. Bank of Almance. Mem. Nat. Guard of N.C. 1904-—, beginning as private; commd. 2d lt., 1906, and advanced through the grades to brig. gen., 1927; comdg. 60th Brig.; inducted into Fed. service, 1940; served as maj., lt. col. and col., 120th Inf., U.S. Army, World War; with A.E.F., 1918-19; awarded Silver Star for bravery. Mem. Kappa Alpha. Presbyn. (deacon). Address: Graham, N.C. Died Feb. 10, 1955.

SCOTT, ERNEST DARIUS, army officer; born Petrolia, Ont., Can., Sept. 6, 1872; s. Alexander Bruce and Margaret (Tweedy) S.; student U. of Neb., 1892-94; B.S., U.S. Mil. Acad., 1898; also grad. Army Sch. of the Line, Army Staff Coll., Field Arty. Sch. of Fire, Army War Coll., Navy War Coll., at various dates, 1908-29; m. Ella von Gerichten, Oct. 8, 1903 (dec. Sept. 12, 1943); children—Florence-May (Mrs. Robert C. Cameron) (dec.), Bruce von Gerichten, Ernest Darius (deceased); m. 2d, Mrs. William S. Baer, May 1, 1944. Came to U.S., 1884, naturalized, 1889. Cadet U.S. Mil. Acad., June 15, 1894; promoted through grades to brig. gen., Dec. 1, 1931; ret. from mil. serivce Sept. 30, 1936. Served in Spanish-Am. War and Philippines, 1898-1901; col. (temp.) in France and Germany, 1917-19; participated in Einville sector, Toul sector, Marne defensive, Marne offensive, St. Mihiel and Meuse

Argonne offensives. Awarded D.S.M. and three silver star citations. Mem. Assn. Grads. U.S. Mil. Acad., Mil. Order of the Carabao, Mil. Order of World War, Nat. Sojourners, Heroes of '76. Mason (32 deg.). Club: Army and Navy (Washington); Bath, Committee of One Hundred (Miami Beach, Fla.). Co-author: Studies in Minor Tactics, 1915; Troop Leading, Division, 1916. Home: 590 Melaleuca Lane, Bay Pt., Miami 38 FL

SCOTT, FITZHUGH architect; b. Milw., Nov. 9, 1881; s. Frederick Meyer and Mary Evelyn (Caswell) S.; B.S. in Architecture, Columbia, 1905; m. Elise Marshall Landrum, Dec. 9, 1908; children—Fitzhugh, William F., Elise (Mrs. Robert Swansen). Works include Blatz Temple of Music, Milw., Milw. Childrens Hosp., Allen-Bradley Co. plants in Milw. and Galt Can., YMCA's in Milw. and Racine, Milw. Country Day Sch. Served as capt. Q.M.C., U.S. Army, World War I. Fellow A.I.A. Home: 7800 N. River Rd., Milw. 17. Office: 5623 N. Lake Dr., Milw. 17. Died Oct. 12, 1957.

SCOTT, HENRY D(ICKERSON) steel mfr.; b. Bridgeport, O., Feb. 26, 1893; s. Isaac MacBurney and Flora Belle (Dickerson) S.; student Hotchkiss Sch., Lakeville, Conn., 1907-10, Yale, 1910-14; m. Lillian Elizabeth Malone, 1919. Bookkeeper Buckeye Rolling Mill Co., Steubenville, O., 1914-15; accountant Wheeling Steel & Iron Co., 1915-17; supt. Wheeling Steel Corp., 1919-26, asst. v.p., 1926-30, v.p. in charge operations, 1937-43; chmn. Scott Lbr. Co., Bridgeport, O., since 1943, Steel Service Inc., The Parkersburg (W.Va.) Steel Co.; president Sharon (Pa.) Tube Co. since 1930. Entered O.T.C., 1917; commd. capt. field arty. U.S. Army, 1918, with A.E.F., 1917-18. Decorated with Croix de Guerre (France). Mem. Am. Legion, Am. Iron and Steel Inst., Am. Petroleum Inst., Phi Beta Kappa, Psi Upsilon. Republican. Presbyterian. Clubs: Ft. Henry, Wheeling Country (Wheeling); Country (Youngstown); Yale (New York). Author: Iron and Steel in Wheeling, 1928. Home: 36 Orchard Rd. Office: Wheeling Steel Corp., Wheeling, W.Va. Died Apr. 21, 1947.

SCOTT, HUGH LENOX officer U.S.A.; b. Danville, Ky., Sept. 22, 1853; s. Rev. Wm. M. Scott and Mary E. Hodge, g.g.d. of Benjamin Franklin; grad. U.S. Mil. Acad., 1876; L.H.D., Princeton, 1910; LL.D., Columbia; L.M.S., Chester (Pa.) Mil. Acad., 1916; m. Mary, d. Gen. Lewis Merrill, June 1880; children—David Hunter, Anna Merrill, Lewis Merrill, Mary Blanchard, Sarah H. Merrill. Second lt. 9th Cavalry, June 15, 1876; transferred to 7th Cavalry, Jne 26, 1876; promoted through grades to maj. gen. U.S.A., April 30, 1915. Served in the Sioux expedition, 1876; Nez Percé expedition, 1877; Camp Robinson, Neb., and Cheyenne expdn., 1878; routine duty, principally with Indians of the Plains, 1878-91; hon. mention from War Dept., Okla., 1891; in charge in investigation of Ghost Dance disturbances, 1890-91; enlisted and comd. Kiowa, Comanche and Apache Indians, troop L, 7th Cav., 1892, until mustered out after 5 yrs.' enlistment (last Indian troop mustered out); in charge Geronimo's band Chiricahua Apaches, 1894-97. On duty at Bur. Ethnology, Smithsonian Instn., writing work on sign language, Plains Indians, N. America, Nov. 1897; adj. gen. of Cuba, 1898-1903; gov. Sulu Archipelago and comdg. military post of Jolo, P.I., 1903-06; abolished slavery and the slave trade in the Sulu Archipelago; supt. and comdt. U.S. Mil. Acad., with rank of col., Sept. 1, 1906-Aug. 31, 1910. On duty, Mar. and Apr. 1908, settling troubles of Navajos in N.M. and Mexican Kickapoos in Ariz. for Interior Dept.; again in 1911, for same dept., trouble with Hopi Indians at Hotevilla, Ariz.; engaged in settlement, for War and Interior depts., of Apache prisoners of war, Okla. and N.M., 1912; comdg. 3d Cav., Ft. Sam Houston, Tex., 1912; comdg. 2d Cav. Brigade and patrol on Mexican border, 1913-14. Settled by diplomacy Navajo Indian trouble at Beautiful Mountain, Ariz., Nov. 1913; asst. chief of Gen. Staff, U.S.A., Apr. 22, 1914; settled by diplomacy impending conflict on Mexican border at Naco, Ariz., Jan. 1915, as well as on two other occasions at El Paso, Tex.; settled Piute Indian trouble, Bluff, Utah, Mar. 1915; recovered property of foreigners confiscated by General Villa in Mexico, Aug. 1915. Chief of staff U.S.A., Nov. 17, 1914-Sept. 22, 1917 (laid basis for participation of U.S. in war with Germany); retired by operation of law, Sept. 22, 1917, but retained on active duty to May 12, 1919; chmn. State Highway Commn. of N.J., 1923-—. Mem. U.S. Commn. to Russia, 1917; apptd. comdr. 78th Div. and Camp Dix, N.J., Dec. 26, 1917; served with a British div. in the front line at Arras and with a French div. in front line at Chalons; present at battle for Passchendal Ridge, 1917; inspected line from Verdun to Ypres. Awarded D.S.M., 1918. Mem. Bd. of Indian Commrs., 1919-—. Hon. mem. many socs. and clubs, and of various Indian tribes. Mason (33 deg.). Author: Some Memories of a Soldier, 1928; also various monographs and reports relating to Plains Indians. Home: Princeton, N.J. Died Apr. 30, 1934.

SCOTT, JAMES BROWN lawyer, educator; b. Kincardine, Bruce County, Ontario, June 3, 1866; s. John and Jeanette (Brown) S.; A.B., Central High School, Philadelphia, Pa., 1885; A.B., Harvard U., 1890, A.M., 1891; Parker fellow, Harvard U., specializing in internat. law, 1891-94; studied Berlin, Heidelberg and Paris; J.U.D., Heidelberg, 1894; m. Adele C. Reed, 1901 (died Oct. 15, 1939). Formerly engaged in academic work. Solicitor Dept. of State, 1906-10; trustee Carnegie Endowment for Internat. Peace since 1910, sec. of orgn. and dir. Division of International Law, 1910-40, sec. emeritus since 1940; tech. del. to 2d Hague Peace Conf., 1907; spl. adviser Dept. of State, chmn. Joint State and Navy Neutrality Bd., 1914-17; tech. del. to Paris Peace Conf., 1919; tech. adviser to Arms Conf., 1921-22. Pres. Am. Inst. International Law since 1915; president Inst. International Law, 1925-27, 1928-29; sec. Am. Soc. Internat. Law, 1906-24, pres., 1929-39, hon. pres. since 1939; editor in chief Am. Jour. Internat. Law, 1907-24; chmn. U.S. Pan-Am. Com. of Jurists to prepare codes of private and pub. internat. law, Rio de Janeiro, 1927; del. to 6th Pan-Am. Conf., Havana, 1928; chmn. Am. del. to Congress of Rectors, Deans and Educators, Havana, 1930; del. to 4th Pan-Am. Commercial Conf., Washington, 1931. Pvt. and corporal Co. C, 7th Calif. Inf., Spanish-Am. War, 1898; maj. and judge advocate U.S. Army, 1917-19. Commr. of U.S. on the commn. created under the Bryan Treaty for the Advancement of Peace between the U.S. and Norway, 1928; prs. Permanent Commn. Conciliation, Belgium and Switzerland, 1928; designated by Guatemala as mem. Central Am. Internat. Tribunal, 1928; apptd. pres. Danish-Polish Conciliation Commn., 1929; mem. Polish-Brazilian Conciliation Commn., 1935, Commn. of Investigation and Conciliation between Cuba and Peru, 1936, Dano-Venezuelan Permanent Commn. of Conciliation, 1937, Permanent Commission of Conciliation between Belgium and Switzerland, 1937; appointed chairman Permanent Commn. of Conciliation between Chile and Poland, 1937. Mem. Am. Philos. Soc. Author: The Hagues Peace Conferences of 1899 and 1907 (2 vols.), 1909; An International Court of Justice, 1916; Peace Through Justice, 1917; Survey of International Relations Between the United States and Germany (Aug 1, 1914-Apr. 6, 1917), 1918; James Madison's Notes on Debates in the Federal Convention of 1787 and Their Relation to a More Perfect Society of Nations, 1918; The United States of America, 1920; Robert Bacon, Life and Letters, 1923; Le Français—Langue Diplomatique Moderne, 1924; Sovereign States and Suits, 1925; Cuba, La America Latina, Los Estados Unidos, 1926; The United States and France: Some Opinions on International Gratitude, 1926; Le Progrès de Droit des Gens, 1930, 31, 34; De Grasse à Yorktown, 1931; The Spanish Origin of International Law—Part I; Francisco de Vitoria and His Law of Nations, 1934; The Catholic Conception of International Law, 1934; The Spanish Conception of International Law and of Sanctions, 1934; Conferencias—en homenaje a la Universidad Mayor de San Marcos, Lima, Peru, 1938; Law, the State and the International Community, 2 vols., 1939. Clubs: Century (New York); Army and Navy, Metropolitan, Cosmos (Washington). Home: Wardour, Anne Arundel County, Md. Office: 700 Jackson Pl., Washington, D.C. Died June 25, 1943.

SCOTT, JAMES HUTCHISON ex-lt. U.S. Revenue Cutter Service; b. E. Liberty, Pa., Feb. 11, 1868; s. Thomas and Matilda Dallas (Sanders) S.; common sch. and academic edn.; entered Naval Acad., 1884, bur resigned because of ill health; served in merchant vessels; grad. Cadet School of Revenue Cutter Service, May, 1890; m. Aug. 19, 1892, Edith, d. Thomas Graham, of Phila. On graduation, 1890, was made acting 3d lt. U. S. S. Woodbury, later of U. S. S. McLane, etc. At beginning of war with Spain assigned as exec. officer to revenue cutter Hudson, which took distinguished part at battle of Cardenas Bay, Cuba, May 11, 1898, by shielding the disabled and unmanageable torpedo boat Winslow and towing her clear of all danger. Recommended by President McKinley to receive thanks of Congress and medal for gallantry during war. After war assigned to revenue cutter Manhattan; later had temporary command of revenue cutter Washington. Navigator U. S. S. Gresham when she rescued the Portuguese bark Fraternidada, saving 113 lives; later exec. officer U. S. S. Perry; resigned July 1, 1901, receiving the first official letter of regret ever sent to an officer. Agent for Harlan & Hollingsworth Corp. Mem. Caribbean Soc., Nat. Geog. Soc. (Clubs: Markham, Railroad. Address: 11 Broadway, New York.

SCOTT, NORMAN naval officer; b. Aug. 10, 1889; entered U.S. Navy, June 1907; advanced to rear admiral, July 1939. Awarded Navy Cross, Congressional Medal of Honor. Address: Indpls. Died Nov. 13, 1942; went down with his ship U.S.S. Atlanta at Guadacanal.

SCOTT, NORMAN, opera, concert singer; b. N.Y.C., Nov. 30,21928; 1928; Maurice and Flora (Silvern) S.; B.B.A., City College of New York; married Erica Glanz; 1 dau., Monika. Sang with N.Y.C. Opera Co., 1948-51, Vienna State Opera, Sept.-Oct., 1956, Metropolitan Opera Co. (bass singer), 1951-68; has appeared with leading opera cos., Pitts., New Orleans, Phila., San Antonio, Havana, Cuba, etc., 1949-51; with Symphony orchestras. N.B.C. Symphony (under Toscanini) in Beethoven 9th (twice), Verdi Requiem, Aida, Falstaff; concertized throughout U.S.; guest artist TV shows; in 1st Am. performances of Christopher Columbus, N.Y. Philharmonic, 1952, The Rake's Progress, with Met. Opera, 1953; guest appearance, Chile, 1959, Argentina, 1960. Commd. ensign, USN, 1943, served South Pacific, disch. lt., 1946. Recipient Presdl. Citation. Mem. Am. Guild Mus. Artists. Recorded with M.G.M., R.C.A. Victor, Columbia, and Remington records; recorded Boris Godunov with Met. Opera. Home: New York City NY Died Sept. 22, 1968; buried Ferncliff Cemetery NY

SCOTT, PHILIP B(EETON) business exec.; b. N.Y. City, Feb. 23, 1912; s. Lester Francis and Margot (Beeton) S.; B.S., Hamilton Coll., Clinton, N.Y., 1934; m. Anne Lightfoot Coleman, Dec. 27, 1939; children—Philip Coleman, David Gordon, Mary Beeton. With Kennedy & Co., 1934-36, Gen. Pub. Service Corp., 1937-41, vice pres., 1941-42, dir. since 1941; dir. Stone & Webster Securities Corp. since 1947. vice president Stone & Webster, Incorporated, 1947-45, executive v.p., 1956-—; peres., dir. Stone & Webster Canada, Limited; director Bates-Thompson Hat-Corporation. Served with Ordnance Dept., U.S. Army, 1942-46, disch. with rank of major. Mem. Alpha Delta Phi, St. Andrews Soc. of N.Y. Republican. Presbyn. Club: Recess. Home: 263 Harwood Av., North Tarrytown, N.Y. Office: 90 Broad St., N.Y. City 4. Died May 7, 1961; buried Ferncliff, Greenburgh, N.Y.

SCOTT, ROBERT KINGSTON governor; b. in Armstrong County, Pa., July 8, 1826; ed. at common schools in Pa. and Central Coll. of Ohio; studied medicine at Navarre, O., and subsequently attended lectures at Starling Med. Coll., Columbus, O. In Calif., 1850-51; engaged in milling and medical practice; 1851-57 practiced medicine in Henry County, O.; then a merchant until 1861. Served in Union army, 1861-65 maj. to bvt. maj. gen.; then, Jan. 2, 1866 to 1868, asst. commr. Freedmen's Bur. in S.C.; gov. of S.C., 1868-72; in real estate business in Columbia, S.C., 1872-77; in like business in Ohio, 1877-—. Address: Napoleon, Henry County, O. Died 1900.

SCOTT, ROBERT NICHOLSON army officer; b. Winchester, Tenn., Jan. 21, 1838; son of W. A. Scott. Accompanied father to Cal., 1854; commd. lt. 4th U.S. Inf., 1857; sent on duty with Army of Potomac as acting adjutant gen. 1st Brigade, U.S. Inf., 1861; promoted capt. U.S. Army, 1861, brevetted maj., 1862; sr. aide to Gen. Henry Halleck, 1863-64, 67-72; instr. mil. science Shattuck Sch., Faribault, Minn., 1872-73; comdr. of Ft. Ontario, N.Y., 1873-77; promoted maj. U.S. Army, 1879, lt. col. 1885; on duty with publications of U.S. Army, also mem. com. to reorganize Army for a time, 1877-87. Author: Digest of The Military Laws of the United States, 1872. Died Washington, D.C., Mar. 5, 1887.

SCOTT, THOMAS ALEXANDER railroad exec.; b. Ft. Loudon, Franklin County, Pa., Dec. 28, 1823; s. Thomas and Rebecca (Douglas) S.; m. Anna Margaret Mullison, 1847; m. 2d, Anna Dike Riddle, 1865; 6 children. Chief clk. Office Collector of Tolls, Phila., 1847-49; station agt. Pa. R.R., Duncansville, 1850, apptd. 3d asst. supt. in charge of division starting westward from Altoona (Pa.) with office at Pitts., 1852, gen. supt., 1858, 1st v.p., 1860; commd. col. U.S. Volunteers, 1861; apptd. asst. U.S. sec. of war to supervise all govt. rys. and transp. lines, 1861; given temporary appointment col. and asst. q.m. gen.; pres. Pennsylvania Co., 1870, U.P. R.R., 1871-72, T. & P. Ry., 1872-80, Pa. R.R. Co., 1874-80. Died "Woodburn," Darby, Pa., May 21, 1881.

SCOTT, THOMAS MORTON soldier; b. Cadiz. O., June 25, 1824; s. James and Harriet (Arnold) S.; lineal descendant of Thomas Scott, mem. English Parliament, and one of com. which signed death warrant of Charles I; acad. edn.; moved to Louisville, Ky., 1844; m. sister of Capt. Z. M. Shirley, May 1851. Sergt. maj., 1st Ky. Inf., in Mexican War; participated in battles of Monterey and Buena Vista; in Calif., 1849-51; comd. troop of vols. against hostile Indians. Lived in Tex., 1852-—; raised Co. I, 9th Tex. Inf., C.S.A.; served through war as capt. and a.a.g.; assisted in making peace treaties with 160 wild Indian tribes who had been depredating in Tex., May 1865. Mem. bd. of dirs. State Agrl. and Mech. Coll. and Prairie View Normal Sch., 1876-86; bus. agt. same, 1886-90; col. on Gov. Roberts' staff 2 yrs.; mem. bd. trustees and financial agt. Add Ran Christion U., Texas, 1892-97-—; again mem. bd. of trustees, June 1898-—. Apptd. lt. col. and a.d.c. on staff Gov. Lanham, 1903; lt. col. and chief q.m. on staff Maj. Gen. K. M. Van Zandt, comdg. Tex. Div. U.C.V.; v.p. for Tex. Nat. Assn. Mexican War Vets.; bvtd. maj. gen. U.C.V., 1906. Address: Melissa, Collin County. Tex. Died Mar. 6, 1911.

SCOTT, WALTER DILL educator; b. Cooksville, Ill., May 1, 1869; s. James Sterling and Henrietta (Sutton) S.; grad. Ill. State Normal U., 1891; A.B., Northwestern U., 1895; grad. McCormick Theol. Sem., 1898; Ph.D., University of Leipzig, 1900, (honorary), Northwestern University; LL.D., Cornell Coll., 1921; LL.D., U. of Southern Calif., 1932; m. Anna Marcy Miller, July 21, 1898; children—John Marcy, Sumner Walter. Asso. prof. psychology and edn., and dir. psychol. lab., Northwestern U., 1901-08, prof. psychology, 1908-20, pres., 1920-39, pres. emeritus, 1939-—; dir. Bureau of Salesmanship Research, Carnegie Inst. Tech., 1916-17. Pres. The Scott Co., consultants and engrs. in industrial personnel, 1919-21. Dir. com. on classification of personnel in the army, 1917-18; col. U.S. Army, 1918-19; now col., U.S.R. Awarded D.S.M. for "devising, installing and supervising the personnel system in the

U.S. Army." Cross Legion of Honor (France), 1933, Chevalier, 1938. Trustee Wesley Memorial Hosp., Presbyn. Theol. Sem. of Chicago; mem. bd. trustees of Century of Progress, 1933, 34. Chmn. solid fuels advisory war council 1941-46; chmn. editorial board, American Peoples Ency., 1948. Mem. Am. Council on Edn., (chmn. 1927), Am. Psychol. Assn. (pres. 1918-19), Phi Beta Kappa, Delta Mu Delta, Sigma Xi, Phi Delta Kappa, Am. Legion. Presbyterian. Clubs: University (Chicago, Winter Park, Evanston); Commercial, Union League; Glenview Golf; etc. Author: Die Psychologie der Triebe, 1900; Theory of Advertising, 1903; Psychology of Public Speaking, 1907; Psychology of Advertising, 1908; Influencing Men in Business, 1911; Increasing Human Efficiency, 1911; Psychology of Advertising in Theory and Practice, 1921; Science and Common Sense in Working with Men, 1921; Personnel Management, 1941; The Life of Charles Deering, 1929; Biography of John Evans, 1939; Life of John Evans; Life of Charle Deering. Joint Author: The Personnel System of the U.S. Army, Vol. I, History of the Personnel System, Vol. II, The Personnel Manual, 1919; Personnel Specifications, 10 vols., 1918-19; Dwellers by the Road, 1911; Aids in Selecting Salesmen, 1916; Stabilizing Business, 1923; Man and His Universe, 1929; Society Today, 1929; Life of Walter P. Murphy, 1947. Home: North Shore Hotel, Evanston, Ill. Died Sept. 23, 1955; buried Meml. Park Cemetery, Evanston.

SCOTT, WENDELL G(ARRISON), physician; b. Boulder, Colo., July 19, 1905; s. Ira Dudley and Callie (Soper) S.; A.B., U. Colo., 1928, Sc.D. (honoris causa), 1954; M.D., Washington U., 1932; m. Ella Johnson, June 29, 1929; children—Horace Wendell, Ann (Mrs. Michel TerPogossian), Sarah Jane (Mrs. C. H. Wallace). Served his internship at the Barnes Hosp., St. Louis, 1933-34, asso. radiologist, 1938; instr. sch. medicine Washington U., St. Louis, 1934-38, asst. prof. radiology, 1938-40, asst. prof. clin. radiology, 1940-41, asso. professor, 1941-56, prof., 1956-72; mem. alumni rep., dir. Washington U., 1954-58. Cons. radiology Oak Ridge Inst. Nuclear Studies, 1955-62, mem. cancer control com. Nat. Cancer Inst. USPHS, 1958-60, 66-70, mem. nat. radiation adv. com., 1960-64; mem. dependents med. care adv. com. Dept. of Defense, 1958-67; mem. com. radiol. NRC, 1947-52, 54, chmn. 1955-64; cons. spl. med. adv. bd. Vets. Administration, 1952-57, chmn. 1954-56, area cons. radiol., 1957-72; cons. radiol., pathology, Armed Forces Inst. Pathology, 1953-58. Served as lt. to capt., med. corps USNR, 1942-46; rear adm. Med. R.C., 1958-65; res. consultant radiology Bur. Medicine and Surgery, Navy Dept., 1946-72; mem. adv. commn. cancer control br. U.S.P.H.S., Health, Edn., Welfare, Chmn. Genitourinary Task Force; mem. adv. bd. for conquest cancer U.S. Senate, 1970-71; mem. Nat. Cancer Adv. Bd., 1971-72, President's Nat. Cancer Adv. Bd. Dir. Am. Cancer Soc., 1957-72, pres., 1963-64. Recip. numerous awards, citations for sci. contbns. by med. socs. Diplomate Am. Bd. Radiology. Fellow Am. Coll. Radiology (chmn. commn. on pub. relations 1950-60, chancellor 1960-64, recipient gold medal 1965, chmn. com. mammography); mem. A.M.A. (chmn. section radiology 1958, del. 1966-72), Mo., So. med. assns., Detroit Medical Soc. (honorary), St. Louis Soc. Radiologists (pres. 1946-48), Am. Radium Soc. (v.p.), Am. Roentgen Ray Soc. (treas. 1947-56, pres. 1958-59), Radiol. Soc. N.A. (vice president 1944), U.S. Assn. Mil. Surgeons (exec. council 1946), Med. Cons. World War II, Tex., Rocky Mountain radiol. socs. (hon.), Washington U. Sch. Medicine Alumni Assn. (pres. 1954). Sociedad de Cancerologia de Guadalajara (hon.), also fraternities of Sigma Xi and Alpha Omega Alpha. Clubs: University, Bellerive Country, Racquet, St. Louis, Clayton, (St. Louis). Author articles medical journals. Editor: Genetics, Radiobiology, and Radiology (Charles C. Thomas), 1959; Planning Guide for Radiologic Installations; associate editor American Journal. Roentgenology and Radium Therapy, 1949-66. Editor Your Radiologist, 1956-68, Cancer, 1964-72. Home: St Louis MO Died May 4, 1972; buried Oak Grove Cemetery St Louis MO

SCOTT, WILLIAM SHERLEY army officer; b. McKinney, Tex., Jan. 12, 1856; s. Col. Thomas M. and Elizabeth M. (Sherley) S.; m. Nelle Z. Hastings, Nov. 30, 1887 (dec.). Grad. U.S. Mil. Acad., 1880, Inf. and Cav. Sch., 1887; Army War Coll., 1908. Commd. 2d lt. 1st Cav., June 12, 1880; promoted through the grades successively to rank of brig. gen. U.S.A., Oct. 14, 1918; retired by operation of law, Jan. 12, 1920, age of 64. Commd. capt. asst. adj. gen. vols., May 9, 1898; maj. A.A.G., Sept. 17, 1898-May 12. 1899; lt. col. 44th Vol. Inf., 1899-1901; col. and asst. chief Philippine Constabulary, 1903-06; brig. gen. N.A., Aug. 5, 1917, vacated by apptmt. to brig. gen. regular army, Oct. 1918. Sec. Inf. and Cav. Sch., 1890-94; adj. 1st Cav., 1894-98; asst. adj. gen. 7th Army Corps, 1898-99, of Philippine Div., 1902-03; adj. gen. Dept. of Tex., 1910-13; in charge militia affairs Southern Dept., adj. 1st Cav. Brigade, and chief of staff 15th Militia Div., 1913-16; comdg. 1st O.T.C., Leon Springs, Tex., May-Aug. 1917. Participated in Sioux Indian Campaign, 1890-91, in Cuba and Puerto Rico, Spanish-Am. War, 1898-99, Philippine Insurrection, 1899-1901; recommended for brig. gen. vols. for suppressing insurrection and securing surrender insurgent forces, World War I; comdg. 59th Brigade Aug.-Sept. 22, and 30th div., Camp Seiver,

Greenville, S.C., to Nov. 8, 1917; comdg. Base Sect. 2, Bordeaux, France, Dec. 3, 1917-Aug. 10, 1918; in charge constrn. and training area of S.W. France, commdg. 41st Div. in France, Aug.-Nov. 1918, 153d Depot Brigade, Camp Dix, N.J., to Dec. 15, 1918; comdg. Ft. Oglethorpe, Ga., and demobilization center, Dec. 18, 1918-Oct. 26, 1919; comdg. Ft. Sam Houston, Tex., to Jan. 12, 1920. Decorations: Gold Medalist Army Team; medals Indian Wars, Spanish-Am. War, Cuban Occupation. Puerto Rican Campaign, Mexican Border, World War; Officer Legion of Honor (France), 1919. V.p. Sam Houston State Bank & Trust Co., 1920-23, pres., 1923-32; chmn. bd. Nat. Bank of Fort Sam Houston, 1932-——. Address: San Antonio, Tex. Died Aug. 31, 1941.

SCOTT, WINFIELD army officer; b. Laurel Branch, Va., June 13, 1786; s. William and Ann (Mason) S.; attended Coll. William and Mary, 1805-06; m. Maria D. Mayo, Mar. 11, 1817, 7 children. Commd. lance cpl. in Petersburg (Va.) troop of cavalry, 1807; commd. capt. of light artillery U.S. Army, May 3, 1808; court martialled for criticizing superior officer Gen. James Wilkinson, 1809, suspended from Army for 1 year; served on staff brig. gen. Wade Hampton, New Orleans, 1811-12; promoted to lt. col., 1812; captured by British at battle of Queenstown, N.Y., Oct. 1812; paroled, Nov. 1812; promoted col., Mar. 1813; led forces which captured Ft. George and defeated British at Upholds Creek, N.Y.; promoted brig. gen., Mar. 9, 1814; led Am. troops at battle on Chippewa River at Lundy's Lane. N.Y.; directed writing of 1st standard set of drill regulations for army Rules and Regulations for the Field Exercise and Maneuvers of Infantry, 1815; head of board to determine which officers would be discharged from army after War of 1812; studied French mil. methods in Europe, 1815-16; early temperance leader, wrote scheme for Restricting the Use of Ardent Spirits in the United States, 1821; pres. boards of tactics, 1815, 21, 24, 26; revised and enlarged Infantry-Tactics for army, 1835; given command in Black Hawk War, 1832 (troops rendered inactive by cholera epidemic); sent by Pres. Jackson to S.C. during nullification troubles; sent to Fla. to conduct campaign against Creek and Seminole Indians, 1835; recalled by President Jackson, 1837, returned to command of Eastern Div. in N.Y., 1837; commd. to restore order on Canadian border in Caroline affair (in which U.S. citizens gave aid and sympathy to rebels in Canada who demanded more democratic govt.), 1838; transported 16,000 Cherokee Indians from Tenn. and S.C. to new lands west of Mississippi River, spring 1838; sent again to Canadian border to settle boundary dispute between Canada and Me., fall 1838; gen.-in-chief U.S. Army, 1841-61; dissatisfied with accomplishments of Gen. Zachary Taylor in Mexican War, personally led forces in Mexico; captured Vera Cruz, Mar. 26, 1847; led troops in victories at Cerro Gordo, Contreras, Churubusco, Molina del Rey and Capultepec; occupied Mexico City, Sept. 14, 1847; Whig candidate for Pres. U.S., 1852, defeated by Franklin Pierce; lt. gen., 1855; settled Anglo-Am. dispute over possession of San Juan Island in Puget Sound, 1859; retired due to infirmities and age, Nov. 1, 1861; remained loyal to U.S. during Civil War, although Confederacy sought his services. Died West Point, N.Y., May 29, 1866; buried National Cemetery, West Point.

SCREWS, WILLIAM PRESTON, army officer; b. Montgomery, Ala., Jan. 1, 1875; s. Henry Preston and Nora (Canty) S.; student Savage Sch., Starke's Univ. Sch., Montgomery, Ala., Marion (Ala.) Mil. Inst., Infantry Sch., Ft. Benning, Ga., 1925, Army War Coll., Washington, 1929; m. Josephine W. Lahey, Nov. 17, 1901; 1 son, James Lahey. Commd. as 2d lt., 1899, advanced through grades to brig. gen., 1940: asst. gov. Mindinao, 1905-07; comd. 167 Inf., 84 Inf. Brig., 42 Div. (Rainbow) World War I; ret., June 1940. Awarded D.S.M.; mem. French Legion of Honor; Citation Comdr. in Chief, A.E.F. City commr. Montgomery, Ala., 1931-47; mem. Ala. Alcoholic Beverage Control Bd. since 1948. Mem. Am. Legion, Rainbow Veterans, Vets. Fgn. Wars, Spanish Am. Vets. Democrat. Presbyterian. Mason (K.T., Shriners, 33 deg., Scottish Rite). Clubs: Rotary (hon.), Army-Navy (Washington), Beauvoir Country. Home: 208 Fairview Av., Montgomery AL

SCRIBNER, GILBERT HILTON corp. exec.; b. New Rochelle, N.Y., Oct. 17, 1890; s. Gilbert Hilton and Josephine Romeyn (Brown) S.; Ph.B., Yale Sci. Sch., 1912; LL.D., U. Kansas City; m. Nancy D. Van Dyke, May 7, 1917 (dec. 1962); children—Gilbert Hilton (U.S. Navy), William V. D. (killed in action in Germany, Apr. 1945), Gertrude Hunter (Mrs. Robert S. Smith), Nancy Brown (Mrs. William T. Kirk, Jr.), Mary (Mrs. Robert D. Judson) m. 2d, Josephine Sidley Kennedy, Sept. 2, 1964. Engaged in central bus. real estate and bldg. mgmt. since 1912; dir. Wm. Wrigley, Jr., Co. IBM Corp., First Nat. Bank Chgo., Clearing Indsl. Dist., Midland Warehouses, Inc., Abercrombie & Fitch; pres. Scribner & Co. Commd. capt. 41st Brigade Army Arty., World War I; 1st Ill. F.A., 1914-16. Trustee Northwestern U., Mut. Life Ins. Co. N.Y. Republican. Episcopalian. Clubs: Commercial, Chicago, University, Indian Hill, Old Elm. Home: 812 Ash St., Winnetka, Ill. Office: 38 S. Dearborn St., Chgo. Died Dec. 31, 1966.

SCRIVEN, GEORGE PERCIVAL army officer; b. Philadelphia, Pa., Feb. 21, 1854; s. Charles Henry and Elizabeth (Shuff) S.; entered U. of Chicago, class 1875, Rensselaer Poly., Troy, N.Y., class 1876, leaving after 2 yrs. to enter U.S. Mil. Acad., from which grad. 1878 (5th in class); m. Bertha, d. Gen. Edward S. Bragg, Feb. 7. 1891 (died 1914); m. 2d, Elizabeth, d. Peter McQuade, Oct. 6, 1915. Second lt. 8th Infantry, June 14, 1878; trans. to Arty. and to the Signal Corps, Dec. 18, 1890; capt., June 14, 1892; maj. Signal Corps; promoted through grades to brig. gen., and chief signal officer of the Army, Mar. 5, 1913; retired Feb. 3, 1917. Served at various posts; mil. attaché, Mexico City, 1894, Rome, 1894-97; present at coronation of Emperor of Russia, 1896; detailed with Turkish forces, 1897; chief signal officer, Dept. of Gulf, Spanish-Am. War, May-June 1898; with 4th Philippine Expdn., 1898; on staff of Gen. Wesley Merritt, in Philippines; served in Cuba, 1899, and in Philippines; chief signal officer of the Visayas, and chief signal officer China Relief Expdn., Aug.-Nov. 1900; in Philippines to May 1901; on duty St. Louis Expn., 1904; chief signal officer Dept. of East, 1904-09, Philippines Div., 1909-11; asst. to chief signal officer of the army, July 1911-Feb. 1913. Cited "for gallantry in action" against Chinese Boxer forces at Yang-Tsun, Aug. 6, 1900, and "for gallantry in action" against Boxer forces at Peking August 14-15, 1900; medal, War Dept., for gallantry in the field. Catholic. Mem. orders of the Dragon and the Cara; bao; badges: Spanish-Am. War, Philippines, Army of Cuban Occupation. China Relief Expdn. (with 2 silver stars), Mexican Expdn., foreign service Great War. Recommended by Gen. Chaffee for bvtd. lt. col. "for gallant conduct" at Yang'Tsun, Aug. 6, 1900, and at Peking, Aug. 14 and 15, 1900. Apptd. by the President mem. Nat. Advisory Com. for Aeronautics, and elected chmn. Applied for retirement after more tan 42 yrs.' service, Dec. 30, 1916; retired Feb. 13, 1917; applied for active service in case of war, same date; on active duty under instructions from the President, Sept. 17, 1917; designated by Sec. of State at request of Sec. of War, Sept. 24, 1917, as mil. attaché to Am. Embassy at Rome, Italy; reported at Rome, Nov. 15, 1917, proceeded to the Italian front along the Piave River, later detailed as observer with the Italian armies; served with Italian troops in the Balkans, and awarded decoration Grand Officer Crown of Italy; on duty War Coll., Washington, July 1-Sept. 27. 1918. Awarded gold medal by Mil. Service Instn. for article "Nicaragua Canal and Its Military Aspects," 1893; wrote (brochure) "Transmission of Military Information," 1908; "The Story of the Hudson Bay Company." Address: Washington, D.C. Died Mar. 7, 1940.

SCRUGHAM, JAMES GRAVES (skrug'am), U.S. senator; b. Lexington, Ky., Jan. 19, 1880; s. James Grinstead and Theodotia (Allen) S.; B.M.E., State U. of Ky., 1900, M.E., 1906; m. Julia McCann, Aug. 4, 1904; children—James G., Martha. Successively with Creaghead Engring. Co. (Cincinnati), Met. West Side Elevated Ry. Co. (Chicago), Abner Doble Co. (San Francisco), 1899-1903; prof. of mech. engring., Engineering College, University of Nevada, 1903-14, dean, 1914-17; state engineer of Nevada, 1917-23. Pub. service commr., State of Nev., 1919-23; gov. of Nev., term 1923-27; spl. adviser to the sec. of the Interior, on Colorado River development projects, 1927; mem. 73d to 77th Congresses (1933-43), at large, Nev.; chmn. subcom. on Naval Appropriations, Ho. of Reps.; elected U.S. senator from Nev., Nov. 1942. Associate member of U.S. Naval Consulting Bd., 1916. Commd. maj., O.R.C., 1917; lt. col. U.S. Army, 1918; lt. col. 517th Regt. Coast Arty., U.S. Army Res. Commr. exhibits for Nev., San Francisco Expn., 1915; Nevada agt. and signatory Colorado River Compact, 1922; Nat. v. comdr. Am. Legion, 1920-21 (State comdr., 1919-20). Mem. Tau Beta Pi, Sigma Chi, Phi Kappa Phi. Democrat. Mason, Elk. Former pub. Nevada State Journal, Reno. Address: Reno, Nev. Died June 2, 1945.

SCUDDER, NATHANIEL army officer, Continental congressman; b. Monmouth County, N.J., May 10, 1733; s. Jacob and Abia (Rowe) S.; grad. Coll. of N.J. (now Princeton), 1751; m. Isabella Anderson, Mar. 23, 1752, 5 children. Elder, Tennent Ch., nr. Freehold, N.J.; trustee Princeton, 1778-81; became mem. local com. of safety; del. to 1st N.J. Provincial Congress, New Brunswick, 1774; speaker N.J. Gen. Assembly, 1776; lt. col. 1st Monmouth County Regt., N.J. Militia, 1776; commd. col., 1781; del. Continental Congress, 1777-1779; present at Battle of Monmouth; his most important service was writing letter to John Hart (speaker N.J. Legislature), strongly urging that state's delegates to Congress be empowered to ratify and sign Articles of Confederation, 1778. Killed while resisting invading party of Brit. Army at Blacks Point nr. Shrewsbury, N.J., Oct. 16, 1781; buried Tennent Churchyard, Monmouth Battlefield, N.J.

SCULLY, C(HARLES) ALISON banker; b. Pitts., Oct. 17, 1887; s. Charles D. and Mary (Scott) S.; B.S., U. Pa., 1909, LL.B., 1912; m. Elizabeth G. Williams, Nov. 2, 1920; children—Scott Williams, David Williams, Elizabeth Alison, John Alison. Admitted to Pa. bar, 1912, and practiced in Phila., 1912-17; trust officer Corn Exchange Nat. Bank of Phila., 1920-23; 2d v.p. Nat. Bank of Commerce, N.Y.C., 1923-26, v.p., 1926-29; v.p Bank of the Manhattan Co., N.Y.C., 1929-42; exec. v.p., dir. Corn Exchange Nat. Bank & Trust

Co. of Phila., 1942-51; pres. Corporate Fiduciaries Assn. of N.Y.C., 1932, 33. Served as capt. and adj. 51st Inf. 6th Div., U.S. Army, later Courier Service with AEF, 1917-19. Mem. S.R., Soc. Colonial Wars, Am. Acad. of Polit. and Social Science, Assn. Bar City of N.Y., Phila. Bar Assn., Phila. Orchestra (dir.), Pa. Academy Fine Arts (dir.), Psi Upsilon. Republican. Presbyn. Clubs: University, Century (N.Y.C.); Philadelphia, Rittenhouse, Orpheus, University Barge, Merion Cricket (Phila.). Author: Insurance Trusts, 1927; Business Life Insurance Trusts (with F. W. Ganse), 1930; The Course of the Silver Greyhound, 1936; The Purchase of Common Stocks as Trust Investments, 1937. Home: Boxwood, Conestoga Rd., Box 127, Bryn Mawr, Pa. Died Nov. 8, 1954.

SCULLY, JAMES WALL brig. gen. U.S.A.; b. Kilkenny, Ireland, Feb. 19, 1838; s. Thomas Sadlier and Eleanor Cairns (Wall) S.; ed. St. Kiernan's Coll., Kilkenny, 1848-51; studied surveying under father, in Ulster County, N.Y., and Gallatin, Tenn., 1852-56; m. Mary Adelaide Cuddy, 1862. Served pvt., corporal and sergt., Co. K, 1st Arty., 1856-61; in vols. as 1st lt. and regimental q.m., 10th Tenn. Inf., July 14, 1862; lt. col., Aug. 21, 1863; col., June 6, 1864; hon. mustered out of vol. service, May 25, 1865; apptd. capt. a.q.m. U.S.A., Sept. 27, 1865; maj. q.m., Jan. 25, 1883; lt. col. deputy q.m. gen., Sept. 12, 1894; col. a.q.m. gen., Feb. 4, 1898; retired at own request, Nov. 1, 1900; advanced to rank of brig. gen. re- tired, by act of Apr. 23, 1904. Bvtd.: maj. (for Mill Springs, Ky.), lt. col. (for Shiloh), and col. (for Nashville), Sept. 27, 1865. Roman Catholic. Address: Atlanta, Ga. Died June 2, 1918.

SCULLY, WILLIAM AUGUSTINE b. New York City. Aug. 24. 1886; s. Daniel Joseph and Julia (Browne) S.; ed. pub. schs., business coll., under pvt. tutor and Georgetown U.; m. Asenath Genevieve Hall, June 1913; children—Kate Hyde, William Hall. Began as bank and stock broker, New York, later newspaper reporter and special newspaper corr.; officer or dir. mfg. and banking corps.; v.p. Ridgway Pub. Co.; dir. Washington Rapid Transit Co.; advisory editor Text Book of Aerial Laws. Spl. attaché for polit.-economic affairs, Div. of Western European Affairs, Dept. of State, 1919-20; Eastern dir. Foreign Language Bur. of Rep. Nat. Com., 1923. Sec. El Paso County (Colo.) Rep. Com., 1910; asst. Eastern dir. of publicity under Republican Nat. Com., campaign, 1923; alternate del. Rep. Conv., N.Y. State, from 1st Assembly Dist., 1926, 27. Served 3 yrs. as mem. 3d Battery, F.A., 2 yrs. with Troop C, Cav. N.Y.N.G., and of Denver City Troop, 2 yrs. Capt. Aviation Sect., Signal Corps, and maj. Air Service, assigned to Gen. Staff, World War I, served 1917-20 as spl. operative, Office of Naval Intelligence; mem. Clearance Com. of War Industries Board, Washington, and mem. Council Nat. Defense, Washington, 1917; lt. col. Mil. Attaché Sect., Mil. Intelligence, O.R.C., 1921-—. Mem. American Acad. of Political and Social Science, Am. Political Science Association. Catholic. Home: Washington, D.C. Deceased.

SEABURY, GEORGE TILLEY sec. Am. Soc. of Civil Engrs.; b. Newport, R.I., Apr. 12, 1880; s. T. Mumford and Mary S. (Tilley) S.; S.B. in Civil Engring., Mass. Inst. Tech., 1902; m. Margaret Howard Knight, Sept. 6, 1904; children—Howard Knight (dec.), T. Mumford III (dec.), Mary Knight (Mrs. Mary Seabury Ray). Field engr. for contractors and construction engr. on subways, Riverside Drive, Grand Central Terminal, etc., N.Y. City, 1902-06; engr. with Bd. of Water Supply, N.Y. City, on Catskill Aqueduct, 1906-15; div. engr. Water Supply Bd., Providence, R.I., on new water supply development, 1915-18; maj. Q.M.C., U.S. Army, and supervising constrn. q.m., Apr. 1918-June 1919; pres., gen. mgr. George T. Seabury, Inc., gen. constrn., 1919-23; sec. Am. Soc. C.E. since Jan. 1, 1925. Mem. Am. Soc. C.E., Engring. Inst. of Can.. Delta Upsilon, Chi Epsilon (nat. hon.). Episcopalian. Office: 33 W. 39th St., New York, N.Y. Died May 25, 1945.

SEAGRAVE, LOUIS H. investment banker; b. Council Bluffs, Ia., May 15, 1892; s. Alfred Amos and Helen M. (Kinne) S.; A.B., U. Wash., 1917; m. Clare E. Nelson, Nov. 24, 1917; 1 son, John Dorrington. Mem. staff Seattle Post Intelligencer, 1915-16, Seattle Times, 1916-17; mgr. Seattle office Lumbermen's Trust Co., 1918-21, v.p., cashier, 1921; sales mgr. First Nat. Corp., Boston, 1923-25; pres. Am. Founders Corp. and United Founders Corp., N.Y.C. from orgn. to 1935 when consolidated into Am. Gen. Corp. of which was dir. and chmn. bd. to 1940; dir. Standard Power & Light Corp., Torque Corp.; pres., chmn. bd. Consol. Va. Mining Co.; dir., chmn. bd. Nat. Machine Products, mfrs. parts and accessories for mil. airplanes, Los Angeles, 1941-45; owner L. H. Seagrave Co., Corporate Finance; pres. Petroleum Properties Inc.; chmn. bd., dir. Prodn. Aids, Inc., Golden Valley Land Co., Ariz.; sec.-treas. Golden Valley Devel. Co., Cal.; dir. Electronic Prodn. and Devel., Inc., Los Angeles. Chmn. bd. Cal. Inst. Cancer Research, 1945-54. Served as maj., inf. U.S. Army, 1918. Mem. Acad. Polit. Sci., Am. Legion (mem. exec. com. 1921), Delta Tau Delta, Sigma Delta Chi. Clubs: University (N.Y.C.); Annandale (Pasadena, Cal.); California (Los Angeles). Home: 369 E. Calaveras St., Altadena, Cal. 91001. Office: 1801 Beverly Blvd., Los Angeles 57. Died Nov. 23, 1966.

SEALS, CARL H. army officer; born Eufaula, Ala., Dec. 31, 1882; commd. 1st lt. Inf., Ala. Nat. Guard, July 1904, and advanced to maj. 1914; called into Fed. service, 1916, duty on Mexican Border; overseas, World War I. Comd. maj. Inf. Regular Army, Sept. 1920, and advanced to brig. gen., Jan. 1942; served with Mil. Intelligence Div., War Dept. Gen. Staff, Washington, D.C., 1931-35, also chief of Pub. Relations Br. and for 2 yrs. in charge of War Dept. Press Section; ordered for duty as adjutant gen., Philippines, Sept. 1935-37; on duty in Hdqrs., Fourth Corps Area, Atlanta, Ga., 1937-40; returned to Fort William McKinley, as adjutant gn. of the Philippine Div., Philippine Islands, June 1940; brig. gen., Army U.S., since Jan. 1942; Adjt. Gen. U.S. Army Forces in the Far East, Manila, July 1941 to surrender May 1942; prisoner of war, Japanese army, May 1942-Sept. 1945. Awarded Distinguished Service Medal. Ret. Oct. 1946. Mem. Am. Legion. Mason (Shriner). Home: 314 Riverview Blvd., Daytona Beach, Fla. Died Oct. 29, 1955.

SEAMAN, GILBERT EDMUND M.D.; b. Alpena, Mich., Sept. 19, 1869; s. Ami L. and Jessie (Gordon) S.; grad. Episcopal Acad. of Michigan, 1886; student Detroit College of Medicine; M.D., Mich. College of Medicine and Surgery, 1889; studied univs. of Würzburg and Berlin. Began practice at Milwaukee, 1892; now med. supt. Winnebago State Hosp. Captain and asst. surgeon, U.S. Vols., Spanish-Am. War, serving in P.I.; maj. and surgeon, Wis. N.G., 1903-13; surgeon gen. of Wis., 1913-—; col. Med. Corps, chief surgeon 32d Div. and chief surgeon, 6th Army Corps. A.E.F. Regent at-large U. of Wis.; mem. Wis. State Bd. Edn.; dir. Div. Mental Hygiene State Dept. Public Welfare; former clin. dir. Shorewood Hosp. Sanitarium. Fellow Am. Coll. Surgeons, Royal Inst. Public Health. Awarded D.S.M. (U.S.); mem. Legion of Honor (France). Republican. Protestant. Author: Compendium for Medical Officers, 1917; History Medical Dept. 32d Division; Lister as a Scientist; Problems Relating to Care of Insane in Wisconsin. Home: Madison, Wis. Died May 25, 1941.

SEARBY, EDMUND WILSON (ser'bi), army officer; b. Berkeley, Calif., Mar. 7, 1896; s. Frederick Wright and Ellen (Porter) S.; U. of Calif., 1914-16; B.S., U.S. Mil. Acad., 1918; grad. Field Arty. Sch., 1928; Command and Gen. Staff Sch., 1940; Cav. Sch., 1929; attended Ecole d'Application d'Artillerie, 1920-21; m. Muriel MacLeod, Aug. 26, 1930; children—Lucy Carter, Frederick Wright, Daniel MacLeod. Commd. 2d lt. F.A., 1918; promoted through grades to brig. gen., 1943; comdg. gen. 80th Div. Arty. Awarded Victory medal. Mem. Delta Chi. Home: Sebastopol, Calif. Died Sept. 14, 1944.

SEARS, CLINTON BROOKS brig. gen. U.S.A.; b. Penn Yan, N.Y., June 2, 1844; s. Clinton William and Angeline (Brooks) S.; ed. pub. and high schs., and Ohio Wesleyan U., to 1862; grad. U.S. Mil. Acad., 3d in class of 63, 1867; (hon. A.B., Ohio Wesleyan, 1881, A.M., 1884); m. Lydia Evelyn Smith, Oct. 22, 1873; 2d, Mrs. Alice (Bullock) Peevers, Feb. 11, 1902. Served as pvt., corporal and acting color sergt. Co. G, 95th Ohio Inf., July 24, 1862-Sept. 15, 1863, commd. 2d lt. and 1st lt., U.S. Engrs., June 17, 1867; capt., Apr. 9, 1880; maj., Sept. 20, 1892; lt. col., Apr. 21, 1903; col., Jan. 11, 1907. Recommended to the President as cadet to U.S. Mil. Acad. by Gens. Grant and Sherman, after competitive exam, from 15th Army Corps; has served in U.S. and P.I. in constrn. of river and harbor works, fortifications, roads. bridges, canals, locks, dams, etc.; asst. prof. civ. and mil. engring., 1876-77, geography, history and ethics, 1877-78, mechanics, acoustics, optics and astronomy, 1878-82, U.S. Mil. Acad.; instr. submarine mining, U.S. Engr. Sch., Willets Point, N.Y., 1891-92; chief engr. div. of the Philippines, 1901-03; mem. and pres. Miss. River Commn., engr. 15th light house dist. and in charge of improvement of Miss. River from St. Louis to Cairo; pres. spl. bd. to report upon 14 ft. water way project from Chicago to the Gulf; retired, June 1, 1908, with rank of brig. gen. U.S.A. Fellow Nat. Acad. Design. Author of numerous official reports. 1870-—, and of Ransom Genealogy. Home: Newton Centre, Mass. Died 1912.

SEARS, JAMES HAMILTON commodore U.S.N.; b. Binghamton, N.Y., Jan. 6, 1855; s. Charles William and Augusta (Howe) S.; grad. U.S. Naval Acad., 1876; m. Rosa Helen Ranlett, Feb. 4, 1885. Promoted ensign, Apr. 1879; lt., jr. grade, Dec. 1884; lt., Sept. 1892; lt. comdr., May 1899; comdr., Jan. 1905; capt., August 1908; commodore and voluntarily retired, June 30, 1910. Served in Yantic, Kearsarge and Tennessee, China squadron, 1876-78; Kearsarge, N. Atlantic squadron, U.S. Naval Acad. and Navy Yard, Boston, 1879-81; Monitor Montauk, 1881-82; Training Ship Portsmouth, 1883-85; Naval Observatory, 1885-86; Schoolship St. Mary, 1887-89; Baltimore, 1890-92; spl. duty, Navy Dept. and Staff War College, Newport. R.I., 1892-93; U.S. Coast and Geod. Survey, 1894-97; U.S. Naval Home, Phila., 1897-98; flag lt. Brooklyn, on staff Commodore W. S. Schley, in W.I. and spl. duty with Puerto Rico Commission during and afterwards, Spanish-Am. War, 1898; U.S.S. Indiana, torpedo sta., Newport, 1898-99; flag lt., staff Rear Admiral W. S. Schley on Chicago, S. Atlantic Sta., 1900-01; in charge hydrographic office, New York, 1901-02; exec. officer Brooklyn, Mediterranean Squadron, and in command Alliance, Vixen, Gloucester, 1903-04; insp. 8th lighthouse dist., Gulf of Mex., 1905-07; China squadron, 1907-08, naval attaché, U.S. Embassy, Tokyo and Am. Legation, Peking, 1909-10. Author: The Chilian Revolution of 1891; War on the Coast. Died Dec. 8, 1915.

SEATON, ROY ANDREW, educator, engineer; b. Glasco, Kan., Apr. 17, 1884; s. Oren Andrew and Sarah Elizabeth (Bartley) S.; B.S. in Mech. Engring., Kan. State Coll., 1904, M.S., 1910; studied U. of Wis., summer 1908; S.B. in Mech. Engring., Mass. Inst. Tech., 1911; Sc.D., honorary, Northeastern University, 1942; m. Gay Perry, June 26, 1913 (died Oct. 4, 1918); 1 son, James Newell; m. 2d, Elnora Wanamaker, June 14, 1921; children—Sarah Frances, Robert Wanamaker, Elnora Margaret, Roy Andrew, II. With Kan. State Coll. most of time, 1904-70, instr. asst. prof. of mathematics, 1904-06, instr. and asst. prof. mech. engring., 1906-10, prof. applied mechanics and machine design, 1910-20, dean school of engring. and architecture and director Engineering Experimental Station, 1920-49; prof. applied mechanics Kan. State Coll., 1949-70; on leave of absence as director of Engineering, Science and Management Defense Training, U.S. Office of Edn., 1940-42; acad. dir. Air Force Inst. Tech., Wright-Patterson AFB, O., 1953-57; designing draftsman steam turbine dept. Gen. Electric Co., 1911-12. Served as capt. engring. div. Ordnance Office, U.S. Army, Washington, D.C., designing arty. ammunition Jan.-Dec. 1918. Chmn. Kan. Registration Bd. for Professional Engrs., 1931-47; chmn. Kansas Bd. Engring. Examienrs since 1947; director Nat. Council of State Bds. of Engring. Examiners, 1935-37; rep. of Soc. for Promotion Engring. Edn. on Engrs. Council for Professional Development, 1937-42; mem. Com. on Professional Training, Engrs. Council for Professional Development, 1933-38. Mem. Am. Soc. Mech. Engrs. (past vice chmn. Mid-Continent sect.), Soc. for Promotion Engring. Edn. (pres. Neb.-Kan. Sect. 1923-24; mem. council 1926-29; v.p. 1930-31; pres. 1932-33; awarded Lamme medal, 1942), Kan. Engring. Soc. (v.p. and acting pres. 1929-30; pres. 1930-31), Engring. Sect. Assn. Land Grant Colls. and Univs. (sec. 1925-29; chmn. 1929-30), Am. Assn. U. Profs. (hon.), Phi Kappa Phi, Sigma Xi, Sigma Tau, Acacia. Mason. Clubs: Manhattan Country, Rotary. Author: Concrete Construction for Rural Communities, 1916; also bulletins, arts. in tech. press, etc. Editor Engring. Expt. Sta. Record Quarterly, 1925-29, Engring. Expt. Sta. Record Summary, 1929. Home: Manhattan KS2Died May 23, 1970; buried Sunset Cemetery Manhattan KS

SEAY, WILLIAM ALBERT, coll. dean; b. Charleston, Mo., Sept. 12, 1920; s. William Arthur and Rui (Brooks) S.; B.S.A., U. Ky., 1942, M.S., 1948; Ph.D. in Soils, U. Wis., 1950; m. Lyda Maxine Short, June 27, 1943; children—Edward Allen, Sally Brooks, Jeffrey Short. Asst. prof. agr. U. Ky., 1949-52, asso. prof., 1952-54, prof., 1954-56, adminstrv. asst. to dean, 1956-57, vice dir. Agrl. Expt. Sta., Lexington, 1957, acting dean Coll. Agr. and Home Econs., also acting dir. Ky. Extension Service and Ky. Agr. Expt. Sta., 1958-59, 61-62, dean and dir., 1962-69. Served to lt. col. AUS, 1942-46. Mem. A.A.A.S., Am. Soc. Agronomy, Internat. Soil Sci. Soc., Soil Sci. Soc. Am., Association Southern Agrl. Workers (pres. 1967), Ky. Acad. Sci., Sigma Ki, Alpha Zeta, Gamma Sigma Delta. Contbr. articles profl. jours. Home: Lexington KY Died Feb. 1, 1969.

SEBREE, EDMUND B(OWER) army cons.; b. Olney, Ill., Jan. 7, 1898; s. Milton Eddy and Catella (Bower) S.; ed. Cornell, 1916-17; B.S., U.S. Mil. Acad., 1919; Inf. Sch., 1919-20; Signal Sch., 1926-27; Command and Gen. Staff Sch., 1936-37; m. Pauline Barbara Weber, Feb. 10, 1920; children—Elizabeth Bower (Mrs. Mark F. Brennan), Martha, (Mrs. R. C. McAlister), Pauline Carlsen (Mrs. John L. Olow III). Commd. 2d lt. 1918, advanced through grades to maj. gen., 1951; prof. mil. sci., tactics Western Mil. Acad., Alton, Ill., 1928-32; Gen. Staff duty with troops, 1940; with War Dept., Gen. Staff, 1942; combat service on Guadalcanal, Solomon Islands; comdg. gen. Americal Div., Jan.-June 1943; asst. Div. Comdr. 35th Inf. Div., 1943; Army attache to Australia, 1946; comdg. gen. II Constabulary Brigade, 1946-48; comdg. gen. Munich (Germany) Mil. Post, 1947-51; comdg. gen. U.S. troops Trieste, 1951-52; comdg. gen. 5th Armd. Div., Camp Chaffee, Ark., 1952-53; dep. comdg. gen. 1st Army, Governor's Island, N.Y., 1953-54; comdg. gen. 7th inf. div., Korea, 1954-55; chief of staff CONARC, Ft. Monroe, Va., 1955-57, ret.; cons. George Washington U. HumRRO Unit No. 5, 1957-—. Decorated D.S.M., Silver Star; Oak Leaf Cluster to D.S.M.; Legion of Merit; Bronze Star Medal; Purple Heart. Mem. Assn. grads. U.S. Mil. Acad. S.A.R. Mason. Elk. Home: P.O. Box 1975, Carmel, Cal. 93921. Died June 25, 1966; buried San Francisco Nat. Cemetery, Presidio San Francisco.

SEBREE, URIEL rear admiral U.S.N.; b. Fayette. Mo., Feb. 20, 1848; s. John P. and Louisa (Daly) S.; early edn. in schools of Fayette, Mo.; grad. U.S. Naval Acad., 1867; m. Annie Bridgman, June 16, 1886. Leaving Naval Acad. as midshipman in June 1867, served in divers duties and grades as naval officer in various parts of the world until promoted capt., Oct. 9, 1901; rear admiral, July 8, 1907. Was on Arctic relief expdn. on S.S. Tigress, 1873, under Comdr. Greer; on Greely relief expdn., 1884, under Comdr. Schley; on U.S.S. Baltimore, under command of Capt. Schley, 1889-92; light house insp., Portland, Ore., 1885-89, San Francisco, 1898-1901; comd. gunboat Wheeling, in Behring Sea, 1897-98; comd. Naval Sta., Samoan Islands, 1901-02; comd. battleship Wisconsin, 1903-04; naval sec., Lighthouse Bd., 1904; comdg. 2d div. Pacific Fleet, 1907-09; comdr.-in-chief Pacific Fleet, 1909-10; retired, Feb. 20, 1910. Home: Coronado, Calif. Died Aug. 6, 1922.

SEDDON, JAMES congressman, Confederate sec. of war; b. Fredericksburg, Va., July 13, 1815; s. Thomas and Susan (Pearson) S.; grad. Law Sch., U. Va., 1835; m. Sarah Bruce, 1845. Admitted to bar, 1838; mem. U.S. Ho. of Reps. from Va., 29th, 31st congresses, 1845-47, 49-51, supported John Calhoun; mem. com. on resolutions Peace Conv., Washington, D.C., 1861, introduced minority report which recognized right of peaceful secession; elected to 1st Confederate Congress, 1861; sec. of war Confederate States Am., 1862-65, exerted considerable influence over Pres. Jefferson Davis until 1863, worked closely with Gen. Robert E. Lee, approved his movement to take offensive at Battle of Gettysburg, 1863, performed duties of office with tact, indecisive in settling adminstrv. problems, resigned at time of cabinet reorgn., 1865; ret. to estate "Sabot Hill," Goochland County, Va. Died "Sabot Hill," Aug. 19, 1880; buried Hollywood Cemetery, Richmond, Va.

SEDGWICK, JOHN army officer; b. Cornwall Hollow, Conn., Sept. 13, 1813; s. Benjamin and Olive (Collins) S.; grad. U.S. Mil. Acad., 1837. Served with arty. U.S. Army during Seminole War, assisted in moving Cherokee Indians west of the Mississippi River; served on No. frontier during Canadian border disturbances; joined Gen. Zachary Taylor's army on Rio Grande River, 1846; participated in all battles of Mexican War; brevetted capt. and maj. for services at battles of Churubusco and Chapultepec respectively; maj. 1st Regt. of Cavalry, 1855; participated in Utah Expdn., 1857-58, also in warfare with Kiowa and Comanche Indians, 1858-60; lt. col. 2d Cavalry, 1861; col. 1st Cavalry, U.S. Army, 1862; transferred to 4th Cavalry; commd. brig. gen. U.S. Volunteers, 1862; commanded div. of Sumner's 2d Corps. during Va. peninsular campaign of 1862, participated in siege of Yorktown, pursuing Confederate Army up the peninsula; distinguished at battles of Fair Oaks, Savage Station, Glendale, Antietam; apptd. maj. gen. U.S. Volunteers in command 9th Corps, 1862, transferred to command 6th Corps, 1863; distinguished in Rappahannock campaign, Pa. campaign of 1863, as comdr. right wing of U.S. Army in battles of Chancellorsville, Fredericksburg, Gettysburg; distinguished in battles of Wilderness and Spotsylvania in Richmond campaign, 1864. Killed at battle of Spotsylvania (Va.), May 9, 1864; buried Cornwall Hollow.

SEDGWICK, ROBERT colonist, army officer; b. Wobwen, Bedfordshire, Eng., 1613; s. William and Elizabeth (Howe) S.; m. Joanna Blake. One of 1st settlers of Charlestown (Mass.); chosen capt. Charlestown Militia, 1637; an organizer Military Co. of Mass., capt., 1640, 45, 48; granted (with 6 others) a monopoly of Indian trade of Mass. Colony, until 1665; elected maj. gen. Mass. Colony, 1652; given charge of 12 ships and 800 men, sent to reinforce expdn. of William Penn, operating against Spanish West Indies. Died Jamaica, B.W.I., May 24, 1656.

SEELBACH, LOUIS, lawyer; b. Louisville, Mar. 29, 1890;2s. Louis and Marie Helen (Durbeck) S.; student Louisville Male High Sch., 1903-07; A.B. Centre Coll., Danville, Ky., 1910; LL.B., Harvard, 1914; m. Daisy A. Peck, Oct. 5, 1916; children—Harriet B. (Mrs. Warner L. Jones, Jr.), Helen L. (Mrs. Lewis R. Hardy, Jr.), Louis, Albert P. Admitted to Ky. bar, 1914 and since practiced in Louisville; mem. Middleton, Seelbach, Wolford, Willis & Cochran; gen. counsel Standard Oil Co. (Kentucky), 1956-63; pres. Bourbon Stock Yard Co., 1950-69, chairman of the board, 1969-71; division counsel Southern Ry. Company, from 1949. Mem. Louisville and Jefferson Co. Air Bd., 1930-41. Mem. bd. of trustees Center College, Ky., 1952-56. Served as 2d lieutenant F.A., U.S. Army, 1918. Mem. Am., Ky. and Louisville bar assns., Sigma Alpha Epsilon. Mason. Clubs: Pendennis, Louisville Country. Home: Louisville KY Died May 24, 1971; buried Cave Hill Cemetery Louisville KY

SEELY, HERMAN GASTRELL financial editor, writer; b. Chicago, Ill., Sept. 27, 1891; s. Herman Barker and Frances Anna (Edsall) S.; grad. Hyde Park High Sch.; spl. courses Northwestern U.; m. Gladys Frackelton, June 30, 1920; 1 dau. Marcia. Reporter, Chicago Herald, 1915-17; feature writer, Chicago Eve. Post, 1919-31, covering nat. politics editorially, 1920 and 1924 campaigns, asst. editorial writer, 1932-35, financial editor, 1925-30, chief editorial writer, 1931; with Chicago Daily News as editorial and financial writer since 1932 (following merger of Post and News); financial editor Chgo. Daily News, 1943-57, ret. Mem. 1st O.T.C., Ft. Sheridan, Ill., 1917; enlisted later in year, overseas 13 mos., winning commn. as 2d lt., Ordnance Corps, U.S. Army, 1918. Mem. Kenilworth Village bd. trustees, 1934-45, chmn. planning commn. since 1947. Mem. Westerners. Episcopalian. Clubs: Chicago Press Veterans Assn., Am. Legion, Wilmette Post No. 46. Author: A Son of the City (1917); Sagebrush Dentist (with Will Frackelton), 1941. Contbr. financial articles to various magazines, ann. supplement World Book Encyclopedia, and American Peoples Encyclopedia. Speaker on business subjects. Home: 700 Kent Rd., Kenilworth, Ill. Office: Chicago Daily News, 400 W. Madison St., Chgo. Died Feb. 17, 1958; buried Forest Home Cemetery, Milw.

SEELYE, THEODORE EDWARD cons. engr.; b. New Orleans, La., Nov. 7, 1887; s. Abram Booth and Mary (O'Connor) S.; spl. student, civil engring., U. of Mich., 1909-12; m. Georgia Reily Bailey, Nov. 6, 1922 (dec.); children—Caroline Reily (Mrs. Henry Cadwalader), James Bailey. With United States Engineer Department, 1906-09; hydraulic engr. Electric Bond & Share Co., 1913; div. engr. Water Supply Commn. of Pa., 1914-15; v.p. Gannett, Seelye & Fleming, Inc., 1916-32; director of Day & Zimmermann, Inc., 1933-—; pres. North Pa. R.R. Co.; dir. Girard Trust Corn Exchange Bank, Delaware & Bound Brook R.R. Co., Fidelity Mut. Life Ins. Co. Served as captain and major, Engineers, U.S. Army, 1917-19, with 30th Division, War Damages Board of American Peace Commission and G5 General Staff. Mem. bd. mgrs., Phila. Zoological Society, Pa. Hosp. Mem. Am. Soc. C.E., Newcomen Soc., Soc. American Military Engineers, Engineers Soc. Pa. Clubs: Rittenhouse, Philadelphia (Philadelphia); State (Schuylkill, Pa.). Home: Morris Rd., Ambler, Pa. Office: 1700 Sansom St., Philadelphia 3. Died Mar. 7, 1963.

SEIBELS, GEORGE GOLDTHWAITE, naval officer; b. Montgomery, Ala., Jan. 4, 1872; s. Emmet and Anne (Goldthwaite) S.; ed. Coll. Prep. Sch., Culpeper County, Va., 1886-88, Starke Univ. Sch., Montgomery, Ala., to 1896; m. Aileen Pettit, May 7, 1907; children—Mabel Pettit, Emmet, George Goldthwaite. Asst. paymaster U.S. Navy, 1896; advanced through grades to highest grade of Supply Corps and commd. pay dir. with rank of rear adm., Sept. 1933; retired from active service, Feb. 1, 1936. Decorated Dewey medal (Battle of Manila Bay), Spanish-Am. War, Philippine Campaign, Mexican Campaign and World War medals. Episcopalian. Home: 711 S. Perry St., Montgomery AL

SEIDEMANN, HENRY PETER (si'de-man), consultant, pub. adminstrn.; b. La Vernia, Tex., Apr. 4, 1883; s. William Joseph and Julia (Curtis) S.; B.C.S., D.C. Coll., 1923, M.C.S., 1925; LL.D., Southeastern U., 1938; m. Mabel Estelle Lyman, Sept. 21, 1910. Chief fiscal insp., U.S. Reclamation Service, 1910-13, chief accountant, 1914-15, chief clk., 1916; chief of accounting staff, Inst. for Govt. Research, 1916-17; tech. dir. Commn. on Pub. Accountancy, Ty. of Hawaii, 1924-27; chief of staff, financial and accounting research, Inst. for Govt. Research, Brookings Institution, 1927-48, retired 1948; treas. Brookings Institution to June 30, 1948; coördinator Federal Social Security Bd., 1935-36; dir. Bureau Old-Age Benefits, 1936-37; consultant Hoover Commn. for reorgn. Fed. Govt., 1948-49; management consultant O.P.S., 1951-52. Assistant treasurer American Red Cross, 1917-18; maj., U.S. Army, European comptroller American Red Cross headquarters, Paris, 1918-19, deputy director, Army Specialist Corps, with rank of brigadier general, 1942-43. Member (Dawes) Dominican Economic Commission, 1929; director survey of state and county government of N.C., 1930, Ala., 1931, N.H., 1932, and participated in other govtl. surveys of state and county govts. of Ia., 1933, Okla., 1935, Montgomery County, Md., 1941. Fellow D.C. Institute C.P.A.; mem. Am. Inst. Accountants, Political Sci. Association, Am. Acad. of Polit. and Soc. Sci., Soc. for Advancement of Management, Am. Inst. of Management (associated), Governmental Research Assn., Vets. of Foreign Wars of the U.S. Decorated Officer Crown of Rumania with swords, and Officer Star of Rumania with swords. Catholic. Club: Columbia Country (Washington). Joint Author: Puerto Rico and Its Problems, 1930. Author: Manual of Accounting and Reporting for the Operating Services of The National Government, 1926; Manual of Accounting, Reporting and Business Procedure for the Territorial Government of Hawaii, 1928; Curtailment of Non-Defense Expenditures, 1941. Assisted in reorganization of financial and accounting methods of American Red Cross to meet war conditions; installed budget and accounting systems in League of Red Cross Socs., Geneva, Switzerland; formulated plan of presentation of 1st and 2d nat. budgets, presented to Congress, 1921, 22; devised uniform accounting and reporting system for comptroller gen. of U.S.; organized auditing, accounting and disbursing depts. of Agrl. Adjustment Adminstrn., 1933; assisted in orgn. of all activities of the Social Security Board and supervised the preparation of all procedures having to do with registration and wage records of the 40 million eligibles under Title II of the Social Security Act; installed budget systems and uniform accounting methods in governments of Ty. of Hawaii, Dominican Republic and State of N.H. Home: The Ontario. Office: 2853 Ontario Rd., N.W., Washington. Died May 1954.

SEITZ, ALBERT BLAZIER fgn. service officer; b. Springfield, O., Aug. 16, 1898; s. Albert and Clara Edwards (Blazier) S.; student Wittenberg Coll., 1916-17, U.S. Mil. Acad., 1918-19, U. Wis., 1924-25, Franklin U., 1933-34, Ohio State U., 1934-35; certificate U. Va. Sch. Mil. Govt., 1942, Columbia, 1946; m. Mildred Ann Dodson, Sept. 4, 1920; children—Albert Blazier III, Sally Ann (Mrs. Edward Lewis (Ramsey), Robb Leigh. With Royal N.W. Mounted Police, Can., 1919-20; engr. Ohio Fuel Gas Co., 1926-28; engr. Pub. Utilities Commn. of Ohio, 1928-40; co-owner D & S Lumber & Tie Co., Columbus, O., 1949-—. With CIA, 1949-52; author, 1952-57; with ICA, 1957-—, chief Laos Tng. Assistance Group, U.S. Operations Mission, 1957-—. Served from capt. to col., AUS, 1940-49; chief OSS mission to Mihailovic, Yugoslavia, 1943-44, mem. French Resistance, 1944, mil. rep. Allied Control Commn., Rumania, 1946, chief civil censorship, Berlin, 1947, asst. mil. attache, Greece, 1947-49. Decorated Legion of Merit (U.S.); Order White Eagle with Swords (Serbia), 1944. Profl. engr., Ohio. Mem. Am. Soc. Profl. Engrs., S.A.R., Phi Kappa Psi. Author: Milhailovic—Hoax or Hero?, 1952; Children of the Mist (Civil War Guerrillas), 1960. Home: 4506 Longfellow St., Tampa, Fla. Office: USOM/PEO, care American Embassy, Vientiane, Laos. Died July 16, 1962; buried Riverside Cemetery, Columbus, O.

SEITZ, FRANK NOAH, gas co. exec.; b. St. Louis County, Mo., Sept. 25, 1909; s. Frank Lee and Catherine (Felchlin) S.; B.S. in Civil Engring., Washington U., St. Louis, 1933; m. Caroline Ruth Garrell, May 5, 1937. With So. Cal. Gas Co., 1939-50; with So. Counties Gas Co., Los Angeles, 1950-69, vice president, 1955-63, senior vice president, 1963-69, also director. Div. leader campaigns Santa Monica chpt. A.R.C., Los Angeles chpts. Am. Heart Assn. and Community Chest. Mem. Cal. Republican Central Com., 1958-69. Served to lt. col. AUS, 1940-46. Mem. Am., Pacific Coast gas assns., Am. Mgmt. Assn., Sales and Marketing Assn. Los Angeles (past dir.), U.S., Cal. chambers commerce, Sigma Xi. Presbyn. (past chmn. trustees). Mason. Home: Santa Monica CA Died Nov. 7, 1969.

SEITZ, GEORGE ALBERT naval officer; b. Mar. 13, 1897; entered U.S. Navy, 1916, and advanced through the grades to commodore, 1944. Address: care Chief of Naval Personnel, Navy Department, Washington 25, D.C. Died Nov. 1947.

SEITZ, IRA JAMES, physician; b. Mandan, N.D., Apr. 30, 1898; s. William H. and Fannie M. (Robbins) S.; student Hedding Coll., 1917-19; A.B., Asbury Coll., 1922; M.S., Northwestern U., Chgo., 1927, M.D., 1930; m. Jennie S. Garvey, June 26, 1922. Intern Wesley Meml. Hosp., Chgo., 1930-31; pvt. practice medicine, Roseburg, Ore., 1931-71; mem. officer VA, 1931-64; cons. gen. surgery urology, med. adminstrn. VA Hosp., Roseburg, 1964-71; mem. staffs Wahoe County, St. Mary's hosps., 1942-48. Served with AUS, 1918; served to lt. col., M.C., AUS, 1944-46. Recipient citation V.F.W. for work with Cal. vets. at VA Hosp., Fresno, 1952. Fellow A.C.S.; mem. A.M.A., Cal. Med. Soc., S.A.R., Mayflower Soc., Am. Legion, D.A.V., Sigma Xi. Methodist. Mason (Shriner), Kiwanian. Author: Studies in Avian Diabetes Mellitus, 1927. Home: Roseburg OR Died Sept. 3, 1971.

SELFRIDGE, THOMAS OLIVER rear admiral, U.S.N.; b. Boston, Apr. 24, 1904; m. Louisa Cary, d. John Soley, Charlestown, Mass., 1834. Apptd. to navy, Jan. 1, 1818; commissioned lt., Mar. 3, 1827; comdr., Apr. 11, 1844; capt., Sept. 14, 1855; commodore, July 16, 1862; placed on retired list, Apr. 24, 1866; promoted rear admiral, July 25, 1866. Comd. the sloop "Dale" of the Pacific squadron, 1847-48; he took part in engagement and capture of Matanzas and Guaymas; at latter place received a severe wound, which incapacitated him for sea duty. During Civil war comd. a few months the steam-frigate "Mississippi" in Gulf squadron; later comd. Mare Island Navy Yard, San Francisco; pres. examining bd., 1869-71; now senior officer on navy retired list. Home: Washington, D.C. Died 1902.

SELFRIDGE, THOMAS OLIVER rear admiral U.S.N.; b. Boston, Feb. 6, 1836; s. late Rear Admiral Thomas Oliver and Louisa Cary (Soley) S.; apptd. acting midshipman U.S. Naval Acad., from Mass., Oct. 3, 1851, grad. 1854; m. Ellen F., d. Judge George F. Shepley, of Portland, Me., Aug. 1895. Promoted passed midshipman, Nov. 22, 1856; advanced through grades to commodore Apr. 11, 1894; rear admiral, Feb. 28, 1896. Served on Independence and Nautilus, 1854-57; on Vincennes as acting master on the coast of Africa, 1858-60; on Cumberland, 1860-61, was on board when she was sunk by Confederate Iron Clad Merrimac; flag lt. N. Atlantic Sta. and comd. submarine boat Alligator, 1862; comd. Cairo, Miss., Squadron, which was blown up by torpedo; comd. a battery at capture of Vicksburg; comd. Huron at engagements at Ft. Fisher; on duty Naval Acad., 1865-68; comd. Nipsic, 1868-70; comd. survey of the Isthmus of Darien to select a route for an interoceanic ship canal, 1869-74; Navy Yard, Boston, 1873-75; torpedo instrn., 1877; comd. Enterprise, 1878-80; in charge Torpedo Sta., Newport, 1881-84; comd. Omaha, 1885-87; spl. duties, 1888-90; commandant Navy Yard, Boston, 1890-93; pres. Bd. Inspection and Survey, 1894-95; comdr.-in-chief European Squadron, 1895-97; retired, Feb. 6, 1898. Chevalier Legion of

Honor, France; awarded gold medal by Czar of Russia in honor of his coronation. Home: Washington, D.C. Died Feb. 4, 1924.

SELIG, LESTER NORTH, ofcl. Gen. Am. Transportation Corp.; b. Brooklyn, N.Y., Sept. 10, 1893; s. Louis N. and Bertha (Norden) S.; prep. edn. Boys' High Sch., Brooklyn; grad. Brooklyn Law Sch., 1914; m. Helen Montgomery, Mar. 8, 1925; 1 dau., Shirley Selig Frey; m. 2d, Vera Sellwood, Oct. 11, 1946; children—Leslie Veva, Louis North. Began as workman in shops of Gen. Am. Tank Car Corp., Chgo., 1914; now chmn. exec. com. Gen. Transp. Co., Chgo.; dir. Gen. Am. Transp. Company. Chmn. bd. trustees Chgo. Med. School, 1948-56. mem. Palm Springs Airport Commn. Mem. Palm Springs City Council, 1966-68. Served as enlisted man, advancing to 2d lt., 1st lt. and capt., engrs., U.S. Army, 1917-18; with A.E.F., May 1918-June 1919. With W.P.B., 1942-45; mem. tech. adv. com. Q.M.C., 1943-45. Decorated Legion of Honor (France). Mem.Am.-Ry. Car Inst. (pres. 1954-56), Art Inst. Chicago (life), Phi Alpha. Republican. Jewish. Clubs: Standard, Tavern, Cloud; Tamarisk County (Palm Springs, Cal.); Palette. Home: Palm Springs CA Died Nov. 23, 1968; buried San Gorgonio Meml. Park, Banning CA

SELKE, GEORGE ALBERT, educator, govt. ofcl.; b. LaCrosse, Wis., June 28, 1888; s. Albert and Wilhelmina (Wokkenfus) S.; grad. State Tchrs. Coll., St. Cloud, Minn., 1913; A.B., U. Minn., 1916; A.M., Columbia, 1926; honorary degree University of Vienna, 1946; LL.D. (honorary), University of North Dakota, 1947; married Eda Carol Ehri, 1920. Teacher rural schs., S.D., 1907-08; prin. village sch., Sartell, Minn., 1908-10; county supt. schs., Benton County, 1910-13; supt. schs., Mabel and Chokio, 1913-18; dir. elementary and high schs., Minn. State Dept. Edn., 1920-24; successively assistant professor, lecturer, U. of Minn., 1924-27; pres. State Teachers Coll., St. Cloud, 1927-46; chancellor U. of Montana 1946-51; deputy chief edn. and cultural relations div., High Commn. for Germany, 1951, chief div. of cultural affairs, office of public affairs, 1952-70. Private, depot brigade, United States Army, 1918; maj., U.S. Army, Military Government, England, Italy and Austria, 1943-46; cultural and educational dir. Salzburg, Austria, 1945; endl. mission to Korea for U.S. War Dept., 1948. Director Nat. Youth Admn. for Minn., 1935-39, Minn. State dir. War Manpower Commn., 1943. Gov. Minn-Dakotas Dist. of Kiwanis International, 1941 (chairman. Internat. Com. on Boys and Girls Work, 1942); pres. Am. Assn. of Teachers Colls., 1941-42; mem. Nat. Commn. on Colleges and Civilian Defense. Mem. N.E.A., Phi Delta Kappa, Kappa Delta Pi. Presbyn. Author: (with Julius Boraas) Rural School of Administration and Supervision, 1926; Handbook for County Superintendents of Schools (with C. B. Lund), 1935. Home: Bad Godesberg Germany Died Oct. 1970.

SELLERS, DAVID FOOTE naval officer; b. Fort Austin, Austin, Tex., Feb. 4, 1874; s. Maj. Edwin Elias and Olive Lay (Foote) S.; B.S., U.S. Naval Acad., 1894; grad. U.S. Naval War Coll., 1917; LL.D., St. John's Coll., Annapolis, Md.; D.Sc., U. of Southern Calif.; m. Anita Clay Evans, Nov. 1, 1905. Commd. ensign U.S. Navy, July 1, 1896; advanced through grades to rear admiral, June 2, 1927; advanced to admiral on retired list, June 16, 1942. Served on Alliance and Philadelphia, Spanish-Am. War, taking part in Samoan campaign, 1899; served on New York, Philippine campaign, 1901-02; comdr. battleship Wisconsin, also transport Agamemnon (had engagement with German submarine), World War. Naval aide at White House, 1903-04; on duty Bureau Navigation, Navy Dept., 1907-09; aide to sec. of navy, 1921-22; comdg. officer Naval Tr. Sta., San Diego, Calif., 1923-26; became comdr. Special Service Squadron, of 5 cruisers, 1927; judge advocate gen. of the Navy, 1929-31; comdr. in chief of the United States Fleet, 1933-34; supt. Naval Acad., Annapolis, until retired, Mar. 1, 1938. Decorated D.S.M. for "exceptionally meritorious services in Nicaragua"; Navy Cross, with citation "for exceptionally meritorious service in a duty of great responsibility"; Victory medal with star, Spanish Campaign, Philippine Campaign, Mexican Service medals (all U.S.); medal El Merito (Nicaragua); Order of Abdon Calderon (Ecuador). Episcopalian. Clubs: Army and Navy, Army, Navy and Marine Corps Country, Chevy Chase (Washington); University, New York Yacht (New York); University (Buffalo). Author: Unofficial Navy Code, 1909. Home: 2216 Wyoming Av., Washington. Address: Navy Dept., Washington. Died Jan. 27, 1949; buried in Arlington National Cemetery.

SELSER, JAMES CLYDE, JR., air force officer; b. Alexandria, La., Sept. 10, 1912; s. James Clyde and Ernestine (Gourrier) S.; B.S. in Aero. Engring., Ga. Sch. Tech., 1933; grad. Command and Gen. Staff Sch., Ft. Leavenworth, Kan., 1944, Army-Navy Staff Coll., 1945; m. Mary Garland, Nov. 12, 1935; children—Mary Victoria, James Clyde III, Christopher Garland. Commd. 2d lt., inf., U.S. Army, 1933, 2d lt., AAC, 1936, advanced through grades to maj. gen., 1951; assigned 8th Pursuit Group, Langley Field, Va., 1933-36; flying instr. Randolph Field, Tex., 1936-40; mem. U.S. Air Mission to Brazil, 1940-43; mil. air attache to Brazil, 1943, also sr. Air Force mem. Joint Brazil-U.S. Def. Commn.; assigned G-2 for Air, 10th Army Hdqrs., T.H., 1945; comdr. 444th Bomb Group, Tinian, 1945; comdr. Davis-Monthan Air Force Base, 1946-50; dep. dir. operations Strategic Air Command, Offut Air Force Base, Omaha, Neb., 1950-53; comdr. 7th Air Div., Eng., 1953-54; dep. comdr. 8th Air Force, 1954-56; dep. dir., net evaluation subcom. NSC, 1956—. Decorated Legion of Merit, D.F.C., Bronze Star Medal, Air Medal, Presdl. Unit Citation; Brazilian War Medal, Order So. Cross, Brazilian Order Aero. Merit; Portuguese Order of Avis. Mem. Delta Tau Delta, Omicron Delta Kappa, Pi Delta Epsilon. Roman Catholic. Rotarian. Home: Quarters 84, Bolling Air Force Base, Washington. Died Nov. 18, 1956.

SEMMES, ALEXANDER JENKINS physician, clergyman, coll. pres.; b. Georgetown, D.C., Dec. 17, 1828; s. Raphael and Matilda (Jenkins) S.; A.B., Georgetown Coll., 1850; M.D., Med. Dept., Columbian Coll., D.C., 1851; attended Pio Nono Coll., nr. Macon, Ga., also Benedictine monastery of St. Vincent, Latrobe, Pa.; m. Sarah Berrien, Oct. 4, 1864. Resident physician Charity Hosp., New Orleans; surgeon 8th La. Inf., during Civil War; commd. surgeon Confederate Army; surgeon La. Brigade in Gen. Thomas J. (Stonewall) Jackson's corps Army of No. Va.; med. insp. Dept. No. Va., insp. hosps.; mem. exam. bds. La., Jackson, Stuart, Winder hosps. (all Richmond, Va.); prof. physiology Savannah (Ga.) Med. Coll., 1870-76; ordained priest Roman Catholic Ch., Macon, 1878; pres., lectr. English and Am. lit. and history Pio Nono Coll., 1886-91; chaplain of sch. and asylum of Sisters of St. Joseph, Sharon, Ga., 1891-95, Author: Report on the Medicolegal Duties of Coroners, 1857; contbr. articles to publs. including Poisoning by Strychnia—The Gardiner Case, published in Stethoscope, 1855; Reports of Cases of Gunshot Wounds. published in London Lancet, 1864. Died Hotel Dieu, New Orleans, Sept. 20, 1898.

SEMMES, RAPHAEL naval officer; b. Charles County, Md., Sept. 27, 1809; s. Richard Thompson and Catherine (Middleton) S.; studied law; m. Anne Spencer, May 5, 1837, 6 children. Commd. midshipman U.S. Navy, 1826; served in Mediterranean Squadron, 1826; passed for promotion, 1823; commd. lt., 1837; admitted to Md. bar, 1834; practiced law, Md. and Ohio; held 1st command, spent time on survey duty on So. coast, Gulf of Mexico on ships Consor, Poinsett; commanded brig. Somers on blockade of the Eastern coast of Mexico, 1846; commd. comdr., 1855, resigned, 1861; became a comdr. from Ala. in Confederate States Navy, 1861; made chief Light House Bur. (Dept. Treasury), Apr. 4-18, 1861; given command of C.S.S. Sumter, 1861-62; promoted capt., voted thanks of Confederate Congress, 1862; commanded ship Alabama, 1862-64; sank U.S.S. Hateras, 1863; commd. rear adm. Confederate Navy, 1864; ship Alabama sunk by U.S. Kearsarge off Cherbourg, France, June 19, 1864; assigned as rear adm. to command James River Squadron, 1865; probate judge Mobile County, Ala., 1866; prof. moral philosophy and English literature La. State Sem. (now La. State U.), Baton Rouge, 1866-67; editor Memphis (Tenn.) Daily Bull.; practiced law Mobile, Ala., 1867-77. Author: Service Afloat and Ashore during the Mexican War, 1851; The Campaign of General Scott in the Valley of Mexico (an abridgement of his earlier work), 1852; Memoirs of Service, Afloat, during the War between the States, 1869; published his papers as The Cruise of the Alabama and the Sumter From the Private Journals and Other Papers of Commander R. Semmes, C.S.N. and Other Officers, 2 vols., 1864 (translated into French, 1864, Dutch, 1865). Died at home Point Clear, Mobile Bay, Ala., Aug. 30, 1877; buried Catholic graveyard, Mobile.

SENN, NICHOLAS physician, surgeon; b. Buchs, Canton of St. Gall, Switzerland, Oct. 31, 1844; brought to U.S. by parents, 1853; settled at Ashford, Fond du Lac Co., Wis.; grad. Fond du Lac High School, 1864; taught school; grad. Chicago Med. Coll., 1868; Univ. of Munich, 1878; house physician, Cook Co. Hosp.. 1868-69; practiced medicine, Fond du Lac, 1869-74; Milwaukee, 1874-93; was surgeon-gen. of Wis.; engaged in practice at Chicago; surgeon-gen. Ill. Nat. Guard; well known specialist in surgery; attending surgeon, Presbyn. Hosp., and surgeon-in-chief, St. Joseph's Hosp., Chicago, until apptd., May 1898, chief surgeon 6th army corps, with rank of lt. col., U.S. vols., and chief of operating staff with army in the field; served until Sept.; prof. surgery, Coll. of Phys. and Surg., Chicago, 1884-85; prof. principles of surgery, 1887-90; from 1890 prof. practical and clinical surgery, Rush Med. Coll., also prof. surgery, Chicago Policlinic; professorial lecturer on mil. surgery, Chicago Univ.; del. Internat. Med. Congress, Berlin, 1890, Moscow, 1897, Madrid, 1903. Author: Four Months Among the Surgeons of Europe; Experimental Surgery; Intestinal Surgery; Surgical Bacteriology; Principles of Surgery; Pathology and Surgical Treatment of Tumors; Tuberculosis of Bones and Joints; Tuberculosis of the Genito-Urinary Organs; Syllabus of Practice of Surgery; Practical Surgery; Surgical Notes of the Spanish-American War; Medico-Surgical Aspects of the Spanish-American War; Practical Surgery; Nurses's Guide for the Operating Room, 1902; Around the World via Siberia; Our National Recreation Parks; Around the World via India—A Medical Tour. Home: Chicago, Ill. Died 1908.

SENN, THOMAS J. naval officer; b. S.C., Dec. 21. 1871; grad. U.S. Naval Acad., 1891. Commd. ensign U.S. Navy, 1891; promoted through grades to rear admiral, June 1924, now retired. Address: 1021 Adella Av., Coronado, Calif.* Died Feb. 11, 1947.

SENSENICH, ROSCOE LLOYD physician; b. Wakarusa, Ind., Nov. 20, 1882; s. Dr. Aaron Stauffer and Martha M. (Brubaker) S.; M.D., Rush Med. Coll., U. Chgo., 1905; m. Helen Frances Daugherty, Apr. 10, 1917; 1 dau., Helene Marjorie. Interne, Presbyn., St. Joseph hosps., Chgo.; practiced medicine, South Bend, Ind. since 1907; mem. med. staff Meml., St. Joseph hosps., South Bend; pres. bd. mgrs. St. Joseph County Tb Hosp. and South Bend Med. Found. (lab., research, edn.). Mem. adv. com. to div. of services for crippled children Ind. State Dept. Pub. Welfare, 1936-44; mem. fed. govt. com. on allocation med. personnel to armed forces and civilian population; mem. adv. com. to Selective Service, World War II; cons., mem. com. on phys. fitness FSA, 1944-45; mem. NRC, 1947-50; hon. cons. USN surgeon gen. Served as maj. M.C., U.S. Army, World War I. Diplomate Am. Bd. Internal Medicine. Fellow A.C.P.; mem. A.M.A. (chmn. bd. trustees, pres. 1948-49), Ind. (past pres.), St. Joseph County (pres. 1920) med. assns., Ind. State Tb Assn. (past pres.), Central Soc. for Clin. Research, Soc. Internal Medicine (Chgo.), Chgo. Inst. Medicine, Phi Rho Sigma, Alpha Omega Alpha. Clubs: University (Chgo.); Chain O'Lakes Country (South Bend). Contbr. research articles on undulant fever and studies in digestive disorders, also numerous articles on med. care to med. jours. and lay publs. Home: 128 S. Scott St., South Bend 46625. Office: 108 N. Main St., South Bend 5, Ind. Died Jan. 18, 1963; buried Riverview Cemetery, South Bend.

SERAKOFF, LEONARD, stock broker; b. St. Louis, Feb. 13, 1921; s. Morris and Anna (Zlotnikov) S.; B.A., U. Mo., 1942; m. Peggy Barbarash, Jan. 8, 1950; children—Charlene (Mrs. Teifeld), Betty Ann, Diane Lynn. Gen. partner Friedman, Brokaw & Co., St. Louis, 1950-61; v.p., dir. Semple, Jacobs & Co., Inc., St. Louis, 1961-65; gen. partner Kohlmeyer & Co., Chgo., 1965-66; asst. v.p. A. G. Becker & Co., Inc., Chgo., 1967. Bd. dirs., mem. exec. com. Midwest Stock Clearing Corp., Chgo., 1961-67; bd. govs. Midwest Stock Exchange, 1961-67, chmn. com. floor procedure, 1964-67; allied mem. N.Y. Stock Exchange, 1951-67; mem. Chgo. Bd. Trade, 1951-61. Mem. Chgo. Natural History Museum. Served to capt. AUS, 1942-46. Home: Wilmette IL Died Feb. 19, 1967.

SERRELL, EDWARD WELLMANN civil and mil. engr.; b. abroad (but a citizen of U.S. by birthright), Nov. 5, 1826; academic edn.; m. Jane, d. Rev. Jesse Pound. Apr. 6, 1848 (died 1896); 2d, Marion Seaton Roorbach, Sept. 6, 1900 (died Nov. 1904). Began engring. profession under his father and elder brother. Was asst. engr. to commrs. of Erie R.R.; asst. to chief of Topog. Engrs., U.S.A.; asst. engr., 1848, Panama Survey; engr. Central R.R. of N.J.; chief engr. Niagara bridge, 1850; chief engr. St. John bridge, Hoosac tunnel and many other public works. In Civil War organized and comd. 1st regt. vol. engrs., U.S.A., becoming col. engrs.; chief engr. 10th corps, U.S.A.; chief engr. and chief of staff, Army of the James; chief engr. Dept. of the South, U.S.A.; was at capture of Fort Wagner; devised and built Swamp Angel batteries; was in 126 actions, becoming bvt. brig. gen. Made many useful inventions, in long wire, armor plate, impromptu gun carriages, electric coast defenses, iron viaducts, etc. Published many reports on railroads and canals. Is consulting engr. to several corps.; has projected an interoceanic canal from San Blas to Pearl Island Harbor. Consulting engr. Am. Isthmus Ship Canal Co. Home: West New Brighton, N.Y. Died 1906.

SEVEY, ROBERT (se've), bus. consultant; b. Cleveland, O., July 5, 1898; s. George Edwin and Mary Jane (Murray) S.; ed. pub. and private schs., Chicago, Ill., and Culver, Ind.; student U. of Pa., 1919-23; unmarried. With engring. dept. N.Y. Central Lines, 1923-27; passenger and freight agent U.S. Lines, Chicago, 1927-30; publisher, Histomaps, Chicago, 1930-33; mgr. Chicago office N.R.A. (Ill. and Wis.), 1933-34; dist. mgr. U.S. Dept. Commerce, Chicago, 1934-35; chief, Dist. Office Service, U.S. Dept. Commerce, 1935-42. Served in U.S. Navy, 1917-19. Commd. maj., Air Corps, Sept. 1942; on staff, comdg. gen. Air Transport Command, comdg. gen. E.T.O., London, 1943-44. Adviser to exec. dir., Office of Internat. Trade Operations, Washington, 1945; spl. asst. to Wilson W. Wyatt, housing expediter, 1945-47; consultant to several U.S. bus. firms. Club: Nat. Press (Washington). Home: Westchester Apts., Washington 16. Office: National Press Bldg., Washington. Deid Sept. 19, 1951; buried Piqua, O.

SEVIER, JOHN gov. Tenn., congressman, army officer; b. nr. New Market, Va., Sept. 23, 1745. s. Valentine and Joanna (Goade) S.; m. Sarah Hawkins, 1761; m. Catherine Sherrill, Aug. 14, 1780, Served as capt. Va. Colonial Militia under Washington in Lord Dunmore's War, 1773-74; commr. Watauga Assn., Knoxville, N.C. (now Tenn.); mem. Knoxville Com. of Safety, 1776; elected rep. N.C. Provincial Congress, then apptd. lt. col. N.C. Militia; led 240 men to victory over British at Battle of King's Mountain, Oct. 7, 1780;

made 3 raids against Indians, 1781-82; established (with William Blount) settlement at Muscle Shoals, Ala., circa 1783; elected gov. State of Franklin, 1785-88, regime collapsed following battle with Tipton faction, 1788; elected to N.C. Senate, 1789; mem. N.C. Conv. which ratified U.S. Constn., voted for ratification; commd. brig. gen. N.C. Militia, 1791; mem. U.S. Ho. of Reps. from N.C., 1st Congress, 1789-Sept. 24, 1791; active land speculator in West during 1790's; trustee Washington Coll. (Tenn.), Blount Coll. (now U. Tenn.); 1st gov. Tenn., 1796-1801, re-elected, 1803-09; mem. Tenn. Senate, 1809-11; mem. U.S. Ho. of Reps. from Tenn., 12th-13th congresses, 1811-15; apptd. mem. commn. to survey boundary of Creek Cession, 1815. Died Ala., Sept. 24, 1815; buried Knoxville.

SEWALL, LEE GOODRICH, hosp. adminstr.; b. Marlin, Tex., Aug. 25, 1907; s. Francis Bates and Mary (Goodrich) S.; B.A., U. Tex., 1927, M.D., 1931; M.S. in Hosp. Adminstrn., Northwestern U., 1954; m. Mary Eleanor Andrews, Mar. 9, 1940; children—Murphy Andrews, Frank Bates. Intern Cleve. City Hosp., 1931-32; resident Deaconess Hosp., Cleve., 1932-33, Lakeside Hosp., Cleve., 1933-34; gen. practice medicine, Waco, Tex., 1934-38; med. officer VA Hosp., North Little Rock, Ark., 1938-42; sr. med. officer VA Hosp., Ft. Custer, Mich., 1942-44; clin. dir. VA Hosp., Lyons, N.J., 1944-46; chief psychiatry and neurology service VA br. office, St. Louis, 1946-47; dir. profl. services VA Hosp., Roanoke, Va., 1947-51; mgr. VA Hosp., Downey, Ill., 1951-55, Leech Farm, Pitts., 1955-57; hosp. dir. VA Hosp., Perry Point, Md., 1957-65, Consol. VA Hosp., Little Rock, 1965-71; director med. audit research project VA Hosp., Perry Point, 1948-64; assistant prof. public health administration School Hygiene and Public Health, Johns Hopkins, 1958-65; clin. prof. psychiatry Arkansas School Medicine, 1966-71. Served from major to lieutenant colonel, M.C., AUS, 1944-46. Diplomate Am. Bd. Psychiatry and Neurology. Fel. Am. Psychiat. Assn.; mem. A.M.A., Group For Advancement Psychiatry, Am. Coll. Hosp. Adminstrs., North Lake County Mental Health Soc. (past pres., dir.), Western Pa. Mental Health Assn. (dir.), Alpha Omega Alpha. Home: Little Rock AR Died Feb. 12, 1971.

SEWARD, HERBERT LEE educator, naval architect, marine engr., maritime cons.; b. Guilford, Conn., Apr. 17, 1885; s. Leonidas C. and Addie A. (Page) S.; Ph.B., Sheffield Sci. Sch. (Yale), 1906, M.E., Yale, 1908; m. Effie May Scranton, Aug. 4, 1909 (died Nov., 1958); children—Ruth, Marion, Dana (all dec.); m. 2d, Anna C. Bronson, Apr. 1959. Instr. mech. engring. Yale, 1908; prof., 1928; asst. to pres. Am. Bur. of Shipping, N.Y.C., 1929-32; mem. adv. com. U.S. Lines, Inc., Fuel Conservation com. U.S. Shipping Bd.; spl. expert and econ. adviser U.S. Maritime Commn.; maritime asst. to Sec. Commerce, 1937-38 (sabbatical leave Yale); cons. Electric Boat Co., Groton, Conn., others; sr. cons. Woods Hole Oceanographic Inst. Mem. OPM Com. on Shipyard Labor. Cons. to and expert for sec. navy in salvaging S.S. Normandie. Organized and operated as exec. officer USN Steam Engring. Sch., at Stevens Inst. Tech., Hoboken, N.J., World War I; served as 3d asst. engr. and asst. navigator S.S. Leviathan, and as comdg. officer U.S.S. Eagle 27; comdr. USNR, ret., naval aide, comdr. on staff of gov. Conn., 8 years. Licensed master of steam vessels, also licensed chief engr. (unlimited). Sec. of U.S. Dept. of Commerce Com. to Coördinate Marine Boiler Rules, 1929-36; tech. advisor to dir. U.S. Shipping Board Bur., U.S. Dept. Commerce; mem. tech. com. Am. Bur. Shipping, Dir. N.Y. Shipbldg. Corp., Camden, N.J., 2 yrs. Chmn. adv. bd., head dept. of Maritime Econs., USCG Acad. 16 yrs. Confidential cons. to Sec. Navy, World War II; asst. to State Dept. on radio aids nav., 1947; mem. tech. com. four experts study and report on collision of M.V. Stockholm and S.S. Andrea Doria. Chmn. Town Beach Erosion Bd., Old Saybrook. Fellow Am. Soc. M.E.; hon. v.p. Soc. Naval Architects and Marine Engrs.; mem. Am. Soc. Naval Engrs., Am. Soc. Engring. Edn., U.S. Power Squadrons, Propeller Club U.S., Sigma Xi (past pres. Yale chpt), Tau Beta Pi, Phi Gamma Delta, Conglist. Mason. Clubs: Whitehall (N.Y.); Grad., Rotary (ex-pres.), Sojourners (New London); Army and Navy (Washington). Author: Constrn. of Diagrams for Engring. Formulas (text book), 1923; also articles in marine mags., tech. papers, bulls., rules for ship constrn., others. Editor-in-chief: Soc. N.A. and M.E. Text Books on Marine Engineering. Sole arbitrator Greek vs. Japanese and other internat. coml. cases. Home: P.O. Box 517, Sea Lane, Old Saybrook, Conn. 06475. Died July 1966.

SEWARD, SAMUEL SWAYZE clergyman; b. Mendham, N.J., Apr. 16, 1838; s. George W. and Tempe Wicke (Leddell) S.; bro. of George Frederick S.; entered Union Coll., 1853, but did not graduate; admitted to Calif. bar, 1861; grad. New Church Theol. Sch., Waltham, Mass., 1868; m. Crissie F. Kimber, Oct. 13, 1864. Lt. 3d N.Y. Heavy Arty., 1861; a.d.c. on staff of Brig. Gen. E. O. C. Ord throughout the war; promoted capt. and maj., with two bvts., lt. col. and col., resigning Oct. 1865. Ordained New Jerusalem (Swedenborgian) ministry, 1869; pastor Poughkeepsie, N.Y., 1868-69, N. Bridgewater, Mass., 1870-75, Wilmington, Del., 1875-78, New York, 1878-97. Sec. Gen. Conv. of the New Jerusalem in the U.S.A., 1877-92; chmn. Council of Ministers, 1892-97 (v.p., 1897-1900, pres., 1900-1911); mem. bd. mgrs. Am. Swedenborg Printing & Pub. Co., 1878-—(pres. 1900-—); dir. Bd. of Publication, New Jerusalem Ch.; mem. bd. mgrs. New Ch. Theol. Sch. Home: Pittsfield, Mass. Deceased.

SEWARD, WILLIAM bvt. brig. gen. N.G.N.Y.; b. New Hackensack, Dutchess Co., N.Y., Aug. 19, 1837; s. Wm. S.; ed. high school, Newark, N.J.; m. Louisa M. Lockwood, Oct. 11, 1864. Joined N.Y. Nat. Guard, Oct. 1, 1858; served in Civil war, 1861-63; commd. 1st lt. while in service of U.S., 1862; adj. 9th regt., 1866; maj. same, 1868; asst. adj. gen. 3d brigade, N.Y.N.G., Apr. 1870; bvt. col., Jan. 31, 1879; col. 9th regt., N.G.N.Y., Apr. 1882; brig. gen. bvt., May 1898; retired at own request (total service, 38 1/2 yrs.). Republican. Home: New York, N.Y. Died 1905.

SEWARD, WILLIAM HENRY soldier, banker; b. Auburn, N.Y., June 18, 1839; s. William Henry (Sec. of State) and Frances A. (Miller) S.; bro. of Frederick William S.; pvt. edn.; m. Janet M. Watson, June 27, 1860 (died 1913). Apptd. Sept. 12, 1862, lt. col., 138th N.Y. Vols.; afterward col. 9th N.Y. Heavy Arty.; participated in battles of Monocacy, Petersburg, Cold Harbor, Opequan and others; promoted for gallantry, Sept. 1863, to brig. gen. comdg. 1st Brigade, 3d Div., Dept. of Shenandoah; resigned, June 1, 1865. Head of banking firm of William H. Seward & Co., 1860-—; trustee Cayuga Co. Savings Bank. Pres. Seymour Library. Republican. Pres. N.Y. electoral coll., 1888. Home: Auburn, N.Y. Died Apr. 26, 1920.

SEXTON, THOMAS SCOTT, life ins. co. exec.; b. Sistersville, W.Va., May 5, 1913; s. Michael P. and Josephine (Scott) S.; A.B., U. W.Va., 1935; M.D. (certificate of honor), U. Md., 1939; m. Elizabeth Ann Johnson, Nov. 23, 1940; 1 dau., Deborah Dudley (Mrs. James P. O'Callaghan). Intern Mercy Hosp., Balt., 1939-40; fellow Mayo Found., 1941, 45-47; asst. med. dir. Mass. Mut. Life Ins. Co., Springfield, 1947-51, asso. med. dir., 1951-56, med. dir., 1956-59, v.p., 1959-62, v.p., chief med. dir., 1962-68, sr. v.p., 1968-73, dir., 1965-73. Served to maj., M.C., USAAF, 1941-45. Mem. Assn. Life Ins. Med. Dirs. Am. (v.p., pres. 1969-70), Am. Life Conv., New Eng. Med. Dirs. Group, Home Office Life Underwriters Assn., Mayo Found. Alumni Assn., Kappa Alpha (So.). Home: Granby MA Died Jan. 9, 1973; buried Springfield MA

SEXTON, WALTON ROSWELL naval officer; b. Monmouth, Ill., Sept. 13, 1876; s. William Harvey and Marian (Burlingim) S.; grad. U.S. Naval Acad., 1897, U.S. Naval War Coll., 1915; unmarried. Ensign U.S. Navy, July 1, 1899; advanced through grades to rear adm., Mar. 31, 1830. Comdr. Destroyer Squadrons, Scouting Force, 1929-31; asst. chief of naval operations, 1931-33; vice adm., comdr. battleships, U.S. Fleet, 1933-34; mem. Gen. Bd., 1934-37; comdr. destroyers Battle Force, 1937-39; chmn. Gen. Bd., 1939. Awarded medals Spanish-Am. War, Philippine Insurrection, Occupation Vera Cruz, World War; decorated Navy Cross. Baptist. Clubs: Army and Navy, Army and Navy Country (Washington); Chevy Chase; New York Yacht. Home: Monmouth, Ill. Address: Navy Dept., Washington, D.C. Died Sep. 9, 1943.

SEXTON, WILLIAM HENRY lawyer; b. Chgo., Mar. 22, 1875; s. Austin Oliver and Mary Ignatius (Lyons) S.; grad. Lake Forest U. Law Sch., 1895; LL.D., U. Dayton, 1925, De Paul U., 1935; K.S.G., Papal, 1934; m. Alice M. Lynch, Oct. 26, 1898 (died Mar. 13, 1945); children—Andrew William, Alice Mary (Mrs. William D. Kavanaugh). Asso. in practice with father, 1895-97; asst. corp. counsel Chgo., 1897-1902, 1st asst., 1902-05; mem. Tolman, Redfield & Sexton, 1905-11; corp. counsel Chgo., 1911-14; spl. traction counsel Chgo., 1914-15, 1921-25; mem. Tolman, Redfield & Sexton, later Tolman, Sexton & Chandler, 1914-31; corp. counsel Chgo., 1931-35; resigned to become spl. traction counsel Chgo., to draft comprehensive ordinance for unification and modernization of local tiansp. systems including Metro. area; also handles all legal matters for City in constrn. of City-owned Initial System of Subways, and Comprehensive System of Superhwys. within City; mem. Ill. Emergency Relief Commn. and its successor Ill. Pub. Aid Commn. by appointments of Govs. Emmerson, Horner, Green and Stevenson since 1932. Pres. Cath. Lawyers Guild (Chgo.), 1934-50, emeritus 1950. Served as capt., judge adv., World War I; lt. col., judge adv. gen. of Reserves, now ret. Mem. Cath. Charities Chgo. (bd. dirs.), Am. and Ill. State bar assns., Chgo. Bar Assn. (pres. 1923-24), Am. Legion. Roman Catholic. Clubs: Iroquois, Law. Office: City Hall, Chgo. 60602. Died Jan. 1963.

SEYMORE, TRUMAN army officer; b. Burlington, Vt., Sept. 24, 1824; s. Truman and Ann (Armstrong) Seymour; grad. U.S. Mil. Acad., 1846; m. Louisa Weir, circa 1852. Brevetted 2d lt. U.S. Army, 1846; brevetted 1st lt., then capt. for bravery in Mexican War; asst. prof. drawing U.S. Mil. Acad., 1850-53; served in Seminole War, Fla., 1856-58; brevetted maj. for gallant conduct as arty. capt., Ft. Sumter, 1861; comdr. tng. camp, Harrisburg, Pa., served in defense of Washington, D.C., autumn 1861; commd. brig. gen. U.S. Volunteers, 1862, served with distinction at battles of Beaver Dam Creek, Malvern Hill and Antietam; brevetted lt. col. and col. U.S. Army for gallantry at Antietam; comdr. unsuccessful attack on Battery Wagner, Charleston Harbor, 1863, expdn. to Fla., 1864, defeated at Olustee Station; taken prisoner in Battle of Wilderness, exchanged, 1864; comdr. div. 6th Corps, Shenadoah Valley, late 1864; recipient 3 brevet commns. (maj. gen. Volunteers, brig. and maj. gen. U.S. Army), 1865; arty. maj. in coastal ports Ft. Warren (Mass.) and Ft. Preble (Me.), following Civil War; ret., 1876. Died Florence, Italy, Oct. 30, 1891.

SEYMOUR, HAROLD J., consultant on unconstitutional finance and public relations; born in St. Paul, Minnesota, August 24, 1894; son of Frederick and Bessie (Townsend) Seymour; B.S., Harvard, 1916; m. Martha M. Andrews, April 10, 1920; children—Martha B. (Mrs. M. K. Smith), Mary Madison (Mrs. Sidney H. Paige), John Andrews. Vice president and director of the John Price Jones Corporation, New York, New York, 1919-43. Served as ensign, U.S. Naval Air Service, 1917-19. Campaign manager, U.S.O., 1941, 1942; campaign manager National War Fund, 1943, general manager, 1944-46; dir. Northern Valley Savings & Loan Association. Past pres. Tenafly (N.J.) Community Chest; past vice pres. Englewood (N.J.) Hosp. Mem. Am. Assn. Fund Raising Counsel (past pres.). Republican. Episcopalian. Clubs: Harvard (N.Y.). Knickerbocker Country. Author: Design for Giving, 1947; Design for Fund-Raising, 1966. Home: Tenafly NJ2Died Apr. 10, 1968.

SHACKELFORD, JAMES M. lawyer; b. Lincoln Co., Ky., July 7, 1827; s. Edmund and Susan S.; academic edn. at Springfield, Ky.; admitted to bar, 1853; was lt. Co. I, 4th Ky. regt., in Mexican war; admitted to Ky. bar, 1853; col. 25th Ky. inf., and later of 8th Ky. cav., in Union army; became brig. gen., March 17, 1863; captured Confederate Gen. John H. Morgan and command, July 20, 1863, and later comd. a cav. army corps, the Army of the Ohio, consisting of 16 regts. Was Rep. elector for Ind., 1880 and 1888; judge U.S. court, Ind. Ty., 1889-93, then engaged in law practice there; atty. for the Choctaw Nation. Republican. Died 1909.

SHAFROTH, JOHN FRANKLIN ret. naval officer; b. Denver, Mar. 31, 1887; s. John Franklin and Virginia (Morrison) S.; B.S., U.S. Naval Acad., 1908; student Naval War Coll.; 1925-26, Army War Coll., 1926-27; LL.D., Denver U. m. Helena Marshall Fischer, Apr. 29, 1911; 1 dau., Helena Mrorison. Commd. ensign U.S. Navy, 1910, ret. as vice adm., 1941; exec. officer U.S.S. Jenkins, 1914, operating off Tampico during Mexican Campaign comdr.; Destroyer Terry, 1917-18, Sub-Chaser Squadron 6, 1919; on staff comdr. Spl. Service Squadron operating in Central Am. waters, 1922-23; staff comdr.-in-chief U.S. Fleet, 1923-25; navigator Battleship Arkansas, 1928-30; exec. officer Battleship West Virginia, 1933-35; comdg. officer Cruiser Indianapolis, 1938-40; faculty Army War Coll., 1927-28; with Bur. Nav., 1940-41; comdr. Southeast Pacific Force, 1942, later dep. comdr. South Pacific area; comdr. battleship div. that bombarded Japan, 1945; comdt. Panama Sea Frontier and 15th Naval Dist., 1946-47; chmn. gen. bd. U.S. Navy, 1948-49. Pres. U.S. Naval Acad. Alumni Assn., 1955-57, Naval Hist. Found., 1961-—. Decorated Navy Cross, Legion of Merit with 3 gold stars, Mexican Campaign medal, World War Campaign medal: Order of El Sol (Peru); Order of Ayachucho; Order of Abdon Calderon (Ecuador); Order of Boyaca (Colombia); Order of Vasco Nunez de Balboa (Panama). Episcopalian. Clubs: Chevy Chase, Army and Navy, Army and Navy Country (Washington); New York Tacht. Author articles on mil. and naval subjects. Home: 3133 Connecticut Av. N.W., Washington. Died Sept. 1, 1967; buried Arlington Nat. Cemetery.

SHAFTER, WILLIAM RUFUS maj. gen. U.S.A., retired; b. Galesburg, Mich., Oct. 16, 1835; s. Hugh M. and Eliza (Sumner) S.; lived on farm and attended com. schs.; taught sch. 3 yrs. prior to 1861; m. Harriet Grimes, Sept. 11, 1862 (died 1898). Entered Union army as 1st lt. 7th Mich. inf., Aug. 22, 1861; maj. 19th Mich. inf., Sept. 5, 1862; lt. col., June 5, 1863; col. 17th U.S. colored inf., Apr. 19, 1864; bvt. brig. gen., Mar. 13, 1865, for gallant and meritorious services during the war; mustered out of vol. service, Nov. 2, 1865; entered regular army as lt. col., Jan. 26, 1867; bvtd. col., U.S.A., Mar. 2, 1867, and given Congressional medal of honor for gallant and meritorious services at battle of Fair Oaks, Va.; assigned to 24th inf., Apr. 14, 1869; col., Mar. 4, 1879; assigned to 1st inf.; brig. gen., May 3, 1897, in charge dept. of Calif.; maj. gen. vols., May 1898; went to Tampa, Fla.; thence to Cuba, where he comd. the mil. operations ending in capitulation of Gen. Linares' army and surrender of Santiago de Cuba, July 1898; comdg. Depts. of Calif. and Columbia, 1899-1901; retired June 30, 1901, as maj. gen. Home: Bakersfield, Calif. Died 1906.

SHALER, ALEXANDER soldier; b. Haddam, Conn., Mar. 19, 1827; s. Ira and Jerusha (Arnold) S.; grad. Brainerd Acad., Haddam, Conn., 1844; m. Mary McMurray, Mar. 31, 1847. At 17 employed by his father, and 3 yrs. later became propr. of a stone business, continuing until 1861. Joined Washington Grays (later 8th Regt., N.Y. State Militia), 1845; transferred to 7th Regt., 1848; promoted sergt., and 1st lt., and took part in suppressing Astor Place riots, 1849; captain, 1850-60; major 7th Regt., N.G.S.N.Y., 1860-61. Commd. of

President lt. col. 1st U.S. Chasseurs, afterward 65th N.Y. Vols., June 1, 1861; col., July 17, 1862; brig. gen., May 26, 1863; maj. gen. U.S.V., July 27, 1865, "for meritorious services during war." Maj. gen. 1st Div. N.G.S.N.Y. and mem. bd. to provide armories for city troops; hon. disch., May 21, 1886. Awarded Congressional Medal of Honor, Nov. 25, 1893, "for distinguished gallantry at battle of Marye's Heights"; was 3 mos. in Confed. prison, 1864. Founder and propr. Hudson Heights, N.J., and of other properties at Ridgefield, N.J. Mem. New York bd. supervisors, 1866; fire commr., 1867-73, and pres., 1867-70, fire dept., New York; spent 3 mos. after great fire of 1871 reorganizing Chicago Fire Dept. at invitation of city authorities; pres. New York Bd. Health, 1883; mayor Borough of Ridgefield N.J., 1899-1901; pres. N.Y. City Assn. Union Ex-Prisoners of War, 1887-96; one of organizers (4 yrs. v.p. and pres.) Nat. Rifle Assn.; comdr. Mil. Order Loyal Legion. Home: Ridgefield, N.J. Died 1911.

SHALER, CHARLES brigadier gen. U.S.A.; b. Pittsburgh, May 23, 1843; s. Charles and Mary Anne (Riddle) S.; ed. U.S. Mil. Acad.; m. Florence Stidham, Apr. 27, 1896. Enlisted as sergt. Co. I, 12th Pa. Inf., Apr. 25, 1861; discharged, Aug. 5, 1861; cadet U.S. Mil. Acad., 1863-67; commd. 2d lt. 5th U.S. Arty., June 17, 1867; transferred to Ordnance Dept., July 5, 1867; 1st lt., June 23, 1874; capt., Mar. 4, 1879; maj., Feb. 22, 1897; lt. col., Feb. 18, 1903; col., Sept. 17, 1904; brig. gen. and retired at own request after 40 years' service, Jan. 19, 1905. Episcopalian. Home: Indianapolis, Ind. Died Mar. 26, 1915.

SHALLENBERGER, MARTIN C(ONRAD) ret. army officer; b. Osceola, Neb., July 6, 1886; s. Ashton Cockayne and Eliza (Zilg) S.; student U. Neb., 1901-04; distinguished grad. Command and Gen. Staff Sch., 1927; grad. Army War Coll., 1931; m. Ina Hamilton Dowdy, May 11, 1910; children—Sarah Elizabeth (Mrs. W. L. Lyons Brown), Martin Conrad. Commd. in U.S. Army from Nat. Guard, 1908; aide de camp to Gen. Pershing, 1915-18; gen. staff officer, 5th Div., 3d Corps, 1918-19; mil. attaché Am. legations, Portugal, Greece, Jugoslavia, 1919-24; sec. Am. Commn. for Tacna Arica Plebiscite, 1925-26; mil. attaché Am. legations, Austria, Hungary, 1933-37; asst. comdt. Command and Gen. Staff Sch., 1939-44; comdg. officer, Camp Sutton, N.C., and Camp Rucker, Ala., 1944-46; retired in rank of gen., Aug. 1946. Decorated D.S.M., Legion of Merit with oak leaf cluster, Order of Commendation with cluster (U.S.), Officer Legion of Honor (France), Officer of Black Star, Officer of White Eagle, Officer of Polonia Resituta, Comdr. of Order of Daneborg, Austrian Order of Merit, Hungarian Order of Merit. Home: Harrods Creek, Ky. Died Feb. 12, 1951; buried Zachary Taylor Nat. Cemetery.

SHANDS, COURTNEY, ret. naval ofcr.; b. Ferguson, Mo., Dec. 1, 1905; s. Claire Walton and Carey Jacqueline (Risque) S.; B.S., U.S. Naval Acad., 1927; student Nat. War Coll., 1951-52; m. Elizabeth Worthen Jones, June 6, 1927; children—Courtney, Carey (Mrs. Richard Lane). Commd. ensign U.S. Navy, 1927, advanced through grades to rear adm., 1955; naval aviator, 1929; participated Atlantic operations, including Malta, 1942, invasion Guadalcanal, 1942; comdr. aircraft carrier U.S. Oriskany, 1952-53; commander Carrier Division 18, 1957-58; director atomic energy div. Navy Dept., 1954-57; dep. comdr. Field Command Armed Forces, Spl. Weapons Project, Sandia Base, Albuquerque, N.M., 1958-61, dep. comdr. Def. Atomic Support Agy., 1961-62; ret., 1962. Decorated Navy Cross, Legion of Merit, Bronze Star, Presidential Unit Citation, Air Medal; Presidential Unit Citation (Korea), Purple Heart. Home: Alexandria VA Died Nov. 21, 1968; buried Arlington Nat. Cemetery, Arlington VA

SHANKS, DAVID CAREY army officer; b. Salem, Va., Apr. 6, 1861; s. David Carey and Sarah (Boone) S.; student Roanoke Coll., Salem, Va., 1874-78; grad. U.S. Mil. Acad., 1884; m. Nancy Chapman, Oct. 5, 1893; children—Katharine Chapman (wife of William E. Malloy, U.S.N.), Sarah Chapman (wife of Stephen J. Chamberlin, U.S.A.). Commd. 2d lt. 18th Inf., June 15, 1884; brig. gen., May 15, 1917; maj. gen. N.A., Aug. 5, 1917; maj. gen. U.S.A., Mar. 7, 1921; retired Jan. 17, 1925. Hon. sec. Am. Foundation for the Blind. Adj. 18th Inf., 1890-94; participated in campaigns, Philippine Insurrection, islands of Negros and Panay, 1899-1901; gov. Cavite Province, P.I., 1903-05; comdr. Port of Embarkation, Hoboken, N.J., Aug. 1, 1917-Sept. 9, 1918, and Dec. 5, 1918—; comd. 16th Div., Camp Kearny, Calif., Sept.-Nov. 30, 1918. Awarded D.S.M. (army), 1919, D.S.M. (navy), 1920. Author: Management of the American Soldier; As They Passed Through the Port, 1927. Home: Washington, D.C. Died Apr. 10, 1940.

SHANLEY, JAMES ANDREW ex-congressman, judge; b. New Haven, Apr. 1, 1896; s. Bernard A. and Rose (Kelley) S.; A.B., Yale, 1919, LL.B., 1923; m. Mildred Fleming, Oct. 21, 1933; children—James Andrew, Mary Louise. Tchr., Carleton Acad., Summit, N.J., 1920-21, Hillhouse High Sch., 1921-35; admitted to Conn. bar, 1928, U.S. Supreme Ct. bar; in practice at New Haven; mem. Feldman & Shanley since 1928; mem. 74th to 77th Congresses (1935-43), 3d Conn. Dist.; receiver Hartford Empire Co., 1942-46; now probate judge New Haven Dist. Lectr., Cath. U. Am., 1941-44, John Carroll Forum, Chgo. Dir. Grace-New Haven Community Hosp.; pres. Human Relations Council. Served as lt. F.A., A.U.S., World War I; adj. 1st Bn., 102d Inf., Conn. N.G., 1929-35; capt. F.A. Res., 1923-35; capt. Inf. Res. since 1935; Athletic ednl. and publicity dir. New Haven Boys Club, 1926-28, now dir. Mem. Am. Soc. Internat. Law, Am. Irish Hist. Soc. Democrat. Catholic. K.C., Elks, Eagles, Knight of St. Patrick. Club: Union League. Home: 1666 Boulevard, New Haven. Died Apr. 4, 1965.

SHANNON, RICHARD CUTTS congressman; b. New London, Conn., Feb. 12, 1839; s. Charles Tebbets and Jane Randell (Stanwood) S.; A.B., Colby Coll., 1862, A.M., 1866; LL.B., Columbia, 1885; (LL.D., Colby, 1892); m. Martha A. Greenough, Sept. 19, 1887. Sergt. Co. H, 5th Me. Inf., June 24, 1861; 1st lt., Oct. 10, 1861; capt. a.a.g. vols., Oct. 2, 1862; bvtd. maj. and lt. col. of vols. for his services. Sec. U.S. Legation to Brazil, 1871-75; asst. treas., v.p. and gen. mgr. and later pres., Botanical Garden R.R. Co., An Am. enterprise in Brazil, 1876-83; admitted to N.Y. bar, 1886; E.E. and M.P. to Nicaragua, Costa Rica and Salvador, 1891-93; mem. 54th and 55th Congresses (1895-99). Republican. Alumni trustee Colby College. Home: Brockport, N.Y. Died Oct. 7, 1920.

SHARP, GEORGE CLOUGH, lawyer; b. Flyria, O., Sept. 19, 1897; s. William Graves and Hallie (Clough) S.; diploma, Ecole libre des Sciences Politiques, 1918; LL.B., Columbia, 1922; m. Ruth Baldwin, Apr. 30, 1936; children—Anna, George. Pvt. sec. to U.S. ambassador to France, 1914-19; admitted to N.Y. bar, 1923, since practiced in N.Y.C.; partner firm Sullivan & Cromwell, 1929-71. Trustee French Inst.; bd. dirs., v.p. Am. Friends of France, Inc. Served as lt. col. AUS, OSS, 1943; legal adv. SHAEF Mission to France, 1944-45. Decorated Order of Pologna Restituta (Poland); Legion of Honor, Croix de Guerre (France). Mem. Assn. Bar City of N.Y., N.Y. County Lawyers Assn., Am., N.Y. State bar assns., Am. Judicature Soc., Council Fgn. Relations, Inc., Sigma Chi. Clubs: Knickerbocker, Downtown Assn. (N.Y.C.); Bedford (N.Y.) Golf and Tennis. Home: Katonah NY Died Dec. 31, 1972.

SHARP, GEORGE GILLIES cons. naval architect; b. Cheshire, Eng.; s. William and Catherine (Bannatyne) S.; grad. naval architect Royal Tech. Coll., Glasgow, Scotland, 1896; m. Rebecca Locke Blackburn, Jan. 20, 1914; 1 dau., Jane Bannatyne; came to U.S., 1902, naturalized, 1919. Apprentice ship draftsman D. & W. Henderson, Glasgow, 1892-97, Fairfield Shipbuilding & Engring. Co. on Clyde, 1897-1901; chief draftsman Eastern Shipbuilding Co., New London, Conn., 1902-07, Bethlehem Shipbuilding Co., Wilmington, Del., 1907-11, also 1913-16, Seattle Constrn. & Dry Dock Co., 1912-13; chief surveyor Am. Bur. Shipping, N.Y.C., 1916-21; cons. practice since 1921; mem. tech. com., Am. Bur. Shipping, V.p. St. John's Guild, N.Y.C. Awarded Capt. Joseph H. Linnard prize, 1937; awarded David W. Taylor Meal, 1949. Mem. Soc. Naval Architect and Marine Engrs. N.Y., Inst. Naval Architects, London, N.-E. Coast Inst. Engrs. and Shipbuilders (Newcastle on Tyne). Clubs: Engrs., Railroad and Machinery (N.Y.C.); British Schools and Universities; Whitehall (N.Y.). Home: 185 Sagamore Rd., Milburn, N.J. Office: 30 Church St., N.Y.C. Died Oct. 21, 1960.

SHARP, WILLIAM F. army officer; b. Yankton, S.D., Sept. 22, 1885; grad. Sch. of the Line, Ft. Leavenworth, 1922, Command and Gen. Staff Sch., Ft. Leavenworth, 1925, Chem. Warfare Sch., Edgewood Arsenal, Md., 1926. Enlisted as private Co. G, 2d Batt. Engrs., U.S. Army, Aug. 29, 1904; commd. 2d lt. Regular Army, 1907, and advanced through the grades to maj. gen. (temp.), October 1945. Served with 14th Inf., Vancouver Barracks, Wash., 1st F.A., Ft. Sill, 2d F.A., Ft. Russel, Wyo., 1907-10; in Philippines, 1910-13; then with Nat. Guard, Denver; inspector Nat. Guard, Kansas City, Mo., Yankton, S.D., Topeka, Kans., 1917; instr. Ft. Leavenworth, 1917; sailed as lt. col. with 11th F.A., with A.E.F., July 4, 1918; comdg. officer 11th F.A., later 78th F.A., France, 1918; took part in Meuse-Argonne offensive; returned to U.S. in command 318th F.A.; prof. mil. science. Ore. Agrl. Coll., Corvallis, 1919-21; instr. F.A. Sch., Ft. Sill, 1922-23; with 6th F.A., Ft. Hoyle, 1926-28; at Holabird Q.M. Depot, Md., then Aberdeen (Md.) Proving Ground, 1918; plans and training officer, 3d Corps Area, 1928-32, dir. extension courses, 1932-35; with 10th F.A., Ft. Lewis, 1935-36; dist. recruiting officer, Seattle, 1936-37; supply officer 4th Army, San Francisco, 1937-40; in charge civilian component affairs, 9th Corps Area, San Francisco, 1940-41; assigned duty with F.A., Philippine Dept., Mar. 17, 1941; Comdr. U.S. Forces, on Mindanao, P.I., and surrendered to Japanese Army, May 1942; prisoner of war with Gen. Wainwright, released Aug. 1945. Awarded D.S.M., Nov. 1942. Home: Monkton, Md. Died March 30, 1947; buried National Cemetery, Fort Leavenworth, Kan.

SHARPE, ALFRED CLARENCE army officer; b. Delaware, O., Sept. 12, 1850; s. George Washington and Caroline Rebecca (Snider) S.; bro. of (Anne) Virginia Sharpe Patterson; ed. Ohio Wesleyan U.; cadet U.S. Mil. Acad., 1872-75; (hon. A.M., U. of Wooster, 1888; LL.D., U. of S.D., 1905); m. Margaret Plunket Richardson, Dec. 27, 1877. Commd. 2d lt. 10th Cav., June 21, 1876; transferred to 22d Inf., July 28, 1876; 1st lt., June 30, 1881; capt., Feb. 1, 1893; maj. a.a.g. vols., May 12, 1898; hon. disch., Apr. 17, 1899; maj. insp. gen. vols., Apr. 17, 1899; maj. a.a.g. U.S.A., Feb. 2, 1901; lt. col. inf., Mar. 29, 1904; a.a.g., Apr. 7, 1904; assigned to 30th Inf., Mar. 16, 1905; detailed General Staff, June 27, 1907; col., May 9, 1908, assigned to 23d Inf. Brevetted 1st lt., Feb. 27, 1890, for action against Indians at Spring Creek, Mont., Oct. 15, 16, 1876; recommended for bvts. lt. col., and col. for action in battles before Santiago, 1898. Admitted to Mich. bar, 1879; prof. mil. science, U. of Wooster, 1884-88, U. of South Dakota, 1891-93; judge advocate Dept. Ariz. and Colo., 1893-97; sec. of justice of P.R. during reconstruction period, 1899-1900; comd. Dist. of Zamboanga, Mindanao, 1908-09. Post of Parang, 1909-10, Dist. of El Paso, Tex., during Madero revolution, 1911; on duty with gov. of Ohio, 1911-12; with gov. of Colo., 1913-14. Retired, age limit, Sept. 12, 1914. Recalled to active duty in war with Germany, Sept. 1918-Mar. 1919. After retirement engaged in orange growing in Calif. Gold medalist and life mem. Mil. Service Instn., 1887. Home: Palo Alto, Calif. Died 1922.

SHARPE, HENRY GRANVILLE army officer; b. Kingston, N.Y., Apr. 30, 1858; s. Gen. George Henry and Caroline (Hasbrouck) S.; grad. U.S. Mil. Acad., 1880; hon. M.Sc., Rutgers, 1917; m. Kate H. Morgan, June 2, 1887. Apptd. 2d lt., 4th inf., June 12, 1880; resigned June 1, 1882; reapptd. in army as capt. staff commissary of subsistence, Sept. 12, 1883; promoted through grades to brig. gen. commissary gen. U.S. Army, Oct. 12, 1905; brig. gen. Q.M. Corps, Aug. 24, 1912; maj. gen., Sept. 16, 1916; q.m. gen. U.S. Army, 1916; maj. gen. line of the army, July 12, 1918; retired, May 1, 1920. Commissary in relief of flood sufferers at Cairo, Ill., and Memphis, Tenn., 1897; chief commissary Camp George H. Thomas, Chickamauga Park, Ga., Apr.-July 1898, 1st Army Corps, July-Oct. 1898, Dept. Porto Rico, Oct. Dec. 1898; purchasing and depot commissary, San Juan, P.R., Oct. Nov. 1898; chief commissary Div. of Philippines, 1902-04. Comdg. Southeastern Dept., June 13, 1918-May 28, 1919; in France, June 4-Sept. 1919. Author: The Art of Subsisting Armies in War; The Art of Supplying Armies in the Field as Exemplified During the Civil War (gold medal prize essay Mil. Service Instn. for 1895); The Provisioning of the Modern Army in the Field; The Quartermaster Corps in the Year, 1917, in the World War, 1921. Address: Navy Club, Washington, D.C. Died July 13, 1947.

SHARPE, HORATIO colonial gov.; b. Hull, Yorkshire, Eng., Nov. 15, 1718. Gov. Md., 1753-69, responsible for providing men and supplies for approaching French and Indian War; royal comdr.-in-chief during war, gathered supplies, inspected mil. posts, strengthened Ft. Cumberland, erected 4 small fts.; mem. mil. councils in N.Y. and Phila., 1755-57; in conflict with lower house about appropriation bills throughout term; in communication to Lord Baltimore outlined concise plan that is prototype of Stamp Act, 1754, warned ministry that Stamp Act could be enforced only by troops; arrived at boundary agreement between Md. and Va., 1760; returned to Eng., 1773. Died Eng., Nov. 9, 1790.

SHATTUCK, EDWARD STEVENS lawyer, mem. Republican Nat. Com.; b. Los Angeles, June 9, 1901; s. Edward Stevens and Grace Corrine (Stoddard) S.; B.S., U. Cal. at Berkeley, 1923; J.D., U. So. Cal., 1926, Dr. Sci. Law, 1927; m. Mary Jane Walker, Nov. 21, 1940 (dec. 1961); children—Georgia Marie (Mrs. John C. Culhane), Elizabeth Eulette (Mrs. Henry W. Kaak, Jr.); m. 2d, Eleanor Dofflemyre, Sept. 29, 1961. Admitted to Cal. bar, 1927; asst. sec. Cal. State Bar, charge Los Angeles Office, 1929-32; dep. city atty., Los Angeles, 1932-34; mem. firm Shattuck, Davis & Story, Los Angeles, 1934-40, Guthrie, Darling & Shattuck, 1946-56, Darling, Shattuck & Edmonds, 1956-62, Darling, Shattuck, Hall & Call, 1962—. Dir. Luber-Finer, Inc., Central Cal. Communications Corp., Selling Products. Mem. U.S. delegation, ofcl. rep. Am. Bar Assn., sect. on criminal law, 1st Internat. Congress on Crime Prevention and treatment of Offenders, Geneva, Switzerland, 1955. Del. Republican Nat. Conv., 1936, alternate del., 1940, vice chmn. Cal. delegation, 1948, del., 1956; mem. Nat. Rep. Policy Com., 1948-50; chmn. Rep. State Central Com., 1948-50. Trustee Redlands U. Served as pvt. 29th Combat Engrs., U.S. Army, World War I; as col. AUS, World War II; gen. consul SSS; asso. gen. counsel War Manpower Commn. Decorated Bronze Star medal, Legion of Merit. Mem. Jr. Barristers of Los Angeles (pres. 1928), Am. (mem. ho. of dels. 1964—), Los Angeles, Los Angeles County (trustee 1959—, sr. v.p. 1964) bar assns., State Bar of Cal., Am. Law Inst., Am. Judicature Soc., Cal. Jr. (pres. 1935), Los Angeles Jr. (pres. 1932) chambers commerce, Am. Legion, Los Angeles World Affairs Council, Internat. Assn. 29-30 Clubs (pres. 1931-32), V.F.W., Native Sons Golden West, Econ. Round Table of Los Angeles, Phi Delta Phi, Delta Tau Delta. Clubs: Rotary, Town Hall, Lincoln, California, Greater Los Angeles Press (Los Angeles); Commonwealth (San Francisco); Los Angeles Country. Home: 1456 Club

View Dr., Los Angeles 90024. Office: 523 W. 6th St., Los Angeles 14. Died Dec. 14, 1965; buried Forest Lawn Meml. Park, Glendale, Cal.

SHATTUCK, SAMUEL WALKER univ. prof.; b. Groton, Mass., Feb. 18, 1841; s. Walter and Roxana (Fletcher) S.; B.S., Norwich U., 1860; A.M., 1867, C.E., 1871 (LL.D., Norwich U., 1907, U. of Illinois, 1912); m. Adelaide L. White, Aug. 14, 1866. Served in U.S.V., 1861-65; sergt. maj. 6th Mass. Vols.; capt. 8th Vt. Vols.; brigade adj. and insp. gen. on several staffs; insp. gen. of Vermont, 1867-68. Instr. mathematics, 1860, adj. prof. mathematics and mil. tactics, 1865-66, pres. pro tem, 1865-66, v.p., 1866-68, Norwich U., Vt.; asst. prof. mathematics and instr. mil. tactics, 1868, prof. civ. engring., 1870, head dept. mathematics, 1868-1906, prof. mathematics, 1871-1912 (emeritus), comptroller, 1905-12, U. of Illinois. Home: Urbana, Ill. Died Feb. 13, 1915.

SHAW, FRANK L. ex-mayor; b. near Warwick, Ont., Can., Feb. 1, 1877; s. John and Katherine (Roche) S.; brought to U.S., 1883; ed. pub. and pvt. schs., Denver, Colo., and Joplin, Mo.; m. Cora H. Shires, Feb. 5, 1905. Engaged in wholesale and retail merchandising business, 1895-1925; mem. Council of City of Los Angeles, 1925-28; mem. Bd. of Supervisors, Los Angeles County, 1928-33, chmn., 1932-33; became mayor of City of Los Angeles, July 1, 1933 (all these offices non-partisan). Hon. colonel, 977th Coast Artillery, U.S. Army. Mem. C. of C. (Los Angeles), United Commercial Travelers of Am. Presbyn. Mason (32 deg., Shriner), Elk, K.P., Moose, Eagle, Maccabee. Clubs: Los Angeles Athletic, Jonathan. Home: 110 W. 59th Pl., Los Angeles, Calif. Died Jan. 1958.*

SHAW, FREDERICK BENJAMIN, army officer; b. Burlington, Pa., June 24, 1869; s. Charles D. and Margaret H. (Dickinson) S.; m. Mary B. Davis, July 8, 1908 (died May 1, 1946); children—Marion (wife of Brig. Gen. H. L. Peckham), Barbara (wife of Lt. Col. F. M. Hinshaw), Frederick B., Robert C., Daniel J. Enlisted in U.S. Army, 1892, commd. 2d lt., and advanced through grades to brig. gen.; retired as brig. gen., 1933; served in Puerto Rica, Cuba, Philippine Islands, Mexican Border and World War I. Author: History of the 2d Infantry U.S. Army (genealogy). Record of the descendants of Anthony Shaw, Boston, 1653. Home: 1920 Queen's Lane, Arlington VA

SHAW, FREDERICK WILLIAM prof. bacteriology; b. Halifax, Eng., Dec. 14, 1882; s. Rowland and Ellen (Stansfield) S.; M.D., U. of Kan., 1906; B.Sc., U. of Mo., 1921, M.Sc., 1921; m. Elizabeth Martin, Nov. 10, 1909; 1 dau., Elizabeth. Came to U.S. 1887, naturalized, 1897. Intern Bethany Hosp., Kansas City, Kan., 1906-07; govt. service as physician, 1907-16; physician Mo. State Sanatorium, 1916-17; asso. prof. hygiene, U. of Mo. Sch. of Mines, 1919-22, prof., 1922-24; asso. prof. bacteriology, Med. Coll. of Va.. 1924-29, prof. bacteriology and parasitology since 1929. Maj. Med. Corps, U.S. Army, 1917-18. Richmond Acad. Medicine, Va. Med. Soc., A.M.A., Socio Fundador. Sanatorio Belem, Porto Alegre, Brazil. Phi Beta Pi, Sigma Zeta. Clubs: Deep Run Hunt (Richmond, Va.); Army and Navy (Washington, D.C.) Collaborator: Approved Laboratory Technic. Contbr. to Physicians Library, Practice of Allergy, also to med. jours. Home: 2312 Stuart Av., Richmond, Va.; (summer) Rolla, Mo. Died May 29, 1945.

SHAW, GARDINER HOWLAND fgn. service officer; b. Boston, June 15, 1893; s. Henry Russell and Grace (Rathbone) S.; A.B., Harvard, 1915, A.M., 1917; LL.D., Holy Cross Coll., 1943; D.C.L., Boston Coll., 1944; L.H.D., Bucknell U., 1944; LL.D., Western Res. U., 1945; LL.D., U. Portland, 1958. Asst. to counselor U.S. Dept. State, 1917; apptd. 3d sec. embassy or legation and assigned to Dept. State, 1918, to Am. Commn. to Negotiate Peace, Paris, 1919; exec. asst. to sec. of state, 1920; 2d sec. of embassy with Am. High Commn., Istanbul, Turkey, 1921; with Am. Mission at Lausanne Conf., 1923; Am. del. Ankara, Turkey, 1924; 1st sec. of embassy, Istanbul, 1924; chief, Div. of Near Eastern Affairs, Dept. State, 1926-29; mem. exec. com. Fgn. Service Personnel Bd., 1927-29; counselor Am. Embassy, Istanbul, 1930-37; chargé d'affaires, Paris, Nov.-Dec., 1931; mem. Am.-Turkish Claims Commn., 1933; consul gen. 1936; chief div. of fgn. service personnel Dept. State, 1937-41; asst. sec. state, 1941-44. Mem. bd. trustees and bd. visitors Nat. Tng. Sch. for Boys, Washington, v.p., dir. Children's Village, Dobbs Ferry, N.Y. until 1957; mem. adv. com. Juvenile Ct. D.C.; pres. Osborne Assn., Am. Found. for Mental Hygiene. Mem. or officer numerous profl. orgns. in sociol. field; active in juvenile orgns. Awarded Laetare medal Notre Dame U., 1945; Leo XIII medal Sheil Sch. Social Studies (Chgo.). Mem. several profl. socs. Roman Catholic. Clubs: Metropolitan, University (Washington); Century Union, Harvard, Racquet and Tennis (New York); Somerset, Tavern (Boston). Home: 2723 N. St., N.W., Washington 7, D.C. Died Aug. 15, 1965.

SHAW, JOHN naval officer; b. Mountmellick, Queens County, Ireland, 1773; s. John and Elizabeth (Barton) S.; m. Elizabeth Palmer; m. 2d, Mary Breed, Oct. 13, 1820; 7 children. Came to N.Y.C., 1790; commd. lt. U.S. Navy, 1798; commanded the George Washington on mission to Algiers, 1801; promoted comdr., 1804, in command the John Adams, 1805; commd. capt., 1807, in charge Norfolk (Va.), Navy Yard, 1808-10, in command naval squadron blockaded by British nr. New London, Conn., 1814; joined Mediterranean Squadron, 1815, ordered to reach settlement with Algiers, remained in Algiers to protect Am. interests, until 1817; in charge of Boston Navy Yard, 1820's, later Naval Station, Charleston, S.C. Died Phila., Sept. 17, 1823.

SHAW, PHILLIPS BASSETT pub. utility exec.; b. New York, N.Y., Jan. 14, 1895; s. John Balcom and Allena (Bassett) S.; A.B., Williams Coll., 1916; student Columbia U. Law Sch., 1917; grad. Sch. of Mil. Aeronautics, Atlanta, Ga., 1918; m. Olive Greene, June 15, 1921; children—Murray H., William C.; married 2d, Jane Bales, August 20, 1946. Began in public utility field, Summit, New Jersey, 1920; operating v.p., Nat. Electric Power Co., and affiliated cos., 1923-25, v.p. and dir., 1925-27; pres. North Amer. Gas & Electric Co., 1929-36; pres. Ariz. Edison Co., Inc., since 1937; mng. dir. Ohio Service Holding Corp., and subsidiaries, 1936-43. Served as 2d lt. arty., later Air Service, U.S. Army, Aug. 1917-Jan. 1919. Mem. Phi Delta Theta. Democrat. Presbyterian. Clubs: Bankers (N.Y.); Williams, Phoenix Country. Home: 2939 E. Manor Drive. Office: Title and Trust Bldg., Phoenix, Ariz. Died Nov. 10, 1947.

SHAW, SAMUEL army officer, diplomat; b. Boston, Oct. 2, 1754; s. Francis and Sarah (Burt) S.; m. Hannah Phillips, Aug. 21, 1792. Commd. 1st lt. 3d Continental Arty., 1766; aide-de-camp to Gen. Knox, 1779; commd. capt., 1780; assisted in arranging disbandment of Continental Army; sec. com. of officers that formed Soc. of Cincinnati; held post on Empress of China, 1st Am. vessel sent to Canton, 1784; 1st sec. (apptd. by Gen. Knox) War Dept., 1785-86; 1st Am. consul in China, 1786-89, 90-92. Died at sea, Cape of Good Hope, May 30, 1794.

SHAWN, EDWIN M. (TED SHAWN), b. Kansas City, Mo., Oct. 21, 1891; s. Elmer Ellsworth and Mary Lee (Booth) S.; student U. of Denver; hon. M.P.E., Springfield (Mass.) Coll., 1936; m. Ruth St. Denis, Aug. 13, 1914. Began as teacher and professional dancer, Los Angeles, Calif., 1912; founded, with Ruth St. Denis, the Denishawn Sch., Los Angeles, 1915, later moved to N.Y. City; toured U.S. and England with Denishawn Dancers, 1922-25, the Orient, 1925-26, toured America, 1931, 32; appeared alone in Germany and Switzerland, 1930, 31; formed 1st company of men dancers, 1933, since toured America with same, also showed in London, 1935; seventh consecutive season with men dancers, 1930-40; dir. Summer School of Dance, Graduate School of Physical Edn., George Peabody Coll. for Teachers, Nashville, Tenn.; managing dir. of Jacob's Pillow Dance Festival, Inc., and University of the Dance, from Oct. 1941. Built and operated first theatre in U.S. designed and used exclusively for art of the dance. Decorated Cross of Dannebrog (Denmark); recipient of Capezio Dance award, 1956; citation Men's Garden Clubs Am., 1964, New Eng. Regional Theatre Conf., 1964, Nat. Fedn. Music Clubs, 1965; medal Nat. Soc. Arts and Letters, 1965. Served as second lieutenant, Company I, 32d Infantry, U.S. Army, 1918. Mem. National Society of Arts and Letters (adv. board), Sigma Phi Epsilon. Author: Ruth St. Denis, Pioneer and Prophet, 1920; The American Ballet, 1926; Gods Who Dance, 1929; Fundamentals of a Dance Education, 1937; Dance We Must, 1940; How Beautiful Upon the Mountain, 1943; Every Little Movement: A Treatise on Francois Delsarte, 1954; 16 Dances in 16 Rhythms, 1956; Thirty Three Years of American Dance, 1959. One Thousand and One Night Stands, 1960. Address: Lee MA also Eustis, Fla. Died Jan. 9, 1972; buried Jacob's Pillow Becket MA

SHAYS, DANIEL army officer, insurgent; b. Hopkinton, Mass., circa 1747; s. Patrick and Margaret (Dempsey) Shay (changed spelling); m. Abigail Gilbert, 1772. Served as ensign in battles of Bunker Hill, Ticonderoga, Saratoga, Stony Point; commd. capt. 5th Mass. Regt., 1777; mem. Pelham (Mass.) Com. of Safety, 1781, 82; prominent in insurrection in West Mass. known as Shays' Rebellion, (caused by econ. depression), demanded redress of grievances; chmn. com. which drew up resolutions that Mass. Supreme Ct. should be allowed to sit, provided it dealt with no case involving indictments of insurgents or debts; leader force of 1,000 insurgents, Wilbraham, Mass., 1787, attacked U.S. arsenal, Springfield, Mass. (protected by Gen. William Shepard), defeated by Mass. Militia, routed by Gen. Lincoln at Petersham; fled to Vt. after defeat; condemned to death, 1787; petitioned for pardon, 1788, pardon granted; ret. to Sparta, N.Y.; Shays' Rebellion took his name even though many others participated who were equally prominent. Died Sparta, Sept. 29, 1825.

SHEAR, THEODORE LESLIE archeologist; b. New London, N.H., Aug. 11, 1880; s. Theodore R. and Mary Louise (Quackenbos) S.; A.B., New York U., 1900, A.M., 1903; Ph.D., Johns Hopkins, 1904; studied Am. Sch. at Athens, 1904-05, U. of Bonn, 1905-06; L.H.D., Trinity Coll., Hartford, Conn., 1934; m. Nora C. Jenkins, June 29, 1907 (died Feb. 16, 1927); 1 dau., Chloe Louise; m. 2d, Josephine Platner, Feb. 12, 1931; 1 son, Theodore Leslie, Jr. Instr. Greek and Latin, Barnard Coll., N.Y. City, 1906-10; asso. in Greek, Columbia, 1911-23; lecturer on art and archeology, Princeton U., 1921-27, prof. classical archeology since 1928; also curator of classical art in Museum of Hist. Art. Trustee Am. Sch. of Classical Studies, Athens, 1936-42; dir. excavation of Athenian Agora, 1930-42. Served as 1st lt. Air Service, U.S. Army, 1917-18. Mem. Archeo. Inst. America, Am. Philol. Assn., Am. Oriental Soc., Am. Numismatic Soc., Royal Soc. of Arts (London), Hellenic Soc. (London), Assn. des Etudes Grecques (Paris), Am. Geog. Soc., Psi Upsilon, Phi Beta Kappa; hon. mem. Greek Archeol. Soc. (Athens); fellow Am. Acad. Arts and Sciences, Am. Philos. Soc. Republican. Episcopalian. Clubs: Century Assn., (New York); Nassau (Princeton). Conducted archeol. excavns. at Cnidus, 1911, Sardis, 1922, Corinth, 1925-31. Athens, 1931-40. Author: Influence of Plato on St. Basil, 1907; Sardis—Architectural Terracottas, 1925; Corinth—The Roman Villa, 1930; also numerous articles in archeol. periodicals. Home: Princeton, N.J. Died July 3, 1945.

SHEARER, JOHN SANFORD physicist; b. New York, Oct. 20, 1865; B.S., Cornell, 1893, Ph.D., 1900; m. Minnie Lee, June 20, 1888. Instr. physics, 1893-1902, asst. prof., 1902-09, Cornell; prof. physics, Columbia, 1909-10, Cornell, 1910-—. Pres. Cornell Coöperative Soc. Commd. maj., Sanitary Corps N.A., 1917, lt. col., 1918; consultant in roentgenology, A.E.F., France. Republican. Conglist. Author: Notes and Questions on Physics, 1900; Lecture Outlines and Notes, 1906. Joint author: U.S.A. X-Ray Manual. Asso. editor Am. Jour. of Roentgenology. Home: Ithaca, N.Y. Died May 1922.

SHEEHAN, JOSEPH RAYMOND pres. Am. President Lines; b. Boston, Mass., Nov. 22, 1888; s. David James and Elizabeth Agnes (Cody) S.; grad. Boston Latin Sch., 1906; A.B., Harvard, 1910; m. Reina Jane Finn, June 24, 1925; children—Jane Patricia, Virginia. Clerk Foreign Office, Jordan Marsh Co., Boston, 1910-11; clerk Burton Pierce Co., Boston, 1911-12; mgr. D. J. Sheehan & Co., Boston, 1912-17; personnel mgr. and asst. to v.p. All America Cables, Inc., New York, 1920-34; administrative co-ordinator Securities and Exchange Commn., Washington, D.C., 1934-36; asst. to Joseph P. Kennedy, New York, 1936-37; exec. dir. U.S. Maritime Commn., Washington, D.C., 1937-38; pres. Am. President Lines, Ltd. (formerly Dollar Steamship Lines, Ltd., Inc.), 1938-—. Served in Harvard Regt., May-Aug. 1917, Plattsburg O.T.C., Aug.-Nov. 1917; capt. 304th Inf., 76th Div., U.S. Army, later capt. 320th Inf., 80th Div., 1917-19, with A.E.F., July 1918-June 1919. Democrat. Catholic. Home: San Francisco, Calif. Deceased.

SHEEHAN, ROBERT FRANCIS JR. (she-han'), physician; b. Buffalo, N.Y., Dec. 5, 1879; s. Robert F. and Pauline (Hitschler) S.; grad. St. Joseph's Collegiate Inst., 1900; M.D., U. of Buffalo, 1904; M.Sc., Manhattan Coll., New York, 1906; grad. U.S. Naval Med. Sch., Washington, D.C., 1910; m. Irene Scholl, Sept. 27, 1921; 1 son, Robert Francis III. Began practice at Buffalo, 1904; psychiatrist U.S. Naval Med. Sch. and Naval Med. Officer Govt. Hosp. for the Insane, Washington, D.C., 1914-16; psychiatrist, 3d Naval Dist., 1918-21; prof. of psychiatry, Fordham Univ., 1937-39; attending neurologist St. Mary's Hosp., Brooklyn, 1935-44; cons. neuropsychiatrist Kings Park State Hospital, U.S. Naval Hospital, Harlem Valley State Hospital; chief neurologist, St. Vincent's Hosp. 1924-46, Community Hosp., N.Y.; consulting neurologist Misericordia Hospital and St. Clare's Hospital, New York City; dir. child guidance clinic, St. Vincent's Hosp., 1934-42; cons. psychiatrist to St. Vincent's Retreat; cons. neurologist Benedictine Hosp.; pres. bd. of visitors of Harlem Valley State Hosp., 1928-35. Lieutenant commander Med. Corps, U.S. Navy, 1910-22, serving in Mexican Expdn. and World War. Fellow A.A.A.S., Am. Psychiatric Assn., A.M.A.; mem. Med. Soc. State of N.Y., New York County Med. Soc., Dutchess County Psychiatric Soc., Assn. Mil. Surgeons of U.S., Eugenics Research Assn., N.Y. Soc. Clin. Psychiatry, Soc. Medical Jurisprudence, Nu Sigma Nu. Catholic. Clubs: Catholic (New York); University (Buffalo); Army and Navy (Washington, D.C.); Larchmont Yacht. Contbr. on military psychiatry. Home: 48 Hampton Rd., Scarsdale, N.Y. Died April 16, 1947.

SHEEHAN, TIMOTHY J. soldier, U.S. officer; b. County Cork, Ireland, Dec. 21, 1835; s. Jeremiah and Ann (McCarthy) S.; parents died in 1838, and he was reared by his paternal grandfather; ed. in National Schs.; m. Nov., 1866, Jennie Judge. Came to U.S., 1850; attended sch. Glens Falls, N. Y.; worked there and, 1855, went to Dixon, Ill., worked in saw mill summer and attended sch. winter. Went to Albert Lea, Minn., 1857; made a homestead; tp. clerk, Albert Lea, 1860-61; resigned and enlisted, Oct. 11, 1861, pvt. Co. F, 4th Minn. inf.; became 1st lt. Co. C, 5th Minn., Feb. 18, 1862; was sent July, 1862, after hostile Indians, Inkupadutas band, and drove them from Yellow Medicine Agency; recalled to Ft. Ridgely; commanded in the heroic defense of that fort, Aug. 19-27, 1862, until relieved by volunteer force; promoted capt., Aug. 31, 1862; served in Tenn., Miss., Ark., and Mo. and Ala., Dec., 1862, to Sept., 1865, commissioned lt.-col. and honorably discharged; wounded twice at Ridgely and twice at Nashville. Resumed farming in Minn.; sheriff Freeborn Co., 1871-83; agt. Chippewa Indians at White Earth Agency, Minn., 1885-89; deputy U. S. Marshal since May, 1890; had charge of right flank in battle with Chippewa Indians at Sugar Point, Oct., 1898 (wounded three times). Address: 831 Ashland Av., St. Paul.

SHEEHY, JOE WARREN U.S. dist. judge; b. Saratoga, Tex., Oct. 21, 1910; s. Joseph T. and Inez (Warren) S.; student U. Tex., 1927-29; LL.B., Baylor U., 1934; m. Mabel Putman, Jan. 1, 1940; children—Joseph William, Michael James. Admitted to Tex. bar, 1934, since practiced in Tyler as mem. firm Ramey, Calhoun, Marsh, Brelsford & Sheehy; asst. atty. gen. Tex., 1934; U.S. dist. judge for Eastern Dist. Tex., Tyler, since 1951, chief judge, 1965-—. Mem. C. of C., Fellows Am. Bar Found. Served as maj. USAAF, 1942-45. Mem. Am., Tex., Smith County (pres., 1942) bar assns., Am. Legion, Am. Judicature Soc. Democrat. Elk, Kiwanian (pres. 1949), Willow Brook Country. Home: 2312 S. Chilton St. Office: Federal Building, Tyler, Tex. Died Feb. 23, 1967.

SHELBY, EVAN army officer, state senator; b. Tregaron, Cardiganshire, Wales, 1719; s. Evan and Catherine (Davies) S.; m. Laetitia Cox, 1744; m. 2d, Isabella Elliott, 1787; at least 1 son, Isaac. Came to Am., circa 1734, settled in Hagerstown, Md.; laid out part of road from Ft. Frederick to Ft. Cumberland in Gen. Braddock's campaign, 1755; commd. capt. of co. of rangers, also capt. Pa. Militia; served under Gen. John Forbes in capture of Ft. Duquesne, 1758; mgr. Potomac Co. for Md., 1762; moved to Va., 1773, became landowner, Fincastle County (Va.); commanded Fincastle Co., Va. Militia in Lord Dunmore's War, 1774; commd. maj. Va. Militia, 1776; col. Washington (Va.) Militia, 1776; led expdn. of 2000 men against Chickamauga Indian towns on lower Tenn. River, 1779; mem. N.C. Senate, 1781; brig. gen. Washington Dist. (N.C.) Militia, 1786-87; commr. for N.C. to negotiate temporary truce with Col. John Sevier, 1787; refused position of gov. State of Franklin, 1787; resigned as brig. gen., 1787. Died Bristol, Sullivan County, Tenn., Dec. 4, 1794; buried East Hill Cemetery, Bristol.

SHELBY, ISAAC army officer, gov. Ky.; b. North Mountain, Washington County, Md., Dec. 11, 1750; s. Evan and Laetitia (Cox) S.; m. Susannah Hart, Apr. 19, 1783, 11 children. Served as lt. Fincastle Company at Battle of Point Pleasant, 1774; commanded garrison Ft. Blair, 1774-75; attended proceedings of L.I. Treaty with Cherokee Indians; mem. Va. Legislature, 1779; col. Sullivan County (N.C.) Militia, 1780; organized a force, joined Gen. McDowell at Cherokee Ford (S.C.), 1780; captured Ft. Anderson on headwaters of Pacolet River, 1780; went to aid of Gen. Greene, 1781; mem. N.C. Legislature, 1781, 85; trustee Transylvania Sem. (now U.), 1783; mem. bd. War for Dist. of Ky., 1791; mem. Ky. Constl. Conv., 1792; 1st gov. Ky., 1792-96, 5th gov., 1812-16; assembled and led Ky. Volunteers to join Gen. Harrison in N.W. for invasion of Can.; apptd. (with Gen. Andrew Jackson) to make a treaty with Chickasaw Indians for purchase of lands west of Tennessee River; declined appointment as U.S. sec. of war, 1818; chmn. 1st bd. trustees Centre Coll., 1819-26; counties in 9 states named for him. Died July 18, 1826; buried "Traveller's Rest," nr. Stanford, Ky.

SHELBY, JOSEPH ORVILLE army officer; b. Lexington, Ky., Dec. 12, 1830; s. Orville and Anna M. (Boswell) S.; studied Transylvania U., 1846-49; m. Elizabeth N. Shelby, 1858, 7 children. Founder, rope factory, Waverly, Mo., 1852; commd. capt. Confederate Army, 1861; organizer cavalry brigade, 1862, became prominent cavalry comdr., invaded Mo. each year, 1862-64, held own against superior Union forces; brevetted brig. gen., 1864; crossed border to Mexico, 1865, his men voted to support Maximilian, who gave Shelby land upon which colony named Charlotta was formed; returned to Bates County, Mo., circa 1867; apptd. U.S. marshal for western dist. of Mo. by Pres. Cleveland, 1893. Died Adrian, Mo., Feb. 13, 1897; buried Forest Hill Cemetery, Kansas City, Mo.

SHELDEN, CARLOS DOUGLAS congressman 12th Mich. dist.; b. Walworth, Wis., June 10, 1840; removed with his parents to Houghton Co., Mich., 1847; ed. Union School, Ypsilanti, Mich.; served through Civil War as capt. 23d Mich. inf. Mem. Mich. legislature, 1892-94; State senate, 1894-96; mem. of Congress, 1897-1903, 12th Mich. dist. Republican. Home: Houghton, Mich. Died 1904.

SHELDON, GEORGE LAWSON ex-governor; b. Nehawka, Neb., May 31, 1870; s. Lawson and Julia A. (Pallord) S.; B.L., U. Neb., 1892; A.B., Harvard, 1893; m. Rose Higgins, 1895. Engaged in farming. Capt. Co. B, 3d Neb. Inf., Spanish-Am. War, 1898. Gov. of Neb., 1907-09; received 10 votes for vice-presidential nomination in Rep. Nat. Conv., Chgo., 1908. Mason. Address: Nehawka, Neb. Died Apr. 5, 1960.

SHELDON, JOHN M. physician; b. Percival, Ia., Nov. 2, 1905; s. Tilley Walter and Carrie (McFarland) S.; A.B., U. of Neb., 1927, M.D., 1930; m. Eloise Herzog, Arp. 4, 1934. Interne U. of Mich. Hosp., 1930-31, asst. resident, Dept. Internal Medicine, 1931-32, resident, 1932-33; instr., U. of Mich. Med. Sch., Univ. Hosp., 1933-37, asst. prof. in internal medicine, 1937-46; asso. prof., U. of Mich. Med. Sch., 1946-50, professor of internal medicine, 1950-—, chmn. department postgraduate medicine, 1954-—, in charge of allergy section, University Hospital; allergist, health service, U. of Mich., since 1950; pvt. practice internal medicine, Ann Arbor, Mich., 1950-—; medical consultant to the Armed Forces. Entered M.C., U.S. Army, 1942; commanding officer, 298th Gen. Hosp. (U. of Mich. affiliated unit); disch. rank of col., Jan. 1946. Fellow Am. Coll. Physicians, Am. Acad. Allergy (pres. 1954-55); mem. World Med. Assn., A.M.A., Central Soc. Clin. Research, Washtenaw County Med. Soc., Mich. Allergy Soc., Sigma Xi. Episcopalian. Clubs: International Correspondence of Allergy; Junior Research. Author: A Laboratory Manual on Allergy, 1951. Contbr. many articles in med. jours. Home: 2121 Tuomy Rd., Ann Arbor. Office: 1405 E. Ann St., Ann Arbor, Mich. Died Feb. 12, 1967; buried Forest Hills, Ann Arbor, Mich.

SHELDON, LIONEL ALLEN governor; b. Worcester, N.Y., Aug. 30, 1831; s. Allen and Anna Maria (de les Dernier) S.; Oberlin Coll., 1848-50; admitted to bar, 1853; LL.B., Fowler Law Sch., Poughkeepsie, N.Y., 1853; m. Mary Greene Miles, Dec. 29, 1868. Probate judge, Lorain Co., O., 1856-57; practiced law, 1857-61; lt. col. 42d Ohio Inf., Nov. 27, 1861 (James A. Garfield, col.); col., Mar. 14, 1862; bvtd. brig. gen. vols., Mar. 13, 1865, "for faithful and meritorious services during the war"; served in W.Va., Ky., E. and W. Tenn., Ark., Miss. and La.; was in battles of Middle Creek, capture Cumberland Gap, Chickasaw Bayou, Arkansas Post, Port Gibson (wounded), Champion Hill, Big Black, Siege of Vicksburg, and (in command) Comite River, La.; mustered out at New Orleans, Dec. 2, 1864. Practiced law, New Orleans, 1864-79; mem. 41st to 43d Congresses (1869-75), 2d La. Dist.; represented govt. as atty. in cases from Gulf Coast before Alabama Claims Commn., and commn. to revise customs regulations for Gulf Coast; presdl. elector, 1876; gov. of N.M., 1881-85; receiver of Tex. & Pacific Ry., 1885-87; sold it Nov. 1887, and removed to Calif.; in practice at Los Angeles, 1887-—. Home: Pasadena, Calif. Died Jan. 17, 1917.

SHELLABARGER, SAMUEL (shel'a-bär'ger), author, educator; b. Washington, D.C., May 18, 1888; s. Robert Rodgers and Sarah Rivera (Wood) S.; A.B., Princeton U., 1905-09; student Munich U., Germany, 1910-11; Ph.D., Harvard, 1917; m. Vivan Georgia Lovegrove Borg, June 14, 1915; children—Ingrid Rivera (Mrs. William Holdship Rea), Marianne Jenner (Mrs. John Jeppson), John Eric (dec.). Instr. in English, Princeton U., 1914-16, asst. prof. in English, 1919-23; author, 1923-38; headmaster, Columbus (O.) Sch. for Girls, 1938-46. Served as 1st lt. Ordnance Dept., U.S. Army, 1917; capt. Military Intelligence, as assistant military attaché, U.S. Legation, Stockholm, Sweden, 1918-19. Republican. Episcopalian. Clubs: Tower, Nassau (Princeton); University, Centur Club (N.Y.). Author: The Chevalier Bayard (biography), 1928; The Black Gale (novel), 1929; Lord Chesterfield (biography), 1935; Captain from Castile (novel), 1945; Prince of Foxes (novel), 1947; The Kings Cavalier, 1950; Lord Chesterfield and His World (biography, rev. edit.), 1951; Lord Vanity, 1953; Tolbecken, 1955 (posthumously); The Token, 1956 (posthumously) (mystery stories under name of John Esteven) The Door of Death, 1928; Voodoo, 1930; By Night at Dinsmore, 1935; While Murder Waits, 1937; Graveyard Watch, 1938; Assurance Double Sure, 1939; (novels under name of Peter Loring) Grief Before Night, 1938; Miss Rolling Stone, 1939. Contbr. fiction to McCall's Mag., Cosmopolitan. Home: 107 Library Pl., Princeton, N.J. Died Mar. 20, 1954.

SHELLEY, TULLY naval officer; b. Washington, Sept. 9, 1892; ed. Jackson Sch. and Staunton (Va.) Mil. Acad.; grad. U.S. Naval Acad., 1915; m.; 1 son, Tully; m. 2d, Hazel Shelley. Commd. ensign 1915, advanced through grades to rear adm., 1949; served in U.S.S. Wyoming, operating with Brit. Grand Fleet, 1915-20; served in, and later comd. U.S.S. H-4, 1921; comd. Battle Fleet Bluejacket Bn. ashore in Nicaragua during presdl. election, 1928; in Office of Chief of Naval Operations, 1941-43; comd. U.S.S. Augusta, which operated out of east coast ports and, later in year, joined Brit. Home Fleet in U.K. waters, Feb.-Dec. 1943; asst. naval attaché Am. Embassy, London, Eng., 1943; naval attache, 1945; then mng. dir. Lummus Co.; Ltd.; apptd. spl. rep. Europe, Western Union Telegraph Co. Decorated Victory Medal with fleet clasp, Am. Def. Service Medal with fleet clasp, 2d Nicaraguan Campaign and China Service medals, Legion of Merit, Bronze Star Medal, Order Comdr. Brit. Empire, Belgian Croix de Guerre with palm, French Croix de Guerre, Greek Order of Geo. 1st with swords, Italian Order of Crown of Italy, Silver Medal of Mil. Valor. Home: Blue Water Hill, Westport, Conn. Died Sept. 6, 1966.

SHELMIRE, HORACE WEEKS army officer; b. Phila., Sept. 7, 1886; s. David and Alice Anne (Ramsey) S.; grad. Lower Merion High Sch., Ardmore, Pa., 1904; grad. F.A. Sch., La Valdahon, France, 1918; Battery Officers Sch., Phila., 1926, Command and Staff Sch., 1932, Aerial Gunnery Sch., Panama City, Fla., 1943; hon. LL.D., Hahnemann Med. Coll., Phila., 1943; m. Anna Dorothy Wolfe, May 15, 1918 (dec.); children—Dorothy Alice (Mrs. Franklin Collins), Eleanor Anne (dec.), Richard Horrace (dec.); m. 2d, Dorothy MacDonald, January 28, 1948. Began as clk. with Hess-Bright Mfg. Co., Phila., Oct. 1904; asst. paymaster Baldwin Locomotive Works, Phila., 1905-10; ind. ins. broker, Phila., 1910-41. Pvt. inf. Pa. N.G., 1903-09, Plattsburg, 1915-16; 1st lt., capt., major, F.A., 81st Div., France, 1917-19; lt. col., col., F.A. Res., 1920-41 (comd. 311th F.A. Regt., 79th Div.); Fed. service since Sept. 1941; exec. asst. to comdg. gen. USAAF, Washington, Sept. 15, 1941-43; transferred Nov. 1943; asst. chief of staff, 73d wing, 20th Air Force, 1943-46. Awarded Victory (2 stars), 2 Bronze stars, Def., Army Occupation, Defenders of Verdun (France), Pa. Victory, N. Am. Theater, Asiatic Theater (6 stars), African Theater (1 star) medals. Mem. Am. Legion (Wayne, Pa.). Club: Explorers. Mason. Author numerous mil. articles and speeches for mil. personnel. Home: Forge Farm, Downington, Pa. 19335. Address: Office Comdg. Gen. USAF, Pentagon Bldg., Washington. Died Mar. 4, 1965.

SHEPARD, EDWIN M. rear admiral U.S.N., retired; b. Oswego, N.Y., Sept. 16, 1843; s. Elisha H. and A. K. (Gray) S.; ed. Naval Acad., 1859-61; m. Alice Stevens, Dec. 9, 1868. Apptd. ensign. Nov. 22, 1862; lt., Feb. 22, 1864; lt. comdr., July 25, 1866; comdr., June 1878; capt., May 15, 1893; rear admiral, Mar. 3, 1901; retired, 1902, after 40 yrs. service as officer. Served on sloop Vincennes, 1861-62, at passes of Mississippi River; on sloop Mississippi, 1862-63, until her destruction; on gunboat Essex in siege of Port Hudson and with naval battery of 9-inch guns on shore for several weeks; on monitor Mahopac at siege of Charleston, S.C., and on James River; on Wachusett, capture of privateer Florida, Oct. 7, 1864; varied services on sea and land, after the war; light-house insp., Apr. 1898. Home: Washington, D.C. Died 1904.

SHEPARD, GEORGE WANZOR naval surgeon; b. Freedom, O., June 11, 1878; s. Sheridan Wells and Fannie Annette (Hopkins) S.; M.D., Western Reserve U. Med. Coll., 1903; m. Frankie Gail Daniels, June 30, 1903; 1 son, Richard Daniels. Surg. intern, Lakeside Hosp., Cleve., 1903-04; in practice, Ravenna, O., 1904-07; commd. asst. surgeon U.S. Navy, Oct. 25, 1907; advanced through grades to capt. Med. Corps, 1929. Med. insp. U.S. Navy, 1921; chief of surg. service, U.S. Naval Hosp., San Diego, Cal., 1922-25; same, U.S. Naval Hosp., Mare Island, Cal., 1927-31; sr. med. officer U.S. hosp. ship Relief, 1931-33; sr. med. officer Am. Embassy Guard, Peiping, China, 1935-37; comdg. officer U.S. Naval Med. Supply Depot, Mare Island, Cal., 1937-42; spent many years at sea on ships of the fleet, ret., 1942. Recalled to active duty in connection with Navy V-12 Training program, 1943. Fellow A.M.A., Am. Coll. Surgeons. Republican. Mason. Address: 115 Camino Alta, Vallejo, Cal. Died Feb. 3, 1958; buried San Bruno Nat. Cemetery, San Francisco.

SHEPARD, WALTER JAMES educator; b. Salt Lake City, Utah, Nov. 10, 1876; s. James Rea and Josephine Amelia (Lockley) S.; A.B., Willamette U., Salem, Ore., 1900, and Harvard, 1902; grad. study Harvard, Heidelberg U. and U. of Berlin, 1903-07; m. Emma Alice Adams, June 26, 1903; children—Max Adams, Mildred Martha. Instr. polit. science, U. of Wis., 1907-09; asst. prof. polit. science, Ohio State U., 1909-11; successively asst. prof. polit. science, asso. prof., U. of Mo., 1911-21; prof. polit. science, Ohio State U., 1921-23, Washington U., 1923-24, Robert Brookings Grad. Sch. of Economics and Govt., Washington, D.C., 1924-28; dean of Coll. Arts and Sciences, Ohio State U. Mem. City Council, Columbia, Mo., 1914-16. Served as 1st lt. and capt., Ordnance Dept., U.S.A., 1917-18. Chmn. Ohio State Planning Bd. Co-author and co-translator of H. Krabbe's The Modern Idea of the State, 1922. Home: Columbus, O. Died Jan. 25, 1936.

SHEPHERD, HAROLD, legal educator; b. Paris, Ida., Nov. 28, 1897; s. Joseph Russell and Rose (Budge) S.; A.B., Stanford University, 1919, J.D., 1922; LL.D., Tulane University, 1946; m. Eleanor Stahman, June 9, 1921 (dec.); m. 2d, Marian Graham McCracken, Feb. 18, 1959. Prof. of law and dean, Law Sch., U. of Wyoming, 1922-23; asso. prof. law, Stanford, 1923-26, prof., 1926-30; prof. law, U. of Chicago, 1930-31; prof. law and dean, Law Sch., U. of Wash., 1931-36; Wald prof. of contracts, U. of Cincinnati, 1936-39; professor law, Duke University 1940-42, dean law sch., 1947-49; William Nelson Cromwell Prof. law Stanford U.; also visiting prof. of law, Columbia Univ., summer 1929, Univ. of Chicago, 1929-30, U. of Minn., summer 1930, Stanford, summer 1932; visiting prof. Duke U., 1939-40; professor law Stanford U., 1949-61, prof. law emeritus, 1961-71; vis. prof. law U. Utah, 1961-62. Secretary Assn. of Am. Law Schools, 1937-40; pres., 1941. Second lt., U.S. Army, World War I. Serving as major, lt. col. and col., Army of U.S., World War II; chief Contract Termination Br., later of Legal Div., Office Chief of Ordnance. Mem. Am., Wyo., Wash. and Ohio bar associations, Phi Beta Kappa, Order of Coif (national president 1959-61), Phi Alpha Delta, Theta Chi. Author: Cases and Materials on Contracts; Contracts and Contract Remedies (with H. Wellington), 1957; Introduction to Freedom of Contract (with B. Sher), 1960. Home: Santa Cruz CA Died Oct. 2, 1971; buried Oakwood Cemetery Santa Cruz CA

SHEPPARD, LAWRENCE BAKER, business exec.; born Baltimore, Md., Dec. 13, 1897; s. Harper Donelson and Henrietta Dawson (Ayres) S.; grad., Haverford Sch., 1917; LL.B., U. of Va., 1921; m. Charlotte Newton, June 12, 1919; children—Charlotte Newton (Mrs. William Todd DeVan), Lawrence Baker (deceased), Alma (Mrs. Lorne Tolhurst), Patricia Anne (Mrs. William J. Winder). With Hanover (Pa.) Shoe, Inc., 1921-68, v.p., gen. mgr., dir., pres., then chmn. bd.; chmn. bd., dir. Sheppard and Myers, Incorporated; chmn. bd. Nat. Bank & Trust Company of Central Pa.; president, general manager Hanover Shoe Farms; president Standardbred Horse Sales Co., Harrisburg, Pa. Mem. Albemarle County bar. V.p. Nat. Footwear Mfrs. Assn.; mem. exec. committee, U.S. Trotting Association; v.p., Hambletonian Soc.; steward, Trotting Horse Club of America, Incorporated; director Hanover Gen. Hosp. Served as cons., Leather and Shoe Sec., W.P.B., dept. chief of div., asst. dir. Textile, Clothing and Leather Bur., World War II. Served as ensign in the U.S. Navy, World War I. Recieved Medal of Freedom, hdqrs. U.S. Forces European Theatre, 1945; certificate of appreciation from War Dept., 1946; T. Kenyon Holly Memorial Award by Philanthropic Foundn. of Shoe and Leather Industry, 1948. Republican. Mem. Pa. State Chamber of Commerce (director), American Legion. Phi Gamma Delta. Mason (K.T., Shriner), Elk. Clubs: Country, Arcadian, Republican (Hanover); Army and Navy (Washington, D.C.). Home: Hanover PA Died Feb. 26, 1968.

SHERBURNE, JOHN HENRY lawyer; b. Boston, Mass., Jan. 29, 1877; s. John Henry and Elizabeth Thayer (Nye) S.; A.B., Harvard, 1899, LL.B., 1901; m. Mary Patterson Harris, Nov. 26, 1901; children—John, Alice, Elizabeth, Sidney Hall; m. 2d, Helen Kemp, Sept. 23, 1931. Admitted to Mass. bar, 1901, and began practice at Boston; mem. firm Sherburne, Powers & Needham; dir. Columbia Nat. Life Ins. Co. Served as col. Mass. F.A., on Mexican border, 1916; col. and brig. gen. U.S. Army, A.E.F., 1917-19; brig. gen., U.S.R. Mem. Mass. Ho. of Rep., 1912-17; del. to Rep. Nat. Conv., 1920, 24, 28; food adminstr., Mass., 1919-20; chmn. com. on revision of highway laws, 1924. Chmn. bd. trustees Howard U., Washington, D.C., 1926-31. Mem. Am. Bar Assn., Bar Assn. City of Boston, Am. Legion (chmn. nat. legislative com. 1929). Decorated Silver Star, Purple Heart (U.S.); Comdr. Legion of Honor, Comdr. Etoile Noir (French); Hon. Citizen of Chateau Thierry and Belleau, France. Pres. Mass. Safety Council, 1930-40; dir. Mass. Com. on Pub. Safety. Adjutant gen. of Mass. July 1942-May 1943. Episcopalian. Mason (32 deg.). Club: Brookline Country (Boston). Home: Longwood Towers, Brookline, Mass. Office: 75 Federal St., Boston. Died July 25, 1959; buried Mt. Auburn Cemetery, Cambridge, Mass.

SHERIDAN, LAWRENCE VINNEDGE, landscape architect, consultant on city and regional planning; b. Frankfort, Ind., July 8, 1887; s. Harry C. and Margaret (Vinnedge) S.; B.S. in C.E., Purdue U., 1909, C.E., 1912; student Harvard Sch. of Landscape Architecture, 1916-17; m. Grace Emmel, Dec. 15, 1919; children—Roger Williams, Roderick Kessler, Harry C. II, Philip. Transitman, insp., chief insp., Bd. of Park Commrs., Indianapolis, 1911-14; Bureau Municipal Research, N.Y., 1914-16; planner Camp Pike, Ark., 1917; engr. Dallas Property Owners Assn., 1919-21; exec. sec. City Plan Commn., Indianapolis, 1921-23; private practice in landscape architecture and city planning since 1923; pres. Met. Planners, Inc., 1953-56, planning counselor, 1956-72; tchr. history of landscape architecture Purdue U.; cons. planning and zoning USAF, 1955-72; cons. landscape architect for Purdue U., Crown Hill Cemetery, Indpls.; cons. to Ind. and Ky. State Planning Bds., 1934-37; regional counselor Nat. Resources Planning Bd. for Ind., Ill., Ohio, Wis., Mich., Ky., and W.Va., 1937-41; redesigned Camp Robinson, Ark., on site of Camp Pike, 1940; camp development or site plans for Ft. Eustis, Va., Billings Gen. Hosp., Ft. Benjamin Harrison, Ind., Camp Chaffee, Ark., and Camp Atterbury, Ind., 1940-41. Served as 2d lt., F.A., A.E.F., 1918-19; commd. 2d lt. Coast Arty. Reserve, 1923, and advanced to grade of lt. col., Construction Div., Q.M. General's Office, 1941; Deputy Service Command Engr., 9th Service Command, 1942-45; colonel, Corps Engrs., Army U.S., August 1942-46; resumed practice city and regional planning, and landscape architecture. Recipient of the Distinguished Service award by the American Institute of Planners, 1957. Fellow American Society of Landscape Architects, American Soc. of Civil Engineers (life); mem. American Inst. of Planners (pres. 1940), Ind. Engring. Soc. (past pres.), Indiana Society of Pioneers, Sigma Phi Epsilon. Christian Scientist. Club: Service (Indpls.). Home: Indianapolis IN Died Jan. 26, 1972.

SHERIDAN, MICHAEL VINCENT brig. gen. U.S.A.; b. Somerset, O., May 24, 1840; s. John and Mary (Miner) S.; youngest brother of late Gen. Philip H. S.; ed. St. Joseph's Coll., Somerset. Served as vol. aide to Gen. P. H. S., at battles of Perryville, Ky., and Stone River, Tenn., Oct. 1862-Jan. 1863; apptd. 1st lt. 2d Mo. Inf., Sept. 7, 1863; capt. a.d.c., May 18, 1864; hon. mustered out of vol. service, Aug. 1, 1866; apptd. 2d lt. 5th U.S. Cav., Feb. 23, 1866; capt. 7th Cav., July 28, 1866; maj. a.a.g., June 7, 1883; lt. col., July 9, 1892; col., Jan. 25, 1897; brig. gen. vols., May 27, 1898; hon. disch. from vols., May 12, 1899; brig. gen. U.S.A., Apr. 15, 1902; retired at own request, over 30 yrs.' service, Apr. 16, 1902. Bvtd.: maj. vols., Mar. 13, 1865, "for gallant and meritorious services"; maj., Mar. 2, 1867, for battle of Opequan, Va.; lt. col., Mar. 2, 1867, for battle of Fisher's Hill, Va. Participated in battles of Chickamauga, Missionary Ridge, in Grant's campaign around Richmond, in Shenandoah, Appomattox campaigns, etc. Lt. col. a.d.c. to Lt. Gen. Sheridan, 1870-78, and his mil. sec., 1878-88; adj. gen. Dept. of the Platte, 1889-93; a.a.g. Dept. of the Mo., 1897-98; adj. gn. vols. at Camp Thomas, Ga., Apr.-July 1898; chief of staff to Gen. Brooke in P.R. expdn., July-Dec. 1898, and in charge civil affairs, Aug.-Dec. 1898; comd. Dept. of the Lakes, 1898-99, adj. gen. same, 1899-1900, Dept. of the East, 1900-02. Died Feb. 21, 1918.

SHERIDAN, PHILIP HENRY army officer; b. Albany, N.Y., Mar. 6, 1831; s. John and Mary (Meenagh) S.; grad. U.S. Mil. Acad., 1853; m. Irene Rucker, June 3, 1875. Served in Rio Grande and N.W., 1853-60; commd. capt. 13th Inf., U.S. Army, S.W. Mo., 1861, col. 2d Mich. Cavalry, 1862; commd. brig. gen. U.S. Volunteers, 1862, promoted maj. gen. (for saving Rosecrans at Stone River), 1862; won Battle of Cedar Creek, 1862; commanded the Twentieth Corps of the Army of the Cumberland at battles of Chickamauga and Chattanooga, 1863; given command of cavalry Army of Potomac by Gen. Grant, 1864, participated in battles of Spotsylvania Ct. House, Cold Harbor; raided Confederate supply lines nr. Richmond, destroyed railroads, 1864; commanded Army of Shenandoah, destroyed all supplies in Shenandoah Valley on which Confederate Army had depended, in the year 1864; commissioned major general of U.S. Army, 1864; led raid from Winchester to Petersburg, destroyed Confederate railroads and depots, inflicted further defeat upon Gen. Early at Waynesboro, 1865; position of his forces at Battle of Five Forks made possible the turning of Confederate flank, 1865, forced evacuation of Petersburg by Lee's Army, cut off Confederate retreat at Appomattox; cmdr. Div. of Gulf, 1865-67; mil. gov. 5th Mil. Dist. (comprised La. and Tex.), 1867; transferred to Dept. of Mo. by Pres. Johnson because of harshness of his adminstrn., settled hostile Indians on allotted reservations, 1867; promoted lt. gen., 1869; observed operations in Franco-Prussian War, 1870-71; commanded Western and Southwestern divs., 1878; became comdr. gen. U.S. Army, 1884; given rank of gen. by U.S. Congress, 1888. Author: Personal Memoirs, 2 vols., 1888. Died Nonquitt, Mass., Aug. 5, 1888; buried Arlington (Va.) Nat. Cemetery.

SHERMAN, BUREN ROBINSON lawyer; b. Phelps, N.Y., May 28, 1836; grad. Elmira, N.Y., 1853 (LL.D., Univ. of State of Iowa, 1883). Removed to Iowa, April 1855; admitted to bar, April 1859, locating at Vinton, Benton Co. Entered Union army, July 1861, as 2d lt. Co. E, 13th Iowa vol. inf.; severely wounded at Shiloh, April 6, 1862; promoted capt., April 11, 1862; resigned on account of wounds received in battle, April 11, 1863. Auditor of State, Iowa, 1875-81; gov. Iowa, 1882-86. Republican. Home: Vinton, Ia. Died 1904.

SHERMAN, FORREST PERCIVAL naval officer; b. Merrimack, N.H., Oct. 30, 1896; s. Frank James and Grace (Allen) S.; student Mass. Inst. Tech., 1913-14; B.S. (Distinguished Grad.), U.S. Naval Acad., 1917; grad. Naval War Coll., 1927; m. Dolores Brownson, Apr. 2, 1923; 1 dau., Elizabeth Ann. Commd. ensign, U.S. Navy, 1917, and advanced through the grades to Admiral, Nov. 1949, served on U.S.S. Nashville, in Mediterranean, 1917-18, on U.S.S. Murray on French Coast, 1918-19; commd. U.S.S. Barry, 1921; student naval aviation, Naval Air Station, Pensacola, 1922, designated naval aviator; exec. officer Fighting Plane Squadron 2, 1923; Officer in charge combat training, Pensacola, 1924-26; student Naval War Coll., 1926-27; asst. air officer, U.S.S. Lexington, 1927; comd. Scouting Squadron 2, U.S.S. Lexington, 1928-29; staff comdr. aircraft, 1929-30; instr. in flight tactics, U.S. Naval Acad., 1930-31; tactical officer, staff of comdr. of aircraft, U.S. Fleet, 1931-32; wing comdr. Fighting Wing, 1932-33; in charge aviation ordnance, Navy Dept., 1933-36; navigator, U.S.S. Ranger, 1936-37; fleet aviation officer, staff comdr. in chief, U.S. Fleet, 1937-40; office of chief of naval operations, 1940; became deputy chief for operations, December, 1945. Apptd. as U.S. rep. in naval aviation on U.S.-Canadian Permanent Joint Bd. on Defense, Aug. 1940; member Army-Navy Joint Planning Com., 1940, Navy Dept. Research Council, 1940; U.S. naval aviation advisor, Atlantic Conf., 1941; chief of staff, Air Force; Pacific Fleet, 1942; mm. Joint Strategic Com., 1942; comd. U.S.S. Wasp, 1942; Deputy chief of staff, comdr. in chief, Pacific Ocean Areas, 1943; Comd. Carrier Div. One, 1945; Dep. Chief, Naval Operations, 1946; commander of the Naval Forces in the Mediterranean, 1948; commander of the U.S. Sixth Task Fleet, 1948; appointed chief of naval operations, Nov. 1949. Awarded Navy Cross, D.S.M., Legion of Merit, Purple Heart, Victory Medal, Philippine Liberation Medal, American Defense Medal, American and Asiatic Theater Ribbons, Occupation Medal, U.S. Grand Cross, Order of Phoenix (Greece), Grand Cross Mil. Order of Italy, Companion of the Bath (England), Grand Cross Naval Order of Merit (Brazil), Grand Cross Naval Order of Merit (Chile). Mem. U.S. Naval Inst. Episcopalian. Clubs: New York Yacht; Army and Navy Country (Washington, D.C.). Home: 4611 Kenmore Dr., Washington. Died July 22, 1951.

SHERMAN, FREDERICK C. ret. naval officer; b. Port Huron, Mich., May 27, 1888; s. Frederick Ward and Charlotte Esther (Wolfe) S.; B.S., U.S. Naval Acad., 1910; grad. Naval War Coll., Jr. Course, 1925, Sr. Course, 1940; rated naval aviator, 1936; m. Fanny Jessop, Nov. 22, 1915; 1 son, John Jessop. Commd. ensign USN, 1912, and advanced through grades to adm.; officer U.S. Submarine 0-7, World War I; became comdr. U.S. Aircraft Carrier Lexington, June 1940, comdg. officer at Battle of Bougainville, Feb. 20, 1942, Battle of Salamaua, Mar. 10, 1942, Battle of Coral Sea, May 7-8, 1942, when Lexington was disabled and sunk; commanded Carrier Task Forces, Pacific area, Nov. 1942-Mar. 1944 and Aug. 1944-Sept. 1945; participated in all major actions in Pacific during this time and surrender and occupation of Japan; comdr. 5th Fleet 1945-46; ret. 1947. Staff writer Chicago Tribune, 1946-48; free lance, 1948-—. Decorated Navy Cross (3); Nicaraguan campaign, Mexican campaign, World War I, Nat. Defense and Distinguished Service (3) medals; Asiatic Pacific campaign medal with 17 bronze stars; Philippine Lberation; Presdl. Unit Citation with bronze star. Mason (32 deg.). Clubs: Army and Navy Country (Washington); Cuyamaca (San Diego). Author book on Pacific war. Address: 3118 McCall St., San Diego, Cal. Died July 27, 1957.

SHERMAN, HARRY MITCHELL surgeon; b. Providence, R.I., Nov. 23, 1854; s. Richard Mitchell and Sally Smith (Mauran) S.; A.B., Trinity Coll., 1877, A.M., 1880; M.D., Coll. Phys. and Surg. (Columbia), 1880; m. Matilda A. Barreda, Apr. 8, 1890 (died 1895); m. 2d, Lucia Hamilton Kittle, July 7, 1900. Mem. house staff Bellevue Hosp., New York, 1880-81; asst. surgeon West Point Foundry, Cold Spring, N.Y., 1881-84; orthopedic surgeon Children's Hosp., San Francisco, 1886-—; clin. prof. orthopedic surgery, 1896-99, prof. principles and practice of surgery, 1899-1912, U. of Calif.; surgeon to St. Luke's Hosp., 1901-—, to Univ. of Calif. Hospital, 1907-12. Fellow Am. Surg. Assn., A.M.A. Maj., M.C. U.S.A., Apr. 1917-Dec. 1918; chief of surg. service, Ft. Rosecrans, Calif., July-Dec. 1918. Home: San Francisco, Calif. Died May 15, 1921.

SHERMAN, HOYT banker; b. Lancaster, O., Nov. 1, 1827; s. Charles R. and Mary (Hoyt) S., brother Gen. W. T. and Senator John Sherman; grad. Howes Acad., Lancaster, O., 1842; studied law, 1848-50, admitted to practice by Ia. Supreme Court, 1850; m. Sarah Moulton, Dec. 25, 1855. In early life learned printer's trade; followed it until 1847 in office of Cincinnati Gazette; postmaster Des Moines, 1849-53; clerk of court 2 terms; maj. and paymaster, 1861-64. Aided in establishing a leading life ins. co. for many yrs.; mem. 11th gen. assembly Iowa, 1865-66. Author of statute regulating life ins. cos., and pres. Equitable Life of Iowa, 1874-88. Republican. Comdr. Iowa Commandery Loyal Legion, U.S.A., 1889-91. Home: Des Moines, Ia. Died 1904.

SHERMAN, THOMAS B., editor; b. Augusta, Ga., Sept. 4, 1891; s. Albert G. and Annie Lee (Hood) S.; student Acad. of Richmond County, Ga., 1902-06; Univ. Ga., 1907-09; m. Chloe Wachmann, Nov. 20, 1928; 1 s., William C. Reporter, rewrite man, Music Critic Atlanta Constitution, 1909-11, Birmingham News8 1911-16, Atlanta Journal, 1916-17. Mag. editor, King Features, hdqrs. New York, 1920-26; music critic St. Louis Post-Dispatch, 1926-65, editor Sunday mag., 1926-38, editor Pictures, 1938-44, editor editorial title page, 1944-47, contbg. editor and music critic, 1965-68, literary editor and editor Post-Disptach Sunday book page, 1947-68, also music and arts editor, 1956-68, also was editor Post Dispatch 75th Anniversary Supplement. Mem. Washington University adv. council, 1958-59. Served as capt., Arty., AUS, 1917-19; overseas, 1918. Recipient Gold medal from chpt. A, Daus. of Confederacy, 1906; gold medal St. Louis chpt. Nat. Soc. Arts and Letters, 1967. Former v.p. Am. Newspaper Guild. Mem. Am. Music Critics Association (pres. 1960-62), Sigma Alpha Epsilon. Democrat. Home: Clayton MO Died Sept. 28, 1968.

SHERMAN, THOMAS WEST army officer; b. Newport, R.I., Mar. 26, 1813; s. Elijah and Martha (West) S.; grad. U.S. Mil. Acad., 1836; m. Mary Shannon, circa 1850, at least 1 child. Commd. 2d lt. U.S. Army, 1836; served in Cherokee Indian Territory during Fla. War, 1836-38; became q.m., 1846; served as capt. under Gen. Zachary Taylor, Mexican War, 1846; brevetted maj. for service in Battle of Buena Vista, 1848; commanded expdn. to Yellow River, Minn.; served in expdn. to Kettle Lake, Dakota, 1859; maj. and lt. col. U.S. Army, brig. gen. U.S. Volunteers, 1861; seized Bull's Bax, S.C. and Fernandina, Fla., 1861; commanded land forces Port Royal expdn., Oct. 1861-Mar. 1862, captured Port Royal; commanded div. under Gen. Henry W. Halleck, 1862; col. 3d Arty., 1863; brevetted brig. gen. U.S. Army for gallant service at capture Port Hudson, 1864; successful in command of defenses of New Orleans, So. and Eastern Dists. of La.; maj. gen. U.S. Volunteers, circa 1865; ret. as maj. gen. U.S. Army, circa 1871. Died Newport, Mar. 16, 1879.

SHERMAN, WILLIAM TECUMSEH army officer; b. Lancaster, O., Feb. 8, 1820; s. Charles Robert and Mary (Hoyt) S.; grad. U.S. Mil. Acad., 1840; m. Ellen Ewing, May 1, 1850, 8 children. Commd. 1st lt. U.S. Army, 1841; served in Ga., 1844-45; served as aide to Gen. Philip Kearny during Mexican War; resigned commn., 1853, entered banking bus., San Francisco; became supt. new mil. acad., Alexandria, La., 1859; pres. of a street ry. co., St. Louis, 1861; commd. col. 13th Inf., U.S. Army, commanding brigade under Gen. McDowell at 1st Battle of Bull Run; brig. gen. U.S. Volunteers, comdr. Dept. of Cumberland, 1861; served in Dept. of Mo., 1861-62; served with distinction under Gen. Grant at Shiloh for which promoted maj. gen. U.S. Volunteers, 1862; commanded Dist. of Memphis, 1862; promoted to brig. gen. U.S. Army for leadership XV Corps in advance on Vicksburg, 1863; comdr. Army of Tenn., participated in Chattanooga campaign, relieved Gen. A. E. Burnside of his command of Army of Potomac, Knoxville, 1863; supreme comdr. in West, led attack on Atlanta which fell by siege, 1864, for this victory given rank maj. gen. U.S. Army; his famed March to the Sea followed, for which he received harsh criticism (although the orders he gave in this campaign were to destroy mil. installations and mfg. facilities only, great destruction of pvt. property took place); his view held that the paralysis of the enemy and quick end of the war could best be accomplished by impressing civilian population with futility of resistance through destruction of property rather than lives; this policy of devastation continued with greater vigor in S.C., 1865, until surrender of Gen. Joseph Johnston, 1865; offered Johnston liberal terms (illustrating Sherman's understanding of conditions in South); received command Div. of Mississippi after Civil War, instrumental in constrn. transcontinental railroad; promoted lt. gen. U.S. Army, 1866, sent on diplomatic mission to Mexico, 1866; comdg. gen. U.S. Army, 1869-83; established mil. sch., Ft. Leavenworth (Kan.), 1881; ret. from active service, 1883. Author: Memoirs, 1875. Died N.Y.C., Feb. 14, 1891.

SHERRARD, GLENWOOD JOHN (sher-ärd'), hotel operator; b. Dorchester, Mass., July 20, 1895; s. J. Alfred and Catherine M. (McLean) S.; student Moses Brown School, Providence, R.I., 1909-13; D.C.S. (honorary), Boston U., 1951; married Jessie A. Lumsden, Nov. 15, 1924; children—Glenwood J., Jr., Andrew Alfred. Engaged in hotel business continuously since 1914; mgr. Ft. Steuben Hotel, Steubenville, O., 1924; mng. director Hamilton Hotel, Hamilton, Bermuda, 1924-33; pres. The Parker House, Boston, Mass., since 1933, G. J. Sherrard Co. since 1933, Bellevue Hotel Company, 1934-—, also president of the Lincolnshire Hotel, Boston. Trustee Suffolk Savings Bank, Boston; now with ODM. Served as enlisted pvt., advancing through the grades to capt. engrs., U.S. Army, 1917-19. Trustee Deaconess Hosp. Mem. Am. (life dir.; past pres.), Mass. (past pres.), N.E. (past pres.) hotel assns., U.S. C. of C. (dir.). Mason, (K.T., 32 deg., Shriner). Clubs: Algonquin (Boston); Brae Burn (Newton). Home: Buzzards Bay, Mass. Office: The Parker House, Boston. Died Aug. 12, 1958; buried Forest Hills Cemetery, Boston.

SHERRILL, CLARENCE OSBORNE, born in Newton, N.C., May 24, 1876; son of Miles Osborne and Sarah Rosanna (Bost) S.; student Trinity Coll. (Duke U.), 1895-97; honor grad. U.S. Mil. Acad., 1901, Army Sch. of Line, Fort Leavenworth, Kan., 1906; grad. Army War Coll., 1907; m. Geraldine Caldwell Taylor, Nov. 30, 1905; children—Clarence Caldwell, Minnie Elizabeth. Commd. 2d lt., Corps Engrs., U.S. Army, Feb. 18, 1901; advanced through grades to col., Engrs., N.A., Aug. 5, 1917; lt. col., U.S. Army, July 1, 1920; resigned, Dec. 31, 1925; col. U.S. Engr. Reserve Corps, 1926-49; colonel Honorary Reserve U.S. Army since 1950. City manager, Cincinnati, 1926-30 and 1937-44; now retired. Vice pres. Kroger Grocery & Baking Co., 1930-35; pres. Am. Retail Fedn., 1935-37. Served in Philippine Insurrection, 1901-03; col. engrs., chief of staff, 77th Div., France, World War. Awarded D.S.M. (U.S.); Croix de Guerre with Palm (France). Service in Army also included mil. and engring. assignments; in charge river and harbor improvements, flood control, levee constrn., bridge bldg.; dir. pub. bldgs. and parks, Washington, D.C., 1921-25; mil. aid to Presidents Harding and Coolidge; etc. Chmn. Cincinnati Com. on Co-ordination and Cooperation; chmn. Cincinnati Employment Advisory Council, 1928-32; mem. City Planning Commn., Cincinnati, 1926-30 and 1937-44. Mem. Am. Soc. C.E., Cincinnati Chamber of Commerce (hon. life mem.), Am. Mil. Engrs. Methodist. Clubs: Commonwealth, Cincinnati Country, Engineers (Cincinnati); Army and Navy, Chevy Chase (Washington, D.C.). Author: Military Map Reading, 1910; Topographical Surveying, 1910; Rapid Sketching, 1910. Home: 2211 E. Hill Av., Hyde Park, Cincinnati 8 OH

SHERRILL, ELIAKIM congressman; b. Greenville, Ulster County, N.Y., Feb. 16, 1813; attended public schs. Tanner and farmer; held several local offices; served as maj. N.Y. Militia; mem. U.S. Ho. of Reps. (Whig) from N.Y., 30th Congress, 1847-49; mem. N.Y. Senate, 1854; organized, served as col. 126th N.Y. Volunteer Regt. during Civil War, wounded at Harpers Ferry; commanded 3d Brigade, 3d Div., 2d Army Corps at Battle of Gettysburg. Mortally wounded at Gettysburg, July 3, 1863, died next day; buried Washington Street Cemetery, Geneva, N.Y.

SHERRILL, STEPHEN H. ret. army officer; b. East Hampton, L.I., N.Y., Mar. 13, 1893; s. Abram E. and Nettie (Glover) S.; B.S., U.S. Mil. Acad., 1917; post grad. work, Yale, Sheffield Sci. Sch., 1920-21, Command and Gen. Staff Sch., 1930-32, Army War Coll., 1938-39; m. Dorothy M. Roberts, Jan. 26, 1918; 1 son, Stephen H. Commd. 2d lt., 1917, and advanced through grades to brig. gen., 1942; comdg. Troop I, 2d Cav.; instr. equitation Plattsburg Tng. Camp, 1917; AEF, France and Germany, 1918-19; transferred to Signal Corps, 1923; War Dept. Gen. Staff, 1939-42; comdg. gen. Western Signal Corps Tng. Center, Camp Kohler, Sacramento; comdg. gen. Aircraft Warning Unit Tng. Center, 3d Air Force, Drew Field, Fla., Eastern Signal Corps Tng. Center, Fort Monmouth, N.J.; ret. 1946. Vice pres. First Nat. Bank of Arlington, Va., in charge Pentagon br. Decorated Legion of Merit with oak leaf cluster, French Legion of Honor. Editor "Signals", 1946-—. Home: 3015 45th St., Washington 16. Died June 28, 1956; buried Arlington Nat. Cemetery.

SHERWIN, THOMAS businessman; b. Boston, July 11, 1839; s. Thomas and Mary King (Gibbens) S.; ed. Boston Latin Sch. and Harvard; m. Isabel Fiske Edwards, Jan. 18, 1870. First lt. and adj. 22d Mass. Inf., Oct. 8, 1861; maj., June 28, 1862; lt. col., Oct. 17, 1862; bvtd. col. vols., Sept. 30, 1864, "for gallant services at battle of Peebles Farm, Va."; brig. gen. vols., Mar. 13, 1865, "for distinguished gallantry at battle of Gettysburg, and for gallant and meritorious services during the war"; hon. mustered out, Oct. 17, 1864. Chmn. bd. N.E. Telephone & Telegraph Co., 1909-—; officer or dir. in other corps. Home: Jamaica Plain, Mass. Died Dec. 20, 1914.

SHERWOOD, ISAAC R. congressman; b. Stanford, N.Y., Aug. 13, 1835; s. Aaron and Maria (Yeomans) S.; student Antioch Coll., O., 1854-56, LL.B., Ohio Law Coll., Cleveland, 1859; m. Katharine Margaret Brownlee, Sept. 1, 1859. Pvt. 14th Ohio Inf., Apr. 22-Aug. 13, 1861; 1st lt. adj. 111th Ohio Inf., Sept. 6, 1862; maj., Feb. 13, 1863; lt. col., Feb. 12, 1864; bvtd. brig. gen. vols., Feb. 27, 1865, "for gallant and meritorious services" at Resaca, June 14, 1864, Franklin, Tenn., Nov. 30, 1864, and at Nashville, Dec. 15, 1864; hon. mustered out, Oct. 8, 1865. Editor Toledo Commercial, 1865, Cleveland Leader, 1865-66, Toledo Journal, 1874-83, Canton News-Democrat, 1888-98. Sec. of state of Ohio, 1869-73; mem. 43d Congress (1873-75), 6th Ohio Dist.; probate judge, 1878-84; mem. 60th to 66th Congresses (1907-21) and 68th Congress (1923-25), 9th Ohio Dist. Author of the "Sherwood Dollar-a-Day Bill" and "Medal of Honor Bill." Elk. Home: Toledo, O. Died Oct. 15, 1925.

SHERWOOD, ROBERT EMMET writer; b. New Rochelle, N.Y., Apr. 4, 1896; s. Arthur Murray and Rosina (Emmet) S.; Harvard Univ., 1914-17; Litt.D., Dartmouth College, 1940, Yale Univ., 1941, Harvard, 1949; D.C.L., Bishop's Univ., 1950; m. Mary Brandon, Oct. 29, 1922; 1 dau., Mary J.; m. 2d, Madeline Hurlock, June 15, 1935. Was dramatic editor of Vanity Fair, 1919-20; associate editor "Life," 1920-24, editor, 1924-28; also motion picture editor "Life" and New York Herald. Enlisted in 42d Batn., Black Watch, Can. Expdn. Force, 1917; hon. disch., Feb. 1919. Spl. Asst. to Sec. of War, 1940, Sec. of Navy, 1945. Served as dir. overseas branch O.W.I.; resigned in September 1944. Clubs: Harvard, Garrick (London). Author: (plays) The Road to Rome, 1927; The Queen's Husband, 1928; Waterloo Bridge, 1929; This Is New York, 1930; Reunion in Vienna, 1931; The Virtuous Knight (novel), 1931; Acropolis, 1933; The Petrified Forest, 1934; Idiot's Delight, 1936; Abe Lincoln in Illinois, 1938; There Shall Be No Night, 1940; The Rugged Path, 1945; Roosevelt and Hopkins (biography), 1948; Miss Liberty, 1949. Contbr. fiction and articles to mags. Pulitzer prize, 1936, 39, 41, gold medal for drama. Nat. Inst. of Arts and Letters, 1941, Bancroft prize for distinguished writings in Am. hist., 1949; Pulitzer prize, 1949. Address: 1545 Broadway, N.Y.C. 36. Died Nov. 14, 1955.

SHERWOOD-DUNN, BERKELEY, M.D., banker; b. Rushford, N.Y.; s. William Erwin and Harriet Elizabeth (Peterson) Dunn; M.D., New York U., 1884; Bach. es lettres, U. of Paris, France, 1884, Dr. of Medecine, 1889; m. at Nice, France, Louise Lacy, d. Royal C. Knapp, of Rochester, N.Y., 1892; children—Gladys (dec.), Yerkes and Hamilton (twins), Dorothy; m. 2d, Princess Guerke, 1923. Practiced at Paris, 1888-97; asst. prof. gynecology, Tufts Coll. Med. Sch., Boston, 1900; surgeon to Cushing Hosp., Boston; joint owner and editor Annals of Gynecology and Pediatrics, Boston, 1900; between 1902-14, was sec. Century Trust Co. and dir. Bankers Life Ins. Co.; pres. European-Am. Bk., Del. & Northampton Ry., N.Y. & Del. Riv. Ry., and was officer or dir. numerous other corpns. and banks at New York and in S.C. Author of numerous med. papers and books. Nat. committeeman for S.C. Progressive Party, 1912. Apptd. dir. A.R.C. Hosp., Amiens, France, 1915; French Army med. service, front line, title benevole, grade of col., Oct. 1915; wounded, Nov. 1915; service at Paris, 1916-19; asst. to l'Hopital Cochin, Paris, 1916-18. Awarded eight decorations, including Legion of Honor. Founder and pres. Washington-Lafayette Com. Mem. various Am. and European med. socs., Soc. Alliance Francaise; v.p. Am. Civic Alliance. Episcopalian. Clubs: Automobile, Athletic, Lawyers' (New York); Aiken (S.C.) Gun; American (founder and pres.), Nice Golf (France). Home: Waldorf Hotel, New York NY Office: 54 Boul. Victor Hugo, Nice France

SHIELDS, EDMUND CLAUDE lawyer; b. Howell, Mich., Dec. 30, 1871; s. Dennis and Lydia (Lonergan) S.; B.L., U. of Mich., 1894, LL.B., 1896; m. Mary Foley, Dec. 28, 1900. Admitted to Mich. bar, 1896; pros. atty., Livingston County, 1901-04; chmn. commn. to compile Mich. state statutes, 1915; mem. Shields, Ballard, Jennings & Tabor; pres. Central Trust Co., Lansing, Mich., Mich. Surety Co.; v.p. W. S. Butterfield Theatres, Inc., Bijou Theatrical Enterprise Co.; dir. Motor Wheel Corp., Grand Trunk Western R.R., Melling Forging Co., Duplex Truck Co. Served as 2d lt., 35th Regt., Spanish-American War. Mem. Dem. Nat. Com. Regent U. of Mich. Mem. Am., Mich. and Ingham County bar assns., Phi Delta Phi. Democrat. Catholic. Clubs: City, Country; Chemung Hills (Howell). Home: Hotel Olds. Office: 1400 Olds Tower, Lansing, Mich. Died Jan. 6, 1947.

SHIELDS, GEORGE ROBERT lawyer; b. Pigeon Forge, Tenn., Oct. 21, 1879; s. William Jesse and Sarah Ellen (Carter) S.; B.S., Murphy Collegiate Inst., Sevierville, Tenn., 1898; student Peabody Coll. for Teachers. 1899-1900; LL.M., Nat. U. Law Sch., 1912; m. Agnes Richardson Hill, Nov. 14, 1902; children—Frederick Wyatt, Mary Elizabeth, Roger Denton (killed in Germany, Feb. 7, 1945). Teacher public schools of Tennessee, 1897-1901; admitted to bar, D.C., 1911; legal aide, Office of Comptroller U.S. Treasury, 1912-16; with King & King, attys., Washington, D.C., 1917-19, mem. of firm (sr. member), 1920-47; retired. Specialist in matters involving suit or claim against the Federal Government. Served as capt., U.S. Army, aide to Brig. Gen. Herbert M. Lord, 1918-19. Mem. Am. and D.C. bar assns., Soc. Am. Mil. Engrs. Republican. Clubs: University, Columbia Country, National Press. Contbr. to Income Tax Mag., The Constructor, Engineering News-Record, etc. Home: The Baronet, 1737 H St., Washington 6, D.C. Died Nov. 20, 1947.

SHIELDS, JAMES senator; b. Altimore, County Tyrone, Ireland, May 10, 1810; s. Charles and Katherine (McDonnell) S.; m. Mary Ann Carr, 1861, at least 3 children. Came to N.Y.C., circa 1826; mem. Ill. Ho. of Reps., 1836; state auditor Ill., 1839, helped correct state's disordered finances; mem. Supreme Ct. Ill., 1843-45; commr. to gen. land office, Washington, D.C., 1845-47; served as brig. gen. Ill. Volunteers, brevetted maj. gen. for gallantry at Cerro Gordo, Mexican War, 1847; apptd. gov. Ore. Territory, 1849, resigned immediately to become mem. U.S. Senate from Ill., Oct. 27, 1849-55; settled in Minn. Territory, 1855, encouraged Irish immigration into region by organizing twps. of Shiedsville, Erin, Kilkenny, Montgomery; founded (with Alexander Faribault) Faribault Twp.; mem. U.S. Senate from Minn., May 11, 1858-59; went to San Francisco, 1859; mine mgr., Mazatlan, Mexico 1861; served as brig. gen. Ill. Volunteers in Shenandoah Valley campaign during Civil War, 1861-63; railroad commr. in Cal., 1863-66, moved to Mo., 1866; mem. Mo. Legislature, 1874, 79; adjutant gen. Mo., 1877; mem. U.S. Senate from Mo., Jan. 22, Mar. 3, 1879. Died Ore., June 1, 1879; buried St. Mary's Cemetery, Carrollton, Mo.

SHIELS, GEORGE FRANKLIN surgeon; b. San Francisco, Calif., Apr. 15, 1863; s. William and Sarah Esdale (Lynham) S.; M.D., M.B., M.S., Edinburgh U., 1878-86; fellow Royal Coll. Surgeons, Edinburgh, 1880-86; post-grad. studies, Berlin, Paris, Vienna, and London; m. Emily Mead, 1902 (died 1913). Began practice at San Francisco, 1888; lecturer on med. jurisprudence, U. of Calif., 1890-92, prof. surgery, 1892-98; prof. clin. surgery, post-grad. dept., 1894-98; asst. lecturer on surgery, New York Polyclinic, 1904-06; prof. surgery, Fordham U., 1905-07; dir. Shiels Estate Co., San Francisco, Maj. and brigade surgeon, Spanish-Am. War, 1898; on staffs of Gens. Otis, King, Wheaton, Grant and MacArthur; hon. mustered out 1900; maj. M.C., World War, 1917-19; now col. M.R.C. Fellow Am. Coll. of Surgeons, Calif. Acad. of Medicine; member A.M.A., Calif. State and San Francisco County med. socs., Mil. Order Fgn. Wars. Naval and Mil. Order Spanish-Am. War, Assn. Army of U.S., Mu Sigma Mu. Awarded Congressional Medal of Honor "for most distinguished gallantry in action"; Spanish-Am. War, Philippine Insurrection, and Victory medals; 3 citations "for distinguished gallantry," World War (U.S.); Croix de Guerre with 2 Palms, Cheva(lier Légion d'honneur (French); 3 Silver Star citations. Republican. Protestant. Clubs: Pacific Union (San Francisco); Army and Navy (New York). Contbr. papers on professional subjects. Home: 337 Hopkins Av., Redwood City, Calif. Died Oct. 26, 1943.

SHINGLER, DON GILMORE retired army officer, consulting engr.; b. Perry Center, N.Y., Oct. 25, 1896; s. John Jay and Anna (Gilmore) S.; B.A., Wyo. U., 1917; B.S., U.S. Mil. Acad., 1919; B.S. in Civil Engring., Mass. Inst. Tech., 1921; grad. Engr Sch., 1930-31, Command and Gen. Staff Sch., 1934-36, Army War Coll., 1939-40;

m. Beatrice Clark, June 16, 1924. Commd. 2d lt. U.S. Army, 1919, advanced through grades to brig. gen.; asst. to U.S. dist. engr., Detroit, 1921-22; asst. to chief Inland and Coastwise Waterways Service, Washington, 1923-24; instr., then asst. prof. math. U.S. Mil. Acad., 1925-30; chief of staff U.S. Mil. Iranian Mission to Iran and Iraq, 41-42; chief Iranian Mission (Basra, Iraq), 1942; dir. Motor Transport Service (Persian Gulf) 1943; dir. internat. div. A.S.F., 1944-45; chief engr. European Theatre, 1946-49; mem. Miss. River Commn., 1950-51; div. engr. Mo. River and later N. Pacific divs. C.E. until retirement, 1954; with Tippetts-Abbett-McCarthy-Stratton Engrs., gen. mgr. Korea office, 1954-56, Iraq, 1956-58; with Inst. Def. Analysis, 1959. Decorated Legion of Merit, D.S.M. (U.S.); Order British Empire; Legion of Honor (France). Mem. Alpha Tau Omega, Delta Sigma Rho. Clubs: Army and Navy (Washington). Home: P.O. Box 61, Lexington, S.C. Office: 4000 Cathedral Av. N.W., Washington. Died Oct. 29, 1963; buried Arlington Nat. Cemetery.

SHINKLE, EDWARD MARSH army officer; b. Higginsport, O., Jan. 9, 1878; s. Michael Eugene and Sarah Blaisdell (Marsh) S.; student Ohio Wesleyan U., 1894-95; grad. U.S. Mil. Acad., 1901; Army War Coll., 1920; m. Margery Gibbons, May 3, 1905; children—Margery (Mrs. Frederic W Farrar), Edward Gibbons, John Gardner. Commd. 2d lt. arty., Feb. 18, 1901; advanced through grades to brig. gen., Sept. 1, 1934; asst. chief ordnance U.S. Army, Washington, Sept. 1, 1934-Aug. 31, 1938; comdg. officer Picatinny Arsenal, Sept. 1, 1938-Oct. 31, 1941; gen. mgr. Ia. Div. Day and Zimmerman, Inc., Phila., July 19, 1942-Sept. 15, 1945. Awarded D.S.M. and L.M. (U.S.). Clubs: Army and Navy (Washington); Chevy Chase (Md.). Address: 66 Cleary Ct., San Francisco. Died Nov. 8, 1966; buried Arlington, Va.

SHIPP, SCOTT educator; b. Warrenton, Va., Aug. 2, 1839; student Westminster Coll., Mo.; grad. Va. Mil. Inst., 1859 (Litt.D., 1883; LL.D., Washington and Lee U., 1890); m. Anne Alexander, d. Arthur A. Morson, Aug. 19, 1869. Asst. prof. mathematics, later of Latin, Va. Mil. Inst.; lt., capt., maj. and lt. col., C.S.A.; ordered, 1862, by Confed. sec. of war to report as commandant of cadets and instr. of Va. Mil. Inst.; comd. cadets at battle of New Market, where was wounded; after war, grad. in law; reapptd. to Va. Mil. Inst., was supt. same (supt. emeritus). Declined presidency Va. Agr. and Mech. Coll.; mem. bd. of visitors U.S. Mil. Acad., 1890; pres. bd. of visitors U.S. Naval Acad., 1894. Retired under Carnegie Foundation, July 1907. Home: Lexington, Va. Died Dec. 7, 1917.

SHIPPEN, EDWARD medical dir. U.S.N.; b. in N.J., June 18, 1826; A.B., Princeton, 1845, A.M., 1848; M.D., U. of Pa., 1848. Apptd. to U.S. Navy, from Pa., 1849, as asst. surgeon, commd. surgeon, Apr. 26, 1861; promoted med. dir., Mar. 17, 1876; retired June 18, 1888; rear admiral retired, 1907. Principal naval service in China and on coasts of Africa and S. America; on European sta. 4 yrs.; was on the Congress when destroyed by Merrimac; on New Ironsides in both battles of Fort Fisher; at Bermuda Hundred, defending Grant's right flank; chief med. officer, Naval Acad., Annapolis; fleet surgeon, European squadron; nearly 7 yrs. in charge of Naval Hosp., Phila. Companion Mil. Order Loyal Legion; fellow Coll. Physicians of Phila.; gov. Pa. Soc. of Colonial Wars; pres. Geneal. Soc. Pa. Author: Thirty Years at Sea; A Christmas at Sea; Naval Battles of America, 1905; Naval Battles of the World, 1905. Home: Philadelphia, Pa. Died 1911.

SHIPPEN, WILLIAM physician, educator; b. Phila., Oct. 21, 1736; s. William and Susannah (Harrison) S.; grad. Princeton, 1754; M.D., U. Edinburgh (Scotland), 1761; m. Alice Lee, 1760, 1 child. Pioneer in establishing courses in midwifery and anatomy using dissection, Phila., 1762; prof. anatomy and surgery med. school Coll. of Phila., 1765; chief physician, dir. gen. Continental Army hosp. in N.J., 1776; chief med. dept. Continental Army, 1777; submitted plan for reorgn. army med. dept. to Continental Congress, 1777 (adopted 1777); physician Pa. Hosp., 1778-79; prof. anatomy U. State of Pa., 1779; prof. anatomy, surgery and midwifery U. Pa., Phila., 1791; a founder Coll. of Physicians of Phila., pres., 1805-08. Died Phila., July 11, 1808.

SHIPTON, JAMES ANCIL army officer; b. Ohio, Mar. 10, 1867; grad. U.S. Mil. Acad., 1892, Sch. of Submarine Defense, 1906. Commd. add. 2d lt. 4th Arty., June 11, 1892; promoted through grades to brig. gen. N.A., Aug. 5, 1917; col. Coast Arty. Corps, May 29, 1918. Served with battery during railroad strikes, Chicago, 1894; mil. attaché Am. Legation, Petropolis, Brazil, 1898-99; in Philippine Islands, 1899-1901; participated in Gen. Kobbe's expdn. to open hemp ports of Luzon; comdg. various dists., P.I., 1900-01; comd. 52d Co., Coast Arty., Governor's Island, N.Y., 1901-02; spl. instrn., Gen. Electric Co., Schenectady, N.Y., 1906-07; comdr. Torpedo Depot and disbursing officer same, 1908; mil. attaché, Argentina, 1912-14; grad. Army War Coll., 1915-16; instr. same, 1916-17; served in France, July 1917-Aug. 1919; organized Anti-Aircraft Service and chief of same until July 1, 1918; comd. 55th Brig. F.A.; comd. divisional arty., 89th Div. in attack on St. Mihiel and divisional arty. 37th Div. in attack in Meuse-Argonne; comd. S.O.S. troops, region of Nancy, to June 1, 1919. Retired at own request, after 30 yrs.' service, Feb. 20, 1920. Officer French Legion of Honor. Married Georgia L. Lincoln, Dec. 17, 1902. Died Feb. 15, 1926.

SHIRLEY, WILLIAM colonial gov.; b. Preston, Sussex, Eng., Dec. 2, 1694; s. William and Elizabeth (Godman) S.; A.B., Pembroke Coll., Cambridge (Eng.) U., 1714-15; m. Frances Barker, circa 1718; m. 2d, Julie Shirley, circa 1751; 9 children including Thomas. Admitted to English bar, 1720; came to Boston, 1731; judge of admiralty, 1733; advocate gen., circa 1735; gov. Mass., 1741-49, 53-56, abolished land bank, 1741, stabilized paper currency, planned expdn. to Louisbourg (fortress captured largely through his efforts and administrn; 1745; used reimbursement from Parliament for Mass. war effort (1744-45) to retire paper currency and establish sound finances; commd. col. Brit. regt. to be raised from New Eng. provincial troops, 1746; mem. commn. in Paris to determine boundary line between French N.Am. and New Eng., 1749-53; maj. gen. at outbreak French and Indian Wars, 1755; one of 5 govs. who attended council on war with Gen. Braddock, Alexandria, Va., Apr. 1755; became comdr. all Brit. forces after Braddock's death, July 1755; failed in Niagara expdn. because of lack of supplies and troops, end of 1755, superseded as comdr.; went to Eng., 1756, malfeasance charges against him dropped; commd. lt. gen., 1757; gov. Bahama Islands, 1761-67. Died Shirley Place, Roxbury, Mass., Mar. 24, 1771.

SHOALS, GEORGE (RALPH) (sho'äls), editor; born Cortland, N.Y., Sept. 8, 1903; s. Frederick Clinton and Bessie Lynn (Angell) S.; B.S., Syracuse Univ., 1926; m. Ruth Streun, Nov. 27, 1926; 1 dau., Lynn Gretchen. Reporter, copyreader, Sunday editor, and other posts on Rome (N.Y.) Sentinel, 1926-27, Worcester (Mass.) Telegram, 1928-29, Bay Shore (N.Y.) Journal, 1927-28; Cortland Standard, 1927-27, Rochester (N.Y.) Journal, 1929-35, Rochester American, 1929-35; mng. editor, Rochester Democrat and Chronicle, since 1941. Served with U.S. Army, advancing from lt. to maj., 1943-46; service in Africa, Middle East theater, 1944-46. Mem. Rochester Chamber of Commerce, Asso. Press Managing Editors Association, Sigma Delta Chi. Methodist Episcopal. Mason; Elk; Moose. Clubs: Ad, Oak Hill Country (Rochester). Home: 99 Penfield Rd., Rochester 10. Office: The Rochester Democrat and Chronicle, 61 Main St. E., Rochester 4, N.Y. Died Apr. 21, 1960; buried Cortland, N.Y.

SHOCK, THOMAS MACY naval officer (ret.); b. Olympia, Wash., May 16, 1892; s. Thomas Alexander Wharton and Olive Caverno (Macy) S.; B.S., U.S. Naval Acad., 1913; student Naval War Coll., 1939-40; m. Evelyn Friddy, Nov. 25, 1919. Commd. ensign USN, 1913, advanced through grades to rear adm., 1947; U.S. Naval Attache to China, 1934-37; war plans, 11th Naval Dist., San Diego, 1940-41; comdr. U.S.S. Chester, 1941-42, U.S. Naval bases, Solomons, 1942-43; mem. staff Naval War Coll., 1943-46; ret. from active duty, 1947; adminstrv. asst. to v.p., Sidney Blumenthal and Co., Inc., N.Y.C. since 1947. Awarded D.S.M. (Army), Legion of Merit, letters of commendation. Episcopalian. Home: 12 Leroy Av., Newport, R.I. Died Oct. 4, 1962.

SHOCK, WILLIAM HENRY engineer-in-chief U. S. navy; retired June 15, 1883; b. Baltimore, June 15, 1821; entered navy as 3d asst. engr., Jan. 18, 1845; served in Mexican war; promoted 2d asst. engr., July 10, 1847; 1st asst. engr., Oct. 31, 1848; chief engr., March 11, 1851; superintended construction of machinery of various naval steamers, the marine engines at West Point, N.Y.; pres. examining bd. engrs., 1860-62; supt. building river monitors at St. Louis, 1862-63; fleet engr. under Admiral Farragut at Mobile and later under Admiral Thatcher, 1863-65; engr.-in-chief of navy, 1877-83; invented and patented numerous improvements in guns, steam devices, and a relieving cushion for wire rigging. Author: Steam Boilers: Their Design, Construction and Management. Address: 1404 15th St., Washington.

SHOCKLEY, M. AUGUSTUS WROTEN, med. officer, U.S. Army; b. Ft. Scott, Kan., May 13, 1874; s. William Bridges and Anna Gertrude (Alexander) S.; student U. of Kan., 1892-93, U.S. Naval Acad., 1894-95; M.D., Kan. City Med. Coll. (U. of Kan.), 1898; grad. Gen. Staff Sch., 1922; m. Irene Brown, 1948. Began as 1st lt., asst. surgeon, 7th U.S. Volunteer Inf., 1898, and promoted through grades to brig. gen., regular army, 1935; dir. Field Service and Corr. Sch. for Med. Officers, U.S. Army, 1915-17; instr. Sch. of the Line and Staff Coll., U.S. Army, 1919-22; prof. mil. hygiene, U.S. Mil. Acad., 1927-31. Fellow Am. Coll. Surgeons; mem. Assn. Mil. Surgeons, A.M.A., Sigma Chi. Awarded D.S.M. (U.S.); Officer Legion of Honor (France). Author: Outline of the Medical Service of the Theatre of Operations, 1922. Home: 2035 W. Olive Av., Fresno CA

SHOEMAKER, HENRY WHARTON newspaper pub.; b. N.Y. City, Feb. 24, 1882; s. Henry Francis and Blanche (Quiggle) S.; ed. private tutors, at Dr. E. L. Lyon's Classical School (now under title of Allen-Stevenson School), New York, and Columbia U., 1897-1900; Litt.D., Juniata Coll., Huntingdon, Pa., 1917, Franklin and Marshall Coll., 1924; m. Beatrice, d. George B. Barclay, June 12, 1907; 1 son, Commander Henry F. (U.S.N.R.); m. 2d, Mabelle Ord, May 10, 1913. Began bus. career with C. H. & D. Railway, Cincinnati and N.Y., 1900-04; sec. American Legation, Lisbon, Portugal, 1904; 3d sec. Am. Embassy, Berlin, 1904-05; mem. N.Y. banking house of Shoemaker, Bates & Co., 1905-11; became publisher of daily morning and evening newspapers, Pa. and Conn., 1905; president Altoona (Pennsylvania) Times Tribune, 1912-50, columnist six days weekly, 1915-50; apptd. E.E. and M.P. to Bulgaria, 1930, retired 1933. Officer, New York, later Pa. National Guard, 1907-19; with Gen. Staff U.S. Army, 1918-19; spl. rep. Nat. Guard Pa. in Europe, 1918; lt. col. O.R.C., 1924, col. since 1933; historian Pa. War Memorial Commn. in Europe, 1928; mem. Gov. of Pa.'s Commn. for Nat. Defense, and Com. Pub. Safety, 1917-18. Mem. State Forest Commn. of Pa., 1918-30; comn. State Hist. Commn. of Pa., 1923-30, mem. of commn., 1936-40; mem. State Geographic Bd. of Pa., 1924-30; dir. State Archives of Pennsylvania, 1937-48; dir. Pa. State Division of Fblk History, 1948-—; director Pa. State Museum, 1939-40; mem. advisory bd. Pennsylvania Council of Nat. Defense, 1941-46. Mem. Pa. Tuberculosis Soc. (2d v.p.), Pa. Parks Assn., Conrad Weiser Park, etc. Decorated Grand Officer Order of the Redeemer (Greece); Grand Cordon Order of Civil Merit (Bulgaria); Comdr. Order of the Crown (Italy); Officer Order of Compassionate Heart (Russia); Knight Order of Nicholas II (Russia); Order of Meritoious Service (Pa.); received War Department citation, 1943. Fellow American Geog. Society, Royal Geog. Society (London); mem. Society Am. Foresters, Netherlands Soc. of Phila. (v.p. 1915-29), Huguenot Soc. of Pa. (pres. 1919-20), Waldensian Hist. Soc. of Pa. (v.p. 1925-30), Pa. Federation Hist. Socs. (pres. 1925-26), Pa. Folk Lore Soc. (pres. 1930-—), S.R., Soc. Fgn. Wars, Mil. Order World War, Sons of Union Vets., Am. Legion, Sojourners, Loyal Legion, etc. Mason. Rotarian. Club: Boone and Crockett, Ends of the Earth (all New York). Author: (biographies) General William Sprague, 1916; Chief John Logan, 1917; Gifford Pinchot, 1922; John Brown (in Pennsylvania), 1931; also several books of verse and many books, articles and brochures on Pa. history, Indians, folklore, folksongs, proverbs, old words, wild life. Home: "Restless Oaks," McElhattan, Pa. Office: 911 N. Front St., Harrisburg, Pa. Died July 14, 1958; buried Highland Cemetery, Lock Haven, Pa.

SHOEMAKER, WILLIAM RAWLE naval officer; b. Staten Island, N.Y., Feb. 10, 1863; s. Capt. Comdt. Charles F. (U.S.R.C.S.) and Mary Augusta (Cole) S.; grad. U.S. Naval Acad., 1884; post-grad. work in electricity, Johns Hopkins, 1889-92; m. Jennie D., d. Morton Cheeseman, of N.Y. City and San Francisco, June 2, 1896; children—William Rawle, Carolyn (Mrs. A. B. Hepler), Katherine (Mrs. Arthur Caley Davis). Commissioned ensign, U.S.N., July 1, 1884; promoted through grades to rear adm., Dec. 24, 1917. Instr. U.S. Naval Acad., 1896-98; comdr. U.S.S. Talbot, Spanish-Am. War, 1898-99, U.S.S. Arayat, Philippine Insurrection, 1900-02; instr. Naval Acad., 1902-04; navigator U.S.S. Alabama; exec. officer U.S.S. Maine and Connecticut; in charge enlisted personnel of navy, Bur. Navigation, 1907-09; comd. scout cruiser Chester, 1909-10; chief-of-staff, Atlantic Fleet, 1910-12; mem. Gen. Bd. of Navy, 1912-14; comd. U.S.S. Arkansas, 1914-16; mem. Gen. Bd., 1917-19; apptd. comdr. battleship div. 3, Atlantic Fleet, Jan. 29, 1919, battleship force 1, Atlantic Fleet, Apr. 1, 1919, battleship div. 3, Pacific Fleet, July 1, 1919, cruiser force, Pacific Fleet, July 8, 1920; comdt. 14th Naval Dist. (Hawaii), Jan. 14, 1921; v. adm. and comdr. battleship force, Pacific Fleet, July 8, 1921-—; dir. war plans operations, Navy Dept., June 26, 1923-24; chief of Bur. of Navigation, June 7, 1924-Feb. 10, 1927, retired. Died May 30, 1938.

SHOLTZ, DAVID (sholts), former governor; b. Brooklyn, N.Y., Oct. 6, 1891; s. Michael and Anne (Bloon) S.; A.B., Yale, 1914; LL.B., Stetson U., Deland, Fla., 1915, hon. M.A., 1921, LL.D., 1933; hon. D.C.L., U. of Tampa, 1936; m. Agatha M. Roberts, June 1919; m. 2d, Alice Mae Agee, Dec. 28, 1925; children—Mitchell, Carolyn, Lois, Eugene. Admitted to Fla. bar, 1915, Fed. Court, No. Dist. Fla., 1915, U.S. Supreme Ct., 1921, N.Y. bar, 1947; mem. Fla. Legislature, 1917; states atty. 7th Jud. Circuit of Fla., 1919-21; municipal judge, Daytona, 1921; became mem. Sholtz, Green & West, 1925; gov. State of Fla., 1933-37. Director, World Trade Corp.; pres. also director of the Transport Steamship Lines, Incorporated, Florida East Coast Land & Investment Corp.; counsel to law firm of E. Albert Pallot. Ensign U.S. Navy, World War I, now lt. comdr. U.S.N.R. (inactive). Past v. chmn. Laymen's Nat. Com. Past pres. Florida State C. of C., Daytona Beach C. of C., Assn. of Chambers Commerce, East Coast of Fla.; mem. American, Florida State and Volusia County (past pres.) bar assns., Am. Legion, Military Order World Wars (commander-in-chief, 1944-45), 40 and 8, Royal Order Scotland, Nat. Sojourners, Beta Theta Pi, Phi Alpha Delta, Acacia. Democrat. Mason (K.C.C.H., 33 deg., Shriner); Elk (past grand exalted ruler; treas. Nat. Vets. Service Commn.). Clubs: Bankers, Yale, Nat. Dem., Grover Cleveland Dem. (N.Y.C.); Rotary (past pres.; Daytona Beach); Nat. Press, Army and Navy (Washington); Com. of 100 (Miami Beach, Fla.). Home: 50 Glendale Road, Asheville, N.C.; Star Island, Miami Beach, Fla. Office: DuPont Bldg., Miami 32, Fla., and Savoy Plaza Hotel, 767 5th Av., N.Y.C. 22. Died March 21, 1953.

SHOOK, CHARLES FRANCIS army officer, physician; b. Omaha, June 11, 1894; s. Charles Lincoln and Mary Belle (Harris) S.; M.D., John A. Creighton Med. Coll., Omaha, 1916; hon. grad. Sch. for Flight Surgs., 1921; grad. Army Indsl. Coll., Washington, 1937; m. Bertha F. Elkins, June 18, 1915 (dec.); son, Charles Francis (dec.). Intern Omaha Gen. Hosp., 1916; entered M.C., U. S. Army, Aug., 1917, comd. 1st lt., June, 1917, advanced through grades to col., 1942; dep. chief surg. Mediterranean and E.T.O., World War II, ret., 1946; med. dir. Owens Ill. Glass Co., Toledo, since 1946. Decorations: Victory medals, World War I and II, Legion of Merit with palm, Bronze Star, O.B.E. (Britain), Cross of War with palm, France, Legion of Merit, Govt. Brazil; four battle stars, World War I, two battle stars, World War II; service ribbons. Diplomate Am. Bd. Preventive Medicine. Mem. A.M.A., Am. Acad. Gen. Practice, Indsl. Med. Assn., Ohio State, Lucas Co. med. assns., C. of C., Phi Rho Sigma. Mason. Home: 3620 Douglas Rd., Toledo 13. Office: Toledo 1. Died Nov. 1966.

SHOR, GEORGE GERSHON, editor; b. Vienna, Austria, Sept. 1, 1884; s. Elias Philip and Helen Fannie (Weirauch) S.; came to U.S., 1893; A.B., Brown U., 1906; m. Lelah Luther, Mar. 25, 1913; 1 son, Francis Marion Luther; married 2d Dorothy Williston, September 8, 1917 (dec. Nov. 1971); children—Samuel Wendell Williston, Dorothy Hathaway (Mrs. Philip D. Thompson), George G. Jr. Began as reporter for Providence Journal, Boston Herald, Boston American, 1906-09; news editor and acting mng. editor Boston American, 1913; mng. editor Phila. Evening Times, 1914; with Chicago Herald until 1917; editor and mgr. Internat. News Service, Inc., and Cosmopolitan News Service, 1921-27; managing editor Philadelphia Record, 1928-29, American Weekly, 1929-53, retired. First lt. U.S. Army, Aug. 15, 1917; assigned adjutant's office, 33d Div., Camp Logan, Tex.; capt. Jan. 1918; went to France with 33d Div.; trans. to 1st A.C., A.E.F.; organized personnel adjutant's sect. First Am. Field Army and personnel adj. with rank of maj.; commd. maj. Army of U.S., Mar. 11, 1943; assigned to Office Strategic Services, Washington, D.C.; promoted to lieut. col., Feb. 11, 1944; ret. Oct. 1, 1944. Member of the Society of American Legion Founders, Phi Beta Kappa, Phi Sigma Kappa. Mason. Club: Overseas Press of Am. Address: Cold Spring NY Died June 20, 1967; buried Arlington Nat. Cemetery, Arlington VA

SHORT, WALTER CAMPBELL army officer; b. Fillmore. Ill.. Mar. 30, 1880; s. Hiram Spait and Sarah Minerva (Stokes) S.; A.B., U. of Ill., 1901; m. Isabel Dean, Nov. 4, 1914; 1 son, Walter Dean. Commd. 2d lt. U.S. Army, 1902, and advanced through grades to maj. gen., 1936; served in France with 1st Div. on Gen. Staff at G.H.Q. and as asst. chief of staff, 3d Army, during World War; comd. 2d Brigade, Fort Ontario, N.Y., 1937-38; comd. 1st Div., Fort Hamilton, N.Y., 1938-40; comd. 4th Army Corps, March-June 1940, 1st Army Corps, Oct.-Dec. 1940; promoted to lt. gen. Feb. 1941, comdg. Hawaiian Department, Feb. to Dec. 1941. Assigned to head traffic dept., Ford Motor Co., Dallas, Tex., Sept. 1942. Decorated D.S.M. (U.S.); Officer Legion of Honor (France). Mem. Phi Beta Kappa. Republican. Clubs: Army and Navy, Army and Navy Country (Washington, D.C.). Author: Employment of Machine Guns, 1922. Home: 3141 Southwestern Blvd., Dallas 5, Tex. Died Sept. 3, 1949; buried in Arlington National Cemetery.

SHORTER, ELI SIMS congressman, lawyer; b. Monticello, Ga., Mar. 15, 1823; grad. in law Yale, 1844. Admitted to bar, began practice of law, Eufaula, Ala., 1844; also engaged in agriculture; mem. U.S. Ho. of Reps. (Democrat) from Ala., 34th-35th congresses, 1855-59; served as col. 18th Regt., Ala. Volunteer Inf., Confederate Army, during Civil War. Died Eufaula, Apr. 29, 1879; buried Fairview Cemetery.

SHOULDERS, HARRISON H. surgeon; b. Whitleyville, Tenn., Feb. 27, 1886; s. Leonard Hogg and Belle M. (Clark) S.; student Potter Bible Coll., 1909; m. Virginia Swiggart, Dec. 5, 1922; children—Harrison H., Virginia Hale (Mrs. R. W. Youngblood, Jr.) Mary Swiggart (Mrs. Bart Wooldridge), Began as physician, Nashville, 1909; interne St. Thomas Hosp., Nashville, 1910; resident surgeon Forts Infirmary, Nashville, 1910-12; asst. sec. and exec. officer Tenn. Dept. Health, 1912-17; post-grad. work N.Y. Post Grad. Hosp., 1919-20; resident surgeon St. Luke's Hosp., N.Y.C., 1920; house surgeon Hosp. for Ruptured and Crippled, N.Y.C., 1921; in practice at Nashville since 1921; mem. staff Vanderbilt U., Bapt., St. Thomas Hosps. Served as capt. M.C., U.S. Army, overseas, 1917-19. Certified as mem. Founders Group Am. Bd. Surgery. Fellow A.M.A. (speaker Ho. of Dels., pres. 1946-47), A.C.S.; mem. Tenn. Med. Assn. (sec.-editor), Nashville Surg. Club (pres. 1940), So. Med. Assn., Alpha Omega Alpha. Republican. Mason (K.T., Shriner). Club: Belle Meade Country (Nashville). Contbr. editorials to Jour. Tenn. Med. Assn. Home: 4512 Granny White Rd. Office: 508 Doctors Bldg., Nashville. Died Nov. 17, 1963.

SHOUP, FRANCIS ASBURY army officer, clergyman; b. Laurel, Ind., Mar. 22, 1834; s. George Grove and Jane (Conwell) S.; grad. U.S. Mil. Acad., 1855; m. Esther Habersham Elliott, 1870, 3 children. Admitted to Indpls. (Ind.) bar, 1860, St. Augustine (Fla.) bar, 1861; erected Confederate battery, Fernandina, Fla.; lt. arty.; maj., 1861; chief of arty. under Hardee, 1861, played important part in capture of Prentiss' command; commd. birg. gen., 1862; commanded La. brigade at Vicksburg; supr. works constructed at Chattahochee River, 1863-64; chief of staff under Hood, 1864-65; prof. applied mathematics U. Miss., Oxford, 1865-69, prof. mathematics, 1869-75; took orders in Episcopal Ch., 1868, rector chs. in Waterford, N.Y., Nashville, Tenn., Jackson, Miss., New Orleans, 1875-83; prof. metaphysics U. of South, Sewanee, Tenn., 1883-88, also chaplain, prof. engring. and physics, later prof. mathematics, until 1896. Author: Infantry Tactics, 1862; Artillery Division Drill, 1864; The Elements of Algebra, 1874; Mechanism and Personality, 1891. Died Columbia, Tenn., Sept. 4, 1896.

SHOUP, GEORGE LAIRD stock raiser, merchant; b. Kittanning, Pa., June 15, 1836; ed. public schools; farmer and stock raiser nr. Galesburg, Ill., 1852-59; miner and mcht., Colo., 1859-61; enlisted in a co. of scouts, Sept. 1861; served in Colo. and N.Mex.; later lt. 1st Colo. cav., promoted until he became col. 3d Colo. cav.; on leave of absence, 1864, to serve 30 days as mem. Colo. constitutional conv.; established stores, 1866, at Virginia City, Mont., and Salmon City, Ida.; 2 terms mem. Idaho legislature; gov. of Territory, 1889-90; elected gov. of State, 1890; U.S. senator, 1890-1901. Republican. Died 1904.

SHUBRICK, JOHN TEMPLER naval officer; b. Charleston, S.C., Sept. 12, 1788; s. Col. Thomas and Mary (Branford) S.; m. Elizabeth Matilda Ludlow, 1814, 1 son, Edward Templer. Commd. lt. U.S. Navy, 1812; served in ship Constitution during her victory over Guerriere, Aug. 1812, and defeat of Java, Dec. 1812; 1st lt. in Hornet in capture of Peacock, 1813; an outstanding young naval officer of War of 1812, received 3 medals from Congress; 1st lt. in Decatur's flagship Guerriere against Algiers, in capture of Algerian frigate Mashuda, 1815; given command of Epervier to carry home treaty of 1815, ship never heard of again. Lost at sea, July 1815.

SHUBRICK, WILLIAM BRANFORD naval officer; b. "Belvidere," Bull's Island, S.C., Oct. 31, 1790; s. Thomas and Mary (Branford) S.; attended Harvard, 1805; m. Harriet Cordelia Wethered, Sept. 1815, 1 child. Commd. midshipman U.S. Navy, 1806, lt., 1813; served as 3d lt. in ship Constitution in capture of Cyane and Levant, 1815; decorated Congressional Medal, 1815; commd. capt., 1831; in command West Indies Squadron, 1838-40; in command Norfolk Navy Yard, also commanded adminstrn. Bur. Provisions and Clothing, 1845-46; in command Cal. coast, 1846-48; head Phila. Naval Yard, 1849, later head Bur. Constrn. and Repair; chmn. Lighthouse Bd., 1852-71; in command expdn. sent to settle comml. and other difficulties with Paraguay, 1858; commd. rear adm., ret., 1862. Died Washington, D.C., May 27, 1874.

SHUFELDT, ROBERT WILSON navy officer; b. Red Hook, N.Y., Feb. 21, 1822; s. George Adam and Mary (Wilson) S.; m. Sarah Abercrombie, Oct. 16, 1847, 6 children. Apptd. midshipman U.S. Navy, 1839, passed midshipman, 1845, chief officer mail steamers Atlantic and Georgia, 1849-51, lt., 1853, resigned, 1854; comdr. Collins Line steamer Liverpool, 1854-56; consul gen. to Cuba, until 1863; comdr. U.S. Navy, 1862, sr. naval officer in joint operations, St. Marks, Fla., 1865, capt., 1869, comdr. Miantonomah expdn. surveying Isthmus of Tehuantepec canal route, 1870-71; chief Bur. of Equipment and Recruiting, 1875-78, reorganized naval apprentice system; rep. U.S. and Britain in settlement of Liberian boundary dispute, 1878-79; naval attache in China, 1881, negotiated treaty of 1882 establishing diplomatic relations, extraterritoriality and trade privileges to Americans; pres. Naval Adv. Bd., 1882-84; supt. Naval Observatory; rear adm., 1883-84. Died Washington, D.C., Nov. 7, 1895; buried Arlington (Va.) Nat. Cemetery.

SHUFELDT, ROBERT WILSON author; b. New York, Dec. 1, 1850; s. Rear Adm. Robert Wilson and Sarah H. (Abercrombie) S.; Cornell, class of '74; M.D., Columbian (now George Washington) U., 1876; m. Catherine Babcock, Sept. 12, 1876; m. 2d, Florence, g.d. J. J. Audubon, Sept. 5, 1895; m. 3d, Alfhild Dagny Lowum, Mar. 14, 1898. Served on U.S.S. "Proteus" in E. Gulf Squadron, Civil War, 1864-65, as captain's sec. and signal officer, with the rank of midshipman; commd. 1st lieut. medical dept. U.S.A., Aug. 5, 1876; capt., 1881; maj., Apr. 23, 1904; retired for disability, 1891. Surgeon with Gens. Merritt, Crook and Sheridan in frontier Indian wars, 1876-81; curator Army Med. Mus., Washington, 1882; hon. curator Smithsonian Instn., under Baird, and in 1895; judge Chicago Expn. Active list M.C. U.S.A., Jan. 8, 1918-Jan. 9, 1919, and in charge classification of war collections of Army Med. Museum. Mem. numerous scientific societies. Author: Contributions to the Anatomy of Birds, 1882; The Osteology of Amia calva, 1885; Outlines for a Museum of Anatomy, 1885; Contributions to the Study of Heloderma, 1890; The Myology of the Raven, 1890; Scientific Taxidermy for Museums, 1894; Lectures on Biology, 1892; Chapters Natural History of U.S., 1897; Osteology of Owls, 1900; Osteology of Herodiones, 1901; Osteology of Pigeons, 1901; Studies of the Human Form, 1907; The Negro, 1907; Osteology of Birds, 1909; (with present wife) Folk-Lore Tales of Moe and Asbjornsen; An Arrangement of the Families and the Higher Groups of the Mammalia, 1911; Racial Types of Beautiful Women as So Considered by Their People, 1911; Review of the Fossil Fauna of the Desert Region of Oregon, 1913; Further Studies of Fossil Birds with Descriptions of New and Extinct Species, 1913; America's Greatest Problem—The Negro, 1915. Editorial naturalist of Nature Magazine, Washington, 1923-—. Home: Washington, D.C. Deceased.

SHULMAN, CHARLES E., clergyman; b. Ukraine, July 25, 1900; s. Maurice and Rachel S.; ed. Ohio Northern U., 1916-20 (LL.B.), LL.D., 1954; student U. Cin., 1922-23, U. Chgo., 1923-24 (Ph.B.), 1924-27 (A.M.), Hebrew Union Coll., 1922-27 (ordained rabbi, 1927); D.D., Hebrew Union Coll.-Jewish Inst. Religion, 1956; D.D., Boston U., 1967; m. Avis Clamitz, June 27, 1929; 1 dau., Deborah Louise. Admitted Ohio bar, 1920; worked in law dept. N.Y. Central R.R., Cleve., 1920, Santa Fe R.R. Albuquerque, N.M., 1921; rabbi, Johnstown Pa., 1926-27, Wheeling, W.Va., 1927-31, North Shore Congregation Israel, Glencoe, Ill., 1931-47, Riverdale Temple, N.Y.C., Sept. 1, 1947-68. Chaplain with rank of lt. comdr., USN, 1943; active duty, naval training stations at Bainbridge, Md., Newport, R.I.; on staff comdr. Seventh Fleet as Jewish chaplain, in Southwest Pacific. Pres. Chgo. Rabbinical Assn., 1942; mem. nat. adv. bd. Anti-Defamation League of B'nai B'rith; mem. exec. bd. Mt. Council N.Y. Anti-Defamation League; mem. nat. adminstrv. com. Am. Jewish Congress; mem. nat. adv. council Jewish Nat. Fund. Chmn. com. on pub. schs. N.Y. Bd. of Rabbis; mem. exec. bd. Henry Hudson Sch. for Brain Injured Children, N.Y.C. Lect. on Jewish Theology, Oberlin Coll. Grad. Sch., 1953. Trustee Hadley Corr. Sch. for the Blind. Mem. USO Council of Chgo.; mem. Nat. Jewish Welfare Bd. (com. on Army-Navy Religious Activities). Traveling rep. United Jewish Appeal to Europe, N. Africa, Israel, 1952-53. Chmn. Bronx Urban League; mem. exec. bd. Urban League Greater New York, Boy Scouts of Bronx; exec. bd. Bronx sect. Nat. Conf. Christians and Jews. Recip. Geo. Washington medal Freedoms Found., 1953, 54, 55, 61, 63, 65, 66. Author: Problems of Jews in the Contemporary World, 1934; Europe's Conscience in Decline, 1939; Religion's Message to a War-torn World, 1942; The Test of a Civilization, 1947; On Being a Jew, 1954; A People That Did Not Die, 1956; The Best Years of Our Lives, 1958; What it Means to be a Jew, 1960; Humanity's Unfinished Business, published, 1964. Member of the editorial board Reconstructionist; chairman editorial board The American Zionist. Contributor to religious journals. Home: New York City NY Died June 2, 1968.

SHUMBERGER, JOHN CALVIN business exec.; b. West Fairview, Pa., Mar. 11, 1873; s. Simon and Sarah (Eckert) S.; grad. Keystone Bus. Coll., Pa., 1898; LL.D., Muhlenberg Coll., 1944; m. Euphemia Stein, Aug. 18, 1903 (died Oct. 1920); children—John Calvin, Euphemia Stein (Mrs. Clyde Good), Anna Ried (Mrs. Alfred Ryan); m. 2d, Mary Lou Irwin, Jan. 26, 1922. Pres., Lehigh Valley Broadcasting Co., 1937-50; pres., v.p., controller Call-Chronicle newspapers, Inc., 1917-51, chmn. since 1952, chmn. Allentown Steam Heating & Power Co. since 1953; organized Lebanon (Pa.) Bus. Coll., Carlisle (Pa.) Comml. Coll., Sch. of Commerce, Harrisburg (Pa.). Pub. accountant and auditor, 1892-1916; accountant and controller Lehigh Portland Cement Co., 1917-37; dir. Allentown Nat. Bank; trustee Pa. State Hosp., 1939-49; estates of Harry C. and Mary M. Trexler, Cedar Crest Coll., YWCA. Served in Pa. N.G., 1897-1917; corpl. Spanish-Am. War, 1898; Mexican border, 1916-17; major, q.m., and paymaster U.S. Army. Mem. United Spanish War Vets., Commandery Mil. Order Fgn. Wars; pres. Controllers Inst. Am. (N.Y., 1935), mem. adv. council; past pres. Hon. First Defenders; chmn. bd. Family Welfare; gen. chmn. Community Chest campaign 1935. Mem. Nat. Tax Assn., Nat. Assn. Cost Accountants, Hist. Soc., C. of C. (dir.), Nat. Municipal League, Am. Inst. Banking. Republican. Presbyn. (moderator Lehigh Presbytery, 1944-45, ruling elder 1st Presbyn. Ch., charter trustee Westminster Found. Pa. State Coll.; mem. exec. com. Pa. synod). Mason (32 deg., K.T., Shriner). Clubs: Lehigh Valley Torch, Lehigh Valley Country, Circus Saints and Sinners. Home: 2602 Tilghman St. Office: Call-Chronicle, Allentown, Pa. Died Sept. 15, 1958.

SHUMWAY, WALDO college dean; b. New Brunswick, N.J., May 8, 1891; s. Edgar Solomon and Florence (Snow) S.; A.B., Amherst Coll., 1911; A.M., Columbia, 1913, Ph.D., 1916; Mining Engr. (hon.), Stevens Inst. of Tech., 1954; m. Helen Davis, Nov. 20, 1920; 1 dau., Jean (Mrs. Peter Ferguson). Field worker, Amherst Coll. Biol. Expdn. to Patagonia, 1911-12; asst. in zoology, Columbia, 1914-15; asst. in biology, Amherst, 1915-16, instr. in biology, 1916-17; asst. prof. biology, Dartmouth, 1919-22; asso. prof. zoölogy, U. of Ill., 1922-29, prof., 1929-47; asst. dean Coll. Liberal Arts and Scis., 1926-31; dean Stevens Inst. Tech., 1947-—, sec. bd. trustees 1947-55, provost, 1955-—. Served as 1st lt. inf., U.S. Army, France, 1917-19; maj., lt. col., col. inf. (gen. staff corps since Dec. 1944); assigned to War Dept., Wash., D.C., 1942-46, retired 1951. Decorated Victory medal with 4 battle clasps; Purple Heart, Army Commendation Ribbon, Bronze Star, Legion of Merit. Fellow A.A.A.S.; mem. American

Society Zoölogists, American Society Engineering Edn., Am. Soc. Mil. Engrs., Am. Assn. Anatomists, Am. Soc. Naturalists, Am. Soc. Growth and Development, Theta Xi, Phi Beta Kappa, Sigma Xi, Gamma Alpha, Scabbard and Blade. Reserve Officers Assn. Republican. Mason. Clubs: Chaos (Chgo.); University, Amherst, Stevens (N.Y.C.); Cosmos (Washington). Author: Vertebrate Embryology, 1927; The Frog, a Laboratory Guide, 1928; Textbook of General Biology, 1931; Laboratory Manual for Vertebrate Embryology (with F. B. Adamstone), 1939. Contbr. to sci. and ednl. jours. Address: Stevens Inst. of Technology, Hoboken, N.J. Died Mar. 8, 1956; buried Arlington Nat. Cemetery.

SHUNK, WILLIAM ALEXANDER army officer; b. Westville, Ind., Dec. 23, 1857; s. Francis Rawn and Cannarissa (Logan) S.; grad. U.S. Mil. Acad., 1879; honor grad. Inf. and Cav. Sch., Ft. Leavenworth, Kan., 1887; grad. Army War Coll., Washington, D.C., 1912; m. Caroline S. Merrill Pratt, June 14, 1885. Commd. 2d lt. 8th Cav., June 13, 1879; 1st lt., July 23, 1885; capt., Oct. 5, 1892; maj. engr. officer vols., May 19, 1898; hon. disch. vols., Mar. 13, 1899; maj. 34th Vol. Inf., July 5, 1899; hon. mustered out vols., Apr. 17, 1901; maj. U.S. Army, June 28, 1902; lt. col. 1st Cav., Nov. 20, 1908; col., Aug. 2, 1912; assigned to 15th Cav., Aug. 15, 1915. Served in campaigns against Victorio in Tex. and N.M., against Geronimo in N.M., also many minor Indian operations; instr. in mil. art, Inf. and Cav. Sch., Ft. Leavenworth, Kan., 1889-93; participated in suppressing Philippine Insurrection, 1899-1901; in Cuba, 1901-02; comd. Central Dept., Chicago, 1913-14. Medals for Indian Wars, Cuban Service, Philippine Insurrection. Home: Fort Leavenworth, Kan. Died Dec. 23, 1921.

SHURLY, BURT RUSSELL, laryngologist, otologist; b. Chicago, Ill., July 4, 1871; s. Col. Edmund R. P. and Augusta (Godwin) S.; B.S., U. of Wis., 1894; M.D., Detroit Coll. of Medicine, 1895; post-grad. course, U. of Vienna; m. Viola Palms, June 28, 1905; children—Marie G., Beatrice A., Burt Russell, Edmund R. P., Fredricka P. Practiced, Detroit, since 1895; prof. laryngology and medicine, Detroit Coll. Med.; cons. laryngologist Harper Hosp.; chief of staff Shurly Hosp.; laryngologist and otologist Woman's Hosp.; pres. Detroit Tuberculosis Sanatorium. Actg. asst. surgeon U.S. Army and U.S. Navy, Spanish-Am. War; passed asst. surgeon, chief surgeon Mich. Naval Brig.; lieut. col. M.R.C.; med. dir. comdg. Detroit Coll. of Medicine and Surgery Base Hosp. No. 36, service in France, 1917-19; col. Med. R.C. Mem. Bd. of Edn., Detroit (pres.). Fellow Am. Coll. Surgeons, Am. Coll. Physicians, Am. Acad. Medicine; mem. A.M.A., Mich. State Med. Soc., Am. Laryngol. Assn. (pres. 1935), Am. Otol. Soc., Am. Climatol. and Clin. Assn. (ex-pres.), Am. Acad. of Ophthalmology and Otolaryngology (ex-pres.), Am. Assn. Rhinology, Laryngology and Otology, American Rhinol., Laryngol. and Otol. Assn. (ex-pres.); v.p. Am. Board of Otolaryngology. Republican. Episcopalian. Mason. Member Loyal Legion, Am. Legion, Military Order World War (former surgeon-general; comdr. Detroit Chapter). Clubs: Detroit, Detroit Athletic, University, Intercollegiate Alumni, Country, Grosse Pointe, Grosse Ile Country, Prismatic, Grist Mill. Mem Order of Purple Heart. Home: 1027 Seminole Av. Office: 62 Adams Av. W., Detroit MI*

SHURTLEFF, ROSWELL MORSE artist; b. Rindge, N.H., June 14, 1838; s. Asahel Dewey and Eliza (Morse) S.; grad. Dartmouth Coll., 1857 (hon. B.S., 1882); took charge architect's office, Manchester, N.H., 1857; worked at lithography, Buffalo, 1858-59; in Boston, drawing on wood and attending evening classes Lowell Inst., 1859; worked as illustrator and attended Acad. of Design, New York, 1860-61; enlisted Apr. 16, 1861, 99th N.Y. Vols.; promoted lt. and adj.; 1st federal officer to be shot and taken prisoner (July 19, 1861); in Southern hosps. and prisons nearly 8 months; released on parole; m. Clara E., d. Joseph B. and Eleanor (Carrier) Halliday, of Hartford, Conn., June 14, 1867. Began to paint in oil, 1870, at first animal pictures, later landscapes in both oil and water colors. Home: New York, N.Y. Died June 6, 1915.

SHUTE, EMMETT R. banking exec.; b. Coal City, Ind., May 26, 1889; s. Joseph Tipton and Cora Virginia (Bealmear) S.; B.S. in E.E., Purdue U., 1912; m. Aline Louise Hurrell, Oct. 3, 1914; 1 son, Alden Hurrell. Telegraph operator, 1900-12; engring. asst. Western Union Telegraph Co., N.Y.C., 1912-17, asst. traffic engr., 1917-19, gen. supr. traffic and consts, 1919-21, operating engr., 1921-28, gen. supt. traffic, 1928-38, v.p. traffic, 1938-49, v.p., charge comml. and traffic depts., 1949-50, v.p. charge operation, 1950-54; pres. Serial Fed. Savs. & Loan Assn. N.Y., 1954-61, chmn. bd., 1961-—; dir. Gold & Stock Telegraph Co. and 18 subsidiaries, 1938-54; licensed profl. engr., N.Y.; dir. Ramp Bldgs. Corp., Motoramp Garages of Md. Served lt. col. Signal Corps, AUS. Mem. Chief Signal Ofcrs. Adv. Council, 1941-44; awarded a chief signal officers Certificate of appreciation, 1944; awarded Dept. of Army certificate of appreciation, 1954. Chmn. Telegraph Com., Bd. War Communications, 1940-47. Mem.-at-large Nat. council Boy Scouts Am. (Silver Beaver award). Fellow Am. Inst. E.E.; sr. mem. I.R.E.; mem. Newcomen Soc., Nat. Audubon Soc. Republican. Methodist. Mason. Clubs: University, Purdue, N.Y. Railroad-Machinery (N.Y.C.); Army and Navy (Washington), Skytop (Pa.). Home: 137 Hampton Rd., Garden City, L.I., N.Y. Office: 70 Church St., N.Y.C. 7. Died July 21, 1965.

SHUTE, SAMUEL colonial gov. Mass.; b. London, Eng., Jan. 12, 1662; s. Benjamin and Caryl Shute; fellow commoner Christ's Coll. Cambridge (Eng.) U., 1683. Admitted to Middle Temple, 1683; lt. col. 3d Dragoon Guards, 1712; gov. Mass. Bay and N.H., 1716-27, engaged in continuous dispute with Assembly over his rights and powers; opposed issues of paper money but over-powered by Assembly; quarrelled with Assembly over his right to disapprove choice of speaker (was forced to accept explanatory charter defining this right of the gov., 1725); requested that Assembly provide fortifications as protection against Indians (assembly refused); made treaty of friendship with Indians at Arrowsick Island, 1717; went to England, 1723, presented grievances to Privy Council and attempted to collect salary in arrears; given pension following expiration of commn., 1727. Died Eng., Apr. 15, 1742.

SHUTTS, FRANK BARKER (shuts), lawyer; b. Dearborn County, Ind., Sept. 11, 1870; s. Abram P. and Amanda (Barker) S.; grad. high sch., Aurora, Ind., 1887; LL.B., DePauw U., 1892; m. Agnes John, June 8, 1910; children—Marion Julia (Mrs. Shutts Stevens), Elinor (Mrs. Bernard R. Baker II). Began practice of law at Aurora, Illinois, 1891; moved to Miami, Florida, 1910; organizer and now senior member Shutts, Bowen, Simmons, Prevatt & Julian; founder, and formerly president and publisher Miami Herald; former dir. First Nat. Bank of Miami; former director Miami Beach First Nat. Bank; dir. Miami Bridge Co.; pres. South Atlantic Telephone & Telegraph Co., 1917-25 (when it was acquired by the Southern Bell Tel. & Tel. Co.); gen. counsel Dade County Defense Council. Lt. col. on staff of Gov. Cary A. Hardee, of Florida, 1921-25. Local chmn. Advisory Board of Salvation Army. Chmn. bd. trustees Jackson Memorial Hosp. Mem. Am. and Fla. State bar assns., Com. of 100 (Miami Beach), Phi Gamma Delta, etc. Democrat. Methodist. Mason, Elk. Clubs: Surf, Bath, Indian Creek Country (Miami Beach). Home: 1438 S. Bay Shore Drive. Office: First National Bank Bldg., Miami, Fla. Died Jan. 7, 1947.

SHY, GEORGE MILTON physician; b. Trinidad, Colo., Sept. 30, 1919; s. James C. and Zella (Henderson) S.; B.S., Ore. State Coll., 1940; M.D., U. Ore., 1943; M.S., McGill U., 1949; m. Doreen Henderson, Jan. 21, 1944; children—Michael E., Kathleen E. Extern in surgery, intern Coffee Meml. Hosp., Portland, Ore., 1942-43; asst. resident internal medicine Royal Victoria Hosp., Montreal, Can., 1943-44; asst. resident Montreal Neurol. Inst., 1944, sr. resident, demonstrator neurology and neurosurgery, 1949-50; house officer, 1st assit. to med. research council Nat. Hosp., London, Eng., 1947-49; sr. fellow NRC (Can.), 1950-51; asst. prof. neurology U. Colo., 1951-52, asso. prof., 1953; clin. asso. prof. Georgetown U., 1953; neurologist Colo. Gen. Hosp., Denver Gen. Hosp., 1951; attending physician VA Hosp., Denver; cons. neurologist Nat. Jewish Hosp., Denver, VA hosps., Grand Junction, Colo., Albuquerque, N.M., 1951-53; clin. dir. Nat. Inst. Neurol. Diseases and Blindness, Nat. Insts. Health USPHS, Bethesda, Md., 1953-60, asso. dir. intramural research, 1960-62; prof. and chmn. dept. neurology U. Pa. Hosp.; cons. neurologist Naval Med. Center, 1955; vis. staff D.C. Gen. Hosp., 1956. Served from 1st lt. to maj., M.C., AUS, 1943-46. Diplomate Am. Bd. Neurology and Psychiatry; certified internal medicine and neurology Royal Coll. Physicians. Mem. Canadian Neurol. Soc., Royal Soc. Medicine, Am. Acad. Neurology, Soc. Nuclear Medicine, Washington-Balt. Neurophysiology Club, Assn. Research Nervous and Mental Disease (v.p. 1958), Am. Assn. Neuropathologist. Clubs: Cosmos. Author: (with others) Atlas of Muscle Pathology, 1957. Contbr. articles med. jours. and textbooks. Home: 28 Beachmont, Bronxville, N.Y. Died Sept. 1967.

SIBERT, WILLIAM LUTHER army officer; b. Gadsden, Ala., Oct. 12, 1860; s. William J. and Marietta (Ward) S.; U. of Ala., 1878-80; grad. U.S. Mil. Acad., 1884; m. Mary Margaret Cummings, Sept. 1887; children—William Olin, Franklin Cummings, Harold Ward, Edwin Luther, Martin David, Mary Elizabeth; m. 2d, Evelyn Clyne Bairnsfather, of Edinburgh, Scotland, June 8, 1922. Apptd. 2d lt. engrs., June 15, 1884; grad. Engr. Sch. of Application, 1887; 1st lt., Apr. 7, 1888; capt., Mar. 31, 1896; maj., Apr. 23, 1904; lt. col., 1909; brig. gen. U.S.A. and extended the thanks of Congress by act approved Mar. 4, 1915; maj. gen., June 28, 1917; retired, Apr. 4, 1920. Asst. engr. river work in Ky., 1887-92; in constrn. ship channel connecting Great Lakes, 1892-94; in charge engring. river and harbor dist. (Ark.), 1894-98; instr. civ. engring., Engr. Sch. of Application, 1898-99; chief engr. 8th Army Corps, and chief engr. and gen. mgr. Manila & Dagupan R.R., 1899-1900; in charge engring. river and harbor dists. (hdqrs. Louisville and Pittsburgh), 1900-07; mem. Isthmian Canal Commn., Mar. 1907-Apr. 1914. Built the Gatun Locks and Dam, Panama Canal, the west breakwater, Colon Harbor, and excavated channel from Gatun to Atlantic Ocean. Under the joint auspices of the Am. Nat. Red Cross and the Chinese Govt., served as chmn. bd. engrs. on flood prevention problem, Huai River Valley, China, June-Oct. 1914. Assigned as comdr. 1st Div., Am. troops in France, under Maj. Gen. Pershing, June 1917; comdr. Southeastern Dept., at Charleston, S.C., Jan.-May 1918; dir. Chem. Warfare Service, U.S.A., which he organized, May 1918-Feb. 1920. Chmn., chief engr. Ala. State Docks Commn., Nov. 26, 1923-—; chmn. bd. engrs. and geologists apptd. July 1928, with approval of President of the U.S., to report on economic and engineering feasibility of Boulder Dam. Pres. Am. Assn. of Port Authorities, 1929-30. D.S.M. (U.S.); Comdr. Legion of Honor (French). Home: Bowling Green, Ky. Died Oct. 16, 1935.

SIBLEY, FREDERICK W. colonel U.S. Army; b. at Ft. Phantom Hill, Texas, Oct. 17, 1852; s. Gen. C. C. (U.S.A.) and Nancy (Davenport) S.; grad. U.S. Mil. Acad., 1874; m. Fannie, d. Col. E. D. Lane, U.S.A., 1877. Second lt. 2d Cav., June 17, 1874; promoted through grades to col. 14th Cav., Mar. 3, 1911. Served for ten years against the Indians, in Rocky Mountains and on the plains; participated in nearly all of General Crook's engagements with the Sioux and Cheyennes; breveted, "for gallantry in action on the Little Big Horn River," in July 1876, and later "for distinguished gallantry in action against Crazy Horse's camp" on Powder River, Mont., Mar. 17, 1876; was recommended for medal of honor; adj. 2d Cav., 1889-93, 1899-1900; insp. gen. Dept. of Tex., 1900-01. During war with Spain commanded headquarters guard, 4th Army Corps under Maj. Gen. John Coppinger; adj. gen. and a.a.g. Dept. of Luzon, P.I., 1903, 1904; in command of squadron of 2d Cav. and battalion of 7th Inf., which suppressed the Ladrones of Cavite and Bantangas provinces, 1905, returning invalided to U.S.; selected for detail on Gen. Staff, declined, Dec. 1908; comdt. U.S. Mil. Acad., Feb. 1, 1909-Feb. 1, 1911. Died Feb. 17, 1918.

SIBLEY, HENRY HASTINGS gov. Minn., congressman; b. Detroit, Feb. 29, 1811; s. Solomon and Sarah Whipple (Sproat) S.; m. Sarah Jane Steele, May 2, 1843, 9 children. Clk., Am. Fur Co., Mackinac, Mich., 1829-34; became partner in operating a co. post, Mendota, nr. Ft. Snelling, Minn., 1834, managed trade with Sioux Indians from Lake Pepin to Canadian boundary; mem. U.S. Congress from Territory of Wis., 30th Congress, Oct. 30, 1848-49; promoted orgn. of Minn. Territory, 1849; mem. U.S. Congress from Minn. Territory, 31st-32d congresses, July 7, 1849-53; 1st gov. Minn. (Democrat), 1858-60; regent Minn. State U., 1860-69, pres. bd., 1876-91; led volunteer mil. forces of Minn. against Indians in Sioux uprising in Minn., 1862; served as brig. gen. U.S. Volunteers in Civil War, 1862-63, 63-65; fought at Battle of Wood Lake, 1862; commanded expdns. against Sioux in Dakota region, 1863, 64; brevetted maj. gen. U.S. Volunteers, 1865; went to St. Paul, Minn., circa 1868; pres. St. Paul Gas Co., 1866, also insurance co. and bank in St. Paul; mem. Minn. Legislature, 1871; pres. Minn. Hist. Soc., 1879-91. Died St. Paul, Feb. 18, 1891; buried Oakland Cemetery, St. Paul.

SICARD, MONTGOMERY rear admiral U.S.N., retired Sept. 30, 1898; b. New York, N.Y., Sept. 30, 1836; apptd. to navy Oct. 1, 1851; Naval Acad., 1851-55; promoted master Nov. 4, 1858; commd. lt., 1861; lt. commander, July 16, 1862; comdr., 1870; capt., Aug. 1881; commodore, 1894; rear admiral, April 1897. Served as executive officer Oneida, West Gulf squadron, 1862-63, taking part in bombardment and passage of Forts Jackson and St. Philip; destruction of Confederate flotilla and gunboats; capture of Chalmette batteries; capture of New Orleans; engagements with Vicksburg batteries, with Confederate ram Arkansas, July 1862; commanded Seneca at both attacks and capture of Fort Fisher and left wing 2d div. in naval land assault on same, Jan. 15, 1865; bombardment of Ft. Anderson, etc.; chief of Bureau of Ordnance, 1881-90, and introduced steel high-power ordnance into the navy; comdr.-in-chief, 1897-98, U.S. naval force North Atlantic station; placed on sick leave; after partial recovery pres. Naval War Bd. for war with Spain. Home: Westernville, N.Y. Died 1900.

SICKELS, DAVID BANKS author; b. New York, N.Y., Feb. 8, 1837; s. Dr. John and Hester Ann (Ellsworth) S.; ed. by pvt. tutors; grad. Kennett Square Inst., Pa., as civ. engr., which profession he followed for several yrs. War corr. for Eastern and Western newspapers during Civil War; apptd. a.d.c. on staff of gov. of Ark., 1870, with rank of col.; was intimate friend of Gen. Sheridan; mem. and represented banking firm of Clark, Walcott & Co., abroad several yrs.; fiscal agt. State of Ark., 1866-70; traveled extensively in Far East and was diplomatic rep. of U.S. to Siam, 1876-81; also acting consul of Royal Netherlands Govt.; with Lyman W. Briggs, founded Am. Surety Co., 1882, of which was 1st sec., then treas. and v.p. until retired, 1906, to engage in lit. work; now v.p. 23d Ward Bank of New York, which he organized; treas. Universal Trust Co. Lecturer on Oriental subjects and Eastern religions. Life mem. Y.M.C.A. (parent soc.); mem. numerous societies. Mason. Author: Leaves of the Lotos, 1896; Land of the Lotos, 1899; Flowers from the Wayside, 1914. Eastern corr. of western newspapers. Home: Paterson, N.J. Died Dec. 19, 1918.

SICKLES, DANIEL EDGAR major gen. U.S.A.; b. New York, N.Y., Oct. 20, 1825; s. George Garrett and Susan (Marsh) S.; ed. New York U.; learned printer's trade; studied law, and admitted to bar, 1846. Practiced in New York, 1846-53; mem. legislature, 1847; maj. 12th Regt. N.G.S.N.Y.; corp. atty., New York, 1853; resigned to become sec. of legation at London, 1853-55; state senator, 1856-57; mem. Congress, 1857-61. Apptd. col. 1st Regt. U.S.V., June 20, 1861; brig. gen. vols., Sept. 3, 1861; maj. gen. vols., Nov. 29, 1862; hon. mustered out of vol. service, Jan. 1, 1868; col. 42d U.S. Inf., July 28, 1866; retired with rank of maj. gen. U.S.A., Apr. 14, 1869. Comd. 2d Brigade, 2d Div., 3d Army Corps, under Gen. Hooker, later succeeded him as comdr. 2d Div., 3d Corps; served in battles of Fair Oaks, Malvern Hill, Antietam, 7 days' battle before Richmond, etc.; comd. 3d Army Corps, Army of the Potomac, participating in Chancellorsville campaign and battle of Gettysburg. Bvtd. brig. gen., Mar. 2, 1867, "for gallant and meritorious services at battle of Fredericksburg, Va."; maj. gen., Mar. 2, 1867, for same at battle of Gettysburg, Pa. (wounded in right leg, necessitating amputation); awarded Congressional Medal of Honor, Oct. 30, 1897, "for most distinguished gallantry in action at Gettysburg, July 2, 1863, displayed on the field of battle before and after the loss of his leg, while comdg. 3d Army Corps." Sent on spl. mission to S. America, 1865; comd. Mil. Dept. of the South, 1865, Dept. of the Carolinas, 1866-67; apptd. U.S. minister to Holland, 1866, to Mexico, 1869, declined; U.S. minister to Spain, 1869-73; mem. Congress, 1892-94; pres. N.Y. State Bd. of Civil Service Commrs., 1888-89; sheriff New York, 1890. Comdr. Medal of Honor Legion, 1902; decorated by Republic of France Commander Legion of Honor of France, 1879. Home: New York, N.Y. Died May 2, 1914.

SIDELL, WILLIAM HENRY army officer; b. N.Y.C., Aug. 21, 1810; s. John Sidell; grad. U.S. Mil. Acad., 1833. Brevetted 2d lt. U.S. Army, 1833, resigned, 1833; engr., various civil engring. posts, 1833-39; engr. with various railroads, U.S. and Mexico, 1840-60; acting asst. provost marshal gen. for Ky., also chief mustering and disbursing officer, Louisville, Ky., 1863-65; commd. lt. col. 10th Inf., 1864; brevetted col. and brig. gen., 1865, ret., 1870. Died N.Y.C., July 1, 1873.

SIEGEL, IRWIN, physician; b. Cleve., Sept. 13, 1924; s. Morris and Molly (Binder) S.; M.D., Western Res. U., 1947; m. Jean Marie Lafaye, June 24, 1952; children—Suzanne Lynn, Judith Ann, Laurel Alice. Intern, Michael Reese Hosp., Chgo., 1947-48; postgrad. dept. biochemistry Western Res. U., Cleve., 1948-50; resident in medicine Crile VA Hosp., Cleve., 1950-52, staff physician dept. medicine, 1955-56; asst. physician outpatient clinic Mr. Sinai Hosp., Cleve., 1955; asso. attending physician Central Dispensary and Emergency Hosp., 1957; mem. staff Washington Hosp. Center, 1958-60; asst. dir. new drug br. FDA, Washington, 1959, asso. dir., 1960, dep. med. dir. 1961-63; asst. chief Psychopharmacology Service Center, Nat. Inst. Mental Health, NIH, Bethesda, Md., 1963-65, asst. chief artificial kidney and chronic uremia program Nat. Inst. Arthritis and Metabolic Disease, 1965-70. Served from 1st lt. to capt., M.C., AUS, 1952-54. Diplomate Am. Bd. Internal Medicine. Fellow A.C.P.; mem. A.M.A., A.A.A.S., Am. Soc. for Artificial Internal Organs. Home: Bethesda MD Died Feb. 28, 1970; buried Washington DC

SIELAFF, GUSTAV JULIUS geologist; b. Gold Hill, Nev., June 18, 1878; s. August Julius Emil and Alwine Augusta (Lietz) S.; B.S., Sch. of Mines, U. Nev., 1900; m. Villa May McDonald, Apr. 15, 1916; 1 dau., Alwine Lorraine. Miner and assayer, Virginia City, Nev., 1900-02; assayer and mill foreman, Abangarez Gold Fields, Costa Rica, 1902-03; gen. mgr. Boston Mines Co., Costa Rica, 1903-05; cons. engr., Reno, Nev., 1906-12; supt. Gongolona & Boston Mines, Costa Rica, 1912-13; gen. mgr. Abangarez Gold Fields, 1914-15; with Southern Pacific Co., 1919-48, chief geologist, 1925-48. Served as capt. Engr. Corps, U.S.A., World War; capt. Chem. Warfare Service, 1919. Mem. Am. Inst. Mining and Metall. Engrs., Seismol. Soc. Am. Republican. Mason (K.T., Shriner). Club: Engineers (San Francisco). Home: 2045 University Av., Berkeley, Calif. Office: 65 Market St., San Francisco. Died Sept. 21, 1956.

SIFTON, VICTOR publisher; b. Ottawa, Ont., Can., Mar. 17, 1897; s. Sir Clifford and Anna (Burrows) S.; student Ottawa Collegiate Inst., U. Toronto; LL.D., U. Man., 1952; m. Louise Macdonald, Jan. 16, 1925; children—John, Carolyn, Arma. Pub. Regina (Sask.) Leader-Post, 1928-35; gen. mgr. Winnipeg Free Press, 1935-40, pub. since 1944; chairman of board F. P. Publs. Limited, 1959-61; v.p. Gt.-West Life Assurance Co.; pres. Winnipeg Free Press; chancellor U. Man., 1952-59. Joined Canadian army, 1914; served in France with Can. Inf.; disch. with rank of maj., 1919; lt. col. reserve, 1925. Master-gen. of Ordnance, Canadian Army, 1940-42. Created Comdr. Distinguished Service Order, Comdr. Order of British Empire. Mem. United Ch. of Can. Clubs: Winter, Manitoba (Winnipeg); University, R.C.Y.C., Toronto. Home: 514 Wellington Crescent. Office: 300 Carlton St., Winnipeg, Man., Can. Died Apr. 21, 1961; buried Mt. Pleasant Cemetery, Toronto, Ont., Can.

SIGEL, FRANZ soldier; b. Sinsheim, Baden, Nov. 18, 1824; grad. Mil. School, Carlsruhe, 1843; lt. in army of Baden, 1843-47; challenged to a duel, 1847; severely wounded his antagonist and resigned from army for political reasons; was a leader in Baden revolution, 1848 and 1849, becoming sec. of war; adj. gen. with Gen. Microslawski, then chief in command, and leading retreat of defeated army to Switzerland; was in Switzerland, 1849-51; in England, 1851-52; came to U.S. in May 1852; taught and published a mil. mag., New York, 1852-58; teacher and elected dir. of public schools, St. Louis, 1858-61; organized a regt. and a battery at beginning of Civil war; commd. brig. gen., May 1861; maj. gen., March 1862; served 1st in Mo.; instrumental in gaining the battle of Pea Ridge; in 1862 comd. troops at Harper's Ferry; comd. reserve army of Pa., June 1863; dept. and Army of W.Va., 1864; participated in many battles; resigned commn., May 1865; edited Baltimore Wecker, 1865-67; removed to New York; Republican candidate for sec. of State of N.Y., 1869; apptd. collector internal revenue, May 1871; elected register of city of New York for the term of 1871-74; lectured and edited a weekly paper after that; affiliated with Democratic party, 1876-96, but took sides with McKinley in latter year. He became an advertising bureau and publisher and editor of the New York Monthly. Home: New York, N.Y. Died 1902.

SIGSBEE, CHARLES DWIGHT rear adm. U.S.N.; b. Albany, N.Y., Jan. 16, 1845; s. Nicholas and Agnes (Orr) S.; apptd. to U.S. Naval Acad. from N.Y., 1859, grad. 1863; m. Eliza Rogers Lockwood, Nov. 1870. Ensign, Oct. 1, 1863; master, May 10, 1866; promoted through grades to rear adm., Aug. 11, 1903—. Served on the Monongahela and Brooklyn, W. Gulf Blockading Squadron, 1863-64; participated in battle of Mobile Bay, Aug. 5, 1864; N. Atlantic Blockading Squadron, 1865; both attacks, and final assault, on Ft. Fisher; Wyoming and Ashuelot, Asiatic Squadron, 1865-69; Naval Acad., 1869-71, 1882-85, 1887-90; Worcester, 1871-73; Hydrographic Office, 1873-74, 1878-82; coast survey, 1874-78, sounded and explored Gulf of Mex.; comd. practice ship Dale, during practice cruises, 1883-84; comd. Kearsarge, 1885-86; spl. duty, Navy Dept., 1887; mem. Examining and Retiring Bds., 1887; comd. training-ship Portsmouth, 1891-93; hydrographer, Navy Dept., 1893-97; comd. Maine, Apr. 10, 1897, until she was blown up and destroyed in Havana harbor, Feb. 15, 1898; comd. St. Paul in Cuban and Porto Rican waters, 1898-1900; advanced 3 numbers in rank "for extraordinary heroism displayed during war with Spain, and on the occasion of the wreck of Maine"; chief intelligence officer, 1900-03; comdt. Navy Yard, League Island, 1903-04; comd. S. Atlantic Squadron, 1904-05, 2d Div. of N. Atlantic Fleet, 1905-06; spl. duty, 1906; retired Jan. 16, 1907. Introduced numerous inventions and new methods in deep sea exploration, for which he later received decoration of Red Eagle of Prussia from Emperor William I, and received gold medal from abroad. Author: Deep Sea Sounding and Dredging, U.S. Coast Survey, 1880; Personal Narrative of the Battleship Maine, 1899. Home: New York, N.Y. Died July 19, 1923.

SILVESTER, LINDSAY MCDONALD army officer; b. Portsmouth, Va., Sept. 30, 1889; s. Lindsay McDonald and Virginia (Hurst) S.; B.S., Md. Agrl. Coll., 1911; grad. Advance Course Inf. Sch. 1923, Command and Gen. Staff Sch., 1924, Army War Coll., 1930; m. Mildred Turner Draper, Feb. 7, 1920; children—Lindsay McDonald, Edward McGuire. Commd. 2d lt. U.S. Army, 1911, advanced through grades to maj. gen., 1942; served with 2d Inf., Hawaii, 1912-15; with 24th Inf., Mexican Punitive Expdn., 1916; capt., maj. 30th Inf. and 7th Inf., with AEF, 1918; participated in Aisne, Champagne-Marne, St. Mihiel, Meuse-Argonne offensives, wounded Oct. 11, 1918; on duty with Am. commr., Berlin, Germany, insp. prison of war camps, 1919; with M.I. Div., Washington, 1919-22; instr. Inf. Sch., Fort Benning, Ga., 1924-27; with 16th Inf., Fort Wadsworth, N.Y., 1927-49; R.O.T.C. instr. N.C. State Coll., later instr. D.C. N.G., 1931-35; with 66th Inf. (light tanks), 1935; mem. Inf. Board, 1937-38; chief tanks sect. Inf. Sch., Fort Benning, 1939-40; comd. 67th Inf. (medium tanks), 1940; comd. 69th Armored Regt., Fort Knox, June 1940-Mar. 30, 1941; now comdg. 1st Tank Group, G.H.Q. Res. Decorated D.S.C., Silver Star Citation, Purple Heart (U.S.); Legion of Honor (France). Clubs: Army and Navy (Washington); Army and Navy Country (Arlington, Va.). Died Aug. 4, 1963; buried Arlington Nat. Cemetery.

SIMLER, GEORGE BRENNER, air force officer; b. Johnstown, Pa., Feb. 16, 1921; s. George Brenner and Katharine (Taggart) S.; B.S., U. Md., 1948; grad. Nat. War Coll., 1961; m. Eleanor Bergeron, Nov. 15, 1942; children—George B., Pierre, Catherine, Eleanor, Michael. Commd. 2d lt. USAF, 1942, advanced through grades to gen.,, 1972; stationed ETO, 1943-44, Hdgrs., Washington, 1948-51, U.S. Air Force Acad., 1957-60, S.E. Asia, 1965-66; vice comdr. in chief U.S. Air Forces Europe, 1969-70; comdr. Air Tng. Command, Randolph AFB, Tex., 1970-72, sr. mil. rep. permanent joint bd. for def. Can./U.S., 1967-72. Decorated D.S.M., with two oak leaf clusters, D.F.C., Air medal, Purple Heart, Legion of Merit. Mem. Phi Delta Theta. Home: Colorado Springs CO Died Sept. 9, 1972; buried U.S. Air Force Academy CO

SIMMONS, JAMES STEVENS univ. prof., dean, retired army officer; b. Newton, N.C., June 7, 1890; s. James Curtley and Angie Mary (Stevens) S.; B.S., Davidson (N.C.) Coll., 1911, hon. Sc.D., 1937; student Univ. of N.C., School of Medicine, 1911-13; M.D., Univ. of Pa., 1915; grad. Army Medical School, 1917; Ph.D., George Washington Univ. Medical Sch., 1934; Dr. P. H., Harvard School Public Health, 1939; hon. Sc.D., Duke Univ., 1943, U. of Pa., 1943, Marquette U., 1944, U. of N.C., 1946, Harvard, 1952; m. Blanche Scott, June 29, 1920; 1 dau., Frances Scott (Mrs. Frances Simmons McConnell). Resident and chief resident physician U. of Pa. Hosp., 1915; bacteriologist Wm. Pepper Lab., U. of Pa., 1916. Served as 1st lt., M.R.C., 1916, 1st lt., M.C., U.S. Army, 1917, advancing through grades to brig. gen., 1943; retired from service, 1946; dean and prof. Harvard Sch. of Pub. Health, Boston, Mass., 1946—. Served as chief of laboratory services in various U.S. Army hospitals, also as commanding officer of various dept. labs., 1917-24; assistant dir. laboratories, Army Medical Sch., also chief bacteriol. dept. Army Med., Dental and Vet. Schs., 1924-28; pres. Army Med. Dept. Research Bd. Bur. of Science, Manila, 1928-30; mem. Advisory Com. for Control of Leprosy in P.I., 1929; chief of dept. of bacteriology, Army Medical School, 1930-34, also dir. department preventive medicine, 1932-34; dir. of labs. Army Med. Center, 1932-34; president Army Medical Research Board, Ancon, Canal Zone, 1934-35; asst. Corps Area surgeon, I.C.A., 1936-40; chief Preventive Medicine Service, Office of Surgeon Gen., U.S. Army, 1940-46, sr. consultant in preventive medicine to the surgeon gen., 1946—; cons. in epidemiology U.S.P.H.S., in global preventive medicine U.S.A.F., Randolph Field, 1949-52; lecturer on public health Yale Med. Sch., George Washington Univ. Med. Sch., and Univ. of Mich. Sch. of Public Health, 1940-46. Army mem. committee on med. research, Office of Scientific Research and Development, 1941-46; U.S. rep. 8th Am. Sci. Congress, 1940; mem. Div. Med. Scis., Nat. Research Council, 1941-46. Mem. sci. advisory com. Gorgas Memorial Inst., 1941-51; member advisory board, Com. on Health, Institute Inter-Am. Affairs, 1942—; mem. com. on health, Office of Foreign Relief and Rehabilitation; mem. adv. com. Nat. Foundation Infantile Paralysis; mem. Nat. Advisory Health Council, U.S.P.H.S., 1945-46. Mem. Nat. Bd. Med. Examiners, 1933-39, Armed Forces Epidemiol. Bd.; pres. Asso. Schs. Pub. Health, 1948-51; chief cons. tropical medicine Vets. Adminstrn., 1946. Acting editor in chief Abstracts of Bacteriology, 1924-26; editor sect., Medical Bacteriology, in Biol. Abstracts, 1926-48; assistant editor Philippine Journal of Science, 1929-30. Fellow A.A.A.S., Am. Coll. Physicians, A.M.A. (mem. bd. on preventive medicine); mem. Assn. Am. Physicians, Assn. Mil. Surgeons, Am. Assn. Pathologists and Bacteriologists, Soc. Am. Bacteriologists, Am. Society Tropical Medicine (pres. 1946), Am. Academy Tropical Medicine (pres. 1946), Am. Foundation Tropical Medicine, Society Experimental Biology and Medicine, D.C. Society Bacteriology (pres. 1932-33), Washington Acad. Sciences, Med. Assn. Isthmian Canal Zone (sec., 1935, pres., 1936), Nat. Malaria Com. (pres. 1942), Council Indsl. Medicine, A.M.A., 1943—; Governing Council, A.P.H.A., 1944-51, Epidemiological Soc., Soc. Colonial Wars, Heroes of '76, Kappa Sigma, Phi Chi, Sigma Xi, Delta Omega. Presbyterian. Author of books and articles on experimental bacteriology, preventive medicine and tropical medicine. Recipient Sternberg medal, 1940; Sedgwick Memorial medal, 1943. U.S.A. Typhus Commn. medal, 1943, Carlos J. Finlay medal, 1943, Walter Reed medal, 1944; D.S.M., 1945; Bruce Medal, 1948; Charles V. Chapin medal, 1952; Gorgas award, Assn. Military Surgeons of United States, 1952. Clubs: Army and Navy (Washington); Harvard (Boston and New York); Tavern (Boston). Home: Longwood Towers, Brookline, Mass. Office: 55 Shattuck St., Boston. Died July 31, 1954; buried Arlington Nat. Cemetery.

SIMMONS, JOHN F. foreign service officer; b. Orange, N.J., Jan. 3, 1892; s. Edwin S. and Elizabeth Stockton (MacLaren) S.; grad. Pingry Sch., Elizabeth, N.J., 1909; A.B., Princeton U., 1913; m. Nancy Robinson, Dec. 6, 1924; 1 dau., Anne (Mrs. John G. Finley); m. 2d, Caroline Huston Thompson, Nov. 11, 1936; children—John Farr, Huston Thompson, Malcolm MacLaren. Teacher, Birmingham, England, and Switzerland, 1914-15; with Simmons Brothers Co., manufacturers, Phila., Mar.-Sept. 1916; apptd. vice counsel, at Vienna, Austria, Jan. 19, 1917; vice consul, Paris, 1917; trans. back to Vienna, as vice consul and Am. del. to Interallied Trade Commn.; returned to Paris, 1921, to take charge of Am. passport office, apptd. consul, at Paris, 1923, trans. as consul to Riga, May 6, 1925; assigned for duty at Dept. of State, Washington, D.C., Aug. 17, 1927; apptd. Chief of Visa Office, Dept. of State, Feb. 1, 1929; apptd. 1st sec. Am. Embassy, lMexico City, June 13, 1930; apptd. consul gen., at Cologne, Germany, July 5, 1932; trans. for duty at Dept. of State, Washington, Nov. 1933; apptd. chief of Visa Div., Dept. of State, Feb. 12, 1934; apptd. counselor Legation, Ottawa, Can., Dec. 27, 1937; counselor of Embassy, Rio de Janeiro, June 11, 1941; became ambassador to El Salvador, Sept. 21, 1944, ambassador to Ecuador, 1947-50; chief of protocol Dept. of State, 1950-57; chmn. Fgn. Service Selection Bd., 1954; Washington rep. of Blaw-Knox Co., Pitts.,

1957-60. Trustee International House, New York City. Member board Washington Symphony Orchestra. Decorated Grand Officer, Order of Orange-Nassau (Netherlands); Grand Officer, Order Al Merito della Republica(de Italia; Grand Cross, Order of St. Olav (Norway); Grand Officer, Mil. Order of Christ (Portugal); Comdr. Legion d' Honneur (France); Grand Cordon, Order Sacred Treasure (Japan); Grand Cross Merit (Germany); Grand Cross of Phoenix (Greece); Grand Cross, Order of Quetzal (Guatemala). Member Am. Fgn. Service Assn. (pres. 1951). Presbyn. Clubs: Chevy Chase (Washington); Cap and Gown (Princeton); Metropolitan (Washington). Home: 2915 44th St., Washington 16. Office: 1001 Connecticut Av., Washington. Died Jan. 1, 1968.

SIMMONS, THOMAS J. jurist; b. Crawford County, Ga., June 25, 1837; s. Allen G. and Mary (Cleveland) S.; did not attend coll.; admitted to bar, 1857; served in C.S.A. as 1st lt., lt.-col., col. and brig.-gen. Del. to State constl. conv., 1865; State senator, 1865; re-elected, 1871, 1873, and was pres. of senate. Mem. Constl. Conv., 1877. Chmn. of finance com. and reported present financial article of constitution. Judge of superior cts., 1878-87; asso. justice Supreme Ct. of Ga., 1887-94; chief justice, 1894-—. Address: Atlanta, Ga. Died Sept. 12, 1905; buried Rose Hill Cemetery, Macon, Ga.

SIMMONS, THOMAS JEFFERSON jurist; b. Hickory Grove, Ga., June 25, 1837; s. Allen G. and Mary (Cleveland) S.; studied law under A. D. Hammond, Forsyth, Ga.; m. Pennie Hollis, 1859; m. 2d, Lucille Peck, 1867; m. 3d, Nannie R. Renfro, 1888; 3 children. Admitted to Ga. bar, 1857; commd. lt. 6th Ga. Inf., Confederate Army, 1861, lt. col., then col., 1862; served in Va. throughout Civil War, mainly in A.P. Hill's Div. of Gen. James Longstreet's Corps; del. Ga. Constl. Conv., to 1865; mem. Ga. Senate, 1865, 71-77, pres. 1875, chmn. com. on finance and bonds; judge Macon (Ga.) Circuit, 1878-87; judge Ga. Supreme Ct., 1887-1905, chief justice, 1894-1905. Died Sept. 12, 1905.

SIMMONS, WILLIAM MARVIN lawyer, educator; b. Stanwood, Ia., Apr. 20, 1885; s. Marvin Lewis and Nellie (Bush) S.; B.S., Cornell Coll., Mt. Vernon, Ia., 1906; LL.B., Harvard, 1911; unmarried. Admitted to Calif. bar, 1911, and began practice in legal dept. Western Pacific Ry. Co., San Francisco; practiced with William C. Crittenden, 1912-14, partner Crittenden & Simmons, 1914-17; in U.S. Army, May 1917-July 1919; hon. discharged as capt.; mem. Bell, Brookman, Simmons & Creech, 1919-24; dean Hastings Coll. of Law, July 1, 1925-—. Home: San Francisco, Calif. Died July 25, 1940.

SIMMS, WILLIAM ELLIOT congressman; b. nr. Cynthiana, Harrison County, Ky., Jan. 2, 1822; s. William Marmaduke and Julia (Shropshire) S.; grad. law dept. Transylvania U., 1846; m. Lucy Ann Blythe, Sept. 27, 1866, 3 children. Began practice law, Ky., 1846; raised company of 3d Ky. Regt. of Inf. in Mexican War, 1846; mem. Ky. Ho. of Reps. (Democrat), 1849; editor Ky. State Flag, 1857; mem. U.S. Ho. of Reps. from Ky., 36th Congress, 1859-61, defeated for re-election, 1860; joined Confederate forces of Humphrey Marshall, 1861; col. Ky. Cavalry, served in eastern Ky. and western Va.; resigned from army to serve as mem. Confederate Senate, 1862. Died June 25, 1898.

SIMON, NAIF LOUIS, anesthesiologist; b. Quincy, Mass., Oct. 31, 1914; s. Louis P. and Latifa (Boulus) S.; B.S., Boston U., 1937, M.D., 1942; m. Beverly Mary Dorley, Sept. 22, 1949; 1 dau., Lynne Marie. Intern, Lynn (Mass.) Hosp., 1942-45; resident during mil. service, 1942-46; with Quincy City Hosp., 1946-68, dir. anesthesiology dept., 1946-68, dir. inhalational therapy, 1946-68, founder, dir. Sch. Nurse Anesthetists, 1947-68, med. dir. intravenous therapy dept., 1946-68, lectr. Sch. Nursing, 1946; anesthesia privileges Milton (Mass.) Hosp., Cape Cod Hosp., Hyannis, Mass. Served to capt. M.C., AUS, 1943-46. Fellow Am. Coll. Anesthesiology, Internat. Coll. Surgeons, Am. Geriatrics Soc.; mem. Am., Mass. (cons. hypnosis 1960) med. assns., Norfolk S. Dist., Pan-Am. med. socs., Am., New Eng., Mass. socs. anesthesiology, Am. Soc. Clin. Hypnosis, Internat. Anesthesia Research Soc., Sons of Lebanon, Boston U. Alumni Assn., Phi Chi. K.C. Home: Quincy MA Died Nov. 26, 1968; buried Blue Hill Cemetery Braintree MA

SIMONDS, ALVAN TRACY mfr.; b. Fitchburg, Mass., Dec. 23, 1876; s. Daniel and Ellen M. (Gifford) S.; A.B., Harvard, 1899; hon. Sc.D., Boston U., 1931; studied at School of Metallurgy, Sheffield, Eng., 1900; m. Susan Gansevoort Lansing, Apr. 16, 1901; m. 2d, Virginia Chalavaya Fildes, Sept. 4, 1926. Pres. Simonds Saw & Steel Co., 1913-—; pres. Abrasive Company, Phila., 1927-—. Captain Ordnance Dept., U.S.A., Washington, D.C., in charge purchase and production of helmets and body armor, World War, 1917. Assistant Chief of Ordnance of 1st Dist., 1938. Member advisory com. Grad. Sch. of Business Administration, Harvard. Has offered prizes annually for best essays on economic subjects by pupils high schs., normal schs. and trade schs., U.S. and Can., 1921-—. Republican. Conglist. Author: Business Fundamentals, 1923. Lecturer. Home: Jamaica Plain, Mass. Died Sept. 2, 1941.

SIMONDS, GEORGE SHERWIN army officer; b. Cresco, Ia., Mar. 12, 1874; s. William O. and Ellen Augusta (Sherwin) S.; grad. U.S. Mil. Acad., 1899; grad. Inf. and Cav. Sch., 1904; grad. Army War Coll., 1920; m. Minnette Lomas, July 7, 1903 (died 1904); m. 2d, Florence Page, May 9, 1906; children—Marjorie Louise (wife of William F. Ryan, officer of U.S. Army), Frances Page (wife of N. A. Costello, officer of U.S. Army). Commd. 2d lt. 22d Inf., Feb. 15, 1899; promoted through grades to maj. gen., Feb. 11, 1933; served as maj., lt. col., col. and brig. gen. N.A., World War. With regt. in Philippines, 1899; comdg. gunboat Oeste, in Philippines, 1899, gunboat Florida, 1900, gunboat Laguna de Bay, 1900-01; in China, Jan.-May 1901; returned to U.S., Feb. 1902; with regt. in Neb. and Okla., 1902-03; at Inf. and Cav. Sch., 1903-04; instr. dept. of law and history, U.S. Mil. Acad., 1904-05, dept. of tactics, 1905-08; in Alaska, 1908-10; on Mexican border, 1910-15; instr. dept. of tactics, U.S. Mil. Acad., 1915-17; arrived in France, June 1917; served as adj. 26th Div., on Gen. Staff at Gen. Hdqrs. as chief of staff, 2d Army Corps, and as chief of staff, and in comd. Am. Embarkation Center, at Le Mans; participated in major operation, Somme defensive, Mar.-Apr. 1918, Lys defensive, Apr., Ypres-Lys offensive, Sept., and in Somme offensive, Aug. 1919; served as student officer, instr. and asst. comdt. Army War Coll., 1919-24; comdr. Tank School, Camp Meade, Md., Sept.-Dec. 1924; comdg. inf. brigade in Canal Zone, Jan. 1925-Sept. 1927; asst. chief of staff, War Plans Div., War Dept., 1927-31; duty with Geneva Disarmament Conf., 1931-32; comdt. Army War Coll., 1932-35; deputy chief of staff War Dept., 1935-36; comdg. gen. 4th Army and 9th Corps Area, June 20, 1936-—. Awarded D.S.M. (U.S.); Companion of the Bath (British); Order of the Crown (Italian); Officer Legion of Honor (French). Home: Cresco, Ia. Died Nov. 1, 1938.

SIMONTON, CHARLES H. U.S. judge 4th circuit, 1893-—; b. Charleston, S.C., July 11, 1829; s. Charles S. and Elizabeth (Ross) S.; grad. S.C. Coll. with 1st honors of class (LL.D.; also D.C.L., U. of the South); taught school 1 yr.; studied law; practiced at Charleston; mem. S.C. legislature, 1858-86 (except during Civil war and Reconstruction period); was speaker and later chmn. judiciary com. Served in C.S.A., capt. Washington light inf.; later col. 25th S.C. vols.; prisoner at Ft. Delaware during last 6 months of war. U.S. dist. judge, Dist. of S.C., 1886-93. Author: Lectures on Jurisdiction and Practice of U.S. Courts; Digest of the Equity Decisions, State of S.C., 1857; The Federal Courts, Organization, Jurisdiction and Procedure, 1898. Home: Charleston, S.C. Died 1904.

SIMPSON, EDWARD naval officer; b. N.Y.C., Mar. 3, 1824; s. Edmund Shaw and Julia Elizabeth (Jones) S.; grad. U.S. Naval Acad., 1846; m. Mary Ann Ridgely, 1853, 5 children. Served in Mexican War, 1846-48; instr. in gunnery U.S. Naval Acad., 1853-54, in charge ordnance instrn., 1858-62, 1st head that dept., 1860, comdt. of midshipman, 1862; promoted to lt., 1855; commd. lt. comdr., 1862; in command ship Passaic in attacks of fts. Wagner and Sumter and in campaign off Charleston, S.C., 1863; commd. comdr., 1865; acted as fleet capt. under Rear Adm. Thatcher in operations below Mobile until after its capitulation, 1865; made reputation in area of naval ordnance; asst. chief Ordnance Bureau, 1869-70; commd. capt., 1870, commodore, 1878, rear adm., 1884; commanded New London (Conn.) Station, 1878-80, League Island Navy Yard, 1880-83; pres. gun foundry bd., 1883-84, naval adv. bd., 1884-85, bd. of inspection and survey, 1885-86; pres. U.S. Naval Inst., 1886-88. Author: Treatise on Ordnance and Naval Gunnery, 1859; Report on a Naval Mission to Europe Especially Devoted to the Material and Construction of Artillery, 1873. Died Washington, D.C., Dec. 1, 1888; buried Cypress Hills Cemetery, L.I., N.Y.

SIMPSON, EDWARD naval officer; b. Annapolis, Md., Sept. 16, 1860; s. Edward (rear admiral U.S.N.) and Mary Ann (Ridgely) S.; grad. U.S. Naval Acad., 1880; m. Camilla M. Ridgely, Dec. 3, 1890; 1 son, Edward Ridgely. Ensign, jr. grade, Mar. 3, 1883; promoted through grades to rear admiral U.S. Navy, July 1, 1919; retired Sept. 16, 1924. Served on Brooklyn during Spanish-Am. War, 1898; assisted in subduing Philippine Insurrection, 1899-1901; exec. officer, Arkansas, 1902-05; duty with Bur. of Ordnance, Navy Dept., 1905-08; comd. Montgomery, 1908-09; naval attaché Am. Embassy, London, Eng., 1909-12; comd. Minnesota, 1912-14; at Naval War Coll., Newport, R.I., 1915; apptd. comdt. naval stas., Olongapo and Cavite, P.I., Feb. 7, 1916. Apptd. hydrographer of the Navy, 1919. Comdr. train, Atlantic Fleet, 1920-21; comdt. 14th Naval Dist., T.H., 1921-23; comdt. 12th Naval Dist., San Francisco, 1923-24. Episcopalian. Home: Ruxton, Md. Died Sept. 6, 1930.

SIMPSON, JAMES HERVEY army officer; b. New Brunswick, N.J., Mar. 9, 1813; s. John Neely and Mary (Brunson) S.; grad. U.S. Mil. Acad., 1832; m. Jane Champlin; m. 2d, Elizabeth (Borup) Champlin, 1871; 4 children. Served with Topog. Engrs., U.S. Army, on road constrn. in East and South. 1838-60; commd. capt., 1853, maj., 1861; chief Topog. Engrs. in Shenandoah and Ohio depts. 1861-63; in charge fortifications and projects in Ky., 1863-65; brevetted col. and brig. gen., 1865; chief engr. Dept of Interior, 1865-67, in charge of direction of U.P.R.R. and govt. wagonroads; author reports including: The Shortest Route to California, 1869; Coronado's March in Search of the Seven Cities of Cibola, 1871. Died St. Paul, Minn., Mar. 2, 1883.

SIMPSON, JOHN brigadier gen. U.S.A.; b. Bethel, O., Jan. 21, 1840; s. Samuel and Elizabeth (Griffith) S.; ed. pub. schs. of Ohio; m. Laura S. Chafee, Oct. 21, 1869. Enlisted pvt. 5th Ohio Cav., Sept. 27, 1862, and served until May 25, 1865; from July 1863, to close of war on duty at hdqrs. Dept. of the Tenn., and Mil. Div. of the Mississippi. Apptd. 2d lt. 4th Arty., Aug. 17, 1867; promoted through grades to col. and asst. q.m. gen., Feb. 2, 1901; brig. gen. U.S.A., Aug. 17, 1903; retired Aug. 18, 1903. Died Oct. 30, 1914.

SIMPSON, KENNETH FARRAND lawyer; b. New York, N.Y., May 4, 1895; s. William Kelly (M.D.) and Anna (Farrand) S.; student Hill Sch., Pottstown, Pa., 1910-13; B.A., Yale, 1917; LL.B., Harvard, 1922; m. Helen Louise Knickerbacker Porter, June 25, 1925; children—William Kelly, Helen-Louise Knickerbacker, Elizabeth Carroll, Sarah Pierpont Fleurnoy. Admitted to N.Y. bar, 1922; associated with Cadwalader, Wickersham & Taft, 1922-25; asst. U.S. atty., Southern Dist. of N.Y., 1925-27; mem. Barnes, Richardson & Halstead, 1928-33, Hunt, Hill & Betts, 1934-39; sr. partner Simpson, Brady & Noonan, 1939-—. Chmn. Rep. County Com., N.Y., 1935-—; mem. Rep. Nat. Com., N.Y. State, 1937-—; Rep. dist. leader 15th Assembly Dist., N.Y. County, 1933-38; del. Rep. Nat. Conv., 1936; mem. N.Y. Rep. State Com. and Rep. State Exec. Com., 1935-—. Served as capt. F.A., U.S. Army, 1917-19, with A.E.F., 1 yr.; comdt. Am. Sch. Detachment, U. of Aix-Marseilles, 1919. Decorated Palmes Academiques, by French Minister of Pub. Instrn. and Beaux Arts. Former trustee Pub. Edn. Assn. Episcopalian. Home: New York, N.Y. Died Jan. 25, 1941.

SIMPSON, KIRKE LARUE, newspaper man; b. San Francisco, Calif., Aug. 14, 1881; s. Sylvester C. and Frances Marion (McFarland) S.; ed. pub. schs.; m. Ella May Field, Apr. 6, 1945 (dec. Oct. 1952); m. 2d, Irene L., Oct. 1953. Began newspaper work in Tonopol, Nev. and San Francisco, 1906; with Associated Press, Washington, 1908-45. Served in 1st Calif. Vol. Inf., Philippine campaigns, during Spanish-Am. War and Philippine Insurrection, 1898-99; commd. maj. Mil. Intelligence O.R.C., U.S. Army, 1921. Club: Nat. Press, The Gridiron. Awarded Pulitzer prize, 1921, for article on the "Unknown Soldier." Home: Los Gatos CA Died June 16, 1972; cremated, ashes interred Los Gatos Memorial Park Los Gatos CA

SIMPSON, MARCUS DE LAFAYETTE army officer; b. Esperance, N.Y., Aug. 28, 1824; s. William and Lydia S.; grad. U.S. Mil. Acad., 1846; m. Clara B. Barnum, Sept. 29, 1892. Bvt. 2d lt. 2d Arty., July 1, 1846; 2d lt., Mar. 3, 1847; promoted through grades to col. asst. commissary gen. of subsistence, June 23, 1874; retired by operation of law, Aug. 28, 1888; advanced to rank of brig. gen. retired, by act of Apr. 23, 1904. Bvtd. 1st lt., Aug. 20, 1847, for battles of Contreras and Churubusco, Mex.; capt., Sept. 13, 1847, for battle of Chapultepec, Mex.; col., brig. gen. and maj. gen., Mar. 13, 1865, for services during Civil War. Home: Riverside, Ill. Died 1909.

SIMPSON, ROBERT TENNENT judge; b. Florence, Ala., June 5, 1837; s. John and Margaret (Patton) S.; A.B., Princeton, 1857, A.M., 1887; LL.B., Cumberland U., Lebanon, Tenn., 1859; m. Mattie Collier, Sept. 2, 1861. Began practice at Des Arc, Ark., 1859; entered C.S.A. as pvt. 4th Ala. Regt., Apr. 1861; in service during entire war, until paroled as capt. 63d Ala. Regt., May 10, 1865. Practiced at Camden, Ala., 1865-70, at Florence, 1870-1904; mem. Ala. Ho. of Rep., 1882-83 and 1903, Senate, 1884-87; asso. justice Supreme Ct. of Ala., 1904-—. Dir. Ala. Trust and Savings Bank, Florence. Democrat. Presbyn. Home: Florence, Ala. Deceased.

SIMPSON, SIDNEY POST lawyer; b. Galesburg, Ill., Aug. 4, 1898; s. James Clarke and Harriette Helene (Post) S.; A.B., Knox Coll., 1917; LL.B., Harvard, 1922. Practiced law in Washington, D.C., 1922-25, New York City, 1925-31, and since 1944; partner Hines, Rearick, Dorr, Travis & Marshall, 1930-31; consultant on cost of crime National Commission on Law Observance and Enforcement, 1929-31; professor law, Harvard University, 1931-46 (on leave since 1940); professor School of Law, New York University, since 1946. Special asst. to asst. secretary of war, 1940; principal business specialist Office of Price Adminstr., 1941; dir. Survey Legal Edn., State Bar Calif., 1948-49; gen. counsel Melpar, Inc. (electronics), since 1947. Served as private, Ordnance Department, later 2d lt., F.A., World War I; mem. O.R.C. since 1919, becoming major, F.A., 1936; active duty as major and lt. col., F.A., World War II. Fellow Am. Acad. Arts and Sciences; mem. Am. Bar Assn. (chmn. com. on continuing edn. of bar, 1946-47), Phi Beta Kappa. Republican. Club: Harvard (N.Y.). Author: Report on the Cost of Crime (with G. H. Dorr(, 1931; Cases on Equity (with Z. Chafee, Jr.), 1934, N.Y. edit. (with Z. Chafee, Jr. and J. P. Maloney), 1939; Cases on Judicial Remedies (with A. W. Scott), 1938; Law and Society (with Julius Stone), 1948; articles in legal periodicals. Mem. editorial bd. Modern Law Review, London, England. Address: 26 W. 9 St., New York 11. Died Oct. 6, 1949.

SIMPSON, SLOAN, b. Weatherford, Tex., Oct. 25, 1876; s. John Nicholas and Susan Elizabeth (Sloan) S.; A.B., Harvard, 1899; m. Eleanora Laurenson Myer, of Baltimore, Md., Jan. 11, 1911; 1 dau., Elizabeth Laurenson. Left college junior year to join 1st U.S. Vol. Cav. ("Rough Riders"); served as pvt. and corpl.; participated in battles of Las Guasimas and San Juan, Cuba; transferred to regular army as 2d lt. 10th Inf.; resigned Oct. 13, 1898, and returned to college. Commissioned maj. and asst. insp. Tex. N.G., 1900; also served as capt. and adj. 4th Inf. Tex. N.G., unitl retirement, 1913; commd. maj. 133d F.A., 1917; promoted lt. col. and assigned to 133d F.A.; served in France as lt. col. and chief of staff of 61st F.A. Brig. Mgr. Bailey County Cattle Co., Tex., 1900-07; postmaster of Dallas, Tex., 1907-12; partner with William Pagen and Son, cotton exporters, 1913-17, now mem. Sloan Simpson & Co., bankers, brokers. Republican. Catholic. Mason (32 deg.). Clubs: Harvard (New York), Dallas, Dallas Country, Brook Hollow Golf. Home: 4605 Abbott Av. Office: First Nat. Bank Bldg., Dallas TX

SIMPSON, VIRGIL EARL physician; b. Jefferson County, Ky., May 11, 1875; s. Grandison Scott and Jennie (James) S.; student Danville Normal Sch., 1896-98; A.B. and M.D., U. of Louisville; married. Teacher high sch., 1895-97; instr. pharmacology and therapeutics, U. of Louisville Med. Sch., 1903-05, asso. prof., 1906-08, prof., 1908-24, prof. clin. medicine since 1920; mem. staff Louisville City Hosp., Baptist Hosp., St. Joseph's Infirmary, Norton Memorial Infirmary; consultant Kosair Crippled Children's Hospital. Member revision committee of United States Pharmacopeia, XI-XII; member house of delegates American Medical Association, 1930-43. Capt. Med. Corps, Ky. Nat. Guard, 1911-17; maj. Med. Corps, U.S. Army, 1918-19; comdg. officer Camp Hosp. No. 8, Montigny le Roi, France, 1918-19. Fellow Am. Coll. Physicians; mem. Am. Heart Assn., Am. Gastro-Enterol. Assn., Southern Med. Assn., Ky. State Med. Assn., Am. Med. Assn. Fellow Am. Coll. Chest Physicians. Democrat. Scottish Rite. Mason. Club: Louisville Country. Home: Heathen Hall, Shelbyville, Ky. Office: Brown Bldg., Louisville, Ky. Died May 3, 1943.

SIMPSON, WILLIAM AUGUSTUS army officer; b. Brooklyn, Feb. 11, 1854; s. George W. and Caroline L. S.; ed. Brooklyn Poly. Inst., 1866-70; grad. U.S. Mil. Acad., 1875; m. Laura Lee of Shepherdstown, W.Va., Apr. 14, 1880 (died Sept. 18, 1895). Apptd. 2d lt. 2d Arty., June 16, 1875; grad. Arty. Sch., 1882; 1st lt., Nov. 8, 1882; capt. 7th Arty., Mar. 8, 1898; maj. a.-a.-g. vols., May 20-Aug. 26, 1898; maj. a.-a.-g. U.S.A., July 8, 1898; lt.-col. a.-a.-g., Apr. 18, 1901; col. a.-a.-g., Aug. 18, 1903. On Gen. Merritt's staff, Philippine expdn., 1898; in charge mil. information div., Washington, 1898-1903; adj.-gen. Philippines Div., 1903-05, Dept. of Cal., 1906-10, Dept. of the Lakes, Chicago, 1910-11, Central Div., Chicago, June 30, 1911-Sept., 1912, Eastern Div. and Eastern Dept., Governor's Island, N.Y., Sept. 1912-—. Clubs: Metropolitan, Army and Navy (Washington); University (New York); Hamilton (Brooklyn). Address: War Dept., Washington.

SIMPSON, WILLIAM DUNLAP gov. S.C.; b. Laurens Dist., S.C., Oct. 27, 1823; s. John W. and Elizabeth (Saterwhite) S.; grad. S.C. Coll. (now U. S.C.), 1843; m. Jane Young, Mar. 1847, 8 children. Admitted to S.C. bar, 1846; mem. S.C. Legislature, circa 1850; served in siege of Ft. Sumter and 1st Battle of Manassas; maj., later lt. col. Confederate Army, circa 1862; mem. Confederate Congress from S.C., 1863-65; del. Nat. Democratic Conv., 1868; elected to U.S. Congress, 1868, denied seat; acting gov. S.C., 1878-79, gov., 1879-80; chief justice S.C., 1880-90. Died Dec. 26, 1890.

SIMS, WILLIAM SOWDEN naval officer; b. Port Hope, Can., Oct. 15, 1858; s. Alfred William and Adelaide (Sowden) S.; apptd. from Pa. to U.S. Naval Acad. and grad., 1880; LL.D., Yale, Harvard, Tufts, and Juniata, 1919, U. of Pa., Columbia and Williams, 1920, Cambridge (Eng.), 1921; Sc.D., Stevens, 1921; LL.D., Union, McGill, and Queen's (Can.), 1922, U. of Calif., Wesleyan, 1923; m. Anne, d. late Sec. of Interior Ethan Allen Hitchcock, of St. Louis, Nov. 21, 1905. Promoted through grades to rear adm., Jan. 5, 1917; vice adm. May 28, 1917; admiral, Dec. 4, 1918 (reverting to permanent rank of rear adm. upon relinquishment of command U.S. naval forces operating in European waters, Mar. 31, 1919); retired Oct. 15, 1922. Naval attaché, Am. embassies, Paris and St. Petersburg, Mar. 1897-Nov. 1900; Kentucky, China Sta., Nov.-Mar. 1900-01; Monterey, China Sta., Mar.-Oct. 1901; Brooklyn, aide on staff comdr. in chief Asiatic Fleet, Oct. 1901-Feb. 1902; fleet intelligence officer and insp. target practice, Asiatic Fleet, on bd. New York, Feb.-Oct. 1902; Bur. Navigation, Navy Dept., Nov. 1902-Feb. 1909; additional duty as naval aide to the President, Nov. 1907-Feb. 1909; comdg. Minnesota, Mar. 1909-Apr. 1911; Naval War Coll., Newport, R.I. (student), May 1911-June 5, 1913; comdg. Atlantic Torpedo Flotilla, 1913-15; battleship Nevada, Nov. 22, 1915-Dec. 31, 1916; pres. Naval War Coll., Feb. 1917 to commencement of hostilities; comdg. Am. naval operations in European waters, Apr. 28, 1917, until end of war; resumed presidencey of Naval War Coll., Apr. 7, 1919. Made extensive report, 1920, to U.S. Senate naval affairs sub-com., alleging grave errors on the part of U.S. Navy Dept. in management of naval operations during the war. Declined D.S.M. (U.S.), 1919; awarded Grand Cross Order St. Michael and St. George (British), 1918; Grand Officer Legion Honor (French), 1919; Grand Cordon, First-Class, Order Rising Sun (Japan), 1920; Grand Cordon Order Leopold (Belgium), 1920; Grand Officer Crown of Italy, 1921. Episcopalian. Home: Newport, R.I. Died Sept. 25, 1936.

SINCLAIR, WILLIAM brig. gen. U.S.A., retired; b. nr. St. Clairville, O., Feb. 15, 1835; s. John and Mary A. S.; grad. West Point, 1857; m. Eugenia McDonald, Dec. 11, 1865. Bvt. 2d lt. arty., July 1, 1857; 2d lt., 1858; 1st lt., 1861; bvt. capt., May 4, 1862, for gallant and meritorious services at siege of Yorktown, Va.; col., 6th Pa. Reserve vols., June 27, 1862; bvt. maj., Dec. 13, 1862, for gallantry at battle of Fredericksburg; resigned vol. commn., June 6, 1863; lt. col., staff U.S.V., 1863-65; capt., 3d arty., Dec. 11, 1865; maj., 2d arty., Apr. 6, 1886; lt. col., 5th arty, June 6, 1896; col., 7th arty., Mar. 8, 1898; brig. gen., U.S.A., Feb. 8, 1899; retired at own request after 40 yrs. service, Feb. 13, 1899. Took part in principal battles of Army of Potomac, 1861-62, and afterward in Vicksburg campaign, Army of Western La., etc.; wounded at Manassas, Aug. 29, 1862, and at Fredericksburg, Dec. 13, 1862; was in service in Pa., quelling ry. disturbances, 1877. Home: Washington, D.C. Died 1905.

SINGER, FREDERIC rear admiral U.S.N.; b. Carlsruhe, Baden, Germany, May 3, 1847; s. Joseph and Frederica (Winterwerber) S.; came to America with parents, 1848; grad. U.S. Naval Acad., 1868; unmarried. Midshipman on U.S. frigate Macedonian, 1864; served on Nipsic, 1868-69; commd. ensign, Apr. 19, 1869; promoted through grades to capt., Feb. 4, 1904, rear admiral and retired, June 26, 1906. Served in various capacities; in naval intelligence office, Washington, 1888-90, 1893-94; in charge of diplomatic corps on board coast survey steamer Blake, representing Navy Dept. at Internat. Naval Review, New York, Apr. 1893; chief intelligence officer of the navy and mem. Bd. of Constrn., 1895-96; took part in battle of Manila Bay, as exec. officer cruiser Raleigh, May 1, 1898; comd. captured transport, Manila, fitted her as a gunboat with 8 guns taken from wrecks of Spanish fleet, July 1898-June 1899; commandant, U.S. naval sta., New Orleans, June 1, 1904-June 1, 1909. Received medal voted by Congress and was promoted 5 numbers for eminent and conspicuous conduct in battle of Manila Bay; Civil, Spanish and Philippine war medals. Died Jan. 4, 1923.

SINGLETON, ASA LEON army officer, educator; b. Taylor County, Ga., Aug. 31, 1876; s. Franklin Parnell and Mildred Leonard (Hayes) S.; grad. Reynolds (Ga.) High Sch.; student Emory U.; grad. Command and Gen. Staff Sch., 1908, Army Signal Sch., 1910, Army War Coll., 1921; m. Elizabeth Forrest Day, June 26, 1903. Enlisted as private in U.S. Army during Spanish Am. War; commd. 2d lt. of infantry, 1901, and advanced through the grades to brig. gen., 1936; served in Philippines during Spanish-Am. War; went with A.E.F., Dec. 1917, as lt. col. and chief of staff, 41st Div., later col. G.S.C. with 8th and 4th Divs.; Gen. Staff, War Dept., after World War, also mem. Army and Navy Joint Planning Com.; Office of Chief of Inf., Washington, D.C., in charge of training and personnel, 1930-35; comd. 29th Inf., 1935-36; comdt. Inf. Sch., Ft. Benning, Ga., 1936-40; retired from active service Aug. 31, 1940; supt. Manlius (N.Y.) Sch. since Oct. 1, 1940. Decorated D.S.M. (U.S.); Legion of Honor (France). Mem. Sigma Nu. Methodist. Mason. Address: Manlius, N.Y. Died June 7, 1943; buried in Arlington National Cemetery.

SINGLETON, WILLIAM DANIEL, auto mfg. exec.; b. Dallas, Feb. 7, 1908; s. John B. and Martha (Stollie) S.; B.S., Tex. A. and M. Coll., 1929; m. Sara Z. Bowers, Feb. 16, 1949; children—William Daniel, Sally (Mrs. Sally Bowers MacDonald). Asst. gen. mfg. mgr. Ford div. Ford Motor Co., 1951-55, mgr. def. prodn. operations, 1952-55, gen. mfg. mgr. Lincoln div., 1955-57, plant mgr. Lincoln plant, 1958-63, regional operations mgr., Automotive Assembly div., 1963-65, spl. asst. to gen. mgr. automotive assembly div., 1965-69. Served as lt. col. AUS Res., 1941-46. Decorated Purple Heart. Mem. Soc. Automotive Engrs., Tau Beta Pi. Home: Bloomfield Hills MI Died July 29, 1969.

SINK, ROBERT FREDERICK army officer; b. Lexington, N.C., Apr. 3, 1905; s. Frederick Obediah and Mary Wilson (Cecil) S.; student Trinity Coll., N.C., 1922; B.S., U.S. Mil. Acad., 1927; grad. Nat. War Coll., 1949; m. Margaret Elizabeth Coe, Sept. 2, 1932; children—Mary Sink Twohey, Margaret Moyer, Robin. Commd. 2d lt. inf. U.S. Army, 1927, advanced through grades to lt. gen., 1959; co. officer various posts in U.S., 1927-40; activated, in charge 506th Parachute Inf. Regt., 101st Airborne Div., 1942-45; organized, in charge 1802d Spl. Regt. U.S. Mil. Acad., 1946-48; asst. div. comdr. 7th Div., Korea, 1951, 11th Airborne Div., 1952-53; div. comdr. 7th Armored Div., 1953; comdg. gen. 44th Inf. Div., Ft. Lewis, Wash., 1953-54; dir. Joint Airborne Troop Bd., Ft. Bragg, N.C., 1954; comdg. gen. XVIII Airborne Corps, Ft. Bragg. Decorated Silver Star with 2 oak leaf clusters, 2 distinguished unit citations, Distinguished Service Order (Eng.), Order of Lion (Holland), Order of Leopold (Belgium), Croix de Guerre (France); Order Mil. Merit (Brazil). Home: 307 E. Center St., Lexington, N.C. Died Dec. 1965.

SIPLE, PAUL ALLMAN, explorer, author, geographer; b. Montpelier, O., Dec. 18,21908; s. Clyde L. and Fannie Hope (Allman) Siple; B.S., Allegheny College, 1932, D.Sc. (honorary), 1942; Ph.D. (Geography), Clark U., 1939; D.Sc., U. Mass., 1958, Boston U., 1958, Clark U., 1958, Bowling Green State U., 1959, Kent State Coll., 1968; hon. grad. Phila. Textile Inst., 1946; LL.D., Gannon Coll., 1958; married Ruth I. Johannesmeyer, Dec. 1936; children—Ann Byrd, Jane Paulette (Mrs. Wertime), Mary Cathrin (Mrs. Remmington). Youngest mem. Admiral Byrd's Antarctic Expdn., chosen after tests among 600,000 Boy Scouts of America; in charge of biol. and zool. work of expdn., bringing back specimens of penguins, seals for Am. Museum of Natural History, 1928-30, head of biological dept. Adm. Byrd's 2d expdn., 1933-35, and mem. Byrd's personal staff; in charge erecting and equipping the base in which Byrd lived alone 4 1/2 mos. in 1934; leader Marie Byrd sledging party into newly discovered land; toured Europe, Asia Minor and N. Africa, off the beaten paths, 1932-33; geographer Div. Territories and Island Possessions, Dept. of Interior, assigned to U.S. Antarctic Expdn. as leader of West Base, Little America, 1939-41; geographer and tech. supervisor of supplies and equipment; on furlough, 1941, from U.S. Antarc. Expdn. and employed by the War Dept. as a civilian expert on design of cold climate clothing and equipment; head research and map projects for U.S. Antarctic Service, 1941-42; commd. capt. Q.M. Corps, AUS, July 1942; discharged as lt. col., Aug. 1946. Mil. Geographer, sci. adviser Office Chief of Research and Devel., Dept. Army Gen. Staff, 1946-63, leader winter environmental teams, 1951-53; sci. attache for Australia, New Zealand, Am. embassy, Canberra, Australia, 1963-66; spl. sci. adviser U.S. Army Research Office, Arlington, Va., 1967-68. Sr. war dept. rep. Navy Antarctic Expdn. Highjump, 1946-47; dep. to Admiral Byrd, U.S. Antarctic Programs, sci. adviser Operation Deep Freeze I, 1955-56; sci. leader U.S. IGY Amundsen-Scott South Pole Sta., 1956-57; mem. numerous arctic, sci. coms. Mem. nat. council and camping com. of Boy Scouts of Am. Awarded Congl. medals, 1930, 37, 46; Heckel sci. prize, Hatfield award, 1931, Legion of Merit Award, 1946; exceptional civilian service award, Dept. Army, 1957; David Livingstone Centenary medal, Am. Geog. Soc., 1958; Hubbard medal, Nat. Geog. Soc., 1958; Distinguished Civilian Service award, Dept. Def., 1958; Patron's medal, Royal Geog. Soc. 1958; Hans Egede medal, Royal Danish Geographical Society, 1960, numerous other medals and awards; Mt. Siple and Siple Island named for him by New Zealand govt. Fellow Arctic Institute of America, American Geographic Society; mem. Antarctican Soc. (past pres.), Australian Antarctic Club, A.A.A.S., Am. Polar Soc. (1st pres.), Assn. Am. Geographers (v.p. 1958, pres. 1959), Am. Geophys. Union, International Geophysical Year (U.S. com.), Vets. Fgn. Wars (hon.), Clark University Geography Society numerous other arctic and sci. socs., Phi Beta Kappa, Sigma Xi, Alpha Chi Rho, Omicron Delta Kappa, Phi Beta Phi, Alpha Phi Omega. Methodist. Clubs: Exchange (Erie, Pa.); Kiwanis (Bloomington, Ill.); Explorers. Lecturer. Author: A Boy Scout with Byrd, 1931, Exploring at Home, 1932; Scout to Explorer, 1936; The Second Byrd Antarctic Expedition—Botany Report, 1938; Adaptations of the Explorer to the Climate of Antarctica, 1939; 90 deg. South, 1959. Originator Wind-Chill Index; co-designer principles leading to devel. thermal boot; researcher design climate controlled housing; patentee in field. Home: Arlington VA Died Nov. 25, 1968; buried Nat. Meml. Park, Falls Church VA

SIQUELAND, TRYGGVE ALBERT banking, lawyer; b. Stavanger, Norway, June 16, 1888; s. Ludwig Albert and Hanna (Aske) S.; grad. Latin Sch., Stavanger; grad. Chicago Law Sch., 1909; LL.B. cum laude, Northwestern Sch. of Commerce, 1912; m. Lovey Mabel Ida Thorp, Dec. 24, 1910; children—Alyce Victoria, Margo Ida. Came to U.S., 1904, naturalized citizen, 1910. Admitted to Ill. bar, 1909, then in pvt. and corp. practice at Chicago; mgr. foreign dept. and 2d v.p. State Bank of Chicago, 1919-29; v.p. Foreman-State Nat. Bank, 1929-31; asst. v.p. First Nat. Bank of Chicago, 1931-—. Mem. I.N.G., 1905-14; served as capt. and promoted to maj. and lt. col. U.S.A., World War; now col. cav., U.S. Army, commanding 317th Cav. Regt.; mem. advisory council 6th Corps Area, U.S.A. Military attaché U.S. Legation, Copenhagen, Denmark, and Oslo, Norway, 1917-19. Treas. and dir. Henry Booth House, Chicago. Decorated Victory Medal (U.S.); Comdr. Mil. Div. Order of British Empire; Comdr. Order of Vasa (Sweden); Comdr. Order of Crown (Roumania); Commander of the Order of Saint Olav (Norway); Knight Order of Dannebrog, and Slesvig Medal (Denmark); Officer Order Crown of Italy; Officier d'Instruction de Perse (Persia); Officier Cruz de Melba de Portuguese (Portugal); gold medal of merit Cross of Malta of the Order of St. John of Jerusalem; Order of the Red Cross (Japan); gold medalist, Geog. Soc. of Persia. Chairman Chicago

George Washington Bi-Centennial Commission; awarded George Washington Bi-Centennial gold medal. Lutheran; trustee Lutheran Deaconess Home and Hospital. Mason. Aide de camp to Queen Marie of Rumania during visit to U.S., 1926, to Crown Prince Gustav Adolf of Sweden during visit to U.S., 1926, to the Maharajah of Karputhala of India, during visit to U.S., 1929, to Gen. Italo Balbo and Maharajah of Baroda, 1933. Lecturer on mil., econ., financial, commercial and art subjects. Home: Bridgman, Mich. Died Feb. 7, 1937.

SIROIS, EDWARD D. (sir-roy'), ins. exec.; b. Lawrence, Mass., Dec. 18, 1898; s. George Arthur and May Monica (Devlin) S.; law student Northeastern U., 1921-22; grad. Command and Gen. Staff Coll., Advance Tank Destroyer Tactical Sch.; student Q.M., Engrs. schs.; m. Margaret Helene Noonan, 1929; children—Eileen M. (Mrs. Albert E. Getchell, Jr.), Edward D., George A. Asst. circulation mgr. Lawrence Telegram, 1915-16; service clk. City of Lawrence, 1920-21; mgr. Lawrence sub-dist. office U.S. Vets. Bur., 1921-26; pres., treas. Winter Garden Flower Shop & Greenhouses, 1926-35; dep. disbursing officer U.S. Govt., 1932-35; exec. v.p. Mut. Fire Ins. Assn. N.E., Boston, since 1946; sec. Gov. Leverett Saltonstall, 1939-40; mem. Gov.'s Advisory Council on Civil Defense. Mem. Gen. Staff (U.S. Army) com. on N.G. and U.S. Army Reserve Policy, 1952-—; mem. Armed Forces Advisory Committee (Northeast area). Mem. Republican State Committee, since 1938. chmn., 1939-40, del. Rep. Nat. Conv., Chgo., 1952. Enlisted as pvt. 1st F.A., Mass. N.G., 1916, served Mexican Border campaign-1916, commd. 2d lt., 1919, advanced through grades to maj. gen., 1952; with 26th Div. 102d F.A., France, World War I; comdg. officer 1st Bn., 102d F.A., 26th Div., 1941-42, asst. G-3, 26th Inf. Div. 6th Army Corps, 1942; assigned G-2, Burma, China, Chinese Combat and Tng. Center. A. P. Hill Mil. Res., Va., 1942-43; now sr. mem. N.G. Decorated Chinese Nationalist Govt.; Legion of Merit (U.S.). lMem. N.G. Assn. (past pres. Mass., nat. chmn.-finance com., chmn. bd. trustees). A.I.M. Clubs: Middlesec (past pres.); Republican (dir. since 1945). Home: 82 Wachusett Av., Lawrence, Mass. Died Feb. 28, 1968.

SISSON, CHARLES NEWTON (sis'un), prof. history; b. Jacksonville, Ala., Oct. 1, 1892; s. William Anderson and Nancy Anne (Hamilton) S.; grad. Jacksonville Normal Coll., 1914; A.B., highest honors, Roanoke Coll., Salem, Va., 1916; A.M., Princeton, 1917; diploma, Sorbonne, Paris, 1919; Ph.D., U. of N.C., 1933; student summer sch. Harvard Univ., 1940-41; m. Louise Hendrick, Aug. 4, 1920. Prof. history and French, Marion (Ala.) Inst., 1919-21, prof. history, politics and French, 1922-24, supt., 1924-27; also head of depts. of history and French, Northwestern Mil. Acad., Lake Geneva, Wis., 1921-22; prof. history, polit. science and French, Lee Sch. for Boys, Blue Ridge, N.C., Sept.-Nov. 1929, headmaster, Nov. 1929-33; head dept. of history Coker Coll., since 1933; hist. research staff, U. of Chicago, summer 1934. Capt. inf., U.S. Army, World War; wounded at Ramboucourt, July 30, 1918; participated in St. Mihiel and Meuse-Argonne offensives. Awarded D.S.C. "for bravery in action"; received 3 gen. citations; decorated Croix de Guerre with Palm (France); Merito di Guerra (Italy). Mem. Am. Acad. Polit. Sc., Am. Hist. Assn., S.C. Hist. Assn., Southern Hist. Assn., Am. Legion (commander Marion post 1924-25). Democrat. Methodist. Author: History of the World War, 1921; Outline of American History, 1925; Creation, Organization and Mobilization of the Army of the French Revolution, 1933. Contbr. to Dictionary of Am. History. Home: Hartsville, S.C. Died Dec. 2, 1947.

SISSON, CHARLES PECK lawyer; b. Providence, R.I., Feb. 9, 1890; s. Charles and Elizabeth D. (Eyre) S.; A.B., Brown U., 1911; LL.B., Harvard, 1914; m. Margaret A. Gifford, June 17, 1916; children—Mary Eyre, Hope. Admitted to R.I. bar, 1914; asst. city atty., Providence, 1916-19; asst. atty. gen. of R.I., 1919-22, atty. gen., R.I., term 1925-29, reëlected for term, 1929-30, res. June 10, 1929; asst. atty. gen. U.S., 1929-32; gen. counsel Fed. Home Loan Bank Bd., 1932; mem. Sisson, Fletcher, Worrell and Hodge. Chmn. Rep. City Com., Providence, 1923-24; chmn. Rep. State Central Com., R.I., 1933. Delegate Republican National Conventions, 1928, 1936. Vice president, Mt. Hope Bridge Corp.; dir. Personal Finance Companies, Columbus National Bank. Lt. col., Air Corps Allied Mil. Govt. in Italy and Germany World War II. Trustee Brown University, Lincoln School, Moses Brown School. Chairman City of Providence Charter Commn., 1939. Mem. American Bar Assn., R.I. Bar Assn., Alpha Delta Phi, Phi Beta Kappa. Clubs: Turks Head, Art, Agawam Hunt. Home: 117 Everett Av. Office: Turks Head Bldg., Providence, R.I. Died Aug. 2, 1947.

SITGREAVES, CHARLES congressman, businessman; b. Easton, Pa., Apr. 22, 1803; studied law. Admitted to bar, Easton, 1824, began practice of law, Phillipsburg, N.J.; mem. N.J. Gen. Assembly, 1831-33; maj. commandant N.J. Militia, 1828-38; mem. town council, 1834-35; mem. N.J. Senate, 1851-54; pres. Belvidere & Del. R.R. Co.; mayor Phillipsburg, 1861-62; pres. Nat. Bank of Phillipsburg, 1856-78; mem. U.S. Ho. of Reps. (Democrat) from N.J., 39th-40th congresses, 1865-69. Died Phillipsburg, Mar. 17, 1878; buried Seventh Street Cemetery, Easton.

SITGREAVES, JOHN Continental congressman; b. Eng., 1757; attended Eton Coll.; came to U.S., studied law. Admitted to bar, began practice of law, New Bern, N.C.; served to lt. during Revolutionary War, later served as mil. aide to Gen. Caswell; commr. in charge of confiscated property; clk. N.C. Senate, 1778-79; mem. Continental Congress from N.C., 1784-85; mem. N.C. Ho. of Commons, 1784, 86-89, speaker, 1787-88; U.S. dist. judge for N.C., 1789-1802. Died Halifax, N.C., Mar. 4, 1802; buried City Cemetery, Raleigh, N.C.

SITTING BULL Indian chief; b. Grand River, S.C., circa 1834; s. Sitting Bull. Medicine man, polit. leader Sioux, Arapaho, Cheyenne Indians, from circa 1870; became leader of war council of Sioux Confederacy by 1875 (camp attracted large number of disaffected warriors of the Sioux, Araphoe, Cheyenne Indians); did no fighting at Battle of Little Big Horn, 1876; took refuge in Can., circa 1876-circa 1881; surrendered to U.S. Army Ft. Byford, 1881; took active part in Messiah agitation, 1890; known as a stalwart antagonist of white rule and of settlement of Indians on reservations, used his position as a medicine man to gain influence among Indians. Arrested by Indian police, shot and killed S.D., Dec. 15, 1890; buried Mil. Cemetery, Ft. Yates, S.D.

SIZER, THEODORE prof. history of art; b. N.Y.C., Mar. 19, 1892; s. Robert Ryland and Mary Theodora (Thomsen) S.; grad. Pomfret (Conn.) Sch., 1911; B.S. in Fine Arts, cum laude, Harvard U., 1915, as of 1916; hon. A.M., Yale U., 1931; m. Caroline Wheelwright Foster, Oct. 14, 1916; children—Caroline (Mrs. Alexander S. Cochran), Hilda Foster (Mrs. Sturgis Warner), Mary Theodora (Mrs. John E. Ecklund), Elizabeth (Mrs. Yorke Allen, Jr.), Alice (Mrs. Caleb Warner), Theodore Ryland. Export-import business, 1915-17 and 1919-22; curator, Cleve. Mus. of Art, 1922-27; lectr. Western Reserve U., 1924-27; asso. prof. history of art, Yale, 1927-31, prof. since 1931, asso. dir., dir., 1929-47, Yale U. Art Gallery; fellow Davenport Coll., since 1932; prof. U. of Penn. Summer Sch., 1937, 38; Oberlaender Fellow, 1937; Guggenheim Fellow, 1947. Served N.G. of Mass., N.Y. and Ohio, O.R.C., and World Wars I and II; maj. U.S.A.F., in MTO and ETO with Monuments, Fine Arts, Archives Sect. Mil. Govt., lt. col. U.S.A.F. Corona d'Italia with rank of Commendatore. Uem. Am. Antiquarian Soc., Walpole Soc., N.Y., Mass. hist. socs., Conn. Acad. Club: Century Assn. Author: Works of John Trumbull, 1950. Editor: Autobiography of Col. John Trumbull, 1953. Contbr. D.A.B., art and hist. periodicals. Home: Litchfield Turnpike, Bethany, R.F.D. 2, New Haven 15, Conn. Died June 21, 1967.

SKENANDOA Indian chief; b. 1706. Born into another tribe, adopted by Oneida Indians at early age; converted to Christianity by Samuel Kirkland, 1755; fought against French in French and Indian Wars; instrumental in keeping Oneida and Tuscarora Indians from joining rest of Iroquois Confedn. in fighting for British, 1775; persuaded Oneida Indians to remain neutral, 1775; influenced many Oneida and Tuscarora Indians to join Americans, 1775-76. Died nr. Oneida Castle, N.Y., Mar. 11, 1816; buried Clinton, N.Y., reinterred graveyard Hamilton Coll., Clinton.

SKIDMORE, HUBERT STANDISH author; b. Webster Springs, W.Va., Apr. 11, 1911; s. Neil Patrick and Daisy (Mollohan) Skidmore; student University of Michigan, 1930-35; married Maritta M. Wolff, Nov. 25, 1943. Received Avery Hopwood award ($1500), 1935. Commissioned 2d lt. Army of U.S., Signal Corps, Oct. 16, 1942. Author: I Will Lift Up Mine Eyes, 1936; Heaven Came So Near, 1938; River Rising!, 1939; Hill Doctor, 1940; Hawk's Nest, 1941; Hill Lawyer, 1942; also articles. Lecturer on folklore, customs and history of Blue Ridges. Home: 1317 1/2 Lake St., Elmira, N.Y. Died Feb. 2, 1946.

SKILTON, JOHN DAVIS clergyman; b. Monroeville, O., Mar. 15, 1867; s. Alvah Stone and Amanda Jane (Davis) S.; A.B., Kenyon Coll., Ohio, 1888, A.M., 1891; grad. Phila. Div. Sch., 1892, B.D., 1914; S.T.D., Temple U., 1920, and all degrees in course; m. Ida Beistle, June 24, 1902 (dec.); children—Henry Alstone, Jane Davis (dec.), John Davis. Deacon, 1892, priest, 1893; curate St. Paul's Ch., Cleveland 1892-97, Am. Ch., Nice, France, 1897-98; Diocese of O., asst. sec. of Conv., 1893-97, registrar, 1896-98. Prin. Cheltenham Mil. Acad., Ogontz, Pa., 1899-1903; head master Melrose Acad., Oak Lane, Phila., 1903-05; house master Chestnut Hill Acad., Chestnut Hill, Pa., 1905-07; head master and chaplain The Cheshire (Conn.) Sch., 1907-11; prin. School of the Lackawanna, Scranton, Pa., 1911-18; asso. field dir. Am. Red Cross, 1918-19; head master Tower Hill Sch., Wilmington, Del., 1919-23; resident head master, Green Vale Sch., Roslyn, L.I., N.Y., 1923-24; rector St. Peter's Church, Cheshire, Conn., 1924-38, rector emeritus since Dec. 1, 1938; chaplain Conn. Reformatory, Cheshire, Dec. 1924-Jan. 1940. Trustee Episcopal Acad. of Conn. since 1927; dir. Conn. Temperance Union, 1934-44. Sec. Permanent Commn. on Parochial Archives, Diocese of Conn., since 1929, examining chaplain since 1936; dir. Church Scholarship Soc., 1935, sec. 1937; chmn. bd. of trustees, Cheshire Acad., 1941. Mem. Troop A, Ohio N.G., 1893-96; capt. and chaplain 3d Inf., N.G. Pa., 1903-07. Mem. Psi Upsilon, Phi Beta Kappa, S.R., Grange. Mason. Clubs: Monday Evening, University (Phila.); Psi Upsilon, Transportation (New York). Editor of "Dr. Henry Skilton and His Descendants," 1921. Co-editor: (with Henry Alstone Skilton) "The Doctor Henry Skilton House, Southington," 1929. Home: 3282 Congress St., R.F.D. 2, Fairfield, Conn. Died July 9, 1951; buried Riverside Cemetery, Monroeville, O.

SKINNER, HAROLD STANFIELD oil co. exec.; b. Wetumka, Okla., May 17, 1907; s. Jasper L. and Gertrude K. (Adair) S.; B.A., Mo. U., 1929; LL.B., Okla. U., 1932; m. Helen Marie Cordell, Apr. 4, 1942; children—Reed (Mrs. Joseph J. McCain, Jr.), Clark R. Admitted to Okla. bar, 1932; practice in Holdenville, 1932-48; v.p. Continental Oil Co., N.Y.C., 1948-—. Served to lt. comdr. USNR, 1942-45. Mem. Okla., Tex. bar assns., Phi Beta Kappa, Sigma Nu. Home: 28 Crooked Mile, Darien, Conn. 06820. Office: 30 Rockefeller Plaza, N.Y.C. 10020. Died Aug. 13, 1967.

SKINNER, LAURENCE HERVEY univ. prof.; b. Arcola, Ill., Dec. 12, 1897; s. Samuel Robert and Eleanor Delia (Hervey) S.; A.B., U. of Fla., 1919; certificate, U. of Grenoble, France, 1922; diploma, U. of Caen, France, 1923; A.M., Ohio State U., 1927; Ph.D., Columbia U., 1933; m. Virginia Kerr, Jan. 30, 1926. Instr. Barnes Sch., Montgomery, Ala., 1921-22; exchange fellow, Ecole Normale d'Instituteurs, Valence, France, 1922-23; asso. headmaster, Castle Heights Mil. Acad., Lebanon, Tenn., 1923-25; asst. prof. Romanic langs., Miami U., 1925-34, asso. prof., 1934-40, prof. since 1940. Served as 2d lt., Inf., U.S. Army, 1918. Mem. Modern Lang. Assn. America, Nat. Fedn. Modern Lang. Teachers, Am. Assn. Teachers of French (ex-sec. Ohio Chapter), Kappa Alpha, Beta Pi Theta. Democrat. Baptist. Author: Collin d'Harleville, Dramatist, 1933. Editor: Notre-Dame de Paris (Hugo), 1930; Quinze Conteurs, 1940. Joint editor: Le Comte de Monte-Cristo (Dumas), 1928; La Tulipe Noire (Dumas), 1929; Gil Blas (Le Sage), 1938; Vingt Contes Divers, 1938. Contbr. articles and professional reviews to Romanic Review, Modern Lang. Jour., Books Abroad, etc. Home: 204 N. Bishop St., Oxford, O. Deceased.

SKINNER, WILLIAM CONVERSE realtor; born Hartford, Conn., Dec. 27, 1888; s. William Converse and Florence Clarissa (Roberts) S.; student The Hill Sch., Pottstown, Pa., 1904-05; B.S., Trinity Coll., Hartford, 1911; m. Edith King, July 1, 1911; children—Calvin Converse, Sally (Mrs. F. P. Kearney), Susanne (Mrs. J. M. Deming); m. 2d, Eleanor Bartlett, April 7, 1938. Real estate, Hartford, Conn., 1915-—; dir. Travelers Indemnity Co., Travelers Ins. Co., Charter Oak Fire Insurance Company, Travelers Life Insurance Co. Pres., dir. Governmental Research Inst., 1940-41. Civilian aide to The Sec. of Army Conn., 1948-53; pvt., corpl., Inf., 26th Div., U.S. Army, 1917-19; capt. and major, A.G.D., U.S. Army, 1942-45. Dir. Hartford Better Bus. Bur., Hartford C. of C., 1935-38. Home: Smith Hill Rd., Cole Brook, Conn. Office: 15 Lewis St., Hartford, Conn. Died Oct. 16, 1962; buried Cedar Hill Cemetery, Hartford.

SLADE, ARTHUR JOSEPH, management cons.; b. Toronto, Ont., Feb. 20, 1893; s. Joseph and Eva K. (Worsley) S.; extension student Queens U., 1913-14; m. Kathleen M. Morrison, Dec. 29, 1919. Came to U.S., 1923, naturalized, 1953. Clk. Mchts. Bank of Can., 1911-15, br. mgr., 1919-20; exec. v.p., gen. mgr. Slade Mfg. Co., Ltd., 1920-23; salesman, sales mgr. automobiles, hardware, advt. and indsl. service firms, 1923-25; sales mgr., dir. Am. Dist. Steam Co., 1923-25; v.p., gen. mgr., dir. Canadian Dist. Steam Co., Ltd., 1928-35, Northeastern Piping & Constrn. Corp., 1929-35; operator Thermalite Insulation Co., 1935-37; spl. assignment Robert Gair Corp., 1937-39; partner Rogers & Slade, 1939-51, Rogers, Slade & Hill, 1951-63. Past pres. YMCA, Community Chest. Pres. Carlton Found., Inc. Served as maj. Canadian Army, World War I. Decorated Distinguished Service Order, Mil. Cross. Mem. C. of C. (past pres.), Am. Mgmt. Assn., N.A.M., Nat. Indsl. Conf. Bd., Assn. Consulting Mgmt. Engrs. Clubs: Canadian (N.Y.C.); Monticeto Country; Channel City; Cosmopolitan. Home: Santa Barbara CA Died June 6, 1971.

SLADEN, FRED WINCHESTER army officer; b. Mass., Nov. 24, 1867; s. late Maj. Joseph A. (U.S. Army) and Martha (Winchester) S.; grad. U.S. Mil. Acad., 1890; m. Elizabeth Lefferts, Oct. 8, 1903; children—Elizabeth Morris, Fred Winchester. Commd. 2d lt. 14th inf., June 12, 1890; promoted through grades to major gen., Jan. 19, 1924. Duty in Ore., Wash. and Ida., to 1897; aide to Maj. Gen. E. S. Otis, on Pacific Coast and while mil. gov. of Philippines, 1897-1900; duty U.S. Mil. Acad., 1900-04; relief work, San Francisco, after earthquake and fire, Apr.-June 1906; sec. Gen. Staff Corps, 1907-11; comdt. of cadets, U.S. Mil. Acad., 1911-14; in China, 1914-16; on Mexican border, 1916-17; comdt. 1st and 2d O.T.C., Presidio, San Francisco, May-Oct. 1917; sec. War Dept. Gen. Staff, 1917-18; comd. 5th Inf. Brig., 3d Regular Div., France and Germany, Apr. 1918-Aug. 1919, during Aisne defensive, Château Thierry defensive sector,

Champagne-Marne defensive, Aisne-Marne offensive, St. Mihil and Meuse-Argonne offensives, and march into and occupation of Germany; comd. 1st Brig. Am. Forces in Germany, Sept. 1919-July 1921; comd. Ft. Sheridan, Oct. 1921-Apr. 1922; supt. and comdt. U.S. Mil. Acad., July 1922-Mar. 23, 1926; comdg. Philippine Dept., Manila, 1926-28, 3d Corps Area, Baltimore, Md., 1928-31; retired, Nov. 30, 1931. Clubs: University (N.Y.); Army and Navy, Chevy Chase (Washington). Home: New London, New Hampshire. Died July 10, 1945.

SLARROW, MALCOLM G(ORDON) naval officer; b. Belair, Md., May 18, 1891; s. John Morrison and Mary Florence (Gordon) S.; B.S., George Washington U., 1913, C.E., 1915; m. Dorothy Gould, May 6, 1916; children—Dorothy (Mrs. Burbeck Benton Gilchrist), Margaret (Mrs. Alfred Coningsby Jackson). Ensign, Supply Corps, 1916; promoted through grades to rear adm., 1943; now gen. inspector Supply Corps, U.S.N. Mem. Theat Delta Chi. Club: Army and Navy (Washington). Home: Kennedy-Warren Apts., Washington. Died Sept. 29, 1958; buried Arlington Nat. Cemetery.

SLATER, HUGHES DE COURCY, newspaper man; b. Marion, Smythe Co., Va., Apr. 12, 1874; s. John S. and Anna Maria (Rothwell) S.; grad. Central High Sch., Washington, D.C., 1891; student Columbian (now George Washington) U., 1891-92; European travel and study, 1919-20; m. Elsie Pomeroy, d. John McElroy, of Washington, D.C., Mar. 30, 1899; children—Elsie McElroy (dec.), John McElroy. Editor Public Opinion (now merged with Literary Digest), 1894-96; civ. engr. and railroad reconnoissance, Northern Mexico, 1897; editor and pub. El Paso Hearld (evening), 1898-1929, and of The El Paso Times (morning and Sunday), 1925-29. Served as capt. inf., 90th Div., U.S.A., A.E.F., France and Germany, 1917-19. Independent Republican. Author of treaty of 1906 with Mexico by which long-standing Rio Grande claims were adjusted. Home: El Paso TX

SLAVENS, THOMAS HORACE (sla'venz), army officer; b. Portland Mills, Ind., Jan. 18, 1863; s. Zenas L. and Irene (Stanley) S.; B.S., U.S. Mil. Acad., 1887; hon. grad. U.S. Inf. and Cav. Sch., 1893; m. Alice Goodrich, Dec. 3, 1890; 1 son, Stanley G. Commd. 2d lt. 4th Cavalry, 1887; promoted through grades to brig. gen., 1923; ret., 1927. Participated in Ind. campaigns, Spanish-Am. War, Philippine Insurrection, Mexican Punitive expdn., Cuban occupation, World War I. Awarded D.S.M., also war medals and Silver Star citations. Mem. S.A.R., Soc. War of 1812, Soc. Indian Wars in U.S., Soc. Foreign Wars, Mil. Order Carabao, Loyal Legion, Am. Legion. Episcopalian. Part Author: Manual of Military Field Engineering, 1895; Military Topography and Sketching, 1897; History of Military Posts in the United States, 1905. Author: San Carlos, Arizona in the Eighties, the Land of the Apache, 1944, Incidents of Cuban Occupation by U.S. Troops, (1898) 1946; Scouting in Northern Luzon, P.I. (1899-1900), 1947. Address: 234 West King's Highway, San Antonio. Died Dec. 24, 1954; buried Fort Sam Houston Nat. Cemetery, San Antonio.

SLEMONS, J(OSIAH) MORRIS (slem'unz), obstetrician, gynecologist; b. Salisbury, Md., Nov. 9, 1876; s. Francis Marion and Martha Ann (Morris) S.; A.B., Johns Hopkins, 1897, M.D., 1901; grad. student U. of Berlin, 1907; A.M., Yale, 1915; m. Anne M. Goodsill, Aug. 2, 1905. Instr. in obstetrics, Johns Hopkins U., 1901-09, asso. prof., 1909-13; prof. obstetrics and gynecology, U. of Calif., 1913-15; prof. obstetrics and gynecology, Yale Med. Sch., 1915-20; removed to Los Angeles, Calif.; attending obstetrician and gynecologist, Good Samaritan Hosp. Dir. Obstet. Survey of France, Am. Red Cross, 1917; maj., M.C., U.S. Army, 1918-19. Fellow Am. Coll. Surgeons; mem. Pacific Coast Soc. Obstetrics and Gynecology, Phi Gamma Delta; Nu Sigma Nu, Phi Beta Kappa, Sigma Xi. Author: The Prospective Mother; The Nutri- tion of the Fetus; John Whitridge Williams, Academic Aspects and Bibliography, Progress in Obstetrics (1890-1940); A Cross-light on Doctor Holmes and His Investigation of Childbirth Fever; also numerous med. monographs. Home: 309 S. Westmorland Av., Los Angeles 5, Calif. Died April 30, 1948.

SLEMP, CAMPBELL congressman; b. Turkey Cove, Va., Dec. 2, 1839; s. S. S. and Margaret (Read) S.; ed. Turkey Cove, until 1856, Emory and Henry Coll., 1856-59; m. Nannie B. Cawood, June 9, 1865. Entered C. S. A., 1861; served as capt., lt. col. and col. 64th Va. regt. Mem. Va. legislature, 1879-83; was on Mahone ticket for lt. gov. in 1889, on Harrison ticket as elector, 1888; on McKinley electoral ticket, 1896; mem. Congress, 9th Va. dist., 1903-07. Farmer and real estate dealer. Home: Big Stone Gap, Va. Died 1907.

SLINGLUFF, JESSE (sling'luf), lawyer; b. Balt. County, Md., June 7, 1870; s. Charles Bohn and Valerie (von Dorsner) S.; LL.B., U. Md., 1897; m. Kathleen Kernan, Sept. 3, 1902; children—Kathleen Kelso, Jesse, Jr., Silvine von Dorsner (Mrs. Charles C. Savage, Jr.), John Kernan. Admitted to Md. bar, 1897, and since engaged in gen. practice of law at Balt.; mem. firm Marbury, Miller & Evans; law at Balt.; mem. firm Marbury, Miller & Evans; dir. Equitable Life Assurance Soc. of U.S., N.Y.C., Balt. Brick Co.; former v.p., dir. Cottman Co., Balt. Served as 1st lt. inf., 1918-21. Mem. Am. Bar Assn., Md. State Bar Assn., Bar Assn. of Balt. City. Democrat. Roman Catholic. Clubs: Elkridge, Bachelor's Cotillon (Balt). Home: 2925 N. Calvert St. Office: Maryland Trust Bldg., Balt. 2. Died Apr. 3, 1957; buried Balt.

SLOAN, GEORGE A. industrial exec.; b. Nashville, Tenn., May 30, 1893; s. Paul Lowe and Anne (Joy) S.; LL.B., Vanderbilt U., 1915; LL.D. (hon.) U. of Chattanooga, 1945, N.Y.U., 1951; m. Florence Lincol (Rockefeller), Nov. 30, 1929; children—Florence Lincoln, Anne. Admitted to Tenn. bar, 1915; asst. to chmn. Am. Nat. Red Cross, 1919-22; pres. Cotton Textile Inst., 1929-35, chmn. 1932-35; pres. Blue Ridge Mut. Fund, Inc.; chmn. Cotton Textile Code Authority, which submitted 1st Code under N.R.A., July 7, 1933-May 21, 1935; commr. of commerce, New York City, and chmn. Mayor's Business Com., 1940-44; chairman of the board Southern Agriculturist, Oct. 1, 1944-50. Dir. (member finance com.), United States Steel Corp.; dir. Goodyear Tire & Rubber Co., Middle South Utilities, Inc., Distillers Corp.-Seagram, Ltd., Montreal, Great American Insurance Co.; mem. adv. com. Bankers Trust Co. Pres. Metropolitan Opera Assn., 1941-45, chmn. bd. since 1946; pres. and public trustee The Nutrition Foundation, Inc. (New York). Member of President Hoover's Committee on Unemployment Relief, 1931-32; past chmn. U.S. Council Internat. C. of C.; mem. bus. adv. council for Dept. of Commerce, Washington, 1935-42. Served as 1st lt. inf., A.E.F., later capt. inf., U.S. Army, World War I; maj. inf., O.R.C.; col. Gov.'s staff, Tenn. Nat. Guard; lt. col., Gov.'s staff Ga. Nat. Guard. Received Annual Award, Nat. Com. for Music Appreciation, 1940; Chevalier, Legion of Honor (France). Trustee, Milbank Memorial Fund, Inst. for the Crippled and Disabled; member board of trust, Vanderbilt U.; life mem. Corp., Mass. Inst. of Tech.; mem. adv. council So. Research Inst., Birmingham, Ala. Mem. Am. Acad. Polit. Sci., Nat. Inst. Social Sciences, Southern Soc. of N.Y. (pres. 1943-44), Am. Acad. Arts and Scis., Am. Italy Soc. (trustee), Phi Beta Kappa, Kappa Alpha. Episcopalian. Clubs: Century Assn., Downtown Assn., Racquet and Tennis (New York); Maligne River Anglers (Alberta); Round Hill (Greenwich, Conn.); Blind Brook (Port Chester, N.Y.); Metropolitan Opera (hon.); St. Andrews Soc. Writer on economic and social problems. Home: Vineyard Lane, Greenwich, Conn., and 340 Park Av., N.Y. City 22. Office: Chrysler Bldg., N.Y.C. 17, and 14 Wall St., N.Y.C. 5. Died May 20, 1955; buried Greenwich, Conn.

SLOAN, WILLIAM FRANKLIN cons. engr.; b. Bozeman, Mont., July 26, 1879; s. Washington Franklin and Blanche Alpine (Daugherty) S.; B.S. in E.E., Mont. State Coll., 1903, U. of Wis., 1904; m. Mary Elizabeth Moffat, May 22, 1912 (dec.); 1 dau., Mary Elizabeth (now deceased); married 2d, Geneva Groves, December 1940. Successively with Montana Power Co., Union Light and Power Co., of St. Louis, Commonwealth Edison Co., of Chicago, and B. J. Arnold Co., of Chicago, 1904-07; appraisal engr. Wis. R.R. Commn., 1907-13; cons. engr., 1913-55, successively as mem. firms Sloan, Huddle & Co., Sloan, Huddle, Feustel & Freeman, Sloan & Cook, now Sloan, Cook & Lowe, ret.; appraisals of investigations City Los Angeles, City of Louisville, Ky., R.I. Pub. Utilities Commn., Manitoba Commn., Province of Alberta, City of St. John, New Brunswick, etc.; has made appraisals for telephone, telegraph, street railway and power companies; chief equipment prodn. sect., communication div. of War Prodn. Bd., Jan. 1942-45. Served as capt. U.S. Army in aircraft production, and as tech. adviser to Postmaster-Gen. during period of govt. operations of wire system during World War I. Mem. Am. Inst. E.E. Presbyterian. Mason, K.P. Clubs: Cosmos (Washington, D.C.); Union League (Chgo.). Home: 1550 N. State Parkway, Chgo. Died July 20, 1958.

SLOANE, RUSH RICHARD, lawyer, capitalist; b. Sandusky, O.; s. John Nelson and Cynthia (Strong) S.; m. Elyria O., Helen F. Hall. City clerk 2 terms; probate judge 2 terms; apptd. by President Lincoln gen. agt., Postoffice Dept., March, 1861. Was delegate to Pittsburg Conv., 1856, which organized the Rep. party, and was invited guest at Phila. Rep. Nat. Conv., June, 1900. Aided in organizing the "Cassius M. Clay brigade," April, 1861, to protect City of Washington, was a mem. of the brigade; chmn. Rep. State Com. of Ohio, 1865-6; candidate of Liberal (Greeley) party for Congress, 1872; mayor Sandusky, 1879-81. In 1852 was sued for $6,000 damages in U.S. court for professional services as a lawyer in defending 6 slaves, escaping to Canada, under the Fugitive Slave Act of 1850; was mulcted in damages and paid the judgment. Was railroad pres. 10 yrs. Built the "Big Four" R.R. between Springfield and Columbus, O. Owned much valuable real estate in Chicago, Ind., Mass., Toledo and Sandusky, O., where he has built the largest hotel (Sloane House) and block and dwelling house in the city; pres. The Firelands Hist. Soc. Mem. S.A.R.; life mem. Ohio State Archaeol. and Hist. Soc.; mem. Ohio State Centennial Comm'n; one of the speakers at Ohio Centennial Celebration, May, 1903, at Chillicothe, O. Address: Sandusky OH

SLOAT, JOHN DRAKE naval officer; b. Goshen, N.Y., July 26, 1781; s. Capt. John and Ruth (Drake) S.; m. Abby Gordon, Nov. 27, 1814, 3 children. Served as master U.S. Navy, 1812, commd. lt., 1813; received 1st naval command in schooner Grampus, 1823; cruised Windward Islands suppressing piracy, 1824-25; commd. master comdt., 1826, capt., 1837; comdt. Portsmouth (Va.) Navy Yard, 1840-44; comdr. Pacific Squadron, 1844-46, landed detachment of marines, took possession of Cal., 1846; sent one of officers to take possession of San Francisco, 1846; comdt. Norfolk (Va.) Navy Yard, 1848-51; on spl. duty with bur. Constrn. and Repair, 1852-51; on spl. duty with bur. Constrn. and Repair, 1852-55; promoted to commodore, 1862, rear adm., 1866 (both ret.). Died Staten Island, N.Y., Nov. 28, 1867; buried Greenwood Cemetery, Bklyn.

SLOCUM, CLARENCE ALFRED assn. exec.; b. Arnette, Okla., May 16, 1904; s. Ben and Nellie Elizabeth (Griggs) S.; B.S., Okla. A. and M. Coll., 1928, M.S., 1931; Ph.D., Ohio State U., 1953; m. Rose Richardson, Mar. 30, 1934 (dec. 1937); children—Clarence Alfred, Donna Rose. Commerce tchr. Panhandle A. and M. Coll., Goodwell, Okla., 1931-33, Pikeville (Ky.) Coll., 1936-37; tchr. management Kent State U., 1937-47; head management dept. U. Tenn., 1947-50; nat. exec. dir. Soc. Advancement of Management, 1950; editor in chief Advanced Management, 1952; pres. Operations Research Institute, Inc., publisher, mng. editor Management's Operations' Research Digest. Served as lt. comdr. U.S.N.R., World War II. Mem. Acad. Management, Am. Arbitration Assn. Panel, Nat. Management Council, Am. Assn. U. Profs., Beta Gamma Sigma, Delta Sigma Pi, Kappa Kappa Psi, Acacia. Presbyn. Mason. Club: Kiwanis. Contbr. articles profl. jours. Home: 25 Haslet Av., Princeton, N.J. Office: 41 Fifth Av., N.Y.C. 3. Died May 3, 1957. Buried Arlington National Cemetery.

SLOCUM, HENRY WARNER congressman, army officer; b. Delphi, Onondaga County, N.Y., Sept. 24, 1827; s. Matthew Barnard and Mary (Ostrander) S.; grad. U.S. Mil. Acad., 1852; m. Clara Rice, Feb. 9, 1854, 4 children. Commd. 1st lt. U.S. Army, 1855; admitted to N.Y. bar, 1858; mem. N.Y. State Assembly, 1859; col. 27th N.Y. Inf., 1861; commd. brig. gen. U.S. Volunteers, 1861, maj. gen., 1862, in command XII Army Corps; fought at Battle of Gettysburg, 1863; commanded dist. of Vicksburg, 1864 and participated in march through Ga. and Carolinas commanding XIV and XX Corps comprising left wing of Sherman's forces; command of Dept. of Miss., 1865; mem. U.S. Ho. of Reps. (Democrat) from N.Y., 41st-42d, 48th congresses, 1869-73, 83-85; commr. pub. works Bklyn., 1876. Died N.Y.C., Apr. 14, 1894.

SLOCUM, HERBERT JERMAIN army officer; b. in Ohio, Apr. 25, 1855; grad. U.S. Mil. Acad., 1876, Inf. and Cav. Sch., 1883. Commd. 2d lt. 25th Inf., June 21, 1876; trans. to 7th Cav., July 28, 1876; 1st lt., Sept. 22, 1883; capt., Aug. 26, 1896; maj. insp. gen. vols., May 12, 1898; hon. disch. vols., May 12, 1899; q.m. U.S.A., July 25, 1902; maj. 1st Cav., Aug. 26, 1903; trans. to 2d Cav., Oct. 16, 1903, to 7th Cav., Feb. 26, 1908; lt. col. of cav., Mar. 3, 1911; col., Aug. 2, 1912; assigned to 13th Cav., Sept. 1, 1914; duty on Mexican border, 1916-17. Died Mar. 29, 1928.

SLOCUM, JOSHUA sea-farer; b. in Wilmot Tp., Annapolis Co., N. S., Can., Feb. 20, 1844; s. John Slocomb of the American Quaker family of Slocum, Slocomb or Slocumbe; gained his edn. principally at sea and in travels; spl. studies in nautical astronomy and marine architecture; m., 1st, Sydney, New South Wales, Jan., 1871, Virginia A. Walker; 2d, Boston, Feb., 1886, Henrietta M. Elliott. Sailor from boyhood; sailed only in ships belonging in U. S. and Great Britain except one, the "Destroyer," a war vessel which he comd. under the Brazilian flag, from New York to Brazil. His several other commands were all under the flag of U. S.; 1st command on the coast of Calif., 1869; sailed 13 yrs. out of San Francisco, to China, Australia, the Spice Islands and Japan. Built a steamer of 90 tons' register at Olongapo, Subig Bay, Luzon, in 1874; built the "Spray," 9 tons' register, at Fairhaven, Mass., in 1892, and completed a voyage around the world in it alone, 1898. Author: The Voyage of the "Liberdade" from Brazil to New York, 1891 R5; Voyage of the "Destroyer" (pamphlet), 1894 A7; Sailing Alone Around the World, Century Mag., 1899-1900; The Voyage of the Destroyer from New York to Brazil, McClure's Mag., 1900. Address: W. Tisbury, Mass.

SLUSS, JOHN WILLIAM surgeon; b. Cloverdale, Ind., Aug. 27, 1867; s. David E. and Nancy D.A. (Sandy) S.; B.S., DePauw U., 1890, A.M., 1894; M.D., Ind. U., 1893; hosp. courses London and Paris, 1905; m. Cora Mabel Hart, Oct. 14, 1896 (dec.); children—David Hart, Mary Helen Hall. Practiced at Indpls. since 1893; demonstrator anatomy, 1894-1900, prof. anatomy, 1900-05, clin. surgery since 1905, Ind. U. Med. Sch.; supt. City Hosp., 1912-15. Capt. and asst. surgeon Ind. N.G., 1906-15; maj. Med. R.C., 1917; chief surg. service Camp Grant; adj. Base Hosp., Camp Cody; lt. col. Med. R.C., 1918; zone surgeon U.S. Fidelity & Guarantee Ins. Co., Balt., 1925. Fellow A.C.S.; mem. A.M.A., Delta Upsilon, Phi Rho Sigma. Republican. Methodist. Mason, Elk. Clubs: Marion, Columbia,

Whist. Author: Emergency Surgery, 1908, 5th edit., 1933. Home: 3657 Washington Blvd., Indpls. Ret. Dec. 20, 1961.

SMADEL, JOSEPH EDWIN research physician; born Vincennes, Ind., Jan. 10, 1907; s. Joseph William and Clara (Green) S.; A.B., U. of Pa., 1928; M.D., Washington U., 1931; M.S. (hon.), Yale, 1950; D.Sc. Jefferson Med. Coll., 1955, U. Md., 1962; m. Elisabeth Moore, July 1, 1936. Intern Barnes Hosp., St. Louis, 1932-33; asst. pathology Washington U., 1931-32, asst. medicine, 1933-34; staff asst. Hosp. of Rockefeller Inst. for Med. Research, 1934-36, asso., 1936-42, asso. mem., 1942-46 (leave of absence for mil. duty, 1942-46); staff Army Med. Service Grad. Sch., Washington, 1946-56, chief, dept. virus and rickettsial diseases, 1946-56, tech. director research (communicable and parasitic diseases) 1950-56; vis. lectr. virology U. Md., 1950-54; visiting prof. rickettsial diseases U. Pa. Sch. Med., 1950-56; asso. dir. Nat. Insts. Health. Bethesda, Md., 1956-60, chief laboratory of virology and rickettsiology Division of Biologics Standards, 1960-—. Entered M.C., A.U.S. as captain, 1942; discharged as lt. colonel, 1946. Awarded United States of America Typhus Commn. medal, 1946, Gordon Wilson medal, 1949; Exceptional Civilian Service award, 1950; Howard Taylor Ricketts medal, 1953; Alumni citation Washington University, 1956; James D. Bruce Memorial award and Stitt award, 1959; Albert Lasker award for clinical research, 1962. Dir. commn. immunization, Armed Forces Epidemiological Board, 1947-52, dir. Commn. Hemorrhagic Fever, 1952-54, director Commission Rickettsial Diseases, 1958-60; mem. virus and rickettsial study sect. USPHS, 1946-51. Mem. com. on virus research and epidemiology and research fellowship in virology Nat. Found. Infantile Paralysis, 1948-—. Fellow Am. Public Health Assn., A.A.A.S., N.Y. Acad. Sci.; member American Epidemiol. Soc., Am. Soc. Exptl. Pathology, Am. Soc. Clin, Investigation, Am. Soc. Pathologists and Bacteriologists, Soc. Exptl. Biol. and Medicine, Soc. Am. Bacteriologists, Harvey Soc., Am. Assn. Immunologists (president 1958), New York Academy of Medicine, American Association of Physicians, National Academy Science, Am. Soc. Tropical Medicine and Hygiene (mem. council 1957-61). Home: 1440 Hemlock St. N.W., Washington 20012. Office: Nat. Insts. Health, Bethesda, Md. Died July 21, 1963; buried Vincennes, Ind.

SMALL, ERNEST GREGOR naval officer; b. Feb. 15, 1888; entered U.S. Navy, 1907, and advanced through the grades to rear adm., 1942. Decorated Distinguished Service Medal, Navy Cross, Legion of Merit (3). Address: Navy Dept., Washington 25. Died Dec. 26, 1944; buried in Arlington National Cemetery.

SMALL, JOHN D. business exec.; b. Palestine, Tex., Oct. 11, 1893; s. John Clay and Louise Moran (Lynch) S.; grad. U.S. Naval Acad., 1915; M.S., Columbia U., 1920; m. Gwendolyn Davies, Mar. 8, 1928; children—Gwendolyn (Mrs. Preston Marshall), Joan (Mrs. R. Walter Silbersack), Storm (Mrs. Jackson Ream). Commd. ensign, USN, 1915, advanced through grades to lieut. commander, inactive 1926; v.p. Dry Ice Corp. 1926-31; western mgr., Publicker, Inc., Chicago, 1932-41. Commd. comdr., U.S. Navy, 1942, advanced through grades to rear adm., served successively as deputy director, Army and Munitions Bd., 1942-43, materials control officer and landing craft coordinator, U.S. Navy Dept., 1943-44. exec. officer, War Prodn. Bd., 1944-45. chief of staff, Apr.-Nov., 1945, adminstr., Civilian Prodn. Adminstrn., 1945-46, ret. 1947; pres. Maxson Food Systems, Inc., 1947-49; chmn. Chmn. Mercantile Sect. N.Y. Bd. Trade, 1947-49, v.p., dir., 1949-50; v.p. Emerson Radio & Phonograph Corp., 1949-50, 55-—; chmn. munitions bd. Dept. Def., Washington, 1950-53; v.p. Quiet-Heet Mfg. Corp., subsidiary of Emerson Radio, 1953-54, pres., 1954-55; chairman of the board Emertron, Inc., 1960-—. Dir. N.Y. Bd. Trade, 1953-54. Democrat. Episcopalian. Clubs: University (N.Y.C.); Columbia Country, Army-Navy (Washington). Office: 1140 East West Hwy., Silver Spring, Md. Died Jan. 23, 1963; buried Arlington Nat. Cemetery.

SMALL, SAM(UEL) (WHITE) journalist; b. Knoxville, Tenn., July 3, 1851; s. Alexander Benson and Elizabeth Jane (White) S.; A.B., Emory and Henry Coll., Va., 1871, A.M., 1887; Ph.D., Taylor U., Upland, Ind., 1894; D.D., Ohio Northern U., 1894; m. Annie I. Arnold, 1873 (died 1915); children—Sam W., Robert Toombs. Stenographer and newspaper reporter; sec. President Andrew Johnson during his post-presidential political campaigns; on the editorial staff of Atlanta Constitution, 1875-—, and now its editorial writer. Official reporter, Georgia Constl. Conv., 1877; sec. Am. Commn. to Paris Expn., 1878; com. reporter U.S. Senate, 1879-81; was founder the Norfolk (Va.) Daily Pilot, later founded Daily Oklahoman, Oklahoma City, Okla. Entered evangelistic work at Atlanta, Ga., Sept. 15, 1885; associated in many campaigns with Sam Jones, later alone, and as reform lecturer. Reserve soldier C.S.A., Jan. 19-Apr. 20, 1865; lt. col. and a.d.c. Ga. N.G.; capt. and chaplain 3d U.S. Vol. Engrs., Spanish-Am. War in Cuba, 1898-99. Chaplain in chief Naval and Mil. Order Spanish-Am. War. Democrat. Methodist. Mason, Odd Fellow, K.P., Red Man. Author: Old Si's Savings, 1886; Pleas for Prohibition, 1889; The White Angel of the World, 1891. Home: Livingston Heights, Va. Died Nov. 21, 1931.

SMALLS, ROBERT congressman; b. Beaufort, S.C., Apr. 5, 1839; s. Robert and Lydia Smalls; m. Hannah, 1856; m. 2d, Annie Wigg, Apr. 9, 1890; at least 2 children. A slave, impressed by Confederacy into service as crewman in steamer The Planter in Charleston harbor, 1861; became nationally famous when he guided The Planter past Charleston forts into U.S. Squadron blockading the harbor, May 1862; became pilot U.S. Navy; capt., comdr. The Planter, 1863-66; del. S.C. Constl. Conv., 1868; mem. S.C. Ho. of Reps., 1868-70, S.C. Senate, 1870-74; mem. U.S. Congress (Republican) from S.C., 44th-45th, 47th-49th congresses, 1875-79, July 19, 1882-83, 84-87; supported bill to provide equal service for all races in interstate travel; opposed civil service reform, attempted to have compensation of $30,000 voted to him for his capture of The Planter; served to maj. gen. S.C. Militia, 1865-77; port collector, Beaufort, 1889-93, 97-1913; convicted of accepting $5,000 bribe, 1877, sentenced to 3 years in prison, but pardoned by Gov. Simpson; del. S.C. Constl. Conv., 1895. Died Beaufort, Feb. 22, 1915; buried Tabernacle Bapt. Ch. Cemetery, Beaufort.

SMALLWOOD, WILLIAM army officer, gov., Md.; b. Charles County, Md., 1732; s. Bayne and Priscilla (Heaberd) S. Mem. Md. Assembly, 1761; del. to Md. Conv. of 1775; joined Assn. of Freemen of Md., 1775; commanded a regt. Md. Militia, 1776; served in Battle of L.I.; commd. brig. gen Continental Army, 1776; protected Gen. Washington's stores near head of Elk River, Wilmington, Del., suppressed Tory revolt on Eastern Shores of Md., 1778-79; commd. maj. gen., 1870; sent to Md. to obtain supplies and reinforcements, 1780-83; served as drill master, raised troops and supplies; gov. Md., 1785-88, called Md. Conv. which ratified U.S. Constn. Died Prince George's County, Md., Feb. 12, 1792; buried Charles County, Md.

SMART, CHARLES soldier, physician; b. Aberdeen, Scotland, Sept. 18, 1841, s. Alexander and Anne (Kelman) S.; ed. Keith, Banffshire and Marischal Coll.; grad. Univ. of Aberdeen, M.B., C.M., 1862; m. Dora, d. Dr. John Purcell, New York, 1869. Came to U.S., 1862; enlisted as asst. surgeon, 63d N.Y. vols., 1862; served with Army of Potomac, 1863-64; apptd. asst. surgeon, U.S.A., Mar. 30, 1864; btvd. capt., Dec. 2, 1864, for meritorious services in the field being the 1st asst. surgeon in U.S.A. to receive the honor; capt., 1866; maj., 1882; later lt. col., and col., Feb. 2, 1902-—; served various stas. after Civil War; now asst. surgeon gen. U.S.A. Author: (novel) Driven from the Path, 1872; Handbook for Hospital Corps, U.S.A., 1898. Home: Washington, D.C. Died 1905.

SMART, EPHRAIM KNIGHT congressman, lawyer; b. Prospect (now Searsport), Me., Spet. 3, 1813; attended Me. Wesleyan Sem., Readfield; studied law. Admitted to bar, 1838, practiced in Camden, Knox County, Me.; apptd. postmaster Camden, 1838, 45; mem. Me. Senate, 1841-42, 62; apptd. a.d.c. with rank of lt. col. on staff Gov. Fairfield, 1842; moved to Mo., 1843, practiced law; returned to Camden, 1844; mem. U.S. Ho. of Reps. (Democrat) from Me., 30th, 32d congresses, 1847-49, 51-53; collector customs, Belfast, 1853-58; founded Me. Free Press, 1854, editor 3 years; mem. Me. Ho. of Reps., 1858; unsuccessful candidate for gov. Me., 1860; moved to Biddeford, York County, Me., 1869, founded Me. Democrat. Died Camden, Sept. 29, 1872; buried Mountain Street Cemetery.

SMEALLIE, JOHN MORRIS navy officer; b. Sept. 5, 1886; promoted through grades to rear adm., June 23, 1938. Died Nov. 24, 1947.

SMEDLEY, AGNES author; b. Northern Mo., 1894; d. Charles H. and Sarah (Ralls) Smedley; student summer sch. U. Cal., 1915, N.Y. U. night sch., U. of Berlin, 1927-28; divorced. Has spent 23 yrs. in foreign countries, of these, 12 yrs. in China; in war zones of China, with regular and guerrilla armies, and Chinese civilian orgns. engaged in war work, 1937-40; special corr. in Far East for the Frankfurter Zeitung of Germany until Hitler's rise to power; spl. war-time corr. for Manchester Guardian of England, 1938-41. Has been fgn. corr., field worker for Chinese Red Cross Med. Corps, lectr. in Chinese armies. Interpreter of China to western world and vice versa. Active participant in China's war for liberation. On death list of Japanese Secret Service during World War II. Mem. Progressive Citizens of Am., Am. Vet. Com., East and West Asso., P.E.N. Author: Daughter of Earth, 1929; Chinese Destinies, 1933; China's Red Army Marches, 1935; China Fights Back, 1939; Battle Hymn of China, 1943; The Great Road; The Life and Times of Chu Teh (in press); Chapter XI of China, The United Nations Series, edited by Harley F. MacNair. Contbr. to Asia, New Republic, Nation, Vogue, etc. Lecturer. Address: Palisades, N.Y. Died May 6, 1950; buried Peking, China.

SMILEY, DEAN FRANKLIN, physician, educator; b. Cheyenne, Wyo., July 7, 1894; s. Elmer Ellsworth and Edith Constance (House) S.; A.B., Cornell, 1916, M.D., 1919; m. Alice Dimon, Sept. 10, 1919; children—Jane Constance (Mrs. Parker Hart), Beth Anne (Mrs. Henry Borst). Interne N.Y. Hosp., 1919-20; mem. faculty, student Health Service Cornell U. 1920-42, prof. dept. hygiene and preventive medicine, 1928-42; cons. in health and fitness, A.M.A., Chicago, 1946-48; sec. Assn. Am. Med. Colleges, Chicago, 1948-57; exec. dir. Edn. Council Fgn. Med. Grads., 1957-63. Served as comdr. M.C., U.S. Navy, 1942-46. Diplomate Am. Bd. Preventive Medicine. Fellow Am. Pub. Health Assn. (mem. com. on survey med. edn.); mem. Am. Med. Writers Assn. (pres. 1956-57), Sigma Xi, Alpha Omega Alpha. Editor Jour. of Med. Edn., 1951-57. Pub. (with A. G. Gould) Your Health, 1951; Your Community's Health, 1952. Address: Evanston IL Died Nov. 20, 1969; cremated.

SMITH, ABIEL LEONARD army officer; b. Fayette, Howard County, Mo., July 14, 1857; s. Joseph D. and Martha (Leonard) S.; grad. U.S. Mil. Acad., 1878; Army War Coll., 1914; m. Florence Comptoh, June 19, 1890; children—Abiel Leonard, Dorothy, Charles Compton, Margaret. Commd. 2d lt. 19th Inf., June 28, 1878; brig. general, Sept. 22, 1916; retired Jan. 3, 1918. Participated in campaigns against Indians, 1878-86; Spanish-Am. War, 1898; also in World War. Brevetted capt., Feb. 27, 1890, "for gallant and meritorious service" in Geronimo Campaign, 1886. Episcopalian. Home: Carmel, N.Y.* Died Apr. 24, 1946.

SMITH, ALEXANDER WYLY lawyer; b. Habersham Co., Ga., June 24, 1861; s. Henry Lamar and Sarah Amelia (Wyly) S.; student U. of Georgia, through junior yr., 1876-78; m. Ida Kendrick, Sept. 10, 1885. Admitted to Ga. bar, 1883, and began practice at Atlanta; mem. Abbott & Smith, 1885-92, Alexander W. and Victor L. Smith, 1892-99, Smith, Hammond & Smith, 1899-—. Spl. counsel to the dir. gen. of railroads, Washington, Apr. 1, 1920-—. Mem. of standing coms. on railroads, tariff and federal trade of Chamber Commerce U.S.A. Maj., U.S.R. Ordnance Div. Gen. mgr. Cotton States and Internat. Expn., Atlanta, 1895. Democrat. Episcopalian. Home: Atlanta, Ga. Died Jan. 12, 1925.

SMITH, ALFRED THEODORE army officer; b. Washington, D.C., Nov. 25, 1874; s. Theodore Smith and Lydia Justine (Kilp) S.; ed. pub. and pvt. schs., Washington, D.C.; grad. army Sch. of the Line, 1915, Gen. Staff Coll., 1922, Army War Coll., 1921; m. Anne Yvonne Pike, Feb. 24, 1903. Successively pvt., corpl. and sergt., U.S.A., 1894-97; commd. 2d lt., 1897; promoted through all grades to brig. gen., May 24, 1933. Served in Santiago Campaign in Cuba, 1898, in Philippine Insurrection, 1899-1901, Philippine Samar Expdn. against bandits, 1905, Mexican border, 1912-14; mil. attaché U.S. Embassy, Buenos Aires, Argentina, 1916-19, The Hague Conf., 1919; comdg. 54th U.S. Inf., 1919-20; gen. staff, hdqrs. 3d Corps Area, 1922-26; in charge N.G. affairs, same hdqrs., 1926-28; comdg. 34th U.S. Inf., 1928-31; asst. chief of staff and chief mil. intelligence div., War Dept. Gen. Staff, 1931-—. Awarded Silver Star and cited for gallantry in action at El Caney, Cuba; Comdr. Order of the Crown (Italian). Died Nov. 27, 1939.

SMITH, ALLEN brigadier gen. U.S.A.; b. Ft. Marion, St. Augustine, Fla., Apr. 21, 1849; s. Maj. Gen. Charles Ferguson (U.S.A.) and Fanny (Mactier) S.; cadet U.S. Naval Acad., 1863-66; m. Julia Stephens, July 2, 1874. Apptd. from Pa., 2d lt. 1st Inf., July 18, 1866; 1st lt., Apr. 22, 1868; capt., May 21, 1880; transferred to 4th Cav., Dec. 6, 1880; maj. 1st Cav., Nov. 21, 1897; lt. col., Feb. 2, 1901; col. 6th Cav., June 28, 1902; brig. gen. and retired at own request after 40 yrs.' service, Mar. 18, 1905. Home: Spokane, Wash. Died Oct. 30, 1927.

SMITH, ALLEN JOHN M.D.; b. York, Pa., Dec. 8, 1863; s. Gibson and Susan (Fahs) S.; A.B., Pa. Coll., 1883, A.M., 1886, Sc.D., 1910, LL.D., 1921; LL.D., McGill, 1911; M.D., U. of Pa., 1886; m. Harriet W. Brooke, 1888 (died 1896); 1 son, Gibson; m. 2d, Pearl L. Pierce, 1899. Resident phys., Phila. Hosp., 1886-87; asst. demonstrator pathology, U. of Pa., 1887-91; prof. pathology, etc., med. dept. U. of Texas, 1891-1903; prof. pathology, 1903-10, prof. comparative pathology and dir. courses in tropical medicine, 1910-—, prof. pathology, 1911-—, U. of Pa. Commd. maj., M.R.C., U.S.A., Apr. 11, 1917; active service, base hosps., Camp Dix, N.J., and Camp Pike, Ark., June 20, 1918-Mar. 22, 1919; lt. col., May 19, 1919. Author: Lessons and Laboratory Exercises in Bacteriology, 1902, etc. Home: St. Davids, Pa. Died Aug. 19, 1926.

SMITH, ANDREW HEERMANCE physician; b. Charlton, N.Y., Aug. 27, 1837; s. Archibald and Cornelia (Heermance) S.; ed. Ballston Spa Inst., Union Coll., A.M., Coll. Phys. and Surg., New York, M.D., 1858; univs. of Göttingen and Berlin; m. Jane T. Sheldon, 1884. Practiced medicine, 1859-61; entered army as asst. surg. 43d N.Y. vols., 1861; surg. 94th N.Y. vols., 1862; asst. surg. U.S.A., 1862-68; bvtd. maj., U.S.A., 1867. Began practice of medicine in New York in 1868. Has been physician to St. Luke's and Presbyn. hosps., and surgeon to Manhattan Eye, Ear and Throat Hosp. Now cons. physician St. Luke's, Presbyn., St. Mark's, Woman's, Post-Graduate and Ruptured and Crippled hosps.; v.p. Post-Grad. Med. Sch. and Hosp. Pres. N.Y. Acad. Medicine, 1903-04; del. to Internat. Med. Congress, Berlin, 1890, Madrid, 1903. Episcopalian. Republican. Home: New York, N.Y. Died 1910.

SMITH, ANDREW JACKSON army officer; b. Buckingham, Pa., Apr. 28, 1815; s. Samuel and Mrs. (Wilkinson) Smith; grad. U.S. Mil. Acad., 1838; m. Ann Mason Simpson. Served in expdn. to South Pass of Rocky Mountains, 1840; commd. 1st lt. U.S. Army, 1845, capt., 1847; maj. 1st Dragoons, 1861; col. 2d Cal. Cavalry, 1861; became chief of cavalry under Henry Wagner Halleck, 1861, served in Corinth campaign, 1862; brig. gen. U.S. Volunteers, 1862, commanded div. in Vicksburg campaign, 1863; maj. gen. U.S. Volunteers, 1864, defeated Nathan Bedford Forrest at Tupelo, Miss., served in Battle of Nashville (Tenn.); commd. lt. col. U.S. Army, 1864; comdr. XVI Corps in Mobile campaign, 1865; col. 7th Cavalry, 1866; postmaster St. Louis, 1869, city auditor, 1877-89; commanded militia brigade during strikes in St. Louis, 1877; col. (ret.) U.S. Army, 1889. Died St. Louis, Jan. 30, 1897.

SMITH, ARTHUR congressman, lawyer; b. Windsor Castle, nr. Smithfield, Isle of Wight County, Va., Nov. 15, 1785; grad. Coll. William and Mary; studied law. Admitted to bar, 1808, practiced in Smithfield; also became farmer; served as col. in War of 1812; mem. Va. Ho. of Dels., 1818-20, 36-41; mem. U.S. Ho. of Reps. from Va., 17th-18th congresses, 1821-25. Died Smithfield, Mar. 30, 1853; buried family burying ground on Windsor Castle Estate.

SMITH, ARTHUR ST. CLAIR rear admiral; b. Cedar Rapids, Ia., Dec. 31, 1873; s. Arthur St. Clair and Harriet Rogerson (Baker) S.; grad. U.S. Naval Acad., 1899; m. Anne Salley, June 8, 1907; children—Anne St. Clair, Donald Bruce. Commd. ensign U.S. Navy, June 1897, and advanced through grades to capt., June 1921; rear admiral, May 1930. Served in Spanish-Am. War, Philippine Insurrection; comdr. Lafayette Radio Station, Bordeaux, France, 1918-19; commander of Battleship Idaho, 1925-27; chief of staff to comdr. battleships, 1928-29; chief staff to comdr. in chief of Battle Fleet, 1929-30; apptd. comdr. Spl. Service Squadron, Canal Zone, 1930, later apptd. comdt. Norfolk Navy Yard, Portsmouth, Va. Comdr. Battleship Div. 3, Comdt. 12th Naval Dist.; retired Jan. 1, 1938. Awarded 6 campaign badges and medals (U.S.); Officer of Legion of Honor (France). Presbyterian. Clubs: Army and Navy (Washington); University (New York). Home: 6 Southgate Av., Annapolis, Md. Address: Navy Dept., Washington, D.C. Died Mar. 26, 1942.

SMITH, ASHBEL state ofcl.; b. Hartford, Conn., Aug. 13, 1805; s. Moses and Phoebe (Adams) S.; grad. Yale, 1824, M.D., 1828; studied medicine, Paris, France, 1831-32. Editor and part owner of nullification newspaper Western Carolinian, 1832; surgeon gen. Army of Republic of Tex., 1837; a commr. to negotiate treaty with Comanche Indians, 1838; Tex. minister to Eng. and France, 1842-44; sec. of state Republic of Tex., 1845, negotiated Smith-Cuevas Treaty by which Mexico recognized Tex. independence; mem. Tex. Legislature, 1855, 1866, 78, leader in movements for advancement of edn. in Tex.; served as capt. Bayland Guards, then lt. col. and col. 2d Tex. Volunteer Inf., Civil War; brevetted brig. gen., commanded forces at Matagorda Peninsula, later commanded defenses of Galveston (Tex.); pres. bd. trustees Galveston Med. Sch.; commr. to locate Agrl. and Mech. Coll. for colored youths; a founder, pres. bd. regents U. Tex.; mem. Phi Beta Kappa. Author: An Account of the Yellow Fever Which Appeared in the City of Galveston, 1839. Died Evergreen plantation, Tex., Jan. 21, 1886; buried State Cemetery, Austin, Tex.

SMITH, BENJAMIN M. army officer; b. Hull, Ala., September 10, 1900; son of Benjamin Alexander and Dovie (Mitchell) Smith; graduate of Company Officer's Course, Ft. Benning, Ga., 1929, Field Officers' Course, 1933, Command and Gen. Staff Sch., Ft. Leavenworth, Kan., 1936; m. Mary Montgomery, Aug. 17, 1927. Served as private, 1919, and advanced through the grades to brig. gen., Ala. Nat. Guard, Jan. 1939; Federal Service since 1939. With Tenn. Coal, Iron, and R.R. Co., Birmingham, Ala., 1919-35; Protective Life Ins. Co., 1935-37; Ala. rep., Seagram's Distellery Corp., 1937-39; adj. gen., State Mil. Dept. since 1939, Ala. State dir. Selective Service, 1940-46, retired; now a member G.M.S. General Sales and Mfrs. Agents. Sec. Armory Commn., Ala.; mem. Ala. State Defense Council. Awarded Victory medal, Ala. Faithful Service medal with 5 crosses, Ala. Special Service medal, Ala. Veterans' Servcie medal. Mem. Ala. State Rifle Assn. (pres.), Nat. Guard Officers Assn. of Ala. Mason (York Rite, Shriner). Club: Country (Montgomery, Ala.). Home: 3294 S. Perry St., Montgomery 6. Office: 811 Shepherd Bldg., Montgomery 4, Ala. Died Apr. 13, 1949; buried Greenwood Cemetery, Montgomery.

SMITH, BEVERLY WAUGH, JR., writer and lawyer; b. Balt., Aug. 9, 1898; s. Beverly Waugh and Eleanor (Euker) S.; A.B., Johns Hopkins, 1919; postgrad. Harvard Law Sch., 1919-20; grad. final honours Sch. of Jurisprudence, Oxford U. (Rhodes scholar 1920), 1922; M.A., 1968; M. Grace Cutler, May 21, 1926. Admitted to N.Y. State bar; practiced in N.Y.C., 1923-26; reporter, later fgn. corr. and columnist, N.Y. Herald Tribune, 1926-31; with American Mag., staff writer and asso. editor, 1931-46; Washington editor, senior contbg. editor Sat. Eve. Post, 1946-64, contbg. writer, 1964-69; admitted to D.C. bar, 1964. Served as 2d lt., arty., U.S. Army, 1918. Mem. Phi Beta Kappa, Omicron Delta Kappa, Alpha Delta Phi. Clubs: Nat. Press, Cosmos (Washington). Author: (with Grace Cutler Smith) Through the Kitchen Door, 1938. Contbr. articles and fiction to Am. Mag., Reader's Digest, New Yorker, other mags. Home: Baltimore MD Died Oct. 22, 1972.

SMITH, BRUCE D(ONALD) banker; b. Lake Forest, Ill., Aug. 13, 1885; s. Byron Laflin and Carrie Cornelia (Stone) S.; grad. Hill Sch., 1902; B.A., Yale, 1906; m. Pauline Mackay, 1909 (divorced 1920); m. 2d, Florence Mann Fisher, June 1921. With Northern Trust Co., Chicago, 1907-19, resigned as vice pres., 1919; mem. bd. dirs. United Corp., Lehigh Coal and Nav. Corp., South N.J. Gas Co.; dir. Lehigh and New England R.R., 1944-46. Mgr. central div. Am. Red Cross, 1917-18; with Emergency Unemployment Relief Commn., N.Y. City, 1932-33; spl. asst. to chmn. A.R.C., 1933-35; supervisor orgn. and constrn. A.R.C.-Harvard Hosp., 1940-41, in Eng., 1941; asso. N.Y. state adminstr. War Bonds Com., 1941-43; spl. asst. to chmn. War Manpower Commn., 1943-45; cons. to gen. mgr. Atomic Energy Commn., 1948, mem. personnel security review bd., 1949. Served as 1st lt., 1st Ill. F.A., 1914-17; capt. Chem. Warfare Service, 1918-19. Republican. Clubs: Yale, Metropolitan (New York); Chevy Chase, 1925 F Street, Army-Navy (Washington); Reading Room, Clambake, Spouting Rock Beach (Newport, R.I.). Address: Bellevue Av., Newport, R.I.; also 36 E. 72d St., N.Y.C. 21. Died May 29, 1952.

SMITH, CHARLES EDWARD univ. dean; b. St. Joseph, Mo., Sept. 7, 1904; s. Charles Madison and Mabel Ellen (Kates) S.; student Sacramento Jr. Coll., 1923-25; A.B., Stanford, 1927, M.D., 1931; D.P.H., U. Toronto, 1934; m. Elizabeth Laidlaw, June 14, 1930; children—Edward Laidlaw, Charles Laidlaw. House officer, Alameda County Highland Hospital, 1931-32; instructor department pub. health and preventive medicine, Stanford U. Sch. Medicine, 1932-34, asst. prof., 1934-37, asso. prof., 1937-42, prof., 1942-49, prof., chmn. dept. U. Cal. Sch. Pub. Health since 1949; dean since 1951; spl. cons. to Surgeon Gen. USPHS, 1946-56, cons. communicable disease center USPHS, 1952-54; fellow internat. health div., Rockefeller Found., 1933-34; asso. Rockefeller Found. in Study of Teaching of Preventive Medicine and Pub. Health in N.Am. and Europe, 1936-37. Mem. Cal. State Bd. Health, 1940-—(pres. 1944-64); cons. Surgeon Gen. 6th U.S. Army, Letterman Gen. Hosp., to sec. of war for epidemic diseases, 1941-46. Cons. to Sec. of War, then Sec. of Army, 1947-55; now cons. Surgeon Gen. Army, hon. cons. Surgeon Gen. Navy, nat. cons. Surgeon Gen. Air Force; dir. Armed Forces Epidemiological Bd. environmental hygiene commn., 1954-55, mem. commn. acute respratory disease, member of central board. Bd. dirs. Florence Crittenton Home, San Francisco. Recipient Bronfman prize Am. Pub. llealth Assn. Mem. A.M.A., Am. Pub. Health Assn. (past mem. exec. bd., chmn. com. profl. edn., mem. tech. devel. bd.), Nat. Adv. Health Council, Nat. Commn. Community Health Services, San Francisco Social Hygiene and Health Assn. (pres.), Am. Epidemiological Soc., Soc. Am. Bacteriologists, Am. Fedn. Clin. Research, Phi Beta Kappa, Sigma Xi, Alpha Omega Alpha, Alpha Kappa Kappa. Theta Chi. Mem. editorial bd. California Medicine. Contributor to tech. jours. Home: 12 W. Clay Park, San Francisco 21. Office: University of California School of Public Health, Berkeley 4, Cal. Died Apr. 1967.

SMITH, CHARLES FERGUSON army officer; b. Phila., Apr. 24, 1807; s. Samuel Blair and Mary (Ferguson) S.; grad. U.S. Mil. Acad., 1825; m. Fanny Mactier, 3 children. Instr. inf. tactics U.S. Mil. Acad., later adjutant, then comdr. of cadets, 1829-43; commd. 1st lt. 2d Arty., U.S. Army, 1832, capt., 1838; in command of battalion, distinguished in battles of Palo Alto and Resaca de la Palma (Tex.), 1846; brevetted maj. and lt. col. for service in Mexican campaign, 1846; brevetted col., 1847; commd. maj. 1st Arty., 1854; lt. col. 10th Inf., 1855; led expdn. to Red River of North, 1856; in command of Dept. of Utah, 1860-61; commd. brig. gen. U.S. Volunteers, also col. U.S. Army, 1861, commanded Dist. of W. Ky.; commanded 2d Div., Grant's Army, fts. Henry and Donelson (Tenn.) and Ft. Heiman (Ky.); commd. maj. gen. U.S. Volunteers, 1862. Died Savannah, Tenn., Apr. 25, 1862.

SMITH, CHARLES HENRY col. and bvt. maj. gen., U.S.A., retired; b. Hollis, Me., Nov. 1, 1827; s. Aaron and Sally (Gile) S.; grad. Waterville Coll. (now Colby), Me., 1856 (A.M.); taught school; studied law at Eastport, Me.; m. Mary Richards Livermore, July 28, 1864. Entered vol. service, 1861; served until 1865; capt. to bvt. maj. gen. Was in 63 battles and engagements and 3 times wounded; mustered out, Aug. 11, 1865. Admitted to bar, 1865; State senator, Me., 1866. July 28, 1866, apptd. col. 28th U.S. inf.; transferred to 19th U.S. inf., 1869; promoted to bvt. brig. gen. and bvt. maj. gen., U.S.A.; retired from active service, Nov. 1, 1891. Died 1902.

SMITH, CHARLES HENRY ("BILL ARP") author; b. Lawrenceville, Ga., June 15, 1826; s. A. R. and Caroline Ann (Maguire) S.; grad. Franklin Coll., Athens, Ga., 1848; studied law, 1849; m. Octavia, d. Judge Hutchins, 1849. Removed to Rome, Ga.; practiced there 27 yrs.; now lives in Cartersville. Has been writing weekly letters to Atlanta Constitution and Home and Farm of Louisville for 30 yrs.; served in C.S. army, 1861-65, becoming maj. on staff Brig. Gen. G. T. Anderson, 3d Ga. brigade. Author: Bill Arp's Letters; Bill Arp's Scrap-Book; The Farm and the Fireside; A Side Show of the Southern Side of the War; Fireside Sketches, 1890; Georgia as a Colony and State, 1733-1893, 1890. Home: Cartersville, Ga. Died 1903.

SMITH, CHARLES LYSLE, lawyer; b. Chgo., Jan. 13, 1895; s. Charles George and Alta (Williams) S.; B.S., Northwestern U., 1917, LL.B., 1920; m. Ruth Graves, Aug. 26, 1924; 1 dau., Ellen Graves (Mrs. Smith Simmons). Admitted to Illinois bar, 1920, practiced in Chgo., asso. Wilson, McIlvaine, Hale & Templeton, 1920-24, pvt. practice, from 1925; sr. partner firm Winston Strawn, 1967. Trustee Village of Glencoe, 1940-48. Trustee Northwestern U., 1956-60. Lt. (j.g.), USN, World War I. Recipient Norman Waite Harris polit. sci. prize, 1917. Mem. Northwestern U. Associates, Soc. Mayflower Descs. (gov. Ill. soc. 1963-66), Phi Delta Theta, Phi Delta Phi. Clubs: University, Legal, Law, Mid-day (Chgo.); Skokie Country; Lake Zurich (Ill.) Golf. Home: Glencoe IL Died May 8, 1972; buried Memorial Park Skokie IL

SMITH, CHARLES SHALER bridge engr.; b. Pitts., Jan. 16, 1836; s. Frederick Rose and Mary Anne (Shaler) S.; m. Mary Gordon Gairdner, May 23, 1865, several children. Asst. engr. Louisville & Nashville R.R., 1855, resident engr. on Memphis br., 1856, supr. track and bridge constrn. for Memphis div., 1859; chief engr. of bldgs. and bridges Wilmington, Charlotte & Rutherford R.R. (N.C.), 1860-61; served as capt. engrs. Confederate Army in Civil War, built powder mill in Augusta dist.; partner (with Benjamin H. and Charles H. Latrobe) in Balt. Bridge Co., 1866; built series of iron trestles on Louisville, Cincinnati & Lexington R.R. and Elizabethtown & Paducah R.R.; 1st to use metal viaducts; built Ky. River Bridge for Cincinnati So. R.R. (his most notable structure), 1876-77; cantilever became dominant type for long-span constrn. as result of his work; most eminent bridge engr. in Am. Author: Comparative Analysis of the Fink, Murphy, Bollman and Triangular Trusses (treatise), 1865; Wind Pressure Upon Bridges (paper), 1881. Died St. Louis, Dec. 19, 1886.

SMITH, CHARLES SIDNEY brigadier gen. U.S.A.; b. St. Albans, Vt., Dec. 26, 1843; s. Rev. Worthington and Mary Ann (Little) S.; apptd. to U.S. Mil. Acad. from Ill., 1862, grad. 1866; m. Miss E. L. Northrop, 1891 (died 1891). Apptd. 2d lt. 4th Arty., June 18, 1866; 1st lt., July 28, 1866; transferred to ordnance dept., Nov. 1, 1874; capt., Aug. 2, 1879; maj., July 7, 1898; lt. col., Apr. 5, 1903; col., Jan. 19, 1905; brig. gen., Oct. 9, 1907; retired Dec. 26, 1907. Died Nov. 9, 1922.

SMITH, CLARENCE JAMES newspaperman; b. Easton, Pa., July 29, 1874; s. John Jackson and Sue (Bonstein) S.; grad. high sch., Easton, 1891; m. Edith Clappison, Apr. 30, 1906; children—Jack Clappison, Clarence James. Reporter Easton Daily Argus, 1893-1904, editor, 1904-10; city editor Allentown (Pa.) Morning Call, 1910-19, owner, v.p. and mng. editor, 1920-34; now connected with Pa. Power & Light Co.; founder and pub., 1919, Allentown Morning Herald. Served as 1st sergt. Pa. Inf., Spanish-Am. War, capt. and regtl. q.m., 1912-17; capt. on Mexican border, 1916; organizer 103d Am. Train, 28th Div., A.E.F., serving as maj. inf. in France, 1918-19; lt. col. inf., Pa. N.G., 1920-23; col. C.A., 1923-—. Mem. Pa. Editorial Assn. (pres.), Interstate Circulation Mgrs. Assn. (pres.), Allentown Chamber Commerce (pres.). Republican. Episcopalian. Odd Fellow, Elk. Home: Allentown, Pa. Died Aug. 28, 1940.

SMITH, COURTNEY CRAIG, coll. pres.; b. Winterset, Ia., Dec. 20, 1916; s. Samuel Craig and Myrtle (Dabney) S.; A.B., Harvard, 1938, A.M., 1941, Ph.D., 1944; student (Rhodes Scholar), Oxford U., 1938-39; LL.D., U. Pa., 1958, Temple U., 1959, U. Pitts., 1960; L.H.D., Bucknell U., 1958; D.Litt., W.Va. University, 1959; Doctor of Laws, La Salle College, 1967; m. Elizabeth Bowden Proctor, Oct. 12, 1939; children—Courtney Craig Jr., Elizabeth Bowden (Mrs. Gregory K. Ingram), and Carol Dabney. Teaching fellow, tutor of English, Harvard, 1939-43; instr. English, Princeton, 1946-48, asst. prof., 1948-53, bicentennial preceptor, 1951-53; nat. dir. Nat. Woodrow Wilson Fellowship Program, 1952-53; Am. sec. Rhodes Scholarships 1953-69, pres. Swarthmore Coll., 1953-69; bd. dirs. Phila. Sav. Fund Soc.; bd. electors George Eastman vis. professorship, Oxford U. Mem. bd. Pa.-N.J.-Del. Met. Project, Inc., 1958-65. Trustee Eisenhower Exchange Fellowships, Inc.; mem. bd. overseers Harvard, 1955-61, now mem. vis. com. dept. English; vis. com. for humanities Johns Hopkins; commn. internat. edn. Am. Council on Edn., 1962-65; dir. Markle Found.; dir. Assn. Am. Colls., 1957-61. Served ensign to lt. (j.g.), USNR, 1944-46. Decorated Hon. Officer Order British Empire. Mem. Modern Lang. Assn., Am. Assn. U. Profs. (asso.). Assn. Am. Rhodes Scholars (bd. dirs.), Phi Beta Kappa. Mem. Soc. of Friends. Clubs: University, Century (N.Y.C.); Rolling Green Golf; Harvard, Sunday Breakfast, Ozone (Phila.). Home: Swarthmore PA Died Jan. 16, 1969.

SMITH, DAN MORGAN lecturer, soldier, lawyer; b. Orange, Va., Oct. 2, 1873; s. Dan Morgan (M.D.) and DeLacy (Cave) S.; cadet Fla. State Coll. (now U. of Fla.), and under pvt. teacher 6 yrs.; m. Frances McKinney, Dec. 27, 1897. Admitted to bar, Fla., 1892, Ga., 1897, Ill., 1899, U.S. Supreme Court, 1908; Dem. nominee for Congress, 3d Ill. Dist., 1902; spl. asst. corp. counsel, City of Chicago, 1905-06; judge adv. State of Ill., 1914-16; spl. asst. U.S. atty., 1915-16. Engaged in "gun running" for Cubans; lt. Fla. Nat. Guard, 1891-98; 1st lt. 3d U.S.V. during Spanish-Am. War; lt., capt., maj., Ill. Nat. Guard, 1900-17; served on Mexican border as capt. Co. D, 7th Ill. Nat. Guard, 1916-17; enlisted as pvt., United States Army, 1917; commd. maj. inf., September 15, 1917; assigned to 357th Inf. and sent to France; major commanding "Battalion of Death" (1st Battalion) 358 Infantry, 90th Division; participated in St. Mihiel drive, Fey en Haye, Hill 350.4, Vilsey, Les Quatres Chemins, Les Huit Chemins, Prany, Meuse-Argonne, Verdun sector Argonne Forest; twice wounded; promoted lt. col. "for gallantry in action"; commd. col. of inf., R.C., Army of U.S. Grad. Am. Field Officers' Sch., Langres, France. Mem. S.R., Veterans of Foreign Wars, Am. Legion, Army Assn. of United States. Author of short stories and treatises—"America," "The Constitution," "Who's Running This Country?" etc. Lecturer on "Better Americanism," "Courage or Cowardice," etc. Home: Nuestro Ranchito. Covina Highlands, Covina, Calif. Died Dec. 8, 1947.

SMITH, DANIEL senator; b. Stafford County, Va.; Oct. 28, 1748; s. Henry and Sarah (Crosby) S.; attended Coll. William and Mary; m. Sarah Michie, June 20, 1773, 2 children. Deputy surveyor, 1773; justice of peace, 1776; aided in orgn. Washington County, Va., 1777, became maj. county militia; a surveyor who extended boundary between Va. and N.C., 1779 (established disputed Walker's Line); high sheriff Augusta County, 1780; col. militia, 1781; moved to Cumberland Settlements (now part of Tenn.), 1783; dir. for laying out Town of Nashville (Tenn.), 1784; trustee Davidson Acad., 1785; brig. gen. Mero Dist. (N.C.) Militia, 1788; mem. N.C. Conv. that ratified U.S. Constn., 1789; sec. territory southwest of Ohio River, 1790; made 1st map Tenn., published 1794; mem. Tenn. Constl. Conv., 1796; mem. U.S. Senate from Tenn., 1798-88, 1805-09. Author: A Short Description of the Tennessee Government, 1793. Died "Rock Castle," Sumner County, Tenn., June 6, 1818.

SMITH, DANIEL FLETCHER, JR., naval officer; b. Pittsburgh, Tex., Mar. 31, 1910; s. Daniel Fletcher and Nannie Lou (Hightower) S.; B.S., U.S. Naval Acad., 1932; grad. Nat. War Coll., 1953; m. Virginia Griggs, Apr. 16, 1947; stepchildren—Stephen Griggs Mace, Barbara Virginia (Mrs. Byron C. Campbell). Commd. ensign U.S. Navy, 1932, advanced through grades to rear adm., 1960; service in Pacific Fleet, 1932-35; designated naval aviator, 1936; service aboard carriers U.S.S. Enterprise, Lexington and Independence, World War II; comdr. U.S.S. Randolph, 1956-57; chief navy information, Navy Dept., 1960-62; comdr. Carrier Div. 3, U.S. Pacific Fleet, 1962-64; chief naval air base tng., Pensacola Fla., 1964-67; comdr. Naval Air Test Center, Patuxent River, Md., 1967-71. Decorated D.F.C. with 3 gold stars, Air medal with 1 gold star. Home: Jacksonville FL Died Oct. 5, 1971.

SMITH, EARL BALDWIN educator; b. Topsham, Me., May 25, 1888; s. Frank Eugene and Nellie Frances (Baldwin) S.; grad. Pratt Inst., Bklyn., 1906; A.B., Bowdoin, 1911, L.H.D., 1931; A.M., Princeton, 1912, Ph.D., 1915; m. Ruth Preble Hall, Jan. 27, 1917 (dec. 1927); children—Mary Baldwin, Lacey Baldwin; m. 2d, Helen H. Hough, June 19, 1930; children—Nathaniel Baldwin, Susan Baldwin. Prof. art and archeology Princeton, 1916-—, chmn. 1945; instr. Naval Air Combat Intelligence School, Quonset, R.I.; lectr. on Charles T. Mathews Found., Columbia, 1940. Served as capt., inf., U.S. Army, World War I. Chmn. arts and skills program, Tilton Hosp., Fort Dix; v.p. Princeton Red Cross. Mem. Athenaeum, Archeol. Inst. America, Coll. Art Assn. (dir.), Am. Inst. for Iranian Art and Archeology (dir. 1936-40), Phi Beta Kappa, Psi Upsilon. Clubs: Nassau (Princeton); Princeton (New York); Mountain View Country (ex-pres.). Author: Early Christian Iconography, 1918; Early Churches in Syria, 1929; Egyptian Architecture, 1938; The Dome, 1950; Architectural Symbolism, 1956. Contbr. to Am. Jour. Archeology, Art Studies, Art and Archeology, The Art Bulletin; also chapter on Fine Arts in Roads to Knowledge. Home: 211 Prospect Av., Princeton, N.J. Died Mar. 7, 1956.

SMITH, EDMUND KIRBY army officer, educator, univ. pres.; b. St. Augustine, Fla., May 16, 1824; s. Joseph Lee and Frances (Kirby) S.; grad. U.S. Mil. Acad., 1845; m. Cassie Selden, Sept. 24, 1861, 11 children. Brevetted 2d lt. U.S. Infantry, 1845; brevetted for gallantry at Cerro Gordo and Contreras in Mexican War, 1846-48; asst. prof. mathematics U.S. Mil. Acad., 1849-52; promoted capt. 2d Cavalry, 1855, maj., 1860; commd. lt. col. of cavalry Confederate Army, 1861; brig. gen. in command 4th Brigade, Army of Shenandoah, 1861; commd. maj. gen., 1861; in command dept. of East Tenn., Ky., North Ga., Western N.C., 1862; lt. gen., 1862; in command Trans-Miss. dept., 1863; commd. gen., 1864; last Confederate officer to surrender his force; pres. insurance co.; pres. Atlantic & Pacific Telegraph Co., 1866-68; active layman Protestant Episcopal Ch.; pres. U. Nashville, 1870-75; prof. mathematics U. of South, Sewanee, Tenn., 1875-93; last surviving full general of either U.S. or Confederate Army. Died Sewanee, Mar. 28, 1893.

SMITH, EDWARD HANSON coast guard officer; b. Vineyard Haven, Mass., Oct. 29, 1889; s. Edward Jones and Sarah Elizabeth (Pease) S.; student, Mass. Inst. Tech., 1909-10; grad. U.S. Coast Guard Acad., 1913; A.M., Harvard, 1924, Ph.D., 1934; m. Isabel Brier, July 12, 1924; children—Porter Hulsart, Stuart Edward, Jeremiah. Commd. ensign U.S. Coast Guard, 1913, and advanced through grades to rear adm., 1942; engaged in oceanographic studies at Geo-Physical Inst., Bergen, Norway, 1924; with Brit. Meteorol. Office, London, 1925; comdr., Coast Guard Marion Expedition conducting oceanographic survey of Labrador Sea and Baffin Bay, 1928; mem. sci. staff, Graf Zeppelin Polar Expedition, 1931; comdr., Internat. Ice Patrol force, 1939-40, Task Force 24, 1943-45. Eastern Area, U.S. Coast Guard, also Coast Guard Dist. 3, and capt., since 1945, also comdr. Eastern Area, 1946-50; director Woods Hole Oceanographic Inst., 1950-56. Decorated Cross of Condr., Order of Dannebrog, 1st class (Denmark), Navy D.S.M., Victory Medal with escort clasp, Am. Def. and Victory medals (U.S.). Fellow Arctic Inst. of N. Am.; mem. American Geophysical Union. Episcopalian. Mason. Club: N.Y. Yacht (New York). Died Oct. 1961.

SMITH, ERNEST G(RAY), newspaper pub.; b. Martins Ferry, O., Oct. 26, 1873; s. Hiram Wolfe and Evangaline (Lash) S.; Ph.B., Lafayette Coll., Easton, Pa., 1894, honorary Litt.D., 1943; M.S., 1897; LL.B., Yale University, 1896; married Marjorie Harvey, October 14, 1913; children—Harrison Harvey, Lois Gray, Andries DeWitt. Began as pub. Wilkes-Barre Times Leader, 1905; pres. Wilkes-Barre Pub. Co., T. L. Printery, Inc., Wilkes-Barre Airport Co., Lafayette Press, Inc., Easton, Pa.; dir. Second Nat. Bank, Wilkes-Barre Hotels Corp., Lehigh Valley Railroad, Wyoming Valley Building and Loan Association; vice chmn. Luzerne County Civilian Defense Council; chmn. Luzerne County Blood Plasma and Victory Garden Coms.; mem. Fed. Reserve Bank Bond Sale Com. Served as private and 2d lieutenant infantry U.S. Army, Cuba and Philippines, 1898-1902; major and lieutenant colonel, infantry World War I. President Wilkes-Barre Playground and Recreation Association; v.p. Pa. Parks Assn.; president board trustees F. M. Kirby Am. Legion Foundation; trustee Luzerne County Industrial School; life trustee Lafayette College. Awarded Certificate for long and meritorious service in newspaper work, P.N.P.A. Convention, Waldorf Astoria, New York City, 1943. Co-author Harvey-Smith History of Wilkes-Barre. Decorated D.S.M. (U.S.), 1919; Officer Black Star (France), 1919. Author: History of Northeastern Pennsylvania. Home: 4 Riverside Drive. Address: Times-Leader Bldg., Wilkes-Barre, Pa. Died Dec. 27, 1945.

SMITH, EUGENE ALLEN geologist; b. Autauga County, Ala., Oct. 27, 1841; s. Dr. Samuel P. and Adelaide Julia (Allen) S.; A.B., U. of Ala., 1862; Ph.D., Heidelberg, 1868; attended one semester in Berlin, one in Göttingen, 1865-66, and two in Heidelberg, 1866-68; LL.D., U. of Miss., 1899, U. of Ala., 1906; m. Jennie H., d. of Chancellor Landon C. Garland, of U. of Ala., July 10, 1872. Second lt. Co. K, 33d Ala., C.S.A., 1862; capt. and instr. tactics, 1862-65, prof. geology and mineralogy, 1871-74, chemistry, geology and natural history, 1874-78, chemistry, mineralogy and geology, 1878-90, mineralogy and geology, 1890-—, U. of Ala. State geologist of Ala., 1873-—. Hon. commr. to Paris Expn., 1878; spl. agt. on cotton culture, 10th Census, 1880; mem. Am. Com. Internat. Geol. Congress, 1884-89; mem. jury of awards, expns. at Atlanta, 1895, Nashville, 1897, St. Louis, 1904. Fellow A.A.A.S. (chairman Sect. E, 1904), Geol. Soc. America (council, 1892-95, 2d v.p. 1906, pres. 1913). Mem. State Highway Commn., 1911-23. Home: University, Ala. Died Sept. 7, 1927.

SMITH, F. JANNEY, physician; b. Baltimore, Md., Nov. 18, 1888; s. Dr. B. and Frances Gist (Hopkins) S.; A.B., Johns Hopkins, 1909, M.D., 1913; special course Rockefeller Inst., 1917; m. Jeanie Wilmer Smart, Feb. 14, 1917 (dec.); children—Martha Janney (Mrs. Charles A. McGowan), Virginia Carter, F. Janney (deceased), Robert Gibbons; m. 2d, Colleen F. Forney, May 22, 1948; children—Steven, Holly. Medical House office, Johns Hopkins Hospital, 1913-14; assistant resident physician and instructor in medicine in Johns Hopkins Medical School, 1914-15; first resident physician Henry Ford Hospital at its opening in 1915, physician in charge of cardio-respiratory division, 1919-66, senior consultant in cardiology, 1953-66; private practice of cardiology, 1959-66. Diplomate American Board of Internal Medicine, 1937. 1st lt., captain, M.C., U.S. Army, 1917-19. Fellow American Coll. of Physicians; mem. Am. Clin. and Climatol. Assn., Central Soc. for Clin. Research, Am. Trudeau Soc., Mich. Trudeau Soc., Am. Heart Assn., Wayne County Med. Soc., A.M.A., Johns Hopkins Med. and Surg. Assn., Pithotomy Club, Phi Gamma Delta, Phi Beta Kappa, Alpha Omega Alpha. Clubs: Detroit Boat; Country (Grosse Pointe, Michigan); Witenagemote. Contbr. numerous articles to med. jours. Home: Grosse Pointe Farms MI Died Nov. 9, 1966; buried Woodlawn Cemetery Detroit MI

SMITH, FRANCIS ASBURY lawyer; b. E. Salisbury, Mass., Nov. 29, 1837; s. James Gilman and Polly (Leavitt) S.; A.B., Wesleyan U., Conn., 1859; m. Julia M. Scott, Apr. 11, 1863. Served 2 yrs. in Civil War as 2d lt. 3d N.Y. Inf.; began practice 1864; county judge Essex County, N.Y., 1879-91; mem. law firm of Smith & Wickes, 1898-—. Author: The Critics versus Shakspere, 1907. Address: Elizabethtown, N.Y. Died Oct. 12, 1915.

SMITH, FRANCIS HENNEY army officer, educator; b. Oct. 18, 1812; s. Francis and Ann (Marsden) S.; grad. U.S. Mil. Acad., 1833; m. Sarah Henderson, 1834, 7 children. Tchr., geography, history and ethics U.S. Mil. Acad., 1835, resigned from U.S. Army, 1836; prof. mathematics Hampden-Sydney (Va.) Coll., 1836-39, prin. prof., 1839; supt. Va. Mil. Inst., Lexington, 1840-89, arranged system of instrn. exchange with Washington Coll. (now Washington and Lee U.), 1840-46, recommended expansion of Inst. into gen. scientific sch., 1859; founder Episcopal Ch., Lexington; col. Va. Militia, commanding officer at John Brown's execution; mem. Va. Gov.'s Adv. Bd., 1861; commd. maj. gen. Va. Volunteers, Confederate Army, 1861, in command Craney Island, Va.; returned to head Va. Mil. Inst., 1862, urged immediate rebuilding and reorgn. (after destruction of Inst. in Civil War), 1865, opposed classic edn. prevalent before war, emphasized program of practical studies. Author series of math. textbooks including An Elementary Treatise on Analytical Geometry, 1840. Died Lexington, Va., Mar. 21, 1890.

SMITH, FRANKLIN GUEST brig. gen. U.S.A.; b. nr. Blossburg, Pa., Feb. 16, 1840; s. Franklin R. (M.D.) and Mary (Guest) S.; C.E., Rensselaer Poly. Inst., 1859; m. Frances L. Dauchy, Feb. 8, 1866; m. 2d, Georgiana Dauchy, of San Francisco, Sept. 4, 1881. Pvt. sec. to gen. supt. Ohio & Miss. R.R., 1860-61; pvt. sec. Maj. Gen. George M. McClellan, spring of 1861-Aug. 5, 1861, when apptd. 2d lt. 4th U.S. Arty.; promoted 1st lt., as of same date, and joined army comd. by Gen. D. C. Buell at Louisville, Ky., Jan. 1862; served with that army under Gens. Buell, Rosecrans and Thomas until close of Civil War. Bvtd. capt., Dec. 31, 1862; maj., Sept. 20, 1863. Capt. U.S.A., Feb. 5, 1867; maj. 2d Arty., Aug. 28, 1891; lt. col. 6th Arty., Mar. 8, 1898; col. Arty. Corps, Feb. 2, 1901; brig. gen., Aug. 3, 1903; retired Aug. 4, 1903. Participated in Indian campaigns against Sioux and Cheyennes, 1876-77, against Bannocks, 1878, and against Apaches, 1881; during war with Spain arty. insp., Dept. of the South, and in command of siege train of 100 guns organized at Port Tampa, Fla., for possible use in siege of Havana, but which never left U.S., owing to sudden close of war. From Jan. 1894, to July 1908 (except during war with Spain), commr. and sec. Chickamauga and Chattanooga Nat. Park Commn. Home: Washington, D.C. Died Oct. 7, 1912.

SMITH, FRED M. physician; b. Yale, Ill., May 31, 1888; s. John Alfred and Sarah Ellen (Newlin) S.; student Eastern Ill. State Normal Sch., 1905-09; B.S., U. of Chicago, 1914; M.D., Rush Med. Coll., 1914; post-grad. work, Vienna, 1927; m. Helen Louise Bushee, May 9, 1917; children—Fred Richard, Barbara, James Herrick. Asst. in medicine, Rush Med. Coll., 1916-18, asso., 1918-20, instr., 1920-24, asst. prof. clin. medicine, 1924; prof. theory and practice of medicine and head of dept., State U. of Ia., 1924, prof. internal medicine since 1924. First lt. Med. Corps, 1918-19. Fellow Am. Coll. Physicians; mem. A.M.A., Assn. of Am. Physicians, Am. Soc. for Clin. Investigation, Am. Physiol. Soc., Soc. Exptl. Biology and Medicine, Chicago Inst. of Medicine, Chicago Society Internal Medicine, Association of American Pilgrims (recorder), Phi Delta Theta, Phi Rho Sigma, Sigma Xi. Democrat. Episcopalian. Wrote "The Coronary Arteries" in Cyclopedia of Medicine, 1932; "Diseases of the Heart" in Text Book of Medicine by Musser, 1932; extensive contbr. to med. jours. Editor in chief of American Heart Jour. Home: Ridge Road. Address: University Hospital, Iowa City, Ia. Died Feb. 23, 1946.

SMITH, FREDERICK APPLETON brig. gen. U.S.A.; b. Craigville, N.Y., May 15, 1849; apptd. from N.Y., and grad. U.S. Mil. Acad., 1873; m. Wilhelmina Fowler, Oct. 3, 1878. Commd. 2d lt. 12th Inf., June 13, 1873; 1st lt., June 28, 1878; capt., Dec. 29, 1890; maj. chief commissary subsistence vols., July 16, 1898-June 13, 1899; maj. 1st U.S. Inf., June 20, 1899; detailed insp. gen., Feb. 28, 1901; lt. col. 29th Inf., July 14, 1902; detailed insp. gen., July 30, 1902; col. 8th Inf., Jan. 24, 1904; brig. gen. U.S.A., Oct. 24, 1908. Served in Indian campaigns on Western frontier in Ariz., Dakotas and Nev. Acting asst. adj. gen., hdqrs. Div. of Cuba, July 28-Oct. 1899; comdg. Dist. of Guanajay, Cuba, Oct. 11, 1899-Aug. 1900; in P.I., Sept. 1900-Feb. 1903; detailed insp. gen., Feb. 28, 1901, Dept. Visayas, Aug. 2, 1901, Dept. S. Philippines, Dec. 1901, Dept. Visayas, Sept. 1902-Feb. 1903; insp. gen.'s office, Washington, Feb.-Apr. 1903; gen. staff, Apr. 17, 1903; revising inf. drill regulations, Sept. 9, 1903-July 1904; at Govs. Island, N.Y., July 1904-Feb. 1906; in P.I., Apr. 1906-Apr. 1908; Ft. McDowell, Angel Island, Calif., May 12-Sept. 1908; comdg. Dept. Calif., Oct. 26, 1908-Jan. 13, 1909;

Ft. D. A. Russell, Wyo., Apr. 25, 1909-Mar. 16, 1910; Dept. of the Mo., Mar. 18, 1910-Feb. 15, 1913; Central Div., Chicago, Oct. 31-Nov. 29, 1912; 5th Brig., 2d Div., Feb. 15-Apr. 29, 1913; retired May 15, 1913. Home: New York, N.Y. Died Feb. 4, 1922.

SMITH, GEORGE ALBERT, JR., educator; b. Salt Lake City, Sept. 10, 1905; s. George Albert and Lucy E. (Woodruff) S.; A.B., U. Utah, 1926; M.B.A., Harvard, 1934, D.C.S., 1937; m. Ruth H. Nowell, July 6, 1935; children—George Albert, III, Samuel N., Robert N. Missionary, adminstrv. officer Swiss-German Mission Ch. Jesus Christ of Latter-day Saints, Basel, Switzerland, 1926-29; in business, 1929-32; mem. faculty, grad. sch. bus. adminstrn. Harvard, 1934-69, prof. bus. adminstrn., 1945-69, sr. asst. dean, 1939-45; vis. instr. bus. adminstrn. Yale Law Sch., 1937-38; visiting professor Stanford University, 1954; vis. professor University Hawaii, summer 1964; special cons. business orgns., ednl. instns. and U.S. Government Depts. and agencies, 1936-69. Served as capt., chaplain corps, 222 F.A., Utah, N.G., 1930-33; asst. dir., dir. Spl. Navy Supply Corps O.T.S., 1942-46. Mem. Am. Econ. Assn., Am. Acad. Polit. Sci., Am. Soc. Pub. Admintrn. Am. Petroleum Inst., Sigma Chi, Phi Kappa Phi. Author: Policy Formulation and Administration, 1950. Co-author rev. editions 1955, 59, 62; Managing Geographically Decentralized Companies, 1958; Business, Society & the Invididual, 1962. Home: Belmont MA Died Oct. 12, 1969; buried Salt Lake City Cemetery.

SMITH, GEORGE MILTON surgeon; b. Hong Kong, China, July 5, 1879; s. Jay Henry and Elisabeth (Connor) S.; A.B., Yale University, 1901, honorary LL.D., 1947; M.D., Columbia University, 1905; married Lucy Clare Young, May 21, 1910; 1 daughter, Clare Connor (Mrs. Sidney Webb Noyes, Jr). Came to U.S., as child, parents U.S. citizens. Interne Presbyn. Hosp., and Sloan Maternity Hosp., N.Y. City, 1905-09; asso. prof. pathology Washington U., St. Louis, Missouri, 1909-16; dir. Barnard Free Skin and Cancer Hospital, St. Louis, Missouri, 1916; research asso. rank prof. emeritus Yale since 1948. Served as capt. med. corps mobile hosp. 39, U.S. Army, 1917-19, with A.E.F. Med. dir. Anna Fuller Fund since 1933; mem. bd. sci. advisors Jane Coffin Childs Meml. Fund Med. Research; med. dir. Conn. State Defense Council, 1941-43, Conn. War Council, 1943-45; chmn. sub-com. on armored vehicles, Nat. Research Council, 1942-46; consultant to surg. gen. of Army, 1944-46. Pres. Conn. State Med. Soc., 1943-44. Mem. Nat. Adv. Cancer Council 1939-46; exec. dir. 1944-46; special consultant, 1947-—. Recipient citations War Dept.; medal American Cancer Soc., 1949; Bertner Found. award (posthumously), 1952; decorated Cross of Knighthood of Dannebrog (Denmark). Mem. Am. Assn. Anatomists, Pathol. Soc. Great Brit. and Ireland; fgn. corr. French Assn. for Study of Cancer. Episcopalian. Contbr. research papers on cancer to med. jours. Home: Pine Orchard, Conn. Office: 333 Cedar St., New Haven. Died Feb. 26, 1951; buried Center Cemetery, Branford, Conn.

SMITH, GEORGE RODNEY army officer; b. at Smith's Mills, Chautauqua Co., N.Y., May 7, 1850; s. Hiram and Melissa Phelps (Love) S.; grad. Collegiate Inst., Jamestown, N.Y., 1869; grad. of the U.S. Mil. Acad., 1875; m. Corinne Barrett, of Jamestown, Aug. 19, 1879. Commd. 2d. lt., 12th U.S. Inf., June 16, 1875; 1st lt., Jan. 11, 1881; maj. and p.m., July 5, 1882; lt.-col., deputy p.m.-gen., Jan. 25, 1904; col., asst. p.m.-gen., Apr. 7, 1908; p.m.-gen., Feb. 16, 1912; brig.-gen., Q.M. Corps, Nov. 1, 1912; retired, Feb. 15, 1913. Mem. Loyal Legion, Mil. Order of Carabao. Campaign badges for service against Apache Indians and druing insurrection in the Philippines. Clubs: Army and Navy, Chevy Chase. Address: The Parkwood, Washington.

SMITH, GILES ALEXANDER army officer; b. Jefferson County, N.Y., Sept. 29, 1829; s. Cyrus and Laura (Wales) S.; m. Martha McLain, July 31, 1856. Commd. capt. 8th Mo. Volunteer Regt., 1861, lt. col., 1862, col., 1862; in command of brigade in Vicksburg campaign; commd. brig. gen. U.S. Volunteers, 1863; in command 2d div. XVII Corps, U.S. Army, 1864; brevetted maj. gen. U.S. Volunteers 1865; mustered out, 1865; 2d asst. postmaster gen. U.S. 1869-72. Died Bloomington, Ill., Nov. 5, 1876.

SMITH, GREEN CLAY congressman, clergyman; b. Richmond, Madison County, Ky., July 4, 1826; s. John Speed Smith; grad. Transylvania U., Lexington, Ky., 1849; studied law. Served as 2d lt. 1st Regt. Ky. Volunteer Infantry in Mexican War, 1846-47; admitted to bar, 1852, practiced in Covington, Ky.; sch. commr., 1853-57; mem. Ky. Ho. of Reps., 1861-63; commd. col. 4th Regt., Ky. Volunteer Cavalry during Civil War, 1862; brig. gen. Volunteers, 1862, resigned, 1863; brevetted maj. gen. of Volunteers, 1865; mem. U.S. Ho. of Reps. (Union Party) from Ky., 38th-39th congresses, 1863-66 (resigned); gov. Mont. Territory (apptd. by Pres. Johnson), 1866-69; moved to Washington, D.C., ordained to ministry Baptist Ch.; became evangelist; Nat. Prohibition Party candidate for Pres. U.S., 1876; pastor Met. Bapt. Ch., Washington, 1890-95. Died June 29, 1895; buried Arlington (Va.) Nat. Cemetery.

SMITH, GUSTAVUS WOODSON army officer, engr.; b. Georgetown, Scott County, Ky., Mar. 1822; s. Byrd and Sarah Hatcher (Woodson) S.; grad. U.S. Mil. Acad., 1842; m. Lucretia Bassett, Oct. 3, 1844. Instr. civil, mil. engring. U.S. Mil. Acad., 1844-46; brevetted 1st lt., then capt., maj. U.S. Army for services at Vera Cruz, Cerro Gordo, Contreras, Churubusco, Mexico City, 1846-48; asst. prof. engring. U.S. Mil. Acad., 1848-54; designated by Treasury Dept. to supervise repairs to the Mint, and constrn. Marine Hosp., New Orleans, 1855; chief engr. Trenton Iron Works, 1856-58; street commr., N.Y.C., 1858-61; commd. maj. gen. 2d Corps, Confederate Provisional Army, 1861; commanded a wing of Army of No. Va. until conclusion Peninsular Campaign; commanded sector from right of Lee's theatre of operations on the Rappahannock to Cape Fear River with hdqrs. Richmond, 1862; sec. of war Confederate States Am., 1862; resigned commn. as maj. gen. Confederate Army, 1862; commd. maj. gen. to command 1st Div., Ga. Militia, 1864, assigned a sector in Dept. of S.C., Ga., Fla.; surrendered 1865; gen. mgr. Southwestern Iron Co., Chattanooga, Tenn., 1866-70; 1st ins. commr., Ky., 1870-75. Author: Notes on Life Insurance, 1870; Confederate War Papers, 1884; The Battle of Seven Pines, 1891. Died N.Y.C., June 24, 1896.

SMITH, HAROLD LEONARD, lawyer; b. Shelton, Conn., Dec. 30,21896; s. Leonard Charles and Elizabeth Evalena (Burke) S.; Bachelor Arts, Trinity College, 1922, Doctor of Laws (honorary), 1958; LL.B., Harvard, 1925; m. Emma Marie Teitscheid, July 30, 1927; 1 son, Harold Leonard. Newspaper reporter Eve. Sentinel, Derby, Conn., 1915-17; admitted to N.Y. bar, 1926, Conn., 1927; in gen. practice law, N.Y. City, 1926-71; asso. Hughes, Schurman & Dwight, 1925-34, mem. firm. 1934-37; mem. of law firm Hughes, Hubbard and Reed, 1937-71. Mem. bd. trustees Scarsdale (N.Y.) Sch. Dist., No. 2, 1940-43; bd. sch. dirs., 2d Supervisory Sch. Dist., Westchester Co., N.Y., 1941-48; mem. bd. trustees Village of Scarsdale, 1948-51, mayor of village, 1951-53. Alumni mem. bd. trustees Trinity Coll., 1947-53. Served as 2d lt., F.A., U.S. Army, World War I; mem. Squadron A, N.Y. N.G., 1926-30. Mem. Am. and N.Y. State bar assns., Assn. Bar City of N.Y., N.Y. Co. Lawers Assn., Am. Legion, Phi Beta Kappa, Sigma Nu. Republican. Presbyn. Clubs: Downtown Athletic, Down Town Assn., Squadron A Ex-Members Association (N.Y.C.); Skytop (Pa.). Home: Edmonds WA Died Aug. 17, 1971.

SMITH, HAROLD TRAVIS naval officer; b. Mpls., June 7, 1887; B.S., U.S. Naval Acad., 1909, grad. work, 1914; M.S., Columbia, 1915. Commd. as ensign U.S. Navy, 1909, and advanced through the grades to rear admiral, 1945; instr. engring., U.S.S. Fulton, 1915-17; in charge fitting out U.S.S. 0-5, 1917-18; engring. aide on staff comdr. submarine force Atlantic fleet U.S.S. Chgo. flagship, 1918; on duty at periscope sch., Portsmouth, Va., 1918; attached to naval hdqrs., London, Eng., 1918-19; assigned U.S.S. Bushnell, assigned U.S.S. Fulton with spl. duty on German subs, 1919; tour of duty Bur. of Engring., Navy Dept., Washington, 1919-21; in charge outfitting U.S.S. Omaha, Todd Dry Dock & Constrn. Co., Tacoma, 1921-23; engr. officer U.S.S. Omaha, 1923-25; assigned to Navy Yard, Portsmouth, N.H., 1925-26; tour of duty bur. engring., Navy Dept., Washington, 1926-30; aide and engr. officer staff comdr. cruisers, scouting force U.S. Fleet, 1930-32; in charge central draughting office N.Y. Navy Yard, 1932-35; Bur. Engring., Navy Dept., Washington, 1935-39; naval insp. machinery and navigation material, Bethlehem Steel Co., Quincy, Mass., 1939-40; became supervisor shipbuilding and naval insp. of ordnance Bethlehem Steel Co., Quincy, Mass. and other shipbldg. and ordnance plants in R.I. and Mass., 1940; now mem. staff Comdr.-in-Chief Pacific Fleet. Decorated Victory Medal, Escort Clasp, U.S.S. Chicago, Am. Defense Service Medal, Address: Navy Dept., Washington. Deceased.

SMITH, HAROLD WELLINGTON naval med. officer; b. Boston, Mass., May 30, 1878; s. Wellington and Mary Eleanor (Dodge) S.; student Harvard Coll., 1897-97, M.D., Med. Sch., 1901; m. Mary Currier Eaton, Nov. 10, 1913 (died 1924); children—Margaret (Mrs. W. F. LaMond), Stephen Currier. Commd. asst. surgeon, U.S. Navy, 1904, and advanced through ranks to rear adm., Med. Corps, 1936. Mem. Med. Com. of Office of Scientific Research and Development. Mem. A.M.A. (house of dels.), Assn. Mil. Surgeons (mem. exec. council), Am. Coll. Surgeons (mem. bd. of govs.), Am. Acad. Tropical Medicine (councillor), U.S. Naval Inst. Unitarian. Clubs: Harvard, Army and Navy (Washington). Author med. articles for U.S. Naval Med. Bulletin. In charge of med. research in U.S. Navy. Home: 4000 Cathedral Av. Office: Bureau Medicine and Surgery, Navy Dept., Washington. Died Feb. 4, 1952; buried Forest Hills Cemetery, Jamaica Plains, Boston.

SMITH, HARRY ALEXANDER army officer; b. Atchison, Kan., June 18, 1866; s. Henry T. and Anna S.; grad. U.S. Mil. Acad., 1891; distinguished grad. Army Sch. of the Line, 1908; grad. Army Staff Coll., 1909; m. Harriet Newcomb, Oct. 27, 1892; children—Newcomb, William A. Commd. 2d lt. 1st Inf., June 12, 1891; promoted through grades to col., Aug. 5, 1917; brig. gen. N.A., June 26, 1918-July 31, 1919; brig. gen. regular army, May 10, 1922; maj. gen., Sept. 20, 1926. With regt. in Calif., 1891-96; on duty with Kan. Nat. Guard, 1896-98, maj. 21st Kan. Vols., Apr. 26-Dec. 10, 1898; in Cuba, 1899-1900; in Philippines, 1900-02, 1905-07; sr. instr., dept. of law, Army Service Schs., 1909-12; instr. dept. of mil. art, Army Service Schs., 1912-14; in charge dept. of justice and of pub. safety, Vera Cruz, Mexico, May 1-Nov. 21, 1914; adj. 5th Brigade, Galveston, Tex., Jan.-Oct. 1915; in China, Apr. 1916-Aug. 1917; duty Gen. Staff, War Dept., Sept. 26-Nov. 19, 1917; arrived in France, Nov. 26, 1917; asst. comdt. Army Service Schs., France, Feb.-May 1918, comdt. May 1-Nov. 11, 1918; in charge civil affairs, Germany, Nov. 11, 1918-July 9, 1919; asst. comdt. Gen. Staff Coll., Washington, D.C., Aug. 1, 1919-Oct. 1, 1922; comdg. 16th Inf. Brig., Oct. 1, 1922-June 30, 1923; comdt. Gen. Service Schs., Ft. Leavenworth, Kan., 1923-25; apptd. asst. chief of staff, War Plans Div., July 1, 1925; mil. del. to Limitation of Arms Conf., Geneva, May 1926; rep. of U.S. Government at coronation of Shah of Persia, Apr. 26, 1926; comdg. gen. 7th Corps Area, June 1, 1927-—. Awarded D.S.M.; Legion of Honor (French); Companion of the Bath (British); Comdr. Order of the Crown of Oak (Luxemburg); Comdr. Order of Solidaridid (Panama). Presbyn. Home: Atchison, Kan. Died May 26, 1929.

SMITH, HARRY EATON naval officer; b. Fremont, O., Dec. 28, 1869; s. Henry Bishop and Eta Beary (Dalton) S.; grad. U.S. Naval Acad., 1891; m. Fanny, d. of ex-President Hayes, Sept. 1, 1897; 1 son, Dalton Hayes; m. 2d, Olga, d. C. A. Bengtson, 1920; children—Harry Eaton, Robert Giesé. Commissioned ensign U.S.N., 1893; lt. (j.g.), 1899; lt., 1900; lt. comdr., 1906; transferred to corps of profs. of mathematics, 1906; comdr., Aug. 10, 1907; capt., 1919. Duty U.S. Naval Acad., 1903-15, and head of dept. mathematics, 1912-15; U.S. Naval Obs., 1915; retired, Mar. 30, 1920. In charge of a group of gold mines, Shasta, Calif. Author: Strength of Material, 1908; Theoretical Mechanics (text-books for midshipmen). Home: Shasta, Calif. Died Mar. 26, 1931.

SMITH, HENRY GERRISH shipbuilder; b. Warrensville, O., Apr. 9, 1870; s. Erastus and Martha (March) S.; grad. U.S. Naval Acad., 1891; studied Royal Naval Coll., Eng., 1891-94; m. Betty Dent, Oct. 9, 1895 (dec.); children—Mrs. Betty Dent Walker, Charles Raymond; m. 2d, Lucy Margaret Gleason, Sept. 24, 1936. Midshipman U.S. Navy, 1887-93; naval constructor U.S. Navy, at Royal Naval Coll., Cramps Shipyard, N.Y. Navy Yard, Bur. of Construction and Repair, Navy Dept., Washington; resigned from Navy, 1903, to become mgr. Fore River Shipbuilding Co. (later Fore River Shipbuilding Corp.), v.p., gen. mgr., 1913-17; mgr. Bethlehem Shipbuilding Corp., Ltd., 1917-21, asst. to pres. 1921, v.p., 1923-32; pres. Shipbuilders Council of Am., 1929-50, chmn. bd., 1950-—. Mem. classification Lloyds, U.S. del. to Internat. Conv. of Safety of Life at Sea, London, 1929. Mem. Soc. Naval Architects and Marine Engrs., 1893-— (sec.-treas. 1932-39; pres. 1939 and 1940); bd. mgrs. Am. Bur. Shipping. Chmn. Shipbldg. and Ship Repairing Industry Code Authority, 1933-35. Rep. Episcopalian. Home: Bronxville, N.Y. Address: 21 West St., N.Y.C. Died June, 1959.

SMITH, HENRY LEE, JR., educator; b. Morristown, N.J., July 11, 1913; s. Henry Lee and Elise Garr (Henry) S.; A.B. summa cum laude, Princeton, 1935, M.A., 1937, Ph.D., 1938; Litt.D., Wagner Coll., S.I., 1961; m. Virginia von Wodtke, Aug. 10, 1946; children—Heather, Marshall, Randolph, Letitia. Lectr. English, Barnard Coll., Columbia, 1938-40; instr. English, Brown U., 1940-42; condr. program Where Are You From, radio sta. WOR, 1939-41; asst. chief div. tng. service Dept. State, 1946-47, asst. dir. Fgn. Service Inst., dir., prof. linguistics sch. langs. and linguistics Fgn. Service Inst., 1947-53, dean sch. langs., 1955-56, prof. linguistics and English, State U. N.Y. at Buffalo, 1956, acting dir. program in linguistics, 1967-68, chmn. dept. anthropology, 1956-65; vis. prof. linguistics U. State N.Y., 1949, 61, dir. communications workshop, 1950, 61; vis. prof. Linguistic Inst., Ind. U., 1951; vis. prof. linguistics U. Pa., 1965-66; adv. com. Fulbright and Smith-Mundt applicants English, 1953-57; Inglis lectr. Harvard, 1954. Mem. grad. adv. council Princeton U. Dept. Oriental Studies, 1961-70; cons. Ford Found., 1960-61. Served as maj., edn. br., information and edn. div., AUS, 1942-45; with Office Provost Marshal Gen., 1945-46. Fellow A.A.A.S. (mem. council), Am. Anthrop. Assn. (del. to div. anthropology and psychology NRC and Nat. Acad. Sci. 1960-63); mem. Washington Acad. Sci., Linguistic Soc. Am. (exec. com. 1960-63, 69), N.Y. Council Tchrs. English (chmn. com. linguistics 1961-66), Soc. Gen. Semantics, Anthrop. Soc. Washington, Am. Council Learned Socs. (com. lang. program 1946-59), Soc. Colonial Wars, S.R., Phi Beta Kappa. Clubs: Saturn, Buffalo Canoe (Buffalo); Princeton University Elm; Princeton (N.Y.C.); Cosmos (Washington). Author: An Outline of English Structure (with George L. Trager), 1951; Linguistic Science and the Teaching of English, 1956; Linguistic Readers series, 1963-67; English Morphophonics; Implications for the Teaching of Literacy, 1968; also numerous ednl. TV films on lang. and linguistics, 1959. Contbr. profl. publs; linguistic adv. panel Am. Heritage Dictionaries, 1966-69. Del. 3d, 4th UNESCO Nat. Confs., 1951, 53, Home: Buffalo NY Died Dec. 13, 1972.

SMITH, HOLLAND MCTYEIRE marine Corps officer; b. Russell County, Ala., Apr. 20, 1882; s. John V. and Corrie E. (McTyeire) S.; B.S., LL.D., Ala. Poly. Inst., 1901; LL.B., U. Ala., 1903; m. Ada B. Wilkinson, Apr. 12, 1909; 1 son, John Victor. Admitted to Ala. bar, 1903, began practice law; commd. 2d lt. U.S. Marine Corps, 1905; promoted through grades to col., 1934, brig. gen., 1938, maj. gen., Feb. 1941; Lt. Gen., Feb. 1944; gen. Aug. 1, 1946, ret.; hon. sgt. 30th Bn., Chaussers a Pied, French Army; asst. comdt. U.S. Marine Corps, Apr.-Sept. 1939; dir. operations and tng., 1937-39; comdg. gen. Amphibious Force, Atlantic Fleet, 1941; comdr. Amphibious Corps, Aleutian Islands, 1943; assult comdr. Gilbert Islands, Marianna Islands, Marshall Islands, Feb. 1944; comdg. gen. in capture Iwo Jima, Feb. 1945. Decorated Croix de Guerre with palm, Santo Domingo medal, Mexican medal, Victory medal, Purple Heart, Marine Corps Expeditionary 3 stars, Order of Merit, D.S.M. with 3 gold stars; 1st class (Rep. Santo Domingo), Comdr. the Bath (Brit.). Mem. Alpha Tau Omega. Democrat. Methodist. Clubs: Bohemian (San Francisco); Army and Navy (Washington); Army and Navy Country (Arlington, Va.). Home: 1821 Viking Way, LaJolla, Cal. Died Jan. 12, 1967; buried Fort Rosecrans Nat. Cemetery, San Diego.

SMITH, HUBERT WINSTON, educator; born Tex., May 18, 1907; s. Thomas and Myrtle (Hawkins) S.; A.B., U. Tex., 1927, M.B.A., 1931; student U. Edinburgh, 1936-38; LL.B., Harvard (Faculty scholarship), 1930, M.D. (Henry Cabot Jackson fellow 1939-41), 1941; m. Catherine Hall McKinley, Aug. 26, 1936; children—Charles McKinley, Alan Winston, Stephen Hall, James Jackson. Asso. Price Waterhouse & Co., accts., Boston, 1928-29; admitted to Tex. bar, 1930; asso. Thompson, Knight, Baker & Harris, Dallas, 1930-34; partner Smith & Carter, 1934-36; prof. law Jefferson U., eves. 1930-35; demonstrator anatomy, med. sch. U. Edinburgh, 1936-37; Research fellow Rockefeller Found., asso. med.-legal research, law and med. schs. Harvard, 1941-44, prof. legal medicine U. Ill., 1945-49; research prof. law and medicine, prof. law and legal medicine, dir. law-sci. program Tulane U., 1949-52; lecturer legal medicine, med. school La. State U., 1951-52; professor law, sch. law, prof. legal medicine, sch. medicine (Galveston), and dir. law-sci. inst. U. Tex., 1952-67; chancellor of Law-Science Acad., 1967-71; dir. inter-profl. studies Coll. Law U. Okla., Norman, also cons. prof. dept. psychiatry and behavioral scis., U. Okla. Med. Center, Oklahoma City, 1968-71; lectr. legal aspects of psychiatry Menninger Clinic and Found. Member Nat. Bd. Med. Examiners. Cons. legal medicine V.A. Hosp., Houston; sometime cons. forensic psychiatry U.S. Pub. Health Hosp., Ft. Worth and V.A. Hosp., Gulfport, Tex. Mem. Coroner's Commn., Orleans Parish. Nat. adv. Am. Assn. Psychiatric Treatment Criminal Offenders; founder Law-Sci. Movement, Law-Sci. Short Course for trial lawyers; chmn. com. mental states and law La. State Inst., 1951-52. Mem. White House Conf. Problems Children and Youth, 1951; mem. com. on reform of Law of Evidence (Tex.); com. on cooperation of Tex. State Bar with med. profession. Served as lt. officer charge legal med. br. Bur. Medicine and Surgery, U.S.N., 1944-45. Awarded Sir Wright Smith prize in med. botany, 1937; Foster award, med. sch. Harvard, 1938; Milton award in sci. research, 1942-43; Gold medal, citation Law-Science Academy, 1959. Research fellow Rockefeller Found., 1941-44; fellow and chancellor Law Sci. Acad. Am.; pres. Law Sci. Found. Am. Mem. Nat. Bd. Med. Examiners. Fellow Internat.Academy Trial Lawyers and the New York Academy of Medicine; member Am. Soc. Science, Research, Mass. Soc. C.P.A. (hon.), Law-Sci. Acad. Am., Law-Sci. Found. Am. (pres.), Scribes, Phi Beta Kappa, Beta Alpha Psi, Beta Gamma Sigma, Order of Coif, Phi Delta Phi. Episcopalian. Author numerous monographs and articles in medico-legal field. Editor: National Symposia on Scientific Proof and Relations of Law and Medicine, 1941, 46; asso. editor Jour. Criminal Law and Criminology, 1946-60. Editor-in-chief, coordinator, contbr. Symposium on Law and Science, 1969. Home: Norman OK Died July 9, 1971; buried Sparkman-Hillcrest Meml. Park, Dallas TX

SMITH, HUGH CARNES army officer; b. Trenton, Mo., Apr. 17, 1873; s. George Washington and Rose Margaret (Carnes) S.; LL.B., U. of Michigan, 1894; LL.M., American U., Washington, D.C., 1924; m. Leona Conover, Sept. 26, 1899; children—Conover Carnes (officer U.S. Army), Hule Austin (officer U.S. Army). Admitted to Mo. bar, 1894, Supreme Court of U.S., 1919, dist. court of D.C., 1937, U.S. Court of Appeals for D.C., 1939; in gen. practice of law, Trenton, Mo., 1894-1905; prosecuting atty., Grundy County, Mo., 1899-1903; general practice of law, St. Joseph, Mo., 1905-10; 1st asst. U.S. atty. Western Dist. Missouri, 1910-13; in gen. practice of law, Kansas City, Mo., 1913-18, also lecturer on medical jurisprudence, Kansas City Dental Coll.; in mil. service, 1918-37; gen. practice of law, Washington, D.C., also asst. gen. counsel in U.S. for Puerto Rico, 1937-40; mil. service since 1940; dir. Richards & Conover Hardware Co., Kansas City, Mo., and Oklahoma City, Okla. Served as major, Judge Adv. Gen.'s Dept., U.S. Army, 1918; asst. judge adv., G.Q.H., A.E.F., 1918-19, disch., 1920; commd. lt. col., 1920; gen. counsel and later mem. War Dept. Bd. of Contract Adjustment, 1920-21; served as mem. mil. justice sect. Judge Adv. Gen.'s Dept., later chief of sect., mem. review bd., 1920-24, corps area judge adv., III Corps Area, Baltimore, Md., 1924-25, dept. judge advocate, Philippine Dept., 1925-27; chief civil affairs sect. and chief contract and reservations sect., Judge Adv. Gen.'s Office, 1927-31, head of commn. to Europe to investigate foreign patent claims, 1929; promoted to colonel, May 1, 1931; corps area judge advocate, IX Corps Area, San Francisco, California, 1931-34; the assistant judge advocate general and intermittently acting judge advocate general, 1934-37; retired, 1937; recalled to active duty, 1940; chief legal sect. purchase and contracts branch office, asst. secretary of war (later office under sec. of war), chmn. advisory com. on claims Mar.-Aug. 1942; pres. War Dept. Bd. of Contract Appeals since Aug. 1942. Awarded Legion of Merit, Sept. 1945. Mem. Am., Mo., Fed. and D.C. bar assns., Am. Judicature Soc., Am. Soc. Internat. Law, Sigma Chi. An organizer Inter-Am. Bar Assn. Club: Army and Navy (Washington). Home: 4343 Cathedral Av. N.W., Washington 16, D.C. Colonel Hugh Carnes Smith died March 30, 1946.

SMITH, JACOB HURD brig. gen. U.S.A.; b. Jackson, Iron Furnace, O., Jan. 29, 1840; s. J. M. G. S.; grad. Collegiate and Commercial Inst., New Haven, Conn., 1858; m. Adelaide M. Hall, of Topeka, Kan., Feb. 4, 1885. Enlisted for Civil War, May 8, 1861; 1st lt. 2d Ky. Inf., June 5, 1861; capt., Jan. 28, 1862; hon. mustered out, June 29, 1863; capt. Veteran Reserve Corps, June 25, 1863; hon. mustered out, Oct. 21, 1865; capt. 13th Inf. U.S.A., Mar. 7, 1867; maj. judge advocate May 25, 1869; aj. 2d Inf., Nov. 26, 1894; lt. col. 12th Inf., June 30, 1898; lt. col. 17th Inf., Oct. 20, 1899; brig. gen. vols., June 1, 1900; brig. gen. U.S.A., Mar. 30, 1901; retired, July 17, 1901. Bvtd. maj. Mar. 7, 1867, "for gallantry in battle of Shiloh, Tenn., Apr. 6, 1862"; twice wounded; in Indian wars of frontier, 1867-98; participated in Spanish-Am. War, 1898, in Philippines, 1899. Address: Washington, D.C. Died Mar. 2, 1918.

SMITH, JAMES pioneer, army officer, author; b. Conococheague Settlement, Franklin County, Pa., 1737; m. Anne Wilson, May 1763; m. 2d, Margaret (Rodgers) Irvin, 1785; 7 children. Frontier leader, settled Franklin County, Pa., 1760; leader "Black Boys" whose purpose was to defend frontier settlements, 1763, 65, 69; lt. in Bouquets' expdn. against Ohio Indians, 1764; served in militia to defend Pa. frontier from Indians, 1760's; mem. bd. commrs. Bedford County (Pa.), 1771, Westmoreland County (Pa.), 1773; active Westmoreland County govt., 1771-77; moved to Ky., 1788; mem. Ky. Constl. Conv., 1792; mem. Gen. Assembly of Ky.; An Account of the Remarkable Occurences in the Life and Travels of Col. James Smith, During his Captivity with the Indians in the Years, 1755-59, published 1799, also a pamphlet about Shakers, 1810. Died Washington County, Ky., 1813.

SMITH, JAMES ARGYLE marshal State Supreme Court of Miss.; b. July 1, 1831; ed. common schools until 1848, when was apptd. at large to U. S. Mil. Acad.; whence he was grad. July 1, 1853; apptd. 2d lt. 6th U. S. inf.; served on Western frontier and Pacific coast until March, 1861, when resigned and entered Confederate service as 1st lt.; passed through different grades and was apptd. brig.-gen., Nov. 19, 1863. Since the war engaged principally in ednl. work; State supt. of edn. of Miss., 1878; re-elected, 1882; in U. S. Indian service, 1893-97; Democrat. Address: Jackson, Miss.

SMITH, JAMES FRANCIS judge; b. San Francisco, Calif., Jan. 28, 1859; s. Patrick and Anne S.; grad. Santa Clara Coll., 1878, A.M.; studied law Hastings Law Sch., Calif.; admitted to bar, Jan. 1881; m. Lillie A. Dunnigan, Aug. 13, 1885 (dec.); 1 son, Cyril J. Became col. 1st Calif. Regt., U.S.V., Apr. 1898; served 1st expdn. to Philippines, arriving June 30, 1898; was in battle of Malate Trenches, July 31, 1898, taking of Manila, Aug. 13, 1898; dep. provost marshal, Manila, Aug. 1898; pres. Mil. Commn., Oct. 12, 1899; comd. 1st Brigade, 1st Div. 8th Army Corps, Oct. 22, 1898; mem. commn. to confer with commn. from Aguinaldo, Jan. 1899; in battle of Santa Aña, Feb. 5, 1899; in fighting at San Pedro Mecati, Pateros and Taguig, Feb. 15, to Mar. 1, 1899; commended for gallantry in dispatches; in command Island of Negros, March 1, 1899; brig. gen. U.S.V., Apr. 24, 1899; comd. Dept. Visayas, Apr. 1899; mil. gov. Island of Negros, July 24, 1899; collector customs, Philippine Archipelago, Oct. 1900; hon. discharged, June 17, 1901. Asso. justice Supreme Court of P.I., June 17, 1901; mem. Philippine Commn. and sec. of Pub. Instrn., P.I., Jan. 1, 1903-06; gov. gen. of P.I., Sept. 20, 1906-Nov. 11, 1909 (resigned); apptd. asso. judge U.S. Ct. of Customs Appeals, 1910. Home: Cloverdale, Calif. Died June 29, 1928.

SMITH, JAMES POWER clergyman; b. New Athens, O., July 4, 1837; s. Rev. Joseph (D.D.) and Eliza (Bell) S.; B.A., Jefferson Coll., Pa., 1856; grad. Union Theol. Sem., Va., 1861; (D.D., Hampden-Sidney College, Va.); married Agnes Lacy, of Chatham (Fredericksburg), Va., Apr. 25, 1871. Served in Confederate Army as corporal in Rockbridge Arty. and ad capt. and a.-d.-c. staff of Gen. Stonewall Jackson and Lt.-Gen. Ewell. Ordained Presbyn. ministry, 1866; pastor Roanoke, Va., 1866-69, Fredericksburg, 1869-92; editor Central Presbyterian, Richmond, Va., 1893-1911. Stated clerk, Synod of Va., 1870-—; pres. Presbyn. Bd. of Publication. Chaplain Battalion Va. Arty., N.G.; chaplain Lee Camp No. 1, C.V., Richmond; pres. Jackson Monument Assn. Mem. Southern Hist. Soc. (sec.), Alpha Chapter Phi Beta Kappa (William and Mary Coll., Va.). Author: Brightside Idyls, 1896; Stonewall Jackson at Chancellorsville; General Lee at Gettysburg; Both a King and a Father, 1898. Address: 10 N. 4th St., Richmond, Va.

SMITH, JEREMIAH JR. lawyer; b. Dover, N.H., Jan. 14, 1870; s. Jeremiah and Hannah (Webster) S.; A.B., Harvard, 1892, LL.B., 1895; unmarried. Sec. to Justice Gray, of Supreme Ct. of U.S., 1895-96; practiced in Boston, 1896-—; mem. firm of Herrick, Smith, Donald & Farley. Served with A.E.F. as capt. Q.-M. Corps; with Am. Mission to Negotiate Peace as counsel to Treasury Dept. and an adviser on financial questions; commr. gen. League of Nations for Hungary, 1924-26, in charge of financial reconstruction of Hungary. Trustee Phillips Exeter Acad., N.H.; fellow Harvard Coll. Democrat. Home: Cambridge, Mass. Died Mar. 12, 1935.

SMITH, JOHN adventurer, colonial gov. Va.; b. Willoughby, Lincolnshire, Eng., Jan. 1579; s. George and Alice S. Mil. adventurer in war against Turks, circa 1597-1604; a promoter and organizer Va. Company of London, 1606, arrive Jamestown; Va., May 1607, mem. governing council of colony; taken prisoner by Indians while on expdn. to obtain food, 1607, sentenced to death, according to legend saved by Pocahontas, dau. of Powhatan; returned to Jamestown, 1608, arrested and condemned to hang, but soon released and restored to place on council; explored Potomac and Rappahannock rivers and Chesapeake Bay, summer 1608; pres. council, gov. Va., 1608-09, saved settlers from starvation by getting corn from Indians; sailed for Eng., 1609; sailed to New Eng., 1614, explored coast, returned with cargo of furs and fish, pointing up value of trade and colonization. Author: A Map of Virginia, With a Description of the Country, the Commodities, People, Government and Religion, 1612; A Description of New England (containing highly useful map of New Eng.), 1616; New England Trials, 1620; The General Historie of Virginia, New England, and the Summer Isles, 1624; The True Travels, Adventures, and Observations of Captaine John Smith, in Europe, Asis, Affrica, and America, 1630; Advertisements for the Inexperienced Planters of New England (which offered advice on settlement in colonies based on experience as explorer), 1631. Died June 21, 1631.

SMITH, JOHN congressman, army officer, farmer; b. Shooter's Hill, nr. Locust Hill, Middlesex County, Va., May 7, 1750. Moved to Frederick County, Va., 1773, became planter at Hackwood, nr. Winchester, acquired large land holdings; commd. by gov. as one of King's justices, 1773; apptd. col. by Va. Council of Safety, 1776; promoted lt. of county militia by Gov. Patrick Henry, 1777; commd. lt. col. commandant by Gov. Henry Lee, 1793, brig. gen. by Gov. James Monroe, 1801, maj. gen. 3d Div., Va. Troops, 1811-36; served in Dunmore's War with Indians, 1774, Revolutionary War and War of 1812; mem. Va. Ho. of Dels., 1779-83; mem. Va. Senate, 1792-95, 96; mem. U.S. Ho. of Reps. (Democrat) from Va., 7th-13th congresses, 1801-15. Died at Rockville, nr. Middletown, Frederick County, Mar. 15, 1836; buried family burying ground at Hackwood; reinterred Mt. Hebron Cemetery, Winchester, 1890.

SMITH, JOHN senator, congressman; b. Mastic, L.I., N.Y., Feb. 12, 1752; completed prep. studies. Mem. N.Y. State Assembly, 1784-99; del. N.Y. State Conv. to ratify U.S. Constn., 1788; mem. U.S. Ho. of Reps. (Democrat, filled vacancy) from N.Y., 6th-8th congresses, Feb. 6, 1800-Feb. 23, 1804 (resigned); mem. U.S. Senate (filled vacancy) from N.Y., Feb. 23, 1804-13; U.S. marshal for Dist. of N.Y., 1813-15; maj. gen. N.Y. State Militia. Died Mastic, Aug. 12, 1816; buried Smiths Point, N.Y.

SMITH, JOHN ADDISON BAXTER rear admiral U.S.N.; b. Baltimore, Mar. 21, 1845; s. John A. and Sophia F. S.; ed. Dickinson Sem., Pa.; served apprenticeship, machine shop, Baltimore; course of engring., Baltimore; m. Ella E. Smith. Apptd. 3d asst. engr. U.S.N., Apr. 21, 1863; promoted 2d asst. engr., Sept. 28, 1864; 1st asst. engr., 1868; chief engr., 1892; comdr., 1899; capt., June 1902; retired, Mar. 21, 1905, with rank of rear admiral, and apptd. gen. insp., Bur. Steam Engring., Navy Dept. Served off Charleston, S.C., during Civil War; attached to U.S.S. Housatonic when that vessel was blown up by Confederate torpedo. Served with Shufeldt Expdn., surveying Isthmus Tehuantepec; head of dept. steam engring., Norfolk Navy Yard, 1896-99; same New York Navy Yard, 1899-1905; had full charge of reconstructing the building and machinery of the dept.; built machinery of battleship Connecticut. Served on following vessels: Housatonic, Paul Jones, Wabash, Mohongo, Saco, Seminole, Mayflower, Hartford, Saugus, Wyandotte, Tallapoosa, Atlanta, Montgomery, Texas; served as gen. insp. of machinery, and pres. bd. on changes in machinery of vessels building on Atlantic Coast until Aug. 1908. Republican. Address: Atlantic City, N.J. Died Mar. 9, 1918.

SMITH, JOHN BLAIR clergyman, coll. pres.; b. Pequea, Pa., June 12, 1756; s. Rev. Robert and Elizabeth (Blair) S.; grad. Coll. of N.J. (now Princeton), 1773; m. Elizabeth Nash, 1779, 6 children. Tutor, Hampden-Sydney Acad. (rechartered as Hampden-Sydney Coll.), 1775-79, pres. 1779-89; an early supporter of movement for Am. independence, became capt. co. of Hampden-Sydney students in Va. Militia, circa 1778; ordained to ministry Presbyn: Ch. by Hanover (Va.) Presbytery, 1779, leader revival movement in Va., 1789-91; pastor 3d Presbyn. Ch. of Phila., 1791-95, 99; pres: Union Coll:, Schenectady, N.Y., 1795-99; pres. Presbyn. Gen. Assembly, 1798. Died Phila., Aug. 22, 1799.

SMITH, JOHN CORSON soldier; b. Phila., Feb. 13, 1832; s. Robert and Sarah (Harvey) S.; ed. pub. schs., Phila.; m. Charlotte A. Gallaher, Mar. 24, 1856. Enlisted pvt. 74th Ill. Vols., 1862; raised Co. I, 96th Ill. Inf., and elected maj., Sept. 6, 1862; lt. col., Sept. 20, 1863; bvtd. col. vols., Feb. 20, 1865; brig. gen. vols. "for meritorious services," June 20, 1865; hon. mustered out, June 10, 1865. Participated in 2d battle of Fort Donelson, battles of Franklin, Liberty Gap, Chickamauga, Lookout Mountain, Missionary Ridge, Resaca, Kingston, Cassville, New Hope Church, Dallas, Pumpkinvine Creek, Pine Mountain, and at Kenesaw Mountain, where was severely wounded, also Nashville. In internal revenue service, 1865-74; chief insp. grain, Ill., 1875-77; commissioner Centennial Exposition, 1876; state treas., 1879-81, 1883-85, lt. gov. of Ill., 1885-89; del. Rep. Nat. convs., 1872, 76. Republican. 33 deg. Mason; Past Grand Master Grand Lodge of Ill. A.F. & A.M., and I.O.O.F. Author: History of Freemasonry in Illinois, 1903; also many pamphlets. Home: Chicago, Ill. Died 1910.

SMITH, JOHN EUGENE army officer; b. Berne, Switzerland, Aug. 3, 1816; s. John Banler Smith; m. Aimee A. Massot, 1836. Came to U.S., settled in Phila., 1817; moved to Galena, Ill., 1836, established jewelry business; treas. Jo Daviess County, Ill., 1860; organized 45th Ill. Infantry, 1861; commd. col. 45th Ill. Inf., U.S. Army, 1861; served at Battle of Shiloh, 1862; commd. brig. gen. U.S. Volunteers, 1862; in command div. under Gen. Grant throughout Vicksburg campaign, 1863, led charge at Missionary Ridge, Tenn.; largely responsible (through swift deployment of his div.) for forcing Confederate Army to evacuate Savannah, Ga., 1864; brevetted maj. gen. U.S. Volunteers, 1865; in command Dist. of Western Tenn., 1865-66; commd. col. 27th Inf., U.S. Army, 1866; brevetted brig. gen., maj. gen. U.S. Army (for gallant service at Vicksburg and Savannah), 1867. Died Chgo., Jan. 29, 1897; buried Galena, Ill.

SMITH, JOHN LEWIS lawyer; b. Washington, Jan. 25, 1877; s. John Ambler and Nannie (Lewis) S.; student Columbian (now George Washington) U.; LL.B., Nat. U., 1902, LL.M., 1903; m. Marie Baggaley, Oct. 1, 1901 (died 1902); 1 dau., Mary Ambler (wife of Brig. Gen. Percy L. Sadler, U.S. Army); m. 2d, Claribel Cassin, June 1, 1909; 1 son, John Lewis. Lawyer, former assistant United States attorney. Began practice of law, Washington, 1903; president National Tribune Corp. Served as private Dist. Columbia Vol. Inf., Spanish-Am. War; capt. Mil. Intelligence Div., U.S. Army, World War. Mem. Am. Bar Assn., D.C. Bar Assn. (ex-pres), United Spanish War Vets. (past comdr. in chief), Am. Legion (past dept. comdr.). Republican. Episcopalian. Mason. Clubs: Chevy Chase, Army and Navy. Home: 2424 Tracy Pl., N.W. Office: 729 15th St. N.W., Washington. Died Nov. 9, 1950; buried Arlington Nat. Cemetery.

SMITH, JOHN P. army officer; b. Jan. 28, 1883; E.E., Pa. State Coll. 1907; distinguished grad. Coast Arty. School 1914; grad. Command and Gen. Staff School 1925, Army War Coll. 1926, Naval War Coll. 1932; m. Cornelia Parmelee, Long Island, 1912. Commd. 2d lt. Coast Arty. Corps, Sept. 25, 1908; promoted through grades to Maj. Gen. April 1941. Service in the U.S., Hawaii, Philippines, and France (W.W.I). Active in battles Aisne-Marne, St. Mihiel and Meuse-Argonne offensives. Mem. Gen. Staff Corps 1920-24, 1932-36, 1939-40. Commanded Fourth Corps Area Oct. 1940 to March 1942, Chief of Administrative Services War Dept., mem. Permanent Joint Board on Defense, Canada-United States, and Joint Mexican-United States Defense Commn. Army Mem. Planning Group, O.S.S. Awarded Distinguished Service Medal, Purple Heart and Victory Medal (W.W.I.) with four stars and bars. Died Nov. 4, 1948.

SMITH, JOHN SPEED congressman, lawyer; b. nr. Nicholasville, Jessamine County, Ky., July 1, 1792; attended pvt. sch., Mercer County; studied law; at least 1 son, Green Clay. Served as pvt. in Indian Campaign of 1811; admitted to bar, 1812, practiced in Richmond, Ky.; enlisted as pvt. in War of 1812; promoted maj.; a.d.c. to Gen. Harrison with rank of col.; mem. Ky. Ho. of Reps., 1819, 27, 30, 39, 41, 45, speaker, 1827; mem. U.S. Ho. of Reps. (Democrat, filled vacancy) from Ky., 17th Congress, Aug. 5, 1821-23; U.S. dist. atty. for Ky., 1828-32; mem. Ky. Senate, 1846-50. Died Richmond, June 6, 1854; buried Richmond Cemetery.

SMITH, JONATHAN BAYARD Continental congressman; b. Phila., Feb. 21, 1742; s. Samuel Smith; grad. Princeton, 1760; m. Susannah Bayard, at least 1 child, Samuel Harrison: Mem: Pa. Provincial Conf., 1774, sec. Pa. Provincial Conv., 1775, sec. Pa. Provincial Conf., 1776; helped overthrow old provincial govt., 1776; mem.. sec. Com. of Safety, 1775-77; lt. col. of a bn. of "Associators" served in Brandywine campaign, 1777; mem. Continental Congress, 1777-78; mem. Bd. of War, 1778; prothonotary of Ct. Common Pleas for City and County of Phila., 1777-79, justice, 1778; auditor gen. Pa., circa 1794. Trustee U. Pa., also Princeton, 1779-1808; mem. Am. Philos. Soc. Died Phila., June 16, 1812.

SMITH, JOSEPH naval officer; b. Hanover, Mass., Mar. 30, 1790; s. Albert and Anne Lentham (Eels) S.; m. Harriet Bryant, Mar. 1, 1818, 4 children including Joseph Bryant. Commd. in U.S. Navy, 1814; served in Battle of Lake Champlain; participated in engagements with Algerines in Barbary War, 1815; master commandant, 1827; capt., 1837, aided in fitting out the Wilkes exploring expdn.; chief Bur. Navy Yards and Docks, 1846-69; ranking naval officer on a naval bd. on ironclad constrn., 1861, instrumental in bldg. ironclad ship Monitor; rear adm. on ret. list, 1862; pres. retiring bd., 1870-71. Died Washington, D.C., Jan. 17, 1877.

SMITH, JOSEPH ADAMS rear admiral, U.S.N.; b. Machias, Me., Sept. 1, 1837; s. George S. and Delia T. (Adams) S.; ed. Machias pub. sch., Bucksport Sem., Me., Plymouth, N.H., and at Harvard Law Sch., LL.D.; m. May Hamlin Bartlett, Jan. 26, 1881. Apptd. to U.S.N. from Me., 1861, as asst. paymaster; served Kearsarge, comd. powder div., in fight with Confederate Stmr. Alabama, July 19, 1864; paymaster, 1862; pay inspector, 1879; paymaster-gen., U.S.N., 1882-86; pay dir., 1891; retired with rank rear admiral, Sept. 1, 1899. Died 1907.

SMITH, JOSEPH EARL, economist; b. Howard, Kan., Sept. 23, 1888; s. Henry L. and Anna Dilla (Raper) S.; A.B., Cotner Coll., Neb., 1908; B.A. (Rhodes scholar from Neb.), Oxford Univ., 1911; A.M., U. of Neb., 1914; Ph.D., Wallas Coll. England, 1930; m. Mary E. Boyer, Nov. 22, 1939. Prof. of economics, Hiram Coll., Ohio, 1920-37; prof. economics, Youngstown (O.) Coll., 1937-48, dean, 1949-70. Served at lt., inf., U.S. Army, World War I; area dir., War Manpower Commn., World War II. Mem. Am. Econ. Assn. Home: North Jackson OH Died Aug. 28, 1970; buried Hillside Cemetery Cortland OH

SMITH, JOSEPH ROWE brig. gen., U.S.A.; b. Madison Barracks, N.Y., Apr. 18, 1831; s. Gen. Joseph R. and Juliet Philipps (de Hart) S.; A.B., U. of Mich., 1848, A.M., 1851; M.D., U. of Buffalo, 1853; LL.D., U. of Mich., 1900; m. Claramond Colquhoun Cleemann, Dec. 17, 1857. Civ. engr., locating ry. bet. Watertown and Sacketts Harbor, 1847; laying out boundary between Creeks and Cherokees, 1850; laying out territorial rds. in Minn., 1851. Asst. surgeon U.S.A., Dec. 15, 1854; maj. surgeon, June 11, 1862; lt. col. surgeon, Jan. 9, 1885; col. surgeon, Feb. 9, 1890; retired, Apr. 18, 1895; advanced to rank of brig. gen. retired, by act of Apr. 23, 1904. In Tex. and on expdn. against hostile Indians, 1854-58; chief med. officer 6th column, Utah forces, 1858, then with Gen. Sumner pursuing Cheyennes; organized gen. hosps. in Washington and Georgetown, 1861, for reception of wounded from 1st Bull Run; acting surgeon gen. U.S.A., 1862-63; bvtd. lt. col., Mar. 13, 1865, "for superior ability and excellent management" of the affairs of his dept., and col., Nov. 22, 1866, for "meritorious services and devotion to the sick during the prevalence of cholera at Little Rock, Ark." Del. Internat. Med. Congress, Phila., 1876, Washington, 1887, Rome, 1894, Pan-Am. Med. Congress, Washington, 1893 (hon. pres. to represent U.S.A.); corporator New York Post-Grad. Med. Sch. and Hosp. Fellow Am. Acad. Medicine, Am. Statis. Assn.; mem. Am. Acad. Polit. and Social Science, Dept. Archaeology U. of Pa. Contbr. of papers to Wood's Reference Hand-Book of Medical Sciences, on duties of military surgeons; also many other scientific and professional papers. Home: Philadelphia, Pa. Died 1911.

SMITH, JOSEPH THOMAS marine corps officer; b. Livermore, Cal., Aug. 11, 1895; s. Daniel Alexander and Elizabeth (Twohey) S.; A.B., U. Cal., 1917; m. Loretta Taylor, Nov. 10, 1944; children (by previous marriage)—Josep & Agate, 1919-26; assistant attorney American Can Company, 1930-33, gen. counsel from 1933 to 1946. Since Jan. 1, 1947, in private practice. Served with Squadron A. Nat. Guard of N.Y., 1903-13, 1st lt. and capt. 1st F.A., 1913-16, maj. and adj., N.Y.F.A. Brigade, 1916-17; insp.-instr. F.A. 34th Div., U.S. Army, 1917-18; batt. comdr. 125th F.A., later 127th F.A., 1918-19. Mem. Am. Bar Assn., Assn. of Bar City of New York, Am. Foreign Law Assn. Republican. Clubs: University, Lawyers (N.Y.). Home: 2 Gramercy Park, N.Y.C. 3. Office: 149 Broadway, N.Y.C. 6. Died Apr. 26, 1957.

SMITH, LEONARD BACON lawyer; b. N.Y.C., May 18, 1873; s. Eugene and Katharine Wadsworth (Bacon) S.; student Phillips Acad., 1889-90; A.B., Yale, 1894; LL.D. with honor N.Y. Law Sch., 1896; m. Simone Alibert, May 27, 1919; children—Marcel Alibert, Marie Anne (Mrs. Jacques Chabrier), Denyse Bacon, Leonard Eugene, Simone Madeleine. Admitted to N.Y. bar, 1896; mem. firm of Price & Smith, New York, 1897-1908, Strong, Smith & Strong, 1908-19, Smith & Agate, 1919-26; asst. atty. Am. Can Co., 1930-33, gen. counsel, 1933-47; pvt. practice, 1947-—. Served with Squadron A. N.G. of N.Y., 1903-13, 1st lt. and capt. 1st F.A., 1913-16, maj. and adj., N.Y.F.A. Brigade, 1916-17; insp.-instr. F.A. 34th Div., U.S. Army, 1917-18; batt. comdr. 125th F.A., later 127th F.A., 1918-19. Mem. Am. Bar Assn., Assn. Bar City of New York, Am. Fgn. Law Assn. Republican. Clubs: University, Lawyers (N.Y.). Home: 2 Gramercy Park, N.Y.C. 3; (summer) "Willowfield," Norfolk, Conn. Office: 149 Broadway, N.Y.C. 6. Died Apr. 26, 1957; buried Center Cemetery, Norfolk, Conn.

SMITH, LILLIAN author; b. Jasper, Fla., 1897; student Piedmont Coll., Peabody Conservatory, Teachers' Coll., Columbia; hon. Dr. Letters, Oberlin Coll., D.H.L., Howard, 1950; Litt.D. (honorary), Atlanta University, 1957; D.Litt. (hon.), Western Md. Coll., 1964. Taught at Virginia School, Huchow, China. Dir. of Laurel Falls Camp, 1925-49; co-editor South Today, 1936-45. Mem. Nat. Bd. Am. Civil Liberties Union. Methodist. Author: Strange Fruit, 1944; Dramatization of Strange Fruit, 1945; Killers of the Dream, 1949, rev., 1961; The Journey, 1954; Now Is the Time, 1955; One Hour, 1959; Memory of a Large Christmas, 1962; Our Faces, Our Words, 1964. Recipient special citation Distinguished Contbn. Am. Letters, Nat. Book Award Com., 1950; So. Author's Award, 1950; Sidney Hillman award for mag. writing, 1962; Queen Esther award, Women's div. Am. Jewish Congress, 1965; Charles Spurgeon Johnson award for distinguished contbn. to human relations, 1966. Contbr. nat. publs. Address: P.O. Box 766, Clayton, Ga. Died Sept. 28, 1966.

SMITH, LOWELL H. army officer; b. Santa Barbara, Calif., Oct. 8, 1892; s. Jasper G. and Nora M. (Holland) S.; ed. high sch., San Fernando, Calif., and San Fernando Academy; m. Madelaine Symington, June 12, 1926. With the Aviation Service of Mexican Army, 1915; mechanical engineer, silver mines of Nevada, 1916-17; enlisted as private Aviation Service, N.A., Apr. 1917; commd. 1st lt., Dec. 1917; capt., Oct. 1918; participated in endurance test, New York to San Francisco, 1919; commd. capt. U.S. Army (regular army), July 1, 1920; comdr. round the world airplane flight, 1924, a distance approximately of 26,103 miles in 365 hours 11 minutes flying time, and a total period of 175 days between departure from Seattle, Wash., Apr. 6, and return to Seattle, Sept. 28. Held 16 world flying records for speed, duration and distance. Awarded D.S.M. (U.S.), "for distinguished service" in World War; Mackay medal, 1919 and 1924, as the outstanding mil. flyer during those yrs.; D.S.M. for world flight, 1924; Distinguished Flying Cross for first refueling of airplanes in flight, 1924; Helen Culver gold medal, "for distinction in broadening the boundaries of world knowledge," 1925. Officer Legion of Honor (France). Advanced 1,000 files in promotion list of U.S. Army, Feb. 25, 1925; became Air Corps rep. at Curtiss Consolidated Corp. and Keystone Aircraft Corp., 1929; advanced to col., Feb. 1942. Protestant.* Deceased.

SMITH, LURA EUGENIE BROWN author; b. Rochester, N.Y., June 23, 1854; d. Leverett Russell and Catharine (Ostrander) Brown; went to Little Rock, Ark., 1883; edited Arkansas Life and was corr. for various papers; m. Sidney Smith, editor Iowa Masonry, Cedar Rapids, Ia., Apr. 20, 1892. Mem. Am. Acad. Polit. and Social Science, League Am. Pen Women. Author: The Autocrat of Arkansas; On the Track and Off the Train, 1892; also short stories, poems, editorial work, etc. Address: P.O. Box 1197, Seattle, Wash.

SMITH, LUTHER ELY lawyer; b. Downers Grove, Ill., June 11, 1873; s. Luther Rominor and Adeline (Ely) S.; prep. edn., Thompson's Grove Public School, Monmouth County, N.J.; Emerson Inst., Washington, D.C.; grad. Williston Acad., Easthampton, Mass., 1890; A.B., Amherst, 1894; LL.B., Washington U., 1897; LL.D., Amherst College, 1942; m. SaLees Kennard, Nov. 17, 1909; children—Adeline Ely (Mrs. Ingram F. Boyd, Jr.), Luther Ely, SaLees Kennard (Mrs. John W. Seddon). Teacher English, Smith Academy (Washington Univ.), 1897-98; admitted to Mo. bar, 1897, in practice at St. Louis, 1899-—; mem. Gilliam & Smith, 1900-04, Klein & Hough, 1904-07, Smith & Pearcy, 1913-37, Luther Ely Smith & Associates, 1937-—; lecturer on contracts, St. Louis U. Law Sch., 1908-13. Served as lt. 3d U.S. Vol. Engrs., Spanish-Am. War, 1898-99; capt. F.A., U.S. Army, 1917. Chmn. Citizens City Plan Com. 1916-22; Civic Development Bur. of St. Louis C. of C., Council Civic Needs, 1929-38; sec. Pageant Drama Assn. of St. Louis, 1913-14; mem. George Rogers Clark Fed. Sesquicentennial Commn., 1928-40. Chmn. State Orgn. Com., Mo. Non-Partisan Court Plan, 1939-41. Recipient of the St. Louis Award, 1941. Mem. Am., Mo., St. Louis (sec. 1905-07) bar assns., Assn. Bar City of New York, Mo. Hist. Soc., Jefferson Nat. Expansion Meml. Assn. (pres. 1934-49), U.S. Territorial Expansion Meml. Commn. (chmn. exec. com., 1934-—), St. Louis Bird Club (pres. 1925-27, v.p., 1945-—), Civil Service Commn. of St. Louis (vice chmn., 1941-45; chmn., 1945-—), 3d U.S. Vol. Engr. Assn. (sec., 1900-—), Phi Beta Kappa, Psi Upsilon, Order of the Coif. Republican. Episcopalian. Editor biographies of David DuBose Gaillard, Walter Henry Sanborn. Home: 4969 Pershing Av. Office: 411 N. 7th St., St. Louis 1. Died Apr. 2, 1951.

SMITH, LYBRAND PALMER naval officer, prof.; b. Decatur, Ill., Jan. 24, 1891; s. Charles Ellsworth and Jennie Agnes (Palmer) S.; ed. Acad. of James Milliken U., 1905-07; B.S., U.S. Naval Acad., 1911; student U. of Santo Domingo, 1919-20; Sc.D., Am. Univ., 1935; m. Katherine Snowden Atwater, April 20, 1912; children—Damaris (wife of Col. A.J. Shower), Towneley (Mrs. Warren M. Rohsenow), Rosalind (wife of Comdr. Robert L. Neyman), Lybrand Palmer. Past midshipman, U.S. Navy, 1911, advanced through grades to capt.; at sea, 1911-19; during mil. occupation of Santo Domingo, held cabinet posts, minister of finance and commerce, sec. state for fgn. affairs, minister of improvements and communications 1919-21; engring, duty (including command of 2 destroyers), 1923-43; asst. coordinator research and development, Office sec. of Navy, July 15, 1941-45; mem. Nat. Defense Research Com., July 1941-45; Navy Dept. mem. uranium com., 1941-45; mem. war metallurgy com., 1941-45; sr. naval liason officer on Com. Selection and Training of Service Personnel and Com. Applied Math. Statistics, 1942-45; ret. because of phys. disability, 1945; now prof. naval engring. Grad. Sch. Mass. Inst. Tech. Served in Mexican, Haitian, Dominican campaigns, World Wars I and II. Decorated Mexican Campaign Medal, Victory Medal with Silver Star, Haitian Campaign, 2d Marine Expdn. medal, Am. Defense medal, Legion of Merit, Am. Theater Victory Medal, World War II. Registered professional engr., Md. Fellow A.A.A.S.; mem. Am. Soc. Naval Engrs. (mem. council 1936-40), Soc. Naval Architects and Marine Engrs., Soc. Colonial Wars, Chi Psi Omega. Clubs: Army and Navy (Washington, D.C., bd. govs. 1936); Algonquin (Boston). Contbr. tech. papers to professional jours. Address: Massachusetts Institute of Technology, Cambridge, Mass. Died Nov. 25, 1948.

SMITH, MARTIN LUTHER army officer; b. Danby, Tompkins County, N.Y., Sept. 9, 1819; s. Luther Smith; grad. U.S. Mil. Acad., 1842; m. Sarah Nisbet, 1846. Served as lt. topog. engrs. in Mexican War; commd. 1st lt. U.S. Army, 1853, capt., 1856; chief engr. Fernanda & Cedar Key R.R., 1856-61; maj. of engrs. Confederate Army, 1861; aided in planning fortifications commanded troops in defense of New Orleans and Vicksburg, 1862, 63; col. 21st La. Inf., 1862; commd. brig. gen., then maj. gen., 1862; chief engr. Army of Northern Va. and Hood's Army of Tenn., 1864, constructed field works used in their campaigns; chief engr. to Beauregard, 1864-65; in command Western theatre, strengthened defenses of Mobile, Ala., 1864-65. Died Savannah, Ga., July 29, 1866.

SMITH, MELANCTON Continental congressman, merchant, lawyer; b. Jamaica, L.I., N.Y., May 7, 1744; s. Samuel and Elizabeth (Bayles) S.; at least 1 son, Melancton. Sheriff, Dutchess County (N.Y.), 1744, 77, 79; del. from Dutchess County in 1st N.Y. Provincial Congress, 1775; organized and capt. 1st company of Rangers of Dutchess County Minutemen; mem. commn. for inquiring into, detecting and defeating all conspiracies . . . against liberties of America, 1777; apptd. to commn. to settle disputes between army and contractors at West Point, N.Y., 1782; moved to N.Y.C., 1785, entered upon extensive merc. enterprises and law practice; mem. Continental Congress, 1785-88; anti-Federalist del. to Poughkeepsie Conv. of 1788 to consider ratification of U.S. Constn.; mem. N.Y. State Assembly, 1791; circuit judge N.Y., 1792. Died N.Y.C., July 29, 1798; buried Jamaica Cemetery.

SMITH, MORGAN LEWIS army officer; b. Mexico, Oswego County, N.Y., Mar. 8, 1821; s. Cyrus and Laura (Wales) S.; m. Louise Genella, Dec. 18, 1866. Enlisted as pvt. U.S. Army, 1843; sgt., drill instr. recruit depot, Newport, Ky., 1845-50; organized 8th Mo. Volunteer Inf., commd. col., 1861; as brigade comdr. fought at Ft. Donelson, Tenn., also in expdn. up Tennessee River and in battles of Shiloh, Corinth praised for courage by Lew Wallace, Sherman, Grant; commd. brig. gen. U.S. Volunteers, 1862; took part in Sherman's campaign against Vicksburg as comdr. 2d div.; comdr. 2d div. XV Corps, 1863, fought at Battle of Missionary Ridge; temp. cmdr., Dist. Vicksburg, brought peace to city; U.S. consul gen., Honolulu, Hawaii, 1867-69; counsel in Washington, D.C. for collection claims of applicants for U.S. Govt. pensions. Died Jersey City, N.J., Dec. 28, 1874.

SMITH, NEWMAN banker, govt. ofcl.; b. Dothan, Ala., Oct. 23, 1889; s. William Jackson and Ella (de Shazo) S.; student Newton Inst., 1902-06, Howard Coll. (Ala.), 1906-07, Massey's Bus. Coll., 1910, N.Y.U., 1919-20; m. Rosalind Sayre Oct. 8, 1917. With First Nat. Bank, Montgomery, Ala., 1912-16; auditor Guaranty Trust Co. of N.Y., N.Y.C., since 1919, auditor-controller, Constantinople, Turkey, Brussels and Antwerp, Belgium, since 1920, exec. sec., Brussels, 1924-28; pres., mng., dir. Comml. Investment Trust, S.A. Brussels, 1928-34; v.p. C. I. T. Corp., N.Y.C., 1934-42; adminstrv. officer loan guaranty div. V.A., 1946-50; asst. to under sec. Dept. of Commerce, Jan. 1950, spl. asst. to Sec. of Commerce and Dir. Security since May 1950. Served as non-commd. officer 6th Cav., U.S. Army, Moro Insurrection. Mindanao, P.I., 1907-09; comdr. MG Co. 4th Ala. Inf., Mexican Border, 1916-17, MG Co., 167th Inf., 150th MG bn. 42 Rainbow Div., A.E.F., France, participating in 5 major battles, 1917-18, G-3 Gen. Staff 2d Army, included Eligible List, WD. 1920; commd. capt. U.S. Army, 1917, advncd through grds to maj., 1919; mil. aide to U.S. food adminstr. Herbert Hoover, Paris, 1919; lt. col. to col. U.S. Army, 1942-46, assigned intelligence div. War Dept. Gen. Staff and Office of U.S. Joint Chiefs of Staff, 1942-46, ret. 1949. Decorated Legion of Merit, Army Commendation medal, Am. Theatre medal, World War I medal with 5 bars, World War II medal, Mexican Border medal, Philippine Insurrection medal; U. D.C. Cross of Mil. Service. Mem. Mil. Order World Wars, Mil. Order Carabao, Rainbow Div. Vets. Assn., Newcomen Soc. N.A. Episcopalian. Mason (32 deg.). Club: Army-Navy (Washington). Died July 28, 1964; buried Greenwood Cemetery, Montgomery, Ala.

SMITH, NICHOLAS author; b. Blackburn, Eng., Oct. 31, 1836; s. William and Sarah (Bailey) S.; never attended sch.; went to Wis., 1844; worked in lead mines winters and on the farm summers, 1847-60; studied law; admitted to bar, 1862; m. Julia Clara, d. Dr. Moses Meeker, Aug. 14, 1862. Pvt. 33d Wis. Inf., Aug. 1862; 2d lt., Oct. 1862; 1st lt., May 1863; capt., Aug. 1863. Took part in Grant's and Sherman's expdn. through Central Miss., 1862-63; siege of Vicksburg and capture of Jackson, 1863; mil. comdr. ill-fated steamer John Warner on Red River expdn., spring of 1864; on expdn. against Marmaduke, fall of 1864; resigned Jan. 1865, on account of disability; began newspaper work on Waukesha (Wis.) Freeman, 1869; editor Janesville (Wis.) Daily Gazette, 1874-91, Fond du Lac Daily Commonwealth, 1895-99. Chmn. Rep. State Central Com., 1891-94; commd. col. on Gov. W. E. Smith's staff, 1880; mem. state bd. supervision of charitable, reformatory and penal instns., 1885-91. Author: Stories of Great National Songs, 1899; Hymns Historically Famous, 1901; Songs from the Hearts of Women, 1903; Our National Flag—In History and Incident; Masters of Old Age, 1905; Grant—The Man of Mystery. Spl. contbr. to History of Milwaukee, 1894. Address: Milwaukee, Wis. Died 1911.

SMITH, NORMAN MURRAY, educational adminstrator; born Williston, S.C., November 16,-21883; son Dr. Winchester C. and Eugenia Kanapau (Murray) S.; graduate U.S. Naval Academy, 1906; C.E., Rensselaer Poly. Inst., 1909; grad. Naval War Coll., 1926; hon. Dr. Eng. Rensselaer Poly. Inst., 1939; m. Genevieve Thompson, June 11, 1921. Around the world as midshipman on U.S.S. Colorado, transferred as jr. lieut. Civ. Engr. Corps, Apr. 20, 1907; promoted through grades to rear adm., Dec. 3, 1933; chief of Bur. of Yards and Docks and chief civil engr. of the Navy, 1933-38. Engaged on constrn. and maintenance of Training Sta. (Great Lakes, Ill.), Navy Yards of Puget Sound and Mare Island; built naval base, Pearl Harbor, 1914-17; built plants, hospitals, dredged harbors and developed waterfronts in 6th and 11th Naval Dists., World War I; duty in naval dists. and Bur. Yards and Docks, at San Diego, Norfolk, Washington, and Boston, 1913-33; built air sta. and all naval establishments within San Diego Naval Base, 1918-23; adminstr. Works Progress Adminstrn., 1935-38; retired Dec., 1937; returned to active duty with Naval Constrn. Battalions, Camp Parks, Calif., 1942; ret., 1945; pres. Univ. of South Carolina, 1946-52. Mem. Am. Soc. C.E., Am. Mil. Engineers, Nat. Soc. Professional Engrs., Mil. Order of the Carabao, Theta Xi. Democrat. Mason, K.T. Clubs: Athenian (Oakland, Calif.); Union (Boston); Arlington (Portland, Ore.); Army and Navy, Army-Navy Country (Washington); Chevy Chase, Cuyamaca (San Diego, Calif.). Home: Williston SC Died Nov. 1968.

SMITH, ORLANDO JAY editor; b. nr. Terre Haute, Ind., June 14, 1842; s. Hiram S.; grad. Asbury (now DePauw) Univ., LL.D., DePauw; m. Evelyn V. Brady, Mar. 28, 1881. Served in armies of the Potomac, Ohio and Cumberland in 16th Ind. Vol. Inf. and 6th Ind. Cav., Apr. 21, 1861 to Sept. 1865, as pvt., sergt., lt., capt., maj.; wounded nr. Atlanta, Aug. 3, 1864. Editor Terre Haute Mail, Terre Haute Express, Chicago Express, pres. Am. Press Assn., 1882-—. Author: A Short View of Great Questions, 1899; The Coming Democracy, 1900; Eternalism, 1902; Balance, 1904. Mem. Loyal Legion. Residence: Dobbs Ferry, N.Y. Office: New York, N.Y. Died 1908.

SMITH, PAUL KENNETH educator; b. Brashear, Mo., Sept. 10, 1908; s. William Robert and Virginia (Johnston) S.; A.B., Westminster Coll., 1930; Ph.D., Yale, 1934; m. Elizabeth Robison Baker, Sept. 12, 1931; children—Robert Kenneth Robison, Katharine Virginia Rice, James Calvin Henderson. Asst. chemistry Westminster Coll., 1926-30; asst. physiol. chemistry, Yale, 1932-34, research fellow pharmacology, 1934-36, instr., 1936-38, asst. prof., 1938-41, chief pharmacology and biochemistry, sch. aviation med., 1942-46; prof. pharmacology and head dept. school medicine George Washington U. since 1946. Consultant therapeutics, University, D.C. General hosps. Served as capt. to colonel, USAF, 1941-46; mobilization assignment (colonel). Office Director Research, U.S.A.F. Delegate International Chemistry Union, London, 1947. Fellow New York Academy Sciences; member American Assn. Cancer Research, Am. Chem. Soc., Soc. Exptl. Biol. Med., Am. Soc. Biol. Chemists, Am. Soc. Pharmacol. Exptl. Therapeutics (councilor 1955-58), A.A.A.S., Aero-Medical Assn. Washington Acad. Medicine, Sigma Xi (chpt. pres. 1950-51), Phi Chi. Club: Cosmos. Author articles on pharmacology, biochemistry, radiobiology and chemotherapy. Home: 4323 Murdock Mill Rd., Washington 16. Office: 1335 H St., Washington 5. Died Oct. 6, 1960; buried Arlington Nat. Cemetery.

SMITH, PERSIFOR FRAZER army officer; b. Phila., Nov. 16, 1798; s. Jonathan and Mary Anne (Frazer) S.; A.B., Princeton, 1815; m. Frances Jeanette Bureau, Jan. 19, 1822; m. 2d, Anne Monica (Millard) Armstrong, Apr. 18, 1854; at least 1 child. Adj. Gen. La., circa 1820; col. La. Volunteers in Seminole War, 1836-38; judge City of Lafayette (La.), 1838, later Parish of Jefferson; col. rifle regt. U.S. Army, 1846; brevetted brig. gen. for service at Monterey, 1846; made surprise attack 1847 which resulted in destruction of Valencia's army; distinguished at Churubusco and Contreras, 1847; brevetted maj. gen., 1848; mil. gov. Mexico City, 1848; brevetted maj. gen., 1849; in command of Pacific Div., 1848-50, then Department of Tex. and Cal., 1850-56, Western Dept., 1856; commd. brig. gen., 1856; assigned to command Dept. of Utah, 1858, died before reaching there. Died Ft. Leavenworth, Kan., May 17, 1858; buried Laurel Hill Cemetery, Phila.

SMITH, PHILLIPS WALLER mfr. aircraft and missile components; b. St. Paul, June 28, 1906; s. Albert Horace and Marie Ada (Cholvin) S.; student St. John's Mil. Acad., 1921-23; B.S., U.S. Mil. Acad., 1930; M.S., Mass. Inst. Tech., 1935; M.B.A., Harvard, 1940; m. Veronica Bernadette McVeigh, June 12, 1930; children—Ann (wife Dr. Henrik A. Hartmann), Veronica (Mrs. George P. Koss), Sandra Jane, Phillips Waller. Commd. 2d lt. U.S. Army, 1930, advanced through grades to col., 1947, USAF, 1947-55, brig. gen., 1950-53, maj. gen., 1953-55, now ret.; exec. v.p. Bowser, Inc., Chgo., 1955-56; pres. Jack & Heintz, Inc., Cleve., 1960-—. Decorated D.S.M., Legion of Merit with cluster. Mem. Old Boys Assn. St. John's Mil. Acad. (nat. pres. 1958-59), U.S. Mil. Forum. Club: Chgo. Athletic Assn. Home: 13605 Shaker Blvd., Cleve. 20. Office: 17600 Broadway, Cleve. 1. Deceased.

SMITH, RALPH M. former dir. selective service; b. Provincetown, Mass., June 23, 1883; s. Franklin N. and Emma M. (Holmes) S.; LL.B., Northeastern Coll. of Law, 1904; m. Ethel M. Coman, June 22, 1907. Admitted to Mass. bar, 1904; in practice of law, Somerville, Mass., 1904-40; special justice, Somerville Dist. Court, since 1922; asst. city solicitor, Somerville, 1923-28; with West Somerville Cooperative Bank (now Middlesex Federal Savings and Loan Assn.) since 1928, successively as treas., v.p., pres., and chmn. of the bd.; dir. Federal Home Loan Bank of Boston. Mem. bd. aldermen, Somerville, 1909-12; mem. Mass. State Legislature, 1913-15. Mem. Mass. Nat. Guard since 1902, advancing through the grades from pvt. to lt. col.; state judge adv., 1920-45; serving with U.S. Army, 1940-45; assigned as state dir. selective service, 1942-46, rank of col.; past pres. U.S. Savs. & Loan Assn.; mem. Council Internat. Union Bldg. Socs. Trustee Follen Ch. Member Somerville, Middlesex, Mass., and Am. bar assns., Judge Advocates Assn. Mason (Shriner, K.T.). Clubs: Boston (Mass.) City; Army and Navy (Washington). Awarded D.S.M. Home: 1162 Massachusetts Av., Lexington 1, Mass. Office: 421 Highland Av. W., Somerville, Mass. Died Oct. 10, 1951.

SMITH, RAYMOND ABNER, coll. prof.; b. Gibson County, Ind., Jan. 14, 1875; s. William Franklin and Rosa Frances (Williams) S.; A.B., Butler U., Indianapolis, 1900, A.M., 1904; grad. student U. of Pa., 1902-03; B.D., Yale University, 1905; LL.D., Texas Christian University, 1944; m. Grace Jean Clifford, Dec. 27, 1905; children—Raymond Clifford, Marian Frances, Ralph Emerson. Prof. edn., Atlantic Christian Coll., Wilson, N.C., 1905-06, pres., 1916-20; mfg. business, 1906-13; supt. Beckley (W.Va.) Inst., 1913-16; prof. edn., Tex. Christian U., Fort Worth, since 1920, dir. sch. of edn. since 1923, dean since 1943. First sergeant, later 2d lieut., 159th Indiana Volunteer Infantry, Spanish-American War. Member A.A.A.S., N.E.A., Progressive Education Assn., Am. Assn. Univ. Profs., Nat. Soc. for Study of Edn., Nat. Soc. College Teachers of Edn., Nat. Soc. for Curriculum Study, Pi Gamma Mu. Club: Torch. Home: 2625 Cockrell Av., Fort Worth 9 TX

SMITH, REX editor; b. Gate City, Scott County, Va., June 17, 1900; s. William Daniel and Sallie Lou (Minnich) S.; ed. Shoemaker Prep. Sch. (Gate City), U. of Va., Coll. of William and Mary and San Marcos U. (Lima, Peru); m. Alice Buchanan, 1925 (divorced 1929); 1 dau., Sally Lou; m. 2d, Jessie Royce Landis 1937 separated 1940, divorced 1944); m. 3d, Izetta Jewel, 1944; children—Rex, Izetta. With Detroit News, 1918, Washington Herald, 1919-20; entered U.S. Foreign Service and served as vice consul, San Jose, Costa Rica, 1920-21, Lima, Peru, 1922-23; then with San Francisco Examiner, 4 years, Los Angeles Times, 2 years; wrote for motion pictures, Hollywood, 1927; journalistic assignments in Italy, Balearic Islands, Germany, Bavaria, 1929; then corr. for Paris edition, N.Y. Herald-Tribune, France and Europe generally for 2 years; fgn. news editor for Associated Press, 1931; chief of Spanish bur. Asso. Press, Madrid, to 1935; while in Spain organized Asso. Press news service for Europe; became foreign editor Newsweek, 1936, later asst. to pres. and worked out editorial formula, then editor to

1941; editor The Chicago Sun, 1941-42; vice pres. public relations Am. Airlines 1946-58, ret. Served in O.T.C., University of Michigan, World War I; maj. A.C., Apr. 1942; lt. col., asst. to comdg. gen., Air Transport Comd., 1942-44; promoted to col., named chief, office of information, Hdqrs., Army Air Forces, Washington, D.C., 1944. Mem. Kappa Sigma, Sigma Delta Chi. Clubs: National Press (Washington); Overseas Press, Wings (New York), Racquet (Chicago). Address: N.Y.C. Died May 1959.

SMITH, RICHARD SOMERS army officer, coll. pres.; b. Phila., Oct. 30, 1813; grad. U.S. Mil. Acad., 1834; m. Ellen Clark, 6 children. Commd. 1st lt. U.S. Army, 1846; instr., asst. prof. drawing U.S. Mil. Acad., 1840-55; quartermaster, 1846-51; prof. mathematics, engring., drawing Bklyn. Collegiate and Poly. Inst., 1856-59; commd. maj. 12th Inf., 1861; with Army of Potomac, 1862; pres. Girard Coll., Phila., 1863-67; prof. engring. Polytechnic Coll. of Pa., Phila., 1868-70; prof. mathematics U.S. Naval Acad., Annapolis, Md., 1870-77, prof. drawing, 1873-77, Author: Manual of Topographical Drawing, 1853; Manual of Linear Perspective, 1857. Died Annapolis, Jan. 23, 1877.

SMITH, ROBERT clergyman; b. Worstead, Norfolk, Eng., June 25, 1732; s. Stephen and Hannah (Press) S.; B.A., Gonville and Caius Coll., Cambridge (Eng.) U., 1754, fellow, 1755; m. Elizabeth Pagett, July 9, 1758; m. 2d, Sarah Shubrick, early 1774; m. 3d, Anna Maria (Tilghman) Goldsborough, after 1779; 3 children. Ordained deacon Protestant Episcopal Ch., 1756, priest, 1756; came to Charleston, S.C., 1757; rector St. Philip's Ch., Charleston, 1759-75, 83-1801; served as chaplain 1st S.C. Regt., also Continental Hosp., Charleston, 1776; chaplain-gen. So. dept. Continental Army, circa 1778; imprisoned by British, Charleston, 1780; later banished to Phila.; returned to Charleston, 1783; founded sch. (known as Coll. of Charleston after 1790) circa 1785, prin., 1790-98; instrumental in summoning S.C. conv. Protestant Episcopal Ch. which sent dels. to Gen. Conv., 1785; consecrated 1st Protestant Episcopal bishop S.C., 1795. Died Charleston, Oct. 28, 1801; buried St. Philip's Cemetery, Charleston.

SMITH, ROBERT cabinet officer; b. Lancaster, Pa., Nov. 3, 1757; s. John and Mary (Buchanan) S.; grad. Coll. of N.J. (now Princeton), 1781; m. Margaret Smith, 8 children. Admitted to Balt. bar, circa 1784; mem. Md. Senate, 1793-95, Md. Ho. of Dels., 1796-1800; mem. Balt. City Council, 1798-1801; Republican; U.S. sec. of navy, 1802-05, maintained blockading squadron in Mediterranean during war against Barbary states; acting atty. gen., 1805; Jefferson's rep. in diplomatic negotiations with British concerning impressment of U.S. seamen, 1808; U.S. sec. state under Madison, 1809-11, resigned after criticism from Pres. Madison, 1811; received positions due in part to influence of brother Gen. Samuel Smith. Died Balt., Nov. 26, 1842.

SMITH, ROBERT congressman, businessman; b. Peterborough, Hillsboro County, N.H., June 12, 1802; attended public schs., New Ipswich Acad.; studied law. Taught sch.; became mcht., 1822, manufactured textile goods, Northfield, N.H., 1823; admitted to bar, practiced law; moved to Ill., settled in Alton, 1832, became mcht.; elected capt. Ill. Militia, 1832; extensive land owner, in real estate business; mem. Ill. Ho. of Reps., 1836-40, elected enrolling and engrossing clk., 1840, 42; mem. U.S. Ho. of Reps. (Democrat) from Ill., 28th-30th, 35th congresses, 1843-49, 57-59; served as paymaster during Civil War; engaged in water-power devel. and railroad enterprises. Died Alton, Dec. 21, 1867; buried Alton City Cemetery.

SMITH, ROBERT HARDY lawyer, Confederate legislator; b. Camden County, N.C., Mar. 21, 1813; s. Robert Hard and Elizabeth (Gregory) S.; m. Evelina Inge, Jan. 12, 1839; m. 2d, Emily Inge, Nov. 25, 1845; m. 3d, Helen Herndon, Apr. 9, 1850; 13 children. Admitted to Ala. bar, 1835; rep. from Sumter County in Ala. Legislature, 1849-51; a Whig leader in Ala.; del.-at-large, mem. Provisional confederate Congress, 1861, assisted com. which framed permanent constn. for Confederacy; organizer, col. 36th Ala. Inf., 1862. Author: An Address to the Citizens of Alabama on the Constitution and Laws of the Confederate States of America, 1861. Died Mobile, Ala., Mar. 13, 1878.

SMITH, ROBERT SHUFELDT army officer; b. Stamford, Conn., Feb. 4, 1861; s. Truman and Mary A. (Dickinson) S.; ed. pub. schs.; m. Bertha Warner, of Denver, Colo., Apr. 30, 1907. Enlisted as pvt. Co. G, 8th N.Y. Inf., May 17, 1898; commd. maj. add. p.-m., same date; hon. discharged vols., May 20, 1901; capt. p.-m., U.S.A., Feb. 7, 1901; maj., Feb. 19, 1903; lt. col., Mar. 27, 1914; col., Oct. 8, 1917. Served in Cuba, Aug. 1898-Feb. 1900; in Philippine Islands, 1900-02, and 1910-13; duty at Denver, Colo., 1903-07, Ft. Benjamin Harrison, Indianapolis, Ind., 1913-16; duty Eastern Dept., Governors Island, N.Y., 1917. Republican. Episcopalian. Clubs: Union League (New York), Columbia (Indianapolis). Address: War Dept., Washington, D.C.

SMITH, RODNEY brig. gen. U.S.A.; b. in Vt., Jan. 3, 1829; s. Israel and Delia (Ferguson) S.; m. Julia Ellen Coates, Sept. 22, 1875. Apptd. from Ky., maj. p.m. U.S.A., Feb. 23, 1864; lt. col. deputy p.m. gen., Jan. 24, 1881; col. asst. p.m. gen., Dec. 8, 1886; retired by operation of law, Jan. 3, 1893; advanced to rank of brig. gen., retired, by act of Apr. 23, 1904. Served in Civil War in Army Potomac, and in Dept. of the South. Home: Orwell, Vt. Died Nov. 12, 1915.

SMITH, ROY CAMPBELL naval officer; b. Ft. Mason, Tex., July 16, 1858; s. Charles Henry and Maria McGregor (Campbell) S.; grad. U.S. Naval Acad., 1878; m. Margaret Aldrich Sampson, Oct. 11, 1887. Promoted ensign, Apr. 8, 1882; lt. jr. grade, May 12, 1889; lt. Feb. 22, 1894; lt. comdr., Mar. 3, 1901; comdr., Jan. 7, 1906; capt., Dec. 27, 1909. Duty at Naval Acad., 1885-88, Torpedo Sta., 1892-95; served on Indiana, at Battle of Santiago, July 3, 1898; at Harvard U., 1899-1900; on Massachusetts, 1901-03; naval attaché, Paris and St. Petersburg, 1903-06; comd. Chattanooga, 1906-08; at Naval War Coll., 1908-10; duty Navy Dept., Washington, D.C., 1910-12; comd. Arkansas, 1912-14; participated in occupation of Vera Cruz, Mexico, 1914; dir. target practice and engring. competitions, Navy Dept., 1914-15; supervisor New York Harbor, 1915-16; apptd. gov. Guam and comdt. Naval Sta., Guam, May 30, 1916. Mem. U.S. Naval Inst. (gold medal), Naval History Soc.; officer Legion of Honor. Santiago and Cuban campaign medals. Home: Richmond, Va. Died Apr. 10, 1940.

SMITH, SAMUEL senator; b. Carlisle, Pa., July 27, 1752; s. John and Mary (Buchanan) S.; grad. Princeton; m. Margaret Spear, 1778, 8 children. Served as capt., maj., lt. col., organized co. of volunteers, 1775; participated in battles of Long Island and Monmouth; helped suppress the "Whiskey Rebellion", 1791; commd. brig. gen. militia, 1794; mem. U.S. Ho. of Reps. from Md., 3d-7th, 14-17th congresses, 1793-1803, Jan. 31, 1816-Dec. 17, 1822; acting sec. navy U.S., 1801; mem. U.S. Senate from Md., 1803-15, Dec. 17, 1822-33, pres. pro tem., 1805-08; leader in opposing nomination of Madison 1808; author non-importation legislation of 1806; maj. gen., head forces which defended Balt. from the British during War of 1812; Federalist, became a Jeffersonian Republican; mayor Balt., 1835-38. Died Balt., Apr. 22, 1839; buried Old Westminster Burying Ground, Balt.

SMITH, S(AMUEL) CALVIN M.D.; b. Hollidaysburg, Pa., Feb. 28, 1881; s. Geo. W. (M.D.) and Eliza Blodgett (Calvin) S.; B.S., Bucknell U., 1901, M.S., 1905, Sc.D., 1928; M.D., Jefferson Med. Coll., 1905; m. Louise Voorhes Warriner, May 28, 1905. In gen. practice at Hollidaysburg, Pa., 1905-16; instr. in medicine, Jefferson Med. Coll., Phila., Pa., 1920-22; cons. cardiologist Misericordia Hosp., 1925-30, West Chester Hosp., 1925-30, Coatesville U.S. Vets. Hosp., 1931-32. Served as maj. M.C., U.S.A. in Am. camps and with A.E.F. in France, World War I. Fellow Am. Coll. of Phys.; mem. Am. Med. Assn. (mem. spl. com. for the presentation of Modern Methods of Heart Study, 1924-28). Republican. Episcopalian. Author: Heart Affections—Their Recognition and Treatment, 1920; Heart Records—Their Interpretation and Preparation, 1923; How Is Your Heart?, 1924, Eng. edit., 1925; That Heart of Yours, 1934. Contbr. articles to jours. Home: Philadelphia, Pa. Died July 31, 1939.

SMITH, SIDNEY lawyer; b. Louisville, Ky., Feb. 12, 1883; s. Milton Hannibal and Annette M. (Jones) S.; A.B., Johns Hopkins, 1902; LL.B., Harvard, 1905; m. Saidee Kempshall, Oct. 2, 1917; 1 son, Milton Hannibal II. Admitted to Tenn. bar, 1905, Ky. bar, 1906; engaged in private practice of law, Louisville, Ky., 1906-16; gen. atty. Louisville and Nashville R.R. Co., 1920-40, asst. gen. counsel, 1940-44, v.p. 1944-53, gen. counsel, 1944-48, dir., 1945-57. With Ky. Nat. Guard, 1908-16; and 1921-40; served as capt., later major, F.A., U.S. Army, 1916-19. Mem. Beta Theta Pi. Clubs: Pendennis, Louisville Country (Louisville); Boston (New Orleans). Home: 125 Indian Hills Trail, Louisville 7. Office: 908 W. Broadway, Louisville 1. Died Oct. 25, 1958; buried Cave Hill Cemetery, Louisville.

SMITH, THOMAS Continental congressman; b. nr. Cruden, Aberdeenshire, Scotland, 1745; attended U. Edinburgh (Scotland); studied law. Came to Am., settled in Bedford, Pa., 1769; dep. surveyor, 1769; admitted to bar, practiced law, 1772; dep. register of wills and prothonotary, 1773; justice of peace, 1774; mem. Com. of Correspondence, 1775; served as dep. col. of militia in Revolutionary Army; del. Pa. Constl. Conv., 1776; mem. Pa. Ho. of Reps., 1776-80; mem. Continental Congress from Pa., 1780-82; judge Ct. Common Pleas, 1791, Pa. Supreme Ct., 1794-1809. Died Phila., Mar. 31, 1809; buried Christ Churchyard.

SMITH, THOMAS ADAMS army officer; b. Essex County, Va., Aug. 12, 1781; s. Francis and Lucy (Wilkinson) S.; m. Cynthia Berry White, Sept. 17, 1807, 8 children including Lucy Anne Tucker. Commd. 2d lt. arty; U.S. Army, 1803, capt. rifles, 1808, lt., then col., col. of the regt. during War of 1812; engaged at battles of Plattsburg, Sacketts Harbor, and Burlington; promoted brig. gen., 1814; col., comdr. rifle regt., 1815; comdr.-in-chief Territories of Mo. and Ill: with hdqrs. at Bellefontaine, nr. St. Louis, 1815; receiver of public monies (apptd. by Pres. Monroe), Franklin, Mo., 1818-26; Ft. Smith (Ark.) named for him. Died June 25, 1844.

SMITH, THOMAS FRANKLIN physician; b. New York, Apr. 26, 1833; s. John T. S. and Amelia (Franklin) S.; ed. high sch., New York; degree Doctor in Medicine, New York Med. Coll., 1860; m. Emma Louisa Clark, Aug. 1, 1854. Enlisted in 7th Regt., N.G. N.Y., 1857; transferred to staff of 8th Regt., 1860, and commd. surgeon's mate, with rank of 1st lt.; promoted to surgeon with rank of maj.; mustered with regt. into U.S. service, Apr. 1861, as chaplain, and served 90 days; reënlisted as acting asst. surgeon U.S.A., Dept. of Va., for 15 mos.; participated in 1st battle of Bull Run and several skirmishes; hon. mustered out; later practiced in New York. Mem. Am. Inst. Homoepathy (sr. mem. and treas. 23 yrs.). Second v.p. Jennie Clarkson Home for Children, Valhalla, N.Y.; mgr. for many yrs. of Assn. for Improving Condition of the Poor. Republican; cast first vote for John C. Fremont for President of U.S. Baptist; elk. Southern N.Y. Bapt. Assn. 22 yrs. Home: New York, N.Y. Died June 1916.

SMITH, THOMAS KILBY army officer, diplomat; b. Boston, Sept. 23, 1820; attended mil. acad., Cincinnati; studied law under Chief Justice Chase. Apptd. spl. agt. Post Office Dept., 1853; served to maj. gen. U.S. Army during Civil War, in charge of dept. of So. Ala. and Fla.; apptd. U.S. consul in Panama, 1866; later engaged in journalism in N.Y. Died N.Y.C., Dec. 14, 1887.

SMITH, T(HOMAS) V(ERNOR) educator; b. Blanket, Tex., Apr. 26, 1890; s. John Robert and Mary Elizabeth (Graves) S.; A.B., U. of Tex., 1915, A.M., 1916; Ph.D., U. of Chgo., 1922; LL.D., Miami U., 1938, Fla. So. Coll., 1940, Toledo U., 1948; D.Litt., Union Coll., 1941; m. Nannie Stewart, June 6, 1917; children—Gayle Stanley, Nancy. Prof. English literature, Texas Christian U., 1916, prof. philosophy, 1917; instr. in philosophy, U. Tex., 1919-21; prof. philosophy, U. Chgo., 1926-48, dean of colleges, 1923-26; asso. dean of colleges, 1926-27; Maxwell prof. of citizenship and philosophy Syracuse U., 1948-56, emeritus; editor Internat. Journal of Ethics; mem. Ill. State Senate, 1935-38; chmn. Ill. Legislative Council, 1937-38; mem. 76th Congress (1939-41), Ill. at large. Served as pvt. in U.S. Army, 1918, lt. col. and col., A.U.S., 1943-45. Dir. of Edn., Allied Control Commn., Italy, 1944; dir. Democratization, Select German Prisoners of War, 1945; mem. U.S. Edn. Mission to Japan and Germany, 1946. Mem. Am. Philos. Assn., Am. Polit. Sci. Assn., Phi Beta Kappa, Delta Sigma Rho. Author or co-author numerous books, including: The Democratic Way of Life, 1925, (new edit. with Eduard C. Lindeman 1951); Am. Philosophy of Equality, 1926; Philosophers in Hades, 1932; Beyond Conscience, 1934; Creative Sceptics, 1934; Foundations of Democracy (with Robert A. Taft), 1939; Politics and Public Service (with Leonard D. White), 1939; Lincoln: Living Legend, 1940; Discipline for Democracy, 1942; Atomic Power and Moral Faith, 1946; Constructive Ethics, with Contemporary Readings, 1948; A Study of Power (with C.E. Merriam and H.D. Lasswell), 1950; Abraham Lincoln and the Spiritual Life, 1951; Live Without Fear, 1956; Ethics of Compromise and the Art of Containment, 1956; A Non-Existent Man: an Autobiography, 1962. Home: 4005 Tennyson Rd., Hyattsville, Md. Died May 24, 1964; buried Arlington Nat. Cemetery.

SMITH, WALTER BEDELL corp. exec., ret. army officer; b. Indpls., Oct. 5, 1895; s. William Long and Ida Frances (Bedell) S.; grad. Inf. Sch., 1930, Command and Gen. Staff Sch., 1935, Army War Coll., 1937; Litt.D. (hon.), Louvaine, 1945; D.Sc. Mil. (hon.), Pa. Mil. Coll., 1949; D.C.L. (hon.), Colgate U., 1950; LL.D., Duquesne U., 1949, Hofstra Coll., 1949, Butler U., 1950, Amherst Coll., 1951, Wesleyan U., 1952, Washington and Jefferson Coll., 1953, U. of N.H., 1953, U. of S.C., 1953; LL.D., Lafayette Coll., 1954; LL.D., Yale, 1955; LL.D., N.Y.U., 1955; LL.D., U. Cal., 1955; m. Mary Cline, July 1, 1917. Served as private, advancing to first sergeant, Indiana National Guard, 1910-15; commd. 2d lt., Inf., Officers Reserve Corps, Nov. 1917, 1st lt., U.S. Army, Sept. 10, 1918; advanced through the grades to lt. gen. (temporary), January 11, 1943; maj. gen. (permanent), Oct. 1945; general, 1951. Gen. Staff Corps, 1940; U.S. sec. Combined Chiefs of Staff and sec. U.S. Joint Chiefs of Staff, 1941-42; Chief of Staff, Allied Force Hqrs., N. Africa, 1942-44, S.H.A.E.F., E.T.O., 1944-45, U.S. Forces, European Theater, June-Dec., 1945; U.S. Ambassador, Union of Soviet Socialist Republics, 1946-49; director of Central Intelligence Agency, 1950-53; Undersecretary of State 1953-54; vice chmn. Am. Machine and Foundry Co., 1954-—; member of the board of directors, NBC, RCA, United Fruit Co., Corning Glass Works. Decorations: Order of Merit (Chile); Most Exalted Order of White Elephant 1st class (Thailand); Distinguished Service Medal with 2 oak leaf clusters, Distinguished Service Medal (Navy), National Security Medal, Legion of Merit, Bronze Star; Knight Comdr., Order of the Bath, Knight Grand Cross, Order of British Empire (Gt. Britain); Grand Officer, Legion of Honor, Croix de Guerre (2) (France); Order of Kutuzov, 1st class (U.S.S.R.); Knight Grand Cross, Order of Lions (Netherlands); Grand Cross of Order of Crown, Croix de Guerre (Belgium); Grand Officer, Order of Polonia Restituta, Silver Cross of Order of Virtuti Militari (Poland); Grand Officer, Order of White Lion, Croix de Guerre (Czech); Grand Cross, Order of Cauronne de Chene, Croix de Guerre (Luxembourg); Grand Officer,

Order of Mil. Merit (Brazil); Grand Officer, Order of Alouite (Morocco); Grand Officer, Order of Nishtan Iftikar (Tunisia); hon. citizen of Brussels, Schaubeek; Silver Medal, Cities of Amsterdam and N.Y. Author: My Three Years in Moscow; Eisenhower's Six Great Decisions: Europe (1944-45), 1956. Address: 4400 Garfield St. N.W., Washington 6. Died Aug. 9, 1961; buried Arlington Nat. Cemetery.

SMITH, WALTER DRISCOLL army officer; b. Cumberland, Md., Nov. 16, 1875; s. Page John and Sarah Dorothy (Ways) S.; A.B., St. Johns Coll., Annapolis, 1897; B.S., U.S. Mil. Acad., 1901; student Staff Coll., Ft. Leavenworth, Kan., 1922-23, War Coll., Washington, 1921, Naval War Coll., 1924; m. Florence Beverly Egerton, Mar. 27, 1901 (dec. Mar. 8, 1948); children—Beverly Egerton (Mrs. F. B. Kane), Charles Calvert Egerton, Dorothy Egerton (Mrs. R. H. Berry), Page Egerton. Commd. 2d lt., 1901, advanced through grades to brig. gen., 1939; instr. U.S. Mil. Acad., 1905-09, tactics officer, 1915-17; duty on constrn. of Panama Canal, 1909-13; duty with regiment, 1913-15; duty at G.H.Q., France, 1917-19; with Gen. Staff, Washington, 1924-28; instr. and dir. Staff Coll., 1930-31; chief hist. sect. Army War Coll., 1931-35; chief of staff, 82d Res. Div., 1935-39; with U.S. War Dept., 1941-46. Decorated Roosevelt Medal for Constrn. of Panama Canal, Purple Heart; French Legion of Honor. Clubs: Army and Navy (Washington), Army and Navy Country (Arlington, Va.). Home: 1805 Army-Navy Dr., Arlington, Va. Died Sept. 20, 1955; buried Arlington Nat. Cemetery.

SMITH, WAYNE CARLETON army officer; b. St. Joseph, Mo., Dec. 4, 1901; s. Carl Oswald and Clara Elizabeth (Heffelfinger) S.; B.S., U.S. Mil. Acad., 1925; grad. Inf. Sch., Ft. Benning, Ga., 1931, Command and Gen. Staff Sch., 1940; m. Mildred Louise Little, Dec. 27, 1925; children—Wayne Carleton, Robert Morris, Carl Richard. Served with Co. E, 1st Gas. Regt., Chem. Warfare Service, 1920-21; commd. 2d lt. inf. U.S. Army, advancing through the grades to maj. gen., 1952; served overseas, in China, 1931-34, Hawaiian Dept., 1937-39, Central Pacific Area, 1943; asst. and chief-of-staff G-4, VII Army Corps., 1941-43; chief of staff, Army Port and Service Comd., 1943-44, Central Pacific Area, Aug. 10, 1943 to June 30, 1944, chief-of-staff, Central Pacific Base Command, July 1944-Nov. 1945, comdg. gen. Schofield Barracks, 1945-47; asst. comdg. gen. Ninth Inf. Div., Ft. Dix, 1947-49; asst. div. comdr. 11th Airborne Div., 1949-51; asst. corps comdr. IX Corps, asst. div. comdr. 45th Div. and comdg. gen. 7th Inf. Div., Korea, 1952-53; comdg. gen. 11th Airborne Div. and comdg. gen. Ft. Campbell, Ky., 1953-55; chief military adv. group Republic of Philippines, 1955-56, ret.; with Me. Agy. of United Services Life Ins. Co., 1957-62. Decorated D.S.C., D.S.M., Air Medal, Legion of Merit, Bronze Star medal, Am. Defense, Am. Theater, Asiatic Pacific Theater ribbons. Master Parachutist and Gliderist badge, Colombian Inf. Combat badge, Korean Service ribbon with 3 stars, U.N. ribbon; Order of Taeguk (Korea); Cruz de Boyaca (Colombia); Order of Crown of Thailand, 2d class; D.S.C.; Soldiers Medal; Ulchi D.S.M. (Korea); Order of Star of Ethiopia with Cordon; A.R.C. Award. Mason. Clubs: Officers Mess, Golf Assn., Rod and Gun (Ft. Campbell); Clarksville (Tenn.) Country; Army and Navy Country (Washington); Wilson Lake Country (Wilton, Me.). Co-author: Manual of the Riot Stick, 1936. Editor: Judo Notes, 1932. Editor of Sentinel (weekly), Tientsin, China, 1932-34, Post Commander's Corner Redlander, 1945-47. Address: No-Reveille, Box 446, Wilton, Me. 04294. Died Nov. 13, 1964; buried U.S. Mil. Acad. Cemetery, West Point, N.Y.

SMITH, WILLIAM gov. Va.; b. "Marengo," King George County, Va., Sept. 6, 1797; s. Col. Caleb and Mary (Waugh) S.; m. Elizabeth H. Bell, 1821. In law practice, Culpeper, Va., 1818; established a daily post service from Washington, D.C. to Milledgeville, Ga., 1834; mem. Va. Senate, 1836-41; mem. U.S. Ho. of Reps. from Va., 27th, 33d-36th congresses, 1841-43, 1853-61; presdl. elector, 1844; gov. Va., 1846-49, 64-65, signed the act accepting the retrocession to Va. of the part of D.C. south of Potomac River, 1847; commd. col. 49th Va. Inf., Confederate Army, 1861, brig. gen., 1862; mem. Con federate Congress, 1862; brevetted maj. gen., 1863; mem. Va. Ho. of Dels., 1877-79. Died "Monterosa" nr. Warrenton, May 18, 1887; buried Hollywood Cemetery, Richmond, Va.

SMITH, WILLIAM brig. gen. U.S.A.; b. Orwell, Vt., Mar. 26, 1831; s. Israel S. and Delia (Ferguson) S.; A.B., U. of Vt., 1854, A.M., 1856; m. Mary O. McAllister, Oct. 10, 1867. Additional p.m. vols., Aug. 29, 1861; bvtd. lt. col., Mar. 13, 1865; hon. mustered out, July 20, 1866; apptd. from Minn., maj. p.m. U.S.A., Jan. 17, 1867; lt. col. deputy p.m. gen., Sept. 6, 1888; brig. gen. p.m. gen., Mar. 10, 1890; retired by operation of law, Mar. 26, 1895. Home: Pelham Manor, N.Y. Died 1912.

SMITH, WILLIAM EPHRAIM congressman, lawyer; b. Augusta, Ga., Mar. 14, 1829; had academic course; studied law. Admitted to bar under spl. act of Ga. Legislature, 1846, practiced in Albany, Ga.; also became planter; ordinary of Dougherty County, Ga., 1853; solicitor gen. of S.W. Circuit, 1858-60; enlisted as 1st lt. 4th Ga. Volunteer Infantry in Confederate Army during Civil War, elected capt., 1862; elected to Ho. of Reps. of 2d Confederate Congress, 1863; mem. U.S. Ho. of Reps. (Democrat) from Ga., 44th-46th congresses, 1875-81; pres. Ga. Dem. Conv., 1886; mem. Ga. Senate, 1886-88. Died Albany, Mar. 11, 1890; buried Oakview Cemetery.

SMITH, WILLIAM FARRAR mil. and civil engr.; b. St. Albans, Vt., Feb. 17, 1824; s. Ashbel and Sarah (Butler) S.; apptd. to West Point, 1841; grad. in topog. engrs., 1845; m. Sarah Ward, Apr. 24, 1861. Served on survey of Upper Lakes, 1845-46; dept. mathematics, West Point, 1847-48; surveys in Texas, 1849-50, and of Mexican boundary, 1850-51; of Florida ship canal, 1853, and other engr. duties, 1861. Served under Gen. Butler to June 20, 1861; col. 3d Vt. vols., July 23, 1861, in defense of Washington; brig. gen. U.S. vols., Aug. 13, 1861; comd. div. in Army of Potomac in siege of Yorktown, battles of Lee's Mills, Williamsburgh, Golding's farm, Malvern Hill, Crampton's Gap, Antietam, etc.; comd. 6th corps at Fredericksburg, 1862; 9th corps, Mar. 17, 1863; comd. div. of N.Y. and Pa. militia at Gettysburg; chief engr. of army of the Cumberland, Oct. 3, 1863; planned and executed capture of Brown's Ferry, Tenn., Oct. 27, 1863, opening shorter line of communication for supplies; chief engr. div. of Miss., Nov. 16, 1863; planned battle of Missionary Ridge. Threw a bridge 1,500 feet long across the Tennessee River for Sherman's army. In command 18th army corps, Apr. 1864; in battles of Drury's Bluff and Cold Harbor; assaulted and carried line of fortifications at Petersburg, June 15, 1864, etc. Resigned as maj. gen. vols., Nov. 4, 1865; resigned from army, Mar. 7, 1867. Pres. Internat. Ocean Telegraph Co., 1865-73; pres. New York Bd. of Police, 1877; civil engr., 1881—. Author: From Chattanooga to Petersburg, under Generals Grant and Butler. Address: Philadelphia, Pa. Died 1903.

SMITH, WILLIAM JONES architect; b. Phila., Pa., May 26, 1881; s. Uselma Clarke and Fanny (Mitcheson) S.; B.S. in architecture, U. of Pa., 1903; A.D.G. architecte diplomé par le Gouvèrnement Francais, Ecole des Beaux Arts, Paris, 1907; m. Mary Van Horne, June 30, 1914; children—William Mitcheson, Van Horne, Sidney Stockton. With Cass Gilbert, architect, N.Y., 1907-09; Holabird & Roche, Chicago, 1909-12; mem. firm Childs & Smith, 1912—, firm architects for ins., office, univ. bldgs. such as Northwestern U. Chicago Campus, high and elem. schs. as Davenport, Ia., Freeport and Kankakee, Ill., med. and dental colls., The Mather Home, Evanston, Ill., Hardware and Employers Ins. Bldg., Wis., Marathon Co. Court house, Wausau, Wis., Evanston Schools, asso. prof. in charge of senior design, Armour Inst. Tech., 1924-29. Served as capt. 319th Engrs., U.S. Army, 1917-18; engr. War Dept., 1942-43; field rep. O.S.S., 1944. Licensed architect 14 states. Fellow A.I.A.; mem. Grad's of Beaux Arts, BAID, Ill. Soc. Architects, Pa. Hist. Soc., Art Inst. Chicago, Burnham Library Com., Am. Soc. Testing Materials, Sigma Xi. Episcopalian. Mason. Club: University (Chicago). Home: 435 Linden St., Winnetka, Ill. Office: 20 N. Wacker Dr., Chgo. Died Jan. 22, 1958; buried Churchyard Christ Church, Winnetka.

SMITH, WILLIAM OLIVER mil. orgn. nat. comdr.; b. Liberty, Mo., Aug. 28, 1894; s. Charles Lee and Sallie Lindsay (Jones) S.; A.B., U. N.C., 1916; m. Vandelia Elizabeth Drew, Oct. 26, 1921; children—William Oliver, Vandelia Drew. Treas., Edwards & Broughton Co., Raleigh, N.C., printers, lithographers, engravers, 1919-51, pres., 1951—. Nat. comdr. Army and Navy Legion of Valor, U.S.A., 1954-55, chief of staff, 1957-59. Served from 2d lt. to 1st lt., inf., U.S. Army, 1917-19; maj., inf., AUS, 1940-44. Decorated Purple Heart, D.S.C.; Croix de Guerre with palm. Mem. Am. Legion (past dist. comdr. N.C.), 40 and 8, Nat. Office Mgmt. Assn. (past pres. Raleigh chpt.), Carolinas Master Printers Assn., Mil. Order World Wars (comdr. N.C. 1954-55), N.C. Soc. of Cincinnati, N.C. Soc. S.A.R. (past treas., past pres., past nat. trustee), Kappa Sigma, Baptist (deacon). Club: Executives (Raleigh). Home: 917 Holt Dr. Office: 1821 N. Boulevard, Raleigh, N.C. Died Jan. 17, 1960.

SMITH, WILLIAM RUTHVEN army officer; b. Nashville, Tenn., Apr. 2, 1868; s. Robert McPhail and Lititia Clark (Trimble) S.; student Vanderbilt U. 2 yrs.; grad. U.S. Mil. Acad., 1892, Sch. of Submarine Defense, Ft. Totten, N.Y., 1908; m. Mary Prince, d. Gen. George B. Davis, U.S.A., Dec. 4, 1901; children—Katharine Alexander, William Ruthven. Commd. additional 2d lt. 1st Arty., June 11, 1892; 2d lt. 1st Arty., Sept. 23, 1892; 1st lt., Mar. 2, 1899; capt. Arty. Corps, May 8, 1899; maj. Coast Arty. Corps, Mar. 31, 1909; lt. col., July 1, 1916; col., May 15, 1917; brig. gen. N.A., Aug. 5, 1917; maj. gen. N.A., June 26, 1918; hon. discharged temp. apptmts., July 15, 1919; Gen. Staff, Aug. 22, 1919; chief of staff Philippine Dept., rank brig. gen. U.S.A., Apr. 27, 1921; maj. gen., July 23, 1924. Instr. and asst. prof. mathematics, natural and exptl. philosophy, ordnance and gunnery, U.S. Mil. Acad., 11 yrs.; asst. to chief of Coast Arty., Washington, D.C., 4 yrs.; dir. Dept. of Electricity and Mine Defense, School of Mine Defense, Ft. Monroe, Va., 3 yrs.; in charge of building and placing first submarine net put down in U.S., Feb. 1917; assigned to Camp Sheridan, Ala., 1917; comd. 62d Arty. brigades, 37th Div. Ohio N.G. and 37th Div. N.G.; comdr. 36th Div. (Tex. and Okla. N.G.), A.E.F., Meuse-Argonne campaign; comdt. coast Arty. Sch., Fort Monroe, Va., 1923-24; comdg. gen. Hawaiian Div., Schofield Bks., 1925-27; dept. comdr. Honolulu, Aug. 1927-Jan. 1928; supt. U.S. Mil. Acad., West Point, 1928-Apr. 30, 1932 (retired); supt. Sewanee Mil. Acad., Aug. 1, 1932—. D.S.M. (U.S.); Comdr. Legion of Honor (France); Croix de Guerre (France). Episcopalian. Address: Sewanee, Tenn. Died July 15, 1941.

SMITH, WILLIAM SOOY civil engr.; b. Tarlton, O., July 22, 1830; s. Sooy and Ann (Hedges) S.; A.B., Ohio U., 1849, later A.M.; grad. U.S. Mil. Acad., 1853; m. Elizabeth Haven; m. 2d, Josephine Hartwell, 1884; father of Charles Sooysmith. Apptd. 2d lt. 3d Arty. U.S.A.; promoted 2d lt. 3d Arty. U.S.A., and stationed in N.M.; resigned; went to Chicago, 1854, entered engring. service of I.C. R.R. Co.; soon afterward apptd. asst. engr. to Col. Graham, U.S. engr. in charge of improvements of Lake Michigan harbors, but resigned because of dangerous illness; conducted select sch. at Buffalo, 1855-57; practiced as civ. engr., 1857-59; chief engr. of co. building iron bridge across Savannah River for Savannah & Charleston R.R. Co., 1860-61; served as lt. col., col. and brig gen. U.S.A., Apr. 1861-Sept. 1864, when resigned because totally disabled by inflammatory rheumatism. When sufficiently recovered resumed practice as civ. engr. at Chicago. Did much difficult work as engr. and contractor for U.S. Govt. and ry. cos., including reconstruction of Waugoshanee Light House at western entrance of Straits of Mackinac; built 1st all-steel ry. bridge in world (Glasgow, Mo.), and substructures of 6 other bridges, by pneumatic process, which developed and greatly improved; with son, Charles Sooysmith, introduced into this country freezing process for difficult subaqueous work, and sank 2 shafts through quick-sands and boulders, to depth of 100 feet, which could not have been put down by any other known method. Completely changed methods of constructing foundations for heavy buildings in Chicago, carrying the loads down through mud and soft earth to hard bottom, 50 feet or more, by means of piles cut off below water surface, and where these could not be driven without endangering foundations of adjacent buildings, by sinking columns of concrete to hard bottom and resting the bldgs. on them; aided in development of plans of high steel bldgs. in Chicago and throughout world; leader in urging Govt. to create bd. to test Am. metals and mem. of that bd. during the 3 yrs. of its existence. Invented the 1st pneumatic caisson ever built; designed new system of fireproof building. Address: Medford, Ore. Died Mar. 4, 1916.

SMITH, WILLIAM STEPHENS army officer, congressman; b. L.I., N.Y., Nov. 8, 1755; s. John and Margaret (Stephens) S.; grad. Princeton, 1774; m. Abigail Amelia Adams, June 12, 1786, 3 children. Aide-de-camp to Gen. Sullivan as maj. 1776; participated in Battle of White Plains; lt. col. in William R. Lee's Regt.; fought at battles of Monmouth and Newport, 1778; insp. and adjutant to a corps of light inf. under Gen. Lafayette, 1780-81; served in 22 engagements in Revolutionary War; aide to George Washington, 1781; charged with supervision of evacuation of N.Y.C. by British in accordance with treaty of peace, 1781; sec. legation, London, Eng., 1785-88; visited Prussia to study orgn. of Frederick the Great, circa 1786; sent on diplomatic mission to Spain and Portugal, circa 1787; was fed. marshal, supr. of the revenue, surveyor Port of N.Y., 1789-1800; commanded 12th Inf., 1798; mem. U.S. Ho. of Reps. (Federalist) from N.Y., 13th Congress, 1813-15, presented his credentials of election to 14th Congress, did not qualify and Westel Willoughby, Jr. successfully contested his election, Dec. 1815; a founder Soc. of Cincinnati in N.Y., pres., 1795-97. Died Lebanon, N.Y., June 10, 1816.

SMITH, WILLIAM STEVENSON, archaeologist; b. Indianapolis, Feb. 7, 1907; s. Louis Ferdinand and Edna Wirth (Stevenson) S.; student U. Chicago, 1924-26; A.B., Harvard, 1928, Ph.D., 1940. Asst. to George A. Reisner, Harvard, 1889; with Egyptian Expdn., Giza Pyramids, 1930-39, 46-47; asst. curator, department of Egyptian art. Museum of Fine Arts, Boston, 1941-54, asso. curator, 1954-56, curator, 1956-69; lecturer in Egyptian art Harvard, 1948-69; director American Research Center in Egypt, Cairo, 1951. Served as lieutenant commander U.S.N.R., active duty 1942-46. Fellow American Acad. Arts. and Scis.; mem. Archeol. Inst. Am., German Archaeological Institute, American Oriental Soc. Author: Ancient Egypt as represented in the Museum of Fine Arts, 1942; A History of Egyptian Sculpture and Painting in the Old Kingdom, 1946; A History of the Giza Necropolis, Vol. 2 (with George A. Reisner), 1955; The Art and Architecture of Ancient Egypt, 1958; Interconnections in the Ancient Near East, 1965. Home: Cambridge MA Died Jan. 13, 1969.

SMITH, WILLIAM STROTHER naval officer; b. Richmond, Va., Sept. 15, 1857; s. Samuel Brown and Margaret (Strother) S.; grad. U.S. Naval Acad., 1880; m. Irma St. Clair-Abrams, Dec. 2, 1891. Asst. engr., June 10, 1882; promoted through grades to rear adm., Mar. 20, 1918; retired, Sept. 15, 1921. Served on Columbia and Yankee, Spanish-Am. War, 1898; asst. insp. machinery, Newport News, Va., 1903-05; on West Virginia, 1905-06; duty Bur. Steam Engring., Navy Dept., 1906-09, Bd. of Inspection and Survey, 1909-12; engr. officer Navy Yard, Phila., 1912-15; detailed spl.

duty Navy Dept., Dec. 7, 1915; served as mem. Submarine Bd., Commn. for Laws Relating to Safety of Life at Sea, and Bd. of Inspection and Survey on Ships. Episcopalian. Home: Jacksonville, Fla. Died Sept. 7, 1927.

SMITH, WILLIAM WARD naval officer, mfg. exec.; b. Newark, Feb. 8, 1888; s. Samuel H. and Elizabeth (Selander) S.; B.S., U.S. Naval Acad., 1909; m. Elizabeth Virginia Purdy, Sept. 2, 1913; children—Virginia Elizabeth (dec.), William Ward (A.U.S.). Passed midshipman, June 1909, and advanced through the grades to v. admiral, 1945; comdr. of destroyers, on staff of Comdr. Naval Forces, European Waters, based Queenstown, Ireland, World War I; service in Atlantic and Pac. Fleets, Asiatic, C.A. and S.A. waters; head of dept. of mathematics, Naval Acad., 1936-39; comd. cruiser U.S.S. Brooklyn, 1939-40; chief of staff, U.S. Pacific Fleet, 1941; comd. cruisers of Pacific Fleet Task Force, 1942; Battle of Coral Sea, Battle of Midway; comd. cruisers and destroyers operating in Aleutian waters; comd. Task Force in bombardment of Kiska, 1942; dir. Naval Transp. Service, Naval Operations, Washington, D.C., Jan. 1943-Mar. 1945; comdr. Service Force, U.S. Pacific Fleet, Mar.-Dec. 1945; ret., 1946. Chmn. U.S. Maritime Commn., 1946-49; v.p. Fruehauf Trailer Co., Detroit, since 1950. Decorations for World War I (Destroyers); Expeditionary Force (China.); Nicaragua (2d Campaign); Order of Merit (Nicaragua); Order of Leopold of Belgium; Expert Rifle and Pistol awards, D.S.M. Coral Sea and Midway), American Theater, Pacific Theater and Victory Ribbons. Mem. Soc. Naval Architects and Marine Engrs. Clubs: Army and Navy; Columbia Country (Chevy Chase, Md.). Author: Midway: Turning Point of the Pacific, 1966. Home: 3410 Newark St., Washington 20016. Office: Tower Bldg., 14th and K Sts. N.W., Washington. Died May 6, 1966; buried U.S. Naval Acad. Cemetery, Annapolis, Md.

SMITH, WINFORD HENRY hosp. dir.; b. West Scarboro, Me., July 11, 1877; s. George Prey and Carrie P. (Burnham) S.; A.B., Bowdoin, 1899, Sc.D., 1918; M.D., Johns Hopkins, 1903; m. Jean Maguire, June 29, 1905. Intern and resident gynecologist Lakeside Hosp., Cleveland, 1903-05; hosp. physician N.Y. City Health Dept., 1905-06; supt. Hartford (Conn.) Hosp., 1906-09; gen. med. supt. of Bellevue and Allied hosps., N.Y.C., 1909-11; dir. Johns Hopkins Hosp., Balt., 1911-46. Cons. on hosp. orgn. and planning. Commd. col., M.C., AUS, World War I; apptd. chief hosp. div., staff of surgeon gen., Washington. Decorated D.S.M. (U.S.). Mem. A.M.A., Am. Hosp. Assn. (pres. 1916; awarded gold medal for outstanding achievement in hosp. adminstrn.), Am. Coll. Hosp. Adminstrs. Republican. Episcopalian. Club: Elkridge Hunt. Author: of numerous papers relating to hosp. orgn., adminstrn. and mgmt. Home: 100 W. University Pkwy., Balt. 10. Died Nov. 13, 1961.

SMITH, ZEMRO AUGUSTUS editorial writer Indianapolis Journal; b. Wiston, Me., Aug. 26, 1837; A.M., Waterville Coll., 1862; m. Jane Steele, Oct. 8, 1891. Capt. maj., lt. col., 1st Me. heavy arty., regt. losing most men of any in Union army; bvtd. col. U.S.V. Republican. Address: Indianapolis, Ind. Deceased.

SMITHER, HENRY CARPENTER army officer; b. Ft. Sill, Okla., July 28, 1873; s. Robert Gano and Mary Virginia S.; grad. U.S. Mil. Acad., 1897; m. Helen Lytle, June 28, 1900; children—Bernice Lytle (Mrs. George W. Gering), Henrietta Carpenter (Mrs. Paul L. Armel), Henry Carpenter. Commissioned 2d lieut., 8th Cavalry, June 11, 1897; promoted through grades to maj., January 30, 1917; colonel Signal Corps (temp.), October 10, 1917; colonel U.S.A., July 1, 1920; brig. gen., June 18, 1925. Served in Cuba, Spanish-Am. War, later in Philippines; mem. Gen. Staff Corps, 1913-15; asst. chief of staff, chief of 4th Sect., Service of Supply, A.E.F., 1918-19; chief of staff, 3d Div., Sept. 1920-July 1921. Selected by Gen. Dawes and appointed by the President to assist in making up Budget of U.S., 1921; apptd. by exec. order of the President, July 27, 1921, chief coördinator; retired Jan. 1, 1929. Decorated D.S.M. (U.S.); Officer Legion of Honor (French); D.S.M. (Republic of Panama). Address: Washington, D.C. Died July 13, 1930.

SMITHEY, LOUIS PHILIPPE architect; b. Mecklenburg County, Va., June 7, 1890; s. William Rosser and Nannie Jane Elizabeth (Greene) S.; A.B., Randolph-Macon Coll., 1909, A.M., 1910; student Va. Poly. Inst., 1910-14, Mass. Inst. Tech., 1914-15; m. Dorothy Terrill, June 11, 1938; 1 dau., Nancy Terrill. Partner, Smithey & Tardy, architects and engrs., Roanoke, Va., 1922-27; pvt. practice, Roanoke, 1927-35; partner Smithey & Boynton, architects and engrs., Roanoke, 1935-—; projects include home office Shenandoah Life Ins. Co., 1st Presbyn. Ch., South Roanoke Meth. Ch., Huntington Court Meth. Ch., Municipal Stadium (all Roanoke), brick dormitory group Va. Poly. Inst., Blacksburg, Va., others. Mem. Roanoke Bd. Zoning Appeals, 1953-64. Served in U.S. Army, World War I and II, advanced to rank of lt. col. Fellow A.I.A. (pres. Va. chpt. 1940); mem. Roanoke C. of C. (dir. 1947-48, pres. 1947), Roanoke Valley Heart Assn. (pres. 1952), Phi Beta Kappa, Kappa Alpha. Methodist (chmn. ofcl. bd.). Elk. Clubs: Kiwanis (pres. 1941), Shenandoah (Roanoke). Home: 2912 Wycliffe Av. S.W. Office: 319 McClanahan St. S.W., Roanoke, Va. Died Aug. 18, 1966.

SMOHALLA Indian chief, religious leader; b. circa 1815. Became chief of Wanapum branch Nez Percés Indians; also noted as medicine man; fought against Whites in Yakima War, 1855-56; believed to have been killed in fight with neighboring tribe, left for dead, but rescued by some white men; rather than immediately returning to his people, wandered throughout Cal., Ariz., Mexico and Utah; then returned home and was thought by his people to have returned from the dead; founded Dreamer religion which claimed that Indians were only true people on earth and would eventually control whole earth; very influential during Nez Percé War of 1877. Died 1907.

SMYKAL, RICHARD army officer; b. Chicago, Ill., Dec. 29, 1900; s. Edward J. and Bessie (Rusy) Smejkal; B.S. in indsl. adminstrn., U. of Ill., 1922; student Chicago-Kent Coll. of Law, 1923-24; m. Helen Holpuch, Feb. 4, 1925; children—Ralph, Susan. Commd. 2d lt., inf., Officer Res. Corps, 1922, and advanced through grades to maj. gen., 1948; served in China, Burma, India Theatre and in European Theatre of Operations during World War II; assigned comdg. gen., 33d Inf. Div., Ill. Nat. Guard, 1948. Exec. in building industry; pres. Richard Smykal, Inc., Wheaton, Ill., 1924-—. Commissioner (chmn.) Community Conservation Bd., Chgo. Awarded Legion of Merit, Bronze Star Medal, Am. Defense Service Medal, Asiatic-Pacific Theatre Medal with 3 bronze stars, European, African, Middle Eastern Theatre, Am. Theatre and Victory medals (U.S.); Breast Order Yun Hwei (Cloud Banner), Army, Navy, Air Forces Medal (China). Mem. Am. Legion, Vets. of Fgn. Wars, Mil. Order World Wars, Lions Internat., Lambda Alpha, Lambda Chi Alpha, Phi Delta Phi, Scabbard and Blade. Presbyterian. Club: University (Chicago). Home: 1010 E. Illinois Street. Office: 100 N. West St., Wheaton, Ill. Died Apr. 4, 1958; buried Wheaton, Ill.

SMYTH, ALEXANDER congressman, army officer; b. on island of Rathlin, off Ireland, 1765; s. Rev. Adam Smyth; m. Nancy Binkley, Jan. 1791, 4 children. Came to Va., 1775; dep. clk. Botetourt County (Va.), 1785; licensed and admitted to Va. bar, 1789; practiced in Abingdon, Va., 1789; mem. Va. Ho. of Dels., 1792-96, 1801-02, 04-08, 16-17, 26-27; mem. Va. Senate, 1808-09; col. S.W. Va. Rifle Regt., 1808-11; ordered to Washington (D.C.) to prepare system of army discipline, 1811; insp. gen. U.S. Army ith rank of brig. gen., 1812; in command of brigade of regulars ordered to Niagra for projected invasion of Canada, 1812, took command of Stephen Van Rensselaer's force at Buffalo, N.Y., failed to invade Canada because of lack of trained troops; mem. U.S. Ho. of Reps. from Va., 15th-18th, 20th-21st congresses, 1817-25, 1827-30. Died Washington, D.C., Apr. 17, 1830; buried Congressional Cemetery, Washington.

SMYTH, CLIFFORD newspaper man; b. N.Y. City, Nov. 13, 1866; s. Joseph Kennedy and Julia Gabriella (Ogden) S.; Urbana (Ohio) U., 1885-87; New Ch. Theol. Sch., Boston, 1888-89; m. Beatrix, d. Julian Hawthorne, of N.Y. City, Aug. 2, 1905; children—Julian Clifford, Hawthorne Lewis, Sylvia Hawthorne. Began writing for New York papers, 1889; editor Yonkers (N.Y.) Daily Herald, 1890-94; Am. consul at Cartagena, Colombia, 1894-98; tramp trip, New York to Atlanta, principally in Ky. and W. Va. mountains, writing for magazines and newspapers; on Atlanta Constitution until 1903; sent by syndicate of Southern papers to Bogota, Colombia, to report on Panama trouble, 1903; sent to Panama, by Dem. Nat. Com., presdl. campaign, 1904; with New York Times Sunday Mag., 1905-13; editor New York Times Book Review, Feb. 1913-Nov. 1922; editor Literary Digest Internat. Book Review, Nov. 1922-Nov. 1926; lit. adviser Funk & Wagnalls Co. since Nov. 1926. Democrat. Mem. Authors' League America. Clubs: Authors, P.E.N., Century. Author: The Gilded Man, 1918; Builders of America, 24 vols., a series of biographies, including Columbus, Washington, Jefferson, Webster, Lincoln, Lee, Wilson, etc., 1931. Home: 321 S. 5th Av., Mt. Vernon, N.Y. Office: 354 4th Av., New York, N.Y.

SMYTH, GEORGE WASHINGTON congressman; b. N.C., May 16, 1803; attended college, Murfreesboro, Tenn. Moved to Tex. (then part Republic of Mexico), 1828, settled in municipality of Bevell, Zavalas Colony (now Jasper County); apptd. by Mexican Govt. as surveyor, later made commr. of titles; del. Gen. Consultation of Tex., San Felipe de Austin, 1835; mem. Tex. State Conv., signer Tex. Declaration of Independence, 1836, also signed Republic of Tex. Constn.; apptd. by Pres. Lamar of Tex. as commr. in charge of boundary line between Republic of Tex. and U.S.; became farmer; dep. Congress of Republic of Tex., 1845, assisted in framing Constn. State of Tex.; elected commr. Tex. Gen. Land Office, 1848; mem. U.S. Ho. of Reps. (Democrat) from Tex., 33d Congress, 1853-55; served in Confederate Army during Civil War; mem. Tex. Constl. Conv., 1866. Died Austin, Tex., Feb. 21, 1866; buried State Cemetery.

SMYTH, WILLIAM congressman, lawyer; b. Eden, County Tyrone, Ireland, Jan. 3, 1824; came to U.S., 1838; attended U. Ia.; studied law. Admitted to bar, 1847, practiced in Marion, Ia.; pros. atty. Linn County, 1848-53; judge dist. ct. for 4th Jud. Dist. of Ia., 1853-57; chmn. commn. to codify and revise Ia. laws, 1858; col. 31st Regt., Ia. Volunteer Infantry in Union Army during Civil War for 2 years; mem. U.S. Ho. of Reps. (Republican) from Ia., 41st Congress, 1869-Sept. 30, 1870. Died Marion, Sept. 30, 1870; buried Oak Shade Cemetery.

SMYTHE, GEORGE WINFRED, army officer; b. Norristown, Pa., Aug. 4, 1899; s. David N. and Laura Virginia (Brooks) S.; student West Chester Normal Sch., 1918, Muhlenberg Coll.; Allentown, Pa., 1919-20; B.S., U.S. Mil. Acad., 1924; Inf. Sch., Fort Benning, Ga., 1927-28; Command and Gen. Staff Sch., Fort Leavenworth, Kan., 1935-36; m. Susie Hubbell Coley, Aug. 12, 1924; children—George W., John David. Commd. 2d lt., U.S. Army, June 12, 1924, and advanced through grades to maj. gen.; served as company officer 29th inf., Fort Benning, Ga., 1924-27; prof. Mil. Science and Tactics. Staunton (Va.) Mil. Acad., 1928-32; co. officer 33d inf., Fort Clayton, Canal Zone, 1932-34, 4th inf., Fort George Wright, Spokane, Wash., 1934-35; dir. phys. edn., U.S. Mil. Acad., 1936-40; staff officer 27th inf., Hawaiian dept., Schofield Barracks, T.H., 1940-42; mem. gen. staff Army Service Force Mil. Lend Lease, Washington, D.C., 1942-43; comdg. officer 47th Inf., 9th Inf. Div., North Africa, Sicily, Eng., France, Belgium and Germany, 1943-44; asst. div. comdr., 80th Div., Germany, 1945; with hdqrs. Army Ground Forces, Fort Monroe, Va., 1945; chief of staff 3d Army, Ft. McPherson, 1947; asst. division comdr. 1st Inf. Division, 1949. Decorated Purple Heart with cluster, Silver Star Medal (cluster 1945), Distinguished Service Cross, 1944, Bronze Star (U.S.); Chevalier Legion of Honor, Cross of War with palm, 1945 (France); Russian Medal of Bravery, 1945; O.B.E. (Eng.), 1946; Office Order of Leopold, with palm, Cross of War, 1940 (palm, 1946) (Belgium). Mem. Alpha Tau Omega. Mason. Awarded Edgerton Sabre by U.S. Mil. Acad. for best all round athlete, class 1924. Home: Arlington VA Died Jan. 1969.

SNAVELY, JOHN ROBERT physician, educator; b. Sterling, Ill., Feb. 16, 1913; s. John Louis and Ada Julia (Weaver) S.; A.B., Grinnell Coll., 1935; M.D., U. Chgo., 1939; m. Martha Keith, Dec. 21, 1945. Intern, Charity Hosp., New Orleans, 1939-40, resident in medicine, 1940-42, vis. physician, 1947-54, sr. physician, 1954-55; asst. prof. medicine Tulane U., 1947-52, asso. prof. medicine, 1952-55; cons. internist USPHS, New Orleans, 1951-55; prof., chmn. dept. medicine U. Miss., 1955-—, asst. dean Sch. Medicine, 1956-—; physician in chief U. Miss. Hosp., 1955-—; cons. medicine VA Hosp., Jackson, Miss., 1955-63. Served from 1st lt. to maj., AUS, 1942-46. Decorated Bronze Star. Diplomate Am. Bd. Interal Medicine. Fellow A.C.P.; mem. Central, So. socs. clin. research, A.M.A., Phi Beta Kappa, Sigma Xi, Alpha Omega Alpha. Home: 2026 Meadowbrook Rd., Jackson, Miss. Died June 12, 1964; buried Sterling, Ill.

SNEAD, THOMAS LOWNDES army officer, Confederate congressman; b. Henrico County, Va., Jan. 10, 1828; s. Jesse and Jane (Johnson) S.; grad. Richmond Coll., 1846; grad. U. Va., 1848; m. Harriet Vairin Reel, Nov. 24, 1852, 2 surviving children. Admitted to Va. bar, 1850; mem. staff St. Louis Bulletin, 1860, 61; aide to Gov. Jackson of Mo., 1861; acting adjutant-gen. with rank of col. Mo. State Guard; one of Mo.'s 2 commrs. in mil. conv. with Confederate States, 1861; asst. adjutant gen. with rank of maj. Confederate Army, 1862, chief of staff to Gen. Sterling Price in S.W.; rep. from Mo. to Confederate Congress, 1864-65; mng. editor N.Y. Daily News, 1865-66; admitted to N.Y. bar, 1866. Author: The Fight for Missouri, 1886. Died Hotel Royal, N.Y.C., Oct. 17, 1890; buried Bellefontaine Cemetery, St. Louis.

SNEED, ALBERT LEE army officer; b. Conway, Ark., Apr. 24, 1884; s. Charles Robert and Vena (Lee) S.; m. Dorothy Ryman, Montgomery, Ala., Dec. 31, 1942; student U. of Ark., 1902-04; B.S., U.S. Mil. Acad., 1908. Commd. 2d lt., 1908, advanced through the grades to brig. gen., June 1942; foreign service in P.I., 1909-10, 1934-37, Hawaii, 1913-14, Constantinople, Turkey, 1922-23, Australia, Feb.-Sept. 1943; now in command Army Air Forces Western Technical Training Command. Awarded Silver Star. Mason. Address: 1108 15th St., Denver, Colo. Died Nov. 1967.

SNEED, JOHN LOUIS TAYLOR jurist; b. Raleigh, N.C., May 12, 1820; s. Maj. Junius and Julia Rowan (Taylor) S.; academic edn.; m. Mary Ashe Shepherd, Aug. 1848. Admitted to Tenn. bar, 1841; mem. Tenn. gen. assembly, 1845-46; officer in Mexican war, 1846-47; dist. atty. gen., 1851-54; atty. gen. of Tenn. and Supreme Court reporter, 1854-59; brig. gen. provisional army of Tenn., 1861; judge Supreme Court, 1870-78; judge Ct. of Arbitration, 1879; Dem. elector for State-at-large, 1880; judge Court of Referees, 1883-84; chancellor 11th Chancery Div. of Tenn., 1894-1900 (resigned Jan. 3, 1900, retiring to private life). Edited 5 vols. Sneed's Tenn. Reports. Pres. Memphis Law School, 1887-93. Address: Memphis, Tenn. Died 1901.

SNEED, WILLIAM LENT orthopedic surgeon; b. Nashville, Tenn., Mar. 21, 1881; s. William Lent and Mary Lucy (Waller) S.; student Nashville Bible Coll., 1904-06; M.D., Vanderbilt Med. Sch., 1910; m. Marion E. Stokes, June 19, 1920; children—William Lent, Constance Blake, Pamela Ann Waller. Instr. in anatomy, Vanderbilt U., 1910-11; became attending surgeon orthopedic dept., Hosp. for Ruptured and Crippled, New York, 1912; now cons. surgeon Hosp. for Ruptured and Crippled and Meadow Brook Hosp. (Hempstead, L.I.); instr. in applied anatomy, Cornell U. Med. Coll., since 1917; cons. orthopedic surgeon Nassau County, French and North Shore Community hosps. Lt. Med. Corps, World War. Fellow Am. Coll. Surgeons; mem. A.M.A.; Acad. of Medicine, N.Y. Southern Soc., Tenn. Soc. of N.Y. Democrat. Clubs: Cornell, Racquet and Tennis (New York); Golf. Author: Orthopedics in Childhood, 1931. Home: 570 Park Av. Office: 654 Madison Av., New York, N.Y. Died Dec. 7, 1941.

SNELL, ALBERT M. physician; b. Lake Park, Minn., June 9, 1896; s. Albert M. and Anna (Markley) S.; B.S., U. Minn., 1916, M.D., 1918, M.S. in Medicine, 1927; m. Alice I. Morrow, Nov. 11, 1944. Grad. work in charge clin. labs. U. Minn. Hosp., Nov. 1919-Mar. 1920; practiced internal medicine, Mankato (Minn.) Clinic, Apr. 1920-Jan. 1924; 1st asst. in medicine, Mayo Clinic, Feb. 1, 1924-July 1925, consultant div. of medicine, July 1925-29, head sect. in div. of medicine since 1929; instr. in medicine, Mayo Foundation Grad. Sch., U. Minn., 1929-32, asst. prof., 1932-35, asso. prof., 1935-39, prof. of med., 1929-50; clin. prof. of medicine U. Cal., 1950-58; clin. prof. of medicine Stanford U., 1958. Entered medical corps., U.S.N.R., lt. (j.g.), served in U.S. Naval Hosp., Great Lakes, Ill., as med. officer and on U.S.S. K. I. Luckenbach, disch. June 9, 1919; entered med. corps U.S.N.R., as comdr., Dec. 29, 1941, served in U.S. Naval Hosp., Corona, Cal. and as sr. med. officer, U.S.S. Tryon, chief of medicine, U.S. Naval Hosp., Oakland, Calif.; disch. rank of capt., Feb. 16, 1946. Mem. professional Services Div. and section chief Vets. Adminstrn. 1946-56, v. chmn. 1948, chmn. 1953. Commended by sec. of navy for meritorious service. Mem. A.M.A., Am. Gastro-enterological Assn., Am. Soc. for Clin. Investigation, Assn. Am. Physicians, Am. Soc. for Exptl. Pathology, Pacific Interurban Clinical Club, Central Soc. of Clinical Research (pres. 1932), Sigma Xi, Alpha Omega Alpha, Alpha Kappa Kappa. Author: two books and numerous articles on med. subjects. Home: 750 Northampton Av. Office: 300 Homer Av., Palo Alto, Cal. Died Feb. 1960.

SNELL, JOHN LESLIE, educator, historian; b. Plymouth, N.C., June 2, 1923; s. John Leslie and Lessie Ann (McLamb) S.; A.B., U. N.C., 1946, A.M., 1947, Ph.D., 1950; m. Maxine Pybas, Dec. 18, 1943; children—Marcia Ruth, John McCullough, Leslie Ann. Instr. history U. N.C., 1946-49; asst. prof. history U. Wichita, 1949-51; faculty history Tulane U., 1953-66, prof., 1959-66, dean of Grad. Sch., 1963-66; prof. history University Pennsylvania, 1966-68; Univ. Distinguished prof. U. N.C., Chapel Hill, 1968-72; summer tchr. U. Tenn., U. Mich., Vanderbilt U., Standford U. Mem. Friends of Library, U. N.C. Served to 1st lt. USAAF, 1943-45; ETO. Decorated Air medal, Distinguished Flying Cross. Scholar for hist. research Am. Council Learned Socities, 1951-53. Mem. Am. (dir. study grad. edn. history 1958-60), So. hist. assns., Am. Assn. U. Profs., U. N.C. Alumni Assn., Omicron Delta Kappa, Phi Alpha Theta. Methodist. Author: Wartime Origins of the East-West Dilemma Over Germany, 1959; Illusion and Necessity; The Diplomacy of Global War, 1939-1945, 1963. Co-author, editor: The Meaning of Yalta, 1956; The Nazi Revolution, 1959; The Education of Historians in the United States, 1961; The Outbreak of the Second World War; Design or Blunder, published in 1962; Critical Issues in History, 1967. Editor: European History in the South, 1959. Contbr. Ency. Americana, numerous articles profl. jours. Home: Chapel Hill NC Died May 27, 1972.

SNELLING, JOSIAH army officer; b. Boston, 1782; m. Elizabeth Bell, Aug. 29, 1809; m. 2d, Abigail Hunt, 1812; at least 5 children including William Joseph, Henry Hunt. Commd. 1st lt. 4th, later 5th Inf. U.S. rmy, 1808, capt., 1809; distinguished at Battle of Tippecanoe, 1811, Battle of Brownstone, 1812; maj., asst. insp. gen., then lt. col. 4th Rifles, col., insp. gen., 1813-14, lt. col. 6th Inf., 1814, col. 5th Inf., 1819; acted as mil. comdr. and constructing engr. during and after bldg. of Ft. St. Anthony (adjacent to cities of St. Paul and Mpls.), 1820-28, responsible for governing settlement, name changed to Ft. Sneeling (in his honor) by War Dept., 1825. Died Washington, D.C., Aug. 20, 1828.

SNIFFEN, CULVER CHANNING army officer; b. N.Y. City, Jan. 1, 1844; s. John and Margaret Melissa (Thompson) S.; ed. Coll. Grammar Sch., Brooklyn; m. Rebecca Sarah Ruan, Sept. 3, 1873 (died 1907); m. 2d, Zenobia Blanche Richardson, June 26, 1909. Exec. clk., 1869, and asst. sec., 1873-77, to President Grant. Apptd. from N.Y., maj. p.-m. U.S.A., Mar. 3, 1877; lt. col. deputy p.-m.-gen., Mar. 31, 1899; col. asst. p.-m.-gen., May 3, 1901; brig. gen. p.-m.-gen. U.S.A., Sept. 11, 1906; retired Jan. 1, 1908. Chief p.-m. 5th Army Corps, Santiago, Cuba, and Montauk Point, L.I., Aug. 1-Sept. 8, 1898. Republican. Mason. Home: Washington, D.C. Died July 28, 1930.

SNOW, ALBERT SYDNEY naval officer; b. Rockland, Me., Nov. 18, 1845; apptd. to U.S. Naval Acad. from Me., 1861, grad. 1865; m. Frances M. Keating, Mar. 13, 1873. Ensign, Dec. 1, 1866; promoted through grades to rear adm., Feb. 21, 1905; retired Nov. 18, 1907. Summer of 1864, on board the Marblehead in pursuit of Confederate steamers Florida and Tallahassee; on bd. Pensacola, 1866-69, Alaska, 1870-73; duty Torpedo Sta., Newport, 1873; on bd. Congress, 1874-76, receiving-ship, Wabash, 1877-78; duty Navy Yard, Boston, 1878-79, 1882-83; exec. officer Portsmouth, 1879-81; coast survey duty, 1883-87; spl. duty at Newport, R.I., 1887; mem. Bd. Inspection and Survey, 1888-90; comd. Essex, 1890-92; duty Naval Acad., 1893-94; light house insp. 3d dist., 1895-98; duty Navy Yard, Portsmouth, 1898; comd. Badger during Spanish-Am. War, 1898; comdt. Naval Sta., San Juan, P.R., 1898-99; comd. New York, 1899-1900; duty Navy Yard, New York, 1900-01; comd. receiving-ships Vermont, 1901, Columbia, 1901-03, Hancock, 1903-04; duty Navy Yard, Boston, 1904-05, comdt. 1905-07. Pres. Gen. Court Martial, Navy Yard, Boston, 1918-19. Home: Brookline, Mass. Died July 14, 1932.

SNOW, LESLIE W(HITMORE) banker; born Snowville, N.H., Dec. 9, 1890; s. Leslie Perkins and Susan E. (Currier) S.; A.B. cum laude, Dartmouth College, 1912; B.S., Mass. Inst. Tech., 1914; m. Emily Royer, June 4, 1921; children—Shirley (Mrs. Douglas King Blue), Janet, Elizabeth (Mrs. Bruce Douglas Knowlton). With Chase Securities Corp., N.Y. City, 1923-31, assistant sec., 1927, assistant vice president, 1928; vice pres. Chase Harris Forbes Corp., 1931-33; 2d vice pres. The Chase Nat. Bank, 1933-45, v.p., 1945-55. Trustee Village of South Orange, N.J., 1949-55. Served as 1st lt., capt. and maj., ordnance dept., U.S. Army, 12 mo. overseas, World War I. Mem. Theta Delta Chi (pres. and dir. Founders Corp.; v.p., trustee Theta Delta Chi Ednl. Foundn.); former mem. Dartmouth Alumni Council. Republican. Presbyterian (elder). Mason. Clubs: Union League, Dartmouth College (N.Y. City); Orange Lawn Tennis (South Orange, N.J.). Home: 49 University Court, South Orange, N.J.; also Snowville, N.H. Died Aug. 15, 1959; buried Rochester, N.H.

SNOW, WILLIAM FREEMAN public health adminstr.; b. Quincy, Ill., July 13, 1874; s. William and Emily M. (Streeter) S.; B.A. in Chemistry, Stanford, 1896, M.A. in Physiology, 1897; M.D., Cooper Med. Coll., San Francisco, 1900; postgrad. Johns Hopkins, 1901-02; m. Blanche Malvina Boring, Aug. 15, 1899; children—William Boring, Richard Boring. Univ. physician, Stanford, 1900-01, asst. prof. hygiene, 1902-03, asso. prof., 1903-09, prof. hygiene and pub. health, 1909-19; gen. dir., chmn. bd. dirs. Am. Social Hygiene Assn., 1914-—; pres. Nat. Health Council, 1927-34. Lectr. in health edn. Columbia, 1928-40; spl. cons. USPHS, 1936-—; mem. U.S. Interdepartmental Venereal Disease Com., 1942-—; mem. nat. adv. com. Nat. Youth Adminstrn.; lectr. on preventive medicine N.Y.U., 1930-36. Epidemiologist, 1903-09; mem. and exec. officer Cal. Bd. of Health, 1909-14; lectr. Sch. of Hygiene and Pub. Health, Johns Hopkins, 1920-26. Investigations health adminstrn., Europe, 1912; mem. sec. Gen. Med. Bd., Council Nat. Defense, 1917-19; chmn. exec. com. U.S. Interdepartmental Social Hygiene Bd., 1918, rank of major; lt. col. M.C., U.S. Army, active duty, 1917-19; col. Med. Res. Corps, 1920-—. Chmn. League of Nations Com. to Study Traffic in Women and Children, 1924-28. Pres. Union Internationale Contre le Péril Vénérin, 1946, Assn. State and Prov. Bds. Health, 1912-13; fellow Am. Pub. Health Assn., A.A.A.S., A.M.A., N.Y. Acad. Medicine. Clubs: Century, Faculty, Cosmos. Home: 464 Riverside Dr. Office: 1790 Broadway, N.Y.C. 19. Died June 12, 1950.

SNOW, WILLIAM JOSIAH army officer; b. in New York, Dec. 16, 1868; s. William Dunham and Mary Elizabeth (Newell) S.; grad. U.S. Mil. Acad., 1890, Arty. Sch., 1898; Army War Coll., 1908; LL.D., Yale, 1919; m. Isabel Locke, Apr. 19, 1892; 1 son, William Arthur (deceased). Commd. 2d lieut. 1st Arty., June 12, 1890; promoted through grades to maj. gen., June 28, 1918; served as brig. gen. N.A., 1917-18. Duty at forts Hamilton, Slocum and Monroe until 1898; regimental q.-m. 7th Arty., 1898-99; with regt. in Philippine Islands, 1900-01; organized, and comd. 20th Battery, Field Arty., at Ft. Riley, Kan., and Ft. Robinson, Neb., to Dec. 1905; sec. Sch. of Application for Cav. and Field Arty., 1906-07; duty with War Dept., 1910-14; on Mexican border, 1917; in P.I. and Hawaii, 1915-17; reorganizing Sch. of Fire for F.A., Ft. Sill, Okla., 1917; apptd. comdr. 156th Field Arty. Brig., Camp Jackson, Columbia, S.C., Sept. 1917; chief of F.A., U.S. Army, Feb. 10, 1918-Dec. 19, 1927 (retired). Awarded D.S.M.; Comdr. Legion of Honor; Companion of the Bath. Home: 2220 20th St. N.W., Washington, D.C.; (summer) Blue Ridge Summit, Pa. Died Feb. 27, 1946.

SNOWDEN, A(RCHIBALD) LOUDON diplomat; b. Cumberland County, Pa., Aug. 11, 1837; s. Dr. Isaac Wayne and Margery (Loudon) S.; A.B., Jefferson Coll., Pa., 1856; A.M., 1888, LL.D., Washington and Jefferson, 1902; read law under David Webster, Phila., and law dept. U. of Pa.; m. Elizabeth Robinson Smith, Feb. 16, 1864. Served as lt. col. in Pa. Vols.; participated in various battles during Civil War. Register, and later chief coiner, U.S. Mint, Phila.; postmaster, Phila., 1877-79; supt. U.S. Mint, Phila., 1879-85; twice declined directorship of all U.S. mints, tendered by President Hayes; minister resident and consul gen. to Greece, Roumania and Servia, 1889-91; minister to Spain, 1891-93. Commr. and pres. Fairmount Park, Phila.; orator and writer; authority on coins and coinage and author many papers on those and other subjects. Decorated with Grand Cordon of the Saviour (Greece), Grand Cordon of the Crown (Roumania), Grand Cordon of Isabella the Catholic (Spain). Home: Philadelphia, Pa. Died Sept. 9, 1912.

SNOWDEN, JAMES ROSS govt. ofcl., numismatist; b. Chester, Pa., Dec. 9, 1809; s. Rev. Nathaniel Randolph and Sarah (Gustine) S.; ed. Dickinson Coll.; m. Susan Patterson, Sept. 13, 1848, 5 children. Admitted to Pa. bar, 1829; dep. atty. gen. (dist. atty.) Venango County (Pa.), circa 1831; mem. Pa. Ho. of Reps., 1838-44, speaker, 1842-44; col. Pa. Militia, circa 1830; presided Pa. Mil. Conv., Harrisburg, 1845; treas. State of Pa., 1845-47, improved state loans; treas. U.S. Mint, also asst. treas. U.S., Phila., 1848-50; solicitor Pa. R.R. Co., 1850; dir. U.S. Mint, Phila., 1854-61 prothonotary Pa. Supreme Ct., 1861-73. Author: (pamphlet) A Measure Proposed to Secure a Safe Treasury and a Sound Currency, 1857; A Description of Ancient and Modern Coins in the Cabinet Collection at the Mint of the United States, 1860. Died Hulmeville, Pa., Mar. 21, 1878.

SNOWDEN, THOMAS naval officer; b. Peekskill, N.Y., Aug. 12, 1857; grad. U.S. Naval Acad., 1879; married; 1 son, Thomas. Ensign jr. grade, Mar. 3, 1883; promoted through grades to rear adm., July 1, 1917; retired Aug. 12, 1921. Served on Dolphin, Spanish-Am. War, 1898; navigation officer, Illinois, 1902-05; duty Office of Naval Intelligence, Navy Dept., 1905-06; Compass Office, Bur. of Equipment, 1906-08; comd. Mayflower, 1908-10; mem. Board Inspection and Survey of Ships, Navy Dept., 1910-11; comd. South Carolina, 1911-13; at Naval War Coll., Newport, R.I., 1913-14; comd. Navy Yard and Sta., Portsmouth, N.H., 1915; comd. Wyoming, 1915-16; apptd. hydrographer Navy Dept., June 21, 1916. Home: Washington, D.C. Died Jan. 27, 1930.

SNYDER, CHARLES PHILIP naval officer; b. Charleston, W.Va., July 10, 1879; s. Charles Philip and Jane (Goshorn) S.; grad. U.S. Naval Acad., 1900; LL.D., Washington and Lee U., 1943; m. Cornelia Lee Wolcott, June 10, 1902 (dec. 1944); children—Elizabeth Lee (wife of Captain Ethelbert Watts, U.S. Navy), Captain Philip Wolcott, (C.C., U.S. Navy), Jane Logan (wife of Comdr. William M. Collins, U.S. Navy); m. 2d, Edith Hanlon Christian, Oct. 11, 1949. Commd. ensign, 1902, advanced through grades to rear admiral, 1933, vice admiral, 1939, admiral, 1940; commanded Argonne, Concord and Tennessee; chief of staff, U.S. Fleet, 1933-34, comdt. Navy Yard, Portsmouth, N.H., 1934-35; comd. Cruiser Div. Six, Scouting Force, U.S. Fleet 1935-36; pres., U.S. Naval War Coll., Newport, R.I., Jan. 1937-June 1939; vice adm., 1939, assigned to command Battleships, U.S. Fleet; assigned to command Battle Force, U.S. Fleet, Jan. 1940; with rank of adm.; apptd. Naval Inspector Gen., May 1942; ret., 1943; insp. gen. of Navy, 1942-47; placed on inactive duty on Retired List, 1947. Mem. Gen. Board, Navy Dept., Washington, 1941-42; comdr. U.S. Battleship Oregon, Transport Mongolia, Cruiser Minneapolis, during World War I. Awarded Navy Cross, World War and special letter commendation from War Dept., D.S.M., World War II. Mem. Sigma Chi. Club: Army and Navy. Home: 1870 Wyoming Av. N.W., Washington 20009. Died Dec. 3, 1964; buried Arlington Nat. Cemetery.

SNYDER, HOWARD MCC., army med. officer; b. Cheyenne, Wyo., Feb. 7, 1881; s. Albert Campbell and Priscilla McClelland (McCrum) S.; student U. Colo., 1899-1901; M.D., Jefferson Med. Coll.; hon. grad. Army Med. Coll., 1908; hon. grad. U.S. Mil. Acad., 1929; Research Bd. Tropical Medicine, P.I., 1909-11; grad. study Mayo Clinic, 1924, Sch. Tropical Medicine, San Juan, P.R., 1930-32, N.Y.U. and Bellevue Hosp., 1934; grad. Army Med. Field Service Sch., 1932; m. Alice Elizabeth Concklin, July 12, 1910; children—Howard McCrum, Richard Concklin. Intern Presbyn. Hosp., Phila., 1905-06; commd. 1st lt. M.C., U.S. Army, 1908, advancing through grades to maj. gen., 1943; sr. med. advisor N.G. of U.S., 1936-40; asst. insp. gen. War Dept., 1940-46; mem. com. to Pres. of U.S. on Integration and Improvement of U.S. med. and Hosp. Services, 1946; mem. Chief of Staff's adv. Group, 1946-48; research asso., conservation of human Resources Project and Manpower Council, Columbia U., N.Y.C., 1948-50; sr. med. officer S.H.A.P.E., 1951-52; physician to Pres. of U.S., 1953-61. Recipient Fed. Hosp. Certificate of Recognition, Am. Hosp. Assn., 1958, U.S. Health award, Met. Washington Bd. Trade and Med. Soc. D.C., 1960; decorated D.S.M.; Grand Comdr. Order Ouissam Alouite (Morocco); Grand Comdr. Order of So. Cross (Brazil). Fellow A.C.S., A.P.A. (hon.); mem. A.M.A., N.Y. Soc. Mil. and Naval Ofcrs. of World War, Mil. Order of Carabao, Assn. Mil. Surgeons of U.S. Home: Washington DC Died Sept. 22, 1970; buried U.S. Mil. Acad., West Point NY

SNYDER, MURRAY, public relations executive; born in Brooklyn, New York, June 20, 1911; the son of Edward and Ida (Schneider) S.; student pub. schs., San

Antonio Jr. Coll., Columbia U.; m. Betty Gathings, Jan. 3, 1943; children—Susan, Diana. Reporter San Antonio Light, 1928-29; polit. writer Albany and Washington corr. Bklyn. Eagle, 1931-37; press aide Borough Pres. of Bklyn., 1938-39; polit. writer N.Y. Post, 1940-41; polit. writer N.Y. Herald Tribune, 1946-52, Albany corr., 1951-52; asst. press sec. White House, 1953-57; Asst. Sec. of Def. for Public Affairs, 1957-61; pres. Murray Snyder Assos., pub. relations, 1962-69; asst. adminstr. for pub. affairs FAA, Washington, 1969. Served as pvt. to capt. Inf., U.S. Army, 1942-46. Mem. Silurians, Sigma Delta Chi. Club: Nat. Press. Home: Washington DC Died Nov. 2, 1969; buried Rock Creek Cemetery, Washington DC

SNYDER, SIMON brig. gen., U.S.A.; b. Selinsgrove, Pa., Feb. 9, 1839; s. Henry W. and Mary C. (Smith) S.; m. Mary T. Wardwell, Oct. 9, 1869. Apptd. from Pa. 2d lt. 5th U.S. Inf., Apr. 26, 1861; 1st lt., June 25, 1861; capt., July 1, 1863; maj. 11th Inf., Mar. 10, 1883; transferred to 5th Inf., May 17, 1883; lt. col. 10th Inf., Jan. 2, 1888; col. 19th Inf., Sept. 16, 1892; brig. gen. vols., May 4, 1898; hon. discharged from vols., May 12, 1899; brig. gen. U.S.A., Apr. 16, 1902; retired at own request after 40 yrs.' service, May 10, 1902. Bvtd. maj., Feb. 27, 1890, for action against Indians at Bear Paw Mountains, Mont., Sept. 30, 1877. Comd. 1st Brigade, 1st Div., 1st Army Corps, and en route to Province of Santa Clara, Cuba, Nov. 1898, to Jan. 1899; gov. Province of Santa Clara, Dec. 6, 1898-Jan. 25, 1899; later on spl. duty to Ponce, P.R.; on duty with regt. at Manila, P.I., Aug. 21-Sept. 15, 1899, comdg. U.S. troops and sub-dist. Cebu, P.I., Sept. 1899-Apr. 2, 1900; acting insp. gen. Dept. of the Lakes, 1900-01; en route to Philippines, Aug.-Oct. 1901; comd. regt., Oct.-Dec. 1901; comd. 5th Separate Brigade, Div. of the Philippines, Dec. 1901, to May 1902. Home: Reading, Pa. Died Apr. 12, 1912.

SOILAND, ALBERT physician; b. Stavanger, Norway, May 5, 1873; s. Edward and Axelina Christine (Halvorsen) S.; brought to U.S., 1883; student U. of Ill., 1895-97; M.D., U. of Southern Calif., 1900; D.M.R.E., U. of Cambridge, Eng., 1926; m. Dagfine Berner Svendsen, Sept. 17, 1902. Practiced in Los Angeles since 1900; dir. of group specializing in the study and treatment of neoplastic disease, Los Angeles Tumor Institute; chief roentgenologist A.T.&S.F. Ry.; cons. radiologist S.P. Co., Pacific Electric Ry. Co.; dir. and mem. senior staff Calif. Hospital. Est. Albert Soiland Cancer Foundn. for cancer research and fellowships in cancer study, Apr. 1946. Asst. surgeon Med. R.C., World War; now on active duty as capt., Medical Corps, U.S. Naval Reserve. Fellow Am. Coll. Phys., Am. Coll. Radiology, Los Angeles Clin. and Pathol. Soc.; hon. fellow Northern Soc. for Med. Radiology (Europe); hon. prof. U. of Guadalajara, Mexico; mem. A.M.A. and constituent societies, Military Surgeons World War I, American Radium Soc., Am. Roentgen Ray Soc., Radiol. Soc. of N.A. Republican. Lutheran. Clubs: California, Army and Navy, Athletic Club group; Newport Harbor Yacht Club, Los Angeles Yacht, Santa Barbara Yacht (hon.), Transpacific Yacht (hon. commodore), Corinthian Yacht (hon.), Royal Norwegian Yacht, Pacific Coast Yachting Assn., Southern Calif. Yachting Assn. Home: 1407 S. Hope St., Los Angeles, Calif. Died May 15, 1946; ashes in Stavenger, Norway.

SOLBERT, OSCAR NATHANIEL army officer, dir. George Eastman House, Inc.; b. Westmanland, Sweden. s. John and Mary (Johnson) S.; came to U.S., 1893; student Worcester (Mass.) Poly. Inst., 1904-06; grad. U.S. Mil. Acad., 1910; student U.S. Engring. Sch. of Application, Washington, 1912-13; m. Elizabeth F. Abernathy, Dec. 25, 1915; children—Peter O. A., Romaine G. Commd. 2d lt., corps of engrs., U.S. Army, 1910, and advanced through grades to brig. gen., 1944; instr. engring. U.S. Mil. Acad., 1914-17; served A.E.F., World War I; mil. attache, Great Britain, 1919-24; presidential mil. aide to Pres. Coolidge, 1924-26; aide to Prince of Wales on U.S. visit, 1924, to Crown Prince of Sweden on U.S. visits, 1926, 1938; resigned 1926; recalled to active duty, 1942, spl. services chief, E.T.O., 1943-45. Asst. to v.p., Eastman Kodak Co., Rochester, N.Y., 1926-49, dir. Eastman House, Inc., 1949-—. Decorated D.S.M. Legion of Merit, Bronze star, Commendation, Victory and E.T.O. medals (U.S.); Comdr. St. Michael and St. George, Comdr. Order Brit. Empire (Gt. Britain); Chevalier Legion of Honor. Croix de Guerre (France), Comdr. of Nassau (Netherlands); Comdr. of St. Olaf (Norway); Comdr. of Vasa, Comdr. of Sword, King's medal (Sweden); Polonia Restituta (Poland); Croix de Guerre (Czechoslovakia); Comdr. White Eagle (Yugoslavia); Comdr. Danneborg (Denmark); Croix de Guerre (Belgium). Mem. Theta Chi. Clubs: Metropolitan, Army and Navy (Washington); Genesee Valley, Country of Rochester, Genesee Fox Hunt. Home: George Eastman House, Rochester 7. Office: 900 East Av., Rochester, 7, N.Y. Died Apr. 16, 1958; buried Arlington National Cemetery.

SOMERS, ORLANDO ALLEN soldier; b. Middletown, Ind., Jan. 24, 1843; s. Valentine and Mary McClain (Williams) S.; ed. Howard Coll., Ind.; m. Mahala Ellen, d. William Burton Morris, Apr. 5, 1866; m. 2d, Emma, d. John Osborne Heaton, Mar. 24, 1887. Teacher and supt. schs., Howard County, Ind.; postmaster, Kokomo, 1879-85; county commr., 1892-95; mem. Ind. Ho. of Rep., 1898-1900; supervisor 12th Decennial Census, 11th Dist., Ind.; pub. instr. in highway constrn. and maintenance, conservation of soils, coöperative production, and sale of farm products, Purdue U. Pvt. 39th Regt. Ind. Vols. and 8th Regt. Ind. Vet. Cav., 1861-65; participated in battles of Shiloh, Stone's River, Chickamauga, and many minor engagements. Orator Soc. Army of the Cumberland, 1904, sec., 1905-13, pres., 1913-18 (only pvt. soldier that has held any office in this soc.); post comdr. G.A.R., at age of 24; comdr. Dept. of Ind., 1909-10; comdr. in chief G.A.R., 1917-18. Republican. Unitarian. Home: Kokomo, Ind. Died June 8, 1921.

SOMERVELL, BREHON BURKE business exec.; b. Little Rock, Ark., May 9, 1892; ed. U.S. Mil. Acad.; holds degrees: LL.D., D.Sc., D.Eng., D.M.S.; m. Anna Purnell (died 1942); married second, Louise Hampton Wartmann, 1943; children—Elizabeth Anne (Mrs. Swager Sherley, Jr.), Mary Louise (Mrs. H. P. Van Lear, Jr.), Mary Anne (Mrs. William S. Brenza), Mildred Alice (Mrs. Albert O. Waldon), Susan (Mrs. John W. Griswold), Constance Joscelyn (Mrs. E. M. Matter). Commd. 2d lt., U.S. Army, 1914, advanced through grades. to gen., 1945, ret., 1946. Now chmn. and pres. Koppers Co., Inc., Pittsburgh; dir. Montreal Coke & Mfg. Co., Westinghouse Air Brake Co., Carborumdum Co. Survey on Rhine and Danube Rivers for League of Nations, asst. Walker D. Hines, 1925; collaborated economic survey Turkey, in charge field work, 1933-34. Awarded D.S.C., D.S.M. with 2 oak leaf clusters, Legion of Merit, and other army and navy decorations (U.S.), also several fgn. decorations. Home: 920 E. 5th St., Ocala, Fla. Died Feb. 13, 1955; buried Arlington Nat. Cemetery.

SOMERVILLE, JAMES FOWNES British royal naval officer; b. Weybridge, Eng., July 17, 1882; s. Arthur Fownes and Ellen (Sharland) S.; ed. Fairfield Sch., Malvern, Eng.; naval training, H.M.S. Brittania, 1897-98; m. Mary Kerr Main, Jan. 7, 1913; children—John Fownes, Rachel Fownes. Entered British Royal Navy, 1897, advancing through the grades to admiral of the fleet, 1945; served at Dardanelles (World War I), 1915-16; dir. signal dept., Admiralty, 1925-27; flag capt. to Vice Adm. John D. Kelly, 1927-29; naval instr., Imperial Defence Coll., 1929-31; in H.M.S. Norfolk, 1931-32; commodore of Royal Naval Barracks, Portsmouth, 1932-34; dir. personal services, Admiralty, 1934-36; comdg. destroyer flotillas, Mediterranean Fleet, 1936-38; comdr. in chief, East Indies, 1938-39; spl. service, Admiralty, 1939; comdr. in chief Eastern Fleet, 1942-44; served as head of British Admiralty delegation, Washington, D.C., 1944-45. Lord Lieut. County of Somerset. Decorated Knight Grand Cross of the Bath, Knight Grand Cross Order of British Empire, Distinguished Service Order. Clubs: Junior United Service, Royal Cruising (London). Home: Dinder House, Dinder, Wells, Somerset, Eng. Died March 19, 1949.

SOMMERS, MARTIN reporter, editor; b. St. Louis, Mo., June 3, 1900; s. Martin Samuel and Laura (Brinkmeyer) S.; m. Betty Stanley, March 1, 1930; children—Jetta Priscilla, Sally. Reporter Parkersburg (W.Va.) News, 1919-20, East Liverpool (O.) Tribune, 1920; city editor Cincinnati (O.) Commercial-Tribune, 1920-22; with Chicago Tribune European edition, Paris, France, 1922-23; asst. city editor New York Daily News, 1923-24, night city editor, 1933-35; with Paris Times, Paris, France, 1924-26; reporter, re-write man, night city editor New York Daily News, 1926-31; covered undeclared war Manchuria, Shanghai, for United Press, 1931-32; asso. editor Saturday Evening Post, 1936-42, fgn. editor, 1945-62. Served as pvt. U.S. Army, World War I; served as maj., lt. col., A.F.H.Q., Algiers, and in War Dept., Washington, D.C., 1943-44. Lutheran. Clubs: Type and Print (N.Y. City); Peking (Peiping, China); Tokyo (Japan) Correspondents; Merion Cricket (Haverford, Pa.). Contbr. articles to mags. Address: St. Davids, Pa. Died July 17, 1963; buried Valley Forge Gardens, King of Prussia, Pa.

SONFIELD, ROBERT LEON, lawyer, assn. ofcl.; b. Nacogdoches, Tex., Mar. 6, 1893; s. Leon and Martha (Chapman) S.; LL.B., U. Tex., 1915; grad. student, Columbia, 1915-16; m. Dorothy Huber, Sept. 15, 1927 (dec. Dec. 1949); children—Robert Leon, Richard Huber; m. 2d, Margie Whitson Erwin, Aug. 24, 1952; 1 stepson, Thomas Sidney Erwin. Admitted Tex. bar, 1915; practice in Beaumont, 1916-17, in Houston, 1921-70; mem. firm Sonfield & Sonfield, 1958-70, Sonfield & Hasse, Brownsville, Tex., 1970-72; pres. Republic Title Company Houston (Texas); chmn. legal research group Houston Commn. Zoning, 1961-62. Mem. S.A.R., 1918-72, pres. Tex., 1960-61, nat. trustee for Tex., 1959-60, chancellor gen., 1961-63, pres. gen., 1963-64. Independent candidate for justice Tex. Ct. Civil Appeals, 1948. Served with 36th Div., U.S. Army, 1917-21; AEF in Germany; served to lt. col. AUS, 1942-47. Mem. State Bar Tex., Cameron County Bar Assn., Sons Confederate Vets., Am. Legion (dist. comdr. 1940-41), Freedom's Found. Valley Forge, Am. Judicature Soc., Patriotic Edn., Inc. Methodist. Club: Knife and Fork (Houston), Houston Turn-Verein (life). Valley Inn and Country (Brownsville). Home: Brownsville TX Died June 24, 1972.

SONNETT, JOHN FRANCIS, lawyer; b. Throgs Neck, N.Y., July 14, 1912; s. John A. and Margaret (McLaughlin) S.; B.S., Fordham U., 1933, LL.B., 1936; m. Monya Karpeshuk, June 24, 1939; children—John Peter, Stephen Franklin. Admitted to N.Y. bar, 1936; asso. firm Cotton, Franklin, Wright & Gordon, N.Y.C., 1936-41; exec. asst. to U.S. atty. So. Dist. N.Y., 1941-43; chief asst. U.S. atty., 1943; civilian spl. asst. to sec. navy, 1945; asst. U.S. atty. gen. charge claims div. Dept. Justice, 1945-47, asst. U.S. atty. gen. charge anti-trust div., 1947-48; partner firm Cahill, Gordon, Sonnett Reindel & Ohl, N.Y.C., 1948-66, sr. partner, 1967-69. Dir. Perkins Services N.V., Massey Ferguson Services N.V., FOSECO, Inc. Served to lt. comdr. USNR, 1943-45. Clubs: University, India House (N.Y.C.); Army and Navy Nat. Lawyers (Washington); Coral Ridge Yacht (Ft. Launderdale, Fla.). Home: New York City NY Died July 31, 1969.

SONTAG, RAYMOND JAMES, prof. of history; b. Chgo., Oct. 2, 1897; s. Anthony Charles and Mary Elizabeth (Walsh) S.; B.S., U. Ill.; 1920, A.M., 1921; Ph.D., U. Pa., 1924; Litt.D., Marquette U., 1959; LL.D., Notre Dame, 1960, U. Cal., 1966; m. Dorothea Agar, June 17, 1927 (dec. Apr. 1965); children—John Philip, Mary Agnes (Mrs. R.E. Johnson), William Robert, James. Instr., U. Iowa, 1921-22; instr. history Princeton U., 1924-25, asst. prof., 1925-30, asso. prof., 1930-39, Henry Charles Lea prof. and chmn. dept. history, 1939-41; Sidney Hellman Ehrman prof. European history U. Cal. at Berkeley, 1941-65, emeritus, 1965-72. Chief of German War Documents Project. Dept. State, 1946-49. Served as 2d lt. inf., U.S. Army, 1918. Mem. Am. Philos. Soc., Am. Catholic Hist. Assn. (pres. 1952), Am. Hist. Assn. (pres. Pacific Coach br. 1959). Council on Fgn. Relations. Author: (with D. C. Munro) The Middle Ages, 1928; European Diplomatic History, 1871-1932, 1933; Germany and England-Background of Conflict, 1938; A Broken World, 1919-1939, 1971. Editor: Documents on German Foreign Policy, 1918-45, (Am. editor-in-chief), 1949; Nazi-Soviet Relations (with J. S. Beddie), 1948. Address: Berkeley CA Died Oct. 27, 1972; buried St. Joseph's Cemetery, San Pablo CA

SOPER, JOHN HARRIS business man; b. Plymouth, Eng., Nov. 17, 1846; s. Thomas Harris and Mary (Kipling) S.; came to U.S. in childhood; ed. Normal Sch., Bloomington, Ill., 1857-61; m. Mary Wundenberg, Sept. 11, 1871; children—John Frederick (dec.), William Henry, Josephine Mary, Blanche Ethel, Ruth Constance. Was miner, prospector, farmer, and plantation mgr., 1863-84. Marshal Hawaiian Kingdom, 1884-86, 1888-90; comdr.-in-chief mil. forces, Provisional Govt. of Hawaii, Jan. 17, 1893; adj. gen., chief of staff, 1894-1907; retired Apr. 2, 1907, with rank of brig. gen. N.G. of Hawaii, by authority of the War Dept., Washington. Republican. Home: Honolulu, H.T. Deceased.

SOPHIAN, LAWRENCE HENRY physician; b. N.Y.C., June 26, 1903; s. Michael and Cecelia (Frank) S.; B.A., Coll. City N.Y., 1921; M.D., Harvard, 1925; m. Josephine W. Smith, June 25, 1952; children—Celia, Catherine. Instr. Harvard Med. Sch., 1928-29; asso. prof. N.Y. Post-Grad. Med. Sch., 1930; pathologist Roosevelt Hosp., N.Y.C., 1930-39; served from lt. comdr. to capt., USPHS, 1939-52; dir. labs. U.S. Marine Hosps. med. dir. USPHS (ret.); asso. dir. med. lit. Lederle Labs., 1952-53; v.p., med. dir. William Douglas McAdams, Inc., med. advt., N.Y.C., 1953-—. Mem. A.M.A., Am. Assn. Pathologists and Bacteriologists, Coll. Am. Pathologists. Club: Harvard (N.Y.C.). Contbr. articles profl. jours. Home: 171 Indian Head Rd., Riverside, Conn. Office: 130 E. 59th St., N.Y.C. 22. Died July 8, 1959; buried Arlington Nat. Cemetery.

SORDONI, ANDREW JOHN, JR., bldg. and electric line constrn. co. exec.; b. Forty Fort, Pa., Dec. 29, 1916; s. Andrew John and Ruth (Speece) S.; student U. Pa., 1935-38; m. Margaret Barnard, July 26, 1941; children—Andrew John III, William, George, Stephen. Founder, 1946, now chmn. bd. Sterling Products Co., Kingston, Pa.; founder, 1947, now chmn. bd., dir. Sterling Truck Sales; chmn. bd., pres., dir. Commonwealth Telephone Co., Dallas, Pa., 1964-67; pres. Harvey's Lake Light Co., Dallas, Pa., 1948-67, Sterling Engring. & Mfg. Co., Wilkes-Barre, Pa., 1949-67, Sordoni Constrn. Co., Forty Fort, 1955-67, Sterling Hotels System, Wilkes Barre, 1958-67, pres., dir. Nat. Tree Surgeons, Inc., Forty Fort, Pub. Service Enterprises of Pa., Inc., Sordoni Enterprises, Inc.; gen. mgr. Lacy, Atherton & Davis, Wilkes-Barre, Sterling Farms, Alderson; dir. Pa. Mfrs. Assn. Ins. Co., United Gas Improvement Co. Pres. Andrew J. Sordoni Found., Inc.; dir., exec. com., finance com. Samuel H. Kress Found., N.Y.C. Trustee, past pres. Wyo. Valley Hosp. Wilkes-Barre. Served to capt. USAF, 1942-46. Mem. Pa. C. of C. (past pres., dir.), Pa. Ind. Telephone Assn. (dir.), Luzerne County (v.p.), Pa. (gov.) mfrs. assns., Navy League U.S. (charter) V.F.W., Am. Legion, Beta Theta Pi. Republican. Mason (Shriner, Jester), Rotarian. Clubs: Marco Polo; Union League (Phila.); Westmoreland. Home: Forty Fort PA Died July 9, 1967.

SOROKIN, PITIRIM ALEXANDROVITCH (so-ro'kin), prof. sociology; b. Village of Touria, Russia, Jan. 21, 1889; s. Alexander P. and Pelageia V. (Rimskych) S.; ed. Teachers Coll., Kostroma Province, Russia,

1903-06, evening sch., St. Petersburg (now Leningrad), Russia, 1907-09, Psycho-Neurol. Inst., St. Petersburg, 1909-10, U. of St. Petersburg, 1910-14; Magistrant of Criminal Law, 1915, Dr. of Sociology, 1922; hon. Ph.D., 1950; m. Elea Petrovna Baratynskaia, May 26, 1917; children—Peter, Sergei. Come to U.S., 1923, naturalized, 1900. Privat-dozent Psycho-Neural Inst., 1914-16; U. of St. Petersburg, 1916-17, prof. sociology, 1919-22; prof. sociology, Agrl. Acad., 1919-22, U. of Minn., 1924-30; prof. sociology Harvard U. 1930-64, emeritus prof., 1964—; now dir. Research Center Creative Altruism. Co-editor New Ideas in Sociology, 1913-15; editor in chief Volia Naroda, newspaper, at Petrograd, 1917. Mem. exec. com. All-Russian Peasant Soviet, 1917; mem. Council of Russian Republic, 1917; sec. to prime minister, 1917; mem. Russian Constl. Assembly, 1918; pres. Internat. Congress Sociology, 1937. Mem. Internat. Soc. Comparative Study of Civilizations (pres. 1961-64), Am. Acad. Arts and Scis., American Sociological Assn. (pres. 1965—); hon. member Internat. Inst. Social Reform, Internat. Inst. Sociology, Czecho-Slovak Acad. Agr., German Sociological Soc. Belgian Royal Acad., Roumanian Royal Acad., Mem. Greek Orthodox Ch. Author numerous books since 1914; latest publs.: Altruistic Love, 1950; Social Philosophies of an Age of Crisis, 1950; Explorations in Altruistic Love and Behavior, 1950; S.O.S.; The Meaning of Our Crisis, 1951; The ways and Power of Love, 1954; Forms and Techniques of Altruistic and Spiritual Growth, 1954; Fads and Foibles in Modern Sociology, pub. 1956; American Sex Revolution, 1957; Power and Morality, 1958; A Long Journey, 1963; The Basic Trends of Our Time, 1963; Sociological Theories of Today, 1966. Contbr. jours. Condemned to death and finally banished by Communist Govt., 1922. Home: 8 Cliff St., Winchester, Mass. Died Feb. 11, 1968.

SOSMAN, MERRILL C(LARY) (sôs'man) roentgenologist; b. Chillicothe, O., June 23, 1890; s. Francis Asbury and Mollie (Browning) S.; A.B., U. Wis., 1913; M.D., Johns Hopkins, 1917; M.A. (hon.), Harvard, 1949; m. Arline Clark Adams, June 27, 1918; children—John Leland, Barbara Clark. Resident physician, U.S. Soldiers Home Hosp., Washington, 1917; grad. student, Mass. Gen. Hosp., Boston, 1921-22; became roentgenologist in chief, Peter Bent Brigham Hosp., Boston, 1922, now chmn. emeritus; cons. roentgenologist Childrens Hosp., Psychopathic Hosp., N. E. Peabody Home for Crippled Children (Boston), Cape Cod Hosp. (Hyannis). Instr. in roentgenology, Harvard Med. Sch., 1922-28, asst. prof., 1928-40, clin. prof., 1940-44, clin. prof. radiology, 1944-48, became prof. of radiology 1948, now prof. emeritus; now cons. radiology, Mass. Gen. Hosp. Served as 1st lt. Med. Corps, U.S. Army, 1917; capt., 1918-22. Recipient gold medal, Radiol. Soc. of Am. Diplomate Am. Bd. Radiology. Fellow A.A.A.S.; mem. A.M.A., N.E. Roentgen Ray Soc. (past pres.; George W. Holmes lectr., 1947), Radiol. Soc. N.A., Am. Roentgen Ray Soc. (past pres.; Caldwell lectr. 1947), Harvey Cushing Soc. (past pres.), Am. Coll. Radiology, Mexican Soc. Radiol. and Phys. Therapy (hon.), Venezuela Radiol. Soc., Am. Acad. Arts Scis., Sigma Xi., A.O.A. Mason. Clubs: Harvard (Boston); Country (Brookline). Contbr. of numerous articles on diagnosis and treatment of diseases or tumors by X-ray to sci. publs. Home: 24 Lee Rd., Chestnut Hill 67, Mass. Office: 721 Huntington Av., Boston 15. Died Mar. 28, 1959; buried Chillicothe, O.

SOUCEK, APOLLO (so'chek), naval officer; b. Lamont, Okla., Feb. 24, 1897; s. John Gothard and Lydia (Pishny) S.; grad. U.S. Naval Acad., 1921; m. Agnes Eleanor O'Connor, May 27, 1930. Commd. ensign U.S. Navy, 1921, and advanced through grades to capt. capacity of comdg. officer, Oct. 27, 1945. Promoted to flag rank, Mar. 2, 1946; qualified as naval aviator Oct. 1924; established world's aircraft altitude record, 39,140 feet, June 4, 1929, seaplane, 38,800 ft. (approximately), June 8, 1929, re-established world's altitude record, any type aircraft, 43,166 feet, June 8, 1930; commd. aircraft carrier U.S.S. Franklin D. Roosevelt as capt., U.S. Navy, Oct. 27, 1945; air officer U.S.S. Hornet-CV-8, exec. officer when ship sunk, battle Santa Cruz Islands, 1941-42; operations officer Vice Admiral Tower's staff, 1943; comdr. Fleet Air Wing One, 1946-47, asst. chief naval operations for aviation plans, 1949-51; naval attache and naval attache for air London July-Nov. 1951; chief bur. aeronautics Navy Dept., 1953—. Awarded Distinguished Flying Cross, Silver Star medal, Legion of Merit with gold star, Bronze Star medal. Home: Medford, Okla. Died July 22, 1955.

SOUERS, SIDNEY WILLIAM, business exec.; b. Dayton, O., Mar. 30, 1892; s. Edgar D. and Catherine (Rieker) S.; student Purdue U., 1911-12; A.B., Miami U., 1914, LL.D., 1953; LL.D., Lindenwood Coll., 1966; m. Sylvia Mettell, May 28, 1943. Pres. Mortgage & Securities Co., New Orleans, 1920-25, Piggly Wiggly Stories, Memphis, Mar. 1925-Oct. 1926; exec. v.p. Canal Bank & Trust Co., New Orleans, La., 1925-30; financial v.p. Mo. State Life Ins. Co., St. Louis, 1930-33; v.p. General Am. Life Ins. Co., 1933-37, dir., exec. com., 1936-73, exec. v.p., 1937-41, chmn. exec. com., 1953-54, chmn. bd., 1954-57, pres., chmn. 1957-58, chmn., chief exec. officer, 1958-65, chmn. bd., chmn. exec. com., 1965-69, chmn. emeritus, dir., exec. com., 1969-73; dir., past chmn. bd. Nat. Service Industries, Inc., Atlanta; dir. Volkswagan Ins. Co., Transit Casualty Co., hon. dir. McDonnell Douglas Corp. Commr., treas., chmn. finance com. Bi-State Devel. Agy. Trustee Jefferson Nat. Expansion Meml. Assn.; bd. dirs. United Fund of Greater St. Louis. Dir. emeritus Lindenwood College, St. Charles, Mo.; trustee Westminster Coll., Govtl. Research Inst.; hon. trustee George Washington Coll., Govtl. Research Inst.; hon. trustee George Washington U. Exec. sec. Nat. Security Council, 1947-50; spl. cons. (mil.-fgn.) to Pres. of U.S., 1950-53. Served to rear adm. USNR, 1940-46; first dir. of CIA. Decorated D.S.M. (Navy), Legion of Merit. Mem. Res. Officers Assn., Mil. Order World Wars, Navy League (bd. councilors St. Louis Council), World Affairs Council Greater St. Louis, U.S. Naval Acad. Found. (bd. govs.), Automobile Club Mo. (gov.), Ret. Officers Assn., Advt. Club Greater St. Louis, Mo. Acad. Squires, Delta Kappa Epsilon. Democrat. Presbyn. Clubs: La Coquille (West Palm Beach, Fla.); University; Boston (New Orleans, La.); Capital City Country (Atlanta); Armed Forces Officers, Mo. Athletic Assn., Noonday, Bogey Golf Roundtable, St. Louis, Media, Old Warson Country (St. Louis); Army and Navy, Metropolitan, Chevy Chase Country (Washington); Garden of Gods (Colorado Springs). Home: 625 S Skinker Blvd St Louis MO Died Jan. 14, 1973.

SOULE, PIERRE senator, jurist, diplomat; b. Castillonen-Couserans in French Pyrenees, Aug. 28, 1801; s. Joseph and Jeanne (Lacroix) S.; attended College de l'Esquille, Toulouse until 1816; Bachelor's degree, U. Bordeaux, 1819; m. Armantine Mercier, 1828, 1 child. Practiced law in France, 1822; arrested for polit. activities, escaped and came to U.S., 1825; settled in New Orleans, admitted to La. bar; de. to conv. of 1844 for revising La. constn.; mem. La. Senate, 1846; mem. U.S. Senate from La., 1847-Apr. 11, 1853, leader at states rights wing of Southern Democracy in Senate; U.S. minister to Spain, 1853-55, sought acquisition of Cuba by purchase, by favor of Queen Mother, or as collateral for a royal loan; author (with James Buchanan and John Y. Mason) Ostend Manifesto, 1854, proposed acquisition of Cuba by purchase or force, resigned, 1855, a scapegoat for administration's change of policy in affair; arrested by fed. forces in New Orleans, 1862; during Civil War served on Beauregard's staff, commd. brig. gen. Died New Orleans, Mar. 26, 1870; buried St. Louis Cemetery Number 2.

SOULE, ROBERT HOMER (sol), army officer; b. Laramie, Wyo., Feb. 10, 1900; s. Justus Freeland and Isabel Dora (Simpson) S.; student U. of Wyoming, 1916-18; grad. Inf. Sch., company officers course, 1927, Command and Gen. Staff Sch., 1940; m. Genevieve Marie Hoffman, Jan. 4, 1922; 1 dau., Genevieve Ann. Commd. 2d lt., inf., U.S. Army, 1918, and advanced through grades to maj. gen., 1950; served with 31st Inf., A.E.F., Siberia and Philippine Islands, 1918-22; Chinese language student and attaché Am. Legation, Peking, China, 1929-33; with War Dept. Gen. Staff, Mar. 1941-Dec. 1942; comdg. officer 11th Airborne Div., 188th Paratroop Glider Inf., 1943-45; became asst. div. comdr. 38th Inf. Div., Mar. 1945, also asst. div. comdr., 11th Airborne Div., Sendai, Japan, 1945-46, mil. attaché Nanking, China, 1946-50; later comdg. gen. 3d Inf. Div., Korea, and then insp. inf., Army Field Forces, Ft. Monroe, Va. Decorated D.S.C. (two), D.S.M., Legion of Merit, Silver Star (two), Bronze Star Medal with oak-leaf cluster, Purple Heart, Combat Inf. Badge, Parachute Badge, Air Medal, Presidential Citation. Mem. Sigma Alpha Epsilon. Mason (Shriner). Home: Carmel, Cal. Died Jan. 26, 1952; buried Arlington Nat. Cemetery.

SOUTHARD, ISAAC congressman; b. Basking Ridge, Somerset County, N.J., Aug. 30, 1783; s. Henry Southard; ed. at classical sch., Basking Ridge. In gen. merchandise business until 1814; apptd. dep. collector internal revenue Somerset County; apptd. maj. 2d Battalion, 2d Regt., Somerset Brigade, 1815, promoted lt. col., 1816, col., 1817; served as aide to Maj. Gen. Peter I. Stryker of Uniformed Militia, 3d Div. as late as 1829; dir. State bank at Morristown, N.J.; apptd. a lay judge Somerset Ct. Common Pleas, 1820; commd. justice of peace, 1820; moved to Sommerville, N.J.; clk. Somerset County, 1820-30; mem. U.S. Ho. of Reps. (Clay Democrat) from N.J., 22d Congress, 1831-33; apptd. master and examiner in chancery by Gov. Elias P. Seeley, 1833; col. N.J. Militia; treas. N.J., 1837-43 lived in Trenton, N.J. several years. Died Somerville, Sept. 18, 1850; buried Old Cemetery.

SOUTHERLAND, WILLIAM HENRY HUDSON naval officer; b. New York, N.Y., July 10, 1852; s. William and Phoebe E. S.; grad. U.S. Naval Acad., 1872; m. Mary Rodman, Aug. 1, 1877; children—Harriet Rodman (Mrs. J. Butler Wright), Mary Rodman (Mrs. Louis Bacon). Ensign, 1872; promoted through grades to rear adm., May 4, 1910. Served in Spanish-Am. War on Cuban coast, in command U.S.S. Eagle; mem. Bd. of Inspection and Survey, 1906-07, Naval Examining and Retiring Bd., 1910. Comdg. 2d Div., Pacific Fleet, 1911-12; comdr.-in-chief Pacific Fleet, 1912-13, and in command of expeditionary landing force in Nicaragua, Aug.-Oct. 1912; mem. Gen. Bd., 1913-14; retired by operation of law, July 10, 1914. Author: (with Comdr. S. Schroeder, U.S.N.) Azimuth Tables (U.S. Hydrographic Office). Wrote: Nautical Monograph No. 4—The North Atlantic Cyclone of August 1883. Home: Washington, D.C. Died Jan. 30, 1933.

SOWELL, INGRAM CECIL naval officer; b. Lawrenceburg, Tenn., Aug. 3, 1889; s. Henry Bascomb and Eustatia (Goodloe) S.; Columbia Military Acad., 1906-08; B.S., U.S. Naval Acad., 1912; grad. U.S. Naval War Coll., 1935; m. Frances Jack, Apr. 17, 1917; children—Mary Ellen (Mrs. Henry Wells Lawrence), Frances Jack (Mrs. Walter Lee Wood), Ingram Cecil, Jr. Passed midshipman, 1912 and advanced through the grades to rear admiral, Sept. 1942; served in armored cruisers, 1912-16; student, Submarine School, New London, Connecticut, 1917, Submarine K-2, 1917; commanded U.S.S. L-2, 1918, U.S.S. S-3, 1919, U.S.S. 49, 1921-24; Navy Department, 1920-21; instructor Naval Academy, 1925-37; commanded U.S.S. Henshaw and U.S.S. Wasmuth, 1927-30; recruit training officer, Great Lakes Training Station, 1930-32; comd. Submarine Div. Four, 1932-34; student, Senior War Coll., 1934-35; Navy Dept., 1935-36; exec. officer, U.S.S. New Orleans, 1936-38; training station, San Diego, 1938-39; comd. U.S.S. Concord, 1940-42; comdt. U.S. Naval Training Station, Farragut, Ida., 1942-43; comdt. Activity No. 1, Navy No. 138, overseas, since Apr., 1943. Awarded Navy Cross, Nicaragua, Mexican Campaign medals (World War I); Victory medal, World War II. Mem. Vets. of Foreign Wars. Home: Lawrenceburg, Tenn. Address: Bureau of Navy Personnel, Navy Dept., Washington. Died Dec. 21, 1947.

SPAFFORD, EDWARD ELWELL b. Springfield, Vt., Mar. 12, 1878; s. Hiram Duncan and Georgiana (Fowler) S.; grad. U.S. Naval Acad., 1901; student law, Columbia Univ., 1915-16; m. Lucille Stevens, May 23, 1912 (died 1914); 1 dau., Lucille. Resigned from U.S. Navy as lt. comdr., 1914; returned to Navy and served in the Mediterranean, World War. Served as chmn. naval affairs of Am. Legion 3 yrs., as comdr. Dept. of N.Y., 1923-24; elected nat. comdr., term 1927-28. Awarded D.S.M. (U.S.); Comdr. Legion of Honor (France); Comdr. Order of Crown of Italy; Comdr. Order of Phoenix (Greece). Republican. Episcopalian. Mason. Clubs: University, New York Yacht, Sleepy Hollow Country, Army and Navy (Washington); Chevy Chase (Chevy Chase, Md.). Died Nov. 13, 1941.

SPAHR, BOYD LEE, lawyer; b. Mechanicsburg, Pa., Apr. 18, 1880; s. Murray Hurst and Clara (Koser) S.; Ph.B., Dickinson, 1900, A.M., 1903; LL.B., U. of Pa., 1904, LL.D., 1952; LL.D., Lafayette, 1933; D.C.L., Dickinson Coll., 1950; married Katharine Febiger, Oct. 8, 1908 (dec. June 1965); children—Boyd Lee, Christian C.F., John F. Admitted Pa. bar, 1904; in practice at Phila.; sr. mem. Ballard, Spahr, Andrews and Ingersoll. Served as major and member of the General Staff in United States Army, 1918. Trustee Dickinson Coll., 1908-70, pres. board, 1931-62, hon. pres., 1962-70. Mem. Hist. Soc. Pa. (past pres.), Society War 1812, Phi Kappa Sigma (nat. pres. 1920-23), Phi Beta Kappa. Episcopalian. Republican. Clubs: Rittenhouse, Union League, Merion Cricket; Century (N.Y.); Bar Harbor (Me.), The Pot and Kettle; Philadelphia. Home: Haverford PA Died Aug. 14, 1970.

SPALDING, ALBERT (spawl'ding), violinist; b. Chicago, Ill., Aug. 15, 1888; s. J. Walter and Marie (Boardman) S.; ed. New York, Florence and Paris; m. Mary Vanderhof Pyle, July 19, 1919. Début in Paris, 1905; made tour of principal cities of Europe; Am. début with Damrosch Orchestra, Carnegie Hall, New York, Nov. 8, 1908, followed by concert tour of U.S.; visited Russia, 1910; since then toured Holland, Belgium, Germany, Austria, Italy, Egypt, France, England, Switzerland, Norway, Sweden, Denmark, Cuba, and W.I.; 2d Am. tour, 1912, 3d, 1914, 4th, 1915. Composer of music for violin. Joined Aviation Corps U.S. Signal Service, June 1917, and served as liaison officer; commd. lt.; with OWI, psychol. warfare, Italy, 1944, in chg. radio Rome for Allied Powers, 1944. Mem. Am. Acad. Arts and Letters, Am. Soc. Composers, Authors and Publishers. Club: Century. Address: 3 E. 77th St., N.Y.C. Died May 26, 1953.

SPALDING, GEORGE R., army officer; b. Monroe, Mich., Jan. 25, 1877; s. Gen. George and Augusta (Lewis) S.; B.S., U.S. Mil. Acad., 1901; grad. Engr. Sch. of Application, 1905, Field Engring. Sch., 1911, Army War Coll., 1920; m. Alice Minnie Ruff, Sept. 17, 1904; children—George, Alice (Mrs. L. R. Wirak), Albert Ruff. Commd. 2d lt., Corps Engrs., 1901, and advanced through the grades to brig. gen., 1936; served in P.I., 1901-03; mapping and camp layout, Va. maneuvers, 1904; locks and dams, Ohio River, 1905-06; improvement Great Lakes and connecting channels, 1907; river and harbor works, Fla., 1908-11; instr. field engring., Command and Gen. Staff Sch., 1911-15; Ohio River Improvement, Cincinnati and Louisville, 1916-17; with A.E.F., as comdg. officer, 305th Engrs., div. engr., 80th Div., corps engr., 5th Corps.; chief engr., 1st Army and 3rd Army; deputy chief engr. A.E.F.; instr. Army War Coll., 1919-20; dir. course supply and transportation, 1920-23; charge, construction Wilson Dam, Tenn. River, 1923-25; Ohio River locks and dams, 1925-29; div. engr., improvement of Missouri, Upper Mississippi, Illinois and Ohio, 1929-33; comd. Engr. Sch. and Post, Ft. Belvoir, Va., 1933-34; div. engr.

N.Y., 1935-36; asst. chief of staff, War Dept., 1936-38; retired for disability, 1938; recalled to Office of Chief of Staff in organization of Lend-Lease Adminstrn., 1941; army service forces in liaison with various civilian agencies; office of Chief of Staff, assisting in organization of Public Works Adminstrn., 1932. Awarded Officer Order of Leopold (Belgium), Legion of Honor (France); D.S.M., U.S. Life Saving medal. Awarded D.S.M., Oak Leaf Cluster. Returned to disability list, Jan. 7, 1945, and ordered home. Mem. Soc. Am. Military Engrs. Home: 202 N. 18th St., Bradenton FL

SPANG, JOSEPH PETER, JR., co. director; b. Boston, Feb. 1, 1893; s. Joseph Peter and Anna (Bosse) S.; Harvard, Class of 1915; L.H.D., Tufts Univ., 1954; LL.D., Northeastern Univ., 1948; married Gwendolen Green, Nov. 6, 1926 (dec.); children—Thomas Johnston Green, Joseph Peter, III. With Swift & Co., 1915-38, v.p. in charge of sales 1930-38; pres. Gillette Co., 1938-56, chmn. bd., 1956-58, past dir.; dir. N.Y. World's Fair 1964-65 Corporation; trustee of the Central Aguirre Sugar Company; director of Sheraton Corporation Am., U.S. Steel Corp., Internat. Packers, Ltd.; mem. corp. Northeastern U. Mem. Bus. Council; overseas econ. operations task force Hoover Commn.; chmn. sponsoring com. 1st Internat. Conf. Mfrs., N.Y., 1951, presided one session 2d conf., Paris, 1954; headed mission to France to evaluate Mut. Security Program, 1953; mem. group businessmen visiting Jugoslavia to study industry, make recommendations, 1954. Nat. chmn. Community Chests and Councils of Am., 1955-56; nat. chmn. United Community Campaigns of Am., 1955-56; pres. Greater Boston United Fund, 1957-59. Trustee, past chairman of finance committee Committee for Econ. Development; trustee of the Vincent Hosp., N.E. Deaconess, Mass. Meml. Hosps., U.S. Council Internat. C. of C.; director Boys' Club of Boston, Jr. Achievement. Served as lt. Balloon Service, U.S. Army. Decorated Chevalier Legion D'Honneur (France). Member of N.A.M., Legion of Honor. Clubs: Harvard, Union (Boston); The Links, Racquet and Tennis, The Brook (N.Y.C.); The Country (Brookline, Mass.). Home: Milton MA Died Dec. 19, 1969; buried Manchester-by-the-Sea MA

SPANGLER, JACOB congressman; b. York, Pa., Nov. 28, 1767; attended York County Acad. Became surveyor; served as trumpeter in Capt. McClellan's Light Horse Co. of York, 1799; county commr., 1800, 14; postmaster York, 1795-1812; dep. surveyor York County, 1796-1815; mem. U.S. Ho. of Reps. (Federalist) from Pa., 15th Congress, 1817-Apr. 20, 1818 (resigned); surveyor gen. Pa., 1818-21, 30-36; comdr. Pa. Militia with title of gen.; clk. York County Ct. until 1830. Died York, June 17, 1843; buried Prospect Hill Cemetery.

SPARKS, N(ORMAN) R(OBERT), coll. prof.; born Alameda, Calif., May 22, 1900; s. Alfred Ethbert and Ellen Morrell (Lavell) S.; B.S., Clarkson Coll. of Tech., 1923, M.E., 1926; m. Ruth Ernestine Barbur, Sept. 2, 1923; 1 dau., Joan Louise. In motive power dept., N.Y.C.R.R., 1923-24; instr. mech. engring., Pa. State Univ., 1924-29, asst. prof., 1929-32, asso. prof., 1932-41, prof., 1941-72, head of dept. of mech. engring., from July 1946; various cons. and tech. adv. positions. Commd. lt., U.S.N.R., 1936; on active duty, advancing to grade of comdr., 1941-46, capt., 1951. Member Am. Soc. M.E., Am. Soc. Naval Engineers, Am. Society Engineering Education, Sigma Xi. Pi Tau Sigma (honorary M.E.). Theta Xi. Republican. Author: Theory of Mechanical Refrigeration, 1938. Contbr. articles to tech. jours. and mags. Home: State College PA Died Jan. 23, 1972.

SPARROW, CARROLL MASON physicist; b. Baltimore, Md., Jan. 10, 1880; s. Leonard Kip and Anne Elizabeth Temple (Magill) S.; A.B., Johns Hopkins, 1908, Ph.D., 1911; m. Lettice Latané, Dec. 14, 1912. With U.S. Coast and Geodetic Survey, 1901-07; adj. prof. physics, U. of Va., 1911-17, asso. prof., 1917-20, prof., 1920-—. Served as capt. Air Service (science and research div.), U.S.A., July 31, 1918-Sept. 3, 1919. Fellow Am. Physical Soc., A.A.A.S. Democrat. Contbr. to scientific jours., mainly on spectroscopy. Asso. editor Physical Rev., 1920-23; asso. editor Virginia Quarterly Rev. Home: University, Va. Died Aug. 30, 1941.

SPAULDING, FRANCIS TROW edn. commnr.; b. Ware, Mass., Nov. 23, 1896; s. Frank Ellsworth and Mary Elizabeth (Trow) S.; A.B., Harvard, 1916, Ed.M., 1921, Ed.D., 1926; A.M., Columbia Tchrs. Coll., 1926; LL.D., Lawrence Coll., 1943, Northeastern U., U. Buffalo, 1946, Alfred U., Rensselaer Polytech. Inst., 1949; Litt.D., Colgate U., 1948; m. Susan Chambers Thompson, June 19, 1922; children—Margaret Montague, Joan Stewart. Tchr., adminstrv. positions, various schs., 1916-17, 1919-24; instr. edn. Harvard, 1924-25, asst. prof., 1926-29, asso. prof., 1929-36, prof., 1936-45, asso. dean grad. sch. edn., 1939-40, dean, 1940-45; commnr. edn., pres. U. State N.Y., 1946-—; lectr. secondary edn. Columbia Tchrs. Coll., 1928-29; specialist in sch. orgn. Nat. Survey Secondary Edn., 1930-32; dir. study secondary edn. N.Y. State Regents Inquiry, 1936-38; trustee Gen. Edn. Bd., 1939-42; mem. Mass. State Adv. Bd. Edn., 1941-44. Sponsor Harvard Found. Advanced Study and Research, 1949-—; chmn. div. edn. study Ford Found. on Policy and Program, 1948-49. Mem. War-Navy Commn., USAFI, 1946-47, one of founders USAFI; mem. N.Y. Vets. Affairs Commn., Commn. Accreditation of Service Experiences, Am. Council Edn., 1946-48; mem. VA Adminstrs. Spl. Commn. Vocational Rehabilitation, Edn., Tng. Problems, 1947-50. Mem. Bd. Visitors Air U.; mem. State Dept. Bd. Fgn. Scholarships. Trustee Am. Mus. Natural History. Served in U.S. Army Med. Dept., 1918-19; col. AUS, chief edn. br., 1942-46. Fellow Am. Acad. Arts and Scis.; mem. Am. Assn. Sch. Adminstrs., N.E.A., Nat. Soc. Study Edn., Phi Beta Kapp, Phi Delta Kappa, Kappa Delta Pi. Author numerous monographs, articles and reports on secondary edn. Home: 317 Loudenville Rd., Albany, N.Y. Office: State Edn. Dept., Albany 1, N.Y. Died Mar. 25, 1950.

SPAULDING, OLIVER LYMAN asst. sec. of Treasury; b. Jaffrey, N.H., Aug. 2, 1833; s. Lyman and Susan (Marshall) S.; A.B., Oberlin, 1855; m. Mary Cecilia Swegles, Aug. 12, 1862. Admitted to bar, 1858. Capt. Co. A, 23d Mich. Inf., Aug. 1, 1862; maj., Feb. 13, 1863; lt. col., Apr. 6, 1863; col., Apr. 16, 1864; bvtd. brig. gen. vols., June 25, 1865, "for faithful and meritorious services during the war"; mustered out, June 28, 1865. Regent U. of Mich., 1859-64; sec. of state, Mich., 1866-70; declined appmt. U.S. dist. judge, Utah Ty., 1871; mem. Mich. State Rep. Com., 1871-78; spl. agt. U.S. Treasury, 1875-81; mem. 47th Congress (1881-83), 6th Mich. Dist.; chmn. U.S. Govt. commn. sent to Sandwich Islands to investigate matters pertaining to Hawaiian reciprocity treaty, 1883; again spl. agt. U.S. Treasury, Jan.-Dec. 1885 and 1889-90; declined appmt. as circuit judge, 1889, tendered by gov. of Mich.; asst. sec. of the treasury, 1890-93 and 1897-1903. Pres. 1st Pan-Am. Customs Congress, 1903; del. Rep. Nat. Conv., 1896. Home: St. John's, Mich. Died July 30, 1922.

SPAULDING, OLIVER LYMAN army officer; b. St. Johns, Mich., June 25, 1875; s. Oliver Lyman and Mary Cecilia (Swegles) S.; A.B., U. of Mich., 1895, LL.B., 1896; LL.D., 1938; A.M., Harvard U., 1932; grad. Arty. Sch., Ft. Monroe, Va., 1903, Army Staff Coll. Ft. Leavenworth, 1905; graduate Army War Coll., Washington, 1911, 1925; m. Alice Chandler, Dec. 29, 1902; 1 son, Edward Chandler. Commd. 2d lt., arty., U.S. Army, 1898; promoted through grades to col., field arty., 1920; retired as brig. gen., 1939; recalled to active duty, 1941; served in N.W. Alaska, 1898-99, China Relief Expdn., 1900, Philippine Insurrection, 1900-01, Panama, 1908, Mexican Border, 1913-15, P.I., 1915-17; brig. gen. with A.E.F. in France, Luxemburg and Germany, 1918-19; served in Hawaii, 1926-29. Instr. Army Service Schs., Ft. Leavenworth, 1905-10; asst. comdt. Field Arty. Sch., Ft. Sill, Okla., 1917-18; prof. mil. science, Harvard U., 1931-35; lecturer in mil. history, Lowell Institute, Boston, 1939, and George Washington University, 1939-41; chief historical section, General Staff, A.E.F., 1919, Army War Coll., 1919-24, 1935-39 and since 1941. Decorated: Distinguished Service Medal, Legion of Merit (U.S.); Commander Order of the Black Star (French). Mem. Phi Beta Kappa, Beta Theta Pi, Phi Delta Phi. Episcopalian. Mason. Clubs: Army and Navy (Washington and Manila); Cosmos (Washington). Author: Notes on Field Artillery, 4th edit., 1918; Warfare (with Hoffman Nickerson and John Womack Wright), 1925, 2d edit., 1937; The United States Army in War and Peace, 1937; Pen and Sword in Greece and Rome, 1937; The Second Division, A.E.F., in France, 1917-19 (with John Womack Wright), 1937; Ahriman, A Study in Air Bombardment, 1939. Writer of articles on mil. and hist. subjects. Home: 1870 Wyoming Av. Address: War Dept., Washington, D.C. Died Mar. 27, 1947.

SPEAKS, JOHN CHARLES ex-congressman; b. Canal Winchester, O., Feb. 11, 1859; s. Charles W. and Sarah (Hesser) S.; ed. pub. schs.; m. Edna Lawyer, 1889; children—Charles, Stanford, John, Margaret. Milling and lumber business. Fish, game and conservation officer of Ohio, 1907-18; mem. 67th to 71st Congresses (1921-31), 12th Ohio Dist. Mem. of the Ohio N.G. 40 yrs., advancing from pvt. through grades to brig. gen.; maj. 4th Ohio Vol. Inf., Spanish-Am. War, participating in Porto Rican Campaign; comdr. 2d Brig., Ohio N.G., on Mexican border, 1916; comdr. 73d Brigade 37th Div., from call of troops, World War, until Mar. 1, 1918. Mason (32 deg., K.T., Shriner), K.P. Republican. Methodist; del. to Gen. Conf., 1936. Rotarian. Home: 309 King Av., Columbus, O. Died Nov. 6, 1945.

SPEAR, ELLIS solicitor of patents; b. Warren, Knox County, Me., Oct. 15, 1834; s. James Marston S.; A.B., Bowdoin, 1858, LL.D. Capt. 20th Me. Inf., Aug. 29, 1862; maj., Aug. 28, 1863; col., May 29, 1865; bvtd. lt. col. vols., Sept. 30, 1864, "for gallant and distinguished services at battle of Peebles' Farm, Va."; col. vols., Mar. 29, 1865, "for gallant and meritorious services at battle of Lewis' Farm, Va."; brig. gen. vols., Apr. 9, 1865, "for faithful and meritorious services during campaign ending in surrender of Army of Northern Va."; hon. mustered out, July 16, 1865. Asst. examiner ry. and civ. engring, 1865-68; examiner, 1868-72, examiner-in-chief, 1872-74, U.S. Patent Office; asst. commr. of patents, 1874-76; resigned. Engaged in pvt. business, 1876, until Jan. 1877, when was apptd. commr. patents, serving until Nov. 1878; atty. and solicitor of patents, 1878-—. V.p. Washington Loan & Trust Co., Equitable Coöperative Bldg. Assn. Overseer Bowdoin Coll. Home: Washington, D.C. Died Apr. 3, 1917.

SPEARS, WILLIAM OSCAR naval officer; b. Jasper, Tenn., Sept. 18, 1885; s. William Douglas and Lou Ross (Hall) S.; B.S., U.S. Naval Acad., 1905; grad. U.S. Naval War Coll., 1923; m. Blanche Fouché Snodgrass, Apr. 5, 1914; children—William Oscar, John Pratt (dec.), Morton Fouche. Commd. rear adm., 1942; served on U.S. Naval Missions to Brazil, 1918-21, 1923-26, to Peru, 1929-33; served continuously on active duty in U.S. Navy until 1940, ret., 1940; comdr. Battleship West Virginia, 1937-38; dir. Pan Am. Div., Office Naval Operations, Navy Dept., Mar. 1942. Sr. naval mem. joint Brazilian-U.S. Defense Commn.; joint Army-Navy adv. bd. Am. Republics. Awarded Legion of Merit, Mexican Campaign, Philippine Campaign, World War I and II Service medals; Expeditionary (Naval); Order of Merit (Cuba), Order of Naval Merit, Grand Officer So. Cross (Brazil); Grand Officer Order of Naval Merit (Chile), Order of Boyaca (Colombia); Naval Merit (Mexico); Order of Libertador (Venezuela); Abdon Calderon, (Ecuador); Order of Sun, Grand Master of Military Order of Ayacucho, Aviation Cross (Peru). Home: Woodley Park Towers, 2737 Devonshire Pl., Washington. Died May 27, 1966; buried Arlington Nat. Cemetery.

SPEED, JAMES BRECKINRIDGE, mcht.; b. Louisville, Ky.; s. William P. and Mary Ellen (Shallcross) S.; ed. public schools; bank clerk Louisville and Chicago until 1861; served in Union army, pvt. and later adj. 27th Ky. inf., 1861-5, serving in all the campaigns in the West; m. 1868, Cora, d. George W. Coffin, Cincinnati. In business in Louisville since war; pres. Louisville Cement Co., Louisville Street Ry. System, Ohio Valley Telephone Co.; head of J. B. Speed & Co., cement, etc., and Byrne & Speed, coal. Address: Louisville KY

SPEED, KELLOGG surgeon; b. Cleve., Jan. 17, 1879; s. Henry Bryant and Anna (Robb) S.; B.S., U. Chgo., 1901, grad. scholar in chemistry, 1901-02; M.D., Rush Med. Coll., 1904; m. 2d, Margaret Rudd, Mar. 14, 1918; children—(1st marriage) Bertha Brown (Mrs. Wm. J. Pringle, Jr.), Janet Brown (Mrs. Francis Woodworth); (2d marriage) Patricia Rudd, Helen Marjorie (Mrs. Jas. H. Hensinger), Ann (Mrs. E. O. Booth, Jr.). Began practice at Chgo., 1905; former prof. surgery, U. Ill. (Rush), now clin. prof. surgery emeritus; attending surgeon Presbyn. Highland Park, Lake Forest hosps.; cons. surgeon U.S. Naval Hosp., Great Lakes, Ill. Hon. lt. col. R.A. M.C., British E.F., France, in charge surg. div. Gen. Hosp. No. 23, 1916; maj. and lt. col. MC., A.E.F., in France, 1917-19 Citation U. Chgo. Alumni Assn., 1942. Trustee Rush Med. College. Diplomate Am. Bd. of Surgery (Founder's mem.), Am. Bd. Orthopedic Surgery. Fellow A.C.S. (mem. bd. govs.); mem. Am., Western (pres. 1927-28), Central surg. assns., Chgo. Surg. Soc. (pres. 1925-26), Am. Orthopedic Assn., Am. Assn. for Surgery of Trauma (1st pres. 1938-39). Société Internat. de Chirurgie, Beta Theta Pi, Nu Sigma Nu, Alpha Omega Alpha, Sigma Xi; hon. mem. Los Angeles Mpls., Seattle surg. socs., Am. Acad. Orthopedic Surgeons. Republican. Presbyn. Clubs: University, Tavern, Chicago, Exmoor Country. Author: Text Book of Fractures and Dislocations, 1916 (4 edits.); Taumatic Injuries of the Carpus, 1925; Primer on Fractures for A.M.A. (6 edits). Mem. editorial bd. Ill. State Med. Jour. Home: 1502 Sheridan Rd., Highland Park, Ill.; also 1907 Ocean Way, Laguna Beach, Cal. Died July 2, 1955; buried Chgo.

SPEED, THOMAS congressman; b. Charlotte County, Va., Oct. 25, 1768; taught by his father. Worked in Office Clk. of Gen. Ct.; became mcht.. Danville, Bardstown, Ky., 1790; became farmer; clk. Bullitt and Nelson circuit cts.; served as maj. of Volunteers in War of 1812; mem. U.S. Ho. of Reps. from Ky., 15th Congress, 1817-19; contbr. articles to Nat. Intelligencer, Washington, D.C.; mem. Ky. Ho. of Reps., 1821-22, 40; became mem. Whig Party when it was organized. Died on his farm Cottage Grove, nr. Bardstown, Feb. 20, 1842; buried on his farm.

SPENCER, FRANK ROBERT physician and surgeon; b. Burlington, Ia., June 12, 1879; s. Dr. Robert Spencer and Alice (Kendall) S.; A.B., U. Mich., 1900, M.D., 1902; m. Edith Clayton, Apr. 5, 1911; children—Donald Clayton, John Robert. Began as physician and surgeon, 1902; asst., Med. Faculty, U. Mich., 1902-04; mem. Med. Faculty, U. Colo., 1905-—; now prof. emeritus otolaryngology. Served as capt., Med. Corps, U.S. Army during World War I. Pres. Colo. State Bd. of Med. Examiners, 1924-26. Fellow Am. Coll. Surgeons, Am. Otol. Soc., Am. Laryngol. Assn. (pres. 1947), Am. Laryngol., Rhinol. and Otol. Soc., Am. Acad. of Ophthalmology and Otolaryngology (pres. 1941; mem. sect. on instrn., 1923-26), Sect. of Laryngology, Otology and Rhinology of A.A. (chmn. of sect., 1928). Charter mem. Am. Bd. of Otolaryngology; mem. Colo. Otolaryngol. Soc. (past pres.). Colo. State Med. Soc. (past pres.), Denver Clin. and Pathol. Soc. (asso.), Sigma Xi, Phi Gamma Delta, Nu Sigma Nu (former mem. exec. grand council). Republican. Episcopalian. Clubs: Boulder Rotary (past pres.). Author of textbook on Laryngeal Tuberculosis; also author more than 75 articles in med. jours.; contbr.

to textbook on nose, throat and ear and their diseases; also to Ency. of Medicine. Formerly mem. editorial bd. of Laryngoscope, St. Louis. Home: 427 Pine St. Office: Physicians Bldg., 2111 14th St., Boulder, Colo. Died 1957.

SPENCER, GEORGE ELIPHAZ senator; b. Champion, Jefferson County, N.Y., Nov. 1, 1836; attended Montreal (Can.) Coll.; studied law. Moved to Ia.; sec. Ia. Senate, 1856; admitted to bar, 1857, practiced law; entered U.S. Army as capt. during Civil War, brevetted brig. gen. for gallantry on field when he resigned, 1865; practiced in Decatur, Ala.; apptd. register in bankruptcy for Ala. 4th Dist., 1867; mem. U.S. Senate (Republican) from Ala., July 13, 1868-79; retired to his ranch in Nev. Died Washington, D.C., Feb. 19, 1893; buried Arlington (Va.) Nat. Cemetery.

SPENCER, HERBERT LINCOLN found. exec.; born Whitney Point, N.Y., July 13, 1894; s. William Henry and Ida Dell (Adriance) S.; B.S., Carnegie Inst. Tech., 1921; LL.D., Pa. Coll. for Women, 1946; M.A., Ph.D., U. Pitts., 1934, LL.D., 1948; L.H.D., Bucknell, 1953; m. Mildred Louise Pollard, June 6, 1916; children—Nancy Lynn (Mrs. L. D. Schaller), Sally Louise. Mech. engr. various indsl. orgns., 1916-21; vice prin. and tchr., Latimer Jr. High Sch., Pitts., 1922-27; vice-prin. Henry Clay Frick Tng. Sch. for Tchrs., Pitts., 1927-28, prin. 1928-34; dean Coll. Liberal Arts and Sciences, U. Pitts., 1934-35; pres. Pa. Coll. for Women, Pitts., 1935-45; pres. Bucknell U. (Lewisburg), 1945-49; exec. v.p. and trustee Samuel H. Kress Found., N.Y.C. 1949-—; dir. Chemecon Corp., Log Cabin Assoc., N.C., N.Y.U. Bellevue Med. Center Coordinator Pitts. Engineering, Science and Management War Training, U.S. Office of Education, 1941-44; ednl. expert for U.S. Army's A.S.T.P.; apptd. to 4th Naval Dist. Navy Manpower Survey Com., U.S. Navy; chmn. coll. and univ. sect. Pittsburgh Defense Council, 1941; chmn. edn. div., blood donors com., Pitts. A.R.C.; mem. Pa. Aero. Commn. Civilian engr., A.C., U.S. Army, World War I. Trustee Bucknell U., Crozer Theol. Sem.; dir. Devitt's Camp. Pres. Pitts. Child Guidance Clinic, Inc., Pitts., Personnel Assn. Dir. Metropolitan Y.M.C.A., Fedn. Social Agencies, Frick Ednl. Commission, Pitts. Acad. Science and Art, Lewisburg Trust & Safe Deposit Bank, Geisinger Hospital; pres. Pa. Assn. Colls. and Univs., 1948; mem. Joint State Govt. Commn. on Higher Education; chmn. Pittsburgh Edn. Com. of Nat. Assn. Mfrs., Exceptionally Able Youths Com., Civic Club of Allegheny County. Mem. N.E.A., A.A.A.S., Pa. State Edn. Assn., mem. Pa. Displaced Persons Commn., Am. Society Mechanical Engineers, Am. Society Engineering Education, Society Advancement Management, Regional War Labor Bd., bd. trustees, Kiskiminetas Springs Sch., Photographic Soc. of Am., Pa. Society of New York, Phi Beta Kappa, Phi Eta Sigma, Phi Delta Kappa, Kappa Phi Kappa, Iota Lambda Sigma, Phi Kappa Phi, Phi Sigma Pi, Delta Tau Deta, Omicron Delta Kappa. Tau Beta Pi, Phi Beta Kappa Assos., Scabbard and Blade. Registered profl. engr. Pa. Mason (33 deg.). Clubs: Century Associates, Rotary (dir.), University (dir.). Home: Newfoundland, Pa. Office: 221 W. 57th St., N.Y.C. Died Jan. 1960.

SPENCER, JAMES BRADLEY congressman; b. Salisbury, Conn., Apr. 26, 1781. Moved to Franklin County, N.Y., settled in Ft. Covington; raised company for War of 1812; served as capt. 29th U.S. Inf.; apptd. local magistrate, 1814; surrogate Franklin County, 1828-37; apptd. loan commr., 1829; mem. N.Y. State Assembly, 1831-32; Democratic presdl. elector, 1832; mem. U.S. Ho. of Reps. (Dem.) from N.Y., 25th Congress, 1837-39. Died Ft. Covington, Mar. 26, 1848; buried probably in Old Cemetery, nr. Ft. Covington.

SPENCER, JOHN CANFIELD congressman, cabinet officer; b. Hudson, N.Y., Jan. 8, 1788; s. Ambrose and Laura (Canfield) S.; grad. Union Coll., Schenectady, N.Y., 1806; m. Elizabeth Scott Smith, May 20, 1809, 3 children including Philip. Admitted to N.Y. bar, 1809; judge adv. gen. in active service along frontier, 1813; postmaster Canandaigua (N.Y.), 1814; asst. atty. gen. and dist. atty. for 5 western counties of N.Y., 1815; mem. U.S. Ho. of Reps. from N.Y., 15th Congress, 1817-19; mem. N.Y. Gen. Assembly, 1820, 21, 22, 33, 38, speaker, 1820; mem. N.Y. State Senate, 1825-28; asso. with Anti-Masonic Party; spl. pros. officer to investigate abduction of William Morgan, 1839; U.S. sec. of war, 1841-43; U.S. sec. of treas-joined Whig Party during 1830's; sec. of state N.Y., 1839; U.S. sec. of war, 1841-43; U.S. sec. of treasury, 1843-44, resigned over opposition to annexation of Tex.; defended Dr. Eliphalet Nott (pres. Union Coll.) against charge of misappropriating Coll. funds. Author; a portrait of Free Masonry, 1832; editor Democracy in America (De Tocqueville), 1838, Died Albany, N.Y., May 18, 1855; buried Albany Rural Cemetery.

SPENCER, JOSEPH Continental congressman, army officer; b. Haddam, Conn., Oct. 3, 1714; s. Isaac and Mary (Selden) S.; m. Martha Barainerd, Aug. 2, 1738; m. 2d, Hannah Brown Southmayd, 1756; 13 children. Dept., Conn. Assembly, 1750-66; probate judge, Haddam, 1753-89; commd. H. Conn. Militia, 1747, maj., 157, lt. col., 1759, col., 1766; commd. brig. gen. Conn. Militia, Continental Army, 1775, resigned after Continental Congress promoted Israel Putnam over him, 1775, returned to service with Continental Army in Boston and N.Y. State, later in year; commd. maj. gen., 1776, served in Providence, R.I., 1777, attempted unsuccessful movement against enemy, investigated by spl. ct. of inquiry, cleared; resigned from Continental Army, 1778; mem. Continental Congress from Conn., 1779; mem. Conn. Council of Safety, 1780-81. Died East Haddam, Conn., Jan. 13, 1789; buried East Haddam.

SPENCER, LEE BOWEN, librarian; b. El Paso, Tex., Jan. 2, 1914; s. Lee Babers and Annabel (Bowen) S.; A.B., Okla. Baptist U., 1934; B.S. in L.S., U. Ill., 1940; M.A., U. Okla., 1946; m. Willa Belle Carter, Aug. 19, 1939; children—Lee Bowen, Mary Ann, Sarah Margaret. Asst. Carnegie Pub. Library, Shawnee, Okla., 1934-36; librarian Okla. Bapt. U., 1936-63, prof. library sci., 1946-63; librarian, prof. library science State College of Ark., Conway, 1963-70; chief acquisitions librarian Air Univ., 1947; vis. prof. Okla. State U., summers 1948, 49; dean men Okla. Bapt. U., 1951-54. Mem. hist. commn. So. Bapt. Conv., 1962-63. Bd. dirs., blood drive chmn. Pottawatomie County chpt. A.R.C., 1950-63; bd. dirs. Carnegie Pub. Library, 1961-63. Served to 1st lt. USAAF, 1942-46; lt. colonel Reserve. Member American, Southwestern, Arkansas (president 1969-70), Okla. (1950-51) library assns., S.A.R. (chaplain Oklahoma 1962-63), Res. Officers Assn. (pres. Shawnee 1961-62), Okla. (foundling mem., v.p. 1956-57), Ark. (pres. 1965-66) geneal. socs., Faulkner County Hist. Soc. (bd. dirs. 1963-—), Kappa Delta Pi, Phi Delta Kappa. Democrat. Baptist (deacon). Mason (K.T. Shriner), Rotarian (dist. gov. 1969-70; dir.). Contbr. profl. jours. Home: Conway AR Died June 12, 1970; buried Conway AR

SPENCER, LORILLARD aircraft mfr.; b. N.Y. City, July 4, 1883; s. Lorillard and Caroline Suydam (Berryman) S.; prep. edn., St. Paul's Sch., Concord, N.H.; student Columbia; m. Mary R. Sands, Sept. 19, 1905 (divorced); 1 son, Lorillard; m. 2d, Katherine Emmons Force, Dec. 6, 1922; children—Katherine Talmage Lorillard, Stephen Wolcott, William H. Force. With Pedersen Manufacturing Co., 1907-10, Colo. Fruit Products Co., 1913-14; pres. Somma Shops, Inc., 1913-25; pres. Austral Window Co., 1913-29; pres. Panama Engring. Co., 1914-16; dir. Advocate Realty Co., 1916-17; pres. Wittemann Aircraft Corp., 1921-22; pres. Atlantic Aircraft Corp., 1923-28; pres. Sixty-Third Street Corp., Fokker Aircraft Corp. of America, 1927-28, Aviation Consolidated, Inc., Color Pictures, Inc.; dir. Austral Sales Corp. Member Squadron A, N.Y. Cavalry, 1909-12; 2d lieutenant C.A.C. N.Y.N.G., 1912, 1st lieutenant, 1913, capt. 1915; lt. col. inf., N.Y.N.G., 1916, maj., 1917; mil. sec. to gov. of N.Y., 1915-17; served as maj. inf., U.S.A., World War I; received citations for Distinguished Service Cross (U.S.), Croix de Guerre and Cross of Legion of Honor (France) for "extraordinary heroism in action in Champagne sector on Sept. 26, 1918." Mem. bd. mgrs. Am. Soc. for Prevention of Cruelty to Animals; mem. bd. govs. and hon. scout commr., Manhattan Council Boy Scouts of America (one of founders of movement in U.S.); trustee French Inst. in U.S. and Moro Ednl. Foundation. Republican. Episcopalian. Mason. Home: New York, N.Y. Died June 9, 1939.

SPENCER, LYLE MANLY, publisher; born Atlanta, Georgia, May 10, 1911; s. M. Lyle and Lois (Hill) S.; A.B., U. Wash., 1933, M.A., 1935; fellow sociology U. Chgo., 1936-37, Marshall Field fellow, 1937-38; Doctor of Laws degree, Syracuse U., 1967. Round-the-world debator, under auspices U. Wash. and U.S. Office Edn., 1933-34; instr. sociology U. Wash., 1934-35; pres. Sci. Research Assos., 1938-42, 45-68; dir. IBM. Mem. council advisers Nat. Scholarship Service and Fund for Negro Students, 1958; mem. adv. com. library research and tng. projects Dept. Health Edn. and Welfare Chmn. trustees Roosevelt U.; trustee Menninger Found., 1950-—, U. Chgo., Midwest Research Inst., Young Presidents' Found.; governing mem. Library Internat. Relations; trustee Center for Study Dem. Instns., Lawrence U., Center for Study Liberal Edn. Adults; bd. dirs. Adlai Stevenson Inst. Internat. Affairs, 1968. Served as lt. col. information, edn. div., AUS, 1943-45. Decorated Legion of Merit, Bronze Star; named one of 10 outstanding young men. U.S. Jr. C. of C., 1940. Fellow Am. Sociol. Soc.; mem. Young Pres.'s Orgn. (chmn. Chgo. chpt. 1952, nat. v.p. 1953), Am. Psychol. Assn., Am. Statis. Assn., Am. Textbook Pubs. Inst. (gen. com. testing), Phi Beta Kappa. Office: Chicago IL Died Aug. 21, 1968; buried Appleton WI

SPENCER, M(ATTHEW) LYLE, univ. dean; b. Batesville, Miss., July 7, 1881; s. Rev. Flournoy Poindexter and Alice Eleanor (Manes) S.; A.B., Kentucky Wesleyan Coll., 1903, A.M., 1904, Litt.D., 1942; A.M., Northwestern University, 1905, LL.D., 1928; Ph.D., University of Chicago, 1910; Litt.D., College of Puget Sound, Tacoma, Washington, 1932; LL.D. and Litt.D., Syracuse Univ., 1951; married Helen McNaughton, Sept. 8, 1920. Physical dir. Ky. Wesleyan College, 1901, instructor English, 1902, professor, 1903-04; fellow in English, U. of Chicago, 1905-07, 1910-11; asst. prof. English, Wofford Coll., S.C., 1907-10; prof. English, Woman's Coll., of Ala., Montgomery, 1910-11; prof. English, Lawrence Coll., Appleton, Wis., 1911-17; reporter, copy reader, editorial writer, Milwaukee Journal, 1913, 1917-19; capt. U.S. Army, 1918; lectr. in journalism U. of Wis., summer, 1919; dir. Sch. of Journalism, U. of Wash., 1919-26; pres. U. of Wash., 1927-33, dean Sch. of Journalism, Syracuse U., 1934-51, emeritus dean, 1951-69 awarded D.S.M., sch. journalism, 1951. Vis. prof. Am. U., Cairo, Egypt, 1937, 1945-46; lecturer, Oriental Culture Coll., Tokyo, Japan, 1940. Dir. Seattle Trust Co., 1924-31, Univ. Nat. Bank, 1925-27. Dir. Seattle Chamber of Commerce, 1925-33. Mem. S.A.R., Kappa Alpha. Phi Beta Kappa, Tau Kappa Alpha, Sigma Delta Chi, Alpha Delta Sigma; hon. mem. Washington Pub. Association, New York Press Association. Editor: Simms's Yemassee, 1911; N.Y. Laws Relating to Publications, 1943. Author: Corpus Christi Pageants in England, 1911; Practical English Punctuation, 1913; News Writing, 1917; Editorial Writing, 1924. Home: Fayetteville NY Died Feb. 1969.

SPENCER, THOMAS physician; b. Great Barrington, Mass., 1793. Founder, Med. Inst. (now part of Hobart Coll.), Geneva, N.Y., 1835, prof. theory and practice of medicine, 1835-50; later taught at med. schs., Phila. and Chgo.; served as surgeon in U.S. Army during Mexican War; pres. N.Y. State Med. Assn. Author: Observations on Epidemic Diarrhea, Known as Cholera, 1832; Lectures on Vital Chemistry, or Animal Heat, 1845; The Atomic Theory of Life, 1853. Died Phila., May 30, 1857.

SPENCER, WILLIAM BRINERD congressman, lawyer; b. Home Plantation, Catahoula Parish, La., Feb. 5, 1835; grad. Centenary Coll., Jackson, La., 1855; grad. law dept. U. La., 1857. Admitted to bar, 1857, practiced in Harrisonburg, La.; served in Confederate Army with rank of capt. until 1863, captured, remained prisoner of war at Johnsons Island (O.) until close of Civil War; practiced in Vidalia, La., 1866; mem. U.S. Ho. of Reps. (Democrat, contested election) from La., 44th Congress, June 8, 1876-Jan. 8, 1877 (resigned); asso. justice La. Supreme Ct., 1877-80; practiced in New Orleans. Died Japla, Mexico, Feb. 12, 1882; buried Magnolia Cemetery, Baton Rouge, La.

SPERRY, CHARLES STILLMAN rear admiral U.S.N.; b. Brooklyn, Sept. 3, 1847; s. Corydon Stillman and Catherine Elizabeth (Leavenworth) S.; grad. U.S. Naval Acad., 1866; LL.D., Yale, 1909; m. Edith, g.d. Gov. William L. Marcy, of N.Y., Jan. 11, 1877. Ensign, Mar. 12, 1868; master, Mar. 26, 1869; lt., Mar. 21, 1870; lt. comdr., Mar. 1, 1885; comdr., June 22, 1894; capt., July 1, 1900; rear admiral, May 26, 1906; retired, Sept. 3, 1909. Pres. U.S. Naval War Coll. and mem. Gen. Bd. U.S.N., 1903; mem. Nat. Coast Defense Bd., 1905; comd. Atlantic Battleship Fleet on cruise around the world, 1908-09. Del. Geneva Conf. for Revision of Geneva Conv. for Treatment of Sick and Wounded, June 1906; del. 2d Hague Conf., June, 1907. Home: Waterbury, Conn. Died 1911.

SPEYERS, ARTHUR BAYARD rear admiral U.S.N.; b. New York, Aug. 15, 1846; s. James and Fanny (Pigot) S.; grad. U.S. Naval Acad., 1868; unmarried. Midshipman U.S.N., 1868; promoted through the various grades to rear admiral and retired, Jan. 11, 1905. Comd. U.S.S. Caesar in southern blockade of Cuba during Spanish-Am. War. Address: New York, N.Y. Died Nov. 19, 1918.

SPICER, HENRY RUSSELL, air force officer; b. Colorado Springs, Colo., Feb. 16,21909; s. Carroll Atchison and Bertha Agnes (Watson) S.; B.S., U. Ariz., 1931; student AC Flying Sch., 1934-35; m. Louise Frances Leonard, June 11, 1938; children—Henry A., Leonard R., Susan, James R. Commd. 2d lt. AC, 1935, advanced through grades to maj. gen. USAF, 1953; comdr. 357th Fighter Group, Eng., 1944; prisoner of war, Germany, 1944-45; comdr. 36th Fighter Group, Panama and Germany, 1946-48; instr. Armed Forces Staff Coll., 1949-50; comdr. Williams AFB, Ariz., 1950-51; comdr. Wichita AFB, Kan., 1951-53, Nellis AFB, Nev., 1953; dep. comdr. Crew Tng. Air Force, 1954; insp. gen. Air Tng. Command, 1954-56, chief of staff, 1956-57, vice commander, 1957; commander of Flying Training Air Force, 1957-58; commander 17th Air Force, 1958-62, 25th Air Division (SAGE), McChord Air Force Base, Washington, 1962-64, ret., 1964. Decorated Distinguished Flying Cross, Bronze Star, Air Medal with clusters, Purple Heart, Legion of Merit with Cluster (U.S.); Croix de Guerre (France). Mem. Assn. Am. Rod and Gun Clubs (pres. Europe), Sigma Chi. Rotarian. Home: Tucson AZ2Died Dec. 4, 1968; buried Nat. Cemetery, Ft. Sam Houston TX

SPILLERS, CHARLES LEE judge; b. Russellville, Ark., Aug. 6, 1901; s. Henry Franklin and Loula Ellen (Shinn) S.; B.S., Washington and Jefferson Coll., 1925; LL.B., Harvard, 1928; m. Elizabeth Reymann, Dec. 2, 1933; children—Charles Lee, George Lawrence, James Reymann, Ann Keating. Admitted to W.Va. bar, 1928, pros. atty. Ohio Co., 1936-40, sheriff 1941; judge of the intermediate court of Ohio County; board of directors National Bank W.Va., Wheeling, Wheeling Coca-Cola Bottling Works, Community Broadcasting. Mem. W.Va. State Senate, 1935-36; U.S. dist. atty. northern dist. W.Va., 1947-52. Trustee Linsley Inst., Washington and Jefferson Coll. Mem. W.Va. Conservation Commn., 1953-54, Bd. Edn., 1955-—, Bd. Law Examiners, 1955-—. Served as sgt., USMC, 1917-19; comdr., USNR, 1941-45, now capt. Mem. Am. Judicature Soc., Am. Bar Assn. Am. Legion. Democrat. Episcopalian.

Elk, Mason. Club: Kiwanis. Home: 38 Poplar Av., Wheeling 26003. Office: Riley Law Bldg., Wheeling, W.Va. Died Nov. 18, 1962.

SPILMAN, ROBERT SCOTT, JR., lawyer; b. Charleston, W.Va., Jan. 6, 1908; s. Robert Scott and Eliza (Dillon) S.; B.A., Va. Mil. Inst., 1928; LL.B., Harvard, 1932; m. Ann Hatfield, Apr. 18, 1941; 1 son, Robert Scott III (dec.). Instr. Am. history Va. Mil. Inst., 1928; admitted to W.Va. bar, 1932, since practiced in Charleston; partner firm Spilman, Thomas, Battle & Klostermeyer, 1937-69. Dir. Kanawha Banking & Trust Co., Charleston, Peerless Eagle Coal Co., Summersville, W.Va., James River Hydrate & Supply Co., Buchanan, Va. Mem. city council, Charleston, 1935-39, 47-51; mem. Charleston Municipal Planning Commn., from 1956, chmn., 1958-66. Bd. dirs. Charleston Community Chest, 1958-62; trustee Greater Kanawha Valley Found., 1960. Served to lt. col. USAAF, 1942-46. Mem. Am., W.Va. (exec. council 1966-69) bar assns., Am. Law Inst., Am. Judicature Soc., Kappa Alpha. Democrat. Episcopalian (vestryman). Clubs: Edgewood Country, Army and Navy, Press (Charleston); Farmington Hunt (Charlotteville, Va.); Springdale Hall (Camden, S.C.). Home: Charleston WV Died Nov. 3, 1969.

SPINGARN, ARTHUR B., lawyer; b. N.Y. City, March 28, 1878; s. Elias and Sarah (Barnett) S.; A.B., Columbia, 1897, A.M., 1899, LL.B., 1900; LL.D., Howard University, 1941; L.H.D., Long Island University, 1966; m. Marion Mayer, Jan. 27, 1918 (dec.). Admitted N.Y. bar, 1900, practiced N.Y. City since 1900. Served as capt. San. corps. U.S. Army, 1917-19; with A.E.F. Mem. Amer., N.Y. State, City N.Y., N.Y. Co. bar assns. Pres. Nat. Assn. for Advancement Colored People, 1940-66 (chmn. nat. legal com. and v. pres., 1911-40, pres. N.A.A.C.P. Legal and Ednl. Fund, Inc. 1940-57), chmn. legal com. Social Hygiene Div. N.Y. Tb and Health Assn.; mem. Manhattan Council State Commn. of Human Rights; past mem. legal com. N.Y. Probation Assn. Mem. Bibliog. Soc. (London). Oxford, Cambridge, Va. bibliog. socs., Society of Peintres Graveurs (France), Legion Fgn. Wars, Am. Legion (past post commdr.). Clubs: City, New York. Author: Laws Relating to Sex Morality in N.Y., 1915, rev. 1926; Legal and Protective Measures (with J. Goldberg), 1950. Contbr. articles and pamphlets on the Negro to nat. mags. Founder Springarn Collection of Negro Lit. at Howard U. Home: New York City NY Died Dec. 1, 1971.

SPINGARN, J(OEL) E(LIAS) author, publicist; b. N.Y. City, May 17, 1875; s. Elias and Sarah (Barnett) S.; A.B., Columbia, 1895, Ph.D., 1899; Harvard, 1895-96, Phi Beta Kappa Poet, Columbia, 1901. Asst. and tutor comparative lit., 1899-1904, adj. prof., 1904-09, prof., 1909-11, Columbia. Owner Amenia (N.Y.) Times, 1911-26. Rep. cand. for Congress, 18th N.Y. District, 1908; del. Prog. Nat. Conv., Chicago, 1912, 1916. Maj. inf., U.S.A., 1917-19; with A.E.F., France, 1918-19; lt. col. O.R.C. One of founders and lit. adviser Harcourt, Brace & Co., pubs., 1919-32. Chmn. dirs. Nat. Assn. Adv. Colored People, 1913-19, treas., 1919-30, pres., 1930—; founded movement for rural coop. recreation, 1910-15; founded Spingarn medal, 1913. Hon. citizen U. of Munich, 1924. Mem. bd. mgrs. New York Bot. Garden; dir. Hort. Soc. of N.Y.; awarded Jackson Dawson Memorial Medal by Mass. Hort. Soc., 1937. Author: A History of Literary Criticism in the Renaissance, 1899 (Italian transl., 1905, with introduction by Benedetto Croce); The New Criticism, 1911; The New Hesperides and Other Poems, 1911; Creative Criticism, 1917; Poems, 1924; Poetry and Religion, 1924; Creative Criticism and Other Essays, 1931; Henry Winthrop Sargent and the Early History of Landscape Gardening and Ornamental Horticulture in Dutchess County, N.Y., 1937. Editor: Critical Essays of the Seventeenth Century (3 vols.), 1908-09; Temple's Essays, 1909; A Renaissance Courtesy Book, the Galateo of Della Casa, 1914; Goethe's Literary Essays, 1921; Criticism in America, 1924; European Library (25 vols.), 1920-25; Troutbeck Leaflets, 1924-31. Contbr. to Civilization in the U.S., Dicitionary of American Biography, Cambridge History of English Literature, Taylor's Garden Dictionary, Markham's Clematis. Home: New York, N.Y. Died July 26, 1939.

SPINNER, FRANCIS ELIAS treas. U.S., congressman; b. German Flats, N.Y., Jan. 21, 1802; s. John Peter and Mary (Brument) S.; attended shcs. in Mohawk Valley, N.Y.; m. Caroline Caswell, June 22, 1826, 3 daus. Mcht., Herkimer, N.Y., circa 1820; served as maj. gen. N.Y. State Militia, 1830's; cashier, later pres. Mohawk Valley, Herkimer; active in Democratic Party; auditor Port of N.Y., 1845-49; mem. U.S. Ho. of Reps. from N.Y., 34th Congress (as anti-slave Democrat), 1855-57, 35th-36th congresses (as Republican), 1857-61; treas. U.S. (apptd. by Pres. Lincoln), 1861-75, responsible for 1st employment of women in Civil Service, resigned in personal dispute with Treasury Dept., 1875; lived in retirement, Jacksonville, Fla., 1875-90. Died Jacksonville, Dec. 31, 1890.

SPINOLA, FRANCIS BARRETTO congressman; b. Stony Brook, L.I., N.Y., Mar. 29, 1821; attended Quaker Hill Acad., Dutchess County, N.Y.; studied law. Admitted to bar, 1844, practiced in Bklyn.; elected alderman 2d Ward, Bklyn., 1846, 47, reelected 1849, served 4 years; mem. N.Y. State Assembly, 1855; mem. N.Y. State Senate, 1858-61; del. Nat. Democratic Conv., Charleston, 1860; harbor commr.; apptd. brig. gen. Volunteers for "meritorious conduct in recruiting and organizing brigade of 4 regiments and accompanying them to the field" in Civil War, 1862, wounded twice, discharged, 1865; alternate del. Nat. Dem. Conv., Chgo., 1884; in insurance business and banking; mem. U.S. Ho. of Reps. (Dem.) from N.Y., 50th-52d congresses, 1887-Apr. 14, 1891. Died Washington, D.C., Apr. 14, 1891; buried Greenwood Cemetery, Bklyn.

SPOFFORD, W(OLCOTT) E(DWARD) naval architect and shipbuilder; b. near Alex, Va., Sept. 17, 1895; s. Edward Coggeshall and Lydia (Riley) S.; grad. Univ. Prep. Sch., Washington, 1916; student Webb Inst. Naval Architecture and Marine Engring., N.Y. City, 1916-17, 1919-20, Franklin Inst., Phila., 1920-21; also spl. univ. courses; m. Dorothy Lincoln Hale, Apr. 20, 1922; 1 dau., Elizabeth Ann (Mrs. John Hyatt). Draftsman, Internat. Mercantile Marine, N.Y. City, 1921; draftsman United States Lines, N.Y. City, 1921-22, designer, 1922-23; vice pres. and naval architect Henry C. Grebe & Co., naval architects and yacht brokers, Chicago, 1924-25; designer, cost estimator and constructor, merchant and naval vessels Newport News (Va.) Shipbldg. & Dry Dock Co., 1926-31; asso. naval architect, Navy Yard, N.Y. City, 1931-37; naval architect U.S. Maritime Commn., Washington, 1937-39, regional dir. constrn. Great Lakes Area, Chicago, 1942-44, tech. consultant U.S. Maritime Commn., 1944-45, asst. to vice chmn., 1945-46, liaison officer Bur. Res. Fleet, 1946-48, chmn. claims review bd. Maritime Commn., Washington, 1948-50; supt. U.S. Maritime Adminstrn. Res. Fleet, Olympia, Wash., 1950-56; naval architect Puget Sound Naval Shipyard, Bremerton, 1957, ret.; now engring. aide bridge division Wash. Hwy. Dept.; naval architect and asst. chief engineer Consolidated Steel Corp., Los Angeles, 1939-42. Am. observer Internat. Conf. on standardization of screw threads, Ottawa, Can., 1945; marine cons. loaned to Internat. Training Adminstrn., Inc., for training 22 Chinese naval ensigns in technique of Am. shipbldg., 1946; Am. del. to Internat. Conf. on safety of life at sea, London, 1948. Enlisted in U.S. Army, 1917; commd. 2d lt., 1918; comdg. officer 114th Inf., N.J.N.G., 1920-21. Mem. Soc. Naval Architects and Marine Engineers, American Soc. Naval Engrs., Am. Legion, Webb Inst. Naval Architecture and Marine Engring. Alumni Assn. (sec.-treas. 1933-35). Profl. engr., Texas, Wash. Contbr. articles to maritime tech. mags. Died Oct. 18, 1961; buried Arlington Nat. Cemetery.

SPOONER, CHARLES HORACE univ. pres.; b. Charleston, N.H., August 6, 1858; s. Stephen and Sophia L. (Hull) S.; S.B., Norwich U., 1878, completed arts course, 1879 (hon. A.M., 1895; LL.D., U. Vt., 1904); m. Inez G. Davis, Nov. 15, 1882. Instr. English and mil. tactics, St. Augustine's Coll., Benicia, Cal., and maj. N.G. Cal., 1879-81; instr. mathematics and mil. tactics, Vt. Acad., Saxtons River, 1881-89; maj. Vt. N.G., 1888-89; prin. sch. Fitchburg, Mass., 1889-91; instr. mathematics, Manual Tng. Sch. of Washington U., 1891-1904; pres. Norwich U., 1904-15, emeritus, 1916. Address: Charlestown, N.H. Deceased.

SPOONER, JOHN COIT senator; b. Lawrenceburg, Ind., Jan. 6, 1843; s. Judge Philip L. and Lydia (Coit) S.; removed to Madison, Wis., 1859; A.B., U. of Wis., 1864, hon. Ph.B., A.M., 1869, LL.D., 1895; LL.D., Yale, 1908, Columbia, 1909; m. Annie E. Main, Sept. 10, 1868. Served pvt. Co. A, 40th Wis. Inf.; capt. and bvt. maj. 50th Wis. Inf.; pvt. and mil. sec. to Gov. Lucius Fairchild, of Wis., 1866-67. Admitted to bar, 1867; asst. atty. gen. of Wis., and in gen. practice at Madison, 1867-70; practiced at Hudson, Wis., 1870-84; regent U. of Wis., 1882-85; mem. Wis. Assembly, 1872; U.S. senator, 1885-91, and 1897-1907, resigned, Mar. 3, to take effect May 1, 1907; in law practice at New York, 1907—. Chmn. Wis. delegation Rep. Nat. convs., 1888, 92; candidate for gov. of Wis., 1892; tendered portfolio of Sec. of the Interior by President McKinley, 1898, membership on British-Am. Joint High Commn., 1898, and portfolio of Atty. Gen. of U.S., 1901, but declined. Address: New York, N.Y. Died June 11, 1919.

SPOTSWOOD, ALEXANDER colonial ofcl.; b. Tangier, Africa, 1676; s. Robert and Catherine (Mercer) Elliott Spotswood; m. Anne Butler Brayne, 1724, 4 children. Served as ensign English Army in War of Grand Alliance, 1693; served under Lord Cadogan, rose to rank lt. col., during War of Spanish Succession, 1703-13; apptd. lt. gov. Va., 1710-22, served under nominal gov. George Hamilton (Earl of Orkney), tried to regulate and stabilize fur trade and finance enlightened Indian policy by organizing Va. Indian Co. with hdqrs. at Ft. Christanna, 1714 (reforms not supported by council and Ho. of Burgesses because they thought he had usurped their power); tried to protect colony from Iroquois raids by establishing settlements of friendly Indians powerful enough to resist attack; concluded treaty with Iroquois stipulating that they keep North of Potomac and West of Blue Ridge Mountains, 1722; after he was removed from office he retired to Germanna (colony Germans organized as part of scheme of frontier defense); bought or granted to himself (while gov.) over 70,000 acres of land in Va., most of which according to his instructions from the Brit. Govt. was not to be sold to anyone; removed from office because he had acquired such a large stock in lands of Va. that he was more on colonist side than that of Royal Govt. in London; title to his lands challenged and went to Eng. to adjust it, 1724; apptd. postmaster-gen. for Am. colonies, 1724, served until 1740; apptd. maj. gen. in charge of recruiting regt. of colonist that would serve under Lord Cathcart, 1740. Died in course of duties, Annapolis, Md., June 7, 1740.

SPRAGINS, ROBERT L. army officer; b. Huntsville, Ala., Nov. 12, 1890; s. Robert Elias and Susan Patton (Echols) S.; ed. U. Ala., 1906-07; U. Va., 1908-09; B.S., U.S. Mil. Acad., 1913; m. Marguerite Stephens Van Vliet, Jan. 27, 1915; children—Robert Beirne, Charles Echols, Stewart Van Vliet. Commd. 2d lt., Inf., 1913, advanced through grades to maj. gen., 1943; ret., Aug. 1945. Decorated Distinguished Service Medal with oak leaf cluster, Silver Star, Purple Heart with oak leaf cluster, Army unit citation, U.S. Coast Guard Silver Medal of Honor. Dir. 1st Nat. Bank, Huntsville Ice & Coal Co., Phillips Brick & Tile Co. (all of Huntsville). Home: 425 McClung St., Huntsville, Ala. Died Dec. 26, 1965.

SPRAGUE, ALBERT ARNOLD (sprag), wholesale grocer; b. Chicago, Ill., May 13, 1874; s. Otho Sylvester Arnold and Lucia Elvira (Atwood) S.; A.B., Harvard U., 1898; LL.D., Northwestern U., 1938; m. Frances Fidelia Dibble, June 22, 1901; children—Albert Arnold, Laura, Otho S.A. Chairman bd. of directors, Consolidated Grocers Corp.; director Continental Ill. Nat. Bank & Trust Co., Internat. Harvester Co., Clearing Industrial Dist., B.&O. R.R. Co., Wilson & Co., Marshall Field & Co., B. F. Goodrich Co.; trustee Chicago Rapid Transit Company, Trustee Chicago Natural History Museum, John Crerar Library, Children's Memorial Hosp., Chicago Symphony Orchestra, Shedd Aquarium, Mus. of Sci. and Industry, Sprague Meml. Institute. Student, O.T.C., Ft. Sheridan, Ill.; command. maj. inf., Nov. 27, 1917; assigned to 341st Regt. Inf., 86th Div., and detailed to hdqrs.; sailed for France, July 1918; lt. col. Nov. 9, 1918; returned to U.S., Mar. 1919; hon. discharged, Mar. 28, 1919; col. O.R.C. Commr. of pub. works, Chicago, 1923-27 and 1931-33. Dem. candidate for U.S. Senate, 1924. Episcopalian. Clubs: City, Chicago, Mid-Day, Commercial, Saddle and Cycle, Old Elm Club (Chicago); Harvard, Racquet (New York); Harvard (Boston). Home: 1130 Lake Shore Drive. Office: 72 W. Adams St., Chicago. Died Apr. 6, 1946.

SPRAGUE, ALBERT TILDEN, JR., naval officer, educator; b. Revere, Mass., Mar. 13, 1898; s. Albert Tilden and Ella Worcester (Baker) S.; B.S., U.S. Naval Acad., 1918; M.S., Harvard, 1925; m. Ebba Briand, Sept. 15, 1920 (dec. Nov. 1938); children—June Elizabeth, Albert Tilden, Evageline Joy; m. 2d, Marie Ancona Robertson, June 6, 1940; children—Katharine Ancona, Caroline Robertson. Commd. ensign U.S. Navy, 1918, and advanced through grades to commodore Nov., 1945, ret. as rear adm., 1949; comd. U.S.S. Beaver (AS-5) and U.S.S. Raleigh (CL7) 1940-44; served as chief of staff comdr. amphibious group 8, 1944-45; comdr. 5th amphibious force, 1945; dep. commandant, Armed Forces Staff Coll., until 1949; asso. prof. elec. engring. Auburn (Ala.) U., 1949-67, prof. emeritus, 1967-68. Awarded Legion of Merit medal, 1944, Gold Star in lieu 2d medal, for services amphibious force. Baptist. Home: Auburn AL Died Apr. 8, 1968; buried Arlington Nat. Cemetery, Arlington VA

SPRAGUE, AUGUSTUS BROWN REED soldier, banker; b. Ware, Mass., Mar. 7, 1827; s. Lee and Lucia (Snow) S. (Mayflower descendant in 7th generation); ed. pub. and pvt. schs.; m. Elizabeth Janes Rice, 1846; m. 2d, Mary Jennie Barbour, Oct. 23, 1890. Clerk in stores in Worcester, 1842-46; in mercantile business for himself, 1846-61; served in Civil War 3 yrs. and 9 mos. as capt., lt. col. and col., Mass. vols.; bvtd. brig. gen. "for gallant and meritorious service during the war." U.S. collector internal revenue, 8th Mass. Dist., 1867-72; sheriff Worcester County, 1871-90; mayor Worcester, 1896-97. Republican. Pres. Worcester Mechanics' Savings Bank, Jan. 1900—; pres. Worcester Electric Light Co., Sept. 1901—. Mem. G.A.R. (comdr. Dept. of Mass., 1868), Loyal Legion, etc. Address: Worcester, Mass. Died 1910.

SPRAGUE, CHARLES EZRA banker; b. Nassau, N.Y., Oct. 9, 1842; s. Ezra and Elisabeth B. (Edgerton) S.; A.B., Union Coll., 1860, A.M., 1884, Ph.D., 1893; Litt.D., Olivet (Mich.) College, 1910; m. Ray Ellison, Apr. 2, 1866. Served in Union Army, becoming bvt. col., N.Y. Vols.; wounded and disabled at battle of Gettysburg. Certified pub. accountant under law of 1896; pres. Bd. Examiners for Public Accountants, 1896-98; connected with Union Dime Savings Bank, New York, 1870—, pres. 1892—. Prof. of accountancy, New York U. (Sch. of Commerce, Accounts and Finance), 1900. Inventor of devices and systems for savings bank and other bookkeeping. Mem. Am. Bankers' Assn. (pres. Savings Banks Sect. 1904-05). Author: Hand-Book of Volapük, 1888; The Accountancy of Investment, 1904; Extended Bond Tables, 1905; The Philosophy of Accounts, 1907; also many articles on lang. and bookkeeping. First Am. advocate of Volapü. Home: New York, N.Y. Died Mar. 21, 1912.

SPRAGUE, CLIFTON ALBERT (spreg), naval officer; b. Dorchester, Mass., Jan. 8, 1896; s. Henry Bruno and Hazel Williams (Furlow) S.; B.S., U.S. Naval Acad., 1917; m. Annabel Fitzgerald, Apr. 12, 1925; children—Hazel Courtney (Mrs. Daniel Vaughan), Patricia (Mrs. Travis Reneau). Commd. ensign USN, 1917, advanced through grades to rear adm., 1944; comd. jeep carrier div. at Leyte Gulf battle, Oct. 1944; comdr. Alaskan Sea Frontier, comdt. 17th Naval Dist., retired as vice adm., 1951. Address: Quarters B, Naval Station, Kodiak, Alaska. Died Apr. 11, 1955; buried Rosecrans Nat. Cemetery, San Diego, Cal.

SPRAGUE, EZRA KIMBALL med. director U.S.P.H.S., sanitarian; b. Milo, Me., May 26, 1866; s. Dr. Seth Billington and Maria Edgeworth (Kimball) S.; A.B., Bates College, Me., 1887; M.D., Coll. Phys. and Surg., Boston, 1890; post-grad. work, Post-Grad. Med. Sch., New York, 1891-92, Harvard Med. Sch., 1897; m. Clara Rebecca Blaisdell, Aug. 22, 1893; children—Kimball Deering, Olive. Commd. asst. surgeon U.S.P.H.S., 1893; promoted to higher grades and retired as colonel in 1931; served in U.S. and at Antwerp (Belgium) and Calcutta; prof. tropical medicine, Detroit Med. Coll., 1901-02; made a study of bubonic plague, Calcutta, 1903-04; chief medical officer, Ellis Island, 1925-28; dir. No. Atlantic Dist. U.S.P.H.S., 1928-32. In charge extra cantonment zone sanitation, Camp Dodge, Des Moines, and Camp Devens, Ayer, Mass., during World War. Mem. A.M.A. Republican. Episcopalian. Mason. Brought about installation of filtration plant at Washington, D.C., as result of reports on drinking water, 1898. Author of articles and addresses on bacteriology, pub. health and sanitation. Club: Army and Navy (New York). Home: 462 Rugby Rd., Flatbush, Brooklyn, N.Y. Died Feb. 2, 1943.

SPRAGUE, HOMER BAXTER educator, lecturer, author; b. Sutton, Mass., Oct. 19, 1829; s. Jonathan and Mary Ann (Whipple) S.; descended in direct line from William (youngest son of Edward Sprague, of Upway, Dorsetshire, Eng.), who was joint founder of Charlestown, Mass. (1628-29) and of Hingham (1636); A.B., Yale (class valedictorian), 1852, A.M., 1855; student Yale Law Sch., 1853-54, also with Mayor Chapin, of Worcester, Mass.; admitted to bar, 1854; Ph.D., U. of New York, 1873; LL.D., Temple U., 1916; m. Antoinette E. Pardee, Dec. 28, 1854 (died 1913). Practiced law at Worcester, 1855-56; principal Worcester High School, 1856-59, practiced law at New Haven, Conn., 1859-61; mem. New Haven Board of Edn., 1860-61. Raised 2 mil. cos. for war, 1861; served as capt., maj., lt. col., 13th Conn. Inf., 1862-66; wounded in action, Irish Bend, La., Apr. 14, 1863; mem. of two "forlorn hopes"; bvtd. col. for conduct at Port Hudson; recd. commn. col. 11th C.D.A.; prisoner of war (battle of Winchester), Sept. 19, 1864-Feb. 1865; served on courts martial, mil. commns., cdnl. supt., freedmens courts, etc., 1865-66; mustered out, Apr. 28, 1866. Prin. Conn. Normal Sch., 1866-67; mem. Conn. Ho. of Rep., 1868; secured abolition of the odious tuition "rate bills," thus making the pub. schs. free, the reopening of State Normal Sch., and the trebling of the annual appropriation for teachers' inst.; prof. rhetoric and Eng. lit., Cornell U., 1868-70; prin. Adelphi Acad., Brooklyn, 1870-75; headmaster Girls' High Sch., Boston, 1876-85; founder and 1st pres. Martha's Vineyard Summer Inst., 1879-82; pres. Mills Coll., Cal., 1885-86; pres. U. of N.D., 1887-91; univ. extension lecturer, 1892-96; prof. and lecturer, Drew Theol. Sem., 1896-1900; editor dept. rhetoric, Students' Journal, 1898-1903; strongly supported for U.S. senator, N.D., 1889. Pres. Am. Inst. Instrn., 1883-85 (dir.); councillor N.E.A., 1887-88; asso. founder and 1st pres. N.D. Teachers' Assn. Author: American Liberty, 1900; The Two Parties, 1900; The Assassination, 1901; Alleged Law Blunders in Shakespeare, 1902; The Nation's Honor Roll, 1902; Right and Wrong in Our Civil War, 1903; The People's Party, 1904; Recollections of Henry Ward Beecher, 1905; The True Macbeth, 1909; Appreciation of Daniel C. Gilman, 1910; War Pensions and Promises, 1910; Caesar and Brutus, 1911; The Elevation of His Satanic Majesty, 1912; Metrical Version of the Book of Job, 1913; The European War—Its Cause and Cure, 1914; Lights and Shadows in Confederate Prisons, 1915; also many annotated masterpieces. Editor Yale Lit. and took 1st De Forest gold medal. Home: Newton, Mass. Died Mar. 23, 1918.

SPRAGUE, HOWARD B., physician; b. Swampscott, Mass., Nov. 3, 1895; s. Henry Breed and Laura Loring (Brown) S.; A.B., Harvard, 1918, M.D., 1922; m. Lucy Sprague, June 14, 1919 (dec. Mar. 7, 1958); children—Priscilla Bulfinch Goldthwait, Elizabeth Howard Manson (M.D.), Howard B., Jr.; m. 2d, Marian B. Norton, Sept. 19, 1958. Intern Mass. Gen. Hosp., Boston, Mass., 1922-24, cardiac residency, 1924-25, asso. physician, 1931-53, physician, 1953-56, bd. consultants, 1956-67, hon. physician, 1967-71; physician specializing in diseases of heart, Boston, from 1925; former chief of staff House Good Samaritan; lectr. medicine Harvard Med. Sch., 1956-56; mem. nat. adv. heart council USPHS, 1954-59; sr. cons. in internal med. to U.S. Naval Hosp., Chelsea, Mass.; area chief in cardiology, New England area, Vets. Adminstrn., 1946-

58. Served with Medical Corps, United States Naval Reserve, on active duty, 1941-45; promoted comdr., 1942, capt., 1943; on overseas service in Pacific, 17 mos. Decorated Asiatic-Pacific Theater Medal, Naval Reserve Medal (10 yrs. Service); Am. Theatre World War II Victory medal; gold-heart award of American Heart Assn., 1954; gold medal Am. Coll. Cardiology, 1965; Theodore and Susan Cummings humanitarian award, 1967. Trustee, treasurer Boston Med. Library, 1946-58, president, from 1958; mem. bd. directors Inter-Am. Soc. Cardiology, from 1946 (v.p. 1952); treas. Internat. Cardiology Found., from 1964. Diplomate Am. Bd. Internal Medicine (Cardiology). Fellow Am. College of Physicians, American College of Cardiology; honorary mem. Mex., Chilean socs. of cardiology, Med. Soc. Santiago, Chile, med. faculty U. Chile; mem. Assn. Am. Physicians, Beacon Soc. Boston vice president 1952; president 1953-55), S.A.R., Soc. Colonial Wars, Harvard Alumni Assn. (dir. 1962-64), Bostonian Society, Am. Heart Assn. (sec. 1937-47, pres. 1950-51), Mass., N.E. Heart Assn. (pres. 1941-48), Mass. Med. Society, Am. Med. Assn., Am. Clin. and Climatol. Assn., Internat. Acad. Pathology, N.E. Cardiovascular Soc. (exec. com.), Internat. Soc. Cardiology, Phi Beta Kappa, Alpha Omega Alpha. Clubs: Harvard (Boston and N.Y.); Country (Brookline); Anglers (N.Y.C.); Cruising of Am. Contbr. numerous papers on diseases of circulation to med. publs. Home: Duxbury MA Died Nov. 4, 1971; buried Pine Grove Cemetery Lynn MA

SPRAGUE, JOHN TITCOMB army officer; b. Newburyport, Mass., July 3, 1810. Apptd. 2d lt. Marine Corps, 1834, served in war against Seminole Indians, 1838-39; brevetted capt., 1839; served in Tex., commanded Dept. of Fla., 1846, brevetted maj. while serving in Tex., 1848; promoted maj. 1st U.S. Inf., 1861; stationed in Tex., arrested and paroled, 1861; commd. brig. gen. N.Y. State Militia, 1862-65, served as mustering and disbursing agt.; adj. gen. of state, 1862-65; brevetted col. 7th U.S. Inf., 1865, served as mil. gov. Fla., 1865-66; retired from U.S. Army, 1870. Author: Origin, Progress, and Conclusion of the Florida War, circa 1848. Died N.Y.C., Sept. 6. 1878; buried N.Y.C.

SPRAGUE, THOMAS LAMISON, naval officer ret.; b. Lima, O., Oct. 2, 1894; s. Grant M. and Livia (Lamison) S.; B.S., U.S. Naval Acad., 1917; m. Evelyn Curry, Feb. 23, 1920; children—Isabel Curry (wife of Lt. Comdr. Louis Piollet Spear, U.S. Navy), Thomas Lamison (died Sept. 1, 1933), Martin Curry. Commd. ensign, U.S. Navy, advancing through the grades to vice adm., 1949; naval aviator (heavier than air) on staff of comdr. air force Pacific Fleet, 1921-22; sr. aviator U.S.S. Maryland, 1926-28; comd. Scouting Squadron 6, 1931, Scouting Squadron 10, 1932; asst. air officer, later air officer, U.S.S. Saratoga, 1935; navigator U.S.S. Langley, 1936; supt. aviation training, Naval Air Sta., Pensacola, Fla., 1937-40; exec. officer U.S.S. Ranger, 1940; comd. U.S.S. Pocomoke, 1941, U.S.S. Charger, 1942; chief of staff to comdr. fleet air, Quonset Point, R.I., Jan.-Feb. 1943, to comdr. air force Atlantic Fleet, Feb.-June 1943; comd. U.S.S. Intrepid, June 1943-Mar. 1944; comdr. fleet air, Alameda, Calif., 1944; comd. Carrier Div. 22, July 1944; comd. escort carrier group composed of 18 carriers with accompanying destroyers and escort vessels during battle for Leyte Gulf, 1944; comdr. carrier training squadron U.S. Pacific Fleet, Jan. 1945-46; comd. Task Group 38-I May-Dec. 1945; chief of naval personnel Feb. 1947; vice adm. serving under Presidential designation as comdr. Air Force, United States Pacific Fleet, 1949-52, retired with rank of admiral, April 1952. Decorated World War I Victory medal, Defense medal, Am. Area, Pacific Area, World War II Victory, Philippine Liberation, Navy Occupation, Navy Unit Citation, Presidential Unit Citation, Bronze Star, Legion of Merit with Gold Star, Distinguished Service medal, Navy Cross. Home: Oakland CA Died 1972.

SPRINGER, RAYMOND SMILEY congressman; b. Rush County, Ind., Apr. 26, 1882; s. Lorenzo D. and Josephine (Smiley) S.; student Earlham College, 1901-02, Butler U., 1903-04; LL.B., Indiana Law School, 1904; m. Nancy Emmons, Sept. 18, 1904. Admitted to Ind. bar, 1904; county atty., 1908-14; judge 37th and 73d Circuits, 1916-22; in practice of law, Connersville, since 1922. Rep. candidate for gov. of Ind., 1932 and 1936; mem. 76th to 80th Congresses (1939-49), 10th Ind. Dist. Comd. capt. inf., U.S. Army, World War; now lt. col. Inf. U.S. Res. Corps. Mem. Am. Legion (past state comdr.). Mason, Elk, Eagle, K.P. Club: Columbia (Indianapolis). Home: Connersville, Ind. Died Aug. 28, 1947.

SPRINGS, ELLIOTT WHITE author, mfr.; b. Lancaster, S.C., July 31, 1896; s. Leroy and Grace Allison (White) S.; grad. Culver Mil. Acad., 1913; A.B., Princeton, 1917; student mil. aviation, Oxford U., Eng., 1917; LL.D., U. of S.C., 1949; m. Frances Hubbard Ley, Oct. 4, 1922; 1 daughter, Mrs. H.W. Close, Jr. Test pilot L.W.F. Airplane Co., 1919; flew 1st cross country airplane race, N.Y.C. to Toronto, 1919; began bus. career as cotton weighter, 1919; sec.-treas. Kershaw Cotton Mills, 1920-21, pres., 1931—; pres. Bank of Lancaster, Bank of Heath Springs, Springs Banking & Mercantile Co., Springs Cotton Mills, Columbia Compress, Leroy Springs & Co., Kershaw Cotton Mills, Lancaster Cotton Mills, Fort Mill Mfg. Co., Eureka Cotton Mills, Springsteen Cotton Mills, Springs Mills;

dir. Soc. Ry. Mem. N.Y. Cotton Exchange, S.C. Ednl. Finance Commn., 1951. Pvt. aviation sect. S.R.C., 1917; trained with R.F.C., Oxford U., sergeant, 2d lt., 1st lt., flight comdr., squadron comdr., capt. A.C. Res.; served with 85th Squadron R.F.C., 148th Squadron U.S.A.S.; officially credited with destroying 11 enemy airplanes; mil. aviator; capt. Air Corps, 1941; lt. col. 1942; ret. 1942. Exec. officer, Charlotte Air Base. Decorated with D.S.C., Distinguished Flying Cross (British), Medal of Honor (Aero Club of Am.). Pres. Marion Sims Meml. Hosp., 1939. Mem. Quiet Birdmen, Nat. Aeronautical Assns., Res. Officers' Assn., Authors' League Am., Dramatist's Guild, Am. Legion. Democrat. Presbyn. Mason. Clubs: Players, Racquet and Tennis, Princeton (N.Y.C.). Author: Nocturne Militaire, 1927; Leave Me with a Smile, 1928; Above the Bright Blue Sky, 1928; Contact, 1930; In the Cool of the Evening, 1930; The Rise and Fall of Carol Banks, 1931; Pent-Up on a Penthouse, 1931; Warbirds and Ladybirds, 1931; Clothes Make the Man, 1948. Address: Fort Mill, S.C. Died Oct. 15, 1959.

SPRINGS, HOLMES BUCK real estate, banker; b. Bucksville, S.C., Aug. 14, 1879; s. Albert Adams and Alice (Buck) S.; student The Citadel, 1895-98; grad. Spartanburg Bus. Coll., 1898; m. Louise Wilson, Oct. 22, 1919; children—Louise Wilson, Holmes Buck, Jr., David Albert, Wilson Baker, Alice Italine, Albert Adams, III. Organizer, pres. Springs & Siau Co., real estate and ins. Georgetown, S.C., 1904-17; organizer, pres. Farmers and Merchants Bank, Georgetown, 1913-19; mem. Serial Bldg. & Loan Assn., 1912-19; mem. Parrish, Gower & Springs, 1919-22; v.p. Woodside Nat. Bank, 1922-29, Pioneer Life Ins. Co., 1925-32; v.p., mgr. Myrtle Beach Investment Co., 1926-32; organizer, pres. H. B. Springs Co., Inc., real estate; State dir. Selective Service, 1940-47; mem. Gov.'s Adv. Counsel Nat. Def., 1940——. Chmn. State Adv. Com. Adult Edn., 1947. Was pres. C. of C. Georgetown and Greenville; mem. S.C. Ins. Commn., 1919——; mem. advisory council Nat. Rivers and Harbors Congress; mem. exec. council Southeastern States Development Commn.; pres. Kings Highway Assn., 1928-35; dir. Atlantic Coastal Hwy. Assn. (1930-35), Ocean Hwy. Assn. Trustee U. S.C., 1919-20; trustee Columbia (Female) Coll., 1940-48. Awarded Presidential citation (Certificate of Merit), 1946; Am. Legion Distinguished Service Plaque, Horry County, 1946. Served as pvt. to col., S.C. Nat. Guard; col., 2d S.C. Inf. on Mexican border, 1916-17; col. Inf. U.S. Army; duty with 30th Div. staff, A.E.F., France, England, Belgium, 1917-19; ret. brig. gen., Apr. 25, 1919; cited for war service. Pres. 2d S.C. Inf. Assn.; mem. 30th Div. Assn. (organizer; 1st pres.). Mem. S.C. Soc. S.A.R., S.C.V., Am. Legion, Yypres League (London), Mil. Order of World War; hon. mem. O.D.K. Leadership Fraternity, 1941. Democrat. Methodist. Mason (K.T., Shriner). Clubs: Rotary, Country, Pinetree Hunt (hon.). Home: Myrtle Beach, S.C. Died Jan. 31, 1951; buried Myrtle Beach, S.C.

SPRUANCE, RAYMOND AMES, admiral; b. Baltimore, Md., July 3, 1886; s. Alexander Peterson and Annie Ames (Hiss) S.; prep. edn. Stevens Prep. Sch., Hoboken, N.J.; grad. (with class of 1907), U.S. Naval Acad., 1906; m. Margaret Vance Dean, Dec. 30, 1914; children—Edward Dean (U.S.N.), Margaret (Mrs. Bogart). Commd. ensign, U.S. Navy, 1908, and advanced through the grades to admiral, 1944; comd. U.S.S. Mississippi, 1938-40; comdt. 10th Naval Dist., San Juan, P.R., 1940-41, with additional duty as comdr. Caribbean Sea Frontier, July-Aug. 1941; became comdr. Cruiser Div. 5, 1941; 2d in command operations in Marshall Islands, Wake Island and Marcus Island, 1942; jr. task force comdr. Battle of Midway, this force being built around carriers Enterprise and Hornet, 1942; chief of staff and aide to comdr. in chief Pacific Fleet, June-Sept. 1942; dep. comdr. in chief Pacific Fleet, Sept. 1942-Aug. 1943; comdr. Central Pacific Force, later known as Fifth Fleet, 1944-45, in overall command of occupation of Gilbert Islands, invasion of Marshall Islands, in strikes against Truk, Palau, Yap and Woleai, also in operations for capture of Saipan, Guam and Tinian (including Battle of Philippine Sea), and of Iwo Jima and Okinawa; comdr. in chief Pacific Fleet and Pacific Ocean Areas, Nov. 1945-Feb. 1946; pres. Naval War Coll., Newport, 1946; retired July 1, 1948; ambassador to the Philippines, 1952-55. Decorated D.S.M. with 2 gold stars (Navy), D.S.M. (Army), Presdnl. Unit Citation (Enterprise), Navy Cross, Victory, Am. Defense, Fleet Clasp, Asiatic-Pacific Area Campaign and World War II Victory medals (U.S.); Gold Cross of Chevalier of Order of Savior (Greece); Hon. Companion Order of Bath (Gt. Britain); Grand Officer de l'Ordre de Leopold with palm, Croix de Guerre with palm, 1940 (Belgium). Address: Pebble Beach CA Died Dec. 13, 1969.

SPRUANCE, WILLIAM CORBIT electrical engr.; b. Wilmington, Del., Sept. 26, 1873; s. William Corbit and Maria Louisa (Spotswood) S.; grad. Friends' Sch., Wilmington 1890; Princeton Univ., 1894, E.E., 1895; m. Alice Moore Lea, May 4, 1907. Cons. practice until 1903; with duPont Co., 1903——, except mil. service; v.p. and dir. E. I. du Pont de Nemours & Co. Commd. maj. Ordnance R.C., U.S.A., Dec. 1917; lt. col. N.A., Jan. 1918; col. U.S.A., Oct. 1918; served as chief of explosives and loading div. Ordnance Dept.; mem. commodity sect. on explosives War Industries Bd. and com. on explosives investigation Nat. Research Council; hon. discharged, Feb. 1919. Awarded D.S.M. (U.S.), 1919. Republican. Presbyn. Home: Wilmington, Del. Died Jan. 9, 1935.

SPURGIN, WILLIAM FLETCHER army officer; b. Carlisle, Ky., Oct. 18, 1838; s. David McKendree and Amanda (Secrest) S.; ed. in Ky. and Asbury (now DePauw) Univ., to junior yr.; studied West Point, July 1, 1858, to Mar. 12, 1861 (A.M., DePauw); m. Martha L. Hair, Dec. 31, 1861, Martha L. Hair. In Civil war served 1st lt., and adj. 54th Ind. vols., June 10, 1862, to Sept. 26, 1862; capt. 15th U.S. colored inf., 9th, Apr. 1864, 100th U.S. colored inf., June 9, 1864; hon. mustered out Dec. 26, 1864; bvtd. maj. vols. for spl. gallantry at Johnsonville, Tenn., Nov. 1864, and Nashville, Tenn., Dec. 16, 1864; 1st lt. 38th U.S. inf., July 28, 1866; capt. 21st inf., June 2, 1876; maj. 23d inf., Dec. 2, 1897; lt. col. 16th inf., May 4, 1899; col. 4th inf., Mar. 1, 1901; brig. gen., May 16, 1902; retired at own request, after 40 yrs. service, May 29, 1902. Took part in Nez Percé campaign, 1877, Bannock campaign, 1878; U.S. Mil. Acad., Sept. 2, 1881, to May 15, 1899; collector customs Philippine Islands, Sept. 1899, to Oct. 1900; comd. dept. Texas, Apr. 3, 1902, to retirement. Died 1904.

SQUIBB, EDWARD ROBINSON pharmacist, chemist, physician; b. Wilmington, Del., July 4, 1819; s. James R. and Catherine H. (Bonsal) S.; studied pharmacy under Warder Morris, Phila., 1837, under J. H. Sprague, Phila., 1837-42; M.D., Jefferson Med. Coll., 1845; m. Caroline F. Lownds, Oct. 7, 1852, 3 children. Commd. asst. surgeon U.S. Navy, 1847; med. officer in ships Perry, Erie, Cumberland, 1847-51; assigned to duty Bklyn. Naval Hosp., 1851; authorized by Navy Dept. to establish his own lab. for manufacture pharmaceuticals and chemicals, 1852; resigned U.S. Navy, 1853, became mfg. co-partner in firm Thomas E. Jenkins & Co. (known as Louisville Chem. Works), Louisville, Ky.; established chem. and pharm. lab. under name Edward R. Squibb, M.D., Bklyn., 1858, severely injured when lab. burned, 1858, later rebuilt factory, admitted his 2 sons as co-partners, 1892, changed name to E. R. Squibb & Sons; contbr. many articles to Am. Journal of Pharmacy. Died Bklyn., Oct. 25, 1900.

SQUIER, GEORGE OWEN army officer; b. Dryden, Mich., Mar. 21, 1865; s. Almon Justice and Emily (Gardner) S.; grad. U.S. Mil. Acad., 1887; fellow, Johns Hopkins, 1902-03 and 1903-04, Ph.D., 1903; hon. D.Sc. from Dartmouth College, 1922; unmarried. Apptd. 2d lieut. 3d Artillery, June 12, 1887; 1st lt., June 30, 1893; capt. signal officer vols., May 20, 1898; lt. col. signal officer vols., July 18, 1898; hon. disch. from vols., Dec. 7, 1898; 1st lt. signal corps U.S.A., Feb. 23, 1899; capt. signal officer vols., Apr. 17, 1899; hon. disch. from vols., June 30, 1901; capt., signal corps U.S.A., Feb. 2, 1901; maj., Mar. 2, 1903. Comd. U.S. Cable-ship Burnside, 1900-02, during laying of Philippine cable-telegraph system. U.S. mil. attaché at London, Eng., 1912; commd. lt. col. Signal Corps, Mar. 17, 1913; brig. gen., chief signal officer U.S.A., Feb. 14, 1917; maj. gen., Oct. 6, 1917; in charge of army air service, May 20, 1916-May 20, 1918. Mem. nat. council Boy Scouts of America. D.S.M. (U.S.); Knight Comdr. St. Michael and St. George (Great Britain); Commander Order of the Crown (Italy); Commander Legion of Honor (France). Elliott Cresson gold medal, Franklin medal. Researches: Electrochemical effects due to magnetization; the polarizing photochronograph; the sine wave systems of telegraphy and ocean cabling; the absorption of electro-magnetic waves by living vegetable organisms; multiplex telephony and telegraphy; tree telephony and telegraphy, multiplex telephony and telegraphy, over open circuit bare wires laid in the earth or sea. Inventor of the monophone for broadcasting over telephone wires and over power wires, also wired wireless, 1910; inventor of "Quickaid," a first aid kit for Army and Red Cross use. War Department rep. and technical adviser to Am. delegation at Internat. Conf. on Elec. Communications, Washington, 1920; rep. dept. of State at sessions of Provisional Tech. com. of Internat. Conf. on Elec. Communications, Paris, 1921; designated an expert asst. to Am. Commrs. at Conf. on Limitation of Armament, Washington, 1921; ex-officio mem., representing War Dept., of U.S. Nat. Com. Internat. Electrotech. Commn. Founder, 1918, of "A Country Club for Country People," Dryden, Mich. Died Mar. 24, 1934.

SQUIRE, FRANCIS HAGAR educator; born Westfield, Mass., Dec. 23, 1902; s. Francis Freeman and Mertie (DeLaVergne) S.; A.B., Yale, 1925, Ph.D., 1935; m. Marjorie Johnson, Sept. 15, 1932. Instr. in history, U. of Del., 1927-28, asst. prof., 1928-30; instr. in history, Yale, 1930-31; asso.prof. of history, U. of Del., 1932-43, chmn., dept. of history, 1942-43, dean of the univ. and dean sch. of arts and science since Dec. 1945. Served with Naval Aviation Training Command, U.S.Navy, 1943-45; disch. to U.S.N.R. as lt. comdr. Mem. Res. Officers Assn., Am. Hist. Assn., Sons Colonial Wars, Naval Order U.S. Del. Hist. Assn., Omicron Delta Kappa, Phi Kappa Phi, Phi Kappa Tau, Alpha Phi Omega. Clubs: Lincoln (Delaware); Elizabethan (New Haven). Episcopalian. Home: 38 Winslow Rd., Newark, Del. Died Apr. 26, 1956; buried Welsh Tract Cemetery, Newark.

SQUIRE, WATSON CARVOSSO senator; b. Cape Vincent, N.Y., May 18, 1838; s. Rev. Orra and Erretta (Wheeler) S.; A.B., Wesleyan U., 1859; prin. Moravia, N.Y., Inst., 1859-61; LL.B., Cleveland (O.) Law Sch., 1862; LL.D., Wesleyan U., Conn., 1911. Pvt. and 1st lt., Co. F, 19th N.Y. Vols., 3 mos., 1861; raised, Oct. 1862, 7th Independent Co. of Ohio Sharpshooters, afterward known as "Gen. Sherman's Body Guard," comd. it in Army of the Cumberland; comd. battalion of sharpshooters Chickamauga campaign; judge advocate, dist. of Tenn., 1864-65; bvtd., July 1866, by President and U.S. Senate, lt. col. and col. "for gallant and meritorious services," mustered out, Aug. 1865; m. Ida, d. Philo Remington, Dec. 23, 1868; children—Philo Remington, Shirley, Aidine (Mrs. Arthur V. White), Marjorie (Mrs. John F. Jennings). Mgr. Remington Arms Co., New York, 1866-79; moved to Seattle, Wash., 1879, inaugurating extensive business enterprises there and a large dairy farm; pres. Union Trust Co., Squire Investment Co. Gov. of Washington Ty., 1884-87; pres. State Conv., 1889; elected U.S. senator, Nov. 21, 1889, under act of Congress admitting Wash Ty. to the Union, reëlected, 1891, for term, 1891-97. Republican. Died June 7, 1926.

STACK, JOSEPH MICHAEL ex-commdr.-in-chief Vet. of Foreign Wars of U.S.; b. Pittsburgh, May 15, 1895; s. John and Katherine (O'Leary) S.; m. Alice M. Dugan, Aug. 21, 1919; children—Dorothy Alice (Mrs. Thayer G. Wiesner), Irene Elizabeth, Mary Helen. Clerk Arbuthnot Stephenson Co., Pittsburgh, 1910-25; mem. firm Stack and Durning, hatters, Pittsburgh, 1925-27; buyer and dept. mgr., The Rosebaum Co., Pittsburgh, 1927-35; investigator for dist. atty., Allegheny County, Pa., 1935-43; chief Allegheny County Detective Bureau, Pittsburgh, since 1943; commander-in-chief, Veterans of Foreign Wars of U.S., 1945-46; chmn. draft bd. since its inception. Served with Co. F, 357th Inf., 90th Div., A.E.F., U.S. Army, World War I. Former pres. Lincoln Civic Club, Pittsburgh; former vice pres. and mem. bd. mgrs., Soldiers and Sailors Memorial Hall, Pittsburgh. Mem. Pa. Chiefs of Police Assn., Fraternal Order of Police, Am. Legion. K.C., A.O.H. Club: Variety (Pittsburgh). Home: 6929 Churchland St., Pittsburgh 6, Pa. Offices: Broadway at 34th St., Kansas City 2, Mo. 303 Allegheny County Court House, Pitts. Died Mar. 7, 1952; buried Mt. Carmel Cemetery.

STACKHOUSE, ELI THOMAS congressman; b. Little Rock, Marion County, S.C., Mar. 27, 1824; attended common schs. Worked on father's farm; taught sch. several years; became farmer; enlisted in Confederate Army, 1861, served throughout Civil War, commd. col. 8th Regt., S.C. Volunteers wounded in battles of Antietam, Gettysburg and Chickamauga; mem. S.C. Ho. of Reps., 1862-68; mem. 1st bd. trustees Clemson A. and M. Coll., 1887; 1st pres. S.C. Farmers' Alliance, 1888; mem. U.S. Ho. of Reps. (Democrat) from S.C., 52d Congress, 1891-June 14, 1892. Died Washington, D.C., June 14, 1892; buried Little Rock Cemetery.

STACKPOLE, ALBERT HUMMEL, editor; b. Harrisburg, Pa., June 28, 1897; s. Edward James and Kate (Hummel) S.; grad. Harrisburg Acad., 1915; student Yale U., 1915-17, 1919; Doctor of Laws, Dickinson Law School, 1969; m. Mary Creighton, Oct. 9, 1920; children—Mary, Creighton. Reporter, city editor, publisher and columnist since 1919, vice pres., Telegraph Press, Inc.; pres. WHP, Incorporated, 1963-69, chairman of the board of directors, 1969-71. Del. Rep. National Conv., Phila., June 1948. Served with U.S. Army in A.E.F., 1917-19; commn. 1st lt. to col., 104th Cavalry, Fed. service, 1921-46; 2 yrs. in China with Chinese Combat Command, 1944-45; now ret. maj. gen. Reserve. Awarded Legion of Merit, Bronze Star; Yaun-Hui (Chinese). Mem. Reserve Officer's Assn., Alpha Delta Phi. Republican. Episcopalian. Clubs: Quiet Birdmen, Kiwanis. Office: Harrisburg PA Died July 31, 1971; buried Arlington Nat. Cemetery, Arlington VA

STACKPOLE, EDWARD J(AMES) publisher; b. Harrisburg, Pa., June 21, 1894; s. Edward James and Maria Kate (Hummel) S.; student Harrisburg Acad., 1909-11; A.B., Yale U., 1915; Litt.D. (honorary), Gettysburg Coll., 1961; m. Frances Bailey, August 17, 1917 (dec. Nov. 1948); 1 daughter, Mary Frances (Mrs. Meade D. Detweiler III). Salesman Telegraph Press, Harrisburg, Pa., 1915-17, general mgr., 1921-36, pres., 1936-63, chmn. bd., 1963-—, also dir.; pres., treas., dir. Radio-TV Sta. WHB, Telegraph Bldg. Corp., Stackpole Co., book pubs.; dir. Harrisburg Trust Co., Penn-Harris Hotel Co., Harrisburg Hotel Co. Served capt. inf., USA, World War I; orgn. and comd. 104th cav. 52d cav. brigade and 22d cav. div. Nat. Guard Pa.; 1922-40; served throughout World War II as brig. gen. of the line; reorganized Pa. N.G., major gen. comdg. 28th Inf. Div., 1946-47; ret. 1947, lt. gen. ret. 1956. Decorated D.S.C., Purple Heart with 2 clusters, World War I; Legion of Merit, World War II; recipient Pa. D.S.M., 1946; D.S.M. N.G. Assn. U.S., 1955. Mem. bd. trustees Harrisburg Hosp. Republican. Presbyn. Mason. Author: They Met at Gettysburg, 1956; Drama on the Rappannock: The Fredericksburg Campaign, 1957; Chancellorsville, Lee's Greatest Battle, 1958; From Cedar Mountain to Antietam, 1959; Sheridan in the Shenandoah, 1961. Home: Green Meadows Farm, Dauphin, Pa. Office: Telegraph Bldg., Harrisburg, Pa. Died Oct. 1, 1967.

STACKPOLE, PIERPONT L(ANGLEY) lawyer; b. Brookline, Mass., Feb. 16, 1875; s. Stephen Henry and Julia Langley (Faunce) S.; prep. edn., Colgate Acad., Hamilton, N.Y.; student Colgate U., 1892-95; A.B., Harvard, 1897, LL.B., 1900; m. Mrs. Laura McGinley Knowles, May 10, 1922. Admitted to Mass. bar, 1900, and began practice at Boston; mem. Warner, Stackpole & Bradlee; director and mem. exec. com. Crompton & Knowles Loom Works. Served as lt. col. F.A., U.S.A.; with A.E.F., Sept. 1917-Sept. 1919; civilian aide to sec. of war, 1st Corps Area, 1922-29. Trustee South End House Assn., Children's Aid Assn., N.E. Conservatory of Music, Boston Symphony Orchestra. Awarded D.S.M. (U.S.); Officier Etoile Noir du Bénin (France); Officier Ordre de la Couronne (Belgium). Home: Boston, Mass. Died Dec. 26, 1936.

STAGER, ANSON telegraph pioneer, army officer; b. Ontario County, N.Y., Apr. 20, 1825; m. Rebecca Sprague, Nov. 14, 1847, 3 children. Worked in office Rochester (N.Y.) Daily Advertiser owned by Henry O'Reilly, 1841, bookkeeper by 1845; studied telegraphy in spare time; apptd. telegraph operator at Lancaster (Pa.) office, 1847 (after O'Reilly had contracted with Samuel F. B. Morse to build telegraph from Phila. to Middle West, circa 1845); mgr., Pitts. office, 1847; mgr. operating dept. of Pitts., Cincinnati & Louisville Telegraph Co., 1847-51; apptd. gen. supt. N.Y. & Mississippi Valley Printing Telegraph Co., 1852-56; gen. supt. Western Union Telegraph Co., 1856-61, assigned to rearrange many telegraph lines and establish good relations with railroads, established hdqrs. at Cleve.; commd. capt. and asst. q.m. gen. U.S. Army, 1861, placed in Washington (D.C.) as chief U.S. mil. telegraphs; promoted col., assigned as a.d.c. to Gen. Henry W. Halleck at War Dept., 1862; brevetted brig. gen. for meritorious services, 1865, discharged, 1866; became supt. Central div. Western Union Telegraph Co. with hdqrs. at Cleve., later at Chgo., v.p. until 1881; pres. Western Edison Electric Light Co. from its formation until 1885. Died Chgo., Mar. 26, 1885.

STAGG, AMOS ALONZO physical dir.; b. West Orange, N.J., Aug. 16, 1862; s. Amos Lindsley and Eunice (Pierson) S.; A.B., Yale Univ., 1888; grad. Internat. Y.M.C.A. Coll., Springfield, Mass., 1891, hon. degree Master of Physical Education, 1912; hon. degree A.M., Oberlin College, 1923; LL.D., College of Wooster, Ohio, 1933; Pd.D. (honorary), Susquehanna University, 1949; HH.D. (hon.), Pacific University, 1951; Dr. Public Service, University Denver, 1955; married Stella Robertson, September 10, 1894; children—Amos Alonzo, Ruth, Paul. Dir. of athletics, Northfield (Mass.) Students' Conf. and Lake Geneva (Wis.) Students' Conf., summers, 1889-91; asso. prof. and dir. dept. physical culture and athletics, U. of Chicago, 1892-1900, prof. and dir., 1900-33, prof. emeritus 1933; football coach, Coll. of the Pacific, 1933-46, prof. emeritus 1947; co-coach football Susquehanna U., 1947-52; adv. coach football, Stockton Coll., 1953-59. Represented U. of Chicago at Inter-collegiate Conf. of Faculty Reps., 1896-1911; mem. football rules com., 1904-32, apptd. mem. for life 1932; mem. Am. com. Olympic Games, 1906-32; chmn. track and field records com., Nat. Collegiate Athletic Assn., 1922-44. Del.-at-large of Amateur Athletic Union, 1943. Fellow Am. Phys. Edn. Soc.; mem. S.A.R., Nat. Coll. Athletic Assn., Psi Upsilon, Skull and Bones (both of Yale). Clubs: Quadrangle, University, Olympia Fields Country of Chicago (pres. 1916-19); Rotary (hon; Stockton). Author: (Stagg, Williams) Treatise on Football, 1893; Touchdown! (with Wesley Winans Stout), 1927. Honors and awards include: Stagg Field, U. Chgo., 1914; Stockton (Cal.) YMCA gymnasium, 1951; Silver Buffalo, Boy Scouts Am., 1935; Am. Ednl. award, 1933; bronze plaque by Am. Football Coaches Assn., 1939; N.Y. City Touchdown Club award for 1940; Edward N. Tarbell Medallion by Springfield College, 1941; Northwestern University Centennial award, 1951; Coach of the Year, America's football coaches, 1943; Football's Man of the Year for service, 1943, by the Football Writer's Assn. Am.; Christian Athletes Found. Award, 1950, All Time Christian Coach; Fellow American Academy of Physical Education, 1946; Nat. Football Hall of Fame, 1951; Stagg Field, West Orange, N.J., 1954; Amos Alonzo Stagg Sr. High Sch., Stockton, Cal., 1959; Great Living Am. award U.S. C. of C., 1959; Nat. Football Found. and Hall of Fame award, 1960; named to Basketball Hall of Fame, 1959. Home: 127 W. Euclid Av., Stockton 4, Cal. Died Mar. 17, 1965.

STAHEL, JULIUS soldier; b. Hungary, Nov. 5, 1825; s. Andreas and Barbara (Nag) S.; ed. Budapest; unmarried. Fought in struggle for Hungarian independence, under Louis Kossuth, 1848, and was wounded and decorated for gallantry; came to America, 1856; in newspaper work at New York, 1856-61; lt. col. 8th N.Y. Inf., Apr. 17, 1861; col., Aug. 27, 1861; brig. gen. vols., Nov. 12, 1861; maj. gen. vols., Mar. 14, 1863; resigned Feb. 8, 1865. Awarded medal of honor, Nov. 4, 1893, for leading his division after he was severely wounded, and turned the enemy's flank, at Piedmont, Va., June 5, 1864. Covered retreat of Union Army at head of his regt. at 1st battle of Bull Run; comd. advance column of Gen. Fremont's army in Shenandoah Valley;

comd. brigade, 1st div., 2d battle of Bull Run; placed in command 11th Army Corps, Jan. 15, 1863; sent for by Pres. Lincoln and assigned to command in front of Washington, Mar. 13, 1863. Apptd. consul at Yokohama, Japan, and consul gen. at Shanghai, China, 1884; resigned, 1885, on account of ill health. Died Dec. 4, 1912.

STAKELY, CHARLES A., lawyer; b. Montgomery, Ala., Apr. 30, 1903; A.B., LL.B., U. Ala. Admitted to Ala. bar, 1926, since practiced in Montgomery; mem. firm Rushton, Stakely & Johnson. Mem. Ala. Senate, 1938-42, 42-46. Served to comdr. USNR, 1943-46. Mem. Am., Ala., Montgomery County bar assns., Phi Beta Kappa, Phi Delta Phi. Office: Montgomery AL Died June 2, 1965.

STALEY, A. ROLLIN, mfg. exec.; b. Baltimore, May 16, 1907; s. Augustus Eugene and Emma L. (Tressler) S.; student Staunton (Va.) Mil. Acad., 1923-24, Culver (Ind.) Mil. Acad., 1924-25, 1925-26; U. of Ill., 1926-29; married Nettie Lou Salisbury, July 24, 1949. Sales promotion mgr., A.E. Staley Mfg. Co., Decatur, Ill., then v.p. charge customer relations, resigned 1956; pres. Skylark Charter Lines. Dir. Decatur and Macon County Hosp.; trustee Naples Community Hospital; member U. Ill. Found. Served as 1st lt. USAF, 1942-44. Mem. Assn. of Commerce (recipient Civic Service award, 1940), Airplane Owners and Pilots Assn. (charter mem.), Alpha Tau Omega. Presbyn. Mason (K.T., Shriner). Clubs: Metropolitan (N.Y.C.); Jonathan (Los Angeles); Country, Decatur (dir.), Shrine, City (Decatur); Hole-in-the-Wall-Golf, Port Royal Beach (Naples, Fla.). Holder pilots license. Home: Naples FL Died Oct. 11, 1968; buried Fair Lawn Cemetery, Decatur IL

STANDEVEN, JAMES WYLIE, hosp. supt.; b. Hancock, Ia., Jan. 25, 1916; s. John Frank and Elsie (Wylie) S.; B.S., State U. Ia., 1940, M.D., 1940; m. Jean E. Beckwith, Apr. 30, 1960; children—John, Steven. Intern Neb. Meth. Hosp., Omaha; gen. practice medicine, Oakland, Ia., 1946-57; with VA, 1957-70, dir. VA Hosp., Montgomery, Ala., 1968-70. Mem. Gov. Ala. Com. Employment Handicapped. Councilman, Oakland, Ia., 1950-54. Bd. dirs. local A.R.C. Served to capt. USAAF, 1941-45. Mem. Am. Coll. Hosp. Adminstrs., A.M.A., Aerospace Med. Assn., Fed. Execs. Assn., Alpha Omega Alpha, Alpha Kappa Kappa. Rotarian. Home: Tucson AZ Died May 20, 1972.

STANDLEY, WILLIAM HARRISON naval officer (ret.); b. Ukiah, Cal., Dec. 18, 1872; s. Jeremiah M. and Sarah Jane (Clay) S.; grad. U.S. Naval Acad., 1895, B.S., 1937; grad. U.S. Naval War Coll., 1921; LL.D., U. of Cal., 1944; m. Evelyn C. Curtis, May 28, 1898; children—Vivian B. (Mrs. Charles B. Wincote), William Harrison, Helen T. (dec.), Marie (Mrs. Edwin W. Herron), Evelyn (Mrs. James A. Hoyt). Commd. ensign U.S. Navy, 1897, and advanced through grades to adm., 1933; asst. chief naval operations, 1928-30; comdr. destroyers, Battle Fleet, 1930-31, cruisers, U.S. Fleet and Scouting Force, 1931-33; comdr. battle force, 1933; chief of naval operations, Washington, 1933-37; ret. from active duty, Jan. 1, 1937; dir. and consultant, Electric Boat Co., 1939-41; dir. Pan Am. Airways since 1939; recalled to active duty with U.S. Navy, Feb., 1941; mem. planning bd. O.P.M.; U.S. ambassador to U.S.S.R., 1941-43; recalled to active duty with Planning Group, Office Strategic Services, 1944-45; retired since 1945. Mem. Beaverbrook-Harriman mission to Moscow, 1941. Robert's Commn. to investigate Pearl Harbor, 1941; dir. foreign participation, N.Y. World Fair, 1937-39; chmn. Cal. gov.'s organized crime commn., 1947; active nat. and local levels A.R.C. Awarded D.S.M. 1942; received letter of commendation for conduct in Philippine insurrection and World War I, spl letter of appreciation from Pres. upon termination of active service, Jan. 1, 1937; decorated with Cross of Italy, 1934, and Cross of Abdon Calderon, 1936; also numerous campaign medals. Mem. Navy League U.S., V.F.W., U.S. Naval Inst., Naval Hist. Soc., Nat. Geog. Soc., Am. Legion, Mil. Order of World Wars, Ret. Officers' Assn., U.S. Naval Acad. Alumni Assn., Am. Soc. Naval Engrs. Democrat. Episcopalian. Clubs: Nat. Rotary, Army Navy, Army Navy Country (Washington), Chevy Chase (Md.), Garden City Golf (L.I., N.Y.), Chulla Vista Golf (San Diego), Ends of the Earth. Author: Admiral Ambassador to Russia, 1955. Home: 862 G Av., Coronado, Cal. Died Oct. 25, 1963; buried Arlington Nat. Cemetery.

STANFORD, ALBERT CLINTON army officer; b. Chatsworth, Ill., Mar. 25, 1895; s. Fred Clinton and Ettie Nora (Tilden) S.; B.S., U.S. Mil. Acad., 1917; M.S., Yale, 1925; grad. Signal Corps Sch., 1923, F.A., Sch., 1929, Command and Gen. Staff Sch., 1941; m. Florence C. Busbee, Mar. 6, 1918; 1 son, Frederick Clinton. Commd. 2d lt. Cav., 1917; promoted through grades to brig. gen. July 1942; transferred to Signal Corps, 1920, to F.A., 1927; prcf. mil. science and tactics, Mich. State Coll., 1936-40; assigned 34th Inf. Div., Aug. 1942; later assigned for overseas station; retired 1946. Home: 301 W. State St., Trenton, N.J. Died Nov. 7, 1952; buried Fort Sam Houston Nat. Cemetery.

STANFORD, HOMER REED naval officer; b. June 26, 1865; entered U.S. Navy, 1898, and advanced through the grades to rear adm., 1938; retired, 1939. Address: Navy Dept., Washington 25. Deceased.

STANLEY, DAVID SLOANE brig. gen. U.S.A., retired June 1, 1892; b. at Chester, O., June 1, 1828; s. John B. and Sarah (Peterson) S.; ed. public schools, Canaan Acad. and West Point, graduating, 1852; m. Anna M. Wright (died 1895). Consecutively 2d lt. 2d dragoons, 1st lt. 1st cav., capt. 4th cav., maj. 5th cav. During war was brig. gen and maj. gen. vols.; comd. 4th corps, Army of the Cumberland, and took part in many battles, notably in the fights in and around Corinth and the battles of the Atlanta campaign and until he was severely wounded at Franklin in a desperate hand-to-hand conflict; was active in the engagements around Nashville. After war was col. 22d U.S. inf. and brig. gen. U.S.A. Died 1902.

STANLEY, EMORY DAY naval officer; b. Hooper, Neb., Nov. 16, 1881; s. Charles Castle and Katherine Barbara (Basler) S.; A.B., U. of Neb., 1904; LL.B., Georgetown Univ., 1922; m. Eva Cooper, Dec. 19, 1908; children—Katherine (Mrs. Frank Virden), Dorothy (Mrs. K. F. VanSant), Emory Day (U.S. Navy). Commd. ensign, 1905, and advanced through the grades to rear admiral, 1942; Navy Yard, Brooklyn, N.Y., 1909-10; U.S. Asiatic Station, 1911-13; Navy Yard, Puget Sound, Wash., 1913-15; U.S.S. Pueblo and staff of comdr. in chief, Pacific Fleet, 1915-18; Navy Dept., Washington, D.C., chmn. exec. com., Food Purchase Bd., 1918-21; coordinator of purchase, U.S. Govt., 1922; mem. U.S. Naval Mission to Peru; dir. or administrn., Peruvian Navy, 1922-26; staff of comdr. aircraft, Atlantic Fleet, 1926-28; supply officer, Naval Aircraft Factory, Phila., 1928-32; Naval Air Station, Sunnyvale, Cal., 1932-34; gen. Inspector, Supply Corps, 1934-36; fleet supply officer, staff comdr. in chief, Asiatic Fleet, 1937-38; mem. U.S. Naval Mission to Peru, financial adv. to Peruvian Navy and Air Corps, 1938-40; supply officer in comd. Naval Supply Depot, Bayonne, N.J., 1940-45; rear adm. Supply Corps, 1942-45, ret., 1945. Elected Township Commr., Cranford, N.J., 1948. Awarded Mexican Service medal, Victory medal with silver star, China medal, Am. Defense Service medal; Polonia Restituta; Knight Comdr. El Sol del Peru; Distinguished Service Award, U. of Neb., 1943. Mem. Phi Gamma Delta. Mason. Home: 316 Casino, Cranford, N.J. Died Feb. 7, 1968.

STANSBURY, HOWARD army officer; b. N.Y.C., Feb. 8, 1806; s. Arthur Joseph and Susanna (Brown) S.; m. Helen Moody, Sept. 1, 1827, at least 2 children. Surveyor route of Mad River & Lake Eire R.R., 1832-35, lower part James River, Va., 1836, proposed railroad route from Milw. to Mississippi River, 1838; commd. lt. Topog. Engrs., U.S. Army, 1838, capt., 1840, surveyed harbor, Portsmouth, N.H.; in charge exploring expdn. to Gt. Salt Lake area, 1849; builder mil. roads in Minn., 1851-61; must Southern control), until 1862, supported Wilmot Proviso, Dred Scott decision; strict constitutionalist and Unionist after 1860; U.S. sec. of war, 1862-68, instituted changes in orgn. of dept. to increase honesty and efficiency; received Congressional sanction for governmental control of railroads and telegraph; maintained close relations with joint Senate-House on conduct of war; reputation as adminstr. based on grasp of detail and quickness of decision; his dispatch of support to Rosecrans in Chattanooga (Sept. 1863) considered one of greatest adminstrn. achievements of war; frequently interferred in plans of field commanders, disliked because of dictatorial and arrogant manners; suppressed evidence tending to show defendent's innocence in trial of Mary Surratt before mil. court; approved Pres. Johnson's reconstrn. policies in cabinet (but evidence indicates that he connived with adminstrn. opposition in Congress); supported Mil. Reconstrn. Act of 1867; author of requirement that all Presdl. army orders be issued through War Dept., 1867; opposed Tenure of Office Act as unconstl.; resisted pressures to resign (although Pres. Johnson opposed his presence in cabinet after 1866), flatly refused Johnson's request for resignation, Aug. 1867; supported by Senate under Tenure of Office Act in this refusal, but resigned in May 1868 following acquittal of Pres. Johnson in impeachment trial; supported Grant in 1868 campaign; nominated to U.S. Supreme Ct. by Grant, 1869, confirmed, Dec. 1869, died before serving. Died Washington, D.C., Dec. 24, 1869; buried Washington.

STANTON, JOSEPH JR. senator, congressman; b. Charlestown, R.I., July 19, 1739. Served in expdn. against Canada, 1759; mem. R.I. Ho. of Reps., 1768-74, 94-1800; served as col. in Revolutionary Army; del. R.I. Constl. Conv., 1790; mem. U.S. Senate (Democrat) from R.I., June 7, 1790-93; mem. U.S. Ho. of Reps. (Dem.) from R.I., 7th-9th congresses, 1801-07. Died Charlestown, 1807; buried family cemetery.

STANTON, OSCAR FITZALAN rear admiral U.S.N.; b. Sag Harbor, N.Y., July 18, 1834; s. Joseph and Elizabeth (Cooper) S.; m. Caroline Eliza Gardiner, July 6, 1859. Apptd. midshipman U.S.N., Dec. 29, 1849; promoted through grades to commodore May 19, 1891; rear admiral, July 21, 1894. Served on St. Mary's, Pacific Squadron, 1860-62; exec. officer Tioga in James River and Potomac flotilla and West Indies Flying Squadron, 1862-63; comd. gunboat, West Gulf Blockading Squadron, 1863-64; present at battle of Mobile Bay; New York Navy Yard, 1864-65; on Powhatan and Tallapoosa, 1865; Naval Acad., 1865-67; comd. Tahoma, 1867; Purveyor, 1867-68; receiving-ship Vandalia, 1870-71; Monocacy and Yantic, Chinese and Japanese waters, 1872-74; Norfolk Navy Yard, 1874-77; Newport, R.I., Torpedo Sta., 1878; comd. training ship Constitution, 1879-81; was at Naval Asylum, Phila., 1881-84; comd. flagship Tennessee, N. Atlantic Sta., 1884-85; naval sta., New London, Conn., 1885-89; training sta., Newport, R.I., 1890-91; gov. Phila. Naval Home, 1891-93; comd. flagship Newark, S. Atlantic sta., 1893; comd. N. Atlantic Squadron and was on bd. Kearsarge when she was wrecked, Feb. 2, 1894; later comd. San Francisco; retired July 30, 1894. Home: New London, Conn. Died July 5, 1924.

STANTON, THADDEUS H. brig. gen. U.S.A.; b. in Indiana; was private, 3d battalion, D.C. inf., April to July 1861; capt. 19th Iowa inf., Aug. to Dec. 1862; became additional paymaster, U.S.V., Dec. 18, 1862, to April 8, 1867. Apptd. maj. paymaster, U.S.A., Jan. 17, 1867; lt. col., dept. paymaster gen., March 15, 1890; col. asst. paymaster gen., Jan. 22, 1893; brig. gen. and paymaster gen., U.S.A., March 27, 1895. Brevets: lt. col. vols., March 13, 1865, for faithful and meritorious services during Civil war; lt. col., U.S.A., Feb. 27, 1890, for gallantry in action against Indians under Crazy Horse on Powder Horn River, March 17, 1876. Home: Washington, D.C. Died 1900.

STANTON, WILLIAM brig. gen. U.S.A.; b. in N.Y., Oct. 13, 1843; s. Gen. Henry and Alexandrine (Macomb) S. Private, corporal and sergt. Co. G, 43d Ohio Inf., Sept. 3, 1862-Mar. 11, 1863; apptd. from Mich., 2d lt. 2d U.S. Arty., Sept. 3, 1867; grad. Arty. Sch., 1871; 1st lt., Nov. 16, 1874; transferred to 6th Cav., Feb. 9, 1877; capt., May 21, 1886; maj. 8th Cav., June 9, 1899; lt. col. 11th Cav., Sept. 13, 1902; col. 6th Cav., Mar. 18, 1905; brig. gen. and retired, Mar. 7, 1906. Present at siege of Santiago, Cuba, comdg. a cav. squadron, July 1-Aug. 6, 1898. Home: New York, N.Y. Died Apr. 7, 1927.

STARBIRD, ALFRED (ANDREWS) ret. army officer; b. Paris, Me., July 15, 1875; s. Winfield Scott and Emeline Hardy (Roberts) S.; B.S., U. Me., 1898; m. (Mary) Ethel Dodd, July 20, 1911; children—Alfred Dodd, Catharine Andrews (Mrs. Edward Jennison), Ethel Allan. Enlisted as sgt., 1st Me. Inf., 1898; commd. as 2d lt. U.S. Army, 1898 with artillery; advanced through grades to brig. gen., 1930; saw service in U.S., Philippine Islands, Europe; retired, 1930; genealogist, 1931-41. Awarded Distinguished Service Medal, various campaign medals. Fellow Inst. Am. Genealogy. Republican. Mason (32 deg.). Author: Geneaology of Starbird Family, 1940, 43. Home: R.F.D., Underhill, Vt. Died Dec. 9, 1956.

STARK, EDWIN JACKSON nurseryman; b. Louisiana, Mo., Sept. 28, 1898; s. Eugene W. and Anne (Withrow) S.; student Culver Mil. Acad., U. Mo., 1919-21; m. Willeyne Crewdson, Aug. 27, 1925. Pres. Stark Brothers Nurseries & Orchards Co., Louisiana, Mo., 1953—, Missouri State Fruit Expt. Sta., Mountain Grove, Mo., 1942—; v.p., dir. Louisiana (Mo.) Press Jour.; dir. Bank of Louisiana. Chmn. Pike County Civilian Def. Com., 1942-46. Vice pres. Great Rivers council Boy Scouts Am.; chmn. USO drive, Pike County, Mo., also state chmn. finance, quota, admission coms., 1945-47; adv. council div. agrl. scis. Mo. Agrl. Coll., U. Mo.; trustee Hannibal La Grange Coll., Phi Delta Theta Fidelity Ednl. Found., Columbia, Mo.; chmn. addition com. Pike County Hosp.; mem. Gov.'s Adv. Com. Indsl. and Econ. Devel. Member bd. of curators University Missouri. Served with U.S. Army, World War I. Named col., Mo. Mem. Nat. Assn. Direct Selling Cos. (dir.), Am. (pres. 1941-42), Western (pres. 1939-40) assns. nurserymen, Am. Legion, Phi Delta Theta. Baptist (deacon). Mason (Shriner), Elk. Club: Pike County Country (Louisiana, Mo.). Home: 417 Main St. Office: Stark Brothers Nurseries & Orchards Co., Louisiana, Mo. 63353. Died Oct. 13, 1964; buried Riverview Cemetery, Louisiana.

STARK, EDWIN M. financial and business cons.; b. Mansfield, Ohio; s. W. W. and Virginia (Wilson) S.; ed. Stanford, also U. Cal.; m. Constance Richardson. Chmn. bd., chmn. exec. com., dir. Horder's Inc.; chmn., dir. Alison Bowes Co., Lancaster Corp., Wood Bros. Constrn. Co., Kingsbury Breweries Corp.; pres., dir. Central West Co.; chmn. reorgn. com. Wood Bros. Corp., St. Louis Gas & Coke Co.; dir. finance, bd. dirs. Magnet Mills, Inc.; exec. com., dir. Butler Bros., Chgo. Terminal Nat. Bank, Gen. Finance Co.; mem. reorgn. com. Western Light & Telephone Co.; v.p., treas., dir. Am. Column & Lumber Co.; v.p., treas., dir. N.Am. Watch Co.; v.p., exec. com., dir. Foreman-State Corp.; v.p. Foreman Trust & Savs. Bank; partner Redmond & Co., mems. N.Y. Stock Exchange; dir. Asso. Stationers Supply Co., No. States Power Co., Chgo. Ry. Equipment Co., Utility and Indsl. Corp., Woods Bros. Securities Co., Central Electric & Telephone Co., Wilson, Jones & Co., Standard Timber Co., Bear Fork Royalty Co., Nachmann Spring-Filled Corp., Alfred Decker & Cohn Co., Bklyn. Nat. Corp., L.G.S. Tools, Inc., Wexstark Radio Stores, Inc., Kinco, Inc., Louisiana Consolidated Mining Co., Federated Metals Corp., Pinebond Corp.; engr. Sanderson and Porter,

N.Y.C. Bd. dirs. Cook County Sch. Nursing, Benton House. Served from lt. (s.g.) to lt. comdr. Flying Corps, U.S. Navy, World War I. Mem. Nat. Hardwood Lumber Assn. (dir.), Mansfield (dir.), N.Y. State (dir.) chambers of commerce, Ohio Soc. of N.Y., Chi Psi. Republican. Clubs: Indian Hill (Winnetka, Ill.); Attic, Bond, Racquet, Mid-day (Chgo.); City Midday, Nat. Arts, Rocky Mountain (N.Y.C.); Racquet (Phila.); Skokie Country (Glencoe, Ill.); Edgewood Country (Charleston, W.Va.); Westbrook Country (dir.), Our (dir.) (Mansfield); Scioto Country, Crichton (Columbus, O.); Scarsdale (N.Y.) Golf. Author articles. Home: 177 Scott Av., Hubbard Woods, Ill. Office: First Nat. Bank Bldg., Chgo. 60603. Died May 7, 1967.

STARK, HAROLD RAYNSFORD, naval officer; b. Wilkes-Barre, Pa., Nov. 12, 1880; s. Benjamin Franklin and Mary Frances (Warner) S.; grad. U.S. Naval Acad., 1903; m. Katharine Adele Rhoads, July 24, 1907; children—Mary (Mrs. Edwin Walker Semans). Katharine Rhoads (Mrs. Harold Perot Gillespie). Commd. ensign, U.S. Navy, Feb. 2, 1905; promoted through grades to admiral, August 1, 1939. Served on various ships and stations, 1903-17; aide on staff of Adm. Sims, comdg. U.S. Naval Forces operating in European waters, 1917-19; inspector in charge of ordnance, Naval Proving Ground, Dahlgren, Va., and Naval Powder Factory, Indian Head, Md., 1925-28; aide on staff and chief of staff, Destroyer Squadrons, Battle Fleet, 1928-30; aide to Sec. of Navy, Washington, D.C., 1930-33; comdg. U.S.S. West Virginia, 1933-34; chief of Bur. of Ordnance, Navy Dept., Washington, D.C., 1934-37; comdg. cruiser div. U.S. Fleet, 1937-38; comdg. cruisers, Battle Force, 1938-39; chief of naval operations, rank of admiral, August 1, 1939; comdg. U.S. Naval Forces in Europe, March 1942-August 1945; retired from active duty April 1, 1946. Decorated Mexican Campaign, and Dominican Campaign medals, World War Medal (U.S.); Expeditionary medal, D.S.M. (United States Navy) with three citations; Order of Crown of Italy; National Order of Southern Cross (degree of Grande Official) (Brazil); Distinguished Service Medal (U.S. Army); Hon. Knight of the Grand Cross, Military Division, Order of the British Empire; Comdr., Legion of Honor, Croix de Guerre with Palm (French); Grand Gross, Order of St. Olav (Norwegian). Episcopalian. Clubs: Army and Navy, Army and Navy Country, U. (Washington); Chevy Chase, Manor Country (Md.); Army and Navy (San Franciso); N.Y. Yacht, Westmoreland (Wilkes-Barre, Pa.). Home: Washington DC Died Aug. 20, 1972; buried Arlington Nat. Cemetery, Arlington VA

STARK, JOHN army officer; b. Londonderry, N.H., Aug. 28, 1728; s. Archibald and Eleanor (Nichols) S.; m. Elizabeth Page, Aug. 20, 1758. Leader exploring expdns.; served at Crown Point and Ticonderoga in French and Indian War, 1759; col. at Battle of Bunker Hill, 1775; resigned commn., 1777; promoted to brig. gen. Continental Army, 1777; captured Ft. Edward; in command No. Dept. twice; joined George Washington in Battle of Short Hills, Morristown, N.J., 1778; served with Gates in R.I., 1779; served in Battle of Springfield, 1780; brevetted maj. gen., 1783. Died Manchester, N.H., May 2, 1822.

STARK, LLOYD CROW, ex-gov. of Mo.; b. Louisiana, Mo., Nov. 23, 1886; s. Clarence McDowell and Lilly (Crow) S.; B.S., U. S. Naval Acad., 1908; LL.D., Westminster Coll., U. of Mo., 1937, Central Coll., Fayette, Mo., 1939, Beloit (Wis.) Coll., 1941, Washington U., St. Louis, 1941; m. Margaret Pearson Stickney, Nov. 11, 1908 (died Oct. 12, 1930); children—Lloyd Stickney (Lt. Comdr., Killed on duty, 1946), John Wingate (major in Air Corps Reserve); m. 2d, Katherine Lemoine Perkins, Nov. 23, 1931; children—Mary (Mrs. Richard Strassner), Katherine (Mrs. Richard Clark Bull). Naval officer, 1904-12, serving in Turkey, 1909; South Am. waters, 1910; Submarines 1911; v.p., gen. mgr. Stark Brothers Nurseries, 1912-17, 1919-35, chmn. bd., 1935-37, 41-71, emeritus chmn. bd., 1971-72, also chief executive officer, nat. sales div. Discovered Stark Golden Delicious apple, 1913. Gov., State of Missouri, 1937-41. Chairman Governor's Conf. of United States, 1939; pres. Council of State Govts., 1939; member bd. of mgrs., 1941-47. Served as maj., batt. comdr. and (acting) asst. divisional chief of staff, 80th Div. and commanded 315th F.A., A.E.F., in Argonne, 1917-19. Decorated Victory medal and two battle clasps. Recipient Hall of Fame award, Am. Assn. Nurseymen, 1967; Patriots award S.R., 1969. Vice pres. and dir. Mo. State Chamber of Commerce, 1935-39; mem. exec. bd. Mo. Council Boy Scouts of Am., 1941, mem. at large Nat. Council; mem. nat. adv. council Arboretum, Washington, 1946-70; hon. life mem. Am. Assn. Nurserymen (pres. 1917, 1920), Fed. Garden Clubs of Mo., Mo. Soc. (Wash., D.C.); mem. Naval Inst., Mo. Hist. Soc. (past dir.), State Hist. Soc. of Mo., Garden Clubs of America, S.R., Am. Saddle Horse Breeders Assn. (past dir.), Naval Acad. Grads. Assn., Navy Athletic Assn., Navy League of the U.S. (v.p. and dir. 1941-46), Pan Am. Soc. (St. Louis com., 1941), Mo. Acad. Squires. Democrat. Episcopalian. Clubs: St. Louis Country, University (St. Louis); Army and Navy (Washington); Rotary. Home: Eolia MO Died Sept. 17, 1972; buried Riverview Cemetery, Louisiana MO

STARK, OTTO artist; b. Indianapolis, Jan. 29, 1859; s. Gustav S. and Leona (Jonas) S.; ed. Cincinnati Art Sch., Art Students' League, New York, Acad. Julien, and under M. F. Carmon, Paris, France; m. Maria Nitschelm, of Paris, Dec. 15, 1886 (died 1892). Located in Indianapolis, Ind., 1895; was head of the art dept. of the Manual Training High School, and instr. in composition, John Herron Art Inst., Indianapolis, resigned. Exhibited twice in Paris Salon, at Internat. Expn. of Art and History, Rome, and in many exhbns. in U.S. Winner of Foulke prize, Richmond, Ind., 1908; 1st Holcombe prize, annual exhbn. of Ind. artists, 1915. Exhibited San Francisco Expn., 1915 (mem. advisory com.), San Diego Expn., 1916. First pres. Ind. Artists Club, 1916-17. Home: Indianapolis, Ind. Died Apr. 14, 1926.

STARNES, JOE (stärnz), ex-congressman; b. Guntersville, Ala., Mar. 31, 1895; s. John Walker and Mary Boyd (Perkins) S.; LL.B., U. of Ala., 1921; m. Del Clark Whitaker, Apr. 10, 1918; children—Joe, Paul Whitaker. Teacher Ala. pub. schs., 1912-17. Admitted to Ala. bar, 1921; in practice at Guntersville; mem. 74th to 78th Congresses (1935-45), 5th Ala. Dist.; (mem. House Appropriations Com., 75th to 78th Congress; mem. Spc. Com. for Investigating un-American Activities, 75th to 78th Congress); author Veterans Preference Act, 1944. Mem. bd. trustees Snead Jr. Coll., Kate Duncan Smith Daus. Am. Revolution Sch. Mem. bd. edn. N. Ala. Conf. Meth. Ch.; mem. Ala. State Mil. Adv. Bd. Served as 2d lt. Infantry, U.S. Army, in Eng., France and Germany, World War I; capt., then major, Ala. Nat. Guard, on inactive duty, 1941-45; colonel U.S. Army, 1945-46. Awarded Silver Star citation (United States). Mem. Ala. State Bd. Edn. Mem. Ala. State Bar Assn., Am. Legion (dept. comdr. Alabama Dept. 1951-52), Civitan (gov. Ala. Dist. North 1952-53, internat. pres. 1959-60), Vets. Fgn. Wars, Mil. Order World War, Nat. Rifle Assn., U.S. Infantry Assn., Pi Kappa Phi, Phi Delta Phi. Dem. Methodist. Mason, Shriner, K.T., K.P. Home: Guntersville, Ala. Died Jan. 9, 1962.

STARR, HENRY FRANK, life ins. exec., physician; b. Greensboro, N.C., Feb. 1,21894; s. Henry Francis and Annie Caroline (Young) S.; student U. N.C., 1911-14; M.D., Jefferson Med. Coll., 1916; m. Virginia Morton Goode, May 5, 1920; children—Elizabeth Frances (Mrs. James M. Jackson) (dec.); Henry Frank. Intern N.Y.C. Hosp., 1916; med. dir. Pilot Life Ins. Co., Greensboro, 1917-45, mem. bd. dirs., 1926-45, v.p., 1933-45; med. dir. Jefferson Standard Life Ins. Co., Greensboro, 1945-69, dir., 1947-51, v.p., 1951-69. Served as capt., 78th Div., U.S. Army, World War I. Mem. Assn. Life Ins. Med. Dirs. Am., Am. Life Conv., A.M.A., N.C. Med. Soc, Tri-State, So. med. assns. Presbyn. Kiwanian. Author articles on life ins. medicine. Home: Greensboro NC Died Sept. 24, 1969; buried Forest Lawn Cemetery Greensboro NC

STARRING, FREDERICK A(UGUSTUS) civil and mining engr., lawyer, soldier; b. Buffalo, N.Y., May 24, 1834; s. Capt. Sylvenus Seaman and Adeline (Williams) S.; ed. Buffalo, Paris, Heidelberg, Vienna and grad. Harvard, class of 1865-66; admitted to bar, 1859; m. Louise Perle Whitehouse, July 21, 1889. Engr. on Ill. Central, location surveys and boundary line surveys, Tex. & Ind. Ter., etc. Sec. Cairo & Fulton R.R. Co. of Ark. and Mo., 1859-61. Served Civil war, maj. 46th Ill. inf., maj., 2d Ill. light arty., col. 72d Ill. inf. (Chicago Bd. of Trade regt.); brig. gen. comdg. 1st, 2d and 3d brigades, Army of Tenn., and maj. gen. and provost marshal gen., dept. of the Gulf. U.S. diplomatic and consular agt. Europe and other foreign countries, 1869-83. Home: New York, N.Y. Died 1904.

STASON, E(DWIN) BLYTHE, lawyer, educator; b. Siouy City, Ia., Sept. 6, 1891; s. Edwin J. and Anna (Blythe) S.; A.B., U. of Wis., 1913, B.S., Mass. Inst. of Tech., 1916, J.D., U. of Mich., 1922, LL.D., 1970; m. Adeline Boaz, Sept. 14, 1921; children—Edwin Blythe, William Boaz. Instr. elec. engring., U. of Pa., 1916-17; asst. prof. elec. engring. U. of Mich., 1919-22; practiced law Sioux City, Ia., as mem. firm Stason & Stason, 1922-24; prof. of law, U. of Mich., from 1924, provost of the Univ. 1938-44, dean of the Law Sch., 1939-60; adminstr. American Bar Found., Chgo., 1960-64; prof. law Vanderbilt U., Nashville, 1964-67, Frank C. Rand professor of law, 1967-70. Michigan commissioner in Nat. Conf. of Commrs. on Uniform State Laws; member Michigan Constitution Revision Study Com., 1941; Mich. tax study commn., 1945; chmn. Michigan anti-subversive study com., 1950. Mem. United States Attorney Genls. Com. on Administrative Procedure 1939-41; cons. Pres.' Conf. on Adminstrv. Procedure, 1953-54, Hoover Commn. Task Force on Legal Services and Practices of Exec. Br. U.S. Govt., 1953-54; mng. dir. Fund for Peaceful Atomic Development, from 1955; trustee Power Reactor Development Co., from 1955; dir. Inst. for Tng. in Citizenship, N.Y. U., 1956-59; chmn. Mich. Commn. on Tax Administration, 1957-58; mem. of Council on Foreign Relations, from 1958. Served as capt. C.E., AUS, 1917-19. Recipient of award for outstanding research in law and government American Bar Found., 1965. Fellow Am. Bar Found.; mem. Am. Law Inst., Am. Judicature Soc. (dir. 1940-52), Univ. of Michigan Musical Society (dir. from 1938), Inter-Am. (council 1950), Am., Mich. (sec., editor Jour. 1929-35; com.-at-large 1946-61) bar assns., S.A.R., American Enterprise Inst. (adv. bd.), Order of the Coif, Gamma Eta Gamma. Republican. Presbyn. Clubs: University (Ann Arbor, Mich.); Detroit (Detroit); University (Nashville). Author: Cases and Materials on Municipal Corporations, 1935, rev. edit. 1959; Cases and Materials on Administrative Tribunals, 1937, revised 1956: (with S. D. Estep and W. J. Pierce) Atoms and the Law, 1959. Home: Ann Arbor MI Died Apr. 10, 1972; buried Ann Arbor MI

STATHERS, BIRK SMITH (sta'therz), lawyer; b. Middlebourne, Tyler County, W.Va., July 13, 1884; s. Walter E. and Mary (Smith) S.; A.B., W.Va. U., 1906, LL.B., 1907; m. Margaret Anne Richards, July 3, 1923; children—Mary Jeannette, Margaret Annette, Birk Smith, Jr. Admitted to W.Va. bar, 1907; asso. in practice of law with Hon. W. W. Brannon, Weston, W.Va., 1907-23; mem. and chmn. W.Va. Pub. Service Commn., 1923-25; judge 15th Judicial Circuit of W.Va., 1925-36; returned to practice of law, 1937, and since sr. mem. firm Stathers, Stathers & Cantrall, Clarksburg, W.Va. Commd. capt. inf., Nov. 27, 1917; capt. Co. D, 332d Inf., 83d Div., May 1918-May 1919; with A.E.F., June 1918-Apr. 1919; hon. discharged May 19, 1919. Mem. Am., W.Va. State and Harrison County bar assns., Phi Beta Kappa, Sigma Chi. Episcopalian. Mason. Home: 600 Stanley Av. Office: Goff Bldg., Clarksburg, W.Va. Died Dec. 28, 1915.

STATON, ADOLPHUS real estate exec., naval officer; b. Tarboro, N.C., Aug. 28, 1879; s. Lycurgus Lafayette and Kate Elony (Baker) S.; student Va. Mil. Inst., 1896-97, U. N.C., 1897-98; B.S., U.S. Naval Acad., 1902; LL.B., George Washington, U. Law Sch., 1917; grad. Navy War Coll., 1921, Army War Coll., 1932; m. Edith Blair, July 28, 1917; 1 dau., Lucy. Began as naval officer, 1902, held successively commissions as ensign, lt., lt. commdr., capt. and retired as rear adm., 1937; turret officer, U.S.S. Connecticut, 1906-07; exec. officer, U.S.S. Mount Vernon and U.S.S. Leviathan, transports, during World War; comd. naval ships Dubuque, Argonne, Asheville, Black Hawk, Nevada, and destroyer squadrons. Admitted to D.C. bar 1917, Md. bar, 1939; exec. v.p. Falkland Properties, Inc., and The Falkland Co., real estate, Silver Spring, Md., since 1937. Awarded Medal of Honor, 1915, Navy Cross, 1920, Spanish Am. War medal, 1898, Mexican Campaign medal, 1914, Cuban Army of Pacification medal, 1906, World War medal, 1918. Clubs: N.Y. Yacht (N.Y.C.); Army and Navy Country (Washington); Chevy Chase (Md.; mem. bd. of govs.). Home: 11 E. Bradley Lane, Chevy Chase, Md. Office: 8305 16th St., Silver Spring, Md. Died June 1964.*

STAUFFER, DONALD ALFRED (staw'fer), prof. of English; b. Denver, Colo., July 4, 1902; s. Alfred Vincent and Carrie Ella (Macdonald) S.; A.B., Princeton, 1923, A.M., 1924; Ph.D., Oxford (Rhodes scholar) 1928. Instr., asst. prof., asso. prof., prof., chmn. dept. of English, Princeton, since 1927; summer sessions U. of Colo., 1938, Bread Loaf Sch., 1941-42, U. of Calif., 1949; George Eastman prof. U. of Oxford, 1951-52. Served with U.S. Marines, capt., major, 1942-45; South and West Pacific as Air Combat Intelligence office, 1934-44. Mem. editorial bd. Princeton U. Press; nat. senator Phi Beta Kappa. Mem. Modern Assn. (mem. exec. council). Club: Nassau (Princeton, N.J.). Author: English Biography Before 1700, 1930; Art of Biography in 18th Century, 1941; The Intent of the Critic, 1941; Nature of Poetry, 1946; Saint and the Hunchback, 1946; The Golden Nightingale, 1949; A World of Images, 1949. Home: 14 Alexander St., Princeton, N.J. Died Aug. 8, 1952.

STAUFFER, HERBERT MILTON, physician; educator; b. Phila., Apr. 26, 1914; s. Milton F. and Anna (Hood) S.; M.D., Temple U., 1939, M.Sc., 1945; m. Joan Dunbar; 1 son, Scott. Intern, Temple U. Hosp., Phila., 1939-41, fellow in radiology, 1941-43; roentgenologist Univ. Hosp., Mpls., 1946-49; asst. prof. radiology U. Minn., Mpls., 1946-49; asso. prof. radiology Temple U., 1949-52, prof., 1952-70, head dept. radiology, 1957-70. Mem. radiation study sect. NIH, 1959-62, mem. internat. fellowship rev. panel, 1964-67, mem. diagnostic radiology tng. com., 1967-68; program USPHS. Bd. govs., mem. profl. edn. com. Heart Assn. Southeastern Pa., 1968-70. Served to lt., M.C., USNR, 1943-46. Diplomate Am. Bd. Radiology. Fellow Am. Coll. Radiology; mem. Assn. Univ. Radiologists (pres. 1963-64), Radiol. Soc. N.Am. (program com. 1964-66, dir. 1967-69, chmn. bd. dirs. 1970, pres.-elect. 1970), Am. (chmn. exec. council 1966, 2d v.p. 1969), Phila. (pres. 1969) roentgen ray socs., Phila. Tb and Respiratory Disease Assn. (dir. case detection com. Tb control adv. com. 1968-70). Contbr. numerous articles to med. jours., also chpts. to books. Home: Philadelphia PA Died Dec. 18, 1970.

STAUNTON, SIDNEY AUGUSTUS naval officer; b. Ellicottville, N.Y., June 7, 1850; s. Joseph Marshall and Mary Elizabeth (Wilber) S.; grad. U.S. Naval Acad., 1871; m. Emily Duncan Biddle, Sept. 23, 1886 (died 1892). Ensign, July 1872; promoted through grades to rear adm., Feb. 20, 1910; retired June 7, 1912. Served on Iroquois, Congress, Wabash, Plymouth, Franklin, Powhatan, Marion, Trenton, Swatara, Pensacola, Chicago, Iowa, New York, Yankton, Rainbow, Helena, Colorado (in command of last 4) and various duties on shore, including service on Gen. Bd. of the Navy, and

Joint Bd. of Army and Navy. On staff of Rear Admiral Sampson, comdr.-in-chief of Atlantic Fleet, during Spanish-Am. War; mentioned by that officer in dispatches and recommended for advancement. Comdr.-in-chief special service squadron sent to the Argentine Republic, Apr.-July 1910, to assist in the celebration of the first centennial of Argentine independence, and naval representative of the U.S. at that celebration. Comd. 5th div. Atlantic Fleet, July 1910-Aug. 1911; mem. spl. commn. sent by the President to Europe, May-June 1912, to encourage participation by foreign govts. in the Panama-Pacific Expn. Home: Washington, D.C. Died Jan. 11, 1939.

STAYTON, EDWARD M(OSES) civil engr.; b. Independence, Mo., Sept. 4, 1874; s. Thomas and Louisa Matilda (Corn) S.; grad. Independence High Sch., 1891; student in engring. U. of Mo., 1892-94; m. Bitha Estella Compton, July 26, 1898; 1 son, George Edward. Civil engr. engaged in railroad location and const. in Southwest and in Honduras, 1895-1911; locating and building highway and interurban railways in Kansas City area, 1911-17; building highways in Clay County, 1919-20; mem. bd. control Kansas City Street Ry. Co., 1920-26; design and constrn. Blue River sewer, Kansas City, 1925-27; cons. engr., Jackson County highways, 1928-33; street railway commr., Kansas City, Mo., 1926-40. Served as capt., 1910-14, major, 1914-17, Mo. Nat. Guard; maj. and lt. col. engrs., U.S. Army, with A.E.F., 1917-19; col. engrs. Mo. Nat. Guard, 1920-33, brig. gen., 1933-37, maj. gen., 1938, retired Sept. 1938. Mem. Nat. Defense Com. Mem. U.S. Chamber Commerce 1940-42. Awarded D.S.M. of Society of American Military Engineers; also Missouri Distinguished Service Medal; Master Conservationist Award of Mo. Conservation Commission 1946. Past State Comdr. Am. Legion; dir. Am. Legion Endowment Corp., 1929-42, pres., 1937-41. Delegate to Missouri Constl. Convention, 1943-44. Chmn. Mo. Statewide Forestry Com., 1946-50. Mem. Am. Soc. of Civil Engrs., Soc. of Country, Engineers (Kansas City). Am. Mil. Engrs., Mo. Acad. Science. Democrat. Mason (32 deg., Shriner). Clubs: Kansas City, Military. Home: 637 Procter Pl., Independence, Mo. Died Mar. 2, 1954; buried Woodlawn Cemetery, Independence.

STAYTON, JOHN WILLIAM jurist; b. Washington County, Ky., Dec. 24, 1830; s. Robert G. and Harriet (Pirtle) S.; LL.B., U. Louisville, 1856; m. Eliza Jane Weldon, 3 children. Moved to Tex., 1856; dist. atty. San Antonio County (Tex.), 1858-62; enlisted as pvt. Confederate Army, 1862, later commd. capt. cavalry; founder law firm with Samuel C. Lackey, 1866; mem. Tex. State Constl. Conv., 1875; asso. justice Tex. Supreme Ct., 1881-88; chief justice, 1888-94. Died Tyler, Tex., July 5, 1894.

STEALEY, SYDNOR LORENZO, seminary pres.; b. Martinsburg, W.Va., Mar. 7, 1897; s. Clarence Perry and Anna (Jamieson) S.; A.B., Okla. Baptist U., 1920, D.D., 1943; Th.M., So. Bapt. Theol. Sem., 1927, Ph.D., 1932; D.D., Wake Forest Coll., 1953; D.D., Furman U., 1954; LL.D., William Jewell Coll., 1959; m. Jessie Wheeler, Oct. 16, 1920; children—Jessie Louise (Mrs. Frank K. Vance), Sydnor Lorenzo. Tchr. high sch., 1920-22, coll., 1922-24; ordained to ministry Bapt. Ch., 1922; pastor in Mo., Ky., Ind., Va., N.C., 1925-42; tchr. ch. history So. Bapt. Sem., 1942-51; pres. Southeastern Bapt. Sem., Wake Forest, N.C., 1951-63, pres. emeritus, 1963-69; tchr. Bapt. Sem., Zurich, Switzerland, 1950, 55. Mem. exec. com. So. Bapt. Conv., 1938-44. Served to 2d lt. U.S. Army, World War I. Mem. Am. Soc. Ch. History. Lion. Club: Watauga (Raleigh). Editor: A Baptist Treasury, 1958. Home: Raleigh NC Died July 24, 1969; buried Wake Forest NC

STEARLEY, RALPH F., ret. air force officer; b. Brazil, Indiana, July 25, 1898; son William F. and Ella Lena (Kaelber) S.; B.S., U.S. Mil. Acad., 1918; student Yale U., 1920-21; m. Mildred S. Volandt, Sept. 19, 1931. Commd. 2d lt., U.S. army, 1918, and advanced through the grades to major general (temp.), Sept. 1949; Mil. Cav. School, 1920, Air Service Primary Flying Sch., 1925; Air Service Advanced Flying Sch., 1926; Air Corps Tactical Sch., 1935, Command and Gen. Staff Sch., 1936; Chemical Warfare Sch., 1938; asst. exec. officer, Office of Chief of Air Corps, Wash., D.C., 1940; mil. intelligence officer Flying Training Command, 1942; dir. of Air Support, Hdqrs. Army Air Forces, 1942; A-3 with 9th Air Force, E.T.O., May-Aug. 1944; G-3, 1st Allied Airborne Army, E.T.O., Aug. 1944-Mar. 1945; comdg. gen. 9th Tactical Air Command, E.T.O., Mar.-Sept. 1945; comdr. Air Sect., 15th Army Theater Gen. Bd., E.T.O., Sept. 1945-Jan. 1946; dep. chief War Dept. Spl. Staff Legislative and Liaison Div. 1946-48, chief, Air Force, 1948; comdg. general 14th Air Force, 1948-50; commanding gen. 20th Air Force, 1950-53, ret. as maj. gen. USAF, 1953; mil. advisor Twigg Industries, Martinsville, Ind. Chmn. Indiana Aeros. Commission. Rated command pilot and command observer. Decorations: D.S.M., second D.S.M. (with cluster), 1953, Legion of Merit, Air Medal, Bronze Star, L'Ordre de la Legion d' Honneur, degree de Chevalier, Croix de Guerre avec Palm (France); L'Ordre de Leopold II, Grede de Commandeur avec Palme, Croix de Guerre avec Palme (Belgium); Comdr. of Order of Orange-Nassau (Netherlands); Commander of Order British Empire. Mem. V.F.W., Am. Legion, C. of C. (pres.). Methodist. Mason, Elk. Clubs: Rotary; Terre Haute (Ind.) Country; Army and Navy (Washington). Home: Brazil IN Died Feb. 3, 1973.

STEARNS, ALBERT WARREN (stûrnz), professor; b. Billerica, Mass., Jan. 26, 1885; s. George Edwin and Helen Maria (Proctor) S.; preparatory education, Howe Sch., Billerica; student Tufts Coll., 1905-06, M.D., Med. Sch. of same, 1910; Sc.D., Tufts College, 1943; married Francis Matsell Judkins, December 28, 1912; children—Albert Warren (dec.), Charles Edward. Began practice at Boston, 1910; consultant U.S. Naval Hosp., Chelsea, Mass., 1923-29; prof. psychiatry and dean of Tufts Coll. Med. Sch., 1927-45, commr. of correction, State of Mass., 1929-33; asso. commr. Dept. of Mental Disease, 1935-38; chief of neurology service, Boston Dispensary 1921-45; prof. sociology, Tufts Coll., 1945-55, dean emeritus, 1955-59. Lt. M.C., USN, 1917-19; capt. World War II. Mem. Am. Med. Assn., Boston Soc. Psychiatry and Neurology (pres. 1934), Am. Psychiatric Assn., N.E. Soc. Psychiatry, Mass. Psychiatric Soc. (pres. 1931), Am. Acad. Arts and Sciences, Mass. Med. Soc. (v.p. 1938-40). Republican. Unitarian. Author: Personality of Criminals, 1931; also monographs in psychiatry and criminology. Home: Billerica, Mass. Died Sept. 24, 1959; buried Fox Hill Cemetery, Billerica, Mass.

STEARNS, GEORGE LUTHER anti-slavery leader; b. Medford, Mass., Jan. 8, 1809; s. Luther and Mary (Hall) S.; m. Mary Train, Jan. 31, 1836; m. 2d, Mary L. Preston, Oct. 12, 1843. A leader in movement that put Charles Sumner in U.S. Senate, 1851; raised subscription to equip free state forces in Kan. with Sharpe's rifles, 1856, made John Brown agt. to receive arms and ammunition for defense of Kan., 1857; maj., recruited many negro soldiers for Mass. regts. in Civil War, 1863, 64; founder Right Way (paper supporting radical Republican policies), 1865. Died N.Y.C., Apr. 9, 1867; buried Mt. Auburn Cemetery, Cambridge, Mass.

STEARNS, GUSTAV clergyman; b. New Richland, Minn., Mar. 23, 1874; s. Halvor and Bergit (Sevats) S.; B.A., St. Olaf Coll., Northfield, Minn., 1896; C.T., Luth. Theol. Sem., St. Paul, Minn., 1899, Master of Theology, 1929; D.D., Augustana Coll., Sioux Falls, S.D., 1931; m. Reidun Moe, June 22, 1920. Ordained ministry Lutheran Ch., June 25, 1899; pastor Evang. Lutheran Church of the Ascension, Milwaukee, 1899-1934; dedicated new church building, 1923; full time U.S. Govt. Vet. Adminstrn. chaplain, Nat. Soldiers Home, Milwaukee, 1934-47. Chaplain, 1st lt., 1st Wis. Inf., Mexican border service, 1916; chaplain, capt., 127th Inf., 32d Div., U.S. Army, 22 mos., World War; overseas 15 mos.; wounded at Badricourt, France, July 12, 1918; engaged in battles, Haute-Alsace sector, May 18-July 21, 1918, Aisne-Marne offensive, July 30-Aug. 6, 1918, Oise-Aisne offensive, Aug. 28-Sept. 6, 1918; chaplain, rank of maj., Wis. Nat. Guard and Reserves, Jan. 1, 1925; lt. col. and chaplain, Nat. Guard of U.S. and State of Wis., 1931-38; v.p. Chaplains' Assn. Army of U.S., 1931, pres., 1932. Awarded service medal by State of Wis. Cited by Gen. Pershing "for gallantry in action" near Juvigny, France, Sept. 1, 1918, in burying dead under heavy shell fire. Decorations (U.S.): Purple Heart medal for wound received in action; Silver Star medal for gallantry in action. In period since 1936, with cooperation of U.S. consuls in foreign service, he assembled largest flag collection in the U.S., including national flags sent from 116 foreign countries. Collection is property of Nat. Soldiers Home Chapel, Wood, Wis. Mem. Am. Legion, Pi Gamma Mu, 1928. Author: From Army Camps and Battlefields, 1919. Contbr. short stories to mags. Home 1727 South 30th St., Milw. 15. Died Apr. 21, 1951; buried Forest Home Cemetery, Milw.

STEARNS, OZORA PIERSON senator, jurist; b. De Kalb, St. Lawrence County, N.Y., Jan. 15, 1831; attended Oberlin Coll.; grad. U. Mich., 1858, grad. law dept., 1860. Admitted to bar, 1860, practiced law, Rochester, Minn.; elected pros. atty. Olmstead County, 1861; mayor Rochester, 1866-68; served as lt. 9th Regt., Minn. Volunteer Inf. in U.S. Army during Civil War, also col. 39th Regt., U.S. Colored Troops, until 1865; mem. U.S. Senate (Republican, filled vacancy) from Minn., Jan. 23-Mar. 3, 1871; moved to Duluth, Minn., 1872, practiced law; judge Minn. 11th Jud. Dist., 1874-95; regent U. Minn., 1890-95. Died Pacific Beach, Cal., June 2, 1896; remains cremated in Los Angeles, ashes interred Forest Hill Cemetery, Duluth.

STEBBINS, HOMER ADOLPH lawyer; b. Syracuse, N.Y., May 6, 1884; s. Morris William and Rebecca (McCabe) S.; Ph.B., Syracuse U., 1906, Ph.M., 1907; LL.B., 1908; Ph.D., Columbia, 1913; J.S.D., New York U., 1917; auditor University of Marburg, Germany, summer 1911; m. Elizabeth Alden Seabury Tredwell, July 3, 1912; children—Roger Morris, Ruth Rebekah, Seabury Tredwell, and (adopted) Viola Virginia Hanson (Mrs. Maurice Paul Bellemans). Admitted to N.Y. bar, 1908; practiced N.Y.C., 1914-—, alone 1933-—, specializing in internat. and pub. law; former tchr. and lectr. law several schs. and colls. Served as capt., Gen. Staff Mil. Intelligence Div., AUS, as political specialist on Near and Far East, 1918-19; in Army Res. Corps 29 yrs.; maj., M.I. Service, U.S. Army, 1941-45; various assignments including A.M.G., 1943-45. Adv. on Internat. Law to U.S. Allied Commn. to Austria, with headquarters at Vienna, Oct. 1945-Dec. 1946. Dem. candidate for Congress, 1934, 36, 37, 38, 40; alternate delegate Democratic N.Y. State Conv., 1938. Acting judge Village Court, Hastings-on-Hudson, N.Y., 1940, 41. A founder Woodrow Wilson Found. Fellow Am. Geog. Soc. of N.Y.; mem. nat., state and local profl. assns., also hon. mem. several socs. Episcopalian. Club: Syracuse Univ. (N.Y.C.). Author books and monographs, covering party politics in U.S. Address: 22 Minturn St., Hastings-on-Hudson, N.Y. 10706. Died Nov. 4, 1962; buried Oaklawn Cemetery, Southport, Conn.

STECK, DANIEL FREDERIC ex-senator, lawyer; b. Ottumwa, Ia., Dec. 16, 1881; s. Albert Clark and Ada (Washburn) S.; LL.B., U. Ia., 1906; m. Lucile Oehler, June 30, 1908. Admitted to Ia. bar, 1906, and began practice at Ottumwa; U.S. senator from Ia., for term ending 1931 (seated 1926, after contest with Smith W. Brookhart); spl. asst. to atty. gen. U.S., 1933-47. Hon. mem. Internat. Printing Pressmen and Assts. Union N.A. Served in World War as capt. 109th Field Signal Batt., U.S. and France. Mem. Am. Legion; comdr. Dept. Ia., 1921-22; chmn. Nat. Legislative Com. of Am. Legion, 1921-22. Mem. Sigma Nu, Phi Delta Phi. Democrat. Episcopalian. Mason (32 deg.). Home: Ottumwa, Ia. Died Dec. 31, 1950.

STEDMAN, CHARLES MANLY congressman; b. Pittsboro, N.C., Jan. 29, 1841; grad. U. of N.C., 1861; m. Catherine de Rosset, d. Joshua G. Wright of Wilmington, N.C., Jan. 8, 1866. Enlisted as pvt. Fayetteville (N.C.) Independent Light Inf. Co., 1st N.C. Inf.; lt., capt. and maj. 44th N.C. Inf. to end of war; served in Gen. R. E. Lee's army during entire war; thrice wounded. Admitted to bar and practiced at Wilmington, 1867-98, Greensboro, N.C., 1898-—; sr. mem. Stedman & Cooke. Lieut. gov. N.C., 1885-89; candidate for Dem. nomination for gov., 1888; mem. 62d to 71st Congresses (1911-31), 5th N.C. Dist. Dir. (state appmt.) N.C. R.R. Co., 1909, pres., 1910; former trustee U. of N.C.; dir. Guilford (N.C.) Battle Ground Co. Home: Greensboro, N.C. Died Sept. 23, 1930.

STEEDMAN, CHARLES naval officer; b. Parish of St. James, Santee, S.C., Sept. 20, 1811; s. Charles John and Mary (Blake) S.; m. Sarah Bishop, Feb. 7, 1843, 6 children. Commd. midshipman U.S. Navy, 1828, passed midshipman, 1834, advanced through grades to rear adm., 1871; served in naval operations on Gulf Coast during Mexican War; ordered to duty in Chesapeake Bay, 1861; commanded ship Bienville, participated in Port Royal expdn., 1861; served in ship Paul Jones, 1862, reduced batteries on St. John's Bluff, Fla.; commanded ship Ticonderoga in cruise against Confederate raiders, 1863; participated in attacks on Ft. Fisher (N.C.); in charge Boston Navy Yard, 1869-72, South Pacific Squadron, 1872-73; ret., 1873. Died Nov. 13, 1890.

STEEDMAN, JAMES BLAIR army officer, state ofcl.; b. Northcumberland County, Pa., July 29, 1817; s. Mellum and Margaret (Blair) S.; m. Miranda Stiles, 1838; m. 2d, Rose Barr; m. 3d, Margaret Gildea. Became mem. Ohio Legislature, 1847; del. to numerous Democratic convs.; commd. col. 14th Ohio Inf., 1861, brig. gen. U.S. Volunteers, 1862; commanded div. which came to rescue of George Henry Thomas at Battle of Chickamauga; maj. gen. volunteers, 1864, served at Battle of Nashville; resigned commn., 1866; collector internal revenue New Orleans, 1866-69; editor No. Ohio Democrat; mem. Ohio Senate; chief of police Toledo (O.). Died Toledo, Oct. 18, 1883.

STEELE, FREDERICK army officer; b. Delhi, N.Y., Jan. 14, 1819; s. Nathaniel Steele; grad. U.S. Mil. Acad., July 1, 1843. Commd. 2d lt., 2d Inf., U.S. Army, 1843, served in Mexican War. Twice brevetted for gallant conduct; promoted 1st lt., 1848; served as maj. 11th Inf., 1855-61, col. 8th Ia. Inf., 1861-62; commd. brig. gen., then maj. gen. U.S. Volunteers, 1862; served in Ark., Vicksburg and Mobile campaigns; in command Dept. of Columbia, 1865-68; commd. lt. col. U.S. Army, 1863, col., 1866. Died San Mateo, Cal., Jan. 12, 1868.

STEELE, GEORGE WASHINGTON congressman; b. Fayette Co., Ind., Dec. 13, 1839; s. Asbury and Mary Louisa S.; student Ohio Wesleyan U., 1 term, 1860; admitted to bar, 1861; m. Marietta E. Swayzee, Oct. 11, 1866. Enlisted in 8th Ind. Inf., Apr. 19, 1861, not mustered; state service, May 2, 1861; 1st lt. 12th Ind. Inf., July 20, 1861; hon. mustered out, May 19, 1862; 1st lt. 101st Ind. Inf., Sept. 2, 1862; capt., Sept. 6, 1862; maj., Jan. 27, 1863; lt. col., May 31, 1863; hon. mustered out of vol. service, June 24, 1865; 2d and 1st lt. 14th U.S. Inf., Feb. 23, 1866; resigned, Feb. 1, 1876. Pres. First Nat. Bank, Marion, Ind., 1890. Member 47th to 50th and 54th to 57th Congresses (1881-89, 1895-1903), 11th Ind. Dist.; 1st gov. of Okla. Ty., 20 mos., 1890, 91. Republican. Mem. bd. mgrs. Nat. Home Disabled Vol. Soldiers, 1890-1904; now gov. Nat. Soldiers' Home, Indiana. Died July 13, 1922.

STEELE, HARRY LEE army officer; b. Benton Co., Ark., June 28, 1874; s. John Bell and Mary (Van Winkle) S.; grad. Rogers (Ark.) Acad., 1894, Army War Coll., 1928; m. Cornelia Elizabeth Lundeen, Dec. 25, 1901; children—Lee, John Chandler, Lundeen Van

Winkle, Ruth. Enlisted as pvt., Battery A, 5th Arty., U.S.A., Aug. 27, 1895, and promoted through grades to maj. gen., chief of coast arty., Feb. 9, 1935. Served in Q.M. Corps in P.I. and China, 1915-16, in Panama, 1919-22, Hawaii, 1931-34. Home: Washington, D.C. Died Mar. 31, 1938.

STEELE, HIRAM ROSWELL lawyer; b. Stanstead, Can., July 10, 1842; s. Sanford and Mary (Hinman) S.; acad. edn., St. Johnsbury, Vt.; capt. Co. K, 10th Vt. Inf., Aug. 12, 1862; bvtd. maj. vols., Dec. 19, 1865, "for faithful services in subsistence dept."; hon. mustered out, Jan. 4, 1866; m. Mary E. Porter, Sept. 19, 1877. Admitted to bar, 1868; judge Parish Court, La., 1868-72; judge Superior Criminal Court, New Orleans, 1875-76; dist. atty., La., 1872-75; asst. atty. gen. of La., 1875; mem. La. Constl. convs., 1868, 79; in law practice at New York, 1890-—; senior, Steele, DeFriese & Steele; trustee New York Life Ins. Co., South Brooklyn Savings Instn. Dist. atty. Kings Co., 1899. Republican. Home: Brooklyn, N.Y. Deceased.

STEELE, JOEL DORMAN educator; b. Lima, N.Y., May 14, 1836; s. Rev. Allen and Sabra (Dorman) S.; grad. Genesee Coll. (now Syracuse U.), 1858; m. Esther Baker, July 7, 1859. Taught in dist. schs. to finance his coll. edn.; instr., then prin. Mexico (N.Y.) Acad., 1858-61; raised 81st N.Y. Volunteers, 1861, capt.; wounded at Battle of Seven Pines, 1862, forced out of war; prin. high school, Newark, N.J., 1863-66, Elmira Free Acad., 1866-72; did not use regular textbooks, substituted his own outlines which grew into his Fourteen Weeks series of texts (1st published 1867); at request of Alfred Cutler Barnes, his friend and publisher, devoted rest of life to writing textbooks, 1872-86. Author: Barnes Brief History Series (most famous: A Brief History of the United States for Schools, 1871). Died May 25, 1886.

STEELE, JOHN congressman; b. Salisbury, N.C., Nov. 1, 1764; s. William Gillespie and Elizabeth (Maxwell) Steel (or Steele); m. Mary Nesfield, Feb. 9, 1783, at least 3 children. Assessor, Town of Salisbury, 1784, town commr., 1787; mem. N.C. Ho. of Commins, 1788, 94, 95, 1806, 11-13-speaker, 1811; commr. to negotiate with Cherokee and Chickasaw Indians, 1788; Federalist mem. conv. to consider U.S. Constn., Hillsboro, N.C., 1788; del. Fayetteville (N.C.) Conv. which ratified U.S. Constn., 1789; mem. U.S. Ho. of Reps. from N.C., 1st, 2d congresses, 1789-93; maj. gen. N.C. Militia, 1794; comptroller U.S. Treasury (apptd.) by George Washington, 1796-1802; mem. commn. to determine boundary between N.C. and S.C., 1805, 14. Died Salisbury, Aug. 14, 1815.

STEESE, JAMES GORDON (stes), civil engr.; b. Mt. Holly Springs, Pa., Jan. 21, 1882; s. James Andrew and Anna Zug (Schaeffer) S.; A.B., Dickinson College, 1902, A.M., 1906; B.S. (1st honors), U.S. Mil. Acad., 1907; studied U. of Calif., 1908; grad. U.S. Engr. Sch., Washington, 1910; Sc.D., U. of Alaska, 1932; unmarried. Commd. 2d lt. engrs., June 14, 1907; promoted through grades to col., June 18, 1918; brigadier general and adjutant general Alaska N.G., 1926-27; retired Oct. 1927. Asst. engr. San Diego and San Francisco bays, Calif., 1907-08; asst. engr. Panama Railroad Co. and Panama Canal, 1908-12; chief engr. 5th (expeditionary) Brig., Tex., 1913; instr. and asst. prof. engring., U.S. Mil. Acad., 1913-17; spl. rep. of gen. mgr. West Md. Ry., June-Sept. 1916; organized O.T.C., Ft. Riley, Kan., and instr. Engr. O.T.C., Ft. Leavenworth, Kan., 1917; asst. chief of engrs., U.S. Army, 1917-18; detailed on General Staff and chief of section, Sept. 1918-June 1920; spl. mission to Adriatic and Balkan countries, 1919; pres. Alaska Road Commn., 1920-27, also chief engr., 1924, 27; dist. and acting div. engr. for rivers and harbors, Alaska Dist., 1921-27; cons. engr. Dept. Commerce, 1921-27, also for Ty. of Alaska, 1921-23; mem. spl. commn. to investigate Russian, Japanese, and Am. fur seal rookeries, June-Sept. 1922; dir. pub. works, Alaska, 1923-27; chmn. Alaska R.R., 1923-24, also chief engr., Mar.-Oct. 1923; with Gulf Oil Corp. as gen. mgr. foreign subsidiary co., 1927-32; chmn. bd. and pres. Guajillo Corp. and affiliated cos., 1932-41; pres. Slate Creek Placers, Inc., 1936-41; recalled to active duty, Corps of Engrs., U.S. Army, detailed as asst. engr. of maintenance, Panama Canal, and asst. to 2d v.p. Panama Ry. Co., Jan. 1941-Mar. 1946; asst. to Gov., Panama Canal and asst. to pres., Panama Ry. Co., 1946-47; cons. engr. N. Am. Car Corp., 1947-50; lieutenant gen. a.d.c. to Gov. of Alaska, 1953-55; Brig., general, a.d.c., Alaska National Guard, 1935-37. In charge Pres. Harding's tour of Alaska, 1923. Trustee Dickinson College, 1919-—, Amelia S. Givin Free Library, 1921-—. Fellow Royal Geog. Soc. (London), Am. Geog. Soc., A.A.A.S.; mem. Am. Soc. C.E. (life), Soc. Am. Mil. Engrs., Phi Beta Kappa, Phi Kappa Sigma, Am. Legion. Decorated Distinguished Service Medal, Legion of Merit (U.S.); Distinguished Service Medal, 2d Class (Panamanian); Officer, later Comdr. Order of Prince Danilo I, and silver medal for bravery (Montenegrin); Croix de Guerre, 2d Class (Grecian); Officer of Public Instruction (French); Khamés de l'Ahal Saxaoul, French Sahara; Knight of Order of Compassionate Heart, Comdr. Imperial Order of St. Nicholas (Russia); Interallied Victory Medal, American Defense Medal with star, and American Theatre Medal (U.S.); specially commended in Senate and House of Rep. of United States, and salary raised by spl. act of Congress, 1926; mil. road from Fairbanks, Alaska, to Yukon River at Circle officially named Steese Highway by War Dept. Del. U.S. Govt. to XIV Internat. Navigatn. Congress, Cairo, Egypt, 1926 (sec. Am. sect.), XV Internat. Navigatn. Cong., Venice, Italy, 1931, XVI Cong., Brussels, Belgium, 1935 XVII Congress, Lisbon 1949 XVIII Congress, Rome Italy, 1953; delegate International Geographic Congress, Paris, France, 1931, XVI Cong., Lisbon, 1949; del. U.S. Govt. to 5th Internat. Congress of Surveyors, London, Eng., 1934 (chmn. Am. section), to Internat. Geog. Congress, Warsaw, Poland, 1934 (pres. sec. I-cartography), to 4th Internat. Congress and Expn. of Photogrammetry, Paris, France, 1934 declined), to Second World Petroleum Congress, Paris, 1937, Internat. Geog. Congress, Amsterdam, Netherlands, 1938. Republican. Episcopalian. Mason (33 deg.), Elk. Clubs: Army and Navy (Washington); West Point Army Mess; University (N.Y.). Author of numerous articles in tech. periodicals and daily press. Address: Mt. Holly Springs, Cumberland County, Pa. Died Jan. 11, 1958.

STEICHEN, EDWARD, photographer, artist, plant breeder; b. Luxembourg, Mar. 27,21879; s. Jean Pierre and Marie (Kemp) S.; came to U.S., 1880; hon. M.A., Wesleyan U., Conn., 1942; A.F.D., U. Wis., 1957, U. Hartford, 1960, Lincoln Coll., 1962; L.H.D., Bard Coll., 1966; hon. degree Fairfield (Conn.) U., 1967; m. Clara Smith, 1903; children—Mary (Mrs. F. Calderone), Kate Rodina; m. 2d, Dana Glover, 1923 (dec. 1957); m. 3d, Joanna Taub, March 1960. One of the first to realize the possibilities of the "new photography" and has produced many notable plates; has exhibited photographs and paintings at the great art centres of America and Europe; retrospective exhbn. photographs Mus. Modern Art, N.Y.C., 1961; paintings in Luxembourg (Paris), Met. Mus. (N.Y.C.), Whitney Mus. Am. Art, Portland Mus. Art, Toledo Mus. Art, numerous pvt. collections; chief photographer Conde Nast Publs., 1923-38; dir. dept. photography Mus. Modern Art, N.Y.C., 1947-62, dir. dept. emeritus, 1962-73. Made photographic mural decoration, subject aviation, in New Roxy Theatre, Radio City, N.Y.C., Commd. Photographic Div., Air Service, U.S. Army, World War I, with A.E.F., rank lt. col. Decorated Chevalier Legion d'Honneur (France). Served as capt., USNR, World War II; commd. U.S. Navy combat photography, dir. Navy Photographic Inst. Decorated D.S.M., Presdl. Medal of Freedom; grand officer de l'Ordre de Merit (Luxembourg). Directed making Road to Victory exhbn. for Museum of Modern Art, 1942; Power in the Pacific, 1944; supervised the photography of film, Fighting Lady. Recipient Ann. Advt. award, 1937; Fine Arts medal A.I.A., 1950; achievement award U.S. Camera Mag., 1949, Photography Mag., 1952; Internat. award Photog. Soc. Am., 1957; Silver Progress medal Royal Photog. Soc. (Eng.), 1960; spl. award Am. Soc. Mag. Photographers, 1961; Presdl. medal of freedom, 1963; Internat. Photog. Exposition award, 1965; award of merit medal Lotos Club, N.Y.C., 1965. Began cross-breeding of flowers, specializing in delphinium, 1910; one-man flower exhibit. Mus. Modern Art, 1936. Hon. pres. Am. Delphinium Soc.; hon. fellow Royal Photog. Soc. Great Britain, Photo. Soc. America. Created for Mus. Modern Art the Family of Man exhibition, 1955; recipient awards from Newspaper Guild, Am. Soc. Mag. Photographers, Phila. Mus. Art Urban League. Author: A Life in Photography, 1963. Editor: Sandburg Photographers View Carl Sandburg, 1966. Home: West Redding CT Died Mar. 25, 1973.

STEIGERS, WILLIAM CORBET soldier, newspaperman; b. St. Louis, Sept. 15, 1845. Served in 8th Mo. Regt., later sergt. U.S. Signal Corps, Civil War; discharged for physical disability after siege of Vicksburg. Joined St. Louis Dispatch, 1868, and in 1878, when the paper was consolidated with the Post as St. Louis Post-Dispatch, became adv. mgr.; business mgr. and v.p. same, 1898-—. Died May 25, 1923.

STEINBACH, MILTON, business exec.; b. New Haven, 1902; s. Abdul D. and Ray (Hoffman) S.; grad. Phillips Andover Acad., 1920; grad. Yale, 1924; m. Ruth Adler, Dec. 8, 1925. Partner Wertheim & Co., N.Y.C., 1933-70; dir. Armour & Co., Baldwin-Lima-Hamilton Corp., Barber Oil Corp., Greyhound Corp. Gov. N.Y. Stock Exchange, 1964-69. Asso. treas. Fedn. Jewish Philanthropies N.Y. Trustee Mt. Sinai Hosp.; pres. Mt. Sinai Sch. Medicine; charter trustee Phillips Acad., Andover, Mass. Served as maj. AUS, 1942-45. Clubs: Harmonie (N.Y.C.); Century Country. Home: Rye NY Died Dec. 1970.

STEINER, ROBERT EUGENE lawyer; b. near Greenville, Ala., May 9, 1862; s. Joseph and Margaret Matilda (Camp) S.; A.B., U. of Ala., 1880, A.M., 1881, LL.D., 1919; LL.B., Harvard, 1884; m. May Flowers, Dec. 16, 1884. Practiced in Greenville, 1884-92, since at Montgomery; mem. Steiner, Crum & Weil (now Steiner, Crum & Baker), 1905-—; dir. and gen. counsel, Western Ry. of Ala.; dir. and Ala. atty. Central of Ga. Ry.; counsel aa Montgomery for Gulf, Mobile & Ohio R.R. Co., The Seaboard Air Line; dist. atty. for Alabama for L.&N. R.R. Co. Mem. Ala. House of Representatives, 1886, Senate, 1892; city atty., Montgomery, 1895; del. Dem. Nat. Conv., St. Louis, 1904; v. chmn. Ala. State Docks Commission. Served as capt. Greenville Guards and maj. 2d Regt. Ala. N.G.; raised regt. of cav., 1916, apptd. col., and served with it on Mexican border; promoted brig. gen., N.G., Mar. 19, 1917; brig. gen. U.S. Army, Aug. 5, 1917, and comdg. 62d Inf. Brig., 31st Div.; went to France in command 62d Inf. Brig., returned in command of 31st Div. Reapptd. brig. gen. N.G. Ala., 1919, also brig. gen. on reserve, by President, Aug. 1919. Mem. Sigma Nu. Methodist. Mason; Odd Fellow; K.P. Club: Beauvoir Country (Montgomery). Home: 220 S. Hull St. Office: First Nat. Bank Bldg., Montgomery 1, Ala. Died Sept. 26, 1955; buried Montgomery.

STEINLE, ROLAND JOSEPH, lawyer; born Milw., Mar. 21, 1896; s. Joseph L. and Elizabeth (Baldauf) S.; student Marquette Coll. Law, 1920; m. Helen Sharpe, May 3, 1923; (dec. Dec. 1953); children—Roland Joseph, Betty (Mrs. David Labissoniere), Rosemary (Mrs. Joseph McCarthy); m. 2d, Nancy Sharpe, Decmeber 28, 1963. Admitted to Wis., bar, 1920; practice, Milw., 1920-40, 58-66; spl. asst. dist. atty. Milw. County, 1923-24, Forest County, 1925-26, County, Waukesha 1938-39, Dodge County, 1937; ct. commnr. Milw. County, 1937-40; circuit judge 2d Judicial Circuit Wis., 1940-54; asso. justice Wis. Supreme Ct. 1954-58; conciliator Circuit Ct. Milw. County, from 1958; instr. jurisprudence Marquette U., 1928-53; chmn. Bd. Circuit Judges Wis., 1946. Wis. chmn. Nat. Conf. Christians and Jews, 1956-57; twice mem. awards jury Freedom's Found. Chmn. Milw. County Republican Com., 1934-35; Rep. candiate lt. gov. Wis., 1936; Rep. candidate U.S. Senator from Wisconsin, 1958. Served from 2d lt. to 1st lt., inf., U.S. Army, 1917-18. Recipient Distinguished Service medal Vets. Fgn. Wars, 1928, citation Nat. Conf. Christians and Jews, 1956. Mem. Wis., Milw. (past pres.) bar assns., Am. Legion (1st judge adv. Wis.). K.C. (past dist. dep.), Cath. Knights Wis. (past v.p., dir.), Elk, Eagle, Moose. Home: Milwaukee WI Died Dec. 22, 1966.

STEINMAN, JAMES HALE newspaper pub.; b. Lancaster, Pa., Oct. 22, 1886; s. Andrew Jackson and Caroline Morgan (Hale) S.; A.B., Yale, 1908; LL.B., U. of Pa., 1911; LL.D., Franklin and Marshall College, 1946; m. Louise McClure Tinsley, Feb. 2, 1922; children—Louise Tinsley (Mrs. T. Peter Ansberry), Caroline Morgan Hale (Mrs. Thomas B. Nunan), Beverly Randolph. Asso. with brother as pub. Lancaster New Era, Intelligencer-Journal and Lancaster Sunday News since 1911; pres. Lancaster Newspapers, Inc., Steinman Development Co., Steinman Stations; dir. Hamilton Watch Co.; mem. Pa. State Planning Bd.; chmn. Defense Council of Lancaster Co., 1940-44. Dir. printing and pub. div. WPB, 1944-46. Admitted to Pa. bar, 1911. Dir. Lancaster County Civil Defense, 1951-52. Mem. bd. trustees Franklin and Marshall Coll., chmn. bd. trustees Henry G. Long Home. Served as asst. adj., div. adj. and lt. col. U.S. Army, 1917-19, in France, July 1918-Aug. 1919. Mem. Lancaster Bar Assn., Soc. of Colonial Wars, Pa. S.R., Am. Newspaper Pubs. Assn. (dir., treas.; dir. bur. advt. 1950-—), Soc. Colonial Wars, Psi Upsilon. Episcopalian. Clubs: Yale, Racquet (N.Y.C.); Metropolitan, Chevy Chase, The 1925 F Street, Press, Army and Navy (Washington); Hamilton; Lancaster Country; Porcupine, Bath and Tennis (Everglades, Fla.); Lyford Cay (Nassau); Travellers (Paris). Home: 1616 Marietta Pike. Office: 8 W. King St., Lancaster, Pa. Died Dec. 31, 1962; buried Woodward Hill Cemetery.

STELLE, CHARLES CLARKSON (stel), govt. official; b. Peking, China. Oct. 25, 1910; s. William Bergen and Elizabeth (Sheffield) S.; ed. Phillips Acad. (Andover, Mass.), 1925-27; student, Amherst Coll., 1927-30, Coll. of Chinese Studies, Peking, 1932-34; A.B., U. of Chicago, 1936, Ph.D., 1938; Rockefeller Found. fellow, Harvard, 1938-40; m. Jane Elizabeth Kellogg; 1 son, Kellogg Sheffield. Sec., Harvard-Yenching Inst., China, 1940-41; with Office of Strategic Services, 1941-43; chief, div. of research for Far East, U.S. Dept. of State, 1946-48; acting chief director international and functional intelligence, 1950; deputy director Office Intelligence Research, 1951; member Policy Planning Staff, 1951-56, dep. assistant sec. state for policy planning, 1956-57, counselor of American Embassy, Tehran, 1957-60; dep. U.S. rep. 10-Nation Disarmament Conf., 1960; acting U.S. rep. to Nuclear Test Ban Conf., 1960; dep. U.S. representative 18-Nation Disarmament Conference, personal rank of ambassador, 1962. Served with U.S. Army, India, Burma, China, 1943-46. Awarded Bronze Star with oak leaf cluster. Mem. Phi Beta Kappa, Delta Tau Delta. Clubs: Metropolitan, Kenwood Golf and Country. Office: U.S. Dept. of State, Washington 25. Died June 11, 1964; buried Arlington Nat. Cemetery.

STELLE, JOHN comdr. Am. Legion; b. McLeansboro, Ill., Aug. 10, 1891; student Western Mil Acad., Alton, Ill., and Washington U. Law Sch.; m. Wilma Wiseheart, 1912; children—Lt. John Albert, Lt. Russell. Admitted to Ill. bar; asst. state treas. of Ill., 1913-31; asst. state auditor, 1933-34; state treas., 1934-36; elected lt. gov., 1936; on the death of Gov. Henry Horner, Oct. 6, 1940, became gov. of Ill. and served for the unexpired term to Jan. 1941. Pres. Arketex Ceramic Corp. (Brazil, Ind.), Evansville (Ind.) Coals Co., Inc., McLeansboro Creamery, McLeansboro Shale Products Co., Cahokia Race Track, East St. Louis, Ill.; owner Stelle Farm. Helped organize Dem. Service Men's Orgn., 1926. Enlisted in U.S. Army, spring 1917, served as 1st lt. Co. B, 115th Machine Gun Battalion, 30th Div.; with

A.E.F., 17 months; wounded and gassed; disch. as capt., 1919. Elected comdr. Am. Legion, 1945. Address: McLeansboro, Ill. Died July 5, 1962; buried McLeansboro.

STELLWAGEN, SEITORDE MICHAEL (stel'wag-en), lawyer; b. St. Ignace, Mich., Dec. 2, 1890; s. Michael Frederick and Lillie Anderson (Pierson) S.; A.B., U. of Minn., 1915; LL.B., 1915; grad. student in law, Harvard, 1915-16; m. Elinor Walker Lynch, Aug. 20, 1918; 1 dau., Barbara Pierson. Admitted to Minn. bar, 1915, and practiced in Minneapolis; atty. for Alien Property Custodian, Washington, D.C., 1917-18, 1919-20; sec. Ry. Loan Advisory Com. to Federal Res. Bd., 1920-21; asso. with former atty. gen. of U.S., A. Mitchell Palmer, and others in practice of law since 1921; firm name Palmer, Stellwagen & Neale since 1939; prof. law, Knights of Columbus Law Sch., Washington, D.C., 1924-25, Columbus U., Washington, D.C., since 1938; counsel Tacna-Arica Plebiscitary Commn., Arica, Chile, 1926. Served as private and 2d lt. field arty., U.S. Army, 1918-19. Trustee Legal Aid Bur. Dist. of Columbia. Mem. Am. Dist. of Columbia, and Federal bar assns., Am. Legion, Alpha Delta Phi, Phi Delta Phi. Democrat. Methodist. Club: Cosmos (Washington, D.C.). Home: 5124 Loughboro Road N.W., Washington 16. Office: 815 15th St. N.W., Washington 5, D.C. Died Nov. 25, 1946.

STEMBEL, ROGER NELSON rear admiral U.S.N., retired; b. Middleton, Md., Dec. 27, 1810; entered navy, midshipman, Mar. 27, 1832; was in cruiser Porpoise, wrecked near Vera Cruz, 1833; on duty, naval school, New York, 1834-38; passed midshipman, June 23, 1838; lt., Oct. 23, 1843; on coast survey until 1847; then on various stations until beginning of Civil war; fitted out gunboats at Cincinnati and served in Mississippi River flotilla; commanded river gunboat Lexington; was in numerous engagements; commanded Cincinnati, which was sunk in action with rams at Fort Pillow, when he was seriously wounded; commd. capt. July 25, 1866, commodore July 13, 1870; retired Dec. 27, 1872; promoted rear admiral on retired list, June 5, 1874. Home: Washington, D.C. Died 1900.

STEPHENS, ALEXANDER HAMILTON Confederate govt. ofcl., congressman; b. Wilkes County (later Taliaferro County), Ga., Feb. 11, 1812; s. Andrew and Margaret (Grier) S.; grad. U. Ga., 1832. Admitted to Ga. bar, 1834; elected to Ga. Legislature, 1836-40, 42; mem. U.S. Ho. of Reps. from Ga., 28th-35th congresses, 1843-59, opposed dispatch of troops to Rio Grande in 1846, Wilmot Proviso and Clayton Compromise, 1848, supported Compromise of 1850 while proclaiming right of secession of any state; always Whig by convenience, repudiated Whig nat. ticket, 1852, joined Democratic party soon after; friend of Stephen Douglas, supported Kan.-Neb. Act of 1854, had major role in securing its passage in Congress; defended slavery in many speeches in 1850's; following election of Lincoln in 1860 urged moderation and secession only as last resort; as del. from Ga. attended convention in Montgomery (Ala.) to frame constn. for Confederacy, elected v.p. of Confederacy by Provisional Congress, Feb. 9, 1861, became leader opposition to Davis government, against conscription, suspension of habeas corpus, and local mil. govts.; attempted peace negotiations with Lincoln, June 1863, met Lincoln and Seward near Fortress Monroe but unable to agree on peace terms, Feb. 3, 1865; elected to U.S. Senate, Jan. 1866, denied entrance; denied power of Fed. Govt. to enfranchise Negroes; purchased interest in newspaper The Southern Sun, 1871, opposing fusion of Liberal Republicans and Democrats in 1872; elected to United States House of Representatives from Ga., 43d-47th congresses, 1873-82; elected gov. of Ga., 1882; published A Constitutional View of the Late War Between the States, 1870, expounding doctrines of state sovereignty; wrote sch. history A Compendium of the History of The United States, 1872. Died Atlanta, Ga., Mar. 4, 1883.

STEPHENS, CLYDE HARRISON business exec.; b. Burlington, Ia., July 1, 1890; s. Thornton Lemuel Louvarie Hulda (Owens) S.; ed. pub. schs. Burlington, Ia.; m. Estelle Uttry, Nov. 18, 1914; children—Clyde H., Jr., Ruth F. (Mrs. R. F. O'Neill), Mark, Hugh, George, Patricia (Mrs. P. C. Wolfe), Joan M., Thomas T., James R. V.p. Phila. Reading Coal & Iron Co. Served with U.S. Army in France, World War I; discharged as capt., F.A. Mem. Mil. Order World Wars (Monmouth chpt., N.J.), Nat. Rifle Assn. (life). Republican. Baptist. Clubs: Downtown Athletic (N.Y.C.); Red Bankers (Red Bank, N.J.); Manasquan River Golf (Brielle, N.J.). Home: 223 Trenton Blvd., Sea Girt, N.J. 08750. Office: 721 Reading Terminal Bldg., 12th and Market Sts., Phila. 5. Died Sept. 13, 1965.

STEPHENS, LEROY denominational sec.; b. at Whitely, Greene Co., Pa., Jan. 20, 1841; s. Washington and Joanna (Steel) S.; B.A., Bucknell U., Pa., 1868, M.A., 1871; grad. Crozer Theol. Sem., Chester, Pa., 1871; (D.D., Bucknell, 1891); m. Mary A. Hakes, of Worcester, Mass., Sept. 26, 1871 (died Mar. 1892); 2d, Nanna J. Wilson, of Beaver Falls, Pa., Dec. 25, 1895. Volunteered for 100 days' service in Union Army, July 18, 1864; sergt. Capt. Bruce Lambert's Independent Cav.; hon. discharged, Nov. 25, 1864. Ordained Bapt. ministry, 1871; pastor Morgantown, W.Va., 1871-72, Mt. Pleasant, Pa., 1872-79; pres. Mt. Pleasant Inst., 1879-94; sec. Pa. Bapt. Ministerial Edn. Soc., 1894-—. Trustee Bucknell U. Address: Lewisburg, Pa.

STEPHENSON, BENJAMIN congressman; b. Ky. Moved to Ill. Territory, 1809, settled in Randolph County; apptd. 1st sheriff Randolph County by Gov. Edwards, 1809; moved to Edwardsville, Ill., became mcht.; apptd. adjutant gen. Ill. Territory, 1813; served as col. in 2 campaigns during War of 1812; mem. U.S. Congress (Democrat) from Ill. Territory, 13th-14th congresses; receiver public moneys Land Office, Edwardsville, 1816-22; del. conv. to frame 1st Ill. Constn., 1818; pres. Bank of Edwardsville, 1819. Died Edwardsville, Oct. 10, 1822.

STEPHENSON, BENJAMIN FRANKLIN physician, assn. founder; b. Wayne County, Ill., Oct. 3, 1823; s. James and Margaret (Clinton) S.; grad. Rush Med. Coll., Chgo., 1850; m. Barbara B. Moore, Mar. 30, 1855, at least 3 children. Lectr. on gen., spl., surg. anatomy in med. dept. State U. of Ia., Keokuk, 1855-57; joined 14th Ill. Volunteers, 1861, regtl. surgeon, mustered out, 1864; a founded Grand Army of Republic (nat. assn. Union vets.), organized Post Number 1, Decatur, Ill., 1866, issued the call for a nat. conv. to meet at Indianapolis, Ind., 1866, became adjutant-gen.; monument erected in his honor, Washington, D.C., 1909. Died Aug. 30, 1871.

STEPHENSON, C(HARLES) S. naval officer, ins. exec.; b. Aetna, Tenn., May 21, 1887; M.D., Vanderbilt, 1912; M.S., Columiba, 1932; Army Indsl. War Coll., 1936; D.Sc., Duke, 1944; m. Naomi A. Ackley; children—Stephen G., Suzanne Florence. Instr. Peiping, 1927; Medical Corps, U.S. Navy, 1913-36; capt. in charge div. preventive medicine, Bur. Med. and Surgery, Navy Dept., 1936-42, rear 1942-—, now ret.; head dept. hygiene and preventive medicine U.S. Naval Medical School, 1936-44; lectr. Johns Hopkins U., 1940-48; v.p., med. dir. United Services Life Ins. Co., Washington; liaison officer, sec. for health relations USPHS; naval observer, Am. embassy (London, Eng.). Adv. councilor USPHS; div. health and safety TVA; dir. U.S. Typhus Commn.; liaison officer, med. sciences div. NRC; mem. Fed. Interdept. Safety Council, Interdept. com. Venereal Diseases; med. dir. D.A.V.; mem. adv. scientific bd. Gorgas Meml. Inst. of Tropical and Preventive Medicine. Decorated Order Purple Heart, 1918; awarded U.S. Typhus Commn. medal, 1944, Legion of Merit, Gorgas medal, 1951. Acting mng. dir. Am. Cancer Soc., Inc., 1945. Mem. Soc. Tropical Medicine, Public Health Assn., Am. Med. Assn., Am. Physicians, Social Hygiene Assn., Royal Soc. Health. Author numerous sci. papers. Editor, Science, 1944 (resigned). Retired for physical disability incurred in line of duty, 1944. Home: 4457 Q St. N.W., Washington 30007. Died Feb. 9, 1965; buried Arlington Nat. Cemetery.

STEPHENSON, FRANKLIN BACHE physician; b. Greenville, Pa., Mar. 28, 1848; s. Robert Gibson and Jane Welch (Porter) S.; A.B., Allegheny (Pa.) Coll., 1870, A.M., 1873; M.D., U. of Pa., 1873; (LL.D., Bucknell U., Pa., 1905); m. Rosalie Carnes Wilson, g.d. late Commodore Joseph Wilson, U.S.N., of Boston, Nov. 21, 1882. Entered med. corps U.S.N., Mar. 14, 1873; promoted through the various grades to med. insp. with rank of comdr. and retired, Jan. 3, 1903. Frequent contbr. to med. and secular press; translator from the French, German, Latin, Greek, Russian, Finnish, Japanese, Spanish, Italian, Portuguese, Dutch, Swedish. Life mem. Asiatic Soc. Japan, Société d'Anthropologie de Paris; mem. Am. Academy Arts and Sciences, Acad. Natural Sciences Phila., Mass. Med. Soc., Phi Beta Kappa. Mason (K.T.). Home: Claremont, Cal.

STEPHENSON, S(EYMOUR) TOWN physicist; born San Jose, Calif., Nov. 28, 1910; s. Rufus Town and Mary Eliza (Baldwin) Stephenson; B.A., DePauw Univ., 1930, D.Sc. (honorary), 1951; Ph.D., Yale, University, 1933; married Mildred May McFall, Sept. 7, 1933; children—David Town, John Rufus, Robert Bruce, Mary Elizabeth. Teaching fellow DePauw U., 1929-30, Yale 1931-32; mem. faculty Wash. State Univ., 1933-42, 47-—, prof., chmn. div. phys. Sciences, 1947-52, professor, dean faculty, 1950-64, academic vice president, 1964. Nat. Defense Research com. of U.S. O.S.R.D., 1942-45; spl. consultant U.S. Navy Radio and Sound Lab., 1945. Mem. Wash. State Weather Modification Bd. Recipient Certificate of Appreciation from War and Navy Depts., 1948. Fellow Am. Phys. Soc.; mem. Soc. Sigma Xi, Phi Beta Kappa, Delta Tau Delta. Methodist. Contbr. articles and abstracts on x-ray spectroscopy. Home: 1814 D St., Pullman, Wash. 99163. Died Dec. 15, 1964; buried City Cemetery, Pullman.

STEPHENSON, WILLIAM surgeon U.S.A.; b. in Me., Mar. 3, 1856; M.D., Coll. Phys. and Surg. (Columbia), 1880. Apptd. asst. surgeon U.S.A., Dec. 3, 1883; capt. asst. surgeon, Dec. 3, 1888; maj. brigade surgeon vols., June 4, 1898; hon. discharged vols., Apr. 30, 1899; maj. surgeon and maj. Med. Corps, U.S.A., Apr. 28, 1900; lt. col., May 1, 1908; col., Apr. 12, 1912. Duty at Central Dept., Chicago, 1916-17. Address: War Dept., Washington, D.C.

STEPHENSON, WILLIAM BENJAMIN lawyer; b. Newport, R.I., Sept. 15, 1915; s. William Henry and Maud Josephine (Stephenson) S.; student San Diego State Coll., 1932-33; B.A., U. Hawaii, 1935; LL.B., U. Mich., 1938; m. Ellen Foster Rhea, Aug. 2, 1941; 1 son, John William. Instr. U. Hawaii, 1938-40; admitted to bar, Hawaii, 1939, U.S. Supreme Ct., 1948; practice of law, Honolulu, 1938-—; exec., counsel Territorial Commn. on Subversive Activities, 1950-52, chmn., 1953-—; dist. magistrate Dist. of Wahiawa, Oahu, 1952-59. Sec., dir. Honolulu Mortgage Co., Ltd. Served as officer USNR, 1941-46; capt. res. Mem. Bar Assn. Hawaii (pres. 1955), Am. Bar Assn. (ho. of dels. 1955), U.S. Naval Inst., U. Hawaii Found., Phi Kappa Phi. Home: 4000 Old Pali Rd., Honolulu 96817. Office: 235 Queen St., Honolulu 96813. Died Sept. 8, 1964; buried Nat. Cemetery of Pacific.

STERETT, ANDREW naval officer; b. Balt., Jan. 27, 1778; s. John and Deborah (Ridgley) S. Commd. lt. U.S. Navy, 1798; exec. officer frigate Constellation at capture of Insurgente; given command schooner Enterprise, 1800, captured L'amour de la Patrie in West Indies, 1800; commanded the Enterprise during Tripolitan War in Mediterranean, 1801, greatest exploit was capture of ship Tripoli due to superior maneuvering, 1801; received a commendation and a sword from U.S. Congress; promoted master comdt., placed in command of brig. under constrn., Balt.; resigned to enter U.S. Mcht. Marine, 1805; U.S. destroyer named for him. Died Lima, Peru, Jan. 9, 1807.

STERETT, SAMUEL congressman; b. Carlisle, Pa., 1758; grad. U. Pa. Held several local offices, Balt.; mem. independent mil. co. of Balt. mchts., 1777; apptd. pvt. sec. to pres. of Congress, 1782; mem. Md. Senate, 1789; mem. U.S. Ho. of Reps. (Anti-Federalist) from Md., 2d Congress, 1791-93; sec. Md. Soc. for Promoting Abolition of Slavery, 1791; mem. Balt. Com. of Safety, 1812; served as capt. independent company at Battle of North Point, 1814; wounded at Battle of Bladensburg; grand marshal at laying of found. stone of B. & O. R.R., 1828. Died Balt., July 12, 1833; buried burying ground Westminster Ch.

STERN, EDGAR BLOOM born New Orleans, Louisiana, January 23, 1886; son Maurice and Hanna (Bloom) S.; prep. edn., McDonogh high sch., New Orleans; student Tulane U., 1902-03; B.A., Harvard, 1907, M.A., 1908; m. Edith Rosenwald, June 29, 1921; children—Edgar Bloom, Jr., Audrey, Philip Maurice. Treasurer Lehman, Stern and Company, Ltd., 1911-36; dir. Sears Roebuck & Co.; chmn. WDSU Broadcasting Corp. Chmn. bd. trustees Dillard U.; trustee Tulane Univ., Howard Memorial Library; trustee Julius Rosenwald Fund, 1932-48. Mem. Charter Revision Com. City of New Orleans, 1951-52; chairman development committee United Fund, 1952; mem. Pres.'s Com. Edn. Beyond High Sch., 1956-58. Member New Orleans School Board, 1912; member bd., State Charity Hosp., 1912-16; pres. New Orleans Association Commerce, 1915; trustee Tuskegee Institute, 1924-34; president New Orleans Community Chest, 1927; president New Orleans Cotton Exchange, 1927, 28; dir. New Orleans Municipal Pub. Belt R.R., 1916-19; Class A dir. Federal Reserve Bank of Atlanta, 1917, 18; director New Orleans Parkway Com., 1929-34; mem. Public Welfare Commn. of La., 1940-41; chairman Economic Development Committee of Louisiana, 1942-43; liaison officer to Bd. of Economic Warfare, Office of Production Management, 1941; chmn. transportation com. War Production Board, 1942; mem. College Grants Adv. Com. Ford Found. 1955; chmn., Mayor's Advisory Com. City of New Orleans. Captain Ordnance Department, United States Army, 1918-19. Times-Picayune Loving Cup Civic Award, 1931. Member Phi Beta Kappa. Jewish religion. Clubs: Metairie Country, New Orleans Country, Lakewood Country; Recess, Harvard (N.Y.C.); Stockbridge (Mass.) Golf; Century Country (White Plains, N.Y.). Home: 11 Garden Lane. Office: 521 Royal St., New Orleans. Died Aug. 24, 1959; buried Metairie Cemetery, New Orleans.

STERN, HENRY ROOT lawyer; b. N.Y.C., Sept. 22, 1882; s. Simon Hunt and Sara Stern; grad. Phillips (Andover) Acad., 1899; A.B., Yale, 1903; LL.B., M.A., Columbia, 1906; m. Elsie Weston Lazarus, Apr. 29, 1909 (dec. July 1947); 1 son, Henry Root. Admitted to N.Y. bar, 1905; pvt. practice of law, 1906-—; counsel to Sprague and Stern, Mineola, N.Y.; counsel Mudge, Stern, Baldwin & Todd (formerly Mudge, Stern, Williams & Tucker), N.Y.C. Mem. N.Y. Temporary Emergency Relief Adminstrn., 1932-34; chmn. N.Y. Bd. Social Welfare, 1946-54. Treas. N.Y. Rep. State Com., 1934-36; permanent pres. Electoral Coll. N.Y. State. Served from first lieutenant to captain, 311th Infantry, U.S. Army, 1918. Decorated D.S.C. Mem. Am., N.Y. State, Nassau Co. bar assns., Assn. Bar City N.Y., N.Y. County Lawyers Assn., Psi Upsilon. Clubs: Yale, Broad Street, Regency, Adventurers (N.Y.C.). Home: Old Court House Rd., New Hyde Park, L.I. Office: 220 Old Country Rd., Mineola, N.Y. Died May 4, 1959.

STERN, HORACE, judge; b. Phila., Pa., Aug. 7, 1878; s. Morris and Matilda (Bamberger) S.; A.B., Central High Sch., Phila., 1895; B.S., U. of Pa., 1899, LL.B., summa cum laude, 1902, LL.D., 1933; Hahnemann

Med. Coll., 1937 D.H.L., Dropsie Coll. Hebrew and Cognate Langs., 1948, Jewish Theological Seminary of America, 1956; LL.D., Pa. Mil. Coll., 1953, Temple University, 1954, Lafayette College, 1955, Villanova University, 1956; married Henrietta Pfaelzer, Feb. 12, 1906; 1 dau., Sophie S. (Mrs. Henry J. Friendly). Admitted to Pa. bar, 1902, practicing in Phila.; mem. Stern & Wolf, 1903-20; apptd. judge Court of Common Pleas, by Gov. Sproul, 1920, and elected to same office, 1922, term of 10 yrs.; pres. judge, 1924, reelected, 1932, term of 10 yrs.; elected justice Pa. Supreme Court, term 21 yrs., 1935; chief justice Supreme Court of Pa., 1952-56; lecturer University of Pennsylvania Law School, 1902-17; Trustee Dropsie College (vice president), University of Pennsylvania, Jewish Pub. Soc. Am. (v.p.); dir. Federation Jewish Charities of Phila. (honorary president). Maj. Ordnance Dept., U.S. Army, 1918-19. Mem. Am. Bar Assn., Pa. Bar Assn., Bar Assn. of Phila., Am. Judicature Soc., Am. Law Inst., Am. Acad. Polit. and Social Science, Hist. Soc. of Pa., Acad. Natural Sciences of Phila., Pennsylvania Society, Am. Jewish Hist. Soc., Am. Legion, Phi Beta Kappa, Beta Gamma Sigma, Order of the Coif. Republican. Mason. Clubs: Lawyers, Contemporary, Midday, Philobiblon, Univ. Home: Philadelphia PA Died Apr. 14, 1969.

STERN, JO. LANE soldier, lawyer; b. Caroline Co., Va., Dec. 23, 1848; s. L. and Elizabeth (Hall) S.; prep. edn., Fontaine Hill Acad., Caroline Co., and Squire's Sch., Richmond, Va.; B.P., Washington Coll. (now Washington and Lee U.), 1869, LL.B., 1870; unmarried. Admitted to Va. bar, 1870, and began practice in Caroline County; settled in Richmond, 1871; partner with Hon. James Lyons (mem. Confederate States Congress), 1872-79; chmn. State Council of Defense, 1918-19; mem. War History Commn. of Va. Served in C.S.A. of Northern Va. 3 yrs.; paroled at Richmond, May 2, 1865. Enlisted in Va. N.G., 1871, and actively identified with that organization for 51 yrs.; promoted through grades to lt. col. 1st Inf.; insp. gen., 1884-1918; acting adj. gen. Spanish-Am. War; adj. gen. and draft executive, World Wa, rank of brig. gen., 1918-22; retired as maj. gen., Mar. 15, 1922. Democrat. Compiler of Roster of Commissioned Officers of Va. Vols., 1871-1920; Reports A.G.O. and Selective Draft, 1918-21. Adj. gen. Army of Northern Va., Dept. U.C.V. Home: Richmond, Va. Died May 3, 1932.

STERNBERG, GEORGE MILLER brigadier gen. U.S.A.; b. Hartwick Sem., Otsego Co., N.Y., June 8, 1838; s. Levi (D.D.) and Margaret Levering (Miller) S.; bro. of Charles Hazelius S.; M.D., Coll. Phys. and Surg. (Columbia), 1860; (LL.D., U. of Mich., 1894, Brown U., 1896); m. Martha L. Pattison, 1869. Apptd. asst. surgeon U.S.A., May 28, 1861; capt. asst. surgeon, May 28, 1866; maj. surgeon, Dec. 1, 1875; lt. col. deputy surgeon-gen., Jan. 12, 1891; brig. gen. surgeon gen., May 30, 1893; retired June 8, 1902. His service began in the army of the Potomac, and later was in Dept. of the Gulf; at end of Civil War was in charge of U.S. Gen. Hosp., Cleveland, O.; served through cholera and yellow fever epidemics; had command of med. service in war with Spain, 1898; was mem. and sec. Havana Yellow Fever Commn. Nat. Bd. of Health, 1879. Author: Photo-Micrographs, and How to Make Them, 1883; Bacteria; Malaria and Malarial Diseases, 1884; Manual of Bacteriology, 1893; Text-Book of Bacteriology, 1895; Immunity, Protective Inoculations, and Serum-Therapy, 1897. Home: Washington, D.C. Died Nov. 3, 1915.

STERNE, THEODORE EUGENE, physicist; b. N.Y.C., Nov. 23, 1907; s. Eugene Washington and Dora (Kohn) S.; B.Sc., Princeton, 1928; Ph.D., Trinity Coll., Cambridge U., 1931; NRC fellow physics, Harvard and Mass. Inst. of Tech., 1931-33; M.A., Harvard, 1956; m. Grace Isabel DeRoo, Aug. 5, 1932; children—Theodore Drummond, John Robert; m. 2d Lois Cremins Isenberg, on Nov. 28, 1964. Research asso. Harvard Obs., 1933-34, astronomer, 1934-41, lecturer astrophysics, tutor Harvard, 1934-41, Simon Newcomb professor astrophysics, 1956-59; chief ballistician Ballistic Research Labs., Aberdeen Proving Ground, Md., 1946-56, chief spl. prob. br., 1941-45, comptng. lab., 1945-47, 52-53, term. ballistic lab., 1946-52, sci. adviser to dir., 1953-56; cons. operations research office Johns Hopkins, 1954-59; staff mem. Research Analysis Corp., 1961-65, Inst. Def. Analyses, Arlington, Va., 1965-70. Asso. director Astrophys. Obs., Smithsonian Instn., 1956-59; staff member of Johns Hopkins University Operations Research Office, Bethesda, Maryland, 1959-61, acting chief Air Def. division, 1960-61. Served from first lieut. to lieut. col., F.A., Ordnance Corps, AUS, 1941-46; col. Res. Fellow Am. Acad. Arts and Scis., A.A.A.S., Am. Physics Soc., Royal Astron. Soc.; mem. Am. Astron. Soc., Astron. Society of Pacific Operations Research Society of America, Cat Fanciers of Washington (pres. 1966-67), also Phi Beta Kappa, Sigma Xi. Club: Cosmos (Washington). Author: Introduction to Celestial Mechanics, 1960. Contbr. articles sci. jours., govt. publs. Home: Chevy Chase MD Died Feb. 6, 1970; buried Arlington Nat. Cemetery, Arlington VA

STETTEN, DEWITT surgeon; b. New York, N.Y., Jan. 22, 1881; s. Joseph and Bella (Rosenthal) S.; M.D., Coll. Physicians and Surgeons (Columbia), 1901; house staff German hosp., New York, 1901-03; studied Vienna, Prague and Breslau, 1904-05; m. Magdalen Ernst, Apr. 23, 1906; children—Margaret (Mrs. Maximilien Vanka), DeWitt, Jr.; m. 2d, Alice Mayer, May 5, 1930. Asst. and attdg. surgeon, German Dispensary, New York, 1905-11; anesthetist, German Hospital, New York, 1905-08; asso. surgeon German Hospital, later Lenox Hill Hospital, New York, 1908-21, actg. attending surgeon, 1921; attending surgeon Lenox Hill Hospital, 1922-46; Beth Israel Hospital, New York, 1930-33; cons. surgeon, Lenox Hill Hospital since 1946; instr. clin. surgery, Coll. Phys. and Surg., 1909-18; clin. prof. surgery, New York University Coll. of Medicine, 1931-46. Member Hospital Corps, 1st Batt., N.Y. Naval Milita, 1898-1902; 1st lt. M.R.C., U.S. Army, 1915-17, capt. 1917-18, maj. M.C., U.S. Army, 1918-19. With Neurol. Sch., U. of Pa., Sept.-Dec. 1917; asst. chief and acting chief of surg. service U.S. Army Gen. Hosp. No. 1, Williamsbridge, N.Y., Jan.-Oct. 1918; chief of surg. service U.S. Army Embarkation Hosp. No. 4, New York, 1918-19; acting comdg. officer same, Feb. 13-22, 1919. Fellow Am. Coll. Surgeons, A.M.A., New York Acad. Medicine, N.A.D., Am. Geog. Soc.; mem. Nat. Audubon Soc., Internat. Soc. of Gastro-Enterology, Am. Gastro-Enterol. Assn., Am. Assn. Thoracic Surgery, Nat. Tuberculosis Assn., Am. Cancer Soc., Assn. Military Surgeons of U.S., A.A.A.S., Acad. Polit. Sci., Fgn. Policy Assn., Med. Soc. State of N.Y., Med. Soc. County of New York (pres. 1929, trustee, 1932-35, chmn. bd. 1935), New York Surg. Soc., N.Y. Soc. for Thoracic Surgery, N.Y. Gastro-Enterological Assn., N.Y. Pathol. Soc., Military Order of the World Wars, Am. Legion, etc. Pres. bd. trustees Blood Transfusion Assn. of New York; mem. and sec. bd. dirs. United Med. Service, Diplomate founders group Am. Bd. of Surgery. Club: Dachshund Club of America. Contbr. more than 90 papers on surgical subjects. Address: 850 Park Av., New York 21, N.Y.; (summer) White Bridge Farm, Rushland, Bucks County, Pa. Died Nov. 10, 1951.

STEUART, GEORGE HUME soldier; b. Baltimore, Aug. 24, 1828; grad. U.S. Mil. Acad., 1848; lt. 2d Dragoons, Nov. 1849; 1st lt., 1st cav., March 1855; capt., Dec. 1855. Resigned April 1861, and entered C.S.A.; lt. col. 1st Md. inf., June 1861, col., July 1861, brig. gen., March 1862; led cav. with Stonewall Jackson in advance upon Gen. Banks, and later in command of inf. brigade; wounded at Cross Keys, June 8, 1862; took part in attack on Culp's Hill, Gettysburg; defended the "bloody angle" at Battle of the Wilderness; taken prisoner, but exchanged some months later. Retired to private life after the war. Home: South River, Anne Arundel Co., Md. Died 1903.

STEVENS, AARON FLETCHER congressman; b. Londonderry, Rockingham County, N.H., Aug. 9, 1819; attended Pinkerton Acad., Derry, N.H., Crosby's Nashua (N.H.) Literary Inst.; studied law. Machinist's apprentice, journeyman for several years; admitted to bar, practiced law, Nashua; mem. N.H. Ho. of Reps., 1845, 76-84; held several local offices; served as maj. 1st Regt., N.H. Volunteer Inf. in Union Army during Civil War, also col. 13th N.H. Volunteer Inf., brevetted brig. gen.; del. Nat. Whig Conv., Balt., 1852; pres. Nashua Common Council, 1853-54; solicitor Hillsborough County, N.H., 1856-61; solicitor Nashua, 1859-60, 65, 72, 75-77; mem. U.S. Ho. of Reps. (Republican) from N.H., 40th-41st congresses, 1867-71. Died Nashua, May 10, 1887; buried Nashua Cemetery.

STEVENS, ALEXANDER RAYMOND, physician; b. Baltimore, May 9, 1876; s. George O. and Rebecca R. (Tibbetts) S.; A.B., Johns Hopkins, 1896, M.D., 1903; m. Mary Lane Davis, Oct. 25, 1919; 1 son, Alexander Raymond. Intern Johns Hopkins Hosp. (Baltimore) and Presbyn. Hosp. (N.Y. City), in practice in N.Y. City from 1909; mem. vis. staff Bellevue Hosp., 1909-37, attending surgeon in charge urol. dept., 1923-37; attending surgeon New York Hosp., also prof. urology Cornell U. Med. Sch., 1935-46; cons. urologist Bellevue, St. Vincent's, Beckman, St. Mary Immaculate (Jamaica), Tarrytown, Englewood, Stamford and Sharon hosps. Served as capt. to maj., Med. Corps, U.S. Army, France, 1917-19. Fellow A.C.S.; mem. A.M.A., Am. Urol. Assn., N.Y. Acad. Medicine. Club: Century (N.Y. City). Contbr. articles and chpts. on urologic surgery to med. publs. Home: Alstead NH Died June 1968.*

STEVENS, CLEMENT HOFFMAN army officer; b. Norwich, Conn., Aug. 21, 1821; s. Clement W. and Sarah J. (Fayssoux) S.; m. Annie Bee, several children. Designed and built battery on Morris Island (1st armored fortification ever constructed); elected col. 24th S.C. Inf., 1862; contributed greatly to Confederate victory at Secessionville, 1862; participated in Vicksburg Campaign, 1863; promoted brig. gen., 1864, commanded a Ga. brigade during Atlanta campaign. Killed at Battle of Peach Tree Creek (Ga.), July 25, 1864.

STEVENS, HAZARD lawyer; b. Newport, R.I., June 9, 1842; s. Gen. Isaac Ingalls and Margaret L. S.; Phillips Acad., Andover, Chauncy Hall Sch., Boston, and Harvard Coll., freshman yr.; (hon. A.M., Harvard, 1900); unmarried. First lt. adj. 79th N.Y. Inf., Aug.-Sept. 12, 1861; capt. a.-a.-g. vols., Oct. 16, 1861; maj., Oct. 13, 1864; hon. mustered out, Sept. 30, 1865. Bvtd.: lt. col. vols., Aug. 1, 1864, "for gallantry and distinguished services in campaign before Richmond"; col. vols., Oct. 19, 1864, "for gallant and meritorious services in battles of Winchester, Fishers Hill and Cedar Creek, Va."; brig. gen. vols., Apr. 2, 1865, for same before Petersburg, Va.; awarded Congressional Medal of Honor, June 13, 1894 "for having led a party that captured Ft. Huger, Va., Apr. 19, 1863." Admitted to bar, 1870; pres. Olympia (Wash.) Light & Power Co. Collector internal revenue, Washington Ty., 1868-70; commr. on British claim on San Juan Archipelago, 1874-75; mem. Mass. Ho. of Rep., 1885-86. Gold Democrat. Made 1st ascent of Mount Tacoma or Rainier, State of Washington, Aug. 17, 1870. Sec. Am. Free Trade League, 1901-03. Independent candidate for Congress, 10th Congressional Dist., Mass., 1908. Author: Life of Isaac Ingalls Stevens, 1900. Established a dairy farm ("Cloverfields Farm") at Olympia, Wash. Home: Olympia, Wash. Died Oct. 11, 1918.

STEVENS, HENRY LEONIDAS, JR., judge; b. Warsaw, N.C., Jan. 27, 1896; s. Henry Leonidas and Fannie (Walker) S.; grad. Porter Mil. Acad., Charleston, S.C., 1913; student U. of N.C., 1913-17, Harvard Law Sch., 1919-20; m. Mildred Anderson Beasley, June 21, 1922; 1 son, Henry Leonidas III. Admitted to N.C. bar, 1921; jr. mem. Stevens, Beasley & Stevens, 1921-27; mem. Beasley & Stevens since 1927. Judge county ct., 1929-31; nat. comdr. Am. Legion, 1931-32; pres. Am. Legion Pub. Co., 1931-32, now dir.; judge of Superior Court of N.C. (resident judge 4th Jud. Dist.), 1938-62, emergency judge N.C. for life, 1963-71. Served as lt. World War; in action St. Die sector and Meuse-Argonne; now lieut. colonel of Specialist Reserve. Mem. Golden Fleece, Phi Delta Phi, Kappa Sigma, La Societe des Quarante Hommes et Huit Chevaux, Society of the Cincinnati. Comdr. Legion of Honor (France); N.C. Mil. D.S.M., 1971; brevet col. N.C. N.G., 1971; hon. chief Blackfeet Indians. Democrat Presbyn. (elder). Mason, Jr. Order United Am. Mechanics. Clubs: Army and Navy (Washington, D.C.); Indianapolis Athletic; Harvard of N.C. Home: Warsaw NC Died Aug. 5, 1971; buried Devotional Gardens, Warsaw NC

STEVENS, ISAAC INGALLS territorial gov., congressman, army officer; b. Andover, Mass., Mar. 25, 1818; s. Isaac and Hannah (Cummings) S.; grad. U.S. Mil. Acad., 1839; m. Margaret Hazard, Sept. 8, 1841, 5 children. Commd. 2d lt. of engrs. U.S. Army; engaged in constrn. or repair of fortification on New Eng. coast; commd. 1st lt., 1840; engr. adjutant on Scott's staff in Mexico during Mexican War; at Battle of Contreras, siege of Vera Cruz, battles of Cerro Gordo, Churubusco, and Chapultepec, brevetted capt. and maj.; reassigned to engring. duties in coastal fortifications after war, 1848-49; apptd. exec. asst. in U.S. Coast Survey, 1849-53; gov. Wash. Territory, circa 1853-57, helped pacify Indians; dir. of exploration for No. route of Pacific Ry. surveys, 1853, determined navigability of Missouri and Columbia rivers; made treaties with Indians, 1854-55; concluded lasting peace with Blackfoot Indians, 1855; elected territorial del. to U.S. Congress, 1857; del. to Democratic Nat. Conv., Charleston, 1860; at outbreak of Civil War became col. 79th Regt. of N.Y. Volunteers (The Highlanders); promoted to brig. gen., 1861, maj. gen., 1862, Author: Campaigns of the Rio Grande and Mexico, 1851; Report of Exploration for a Route for the Pacific Railroad, 1855. Killed in action at Battle of Chantilly, Sept. 1, 1862; buried Island Cemetery, Newport, R.I.

STEVENS, JOHN Continental congressman; b. Perth Amboy, N.J., 1715. Mcht. and shipowner, in trade with West Indies and Madeira; large landowner and mine owner, Hunterdon, Union, Somerset counties (N.J.); mem. Gen. Colonial Assembly, 1751; active in raising troops and money for Crown Point in French and Indian War, 1755; helped build blockhouses at Drake's Ft., Normenach, Philipsburg; mem. def. com. to protect N.Y. and N.J. against Indian attacks; commr. to Indians, 1758; paymaster Col. Schuyler's Regt., the Old Blues, 1756-60; mem. com. of 4 who prevented issued of stamps under Stamp Act, N.Y.C., 1765; apptd. commr. to define boundary line between N.Y. and N.J., 1774; v.p. N.J. Council, 1770-82; pres. Council East Jersey Proprs., 1783; mem. Continental Congress from N.J., 1783-84; presided over N.J. Constl. Conv., 1787. Died Hoboken, N.J., May 10, 1792; buried Frame Meeting House Cemetery, Bethlehem Twp., Hunterdon County.

STEVENS, JOHN engr., inventor; b. N.Y.C., 1749; s. John and Elizabeth (Alexander) S.; grad. Columbia, 1768; m. Rachel Cox, Oct. 17, 1782, at least 7 children including John Cox, Robert Livingston, Edwin Augustus, Mary, Harriet. Studied law, 1768-71, apptd. an atty., N.Y.C., 1771; served from capt. to col., obtaining loans for Continental Army during Revolutionary War; loan commr. for Hunterdon County (N.J.); treas. N.J., 1776-79; surveyor gen. Eastern div. N.J., 1782-83; instrumental in framing 1st patent laws, 1790; became cons. engr. for Manhattan Co. (organized to furnish adequate water supply to N.Y.C.), circa 1800; became pres. Bergen Turnpike Co., 1802; received patent for multitubular boiler, 1803; his steamboat Little Juliana (operated by twin screw propellers) put into use on Hudson River, 1804; attempted to operate regular line of steamboats on Hudson between N.Y.C. and Albany and on other inland rivers, prevented by lawsuits; sent the Phoenix (1st sea-going steamboat in world) to Phila., 1809; built the Juliana, began regular ferry service, 1811; obtained 1st Am. railroad authorization from N.J. Assembly in 1815; authorized by Pa. Legislature to build Pa. R.R., 1823; designed, built exptl. locomotive on his estate in Hoboken, N.J. (1st Am.-made steam locomotive though never used for actual service), 1825; proposed a vehicular tunnel under the Hudson as well as an elevated railroad system for N.Y.C. Died Hoboken, Mar. 6, 1838.

STEVENS, LESLIE CLARK naval officer; b. Kearney, Neb., Feb. 19, 1895; s. Leslie and Amelia Jane (Phillips) S.; A.B., Neb. Wesleyan, 1913; grad. U.S. Naval Acad., 1918; M.Sc., Mass. Inst. of Tech., 1922, m. Nell Millikin, June 6, 1918; 1 son, Leslie Clark. Served in Queenstown destroyer forces, World War I; naval aviator, 1924; in U.S.S. Langley, 1925-26; in charge ship's installations Bur. of Aeronautics, Navy Dept., Washington, D.C., 1926-30; assembly and repair officer Naval Air Sta., San Diego, Calif., 1930-34; asst. naval attache for air, London, 1934-37; tech. adviser to London Disarmament Conf., 1936; in charge expts. and developments Bur. Aeronautics, 1937-44; staff, comdr. Aircraft Forward Area (Pacific), 1944; staff, comdr. Aircraft (Pacific), 1944-45; asst. chief Bur. Aeronautics for research development and engring., Washington, D.C., 1946-47; naval attaché and naval air attaché, Moscow, 1947-49; with Joint Chiefs of Staff, 1949-51; chmn. Am. Com. Liberation from Bolshevism, 1952-54; mem. national advisory com. for aeros., 1946-47. Advanced through grades to rear admiral, U.S. Navy, 1946, retired as vice admiral, 1951. Awarded: Legion of Merit, Bronze Star, Commendation Ribbon (United States); Commander Mil. Div. Order of British Empire (Eng.). Mem. Inst. Aero. Sci., Am. Anthrop. Assn., Archaeol. Inst. Am. Clubs: Explorers, New York Yacht (N.Y.C.); P.E.N., Army and Navy, Army-Navy Country (Washington). Author: Russian Assignment. Contbr. publs. Home: 213 King George St., Annapolis, Md. Died Nov. 30, 1956; buried Arlington Nat. Cemetery.

STEVENS, ROBERT SPROULE, educator; b. Attica, N.Y., May 29, 1888; s. Frederick C. and Isabel C. (Sproule) S.; A.B., Harvard, 1910, LL.B., 1913; m. Pauline Croll, Aug. 16, 1922 (dec.); 1 son, Robert Croll; m. 2d, Eva Howe, March 30, 1940. Admitted to N.Y. bar, 1913, and practiced at Buffalo; with Rogers, Locke, & Bancock, 1913-16; mem. Stevens & Reynolds, 1916-17; lecturer Cornell Law Sch., 1919-21, prof. law, 1921-54, emeritus, 1954-68, acting dean, 1930, 34, dean 1937-54. N.Y. commr. Nat. Conference on Uniform State Laws, 1926-48; spl. asst. to U.S. atty. gen., 1935; spl. consultant to N.Y. State Law Revision Com., 1936; asst. gen. counsel Office of Lend Lease Adminstrn., 1942-43, Fgn. Econ. Adminstrn., 1943-45; chmn. Appeal Bd., Office of Contract Settlement, 1945; chief consultant to the joint legislative committee appointed to revise corp. laws of N.Y., from 1957. Served as 2d lt., F.A. and A.S., U.S. Army, 1917-19. Trustee Hackley Sch., Tarrytown, N.Y., 1937-41; faculty rep. to bd. trustees, Cornell U., 1934-39. Mem. Am., N.Y. State and Tompkins County bar assns., Am. Law Inst., Am. Judicature Soc., Order of Coif, Delta Theta Phi, Phi Kappa Phi. Republican. Mason. Author: Stevens on Corporations, 1936; Stevens and Larson Cases and Materials on the Law of Corporations, 1947. Contbr. to law revs. Home: Ithaca NY Died Nov. 1968.

STEVENS, THOMAS HOLDUP naval officer; b. Charleston, S.C., Feb. 22, 1795; m. Elizabeth Sage, Nov. 1815, 6 children. A leader of detachment which captured 2 enemy guns, Niagara frontier, Nov. 27-28, 1812; made acting lt. U.S. Navy, 1813; commanded sloop Trippe in Battle of Lake Erie, recipient Silver medal awarded by Congress to officers in the action; 1st lt. of ship Niagara, 1814; duty on ships Alert and Constellation at Norfolk, 1818-20; commd. master comdt., 1825; served in ship Ontario, Mediterranean Squadron, 1829-31; in charge of Boston naval rendezvous, 1832-36; commd. capt., 1836, in command of Washington (D.C.) Navy Yard. Died Washington, Jan. 21, 1841; buried Arlington (Va.) Nat. Cemetery.

STEVENS, THOMAS HOLDUP naval officer; b. Middletown, Conn., May 27, 1819; s. Thomas Holdup and Elizabeth (Sage) S.; m. Anna Maria Christie, Nov. 2, 1844, 9 children including Thomas H. Entered U.S. Navy as midshipman, 1836, passed midshipman, 1842; aide to Pres. Tyler; naval storekeeper, Honolulu, Hawaii, 1845-48; in Chilean ship Maria Helena wrecked on Christmas Island, 1848, remained there nearly 3 months before rescued; served with Colo. Home Squadron, 1858-60; commanded gunboat Ottawa in capture of Port Royal in Civil War, 1861; commanded monitor Patapsco around Charleston, Aug.-Sept. 1863; in charge of night attack on Ft. Sumter, Sept. 1863; in ship Winnebago in Battle of Mobile; sr. officer operating off Tex., 1865; commd. capt., 1866, lighthouse inspector, 1867-70; in command of ship Guerriere in European Squadron, 1870-71; commd. commodore, 1872, rear adm., 1879; on duty in Norfolk, Va., 1873-80; in command of Pacific Squadron, 1880-81; ret., 1881, Contbr. article Service under Du Pont to Times, Phila., 1886. Died Rockville, Md., May 15, 1896; buried Arlington (Va.) Nat. Cemetery.

STEVENS, THOMAS HOLDUP 3D rear admiral U.S.N.; b. Honolulu, H.I., July 12, 1848; s. Thomas Holdup, 2d, and Anna Maria (Christie) S.; grad. U.S. Naval Acad., 1868; m. Washington, Cara de la Montaigne, d. late A. Oakey Hall, Apr. 29, 1903. Entered U.S.N., Oct. 1, 1863; after 22 yrs.' sea service and 40 yrs.' service, was advanced to rank of rear admiral and retired at own request, Feb. 11, 1905 (third of same name to attain flag rank in U.S.N.). Served in Civil War and in P.I. during insurrection. Youngest original naval mem. Mil. Order Loyal Legion U.S.; mem. S.R., Mil. Order of the Carabao. Died Oct. 3, 1914.

STEVENS, WALLACE poet, ins. exec.; b. Reading, Pa., Oct. 2, 1879; s. Garrett Barcalow and Mary Catherine (Zeller) S.; student Harvard Univ., N.Y. Law School; married to Elsie V. Kachel, September 21, 1909; one daughter, Holly Bright. Admitted to N.Y. bar, 1904, and engaged in gen. practice of law at New York, N.Y.; asso. with Hartford Accident and Indemnity Co., Hartford, Conn., 1916—, v.p., 1934—. Author: (poems) Harmonium, 1924; Ideas of Order, 1936; Owl's Clover, 1936; Man with the Blue Guitar, 1937; Parts of a World, 1942; Notes Toward a Supreme Fiction, 1942; The Auroras of Autumn, 1950; The Necessary Angel, 1951. Recipient of Bollingsen Prize in Poetry from Yale University Library, 1949. Member of the National Inst. Arts and Letters, 1946; Transport to Summer, 1947. Home: 118 Westerly Terrace. Office: 690 Asylum Av., Hartford, Conn. Died Aug. 2, 1955; buried Cedar Hill Cemetery.

STEVENS, WALTER HUSTED army officer; b. Penn Yan, N.Y., Aug. 24, 1827; s. Samuel Stephens; grad. U.S. Mil. Acad., 1848; married. Commd. in Corps Engrs., U.S. Army, 1848, promoted to 1st lt., 1855, resigned commn., 1861; apptd. capt. engrs. Confederate Army, 1861; promoted maj. at Battle of Bull Run, made chief engr. Army of No. Va., 1862; col. in charge of defenses of Richmond (Va.), circa 1862; commd. brig. gen., 1864, also chief engr. Lee's Army until its surrender, 1865; became supt., constructing engr. of a railroad between Vera Cruz (Mexico) and Mexico City, 1865, subsequently chief engr. Died Vera Cruz, Nov. 12, 1867.

STEVENS, WAYNE EDSON educator, historian; b. Avon, Ill., July 24, 1892; s. Willis Edson and Edith Quincy (Belding) S.; A.B., Knox Coll., 1913; M.A., U. Ill., 1914, Ph.D., 1916; m. Ann Baumler Francis, Sept. 4, 1933. Instr. history U. Minn., 1916-17; sec. war records sect. Ill. State Hist. Library, 1919-20; historian U.S. Army A.S., 1920-21; instr. history Dartmouth, 1921-23, asst. prof., 1923-30, prof., 1930—; mem. adv. bd. hist. sect. U.S. Army War Coll., 1929-31. Served as 1st lt. U.S. Army, 1917-19, as maj. specialist res., 1929-31. Mem. American Hist. Association, Phi Beta Kappa, Sigma Phi Epsilon. Conglist. Club: Author: The Northwest Fur Trade, 1763-1800, 1928; European Militarism in a New Phase, 1926. Editor: History of the 151st Field Artillery, Rainbow Division (Louis L. Collins), 1924. Contbr. to Dictionary Am. Biography. Home: 4 N. Park St., Hanover, N.H. Died July 20, 1959; buried Pine Knoll Cemetery, Hanover, N.H.

STEVENSON, ALEC BROCK, investment banker; b. Toronto, Ont., Dec. 29, 1895; s. James Henry and Evelyn (Sutherland) S.; brought to U.S., 1896, naturalized, 1920; B.A., Vanderbilt U., 1916; m. Florence Elise Maney, Nov. 10, 1920; children—Alec Brock, Florence Elise. Newspaper reporter, 1916-17, 19; asst. sec. Am. Nat. Co., investment bankers, Nashville, 1920-33; v.p. Gray, Shillinglaw & Co., investment bankers, 1933-40; v.p., trust officer Am. Nat. Bank of Nashville, 1940-51, dir., 1944-51; with Vance, Sanders and Co., sponsors mut. investment funds, Boston, 1951-59, partner, 1953-59; vice president Vance Sanders & Co., Inc., 1959-69. Commr., vice mayor, Belle-Meade, Tenn., 1938-40. Pres. Community Chest of Nashville and Davidson Co., 1950-51. Trustee Vanderbilt U., Joint U. Libraries Sgt. to lt. F.A., A.E.F., 1917-19. Mem. Phi Beta Kappa, Sigma Chi, Omicron Delta Kappa. Methodist. Club: Bellemeade Country, Cumberland (Nashville). Author: Shares in Mutual Investment Funds, 1946; Investment Company Shares, 1947. Mem. group. editing and pub. The Fugitive, a mag. of verse, Nashville, 1922-25. Home: Nashville TN Died May 27, 1969; buried Mt. Olivet Cemetery Nashville TN

STEVENSON, CARTER LITTLEPAGE army officer; b. nr. Fredericksburg, Va., Sept. 21, 1817; s. Carter Littlepage and Jane (Herndon) S.; grad. U.S. Mil. Acad., 1838; m. Martha Griswold; Commd. 2d lt. 5th Inf., U.S. Army, 1838; fought in Mexican War; promoted to capt., 1836; served in Utah expdn., 1858; commd. lt. col. inf. Confederate Army, 1861, then col. 53d Va. Inf.; apptd. brig. gen., sent to West, 1862, commd. maj. gen., 1862; fought at battles of Champion's Hill and Big Black Ridge in Vicksburg campaign, at Battle of Missionary Ridge in Hardee's corps, also with Hood's corps in Atlanta Campaign; participated in campaign of the Carolinas, also at Battle of Bentonville; civil and mining engr. after Civil War. Died Caroline County, Va., Aug. 15, 1888.

STEVENSON, ELDON, JR., ins. exec.; b. Nashville; s. Eldon Boisseau and Minnie (Gleaves) S.; B.S., Vanderbilt U., 1914; m. Sarah Shannon, June 2, 1920. With Nat. Life and Accident Ins. Co., 1913-72, beginning as agent successively branch office cashier, inspector, supervisor and dist. mgr., later transferred to home office and made asst. mgr. of ordinary dept., later mgr. and then v.p. in charge of ordinary, dir. of co., 1925-72, exec. v.p., 1938, pres., 1953-72, vice chmn. corp., 1963-65, hon. vice chmn., 1965-72, cons. to co., 1970-72; vice chmn. bd. Radio WSM and WSM-TV; also past chmn. Combination Cos. Past chmn. bd. Life Ins. Sales Research Bur., Hartford, Conn.; mem. bd. Life Insurers Conf., Richmond, Va., 1948-72, pres., 1954-55. Trustees, hon. v.p. bd. trust Vanderbilt U. Enlisted USN, World War I; commd. ensign; instr. U.S. Naval Acad.; officer in U.S.S. George Washington. Mem. Vanderbilt Alumni Assn. (past mem. bd., exec. com. and nat. pres.), Phi Delta Theta. Mason. Clubs: Links, Brook, (N.Y.C.); Cumberland, Belle Meade Golf and Country (Nashville); Linville (N.C.) Golf; Augusta (Ga.) National Golf; Everglades and Mountain Lake Colony (Fla.). Home: Nashville TN Died Nov. 23, 1972.

STEVENSON, HOLLAND NEWTON naval officer; b. Cambridge, N.Y., Sept. 3, 1844; s. John M. and Seraph H. S.; C.E., Rensselaer Poly. Inst., 1866; apptd. to Naval Acad. from N.Y. as acting 3d asst. engr., Oct. 10, 1866; grad. spl. course in engring., 1868; 3d asst. engr., June 2, 1868; 2d asst. engr., June 2, 1869; passed asst. engr., Dec. 13, 1874; chief engr., Dec. 14, 1892; comdr., Mar. 3, 1899; capt., Feb. 10, 1903; retired as commodore, June 30, 1905. At Naval Acad., 1866-1868; Navy Yard, N.Y.C., 1867; Dacotah and Saranac, 1868-71; Bur. of Steam Engring., 1871-72; spl. duty, N.Y.C., 1872-74; Swatara, 1874-75; coast and geodetic survey, 1875-78; Morgan Iron Works, N.Y.C., 1878-79; Trenton, 1879-81; Wyo., 1882; coast survey, 1883-87; insp. of machinery, 1888-91; Alliance, 1891-94; Constellation, 1894-95; insp. of machinery, Bath Iron Works, 1895-97; Monterey, 1897-99; insp. of machinery for the Navy at Union Iron Works, San Francisco, 1899-1908. Home: 1482 Sutter St., San Francisco. Died Jan. 11, 1959.

STEVENSON, JAMES ethnologist, explorer; b. Maysville, Ky., Dec. 24, 1840; m. Matilda Coxe Evans, Apr. 18, 1872. Spent several winters among Blackfoot and Sioux Indians; participated in survey of Yellowstone region, 1871, leader in making it a nat. park; in charge of exploration of Snake and Columbia rivers in Ida. and Wyo. territories, 1872, prepared maps of region; in survey trip of 1872 climbed Great Teton (1st white man known to have reached ancient Indian altar on its summit); served as col. with 13th N.Y. Volunteers, Union Army, 1861-65; engaged in research among Pueblo Indians and the remains of their former settlements for Bur. Ethnology at its inception, 1879; outfitted, conducted expdns. investigating ancient ruins and the living Navaho, Zuni, Hopi, other Indian tribes; published 1st studies among the Navaho as "Ceremonial of Hasjelti Dailjis and Mythical Sand Painting of the Navajo Indians;" his ornithol. collections in U.S. Nat. Mus., Smithsonian Instn. Died N.Y.C., July 25, 1888.

STEWARD, LEROY T. (stu'erd); b. Dayton, O., Mar. 24, 1860; s. Thomas L. and Frances (Garber) S.; ed. pub. schs.; m. Florence Donovan, Apr. 14, 1895 (died Nov. 1921); m. 2d, Helen Gertrude Scott, Apr. 13, 1935. Supt. Chicago Post Office and general supt. City mail delivery, 1897-1909; gen. supt. police, Chicago, 1909-11; returned to former position in post office (retired 1925). Served in Ohio Nat. Guard, 1877-79, and as an officer 1st and 2d regts. Ill. Nat. Guard, advancing to rank of col.; brigadier general Ill. Reserve, 1917-20. Organized 1st ship's crew, Ill. Naval Militia, and 1st squadron of cav., Ill. Nat. Guard; served on Cook County Mil. Affairs Com. during war period, and was active in the organization of reserve troops, etc. Chmn. com. on pub. information, Chicago Expn., 1893; active in securing filling of "lake front," at Chicago, also in securing park lagoons and street renumbering. Scout commr. Boy Scouts of America, Chicago, Ill., 1918-27, now Chief Scout, Chicago; has been actively identified for many years with public welfare, organization and boys' work. Mem. Ohio Soc. (pres. 1919-20). Republican. Presbyterian. Mason (32 deg., Shriner). Clubs: Hamilton, Union League. Home: Watervliet, Mich. (R.F.D. No. 1). Died Apr. 26, 1944.

STEWART, ALEXANDER P. commr. Chickamauga Nat. Park, Sept. 1890—; b. Rogersville, Tenn., Oct. 2, 1821; s. William and Elizabeth (Decherd) S.; prep. edn. in Tenn.; grad. U.S. Mil. Acad., West Point, N.Y., June 1842 (LL.D., Cumberland Univ.); m. Harriet Byron Chase, Aug. 7, 1845 (died 1898). Apptd. 2d lt. 3d U.S. Arty., June 1842; an asst. to prof. mathematics, U.S. Mil. Acad., 1843; resigned, 1845; prof. mathematics and natural philosophy in Cumberland and Nashville univs., 1845-60; volunteered in State Army of Tenn.; apptd. by gov. maj. arty. corps; transferred to C.S.A., 1861 commd. brig. gen., Nov. 1861; maj. gen., 1863; lt. gen., 1864; in command Army of Tenn. at close of the war; chancellor Univ. of Miss., 1874-86; Southern mem. Chickamauga Park Commn., 1890—. Home: Biloxi, Miss. Died 1908.

STEWART, CHARLES Continental congressman; b. Gortlea, County Donegal, Ireland, 1729. Came to Am., 1750; became farmer; commd. lt. col. Hunterdon County (N.J.) Militia, 1771; active in pre-Revolutionary movements; commd. col. battalion of Minutemen, 1776; apptd. commissary gen. of issues by Continental

Congress, 1777; mem. Continental Congress from N.J., 1784-85. Died Flemington, N.J., June 24, 1800; buried Old Stone Ch., Bethlehem Twp., Hunterdon County.

STEWART, CHARLES naval officer; b. Phila., July 28, 1778; s. Charles and Sarah (Ford) S.; m. Delia Tudor, Nov. 25, 1813, 2 children. Commd. lt. U.S. Navy, 1798, in command schooner Experiment, 1800, command brig Siren, 1802; served in war with Tripoli and Tunis; commd. capt., 1806, supr. constrn. gunboats, N.Y., 1806-07; comdr. ship Constellation, 1812, ship Constitution, 1813, ship Franklin, 1816; commodore squadron in Pacific, 1824; naval commr., 1830-32; in charge Phila. Navy Yard, 1838-41, 46, 54-61; sr. commodore, 1856, rear adm.. ret., 1862. Died Bordentown, N.J., Nov. 6, 1869.

STEWART, CHARLES SEAFORTH col. U.S.A., retired, Sept. 16, 1886; b. at sea, April 11, 1823; s. Rev. Charles Samuel S. (chaplain U.S.N.) and Harriet Bradford (Tiffany) S.; m. Cecilia Sophia de Louville Tardy, April 15, 1857 (died 1886). Grad. West Point, 1846; asst. engr. fortifications New London and Boston Harbor, 1846-49; acting asst. prof. engineering, West Point, 1849-54; 1st lt. engrs., 1853; capt., 1860; maj., 1863; lt. col., 1867; col., 1882. Asst. engr., 1854-57; superintending engr. construction fortifications Boston Harbor, 1857-61; same, construction defenses Hampton Roads and Ft. Monroe, Va., 1861-64, in charge defenses, Delaware River and Bay, and of construction river and harbor work there, 1865-70. Bvtd. lt. col., Feb. 25, 1865, for long, faithful and efficient services; bvt. col., March 13, 1865, for gallant and meritorious services during the Rebellion—declined. Mem. bd. engrs. for fortifications on Pacific Coast, 1870-86; superintending engr. construction fortifications Fort Point, Point San José and Angel Island, San Francisco Harbor, 1870-86; Ft. San Diego, Calif., 1873-86; improvement San Diego Harbor, 1875-86; mem. various engring. bds., 1866-86; retired on own application having served 40 yrs. as commd. officer. Home: Cooperstown, N.Y. Died 1904.

STEWART, EDWIN paymaster gen. U.S.N.; b. New York, May 5, 1837; s. John and Mary (Aikman) S.; bro. of John Aikman S.; A.B., Williams, 1862, A.M., 1882 (LL.D., 1898); m. Laura S. Tufts, Aug. 24, 1865; 2d, Susan M. Estabrook May 17, 1877. Apptd. from N.Y., asst. p.-m., Sept. 9, 1861; p.-m., Apr. 14, 1862; war service in battles of Port Royal, Port Hudson and Mobile Bay; promoted pay-insp., Mar. 8, 1870; pay dir., Sept. 12, 1891; paymaster-gen., May 16, 1890; re-apptd., May 16, 1894; again re-apptd., May 16, 1898; rear adm., Mar. 3, 1899, and retired, May 5, 1899. Elected comdr. D.C. Commandery Loyal Legion, 1900, N.Y. Commandery, 1913-17; sr. v. comdr.-in-chief, 1912, 17; mem. Loyal Legion, Soc. Am. Wars. Home: South Orange, N.J. Died Feb. 28, 1933.

STEWART, FRANK MANN prof. polit. science; b. Sherman, Tex., Apr. 8, 1894; s. John Wiley and Mary Josephine (Mann) S.; student Austin Coll., Sherman, Tex., 1911-12; A.B., U. of Tex., 1915, A.M., 1917; student Inst. Pub. Adminstrn., New York, 1920-21; Ph.D., U. of Chicago, 1928; m. Martha Roberta Dulin, Oct. 30, 1921. Tutor, U. of Tex., 1916-17, instr., 1919-23, adjunct prof., 1923-26, asso. prof., 1926-29, prof. of govt., 1929-32, chmn. of dept., 1929-30, 1931-32; prof. of political science, U. of Calif. at Los Angeles, since 1932, chmn. of dept., 1935-39; dir. Bureau of Govt. Research, U. of Calif. at Los Angeles, 1937-48. Exec. sec. League of Tex. Municipalities, 1919-24; mem. Com. on Govt. Simplification, Los Angeles County, 1933-36 and mem. Citizens Com. on Govtl. Reorganization, Los Angeles City, 1935-36; v. chmn. Los Angeles Charter Revision Com., 1940-41, 2d lt., 1st lt. and capt., U.S. Army, 1917-18. Mem. Town Hall (charter mem.), Am. Political Science Assn. (council, 1931-34; vice-pres., 1941), Nat. Municipal League, Am. Assn. Univ. Profs., Internat. City Mgrs. Assn., Am. Soc. for Public Adminstrn., Pacific Southwest Acad. (v.p., 1932-33; mem. of dirs., 1935-41, advisory council since 1941), Western Governmental Research Association (exec. com. 1937-38, 1942-46; president 1941-42). National Civil Service Reform League (council since 1930), Phi Beta Kappa, Pi Gamma Mu, Pi Sigma Alpha. Democrat. Member Disciples of Christ Ch. Author: The Reorganization of State Administration in Texas, 1925; The National Civil Service Reform League, 1929; Constitution and Government of Texas (with J. L. Clark), 1930; Highway Administration in Texas, 1934; A Half Century of Municipal Reform, 1950. Contributor to Am. Political Science Review and other jours. Contbg. editor Public Management, 1936-40. Editor of Texas Municipalities, 1919-24; editor in charge Southwestern Polit. Science Quarterly, 1922-23. Home: 908 Malcolm Av., Los Angeles 24. Died Oct. 17, 1961; buried Forest Lawn Meml. Park, Glendale, Cal.

STEWART, GEORGE, author, minister, soldier; b. Webb City, Mo., Feb. 11, 1892; s. George and Fanny (Meade) S.; A.B., Linfield Coll., McMinnville, Ore., 1914, Litt.D., 1928; A.B., Yale, 1915, LL.B., 1917, Ph.D., 1921, D.D., 1939; Dr. Theol., Faculte Libre de Theologie Protestante de Paris, 1927; L.H.D. (honorary), Temple U., 1955; LL.D., Norwich U., 1963; m. Sarah Malcolm Klebs, May 20, 1925 (dec. July 1957); children—Mary (Mrs. James Meath), Anne, Jane (Mrs. William McDermott), Sarah (Mrs. Kendall Preston); m. 2d, Leni Loosli, Sept. 16, 1958. Gen. sec. YMCA, 1919-21; asso. pastor, Madison Av. Presbyn. Ch., N.Y. City, 1921-28; minister of First Presbyn. Ch., Stamford, Conn., 1928-44; Turnbull Trust preacher Scots Church, Melbourne, Australia, 1941; lecturer Yale Divinity School, 1930-36. Private, non-commd. officer and capt., World War; vol. student relief work, Europe part time, 1918-25. Mem. com. on worship Federal Council of the Chs. of Christ in America; mem. bd. trustees Community Chest, Stamford; mem. bd. trustees Ferguson Library, Stamford; mem. Am. Com. on Religious Rights and Minorities; mem. Am. Com. of the Paris Theol. Sem.; past mem. numerous govtl. and orgn. coms. in social field; mem. subcom. on hist. records, Nat. Research Council, 1942-44; mem. bd. dirs. Am. Waldensian Aid Soc.; mem. Oecumenism Commn. World Student Christian Feln.; mem. Am. sect. World Council of Churches. Commander, Legion of Honor; medaille Militaire (France); Orders of St. George and St. Vladamir (Russia); Golden Cross of Merit with Crossed Swords, Officer Order Polonia Restituta (Poland) Grand Officer Order of the Crown, Military Cross; Criox d' Honneur, Union Franco-Belge Devouement, Croix de laFrance Leberee, Croix d'Honneur Le Ligue Entriaide Francaise de Merite, Cuique, Croix de Commander Societe d' Encouragement on De-voncment (France), Soldat premiere Classe Honor dise de la Legion Entrangere, Croix de Commandeur Ligne Universelle du Bien Public (France), Grand Cross, Order of The Holy Sepulchre. Fellow fo the Royal Geographical Society; member several profl. and geneol. socs. Clubs: Century Association (N.Y.C.); Dublin Lake (New Hampshire). Author: Soldiers' Spirit, 1917; (with Professor Henry B. Wright of Yale) The Practice of Friendship, 1918; (with same) Personal Evangelism Among Students, 1919; A History of Religious Education in Connecticut to the Middle of the Nineteenth Century (winner John Addison Porter prize at Yale University), 1921; Life of Henry B. Wright, 1925, also God and Pain; The Incarnation in Our Street; The Crucifixion in Our Street; The Resurrection in Our Street; Redemption—An Anthology of the Cross; Protestant Europe—Its Crisis and Outlook (with Adolh Keller), 1927; Ask Me a Bible Question, 1927; The Sanctuary, 1928; The Letters of Maxwell Chaplin, 1928; Can I Teach My Child Religion?, 1929; Jesus as a Friend, 1931. Compiler and editor of Dedication—An Anthology of the Will of God, 1931; The White Armies of Russia, 1933; Jesus Said "I Am," 1934; Reluctant Soil, 1936; The Church, 1938; God in Our Street, 1939; I Met Them Once, 1940; A Face to the Sky, 1940; The Story of a Carillon, 1944. Contbr. to mags.; mem. editorial bd. Presbyterian Tribune. War missions in 37 countries, rank of col. Hon. chaplain to British armies; Col., USAF (Reserve) (Ret.). Home: Dublin NH Died Feb. 19, 1972.

STEWART, GILBERT HENRY army officer; b. Wichita, Kan., Nov. 12, 1878; s. Samuel Hamilton and Mary Ibela (Hair) S.; B.S., U.S. Mil. Acad., 1902; grad. Ordnance Sch. of Tech., 1913, Army War Coll., 1922, Army Indsl. Coll., 1932; m. Elizabeth Finley Barnard, June 7, 1909; children—Jane Semple (Mrs. Alfred J. Ronk), Charles Barnard, Gilbert Henry, Hamilton. Commd. 2d lt., inf., 1902; commd. 1st lt., Ordnance Dept., 1904, and advanced through the grades to brig. gen., 1940; works mgr., Rock Island Arsenal, 1923-26; in command Augusta (Ga.) Arsenal, 1926-28, Hawaiian Ordnance Depot, 1928-31, Watervliet (N.Y.) Arsenal, 1932-38, Springfield (Mass.) Armory, 1938-42; retired June 1942. Awarded Legion of Merit, 1943. Clubs: University (Phila.); Army and Navy (Washington). Home: 142 Randolph Pl., West Orange, N.J. Died Aug. 4, 1957; buried West Point, N.Y.

STEWART, JACOB HENRY congressman, physician; b. Clermont, Columbia County, N.Y., Jan. 15, 1829; grad. Phillips Acad., Peekskill, N.Y.; attended Yale; grad. U. Med. Coll. of N.Y.C., 1851. Practiced medicine, Peekskill; moved to St. Paul, Minn., 1855; med. officer Ramsey County, 1856; mem. Minn. Senate, 1858-59; served as surgeon in Union Army in Civil War, 1861; captured at 1st Battle of Bull Run, paroled, cared for wounded at Sudley Ch. Hosp.; surgeon gen. State of Minn., 1857-63; mayor St. Paul, 1864, 68, 72-74, postmaster, 1865-70; mem. U.S. Ho. of Reps. (Republican) from Minn., 45th Congress, 1877-79; surveyor gen. Minn., 1879-82. Died St. Paul, Aug. 25, 1884; buried Oakland Cemetery.

STEWART, JOHN ALEXANDER, banker; b. Bay City, Mich., May 23, 1900; s. John A. and Margaret (MacDonald) S.; A.B., U. Mich., 1921; m. Mary K. Martin, Oct. 11, 1928; children—Albert W., John A., Dennis M., Robert M. With Second Nat. Bank of Saginaw, 1921-68, beginning as clk., successively asst. cashier, v.p., v.p. and cashier, exec. v.p., cashier, 1921-57, pres., 1957-65, chmn. bd., 1965-68, also director; director Morley Brothers, Michigan Sugar Company. Treas., v.p., dir. Saginaw Community Chest, 1956; dir. Children's Home Family Soc.; bd. dirs. Saginaw YMCA, 1958-68, pres., 1963-65; trustee Delta College. Served as pvt., infantry, United States Army, 1918, later lt. U.S. Coast Arty. Mem. Mich. Bankers Assn. (exec. com. 1937-40), Saginaw C. of C. (treas., dir. 1947-58), Newcomen Soc., Navy League. Republican. Conglist. Mason (Shriner). Clubs: Saginaw, Saginaw Country, Saginaw Kiwanis; Economic, Detroit (Detroit). Home: Saginaw MI Died May 20, 1968.

STEWART, JOHN DAVID congressman; b. nr. Fayetteville, Fayette County, Ga., Aug. 2, 1833; attended Marshall Coll., Griffin, Ga.; studied law, theology. Taught sch., Griffin for 2 years; admitted to bar, 1856, practiced law, Griffin; probate judge Spalding County, 1858-60; lt. and capt. 13th Ga. Regt., during Civil War; mem. Ga. Ho. of Reps., 1865-67; ordained to ministry Baptist Ch., 1871; mayor Griffin, 1875-76; judge Superior Ct., 1879-86; mem. U.S. Ho. of Reps. (Democrat) from Ga., 50th-51st congresses, 1887-91. Died Griffin, Jan. 28, 1894, buried Oak Hill Cemetery.

STEWART, JOHN LESLIE, lawyer; b. Toronto, Ont., Can., Sept. 24, 1911; s. John Leslie and Mary Frances (Nicholson) S.; B.A., U. Toronto, 1932; B.C.L., U. Oxofrd, 1934, diploma politics and economics, 1935; m. Winifred Muriel Gibson, Dec. 6, 1941; children—Margaret Ann, John Leslie, Gordon Fraser, Robert David Roy, Janet Elizabeth Mary. Called to bar, London, Eng., 1935, Ont., 1936, apptd. Queen's Counsel, 1950; with Fraser & Beatty, and successor firms, Toronto, 1936-71, partner, 1936-71; dir. various Canadian corps. Exec. com. corp. Trinity Coll., Toronto; sec. Can. Rhodes Scholarship Trust. Legal adviser Royal Commn. on Taxation. Served as lt. col. Canadian Army, World War II. Decorated Order Brit. Empire; Officer Order Orange Nassau (Netherlands). Mem. Alpha Delta Phi. Clubs: University, Badminton and Racquet, Granite, Toronto, Lambton Golf, Toronto Golf. Editor: Fraser and Stewart Handbook on Canadian Company Law, 5th edit., 1960; Company Law of Canada, 5th edit., 1962. Home: Toronto Ontario Canada Died 1971.

STEWART, JOHN TRUESDALE civil engr.; b. Loda, Ill., Jan. 13, 1868; s. William R. and Nancy (Barr) S.; B.S., in C.E., U. of Ill., 1893, C.E., 1909; m. Ida Belle Wilson, Jan. 1, 1900. In pvt. practice to 1897; field asst., topographic corps, U.S. Geol. Survey, 1898-1903; drainage engr., U.S. Dept. Agr., 1904-08; prof. and chief div. of agrl. engring., U. of Minn., 1908-17. Cadet officer U. of Ill.; bvt. capt. Ill. N.G., 1893; organized and drilled company for Spanish-Am. War, 1898, but not called into service; maj., Engrs. U.S.R., on active duty, May 26, 1917; lt. col. engrs., Oct. 18, 1918; hon. disch., Oct. 13, 1919; lt. col. E.O.R.C., Jan. 31, 1920, col. Jan. 14, 1924. In charge of ednl. activities in schools and colleges for Portland Cement Assn., Jan. 1921-Mar. 1922; consulting engr., drainage and wet land development, Apr. 1922—. Presbyn. Senior author of Engineering on the Farm. Home: St. Paul, Minn. Died June 9, 1928.

STEWART, MALCOLM CHILSON, lawyer; b. Brookline, Mass., Jan. 10, 1913; s. Ralph Aldace and Mary Wallace(Guilford) S.; student St. Mark's Sch., Southborough, Mass., 1924-30; A.B., Harvard, 1934, LL.B., 1937; m. Marian deForest Clark, Dec. 14, 1941. Admitted to Mass. bar, 1937, asso. mem. Choate, Hall & Stewart, Boston, 1937-41, 46-49; legal dept. Gillette Co. (formerly Gillette Safety Razor Co.), 1949-70, gen. counsel 1951-56, dir., 1956-70, treas., 1955-66, v.p., 1959-65, sr. v.p., 1965-66, vice chairman of the board, 1968-70; mem. bd. directors Mchts. Nat. Bank Boston. Dir., exec. com. Boston Municipal Research Bur.; director National Foreign Trade Council. Director Mutual Security, special mission to France, 1953; mem. Nat. Indsl. Conf. Bd. Trustee Peter Bent Brigham Hosp., Affiliated Hosps. Center, Inc., Boston. Served as lieut. col. F.A., AUS, 1941-45. Decorated Bronze Star, Air Medal. Mem. Am., Mass. State, Boston bar assns., Boston C. C. (dir.), Nat. Assn. Mfrs. Clubs: Myopia Hunt (Hamilton, Mass.); Somerset (Boston); Racquet (Chgo.). Home: Prides Crossing MA Died Apr. 3, 1970; buried Westport, Essex County NY

STEWART, MERCH BRADT army officer; b. Mitchell Sta., Va., June 24, 1875; s. James Robinson and Grace Alice (Bushong) S.; prep. edn. Glens Falls (N.Y.) Acad.; grad. U.S. Mil. Acad., 1896; m. Nan Wheelihan, Feb. 16, 1898; 1 son, Peter. Commd. add. 2d lt. inf., June 12, 1896; promoted through grades to brig. gen. Dec. 16, 1925; maj. gen., Oct. 2, 1927; retired, Oct. 3, 1927; col., later brig. gen. N.A., Aug. 15, 1917-Aug. 15, 1919. Active service in Spanish-Am. War, Philippine Insurrection and World War; mem. Gen. Staff 4 yrs.; mem. Inf. Equipment Bd., 1909-10, Inf. Drill Regulation Bd., 1911, Land Defense Bd., Panama Canal, 1915-16; comdt. cadets, U.S. Mil. Acad., 1923-26; supt. of same, 1926-27, retired. Awarded D.S.M. (U.S.); Officer Legion of Honor and Croix de Guerre, with Palm (French). Presbyn. Author: The Nth Foot in War, 1898; Military Character, Habit, Deportment, Courtesy and Discipline, 1913; Physical Development of the Infantry Soldier, 1913. Co-author: Junior Military Manual, 1917; Thirty Minute Talks, 1920; The Drillmaster, 1921. Died July 3, 1934.

STEWART, PAUL MORTON ret. coast guard officer; b. Belle Center, O., Sept. 5, 1888; s. James Irwin and Rebecca (Perrine) S.; M.D., U. Cin., 1914; m. Norma Pellegrini, Dec. 13, 1919; children—Robert Pellegrini (dec.), Paul Morton, Giovanna, Stewart Kirby, James Alexander. Commd. asst. surgeon USPHS, 1915, passed asst. surgeon, 1919, surgeon, 1926, sr. surgeon, 1935; mem. dir. U.S. Employees Compensation Commn.,

1936; asst. surgeon gen., 1939, chief inspector, 1944; chief med. officer, with rank of rear adm. USCG, 1946-52, ret. Fellow A.M.A. Clubs: Columbia Country, Chevy Chase (Washington). Home: 2210 Wyoming Av., Washington. Died Aug. 24, 1957; buried Arlington Nat. Cemetery.

STEWART, ROBERT WRIGHT corp. executive, lawyer; b. Cedar Rapids, Ia., Mar. 11. 1866; s. William and Eliza Mills (Lucore) S.; B.S., Coe Coll., Ia., 1886; LL.B.. Yale, 1888; LL.D., Blackburn Coll.. 1922, Coe Coll., 1927; m. Maude Bradley Elliott, July 14, 1906; children—Donald William, John Eliliott; (by first marriage) Robert Giffen, James Wright. State's atty., Hughes County, S.D., 1893-95; Supreme Court reporter, 1893-98; mem. S.D. Senate, 1899-1903; gen. atty., 1907-15, general counsel. May 1, 1915-Oct. 1918, and chmn. bd. dirs. Standard Oil Co. of Ind., Chicago, 1918-29; dir. Hanover Fire Ins. Co., Fulton Fire Ins. Co. (New York), National City Bank (New York), 1921-31, Continental Ill. Nat. Bank & Trust Co. (Chicago), 1918-34. Maj. 3d U.S. Vol. Cav. ("Rough Riders"), May-Oct. 1898; col. 4th Regt., S.D. Nat. Guard, 1899-1907. Home: Chicago, Ill. Died Feb. 24, 1947.

STEWART, THOMAS JAMISON soldier; b. Belfast, Ireland, Sept. 11, 1848; s. John and Eliza. S.; came to America with parents, 1849; ed. pub. schs., Norristown, Pa.; m. Mrs. A. R. Weaver, Nov. 28, 1901. Pvt. 138th Pa. Vols., Civil War; officer N. G. of Pa., 1868-—; sec. internal affairs of Pa., 1886-95; adj. gen. of Pa., Jan. 1895-—. Asst. adj. gen. G.A.R. of Pa., 1882-89; comdr. Pa. Dept. G.A.R., 1890; adj. gen. G.A.R., 1898-1900, comdr.-in-chief, 1902-03. Republican. Home: Harrisburg, Pa. Died Sept. 11, 1917.

STEWART, WILLIAM HENRY chaplain U.S.N.; b. Andover, Mass., July 11, 1831; s. John and Dorcas (Baxter) S.; m. Roline Mayo, July 11, 1860; m. 2d, Azuba E. Tolles, Jan. 20, 1885. Apptd. chaplain U.S.N., Mar. 10, 1863; served at naval sta., Cairo, Ill., 1863-65, Naval Acad., 1866-67, and later on various vessels and at various stas.; retired, July 11, 1893; advanced to rank of rear adm., retired, June 29, 1906; for services during Civil War. Home: De Land, Fla. Died Mar. 31, 1913.

STEYNE, ALAN NATHANIEL (stin), foreign service Officer; b. New York City, Nov. 19, 1898; s. Abram and Nina (Herzog) S.; student Phillips Andover; Ph.B., Yale, 1921; unmarried. Advertising and asst. sales mgr., 1922-27; metal export business, China, 1928-29; vice consul, Montreal, Can., 1930-31; vice consul, Hamburg, 1931-35; consul, Hamburg, 1935-36. Dept. of State, Div. Trade Agreements, 1836-37; 2d sec. (consul), Am. embassy, London, 1937-43 1st. sec., 1943. Assigned to Dept. of State, Sept. 1943. Special asst. to Dir. Gen. UNRRA, first session of the United Nations Relief and Rehabilitation Administrn, 1943; Division of Commercial Policy, Dept. of State, Sept. 1943-Mar. 1944; sec. exec. com. on Economic Fgn. Policy, Mar.-Apr. 1944. Asst. chief of planning staff, Office of Foreign Service, May-Dec. 1944; special asst. to dir., Office of Foreign Service, Jan.-Mar. 1945; exec. asst. to dir. Office of Foreign Service, Apr. 1945. Am. mem. Inter-Allied Com. on Postwar Requirements, 1941-43; Am. del. Internat. Sugar Council, 1941, Consumers Panel, Internat. Tin Com., 1941; chmn. Joint Survey Group for Improvement Fgn. Service Reporting, 1944-45. Served as corpl., 16th Field Arty., 4th Div., 2d lt. aerial observer, 90th Aero Squadron, 3d Army Corps, A.E.F., 1918-19, World War I. Clubs: Metropolitan. Cosmos (Washington); Yale (New York); Reform, St. James, Bath (London); Guana Island (Virgin Islands, B.W.I.). Address: Metropolitan Club, Washington, D.C. Died May 22, 1946.

STICKNEY, ALBERT lawyer; b. Boston, Feb. 1, 1839; grad. Harvard, 1859; Harvard Law School, 1862. Served as lt. col., 47th Mass. vols., Civil war; aide on staff of Maj. Gen. Banks and insp. gen. on staff of Maj. Gen. Emory. Author: The Lawyer and His Clients; A True Republic; Democratic Government; a Study of Politics; The Political Problem; The Transvaal Outlook, 1900; Organized Democracy, 1906. Home: New York, N.Y. Died 1908.

STICKNEY, AMOS brig. gen. U.S.A.; b. St. Louis, Mo., Aug. 27, 1843; s. Benjamin and Sarah J. S.; grad. U.S. Mil. Acad., 1864; m. Virginia Fetter, July 10, 1866. Commd. 1st lt. engrs., June 13, 1864; capt., Mar. 7, 1867; maj., Jan. 2, 1881; lt. col., May 18, 1893; col., May 2, 1901; brig. gen. and retired by operation of law, Aug. 27, 1907. Bvtd. capt., Dec. 21, 1864, for campaign in Georgia, 1864; maj., Mar. 13, 1865, for campaign through Georgia and Carolinas. Engr. on staff comdg. gen., Dept. of the Mo., June-Aug. 1864, and on staff Gen. Cullum, at Nashville, Aug.-Sept. 1864; asst. engr., Oct. 1864-June 1865, and chief engr., June-July 1865, Army of the Tennessee, and engaged in various movements and operations of Ga. and Carolina campaigns; served on constrn. of forts until 1866; prof. engring., West Point, 1866-67; chiefly occupied with work of river and harbor improvement from 1868; pres. Mo. River Commn., 1896-1902, Miss. River Commn., 1901-03; chmn. of commn. to establish and mark the boundary line between the States of Ky. and Ind. under the orders of the U.S. Supreme Court. Home: New York, N.Y. Died Oct. 25, 1924.

STICKNEY, HERMAN OSMAN naval officer; b. Pepperell, Mass., Dec. 10, 1867; s. Walter Brooks and Lydia Jane (Edwards) S.; grad. U.S. Naval Acad., 1888; m. Jennie Griffin Milhado, Oct. 16, 1895. Assistant engr., July 1, 1890; trans. to line and promoted through grades to rear adm., Dec. 22, 1919; retired, Dec. 27, 1921. Served on Iowa, Spanish-Am. War, 1898; on Princeton, Philippine Insurrection, 1899-1901; Navy Yard, Norfolk, Va., 1901-02; navigator Texas, 1902-05; at U.S. Naval Acad., 1905-06; duty Navy Yard, Norfolk, Va., 1906-07; exec. officer South Dakota, 1908-10; insp. in charge 4th Light House Dist., Phila., 1910-12; comd. Massachusetts, 1912; at U.S. Naval Acad., 1912-13; comd. Prairie, 1913-14; adminstr. of customs, Vera Cruz, Mexico, 1914; at Naval War Coll., Newport, R.I., 1915; comd. Vermont, 1915-18; Bd. of Inspection and Survey, Washington, 1918; sr. mem. Pacific Coast Bd. of Inspection, San Francisco, 1919; comdr. train, Pacific Fleet, July 1921; U.S. commr. to Sesquicentennial Expn., Phila., 1926-27, in charge all federal participation in that expn. Atty. at law; admitted to practice in Va., June 27, 1923. Home: Norfolk, Va. Died Sept. 13, 1936.

STICKNEY, JOSEPH L. journalist; b. "The Mines," nr. Marion, Ky., July 12, 1848; s. John Charles and Abby Anna (Clifford) S.; grad. U.S. Naval Acad., 1867; m. Edith Lucy Cooley, June 1900. Entered navy as midshipman, Sept. 25, 1862; in Civ. War, served as midshipman aboard Marion, Franklin with Admiral Farragut, Frolic, Guard, Ohio, Congress and Nantasket; resigned as lt., 1871. Began as reporter, 1873; corr. Chicago Tribune, Russo-Turkish War, 1877-78; editorial writer Phila. Record, 1881-82; mng. editor Milwaukee Centinel, 1883-84; editor and prop. Detroit Post, 1884-85; foreign editor and editorial writer, New York Herald, 1887-98. Aide to Commadore Dewey at battle of Manilla Bay, May 1, 1898, receiving personal mention in Commadore's official report of that battle; corr. in Pip I So. Africa, 1899-1908. Home: Chicago Ill. Died 1907.

STIGLER, WILLIAM G. congressman; b. Stigler, Indian Territory (now Oklahoma), July 7, 1891; s. Joseph S. and Mary Jane (Folsom) S.; grad. Northeastern State Coll., Tahlequah, Okla., 1912 (life teacher's certificate); U. of Okla., 1915; student U. of Grenoble, France, 1919; m. Ona Beller, June 7, 1925; children—Denyse, Elaine. Admitted to Okla. bar, 1920; practice before state dist. courts, Supreme Court of Okla., U.S. Dist. Court of Eastern Okla., U.S. 10th Circuit Court of Appeals, U.S. Court of Claims and Supreme Court of U.S.; city atty., Stigler, Okla., 1920-24; elected state senator, 27th senatorial dist. Okla., 1924, reelected, 1928; pres. pro tem. of Okla. State Senate, 1931; nat. atty. for Choctaw Nation (Indian) 1937-44; mem. 78th to 82d Congresses (1944-53), 2d Okla. District. Served with 90th Div., as 2d lt., 357th Inf. A.E.F., during World War I; participated in offensives St. Mihiel and Meuse-Argonne; with Army of Occupation, Germany; lt. col., 45th Div., Okla. Nat. Guard, 1925-38. Mem. Soldiers Relief Commn. of Okla., 1932; former mem. state pardon and parole advisory board; former chmn. war finance com. of Haskell County; an exec. vice pres. Choctaw area council Boy Scouts of America, 1942-45. Nat. pres. 90th Div. Assn., 1935. Mem. Choctow Tribe of Indians. Mem. Am. Legion (dept. comdr., Okla., 1933; mem. nat. exec. com., 2 yrs.), 40 and 8, Vets. Fgn. Wars, Sigma Alpha Epsilon. Methodist (mem. bd. stewards). Mason (32 deg.) Shriner, Odd Fellow, Modern Woodman. Home: Stigler, Okla. Died Aug. 21, 1952.

STILES, WILLIAM HENRY congressman, lawyer; b. Savannah, Ga., Jan. 1, 1808; studed law Yale. Admitted to bar, 1831, practiced in Savannah; solicitor gen. Eastern Dist. Ga., 1833-36; mem. U.S. Ho. of Reps. (Democrat) from Ga., 28th Congress, 1843-45; chargé d'affaires to Austria (apptd. by Pres. Polk), 1845-49; mem. Ga. Ho. of Reps., speaker, 1858; del.-at-large from Ga. to Comml. Congress, Montgomery, Ala., 1858; del. Dem. Nat. Conv., Balt., 1860; served as col. in Confederate Army during Civil War. Died Savannah, Dec. 20, 1865; buried Laurel Grove Cemetery.

STILLWELL, LEANDER lawyer; b. Jersey Co., Ill., Sept. 16, 1843; s. Jeremiah O. and Ann Eliza (White) S.; ed. common schs.; LL.B., Albany Law Sch. (Union U.), 1868; m. Anna L. Stauber, of Erie, Kan., May 9, 1872 (died Apr. 9, 1909); children—Rena, Nora, Hubert, Charles Rodney (dec.), Jeremiah E. Enlisted Co. D, 61st Ill. Inf., Jan. 7, 1862, and advanced to 1st sergt.; reenlisted in same regt., at Little Rock, Ark., Feb. 1, 1864, as vet. volunteer; commd. 2d lt., July 18, 1865; 1st lt., Aug. 21, 1865; hon. mustered out, Sept. 8, 1865; participated in Battle of Shiloh, siege of Vicksburg, and many minor engagements. Began practice at Erie, Kan., 1868; mem. Kan. Ho. of Rep., 1876; judge 7th Jud. Dist. of Kan., 6 terms, 1884-1907 (thrice elected without opposition); resigned; 1st dep. commr. pensions by appmt. of President Taft, 1909-13. Republican. Author: The Story of a Common Soldier, 1917. Home: Erie, Kan.

STILWELL, JOSEPH W. army officer; b. Florida, Mar. 19, 1883; B.S., U.S. Mil. Acad., 1904; grad. Advance Course, Inf. Sch., 1924, Command and Gen. Staff Sch., 1926; married; 3 daus., 2 sons. Comd. 2d lt., June 15, 1904; promoted through grades to maj. gen., Oct. 1, 1940; lt. gen., Feb. 1942, gen., Aug. 1, 1944; with 12th Inf., P.I., 1904-06 and 1911-12; instr. U.S. Mil. Acad., 1906-10, 1913-17; with A.E.F. General Hdqrs. and as asst. chief of staff, 4th Corps to May 1919; studied Chinese language, U. of Calif., 1 year, and in Peking, China, 3 years, 1920-23; served in Tientsin, China, 1926-29; instr. Inf. Sch., Fort Benning, 1929-33; mil. attache, Peiping, China, 1935-39; com. 3d Inf. Brigade, Fort Sam Houston, 1939, 7th Div., Fort Ord, Calif., 1940-41, 3d Army Corps, Presidio of Monterey, Calif., 1941-42; apptd. comdr. 5th and 6th Chinese Armies in Burma by Chiang Kai-Shek, Mar. 1942; comdg. gen. U.S. Forces in China-Burma-India, 1942-44; relieved, Nov. 1944; apptd. comdr. U.S. ground forces, Jan. 1945. Apptd. comdr. 10th army, Pacific Theater, June, 1945. Awarded D.S.C.; D.S.M. with Oak Leaf Cluster; Legion of Merit; Philippine Campaign; Victory Medal, 2 Stars; China Service Ribbon, Navy Decoration; American Defense Service; Asiatic-Pacific, 3 stars; French Chevalier de Legion d'Honneur; La Solidaridad (2nd Class), Panama. Home: Carmel, Calif. Died Oct. 12, 1946.

STIMSON, HENRY LEWIS former secretary of war; b. N.Y. City, Sept. 21, 1867; s. Lewis Atterbury and Candace (Wheeler) S.; A.B., Yale Univ., 1888; A.M., Harvard Univ., 1889; Harvard Law Sch., 1889-90; m. Mabel Wellington White, July 6, 1893. Admitted to bar, 1891; became mem. Root & Clarke, 1893, Root, Howard, Winthrop & Stimson, 1897, Winthrop & Stimson, 1901, Winthrop, Stimson, Putnam & Roberts since 1927; U.S. atty. Southern Dist., N.Y., 1906-09; Rep. candidate for gov. of N.Y., 1910; sec. of war in Cabinet of President Taft, May 1911-Mar. 5, 1913. Del. at large, New York Constl. Conv., 1915; special rep. of President to Nicaragua, 1927; gov. general of Philippine Islands, 1927-29; sec. of state in Cabinet of President Hoover, Mar. 1929-33; secretary of war in Cabinet of President Roosevelt, July 1940-Apr. 1945, President Truman's Cabinet, Apr.-Sept. 1945; retired Sept. 1945. Chmn. Am. delegation to London Naval Conf., 1930; chmn. Am. delegation to Disarmament Conf., 1932. Commd. maj. judge advocate U.S. Res., Mar. 1917; lt. col. 305th F.A., Aug. 1917; col. 31st F.A., Aug. 1918; with A.E.F. in France, Dec. 1917-Aug. 1918. Republican. Presbyterian. Mem. Am., city and state bar assns., Psi Upsilon, Skull and Bones (Yale). Clubs: Century, University, Republican, Down Town (New York); Metropolitan (Washington). Office: 40 Wall St., N.Y. City. Died Oct. 20, 1950.

STIMSON, JULIA CATHERINE nurse; b. Worcester, Mass., May 26, 1881; d. Henry A. (D.D.) and Alice Wheaton (Bartlett) Stimson; prep. edn., Brearley Sch., N.Y. City; A.B., Vassar Coll., 1901; A.M., Washington U., 1917; hon. Sc.D., Mt. Holyoke Coll., S. Hadley, Mass., 1921; unmarried. Grad. as nurse, New York Hosp., 1908; supt. nurses, Harlem Hosp., N.Y. City, 1908-10; adminstr. of hosp. social service, Washington U., 1911-12; dir. Sch. of Nursing, St. Louis, 1913-17; chief nurse Base Hosp. No. 21, A.E.F., 1917-18; dir. nursing service, A.E.F., 1918-19; supt. Army Nurse Corps, U.S. Army, since 1919; rank of maj. since Nat. Defense Act, June 4, 1920. Retired from active service, May 30, 1937; recalled to active duty in Army Nurse Corps, 1943-44; advanced to col. U.S. Army Nurse Corps, ret., June 1948. Member Am. Nurses Assn. (pres. 1938-44). Decorations: D.S.M. (U.S.); Royal Red Cross, 1st Class (Great Britain); Medaille de la Reconnaissance (France); Florence Nightingale medal, Internat. Red Cross Com. Democrat. Congregationalist. Club: Army-Navy Country (Washington, D.C.). Author: Nurses' Handbook of Drugs and Solutions, 1910; Finding Themselves (war letters), 1918. Home: Horse-chestnut Road, Briarcliff Manor, N.Y.; (summer) Rockland, Me. Died Sept. 30, 1948.

STIMSON, LEWIS ATTERBURY surgeon; b. Paterson, N.J., Aug. 1844; s. Henry C. and Julia M. (Atterbury) S.; brother of Henry Albert and John Ward S.; A.B., Yale, 1863; M.D., Bellevue Hosp. Med. Coll. (New York U.), 1874; (LL.D., Yale, 1900); served in Union Army in Civil War as capt. and a.-d.-c., 1864-65; traveled and studied abroad until 1873; m. Candace Wheeler, Nov. 1866; father of Henry Lewis S. Prof. of physiology, 1883-85, anatomy, 1885-89, surgery, 1889-98, New York U.; prof. surgery, Cornell U. Med. Coll., 1898-—. Regent U. State of N.Y., 1893-1904. Author: Operative Surgery, 1900; Fractures and Dislocations (6th edit.), 1910. Home: New York, N.Y. Died Sept. 17, 1917.

STIMSON, PHILIP MOEN, pediatrician; b. St. Louis, Mo., Nov. 1, 1888; s. Henry Albert and Alice Wheaton (Bartlett) S.; ed. The Hill Sch.; A.B., Yale, 1910; M.D., Cornell, 1914; m. Elizabeth Baldwin, June 5, 1920. Interne N.Y. Hosp., 1914-16; asst. resident in pediatrics, St. Louis Childrens Hosp., 1916-17; dir. Poliomyelities Service, Knickerbocker Hosp., 1945-49; med. dir. Floating Hosp. of St. John's Guild at N.Y. City, from 1927; attending physician Willard Parker Hosp., N.Y.C., 1924-55; consulting pediatrician Meadowbrook, Bergen Pines, Norwegian, New York, Roosevelt, Horton Memorial and the St. Francis hosps.; prof. emeritus clin. pediatrics Cornell University Medical College. Served lieutenant to captain, United States Army, 1917-19. Awarded Purple Heart with oak leaf. Diplomate American Bd. Pediatrics; fellow Am. Acad. Pediatrics, A.M.A. life fellow in pediatrics, N.Y.

Acad. Med. (chmn. Pediatrics Sect., 1938-39); founder mem. Clin. Research Soc., Pediatric Travel Club. Trustee The Hill Sch.; pres. of bd. of trustees St. John's Guild since 1951; member of the advisory committee of the Intercollegiate br., Y.M.C.A. Mem. The Century Assn. Author: (with Hodes) Common Contagious Diseases, 5th edit., 1956. Contbr. articles to various jours. Home: Hightstown NJ Died Sept. 13, 1971; inurned Columbarium, Riverside Ch., New York City NY

STINCHFIELD, FREDERICK HAROLD lawyer; b. Danforth, Me., May 8, 1881; s. Amaziah and Rose Brown (Foss) S.; A.B., Bates Coll., 1900, LL.D., 1937; LL.B., Harvard, 1905; LL.D., Bowdoin Coll., 1937, LL.D., American U., 1938; m. Elizabeth Shrader, Oct. 31, 1928. Admitted to N.Y. bar, 1906, and began practice at N.Y. City; moved to Minneapolis, 1908; mem. Jamison, Stinchfield & Mackall, 1918-29, Stinchfield, Mackall, Crounse, McNally & Moore, 1929-40, Stinchfield, Mackall, Crounse & Moore since 1940; dir. and counsel Twin City Federal Savings & Loan Assn.; director Public Markets Inc., United Fur Ranches. Major, judge advocate general's dept., U.S. Army, 1918. Mem. Draft Board, Minneapolis, World War I. Member American Bar Association, president 1936-37), Minn. State Bar Assn. (ex-pres.), Hennepin County Bar Assn. (ex-pres.), Am. Law Institute (charter member), Nat. Econ. League, Am. Liberty League (advisory council), Am. Judicature Soc. Republican. Baptist. Mason (Shriner). Clubs: Minneapolis, Minikahda (ex-pres.), Minneapolis Athletic. Home: 1819 Mt. Curve Av. Office: 1100 First Nat. Soo Line Bldg., Minneapolis, Minn. Died Jan. 15, 1950; buried Lakewood Cemetery, Minneapolis.

STIRLING, YATES naval officer; b. Baltimore, Md., May 6, 1843; s. Archibald and Elizabeth Ann (Walsh) S.; apptd. to U.S. Naval Acad. from Md., 1860, grad. 1863; m. Ellen Salisbury Haley, Aug. 29, 1867; children—Helen, Marie Yates (Mrs. J. Lee Tailer), Yates, Margaret Yates (Mrs. J. Pembroke Thom), Archibald, Alice, Walter (dec.). Ensign, May 28, 1863; promoted through grades to rear adm., June 8, 1902; retired May 6, 1905. Served on Shenandoah, N. Atlantic Blockading Squadron, 1863-65; participated in both attacks on Ft. Fisher; on bd. Mohongo, Pacific Squadron, 1865-67, Wampanoag, Jan.-Mar. 1868, Contoocook, 1868-69; duty Hydrographic Office, 1870; on bd. receiving ship Independence, 1871-72; exec. officer receiving ships New Hampshire, 1875, Worcester, 1876; torpedo duty, 1877; ordnance duty, Navy Yard, Washington, 1878, 1882-84; exec. officer Lackawanna, 1878-81; comd. Iroquois, 1884-86, receiving-ship Dale, 1887-89, Dolphin, 1890-91; light house insp. 5th dist., 1892-94; comd. Newark, 1895-96, Lancaster, 1896-97; mem. Lighthouse Bd., 1898-1900; comdt. Naval Sta., San Juan, P.R., 1900-02, Navy Yard, Puget Sound, 1902-03; comd. Philippine Squadron, Asiatic Fleet, 1902-03, Cruiser Squadron, Asiatic Fleet, 1904; comdr.-in-chief Asiatic Fleet, 1904-05. Home: Baltimore, Md. Died Mar. 5, 1929.

STIRLING, YATES JR. naval officer, author; b. Vallejo, Calif., Apr. 30, 1872; s. Rear Admiral Yates and Ellen Salisbury (Haley) S.; grad. U.S. Naval Acad., 1892; Naval War Coll., 1912; m. Adelaide Egbert, Dec. 12, 1903; children—Yates, Ellen E., Adelaide Y., Harry E., Kathrin G. Midshipman, 1892-94; promoted through grades to capt., Aug. 1917. Participated in expedition for recovery of Spanish contact mines in Guantanamo Harbor, 1898; served in Philippines during insurrection there, comdg. gunboat Paragua; made world's cruise in battleship Connecticut, 1907-08; comd. destroyer Paulding, 1910-11; staff, Naval War Coll., 1912-13, exec. officer battleship Rhode Island, 1913-14; comd. submarine flotilla, Atlantic fleet, 1913; comd. monitor Ozark, 1914, cruiser Columbia, 1918, and submarine flotilla and base at New London, Conn., 1916; at outbreak of war fitted out and comd. navy transport President Lincoln, 1917; comd. auxiliary cruiser Von Steuben (ex-German Crown Prince Wilhelm), 1917-18; chief of staff Naval Dist., New York, 1918-19; comd. battleship Connecticut, 1919; duty Navy Yard, Phila., 1920. Comdg. battleship New Mexico, 1922-24; at Navy Yard, Washington, D.C., 1925; promoted to rear admiral 1926; apptd. chief of staff, U.S. Fleet, 1927; then comdr. Yangtze Patrol, China; later comdt. 14th Naval Dist., hdqrs. Pearl Harbor, T.H.; comdt. 3d Naval Dist., New York; retired, Apr. 30, 1936. Service Medals: Spanish War, Santiago Campaign; Philippine insurrection; Mexico, 1914; World War, Legion of Honor (France), Navy Cross; Comdr. Order of Bolivar (Venezuela). Presbyn. Clubs: Army and Navy (Washington); New York Yacht. Author: U.S. Midshipman Series (5 vols.); Fundamentals of Naval Service; Sea Duty; How to Be a Naval Officer; Why Seapower Will Win the War. Address: 375 Park Av., New York, N.Y.* Died Jan. 27, 1948.

STITT, EDWARD RHODES rear adm. med. Corps, U.S. Navy; b. Charlotte, N.C., July 22, 1867; s. William Edward and Mary (Rhodes) S.; A.B., U. of S.C., 1885; M.D., U. of Pa., 1889; studied London Sch. of Tropical Medicine, 1905; LL.D., Univ. of S. Carolina, 1917, U. of Mich., 1921; Sc.D., Jefferson Med. Coll., 1920; Ph.M., Phila. Coll. of Pharmacy and Science, 1921; Sc.D., U. of Pa., 1924; m. Emma Woodruff Scott, July 19, 1892; children—Edward Wynkoop, Mary Raguet, Emma Scott; m. 2d, Laura Armistead Carter, June 22, 1935; m. 3d, Helen Bennett Newton, May 3, 1937. Apptd. asst. surgeon U.S. Navy, Mar. 27, 1889; passed asst. surgeon, Mar. 27, 1892; surgeon, June 7, 1900; med. dir. with rank of rear adm., Oct. 15, 1917. Has specialized in tropical diseases; teacher in U.S. Naval Med. Sch. and in service in Philippines; prof. tropical medicine, Georgetown U., and George Washington U.; lecturer on tropical medicine, Jefferson Med. Coll., Phila.; comdg. officer U.S. Naval Med. Sch., 1916-20; apptd. surgeon general, Nov. 30, 1920, re-appointed Nov. 30, 1924, retired Aug. 1, 1931. Mem. Nat. Bd. of Medical Examiners, 1915-29, pres., 1926-28. Consultant on tropical medicine to Sec. of War since 1941. Hon. Fellow Am. Coll. Surg.; mem. Am. Med. Assn., Assn. of American Physicians, American Coll. Physicians, Southern Med. Assn., Am. Soc. Tropical Medicine (pres., 1912), American Assn. Military Surgeons (pres. 1925-26), Royal Soc. Medicine, Sigma Alpha Epsilon, Phi Beta Kappa, Sigma Xi. Episcopalian. Clubs: Army and Navy, Cosmos (Washington); Rittenhouse, University (Phila.); New York Yacht. Author: Practical Bacteriology—Haematology and Animal Parasitology, 9th edit., 1938; Diagnostics and Treatment of Tropical Diseases, 5th edition, 1929. Home: 1625 R St. N.W., Washington 9, D.C. Died Nov. 13, 1948.

STIVERS, EDWIN JACOB major U.S.A.; b. Brooklyn, O., June 14, 1835; s. Jacob and Polly (Bankson) S.; ed. pub. schs. and Eastman Commercial Coll., Rochester, N.Y.; studied mathematics, French and Spanish under pvt. tutors; m. Kazia A. Rawson, of Chicago, Nov. 25, 1855. Fifer and pvt. Co. K, and fife maj. and sergt.-maj. 89th Ill. Inf., Aug. 7, 1862-Dec. 1, 1863; 2d lt. U.S.C.T., Dec. 2, 1863; 1st lt., Feb. 5, 1864; capt., Aug. 2, 1865; hon. mustered out of vol. service, Nov. 3, 1866; apptd. from Ill., 2d lt. 40th Inf., July 28, 1866; 1st lt., Sept. 15, 1868; transferred to 25th Inf., Apr. 20, 1869; capt., Feb. 19, 1883; retired for disability in line of duty, Feb. 24, 1891; advanced to rank of maj. retired, by act of Apr. 23, 1904. Bvtd. 1st lt., U.S.A., Mar. 2, 1867, "for gallant and meritorious services" in battle of Nashville; hon. mentioned by Gen. Rosecrans "for conspicuous gallantry in battle of Chickamauga." Mem. Loyal Legion; artist mem. Salmagundi Club; mem. American Club, Paris. Address: Care Am. Express Co., Paris, France.

STOBO, ROBERT army officer; b. Glasgow, Scotland, 1727; s. William Stobo; attended U. Glasgow, circa 1742. Capt., Va. Militia, fought with George Washington at Fort Necessity, 1754, captured by French; tried for treason by French, 1755, sentenced to be executed (sentence never confirmed); escaped down St. Lawrence River, 1759; received thanks of Va. Ho. of Burgesses and gift of 1000 pounds, 1759; capt. Foot's 15th Regt.; his life served as model for character of Tismahago in Smollett's The Expedition of Humphrey Clinker. Author: Memoirs of Major Robert Stobo of the Virginia Regiment, published posthumously, 1800. Died circa 1772.

STOCKDALE, GRANT ambassador; b. Greenville, Miss., July 31, 1915; s. Levert and Lydia (Virgin) S.; B.B.S., U. Miami (Fla.), 1940; m. Alice Boyd Magruder, May 30, 1940; children—Sally, Ann, Grant, Lee Lawson, Susan. Congl. adminstrv. asst., 1946-48; mem. Fla. Ho. of Reps. from Miami, 1948-49; mem. bd. commnrs. Dade County, Fla., 1952-56; organizer, owner Grant Stockdale and Assos., real estate, 1956-—; v.p. Automatic Vending Co., Inc., Miami; U.S. ambassador to Ireland, 1961-—. Served to capt. USMCR, 1943-46; PTO. Recipient Good Govt. award as Dade County commnr., 1956. Mem. Miami Jr. C. of C. (pres. 1943), Alumni Assn. U. Miami (pres. 1948). Home: 611 N. Greenway Dr., Coral Gables, Fla. Office: American Embassy, Dublin, Ireland. Died Dec. 2, 1963; buried Miami, Fla.

STOCKDALE, THOMAS RINGLAND congressman; b. Greene County, Pa., Mar. 28, 1828; s. William and Hannah (McQuaid) S.; grad. Jefferson (now Washington and Jefferson) Coll., 1856; law degree, U. Miss., 1858; m. Fannie Wicker, Feb. 13, 1867, at least 1 son, 1 dau. Moved to Miss., 1856; admitted to Miss. bar practiced law, Holmesville, Miss.; became pvt. Quitman Guards, Miss. Militia, 1861, rose to lt. col., served during Civil War; returned to practice law, 1865; mem. Democratic Nat. Conv., 1868; Dem. presdl. elector, 1872-84; mem. U.S. Ho. of Reps. (Democrat) from Miss., 51st-53d congresses, 1887-95; asso. judge Miss. Supreme Ct., 1896-97. Died Summit, Miss., Jan. 8, 1899; buried Woodlawn Cemetery.

STOCKTON, CHARLES HERBERT rear admiral U.S.N.; b. at Phila., Oct. 13, 1845; s. Rev. William R. and Emma T. S.; apptd. to U.S. Naval Acad. from Pa., 1861, grad. 1865; LL.D., George Washington U., 1909; m. Cornelia Carter; m. 2d, Pauline Lentilhon King, Nov. 23, 1880. Ensign, Dec. 1, 1866; master, Mar. 12, 1868; lt., Mar. 26, 1869; lt. comdr., Nov. 15, 1881; comdr., Apr. 3, 1892; capt. July 8, 1899; rear admiral, Jan. 7, 1906. Summer of 1864, on board the Macedonian, in pursuit of Confederate steamers Florida and Tallahassee; served on Dacotah, Chattanooga and Mohican; service Navy Yard, Phila., 1869-70, 1873, 1874; Congress and Brooklyn, 1870-73; Dictator, 1873; Swatara, 1874-75; Hydrographic Office, 1875-76; Plymouth, 1876-79; Navy Yard, New York, 1879-80; Navy Yard, Washington, 1880-82; Iroquois, 1882-85; Bur. of Yards and Docks, 1885-89; comd. Thetis, 1889-91; Naval War Coll., 1891-94; spl. duty, 1894-95; comd. Yorktown, 1895-97; pres. Naval War Coll., 1898-1900; comd. Kentucky, 1901-03; naval attaché, Am. Embassy, London, 1903-06; pres. Bd. Inspection and Survey, 1906; pres. Naval Examining and Retiring Bds., 1906-07; comdg. Spl. Service Squadron, visiting Bordeaux, France, for the maritime expn., 1907; retired, Oct. 13, 1907. Pres. George Washington U., 1910-18. First U.S. del. to London Naval Conf., 1908-09. Author of U.S. Naval War Code, and various works and papers on internat. law. Home: Washington, D.C. Died May 31, 1923.

STOCKTON, EDWARD A. JR. army officer; b. Phila., Pa., Apr. 22, 1886; s. Edward A. and Sara E. (Mann) S.; A.B., Central High Sch., Phila., Pa., 1904; B.S., U.S. Mil. Acad., 1908; grad. Coast Arty. Sch., Fort Monroe, Va., 1927, Command and Gen. Staff Sch., 1928, Army War Coll., 1931; m. Theodosia Roberts, Mar. 25, 1908; 1 dau., Marion Roberts (Mrs. Donald C. Graves). Commd. 2d lt., Coast Atty. Corps, U.S. Army, 1908; advanced through the grades to brig. gen., 1941; later comdg. gen. Harbor Defenses of San Francisco; comdg. Antiaircraft Replacement Training Center, Fort Eustis, Va. Decorated Legion of Merit, French Croix de Guerre with gilt and silver stars. Member Sons of Am. Revolution. Club: Army & Navy (Washington, D.C.). Address: War Dept., Washington 25, D.C. Died July 13, 1948.

STOCKTON, HOWARD lawyer, financier; b. Phila., Pa., Feb. 15, 1842; s. Philip Augustus and Mary Ann (Remington) S.; silver medalist, Royal Saxon Poly. Inst., Dresden, 1862; m. Mary Mason, Jan. 6, 1870; 1 son, Philip S. Apptd. capt. U.S.V., June 9, 1862; 1st lt., 3d R.I. Cav., Mar. 17, 1864; 2d lt., Ordnance Corps U.S.A., May 23, 1864; bvtd. 1st lt., and capt., Sept. 14, 1866; 1st lt. Ordnance Corps U.S.A., May 13, 1867; resigned from army June 1, 1871. Lawyer at Boston, Sept. 26, 1871-—. Treas. Cocheco Mfg. Co., 1876-87, Salmon Falls Mfg. Co., 1880-87; pres. Am. Bell Telephone Co., 1887-89; v.p. Old Colony R.R. Co.; dir. Merchants Nat. Bank, Boston Mfrs.' Mut. Fire Ins. Co.; treas. Merrimac Mfg. Co., 1889-1900, Essex Co., Boston, 1880-—; actuary Mass. Hosp. Life Ins. Co. Pres. Boston Athenaeum; trustee Mass. Inst. Tech.; del. to Diocesan convs., 1888-92; mem. Standing Com. Diocese of Mass., 1892. Home: Boston, Mass. Died Apr. 22, 1932.

STOCKTON, JOSEPH soldier, transportation agt.; b. Pittsburgh, Pa., Aug. 10, 1833; ed. schs. of Pittsburgh; moved to Chicago, 1851; clerk in commn. house, then in Am. Transportation Co., and Ft. Wayne R.R., 1851-62. Enlisted, July 1862, in 1st Bd. of Trade regt. (72d Ill. inf.), serving as 1st lt. to lt. col., 1862-65; wounded in battle of Franklin, Tenn., Nov. 30, 1864; bvtd. col. and brig. gen. for meritorious services. Agt. Empire Transportation Co., 1866-—. Mem. Bd. Commrs. Lincoln Park, 1869-93, and leader in securing completion of Grant Memorial. Republican. Home: Chicago, Ill. Died 1907.

STOCKTON, ROBERT FIELD naval officer, senator; b. Princeton, N.J., Aug. 20, 1795; s. Richard and Mary (Field) S.; attended Princeton, 1808; m. Harriet Maria Potter, 1823/24, 9 children including John Potter. Commd. midshipman U.S. Navy, 1811, lt., 1812; 1st lt. in ship Spitfire in War with Algiers, 1815; interested in Am. Colonization Soc., carried Dr. Eli Ayres (agt. for soc.) to West Coast of Africa and obtained by treaty new site for agency Cape Mesurado (later Liberia); employed in suppressing piracy in West Indies, 1822; had surveying duties, 1823-24, 27-28; invested in Del. & Raritan Canal, circa 1829, 1st pres.; invested in Camden & Amboy R.R.; owned racing horses; organized N.J. Colonization Soc., 1st pres.; commd. master comdt., 1830, capt., 1838; in command of Ohio as fleet capt. and capt., 1838; campaigned for Harrison in presdl. election, 1840; assisted in constrn. of steamer Princeton, 1st comdr., 1843-45; in command land operations in Cal., 1846; combined forces of navy and army, entered Los Angeles and claimed it for U.S.; organized civil and mil. govt. as gov. and comdr. in chief, resigned, 1850; mem. U.S. Senate (Democrat) from N.J., 1851-Jan. 10, 1853, introduced bill providing for abolition of flogging in navy and urged adequate harbor defenses; pres. Del. & Raritan Canal Co., 1853-66. del. to Peace Conf., Washington, D.C., 1861. Died Princeton, Oct. 7, 1866; buried Princeton Cemetery.

STODDARD, AMOS army officer, territorial gov.; b. Woodbury, Conn., Oct. 26, 1762; s. Anthony and Phebe (Reade) S.; never married. Enlisted in inf., 1779; asst. clk. Supreme Ct., Mass., 1784; commd. officer in suppression of Shay's Rebellion, 1787; admitted to Mass. bar, 1793; mem. Mass. Legislature, 1797; served with Mass. Militia, 1796-98; commd. capt. 2d Regt. Artillerists and Engrs., U.S. Army, 1798, maj., 1807; commd. 1st civil and mil. comdt. Upper La., 1803; agt. and commr. of France at transfer of Upper La. Territory from Spain to France to U.S., 1804; acting gov. La. Territory, 1804-12; defended Fort Meigs (O.) in War of 1812. Author: The Political Crisis, 1791. Died Fort Meigs, May 11, 1813.

STODDARD, FRANCIS RUSSELL lawyer; b. Boston, Mass., July 26, 1877; s. Francis Russell and Mary Frances (Baldwin) S.; prep. edn., schs. in France, Germany, Italy, and Hopkinson Sch., Boston; A.B., Harvard, 1899; law study Harvard and Buffalo law Sch.; m. Eleanor Sherburne Whipple, Nov. 8, 1909; children—Margery Pepperell, Howland Bradford, Anna Bailey (Mrs. Renwick Washington Hurry), Dudley Wentworth, Frances LeBaron (Mrs. Edward Delaney Dunn, Jr.). In law department Brooklyn Rapid Transit Company, 1902-09; with law firm Greene & Hurd, 1909-37, partner, 1915-49; now of counsel in succeeding firm Hamlin, Hubbell and Davis; special deputy attorney general of New York, 1910; mem. New York State Assembly, 1912, 14, 15; deputy superintendent of insurance, in charge New York City office of N.Y. State Insurance Department, 1915-21; state supt. ins., 1921-24; chmn. N.Y. State Pension Commn., 1921-24; chmn. exec. com. Nat. Conv. of Ins. Commrs., 1922-24; employed by N.J. Legislature to reorganize N.J. State Banking and Ins. Dept. and to revise ins. laws, 1925-26; spl. dep. atty. gen. of N.Y., 1925-28; arbitrator, Greater New York, for fidelity and surety companies of U.S., 1927-49, and for casualty companies, 1936-49; member N.Y. State Ins. Bd., 1933-—; counsel Eastern Life Insurance Company of N.Y., 1926-—, United Mutual Life Ins. Co., 1934-—. Vice president of Grant Monument Association. Served in Spanish-American War, 1898, Mexican border, 1916; major 9th Coast Arty., N.Y.G., 1917-18; on artillery mission at front with British and French Armies; maj. 17th Div., U.S. Army, 1918-19; lt. col. Ordnance O.R.C., 1919-23; colonel comdg. 533d C.A., 1923-35; now colonel retired. Organized New York City Patrol Corps; military aide of Mayor La Guardia during World War II. Republican leader 10th Assembly Dist., 1919-27; mem. N.Y. State Rep. Com., 1926-28. Mem. Sons of Revolution, Society Mayflower Descendants in State of N.Y. (ex-gov. and gov. gen. of gen. soc.), Soc. Colonial Wars in N.Y. State (ex-gov. and gov. gen.; now hon. gov. gen. of the gen. soc.), Soc. of the Cincinnati, St. Nicholas Soc. (ex-pres.), Naval and Military Order of Spanish American War, United Spanish War Veterans, American Legion, Military Society of the Loyal Legion, Phi Delta Phi. Episcopalian. Mason. Clubs: Union, Down Town, Badminton of City of N.Y. (ex-president). Author: The Stoddard Family, 1912; War Time France, 1918; The Pilgrims, 1935; The History of Acquisition Cost in the State of New York, 1914; The Truth About the Pilgrims, published, 1952. Contbr. numerous tech. articles on ins. Home: 791 Park Av., New York, N.Y.; and Cold Spring Harbor, L.I. Office: 386 Fourth Av., N.Y.C. 16. Died Oct. 11, 1957; buried Cold Spring Harbor, L.I., N.Y.

STODDERT, BENJAMIN sec. navy; b. Charles County, Md., 1751; s. Thomas and Sarah (Marshall) S.; m. Rebecca Lowndes, June 17, 1781. Served as capt. Pa. Regt., 1777, resigned, 1779; began career as mcht. in firm Forrest, Stoddert & Murdock, Georgetown, Md.; incorporator, later pres. Bank of Columbia, organized 1794; aided gov. in acquisition lands in D.C. at fair prices; 1st sec. navy, May 1798-1801, apptd. by Pres. John Adams; organized fleet of 50 ships during war scare with France, 1798-99, drew up bill for governing of Marine Corps, began constrn. naval hosp. at Newport, began work of locating docks and the establishment of navy yards. Died Bladensburg, Md., Dec. 7, 1813.

STOESSEL, ALBERT (stes'el), conductor; b. St. Louis, Mo., Oct. 11, 1894; s. Albert J. and Alfreda (Wiedmann) S.; ed. pub. schs., St. Louis; studied music, Berlin Hochschule; hon. M.A., New York, U., 1924; m. Julia Pickard, June 27, 1917; children—Albert Frederick (dec.), Edward Pickard, Frederick. Violin virtuoso since 1913; début Berlin, later Paris and New York; mem. faculty Inst. Musical Art, New York, 1919; musical dir. Symphony at Chautauqua Instn., summers since 1920; condr. N.Y. Oratorio Soc. since 1921; head of music dept. New York U., 1923-30; condr. Worcester (Mass.) Festival, 1925, Westchester (N.Y.) Festival, 1927-33; dir. opera and orchestra depts., Juilliard Grad. Sch. Served as 2d lt., 301st Inf., U.S. Army, 1917-19; dir. A.E.F. Bandmasters' Sch., Chaumont, France. Mem. Am. Soc. Composers, Authors Pubs., Nat. Inst. Arts and Letters; U.S. sect. Internat. Soc. for Contemporary Music. Officier d'Académie, France. Clubs: Town Hall, Century, Bohemians. Author: Technique of the Baton, 1919. Composer: Sonata in G (violin and piano); suite for 2 violins and piano; suite Antique for orchestra; Hispania (suite for piano); Garrick Opera in 3 acts; Concerto Grosso for Strings; also songs, choruses, orchestral and violin pieces, pedagogical works. Home: 14 E. 90th St. Office: 113 W. 57th St., New York, N.Y. Died May 12, 1943.

STOKES, CHARLES FRANCIS M.D., surgeon; b. N.Y. City, Feb. 20, 1863; s. Charles and Helen (Durham) S.; Adelphi Acad. and Poly. Inst. of Brooklyn; M.D., Coll. Phys. and Surg. (Columbia U.), 1884, Sc.D., 1911; LL.D., Jefferson Med. Coll., Phila., 1911; M.A., Harvard, 1912; m. Charlotte Bermingham, Apr. 18, 1892; 1 son, John Fraser. Entered U.S. Navy as asst. surgeon, Feb. 1, 1889; promoted surgeon, May 31, 1900, later med. insp. and med. dir.; retired Jan. 10, 1917. Surgeon gen. U.S.N. and chief Bur. Medicine and Surgery, with rank of rear admiral, Feb. 5, 1910-14. Later practiced in N.Y. City. Fellow Am. Coll. Surgeons (mem. original bd. of regents, 1913); pres. Am. Electrotherapeutic Assn. Home: New York, N.Y. Died Oct. 29, 1931.

STOKES, HAROLD PHELPS, newspaper man; b. N.Y.C., Jan. 10, 1887; s. Anson Phelps and Helen Louisa (Phelps) S.; grad. Groton (Mass.) Sch., 1904; B.A., Yale, 1909 (Phi Beta Kappa); traveled and studied in Europe, 1904-05, and in Far East, 1909-10; m. Elizabeth Miner King, Sept. 17, 1920; children—Helen Elizabeth, Lydia King, Anne Cornelia. Reporter N.Y. Evening Post, 1911-13; Albany corr., 1913-17; corr. for Evening Post at Peace Conf., Paris, France, 1919; Washington corr. Evening Post, 1919-23; sec. to Herbert Hoover, 1924-26; editorial staff N.Y. Times, 1926-37. Student 1st Plattsburg O.T.C., 1917; commd. 2d lt., Aug. 15, 1917; 1st lt., Sept. 2, 1918; served with 306th F.A., 77th Div., A.E.F., Sept. 1917-Apr. 1919; participated in Oise-Aisne and Meuse-Argonne campaigns. Trustee Trudeau (N.Y.) Sanatorium, 1913-38. Sec. Class of 1909, Yale, 1909-21. Episcopalian. Clubs: Yale, Century; Metropolitan (Washington). Home: Washington DC Died June 3, 1970.

STOKES, J(AMES) G(RAHAM) PHELPS publicist; b. N.Y.C., Mar. 18th, 1872; s. Anson Phelps and Helen Louise (Phelps) S.; Ph.B., Sheffield Sci. Sch., Yale, 1892; M.D., Coll. Phys. and Surg., Columbia, 1896, grad. work Sch. Polit. Sci., 1896-97; m. Rose Harriet Pastor, July 18, 1905; m. 2d, Lettice Lee Sands, Mar. 13, 1926. Pres. Austin Mining Co., 1897-1900, Nev. Central R.R. Co., 1897-1938, Nev. Central Motor Lines, Inc., 1928-49, The Nevada Co., 1897-—, Phelps Stokes Corp., 1927-—; v.p. State Bank of Nev., 1899-1904. Many yrs. mem. governing bds. of numerous ednl., philanthropic and sociol. orgns., including governing bds. and coms. of YMCA's in N.Y.C., at Yale, Columbia, and Governor's Island (U.S. Army br.), 1889-1947; founder of Y at Sheffield Sci. Sch., 1892, Coll. Phys. and Surg., 1895, West Side Branch, N.Y.C., 1896; mem. centennial com. YMCA of N.Y., 1944. Mem. bd. trustees Univ. Settlement Soc. of N.Y., 1897-1903, Hartley House, 1896-—; chmn. bd. trustees People's Inst., N.Y., 1897-1902; trustee Tuskegee (Ala.) Normal and Indsl. Inst., 1898-1907; dir. Burnham (Berkshire) Indsl. Farm, Cannan, N.Y., 1897-1909, N.Y. Juvenile Asylum (and Children's Village, Dobbs Ferry, N.Y.), 1900-06; treas. Manhattan Trade Sch. for Girls, 1902-03; trustee Northern Dispensary, N.Y.C., 1944-—, v.p., 1947-—. Treas., exec. com. Outdoor Recreation League of N.Y., 1899-1907; exec. com. Armstrong Assn. (for Hampton Inst., Va.), 1899-1907; mem., treas. N.Y. Child Labor Com., 1902-97; mem. exec. com. Prison Assn. of N.Y., 1899-1906; treas., mem. exec. com. (1904 incorporator) League for Polit. Edn. (later known as Town Hall, Inc.), 1903-07. Treas. Nat. Conf. Charities and Correction, 1904-05; rep. N.Y. Assn. for Improving Condition of Poor, at 1st N.Y. State Conf. Charities and Correction, at the capitol, Albany, N.Y., 1900; apptd. by 1st and 2d confs., mem. for 1901 of com. on care and relief of needy families in their own homes, apptd. by 4d and 5th confs., chmn. com. on preventive social work for 1904, mem. N.Y.C. com. for 6th N.Y. State Conf., 1906. Vice chmn., also its candidate for pres. bd. of aldermen of N.Y., Municipal Ownership League, 1905; v.p. Electoral Laws Improvement Assn., 1905; vice chmn. Independence League, 1905-06. Presdl. elector Populist ticket, 1904; mem. Socialist Party, 1906-17, mem. nat. exec. com., 1908, mem. state exec. com., Conn., 1911, Party candidate for N.Y. Assembly, 1908, for mayor of Stamford, Conn., 1912; pres. Intercollegiate Socialist Soc., 1907-18 (withdrew from soc. 1918); vice chmn. Nat. Party, 1917; sec.-treas. Social Dem. League of Am., 1917, treas., 1917-19; treas. Am. Alliance for Labor and Democracy, 1917-19. Hon. adviser Roerich Mus., N.Y., 1931-33. Mem. Squadron A, N.Y.N.G., 1898-1901; pvt., cav., U.S. Army, 1898-99; enlisted Vet. Corps of Arty., N.Y., Aug. 1917; trans. to 9th C.A.C., N.Y.G., Oct. 1917; promoted 2d lt., Mar. 1919, 1st lt., Aug. 1919, capt., Dec. 1919; capt. C.A.C., N.Y.N.G., 1920; capt. C.A., O.R.C., U.S., 1922; capt. adj., 244th Arty, C.A.C., U.S., Feb. 1924, maj., May 1924; maj. C.A., U.S., Aug. 1924; trans. to N.Y. State Res. List, 1926, State Ret. List, 1936. Awarded Mil. Cross of State of N.Y. (Conspicuous Service Cross), also N.Y. State decorations for long and faithful service and for service in aid of civil authority, 1922. Hon. councillor Russian Information Bureau in U.S., 1917-22; pres. Constitutional Democracy Assn., 1937-38; mem. adv. bd. Defense Soc., 1937, bd. trustees, 1938-40; mgr. Disaster Relief Service, 6th Precinct, A.R.C., N.Y.C., 1942. Fellow Am. Geog. Soc., N.Y. Acad. Scis.; mem. S.R., S.R. in State of N.Y. (sec. 1925-26), Soc. Am. Wars (sr. vice comdr. 1931), Soc. Colonial Wars, Naval and Mil. Order Spanish-Am. War (council 1953-—), N.Y. Soc. Mil. and Naval Officers World Wars (standing com. 1923-26), Soc. Am. Mil. Engrs., Soc. of Massing of the Colors, Am. Mus. Natural History (patron 1906-—), Met. Mus. Art, Pilgrims (N.Y. and London), India Soc. (Royal India and Pakistan Soc.) (London), Sulgrave Instn. (founder 1920), N.Y. State C. of C., Mus. of City of N.Y. (founder 1938), Archaeol. Inst. of Am., Société Francaise des Amis de l'Orient (Paris), Oriental Inst. (U. Chgo.), Am. Oriental Soc., Chelsea Post Am. Legion (hon.), Res. Officers Assn. (mem. council Manhattan chpt. 1941-42), Soc. Ex-members Squadron A, France-Am. Soc., Netherland-Am. Found., Italy-Am. Soc., China Soc. Am. (hon.), Acad. Polit. Sci. (life) Am. Hist. Assn., Am. Acad. Polit. and Social Sci., Delta Psi. Clubs: Century, University, Yale, Columbia, Military-Naval (bd. govs.; chmn. com. nat. defense, 1937-46), City, Drug and Chemical (hon.), Church. Vestryman Grace Episcopal Ch. Traveled around world, 1892-93. Mem. com. apptd. by gov., 1921, to represent State of N.Y. in welcoming to N.Y.C. representatives from European countries arriving in U.S. to attend Internat. Conf. on Limitation of Armaments, Washington. Home: 88 Grove St., N.Y.C. 14. Office: 235 Fourth Av., N.Y.C. 3. Died Apr. 8, 1960.

STOKES, JOHN HARRISON, JR., army officer; b. Freehold, N.J., Oct. 27, 1895; s. John Harrison and Elizabeth (Ayres) S.; B.S., U.S. Mil. Acad., 1918; m. Marion Elizabeth Mitchell, July 25, 1934; 1 son, John Harrison, III. Commd. 2d lt., U.S. Army, 1918, advanced through grades to maj. gen., 1953; served as chief of staff and asst. div. comdr. 2d Inf. Div., 1941-45, chief of staff XV Corps, 1945-46; dep. comdr. Allied Control Commn., Hungary, 1946-47; mil. attache. Hungary, 1947-49; chief of staff 6th Army, 1950-51; asst. chief of staff plans and operations Allied Forces So. Europe, Naples, Italy, 1951-53; mem. Sec. of Army's Review Bd. Council, 1953-54; comdg. gen. Mil. Dist. of Washington, 1954-56. Decorated Silver Star with oak leaf cluster, Legion of Merit with oak leaf cluster, B.S.M.; Legion of Honor, Croix de Guerre with palms (France); Russian Order of the Fatherland; War Cross (Czechoslovakia). Mem. Delta Tau Delta. Home: Menlo Park CA Died Nov. 1968; buried Presidio Nat. Cemetery CA

STOKES, MONTFORT senator, gov. N.C.; b. Lunenberg County, Va., Mar. 12, 1762; s. David and Sarah (Montfort) S.; m. Mary Irwin; m. 2d, Rachel Montgomery; children include Montfort S. Enlisted in Continental Navy, 1776, soon captured and imprisoned by British; clk. N.C. Senate, 1786-91; clk. Superior Court of Rowan County (N.C.), 1790; trustee U. N.C. 1805-38; Democratic presdl. elector, 1804, 12, 24, 28; served as maj. gen. N.C. Militia in War of 1812; mem. U.S. Senate from N.C., Dec. 4, 1816-23; pres. N.C. Constl. Conv., Raleigh, 1823; mem. N.C. Senate, 1826-29, N.C. Ho. of Commons, 1829-30; gov. N.C., 1830-32; a commr. to investigate conditions in present state of Okla., 1832; sub-agt. for Cherokee, Seneca and Shawnee Indians in Ark., 1836, agt., 1837-41. Died Ft. Gibson, Ark., Nov. 4, 1842; buried with mil. honors, Ft. Gibson Cemetery.

STOKES, WILLIAM BRICKLY congressman; b. Chatham County, N.C., Sept. 9, 1814; attended common schs.; studied law. Moved to Tenn., became farmer; mem. Tenn. Ho. of Reps., 1849-52; mem. Tenn. Senate, 1855-56; mem. U.S. Ho. of Reps. from Tenn. (as Whig) 36th, (as Republican) 39th-41st congresses, 1859-61, July 24, 1866-71; served as maj. Tenn. Volunteers in U.S. Army during Civil War, 1862, brevetted maj. gen., discharged, 1865; admitted to bar, 1867, practiced law, Alexandria, Tenn.; supr. internal revenue for Tenn. Died Alexandria, Mar. 14, 1897; buried East View Cemetery.

STOLLER, MORTON JOSEPH elec. engr., govt. ofcl.; b. N.Y.C., May 23, 1917; s. Samuel Bernard and Anna Estelle (Selman) S.; B. Elec. Engring., Coll. City N.Y., 1938; M. Elec. Engring., U. Va., 1949-52; m. Ruth Klarberg, Oct. 3, 1939; children—Peter J. and Robert N. (twins), Nancy E. With NASA, and predecessor, 1939-—, head radio control and telemetering sect., 1946-47, asst. chief instrument research div., 1947-58, chief space sci. projects. Office Space Flight Devel., 1958-60, asst. dir. satellite and sounding rocket programs, 1960-61, dep. dir. Office Applications, 1961-62, acting dir., 1962, dir., 1962-—. Mem. working group telemetering Research and Devel. Bd., 1946-50, chmn. working group precision tracking radar, 1948-50; mem. pane unmanned spacecraft Aero. and Astronautics Coordinating Bd., 1960-—, chmn., 1961-—. Mem. Am. Inst. E.E., I.R.E., Am. Geophys. Union, Assn. Computing Machinery. Home: 6212 Bannockburn Dr., Bethesda, Md. 20034. Office: 400 Maryland Av. S.W., Washington 25. Died June 13, 1963.

STONE, CALVIN PERRY prof. psychology; b. Portland, Ind., Feb. 28, 1892; s. Ezekiel and Emily (Brinkerhoff) S.; A.B., Valparaiso U., 1913; M.A., Indiana University, 1916, Doctor of Science (honorary), 1954; Ph.D., U. of Minn., 1921; married Minnie Ruth Kemper, June 30, 1917; children—James Herbert, Robert Kemper, Barbara Ruth. High sch. prin. and supt., 1910-14; teaching fellow, U. of Minn., 1916, 1919-21; dir. research Psychol. Lab. of Ind. Reformatory, 1916-17; instr. psychology and histology, U. of Minn., 1921-22; asst. prof. psychology, Stanford, 1922-25, asso. prof., 1925-29, prof. since 1929. Inst. Juvenile Research, 1928-29; research, New York Psychiatric Institute, 1945; Columbia U., summer 1945; U. of Wisconsin, summer 1947. Served as lieut., later capt. U.S. Medical Corps, World War I. Fellow A.A.A.S. (v.p. sect. I, 1938-39); mem. Western Psychol. Assn. (pres. 1931-32), Am. Psychol. Assn. (pres. 1941-42), Am. Assn. Univ. Profs., Am. Assn. on Mental Deficiency, Calif. Acad. Science, Western Naturalists, Soc. Exptl. Biology, Nat. Acad. Science, Sigma Xi. Republican. Author of many articles on exptl. studies of instinct, sex behavior, learning, memory, and genetic psychology. Editor Jour.

Comparative and Physiol. Psychology, 1947-50; Annual Review of Psychology since 1948; editor, Comparative Psychology, 1951. Home: 668 Alvarada Row, Stanford, Calif. Died Dec. 28, 1954; buried Alta Mesa Cemetery, Palo Alto, Cal.

STONE, CHARLES POMEROY army officer, engr.; b. Greenfield, Mass., Sept. 30, 1824; s. Dr. Alpheus Fletcher and Fanny Lincoln (Cushing) S.; grad. U.S. Mil. Acad., 1845; m. Maria Louisa Clary, 1853; m. 2d, Annie Granier Stone, 1863; 6 children. Served as 1st lt. U.S. Army in Mexican War, 1846; resigned commn., 1856; commd. col. D.C. Volunteers, 1861, col. 14th Inf., U.S. Army, 1861, brig. gen. U.S. Volunteers, 1861; unjustly blamed for death of ex-senator Baker (col. in command at Battle of Ball's Bluff 1861) arrested 1862, imprisoned in Ft. Layfayette, released, 1862; served at Ft. Hudson and in Red River campaign; mustered out of volunteer commn., commd. col. U.S. Army; assigned to Army of Potomac, resigned, 1864; eng., supt. Dover Mining Co., Goochland County, Va., 1865-69; served in Egyptian army, 1870-83, chief of staff, lt. gen.; chief engr. Fla. Ship Canal Co., 1883-84; constructing engr. for foundations of Statue of Liberty. Died N.Y.C., Jan. 24, 1887; buried West Point, N.Y.

STONE, DAVID LAMME, army officer; b. Stoneville, Miss., Aug. 15, 1876; s. David Lamme and Katie (Hunt) S.; grad. U.S. Mil. Acad., 1898; m. Helen Hoagland, Oct. 3, 1903; children—David Lamme, Mrs. Mark A. Devine, Mrs. John Theimer; m. 2d, Ruth B. Warfield, Dec. 20, 1931; m. 3d, Anita Thorne Corse, Jan. 1, 1936. Commd. 2d lt. inf., U.S. Army, Apr. 26, 1898; advanced through grades to major general, Oct. 1, 1936. Served in Cuba, 1898, Philippines, 1899-1903, with A.E.F., France, 1918-19. In charge mil. constrn. H.I.; built Camp Lewis, Wash., at beginning of World War; with 3d Div. in France in Marne, Chauteau Thierry, St. Mihiel, Argonne campaigns; staff Army of Occupation, Germany, 1919; Am. rep. on Inter-Allied Rhineland High Commn., Coblenz, 1919-23; Gen. Staff, 1923-25; comd. 6th Inf., Jefferson Barracks, Mo., 1925-26; exec. officer for asst. sec. of War in charge organized reserve affairs, 1926-30; comdg. 3d Inf., Ft. Snelling, 1931-32; prof. mil. science and tactics, U. of Ill., 1932-33; comdg. Ft. Snelling, 88th Div. Organized Res. and Civilian Conservation Corps, Northern Minn., 1933-35; comdg. gen. 3d Div., Ft. Lewis, Wash., 1935-36; dept. comdr. Panama Canal Dept., 1936-40; retired. Awarded D.S.M.; Silver Star Medal for gallantry against Philippine Insurgents (woulded in action); Maple Heart Decoration (U.S.); Comdr. Legion of Honor (France); Officer of Order of Leopold I (Belgium); Croix de Guerre (France). Episcopalian. Clubs: Chevy Chase, Army and Navy (Washington); Minnesota, University, Somerset (St. Paul); Minneapolis Club. Home: Thornewood, Tacoma WA*

STONE, EBENEZER WHITTIER army officer; b. Roxbury, Mass., June 1801. Served with U.S. Army, 1817-21; became officer Mass. Militia, 1822; mem. lower house Mass. Legislature, 1840-41, mem. mil. com.; adj. gen. Mass., 1851-60; organized light arty. battery Mass. Militia (1st battery of light arty. outside of U.S. Army), 1853; secured adoption of rifled musket in Mass. Militia, 1855; designed 1st rifled cannon for U.S. Army, 1859; chief ordnance officer Mass. Militia, 1861. Author: Digest of the Militia Laws of Massachusetts, 1851; Manual of Percussion Arms, 1857. Died Boston, Apr. 18, 1880.

STONE, GEORGE WHITEFIELD b. Moravia, N.Y., Feb. 29, 1840; s. Jacob Thompson and Mary (Bennett) S.; grad. Cortland Acad., Homer, N.Y., 1860; m. Catherine Cushing Graupner, Feb. 28, 1865; m. 2d, Jane E. Stikeman, Oct. 13, 1920. Enlisted in Union Army, Apr. 1861; commd. capt. 12th N.Y. Vols., May 1, 1861; apptd. actg. asst. p.m., U.S.N., Aug. 1861; detailed as judge advocate during last 2 yrs. of war. In merc. bus. till 1889; nat. bank examiner, 1889-95 (resigned); apptd. treas. Am. Unitarian Assn., 1895; ordained Unitarian ministry, 1898; field sec. Unitarian Ch. for Pacific Coast, 1898-1907 (resigned); mayor of Santa Cruz, Calif., July 1911-July 7, 1913. Apptd. by Gov. Johnson mem. State Bd. of Edn., Aug. 29, 1913, reapptd. term 1917-21. Contbg. editor Santa Cruz Sentinel. Mason. Home: Santa Cruz, Calif. Died Mar. 19, 1923.

STONE, HARRY R. business exec.; b. Macon, Ga., Oct. 7, 1896; s. William T. and Ida (Lowrey) S.; student Emory Coll., Oxford, Ga., 1910-12; extension student Ga. Inst. Tech., Atlanta, 1912-14; m. May Gunter, Sept. 29, 1920; children—Elizabeth Davis (Mrs. J. Lamar Pierson), Harry Harlan. With So. Bell Tel. & Tel. Co., 1912-—, auditor disbursements, 1930-39, gen. auditor, 1939-44, comptroller 1944-—, v.p., 1952-—. Served as sgt. Ga. N.G., 1913-15; 2d lt. F.A., U.S. Army, World War I. Episcopalian. Mason. Clubs: Capital City, Civitan (Atlanta). Home: 3824 Vermont Rd. N.E. Office: So. Bell Tel. & Tel. Co., Atlanta. Died Mar. 16, 1965; buried Oxford (Ga.) Cemetery.

STONE, HERBERT LAWRENCE editor; b. Charleston, S.C., Jan. 18, 1871; s. William and Mary A. (Taylor) S.; ed. private schs., N.Y. City; m. Redelia Gilchrist. Asst. p.m. N.Y.C. R.R., until 1907; editor Yachting since 1908; president Yachting Publishing Corp. since 1938. Lt. (sr. grade) U.S.N.R.F., April 1917-August 1919; served as navigating officer cruiser Montgomery, transport Pastores; comdr. U.S.S. Onward, Squadron 1, Sub Chasers. Clubs: Cruising Club America, New York Yacht, Larchmont Yacht, Stamford Yacht, Royal Ocean Racing. Author: America's Cup Races, 1914, 30; The Yachtman's Handbook (with others), 1915; Millions for Defense, 1934; The A.B.C. of Boat Sailing, 1946. Editor: Ice Boating, 1916. Home: Pound Ridge, N.Y. Office: 205 E. 42nd St., N.Y.C. Died Sept. 27, 1955.

STONE, JOHN HOLDEN lawyer; b. Boston, Mass., Aug. 22, 1881; s. Oscar Perry and Martha Alice (Rice) S.; grad. high sch., Malden, Mass., 1900; A.B., Harvard, 1904, LL.B., 1907; m. Louise Freeman, May 19, 1908; children—John Freeman, Paulina, Harriet. Admitted to Mass. bar, 1907, and began practice with Choate, Hall & Stewart at Boston; gen. practice, 1908-18; gen. counsel Atlantic Refining Co., Phila., and its subsidiaries; pres. Atlantic Co. City counsel, Everett, 1909; mem. Ho. of Reps., Mass., 1913. Served as maj. Judge Adv. General's Dept., U.S.A., in France and Belgium, 1918-19. Republican. Unitarian. Mason. Home: Wayne, Pa. Died Apr. 7, 1935.

STONE, JOHN PITTMAN, lawyer; b. Carroll County, Miss., Oct. 9, 1890; s. Isaac Burgess and Katherine (Farmer) S.; B.S., U. Miss., 1913, LL.B., 1916; M. Ruth Sisler, Nov. 7, 1933; children—Nancy Ruth (Mrs. John E. Kimbrough), John Burgess. Admitted to Miss. bar, 1916; local atty. I.C. R.R., 1920-69; organized Tallahatchie Valley Electric Power Assn., 1936, gen. counsel, 1936-61; atty. Bank of Water Valley, Miss., municipality atty., Coffeeville, Miss.; assisted orgn. Oxford Prodn. Credit Assn., 1934, v.p., dir., 1934-44; organized Yalobusha County Soil Conservation Dist., 1938, now dir.; mem. stockholders com. of nine Nat. Farm Loan Assns., 1950-59; nat. adv. committeeman Fed. Loan Bank Assns., 5th Farm Credit Dist., 1950-59, chmn. nat. adv. com., 1955-56; mem. Fed. Farm Credit Bd., 1959. Mem. Miss. Legislature, 1920-28; sec. County Democratic Exec. Com., 1943-69. Served as lt., Air Corps, U.S. Army, 1917-19. Named col. staff gov. Miss. Mem. Miss. Bar Assn., Coffeeville C. of C., Am. Legion, Miss. Farm Bur., Phi Kappa Psi. Mason. Home: Coffeeville MS Died Aug. 22, 1969.

STONE, LEWIS actor; b. Worcester, Mass., Nov. 15, 1879; s. Bertrand and Lucy S.; student Columbia U.; m. Hazel Woof, Oct. 15, 1930; children—Virginia, Barbara. Starred on stage in N.Y.C., also in Belasco Theatre, Los Angeles; has starred in motion pictures, 1915-—; plays in all "Andy Hardy Family Series." Served in U.S. Army in Spanish-Am. War and World War, advancing to rank of maj. Home: San Fernando, Cal. Address: care Metro-Goldwyn-Mayer, Culver City, Cal. Died Sept. 12, 1953.

STONE, RALEIGH WEBSTER, economist; b. Portland, Ind., Dec. 18, 1889; s. Ezekiel and Emily (Brinkerhoff) S.; S.M., Valparaiso (Ind.) U., 1914; Ph.D., U. of Chicago, 1919; m. Ursula Chase Batchelder, Sept. 1, 1928; children—Mary Alzina, George Batchelder. Public sch. teacher, Portland, Ind., 1906-07, Union City, Ind., 1910, Bryant, Ind., 1913; asst. prof. social science Goucher Coll., Baltimore, 1920; asst. prof. economics, U. of Ia., 1920-23; dir. of research Nat. Industrial Conf. Bd., 1923-24; prof. indsl. relations U. of Chicago from 1924. Econ. counselor, Div. of Review, N.R.A., 1935-36. Cons. to bus. and union orgns. Served as capt., inf., U.S. Army, 1917-19. Mem. Am. Econ. Assn., Indsl. Relations Assn. of Chicago (mem. exec. com.). Club: Quadrangle (Chicago). Author: Financing Education (with William F. Russell and others), 1925; The Baking Industry under N.R.A. (with U. B. Stone), 1936. Editor: Problems in Collective Bargaining, 1938. Home: Chicago IL Died Apr. 29, 1969.

STONE, ROYAL AUGUSTUS judge; b. LeSueur, Minn., June 26, 1875; s. Herman Ward and Polly (Wells) S.; student Carleton Coll., 1892-94, U. of Minn., 1895; LL.B.. Washington U., 1897; m. Edith Olive Whiting, Aug. 14, 1901. Admitted to Minn. bar, 1897, and began practice at Morris; asst. atty. gen. of Minn., 1905-07; mem. O'Brien, Stone, Horn & Stringer, St. Paul, 1907-23, except during war; apptd. by gov. asso. justice Supreme Court of Minn., 1923, and elected to same office, 1924, 1930 and 1936, 3d term ending 1942. Served as pvt. and sergt. 15th Minn. Vol. Inf., 1898, Spanish-Am. War; also as capt. and maj. 349th Inf., 88th Div., and 14th Inf., 19th Division, United States Army, World War. Chairman Minnesota Judicial Council. Member American, Minn. State and Ramsey County bar assns., Am. Law Inst. Conglist. Mason. Clubs: Minesota, St. Paul Athletic. Home: 903 Goodrich Av. Address: State Capitol, St. Paul, Minn. Died Sep. 13, 1942.

STONE, WILLIAM colonial gov.; b. Northamptonshire, Eng., 1605; m. Virlinda Cotton, 7 children. Came to Va. before 1628; justice Accomac County (Va.), 1633; sheriff of Northampton, 1 term; gov. Md., 1648, Toleration Act of 1649 (which required oath to England) passed under his administration, 1649; opposed by Puritan parliamentary commn. from Eng., 1652-54, forced by them to resign, 1654; under orders from Lord Baltimore gathered small force and met Puritans in Battle of the Severn, 1655, defeated, wounded and captured, sentenced to death by council of war but saved by friends among the Puritans; mem. Gov. Josias Gendall's Council, 1657. Died on estate, Charles County, Md., circa 1660.

STONE, WILLIAM congressman; b. Sevier County, Tenn. (then N.C.), Jan. 26, 1791; completed prep. studies. Held several local offices; served as capt. in Creek War, commd. brig. gen. for gallantry at Battle of Horseshoe; served with Gen. Jackson in Battle of New Orleans; presented cane by Congress for bravery at Battle of Tippecanoe; mem. U.S. Ho. of Reps. (filled vacancy) from Tenn., 25th Congress, Sept. 14, 1837-39. Died Delphi (later Davis), Sequatchie County, Tenn., Feb. 18, 1853; buried family burying ground at Delphi.

STONE, WILLIAM ALEXIS gov. Pa., congressman, lawyer; b. nr. Wellsboro, Tioga County, Pa., Apr. 18, 1846; attended Pa. Normal Sch., Mansfield; studied law, Wellsboro, Pa. Served in Civil War as 2d lt. Company A, 187th Regt., Pa. Volunteer Inf.; became lt. col. Pa. Nat. Guard after war; admitted to bar, 1870, practiced in Wellsboro and Pitts.; dist. atty. Tioga County, 1874-76, resigned, moved to Pitts.; U.S. atty. for Western Dist. Pa., 1880-86; mem. U.S. Ho. of Reps. (Republican) from Pa., 52d-55th congresses, 1891-Nov. 9, 1898 (resigned); gov. Pa., 1899-1903; prothonotary Eastern Dist. Pa., 1916-20. Died Phila., Mar. 1, 1920; buried Wellsboro Cemetery.

STONE, WILLIAM S(EBASTIAN), air force officer; b. Cape Girardeau, Mo., Jan. 6, 1910; s. William M. and Emma (Albert) S.; B.S. in Engring., U.S. Mil. Acad., 1934; M.S. in Meteorology, Cal. Inst. Tech., 1938; M.A. in Econs., Columbia, 1949; m. Myra McCarthy, Sept. 15, 1937; children—Susan, William McCarthy. Commd. 2d lt. U.S. Army, 1934, advanced through grades to gen., 1966; with meteorol. service USAAF, 1937-40, 42-47; instr. econs. and govt. U.S. Mil. Acad., 1940-42, asso. prof. social scis., 1947-50; assigned Nat. War Coll., 1950-51; with plans div. Hdqrs USAF, Europe, 1951-53; directorate personnel plans, asst. dep. chief staff, personnel Hdqrs. USAF, Washington, 1953-57; comdr. Eastern Air Force Transport, Mil. Air Transport Service, McGuire AFB, N.J., 1957-59; supt. USAF Acad., Colo., 1959-62; dep. chief staff, personnel Hdqrs. USAF, Washington, 1962-66; air dep. to supreme allied comdr. Europe, Paris, France, 1966-68. Mem. Order Daedalians. Clubs: Belle Haven (Va.) Country; Army and Navy (Washington); Rotary (hon.) (Colorado Springs). Author: Meteorology for Pilots, 1938; Strategic and Critical Raw Materials, 1950. Co-author: Economics of National Security, 1950; Contemporary Foreign Governments, 1940. Died Dec. 1968.

STONEMAN, GEORGE army officer, gov. Cal.; b. Busti, N.Y., Aug. 8, 1822; s. George and Catherine (Cheney) S.; grad. U.S. Mil. Acad., 1846; m. Mary Oliver Hardisty, circa 1865, 4 children. Brevetted 2d lt. 1st Dragoons (now 1st cavalry); q.m. "Mormon Battalion," a part of Gen. Kearney's expdn. to Cal., 1846; served in Southwest until 1855; capt. 25th U.S. Cavalry; maj. 4th Cavalry, 1861, on Gen. McClellan's staff; brig. gen. volunteers, cavalry officer Army of Potomac; in command 1st div. III Corps, Peninsular Campaign of 1862; maj. gen. U.S. Volunteers, 1862; commd. col. U.S. Army, served in battles of Fredericksburg, then Chancellorsville, 1863; chief Cavalry Bur., Washington, D.C., 1863; served in cavalry corps Army of the Ohio, 1864, with Sherman in march through Ga., captured Aug. 1864, exchanged, Oct. 1864; brevetted brig. gen. and maj. gen. U.S. Army, 1865; commanded in Petersburg and Richmond, 1865-69; col. 21st Inf., 1866, commanded Dept. of Ariz., 1869-71; gov. Cal. (Democrat), 1883-87; ry. commr., 1879, opposed influence of Pacific rys. in state affairs; restored to army list as col., ret., by spl. act of Congress, 1891. Died Buffalo, N.Y., Sept. 5, 1894; buried Lakewood, Chaletauqua Lake, N.Y.

STONER, FRANK E. army officer; b. Vancouver, Wash., Dec. 25, 1894; s. Frederick Mayer and Alice A. (La Voy) S.; student U.S. Mil. Acad., 1915-16; grad. Signal Corps Sch., 1928, Command and Gen. Staff Sch., 1937, Army Indsl. Coll., 1940; m. Deah D. Gilroy, Aug. 31, 1917; children—Frank Gilroy, Larry Ballard. Began as pvt. 145t Inf., U.S. Army, 1914; sgt., 1916; commd. 2d lt., Philippines Scouts, 1917; advanced through grades to maj. gen., 1944; service in Philippines, 1917-24; prof. mil. sci. and tactics, Dallas High Sch., 1922-23; in charge War Dept. Message Center and War Dept. Radio Net., Washington, 1928-32; duty with Washington-Alaska Mil. Cable and Telegraph System, Seattle, 1932-36; signal officer 5th Army Corps, 1940; signal officer 3d Army, 1941; assigned to Office of Chief Signal Officer, Washington, 1942; became asst. chief signal officer, 1945; apptd. dir. telecommunications UN, 1947; cons. Dept. State, 1952-—. Decorated D.S.M., World Wars I and II; North Am. and Victory ribbons, Army of Occupation Ribbon, European Service ribbon, World War II; Mexican Border and Def. Service medals (U.S.); Officer Legion of Honor (French); Comdr. Cross of Brit. Empire. Awarded: Marconi Distinguished Soc. medal, 1946. Home: 4742 W. Ruffner St., Seattle. Died May 1965.

STORER, CLEMENT senator, congressman; b. Kennebunk, Me., Sept. 20, 1760; completed prep. studies; studied medicine, Portsmouth, N.H., also

Europe. Practiced medicine, Portsmouth; served from capt. to maj. gen. of militia; mem. N.H. Ho. of Reps., 1810-12, speaker 1 year; mem. U.S. Ho. of Reps. from N.H., 10th Congress, 1807-09; mem. U.S. Senate (filled vacancy) from N.H., June 27, 1817-19; high sheriff Rockingham County, 1818-24. Died Portsmouth, N.H., Nov. 21, 1830; buried North Cemetery.

STORER, ROBERT TREAT PAINE cons. finance; born Boston, Apr. 17, 1893; s. John Humphreys and Edith (Paine) S.; grad. Noble and Greenough Sch., Boston, 1910; A.B., Harvard, 1914; m. Dorothy Paine, June 14, 1919; children—Dorothy (widow of William B. Long, Jr.), Robert T.P., Elizabeth. With Stone and Webster, Inc., and affiliates, 1914-17, 1919-23; treas., dir. Putnam and Storer, Inc., investment bankers, 1923-28; partner Jackson, Storer & Schwab and Wm. Schall & Co., 1928-30; with E. A. Pierce & Co., 1930-40; mfrs. rep., 1940-45; pres., treas. The Storer Assos., Inc., financial cons., Boston, 1945-—; dir. Am. Locker Co., Specialty Convertors, Inc. Mem. national council YMCA's, 1935-38 and 1945-54, exec. com. Mass. and R.I., 1946-—, pres. Boston, 1936-56, dir. Mem. Cambridge Municipal Def. Bd., Mass. chmn. U.S.O., 1942-46, vice chmn. nat. council U.S.O., 1944-46; trustee and mem. corp. Northeastern U.; bd. govs. Huntington Sch.; mem. Harvard Fund Council, 1950-56. Served as capt. and maj. 305th F.A., 77th Div., AEF, France, World War I. Decorated Silver star, World War I. Member Robert Treat Paine Association (dir.). Republican. Clubs: Harvard (N.Y.C., N.Y.); Cambridge (Mass.). Home: 133 Coolidge Hill, Cambridge 38, Mass. Office: 60 State St., Boston 9. Died Feb. 5, 1962.

STOREY, ROBERT GERALD JR. lawyer; b. Tyler, Tex., Apr. 27, 1921; s. Robert Gerald and Hazel (Porter) S.; B.A., U. Tex., 1941; indsl. adminstr. degree, Harvard Bus. Sch., 1942; LL.B., So. Meth. U., 1948; m. Elizabeth Anne Toline, Sept. 12, 1942; children—Robert Gerald III, John Charles, Frances Elise. Admitted to Tex. bar, 1948; partner Storey, Sanders, Sherrill & Armstrong, 1948-51, Storey, Armstrong & Steger, Dallas, 1952-—; dir. C. H. Collier Co. Mem. Greater Dallas Planning Council, Dallas Council on World Affairs, Dallas Citizens Traffic Commn. Mem. bd. mgrs. YMCA Boys Camp, East Dallas YMCA. Served as lt., USNR, 1942-45. Mem. Am. (chmn. jr. bar conf., house dels. 1957-—), Tex., Dallas (dir.) Inter-Am. bar assns., Am. Law Inst., Am. Judicature Soc., Dallas Assn. UN (pres. 1961), Delta Theta Phi. Mem. Christian Ch. Mason (32 deg.). Clubs: Kiwanis, Lakewood Country (bd. govs. 1958-60), Chaparral (Dallas). Home: 2531 Winsted Dr., Dallas 14. Office: Republic Nat. Bank Bldg., Dallas 1. Died Apr. 18, 1962; buried Restland Meml. Park, Dallas.

STORY, JOHN PATTEN major gen. U.S.A.; b. Waukesha, Wis., Aug. 25, 1841; s. John Patten and Elizabeth (Quarles) S.; grad. Carroll Coll., Waukesha, Wis., 1857, U.S. Mil. Acad., 1865; m. Caroline Sherman, Sept. 10, 1868. Apptd. 2d and 1st lt. 16th Inf., June 23, 1865; trans. to 34th Inf., Sept. 21, 1866; assigned to 2d Arty., Dec. 15, 1870; trans. to 4th Arty., Jan. 1, 1871; capt. 4th Arty., Sept. 14, 1883; maj. 7th Arty., Mar. 8, 1898; lt. col. arty. corps, May 8, 1901; col., Oct. 15, 1902; brig. gen. chief of arty. U.S.A., Jan. 22, 1904; maj. gen., June 17, 1905; retired at own request after 40 yrs.' service, June 19, 1905. Instr. in Arty. School, Ft. Monroe, Va., 1888-98; arty. insp., Atlantic coast, 1898-1902; comdt. Arty. Sch., 1902-04; gen. officer Gen. Staff U.S.A. and mem. Joint Army and Navy Bd., 1902-04; mem. Bd. Ordnance and Fortification, 1901-02, 1904-05; mem. Nat. Coast Defense Bd., 1905-07. Home: Pasadena, Calif. Died Mar. 25, 1915.

STORY, WALTER P. army officer; b. Bozeman, Mont., Dec. 18, 1883; s. Nelson and Ellen S.; ed. pvt. and pub. schs., Mont. and Cal.; Eastman Coll., 1902; Shattuck Mil. Acad., 1903; U.S. Army War Coll., 1933; Leavenworth 9th Corps Area, 1939; Gen. Officers Course, Ft. Benning, 1940; m. Lorenza Lazzarini, May 17, 1923. Enlisted as private in infantry, World War I; commd. capt. Infantry, Calif. National Guard, Dec. 1920, maj., 1921, col., 1922; organized and comd. 160th Infantry; brig. general of the line, July, 1926; comd. Long Beach, Calif. Area, during earthquake, 1933; major gen., July 1937; comd. 9th Army Corps, Ft. Lewis, summer 1940; entered Fed. Service Mar. 1941, assigned command of 40th Div. in training, Camp Merriam, Calif., relieved from comd. due to protracted illness, Sept. 1941, retired from active list July, 1942; maj. gen. Hon. Res., by order of sec. of army placed on A.U.S. ret. list, grade maj. gen., 1948. Decorations: Victory Medal, over 25 yrs. service medal; Medal of Merit; Pre-Pearl Harbor medal; Am. Def. Service Ribbon; Order Crown of Italy. Bookkeeper and teller, Comml. Nat. Bank, Bozeman, Montana; moved to Los Angeles, 1905, managed and pioneered first motor transit lines in West, in Tonopah-Goldfield, Nev., 1906; real estate business, Los Angeles, 1907-—; former v.p. L.A. Realty Bd., former mem. L.A. Fire and Police Pension Commn.; former dir. 6th Dist. Agrl. Assn., State of Cal.; chmn. bd. Mullen & Bluett Clothing Co.; pres. Building Owners and Mgrs. Assn. Los Angeles. Mem. S.R., Colonial Wars, Am. Legion (past comdr.), Spanish-Am. War Vets. (hon.), former mil. chmn. Los Angeles C. of C. Clubs: California, Bel Air Bay, Bohemian (San Francisco); Rancho Visitadores (Santa Barbara). Home: Penthouse, Story Bldg.; and 3405 Laurel Canyon Blvd., North Hollywood. Office: Walter P. Story Bldg., 6th and Broadway, Los Angeles 14. Deceased.

STOTESBURY, LOUIS WILLIAM (stots' ber-i), lawyer; b. Beacon, N.Y., Oct. 21, 1870; s. William, Jr., and Charlotte F. (Meyer) S.; B.S., Rutgers Coll., 1890, M.S., 1893; LL.B., New York U., 1892; m. Helen Mathers Tompkins, Oct. 7, 1897; 1 dau., Helen Mathers. Practiced N.Y. City, since 1892; counsel to N.Y. State Transit Commn., 1924. Served in 7th Inf. Nat. Guard N.Y., 1892-1912; a.d.c. staffs of Govs. Hughes and White; insp. gen. N.Y. Div. Nat. Guard, 1912-14; adj. gen. State of N.Y., 1915-17; commd. maj. Insp. General's Dept., U.S. Army, 1918, duty with Gen. Staff U.S. Army, 1918; lt. col. Insp. General's Sect. U.S.R., 1919, col., 1923. Trustee Rutgers Coll.; pres. bd. Collegiate School; bd. of management Y.M.C.A. Mem. S.A.R., Sons of Vets., Loyal Legion, Mil. Service Instn. of U.S., Naval Order of U.S., 7th Regt. Vet. Assn. (pres.), Delta Upsilon, Colonial Wars, Nicholas Soc., Officers of Foreign Wars, Military and Naval Officers World's War, Humane Soc. of New York (pres.). Trustee Excelsior Savings Bank. Republican. Mem. Dutch Ref. Ch. Clubs: Union League, Republican, University, Southern Dutchess Country, City, New York Athletic. Home: 154 W. 74th St. Office: 505 5th Av., New York, N.Y. Died June 25, 1948.

STOUFFER, GORDON A. restaurant ofcl.; b. Cleve., May 7, 1905; s. A. E. and Mahala (Bigelow) S.; student Mercersburg (Pa.) Acad., Cheshire (Conn.) Acad., U. Sch., Cleve.; married 2d, Mary Augusta Biddle, May 7, 1952; stepchildren—Elizabeth Wood, Mary Seton, Christopher Fleming. Exec. v.p., gen. mgr., dir. Stouffer Corp., 1930-53, chmn., 1953-—; pres., dir. Portersville (Pa.) Stainless Equipment Corp. Bd. control Cleve. Zool. Park. Mem. Hoover Commn. Task Force on Subsistence Services. Served as col. USAAF, World War II. Decorated Legion of Merit. Mem. C. of C. (del. Internat. C. of C. meeting, Japan, 1955). Episcopalian. Clubs: Union, Pepper Pike Country, Kirtland, The Country, City (Cleve.); Metropolitan, Canadian (N.Y.C.); Cat Key (Cat Cay, Bahamas); Fin 'n Feather (Dundee, Ill.). Home: Rte. 3, Chagrin Falls, O. Office: 1375 Euclid Av., Cleve. 15. Died June 3, 1956; buried Knollwood Cemetery.

STOUGHTON, WILLIAM LEWIS congressman, lawyer; b. Bangor, N.Y., Mar. 20, 1827; attended Kirkland, Painesville, Madison (O.) acads.; studied law, Ohio, Ind., Mich., 1849-51. Admitted to bar, practiced law, Sturgis, Mich., 1851; pros. atty., 1855-59; del. Republican Nat. Conv., Chgo., 1860; apptd. by Pres. Lincoln as U.S. dist. atty. for Mich. dist., 1861, resigned few months later; served as col. and brig. gen. U.S. Army, during Civil War, brevetted maj. gen., resigned because of ill health, 1864; mem. Mich. Constl. Conv., 1856; atty. gen. Mich., 1867-68; mem. U.S. Ho. of Reps. (Rep.) from Mich., 41st-42d congresses, 1869-73. Died Sturgis, June 6, 1888; buried Oak Lawn Cemetery.

STOUT, JOSEPH DUERSON neuropsychiatrist; b. Washington, D.C., Nov. 20, 1886; s. Henry Isaiah and Nellie Wallace (Duerson) S.; A.B., George Washington U., 1910, M.D., 1913, A.M., 1914, Ph.D., 1915; grad. Army Med. Sch., 1918; m. Agnes Josephine Mills, July 14, 1921; children—Betty Jane, Joseph Duerson, Henry Wallace, Robert West. Prof. of physiology, dept. of dentistry, and prof. pharmacology and asso. prof. of physiology, dept. of medicine, George Washington U., 1913-17, prof. nervous diseases, 1920-27; pvt. practice as neuropsychiatrist, Washington, since 1920. Asst. surgeon U.S. Pub. Health Service, 1916-17; 1st lt. Med. Corps, U.S. Army, 1917; lt. col. Med. R.C., 1932-34, M.I. Res. since 1934; on extended active duty with U.S. Army, at Army Med. Center, Washington, Mar. 1941; lt. col. M.C., Sept. 30, 1942, col. Med. Corps, U.S. Army, Dec. 9, 1942; comdg. officer, 136th Sta. Hosp., Oct. 10, 1942. Mem. Washington Soc. Nervous and Mental Diseases, Phi Chi. Republican. Baptists. Mason (32 deg., K.T., Shriner). Home: 3530 Porter St. N.W., Washington, D.C.* Died Nov. 6, 1944.

STOVER, JOHN HUBLER congressman; b. Aaronsburg, Center County, Pa., Apr. 24, 1833; completed prep. studies Bellefonte (Pa.) Acad.; studied law. Admitted to bar, 1857, practiced law, Bellefonte; held several local offices; dist. atty. Center County, 1860-62; enlisted in U.S. Army as pvt. during Civil War, 1861, commd. capt., maj; commd. col. 184th Regt., Pa. Volunteer Inf.; after war moved to Versailles, Morgan County, Mo., practiced law; dist. atty. Morgan County, 1866-68; mem. U.S. Ho. of Reps. (Republican, filled vacancy) from Mo., 40th Congress, Dec. 7, 1868-69; in real estate business, mining activities, Versailles; del. Centennial Expn., Phila., 1876. Died Aurora Springs, Mo., Oct. 27, 1889; buried City Cemetery, Versailles.

STRAHM, VICTOR H. army officer; b. Nashville, Oct. 26, 1895; s. Franz Joseph and Alice Elizabeth (Jones) S.; student Western Ky. Tchrs. Coll., 1911-15, U. Ky., 1915-17, U. Wis., 1919-20, Air Force Engring. Sch., 1923-24, Air Force Tactical Sch., 1931-32, Command and Gen. Staff sch., 1935-26, Army War Coll., 1938-39. Commd lt. (pilot), Oct. 26, 1917, and advanced through the grades to brig. gen., 1942; Ace (credited with destruction over five enemy aircraft), World War I; comd. 91st Aero Squadron, Army of Occupation, Coblenz, 1919; served in various capacities at Army Air Corps and Air Force stations after World War I; chief of staff, 9th U.S. Air Force, Sept. 30, 1942-—; now stationed overseas. Awarded D.S.C., Silver Star, French Croix de Guerre with Two Palms, Legion of Merit. Mem. Sigma Alpha Epsilon. Home: 1349 College Av., Bowling Green, Ky. Died May, 1957.

STRAIN, ISAAC G. naval officer, explorer; b. Roxbury, Pa., Mar. 4, 1821; s. Robert and Eliza (Geddes) S.; attended naval sch., Phila., 1842-43. Became midshipman U.S. Navy, 1837; served in W.I. and S.Am., 1837-42; on leave of absence, 1843-44, led expdn. partially financed by Acad. Natural Scis. of Phila. to Brazil; served in frigate Constitution in East Indies, 1844; served in ship Ohio during Mexican War, 1848; crossed S.Am. from Valparaiso to Buenos Aires, 1848-49; served to Mexican boundary commn. of Dept. of Interior, 1850; led exploration of Isthmus of Darien to evaluate route for possible canal, 1853; joined Lt. O. H. Berryman's expdn. in ship Arctic to investigate possibility of laying submarine cable between U.S. and Gt. Britain, 1856. Author: Cordillera and Pampa, Mountain and Plain, 1853; A Paper on the History and Prospects of Interoceanic Communication by the American Isthmus, 1856. Died May 14, 1857.

STRAIT, THOMAS JEFFERSON M. D.-ex-congressman b. in Chester District, S. C., Dec. 25, 1846; ed. at Mayville, S. C., and Cooper (Miss.) Inst. Entered Confederate army, 1862, in 15th year; served private and serg. to end of war; grad. S. C. Med. Coll., 1885; State senator, 1890; member Congress, 1893-99; Democrat. Address: Lancaster, S. C.

STRANDJORD, NELS MAGNE, radiologist, educator; b. Grenora, N.D., Aug. 18, 1920; s. Selmer J. and Eunice (Langeland) S.; B.A., Luther Coll., 1942; M.D., U. Chgo., 1946; m. Margaret E. Fry, Sept. 10, 1944; children—David Christian, Sarah Eunice, Mark Charles, Daniel Theodore. Intern, Ancker Hosp., St. Paul, 1946-47; gen. practice medicine, Virginia, Minn., 1948-51; resident U. Chgo., 1955-57, instr. radiology, 1958-59, asst. prof., 1959-61, asso. prof., 1961-65; prof., chmn. dept. radiology U. Kan., Kansas City, 1965-67; asso. prof. radiology U. Chgo., 1967-68. Vis. prof. Nat. Def. Med Center, Taipei, Taiwan, 1960-61; mem. physicians team Care-Medico and Department of State, Algiers, 1962; Project Vietnam, 1966. Served to captain in Medical corps, AUS, 1951-54. Recipient James A. McClintock award for outstanding teaching U. Chgo., 1960. Picker scholar in radiol. research, 1959-62. Diplomate Am. Bd. Radiology. Mem. Am. Coll. Radiology, Assn. U. Radiologists, Chgo. Roentgen Soc., Sigma Xi. Contbr. profl. jours. Home: Chicago IL Died Sept. 11, 1968; buried Belview MN

STRASSBURGER, RALPH BEAVER publisher, diplomat; b. Norristown, Pa., Mar. 26, 1883; s. Jacob Andrew and Mary Jane (Beaver) S.; graduate Philips Exeter Academy, also United States Naval Acad., 1905; LL.D., Ursinus Coll., Collegeville, Pa., 1930; m. May Bourne, 1911; 1 son, Johann Andreas Peter. Resigned from Navy, 1909; apptd. by President Taft counsel gen. and sec. of Legation to Roumania, Bulgaria and Serbia, 1913, later 2d sec. Embassy, Tokio; jr. and sr. lt. U.S. Navy, World War; pub. Norristown Times Herald; owner Normandy Farm, breeder of thoroughbred and hunting horses and Ayrshire cattle; owns racing stables in America, France, England and Ireland. Decorated Chevalier French Legion of Honor; Caporal d'Honneur Escadron 2/17 Valois, French Air Force. Active supporter Rep. party in state and nat. affairs; del. at large from Pa. to Rep. National Convention, 1924; del. to 17th Pa. Rep. National Conv., 1936. Mem. Huguenot Soc. of Pa. (pres.), Colonial Soc. of Pa. (councillor), S.R., Soc. Foreign Wars, Hist. Soc. Pa., Gen. Soc. Pa., Pa. German Soc. (pres.), Am. Soc. M.E. Clubs: Bryn Mawr Polo, Racquet Club, White Marsh Valley Hunt, University, Recess, Army and Navy, Press, Racquet and Tennis, New York Yacht (New York); Metropolitan, Army and Navy (Washington, D.C.); Travelers (Paris); Cercle de Deauville; life mem. St. Cloud, Chantilly (France); Epsom (Eng.); others U.S. and Europe. Author: The Strassburger Family and Allied Families in Pennsylvania, 1922; The Pennsylvania German Pioneers (3 vols.), 1934; et. Addresses: Normandy Farm, Gwynedd Valley, Pa. 19437; 3, Av. de Tourville, Paris, 7e France; (summer) La Ferme du Coteau, Deauville, France; Haras des Monceaux, Lisieux, France; Villa Pennsylvanie, Chantilly, France. Office: 26 Av. des Champs-Elysees, Paris, Se France. Died Feb. 26, 1959.

STRATEMEYER, GEORGE E., air officer; b. Nov. 24, 1890; B.S., U.S. Mil. Acad., 1915; grad. Air Corps Tactical Sch., 1930; Command and Gen. Staff Sch., 1932, Army War Coll., 1939. Commd. 2d lt., June 12, 1915; promoted through grades to lieutenant general, 1945; chief of staff for the Army Air Forces, 1942; commander Army Air Forces, India-Burma sector, 1943; air comdr. Eastern Air Comd., 1944; comdg. gen., Army Air Forces China Theater, 1945; comdg. gen., Air Defense Comd., 1946-48; comdg. gen. Continental Air Comd., 1948; comdr. Far East Air Force in Korea, 1950-51, ret., 1952. Recipient Republic of Korea Order Mil. Merit with Gold Star. Address: Winter Park FL Died Aug. 1969.*

STRATTON, CLIF (CLIFTON JARIUS), newspaperman; b. Reading, Kan., May 20, 1886; s. Jairus Litchfield and Martha J. (Hultz) S.; B.S., Kan. State Agrl. Coll., 1911; m. Lenore Monroe, Aug. 20, 1917; children—Clifton Jairus, Lee Monroe. In circulation dept. Topeka (Kan.) Daily Capital, 1911-12, reporter, 1912-13, state house reporter, 1913-17, 1919-20; sec. Kan. State Agrl. Coll. Alumni Assn., 1920-22; mng. editor Topeka Daily Capital, 1926-58, Clif Stratton Writes; ret. Oct. for Capper Publs. Trade Union Courier, Ohio Farmer, Kansas Farmer, Mo. Ruralist; editorial page column Capital, 1926-58, Clif Stratton Writes; ret. Oct. 1958. Served in 1st O.T.C., 1917; 1st lt., Inf., U.S. Army, 1917-19; successively 2d lt., capt., maj., Kan. Nat. Guard, 1920-30. Mem. Delta Tau Delta, Sigma Delta Chi. Republican. Conglist. Mason (Shriner). Clubs: National Press (Washington); Topeka Press. Home: Topeka KS Died Dec. 22, 1970; buried Mount Hope Cemetery Topeka KS

STRATTON, SAMUEL WESLEY physicist; b. Litchfield, Ill., July 18, 1861; s. Samuel and Mary B. (Webster) S.; B.S., U. of Ill., 1884, D.Eng., 1903; D.Sc., Western U. of Pa. (now U. of Pittsburgh), 1903, Cambridge, 1909, Yale, 1919; L.D., Harvard, 1923; Ph.D., Rensselaer Poly. Inst., 1924; unmarried. Instr. mathematics, asst. prof., and prof. physics and elec. engring., U. of Ill., 1885-92; successively asst. prof., asso. prof. and prof. physics, U. of Chicago, 1892-1901; dir. Nat. Bur. of Standards, Washington, 1901-23; pres. Mass. Inst. of Tech., 1923—. Ensign, lt. jr. grade, lt., and lt. comdr. Ill. Naval Militia, 1895-1901; lt. U.S.N., during Spanish-Am. War, May-Nov. 1898; comdr. comdg. D.C. Naval Militia, 1904-12. Mem. Internat. Com. on Weights and Measures, Am. Inst. Elec. Engrs., Nat. Acad. Sciences, Nat. Advisory Com. for Aeronautics. Chevalier Legion of Honor, 1909, Officer, 1928. Home: Cambridge, Mass. Died Oct. 18, 1931.

STRAUB, OSCAR ITIN army officer; b. in Pa., Feb. 19, 1865; grad. U.S. Mil. Acad., 1887, Arty. Sch., 1892. Commd. add. 2d lt. 1st Arty., June 12, 1887; 2d lt., Aug. 11, 1887; 1st lt., 5th Arty., Jan. 3, 1894; capt. Arty. Corps, Feb. 12, 1901; maj., Jan. 25, 1907; lt. col. Coast Arty. Corps, July 28, 1911; col., Aug. 9, 1915. Participated in campaign in Puerto Rico, with Light Battery D, 5th Arty., July-Aug., 1898; in engagement at Harmigueros, Aug. 10, 1898; comd. 28th Battery, Field Arty., Ft. Snelling, Minn., 1904-07; duty at Ft. Howard, Md., 1917. Address: Washington, D.C. Died July 9, 1922.

STRAUS, ROGER WILLIAMS metal processing exec.; b. N.Y.C., Dec. 14, 1891; s. Oscar S. and Sarah L. (Lavanburg) S.; student Collegiate Sch., N.Y.C., Lawrenceville (N.J.) sch.; Litt.B., Princeton, 1913; L.H.D., Bucknell U., 1936; D.H.L., Hebrew Union Coll., 1943; LL.D., Jewish Theol. Sem., 1950; L.H.D., N.Y.U., 1953; m. Gladys Guggenheim, Jan. 12, 1914; children—Oscar S., Roger Williams, Florence G. (Mrs. Max A. Hart). With Am. Smelting & Refining Co., 1914—, dir., 1916—, pres., 1941-47, chmn. bd., 1947—; dir., chmn. exec. com. Revere Copper & Brass, Inc., Gen. Cable Corp.; dir. N.Y. Life Ins. Co., N.Y. Telephone Co. Hon. pres. Nat. Fedn. Temple Brotherhoods; trustee John Simon Guggenheim Meml Found., Daniel and Florence Guggenheim Found., Theodore Roosevelt Assn., Nat. Found. for Infantile Paralysis; trustee, mem. exec. bd. Union Am. Hebrew Congregations; hon. vice chmn. United Jewish Appeal of Greater N.Y., 1940-56; bd. govs. Am. Financial and Development Corp. for Israel; pres. Fred L. Lavanburg Found.; co-chmn. Nat. Conf. Christians and Jews, chmn. 25th anniversary 1953; gen. chmn. Brotherhood Week, 1953; mem. gen. com. Am. Jewish Com.; mem.-at-large Nat. Council Boy Scouts Am.; Chancellor bd. regents U. State N.Y. Mem. U.S. Delegation 9th session UN Gen. Assembly. Served as capt., intelligence officer, comdg. gen.'s staff in Siberia, World War I; maj. O.R.C., 1920-34. Recipient Am. Soc. for Metals medal for advancement research, 1935, Class Cup (Princeton 1913), 1936. Mem. Am. Inst. Mining and Metall. Engrs., Am. Legion. Jewish religion, (congregation trustee). Clubs: Nat. Republican, Princeton, Bankers of Am., Lotos (N.Y.C.); Cosmos (Washington). Author: Religious Liberty and Democracy, 1939; also articles on religious liberty. Co-editor: The American Way, 1936. Home: 6 E. 93d St., N.Y.C. Died July 28, 1957.

STRAUSS, JOSEPH naval officer; b. Mt. Morris, New York, November 16, 1861; graduate United States Naval Academy, 1885. Ensign, June, 1887; junior lieut., June 1896; promoted through grades to rear admiral, February 1, 1918; admiral on the retired list, June 21, 1930. Cruised in various parts of the world, 1885-87; engaged in hydrog. surveys on east and west coast of U.S. and in Alaska, 1887-90; cruising, 1890-93; in Bur. of Ordnance, Navy Dept., 1893-96; invented superposed turret system of mounting guns on battleships, 1895; cruised in S. America, 1896-1900, and engaged in blockade of Cuban Coast; in charge of U.S. Naval Proving Ground, 1900-03; insp. ordnance Naval Proving Ground, 1906-08; comdr. cruiser Montgomery in experimental work on torpedoes, 1909-10; asst. aid for material, Navy Dept., 1910-12; comd. Battleship Ohio, 1912-13; chief Bur. Ordnance, with rank of rear-admiral, Oct. 1913-Dec. 1916; apptd. comdr. Battleship Nevada, Dec. 1916; apptd. comdr. mine force Atlantic Fleet, Mar. 1918; laid mine barrage across North Sea, Norway to Scotland, planting over 56,000 Am. mines; comd. expdn. that cleared North Sea of Mines, completing the work, Sept. 30, 1919; mem. Gen. Bd., 1920; comdr.-in-chief Asiatic Fleet, Feb. 1921-Sept. 1922; was mem. Gen. Bd. Sampson medal for Spanish-Am. War; U.S. Navy D.S.M.; Knight Comdr. St. Michael and St. George; Comdr. Legion of Honor of France; Comdr. Order of Sacred Treasure of Japan. Comdr. Order of Wen Hu, first class of China. Mem. Commn. to finally determine cause of destruction of Maine after she had been uncovered in Havana Harbor. Retired by operation of law, Nov. 16, 1925; recalled to active service as mem. bd. on Safety and Salvage of Submarines, June 1928-Mar. 1929, and again in 1937 as mem. of board to pass upon the design for new battleships. Has written various articles on ordnance and ballistics. Home: 2208 Mass. Ave. N.W., Washington. Died Dec. 30, 1948; buried in Arlington National Cemetery.

STRAWBRIDGE, JAMES DALE congressman, physician; b. Liberty Twp., Mountour County, Pa., Apr. 7, 1824; grad. Princeton, 1844; grad. med. dept. U. Pa., 1847. Practiced medicine at Danville, Pa.; served as brigade surgeon of Volunteers in Civil War, imprisoned in Libby Prison, 3 months; mem. U.S. Ho. of Reps. (Republican) from Pa., 43d Congress, 1873-75. Died Danville, July 19, 1890; buried Fairview Cemetery.

STRECKER, EDWARD ADAM prof. psychiatry; b. Phila., Pa., Oct. 16, 1887; s. Adam and Mary (Weiler); prep. edn., St. Joseph's Coll., Phila., hon. Sc.D., 1935; B.A., LaSalle Coll., Phila., 1907, M.A., 1911, Litt.D., 1938; M.D., Jefferson Med. Coll., 1911; LL.D., Franklin and Marshall Coll., Boston Coll.; L.H.D., St. Bonaventure U., 1956; m. Elizabeth Kyne Walsh, Jan. 1917. Res. physician St. Agnes Hosp., Phila., 1911-15; asst. phys. Pa. Hosp. Dept. for Nervous and Mental Diseases, 1913-17, med. dir., 1917—, and dir. of clinic; staff neurologist, Pa., Phila. and Germantown hosps.; prof. of nervous and mental diseases, Jefferson Med. Coll., 1925-31; prof. and head dept. psychiatry, U. of Pa., 1931-53, emeritus prof. psychiatry Schools of Medicine, clin. prof. psychiatry and mental hygiene, Yale U., 1926-32; chief of service and consultant, Inst. for Mental Hygiene, Pa. Hosp., Phila.; cons. Sec. War in psychiatry for Army; cons. surgeon Gen. of Navy, World War II; cons. U.S.P.H.S.; 17th Pasteur lecturer; also consultant to Bryn Mawr Coll., and U.S. Veterans Bureau; Thomas William Salmon Memorial Lecturer, 1939; Pasteur, Menas Gregory Memorial, Bernard McGhie Memorial lectures, 1946; consultant in mental hygiene, U.S.P.H.S. Commd. from 1st lt. to maj., Medical Corps, U.S. Army, 1917-19. Mem. Commn. to administer the U.S.P.H.S. Bill for Psychiatry and Mental Hygiene. Fellow A.C.P.; mem. Am. Neurol. Assn., Am. Psychiatric Assn., Alpha Omega Alpha, Sigma Phi Epsilon, Alpha Kappa Kappa, etc. Republican. Catholic. Author: Clinical Psychiatry, 1925; Clinical Neurology, 1927; Discovering Ourselves, 1931; Practical Examination of Personality and Behavior Disorders, 1936; Alcohol One Man's Meat, 1938; Beyond the Clinical Frontiers (Salmon lecture), 1940; Fundamentals of Psychiatry, 1942; Their Mothers' Sons, 1946; Their Mothers' Daughters (with V. T. Lathbury), 1956; also numerous articles and papers on nervous and mental disorders. Spl. researches in behavior disorder of children and normal and abnormal psychology of childhood. Address: 111 N. 49th St., Phila. Died Jan. 2, 1959; buried Greenmount Cemetery, Phila.

STREET, RANDALL S. congressman, lawyer; b. Catskill, N.Y., 1780; studied law. Admitted to the bar, began practice law in Poughkeepsie, N.Y.; dist. atty. for 2d jud. dist., 1810-11, 13-15; lt. col. N.Y. Militia, War of 1812; mem. U.S. Ho. of Reps. (Democrat) from N.Y., 16th Congress, 1819-21; moved to Monticello, N.Y., circa 1825, continued practice law. Died Monticello, Nov. 21, 1841; buried Poughkeepsie.

STREETER, EDWARD CLARK, M.D.; b. Chicago, Ill., Nov. 10, 1874; s. John Williams and Mary (Clark) S.; A.B., Yale, 1898; M.D., Northwestern U., 1901; studied Harvard, Paris, Vienna and Berlin; m. Alice Martha Chase, of Waterbury, Conn., 1906; children—Helen Chase, John Williams, Gordon Chase, Edward Clark. Began practice at Chicago, 1901; settled in Boston, 1907; lecturer on med. history, Harvard, since 1921. Capt. Q.M.C., U.S.A., 1917-19; with A.E.F., Aug. 23, 1917-Jan. 22, 1919. Trustee Congl. Foundation for Edn. Republican. Clubs: Yale (Boston, New Haven, New York); St. Botolph, Odd Volumes (Boston). Asst. editor History of Anatomic Illustration, 1920, Osler's Evolution of Modern Medicine, 1921. Asso. editor Annals of Medical History. Contbr. numerous med.-hist. studies revs. Home: 280 Beacon St., Boston MA

STREETT, ST. CLAIR, army officer; b. Washington, D.C., Oct. 6, 1893; s. Shadrack Watkins and Lydia Ann (Coggins) S.; m. Mary Lois Williams, Jan. 18, 1922; 1 son, St. Clair. Military airplane pilot, 1916; commd. 1st lt. Aviation Sect., Signal Corps Reserve, 1917; advanced through the grades to maj. gen., Dec. 1942; grad. Command and General Staff Sch., Army War Coll., Naval War Coll.; comdr. of Army Alaskan flight, New York to Nome, Alaska, and return, 1920; became comdg. gen. 3d Air Force, Dec. 1942, 2d Air Force, Sept. 1943, 13th Air Force, S.W. Pacific, Apr. 1944; became dep. comdg. gen. Continental Air Force, Feb. 1945, Strategic Air Command, Mar. 1946; assigned chief, Mil. Personnel Procurement Service, AGO, Jan. 1947; assigned dep. inspector gen. U.S.A.F., Jan. 1948; assigned dep. comdg. gen. Air Materiel Comd., 1949; ret., 1952. Awarded Distinguished Flying Cross, Purple Heart, Air Medal, Mackay Trophy, D.S.M. with 2 oak leaf clusters, Legion of Merit; Italian Order of the Court in the Grade of Officer (Italy). Died Sept. 1970.

STRENG, J(AMES) TRUMAN ins. exec.; b. Holland, Mich., May 14, 1896; s. Henry P. and Mary (Cook) S.; student Philadelphia Textile Sch., 1915-16; student Northwestern U. Night Sch., 1932; M.A.I., Am. Inst. of Real Estate Appraisers case study courses, 1940; m. Katherine M. Perkins, Nov. 28, 1931. Entered real estate and mortgage field. Chicago, 1923; joined real estate dept. of Mass. Mutual Life Ins. Co., 1936, successively city property mgr., dist. mgr., vice pres., 1951, managing co's. mortgage loan and real estate dept. in U.S.; non-resident lecturer, U. of Mich. Sch. Bus. Adminstrn. Served as 1st lt., Inf., Am.-North Russian Expeditionary Force, World War I; re-commd. in Res. Corps, 1920, major, 1936. Mem. bd. govs. and mem. New Eng. chapter, Am. Inst. Real Estate Appraisers, Springfield (Mass.) Real Estate Bd. (mem. central bus. dist. council, trustee Urban Land Inst.), Springfield C. of C., Vets. Fgn. Wars; Polar Bear Assn. (past pres.). Conglist. Club: Longmeadow (Mass.) Country. Home: 60 Summit Av., Longmeadow 6, Mass. Office: 1295 State St., Springfield, Mass. Died Apr. 8, 1953.

STRICKER, FREDERICK DAVID, health officer; b. Detroit, Mich., Mar. 24, 1875; s. Frederick D. and Loida (Wegener) S.; M.D., Detroit Coll. of Medicine, 1900; m. Bertha Stewart, Jan. 15, 1904; 1 dau., Rosamond. Resident Physician Grace Hosp., Detroit, 1900-02; practicing physician and county health officer, Josephine County, Ore., 1903-17; in practice at Tucson, Ariz., 1919-21; state health officer and exec. sec. State Bd. of Health, Ore., 1921-45; now retired. Served as capt. Med. Corps, U.S. Army, 1917-19; now lt. col. Med. Res. Corps, U.S. Army. Fellow Am. Pub. Health Assn. (pres. Western Branch 1939-40), Am. Med. Assn., Portland Acad. of Medicine. Republican. Mason. Clubs: City, University. Home: Route 1, Box 601, San Rafael CA

STRICKLER, CYRUS WARREN, SR., physician; b. near Fisherville, Augusta County, Va., Nov. 1, 1873; s. Rev. Givens Brown and Mary Frances (Moore) S.; student Washington and Lee U., 1891-94; M.D., with first honor, Atlanta Med. Coll. (now Emory U. Sch. of Med.), 1897; m. Anne Virginia Williams, Feb. 24, 1903; children—Givens Brown, II, Cyrus Warren. Served as intern and resident Grady Hosp., Atlanta, Ga., 1897-99; resident Elkin-Cooper Sanatorium, 1899-1901; out-patient dept., Atlanta Med. Coll., 1901-11, lecturer minor surgery, 1903-05, quiz master in surgery, 1903-05; asso. prof. of medicine, Atlanta Coll. Physicians and Surgeons, 1911-16; prof. of medicine, Emory U. Sch. of Med., 1916-30. Now emeritus prof. of clin. med., Emory Univ. Sch. of Medicine. On the visiting staff Emory Univ. Hosp. and Grady Memorial Hosp. and consultant on staff of St. Joseph's Infirmary. Consultant Grady Memorial Hospital. Served as chief Medical Service, with Base Hospital No. 43; later lieutenant colonel, executive officer of hospitals at Blois, France, 1918-19. Decorated Officer d'Academie. Fellow American Coll. Physicians; diplomate Am. Bd. of Internal Med.; mem. Fulton County and Fifth Dist. med. socs., Ga. State Med. Assn., Southern Med. Assn., A.M.A., Mil. Surgeons U.S., Assn. Study Internal Secretions, Am. Legion, Phi Chi, Phi Beta Kappa, Alpha Omega Alpha. Democrat. Presbyterian. Clubs: Atlanta Athletic, Druid Hills Golf, Capital City, Kiwanis (Atlanta). Contbr. to med. jours. Home: 871 Oakdale Road N.E., Atlanta GA Office: 123 Forrest Av. N.E., Atlanta 3 GA

STRICKLER, GIVENS BROWN theologian; b. Strickler's Springs, Rockbridge County, Va., April 25, 1840; s. Joseph and Mary Jane (Brown) S.; student Washington and Lee U., 1868, Union Theol. Sem., Va., 1868-70; D.D., Washington and Lee, 1878; LL.D., Davidson Coll., N.C., 1894; capt. Co. I, 4th Va. Regt., "Stonewall Brigade," C.S.A., 1861-65; m. Mary Frances Moore, Nov. 6, 1871 (died 1905). Ordained Presbyn. ministry, 1870; pastor Tinkling Spring Ch., Augusta County, Va., 1870-83, Central Ch., Atlanta, Ga., 1883-96; prof. systematic theology, Union Theol. Sem., 1896—. Address: Richmond, Va. Deceased.

STRICKLER, THOMAS JOHNSON pub. utility exec.; b. Topeka, Kan., May 21, 1883; s. Jacob Nissley and Mary (Johnson) S.; grad. Wentworth Mil. Acad., Lexington, Mo., 1900, grad. study, 1901; B.S. in C.E., U. Kan., 1906; student of Washburn Law School; m. Lillian Foster, Nov. 14, 1919 (dec.); m. 2d, Margaret Jane Armstrong, Aug. 8, 1929 (dec. Jan. 1958). With U.S. Reclamation Service, 1902-10; asst. mgr. and engr. Fed. Betterment Co., Cherryvale, Kan., 1910-11; asst. engr. Kan. Pub. Utilities Commn., 1911-13, chief engr., 1913-20; admitted to Kansas bar, 1927, consulting engr. Empire Gas & Fuel Co., Bartlesville, Okla., 1920-22, Henry L. Doherty & Co., N.Y. City, 1922-24, at Kansas City, Mo., 1924-25; cons. engr. Gas Service Co., and vice-pres. or dir. 30 subsidiaries in Kan., Okla. and Mo., 1925-27; v.p. and gen. mgr. Kansas City (Mo.) Gas Co.

1927-47; dir. Gas Service Co., 1926-36, v.p., dir., mgr. Kansas City (Missouri) Division 1947—. Served as capt. Engineer Corps, U.S. Army, 1917. Mem. Kansas State Water Commn., 1917-20; gen. chmn. Kansas City Charities Fund campaigns, 1928 and 1929; mem. bd. govs. Am. Royal Live Stock Show, 1928-42; pres. Kan. City Safety Council, 1928, 1929, mem. bd. govs. 1929—; v. chmn. Club Presidents' Round Table, 1929; trustee Liberty Memorial Assn., 1938—, bd. govs., 1951—; Greater K.C. Com. Econ. Development, 1943—; v.p., trustee Kansas City Conservatory of Music, 1934—; mem. bd. of govs. Patriots and Pioneers Memorial Foundation, 1936—, Citizens Regional Planning Council of K.C., 1945—; mem. adv. council, Region No. 7, War Labor Bd., 1942-43; mem. adv. bd. Salvation Army, 1935—; 2d vice pres. Kansas City Art Inst., 1939-49, 1st v. chmn. bd. govs., 1949, chmn., 1952—; mem. exec. com., bd. trustees Kansas City Philharmonic Orchestra, 1933-44; mem. Defense Savings Com., State of Mo., 1941-46; mem. nat. gas and gasoline com., dist. 2, Petroleum Industry War Council 1942-46; mem. com. Internat. Econ. Policy in coop. with The Carnegie Endowment for Internat. Peace, 1943—; pres. Kan. City War Chest Fund, Inc., 1941-46; dir. Mo. War Chest, 1943-47; v.p. Community Chest of K.C., Mo., 1946, mem. exec. com., 1946-48, trustee, 1946—. Registered profl. engr. Mo. and N.Y. Mem. Mo. Soc. Profl Engrs., U.S. C. of C. (dir. 1934-46), Am. Soc. C.E. (v.p. Kansas City Chapter 1931; pres. 1933), Midwest Research Inst. (v. chmn. bd. govs., mem. exec. com., chmn. development com. 1946-48, trustee), Soc. Am. Mil. Engrs., Am. Gas Assn. (pres. 1940-41; chmn. natural gas dept. 1932; nat. advertising com., 1936-42), Mo. Association Pub. Utilities (pres. 1929-30), Kansas City C. of C. (v.p. Civics 1931 and 1934), Am. Legion (comdr. local post 1928; chmn. vets. welfare com. 1929; comdr. Dept. Mo. 1929-30), Forty and Eight, Mil. Order World War (comdr. Kansas City Chapter 1938-39), S.R. (1st v.p. K.C. Chapter 1940-43), Kan. U. Alumni Assn. (pres. 1934-35; bd. dirs. World War II Meml. Bldg., 1951—), Sigma Chi (grand trustee, 1944-48), Tau Beta Pi. Pres. Kan. Engr. Soc., 1915. Mason 32 deg., K.T., Shriner). Clubs: University (vice pres. 1929), Kansas City, Rotary, Mission Hills Country, Advertising and Sales Executives. Home: 5760 Ward Parkway, Kansas City 2. Office: Scarritt Bldg., 824 Grand Av., Kansas City 13, Mo. Died Nov. 19, 1958.

STRINGFELLOW, HENRY MARTYN horticulturist, b. Winchester, Va., Jan. 21, 1839; s. Horace and Harriet Louisa (Strother) S.; A.M., William and Mary Coll., Va., 1858; Theol. Sem., Alexandria, Va., 1859-61; m. Alice Johnston, Dec. 15, 1863. Voted against secession, 1861; enlisted in C.S.A. as pvt., June 1861; participated in campaign at Yorktown, Va., and around Richmond, 1862; went to Tex. with Gen. Magruder, fall of 1862; was in battle of Galveston, and capt. in ordnance dept. at close of war. Pioneer in discovering value of gulf coast of Tex. for raising fruit and vegetables; planted first pear orchard on coast, 1882; planted first Satsuma oranges in Tex., 1884; in nursery business until 1895, later devoting attention to experiments in horticulture; moved to Fayetteville, Ark., 1909, and set out the first English walnut grove of 500 trees, in the state. Democrat. Spiritualist. Author: The New Horticulture, 1896. Address: Fayetteville, Ark. Died June 17, 1912.

STRINGHAM, SILAS HORTON naval officer; b. Middletown, N.Y., Nov. 7, 1797; s. Daniel and Abigail (Horton) S.; m. Henrietta Hicks, 1819, 4 children. Commd. midshipman U.S. Navy, 1809; served in War of 1812, then in 2d war with Algiers pirates; served on patrol duty off African coast to suppress slave trade, 1820-22; exec. officer on brig. Hornet in West Indies, 1822-24; commanded ship-of-the-line Ohio in Mexican War, 1847; commanded Mediterranean Squadron, 1853-55; apptd. to head Ft. Sumter relief fleet which never took place; in command of successful naval expdn. against Hatteras, Va.; commanded Atlantic Blockade Squadron in Civil War, 1861, asked to be relieved of assignment, 1861; rear adm., 1862, in command of Boston Navy Yard, 1862-64. Died Bklyn., Feb. 7, 1876.

STRODE, GEORGE KING (strod), hygienist; b. Chester County, Pa., Jan. 16, 1886; s. Richard Henry and Hannah Mary (King) S.; Sc.B., Haverford Coll., 1908; M.D., U. Pa., 1912; M.P.H., Havard, 1927; Sc.D., Haverford, 1942; m. Elizabeth J. Coombs, May 22, 1919 (died 1937); m. 2d, Josephine Clark Dillard, June 29, 1944. Hygienist Pa. State Dept. Health, 1915-16 and 1919-20; member International Health Division of Rockefeller Foundation, 1916-17 and, 1920—, rep. in Brazil, 1920-26, also asst. dir. activities in Europe and the Near East, 1927-38, asso. dir., 1938-44, dir. 1944-51, also chmn. Paris (France) office, 1932-38. Served as captain, Med. Corps, U.S. Army, 1917-19. Fellow Am. Pub. Health Assn.; mem. Am. Soc. and Acad. Tropical Medicine, New York Society Tropical Medicine, A.A.A.S., Alpha Omega Alpha, Delta Omega. Hon. fellow Soc. of Med. Officers of Health of Great Britain. Decorated by governments of Norway, Denmark, Bulgaria, Portugal, France, Rumania and Sweden. Presbyterian. Now retired. Died Oct. 27, 1958.

STROH, DONALD ARMPRIESTER (stro), army officer; b. Harrisburg, Pa., Nov. 3, 1892; B.S., Mich. Agrl. Coll., 1915; m. Annie Imogene Finger, Hickory, N.C., June 13, 1917; children—Imogene Covert (Mrs. Robert H. Stumpf), Harry Richard (killed in action, Aug. 1944). Commd. 2d lt. Cav., June 1917; promoted through grades to maj. gen., 1944; became intelligence officer, G-2, 4th Army hdqrs. Presidio of San Francisco, July, 1940, serving also as aide to Lt. Gen. John L. DeWitt, comdg. gen. 4th Army; mil. observer London, Eng., May-June, 1941, also attended Brit. Intelligence Sch.; returned 4th Army as intelligence officer, July 1941; assigned 85th Inf. Div., comdg. officer 339th Inf., Feb. 1942, upon its activation; assigned 9th Inf. Div., asst. to comdg. gen., July 1942. Served in French Morocco and through campaigns So. and No. Tunisia, Sicily and Normandy; assigned to comd. 8th Inf. Div. July 1944; promoted maj. gen. Aug. 1944. Participated in campaigns of No. France and Germany; transferred to comd. 106th Inf. Div., Feb. 1945. Awarded D.S.M., Legion of Merit with Oak Leaf Cluster, Bronze Star Medal, French Legion of Honor (officer), Croix de Guerre with palm. Home: 3133 Connecticut Av., Washington. Died Dec. 20, 1953; buried Arlington Nat. Cemetery.

STROMBERG, GUSTAF (BENJAMIN) astronomer; b. Gothenburg, Sweden, Dec. 16, 1882; s. Bengt Johan Gustaf Lorentz and Johanna Elisabeth (Noehrman) S.; prep. edn., Real Sch., Gothenburg, 1892-1902; student U. Kiel, Germany, 1904-05; Candidate of Philosophy, U. Stockholm (Stockholms Högskola), 1915., Licentiate of Philosophy, 1915; Ph.D., U. Lund, Sweden, 1916; m. Helga Sofia Henning (pen name Sister Benediction), May 11, 1914. Came to U.S., 1916, naturalized, 1922. Instr. in astronomy, U. Stockholm, 1906-13; asst., Stockholm Obs., 1906-13; astronomer Mt. Wilson Obs., 1917-46. Sci. research work for U.S. Navy and Air Force 1943-45. Mem. Am. Astron. Soc., A.A.A.S., Internat. Astron. Union, Royal Astron. Soc., Eng. Am. Phys. Soc., Royal Soc. Scis. Sweden, Sigma Xi. Club: University. Author of sci. papers most of which deal with statis. astronomy, stellar motions, the intrinsic brightness of the stars, and the philosophy of science. Listed among citizens of foreign birth who have made outstanding contributions to American culture in the Wall of Fame at the N.Y. World's Fair, 1940. Author: The Soul of the Universe, 1940; The Searchers, 1947; A Scientist's View of Man, Mind, and the Universe, 1966. Home: 1383 N. Marengo Av., Pasadena, Cal. 91103. Died Jan. 30, 1962; buried Pasadena Mausoleum.

STRONG, EDWARD TRASK rear admiral U.S.N.; b. Ipswich, Mass., Feb. 10, 1840; s. Simeon E. S., M.D.; ed. Andover, Mass.; m. June 11, 1867. Entered navy, vol. officer, Nov. 24, 1862; served through remainder of Civil war; commissioned ensign in regular navy, March 12, 1868; master, Dec. 18, 1868; lt., March 21, 1870; lt. comdr., July 2, 1882; comdr., Jan. 9, 1893; capt., Oct. 10, 1899; retired with rank of rear admiral Nov. 21, 1900. Served at sea on the North Atlantic, Pacific, European and Asiatic stas. Address: Albany, N.Y. Died 1909.

STRONG, FREDERICK SMITH army officer; b. Paw Paw, Mich., Nov. 12, 1855; s. Samuel Filer and Anna Maria (Fish) S.; grad. Kalamazoo (Mich.) High Sch., 1876, U.S. Mil. Acad., 1880, U.S. Arty. Sch., 1884; m. Alice Marion Johnston, Oct. 3, 1883; 1 son, Frederick Smith. Commd. 2d lt. 4th Arty., June 12, 1880; promoted through grades to brig. gen., May 4, 1915; maj. gen., Aug. 5, 1917. Served in Spanish-Am. War, 1898; comd. 40th Div., Aug. 25, 1917-Apr. 20, 1919; in France, Aug. 12, 1918-Mar. 3, 1919; retired from active service at own request, Aug. 17, 1919. Home: San Diego, Calif. Died Mar. 9, 1935.

STRONG, GEORGE CROCKETT army officer; b. Stockbridge, Vt., Oct. 16, 1832; grad. U.S. Mil. Acad., 1857. Asst. ordnance officer Watervliet Arsenal, 1859-61, chief ordnance officer, 1861; commd. maj., asst. adj. gen. U.S. Volunteers, 1861; served at Battle of Bull Run; chief of staff for Gen. Benjamin F. Butler, 1862; promoted brig. gen. U.S. Volunteers, 1862; led 2 expdns. into Miss., 1862; promoted capt. ordnance U.S. Army, 1863; 1st to reach enemy positions in Battle of Morris Island, 1863; mortally wounded in defense of Battery Wagner, July 18, 1863. Died N.Y.C., July 30, 1863.

STRONG, GEORGE VEAZEY army officer; b. Chicago, Mar. 14, 1880; s. John Winder and Elizabeth (Veazey) S.; student Mich. Mil. Acad., 1898-1900; B.S., U.S. Mil. Acad., 1904; LL.B., Northwestern U., 1916, LL.D., 1943; grad. Army War Coll., 1924, Command and Gen. Staff Sch., 1931; m. Gerda E. Loenholm, June 2, 1909; children—George Loenholm, Elizabeth Veazey (dec.), William Ronald, Commd. 2d lt. cav., U.S. Army, June 15, 1904, and advanced through the grades to maj. gen. Apr. 1941; retired Feb. 1944; became asst. chief of staff, Oct. 1938; comdg. gen. 8th Army Corps, May, 1941; apptd. head Military Intelligence, June, 1942; Joint chiefs of staff, Apr. 1944-45. Decorated D.S.M. with Oak Leaf Cluster, Legion of Merit, Purple Heart (U.S.), Legion of Honor (France). Adviser to Traffic in Arms Conf., Geneva, Switzerland, 1925; tech. adviser Preparatory Commn., 1927-30; mil. adviser, Disarmament Conf., 1930-34. Adviser, Dumbarton Oaks Conf., 1944, Pan-Am. Conf., Mexico City, 1945. Episcopalian. Mason. Clubs: Army and Navy (Washington, D.C.); Army-Navy Country (Arlington, Va.). Author: Japanese-English Military Dictionary, 1911; Common Chinese-Japanese Characters, 1911. Address: New War Dept. Bldg., Washington. Died Jan. 10, 1946; buried at West Point, N.Y.

STRONG, JAMES HOOKER naval officer; b. Canandaigua, N.Y., Apr. 26, 1814; s. Elisha Beebe and Dolly (Hooker) S.; attended Polytechnic Sch., Chittenango, N.Y.; m. Maria Louisa Von Cowenhoven, 1844. 2 children. Commd. midshipman U.S. Navy, 1829, participated in expdn. which apprehended pirate Vernet in Falkland Islands, 1832; comdr. ship Mohawk, 1861, steamer Flag in South Atlantic Blockading Squadron, 1862; in command ships Monogahela, Owasco and Virginia, 1863, convoyed expdn. of 9,000 men to mouth of Rio Grande, capturing Brownsville, Corpus Christi and Arkansas Pass; won surrender of ram Tennessee at Battle of Mobile, 1864; commd. capt., 1865; insp. Bklyn. Navy Yard, 1866-67; commanded steam-sloop Canandaigua in European Squadron, 1868-69; promoted commodore, 1870; house insp., 1871-73; in command South Atlantic Station, 1874; commd. rear adm., 1873, ret., 1876. Died Columbia, S.C., Nov. 28, 1882.

STRONG, L(ESTER) CORRIN U.S. ambassador; b. Tacoma, Nov. 25, 1892; s. Lester B. and Hattie Maria (Corrin) Lockwood; student Hill Sch., 1907-09, Haollock Sch., Great Barrington, Mass., 1911-13; Ph.B., Yale, 1916; postgrad. Columbia Law Sch., 1924-25; LL.D. (hon.), Keuka (N.Y.) Coll.; m. Alice Trowbridge, Sept. 23, 1922; children—Henry, Trowbridge, Corrin Peter. Trust dept. Guaranty Trust Co., N.Y.C., 1925-27, Nat. Savs. & Trust Co., Washington, 1927-29; organized and established Hattie M. Strong Found. (of which mother Mrs. Henry Alvah Strong is founder), 1928 and since served as pres. Dir. Nat. Savings & Trust Co. Trustee Rollins Coll., Children's Hosp., 1932-36; adv. trustee YWCA, 1939-41. Served as chmn. exec. com. Washington Cathedral Bldg. Fund, 1946. Dir. loan div. ECA, 1948; dep. dir. Internat. Trade Promotion Div., 1949-50; U.S. ambassador to Norway, 1953-57. Trustee George Washington U.; bd. dirs. Washington Schpt. Boy Scouts Am., 1938-41. Served as 2d lt. French Arty., 1917-18; maj. U.S. Army Ordnance dept., 1941; as col. gen. staff corps, served as chief liaison br. internat. div. Army Service Forces, 1943-46. Decorated Legion of Merit (U.S.); Officer, Legion of Honor (France); Order of the White Cloud Banner (China); Cross of Liberation (Norway); Grand Officer, Order Orange Nassau (Netherlands); Officer, Order of Leopold (Belgium); Grand Cross of the Norwegian Order of St. Olav. Mem. Nat. Symphony Orchestra Assn. (pres. 1939-41). Republican. Episcopalian. Clubs: Yale, Coffee House (N.Y.); Metropolitan, Chevy Chase (Washington). Home: Route 2, Whitehall Rd., Annapolis, Md. Died Sept. 1966.

STRONG, ROBERT ALEXANDER prof. pediatrics, med. editor; b. New Orleans, Nov. 17, 1884; s. Robert and Joanna (O'Connor) S.; M.D., Tulane, 1907; grad. study, London, and at various German pediatric centers; m. Elmire Delbert, Apr. 3, 1907; 1 son, Delbert. Asst. prof. pediatrics, Tulane U., 1917-20, clin. prof. pediatrics, 1920-23, prof. and head dept. pediatrics, 1929-44, prof., head of pediatrics, Dept. Graduate Studies, 1937-44, on military leave of absence, 1941-44; surgeon, U.S. Pub. Health Service (consultant), 1920-23. Vis. physician Charity and Bapt. hosps., Touro Infirmary. First lt., later capt. and maj., U.S. Med. Corp during World War I; lt. col. Med. Res. Corps, 1919-39, col. 1939—; active duty with rank of col., as med. officer, 3d Mil. Area of the 4th Corps, New Orleans, Apr. 1941—; comdg. officer Station Hosp., Gulfport Field, Miss., - 1942-43; inactive Reserve 1943. Pres. La. State Pediatrics Soc., 1930-31; La. state chmn. for Region II, Am. Acad. Pediatrics, 1930-40. Diplomat Am. Bd. of Pediatrics. Fellow and charter mem. Am. Acad. Pediatrics (emeritus 1947); formerly mem. A.M.A., So. Med. Assn., La. Med. Soc., La. and Central States pediatric socs., Alpha Omega Alpha, Phi Rho Sigma, Pi Kappa Alpha. Democrat. Co-author of Tice's Practice of Medicine and Brennemann's Pediatrics. Editor Internat. Med. Digest, 1924—; mem. editorial board Jour. of Pediatrics, 1932-46. Advances in Pediatrics, American Jour. of Syphilis (1930-35), Aviation Medicine (1930-34). Contbr. many articles to professional and assn. jours. Home: 997 East Beach Blvd., Pass Christian, Miss. Died 1955.

STROTHER, DAVID HUNTER (pen name Porte Crayon), writer, illustrator; b. Martinsburg, W.Va., Sept. 26, 1816; s. Col. John and Elizabeth (Hunter) S.; attended Jefferson Coll., Canonsburg, Pa.; studied art in Phila., Italy, France, 1840-43; m. Anne Wolfe, 1849; m. 2d, Mary Hunter; 3 children including Emily (Strother) Walker. Illustrated 1851 edition of Swallow Barn; did drawings for The Blackwater Chronicle, 1853; contbd. to Harper's New Monthly Mag., 1853; did series of articles, entitled "North Carolina Illustrated" for Harper's, 1857, "A Winter in the South," 1857-58, "A Summer in New England," 1860-61; served in Topog. Corps as asst. adjutant gen. and mem. staffs of Gens. McClellan, Banks, Pope, and Hunter; became col. 3d W.Va. Cavalry; resigned, 1864; brevetted brig. gen., 1865; contributed series of articles "Personal Recollections of the War by a Virginian" to Harper's, 1866-68; U.S. consul gen. in Mexico City, 1879.

Author: Virginia Illustrated, by Porte Crayon (collected sketches) 1857. Died Jefferson County, W.Va., Mar. 8, 1888.

STROTHER, JAMES H. marine officer; b. Dadeville, Ala., Sept. 11, 1896; grad. U.S. Naval Acad., 1920; m. Elizabeth Ellen Wright; 4 children, including James W. (dec. May 1953). Commd. 2d lt., USMC, 1920, and advanced through grades to brig. gen., 1949; comdg. gen. Marine Corps Depot of Supplies, Phila.; ret., 1952; now pres. Dadeville Industries, Inc. Mem. C. of C. Decorated Legion of Merit. Mem. S.A.R. (pres. Ala.). Club: (founder mem.) Army-Navy Country (Washington). Mason, Elk, Kiwanian. Home: 709 Columbus St., Dadeville, Ala. 36853. Died Jan. 27, 1966; buried Dadeville Cemetery.

STROVER, CARL BERNHARD WITTEKIND lawyer, author; b. Wedigenstein, Prussia, Dec. 11, 1865; s. Bernhard and Caroline (Boedecker) S.; grad. Gymnasium, Minden, Prussia, 1884; studied agriculture, politics and economics, U. of Berlin, 1888-90; LL.B. and M.A., Univ. of Wis., 1894; m. Martha Gross, 1904; children—Dorothy and Warren (both adopted). Served in the Prussian Inf., 1887-91, commd., 1890, lt. 54th Prussian Inf.; came to U.S., 1891; naturalized citizen, 1896. Admitted to Wis. and Ill. bar, 1894, U.S. Supreme Ct., 1910; maj. Ill. vols. Spanish-Am. War, 1898. Author: The Hawaiian Problem, 1898; Monetary Reconstruction, 1922; Hard Times Can Be Ended, 1930; Monetary Progress, 1937. Home: Chicago, Ill. Died Apr. 19, 1941.

STRUM, LOUIE WILLARD judge; b. Valdosta, Ga., Jan. 16, 1890; s. Louis Henry and Dora Lee (Ramsey) S.; grad. St. Petersburg (Fla.) Mil. High Sch., 1906 (capt. of cadets); LL.B., Stetson U., 1912, LL.D., 1934; m. Ophelia Wilson Gray, June 6, 1917; children—Louie Willard, Charles Gray, Ophelia Gray; married 2d, Grace Hilditch Holt, October 6, 1951. Admitted to Fla. bar, 1912, and began practice Jacksonville; city atty., Jacksonville, 1921-25; justice Supreme Court of Fla., 1925-31; chief justice, Jan.-Mar. 1931; judge U.S. Dist. Court, Southern Dist. of Fla., 1931-50, U.S. Court of Appeals, 5th Jud. Circuit, Oct. 1950—. Served in U.S. Navy, 1906-10; lt. comdr. Apr. 6, 1917-July 2, 1919, World War, Mem. Am. Legion (past post comdr.), Sigma Nu, Phi Delta Phi. Democrat. Episcopalian. Mason (32 deg., K.T., Shriner). Clubs: Tallahassee Country (Tallahassee); Timuquana, Seminole, Fla. Yacht (Jacksonville). Home: George Washington Hotel. Office: Federal Bldg., Jacksonville, Fla. Died July 26, 1954; buried St. Petersburg, Fla.

STRUVE, GUSTAV journalist; b. Munich, Germany, Oct. 11, 1805; s. Johann Gustav and Friederike (von Hockstetter) von S.; attended Karlsrube; studied law Gottingen and Heidelberg (Germany), univs.; 1824-26; m. Amalie Dusar, 1845; m. 2d, Frau von Centener; 3 children. Sec. Oldenburg legation, Frankfort, circa 1826; judge, Jinver; lawyer, Mannheim; founded publ. Zeitschrift fur Phrenologie, 1843; editor polit. jour. Das Mannheimer Tageblatt, 1845; founder, owner Deutsher Tuschaver (favored agitation for German Republic which culminated in Revolution of 1848), 1846-48; a leader in calling mass meeting, Offenburg, Baden, 1848; mem. Vorparlament; led armed revolt, 1848, exiled; came to Am., 1851; editor socialist publ. Die Sociale Republik, 1858, 59; worked for cooperation of labor groups, N.Y.C., Phila.; served from pvt. to capt. 8th German Vol. Regt., U.S. Army, 1861-62; returned to Germany, 1863. Author: Weltgeschichte (written in U.S., presented view that progress in Am. due to absence tyrannical restrictions), 1852-60; (autobiographical) Diesseits und Jenseits des Oceans, 1863. Died Vienna, Austria, Aug. 21, 1870.

STRUVE, OTTO (stroo've), astronomer; b. Kharkov, Russia, Aug. 12, 1897; s. Ludwig and Elisabeth (Grohmann) S.; student Michael Artillery Sch., Petrograd, Russia, 1916-17; Diploma of First Rank, U. of Kharkov, 1919; Ph.D., U. Chgo., 1923; hon. Sc.D., Case Sch. Applied Sci., 1939, U. Pa., 1956; Ph.D., (hon.), Copenhagen, 1946, U. Mexico, 1951; D.Sc. (hon.), Liege U., 1949; Wesleyan U., 1960; D. Phil., Kiel U., 1960; married Mary Lanning, May 21, 1925. Came to America, 1921, naturalized, 1927. Asst. in astronomy, Yerkes Obs., 1921-23, instr., 1924-27, asst. prof., 1927-30, asso. prof., 1930-32, asst. dir., 1931-32, dir. 1932-47, chmn. and hon. dir., 1947-50; prof. astrophysics, U. of Chicago, 1932-47, Andrew MacLeish Distinguished Service prof., 1946-50; dir. McDonald Observatory of University of Texas, 1932-47, honorary director, 1947-50, chairman astronomy dept., 1947-49; professor of astrophysics, chmn. dept. dir. Leuschner Obs. U. Calif. at Berkeley, 1950-59; director National Rario Astronomy Obs., 1959—; editor: The Astrophysical Journal, 1932-47; fellow International Education Board, Mt. Wilson Observatory, 1926; Guggenheim Foundation fellow, Cambridge (England) U., 1928. Trustee Associated Universities of N.Y., 1957-59, Associated Universities Incorporated of N.Y., 1959. Served as lt. in Imperial Russian Army, 1916-17; lt. White Russian Army, 1919-21. Fellow A.A.A.S.; mem. Nat. Acad. of Sciences, Am. Philos. Soc., Am. Astron. Soc. (pres., 1946), Astron. Soc. of Pacific (pres. 1951), Am. Phys. Soc., Wis., Cal. acads. sci., Am. Acad. Arts and Sci., Sigma Xi, Internat. Astron. Union (pres., 1952-55), Amsterdam, Stockholm and Oslo Acads., Uppsala Soc. Scis., Society Astr. de France, Astr. Gesellschaft; corr. mem. Société Royale des Sciences de Liége, Acad. Sci., Copenhagen, Haarlem (Holland) Soc. of Sciences; fgn. asso. mem. Royal Astron. Soc. (Eng.); fgn. mem. Royal Soc. London, Edinburgh; hon. mem. Royal Astr. Soc. Can. Decorated Chevalier, Comdr. Order of Crown (Belgium); Gold Medal, Royal Astr. Soc. (London), 1944; Bruce Gold Medal, San Francisco, 1948; Draper Gold Medal, Nat. Acad. Sci., 1950; Rittenhouse Medal, Phila., 1954; Janssengold medal Paris Acad. Sci., 1955; Bruce Blair award, 1956. Address: 853 Station Pl., Berkeley 7, Cal. Died Apr. 6, 1963.

STRYKER, LLOYD PAUL (strik'er), lawyer; b. Chicago, Ill., June 5, 1885; s. Melancthon Woolsey and Elizabeth (Goss) S.; A.B., Hamilton Coll., 1906; A.M., 1909, L.H.D., 1933; m. Katharine Truax, Apr. 30, 1910; 1 dau., Katharine S. Dunn. Admitted to N.Y. bar, 1909, and practiced since at N.Y. City; asst. dist. atty. N.Y. County, 1910-12. Served as 2d lt., later 1st lt. and capt., F.A., U.S. Army, World War. Rep. nominee for judge of City Court, New York, 1914; apptd. judge U.S. Dist. Court, Southern Dist. N.Y., by President Coolidge, Mar. 1, 1929, but Senate adjourned without ratifying appointment. Fellow, American College of Trial Lawyers. Member Am. N.Y. State and N.Y. County bar assns., Assn. Bar City New York, New York Hamilton Coll. Alumni Assn., N.Y. Soc. Mil. and Naval Officers of World War, St. Nicholas Society; life mem. Tenn. State Bar Assn. Episcopalian. Clubs: University, Manhattan. Down Town, Piping Rock. Author: Andrew Johnson—A Study in Courage, 1929; Courts and Doctors, 1932; For The Defense (A Biography of Thomas Erskine), 1947; The Art of Advocacy, 1954. Home: 31 E. 72d St., N.Y.C. 21. Office: 40 Wall St., N.Y.C. Deceased.

STRYKER, WILLIAM SCUDDER pres. N.J. Hist. Soc.; b. Trenton, N.J., June 6, 1838; grad. Princeton, 1858; studied law; assisted in organizing 14th N.J. vols.; in Feb. 1863, aide to Gen. Quincy A. Gillmore, with rank of maj.; took part in capture of Morris Island and in the night attack on Ft. Wagner; later sr. paymaster in charge of disbursements dist. of Columbus, O.; bvtd. lt. col.; resigned, June 30, 1866; later on mil. staff gov. N.J.; commissioned adj. gen., N.J., Apr. 12, 1867; admitted to bar, 1866. Pres. Trenton Banking Co. Pres. Trenton Saving Fund Soc.; pres. Trenton Battle Monument Assn.; pres. Soc. of the Cincinnati in the State of N.J. Author: Officers and Men of New Jersey in the Civil War; The Battles of Trenton and Princeton. Address: Trenton, N.J. Died 1900.

STUART, CHARLES abolitionist, author; b. Jamaica, B.W.I., 1783. Served as lt. B.W.I. Co., 1801-14, ret. on pension with rank of capt., 1814; traveled at own expense through B.W.I. lecturing against slavery, 1828, also wrote pamplets on subject; successfully opposed 1831 campaign of Am. Colonization Soc.; lectr. for Am. Anti-Slavery Soc. in Ohio, Vt., N.Y., 1834-38; visited W.I. to study freed men, 1838-40; agt. Am. Anti-Slavery Soc. at World Anti-Slavery Conv., 1842. Author: Is Slavery Defensible from Scripture, 1831; A Memoir of Graham Sharp, 1836. Died Lake Simcoe, Can., 1865.

STUART, CHARLES EDWARD senator, congressman, lawyer; b. nr. Waterloo, N.Y., Nov. 25, 1810; studied law. Admitted to the bar, 1832, began practice law, Waterloo; moved to Kalamazoo, Mich., 1835; mem. Mich. Ho. of Reps., 1842; mem. U.S. Ho. of Reps. (Democrat, filled vacancy) from Mich., 30th, 32d congresses, Dec. 6, 1847-49, 51-53; mem. U.S. Senate from Mich., 1853-59; del. Democratic nat. convs., Charleston, S.C. and Balt., 1860, Nat. Conv. of Conservatives, Phila., 1866; organizer, col. 13th Regt., Mich. Vol. Inf. during Civil War, resigned commn. because of poor health. Died Kalamazoo, May 19, 1887; buried Mountain Home Cemetery.

STUART, CHARLES JENCKES BARNES b. Chgo., Oct. 28, 1891; s. George and Elizabeth Aborn (Barnes) Stuart; prep. edn., 1912; A.B., U. Mich., 1915; married. Vice-pres., Halsey Stuart & Co., investment bankers. Served on Mexican border, 1916, with Battery C, 1st Ill. F.A.; capt. Battery E, 331st F.A., AEF, 1917-19. Mem. Delta Kappa Epsilon, Soc. Colonial Wars, Am. Legion. Clubs: Chicago, University, Bond (Chicago); University, D.K.E., Broad Street, Recess, Sleepy Hollow Country, City Midday (N.Y.). Home: Drifton-Grove Point Rd., Savannah, Ga. Address: 35 Wall St., N.Y.C. Died Sept. 18, 1964.

STUART, DANIEL DELEHANTY VINCENT rear admiral U.S.N.; b. Albany, N.Y., Sept. 15, 1847; s. John and Mary (Delehanty) S.; student Albany Acad., 1861-62; midshipman in active service during Civil War; grad. U.S. Naval Acad., 1869; m. Alicia A. Smith, Sept. 26, 1883; children—Daniel Delehanty Vincent, Bartlett Gregory (dec.). Promoted through the various grades to rear admiral, Sept. 3, 1900; retired by operation of law, Sept. 15, 1909. During Spanish-American War comd. Mangrove; during Philippine campaign comd. Isla de Luzon, Don Juan de Austria, and Yorktown. Medals for Civil War, Spanish campaign, Philippine campaign and for service while in command of Mangrove. Home: Washington, D.C. Died Apr. 13, 1932.

STUART, DAVID congressman; lawyer; b. Bklyn., Mar. 12, 1816; studied law. dmitted to the bar, began practice law in Detroit; mem. U.S. Ho. of Reps. (Democrat) from Mich., 33d Congress, 1853-55; moved to Chgo.; commn. lt. col. 42d Regt., Ill. Vol. Inf., U.S. Army, 1861, col. 55th Regt., Ill. Vol. Inf., 1861, apptd. brig. gen. Volunteers, 1862 (nomination declined by U.S. Senate, 1863), resigned from army. 1863; resumed practice law, Detroit. Died Detroit, Sept. 12, 1868; buried Elmwood Cemetery.

STUART, EDWARD sanitarian (ret.); b. Boston, Sept. 1, 1888; s. Edward and Emma Sophie (Wornle) S.; S.B., in Sanitary Engring., Mass. Inst. Tech., 1910; studied Technical School of Public Health Harvard, 1914-15; m. Helen Louise Fox, June 21, 1911; children—Edward, Virginia Sedgwick (Mrs. Emmett W. Wood). Sanitary engr. Oklahoma, and Brazil, South America, 1910-14; sanitary engineer, later dir. Am. Red Cross Sanitary Commn. in Serbia, 1915; dir. relief work of Am. Red Cross in the Balkans, 1916-17; with earthquake expn. to Guatemala, 1918; maj. Sanitary Corps, U.S. Army, 1918-19; mem. Rockefeller Tuberculosis Commn. in France, 1919-21; nat. dir. disaster relief, Am. Red Cross, 1922; producer of ednl. motion pictures for Rockefeller Foundation and Internat. Edn. Bd., 1923-25; in charge of malaria control, Cal. State Dept. Pub. Health, 1926-32. Mem. bd. dirs. Am. Yugoslav Soc. Mem. Am. Pub. Health Assn., Beta Theta Pi; asso. mem. Am. Soc. C.E. Episcopalian. Clubs: Explorers (N.Y.C.); Cosmos (Washington, D.C.). Contbr. to Am. Jour. Pub. Health, Nation's Health, etc. Home: 34 Marmion Way, Rockport, Mass. Died Nov. 25, 1953.

STUART, EDWIN ROY army officer; b. Arnettsville, W.Va., Aug. 19, 1874; s. Samuel Calvin and Sarah Emeline (Cox) S.; grad. U.S. Mil. Acad., 1896; m. Emma Smith Jervey, Jan. 4, 1900. Commd. add. 2d lt. engr. corps, June 12, 1896; 2d lt., July 31, 1897; 1st lt., July 5, 1898; capt., Apr. 23, 1904; maj., Oct. 16, 1909; prof. drawing, U.S. Mil. Acad., rank of lt. col., Oct. 4, 1911. On duty U.S. Engr. Office, Charleston, S.C., 1896-97; student officer U.S. Engr. Sch., 1897-99; instr. Dept. of Engring., U.S. Mil. Acad., 1899-1903; adj. 1st Battalion Engrs., 1903-04; instr. Engring. Staff Coll., Ft. Leavenworth, Kan., 1904-07; in charge U.S. Engr. Office, Charleston, S.C., 1907-08; in charge mil. surveys of P.I., 1908-10; at Staff Coll., Ft. Leavenworth, 1910-11; assigned as prof. at U.S. Mil. Acad., 1911. A joint editor Internat. Mil. Digest. Author: Individual and Combined Military Sketching, 1907. Home: West Point, N.Y. Died Mar. 6, 1920.

STUART, HARRY ALLEN naval officer; b. Tazewell, Va., June 16, 1882; s. Stuart James and Armie Lee (Miller) S.; student Tazewell Coll., 1898-1900; B.S., U.S. Naval Acad., 1904; m. Marie D. Blandin, Oct. 8, 1913; children—Marie Blandin (Mrs. Thomas J. Wacker), Anna Lee, Valerie Corinne. Commd. ensign, U.S. Navy, 1906, and advanced through grades to rear admiral, May 19, 1939. Democrat. Catholic. Clubs: Army and Navy Country (Washington). Deceased.*

STUART, JAMES AUSTIN marine corps officer; b. Spokane, Mar. 11, 1899; s. James Wiley and Effie Ann (La Rue) S.; B.S., U.S. Naval Acad., 1922; student Nat. War Coll., 1950; m. Sara Raby Cross, May 24, 1924; children—James Austin, Thomas Rodney, Jerome Carroll. Commd. 2d lt. USMC, 1922, advanced through grades to maj. gen., 1950; exec. officer 9th Marines, Bougainville campaign World War II; operations officer 3rd Marine Div., Guam campaign, comdg. officer Iwo Jima campaign World War II; Joint U.S. Mil. Adv. and Planning Group in Greece, 1947-48; dir. Marine Corps Edn. Center, 1951; presently Marine Corps liaison officer Office Chief Naval Operations. Decorated Legion of Merit, Bronze Star, Presdl. Unit Citation with Star, Navy Unit Commendation with 2 Stars, Comdr. Order of Phoenix (Greece). Mason. Home: Anniversary Hill, Edgewater, Md. Office: Office Chief Naval Operations, Pentagon, Washington 25. Died Mar. 1967.

STUART, JAMES EWELL BROWN (JEB STUART) army officer; b. "Laurel Hill" plantation, Patrick County, Va., Feb. 6, 1833; s. Archibald and Elizabeth (Pannill) S.; attended Emory and Henry Coll., 1848-50; grad. U.S. Mil. Acad., 1854; m. Flora Cooke, Nov. 14, 1855, 3 children. Commd. 2d lt. U.S. Army, 1854, 1st lt., 1855, capt., 1861; patented device for attaching cavalry sabre to belt, 1859; resigned to become lt. col. Va. Inf. and capt. cavalry Confederate Army, 1861; promoted brig. gen. for role in 1st Battle of Manassas, 1861; fought with well-organized cavalry outpost in engagement at Dranesville, Va., Dec. 1861; covered army retreat to Chickahominy during Peninsular campaign, 1862; executed reconnaissance mission to McClellan's right (exemplary in method, results), June 1862; led rash attack from Evelington Heights, during Seven Days campaign, July 1862; raided Pope's hdqrs. at 2d Battle of Manassas, Aug. 1862 (praised by Lee); made highly successful raid into Pa. (riding around Fed. troops), Sept. 1862; conducted skillful arty. attack from Confederate right at Battle of Fredericksburg; informed Lee of Hooker's movements at beginning of Chancellorsville campaign, became key intelligence source to Lee; played disputed role in Gettysburg campaign (because of failure to join main body Confederate Army until 2d day of battle); his cavalry activity declined in 1864 due to lack of supplies, but he managed to successfully block movement of Gen. Sheridan's forces toward Richmond, Va., May 9, 1864. Equestrian statue erected in his honor, Richmond, 1907. Died of wounds received in action, Richmond, Va., May 12, 1864; buried Hollywood Cemetery, Richmond.

STUART, JOHN army officer, supt. Indian affairs; b. Scotland, 1700; m. Miss Fenwick before 1759, at least 1 son, Lt. Gen. Sir John. Came to U.S., circa 1748; capt. S.C. Provincial Militia 1757; supt. Indian affairs for So. dist. S.C, 1762, responsible to secs. of state in Eng. following proclamation of 1763; in Floridas, 1764, named mem. East Fla. governing council by Gov. James Grant; gained imperial status (responsible to King, rather than secs. of state) for his dept., 1765; became refugee in Floridas, arrest ordered by S.C. Assembly on charge of attempting to incite Catawba and Cherokee Indians in Brit. interest, 1775; organized 3 cos. of refugees to further Brit. interest in South, 1778. Died Pensacola, Fla., Mar. 25, 1779.

STUART, PHILIP congressman, army officer; b. nr. Fredericksburg, Va., 1760; prep. edn. Moved to Md.; served in Continental Army as lt. 3d Continental Dragoons, wounded at Eutaw Springs, 1781, transferred to Baylor's Dragoons, 1782, lt. Second Artillerists and Engrs., 1798-1800; served in War of 1812; mem. U.S. Ho. of Reps. (Federalist) from Md., 12th-15th congresses, 1811-19. Died Washington, D.C., Aug. 14, 1830; buried Congressional Cemetery.

STUART, ROBERT YOUNG forester; b. S. Middleton Tp., Cumberland County, Pa., Feb. 13, 1883; s. William Chalmers and Janet (Morris) S.; A.B., Dickinson Coll., 1903, A.M., 1906; M.F., Yale, 1906; m. Janet Mary Agnes Wilson, Dec. 9, 1907; children—Janet Crichton, Helen. Asst., U.S. Forest Service, Mont., Ida., Wyo., later chief of timber sale and planting, Missoula (Mont.) dist., 1906-12; forest insp., Washington, D.C., 1912-17; dep. commr. forestry, Pa., 1920-22, commr., 1922-23; sec. of forests and waters, Pa., 1923-27; chief of pub. relations, U.S. Forest Service, 1927-28; chief of U.S. Forest Service, May 1, 1928-—. Served as capt., later maj., Forest Engrs., U.S.A., 1917-19; citation from Gen. Pershing for work with A.E.F. Mem. Tri-State Delaware River Treaty Commn., 1923-27; chmn. Pa. Sesquicentennial Commn.; 1926; mem. Nat. Capital Park and Planning Commn. Episcopalian. Mason. Home: Chevy Chase, Md. Died Oct. 23, 1933.

STUECK, FREDERICK (stook), govt. ofcl.; b. St. Louis, Jan. 8, 1906; s. John and Etta (Wagner) S.; LL.B., Washington U., 1929; m. Camilla Cuningham, June 25, 1931. Admitted to Mo. bar, 1929; practice of law, St. Louis, 1929-41, 50-54; exec. asst. Gov. Forrest C. Donnell, Mo., 1941; chmn. State of Mo. Pub. Service Commn., 1941-43; mgr., v.p. in charge operations Transit Casualty Co., 1946-50; commr. Fed. Power Commission, Washington, 1954-—. Vice chmn. 1957-58. Served as captain, AUS, 1943-46. Member Am., Fed., St. Louis, St. Louis Co. bar assns., Am. Judicature Soc., Mo. State Hist. Soc., Am. Legion (past comdr. St. Louis), Washington U. Law Alumni Assn., Res. Officers Assn., Delta Theta Phi (past dist. chancellor). Republican. Mason (past master). Clubs: Rotary, Missouri Athletic (St. Louis); Congressional Country (Washington, Dist. Columbia); John Marshall Lawyers (past pres.). Home: 2936 Garfield Terrace, N.W., Washington; also 21 Balmagoun, Kirkwood, Mo. Office: 441 G St., Washington 25. Died July 15, 1961.

STUMM, RICHARD A(UGUST) indsl. exec.; b. St. Louis, July 18, 1896; s. Ernest C. and Augusta (Eschle) S.; student U. Cal. at Berkeley, 1914; m. Pauline Borradaile, Dec. 15, 1917; children—Richard A., John B. With Paraffine Cos., Inc., 1921-26, Los Angeles Mfg. Co., 1926-32; founder, pres. to chmn. bd. Southern Pipe & Casing Co., Azusa, Cal., 1932-60; mgmt. cons., Glendora, Cal., 1960-—. Served from 2d lt to 1st lt., U.S. Army, 1917-19. Clubs: California (Los Angeles); Annandale Golf, Overland (Pasadena, Cal.); Family (San Francisco). Home: 1802 Blue Bird Rd., Glendora, Cal. Office: P.O. Box 336, Glendora, Cal. Died Mar. 5, 1963.

STUMP, FELIX BUDWELL, ret. naval officer; b. Parkersburg, W.Va., Dec. 15, 1894; s. John Sutton and Lily (Budwell) S.; B.S., U.S. Naval Acad., 1917; M.S., Mass. Inst. Tech., 1924; m. Myra Morgan, Dec. 22, 1923; 1 son, John Morgan; m. 2d, Elizabeth Smith, Aug. 11, 1937; children—Frances, Felix. Commd. ensign USN, 1917, advanced through grades to adm., 1953; navigator U.S.S. Cincinnati, World War I; flight tng. Naval Air Sta., Pensacola, Fla., 1919-20; comdr. exptl. squadron Naval Air Sta., Norfolk, Va., 1921-22; staff comdr. Air Bat. For., 1924-25; with torpedo plane squadron U.S.S. Langley, 1925-27; staff Naval Air Sta., Norfolk, 1927-30; comdr. cruiser scouting squadrons, 1930-32; with bur. aero. Navy Dept., 1932-34; comdr. dive bombing squadron U.S.S. Saratoga, 1934-36; navigator U.S.S. Lexington, 1936-37; with bur. aero. Navy Dept., 1937-40; exec. U.S.S. Enterprise, 1940-41; comdr. U.S.S. Langley, 1941; dir. combined operations, intelligence center Am., Brit., Dutch, Aus. Com. Java, 1942; capt. new U.S.S. Lexington, 1943-44; comdr. Carrier Div. 24, 1944-45; chief naval air tech. tng., 1945-48; comdr. Air Force, Atlantic Fleet, 1948-51, 2d Fleet and NATO Striking Fleet, 1951-53; comdr.-in-chief Pacific and U.S. Pacific Fleet, 1953-58; chairman of the board of Air America, Incorporated, Air Asia Co., Ltd., from 1959. Decorated Navy Cross with gold star, D.S.M. War and Navy depts., Legion of Merit with gold stars, Silver Star medal, also fgn. decorations. Address: McLean VA Died June 13, 1972; buried Arlington Nat. Cemetery, Arlington VA

STURDEVANT, CLARENCE L. (stûr'de-vant), army officer; b. Aug. 1, 1885; B.S., U.S. Mil. Acad., 1908; grad. Engring. Sch., 1911; grad. Command and Gen. Staff Sch., 1926, Army War Coll., 1931. Commd. 2d lt., 1908; promoted through grades to maj. gen., 1945; Asst. Chief of Engrs., Washington, D.C., 1940; comdg. gen., New Guinea Base Section, SOS, June 1944; Deputy Chief of Staff, Am. Forces Western Pacific, July 1945; retired in grad of maj., gen., Sept. 1945; supr. Alcan Highway. Legion of Merit; Bronze Star; Distinguished Service Medal. Home: Route 4, Rockville, Md. Died Apr. 1958.

STURGES, WESLEY A. dean; b. Fairfield, Vt., Nov. 3, 1893; s. Rev. Alba H. and Alma F. (McGowan) S.; Ph.B., U. of Vt., 1915; LL.B., Columbia, 1919; J.D. cum laude, Yale, 1923, hon. A.M.; hon. D.C.L., U. of Vt., 1947; LL.D., Tulane University, 1948; LL.D., Columbia University, 1954; married B. Almira Watts, June 22, 1918 (div.); children—William Watts, Douglas Watts; m. 2d, Clare J. Campbell, June 23, 1951. Admitted to bars of Conn., South Dakota, Vt.; asst. prof. of law, University S.D., 1920-22, U. of Minn., 1923-24; with Yale since 1924, as asst. prof. of law, 1924-26, asso. prof., 1926-28, Phelps prof. of law, 1928-61, Edward J. Phelps professor of law emeritus, 1961-—, dean, 1945-54; dean of University of Miami Law School, 1961-—; on leave, 1942-45, to act as adminstr. Conn. State Defense Council, and as State fuel administrator, 1942-43; chief representative Office Economic Warfare, for French North and West Africa and prin. rep. U.S. Commercial Co., Algiers, Algeria, 1943-44; sub-area economic coordinator for Sicily, 1943-44; vis. prof. U. Wash., summer 1949, Tulane U., 1954, U. Miami, 1955, 1956, 57, 58, 59. Gen. counsel Surplus Property Bd., Mar.-July 1945; exec. dir. Distilled Spirits Inst., Inc., 1938-40. Chmn. panel to study stock options Salary Stblzn. Bd.; spl. rep. A.A.A., Hawaii, 1935; served as impartial mem. New Haven Grievance Bd. Motion Picture Code Authority; mem. Administrative Com., Motion Picture Arbitration System. Served with 1st Infantry, Vt. National Guard, 1917-19; discharged as captain O.R.C. Mem. American Bar Assn., Connecticut Bar Association, Assn. Am. Law Schs. (pres.-elect, 1954, pres. 1955). Kappa Sigma. Clubs: Century Association (N.Y.C.); Morys (New Haven); Coral Gables Country (Miami, Florida). Author: Commercial Arbitrations and Awards, 1930; Cases and Materials on Credit Transactions, 3d edit., 1947; Cases and Materials on Debtor's Estates, 3d edit. (Poteat and Rostow), 1940; Cases on Arbitration Law, 1953. Contributor to the Arbitration Journal and also to law reviews. U.S. mem. permanent com. of jurists to study and prepare the unification of the civil and commercial laws of the American republics. Am. collaborator on Internat. Year-book on Commercial Arbitration. Home: 5865 S.W. 114 Terrace, Miami, Fla. Office: U. Miami, Coral Gables, Fla. Died Nov. 9, 1962.

STURGIS, HENRY SPRAGUE, ret. banker; b. Cheyenne, Mar. 1, 1892; s. William and Anna Louisa (Sprague) S.; prep. edn., Phillips Acad., Andover, Mass.; A.B. cum laude, Harvard, 1915; m. Gertrude Lovett, June 19, 1916; children—Elizabeth Moorfield (Mrs. T. Suffern Tailer), Henry Sprague, Robert Lovett; m. 2d, Catharine Bartholomay Osborne, 1941. Began business career in association with father, 1915-17; with Spencer, Trask & Co., 1919-24; with First Nat. City Bank N.Y., 1925-56, v.p., 1928-56; asso. with Sanderson & Porter, bus. consultants, 1956-73; chmn. exec. com. Erie Railroad; bd. dirs. Gen. Mills, Inc. Asst. to Gov. of Ariz. for Indsl. Devel. Mem. bd. St. Joseph's Hosp., Phoenix. Sr. bd. mem. Nat. Indsl. Conf. Bd. Served from pvt. to capt., AS, U.S. Army, Sept. 1917-March 1919. Vice-pres. New York Hospital. Clubs: Harvard, Knickerbocker, Rockaway Hunting; Royal and Ancient Golf (St. Andrews, Scotland); Paradise Valley Country. Author: Investment—A New Profession, 1924; A New Chapter of Erie, 1948. Address: Scottsdale AZ Died Mar. 19, 1973.

STURGIS, RUSSELL merchant; b. Boston, Mass., Aug. 3, 1831; ed. Harvard; his father was a merchant in China trade, at Canton, and after graduation he went there; was U.S. consul at Canton, but returned to U.S. and engaged in business in Boston; capt. and maj. 45th Mass. regt., 1862-63; active in Y.M.C.A., 1858-—, as pres. of the Boston Assn., chmn. State com. and member Internat. com. Address: Boston, Mass. Died 1899.

STURGIS, SAMUEL DAVIS army officer; b. Shippensburg, Pa., June 11, 1822; s. James and Mary (Brandenburg) S.; grad. U.S. Mil. Acad., 1846; m. Jerusha Wilcox, 1 son, Samuel Davis. Joined 2d Dragoons; fought in Mexican War; served as 1st lt., 1st Dragoons in West, 1853; capt. with 1st (now 4th) Cavalry, 1855; mem. Utah expdn., 1858; maj., 1861, fought at Wilson's Creek; brig. gen. U.S. Volunteers, 1861; in charge of dist. of Kan.; served at 2d Battle of Bull Run, Battle of Antietam; mustered out of volunteer service, 1865; lt. col. 6th Cavalry, col. 7th Cavalry, 1869. Author: The Other Side as Viewed by Generals Grant, Sherman, and Other Distinguished Officers, Being a Defence of His Campaign into N.E. Mississippi in Year 1864, 1882. Died St. Paul, Minn., Sept. 28, 1889.

STURGIS, SAMUEL DAVIS army officer; b. St. Louis, Mo., Aug. 1, 1861; s. Samuel Davis and Jerusha (Wilcox) S.; student Washington U., St. Louis; grad. U.S. Mil. Acad., 1884; m. Bertha Bement, July 29, 1896; children—Samuel Davis, Elizabeth Tracy (Mrs. Hugh A. Murrill, Jr.), Robert Bement. Commd. 2d lt. 1st Arty., June 15, 1884; promoted through grades to brig. gen., July 1, 1917; maj. gen. N.A., Aug. 24, 1917; maj. gen. regular army, Oct. 7, 1921. Aide to Brig. and Maj. Gen. Wesley Merritt, 1891-96; asst. adj. gen. Dept. of Pacific and 8th Army Corps, 1898; participated in campaign against Manila, P.I., 1898; adj. gen. Dept. of Pinar del Rio, Cuba, Jan.-May 1899; asst. adj. gen. Philippine Div., 1899-1901; mem. Gen. Staff Corps, 1907-11; with 3d F.A., at Ft. Sam Houston, Tex., 1911-13; col. 1st Field Arty., in Hawaiian Islands, 1913-16; organized 7th Field Arty. at San Antonio, Tex., July 1916; comd. Camp Funston, Leon Springs, Kan., until Aug. 24, 1917; apptd. comdr. 87th Div., N.A., Camp Pike, Little Rock, Ark., Aug. 25, 1917; arrived in France, Sept. 11, 1918; detached service, with 1st and 42d divs. in Meuse-Argonne operations, Oct. 4-18, 1918; comd. 80th Div., Nov. 18, 1918-Apr. 12, 1919; comd. Camp Gordon, Atlanta, Apr. 30-July 2, 1919, Camp Pike, July 3-Nov. 10, 1919; comd. Camp Sherman, O., 1920-21; comd. Panama Canal Dept., 1921-24; comd. 3d Corps Area, 1924-25; retired from active service Aug. 1, 1925. Roman Catholic. Address: Washington, D.C. Died Mar. 6, 1933.

STURGIS, SAMUEL DAVIS JR. army officer; b. St. Paul, July 16, 1897; s. Maj. Gen. Samuel Davis and Bertha (Bement) S.; student U. Minn., 1915; B.S., U.S. Mil. Acad., 1918; grad. Engr. Sch. Application, 1920, Command and Gen. Staff Sch., 1935, Army War Coll., 1940; D.Engring., Rose Poly. Inst., 1955; m. Frances Jewett Murray, Jan. 28, 1922; 1 dau., Harriet (Mrs. Richard G. Knox). Commd. 2d lt., C.E., U.S. Army, 1918, advanced through grades to lt. gen., 1955; served P.I. in constrn. original trails in Bataan, 1926-29; at Passamaquoddy Power Project, Eastport, Me., 1935-37; exec. officer, navigation and flood control projects, U.S. Engr. Dist., Huntington, W.Va., 1937-39; dist. engr., flood control and war plant, airdrome and camp constrn., Vicksburg, Miss., 1940-42; corps. engr., XIII Corps., 1943; chief engr., 6th Army, in offensive from Australia to Luzon, 1943-45; chief engr. USAF, 1946-48; div. engr. Mo. River Div., C.E., in charge constrn. under Pick-Sloan Plan, 1949-51; comdg. gen. 6th Armored Div., Ft. Leonard Wood, Mo., 1951-52; comdg. gen. Army Communication Zone, France, 1952-53; chief engrs. Dept. Army, 1953-56; ret. 1956; chmn. U.S. section of the International Passamaquoddy Engineering Bd. Decorated Legion of Merit, also Bronze Star, Silver Star, D.S.M. with oak leaf cluster; recipient special award from Beavers, 1956. Mem. Chi Psi. Home: 3025 Cleveland Av., Washington 20008. Died July 5, 1964; buried Arlington Nat. Cemetery.

STURTEVANT, EDWARD LEWIS agrl. scientist; b. Boston, Jan. 23, 1842; s. Lewis W. and Mary (Leggett) S.; grad. Bowdoin Coll., 1863; grad. Harvard Med. Sch., 1866; m. Mary Mann, Mar. 9, 1864; m. 2d, Hattie Mann, Oct. 22, 1883; 5 children including Grace. Commd. lt., Co. G, 24th Me. Volunteers, 1861, later capt.; with brother purchased and began devel. of Waushakum Farm, South Framingham, Mass., 1867; conducted numerous agrl. expts., particularly interested in physiology of milk and milk secretion (gained acceptance for his research); editor or co-editor Scientific Farmer, 1876-79; erected 1st lysimeter in Am. at Waushakum Farm; studied history of edible plants; 1st dir. N.Y. Agrl. Expt. Station at Geneva, 1882; leader movement for expt. stas. Author: (with brother Joseph) The Dairy Cow: A Monograph on the Ayrshire Breed, 1875; North American Ayrshire Register, 4 vols., 1875-80; Sturtevant's Notes on Edible Plants (edited by U. P. Hedrick), 1919. Died South Framingham, July 30, 1898.

STYER, HENRY DELP (stir), army officer (retired); b. Sellersville, Pa., Sept. 21, 1862; s. William Barrett and Katherine (Delp) S.; student Franklin and Marshall Coll., Lancaster, Pa., 1877-79; grad. U.S. Mil. Acad., 1884, Army War Coll., 1914; m. Bessie Wilkes, g.d. Admiral Charles Wilkes, June 3, 1891. Commd. 2d lt. 21st Inf., June 15, 1884; 1st lt. 22d Inf., May 19, 1891; transferred to 13th Inf., July 20, 1891; capt. inf., Oct. 4, 1898; assigned to 13th Inf., Jan. 1, 1899; trans. to 11th Inf., Mar. 8, 1907; maj. 29th Inf., May 6, 1907; lt. col. 17th Inf., Nov. 12, 1912; col., July 1, 1916; brig. gen. N.A., Aug. 5, 1917. Served in Wyo., Utah, Ind. Ty. and at Ft. Niagara, N.Y., 14 yrs.; as capt. in Philippine Islands, 1899-1902, mentioned in orders for capture of Vicente Prado, notorious guerilla leader; prof. mil. science and tactics, Utah Agrl. Coll., 1892-96, 1903-06; comd. Ft. Niagara, 1909-12; duty with 2d Div., in Tex., 1913; on Mexican border at Eagle Pass, 1914, at Yuma, 1917; apptd. comdr. 181st Inf. Brigade, Camp Lewis, Tacoma, Wash., Sept. 4, 1917; first comdr. A.E.F., Siberia, Aug. 1918: comdr. Am. Zone of Advance on Amur River, to Apr. 1919; retired at his own request, Apr. 10, 1919; on active duty, Detroit, Nov. 1919 to

Aug. 1922. Decorated Order of Rising Sun (Yoshihito); War Cross (Czechoslovakia). Elected nat. comdr. Nat. Assn. Vets, of A.E.F. in Siberia (1918-20), 1941. Mem. mil. affairs com., San Diego Chamber of Commerce. Mem. German Reformed ch. Mason. Address: 400 2d St., Coronado, Calif. Died May 11, 1944.

STYGALL, JAMES HENRY physician; b. Buffalo, Mar. 10, 1887; s. James Sadler and Emma (Greiner) S.; M.D., U. Buffalo, 1910; m. Della E. Curry, June 15, 1915; 1 son, James Sadler. Supt. Rocky Chest Sanatorium, Olean, N.Y., 1919-21; med. supt. Ind. Tb Assn., 1921-24, pres., 1928; established Tb clinics in Ind. counties; chief staff Flower Mission Hosp.; Tb controller Indpls. and Marion counties; asst. prof. medicine Ind. U.; staff Meth., St. Vincent's, Gen. hosps. Served as capt. M.C., U.S. Army, World War I; chest cons. Selective Service, 1941-45. Fellow Am. Coll. Chest Physicians (founder council research; pres. 1955-56), A.C.P.; mem. A.M.A., Am. Trudeau Soc., Nat. Tb Assn. Republican. Episcopalian. Kiwanian. Home: 4311 N. Meridian St. Office: 1221 N. Delaware St., Indpls. Died Oct. 19, 1959.

SUGG, REDDING STANCIL (sug), dean, Sch. Vet. Medicine; b. Old Sparta, N.C., Oct. 19, 1893; s. William Edgar and Jane Leona (Stancil) S.; student, N.C. State Coll., 1910-13, B.S. in Agr., Ala. Polytech. Inst., 1914, D.V.M., 1915; m. Katherine Maude Miller, Oct. 31, 1918; 1 son, Redding Stancil. Vet. practitioner, 1915-16; with Sch. Vet. Medicine, Ala. Polytech. Inst. since 1916, as instr., bacteriology and pathology, 1916-17, asst. prof. bacteriology, 1919-28, prof., 1930-31; dean of school since 1940; state veterinarian since 1940; extension animal husbandman, Ala. Extension Service, 1928-30, 1931-40. Commd. 2d lt. Vet. Corps, 1917, promoted to capt., 1918; with Officers Reserve Corps, lt. col., 1930; active duty as lt. col., Vet. Corps, 1942; chief, Vet. Service Branch, Camp Shelby, Mississippi, 1942-46; colonel Vet. Reserve, inactive, since 1946. Member American Vet. Med. Assn., U.S. Livestock Assn., Ala. Vet. Med. Assn., Assn. Mil. Surgeons, Alpha Psi, Epsilon Sigma Phi, Phi Kappa Phi, Phi Zeta. Mason. Club: Kiwanis (Auburn, Ala.). Recipient 12th Internat. Vet. Congress award, 1951. Home: 408 W. Magnolia Av., Auburn, Ala. Died Jan. 4, 1958.

SULLENS, FREDERICK editor; b. Versailles, Mo., Nov. 12, 1877; s. John Perry and Ann Elizabeth (Waddell) S.; student U. of Mo., 1894-96; m. Anne Kirkpatrick Lemon, Nov. 25, 1903; 1 dau., Ann Kirkpatrick; m. 2d, Barbaara Barber, May 15, 1939. Began with Jackson Daily News, Jackson, Miss., 1904, editor, 1905-—. Served as capt. Mil. Intelligence Div., Gen. Staff, U.S. Army, World war; maj. Mil. Intelligence, O.R.C. Mem. Am. Soc. Newspaper Editors. Mem. Associated Press, Southern Newspaper Pubs. Assn., Reserve Officers' Assn. of Miss. Democrat. Presbyn. Clubs: Rotary, Elks, Pioneer, Travelers, Newcomen, National Press, Army and Navy of Washington, Colonial Country, Union League. Home: 3806 Kings Highway. Address: Daily News Bldg., Jackson, Miss. Died Nov. 20, 1957; buried Lakewood Meml. Park.

SULLIVAN, DONAL MARK, journalist; born Boston, Massachusetts, Oct. 25, 1910; s. John Andrew and Mary Elizabeth (Donovan) S.; A.B., cum laude, Harvard Coll., 1933, student Law Sch., 1933-35; LL.B., Boston U. Law Sch., 1937; m. Annette C. Bandler, Mar. 11, 1936;children—Gail, Marcia. Began as newspaperman, 1929; Harvard corr. Boston Globe, 1929-35, editorial writer, rewrite man, reporter, 1935-71; admitted to Mass. bar, 1937. Pres. Newspaper Guild of Boston, 1937; internat. v.p. Am. Newspaper Guild (Congress Indsl. Orgns.), 1938, 39, pres., 1940-41; pres. Greater Boston Indsl. Union Council, 1939-40; v.p. Mass. State Indsl. Union Council, 1940-42, New England dir., C.I.O. War Relief com., 1942; confidential sec., Mass. Commr. of Mental Health. Served as 2d lt., F.A., O.R.C., U.S. Army, 1933-38. 2d lt. and capt. C.A.C., U.S. Army, 1942-46. Permanent sec. Harvard Coll. Class of 1933. Democrat. Club: Harvard (Boston); Harvard (N.Y. City); Wellesley Country. Home: Wellesley Hills MA Died May 30, 1971.

SULLIVAN, FRANCIS PAUL architect; b. Washington, D.C., June 25, 1885; s. Thomas Joseph and Mary Katherine (Connolly) S.; A.B., Georgetown U., Washington, D.C., 1904; student George Washington U., 1905-09; m. Villette Anderson, June 28, 1911; 1 dau., Mannevillette. Engaged in practice of architecture, Washington, 1926-—, partner with Delos H. Smith and Joseph Whitfield Burnum, 1956-—; cons. architect for work on U.S. Capitol, House and Senate office bldg.; asso. architect with David Lynn (architect of the Capitol) and Harbison Hough, Livingston and Larson (cons.) to design reconstrn. of House and Senate Chambers. Principal works; Afghanistan Embassy, Children's Country Home, East Wing Senate Office Bldg., residence of Chief Justice Harlan F. Stone, Canadian Embassy; U.S. Legation, Tirana, Albania (in collaboration with Nathan C. Wyeth); Carrollsburg Housing Project Nat. Sports Center. Served as 1st lt., Ordnance Reserve, 1918-19; capt., Ordnance Dept., U.S. Army, 1919-20, Finance Dept., 1920-22; in charge of audit of war contracts, rep. of sec. of War in settlements with aluminum industry; comptroller, Post Office Dept., 1922-26. Nat. exec. officer Historic American Buildings Survey, 1934. Mem. constrn. code com. N.R.A., 1933. Fellow A.I.A. (2d v.p., 1935-36; chmn. com. Nat. Capital, 1930-42; chmn. com. pub. works, 1936-38; chmn. com. inter-professional relations, 1938-40; pres. Wash., D.C., chapter, 1933), Am. Geog. Soc.; mem. Soc. Archtl. Historians, Thornton Soc., Columbia Hist. Soc., Am. Planning and Civic Assn. (mem. com. of 100 on Nat. Capital), Phi Sigma Kappa. Del. Internat. Congress of Architects, Paris, 1937. Clubs: Cosmos, University (Washington). Author: The Portion of a Champion, 1916; also numerous articles relating to architecture, art criticism and city planning pub. in mags. and newspapers. Home: 3320 Rowland Pl., Washington 8. Office: 808 17th St., Washington 6. Died Feb. 3, 1958; buried Arlington Nat. Cemetery.

SULLIVAN, JEREMIAH J. banker; b. Fulton, Stark Co., O., Nov. 16, 1845; ed. pub. schs.; m. Selina J. Brown, 1873. Enlisted in 3d Ohio Battery, 1862, and served until after close of Civil War, July, 1865; engaged in gen. mercantile and hardware business, Millersburg, O.; mem. Ohio State Senate, 1879-83, 1885-89; nat. bank examiner for State of Ohio, 1887-90 (resigned); organizer, 1890, treas., mgr., and pres. since 1900, Central Nat. Bank, Cleveland, O.; pres. Superior Savings & Trust Co.; v.p. Pioneer Steamship Co., New England Co.; treas. Cleveland & Aurora Mineral Land Co., Mut. Building & Investment Co.; dir. 1st Nat. Bank (Canton, O.), Smith Steamship Co. (Mentor), Am. Malleable Castings Co. (Marion), Acme Transit Co.; trustee Am. Surety Co., etc. Ex-pres. Ohio State Bankers' Assn., Cleveland Chamber of Commerce; pres. Nat. Bd. of Trade, 1905, 1906. Trustee Soldiers' Home, Sandusky, O. Col. 5th Regt., Ohio N.G., 1893-94. Democrat. Clubs: Union, Country, Roadside, Chagrin Valley Hunt. Home: 4146 E. 99th St. Office: Central Nat. Bank, Cleveland, O.

SULLIVAN, JOHN army officer, Continental congressman, gov. N.H.; b. Somersworth, N.H., Feb. 17, 1740; s. John and Margery (Browne) S. Del. to Continental Congress, 1774, 75, 80-81; apptd. brig. gen. by 2d Continental Congress, 1775; served in siege of Boston, 1775; commd. maj. gen. with command on L.I., 1776; served at Valley Forge, 1777-78; completely routed combined Indian and Loyalst forces at Elmira, N.Y., 1779; resigned commn., 1779; mem. N.H. Constl. Conv., 1782; atty. gen. N.H., 1782-86; speaker N.H. assembly, 1785, 88; gov. N.H., 1786, 87, 89, suppressed paper-money riots; chmn. N.H. Conv. which ratified U.S. Constn., 1788; U.S. dist. judge for N.H., 1789-95. Died Durham, N.H., Jan. 23, 1795; buried in Sullivan family cemetery, Durham.

SULLIVAN, JOHN LAWRENCE lawyer; b. Wilkes-Barre, Pa., July 20, 1891; s. John Martin and Honora (Hurley) S.; LL.B., Georgetown U., 1914; m. Elizabeth Coyne, July 19, 1910 (died Dec. 31, 1927); children—Jonn Francis, Mary Kathleen; m. 2d, Ethel Fisher, Apr. 13, 1936. Admitted to practice law in states of Ariz., Calif., Neb., Ia.; in practice 1915-—; county atty. Prescott, Ariz., 1921-23; atty. gen. of Ariz., 1935-36, 44-—. Served as 1st lt., later capt. U.S. Army, in France and Germany, World War I; served in Provost Marshal Gen. Dept., U.S. Army, 1942-43. State comdr. Vets. Fgn. Wars, 1922, mem. nat. council of adminstrn., 1923-24, nat. juege advocate gen., 1940-41, now chmn. nat. rehabilitation com. Mem. No. Ariz., Ariz., Cal., Am. bar assns., Am. Legion. Democrat. Catholic. K.C. (State Dept.). Home: 313 W. Granada Rd., Phoenix. Died Oct. 13, 1949; buried St. Francis Cemetery, Phoenix.

SULLIVAN, MARK author; b. Avondale, Chester Country, Pa., Sept. 10, 1874; s. Cornelius and Julia (Gleason) S.; grad. Normal Sch., West Chester, Pa., 1892; A.B., Harvard, 1900; LL.B., 1903; hon. Litt.D., Brown U., 1927, Dartmouth, 1928; LL.D., Washington and Jefferson, 1936. Bates, 1936, St. John's, 1937; m. Marie McMechen Buchanan, Oct. 31, 1907 (died Dec. 5, 1940); children—Sydney Buchanan (Mrs. Jameson Parker), Mark, Cornelius (dec.), Narcissa Harvey (Mrs. Dale Siegchrist). Author and commentator, Overseer Harvard, 1928-34; Bromley lecturer Yale, 1929; bd. visitors U.S. Naval Acad., 1929. Col. U.S.M.C. Reserve, 1933. Hon. mem. Phi Beta Kappa. Author: Our Times—The Unites States, 6 vols., 1900-25; The Education of an American (autobiography), 1938. Clubs: Players, Harvard, Century (New York); Metropolitan, Nat. Press, Gridiron (Washington). Address: Avondale, Pa. Died Aug. 13, 1952; buried Balt.

SULLIVAN, PETER JOHN diplomat; b. Cork, Ireland, Mar. 15, 1821; brought to U.S., 1823; attended U. Pa. Served in Mexican War; stenographer U.S. Senate; admitted to Ohio bar, 1848; served as brig. gen. U.S. Volunteers during Civil War; U.S. minister to Colombia, 1865-69. Died Cincinnati, Mar. 2, 1883.

SULLIVAN, PHILIP LEO judge; b. Marengo, Ill., Oct. 2, 1889; s. William B. and Catherine C. (Brickley) S.; LL.B., Loyola U., 1911; m. Daisy Donahue, Nov. 24, 1920; 1 dau., Virginia. Teacher pub. sch., Buena Vista, Ill., 1907-08; admitted to Ill. bar, 1911, and began practice at Chicago; master in chancery, Superior Court, 1916-17; master in chancery, Circuit Court, 1919-21; judge Circuit Court, 1921-33; chief justice Criminal Court of Cook County, Sept. 1933-Dec. 11, 1933, resigned; U.S. dist. judge, Northern Ill. Dist., 1933-57; chief judge U.S. District Court, 1957-—. Enlisted in U.S. Army, 1917; hon. discharged as lt. field arty., 1919. Mem. Am., Ill. State and Chicago bar assns., Am. Legion. Democrat. Clubs: Chicago Athletic, Union League, Illinois Athletic, Lake Shore, Olympia Fields, Standard, South Shore Country. Home: 7321 So. Shore Drive. Address: U.S. Court House, Chicago, Ill. Died June 1960.

SULLIVAN, THOMAS CROOK army officer; b. Montgomery County, O., Nov. 14, 1833; grad. West Point, 1856; 2d lt. 1st Arty., July 1, 1856; unmarried. 1st lt., Apr. 27, 1861; capt. commissary of subsistence, Aug. 3, 1861; lt. col. vols., Aug. 20, 1862-Jan. 27, 1863, and Mar. 21-Aug. 1, 1865; bvtd. maj. and lt. col., Mar. 13, 1865, for faithful and meritorious services during the war; maj., Apr. 14, 1875; lt. col. asst. commissary gen., July 14, 1890; col., Dec. 27, 1892; brig. gen. commissary gen. of subsistence, Jan. 18, 1897; retired Nov. 14, 1897. Home: Troy, O. Died 1908.

SULTAN, DANIEL ISOM army officer; b. Oxford, Miss., Dec. 9, 1885; s. Daniel Isom and Emma Linda (Wohlleben) S.; student U. of Miss., 1901-03; B.S., U.S. Mil. Acad., 1907; grad. Army Engring. Sch., 1909, Command and Gen. Staff Sch., 1923, Army War Coll., 1926; m. Florence Braden, Jan. 29, 1916; children—Sheila, Linda Faser. Commd. 2d lt., June 14, 1907; advanced through grades to brig. gen., Dec. 1, 1938; instr. civil and mil. engring., United States Military Acad., 1912-16; commander Engineer troops and engaged in construction of roads and fortifications in P.I., 1916-17; col. Gen. Staff, World War; dist. engr., Savannah, Ga., 1923-25; mem. Bd. Engrs. for Rivers and Harbors, 1926-29; in command of U.S. Army troops in Nicaragua and mem. Interoceanic Canal Bd., 1929-31; district engineer, Chicago, 1932-34; engr. commissioner, D.C., 1934-38; comdg. 2d Engr. Regiment, Ft. Logan, Colorado, 1938; commanding general 22d Inf. Brigade, Schofield Barracks, T.H., 1939-41; comdg. gen. Hawaiian Div., Mar.-Apr. 1941; comdg. gen. 38th Div., Camp Shelby, Miss., May 1, 1941-Apr. 6, 1942; comdg. VIII Army Corps, Apr. 1942-43; apptd. dep. comdr. in chief China-Burma-India Theater, Jan. 1943-44; comdr. U.S. Forces in India-Burma Theater since Nov. 1944; maj. gen., inspector gen., July 1945. Decorated D.S.M. with Oak Leaf Cluster (U.S.), Presidential Medal of Merit and Congressional Medal of Distinction (Nicaragua). Mem. Am. Soc. Mil. Engrs., Sigma Chi. Presbyterian. Clubs: Army and Navy, Army and Navy Country (Washington). Writer of articles. Address: War Dept., Washington, D.C.* Died Jan. 14, 1947.

SUMMERALL, CHARLES PELOT army officer (ret.) b. Lake City, Fla., Mar. 4, 1867; s. Elhanan Bryant and Margaret Cornelia (Pelot) S.; grad. Porter Mil. Acad., Charleston, S.C., 1885; B. S., U.S. Mil. Acad., 1892; LL.D., Hobart Coll., 1921, Williams Coll., 1927, Coll. of Charleston, 1935, Brown U., 1936; Dr. Mil. Sci., Pa. Mil. Coll., 1927, The Citadel, 1954; m. Laura Mordecai, Aug. 14, 1901; 1 son, Charles P. (U.S. Army). Commd. 2d lt. inf., 1892, transferred to arty., 1893, promoted through grades to col., 1917; brig. gen. N.A., 1917; maj. gen. N.A., 1918; brig. gen. regular army, 1919; maj. gen., 1920; general (as chief of staff), 1929; retired with rank of gen., 1931. A.d.c. to Maj. Gen. Graham, comdr. II Army Corps, 1898, to Brig. Gen. Pennington, comdg. Dept. of Gulf, 1898-99; campaigns, Philippine Islands, 1899-1900; with China Relief Epdn., 1900-01; located and initiated constrn. of Ft. William H. Seward, Alaska, 1902; mem. mil. mission to Eng. and France, Apr.-July 1917; apptd. comdr. 67th F.A. Brig., later 1st F.A. Brig.; joined A.E.F. in France, Oct. 1917; comd. 1st Div., July-Oct. 1918, later V, IX and IV army corps; mem. interallied commn. at Fiume, July-Aug. 1919; on duty with Am. Mission to Negotiate Peace to Aug. 31, 1919; apptd. chief of staff, U.S. Army, 1926. Former mem. Joint Bd. Army-Navy. Pres. The Citadel, Mil. Coll. of S.C., 1931-—. Grand Minister of State Supreme Council. Chairman of Florida Canal Authority. Mem. S.C. Rural Electrification Authority. Decorated D.S.C. for gallantry, Battle of Soissons with 1st Div., World War I, D.S.M. for meritorious and distinguished services, Silver Star, 4 War Dept. citations for gallantry in action Philippines and China, 1900, Victory Medal for 5 major operations A.E.F., Spanish-Am. War Philippine and China Relief Epdn. campaign badges (U.S.); Legion of Honor. Croix de Guerre with two palms (France); Grand Officer Crown of Belgium; Comdr. Order of Crown (Italy); Mil. Medal (Panama); Order of Prince Danilo I (Montenegro); Grand Ribbon Polonia Restituta (Poland); Order Military Merit (Cuba). Mem. Soc. of 1st Div. of A.E.F., Am. Legion, S.A.R., Phi Beta Kappa, Omicron Delta Kappa, Blue Key. Episcopalian. Mason 33 deg.); mem. Supreme Council Scottish Rite (grand treas.), grnad insp. gen. in S.C. Clubs: Army-Navy (Washington); Rumson (N.J.) Country. Home: Aiken, S.C. Died May 14, 1955; buried Arlington Nat. Cemetery.

SUMMERLIN, GEORGE THOMAS diplomatic service; b. Rayville, La., Nov. 11, 1872; s. John S. and Mary (Davis) S.; student La. State U. and A. and M. Coll.; grad. U.S. Mil. Acad., 1896. Served in Puerto Rico, 1898, later in Philippines; resigned from Army as capt. of cav., May 17, 1903; apptd. clk. Dept. of State July 1, 1909; 2d sec. Embassy, at Tokyo, Japan, 1910; 2d sec. Legation, Peking, 1911-14; sec. Legation,

Santiago, Chile, 1914-17; sec. Embassy, Class I, Feb. 5, 1915; assigned to Mexico, Feb. 2, 1917; apptd. counselor of Embassy, Jan. 7, 1918; chargé d'affaires, ad interim, at Mexico City, 1919-24; counselor of Embassy, to Rome until Mar. 1925; E.E. and M.P. of U.S. to Honduras, 1925-29, to Venezuela, 1929-34, to Panama, 1934-37; chief of protocol, Dept. of State, since July 29, 1937; also special asst. to sec. of state, January 1944 with the rank of Minister. Member Kappa Alpha. Presbyterian. Clubs: Metropolitan, Army and Navy, Chevy Chase, Alibi (Washington); India House (New York). Home: Rayville, La. Address: 1718 H St. N.W., Washington. Died July 1, 1947; buried in Arlington National Cemetery.

SUMMERS, JAMES COLLING ("BLUE PETER") writer; b. Southgate, Eng., Feb. 19, 1854; s. Rev. James (prof. Chinese, Brit. Mus.) and Jane (Frankland) S.; ed. English schs. and King's College, London, England; m. Emily Simms, 1881. Served in the British merchant service, 1864-72; mate, master, and pilot U.S. steamers, 1872-81; in N.Y. naval militia, 1890-98; commd. ensign U.S.N., 1898; promoted lt. 1899, during Spanish-Am. War; at age of 62, commd., Feb. 9, 1917, lt. jr. grade U.S.N. (Fleet Reserve Class 1), for duty German-Am. War, in 3d Naval Dist., New York; promoted lt., Dec. 1, 1917. Yachting editor New York Tribune, 1899-1917. Drafted, 1897, bill introduced in Congress by Congressman Adolph Meyer, asking for 6 coast defense monitors for use of naval militia. Mem. The Old Guard (New York), Naval and Mil. Order Spanish-Am. War, Vets. Fgn. Wars, U.S. Revolver Assn., Masonic Vets., United Spanish War Vets. Editor "Who Won?" (ann. official yacht record), 1885-96. Editor and pub. Burgee and Pennant (illustrated yachting weekly), 1893-95; also Yachting (monthly mag.), 1895-98. Contbr. to mags. Home: Brooklyn, N.Y. Died Feb. 2, 1929.

SUMMERS, JOHN EDWARD army officer; b. in Va., Jan. 24, 1822. Apptd. from Va., asst. surgeon U.S.A., Dec. 13, 1847; capt. asst. surgeon, Dec. 13, 1852; maj. surgeon, May 21, 1861; lt. col. med. insp. vols., Feb. 27, 1863; hon. mustered out of vol. service, Oct. 31, 1863; lt. col. surgeon, Mar. 17, 1880; col. surgeon, Jan. 9, 1885; retired by operation of law, Jan. 24, 1886; advanced to rank of brig. gen. retired, by act of Apr. 23, 1904. During Civil War was at Gen. Hosp., Alexandria, Va., 1862-63; hosp. at Memphis, Tenn., 1863; med. dir. Dept. of Tenn. to Oct. 1866, and with Grant's Army in field until Oct. 1865; med. dir. Dept. Dakota to Sept. 1870; post-surgeon to Fortress Monroe, Va., 1870-74; med. dir. Dept. of the Platte, Omaha, Neb., 1874-86. Address: Washington, D.C. Deceased.

SUMNER, CHARLES BURT clergyman; b. Southbridge, Mass., Aug. 17, 1837; s. George and Julia Fisk (Newell) S.; A.B., Yale, 1862 (Phi Beta Kappa); grad. Andover Theol. Sem., 1867; (LL.D., Pomona Coll., Cal., 1910); m. Mary Louise Stedman, of Southbridge, Mass., Oct. 7, 1869 (now deceased); m. 2d, Maria Frost Cole, of N.Y. City, Jan. 26, 1904 (now deceased). Pvt. 45th Mass. Vols., 1862-63; ordained Congl. ministry, 1868; pastor Monson, Mass., 1868-80, West Somerville, 1880-82, Tuscon, Ariz., 1882-84; supt. home missions, Las Vegas, N.M., 1884-86; pastor Pomona, Cal., 1887-88, Claremont, Cal., 1891-93; sec. and business mgr., Pomona Coll., 1888-90; prof. Bibl. lit., Pomona Coll., 1890-99, now trustee. Republican. Clubs: University, Yale (Los Angeles, Cal.). Author: The Story of Pomona College, 1914. Home: Claremont, Los Angeles Co., Cal.

SUMNER, EDWIN VOSE army officer; b. Boston, Jan. 30, 1797; s. Elisha and Nancy (Vose) S.; m. Hannah W. Forster, Mar. 31, 1822, at least 3 children including Brig. Gen. Edwin Vose, Jr., Maj. Gen Samuel Storrow, 1 dau. Commd. 2d lt., 2d Inf., U.S. Army, 1819, promoted 1st lt., 1823, capt., 1833; served with 1st U.S. Dragoons, mainly on frontier duty; commd. maj. 2d Dragoons, 1846, assigned to army under Gen. Winfield Scott in Mexico, 1846; placed in command of 3d Cavalry by Scott; wounded at Cerro Gordo; brevetted for Mexican War service; promoted lt. col. 1st Dragoons, 1848; mil. comdr., acting gov. N.M., 1852; promoted col. 1st Cavalry, 1855; left Ft. Leavenworth for Ft. Laramie, 1855, turned back after marching 400 miles, claimed that further marching would sacrifice horses; charges preferred against him for this action by commanding officer Gen. Harney (War Dept. backed Sumner); commanded Ft. Leavenworth, 1856-57, attempted to keep order between warring pro-slavery and Free Soil factions in Kan.; became comdr. Dept. of West, hdqrs. St. Louis, 1857; promoted brig. gen., 1861; commanded II Corps in Peninsular campaign at S. Mountain and Antietam; apptd. maj. gen. U.S. Volunteers, 1862; relieved from duty at his own request. Died Mar. 21, 1863.

SUMNER, EDWIN VOSE brig. gen. U.S.A.; b. Carlisle, Pa., Aug. 16, 1835; s. Maj. Gen. Edwin Vose and Hannah W. (Forster) S.; brother of Samuel Storrow S.; m. Margaret, d. Gen. John Forster, July 18, 1866. Apptd. from N.Y., 2d lt. 1st U.S. Cav., Aug. 5, 1861; 1st lt., Nov. 12, 1861; maj. a.d.c. vols., May 19, 1863; hon. mustered out of vol. service, Aug. 15, 1863; capt. U.S.A., Sept. 23, 1863; col. 1st N.Y. Mounted Rifles, Sept. 8, 1864; bvtd. gen. vols., Mar. 28, 1865; hon. mustered out of vol. service, Nov. 29, 1865; maj. 5th U.S. Cav., Mar. 4, 1879; lt. col. 8th Cav., Apr. 15, 1890; col. 7th Cav., Nov. 10, 1894; brig. gen. vols., May 27, 1898; hon. discharged from vols., Feb. 24, 1899; brig. gen. U.S.A., Mar. 27, 1899; retired at own request, over 30 yrs.' service, Mar. 30, 1899. Participated in Modoc, Nez Perces and Bannock wars, campaign in southeast Nev., Sioux campaign, 1890-91. Home: Syracuse, N.Y. Died Aug. 24, 1912.

SUMNER, GEORGE WATSON rear admiral U.S.N.; b. Constantine, Mich., Dec. 31, 1841; s. Dr. Watson and Hester Ann (Welling) S.; apptd. to U.S. Naval Acad. from Ky., Sept. 20, 1858, grad. 1861; m. Maudthilde Willis, Feb. 20, 1886. Lt., Aug. 1, 1862; lt. comdr., July 25, 1866; comdr., June 13, 1876; capt., Oct. 2, 1891; rear admiral, Mar. 3, 1899. Served on Colo., W. Gulf Blockading Squadron, 1861; Mortar Flotilla, 1862; participated in bombardments of Fts. Jackson and St. Philip; engagements with Vicksburg batteries, 1862; West Gulf Blockading Squadron, 1863-64; Pensacola, 1864; Naval Acad., May-July, 1864; Massasoit, N. Atlantic Blockading Squadron, 1864-65; comd. Massasoit, Jan. 1865, during the engagement with the Confederate ironclads and batteries at Dutch Gap, James River, Va.; De Soto, Atlantic, 1866-67; Franklin, European Squadron, 1868-71; Hydrographic Office, 1872-77; comd. Monocacy, 1877-80; spl. duty, Washington, 1880-81; Bur. of Ordnance, 1881-86; Naval War Coll., 1887; Torpedo duty, and at Naval War Coll., 1888; comd. Galena, 1888-90; equipment officer, Navy Yard, New York, 1891-93; comd. Baltimore, Feb.-May 1893; gen. insp. of Columbia, 1893; comd. Columbia, 1894-95; comd. Monadnock, 1896-97; capt. of yard, Navy Yard, New York, 1897-99; commandant Naval Sta., Port Royal, 1899-1901, Navy Yard, Phila., 1901-02; comdr.-in-chief S. Atlantic Squadron, 1902-03; retired, Dec. 31, 1903. Home: Patchogue, N.Y. Died Feb. 20, 1924.

SUMNER, JETHRO army officer; b. Nansemond County, Va., circa 1733; s. Jethro and Margaret (Sullivan) S.; m. Mary Hurst, circa 1764; 1 dau., Jacky Sullivan (Sumner) Blount. Served as lt. Va. Militia, 1755-61; commanded Ft. Bedford during French and Indian War; justice of the peace Warren County (N.C.), 1768, sheriff, 1772-77; Warren County rep. N.C. Revolutionary Provisional Congress, 1775, which elected him maj. Minutemen; col. third bn. N.C. Regt., Continental Army, 1776; commd. brig. gen. Continental Army, led brigade to S.C., participated in battle of Stone Ferry, 1779, also recruited in N.C.; assisted in defense of N.C. against Cornwallis' invasion, 1780; in charge of N.C. Militia, 1781-83. Died Warren County, between Mar. 15-19, 1785.

SUMNER, SAMUEL STORROW army officer; b. Carlisle, Pa., Feb. 6, 1842; s. Maj. Gen. Edwin Vose and Hannah W. (Forster) S.; ed. at army posts, pvt. sch., Syracuse, N.Y., and Walnut Hill, Geneva, N.Y.; m. Frederica N. Bennett. Apptd. from N.Y., 2d lt. 2d (later 5th) Cav., June 11, 1861; promoted through grades to brig. gen. vols., May 4, 1898; maj. gen., Sept. 7, 1898; brig. gen. regular army, Feb. 4, 1901; maj. gen., July 26, 1903; retired, Feb. 6, 1906. Bvtd. 1st lt., June 1, 1862, for battle of Fair Oaks, Va.; capt., Sept. 17, 1862, for Antietam; maj., Mar. 13, 1865, for campaign against Vicksburg; lt. col., Feb. 27, 1890, for action against Indians at Summit Springs, Colo., July 11, 1869. Comd. cav. brigade and div. in Cuban campaign, 1898; mil. attaché Am. Embassy, London, 1899-1900; comd. brigade in China during uprising, 1900; comd. dist. Southern Luzon, 1901-02, dist. Northern Luzon, 1902; comd. Dept. Mindanao, P.I., 1902-03; comd. Dept. of the Mo., 1903-04, Southwestern Div., 1904-05, Div. of the Pacific, 1905-06. Silver star citation, Battle of San Juan, Cuba, July 1, 1898. Home: Brookline, Mass. Died July 26, 1937.

SUMTER, THOMAS senator, congressman; b. Hanover County, Va., Aug. 14, 1734; coll. edn. Became a surveyor; moved to S.C., circa 1760, settled on plantation, nr. Stateburg; served as lt. col. 6th Continental Regt., Continental Army; became brig. gen. S.C. Militia, 1780; mem. S.C. Senate, 1781-82; elected to privy council, 1782; del. to S.C. Conv. which ratified U.S. Constn. (which he opposed); mem. U.S. Ho. of Reps. (Democrat) from S.C., 1st-2d, 5th-7th congresses, 1789-93, 1797-Dec. 15, 1801 (resigned); mem. U.S. Senate (Democrat, filled vacancy) from S.C., Dec. 15, 1801-Dec. 16, 1810 (resigned); elected del. State Rights and Free Trade Conv., Charleston, S.C., 1832 (did not serve). Died on his plantation "South Mount," nr. Stateburg, June 1, 1832; buried pvt. burial ground on estate.

SUMTER, THOMAS DELAGE congressman; b. Germantown, Pa., Nov. 14, 1809; grad. U.S. Mil. Acad., 1835. Served from 1st lt. to col. U.S. Army, 1835-41, served in war against Seminole Indians; moved to Stateburg, S.C.; mem. U.S. Ho. of Reps. (Democrat) from S.C., 26th-27th congresses, 1839-43; tchr., surveyor, farmer; agt. S.C. R.R. Co. Died on plantation "South Mount," nr. Stateburg, July 1 1874; buried on estate.

SUNDBERG, CARL ANDREW LAWRENCE locomotive exec.; b. Union Hill, N.J., Nov. 9, 1898; s. Andrew Peter and Olga (Linstrom) S.; student Yale, 1916-17; B.S., U.S. Naval Acad., 1920; m. Evelyn Back, Mar. 29, 1941; children—Carlyn Lorain, Carl Andrew Lawrence. Tchr. science and math. pvt. and pub. schs., 1924-26; employee Nat. Bank of Commerce and successor Guaranty Trust Co., N.Y. City, 1926-40; joined Alco Products, Inc., N.Y. City, 1940, asst. treas., 1942, sec., 1944—; dir., v.p. Alco Products Oil Field Equipment Co., Inc.; treas., sec. Am. Locomotive & Equipment Corp.; sec. Alco Products Export Co.; Eastern adv. bd. Mut. Boiler & Machinery Ins. Co. Served as ensign to lt. (j.g.), U.S. Navy, 1920-24. Mem. N.Y. Elec. Soc., Am. Soc. Corporate Secs., Am. Management Assn., Alpha Kappa Pi. Republican. Baptist, Mason. Clubs: Yale, Railroad Machinery (N.Y. City). Home: Harvey Lane, Upper Saddle River, N.J. Office: 530 Fifth Av., N.Y.C. 36. Died Aug. 10, 1962; buried George Washington Meml. Park.

SUNSTROM, MARK A. business exec.; b. Boone, Ia., Sept. 8, 1897; s. John M. and Selma J. (Wiederberg) S.; student Coe Coll., Cedar Rapids, Ia., 1916-18; m. Gladys Faye Holliday, Mar. 15, 1926; children—Dolores Y., Mark A. Partner, firm Furness & Rogers, real estate and ins. brokers, Enid, Okla., 1920-21; mem. staff of Arthur Andersen & Co., C.P.A.'s, Chgo., N.Y., 1922-26; pres., dir. Internat. Standard Trading Corp.; exec. v.p., exec. com., dir. Internat. Standard Electric Corp.; v.p., dir. Internat. Tel. & Tel. Corp., Internat. Telephone Bldg. Corp.; dir. Standard Telephone et Radio S.A. (Zurich), Standard Electric Cos. (Madrid, Argentina, Tokyo, Stuttgart), United Tel. & Tel. Works, Ltd. Czeija, Nissi & Co. (Vienna), Internat. Tel. & Tel. S.A. (Buenos Aires), Bell Telephone Mfg. Co., Fed. Electric Mfg. Co., Ltd., Standard Electrica (Lisbon), Fed. Telecommunications Labs., Inc., Fed. Telephone & Radio Corp., Internat. Telecommunication Labs., Inc. Served as 2nd lt. inf. World War I. Civilian tech. advisor, USSTAFATI, World War II. Club: Broad Street (N.Y.). Home: 1221 Middle River Dr., Ft. Lauderdale, Fla. 33304. Died Oct. 31, 1960; buried Arlington Nat. Cemetery.

SURLES, ALEXANDER D(AY) (sûrlz), army officer; b. Milwaukee, Wis., Aug. 14, 1886; s. William Henry and Caroline (Pascoe) S.; student U. of Mich., 1906-07; B.S., U.S. Mil. Acad., 1911; grad. Cav. Sch. Advanced Course, 1924, Command and Gen. Staff Sch., 1925, Army War Coll., 1935; m. Anne Lee Gaines, Feb. 27, 1915; children—Alexander Day (U.S. Army), William G. Commd. 2d lt. U.S. Army, 1911, and advanced through the grades to maj. gen. (temp.), Feb. 16, 1942; with 15th Cavalry, U.S., 1911-15, Philippines, 1915-17, A.E.F. (France) Mar. 1918-Aug. 1919; instr. United States Mil. Acad., 1919-23; with 7th Cav., Ft. Bliss, Tex., 1925-27; asst. chief of staff Mil. Intelligence, 1st Cav. Div., Ft. Bliss, 1927-30; chief pub. relations branch, Mil. Intelligence Div., War Dept., 1935-39, with 7th Cav. Brigade (mechanized), later comd. 1st Armored Regt. (light tanks), Armored Force, Ft. Knox, 1939-40; with 1st Armored Div., Ft. Knox, 1940-41; dir. bur. public relations, War Dept., Aug. 1941-45; dir. of information, War Dept., Sept. 1945; mem. Chief of Staff's Adv. Group, Dec. 1945-47. Decorated Distinguished Service Medal, and decorations from France, England, Brazil and Ecuador. Mem. Chi Psi. Clubs: Army and Navy (Washington, D.C.); Chevy Chase Country (Md.). Address: 2022 Columbia Rd., Washington. Died Dec. 6, 1947; buried in Arlington National Cemetery.

SUTER, CHARLES RUSSELL brig. gen. U.S.A.; b. New York, May 5, 1842; s. Alexander F. S. (U.S.A.). Grad. U.S. Mil. Acad., 1862; 2d lt., June 17, 1862, 1st lt., Mar. 3, 1863, corps of engrs. (bvt. capt., July 18, 1863, "for gallant and meritorious services during siege of Morris Island, S.C."); capt. corps of engrs., June 17, 1864 (bvt. maj., Mar. 13, 1865, "for faithful and meritorious services during war"); maj., Oct. 10, 1871; lt. col., Jan. 10, 1887; col., Oct. 12, 1895, corps of engrs.; brig. gen. and retired by operation of law, May 5, 1906. After Civil War engaged as asst. engr. on survey of upper Miss. River, 1873-76, and on various engring. works, river commns., engr. bds.; in charge fortifications and river and harbor works in vicinity of Boston; later at New York. Address: Brookline, Mass. Died Aug. 7, 1920.

SUTER, HERBERT WALLACE JR. paper mfr.; b. Pitts., June 24, 1909; s. Herbert Wallace and Edith Marie (Harris) S.; grad. Mercersburg Acad., 1928; student Miami U., Oxford O., 1929-31; m. Mabel Irene Ritchie, Apr. 26, 1943. With Procter & Collier Co., Cin., 1932-33, A. W. Pohlman Paper Co., N.Y.C., 1934-35, Standard Paper Co., Cin., 1935-37; asst. mgr. Champion Paper & Fibre Co., Cleve., 1937-42, mgr., Detroit, 1945-47, gen. sales mgr., 1947-57, v.p., gen. sales mgr., 1957—. Served as capt. USAAF, 1942-45. Mem. Writing Paper Mfrs. Assn., Printing Paper Mfrs. Assn., Sulphite Paper Mfrs. Assn., Nat. Paper Board Assn. Elk. Club: Detroit Athletic. Home: 209 South D St. Office: 601 North B St., Hamilton, O. Died May 1960.

SUTHERLAND, ARTHUR EUGENE, educator; b. Rochester, N.Y., Feb. 9, 1902; s. Arthur E. and Eleanor (Reed) S.; ed. pub. and pvt. schs. U.S. and Switzerland; A.B., Wesleyan U., Middletown, Conn., 1922; LL.B., Harvard, 1925; J.S.D., Suffolk U., 1960; m. Margaret Adams, Sept. 10, 1927 (dec. Jan. 1958); children—David Adams, Peter Adams, Eleanor Reed, Prudence; m. 2d, Mary Genung Kirk, Feb. 21, 1959. Asso. with Am. Commn. Relief Near East, in Asia Minor and

Thrace, 1919; admitted to N.Y. State bar, 1926, practiced in Rochester, 1926-41; sec. to justice O. W. Holmes, U.S. Supreme Ct., 1927-28; commr. Uniform State Laws of N.Y., 1948-50; prof. law Cornell U., 1945-50; prof. law Harvard 1950-55, Bussey prof. law. 1955-70, emeritus prof. 1970-73; Purington vis. prof. polit. sci. Mt. Holyoke Coll., 1958-59; Fulbright lectr. Oxford U., 1956. Del. N.Y. State Constl. Conv., 1938; mem. N.Y. State Commn. on Elementary and Secondary Edn. 1969-71. Trustee Mt. Holyoke Coll. Served to col. AUS, 1941-45; ETO; MTO Decorated Legion of Merit with oak leaf cluster, Bronze Star Medal (U.S.); Order Brit. Empire: Cross of War (2) (France); Czechoslovakian War Cross: Ouissam Alaouite (Morocco); Volontai della Liberta, Italy. Fellow Am. Acad. Arts and Scis; mem. Am. Law Inst., Am. N.Y. State bar assns. Republican. Episcopalian. Author: Cases and Materials on Commercial Transactions (with others), 1951; Constitutional Law Cases and Other Problems, 1952; The Law and One Man Among Many, 1956; Constitutionalism in America, 1965; Apology for Uncomfortable Change, 1965; The Law at Harvard, 1817-1967, 1967. Editor: The Path of the Law from 1967, 1968. Contbr. articles to various legal publs. Home: Cambridge MA Died Mar. 8, 1973.

SUTHERLAND, JOSEPH HOOKER, chaplain U.S.A.; b. Good Intent. Pa. Apptd. post chaplain, Apr. 4, 1898; Assigned to 23d Inf., Feb. 25, 1901; commd. maj. "for exceptional efficiency," Dec. 29, 1908; transferred to 12th Inf., Aug. 15, 1911; retired on account of disability in line of duty, Mar. 21, 1912; restored to active duty at own request, 1917. Served in Spanish-Am. War, Philippine Insurrection and Moro campaigns; mentioned in orders for gallant conduct under fire. Known as writer, traveler and lecturer. Home: West Alexander PA

SUTHERLAND, RICHARD K. army officer; b. Hancock, Md., Nov. 27, 1893; s. Howard and Effie (Harris) S.; A.B., Yale, 1916; grad. Inf. Sch., 1923, Command and Gen. Staff Schl., 1928, Army War Coll., 1933; student Ecole Superieure de Guerre, Paris, 1928-30; m. Josephine Whiteside, Oct. 1, 1919; 1 dau., Natalie. Commd. 2d lt. Inf., Nov. 28, 1916; promoted through grades to brig. gen. U.S. Army, July 19, 1941, maj. gen., Dec. 19, 1941, lt. gen., Feb. 20, 1944; served with 2d div., AEF 11th, 63d, 29th and 15th Regts. of Inf.; War Dept. Gen. Staff; chief of staff to Gen. Douglas MacArthur, 1939-45. Awarded D.S.C. with Oak Leaf Cluster, D.S.M., Silver Star with oak leaf cluster (U.S.); Distinguished Service Star (Commonwealth of Philippines); Companion of Order of Bath (Gt. Britain). Mem. Alpha Delta Phi. Clubs: University, Chevy Chase, Army and Navy (Washington). Address: War Dept., Washington. Died June 1966.

SUTTON, DALLAS GILCHRIST, med. naval officer; b. Washington, D.C., Sept. 1, 1883; s. Robert Gilchrist and Elizabeth (Fearson) S.; M.D.; George Washington Univ., 1906, Naval Med. Sch., 1907-08; m. Mabel Clara Pimper, Sept. 23, 1911 (dec. Dec. 1940); children—Margaret Virginia (Mrs. Raymond Ringness), Mabel Elizabeth; m. 2d Violet G. Posthoff, Jan. 16, 1946. Resident physician, Emergency Hospital, Washington, D.C., 1906-07; commd. lt. (j.g.) Med. Corps, U.S. Navy, 1907, and advanced through the grades to rear admiral, 1942; instr. psychiatry, Naval Med. Sch., 1916-20; exec. officer, Naval Hosp., Great Lakes, Ill., 1921-24; senior med. officer, U.S. Naval Acad., 1934-36; asst. surgeon gen., U.S. Navy, 1936-41; comdg. officer, Naval Hosp., Portsmouth, Va., 1941-46; retired from U.S. Navy Jan. 1947. Mem. staff, Am. Hosp. Assn. since Sept. 1946. Campaign ribbons, Nicaraguan, Mexican, World War I, and World War II. Mem. Delta Tau Delta. Club: Officers (Naval Acad., Annapolis, Md.). Home: Washington DC Died Sept. 16, 1970; buried Arlington Nat. Cemetery Arlington VA

SUTTON, JOSEPH LEE, univ. pres.; b. Oklahoma City, Mar. 22, 1924; s. Erville Clarence and Carolyn Elizabeth (Hatch) S.; A.B. in Oriental Langs., U. Mich., 1948, M.A. in Oriental Civilization, 1949, Ph.D. in Polit. Sci., 1954; m. Jean Elizabeth Harkness, Aug. 19, 1945; children—James Werner, Geoffrey Joseph, David Harkness, Abigail Jean; m. 2d, Elizabeth Hartke Josephson, Mar. 15, 1971. Instr., Western Res. U., 1952-53; mem. faculty Ind. U., 1953-72, prof. govt., 1962-72, chmn. Asian studies com., also Asian studies program, from 1959, asso. dean Coll. Arts and Scis., 1962-65, dean College of Arts and Scis., 1965-66, v.p., dean faculties 1966-68, pres., 1968-71; chief adviser of pub. adminstrn. Govt. Thailand, 1955-58; mem. fgn. area fellowship nat. com. of Ford Found., Social Sci. Research Council and Am. Council Learned Societies. Cons. to U.S. Ho. of Reps. Republican Policy Com., 1960-62. Served to 2d lt. AUS, 1934-46. Research asst. Center Japanese Studies, U. Mich., 1948-49; World Area fellow Social Sci. Research Council, 1951-52. Mem. Am. Polit. Sci. Assn., Assn. Asian Studies, Club Indiana Univ. Men's Faculty (pres. 1962-63). Contbr. articles profl. jours., chpts. in books. Editor, contbr.: Problems of Politics and Administration in Thailand, 1961. Home: Bloomington IN Died Apr. 28, 1972; buried Oklahoma City OK

SUYDAM, CHARLES CROOKE lawyer; b. New York, June 15, 1836; s. Henry and Almira (Van Nostrand) S.; A.B., Columbia, 1856, A.M., 1859; studied law in office of Kent, Eaton & Davis, New York; m. Eliza Gracie Halsey, of Elizabeth, N.J., Apr. 18, 1860 (died Nov. 17, 1901). Admitted to bar, 1858; served Union Army, in Civil War, Aug., 1861-Nov., 1864, 1st lt. 5th N. Y. Cav.; capt. and lt.-col. (chief of staff, 4th Army Corps, Gen. Keyes); lt.-col. 3d N.J. Cav., 1964. Counsel for U.S. Govt. before Am. Spanish Commn., 1882; asso. counsel U.S. Govt. before Ct. of Commrs. of Alabama Claims, 1882-85. Republican. Mem. Loyal Legion, Holland Soc. Home: Elizabeth, N.J. Office: 206 Broadway, New York.

SWAIN, JAMES journalist; b. N.Y.C., July 30, 1820; s. Joseph and Jerusha (Everts) S.; m. Relief Davis, 1842, children include son Chellis. Began newspaper work on Horace Greeley's The Log Cabin, 1840; ran private printing business; published The Life and Speeches of Henry Clay, 1843; published Hudson River Chronicle and small paper at Sing Sing, 1844-49; asst. N.Y. Tribune; independent printer; city editor N.Y. Times, 1852, corr. at Albany, N.Y., Washington corr., 1860; railroad commr. State of N.Y., 1855-57; established Free State Advocate, 1856; founded Albany Statesman, 1857; introduced correspondent system; apptd. 2d, later 1st lt. N.Y. Militia, 1861; organized 11th N.Y. Cavalry; commd. lt. col., 1862; saw no fighting, dismissed from command, 1864, dismissal revoked, 1866; apptd. engr.-in-chief to Gov. Reuben S. Fenton of N.Y., 1865; conceived triple-decked rapid transit system of N.Y.C.; received charter for Met. Transit Co., 1872, scheme failed; weigher N.Y. Customs House, 1867-71 reporter N.Y. Tribune, 1872, clk. of a com. N.Y. Assembly; editor Hudson River Chronicle, 1876-95. Died May 27, 1895.

SWAN, JAMES revolutionary patriot, financier; b. Fifeshire, Scotland, 1754; m. Hepzibah Clarke, circa 1776, 4 children. Came to Boston, 1765; mem. Sons' of Liberty; participated in Boston Tea Party; aide-de-camp to Gen. Joseph Warren at battle of Bunker Hill; attained rank of maj., later col.; sec. to Mass. Bd. of War, 1777; mem. Mass. Legislature as adj. gen. of commonwealth, 1778; went to France, 1787; gained control of remainder of U.S. debt. to France, 1787, apptd. agt. French Republic; as both agt. France and as broker he profited from having Am. debt obligations from France accepted in payment for supplies furnished or to be furnished the French marine; put in debtor's prison in Paris, 1800. Author: A Dissuasion to Great Britain and the Colonies, from the Slave Trade to Africa, 1773. Died in debtor's prison, Paris, July 31, 1830.

SWAN, JOHN MUMFORD physician; b. Newport, R.I., Jan. 23, 1870; s. John Mumford and Annie Frances Greene (Taggert) S.; grad. Rogers High Sch., Newport, 1887; M.D., U. Pa., 1893; m. Sara Halyday Raymond, Dec. 16, 1896 (died Oct. 13, 1949). Demonstrator osteology and asst. demonstrator anatomy, U. Pa., 1895-1904; instr. clin. pathology and instr. tropical medicine, Phila., Polyclinic and Coll. for Grades. in Medicine, 1904-10; asso. prof. clin. medicine, Medico-Chirurg. Col. of Phila., 1909-10; med. dir. The Glen Springs, Watkins, N.Y., 1910-12. Commd. 1st lt. Med. Res. Corps, AUS, Dec. 9, 1915; maj., Apr. 9, 1917; lt. col., Aug. 20, 1918; comdg. officer Base Hosp. 19, July 1918 to demobilization, May 1919; active service at Vichy, France; chief med. service Base Hosp., Camp Devens, Mass., May-Aug. 1919; discharged Aug. 18, 1919. Citation from comdg. gen. A.E.F., Apr. 1919, "for especially meritorious and conspicuous service at Base Hosp. 19." Field rep. A.R.C., Dominican Republic and Haiti, 1919-20. Col., Med. Res., U.S. Army, May 1923; col. Auxiliary Res., U.S. Army, Jan. 1934. Awarded Purple Heart. Fellow A.C.P., Coll. Physicians Phila.; mem. Am. Climatol. and Clin. Assn., Am. Acad. Polit. and Social Sci., A.M.A., Am. Cancer Soc. (state sec. N.Y. State Div.), Mil. Order Fgn. Wars, Assn. Mil. Surgeons of U.S. Am. Legion Post No. 194 (comdr. 1942), Am. Soc. Tropical Medicine (pres. 1921). Author: A Manual of Human Anatomy, Arranged for Second Year Students, 1898; A Manual of Human Anatomy, Arranged for First Year Students, 1900; Prescription Writing and Formulary, 1910. Address: 457 Park Av., Rochester 7, N.Y. Died Nov. 22, 1949; buried Arlington Nat. Cemetery.

SWANBERG, HAROLD, educator; b. Phila., July 13, 1891; s. William H. and Lillian (Goerz) S.; B.S., Loyola U, 1916, Md., 1916; Harvard, summer 1924; certificate, U. Vienna, 1931; ScD., Carthage (Ill.) Coll., 1963; m. Zoe Johnson, Dec. 10, 1919 (div. 1933); 1 son, William Harold; m. 2d Mildred Wilber Spiva, Feb. 10, 1934; 1 dau., Nancy Gail; step-children—JoAnn Spiva, Mary Spiva. Practice of medicine, 1916-61; resident St. Luke's Hosp., Chgo., also instr. anatomy sch. medicine Loyola U., 1917; radiologist, dir. Quincy X-Ray & Radium Labs., 1919-61, sec., mng. editor. Recipient Distinguished Service award, Miss. Valley Med. Soc., 1946, Am. Med. Writers Assn., 1952; Golden Deeds award, Quincy Exchange Club, 1962. Served as radiologist, lt. to maj. med. R.C., U.S. Army, 1917-19, 24-29. Fellow Am. Pub. Health Assn., A.C.P., A.A.A.S. Am. Geriatrics Soc., Soc. Academic Achievement; mem. A.M.A., Miss. Valley Med. Soc. (founder, sec. 1935-61), Am. Med. Writers' Assn. (founder, sec. 1940-60, hon. pres.), Radiol. Soc. N.A., Am. Roentgen Ray Soc., Society for Academic Achievement (founder, sec.-teas. from 1959), Adams County (past sec., editor, pres., del.), Ill. (past chmn sect. radiology, secs. conf.) med. socs., Chgo. Am. Assn. Ret. Persons (past chpt. pres., v.p., del.), Quincy C. of C., Nat. Edn. Assn. U.S. Council Basic Edn., Med. Assn. Vienna, Hist. Soc. Quincy and Adams County, Am. Legion. Clubs: Art, Kiwanis (past president). Author: The Intervertebral Foramen, 1914; The Intervertebral Foramina in Man, 1915; Radiologic Maxims, 1932; History of American Medical Writer's Assn., 1965; also articles and editorials radiologic and ednl. subjects. Founder and editor Quincy Med. Bull., 1924-30, Miss. Valley Med. Jour., 1924-60; editor; Academic Achievement, from 1959; founder Swanberg Med. Found. 1943, Swanberg Kiwanis Found., 1948, Swanberg Collegiate Education Foundation, 1956. Member of the Golden Key Soc. (U. Vienna). Home: Quincy IL Died June 27, 1970; buried Quincy IL

SWANSON, CLAUDE AUGUSTUS secretary of the Navy; b. Swansonville, Va., Mar. 31, 1862; s. John M. S.; A.B., Randolph-Macon Coll., 1885; LL.B., U. of Va., 1886; engaged in practice at Chatham, Va. Mem. 53d to 58th Congresses (1893-1905), 5th Va. Dist.; reëlected to 59th Congress, but resigned; gov. of Va., 1906-10; apptd. U.S. senator, Aug. 1, 1910, for unexpired term (1910-11) of John W. Daniel, deceased; reapptd., Mar. 4, 1911, until meeting of Gen. Assembly, which elected him for unexpired term ending Mar. 3, 1917; reëlected, 3 terms, 1917-35; resigned to become secretary of Navy, Mar. 4, 1933. Am. del. to Disarmament Conf., Geneva, Switzerland, 1932. Democrat. Died July 7, 1939.

SWARTWOUT, RICHARD HENRY stock broker; b. Morristown, N.J., Oct. 16, 1874; s. William Henry and Meriam (Evans) S.; ed. pub. sch.; m. Ethel Rogers, Oct. 9, 1909; 1 dau., Ethel Victoria. Identified with stock brokerage business N.Y. City, 1893-—; mem. Swartwout & Appenzellar, 1898-1927; chmn. bd. Intertype Corp., Dictaphone Corp.; dir. Norfolk Southern R.R. Served as maj. U.S. Army, World War. Presbyn. Office: 40 Wall St., New York, N.Y. Died July 21, 1938.

SWARTWOUT, SAMUEL army officer, mcht., speculator; b. Poughkeepsie, N.Y., Nov. 17, 1783; s. Abraham and Maria (North) S.; m. Alice Ann Cooper, 1814, 2 children. Asso. with Aaron Burr, 1804-06; delivered famous cipher letter from Burr to Gen. James Wilkinson (used as evidence of Burr's treason), 1806, arrested in New Orleans and sent to Washington (D.C.) for trial as accomplice in Burr's schemes, 1807, tried and acquitted, important witness against Burr, preceded Burr to Eng. to prepare for his favorable reception; involved in scheme to open up trade with Mississippi Valley through Mobile and Pensacola in violation of Jefferson's embargo; served as capt. in War of 1812; asso. with Andrew Jackson from 1814, worked for Jackson's nomination and election to Presidency, his services recognized by his appointment as collector Port of N.Y., 1829-38; later investigations revealed he had used over million dollars in public funds for land and railroad speculations. Died N.Y.C., Nov. 21, 1856.

SWATLAND, DONALD CLINTON lawyer; b. Newark, N.J., May 5, 1895; s. Stephen Seran and Ella Tracy (York) S.; A.B., Princeton, 1916; LL.B., Harvard, 1921; m. Muriel Bacheller, Apr. 7, 1922; children—Suzanne, Judith, Thomas York. Admitted to N.Y. bar, 1921, and since practiced in New York City; with firm Cravath, DeGersdorff, Swaine & Wood, 1921-26, partner, 1926-42. Cravath, Swaine & Moore, since 1945. Director, Minneapolis-Honeywell Regulator Co., Westinghouse Electric Corporation. Director of the Travelers Aid Society of New York, since 1950. Served as 1st lt., inf., A.E.F., U.S. Army, 1917-19; lt. col. to brig. gen., A.A.F., Army U.S., 1942-45; chief procurement division, Air Tech. Service Command, Wright Field, Dayton, O., 1945. Editor Harvard Law Review, 1919-21; president 1920-21. Awarded D.S.M.: Order of the Crown (Roumania): Order of the White Rose (Finland). Member of the Council on Foreign Relations, International Law Association (member American branch), N.Y. State, American bar associations, Bar Association City of N.Y., Phi Beta Kappa. Clubs: Princeton Campus, Princeton, Harvard, Broad St., Economic, Union (New York City); Essex (Newark, New Jersey); Rockaway River Country Club (Denville, New Jersey); Nantucket (Mass.) Yacht; Metropolitan (Washington). Home: 17 Morris Av., Denville, N.J. 07834. Office: 15 Broad St., N.Y.C. Died Apr. 2, 1962; buried Clinton, N.Y.

SWAYNE, WAGER lawyer; b. Columbus, O., Nov. 10, 1834; s. Noah H. S. (asso. justice Supreme Court U.S.); grad. Yale, 1856; Cincinnati Law School, 1859; began practice at Columbus; m. Ellen Harris, Dec. 22, 1868. Apptd. maj., Aug. 13, 1861; lt. col., Dec. 14, 1861; col., Oct. 18, 1862, of 43d Ohio vols.; served through Atlanta campaign and lost a leg at Salkahatchie, S.C.; bvtd. brig. gen. U.S. vols., Feb. 5, 1865, becoming full brig. gen., March 8, 1865, and maj. gen., June 20, 1865; mil. administration in Ala., 1865-68; was made col. 45th regt. inf., July 28, 1866, and bvt. brig. gen. and maj. gen. U.S.A. for gallant and meritorious services during war; retired July 1, 1870. Practiced law in Toledo, O., until 1880; then in New York, where he was for yrs. gen. counsel Western Union Telegraph Co., the Wabash Ry. Co., the Associated Press, and other corporations. Was also pres. Ohio Soc. of New York, New York Commandery Loyal Legion, Am. Ch. Missionary Soc. Died 1902.

SWEARINGEN, LLOYD EDWARD, educator; b. Rosendale, Mo., Aug. 30, 1897; s. William H. and Elizabeth (Trussel) S.; B.S., U. Okla., 1920, M.S., 1921; Ph.D., U. Minn., 1926; m. Lillian Weisenbach, June 12, 1925. Head dept. phys. sci. Southwestern State Coll., Weatherford, Okla., 1921-23; asst. prof. U. Okla., 1923-26, asso. prof., 1926-29, prof. chemistry, from 1929, research prof., 1948-53, v.p. for research and development, from 1953; dir. U. Okla. Research Inst., 1947-49, exec. director, 1953-58, dean of the Graduate College, 1958-59; director of basic sciences research Dept. of Army (on leave from U. Okla.) 1951-53, sci. asst. dep. for research and development Asst. Chief of Staff G-4, Dept. Army, 1952-53. Served as col., U.S. Army, World War. I, also 1942-46; ETO. Decorated Bronze Star (U.S.); Croix de Guerre with palms (France). Recipient Outstanding Achievement award U. Minn., 1955; Lloyd Swearingen Research Park at U. Okla. named in his honor, 1968. Mem. Am. Chem. Soc. Okla. Acad. Sci., Phi Beta Kappa, Sigma Xi, Alpha Chi Sigma, Phi Lambda Upsilon, Alpha Epsilon Delta, Phi Delta Chi. Contbr. profl. jours. Address: Norman OK Died Mar. 9, 1972; interred I.O.O.F. Mausoleum Norman OK

SWEARINGEN, VICTOR CLARENCE, govt. ofcl.; b. Science Hill, Ky., June 1, 1899; s. Charles Clark and Eva Lena (Hubble) S.; A.B., U. Ky., 1922; J.D., Detroit Coll. Law, 1925; post grad., U. Mich. Law Sch., 1928-29; LL.M., George Washington U. Law Sch., 1951; m. Beth Secord Elliott, Aug. 22, 1929; 1 dau., Janet. Admitted to Mich. bar, 1925; in practice of law, Detroit, 1925-36, instr. in internat. law U. Detroit, 1926-31; instr. in legislation Wayne State U., Detroit, 1932-38; asst. atty.-gen., State of Mich., Lansing, 1937-38; atty. Dept. of Agr., Washington, 1939-40; referee on wage rates Dept. of Labor, Washington, 1940-41; Mich. State labor mediator, Detroit, 1941-46; U.S. judge Internat. War Crimes Trials, Nurnberg, Germany, 1946-47; spl. asst. to atty. gen. of U.S., Washington, 1948-56; hearing examiner ICC, Washington, 1956-68. Served as enlisted man U.S. Army, World War I; AAF intelligence officer, 1942-44, comdg. officer 419th troop carrier group, A.A.F., 1944-45, chief of war crimes operations Gen. Staff, U.S. Army, Jan.-Oct. 1946, recalled to active mil. service as col. USAF Res., Mar. 1951, chief, investigations div. Office Insp. Gen., USAF, 1951-53, sec. UN Command-Mil. Armistice Commn., Panmunjom, Korea, 1954-55, colonel U.S. Air Force retired, 1960. Member of Fed., Mich., and Detroit bar assns., Am. Soc. Internat. Law, Am. Legion, S.A.R., Delta Phi Epsilon, Delta Theta Phi. Democrat. Methodist. Mason (K.T., Shriner). Club: Lions. Contbr. articles law and govtl. subjects to various legal pubs. Home: Washington DC Died Jan. 15, 1968.

SWEENEY, ALVIN RANDOLPH med. dir. U.S. P.H.S. (retired); b. Grand Chenier, La., Sept. 2, 1881; s. George C. Carter and Aurelia (Miller) S.; ed. Acadia Coll., Lake Charles, 1900-02; B.S., Tex. Central U., Greenville, 1904; student Vanderbilt U. Med. Sch., 1904-07; M.D., Jefferson Med. Coll., Phila., 1908; m. Rilla Adele Ingram, Dec. 1, 1908; children—Gertrude Elizabeth (Mrs. Clarke Eugene Brown), Alvin Randolph, Edward Chalmers, Ruth Adele. Physician, Lake Arthur, La., 1909-13; asst. surgeon U.S. Pub. Health Service, 1913; promoted through grades to Captain Dist. med. 9th Naval Dist., Cleveland; served at Ellis Island, New Orleans, Galveston, St. Louis, Port Arthur, Boston. In charge of many different quarantine stations and hospitals during service; past supt. Gallinger Municipal Hosp., Wash. D.C. Mem. Washington Health Council. Fellow Am Coll. Physicians; mem. Am. Acad. Polit. and Social Science, A.M.A., Washington Med. Soc., Assn. Mil. Surgeons, Am. Pub. Health Assn., Acad. Polit. Sci. Served in Army during World War I. Mason 32 deg.). Clubs: Washington Board Trade, Boston C. of C. Contbr. articles on health topics. Address: 5126 Bradley Blvd., Chevy Chase 15, Md. Died Apr. 1954; buried Arlington Nat. Cemetery.

SWEENEY, ORLAND RUSSELL coll. prof.; b. Martin's Ferry, O., Mar. 27, 1882; s. Robert Emmet and Elizabeth (Woods) S.; B.S. in Chem. Engring., Ohio State U., 1909, M.A., 1910, Chem. E., 1935; Ph.D., U. Pa., 1916; m. Louella Dubois Smith, Oct. 25, 1919; children—Elizabeth Dubois, Jacqueline. Instr. chem. engring., Ohio State U., 1910, U. Pa., 1910-16; asso. prof. chem. engring., N.D. Agrl. Coll., Fargo, N.D., 1916; head dept. chem. engring., U. Cin., 1919-21, Ia. State Coll. Agr. and Mechanic Arts, 1921-50 (now Iowa State U.); also chem. engr. Engring. Expt. Sta. Capt. ordnance and maj. C.W.S., U.S. Army, Nov. 22, 1917-Feb. 17, 1920; designed constructed and operated chlorpicrine plant at Edgewood (Md.) Arsenal, World War. Mem. Am. Chem. Soc., Ia. Engring. Soc., Am. Inst. Chem. Engs., Sigma Xi, Tau Beta Pi, Phi Lambda Upsilon. Mem. United Presbyn. Ch. Mason. Author: The Commercial Utilization of Agricultural Wastes, 1925. Home: Ames, Ia. Died Apr. 21, 1958; buried Martin's Ferry, O.

SWEENEY, THOMAS WILLIAM army officer; b. County Cork, Ireland, Dec. 25, 1820; s. William and Honora (Sweeny) S.; m. Eleanor Swain Clark; m. 2d, Eugenia Octavia Reagan at least 4 children. Came to U.S., 1832; served as 2d lt. 1st N.Y. Volunteers in Mexican War, 1846, served from Vera Cruz to capture of Churubusco; commd. capt., 1848; participated in operations against the Yuma Indians of the Southwest, or the Sioux of Neb. region, 1848-61; ordered to U.S. arsenal, St. Louis, 1861; commd. brig. gen. of Three Months' Mo. Volunteers, 1861; mustered out of Mo. Volunteers, commd. col. 52d Ill. Regt., 1862, aided in capture Ft. Donelson; served in battles of Corinth, 1862, Kenesaw Mountain, 1864, Atlanta, 1864; commd. brig. gen. U.S. Volunteers, 1862, maj. 16th Inf., 1863, honorably discharged, 1865; leader unsuccessful Fenian raid on Can., 1866; sec. war of "Irish Republic" circa 1865; retired from U.S. Army with rank brig. gen., 1870. Died Astoria, L.I., N.Y., Apr. 10, 1892.

SWEENEY, WALTER CAMPBELL army officer; b. Wheeling, W.Va., Nov. 16, 1876; s. Andrew James and Maria (Hanna) S.; grad. Linsly Inst., Wheeling, 1895; distinguished grad. Sch. of Line, U.S. Army, 1912; grad. Army Staff Coll., 1913, Army War Coll., 1920; m. Anne McConnell, Apr. 20, 1904; children—Elizabeth Josephine (wife of Lt. Col. Richard B. Gayle), Col. Walter Campbell, Anne-Eloise (maj. WAC). Enlisted as pvt. 1st W.Va. Inf. Vols., May 1898, and advanced to 2d lt., Spanish-Am. War; commd. 2d lt. Inf. U.S. Army, June 1, 1899; advanced through grades to maj. gen., June 1, 1938. Served in Philippine Insurrection, 1901, Pulajane campaign, 1906-07, Moro outbreaks, 1910-11; on Mexican Border, 1915-16; chief of Censorship div. Intelligence Sect. on General Staff AEF, duty with Gen. Staff Hdqrs., 5th Corps, St. Mihiel operations, and chief of staff 28th Div., Meuse-Argonne operations, World War I; chief of Inf. Office, Washington, 24; instr. Army War Coll., 1924-28; comdr. 3d Inf., Ft. Snelling, Minn., 1928-30; chief staff 5th Corps Area, 1930-34; comdr. 38th Inf., Ft. Douglas, Utah, 1935, 6th Brig., Ft. Douglas, 1936-38; comdg. gen., 3d Div., Ft. Lewis, Wash., 1938-40; ret. Nov. 30, 1940; recalled to active duty June 4, 1942; comdg. gen. Mil. Forces, Cal., 1942; Hdqrs. Western Def. Command and 4th Army, 1942-43. Awarded D.S.M. for distinguished service Argonne-Meuse offensive; Silver Star for gallantry at Apremont, France, Sept. 28, 1918; Officer Legion of Honor (France); Comdr. with Star Royal Order St. Olav (Norway). Mem. S.A.R., Sojourners, Mil. Order World War, Am. Legion. Presbyn. Mason (Shriner). Clubs: Army and Navy (Washington); Bohemian (San Francisco). Author: Military Intelligence: A New Weapon in War, 1924. Address: San Francisco. Died Dec. 1965.

SWEET, JOSHUA EDWIN prof. surgical research; b. Unadilla, N.Y., Aug. 9, 1876; s. Joshua J. and Emeline G. (Allen) S.; prep. edn., Unadilla Acad.; A.B., Hamilton Coll., 1897, A.M., 1900, hon. Sc.D., 1922; M.D., U. of Giessen, Germany, 1901; studied at Pasteur Inst., Paris, 1901; m. Greta McCauley, June 22, 1904 (died Jan. 2, 1942); 1 dau., Ruth; m. 2d, Florence West, June 6, 1942. With Univ. of Pa., 1906-26, prof. surg. research, 1917-26; prof. research, Cornell U. Med. Coll., 1926-41, emeritus 1941. Lt. col. with A.E.F. in France, as consultant in surg. research, 1917-19; m. staff Base Hosp. No. 10. Fellow Am. Coll. Surgeons; mem. A.M.A., N.Y. State and N.Y. County med. socs., Am. Soc. Exptl. Pathology, Am. Physiol. Soc., Harvey Soc., Society of Exptl. Biology and Medicine, N.Y. Acad. Medicine, N.Y. Surg. Soc., Phila. Acad. Surgery, Surg. Research Soc., Theta Nu Epsilon, Delta Kappa Epsilon, Phi Beta Kappa, Sigma Xi, Alpha Omega, Phi Alpha Sigma. Republican. Presbyterian. Awarded Alveranga prize for essay, "The Surgery of the Pancreas," 1915; delivered annual oration, Phila. Acad. Surgery, 1916; Mütter lecture, "The Gallbladder, Its Past, Present and Future," 1923. Contbr. 75 papers to med. lit. Home: Unadilla, N.Y. Died Apr. 8, 1957; buried Evergreen Hill Cemetery, Unadilla.

SWEET, OWEN JAY brigadier gen. U.S.A.; b. Kent, Conn., Sept. 4, 1845; s. James S. and Aurilla (Duncan) S.; ed. Binghamton, N.Y.; m. Mary E. Bolt, 1873. Apptd. 2d lt. 137th N.Y. Inf., Sept. 6, 1862; served in 3d Brigade, 2d Div., 12th Army Corps, Army of Potomac, serving in many skirmishes, and battles of Fredericksburg, Chancellorsville and Gettysburg; capt. May 21, 1863; served in Army of the Cumberland, 20th Army Corps, taking part in all its battles up to and including the capture of Atlanta, then in Army of Ga., taking part in Sherman's March to the Sea, and the fighting in front of and capture of Savannah, where was the first officer to enter enemy's fortifications; afterwards in Sherman's campaign through the Carolinas; bvtd. maj., Mar. 13, 1865, "for gallant and meritorious services during the war"; mustered out of vol. service, Bladensburg, Md., June 9, 1865. Apptd. 2d lt. 40th Inf., May 27, 1867; 1st lt. 25th Inf., Aug. 19, 1873; promoted through grades to brig. gen. and retired, Sept. 4, 1909. Served through several campaigns against Indians, and in the Philippines, 1899-1901, and 1903-04; comd. 3d mil. dist., comprising the Sulu Archipelago; comd. Ft. Snelling, Minn., 1904-06; comdg. regt. and sta., Matanzas, Cuba, 1906-09. Died Jan. 6, 1928.

SWEITZER, CAESAR, physician; b. Chgo., May 8, 1911; s. Adolph and Katherine (Veron) S.; M.D., U. Ill., 1939; m. Rachel M. Fairbanks, July 1949; children—Caesar, Dean, Richard, David. Intern, Grant Hosp., Chgo., 1938-39, resident in gen. surgery, 1939-40, asso. surg. staff, until 1970; resident in gen. surgery Wesley Meml. Hosp., Chgo., 1946-48, chief resident in surgery, 1948, sr. attending surgeon, until 1970; asso. dept. surgery Northwestern U., Chgo., until 1971. Served to lt. col., M.C., AUS, 1945-46. Decorated Bronze Star. Diplomate Am. Bd. Surgery. Fellow A.C.S.; mem. A.M.A., Internat. Coll. Surgeons. Republican. Home: Wilmette IL Died May 31, 1970; buried Forest Home, Forest Park IL

SWIFT, EBEN army officer; b. Ft. Chadbourne, Tex., May 11, 1854; s. Ebenezer (surgeon U.S.A.) and Sarah Edwards (Capers) S.; student Racine Coll. (Wis.), Washington U., Dickinson Coll., Carlisle, Pa.; grad. U.S. Mil. Acad., 1876; m. Susanne Palmer Swift, May 17, 1880; children—Eben, Innis Palmer, Wesley Merritt, Mrs. Clara Humphrey, Mrs. Katharine McKinney. Commd. 2d lt. 14th Inf., 1876; promoted through grades to brig. gen. regular army, Sept. 30, 1916; served as maj. gen. N.A., 1917-18; retired, May 11, 1918; promoted to rank of major general, retired. Served in Indian campaigns, Wyoming, Mont., Neb., Idaho, Colo., against Sioux, Cheyenne, Bannock and Ute Indians; later a.d.c. to Gen. Wesley Merritt; served in Cuba and Puerto Rico; asst. instr. Inf. and Cav. Sch.; asst. comdt. at Gen. Service and Staff Coll.; dir. Army War Coll.; in campaign against Moros in Philippines; chief of staff Western Dept.; comdt. Army Service Schs.; comdr. 2d Cav. Brigade in Mexico; comdr. cav. div. at El Paso, Tex., 1916; assigned as comdr. Camp Gordon, Atlanta, Ga., 1917; organized and comd. 82d Div. till Dec. 1918; with A.E.F. in France till Feb. 1918; chief Am. mil. mission and comdr. U.S. forces in Italy, Feb.-Aug. 1918. Died Apr. 25, 1938.

SWIFT, HOMER FORDYCE physician; b. Paines Hollow, N.Y., May 5, 1881; s. Charles Fayette and Nancy Maria (Fordyce) S.; Adrian (Mich.) Coll., 1898-1900; Ph.B., Western Res., 1902, student med. dept., 1902-04; M.D., U. and Bellevue Hosp. Med. Coll., 1906; D.Sc., N.Y. U., 1931; received the medallion of Meritorious Service award by Alumni Fedn. N.Y.U., 1933; m. Emma Fordyce MacRae, Apr. 24, 1922; step-dau., Alice MacRae (Mrs. Lester Kissel). Interne Presbyn. Hosp., N.Y., 1906-08; asst. in pathology and dermatology, U. and Bellevue Hosp. Med. Coll., 1908-10; asst. res. physician, Rockefeller Hosp., 1910-12, res. physician, 1912-14; asso. prof. medicine, Columbia, 1914-17; same (on leave), Cornell Med. Coll., 1917-19; asso. mem., Rockefeller Inst., 1919-22, mem., 1922-46, Emeritus mem., 1946-—; physician Hosp. of Rockefeller Inst. Med. Research, 1942-46, emeritus mem., 1946-—. Mem. Council N.Y.U., 1942-46. Mem. bd. dirs. Russell Sage Inst. Pathology 1923-48; Kober lectr. Georgetown U. Med. Sch., 1949. With A.E.F. in France, May 1917-Apr. 1919, attached to B.E.F., May 1917-May 1918; mem. A.R.C. Trench Fever Commn., also cons. in medicine 1st Army Corps and 3d Army (Army of Occupation), A.E.F.; discharged as col. med. corps, World War I. cons. to sec. of war, 1942-46. Spl. investigator OSRD study of streptococci 1942-45. Has specialized in treatment of syphilis of the central nervous system, and in study of rheumatic fever, streptococcus infections and trench fever. Chmn. gen. adv. com. for the cardiac program, N.Y. State Dept. Health, 1941-—. Chmn. Am. Council Rheumatic Fever, 1945-46. Mem. A.M.A., N.Y. State Med. Soc., Assn. Am. Physicians, Am. Soc. Clin Investigation (pres. 1928), N.Y. Acad. Medicine, Soc. Am. Bacteriologists, Am. Soc. Immunology, Harvey Soc. (pres. 1925-26), Alpha Tau Omega, Nu Sigma Nu, Theta Nu Epsilon, Alpha Omega Alpha; fellow A.A.A.S. Club: Century: Collaborator: Trench Fever (report of commn. A.R.C. Research Com.), 1918. Contbr. to Forchheimer's Therapeusis of Internal Diseases, Practical Treatment (Musser and Kelly), Nelson's Loose-Leaf Medicine, Oxford Loose-Leaf Medicine, Text-Book of Medicine (Cecil); Bacterial and Mycotic Infections of Men (Dubos), also numerous articles med. jours. Home: 888 Park Av. Office: Rockefeller Institute Hospital, 66th St. and York Av., N.Y.C. 21. Died Sept. 24, 1953.

SWIFT, INNIS PALMER ret. army officer; b. Fort Laramie, Wyo., Feb. 7, 1882; s. Eben and Susan Bonaparte (Palmer) S.; B.S., U.S. Mil. Acad., 1904; grad. U.S. Mounted Service Sch., 1909, U.S. Cavs. Sch., 1922, Command and Gen. Staff Sch., 1923, Army War Coll., 1930, Army Indsl. Coll., 1931; m. Lucille Genevieve Paddock, Sept. 1908; children—Lucile Paddock (Mrs. Boyd L. Hillsinger), Susanne Palmer (Mrs. Henry Thomas Cherry), Sally Genevieve (Mrs. Ralph Haines, Jr.), Pamela (Mrs. George W. Vaughan). Commd. 2d lt., Cav., U.S. Army, 1904, advanced to maj. gen., 1941; served as maj. of Inf., 1917, lt. col. of cav., 1918, AEF, France. Decorated with campaign medals for service in Philippine Insurrection, Punitive Expdn. Mexico and France, World War I; for service Asiatic-Pacific Theatre, Battle Stars for Bismark Sea, Dutch New Guinea, P.I., World War II; Comd. 8th Cav., 1936-39, 2d Cav. Brigade, 1939-41, 1st Cav. Div., 1941-44; tax force which recaptured the Admiralty Islands, 1944; 1st Army Corps, Dutch New Guinea, 1944-45, during recapture of Luzon, P.I. and occupation of Japan, 1945. Decorated D.S.M. with oak leaf cluster, Legion of

Merit, Silver Star Medal for gallantry in action (U.S.); Order of the Aztec Eagle, First Class (Republic Mexico). Episcopalian. Mason (32 deg., Shriner). Home: 826 Burr Rd., San Antonio 9. Died Nov. 3, 1953; buried Fort Sam Houston Nat. Cemetery, San Antonio.

SWIFT, JOSEPH GARDNER army officer, engr.; b. Nantucket, Mass., Dec. 31, 1783; s. Dr. Foster and Deborah (Delano) S.; grad. U.S. Mil. Acad. (1st graduating class), 1802; m. Louisa Walker, June 6, 1805, 1 son. Served as cadet in corps of artillerists and engrs.. Newport, R.I., 1800, trans. to U.S. Mil. Acad., 1801; commd. 1st lt. Engr. Corps, U.S. Army, 1805, capt., 1806, maj., 1808, lt. col., 1812, became col. and chief engr., 1812; served with Gen. Wilkinson during abortive invasion of Can., 1813, brevetted brig. gen., 1814; charge constrn. of fortifications N.Y.C., 1814; supt. U.S. Mil. Acad., 1816-18; resigned commn., 1818; surveyor Port of N.Y., 1818-26; chief engr. various railroads including Balt. & Susquehanna, New Orleans & Lake Pontchartrain, 1826; civil engr. in U.S. Govt. service, in charge harbor improvement on Gt. Lakes, 1829-45; 1st Am. engr. trained wholly in U.S. Died Geneva, N.Y., July 23, 1865.

SWIFT, WILLIAM rear admiral U.S.N.; b. Windham, Conn., Mar. 17, 1848; s. William and Harriet Gray (Byrne) S.; grad. U.S. Naval Acad., 1867; m. Grace Virginia, d. Commodore George M. Ransom, of Richfield Springs, N.Y., Sept. 18, 1872. On flagship Susquehanna, home sta., 1867; became ensign, 1868; promoted through grades to rear admiral, Jan. 3, 1908. Ordnance duty, Washington Navy Yard, 1886-90; cruiser New York and battleship Indiana, 1894-97; ordnance officer, Navy Yard, New York, 1897-1900; comdg. Prairie, Concord, Yorktown, 1900-02; mem. Gen. Bd., and Army and Navy Joint Board, 1902-06; commandant Navy Yard, Boston, 1907-09; aid for material, Navy Dept., 1909-10; retired, Mar. 17, 1910. Home: Richfield Springs, N.Y. Died May 30, 1919.

SWIFT, WILLIAM HENRY army officer, engr.; b. Taunton, Mass., Nov. 6, 1800; s. Dr. Foster and Deborah (Delano) S.; grad. U.S. Mil. Acad.; m. Mary Stuart, 1825; m. 2d, Hannah Howard, 1844; Commd. 2d lt. arty. U.S. Army, 1st lt., 1824; worked on coastal improvements on surveys for Chesapeake and Ohio Canal for a projected canal across Fla. peninsula; brevetted capt., 1832, also asst. topog. engr.; commd. capt., 1838; prin. asst. in Topog. Bur., Washington, D.C., 1843-49; responsible for constrn. of 1st skeleton iron tower lighthouse in U.S., Black Rock Harbor, Conn., resigned Commn., 1849; became pres. Phila., Wilmington & Balt. R.R., also Mass. Western R.R.; pres. bd. trustees Ill. & Mich. Canal, 1845-71; published report on Chesapeake & Ohio Canal, 1846. Died N.Y.C., Apr. 7, 1879.

SWIGGETT, DOUGLAS WORTHINGTON (swig'et), editor; b. Morrow, O., Sept. 11, 1882; s. Rev. Edward T. and Eleanor Strode (Mansfield) S.; A.B., Harvard, 1906; unmarried. Teacher Marietta O., U. of Mo. and at Cicero, Ill., until 1908; with Longmans, Green & Co., publishers, 1909-11 editorial writer The Journal, Milwaukee, Wis., 1912-17 and 1919-47. Enlisted in U.S. Army, Aug. 27, 1917; commd. 2d lt., F.A., Nov. 27, 1917; served with 53d Arty., C.A.C., Meuse-Argonne offensive and St. Mihiel and Verdun sectors; discharged, Apr. 1, 1919; capt., O.R.C., 1924-29. Mem. Am. Soc. Newspaper Editors. Presbyterian. Clubs: University, City. Editor: Selections from Malory's Morte d'Arthur, 1909. Received hon. mention for distinguished editorial. Pulitzer award, 1938. Home: University Club. Address: 924 E. Wells St., Milwaukee 2. Died Feb. 12, 1950; buried Spring Grove Cemetery, Cincinnati.

SWIM, DUDLEY, corp. exec.; b. Bellingham, Wash., June 15, 1905; s. Arthur L. and Mary (Galbraith) S.; A.B. with great distinction, Stanford, 1926, M.B.A., 1928; m. Katherine Merrill, June 22, 1935; children—Marilyn L., Roger C., Gaylord K. Engaged in ranching; past sr. v.p. Nat. Investors Corp.; dir. Investors Diversified Service, Inc., Mpls., 1952-54; former director., member of exec. committee M.O. Pacific R.R.; now chmn. board National Air Lines, Inc.; now president Twin Falls Mortgage Loan Co., former dir., mem. finance com. Providence Washington Ins. Grp., Del Monte Corp; former chmn., dir. Baker Raulang Co. Former member of the California State Coordinating Council Higher Edn.; internat. advisory committee Information Council of Americas. Member policy bd. USNR, 1946; pres. Carmel Valley (Cal.) Assn., 1957, Monterey Bay Area council Boy Scouts Am., 1957; director of Stanford Research Inst. Trustee of Cordell Hull Found. Internat. Education; mem. national council Pomona Coll.; founder, managing trustee of Arthur L. Swim Found.; chmn. adv. council, nutrition dept. U. Cal. at Berkeley; pres. Monterey County Found. for Conservation; mem. adv. bd. Hoover Instn. on War, Revolution and Peace, Stanford trustee Cal. State Colls., Rockford Coll., Wabash Coll. Served to lt. comdr. USNR, 1942-45. Mem. Free Soc. Assn. (trustee), Am. Legion (nat. vice comdr. 1946), Stanford Alumni Assn. (pres. 1951-52), Phi Beta Kappa, Sigma Nu. Republican. Presbyn., Clubs: Bohemian, Commonwealth (San Francisco); Blue Lakes Country (Ida.); Hope (R.I.). Home: Carmel CA Died 1972.

SWINBURNE, JOHN congressman, physician; b. Deer River, N.Y., May 30, 1820; grad. Albany Med. Coll., 1847. Began practice medicine, 1847; apptd. chief med. officer on staff Gen. John F. Rathbone, 1861, placed in charge of depot for recruits, Albany; served as surgeon Volunteers with rank of med. supt. of N.Y. wounded troops, 1862; taken prisoner of war, 1862; apptd. health officer port of N.Y. by gov. of N.Y., 1864; in charge of Am. Ambulance Corps during siege of Paris by Prussians, 1870-71; elected mayor Albany, 1882; mem. U.S. Ho. of Reps. (Republican) from N.Y., 49th Congress, 1885-87. Died Albany, Mar. 28, 1889; buried Albany Rural Cemetery.

SWINBURNE, WILLIAM THOMAS rear admiral U.S.N.; b. Newport, R.I., Aug. 24, 1847; s. Daniel Thomas and Harriet (Knowles) S. Grad. U.S. Naval Acad., 1866; after graduation on bd. Saco, West Indian Squadron, 1866-67; Kearsarge, S. Pacific Squadron, 1868-70; promoted ensign, 1868; master, 1869; lt., 1870; Michigan, 1870-72; flagship Lancaster, S. Atlantic, 1872-74; torpedo sch., 1875; Hartford, 1875-77; Trenton, China sta., 1883-86; Naval Acad., 1886-90; promoted lt. comdr., 1887; exec. officer Boston, 1890-93; comd. battalion landed in Honolulu, Jan. 16-Apr. 1, 1893; head dept. seamanship, Naval Acad., 1893-97; promoted comdr., 1896; comd. Helena, 1897-99; served in N. Atlantic Fleet during Spanish-Am. War; captured Spanish steamer Miguel Jovar, Apr. 23, 1898; with convoy to Santiago-Cienfuegas blockade, June 1898; engagement of Tunas, July 1 and 2, 1898, Manzanilla, destruction Spanish gunboats and transports, July 18, 1898; joined fleet at Manila under Admiral Dewey, Feb. 1899; convoyed 23d Inf. to Jolo, June 1899; senior officer in command of vessels assisting Gen. Lawton in his campaign, Paranaque and Bacoor (Manila Bay), June 10-13, 1899; Portsmouth Navy Yard, Oct. 1899-1902; promoted capt., Mar. 1901; comd. Texas, 1902-04; mem. General Bd., Washington, 1904-06; rear admiral, July 22, 1906; comdr.-in-chief Pacific Squadron, 1906-09; War Coll., June 10-Oct. 1, 1909; retired, Aug. 24, 1909; m. Katherine Elsie Vincent, Nov. 27, 1875 (died 1904); m. 2d, Mrs. Sophie Cook Poe, Sept. 7, 1905. Home: New York, N.Y. Died Mar. 3, 1928.

SWING, PHILIP DAVID ex-congressman; b. San Bernardino, Calif., Nov. 30, 1884; s. James Wesley and Mary Frances (Garner) S.; A.B., Stanford, 1905; m. Nell C. Cremeens, Aug. 16, 1912 (dec.); children—Mary Margaret (Mrs. James Carry), Phyllis (Mrs. Robert R. Hind). Admitted to the bar and began practice at San Bernardino, Calif., 1906; mem. Eshleman & Swing, 1908-16; El Centro firm organizers and attorneys for Imperial Irrigation District (largest irrigation district in the United States, 420,000 acres under cultivation). Dep. dist. atty. Imperial County, 1908-11, dist. atty., 1911-15; judge Superior Court, Imperial County, 1919-21; mem. 67th to 72d Congresses (1921-33), 11th Calif. Dist.; mem. State Water Resources Bd., 1945-56. Republican. Waived exemption and in U.S. Army, Camp Taylor, Ky., 1918; hon. discharged, Dec. 5, 1918. Mem. Phi Beta Kappa. Mason, Elk, Rotarian. Club: Cuyamaca (San Diego). Office: San Diego Trust & Savings Bldg., San Diego 1, Cal. Died Aug. 3, 1963.

SWISHER, BENJAMIN FRANKLIN lawyer; b. Iowa City, Ia., Jan. 21, 1878; s. Lovell and Elizabeth (Leonard) S.; B.Ph., U. Ia., 1889, LL.B., 1900; m. Helen Field Moulton, Nov. 26, 1902; children—Martha Elizabeth (Mrs. Deam E. Horner), Benjamin F. (dec.), Helen Moulton (Mrs. Richard H. Plock), Charles Franklin. Admitted to Ia. bar, 1900, and since practiced in Waterloo, Iowa; mem. firm Swisher, Cohrt & Swisher; city solicitor, 1910-15; v.p. and general counsel Waterloo. Cedar Falls & Northern R.R.; general counsel, dir. Rath Packing Co. Pres. Bd. of Edn., Waterloo, 1918-24; pres. bd. trustees Iowa Memorial Union. Lieut. colonel Specialist Reserve. Mem. C. of C. (dir.), Am. Bar Assn., Ia. State Bar Assn. (pres. 1926-27), U. of Ia. Alumni Assn. (pres. 1927-30), Reserve Officers Assn., Phi Kappa Psi, Phi Delta Phi. I Club (U. of Iowa). Republican. Conglist. (trustee). Elk. Clubs: Rotary (pres. 1942-43), Sunnyside Country (Waterloo). Home: 410 Sunset Rd. Office: 502-509 Waterloo Bldg., Waterloo, Ia. Died Jan. 22, 1959.

SWOPE, GERARD elec. engr.; b. St. Louis, Mo., Dec. 1, 1872; B.S. in E.E., Mass. Inst. Tech., 1895; hon. D.Sc., Rutgers, 1923, Union Coll., 1924; LL.D., Colgate U., 1927; Dr. Engring., Stevens Inst. Technology, 1929; D.Sc., Washington U., 1932; m. Mary Dayton Hill, 1901; LL.D. (hon.), Dartmouth, 1952; children—Henrietta H., Isaac G., Gerard, David, John. Began as helper Gen. Electric Co., 1893; entered employ Western Electric Co., 1895, mgr. in St. Louis, 1899-1906; trans. to Chicago, 1906, to N.Y. as gen. sales mgr., 1908, and elected v.p. and dir., 1913; elected pres. Internat. Gen. Electric Co., Jan. 1919, chmn. 1922-33, now hon. chmn., pres. General Electric Co., 1922-39, retired, 1939, hon. pres. and dir., 1940-42 and, 1944-— (re-elected pres. 1942-44). Dir. National City Bank, also many foreign corps. First pres. and now mem. bd. of govs. of Nat. Elec. Mfrs. Assn.; mem. first Playground Commn. of St. Louis, 1901-03; chmn. of first public Bath Commn., St. Louis, 1903-06; chmn. N.Y.C. Housing Authority, 1940-42; asst. to sec. of treasury, 1942. Mem. gen. staff U.S. Army, World War I, served as asst. dir. purchase, storage and traffic. Mem. Indsl. Adv. Bd. of N.R.A. (Washington), 1933; first chmn. Bus. Adv. and Planning Council for Dept. of Commerce, 1933; chmn. Coal Arbitration, Bd., 1933; mem. first Nat. Labor Board, 1933; mem. President's Adv. Council on Economic Security, 1934; mem. Adv. Council on Social Security, 1937-38; chmn. Indsl. Relations Commn. to Great Britain and Sweden, 1938; life mem. corp. and mem. exec. com. Mass. Inst. Tech.; mem. vis. com. Dept. of Astronomy, Harvard, 1927-—; former pres. and now dir., Greenwich House (New York); alternate mem. Nat. Defense Mediation Bd., 1941. Chmn. 8th Am. Red Cross Roll Call, 1924; chmn. Nat. Mobilization for Human Needs, 1935-36, gater hon. pres. community chests and councils; organizer and chmn., Com. to Study Budget of Relief Appeals for fgn. countries, 1942; an organizer, mem. exec. com., chmn. and chairman budget com., Nat. War Fund; chmn. Nat. Health and Welfare Retirement Association. F. Am. Inst. Elec. Engrs.; mem. Council on Foreign Relations and various scientific socs.; hon. mem. Tau Beta Pi, 1932. Awarded D.S.M. (for work on procurement program for U.S. Army, 1918), Chevalier Legion of Honor (French); Order of Rising Sun (Japanese). Awarded Gold Medal of Nat. Inst. Social Sciences, 1932; Gold Medal and purse for signal contributions to elec. manufacturing industry, 1932; Hoover medal, 1942, for pub. service in social, civic and humanitarian fields. Clubs: Technology (New York); Mohawk (Schenectady). Author: Stabilization of Industry (often referred to as "Swope Plan"), 1931; Futility of Conquest in Europe, 1943; Some Aspects of Corporate Management. Contbr. papers and articles on unemployment and economic subjects. Home: The Croft, Ossining, N.Y. Office: 570 Lexington Av., N.Y.C. Died Nov. 20, 1957.

SWOPE, GUY J., state official; born Meckville, Pa., Dec. 26, 1892; s. Jeremiah Gerhart and Mary Jane (Smith) S.; student pub. schs. of Pennsylvania and Keystone State Teachers College, Kutztown, Pennsylvania, Columbia U.; married Mayme Catherine Gerberich, October 23, 1909 (died May 6, 1948); children—Marjorie Evelyn (Mrs. Leon Guyer), Harold Wesley, Lee Frederick; married Helen Y. Yoshimura, August 13, 1949. Public school teacher, 1909-13; U.S. internal revenue agt., 1913-18; private accountant, 1918-19; pub. accountant, banker, dept. store comptroller, 1919-35; mem. Swope and Nichols, pub. accountants, 1936-54; budget sec. State of Pennsylvania, 1935-37; mem. 75th Congress (1937-39), 19th Pa. Dist.; auditor of Puerto Rico, Jan. 29, 1940-Feb. 2, 1941; gov. of Puerto Rico, 1941; resigned to become dir. Div. of Territories, Dept. of Interior, July 1941. Dem. chmn. Dauphin County, Pa., 1934-37. Entered on active duty as naval officer July, 1943; Deputy Military Gov. of Saipan, 1944. Mem. General MacArthur's staff as Chief, Legislative Div., Aug., 1945 to Aug., 1946. Retired from active service as captain, November, 1946. Returned to Tokyo Feb., 1947 as Chief, Nat. Govern. Div., General MacArthur's Headquarters, in civilian status; spl. asst. to U.S. High Commr. in Germany, and Chief Displaced Populations div., 1949-54; comptroller Lake Asphalt & Petroleum Co. of Pa., Harrisburg, 1955-61; dep. state treas. Commonwealth of Pa., 1961-65; del. Pa. Constl. Conv., 1967-68. Decorated Legion of Merit; recipient Good Citizenship medal for distinguished pub. service S.A.R. C.P.A., Pa. Democrat. Lutheran. Mason (32 deg., Shriner). Home: Harrisburg PA Died July 25, 1969; interred Hamlin Cemetery Fredericksburg PA

SWOPE, HERBERT BAYARD journalist, policy consultant; b. St. Louis, Mo.; s. Isaac and Ida S.; L.H.D., Hobart, 1924; Litt.D., Colgate University, 1927; married Margaret Honeyman Powell; children—Jane Marion, Herbert Bayard (lt. USNR). Successively reporter on St. Louis Post Dispatch, N.Y. Herald and N.Y. World; war corr. The World and Post Dispatch with German armies 1914-16; in 1914 sent exclusive dispatches of German U-boat U-9, sinking battleships Crecy, Abou-Kir and Hogue; winner Pulitzer prize for best reporting of 1917; upon U.S. war declaration, designated lt. comdr. U.S. Navy; later apptd. to U.S. War Industries Bd., asso. mem. and asst. to B.M. Baruch; chief corr. The World at Paris Peace Conf; chmn. Official Am. Press Delegation; mem. Internat. Press Com. which fought successfully for publicity in conf.; first to publish secret League of Nations Covenant; also first full text of reparation clauses. Exec. editor The World, 1920-29, (during this period paper received 3 Pulitzer medals for pub. service (one for exposure of K.K.K.); retired from The World, 1929; awarded Poor Richard medal, Phila.; U.S. Medal for Merit by President, U.S. Gold Medal by Interfaith In Action, 1950. Major, U.S. Army Res.; personal cons. Sec. of War, 1942-46. Mem. U.S. Delegation to U.N. AEC (Baruch) which prepared Am. plan for Atomic Control. Founder Overseas New Agency; v.p. L.I. Pk. Com.; former chmn. (11 yrs.) N.Y. Racing Com. (voted 3 plaques by turf writers' group for best services to racing); chmn. Turf Com. Am. raising $17,000,000 from Turf for War Relief; a founder and former gov. Am. Soc. Newspaper Editors; dir. Freedom House; sent by Pres. Roosevelt to London Econ. Conf.; exec. com. Citizens Com. Displaced Persons; v. chmn. Citizens Council Civil Rights; cons. Radio Corp. Am., Nat. Broadcasting Company. Chairman God Bless Am. Fund; co. chmn. Greater N.Y. $4,000,000 campaign for Nat. Found. for Infantile Paralysis, 1952; trustee Walt Whitman

Birthplace Assn.; dir. United Service for New Americans; dir. 300th Anniversary celebration N.Y.C., chmn. Mayor's Commn. on Intergroup Relations, N.Y.C.; dir. Nat. Conf. Christians and Jews; mem. Pulitzer Prize Jury for International Reporting, 1957. Decorated Knight Comdr., Republic of Liberia, 1954. Mem. Council Foreign Relations, Vets. Fgn. Wars, Phi Beta Kappa (hon.), Sigma Delta Chi. Clubs: River, Turf & Field, Pilgrims, Oversees Press, National Press, P.E.N. Author: Inside German Empire; War Censorship; Journalism—an Instrument of Civilization; Free Speech, etc. Home: 1060 Fifth Av., N.Y.C.; and Sands Point, L.I. Office: 745 Fifth Av., N.Y.C. Died June 20, 1958.

SYDENSTRICKER, VIRGIL PRESTON physician, educator; b. Hamilton, Mo., July 15, 1889; s. Hiram and Alma (Willis) S.; B.A., Washington and Lee U., 1910, M.A., 1911; M.D., Johns Hopkins, 1915; m. Olive Thompson, May 27, 1920; 1 dau., Anne Willis (Mrs. Joel M. Le Sueur). Intern, asst. resident physician Johns Hopkins Hosp., 1915-17; prof. medicine Med. Coll. Ga., 1923-—. Mem. nutrition com. NRC, 1940-45; cons. Surgeon Gen. of Army, 1940-—; adviser Brit. Ministry of Health, 1942-43, nutrition div. WHO, 1950; head European nutrition sect. UNNRA, 1944-45; mem. internat. health div. Rockefeller Found., 1942-43. Served from 1st lt. to capt., M.C., U.S. Army, 1917-19. Recipient King's Medal for Service, Eng., 1946, citation, U.S. War Dept., 1945, Brit. Govt., 1945, Dutch Govt., 1945. Master A.C.P.; fellow A.A.A.S.; mem. Assn. Am. Physicians, Soc. Exptl. Biology and Medicine, Am. Nutrition Inst., Royal Soc. Medicine (Gt. Britain). Home: 2223 Overton Rd., Augusta, Ga. Died Dec. 12, 1964; buried Augusta.

SYKES, GEORGE (NICKNAME TARDY GEORGE) army officer; b. Dover, Del., Oct. 9, 1822; s. William Sykes; attended U.S. Mil. Acad., 1842; m. Elizabeth Goldsborough. Commd. 2d lt., 3d Infantry, took part in Seminole War, 1842; 1st lt. in war with Mexico from Vera Cruz to Mexico City, 1846; brevetted capt. for gallant conduct at Battle of Cerro Gordo, 1855; maj. in Civil War, served in 1st Battle of Bull Run, 1861; commd. brig. gen. U.S. Volunteers, Sept. 1861; at Malvern Hill, 1862; commanded V Corps in Gettysburg campaign, brevetted brig. gen. U.S. Army; went to Kan., 1864; mustered out of U.S. volunteers as maj. gen., reverted to rank lt. col. 5th Inf., U.S. Army, 1866; col. 20th Inf., Ft. Brown, Tex., 1868. Died Ft. Brown, Feb. 8, 1880; buried West Point, N.Y.

SYLVESTER, EVANDER WALLACE naval officer; b. Alexandria, La., Jan. 2, 1899; s. Ira Wallace and Heloise (Violet) S.; B.S. with distinction, U.S. Naval Acad., 1919; M.S., Mass. Inst. Tech., 1923; m. Frances Edwards, Sept. 5, 1925; children—Ann Baird (Mrs. John Thomas Collins), and Susan Heloise (Mrs. John Teunis). Commissioned ensign United States Navy, June 6, 1919, advanced through grades to rear admiral, Dec. 24, 1946; duty in design, constrn. and repair of naval surface vessels and submarines, 1923-38; in charge installation of carriage tracks and testing equipment, David W. Taylor model basin, Carderock, Md., 1938-40; asst. naval attache, London, 1940-41; Navy Dept. liaison officer to Nat. Defense Research Com., Oct. 1941-June 1942; duty in shipyards and Navy Dept., 1942-46; comdr. Puget Sound Naval Shipyard, Bremerton, Wash., 1946-50; asst. chief Bur. of Ships for field activities 1950-51, for design constrn. and maintenance, 1951-54; now dir. The Mariners Museum, Newport News, Va. Recipient of Legion of Merit for work in Office of Coordinator of Research, Navy Dept., 1941-42; Gold Star in lieu of 2d Legion of Merit for work in prodn. of landing craft and other multiple ship programs during 1942-46. Mem. Am. Soc. Naval Engrs. (pres. 1954), Soc. Naval Architects and Marine Engrs., Chi Phi. Episcopalian. Mason. Clubs: Army-Navy, James River, Army-Navy Country. Home: 101 Museum Pkwy., Newport News 23601. Office: The Mariners Museum, Newport News, Va. Died Aug. 4, 1960; buried Arlington Nat. Cemetery.

SYMES, GEORGE GIFFORD congressman, lawyer; b. Ashtabula County, O., Apr. 28, 1840; studied law. Admitted to bar, practiced law; enlisted as pvt. Co. B, 2d Regt., Wis. Volunteers, U.S. Army, 1861, wounded in 1st Battle of Bull Run, adjutant 25th Regt., Wis. Inf.; served in Sioux Indian (1862), Vicksburg (1863), Atlanta (1864) campaigns, wounded at Battle of Atlanta, 1864, commd. col. 44th Regt., Wis. Volunteers, 1864, commanded post at Paducah, Ky., 1865; began practice law, Paducah, 1865; asso. justice Mont. Territory Supreme Ct., 1869-71; practiced law, Helena, Mont.; moved to Denver, Colo., 1874; mem. U.S. Ho. of Reps. (Republican) from Colo., 49th-50th congresses, 1885-89. Died Denver, Nov. 3, 1893, buried Fairmount Cemetery.

SYMES, J(OHN) FOSTER (simz), lawyer; b. Denver, Feb. 10, 1878; s. George Gifford and Sophie Elizabeth (Foster) S.; Ph.B., Yale, 1900; LL.B., Columbia, 1903; m. Cynthia Edrington, Jan. 26, 1916 (div. 1928); children—Virginia Bethel (Mrs. John G. McMurtry, Jr.), Cynthia Edrington (Mrs. Claude Maer); m. 2d, Florence J. Wade, Sept. 29, 1931 (died Apr. 1942). Practiced at N.Y.C., 1902-06; moved to Denver, 1906; U.S. dist. atty., Dist. Colo., 1921-22; U.S. Dist. judge, Colo., 1922-—. Student 1st Officers' Tng. Camp, Ft. Riley, Kan., Apr. 1917; commd. capt., Aug. 1917; maj., Oct. 1918; served with 355th Inf., 89th Div. and 362d Inf., 91st Div.; hon. discharged, Apr. 1919; participated in St. Mihiel and Argonne operations and Army of Occupation in Germany. Trustee U. Denver. Mem. Am., Colo., and Denver bar assns., Denver Philos. Soc., Mayflower Soc. Republican. Episcopalian. Vestryman St. John's Cathedral. Mason. Clubs: Denver, Denver Country, Mile High (Denver); University (N.Y.C.). Died Apr. 5, 1951.

SYMMONDS, CHARLES JACOBS army officer; b. Holland, Mich., Oct. 6, 1866; s. Robert and Phillis Wey (Jacobs) S.; grad. U.S. Mil. Acad., 1890; m. George Crook, d. Brig. Gen. Earl D. Thomas, U.S.A., Fort McIntosh, Texas, Feb. 21, 1894; children—Robert Earl (killed in action, World War), Katharine, Godfrey, Phillis Wey. Commissioned 2d lt. 18th Inf., June 12, 1890; promoted through grades to brig. gen. Nov. 3, 1923; served as capt. a.q.m., vols., Spanish-Am. War, 1898; comdr. Intermediate Depot, Giévres, France, the principal storage depot of A.E.F. during World War; retired, Oct. 31, 1930. Awarded D.S.M. "for exceptionally meritorious and distinguished service" at Giévres; Officer Legion of Honor (France); Officer Polonia Restituta (Poland). Home: Chevy Chase, Md. Died July 16, 1941.

SYMONDS, FREDERICK MRTIN rear admiral U.S.N.; b. Watertown, N.Y., May 16, 1846; s. Charles F. and Louise S.; apptd. to U.S. Naval Acad. from N.Y., 1862, grad. 1867; m. Annie C. Parker, 1871. Ensign, Dec. 18, 1868; master, Mar. 21, 1870; lt., Mar. 21, 1871; lt. comdr., July 31, 1809; comdr., June 19, 1897; capt., Mar. 16, 1902; retired with rank rear admiral, Dec. 1, 1902. Summer of 1863, was in active service on board Macedonian in pursuit of Confed. steamer Tacony; served on Piscataqua and Delaware, 1867-70; torpedo duty, 1871; on bd. Tuscarora, 1872-75; Minnesota, 1875-78; Jamestown, 1879-81; New Hampshire, 1882-85; Mohican, 1885-88; Michigan, 1889-92; insp. ordnance, Mare Island, Calif., 1893-96; comd. Pinta, 1896-97, Marietta, 1897-99; insp. 9th light house dist., 1899-1902; duty in connection with steamboat inspection service, 1904-05. Home: Galesville, Wis. Died Mar. 14, 1926.

SYMONDS, PERCIVAL MALLON educator; b. Newtonville, Mass., Apr. 18, 1893; s. Joseph Ainsworth and Abbie Kendall (Mallon) S.; A.B., Harvard, 1915; A.M., Columbia, 1920, Ph.D., 1923; m. Johnnie Pirkle, Dec. 25, 1922. Tchr., Punchard High Sch., Andover, Mass., 1915-17, Worcester Acad., 1917-18; asst. Inst. Ednl. Research, Tchrs. Coll., 1921-22; prof. edn. and psychology, U. Hawaii, 1922-24; asso. in edn. Tchrs. Coll., Columbia, 1924-25, asst. prof. edn., 1925-28, asso. prof., 1928-34, prof. 1934-58, prof. emeritus, 1958-—, chmn. div. theory and techniques of measurement and research, 1933-37, head dept. research methods, 1937-42; vis. prof. edn. U. Cal., Los Angeles, summers 1938, 39, 41; U. Wis., summer 1944, U. Miami, 1945. Served in Ordnance Dept., U.S. Army, doing statistical work in ballistics, Aberdeen proving grounds, 1918. Assessment Sch., Office of Strategic Services, U.S. Govt., 1945. Diplomate, fellow Am. Psychol. Assn. (pres. ednl. psychology div. 1947-48). Fellow Am. Orthopsychiat. Assn., A.A.A.S. (sec. Q, 1937-39), Soc. for Projective Techniques, Rorschach Inst.; mem. Am. Ednl. Research Assn. (pres. 1956-57), Soc. for Research in Child Devel., Soc. for Psychol. Study Social Issues, N.Y. State Psychol. Assn. (charter), N.Y. Soc. Clin. Psychologists, Assn. for Family Living, Eastern Psychol. Assn., Phi Beta Kappa, Sigma Xi, Phi Delta Kappa, Kappa Delta Pi. Conglist. Clubs: Appalachian Mountain, Marshall Chess. Author: Measurement in Education, 1927; Ability Standards for Standardized Achievement Tests in High School, 1927; The Nature of Conduct, 1928; Tests and Interest Questionnaires in the Guidance of High School Boys, 1930; Diagnosing Personality and Conduct, 1931; Mental Hygiene of the School Child, 1934; Psychological Diagnosis in Social Adjustment, 1934; Measurement of Personality Adjustments of High School Pupils (with C. E. Jackson), 1935; Education and Psychology of Thinking, 1936; Psychology of Parent-Child Relationships, 1939; Dynamics of Human Adjustment, 1946; Dynamic Psychology, 1949; Adolescent Fantasy, 1949; Dynamics of Parent-Child Relationships, 1949; Ego and the Self, 1951; Dynamics of Psychotherapy, Vol. 1, 1956, Vol. 2, 1957, Vol. 3, 1958; What Education Has to Learn from Psychology, 1958; From Adolescent to Adult, 1961; Pssychology of the Teacher (manuscript), 1960. Contbr. to ednl. and psychol. jours. Mem. editorial bd. Jour. Ednl. Psychology; Jour. Edn. Research; Psychol. Monographs; Sociatry, Personality; Nervous Child. Mem. Riverside Church (N.Y.). Home: 106 Morningside Dr., N.Y.C. 10027. Died Aug. 6, 1960; buried Greenwood Cemetery, Salem, Mass.

SYMONS, THOMAS WILLIAM colonol U.S.A.; b. Keesville, N.Y., Feb. 7, 1849; s. Thomas and Syrena (Eaton) S.; grad. U.S. Mil. Acad., 1874; m. Letitia V. Robinson, Oct. 12, 1884. In service on civ. and mil. engrng. works in Washington, D.C., Ore., Calif., Nev., Wash., Ida., Mont., and the Great Lakes until retired from mil. service, 1898, to devote attention to work of bldg. the New York state canals. Built the largest breakwater in the world, at Buffalo, N.Y.; had charge of U.S. lighthouses from Detroit, Mich., to Ogdensburg, N.Y.; was supt. pub. bldgs. ingrounds and mil. aid to the president; mem. Canal Advisory Board and consulting engr. on canals State of N.Y. Author: The Columbia River, 1882; A Ship Caal from the Great Lakes to the Sea, 1897. Home: Washington, D.C. Died: Nov. 22, 1920.

SYVERTON, JEROME T. physician, educator; b. Courtenay, N.D., Mar. 29, 1907; s. John and Thea (Nelson) S.; A.B., U. of N.D., 1927, B.S., 1928; M.D., Harvard, 1931; m. Mildred Sloulin, June 26, 1932; children—Jane, Gail, Laurie. Instr. in bacteriology, Univ. N.D., 1928; interne and asst. resident in medicine, Duke Univ. Hosp., 1931-32; asst. pathology and bacteriology, Rockefeller Inst. Med. Research, 1932-34; vis. asso. prof. pathology and bacteriology, Vanderbilt Univ., April-Oct., 1942; in str. bacteriology, Univ. of Rochester Sch. Medicine and Dentistry, 1934-37, asst. prof., 1937-39, asso. prof., 1939-47; prof. microbiol. and head dept., La. State U., Sch. Medicine, 1947-48; prof. and head of department of bacteriology U. of Minnesota since 1948. Mem. microbiol. panel Office of Naval Research, 1946-50; cons. surgeon gen. USPHS, 1950-—, as mem. virus, rickettsial and microbiology study sects., 1950-55, National Adv. Allergy and Infectious Diseases Council, 1957-61, adv. panel on viruses and cancer Nat. Cancer Council, 1959-—; mem. scientific advisory board consultants Armed Forces Institute Pathology, 1960-—. Served in Med. Corps, U.S.N.R., 1941-47; active duty April 1944-Jan. 1946 with appointment as vis. investigator Hosp. Rockefeller Inst., Apr.-Nov., 1944; fgn. duty Naval Med. Research Unit 2 in Pacific theater to Jan., 1946. Recipient Lilly award for Research in Bacteriology and Immunology, 1938; Commonwealth Fund Award in Support of Creative Work, 1957. Diplomate Nat. Bd. Med. Examiners. Mem. A.M.A., American Academy of Microbiology, also Society Am. Bacteriologists, Soc. Clin. Investigation, Soc. Exptl. Pathology, Am. Assn. Immunol.; Am. Soc. Tropical Med., Am. Epidemiol. Soc., Tissue Culture Association Central Society Clinical Research, New York Academy of Science, A.A.A.S., Minnesota Med. Assn., Am. Soc. Cancer Research, Soc. Exptl. Biology and Medicine, American Assn. Pathologists and Bacteriologists (exec. council 1959-—), Am. Soc. Cell Biology, Harvey Society (N.Y.), Alpha Omega Alpha, Sigma Xi. Presbyn. Clubs: Campus (U. Minn.); Harvard (Minn.); Lafayette. Author: scientific articles in field of infectious disease for profl. jours. Mem. editorial bd. Bacteriological Reviews, Cancer Research, Proceedings of Soc. for Exptl. Biology and Medicine. Home: Woodbridge Rd., Route 1, Box 18, Wayzata, Minn. Office: 1060 Mayo Meml. Bldg., U. of Minn., Mpls. 14. Died Jan. 28, 1961.

TAFEL, GUSTAV lawyer; b. Munich, Germany, Oct. 13, 1830; early edn. at Ulm, Germany; grad. Latin Acad., Schorndorf, Germany, 1847; m. Therese Dorn, Jan. 19, 1870. Arrived in Cincinnati, Sept. 20, 1847; learned printing trade; engaged in journalistic work; admitted to bar 1858; in 1848 one of founders of first German Gymnastic Assn. ("Turners") in America. Enlisted private 9th Ohio Inf., April 1861; served until July 1865, when mustered out as col. 106th regt. Ohio vol. inf.; elected to legislature, 1865. Mayor Cincinnati, 1897-99. Home: Cincinnati, O. Died 1908.

TAFFE, JOHN congressman, lawyer; b. Indianapolis, Ind., Jan. 30, 1827; studied law. Admitted to bar in Indpls.; moved to Neb., 1856; mem. Neb. Territory Ho. of Reps., 1858-59; mem., pres. territorial council, 1860-61; served as maj. 2d Regt., Neb. Volunteer Cav., U.S. Army, Civil War; mem. U.S. Ho. of Reps. (Republican) from Neb., 40th-42d congresses, 1867-73; receiver of pub. land office, North Platte, Neb. Died North Platte, Mar. 14, 1884; buried Prospect Hill Cemetery, Omaha, Neb.

TAFFINDER, SHERWOODE AYERST naval officer; b. Council Bluffs, Ia., Mar. 18, 1884; s. William Geoffrey and Mina (Ayerst) T.; B.S., U.S. Naval Acad., 1906; m. Margaret Knowlton Brownell, Sept. 28, 1915; children—Sherwoode Ayerst, Margaret Brownell, Constance De Wolf. Commd. ensign, U.S. Navy and advanced through grades to rear adm., 1940; served on Asiatic Station, 1906-09; Pacific, 1909-13; Atlantic, 1913-21; Pacific, 1912-24; with Naval Mission to Peru, S.A., 1924-26; C.Z., 1928-30; War Coll., 1932-35; Navy Dept., 1936-39; chief staff U.S. Fleet, 1940-41; comdr. Cruiser Div. 5, Pacific Fleet, 1941; comdt. Puget Sound Navy Yard, Bremerton, Wash., 1942-43; apptd. vice adm., comdr. Service Force Atlantic Fleet, 1944; comdt. 14th Naval Dist., also Haawaiian Sea frontier, 1945; ret. vice adm., 1947. Decorated World War and Mexican Campaign medals; Def. Service Medal, Fleet Clasp; Legion of Merit with 2 stars, Ordew del Sol del Peru, Grande Official Peru. Episcopalian. Clubs: New York Yacht; Army and Navy (Washington). Address: 20 Sea View Av., Newport, R.I. 02840. Died Jan. 25, 1965; buried Naval Acad. Cemetery.

TAFT, KINGSLEY A., judge; b. Cleveland, O., July 19,21903; s. Frederick L. Taft and Mary Alice (Arter) T.; A.B., Amherst Coll., 1925, LL.D., 1950; LL.B., Harvard, 1928, LL.D., Baldwin Wallace College, 1952, Kenyon Coll., 1969; married Louise Dakin, Sept. 14,

1927; children—Charles K., Kingsley Jr., Sheldon A., David D. In practice of law in Cleveland with McKeehan, Merrick, Arter and Stewart and predecessor firm, 1928-39, partner, 1940-48; dir. Land Title Guarantee and Trust Co. of Cleveland, 1938-63. Mem. Ohio House of Reps., 1933-34. Elected U.S. senator from Ohio, Nov. 1946 to fill unexpired term of Mr. Justice Burton; judge Supreme Court of Ohio, 1948-62, chief justice Supreme Court of Ohio, 1963-70. Trustee Baldwin-Wallace College. Served in Army of the United States, 1942-46, advanced through the grades to major, 1945. Awarded Army Commendation Medal with oak leaf cluster, 1946. Mem. Shaker Heights Bd. of Edn., 1940-42, pres., 1942. Member American Law Institute, Cleveland, Am., Ohio, Cuyahoga, Columbus bar assns., Am. Legion, Sons American Revolution, American Judicature Society, Phi Beta Kappa, Phi Kappa Psi, Phi Alpha Delta. Republican. Methodist. Mason. Clubs: University, Rocky Fork (Columbus); Union (Cleveland). Associate editor Harvard Law Review, 1927-28. Home: Columbus OH Died Mar. 28, 1970; buried Lake View Cemetery Cleveland OH

TAFT, WILLIAM HOWARD twenty-seventh President of the United States; b. Cincinnati, Sept. 15, 1857; s. Alphonso (Atty. Gen., 1876-77) and Louisa Maria (Torrey) T.; grad. Woodward High Sch., Cincinnati, 1874; B.A., Yale, 1878 (2d in class of 121, salutatorian and class orator); LL.B., Cincinnati Law Sch., 1880, dividing 1st prize; LL.D., Yale 1893, U. of Pa., 1902, Harvard, 1905, Miami U., 1905, State U. of Ia., 1907, Wesleyan, 1909, Princeton, 1912, McGill U., 1913, Cambridge, 1922, Aberdeen, 1922; U. of Cincinnati, 1925; D.C.L., Hamilton, 1913; Oxford, 1922; hon. bencher, Middle Temple, 1922; m. Helen, d. John W. Herron, Cincinnati, June 19, 1886. Admitted to Ohio bar, 1880; law reporter Cincinnati Times, and later of Cincinnati Commercial, 1880; asst. pros. atty. Hamilton Co., O., 1881, 82, 83; practiced law at Cincinnati, 1883-87; asst. county solicitor Hamilton Co., 1885-87; judge Superior Ct., Cincinnati, 1887-90; solicitor gen. of U.S., 1890-92; U.S. circuit judge, 6th Circuit, 1892-1900; prof. and dean law dept., U. of Cincinnati, 1896-1900; pres. U.S. Philippine Commn., Mar. 12, 1900-July 4, 1901; first civil gov. of P.I., July 4, 1901-Feb. 1, 1904; sent to Rome by President Roosevelt, 1902, to confer with Pope Leo XIII concerning purchase of agrl. lands of religious orders in the P.I.; twice declined apptmt. from President Roosevelt as asso. justice Supreme Ct. of U.S., 1903; Sec. of War in cabinet of President Roosevelt, Feb. 1, 1904-June 30, 1908; sent to Cuba by President Roosevelt to adjust insurrection there, 1906, and acted short time as provisional gov.; in Mar. and Apr. 1907, visited Panama, Cuba and P.R., by direction of the President, to take up various matters and familiarize himself with conditions; later he visited Japan and P.I., returning to America via Russia. Nominated for President by Rep. Nat. Conv., Chicago, June 1908, and elected Nov. 3, 1908, for term, Mar. 4, 1909-Mar. 4, 1913; received 321 electoral votes against 162 for William Jennings Bryan, the Dem. candidate; renominated for the Presidency June 1912, by Rep. Nat. Conv., Chicago; defeated in Nov. election following by Woodrow Wilson, Dem. candidate. Kent prof. of law, Yale, 1813-21; apptd. and confirmed by the Senate Chief Justice of the U.S., June 30, 1921. Apptd. mem. Nat. War Labor Conf. Bd., Apr. 1918, and co-chmn. same until bd. dissolved Aug. 1919. Pres. Am. Nat. Red Cross, 1906-13, Am. Bar Assn., 1913, Am. Acad. Jurisprudence, 1914; pres. League to Enforce Peace, engaged in promotion and ratification of Treaty of Peace and League of Nations; chancellor Smithsonian Instn., 1923. Author: Four Aspects of Civic Duty, 1906; vol., 1913, containing 8 Yale lectures and 2 addresses before Am. Bar Assn., on Popular Government; The Anti-Trust Act and the Supreme Court, 1914; The United States and Peace, 1914; Our Chief Magistrate and His Powers, 1916; Taft Papers on League of Nations, 1920. Home: Washington, D.C. Died Mar. 8, 1930.

TAGGART, ELMORE FINDLAY army officer; b. Orrville, O., Oct. 6, 1858; s. Samuel Morrow and Sarah J. T.; grad. U.S. Mil. Acad., 1883. Commd. 2d lt. 6th Inf., June 13, 1883; 1st lt. 4th Inf., Feb. 20, 1891; trans. to 6th Inf., July 20, 1891; capt. commissary subsistence vols., May 12, 1898; maj. same, Oct. 28, 1898; hon. discharged, vols., June 10, 1899; maj. 28th Vol. Inf., July 5, 1899; hon. discharged vols., May 1, 1901; capt. of inf., U.S.A., July 1, 1898; assigned to 6th Inf., Jan. 1, 1899; q.m., Dec. 10, 1903; assigned to 8th Inf., July 17, 1905; maj. 24th Inf., June 25, 1906; lt. col. of inf., Sept. 27, 1911; assigned to 4th Inf., Nov. 16, 1911; trans. to 28th Inf., Oct. 4, 1913; col. of inf., Sept. 21, 1915. Participated in campaign against Santiago de Cuba, 1898; in charge distribution of rations to the destitute in Cuba, Nov. 1898; chief commissary, Dept. of Matanzas, Cuba, Jan.-May 1899; chief of police, city of Manila, P.I., under mil. govt., 1901-02; at Shanghai, China, Nov. 1902; comd. 2d Dist. of Leyte, P.I., 1906-07; with 24th Regt. (colored) in P.I., 1910, and with same regt. at Oswego, N.Y., 1910-12; comdg. at Little Rock, Ark., 1913-14; comdr. 28th Inf., on Mexican border, 1914-17, participating in expdn. to Vera Cruz; assigned as comdr. 12th U.S. Inf., Oct. 1917; apptd. comdr. 8th Div. U.S.A., Camp Fremont, Cal., upon its orgn. Mem. Beta Theta Pi. Presbyn. Home: Orrville, O. Address: War Dept., Washington, D.C.

TAIT, GEORGE foreign service officer; b. Spring Garden, Amherst County, Va., Aug. 14, 1893; s. Robt. and Frances (Adams) T.; ed. U. of Va. Law Sch., 1913-17, Georgetown Sch. Fgn. Service, Ecole Libre des Sciences Politiques, University of Grenoble; married Marjorie Percival, June 5, 1947. Admitted to Virginia bar; practiced law, 1917-18, lecturer Georgetown Sch. Fgn. Service, 1931-33. 2d lt. U.S. Army, 1918-19; vice consul Rio de Janeiro, Nov. 1923, Palermo, July 1925, Algiers, March 1927; Malta, May 1927; consul, Rotterdam, Oct. 1927; Dept. of State, July 1930; consul, Paris, Sept. 1933, Manchester, Apr. 1937, Montreal, May 1941; 1st sec. Bern, Apr. 1942; counselor of Embassy and Consul gen., London, 1946; consul general, Algiers, 1949, Antwerp, 1950-—. Address: Dept. of State, Washington. Died Aug. 24, 1952.

TALBOT, M(URRELL) W(ILLIAMS), forester, ecologist; b. Appleton City, Mo., Aug. 18, 1889; s. LeRoy Hitt and Lettie E. (Williams) T.; B.S., U. Mo., 1913; postgrad. U.S. Dept. Agr. Grad. Sch., 1931; m. Zenaida Merriam, Oct. 27, 1928; children—Lee Merriam, Zenaida (Mrs. William Penn Mott III). Various positions U.S. Forest Service and Bur. Plant Industry, 1913-31; sr. ecologist charge range research Pacific S.W. Forest & Range Expt. Sta., Berkeley, Cal., 1931-55, acting dir., 1941-45, also dir., 1946-55, cons., 1955-72; cons. Govt. Spain, Pack Found., Salt River Basin, Ariz., State Cal.; collaborator U.S. Department of Agriculture. Member Alameda County Grand Jury. Served to 2d lt. F.A., U.S. Army, 1918. Recipient Spl. Meritorious award U.S. Dept. Agr., 1945, Alumnus of year citation Merit U. Mo., 1959. Fellow A.A.A.S.; mem. Am. Soc. Range Mgmt. (pres. 1963), Soc. Am. Foresters, Ecol. Soc. Am., Wilderness Soc., Alpha Zeta, Xi Sigma Pi. Republican. Conglist. Mason (32 deg.). Clubs: Faculty University California, Outlook (Berkeley); Commonwealth (San Francisco); Hillside (Berkeley). Author articles in field. Home: Berkeley CA Died Jan. 12, 1972.

TALBOT, SILAS naval officer, congressman; b. Dighton, Bristil County, Mass., Jan. 11, 1751; s. Benjamin and Rebecca (Allen) T.; m. Miss Richmond, 1772; m. 2d, Miss Morris; m. 3d, Mrs. Pintard; at least 4 children. Mcht., Providence, R.I., circa 1772; apptd. capt. R.I. Regt., 1775; commd. capt. Continental Navy, 1775-79, maj., lt. col., 1777-78, captured by British and held prisoner, 1779-81; mem. N.Y. Assembly, 1792-93; mem. U.S. Ho. of Reps. from N.Y., 3d Congress, 1793-95; commd. capt. U.S. Navy, 1794, supt. constrn. of frigate President, N.Y.C.; comdr. Santo Domingo naval station, cruised in West Indies on board ship Constitution. Died N.Y.C., June 30, 1813; buried Trinity Churchyard, N.Y.C.

TALBOTT, HAROLD E. capitalist, ex-sec. air force; b. Dayton, O., Mar. 31, 1888; s. Harry Elstner and Katharine H. (Houk) T.; prep. edn. The Hill School; student Yale U., 1907-09; married Margaret Thayer, Aug. 11, 1925; children—Margaret T., Pauline, John Thayer, Harold E. III. V.p., gen. mgr. The H. E. Talbott Co., 1911-20, in chg. of hydro-elec. dvlpmnt. and indsl. construction; v.p., gen. mgr. Dayton Metal Products Co., 1914-20; pres. Dayton Wright Airplane Co., 1916-20, Dayton Wright Co., 1919-23; chmn. bd. Standard Packaging Corp., North Am. Aviation Co., 1931-32; vice pres. Talbott Corp., dir. and chmn. finance com. of Mead Corp., Electric Auto-Lite Co.; limited partner Paul B. Mulligan & Company; dir. Baldwin-Lima-Hamilton Corp., Chrysler Corp. (mem. finance com.), Russell Mfg. Co., Madison Square Garden Corp. Dir. aircraft prodn. W.P.B., 1942-43; sec. of Air Force, 1953-55. Served as major Airplane Service, 1918. Eastern chmn. Republican Finance Com., 1934, chmn. for Met. New York, 1943, chmn. Republican national finance com., 1948-49. Republican. Clubs: Deepdale, Cloud, Creek, Madison Square Garden (N.Y.C.); Burning Tree (Chevy Chase, Md.); Capitol Hill (Washington). Dayton, Buzfuz, Miami Valley Hunt and Polo (Dayton, O.); Racquet and Tennis, Meadow Brook, Turf and Field, The River, Piping Rock, The Links (New York). Died Mar. 2, 1957; buried Dayton, O.

TALCOTT, ANDREW army officer, engr.; b. Glastonbury, Conn., Apr. 20, 1797; s. George and Abigail (Goodrich) T.; grad. U.S. Mil. Acad., 1818; m. Catherine Thompson, Apr. 1826; m. 2d, Harriet Randolph Hackley, Apr. 11, 1832; 11 children. Brevetted 2d lt. U.S. Army, 1818; 1st lt. Engr. Corps, 1820, capt., 1830; engr., aide-de-camp to Gen. Henry Atkinson in establishment of posts on Upper Missouri and Yellowstone rivers, 1820-21; chief engr. Ft. Delaware, Del., 1824-25; supt. constrn. canal through Dismal Swamp in Va., 1826-28; supervised constrn. Ft. Monroe, Ft. Calhoun, Hampton Roads, Va., 1828-34; astronomer for determining boundaries between Ohio and Mich., 1828-35; chief engr. in charge of Western div. N.Y. & Erie R.R., 1836-37; supt. improvement of delta of Mississippi River, 1837-39; chief engr. Richmond & Danville R.R., 1848-55; astronomer, surveyor for making the northern boundary of Ia., 1852-53; chief engr. Ohio & Miss. R.R. from Cincinnati and St. Louis, 1856-57; located, constructed railroad from Vera Cruz to Mexico City, 1857-60, 61-67; mgr. Sonora Exploring & Mining Co., chief engr. State of Va., 1860-61; elected chief engr. Va., 1861; devised method of determining terrestrial latitudes through the observation of stars near the zenith; mem. Am. Philos. Soc. Died Richmond, Va., Apr. 22, 1883.

TALCOTT, JOSEPH colonial gov.; b. Hartford, Conn., Nov. 1669; s. Lt. Col. John and Helena (Wakeman) T.; m. Abigail Clark, 1693; m. 2d, Eunice (Howell) Wakeman, June 26, 1706; 9 children. Chosen selectman of Hartford, 1692; justice of peace for Hartford County (Conn.), 1705; dep. from Hartford to Conn. Gen. Assembly, 1708, speaker lower house, 1710; maj. 1st Regt., Conn. Militia, 1710-24; mem. upper chamber Conn. Gen. Assembly, 1711-23; judge county ct., ct. of probate Hartford County, 1714; judge Conn. Superior Ct., 1721; dep. gov. Conn., 1723, gov.. 1724-41. Died Hartford, Nov. 11, 1741.

TALIAFERRO, BENJAMIN congressman; b. in Va., 1750; prep. edn. Served as lt., rifle corps commanded by Gen. Morgan, Continental Army, promoted capt., captured by British at Charleston, 1780; settled in Ga., 1785; mem., pres. Ga. Senate; del. Ga. Constl. Conv., 1798; mem. U.S. Ho. of Reps. from Ga., 6th-7th congresses, 1799-1802 (resigned); judge of superior ct.; trustee Ga. U. Died Wilkes County, Ga., Sept. 3, 1821.

TALIAFERRO, HENRY BECKWITH (tol'i-ver), govt. ofcl.; b. Washington, July 15, 1904; s. Henry Addison and Sarah (Ashlin) T.; B.S., U.S. Naval Acad., 1928; m. Dorothy Tower Butts, June 7, 1928. Served as seaman 2d class to ensign, U.S.N., 1923-30, comdr., 1942-47, ret. as capt., 1947; design and test engr. Gen. Electric Co., 1930-31; staff of v.p. and chief engr. Potomac Electric Power Co., 1931-35; elec. engr. El Segondo and Richmond Refineries, Standard Oil Co. of Cal., 1935-37; elec. engr. constrn. and operation govt. of D.C., 1937-39; elec. engr. substa. and transmission line constrn. Bonneville Power Adminstr., 1939-41, asst. to adminstr., Washington, 1941-42; elec. engr., power mgr. U.S. Bur. Reclamation, Sacramento, 1947-51, asst. dir. power utilization, Washington, 1951-52, dir., 1952-56; dir. of power utilization Power Authority State of N.Y., 1956-—. Decorated Legion of Merit, Commendation Ribbon, Unit Citation, Victory Medal. Registered profl. engr., Cal. Mem. Am. Inst. E.E., C.I.G.R.E. Club: Commonwealth. Home: The Westchester, 4000 Cathedral Av., N.W., Washington. Office: Coliseum Tower, 10 Columbus Circle, N.Y.C. 19. Died Nov. 5, 1958; buried Arlington Nat. Cemetery.

TALIAFERRO, WILLIAM BOOTH army officer; b. Belleville, Gloucester County, Va., Dec. 28, 1822; s. Warner and Frances (Booth) T.; grad. Coll. William and Mary, 1841; studied law Harvard; m. Sally Lyons, 8 children. Capt. 11th U.S. Infantry in Mexico; discharged with rank of maj., 1848; mem. Va. Ho. of Dels., 1850-53; col. Confederate Army, 1861, brig. gen., 1862, led brigade under Jackson throughout Valley campaign; defended Battery Wagner of Morris Island during assault on Charleston Harbor, S.C., July 18, 1863; safeguarded garrison of Savannah in escaping from Sherman, 1864; maj. gen., 1865; mem. Va. Legislature, 1874-79; judge Glouester County (VA.). Ct.: 1891-97; mem. bd. vis coll. Wm. and Mary. Died Durham Massic, VA., Feb. 27, 1898; buried cemetery of Ware church Glouchester Co.

TALLMADGE, BENJAMIN army officer, congressman; b. Brookhaven, N.Y., Feb. 25, 1754; s. Benjamin and Susannah (Smith) T.; grad. Yale, 1773; m. Mary Floyd, Mar. 18, 1784; m. 2d Maria Hallett, May 3, 1808; 7 children including Frederick Augustus. Supt., Wetherfield (Conn.) High Sch., 1773-76; apptd. lt. adj. Conn. Militia, 1776, capt., 1776, maj., 1777, brevetted lt. col., 1873; fought in battles of Brandywine, L.I., Monmouth; captured Ft. George, L.I., N.Y., 1780; officer in charge of taking custody of Maj. John Andre; mem. U.S. Ho. of Reps. (Federalist) from Conn., 7th-14th congresses, 1801-17; mem. Soc. of Cincinnati. Died Litchfield, Conn., Mar. 7, 1835; buried East Cemetery, Litchfield.

TALLMADGE, JAMES JR. congressman; b. Stanford, N.Y., Jan. 20, 1778; s. Col. James and Ann (Southerland) T.; grad. R.I. Coll. (now Brown U.), 1798; m. Laura Tallmadge, Jan. 21, 1810; 2 children including Mary (Tallmadge) Van Rensselaer. Sec. to Gov. Clinton of N.Y., 1798-1800; began practice of law, Poughkeepsie, N.Y., circa 1800; Democrat; commd. brig. gen. N.Y. Militia, 1813, commanded defense of N.Y.C., circa 1814; mem. U.S. Ho. of Reps. from N.Y., 15 Congress, June 6, 1817-19, introduced Tallmadge Amendment to bill regarding admission of Mo. to statehood designed to prohibit further introduction of slaves into Mo., 1819 (bill defeated in Ho. of Reps.), del. N.Y. Constl. Conv., 1821, 46; mem. N.Y. State Legislature, 1824; lt. gov. N.Y., 1824-26; a founder N.Y. U., pres. council, 1834-36; founder Am. Inst. of City of N.Y. (for promotion of useful arts), pres., 1837-53; while in Europe obtained removal of some quarantine restrictions which hampered U.S. trade with No. Europe, 1838. Died N.Y.C., Sept. 29, 1853; buried Marble Cemetery, N.Y.C.

TALLMAN, PELEG congressman; b. Tiverton, R.I., July 24, 1764; attended pub. schs. Served in Revolutionary War on privateer Trumbull, lost an arm in naval engagement, 1780, captured, imprisoned in Eng. and Ireland, 1781-83; became a mcht. in Bath, Me. (part of Mass. until 1820); mem. U.S. Ho. of Reps.

(Democrat) from Mass., 12th Congress, 1811-13; overseer Bowdoin Coll., Brunswick, Me., 1802-40; mem. Me. Senate, 1821-22. Died Bath, Mar. 12, 1840; buried Maple Grove Cemetery, reinterred Forest Hills Cemetery, Roxbury, Mass.

TAMMANY Indian chief; b. along Delaware River, Buck County, Pa. Chief of Lenni-Lenape (or Delaware) Indians; attended council between Pa. settlers and Indians, 1694, spoke in favor of friendship with settlers; few records exist of his activities; had become a symbol of Am. resistance to Brit. tyranny by advent of Revolutionary War; became symbol of democracy vs. aristocracy after Am. Revolution; named adopted by Soc. of Tammany of N.Y.C. (founded by William Mooney), 1786.

TANGEMAN, WALTER W(ILLIAM) mfg. exec.; b. Cin., Sept. 16, 1891; s. Charles O. and Emma (Hanhart) T.; M.E., U. Cin., 1913; m. Margaret Core, Sept. 18, 1920; children—Donald (dec.), Ellen (Mrs. Halbert Emerson Payne). With Cin. Milling Machine Co., 1913-—, time study engr., 1914-17, plant asst. supt., 1919-20, sales mgr., 1920-34, v.p., gen. mgr., 1934-50, exec. v.p., 1950-56, chmn. bd., 1956-—, also dir.; dir. Buckeye Tool Co. Mem. indsl. research rev. com. Munitions Bd.; Mem. Second Hoover Commn. Pres. Research Found. U. Cin.; chmn. bd. Wilmington Coll.; mem. bd. mgmt. YMCA. Chmn., Cin. Council World Affairs, 1958-—. Pres. bd. Asso. Health Agys. Mem. bd. trustees Community Chest Agys. Maj., U.S. Army, 1917-19. Mem. Nat. Machine Tool Builders Assn. (pres.), Machinery and Allied Products Inst. (exec. com.), Am. Soc. M.E., Internat. Mgmt. Council, Am. Ordnance Assn. Republican. Episcopalian. Clubs: Queen City, Cincinnati Country, Commercial, Commonwealth. Home: 3524 Holly Lane, Cin. 45208. Office: 4701 Marburg Av., Cin. 9. Died Oct. 12, 1966; buried Evergreen Cemetery, Newport, Ky.

TANNER, ADOLPHUS HITCHCOCK congressman, lawyer; b. Granville, N.Y., May 23, 1833; studied law. Admitted to the bar, 1854, began practice law, Whitehall, N.Y.; capt. U.S. Army, 1862, commd. lt. col. 123d Regt., N.Y. Volunteer Inf., served until end of Civil War; mem. U.S. Ho. of Reps. (Republican) from N.Y., 41st Congress, 1869-71. Died Whitehall, Jan. 14, 1882; buried Evergreen Cemetery, Salem, N.Y.

TANNER, FREDERICK CHAUNCEY lawyer; b. Apr. 7, 1878; s. Edward Allan and Marion (Brown) T.; A.B., Ill. Coll., Jacksonville, 1898, LL.D.; LL.B., N.Y. U., 1901; m. Jane Ogden, Nov. 6, 1915; children—Frederick Chauncey, Jane Ogden Trimingham, Edward Ogden. Began practice in N.Y.C., 1901; 1st dep. atty. gen. of N.Y., 1910, in charge N.Y. office; mem. firm Tanner, Sillcocks & Friend; counsel for Union Dime Savs. Bank, Met. Life Ins. Co., Home Life Ins. Co., John Hancock Mut. Life Ins. Co., City Savs. Bank Bklyn. and others; sec., dir. 660 Park Av. Corp.; mem. adv. com. Met. br. Chase Nat. Bank. Chmn. Rep. State Com., N.Y., 1914-17; mem. Constl. Conv., N.Y., 1915; del. 1912, del. at large, 1916, Rep. Nat. Conv. Served as pvt., corpl. and sgt., 23d Reg. Inf., 2d lt. 12th Regt. Inf., 1st lt. and capt. 14th Regt. Inf.—all N.G., N.Y. Mem. Soc. Mayflower Descs., S.R., Order of the Cincinnati, Soc. Colonial Wars, Am., N.Y. State bar assns., Bar Asity N.Y., Phi Beta Kappa, Phi Delta Phi. Clubs: Union, Manhattan, Piping Rock, Southside Sportsmen's. Home: 1 E. 66th St. Office: 1 Madison Av., N.Y.C. Died June 22, 1963.

TANNER, SHELDON C(LARK) economist, educator; b. Farmington, Utah, May 29, 1900; s. Joseph Marion and Annie (Clark) T.; B.S. cum laude, U. Utah, 1923, A.M., 1925; teaching fellow U. Cal., 1925-27; m. Gladys Green, May 17, 1922; 1 dau., Marilyn (Mrs. Don C. Worthington). Instr. bus. U. Utah, 1920-25; legal technician Pa. State Workmen's Compensation Bd., 1931-35; pres. Am. Bus. Law Assn., 1937; cons. Ednl. Policies Commn., N.E.A. and Am. Assn. Sch. Adminstrns., 1938; vis. prof. Utah State Agrl. Coll., 1938; advisor joint commn. on State Govt., Legislature of Pa., 1941; commr. of conciliation U.S. Dept. Labor, 1942-43; spl. examiner, panel chmn. Nat. War Labor Bd., 1942-43; commd. major, spec.-res. AUS, 1943; regional dir. labor A.M.G., Italy, 1943; labor advisor 15th Army Group, chief labor officer, A.M.G., 5th Army, 1944; exec. officer Labor Br., HNSC, 1945; prof. econs. and head div. bus. mgmt. and law Pa. State U., 1927-50, prof. bus. law, 1950-60, prof. emeritus, 1960-—; lectr. bus. law San Diego State Coll., 1960-62; vis. prof. U. Cal. at Los Angeles, 1962-64; artitrator of labor disputes for many indsl. cos. Mem. Nat. Panel Arbitrators, Am. Arbitration Assn., Am., Pacific S.W. (hon. pres. 1962-63) bus. law assns., Am. Assn. U. Profs., Am. Legion, Delta Nu Alpha, Phi Kappa Tau, Phi Kappa Phi, Pi Gamma Mu, Omicron Delta Gamma, Pi Sigma Alpha, Alpha Kappa Psi, Phi Mu Alpha, Kappa Gamma Psi, Phi Chi Theta (hon.), Beta Gamma Sigma. Republican. Mason. Author: Pennsylvania Business Law, under the Uniform Commercial Code, 6th edit., 1958. Contbr. to profl. jours. Home: 12324 Lomica Rd., San Diego 28. Died Oct. 15, 1966; burried Farmington.

TANNER, ZERA LUTHER comdr. U.S.N., retired; b. Warsaw, N.Y., Dec. 5, 1835; s. Zera and Ruth Emeline T.; common school edn.; followed the sea in merchant marine, 1855-62; in vol. navy, 1862-67; after that in regular navy, through grades to comdr., retiring by reason of age, Dec. 5, 1897; cruised in all parts of the world. On leave of absence, 1874-78, comdg. Pacific Mail Steamers Colon and City of Peking; engaged in scientific deep-sea explorations, 1879-94. During Spanish war, 1898, on duty at Navy Dept., Washington, San Francisco and Honolulu; m. Helen Benedict, Nov. 11, 1884. Home: Warsaw, N.Y. Died 1906.

TAPPAN, BENJAMIN naval officer; b. New Orleans, La., Apr. 12, 1856. Apptd. U.S. Naval Acad. from Ark., Sept. 22, 1871, grad. 1876; midshipman, June 21, 1876; promoted through grades to capt., Oct. 30, 1908. Served on Tennessee, 1876-78; Franklin, 1879; Constellation, 1879-81; New Hampshire, 1882-84; Saratoga, 1884-87; Bur. of Navigation, Navy Dept., 1888-91; Newark, 1891-93; Miantonomoh, 1893-94; equipment duty, Navy Yard, New York, 1895-96; Amphitrite, 1896-97; Raleigh, 1897-98; was advanced 5 numbers in rank for eminent and conspicuous conduct in the battle of Manila Bay, May 1, 1898; comd. Callao, 1898-99; charge branch hydrographic office, Baltimore, 1900-01; staff Iowa, 1901-02, New York, 1902; Naval War Coll., 1903; comd. Petrel, 1903-04; Navy Yard, New York, 1904-05; comd. Newport, 1905-06, Tacoma, 1906-09, Indiana, 1909-10; capt. of yard, Navy Yard, Mare Island, Calif., 1910-11; supervisor naval auxiliaries, 1911; comdt. naval sta., Olongapo and Cavite, P.I., Mar. 15, 1913-16; retired with rank of rear admiral, Apr. 26, 1916. Took part in many engagements during insurrection in Philippines; specially commended in dispatches by Rear Admiral Watson for part taken by Callao at capture of Dagupan, Lingayen Gulf, Luzon, in coöperation with forces under Maj. Gen. Wheaton. Active duty World War, as comdt. Naval Sta., Phila., and comdt. 8th Naval Dist., New Orleans; retired Oct. 1, 1919. Died Dec. 18, 1919.

TAPPAN, MASON WEARE congressman, lawyer; b. Newport, N.H., Oct. 20, 1817; attended Hopkinton and Meriden acads.; studied law. Admitted to the bar, 1841, began practice law, Bradford, N.H.; mem. N.H. Ho. of Reps., 1853-55, 60-61; mem. U.S. Ho. of Reps. (Republican) from N.H., 34th-36th congresses, 1855-61; served as col. 1st Regt., N.H. Volunteer Inf., U.S. Army, Civil War; atty. gen. State of N.H., 1876-86. Died Bradford, Oct. 25, 1886; buried Pleasant Hill Cemetery.

TAPPIN, JOHN LINDSLEY Am. ambassador; b. N.Y.C., Jan. 22, 1906; s. Lindsley and Elise Irving (Huntington) T.; grad. St. Mark's Sch., 1924; student Princeton, 1924-28; m. Helena Maria Krazcek, Feb. 15, 1946; 1 dau., Halina Huntington. Engaged in merchandising, selling, pub. relations, N.Y.C., 1928-40; civilian tech. cons. G-3 div. War Dept., 1940-42; asst. to under sec. commerce, 1947-48; spl. asst. to dep. U.S. spl. rep. in Europe, ECA, 1948-50, spl. asst. to dep. adminstr. in Washington, 1950-52; dir. fgn. origins div. Nat. Citizens for Eisenhower-Nixon Hdqrs., also cons. personal staff Pres.-Elect Eisenhower, 1952-53; cons. to sec. of state, also spl. asst. to under sec. of state for adminstrn., 1953-54; U.S. ambassador to Libya, 1954-—. Served from capt. to col. AUS, 1942-47, ETO; col. Res. Decorated Legion of Merit, Army Commendation Ribbon (U.S.); Order of Brit. Empire; Legion of Honor, Croix de Guerre with palm (France); Comdr.'s Cross Order of Palonia Restituta; Comdr. Crown of Italy; Czechoslovak War Cross; Brazilian Medalha da Guerra. Mem. Soc. Colonial Wars, U.S. Squash Racquets Assn. (exec. com.). Republican. Episcopalian. Clubs: Princeton (N.Y.C., Washington); University (Washington). Home: Washington 16. Office: Am. Embassy, Tripoli, Libya. Died Dec. 1964.

TARACOUZIO (TARACOUS-TARACOUZIO), TIMOTHY ANDREW (tä-rä-koo'ze-o), educator, author; b. Reval, Russia, Jan. 11, 1897; s. Andrei Ivanovich and Varvara Timofeevna (Alekseev) T.; student law shc., U. of St. Petersburg, 1914; grad. Aviation School, Gatchina, Russia, 1916; M.A., Univ. of Southern Calif., 1927; M.A., Harvard, 1928, Ph.D., 1935; m. Evlin Shaw Coleman, Oct. 14, 1933; 1 son, Lon Anthony. Came to U.S., 1923; naturalized, 1929. Successively manual laborer, bank clerk and translator, 1923-27; bibliog. research asst. and in charge Slavic Dept., Harvard Law Library, 1928-42; lecturer on comparative Law, Harvard Law Sch., 1930-31; mem. Bur. Internat. Research, Harvard Univ. and Radcliffe Coll. 1929-42; with U.S. Govt. in wartime gencies, 1942-1943; capt., to lt. col. A.U.S.; overseas, 1943-46; faculty, Nat. War Coll., 1946-47; asso. prof. U.S. Navy Intelligence Sch., 1947, ret. now professor law U. of Florida, 1956-—. Received commn. from Artillery Acad. of Grand Duke Constantin, 1915; grad. Officer's Aviation Sch., 1916; served throughout World War, 1914-17, and Civil War, Russia, 1918-22, successively in arty., air service and Navy, advancing to rank of capt. in the Army. Decorated Order of St. Stanislav (3d and 2d class), Order of St. Anne (4th, 3d and 2d class), Order of St. Validimir (4th class). Mem. American Soc. Internat. Law. Mem. Russian Orthodox. Author: The Soviet Union and International Law, 1935; Soviets in the Arctic, 1938; War and Peace in Soviet Diplomacy, 1940; also articles. Address: Passa-Grill, Fla. Died Mar. 4, 1958.

TARBELL, JOSEPH naval officer; b. Mass., circa 1780; m. Eliza Cassin, 1808, 2 children. Apptd. midshipman U.S. Navy, 1798, lt., 1800; master Washington (D.C.) Navy Yard; 1806; mem. ct. which tried Capt. James Barron after Chesapeake-Leopard affair, 1808; promoted master-comdr., 1808; comdr. ship Siren, 1810-11, enforced embargo, Charleston, S.C., suppressed slave trade at New Orleans; commanded ship Constellation, later gunboat flotilla, Norfolk, Va., during War of 1812; commd. capt., 1813. Died Washington, D.C., Nov. 25, 1815.

TARKINGTON, JOHN STEVENSON lawyer; b. Centreville, Ind., June 24, 1832; s. Rev. Joseph and Maria (Slauson) T.; A.B., Asbury (now De Pauw) U., Greencastle, Ind., 1852, A.M., 1855; m. Elizabeth Booth, Nov. 19, 1857 (died 1909) m. 2d, Linda H. Schulz, Sept. 10, 1910; father of (Newton) Booth T. In law practice at Indianapolis, 1855-—; mem. Ind. Ho. of Rep., 1863; capt. Co. A, 132d Ind. Inf., 1864; judge 7th Jud. Circuit, Ind., 1870-72. Republican. Methodist. Author: The Hermit of Capri, 1910; Auto-Orphan, 1913. Home: Indianapolis, Ind. Died Jan. 30, 1923.

TARR, FREDERICK COURTNEY educator; b. Balt., May 6, 1896; s. Adam Shoop and Anne (Courtney) T.; student Baltimore City Coll., 1908-11; A.B., Johns Hopkins, 1915, A.M., 1917; Ph.D., Princeton U., 1921; m. Martha Louise Slocomb, Sept. 22, 1917 (div. May 1934); 1 dau., Martha Madeline; m. 2d, Sofía de Yturriaga y Manzano, July 28, 1934. Instr. in Spanish, Princeton U., 1920-22, asst. prof., 1922-28, asso. prof., 1928-37, Emory L. Ford prof. of Spanish, 1937-—; vis. prof. Spanish, U. of N.M., 1938. Served from pvt. to capt., U.S. Army, 1917-19. Mem. Modern Lang. Assn. America, Am. Assn. Univ. Profs., Am. Assn. Teachers of Spanish. Awarded John Simon Guggenheim fellowship, 1929-30. Decorated Caballero de la Orden de Isabel la Católica, 1934. Democrat. Asso. editor Hispanic Review. Author: Prepositional Complementary Clauses in Spanish, 1922; A First Spanish Grammar (with C. C. Marden), 1926; A Graded Spanish Review Grammar (with Augusto Conteno), 1933; Impresiones de Espana, 1933; Shorter Spanish Review Grammar, 1937; Romanticism in Spain and Spanish Romanticism, 1939. Contbr. to learned mags. of U.S. and abroad. Home: 1 College Rd., Princeton, N.J. Deceased.

TARRANT, WILLIAM THEODORE, naval officer (ret.); b. Black Hawk, Miss., July 28, 1878; s. Edward William and Anne Wilson (Spencer) T.; ed., U.S Naval Acad., 1898; m. Ruth Gibson, June 13, 1906. Commd. ensign U.S. Navy, 1900 and advanced through grades to vice adm., 1936; comdt. 11th Naval Dist., 1933-36; comdr. scouting force, U.S. Fleet, 1936-38; comdt. 1st Naval Dist., 1938-42; ret., 1942, recalled to active duty, 1943-46. Episcopalian. Club: Army Navy (Washington). Home: Washington DC Died Aug. 2, 1972.

TARSNEY, JOHN C. asso. justice supreme court Oklahoma since 1896; b. Lenawee Co., Mich., Nov. 7, 1845; served in Union army; studied law; settled in practice, Kansas City, Mo.; city atty., 1874-75; member Congress, 1889-96; Democrat. Address: Guthrie, Okla.

TATE, ROBERT steamship co. exec.; b. E. Orange, N.J., May 6, 1911; s. Cecil W. and Laura (Bromell) T.; B.S., Mass. Inst. Tech., 1932; m. Charlotte Busby, Dec. 28, 1940; children—Robert Bruce, Stephen. Engr., Isthmian Steamship Co., N.Y.C., 1932-38; surveyor Am. Bur. Shipping, N.Y.C., 1939; with Matson Navigation Co., San Francisco, 1940-41, 45-62, v.p., 1959-62; prodn. mgr. advanced marine systems orgn. The Boeing Co., Seattle, 1962-—; v.p. Oceanic Steamship Co., 1959-—. Served to comdr. USNR, 1941-45. Decorated Bronze Star. Mem. Soc. Naval Architects and Marine Engrs. (v.p.). Home: 10451 Kenbar Rd., Los Altos, Cal. Office: 215 Market St., San Francisco 5, Cal. Died Oct. 18, 1962; buried Nat. Cemetery, San Bruno, Cal.

TATSCH, J(ACOB) HUGO Masonic author; b. Milwaukee, Wis., Jan. 29, 1888; s. Jacob and Louise Hedwig (Hartmann) T.; student George Washington U., 1923-24; grad. Army Finance Sch., Washington, D.C., 1924; student Coe Coll., Cedar Rapids, Ia., 1925-27; grad. Command and Gen. Staff Sch., U.S.A., 1929; D.Litt., Theosophical U., Pt. Loma, Calif., 1929; M.A., Atlantic U., Virginia Beach, Va., 1933; m. Harriet Hughes, Oct. 3, 1928. With Old National Bank, Spokane, Wash., 1905-19; in foreign depts., Chem. Nat. Bank, N.Y. City and 1st Nat. Bank, Boston, Mass., 1919; asst. cashier Union Bank & Trust Co., Los Angeles, Calif., 1921-22; asst. sec. and asst. editor Nat. Masonic Research Soc., Cedar Rapids, 1923; with Masonic Service Assn. of U.S., Washington, D.C., 1923-24; curator Ia. Masonic Library, Cedar Rapids, and asso. editor Grand Lodge Bulletin (Iowa), 1925-29; v.p. Macoy Pub. Co., New York, 1927-34; pres. Glastonbury Press, Brookline, Mass.; sec., treas. Ednl. Research Associates, Inc., Washington, D.C.; acting librarian, curator, Library Grand Lodge A.F.&A.M., Mass. and Supreme Council, 33 deg., N.M.J., Boston. Capt. N.G., Washington, 1917-18; spl. agt. Mil. Intelligence Div., U.S.A., 1918; capt. finance dept. O.R.C., 1924; maj., 1929. lt. col., 1935; Ia. member 7th Corps Area Advisory Board, U.S.A., 1927-28. Fellow

Nat. Masonic Research Soc. Mason, mem. various Am. and foreign Masonic socs.; awarded European decorations and diploma for Masonic bibliog. and ednl. services. Author: Short Readings in Masonic History, 1926 (Spanish and Russian translations); High Lights of Crescent History, 1926; (with Winward Prescott) Masonic Bookplates, 1928; Freemasonry in the Thirteen Colonies, 1929; A Reader's Guide to Masonic Literature, 1929; The Facts About George Washington as a Freemason, 1931; Lodge Officers' Speech Book, 1934; Books on Freemasonry, 1935; (with Harry Smith) Moses Michael Hays; John James Joseph Gourgas, 1938; (with M. A. Davis) List of Masonic Subject Headings, 1937. Home: Brookline, Mass. Died July 17, 1939.

TATTNALL, JOSIAH senator, gov. Ga.; b. Bonaventure, nr. Savannah, Ga., 1764; attended Eaton Coll., Eng. Served under Gen. Anthony Wayne in Continental Army, 1782; col. regt. Ga. Militia (organized to protect state against Indians), 1793, promoted brig. gen., 1801; mem. Ga. Ho. of Reps., 1795-96; mem. U.S. Senate (filled vacancy) from Ga., Feb. 20, 1796-99; gov. State of Ga., 1801-02 (resigned). Died Nassau, New Providence, B.W.I., June 6, 1803; buried Bonaventure Cemetery, Savannah.

TATTNALL, JOSIAH naval officer; b. "Bonaventure" nr. Savannah, Ga., Nov. 9, 1795; s. Josiah and Harriet (Fenwick) T.; m. Harriette Fenwick Jackson, Sept. 6, 1821, at least 3 children. Apptd. midshipman U.S. Navy, 1812, took part in War of 1812; engaged against Algierian pirates, 1815; promoted lt., 1818; served in Mediterranean and Caribbean against West Indian pirates, 1823-31; comdt. Boston Navy Yard, 1838-40; served in African Squadron, 1843-44; promoted capt., 1850; served in Pacific Squadron, 1854-55, comdr. East India Squadron, 1857-60; commd. sr. flag officer Ga. Navy, 1861; engaged in coastal defense for Confederate Navy; burned iron-clad Merrimac to prevent her capture when Norfolk (Va.) Naval Yard was captured by Union Navy; in charge of Ga. Naval Defenses, 1863-65; resided in Halifax, N.S., Can., 1866-70; insp. Port of Savannah, 1870-71. Died June 14, 1871.

TAUSSIG, EDWARD DAVID rear adm. U.S.N.; b. St. Louis, Nov. 20, 1847; s. Charles and Anna (Abeles) T.; grad. U.S. Naval Acad., 1867; m. Ellen Knefler, Nov. 9, 1873. Ensign, Dec., 1868; promoted through grades to rear adm., May 15, 1908. Commended to dept. by Comdr. Gillis for services during the earthquake at Arica, Aug. 13, 1868. Served on the European and Pacific stations and in the coast survey; comd. the Bennington, Aug., 1898-Aug. 1899; took possession of Wake Island for the U.S. and took charge of Guam on Feb. 1, 1899; served in the Philippines and during the summer of 1900 in North China; comd. Yorktown, June 1900, to June 1901; at Navy Yard, Washington, Nov. 1901, to Jan. 1902, Navy Yard, Boston, to May 1902; comd. Enterprise, May 1902, to Oct. 27, 1902. Navy Yard, Pensacola, Jan.-Oct. 1903; comd. Independence, Oct. 1903-Oct. 1904; comdg. battleship Massachusetts, Nov. 1, 1904; transferred to battleship Indiana, Jan. 6, 1906, Navy Yard, New York, Mar. 15, 1907; comdt. Navy Yard, Norfolk, Va., Dec. 1907; retired, Nov. 20, 1909. Home: Jamestown, R.I. Died Jan. 29, 1921.

TAUSSIG, JOSEPH KNEFLER (taw'sig), naval officer; b. of Am. parentage, Dresden, Germany, Aug. 30, 1877; s. Edward David and Ellen (Knefler) T.; grad. Western High Sch., Washington, D.C., 1895; B.S., U.S. Naval Acad., 1899; grad. Naval War Coll., 1920; m. Lulie Augusta Johnston, Oct. 18, 1911; children—Emily Johnston (Mrs. Henry Wadsworth Whitney), Margaret Stewart (Mrs. George Philip), Joseph Knefler. Commd. ensign in U.S. Navy, Jan. 29, 1901; promoted through grades to rear admiral, July 1, 1931; assistant chief of naval operations, 1933-36; commandant, 5th Naval District and Naval Operating Base, Norfolk, Va., 1938-41; retired as vice admiral Sept. 1, 1941. Participated in Spanish-American War, Philippine Insurrection, Boxer Campaign, Cuban Pacification, World War I, Nicaraguan Campaign of 1927. Recalled to active duty, June 1943; Office of Secretary of Navy, Navy Department, 1945. Chairman Hampton Roads Sanitation Commission. Was awarded Distinguished Service Medal (United States); Sampson medal (Spanish-American War); Life Saving Medal of Honor; Order of Saint Michael and Saint George (England); Order of Merit First Class (Chile); Naval Institute gold medal, 1939; advanced "for eminent and conspicuous conduct in battle," Boxer Campaign, 1900. Unitarian. Clubs: Army and Navy (Washington); Rotary International; New York Yacht; University (Phila.); Wardroom (Boston). Home: Washington, D.C., and Jamestown, R.I. Died Oct. 29, 1947.

TAVENNER, FRANK STACY JR. lawyer; b. Woodstock, Va., July 12, 1895; s. Frank Stacy and Lou Lazear (Stephenson) T.; A.B., Roanoke Coll., Salem, Va., 1916; A.M., Princeton, 1917; LL.B., U. Va., 1922; m. Sarah Ellen Zea, Dec. 28, 1920; children—Hariett Stephenson, Frank Stacy, III. Admitted to Va. bar, 1922, and began practice, Woodstock; asst. U.S. atty. for Western Dist. of Va., 1933-40, U.S. atty., 1940-48; became acting chief of counsel Internat. Prosecution Sect., Tokyo, in trial of maj. war criminals, 1947; chief counsel Ho. of Reps. com. on un-Am. activities. Mem. Va. Law Rev. Bd. Served as 1st lt. Pioneer Inf., U.S. Army, at Aisne-Marne, Oise-Aisne, and Meuse-Argonne offensives in World War I and with Army of Occupation in Germany. Trustee Roanoke Coll., Salem, Va. Mem. Am., Va. bar assns., Am. Legion, V.F.W., Sigma Upsilon, Phi Alpha Delta. Democrat. Presbyn. (elder). Mason, K.P. Club: Rotary (Woodstock). Address: Woodstock, Va. 22664. Died Oct. 21, 1964.

TAWRESEY, JOHN GODWIN (taw're-se), naval officer; b. Odessa, New Castle County, Del., Jan. 23, 1962; s. Joseph Squires and Mary Jane (Rust) T.; grad. U.S. Naval Acad., 1885; student Royal Naval Coll., Greenwich, Eng., 1888-90; m. Edith Jane Haken, Apr. 3, 1892; children—Alfred Purl Haken, John Squires, Harold R., Edith Virginia (Mrs. Alexander Whitney), Mary Constance (Mrs. John Stuart Milne II), Barrett Godwin. Began as cadet engr., 1881; naval cadet, 1883-87; commd. ensign, 1887; became asst. naval constructor, 1889; commd. comdr., Construction Corps, U.S. Navy, 1901, capt., 1917, rear admiral, 1925; retired since 1926. Del. Internat. Conf. of Safety of Life at Sea, London, Eng., 1929, Internat. Conf. on Load Lines, London, 1930. Mem. Soc. Naval Architects and Marine Engrs., Instn. of Naval Architects (London), Am. Soc. of Naval Engrs., U.S. Naval Inst., Franklin Inst. Baptist. Clubs: Army and Navy (Washington); Engineers (Phila.). Address: 514 Cheltena Av., Jenkintown, Pa. Died Feb. 17, 1943.

TAYLOR, ALBERT HOYT physicist, radio engr.; b. Chgo., Jan. 1, 1879; s. Albert H. and Harriet (Getschell) T.; B.S., Northwestern U., 1902; Ph.D., Goettingen U., Germany, 1909; D.Sc. (hon.), U. N.D., 1953; m. Sarah E. Hickman, Aug. 9, 1911; children—Albert H., Barbara M., Harriet, Margaret A. Instr., later asst. prof. physics U. Wis., 1903-08; prof., head physics dept. U. N.D., 1909-17; commd. lt. USNR, 1917, advanced through grades to comdr., 1922, supt. radio div. naval research lab., 1923-45, pioneer research in devel. radar, ret. 1948. Awarded medal of honor by I.R.E., 1941, John Scot medal and premium, 1942, medal for merit by U.S. Pres., 1944. Fellow I.R.E. (pres.), Am. Phys. Soc., A.A.A.S., Am. Inst. E.E.; mem. Naval Inst., Sigma Xi. Club: University. Home: 691 W. 12th St., Claremont, Cal. Died Dec. 11, 1961; buried Arlington Nat. Cemetery, Washington.

TAYLOR, ASHER CLAYTON brig. gen. U.S.A.; b. Fredonia, N.Y., Feb. 21, 1842; s. Joel and Almira (Parrish) T.; ed. Hillsdale Coll., Mich., 1865-66, Ripon Coll., Wis., 1866-67; m. Mary J. Branigan, Oct. 30, 1872. Corporal and sergt. Co. D and sergt. maj. 3d Wis. Inf., Apr. 25, 1861-Oct. 28, 1864; 1st lt. and adj. 3d Wis. Vet. Inf., Oct. 29, 1864; hon. mus. lt. 15th U.S. Inf., Oct. 16, 1867; 1st lt., Aug. 25, 1868; assigned to 2d Arty., Jan. 1, 1871; grad. Arty. Sch., 1876; capt., Jan. 20, 1889; maj. 4th Arty., June 18, 1900; lt. col. arty. corps, Feb. 21, 1902; col., Aug. 10, 1903; brig. gen., Jan. 21, 1904; retired at own request after 40 yrs. service, Jan. 22, 1904. Participated with regt. in capture of the secession legislature of Maryland, Sept. 17, 1861, thereby saving the state to the Union; served in Army of the Potomac, 1861-63, Army of Cumberland, 1863-64; participated in campaigns to Atlanta, Savannah, and from Savannah to Washington, under Gen. Sherman; battles of Winchester, Va., Cedar Mountain, Antietam, Chancellorsville, Gettysburg, Resaca, Dallas, Kenesaw Mountain, Peach Tree Creek; siege and capture of Atlanta, of Savannah, battles of Averysboro, N.C., Bentonville; in campaign from Goldsboro, N.C., to Raleigh, N.C., etc. On reconstruction duty in Ala. and Tex., 1867-69; at Sitka, Alaska, 1871-72; with army of occupation at Havana, 1899-1900, comdg. guard in charge of governor's palace, Jan.-May 1899. Distinguished marksman U.S.A., 1886-—. Republican. Home: Cottonwood, Calif. Died Jan. 20, 1922.

TAYLOR, CHARLES WILLIAM state supt. schs.; b. Red Oak, Ia., June 3, 1874; s. James Henry and Tamar Anne (Ratliff). T.; A.B., U. of Neb., 1898; grad. study same and Columbia; m. Sarah Elizabeth Wert Smith, July 3, 1899; children—Seth Charles Henry, John William, Beth Elaine, Marie Provo (dec.), Hutch Nordel (dec.), James (dec.). Teacher, W. Riverside Rural Sch., Montgomery County, Ia., 1893-94; supt. schs., Ohiowa, Neb., 1898-1901, Geneva, Neb., 1901-07; sec., treas. and mgr. S. R. Smith Furniture Co., Lead, 1907-08; supt. city schs., McCook, Neb., 1908-11; prof. sch. adminstrn., dir. teacher training and prin. Teachers Coll. High Sch., U. of Neb., 1911-27; state supt. pub. instrn., Neb., since 1927. Mem. Ia. Nat. Guard, 1893-96, 2d lt., 1902-03; mem. U. of Neb. cadets, 1894-98; served as capt., inf., later machine gun officer, U.S. Army, 1917-18; capt., inf., O.R.C. Chmn. advisory bd. Salvation Army, Lincoln. Mem. Neb. State Library Commn.; sec. Neb. State Bd. Vocational Edn.; former sec. Neb. State Illiteracy Commn.; now chmn. State Bd. Advisory Com. on Illiteracy; mem. Bd. of Edn. of State Normal Schs.; under constl. amendment, 1940, a member of Board of Educational Lands and Funds; mem. Bishop Clarkson Memorial Hosp. Assn. Life mem. N.E.A. (state chmn. rural life com.); mem. Am. Assn. Univ. Profs., Neb. Ednl. Assn., Neb. State Teachers Assn. (ex-v.p.), Nat. Inst. on Mercenary Crime (dir.), Lincoln Chamber Commerce, Neb. School Master's Club, Sons of the Am. Revolution (state pres.), Sons of Vets. Civil War, Am. Legion (state comdr. 1924), Res. Officers Assn., Phi Delta Kappa, Acacia. Republican. Episcopalian. Mason; mem. O.E.S., Royal Neighbors America. Clubs: Lincoln Auto, Knife and Fork, Lincoln University. Home: 2127 Harwood St. Office: State Capitol Bldg., Lincoln, Neb. Died Jan. 21, 1943.

TAYLOR, DAVID WATSON naval constructor; b. Louisa Co., Va., Mar. 4, 1864; s. Henry and Mary Minor (Watson) T.; Randolph-Macon Coll., Va., 1877-81; grad. U.S. Naval Acad., 1885, head of class and excelled highest record ever made there up to that time; sent to Greenwich in 1885, received highest honors of Royal Coll., 1888, again making the highest record of any student there up to that time; hon. D.Engring., Stevens Inst., Hoboken, N.J., 1907; D.Sc., George Washington U., 1915; LL.D., Randolph-Macon Coll., 1922, U. of Glasgow, Scotland, 1924; m. Imogene Maury Morris, Oct. 26, 1892; children—Dorothy Watson, May Coleman, David Watson, Imogene Morris. Capt. U.S.N., Mar. 4, 1901; promoted to rank of rear admiral, 1917. Awarded gold medal by British Instn. Naval Architects, for best original paper on Ship-Shaped Stream Forms (first American so honored). In 1899 constructed (and had charge of) first experimental tank ever built in U.S. Retained by British Govt. as expert in suit growing out of Hawke-Olympic collision, 1911. Chief constructor U.S.N. and chief of Bur. of Constrn. and Repair, Navy Dept., 1914-22; retired, Jan. 15, 1923; awarded D.S.M. (U.S.); Comdr. Legion of Honor (France). Vice chmn. Nat. Advisory Com. for Aeronautics; mem. Soc. Naval Architects and Marine Engrs. (pres. 1925-27), (British) Instn. of Naval Architects (hon. v.p. 1931). John Fritz Medalist, 1931; gold medalist (British) North East Coast Instn. of Engrs. and Shipbuilders, 1931. Awarded 1st David Watson Taylor Gold Medal (established in his honor) by Soc. Naval Architects and Marine Engrs., 1936; new U.S. David Watson Taylor Model Basin named in his honor, 1937. Author: Resistance of Ships and Screw Propulsion, 1893; Speed and Power of Ships, 1910. Home: Waldrop, Va. Died July 28, 1940.

TAYLOR, EDWY LYCURGUS pub. utilities; b. Albany, N.Y., Sept. 8, 1879; s. Edwy Lycurgus and Elizabeth Ellison (Taylor) T.; Ph.B., Yale 1901, C.E., 1904; m. Helen Very Curtis, Dec. 9, 1911; children—John, William Curtis, Helen Angeline. Asst. instr. Yale, 1901-03, instr., 1904-06; asst. prof., U. of Kan., 1903-04; with engring. dept. N.Y., N.H.,&H. R.R., 1906; with N.Y.C. R.R., 1906-12, maintenance of way dept., 1906-08, asst. engr. electric div., 1908-11, asst. engr. in office of designing engr., 1911-12; with N.Y.,N.H.&H. R.R., 1912-18, 1919-30, asst. engr. 1912-14, contract agt., 1914-18, 1919-25, asst. to v.p., 1925-29, asst. to exec. v.p., 1929-30; asst. to treas. Conn. Savings Bank, New Haven, Jan.-May 1931; mem. Conn. Pub. Utilities Commn., 1931-41, chmn., 1934, 35 and 38; corporator Conn. Savings Bank. Trustees for Receiving Donations for Support of the Bishop of Conn.; col. on Governor's staff, 1931-38. Served as 1st lt. engrs., U.S. Army, with A.E.F., 1918-19; capt. Engrs. Res. Corps, 1920-24, maj., 1924-39, lt. col. since 1939. Mem. Soc. Am. Mil. Engrs., Am. Soc. Civil Engrs., Conn. Sect. Am. Soc. Civil Engrs., Conn. Soc. Civil Engrs. (hon.), Am. Legion, Mil. Order of the World War, Res. Officers Assn., Nat. Assn. of R.R. and Utilities Commrs., Am. Ry. Engring. Assn., Am. Water Works Assn., Am. Gas Assn., New England Regional Planning Commn. (advisory com.), New Haven Colony Hist. Soc., Sigma Xi, Berzelius Soc. (Yale). Democrat. Episcopalian (warden). Clubs: New Haven Lawn, Graduate (New Haven); Yale (N.Y. City); Hartford (Hartford); Army and Navy (Washington, D.C.); Camden Yacht, Megunticook Golf (Camden, Me.). Home: 165 Everit St., New Haven, Conn. Deceased.

TAYLOR, F.W. HOWARD physician, lawyer; author; b. Chicago, Ill., Mar. 14, 1891; s. Frank Wing and Minnie (Cray) T.; student University of Calif., 1910-13; M.D., University of Southern California, 1917; law study, University of Southern California, 1927-31, LL.B.; m. Helen Irene Clark, Sept. 18, 1916; 1 son, Howard Clark; m. 2d, A. Verna Nelson, August 12, 1925; children—Robert Nelson, Verna Belle. Began practice at Los Angeles, 1917; roentgenologist, Clara Barton, French, Angelus, Roosevelt hosps., Pottenger Sanatorium, U.S. Vets. Bur., 1919-29; instr. in x-ray and electrotherapy, U. of Southern Calif., 1919-20; became dir. Coop. Diagnostic Labs., Los Angeles, 1928; vice-pres. Taylor Holding & Investment Corp. Instr. in mil. x-ray and chief roentgenologist, Med. corps, U.S. Army, later lt. comdr., Navy Res., World War. Mem. A.M.A. (adviser to council on hosps. and edn.), Med. Soc. State of Calif., Los Angeles County Med. Society, Am. Radiological Soc., Phi Kappa Sigma, Phi Rho Sigma. Republican. Episcopalian. Clubs: California Yacht, Deauville Beach, Swimming, Fox Hills Country. Author: Lawyers Text and Atlas of the Human Body. Contbr. to med. and legal journals. First research in use of x-ray in whooping cough. Admitted to practice of law; now medico-legal consultant and medical X-ray consultant. Home: 10393 Ilona Av. Office: 1709 W. 8th St., Los Angeles, Calif. Died July 2, 1943.

TAYLOR, FRANK brigadier gen. U.S.A.; b. Calais, France, Apr. 29, 1842; ed. in France and England. Served as pvt. and sergt. gen. service, Oct. 24, 1860-Apr. 1, 1863; apptd. from Iowa, 2d lt. 2d U.S. Inf., Oct. 29, 1867; assigned to 14th Inf., July 31, 1869; 1st lt., Feb. 25, 1876; capt., Mar. 23, 1892; transferred to 8th Inf., Apr. 17, 1900; maj. 15th Inf., Oct. 9, 1900; lt. col.

19th Inf., Aug. 13, 1903; brig. gen., Apr. 9, 1905; retired at own request, Apr. 10, 1905. Served in Civil War, Indian campaigns, and in P.I. Home: Seattle, Wash. Died May 20, 1920.

TAYLOR, HARRY army officer; b. Tilton, N.H., June 26, 1862; s. John Franklin and Lydia T.; grad. U.S. Mil. Acad., 1884, Engr. Sch. of Application, 1887; m. Adele Austin Yates, Oct. 30, 1901. Commd. 2d lt. engrs., June 15, 1884; promoted through grades to maj. gen., June 19, 1924. Engr. duties on Columbia River, and river and harbor works in Ore. and Wash., 1891-96, in charge defense works, Puget Sound, Wash., 1896-1900; in Philippines, 1903; comd. 3d Batln. Engrs., in P.I., 1904; engr. officer Dept. of Luzon, 1903-04; fortification constrn., 1904-05; in charge defenses of eastern entrance L.I. Sound and various improvements, 1906-11; asst. to chief of engrs., War Dept., 1911-16; in charge river and harbor works New York Harbor, Hudson River and Lake Champlain, dept. engr. Eastern Dept., Governors Island, 1916-17; chief engr. A.E.F. in France, May 1917-Sept. 1918; apptd. asst. chief of engrs. U.S.A., Sept. 1918, and chief of engrs., June 1924; retired 1926. Awarded D.S.M. (U.S.); Comdr. Legion of Honor (French). Episcopalian. Home: Washington, D.C. Died Jan. 28, 1930.

TAYLOR, HENRY CLAY rear admiral U.S.N.; b. Washington, Mar. 4, 1O45; apptd. from Ohio, Sept. 20, 1860; Naval Acad., 1863; promoted ensign May 28, 1863; served in Civil war on board the Shenandoah in the actions off Wilmington, 1863, and spring of 1864; then in Iroquois to relieve the Kearsarge in the English Channel; thence searching for Confederate cruisers in E. Indies. Promoted master, Nov. 10, 1865; lt., Nov. 10, 1866; lt. comdr., Mar. 12, 1868; comdr., Dec. 16, 1879; capt.. Apr. 16, 1894; served on many duties and stas.; was pres. Naval War Coll. Newport, R.I., Nov. 1893, to Dec. 1896; later comd. battleship Indiana, in which he served in operations against Spain, 1898, including the destruction of Cervera's fleet; confirmed by Senate as Chief Bureau of Navigation, Apr. 26, 1902. Died 1904.

TAYLOR, J. GURNEY physician; b. Burlington, N.J., May 23, 1872; s. William Shipley and Julia (Kirkbride) T.; student Haverford Coll.; M.D., U. Pa., 1895; m. Mary Richards; children—Ann Richards, J. Gurney, Jr.; m. 2d, Elizabeth Broughton. Practiced in Phila. 1895-1912, Milwaukee, 1913-—; practice limited to internal medicine and pediatrics; cons. physician Milwaukee Children's Hosp., Columbia Hosp., Johnston Emergency Hosp., all Milwaukee. Served as lt. col., med. reserve, U.S. Army, World War I. Chief med. examiner Wis. subsidiary bd. Nat. Bd. Med. Examiners. Fellow A.C.P.; mem. Am. Assn. Med. Milk Commns. (pres., mem. council), A.M.A., Am. Climatol. and Clin. Assn., Am. Acad. Pediatrics, Nat. Tb Assn. (dir.), Wis. Antituberculosis Assn. (dir.), Phi Gamma Delta, Alpha Mu Pi Omega. Episcopalian. Clubs: University, Rotary (Milwaukee). Home: 925 E. Wells St., Milwaukee 2. Office: 324 E. Wisconsin Av., Milwaukee. Died Nov. 30, 1956.

TAYLOR, JACOB B(ACCHUS) telephone exec.; born Perth Amboy, N.J., Oct. 27, 1898; s. Jacob and Margaret Ellen (Fitzgerald) T.; B.S. in Economics, Wharton Sch., U. of Pa., 1921; M.A., U. of N.D.; D. Bus. Adminstrn. (hon.) Bowling Green State University; married Minnie A. Johnson, June 2, 1922; 1 dau., Sylvia Joan (Mrs. Frederick B. Johnston). Instr., U. of N.D., to asso. prof. accounting, 1921-27; asso. prof. accounting, Ohio State U., 1927-32, chmn. dept., 1930-46, prof. accounting, 1932-57, prof. emeritus, 1957, bus. mgr. 1946-57, v.p., 1948-57, treas. 1953-57; v.p. finance Gen. Telephone Corp., N.Y., 1957-59; exec. v.p. finance General Telephone & Electronics Corporation, General Telephone & Electronics Service Corp., 1959-—; vice president General Telephone Credit Company, Incorporated, N.Y., Associated Telephone and Telegraph Co., N.Y., General Telephone & Electronics Laboratories, Inc.; General Telephone & Electronics, Internat., Inc., dir. Leich Electric Co., Leich Sales Corp., General Telephone Credit Co., Inc., General Telephone Co. of the S.E., Philippine Long Distance Telephone Company, the State Savings Company, Columbus, O., Gen. Telephone & Electronics Labs., Inc., Gen. Telephone Co., Gen. Telephone Co. of Southeast Alaska Telephone Corp., Asso. Telephone and Telegraph Co., Lincoln Nat. Life Ins. Co. of New York. Trustee Teachers Ins. & Annuity Asso. of Am. Dir. liquor control, member Ohio governor's cabinet, 1939-43; lieutenant col., finance dept. Audit Div., Office of Fiscal Dir., Hdqrs. Army Service Forces, chief, cost accounting procedures sect., Jan. 1943-Sept. 1945. C.P.A., N.D., 1925, Ohio, N.Y. Served with A.E.F., Engrs., 1917-19. Distinguished Service Award, O. State U., 1952. Member Am. Inst. Accountants, Am. Accounting Assn. (pres., 1937), Ohio Soc. C.P.A., Central Assn. Coll. and U. Bus. Officers (pres. 1954), Beta Alpha Psi (nat. pres., 1931), Beta Gamma Sigma, Delta Sigma Pi. Mason. Methodist. Republican. Clubs: Ohio Society (N.Y.); Faculty (Columbus, O.); Siwanoy Country (Bronxville, N.Y.). Author (with Miller): Intermediate Accounting, 2d edit., 1937: C.P.A. Problems, 4th edit., 1953: Solutions to C.P.A. Problems, 4th edit., 1953. Home: 201 E. 79th St., N.Y.C. 21. Office: 730 3d Av., N.Y.C. 17. Died Mar. 14, 1962; buried Union Cemetery, Columbus, O.

TAYLOR, JOHN THOMAS army officer; b. Phila., June 3, 1885; s. John Barrett and Agnes Jane Taylor; LL.B., Temple U.; law 1914, U. Pa. and Inns of Court, London, Eng.; m. Louise Elizabeth Catlin, Aug. 23, 1926; children—Stewart Fraser (capt. U.S. Army), John Barrett (read adm. U.S. Navy), Gwendolyn H. (Mrs. Charles Critcher). Admitted to practice at Washington, 1911; dir. nat. legislative com. and legislative counsel Am. Legion since its formation Mar. 15, 1919. Enlisted in U.S. Army, attended O.T.C., commd. 1917; served in 27th and 79th divs., overseas, 17 mos.; participated in Oise-Aisne, Aisne-Marne and Argonne offensives, Verdun defensive; commd. brig. gen. Res.; called to active duty as asst. dir., bur. pub. relations, U.S.A., Sept. 1941; engaged in invasions and campaigns Africa, Italy, France (served with First French Army, made Pvt. First Class, Inf. French Fgn. Legion), returned to U.S., 1944, for duty, Office Chief of Staff. Decorated Officer Crown of Leopold (Belgium); Medaille Verdun (France); Officier Corona di Italia (Italy); Officer Polonia Restituta, Polska Obroncy (Poland); Officier Legion of Honor (France); Chateau Thierry medal; Order of Compassionate Heart (Russia); Bronze Star (U.S.), Liberation of France Medal. Mem. Order Lafayette (v.p.), Am., Fed., D.C. bar assns., Soc. Am. Legion Founders, Am. Legion (cons. nat. legislative com.), Mil. Order of World War, Res. Officers Assn., Armed Forces Chem. Assn., Am. Acad. Polit. and Social Sci., Assn. U.S. Army, Sigma Pi. Mason (32 deg., Shriner). Clubs: Army and Navy, University, Officers (bd. govs.), Racquet, Admirals, Post Mortem, Enquirendo, University of Pennsylvania Alumni, Temple University Alumni (Washington); University of Pennsylvania (N.Y.). Home: 7006 Meadow Lane, Chevy Chase 15, Md. Died May 1965.

TAYLOR, JOHN YEATMAN medical dir. U.S.N.; b. E. Nottingham, Pa., Jan. 21, 1829; s. Job and Susanna (Yeatman) T.; acad. edn.; M.D., Jefferson Med. Coll., Phila., 1852; m. Sabella Barr Bryson, Feb. 6, 1878; father of C. Bryson T. Apptd. asst. surgeon U.S.N., Sept. 26, 1853; passed asst. surgeon, Sept. 26, 1858; surgeon, Aug. 1, 1861; med. insp., June 29, 1872; med. dir., Apr. 20, 1879; retired, Jan. 10, 1891; advanced to rank of rear adm., retired, June 29, 1906, for services during Civil War. Fleet surgeon S. Atlantic sta., 1877-79; in charge Naval Hosp., Washington, 1879-83; Norfolk, Va., 1883-86, New York, 1886-88. Home: Washington, D.C. Died 1911.

TAYLOR, MONTGOMERY MEIGS naval officer; b. Washington, Oct. 13, 1869; grad. U.S. Naval Acad., 1890. Ensign, July 1, 1892; lt. jr. grade, Mar. 3, 1899; promoted through grade to rear adm., Oct. 1, 1922. Served on Olympia, Spanish-Am. War, 1898; comd. Hopkins, 1903-05, 2d Torpedo Flotilla, 1905-06, receiving ship Wabash, 1906-08; exec. officer Salem, 1908-09, Milw., 1909-10; comdg. Petrel, 1910-11; aide to comdt. Navy Yard, N.Y.C., 1911-13; comd. Buffalo, 1913-15, Balt., 1915; at Naval War Coll., Newport, R.I., 1915-16; apptd. comdr. Me., June 27, 1916; comdg. Fla., 1918-19; staff Naval War Coll., 1919-21; assigned comdr. Control Force, 1923; dir. fleet tng., comdr. divs. in Battle Fleet; vice adm. in command Scouting Fleet, 1926-27; dir. War Plans, 1928-29; apptd. comdr. Asiatic Fleet, 1930; ret., Nov. 1, 1933; apptd. temp. mem. Maritime Commn., 1936. Awarded medals—Manila Bay, Spanish-Am. War, Philippine Campaign, Victory, D.S.M. Address: The Highlands, Connecticut Av. and California St. N.W., Washington. Died Oct. 21, 1952.

TAYLOR, NELSON congressman, lawyer; b. South Norwalk, Conn., June 8, 1821; grad. law dept. Harvard, 1860. Served as capt. First Regt., N.Y. Volunteer Inf., U.S. Army, 1846-48, sent to Cal. before outbreak of Mexican War, 1846; remained in Cal., engaged in bus., Stockton; mem. Cal. Senate, 1850-56; elected sheriff San Joaquin County, 1855; moved to N.Y.C.; admitted to bar, practiced law; commd. col. 72d Regt., N.Y. Volunteer Inf., U.S. Army, 1861, in command of troops at Harlem during draft riots in N.Y.C.; brig. gen. Volunteers, 1862, resigned, 1863; resumed practice law, N.Y.C.; mem. U.S. Ho. of Reps. (Dem.) from N.Y., 39th Congress, 1865-67; moved to South Norwalk, 1869, practiced law; city atty., several terms. Died South Norwalk, Jan. 16, 1894; buried Riverside Cemetery.

TAYLOR, OLIVER GUY civil engr.; b. Boone County, Ind., Oct. 28, 1883; s. Charles Andrew and Margaret Ann (Kern) T.; B.S., in C.E., Purdue U., 1909; m. Marjorie Edwina Macdougall, May 15, 1915. Topographer U.S. Geol. Survey, 1909-13, 1914-17, 1919-20; civil engr., Republic of Argentine, 1914; park engr., Yosemite Nat. Park, 1920-30; civil engr. charge engring. Eastern Nat. Park Areas, 1930-37; chief engr. Nat. Park Service, 1937-43, regional dir. 1943-44, supr. concessions, 1944-—. Served as 2d lt., 1st lt. and capt., Engrs., U.S. Army, with A.E.F., 1917-18. Mem. Soc. Civil Engrs. Mason. Club: Cosmos (Washington). Home: 6313 Georgia St., Chevy Chase, Md. Office: National Park Service, Washington 25. Died Aug. 26, 1950; buried Arlington Nat. Cemetery.

TAYLOR, ORVILLE, lawyer; born Sioux City, Iowa, the son of Orville J. and Eleanor Sarah (Harris) T.; U. of Chicago; LL.B., Northwestern University Law Sch., 1908; married Catherine E. Apperson, January 19, 1924. Admitted to Illinois bar, 1908; mem. Taylor, Miller, Magner, Sprowl & Hutchings, Chgo.; special asst. atty. gen. U.S., 1922; asst. sec. Army, Germany, 1948; commr. Ill. State Toll Highway Commn.; dir. N.Y. Central System, United Asbestos Co., Ltd. (Canada). Director LaFayette Fellowship Found., Inc.; pres. Am. Legion Founders Ltd., 1966-67; dir. U.S.O., Chgo., Ch. Fedn. Greater Chgo.; chmn. A. Montgomery Ward Found.; trustee Ill. Inst. of Tech.; trustee and founder "Chicago World's Fair Centennial Celebration"; pres. Chicago Bd. of Edn., 1933; mem. Chicago Plan Commn.; mem. Northwestern U. Assos., Citizens Bd., U. of Chgo. Candidate for Republican nomination for United States senator, 1936. Maj. U.S. Army, overseas with 86th Div., World War I. Recipient Order of Lafayette. Trustee, Am. Legion Americanism Endowment Fund, Little League Foundation. Vice pres. and dir. Alliance Francaise; v.p. and dir. France-America Soc.; co-chmn. (Chicago) Treasury Dept. War Loan Drives, 3-8 inclusive; dir. and v.p., Bill of Rights Commemorative Soc.; mem. Am. Branch of Internat. Law Assn., Am., Ill. State and Chicago bar assns., Assn. Bar N.Y. City, English Speaking Union (v.p., dir.), S.A.R. (v.p., dir.), Chicago Law Inst., Am. Judicature Soc., Legion of Honor, Am. Legion, Society of American Legion Founders, Limited, Navy League U.S. (life), Army, Navy and Air Force Vets. in Can. (life), Comarade de Combat (France), Ill. St. Andrew Soc. (life), Beta Theta Pi, Phi Delta Phi. Republican. Episcopalian. Mason, Elk, Moose. Clubs: Chicago, Legal, Law, Saddle and Cycle, Tavern, Casino, Attic (Chgo.); Bohemian (San Francisco); Metropolitan (N.Y.C.). Home: Chicago IL Died Jan. 19, 1969.

TAYLOR, PAUL BENNETT fgn. service officer; b. Neligh, Neb., Aug. 12, 1905; s. Joseph E. and Anna (Bennett) T.; A.B., Doane Coll., 1927; A.M., Ph.D., Columbia, 1951; exchange fellow U. Kiel (Germany), 1931-32; m. Katrina Van Hook, Mar. 6, 1943; children—Joanna, Marcia, Phyllis. Research asso. Carnegie Endowment for Internat. Peace, 1935-37; mem. research staff Fgn. Policy Assn., 1937-39; instr. govt. and internat. relations Wesleyan U., 1939-41; officer Dept. State, 1941-65, fgn. service officer, 1955-65; adviser U.S. delegation UN Gen. Assembly, 1946-54; officer charge UN Gen. Assembly affairs, 1955; counselor Am. embassy, Addis Ababa, Ethiopia, 1955-58; dir. dept. polit. affairs Nat. War Coll., Washington, 1958-59, 59-60; consul gen. Stuttgart, Germany, 1960-63, Munich, Germany, 1963-65; ret., 1965; dir. Washington office Atlantic Inst., 1965-—. Served to 2d lt. Signal Corps, AUS, 1942-45. Home: 26 Grafton St., Chevy Chase, Md. 20015. Died Feb. 1, 1966.

TAYLOR, RICHARD army officer; b. "Springfield," nr. Louisville, Ky., Jan. 27, 1826; s. Gen. Zachary and Margaret (Mackall) T.; attended Harvard; grad. Yale, 1845; m. Louise Marie Myrthe, Feb. 1851, 5 children. Chmn. com. of fed. relations La. Senate, 1865-61, chmn. com. mil. and naval affairs; col. La. 9th Inf., 1861, apptd. brig. gen. in Valley campaign under Stonewall Jackson, 1861; promoted maj. gen., 1862, assigned command Dist. of West La., at Pleasant Hill and Mansfield (Sabine Crossroads), 1864; promoted lt. gen., 1864, assigned to Dept. East La., Miss., Ala.; surrendered the last Confederate army East of Mississippi River, 1865; trustee Peabody Edn. Fund. Author: Destruction and Reconstruction (his reminiscences), 1879. Died N.Y.C., Apr. 12, 1879.

TAYLOR, VICTOR V. army officer; b. Stockton, Calif., July 24, 1893; s. Robert William and Harriet Frances (Vaughan) T.; B.S., U.S. Mil. Acad., 1915; grad. Command and Gen. Staff Sch., Leavenworth, Kan., 1923, Army War Coll., 1939; m. Dorothy Edith Hossie, Apr. 12, 1924; children—Henry L., Victor Vaughan, Jr., Robert Scott. Commd. 2d lt., 1915, and advanced through the grades to brig. gen. Decorated Mexican Service, and Victory (1 star) medals; European Theater ribbon. Clubs: Army-Navy. Home: 4818 Woodway Lane N.W., Washington. Died Sept. 22, 1944; buried in Arlington National Cemetery.

TAYLOR, WALTER HERRON banker; b. Norfolk, Va., June 13, 1838; s. Walter Herron and Cornelia (Wickham) T.; ed. Norfolk Acad., and Va. Mil. Inst.; m. Elizabeth Selden, d. John L. Saunders, U.S.N., of Norfolk, Apr. 3, 1865. Bank officer, 1856-61; served in C.S.A., 1861-65, on staff Gen. Robert E. Lee, part of time as his a.d.c., and part of time as adj. gen. Army of Northern Va.; present at all gen. engagements of the army under Gen. Lee. Mem. Va. Senate, 1869-73; pres. Marine Bank of Norfolk, 1877-—. Author: Four Years with General Lee, 1877; General Lee, 1861-1865, 1906. Home: Norfolk, Va. Died Mar. 1, 1916.

TAYLOR, WILLIAM ROGERS naval officer; b. Newport, R.I., Nov. 7, 1811; s. William Vigneron and Abby (White) T.; m. Caroline Silliman, Apr. 30, 1840, at least 2 children. Apptd. midshipman U.S. Navy, 1828; aboard Hudson in Brazil station, 1829-32; made lt., 1840; during Mexican War took part in the St. Mary's attack on Tampico, 1846; promoted comdr., 1855; promoted capt. and assigned to steam sloop Housatonic on the Charleston blockade, 1862; was Adm. Dahlgren's fleet capt. during offensive against Morris Island, 1863; commanded ship Juniata during 1st attacks on Fort Fisher, 1864; promoted commodore, 1866, rear adm., 1871; commanded Northern squadron of Pacific Fleet, 1869-71; pres. Naval examining bd., 1871-72; had command South Atlantic sta., 1872-73;

pres. bd. to revise navy regulations, 1866-67. Died Washington, D.C., Apr. 14, 1884; buried Congressional Cemetery, Washington.

TAYLOR, WILLIAM VIGNERON naval officer; b. Newport, R.I., Apr. 11, 1780; s. James and Mary (Vigneron) T.; m. Abby White, Dec. 31, 1810, 7 children including William Rogers and Oliver Hazard Perry. Joined navy at Newport, War of 1812; warranted sailing-master, 1813; in command flagship Lawrence in Battle of Lake Erie, 1813; received thanks of Congress and a sword, 1814; sailed on ship Java to the Mediterranean, 1815; Mediterranean cruise aboard the Ontario, 1824-26; service in Brazil station, 1829-30; had command sloops Erie, Warren, Concord, Columbus in Gulf of Mexico in late 1830's; made capt., 1841; during Mexican War (1847) took warship Ohio around Cape Horn for operations on the Mexican west coast until end of war, 1848; placed on reserved list, 1855. Died Newport, R.I., Feb. 11, 1858; buried Island Cemetery, R.I.

TAYLOR, WILLIS RATCLIFFE army officer; b. Parkersburg, W.Va., Feb. 24, 1897; s. Nathaniel Ratcliffe and Josephine (Golden) T.; student, U. of Calif., 1917; m. Anne Addison, Dec. 18, 1920; children—Addison, Jo Anne. Commd. 2d lt., 1918, and advanced through the grades to brig. gen., 1942; Photographic Sch., 1921; serial survey program, Manila, P.I., 1921-23; mapping of northwest territory in Wash. and Ore., 1923-28; Scott Field, Ill., comd. photographic section, 1928-31; comdr. Observation Squadron, Mitchel Field, 1931-34; comdg. officer, Bombardment Squadron, Panama, 1934-37; served on boundary settlement comm. to Guatemala, Honduras and Salvador; comd. 27th Pursuit Squadron, Selfridge Field, Mich., 1937-39; with R.A.F., in England and Scotland, 1939-40; exec. officer, 2d Interceptor Comd., Seattle, Wash., 1941-42; organized Fighter Comd. Sch., Orlando, Fla., 1942; comd. I Fighter command, Mitchel Field, since 1942. Address: Mitchel Field, Hempstead, L.I., N.Y. Died June 14, 1945.

TAYLOR, ZACHARY 12th Pres. U.S., army officer; b. Montebello, Va., Nov. 24, 1784; s. Richard and Mary (Strother) T.; m. Margaret Mackall Smith, June 18, 1810, 6 children including Ann Mackall, Sarah Knox, Mary Elizabeth, Richard Taylor. Commd. 1st lt. 7th Inf., U.S. Army, 1808; served as capt., Ft. Knox, Ky., 1810; defended Ft. Harrison against Indian attack, 1812, brevetted maj.; in command of Ft. Knox, 1814-15; commd. lt. col. 4th Inf., New Orleans, 1819; built Ft. Jessup on La. frontier, 1822; Indian supt. at Ft. Snelling, 1829-32; col. in charge of 1st Regt., Ft. Crawford, 1832; led troops in Black Hawk War, 1838, brevetted brig. gen., received nickname "Old Rough and Ready;" in command of army in Tex., 1845; ordered to march to Rio Grande, 1846, victorious at battles of Palo Alto (defeated force 3 times his own) and Resaca de la Palma, 1846; brevetted maj. gen., 1846; captured at Monterey, Mexico, 1846; defeated Mexicans at Battle of Buena Vista, 1847; Whig; in "Allison" letters, 1848, stated his polit. views: that executive should be coordinate branch of govt., veto used sparingly, Wilmot Proviso was insignificant and that he would be "untrammeled by party schemes"; Whig candidate for U.S. Pres., elected Nov. 1848; gave inaugural address, Mar. 5, 1849, promised honesty and capability as qualifications for office holding, encouragement of commerce and mfg., agr., conciliation of sectional controversies; gave spl. messages, Jan. 21, 23, 1850, urged unconditional admission of Cal., statehood for N.M.; most notable achievement in foreign affairs was Clayton-Bulwer Treaty of 1850; encountered opposition to admission of Cal. which led to Compromise of 1850; determined to reorganize cabinet because of "Galphin Claim" scandal (involving Sec. War Crawford), shortly before his death. Died Washington, D.C., July 9, 1850.

TEACHENOR, FRANK RANDALL neurol. surgeon; b. Kansas City, Mo., Sept. 1, 1888; s. Richard Bennington and Mary Catherine (Givauden) T.; M.D., U. of Kan., 1911; m. Ethel Glevo Heath, July 3, 1920. Interne, Kansas City Gen. Hosp., Kansas City, Mo., 1911-12; pvt. practice medicine, Kansas City, since 1912, specialist in neurol. surgery since 1920; in research, St. Luke's, St. Mary's, Trinity Luth. and Menorah hosps. since 1920; in practice of neurol. surgery U. of Kan. Med. Center since 1924; asst. in surgery U. of Kan. Med. Sch., 1924-28, asst. clin. prof., 1928-35, asso. clin. prof., 1935-39, prof. clin. surgery since 1939. Served as capt., M.C., U.S. Army, 1917-19; service in France Certified Am. Bd. Surgery. 1937, Am. Bd. Neurol. Surgery, 1940. Fellow A.M.A., A.C.S.; mem. Soc. Neurol. Surgeons, Harvey Cushing Soc. (pres. 1947), Western Surg. Assn. (pres. 1934), Jackson County Med. Soc. (pres. 1936), Mo. State Med. Assn., Southern Med. Assn. Contbr. articles on neurol. surgery to med. jours. Home: The Walnuts, 5049 Wornell Road. Office: Plaza Times Bldg., 411 Nichol's Rd., Kansas City 2, Mo. Died Nov. 28, 1953; buried Forest Hill Cemetery, Kansas City, Mo.

TEASDALE, KENNETH, lawyer; b. St. Louis, Feb. 10,21895; s. George Willard and Mamie (Walsh) T.; LL.B., U. Mo., 1918; m. Anne Fulbright, June 25, 1921; children—Suzanne Zorn, Kenneth S. Admitted to practice law 1917; member Armstrong, Teasdale, Kramer & Vaughan and predecessor firms, from 1921; chairman Supreme Court Committee to Revise Mo. Civil Procedure, 1938. Appointed to St. Louis Public Library board, 1956-57; mem. of bd. of Police Commrs. of St. Louis, from 1957. Served as 1st lt., F.A., U.S. Army, World War I. Fellow American College of Trial Lawyers; member American, Mo. (pres. 1936-37) bar assns., Bar Assn. St. Louis (pres. 1935-36), Order of Coif. Clubs: Noonday, Racquet, Bellerive Country, Missouri Athletic, Jefferson (pres. 1926-27). Home: St Louis MO Died Aug. 22, 1970; buried Fayetteville AR

TECUMSEH (also known as Tikamthi or Tecumtha), Indian chief; b. Great Springs, nr. Old Chillicothe (now Oldtown), O., Mar. 1768; s. Pucksinwa. Chief, Sewanee Indians; attempted to stop flow of Westward emigration and preserve Indian lands intact; believed that consent of tribes involved was necessary to render any cession of land legal, based claims on Treaty of Greeneville of 1795; planned to combine all tribes into confederacy to prevent land cessions and strengthen Indian character against temptations offered by white settlers; relied on British mil. aid during period when Gov. W. H. Harrison negotiated numerous cession treaties, 1803-11; his brother (the Prophet) was manuevered into Battle of Tippecanoe during his absence, 1811, idea of confederacy was destroyed with the subsequent Indian defeat; participated in fighting on Brit. side with rank of brig. gen. during War of 1812. Killed at Battle of Thames while leading an Indian force, Oct. 5, 1813.

TEDDER, LORD ARTHUR WILLIAM (BARON TEDDER OF GLENGUIN) chancellor Cambridge U.; s. Sir Arthur John Tedder; B.A., Cambridge U., 1912, LL.D., 1946; LL.D. (hon.), Oxford, Univ. Glasgow, Univ. of Leeds, Sheffield Univ., 1946; m. Rosalinde MacLardy, 1915 (died 1943); children—Arthur R. B. (dec.), Mina U. M., John M.; m. 2d, Marie De Seton Black, 1943 (dec. 1965); 1 son, Richard Seton. In Colonial service, Fiji, 1914; with Dorset regt., 1914, in France, 1915-17, Egypt, 1918-19; transferred to RAF, 1919; squadron comdr., Constantinople, 1922-23; Royal Naval Staff Coll., 1923-24; various appts. Air Ministry, 1924-40; dep. air officer, Comdr. in Chief; air officer, Comdr. in Chief, R.A.F., Middle East, 1940-43; Mediterranean air command, 1943; Allied Dep. Supreme Comdr., SHAEF under General Eisenhower, 1943-45; Chief Air Staff, 1946-50; chmn. Brit. Joint Staff Mission, Wash., and Brit. rep. on Standing Group NATO, 1950-51; chancellor Cambridge University, 1951-—; vice chmn. B.B.C., 1952-54; chairman Standard-Triumph Internat., Ltd., 1954-60, pres., 1960-—; marshal of the RAF, 1961-—; deputy president of Outward Bound Trust. Decorated D.S.M. Chief Comdr. Legion of Merit, European Theatre of Operations medal (U.S.A.); Italian Medaille Militaire (Italy); Croix de Guerre with Palm, Grand Cross of Legion of Honor (France); Order of Kutusov (Russia); Knight of Grand Cross, Order of the Bath, created first baron of Glenguin, 1946 (Eng.); also other decorations. Club: Surrey County Cricket (v.p.). Pres. R.A.F.A. Address: Well Farm, Banstead, Surrey, Eng. Died June 3, 1967.

TELLER, LUDWIG congressman, lawyer; b. N.Y.C., June 22, 1911; s. Morris and Rose (Smolov) T.; A.B., N.Y. U., 1936, LL.B., 1935, LL.M., 1937, J.S.D., 1939; m. Clarice Hilda Schlesinger, Dec. 15, 1938. Expert cons. to Labor Relations Br., War Dept., 1942; arbitrator, mem. law com. Am. Arbitration Assn.; lectr. grad. div. N.Y.U. Law Sch., 1947-51; prof. N.Y. Law Sch., 1951-63, chmn. Grad. Faculties for Advanced Degrees in Law, 1958-63. Mem. N.Y. State Assembly, 1950-56; mem. 85th-86th congresses from 20th Dist., Manhattan. Mem. N.Y. County Dem. Exec. Com., 1955-63. Congl. adviser 2nd Internat. Conf. Peaceful Use of Atomic Energy, Switzerland, 1958. Pres., Central Library for Blind in Israel, 1958-63; bd. dirs. League for Emotionally disturbed Children, 1958-61. Served to lt. USNR, 1943-45; lt. comdr. Res., 1958-64. Mem. temp. state commn. to study organizational structure of N.Y.C., 1953-54, N.Y. Bar 1937-—, bar Fed. Ct., So. Dist. and Circuit Ct. Appeals (2d Circuit) Supreme Ct. of U.S. Mem. N.Y. State Bar Assn., Am. Bar Assn. (chmn. com. to improve adminstrn. of collective bargaining agreements, labor law sect. 1960), Am. Arbitration Assn. (chmn. com. to revise U.S. Arbitration Act), Assn. Bar N.Y.C., N.Y. County Lawyers' Assn., Phi Delta Phi. Club: National Democratic. Author: The Law Governing Labor Disputes and Collective Bargaining (3 vols.), 1940, supplementary vol., 1950; A Labor Policy for America, 1945; Management Functions Under Collective Bargaining, 1946; Law of Contracts, 1947; Law of Torts, 1947; Law of Bills and Notes, 1948; Law of Agency, 1948; Law of Corporations, 1949; Law of Partnership, 1950; Worker Participation in Business Management, 1961. Contbr. to Ann. Survey of Am. Law, 1948-50; also articles on law and labor relations to revs. and mags. Home: 320 Central Park West, N.Y.C. 25. Office: 295 Madison Av., N.Y.C. 17. Died Oct. 4, 1965.

TELLER, STEADMAN naval officer, aviator; b. Kingston, N.Y., Aug. 21, 1903; s. Myron Steadman and Jane (Crosby) T.; B.S., U.S. Naval Acad., 1924; grad. Naval Postgrad. Sch., 1934, Nat. War Coll., 1948; m. Margaret Connable, Sept. 14, 1929; 1 son, Dirck. Commd. ensign, U.S. Navy, 1924; advanced through grades to capt.; served various squadrons and aircraft carriers, 1926-40; asst. naval attache for air, serving with Brit. aircraft carries, Mediterranean, London, 1941; successively in charge fighter dir. tng., airborne radar tng., air combat intelligence, and guided missiles Navy Dept., 1941-43; comd. U.S.S. Steamer Bay, chief staff to Comdr. Aircraft, 7th Fleet, 1944-45; mem. U.S. Strategic Bombing Survey, Japan, 1945-46; comd. U.S.S. Boxer, 1948-49; Navy Sec., Research and Devel. Bd., Def. Dept., 1951-52; chief operations br. Hdqrs. CINC, U.S. Forces, Europe. Decorated Legion of Merit, Commendation ribbon, Bronze Star (Navy). Mem. Naval Order U.S., Holland Soc. N.Y. Clubs: Army-Navy Country (Arlington, Va.); Potomac (Md.) Hunt. Home: R.F.D. 2, Germantown, Md. Office: Navy Dept., Washington 25. Died Feb. 13, 1955.

TEMPLE, WILLIAM GRENVILLE naval officer; b. Rutland, Vt., Mar. 23, 1824; s. Robert and Charlotte Eloise (Green) T.; grad. U.S. Naval Acad., 1846; m. Catlyna Totten, Oct. 7, 1851. Commd. midshipman U.S. Navy, 1840; made 1st cruise on ship Constellation around the world, 1840-44; passed midshipman, 1846; took part in chief naval operations during Mexican War, 1847, capture of Alvarado, occupation of Tuxpan and Tabasco; served on Mediterranean cruise, 1852-55; promoted master, 1854; flag lt. Pacific Squadron, 1859-61; served in U.S. coast survey; commanded steamer Flambeau during Civil War, 1861. ship Pembina on Mobile Blockade, 1862-63; commd. lt. comdr., 1862; fleet capt. Eastern Gulf squadron, 1862-64; commanded side-wheeler Pontoosue, 1864-65, participated in both attacks on Fort Fisher, 1864-65; promoted comdr., 1865, capt., 1870, commodore, 1878; rear adm., 1884; ordnance duty, Portsmouth, N.H., 1866-69; chief of staff European Squadron, 1871-73; capt. N.Y. Navy Yard, 1875-77; mem. Navy Retiring Bd., 1879-84; ret., 1884. Died Washington, D.C., June 28, 1894; buried Congressional Cemetery, Washington.

TEMPLETON, RICHARD HARKNESS, lawyer; b. Buffalo, N.Y., Sept. 23, 1877; s. Thomas and Charlotte (Harkness) T.; prep. edn., Central High Sch., Buffalo; A.B., Syracuse U., 1899, studied law, same univ.; m. Mai Morgan, 1908; children—Richard Harkness, Mary Reese, Jean Morgan. Admitted to N.Y. bar, 1901, and began practice at Buffalo; lecturer on corps., U. of Buffalo, 1910-25; U.S. atty. Western Dist. of N.Y., by appointment of President Coolidge, 1925-35. Major of 74th Inf. of N.Y.N.G. Dir. Buffalo Assn. for the Blind, Legal Aid Bur., Buffalo Mus. of Science. Mem. Am., N.Y. State and Erie County bar assns., Phi Kappa Psi, Phi Delta Phi. Republican. Episcopalian. Mason (32 deg.). Home: 309 Porter Av. Office: White Bldg., Buffalo NY

TEN BROECK, ABRAHAM army officer, jurist; b. Albany, N.Y., May 13, 1734; s. Dirck and Grietja (Cuyler) Ten B.; m. Elizabeth Van Rensselaer, Nov. 1, 1763, 5 children. Mem. Colonial Assembly of N.Y., 1761-65; dep. N.Y. Provincial Congress, 1775-77; mem. N.Y. Constl. Conv. of 1777; served as brig. gen. N.Y. Militia during Am. Revolution; had key role in Battle of Bemis Heights which resulted in forced retreat of Gen. Burgoyne, 1777; resigned commn., 1781; 1st judge Ct. of Common Pleas of Albany County (N.Y.), 1781-94; mayor Albany, 1779-83, 96-99; mem. N.Y. State Senate, 1780-83; pres., dir. Albany Bank. Died Albany, Jan. 19, 1810.

TENBROECK, CARL bacteriologist; b. Parsons, Kan., Sept. 5, 1885; s. Andrew and Carrie (Aldrich) T.; A.B., U. Ill., 1908; M.D., Harvard, 1913; m. Janet Rinaker, Apr. 28, 1917; children—Carlon (dec.), Jane, Nancy. Asso., Rockefeller Inst. for Med. Research, 1914-20, mem. dept. animal pathology, 1927-51, emeritus, 1951-—, dir., 1929-51; asso. prof. bacteriology, Peking (China) Union Med. Coll., 1920-23, prof., head dept. pathology, 1923-27. Cons. to Sec. of War, 1942-46. Served as 1st lt. M.C., U.S. Army, 1917-18. Recipient Medal of Freedom. Mem. A.A.A.S., Am. Soc. Immunologists, Soc. Exptl. Biology and Medicine. Research on animal diseases. Address: Bar Harbor, Me. Died Nov. 1966.

TEN EYCK, ANDREW (ten'ik), lawyer; b. Coeymans, N.Y., Aug. 3, 1888; s. James Barent and Helen (Huyck) T.; desc. Conraet Ten Eyck who came to America from Holland in 1651; A.B., N.Y. Univ., 1911; studied law, Harvard, 1911-12; LL.B. and J.D., N.Y. Univ., 1914; Diploma, U. of Paris, France, Faculte de Droit, 1919; m. Doris Boomer, June 2, 1926. Asst. to chancellor of N.Y. Univ., 1913-14; mem. staff Knickerbocker Press, Albany, 1914-15; sec. to J. H. Finley, N.Y. State commr. of edn., 1915-19; spl. asst. to Elihu Root at N.Y. Constitutional Conv., 1915; dir. 2d and 3d war loans for ednl. instns., 2d Federal Reserve Bank, 1917-18; asst. to F. A. Vanderlip, U.S. Dept. of Treasury, war finance, 1917-18; spl. corr. N.Y. Tribune in London and other European cities, 1920; admitted to N.Y. bar, 1920; instr. internat. relations, N.Y. Univ., 1921; sec. to N.Y. Supreme Court Justice, A. R. Page, 1921-23; practiced law, New York City, 1923-33; counsel N.Y. Stock Exchange, 1923; referee several occasions N.Y. Supreme Ct., 1923-32; assistant secretary Williamstown Inst. of Politics, 1924-32; confidential asst. to Gov. and President-elect F. D. Roosevelt, 1932-33; sr. atty. securities div. Federal Trade Commn., Washington, D.C., 1933-34; sr. atty. Securities and Exchange Commn., 1934-36, detailed asst. to chmn., 1934, and 1934-36, counsel to economic adviser; legislative and general law practice, 1937-38; spl. counsel Federal Marketing Law Survey, 1938-39; counsel on staff Comptroller Gen. of U.S., 1940-42. Served in 310th F.A., 79th Div., U.S. Army, A.E.F., 1918-19; capt. Res. Mil. Intelligence, Gen. Staff U.S. Army, 1922, major, 1941; lt. col. Air Forces, 1942, col., 1947; chief branch special studies and policy, Pub. Relations Office, hdqrs. Army Air Forces, 1942; grad. School of Mil. Govt., U.S. Army, Charlottesville, Va., 1943; chief, review branch Office Air Provost Marshal; Air Force mem. Indusl. Employment Review Board, Under-Sec. of War's office, 1943-44; assistant sec. Air Staff, 1945-46; chief, research section Legislative Services br., Legis. liaison Div., dir. public relations, Dept. of Air Force 1947-48; adviser security and policy Office Sec. of Defense 1949-52; consultant, Department of Defense 1952-53; admitted to D.C. bar, practice of law, Washington, 1953-—. Recipient several decorations and awards. Mem. Holland Soc. of N.Y., Psi Upsilon, Phi Delta Phi. Democrat. Episcopalian. Clubs: Cosmos (Washington); Harvard (N.Y.). Contbr. numerous mag. articles, notably, one in 1924 on British Companies Act which was earliest advocacy of its pattern for Fed. Securities Act of 1933. Editor: Army Air Forces Handbook for Public Relations Officers, 1942; Provost Marshal Public Relations, 1944. Author: Jeeps In the Sky. Home: 1814 37th St. S.W., Washington. Died Apr. 26, 1964; buried Arlington Nat. Cemetery.

TENNEY, HENRY FAVILL, lawyer; b. Chicago, Ill., June 1, 1890; s. Horace Kent and Eleanor Baird (Favill) T.; Williams Coll., 1908-12; M.A. (hon.), 1946, Ph.B., U. of Chicago, 1913, J.D., 1915; m. Eleanor N. Elmer, Dec. 24, 1917. Admitted to Ill. bar, 1915, practiced in Chicago, mem. firm of Tenney, Sherman, Bentley & Guthrie, from 1916; dir. Inland Steel Company, Mid-West Forging &Mfg. Co., Bradner Smith & Company. President Village of Winnetka, Ill., 1927-29; chmn. Chicago chapter Am. Red Cross 1944-46; mem. bd. trustees, U. of Chicago and Wesley Memorial Hosp.; mem. bd. governors Am. Nat. Red Cross, 1948-54, and from 1960; mem. Ill. Civil Service Commn., from 1961; dir. Chicago Boys Club, club, Good Will Industries, Chgo. Community Trust; chmn. Public Aid Commission 1949-52. Capt. 332d F.A., 86th Div., U.S.A., Apr. 1917-Mar. 1919. Mem. Am., Ill. State and Chicago bar assns., Law Club, Legal Club, Chi Psi, Phi Delta Phi. Democrat. Clubs: Univ., Mid-Day, Indian Hill, Tavern, Commercial, Chicago. Home: Winnetka IL Died Sept. 1, 1971.

TERMAN, LEWIS MADISON (tûr'man), psychologist; b. Johnson County, Ind., Jan. 15, 1877; s. James William and Martha Parthenia (Cutsinger) T.; A.B., Central Normal Coll., Danville, 1898; A.B., Ind. U., 1902, A.M., 1903, LL.D., 1929; fellow in psychology and edn., Clark U., 1903-05, Ph.D., 1905; LL.D., U. Cal., 1945, U. So. Cal., 1949; Sc.D., U. Pa., 1946; m. Anna Belle Minton, Sept. 18, 1899; children—Frederick Emmons, Helen Clare. Prin. high schs., Smiths Valley, Ind., 1898-1901, San Bernardino, Cal., 1905-06; prof. psychology and pedagogy, State Normal Sch., Los Angeles, 1906-10; asst. prof. edn., Stanford, 1910-12, asso. prof., 1912-16, prof., 1916-—, exec. head dept. psychology, 1922-42, prof. emeritus, 1942-—. Mem. com. Psychol. Exam. Recruits, Com. on Classification of Personnel, U.S. Army, 1918-19; served as maj. in div. of psychology, Surgeon General's Office, Washington. Fellow A.A.A.S., Brit. Psychol. Soc., Ednl. Inst. Scotland (hon.); mem. Am. Psychol. Assn. (pres. 1923), N.E.A., Am. Sch. Hygiene Assn. (pres. 1917), Nat. Soc. Study Edn., Nat. Acad. Scis., Phi Beta Kappa, Sigma Xi. Mem. bd. 5 psychologists appts. to revise Army mental test methods for use in schs.; author of researches on gifted children. Republican. Author: The Teacher's Health, 1913; The Hygiene of the School Child, 1914; (with Dr. E. B. Hoag) Health Work in the Schools, 1914; The Measurement of Intelligence, 1916; The Stanford Revision of the Binet-Simon Intelligence Scale, 1916; The Intelligence of School Children, 1919; The Terman Group Test, 1920; (with T. L. Kelley and G. M. Ruch) The Stanford Achievement Test, 1923; (with others) Genetic Studies of Genius, Vol. I, 1925, Vol. II (with Catharine M. Cox), 1926, Vol. III (with Barbara Burks and Dortha Jensen), 1930; Children's Reading (with Margaret Lima), 1925; Sex and Personality (with Catharine Cox Miles), 1936; Measuring Intelligence (with Maud A. Merrill), 1937; Marital Happiness, 1938; The Terman-McNemar Test of Mental Ability (with Q. McNemar), 1942; The Gifted Child Grows Up (with Melita Oden), 1947; The Gifted Group at Mid-Life (with Melita Oden), 1959. Editor The Measurement and Adjustment Series; asso. editor Brit. Jour. Ednl. Psychology; Jour. Genetic Psychology; Genetic Psychology Monographs. Address: 761 Dolores St., Stanford University, Stanford, Cal. Died Dec. 21, 1956.

TERRELL, ALEXANDER WATKINS diplomat; b. Patrick County, Va., Nov. 3, 1827; s. Christopher Joseph and Susan (Kennerly) T.; ed. U. of Mo.; married 3 times. Admitted to bar, 1849; began practice at St. Joseph, Mo.; removed to Tex.; judge Dist. Ct., 1857-62; col. of cav., C.S.A.; mem. Tex. Ho. of Reps., 4 yrs., Senate, 10 yrs.; U.S. minister to Turkey, 1893-97. Portrait hung in Tex. Ho. of Rep., 1903, in recognition of prominence as legislator. Home: Austin, Tex. Died Sept. 9, 1912.

TERRELL, SCURRY LATIMER, oculist, aurist; b. Houston, Tex., Dec. 12, 1869; s. Edwin Ruthven and Kate (Scurry) T.; A.B., U. of Ala., 1889; M.D., Coll. Phys. & Surg., Baltimore, 1895; post-grad. work in New York, London, Paris, Vienna and Wurzburg; m. Joe C. Goode, of Fort Worth, Tex., Apr. 30, 1908 (died Apr. 9, 1910); 2d, Homer Collier Gaston, June 21, 1913. Practiced, Dallas, Tex., 1896; formerly surgeon Tex. & Pacific Coal Co.; prof. otology, med. dept., Southern Meth. U.; mem. staff St. Paul's Sanitarium; consulting oculist and aurist various rys.; served as specialist to Col. Theodore Roosevelt, campaign 1912. Maj. Med. Corps Tex. N.G., now U.S.A. Progressive. Episcopalian. Mem. A.M.A., Tex. State Med. Assn., Dallas Co. Med. Soc., Assn. Mil. Surgeons of U.S., Delta Tau Delta, etc. Clubs: Dallas, Dallas Press, Dallas Country. Aurist to Gen. Hosp. 23, British Expeditionary Force, France, summer, 1915. Home: 2807 Forest Av. Office: Wilson Bldg., Dallas TX

TERRIBERRY, WILLIAM S(TOUTENBOROUGH) (ter'i-ber-i), U.S. Pub. Health Service; b. Paterson, N.J., July 3, 1871; s. George W. and Martha Griffith (Stoutenborough) T.; grad. St. Paul's Sch., Garden City, N.Y., 1889; A.B., Yale, 1893; M.D., Columbia, 1896; m. Emilie Varet Reinhart, Oct. 17, 1907. Interne Bellevue Hosp., 1896-98; asst. visiting surg., 1902-13. Asst. surg. (1st lt.) N.J. Vols., 1898; contract surg. U.S. Army, 1896-99; lt. col. Med. Corps, N.Y. Nat. Guard, 1916; lt. col. Med. Corps, U.S. Army, 1918; assigned as comdg. officer Embarkation Hosp., Newport News, Va.; advanced to col., Aug. 1918, hon. discharged, Nov. 1919; commd. asst. surgeon U.S.P.H.S., Dec. 1919, sr. surgeon, Jan. 1920, asst. surgeon gen., July 1920, med. dir. 1930; retired, Nov. 1937. Awarded Conspicuous Service Cross, 1922. Mem. Zeta Psi. Clubs: Yale (N.Y. City); Army and Navy (Washington, D.C.). Home: Old Lyme, Conn. Died Oct. 13, 1948.

TERRY, ALFRED HOWE army officer; b. Hartford, Conn., Nov. 10, 1827; s. Alfred and Clarissa (Howe) T.; attended Yale Law Sch. Admitted to Conn. bar, 1849; commd. col. Conn. Militia, 1861; served in 1st Battle of Bull Run; organized 7th Conn. Volunteers, 1861, commd. col.; promoted brig. gen. U.S. Volunteers, 1862; in command forces on Hilton Head, 1862; assigned to Army of the James, 1863; participated in operations against Richmond and Petersburg, 1864; brevetted maj. gen. U.S. Volunteers, 1864; took Ft. Fisher, N.C., 1865, as result commd. brig. gen. U.S. Army, 1865; commd. maj. gen. volunteers, 1865; assumed command Dept. of Dakota, 1866, head Dept. Dakota during exploration of Black Hills and Sioux War, 1874; commd. maj. gen. U.S. Army, 1866 (only general on army list not a U.S. Mil. Acad. graduate); in command Div. of Mo. with hdqrs. at Chgo., 1866; ret. for disability, 1888; mem. Indian Commn. created by U.S. Congress, 1867; mem. bd. of army officers to review court martial and sentence of Gen. Fitz John Porter. Died New Haven, Conn., Dec. 16, 1890.

TERRY, JOHN YOUNG miner; b. Wytheville, Va., Mar. 23, 1858; s. William and Emma (Wigginton) T.; ed. pvt. schs., Wytheville, Va., and Va. Mil. Inst., A.B., 1879; m. Wytheville, Va., Feb. 3, 1896, Virginia Secessia Withers. Followed civ. engring., 1879-87; employed in Govt. service in U.S. Land Office, at Seattle, Wash., 1887-90; in real estate business, 1890-94; receiver U.S. Land Office, 1894-98; mining since 1898; pres. and treas. Cherry Placer Mining Co.; dir. Buffalo Hump Mining Co. Has taken active interest in politics in State of Wash.; now mem. Dem. Nat. Com. from Wash. Episcopalian. Residence: 1018 E. 55th St. Office: Hinckley Blk., Seattle, Wash.

TERRY, NATHANIEL MATSON physicist; b. Lyme, Conn., Apr. 6, 1844; s. Rev. James Pease and Catharine A. (Matson) T.; A.B., Amherst, 1867, A.M., 1870; Ph.D., U. of Göttingen, 1871; hon. A.M., Yale, 1873; LL.D., Amherst, 1917; m. Frances A. Griswold, Nov. 6, 1878 (died 1915); children—Frances Griswold (wife of A. K. Atkins, U.S.N.), Nathaniel Matson, Louisa Mather. Prof. physics, U.S. Naval Acad., 1872-1917, head of dept. of physics and chemistry, 1886-1913. Commd. prof. mathematics U.S.N., 1913, and ordered to duty in connection with post-grad. course at U.S. Naval Acad.; retired with rank of commodore, U.S.N., 1917. Mem. bd. control Naval Inst., 22 years; trans. to retired list U.S. naval officers, 1917. Mem. exec. com. Navy Athletic Assn., 10 yrs.; hon. mem. U.S. Naval Acad. Graduates' Assn.; pres. First Ecclesiastical Soc. of Old Lyme. Home: Lyme, Conn. Died Oct. 12, 1938.

TERRY, SILAS WRIGHT rear admiral U.S.N.; b. Wallonia, Ky., Dec. 28, 1842; s. Abner R. and Eleanor (Dyer) T.; apptd. to U.S. Naval Acad. from Ky., Sept. 28, 1858, grad. 1861; m. Louisa G. Mason, Oct. 14, 1873. Promoted ensign. Sept. 16, 1862; advanced through grades to rear admiral, Mar. 29, 1900. Served on Dale, Atlantic coast, 1861-62; Wabash and Alabama, 1862; N. Atlantic Blockading Squadron, 1862-63; Miss. Squadron, 1863-64; N. Atlantic Blockading Squadron, 1864-65; participated in battles with Fts. Fisher and Anderson, and other engagements on coast of N.C.; on Ticonderoga, 1865-68; receiving-ship at New York, 1869; Naval Acad., 1869-71; Severn, 1871; Worcester, 1871-73; Naval Observatory, 1873-74; light house insp. 5th dist., 1877-80; comd. Marion, 1881-82; Navy Yard, League Island, 1883-84; comd. Portsmouth, 1884-86, Jamestown, 1886; Navy Yard, Washington, 1887-89; mem. Naval Examining and Retiring Bds., 1887-93; comd. Newark, 1893-95, receiving-ship, Franklin, 1895-98, Iowa, 1898-99; comdt., Navy Yard, Washington, 1900-03, Naval sta., Honolulu, 1903-04; retired, Dec. 28, 1904. During Civil War was engaged in blockading service on Atlantic Coast, 1861-62; in Mississippi Squadron and on Red River expdn., 1863-64; advanced 5 numbers in his grade for gallant conduct on latter; was present during naval operations and serving on staff of Admiral Porter, against Fts. Fisher and Anderson, and capture of Wilmington, Feb. 1865; later on James River; was present at fall of Richmond, accompanied President Lincoln when he entered Richmond. In Jan. 1882, while comdg. the Marion, rescued crew of bark Trinity, which had been wrecked, Oct. 1880, on Heard Island, Indian Ocean, lat. 53 deg. 30 min. S., long. 73 deg. 30 min. E.; in Feb. 1881, while at Cape Town, hauled English ship Poonah off the beach, saving her from total loss, for which he received the thanks of the Govt. of Cape Colony and of the English Govt. Home: Washington, D.C. Died 1911.

TERRY, THOMAS ALEXANDER army officer; b. Abbeville, Ala., Nov. 22, 1885; s. Thomas Alexander and Malinda Caroline (Gamble) T.; B.S., U.S. Mil. Acad., 1908; grad. Coast Arty. Sch., 1926, Command and Gen. Staff Sch., 1927, Army War Coll., 1932; hon. D.Sc., Boston U., 1942; LL.D., U. Del., 1943, Manhattan Coll., N.Y.C., 1944; m. Frances Ruby Holley, Dec. 7, 1911; 1 son, Thomas Alexander. Commd. 2d lt., 1908, advanced through successive ranks to brig. gen., 1940, maj. gen. (temp.), Oct. 1, 1940; stationed various posts in U.S. and Panama C.Z., 1908-18; in France with 58th Coast Arty., 1918-19; assigned to command 2d Service Command, Apr. 1942; apptd. comdg. gen. U.S. Forces, 1945; CBI. Awarded Victory Medal, 1919. Clubs: Army and Navy (Washington, D.C.; Manila, P.I.). Address: Governors Island, N.Y. Died Apr. 1963.

TERRY, WILLIAM congressman, lawyer; b. Amherst County, Va., Aug. 14, 1824; grad. U. Va., 1848; studied law. Taught sch.; admitted to Va. bar, 1851, began practice law, Wytheville, Va.; in newspaper work; served as lt. 4th Regt., Va. Inf., Confederate Army, promoted maj., 1862, col., 1864, was last comdr. of "Stonewall Jackson" brigade; resumed practice law, Wytheville; mem. U.S. Ho. of Reps. (Conservative) from Va., 42, 44th congresses, 1871-73, 75-77; del. Democratic Nat. Conv., Cincinnati, 1880. Drowned while trying to ford creek nr. Wytheville, Sept. 5, 1888; buried East End Cemetery, Wytheville.

TERWILLIGER, CHARLES VAN ORDEN educator; born Albany, N.Y., May 14, 1894; s. Charles Robert and Grace Alida (Ten Broeck) T.; B.Eng., Union Coll., 1916, M.S., 1919; M.S., Harvard, 1922; D.Eng., Johns Hopkins, 1938; m. Susan Gray Bagby, July 13, 1927. Instr. math. Union Coll., 1916-17, 1918-21; mem. engring. test dept. Gen. Electric Co., Schenectady, 1917-18; asst. engr. Gen. Electric engring. lab., summers 1916, 20, 22; instr. elec. engring. Harvard, 1922-24; asst. prof. elec. engring. Ohio State U., 1924-25; asst. prof. elec. engring. U.S. Naval Postgrad. Sch., Monterey, Cal., 1925-28, asso. prof., 1928-38, prof. since 1938, chmn. dept. elec. engring. since 1929. Lt. comdr., U.S. N.R., 1926-40. Fellow Am. Inst. E.E., A.A.A.S.; mem. Holland Soc. N.Y., Am. Assn. U. Profs., Sigma Xi. Home: Shafter Way, Route 1, Box 342A, Carmel. Office: USN Postgraduate Sch., Monterey, Cal. Died Nov. 12, 1962; buried El Encinal Cemetery, Monterey.

TETLOW, PERCY, mem. Bituminous Coal-Commn.; b. Leetonia, O., Dec. 16, 1875; s. William and Ann (Hadfield) T.; ed. pub. schs.; m. Sadie M. Carrier, of Washingtonville, O., July 3, 1900; children—Harry Lester, Percy William, Jessie May. Began as coal miner and became union official; mem. 4th Constitutional Conv. of Ohio, 1912; mem. Ohio Ho. of Rep., 1913; dir. Industrial Relations of Ohio, 1921-22; mem. Bituminous Coal Commn., Washington, D.C., since Sept. 21, 1935, now chmn. Served as pvt. Co. B, 16th Vol. Inf., Spanish-Am. War, 1898; capt. 134th Machine Gun Batt., 37th Div., World War, 1917-19. Republican. Methodist. Home: Columbus OH Address: Investment Bldg., 15th and K Sts. N.W., Washington DC

TEXTOR, GORDON EDMUND army engr.; b. Kasota, Minn., July 9, 1902; s. Charles E. and Louise (Offenloch) T.; B.A., B.M.S., U.S. Mil. Acad., 1924; C. E., Cornell, 1928; married; children—Mary Louise, Gretchen Elizabeth. Served in U.S. Army, Corps of Engrs., 1928-—, advancing to brig. gen., 1945; dir. projects, W.P.A., 1937-39; dir. constrn. and facilitation bur. W.P.B., 1942-43; gen. officer, War Dept. Gen. Staff, 1943-45. Address: 314 Mansion Drive, Alexandria, Va. Died Mar. 30, 1955.

THACH, JAMES HARMON JR. naval officer; b. Pine Bluff, Ark., Dec. 13, 1900; s. James Harmon and Jo Bocage (Smith) T.; B.S., U.S. Naval Acad., 1923; m. Caroline Lee Jewett, July 27, 1929; 1 son, James Harmon. Commd. ensign, U.S. Navy, 1923; advanced through grades to vice adm., 1956; served as gunnery div. officer, U.S.S. Tex. and Concord, 1923-28; mem. staff Adm. William Pratt, U.S. Fleet comdr. in chief,

1928-30; instr. U.S. Naval Acad.; gunnery officer, Asiatic fleet and cruisers, Savannah and Brooklyn, 1930-42; head New Weapons Devel. sect., staff of comdr. in chief, 1942-44; comdr. U.S.S. Montour, Pacific, 1944-45; navy sec. Joint Research and Devel. Bd., 1946-48; comdr. U.S.S. Missouri, 1948-49; naval staff mem. Nat. Security Council, 1949-50; dir. internat. affairs div. Office of Chief of Naval Operations, 1950-52; comdr. cruiser div. VI, U.S. Atlantic Fleet, 1952; comdr. Mil. Sea Transp. Service, Western Pacific area, 1953; chief of staff and aide to Supreme Allied Comdr., Atlantic, 1954-—. Awarded commendation ribbon for devel. work in rockets, Yangtze Campaign medal, China Service medal, Dev. medal with action award, Am. Area Campaign medal, European Area Campaign medal, Asiatic Area medal, World War II medal, China-Japan Occupation medal, Expert Pistol medals, Def. medal with action award (U.S.); Breast Order of Pao Ting (China); Grand Officer Cross of Avis (Portugal); Nat. Def. medal; Korean Service medal; UN medal. Episcopalian. Club: Army and Navy (Washington and Manila); N.Y. Yacht. Home: Topside, Mitchell Hill Rd., Old Lyme, Conn. 06371. Died July 4, 1962; buried Lyme, Conn.

THACHER, ARCHIBALD GOURLAY lawyer; b. Boston, Mass., Jan. 16, 1876; s. George and Isabel Gourlie (Gourlay) T.; A.B. magna cum laude, Harvard, 1897, LL.B., 1900; m. Ethel Davies, Aug. 9, 1902 (died Feb. 24, 1935); children—Alice Davies (dec.), Archibald Gourlay (dec.), Isabel Davies (Mrs. Sanford S. Clark); m. 2d, Edna Marston Beeckman, July 29, 1937. Admitted to New York bar, 1900; asst. with Butler, Notman, Joline & Mynderse, New York, N.Y., 1900-05; became partner firm Butler, Notman & Mynderse, 1905, and of successor firms, Wallace, Butler & Brown, 1907-13, Barry, Wainwright, Thacher & Symmers, 1913-51, Thatcher, Proffitt, Prizer & Crawley, 1951-—; director Am. and Fgn. Insurance Co., Columbia Ins. of N.Y., Eagle Fire Co. of N.Y., Imperial Ins. Co., Norwich Union, Phoenix, and Sun indemnity cos., Patriotic Ins. Co. of America, Sun Underwriters Insurance Company of New York, Seamens Bank for Savings in City of N.Y. (trustee). Served as captain 306th inf., 77th Div., A.E.F., 1917; regimental adjutant, 1917-18; promoted major, comdg. 2d Btn., France, 1918; col., inf., O.R.C., 1920; participated in major campaigns Vesle-Aisne and Argonne-Meuse offensive. Decorated Distinguished Service Cross (U.S.), Legion of Honor (France). Nat. co-chmn. Citizens Com. for Universal Mil. Training of Young Men (chmn. advisory com.). Mem. Am. and N.Y. State bar assns., Assn. Bar City of N.Y., (chmn. com. nat. defense; treasurer and mem. executive com. of war com.), American Society International Law, Grotius Soc., London, Council on Foreign Relations, Ins. Soc. of N.Y., Liverpool Underwriters Assn. Clubs: Knickerbocker, Harvard (New York); Southside Sportsmen's (Oakdale, L.I.). Author: Background of The North Atlantic Treaty (monograph); also pamphlets relating to history of marine ins. and to universal mil. training. Home: 620 Park Ave., New York, N.Y. Office: 72 Wall St., N.Y.C. 5. Died Jan. 1, 1952; buried Mount Auburn Cemetery, Boston.

THACHER, JAMES physician, army officer; b. Barnstable, Mass., Feb. 14, 1754; s. John and Content (Norton) T.; M.D. (hon.), Harvard, 1810; m. Susannah Hayward, Apr. 28, 1785, 6 children. Served with 1st Va. Regt., 1778-79; took part in ill-fated Penobscot Expdn.; acted as surgeon to select corps of light infantry, 1781; at siege of Yorktown and surrender of Lord Cornwallis; retired from army, 1783; began practice medicine and surgery, 1784; kept diary during the American Revolutionary War published under title A Military Journal, 1823, 2d edit., 1826, reprinted as Military Journal, 1854; wrote The American Medical Biography (1st publ. of it kind), 1828; mem. Am. Acad. Arts and Scis., Mass. Med. Soc. Author: Observations on Hydrophobia, 1812: American Modern Practice, 1817. Died Plymouth, Mass., May 23, 1844.

THACKREY, LYMAN AUGUSTUS naval officer; b. Manhattan, Kan., Aug. 6, 1897; s. William Elwood and Bettie (Olsen) T.; student U. N.M., 1915-17; grad. U.S. Naval Acad., 1920, advance course, Naval War Coll., 1949; m. Josephine Murray, Dec. 15, 1930. Commd. ensign U.S. Navy, 1920, advanced through grades to rear adm., 1948; various assignments Atlantic, Pacific, European and Asiatic fleets, 1920-48; command mine sweeper Sunnadin, destroyer Dallas, and Destroyer Div. 63; 1st lt., damage control officer USS North Carolina (participated landing Guadalcanal and Battle Eastern Solomons), 1942, exec. officer rank comdr., 1942; command USS Calvert (APA-32, invasion Sicily), 1943; Naval mem. staff which planned Normandy invasion, London, 1943; U.S. asst. chief staff to Allied Naval Comdr. Expeditionary Force and Sr. Naval planner of Gen. Eisenhower's Supreme Hdqrs., A.E.F., 1943-44; command heavy cruiser U.S.S. Portland, Okinawa, (during surrender Truk), 1945; mem. steering com. formed to give guidance to the Navy Dept. during the period unification of the Armed Services was being negotiated; Secretary's Com. on Unification, 1945-48; command Amphibious Group 4, July 1949-July 1950; comdr. Amphibious Group Three since Aug. 3, 1950; participated amphibious landing Inchon, Korea, Sept. 1950; command amphibious landing Iwon, Oct. 1950; evacuated U.N. forces, Inchon, Jan. 1951; reopened Inchon, Feb. 1951; apptd. chmn. Joint Amphibious Bd., Oct. 1951. Navy dept. liaison officer with Eberstadt Task Force under Hoover Com. studying Modernization govt. structure, 1947-48. Decorated D.S.M., Legion of Merit with Combat V, Navy Unit citation; comdr. Mil. Order of the British Empire; French Legion Honor and Croix de Guerre. Mem. U.S. Naval Inst., Phi Kappa Alpha. Student politico-economic systems and part war has played or will play in their establishment. Home: 320 W. Olive St., San Diego, Cal. Office: Care of U.S. Navy Department, Washington 25. Died Apr. 14, 1955; buried Nat. Cemetery, San Diego.

THARIN, ROBERT SEYMOUR SYMMES lawyer; b. Magnolia, nr. Charleston, S.C., Jan. 10, 1830; grad. Coll. of Charleston, A.M., 1856; LL.B., 1859; m., 1858, nr. Montgomery, Ala., Mary Hart Dhu (died 1897). Was partner in law business of William L. Yancy in Ala., 1858; opposed his late partner's "League of United Southerners" and vigilance 2 committees, advocated 2 colonization of slaves in Liberia, Africa, and was obliged to flee from Ala.; served in Union army in 16th Ind. vols.; mustered out, May 23, 1862; was ordained minister of the gospel, preaching until 1867; returned to S.C. for awhile, but entered civil service; afterward resigning to practice law. Founded, 1896, and is pres. Pro-Armenian Alliance. Was twice defeated for Congress in 2d dist., S.C. Author: Arbitrary Arrests in the South, or Scenes from the Experience of an Alabama Unionist; Pro-Armenian Bulletin; unpublished crimes of Islam; From Patmos to Jerusalem. Address: 1515 29th St. N.W., Washington.

THATCHER, GEORGE WILSON, educator; b. Ogden, Utah, Aug. 1,21913; s. Gilbert and Margret (Folkman) T.; B.S., U. Utah, 1936; Ph.M., U., Wis., 1939, Ph.D., 1951; m. Alberta Riegel Neiswonger, Aug. 17, 1941; children—Karen Margret, Jeffrey Kirk. Grad. asst. U. Wis., 1937-40; faculty Miami University, Oxford, Ohio, 1940-42, 45-71, professor of economics, 1957-71, chairman of the department, 1957-63. Served to lieutenant (s.g.) USNR, 1942; 45. Mem. Am. Econ. Assn., Nat. Tax Assn., Beta Gamma Sigma, Delta Sigma Pi, Omicron Delta Kappa. Home: Oxford OH Died May 9, 1971; buried Oxford Cemetery, Oxford OH

THATCHER, HENRY KNOX naval officer; b. Thomaston, Me., May 26, 1806; s. Ebenezer and Lucy Flucker (Knox) T.; attended U.S. Mil. Acad.; m. Susan C. Croswell, Dec. 26, 1831, 1 adopted child. Apptd. midshipman U.S. Navy, 1823; served in ship United States, 1824-27; made cruise in west Indies as acting master in Erie, 1831; commd. lt., 1833; commanded storeship Relief of Brazil Squadron, 1851-52; exec. officer Naval Asylum, Phila., 1854-55; comdr., 1855; commanded Decatur in Pacific. 1857-59; exec. officer Boston Navy Yard, 1861; in command corvette Constellation for special duty in Mediterranean, Nov. 1861; commodore, 1862; assigned in Colorado of North Atlantic Squadron, 1863; commanded 1st div. of Adm. Porter's fleet and served with distinction at attack on Ft. Fisher, N.C., Dec. 1864-Jan. 1865; apptd. acting rear adm., ordered to take command of West Gulf blockading squadron, 1865; commanded North Pacific Squadron, 1866-68; promoted rear adm., 1866, ret. 1868. Died Boston, Apr. 5, 1880.

THAYER, AMOS MADDEN U.S. circuit judge, 8th circuit, Aug. 9, 1894-—; b. Mina, N.Y., Oct. 10, 1841; s. Ichabod and Fidelia (La Due) T.; grad. Hamilton Coll., Clinton, N.Y., 1862 (LL.D., 1892). Served in Civil war 3 yrs. as 1st lt. U.S. Signal Corps; settled in St. Louis, Feb. 1866; admitted to bar, 1868; circuit judge, St. Louis, 1876-86; U.S. dist. judge, Eastern dist. Mo., from Feb. 24, 1887, until 1894; m. Sidney Hunton Brother, Dec. 22, 1880. Home: St. Louis, Mo. Died 1905.

THAYER, CHARLES W(HEELER), writer; born Villanova, Pa., Feb. 9, 1910; s. George Chapman and Gertrude May (Wheeler) T.; student St. Paul's Sch., Concord, N.H., 1923-28; B.S., U.S. Mil. Acad., West Point, 1933; m. Cynthia Dunn, Mar. 27, 1950; stepdaughter, Diana, 1 son, James Dunn. U.S. fgn. service officer 1933-53; in Moscow, 1933-37, Berlin, 1937-38, Hamburg, 1939-40, Moscow, 1940-42, Kabul, Afghanistan, 1942-43, London, 1943-44; served as lt. col., U.S. Army, chief of mil. mission to Yugoslavia, 1944-45; chief, O.S.S., Austria 1945-46; mem. U.S.-U.S.S.R. Commn. for Korea, 1946; at U.S. Nat. War Coll., 1946; chief, div. internat. broadcasting, Voice of America, 1947-49; polit. liaison officer to German Govt., Bonn, Germany, 1950-51; U.S. consul gen., Munich, 1952-53. Clubs: Metropolitan (Washington). Author: Bears in the Caviar; Hands Across the Caviar; The Unquiet Germans, 1957; Diplomat, 1959; Russia (with others), 1960; Moscow Interlude, 1962; Checkpoint, 1963; Guerrilla, 1963; Muzzy, 1966. Home: Philadelphia PA Died Aug. 27, 1969; buried Bryn Mawr PA

THAYER, EDWIN POPE ex-sec. U.S. Senate; b. Greenfield, Ind., Dec. 15, 1864; s. Hollis B. and Permelia A. (Hart) T.; A.B., DePauw, 1886, A.M., 1889; married; children—George A., Mrs. Roxana H. Smith. In mercantile bus., 1880-1906, irrigated land and mining bus., 1906-16; pres. Arizona Exploration & Development Co. Mem. Ind. N.G. 23 yrs.; served as col. 158th Regt., Ind. Vols., Spanish-Am. War; col. 3d Regt., I.N.G., 1900-12. Chief asst. to sergt. at arms, Rep. Nat. Com., 1904, 08, 12, 16; sergt. at arms, 1920, 24; chief supervisor for U.S. Senate in the Paddy-Mayfield contest (Tex.), 1924, Steck-Brookhart contest (Ia.), 1925, and the Bursum-Bratton contest (N.M.), 1926; sec. of the Senate, 1925-33. Now practicing law, Washington, D.C. Mem. Ind. and D.C. bars. Methodist. Mason 32 deg.). Club: Columbia. Home: Greenfield, Ind. Deceased.

THAYER, FLOYD K. business exec.; b. Castle Rock, Colo., July 22, 1896; s. William H. and Hattie (Kinyon) T.; A.B., U. Denver, 1918; A.M., U. Ill., 1920; m. Edith Fales, July 1921; children—Willard K., Jean E. With the Abbott Labs., 1920, dir., 1938, dir. chem. marketing, sec., mem. exec. com., became v.p., 1953; dir. First Fed. Savs. & Loan Assn. of Waukegan. Cons. drugs and medicines Health Supplies br. WPB, 1942-43. Served in CWS, U.S. Army, 1918; maj., Res., 1924-38. Recipient Marketing Man of Year award Chgo. chpt. Am. Marketing Assn., 1958. Bd. dirs. Ill. State C. of C., 1952-57; mem. Am. Chem. Soc., Chgo. Drug and Chem. Assn., Am. Pharm. Mfrs. (past dir.), Waukegan-North Chicago C. of C. (dir. 1958-61), Beta Theta Pi, Sigma Xi. Republican. Episcopalian. Mason. Club: Rotary. Contbr. to Am. Jour. Pharmacy, Jour. Am. Chem. Soc. Home: 335 Douglas Av., Waukegan, Ill. Office: Abbott Labs., North Chicago. Died Sept. 28, 1965; buried N. Shore Garden of Memories, North Chicago.

THAYER, JOHN MILTON lawyer; b. Bellingham, Mass., Jan. 24, 1820; s. Elias and Ruth T.; grad. Brown Univ.; studied law; admitted to Neb. bar; m. Mary Torrey Allen, 1843. Lived some time in Washington, in Neb., 1854-—; brig. gen. and maj. gen. Territorial forces operating against Indians, 1855-61; captured Pawnees and placed them on reservation, 1859; col. and brig. gen. U.S. vols., 1861-65; assisted Gen. Sherman in operations against Vicksburg; U.S. senator, 1867-71; gov. Wyoming Ty., 1875-79; dept. comdr. G.A.R., Neb., 1886; gov. Neb., 1887-93. Home: Lincoln, Neb. Died 1906.

THAYER, PHILLIP W. educator; Springfield, Mass., Sept. 13, 1893; s. Dwight Ransom and Katharine (Pease) T.; A.B. magna cum laude, Harvard, 1914, LL.B., 1917; m. Barbara Wilson Sears, Sept. 25, 1941; children—George, Jean (Mrs. Alan Osgood Watts), Richard Sears (stepson), Joan Sears (stepdau.). Admitted to Mass. bar, 1917. In export and import business, Far East, 1920-31; research supr. fgn. trade Harvard Bus. Sch., 1925-26; prof. internat. coml. Law Fletcher Sch. Law and Diplomacy, 1933-42; research asso. comparative law Harvard Law Sch., 1936-46; also acting asst. chief Div. World Trade Intelligence, Dept. State, 1941-42; spl. asst. to ambassador, Santiago, Chile, 1942-44; cultural relations attaché Am. embassy, Santiago, 1944-45; prof. law, Sch. Advanced Internat. Studies, Johns Hopkins, 1946-65, prof. emeritus internat. law, 1965-—, dean, 1948-61; vis. prof. U. Rangoon, 1953; expert cons. on legal affairs to sec. of Army, 1948; vis. prof., lectr. U. Wash., Bklyn. Law Sch., U. Concepcion, Chile, U. of Va. Law Sch. Apptd. to commn. on occupied areas and chmn. panel on legal affairs Am. Council on Edn., 1949; advisor on German and Austrian legal exchanges Dept. State, 1950, mem. adv. com. on U.S. Fgn. Relations, 1957-—; cons. ICA on u. edn. in Tunisia, 1958, ICA gen. edn. in Indonesia, 1959. Served as lt. (j.g.) USNRF, 1918-19. Decorated Order of Merit (Chile), 1946, (Italy), 1960. Chmn. com. on internat. and fgn. law Assn. Am. Law Schs., 1947-48. Mem. Am. Soc. Internat. Law, Am. Bar Assn. Club: Cosmos (Washington). Author: The Law Merchant, 1939; also articles on comparative comml. law and Southeast Asia. Editor: Southeast Asia in the Coming World; Nationalism and Progress in South and Southeast Asia, 1955; Tensions in the Middle East, 1957. Home: 1400 29th St., Washington 7. Office: 1740 Massachusetts Av. N.W., Washington 20036. Died Dec. 18, 1966; buried Oak Grove Cemetery, Springfield, Mass.

THAYER, SYLVANUS mil. engr., educator; b. Braintree, Mass., June 9, 1785; s. Nathaniel and Dorcas (Faxon) T.; attended Dartmouth, 1807, LL. (hon.), 1846; grad. U.S. Mil. Acad., 1808; LL.D. (hon.), St. John's Coll., Kenyon Coll., 1846, Harvard, 1857. Commd. 2d lt. Corps Engrs., U.S. Army, 1808; served on Canadian frontier and Norfolk (Va.) during War of 1812; commd. capt., 1813; brevetted maj., 1815; apptd. supt. U.S. Mil. Acad., West Point, N.Y., 1817-33; commd. maj., 1828, col., 1833; engr. in charge constrn. of fortifications at Boston Harbor and improvement of harbors on New Eng. coast, 1833-63; profl. duty in Europe, 1843-46; brevetted brig. gen., 1862; retired from army, 1863; established and endowed Thayer Sch. Engring., Dartmouth Coll., 1867. Author: Papers on Practical Engineering, 1844. Died South Braintree, Sept. 7, 1872; buried West Point.

THAYER, WILLIAM SYDNEY M.D.; b. Milton, Mass., June 23, 1864; s. James B. and Sophia B. (Ripley) T.; A.B., Harvard, 1885 (Phi Beta Kappa; pres. 1929), M.D., 1889; LL.D., Washington Coll., Chestertown, Md., 1907, Edinburg U., 1927; McGill U., 1929; hon. Dr. U. of Paris, 1928; Sc.D. from U. of Chicago; m. Susan Chisolm, d. late Benjamin Huger Read, of Charleston, S.C., Sept. 3, 1901. Visiting phys. Johns

Hopkins Hosp.; prof. emeritus of medicine, John Hopkins U. (Phi Beta Kappa). Mem. Bd. Overseers, Harvard, two terms; mem. Bd. Trustees, Carnegie Inst. of Washington, 1929. Fellow Am. Acad. Arts and Sciences; mem. numerous Am. and fgn. societies. Maj. and dep. commr. Am. Red Cross Mission to Russia, June 1917-Jan. 1918; maj., col. and brig. gen. Med. Corps, U.S.A., and chief consultant med. services, A.E.F., in France, Mar. 1918-Jan. 1919; became brig. gen. Medical Sect. O.R.C., U.S.A.; brig. gen. Auxillary, U.S.A., 1929. Awarded distinction badge, Red Cross of Russia, 1918; D.S.M. (U.S.), 1919; Comdr. Legion of Honor, France, 1928; Bright medalist, Guy's Hosp., London, 1927. Author: Lectures on the Malarial Fevers, 1897; (with Dr. Hewetson) The Malarial Fevers of Baltimore (Johns Hopkins Hosp. Reports), 1895; Studies on Bacterial Endocarditis (pub. by same), 1925; America—1917, and Other Verse, 1926. Home: Baltimore, Md. Died Dec. 10, 1932.

THEISS, PAUL SEYMOUR naval officer, ret.; b. Washington, Oct. 6, 1890; s. Capt. Emil Theiss (USN); grad. U.S. Naval Acad., 1912; m. Ellen Elizabeth Wright Macdonald, June 16, 1948. Commd. ensign, U.S.N., 1912, and advanced through grades to commodore, 1944; served in U.S. ships Montana, Prairie, Castine, Brooklyn and South Carolina, 1914-16, U.S.S. Allen, 1917-18, U.S.S. Laub and U.S.S. Ringgold, 1919, comd. U.S.S. Paul Hamilton, 1927-29, U.S.S. Borie, 1929-31, U.S.S. Fuller (formerly S.S. City of Newport News), 1941-42; assigned to command a transportation div. in Pacific area, participating in initial landings on Guadalcanal (1942), on New Georgia Island (1943); chief of staff and aide to comdr. Fifth Amphibious Force, Pacific Fleet, 1943, later becoming chief of staff to comdr. Amphibious Force, Central Pacific to Oct. 1945; command U.S. Naval Training Station, Newport, R.I., 1946-49; rear adm. ret. 1949. Decorated Am. Defense Service Medal with bronze "A," Navy Cross, Legion of Merit with Star, Victory Medal with destroyer clasp, World War I; D.S.M., American area Philippine Liberation and European-African-Middle East campaign medals, Victory Medal World War II. Mexican Service, Haitian Campaign, Yangtze Service and Asiatic-Pacific Area Campaign (with 10 battle stars) medals; Imperial Order of the Rising Sun, Fourth Class, Japan, 1938. Clubs: Cricket, Racquet, Phila. Country. Home: The Kenilworth, Alden Park, Philadelphia 44. Office: General Baking Co., 56th and Market, Phila. Died June 3, 1956.

THELEEN, DAVID E., naval officer; b. Kenosha, Wis., Nov. 6, 1875; s. Charles G.T.; grad. U.S. Naval Acad., 1897; m. Mary C. Persons, of Auburn, Ala., June 2, 1903. Promoted ensign, July 1, 1899; lt. jr. grade, July 1, 1902; lt., Aug. 10, 1903; lt. comdr., July 1, 1909; comdr., Aug. 29, 1916; capt. (temporary), Feb. 1, 1918. Served on Massachusetts during Spanish-Am. War, 1898; on surveying cruises in West Indies 3 yrs. and with Atlantic Training Squadron 3 yrs.; duty at Naval Proving Gound, Indian Head, Md., and two times at Naval Gun Factory, Navy Yard, Washington, D.C.; comdr. U.S.S. Glacier in U.S. Pacific Fleet, at outbreak of World War; served in Brazil and off East Coast S. America; duty Navy Yard, Washington, D.C., Sept. 1917-19; assigned as comdr. U.S.S. St. Louis, Oct. 8, 1919. Has specialized in ordnance work and engring. Mem. Am. Soc. Naval Engrs., Naval Inst. Republican. Baptist. Mason. Clubs: Army and Navy (Washington, D.C., and Manila). Address: Navy Dept., Washington DC

THEODOROVICH, JOHN VOLODYMYR, clergyman; b. Ukraine, Oct. 6, 1887; s. Volodymyr A. and Agapie (Chervinska) T.; student schs., Zhitomyr, Volynia, Theol. Sem., 1915; m. Julia Kornievich, May 24, 1914 (dec. Aug. 15, 1915); 1 dau., Valentina (Mrs. E.M. Prosen). Came to U.S., 1924, naturalized, 1929. Ordained priest, 1915; served with Army Red Cross, Russia, 1915-17; chaplain Ukranian Army, 1918-19; ordained bishop, Diocese of Podolia, City of Vinnitza, 1921-23; archbishop Ukrainian Orthodox Ch. in U.S., 1924-71, archbishop Ukrainian Greek Orthodox Ch. in Can., 1924-47; metropolitan of the Church, 1950, in jurisdiction affiliated churches, Brazil and Argentina. Address: Bala Cynwyd3PA Died May 1971.

THERREL, CATCHINGS, lawyer; b. Seattle, Nov. 25, 1890; s. Robert S. and Hattie (Catchings) T.; student Vanderbilt U., 1912; LL.B., Atlanta Law Sch., 1915; m. Bessie L. Huggins, Aug. 11, 1923 (dec.); m. 2d, Blanche Ash, 1955 (dec.); m. 3d, Ida M. Pelton, 1967. Admitted to Ga. bar, 1914; practiced in Atlanta, 1914-16, Miami Beach, Fla., 1927-71; mem. firm Copeland, Therrel, Baisden & Peterson. Dir. Miami Beach Abtract & Title Co., Chase Fed. Savs. & Loan Assn., Miami Beach First Nat. Bank; dir., v.p. Community Nat. Bank Bal Harbour. Entered N.G., 1916, served on Mexican Border; commd. capt. U.S. Army, 1917; served overseas with 328th Inf., 82d Div., disch. as maj., 1919. Mem. Am., Fla., Dade County bar assns., Am. Legion (past comdr.), Miami Beach C. of C. (dir.), Com. of 100 Miami Beach, Delta Theta Phi. Episcopalian. Clubs: LeGorce Country (sec.), Surf, Bal Harbour; Rivlera Country. Home: Miami Beach FL Died Sept. 1, 1971; buried Woodlawn Park Cemetery, Miami FL

THIGPEN, CHARLES ALSTON (thi'p'n), opthalmologist; b. Greenville, Ala., Dec. 19, 1865; s. Job and Martha Amanda (Watts) T.; A.M., Howard Coll., Marion, Ala., 1886; M.D., Tulane U., 1889; grad. study Royal London Ophthal. Hosp., 1890-91, U. Vienna, 1892, Augenclinic, Heidelberg, 1892; LL.D., U. Ala.; m. Daisie Lee Bissell, Nov. 17, 1896; children—Dorothy (Mrs. Edmund B. Shea), Elisabeth (Mrs. Wiley C. Hill, Jr.), Charles Alston. Began practice at Montgomery, Ala., 1893. Served as maj. Med. Corps, U.S. Army, 1917-18. Trustee Bryce Hosp., Tuscaloosa, Ala. Fellow A.C.S., A.M.A., Am. Acad. Ophthalmology and Otolaryngology; mem. State of Ala. Med. Assn. (pres.; mem. bd. censors), Montgomery County Med. Assn., World War Vets, Am. Legion. Democrat. Episcopalian. Home: 1420 S. Perry St. Office: 401 S. Court St., Montgomery, Ala. Died Apr. 23, 1958; buried Greenwood Cemetery, Montgomery.

THISTLEWOOD, NAPOLEON B. congressman; b. Kent Co., Del., Mar. 30, 1837; s. Benjamin and Eliza T.; ed. pub. schs., Del.; removed to Ill., 1858; m. Sarah E. Taylor, Sept. 6, 1866. Enlisted in Union Army as pvt., 1862; commd. capt. Co. 3, 98th Ill. Inf., Sept. 24, 1864; served in Wilder's brigade, Army of Cumberland; participated in battles of Stone River, Tullahoma, Chickamauga, Mission Ridge, etc., and Atlanta campaign; wounded, Selma, Ala., Apr. 2, 1865. Mayor of Cairo, Ill., 1879-83, 1897-1901; elected to 60th Congress to fill unexpired term of George W. Smith, deceased; reëlected 61st and 62d Congresses (1909-13), 25th Ill. Dist.; defeated for reëlection, 1912. Republican. Comdr. Dept. Ill. G.A.R., 1901. Home: Cairo, Ill. Died Sept. 16, 1915.

THOMAS, ALBERT congressman; b. Nacogdoches County, Tex., Apr. 12, 1898; s. James and Lonnie (Langston) T.; A.B., Rice U., 1920; LL.B., U. Tex., 1926; m. Lera Millard, Oct. 2, 1922; children—Anne (Mrs. Edward A. Lasater), Lera. Admitted to Tex. bar, 1927, and practiced in Nacogdoches County; county atty., 1927-30; asst. U.S. dist. atty., 1930-36; mem. 75th to 89th congresses from 8th Tex. Dist. Served as 2d lt. U.S. Army. Democrat. Methodist. Home: Houston. Died Feb. 15, 1966; buried Vet's Cemetery, Houston.

THOMAS, BRYAN M. supt. city schools, Feb. 1, 1891—; b. Milledgeville, Ga., 1836; s. John S. T.; ed. Oglethorpe Coll., 1851-54; grad. U.S. Mil. Acad., West Point, 1858; m. Mary Withers, Nov. 14, 1864. Three yrs. in U.S.A., 4 yrs. in C.S.A., passing through various grades from 1st lt. to brig. gen.; engaged in farming and teaching after Civil war. Democrat. Home: Dalton, Ga. Died 1905.

THOMAS, CHARLES MITCHELL naval officer; b. Phila., Oct. 1, 1846; s. Joseph T. and Belinda J. T.; apptd. to U.S. Naval Acad. from Pa., 1861, grad. 1865; m. Ruth, d. Rear Admiral Edward Simpson, U.S.N., Nov. 3, 1874. Promoted ensign, Dec. 1, 1866; advanced through grade to rear adm., Jan. 12, 1905. Served on Shenandoah, 1865-69; Navy Yard, League Island, 1869; on Supply, 1869-70; Guerriere, 1870-71; receiving-ship Potomac, 1872; Ajax and Terror, 1872-73; at Torpedo Sta., Newport, 1873-74; on Dictator, 1874-75; at Navy Yard, Phila., 1875; Centennial Expn., 1875-77; on receiving-ship St. Louis, 1877-78; Constitution, 1878-80; at Naval Acad., 1880-84; exec. officer Hartford, 1884-87; coast survey steamer Patterson, 1887-89; hydrographic insp. coast survey, 1889-91; Bureau of Navigation, 1891-93; comd. Bennington, 1893-95; Naval Home, Phila., 1895-97; Naval War Coll., Newport, 1897; Naval Acad., 1897-98; light-house insp. 5th dist., 1898-99; comd. Lancaster, 1899, Brooklyn, 1900-01, Oregon, 1901-02, receiving-ship Franklin, 1902-04; comdt. Naval Training Sta., Newport, R.I., and 2d naval dist., 1904-05; supt. naval training service, 1905-07; comdg. 2d div. Atlantic Fleet, Jan.-Aug. 1907; comdg. 2d Squadron, Atlantic Fleet, 1907-—. Home: Newport, R.I. Died 1908.

THOMAS, CHAUNCEY naval officer; b. Barryville, N.Y., Apr. 27, 1850; s. Chauncey and Margaret (Bross) T.; apptd. to U.S. Naval Acad. from Pa., 1867, and grad. 3d in class, 1871; m. Carrie Ella Flagg, Sept. 12, 1876. Promoted ensign, 1872; advanced through grades to rear adm., Mar. 10, 1910. Served on various ships and at various stations; in Nautical Almanac Office, Washington, 1878-81, 1885-86; aide to Admiral David D. Porter, 1886-91; at Hydrographic Office, Washington, 1894-96, 1900-01; exec. officer Yorktown, during Philippine insurrection, participating in several engagements; exec. officer battleship Oregon and comd. monitor Monadnock, 1899; comd. Albatross, 1901, and made scientific cruise, of 5 mos., in and about H.I.; comd. Bennington, 1902-03; comd. Maryland, at Woosung, China, 1907-08, leading U.S.N. in small arms target practice, and took battleship trophy for excellence in record target practice, 1908; insp. 3d light house dist., June 25, 1908-Jan. 26, 1910; pres. Bd. Inspection and Survey for Ships, Feb. 1-Oct. 20, 1910; comdr. 2d div. U.S. Pacific Fleet, Nov. 1, 1910-Jan. 16, 1911; then made comdr.-in-chief U.S. Pacific Fleet, flagship California; relieved Mar. 9, 1912, at Honolulu, T.H., transferred flag to U.S.S. West Virginia for passage to Navy Yard, Puget Sound; retired from active service by operation of law, Apr. 27, 1912. Mem. court martial and court of inquiry U.S.N., 1917. Mem. Calif. State Council Defense, 1917. Home: Pacific Grove, Calif. Died May 9, 1919.

THOMAS, DAVID army officer, congressman; b. Pelham, Mass., June 11, 1762; s. David and Elizabeth (Harper) T.; m. Jeannette Turner, 1784. Took part in expdns. of Mass. Militia for relief of R.I., 1777; re-entered Mass. Militia, 1781, served with 3d, 5th regts.; mem. N.Y. Assembly (Anti-Federalist), 1793, 98, 99; served in N.Y. Militia, rose to maj. gen. in command 3d div.; mem. U.S. Ho. of Reps. from N.Y., 7th-10th congresses, 1801-May 1, 1808; treas. State of N.Y., 1808-10; agt. for Bank of Am., 1811. Died Providence, R.I., Nov. 27, 1831.

THOMAS, EARL DENISON brig. gen. U.S.A.; b. McHenry, Ill., Jan. 4, 1847; s. Edwin E. and Naomi (Patterson) T.; ed. Todd's Acad., Woodstock, Ill., 1859-61; grad. U.S. Mil. Acad., 1869; m. Clara M. Church, 1869. Pvt. and corporal Co. H, and sergt. maj. 8th Ill. Cav., Apr. 1, 1862-Apr. 23, 1865; commd. 2d lt. 5th U.S. Cav., June 15, 1869; 1st lt., Mar. 1, 1872; capt., Apr. 1, 1885; maj. insp. gen. vols., May 12, 1898; maj. 8th U.S. Cav., Feb. 14, 1899; hon. disch. from vol. service, Mar. 7, 1899; transferred to 5th U.S. Cav., May 23, 1899; insp. gen., Feb. 28, 1901; lt. col. 13th Cav., Nov. 16, 1901; col. 7th Cav., Apr. 19, 1903; transferred to 11th Cav., Apr. 21, 1903; brig. gen. U.S.A., Apr. 18, 1907. Bvtd. 1st lt., Feb. 27, 1890, "for gallant services in action against Indians nr. Ft. McPherson, Neb., June 8, 1870"; capt. for same in action against Indians at the Caves, Ariz., Dec. 28, 1872, and campaign against Indians in Ariz., 1874. Served at various frontier posts and in Indian country, 1870-98, in Spanish-Am. War, P.R., P.I. and Cuba; second intervention of Cuba, 1906, in comd. 11th U.S. Cav. hdqrs. Pinar del Rio, Cuba; in charge of the Province of Pinar del Rio, 1906-07; in comd. of Dept. of Colorado, 1907-11; in charge of operations on the border of Ariz. and N.M. in Mexican troubles, 1910; retired Jan. 4, 1911. Home: Laurel, Md. Died Feb. 17, 1921.

THOMAS, ELBERT DUNCAN ambassador; born Salt Lake City, Utah, June 17, 1883; s. Richard Kendall and Caroline (Stockdale) T.; A.B., U. of Utah, 1906; Ph.D., U. of Calif., 1924; LL.D., U. of Southern Calif., 1935, University of Hawaii, 1951; Litt.D., National U., 1937; m. Edna Harker, June 25, 1907 (died Apr. 29, 1942); children—Chiyo (Mrs. Horton R. Telford), Esther (Mrs. Wayne C. Grover), Edna Louise (Mrs. Lawrence Lee Hansen); m. 2d Ethel Evans, Nov. 6, 1946. Served as missionary of Latter Day Saints' Ch. in Japan, 1907-12; was traveler and student, Asia and Europe, 1912-13; instr. Latin and Greek, U. of Utah, 1914-16, sec.-registrar, 1917-21; fellow polit. science, U. of Calif., 1922-24; prof. polit. science, U. of Utah, since 1924; mem. of U.S. Senate, 1933-51; U.S. High Commissioner Trust Territory of the Pacific Islands with rank of ambassador since 1951. Major Insp. Gen's. Department, Utah Nat. Guard and U.S. Reserves, 1917-26. Mem. Gen. Board Deseret S.S. Union; del. U.S. Senate Interparliamentary Union, Budapest, 1936, Paris, 1937; chmn. Thomas Jefferson Memorial Commn.; dir. Columbia Institute for the Deaf. Apptd. U.S. del., Internat. Labor Organization Conference Philadelphia, 1944, Paris, 1945, Montreal, 1946, Geneva, 1947, San Francisco, 1948. Mem. Am. Assn. Univ. Profs., Am. Soc. Internat. Law (v.p.), Am. Political Science Assn. (v.p. 1940-41), Utah Alumni Assn. (pres. 1913-14), Coun. Am. Learned Socs., Chinese Polit. and Social Science Assn., Am. Oriental Soc., New Orient Soc., Phi Delta Theta, Phi Kappa Phi, Alpha Pi Zeta, Pi Gamma Mu. Mem. Carnegie Internat. Conf. Am. Profs., 1926, Conf. Teachers of Internat. Law, Washington, D.C., 1925-28. Democrat. Club: Timpanogos. Author: (in Japanese) Sukui No Michi; Chinese Political Thought, 1927; World Unity Through Study of History, 1928, Thomas Jefferson—World Citizen, 1942; The Four Fears, 1944; This Nation Under God, 1950. Contbr. on Oriental affairs and internat. relations. Home: 4758 Aukai Av., Honolulu, T.H. Died Feb. 11, 1953.

THOMAS, FREDERICK LIONEL, lawyer; b. Lansing W.Va., June 14, 1892; s. Ullyses Grant and Cora Alice (Calloway) T.; J.D., W.Va. U., 1917; m. Leafy Woofter, Dec. 24, 1917; m. Virginia Alice (Mrs. Roy H. Jones, Jr.), Frederick Lionel, Robert S. Admitted to W.Va. bar, 1917; with legal dept. United Fuel Gas Co., 1917; partner firm Spilman, Thomas, Battle & Klostermeyer, and predecessors, Charleston, W.Va., from 1920. Pres., dir. Midwale Colliery Co.; dir. Crab Orchard Coal & Land Co., also dir. 8 comml. credit plan companies. Mem. Pub. Assistance Council, Kanawha County, W.Va., 1933-36; chmn. Kanawha Clay chpt. A.R.C., 1943. Served to 2d lt. U.S. Army, World War I. Mem. Am., W.Va., Kanawha County (pres. 1930) bar assns., Charleston Area and W.Va. C. of C. W.Va. State Bar, Order of Coif, Phi Delta Phi, Phi Sigma Kappa. Republican. Baptist. Clubs: Edgewood Country, Army-Navy (Charleston). Home: Charleston WV Died Sept. 9, 1969.

THOMAS, GEORGE HENRY army officer; b. Southampton County, Va., July 31, 1816; s. John and Elizabeth (Rochelle) T.; grad. U.S. Mil. Acad., 1840; m. Frances Lucretia Kellogg, Nov. 17, 1852. Commd. 2d lt. 3d Arty., U.S. Army during Fla. War; brevetted 1st lt. for gallantry in action against Indians; served in several Southern garrisons; commd. 1st lt., 1844; served throughout Taylor's Mexican campaign; brevetted capt. and maj. for gallantry at battles of Monterey and Buena Vista; instr. arty. and cavalry U.S. Mil. Acad., 1851-54; commd. lt. col., 1861; col., 1861; commanded brigade in Shenandoah Valley; commd. brig. gen. U.S. Volunteers, 1861; assumed command 1st Div., Army of Ohio, 1861; won victory at Mill Springs, 1862; promoted maj. gen. volunteers, comdr. right wing of Halleck's army, 1862; commanded XIV Army Corps at Stone's River, 1862-63, became known as "the Rock of Chickamauga" as result of Battle of Chickamauga, 1863; promoted brig. gen. U.S. Army, 1863; Sherman's Atlanta campaign began, 1864, Thomas' Army of Cumberland participated in every offensive move; received surrender of Atlanta; ordered to Nashville, Tenn., 1864; defeated Hood near Nashville, 1864; promoted maj. gen. U.S. Army, 1865; received thanks of U.S. Congress, 1865; name sent by Pres. Johnson to Senate for promotion to rank of maj. gen. U.S. Army, and for brevets of lt. gen. and gen., 1868, declined ranks; assumed command Mil. Div. of Pacific, San Francisco, 1869. Died San Francisco, Mar. 28, 1870.

THOMAS, HENRY BASCOM orthopedic surgeon; b. Elk Garden, Va., Aug. 17, 1875; s. Thaddeus Peter and Sarah (Price) T.; B.S., U. Chgo., 1899; M.D., Northwestern U., 1903; m. Louise Downing Wendell, 1905. Prof. hygiene and physical edn., med. adviser Armour Inst. Tech., 1903-20; instr. orthopedic surgery, Northwestern U., 1911; prof. and head of dept. orthopedic surgery, U. of Ill. Coll. of Med., now emeritus; sr. cons. orthopedic surg. St. Luke's Hosp., Research and Ednl. Hosp., Ill. Surg. Inst. for Children (dir. in charge); chief orthopedic surgeon Cook County Hosp., 10 yrs., Home for Destitute Crippled Children, 10 yrs.,; cons. orthopedic surgeon Municipal Tuberculosis Hosp., Sanitarium and Dispensary, 16 yrs. Orthopedic surgeon, major, U.S. Army, World War. Citation from University of Chicago, St. Luke's Hospital for 25 yrs. of service; certificate of Merit (U.S.A.) for World War II. Mem. A.M.A. (past sec. and pres. orthopedic sect.), Ill., Chicago med. socs., Am. Orthopedic Assn., Chicago Orthopedic Soc. (past pres.), Clinical Orthopedic Soc. (ex-pres.), Am. Acad. Orthopedic Surgery, Inst. of Medicine, Chicago. Mason (Shriner), Elk. Clubs: University, Rotary, City, Olympia Fields Country; Lake Placid (New York). Home: University Club of Chicago, 76 E. Monroe St., Chicago 3. Office: 30 N. Michigan Av., Chgo. Died Mar, 25, 1958; buried Oak Woods Cemetery.

THOMAS, JACKSON MASH psychiatrist; b. Thomasville, Ga., July 29, 1903; S. Jackson Mash and Maud (Walden) T.; B.S., Emory U., 1924, M.D., 1926; m. Julia Bruck, Nov. 20, 1929; children—Jane, Jackson W. Intern Piedmont Hosp., Atlanta, 1926-27; jr. med. officer Boston Psychopathic Hosp., 1927-28, sr. med. officer, 1928-29, chief med. officer, 1936-37; asst. psychiatry Harvard, 1928-36, instr., 1936-37, asso., 1938-47; Commonwealth Fund fellow, 1929-32, study European clinics, 1930-31; chief men's dept. McLean Hosp., Waverly, Mass., 1932-36; asst. prof. psychiatry Boston U., 1936-37; asso. prof. psychiatry U. Louisville, 1937-38; vis. psychiatrist outpatient dept. Peter Bent Brigham Hosp., Boston, 1938—; asst. psychiatrist Mass. Gen. Hosp., 1941—; prof. psychiatry Tufts Coll., 1947—, now chmn. dept. Served from maj. to lt. col. M.C. AUS, 1942-45. Diplomate Am. Bd. Psychiatry and Neurology. Mem. Boston Soc. Psychiatry and Neurology, Mass. (pres.), N.E. psychiat. socs., Mass. Med. Soc., A.M.A., Am. Psychiat. Assn. Club: Harvard (Boston). Contbr. med. jours. Home: 22 Longfellow Rd., Wellesley Hills, Mass. Office: 319 Longwood Av., Boston 15. Died Nov. 9, 1963; buried Sandersville, Ga.

THOMAS, JOHN army officer; b. Marshfield, Mass., Nov. 9, 1724; s. John and Lydia (Waterman) T.; m. Hannah Thomas, 1761, 3 children. Commd. lt. and surgeon's mate, 1755, empowered to enlist volunteers in province; served in N.S. and in expdn. dispatched to Can. under Amherst, 1759-60; apptd. by Gov. Hutchinson as justice of peace, Kingston, Mass., 1770; commd. lt. gen. Mass. Militia, 1775; commd. brig. gen. by Continental Congress, 1775; in command at Roxbury (important post in Am. siege lines) winter 1775-76; seized and fortified strategic site of Dorchester (Mass.), 1776, as result British were forced to evacuate Boston; promoted maj. gen. and ordered North, 1776; summoned council of war at Quebec, Can., 1776, unanimously decided to retreat and fell back to Sorel. Died of smallpox, June 2, 1776; buried Chambly, Que.

THOMAS, JOHN JENKS neurologist; b. Columbus, O., Sept. 6, 1861; s. Alfred and Martha A. (Hoge) T.; A.B., Williams, 1886; M.D. and A.M., Harvard, 1890; studied univs. of Heidelberg, Berlin and Vienna; m. Frances Pickering, d. Rear Admiral John G. Walker, Oct. 21, 1899; children—John G. W., Henry Pickering, Alfred Rebecca Pickering. Dist. phys. and phys. to Boston Dispensary, 1892-97; asst. phys. for nervous system, Boston City Hosp., 1893-1906, phys. same, 1906-25, and consulting physician to same from 1925; asst. neurologist, Children's Hosp., 1893-1913, neurologist, 1913-19, and consulting neurologist to same, 1919—; pathologist, Boston Insane Hosp., 1898-1903; instr. in neurology, 1902-06, asst. prof., 1906-12, prof., 1912-16, prof. emeritus, 1916—, Tufts Coll. Med. Sch.; asso. in neurology, Harvard Grad. Sch. of Medicine; consulting neurologist to Quincy City, Infants' hosps. Served with Harvard Unit at English Base Hosp., 1915, as lt. col. comdg. med. div.; maj. Med. Corps, A.E.F., 1918-19; with Base Hosp. 7, and as consultant in neuro-psychiatry. Joint author: Modern Treatment of Nervous and Mental Diseases; Cerebral Paralyses of Children, in Nelson's Loose Leaf Medicine; "Malingering," in Peterson, Haynes and Webster's Legal Medicine and Psychology. Home: Boston, Mass. Died July 17, 1935.

THOMAS, JOHN PARNELL, congressman; b. Jersey City, N.J., Jan. 16, 1895; s. J. Parnell and Georgianna (Thomas) Feeney; grad. high sch. Ridgewood, N.J., student Univ. of Pa., 1914-17; m. Amelia Stiles, Jan. 21, 1921; children—J. Parnell, Stiles. Bond salesman with Kountze Bros., N.Y. City, 1919-20; with Paine, Webber & Co., N.Y. City, as salesman, 1920-24, as mgr. N.Y. bond department, 1924-38; mem. Thomas & Godfrey, insurance brokers, N.Y. City. Mem. 75th to 81st Congresses (1937-49), 7th N.J. Dist.; mem. Com. on Armed Services House of Representatives, Chairman Committee on Un-American Activities. Mayor of Allendale, 1926-30; mem. N.J. Assembly, 1935-37. Served as 2d and 1st lt. and capt. inf., U.S. Army, with A.E.F., 1917-18. Mem. Psi Upsilon. Republican. Mason. Home: Allendale NJ Died Nov. 19, 1970.

THOMAS, JOHN ROBERT congressman; b. Mt. Vernon, Ill., Oct. 11, 1846; s. Maj. William A. and Caroline (Neely) T.; ed. Hunter Coll. Inst., Princeton, Indiana; (LL.D., McKendree Coll., Ill., 1895); served in Civil War, rising from pvt. to capt.; m. Lottie Culver, Dec. 28, 1870 (died 1880). Admitted to bar, 1869; city atty., Metropolis, Ill., 2 terms, 1869, 1870; state's atty., 1871-74; mem. 46th to 50th Congresses (1879-89); served on various important coms., including com. on Naval Affairs; has been called "father of the modern Am. Navy"; judge U.S. courts, Ind. Ty., 1897-1901; resumed practice, 1901; elected 1st mem. Congress from Ind. Ty. under Sequoyah Constn., 1905; nominated for judge Supreme Ct. by 1st Rep. State Conv. of Okla. (declined); mem. State Code Commn. of Okla., 1909-10. Was Grand Master Masonic Grand Lodge, Ill., and held other Masonic offices; mem. G.A.R. Home: Muskogee, Okla. Died Jan. 19, 1914.

THOMAS, LORENZO army officer; b. New Castle, Del., Oct. 1804; s. Evan and Elizabeth (Sherer) T.; grad. U.S. Mil. Acad., 1823. Commd. maj. 4th Inf., U.S. Army, 1848; quartermaster in Seminole War, 1836-37; adjutant-gen., Washington, D.C., 1838; brevetted maj. 1846-53; joined volunteer div. of Maj. Gen. William O. Butler as chief of staff in Mexican War; designated chief of staff to Lt. Gen. Winfield Scott, 1853; promoted to col. in charge adjutant's office, 1861; made adjutant-gen., given rank brig. gen., 1861-63; organized Negro regts. in Mississippi Valley, 1863-65; brevetted maj. gen., 1865; after adjutant-gen. resumed full charge of bureaus, 1868; sec. ad interim for Johnson, 1868; arrested for violation of Tenure of Office Act, 1868, immediately admitted to bail and discharged; ret. 1869. Died Washington, D.C., Mar. 2, 1875.

THOMAS, PERCY CHAMPION, retired mfr.; b. St. Louis, Mo., Nov. 5, 1874; s. James Stringham and Jane Hunt (Dodge) T.; ed. Rome Free Acad.; m. Mary Minton Hoxsey, Sept. 2, 1902 (died July 1942); children—Louise Hoxsey (Mrs. Earl Martin), Jane Dodge (Mrs. Josiah N. Knowles); m. 2d, Jane Patten Waterbury, April 20, 1946. Began as clerk in railroad offices, Chicago, Ill., and St. Paul, Minn., 1887-91; with Rome Mfg. Company, manufacturers brass, copper, aluminum and steel products, since 1892, advancing through various offices, president, 1920-28, (retired). Major Ordnance Dept., U.S. Army, 1918; Republican presdl. elector, N.Y., 1920; commr. pub. works, Rome, 1921; ex-pres. Rome Community Chest; dir. Rome Chamber Commerce. Episcopalian. Clubs: Rome, Teugega Country (Rome); Tin Whistles (Pinehurst, N.C.); Burlingame (Calif.) Country; Everglades (Palm Beach, Fla.). Home: Delta Farms, Town of Lee, P.O. Box 266, Rome NY

THOMAS, RALPH LLEWELLYN public utilities exec.; b. Marion, O., May 2, 1887; s. Rev. Welling E. and Emma (Mattoon) T.; A.B., Princeton, 1909; S.B. in Elec. Engring., Mass. Inst. Tech., 1913; m. Rebekah Ober, Apr. 22, 1924 (dec. Mar. 1965); children—Ralph L., Jr. (killed in action, France, 1944), Gustavus Ober, Rebekah Elizabeth (dec. May 1966). Student engr. Stone & Webster Mgmt. Assn., Boston and Fall River, Mass. and New London, Conn., 1913-15; asst. engr. later efficiency engr., asst. to gen. supt., asst. gen. supt., gen. supt. Pa. Water & Power Co., Balt., 1915; 38; project engr. Safe Harbor Water Power Corp., 1930-42; exec. engr. Consol. Gas Elec. Light & Power Co. Balt, 1938-42, dir., 1939—, v.p. charge elec. operations, 1942-50, v.p., exec. engr., 1950-54. Served from 1st lt. to capt. 302d Engrs. 77th Div., U.S. Army, 1917-19. Chief utilities service Md. Citizens Def. Corps, 1942-45; mem. Md. Adv. Council for Civil Def., 1950—. Mem. exec. bd. Balt. council Boy Scouts Am.; bd bd. mgrs. Md. Tng. Sch. for Boys. Fellow Am. Inst. E.E.: (chmn. Md. sect. 1936-37), Am. Soc. M.E.; mem. Princeton Engring. Assn., Newcomen Soc. Eng., Phi Beta Kappa, Tau Beta Pi, Kappa Sigma. Republican. Presbyn. (elder). Clubs: Baltimore Engineers (pres., 1939-40), Princeton Terrace. Contbr. to sci. publs. Home: 803 St. Georges Rd., Balt. 21210. Office: Lexington Bldg., Balt. 1. Died Nov. 17, 1965; buried Balt.

THOMAS, SAMUEL capitalist; b. at South Point, O., Oct. 27, 1840; ed. Marietta, O.; clerk with Keystone Iron Co. until 1861; in Union army, 1861-65, pvt. to bvt. brig. gen.; after the war asst. commr. for Miss. and later asst. adj. Freedmen's Bur. until 1867; then in coal and iron interests in Hocking Valley; acquired large ry. interests; became pres. E. Tenn., Va., and Ga. and other Southern roads; pres. Louisville, New Albany & Chicago; pres. Duluth, South Shore & Atlantic; contractor for building the Croton Aquedust, New York. Home: New York, N.Y. Died 1903.

THOMAS, SAMUEL MORGAN, electrical engr.; b. Searcy, Ark., Dec. 12, 1903; s. George Crawford and Annie (Tapscott) T.; B.S., Ga. Sch. Tech., 1926; m. Bebe Wharton, June 21, 1930; 1 son, Samuel Morgan. Employed by Allis Chalmers Mfg. Co., Milw., 1926-31; elec. engr. Corps Engrs., U.S. Army, 1931-40; commd. capt. Signal Corps, Army U.S., 1940 and advanced through grades to brig. gen.; signal dir., Persian Gulf Comd., Teheran, Iran, U.S. Army, 1942-45, chief of staff, 1945; dir. communications and postal service, U.S. Control Group Council, Berlin, Germany, 1945; brig. gen., Signal Corps. Res., 1947; asst. chief engr., RCA Communications, Inc., 1947; v.p., 1947-51; spl. asst. to sec. of army, 1952; v.p. Hazeltine Electronics Corp. 1954-62, sr. v.p. Hazeltine Dir. Internat. div., 1962-73. Decorated Legion of Merit with oak leaf cluster, Bronze Star, Order of Kutuzov (Russia); Order British Empire. Mem. Phi Kappa Phi, Tau Beta Pi, Alpha Tau Omega. Clubs: Greenwich Country; Army and Navy (Washington). Home: Greenwich CT Died Jan. 4, 1973; buried Arlington Nat. Cemetery, Washington DC

THOMAS, WILLIAM NATHANIEL, navy chaplain; b. Rankin County, Miss., Mar. 21, 1892; s. John C. and Annie Laura (Thompson) T.; A.B., Millsaps Coll., Jackson, Miss., 1912, diploma, Seashore Divinity Sch., Gulfport, Miss., 1913-15, Chicago Theological Seminary, 1925, D.D. (hon.) Millsaps Coll., 1935, Am. Univ., Washington, D.C., 1941; m. Martha Ellen Fondren, Feb. 18, 1913; children—William N., John Edward. Began career as Methodist clergymen, 1911; Milsaps Memorial Meth. Ch., Jackson, Miss., 1910-11, Daleville Meth., Ch., Miss., 1912-13; Meth. Ch., Summit, Miss., 1913-17. Apptd. to chaplaincy in 1918, first duty Receiving Ship, Boston, Mass., 1918; U.S.S. Madawaska, 1918-19, U.S.S. Imperator, 1919; Naval Hosp., Fort Lyon, Colo. 1919-22; U.S.S. Pennsylvania, 1922-24; Naval Acad. Annapolis, 1924-27; U.S.S. Raleigh, 1927-29; 14th Naval Dist., 1929-32; U.S.S. West Virginia, 1932-33; Naval Acad., Annapolis, 1933-45; apptd. chief of chaplains, U.S. Navy, with rank of rear adm., 1945, ret. Awarded Victory Medal with Bronze Star—Transport Service, 1918; American Area Campaign Service Ribbon, American Defense Campaign Service Ribbon, Victory Medal, World War II, Legion of Merit. Mem. Internat. Soc. of Theta Phi, Kappa Sigma Frat. Mason. American Legion. Home: Lake Junaluska NC Died Apr. 1971.

THOMPSON, CHARLES FULLINGTON army officer; b. Jamestown, N.D., Dec. 11, 1882; s. John Justin and Ida May (Fullington) T.; student U. of Mich., 1899-1900; B.A., U.S. Mil. Acad., 1904; m. Laura Bell Jenks, Apr. 29, 1909; children—Marjorie Fullington (Mrs. Howard Eugene Engler), Barbara Jenks (Mrs. J. Maury Dove, Jr.). Commd. 2d lt., Inf., June 15, 1904; advanced through grades to maj. gen., Oct. 1, 1940, retired Nov. 30, 1945. Inclusive of 10 yrs. overseas, service comprises 18 yrs. with troops, 14 yrs. on high staffs, 2 yrs. as student and 7 yrs. on faculties. Decorated D.S.M., with two Oak Leaf Clusters; Companion Military Division, Most Honourable Order of the Bath (British), Chevalier Legion of Honor (French). Clubs: Chevy Chase (Md.); Army and Navy (Washington). Home: Kenneday-Warren Apts., Washington 8. Died June 15, 1954; buried Arlington Nat. Cemetery.

THOMPSON, CLARY govt. ofcl.; b. N.C., Sept. 30, 1912; s. Edward Braxton and Newell (McDuffie) T.; student Campbell Coll., Buie's Creek, N.C., 1934-36; A.B., U. N.C., 1938; grad. Nat. War Coll., 1957; m. Jessie Futrell, Dec. 5, 1941; children—Stephen Braxton, Richard Gregory, Laura Elizabeth. Editor, News Dispatch, Sanford, North Carolina, 1938; city editor Sanford (N.C.) Herald, 1938-39; reporter, editorial writer Daily Times-News Burlington, N.C., 1939; polit. reporter Winston-Salem (N.C.) Jour., 1939-42; spl. cons. chief pub. information Dept. Army, 1948, spl. asst. sec. army, 1949; with fgn. service res. Dept. State, 1951—; press attache Am. embassy, Tehran, 1951-52; assigned policy officer Greek, Turkish and Iranian desk, U.S. Information Agy., Washington, 1953, dep. asst. dir. for Near East, South Asia and Africa, Washington, 1953-56; pub. affairs officer, dir. U.S. Information Service, Am. embassy, Athens, Greece, 1957-60, dep. asst. dir. USIA, Washington, 1960—. Served from apprentice seaman to lt. comdr., USNR, 1942-46.

Home: 4509 Western Av. N.W., Washington 16. Office: USIA, Washington 25. Died Feb. 26, 1961; buried Arlington Nat. Cemetery.

THOMPSON, EGBERT naval officer; b. N.Y.C., June 6, 1822; s. Egbert and Catherine (Dibble) T.; m. Emily B. Thompson, at least 1 dau. Served with Wilkes Exploring Expdn. in Antartic, 1838-42; passed midshipman, 1843; in brig Somers; exec. in schooner Bonita during Mexican War; joined Adm. Foote's Miss. flotilla, 1862; commanded gunboat Pittsburg in attack on Ft. Donelson, 1862; ran heavy batteries at Island Number 10 in Mississippi River to aid Polk's army below; commanded ships Commodore, McDonough, later Cimarron on blockade duty, 1864-65; commd. capt., 1867; commanded Dacotah, 1866-67, Canandaigua, 1871-72. Died Washington, D.C., Jan. 5, 1881.

THOMPSON, FRANK E. lawyer; b. Duluth, Minn., Aug. 16, 1875; s. William Andrew and Caroline (Anderson) T.; ed. high sch.; student Chicago Coll. of Law, 1895-98; m. Ella Lewis, Dec. 1903 (now dec.); 1 son, Frank E.; m. 2d, Alice Roth, June 20, 1912; children—Barbara, Dixie (Mrs. Samuel Carnes Collier), William Roth. Practiced at Honolulu, T.H., since 1900; served as 1st referee in bankruptcy, U.S. Dist. Court of Hawaii; admitted to practice Supreme Court of U.S., 1908; specializes in admiralty law and represents various cos.; was atty. for Queen Liliuokalani in claim against U.S. for seizure of her personal crown lands; personal atty. for Princess Abigail Kawananakoa; atty. Matson Navigation Co.; pres. Lines, Isthinian S.S. Co., Royal Hawaiian Hotel, Civic Auditorium, Finance Corp., Consolidated Motors; dir. Hawaiian Contracting Co., Ltd., The von Hamm-Young Co., Ltd., Mfrs. Shoe Co., Ltd. Served in Spanish-Am. War; capt. U.S. Res., 1914-17; served with Draft Bd., Hawaii, World War. Mem. bd. Community Chest Fund, Honolulu, two terms. Mem. Am. Bar Assn., Bar Assn. Ty. of Hawaii (twice pres.); mem. Honolulu Commn. on Uniform laws. Republican. Mason. Clubs: Pacific, University, Waialae, Schofield Barracks Golf, Waialae Golf (Honolulu). Home: 1559 Thurston Av. Office: 5th Floor, Inter-Island Bldg., Honolulu, T.H. Deceased.

THOMPSON, HARRY LEROY naval officer (ret.); b. Gibraltar, Pa., Mar. 18, 1890; s. Heber Clouser and Emma Fawkes (Wicklein) T.; grad. Naval War Coll., 1929, U.S. Naval Acad. Postgrad. Sch., 1930; m. Kathryn Dunleavy, Jan. 5, 1913; children—Harry LeRoy (Comdr. U.S.N.), Leah (Mrs. James Wilbur White), Jordan (M.D.). Enlisted U.S. Navy, 1906, commd. ensign, 1917, advanced through grades to rear adm., 1947; splized. in communications; comdr. U.S.S. Humphreys, 1931-33, U.S.S. Owl, 1930-31, U.S.S. Nevada, 1941-42, U.S.S. Richmond, 1944-45; ret. from active service, Jan. 1, 1947; now engaged in real estate bus. Awarded combat Legion of Merit. Reformed Ch. Home: 1519 Arlington Terrace, Alexandria, Va. Office: 1505 H St., N.W., Washington. Died Aug. 17, 1953.

THOMPSON, HEBER SAMUEL engr.; b. Pottsville, Pa., Aug. 14, 1840; s. Samuel and Elizabeth (Cunningham) T.; A.B., Yale, 1861, A.M., 1871; studied mining engring, in pvt. offices; m. Sarah E. Beck, Jan. 23, 1866. Enlisted, pvt., Apr. 16, 1861, "First Defenders," 1st troops of war of secession to enter Washington (Apr. 18, 1861); later served, 1861-65; lt. and capt. 7th Pa. Cav.; engr. and agt. Girard Estate, Mar. 16, 1874-—. Pres. bd. trustees State Hosp. for Injured, anthracite coal region, Pa., Ashland, Pa. ("Miners' Hosp."); apptd. under act of assembly, by gov. of Pa., on "Coal Waste Commn."—pub. report, 1893. Address: Pottsville, Pa. Died 1911.

THOMPSON, HUGH SMITH gov.; b. Charleston, S.C., Jan. 24, 1836; s. Henry Tazewell and Agnes (Smith) T.; grad. S.C. Mil. Acad., 1856; m. Miss Clarkson, 1858. Lt. and prof. French Arsenal Acad., Columbia, S.C., 1858-60; capt. battalion of State cadets of S.C., C.S.A., 1861-65; prin. Columbia Male Acad., 1866-76; State supt. edn., 1876-82; gov., 1882-86; asst. sec. treasury, U.S., 1886-89; U.S. civil service commr., 1889-92; comptroller New York Life Ins. Co., 1892. Democrat. Home: New York, N.Y. Died 1904.

THOMPSON, JACOB congressman, cabinet officer; b. Leasburg, N.C., May 15, 1810; s. Nicholas and Lucretia (Van Hook) T.; grad. U. N.C., 1831; m. Catherine Jones. Admitted to N.C. bar, 1834; practiced law in Pantotoc, Miss.; mem. U.S. Ho. of Reps. from Miss., 26th-31st congresses, 1839-51; played important part in Nat. Democratic convs., 1854, 56; U.S. sec. of interior, 1857-61, reorganized dept. to increase efficiency; served with Confederate Army until 1863, chief insp. of army under Pemberton; elected to Miss. Legislature, 1863; sent to Can. as Confederate secret agt., 1864, cooperated with "Sons of Liberty," sought to free Confederate soldiers imprisoned nr. Gt. Lakes; took part in plans to burn No. cities including N.Y.C.; charged with complicity in Lincoln's assasination; lived in Can. and Europe until 1868; returned to Oxford, Miss., 1868. Died Memphis, Tenn., Mar. 24, 1885; buried Elmwood Cemetery, Memphis.

THOMPSON, JAMES VOORHEES religious edn.; b. Rock Springs, Pa., May 25, 1878; s. Johnathan MacWilliams and Anna Sara (Carpenter) T.; A.B., Wesleyan U., Conn., 1902; B.D., Drew Thoel. Sem., 1905; grad. study, U. of Pittsburgh, 1912-14; Ph.D., Northwestern, 1928; m. Nora Gray, Aug. 18, 1909; m. 2d Mary Young Ruffin, Aug. 12, 1951. Student pastor Bronxdale M.E. Ch., N.Y. City, 1903-04; asst. minister and dir. religious edn. (first recorded in U.S.), Christ M.E. Ch., Pittsburgh, 1905-07; ordained ministry M.E. Ch., 1907; teacher Shadyside Acad., Pittsburgh, 1908-12, Peabody High Sch., Pittsburgh, 1912-14; supt. young people's dept. Bd. of Sunday Schs., M.E. Ch., 1914-25; instr. dept. religious edn., Boston U., 1918; agt. World's Sunday Sch. Assn. and Bd. of Sunday Schs. M.E. Ch. in Japan, Korea and China, 1920-21; asso. minister and dir. religious edn., First M.E. Ch., Evanston, Ill., 1925-28; asst. prof. religious edn., Northwestern U., 1928-29, asso. prof., 1929-30; prof. adminstr. in religious edn., Drew Theol. Sem., 1930-48; ret.; counselor div. inter-religious activities Am. Jewish Com., N.Y.C., 1948-52; dir. Coll. of Religious Edn. and Missions, same, 1931-35. Active National Conference Christians and Jews. Served as corporal Spanish-Am. War, 1898; chaplain 325th Inf., 82d Div., A.E.F., June-Oct. 1918, sr. chaplain 2d Army Corps, Oct. 1918-19; mem. O.R.C. Decorated capt. Order of the Silver Palms (France), also Officer of Academy. Mem. Religious Edn. Assn., Internat. Council Religious Edn., Alpha Delta Phi, Phi Delta Kappa, Ind. Rep. Mason (32 deg.). Club: University (Evanston). Author: Handbook for Workers with Young People, 1921; The Daily Vacation Church School (with J. E. Stout), 1923, Studied in Religious Education (with Lotz and others), 1931; Orientation in Education (with Schutte and others), 1932; Great Biographies (with Lotz and others), 1938; Making the Gospel Effective (with Anderson and others), 1944. Editor and author of "The Open Door Series" (guidance pamphlets for adolescents and their leaders). Lecturer on religious edn. Home: 22 Irving Pl., N.Y.C. Died. July 1, 1952; buried State College, Pa.

THOMPSON, JOHN FAWDREY, JR., coast guard officer; b. Franklin, N.H., May 30, 1919; s. John Fawdrey and Anna (Hildrebrand) T.; student Syracuse U., 1937-38; B.S., U.S. Coast Guard Acad., 1941; m. Marjorie A. Dunton, July 8, 1956; children—Dan J., Sheri Ann, Mark Dale. Commd. ensign USCG, 1941, advanced through grades to rear adm., 1970; comdg. officer sub chaser, Greenland Patrol, 1942; staff officer antisubmarine warfare, 1943; exec. officer, comdg. officer U.S.S. Harveson, 1943-45; comdg. officer U.S.S. Joyce, Atlantic Fleet, 1945; adminstrv. aide to Chief Mcht. Marine Safety, 1945-48; Industry tng. Esso Co. N.Y., 1948-49; insp. Marine Insp. Office, N.Y.C., 1949-50, 52-53; exec. officer, comdg. officer cutter Mendota, 1950-52; insp., sr. investigating officer Marine Insp. Office, Jacksonville, Fla., 1953-58; comdg. officer cutter Cherokee, 1958-60; officer in charge Coast Guard Mcht. Marine Detail, Yokohama, Japan, 1960-63; exec. officer, officer in charge Marine Insp. Office, Phila., 1963-67; chief operations div., chief staff 7th Coast Guard Dist., 1967-70; supt. U.S. Coast Guard Acad., New London, Conn., 1970-72. Decorated Navy Commendation medal. Mem. Nat. Def. Transp. Assn., Propeller Club U.S., Newcomen Soc. N.Am., U.S. Power Squadrons (bd. govs.). Address: New London CT Died Jan. 19, 1972.

THOMPSON, J(OHN) MILTON brig. gen. U.S.A.; b. Lebanon, N.H., Aug. 1, 1842; s. Ira W. and Cynthia Wheeler (Spalding) T.; ed. pub. and pvt. schs.; hon. A.M., Dartmouth College, 1907; m. Mary Elizabeth Walcott, Mar. 5, 1871; m. 2d, Carrie Alice Ellis, Nov. 21, 1914. Enlisted pvt. 7th N.H. Inf., Nov. 7, 1861; apptd. 2d lt. 33d U.S.C. Inf., Jan. 15, 1863, 1st lt., Jan. 27, 1863, capt., Nov. 7, 1863, until end of Civil War; apptd. 2d lt. 38th U.S. Inf., July 28, 1866, 1st lt., Nov. 4, 1867; capt. 24th Inf., Dec. 23, 1878, maj., Apr. 26, 1898 (col. 42d U.S. Vol. Inf., Aug. 17, 1898); lt. col. 14th Inf., Oct. 19, 1899; col. 23d Inf., Apr. 22, 1901; brig. gen. U.S.A., Aug. 9, 1903, and retired. Bvtd. 1st lt., Mar. 2, 1867, "for gallant and meritorious service at James Island, S.C." Address: Washington, D.C. Died Apr. 6, 1922.

THOMPSON, JOHN TALIAFERRO army officer, mech. engr., inventor; b. Newport, Ky., Dec. 31, 1860; s. Lt. Col. James and Julia Maria (Taliaferro) T.; student Ind. U., 1876-77; grad. U.S. Mil. Acad., 1882; torpedo course, U.S. Engrs.' Sch., 1884; grad. U.S. Arty. Sch., 1890; LL.D., Ind. U., 1922; m. Juliet Estelle, d. Judge M. B. and Almira Lewis Hagans, July 27, 1882; 1 son, Lt. Col. Marcellus Hagans. Commd. 2d lt. arty., June 13, 1882; promoted through grades to col., Oct. 30, 1913; retired, Nov. 2, 1914; brig. gen. ordnance, O.R.C., Army of U.S., 1924. Served various garrisons, Naval Gun Factory, Nat. Armory, etc.; lt. col. U.S. Vols., Tampa, Fla., 1898, and in Cuba; connected with development of service small arms; charged by War Dept. with preparation of war plans of Ordnance Dept., 1908-14, lecturer Army War Coll., 1908-14-—; cons. engr., New York, 1914-17; in charge design and mfr. of all small arms and cartridge for U.S., Apr. 16, 1917-18. Brig. gen. (temp.), Aug. 1918; advisory engr. to chief of ordnance; dir. of ordnance training; dir. of arsenals. Awarded D.S.M., 1919, "For exceptionally meritorious and conspicuous service," as chief of small arms div.; later pres. John T. Thompson Corp., New York. Episcopalian. Writer of various tech, pamphlets and articles. Inventor of firearms, machinery and airplane devices. Home: Great Neck, L.I., N.Y. Died June 21, 1940.

THOMPSON, LAWRANCE ROGER, educator, author; b. Franklin, N.H., Apr. 3, 1906; s. Roger Everett and Lena (Keller) T.; B.A., Wesleyan U., Middletown, Conn., 1928; Ph.D., Columbia, 1939; m. Janet Arnold, Jan. 9, 1945; children—Nathaniel Arnold, Eleanor Ann, Joel, Thomas Neal. Instr. English, Wesleyan U., 1934-35; instr. English and comparative lit. Columbia Grad. Sch., 1935-36, research fellow, 1936-37; curator rare books Princeton U. Library, 1937-42, editor-in-chief Library Chronicle, 1938-42; Guggenheim fellow, 1946-47; asso. prof. English, Princeton, 1947-51, prof., 1951-73, Holmes prof. Belles-lettres, 1968-73. Ford Found. fellow, 1953-54; guest lectr. Salzburg (Austria) Seminar in Am. Studies univs. Ljubljana, Zagreb and Belgrade, Yugoslavia, U. Oslo, Norway, Hebrew Jerusalem, Israel. Trustee Princeton U. Press, 1955-60, chmn. editorial board, 1959-60. Served from lt. (j.g.) to lt. comdr., USNR, 1942-46. Decorated Legion of Merit; recipient Citation for Distinguished service as tchr., scholar, author, Wesleyan U., 1958. Author: Robert Frost: A Chronological Survey of His Work, 1933; Edwin Arlington Robinson: A Catalogue of An Exhibition (with H. Bacon Collamore), 1935; Young Longfellow, 1939; Fire and Ice: The Art and Thought of Robert Frost, 1942; The Navy Hunts the CGR 3070, 1944; Melville's Quarrel with God., 1952; A Comic Principle in Sterne, Meredith, Joyce, 1954; Robert Frost: A Critical Study, 1959; William Faulkner: An Introduction and Interpretation, 1963; Robert Frost; The Early Years (Melville Cane award 1967), 1966; Robert Frost: The Years of Triumph, 1970 (Pulitzer prize in biography 1971). Editor: Tilbury Town; Selected Poems of Edwin Arlington Robinson, 1954; Selected Letters of Robert Frost, 1964; (with Edward Connery Lathem) Robert Frost, Farm-Poultryman, 1963, Robert Frost and the Lawrence, Massachusetts, High School Bulletin, 1966; (with Benton Spruance) Moby Dick: The Passion of Ahab, 1968; (with Arnold Grade) New Hampshire's Child: The Derry Journals of Lesley Frost, 1969. Home: Princeton NJ Died Apr. 16, 1973.

THOMPSON, LEWIS RYERS asst. surgeon gen.; b. LaFayette, Ind., Aug. 6, 1883; s. Lewis Ryers and Laura (Steuben) T.; M.D., Louisville Med. Coll., 1905; married Mabel Cook, February 22, 1908; children—Lewis Ryers, Joyce Ann. Member Philippine Constabulary, 1906-09; United States Public Health Service, 1910-—, assistant surgeon, 1910, passed assistant surgeon, 1914, surgeon, 1921, senior surgeon, 1930, asst. surgeon gen., 1930-42; dir. National Institute of Health, 1937-42, inspection officer 1943, asst. surg. gen. Bureau of State Service, 1943-45; dir. med. div., Strategic Bombing Survey of Japan, 1945; rank of brigadier general; consultant medical services of the American Red Cross 1947-—. Was scientific dir. Internat. Health Div., Rockefeller Foundn. Mem. div. of med. scis. Nat. Rsrch. Council. Fel. Am. Coll. Dentists; mem. A.M.A., Am. Pub. Health Assn., Indsl. Phys. and Surgs., Phi Chi. Episcopalian. Club: Columbia Country. Author of numerous arts. and bulletins on med. subjects. Home: 3917 Virgilia St., Chevy Chase, Md. Address: U.S. Public Health Service, Bethesda Sta., Washington. Died Nov. 12, 1954; buried Arlington Nat. Cemetery, Va.

THOMPSON, MAURICE WYCLIFFE; b. Crawfordsville, Ind., Aug. 27, 1878; s. Will H. and Ida (Lee) T.; student U. Washington, 1896-97; m. Ada Forsey, Mar. 14, 1907; children—Alma (dec. 1918), Wilda (dec.), Betty (Mrs. Carroll Barton McMath, Jr.). Mem. Washington N.G., 1898-—, advanced through grades to rank maj. gen.; appt. adj. State of Wash., with rank of brig. gen., 1914, and served until retirement, 1941; acting adj. gen., 1945-47. Served in adj. gen's. dept. U.S. Army, with rank of maj., World War I. Supt. State Soldiers Home, Orting, Wash., 1941-47; state dir. S.S.S., 1917, 1940-41. Awarded certificate of merit and selective service medal, 1946. Mem. Mil. Order of the World Wars, Am. Legion, S.A.R. Elk. Club: Lions (Orting, Wash.). Address: 9115 Gravelly Lake Drive, South Tacoma, Wash. Died Nov. 3, 1954; buried Lakeview Cemetery, Seattle.

THOMPSON, MELVILLE WITHINGTON financial accountant, lawyer; b. Washington, D.C., Oct. 22, 1871; s. Niles Hibbard and Lucy (Withington) T.; m. Mary L. Glass, 1925. Mem. Thompson & Black, accountants and tax consultants, N.Y. City; pres. Thompson & Black, Incorporated, oil producers, Tulsa, Oklahoma. Commd. lt. col. U.S.A., Aug. 15, 1917; pres. War Credits Bd. of War Dept.; hon. discharged, Nov. 29, 1918; (civilian) gov. War Credits Bd. from Nov. 1918. Awarded D.S.M. Home: Mt. Kisco, N.Y. Died July 15, 1936.

THOMPSON, PERCY WALLACE captain United States Coast Guard, retired; b. at Washington, June 20, 1858; s. Col. M. T. and Mary Gray (Douglas) T. (lineal descendant Col. Ninian Beall, Md., 1654, and Rev. John Orme, "Father of Presbyterianism in America"); ed. Va. Mil. Inst., Md. Agrl. Coll., Columbian (now George Washington) U., Nat. U. Law Sch., Washington; grad. U.S. Revenue-Cutter Service Acad., 1881; m. Nellie Cardozo Snell, of Erie, Pa. (descendant of Richard

Warren of the Mayflower). Exec. officer U.S.S. Rush and exec. and comdg. officer U.S.S. Corwin, attached to Pacific Squadron of Admiral Miller during Spanish-Am. War; has since comd. U.S. steamers Dexter, Hamilton, Appache, Windom, McCulloch, Woodbury, Onondaga. Mem. S.A.R., Naval and Mil. Order Spanish-Am. War, Alpha Tau Omega. Democrat. Presbyn. Clubs: University (Washington); Southern (San Francisco). Contbr. articles on naval, maritime and hist. subjects to Scribner's Magazine, Belford's Monthly, Maritime Register, New York Sun, Boston Herald, Detroit Free Press, etc. Asso. editor Our Army and Navy. Address: "The Anchorage," Palo Alto, Calif.

THOMPSON, RICHARD WIGGINTON sec. navy; b. Culpeper County, Va., June 9, 1809; went to Ky., 1831, becoming clerk in Louisville store; moved to Lawrence County, Ind.; admitted to bar, 1834; member Ind. legislature, 1834-36, senate, 1836-38; short time pres. senate and acting lt. gov.; presdl. elector on Harrison and Tyler ticket, 1840; member Congress, 1841-43 and 1847-49; presdl. elector, 1864; del. Nat. Rep. convs. 1868 and 1876; judge 5th Ind. circuit, 1867-69; sec. navy in Hayes cabinet, 1877-81; became chmn. Am. com., Panama Canal Co., 1881. Author: The Papacy and the Civil Power; Footprints of the Jesuits; History of the Tariff; Personal Recollections of Sixteen Presidents. Address: Terre Haute, Ind. Died 1900.

THOMPSON, ROBERT BRUCE, mfg. exec.; b. Balt., Feb. 2, 1906; s. Robert Bruce and Mary (Pattersen) T.; student Johns Hopkins, 1922-24; m. Helen A. French, Oct. 27, 1928; 1 dau., Janet F. (Mrs. John Knauth). With Am. Can Co., from 1922, successively serviceman, plant operations staff, plant mgr., Balt., mgr. Atlantic div., N.Y.C., gen. mgr., v.p. mfg., 1922-63, v.p. mfg., purchasing and engring, from 1963; civilian cons. to comdg. gen. Munitions Command, U.S. Army, 1966-70. Home: Stamford CT Died Jan. 1970.

THOMPSON, THEODORE STRONG pay dir. U.S.N.; b. Northampton, Mass., April 23, 1842; s. Augustus C. and Sarah Elizabeth (Strong) T.; ed. Williams Coll. Served 9 mos. in U.S. Vols. Civil War; apptd. acting asst. p.m. U.S.N., Oct. 9, 1863; hon. discharged, Aug. 31, 1865; apptd. asst. p.m., July 23, 1866; passed asst. p.m., Feb. 1, 1868; p.m., Jan. 25, 1878; pay insp., July 10, 1898; pay dir., Sept. 21, 1901; retired, Dec. 26, 1903, with rank of rear admiral for services during Civil War. Home: Brookline, Mass. Died July 27, 1915.

THOMPSON, THEOS JARDIN, scientist, nuclear engr.; b. Lincoln, Neb., Aug. 30, 1918; s. Theos Jefferson and Mabel E. (Dow) T.; A.B., U. Neb., 1941, M.A., 1942, Doctor of Science (honorary), 1964; Ph.D. in Nuclear Physics, University of Cal. at Berkeley, 1952; m. Dorothy Sibley, Feb. 14, 1947; children—Jeff, Edward, Robert, Elizabeth. Physicist U. Cal. Radiation Lab., 1948-52, lectr. physics, Berkeley, 1949-52; staff Los Alamos Sci. Lab., 1952-55, reactor design and constrn.; asso. prof. nuclear engring. Mass. Inst. Tech., 1955-58, prof., 1958-—, dir. nuclear reactor for design, constrn. and operation; cons. Mem. AEC adv. com. reactor safeguards, 1959-66, chmn., 1960; co-editor AEC project Safety Information for Technology of Reactors, 1962-70; commr. AEC, 1969-70. Served from 2d lt. to maj., C.W.S., AUS, 1942-46. Recipient E.O. Lawrence Meml. award, Atomic Energy Commn., 1964; Guggenheim Found. fellow, 1963-64. Fellow American Nuclear Soc. (director); mem. Am. Academy of Arts and Sciences, American Phys. Soc., Phi Beta Kappa, Sigma Xi. Home: Winchester MA Died Nov. 25, 1970; buried Lincoln NB

THOMPSON, THOMAS GORDON educator; b. Rosebank, N.Y., Nov. 28, 1888; s. John Haslam and Mary Elizabeth (Langdon) T.; grad. Bklyn. Comml. High Sch., 1906; B.A., Clark U., Worcester, Mass., 1914; M.S., U. Wash., 1915, Ph.D., 1918; m. Hariert Galbraith, June 27, 1922 (dec.); children—Thomas, John Souter, Harriet; m. 2d, Isabel Harris Costigan, July 14, 1954; children (adopted)—Charles Harris, Gary Howard. Lab asst. Am. Brass Co., 1906-11; asst. chemist Am. Steel & Wire Co., 1911; teaching fellow U. Wash., 1914-17, instr. chemistry, 1919, asst., asso., prof., 1919-51, dir. oceanographic labs., 1930-51, prof. oceanography, 1951-—, mil. leave of absence, 1942-46. Pvt., Inf., 1st lt. Ordinance, capt. CWS, 1917-19; maj. CWS Res. 1924-42, active service as lt. col. 1942-45, col. 1945-—; dir. War Dept. Civilian Protection Sch., Seattle, 1942-43; Chem. Warfare Bd., 1943-44; tech. dir. San Jose Project, Panama, 1944-45. Ret. col. AUS, 1946. Rep., Am. Geophys. Union to Internat. Geodetic and Geophys. Union, Stockholm, 1930, Lisbon, 1933, Edinburgh, 1936, Washington, 1939; chmn. internat. com. on Pacific Sci. Congress, 1936-53; chmn. com. on oceanography NRC, 1935-41; mem. oceanographic panel Research and Devel. Bd., 1947-51. Awarded Agassiz Gold medal, Nat. Acad. Scis., 1948; Carnegie Scholar Brit. Iron and Steel Inst., 1915; Rockfellow Found. travel grantee, 1930; 1st State of Wash. Distinguished Service Citation 1960. Fellow Cal. Acad. Scis.; mem. Nat. Acad. Scis., Am. Chem. Soc. (chmn. Puget Sound sect. 1922-25), A.A.A.S. (pres. Pacific Div., 1946-47), Am. Geophysics Union, Oceanographic Sec. (pres. 1935-38), Am. Geog. Soc., Alpha Delta Phi, Sigma Xi, Phi Lambda Upsilon. Club: Cosmos. Author: numerous sci. papers reporting results of original research. Home: 4002 Burke Av. N., Seattle, also McConnell Island, Deer Harbor, Wash. Died Aug. 10, 1961; buried McConnell Island.

THOMPSON, W. STUART, architect; born at N.Y.C., Jan. 25, 1890; s. George and Mary (Stuart) T.; grad. Sch. Arch., Columbia, 1912; grad. study architecture, southeastern Europe, 1913-16; m. M. Gladys Slade, Aug. 22, 1913; children—William Stuart, George Clifford, Isabel F. (dec.). Critic archtl. design Cooper Union, 1917-20; practicing architect, N.Y.C., from 1918; architect: Gennadius Library and Loring Hall, Athens, Greece (J. Van Pelt partner); Pearce Coll.; Corinth Mus.; hosp., Manisa, Turkey (H.S. Churchill partner); Am. Hosp., Istanbul, Turkey; numerous bldgs. in Greece and Near East; pvt. houses, apts. and office bldgs. in U.S., including: State Tower Bldg., Syracuse, N.Y., Crucible Steel Bldg., Chgo.; Sterling Drug Plant, Gulfport, Miss.; Sterling-Winthrop Research Inst., Rensselaer, N.Y.; lab. for Sharp & Dohme, West Point, Pa.; master plan terminal bldgs. Conn. State Airport; sch. bldgs., Greenwich, Conn.; pharm. mfg. bldgs., Rio de Janeiro, Cali, Colombia, Durban, S. Africa; Byzantine chs. Church Holy Cross, Brookline, Mass., Greek Orthodox Ch. of Archangels, Stamford, Conn.; Med. Research Bldg. for Carter Products, Inc., Cranbury, N.J.; architect restoring Stoa Attalos (159 B.C.), Athens (Phelps Barnum, partner), and others; airport designer in def. program U.S. Govt. with Pan-Am. Airways, 1942-43. Archtl. fellow Am. Sch. Classical Studies, Athens, 1913-15. Mem. board Near East Found. Decorated Order of Saviour, 1926, Order of Phoenix, 1956 (Greece); named hon. citizen Athens, 1926, 56. Fellow N.Y. Acad. Sci.; mem. Am. Friends of Greece (sec.). A.I.A., Archaeol. Institute of Am., N.Y. Acad. Scis. (mem. bd.); hon. mem. Archaeological Society of Athens. Mem. various coms. for amelioration Greek people, 40 yrs. Clubs: Indian Harbor Yacht Columbia Univ. (N.Y.C.). Home: Greenwich CT Died Apr. 2, 1968.

THOMPSON, WILLIAM army officer; b. Ireland, 1736. Came to Am., 1756; settled in Carlisle, Pa., became surveyor and justice of peace; served as capt. during French and Indian War, participated in John Armstrong's expdn. against Kittanning; elected mem. Com. of Correspondence for Cumberland County (Pa.), 1774; mem. Pa. Com. of Safety, 1775; in command of a battalion of riflemen raised in Southeastern counties of Pa., 1775; served in 2d Pa. Regt. (1st body of men to reach Boston from South); repulsed attack on Lechmere Point, 1775; commd. brig. gen. Continental Army, 1776, ordered to Can. in charge of detachment of 2,000 men; attempted to attack Three Rivers, 1776, failed because of treachery, made prisoner, exchanged, 1780. Died Carlisle, Sept. 3, 1781; buried Carlisle.

THOMPSON, WILLIAM congressman, army officer, editor; b. Fayette County, Pa., Nov. 10, 1813; attended common schs. Moved to Mt. Pleasant, Ia.; mem. Ia. Territorial Ho. of Reps., 1843; sec. Ia. Constl. Conv., 1846; mem. U.S. Ho. of Reps. (Democrat) from Ia., 30th-31st congresses, 1847-June 29, 1850 (when seat was declared vacant); commd. capt. 1st Ia. Volunteer Cav., U.S. Army, 1861, promoted maj., 1863, col., 1864, brevetted brig. gen. of Volunteers for gallant services, 1865, honorably mustered out, 1866, recommd. capt. 7th Cav., U.S. Army, 1866, brevetted maj., 1867 for gallant services at Prairie Grove, Ark., lt. col. for gallant services in action at Bayou Metoe, Ark., 1867, ret., 1875; became editor Ia. State Gazette. Died Tacoma, Wash., Oct. 6, 1897; buried Tacoma Cemetery.

THOMPSON, WILLIAM BLAINE, JR., railroad ofcl.; b. Falls Church, Va., Aug. 22, 1917; s. William Blaine and Catherine Elizabeth (Foley) T.; A.A., U. Fla., 1940; m. Margaret Louise Covey, Dec. 5, 1958; children—William Blaine III (dec.), Holland McTyeire, Gayle Tigert (Mrs. Carpenter). Asst. cashier Fla. Nat. Bank, Jacksonville, 1940-48; asst. to v.p. Fla. Power and Light Co., 1949; self-employed pub. relations cons., 1952-58, also v.p. Riddle Air Lines; asst. v.p. Assn. Am. Railroads, 1958-60, 64-70; pres. Fla. East Coast Ry. Co., 1961-64, dir., 1961-70; pres., dir. Florida East Coast Highway Dispatch Co., 1961-64; dir. Fla. Nat. Bank and Trust Co., Miami. Sec., asst. treas. Am. Taxpayers Assn., 1963-70. Served to lt. col. USMCR, World War II, Korea. Mem. Am. Legion. Club: Seminole (Jacksonville, Fla.). Home: Arlington VA Died Oct. 12, 1970; buried Falls Church VA

THOMPSON, WILLIAM LELAND wholesale druggist; b. Troy, N.Y., Apr. 4, 1871; s. William Augustus and Harriette (Crosby) T.; A.B., Harvard, 1893; LL.D., Rensselaer Poly. Inst., 1931; m. Martha Groome, Jan. 6, 1909; children—William Leland, Martha E., Peter Schuyler. With John L. Thompson Sons & Co., Troy, 1893-—, treasurer, 1903, president, 1911-54, chairman of the board, 1954-—; chairman of board Nat. City Bank of Troy, Rensselaer Improvement Co., Community Hotel Co.; 1st v.-pres. of the Troy Savings Bank. Rep. candidate for N.Y. Assembly, 1897; mem. Bd. of Edn., Troy, 1906-27 (resigned); regent University State of N.Y., 1927-51. Pres. Associated Sch. Boards of N.Y. State, 1920-22; former pres. board trustees Emma Willard Sch., and Russell Sage Coll.; former mem. bd. Troy Pub. Library; mem. bd. Tuberculosis Relief Assn., Y.M.C.A. Former regent and vice chancellor, Univ. State of N.Y. Mem. Nat. Guard N.Y., 1896-1912, advancing to capt. Co. C, 2d Regt.; served in Spanish-Am. War and as aide to Brig. Gen. Charles F. Roe; aide on staff Gov. Odell of N.Y., 1901-05. Republican. Episcopalian; sr. warden St. John's Church; mem. Standing Com. Diocese of Albany. Mem. N.Y. State Hist. Soc., Am. Assn. Museums, S.R., St. Nicholas Soc., Mil. Order Foreign Wars. Clubs: Institute of 1770, Varsity, Hasty Pudding, Dickey and Spee clubs (Harvard); Harvard (New York); Troy. Home: Red House Farm, Rensselaer, N.Y. Office: 161 River St., Troy, N.Y. Died Oct. 13, 1957; buried Oakwood Cemetery, Troy.

THOMSON, CHARLES GOFF author; b. Little Falls, N.Y., Feb. 9, 1883; s. William Philander and Henrietta (Nellis) T.; D.V.M., Cornell, 1907; m. Hazel Gibbs, Apr. 30, 1912; children—Peter, Robert Dade. Dir. Alabang Serum Lab., P.I., 1908-10; in charge mil. and civilian forces operating against rinderpest in Philippines, 1910-13; asst. dir. prisons for Philippine Govt., 1914-17. Capt. Remount Div., comdg. remount depots at Camp Gordon and Camp Dix, 1917; lt. col. and comdr. all troops at Lux, France, Aug. 1918-May 1919. Became supt. Yosemite Nat. Park, Calif. Author: Terry—A Tale of the Hill People, 1921; Time Is a Gentleman, 1929. Contbr. to mags. Home: Yosemite National Park, Calif. Died Mar. 23, 1937.

THOMSON, JAMES SUTHERLAND, educator, former univ. dean; b. Stirling, Scotland, Apr. 30,21892; s. John and Margaret (Sutherland) T.; student Craig's, Stirling, 1896-1903; Eastbank Acad., Glasgow, 1903-10; M.A., U. Glasgow, 1914, D.D., 1946; student Trinity Coll., Glasgow, 1919-21; D.D., U. Toronto, 1936; LL.D., State Coll. Wash., 1943, McGill U., 1946, Queen's U., 1946, Toronto University, 1947, Manitoba University, 1948, McMaster University, 1948, Alberta University, 1949, U. Sask., 1951; m. Margaret Stewart Troup, June 27, 1922; children—John, Margaret Stewart. Minister, Middle Ch., Coatbridge, Scotland, 1920-24; sec. of edn., Ch. of Scotland, 1924-30; prof. theology, Pine Hill Coll., Halifax, N.S., 1930-37; pres., U. of Saskatchewan, from 1937; prof. philosophy of religion, McGill U., 1949-61, lecturer philosophy of education, 1961-72. Moderator of United Church of Canada, 1956. Served with Queen's Own Cameron Highlanders, 1915-17; capt., Rifle Brigade, 1917-19; now hon. colonel C.O.T.C. Fellow Royal Society Can. Mem. United Ch. of Can. Author: Studies in the Life of Jesus, 1927; The Way of Revelation, 1928; The Hope of the Gospel, 1955; The Divine Mission, 1957; The Word of God, 1959. Contributor of articles to the Dalhousie Review, and other jours. Home: Montreal Quebec Canada Died Nov. 1972.

THOMSON, JAMES WILLIAM chief engr. U.S.N.; b. Wilmington, Del., Nov. 10, 1836; s. James William and Sarah (Peters) T.; acad. edn.; m. Laura N. Troth, Oct. 7, 1862. Apptd. 3d asst. engr. U.S.N., June 26, 1856; 1st asst. engr., Aug. 2, 1859; chief engr., Feb. 2, 1862; retired, June 26, 1896; advanced to rank of rear admiral retired, June 29, 1906, for services during Civil War. Served on various vessels and at various stations during Civil and Spanish wars; mem. bd. Naval Acad., Oct.-Nov. 1875, bd. of inspection, Nov. 5, 1875-Aug. 1, 1876, bd. of examiners, May 12-May 31, 1881, examining bd., Phila., 1885-87. Home: Moorestown, N.J. Died Mar. 17, 1914.

THOMSON, KEITH congressman; born Newcastle, Wyo., Feb. 8, 1919; s. William John and Mary Forbes (Coffey) T.; LL.B., U. Wyo., 1941; m. Thyra Rose Godfrey, Aug. 6, 1939; children—William John II, Bruce Godfrey, Keith Coffey. Mgr. bookstore, storeroom U. Wyo., 1939-41; admitted to Wyo. bar, 1941; partner Henderson & Thomson, Cheyenne, 1946-—; mem. Wyo. Ho. of Reps., 1950-54; mem. 84th-86th Congresses, at large, Wyo.; U.S. senator-elect to the 87th Congress. Lt. col., inf., AUS, 1941-46, comdr. 2d Bn., 362d Regt., 91st Inf. Div. Decorated Legion of Merit, Bronze Star, Purple Heart (U.S.); Cross of Valor (Italy); named outstanding young man of year Cheyenne Junior Chamber of Commerce, 1947. Member American Legion, Vets. Foreign Wars, University of Wyoming Alumni Association (past president), Wyo., Laramie County bar assns., Phi Delta Theta. Republican. Presbyn. Club: Lions. Home: 3902 Dey Av., Cheyenne, Wyo. Office: House Office Bldg., Washington. Died Dec. 9, 1960; buried Arlington Nat. Cemetery.

THOMSON, MARK congressman; b. Norriton Twp., nr. Norristown, Pa., 1739. Became a miller; justice of peace Sussex County, N.J., 1773; mem. provincial conv., 1774; Provincial Congress, 1775; commd. lt. col. 1st Regt., Sussex County Militia, 1775; lt. col. Col. Charles Stewart's Battalion of Minutemen, 1776, col. 1st Regt., Sussex County Militia, 1776, col. Battalion of Detached N.J. Militia, 1776; mem. N.J. Gen. Assembly, 1779; mem. state council, 1786-88; apptd. lt. col. and a.d.c. on staff Gov. Richard Howell of N.J., 1793; mem. U.S. Ho. of Reps. (Federalist) from N.J., 4th-5th congresses, 1795-99. Died Marksboro, Sussex (later Warren) County, N.J., Dec. 14, 1803; buried Presbyn. Ch. Cemetery.

THOMSON, WILLIAM army officer; b. Pa., Jan. 16, 1727; s. Moses and Jane Thomson; m. Eugenia Russell, Aug. 14, 1755, 12 children. Worked on his father's plantation, S.C., also traded with Indians; served as maj. S.C. Militia during Cherokee War (for which Assembly voted him bonus and land); indigo planter, justice of peace, enquirer and collector of taxes, at various times; mem. Ga. Legilsature; served as col. Orangeburg Militia; a commr. to relocate N.C.-S.C. border, 1772; mem. 1st Ga. Provincial Assembly; lt.-col.-comdt. Continental Army, blocked British attempt to land on Sullivan's Island at entrance to Charleston harbor, 1776; received Congressional thanks for this action; promoted col. Continental Army, 1776, resigned, 1778; imprisoned for having broken parole to British following capture of Charlestown, 1781; mem. S.C. Conv. to ratify U.S. Constn., 1788. Died Nov. 2, 1796.

THOMSON, WILLIAM JUDAH naval officer; b. Washington, Apr. 27, 1841; s. William and Mary (Delano) T.; ed. Baltimore schs.; m. Maud Spurgeon, Apr. 25, 1898. Apptd. acting asst. p.m. U.S.N., Mar. 29, 1865; asst. p.m., July 23, 1866; passed asst. p.m., Mar. 20, 1868; p.m., Feb. 16, 1878; pay insp., Apr. 9, 1899; pay dir., Mar. 9, 1902; retired, Jan. 10, 1903, with rank of rear admiral for services during Civil War. Home: Seattle, Wash. Died 1909.

THORNAL, BENJAMIN CAMPBELL, judge; b. Charleston, S.C., Oct. 15, 1908; s. Benjamin Campbell and Henrietta F. (Wagener) T.; LL.B. University Fla., 1930; m. Alyce Carolyn Letton, Nov. 7, 1936; children—Alyce (Mrs. Thomas H. Wyatt), Ben C. Admitted to Fla. bar, 1930, practiced in Orlando, 1930-55; city atty., Orlando, 1938-41. 46-48, 52-55; county atty. Orange County, Fla., 1941-43; justice Supreme Ct. of Fla., 1955-70, chief justice, 1965-67. Legislative aide to gov. of Fla., 1943, 53. Trustee U. Fla. Endowment Corp.; vice chmn. bd. trustees Fla. So. Coll. Served as lt., USNR, World War II. Mem. Am. Law Inst., Fla. Bar, U.S. (dir. 1939-41), Fla. (pres. 1939-40) Jr. C.'s of C., Order of the Coif, also frats. Phi Kappa Phi, Phi Delta Phi, Lambda Chi Alpha, Blue Key. Methodist. Author, compiler: Code City of Orlando, 1948. Home: Tallahassee FL Died Nov. 4, 1970; buried Orlando FL

THORNE, JAMES REYNOLDS, r.r. exec.; b. Spearsville, La., Sept. 19, 1909; s. John William and May (Reynolds) T.; student pub. schs., Fla.; grad. Advanced Mgmt. Program at Harvard Univ.; m. Helen Connor, July 20, 1935. With S.A.L. Ry., 1926-43, successively sec., chief clk. to supt., yardmaster, terminal trainmaster, trainmaster, assistant supt., 1937-43; with Seaboard Air Line R.R. Company, 1946-67, successively asst. supt., supt., asst. gen. mgr., asst. v.p. operations, asst. to pres., 1952-58, exec. v.p., 1958-67; dir., 1960-67; v.p. operations, Seaboard Coast Line R.R. Co., 1967-70, v.p. exec. dept., Jan.-July 1970; exec. vice pres. and/or dir. subsidiaries; v.p. operations Athens Terminal Co., Gainsville Midland R.R. Co., Ga., Fla. & Ala. R.R. Co., Tavares & Gulf R.R. Co., Tampa & Gulf Coast R.R. Co.; exec. v.p., dir. Southeastern Investment Co.; mem. exec. com., dir. Fruit Growers Express Company; dir. Barnett National Bank of Jacksonville (Fla.), Seacoast Transportation Co., also Jacksonville Terminal Co., North Charleston Terminal Co., Duval Connecting R.R. Company, Richmond Terminal Railway Company, Trailer Train Company, Railway Express Agy., Inc., Norfolk & Portsmouth Belt Line R.R. Co. Served as capt., maj. AUS, 1943-46. Mem. Am. Assn. R.R. Supts., Nat. Def. Transportation Assn. Baptist. Mason (Shriner). Clubs: River; Commonwealth (Richmond); Southern and Southwestern Railway. Home: Jacksonville FL Died July 9, 1970; buried Evergreen Cemetery, Jacksonville FL

THORNTON, SIR HENRY WORTH ry. mgr.; b. Logansport, Ind., Nov. 6, 1871; s. Henry Clay and Millamenta Comegys (Worth) T.; grad. St. Paul's Sch., Concord, N.H., 1890; B.S., U. of Pa., 1894, D.Sc., 1923; m. Virginia Dike Blair, June 20, 1901; children—Anna Blair, James Worth; m. 2d, Martha Watriss, Sept. 11, 1926. Began, 1894, as draughtsman in office of chief engr. of Southwest System of Pa. Lines West of Pittsburgh; asst. engr. of constrn., Cleveland & Marietta R.R. (a subsidiary of the Pa. R.R.), 1895-96, and later in field work of Southwest System, supervisor yards at Columbus, O., asst. engr. Cincinnati div. and asst. engr. in spl. work; engr. maintenance of way, Erie & Ashtabula div. Northwest System of Pa. R.R., 1899-1901; supt. Cleveland, Akron & Columbus R.R., 1901-02, Erie & Ashtabula div., 1902-11; asst. gen. supt. L.I. R.R., Feb.-Nov. 1911, gen. supt. 1911-14; apptd. gen. mgr. Gt. Eastern Ry., Eng., 1914. Served on exec. com. of Gen. Mgrs. which, under direction of the Govt., controlled and worked the English railways upon the outbreak of war in 1914; dep. dir. of inland water transportation with rank of col. in Royal Engrs., 1916; asst. dir. gen. of movements of rys. in France, 1917; apptd. dep. dir. gen., same, with rank of brig. gen., Dec. 1917; insp. gen. of transportation with rank of maj. gen., 1918; served on commn. to investigate operations and financial condition of the Metropolitan Water Bd. of City of London, 1920; apptd. chmn. and pres. Canadian National Rys., Oct. 1922. Naturalized British subject, 1919; Knight Comdr. Order British Empire, 1919; Companion Legion of Honor (French); Officer Order of Leopold (Belgian): D.S.M. (U.S.). Address: Montreal, Quebec. Died Mar. 14, 1933.

THORP, FRANK brig. gen. U.S.A.; b. in Me., Mar. 29, 1842. Second lt. 28th Me. Inf., Oct. 14, 1862; hon. mustered out, Aug. 31, 1863; 2d lt. 1st Me. Light Arty., Dec. 30, 1863; hon. mustered out, June 21, 1865; apptd. from Me., 2d lt. 5th U.S. Arty., May 11, 1866; 1st lt., June 6, 1867; grad. Arty. Sch., 1875; capt., Apr. 24, 1891; maj., Jan. 25, 1901; lt. col. Arty. Corps, Sept. 20, 1902; col., Jan. 21, 1904; brig. gen. and retired at own request, over 40 yrs.' service, Feb. 9, 1906. Address: Washington, D.C. Died Aug. 8, 1924.

THORPE, GEORGE CYRUS lawyer, officer U.S.M.C.; b. Northfield, Minn., Jan. 17, 1875; s. George Carleton and Adelaide (Carpenter) T.; B.S. and LL.B., New York U., 1910; grad. Naval War Coll., 1915; A.M., Brown U., 1916; grad. Gen. Staff Coll., 1921; m. Cora Wells, Apr. 8, 1908; children—Amy Elizabeth (Mrs. Arthur J. Pack), Jane Wells, George Wells. Commd. 2d lieutenant U.S. Marine Corps, 1898, and advanced through grades to col. (temp.), July 1918; col. (permanent), Mar. 9, 1919. Served on U.S.S. Yale, Santiago Campaign,.Spanish-Am. War, 1898, and in 1st P.R. Expdn.; Philippine Insurrection, 1899-1901; fleet marine officer, European Fleet, 1892-93; with Am. expdn. to Syria, 1903; comd. marines in expdn. through Abyssinia to make treaty with Menelik; with Army of Cuban Pacification, 1906-08; comd. Naval Prison, Portsmouth, 1911-14; chief of staff 2d Brig. Marines, 1917-18; with Naval War Coll., 1919-20; Gen. Staff Coll., 1920-21; comdg. Marine Barracks, Pearl Harbor, T.H., Aug. 1921; retired. Layer; mem. bars of Mass., N.H., and D.C. Bvtd. captain "for distinguished service and gallant conduct" at Novelta, P.I., Oct. 1899. Decorated with star of Ethiopia, by Menelik. Mason. Author: Pure Logistics, 1917; Recruit Manual, 1918; Preparation of International Claims, 1924; Federal Departmental Organization and Practice, 1925; Prohibition, National and State, 1925. Co-author: Hughes Federal Practice, 1931; Thorpe and Ellis' Federal Securities Act Manual, 1933. Home: Washington, D.C. Died July 28, 1936.

THORPE, SPENCE ROANE farmer; b. at Louisville, Ky., Jan. 20, 1842; s. Thomas J. and Sarah Anna (Roane) T.; ed. Bardstown, Ky., at St. Joseph's Coll.; m. Ft. De Russy, nr. Marksville, La., Jan. 20, 1868, Helena C. Barbin. Practiced law in La., 1866-83; served in C.S.A., 1861-65, becoming capt. Co. A, 2d Ky. cav.; wounded at Drainsville, Va., Dec. 20, 1861, at Cynthiana, Ky., July 16, 1862, at Corydon, Ind., June 9, 1863; was prisoner in hosp. in New Albany, Ind., June to Nov., 1863; prisoner confined on Johnson's Island, Nov., 1863, till exchanged, Oct., 1864; since 1886 farming in Cal. Residence: 333 S. Bunker Hill Av. Office: 213 Grant Bldg., Los Angeles, Cal.

THORSEN, DAVID S., physician; b. Minn.,21916; M.D., U. Minn., 1943. Intern, San Bernardino County Hosp., San Bernardino, Cal., 1943-44; tng. U. Minn., VA Hosp., Mpls., 1946-49; fellow in child psychiatry Wilder Child Guidance Clinic, 1952-53, staff, 1953-67, dir., 1968-69. Served to lt., M.C., USNR, 1944-46. Diplomate Am. Bd. Psychiatry and Neurology. Mem. A.M.A., Am. Psychiat. Assn., Am. Assn. on Mental Deficiency, Alpha Omega Alpha. Home: St Paul MN Died July 4, 1968.

THORSON, TRUMAN C. army officer; b. Hawkins, Wis., Jan. 23, 1895; s. Halvor and Anna T.; grad. Tank Sch., 1926, Inf. Sch., 1930; m. Nadine Moody, Aug. 16, 1926; 1 dau., Margaret. Commd. 2d lt., inf. U.S. Army, 1917, advancing through grades to brig. gen.; served in France during World War I; overseas in Sicily, Eng., European continent since June 6, 1944; assigned Gen. Staff G-3, First U.S. Army, since Oct. 1943. Decorated D.S.M., Legion of Merit, Bronze Star, French Legion of Honor, Croix de Guerre with Palm, Russian Order of Zuvorov. Home: Hawkins, Wis. Died Dec. 1966.

THROCKMORTON, JAMES WEBB gov. Tex., congressman, lawyer, physician; b. Sparta, Tenn., Feb. 1, 1825; studied medicine in Princeton, Ky.; studied law. Practiced medicine in Collin County, Tex.; served as surgeon, Mexican War; admitted to the bar, began practice law, McKinney, Tex.; mem. Tex. Ho. of Reps., 1851-56; candidate as Whig presdl. elector, 1852; mem. Tex. Senate, 1856-61, 65; mem. Tex. Secession Conv., 1861; served as capt. and maj. Confederate Army, 1861-63; brig. gen. Tex. Militia, 1864, comdr. on northwest border of Tex.; del. and presiding officer reconstrn. conv. under Pres. Johnson's proclamation, 1866; elected, inaugurated gov. of Tex., 1866, removed by order of Gen. Sheridan, 1867; resumed practice law, Collin County; mem. U.S. Ho. of Reps. (Democrat) from Tex., 44th-45th, 48th-49th congresses, 1875-79, 83-87; Democratic presdl. elector, 1880; del. Dem. Nat. Conv., Chgo., 1892. Died McKinney, Tex., Apr. 21, 1894; buried Pecan Grove Cemetery.

THRUSTON, GATES PHILLIPS soldier, author; b. Dayton, O., June 11, 1835; s. Hon. R. A. and Marianna (Phillips) T.; A.B. (valedictorian), Miami U., 1855, A.M., 1858; L.H.D., 1899; LL.B., Cincinnati Law Sch., 1859; m. Ida Hamilton, Dec. 21, 1865 (died 1893); m. 2d, Fanny Dorman, Sept. 1894. Capt. 1st Ohio Inf., Aug. 24, 1861; maj. asst. adj. vols., Sept. 4, 1863; lt. col., Nov. 1, 1863; bvtd. lt. col. vols., Mar. 13, 1865, "for faithful and meritorious services during the war"; col. and brig. gen. vols., Mar. 13, 1865, for same and particularly "for gallant and meritorious services at battles of Stone River and Chickamauga"; a.a.g. and chief on staff, 20th Army Corps, at Chickamauga; later judge advocate, Army of the Cumberland; hon. mustered out, Dec. 19, 1865. Settled at Nashville, 1865; chief dept. history and antiquities, Tenn. Centennial Expn. Fellow A.A.A.S.; v.p. Tenn. Hist. Soc.; pres. Soc. Army of the Cumberland, 1906—. Author: Antiquities of Tennessee and Adjacent States, 1890. Contbr. to mags. on antiquarian and mil. subjects. Address: Nashville, Tenn. Deceased.

THURSTON, LLOYD, comdr.-in-chief United Spanish War Vets; b. Osceola, Ia., Mar. 27, 1880; s. S. and Margaret (Maloy) T.; LL.B., State U. Ia., 1902; m. Louella Bolibaugh, 1910. Admitted to Iowa bar, 1902, and began practice at Osceola; county atty. Clarke Co., Ia., 1906-10; mem. Ia. Senate, 1920-24; mem. 69th to 72d Congresses, 8th Ia. Dist.; and 73d to 75th Congresses, 5th Ia. Dist., successively mem. rules, appropriations and ways and means coms. Mem. nat. awards jury Freedoms Founds. at Valley Forge. Served in Spanish-Am. war, Philippine Insurrection and World War I. Mem. Library Bd., Farm Bureau, Am. Legion, United Spanish War Vets. (comdr.-in-chief), Vets Fgn. Wars, Nat. Soc. Army of Philippines, Naval and Mil. Order Spanish War, Pioneer Lawnmakers Assn., Caribou Soc., Isaak Walton League of Am. Republican. Rotarian (past pres.). Home: Osceola IA Died May 7, 1970.

THWAITE, CHARLES EDWARD JR. trust co. exec.; b. Macon, Ga., Jan. 4, 1912; s. Charles Edward and Annie Bell (Godwin) T.; student Ga. Sch. Tech., 1929-33; m. Martha Bunn Zachry, May 16, 1942; children—Charles Edward, III, Robert Zachry, Martha, James, Lila, Walter. With Trust Co. of Ga., 1934—, successively First Nat. Bank & Trust Co., 1934-39, Trust Co. Ga., 1939-40; v.p. First Nat. Bank of Augusta, 1940-46; v.p. Trust Co. Ga., and Trust Co. Ga. Assos., 1946-48; pres. Fourth Nat. Bank, Columbus, 1948-57; pres. Trust Co. Ga., 1957-58, chmn. bd., 1959—, chmn. Trust Co. Ga. Assos., 1959—; dir. Atlantic Steel Co., Creamulsion Co., Coca Cola Co., Columbus Fibre Mills Co. Trustee Com. Econ. Devel., Nat. Fund Med. Edn. Trustee Emory U., Agnes Scott College, Southern Research Institute, Ga. Tech. Foundation. Served from lt. to col., AUS, 1941-46. Decorated Bronze Star; Croix de Guerre. Mem. C. of C., Community Service, Cotton Mfrs. Assn. Ga. Methodist. Clubs: Rotary, Capital City, Piedmont Driving, Peachtree Golf, Augusta Nat. Golf. Home: 2485 Montview Dr. N.W. Office: 36 Edgewood Av., N.E., Atlanta. Died Jan. 31, 1964; buried Arlington Nat. Cemetery.

THYE, EDWARD JOHN, ex-U.S. senator; b. Aberdeen, S.D., Apr. 26, 1896; s. Andrew and Bertha (Wangan) T.; ed. pub. schs. and bus. coll.; LL.D., Carroll Coll.; m. Hazel Ramage, 1921 (dec. 1936); 1 dau., Jean Robertha; m. 2d, Myrtle Oliver, Nov. 1942. Enlisted as pvt. USAAF, 1917; commd. 2d lt. in France, World War I. Slaes force Deere & Webber Co., Mpls., 1919-22; owner, operator farm, Northfield, Minn., 1922-69; appraiser Federal Land Bank, 1933-34; dairy and food commr. and dep. commr. of agr., State Minn., 1939-42; elected lt. gov., Minn., 1942; gov. Minn., 1943-46; U.S. senator from Minn., 1946-59, congl. del. WHO conv., 1958. Pres. Sciota Town and Sch. bd., 1925-39. Pres. Dakota County Farm Bur., 1929-40; dir. Twin City Milk Producers Assn., 1933-40. Mem. bd. dirs. Gallaudet Coll.; mem. bd. vistors USAF Acad.; supported establishment of Nat. Found. Ulcerative Colitis. Recipient citation Am. Cancer Soc., Cerebral Palsy Found., Nat. Epilepsy League; Silver Beaver award Boy Scouts Am.; hon. alumnus U. Minn., Class 1918. Lutheran. Mason. Elk. Club: Minnesota (St. Paul). Home: Northfield MN Died Aug. 28, 1969.

TIBBALS, C(HARLES) AUSTIN JR. (tib'als), educator; b. N.Y. City, July 23, 1881; s. Rev. Charles Austin and Mary Louise (Watkins) T.; student Columbia, 1899-1902; A.B., U. of Wis., 1904, A.M., 1906, Ph.D., 1908; m. Miriam Keith Reed, Dec. 10, 1908 (died Sept. 1925); children—Mary Reed, John Reed. Asst. and instr. chemistry, U. of Wis., 1902-08; later asst. prof., asso. prof. and prof. chemistry and dean of Armour Inst. Technology; dean, Armour Coll. Engring., Ill. Inst. Technology, 1937-43; dean of students, Ill. Inst. Tech., 1943-46; now dean emeritus, Ill. Inst. of Technology (retired Sept. 1946). Served as captain Ordnance Department, United States Army, 1918; engaged in research on high explosives and projectile loading; now capt. Ordnance Res. Fellow A.A.A.S.; mem. Soc. Promotion Engring. Edn., Western Soc. Engrs., Am. Coll. Personnel Assn., Nat. Assn. Deans and Advisers of Men, Am. Chem. Soc., Army Ordnance Assn., Tau Beta Pi, Sigma Xi, Phi Gamma Delta. Episcopalian. Clubs: University (Chicago); University of Wisconsin, Ill. Club of Columbia Alumni. Home: 511 Hawthorn Lane, Winnetka, Ill. Died Dec. 29, 1948.

TIDBALL, JOHN CALDWELL army officer; b. Ohio County, Va. (now W.Va.), Jan. 25, 1825; s. William and Maria (Caldwell) T.; grad. West Point, 1848; m. Mary Langdon Dana, d. of Gen. N. J. T. Dana, U.S.A. Bvtd. 2d lt. 3d arty., July 1, 1848; promoted 2d lt. 2d arty., Feb. 14, 1849; 1st lt., Mar. 31, 1853; capt., May 14, 1861. Bvts. for gallant and meritorious services; Bvtd.

maj., June 27, 1862 (for Gaines' Mill); bvtd. lt. colonel, Sept. 17, 1862 (for Antietam); bvtd. brig. gen. U.S.V., Aug. 1, 1864 (gallant and distinguished services in the battles of the Po. Spottsylvania C.H., and operations before Richmond); bvtd. col. and brig. gen. U.S.A., Mar. 13, 1865 (Ft. Steadman, Va.); bvtd. maj. gen. U.A.V. (Fts. Steadman and Sedgwick, Va.). Served in regular arty. in Civil war until Aug. 28, 1863, then col. 4th N.Y. vol. arty. until mustered out of vol. service Sept. 30, 1864; participated in many battles; maj. 2d arty., Feb. 5, 1867; col. staff aide-de-camp to gen.-in-chief, Jan. 1, 1881, to Feb. 8, 1884; lt. col. 3d arty., June 30, 1882; transferred to 1st arty. Nov. 10, 1882, to 3d arty. Jan. 25, 1884, col. Mar. 22, 1885; in command Arty. Sch. for Practice and Post of Ft. Monroe, Va., Nov. 7, 1883, to Nov. 4, 1888; retired Jan. 25, 1889. Author: A Manual of Heavy Artillery Service, 1880. Address: Montclair, N.J. Died 1906.

TIEDEMANN, TUDOR H.A. (ted'a-man), industrial relations counselor; b. Seattle, Wash., July 17, 1889; s. Tudor J. A. and Mary J. (Suffern) T.; grad. Stanford U., 1912; m. Maybelle Barlow, Aug. 3, 1912 (divorced, 1919); children—Jane, Tudor Alfred; m. 2d, Alice Irwin Hopper, Dec. 1922; 1 son, Tudor H. A. Fire insurance broker, Los Angeles, 1912-16; pres. Jr. Underwriters Assn., 1916; joined Standard Oil Co. of N.J., 1920, for development of employment and personnel program and employee representation in subsidiary cos.; worked on labor relations in Standard Oil Co. of La., Colonial Beacon Oil Co., Humble Oil Co., Carter Oil Co. and various natural gas cos. and southwestern pipe line units; mem. labor com. Am. Petroleum Inst., 1932, later same for petroleum industry at Washington, D.C.; mng. dir. Indsl. Relations Counselors, Inc., N.Y. City (founded and fostered by J. D. Rockefeller, Jr.), 1934-52; exec. asst. to employers panel. War Labor Bd., Washington, 1942; trustee Indsl. Relations Counsellors, Inc., since 1944. Enlisted Calif. Nat. Guard, 1916; served in Mexico; sergt., 2d lt., 1st lt., Co. B, 160th Inf.; sent to Washington, D.C., for conf. on war risk ins. details; capt. 40th Div., Camp Kearny, Calif.; div. personnel adj. in France, later maj. in Adj. Gen.'s Dept.; replacement officer for 1st Army; returned to U.S. as lt. col. and div. adj. Mem. Phi Kappa Psi. Clubs: Rockefeller Center; Bronxville Field; American Yacht Club (trustee; vice commodore, 1940; commodore, 1941, 42); Stanford of New York (trustee), New York Yacht Shenorock Shore, Tred Avon Yacht. Lecturer on labor subjects. Contbr. articles on labor problems. Home: Bald Eagle Point, Tilghman, Md. Office: Americas Bldg., Rockefeller Center, N.Y.C. Died Apr. 15, 1956.

TIERNON, JOHN LUKE army officer; b. Madison, Ind., Jan. 18, 1841; s. Anthony and Katherine (Sendelbach) T.; ed. St. Mary's Sem., Mo., m. Harriet Virginia Pickett, Feb. 1, 1865. Apptd. from Mo., 2d lt. 3d Arty., Feb. 19, 1862; 1st lt., Jan. 20, 1864; grad. Arty. Sch., 1869; capt., July 2, 1877; maj. 1st Arty., Sept. 1, 1896; lt. col. 5th Arty., July 15, 1900; col. arty. corps, Aug. 22, 1901; brig. gen., Aug. 11, 1903; retired at own request after 40 yrs.' service, Aug. 12, 1903. Address: Buffalo, N.Y. Died 1910.

TIFFANY, (LEWIS) HANFORD educator; b. Lawrenceville, Ill., July 29, 1894; s. Charles Edward and Mary Frances (Hull) T.; grad. Eastern Ill. State Tchrs. Coll., 1915, Ph.D. (hon.), 1949; B.S., U. Chgo., 1920; M.S., Ohio State U., 1921, Ph.D., 1923; m. Loel Zehner, Sept. 10, 1921. Began as tchr. in pub. schs., 1912; instr. botany, O. State U., 1920-25, asst. prof., 1925-28, asso. prof., 1928-32, prof., 1932-37; prof. botany, chmn. dept. botany Northwestern U., 1937-49, William Deering prof. botany, 1945-62, William Deering prof. botany emeritus, 1962—; hon. asso. in cryptogamic botany, Chgo. Natural History Mus., 1944—; hon. life mem. Centro Italiano de Studi Anglo-Franco-Americani, 1946—; prof. algology, Stone Lab., summers 1928-36; bus. mgr., Ohio Jour. Sci., 1920-30. Mem. Ill. Bd. Natural Resources and Conservation, vice chmn., sec.; v.p. phycology sect. 8th Internat. Bot. Congress, Paris, 1954. Served as 2d lt. F.A., U.S. Army, 1918. Patron, Smithsonian Inst. Fellow A.A.A.S., Ohio Acad. Sci.; mem. Am. Soc. Naturalists, Bot. Soc. Am., Ecol. Soc. Am., Am. Microscopic Soc. (pres. 1934), Limnol. Soc. Am. (pres. 1939), Am. Soc. Plant Physiology, Am. Soc. Plant Taxonomy, Chgo. Acad. Scis. (bd. govs. 1941—; hon. life mem.), Ill. Acad. Sci., Phycological Soc. Am. (pres. 1949), Cowles Bot. Soc., Sigma Xi, Gamma Alpha. Republican. Clubs: University (Evanston); Chaos (Chgo.). Author: The Oedogoniaceae, 1930; Work Book in General Botany (with E. N. Transeau and H. C. Sampson), 1934; Algae, the Grass of Many Waters, 1938; Text Book of Botany (with E. N. Transeau H. C. Sampson), 1940; The Study of Plants, 1944; chpt. on ecology in Manual of Phycology, 1951; The Algae of Illinois (with M. E. Britton), 1952; Life (with G. G. Simpson and C. Pittendrigh), 1957. Editor: Culturing of Algae (with J. Brunel, G. W. Prescott), 1951. Mem. editorial bd. Ecology, 1950-52. Contbr. to sci. jours. Home: Route 3, Lawrenceville, Ill. Office: Northwestern U., Evanston, Ill. Died Mar. 13, 1965; buried Derr Cemetery, Lawrenceville.

TIGERT, JOHN JAMES (ti'gert), univ. pres.; b. Nashville, Tenn., Feb. 11, 1882; s. John James (bishop M.E. Ch., S.) and Amelia (McTyeire) T.; B.A., Vanderbilt U., 1904, B.A., Honor Sch. of Jurisprudence, Oxford U., Eng., 1907 (1st Rhodes scholar from Tenn.), M.A., 1915; studied Grad. Sch. U. of Minn., 1916; L.L.D., U. of Ky., 1921; Ed.D., Rhode Island, 1923; LL.D., Bates Coll., 1924, U. of N.M., 1924, Dickinson, 1928; D.C.L., Hillsdale, 1928; L.H.D., Muhlenberg, 1928; D.Litt., Fla. Southern College, 1933; LL.D., Rollins College and Stetson University, 1935, Louisiana State University, 1943; m. Edith Jackson, d. of M. C. Bristol, Aug. 25, 1909; children—John James 5th, Mary Jane (Mrs. William Blaine Thompson). Professor of philosophy and psychology, Central College, Fayette, Mo., 1907-09; pres. Ky. Wesleyan Coll., Winchester, 1909-11; prof. philosophy and psychology, U. of Ky., 1911-17, prof. psychology, 1917-21; U.S. commr. of edn., 1921-28; pres. U. of Fla. since 1928. Pres. Assn. of Colls. and Univs. of Ky., 1911; del. 4th Ecumenical Meth. Conf., Toronto, 1911. With Y.M.C.A., A.E.F., June 1918-July 1919; mem. Army Ednl. Corps, Apr.-July 1919; extension lecturer, A.E.F., U. of Beaune, France; lt. col. Spl. Res., U.S. Army, Chmn. edn. sect., 1st Pan-Pacific Conf. on Edn., Rehabilitation, Reclamation and Recreation, Honolulu, 1927; chmn. Federal Council on Citizenship Training, 1925-28, also of Com. on Selection of Rhodes Scholars; vice chmn. Federal Bd. for Vocational Edn., 1924-28; mem. Nat. Com. on Research in Secondary Edn., 2d Pan-Am. Scientific Congress, Federal Bd. of Maternity and Infant Hygiene (1921-28), 6th Industrial Congress for Art Edn., Drawing and Art Industry (v.p.), Am. Council on Edn., Boy Scouts of America (nat. council), President's Outdoor Recreation Conf. (1924), Federal Com. on Overseas Possessions, White House Conference on Child Health and Protection (1930), Nat. edn. com. Thomas Jefferson Memorial Foundation, Nat. Advisory Com. on Illiteracy, Nat. Council of Edn., Assn. of Am. Colleges, Am. Sportsmanship Brotherhood (dir.), Americanism Commn. of Am. Legion, N.E.A. (life dir.), Assn. Land-Grant Colls. and Univs. (exec. com.), Nat. Assn. of State Univs. (mem. exec. com., 1936-42); pres. 1939-40; chmn. Joint Com. on Accrediting representing Assn. Land-Grant Colls. and Univs., Nat. Assn. of State Univs., Assn. of Urban Univs. and Assn. of Am. Univs. Chmn. Conf. State Instns. in South, 1942-43; mem. Advisory Council Inst. of Pacific Relations; mem. Sponsoring Com. of Nat. Conf. for Mental Hygiene; mem. Com. on Inter-Am. Intellectual Cooperation, Department of State; member Southern Council on International Relations (director); member Advisory Council, Inst. of Indsl. Progress; mem. adv. com. Army Specialized Training Program, War Dept.; mem. bd. visitors U.S. Naval Acad., 1944; mem. bd. dirs. Nat. War Fund; chmn. Fla. War Fund; member Fla. School Code Com., Fla. State Chamber of Commerce (dir.), Gainesville (Fla.) Chamber Commerce, Southeastern (Athletic) Conf. (pres. 1935, 36, 46, 47), Southern University Conference (exec. com.; president 1940-41), Phi Beta Kappa (member Senate and Foundation), Phi Delta Theta (past pres.), Alpha Delta Sigma (v.p.), Kappa Delta Pi, Phi Kappa Phi, Kappa Phi Kappa, Phi Alpha Delta, Omicron Delta Kappa, Tau Kappa Alpha (nat. council), Pi Gamma Mu, Blue Key, etc. Trustee Vanderbilt Univ.; dir. Ringling Museum. Awards: George Washington Bicentenary medal; King Christian X (Denmark) Medal of Liberation. Mason. Moose. Clubs: Congressional Country (Washington, D.C.), University, Rotary, Golf and Country (Gainesville), Propeller. Author: Philosophy of the World War (monograph), also many addresses and pub. articles on edn. Co-author: The Child—His Nature and His Needs; The Book of Rural Life; High School Anthology—American Literature, English Literature, and Literary Types. Home: 1200 E Blvd., Gainesville, Fla. Deceased.

TIGHE, LAURENCE GOTZIAN (ti), education; b. St. Paul, Minn., Mar. 19, 1894; s. Ambrose and Harriet (Gotzian) T.; student U. of Minnesota, 1911; A.B., Yale, 1916, A.M., 1938; m. Hester Smith, Feb. 7, 1918; children—Laurence Gotzian, Patricia. Clerk, Equitable Trust Co., New York, N.Y., 1916-17, Kalman, Matteson & Wood, St. Paul, Minn., 1919; asst. treas., F. H. Swift & Co., Inc., Boston, Mass., 1919-21; sales corr., S. W. Straus & Co., Boston, Feb.-Oct. 1921; rep. Stacy & Braun, Boston, 1921-24; with Brown Brothers & Co. and Brown Brothers, Harriman & Co., Boston and New York, 1924-34, partner, 1930-34; vice pres. and dir., Brown, Harriman & Co., New York and Boston, 1934-38; asso. treas., Yale U., 1938-42, treas. since 1942; dir. Pa. Water and Power Co. (mem. finance committee), Connecticut Light & Power Company, National Sugar Refining Company, First Nat. Bank & Trust Co., New Haven, Conn. (mem. trust com.); trustee, corporator New Haven Savs. Bank. Served as capt., 339th F.A., U.S.A., 1917-19; overseas, 1918-19. Treas. bd. trustees Sheffield Scientific Sch. (Yale); treas. Yerkes Labs. of Primate Biology, Inc., (Orange Park, Fla.), Conn. Acad. Arts and Sciences, Interseminary Commn. for Training for Rural Ministry. Trustee New Haven Orphan Asylum and Children's Center. Dir. Am. Red Cross (New Haven chapter). Mem. Phi Beta Kappa, Delta Kappa Upsilon, Skull and Bones. Clubs: Bond (hon.) (Boston); Lawn, Graduates, Faculty, Mory's (New Haven); Yale (New York); Hammonassett Fishing (Madison, Conn.). Home: 31 Hillhouse Av., New Haven 11. Died Dec. 3, 1954.

TILESTON, MARY WILDER author; b. Salem, Mass., Aug. 20, 1843; d. Caleb and Mary Wilder (White) Foote; m. John Boies Tileston, Sept. 25, 1865 (died 1898); children—Mary Wilder, Margaret Harding, Roger, Amelia Peabody, Wilder, Edith, Eleanor Boies. Author: (or compiler) Heroic Ballads, 1883; Daily Strength for Daily Needs, 1884; Sugar and Spice collection of nursery rhymes, 1885; Tender and Ture, 1892; Selections from Isaac Penington, 1892; Prayers, Ancient and Modern, 1897; Joy and Strength for the Pilgrim's Day, 1901; Memorials of Mary Wilder White, 1903; Children's Treasure Trove of Pearls, 1908; The Child's Harvest of Verse, 1910; Caleb and Mary Wilder Foote. 1918; Amelia Peabody Tileston and Her Canteens for the Serbs, 1920. Home: Brookline, Mass. Died July 3, 1934.

TILFORD, JOSEPH GREEN brig. gen. U.S.A.; b. Georgetown, Ky., Nov. 26, 1829; s. Col. Alexander and Agnes T.; grad. U.S. Mil. Acad., 1851; m. Cornelia Van Ness Dean, 1864. Bvt. 2d lt. Mounted Rifles, July 1, 1851; 2d lt., Jan. 27, 1853; 1st lt., June 14, 1858; capt. 3d Cav., July 31, 1861; maj. 7th Cav., Nov. 14, 1867; lt. col., Sept. 22, 1883; col. 9th Cav., Apr. 11, 1889; retired at own request after 40 yrs.' service, July 1, 1891; advanced to rank of brig. gen. retired, under act of Apr. 23, 1904. Bvtd. maj., Feb. 21, 1862, for battle of Valverde, N.M.; lt. col., Mar. 13, 1865, for services during the war. Participated in defense of Ft. Craig, 1862, battle of Valverde, Feb. 21, 1862, skirmish before Albuquerque, actions at Peralta, Apr. 1862, Parugo, May-July 1862, and other operations in N.M.; served with Sherman's expdn. to Chattanooga, Oct.-Nov. 1863; engaged in actions of Cherokee, Ala., Oct. 24, 1863, Tuscumbia, Oct. 27, 1863, Lookout Mountain and Missionary Ridge, Nov. 23-25, 1863, etc. Home: St. Louis, Mo. Died 1911.

TILGHMAN, TENCH army officer; b. "Fausley," Talbot County, Md., Dec. 25, 1744; s. James and Anna (Francis) T.; grad. Coll., Acad. and Charitable Sch. of Phila. (now U. Pa.), 1761; m. Anna Maria Tilghman (cousin), June 9, 1783, 2 children. Mcht., Phila., 1761-75; sec. and treas. to commrs. of Continental Congress Six Nations, 1775; capt. of an independent company which joined Flying Camp, 1776; a.d.c. and personal mil. sec. to Gen. Washington, 1776-81; commd. lt. col. Continental Army for service to Gen. Washington; selected for honor of carrying message of Cornwallis' surrender to Continental Congress, 1781. Died Balt., Apr. 18, 1786; buried St. Paul's Churchyard, Balt.

TILLETT, CHARLES WALTER lawyer; b. Mangum, N.C., Feb. 6, 1888; s. Charles W. and Carrie (Patterson) T.; A.B., U. N.C., 1909; student law sch., 1909-10; m. Gladys Avery, July 21, 1917; children—Gladys (Mrs. Coddington), Charles Walter III, Sara (Mrs. Thomas). Admitted to N.C. bar, 1910 and since practiced in Charlotte; mem. Tillett, Campbell, Craighill & Rendelman. Mem. bd. sch. commrs. City Charlotte, 1919-23; mem. Bd. Law Examiners N.C., 1933-44; city atty., Charlotte, 1941-45. Mem. bd. trustees U.N.C., 1932-36. Served as capt. 50th Inf. Regt., World War I. Mem. Am., N.C. (past pres.) and Meclenburg bar assns., Am. Law Inst., Am. Legion, Phi Beta Kappa, Sigma Alpha Epsilon. Democrat (co. exec. com.; del. nat. conv. 1944). Presbyn. Clubs: Charlotte Country, Charlotte City, Rotary. Author articles. Home: 2200 Sherwood Av., Charlotte 7. Office: Law Bldg., Charlotte 2, N.C. Died Dec. 23, 1952; buried Charlotte.

TILLEY, BENJAMIN FRANKLIN officer U.S.N.; b. Bristol, R.I., Mar. 29, 1848; s. Benjamin Rogers and Susan W. (Easterbrookes) T.; ed. pub. schs., Bristol, R.I.; grad. U.S. Naval Acad., 1867 (No. 1 of class); m. Emily Edelin Williamson, June 6, 1878. Served as midshipman on Franklin, flagship, European fleet, 1867-68, steamer Frolic, 1868-69; promoted ensign, 1868, master, 1870; commd. lt., 1871, lt. comdr., Sept. 1887, comdr., Sept. 1896, capt., Sept. 1, 1901. Comd. U.S.S. Newport, 1897-98, during Spanish-Am. War; captured a number of prizes and was on blockade duty off Havana and other ports; comdt. Navy Yard, Norfolk, Va., 1898-99; comdg. Abarenda, and comdt. Naval Sta., Tutuila, Samoa, 1899-1901; 1st naval gov. of Samoa; capt. Navy Yard, Mare Island, 1902; later comdg. battleship Iowa, N. Atlantic squadron. Address: Washington, D.C. Died 1907.

TILLMAN, JAMES DAVIDSON lawyer, farmer; b. Bedford Co., Tenn., Nov. 25, 1841; s. Lewis and Mary Catherine (Davidson) T.; brother of Abram Martin, Samuel Escue and George N. T. (all q.v.); grad. U. of Nashville, 1860, and attended law sch., Cumberland U., but left for war; m. Mary Frances Bonner, 1865. Entered C.S.A. as lt. in a co. from Shelbyville; taken prisoner at Ft. Donelson; was at Johnson's Island until exchanged, Sept., 1862; elected lt.-col. 41st Tenn. Regt., C.S.A., Sept., 1862; col., 1863; comd. regt. at Chickamauga, where he was severely wounded at Snodgrass Hill; upon recovery resumed command, later col. 3d Consolidated Tenn. regt.; surrendered with Joe Johnston's army in N.C.; removed to Fayetteville and practiced law, 1865-95. Mem. Tenn. Ho. of Rep., 1870, Senate, 1873, 1893, 1901; U.S. minister to Ecuador, 1895-98; State credit and sound money Democrat. Home: Harms, Tenn. Office: Fayetteville, Tenn.

TILLMAN, SAMUEL ESCUE army officer; b. near Shelbyville, Tenn., Oct. 2, 1847; s. Lewis and Mary Catherine (Davidson) T.; grad. U.S. Mil. Acad., 1869; hon. M.A., Yale, 1906; m. Clara Williams, Apr. 20, 1887; 1 dau., Mrs. Katharine Tillman Martin. Second lt. 4th Arty., June 15, 1869; on frontier duty in Kan., 1869-70; asst. prof., 1870-73, and 1879-80, prof. chemistry, mineralogy and geology, with rank of col., 1880-1911, U.S. Mil. Acad.; retired by operation of law, Oct. 2, 1911; recalled to active service, June 6, 1917, and assigned to duty as supt. U.S. Mil. Acad. until June 12, 1919; brig. gen. U.S. Army retired, Mar. 4, 1919. D.S.M., June 11, 1919 "for especially meritorious and conspicuous services as supt. U.S. Mil. Acad. during the period of the emergency." Asst. astronomer U.S. Transit of Venus Expdn., Tasmania, 1874-75; instr. in mechanics, U.S. Mil. Acad., 1875-76; asst. engr. on the U.S. (Wheeler) explorations west of the 100th meridian, 1873-74 and 1876-79. Author: Essential Principles of Chemistry, 1884; Elementary Lessons in Heat, 1889; Elementary Mineralogy, 1894; Descriptive General Chemistry, 1899; Important Minerals and Rocks, 1900. Address: Century Assn., 7 W. 43d St., New York, N.Y. Died June 24, 1912.

TILLSON, JOHN CHARLES FREMONT army officer; b. N.Y., May 26, 1856; grad. U.S. Mil. Acad., 1878; Army War Coll., 1910. Commd. add. 2d lt. 5th Inf., June 14, 1878; 2d lt., June 21, 1878; 1st lt., Mar. 24, 1883; capt. 14th Inf., Mar. 18, 1897; maj. 4th Inf., Mar. 12, 1902; lt. col. 18th Inf., Dec. 7, 1908; col. of inf., Nov. 27, 1911; assigned to 8th Inf., Mar. 28, 1912; trans. to 15th Inf., July 1, 1913. Prof. mil. science and tactics, North Ga. Agrl. Coll., Dahlonega, Ga., 1897-98; comd. Co. F, 14th Inf., China Relief Expdn., 1900; participated in capture of Peking and attack on Forbidden City; provost marshal, Am. Dist., Chinese City, until withdrawal of forces, May 1901; in charge Officers' Sch., Ft. Thomas, Ky., 1905-06; in Philippine Islands, 1908; duty Ft. Jay, N.Y., 1917. Address: War Dept., Washington. Died Dec. 15, 1941.

TILTON, JAMES congressman; b. Kent County, Del., June 1, 1745; M.B., Coll. of Phila. (now U. Pa.), 1768, M.D., 1771. Served as surgeon Del. Regt., Continental Army, 1776; in charge of mil. hosps. at Princeton, Trenton (N.J.), New Windsor (Md.), 1777-80 (to improve san. conditions built "hosp. huts" for each 6 patients); promoted sr. hosp. physician, surgeon, 1780; operated hosp. at Williamsburg, Va. during Yorktown campaign; mem. Continental Congress, also Del. Ho. of Reps., 1783-85; govt. commr. loans, Del., 1785-1801; physician and surgeon-gen. U.S. Army, 1813-15, made tour inspection along No. frontier instituting widespread san. reforms. Author: Economical Observations on Military Hospitals: and the Prevention and Cure of Diseases Incident to an Army, 1813; Regulations for the Medical Department, 1814. Died nr. Wilmington, Del., May 14, 1822; buried Wilmington and Brandywine Cemetery.

TIMBERLAKE, GIDEON urologist; b. Charlottesville, Va., Mar. 6, 1876; s. Crawford G. and Sarah (Garland) T.; M.D., U. of Va., 1902; m. Sallie Virginia Helms, Jan. 19, 1922; children—Virginia Helms (Mrs. A. B. Taylor, Jr.), Martha Ann (Mrs. Wm. J. Haymaker, Jr.). Prof. urology, U. of Md. and Coll. of Physicians and Surgeons, Baltimore; urologist to University, St. Agnes and Franklin Square Hosps., Baltimore, Maryland; cons. urologist to Bay View Hospital, Kernan Hospital for Ruptured and Crippled Children and Med. Center of Venice, Florida; surgeon to staff of Church Home and Infirmary and West Baltimore General hosps. (resigned); mem. staff Mound Park and St. Anthony's hosps., St. Petersburg, Fla.; consultant in urology to Vets. Hosp., Bay Pines, Fla.; consultant to Crippled Children's Hosp., St. Petersburg. Organizer, dir. Army Sch. Urol., Ft. Oglethorpe, Ga., 1918; chief of dept. of urology, Walter Reed Hosp.; maj. Med. Corps, U.S. Army, World War. Founder and diplomate Am. Bd. Urology. Fellow Am. Coll. Surgeons; mem. Am. Urol. Assn., A.M.A., Pinellas County Med. Soc. (St. Petersburg, Fla.). Club: Baltimore. Editor: The Urologic and Cutareous Review. Contbr. med. jours. Inventor several urol. instruments. Home: 455 19th Av. N.E., St. Petersburg, Fla. Died Mar. 1, 1951.

TIMBERLAKE, HENRY army officer; b. Hanover County, Va., 1730; s. Francis and Sarah (Austin) T. Joined Patriot Blues against French and Indians under George Washington, 1756; apptd. to regt. of William Byrd III in campaign against French at Ft. Duquesne, 1758; placed in command Ft. Necessity, Pa., 1759; made 22 day voyage (with Thomas Sumpter) to Cherokee Indian villages, 1761-62, remained 3 months; accompanied a Cherokee chief and 2 warriors on visit to England, 1762; commd. lt. for services; conducted another group of Cherokee warriors overseas, 1764. Author: Memoirs of Lieutenant Henry Timberlake, London (valuable source for ethnologists), 1765. Died London, Eng., Sept. 30, 1765.

TIMM, JOHN A(RREND), prof. chemistry; b. New Haven, Conn., Oct. 31, 1898; s. Rev. John Arrend and Emma (Stein) T.; Ph.B., Sheffield Scientific Sch., Yale, 1919, Ph.D., Grad. Sch., Yale, 1922; m. Marguerite Benedict, June 9, 1923; 1 dau., Mrs. Jane Eagle. Instr. chemistry, Yale, 1922-27, asso. prof., 1927-41; prof. chemistry, chmn. dept., chmn. div. of science, director School of Science, Simmons Coll., 1941-66, prof. emeritus, 1966-69, dir. of summer inst. for high sch. tchrs. chemistry, 1959-69. Served as 2d lieutenant F.A., U.S. Army, 1918; 2d lt. O.R.C., 1918-23. Recipient Honor Scroll, American Institute of Chemists, 1958; James Flack Norris award, 1966. Member American Chemical Society (chairman of Northeast section 1951-52), N.E. Assn. Chemistry Tchrs. (hon. mem.; pres. 1954-55), Sigma Xi, Theta Xi, Alpha Chi Sigma, Gamma Alpha. Unitarian. Author: Charts of the Chemical Reactions of the Common Elements, 1924; An Introduction to Chemistry, 1930, 3d edit., 1938; General Chemistry, 1944, 4th edit., 1966, Spanish and French transl., 1968. Co-author: Laboratory Exercises in General Chemistry, 1930; Development of the Sciences, 1941. Co-editor: Marvels of Science, 1941. Contributor articles to Journal of American Chemical Soc. and Journal Chemical Edn. Co-author: Laboratory Exercises in General Chemistry, 1948. Home: Newton Centre MA Died Mar. 4, 1969; buried Congregational Cemetery Seymour CT

TIMME, ERNST G. auditor for U.S. State and other depts. since Mar., 1897; b. Werden, Prussia, June 21, 1843; came to U.S., 1847; has since resided in Kenosha Co., Wis. Ed. in public schools and commercial coll.; enlisted in 1st Wis. vols., July, 1861, and having lost his left arm in battle of Chickamauga, was honorably discharged in May, 1864. Is a farmer; town clerk and justice of the peace, Wheatland, Wis., 1865-67; co. clerk, 1867-82; sec. State of Wis., 1882-91; 5th auditor U.S. Treasury Dept., July, 1892, to Mar., 1893. Mem. State senate, 1894-97. Home: Kenosha, Wis. Office: Washington.

TIMMERMAN, GEORGE BELL, judge; b. Edgefield County, S.C., Mar. 28, 1881; s. Washington Hodges and Henrietta Maria Wolfe (Bell) T.; grad. Patrick Military Inst., 1900, LL.B., S.C. Coll. (now Univ. South Carolina) 1902, LL.D., (honorary), 1952; m. Mary Vandiver Sullivan, Nov. 22, 1906, children—Margaret, George Bell. Gen. practice of law, 1902-42; appointed U.S. District judge for the Eastern and Western Districts of S.C., 1942. Captain, S.C. Militia, aide on Brigade Staff, 1905. Solicitor 5th Judicial Circuit, 1905-08, 11th Judicial Circuit, 1908-20; mem. House of Rep., Gen. Assembly of S.C., 1923-24; mem. State of S.C. Highway Commn., 1931-39, chmn., 1936-39; chmn. Lexington County, S.C., Dem. Com., 1914-16, Dem. State exec. committeeman, 1930-32, 1938-42; pres. Dem. State Convention, 1932. Chmn. Ridge Dist. Boy Scouts of Am., 1940-43, v.p. Central Council, 1942-44; chairman Batesburg-Leesville Park Commn., 1941-46. Trustee University of S.C., Columbia, S.C., 1941-47. Member S.C. and Am. bar assns., Phi Kappa Sigma, Omicron Delta Kappa. Clubs: Ridge Golf (Batesburg, S.C.), Internat. Assn. of Lions Clubs (dist. gov., dir.). Home: Batesburg SC Died Apr. 22, 1966; buried Batesburg SC

TINGEY, THOMAS naval officer; b. London, Eng., Sept. 11, 1750; m. Margaret Murdoch, Mar. 30, 1779; m. 2d, Ann Bladen Dulany, Dec. 9, 1812; m. 3d, Ann Evelina Craven, May 19, 1817; 3 children. Commanded brig Lady Clausen sailing from St. Croix, V.I. to Europe, 1778; served in Am. mcht. marine, after 1781; commd. capt. U.S. Navy, 1798; commanded 3 vessels in the Windward Passage, 1798-99, rejected demand of Brit. frigate Surprise to have his crew examined for presence of Brit. seamen; sr. officer in W.I., 1799; organizer, comdt. Washington (D.C.) Navy Yard, 1800, 04-14; supt., 1800-03, financial agt., 1803-04, naval agt., 1804-14, burned navy yard when British invaded, 1814. Died Washington, Feb. 23, 1829; buried Congressional Cemetery, Washington.

TINKER, CLARENCE L. army officer; b. Nov. 21, 1887. Commd. 2d lt. inf., June 12, 1924; promoted through grades to lt. col.; temp. rank of brig. gen., Oct. 1940; apptd. comdr. Air Force in Hawaii, Dec. 1941. Address: War Dept., Washington, D.C.* Died June 7, 1942.

TINKER, EDWARD LAROCQUE, author; b. New York, N.Y., Sept. 12, 1881; s. Henry Champlin and Louise (Larocque) T.; prep. edn., Browning Sch., N.Y. City; A.B., Columbia University, 1902, Litt. D. (hon.), 1963; studied at Columbia University Law Sch., 2 yrs.; LL.B., New York Law Sch., 1905; Docteur de l'Universite de Paris (France), 1933; LL.D. (honorary), Middlebury Coll., 1949; Doctor, de la Universidad de Madrid, 1955; married Frances McKee, Jan. 16, 1916. Admitted to N.Y. bar, 1905; counsel Legal Aid Soc. 1 yr.; asst. dist. atty. 3 yrs.; pres. Tinker Realty Co.; installed, operated one of first "safety first" systems in Southwest, El Paso & Southwestern R.R. Co. Excng. prof. Nat. Univ. of Uruguay and Argentina, 1945; prof. extraordinario Nat. U. Mex. Pres. Tinker Found.; adv. council Sch. Internat. Affairs Columbia Bd. dirs. Operation Amigo, The Americas Found. Formerly mem. Squadron A, N.Y.N.G.; lt. U.S. Navy, World War I. Decorated Officer d'Academie (France), 1933; Commendador de la Orden de Isabela Catolica; recipient gold medals by French Acad., 1934, 37, also 1962 award from the Americas Foundation; medal Fedn. French Alliances in the U.S., 1964. Trustee Marine Museum and Museum of City of N.Y. Decorated, Chevalier Legion of Honor, 1939; Order de Mayo al Merito by Argentina. Member of the Louisians Historical Society (honorary life mem.), Am. Antiquarian Society (chancillor), Council on Foreign Relations, Inst. Social Sciences, Soc. Am. Historians, Spanish Inst. (v.p.), Uruguayan-Am. Assn. (pres.), Pan-Am. Soc., Psi Upsilon; trustee Am. Bible Soc., France Am. Soc., Elysee Francaise, Hispanic Soc., Instituto Gonzalo Fernandez de Oviedo, Institute Geografico Historico del Uruguay. Republcan. Episcopalian. Clubs: University, Union, Dutch Treat, Coffee House (N.Y.); Pilgrims; Piping Rock. Author: Lafcadio Hearn's American Days, 1924; Toucoutou, 1928; (with Frances Tinker) Old New Orleans, 1930; Les Cenelles, 1930; Les Ecrites de Langue Francaise en Louisiane au XIXe, Siecle, Paris, 1932; The Palengenesis of Craps, 1933; Bibiliography of the French Newspapers and Periodicals of Louisiana, 1933. Gombo, the Creole Dialect of La., 1936; The Cult of The Gaucho and the Birth of a Literature, 1948; The Horsemen of the Americas and the Literatures They Inspired, 1953; Creole City, 1953; The Life and Literature of the Pampas, 1961; Corridos and Calaveros, 1961; Centaurs of Many Lands, 1963. Contbr. New Edits. Fine and Otherwise N.Y. Times, 1937-42. Vis. lectr. Mex. for Carnegie Endowment for Internat. Peace, 1943. Home: New York 6, July 1968.

TIPPETTS, CHARLES SANFORD, economist, educator; b. in Glens Falls, N.Y., Jan. 16, 1893; s. of William Henry and Emily Katharine (Bell) T.; student Mercersburg (Pa.), Acad., 1910-12; Litt. B., Princeton, 1916, A.M., 1922, Ph.D., 1924; studied law, Harvard, 1916-17; Litt. D. (hon.), Franklin and Marshall Coll., 1941; Sc.D., (hon.) Lafayette Coll., 1954; married Margaret Elizabeth Griffith, Apr. 4, 1920; children—Katherine Bell, Charles Sanford. Inst. economics, Princeton, 1919-21 and 1923-24; asst. prof. economics State U. of Ia., 1924-25, prof., 1925-28; prof. business adminstrn., U. of Wash., 1928-29; prof. economics, U. of Buffalo, 1929-35; dean Sch. of Business Adminstrn., U. of Pitts., 1935-41; headmaster, Mercersburg Acad., 1941-61, emeritus, 1961-67; vis. professor, summer sessions, U. of Wash., 1930, W.Va. U., 1931, Ohio State U., 1932; dir. Fed. Home Loan Bank of Pitts. Mem. State Hwy. Planning Commn., 1949-51, Pa. Citizens Committee for Welfare, 1946-67. Economist National Committee on Monetary Policy. Served as first lieutenant Infantry, 76th Division, A.E.F., 1917-19; captain inf., O.R.C., 1919-34, Decorated Sacred Order of St. Olaf (Norwegian). Mem. American Economic Association, Headmasters Association, Scabbard and Blade, Phi Beta Kappa, Beta Gamma Sigma, Delta Sigma Rho, Alpha Kappa Psi, Omicron Delta Kappa. Presbyn. Mason. Clubs: University, Harvard-Yale-Princeton (Pitts.); Franklin Inn (Phila.). Author: State Banks and Federal Reserve System, 1929; Business Organization and Control (with S. Livermore), 1932. Revisor (with L. A. Froman) of Horace White's Money and Banking, 1935. Contbr. econ. articles. Home: Mercersburg PA Died Aug. 27, 1967.

TIPTON, JOHN army officer, state legislator; b. Baltimore County, Md., Aug. 15, 1730; s. Jonathan and Elizabeth T.; m. Mary Butler, circa 1753; m. 2d, Martha (Denton) Moore, July 22, 1779; 15 children. A founder Woodstock, Dunmore County (later Shenandoah County), Va.; justice of peace Beckford Parish (Va.); an organizer, signer Independence Resolutions, Woodstock, 1774; mem. Dunmore County Com. of Safety and Correspondence, also recruiting officer; mem. Va. Ho. of Burgesses, 1774-81; rep. to Va. Conv., Williamsburg, 1776; commd. lt. col. Va. Militia; high sheriff of Shenandoah County during Revolutionary War; elected to N.C. Assembly in opposition to John Sevier (gov. State of Franklin), 1785; served as col. Washington County (N.C.) Militia; both Sevier and Tipton's factions maintained cts. and militias, raiding parties from both sides carried off ct. records and ofcl. papers, civil war lasted 3 years, Tipton was victorious after a battle at his home nr. Jonesboro, Tenn., 1788; rep. from Washington County in 1st Tenn. Assembly, 1793, 94-95; trustee Washington Coll., 1795; helped draft Tenn. Constn., 1796; mem. Tenn. Senate. Died Sinking Creek, N.C., Aug. 1813.

TIPTON, JOHN senator, army officer; b. Sevier County, Tenn., Aug. 14, 1786; s. Joshua and Jennett (Shields) T.; m. Jennett Shields (his cousin) 1818, 3 children; m. 2d, Matilda Spencer, 1825, 3 children. Served with "Yellow Jackets" of U.S. Army in Tippecanoe campaign, 1809; promoted brig. gen. Ind. Militia, 1811; justice of peace Ind. Territory, 1810; commanded troop of rangers Ind. Militia on Ohio River frontier; elected maj. gen. 2d Div., Ind. Militia, 1822; sheriff Harrison City, Ind. Territory, 1815-19; mem. Ind. Assembly, 1819-23; surveyor Ind.-Ill. boundary, 1821; U.S. Indian agt. for Ft. Wayne dist. Northern Ind., 1823, negotiated important treaties, 1826, 28, 36; land speculator; mem. U.S. Senate from Ind., Jan. 3, 1832-39; a Jacksonian Democrat; wrote journal published in Indpls. News, Apr. 17, May 5, 1879. Died Logansport, Ind., Apr. 5, 1839; buried Mt. Hope Cemetery.

TIPTON, LAURENCE B. educator; b. Selma, Ala., Mar. 27, 1910; s. William Hogan and Mary Wood (Buell) T.; student The Citadel, 1928, 1930; A.B., U. of Ala., 1933; M.A., New York U., 1940, Ed.D., 1941; m. Catharine Randolph, June 2, 1939; children—Laurence B., Catharine. Editor Shelby County (Ala.) Democrat, 1932-33; Ala. state examiner of pub. accounts, 1933-34; Ala. dir. pub. safety, 1934-36; asst. dir. Northwestern U. Safety Inst., 1936-38; prof. and head bur. of safety, Rutgers U., 1938-41; instr. summer sessions, U. of Ala., Penn State Coll., Harvard U., 1936-40; chief training advisor, U.S. Dept. of Labor, 1941-42; lt. col., U.S. Army, assigned as fed. dir. indsl. safety training, 1942-46; ednl. dir. Warner Bros. Pictures, Inc., 1946-—; head Laurence B. Tipton & Associates; v.p. Pathe Pictures, Inc. Mem. Phi Beta Kappa, Phi Delta Kappa, Phi Gamma Delta. Democrat. Episcopalian. Author articles, papers, treatises and bulls. in field. Home: 412 Union St., Selma, Ala. Office: 33 W. 60th St., N.Y.C. Died Jan. 20, 1957; buried Live Oak Cemetery, Selma, Ala.

TIPTON, ROYCE JAY, civil engr.; b. Litchfield, Ill., Mar. 23, 1893; s. Basil Foster and Sarah (Calvert) T.; student U. Colo., 1915-17, C.E. (hon.), 1940; m. Natalie Knight, Aug. 25, 1919 (dec. Oct. 1961); children—John Knight, Robert Royce, Natalie Jean (Mrs. Thomas Milaskey); m. 2d, Jincy Hunt, July 30, 1962. Pvt. practice civil engring., Monte Vista, Colo., 1922-28, Denver, 1933-67; pres. R.J. Tipton & Assos., Inc., 1945-54, Tipton and Kalmbach, Inc., Denver, Colo., 1954-67; designing engr. Rio Mante Project, Mexico, 1928; spl. engr. interstate water problems and water resources studies Colo. Engr.'s Office, 1929-33; assisted negotiation interstate compacts Upper Colo. River, Pecos River, Costilla Creek and Rio Grande, also negotiation Mexican Water Treaty, 1944, Indus Water Treaty, 1960; mem. bd. cons. Pecos River Joint Investigations, 1939-42, Nat. Resources Planning Bd., 1935-42, canal linings U.S. Bur. Reclamation, 1948; mem. task force water resources and power 2d Hoover Commn., 1953-55; cons. Colo. Water Conservation Bd., 1937-58, Colo. Planning Commn., 1933-37, Climax Molybdenum Co., 1935-52; tech. adviser Internat. Boundary and Water Commn., U.S. and Mexico, 1938-67; architect-engr. War Dept. projects, World War II. Served to 2d lt., C.E., U.S. Army, World War I; AEF in France and Germany. Recipient Norlin medal U. Colo., 1958. Mem. Am. geophys. Union Am. Inst. Cons. Engrs., Soc. Am. Mil. Engrs., Colo. Engring. Council (Gold Medal award 1963), Colo. Soc. Engrs., Am. Soc. C.E. (v.p. 1965-67), Internat. Commn. Irregation and Drainage (pres. 1966-67), Internat. Commn. Large Dams, Colo. Hist. Soc., Am. Legion, Alpha Sigma Phi, Tau Beta Pi, Chi Epsilon. Mason. Clubs: Denver Athletic, Denver, University (Denver); Metropolitan (Washington). Home: Denver CO Died Dec. 23, 1967; buried Fairmount Cemetery, Denver CO

TISELIUS, ARNE (WILHELM KAURIN), biochemist; b. Stockholm, Sweden, Aug. 10, 1902; s. Hans J. and Rosa (Kaurin) R.; Dr. phil., U. Upsala, 1931; student Princeton, 1934-35; Dr. honoris causa, univs. of Paris, Bologna, Glasgow, Madrid and Cambridge, Caroline Inst., Stockholm, U. Oxford, Oslo U., U. Lyon, U. Cal., Berkeley, Gustavus Adolphus College; m. Ingrid Margareta Dalen, Nov. 26, 1930; children—Eva, Per. Research asst. in phys. chemistry U. Upsala, 1925, became asst. prof., 1930, prof. biochemistry, 1938-68. Mem. nat. sci. research com. Atomic Energy Research Com., Com. for Reformation of the Univs., Med. Research Council of Sweden, 1944-47; president Swedish Natural Science Research Council, 1946-50; vice president Nobel Foundation, 1947-60, pres., 1960-64, chmn. chemistry com.; head Nobel Inst. of Swedish Royal Acad. Scis.; mem. sci. adv. council Swedish Govt.; pres. Internat. Union Pure and Applied Chemistry, 1951-55. Awarded Nobel Prize in chemistry, 1948. Hon. fellow Royal Inst. Chemistry London; hon. member French Chem. Soc., Swedish Society Physicians, Harvey Soc. N.Y., N.Y. Acad. Scis., N.Y. Acad. Medicine, Royal Inst. Great Britain, Chem. Soc. London, Internat. Assn. Allergists Zurich, Real Sociedad Espanola de Fisica y Quimica Madrid, Soc. Sci. Helsingfors, Consejo Super. de Investigaciones Scientificas Madrid, Am. Acad. Arts and Sci., Royal Dutch, Swiss chem. socs., National Acad. Scis. India; fgn. mem. Royal Soc. and Soc. Chem. Industry London, American Philosophical Society; corresponding member Society Philomat. Paris, Academie des Ciencias de Lisboa, Acad. des Sciences, Paris; mem. Pontificia Sci. Acad. of Vatican, Royal Swedish Acad. Sci., Nobel Com. Chemistry, Royal Acad. Engring. Scis., Royal Soc. Sci. Upsala, Royal Soc. Scis. and Letters Gothenburg, Nat. Acad. Scis. Washington, Royal Danish Sci. Soc., Copenhagen and Accademia Nazionale De quaranta Roma, Polish Acad. Sci., Warsaw, Rumanian Acad. Scis. (hon.); fgn. mem. Czeckoslovak Acad. Sci.; hon. mem. Soc. Electropheresis, Tokyo, Indian Inst. Scis. Liberal. Luth. Home: Upsala Sweden Died Oct. 29, 1971.

TITSWORTH, GRANT lawyer, company exec., assn. ofcl.; b. Newark, Feb. 19, 1908; s. Charles Grant and Elizabeth Linen (Dawson) T.; A.B., Princeton, 1929; LL.B., Harvard, 1932; m. Jane Isherwood Wyckoff, July 17, 1937; children—Linen Jane, Frances Wyckoff, Randolph Grant. Admitted to N.Y. bar, 1933, Conn. bar, 1951; practice of law, N.Y.C., 1933-42, partner Boyd & Holbrook, 1935-42; practice of law, Draien, Conn., 1951-—; asst. sec., then sec.-treas. American Overseas Airlines, Inc., 1946-50; asst. treas. Pan American World Airways, Inc., 1950-51; pres. Pease Co., Stamford, Conn., 1951-—; chmn. Grauer Prodns., Inc. (Riverside Records), 1958-—. Bd. dirs. Nat. Recreation Assn., 1947, v.p., 1956-58, chmn., 1958-—. Adv. council dept. philosophy Princeton, 1939-—. Served from 1st lt. to maj., USAAF, 1942-45. Mem. Conn., Stamford bar assns., Assn. Bar City N.Y., Soc. Mayflower Descendants. Clubs: Princeton (N.Y.C.); Ausable (St. Huberts, N.Y.); Wee Burn (Darien). Home: 11 Beach Dr., Norton, Conn. Office: 1019 Post Rd., Danien, Conn. Died May 14, 1960; buried Mt. Pleasant Cemetery, Newark.

TITTMANN, CHARLES TROWBRIDGE basso; b. Detroit, Mich., Feb. 7, 1883; s. Otto Hilgard and Kate Trowbridge (Wilkins) T.; B.S., Princeton, 1905; LL.B., Harvard, 1908; studied music under Alfred Giraudet and Myron Whitney, Jr.; m. Jean Audenried Crosby, Sept. 19, 1912; children—Louise Audenried (Mrs. William Stanley), Miriam Trowbridge. Admitted to N.Y. bar, 1908; settled in Washington, 1910; asst. solicitor Dept. State, 1920-21. Concert and oratorio soloist much of time, 1916-—; has appeared with Bach Choir, of Bethlehem, Pa., 15 seasons, soloist at many music festivals and toured with N.Y. Symphony Orch. Commd. 1st lt. U.S. Army, 1918, disch. as maj., 1920; served in Judge Adv. Gen.'s Corps. Awarded Cross of Honor by German Red Cross for post-war relief work. Mem. Am. Legion, Mil. Order of World War, S.R. Episcopalian. Clubs: Cosmos, Chevy Chase, Gridiron. Home: 1718 Connecticut Av., Washington; (summer) Leesburg, Va. Died Oct. 8, 1964; buried Leesburg, Va.

TITUS, PAUL obstetrician, gynecologist; b. Batavia, N.Y., May 6, 1885; s. Rev. John Wentworth and Elma Margaret (Titus) Sanborn; adopted by maternal grandparents, Rev. and Mrs. Wicks Smith Titus; M.D., Yale, 1908; m. Mary Cushing. Asst. Universitäts Frauenklinik, Heidelberg, Germany, 1908-10; asst. in obstetrics, Johns Hopkins Hosp., Baltimore, 1910-11; resident obstetrician and gynecologist, Magee Hosp., Pittsburgh, 1911-12; now obstetrician and gynecologist, St. Margaret Memorial Hosp.; cons. obstetrician and gynecologist, Shadyside Hosp. Sec.-treas. and dir. Am. Bd. of Obstetrics and Gynecology; sec.-treas. Adv. Bd. for Med. Specialists, 1933-41, v.p., 1943-45, pres., 1945-47; mem. adv. editorial bd., Ma. Jour. Obstetrics and Gynecology; directing editor, Directory of Medical Specialists, 1937-47. Pres. the Assn. of Yale Alumni in Med., 1942-43. Special agt. for Naval Intelligence, and Mil. Intelligence Sect., War Dept., 1915-19. Consultant to surg. gen., U.S. Army, 1943-44; lt. comdr. to capt., M.C., U.S.N.R., attached to Professional Div., Bur. Med. and Surg., Navy Dept., Washington, 1944-45 and 1946; mem. Reserve Consultants Adv. Bd., Bur. Medicine and Surgery, Navy Dept., since 1946; mem. Armed Forces Medical Adv. Com., 1948-50. Awarded Navy Commendation Ribbon. Fellow Am. Coll. Surgeons, A.M.A., Am. Assn. of Obstetricians, Gynecologists and Abdominal Surgeons (exec. council 1929-35, and 1939-45; pres. 1937-38), Am. Gynecol. Soc. (v.p. 1948-49); mem. Med. Soc. State of Pa., Pittsburgh Acad. Medicine (pres. 1929-30), Allegheny County Med. Soc., Soc. Royale, Belge de Gynécologie et d'Obstetrique, Phi Gamma Delta, Nu Sigma Nu. Awarded Commanders Cross, Order of Merit, Hungary, 1938. Author: Management of Obstetric Difficulties, 1937, 2d edit., 1940, 3d edit., 1945, 4th edit., 1950; Diseases of Women for the General Practitioner, 1937; Atlas of Obstetric Technic, 1943, 2d edit., 1949. Home: Schenley Apts., 5th Av. Office: Highland Bldg., Pittsburgh 6. Died June 28, 1951.

TOBIN, CHARLES MILTON, b. San Antonio, Tex., Mar. 30, 1871; s. William Girard and Josephine (Smith) T.; ed. U. of the South, Sewanee, Tenn.; m. Olivia Prescott, of San Antonio, June 13, 1893. Began as fire ins. agt., San Antonio, 1892; spl. agt., Commercial Union Ins. Co., Ltd., of London, Eng., for Western Dist. of N.Y. and Pa., 1906-14. Capt. Co. I, 3d Tex. Inf., 1886-8; capt. Troop H, 1st N.Y. Cav., 1914-16; service on Mexican border, June 1916-Mar. 1917; maj. 1st N.Y. Cav., Nov. 1916-Mar. 25, 1917; supervising officer for West Central Zone, Mil. Training Commn., State of N.Y., Mar. 1917. Grad. Sch. Musketry and Machine Gunnery, Fort Sill; comd. 102d Supply Train, 27th Div.; arrived in France, July 13, 1918; at Brest until Oct. 1918, when joined div. at front; after armistice on staff of comdg. gen. at Brest. Wrote official history of Am. occupancy of Brest for Gen. Staff U.S.A.; discharged as lt. col., Oct. 8, 1919. Pres. Underwriters' Assn. of N.Y. State, 1914; mem. Delta Tau Delta. Republican. Episcopalian. Mason. Club: Rochester. Author: (with Maj. James K. Parsons, U.S.A.) Complete Infantry Guide, 1917; History of Brest, France, 1920. Home: 52 Vassar St., Rochester NY

TOBIN, RALPH C. army officer; b. N.Y.C., May 5, 1890; student Coll. City of N.Y.; entered Fed. Service with N.Y. Nat. Guard, June 1916, as pvt. serving at McAllen, Tex., with 7th N.Y. Inf. until Dec. 1916 during border crisis; commd. 2d lt. Inf. Res., Oct. 1918; commd. capt. Inf. N.Y. Nat. Guard, Apr. 1921, and advanced to brig. gen., July 1942; entered Fed. service, Feb. 1941 as comdg. officer 207th Coast Arty. (Anti-Aircraft) Camp Stewart, Ga., 1941-42; in command 44th Coast Arty., Brigade (Anti-Aircraft), July 1942-—. Awarded Silver Star, World War I. Address: Washington. Died Aug. 5, 1957.

TOBIN, ROBERT GIBSON naval officer; b. Ronceverte, W.Va., Aug. 17, 1894; s. Robert Emmet and Nellie Theresa (Farrell) T.; student Va. Mil. Inst., 1912-13; B.S., U.S. Naval Acad., 1917; m. Carolyn Cecilia O'Rourke, Jan. 7, 1922; 1 son, Robert G. Commd. ensign U.S. Navy, 1917, and advanced through grades to commodore; served in World War I as engring. and later comdg. officer U.S.S. Hopkins; serced on destroyers, cruiser Marblehead, the Pennsylvania, at sea, and the U.S. Naval Acad. and Bur. of Navigation, Washington, D.C.; served as commander 12 destroyers and as commanding officer, U.S.S. Montpelier in the South Pacific Area, World War II; also in London. Awarded 3 Navy crosses, Bronze star, Navy Expeditionary medal, China service, Victory World War I, Purple Heart, Defense medal, Navy Unit commendation, Am. campaign, European campaign, Pacific campaign (7 battle stars), World War II medal. Catholic. Office: 90 Church St., N.Y.C. 7. Deceased.*

TODD, CHAPMAN COLEMAN rear admiral U.S.N.; b. Frankfort, Ky., Apr. 5, 1848; s. Harry Innes and Jane (Davidson) T.; grad. U.S. Naval Acad., 1866; m. Eliza James, Oct. 1872. Cruised in the Pacific Ocean, 1866-67. Promoted ensign, Apr. 1868; master, Mar. 26, 1869; lt., March 25, 1870; lt. comdr., Nov. 1886; comdr., May 1895; capt., Feb. 11, 1901; rear admiral and retired, Oct. 31, 1902, after 41 yrs.' service. Comd. Wilmington, May 1897, to Aug. 1899, and served as hydrographer from Jan. 22, 1900, until November 1901; comdr. flagship Brooklyn, Asiatic sta., until Sept. 1902. Advanced "for eminent and conspicuous conduct in battle" during war with Spain. Address: Washington, D.C. Died Apr. 28, 1929.

TODD, CHARLES STEWART lawyer, diplomat; b. Danville, Ky., Jan. 22, 1791; s. Thomas and Elizabeth (Harris) T.; grad. Coll. William and Mary, 1809; attended Litchfield (Conn.) Law Sch.; m. Letitia Shelby, June 16, 1816, 12 children. Admitted to Ky. bar, 1811; served as volunteer acting q.m. in left wing of Northwestern Army in War of 1812, commd. col. and insp. gen., 1815; sec. of state Ky., 1816; Franklin County rep. in Ky. Legislature, 1817-18; apptd. by Pres. Monroe as diplomatic agt. in Colombia (S.Am.), 1820; commr. to Presbyn. Gen. Assembly, 1837; campaigned for William Henry Harrison for U.S. Pres., 1840, collaborated with Benjamin Drake in writing campaign biography of Harrison; published Cincinnati Republican; apptd. by Pres. Tyler as U.S. minister to Russia, 1841; a commr. to negotiate with Indian tribes on Mexican border, 1850; editor Louisville Indsl. and Comml. Gazette. Died Baton Rouge, La., May 17, 1871.

TODD, FORDE ANDERSON, naval officer; b. Anderson, S.C., Feb. 20, 1881; s. Albert Whitner and Martha (Anderson) T.; student Richmond Acad., Augusta, Ga., 1896-98, Coll. of Charleston (S.C.), 1899-1900; B.S., U.S. Naval Acad., 1904; m. Sylvia Leland Barnes, June 21, 1917; children—Emily Harrison, Anderson, Dorothy Marilla, John Barnes. Commd. ensign, U.S. Navy, 1906, and advanced through the grades to rear adm., 1938; served as naval aid to Pres. Wilson; exec. officer U.S.S. Utah with Grand Fleet, during World War; naval attache, Rome, Italy, 1926-28; comdg. officer U.S.S. Idaho, 1933-34; comdt. of midshipmen, U.S. Naval Acad., 1935-37; comdr. Atlantic Squadron, 1938; comdg. Cruiser Div. 8, U.S. Fleet, 1938-40; retired for physical disability, May 1, 1941, and ordered Governor Naval Home, Philadelphia. Decorated Victory medal for World War, Mexican Campaign medal. Mem. Alpha Tau Omega. Democrat. Presbyn. Clubs: New York Yacht (New York); Rittenhouse, Racquet (Phila.); Army and Navy, Chevy Chase (Washington, D.C.). Home: Haverford PA Died Aug. 1971.

TODD, HENRY DAVIS naval officer; b. Cambridge, Mass., Aug. 25, 1838; s. John N. Todd (formerly of the Navy); ed. Nyack, N.Y., Acad.; apptd. U.S. Naval Acad., 1853; grad. 1857; m. Flora Johnson, Sept. 28, 1865. Promoted to passed midshipman, June 25, 1860, master, Oct. 24, 1860; lt., April 3, 1861; lt. comdr., Jan. 3, 1863; apptd. prof. mathematics, Sept. 16, 1877. At beginning of Civil war was on Cumberland at burning of Norfolk navy yard, and afterward took part in 11 engagements, heavy batteries and sharp shooters, slightly wounded in gunboat night attack, Appomattox River, 1862; flag lt. with Admiral Wilkes, 1862-63, and on Sacramento during rest of war. Instr. mathematics, Naval Acad., 1865-66; head of dept. physics and chemistry same, 1879-86; on duty at Nautical Almanac Office, 1886-1900, dir., 1899-1900; retired from active service, Aug. 25, 1900, at age limit. Address: Washington, D.C. Deceased.

TODD, HIRAM CHARLES lawyer; b. Saratoga Springs, N.Y., July 17, 1876; s. Vernon Lawrence and Anna Elizabeth (Tefft) T.; Ph.B., Union Coll., Schenectady, 1897; L.H.D., 1932; m. Susan Thomas Lumpkin, Nov. 27, 1901; children—Mary Lumpkin (Mrs. Edward Maguire), Susan (Mrs. Peter Malevsky-Malevitch), Hiram Charles. Admitted to N.Y. bar, 1900; practice Saratoga Springs with Edgar T. Brackett, 1900-17; mem. Brackett, Todd, Wheat & Wait, 1917-22; U.S. dist. atty. No. Dist. N.Y., by apptmt. Pres. Harding, July 1921-Sept. 1922; mem. firm Mudge, Stern, Baldwin & Todd and predecessor firms, N.Y.C., since 1922, one of counsel for mgrs. in impeachment Gov. William Sulzer of N.Y., 1913; spl. asst. to Atty. Gen. Daugherty in prosecution of striking trainmen who deserted trains in desert in Ariz. and So. Cal., Aug. 1922, and in prosecution Gaston B. Means and Thomas Felder for obstructing justice, in prosecution of Thomas W. Miller, alien property custodian, 1923-24; spl. asst.

dist. atty. N.Y. County, 1929, in prosecutions connected with failure of City Trust Co.; spl. asst. atty. gen. N.Y. in prosecution George F. Ewald, et al., 1930-31; spl. asst. atty. gen. N.Y. in N.J. Literage case, 1930-32; spl. asst. atty. gen. N.Y. in Drukman murder case, 1935-38; counsel for petitioners for removal of Dist. Atty. Geoghan of Kings County, N.Y.; spl. asst. atty. gen. of N.Y. in legislative investigation, 1944-45; 2d lt. Co. A, 202d N.Y. Vol. Inf. Spanish-Am. War, 1898; in Cuba 4 mos.; mem. N.Y. N.G. grades pvt. to capt. and a.d.c. staff Brig. Gen. Lloyd; maj. judge adv. 13th Div., World War I. Trustee Union Coll., now emeritus. Fellow Am. Bar Found.; mem. Am., N.Y. State, N.Y. County bar assns., Assn. Bar City N.Y., Delta Phi, U.S. War Vets., Naval and Mil. Order Spanish-American War, Am. Legion, N.Y. Soc. of Mil. and Naval Officers of World Wars. Republican. Episcopalian. Clubs: University, Down Town Assn. Home: University Club, N.Y.C. 22. Office: 20 Broad St., N.Y.C. 5. Died Apr. 7, 1965.

TODD, JOHN BLAIR SMITH congressman, army officer; b. Lexington, Ky., Apr. 4, 1841; grad. U.S. Mil. Acad., 1837; studied law. Commd. 2d lt. Sixth Inf., U.S. Army, 1837, 1st lt., 1837, capt., 1843, served in Fla. War, 1837-42, also in war with Mexico, resigned, 1856; became an Indian trader, settled in Ft. Randall, Dakota; admitted to bar, 1861, began practice of law, Yankton, Dakota; served as brig. gen. Volunteers, Union Army, 1861, 62; mem. U.S. Congress (Democrat) from Dakota Territory, 37th Congress, Dec. 9, 1861-63 (contested election) 38th Congress, June 17, 1865-65; mcht., lawyer in Dakota; speaker Territorial Ho. of Reps., 1866-67. Died Yankton County, Dakota (now S.D.), Jan. 5, 1872; buried Yankton Cemetery.

TODD, LEMUEL congressman, lawyer; b. Carlisle, Pa., July 29, 1817; grad. Dickinson Coll., Carlisle, 1839; studied law. Admitted to Pa. bar, 1841, began practice law, Carlisle; mem. U.S. Ho. of Reps. from Pa., 34th, (as Republican) 43d congresses, 1855-57, 73-75; served as maj., 1st Regt., Pa. Volunteer Res. Corps, U.S. Army, Civil War; insp. gen. of Pa. on gov.'s staff. Died Carlisle, May 12, 1891; buried Ashland Cemetery.

TODD, PAUL HAROLD, business exec.; b. Nottawa, Michigan, September 10, 1887; s. Albert May and Augusta (Allman) T.; B.S., U. Mich., 1909; m. Elizabeth Dewing, June 18, 1931; children—Paul Harold, Thomas A. Dir. Abacus Fund, Inc.; pres., mgr. Farmers' Chem. Co., Kalamazoo, Mich.; pres. Mentha Plantation, Inc. (Mich.); dir. Kalamazoo Spice Extraction Co., First Nat. Bank & Trust Co., Kalamazoo, Michigan. Mayor of City of Kalamazoo, 1937, 38, 49, 50; chairman of the Mich. Public Utilities Commn., 1937, 38; past mem. Mich. Econ. Development Commn. Trustee Kalamazoo Coll. Served as 2d lt., arty., U.S. Army, World War I. Mem. Am. Chem. Soc., A.A.A.S., Am. Pharm. Assn., Am. Pub. Power Assn., Am. Legion, Vets. Fgn. Wars Clubs: Torch, Kiwanis (Kalamazoo); Marshall Chess (N.Y.C.). Home: Kalamazoo MI Died Sept. 3, 1969; buried Mountain Home Cemetery, Kalamazoo MI

TOFTOY, HOLGER NELSON army officer; b. Marseilles, Ill., Oct. 31, 1902; s. Nils and Thea (Thorsen) T.; student U. Wis., 1920-22; B.S., U.S. Mil. Acad., 1926; student Army-Navy Staff Coll., 1942-43; LL.D., Athens Coll., 1955; m. Hazel Eunice Schweikert, Dec. 28, 1926; children—Doris (Mrs. George K. Williams), Charles Nelson. Commd. 2d lt. U.S. Army, 1926, advanced through grades to maj. gen., 1952; instr. U.S. Mil. Acad., 1930-35; chief research and devel. and indsl. divs. Submarine Mine Depot, 1938-44; chief ordnance tech. intelligence teams ETO, 1944-45; chief rocket br. research and development div. Office Chief Ordnance, 1945-52; dir. Ordnance Missile Labs., 1952-54; comdg. gen. Redstone Arsenal, 1954-58; dep. comdr. U.S. Army Missile Comd., 1958; comdg. gen. Aberdeen Proving Ground, Md., 1958—. Nat. com. mem. Aero. Bd., 1945-47; guided missile com. Research and Devel. Bd., 1947-52; mem. tech. com. Nat. Adv. Com. Aeros. Decorated Legion of Merit, Bronze Star (U.S.); Croix de Guerre with palm (France); D.S.M., 1958. Recipient James H. Wyld award for outstanding application of rocket power, Am. Rocket Soc. Fellow Am. Rocket Soc.; mem. Am. Ordnance Assn., Am. Legion, Mil. Order World Wars. Clubs: Rotary (Huntsville); Toastmaster (Redstone). Address, Aberdeen Proving Ground, Md. Died 1967.

TOLBERT, RAYMOND AUGUSTINE lawyer; b. Vernon, Tex., Mar. 17, 1890; s. Judge James R. and Emma Nancy (Gilbert) T.; student Southwestern U., 1907-10; A.B., U. Okla., 1912, LL.B., 1913; m. Irma Rapp, Mar. 7, 1920. Admitted to Okla. bar, 1913; pvt. practice law, Hobart, Okla., 1913-17; asst. atty. Okla., Chgo., Rock Island & Pacific Ry. Co., 1919-22; mem. firm Embry, Crowe, Tolbert, Boxley & Johnson, Oklahoma City, and predecessor firms, 1922—. Dir. State Fuel Supply Co. Regent U. Okla., 1931-33. Served from 1st lt. to capt., USAF Res., 1919-29. Recipient Scroll of Honor, Sigma Delta Chi, 192 Okla. bar assns., U. Okla. Alumni Assn. (pres. 1930), Oklahoma City C. of C., Sigma Alpha Epsilon, Phi Delta Phi, Sigma Delta Chi. Clubs: Men's Dinner, Beacon (Oklahoma City). Home: 516 N.W. 37th St., Oklahoma City 18, Office: First Nat. Bldg., Oklahoma City 2. Died July 10, 1960.

TOLEDO-HERRARTE, LUIS, diplomat; b. Guatemala City, Guatemala, C.A., Mar. 28, 1871; s. Roderico and Jesus (Herrarte) Toledo-Mattei; B.A., Instituts Nacional Central, Guatemala City, 1887; M.D., Faculty of Paris, France, 1894; m. Eugenie Roquejoffre, of France, May 27, 1902. Began practice at Guatemala City, 1894; prof. Faculty of Medicine, Guatemala; dir. Nat. Inst.; twice representative in Guatemalan Congress; lt.-col. med. corps; del. of Guatemala to Med. Congress, Panama, 1905; sec. Guatemalan Legation, Rio de Janeiro, Brazil, 1906; E.E. and M.P. to U.S. and Cuba since 1907; mem. Permanent Ct. of Arbitration of The Hague. Mem. Am. Acad. Polit. and Social Science. Roman Catholic. Clubs: Metropolitan (hon.), Guatemala. Author: El papel de los mosquitos en la transmision de las enfermedades contagiosas. Address: The Highlands, Washington DC

TOLFREE, JAMES EDWARD pay dir. U.S.N.; b. Ithaca, N.Y., Aug. 29, 1837; s. John Edward and Caroline Rebecca (Cole) T.; ed. Ithaca Acad. and in France and Italy under pvt. tutors; m. Caroline Overman, Oct. 9, 1872. Apptd. acting asst. p.m. in the vol. navy from N.Y., Sept. 13, 1862; apptd. asst. p.m. in regular service, Mar. 3, 1865; promoted p.m., Jan. 22, 1866; pay insp., Aug. 10, 1886; pay dir., Feb. 12, 1898; retired as pay dir. with rank of rear admiral, Aug. 29, 1899. Served during the Civil War on Vanderbilt, 1862-67; Savannah, 1868; Richmond, 1869-71; Vermont, 1872-75; in 1875, was advanced 10 numbers in rank "for eminent and conspicuous conduct in battle" during the Civil War; on Colorado, 1875-77; on Trenton and fleet p.m., 1877; naval storekeeper, Ville Franche, 1877-78; navy yard, Washington, 1879; Shenandoah, 1879-82; receiving-ship Colorado, 1882-85; Trenton, Omaha, and Brooklyn, as fleet p.m., Asiatic Fleet, 1885-89; Navy Yard, Norfolk, 1892-93; Navy Yard, New York, 1894-96; in charge navy pay office, New York, 1896-99. Home: New York, N.Y. Died Jan. 10, 1920.

TOLL, ROGER WOLCOTT supt. Yellowstone Nat. Park; b. Denver, Colo., Oct. 17, 1883; s. Charles H. and Katharine E. (Wolcott) T.; grad. Manual Training High Sch., Denver, 1901; student Denver U., 1901-02; C.E., Columbia, 1896; m. Marguerite Cass, Sept. 21, 1910; children—Donald Alan, Natalie, Roger W. With engring. dept. Mass. State Bd. of Health, 1907; with U.S. Coast and Geodetic Survey, Alaska, 1908; in engring. dept., later chief engr. Denver Tramway Co., 1908-16; supt. Mt. Rainier Nat. Park, 1919-20; supt. Rocky Mountain Nat. Park, 1921-29; supt. Yellowstone Nat. Park, Feb. 1, 1929—. Served as capt. and maj. Ordnance Dept., U.S.A.; World War I. Republican. Protestant. Author: Mountaineering in the Rocky Mountain National Park, 1919; The Mountain Peaks of Colorado, 1923. Climbed all of the fifty mountain peaks in Rocky Mountain Nat. Park; made first ascent, with 3 other persons, of Mt. Rainier, by the Kautz Glacier route, June 1920. Died Feb. 1936.

TOLLEFSON, MARTIN dean and univ. prof.; born Pelican Rapids, Minn., June 1, 1894; s. Arnt Cornelius and Manna (Guinn) T.; grad., valedictorian, Red Wing Sem. Acad., 1913; A.B., St. Olaf Coll. (salutatorian), 1916; A.M., U. of N.D., 1917; LL.B., U. of Minn. (scholar, fellow, part-time instr. in polit. science), 1921, Ph.D., 1926; Brandeis Research Fellow, Harvard Law Sch., 1935-36; m. Helen Frances Frisbey, Nov. 26, 1927; children—Teresa (Mrs. Vernon Vermeer), Maurine (Mrs. Charles Sutton). Superintendent of schools, Garrison, North Dakota, 1917-18; admitted bars on Minn., 1921, N.D., 1922, Ia., 1926; in practice of law with firm Leslie & Tollefson, Hillsboro, N.D., trial work in Fargo N.D. and Minneapolis, Minn., 1921-24; instr. polit. science and pub. law, U. of Kan., 1924-25, asst. prof. with appointment to permanent faculty status, 1925-26; prof. law, Drake U., since 1926, acting dean, 1937-41, chmn. Council of Deans (functioning in the absence of a univ. pres., 1941), dean, since 1946. Served as private to cpl., 34th Engrs., A.E.F., U.S. Army, 1918-19; commd. capt. 1934, advanced through grades to col., 1943; chief legal branch, prisoner of war operations div., Provost Marshall General's Office, 1941-43, asst. dir., and chief of legal branch, 1943-44, div. dir., 1944-46; discharged, 1946. Decorated S.W. Commendation Ribbon; Legion of Merit. Mem. Am. Law Inst., Am., Ia., Polk Co. bar assns., Am. Judicature Soc., United Presbyn. Found. (trustee, exec. com.), Phi Beta Kappa, Order of Coif, Phi Alpha Delta. Presbyn. (elder). Mason (32 deg.). Clubs: Drake Faculty (pres. 3 terms); Des Moines U. (dir.). Author: Iowa Probate Law and Practice, 2 vols., 1960. Contbr. Normanden, N.D. State Hist. Colls., and profl. jours. Home: 227 Zwart Rd., Des Moines 50312. Address: Law School, Drake University, Des Moines, Ia. Died Dec. 26, 1963; buried Mt. Hope Cemetery Mausoleum, Topeka.

TOLLEY, HAROLD SUMNER ex-congressman; b. Honesdale, Pa., Jan. 16, 1894; s. Adolphus Charles and Emma Grace (Sumner) T.; A.B., Syracuse U., 1916; student Drew Theol. Sem. 1 yr.; m. Anna Marguerite Germond, Oct. 6, 1917; children—Douglas Germond, Eleanor Grace, Harold Tolley. Asso. with father in retail shoe bus., Binghamton, as A. C. Tolley & Co., 1919—; mem. 69th Congress (1925-27), 34th N.Y. Dist. Dir. Buffalo area, N.Y. State Social Welfare, 1937-56. Enlisted in R.O.T.C., May 13, 1917; commd. 2d lt. 309th Inf., U.S.A., Aug. 15, 1917; 1st lt. Dec. 31, 1917; capt. May 13, 1918; participated with 1st Army in Meuse-Argonne offensive; hon. discharged, July 25, 1919; capt. inf., O.R.C.; capt. F.A., exec. officer 1st Bn., 104th F.A., N.Y.N.G. (resigned Dec. 1924). Mem. Am. Legion, Delta Sigma Rho, Pi Kappa Alpha. Republican. Methodist. Mason. Home: Kenmore, N.Y. Died May 20, 1956.

TOLMAN, EDGAR BRONSON (tol'man), lawyer; b. Nowgong, British India, Sept. 5, 1859; s. Rev. Cyrus Fisher (D.D.) and Mary Ruth (Bronson) T.; A.B., U. of Chicago, 1880, A.M., 1883; LL.B., Union Coll. Law, 1882; LL.D., Northwestern U., 1927; m. Nellie M. Browne, 1883 (died 1888); children—Ruth M., Helen I.; m. 2d, Blanche N. Stevens. 1889 (died 1903); children—Mary L. (Mrs. Eric W. Stubbs), Edgar B., Blanche S. (Mrs. Albert C. Fiedler). Practiced in Chicago since 1882; mem. Tolman, Megan & Bryant. Corp. counsel, Chicago, 1903-06; spl. asst. to U.S. atty. gen., 1934-38. Mem. adv. com. to U.S. Supreme Court to draft and submit federal rules of civil procedure since 1934. Major 1st Ill. Volunteer Inf., Spanish-Am. War; participated in Santiago campaign; maj. of Inf. U.S. Army, assigned to supervise adminstrn. of the draft in Ill., 1917-18; awarded D.S.M. and promoted to rank of lt. col. J.A.G. Awarded Am. Bar Assn. medal, July 12, 1939. Editor-in-chief Am. Bar Assn. Jour., 1920-47, editor-in-chief emeritus since 1946. Mem. Illinois State Bar Assn. (pres. 1917-18), Chicago Bar Assn. (pres. 1911-12), Law Club of Chicago (pres. 1910-11), Am. Law Inst. (council, 1924-47), Ill. Soc. S.A.R. (ex-pres.), Ill. Commandery Soc. Foreign Wars of U.S. (ex-pres.), Ill. branch Soc. Army of Santiago de Cuba, Am. Legion, Delta Kappa Epsilon. Democrat. Clubs: Chicago Athletic, Flossmoor Country, Iroquois, Quadrangle. Home: 5554 Woodlawn Av. Office: 30 N. La Salle St., Chicago, Ill. Died Nov. 20, 1947.

TOMEI, PETER ANDREW, lawyer; b. Chgo., July 12, 1934; s. Felix and Hortense (Schurman) T.; B.A. magna cum laude, Yale, 1956; J.D. cum laude, Harvard, 1959; m. Mary Cleopha Staciva, May 30, 1959; children—Peter Alexander, Jennifer Lee, John Adam, Joshua Ellsworth. Admitted to D.C., Ill. bar, 1959, since practiced in Chgo.; asso. firm Isham, Lincoln & Beale, 1959-67, partner, 1968-71. Del. Ill. Constl. Conv., 1969-70. Served to capt. AUS, 1959-62. Recipient Maurice Weigel award Chgo. Bar Found., 1968; named one of Chgo.'s ten outstanding young men Chgo. Jr. Assn. Commerce and Industry, 1969. Mem. Am., Ill., Chgo. (chmn. com. on constl. revision 1968-69) bar assns., Econ. Club Chgo. Am. Trial Lawyers Assn., Chgo. Hist. Soc., Adlai Stevenson Inst. Internat. Affairs, Phi Beta Kappa. Democrat. Roman Catholic. Contbr. articles on Ill. constl. reform. Home: Chicago IL Died May 16, 1971.

TOMLINSON, WILLIAM GOSNELL, naval officer; b. Leavenworth, Kan., Dec. 17, 1897; s. John Cassett and Medora (Gosnell) T.; grad. U.S. Naval Acad., 1919; m. Katharine Estelle Dent, June 15, 1931. Qualified as naval aviator 1922; early test pilot; participated in development of dive bombing and carrier aircraft tactics; comd. patrol squadron which made early overseas flights; head Reserve Aviation, Bur. Aeronautics, Washington, D.C., 1932-35; in World War II served overseas or on sea duty, holding 4 comds., last—aircraft carrier U.S.S. Belleau Wood (ship received Presdl. Unit citation; chief air readiness, Navy Dept., Washington, D.C.; comdr. Pacific Division Mil. Air Transport Service. Awarded Navy Cross for heroism in action (Iwo Jima); Legion of Merit with gold star in lieu of 2d for action against enemy. Baptist. As racing pilot member Am. Schneider Cup Team, 1926; won Curtiss Marine Trophy, 1929. Home: Washington DC Died Oct. 13, 1972.

TOMPKINS, CHARLES HENRY brig. gen., U.S.A.; b. Ft. Monroe, Va., Sept. 12, 1830; s. Daniel D. and Mary (Pierce) T.; cadet U.S. Mil. Acad., 1847-49; m. Augusta Root Hobbie, Dec. 17, 1862. Served pvt., corpl., and sergt. Co. F, 1st Dragoons, Jan. 21, 1856-Jan. 10, 1861; 2d lt. 2d Cav., Mar. 23, 1861; 1st lt., Apr. 30, 1861; capt. a.q.m., Nov. 13, 1861; col. 1st Vt. Cav., Apr. 24, 1862; resigned, Sept. 9, 1862; lt. col. q.m. vols., July 1, 1865; col. q.m. vols., June 13, 1866; lt. col. deputy q.m. gen. U.S.A., July 29, 1866; col. a.q.m. gen., Jan. 24, 1881; retired by operation of law, Sept. 12, 1894; advanced to rank of brig. gen. retired, by act of Apr. 23, 1904. Bvtd. maj., Mar. 13, 1865, "for gallant conduct at battle of Fairfax C.H., Va., May 31, 1861"; lt. col., Mar. 13, 1865, "for meritorious services in campaigns of Gens. Banks and McDowell, 1862, 1863"; col., Mar. 13, 1865, for same in q.m. dept., 1863-65; brig. gen., Mar. 13, 1865, "for faithful and meritorious services during the war"; awarded Congressional Medal of Honor, Nov. 13, 1893, "for distinguished gallantry in action at Fairfax C.H., Va., June 1, 1861." Home: Washington, D.C. Died Jan. 18, 1915.

TOMPKINS, DANIEL D. vice pres. U.S., gov. N.Y.; b. Scarsdale, N.Y., June 21, 1774; s. Jonathan G. and Sarah (Hyatt) T.; grad. Columbia, 1795; m. Hannah Minthorne, 1797, 7 children. Admitted to bar, 1797; mem. N.Y. Constl. Conv., 1801; mem. N.Y. Assembly, 1803; elected to U.S. Ho. of Reps. 9th Congress, 1804, resigned before taking seat to become asso. justice N.Y. Supreme Ct., 1804-07; gov. N.Y., 1807, 10, 13, prevented establishment Bank of N. Am.; instrumental in passage of law to extinguish slavery in N.Y. State,

1817 (became effective 1827); served as comdr.-in-chief N.Y. Militia, War of 1812; commanded 3d Mil. Dist., including So. N.Y., Eastern N.J., 1814, used personal credit to pay and maintain troops (later accused of irregularities in wartime financial conduct, cleared, compensated for expenditures by Congress); vice. pres. U.S., 1817-25; pres. N.Y. Constl. Conv., 1821; a founder N.Y. Hist. Soc. Died Staten Island, N.Y., June 11, 1825; buried St. Mark's Churchyard, N.Y.C.

TOMS, ROBERT MORRELL jurist; b. La Crosse, Wis., Oct. 14, 1886; s. Frank Phelps and Lark M. (Looney) T.; A.B., U. Chgo., 1907; LL.B., U. Mich., 1910; m. Gladys Bassford Wetmore, Nov. 11, 1914; children—Elinor Bassford (Mrs. Robert M. Jones), Margaret Sprague (Mrs. George C. Cope). Prosecuting atty., Detroit, 1921-29; judge, 3d Judicial Circuit, Mich., 1929—; exec. presiding judge, U.S. War Crimes Courts, Nurnberg, Germany, 1946-47; prof. constl. law, Wayne U., 1932—. Home: 17374 Muirland Av., Detroit. Office: County Bldg., Detroit 26, Mich. Died Apr. 6, 1960.

TOMS, ZACH tobacco co. exec.; b. Durham, N.C., Feb. 9, 1901; s. Clinton White and Mary (Newby) T.; A.B., U. Va., 1921; student Wharton Sch. Finance, U. Pa., 1921-22; m. Frances Coleman, Feb. 4, 1928; children—Zach Toms, Peter Coleman, Mary C. (Mrs. Herbert E. Fitzgerald), Newby. With Liggett-Myers Tobacco Co., 1922—, dir., 1945—, secretary, 1947—, vice president, 1951-59, exec. v.p., 1959-61, pres. 1961—. Served to 2d lt. U.S. Army, 1918-19. Presbyn. (trustee). Clubs: Union (N.Y.C.); Hudson River Country (Greystone, N.Y.); Commonwealth, Country of Va. (Richmond, Va.). Home: 655 Park Av., N.Y.C. 21. Office: 630 Fifth Av., N.Y.C. 20. Died July 9, 1964.

TOOKER, STERLING TWISS, ins. co. exec.; b. Hartford, Conn., May 23, 1913; s. Morris S. and Hazel (Twiss) T.; B.A., Wesleyan U., Middletown Conn., 1935; B. Ins., U. Conn., 1942; m. Alice Miller, Aug. 10, 1940; children—Adlin M., S. Christopher. With Travelers Ins. Companies, Hartford, 1935-68, v.p. exec. dept., 1959-62, exec. v.p., 1962-64, pres., 1964-68, also dir.; dir. Hartford National Bank and Trust Company (Conn.), Standard Screw Co., N.E. Utilities. Bd. dirs. Travelers Research Center, Inc., Am. Sch. Deaf; pres. bd. trustees Kingswood Sch., Hartford; bd. trustees Wesleyan U., Com., Econ. Devel.; mem. council Grad. Sch. Bus., U. Chgo.; dir. v.p. Greater Hartford YMCA; mem. bd. advisers Hartford Grad. Center, Rensselaer Poly Inst. Conn., Inc.; mem. bd. electors Ins. Hall Fame. Served as lt. (j.g.) USNR, 1943-46. Mem. Greater Hartford C. of C. (chmn. edn. com., dir.). Home: West Simsbury CT Died June 6, 1969.

TOOMBS, HENRY JOHNSTON, architect; b. Cuthbert, Ga., Jan. 4, 1896; s. Robert Edwin and Rebecca Seymour (Johnston) T.; B.Arch., U. of Pa., 1921, M.Arch., 1922; m. Frances Bennett, Feb. 10, 1931 (divorced 1946); one son, Michael; married 2d, Adah Knight Hereford, August 11, 1948. Draftsman, Paul P. Cret, Phila., 1922-24, McKim, Mead and White, N.Y. City, 1924-27; practicing architect since 1928; architect for Ga. Warm Springs Foundation, Bridge building for Rich's, Inc., Atlanta, Rhone Cemetery for Am. Battle Monuments Commission, also other pub. and private bldgs. and residences N.Y. and Ga.; partnership with Wm. J. Creighton as Toombs and Creighton, Jan. 1946-49; partner Toombs & Co., 1949-53; Toombs, Amisano & Wells, 1955-67; architect Fed. Reserve Bank Atlanta. Ensign, U.S. Navy, 1917-19. Mem. Bd. of Zoning Appeals, Fulton County, Ga., 1940-44, mem. Co. Planning Commn., 1946-51; mem. Municipal Planning Bd. since 1952; mem. Fulton Co. Grand Jurors Assn. Capt., U.S. Army Air Corps, May 1, 1942, maj., Dec. 17, 1943; retired 1944. Fellow A.I.A. Clubs: St. Anthony, Army and Navy, Washington, D.C.; Century (N.Y.) Home: Atlanta GA Died June 15, 1967; buried Warm Springs GA

TOOMBS, ROBERT AUGUSTUS senator, Confederate ofcl.; b. Wilkes County, Ga., July 2, 1810; s. Robert and Catherine (Huling) T.; attended U. Ga.; grad. Union Coll., Schenectady, N.Y., 1828; m. Julia DuBose, 1830, 3 children. Admitted to bar, 1830; active in Whig Party; mem. Ga. Legislature, 1837-41, 42-43; mem. U.S. Ho. of Reps. from Ga., 29th-32d congresses, 1845-53, did not appear as spokesman for So. interests until 1850 crisis when he threatened secession, but urged support of Compromise of 1850 after passage; mem. U.S. Senate from Ga., 1853-Feb. 4, 1861 (elected Constl. Union Party candidate and Breckinridge supporter, 1858); advocated secession when Crittenden Compromise did not pass in Congress, 1861; Ga. del. to Confederate Provisional Congress, Montgomery, Ala., 1861; sec. of state Confederate States Am., 1861, resigned because of dissatisfaction with leadership of Jefferson Davis; commd. brig. gen. Confederate Army, 1861, served in Va. theater, effectiveness as mil. leader impaired by continued polit. activity; resigned commn. after failure to obtain promotion after Battle of Antietam, 1862; retired to home in Washington, Ga., became a vehement critic of Confederate govt. and conduct of the war; lived in London, Eng., 1865-67; returned to Ga., leading opponent of Radical Reconstrn., urged solution of So. problems through Democratic Party; mem. Ga. Conv. of 1877, repudiated Carpetbag govt. debts and limited Negro suffrage. Died Washington, Ga., Dec. 15, 1885; buried Rest Haven Cemetery, Washington.

TOON, THOMAS FENTRESS farmer; b. Columbus County, N.C., June 10, 1840; s. Anthony Fentress and Mary (McMillan) T.; grad. Wake Forest Coll., N.C., 1861; enlisted in C.S.A., May 20, 1861, as pvt. Co. K, 20th N.C. regt.; promoted 1st lt., June 17, 1861; capt., July 1861; col. 20th regt., N.C. troops, Feb. 26, 1863; brig. gen., May 31, 1864; assigned to command of Johnston's brigade, June 4, 1864; took part in the prominent battles of Civil War; wounded 5 times; m. Carrie E. Smith, Jan. 24, 1866; m. 2d, Rebecca Cobb Ward, Oct. 29, 1891. Elected to N.C. legislature, 1881, to N.C. senate, 1883; State supt. public instruction, N.C., 1900. Address: Lumberton, N.C. Died 1902.

TORBERT, ALFRED THOMAS ARCHIMEDES army officer, diplomat; b. Georgetown, Del., July 1, 1833; s. Jonathan R. and Catherine (Milby) T.; grad. U.S. Mil. Acad., 1855; m. Mary E. Curry, Jan. 17, 1866. Apptd. brevet 2d lt. inf. U.S. Army, 1855; served on frontier, 1856-61; promoted 2d lt., 1856, 1st lt., 1861; commd. col. 1st N.J. Volunteers, 1861; commd. capt. U.S. Army, 1861; participated in siege of Yorktown, battles of West Point, Gaine's Mills; commanded a brigade of VI Corps; brevetted brig. gen. U.S. Volunteers, 1862; assigned command 1st Cavalry div. Army of Potomac, 1864; defeated Confederate Army at battles of Hanovertown, Matadequin Creek, Cold Harbor; apptd. chief of cavalry of middle mil. div. Army of Shenandoah, 1864; brevetted maj. gen. U.S. Army, 1865; U.S. minister to Salvador, 1869-71; consul gen. Havana, Cuba, 1871-73, Paris, France, 1873-78; resigned to enter bus. enterprise in Mexico, 1878. Drowned off coast of Fla., Aug. 29, 1880.

TORGERSEN, HAROLD engr., univ. dean; b. Bklyn., Jan. 2, 1910; s. Anton and Marie (Evensen) T.; B.S., in Elect. Engring., N.Y.U., 1929; student U. Wis., 1932, Columbia, 1933-34; M.S., Harvard, 1939. Test engr. Gen. Electric Co., 1929-30; instr. elec. engring. N.Y.U., 1930-39, supr. power plant, 1935-36, asst. prof., 1939-46, asso. prof., 1946-53, asst. dean evening div. engring., 1946-52, asst. dean engring., 1952-56, prof. elec. engring., 1953-57, asso. dean engring., 1956-57; dean engring. prof. elec. engring. U. Conn., 1957—. Served from lt. (j.g.) to comdr. USNR, 1941-46. Fellow Am. Inst. E.E.; mem. Am. Soc. Engring. Edn., Inst. Radio Engrs., Conn. Soc. Civil Engrs., Harvard Engring. Soc., S.I. Hist. Soc., Perstare et Praestare, Tau Beta Pi, Eta Kappa Nu, Pi Tau Sigma. Clubs: Harvard (N.Y.C.); Nordmanns Forbundet. Home: 24 Whitney Rd., Storrs, Conn. Died Nov. 5, 1961.

TORNEY, GEORGE HENRY surgeon gen. U.S.A.; b. Baltimore, Md., June 1, 1850; s. John P. and Mary M. (Peacock) T.; student Carroll Coll., New Windsor, Md., 1862-67; M.D., U. of Va., 1870; m. Mary A. Johnston, Jan. 22, 1872. Apptd. asst. surgeon U.S.N., Nov. 1, 1871; passed asst. surgeon, Nov. 1, 1874; resigned from navy, June 30, 1875; apptd. 1st lt. asst. surgeon U.S.A., July 1, 1875; promoted capt. asst. surgeon, July 1, 1880; maj. surgeon, June 6, 1894; lot. col. deputy surgeon gen., Aug. 8, 1903; col. Med. Corps, Apr. 23, 1908; surgeon gen. U.S.A., Jan. 14, 1909—. Republican. Catholic. Died Dec. 27, 1913.

TORRANCE, ELL soldier, lawyer; b. at New Alexandria, Pa., May 16, 1844; s. Adam (D. D.) and Eliza (Graham) T.; ed. Eldersridge Acad., Ind. Co., Pa.; m. Anna Mary Macfarlane, Sept. 22, 1868. Enlisted, although under military age, June 26, 1861, pvt. Co. A, 9th Pa. Reserves; served in all battles (except when disabled by wounds) of his regt. and was discharged with regt. at Pittsburgh, May 11, 1864; reentered service, July 9, 1864, 2d lt. Co. K, 193d Pa. Inf.; transferred to 97th Pa. Inf., Oct. 15, 1864; discharged at close of war, June 17, 1865; guarded body of President Lincoln when it lay in state at Baltimore; participated in many campaigns Army Potomac. Read law, Pittsburgh, admitted to bar, 1868; for 42 yrs. in practice in Minneapolis. Del. Rep. Nat. Conv., 1896; president Normal Sch. Bd., Minn., since 1905; ex-chmn. State High School Bd.; trustee McKinley Nat. Memorial Assn. Charter mem. John A. Rawlins Post, G.A.R., Minneapolis; comdr. Dept. of Minn., 1895; comdr.-in-chief G.A.R., 1901-02; comdr. Minn. Commandery Loyal Legion, 1908-09; mem. Minn. Soc. Colonial Wars (ex. gov.), Minn. Soc. S.A.R. (ex-pres.); life mem. Soc. Army of the Potomac. Mem. Board Visitors, U.S. Mil. Acad., 1902. Chmn. Nat. Com. G.A.R. on 50th Anniversary Battle of Gettysburg, 1909-13; also on Lincoln and Grant centennials; chmn. Minn. State War Memorial Commn. Has mil. library relating to the Civil War of 5,000 vols. Presbyn. Republican. Mem. Six O'Clock and Golden Wedding Clubs. Home: The Leamington. Office: New York Life Bldg., Minneapolis, Minn.

TOTTEN, JOSEPH GILBERT army officer, engr.; b. New Haven, Conn., Aug. 23, 1788; s. Peter and Grace (Mansfield) T.; grad. U.S. Mil. Acad., 1805; A.M. (hon.), Brown U., 1829; m. Catlyna Pearson, 1816, 7 children. Commd. 2d lt. engrs. U.S. Army, 1805, 1st lt., 1810, capt., 1812; asst. engr. harbor defenses N.Y.C., 1808, spl. supr. Ft. Clinton, Castle Garden, N.Y.; asst. in defenses of New Haven, New London (Conn.), Sag Harbor; chief engr. U.S. Army of Niagara frontier, 1812; brevetted maj., 1813, lt. col., 1814; engaged in coastal fortifications, 1815-38; promoted maj., 1818, lt. col., 1828, col., 1838; chief engr. U.S. Army, insp. U.S. Mil. Acad., 1838-64; served with Gen. Winfield Scott as chief engr. and mem. so-called Little Cabinet; originated successful plan of operations at Battle of Veracruz during Mexican War; brevetted brig. gen., 1847; mem. Lighthouse Bd., 1851-58, 60-64; instrumental in putting into use system of lighting by Fresnel lenses; commd. brig. gen. U.S. Army, 1863; supr. defensive works around Washington, D.C.; mem. bd. to regulate and fix heavy ordnance, 1861-62; brevetted maj. gen. by U.S. Congress, 1864; published Essays on Hydraulic and Common Mortars and on Lime-Burning, 1838; corporator Nat. Acad. Scis., 1863; studied conchology, 2 shells (gemma and succinca tottenii) named for him; Ft. Totten (N.Y.C. Harbor) named for him. Died Washington, D.C., Apr. 22, 1864.

TOULMIN, HARRY AUBREY JR. (tool'min), lawyer, soldier, author; b. Springfield, Ohio, Nov. 25, 1890; s. Harry Aubrey and Rosamond (Evans) T.; student Wittenberg College, Springfield, Ohio, 1905-06, Litt.D., 1917; B.A., University of Virginia, 1911 (gold medalist); J.D., Ohio State University, 1913; LL.D., Transylvania College, 1930; married Margaret McCarty, July 24, 1919 (div.); 1 dau., Margaret Aubrey; m. 2d, Virginia Bernthal, November 12, 1958. Admitted to Ohio bar, 1913, mem. Toulmin & Toulmin, patent attys.; dir. Commonwealth Engring. Corp., Bus. Corners, Inc., Consol. Corps., Inc., also chmn. bd. Central Pharmacal Co., Seymour, Ind.; officer and dir. numerous corps. Asst. sec. Gen. Munitions Bd. of Council Nat. Def. Served as lt. col. U.S. Army, World War I; A.E.F.; col., A.C., World War II, asst. chief transportation Corps, staff officer charge Atlantic and Pacific Overseas Commands Air Force. Decorated D.S.M. (U.S.), Legion of Merit, Victory medal with French Bar. Mem. nat., state and local profl. socs. and orgns. Democrat. Episcopalian. Clubs: Queen City (Cin.); Engineers (Dayton); Army and Navy, National Press (Washington). Author books, latest: Anti-Trust Laws of the U.S. (7 vols.), 1949; The Law of Food and Drugs (5 vols.). Home: 501 Maysfield Rd., Oakwood, Dayton, O. Office: 11 S. Wilkinson St., Dayton, O.; Springfield Gas & Electric Co. Bldg., Springfield, O.; also Brussels, Belgium. Died Mar. 28, 1965; buried Ferncliff Cemetery, Springfield.

TOULMIN, JOHN EDWIN, banker; b. Brookline, Mass., Nov. 1, 1902; s. John Edwin and Alice Munroe (Barbour) T.; ed. Country Day Sch., Choate Sch. and Harvard; m. Rose Cracroft Loveland, Sept. 25, 1926; children—Peter Noyes, Hugh Huidekoper, Paul Routledge; married 2d Virginia Belcher Campbell, Aug. 26, 1950 (div. 1963). With First Nat. Bank of Boston, 1925-67, v.p., 1932-47, sr. v.p., 1947-59, vice chmn. bd., 1959-67; dir. 1st Nat. Bank Boston, First Bank Boston Internat., Boston Overseas Financial Corp., Massanet Corp., Firstbank Financial Corp., MIF Industries, Inc., McGregor-Doniger, Inc., United Fruit Co., Arthur D. Little Co., 1st Small Bus. Investment Corporation of New England, Badger Company, Inc. Member board of trustees Free Hospital for Women. Col. A. U.S., 1942-45, overseas 1943-44. Member Association Reserve City Bankers, Unitarian. Clubs: Harvard (Boston and New York); Dedham (Mass.) Country and Polo, Harvard Varsity; The Country (Brookline, Mass.). Home: Westwood MA Died Apr. 9, 1968; buried Forest Hills Cemetery, Jamaica Plain MA

TOUPS, ROLAND LEON, sugar co. exec.; b. Thibodaux, La., July 25, 1911; s. Leonidas M. and Maude (Peltier) T.; B.S. in Mech. Engring., Ga. Inst. Tech., 1933; m. Gertrude Daigle, Sept. 27, 1935;children—Roland Michael and Leon Henry (twins), Henry Etta. With Godchaux Sugars, Inc., New Orleans, 1933-42; with South Coast Corp., New Orleans, 1945-69, v.p., gen. mgr., 1953-64, pres., 1964-69; dir. Raceland Bank & Trust Co. (La.), La. Agrl. Credit Corp., New Orleans, Gulf South Financial Advisers, Inc., Thibodaux. Past chmn. St. John and Terrebonne parishes Boy Scouts Am., past mem. exec. bd. New Orleans area; past pres. St. Francis Boys Sch. Fathers Club. Houma, La. Served to lt. col. AUS, 1942-45. Named King Sucrose XXVII for La. Sugar Cane Festival, 1968. Registered profl. engr., La. Mem. Sugar Industry Technicians, Am. Sugar Cane Tech. Assn. (past pres.), La. Engring. Soc., Nat. Soc. Profl. Engrs., Houma-Terrebonne C. of C. (bd. dirs.), Lambda Chi Alpha, Pi Tau Sigma, Scabbard and Blade. Home: Houma LA Died May 9, 1969; interred St. Francis de Sales Mausoleum Houma LA

TOUR, REUBEN S(IMKIN) (toor), chem. engr.; b. Troy, N.Y., Aug. 20, 1889; s. James and Sophia (Simkin) T.; B.S., U. of Mich., 1910, M.S.E., 1915, Ch.E., 1927; m. Margaret Meyer, 1914; 1 son, Robert Louis. Asst. supt., Consolidated Gas Co., N.Y. City, 1911-13; asst. prof. gas engring., U. of Calif., 1913-17; capt. Ordnance Dept., U.S. Army, chief of tech. dept. U.S. Nitrate Plant No. 1, Muscle Soals, Ala., 1917-19; chem. engr. nitrate div. Ordnance Dept., U.S. Army, 1919-21; prof. chem. engring. and head of dept., U. of Cincinnati, since 1921; cons. chem. engr. (industrial gases). Lt. col. Ordnance O.R.C., to 1942. Mem. Am. Inst. Chemical Engrs., Am. Soc. Engineering Educ., A.A.A.S., Am. Assn. Univ. Profs., Sigma Xi, Tau Beta

Pi, Phi Lambda Upsilon. Mason. Contributor of articles on nitrogen fixation and chemical engineering. Address: University of Cincinnati, Cin. 21. Died Aug. 1, 1952.

TOURTELLOT, GEORGE P(LATT) (toor'tĕ-lot), army officer; b. Dows, Ia., Nov. 5, 1895; s. George Mason and Mary Eleanor (Platt) T.; ed. Carroll Coll., 1915-17; Army Flying Sch., 1917-18; Air Corps Engring. Sch., 1928-29; Air Corps Tactical Sch., 1936-37; Command and Gen. Staff Sch., 1939-40; m. Peggy Leota Strane, April 26, 1921; 1 son, George Platt. Commd. 2d lt. Air Service, 1918; promoted through grades to brig. gen., 1943; on duty in France and Germany with combat pursuit units, 1918-19; comdg. officer 75th Service Squadron, Wheeler Field, Hawaii, 1930-33 and aeronautical insp. for Commerce Dept.; aviation instr., Mich. Nat. Guard, 1938-39; comdg. officer 35th Pursuit Group, Hamilton Field, Calif., 1940-41; exec. officer 2d Interceptor Command, Seattle, 1942; comdg. officer 111th Fighter Command, Drew Field, Fla., 1942; comdg. general 24th Composite Wing, 1942-44; comdg. general 72d Fighter Wing, Peterson Field, Colo., 1944; assigned to Hdqrs. A.A.F., Washington, D.C-, 1945; comdr. McDill Field, Fla. until Oct. 15, 1946; comdr. Selfridge Field, Mich., Oct. 16-Oct. 26, 1946. Rated combat pilot and combat observer. Mem. Quiet Birdmen, Daedalians. Address: 3102 Oaklyn Drive, Parkland Estates, Tampa, Fla. Died Oct. 26, 1946; buried in Arlington National Cemetery.

TOWAR, ALBERT SELAH officer U.S.A.; b. Walsingham, Ont., Nov. 10, 1845; s. George Washington and Hannah (Matthews) T., both natives of N.Y. State; ed. in schs. of Tillsonburg, Ont., until 1858; m. Adrian, Mich., Sept. 23, 1873, Kate A. Gambell. Commd. maj. paymaster, U.S.A., Mar. 3, 1875; promoted lt. col., deputy paymaster-gen., U.S.A., Feb. 1, 1899, col. asst. paymaster-gen., Feb. 2, 1901. Served successively at Santa Fe, N.M., 1875-79, Ft. Sanders, Wyo., 1879-80, Ft. D. A. Russell, Wyo., 1880-81, Omaha, Neb., 1881-85, Cheyenne, Wyo., June-Oct., 1885, Detroit, 1885-89, Tucson, Ariz., 1889-91, Albuquerque, 1891-92, Santa Fe, N.M., 1892-94, New York, 1894-95; chief paymaster, Dept. of the Missouri, Omaha, 1895-99; chief paymaster, Div. of the Philippines, Manila, 1899-1901; chief paymaster, Dept. of the Lakes, 1902-07; retired Apr. 15, 1907. Address: War Dept., Washington.

TOWER, GEORGE EDWARD naval officer; b. Ashtabula, O., Apr. 11, 1836; s. Reuben and Clarissa W. (Sheffer) T.; ed. Ashtabula Acad.; m. Phebe Wetherex, Mar. 5, 1863 (died 1895); m. 2d, Jennie MacIntire, Oct. 19, 1897. Began as engr. on Lake Erie, 1856; apptd. 3d asst. engr. U.S.N., Jan. 1862; promoted 2d asst. engr., Oct. 1, 1863; 1st asst. engr., Jan. 1868; comd. chief engr., June 1887; retired, Feb. 1897. Was in N. and S. Atlantic squadrons during Civil War; prin. engagements, at Yorktown and West Point, Va.; with Admiral Farragut at Battle of Mobile Bay and bombardment of Ft. Morgan, and with Admiral Porter in both attacks on Ft. Fisher; served in Spanish-Am. War, May 11-Dec. 22, 1898. Republican. Presbyterian. Died June 9, 1914.

TOWERS, JOHN HENRY naval officer; b. Rome, Ga., Jan. 30, 1885; s. William Magee and Mary (Norton) T.; student Ga. Sch. Tech., 1 yr.; grad. U.S. Naval Acad., 1906; m. Lily Carstairs, Oct. 5, 1915 (div.); children—Marjorie, Charles Stewart; m. 2d, Pierrette Anne Chauvin de Grandmont, Aug. 1930. Commd. ensign U.S. Navy, Feb. 12, 1908, promoted through grades to comdr., June 25, 1918, admiral, Nov. 7, 1945. Aviation duty 1911—; one of earliest officers of Navy in aviation service; twice attached to Am. Embassy, London; asst. dir. Naval Aviation, World War; comdr. transatlantic flight, 1919; asst. chief Bur. Aeros., Navy Dept., 1929-31; comdg. officer U.S.S. Saratoga, 1937-38; chief Bur. Aeros., June 1, 1939-Oct. 7, 1942; comdr. Air Force, U.S. Pacific Fleet, 1942-44; deputy comdr. in chief, Pacific Areas, Feb. 1944-Nov. 1945; comdr. in chief Pacific Fleet and Pacific Ocean Areas, Nov. 1945—; adm. ret.; asst. v.p. Pan-American Airways. Decorated Navy Cross, Royal Air Force (British); comdt. Order of Tower and Sword (Portuguese); spl. medals of Congress; Kt. Comdr. Order British Empire. Clubs: Army and Navy, Chevy Chase, Metropolitan (Washington); New York Yacht, Seawanhaka-Corinthian Yacht. Address: Navy Dept., Washington. Died Apr. 1, 1955; buried Arlington Nat. Cemetery.

TOWLER, THOMAS WILLARD, pub. rep.; b. Chgo., Aug. 20, 1891; s. Edward Thomas and Elizabeth Hadley (Davis) T.; A.B., Dartmouth, 1913; m. Lois Breckenridge, Apr. 27, 1918. Salesman The Knapp Co., N.Y.C., 1913-15; advt. mgr. Westinghouse, Church, Kerr & Co., 1915-17, 19-20, Dwight P. Robinson & Co., 1920-22; advt. rep. Cosmopolitan mag., Chgo., 1922-27; account exec. Ruthrauff & Ryan, N.Y.C., 1927-28; advt. mgr. United Engrs. & Constructors, 1927-33, Am. Architect mag., 1933-38; pub., v.p. Town and Country mag., N.Y.C., 1938-66; pub. rep. Men's Bazaar, also Am. rep. Brit. Bazaar, German Bazaarette, 1966-68; pres. Magazine Space Consultants, 1968-72. Served as 1st lt. C.W.S., U.S. Army, 1918. Mem. Beta Theta Pi. Presbyn. Clubs: University, Dartmouth (N.Y.C.); Baltusrol Golf (Springfield, N.J.). Home: Summit NJ Died June 22, 1972; buried Fairview Cemetery, Westfield NJ

TOWNER, ZEALOUS BATES army officer, engr.; b. Cohasset, Mass., Jan. 12, 1819; s. Nichols and Ann (Bates) T.; grad. U.S. Mil. Acad., 1841. Engaged in mil. constrn. duty U.S. Army, 1841-46; served in Mexican War, 1847-48; brevetted maj. for gallantry, 1847; in charge of San Francisco defenses, 1855-58; commanded Ft. Barrancas (Fla.), 1861; brevetted lt. col. U.S. Army, commd. brig. gen. U.S. Volunteers for defense of ft. against Confederate Army; served in battles of Cedar Mountain and 2d Bull Run, severely wounded, out of field service for 1 year; brevetted col. and brig. gen. U.S. Army, 1862; supt. U.S. Mil. Acad., 1864; in charge of field defense, Nashville, Tenn., 1864; insp. gen. fortifications Dept. of Miss.; brevetted maj. gen. U.S. Volunteers and maj. gen. U.S. Army, 1865; ret., 1883. Died Cohasset, Mar. 20, 1900.

TOWNSEND, CURTIS MCDONALD army officer; b. Brooklyn, Mar. 22, 1856; s. M. L. and A. S. (McDonald) T.; A.B., Coll. City of New York, 1875; grad. U.S. Mil. Acad., 1879; 2d lt., Corps of Engineers United States Army, June 30, 1879; 1st lt., June 15, 1882; capt., Oct. 5, 1889; maj., Jan. 29. 1900; lt. col., Jan. 11, 1907; col., 1909. Has been connected with river and harbor improvements on the east shore of Lake Michigan, on the Mississippi near Rock Island; chief engr. officer Philippine div., in charge of harbor improvements, P.I.; in charge of improvement of harbors of Ohio on Lake Erie; in charge of improvement of waterways connecting the Great Lakes; comd. 12th (Ry.) Engrs., serving with 3d Brit. Army in operations around Cambrai; afterwards engr. purchasing agt. A.E.F.; organized Batn. of Cement Engrs. and operated French cement factories; pres. Miss. River Commn. and div. engr. Western Div.; retired, Feb. 15, 1920, after more than 40 yrs.' service. Awarded French Legion of Honor. Reassigned to duty, Jan. 1, 1924, in charge improvement of mouth of the Miss. River and div. engr. South Western Div., relieved, Oct. 1, 1926. Author: Hydraulic Princ Principles Governing River and Harbor Construction. Died May 26, 1941.

TOWNSEND, DALLAS SELWYN lawyer; b. Fayetteville, N.C., Aug. 2, 1888; s. Richard W. and Mary (McDuffie) T.; student Randolph-Macon Coll., Ashland, Va., 1906-08; A.B., Columbia, 1910; LL.B., 1913, A.M., 1914; m. Adelaide H. Heuermann, Nov. 28, 1917; children—Dallas Selwyn, Elizabeth (Mrs. William A. McFadden), Lewis Raynham, Robert Haines. Admitted to N.Y. bar, 1913, mem. firm Barry, Wainwright, Thacher & Symmers, N.Y.C., 1919-35. Townsend & Lewis, 1935-53; asst. atty. gen. U.S. 1953-60; dir. Office Alien Property, Dept. Justice, 1953-60; counsel to Townsend & Lewis, 1961—; dir. Bankers Nat. Life Ins. Co., Montclair, N.J. Trustee Lalor Found., Wilmington, Del., First Congl. Ch., Montclair, N.J. Served as capt. to lt. col. U.S. Army, 1917-18; col., GSC and mem. War Dept. Gen. Staff, 1943; dep. comdr. Am. Mil. Mission in Hungary, 1945-46. Awarded Legion of Merit, 1946. Mem. Am., N.Y. State bar assns., Assn. Bar City N.Y., N.Y.C. Lawyers Assn., Am. Soc. Internat. Law, Internat. Law Assn., S.A.R., Phi Beta Kappa, Delta Sigma Rho, Kappa Alpha. Mason. Clubs: Racquet and Tennis, Univ., Columbia Univ., Pilgrims, Downtown Assn., Bankers of Am.; Montclair Golf; Metropolitan, Chevy Chase (Washington). Home: 10 Crestmont Rd., Montclair, N.J. Office: 120 Broadway, N.Y.C. 10005. Died May 1966.

TOWNSEND, EDWARD DAVIS army officer; b. Boston, Aug. 22, 1817; s. David S. and Eliza (Gerry) T.; attended Harvard 1 year; grad. U.S. Mil. Acad., 1837; m. Ann Wainwright, May 9, 1848, 5 children. Commd. 2d lt. 2d Arty., U.S. Army, 1837; served in Seminole War; served on Pacific Coast and Washington, D.C., 1846-61; adj. gen. to Winfield Scott, 1860; sr. asst. Adj. General's Dept., 1861; adj. gen. U.S. Army, 1862-65; brevetted maj. gen., 1865; adj. gen. (apptd. by Pres. Grant), 1869-80; collected all war papers, later published as War of the Rebellion: Official Records; ret 1880; mem. Soc. of Cincinnati. Died Washington, D.C., May 10, 1893.

TOWNSEND, EDWIN FRANKLIN army officer; b. New York, July 14, 1833; s. Edwin and Ann Eliza T.; grad. U.S. Mil. Acad., 1854; m. Mary Jane Wadhams, Feb. 8, 1858; 2d, Katherine Claire Durant, Apr. 19, 1899. Bvtd. 2d lt. 3d U.S. Arty., July 1, 1854; commd. 2d lt., Jan. 31, 1855; resigned, Mar. 11, 1856; commd. 1st lt., 14th U.S. Inf., May 14, 1861; capt. 16th Inf., May 14, 1861; transferred to 25th Inf., Sept. 21, 1866; maj. 27th Inf., June 22, 1868; transferred to 9th Inf., Mar. 15, 1869; lt. col. 11th Inf., Mar. 20, 1879; col. 12th Inf., Oct. 13, 1886; retired at own request, Oct. 1, 1895, over 62 yrs. of age; advanced to rank of brig. gen. retired, by act of Apr. 23, 1904. Bvtd. maj., Apr. 7, 1862, for gallant and meritorious conduct in battle of Shiloh; lt. col., Mar. 13, 1865, for continued and faithful service in ordnance dept. In Civil War served in Dept. of the Cumberland, 1861-62; in Tenn. and Miss. campaigns comdg. battalion (Army of the Ohio), engaged in march to Nashville, Pittsburg Landing, battle of Shiloh, siege of Corinth, etc., and in command ordnance depot at Nashville, Tenn., 1862-65; afterward on various duties in South and on frontier until retired. Home: Washington, D.C. Died 1909.

TOWNSEND, FRANCIS EVERETT physician; b. Fairbury, Ill., Jan. 13, 1867; s. George Warren and Sarah Jane (Harper) T.; student rural schs. Livingston County, Ill., 1875-85; grad. Franklin (Neb.) Acad., 1893; M.D., U. Neb., 1903; LL.D., Met. U. Los Angeles, 1950; m. Mrs. Minnie Bogue, Oct. 30, 1906; children—Robert Craig, Marlyn (Mrs. Lester Pennock, dec.). Practiced in S.D., Wyo. and Mont., hdqrs. Belle Fourche, S.D., 1903-19, Long Beach, Cal., 1919-31; served as asst. health officer City of Long Beach; physician to indigent; originator and pres. Townsend Plan, Inc. (monthly pensions, based on a 3 percent gross income tax above $250 mo. exemption, to U.S. citizens over 60 yrs. of age, to include all totally and permanently disabled persons between 18 and 60 yrs. of age, with certain restrictions); pres. Townsend Nat. Weekly, Inc., United Pub. Co.; also pres. and trustee Townsend Found. Served as 1st lt. M.C., World War, 1918. Awarded Wilson Service medal; winner Life Begins at Eighty contest, M.B.S., 1949. Author autobiography, New Horizons; also pamphlets, articles on pension plan. Home: 227 N. New Hampshire St., Los Angeles. Office: 6875 Broadway, Cleve. 5. Died Sept. 1960.

TOWNSEND, JULIUS CURTIS naval officer; b. Athens, Mo., Feb. 22, 1881; s. James William and Harriet Morrison (Curtis) T.; grad. U.S. Naval Acad., 1902; m. Martha B. Gaither, Jan. 14, 1909; children—Harriet Gaither (dec.), Martha Gaither. Commd. ensign, U.S. Navy, 1904, and advanced through the grades to rear adm., 1936; comdr. U.S. Naval Aviation Base, Aghada, Eng., World War; comdr. Cruisers Battle Force, U.S. Fleet, 1936—. Decorated Congl. medal of honor, Navy Cross. Mem. Mil. Order of the Caribou. Episcopalian. Died Dec. 28, 1939.

TOWNSEND, OLIVER HENRY, govt. ofcl.; b. Elyria, O., Jan. 29, 1917; s. Henry and Agnes (Taylor) T.; A., Ohio Wesleyan U., 1939; M.A., U. Cin., 1941; m. Anna Jeanette Sheppard, Feb. 2, 1941. Pub. adminstrn. specialist U.S. Govt. Agys., Washington, 1941-43, 47-51; asst. to chmn. U.S. AEC, Washington, 1951-53; sec. Atomic Indsl. Forum, N.Y.C., 1953-59; dir. N.Y. State Office of Atomic and Space Devel. N.Y.C., 1959-68; mem. U.S. AEC com. of state ofcls., adv. com. on isotopes devel., adv. com. on tech. information. Chmn., mem. N.Y. State Atomic and Space Devel-Authority, 1962-69. Served from ensign to lt., USNR, 1943-47, PTO. Mem. Council on Fgn. Relations, Phi Delta Theta, Omicron Delta Kappa. Presbyn. Club: Coveleigh. Author articles in field. Home: Scarsdale NY Died Dec. 2, 1969; interred Elyria OH

TOWNSEND, ROBERT naval officer; b. Albany, N.Y., Oct. 21, 1819; s. Isaiah and Hannah (Townsend) T.; grad. Union Coll., 1835; attended naval sch., Phila., 1835; m. Harriet Monroe, 1850, 3 children. Apptd. midshipman U.S. Navy, 1837; served in Mediterranean on brig Ohio, 1838-40; served in brig Porpoise, 1846, participated in expdn. against Tampico and capture of Mexican schooner Ormigo; served in seige and occupation of Vera Cruz and San Juan d'Ulua; resigned, 1851; reentered U.S. Navy, assigned to ship Harriet Lane of Potomac flotilla, 1861, later in ship Miami on blockade duty off N.C.; transferred to ship Mississippi, 1863; commanded steamer Essex in capture of Port Hudson; participated in Red River Expdn.; commd. capt., 1866, sent to Chinese Coast, 1866. Died ship off Chin-Kiang-Lu, China, Aug. 15, 1866.

TOWNSEND, WAYNE LASALLE, lawyer, ct. ofcl.; b. Cook, Neb., Dec. 7, 1896; s. Adelbert and Anna (Cook) T.; B.A., U. of Neb., 1918; LL.B., Yale, 1928, J.S.D., 1929; married to Dorothy Pierce, June 7, 1922; 1 daughter, Nancy (Mrs. Marvin E. Pyle). Assistant cashier Minatare (Nebraska) Bank, 1920-22; cashier State Bank of Minatare, 1922-26; instr. law, Yale Sch. of Law, 1929-31; visiting prof. law, Tulane U., 1931-32; prof. law, Western Reserve U., 1932-45; asso. with firm Thompson, Hine and Flory, Cleveland, 1943-45; dean sch. of law and prof. law, Washington U., 1945-51; distinguished service professor of law, 1951-65; Legion Lex Distinguished visiting professor, University of Southern California, 1959-60. Labor arbitrator, Cleve. and St. Louis since 1944; referee court of common pleas, Ohio, 1942; judge, Magistrate Ct. of Jefferson County, Mo., 1963-65; commr. St. Louis Ct. of Appeals, St. Louis, 1965-69. Served as second lt., F.A., U.S.A., 1918. Trustee and vice pres. bd., Cleveland Pub. Library, 1942-45; chmn. McBride Lecture Foundation, Cleveland, 1938-45; trustee Great Lakes Hist. Soc., Cleveland; pres. St. Louis Artists Guild, 1957-58, trustee, 1958-69. Compliance Commr., W.P.B., Cleveland, 1942-44. Fellow Am. Bar Foundation; member Neb., Ohio, Mo. bars, International Society Clinical Laboratory Technologists (chairman accrediting commission), Phi Beta Kappa, Phi Alpha Delta, Alpha Theta Chi, Chi Phi, Sigma Delta Chi. Author and editor: Townsend's Cases and Other Select Materials on the Law of Banking, 1938; Townsend's Ohio Corporation Law, 1961. Home: Dittmer MO also Cook NE Died Apr. 1969.

TOWNSLEY, CLARENCE PAGE army officer; b. DeKalb, N.Y., Sept. 24, 1855; s. Hon. Elias Page and Louisa Ellen (Thompson) T.; grad. State Normal Sch., Potsdam, N.Y., 1872; C.E., Union Coll., 1876, hon. Sc.D., 1913; grad. U.S. Mil. Acad., 1881, Arty. Sch., Ft. Monroe, Va., 1884, Torpedo Sch., Willetts Point, N.Y., 1885; m. Marian Howland, Jan. 7, 1891; children—Marian Page, Helen Howland, Clarence Page. Cadet U.S. Mil. Acad. from Ia., 1877; commd. 2d lt. arty., 1881; promoted through grades to brig. gen., July 1, 1916; maj. gen., N.A., Aug. 5, 1917. Maj. and chief ordnance officer vols., 1898-99; during Spanish-American War on staff of chief of arty. and chief ordnance officer, Dept. of Havana, Cuba, on staff of Gen. Ludlow; comdt. Coast Arty. Sch., Ft. Monroe, Feb. 1909-Sept. 1911, and comdg. 2d Provisional Regt. Coast Arty, in Tex., Mar.-July 1911; supt. U.S. Mil. Acad., Aug. 31, 1912-July 1, 1916; apptd. comdr. 30th Div., N.G., Oct. 13, 1917; retired as brig. gen. U.S.A., Nov. 29, 1918. Episcopalian. Home: Washington, D.C. Died Dec. 28, 1926.

TOY, HARRY STANLEY lawyer; b. Elkhorn, W.Va., Jan. 12, 1892; s. James W. and Mary E. (Beals) T.; LL.B., Detroit Coll. of Law, 1913; m. Lorol E. Murray, Dec. 31, 1912; 1 son, James M. Admitted to Mich. bar, 1913; in gen. practice at Detroit, 1913-21 and 1923-30; asst. pros. atty. Wayne County, 1921-23, pros. atty., 1930-35; atty. gen. State of Mich., Jan. 1, 1935-Oct. 24, 1935; justice of Supreme Court Mich., 1935-37; prof. criminal procedure U. Detroit, 1924-31; police commr. Detroit, 1948-50; partner Toy & Toy; pres. T-W-T Co.; sec.-treas. Howe Hinge Co.; dir. Scullin Steel Co. Served as capt. inf., U.S. Army World War. Mem. Am., Mich. State and Detroit bar assns., Nat. Prosecuting Attys.' Assn. (past pres.), Delta Phi Delta. Republican. Mason (33 deg.). Clubs: Detroit Athletic, Grosse Pointe Yacht. Home: 415 Burns Av. Office: Penobscot Bldg., Detroit. Died Sept. 9, 1955; buried Mausoleum Woodlawn Cemetery Assn., Detroit.

TRABUE, MARION REX, b. near Kokomo, Ind., Apr. 30, 1890; s. Otto A. and Mary Emma (Long) T.; student DePauw U., 1907-08; A.B., Northwestern U., 1911; A.M., Columbia, 1914, Ph.D., 1915; m. Emma Wilkie Small, Apr. 20, 1913; children—Bruce McDougal, Douglas Small. Prin. high sch., Fairbury, Ill., 1911-12, Hinsdale, Ill., 1912-13; with Teacher's Coll. (Columbia), 1913-22, as research scholar, student asst., instr. and asst. prof. edn., 1917-22, dir. Bur. Ednl. Service, 1919-22; prof. ednl. administration, U. of N.C., 1922-37, dir. Bur. Ednl. Research, 1923-37, and dir. consolidated univ. div. of edn., 1935-37; dean Sch. of Edn. and dir. of summer sessions, Pa. State Univ., 1937-56; prof. higher edn. University of Kentucky, 1956-72; exec. sec. com. on diagnosis and training Employment Stabilization Research Inst., U. of Minn., 1931-33. Head of Diagnosis Div. of the Adjustment Service, N.Y. City, 1933; mem. Federal Council of U.S. Employment Service, 1934-39, tech. dir. occupational research, 1934-36; mem. staff Am. Youth Commn., Washington, 1936. Lt. and capt., psychol. examiner and psychologist, U.S. Army, 1917-18. Chmn. Emergency Subcom. on Learning and Training, Nat. Research Council, 1941-43. Mem. nat., state and local scientific and profl. orgns. and assns., has served as pres. or other exec. of several. Author or co-author of several books; latest publication: Language Arts for Boys and Girls series, 1941. Home: Lexington KY Died Jan. 1972.

TRACY, BENJAMIN FRANKLIN secretary of the navy; b. Owego, N.Y., Apr. 26, 1830; s. Benjamin T.; ed. Owego Acad.; m. Delinda E. Catlin, 1851. Admitted to bar, 1851; dist. atty. Tioga Co., 1853-59; one of organizers of Rep. party in N.Y.; mem. N.Y. Assembly, 1862. In July and Aug. 1862, raised 109th and 137th N.Y. Vols.; was made col. 109th, Aug. 28, 1862; col. 127th U.S. C.T., Sept. 10, 1864; comdr. mil. post at Elmira, N.Y., 1864-65; received Congressional Medal of Honor, June 21, 1895. "for gallantry in battle of the Wilderness"; bvtd. brig. gen., Mar. 14, 1865, "for gallant and meritorious services during the war"; hon. disch. June 13, 1865. U.S. dist. atty. Eastern Dist. N.Y., 1866-73; judge N.Y. Ct. of Appeals, 1881-82; sec. of the navy in cabinet of Pres. Harrison, 1889-93; resumed law practice in New York, 1893; pres. of commn. which drafted new charter for Greater New York; defeated as Rep. candidate for mayor of Greater New York, 1897. Home: New York, N.Y. Died Aug. 6, 1915.

TRACY, JOSEPH POWELL army officer; b. Washington, Oct. 4, 1874; s. Burr Ridgway and Anna (Putnam) T.; grad. U.S. Mil. Acad., 1896, Sch. Submarine Def., Ft. Totten, N.Y., 1905, Army War Coll., 1920, Naval War Coll., 1921; m. Jeanne West Wood, Apr. 18, 1899; children—Jeanne Wood, Maxwell Wood. Commd. add. 2d lt. arty., U.S. Army, June 12, 1896; advanced through grades to col., June 27, 1920; brig. gen., May 22, 1931. Served in Cuba, Spanish-Am. War, Philippine Insurrection; with C.A.C. and Adj. Gens. Dept., World War. Mem. Gen. Staff Corps, 1907-11, asst. comdt. Army War Coll., 1930-31; asst. chief staff, War Plans Div., 1931-32; comdg. 3d Coast Arty. Dist. and comdt. Coast Arty. Sch., Ft. Monroe, Va., 1932-36; comdg. 9th Coast Arty. Dist., Presidio San Francisco, 1937-38; ret., Oct. 31, 1938. Awarded D.S.M. (U.S.). Episcopalian. Clubs: Army and Navy, Army, Navy and Marine Corps Country (Washington); Chevy Chase (Md.) Address: 2126 Connecticut Av., Washington. Died May 21, 1950.

TRACY, LEO JAMES railroad ofcl.; b. Omaha, Neb., Feb. 24, 1890; s. Christopher and Julia (Slightam) T.; grad. high sch.; m. Amber M. (Small), Dec. 1, 1910; s. Robert L., Francis D., Arthur J., Mary J. (Mrs. John P. Warren). With U.P. R.R. Co., 1904-14, C.,M. and St.P. R.R., 1914-18; U.S. R.R. Adminstrn., 1918-27; with U.P. R.R. Co., 1927-60, v.p., controller, also dir.; dir. Los Angeles & Salt Lake R.R. Co., Ore. Short Line R.R. Co., Ore.-Wash. R.R. & Navigation Co., St. Joseph and Grand Is. Ry. Co., Union Land Co., Utah Parks Co., Ry. Express Agy., Inc. Mem. Controllers Inst. Am. Republican. Roman Cath. Clubs: Union League (N.Y.C.); Wykagyl Country (New Rochelle, N.Y.). Home: Wykagyl Garden Apts., 1273 North Av., New Rochelle, N.Y. Office: 120 Broadway, N.Y.C. 5. Died Aug. 2, 1960; buried Holy Mount Cemetery, Eastchester, N.Y.

TRACY, (WILLIAM) LEE, actor; b. Atlanta, Apr. 14, 1898; s. William Lindsey and Ray (Griffith) T.; student Union Coll., Schenectady, N.Y., 1917-18; m. Helen Thomas, July 20, 1938. Began as actor, 1919; starred in play, Broadway, in N.Y.C., 1926-27, Front Page, 1928; entered motion pictures, 1928; returned to stage for plays Oh Promise Me, Louder Please, 1930; starred in various talking pictures under contract to Paramount Corp.; now under contract to RKO Radio Pictures; appeared in play The Gag Stays In, New York, 1938; Every Man for Himself, 1940; Idiots Delight, London, 1938; The Traitor, N.Y.C., 1948; Mr. Barry's Etchings, New York City, 1949; Caine Mutiny Court Martial, Sydney, Australia, 1955; The Best Man, New York City, 1960-61; Minor Miracle, 1965; starred in the TV series Martin Kane, N.B.C., 1952-53. Recent pictures: Betrayal from the East, 1945; High Tide, 1947; The Best Man, 1965. Served as 2d lt. inf., AUS, World War I; commd. 1st lt., U.S. Army, 1942; advanced to capt.; with Office of Provost Marshal Gen., War Dept., Washington. Presbyn. Clubs: Green Room (New York); Masquer's (Hollywood). Home: Pacific Palisades CA Died Oct. 18, 1968; buried Evergreen Cemetery, Shavertown PA

TRAER, CHARLES SOLBERG (tra'er), corp. official; b. Chicago, Ill., Nov. 24, 1890; s. Glenn Wood and Ida (Solberg) T.; Ph.B., Yale, 1910; m. Josephine Louise Thomas, July 2, 1931; m. 2d, Marjorie Arnold, Aug. 23, 1940; children—Mary Rose (by former marriage), Patricia Arnold (step-dau.). Began as mining engr. Traer Coal Co., 1910-12; mining engr. Ill. Coal Operators Mut. Employers Liability Ins. Co., 1912-15; treas. and gen. mgr. MacMurray Steel Hoop Co., 1915-17; with Acme Steel Co., Chicago, Ill., since 1919, as mgr. Riverdale Works, 1919-36, also treas., 1922-35, second v.p., 1935-36, v.p. and mgr. Production, 1936-41, pres. since 1941; dir. Truax-Traer Coal Co. During World War I, served as lt. and capt., 10th U.S. Inf. Mem. Am. Iron and Steel Inst., Chi Phi. Clubs: South Shore Country, Swan Lake Gun, Chicago Athletic, La Crosse River Reserve Fishing, Fin 'n' Feather. Home: 5555 Everett Av. Office: Riverdale Station, Chicago 27, Ill. Died Oct. 26, 1949.

TRAIN, CHARLES J. officer U.S.N.; b. in Mass.; apptd. to navy from Mass., Nov. 26, 1861; Naval Acad., 1861-64; promoted master, Dec. 1, 1866; lt., Mar. 12, 1868; lt. comdr., June 30, 1869; comdr., Jan. 1886; capt., Nov. 22, 1898; served on many stas. and duties; was naval officer of Atlanta Expn., 1894-96; comd. U.S.S. Prairie, auxiliary curiser in N. Atlantic patrol squadron, March to Nov. 1898; was comdr. Puritan; later Massachusetts; pres. Bd. of Inspection and Survey, 1901-04; promoted rear admiral, Sept. 12, 1904, and served on Asiatic Station. Died 1906.

TRAIN, HAROLD CECIL, naval officer; b. Kansas City, Mo., Oct. 15, 1887; s. Harry D. and Dora (Langdon) T.; grad. U.S. Naval Acad., 1909; m. May Philipps, May 25, 1916; children—Marian Langdon (wife of Capt. Amos T. Hathaway, USN) (dec.), Harriett Cecil (widow of Lt. Comdr. David S. Wilson, USN, dec.), Harry D., II, Jane Bullen (Mrs. John R. Flynn). Commd. ensign, U.S.N., 1911, and advanced through the grades to rear adm., 1942; exec. officer, U.S.S. Siboney, in transport of troops to Europe, World War I; comd. U.S.S. Borie and U.S.S. Parrott, Asiatic Fleet, also fleet operations officer and aide on staff comdr. in chief Asiatic Fleet, 1924-26; fleet communications officer, staff comdr. in chief, Battle Fleet, 1930-31; tactical officer and aide on staff comdr. in chief U.S. Fleet 1931-32; exec. officer U.S.S. Mississippi, also comd. U.S.S. Vestal, 1935-37; asst. dir. officer personnel, 1937-38, dir., 1938-40; comd. U.S.S. Arizona, 1940-41; chief of staff to comdr. Battle Force, 1941-42, with additional duty as asst. chief of staff comdr. in chief Pacific Fleet, Jan.-Mar. 1942; dir. Naval Intelligence, 1942-43; comdt. 15th Naval Dist., comdr. Panama Sea Frontier, and comdr. Southeast Pacific Force, 1943-44; sr. naval mem. Joint Postwar Com., Joint Chiefs of Staff, Washington, 1944-46, retired. Member American delegations to 3d, 5th and 6th Preparatory Commissions for Reduction and Limitations of Armaments, Geneva; mem. Am. delegation Three Power Naval Conf., Geneva, 1927, London Naval Conf., 1930. One of U.S. reps. Dumbarton Oaks Conf., Washington, D.C., 1944; U.S. naval adviser Conf. Problems War and Peace, Mexico City, 1945; a U.S. naval adviser United Nations Conf. on Internat. Orgn., San Francisco, Calif., 1945. Naval aide to President-elect Herbert Hoover on trip through Central and So. America, 1928-29. Decorations: Legion of Merit with Oak Leaf Cluster, Commendation Ribbon, Nicaraguan Campaign, 1912, Mexican Service, Victory with transport clasp, Am. Defense with fleet clasp, Asiatic-Pacific Area and Am. Area medals (U.S.), World War II, Abdon Calderon (Ecuador), Mil. Order Boyaca (Colombia), Mil. Order Merit (Chile), Mil. Order Vasco Nunez de Balboa (Panama), Mil. Order Ayacucho (Peru), Polonia Restituta (Poland). Clubs: Army-Navy Country (Arlington, Va.); Army-Navy (Washington); Columbia Country (Chevy Chase). Home: Washington DC Died Sept. 7, 1968; buried Naval Acad. Cemetery, Annapolis MD

TRAMBURG, JOHN WILLIAM pub. welfare adminstr.; b. Columbia County, Wis., Feb. 28, 1913; s. John Henry and Helena Bertha (Iwert) T.; student Carroll Coll., 1931-32; B.E., Whitewater State Coll., 1935; grad. student U. Chgo. Sch. Social Service Adminstrn., 1937-38, Columbus U. Law Sch., 1941-43; m. Vera Edith Lange, June 29, 1940; children—Georgene Lou, Robert Steven. Tchr., athletic coach, 1935-36; ednl. adviser Civilian Conservation Corps, 1936-37; probation officer Juvenile Ct., D.C., 1939-42; asst. supt. Indsl. Home Sch., Washington, 1942, supt., 1946-48; dir. Washington Bd. Pub. Welfare, 1948-50; dir. pub. welfare State of Wis., 1950-53, 54-55; commr. social security Dept. Health, Edn. and Welfare, Washington, 1953-54; commr. N.J. Dept. Instns. and Agencies, 1955-63. Mem. N.J. Rehabilitation Commn., N.J. Commn. on Interstate Cooperation, N.J. Welfare Council, Governor's Com. on Refugee Relief Act, Governor's Com. on Inadequate Pensions, Nat. Adv. Com. on Chronic Disease and Health of the Aged; nat. adv. council AFL-CIO Community Services Com. Served as lt. USNR, 1942-46. Recipient good government award Jr. C. of C., Wis., 1952. Mem. National Probation and Parole Association (member of professional council), National Council State Public Assistance and Welfare Adminstrs. (chmn. 1952-53), Am. Pub. Welfare Assn. (pres. 1955-56), Council Social Work Edn. (dir.), Nat. Assn. Social Workers (chmn. commn. on social policy and action 1961. Methodist. Home: Station A., Sullivan Way, Trenton 8. Office: State Office Bldg., Trenton 25, N.J. Died Jan. 14, 1963; buried Fall River, Wis.

TRAMMELL, LEANDER NEWTON member, Oct. 15, 1881-—, and chmn., 1888-—, R.R. commn. of Ga.; b. Nacoochee Valley, Ga., June 5, 1830; brought up on farm; ed. country school; attended law school, Lebanon, Tenn.; admitted to bar; m. Zenobia J. Barclay, Apr. 2, 1856. Represented Catoosa Co. in legislature, 1861-63; capt. quartermaster, Confederate army; member Ga. constl. conv., 1867, 1868 and 1877; State senator and pres. senate; pres. State Dem. conv., 1881; chairman State Democratic exec. com., 1881-82; elector on Tilden ticket, 1876. Home: Marietta, Ga. Died 1900.

TRAMMELL, NILES, business cons.; b. Marietta, Ga., July 6, 1894; s. William and Bessie (Niles) T.; ed. Sewanee (Tenn.) Mil. Acad., 1912-15; Univ. of the South, 1915-17; LL.D., DePauw Univ., 1942; married Elizabeth Huff, Nov. 14, 1923 (divorced, 1945); married 2d, Cleo Murphy Black, April 7, 1945 (dec. 1971). Comml. rep. traffic dept. RCA, San Francisco, Mar. 1923, transferred to Seattle, May 1923; dist. mgr. Pacific Northwest, Radiomarine Corp., Seattle, 1924; asst. sales mgr. Pacific div. RCA, 1925; joined sales staff NBC, Chgo., 1928, mgr. then v.p. in charge Central div., Chicago, 1928-29, exec. v.p., N.Y.C., 1939, pres., 1940-49, chmn. bd., 1949-53; pres., gen. mgr. Biscayne TV Corp., Miami, Fla., 1953-62; gen. bus. cons., Miami, 1962-73. Served as 2d lt. 36th Inf., 12th Div., U.S. Army, 1917; 1st lt., 1918; staff officer under Maj. Gen. Charles G. Morton, Presidio, San Francisco, until Mar. 1923. Mem. Kappa Alpha. Episcopalian. Clubs: University, Links Golf, Twenty-Nine, and River (New York City); Chicago (Chicago); Miami, LaGorce Country, and Indian Creek Country, Bath (Miami); National Golf; Links, South Hampton; Lake Placid; Key Largo Anglers. Home: Miami Beach FL Died Mar. 28, 1973; buried Woodlawn Mausoleum, Miami FL

TRANT, JAMES BUCHANAN, coll. dean; b. Pitts., Fla., Oct. 15,21890; s. Thomas Franklin and Mary Ann (Isler) T.; student Campbell Business Inst., Dothan, Ala., 1911-12; A.B., Howard Coll., Birmingham, Ala., 1920; A.M., Princeton U., 1921; Ph.D., U. of Ill., 1925; m. Pauline Willoughby, June 9, 1924; 1 dau., Jean. Acting prof. of econ. and history, Howard Coll., 1921-22; instr. in economics, U. of Ill., 1922-25; asst. prof. of economics, U. of Tex., 1925-26, asso. prof. of business adminstrn., 1926-28; prof. of banking and dean Coll. of Commerce, La. State U., 1928-56, dean emeritus, 1956-70. Vice pres. Guaranty Income Life Ins. Co., 1957-70. Chmn. compliance bd., President's Re-employment Agreement, Baton Rouge; mem. com. on study of business edn., Am. Assn. of Collegiate Schs. of Bus., 1933-39; also mem. exec. com., 1939-42; consultant Nat. Resources Planning Bd. for Southwestern Dist., La., Ark., Tex., and Okla.; mem. exec. com. in charge of program La. Coll. Conf., Mar. 1939 and 1940; chmn. Selective Service Board No. 2, East Baton Rouge,

Parish, La.; mem. Econ. Development Com. of La. (chmn. subcom. on edn., mem. subcom. on unemployment, ins. and social security, 1943-44; vice chmn. and chmn. subcom. on research, 1944-46). Dir. American Legion High School Oratorical Contest for Louisiana, 1944-46; mem. Research Com., Gulf Southwest Indsl. and Agrl. Conf., 1945-47; vice chmn. bd., Dept. of Commerce and Industry, chmn. subcom. on Ednl. Research and Finance, 1946-48; bd. trustees So. Assn. Sci. and Industry, 1947-48; chmn. Baton Rouge chpt. A.R.C., 1948-49; bd. dirs. C. of C., 1949-51; exec. com. Economists Nat. Com. on Monatary Policy since 1951. Served as pvt., sergeant and lt., San. Corps, U.S. Army, 1917-18. Pres. Legionnaire-Schoolmasters Club, La. Dept. American Legion, 1942-43. Member Mil. Order World War (state commander 1947-48), American Econ. Assn., Royal Econ. Society, Southern Econ. Assn., Southwestern Social Science Assn. (chmn. business adminstrn. sec. 1930-31; v.p. 1936-37, pres. 1937-38), Southern Econ. Assn. (pres. 1932-33), Phi Kappa Phi, Pi Kappa, Tau, Beta Gamma Sigma (exec. com. 1939-42), Pi Gamma Mu (Nat. Adv. Council), Beta Nu Kappa. Democrat. Baptist. Mason (K.T.). Club: Rotary (Baton Rouge). Author: Bank Administration, 1931. Contbr. to jours. Mem. editorial advisory bd. Southwestern Social Science Quarterly, 1930-32. Home: Baton Rouge LA Died Feb. 3, 1970; buried Green Oaks Cemetery Baton Rouge LA

TRAUB, PETER EDWARD (trawb), army officer; b. N.Y.C., Oct. 15, 1864; grad. U.S. Mil. Acad., 1886. Commd. 2d lt. 1st Cav., July 1, 1886; advanced through grades to col. U.S. Army, July 1, 1916; brig. gen. N.A., Aug. 5, 1917; maj. gen. N.A., June 15, 1918; honorary discharge N.A., June 30, 1919; brig. gen. U.S. Army, Apr. 19, 1928; retired Oct. 15, 1928; promoted maj. gen., ret. June 21, 1930. Served in campaign against Crow Indians, Nov. 1887 and against Sioux Indians in S.D., 1890-91; duty dept. of langs., U.S. Mil. Acad., 1892-98, 1902-04; comd. 1st Platoon, Troop G. 1st Cav., Battle of Las Guasimas, Cuba, June 24, 1898; recommended for bvt. of capt. "for gallantry in action," at Las Guasimas and brevet maj. for gallantry at Battle of San Juan, July 1-3, 1898, and siege of Santiago; acting asst. adj. gen. and asst. adj. gen., Dept. Luzon, 1900-01; secured signed agreement of Gen. Guevara to surrender, Apr. 27, 1902; head dept. of langs., Army Signal Sch., Army Staff Coll., 1904-07; on confidential missions fgn. countries, 1904-05; mem. mission, on invitation of Kaiser, to witness German army maneuvers, Breslau, 1906; appt. asso. prof. modern langs., U.S. Mil. Acad., 1907; mem. mission Isthmus of Panama supervise eection pres. of republic, 1908; in P.I., 1911-17; dist. chief Philippine Constabulary, Mindanao-Sulu. 1914-17; apptd. comdr. 51st Inf. Brig., Aug. 16, 1917; served in France, Sept. 1917-19; comd. 35th Div., July 20-Dec. 26, 1918, 41st Div., to Feb. 20, 1919; comd. Camp Pike, Ark., to July 1, 1919, Ft. Thomas, Ky., Nov. 1921. In charge recruiting drive, Washington, Jan.-Apr. 1920. Silver Star Citation, Purple Heart with Oak Leaf Cluster, for wounds in action in France (U.S.); Croix de Guerre with palm; Comdr. Legion of Honor (French). Home: Augusta, Ga. Died Sept. 1956.

TRAUTMAN, GEORGE M(CNEAL) baseball exec.; b. Bucyrus, O., Jan. 11, 1890; s. George B. and Della (McNeal) T.; B.S., O. State, 1914; student Harvard Summer Sch. for Phys. Edn., 1914, 1915; m. Mary Crumit, June 1917 (died Nov. 1940); children—Peggy (Mrs. Peggy T. Larsen), George M., Jr.; m. 2d, Jane Daley Asbury, May 1942. Asst. athletic dir. Ohio State U., 1919-28; dir. convs. and publicity Columbus (O.) Chamber of Commerce, 1929-33; pres. Columbus Baseball Club, 1933-35; pres. Am. Assn. Professional Baseball Clubs, Columbus, O., 1936-45; exec. v.p. and gen. mgr., Detroit (Mich.) Baseball Club, 1946; pres.-treas., Nat. Assn. Professional Baseball Leagues since 1947. Mem. and chmn. Ohio State Commn. for Conservation of Natural Resources, 1939-45; mem. nat. com. on phys. fitness, Fed. Security Commn., 1942-46. Served as athletic dir., Camp Sheridan, Ala., World War I; col. in Army Specialist Corps., 1942. Chmn. Am. Commn. for Living War Memorials, 1944-46. Honorary dir. Am. Bowling Congress; vice pres. Columbus Conv. Bur. Mem. O. State Univ. Alumni Assn. (past pres., mem. bd. dirs.). Bi-partisan. Mem. Lutheran Church. Mason. Elk. Clubs: Columbus, Columbus Country. Home: 28 Meadow Park Av., Columbus 9. Office: 720 E. Broad St., Columbus 15, O. Died June 24, 1963.

TRAVIS, ROBERT FALLIGANT army officer; b. Savannah, Ga., Dec. 26, 1904; s. Maj. Gen. Robert Jesse and Rena (Falligant) T.; student U. Ga., 1923; B.S., U.S. Mil. Acad., 1928; grad. A.C. Engring. Sch., Wright Field, 1933; rated sr. pilot, combat observer, expert aerial gunner, celestial navigator and bombardier; grad. Nat. War Coll.; m. Frances Johnson, Aug. 16, 1929; children—Jane Darracott, Robert Falligant, Jr., John Livingston, Roger Bassett. Commd. 2d lt. Air Force, 1928, and advanced through the grades to brig. gen., 1943; at Mitchell Field, L.I., N.Y., 1929-31, Wright Field, Dayton, O., 1932, Langley Field, Va., 1933-39, Hickam Field, Oahu, T.H., 1939-41, MacDill Field, Tampa, Fla., 1941, Gowen Field, Boise, Ida., 1942-43; comdg. officer, 29th Bombing Group, 1940-42, 15th Tng. Wing, 1942-43, 1st Bombardment Command. 1943, 41st Combat Bombardment Wing, 8th Air Force, 1943; 17th Bombardment Wing, 1944-45; 14th Air Force, 1946; Commander of the Pacific Air Command, 1948-—. Awarded D.S.C., Silver Star with 2 oak leaf clusters, D.F.C. with 3 oak leaf clusters, Air Medal with 3 oak leaf clusters, Purple Heart; Legion of Honor, Croix de Guerre and palm (France); British D.F.C.; Croix de Guerre and palm (Belgium); also numerous service ribbons; Presdl. Citation. Mem. Sigma Alpha Epsilon (Georgia Beta). Mason. Travis Air Base, Cal. so named in his honor. Address: care Adjutant General, War Dept., Washington. Died Aug. 5, 1950.

TRAVIS, WILLIAM BARRET army officer; b. nr. Red Banks, S.C., Aug. 9, 1809; s. Mark and Jemima (Stallworth) T.; m. Rosanna Cato, Oct. 26, 1828, 2 children. Admitted to Ala. bar, 1829; opened law office in San Felipe, Tex., Oct. 1832; apptd. sec. of ayuntamiento (Spanish colonial municipal governing council); leader of war party in local politics, which insisted on preservation of rights of Am. colonists; raised a volunteer co., captured and disarmed garrison at fort at Anahuac, 1835; commanded a scouting co., fall 1835; maj. of arty., Dec. 1835; lt. col. cavalry, circa 1836; joint commander (with James Bowie) of Alamo, San Antonio, Tex., Feb. 13-23, 1836; sole commander, Feb. 23-Mar. 6, when entire garrison of 188 Texans was destroyed by Mexican Army under Gen. Antonio Santa Anna. Killed in Battle of Alamo, Mar. 6, 1836.

TRAWICK, LEONARD M(OSES) (tra' wik), educator; b. Opelika, Ala., Nov. 29, 1904; s. Leonard M. and Sarah (Trawick) T.; B.S., Ala. Polytech. Inst., 1926; A.M., Harvard, 1928; LL.B., U. Ala., 1932; m. Frances Earle, Aug. 6, 1930; children—Leonard M., Sarah Frances. Tchr. English, Clemson (S.C.) Coll., 1928-29; admitted to Ala. bar, 1932, and practiced in Ozark, 1932, Decatur, 1933; atty. Fed. Land Bank of New Orleans, 1933-38; tchr. English, Ala. Poly. Inst., 1939-41; mem. faculty law sch. U. Ala. since 1945, prof. law, dir. Bur. Legal Research, faculty adviser Ala. Law Rev., since 1948. Served with U.S.A.A.F., 1942-45, disch. as capt. Mem. Alpha Tau Omega, Phi Delta Phi. Episcopalian. Home: 228 30th St. E., Tuscaloosa, Ala. 35401. Office: University, Ala. Died July 14, 1964; buried Rose Mere Cemetery, Opelika, Ala.

TRAYLOR, JOHN H. mayor of Dallas, Tex., since 1898; b. Traylorsville, Henry Co., Va., Mar. 27, 1839; reared and ed. in Tishomingo Co., Miss., and Troup Co., Ga.; m. Jefferson, Tex., 1869, Pauline Lockett. Served through Civil war in 4th Ga. inf., Army of Northern Va.; Dole's brigade, Rodes' div., Stonewall Jackson's corps; present at all great battles of that army; wounded at Warrenton Springs, Chancellorsville and Spotsylvania Court House; was within a few yards of Gen. Jackson when he received his death-wound; served as q.m., 1864-65; lived in Jefferson, Tex., 1867-71; Granbury, 1871-87; sheriff and tax-collector Hood Co., 1876-80; mem. legislature, 1880-82; State senator, 1882-87; removed to Dallas, 1887; Democrat. Address: Dallas, Tex.

TREAT, CHARLES GOULD army officer; b. Me., Dec. 30, 1859; grad. U.S. Mil. Acad., 1882, Arty. Sch., 1888; Army War Coll., 1911; married; children—Joseph B., Margaret, Katherine, Godfrey Macdonald (stepson). Commd. 2d lt. 5th Arty., June 13, 1882; 1st lt., Apr. 15, 1889; capt. a.a.g. vols., May 12, 1898; maj. vols., Jan. 10, 1899; hon. discharged vols., May 12, 1899; capt. 7th Arty., Mar. 2, 1899; promoted through grades to brig. gen., Oct. 18, 1916; maj. gen., Aug. 5, 1917. Sr. instr. F.A., U.S.M.A., 1900-01, comdt. cadets same, 1901-05. Apptd. comdr. Camp Sheridan, Montgomery, Ala., Aug. 1917; assigned to Western Dept., San Francisco, Calif., Apr. 1918. Chief of Am. Mil. Mission to Italy, June 1918-May 1919; comdg. Base Sect. 8, and A.E.F. in Italy; Camp Sherman, O., 1919; assigned to duty, Philippine Islands, 1920; retired, Apr. 27, 1922. Died Oct. 11, 1941.

TREECE, ELBERT LEE educator; b. Blue Mound, Kan., Oct. 25, 1892; s. Thomas Jefferson and Nancy Wilmoth (Holland) T.; B.S., U. Kan., 1916, A.M., 1919, Ph.D., 1926; grad. student U. Chgo., 1924; m. Mildred Bacon Foster, Dec. 26, 1917; children—Richard Foster, Robert Lee. Asst. City chemist, Kansas City, Mo., 1917; instr. bacteriology U. Kan., 1917-21, asst. prof., 1921-25, asso. prof., 1925-49, prof., 1949-—, chmn. dept., 1950-57. Capt. San. Corps, Med. Res., 1925-40, Fellow Am. Pub. Health Assn.; mem. Soc. Am. Bacteriologists, A.A.A.S., Kan. Acad. Sci., Sigma Xi, Phi Sigma, Nu. Sigma Nu, Acacia. Republican. Mason (32 deg.). Clubs: Faculty, Willistonian. Contbr. articles sci. jours. Home: 1635 Mississippi St., Lawrence, Kan. Died Apr. 17, 1961; buried Meml. Park, Lawrence.

TREMAIN, HENRY EDWIN soldier, lawyer; b. New York, Nov. 14, 1840; s. Edwin Ruthven and Mary (Briggs) T.; A.B., Coll. City of New York, 1860; LL.B., Columbia, 1867; m. Sarah Brownson Goodrich, June 1, 1869. Pvt. 7th Regt. N.Y. State Militia Apr. 19, 1861; 1st lt. 73d N.Y. Inf., Aug. 14, 1861; capt., Nov. 1, 1862; maj. a.d.c. U.S.V., Apr. 25, 1863. Bvtd.; lt. col., vols., Mar. 13, 1865, "for gallant and meritorious services"; col. vols., June 12, 1865, for same during the war; brig. gen. vols., Nov. 30, 1865, "for faithful and meritorious services"; awarded Congressional Medal of Honor, June 30, 1892, "for distinguished conduct" at battle of Resaca, Ga., May 15, 1864. First asst. U.S. atty., New York, 1873-77; active in Rep. campaigns; col. veterans of 7th Regt., N.G.S. N.Y., 1887-89; pres. Republican Club of City of New York, 1901, 1906. Author: Last Hours of Sheridan's Cavalry, 1904; Two Days of War, 1905; Sectionalism Unmasked, 1907. Also "Fifty Papers," writings and addresses on mil. polit. and legal subjects, and in favor of a protective tariff, municipal ownership, etc. Died 1910.

TRENCHARD, STEPHEN DECATUR naval officer; b. Bklyn., July 10, 1818; s. Capt. Edward and Eliza (Sands) T.; entered Kenyon Coll., Gambier, O., 1829; m. Ann O'Conner Barclay, Dec. 1, 1848, 1 son, Edward. Entered U.S. Navy as midshipman, 1834, passed midshipman, 1840; served in Mediterranean, 1840-44; assigned to coast survey, 1844; joined Commodore Perry's Squadron off Vera Cruz, took part in expdn. against Tabasco, 1847; commd. lt., 1847; in command ship Vixen, 1856, rescued Brit. vessel Adieu off Gloucester, Mass., presented sword by Queen Victoria as reward; commanded ship Keystone State during Civil War, helped save Cumberland from capture, 1861; commanded brig Rhode Island with orders to transport supplies to blockading squadrons, 1861; on blockade duty, 1862; joined Adm. Porter's fleet at Hampton Roads, 1864, participated in both attacks on Fort Fisher; commd. comdr., 1862, capt., 1866; exec. officer N.Y. Navy Yard, 1866-69; made mem. Bd. Naval Examiners, 1872; lighthouse insp., 1873-75; promoted rear adm., 1875; commanded North Atlantic Squadron, 1876-78; ret., 1880. Died N.Y.C., Nov. 15, 1883.

TRENT, WILLIAM JOHNSON coll. pres.; b. Charlotte, N.C., Dec. 30, 1873; s. Edward and Malinda (Johnson) T.; A.B., Livingstone Coll., N.C., 1898; A.M., 1910; student U. Chgo., summers 1926, 27, 28; LL.D., Livingstone Coll., 1945; m. Annabelle Mitchell, Apr. 3, 1904 (died 1907); 1 dau., Altona Malinda (Mrs. Vernon Johns); m. 2d, Maggie Tate, June 30, 1909 (died June 1, 1934); children—William Johnson, Mary Estelle; m. 3d, Hattie Covington, Dec. 22, 1935 (dec. 1952); m. 4th, Cleota Collins, June 19, 1953. YMCA sec., 3d N.C. Regt., Spanish-Am. War, 1898; pres. Greenville (Tenn.) Secondary Sch., 1899-1900; gen. sec. Young Men's Inst. (YMCA), Ashville, N.C., 1900-11; exec. sec. YMCA, Atlanta, 1911-25; pres. Livingstone Coll., Salisbury, N.C., since 1925; elected mem. Sch. Bd. Edn., 1951. Mem. Salisbury Postwar Planning Commn., Salisbury C. of C. Mem. N.C. Assn. Negro Colls. (pres. 1927 and 1941), N.C. Interracial Commn. (mem. exec. com.), Omega Psi Phi. Mason, Odd Fellow. Home: 630 W. Monroe St., Salisbury, N.C. Died June 12, 1963.

TRESOLINI, ROCCO JOHN, educator, author; b. Dolgeville, N.Y., Mar. 17, 1920; s. Oronzo and Albina (Ruggierio) T.; A.B., Hartwick Coll., Oneonta, N.Y., 1942; M.A., Syracuse U., 1947, Ph.D., 1949; m. Virginia Krohn, Sept. 24, 1943; children—Roger Lawson, Carol Patricia, Kevin Karl, Justin Andrew. Instr. polit. sci. Syracuse U., 1948-49; mem. faculty Lehigh U., 1949-67, prof. polit. sci., 1958-67, chmn. dept. govt., 1962-67; lectr. advanced study program Brookings Instn., 1965-67; vis. lectr. Armed Forces Information Sch., A. and M. Coll. N.C. Served to 1st lt. USAAF, 1942-46; ETO. Recipient Hillman award Lehigh U., 1964. Mem. Am. Polit. Sci. Assn., Pa. Pub. Adminstrn. and Polit. Sci. Assn. (sec.-treas. 1956-57, v.p. 1966), Pi Gamma Mu, Phi Alpha Theta. Author: American Constitutional Law, 2d edit., 1965; Justice and the Supreme Court, 1963; These Liberties: Case Studies in Civil Rights, 1968. Sr. editor: Cases in American National Government and Politics, 1966. Home: Coopersburg PA Died June 27, 1967.

TREVOR, JOHN BOND (trev'er), lawyer; b. "Glenview," Yonkers, N.Y., Nov. 19, 1878; s. John Bond and Emily (Norwood) T.; prep. edn., Cutler Sch., N.Y. City; B.A., Harvard, 1902, M.A., 1903; LL.B., Columbia U. Law Sch., 1906; LL.D., University of Rochester, 1932; m. Caroline M. Wilmerding,June 25, 1908; children—John B., Bronson. Admitted to N.Y. bar, 1904; spl. dep. atty. gen. State of N.Y., 1919; asso. counsel for sub-com. of Com. on Foreign Relations, U.S. Senate, 1920. With U.S. Army, Nov. 1917-June 1919; 1st lt., later capt. Mil. Intelligence Div., U.S. Army, May 1918-June 1919, in comd. Office of Mil. Intelligence Div., N.Y. City, Dec. 1918-June 1919. Chmn. of board Am. Coalition of Patiotic Socs., 1927-33; pres. Am. Coalition, 1933-50; active in movement to restrict immigration into U.S. Trustee Am. Museum Nat. History, 1908-25; mem. council New York U., 1927-28; mem. bd. mgrs. Empire State Soc., S.A.R., since 1935; mem. bd. dirs. Eugenics Research Assn., 1937-38. Mem. Chamber Commerce of State of N.Y. (mem. exec. com. 1921-23, 1924-27), France-America Soc., New York Soc. Mil. and Naval Officers World War, S.A.R., New York Chap. Soc. Colonial Wars (mem. council), 1942-45), French Inst. in United States, American Society of French Legion of Honor, Institute of 1770 Harvard), Delta Kappa Epsilon. Decorated Chevalier Legion of Honor (France). Republican. Baptist. Club: Union. Wrote: (brochures) An Analysis of the American immigration Act of 1924; Japanese Exclusion—A Study of the Policy and the Law, 1925; The Crisis, 1931; The Recognition of Soviet Russia by the United States—an American Problem, 1932. Home: Paul Smiths, N.Y. Office: 20 Exchange Pl., N.Y.C. Died Feb. 20, 1956; buried Woodlawn Cemetery, N.Y.C.

TREXLER, SAMUEL GEISS clergyman; b. Bernville, Pa., October 19, 1877; s. Rev. Daniel D. and Agnes A. (Geiss) T.; A.B., Muhlenberg Coll., Allentown, Pa., 1896, D.D., 1919; grad. Luth. Theol. Sem., Phila., 1899; student at U. of Jena, 1913; S.T.D., Syracuse U., 1941, LL.D., Thiel. Coll., 1943. Ordained Lutheran ministry, 1899; pastor Messiah Church, Brooklyn, N.Y., 1899-1912 (which he organized); student pastor of New York and N.E. Synod, 1912-14; organized religious work among Luth. students at Columbia, Harvard, Yale and Cornell univs.; pastor Ch. of the Redeemer, Buffalo, 1914-20; pres. Synod of N.Y. and N.E., 1920-29; first pres. United Lutheran Synod of New York, 1929-34, 1939-44; commr. Lutheran World Fedn. for Russia, 1946; pres. Bd. of Fgn. Missions of United Lutheran Ch. of Am., 1940-44; del. to 3d Lutheran World Conv., Paris, 1935; toured South America to inspect missions and schools, 1941. Chaplain U.S. Army in France and Germany, 1917-19. Univ. Preacher, Columbia and Cornell U.; trustee Hartwick Coll., Josiah Macy Junior Foundation, Endicott Coll. Mem. S.R., Pilgrims, Phi Gamma Delta. Clubs: Univ., Clergy (past pres.). Author: Crusaders of the Twentieth Century, 1926; Out of Thirty-five Years, 1936; John A. Morehead, 1938, A Pastor Wings over South America, 1941. Home: 1170 Fifth Av., New York 29, N.Y. Died May 30, 1949.

TRIGG, JOHN JOHNS congressman; b. nr. Old Liberty (now Bedford), Va., 1748; liberal edn. Became a farmer; raised a co. of militia in Bedford County, Va., 1775; commd. capt. Continental Army, 1778, promoted maj., 1781, served under Gen. George Washington at siege of Yorktown; mem. Va. Conv. which ratified U.S. Constn., 1788; lt. col. Va. Militia, 1791, maj. 2d Battalion, 10th Regt., Va. Militia, 1793; justice of peace, Bedford County; mem. Va. Ho. of Dels., 1784-92; mem. U.S. Ho. of Reps. from Va., 5th-8th congresses, 1797-1804. Died Old Liberty, Bedford County, Va., May 17, 1804; buried on his estate.

TRILLEY, JOSEPH rear admiral U.S.N.; b. in Ireland, Sept. 25, 1838; s. Samuel and Ann T.; ed. Phila., and Baltimore; studied engring. Md. Inst. Sch. of Design; m. Blanche Haynes, Apr. 25, 1868. Apptd. 3d asst. engr. U.S.N., Aug. 11, 1860; 2d asst. engr., July 1862; 1st asst. engr., July 1864; chief engr., Feb. 1871; capt. in the line, Mar. 1899; rear admiral, Sept. 25, 1899, and retired same date. During Civil War took part in engagements at Fort Sumter, burning of Norfolk Navy Yard, Acquia Creek, Hatteras Inlet, Hilton Head, Fernandina, Port Hudson, Donaldsonville, Mobile Bay and several other minor engagements. Served on the West Indian, European (and, as fleet engr.) on the China and Pacific stas.; also as chief engr. of the Portsmouth and Mare Island Navy Yards. Died 1911.

TRIMBLE, HARVEY MARION comdr.-in-chief G.A.R.; b. nr. Wilmington, Clinton Co., O., Jan. 27, 1842; removed to Princeton, Ill., with family, 1843; s. of Mathew and Lydia (Thatcher) T.; ed. common schs. and partial course Eurekea Coll., Ill.; quit coll. to enter army; studied law alone; m. Margaret S. Dakin, Oct. 9, 1866. Deputy clerk Circuit Ct. of Bureau Co., Ill., 1865-67; admitted to Ill. bar, 1867; practiced successfully in firms of Paddock & Trimble, Henderson & Trimble, Henderson, Trimble & Butler, H. M. Trimble, Henderson, Trimble & Colton, and H. M. & Cairo A. Trimble. Master in chancery Circuit Ct. of Bureau Co., 1868-77; county judge of Bureau Co., 1877-90, 1894-97; circuit judge 13th Jud. Circuit, 1897-1903. Mem. Bd. Edn. Princeton, 1878-97, Princeton High Sch. Bd., 1881-86; an organizer, and mem. 1st bd. dirs., 1886-88, Pub. Library, Princeton. Enlisted in Co. K, 83d Regt., Ill. Vol. Inf., Aug. 21, 1862; elected sergt. maj., Sept. 8, 1862; promoted 1st lt. and adj. of regt., Apr. 13, 1864; served as a.-a.-g. of 2 brigades, Mar. 28, May 31, 1865; mustered out of service June 23, 1865; was with regt. on every march (except 10 miles) and in every battle; captured and held prisoner by Confederates 14 days. Comdr. Ferris Post G.A.R., Princeton, 1897-98; comdr. Dept. of Ill., 1902-03; elected comdr.-in-chief G.A.R., Aug. 25, 1911. Republican. Mem. Christian (Disciples) Ch. Mason. Author: History of the Ninety-Third Regiment Illinois Volunteer Infantry, 1898. Home: Princeton, Ill. Died Jan. 10, 1918.

TRIMBLE, ISAAC RIDGEWAY army officer, engr.; b. Culpeper County, Va., May 15, 1802; s. John Trimble; grad. U.S. Mil. Acad., 1822; m. Maria Presstman; m. 2d, Ann Presstman; 2 children. Served with U.S. Army, until 1832; asst. engr. Boston & Providence R.R., 1832-35; successively chief engr. Balt. Susquehanna R.R., Phila., Wilmington & Balt. R.R., Phila. & Balt. Central, 1835-59; gen. supt. Balt. & Potomac R.R., 1859-61; burned bridges to obstruct movement of Union troops to Washington, D.C., 1861; col. of engrs. in Va., 1861; commd. brig. gen. Confederate Army, 1861; constructed defenses of Norfolk, Va.; constructed batteries on Potomac to prevent passage of U.S. vessels, 1861; commanded a brigade in Army of No. Va., 1862; took part in Stonewall Jackson's operations in Shenandoah Valley, 1862; participated in Seven Days' battles, nr. Richmond, 1862; captured Union depot of supplies at Manassas Station, 1862; as maj. gen. led division at Battle of Chancellorsville, 1863; had command of troops in Shenandoah Valley, June 1863, campaigned as far north as Carlisle, Pa.; assigned command of a division of Hill's Corps at Battle of Gettysburg, 1863, lost leg on 3d day of battle; prisoner, 1863-65. Died Balt., Jan. 2, 1888.

TRIMBLE, WILLIAM ALLEN senator, lawyer, army officer; b. Woodford, Ky., Apr. 4, 1786; grad. Transylvania Coll., Lexington, Ky.; studied law. Admitted to the bar, 1811, began practice law, Highland County, O.; adjutant in campaign against Pottawatomie Indians, 1812; maj. Ohio Volunteers, 1812, taken prisoner at capture of Detroit; maj. 26th U.S. Inf., 1813, brevetted lt. col. for gallantry at Ft. Erie where he was severely wounded, 1814; lt. col. 1st U.S. Inf., 1814, transferred to 8th U.S. Inf., 1815-19; mem. U.S. Senate from Ohio, 1819-21. Died Washington, D.C., Dec. 13, 1821; buried Congressional Cemetery.

TRIPP, LOUIS H. constrn. exec.; b. Westport, Mass., June 11, 1884; s. Jonathan Potter and Lucy Ella (Manley) T.; B.S., Mass. Inst. Tech., 1906; m. Florence May Dennis, Apr. 25, 1911 (died Jan. 20, 1939); m. 2d, Hilma Eleanor Swanteson, June 23, 1941. Mech. draftsman, Office Supervising Architect Treasury Dept., 1907-13; mech. engr. Office Q.M. Gen., War Dept., 1913-17; chief constrn. div. Vets. Bur. (dir. constrn. service VA until retirement, 1946). Commd. capt. Q.M.C., U.S. Army, 1917; detailed to cantonment div. (later constrn. service); promoted maj., 1918; disch. Sept. 30, 1920. Mem. Mil. Order World War, Am. Legion. Club: Cosmos (Washington). Home: 202 Hix-Bridge Rd., South Westport, Mass. 02790. Died Sept. 11, 1963; buried Arlington Nat. Cemetery.

TRIPP, WILLIAM HENRY, JR., naval architect; b. N.Y.C., Sept. 22, 1919; s. William Henry and Ethel Mary (Moran) T.; grad. Dwight Prep. Sch., N.Y.C., 1939; m. Alice Shelly Williamson, Sept. 14, 1944; 1 son, William Henry III. Propr. W. H. Tripp & Co., Port Washington, N.Y., from 1954; designer specialized comml. craft, sail and power yachts, racing and cruising sail boats. Served to lt. (j.g.) USCGR, 1942-46; PTO. Mem. Soc. Yacht Brokers and Designers. Clubs: N.Y. Yacht; Manhasset Bay Yacht. Office: Port Washington LI NY Died Oct. 13, 1971; cremated.

TROPER, MORRIS C(ARLTON) certified pub. acct., lawyer; b. N.Y.C., Nov. 18, 1892; s. Abraham and Rose (Schaeffer) T.; A.B., Coll. City of N.Y., 1914; B.C.S., N.Y.U, 1917, M.C.S. cum laude, 1918, J.D., 1925; m. Ethel Dorothy Gartner, Nov. 20, 1919; children—Betty Elise (wife Dr. Alfred Yager), John Gartner. A sr. partner Loeb & Troper, C.P.A.'s, N.Y.C., since 1919; admitted to N.Y. bar, 1926, since practiced in N.Y.C.; ind. auditor Joint Distbn. Com. and affiliates, U.S. and abroad, since 1920; systematized records, accounts, European countries, 1920, chmn. European exec. council Am. Joint Distbn. Com., Paris, France, also Lisbon, Portugal, 1938-41, trips to Israel, 1948, 50, 52; systematized accounts, records, procedures Am. Soc. Jewish Farm Settlements, Russia, 1929, 1936. Officer campaigns United Jewish Appeal, Fedn. Jewish Philanthropies, N.Y.C. Mem. C.P.A. com. on grievances N.Y. State Bd. Regents, 1933-40, chmn., 1935-37. Served in Office of Fiscal Dir., U.S. Army, 1942-46; brig. gen. Res. since 1948. Decorated Legion of Honor (France); Legion of Merit (U.S.); Conspicuous Service Cross (N.Y. State). C.P.A., N.Y., 1922. Mem. N.Y. State Soc. C.P.A.'s (bd. dirs. 1926-33, 39-42, v.p. 1933-37, pres. 1937-39), Am. Inst. Accts., Nat. Assn. Cost Accts., Am. Soc. French Legion of Honor, Delta Mu Delta. Clubs: Beach Point (treas., 1957), Accountants America. Contbr. articles profl. publs. Home: 33 E. 70th St., N.Y.C. 21. Office: 501 Fifth Av., N.Y.C. 17. Died Nov. 17, 1962.

TROTT, CLEMENT AUGUSTUS, army officer; b. Milwaukee, Dec. 14, 1877; s. August Von and Anna (Paul) T.; grad. U.S. Mil. Acad., 1899; honor grad. Inf. and Cav. Sch., Ft. Leavenworth, 1904; grad. Staff Coll., Ft. Leavenworth, 1905, Army War Coll., Washington, 1920; m. Leah Wright, Nov. 28, 1899. Commd. 2d lt. 7th Inf., 1899; promoted through grades to major gen., 1941; 1st lt. inf. Philippine Insurrection, 1901-03, capt. inf. Punitive Expdn., Mexico, 1916, col., chief of staff, 5th Div. in World War, 1917-18, commanding 6th Division, 1939-40; commanding 5th Corps Area, 1940-41; retired, Dec. 31, 1941. Awarded Spanish War Service medal, Philippine Campaign. Mexican Campaign Victory with 4 battle clasps, Silver Star medals, and D.S.M. (all U.S.); Croix de Guerre with palm, and Officer Legion of Honor (France). Clubs: Army and Navy (Washington). University (Chicago). Home: Hawthorne Lane, Geneva IL

TROUP, ROBERT army officer, jurist; b. N.Y.C., 1757; probably s. Robert and Elinor (Bisset) T.; grad. King's Coll. (now Columbia), studied law, circa 1780-83. Served as lt. Continental Army during Am. Revolution, a.d.c. to Brig. Gen. Timothy Woodhull; promoted lt. col., 1777, on staff of Gen. Horatio Gates; present at Battle of Stillwater and at surrender of Burgoyne, 1777; sec. bd. war, 1778; mem. N.Y. State Assembly; supported adoption of U.S. Constn., 1787-88; involved in land speculation in Western N.Y., 1794-1832; judge U.S. Dist. Ct. N.Y., 1796; gave financial aid to the founding of Hobart Coll.; agt. for Pulteney estate, 1801-31. Died N.Y.C., Jan. 14, 1832.

TROUT, HUGH HENRY SR. surgeon; b. Staunton, Va., June 6, 1878; s. Philip H. and Olivia (Benson) T.; M.D., Univ. of Va., 1902; student in Europe, 1907-08; m. Leonora Cocke, 1910; children—Leonora (Mrs. Herman Bolster), Hugh Henry, Philip Cocke; m. 2d, Alice Green, 1926; children—Alice Green, Albert Henry. Intern Johns Hopkins Hosp., 1902-04; surgeon St. Joseph's German Hosp., Baltimore, 1904-05, Union Protestant Infirmary, 1905-08; pres. Jefferson Hosp., Roanoke, Va. Mem. bd. visitors U. of Va., Mary Washington Coll. Served as lt. col. Med. Corps, U.S. Army, 1918-19. Fellow Am. Coll. Surgeons; mem. A.M.A., Southern Med. Assn., Am. Surg. Assn., Southern Surg. Assn. (pres. 1931), Med. Soc. of Va. (pres., 1940), Internat. Surg. Assn., Alpha Omega Alpha, Phi Kappa Psi. Democrat. Episcopalian. Mason. Clubs: Rotary, Shenandoah (Roanoke, Va.). Home: 1301 Franklin Rd. Office: Jefferson Hosp., Roanoke, Va. Died Jan. 13, 1950.

TROXELL, EDWARD LEFFINGWELL, geologist; b. Deshler, Neb., Apr. 15, 1884; s. Jacob and Evelyn Virginia (Leffingwell) T.; prep. edn., Collegiate Inst., Salt Lake City, Utah; A.B., Northwestern U., 1908, A.M., 1911; Ph.D., Yale, 1914; student Sorbonne, Paris, 1919; m. Jane Allen Campbell, Oct. 17, 1917. Research asst., Yale, 1919, research asso. in paleontology, 1920; asst. prof. geology, 1920-25, prof. since 1925, Trinity Coll., dean of Coll., 1925-28; dir. State Geol. and Natural History Survey since 1940; Red Cross first aid instr., 1941; member State Defense Minerals Resources Committee. Joined First O.T.C., Fort Sheridan, Ill., 1917; commd. capt. inf., Aug. 15, 1917; at Camp Custer, Aug. 1917-July 1918; overseas, July 1918-July 1919; with 82d and 86th Divs., Argonne Forest. Fellow Geol. Soc. America, Am. Geog. Soc., Am. Assn. for Advancement of Science, Paleontol. Soc.; mem. Assn. of Am. State Geologists (exec. com.; pres. 1947-48), Am. Soc. Mammalogists, Am. Assn. Univ. Profs., Phila. Acad. Natural Sciences, Sigma Xi, Pi Gamma Mu (vice chancellor), Alpha Delta Phi, Book and Bond of Yale. Congregationalist. Clubs: Hartford Engineers, Twentieth Century, Hartford Golf. Field trips and exploration in the West, specimens now in many museums; important discoveries in fossil reptiles, birds and mammals. Contbr. plans in flood control and engring.; Gildersleeve Canal, etc. Author of about 80 papers, mostly on paleontology, geology and education, in Am. Jour. Science, Scientific Monthly, Yale Alumni Weekly, etc. Inventor. Home: West Hartford CT Died Sept. 21, 1972.

TROXELL, THOMAS FRANKLIN, investment banker; b. Balt., Jan. 9, 1895; s. Frederick W. and Mary K. (Hopkins) T.; A.B., Johns Hopkins, 1915; m. Louise F. Chase, Sept. 22, 1923; children—Thomas Franklin, D. Chase. With Dillon, Read & Co., Inc., N.Y.C., 1925-57, v.p., 1946-57; pres. Nassau Assos., Inc., 1952-57; dir. New Amsterdam Casualty Co., U.S. Casualty Co. Served as capt. 4th Inf., U.S. Army, 1917-19: AEF in France. Decorated Purple Heart. Mem. Phi Beta Kappa. Home: Montclair NJ Died Jan. 8, 1971; buried Loudon Park Cemetery Baltimore MD

TRUBY, ALBERT ERNEST, army officer; b. Otto, N.Y., July 18, 1871; s. John and Minnie (Ackerman) T.; student Cornell, 1890-93; B.S., U. of Pa., 1894, M.D., 1897; m. Elizabeth Downing, Apr. 26, 1906; children—Elizabeth, Barbara, Albert Eliot (deceased), John Orrien. Surgeon Medical Corps, United States Army, 1898; captain, 1903; promoted through grades to brigadier general, Jan. 1, 1933; retired Aug. 1, 1935. Served in Spanish-Am. and World Wars. Fellow Am. Coll. Surgeons; mem. A.M.A. Mason. Author: Memoir of Walter Reed—The Yellow Fever Episode, 1943. Address: 145 Laurel St., San Francisco CA

TRUE, THEODORE EDMOND brig. gen. U.S.A.; b. Coles County, Ill., Dec. 24, 1842; s. Edmond White and Mary Blackburn (Jones) T.; ed. schs. and acads. in Ill.; grad. U.S. Inf. and Cav. Sch., Ft. Leavenworth, Kan., 1883; m. Cynthia L. Bowman, Nov. 29, 1864. Corporal Co. B, 7th Ill., Inf., Apr. 25, 1861; sergt. Co. D, 41st Ill. Inf., July 30, 1861; promoted 2d lt. 41st Ill. Inf., "for meritorious services" at battle of Ft. Donelson, Tenn., where was twice wounded, Feb. 15, 1862; capt. 6th U.S.C. Arty., Nov. 28, 1863; 2d lt. 4th U.S. Inf., July 24, 1866; 1st lt. 4th U.S. Inf., Feb. 26, 1876; capt. a.q.m. U.S.A., Oct. 23, 1889; maj. q.m., Nov. 13, 1898; lt. col. deputy q.m. gen. U.S.A., Feb. 24, 1903; brig. gen. U.S.A., Jan. 23, 1904, and retired. Participated in battles of Civil War, including capture of Ft. Henry, Tenn., battles of Ft. Donelson, Tenn., Big Hatchie River, Tenn., attack on transport fleet near Island 82, Mississippi River, Siege of Vicksburg, Defense of Vidalia, La., etc., and skirmishes with hostile Indians in Wyo. in 1869, 70. Baptist. Republican. Home: Los Angeles, Calif. Died Aug. 30, 1925.

TRUESDELL, KARL (trooz'del), army officer; b. Moorhead, Minn., Aug. 27, 1882; s. Julius Augustus and Cornelia Octavia (Riggs) T.; ed. high sch., Washington, D.C., 1901, Army Signal Sch., 1911-12, Sch. of the Line, 1920-21 (hon. grad.), Staff Sch., 1921-22, Army War Coll., 1925-26, Naval War Coll., 1926-27; m. Mary Maurice Smith, Apr. 15, 1907; children—Karl, Cecil Olive (wife of Edgar Thomas Conley III, U.S. Army). Enlisted in U.S. Army, 1901, commd. 2d lt., 1904, advanced through the grades to maj. gen., 1940; served with 33d, 26th and 1st Divs. and V Army Corps, A.E.F., during World War I; in battles of Siechprey, Cantigny, Soissons, St. Mihiel, Meuse-Argonne; chief budget and legislation, War Dept. Gen. Staff, 1927-31; with 15th Inf., Tientsin, China, 1932-35; dir. Mil. Intelligence Dept., Army War Coll., 1935-37; comdg. officer Ft. Jay, N.Y., and 16th Inf., 1937-38; comdg. gen. 12th Brig., 1938-39, First Div., 1940, 6th Army Corps, 1941; dep. comdr. Panama Dept. to Mar. 1942; comdt. Command and Gen. Staff Sch., Ft. Leavenworth, 1943-45; ret. 1946. Am. mem. of Internat. Allied Radio Commn. Decorated Distinguished Service Medal with oak leaf (U.S.); Croix de Guerre (France); Comdr. Order Brit. Empire; Grance official Order Merit Militar, Order Merit Aeronautico (Brazil); Grand officer Mil. Order Ayacuche (Peru); Comdr. Order Polonia Restituta (Poland). Mem. Am. and Washington philatelic socs., China Stamp Soc., Council Fgn. Relations, N.Y. Genealogical and Biographical Society, Founders and Patriots (governor D.C. dist.), Soc. of the Cincinnati. Mason. Club: Army and Navy (Washington). Author: Military Policy of the United States, 1921; Tactics and Technique of Separate Branches, 1922; Command and General Staff School Correspondence Courses, 1923-26. Lecturer for Council on Foreign Relations. Address: 6312 Beechwood Dr., Chevy Chase, Md. Died July 16, 1955; buried Arlington Mil. Cemetery.

TRUITT, RALPH PURNELL, physician; b. Snow Hill, Md., Aug. 4, 1885; s. George Worthington and Gertrude Duncan (Purnell) T.; grad. high sch., Snow Hill, student Washington Coll., Chestertown, Md.; M.D., U. of Maryland, 1910; m. Eleanor McConnell, Sept. 2, 1920 (died 1946); 1 son, James McConnell. Intern University Hospital, Baltimore, 1909-10; jr. assistant physician N.J. State Hospital, Trenton, 1910-12; psychiatrist in chief City Hosp. (insane department), Baltimore, Maryland, 1912; assistant resident Psychiatrist Johns Hopkins Hosp., 1913-14; clin. dir. La. State Hosp., Jackson, La., 1915; sr. physician N.J. State Hosp., 1916-17; lt., capt. and maj. Med. Corps, U.S. Army, 1917-19; med. dir. Ill. Soc. for Mental Hygiene and asst. prof. neurology and psychiatry, U. of Ill. Med. Dept., 1919-23; dir. Child Guidance Clinic Demonstration under auspices Nat. Com. for Mental Hygiene, Los Angeles, Calif., 1924; dir. Div. on Prevention of Delinquency, Commonwealth Fund Program, New York, 1925-27; asso. prof. psychiatry and dir. psychiatric clinic, U. of Md., 1927-46, prof. clin. psychiatry and chief of psychiatric service, 1946-50, chairman of the department of psychiatry, 1948-50. Mem. Am. Psychiat. Assn., Am. Orthopsychiatric Assn. (pres. 1935-36), Phi Sigma Kappa. Home: Stevensville MD Died June 20, 1966.

TRUMAN, BENJAMIN CUMMINGS soldier, author; b. Providence, R.I., Oct. 25, 1835; s. Henry Hammond and Susan (Cummings) T.; ed. pub. and pvt. schs., Providence and Boston; taught sch., Canterbury, N.H., at age of 17; learned to set type at 18; compositor and proofreader New York Times, 1854-60; reporter Phila. Press, 1861; m. Augusta Mallard, 1869. Went to Nashville, Tenn., as capt. and on staff of Andrew Johnson (then mil. gov. of Tenn.) in Mar. 1862; served in Army of the Cumberland as staff officer, and corr. New York Times. After death of Lincoln was 18 months on President Johnson's staff; went to Calif. as spl. agt. P.O. Dept., 1866-69 and 1877-78; census marshal of Southern Calif., 1870; later spl. agt. Treasury Dept.; went to China, Japan, Hawaii and Alaska for Govt., and 4 times to Europe; also traveled in Egypt, Algiers, Morocco and Palestine, as corr. San Francisco Chronicle; asst. chief floriculture, World's Columbian Expn.; one of Calif. commrs. to Paris Expn., 1900; also Yosemite Valley commr. Author: See How It Sparkles; The South During the War; Semi-Tropical California; Occidental Sketches; Summer and Winter Resorts of California; From the Crescent City to the Golden Gate; Homes and Happiness in the Golden State; The Field of Honor; History of World's Fair in Chicago; Campaigning in Tennessee; Vasquez, the Bandit; Tourists' California Guide; The Missions of California; Pictorial Southern California; Pictorial Los Angeles; Divorced on the Desert. Home: Los Angeles, Calif. Died July 18, 1916.

TRUMAN, HARRY S., 33d Pres. of U.S. (32d man to serve although officially designated 33d President); b. Lamar, Mo., May 8, 1884; s. John Anderson and Martha Ellen (Young) T.; educated in public schools, Independence, Mo.; student Kansas City Sch. of Law, 1923-25. Field Arty. Sch. (Fort Sill, Okla.) 1917-18; m. Bess Wallace, June 28, 1919; 1 dau., Mary Margaret (Mrs. Clifton Daniel). With Kansas City Star, 1901; timekeeper for r.r. contractor, 1902; with Nat. Bank of Commerce and Union Nat. Bank, Kansas City, 1903-05; operated family farm, 1906-17; judge Jackson County Court, 1922-24, presiding judge, 1926-34; elected to U.S. Senate from Mo., 1934, re-elected 1940; served as chmn. Special Com. to investigate Nat. Defense Program; elected v.p. of United States, Nov. 7, 1944; and took office, Jan. 20, 1945; succeeded to presidency on death of Franklin Delano Roosevelt, Apr. 12, 1945; elected Pres. of the U.S. 1949-53. Served as 1st lt. Battery F. and capt. Battery D. 129th Field Atty., 35th Div., U.S. Army, World War I; participated in Vosges operations, St. Mihiel and Meuse-Argonne offensives, A.E.F. discharged as major, May 1919; col. Field Atty., U.S. Res. Corps, since 1927. Baptist. Mason (past grand master, Mo.). Author: Years of Decisions, Vol. I, 1955; Years of Trial and Hope, Vol. II, 1956. Home: Independence MO Died Dec. 26, 1972; buried Garden of Truman Library, Independence MO

TRUMAN, RALPH EMERSON army officer; b. Kansas City, Mo., May 10, 1880; s. William Thomas and Henrietta (Strang) T.; student Brown's Bus. and Tech. Sch., Kansas City, 1902-03; grad. Inf. Sch., 1925, Command and Gen. Staff Sch., 1928; children—(1st marriage) Henrietta Edna (Mrs. Earl G. Davidson), Louis Watson, Corbie Ralph; m. 2d, Olive Lougrette Johnson, Oct. 10, 1932. With Kansas City Union Depot Co., 1904-05; sec. chief of detectives Kansas City Police Dept., 1905-16; asst. chief spl. agt. St.L.-S.F. R.R. Co., 1920-28; spl. agt. Nat. Bd. Fire Underwriters, Western Dist. of Mo., 1928-—. Served with 20th U.S. Inf., Spanish-Am. War; served on Mexican Border with 4th Mo. Inf., 1916-17; commd. 2d lt., 1916, advanced through the grades to maj. gen., 1938, inactive, 1942; served from 1st lt. to maj., Inf., World War I; mem. Mo. Nat. Guard, 1916-—. Decorated Purple Heart. Mem. Am. War Dads (nat. v.p.), Am. Legion, V.F.W., S.R., Order of Blue Goose, 40 and 8, Spanish-Am. War Vets., Mo. Peace Officers Assn. Mason (Shriner, Scottish Rite), Eagle, Sojourner. Club: Officers (Kansas City, Mo., pres.). Home: 5106 Garfield Av., Kansas City, Mo. Address: Chgo. Died 1962.

TRUSCOTT, LUCIAN KING JR. army officer; b. Chatfield, Tex., Jan. 9, 1895; s. Lucian King and Maria Temple (Tully) T.; certificates from Normal Sch., Norman, Okla., 1911, Sapulpa, 1912, Eufaula, 1913; m. Sarah Nicholas Randolph, Mar. 29, 1919; children—Mary Randolph (wife of Capt. Robert Wilbourn, U.S. Army), Lucian King III, James Joseph. Sch. tchr., 1911-17; commd. 2d lt. Cav., 1917; promoted through grades to brig. gen., Oct. 1945; assigned duty ETO. London 1942; apptd. comdg. gen. 3d Inf. Div., Mar. 1943; 6th Corps, Feb. 1944; 15th Army, Oct. 1944; 5th Army, Dec. 1944; 3d Army, Germany, Oct. 1945. Led assault troops in invasion of Southern France, 1944. Decorated D.S.M. with Oak Leaf Cluster, Legion of Merit, D.S.C., Purple Heart (U.S.); Hon. Companion, Order of Bath (Brit.); Comdr. Legion of Honor, Croix de Guerre (France); Silver Medal for Valor, Grand Officer, Order of Saints Maurice and Lazarus, Grand Cross Order of Crown of Italy (Italy); Grand Officer Order of Mil. Merit, War Medal (Brazil); Order of White Lion (First Class), War Cross (Czechoslovakia); Silver Cross (Poland). Home: Alexandria, Va. Died Sept. 12, 1965.

TRUSSELL, C(HARLES) P(RESCOTT), newspaper corr.; b. Chicago, Aug. 3, 1892; s. Homer Milton and Margaret (Shuck) T.; ed. pub. schs. of Md. and Ill.; m. Beatrice W. Tait, June 14, 1923; children—Charles Tait, Galen Douglas. Reporter Baltimore Sun, 1917-19, copyreader, 1919-22, asst. city editor, 1922-25, city editor, 1925-32, mem. Washington Bur., 1932-41; mem. Washington Bur. N.Y. Times, 1941-65. Served as 2d lt., Inf., U.S. Army, World War I. Mem., chmn. standing com. of corrs. U.S. Capitol, 1934-36. Awarded Pulitzer prize in journalism for distinguished reporting on nat. affairs, 1949. Mem. White House Corr. Assn., Sigma Delta Chi. Clubs: National Press (bd. govs. 1946-49), Gridiron. Occasional contbr. to current pubs. Home: Washington DC Died Oct. 2, 1968; buried Rock Creek Cemetery Washington DC

TRUSTY, S(AMUEL) DAVID, lawyer; b. Louisville, Dec. 12, 1913; s. Samuel L. and Dorothy (Lemmon) T.; A.B., U. Mo., 1935, LL.D., 1938; m. Jean Lois Murray, Dec. 22, 1938; children—David Michael, Jean Murray, Scott Townsend, Ann Wilson. Admitted to Mo. bar, 1938, also U.S. Treasury Dept., ICC; mem. firm Trusty, Pugh & Trusty, 1938-41; spl. asst. to dist. atty. for D.C., 1941; spl. atty. OPA, Washington, 1941; mem. firm Popham, Thompson, Popham, Trusty & Conway, and predecessor, Kansas City, 1946-68. Mem. Appellate Judicial Commn. State Mo., 1962-68. Mem. corporate bd. YMCA, Kansas City; bd. mgrs. S.W. br., bd. curators Lincoln U. Served to lt. comdr. USNR, 1942-45. Fellow Am. Coll. Trial Lawyers; mem. Am. Judicature Soc., Am., Fed., Mo., Kansas City (pres.) bar assns., Chancery, Lawyers Assn., Res. Officers Assn., Phi Delta Phi, Sigma Chi, Sigma Gamma Epsilon, Chi Chi Chi. Clubs: Kansas City, Mission Hills Country (Kansas City, Mo.). Home: Kansas City MO Died Dec. 12, 1968.

TRUXTUN, THOMAS naval officer; b. Hempstead, L.I., N.Y., Feb. 17, 1755; s. Thomas and Sarah (Axtell) T.; m. Mary Fundran, May 27, 1775, 13 children. Went to sea at age 12, ship comdr. in mcht. service by age 20; served during Am. Revolution as lt. in privateer Congress, also commanded ships Independence and Mars, captured many prizes, 1777, served in or commanded other privateers; commd. capt. U.S. Navy; took 1st ship (the Canton) from Phila. to China, 1786; commanded frigate Constellation, won 2 important naval engagements during naval war with France, 1797-1800; received Gold medal from U.S. Congress; commd. to lead squadron against Tripoli, 1801, withdrew because his flagship was not given a capt. (withdrawal taken by hostile adminstrn. as resignation); refused offer naval command in Aaron Burr's western scheme, 1806; sheriff Phila., 1816-19. Died Phila., May 5, 1822; buried Christ Churchyard, Phila.

TRUXTUN, WILLIAM TALBOT naval officer; b. Phila., Mar. 11, 1824; s. William and Isabelle (Martin) T. m. Annie Scott, Oct. 15, 1856; m. 2d, Mary Walke, Sept. 2, 1875; 8 children including William. Served in ships Dolphin and Falmouth in Home Squadron, 1841, later in brig Truxton on African coast; passed midshipman, 1847; on Brazilian station, 1847-48; served in Dolphin, 1853; exec. sailing sloop-of-war Dale in North Atlantic Blockading Squadron, 1861; lt. comdr., 1862; commanded the Chocura, 1862-63, Tacony until close of war; in action with batteries at Plymouth, N.C., attacks on Ft. Fisher, 1864, 65; supt. naval coal shipments, 1866-67; in command of Jamestown in North Pacific Squadron, 1868-70, Brooklyn in North and South Atlantic, 1873-75; comdr. Boston and Norfolk (Va.) navy yards, 1876-80; commodore, 1882; in command of Norfolk Navy Yard, 1885-86. Died Norfolk, Feb. 25, 1887.

TRYON, FREDERICK GALE mineral economist; b. Minneapolis, Minn., Mar. 23, 1892; s. Charles John and Isabel (Gale) T.; A.B., U. of Minn., 1914, Shevlin fellow, 1915, A.M., 1916; m. Ruth Wilson, Aug. 16, 1919; children—John Griggs, Richard Gale, Joseph Lee. Geologist, Empire Gas & Fuel Co., 1916. asst. geologist U.S. Geol. Survey, 1917; attached to com. on coal production, Council Nat. Defense; in charge statistics of mineral raw materials for War Industries Bd.; capt. U.S.A., in statistics br., Gen. Staff, Washington, D.C., and G.H.Q., France, 1917-18; maj. Spl. Res., U.S.A. Am. sec. raw materials sect., Supreme Econ. Council, Am. Peace Commn., Paris, Jan.-May 1919; in charge coal statistics, U.S. Geol. Survey, 1919-24; same, Bur. Mines, 1925-34, chief Coal Economics Div., 1834-37; statistician Nat. Bituminous Coal Commn., 1937-—; lecturer U. of Penna., 1924-25, Robert Brookings Grad. Sch. of Economics, 1825-27; on leave Brookings Instn., 1926, 31, 33. Mem. President Harding's fuel distribution com. during 1922 coal strike; statis. adviser U.S. Coal Commn., 1922-23; mem. staff President's Research Com. on Social Trends, 1931, and study of population redistribution, 1935. Fellow American Statis. Assn. Author of official repts. and tech. papers on economics of coal, fuels and power, and collaborator in group studies: Boycotts and Peace, 1932; Recent Social Trends, 1932; America's Capacity to Produce, 1934; Migration and Economic Opportunity, 1936; Technological Trends, 1937. Editor and author (with others): What the Coal Commission Found, 1925; Mineral Economics (Brookings lecturers), 1932. Home: Washington, D.C. Died Feb. 15, 1940.

TRYON, JAMES RUFUS medical dir. U.S.N.; b. Coxsackie, N.Y., Sept. 24, 1837; A.B., Union Coll., 1858, Ph.D., 1891, LL.D., 1895; unmarried. Entered U.S.N. as asst. surgeon, 1863; passed through all grades; apptd. surgeon gen. U.S.N., May 1893; retired as rear adm., Sept. 24, 1899. Address: Coxsackie, New York. Died Mar. 21, 1912.

TSCHAPPAT, WILLIAM H., army officer; b. Aug. 10, 1874; grad. U.S. Mil. Acad., 1896. Commd. add. 2d lt. arty., June 12, 1896; promoted through grades to col., Sept. 4, 1919; served as col. Ordnance Dept., N.A., Jan. 1918-Sept. 1919; apptd. asst. to chief of ordnance with rank of brig. gen. for 4 yrs., beginning June 3, 1930; apptd. maj. gen., chief of ordnance, Mar. 1934; retired Aug. 31, 1938. Mem. Nat. Inventors Council, 1942-45. Home: Box 264, Falls Church VA

TUBMAN, HARRIET abolitionist; b. Dorchester County, Md., circa 1820. Escaped from slavery, 1849; helped over 300 slaves escape via Underground Railroad; nurse and spy for U.S. forces in S.C. during Civil War. Died 1913.

TUCK, SOMERVILLE PINKNEY business exec., fgn. service officer; b. S.I., N.Y., May 31, 1891; s. Judge Somerville Pinkney and Emily Rosalie Snowden (Marshall) T.; prep. edn. Switzerland and Germany, also Ridgefield (Conn.) Sch.; A.B., Dartmouth, 1913; m.; children—James M., David II. Apptd. dept. consul, Alexandria Egypt, 1913; consul, Samsoun, Anatolia, Turkey, 1920-21; mem. staff U.S. high commr. to Turkey, Constantinople, 1921; detailed consul to diplomatic agy., Cairo, Egypt, 1922; consul, Vladivostok, Siberia, 1922-23; detailed to Dept. State, 1923-24; consul, Geneva, 1924-28; first sec. Am. Embassy, Constantinople, 1928-29, Am. Legation, Budapest, 1929-31; chargé d'affairs, Prague, 1932; assigned to Am. Embassy, Paris, 1933; assigned counselor of Embassy, Brussels, 1937, Buenos Aires, 1938, Vichy, France, 1941; detained by enemy, 1942-44; apptd. E.E. and M.P. to Egypt, 1944, first ambassador to Egypt, 1946; ret., 1948. Attended sessions adv. com. on opium League Nations, 1925, 26, 27; mem. Am. delegation to Prep. Commn. for Disarmament, 1927-28; Am. del. to Conf. for Limitation of Naval Armament, 1927; mem. Gen. Disarmament Conf., Geneva, 1932. Lt. comdr. USNR. Decorated Comdr. Legion of Honor (France); Hungarian Order of Merit Class II. Mem. Alpha Delta Phi. Democrat. Episcopalian. Clubs: Racquet and Tennis, The Brook, Century Assn. (N.Y.C.); Metropolitan (Washington); Travelers, Jockey (Paris); White's (London). Address: 7 rue Octare-Feuillet, Paris 16em, France. Died Apr. 22, 1967; buried St. Barnabas Ch., Leeland, Upper Marlborough, Md.

TUCK, WILLIAM HALLAM chem. industry; b. Balt., Mar. 9, 1890; s. Judge Somerville Pinkney and Emily (Marshall) T.; Litt.B., Princeton, 1912; m. Hilda Bunge, Apr. 15, 1920; children—Dorothea (Mrs. Alden Griswold Bigelow), Emily (Mrs. Giles Mills), Edward Hallam. Became dir. Allied Chem. & Dye Corp., N.Y.C., 1929. Vice pres. Belgian Am. Edn. Found., N.Y.C., Foundation Universitaire, Brussels, Belgium; dir. gen. Internat. Refugee Orgn., UN, 1947-49. Served in Brit. Army, 1916-18, maj. F.A., U.S. Army, 1918-19, USNR, 1941-45, capt. Res. Decorated Comdr. Legion of Honor (France); Comdr. Order of Leopold (Belgium). Mem. Soc. of Cincinnati. Republican. Episcopalian. Clubs: Knickerbocker, University (N.Y.C.); Metropolitan, Chevy Chase (Washington). Home: Chateau de Rougemont, Switzerland; also Perrywood, Upper Marlborough, Md. Died Aug. 1966.

TUCKER, BEVERLEY DANDRIDGE, bishop and educator; b. Warsaw, Va., Feb. 4, 1882; s. Rt. Rev. Beverley Dandridge and Anna Maria (Washington) T.; B.A., U. of Va., 1902; Va. Theol. Sem., 1902-05, B.D., 1915, D.D., 1920; Rhodes scholar, from Va. at Christ Church, Oxford U., 1905-08, B.A., 1908, M.A., 1912; D.D., Univ. of Richmond, 1932; LL.D., Univ. of Ala., 1932; Western Reserve Univ., 1939; S.T.D., Kenyon College, 1938; L.H.D., Baldwin-Wallace College, 1945; married Eleanor Carson Lile, April 20, 1915; children—Maud (Mrs. W. H. Drane), Beverley D., Eleanor S., Louisa Lile (Mrs. T. G. Bell), Maria Washington (Mrs. E. S. Bowerfind, Jr.). Ordained deacon, 1908, priest, 1909, P.E. Church; rector St. James and St. Luke's parishes, Mecklenburg County, Va., 1908-11; rector St. Paul's Memorial Ch., U. of Va., 1911-20; prof. practical theology, Va. Theol. Sem., 1920-23; rector St. Paul's Church, Richmond, Va., 1923-38; bishop Diocese of Ohio, 1938-52; deputy to Gen. Conv., P.E. Ch., 1928, 31, 34, 37. Pres. Cleveland Church Fedn., 1947-48. First lt., chaplain, U.S. Army, 1918-19; attached to 17th Engrs. (Ry.), Base Hosp. 41, A.E.F. Mem. bd. dirs. and overseers Sweet Briar (Va.) Coll.; mem. bd. trustees Kenyon Coll., Lake Erie Coll., Western Reserve U. Mem. Alpha Tau Omega, Phi Beta Kappa, Raven Soc. Episcopalian. Democrat. Clubs: Colonnade, Univ. of Virginia, Farmington (Charlottesville, Va.); Union, Kirtland Country (Cleveland). Home: Cleveland Heights OH Died July 4, 1969; buried University Cemetery Charlottesville VA

TUCKER, BEVERLEY RANDOLPH, neuropsychiatrist; b. Richmond, Va., Apr. 26, 1874; s. John Randolph and Fannie Booth (Crump) T.; ed. Va. Mil. Inst., 1890-92; M.D., Med. Coll. of Va., Richmond, 1905; postgrad. work, Phila., New York, London and Vienna; m. Elsie Boyd, Apr. 3, 1907; children—Mary Hannah, Elsie Boyd, Weir Mitchell, Beverley R. Asst. to Dr. S. Weir Mitchell, Phila., 1906, 67; adj. prof. nervous and mental diseases, Med. Coll. of Va., 1907-12, prof. 1912-1938. President and physician in charge Tucker Hospital, Inc.; member State Board of Health, Va. (mem. exec. com., 1917-20; member of board Nemours Foundation. Editor Old Dominion Journal Medicine and Surgery, 1908-14. Member Richmond Light Inf. Blues 2 yrs. Contract surgeon U.S. Army, 1918; mem. med. advisory bd. Selective Service; mem. Am. bd. Am. Hosp., Paris. Pres. Richmond Acad. Medicine, 1942-43. Diplomate Am. Bd. Psychiatry and Neurology. Fellow Am. Coll. Physicians, Am. Psychiatric Assn. Mem. Soc. of Cincinnati (pres. in State of Va., 1933-35), Am. Neurol. Assn., Med. Soc. of Va. (councilor), Tri-State Med. Assn. (pres. 1931-32), Mental Hygiene Soc. of Va. (pres.), Pi Mu, Phi Beta Kappa; Democrat. Episcopalian. Clubs: Commonwealth, Westmoreland (pres. 1924-25), Country; Writers Club of Va. Author: S. Weir Mitchell, 1914; Nervous Children, 1916; Verses of Virginia, 1923; The Lost Lenore (one-act play), 1929; The Gift of Genius, Adolescence; Narna Darrell (hist. novel), 1936; Various Verse, 1938; Tales of the Tuckers, 1942; also of sect. on cranial nerves, Tice's Practice of Medicine, 1920. Contbr. articles to med. publs., poems to newspapers and mags. Home: dd s2700 Monument Av. Office: 212 W. Franklin St., Richmond, Va. Died June 19, 1945.

TUCKER, HARRY highway engr.; b. Amherst County, Va., Feb. 7, 1890; s. Cornelius Sale and Sallie (Stickley) T.; A.B., and B.S., Washington and Lee U., 1910, C.E., 1923; m. Mary Lillian Briggs, May 5, 1918 (died Aug. 24, 1930); children—Harry, Robert Briggs. Admitted to N.C. bar, 1914; instr. in civil engring., N.C. State Coll. of Agr. and Engring., 1910-16, prof. of highway engring. since 1920, dir. Engring. Expt. Sta. since 1932; cons. engr. and tech. expert in civil engring., highway transportation and safety. Served with 105th Engrs., U.S. Army, with A.E.F., advancing from pvt. to to capt., 1917-19. Mem. N.C. Utilities Commn. Mem. Am. Society Civil Engrs., Inst. of Traffic Engrs., N.C. Bar Assn., Sigma Phi Epsilon, Theta Tau, Phi Kappa Phi. Ind. Democrat. Presbyterian. Author: The History of the 105th Engineer Regiment (with W. P. Sullivan), 1919; Highway Accidents in North Carolina and Guides to Safety, 1935; Manual in the Testing of Materials, 1935; Highway Economics (with M. C. Leager). Contbr. many articles on highway transportation, accidents, etc., to jours. Home: 20 Logan Court, Raleigh, N.C. Died Mar. 18, 1942.

TUCKER, JOHN RANDOLPH naval officer; b. Alexandria, Va., Jan. 31, 1812; s. John and Susan (Douglas) T.; m. Virginia Webb, June 7, 1838, 3 children. Commd. midshipman U.S. Navy, 1826, passed midshipman, 1833, lt., 1837; known to sailors as handsome Jack; served as 1st exec. officer, then capt. on ship Stromboli during Mexican War; commissioned comdr., 1855, resigned commn., 1861; commd. comdr. Confederate States Navy, 1861; in charge of naval defenses of James River; commanded steamer Yorktown (converted into cruiser Patrick Henry), until 1862; participated in Battle of Hampton Roads, 1862; had command of ironclad ram Chicora, 1862; commanded Charleston Squadron; capt. Provisional Navy of Confederate States, 1863; served in Battle of Sailor's Creek, 1865; imprisoned at Fort Warren, 1865, released upon taking oath of allegiance to U.S.; commd. rear adm. Peruvian Navy; commanded fleets of Peru and Chile in war with Spain, 1869; head hydrographical commn. to survey upper waters of Amazon River, 1869. Died Petersburg, Va., June 12, 1883.

TUCKER, ST. GEORGE army officer, jurist; b. Port Royal, Bermuda, July 10, 1752; s. Henry and Anne (Butterfield) T.; grad. Coll. William and Mary, 1772; m. Frances (Bland) Randolph, Sept. 23, 1778; m. 2d, Lelia (Skipwith) Carter, Oct. 8, 1791; at least 2 children, Nathaniel Beverley, Henry St. George. Admitted to Va. bar; served as col. Chesterfield County (Va.) Militia, lt. col. Va. Cavalry, during Revolutionary War; served at Battle of Guilford Court House, took part in siege of Yorktown; commr. Annapolis Conv., 1786; judge of Gen. Ct. of Va., 1788-1800; prof. law Coll. William and Mary, 1800-03; judge Supreme Ct. of Appeals of Va., 1803-11; judge U.S. Dist. Ct. for Va., 1813-28; his opinion in Kamper vs. Hawkins (1 Va. Reports, 20) held that state constn. was sovereign act of people, opinion in Turpin vs. Locket (6 Call Reports, 113) sustained constitutionality of 1802 act for relief of poor. Author: Dissertation on Slavery: with a Proposal for its Gradual Abolition in Virginia (pamphlet), 1796, reprinted, 1861; published annotated edition of Blackstone's Commentaries, 5 vols., 1803; Liberty, a Poem on the Independence of America, 1788, The Probationary Odes of Jonathan Pindar, 2 parts, 1796. Died Nelson County, Va., Nov. 10, 1827.

TUCKER, SAMUEL naval officer; b. Marblehead, Mass., Nov. 1, 1747; s. Andrew and Mary (Belcher) T.; m. Mary Gatchell, Dec. 21, 1768. Commanded ship Young Phoenix, 1775; capt. ship Franklin, preyed on Brit. vessels, 1776; transferred to ship Hancock; commd. capt. Continental Navy, 1777; commanded frigate Boston; sailed for France, 1778; carried John Adams to his post as commr. to France, 1778; continued attacks on Brit. commerce, 1778-80; commanded several vessels trading with West Indian and European ports, 1783-85; mem. Mass. Legislature, 1814-18; elected to Me. Ho. of Reps., 2 terms. Died Bremen, Me., Mar. 10, 1833.

TUDOR, RALPH ARNOLD ex-govt. ofcl.; engr.; b. Colorado Springs, Colo., Mar. 19, 1902; s. E. A. and Ida J. (Herzog) T.; B.S., U.S. Mil. Acad., 1923; C.E., Cornell U.; m. Mary Lucile Taylor, 1925; 1 dau., Jean Ellen. Commd. 2d lt., C.E., U.S. Army, 1923, served to 1st lt., 1929, resigned; bridge engr. San Francisco-Oakland bridge, 1929-37, prin. engr., 1939-40; assistant executive officer and chief engineer of Golden Gate International Exposition, 1937-38; lieutenant col., later colonel, Corps of Engrs., U.S. Army, 1941-42; dist. engr., Portland, 1943-45; chief engr. Morrison-Knudsen, engrs., China, 1946; v.p. Morrison-Knudsen Internat. Co., San Francisco, 1947—; president of Tudor Engring. Co., specializing in road and bridge construction, San Francisco, 1947—, also civil engring. projects. Under sec. of Interior, 1953-54. Decorated Legion of Merit. Fellow Am. Soc. Civil Engrs.; mem. Am. Soc. M.E., Assn. Grads. West Point (trustee). Presbyn. Clubs: Engineers (San Francisco); Commonwealth (Cal.). Home: 140 Selby Lane, Atherton, Cal. Office: 595 Mission St., San Francisco 5. Died Nov. 12, 1963; buried U.S. Mil. Acad., West Point, N.Y.

TUGMAN, WILLIAM MASTEN newspaper editor, publisher; b. Cin., Aug. 22, 1893; s. William M. and Alice Marion (Callahan) T.; B.A., Harvard, 1914; m. Genevieve New, Aug. 19, 1920; children—William Masten, Peter New, Janet (Mrs. Jerry Stone), Thomas Anderson. Reporter, Springfield (Mass.) Republican, 1914-15, New Bedford (Mass.) Standard, 1915, Providence Jour., 1916-19, Cleve. Plain Dealer, 1919-27; mng. editor Eugene (Ore.) Register Guard, 1927-50, editor, 1950-54; editor, owner Port Umpqua Courier, 1955—. Mem. Douglas County Library Bd.; chmn. Ore. Hwy. Commn. adv. bd. on travel information; chmn. Gov's. spl. com., chmn. adv. com. Ore. State Parks. Served as capt. F.A., World War I. Recipient Voorhies Award, Ore. Newspaper Pub. Assn., 1944; distinguished pub. service award U. Ore., 1958. Mem. Umpqua Little Theatre, Am. Soc. Newspaper Editors, Ore. Newspaper Publs. Assn., Eugene Very Little Theatre, Eugene Round Table, Order of Antelope. Republican. Episcopalian. Clubs: Commonwealth (San Francisco) Portland (Ore.) City. Converted dramatic poem, Dream of Alcestis (Theodore Morris son), into stage script, 1953. Home: Box 63, Gardiner, Ore. Died May 1960.

TUKEY, HAROLD BRADFORD, horticulturist; b. Berwyn, Ill., Sept. 30, 1896; s. James Bradford and Armenia (Mehrhof) T.; B.S., U. of Ill., 1918, M.S., 1920; Ph.D., U. of Chicago, 1932; D.H.C. (honorary), Hanover, Germany, 1957; m. Margaret Davenport. November 23, 1918 (deceased February 7, 1930); children—Loren Davenport, Lois (Mrs. W. D. Baker, Jr.), Ronald Bradford; married 2d, Ruth Ann Schweigert, Nov. 23, 1932; children—Harold Bradford, Ann. Asst. horticulturist N.Y. State Agrl. Expt. Station, 1920-23; horticulturist in charge Hudson Valley Fruit Investigations, 1923-27; chief in research (horticulture), N.Y. State Agricultural Experimental Station, professor pomology, Cornell University, 1927-45. Head dept. of horticulture, Mich. State U., 1945-62, now prof. emeritus; U.S. tech. adv. Internat. Conf. on Atomic Energy, 1955. Commd. 1st lt. F.A., U.S. Army, 1918, serving W.W. Awarded Jackson Dawson Medal, 1948, Marshall P. Wilder medal 1956, N. J. Colman award, 1956, citation Am. Hort. Council, 1957; Gold medal of Honor, 1967; Liberty Hyde Bailey medal, 1967. Fellow A.A.A.S., Royal Hort. Soc. (Eng.), Am. Inst. Biol. Scis. (organizing bd. 1946-47, v.p.); mem. Am. Pomol. Soc. (bd. mgrs. 1925-28; exec. bd., 1925-48; pres. 1950-52; chairman Wilder Medal Award 1942-56, 59-62), Internat. Soc. Horticultural Sci. (pres. 1962-66), Am. Soc. Hort. Sci. (sec.-treas. 1927-46; pres. 1946; editor proc., 1927-50), Bot. Soc. Am., Am. Society Plant Physiologists, American Society Naturalists, Society Growth and Development, Soc. Nationale d'Horticulture de France (hon.), Mass. Hort. Soc., Michigan Horticultural Soc. American Horticultural Society, Phi Kappa Phi, Pi Alpha Xi, Theta Chi, Sigma Xi, Alpha Zeta. Republican. Presbyterian. Rotarian. Author: (books) The Pears of New York (with others), 1921; The Pear and Its Culture, 1929; Plant Regulators in Agrl., 1954; Dwarfed Fruit Trees, 1964. Contbr. to jours., agrl. press, and bulls. expt. sta. Mem. editorial and exec. staff Rural New Yorker, 1923-64; asso. editor Am. Fruit Grower. Contbr. Fruit Year Book (Eng.). Delivered Amos Meml. Lectr. (Eng.), 1952. Del. Internat. Hort. Congress, London, 1952, Scheveningen, 1955, Brussels, 1962, U.S., 1966, pres. XVIIth, 1966. Home: Woodland MI Died Nov. 1971.

TULLY, JOSEPH MERIT army officer; b. Orange, N.J., Oct. 4, 1893; s. John Martin and Hannah Matilda (Busill) T.; B.S., U.S. Mil. Acad., 1916; grad. Cav. Sch., troop officers course, 1923, Command and Gen. Staff Sch., 1926; m. Fannie Larkin Smith, Apr. 25, 1917; children—Joseph Merit, Frances Smith (Mrs. Harry A. Clark, Jr.), Larkin Smith, Robert Busill. Commd. 2d lt. U.S. Army, 1916, advanced through grades to brig. gen., 1945; served as comdt. of cadets Norwich U., Northfield, Vt., 1931-35. Decorated D.S.M., Silver Star with oak leaf cluster, Bronze Star (U.S.), Legion of Honor, Croix de Guerre with palm (France). Home: San Antonio. Died 1963.

TUOHY, EDWARD BOYCE (too'e), physician; b. Duluth, Minn., March 17, 1908; s. Edward Leo and Ida Mary (Boyce) T.; B.S., U. of Minn., 1925-29; M.D., U. of Pa., 1929-32; M.S. in Anesthesiology, Mayo Foundation Grad. Med. School, U. of Minn., 1933-36; m. Dorothy A. Johnson, April 11, 1934; children—Barbara, Michael, Patrick. Fellowship in anesthesiology, Mayo Foundation; Mayo Clinic staff, 1935, consultant 1935-47; prof. of anesthesiology, Georgetown Med. Center 1947-51; prof. surgery (anesthesiology) U. So. Cal. 1953; pvt. practice anesthethesiology. Mem. Reserve Corps. U.S. Army; active duty, May 1942; disch. rank maj., 1945; cons. USAF, 1954-56. Diplomate Am. Bd. Anesthesiology (mem. bd. 1950-56, del. A.M.A. 1951-55). Mem. Am. Soc. Anesthesiology for Pharmacology and Exptl. Therapeutics (pres. 1947), A.A.A.S., Sigma Xi, Nu Sigma Nu, Chi Psi. Roman Catholic. Contbr. chapters to Surgery and Dental Science and Dental Art by Dean Lewis; also over 100 articles to jours. Address: 2485 Sherwood Rd., San Marino, Cal. Died Jan. 12, 1959; buried Calvary Cemetery, Los Angeles.

TUPOLEV, ANDREI NIKOLAEVICH, aircraft designer; b. Pustomazovo, Tver, USSR Nov. 10, 1888; graduate Moscow Higher Technical Sch. in 1915. Began career as designer wind tunnels, glider; assisted establishment Aerodynamic Aircraft Design Bur., 1916, became Central Inst. Aerodynamics and Hydrodynamics, 1919, then head of designing bureau; dep. directors of the Main Adminstrn. of the Aircraft Industry, USSR People's Commissariat of Heavy Industry, 1932, also dir., chief designer Exptl. Aircraft Constrn. Plant to 1938; polit. prisoner, 1938-43; lt. gen. Air Force Engring. and Tech. Service; designed metal constrn. single-engine monoplane, eight-engine, forty ton aircraft, twin-engine, double-fin dive bomber, 1938, four-engine plane, 1944, super-heavy four-engine bomber, 1945-46; designed, produced jet passenger plane for 50 passengers, 1950; design and exptl. constrn. super-heavy jet aircraft for 170 passengers, 1955-56, deluxe improved design, 1957; designed double-deck airliner with four propjet engines, TU-144 Supersonic Transport. Deputy Supreme Soviet, USSR, 1950, 54. Decorated Order of Lenin; recipient Stalin prize, Lenin prize for aircraft design; Hero of Socialist Labor award (2), others. Mem. USSR Acad. Scis. Address: Moscow USSR Died Dec. 1972.

TUPPER, BENJAMIN army officer, pioneer; b. Stoughton, Mass., Mar. 11, 1738; s. Thomas and Remember (Perry) T.; m. Huldah White, Nov. 18, 1762, 7 children, including Rowena (Tupper) Sargent. Served to sgt. during French and Indian Wars, 1756; commd. lt. Western Mass. Militia, 1774; participated in siege of Boston, destruction of Brit. light house on Castle Island, 1775; commd. lt. col., 1776; col. Mass. Militia in Battle of L.I., Saratoga campaign, Battle of Monmouth; retired with brevet rank brig. gen., 1783; mem. Mass. Legislature, circa 1783; one of Continental officers to sign Newburgh Petition of 1783, seeking creation of new territory in the N.W.; rep. from Mass. on corps of state surveyors sent West by U.S. Congress; conducted preliminary surveying, 1785; aided movement which led to formation of Ohio Co.; accompanied original settlers to Marietta, O., 1788; judge Ct. Common Pleas and Quarter Sessions (1st civil ct. in Ohio Territory), 1788-92. Died June 7, 1792.

TURCHIN, JOHN BASIL soldier farmer; b. in Province of Don, Russia, Jan. 30, 1822; his name being Ivan Vasilevitch Turchininoff, which he anglicized as above. Served in Hungarian campaign and Crimean war in Russian army, reaching rank of col. Came to U.S., 1856; engr. with Ill. Central R.R.; served in Union army in Civil war as col. 19th Ill.; later brig. gen. After war solicitor of patents in Chicago; in 1873 established Polish colony of Radom in Washington County, Ill., where he lived on a farm. Author: The Campaign and Battle of Chickamauga. Address: Radom, Ill. Died 1901.

TURLEY, JAY (tûr'le), engineer; b. Beaver City, Utah, Apr. 16, 1877; s. Omner and Louisa Ann (Woodhouse) T.; both born west of Rocky Mts.; ran away from home at 17 to attend sch.; matriculated in Ore. State Agrl. Coll., 1895; but did not grad.; spl. advanced studies in U. of Tex. and George Washington U.; m. Urna Bradford Hickox, Sept. 7, 1904 (divorced Apr. 28, 1921). Apptd. U.S. dep. surveyor for Ida., 1899, for N.M., 1900-06; formulating extensive irrigation projects in Rio San Juan, N.M., since 1901; made original draft of irrigation laws for State of N.M., 1903-05; cons. engr. for N.M. in suit against Tex. over boundary along Rio Grande, 1913-16, 1921, 25; admitted to practice law, N.M., 1916, D.C., and Supreme Court of U.S., 1921. Mem. Idaho Nat. Guard, 1894-98; capt. engrs., U.S. Army, 1917-19, serving with 316th Engrs., 91st Div., and with 116th Engrs., 41st Div., A.E.F., also spl. staff and liaison service; retired as capt. Engrs., May 20, 1929. Republican. Mason (32 deg.). Opposed, 1925, bldg. of St. Francis Dam, near Los Angeles, Calif., which burst in 1928; reported, 1928, on "astral collision," at Crater Mound, Ariz., contending that it caused fissures forming Grand Canyon of the Colorado; reported, 1929, geological and other conditions for building high dam above Grand Canyon, instead of below at Boulder site; on spl. scientific research and writing up data since 1931; working on case of old Spanish grant community ditches of central N.M. in connection with suit before Supreme Court since 1934 and on development of water supply sources near Albuquerque, N.M. Home: near Albuquerque, N.M. Address: P.O. Box 161, Albuquerque, N.M. Died Sep. 17, 1942.

TURNAGE, ALLEN HAL, marine corps officer; b. Farmville, N.C., Jan. 3, 1891; s. William J. and Ora (Smith) T.; ed. Homer Mil. Sch., Oxford, N.C.; hon. LL.D., U. of N.C., 1946; m. Hannah Pyke Torrey, July 21, 1920. Commd. 2d lt., Marine Corps, 1913; promoted through grades to lt. gen.; comd. 3d Marine Div., July 1943-Sept. 1944; dir. personnel and asst. comdt. U.S.M.C., 1944-46. Decorated Navy Cross, Navy D.S.M., Navy Legion of Merit, Haitian D.S.M., Nicaraguan D.S.M., Medal of Merit, Santo Domingo. Mem. Sigma Nu. Home: Wide Water VA Died Oct. 22, 1971.

TURNBULL, ANDREW WINCHESTER, author, educator; b. Balt., Feb. 2, 1921; s. Bayard and Margaret Carroll (Jones) T.; A.B. with high honors, Princeton, 1942; M.A., Harvard, 1947, Ph.D. in European History, 1954; m. Joanne Tudhope Johnson, Dec. 18, 1954; children—Joanne Tudhope, Frances Litchfield. Clk., ECA, Paris, 1951-52; instr. humanities Mass. Inst. Tech., 1954-58; free-lance writer, 1958-67; Fulbright lectr. Am. lit. U. Bordeaux (France), 1967-68; vis. prof. Brandeis U., also Trinity Coll., Hartford, Conn., 1969, Brown U., 1969-70. Served to lt. USNR, 1942-46, Guggenheim fellow, 1964-65. Presbyn. Author: Scott Fitzgerald, 1962; Thomas Wolfe, 1968. Editor: Letters of F. Scott Fitzgerald, 1963. Address: Cambridge MA Died Jan. 10, 1970; buried Gtencoe MD

TURNBULL, J(OHN) GORDON engr.; b. San Francisco, Nov. 8, 1891; s. Alexander and Margaret (Noakes) T.; specialized tng. engring. U. Louvain, 1907-10; m. Susan Aycock, 1938; children—John Gordon, Alexander, Susan Gay. Draftsman, San Francisco, 1911-13; engr., Portland, Ore., 1913-15; partner W. A. Kramer Co., Portland, and co-adventurer Hans Pederson Co., Seattle, constn. Nisqually Dam, Tacoma Power Plant and transmission lines, Lake Washington Canal Locks, 1915-17; cons. archtl., indsl. engr. for Ford, G.M., Paige, Dodge, Hudson & Packard Motor cos., Curtis-Wright, Chance-Vought Airplane cos., Pratt-Whitney Engine Co., and others, 1918-37; cons. engr. G.M. Corp. (Detroit Diesel, Allison Engine, Electro-Motive plants), 1938-41; pres., chmn. bd., chief cons. J. Gordon Turnbull, Inc., 1941-—, designing and supervising constrn. synthetic rubber plants including, Rubber Res Corp.; tire plants including, Goodyear, U.S. Rubber, Kelly Springfield; aircraft plants including, N.A. Aviation, Lockheed, Goodyear); aluminum reduction and extrusion plants including, Reynolds Metals Co.; def. installations including, Canol Project comprising airfields, highways, pipelines, refineries and dockage: airfields at Ferry Island Groups, Honolulu to New Guinea; master plans U.S.A.F. bases, U.S.A., Eng., and Japan; and other engring. projects for U.S. C.E., AEC, Air Force; headed spl. engring. mission to Europe for U.S. State Dept., Army, Navy and Air Force, 1948. Mem. Am. Soc. C.E. Clubs: Rainier (Seattle); Union (Cleve.). Home: 11499 Bellagio Rd., Los Angeles. Died Apr. 1, 1953; buried Glen Haven Meml. Park, San Fernando, Cal.

TURNBULL, WILLIAM army officer, engr.; b. Phila., 1800; s. William and Mary (Nisbet) T.; grad. U.S. Mil. Acad., 1819; m. Jane Graham Ramsay, 1826, 10 children, including Charles N. Commd. 2d lt. on topog. duty Corps Arty., U.S. Army, 1819-31, 1st lt., 1823; capt. Topog. Engrs. on survey of railroad route in Miss., 1831-32; assigned to constrn. of Potomac Aqueduct across Potomac River at Georgetown, D.C., 1832-43 (one of 1st important Am. engring. works); published Report on the Construction of the Piers of the Aqueduct of the Alexandria Canal across the Potomac River at Georgetown, District of Columbia, 1836, 2d report, 1838; chief topog. engr. on staff of Gen. Winfield Scott, participated in operations from siege of Vera Cruz to capture of Mexico City; brevetted lt. col. for services in battle of Contreras, Churubusco, col. for Battle of Chapultepec; superintending engr. of constrn. custom house, New Orleans, 1848-49; surveyed Whales Back Rock, Portsmouth, N.H. (for a lighthouse site), examined practicability of bridging Susquehanna River at Havre de Grace, 1850-52; mem. bd. to examine feasibility of additional canal around the Falls of the Ohio, 1853-56; engaged in lighthouse constrn., Oswego, N.Y., 1853-55. Died Dec. 9, 1857.

TURNER, CHARLES EDWARD mayor; b. Richardson, Tex., Sept. 13, 1886; s. John Edward and Mary Elizabeth (Heffington) T.; grad. Oak Cliff High Sch., Dallas, 1904; m. Valine Leachman Oct. 28, 1920; 1 dau., Betty. In cattle business 1905-06; in wholesale drug bus., Dallas, 1911-14, real estate bus., 1914-17; pres. firm Chas. E. Turner & Co., Inc., 1919-—; city plan commr., Dallas, 1925-29; mayor of Dallas, 1932-35; pres. Crown Hill Co.; dir. finance and comptroller Tex. Centennial Central Expn.; dir. Dallas Office & Club Bldg. Co.; mem. Advisory Bd. Rivers and Harbors Congress. Served as lt., later capt. inf., U.S.A., in France, World War I. Dir. Dallas Real Estate Bd. Democrat. Baptist. Scottish Rite Mason (33 deg.). Home: Dallas, Tex. Died Mar. 5, 1936.

TURNER, DANIEL naval officer; b. probably Richmond, S.I., N.Y., 1794; m. Catharine Bryan, May 23, 1837, at least 1 dau. Apptd. midshipman U.S. Navy, 1808; served in Constitution, 1809-11; ordered to take command of gunboats at Norwich, Conn., 1812; commd. lt., 1813; given command of Caledonia, participated in defeat of British at Battle of Lake Erie, victory over British, 1813, received silver medal from Congress, sword from N.Y.; commanded Scorpion, 1814, participated in capture of several Brit. vessels on Lake Huron, burning of the fort and barracks at St. Joseph, and attack on Mackinac; captured by enemy while in Scorpion; with frigate Java, 1815-17 cruiser Nonesuch, 1819-24; master comdt., 1825; cruised in West Indies, 1827-30, comdr. ship Erie; commd. capt., 1835; commanded Constitution in Pacific Squadron, 1838-41; commanded Brazil Squadron, 1843-46; comdt. Portsmouth Navy Yard, 1846-49. Died Phila., Feb. 4, 1850.

TURNER, FARRANT LEWIS govt. ofcl.; b. Hilo, Hawaii, July 16, 1895; s. Lewis Farrant and Jessie (Curtis) T.; B.S., Wesleyan U., Middletown, Conn., 1917, M.A. (hon.), 1947; m. Helen Van Inwegen, May 20, 1921; 1 son, Albert Farrant. With sugar plantation, Hawaii, 1919-22; v.p. Building Supply House, Honolulu, 1922-53; sec. Territory of Hawaii, 1953-58; branch manager Small Business Adminstrn., 1958-—. Served from 2d lt. to capt., U.S. Army, 1917-19; lt. col. AUS, 1940-44. Decorated Inf. Combat Badge, Medaille Militaire (Italy), Legion of Merit. Mem. Honolulu C. of C. (past pres.), Psi Upsilon Conglist. Rotarian. Home: 4644 Kolohala St. Office: Finance Factors Bldg., Honolulu. Died Mar. 19, 1959.

TURNER, FRED J. bus. exec.; b. Phila., Jan. 31, 1893; s. Fred and Agnes (Turner) T.; m. Grace Hengge, Dec. 25, 1918; children—Beverley, Fred J. Mgr. Carolinas, So. Bell Tel. & Tel. Co., Charlotte, N.C., later became gen. comml. mgr., has served as v.p., treas. and dir. So. Bell Tel. & Tel. Co., Atlanta, 1943-—. Served as 2d lt. U.S. Army, World War I. Ind. Democrat. Presbyn. Home: 3260 Peachtree St. Office: Hurt Bldg., Atlanta. Died Apr. 1967.

TURNER, GARDNER CLYDE, lawyer; b. Ludlow, Mass., Mar. 3, 1910; s. Clyde A. and G. (Estes) T.; A.B., Harvard, 1932, LL.B., 1935; hon. degree N.H. Sch. Accounting and Commerce; m. Virginia Wells, Aug. 16, 1941. Admitted to N.H. bar, 1937, U.S. Supreme Ct.; asso. pvt. law practice Philip H. Faulkner, Keen, N.H., 1937-43; pvt. practice, Keene, 1946-70; atty. gen. N.H., 1961, also newspaper columnist, polit. writer. Former gen. counsel U.S. Senate Appropriations Com. Investigations Staff; counsel to minority U.S. Senate Appropriations com., spl. asst. to Senator Styles Bridges; mem. N.H. Gen. Ct., 1947, 49-51 (chmn. judiciary com.; mem. rules com.; majority floor leader Ho. Reps.); chairman of the board of selectman Town of Sullivan, 1964-70; mem. N.H. Legislative Council. Past treas., co-owner Brentwood Products, Inc. Member adv. bd. registrants SSS, 1942-70. N.H. atty. War Manpower Commn., 1945; mem. Gov.'s Commn. for Reorgn. State Govt.; chmn. Interim Com. to Study Tax Exempt Property; chmn. exec. com. Cheshire County Legislative Conv.; del. N.H. Constl. Conv., 1948, mem. Bill of Rights Com. Mem. exec. com. N.H. Republican Com.; treas., finance chmn. Cheshire County Republican Com. Chmn. bd. trustees N.H. State Indsl. Sch. 1950-61; chmn. N.H. Bd. of Hosps., Instns. and Corrections, 1956-61; chmn. Gov's. Mental Health Survey Com., 1957-59; bd. dirs. N.H. Citizens Council Gen. Welfare, 1950-52; adv. bd. Spaulding Youth Center, Tilton, N.H.; adv. bd. New Eng. Coll. Served to lt. (j.g.) USNR, 1943-45. Mem. Harvard Alumni Assn., Harvard Law Sch. Alumni Assn., Monadnock Region Assn., Soc. Protection N.H. Forests, S.A.R., Atlantic Union, Am., Fed. N.H., Cheshire County bar assns., Farm Bur. Fedn., N.H. Maple Products Assn., N.H. Council of Towns (past dir.), Keene Jr. C. of C. (past v.p.). Episcopalian. Clubs: Harvard (Lowell, Mass.); Harvard of N.H. (Concord); Boothbay Harbor (Me.) Yacht; Sullivan Golf. Contbr. legal articles to trade jours., polit. feature stories to newspapers. Home: East Sullivan NH also Lowell MA Died Jan. 23, 1970; buried Lowell MA

TURNER, JOHN PICKETT educator; b. Cedar Hill, Tenn., May 5, 1876; s. Rev. William Allen and Mary Jane (Pickett) T.; prep. edn., Webb Sch., Bell Buckle, Tenn.; A.B., Vanderbilt U., 1900 (Class of 1901), fellow in classical philology, 1900-01, A.M., 1901; Ph.D., Columbia, 1910; m. Anna Maria Zemke, Sept. 4, 1907; children—Catharine Pickett (Mrs. Franklin R. Fort), John Pickett (lt. comdr. USNR 1941-45), Fennell Parrish (maj. M.C. AUS, 1941-45), Thomas Bedford (lt. (j.g.) USNR 1943-45). Instr. in various secondary schs., 1901-05; pres. Weatherford Coll., 1905-07; asst. prof. philosophy, Vanderbilt U., 1910-11; instr. philosophy Coll. City of N.Y., 1911, asst. prof., 1913, asso. prof., 1919-28, prof., 1928-30, acting head dept., 1920-21; prof. philosophy, head of dept. philosophy, psychology and anthropology, Bklyn. Coll., 1930-40, prof. philosophy, chmn. dept. philosophy and psychology, 1941-43, prof. philosophy, chmn. dept. 1943-45, emeritus 1946; lectr. U. Wyo., summer 1915, Adelphi Coll., 1918, Columbia, 1928. Established first psychol. lab. at Vanderbilt U., 1910. Served in S.A.T.C. during World War I; lecturing on War Aims. Fellow Inst. Am. Genealogy, A.A.A.S.; mem. Am. Philos. Assn., Am. Psychol. Assn., Am. Assn. U. Profs. (pres. chpt. 1930-32), Sigma Chi, Phi Beta Kappa, Phi Beta Kappa Alumni in N.Y. Club: Quill. Author: Idealistic Beginnings in England, 1910. Home: 430 W. 116th St., N.Y.C. 27. Died July 19, 1960; buried Mt. Hope Cemetery, Franklin, Tenn.

TURNER, JOHN WESLEY army officer; b. nr. Saratoga, N.Y., July 19, 1833; grad. U.S. Mil. Acad., 1855; m. Blanche Soulard, Sept. 18, 1869, several children. Commd. lt. U.S. Army, 1855, capt., 1861; chief commissary under Gen. David Hunter, 1861-62, under Gen. Benjamin F. Butler, New Orleans, 1862; chief commissary and later chief of staff Dept. of the South, 1863; took part in attack on Ft. Sumter, S.C., 1863; brevetted maj. U.S. Army, commd. brig. gen. U.S. Volunteers, 1863; commanded a div. under Gen. Butler in Va., 1864; brevetted lt. col. U.S. Army and maj. gen. Volunteers; chief of staff Army of the James, 1864-65; brevetted col., then brig. gen. and maj. gen. U.S. Army, 1865; commanded dist. of Henrico (including city of Richmond, Va.), 1865-66; resigned from army, 1871; pres. Bogey Lead Mining Co., St. Louis, 1872-77; commr. streets St. Louis, 1877-88; pres. St. Joseph Gas & Mfg. Co., St. Louis 1888-97; dir. Am. Exchange Bank, St. Louis, 1893-99, St. Louis Savs. & Safe Deposit Co. Died St. Louis, Apr. 8, 1899.

TURNER, LEWIS M. colleg dean; b. Heyworth, Ill., Sept. 7, 1898; s. Frank and Harriet (Cogswell) T.; student U. of Michigan, 1919-21; B.S., U. of Illinois, 1923, M.S., 1925; Ph.D., U. of Chicago, 1931; m. Eunice Josephine Brown, July 11, 1925; children—Frederick Brown, Lewis MacDonald. Teacher science, Heyworth (Ill.) High Sch., 1923-24; fellow, dept. botany, U. of Ill., 1924-25, U.S. Dept. Agr., summer 1925; head dept. biology, Blackburn Coll., 1925-29; teaching fellow U. of Chicago, 1929-31; asst. prof. forestry, U. of Arkansas, 1931-36; asso. conservationist, U.S. Forest Service, 1937-38, forester, 1938-39, sr. forester, 1939-43, asst. chief, div. forest influences, branch of research, 1941-43; dean College Forest Range and Wildlife Management, Utah State University, Logan, Utah, 1943-—; U.S. Operations Mission to Iran to establish Nat. Forestry School, 1954, 58. National Forester 1949-—. Served with U.S. Army, 1918-19; 2d lt., Organized Reserves, 1926-31. Fellow A.A.A.S.;

senior member Soc. Am. Foresters (chairman program com. national meeting, 1958); mem. Ecol. Soc. America, Bot. Society Am. Am. Assn. Univ. Profs., Am. Forestry Assn., Ill. and Utah acads. sciences, Kiwanis Internat., N.E.A., Am. Soc. Range Mgrs., Am. Council Forestry Sch. Execs., Am., Utah edn. assns., Sigma Xi, Phi Delta Kappa, Phi Kappa Phi, Xi Sigma Pi. Mason. Author: Articles, bulls. and booklets. Based on original research to sci. publs. Home: 228 N. 4th East St., Logan, Utah. Died Nov. 4, 1960.

TURNER, RICHMOND KELLY naval officer; b. Portland, Ore., May 27, 1885; s. Enoch and Laura Frances (Kelly) T.; grad. U.S. Naval Acad., 1908, Naval Ordnance, 1916, Naval Aviation Sch., 1927; m. Harriet Sterling, Aug. 3, 1910. Commd. ensign, U.S. Navy, June 5, 1910, advanced through grades to adm., May, 1945; naval aviator, 1927; comdr. Aircraft Squadron, Asiatic Fleet, 1928-29; chief planning div. Bur. Aeros., U.S. Navy, 1929-31; naval aviation adviser Am. delegation to Gen. Disarmament Conf., Geneva, 1931-32; exec. officer U.S.S. Saratoga, 1932-34; chief staff Aircraft Battle Force, 1934-35; Naval War Coll., 1935-38. Comdr. U.S.S. Stewart, 1913, U.S.S. Mervine, 1924-25, U.S.S. Jason, 1928-29, U.S.S. Astoria, 1938-40; dir. War Plans Div., Navy Dept., 1940-42; in command amphibious forces in Solomons, Gilbert and Marshall Islands, 1942-43, Mraianas, Iwo Jima and Okinawa, 1944-45, U.S. Naval Rep. to Mil. Staff Com., 1945-47; ret. 1947. Clubs: Army and Navy Country (Washington); New York Yacht; Monterey. Home: Monterey, Cal. Died Feb. 12, 1961; buried (Cal.) Peninsula Country; Manila (P.I.) Golf. Golden Gate Cemetery, San Bruno, Cal.

TURNER, ROSCOE, aviator; b. Corinth, Miss., Sept. 29, 1895; s. Robert Lee and Aquilla (Derryberry) T.; ed. pub. schs., business coll.; m. Carline Stovall, Sept. 29, 1924; m. 2d, Margaret Madonna Miller, Dec. 1946. Chmn. bd. Roscoe Turner Aero Corp.; cons. House Com. Science and Astronautics, 1960, 63, Barnstorming flyer and stunt performer, 1919-27; operated pioneer comml. air field, Richmond, Va., 1927-28; operated world's pioneer high speed air line, 1929-30; holder cross country speed records Nat. Air Races, as winner Bendix Race, 11 hrs. 30 mins. N.Y. to Los Angeles, 1933 (record still standing in 1938); Nat. Air Races as winner Thompson Trophy Race, 1934, 38, 39; finished 2d. Speed Div., Internat. Air Race from London to Melbourne, 1934. Awarded Harmon Trophy by Ligue Internationale des Aviateurs as America's premier aviator for 1932. Served Air Service. World War; disch. 1st lt., 1919. Decorated Distinguished Flying Cross, 1952; recipient Paul Tissandier Diploma, Federation Aeronautique Internationale, (Austria), 1956; Beechcraft Man of Year award, 1960; Spl. Recognition award Ind. Aviation Trades Assn., 1960; Silver Wings award, 1964; Distinguished Citizen award Ind. dept. Am. Legion, 1969; Distinguished Nat. Vets. award Combined Vets. Orgns., 1969; honored with Col. Roscoe Turner Day in City of Indpls., 1969; Roscoe Turner Musuem established in his honor. Formerly col. gov.'s staff of Nev. Nat. Guard, Miss. Nat. Guard, on staff gov. of Cal.; now colonel in Civil Air Patrol. Honorary mem. Los Angeles Police Dept.; Sheriff's Staff, Los Angeles; capt. Aero Police, St. Joseph, Mo.; C. of C. Pitts.; Jr. C. of C., Dayton, O.; New York Detective Endowment Assn. Mem. Quiet Birdmen, Nat. Aeronautic Assn., Racing Pilots Assn. of Nat. Aeronautic Assn., Ind. Soc. of Chgo., Nat. Pilots Assns., Conquistadores Del. Celo. Am. Legion, Ligue Internationale des Aviateurs, Texas Rangers, Ind., Indpls. chambers commerce, Civil Air Patrol, Civil Air Patrol Nat. Aerospace Edn. Assn., Am. Inst. Aeros. and Astronautics, Air Force Assn., Nat. Aviation Traders Assn., Nat. Defense Transp. Assn., Inst. Aero. Scis., Soc. Automotive Engrs., Sigma Alpha Tau, other orgns. Mason (Shriner); mem. Order Eastern Star. Clubs: Flying (Columbus, O.), Kiwanis (Cleve.); Lions (Anderson, S.C.). Home: Indianapolis IN Died June 23, 1970; interred Crown Hill Cemetary Mausoleum, Indianapolis IN

TURNER, SCOTT, mining; b. Lansing, Mich., July 31, 1880; s. James Munroe and Sophie Porter (Scott) T.; A.B., U. of Mich., 1902, D.Eng., 1930; B.S. and E.M., Mich. Coll. Mines, 1904, D.Eng., 1932; Sc.D., Colorado School of Mines, 1930; D.Sc., Kenyon Coll., 1940; m. Amy Prudden, June 25, 1919. Mining engr., Ida. and Ore., 1902, Ariz., 1904, Calif., Panama, Nev. and Colo., 1905; examining engr., Nev., 1906; mining engr., Ida., 1906; asso. editor Mining Scientific Press, 1907; mining engr., Alaska, Wash., 1908; mine geologist, Calif. and Pacific Coast, 1909-10; mine examiner, Europe, 1911; mine mgr., Norway and Spitzbergen, 1912-16; mining engr., Peru, Chile, Bolivia, 1916-17; cons. engr., Can., 1919-25; dir. U.S. Bur. Mines, 1926-34; v.p. and dir. various mining cos., consultant in mining. Mem. Nat. Research Council, tech. com. and Div. Fed. Relations; mem. Nuclear, orgn. and geophys. coms. of Internat. Geol. Congress; mem. research com. Engring. Foundation; Holmes Safety Assn. (past pres.); mem. Geol. Soc. of Am.; mem. Council and Bd., World Power Conf.; mem. tech. adv. com. Fed. Oil Conservation Bd., 1926-34. Sole U.S. del. to Empire Mining Congress, Can., 1928. Apptd. by Dept. of Justice as mem. U.S. Anaconda Smelter Smoke Commn., 1926; apptd. by sec. of state as U.S. del. to World Engring. Congress, Tokyo, 1929; to World Power Conf., Berlin, 1930; to Internat. Congress of Mining, Liege, Belgium, 1930; Apptd. by secy. of treas. to U.S. Assay Commission and other important Fed. posts. Past chmn. Nat. Interfrat. Conf.; chmn. Hoover Medal Bd. of Award; dir. Belgian-Am. Ednl. Foundation; mem. Nat. Technol. Adv. Com. apptd. by sec. of war. Recipient Hoover medal (engring.), 1957. Served as lieutenant (s.g.) USNRF, 1917-19. Mem. Am. Inst. Mining, Metall. and Petroleum Engrs. (past pres.), Am. Inst. of Cunsulting Engrs. (pres.), Mining and Metall. Soc. Am., Canadian Inst. Mining and Metallurgy, Lake Superior Mining Inst., hon. mem. Am. Zinc Inst., Coal Mining Inst. of Am., Am. Rifle Assn., S.A.R., Tau Beta Pi, Psi Upsilon (nat. pres.). Republican. Mason. Clubs: Leash; Hammonasset Fishing; Burning Tree, Chevy Chase, Cosmos, Met. (Washington); Round Hill, Milbrook Gun (pres.), Engineers, River Hills Fishing (Conn.); Turtle Lake (Mich.); University, Century Assn., Mining, Explorers; Camp Fire of Am.; Boone and Crockett; Preston Mountain Club, Incorporated, Verbank Hunting and Fishing, Economic, A.R.A. Assn. (New York). Home: Greenwich CT Died July 30, 1972; buried Mt. Hope Cemetery, Lansing MI

TURNER, WILLIAM HENRY commodore U.S.N.; b. Cincinnati, O., Jan. 28, 1848; s. Samuel and Rachel Sparks (Wiltsee) T.; unmarried. Grad. U.S. Naval Acad., 1869; commd. ensign, July 12, 1870; master, Apr. 12, 1872; lt., May 13, 1875; lt. comdr., May 16, 1897; comdr., Mar. 29, 1900; capt., May 6, 1905; commodore and retired, June 30, 1906. Served in N. and S. Atlantic squadrons, European, Asiatic, and N. and S. Pacific squadrons and several spl. cruises; served on shore duty at New York, Norfolk and Portsmouth navy yards; stationed at Washington, and U.S. Naval Acad. Home: Cincinnati, O. Died June 25, 1926.

TURNEY, PETER lawyer, gov.; b. Jasper, Marion County, Tenn., Sept. 22, 1827; s. Hopkins L. T. (U.S. Senator from Tenn.); ed. pub. and pvt. schs.; admitted to bar, 1848; practiced at Winchester, Tenn.; defeated for atty. gen., 1854; alternate elector, Breckinridge and Lane ticket, 1860; col. Turney's 1st Tenn. regt.; recommended for promotion, but failed to get it because of unfriendliness of Jefferson Davis; judge Supreme Ct. Tenn., 1870-93 (chief justice, Sept. 1886, to Jan. 1893); defeated for U.S. senator, 1876; gov. Tenn., 1893-97. Address: Winchester, Tenn. Died 1903.

TURNLEY, PARMENAS TAYLOR soldier, author; b. Dandridge, Tenn., Sept. 6, 1821; s. John Cunnyngham and Mahala (Taylor) T.; grad. West Point, 1846; joined Gen. Zachary Taylor's army, then on Rio Grande, beginning war against Mexico; served through Mexican war, and until 1852, locating and building mil. stas., along Rio Grande and Marking boundary line bet. Mexico and U.S.; on various duties and details until 1857; on Gen. Albert Sidney Johnston's Utah Expdn., 1857-61; had charge of bldg. mil. post 40 miles from Salt Lake; at work establishing army depots at Annapolis, Md., St. Louis, Cairo, Ill., Columbus, Ky., Memphis, Tenn., 1861-62. Disabled by chronic gastritis and retired by President Lincoln from service, Sept. 17, 1863, "for long and faithful service and disease contracted in line of duty." Resident of Highland Park, Ill., 1881-—, alderman and mayor. Author: Turnley's Narrative from Diary, 1893; "The Turnley's," 1905. Address: Highland Park, Ill. Died 1911.

TURPIN, C. MURRAY ex-congressman; b. Kingston, Pa., Mar. 4, 1878; grad. high sch., Kingston, and Wyoming Sem.; D.D.S., U. of Pa., 1904; m. Anna M. Manley, 1907 (died 1929); 4 children. Carpenter, grocery clk. and steamboat capt. before entering dental practice at Kingston; mem. Bd. of Edn., 6 yrs., burgess of Kingston 4 yrs., prothonotary of Luzerne County, Pa., 4 yrs.; elected to 71st Congress, 1929, to fill vacancy; reëlected to 72d to 74th Congresses (1933-37), 12th Pa. Dist. Corpl. Co. F, 9th Pa. Vol. Inf., Spanish-Am. War, later capt. Pa. N.G. Mem. Veteran Firemen's Assn., Jr; Order United Am. Mechanics, United Spanish War Vets., Westside Vets. Assn., Psi Omega, etc., also hon. life mem. various orgns. Republican. Clubs: Wyoming Valley Automobile, etc. Home: Kingston, Pa. Died June 4, 1946.

TUSKA, GUSTAVE ROBISHER cons. engr.; b. N.Y. City, July 15, 1869; s. Adolph and Elsie (Robisher) T.; B.Sc., Coll. City of N.Y., 1888, M.Sc., 1891; C.E., Sch. of Mines (Columbia), 1891; m. Isabel Pappenheim, Nov. 24, 1902. Asst. engr. Link Engring. Co., 1891-92; bridge engr., L.I. R.R. Co., 1892-93; lecturer on bridge design and masonry constrn., Columbia, 1893-97; resident engr., Knoxville, Cumberland Gap and Louisville R.R. Co., 1894-95; engr. to Health Dept., N.Y. City, 1894-96; resident engr. Central N.Y. and Western R.R., 1896; chief engr. Panama R.R. and superintending engr. Panama S.S. Co., 1896-99; pres. and chief engr. Am. Process Co., in charge constrn. plants handling waste products, 1899-1925; pres. and chief engr. Atlantic Constrn. Co., 1899-1907; lecturer on municipal engring., Columbia, 1915-17. Consultant on municipal engring. work, City of New York, St. Louis, Chicago, Buffalo, Washington, D.C., and water power plants, railroads and piers, N.H., Va., N.Y., etc.; pres. Internat. Engineering Corp., 1923-—. Maj. engrs. U.S.A., Sept. 24, 1917-July 28, 1919, at Camp Lee and Camp Humphrey's, Va., on staff of chief of engrs. U.S.A., and at office of Dir. Gen. Mil. Rys., Washington; lt. col. engrs., Res., U.S.A., 1923. Mem. steel com. War Industries Bd., Washington, 1918; mem. Mexican Com., U.S. Govt., 1919; del. 2d Pan-Am. Congress, Washington, 1920, to 3d Pan-Am. Congress, 1927. Fellow A.A.A.S.; mem. Nat. Inst. Social Sciences, Am. Acad. Polit. and Social Science; trustee Allied Patriotic Socs. Home: New York, N.Y. Died May 28, 1931.

TUTHILL, ALEXANDER MACKENZIE, surg.; b. S. Lebanon, N.Y., Sept. 22, 1871; s. William H. and Christina (Mackenzie) T.; grad. high sch., Los Angeles, Calif., 1890; M.D., U. of Southern Calif., 1895; m. May E. Heimann, Nov. 16, 1896; children—Dorothy Ila Lange, Christine Elizabeth Warbasse. Began practice at Los Angeles, 1895; chief surgeon Detroit Copper Co., Morenci, Ariz., 1903-16; state supt. pub. health of Ariz., 1921-22. Mem. Constl. Conv., Ariz., 1910. Enlisted as pvt. Troop D, N.G. Calif., 1896; capt. Troop A, N.G. Ariz., 1903-10; col. 1st Ariz. Inf., 1910-17; apptd. brig. gen. N.A., Aug. 5, 1917; served on Mexican border, 1916-17; assigned as commdr. 79th Inf. Brig., Camp Kearny; with A.E.F., Aug. 1918-Mar. 1919; later major gen. Nat. Guard Ariz., comdg. 45th Div. (Okla., Colo., N.M. and Ariz.); retired at age limit with rank maj. gen. Ariz. for life and detailed as sr. tactical comdr. and asst. adj. gen., now the adjutant gen. state dir. Selective Service. Mem. A.M.A.; fellow Am. Coll. Surgeons. Mason (32 deg., Shriner). Home: 2 Pasadena Av., Phoenix AZ

TUTT, CHARLES LEAMING investments; b. Colorado Springs, Colo., Jan. 9, 1889; s. Charles Leaming and Josephine (Thayer) T.; St. George's Sch., Newport, R.I., 1903, Thacher School, Ojai, California, 1906; LL.D. (honorary) Colorado College; married Eleanor Armit, Aug. 16, 1908 (now dec.); children—Charles Leaming, William Thayer, Russell Thayer, Josephine Thayer; m. 2d, Vesta Halliday Wood, Feb. 23, 1934; 1 son, John Wood Tutt. Pres. El Pomar Investment Co., El Pomar Found., Securities & Investments Corporation, Pikes Peak Auto Highway Co.; chmn. bd. First Nat. Bank, Colo. Springs, Broadmoor Hotel, Inc., Mt. Manitou Park & Incline Ry. Co., Pikes Peak Automobile Co., Manitou & Pikes Peak Ry. Co., Garden City Co.; director Holly Sugar Corporation, Holly Oil Co. Served as captain, U.S. Army, World War. Mem. Soc. of the Cincinnati, Newcomen Soc. N. Am. Rep. Episcopalian. Clubs: El Paso, Cooking, Cheyenne Mt. Country, Broadmoor Golf (Colo. Springs); Denver Club. Home: Cheyenne Mountain. Office: Broadmoor Hotel, Colorado Springs, Colo. Died Nov. 1, 1961; buried Evergreen Cemetery, Colorado Springs.

TUTTLE, W(ILLIAM) B(UCKHOUT), pub. service exec.; b. Austinburg, O., July 3, 1874; s. Albert H. and Kate (Seeley) T.; student U. of Va.; m. Leila House, 1898. Was student-instr. U. of Va.; asst. to supt. Consol. Gas Co. of N.J., 1896-97, supt., 1898-1902, gen. mgr., 1902-06; asst. to engr. Am. Light & Traction Co., N.Y. City, 1897-98; v.p. and gen. mgr. San Antonio (Tex.) Gas & Electric Co. and San Antonio Traction Co., 1906-16; v.p., gen. mgr. San Antonio Pub. Service Co., 1916-18, v.p., 1918-22, pres.; 1922-35; chmn. bd., 1935-42; chmn. City Pub. Service Bd., 1942-48; cons. engr. since 1948. Chmn., Alamo Soil Conservation Dist. No. 330, San Antonio River Canal and Conservancy Dist. Asso. mem. Naval Consulting Bd., Feb.-Sept. 1916; col. 2d Tex. Cav., Apr.-July 1918; maj. Constrn. Div., Q.M.C., U.S.A., July 1918-Mar. 1919; maj. Engr. O.R.C., 1921-23, lt. col., 1923-26, col. since 1926. Pres. emeritus Alamo Council Boy Scouts of Am. Mem. Am. Soc. M.E., Am. Inst. E.E., Soc. Am. Mil. Engrs., Res. Officers Assn. of U.S., Izaak Walton League America. Mason (Shriner). Clubs: Rotary, San Antonio Country; Army Navy Country, Army and Navy (Washington, D.C.). Home: 185 Terrell Rd. Office: 201 N. St. Mary's St.,2San Antonio TX

TWELLS, ROBERT business exec.; b. Independence, O., Mar. 11, 1895; s. Robert and Hepzibah (Greetham) T.; B.S., U. Ill., 1920; m. Margaret Proudfoot Shaw MacKillop, Sept. 17, 1921; children—Douglas Sinclair, Robert Greetham, John Lawrence, Richard Byron. With Gen. Electric Co., N.Y., 1920-21; ceramic div. Champion Spark Plug Co., Detroit, 1921-33; AC spark plug div. Gen. Motors Corp., Mich., 1933-35; mgr. spark plug div. Electric Auto Lite Co., Toledo, 1935-57, v.p., 1948-57, v.p., group exec. ceramic and spark plug group, 1957-64, (co. merger) now group exec. ceramic and Spark Plug Eltra Corp. First lt. F.A., World War I.; maj. Air Force Res., until 1948. Mem. Am. Ceramic Soc. (past pres.), Nat. Inst. Ceramic Engrs. (v.p.), Ohio Ceramic Industries Assn. (past pres.), Soc. Automotive Engrs., Am. Ordnance Assn., Wildcat (81st) Div. Assn., Brit. Ceramic Soc., Air Force Assn. Am. Legion, Sigma Tau, Tau Beta Pi, Keramos. Mason (32 deg., Shriner). Clubs: Rotary (past pres.), University, Country (Fostoria, O.). Author of articles in profl. jours. Home: 723 West Fremont St., Fostoria, O. Office: The Eltra Corp., P.O. Box 931, Toledo. Died Dec. 14, 1966.

TWIGGS, DAVID EMANUEL army officer; b. Richmond County, Ga., 1790; s. Gen. John and Ruth (Emanuel) T.; m. Elizabeth Hunter; m. 2d, Mrs. Hunt; 2 children. Commd. capt., inf. U.S. Army, 1812; served in War of 1812; commd. maj., 1814, commn. withdrawn at end of War, commd. maj. 1st U.S. Inf., 1825, lt. col.

4th U.S. Inf., 1831, col. 2d U.S. Dragoons, 1836; served in Mexican War; commd. brig. gen. U.S. Army, 1846, brevetted maj. gen. for bravery, 1846; recipient sword for services in Mexican War by vote of U.S. Congress, 1847; mil. gov. Veracruz (Mexico), 1847-48; in command Dept. of Tex., U.S. Army, 1861; a Southern sympathizer, surrendered his command to Confederacy, dismissed from U.S. Army; commd. maj. gen. Confederate Army, assigned to command Dist. of La., too old for active service. Died Augusta, Ga., Sept. 15, 1862; buried Twiggs Cemetery, nr. Augusta.

TWINING, NATHAN CROOK naval officer; b. Boscobel, Wis., Jan. 17, 1869; s. Nathan Crook and Mary Jane (Rennie) T.; grad. U.S. Naval Acad., 1889; m. Caroline Salisbury Baker, Apr. 5, 1899. Commd. ensign U.S.N., July 1, 1891; lt. jr. grade, Aug. 2, 1898; lt., Mar. 3, 1899; lt. comdr., July 1, 1905; comdr., July 1, 1910; capt. July 29, 1915; rear admiral (temp.), Apr. 14, 1920; rear admiral, permanent rank, June 3, 1921. Chief Bur. of Ordnance, with rank of rear admiral, June 7, 1911-Oct. 6, 1913, resigned; comdg. U.S.S. Tacoma, Oct. 18, 1913; attending Naval War Coll., July 26, 1915-Apr. 2, 1917; comdg. Squadron Two, Patrol Force, Atlantic Fleet, April 5, 1917-July 15, 1917; chief of staff to vice admiral comdg. U.S. naval forces in European waters, Aug. 1, 1917-Dec. 20, 1918; comd. U.S.S. Texas, Dec. 31, 1918-July 15, 1919; chief of staff to admiral comdg. Pacific Fleet, July 16, 1919-July 5, 1921; naval attaché, Am. Embassy, London, Aug. 27, 1921-Jan. 31, 1922. Retired Jan. 4, 1923, for physical disability incurred in service. Officer Legion of Honor; Officer Order of Leopold; Companion of the Bath. Mem. U.S. Naval Inst. Episcopalian. Home: Newport, R.I. Died July 4, 1924.

TWITTY, JOSEPH JONES army officer; b. Pelham, Ga., Nov. 24, 1894; B.S. in M.E., Ga. Sch. Tech., 1915; B.S., U.S. Mil. Acad., 1918; grad. Engr. Sch., basic course, 1921, civil engineering course, 1921; married DeLiesseline Durham Wells, February 3, 1934. Commd. 2d lt., U.S. Army, 1918, and advanced through grades to brig. gen., 1944 (ret.); observer, A.E.F., France, 1919; attaché Am. Embassy and lang. student, Tokyo, 1929-33; asst. div. engr. and sec. Miss. River Commn., 1933-34; asst. mil. attaché, Hongkong, China, Sept.-Oct. 1941; engineer mem. U.S. Military Mission to China, Oct.-Dec. 1941, mission rep. to Rangoon, Dec. 1941-Feb. 1942; successively asst. G-2 (intelligence), and G-1 (personnel), Hdqrs., Hawaiian Dept., 1942-43; Pacific Ocean Area, Sept. 1943; intelligence officer Cincpoa-Cincpac, P.H., 1943-45; comdg. gen., Jicpoa, 1943-45; mem. joint Army-Navy Reviewer Bd., ANSCOL, 1946; comdg. gen. 2 engr. spl. brigade Inchon, 1950, Port of Hungnam in evacuation X corps, Dec. 1950; resident engr. Palmer & Baker, 1954-—. Intelligence Inst., Nat. War Coll., Grad. NWC 1947, highest award DSM (Navy), 1946; LM-V (USMC), 1950; DSM (Army), 1952. Home: Covington, La. Office: care of Palmer & Baker, Mobile, Ala. Died 1959.

TWOMBLY, EDWARD BANCROFT, lawyer; b. Summit, N.J., Feb. 25, 1891; s. Henry Bancroft and Frances (Doane) T.; B.A., Yale, 1912; LL.B., Columbia Law, 1914; LL.D. (honorary), Temple University, 1958; married Mildred Hadra, Apr. 14, 1917; children—Doane, Gilmer and Edward B. Asso. with Putney, Twombly, Hall & Skidmore, 1914-69, partner 1919-66, senior partner, 1966-69. Troop C. 1st N.J. Cav., 1914-17; Mexican border service, 1916; commissioned first lieutenant cav. res., 1917; commd. capt., 1917; overseas with Co. B-304th Machine Gun Bn., 77th Div., 1918-19; received Silver Star; maj., inf. res., 1919; lieut. col., inf. res., 1922-37. Mayor, City of Summit, N.J., 1930-32; Common Council, 1922-30, pres., 1926-30; pres. Summit Rep. Club, 1932-38; pres., Organization Rep. Club of Union Co., N.J., 1935-38; chmn., Summit Defense Council, 1940-45; chmn., United Campaign, 1938; Chairman adv. com. National State Bank, Elizabeth, New Jersey, Summit, N.J. branch; director general counsel Distributors Group, Inc., Promenade Mags., v.p. general counsel member board and exec. com. Chemetals Corp., counsel Group Securities, Incorporated; gen. counsel, director Lobsitz Mills Company. Trustee Temple University; now honorary chmn. Berkshire Farm for Boys. Member of Assn. Bar N.Y.C., Am., New York State bar assns., S.A.R., Newcomen Soc. N.Am., English Speaking Union, Skull and Bones, Alpha Delta Phi. Presbyn. (elder). Clubs: Royal Bermuda Yacht; Short Hills, Balustrol Golf; Coral Beach (Bermuda), Down Town Assn. (N.Y.). Home: Short Hills NJ Died June 7, 1969; buried Fairmount Cemetery Chatham NJ

TYDINGS, MILLARD E. (ti'dingz), ex-senator; lawyer; b. Havre de Grace, Md., Apr. 6, 1890; s. Millard F. and Mary B. (O'Neill) T.; B.S. in M.E., Maryland Agricultural College 1910; LLB., University of Maryland, 1913; LL.D., Washington College, 1927; LL.D., St. John's College, 1935; m. Eleanor Davies, 1935; children—Joseph D., daughter (Mrs. J. Schapiro). Admitted to Md. bar, 1913, and began practice at Havre de Grace; mem. Md. Ho. of Del., 1916-17, speaker 1920-22, Senate, 1922; mem. 68th and 69th Congresses (1923-27), 2d Md. Dist.; elected mem. U.S. Senate 4 terms, 1927-51; chmn. Senate Armed Services Com.; mem. Senate Fgn. Relations Com. and Joint Com. on Atomic Energy; member of law firms Davies, Richberg, Tydings, Beebe and Landa, Washington, also Tydings & Rosenberg, Balt. Served as private on Mexican border, 1916; with A.E.F., as officer, advancing to lt. col. 29th Div., Machine Gun Units; participated in Haute-Alsace, Meuse-Argonne offensive. Awarded D.S.M., D.S.C., 3 citations. Mem. Commn. on State War Memorial Bldg., Md. Mem. Am. Legion, Vets. of Foreign Wars. Democrat. Episcopalian. Mason, Elk. Clubs: Maryland; Chevy Chase, Burning Tree, Metropolitan, Sulgrave (Washington). Co-author, Philippine Independence Bill; Rehabilitation Bill after World War II. Home: Oakington, Havre de Grace, Md. Died Feb. 9, 1961; buried Angel Hill Cemetery, Havre de Grace.

TYLER, CHARLES MELLEN clergyman; b. Limington, Me., Jan. 8, 1832; s. Daniel and Lavinia (Small) T.; A.B., Yale, 1855, A.M., 1890, D.D., 1892; Union Theol. Sem., 1855-56; m. Ellen A. Davis, 1857; m. 2d, Kate E. Stark (prof. music, Syracuse U.), 1892. Ordained Congl. ministry, 1857; pastor Galesburg, Ill., 1857-58, Natick, Mass., 1858-67, South Ch., Chicago, 1867-72, First Ch., Ithaca, N.Y., 1872-91; Sage prof. history and philosophy of religion and Christian ethics, 1891-1903, emeritus prof., 1903, Cornell. Mem. Mass. Ho. of Reps., 1861-62; city librarian Ithaca, and trustee of Cornell U., 1886-92, and, 1907-—. Capt. U.S. vols., 1864-65; served through Wilderness and Spottsylvania battles, and about Petersburg. Author: Life of Lt. George Wolcott, U.S.V.; Bases of Religious Belief, Historic and Ideal, 1892. Also of last chapter of Prof. Pfleiderer's Geschichte der Religious Philosophie (Berlin), and various articles in papers and mags. Address: Scranton, Pa. Died May 16, 1918.

TYLER, DANIEL army officer, industrialist; b. Brooklyn, Conn., Jan. 7, 1799; s. Daniel and Sarah (Edwards) Chaplin T.; grad. U.S. Mil. Acad., 1819; attended Arty. Sch., Metz, France, 1828; m. Emily Lee, May 23, 1832, at least 5 children, including Alfred. Went to France to study French mil. system, 1828; translated many French books on arty.; U.S. Army, 1819, supt. insps. of contract arms, 1832, resigned, 1834; pres. Norwich & Worcester R.R., Morris Canal & Banking Co., during 1840's; completed constrn. railroad from Macon to Atlanta (Ga.), 1844-45; comdr. 1st Conn. Regt., U.S. Volunteers, during Civil War, commd. brig. gen., 1861; participated in battles of Bull Run, Corinth, 1862; in command at battles of Md. Heights, also Harpers Ferry, 1863; organized (with Samuel Noble) Woodstock Iron Co. (after examining iron deposits in Eastern Ala.), 1872; pres. Mobile & Montgomery R.R. Died N.Y.C., Nov. 30, 1882; buried Anniston, Ala.

TYLER, FRANK EDWARDS lawyer; b. Clifton, Kan.; s. DeWitt Clinton and Mary Caroline (Edwards) T.; A.B., Kan. U., 1909; LL.B., Harvard, 1913; student Lincoln's Inn, London, Eng., 1920; LL.D., Park Coll., 1960; m. Helen Erma Bowman, Dec. 8, 1920; 1 son, Frank Bowman. Admitted to Mo. bar, since practiced in Kansas City; partner firm Dietrich, Tyler, Davis, Burrell & Dicus, 1930-—. Vice pres., dir. Burgner-Bowman-Matthews Lumber Co., Musserdavis Land Co.; dir. Havens Structural Steel Co. Trustee Robert A. Taft Meml. Found. Served to maj. U.S. Army, World War I. Mem. Am., Mo. bar assns., Kansas City (Mo.) Bar, Lawyers Assn. Kansas City (past pres.), Alpha Tau Omega. Presbyn. (elder). Clubs: Kansas City, Mission Hills Country (Kansas City, Mo.). Home: 1227 W. 66th St., Kansas City 13, Mo. Office: Dwight Bldg., Kansas City 5, Mo. Died Mar. 19, 1964.

TYLER, JOHN 10th Pres. U.S.; b. Greenway, Charles City County, Va., Mar. 29, 1790; s. Judge John and Mary (Armistead) T.; grad. Coll. William and Mary, 1807; m. Letitia Christian, Mar. 20, 1813; m. 2d, Julia Gardiner, June 26, 1844; 14 children including Robert. Admitted to bar, Charles City County, 1809; served as capt. co. of Richmond volunteers in War of 1812; mem. Va. Ho. of Dels., 1811-16, 23, 38; mem. Va. Exec. Council, 1815-16; mem. U.S. Ho. of Reps. (Democrat) from Va., 15th-16th congresses, 1817-21, mem. com. to report on Bank of U.S.; identified with William H. Crawford faction in election of 1824; gov. Va., 1825-26; mem. U.S. Senate from Va., 1827-36, opposed Pres. Andrew Jackson on constl. issues, resigned seat rather than support expunging censure of Jackson, 1836; vice pres. U.S., 1841, became 10th Pres. U.S. (upon death of William Henry Harrison), 1841-45, remained loyal to anti-nationalist views in bank question that created crisis between Pres. and Whig party, 1841, opposed measure to allow a Nat. Bank to establish branches in states without their previous consent, originated and recommended to Congress plan known as exchequer system for govt. funds, (Clay rejected this); reorganized navy; established depot for nautical charts and instruments (later became Nat. Observatory); ended Seminole War; upheld power of Pres. over cabinet (resulted in cabinet's resignation); negotiated the first trade treaty with China; enforced Monroe Doctrine in case of Tex. and Hawaiian Islands; greatest achievements: negotiation of Webster-Ashburn Treaty, 1842; annexation of Tex., 1845; chmn. Washington (D.C.) Peace Conv., Feb. 1861; mem. Va. Secession Conv. 1861, remained loyal to Va. when it seceded; mem. Provisional Congress of Confederacy, 1861; elected to Confederate Ho. of Reps., died before serving. Died Va., Jan. 18, 1862; buried Hollywood Cemetery, Richmond, Va.

TYLER, MASON WHITING lawyer; b. Amherst, Mass., June 17, 1840; s. Prof. William S. and Amelia Ogden (Whiting) T.; grad. Amherst, 1862; served 2d lt. to col. 37th Mass. vols., 1862-65; studied Columbian Coll. Law Sch., 1865-66; m. Eliza M. Schroeder, Dec. 29, 1869. Admitted to bar, Oct. 1866; student and clerk in office of Evarts, Southmayd and Choate, 1866-69; mem. law firm Tremain & Tyler, 1869-94, Tyler & Durand, 1894-1902; law firm of Tyler & Tyler, 1902-—. Pres. bd. directors Plainfield Public Library; mem. bd. trustees Amherst Coll. Home: Plainfield, N.J. Died 1907.

TYLER, ROBERT OGDEN army officer; b. Hunter, Md., Dec. 22, 1831; s. Frederick and Sophia (Sharp) T.; grad. U.S. Mil. Acad., 1853. Commd. 2d lt. 3d Arty., U.S. Army, 1853, 1st lt., 1856; mem. garrison at Ft. Columbus Recruiting Sta. (N.Y.) during Civil War; capt. Q.M. Dept. 1861; served at open supply depot, Alexandria, Va.; commd. col. 1st Conn. Heavy Arty.; participated in battles of Gaines Mill and Malvern Hill, 1862; commd. brig. gen. U.S. Volunteers, 1862; commanded arty, res. of 130 guns during Gettysburg campaign, helped to stop Pickett's charge; his arty. served as inf. throughout Wilderness campaign, 1864; participated in battles of Spotsylvania, Cold Harbor, 1864; brevetted maj. gen., 1865; mustered out of volunteer service, 1866; commd. lt. col. Q.M. Dept., U.S. Army; kept diary published posthumously as Memoirs of Brevet Major Robert Odgen Tyler, 1878. Died Boston, Dec. 1, 1874; buried Hartford, Conn.

TYNDALE, HECTOR mcht., army officer; b. Phila, Mar. 24, 1821; s. Robinson and Sarah (Thorne) T.; m. Julia Nowlen, Aug. 1842. Became partner (with Edward P. Mitchell) in glass importing bus., 1845; mem. 1st Republican Com. in Phila.; commd. maj. 28th Regt., Pa. Volunteers, 1861, served in 43 engagements during Civil War; commanded forces nr. Harper's Ferry, 1861; commd. lt. col., then brig. gen., 1862, served with Gen. Nathaniel Bank's Corps in Shenandoah Valley campaign in Battle of Chantilly and 2d Battle of Bull Run; served at battles of Antietam, Missionary Ridge; resigned, 1864, brevetted maj. gen., 1865; trustee of fund which provided univ. scholarships in physics, including Hector Tyndale scholarship at U. Pa. Died Phila., Mar. 19, 1880.

TYNDALL, ROBERT H. (tin'dal), mayor; born at Indianapolis, Indiana, May 2, 1877; son of William E. and Alice (Boyd) T.; student pub. schs.; married Hazel Dean Spellman, June 24, 1908; children—Ann, Samuel Spellman, Ruth. Formerly vice-pres. Fletcher Am. Nat. Bank, Indianapolis, Ind., also vice-pres. treas. Carl G. Fisher Co. and Subsidiaries, Miami Beach, Florida and Montauk Point, Long Island. Served with 27th Indiana Vols., Spanish-Am. War; col. comdg. 150th F.A., 42d (Rainbow) Div., U.S. Army, World War; commd. major gen. on return from France, and assigned to comd. 38th Nat. Guard Div.; comd. 38th Div. and camp comdr., Camp Shelby, Miss., Jan.-May 1941; retired, May 2, 1941; mayor Indianapolis, Ind., since Jan. 1, 1943; dir. Marion County Civilian Defense Council; dir. Marion County Red Cross. Past pres. Ind. S.A.R.; mem. Am. Legion (nat. treas. 1919-27). Decorated D.S.M. (U.S.); Croix de Guerre with two Palms, Comdr. Legion of Honor (French). Republican. Mason (33 deg.). Clubs: University, Columbia, Athletic, Woodstock, Traiders Point Hunt, Country (Indianapolis). Home: 2016 N. Meridian St. Office: City Hall, Indianapolis, Ind. Died July 9, 1947.

TYNER, GEORGE PARKER, army officer; b. Davenport, Ia., Apr. 26, 1876; s. Henry Richard and Katherine Ellen (Parker) T.; distinguished grad. Army Sch. of the Line, 1915, Army Staff Coll., 1916, Army War Coll., 1922, Field Arty. Sch. (advanced course), 1923; m. Louise Judson, Aug. 7, 1909. Served as capt. 1st Ill. Cav., Spanish-Am. War; 1st lt. 45th Inf. (Vols.), 1899; commd. 2d lt. Cav., U.S. Army, 1901, and promoted through grades to brig. gen., 1936; asst. chief of staff, 1937-40; served in Philippine Insurrection, 1899-1901. Cuban Occupation, 1901-02, on Mexican border, 1916; active duty in France, World War, 1918-19; retired, 1940. Awarded D.S.M.; Officer French Legion of Honor. Episcopalian. Address: 1718 Hoban Rd N.W., Washington

TYNG, EDWARD naval officer; b. Boston, 1683; s. Col. Edward and Miss (Clarke) T.; m. Elizabeth (Southack) Parnel, Jan. 8, 1725; m. 2d, Ann Waldo, Jan. 27, 1731; 7 children. Capt. of south and north batteries and fortifications, Boston, 1740; comdr. vessel Prince of Orange, 1740, cruised after Spanish privateers, chiefly off New Eng. coast, 1741-43; commodore of provincial fleet during King George's War, 1744, captured French privateer commanded by Capt. Delabroitz; in command of frigate Massachusetts, 1745; sr. officer Mass. Navy, participated in taking of the Vigilante, capture of Louisbourg and destruction of St. Ann. Died Boston, Sept. 8, 1755.

TYSON, JOHN AMBROSE, judge; b. Denmark, Tenn., Dec. 12, 1873; s. John A. and Elizabeth (Ewing) T.; B.S., Union U., Jackson, Tenn.; B.L., Cumberland

U., Lebanon, Tenn., 1898; m. Annabel Broadley, Dec. 29, 1908; 1 dau., Elizabeth Nell. Practiced law, Jackson, Tenn., 1898-1904, Greenwood, Miss., 1904-35 (with exception of 3 1/2 yrs.). Commd. maj., Judge Advocate General's Dept., Washington, D.C., 1918; lt. col., 1919, hon. discharge, 1919; served as chief counsel, Bd. Contract Adjustment, War Dept., 1919-21. Mem. Tenn. Legislature, 1903-05; chmn. Ways and Means Com. House of Reps. 1903-05; mem. Miss. Legislature, 1908-10; atty. Yazoo-Miss. Delta Levee Bd., 1923-35; mem. U.S. Bd. of Tax Appeals Dec. 1935-Oct. 1942; judge, Tax Court of U.S. since 1942. Mem. Nat. Press Club (asso.), Sigma Alpha Epsilon. Democrat. Episcopalian. Home: Washington DC Died Nov. 14, 1971; buried Arlington Nat. Cemetery, Arlington VA

TYSON, LAWRENCE DAVIS senator; b. Greenville, N.C., July 4, 1861; s. Richard Lawrence and Margaret Louise (Turnage) T.; grad. U.S. Mil. Acad., 1883; LL.B., U. of Tenn.; m. Bettie Humes McGhee, Feb. 10, 1886. 2d lt. 9th U.S. Inf., June 13, 1883; 1st lt., Oct. 15, 1889; prof. mil. science and tactics, U. of Tenn., 1891-95; admitted to bar, 1895; resigned from U.S.A., Apr. 15, 1896. Pres. Poplar Creek Coal & Iron Co., Lenoir City Co., E. Tenn. Coal & Iron Co.; v.p. Coal Creek Mining & Mfg. Co.; pres. and pub. Knoxville Sentinel Co. Apptd. by President McKinley col. 6th U.S. Vol. Inf., May 20, 1898; served in P.R., during Spanish-Am. War; mustered out Mar. 15, 1899; brig. gen. and insp. gen. on staff gov. of Tenn., 1902-06. Mem. Tenn. Ho. of Reps., 1903 (speaker of House); del. at large Dem. Nat. Conv., 1908; candidate for U.S. Senate before Gen. Assembly of Tenn., 1913, receiving 62 votes, 67 being necessary to elect; elected U.S. Senator for term, 1925-31. Commd. brig. gen. N.A., Aug. 5, 1917 and apptd. comdr. 59th Brigade, 30th Div.; comdr. brigade with British at Ypres and Lys Canal sector, later at breaking of Hindenburg line at Bellicourt and Nauroy in the Somme sector; discharged, Apr. 15, 1919. Awarded D.S.M. "for extraordinary conduct during the war." Episcopalian. Home: Knoxville, Tenn. Died Aug. 24, 1929.

TYSSOWSKI, JOHN (ti-sou'ske) business exec., engr.; b. Washington, Jan. 19, 1887; s. Thaddeus Matthew and Alice Walton (Green) T.; B.S., mining, U. Calif., 1908; m. Catherine Woodward, Oct. 9, 1915. Various positions in mining, 1908-14; asst. to gen. mgr., Childs Co., 1914-16, gen. mgr. and treas. Bennett Day Importing Co., 1922-28; pres. Copper Deoxidation Corp., 1928-38; dir. Woodward & Lothrop, dept. store, Washington, since 1919, v.p., 1942-46, chmn. exec. com., 1946-48, chmn. bd. dirs., 1948-57, chairman of the executive committee; 1957-—; farmer, Cobbler Mt. Farms, Delaplane, Virginia 1941-—. Mem. exec. com., v.p. Atlantic Rural Expostion, Richmond. Mem. board visitors, Va. Polytech. Inst. Served with Squadron A. Cav., Nat. Guard N.Y., on Mexican border, 1916-17; commd. capt. U.S. Army Res.; active duty 1917-19; discharged as lt. col.; col. U.S. Res. Corps; inactive status for phys. disability, 1941; now col. Hon. Reserve. Mem. Va. Hereford Breeders Assn., Inc. (past president), American Institute of Mining Metallurgical and Petroleum Engineers, also mem. Mining and Metal. Soc. Am., Phi Delta Theta, Tau Beta Pi. Author numerous tech. articles in tech. and live stock jours. Home: Cobbler Mt. Farms, Delaplane, Va. Office: Woodward & Lothrop, Washington 13. Died Nov. 24, 1960.

UBICO, JORGE (oo-bek'o). former pres. of Guatemala; b. Guatemala City, Nov. 10, 1878; s. Arturo and Matilde (Castaneda) U.; student Polytechnic School, Guatemala City, and Mil. Acad. of Guatemala. Entered Army service as an officer, 1897, becoming gen. of a div.; participated in mil. campaign against El Salvador, 1906; political chief and comdr. armed forces in Alta Veparaz, 1907-11; chief of sanitation of Pacific Coast region fighting yellow fever, 1918; became mem. war commn. of Nat. Assembly, minister of industry, chief of gen. staff and comdr. city's armed forces, 1920; became minister of war, 1931; candidate for pres. of Guatemala, 1922, 26; pres. as mem. Liberal Prog. party, Feb. 1931-44; while the Constitution prohibits presidential succession, he ordered a plebiscite to extend his term for a second 6-year period. Address: 6 A Avenida Norta No. 4, Guatemala.* Died June 14, 1946.

ULIO, JAMES ALEXANDER (u'li-o), army officer; b. Walla Walla, Wash., June 29, 1882; grad. Command and Gen. Staff Sch., 1921, Army War Coll., 1934; hon. degree, Villanova, 1943. Enlisted as private in Regular Army, 1900; commd. 2d lt. Inf., 1904, and advanced through the grades to brig. gen., 1939, major gen., 1942; served with 1st Inf., P.I., 1906-08, Vancouver Barracks, Wash., 1908-12, Hawaii, 1912-16; with 23d Inf. in U.S., 1917-18; asst. chief of staff for personnel, 35th Div., France, May-June 1918, for IV Corps, July-Nov. 1918; chief Statis. Div., Central Records Office, adjutant General's Office, A.E.F., 1918-19; asst. chief of staff for supply, Mission to Armenia, 1919-20; chief Administrative Div., Am. Red Cross, Athens, 1923; asst. to adjutant gen., 2d Corps Area, N.Y., 1924-26; in Adjutant General's Office, 1926-29, 1931-33, exec. officer, same, 1934-35; aide to comdg. gen. Hawaiian Dept., Honolulu, 1935; chief Service Command Sect., Hawaiian Dept., 1936, chief of staff, 1936-37; asst. adjutant gen., 2d Corps Area, N.Y., 1938; exec. officer, Office of Adjutant Gen., 1938-39, asst. adjutant gen. (brig. gen.), 1939-42, adjutant gen. of the Army (major gen.), 1942-46; retired; v.p. Food Fair Stores, Inc., Phila., 1945-49. Awarded D.S.M., Oak Leaf Cluster (U.S.); Chevalier French Legion of Honor; Comdr. Order of Prince Danillo (Montenegro); Order of White Eagle with swords (Serbia); Knight Order of the Redeemer (Greece); Order of the Crown (Italy); Abdon Calderon, 1st class (Ecuador); La Salidaridad (Panama). Address: The Adjutant General, Dept. of the Army, Washington. Died July 30, 1958; buried Arlington Nat. Cemetery.

ULLMAN, JAMES RAMSEY, author; b. New York, N.Y., Nov. 24, 1907; s. Alexander F. and Eunice (Ramsey) U.; student Phillips Acad., Andover, Mass., 1922-25; B.A., Princeton U., 1929; m. Ruth Fishman, June 27, 1930; children—James Ramsey, William A.; married 2d, Elaine Luria, January 25, 1946; married third, Marian McCown, March 18, 1961. Newspaper reporter, and feature writer, 1929-33; playwright, 1930-35; theatrical producer, 1933-37 (produced 10 Plays on Broadway); co-producer; Mem in White (Pulitzer prize play), 1934; exec. Fed. Theater Project, N.Y. and Calif., 1937-39; free lance writer, 1939-71; partner, editor-at-large Caribbean Beachcomber; 1st lt. Am. Field Service, with Brit. 8th Army, 1942-43; awarded Africa Star. Mem. Am. Mt. Everest Expedition, 1963. Bd. dirs. MacDowell Colony, Peterborough, N.H. Author: Mad Shelley, 1930; Is Nothing Sacred, 1934; The Other Side of the Mountain, 1938; High Conquest, 1941; The White Tower, 1945; River of the Sun, 1951; Windom's Way, 1952; The Island of the Blue Macaws, 1953; The Sands of Karakorum, 1953; Banner in the Sky, 1954; The Age of Mountaineering, 1954; Tiger of the Snows (with Tenzing Norgay), 1955; The Day on Fire, 1958; Down the Colorado with Major Powell; Fia Fia, 1962; Where The Bong Tree Grows, 1963; Americans on Everest, 1964; Straight Up, 1967; (with Al Dinhofer) Caribbean Here and Now, 1968, rev. biannually; And Not to Yield, 1970. Editor: Kingdom of Adventure; Everest 1947. Clubs: Explorers; Nassau (Princeton), Princeton; American Alpine, P.E.N., Overseas Press. Contbr. stories and articles to various mags. Home: Boston MA Died June 20, 1971.

UNCAS Indian chief; b. 1588; s. Oweneco and Meekunump; married twice, at least 3 children. Rebelled against Sassacus (chief sachem of Pequot Indians), defeated and banished, circa 1630; allowed to return, rebelled again causing split in Pequot tribe; followers of Uncas became known as Mohegans; joined English settlers of Mass., Conn. and Narragansett Indians in war against Pequots, 1637; signed peace treaty with English and Narragansetts, Hartford, Conn., 1638; at war with Narragansetts, 1643-45; made uprovoked war of Massasoit, 1661; forced by English to give up captives, stolen goods; forced to surrender arms to English at Boston to prevent him from participating in King Philip's War, 1675. Died 1683.

UNCLES, JOHN FRANCIS army officer; b. Chillicothe, Mo., Sept. 18, 1898; s. Henry Lockwood and Margaret (Glennon) U.; B.S., U.S. Mil. Acad., 1922; grad. F.A. Sch., 1927, Command and Gen. Staff Sch., 1938; m. Elizabeth Banks, Aug. 26, 1926; 1 dau., Margaret (Mrs. Brunside E. Huffman, Jr.). Pvt. 129 F.A., 35th Div., A.E.F., World War I; commd. 2d lt. F.A., U.S. Army, 1922, advanced through grades to lt. gen., 1956; instr. F.A. Sch., 1928-30, 38-40, U.S. Mil. Acad., 1930-34; with office chief F.A., 1940-42; comdr. 34th F.A. Brigade, ETO, World War II; chief staff U.S. Constabulary, Germany, 1948-50; comdr. 4th Inf. Div. Arty., 1950-51; dep. asst. chief staff G-4, Army Gen. Staff, 1952-54; chief of Research and Development, 1953-54; chief staff U.S. Army, Europe, 1954-56; comdg. gen. VII corps. Germany, 1956-58, ret., 1958. Decorated D.S.M. with oak leaf cluster, Legion of Merit, Bronze Star Medal. Address: 4000 Cathedral Av. N.W., Washington 20016. Died Jan. 20, 1967; buried Arlington Nat. Cemetery.

UNDERWOOD, BERT ELIAS publisher of photographs; b. Oxford, Ill., Apr. 29, 1862; s. Rev. Elias and Lavina (Elmer) U.; ed. Ottawa (Kan.) U.; m. Susan Stannard, Dec. 1, 1887; children—Elmer Roy, Esther Lael (Mrs. Charles Evans, Jr.), Robert Stannard. Began selling stereoscopic photographs in Kan., 1882, forming partnership (with brother) of Underwood & Underwood (later incoporated); activities extended to Pacific Coast states, 1884; office opened in Baltimore, 1886, later in Toronto, New York, Chicago, also in many countries of Europe and Asia; began selling pictures with news interest to periodicals, 1896, with photographs and articles descriptive of Greco-Turkish War for Illustrated London News and Harpers Weekly; was the only photographer to take picture of Edward VII and Queen Alexandria wearing coronation crowns and robes; made trips into many parts of the world to develop picture "tours," sets of photographs with descriptions in book form; pres. Underwood & Underwood (from time of incorpn.) until retirement in 1925, now dir.; dir. El Encanto Estates, Inc. Del. Nat. Progressive Conv., Chicago. 1912, 16; mem. of Mayor's Com. of Welcome to City of New York to returning soldiers, 1918-19. Served as maj. Signal Corps, U.S. Army, and comdg. officer of photographic div., during World War. Commr. Gen. Assembly. Presbyn. Ch. 1936. Mem. Am. Legion, S.A.R. (former nat. trustee; state chaplain), Hiram Internat. Ind. Republican. Presbyn. (mem. Nat. Missions Bd. Presbyn. Ch.). Mason. Clubs: Lake Placid (N.Y.); Canoebrook Country (Summit, N.J.). Author: A Stereograph Record of William McKinley, 1901. Home: El Encanto Estates, Tucson, Ariz. Died Dec. 28, 1943.

UNDERWOOD, JOHN COX engr.; b. Georgetown, D.C., Sept. 12, 1840; s. Judge Joseph Rogers (of Ky.) and Elizabeth Threlkeld (Cox) U.; C.E., Rensselaer Poly. Inst., Troy, N.Y., 1862; hon. A.M., Center Coll., Ky., 1876; m. Drue A. Duncan, May 16, 1867. Officer in C.S.A., Civil War, reaching rank of lt. col.; prisoner in Fort Warren nearly a year; mayor of Bowling Green, Ky., 1870-72; city, county and cons. state engr., 1866-75; lt. gov. of Ky., 1875-79. Conservative Democrat. Grand Sire and Generalissimo, I.O.O.F. of World, 1888-90; lt. gen. Patriarchs Militant, 1885-93; maj. gen. United Confederate Vets., and erected monument over Confederate dead at Chicago, 1891-95. Chronol. and geneal. historian. Address: Covington, Ky. Died Oct. 26, 1913.

UNDERWOOD, OSCAR WILDER JR. lawyer; b. Birmingham, Ala., July 27, 1890; s. Senator Oscar Wilder and Eugenia (Massie) U.; student Richmond (Va.) Coll., 1906-09; B.L., U. Va., 1913; m. Ellen Pratt, Apr. 18, 1917 (dec. Jan. 1957); children—Oscar Wilder, Ellen Pratt (Mrs. Jason I. Eckford, Jr.), Virginia Merrill (Mrs. Paul Barringer II). Began as law clerk in office of Donald Harper, Paris, France, 1913; partner Thach & Underwood, Birmingham, 1915-16; jr. partner Covington, Burling & Rublee, Washington, 1919-26; partner Underwood & Kilpatrick, Washington, 1926-36, Underwood, Mills & Kilpatrick, Washington, 1936-40; commr. for U.S., Gen. Claims Commn. U.S. and Mexico, 1934-37. Prof. law sch. U. Va., 1940-50; retired; now engaged in legal and other studies. Mem. Va. bar. Served on Mexican Border and in 42d Div., A.E.F., in grades from pvt. to capt.; wounded 1918. Decorated Mil. Order Purple Heart. Mem. Am. Bar Assn., Phi Kappa Sigma, Sigma Delta Chi. Episcopalian. Clubs: Metropolitan (Washington); Farmington Country (Charlottesville, Va.); Commonwealth (Richmond, Va.). Home: 1801 Westview Rd., Charlottesville, Va. Died Nov. 11, 1962.

UNGERLEIDER, SAMUEL, JR., pulp and paper co. exec.; b. Columbus, O., Apr. 28, 1917; s. Samuel and Selma (Dallet) U.; A.B., Brown U., 1939; m. Joy Gottesman, Dec. 2, 1945; children—Peter, Steven, Jeane, Andrew. With Central Nat. Corp., 1956, v.p., dir., 1957-73; with Gottesman & Co., N.Y.C., 1956-73, v.p., dir., 1958-73; dir. Ungerleider Motors Co. Pres., trustee 92d St. YM-YWHA. Served from pvt. to capt., AUS, AUS, World War II. Clubs: Nat. Press (Washington); Brown University (N.Y.C.); Beach Point Yacht (Mamaroneck, N.Y.). Home: Larchmont NY Died 1973.

UNTERMYER, ALVIN lawyer; b. New York, N.Y., Dec. 1, 1882; s. Samuel and Minnie (Carl) U.; A.B., Princeton, 1904; student Columbia Law Sch., 1905, N.Y. Law Sch., 1906; m. Kate Willis Schall, Nov. 22, 1923 (dec.). Admitted to N.Y. bar, 1906, and began practice at N.Y.C., with Guggenheimer & Untermyer and predecessor firm, partner, 1907-54, now also as counsel; dir. Publication Corp.; past dir. Bethlehem Steel Corp., Sinclair Oil Corp., Crowell-Collier Pub. Co. Pres., dir., chmn. finance com. Andrew Freedman Home. Served as capt. F.A., U.S. Army, World War I. Office: 80 Pine St., N.Y.C. 5. Died Sept. 19, 1963.

UPHAM, FRANCIS B(OURNE) JR. lawyer; b. Bklyn., May 29, 1894; s. Francis Bourne and Fannie Eleanor (Williamson) U.; A.B., Wesleyan U., Middletown, Conn., 1915; LL.B., N.Y. Law Sch., 1917; m. Pamela Hayward, Sept. 9, 1922; children—Francis Bourne III, Hayward. Admitted to N.Y. bar, 1922; gen. practice law, 1922-29; asst. v.p. Central Hanover Bank & Trust Co. (now The Hanover Bank), N.Y.C. 1930; gen. practice of law with Upham, Blasi & Drews and successor firms, now Upham & Meeker, N.Y.C., 1930-—. Trustee Wesleyan U., 1939-—. Served from 1st lt. to capt., inf., U.S. Army, 1917-18. Mem. Am., Westchester County bar assns., Assn. Bar City N.Y., Phi Nu Theta. Republican. Methodist. Mason. Clubs: University, Cloud (N.Y.C.); Apawamis, Shenorock Shore (Rye, N.Y.). Home: 721 Stuart Av., Mamaroneck, N.Y. 10543. Office: 405 Lexington Av., N.Y.C. 17. Died Aug. 17, 1962; buried Chilmark Cemetery, Martha's Vineyard, Mass.

UPHAM, FRANK BROOKS rear admiral; b. Ariz., Sept. 7, 1872; grad. U.S. Naval Acad., 1893. Promoted through grades in U.S.N. to rear adm., June 2, 1927; comdr. Control Force, 1928-30; chief Bur. of Navigation, 1930-33; admiral, comdr. in chief, Asiatic Fleet, 1933-36; chmn. Gen. Bd., Navy Dept., 1936; retired as rear admiral. Awarded Navy Cross; Letter of Commendation War Dept. Address: Washington, D.C. Died Sept. 15, 1939.

UPSHUR, JOHN HENRY rear admiral U.S.N.; b. Northampton County, Va., Dec. 5, 1823; s. John Nottingham and Elizabeth (Parker) U.; student William and Mary Coll.; grad. U.S. Naval Acad., 1848, having previously served on various naval vessels in the Mediterranean, Brazil, and Gulf of Mexico; present at siege and capture of Vera Cruze; promoted master, 1855; lt., Sept. 1855; served with Perry expdn. in opening Japan to Commerce; flag lt. of African Squadron, 1857-59; instr. at Naval Acad. when Civil War began; served 2 yrs. in N. Atlantic Squadron during war; present at capture of Fort Hatteras and Port Royal, S.C., and in minor actions and expdns. on the coast; commd. lt. comdr., July 16, 1862; comd. flagship in N. Atlantic Fleet, 1864; present in actions with and final capture of Fort Fisher, Jan. 1865; commd. comdr., July 25, 1866; capt., Jan. 31, 1872; commodore, July 1880; rear admiral, Oct. 1884. Comd. flagship, Pacific Squadron, 1872-73, flagship S. Atlantic Squadron, 1875-76, Navy Yard, New York, 1882-84; ordered to command naval forces in Pacific when promoted to rear admiral; in May 1885, retired at own application, after 44 yrs.' service. Address: Washington, D.C. Died May 30, 1917.

UPSHUR, WILLIAM PETERKIN (up'shûr), Marine Corps officer; b. Richmond, Va., Oct. 28, 1881; s. John Nottingham and Elizabeth Spencer (Peterkin) U.; grad. Va. Mil. Inst., 1902; law student U. of Va., 1902-03; grad. Command and Gen. Staff Sch., U.S. Army, 1925, Naval War Coll., 1932, Army War Coll., 1933; m. Lucy Taylor Munford, Dec. 20, 1904; 1 son, William Peterkin (died in infancy). Commd. 2d lt., U.S. Marine Corps, 1904, and advanced through the grades to maj. gen., Oct. 1, 1939; has served in nearly all Marine barracks within U.S. and with forces in Haiti, Cuba, Santo Domingo, China, France, Philippines, also on U.S.S., California, Maine, Kearsarge, Rainbow and Buffalo; Force Marine officer Battle Force, U.S. Fleet, 1929-31; service at Navy Department, Washington, D.C., in the office of the Major General, Commandant of the Marine Corps, and of the Chief of Naval Operations; dir. Marine Corps Reserve; became comdg. gen. Fleet Marine Force and Marine Corps Base, San Diego; now comdg. Marine Corps Dept. of the Pacific, San Francisco. Decorated Congl. Medal of Honor, 1915, Haitian Campaign, Cuban Campaign, Santo Domingo Campaign, Expeditionary medals, Victory medal with French clasp. Mem. Mil. Order Foreign Wars, Mil. Order of Carabao. Episcopalian. Clubs: Army and Navy, Army and Navy Country (Washington, D.C.); Aztec Club of 1847. Home: 1613 Grove Av., Richmond, Va. Address: care Headquarters U.S. Marine Corps, Washington, D.C. Died July 1943.

UPSTON, JOHN EDWIN air force ofcr.; b. Tawas City, Mich., Sept. 9, 1890; s. Marshall J. and Frederica (Smith) U.; grad. A.C. Tactical Sch., 1935, Command and Gen Staff Sch., 1937, Army War Coll., 1939; m. Claudia J. Smith, July 7, 1934; 1 son, John Edwin. Enlisted as aviation cadet, aviation sect. Signal Corps, 1917; commd. 2d lt., 1918; promoted through grades to brig. gen. Dec. 1942, to major gen. January, 1950; chief African and Middle Eastern Theater Unit, Operations Div.; dep. chief theatres group, operations div., War Dept. Gen. Staff, Mar. 1942-Feb. 1944; apptd. chief of African and Middle Eastern Theater Unit, Operators Div, War Dept. Gen. Staff, Mar. 1942; operations officer and chief of staff XX Bomber Command; overseas in China-Burma-India Theater, Mar. 1944-Feb. 1945; comdg. gen. 72d Fighter Wing, Mar.-Sept. 1945; assigned Hdqrs. Army Air Forces, Sept. 1945; staff duty Hq. A.F., Sept. 1945-Jan. 1948; apptd. comdg. gen. 4th Air Force, Jan. 1948. Awarded: Distinguished Service Medal; Air Medal; Legion of Merit; rated command pilot, combat observer, Mason (32 deg., Shriner). Clubs: Army and Navy Country (Arlington, Va.), Columbia Country (Chevy Chase, Md.); Army-Navy (Washington); Bohemian, St. Francis Yacht (San Francisco). Home: Sonoma, Cal. Address: Hamilton Air Force Base, Hamilton, Cal. Died Aug. 18, 1952; buried Presedio Nat. Cemetery. S.F.

UPTHEGROVE, FAY R(OSCOE) army officer, b. Port Allegany, Pa., Jan. 28, 1905; s. Frank Ellis and Cora Jane Upthegrove; B.S., U.S. Mil. Acad., 1927; grad. Air Corps Primary Flying Sch., 1928, Advanced Flying Sch., 1928, Tactical Sch., 1939; m. Marcella Gretchen Driscoll, Sept. 6, 1930; children—Sophie-Lou, Mary Jane. Commd. 2d lt., U.S. Army, 1927, advancing through the grades to brig. gen., 1944; served at domestic stations in U.S. and in Hawaii; rated command pilot, aerial navigator, sr. aircraft observer. Decorated Distinguished Service Medal, Silver Star, Distinguished Flying Cross with oak leaf cluster, Air Medal with 9 oak leaf clusters, Am. Defense and Am. Theater ribbons, African-European Theater Ribbon with 5 stars, Presidential Unit Citation. Home: 127 S. 12th St., Olean, N.Y. Died Oct. 22, 1946.

UPTON, EMORY army officer; b. Batavia, N.Y., Aug. 27, 1839; s. Daniel and Electra (Randall) U.; attended Oberlin Coll., 1855-56; grad. U.S. Mil. Acad., 1861; m. Emily Norwood Martin, Feb. 19, 1868. Commd. 2d lt. 4th Arty., U.S. Army, 1861, 1st lt., 5th Arty., 1861, also served in inf., cavalry, often cited for bravery; commd. brig. gen., 1864; brevetted maj. gen. U.S. Army during Civil War; mem. bd. to consider system mil. tactics U.S. Mil. Acad., 1867, comdt. of cadets, instr. arty., cavalry and inf. tactics, 1870-75; went on world trip to study foreign army orgns., 1875-77; wrote plan for Chinese Mil. Acad., 1876; supt. theoretical instrn. arty. sch. Ft. Monroe, Va., 1878-81; commanded 4th Arty. and Presidio of San Francisco; commited suicide because of an incurable disease. Author: A New System of Military Tactics, Double and Single Ranks, Adapted to Am. Topography and Improved Firearms, 1867; The Armies of Asia and Europe, 1878; The Military Policy of the U.S., published posthumously, 1904. Died Presidio of San Francisco, Mar. 15, 1881; buried Ft. Hill Cemetery, Auburn, N.Y.

UPTON, LA ROY SUNDERLAND army officer; b. Decatur, Mich., Oct. 8, 1869; s. Capt. John B. and Julia (Sherman) U.; grad. U.S. Mil. Acad., 1891; honor grad. Army Sch. of the Line, 1914; grad. Army Staff Coll., 1915; m. Agnes Millar, Sept. 4, 1902. Commd. 2d lt., June 12, 1891; promoted through grades to brig. gen. Nov. 5, 1923. Duty various posts in N.Y., 1892-98; recruiting service, Mich., 1898; with regt. at Montauk Pt., L.I., N.Y., 1898; collector customs, Tunas de Zaza and Manzanila, Cuba, 1899-1902; in Philippines, 1908; p.m. N.Y. City, 1911-12; duty Panama Canal, 1912-13, 1915-16, Fort Leavenworth, Kan., 1913-15, Eagle Pass, Tex., 1916-17; arrived in France, June 26, 1917; returned to U.S. May 14, 1919. Awarded D.S.C. "for extraordinary heroism" in action nr. Soissons, France, July 18-19, 1918; D.S.M. "for exceptionally meritorious and distinguished services" in trench sector South of Verdun, and in operations before Chateau Thierry; Croix de Guerre with three palms, on citations dated Oct. 25, 1918, and Mar. 28, 1919, Apr. 25, 1919; Italian War Cross for Merit "for gallantry shown and merit acquired for common cause" June 8, 1919; Companion of St. Michael and St. George, "in recognition of meritorious service rendered the Allied cause"; Officer Legion of Honor (French), May 5, 1919; La Solidaridad medal, 2d class, Panama, "in recognition of meritorious services rendered the Allies cause," 1919. Address: Washington, D.C. Died Mar. 1, 1927.

URELL, M(ICHAEL) EMMET soldier, War Dept. clerk; b. Henagh, Tipperary Co., Ireland, Nov. 8, 1844; s. James T. and Mary U.; came to U.S. in childhood; ed. New York pub. schs., 1854-61; m. Brooklyn, Isabel Helen Walton (died May 7, 1892). Enlisted 2d N.Y. State militia (82d N.Y. vols.), Apr. 17, 1861, engaged in battles Bull Run. Ball's Bluff, Fair Oaks, 7 days' battles Peninsular Campaign (1862); captured at battle Malvern Hill, July 2, 1862; at Antietam, Gettysburg, Bristoe Station, The Wilderness, etc.; at Bristoe Station severly wounded and left on field for dead, awarded Congressional medal of honor for conspicuous gallantry in this action; honorably discharged on account of wounds received in action; promoted through grades to 1st lt., and bvt. capt. and maj. for gallant and meritorious services at Fair Oaks, Bristoe Station and the Wilderness. In civic service of govt. since Aug., 1864. Maj. 1st battalion D.C. inf. U.S.V., war with Spain; took part in campaign in front of Santiago, and at surrender of Spanish army, July 17, 1898, and was commandant of guard of Spanish prisoners of war after surrender. Now col. 2d regt. Nat. Guard D.C., and comdr.-in-chief Nat. Army and Navy Spanish War Vets; mem. G.A.R. (past dept. comdr.); medal of Honor Legion; B.P.O. Elks (Past Ex. Ruler) and Home Club. Address: War Dept., Washington.

USHER, NATHANIEL REILLY naval officer; b. Vincennes, Ind., Apr. 7, 1855; s. Nathaniel and Pamela (Woolverton) U.; grad. U.S. Naval Acad., 1875; m. Anne Usher, July 29, 1891. Ensign, July 18, 1876; promoted through grades to rear adm., Sept. 14, 1911. Comd. Ericsson during Spanish-Am. War; with Gen. Bd., Navy Dept., 1903-04; Bur. of Navigation, 1904-06; comd. St. Louis, 1906-08; asst. to Bur. of Navigation, 1908-09; comd. Michigan, 1910-11; pres. Naval Examining and Retiring Boards, Washington, 1911-12; comd. 4th div., Atlantic Fleet, 1912, 2d div., 1912-13, 3d div., 1913; commandant Navy Yard, Norfolk, Va., 1913-14, Navy Yard, New York, 1914-18; apptd. comdt. 3d Naval Dist., 1914; retired Apr. 7, 1919. Home: Potsdam, N.Y. Died Jan. 8, 1931.

USINGER, ROBERT L(ESLIE), educator, entomologist; b. Ft. Bragg, Cal., Oct. 24, 1912 s. Henry Clay and Edith (Johnson) U.; B.S., U. Cal. at Berkeley, 1935, Ph.D., 1939; m. Martha Boone Putnam, June 24, 1938; children—Roberta Christine (Mrs. Ronald Manuto), Richard Putnam. With Bishop Museum, Honolulu, 1935-36, Cal. Acad. Scis., 1936-39; faculty U. Cal. at Berkeley, 1939-68, entomologist in expt. sta., 1953-68, prof. entomology, 1953-68, chmn. div. entomology and acarology, 1963-68. NIH spl. research fellow Brit. Mus. National History, 1948-49; chmn. Pacific sci. bd. NRC-Nat. Acad. Sci., 1961-63, participant bd.'s Coral Atoll study, Marshall Islands, 1950, Laysan expdn. 1961; chmn. biology div. Pacific Sci. Congress, Honolulu, 1961; mem. comite permanent Internat. Congresses Entomology and Internat. Union Biol. Scis., 1953-68; dir. Galapagos Internat. Sci. project, 1964; participant Congo expdn. Institut pour la Recherche Scientifique en Afrique centrale, 1959. Served to maj. sanitarian, USPHS, 1943-46. Decorated Gold medal King Frederick of Denmark, 1956; medal and award of merit Govt. of Ecuador, 1964; named hon. citizen Guayaquil, Ecuador, 1964. Fellow Royal Entomol. Soc. London, Linnean Soc. London; mem. Entomol. Soc. Am. (pres. 1966), Pacific Coast Entomol. Soc. (pres. 1952), Soc. Systematic Zoology (pres. 1967). Author: Elements of Zoology, 2d edit., 1961; General Zoology, 4th edit. 1965; Methods and Principles of Systematic Zoology, 1953; Classification of Aradidae, 1959; Aquatic Insects of California, 1956; Sierra Nevada Natural History, 1964; Life in Rivers and Streams, 1967; Autobiography of an Entomologist, 1972. Editor Pan-Pacific Entomologist, 1939-49. Home: Berkeley CA Died Oct. 1, 1968; buried Mountain View Cemetery, Oakland CA

UTERHART, HENRY AYRES (u ter-härt), lawyer; b. New York, N.Y., Jan. 5, 1875; s. Henry and Emma Jane (Ayres) U.; B.A., Columbia, 1894, M.A., LL.B., 1896; m. Josephine Stein, Apr. 27, 1903; 1 dau., Josephine H. Practiced at N.Y. City since 1896; counsel L.I. R.R. Co., many yrs.; counsel Commercial Cable Co.; counsel in many important cases. Served as capt. U.S. Army, A.E.F., 1918; mil. attaché to Italy, 1919. Mem. Assn. Bar City of New York, Am. and N.Y. State bar assns., N.Y. County Lawyers Assn., Nassau County Bar Assn. (pres.), Modern Lang. Assn. America, Am. Legion, Mil. Order World War, Theta Delta Chi. Republican. Episcopalian. Mason. Clubs: Lawyers, Republican, Columbia Univ., Piping Rock (New York); The Travellers, L'Etriel (Paris). Home: East Norwich, L.I. and 42 E. 51st St., New York. Office: 36 W. 44th St., New York. Died April 12, 1946; buried in Arlington National Cemetery.

VACHON, JOSEPH PETER (va'shon), army officer; b. Westbrook, Me., Jan. 23, 1887; enlisted in Regular Army and served as pvt., corp., and sergt., Coast Arty.; commd. 2d lt. Philippine Scouts, Feb. 9, 1912; 2d lt. Regular Army, Nov. 1916; m. Lola Ellen Playfair, Jan. 4, 1917 (died Aug. 23, 1948); children—Ross Peter, Patricia Mary Light; married 2d, Mintha Willette Shelton, August 10, 1949. Served through grades to colonel; apptd. brig. gen., Dec. 1941; duty with troops in Philippines, China, and Hawaii; instr. with Ill. Nat. Guard, Conn. Nat. Guard, and Organized Res. Dist., Englewood, N.J.; grad. advanced course, Inf. Sch.; grad. Command and Gen. Staff Schs.; to Philippines Nov. 1, 1941, and given command of 101st Div., Philippine Army, Mindanao, by Gen. MacArthur; organized Mindanao Force, Dec. 7, 1941; prisoner of war from May 10, 1942 (when Philippine Islands were surrendered) to Aug. 1945; retired as brig. gen., U.S. Army, Aug. 31, 1946. Awarded Distinguished Service Medal for exceptionally meritorious service; Silver Star for gallantry in action. Home: R.F.D. 2, Box 605, Central Point, Ore. Died Dec. 31, 1961; buried Presidio Nat. Cemetery, San Francisco.

VAIL, DERRICK TILTON, ophthalmologist; b. Cincinnati, O., May 15, 1898; s. Derrick Tilton and Della (Harriss) V.; A.B., Yale, 1919; M.D., Harvard, 1923; grad. study Oxford U., Eng., 1927; m; Elizabeth Yeiser, Aug. 30, 1921; children—Derrick Tilton, III (Royal Can; Air Force; killed in action, Feb. 22, 1942), David Jameson, Ann Elizabeth, Peter. Ophthalmic interne Mass. Eye and Ear Infirmary, Boston, 1923-24; instr. in ophthalmology, Coll. of Medicine, U. of Cincinnati, 1926-37, prof. of ophthalmology, 1937-45; dir. eye dept. Children's Hosp. and Cincinnati Gen. Hosp., 1937-45; prof. ophthalmology, head dept. Northwestern U. Med. Sch., 1945-66, prof. of ophthalmology emeritus, 1966-73. DeSchweinitz lecturer, 1945, Francis Proctor lecturer, 1947, Montgomery lecturer R.C.S. (Dublin, Ireland) 1952. Served in S.A.T.C., 1918; served as lt. col. to col., U.S. Army, 1942-45. Decorated Bronze Star, Legion of Merit (U.S.); Medaille de Reconnaisance (France); Officer Order Crown of Belgium. Mem. various civic health groups, former mem. council Nat. Institute Neurology & Blindness USPHS; vice president Ill. Soc. Prevention Blindness. Recipient Outstanding Contribution medal A.M.A. (sect. ophthalmology), 1956; Doyne lecture and medal Oxford Ophthalmological Congress (England), 1957; Leslie Dana gold medal, Nat. Soc. Prevention of Blind, 1959; Lucien Howe gold medal Am. Ophthal. Soc., 1960. Decorated Comdr. Knights St. John Jerusalem. Diplomate Am. Bd. Ophthalmology (dir. 1946-54, pres. 1954). Fellow A.C.S.; (2d v.p.); hon. mem. several fgn. profl. socs.; mem. Am. Ophthal. Soc. (pres. 1958-59), Internat. Council Ophthalmology (pres. 1962-66); member other nat., state and local profl. med. socs., past officer of several. Republican. Presbyn. Clubs: Literary, Commonwealth (Cincinnati); University, Commercial, Casino (Chgo.). Author: Truth About Your Eyes, 1950. Editor-in-chief, gen. mgr. emeritus American Jour. of Opthalmology; asso. editor Experta Medica, Ophthalmology; asso. editor Graduate Medicine. Editorial com. L'Annee Therapeutique en Ophthalmologie, Paris. Contbr. to med. jours. Home: Lake Bluff IL Died Apr. 24, 1973.

VALENTINE, EDWARD ROBINSON, bldg. co. exec.; b. Los Angeles, Jan. 23, 1908; s. William L. and Louise C. (Robinson) V.; A.B. Stanford, 1930; m. Mary C. Urmston, May 9, 1936 (dec.); married 2d. Carol Lapham Ophuls, Aug. 5, 1958. Vice pres., treas. Fullerton Oil Co. (Cal.), 1930-54; chmn., pres. J. W. Robinson Co., 1949-54; pres. dir. Robinson Bldg. Co., Los Angeles; dir., mem. exec. com. Security-First Nat. Bank Los Angeles; dir. Cal. Portland Cement Company, Associated Dry Goods Corp.; adv. bd. Am. Mutual Fund. Past chairman and campaign director of Los Angeles area Community Chest; past dir. Community Chest and Councils Am.; trustee Cal. Inst. Tech., chmn. bd., trustees Huntington Meml. Hosp. Served as comdr. USNR, 1942-45. Mem. Cal. C. of C. (past pres., past dir.), Automobile Club of Southern Cal. (dir. and past pres.). Republican. Club: Lincoln (past pres., dir.) (Los Angeles). Home: Santa Barbara CA Died July 21, 1968.

VALENTINE, LEWIS JOSEPH police commr. New York, N.Y.; b. Brooklyn, N.Y., Mar. 19, 1882; s. John and Elizabeth (Daly) V.; student Manual Training High Sch., Brooklyn, 1896-98; m. Elizabeth J. Donohue, Oct. 12, 1904 (died Aug. 18, 1910); children—Elizabeth (Mrs. Charles A. Locke), Edward Lewis (dec.), Dorothy G. (Mrs. William J. McBride, Jr.), Ruth J. (Mrs. William H. Cahill); m. 2d, Teresa A. Donohue, July 6, 1914; 1 dau., Miriam. With delivery dept., Abraham & Strauss Dept. Store, 1898-1903; patrolman, Police Dept., N.Y. City, 1903-13, successively sergt., lt. and capt., 1913-26, dep. inspector and inspector, 1926-28, dep. chief inspector, 1928-34, chief inspector, 1934; apptd. police commr. N.Y. City, Sept. 25, 1934; retired, Sept. 1945; commentator on radio program, Gang Busters, since Sept. 1945. Catholic. K.C. Home: 1650 68th St., Brooklyn, N.Y. Office: 240 Centre St., New York, N.Y. Died Dec. 16, 1946.

VALLEJO, MARIANO GUADALUPE army officer; b. Monterey, Cal., July 7, 1808; s. Ignacio and María Antonia (Lugo) V.; m. María Francisca Felipa Benicia Carrillo, Mar. 6, 1832, 13 to 17 children. Ensign in company at Presidio (now San Francisco), 1827; served against Estanislao Indian Rebellion, 1829; dep. to territorial congress, 1830; comdt. new garrison at Sonoma (Cal.), organized frontier defenses and controlled Indians; adminstr. of Solano mission; supported nephew Juan Bautista Alvarado in rebellion that led to proclamation "free state of California," 1836; comdr. of state forces, 1838; lived in Sonoma as semi-independent chief with Indian allies and Mexican troops devoted to his cause, 1836-46; powerful agent in securing submission of Cal. to U.S.; mem. Cal. Constl. Conv. of 1849; mem. 1st Cal. Senate. Died Sonoma, Jan. 18, 1890.

VALLIANT, LEROY BRANCH judge; b. Moulton, Ala., June 14, 1838; s. Denton Hurlock and Narcissa (Kilpatrick) V.; A.B., U. of Miss., 1856, LL.D., 1898; LL.B., Cumberland U., 1858; m. Theodosia T. Worthington, 1862. Capt. Co. I, 22d Miss. Regt., C.S.A.; moved from Miss. to St. Louis, 1874; judge Circuit Ct., City of St. Louis, 1886-98; asso. justice Supreme Ct. of Mo., 1898-—, becoming chief justice. Democrat. Grand Master of Masons of Mo., 1904-05. Address: St. Louis, Mo. Died Mar. 3, 1913.

VAN ANTWERP, EUGENE IGNATIUS civil engr., mayor; b. Detroit, July 26, 1889; s. Eugene Charles and Cecilia Mary (Renaud) Van A.; ed. U. Detroit; m. Mary Frances McDevitt, June 21, 1911; children—Mary Dolores, Pauline Annetta (Mrs. Robert Denton), Frances Lauretta (Mrs. Julius Aloysius Jaeger), Eugene Ignatius, Francis Joseph, Anthony Gore, Joan Cecilia (Mrs. John Francis Shannon, Jr.), Agnes Carolyn, George Bernard, Rita Dacia, Daniel Janse. Instr., Gonzaga Coll., Spokane, Wash., from 1910 to 1911; constrn. dept. Mich. Central R.R., 1912-13; engring. dept., Grand Trunk Ry., 1913-17, land and tax dept., 1919-26; chief engr. Nat. Survey Service, Detroit, 1926-28; private practice since 1928. Registered profl. engr. and land surveyor, State of Mich. Served as 1st lt. 16th Engrs., U.S. Army, 1917-18; with A.E.F.; capt. staff of chief engrs., Washington, 1918; capt. Engrs., Mich. N.G., 1919-24; maj. 310th Engrs., Reserve, 1924-36. Mem. City Council of Detroit, 1932-47, 50-62; mayor of Detroit, 1948-49; past chmn. Bd. Suprs., Wayne County, Mich.; past chmn. ways and means com. Detroit City Council; trustee Mich. Municipal League; first chmn. Detroit Met. Airport Authority. Mem. V.F.W. (comdr.-in-chief 1938-39; trustee Nat. Security Fund), S.A.R., Holland Soc. of N.Y., Am. Legion, D.A.V., Mil. Order of World War, Engring. Soc. Detroit, Am. Soc. C.E., Mich. Engring. Soc., Mich. Soc. Registered Land Surveyors; hon. pres. Canadian Corps Assn.; hon. mem. French Vets. of Mich. Democrat. Roman Catholic. Elk, K.C. (4 deg.), Knight of St. John (4 deg.), Knight of Equity; Ky. Col.; mem. Ancient Order Hibernians. Home: 16845 Muirland Av. Office: 103 City Hall, Detroit. Died Aug. 5, 1962; buried Holy Sepulchre Cemetery, Detroit.

VAN ARSDALE, NATHANIEL H. editor, clergyman, b. Bound Brook, N.J., Apr. 6, 1838; s. Elias Brown and Sarah (Layton) V.; A.B., Rutgers, 1862 (D.D., 1889); grad. New Brunswick Theol. Sem., 1867; m. Harriet Walton Hasbrouck, of Hill Falls, N.Y., Sept. 1, 1868. First lt. and acting adj. 1st N.J. Vols., Army of Potomac, 1861-64; ordained Reformed Ch. ministry, 1867; pastor Clove, N.Y., 1867-74, Chatham, 1874-80, Congl. Ch., Batavia, Ill., 1880-81, Paterson, N.J., 1881-95, Greenwood Heights, Brooklyn, 1899-1901, Athenia, N.J., 1901-09; on editorial staff Christian Intelligencer, 1882-1917. Mem. N.Y. Commandery Loyal Legion. Home: Clifton, N.J.

VAN AUKEN, WILBUR RICE naval officer; b. Utica, N.Y., Mar. 13, 1882; s. Myron W. and Caroline (Rice) Van Auken; B.S., M.S. U.S. Naval Acad., 1903; Naval War Coll., 1927; m. Pauline Thompson, June 16, 1909; 1 dau., Rosalie (wife of Comdr. Francis Blouin). Promoted through grades to captain, 1926; served as gunnery officer on Flagship Rhode Island (Mexican campaign, 1914) and later on Texas; in World War I, in charge fire control, Bureau Ordnance; naval ordnance observer on staff of Admiral W. S. Sims in Europe; command of Stribling in Mediterranean and Adriatic seas; head of Ordnance and Gunnery Dept. at U.S. Naval Acad., 1921-24; command of Aircraft Tender Aroostook, 1924-26; head Training Div., Bureau of Navigation, 1927-29; command of U.S.S. Vestal, 1929-31; staff of Naval War Coll., 1931-34; in command of Oklahoma, 1934-35; on Naval Examining Bd. Navy Dept., 1935-39; retired 1939; entered investment banking business, Washington, D.C.; returned to active duty (on leave from Merrill Lynch Pierce Fenner & Beane) as chief of naval personnel, Bur. of Ordnance, Navy Dept., Jan. 1941-Sept. 1945. Retired, inactive duty, Navy 1941-Sept. 1945. Retired, inactive duty, Navy Dept., since Sept. 1, 1945. Awarded Mexican Campaign Victory, Army Occupation of Austria, 1918, National Emergency medals; World War II medals and Commendation Ribbon, citation from Sec. of Navy. Mem. Naval Hist. Foundn., Naval Inst., National Geographic Soc., Herkimer Co. (N.Y.) Hist. Soc., Fairfield Sem. Alumni Assn. Former pres. Washington Philatelic Soc. Rep. Presbyterian. Mason. Clubs: Army and Navy, Country, Chevy Chase (Washington, Country); N.Y. Yacht Club. Former mem. Bd. of Control, Naval Inst.; former mem. bd. of mgrs., Navy Relief Soc.; mem. bd. dirs. Navy Mutual Aid Assn., since 1942; chmn. restoration com. Fairfield Coll. and Sem. Chapel. Author: (textbooks) Technical Ordnance; Gunnery and Strategy Textbooks for Navy, Revised "Naval Ordnance," 1942 Edition Encyclopedia Britannica; "Notes on Half Century of U.S. Naval Ordnance, 1939"; Top of the Hill (with Thomas O'Durell) 1953. Contributor articles on naval subjects to mags. Speaker in colls. and Navy training schs., during World War II. Home: Quebec House, 2800 Quebec St. N.W., Washington; Fairfield, Herkimer County, N.Y. Office: 815 15th St., Washington 5. Died Aug. 15, 1953; buried Arlington Nat. Cemetery.

VAN BEUREN, FREDERICK THEODORE JR. (van-bu'ren), surgeon; b. New York, N.Y., Feb. 10, 1876; s. Frederick T. and Elizabeth A. (Potter) Van B.; A.B., Yale, 1898; M.D., Coll. Phys. and Surg. (Columbia), 1902; m. Jessica T. Mohlman, May 26, 1906; children—Frederick T. III, Jessica, Michael M. II, John M. Asso. in anatomy, 1905-13, asso. in surgery, 1920, asst. professor, 1922, asso. prof. clin. surgery since 1929, asso. dean, 1921-34, Coll. of Physicians and Surgeons (Columbia); pres. Morristown (N.J.) Memorial Hosp. since 1933; asst. attending surgeon, Lincoln Hosp., 1910-13, Roosevelt Hosp., 1913-21; attending surgeon Volunteer Hosp., 1915-17, Sloan Hosp. for Women, 1920-38, asso. visiting surgeon Presbyn. Hosp. Mem. Squadron A., Nat. Guard N.Y., 1899-1910, resigned as capt.; 1st lt. M.R.C., U.S. Army, 1910-18; capt. and maj. M.C., U.S. Army, 1918-19; with A.E.F., July 1918-Feb. 1919; hon. disch. Feb. 2, 1919; maj. M.R.C., U.S. Army, 1920-35. Fellow Am. Coll. Surgeons, Am. Surg. Assn., Am. Foundation of Surgery; mem. A.M.A., New York Surg. Soc., Acad. Medicine, Alpha Delta Phi, Wolf's Head. Republican. Presbyterian. Clubs: Century (New York); Morris Country Golf; Yeamans Hall. Home: Morristown, N.J. Office: 65 5th Av., New York, N.Y. Died Mar. 13, 1943.

VAN BUSKIRK, ARTHUR B., business exec.; b. Pottstown, Pa., Mar. 27, 1896; s. Charles C. and Florence (McKinley) Van B.; A.B., Yale, 1918; LL.B., University of Pennsylvania, 1922; LL.D., Thiel College, 1956; LL.D., U. Pittsburgh, Marietta College, 1957; LL.D., Carnegie Institute of Technology, 1959; married Katharine Jones, October 17, 1925; children—George, Joseph, David. Law sec. to Chief Justice of Pa., 1922-24; asso. of Reed, Smith, Shaw & McClay, 1924-34, partner, 1934-41; deputy adminstr. Lend Lease adminstrn., 1942-43; vice-pres. Mellon Securities Corp., 1944-45; vice-pres. and gov. T. Mellon and Sons, from 1945; chmn. and dir. Fed. Reserve Bank Cleve., 1957-61; mem. bd. directors North Star Reinsurance Company, Consolidation Coal Co., Gen. Reinsurance Corp., Koppers Co., Inc., Equitable Life Assurance Soc. U.S.; mem. adv. com. Export-Import Bank of Washington, 1958-60. Trustee Richard King Mellon Found., Com. Econ. Devel., Eisenhower Exchange Fellowship; vice chairman Urban Redevelopment Authority Pittsburgh, 1947-51; chairman Allegheny Conference on Community Development, 1952-56; formerly dir. United Fund of Allegheny County, Pittsburgh, Symphony Society; bd. of mgrs. Children's Hospital of Pitts. Served as 2d lieutenant, with 312th F.A., 79th Div., Aug. 17, 1917 to July 25, 1919. Awarded Presdl. Certificate of Merit, 1947. Member American, Pa. and Allegheny County bar assns., Am. Judicature Soc., Am. Legion. Republican. Episcopalian. Clubs: Duquesne, Fox Chapel Golf (Pitts.); Rolling Rock, Laurel Valley (Ligonier, Pa.); Links (N.Y.C.); Union (Cleve.). Home: Ligonier PA Died Apr. 6, 1972.

VANCE, WILSON editor; b. Findlay, O., Dec. 20, 1845; s. Joseph Colville and Melinda Bromwell (Baldwin) V.; ed. common schs., Harvard Law Sch., 1866-67; m. Rachel E. Johnston, Sept. 5, 1867 (died 1873); m. 2d, Lillie Bell Beall, May 31, 1877. Enlisted as pvt. 21st Ohio Inf., 1861; commd. 2d lt. after battle of Stone River, Tenn., Dec. 31, 1862-Jan. 2, 1863; in same battle won Congressional Medal of Honor; comd. his co. in battle of Chickamauga, Sept. 20, 1863; mustered out Mar. 26, 1866. Managing editor Ohio State Journal, 1870, Indianapolis Journal, 1873, New York Morning Advertiser, 1892-94; Washington corr. Ohio State Journal, Cincinnati Commercial, Chicago Tribune, St. Louis Republic, Phila. Times, St. Paul Pioneer Press, etc., at various times, 1870-81; mgr. The C. W. Post Press, Ltd.; editor The Square Deal, 1904-—. Republican. Episcopalian. Author: Princes' Favors, 1879; Little Amy's Christmas, 1879; God's War, 1899; Big John Baldwin, 1909. Home: Brooklyn, N.Y. Deceased.

VAN CORTLANDT, PHILIP congressman, army officer; b. N.Y.C., Aug. 21, 1749; s. Pierre and Joanna (Livingston) Van C.; grad. King's Coll. (now Columbia), 1768; never married. Mem. Provincial Conv. at the Exchange in N.Y.C., 1775; one of Westchester County's reps. in 1st N.Y. Provincial Congress, 1775; lt. col. 4th N.Y. Regt., 1775; col. 2d N.Y. Regt. at Valley Forge; mem. ct. martial which heard charges preferred by Pa. authorities against Benedict Arnold, 1778; ordered to join Continental forces on lower Hudson in time to take active part in campaign against Cornwallis which culminated in his surrender, 1781; distinguished at Battle of Yorktown under Gen. Lafayette, brevetted brig. gen., 1783; del. to Poughkeepsie Conv., 1788, voted to ratify U.S. Constn.; supr., sch. commr., road master Town of Cortlandt (N.Y.); mem. N.Y. State Assembly, 1788, 90; mem. N.Y. Senate, 1791-93; mem. U.S. Ho. of Reps. from N.Y., 3d-10th congresses, 1793-1809; accompanied Gen. Lafayette on his tour through U.S. in 1831; charter mem. Soc. of Cincinnati. Died Croton, N.Y., Nov. 1, 1831; buried Hillside Cemetery, Peekskill, N.Y.

VAN CORTLANDT, PIERRE state ofcl.; b. N.Y.C., Jan. 10, 1721; s. Philip and Catharine (De Peyster) Van C.; m. Joanna Livingston, May 28, 1748; several children including Philip. Served in provincial militia during French and Indian Wars; mem. N.Y. Assembly, 1768; col. 3d Regt., Westchester Militia, 1775; mem. 2d, 3d, 4th N.Y. provincial congresses; leader in Com. of Safety, 1776; pres. Council of Safety, 1777; presided over 1st N.Y. Constl. Conv.; 1st lt. gov. N.Y. State, 1777-95; mem. bd. regents U. State of N.Y., 1784-95; donated land and subscribed to bldg. fund for local Methodist meeting house. Died Manor House, Croton, N.Y., May 1, 1814; buried family cemetery on estate, Croton.

VAN DEMAN, JOHN D. lawyer, banker; b. Delaware, O., Feb. 12, 1832; s. Rev. Henry and Sarah (Darlinton) V.; A.B., Ohio Wesleyan U., 1851, A.M., 1854; m. Lydia S. Runkle, of West Liberty, Logan Co., O., Oct. 23, 1861. Admitted to Ohio bar, 1853; practiced at Delaware; partner Judge T. W. Powell, 1853-60, then with H. M. Carper, 34 yrs.; retired from law practice, 1903; dir. 1st Nat. Bank, Delaware, 1883-—, resigned as pres., Nov., 1911; dir. Fidelity Bail Assn. and Loan Co.; trustee Cemetery Assn. Served in 145th Ohio Inf., Civil War; mayor of Delaware 3 terms; pros. atty. Delaware Co., 2 terms. Pres. bd. trustees Diocese of Southern Ohio, P.E. Ch., 15 yrs., dir. 37 yrs. Republican. Mem. Phi Gamma Delta. Home: Delaware, O.; (winter) Rockledge, Fla.

VAN DEMAN, RALPH HENRY, army officer; b. Delaware, O., Sept. 3, 1865; s. John Dodridge and Lydia Sieg (Runkle) Van D.; student Ohio Wesleyan U., 1883-86; A.B., Harvard, 1888; M.D., Miami Med. Sch., Cincinnati, 1893; grad. Inf. and Cav. Sch., Fort Leavenworth, Kan., 1895, Army War Coll., Washington, D.C., 1905; m. Irene Kingcombe, Mar. 3, 1917. Commd. 2d lt. inf., U.S. Army, Aug. 1, 1891; advanced through grades to brig. gen., Sept. 28, 1927; maj. gen., May 27, 1929; retired Sept. 3, 1929. Member Harbor Commission, San Diego, Calif. Participated in Spanish-American War, Philippine Insurrection and World War. Awarded D.S.M. (U.S.); Companion of the Bath (British); Officer Legion of Honor (French); Comdr. Crown of Italy. Mem. Phi Kappa Psi. Republican. Episcopalian. Mason (32 deg.). Club: Army and Navy (Washington, D.C.). Home: 3141 Curlew St., San Diego 3 CA

VAN DE MORTEL, J(AN) B(ENEDICTUS) V(ICTOR) M(ARIA) J(OSEPHUS) consul gen. of the Netherlands; b. 'sHertogenbosch, The Netherlands, Aug. 2, 1897; s. Joannes Henricus and Jonkvrouw Cecile (de la Court) van de M.; ed. U. of Nijmegen, Netherlands, 1929; m.; children—Jan Hein Lodewijk, Sabine (Mrs. Vincent Brandt). Apptd. Mayor of Noordwijk, The Netherlands, 1929, dismissed by Germans, 1943, resumed post, 1945; consul gen. of the Netherlands, Chgo., 1946-58. Served as lt., Netherland Cavalry, World War I; commd. maj. Netherland mil. forces, 1944; sent to Brussels and became chief Office of Evacuation, The Netherlands, 1944; dir. office caring for war victims, 1944-45. Roman Catholic. Clubs: Tavern, Casino, The Arts (Chgo.); various clubs in the Netherlands. Home: Chgo. Died Sept., 1962.

VANDENBERG, ARTHUR H(ENDRICK) JR. b. Grand Rapids, Mich., June 30, 1907; s. Arthur H. and Elizabeth (Watson) V.; A.B., Dartmouth, 1928. Adminstrv. asst. to Senator Arthur H. Vandenberg, 1934-48; pub. relations officer, dep. mgr. Internat. Basic Economy Corp., Brazil, 1949-50; cons. Nelson A. Rockefeller, 1951; nat. chmn. Citizens for Eisenhower

Com., 1952; exec. asst. Gen. Dwight D. Eisenhower, 1952; dir. Govt. Affairs Found., Inc., N.Y.C., since 1953; vis. lectr. govt. fgn. policy U. Miami, Coral Gables, Fla. Served as maj. USAAF, 1942-45. Mem. Phi Delta Theta. Editor: Private Papers of Senator Vandenberg, 1952. Home: 431 Brickell Av., Miami, Fla. Office: 30 Rockefeller Plaza, N.Y.C. Died Jan. 18, 1968.

VANDENBERG, HOYT SANFORD air force officer; born Milwaukee, Jan. 24, 1899; s. William Collins and Pearl (Kane) V.; student Columbian School, 1918-19; B.S., U.S. Mil. Acad., 1923; student A.C. Tactical Sch., 1934-35, Command and Gen. Staff Sch., 1935-36, Army War Coll., 1936-39; m. Gladys Rose, Dec. 26, 1923; children—Gloria Rose, Hoyt Sanford. Commd. 2d lt., 1923, U.S. Army Air Corps; promoted through grades to lieut. gen., Mar. 1945, gen., 1947; instr. Fighter Tactics, A.C. Tactical Sch., 1936-38; asst. chief of staff A.A.F., 1940-41; chief of staff, Northwest African Strategic Air Force, 1942-43; dep. chief of staff, 1943; head of air mission to Russia, 1943-44; apptd. dep. comdr. in chief, A.E.F., Apr. 1944; made comdg. gen. U.S. 9th Air Force in France, Aug. 1944; became asst. chief of staff G-2 (Intelligence), War Dept. Gen. Staff, Feb. 1946; apptd. U.S. dir. Cent. Intelligence, June 1946; became dep. comdr. A.A.F. and chief of air staff A.A.F., 1947; vice chief of staff U.S. Air Force, October 1947, chief of staff 1948-53. Awarded Distinguished Service Medal (with Oak Leaf Cluster), Silver Star, Distinguished Flying Cross, Air Medal (4 Oak Leaf Clusters), Legion of Merit, Bronze Star. Home: Washington. Died Apr. 2, 1954.

VANDERBILT, AARON v.p. of Wheeler Condenser & Engring. Co.; b. Staten Island, N.Y., Jan. 29, 1844; s. Isaac Simonson and Sarah A. (Seguine) V.; ed. public and private schools Staten Island and Brooklyn; m., Haledon, N.J., 1869, Lillie L. Wheeler. Ensign U.S.N., on staff Admiral Porter during Civil war; served on blockage service, battles of Fort Fisher, Cape Fear River campaign, taking of Wilmington, N.C.; siege of Petersburg and Richmond, Va.; James River and Appomattox River campaign; at fall of Richmond, an escort to Pres. Lincoln. After war identified with Am. shipping interests; now mfr. machinery; senior officer in command naval force N.Y. State during Spanish-Am. war; treas. Am. Shipping League; chief of ordnance, N.Y. Naval Reserve; now retired as lt.-comdr.; chmn. com. on Ocean Transportation, New York Board of Trade; mem. com. on Am. Mercantile Marine, selected by chmn. Commerce Com. U.S. Senate; v.p. Merchant Marine League of the U.S., Cleveland, O. Promoted establishment of naval militia forces of the country; mem. Army and Navy Club, Washington, Naval Order of the U.S., Soc. Army of the Potomac, Mil. Order Loyal Legion and G.A.R., Soc. Naval Inst., Annapolis; dir. Navy League, U.S.; trustee Hudson-Fulton Celebration Commn. Dir. Cuba and Pan-Am. Express Co. Residence: Westhampton, L.I. Office: 42 Broadway, New York.

VANDERBILT, CORNELIUS III capitalist; b. New York, 1873; s. Cornelius and Alice Claypoole (Gwynne) V.; A.B., Yale, 1895, Ph.B., 1898, M.E., 1899; m. Grace, d. Richard T. Wilson, 1896; children—Cornelius, Jr., Grace. I.C. R.R. Co. Commd. col. 102d U.S. Engrs., 1917; brig. gen. N.A., July 6, 1918; now brig. gen. O.R.C. Home: 640 5th Av. Office: 32 Nassau St., New York, N.Y. Died Mar. 2, 1942.

VANDERBILT, HAROLD STIRLING, capitalist; b. Oakdale, N.Y., July 6, 1884; s. William Kissan and Alvia E. (Smith) V.; A.B., Harvard, 1907; Harvard U. Law Sch., 1907-10. Began active career with N.Y.C. R.R.; for many years dir. various ry. and other corps. Pres. bd. trust Vanderbilt U. Served from lt. (j.g.) to lt. USNRF, 1917-18; comdg. officer Scout Patrol 56, later comdr. Block Island and New London sects., served with submarine chaser detachment 3, Queenstown, Ireland, 1918. Inventor contract bridge, 1925. Home: New York City NY Died July 4, 1970.

VANDERPOOL, WYNANT DAVIS banker, lawyer; b. Newark, N.J., Aug. 15, 1875; s. Wynant and Alice Wayland (Davis) V.; ed. Princeton, 1894-98, Harvard Law Sch., 1898-1901; m. Cornelia Willis, Oct. 17, 1905; children—Eugene, Mary Willis (Mrs. William W. Cochran), Wynant Davis. Admitted to N.J. bar, 1903; v.p. Howard Savings Instn., Newark, 1917, pres. since 1924; pres., mem. bd. mgrs. Howard Savings Instn. of Newark; dir. Nat. Newark & Essex Banking Co., Am. Ins. Co., Mutual Benefit Life Ins. Co., Bankers Indemnity Ins. Co. (all of Newark), Nat. Biscuit Co. of New York, Morristown (N.J.) Trust Co., United N.J. R.R. and Canal Co., Trenton, N.J. Capt. motor transport, U.S. Army, 1918. Trustee Morristown Memorial Hosp., Morristown Library, St. Barnabas Hosp. Mem. Am. and Essex County bar assns., Am. Inst. Banking, Harvard Law Sch. Assn., Holland Soc. of N.Y., N.J. Hist. Soc., The Pilgrims, Newcomen Soc. of England, Bond Club of N.J., Chamber of Commerce. Episcopalian. Home: 86 Miller Rd., Morristown, N.J. Address: P.O. Box 177, Newark, N.J. Died Aug. 19, 1944.

VAN DEUSEN, GEORGE WILLIAM army officer; b. Van Deusen Ville, Berkshire Co., Mass., Feb. 11, 1859; s. William Ingersol and Sarha Ann (Ball) V.; grad. U.S. Mil. Acad., 1880, U.S. Arty. Sch., Fort Monroe, Va., 1892; Field Officers' Class, Mounted Service Sch., Ft. Riley, Kan., 1911; m. Florence L., d. Curtis E. Munn (surgeon U.S.A.), Oct. 18, 1882. Commd. 2d lt. 4th Cav., June 12, 1880; trans. to 1st Arty., Jan. 31, 1884; 1st lt., Aug. 9, 1889; capt. 7th Arty., Mar. 2, 1899; maj. Arty. Corps, Mar. 3, 1906; assigned to 2d Field Arty., June 6, 1907; lt. col., Nov. 15, 1910; col., Sept. 7, 1911; assigned to 3d Field Arty., Aug. 2, 1914; col. 2d Field Arty., Jan. 3, 1916. Duty in Philippine Islands, 1899-1900, 1904-07, 1908-10, 1916-17; comd. recruit dept., Ft. Logan, Colo., 1911-14; assigned duty at Presidio, San Francisco, Oct. 1917. Episcopalian. Club: Union League (New York). Address: War Dept., Washington, D.C.

VAN DEUSEN, ROBERT HICKS, chmn. Stone & Webster Securities Corp.; b. Phila., Pa., July 10, 1891; s. Edwin H. and Adelaide Parmalee (Smith) van D.; ed. public and private schs.; m. Maidza Wakem, Dec. 11, 1920; children—Frederick, Robert H., Maidza. Chmn. and dir. Stone & Webster Securities Corporation (formerly Stone & Webster and Blodget, Inc.), 1932-51, dir., 1926-51. First lt. with 12th F.A., 2d Div., A.E.F. Episcopalian. Clubs: Recess, Knickerbocker (New York). Home: Roxbury CT Died May 1971.

VANDIVER, ALMUTH CUNNINGHAM lawyer; b. Gadsden, Ala., June 21, 1879; s. Wellington and Florence (Cunningham) V.; B.Sc., Ala. Poly. Inst., Auburn, Ala., 1898; LL.B., New York U. Law Sch., 1904; m. Eleanor M. S. Williams, Nov. 30, 1912; children—Almuth II, Wellington II. Dept. asst. dist. atty. New York Co., under William Travers Jerome, 1905-08; associated with Gov. Charles S. Whitman as Whitman & Vandiver, 1908-10; mem. O'Gorman, Battle & Vandiver, 1913-23. Battle, Vandiver, Levy & Van Tine, 1923-27. Capt. 14th Inf. N.Y.G., 1918; maj. ord. dept. N.Y.G., 1918; maj. judge adv. Army of U.S., 1918-19; maj. judge adv. gen's. dept., N.Y.G., 1919-22; maj. J.A.G. (Res.), 61st Cav. Div., Army of U.S. Grand Officer Order of St. Sepulchre (Orthodox). Past sr. v. comdr. in chief Mil. Order World War. Home: New York, N.Y. Died June 21, 1931.

VAN DORN, EARL army officer; b. Port Gibson, Miss., Sept. 17, 1820; s. Peter Aaron and Sophia Ponelson (Caffery) Van D.; grad. U.S. Mil. Acad., 1842; m. Caroline Godbold, 1843. Served in Mexican War; commd. 1st lt., 1847, took part in Seminole War in Fla., 1848-50; capt. 2d Cavalry, U.S. Army, 1855-61, served in Tex. and Indian Territory, promoted maj., 1860; resigned from army, 1861; commd. brig. gen. Miss. Militia, 1861, maj. gen., 1861; col. of cavalry Confederate Army, assigned to duty in Tex.; promoted brig. gen., 1861, maj. gen., 1861; comdr. Trans-Mississippi dist., 1862; raided Union depots at Holly Springs, Miss., captured garrison. Killed at Battle of Spring Hill (Tenn.), May 8, 1863.

VAN DUYN, EDWARD SEGUIN, surgeon; b. at Syracuse, N.Y., Aug. 20, 1872; s. John and Sarah (Faulks) Van D.; M.D., Syracuse U., 1897; m. Lucy Leavenworth Ballard, Feb. 4, 1903; children—Mary L., John, Constance. Practiced at Syracuse since 1897; prof. Syracuse U. Coll. of Medicine, 1917-37, emeritus since 1937; surgeon University Hosp.; cons. surgeon Syracuse Free Dispensary. Pres. bd. visitors Syracuse State Sch., State Dept. Mental Hygiene. Served as lt. col., M.C., U.S. Army, in World War I. Fellow Am. Col. Surgeons; mem. A.M.A., Med. Soc. State of N.Y. Republican. Presbyterian. Club: Century. Home: 607 James St. Office: Medical Arts Bldg., Syracuse NY

VAN DUZER, LEWIS SAYRE officer U.S.N.; b. Elmira, N.Y., June 29, 1861; s. William Henry and Susan Rachel (Sayre) V.; entered U.S. Naval Acad., 1876, grad. 1880; m. Alice Louise Averill, Dec. 19, 1883 (died 1925); m. 2d, Clara L. Van Order, Nov. 2, 1927. Promoted through the various grades to capt., Mar. 3, 1911. Officer U.S.S. Iowa, and present at battle of Santiago and destruction of Cervera's fleet, 1898; also at attack on fortifications of San Juan, P.R., etc.; served in the Philippines throughout the Phillipine Insurrection; went to China at beginning of Boxer rebellion, June 1900; instr. in ordnance, U.S. Naval Acad., 1900-02; commanded U.S.S. Cleveland, 1908-09; comdt. Olongapo Navy Yard, 1909-10; capt. of the yard, Navy Yard, New York, 1910-13; in command of U.S.S. Utah, 1913-14; retired at his own request, Apr. 1914. Served in the cruiser and transport service at New York, 1918. Received medal for services in West Indies, Spanish-Am. War, also medals for Santiago, Philippine Insurrection, Boxer campaign. Nautical and naval editor New Internat. Ency., 1900-31, Nelson's Ency., 1906-17. Home: Horseheads, Chemung County, N.Y. Died Mar. 28, 1936.

VAN DYKE, WILLIAM DUNCAN, JR., corp. exec.; b. Milw., Dec. 13, 1893; s. William Duncan and Gertrude H. (Goodrich) Van D.; grad. The Hill Sch., 1913; A.B., Princeton, 1917; m. Helen Bemis (Mrs. Paul V. Godfrey), Olive Bagley (Mrs. Thomas F. Scannell, Jr.), William Duncan III. Pres., dir. Mineral Mining Co., Milw., 1938—; trustee, mem. finance and exec. coms. Northwestern Mut. Life Ins. Co.; dir., mem. finance com. Marine Nat. Exchange Bank, Northwestern Nat. Ins. Co.; dir. Western Lime & Cement Co. Served as capt., F.A., U.S. Army, World War I. Mem. Am. Inst. Mining and Metall. Engrs., Am. Legion. Presbyn. (trustee). Republican. Clubs: Univeristy, Milwaukee Country, Milwaukee, Beach (Milw.). Home: 7272 N. Bridge Lane, Fox Point, Milwaukee County, Wis. Office: Wells Bldg., Milw. 2. Died Apr. 29, 1959.

VAN EPPS, CLARENCE, physician; b. Aug. 29, 1875; s. Charles H. and Elizabeth Van E.; B.S., Ia. State Coll., 1894; M.D., State U. of Iowa, 1897, Univ. of Pa., 1898; m. Ella P. Parsons, July 6, 1904. Professor and head department of neurology, State University of Iowa, to 1945 (now prof. emeritus). Lieutenant colonel Med. O.R.C., serving General Hosp. No. 54, U.S. Army. Mem. Am. Med. Assn., Iowa State Medical Society, Central Neuropsychiatric Association, Delta Tau Delta, Phi Rho Sigma, Sigma Xi, Alpha Omega Alpha. Home: 128 E. Fairchild, Iowa City IA

VAN EPPS, EUGENE FRANCIS, physician, educator; b. DeWitt, Ia., Jan. 31, 1912; s. Homer Eugene and Anna (Foley) Van E.; M.D., U. Ia., 1935; m. Yola Margaret Came, Sept. 2, 1937; children—Robert Francis, Marcia Ann, William Michael. Intern State U. Ia. Hosps., 1935-36, resident medicine and pediatrics, 1936-39, radiology resident, 1946-49, radiologist, 1949-70, asst. prof., then asso. prof. radiology, 1949-55, prof., head dept., 1955-67, Ia. prof., 1967-68, prof. Duke U. 1968-70. Mem. sch. bd., Iowa City, 1961-64, pres., 1961-62. Served as capt., M.C., AUS, 1942-46. Diplomate Am. Bd. Radiology (vice president 1966-67, treasurer, trustee, pres. 1969-70). Fellow Am. Coll. Radiology; mem. Radiology Society N.A., Ia. Radiol. Soc. (pres. 1957-58), Ia. Med. Soc. (sec., chmn. jud. council 1953-57, pres. 1960-61), Society for Pediatric Radiology, American Roentgen Ray Soc. (exec. council), N.Y. Acad. Scis., Sigma Xi, Alpha Omega Alpha. Home: Albuquerque NM Mar. 11, 1970.

VAN ETTEN, EDGAR railway official; b. Milford, Pa., Apr. 15, 1843; s. Amos and Lydia Cornelia (Thrall) V.; grad. Stillwater (N.J.) Acad., 1858; m. Lillian Frances Cramblett, of Killbuck, O., June 30, 1897. Enlisted as pvt. Civil War, 1861, served 3 yrs., discharged as capt. In ry. service since war, in all capacities, beginning as freight brakeman; gen. supt., 1893-1901, v.p., 1901-07, now advisory officer, N.Y.C.&H.R. R.R.; pres. Cuba Eastern Ry., since Jan., 1908. Mem. Holland Soc., New York, Beacon Soc., Boston, S.A.R., Loyal Legion of Honor. Clubs: Railroad, Transportation (New York), Fort Orange (Albany, N.Y.), Commercial, Merchants, New Algonquin (Boston). Office: 225 5th Av., New York.

VAN HORN, PETER HARRY pres. Nat. Fedn. of Textiles; b. Logan, O., Oct. 1, 1893; s. Jesse and Belle (Tedrow) V.; student Ohio State U., 1912-14, Univ. of Calif., 1915-17; m. Helen Genevieve Prosser, Sept. 20, 1920; 1 son, Peter Van Horn II. Began with Nat. City Bank, N.Y. City, 1919; v.p. Allen Archer Co., Los Angeles, 1920-21; pres. K. W. Kays Co., Los Angeles, Jan.-Oct. 1921; gen. mgr. Columbus Better Business Bur., 1926-34; pres. Nat. Assn. Better Business Bureaus, 1933-34, Nat. Fedn. of Textiles, Mar. 1934—. Served as lt. U.S. Army and as pilot Air Corps, World War, June 1917-March 1919; consultant, staff of NRA, Washington, D.C., 10 weeks, 1935. Protestant. Home: New York, N.Y. Died Dec. 18, 1936.

VAN HORN, ROBERT OSBORN army officer; b. Whipple Barracks, Ariz., Aug. 15, 1876; s. Col. James Hatch and Margaret (Wilson) Van H.; B.S. in Engring., U. of Mich., 1897; grad. Army Sch. of the Line, 1911, Army Staff Coll., 1912; m. Lucretia Blow Le Bourgeois, Oct. 19, 1908; children—Margaret Elizabeth (dec.), Lucretia. Pvt. 12th Inf., 1897; commd. 2d lt. inf., 1899; promoted through grades to brig. gen., Dec. 1, 1933; civil gov. Cotabato Dist., Moro Province, P.I., 1903-05; aide to President Theodore Roosevelt, 1907-08; comdg. 9th Inf., A.E.F. Awarded D.S.M., Silver Star medal with cluster. Died June 26, 1941.

VAN HORN, ROBERT THOMPSON journalist; b. E. Mahoning, Pa., May 19, 1824; went to school winters until 15, then was apprenticed to printing trade; m. Adela H. Cooley, Dec. 2, 1848. Editor Kansas City Journal, 1855-96, except during war interval; lt. col. 25th Mo. Inf. during Civil War; took part in battle and siege of Lexington, Mo., Sept. 1861, battle of Shiloh, and other engagements. Mem. Mo. Senate, 3 yrs.; mem. Congress, 1865-71, 1881-83, 1895-97. Home: Kansas City, Mo. Died Jan. 3, 1916.

VAN HORNE, ISAAC congressman; b. Tollbury Twp., Bucks County, Pa., Jan. 13, 1754; apprenticed as carpenter and cabinetmaker. Became ensign of militia co., 1775; apptd. ensign Continental Army by Com. of Safety, assigned to Col. Samuel McGaw's Regt., Jan. 1776; held prisoner, Nov. 1776-78, exchanged; served from 1st lt. to capt. until end of Revolutionary War; justice of peace Tollbury Twp., several years; coroner Bucks County, 4 years; mem. Pa. Ho. of Reps., 1796-97; mem. U.S. Ho. of Reps. (Democrat) from Pa., 7th-8th congresses, 1801-05; moved to Zanesville, O., 1805; receiver of land office, Zanesville, 1805-26. Died Zanesville, Feb. 2, 1834; buried Woodlawn Cemetery.

VAN HORNE, WILLIAM MCCADDEN brig. gen. U.S. Army; b. Ohio, Aug. 22, 1842. Enlisted as pvt. Co. E, 2d Ohio Inf., Aug. 14, 1861; discharged, Oct. 10, 1864; commd. 2d lt. 184th Ohio Inf., Jan. 4, 1865; transferred to 195th Ohio Inf., Mar. 17, 1865; capt., Mar. 17, 1865; hon. mustered out, Dec. 18, 1865; apptd. from Ohio, 2d lt. 17th U.S. Inf., Feb. 23, 1866; 1st lt., Feb. 23, 1866; capt., Dec. 31, 1872; maj. 22d Inf., May 23, 1896; transferred to 8th Inf., Oct. 24, 1898; lt. col. 18th Inf., Nov. 1, 1898; col. 29th Inf., Feb. 2, 1901; retired on account of disability incurred in line of duty, Oct. 16, 1901; advanced to rank of brig. gen. retired, by act of Apr. 23, 1904. Home: Chicago, Ill. Died Jan. 19, 1923.

VAN KEUREN, ALEXANDER HAMILTON naval officer; b. Howell, Mich., Mar. 9, 1881; s. James Irvin and Fanny Ann (Morgan) Van K.; ed. U. of Mich., 1898-99, U.S. Naval Acad., 1899-1903 (B.S.), Mass. Inst. Tech., 1905-08 (M.S.), Naval War Coll., 1925-26; m. Helen Cuthbert Molten, June 19, 1911; children—Alexander Hamilton, Frances Cuthbert (Mrs. H. G. Pestalozzi). Commd. ensign, U.S. Navy, 1905, advanced through grades to rear adm., 1939; served on the U.S.S. Wisconsin, Oregon, Villalobos, Asiatic Station, 1903-05; duty at Navy Yards, East and West Coasts, 1908-16. Bur. Constrn. and Repair, design div., 1916-20, East and West Coasts, 1920-25; staff Naval War Coll., Newport, R.I., 1926-27; head design div., Navy Dept., Bur. Constrn. and Repair, 1927-36, also tech. adviser London Naval Conf., 1930, Gen. Disarmament Conf., Geneva, 1932; superintending constructor for U.S. Navy, N.Y. Shipbuilding Co., Camden, N.J., 1936-37; mgr. indsl. dept. Navy Yard, Phila., 1937-39; chief constructor and chief Bur. Constrn. and Repair, U.S. Navy (rank read adm. Constrn. Corps), 1939-40; asst. chief Bureau of Ships, 1940-42; Chief Bureau of Ships, 1942; dir. Naval Research Laboratory, Anacostia Sta., 1942-45; Navy Dept. 1945-46; permanent rank of rear adm., 1941, ret., 1946. Mem. Soc. Naval Architects and Marine Engrs., Sigma Chi. Mem. Sojourners. Episcopalian. Club: Chevy Chase (Md.). Home: Washington. Died July 1966.

VAN LEER, CARLOS CLARK, b. Nashville, Tenn., Oct. 15, 1865; s. Samuel and Alice McCorry (Clark) Van L.; LL.B., Vanderbilt, 1895; m. Harriet Draper, Aug. 23, 1905; children—Carlos C., Jr., Anthony Wayne, Leila D. Clerk in post office, Nashville, 1887-97; paymaster's clk., U.S. Navy, 1897; same in office of auditor U.S. Treasury, 1900-15, chief clk., 1915-21; chief of treasury dept. div., gen. accounting office, 1921; investigator, Bur. of the Budget, 1922-27; asst. to dir. of Budget and chmn. Personnel Classification Bd., 1927-32. Served as 1st lt. and capt. Tenn. Vol. Inf., 1898-99. Mem. S.A.R., Sigma Alpha Epsilon. Christian Scientist. K.P. Club: Columbia Country. Home: 1858 Ontario Pl., Washington DC

VAN NESS, JOHN PETER congressman, mayor Washington; b. Ghent, Columbia County, N.Y., 1770; attended Columbia; studied law. Admitted to bar, never practiced law; Democratic presdl. elector, 1800; mem. U.S. Ho. of Reps. (Democrat, filled vacancy) from N.Y., 7th Congress, Oct. 6, 1801-Jan. 17, 1803; apptd. maj. militia in D.C. by Pres. Jefferson; pres. second council, 1803; promoted lt. col. commandant 1st legion of militia, 1805, brig. gen., 1811, maj. gen., 1813; alderman City of Washington (D.C.), 1829, mayor, 1830-34; 2d v.p. Washington Nat. Monument Soc., 1833; pres. commrs. Washington Canal, 1834; pres. branch bank of U.S., Washington; 1st pres. Nat. Met. Bank, 1814-46. Died Washington, D.C., Mar. 7, 1846; buried mausoleum at Oak Hill Cemetery.

VAN NICE, ERRETT, banker; b. Chgo., Apr. 5, 1908; s. Errett I. and Lillian (Blaker) Van N.; A.B., U. Chgo., 1931; m. Ruth Swift, Nov. 22, 1935; children—Ruth, Peter, Paul. With Harris Trust & Savs. Bank, Chgo., 1932-70, v.p., from 1949, later senior vice president; director of the Fred Harvey Company. Active in YMCA, Nat. Found. Infantile Paralysis, Community Fund; bd. dirs., past pres. Tb Inst. Chgo. and Cook County, Children's Meml. Hosp.; asso. mem. United Charities Chgo.; trustee, treas. Adler Planetarium; bd. dirs., treas. Chgo. Crime Commn.; dir.-at-large Nat. Tb and Respiratory Disease Assn.; mem. citizens bd. U. Chgo. Served to comdr. USNR, 1942-45. Fellow Inst. Medicine Chgo.; mem. Am. Enterprise Assn., Chgo. Assn. Commerce and Industry (dir.), Assn. Res. City Bankers, Delta Kappa Epsilon. Clubs: Bankers, Casino, Chicago, Chicago Sunday Evening (v.p., trustee), Chicago Commonwealth (dir., treas.), Economic, Executives, Mid-America, Attic, Commercial, Old Elm, Onwentsia. Home: Chicago IL Died Dec. 9, 1970.

VAN ORNUM, JOHN LANE (van-ôr'num), civil engineer; b. Hartford, Vt., May 14, 1864; s. Adoniram Judson and Sarah Josephine (Lane) Van O.; B.S. in C.E., U. of Wis., 1888, C.E., 1891; m. Carrie Beattie Scott, July 25, 1894; children—Thurwood, Judson (dec.). Municipal engring. work, Milwaukee, Wis., July-Nov. 1888; surveyor and inspector U.S. harbor works, Ga. and Fla. coasts, 1888-90; asst. engr. Milwaukee, Lake Shore & Western R.R., in Mich. and Wis., May-Oct. 1890; U.S. asst. engr. on river surveys, etc., in Ga. and Tenn., 1890-91; chief topographer Mexican Boundary Survey, 1891-94; instr. civ. engring., Washington U., 1894-97; traveled in Europe, 1897-98; capt. and maj. 3d U.S. Vol. Engrs., Spanish-Am. War, 1898-99, assisting in elimination of yellow fever at Cienfuegos, Cuba, etc.; prof. civ. engring., Washington U., 1899-1934, emeritus prof. since 1934. Fellow A.A.A.S.; mem. Am. Soc. Civil Engrs., Am. Soc. Testing Materials, Internat. Assn. Navigation Congresses (life mem.), Soc. for Promotion Engring. Edn., Engineers Club St. Louis (past pres.), Mil. Order Foreign Wars, Sigma Xi, Tau Beta Pi (hon. mem.), Beta Theta Pi, etc. Presbyterian. Author: The Regulation of Rivers, 1914; also many articles in tech. mags. as result of original research, etc. Home: 126 Linden Av., Clayton, Mo. Died Nov. 6, 1943.

VAN PETTEN, JOHN B. educator; b. in Sterling, N.Y., June 19, 1827; s. Peter and Lydia (Bullock) V.; grad. Wesleyan Univ., Conn., 1850; completed conf. course in divinity, 1856 (Ph.D., Syracuse Univ., 1888); m. Mary B. Mason, Aug. 10, 1850. Prin. Fairfield (N.Y.) Sem., 1855-61 and 1866-69. Was clergyman, M.E. Ch. chaplain 34th N.Y. inf., June 15, 1861, to Sept. 22, 1862; lt. col. 160th N.Y. inf., Sept. 25, 1862, to Jan. 20th, 1865; in permanent command of regt. over 2 yrs.; comd. 2d brigade of 1st div., 19th corps, at Pt. Hudson, June 14, 1863; severely wounded at battle of Opequan, Sept. 19, 1864; complimented in gen. orders by Gen. Sheridan for conspicuous gallantry; col. 193d N.Y. inf. and bvt. brig. gen. U.S.V., comdg. dist. of Cumberland in W.Va., June 1865, to Jan. 1866; State senator, 1868-69. Prin. Sedalia, Mo., Sem., 1877-82; prof. Latin and history, Claverack Coll., N.Y., 1885-1900. Home: Oswego, N.Y. Died 1908.

VAN RENSSELAER, HENRY BELL congressman, army officer; b. Manor House, Albany, N.Y., May 14, 1810; son of Stephen Van R.; grad. U.S. Mil. Acad., 1831. Commd. brevet 2d lt. 5th Regt., U.S. Inf., 1831, resigned, 1832; engaged in agriculture, nr. Ogdensburg, N.Y.; mem. U.S. Ho. of Reps. (Whig) from N.Y., 27th Congress, 1841-43; interested in mining enterprises; commd. brig. gen. U.S. Army, chief of staff under Gen. Winfield Scott, at beginning of Civil War; served as insp. gen., with rank of col., 1862-64. Died Cincinnati, Mar. 23, 1864; buried Grace Episcopal Churchyard, Jamaica, L.I., N.Y.

VAN RENSSELAER, SOLOMON VAN VECHTEN congressman; b. Rensselaer County, N.Y., Aug. 6, 1774; s. Henry Kiliain and Alida (Bradt) Van R.; m. Harriet Van Rensselaer (cousin), Jan. 17, 1797, several children. Served as cornet in U.S. Cavalry, 1792, capt. under Gen. Anthony Wayne in Indian campaigns, 1794; commd. maj. U.S. Army, 1799, discharged, 1800; adj. gen. N.Y., 1801-11, 13-21; became aide-de-camp to Maj. Gen. Stephen Van Rensselaer at beginning of War of 1812, served in attack on Queenston, Ont., Can., 1812, wounded; mem. U.S. Ho. of Reps. (Federalist) from N.Y., 16th-17th congresses, 1819-22; postmaster Albany (N.Y.), 1822-39, 41-43; del. from N.Y. to opening of Erie Canal, 1825. Died Albany, Apr. 23, 1852; buried Albany Rural Cemetery.

VAN REYPEN, WILLIAM KNICKERBOCKER medical dir. U.S.N.; b. Bergen, N.J., Nov. 14, 1840; s. Cornelius C. and Christina Cantine (Van Alen) V.; A.B., New York U., 1858, A.M., 1863; M.D., Univ. Med. Coll. (New York U.), 1862; m. Nellis C. Wells, Sept. 21, 1876. Apptd. from N.J., asst. surgeon U.S.N., Dec. 26, 1861; passed asst. surgeon, May 26, 1865; surgeon, May 12, 1868; med. insp., Aug. 16, 1887; med. dir., Mar. 30, 1895. Served at the naval hosp., New York, 1862; on St. Lawrence, East Gulf Blockading Squadron, 1863-64; naval hosp., Chelsea, Mass., 1865, 1869-70; Lenapee, 1865-67; Ticonderoga and Frolic, 1867-69; naval hosps., Norfolk, 1870-71, Annapolis, 1871-72, New York, 1874-77; on Iroquois, 1872-74; Alaska, 1878-80; at Navy Yard, Norfolk, 1880; naval hospital, Brooklyn, 1881-83; Powhatan, 1883-84; asst. chief Bur. of Medicine and Surgery, 1884-92; fleet surgeon Pacific Fleet, 1892-94; mem. Bd. of Inspection and Survey, 1894-97; during Spanish-Am. War designed and fitted out the ambulance ship Solace, the first ever used in naval warfare; surgeon-gen. U.S.N., and chief of Bur. of Medicine and Surgery, with rank of commodore, 1897-99, with rank of rear adm., 1899-1902; retired on own application after 40 yrs.' service, with the rank of sr. rear adm., Jan. 25, 1902. Del. representing U.S.N. at 12th Internat. Med. Congress, Moscow, 1897; del. Red Cross Conf., St. Petersburg, 1902; pres. Am. Nat. Red Cross, 1904-05 (chmn. Central Com., 1905-—). Home: Washington, D.C. Died Dec. 22, 1924.

VAN SCHAICK, GOSEN army officer; b. Albany, N.Y., Sept. 16, 1736; s. Sybrant and Alida (Roseboom) Van S.; m. Maria Ten Broeck, Nov. 15, 1770, 6 children. Served as capt. N.Y. Militia, French and Indian War; served in campaign against Fort Frontenac, 1758; commd. lt. col. 2d Regt., N.Y. Provincials, 1760; lt. col. 1st N.Y. Regt., 1760-62; commd. col. 1st N.Y. Regt., Continental Army, 1776, served in battles of Ticonderoga and Monmouth; led expdn. against Onondago Indians, 1779; brevetted brig. gen., 1783, ret. 1783. Died Albany, July 4, 1789.

VAN SCOYOC, LELAND STANFORD, economist, educator; b. Luray, Kan., Oct. 5, 1900; s. John M. and Lenna M. (Butler) Van S.; B.S., Kan. State U., 1926, M.S., 1935; D. Bus. Administrn., Ind. U., 1953; m. Marthellen Ratcliff, 1947; 1 dau., Jeanette. Tchr., adminstr. pub. schs., Kan. and N.M., 1926-37; instr. Highland (Kan.) Pub. Jr. Coll., 1937-42; asst. prof. econs. U. Dubuque, 1945-46; asst. prof. dept. econs. Bowling Green (O.) State U., 1946-50, asso. prof., 1950-56, prof., 1956-71, prof. emeritus, 1971-72, chmn. dept., 1955-66. Served to maj., Transp. Corps, AUS, 1942-44; faculty Chem. Warfare Sch., 1944-45. Mem. Am. Econ. Assn., Transp. Assn., Am. Phi Delta Kappa, Beta Gamma Sigma. Delta Nu Alpha. Mason. Home: San Diego CA Died Jan. 6, 1972; buried Crown Hill Cemetery, Indianapolis IN

VAN SINDEREN, ADRIAN corporation official, author; born at Brooklyn, New York, February 21, 1887; son of William Leslie and Mary (Brinsmade) Van S.; A.B., Yale, 1910; Doctor of Humane Letters, Syracuse University, 1947; married Annie Jean White, Dec. 9, 1911; children—Adrian, Katharine, Jean, Alfred White. Teacher at St. Paul's Sch., 1910-11; with J. P. Morgan & Co., 1911-13, White, Weld and Co., 1913-15, W. A. & A. M. White since 1915, partner 1916-—. Trustee Brooklyn Savings Bank 1923-58, president 1944-47; director Brooklyn Trust Co., 1930-50, Greenwood Cemetery, N.Y. Telephone Co., Nat. Surety Co., Holmes Elec. Protective Co., 1944-50, Mfrs. Trust Co. (adv. com., trust com.), Cruickshank & Co. Served as captain, later major, assistant dir. Marine operations Port of New York, World War I. Awarded D.S.C. (U.S.N.), 1918; gold medal Downtown Brooklyn Assn., 1932. Pres. Brooklyn Acad. Music, 1921-36, Brooklyn Hosp., 1930-46; v.p. Brooklyn Bur. Charities, 1928-38, Long Island College Medicine, 1930-40; trustee Brooklyn Institute of Arts and Sciences, 1922-53, vice pres. 1927-42, pres. 1942-51; secretary-treasurer Gunnery School (Washington, Conn.), 1923-37. Chmn. bd. American Horse Shows Assn.; dir. National Horse Show of America; chmn. Brooklyn Chapter Am. Red Cross, 1922-23; pres. Brooklyn Soc. for Prevention of Cruelty to Children, 1922-35; past dir. Vis. Nurses Assn., Am. Hackney Soc. Trustee Bklyn. Library Bd., 1933-35, Adirondack Mt. Reserve, Grand Central Art Galleries. Member of the New York City Municipal Art Commission 1944-45; chairman United Rep. Finance Com. of N.Y., 1942; chmn. Citizens for Eisenhower-Nixon, Kings County, N.Y., 1956. Recipient Centennial citation Bklyn. Acad. Music. Mem. Psi Upsilon. Rep. Presbyn. Clubs: Harbour View, Yale, University, Grolier, Union, St. Wilfred's Club of Organists, Rembrandt, India House (N.Y.); Elihu (Yale); Washington (Conn.) Country. Author: Canter, Please, 1935; Important Beginnings, 1936; Christmas Greetings, 1937; Adventures in Experience, 1938; As We Go Galloping On, 1939; Vagaries and Verities, 1940; In Quest of Oases, 1941; A Yuletide Phantasmagoria, 1942; Four Years, A Chronicle of World War II, 1943; The Fifth Year, A Further Chronicle, 1944; Peter Make Believe, 1945. Six Years of Global War, 1946; Neolithic Times, 1947; Isthmus Isthmus Maximus, 1948; The Price of Liberty, 1948; Behind The Scenes at a Horse Show, 1948; Balke, The Mystic Genius, 1949; Africa, Land of Many Lands, 1950; The Country of the Mountains of the Moon, 1951; Foundation Stones, 1952; From the Canal to the Horn, 1953; The Lure of the Middle East, 1954; Passage to India, 1955; An Illustrious Company, 1956; Our Home in the Country Side, 1957; A Voyage through the Agure Seas, 1958; The Other Half of The Earth, 1959. Home: Washington, Conn. Office: 20 Broad St., N.Y.C. 10005. Died Oct. 1, 1963.

VAN VALKENBURGH, ROBERT BRUCE congressman, diplomat; b. Prattsburg, Steuben County, N.Y., Sept. 4, 1821; attended Franklin Acad., Prattsburg; studied law. Admitted to bar, began practice of law, Bath, N.Y.; mem. N.Y. State Assembly, 1852, 57-58; in command of recruiting depot, Elmira, N.Y., organized 17 regts. for Civil War; mem. U.S. Ho. of Reps. (Republican) from N.Y., 37th-38th congresses, 1861-65; served as col. 107th Regt., N.Y. Volunteer Inf., commanded regt. at Battle of Antietam; acting commr. Indian affairs, 1865; minister resident to Japan, 1866-69; settled in Fla.; asso. justice Fla. Supreme Ct., 1874-88. Died Suwanee Springs, nr. Live Oak, Fla., Aug. 1, 1888; buried Old St. Nicholas Cemetery, nr. Jacksonville, Fla.

VAN VLIET, ROBERT CAMPBELL army officer; b. in Kan., Aug. 22, 1857; grad. U.S. Mil. Acad., 1876. Commd. 2d lt. 10th Inf., Dec. 14, 1876; 1st lt., May 7, 1884; capt., Mar. 8, 1898; maj., Oct. 3, 1902; lt. col. 16th Inf., June 12, 1910; col. 25th Inf., Mar. 3, 1911; assigned to 4th Inf., Aug. 30, 1913; brig. gen. N.A., Aug. 5, 1917. Duty on Mexican border, 1916-17; apptd. comdr. 173 Inf. Brigade, Camp Pike, Little Rock, Ark., Sept. 1917. Address: War Dept., Washington. Died Oct. 27, 1943.

VAN VOAST, JAMES brig. gen. U.S.A.; b. Schenectady, N.Y., Sept. 1827; s. John G. and Maria (Teller) V.; student Union Coll., 1846-48, A.M., 1852; grad. U.S. Mil. Acad., 1852; m. Helen Pierce Hoar, 1855; m. 2d, Virginia M. Harris, 1870. Bvtd. 2d lt. 3d Artillery, July 1, 1852; promoted 2d lt., Aug. 22, 1853; advanced through grades to col. 9th Inf., Feb. 20, 1882; retired from active service, Apr. 2, 1883, for disability incurred in line of duty; advanced to rank of brig. gen. retired, by act of Apr. 23, 1904. Early service largely on frontier, among Indians. Was stationed at San Francisco, 1861-64, as mil. provost marshal; then served with regt. on Pacific Coast; after war in various duties and stations until retired. Home: Cincinnati, O. Died July 16, 1915.

VAN VOORHIS, DANIEL (van-vor'ez), army officer; b. Zanesville, O., Oct. 24, 1878; s. Henry Clay and Mary Ann (Brown) Van V.; ed. Ohio Wesleyan U. and Washington and Jefferson Coll.; grad. Inf.-Cav. Sch., 1905, Mounted Service Sch., 1910, Army War Coll., 1929; m. Edith Burbank, Jan. 11, 1911; children—Daniel, Betsy Bell. Enlisted as pvt., 10th Pa. Vol. Inf., Spanish-Am. War, 1898; commd. 2d lt. Cav., U.S. Army, Feb. 1, 1900, and advanced through the grades to brig. gen., 1936, maj. gen., 1938, lt. gen., 1940; served as col. of cavalry, during World War. Decorated D.S.M., Navy Cross, Silver Star (U.S.); Legion of Honor (France); Order of the Sun (Peru); Legion of Merit (Ecuador). Mem. Phi Kappa Psi. Club: Chevy Chase (Md.) Country. Home: Van Voorhis Farm, Nashport, O. Address: War Dept., Washington. Died Jan. 9, 1956; buried Meml. Park, Zanesville, O.

VAN WART, WALTER BRIGHT, steel co. exec.; b. Dallas, Aug. 25, 1900; s. Walter Henry and Eliza Bell (Bright) Van W.; student U. Tex., 1916-18; m. Charlotte Kramolis, Nov. 1, 1923; children—Walter Bright, Charles Donald. With Wyatt Industries, Incorporated, Dallas, 1919-67, v.p., 1938-55, pres., 1955-62, chmn. bd., 1962-67, dir.; dir. Tex. Nat. Bank, Steel Tank Constrn. Co., Austin Bros. Steel Co., Big Three Welding Equipment Co., Spring Branch State Bank. Dir. Mus. Natural Sci., Jr. Achievement, Houston, Cath. Charities Houston, Houston Fat Stock Show, Houston Horse Show, United Fund. Served as 2d lt. U.S. Army, 1918-19. Mem. C. of C. (past dir.), N.A.M. (dir.), Tex. Mfrs. Assn., Steel Plate Fabricators Assn., Beta Theta Pi. Roman Catholic. Home: Houston TX Died Mar. 17, 1967; buried Forest Park Cemetery.

VAN WICKEL, JESSE FREDERICK foreign service officer; b. Bklyn., June 11, 1890; s. Jesse and Rosina (Versfelt) VanW.; ed. N.Y. pub. schs. and bus. schs.; m. Lilian Perry, July 26, 1913; children—Doris Lilian, Jesse Frederick, Jr. Code expert, 1906-12; traffic mgr., export mgr., purchasing agt., 1912-18; branch mgr. in Shanghai for trading companies, 1918-22; special asst. to sugar corp. in Cuba, 1922-23; trade commr. at Batavia, 1923; commercial attaché at The Hague, Sept. 1926; del. 5th Internat. Congress for Sci. Mgmt., Amsterdam, 1932; del. 8th Internat. Road Congress, The Hague, 1938; consul and sec. in the Diplomatic Service, 1939; consul at Batavia, 1940, Sydney, 1942; detailed to the Dept. of Commerce, 1942, Dept. of State, 1942; 1st sec. American Embassy, London, 1944-45; comml. attaché Am. Embassy, The Hague, 1945-47; consul general at Amsterdam since 1947. Clubs: Rotary, Am. Businessmens (both Amsterdam), Royal Netherlands Automobile (The Hague). Address: Am. Consulate, Amsterdam, Netherlands. Died Mar. 1958.

VAN WINKLE, EDGAR BEACH engineer; b. New York, N.Y., Mar. 4, 1842; s. Edgar Simeon and Hannah (Beach) V.; A.B., Union College, 1860, C.E., 1861; m. Elizabeth, d. Judge William Mitchell, June 7, 1876 (died 1894); m. 2d, Mary Flower, d. William Speiden, of New York, June 3, 1899. Employed on Croton water works extension, 1861-62; pvt. and 1st lt., 1862, capt., 1865, U.S.V.; served on staffs of Gens. Viele, Gilmore and Hatch in Civil War. Elected Companion (1st class) Mil. Order Loyal Legion, 1866; recorder N.Y. Commandery, same, 1886; mem. Commandery-in-Chief, same. Col. and division engr., 1st Div. N.G.S.N.Y., 1876-83. As civil engr. employed on sewerage system, New York; also by Erie R.R., Shepaug Valley R.R.; chief engr. Dept. Public Parks, New York, 1878-84. Home: New York, and Litchfield, Conn. Died Apr. 27, 1920.

VAN ZANDT, KHLEBER MILLER b. Franklin Co., Tenn., Nov. 7, 1836; s. Isaac and Frances Cooke (Lipscomb) V.; m. 3d, Octavia Pendleton, Oct. 8, 1885. Began in banking business in Fort Worth, Tex., 1874; pres. Fort Worth Nat. Bank, 1884-—; mem. Tex. Ho. of Rep., 1873. Served as 2d lt., maj., C.S.A., 1861-65; past gen. comdr. Confed. Vets. of U.S. Democrat. Mem. Christian (Disciples) Ch. Home: Fort Worth, Tex. Died Mar. 19, 1930.

VARIAN, DONALD CORD, naval officer; b. Washington County Md., Mar. 7, 1902; s. Walter and Alice Blake (Cord) V.; B.S., U.S. Naval Acad., 1925; m. Lydia Hill, Nov. 6, 1926; 1 dau., Alice Jean (wife of H. L. Blanton, USMC). Commd. ensign, USN, 1925, advanced through grades to rear adm., 1953; various sea and shore assignments, primarily destroyers; staff Office Sec. Def. 1956-61, dir. personnel policy, 1956-61; pres. Varian Internat. Corp., 1961-69. Home: Coronado CA Died Sept. 1969.

VARICK, RICHARD army officer, mayor N.Y.C.; b. N.J., Mar. 25, 1753; s. Johannes and Jane (Dey) V.; m. Cornelia Hoffman Roosevelt, May 8, 1786, no children. Became capt. 1st N.Y. Regt., 1775, mil. sec. to Gen. Philip John Schuyler; promoted lt. col., later dep. mustermaster-gen. No. Dept., Continental Army; became aide to Benedict Arnold, West Point, 1780; recording sec. to arrange, classify and copy all coor. and records of Continental Army (apptd. by Gen. Washington), 1781-83; recorder of N.Y.C., 1784-86; in charge (with Samuel Jones) of codification N.Y. Statutes, 1786; speaker N.Y. Assembly, 1787-88; atty. gen. N.Y., 1788-89; mayor N.Y.C., 1790-1801; pres. N.Y. Soc. of Cincinnati, 1806-31; an appraiser Erie Canal, 1817; a founder Am. Bible Soc., pres., 1828, 31. Died July 30, 1831.

VARNEY, WILLIAM HENRY naval officer; b. Wolfsborough, N.H., Apr. 19, 1838; s. Henry Weed and Ruth Basset (Buffum) V.; ed. Boston pub. schs.; studied naval architecture, and was designer of merchant vessels; m. Boston, Jan. 1, 1863, Mary Elizabeth Hoffman, of Port Huron, Mich. Apptd. asst. naval constr. U.S.N., July 29, 1869; promoted naval constr., Mar. 12, 1875; retired Apr. 19, 1900. Served at various navy yards, and as superintending constr. of several vessels, mem. Bd. of Inspection and Survey, etc. Author: Ship Builders' Manual, 1877 01. Home: 712 N. Carey St., Baltimore.

VARNEY, WILLIAM WESLEY engr., lawyer; b. Boston, Mass., Sept. 17, 1864; s. William Henry (capt. U.S. Navy) and Mary E. (Hoffman) V.; mech. engring. course, Mass. Inst. Tech., 1883-86; LL.B., U. of Md., 1893; m. Edith McDonnal, Sept. 6, 1899; children—William Henry, John Hoffman. Draftsman, superintending constructor's office, U.S. Navy, Cramp's Shipyard, Phila., 1886-89; draftsman in charge superintending constructor's office, U.S. Navy, Baltimore, 1889-92; admitted to bar, federal and state, 1893; cons. engineer, Baltimore, 1893-99; city commissioner, Baltimore, 1899-1900; also city engr., pres. Bd. Pub. Works and mem. Water Bd.; cons. engr., Baltimore City, 1903-17, harbor engr., 1917-18; also in practice as patent lawyer since 1895. Mem. Am. Soc. M.E. (Am. Engring. Council 1925-27), Am. Soc. C.E., Soc. Naval Architects and Marine Engrs. Mem. Christian (Disciples) Ch. Odd Fellow; Grand Master I.O.O.F. of Md., 1910. Club: Maryland Yacht. Pioneer in television; filed application for 2 patents, Jan. 1892, on method of elec. transmission of optical impressions, and transmission of moving pictures in natural colors from life as well as from films. Home: 6017 Bellona Av., Baltimore, Md. Died July 30, 1943.

VARNUM, JAMES MITCHELL army officer, Continental congressman; b. Dracut, Mass., Dec. 17, 1748; s. Maj. Samuel and Hannah (Mitchell) V.; attended Harvard; grad. with honors R.I. Coll. (now Brown U.), 1769; read law in office of Oliver Arnold, R.I.; m. Martha Child, Feb. 8, 1770, no children. Taught sch.; admitted to R.I. bar, 1771; commd. col. Kentish Guards, 1774; col. 1st Regt., R.I. Inf. (later 9th Continental Inf.), 1775; served in seige of Boston, battles of Long Island and White Plains; commd. brig. gen. R.I. Militia, 1776, also brig. gen. Continental Army (confirmed by Gen. Washington); wintered at Valley Forge with Washington, 1777-78; comdr. R.I. Dept., 1779; resigned to revive law practice, 1779; served as maj. gen. R.I. Militia, 1779-88; served irregularly as mem. Continental Congress, 1780-87; early mem. Soc. of Cincinnati; dir. Ohio Co. of Assos.; apptd. U.S. judge for N.W. Territory, 1788-89, assisted in drawing up territorial law. Died Jan. 10, 1789; buried Mound Cemetery, R.I.

VARNUM, JOSEPH BRADLEY senator; b. Dracut, Mass., Jan. 29, 1750; s. Samuel and Hannah (Mitchell) V.; m. Molly Butler, Jan. 26, 1773, 12 children. Served as capt. Dracut Militia, 1770-74; present at Battle of Lexington; served as capt. Dracut Minute-men, 1776-87, served against Burgoyne, 1777, fought in R.I., 1778; mem. lower house Mass. Legislature, 1780-85, Mass. Senate, 1786-88, 95, 1817-21; served in suppression of Shays' Rebellion, 1786; mem. Mass. Conv. to ratify U.S. Constn., 1788; mem. U.S. Ho. of Reps. from Mass., 4th-12th congresses, 1795-1811, speaker, 10th-11th congresses (charged with corrupt election in 1794); mem. U.S. Senate from Mass., 1811-17, only New Eng. supporter of War Hawks (to bring on War of 1812), pres. pro tem, 1813; del. Mass. Constl. Conv., 1820; mem. Mass. Peace Soc. (later Am. Peace Soc.). Author: An Address Delivered to the Third Division of Massachusetts Militia . . . , 1800. Died Dracut, Sept. 11, 1821; buried Varnum Cemetery, Dracut.

VAUGHAN, ALFRED JEFFERSON maj. gen. and State comdr. United Confederate Veterans for Tenn.; b. Dinwiddie Co., Va., May 10, 1830; grad. Va. Mil. Inst., 1851; practiced as civil engr.; made survey of Hannibal & St. Joseph R.R.; later U.S. surveyor for dist. of Calif.; settled in Miss.; m. Martha J. Hardaway, 1856. Settled on farm in Miss.; served, capt. to brig. gen., in Confederate army; lost leg at Chickamauga; farmed in Miss. until 1872; as gen. agt. of Nat. Grange organized State Granges of Miss., Ark. and Tenn.; was master State Grange of Miss.; established in mercantile business in Memphis, 1873; clerk criminal court Shelby Co., 1878-86. Democrat. Home: Memphis, Tenn. Died 1899.

VAUGHAN, GEORGE TULLY surgeon, soldier, teacher; b. Arrington, Va., June 27, 1859; s. Dr. James Walter Washington Lafayette and Frances Ellen (Shields) V.; M.D., U. of Va., 1879; M.D., Bellevue Hosp. Med. Coll. (N.Y.U.), 1880; post-grad. courses in N.Y. Polyclinic, Univ. of Berlin, and Jefferson Med. Coll., Phila.; LL.D., Georgetown U., 1919; m. May Townsend Venable, June 27, 1883; children—Vera V., William W. Asst. surgeon, Jan. 25, 1888, passed asst. surgeon, 1892, surgeon, 1900, asst. surgeon-gen., 1902-06, U.S. Pub. Health and Marine Hosp. Service; maj. and brigade Surgeon, 7th Army Corps, during war with Spain; became prof. surgery, Georgetown U. Med. Sch., 1897; now emeritus professor of surgery; chief surgeon Georgetown University Hospital; surgeon Tuberculosis Hospital and consulting surgeon St. Elizabeth Hosp. and Washington Asylum Hosp., U.S. Vets. Bureau; was operating surgeon in the navy in Mexican imbroglio at Vera Cruz, 1914, and surgeon U.S.S. Leviathan in the World War, 1917-19; comdr. Med. Reserve Corps, U.S.Navy. Pres. Assn. Mil. Surgeons, 1907-08; fellow Internat. Surg. Assn.; mem. A.M.A., Am. Surg. Assn., Am. Coll. of Surgeons (a founder), Washington Acad. Sciences, Washington Surg. Soc. (pres.), Soc. Colonial Wars, Soc. of the Cincinnati, Order of Washington (comdr. gen.), Southern Surg. Assn., S.A.R., Naval and Mil. Order Spanish-Am. War, Mil. Order World War, Am. Legion, Pi Gamma Mu, Kappa Sigma, Phi Chi, Alpha Omega Alpha and Phi Beta Kappa. Clubs: Cosmos, Army and Navy (Washington). Author: Principles and Practice of Surgery, 1903; Papers on Surgery and Other Subjects, 1932. Frequent contbr. on med. and surg. subjects to tech. jours. Address: 1718 I St., Washington, D.C. Died April 26, 1948.

VAUGHAN, GEORGE WILLIAM bus. exec.; b. Oklahoma City, Mar. 21, 1918; s. George Raymond and Audrey Minerva (Aiken) V.; B.A., Stanford, 1940; m. Jean Webb, Mar. 14, 1942; children—George William, Merry. With Wilson & George Meyer & Co., Los Angeles, 1945-46, Admiral Mfg. Co., Bell, Cal., 1947, Howard Auto Co., Los Angeles, 1947-48; v.p., gen. mgr. Howard Buick Co., Beverly Hills, Cal., 1948-50; pres. Vaughan Buick Co., Los Angeles, 1950-59; asst. sec. for legislative affairs Dept. Def., 1959-60; v.p. Utah Constrn. and Mining Company, 1960-—. Served from ensign to lt. comdr., USNR, 1941-45; assigned to sec. state, orgn. UN Conf., San Francisco, 1945. Mem. Buick Dealers Assn. Los Angeles (pres. 1956), Nat. Buick Dealers Council, Delta Kappa Epsilon. Home: 2614 Jackson St., San Francisco 15. Office: 550 California St., San Francisco 4. Died Sept. 14, 1963; buried Los Angeles.

VAUGHAN, GUY W. pres. Curtiss-Wright Corp.; b. Bayshore, L.I., N.Y., Aug. 15, 1884; s. Gustavus and Elmira (Tilden Goetchius) V.; grad. New Rochelle High Sch., 1898; m. Helen Knapp, Oct. 8, 1908; 1 son, Guy. Began with Desberon Motor Co., New Rochelle (N.Y.), 1898; designed and developed the Vaughan automobile, 1909; drove the Decauville racer which won the Gordon Bennett race, 1902, and made other records; became cons. engr. Babcock Electric Works, Buffalo, N.Y., and Olds Motor Works, Lansing, Mich., 1912; asso. with F. B. Stearns Co. as asst. to pres. and exptl. engr. to assit in devel. of Knight car; was made quality mgr. Wright-Martin Aircraft Co., later factory mgr. for same co.; was v.p. and gen. mgr. Van Blerck Motor Co., Monroe, Mich.; later pres. and gen. mgr. Standard Steel & Bearings Co., Phila.; connected with Wright Aeronautical Corp. since 1924, v.p. and gen. mgr. until 1930, pres. and gen. mgr., 1930-35, pres. 1935-46, chmn. bd., 1935-49, pres. Curtiss-Wright Corp. Comdr. U.S. Naval Res. Dir. Aircraft Industries Am.; chmn. of bd. L.G.S. Spring Clutch Corp., Indpls., Victor Animatograph Corp., Davenport, Ia.; Marquette Metal Products Co., Cleve.; dir. Manufacturers Trust Co., N.Y.; dir. and mem. exec. com. Western Elec. Co., N.Y. Mem. Inst. Aero. Scis., Naval Reserve Officers Assn. Clubs: Engineers (New York); Army-Navy (Washington). Address: 720 Pelham Rd., New Rochelle, N.Y. Died Nov. 21, 1966.

VAUGHAN, HARRY BRIGGS JR. cons. engr.; b. Norfolk, Va., July 24, 1888; s. Henry B. and Josie C. (Cannon) V.; B.S. in Civil Engring., Virginia Poly. Inst., 1911, C.E., 1912; grad. Engr. Sch., 1924, Command and Gen. Staff Sch., 1930; m. Marion R. Evans, Feb. 7, 1921; children—Marion Evans (Mrs. William C. Clement), Harry B., David. Engaged in municipal engring., 1912-17, commd. lt., Engr. Corps, U.S. Army, 1917, advanced through grades to maj. gen.; retired 1946. Decorated D.S.M., Legion of Merit, Silver Star, Purple Heart; Companion of the Bath (Eng.); Comdr. of The Couronne (Belgium); Croix de Guerre with Palm (France). Mem. Am. Soc. C.E., Soc. Naval Architects and Marine Engrs., Soc. Mil. Engrs. Clubs: Army and Navy (Washington); Union League, Engineers (Philadelphia); Army Constituency (Fort Leavenworth). Home: Ithan, Pa. Died Mar. 1964.

VAUGHAN, HERBERT HUNTER educator, lecturer; b. Ann Arbor, Mich., Apr. 2, 1884; s. Victor and Dora (Taylor) V.; A.B., U. of Mich., 1903; Ph.D., Harvard, 1906; unmarried. Began instr. Romanic langs., U. of Kan., 1905; teacher, U. of Mich., Dartmouth, U. of Pa., 1912-19; 1st lt. Mil. Intelligence Div., Gen. Staff, U.S. Army, 1918-19; prof. modern langs., U. of Neb., 1919-22; asst. prof. Italian, Yale, 1922-23; prof. Italian, U. of Calif., since 1923. Mem. Modern Lang. Assn. America, Am. Legion, Am. Assn. Teachers of Italian (pres. 1936), Am. Assn. Univ. Profs. Writer of modern lang. textbooks, and studies on Italian dialects. Address: Wheeler Hall, Univ. of California, Berkeley, Calif. Died Jan. 4, 1948; buried Buchanan, Mich.

VAUGHAN, JOHN RUSSELL physician; b. Huntsville, Mo., Mar. 16, 1888; s. William Walter and Ella Mary (Peery) V.; M.D., Washington U., 1910; m. Sara Elizabeth Thomas, Mar. 6, 1912; children—John Russell, William Edward. Intern, Washington U. Hosp., St. Louis, 1910-11; pvt. practice, specializing in obstetrics and gynecology, St. Louis since 1912; staff St. Louis City and Barnes hosps., 1921-35, St. Luke's Hosp. since 1921. Mem. Med. Civil Def., St. Louis, 1941-45, dep. chief, 1943-45, med. exec. com., 1951; mem. Sch. Bd., University City, Mo., 1929-34, pres., 1933-34. Served as capt., med. corps U.S. Army, 1918-19; chief surgery Camp Colt, Gettysburg, Pa., 1918, Base Hosp. 103, Dijon, France, 1918-19. Mem. A.M.A., St. Louis Gynecol. Soc., Mo. State and St. Louis med. socs., Phi Beta Pi, Sigma Nu. Mason. Club: University (St. Louis). Office: 634 N. Grand Blvd., St. Louis 3. Died Dec. 4, 1952.

VAUGHAN, J(OHN) WALTER surgeon; born Mt. Airy, Mo., Aug. 6, 1880; s. Victor and Dora (Taylor) V.; B.S., U. of Mich., 1902, M.D., 1904; m. Gertrude Leffingwell, Dec. 12, 1906. Practiced at Detroit, since 1905; prof. surgery, Detroit Coll. of Medicine and Surgery, 1907-17; attending surgeon Harper Hosp.; mem. Detroit Bd. of Health, 1914-17. Served in Med. Corps, U.S. Army, in France, Aug. 1917-Feb. 1919; with the French at Soissons, with the British at Cambrai, with Americans at Château Thierry, Juvigny and Verdun; hon. discharged as lt. col. Cited by Gen. Pershing "for exceptionally meritorious and conspicuous services" as cons. surgeon 32d Div. Fellow Am. Coll. Surgeons; mem. A.M.A., Mich. State Med. Soc., Detroit Surg. Soc., Detroit Acad. Medicine, Am. Surg. Assn. Episcopalian. Clubs: University, Detroit Athletic, Detroit Boat, Lochmoor Golf. Author: (with V. C. Vaughan and V. C. Vaughan, Jr.) Protein Split Products. Also several short articles upon professional topics. Address: Veterans Administration Hosp., Roanoke, Va. Died Jan. 21, 1949.

VAUGHAN, VICTOR CLARENCE scientist; b. Mt. Airy, Mo., Oct. 27, 1851; s. John and Adeline (Dameron) V.; B.S., Mt. Pleasant Coll., Mo., 1872; M.S., U. of Mich., 1875, Ph.D., 1876, M.D., 1878, LL.D., 1900; hon. Sc.D., U. of Western Pa., 1897; LL.D., Central Coll., 1910; Jefferson Med. Coll., Phila., 1915, U. of Mo., 1923; m. Dora Catherine Taylor, August 21, 1877; children—Victor C. (dec.), John Walter, Herbert Hunter, Henry Frieze, Warren Taylor. Assistant in chem. lab., 1875-83, lecturer med. chemistry, 1879-80, asst. prof., 1880-83, prof. physiol. and pathol. chemistry and asso. prof. therapeutics and materia medica, 1883-87, prof. hygiene and physiol. chemistry, and dir. Hygienic Lab., 1887-1909, dean dept. medicine and surgery, 1891-1921, U. of Mich. in Santiago campaign, 1898, as maj. and surgeon 63d Mich. Vol. Inf.; apptd. div. surgeon, 1898; recommended by President for bvt. of lt. col.; col., M.C. U.S.A., in charge of communicable diseases, 1917-18. Chmn. div. of med. sciences, Nat. Research Council; member Typhoid Commn. Awarded D.S.M. Pres. Assn. Am. Physicians, 1908-09; pres. A.M.A., 1914-15. Knight Legion of Honor, France, 1923. Author: Osteology and Myology of the Domestic Fowl, 1876; Text-book of Physiological Chemistry (3 edits.), 1879-83; Ptomaines and Leucomaines and Cellular Toxins (with Dr. Novy); Protein Split Products (with Victor C. Vaughan, Jr., and J. Walter Vaughan), 1913; (with Henry F. Vaughan and George T. Palmer) Epidemiology and Public Health, 3 vols.; A Doctor's Memories. Mng. editor Jour. Lab. and Clin. Medicine, 1915-23. Home: Detroit, Mich. Died Nov. 21, 1929.

VAUGHAN, WARREN TAYLOR physician; b. Ann Arbor, Mich., Feb. 22, 1893; s. Victor Clarence and Dora Catherine (Taylor) V.; student Lancy, Switzerland, 1908-09; A.B., U. of Mich., 1913, M.D., 1916, hon. M.S., 1941; m. Emma Elizabeth Heath, June 21, 1917; children—Victor Clarence III, Warren Taylor, John Heath, David DuPuy. House officer, Peter Bent Brigham Hosp., Boston, Mass., 1916-17; asst. in preventive medicine and hygiene, Harvard Med. Sch., 1919-20; in practice internal medicine, specializing in allergy, Richmond, Va., since 1920; dir. Vaughan-Graham Clinic. Served as 1st lt., advancing through grades to lt. col. Med. Corps, U.S. Army, 1917-19; chief of med. service, Camp Hosp. 41, A.E.F. Mem. advisory com. to Committee on Costs of Medical Care; mem. com. on aerobiology and food habits of Natural Research Council; mem. Research Council on Problems of Alcohol (dir.); chmn. com. on medicaments and pharmaceuticals, American Academy of Allergy. Fellow A.A.A.S. (council since 1938); mem. Medical Society of Virginia (vice-pres. 1931-32), Southern Medical Assn., A.M.A., Am. Society Clin. Pathologists, Am. Assn. Study Allergy (sec.-treas. 1928-38, pres. 1939), Soc. for Study Asthma and Allied Conditions (pres. 1938-39), Am. Rheumatism Assn., Soc. of Investigative Dermatology, Internat. Soc. Gastroenterology, Inst. of Practice of Medicine, Barcelona, Spain (hon.), Soc. Study Allergy, Argentina (hon.), Va. Acad. Science (chmn. biol. sect., 1931), Huguenot Soc., Beta Theta Pi, Phi Rho Sigma, Sigma Xi, Alpha Omega Alpha. Formerly mem. Assn. Am. Phys., Am. Coll. Physicians. Episcopalian. Clubs: Commonwealth, Harvard Club of Va. (pres. 1940-41). Author: Influenza, An Epidemiologic Study, 1921; Allergy and Applied Immunology, 1931; Practice of Allergy, 1939; Primer of Allergy, 1939; Strange Malady, 1941. Editor in chief Journal Laboratory and Clinical Medicine; asso. editor Jour. of Allergy; mem. editorial bd. Am. Jour. Digestive Diseases, Am. Journal Clin. Pathology; formerly mem. editorial bd. Review of Gastro-enterology, Am. Jour. Syphilis and collaborating editor Folia Clinica Chimica et Microscopica (Bologna, Italy). Contributor of over 150 articles to current med. lit.; also contbr. to Ency. Americana and Oxford Medicine. Office: 201 W. Franklin St., Richmond, Va. Died Apr. 2, 1944.

VAUGHN, SAMUEL JESSE, educator; b. Elkton, Mo., Feb. 12, 1877; s. Alexander Shelton and Mary Elizabeth (Boone) V.; grad. Weaubleau (Mo.) Christian Coll., 1897; A.B., Drury Coll., Mo., 1908; U. of Chicago, summers, 1905-10; m. Florence Rose Perry, of Springfield, Dec. 31, 1900; children—Jesse Wendell, Rebecca Merle. Prin. Dadeville (Mo.) Acad., 1899-1902; supt. schs. in Mo., 1902-05; dir. industrial edn., Springfield, Mo., 1905-08; dir. industrial teacher training, Northern Ill. Teachers Coll., De Kalb, Ill., 1908-20; head dept. industrial edn., U. of Ill., 1920-21; pres. Hardin Coll., Mexico, Mo., 1921-26; pres. Colo. Woman's Coll. since 1926. Editor Industrial Arts Magazine since 1914. Served as 1st lt. Sanitary Corps, reeducation service, Ft. McHenry, Baltimore, World War; asst. editor of "Carry On" for Surgeon General's Office, Washington, D.C. Pres. Western Arts Assn., 1915, Vocational Edn. Assn. of Middle West, 1916; mem. Phi Delta Kappa. Republican. Missionary Bapt. Club: Rotary. Author: Printing and Bookbinding for Schools, 1912; Content and Methods of the Industrial Arts, 1922. Lecturer on ednl., social and economic problems. Address: 2001 Josephine St., Denver CO*

VEBLEN, OSWALD mathematician; b. Decorah, Ia., June 24, 1880; s. Andrew A. and Kirsti (Hougen) V.; A.B., U. Ia., 1898; A.B., Harvard, 1900; Ph.D., U. Chgo., 1903, D.Sc., 1941; hon. D.Sc., Oxford, 1929; hon. Ph.D., U. Oslo, 1929, Hamburg, 1933; LL.D., Glasgow U., 1951; m. Elizabeth M. D. Richardson, 1908. Asso. in math. U. Chgo., 1903-05; preceptor in math. Princeton, 1905-10, prof., 1910-32, prof. Inst. for Advanced Study, Princeton, 1932-50, prof. emeritus since 1950. Pres. Internat. Congress Mathematicians held at Harvard, 1950. Capt. and maj. Ordnance Dept., U.S. Army, 1917-19. Chmn. phys. scis. NRC, 1923-34; Fellow Am. Acad. Arts and Sciences, Am. Phys. Soc., A.A.A.S.; mem. Nat. Acad. Sciences, Am. Philos. Soc., Am. Math. Soc. (pres. 1923-24), Math. Assn. Am.; hon. mem. London Math. Soc., Circolo Mathematico di Palermo, Société Mathematique de France (hon. mem. bureau); fgn. corr., Academia Nacional de Ciencias Exactas, Lima, Peru; hon. fellow, Royal Soc., Edinburgh; mem. Royal Irish Acad. (Dept. Sci.); fgn. mem. Royal Danish Acad. of Sciences; Polish Acad. Scis. and Letters, Accademia dei Lincei; Knight, 1st Class, Royal Order of St. Olav (Norway). Army-Navy Certificate of Merit, 1948. Author: Infinitesimal Analysis (with N. J. Lennes), 1907; Projective Geometry (Vol. I, with J. W. Young), 1910, Vol. II, 1918, Cambridge Colloquium Lectures on Analysis-Situs, 1922; Invariants of Quadratic Differential Forms, 1927; Foundations of Differential Geometry (with J. H. C. Whitehead), 1932; Projektive Relativitätstheorie, 1933; Geometry of Complex Domains (with Wallace Givens), 1936. Home: 452 Herrontown Rd., Princeton, N.J. Died Aug. 10, 1960; cremated.

VENABLE, CHARLES SCOTT educator; b. Prince Edward County, Va., April 19, 1827; grad. Hampden-Sidney, 1842; U. of Va., 1848, LL.D., 1868; studied Berlin, 1852, and Bonn, 1854; prof. mathematics Hampden-Sidney Coll., 1848-56; prof. physics and chemistry, U. of Ga., 1856; of mathematics and astronomy, U. of S.C., 1858-61; capt. engrs., 1861-62; lt. col. and aide-de-camp to Gen. Robert E. Lee, 1862-65, in Army of Northern Va.; prof. mathematics U. of Va., 1865; chmn. of faculty, 1870-73, and again in 1887. Home: Charlottesville, Va. Died 1900.

VENABLE, RICHARD MORTON lawyer; b. Charlotte County, Va., Feb. 8, 1839; s. Richard N. and Magdalen (McCampbell) V.; A.B., Hampden-Sidney Coll., 1857, LL.D., 1888; U. of Va., 1859-60; LL.B., Washington and Lee U., 1868; unmarried. Entered C.S.A. as pvt., Apr. 21, 1861; became maj. of arty. and engrs. serving in Army of Northern Va. and Trans-Mississippi Dept. Prof. engring., U. of La., 1865; prof. mathematics, Washington and Lee U., 1867; in law practice Baltimore, 1869—; mem. Baltimore City Council, 1899-1903; pres. Bd. Park Commrs., Baltimore, Prof. law, U. of Md., 1870-1905. Trustee Johns Hopkins U.; v.p. Johns Hopkins Hosp. Home: Baltimore, Md. Died 1910.

VERBECK, GUIDO FRIDOLIN educator; b. Aurora, N.Y., May 2, 1887; s. William and Katherin (Jordan) V.; grad. St. John's School, Manlius, N.Y., 1905; student Cornell U., 1906-09; Sc.D., Colgate U., 1934; m. Muriel Halcomb, June 1, 1911; children—Guido F., Samuel Sumner, Edith, Nan. Instr. St. John's Sch. (title changed to Manlius Sch., 1925), 1910-12, comdt., 1912-30, supt., 1930, later headmaster, also v.p. and trustee. Served as lt. col. 106th F.A., World War I; col. 368th F.A., Res. Awarded two silver star citations and Conspicuous Service Cross (U.S.). Pres. Assn. of Mil. Colleges and Schools of U.S. Republican. Episcopalian. Mason. Home: Manlius, N.Y. Died July 27, 1940.

VERDELIN, HENRY bank exec.; b. Minneapolis, Aug. 5, 1899; s. John Henry and Olga M. (Anderson) V.; student U. of Minn., 1917-19; LL.D., Minn. Coll. Law, 1923; m. Mildred Eberhart. With First Nat. Bank, Minneapolis, 1917-40, v.p., 1935-40; v.p. Mutual Life Ins. Co. of N.Y. 1940-52; sr. v.p. The San Francisco Bank, 1952, pres. 1953-54; pres. First Western Bank and Trust Co., 1954-57; executive vice president and member board directors Coast Federal Savs. & Loan Assn., 1958—. Lt. col., U.S. Army, 1942-45. Mem. Am. Inst. Banking (pres. 1936-37). Sigma Delta Kappa. Clubs: California, Los Angeles Athletic; Oakmont Country (Glendale); Los Angeles Athletic. Home: 360 Grove St., Pasadena 2, Cal. Office: 855 S. Hill St., Los Angeles 14. Died Mar. 24, 1961; buried Pasadena Mausoleum.

VERHOEFF, FREDERICK HERMAN, ophthalmologist; b. Louisville, Ky., July 9, 1874; s. Herman and Mary Jane (Parker) V.; Ph.B., Yale, 1895; M.D., Johns Hopkins, 1899; LL.D., 1953; A.M., Harvard, 1902; study ophthalmology, in Europe, 1902-03; Margaret F. Lougee, Sept. 17, 1902; children—Mary Josephine (dec.), Margaret. Externe Johns Hopkins Hospital, 1899-1900; asst. surgeon Baltimore Eye, Ear and Throat Charity Hosp., 1899-1900; asst. in pathology, Harvard Med. Sch., 1900-02; asst. ophthalmic surgeon Carney Hosp., Boston, 1902-06; pathologist, Mass. Charitable Eye and Ear Infirmary, 1900-31, asst. ophthalmic surgeon, 1905-13, ophthalmic surgeon, 1913-32, chief of research, 1925-32, cons. chief of ophthalmology since 1932; instr. in ophthalmic pathology, Harvard Med. School, 1907-16, asst. prof. of ophthalmic research 1916-21, asst. prof. ophthalmology, 1921-24, prof. ophthalmic research, 1924-40, emeritus since 1940; scientific dir. Howe Lab. of Ophthalmology, 1931-32, dir. 1932-40. Maj. Med. Corps, U.S. Army, 1918-19. Fellow Am. Acad. Arts and Sciences, A.A.A.S., Am. Coll. Surgeons; mem. Am. Ophthal. Soc. (awarded Howe medal 1932; pres. 1937). A.M.A. (chmn. sect. on ophthalmology, 1932; awarded Knapp medal 1922, ophthalmic research medal, 1930). Awarded Leslie Dana Medal, 1947. Clubs: Harvard, Yale, Longwood Cricket, Algonquin, Eastern Yacht. Home: 61 Monmouth St., Brookline 16 MA Office: 395 Commonwealth Av., Boston 15 MA

VERNON, JAMES WILLIAM physician, psychiatrist; b. Person Co., N.C., July 21, 1886; s. Charles R. and Corinna Josephine (Henry) V.; B.S.; Wake Forest (N.C.) Coll., 1907; M.D., Jefferson Med. Coll., 1909; m. Sarah Cole Taylor, July 17, 1919; children—James Taylor, Livingston, Charles Robertson. Interne, Polyclinic Hosp., Philadelphia, Pa., 1910; asst. physician, Broadoaks Sanatorium, Morganton, N.C., 1910-17, supt. since 1921; cons. psychiatrist Morganton State Hosp.; psychiatrist to Grace Hosp., Morganton; company surgeon to Southern Ry., Morganton. Dir. First Nat. Bank, Morganton, Mayor of Morganton, 1933-37. Examining physician Burke County (N.C.) Local Bd. No. 1 since 1940; N.C. Hospitals Bd. Control (advis. comm.) since 1945. Served as 1st lt., M.C., U.S. Army, 1917, capt. 1918, major 1918; with A.E.F., France. Diplomate Am. Bd. Psychiatry and Neurology. Fellow A.C.P., A.M.A., Am. Psychiatric Assn.; mem. Southern Med. Assn., Fellow Med. Soc. of N.C. (pres. 1943-44), Assn. Southern Ry. Surgeons, Burke County Med. Soc. (pres. 1936), Tri-State Med. Assn., Catawba Valley Med. Soc., N.C. Bd. of Med. Examiners (pres. 1938), N.C. Neuropsychiatric Soc. (pres. 1938), Southern Psychiatric Assn., Am. Ornithologists Union, A.A.A.S., N.C. Academy Science, National Committee for Mental Hygiene, American Legion. Democrat. Presbyterian. Mason (32 deg.). Clubs: Kiwanis, North Carolina Bird. Author: Circular Psychosis, 1926; Psychoneurosis, 1933; Psychiatry and the General Practitioner, 1926; Some Preventive Aspects of Mental Hygiene, 1943; A Challenge to the Doctors of North Carolina, 1944. Home: 209 Valdese Av. Office: Broadoaks Sanatorium, Morganton, N.C. Died July 16, 1955; buried Morganton.

VERRILL, ROBINSON, lawyer; b. Portland, Me., Aug. 22, 1896; s. Harry Mighels and Louise Shurtleff (Brown) V.; A.B., Yale, 1918; LL.B., Harvard Law Sch., 1922; m. Agnes Walton Thompson, Apr. 27, 1925; children—Robinson, Eric. Admitted to Mass. and Me. bars 1922; partner Verrill, Dana, Philbrick, Whitehouse & Putnam, Portland; dir. Coca-Cola Bottling plants, Inc.; chmn. exec. com. Bates Manufacturing Co., Served as Volunteer with Am. Field Service and as 2d lieut. U.S. Army, with A.E.F., World War I; served as maj. and lt. col. with I Troop Carrier Command, 1st Allied Airborne Army, Office of Strategic Services, Air Corps in U.S. and European Theatre, World War II col. USAFR, ret. Decorated Bronze Star. Fellow American Bar Foundation; member American, Maine, Cumberland bar assns., Zeta Psi. Republican. Conglist. Home: Portland ME Died Aug. 13, 1970.

VERY, SAMUEL WILLIAMS rear admiral U.S.N.; b. Liverpool, Eng., Apr. 23, 1846; s. Samuel (Jr.) and Sarah Williams (McKey) V.; pvt. and pub. schs.; U.S. Naval Acad., Newport, R.I., and Annapolis, Md., 1863-66; m.

Martha Bourne Simonds, June 14, 1883. Ensign, Mar. 12, 1868; master, Mar. 26, 1869; lt., Mar. 21, 1870; lt. comdr., Mar. 4, 1886; comdr., Mar. 5, 1895; capt., Feb. 19, 1901; rear admiral, July 22, 1906. Served in numerous vessels of the Navy and at several naval stas., besides engaging in magnetic investigations on part of Coast Survey, 1880-81, and having charge of Transit of Venus Expdn. to Patagonia, 1882-83; comd. steamers Saturn and Cassius, 1898, in operations around Cuba, and the gunboat Castine, 1899-1900, in Philippine and Chinese waters; while comdg. Castine conquered and received surrender of Zamboanga, Mindanao, P.I., with results that were highly commended in report of Rear Admiral J. C. Watson; comd. U.S.S. San Francisco, Mediterranean and Asiatic stas., Nov. 1903-Dec. 31, 1904; comdt. of Naval Sta., Hawaii, July 26, 1906-Apr. 23, 1908; retired Apr. 23, 1908. Home: Chestnut Hill, Mass. Died Jan. 3, 1919.

VESTAL, SAMUEL CURTIS author, army officer; b. Cloverdale, Ind., Apr. 6, 1873; s. William B. and Isis M. (East) V.; grad. U.S. Naval Acad., 1895, Army Staff Coll., 1906, Army War Coll., 1915, Gen. Staff Coll., 1920; m. Olive S. Miller, of Greencastle, Ind., Mar. 29, 1899 (died 1943); children—Mildred (Mrs. M. V. Seeds), William Miller; m. 2d, Bertha Kimmel, Feb. 3, 1946. Pvt., corpl. and sergt., Co. E, 2d Inf., 1895; 2d lt. 7th Artillery, 1898; promoted through grades to colonel, 1920; retired, 1937. With siege train, Spanish-American War; in Puerto Rico, 1903-04; in Philippines, 1909-11, 1924-27; comdr. 339th Regiment F.A., Aug. 1917; arrived in France, Sept. 1918; participated in Meuse-Argonne offensive; insp. 6th Corps, after Armistice; instr. Army War Coll., 1920-24; asst. comdt. Coast Arty. Sch., 1927; chief of historical sect. Army War Coll., 1928-30; prof. mil. science and tactics, Mass. Inst. Tech., 1930-37; asso. mem. Walter Hines Page Sch. of Internat. Relations, Johns Hopkins U., 1929-33. Mem. Am. Hist. Assn., Am. Legion. Mason. Author: The Maintenance of Peace, 1920; Washington, The Military Man, 1931; also numerous mag. articles on mil. and internat., subjects. Home: 554 E. Howard St., Pasadena 6, Cal. Died Nov. 21, 1958.

VICKERY, HOWARD LEROY naval officer, U.S. maritime commr.; b. Bellevue, O., Apr. 20, 1892; s. Willis and Ann (Schneider) V.; B.S., U.S. Naval Acad., 1915; M.S., Mass. Inst. Tech., 1921; grad. Army Indsl. Coll., 1934; m. Margurite Blanchard, Apr. 9, 1917; children—Hugh Blanchard, Barbara Willis. Commd. ensign, U.S.N., 1915; assigned to navy constrn. corps as lt., 1918; rear adm., Apr. 1942, vice admiral, Oct. 1944; assistant to supt. in charge submarine construction Bethlehem Shipbuilding Co., San Francisco, 1920; outside supt., new work supt. and docking supt., Boston Navy Yard, 1921-25; loaned to Govt. of Haiti as treaty engr. and dir. of shop, Supply and Transportation Div., 1925-28; head materials, equipment, and inspection div., Bur. of Construction and Repair, U.S. Navy, 1928-29; tech. adviser on shipping to gov.-gen. of P.I., 1929-33; head War Plan Sect., design branch, Bur. of Construction and Repair, 1934-37; asst. to chmn. of U.S. Maritime Commn., 1937-40; mem. since Sept. 1940; vice chmn., Feb. 1942-Dec. 1945; deputy administrator War Shipping Adminstrn. since June 1942; member production exec. committee War Production Board, and member War Manpower Commn.; chairman Postwar Planning Com., U.S. Maritime Commn. Awarded Morehead Medal, 1945. Decorated Victory medal (Cruiser); Lieut. of Grand Dragon of Anam (French Indo-China); Distinguished Service Certificate, Am., Legion; Distinguished Service Medal (United States Army). Member Council Society Naval Architects and Marine Engineers; member Naval Architecture and Classification Committee, Am. Bureau of Shipping. Chmn. bd. trustees Cleveland Law Sch. Republican. Conglist. Clubs: Chevy Chase Country, Army-Navy (Washington); Army-Navy Country (Arlington, Va.); Polo (manila). Home: 4420 Dexter St. N.W. Office: U.S. Maritime Commission, Washington. Died Mar. 21, 1946; buried in Arlington National Cemetery.

VIDAL, EUGENE LUTHER, aviation official; b. at Madison, S.D., Apr. 13, 1895; s. Felix Louis and Margaret (Rewalt) V.; C.E., U. of S.D., 1916; grad. U.S. Mil. Acad., 1918, U.S. Army Engring., Air Corps Pilot and Observation Schs., 1918-21; Sc.D., (hon.), Lawrence Coll. 1943; m. Nina Gore, Jan. 11, 1921 (div. 1935); 1 son, Gore; m. 2d, Katharine Roberts, 1939; children—Vance, Valerie. Served in U.S. Army, 1918-26, football coach University of Oregon, 1926-27; assistant general manager Transcontinental Air Transport, 1929-30; organizer and general manager Ludington Air Lines, 1930-32; dir. of air commerce, U.S. Dept. of Commerce, Washington, and mem. Nat. Advisory Committee for Aeronautics, 1933-37; aviation consultant Bendix Aviation, 1937-38; pres. Aircraft Research Corp. and Vidal Research Corp. (developing Vidal Process), and dir. and asso. Northeast Airlines since 1937; pres. Vidal Corp., 1943-45. Dir. Metropolitan Aviation Corp., 1946, Northeast Airlines; pres. Vidal Co., 1949-69, aviation adviser to chief of staff U.S. Army, 1955-65; cons. Phillips Petroleum Co., 1962-69, U.S. Army, 1963-69. Mem. U.S. Army Sci. Adv. Panel, also Transportation Corps adv. com., 1957-69, Gov. Flight Safety Found. Mem. Nat. Aero. Assn., Inst. Aero. Sci. Phi Delta Theta. Democrat. Club: Wings (N.Y.). Home: Avon CT Died Feb. 20, 1969.

VIDMER, GEORGE, army officer; born Mobile, Ala., Aug. 16, 1871; s. John and Ella (Redwood) V.; student U. of Ala., 1888-89; grad. U.S. Mil. Acad., 1894, War Coll., 1920; m. Carol Richards, Sept. 5, 1894; children—Eleanor Redwood (wife of Col. Joseph P. Aleshire), Julian Richards. Promoted through grades to brig. gen., Aug. 21, 1933; comd. troops in battle, Santiago, Cuba, Spanish-Am. War, 1898; Army of Cuban Occupation, 1899-1902; in P.I., 1902-04; Army of Cuban Pacification, 1906-09; adjutant U.S. Mil. Acad., 1912-14; on Mexican border, 1914-17; served in France, 1918-19; asst. chief of cavalry, U.S. Army, 1920-24; chief of staff 61st Cav. Div., 1924-29; on staff 7th Corps Area, 1929-31; comdg. 2d Cav. Brig., 1933-35; retired from the active service, Aug. 31, 1935. Twice wounded in action. Awarded D.S.C., D.S.M., Silver Star Citation with oak leaf cluster, Order of Purple Heart (U.S.); Officer Legion of Honor and Croix de Guerre with Palms (France). Mem. Internat. Equestrian Team, 1909-13. Mem. Sigma Nu. Democrat. Methodist. Home: Spring Hill, Mobile AL

VIELÉ, CHARLES DELAVAN brig. gen. U.S.A.; b. Albany, N.Y., Feb. 7, 1841; s. Rufus King and Phebe A. (Gregory) V.; ed. pvt. schs., Albany, N.Y.; m. Nannie D. Minor, Jan. 10, 1872. Apptd. 2d lt. 1st U.S. Inf., Oct. 24, 1861; 1st lt., Apr. 6, 1862; bvtd. capt., July 4, 1863, "for gallant and meritorious service during siege of Vicksburg"; assigned to 10th U.S. Cav., Dec. 31, 1870; maj. 1st U.S. Cav., Aug. 20, 1889; lt. col., Nov. 21, 1897; brig. gen. U.S.V., Sept. 21, 1898; col. 4th U.S. Cav., Sept. 14, 1899; retired from active service, Jan. 23, 1900, for disability in line of duty; brig. gen. U.S.A. retired, Apr. 23, 1904. Served with Regular Div., 5th Corps, Army of Potomac, until June 1862; with Gen. Grant in campaign resulting in capture of Vicksburg, July 4, 1863; participated in Red River campaign, 1864, on staff Gen. Dudley, comdg. 4th brigade of cav.; served in Ind. Ty., Ariz., Tex., Mont., 1871-95, participating in numerous Indian campaigns and scouting parties; on duty at Ft. Riley, Kan., and Ft. Sheridan, Ill., 1895-98; comd. 1st U.S. Cav. during Spanish War, taking part in battle of San Juan and siege of Santiago de Cuba; comd. Ft. Riley, Kan., 1898-99, Ft. Robinson, Neb., Jan.-Sept. 1899, when was ordered to Manila, P.I., where stationed until retired. Republican. Died Oct. 6, 1916.

VIELÉ, EGBERT LUDOVICKUS soldier, engr., author; b. Waterford, N.Y., June 17, 1825; grad. West Point, 1847; served in Mexican War; also in Indian campaigns on Western frontier; resigned as lt., Oct. 26, 1850. Settled in practice in New York as civil engr.; State engr. of N.J., 1854-56; apptd. chief engr., 1856, of Central Park, New York, and prepared original plan which was adopted for the park; engr. Prospect Park, Brooklyn, 1860, but resigned on 1st call for vols., 1861, and comd. force that opened Potomac River to Washington; capt. engrs. 7th N.Y. regt.; commd. brig. gen. vols., Aug. 17, 1861. 2d in command of Port Royal expdn.; comd. at capture of Ft. Pulaski; planned and executed march on Norfolk, Va., mil. gov. Norfolk, May to Oct. 1863; resigned and resumed practice; engr. of many pub. works; commr. of parks, 1883, and pres. dept. parks, 1884; mem. Congress, 1885-87. Democrat. V.p. Am. Geog. Soc.; appeared before Com. of British House of Lords on subject of municipal adminstrn., 1896. Author: Handbook for Active Service; Topographical Atlas of City of New York; etc. Died 1902.

VIGNEC, ALFRED J. physician; b. N.Y. City, Apr. 4, 1905; s. Auguste and Marie (Eigeldinger) V.; B.S., N.Y. U., 1928; M.D., Yale, 1934; m. Wilhelmina Vissers, 1943 (deceased 1952); children—Alfred A., Ann L. (both adopted); married second, Elsie E. Essmuller, 1954; one son, Paul Alfred. Interne, L.I. Coll. Hosp., Brooklyn, 1934-35, resident, 1935-37; research fellow Yale, 1937-39; instr. pediatrics, L.I. Coll. of Medicine, 1939-41; med. dir., pediatrician-in-chief, N.Y. Foundling Hospital since 1944; dir. pediatrics St. Vincent's Hosp., N.Y. City, since 1947; instr. pediatrics Cornell Med. Sch., and asst. pediatrician, N.Y. Hosp., 1944-47; asso. pediatrician St. Clare's Hosp., N.Y. City, 1944-47; clin. prof. pediatrics N.Y. U.-Bellevue Med. Center; cons. pediatrician, N.Y. State Rehabilitation Hosp., West Haverstraw, N.Y., St. Joseph's Hosp., Yonkers, N.Y., St. Agnes Hosp., White Plains, N.Y., St. Clares Hosp., and Misercordia Hospital, New York City; associate pediatrician, University Hospital (Post-Grad.), N.Y.C.; medical dir. Kennedy Child Study Centre, N.Y.C. Mem. pediatric adv. com. Commr. of Health N.Y.C., premature adv. com. Dept. of Health, N.Y.C.; Medical Advisory Board for Dependent Children, N.Y. City Dept. of Welfare. Capt., M.C., U.S. Army, 1942-43. Decorated papal Knight Order of Holy Sepulchre. Fellow Am. Acad. of Pediatrics, A.M.A., N.Y. Acad. Medicine; mem. N.Y. Co. Med. Soc. (mem. milk commn., com. on infant mortality); honorary member of Sigma Xi. Roman Catholic. Clubs: Yale (N.Y.C.) Strathmore-Vanderbilt Country. Contributor articles on poliomyelitis infant nutrition to technical and profl. jours. Home: 119 Mill Spring Rd., Manhasset, N.Y. Office: 39-A, Gramercy Park, N.Y.C. 10. Died Feb. 4, 1962; buried Woodland Cemetery, S.I., N.Y.

VIGUERS, RICHARD THOMSON, hosp. adminstr.; b. Phila., Aug. 25, 1911; s. Frank Rutherford and Mary (Thomson) V.; B.S. in Econs., U. Pa., 1933; LL.B., 1938; student New Sch. for Social Research, 1939-40; H. H. D., Portia Law Sch., 1965, Dr. Humanities, 1965, Calvin Coolidge Coll., 1965; m. Ruth Alfarata Hill, June 2, 1937; children—Deborah Hill (Mrs. Dennis Hughes), Susan Thomson (Mrs. Barnard L. Berman), Doris Kimball. Engaged as a lectr. in economics Central China Coll., Wuchang, China, 1935-37; adminstrator Bound Brook (New Jersey) Hospital; 1939; asso. div. rural hosps. The Commonwealth Fund, N.Y., 1940-46; administrator of the Pratt Diagnostic Clinic, N.E. Center Hosp., Boston, 1947-65, New England Medical Center Hospitals, 1965-69; cons. in hospital adminstrn. Pres. Greater Boston Hospital Council, 1962; chmn. adv. com. Center of Continuing Edn. in Hosp. Adminstrn., Columbia U. Bd. dirs. Chinese br. YMCA, Boston; pres. Human Relations Service, Inc., Wellesley, Mass., 1956-59; lectr. Tufts Sch. Dental Medicine, 1968. Trustee Wellesley Free Library, 1963-69. Served from lt. to lt. col., Med. Adminstrv. Corps, AUS, 1942-46; China-Burma-India Theatre. Fellow Am. Pub. Health Assn., Royal Soc. Health Gt. Britain, Am. Coll. Hosp. Adminstrs.; mem. Am. (mem. council on adminstrv. practice 1955-58), Mass. (pres. 1965) hospital associations, Assn. Am. Med. Colls., New England Hosp. Assembly (pres. 1955), Hosp. Supts. Club (pres. 1959-61), Mass. Health Council (pres. 1961), Hosp. Adminstrs. Study Soc. (pres. 1964-65); asso. mem. Am. Assn. Hospital Cons. Democrat. Episcopalian. Author articles on hosps. adminstrn. Home: Wellesley Hills MA Died Oct. 31, 1969.

VIJITAVONGS, PHYA, diplomatic service; b. Bangkok, Siam, Jan. 31, 1877; ed. in England at Sandhurst Mil. Acad., Sch. of Musketry (Hythe), Sch. of Arty. (Okehampton) and Christ Ch. Coll., Oxford; m. Yubha Singhara, of Bangkok, 1903. Served as lt. gen. Siamese Army; E.E. and M.P. from Siam to U.S. since Sept. 1926. Address: Siamese Legation, 2300 Kalorama Rd., Washington DC

VILAS, WILLIAM FREEMAN U.S. senator, lawyer; b. Chelsea, Vt., July 9, 1840; s. Hon. Levi B. and Esther G. (Smilie) V.; family settled at Madison, June 1851; grad. U. of Wis., 1858; Albany Law Sch., 1860; established practice. In July 1862, recruited Co. A, 23d Wis. vols.; took part in Vicksburg campaign; promoted to lt. col., comdg. his regt. during siege of Vicksburg and 2 months afterward; resigned commn. Aug. 1863; resumed practice; law prof., 1868-85, and 1881-85 and 1897-1905, regent, U. of Wis.; trustee Soldiers' Orphans' Home; mem. commn. to revise statutes of Wis., 1875-78; mem. Dem. Nat. Com., 1876-86; mem. Wis. legislature, 1885; permanent chmn. Nat. Dem. Conv., 1884; Postmaster Gen. U.S., 1885-88; Sec. of the Interior, Jan. 1888 to March 1889; U.S. senator, 1891-97; mem. commn. which built State Hist. Library, 1897-1903; joined the Nat. (gold standard) Dem. party, 1896; chmn. Com. on Resolutions, Indianapolis Conv., 1896. Mem. commn. to build Wis. capitol, 1906-—. Edited (with Ed. E. Bryant), Vols. 1, 2, 4, 6 to 20 Wis. Supreme Ct. Reports. Home: Madison, Wis. Died 1908.

VILJOEN, BENJAMIN JOHANNIS soldier; b. Woodhouse, C. C., S. Africa, Sept. 7, 1868; s. Wynand J. and Susana (Storm) V.; ed. pub. schs., mil. training at Model Acad. and Mil. Sch., Pretoria, Transvaal, S. Africa; m. St. Louis, June, 1905, Myrtle Dickerson. Mem. Transvaal senate 2 yrs.; spl. commandant Johannesburg forces, lt. gen. in Boer War, 2 yrs.; captured by British and exiled to island of St. Helena; released and emigrated to America, 1902; head of Boer settlement, Chamberino, N.M., since 1905. Pres. Western Mesilia Valley Farmers' Union; gen. mgr. Lucerne Farm Co. (inc.) Pres. Boer War Exbn. at World's Fair, St. Louis, 1903. Republican. Author: An Exiled General, 1902 L11; Under the Vier Kleur, 1904 L9. Address: Chamberino, N.M.

VIMEUR, JEAN BAPTISTE DONATIEN DE (comte de Rochambeau), army officer; b. Vendôme, France, July 1, 1725; s. Joseph Charles (comte de Rochambeau) and Claire (Begon) de Vimeur; attended Collège de Vendôme; m. Jeanne d'Acosta, Dec. 1749. Served in War of Austrian Succession, Seven Years War; promoted brig. gen., 1761, became insp. cavalry; apptd. gov. Villefrancheen-Roussillon, 1776; came to Am. as comdr. French troops in Am. Revolution, sailed from Brest to Newport, R.I., with 6,000 men, 1780; joined Continental Army under Washington at White Plains, N.Y., 1781; beseiged Cornwallis at Yorktown, aided in gaining his surrender, Oct. 1781; returned to France, 1783; became comdr. of important mil. dist. with hdqrs. at Calais, France; active mem. Soc. of Cincinnati; mem. 2d Assembly of Notables; made comdr. dist. of Alsace (France); placed in charge of No. Mil. Dept., 1790; created marshal of France, 1791; honored by Napoleon; mem. Legion of Honor. Author: Memoirs, published Paris, 1809, in English, 1838. Died Alsace, May 10, 1807; buried Thoré, France.

VINCENT, CLINTON DERMOTT U.S. Army officer; b. Borden Co., Tex., Nov. 29, 1914; s. Carvin Wyoming and Rose Loins (Burgess) V.; B.S., U.S. Mil. Acad., 1936; grad. Air Corps Advanced Flying Sch., 1937; m. Margaret Thayer Hennessey, Feb. 10, 1938; children—Thayer Ann, Patricia Thayer. Commd. as 2d lt. U.S. Army, 1936; and advanced to lt. col., 1942; mem. 19th pursuit sqdn., Wheeler Field, Hawaii, 1937-40; comdg. officer air base sqdn., Moffet Field, 1940; sqdn. comdr. fighter sqdn., Hamilton Field, Cal., 1940, later group operations officer, group exec., group comdr., 1940-42; exec. to Brig. Gen. F. M. Brady, India, 1942; operations officer, later exec., China air task force, acting chief staff 14th air force under Maj. Gen. Chennault, China, 1943; comdg. officer forward echelon 14th air force and C. G. 68th composite wing since May 1943, participating in fighter and bomber combat missions, combat record 6 Japs planes confirmed, 4 probably destroyed. Spl. mission to U.S., Sept.-Nov. 1943. Decorated Silver Star, Legion Merit, Distinguished Flying Cross with oak leaf cluster, Distinguished Service Medal, Air Medal with 3 oak leaf clusters, (U.S.); Golden Air Hero Medal, Order of Precious Tripod, Order of the Cloud Banner, Spl. Order of Yun Ma (China). Democrat. Methodist. Home: 232 W. Hollywood, San Antonio. Office: care Adjutant General, Washington. Died July 6, 1955.

VINCENT, JESSE GURNEY mech. engr.; b. Charleston, Ark., Feb. 10, 1880; s. Joseph M. and Nellie (Gurney) V.; ed. public schs. and I.C.S.; hon. M. Engring., U. Mich., 1929; m. Clarinda Blood, Oct. 2, 1902 (died 1943); m. 2d, Rachel M. Hawes. Machinist and toolmaker, St. Louis, 1898-1902; supt. inventions Burroughs Adding Machine Co., Detroit, 1903-10; chief engr. Hudson Motor Car Co., 1910-12; v.p. engring., Packard Motor Car Co. since 1912. Commd. maj. U.S. Signal Corps, 1917; lt. col., 1918; col. S.O.R.C., 1919. Built exptl. sta. at McCook Field, later in charge airplane engr. dept., Dayton, O.; apptd. chief Airplane Engring. Div., Bur. Aircraft Prodn., 1918, title of chief of engring.; mem. Joint Army and Navy Tech. Aircraft Bd., 1918; co-designer of Liberty Aircraft Engine. Dir. Am. Standards Assn. to rep. Auto Mfrs. Assn. Mem. Soc. Automotive Engrs., Am. Soc. M.E. Clubs: Detroit Athletic, Detroit Automobile, Detroit Country. Home: 415 Burns Dr., Detroit 14. Died Apr. 1962.

VINCENT, THOMAS MACCURDY army officer; b. nr. Cadiz, O., Nov. 15, 1832; s. Thomas Carleton and Jane (MacCurdy) V.; ed. high sch., Cadiz, O.; grad. U.S. Mil. Acad., 1853; m. Laura Louise Lancaster, Aug. 15, 1857. Bvt. 2d lt. 2d Arty., July 1, 1853; 2d lt., Oct. 8, 1853; promoted through grades to col. asst. adj. gen., Aug. 2, 1890; retired by operation of law, Nov. 15, 1896; advanced to rank of brig. gen. retired, by act of Apr. 23, 1904. Bvtd. lt. col. and col., Sept. 24, 1864, and brig. gen., Mar. 13, 1865, for faithful and meritorious services during the war. At various times acting adj. gen. U.S.A. Pres. Ft. Stevens Lincoln Nat. Mil. Park Assn. During Civil War in charge of organization and miscellaneous bus. of vol. armies, and their disbanding as planned by him, subsequently closing certain War Dept. bureaus, with financial responsibility of $33,000,000. Made official tours observation and inspection to main parts of U.S. and adjoining foreign territory. Author: Staff Organization; Military Power of the United States During the War of the Rebellion; Lincoln and Stanton; Lincoln; Florida Indians in Day of De Soto and Flordia Seminole Wars; Battle of Bull Run, July 21, 1861; official reports on Army and Staff Organization, and many other official reports, 1853-96. Died 1909.

VINSONHALER, FRANK (vin'sun-hä-ler), ophthalmologist; b. Graham, Mo., Apr. 14, 1864; s. George and Sarah (Rea) V.; Northwestern Normal Sch., Oregon, Mo., M.D., Coll. Physicians and Surgeons, Columbia, 1885; student extraordinary U. of Vienna, 1892; Royal Ophthalmic Hosp., London, England; LL.D., U. of Ark., 1929; m. Wrennetta Beidelman, Feb. 9, 1898; children—Marion Wilmer, Frances Rea, George. In practice at Little Rock since 1893; prof. ophthalmology, U. of Ark., since 1893, also dean Med. Sch.; retired. Commd. maj., Med. R.C., 1917; lt. col., 1919; comd. Base Hosp. 109, Vichy, France. Colonel U.S.R. Fellow Am. Coll. Surgeons; pres. Ark. Med. Soc., 1900-01. Awarded medal Columbia Univ., 1935. Mem. Phi Beta Kapa. Home: 500 E. 9th St., Little Rock, Ark. Died Sep. 1, 1942.

VINTON, FRANCIS LAURENS army officer, engr.; b. Fort Preble, Me., June 1, 1835; s. John Rogers and Lucretia (Parker) V.; grad. U.S. Mil. Acad., 1856; attended Ecole des Mines, France, 1856-60. Instr. mech. drawing Cooper Union, N.Y.C., 1860; led expdn. to explore mineral resources of Honduras, 1861; commd. capt. 16th U.S. Inf., 1861, raised 43d N.Y. Volunteers, commd. col., 1861 served in various battles Va. peninsular campaign, 1862, commanded brigade in VI Corps, Army of the Potomac, 1862, wounded in Battle of Fredericksburg, 1862; commd. brig. gen. U.S. Volunteers, 1863, resigned commn., 1863; prof. civil, mining engring. Sch. Mines, Columbia, 1864-77; cons. mining engr., Denver, Colo., 1877-79; Colo. corr. Engring. and Mining Jour. of N.Y. Died Leadville, Colo., Oct. 6, 1879.

VOGDES, ANTHONY WAYNE brigadier-gen. U.S.A.; b. West Point, N.Y., April 23, 1843; s. Gen. Israel (U.S.A.) and G.W. (Berard) V.; Sanders Inst., Phila.; grad. Arty. Sch., Ft. Monroe, Va., 1882; m. Ada A. Adams, of New York, Dec. 7, 1867. Second lt. 100th N.Y. Inf., Aug. 13, 1863; served Light Battery M, 1st U.S. Arty., 1864-65; bvtd. capt. and maj. N.Y. Vols. "for gallant and meritorious services during the war." Apptd. 2d lt. 4th U.S. Inf., Apr. 26, 1866; engaged in constrn. U.P. R.R., 1867-68; 1st lt., May 15, 1867; transferred to 5th U.S. Arty., May 22, 1875; capt., Oct. 1, 1889; served at San Juan, P.R.; maj., Oct. 5, 1900; comdg. arty. dist. San Diego, Cal., and Key West, Fla.; lt.-col., July 20, 1902; col., Nov. 1, 1903; retired May 20, 1904, as brig.-gen. U.S.A. Fellow Am. Geol. Soc., A.A.A.S.; mem. N.Y., Ga., Phila., Chicago and Cal. acads. of science; pres. San Diego Acad. Science; mem. Loyal Legion, S.A.R. Author: Course of Science Applied to Military Art, Part 1, Geology and Military Geography, 1884 (U.S. Arty. Sch.); also various bulls. and papers on geology, palaeontology, etc. Address: 2425 1st St., San Diego, Cal.

VOGEL, CLAYTON BARNEY marine corps officer; b. Phila., Sept. 18, 1882; s. Theodore Knight and Clayonia Woods (Barney) V.; student Rutgers Coll., 1900-01; LL.B., Georgetown U., 1927; m. Margaret Jane Bennett, July 7, 1917; children—Margaret Bennett, Julia Lindsly, Mary Barney. Commd. 2d lt. U.S. Marine Corps, 1904, advanced through grades to brig. gen., 1937; promoted to maj. gen., 1941, comdg. Joint Tng. Force, and Fleet Marine Force, San Diego area; now comdg. Marine Barracks, Parris Island, S.C. Decorated Expeditionary medal, U.S. Marine Corps; Vera Cruz Campaign medal; Victory medal, World War I; 2d Nicaraguan Campaign medal; Medal of Merit (Nicaraugua); D.S.M., Medaille Militaire, Order of Honor and Merit, Medal of Merit (Hiati). Mem. Delta Kappa Epsilon. Clubs: National Press, Army and Navy (Washington); Racquet (Phila.). Address: Parris Island, S.C. Died Nov. 1964.

VOGELBACK, WILLIAM EDWARD cons. engr., business exec.; b. N.Y. City, June 9, 1893; s. Louis and Antonia (Hanosey) V.; ed. civil and elec. engring. various tech. schs., N.Y.; M.B.A., U. Chicago; m. Parthenia Carmichael, concert pianiste, Dec. 25, 1920. Mem. engring. staff Sanderson & Porter, 1914-17, asst. Chgo. mgr., 1920-24; ind. cons. engr. 1924-—; pres. So. States Power Co., 1926, Standard Tel. Co., 1927-28, Boise (Ida.) Water Co., 1927-28, Am. Engring. & Management Corp., 1927-42, Am. States Pub. Service Co. (also pres. or chmn. of its 34 subsidisries and affiliates), 1928-33, and several other corps.; pres. and chmn. bd. Union Gas & Electric Co., 1944-—. Mem. U. of Ill. Citizens Com.; mem. governing bd., trustee Library of Internat. Relations. Cons. engineer, aircraft, W.P.B., Washington, 1942; central field commissioner, Pacific and China, Dept. of State, 1946. Served with 1st Ill. Cav., Mex. Border, 1916; attended Plattsburg (Arty.), 1917, Sch. Mil. Aeronautics (O.S.U.); commd. in Signal Corps (Aviation), 1918. Mem. bd. assos. Northwestern U.; citizens bd. U. Chgo.; mem. bd. Salvation Army, Chgo. Mem. Am. Inst. E.E., Soc. Am. Mil. Engrs., Ill. and Nat. socs. profl. engrs, Beta Gamma Sigma. Profl. engr., N.Y., Ill. Clubs: Racquet, Chicago, Tavern, Chicago Golf; Metropolitan (N.Y.C.). Author: Magnets Light, in Library and Sci. Series, 1933 (editor). Designed and pub. Series Pictorial Maps of various countries; also Panorama Western Theatre of War in Europe, 1940. Home: 232 E. Walton Pl. Office: 230 N. Michigan Av., Chgo. Died Apr. 17, 1960.

VOGELGESANG, CARL THEODORE naval officer; b. N. Branch, Calaveras County, Calif., Jan. 11, 1869; s. Henry John and Anna (Vennigerholz) V.; grad. U.S. Naval Acad., 1890; m. Zenaide Stevens Shepard, Dec. 27, 1899; children—Shepard, Zenaide. Ensign, July 1, 1892; lt. jr. grade, Mar. 3, 1899; promoted through grades to rear admiral, Oct. 15, 1922. Served on Bancroft, Spanish-Am. War, 1898; duty with Bur. Nav., Navy Dept., 1904-06; navigator Louisiana, 1906-07; comdr. Mayflower, 1907-08; navigator Wisconsin, 1908-09, at Naval War Coll., Newport, R.I., 1909-12; exec. officer, Wyoming, 1912-14; comdr. Des Moines, 1914; at Naval War Coll., 1914-17; apptd. chief of staff, Asiatic Fleet, Apr. 14, 1917; chief of naval commn. to Brazil, Jan.-Nov. 1918; comdg. U.S.S. Idaho, Jan. 7, 1919-June 1920; chief of staff U.S. Fleet, July 1, 1920-July 1, 1921; comdt. Navy Yard, New York, and 3d Naval Dist., July 1, 1921-Nov. 27, 1922; chief of U.S. Naval Mission to Brazil, Nov. 27, 1922; comd. midshipman cruise, June 6-Aug. 30, 1925; comdr. Scouting Fleet, 1926. Died Feb. 16, 1927.

VOGELGESANG, SHEPARD, architect; born San Francisco, California Feb. 9, 1901; s. Carl Theodore (rear adm. U.S. Navy) and Zenaide Stevens (Shepard) V.; diploma Phillips Acad., Andover, Mass., 1920; student Mass. Inst. Tech., 1920-26; traveling fellowship in architecture; studied in Vienna, Austria, 1927-28; grad. Mass. Inst. Tech., 1942; m. Camilla Herbert Boone, Aug. 6, 1942 (divorced 1949); 1 dau., Carlyle V. Archtl. draftsman in offices in Boston and New York until 1931; in charge interior color design, Century of Progress, Chicago, 1933, director of color, Century of Progress, 1934; assistant director decorative arts and dir. design Fine Arts Com., Golden Gate Internat. Expn., San Francisco, 1938-39; asso. dir. and designer of "America at Home," N.Y. World's Fair, 1940; color consultant for Fed. Defense Housing, 1941; architectural practice Whitefield, N.H., 1941-69. Registered architect in N.H. and Vt. Lieutenant U.S.N.R., August 1942, comdr. October 1944. Member Beaux Arts Inst. Design (N.Y.C.), A.I.A. (also mem. N.H. chpt.), Dalton Grange, Phi Gamma Delta. Mem. Ch. of England. Rotarian. Contbr. to archtl. mags. Writer, lecturer, designer. Home: Whitefield NH Died Feb. 18, 1969; buried Cushman Cemetery, Dalton NH

VOLLRATH, EDWARD army officer; b. Bucyrus, O., June 28, 1858; s. Charles and Eva Elizabeth (Hocker) V.; A.B., Princeton, 1833, A.M., 1886; m. Millie Wise, June 27, 1888 (died 1910); children—Jeanne Elizabeth, Mrs. Edna Grace Willaman, Charles Victor, Carol Pamilla, Edward Wise. Admitted to Ohio bar, 1885, and practiced at Bucyrus; judge Ct. of Appeals of Ohio, 1904-05. Enlisted as pvt. Co. A, 8th Ohio Inf., Apr. 30, 1884; sergt. maj., June 20, 1884; capt. Co. A, June 30, 1886; maj. 8th Ohio Inf., July 5, 1892; lt. col., Aug. 14, 1899; col., Dec. 22, 1899; brig. gen. N.A., Aug. 5, 1917. Served as maj. 8th Ohio Inf., with 5th Army Corps, at Santiago de Cuba, Spanish-Am. War, 1898; col. same regt. Mexican border service, June 19, 1916-Mar. 22, 1917; responded with regt. to President's call, July 15, 1917; successively apptd. comdr. 66th Depot Brigade, Aug. 1917, 66th Arty. Brigade, 41st Div., Sept. 1917; comd. 82d Inf. Brig. and 41st Div., A.E.F., in France, Dec. 15, 1917-Feb. 11, 1919. Hon. discharged, Mar. 1, 1919, and resumed practice of law at Bucyrus, O. Republican. Evang. Lutheran. K.P. Home: Bucyrus, O. Died Jan. 21, 1931.

VON CHOLTITZ, DIETRICH German army officer; b. Nov. 1894. Cited for bravery for German army service in Poland, invasion of France, and conquest of Russian fortress of Sebastopol on Crimean peninsula; defied Hitler's order in 1944 to destroy Paris before Allies entered city, was central figure in saving Paris from destruction in World War II. Author: Is Paris Burning (inspired later best seller of same name), 1950. Died Baden Baden, Germany, Nov. 5, 1966.*

VON HOFFMANN, BERNARD business executive; b. Milwaukee, Wis., Nov. 3, 1900; s. Albert and Anna (Albrecht) von H.; A.B., Univ. of Mo., 1921; m. Dorothy Elizabeth McClintock, Sept. 6, 1922; children—Bernard, Beverly (Mrs. Wm. H. Macon), Barbara. Pres. and mem. bd. dirs. Von Hoffmann Corp., St. Louis, Mo., since 1928; treas. and mem. bd. dirs. Von Hoffman Press since 1931; pres. and mem. bd. dirs. Von Hoffmann Distributing Co. since 1933; treas. and mem. bd. dirs., Mid-State Printing Co. since 1942; chmn. bd. dirs. Meat Merchandising, Inc., since 1940. Partner Midland Stationery & Printing Co., Jefferson City, Mo., since 1944. Enlisted U.S. Army Air Corps, Apr., 1942; placed in inactive status Aug. 1945, rank of major. Mem. bd. dirs. Jefferson Coll., 1939-42. Dir. St. Louis Aviation Council. Mem. Scabbard and Blade. Elk. Clubs: Algonquin Golf (Webster Groves); Missouri Athletic (St. Louis). Licensed free balloon pilot, 1917; rep. U.S. in Internat. Balloon Races, Brussels, Belgium, 1921; airplane pilot, 1926. Filmed Life of the Djukas of Interior Surinam, Jan.-Apr., 1940. Home: 7730 Mohawk Dr., Clayton, Mo. Office: 105 S. 9th St., St. Louis 2, Mo. Died May 31, 1947; interred Valhalla Crematorium, St. Louis.

VON STEUBEN, FRIEDRICH WILHELM LUDOLF GERHARD AUGUSTIN (Baron von Steuben), army officer; b. Magdeburg, Prussia, Germany, Sept. 17, 1730; s. Wilhelm Augustin and Maria Dorothea (von Jagow) von S. Served as staff officer with rank of capt. under Frederick the Great in Seven Years War; recommended as mil. expert to Am. govt. by Benjamin Franklin and French ofcls.; arrived at Portsmouth, N.H., 1777; directed by Continental Congress to serve under George Washington at Valley Forge; acting insp. gen. Continental Army, highly successful in drilling the army, apptd. insp. gen. with rank of maj. gen., 1778; fought with distinction at Battle of Monmouth; wrote drill manual Regulations for the Order and Discipline of the Troops of the United States (invaluable for tng. Am. volunteers, immediately adopted by Continental Army), winter 1778-79; Gen. Washington's rep. with Continental Congress in efforts to reorganize army, winter 1779-80; in command in Va. under Gen. Greene, 1780-81; commanded a div. at Battle of Yorktown, 1781; served as Washington's aide in mil. planning, helped prepare plan for future defense of U.S., demobilization of Continental Army, spring 1783; honorably discharged, 1784; became Am. citizen by act of Pa. Legislature, 1783, by act of N.Y. Legislature, 1786; prominent founder Soc. of Cincinnati, pres. N.Y. br.; pres. German Soc.; elected a regent Univ. State N.Y., 1787. Died Utica, N.Y., Nov. 28, 1794.

VON TRESCKOW, EGMONT CHARLES, b. Mamaroneck, N.Y., June 18, 1872; s. Egmont and Jane Augusta (Eldredge) von T.; ed. private instrn. and schs. in Austria; LL.B., Univ. of S.C., 1900; student U. of Va., summer, 1900; m. Sadie Belton Kennedy, July 22, 1907. Admitted to S.C. bar, 1900, in practice, 1900-16 and 1919-21; consul at Arica, Chile, 1921-26, Berlin, Germany, 1926-29, Rotterdam, Netherlands, 1929-32, Zagreb, Jugoslavia, 1932-35, St. John, N.B., 1935-37. Retired. Major S.C. Nat. Guard, Mexican border service; served with A.E.F., World War; was lt. col. S.C. Nat. Guard; now lt. col. O.R.C., Inactive List Mem. S.A.R. Associate member of Carlton Branch Canadian Legion of the British Empire Service League. Episcopalian. Home: Camden SC

VOORHEES, PHILIP FALKERSON naval officer; b. New Brunswick, N.J., 1792; m. Anne Randall, May 12, 1835, 2 children. Apptd. midshipman U.S. Navy, 1809; in War of 1812 participated in capture ship Macedonian by brig United States and of Epervier by the Peacock;

awarded silver medal by Congress; on Mediterranean cruise in vessel North Carolina, 1825-27; with rank of capt. sailed for Mediterranean commanding frigate Congress, 1842; joined Brazil squadron under Commodore Daniel Turner, 1843; assisted in rescuing H.M.S. Gorgon stranded in the Rio de la Plata, 1844; court-martialed for his action against Argentine squadron, 1845, sentenced to reprimand and suspension for 3 years, also court-martialed on series of charges, chiefly disobedience to Commodore Turner, found guilty on two specifications, suspended for 18 months, dismissed from service by ct., Aug. 1845, Pres. Polk lessened his sentence to suspension for 5 years, removed suspension, 1847; commanded East India squadron, 1849; placed by naval retiring bd. on res. list with furlough pay, 1855, appealed and received leave pay; petitioned unsuccessfully to return to active duty. Died Annapolis, Md., Feb. 23, 1862.

VOORHEES, STEPHEN FRANCIS (voor'ez), architect; b. Rocky Hill, N.J., Feb. 15, 1878; s. Charles Hagaman and Mary Frances (Skillman) V.; prep. edn., State Model Sch., Trenton, N.J.; C.E., Princeton, 1900; hon. Dr. Engring., Princeton, 1937, Rensselaer Poly. Inst., 1939; A.F.D. (hon.), N.Y. U., 1939; m. Mabel Aleda Buys, Oct. 15, 1907 (dec.). Civil engr. with William P. Field, Newark, N.J., 1900-02; civil engr. and supt. constrn. with Eidlitz & McKenzie, 1902-10; mem. firm McKenzie, Voorhees & Gmelin, 1910-26, Voorhees, Gmelin & Walker, 1926-39, Voorhees, Walker, Foley & Smith, 1939-55, Voorhees, Walker, Smith & Smith, 1955-59; consultant architectural firm Voorhees, Walker, Smith, Smith & Haines, New York City, 1959-64; cons. Smith, Smith, Haines, Lundberg & Waehller, 1964-—; supervising architect Princeton, 1930-49; dir. Marine Midland Trust Co. Rockland Co., Bank N.Y. Principal works: New York Telephone Headquarters Bldg., Western Union Telegraph Bldg., One Wall St. Building (all New York, N.Y.), Bell Telephone Laboratories, Murray Hill, N.J., Prudential Ins. Co. of Am. Headquarters Building, Newark, N.J.; chmn. Board of Design New York World's Fair, 1936-40. Served as corpl. U.S. Vol. Engrs., Spanish-Am. War, 1898-99; maj. Sanitary Corps, U.S. Army, 1917-19; cons. W.P.B., 1940-42. Charter trustee Princeton U., 1943-48, trustee emeritus since 1948. Trustee Stevens Inst. of Tech., Met. Museum of Art, N.Y.C. Fellow Am. Inst. Architects (past pres.), New York chapter, A.I.A. (past pres.); mem. Am. Soc. C.E., Am. Soc. M.E., Princeton Archtl. Assn. (past pres.), Princeton Engring. Assn. (past pres.), Archtl. League N.Y. N.Y. C. of C., Commerce and Industry Assn. of New York, Holland Soc., Royal Inst. British Architects (hon. correspondent). Republican. Elder Dutch Reformed Ch. Clubs: University, Princeton, Union League, Century Association, Rockland Country (New York). Home: Voorhis Point, Nyack, N.Y. Office: 101 Park Av., New York 17, N.Y. Died Jan. 23, 1965.

VOROSHILOV, MAZSHAL KLIMENT YEFREMOVICH, mem. presidium USSR; b. Verkhneye, Drepzopetrovsk region, Feb. 4, 1881. Worker, Lugansk Engine-Building Works; joined Russian Social Democratic Labour Party, 1903; sent to Donbass with plenipotentiary powers by Communist Party Central Com., October Revolution of 1917; participated in rout of white-guard generals and fgn. interventionists during Civil War; mem. Central Com., Russian Communist Party, 1921-61; mem. Polit. Bur., 1926-52; comdr. North Caucasian Mil. area, 1921-24, Moscow Mil. area, 1924-25, people's commissar for mil. and naval affairs, 1925-34, people's commissar of def., USSR, 1934-40. Vice chmn. people's commissars of USSR, chmn. def. com., 1940-46; chmn. Allied Control Commn., Hungary, 1945-47; vice chmn. USSR Council Ministers, 1946-53; pres. Presidium of USSR Supreme Soviet, 1953-60, mem. Presidium, 1960-69. Decorated orders of Lenin, orders of Red Banner, Order of Suvorov 1st class other orders and medals; named marshal of Soviet Union, 1935, Hero of the Soviet Union, 1956, Hero of Socialist Labour, 1960. Author books on mil. sci. and history. Home: Moscow USSR Died Dec. 2, 1969.

VOSE, WILLIAM PRESTON army officer; b. Orrington, Me., July 19, 1839; s. William and Mary Wooderson (Phillips) V.; grad. U.S. Mil. Acad., 1864; m. Bettiea May Williams, Oct. 22, 1874. Apptd. 2d lt., 2d Arty. U.S.A., June 13, 1864; promoted 1st lt., 8th Arty., Mar. 8, 1865, capt., Oct. 2, 1883, maj., 6th Arty., Mar. 8, 1898, lt. col. Arty. Corps, May 8, 1901, col., Dec. 20, 1902, brig. gen. U.S.A., Apr. 23, 1904. Upon graduation was ordered to Army of the Potomac; assigned to Light Battery B, 4th Arty., of Arty. Brigade, 5th Army Corps; took part in all engagements of that army, including different attacks on Petersburg, Weldon R. R., Hatcher's Run, Peebles Farm, Weldon raid, Grovelly Run, Five Forks, Sailor's Creek and Appomattox; comd. battery during Appomattox Campaign until after gen. review of army at Washington. Served in nearly every State and Ty. of U.S., Hawaii, and nearly 3 yrs., 1898-1901, in P.I.; retired for age, 1903. Mem. Assn. Graduates Mil. Acad.; companion Loyal Legion. Died 1906.

VROOM, PETER DUMONT brig. gen. U.S.A.; b. Trenton, N.J., Apr. 18, 1842; s. Gov. Peter D. and Matilda (Wall) V.; C.E., Rensselaer Poly. Inst., 1862. First lt. adj. 1st N.J. Inf., Aug. 13, 1862; resigned, Sept. 19, 1863; maj. 2d N.J. Cav., Sept. 25, 1863; bvtd. col., Mar. 13, 1865; hon. mustered out, Oct. 24, 1865; apptd. from N.J. 2d lt. 3d U.S. Cav., Feb. 23, 1866; 1st lt., July 28, 1866; capt., May 17, 1876; maj. insp. gen., Dec. 10, 1888; lt. col. insp. gen., Jan. 2, 1895; col. insp. gen., Dec. 19, 1899; brig. gen. insp. gen., Apr. 11, 1903; retired at own request after 40 yrs.' service, Apr. 12, 1903. Home: Trenton, N.J. Died Mar. 19, 1926.

WADDELL, CHARLES EDWARD (wa-del'), consulting engr.; b. Hillsboro, N.C., May 1, 1877; s. Francis Nash and Ann Ivy (Miller) W.; ed. Bingham Mil. Sch., N.C., and in shops of Gen. Electric Co.; Sc.D., N.C. State Coll. Agr. and Engring., 1925; m. Eleanor Sheppard Belknap, Apr. 19, 1904; children—Eleanor B. (Mrs. George M. Stephens), Charles E. Built various steam and hydraulic plants along the eastern seaboard; cons. engr. to George W. Vanderbilt, for "Biltmore" (designed and built majority of engring. works at Biltmore); designer, and builder of N.C. Elec. Power Co.'s system, 1903-23; cons. engr. United Electric Securities Co., Boston, 1912; consulting engr. on State water powers for the City of Medellin, Colombia, South America, 1927. Cons. engr. to power sect. Council of Nat. Defense, in surveying and analyzing the power resources of the Southern States for war emergency, 1917; engr. to Q.-M. Dept., U.S. Army, for constrn. of gen. hosps. No. 12 and No. 19, 1918; dir. of conservation for the State of N.C., U.S. Fuel Administration. Chmn. and mem. N.C. Board Engring. Examiners, 1921-26; mem. N.C. Ship and Water Transportation Commn., 1923-24; commr. Biltmore Forest, 1923-27; pres. Biltmore Hosp., 1920-23; cons. engr. City of Asheville, 1925-27; cons. engr. to N.C. Corp. Commn. in readjustment of utility rates, 1932-34. Cons. engr. Tenn. Valley Authority, 1936-38, and for City of Asheville, N.C., 1940; for Ecusta Paper Corp., Pisgah Forest, N.C., since 1941; for Am. Enka Corp., 1943-44. Fellow American Institute Electrical Engrs. (chmn. N.C. Sect. 1936); mem. Am. Soc. C.E. (pres. N.C. sect. 1923-24; hon. mem. N.C. sect. 1943), Am. Soc. M.E., N.C. Soc. Engrs. (pres. 1928; hon. mem. 1942). Clubs: Asheville Civitan (president 1923), Pen and Plate (president 1916), Biltmore Forest Country (gov. 1922-30). Episcopalian. Home: Biltmore, N.C. Office: Asheville, N.C. Died Apr. 20, 1945.

WADDELL, HUGH army officer; b. Lisburn, County Down, Ireland, 1734; s. Hugh and Isabella (Brown) W.; m. Mary Haynes, 1762, 3 children. Served as lt. with regt. of James Innes to help drive French from Ohio, 1754; clk. Gov.'s Council of N.C., 1754-55; on frontier duty in Western Carolina, 1755; as Va. commr. negotiated offensive-defensive alliance with Cherokee and Catawba Indian tribes, 1756; maj. in command 3 cos. to aid expdn. of John Forbes against Fort Duquesne, 1758; col. in command 2 cos. with authority to summon the militia of the frontier counties and cooperate with S.C. or Va., 1759; defended Ft. Dobbs against Indian attack, 1760; foremost soldier of N.C. before Am. Revolution; justice of the peace in Rowan and Bladen (N.C.); rep. N.C. Colonial Assembly from Rowan, 1757, 58, 59, 60, from Bladen, 1762, 66, 67, 71; a leader of colonists against Gen. William Tyron's attempt to enforce Stamp Act, 1765; took part in suppression of Regulator movement in N.C., 1771. Died Bladen County, N.C., Apr. 9, 1773.

WADDELL, JAMES IREDELL naval officer; b. Pittsboro, N.C., July 13, 1824; s. Francis Nash and Elizabeth Davis (Moore) W.; m. Ann Iglehart, 1848. Apptd. midshipman U.S. Navy, 1841; served on ship Somers off Vera Cruz during Mexican War; passed midshipman, 1847, lt., 1855; taught navigation U.S. Naval Acad., 1846-48; secretly entered Confederate lines by way of Balt., 1862; commd. lt. Confederate States Navy, 1862-63; took command of Sea King in 1864 and transformed her into Confederate vessel Shenandoah; on cruise from Melbourne (Australia) in command of Shenandoah destroyed over 30 U.S. whalers in Bering Sea, 1865, landed at Liverpool, Eng.; capt. Pacific Mail Co., 1875; commanded Md. State Flotilla for policing oyster beds, circa 1883-86. Died Annapolis, Md., Mar. 15, 1886.

WADE, JAMES FRANKLIN major gen. U.S.A.; b. Jefferson, O., Apr. 14, 1843; s. Benjamin F. (U.S. senator from Ohio) and Caroline M. (Rosecrans) W.; ed. common schools; m. Clara Lyon, May 27, 1866. Appointed from Ohio, 1st lt. 6th U.S. Cavalry, May 14, 1861; lt. col. 6th U.S. Colored Cav., May 1, 1864; col., Sept. 19, 1864; bvtd. brig. gen., Feb. 13, 1865; hon. mustered out of vol. service, Apr. 15, 1866; capt. U.S.A., May 1, 1866; maj. 9th Cav., July 28, 1866; lt. col. 10th Cav., Mar. 20, 1879; col. 5th Cav., Apr. 21, 1887; brig. gen., May 26, 1897; maj. gen. vols., May 4, 1898; hon. discharged from vol. service, June 12, 1899; maj. gen. U.S.A., Apr. 13, 1903; retired by operation of law, Apr. 14, 1907. Bvtd.: capt., June 9, 1863, "for gallant and meritorious services in battle of Beverly Ford, Va."; maj., Dec. 19, 1864, for same in action at Marion, East Tenn.; lt. col. and col., Mar. 13, 1865, for same during the war; brig. gen. vols., Feb. 13, 1865, "for gallant services in campaign in southwestern Va." Head of Cuban Evacuation Commn., 1898; served in P.I., 1901-04; comd. Div. of Philippines, 1903-04; comd. Atlantic Div., 1904-07. Home: Jefferson, O. Died Aug. 23. 1921.

WADE, JOHN DONALD found. exec.; b. Marshallville, Ga., Sept. 28, 1892; s. John Daniel and Ida (Frederick) W.; A.B., U. Ga., 1914; A.M., Harvard, 1915; Ph.D., Columbia, 1924; m. Julia Floyd Stovall, July 18, 1942 (dec. 1959); 1 dau., Anne; m. 2d, Florence Lester, Oct. 5, 1962. Instr., then asso. prof. English, U. Ga., 1919-25; Guggenheim fellow in Eng., 1926-27; asst. editor Dictionary Am. Biography, 1927-28; prof. English, Vanderbilt U., 1928-34; prof. English, U. Ga., 1934-46, head dept. English, dir. div. lang. and lit., 1939-46, founder, editor Ga. Quar. Rev. (publ. of U. Ga.), 1946-50; founder, pres. Marshallville Found., 1944-—. Lectr. summers, U. N.C., Duke. Chmn. Macon County Library Bd., 1952-—. Served as 2d lt. U.S. Army, 1918-19. Mem. Modern Lang. Assn. Am., Ga. Hist. Soc., Sigma Nu, Phi Beta Kappa. Democrat. Methodist. Author: August Baldwin Longstreet, a Study of the Development of Culture in the South, 1924; John Wesley, 1930; also article in Southern Pioneers, 1925; I'll Take My Stand, 1930; Culture in the South, 1934; Who Owns America, 1936; Literary History of the United States, 1948. Co-editor: Masterworks of World Literature, 1947. Contbr. to Am. Mercury, Am. Review, Va. Quar., So. Rev. Home: Marshallville, Ga. Died Oct. 9, 1963.

WADHAMS, ALBION VARETTE rear adm. U.S.N.; b. Wadhams Mills, N.Y., June 8, 1847; s. William Luman and Emeline Lorette (Cole) W.; apptd. from N.Y., and grad. U.S. Naval Acad., 1868; m. Caroline E. Henderson, Feb. 28, 1870; children—William Henderson, Albion James, Mae Elizabeth (dec.). Ensign, Apr. 19, 1869; master, July 12, 1870; lt. Mar. 25, 1873; lt. comdr., July 21, 1894; comdr., Mar. 3, 1899; capt., Dec. 27, 1903; retired as commodore, June 30, 1907; promoted to rear adm. on the retired list, May 9, 1925, to date from June 30, 1907. Served successively on the Pacific, Atlantic, China stas. in the Tuscarora, Albany, Alaska; at torpedo sta., on bd. Powhatan, and Alert, 1868-75; Naval Acad., 1875-78; coast survey, 1878-79; Nipsic, European sta., 1880-83; Navy Yard, Washington, 1884-86; Essex China sta.; Brooklyn, Monocacy, Marion, 1886-89; insp. 2d light house dist. and mem. Bd. Inspection, 1889-92; exec. officer Mohican, 1893-95, Boston and Monterey, 1895-96; insp. 8th light house dist., 1897-99; during Spanish-Am. War was in charge 8th Coast Defense Dist., comd. Monongahela, Oct., 1899-Dec. 1900; insp. merchant ships and at Navy Yard, New York, 1901; comd. St. Mary's, 1901-02; in charge recruiting sta. and branch hydrographic office, Chicago, 1902-03; comd. Prairie, 1903-05; capt. Navy Yard, Norfolk, 1905-07; apptd. 1907 by Gov. Charles E. Hughes mem. of Bd. of Pardons and Parole for State Prisons; apptd. by Gov. Sulzer, 1913, commr. on new prisons. Called to active duty, 1917, and assigned as rep. of Navy Dept. at Am. Red Cross hdqrs., Washington to Oct. 30, 1919; comd. Naval Prison, Portsmouth, N.H., Mar. 7, 1920-July 6, 1921; duty at Navy Yard, Portsmouth, to Aug. 1, 1921; relieved from active duty; 20 yrs. of sea service: 3 yrs. active service after retirement. Home: Wadhams, N.Y. Died Jan. 14, 1927.

WADLEIGH, GEORGE HENRY rear adm. U.S.N.; b. Dover, N.H., Sept. 28, 1842; s. George and Sarah (Gilman) W., apptd. to U.S. Naval Academy from N.H., 1860, grad. 1863; m. Clara Robinson, Oct. 12, 1869. Ensign, May 28, 1863; promoted through grades to rear adm., Feb. 9, 1902. Served on Lackawanna, W. Gulf Blockading Squadron, 1863-65; present at attack on Fort Powell, Mar. 2, 1864, battle of Mobile Bay, Aug. 5, 1864, surrender of Ft. Morgan, Aug. 23, 1864; served on Richmond, Mar.-July 1865; Ticonderoga, European sta., 1865-69; Naval Acad., 1869-79; torpedo sta., 1870; exec. officer Shawmut, 1871-73; Canonicus, 1873-74, Ohio, 1874, St. Mary's, 1874-76, Pensacola, 1876-78, Navy Yard Portsmouth, 1878-81; comd. Alliance, 1881-82, on spl. Arctic cruise in search of Jeannette and reached latitude 80 deg. 10'; light house insp. 2d dist., 1883-86; Navy Yard, Boston, 1887-89; comd. Mich., 1889-99; Navy Yard, Boston, 1892-94; comd. receiving ship Richmond, 1894; comd. Minneapolis, cruising off coast of Asia Minor to protect Am. missionaries, 1895-97; Navy Yard, Boston, 1897-98; comd. Phila., June-Oct., 1898, receiving ship Wabash, 1898-1902; comdt. Navy Yard, League Island, 1902; pres. Bd. of Inspection and Survey, 1902; retired, June 7, 1902. Home: Dover, N.H. Died July 11, 1927.

WADSWORTH, ARTHUR LITTLEFORD, banker; b. Ft. Thomas, Ky;, July 30, 1910; s. Arthur W. and Bernice (Littleford) W.; Ph. B., U. Wis., 1933; M.B.A., Harvard, 1935; m. Betty Nevin, Feb. 3, 1940; children—Anne, Nancy, Arthur William. With Dillon, Read & Co., N.Y.C., 1935-70, v.p., 1949-63, exec. v.p., 1963-70; chairman executive com., dir. Copperweld Steel Co. (Pitts.); dir. The Jeffrey Co., Columbus, O., Dillon Read & Co., Inc., Grumman Aircraft Corp. Staff, of the WPB, 1942-43. Trustee of Wis. Alumni Research Foundation. Served from lt. (j.g.) to comdr., USNR, 1943-46. Decorated Legion of Merit, Order of Rising Sun 3d class (Japan). Mem. Investment Bankers Assn. Am. (v.p. 1959), Chi Psi. Episcopalian (vestryman 1954-60). Clubs: Creek, Manhasset Bay Yacht (L.I., N.Y.); Harvard, Wall Street, Links (N.Y.C.); Duquesne (Pitts.). Home: Roslyn NY Died June 2, 1970; buried Evergreen Cemetery, Ft Thomas KY

WADSWORTH, JEREMIAH army officer, congressman; b. Hartford, Conn., July 12, 1743; s. Rev. Daniel and Abigail (Talcott) W.; hon. degrees from Yale and Dartmouth; m. Mehitable Russell, Sept. 29, 1767, 3 children. Engaged in mcht. service, 1761-71; commissary gen. to Col. Joseph Trumbull of Revolutionary forces raised in Conn., 1775; dep. commissary gen. of purchases Continental Army, 1777, commissary-gen., 1778-79; at request of Gen. Rochambeau also commissary to French troops in America to end of war; went to Paris to submit report of his transactions, 1783; mem. Continental Congress from Conn., 1787-88; mem. Conn. Conv. to consider ratification of U.S. Constn., 1788; mem. U.S. Ho. of Reps. (Federalist) from Conn., 1st-3d congresses, 1789-95; mem. Conn. Legislature, 1795; mem. Conn. Exec. Council, 1795-1801; founder Bank of N.Am. in Phila. and Hartford Bank (Conn.); dir. U.S. Bank; pres. Bank of N.Y.; a promoter Hartford Mfg. Co., established 1788; established 1st insurance partnership in Conn., 1794; introduced fine breeds of cattle from abroad, engaged in experiments to improve agriculture. Died Hartford, Conn., Apr. 30, 1804; buried Ancient Burying Ground, Hartford.

WADSWORTH, PELEG army officer, congressman; b. Duxbury, Mass., May 6, 1748; s. Peleg and Lusanna (Sampson) W.; grad. Harvard, 1769; m. Elizabeth Bartlett, June 18, 1772, 11 children including Henry, Zilpah (Wadsworth) Longfellow. Capt. of a co. of minute men, 1774; mem. Com. Correspondence of Plymouth County (Mass.); a.d.c. to Artemas Ward, 1776; served under Washington in L.I., N.Y., 1776; served under Sullivan in R.I., 1778; adj. gen. Mass. Militia, 1778, brig. gen., 1779; rep. from Duxbury in Mass. Legislature, 1777-78; 2d in command of expdn. to expel British from Ft. George, Castine, Me., 1779; commanded Eastern Dept. of Mass. with hdqrs. at Thomaston, Me., 1780; raided by party of British, held captive, until 1781; land agt., 1784; mem. Mass. Senate, 1792; selectman of Falmouth (now Portland), Me.; mem. U.S. Ho. of Reps. (Federalist) from Mass., 3d-9th congresses, 1793-1807. Died "Wadsworth Hall" Hiram, Me., Nov. 12, 1829; buried family graveyard at "Wadsworth Hall."

WADSWORTH, WILLIAM AUSTIN farmer; b. Boston, Dec. 8, 1847; s. William Wolcott and Emmeline (Austin) W.; A.B., Harvard, 1870 (honors in chemistry); U. of Berlin, 1871-72; m. Elizabeth Greene Perkins, Sept. 4, 1901. Inherited large landed estate from grandfather. Member Independent Corps Cadets, 2d Regt., Mass. Vol. Militia; maj. and q.m. 8th Army Corps, Spanish-Am. War, 1898, at Manila and San Francisco, on staffs of Generals Merritt and Otis. Pres. N.Y. State Forest, Fish and Game Commn., N.Y. State Agrl. Soc.; trustee State Normal Sch.; pres. Village of Geneseo, Board Supervisors Livingston Co., Good Roads Assn., N.Y. Farmers Assn., Geneseo Pub. Library, Livingston Co. Agrl. Soc.; etc. Republican. Unitarian. Home: Geneseo, N.Y. Died May 2, 1918.

WAESCHE, RUSSELL RANDOLPH (wa'che), admiral U.S. Coast Guard; b. Thurmont, Md., Jan. 6, 1886; s. Leonard Randolph and Mary Martha (Foreman) W.; student Purdue U., 1903-04; grad. U.S. Coast Guard Acad., 1906; m. Dorothy Luke, 1911; children—Russell Randolph, Harry Lee, James Mountford; m. 2d, Agnes Rizzuto, 1933; 1 son, William Alexander. Commd. ensign, U.S. Coast Guard, 1906, and promoted through grades to admiral, 1945; apptd. rear adm. and comdt. U.S. Coast Guard, June 15, 1936, and reappointed, 1940; apptd. vice adm. for temporary service, March 10, 1942; reapptd. comdt., June 1944; member Newcomen Society, National Sojourners, Propeller Club of United States Society of Naval Architects and Marine Engrs., Soc. of Am. Mil. Engrs., Mil. Orders of World War, Am. Legion. Episcopalian. Mason. Clubs: University, Army and Navy (Washington). Home: 7005 Rolling Rd., Chevy Chase, Md. Address: U.S. Coast Guard Hdqrs., Washington, D.C. Died Oct. 17, 1946; buried in Arlington National Cemetery.

WAGNER, ARTHUR LOCKWOOD col. U.S.A.; b. Ottawa, Ill., Mar. 16, 1853; s. Joseph H. and Matilda (Hapeman) W.; grad. West Point, 1875; 2d lt. 6th U.S. inf., June 16, 1875; 1st lt., Oct. 18, 1882; capt., Apr. 2, 1892; maj. and asst. adj. gen., Nov. 18, 1896; lt. col. and asst. adj. gen., Feb. 25, 1898; m. Annie B., d. Andrew Howard, of Pittsburgh, Sept. 5, 1883. Served in Dak., Mont., Colo. and Utah, Sioux campaigns, 1876-77; Ute campaigns, 1880-81; prof. military science and tactics at E. Fla. Sem., Gainesville, Fla., 1882-85, Ft. Douglas, Utah, 1885-86; instr. art of war. U.S. Inf. and Cav. School, Fort Leavenworth, Kan., Nov. 1886, to Apr. 1897; in charge mil. information div., War Dept., Washington, Apr. 1897, to May 1898; on staff Maj. Gen. Miles in war with Spain; detached for duty on staff Maj. Gen. Lawton in campaign in Cuba until surrender of Santiago; with Gen. Miles in Puerto Rico; adj. gen. Dept. Dak., St. Paul, Minn., Jan. to Nov., 1899; adj. gen. 1st div. 8th army corps. Philippine Islands, Dec. 22, 1899, to Apr. 7, 1900, on staff Maj. Gen. Bates in campaign in Province of Cavite; adj. gen. dept. Southern Luzon, Apr. 7, 1900, to Nov. 30, 1901; adj. gen. dept. North Philippines, Nov. 30, 1901, to Mar. 25, 1902; adj. gen. dept. of the Lakes, Chicago, May 7, 1902-—. Author: The Campaign of Königgrätz, 1889; Organization and Tactics, 1895; The Service of Security and Information, 1893; A Catechism of Outpost Duty, 1896. Received gold medal of Mil. Service Instn. of U.S. (1884) for essay on "The Military Necessities of the United States and the Best Provisions for Meeting Them." Died 1905.

WAGNER, LOUIS banker, soldier; b. Giessen, Hesse-Darmstadt, Germany, Aug. 4, 1838; s. Ludwig and Christina (Berg) W.; came to Phila. with family, 1849; ed. Zane St. Grammar Sch., Phila.; learned lithograph business; m. Hattie Slocum, Aug. 4, 1859. Entered Union Army, Aug. 1861; 1st lt. Co. D, 88th Pa. Vols.; promoted capt., 1862, col., 1863, bvtd. brig. gen., 1865; badly wounded at 2d Bull Run, Aug. 1862; wound broke out anew at Chancellorsville, and he was sent home; placed in charge Camp William Penn for organization of colored troops, and sent to the front over 14,000 men. Began in ins. business, 1866; pres. Third Nat. Bank, Phila., July 19, 1891-—; dir. United Firemen's Ins. Co.; trustee N.Y. Life Ins. Co. Mem. council from 22d ward, 1867-73, 1876-78, was 3 times its pres.; mem. bd. edn., 1873-76; recorder of deeds, 1878-82; mem. bd. Guardians of the Poor, 1882; dir. pub. works, 1887-91; pres. bd. dirs. of City Trusts, 1891; chmn. Sinking Fund Commn., City of Phila. Mason. Comdr. in chief G.A.R., 1880-81; treas. bd. trustees Soldiers' and Sailors' Home, Erie, Pa.; chmn. 50th anniversary Battle of Gettysburg Commn., created by act of Legislature of Pa. Home: Germantown, Phila., Pa. Died Jan. 15, 1914.

WAGSTAFF, ALFRED lawyer; b. New York, N.Y., March 1844; s. Alfred and Sarah Platt (Du Bois) W.; LL.B., 1866; m. Mary A. Barnard, Mar. 1880. Capt., maj. and col. 16th Regt. N.G.S.N.Y., 1863-64; lt. col. 15th Regt. N.G.S.N.Y. in service of U.S., July 1864; maj. 91st N.Y. Vet. Vols., 1864-July 1865; chief of staff 3d Div. 5th Army Corps, July 1865; col. and a.d.c. on staff of gov., 1867-69. Admitted to bar, 1866; mem. N.Y. Assembly, 1867-74, Senate, 1876-80; pres. New York & Brooklyn Bridge Co.; clk. Ct. of Common Pleas, N.Y., 1892-95; clk. appellate div. Supreme Ct. 1st dept., 1896-—. Pres. Am. Society Prevention Cruelty to Animals, 1906-—; pres. N.Y. Assn. Protection of Game; trustee Samaritan Home for the Aged. Democrat. Episcopalian. Home: New York, N.Y. Died Oct. 2, 1921.

WAHL, LUTZ army officer; b. Wisconsin, Nov. 2, 1869; grad. U.S. Mil. Acad., 1891; grad. Army War Coll., 1816; grad. Gen. Staff Sch., 1921. Commd. 2d lt. inf., June 12, 1891; promoted through grades to brig. gen. asst. to the adj. gen., May 16, 1924, with rank for 4 yrs., now maj. gen.; served as brig. gen. N.A., Apr. 12, 1918-Oct. 31, 1919. Died Dec. 30, 1928.

WAINWRIGHT, GUY ALWYN mfg. exec.; b. Noblesville, Ind., Nov. 29, 1889; s. Lucius and Victoria (Gray) W.; B.S., Purdue U., 1911; m. Jeanette Harvey, Jan. 3, 1922; children—William Harvey, Stephen Andrew. Pres., gen. mgr. and dir. Diamond Chain Co., Inc., Indpls., 1931-—. Served as lt. col., U.S. Army, World War I. Decorated Croix de Guerre with Palm. Mason. Mem. Sigma Xi, Sigma Chi, Tau Beta Pi. Club: Rotary. Home: 4139 N. Capitol St., Indpls. 8. Office: 402 Kentucky Av., Indpls. 7. Died Sept. 26, 1956.

WAINWRIGHT, JOHN soldier; b. Syracuse, N.Y., July 13, 1839; s. Samuel Force and Maria (Humphrey) W.; ed. pub. schs., New York; m. Emma M. Edwards, of Chester Co., Pa., Apr. 18, 1864. Pvt. Co. G, 2d Pa. Inf., Apr. 18, 1861-July 26, 1861; pvt. Co. F, 97th Pa. Inf., Aug., 1861; 1st sergt., Oct. 3, 1861; 2d lt., Jan. 10, 1862; 1st lt., Mar. 9, 1863; capt., Nov. 1, 1864; lt.-col., Jan. 15, 1865; col., June 1, 1865; mustered out, Aug. 28, 1865. Served in Army of the South, Army of Va., and N.C., Army of the Potomac and Army of the Ohio. Bvtd. capt. and maj. and commended "for gallantry in action before Richmond, Va., Oct. 7, 1864"; awarded Congressional Medal of Honor "for gallant and meritorious services at storming of Ft. Fisher, N.C., Jan. 15, 1865." Gen. claims atty., Wilmington, Del., since 1889. Republican. Unitarian. Mem. City Council, Wilmington, 1893-95; comdr. Dept. of Del. G.A.R., 1882-83; mem. Loyal Legion, Medal of Honor Legion of U.S., S.A.R. Address: 3 W. 7th St., Wilmington, Del.

WAINWRIGHT, JONATHAN MAYHEW naval officer; b. N.Y.C., July 21, 1821; s. Jonathan Mayhew and Amelia (Phelps) W.; m. Maria Page, Dec. 1844, 4 children including Marie, Jonathan Mayhew. Commd. midshipman U.S. Navy, serving on sloop Porpoise, 1837; in ship John Adams on E. Indies cruise, 1838-40; passed midshipman, 1843; on ship Columbia, E. Indies cruise, 1845-46; commd. lt., 1850, served on ship San Jacinto in Mediterranean, 1851-53; spl. service on ship Merrimack, 1858-59; lt. on ship Minnesota in Atlantic Blockading Squadron, 1861; in command Harriet Lane, flagship of W. Gulf Blockading Squadron, 1862, seized Confederate vessel Joanna Ward; participated on ship Harriet Ward in capture of Galveston, Tex., Oct., 1862. Killed during Confederate attack on Galveston, Jan. 1, 1863; buried Trinity Ch. Cemetery, N.Y.C.

WAINWRIGHT, JONATHAN MAYHEW lawyer; b. New York, N.Y., Dec. 10, 1864; s. John Howard and Margaret Livingston (Stuyvesant) W.; A.B., Ph.B., Columbia U., 1884, LL.B., 1886; hon. A.M., 1908; m. Laura Wallace Buchanan, Nov. 23, 1892; 1 dau., Laura F. Admitted to bar, 1886, and practiced at N.Y. City; partner Barry, Wainwright, Thacher & Symmers since 1913. Mem. N.Y. Assembly, 1902-08, Senate, 1909-13; asst. sec. of war, 1921-23; mem. 68th to 71st Congresses, (1923-31), 25th N.Y. Dist Commd. 2d lt., advancing to lt. col., 12th Regt., Nat. Guard N.Y., 1889-1906; capt. 12th N.Y. Vols., Spanish-Am. War; lt. col. insp. gen.'s dept., Nat. Guard, N.Y., Mexican border, 1916; lt. col. and div. insp., N.Y. Div., Feb. 1917; mustered into U.S. service as lt. col., div. insp. 27th Div., U.S. Army, July 15, 1917; served in France and Belgium, participating in all battles and engagements of 27th Div.; hon. discharged Mar. 31, 1919; col. O.R.C., Inf., 1921-29, auxiliary, 1929; col. inactive since Nov. 23, 1937. Decorations: D.S.M., A.E.F. (U.S.); Officier Legion d'Honneur (French); Croix de Guerre with Palm (Belgian); conspicuous Service Cross of State of N.Y., Silver Star medal for "exceptional courage under fire." Awarded Columbia University medal for service, 1934; president Intercollegiate Athletic Association, 1884. Chairman Westchester County Defense Council, 1941. Member board mgrs. St. Luke's Hosp., and Seamen's Ch. Inst., N.Y. City. Mem. bd. trustees Grant Monument Assn. of N.Y. City. V.p. Westchester County Historical Society. Member Assn. Bar City of New York, Westchester County Bar Assn. (pres. 1903-04), Westchester County Park Commn., 1930-37; Mil. and Naval Order Spanish-Am. War, Mil. Order World War, N.Y. Soc. Mil. and Naval Officers of World War, S.R., St. Nicholas Soc., Pilgrims of U.S., United Spanish War Vets., Am. Legion, Delta Psi, Phi Beta Kappa. Mason. Republican. Episcopalian (warden Christ's Ch., Rye, N.Y.). Clubs: Union, Republican (New York); Army and Navy (Washington); Apawamis, American Yacht. Home: Rye, N.Y. Office: 72 Wall St., New York, N.Y. Died June 3, 1945.

WAINWRIGHT, JONATHAN MAYHEW army officer; b. Walla Walla, Wash., Aug. 23, 1883; s. Major Robert Powell Page (U.S. Cav.) and Josephine (Serrell) W.; B.S., U.S. Mil. Acad., 1906; m. Adele Howard Holley, Feb. 18, 1911; 1 son, Jonathan Mayhew V. (officer United States Merchant Marine and U.S. Naval Reserve Force). Commd. 2d lt. cav., 1906; promoted through grades to brig. gen., 1938; temp. rank of maj. general, 1940, lieut. general (temp.), Mar. 19, 1942, promoted to general, September 1945. Served with 1st Cav., Tex., 1906-08; with expedition against Moros, Philippines, 1909-10; with 1st Cav., Ida., Vt., Wyo., 1910-15; attended Mounted Service Sch., Fort Riley, 1915-16; adjutant 1st O.T.C., Plattsburg, N.Y., 1917; with gen. staff, 76th Nat. Army Div., Aug. 1917, sailing for France, Feb. 1918; gen. staff 82d Div. at Toul, St. Mihiel and Meuse-Argonne; gen. staff 3d Army, Germany, Nov. 1918-20; instr. Cav. Sch., Fort Riley, 1920-21; Gen. Staff War Dept., 1921-23; with 3d Cav., Fort Myer, Va., 1923-25; Chem. Warfare Sch., Cavalry Sch., Command and Gen. Staff Sch., 1928-31; Army War Coll., 1933-34; asst. comdt., Fort Riley, 1934-36; comd. 3d Cav., Fort Myer, 1936-38, 1st Cav. Brigade, Fort Clark, Tex., 1938-40; assigned duty in Philippines, Oct. 1940; comd. Philippine Div., Oct. 1940; served throughout the Bataan campaign and assumed command when Gen. MacArthur went to Australia; prisoner of war of Japanese govt.; rescued from Jap prison camp, Manchuria, Aug. 1945; became comdr. 4th Army, Jan. 1946; retired Aug. 31, 1947. Decorated D.S.M., 1920; D.S.C. Feb. 1942; Oakleaf Cluster for D.S.M., Nov. 1942; received Congressional Medal of Honor, Sept. 1945. Now chmn. bd. Hom-Ond Food Stores; mgr. Alamo Stock Farm; v.p. Acme Sash Window Balance Co. Home: Fiddlers Green, 500 Elizabeth Rd., San Antonio. Died Sept. 2, 1953; buried Arlington Nat. Cemetery.

WAINWRIGHT, RICHARD naval officer; b. Charlestown, Mass., Jan. 5, 1817; s. Robert Dewar and Maria (Auchmuty) W.; m. Sally Bache, Mar. 1, 1849, at least 4 children including Richard. Commd. midshipman U.S. Navy, 1831; cruised in Mediterranean, 1833-36; passed midshipman, 1837, commd. lt. 1841; served on ship Vincennes in Home Squadron, 1842-45; with ship Columbia in Brazil Squadron, 1846-47; with Coast Survey, 1848-56; on brig Merrimac of Pacific Squadron, 1857-60; served ordnance duty at Washington (D.C.) Navy Yard, 1860-61; promoted comdr., 1861; commanded the Hartford (flagship of Flag Officer David Farragut), 1861-62. Died on board Hartford, Donaldsville, La., Aug. 10, 1862.

WAINWRIGHT, RICHARD rear admiral U.S.N.; b. Washington, D.C., Dec. 17, 1849; s. Comdr. Richard (U.S.N.) and Sallie Franklin (Bache) W.; brother of Dallas Bache W.; apptd. to U.S. Naval Acad. by the President, at large, 1864; grad., 1868; LL.B., Columbian (now George Washington) U., 1884 (LL.D., 1900); m. Evelyn Wotherspoon, Sept. 11, 1873. Promoted ensign, Apr. 19, 1865; master, July 12, 1870; lt., Sept. 25, 1873; lt. comdr., Sept. 16, 1894; comdr., Mar. 3, 1899; capt., Aug. 10, 1903; rear admiral, July 11, 1908. Served on Jamestown and Colorado; at Hydrographic Office; coast survey on Asiatic Sta., and Richmond, 1868-80; Bur. of Navigation, 1880-84; Tennessee, 1884-86; Galena, 1886-87; Naval Acad., 1887-90; Alert, 1890-93; Hydrographic Office, 1893-96; chief, Intelligence Office, 1896-97; exec. officer Maine, Nov. 17, 1897, until she was blown up in Havana harbor, Feb. 15, 1898; comd. Gloucester during Spanish War and took part in the destruction of Admiral Cervera's squadron off

Santiago, Cuba, July 3, 1898; was advanced 10 numbers in rank "for eminent and conspicuous conduct in this battle," presented with a silver loving cup by citizens of Gloucester, Mass., and a sword by citizens of Washington; comd. ships at Naval Acad., 1899-1900; supt. Naval Acad., 1900-02; comd. Newark, 1902-04; mem. Gen. Bd., 1904-07; comdg. Louisiana, 1907-08, 2d div. Atlantic Fleet, 1908-09, 3d div., 1909-10; aid for operations to Sec. of the Navy, 1910; retired by operation of law, Dec. 17, 1911. Died Mar. 6, 1926.

WAITE, HENRY MATSON civil engr.; b. Toledo, O., May 15, 1869; s. Henry Selden and Ione (Brown) W.; grad. Toledo High Sch.; student Mass. Inst. of Tech.; LL.D., Univ. of Miami; Dr. of Engring., Univ. of Cincinnati; m. Mary Mason Brown, Apr. 15, 1914. With C.,C.,C.&St.L. Ry. as transitman, 1890-92, engr. maintenance of way, 1892-93; div. engr. C.,N.O.&T.P. Ry., 1893; bridge engr., roadmaster and supt. Cincinnati div., same rd., 1899-1905, supt. Chattanooga div., 1905-07; supt. Seaboard Air Line Ry., 1907-09; v.p. and chief engr. Clinchfield Coal Corp., Dante, Va., 1909-12; chief engr. City of Cincinnati, 1912-14; city mgr., Dayton, 1914-18; v.p. and chief engr., Lord Constrn. Co., N.Y., 1919-20; pres. Lord Dry Dock Corp., N.Y., 1920; in private practice at N.Y., 1920-27; chief engr. Cincinnati Union Terminal Co., 1927-1933; dep. adminstrn. of Public Works, July 1933-Sept., 1934; dir. Regional Dept. of Economic Security, Cincinnati, since Sept. 1934; private practice cons. engr. since 1937; chmn. Chicago Subway Commn., Public Works Adminstrn.; chmn. public works com. Nat. Resources Com., Col. of engrs. Transportation Corps, U.S.A., with A.E.F., 1918-19; served as chief engr. Trans. Corps, asst. dep. gen. of transportation, 2d Army, in Advance Zone, and as a.d.g. Trans., 3d Army in Germany; one of members of Am. Bridgehead Commn. at Coblenz before arrival of Am. Army, asst. to officer in charge civ. affairs at advanced G.H.Q. at Treves, Germany. Mem. Am. Soc. C.E., Am. Inst. Mining and Metall. Engrs., Am. Ry. Engring. Assn. Awarded D.S.M. (U.S.); Officer Légion d'Honneur (French). Club: Engineers. Home: 3515 Cornell Place, Cincinnati. Died Sept. 1, 1944.

WAITE, SUMNER army officer; b. Westbrook, Me., Sept. 6, 1888; s. John L. and Annie (Gowen) W.; A.B., U. of Maine, Orono, Me., 1911; grad. Inf. Sch., Ft. Benning, Ga., 1923, Command and Gen. Staff Sch., 1926, Army War Coll., 1932; Ecole Superieure de Guerre, Paris, France, 1928; Master of Arts, George Washington University, 1950; m. Elizabeth Carrison, Nov. 7, 1923; children—Elizabeth C., Sumner, Jordan C. Commd. 2d lt., 5th Inf., U.S. Army, 1911, promoted through the grades to brig. gen., 1944. Decorated D.S.M., Commendation Ribbon, Legion of Merit (U.S.); Commander Legion of Honor, Croix de Guerre with palm (France), Croix de Guerre, Mil. Cross 1st Class (Belgium). Mem. Phi Gamma Delta. Club: Army and Navy (Washington). Address: care The Adjutant General's Office, War Dept., Washington 25. Died June 7, 1952.

WALCUTT, CHARLES C. JR. army officer; b. in Ohio, June 20, 1861; grad. U.S. Mil. Acad., July 1, 1886, Inf. and Cav. Sch., 1893; Army War Coll., 1912. Commd. 2d lt. 8th Cav., July 1, 1886; 1st lt. 3d Cav., Aug. 16, 1892; trans. to 8th Cav., Dec. 5, 1892; capt. a.q.m. vols., May 12, 1898; vacated Sept. 18, 1899; maj. 44th Vol. Inf., Aug. 17, 1899; hon. disch. vols., June 30, 1901; capt. 2d Cav. U.S.A., Feb. 2, 1901; q.m., Oct. 29, 1901; assigned to 5th Cav., Nov. 3, 1905; maj., Mar. 3, 1911; col., July 1, 1916; brig. gen. N.A., June 26, 1918. Ordered to Manila, P.I., 1898; depot q.m., Manila, 1890-1901; duty at Washington, D.C., 1901-02; constructing q.m. Whipple Barracks, Ariz., 1902; detailed as col., Bur. Insular Affairs, Washington, D.C., 1912, serving as asst. chief, later acting chief and chief of same. Died June 20, 1925.

WALDEN, AUSTIN THOMAS municipal judge; b. Ft. Valley, Ga., Apr. 12, 1885; s. Jeff and Jennie (Tomlin) W.; A.B., Atlanta U., 1907, LL.D., 1950; LL.B., U. Mich., 1911; L.H.D., Morehouse Coll., Atlanta, 1950; m. Mary E. Denny, May 18, 1918; children—Jenelsie M. (Mrs. Charles Holloway), Austella M. (Mrs. Richard D. Colley). Admitted to Ga. bar, 1912; practice in Macon., Ga., 1912-17, Atlanta, 1919-62; civic counselor, Atlanta, 1963-—; prohac vice judge Municipal Cts., Atlanta, 1964-—. Counsel, Citizens Trust Co., Atlanta, 1929-—, pres., 1931-38, also trust officer, dir.; a founder, pres. Consol. Mortgage Investment and Loan Assn., Atlanta, 1956-—; asso. counsel, dir. Mut. Fed. Savs. & Loan Assn., Atlanta, 1952-—. Mem. Am. Battle Monument Commn., 1962-—; co-founder, chmn. Atlanta Negro Voters League, 1937-57. Mem. Atlanta City Exec. Com., 1954-62, atty. parliamentarian, 1954-62. Mem. Democratic Exec Com. Ga., 1962; del. Dem. Nat. Conv., 1964; founder, pres. So. Dem. Conf., 1962-—. Chmn. bd. dirs. Butler Street YMCA, Atlanta, 1931-42, Atlanta Urban League, 1937-57. Served as capt. inf. U.S. Army, 1917-19; AEF in France. Recipient award Butler St. YMCA, 1957. Human Relations award Phi Beta Sigma, 1960, award Nat. Urban League, 1960, Outstanding Achievement award U. Mich., 1964. Mem. Am., Ga., Atlanta, Gate City (organizer, 1st pres. 1946) bar assns., N.A.A.C.P. (v.p. 1962, mem. nat. legal com. 1952-—; pres. Atlanta bar, 1922-34; award 1957), Atlanta U. Alumni Assn., Alpha Phi Alpha (award 1957), Sigma Pi Phi (v.p. 1960). Baptist (chmn. trustees). Home: 980 Westmoor Drive, N.W., Atlanta 30314. Office: Walden Bldg., Atlanta 30303. Died July 2, 1965.

WALDEN, MADISON MINER congressman; b. nr. Scioto, Brush Creek, O., Oct. 6, 1836; attended Denmark Acad., Ia., also Wesleyan Coll., Mt. Pleasant, Ia.; grad. Wesleyan U., Delaware, O., 1859. Served as capt. 6th Regt., Ia. Volunteer Inf., also 8th Regt., Ia. Volunteer Cavalry, during Civil War, 1861-65; taught sch.; publisher Centerville (Ia.) Citizen, 1865-74; mem. Ia. Ho. of Reps., 1866-67, Ia. Senate, 1868-69; lt. gov. Ia., 1870; mem. U.S. Ho. of Reps. (Republican) from Ia., 1871-73; engaged in agriculture, coal mining, Centerville; apptd. chief clk. in office of Solicitor of Treasury, Washington, D.C., 1889. Died Washington, July 24, 1891; buried Oakland Cemetery, Centerville.

WALDEN, WALTER, author; b. Milan, Ill., June 1, 1870; s. Lars P. Bergstrom and Dorothea Amelia (Axelson) W.; student Augustana Coll., Rock Island, Ill., 1888-90, Northwestern U., 1890-1892; M.D., Northwestern U. Med. Sch., 1896; m. Henri Albertine Wilhelm, of Chicago, Dec. 3, 1902; children—Viola, Walford. Began practice at Chicago, 1896. Commd. capt. M.C., U.S.A., Jan. 7, 1918; apptd. comdg. officer med. detachment 1st Div., Field Arty., Oct. 15, 1919; hon. discharged Sept. 14, 1920; passed asst. surgeon, U.S.P.H.S. Reserve, Nov. 1920; capt. O.R.C., U.S.A., Feb. 1921; hon. discharged U.S.P.H.S., Aug. 17, 1923; maj. Auxiliary Res. since June 1, 1934. Mem. Soc. Midland Authors, Am. Legion. Episcopalian. Author: Boy Scouts Afloat, 1918; The Hidden Islands, 1920; The Voodoo Gold Trail, 1922. Contbr. serials and short stories to Boy's Life Mag., Boy Scouts' Year Book, etc. Home: Campbell's Island, P.O. East Moline IL

WALDO, RICHARD H. editor; b. New York, N.Y., Sept. 28, 1878; s. Howard Lovett and Clara Waldo (Sullivan) W.; ed. Friends Acad., Locust Valley, N.Y., Hawkins Collegiate Inst., New Brighton, N.Y.; married; children—Allan Stone, William Stone, Howard Lovett, Thayer Everett. Advertising rep. Harper & Brothers, 1902-05; adv. and business mgr. Good Housekeeping Mag., 1905-14; established and developed Good Housekeeping Inst. with licensing of mfrs.; sec. and associate gen. mgr. N.Y. Tribune, 1914-17. Created and caused to be adopted "Truth" emblem by Associated Advertising Clubs of the World (Advertising Fedn. of America), 1909-14. Chmn. publicity com. Chamber Commerce U.S.A., 1913-17; established and staffed The Nation's Business, Washington, D.C. Commd. capt. Inf. U.S.R., Plattsburg, N.Y., Nov. 8, 1917; duty A.E.F., Dec. 1917-Aug. 1919; organized War Risk Insurance in Gt. Britain and Ireland; as business mgr. organized "The Stars and Stripes," G.-2, Chau-mont; comd. troops 111th Inf., 28th Div., field service; also sec. and organizing officer Inter-allied Games, Paris, 1919, G.-5, Chaumont. U.S. Army, 1919. Decorated Order of the Holy Redeemer (Greece), 1919. Pub. Hearst's Internat. Mag., New York, 1921-23; adv. counsel and management, John Wanamaker New York, 1923-28; pres. and editor McClure Newspaper Syndicate since 1928. Dir. Pollak Foundation for Econ. Research since 1929. Treas. Grand Jury Assn., N.Y. County, 1934-37; historian N.Y. Chapter Mil. Order World War, 1935-39, nat. historian, 1939-40; dir. Sales Execs. Club of N.Y. since 1939. Clubs: Atlantic Beach, Mil.-Naval, Metropolitan (New York). Home: 37 Washington Sq. W. Office: 75 West St., New York, N.Y. Died June 11, 1943.

WALDORF, ERNEST LYNN bishop; b. South Valley, Otsego County, N.Y., May 14, 1876; s. David Hiram and Mercy Ann (Thrall) W.; A.B., Syracuse U., 1900; D.D., Syracuse, 1915; LL.D., Kan. Wesleyan and Albion (Mich.) Coll., 1920; also LL.D. from De Pauw U., 1934; m. Flora Janet Irish, Jan. 1902; children—Lynn Osbert, Ethel Margaret, Paul Douglas, John David, Robert James. Ordained M.E. Ministry, 1900; pastor Shortsville, N.Y., 1900-02, Union Springs, 1902-03, Phelps, 1903-05, Clyde, 1905-07, Centenary Ch., Syracuse, 1907-11, Plymouth Ch., Buffalo, 1911-15, 1st. Ch., Cleveland, O., 1915-20; bishop M.E. Ch., 1920-24, in charge states of Kan., Okla., Tex., and La.; of Kansas City area, covering Kan., Okla., Tex., La., Ark. and Mo., 1924-32; assigned to Chicago Area (covers work of M.E. Chs. in Ill. together with bilingual confs. of Swedish and Norwegian-Danish work between Atlantic Ocean and Rocky Mountains), May 1932. Chaplain 74th Rgt., Nat. Guard N.Y., Buffalo, 1911-15. Trustee Garrett Biblical Inst., Ill. Wesleyan Coll., McKendree Coll. Mason, K.P. Club: Union League. Home: 941 Sheridan Rd., Wilmette. Address: 77 W. Washington St., Chicago, Ill. Died July 27, 1943.

WALDSEEMULLER, MARTIN cartographer; b. Freiburg, Germany, circa 1470; studied theology U. Freiburg. Became interested in cartography and geography as a youth; published map of world, Universalis cosmographia (contains 1st mention of name America, shows S.Am. as island) and Cosmographiae introductio (contains explanation of use of name America, suggests this name for New World), 1507 (a 1st edit. now in N.Y. Public Library); published Latin translation of 4 voyages of Amerigo Vespucci; produced Carta itineraria Europae (1st printed wall map of Europe), 1511; helped prepare 1513 edit. of Ptolemy's Geography (considered 1st modern atlas); apptd. canon of St. Dié, Lorraine, France, 1514; produced Carta marina navigatoria, 1516; often signed his maps with Greek spelling of his name, Illacomilus. Died St. Dié, circa 1522.

WALES, PHILIP SKINNER M.D., medical dir. U.S.N.; b. Annapolis, Md., Feb. 27, 1837; ed. Univ. of Md. and in its med. dept.; also M.D. Univ. of Pa.; settled in Baltimore and later in Washington. Entered navy as asst. surgeon, Aug. 7, 1856; commissioned surgeon, Oct. 12, 1861; served in U.S.S. Fort Jackson of North Atlantic and Western Gulf squadrons, 1862-65. Member Bd. of Examiners, 1873-74; medical inspector. 1873-80; surgeon gen. of navy and chief of bureau of medicine and surgery, 1880-84; assisted in attendance on President Garfield after he had been shot. Author: Mechanical Therapeutics. Died 1906.

WALES, WELLINGTON newspaper editor; b. Hollywood, Cal., July 16, 1917; s. Wellington Edward and Ethel Franklin (Oborn) W.; A.B., Dartmouth, 1938; M.S., Columbia, 1941; m. Helen Woolsey, Sept. 13, 1941; children—Heathcote, Samuel Gardner, Jane MacGregor Keep. Asst. dir. coll. promotion N.Y. Times, 1938-39, editorial writer, 1965-—; newspicture editor Acme Newspictures, 1941-42; makeup editor N.Y. Times Mag., 1946-49; copy editor Reporter mag., 1949; editor Citizen-Advertiser, Auburn, N.Y., 1949-54; reporter Boston Herald, 1954-55; mng. editor Woman's Day, N.Y.C., 1955-57; dir. publicity, N.Y. State, 1957-58; asso. editor Daily News of V.I., 1960-62; chief editorial writer Knickerbocker News, Albany, N.Y., 1962-64, editor editorial page, 1964-65. Nieman fellow, Harvard, 1950-51; Pulitzer Prize juror, 1953-54; moderator Starring the Editors, TV series, 1952. Mem. 7th Regiment N.Y. N.G., 1939-40; capt. U.S. Army, 1942-45, ETO, PTO, supervision of all Korean newspapers, 1945-46. Mem. Nat. Conf. Editorial Writers. Democrat. Clubs: Ft. Orange (Albany, N.Y.); Harvard of N.Y.; Schuyler Meadows (Loudonville, N.Y.). Address: 236 E. 32d St., N.Y.C. 10016. Died Apr. 10, 1966; buried Dosoris Cemetery, Glen Cove, L.I., N.Y.

WALKE, HENRY naval officer; b. "The Ferry," Princess Anne County, Va., Dec. 24, 1808; m. Sara J. Aim; m. 2d, Jane Ellen Burges; m. 3d, Julia Reed; at least 4 children. Commd. midshipman U.S. Navy, 1827; served in Natchez, 1827, in Ontario, 1829; commd. lt., 1839, sailed around world in ship Boston, 1840-43; exec. of brig Vesuvius against Vera Cruz, Alvarado, Tuspan and Tabasco in Mexican War; with Commodore Foote's Flotilla on Upper Mississippi River, 1861-63; in Carondelet in attack on Ft. Henry (Tennessee River), 1862; in attack on Ft. Donelson (Cumberland River), carried on alone 6-hour bombardment; most celebrated exploit was running of batteries at Island Number 10 (one of most famous events of Civil War); capt. in command ironclad Lafayette, 1862; served under Porter in passing of Vicksburg batteries and 5-hour action at Grand Gulf, 1863; commanded Sacramento, 1863-65; commd. commodore, 1866; commanded Mound City Naval Station, 1868-69; commd. rear adm., 1870-71; ret. to Bklyn., 1871. Author: Naval Scenes and Reminiscences of the Civil War, 1877. Died Bklyn., Mar. 8, 1896.

WALKE, WILLOUGHBY officer U.S.A.; b. Norfolk, Va., Jan. 28, 1859; s. Richard and Mary Diana (Talbot) W.; grad. U. of Va., 1879, U.S. Mil. Acad., 1883, Arty. Sch., 1888; m. Julia Armstead Sharp, Nov. 28, 1883. Promoted 2d lt. 2d Arty., June 13, 1883; 1st lt. 5th Arty., Apr. 24, 1891; transferred to 7th Arty., Mar. 8, 1898; maj. 3d U.S. Vol. Engrs., June 28, 1898-May 29, 1899; capt. 2d Arty., Aug. 28, 1899; maj. Arty. Corps, Oct. 1, 1906; lt. col., Coast Arty. Corps, Mar. 3, 1911; col., Aug. 3, 1912. Served in southern camps and in army of occupation at Matanzas, Cuba; comdr. Middle Atlantic Coast Arty. Dist., Sept. 1, 1917-Feb. 1919. Fellow Royal Chem. Soc. Author: Essentials of Chemistry; Lectures on Explosives, 1894; Gunpowder and High Explosives; Comparative Strength of High Explosives. Died Dec. 16, 1928.

WALKER, ALFRED dentist; b. New York, N.Y., May 22, 1876; s. Alfred and Jane (Finnegan) W.; D.D.S., New York Coll. of Dentistry, 1897; m. Elizabeth Muir, Jan. 24, 1912; children—Alfred, John Muir. Practiced in N.Y. City since 1897; formerly mem. Bd. of Dental Examiners, State of N.Y.; prof. emeritus of pulp canal therapy, New York Univ. Coll. of Dentistry. Served as pvt. 7th Regt., Nat. Guard N.Y., 1901-11; 1st lt. and capt. 107th Inf., Nat. Guard N.Y., 1918-23; lt. comdr. U.S. Naval Res. (hon. retired list). Hon. trustee Boys' Club. Pres. dental sect. Pan Am. Med. Assn. Recipient of N.Y. U. Alumni Federation Medallion, 1935. Pierre Fauchard Medal Award, 1940. Fellow Am. Coll. Dentists, N.Y. Acad. Dentistry, Internat. Coll. Dentists; mem. Am. Dental Assn. (life), Dental Soc. State N.Y. (pres. 1930-31, life mem.), 1st Dist. Dental Soc. (pres. life mem.), Florida State Dental Society, Miami Dental Society, F.A.A.A.S., New York Academy Sciences, Psi Omega, Omicron Kappa Upsilon. Democrat. Author of numerous papers and repts. on dental subjects. Co-author, vol. on Dental Practice Management; co-author, vol. on Oral Diagnosis and Treatment. Home: 2131 Biarritz Drive. Office: 420 Lincoln Rd., Miami Beach, Fla. Died Oct. 16, 1948.

WALKER, ASA rear adm. U.S.N.; b. Portsmouth, N.H., Nov. 13, 1845; s. Asa T. and Louisa W.; grad. U.S. Naval Acad., 1866; m. Miss A. W. Grant, June 11, 1890. Ensign, Mar. 12, 1868; promoted through grades to rear adm., Jan. 7, 1906. Has served on various stas., and 1873-76, 1879-83, 1886-90 and 1893-97 at the Naval Acad.; took command U.S.S. Concord, May 23, 1897, participating in battle of Manila Bay, May 1, 1898; advanced 9 numbers "for eminent and conspicuous conduct in battle," June 10, 1898; on duty at the Naval War Coll., Newport, R.I., 1899-1900; mem. Naval Examining Bd., 1900-01; comdg. U.S.S. San Francisco, Jan. 2, 1902-Nov. 21, 1903; mem. Gen. Bd., Jan.-Oct. 1904; commanded U.S.R.S. Wabash, 1904-05; apptd. supt. Naval Obs., Washington, Feb. 28, 1906. Retired, Nov. 13, 1907. Died Mar. 7, 1916.

WALKER, C. IRVINE b. Charleston, S.C., Feb. 14, 1842; s. Joseph and Cornelia M. W.; grad. S.C. Mil. Acad., Charleston, S.C., April 1861; m. Orie St. Clair, of Georgetown, S.C., June 20, 1866. Entered C.S.A., Apr. 1861, and rose to rank of lieutenant-colonel 10th S.C. Regt.; established business of Walker, Evans & Cogswell, Charleston, S.C., 1868, and continued at its head until May 1900. Lt.-gen. comdg. Army Northern Va. Dept. U.C.V. since 1902, and succeeded Gen. George W. Gordon as comdr. U.C.V., on latter's death, Aug. 1911; now honorary commander-in-chief U.C.V.; mem. S.C. Chickamauga Monument Commn.; prominent in movement for monuments to the Women of Confederacy; chmn. S.C. Woman's Monument Commission, chairman U.C.V. Rutherford Com. Democrat. Wrote: Sketch of 10th S.C. Regt., Confederate Army, 1881; Romance of Lower Carolina; Life of Lt. Gen. Richard H. Anderson, of the Confederate Army; History of the Agricultural Society of South Carolina; History of South Carolinians in the Confederate War, 1925; also many articles for press. Southern rep. Gettysburg Semi-Centennial Commn., 1913. Home: Charleston, S.C.

WALKER, CHARLES SWAN b. Cincinnati, O., Oct. 7, 1846; s. Samuel Swan and Harriet N. (Fowles) W.; A.B., Yale, 1867, A.M., B.D., 1870; Andover Theol. Sem., 1868-69; Ph.D., Amherst, 1885; m. Alice M. Morehouse, of Darien, Conn., 1873; children—Claude Frederic, Charles Morehouse. Served 100 days as mem. 137th Regt., U.S. Vols., Civil War. Ordained Congl. ministry, 1871; pastor Darien, 1871-72, Huntington, W.Va., 1873-74, Holyoke, Mass., 1874-76, South Ch., Amherst, 1876-79, 1881-86, Vineland, N.J., 1879-81; prof. mental and polit. science, Mass. Agrl. Coll., 1886-1906, also chaplain. Writer, lecturer, newspaper corr. Mem. Am. Acad. polit. and Social Science, Am. Econ. Assn., Amherst Hist. Soc. (pres.), Phi Beta Kappa, Chaplain State Grange, Mass., 14 yrs. Republican. Mason. Author: Samuel Minot Jones—the Story of an Amherst Boy, 1922. Home: St. Petersburg, Fla.

WALKER, DOW VERNON lawyer; b. Greensprings, O., Dec. 28, 1885; s. Lindsey E. and Lillie Belle (Harris) W.; grad. Ore. State Coll., 1906; LL.B., U. of Ore., 1912; m. Mabel Davis, Dec. 15, 1906; children—Marshall Vernon, Dow Edwin. Cashier Northern Pacific Terminal Co., Portland, Ore., 1906-08; mgr. Multnomah Amateur Athletic Club, Portland, Ore., 1908-19; admitted to Ore. bar, 1912 and since practiced in that state; county commr., Multnomah Co., Ore., 1921-24. Nat. comdr. Disabled Am. Veterans, 1945-46, mem. finance com. since 1942; trustee Disabled Am. Vets. Service Foundation since 1942. Served as div. staff officer, 39th Div., U.S. Army, 1917; with French gen. staff, 1918; mem. Gen. Pershing's hdqrs. staff. Adj. Gen.'s Office, Chaumont, France, 1918; assigned to G-3, in charge moving 41st Div., U.S. Army, to U.S., 1919. Mem. Am. Legion, Veterans Fgn. Wars, Mil. Order of World Wars, Phi Delta Phi. Elk. Club: Multnomah Amateur Athletic (hon. life mem.). Address: Box 276, Newport, Ore. Died July 25, 1947.

WALKER, FRANK BUCKLEY entertainment corp. exec.; b. Fly Summit, N.Y., Oct. 24, 1889; s. Solomon and Mary (Buckley) W.; m. Laura Boyne, Sept. 9, 1919; children—John, Joan, Jean. With Nat. Savs. Bank, Albany, N.Y., 1908-12, W. N. Coler & Co., N.Y.C., 1912-15; pres. Central Concert Co., Detroit, Chgo., St. Louis, 1919-21; dir. Columbia Phonograph Co., N.Y.C., 1921-32; v.p. RCA-Victor Co., Camden, N.J., 1933-44; exec. dir. record div. Metro-Goldwyn-Mayer, N.Y.C., 1945-56, now cons.; v.p. Loew's, Inc., N.Y.C., 1956—. Dir. Phila. Opera Co., Merchant Marine Vets. Foundation; mem. popular award panel A.S.C.A.P.; panel Country Music Assn. Served as capt., U.S. Army, Mexican Border, 1917; lt., USN, 1917-19. Mem. Am. Legion, Record Industry Assn. Am. (pres. 1956), Alhambra, K.C., Elk. Clubs: Advertising, Lotos (N.Y.C.); North Hills Golf (Douglaston, N.Y.). Office: 1540 Broadway, N.Y.C. Died Oct. 15, 1963.

WALKER, FRED LIVINGOOD, army officer; b. Fairfield County, O., June 11, 1887; s. William Henry and Belle (Mason) W.; E.M., Ohio State U., 1911; grad. Infantry Sch., 1923, hon. grad. Command and Gen. Staff Sch., 1927; grad. Army War Coll., 1933; m. Frances M. Messmore, Aug. 19, 1911; children—Mary Elizabeth (dec.), Fred Livingood, Charles. Commd. 2d lt. Inf., 1911; promoted through grades to major gen., Jan. 1942; Comdt. The Inf. Sch., July 1944-45; retired from active service Apr. 30, 1946. Served in P.I., Mexico, China and with A.E.F. in France, Italy and Germany; instr. Army War Coll., 1933-37. Decorated D.S.C. with oak leaf cluster, D.S.M., Purple Heart with oak leaf cluster. Author: From Texas to Rome, 1969. Home: Charleston OH Died Oct. 1969.

WALKER, GEORGE HENRY, army officer; b. Muskogee, Okla., Apr. 2, 1914; s. George H. and Estelle (McRae) W.; B.S., U.S. Mil. Acad., 1937; M.S. in Civil Engring., U. Cal. at Berkeley, 1941; grad. Army War Coll., 1955; grad. Advanced Mgmt. Program, Harvard, 1961; m. Jo Dorsey Ballantine, Apr. 9, 1938; children—Joan VanNess (Mrs. Thomas H. O'Connor), George Henry III. Commd. 2d lt. U.S. Army, 1937, advanced through grades to maj. gen., 1964; served in PTO, also comdr. 1103d Engr. Combat Group, ETO, World War II; staff and command assignments Dept. Army, also U.S. Army Europe, 1945-52; dist. engr. U.S. Army, Engrs., San Francisco, 1952-54; corps engr. I U.S. Army Corps, Korea, 1957-58; asst. comdr. Army Engr. Sch., 1961-63; div. engr. Mo. River div. U.S. Army Engrs., 1963-65, S. Atlantic div., 1965-69. Mem. Miss. River Commn., Bd. Engrs. for Rivers and Harbors, Coastal Engring. Research Bd. Decorated Legion of Merit, Bronze Star for valor with oak leaf cluster; Croix de Guerre (France). Registered profl. engr., Neb. Mem. Soc. Am. Mil. Engrs. Home: Atlanta GA Died Sept. 1969.

WALKER, HARVEY, prof. polit. sciences; b. Des Moines, Ia., Feb. 24, 1900; s. Marion McCreary and Lillie May (Harvey) W.; A.B., U. of Kan., 1923; M.A., University of Minnesota, 1927, Ph.D., 1928; LL.B., Ohio State University, 1948; m. Myra Lois Lingenfelter, May 18, 1924; children—Harvey, John Vaughan, Jeanne Carolyn. Instr. polit. science, U. of Kan., 1924-25, prof., 1969-70; instr. U. of Minn., 1927-28; asst. prof. polit. science, Ohio State U., 1928-30, asso. prof., 1930-33, professor, 1933-67, prof. emeritus, 1967-71; also engaged in practice of law; superintendent of budget of State of Ohio, 1928-31; lt. col. Finance Reserve, U.S. Army; deputy finance officer and finance officer, Columbus, O., 1941-42; asst. Corps Area finance officer, 5th Corps Area, Fort Hayes, O., 1942; finance officer South Atlantic Ferrying Wing, Air Transport Command, 1942-43; finance officer, Services of Supply, U.S. Army Forces South Atlantic, 1943-44, chief Administrative Management Section, Office of Fiscal Dir. War Dept., 1944. Chief, Employee Relations Section, Indusl. Personnel Div., Army Service Forces, 1944; relieved from active duty, Aug. 1944; with UN Tech. Assistance Adminstrn., Rio de Janeiro, Brazil, 1951-52, C.Am., 1956-57. Fellow Social Sciences Research Council, 1932-33. Fellow Inst. Public Adminstrn. (London); mem. Internat. City Mgrs. Assn. (affiliate), Am. Polit. Science Assn. (secretary-treas.), Am. Acad. Polit. and Social Science, Am. Soc. for Public Adminstrn., Am. Assn. University Profs., Columbus, Ohio State and Am. Bar Assos., Order Coif, Phi Beta Kappa, Delta Sigma Pi, Pi Sigma Alpha, Acacia, Republican. Unitarian. Mason, K.T. Club: Faculty. Author, co-author, translator of books relating to field, also tech. articles. Home: Worthington OH Died May 22, 1971; cremated.

WALKER, HENRY LEE r.r. exec.; b. Goshen, N.Y., Feb. 17, 1905; s. H. Lee and Laura McChord (Rav) W.; student George Washington U., 1922-24; LL.B., Georgetown U., 1927; m. Corinne Lund, Nov. 22, 1940; children—Wickliffe Wade, Judith Rav. Admitted to D.C. bar, 1927; with U.S. Lines, 1921-23, Bonbright & Co., Washington, 1924-27; with So. Ry. Co., 1927—, gen. solicitor, 1951-56, became v.p., gen. counsel, 1956, v.p. law, 1963-ret., 1963; with Covington & Burlington, Washington, 1963—; prof. law Nat. U., 1931-54. Served to lt. comdr. USNR, 1942-45. Mem. Am., D.C. bar assns., Assn. ICC Practitioners. Republican. Presbyn. Clubs: Chevy Chase (Md.); Metropolitan (Washington). Contbr. to legal, financial publs. Home: 1419 33d St. N.W., Washington 20007. Office: Union Trust Bldg., Washington. Died Dec. 7, 1964; buried Arlington Cemetery.

WALKER, HERBERT WILLIAM newspaper exec.; b. Atchison, Kan., June 4, 1895; s. Jacob William and Clara Anastasia (Rank) W.; A.B., Midland Coll., 1915; B. J., U. Mo. Sch. Journalism, 1917; LL.D., Midland Coll., 1950; m. Lynn Curry, Apr. 9, 1921. Reporter, Atchison (Kan.) Globe and Kansas City Star, 1917; mgr. Washington Bur., United Press, 1921-23; mng. editor Washington News, 1923-25; editor Newspaper Enterprize Assn., Inc., 1927-31, bus. mgr., 1931-35, v.p., gen. mgr., 1935-58, pres., gen. mgr., Cleve., 1958-63, adv. service, 1963—. Recipient award for distinguished service in journalism U. Mo. Served as ensign, Naval Air Force, 1918. Mem. Sigma Delta Chi, Acacia. Lutheran (United). Clubs: Canterbury, Cleveland Athletic, (Cleve.). Home: 2722 Belvoir Blvd., Shaker Heights 22, O. Office: 1200 W. 3d St., Cleve. 13. Died Jan. 1967.

WALKER, IVAN N. comdr.-in-chief G.A.R.; b. Rush Co., Ind., 1839; s. James and Jane W.; served 1861-65, capt. to col., 73d Ind. vols., except nearly a year, 1863-64, in Libby prison, escaping through the tunnel, Feb. 1864; bvtd. brig. gen. U.S.V. Mem. G.A.R., 1867—; asst. adj. gen., 1887-91; dept. comdr., 1891-92, Ind. Dept. G.A.R.; comdr.-in-chief, 1895-96; State tax commr. Ind.; pres. bd. control State Soldiers and Sailors Monument. Home: Indianapolis, Ind. Died 1905.

WALKER, JOHN GRIMES rear admiral U.S.N., retired; b. Hillsborough, N.H., Mar. 20, 1835; s. Alden and Susan (Grimes) W.; apptd. to navy from Iowa, Oct. 5, 1850; grad. U.S. Naval Acad., 1856; promoted master, Jan. 22, 1858; lt., Jan. 23, 1858. In blockading service and Mississippi squadron during Civil war; became lt. comdr., July 16, 1862, comdr., July 25, 1866; capt., June 25, 1877; commodore, Feb. 1889; rear admiral, Jan. 1894; retired at age limit, 1897; m. Rebecca W. Pickering, Sept. 12, 1866. During Civil war participated in the capture of New Orleans; was in operations against Vicksburg, summer of 1862, including passage of batteries both way; comd. iron-clad Baron de Kalb in Mississippi squadron in several engagements; comd. naval battery, 15th army corps, in siege of Vicksburg; later comd. gunboat in N. Atlantic squadron at capture of Wilmington, N.C., etc. Specially promoted, 1866, for war service; sec. to Light-House Bd., 1873-78; chief Bur. of Navigation, Navy Dept., 1881-89. Comd. squadron of evolution, 1889-93, during which time comd. the European Sta., the S. Atlantic Sta. and the N. Atlantic Sta. In 1894 ordered to command Pacific Sta., being particularly charged with maintenance of peace and good order in Hawaiian Islands. Later chmn. of Light-House Bd., 1895-96, and 1896-97 was chmn. of commn. for location of deep water harbor on coast of Southern Calif. Pres. Nicaragua Canal Commn., 1897-99; pres. Isthmian Canal Commn., 1899—. Died 1907.

WALKER, JOSEPH ALBERT test pilot; b. Washington, Pa., Feb. 20, 1921; s. Thomas Jefferson and Pauline Sharp (Smith) W.; B.A. in Physics, Washington and Jefferson Coll., 1942, D.Aero. Scis. (hon.), 1962; m. Grace McClarv, Apr. 16, 1949; children—Thomas Daniel, James Paul, Joseph Brian, Elizabeth Ann. With NASA, 1945—; project pilot on D-558, X-1E, X-3, X-5, X-15; research on F-100, F-101, F-102, F-104, B-47; 1st flight on 15, 1960, since then 25 more; attained speed 4104 Miles per hour, 1962, altitude 348,700 feet, 1963; flight tested Lunar Landing Research Vehicle. Mem. Adv. Commn. Aviation, County Los Angeles. Served to capt. USAAF, 1942-45. Decorated D.F.C., Air medal with 7 oak leaf clusters; recipient Robert J. Collier trophy, 1961, Harmon Internat. trophy for aviators, 1961, Kincheloe award, 1961, Octave Chanite award, 1961, pilot of year award Nat. Pilots Assn., 1963, Henry De Lavaulx prix Fedn. Aero. Internat., 1963. Charter mem. Sox. Exptl. Test Pilots (v.p. 1963-64); mem. Aero-Space Profls., Phi Gamma Delta. Home: 1309 West Av. L-4, Lancaster, Cal. 93534. Office: care NASA, Edwards AFB, Cal. Died June 8, 1966.

WALKER, KENNETH N. army officer; b. Cerrillos, N.M., July 17, 1898; grad. Air Service Observation Sch., 1922, Air Corps Tactical Sch., 1929, Command and Gen. Staff Sch., 1935; rated, command pilot, combat observer. Enlisted as private 1st class, Aviation Sect., Signal Enlisted Reserve Corps, 1917, called to active duty 1918; commd. 2d lt., U.S. Army, 1918, and advanced through the grades to brig. gen., 1942; served as comdr. 5th Bomber Command, Solomon Islands; reported missing in action leading bombing attack on Japanese shipping at Rabaul, New Britain, Jan. 5, 1943. Awarded Congl. Medal of Honor for conspicuous leadership and Personal valor and intrepidity at an extreme hazard to life, Mar. 1943. Died Dec. 12, 1945.

WALKER, KENZIE WALLACE army officer; b. LaGrange, Tex., Dec. 25, 1870; s. William Wallace and Emma (Routh) W.; grad. U.S. Mil. Acad., 1893; m. Helen Hobart Whitman, Oct. 17, 1895 (dec.); children—Augustine Whitman (dec.), Dorothy Whitman. Commd. add. 2d lt. cav., 1893; 2d lt., 1893; promoted through grades to col. of inf., N.A., 1917, and to col. of cav., U.S. Army, 1920; apptd. chief of finance, U.S. Army, with rank of brig. gen., 1922; reappted. chief of finance, with rank of maj. gen., 1925; retired 1928. Cited for service in Spanish-Am. War; D.S.M., World War. Mem. Mil. Order Fgn. Wars, M.O. World War, Am. Legion, Sojourners, Mason. Clubs: Army and Navy (Washington, D.C. and New York); Chevy Chase (Chevy Chase, Md.). Home: 2962 2d Av., North, St. Petersburg, Fla. Died June 18, 1958; buried Arlington Nat. Cemetery.

WALKER, MERIWETHER LEWIS army officer; b. Lynchburg, Va., Sept. 30, 1869; s. Thomas Lindsay (M.D.) and Catherine Maria (Dabney) W.; grad. U.S. Mil. Acad., 1893; grad. U.S. Engr. Sch., 1896, Army War Coll., 1920; m. Edith, d. Gen. A. B. Carey, Sept. 28, 1904; 1 dau., Cary Dabney (Mrs. R. B. Luckey). Commissioned additional 2d lt. Corps of Engineers, June 12, 1893; promoted through regular grades to col., July 1, 1920; col. and brig. gen. N.A., World War. Dir. Army Field Engr. Sch., 1912-14; prof. practical mil. engring., U.S. Mil. Acad., 1914-16; chief engr. Punitive Expdn. into Mexico, 1916-17; went to France as chief engr. 41st Div., Nov. 1917; prin. asst. to chief engr. A.E.F., Jan.-July 1918; dir. Motor Transport Corps, A.E.F., Aug. 1918-Aug. 1919; instr. Army War Coll., 1919-20; comdr. U.S. Engr. Sch., 1920-21; engr. of maintenance, Panama Canal, 1921-24; apptd. gov. Panama Canal, Oct. 16, 1924; promoted to brigadier general, July 1, 1927; comdg. 18th Brig., U.S. Army, Boston, Oct. 16, 1928-Aug. 16, 1933; retired, Sept. 30, 1933. Decorated D.S.M. (U.S.); Officer Legion of Honor (French). Episcopalian. Home: Vineyard Haven, Mass. Died July 29, 1947.

WALKER, NELSON MACY army officer; b. Pittsfield, Mass., Sept. 27, 1891; s. Elliot and Alice (Macy) W.; ed. Infantry Sch., Ft. Benning, Ga., 1923-24; Command and Gen. Staff Sch., Ft. Leavensworth, Kan., 1928-30; Army War Coll., Washington, D.C., 1932-33; m. Doris Katherine Wyke, June 21, 1921; children—Perrin, Nancy Ann (twins). Commd. 2d lt. Inf., 1917, and advanced through the grades to brig. gen., Sept. 1942; with 47th Inf. France, as regimental signal officer, 1918; aide de camp to Gen. Hines, Camp Jackson, S.C., 1920; assigned to 30th Inf. at Presidio, San Francisco, 1930-32; Operations and Training Div., G-3, 1933-37; Office of Chief of Inf., Washington, D.C., 1937; plans and training officer, 15th Inf., Tientsin, China, 1937-38; prof. mil. tactics and science, Manlius Sch., Manlius, N.Y., 1938-40; Operations and Training Div., G-3, War Dept. Gen. Staff, Washington, D.C., 1940-42; hdqrs., army ground forces, Washington, D.C., 1942; assigned to 84th Inf. Div., Aug. 1942. Awarded Purple Heart. Address: 275 South St., Pittsfield, Mass. Killed in action July 9, 1944.

WALKER, REUBEN LINDSAY army officer, civil engr.; b. Logan, Va., May 29, 1827; s. Meriwether Lewis and Maria (Lindsay) W.; grad. Va. Mil. Inst., 1845; m. Maria Eskridge, 1848; m. 2d, Salley Elam, 1857; 8 children. Commd. capt. in Confederate Army in Civil War, 1861; maj. chief arty., A.P. Hill's div., 1862, connected with Hill's command throughout war, promoted col., chief of arty. when Hill became comdr. III Army Corps; brig. gen. arty., 1865; supt. Marine and Selma R.R., 1872-74; employed by Richmond & Danville R.R., 1876-77; supt. Richmond (Va.) street railways; constrn. engr. Richmond & Alleghany R.R.; superintended building of women's dept. Va. State Penitentiary; supt. constrn. Tex. State Capitol, 1884. Died on his farm at fork of Rivanna and James rivers, Va. June 7, 1890.

WALKER, THEODORE C. editor; b. Paw Paw, Mich., July 29, 1839; ed. pub. schs. Served in Union Army 3 yrs., Civil War; ordained Congl. ministry; settled in Aurora, Mo., 1890; was newspaper reporter and corr. for city dailies; editor The Menace (anti Roman Catholic weekly) since its initial issue, 1911-19 (plant and business destroyed by fire, 1919). Home: Aurora, Mo.

WALKER, THEODORE PENFIELD pres. Commercial Solvents Corp.; b. Penfield, O., Sept. 4, 1886; s. Theodore C. and Emma Louise (Catt) W.; B.S., Drury Coll., 1908; LL.D., Drury Coll., 1939; student Philippine Constabulary Acad., 1908; m. Eugenie Grandblaise Revel, May 7, 1919. Officer of Philippine Constaulary, 1908-16; with Standard Oil Co. of N.Y., Dutch East Indies, 1916-17, Am. Metals Co., Ltd., Java, 1919-22; with Commercial Solvents Corp. as exec. v.p. and dir., 1922-38, pres., dir., 1938-47, chmn. bd. since 1947; chmn. bd. Thermatomic Carbon Co.; dir. Corn Products Refining Company. Served as lieutenant, advancing to captain, major, Air Corps, U.S. Army, during World War. Mem. bd. of trustees, Drury College. Member Manufacturing Chemists Assn., Kappa Alpha, Phi Lambda Upsilon. Clubs: Creve Coeur (Peoria, Ill.); Uptown, University (New York). Home: 710 Park Av. Office: 17 E. 42d St., N.Y.C. Died Nov. 28, 1951; buried Blue Hill, Me.

WALKER, WILLIAM HENRY TALBOT army officer; b. Augusta, Ga., Nov. 26, 1816; s. Freeman and Mary Washington (Creswell) W.; grad. U.S. Mil. Acad., 1837; m. Mary Townsend, 4 children. Commd. 2d lt. 6th Inf., U.S. Army, 1837; served in Fla. Indian War. brevetted 1st lt. for gallant conduct at Battle of Okeechobee; resigned from army, 1838, reappointed, 1840, rejoined his regt. and served through Fla. war; commd. capt., 1845; participated in all battles of Mexican War, brevetted maj. for heroic conduct at Contreras, 1847, lt. col. for gallantry at Molino del Rey, 1847; presented with sword of honor by State of Ga., 1849; in recruiting service, 1847-52, dep. gov. of mil. asylum, East Pascagoula, Miss., 1852-54; comdt. of cadets, instr. mil. tactics U.S. Mil. Acad., 1854-56; commd. maj., 1855; resigned from U.S. Army, 1860, entered Confederate service; commd. maj. gen. Ga. Volunteers, 1861, brig. gen. Confederate Army, 1861; brigade comdr. in Northern Va.; resigned commn., 1861; maj. gen. Ga. Militia, Nov. 1861; reentered Confederate service as brig. gen., 1863, promoted maj. gen., 1864; in command reserves at Battle of Chickamauga; with Army of Tenn. during campaign in Northern Ga. Killed in action, July 22, 1864; buried family burial ground, Summerville (now part of Augusta), Ga.

WALKER, WILLIAM HULTZ chemical engr.; b. Pittsburgh, Pa., Apr. 7, 1869; s. David H. and Anna (Blair) W.; B.S., Pa. State Coll., 1890; A.M., Ph.D., U. of Göttingen, 1892; Sc.D., U. of Pittsburgh, 1915; m. Isabelle Luther, Sept. 15, 1896. Prof. industrial chemistry, now chem. engring., Mass. Inst. Tech., 1894-1921; lecturer on industrial chemistry, Harvard, 1905-08; cons. chem. engr., 1900—; mem. Little & Walker, 1900-05; dir. research lab. applied chemistry, Chem. Products Co. Professional work has been principally in the production of art glass, the mfr. of sterling silver, the chemistry of cellulose and its industrial applications and uses, the cause and prevention of the corrosion of iron and steel, and the technology of petroleum. Has invented and introduced numerous industrial processes of value. Commd. lt. col. N.A., 1917; chief of chem. service sect.; promoted col. U.S.A., in charge Gas Offense Div. Chem. Warfare Service; comdr. officer Edgewood Arsenal. Fellow Am. Acad. Arts and Sciences, Am. Iron and Steel Inst., Am. Electrochem. Soc. (pres. 1910-11), Am. Chem. Soc. (pres. Eastern Sect. 1904), Am. Soc. for Testing Materials, Soc. Chem. Industry (London). Awarded Nichols medal, 1908. Presbyn. Awarded D.S.M., 1919. Home: Pasadena, Calif. Died July 9, 1934.

WALL, WILLIAM GUY consulting engr.; b. Baltimore, Md., Aug. 7, 1876; s. William Edward and Mary Catherine (Dade) W.; grad. in Civ. Engring., Va. Mil. Inst., 1894; B.S., Mass. Inst. Tech., 1896; m. Minnie Tyndall, 1909 (died 1931); m. 2d, Helen Wessel, 1934. Practiced at Indianapolis, 1900—; founder, v.p. and chief engr. Nat. Motor Car Co.; cons. engr. for several prominent automobile companies. Maj. and lt. col., U.S.A., World War; col. Res. Secretary, Am. Legion Endowment Fund Corp. Democrat. Episcopalian. Home: Indianapolis, Ind. Died Jan. 16, 1941.

WALLACE, DAVID A., automobile exec.; b. Castleton, Kan., Mar. 1, 1888; student Highland Park Coll. Engring.; E.D. (hon.), Mich. Coll. Mining and Tech., 1951. Employee A.T. & S.F. R.R. Shop, Dodge City, Kan., 1906; machinist, tool designer, service and sales rep. Buick Automobile Co., Flint, Mich. and Tex.; mech. supt. Concheno Mining Co., Mexico; tool room foreman, master mechanic, supt. Hart-Parr Tractor Co., Charles City, Ia.; master mechanic, supt., woris mgr. John Deere Tractor Co., Waterloo, Ia.; staff master mechanic Chrysler Corp., Detroit, 1929, v.p. in charge mfg. Chrysler div., 1930, pres. Chrysler Marine and Indsl. Engine Div., 1936-48, Chrysler div., 1937-53, Pekin Wood Products Co., Helena, Ark., 1932-48, Walco, Inc.; dir. Chrysler Sales Corp., Chrysler Export, Pekin Wood Products Indsl. Engine Div., Detroit Trust Co. Served as pvt. to capt., with Motor Transport, U.S. Army, World War I. Clubs: Detroit Athletic (pres.), Grosse Pointe Yacht, Country, Detroit, Yondotega (Detroit); Gulfstream Bath and Tennis, Gulfstream Golf, Little (Delray Beach, Fla.). Address: Grosse Pointe Farms MI Died Jan. 21, 1970; buried Nat. Chapel Cemetery, Lontana FL

WALLACE, GEORGE BARCLAY prof. pharmacology; b. Detroit, Mich., Sept. 21, 1874; s. Hugh W. and Catherine (Barclay) W.; U. of Ore., 1890-92; M.D., U. of Mich., 1897; hon. A.M., U. of Mich., 1935; hon. Sc.D., N.Y.U., 1941; m. Georgina Burns, 1912; children—Craig, Virginia. Prof. emeritus pharmacology, Univ. and Bellevue Hosp. Med. Coll. Editor, Jour. Pharm. and Exptl. Therapy, 1943-46. Editor, Jour. Pharm. and Exptl. Therapy, 1943-46. Maj. M.C., 1917-19; served as director A.R.C. Hosp. 1, in France; col. Med. R.C. Mem. Soc. Exptl. Biology and Medicine (pres. 1921-23), Harvey Soc. (pres. 1915-17), Am. Physiol. Soc., Am. Soc. Biol. Chemistry, Am. Pharmacol. Soc. (pres. 1929-31), A.M.A., N.Y. Acad. Medicine (trustee, 1925-28), A.A.A.S., Am. Soc. Naturalists, Am. Soc. Anaestetists (hon.), Nu Sigma Nu, Sigma Xi. Decorated by Chinese govt. Republican. Presbyterian. Club: Century. Contbr. to med. and scientific jours. Home: 145 E. 54th St., New York, N.Y. Died Jan. 15, 1948.

WALLACE, JAMES M. congressman; b. Lancaster (now Dauphin) County, Pa., 1750; attended sch. in Phila. Served with various cos. in Revolutionary War, maj. battalion of Associators at end of war; commanded co. of rangers in defense of frontier, 1779; commd. maj. Dauphin County Militia, 1796; a commr. Dauphin County, 1799-1801; mem. Pa. Ho. of Reps., 1806-10; mem. U.S. Ho. of Reps. (filled vacancy) from Pa., 14th-16th congresses, Oct. 10, 1815-21; retired to his farm. Died nr. Hummelstown, Pa., Dec. 17, 1823; buried Old Derry Church Graveyard, Derry (now Hershey), Pa.

WALLACE, LEWIS ("Lew Wallace"), lawyer, soldier, diplomat, author; b. Brookville, Ind., April 10, 1827; s. Gov. David W.; self-educated; began study of law; served in Mexican war, 2d lt. Co. H, 1st Ind. inf.; resumed study of law; located in Covington, and later in Crawfordsville, Ind.; m. Susan Arnold Elston, 1852. At beginning of Civil War apptd. adj. gen. of Ind.; soon after col. 11th Ind. vols.; served in W.Va.; became brig. gen. vols., Sept. 3, 1861; comd. div. at Donelson; maj. gen., March 21, 1862; comd. a div. at Shiloh; prepared defenses of Cincinnati in 1863 and saved city from capture by Gen. Edmund Kirby Smith; later comd. Middle dept. and 8th army corps; intercepted march of Gen. Jubal A. Early on Washington; fought battle of Monocracy, and saved Washington from capture, July 9, 1864; was second mem. of the court that tried the assassins of President Lincoln, and pres. of court which tried and convicted Henry Wirz, comdt. of Andersonville prison; mustered out, 1865. Gov. New Mexico, 1878-81; U.S. minister to Turkey, 1881-85. Author: Ben Hur, a Tale of the Christ, 1880; Life of General Benjamin Harrison, 1888; The Fair God, 1873; The Boyhood of Christ, 1889; The Prince of India, 1893; The Wooing of Malkatoon, 1898. Home: Crawfordsville, Ind. Died 1905.

WALLACE, RUSH RICHARD commodore U.S.N.; b. Pond Spring, Tenn., Nov. 7, 1835; apptd. to U.S. Naval Acad. from Tenn., 1852; promoted passed midshipman, Apr. 29, 1859; advanced through grades to commodore, Nov. 11, 1894; retired, Nov. 7, 1897. Served on bd. St. Lawrence, Brazilian Squadron, 1856-59; Crusader, 1859-61; Constellation, Mediterranean Squadron, 1861-63; Shenandoah, N. Atlantic Blockading Squadron, 1863-64; participated in both attacks on Ft. Fisher; Fort Jackson, W. Gulf Blockading Squadron, 1864-65; Naval Acad., 1865-67; Guerriere, S. Atlantic Squadron, 1868; Richmond, European Fleet, 1869; comd. store-ship Idaho, 1870-71; Ashuelot, 1872-73; insp. ordnance, Navy Yard, Norfolk, 1873-74; light house insp. 15th dist., 1875-79; Torpedo Sta., Newport, 1881; spl. duty Navy Dept., 1881-82; comd. Vandalia, 1882-84; capt. of yard, Navy Yard, Washington, 1884-87; comdt. Navy Yard, Washington, 1887; mem. Naval Examining Board, 1887-91; comd. receiving-ship Franklin, 1892-93, Miantonomoh, 1893-94, Naval Sta., Newport, 1894-97; spl. duty and member Lighthouse Bd., 1898; mem. Board on Awards, 1902-05. Home: Washington, D.C. Died June 12, 1914.

WALLACE, WILLIAM MCLEAN, physician; b. Montclair, N.J., Jan. 12, 1912; s. Albert Howard and Ethel (McLean) W.; A.B., U. Pa., 1934, M.D., 1938; m. Patricia Raymond, July 2, 1949; children—William, Andrew, Jane, Harriet, Patricia. Intern Robert Packer Hosp., Sayre, Pennsylvania, 1938-39; NRC fellow Harvard, 1939-41, Rockefeller Found. fellow, 1946-48, asst. prof. pediatrics, med. sch., 1948-51; intern, resident Children's Hosp., Boston, 1941-42; prof. pediatrics Western Res. U. Sch. Medicine, 1951-68; dir. pediatrics Univ. Hosp., Cleve., 1951-68. Mem. human embryology and devel. study sect. NIH. Served from 1st lt. to maj. M.C., AUS, 1941-45. Decorated Silver Star, Bronze Star, Purple Heart. Diplomate Am. Bd. Pediatrics. Mem. A.M.A., Am. Soc. Clin. Investigation, Soc. Pediatric Research, Am. Pediatric Soc., American Institute Nutrition, Am. Assn. Advancement Sci., Am. Acad. Pediatrics, Home: Cleveland Heights OH Died Nov. 9, 1968; cremated.

WALLACE, WILLIAM MILLER brig. gen. U.S.A.; b. Prairie du Chien, Wis., Jan. 9, 1844; s. Lt. Col. George Weed (U.S.A.) and Susan H. (Salter) W.; ed. Bowens and Loomis schools, Washington, and Georgetown, D.C., and Churchill's Mil. School, Sing Sing, N.Y.; m. Alice Knight, Jan. 18, 1871. First lt. N.Y. Arty., Mar. 29, 1864; hon. mustered out, May 6, 1864; apptd. from N.Y., 2d lt. 8th U.S. Inf., Oct. 2, 1866; 1st lt., Sept. 25, 1867; assigned to 6th Cav., Dec. 15, 1870; capt., May 17, 1876; maj. 2d Cav., Nov. 10, 1894; lt. col., Oct. 18, 1899; col. 15th Cav., Mar. 1, 1901; brig. gen. and retired at own request, over 40 yrs.' service, Oct. 2, 1906. Died Nov. 5, 1924.

WALLACK, JAMES WILLIAM actor, theatrical mgr.; b. London, Eng., Aug. 24, 1795; s. William H. and Elizabeth (Field) Granger Wallack; attended Academic Theatre, Leicester Square, London; m. Susan Johnstone, 1817, at least 2 children, John Lester, Charles. With Company of Drury Lane Theatre, London, Royal Hibernian Theatre, Dublin, Ireland; made Am. debut as Macbeth at Park Street Theatre, N.Y.C., 1818; toured Am.; played Don César de Bazan, Capt. Bertram in Fraternal Discord, Massaroni in The Brigand, Don Felix in The Wonder; played season in England, 1820, returned to Am.; played Hamlet, Rolla, Macbeth, Richard III, and Romeo in N.Y.C.; appeared at Arch Street Theater, Phila., 1828; mgr. National Theatre, N.Y.C., 1837; managed Niblo's Garden, 1839; appeared at Park Street Theatre, 1844; owner, mgr. Brougham's Lyceum, N.Y.C., 1852-61; with son Lester opened New Wallack's Theatre at Broadway and 13th St., N.Y.C., 1861; made frequent appearances in Eng. throughout career. Died N.Y.C., Dec. 25, 1864.

WALLER, CURTIS L. judge; b. Silver Creek, Miss., Jan. 9, 1887; s. William Mikell and Clara Cordelia (Longino) W.; Ph.B., Miss. Coll., 1908; LL.B. Millsaps Coll., 1910; grad. Sch. Mil. Aeros., Tex., 1918; m. Lucy McGinn, Dec. 8, 1920; 1 dau., Mary Ann. Admitted to Miss. bar, 1910; pvt. sec. to Pat Harrison, mem. Congress, 1911; mem. firm Gex and Waller, Bay St. Louis, Miss., 1914-27; Waller and Pepper, 1930-37, Waller and Meginniss, 1937-40, Tallahassee, Fla., apptd. U.S. Dist. judge, No. and So. dists. Fla., 1940; apptd. U.S. circuit judge, Fifth Circuit, 1943. Served in World War I; lt. col. U.S. Res. Corps. Mem. Miss. Legislature, 1924, Fla. Legislature, 1933; states atty., Fla., 1932. Mem. Fla. State, Am. bar assns., Kappa Alpha; hon. mem. Phi Alpha Delta, Elks, Am. Legion. Club: Army and Navy (Washington). Home: 416 E. Williams St. Office: Federal Bldg., Tallahassee, Fla. Died July 11, 1950; buried Tallahassee.

WALLER, JOHN ROBERT lawyer, banker; b. Dubuque, Ia., Feb. 1, 1883; s. John Robert and Mary Ellen (Cooper) W.; student State U. of Ia., U. of Chicago, St. Catharines Coll., Oxford U., England; Institute Fauvel, Paris; LL.B., Yale, 1905, B.C.L., 1906; LL.M., U. of Mich., 1907; m. Margaret Tredway, June

20, 1921; one daughter, Margaret Roberta (Mrs. James Donald Griffin, Junior). Admitted to bars, Mich. and Iowa, 1907, Dist. of Columbia 1918; practiced at Dubuque, 1907-18; organized several corps., Ia., 1907-19; organized Internat. Bank, Washington, D.C., 1919, former chmn. bd., now dir.; pres. Interstaate Properties, Inc.; pres., dir. Rutland Railroad (1949-50); orgn. bd. Hotel Walker, now Mayflower, 1922; dir. Am. Securities Co., Pierce Oil Corp., Internat. Bank, Pitts. Terminal Warehouses, other corps.; pres. I-B Corp., Washington. Active community projects such as arthritis fund drives. Served as capt., U.S. Army, 1918-19. Mem. numerous profl. orgn. and assns. including C. of C., S.R., Am. Legion, bar assns., Greek letter socs. Clubs: National Press, Yale, Army and Navy, University, Book and Gavel, Congressional Country, Racquet, Inquerendo (Washington); Metropolitan (N.Y.C.); Farmington Country (Charlottesville, Va.); American (London, Eng.). Author several books 1910-41. Musical compositions: Silver Wedding Prelude, 1946; Christmas Carol Fantasy, 1948; Chords and Counterpoint, 1951; The Lord's Prayer, 1954; American Hymn, 1955; Etude for Organ, 1956; A Toast to Zeta Psi, 1958; Christmas Serenade, 1959. Home: 4900 Edgemoor Lane, Bethesda 14, Md. Office: The Washington Bldg., Washington 5. Died Sept. 30, 1961; buried Linwood Cemetery, Dubuque, Ia.

WALLER, LITTLETON WALLER TAZEWELL officer U.S. M.C.; b. York Co., Va., Sept. 26, 1856. Apptd. 2d lt. U.S.M.C., June 16, 1880; promoted through grades to brig. gen., Aug. 29, 1916; major gen., Aug. 29, 1918. Participated in naval battle at Santiago, Cuba, July 3, 1898; in charge recruiting, Pa., Del. and western N.J., 1902-03; comd. Provisional Regt. Marines, Isthmus of Panama, 1904; comd. expeditionary forces for service in Cuba, 1906; comd. Provisional Brigade of Marines, in Cuba, 1911; duty Marine Barracks, Mare Island, Calif., 1911-14, Phila., 1914; comd. 1st Brig. of Marines for service in Mexico, 1914; comd. marine expeditionary forces ashore in Haiti, 1915-16; apptd. comdr. Advanced Base Force, Phila., Jan. 8, 1917. Bvtd. lt. col., Mar. 28, 1901, "for distinguished conduct and pub. service," in presence of enemy nr. Tientsin, China, and advanced 2 numbers in grade "for eminent and conspicuous conduct" in Battle of Tientsin. Retired June 1920. Home: Philadelphia, Pa. Died July 13, 1926.

WALLER, LITTLETON W.T. marine corps officer; b. Norfolk, Va., Sept. 18, 1886; s. Littleton W. T. and Clara E. (Wynn) W.; ed. Woodberry Forest, Orange, Va., U.S. Naval Acad., Marine Corps Tech. Schs.; m. Sadie E. Carnill, June 12, 1920 (dec.); married 2d, Cecile Howell Rowland, May 15, 1948 (dec. Aug. 1953). Midshipman, 1904; 2d lt. U.S. Marine Corps, 1907, promoted through capt. to maj., resigned, 1925, enrolled in Marine Corps Reserve, promoted lt. col. reserve, called to active duty in June 1941; advanced through all grades to brig. gen., served as dir. Personnel, Marine Corps and later as commanding general Marine Garrison Forces, Pacific. Retired as maj. gen., 1947. Formerly with du Pont Company of Wilmington, Delaware, resigned when ordered to active duty. Awarded Navy Cross, Purple Heart, Croix de Guerre, Legion of Honor, Marine Expeditionary Medal, Mexican Campaign, Victory Medal 5 stars, German Occupation, American Defense Medal, Asiatic-Pacific Area Campaign, Legion of Merit, World War II Victory. Bd. of trustees Abington Memorial Hosp. Mem. M.O.F.W., W.O.W.W., Sons of the American Revolution. Clubs: Army and Navy (Washington), Racquet, Huntington Valley Country (Philadelphia). Home: Meadowbrook, Pa. Died Apr. 1967.

WALLERSTEIN, EDWARD, business cons.; b. Kansas City, Mo., Dec. 9, 1891; s. David and Helen (Coons) W.; ed. Germantown Acad., Phila.; A.B., Haverford Coll.; m. Helen Perry Ault, Sept. 2, 1927; children—E. Perry, Jane Hastings, David V. Eastern mgr. music div. Brunswick-Balke-Collender Co., 1925-30; sales mgr. Brunswick Record Corp., 1930-32; mgr. record div. R.C.A. Victor, 1933-38; pres. Columbia Records, Inc., and all its subsidiaries, 1939-48, 49-59, chmn. bd., 1948-59; head Belock Recording Co. div. Belock Instrument Corp., also v.p. of corp., 1959-60; business cons., 1961-70. Served as 1st lt., inf., World War I. Club: Brodheads Forest and Stream (Stroudsberg). Home: Pomono Beach FL Died Sept. 1, 1970.

WALLGREN, MONRAD C. gov. of Wash.; b. Des Moines, Apr. 17, 1891; ed. pub. schs. and bus. coll.; grad. Wash. State Sch. Optometry, 1914; m. Mabel C. Liberty, Sept. 8, 1914. Engaged in retail jewelry and optical bus.; mem. 73d to 76th Congresses (1933-41), 2d Wash. Dist.; elected U.S. Senate, Nov. 1940; apptd. to succeed Senator L. B. Schellenbach, who resigned, 1940 (for unexpired term to 1941); elected for term, 1941-47; resigned to become gov. of Wash., 1945; apptd. chmn. Fed. Power Commn.; resigned 1951. Served to lt. U.S. Army during World War I. Mem. State Retail Jewelers Assn. (pres. 1921-22), Am. Legion, Forty and Eight. Democrat. Mason, K.T., Elk, Eagle, Rotarian. Home: 73-510 Pinyon St., Palm Desert, Cal. Died Sept. 18, 1961; buried Everett, Wash.

WALLING, WILLIAM HENRY, printer; b. Potsdam, N.Y., Mar. 17, 1895; s. William W. and Ada (Coats) W.; student Hamilton Coll., 1913-14; grad. U. Ill. Sch. Mil. Aeros., 1917; m. Peggy Wood, Oct. 1, 1946; children—Janet Barclay, Ann Jermain. Asst. to advt. mgr. Packard Motor Car Co., 1919-20; v.p. Mortimer & Walling, printers, N.Y.C., 1920-73, dir. Dirs. Co., 1931-58, pres., 1958-73; chmn. Rogers Kellogg-Stillson, Inc., 1946-55, Hawley-Lord, Inc., Somerset Pub. Co., Shelter Industries; chmn. bd. dirs. Graphic Arts Mut. Ins. Co., 1957-73; pres. Boreal, Inc., 1964-73, Kewal Paper Co., 1957-73, Graphic Arts Mgmt. Corp., 1964-73, Overseas Devel. Services, Inc., 1966-73; dir. Utica Mut. Ins. Co. Served to lt. col. USAF. Decorated Bronze Star medal, Air medal. Mem. N.Y. Employing Printers Assn., Printing Industry Am. (pres., dir.), Printers League N.Y., Mayflower Descs., Colonial Wars, Air Force Assn., Soc. Am. Wars, Quiet Birdmen. Clubs: Metropolitan, Players, Saint Nicholas of New York, Turf and Field, Dutch Treat (N.Y.C.). Author: Backgammon Standards, 1930. Home: Stamford CT Died Feb. 5, 1973.

WALLS, FRANK XAVIER, physician; b. Toronto, Can., Dec. 3, 1869; s. Thomas and Catherine (Ahern) W.; South Division High Sch., Chicago; M.D., Northwestern U. Med. Sch., 1891; m. Cecelia Cunningham, of Chicago, June, 1896; m. 2d, Mrs. Elizabeth G. Dickason, Sept. 1917. Attending phys. Cook Co., St. Luke's and Wesley hosps.; prof. pediatrics, Northwestern Univ. Med. Sch., since Feb. 1911. Mem. Chicago Med. Soc.; apptd. 1st lt. Med. R.C., U.S.A., 1911. Home: 999 Lake Shore Drive. Office: 30 N. Michigan Av., Chicago IL

WALSH, ARTHUR exec. v.p. Thomas A. Edison, Inc.; b. Newark, N.J., Feb. 26, 1896; s. Michael Joseph and Mary Ann (Shane) W.; ed. Newark pub. schs. and by private tutor; New York U. Sch. of Commerce; m. Agnes Mulvey, June 8, 1920; 1 dau., Barbara Louise (Mrs. Millard Carnick, Jr.) Recording violinist for Thomas A. Edison, 1915; successively advertising mgr., v.p. and gen. mgr. phonograph div., Thomas A. Edison, Inc., 1924-31, vice-president on general staff and director since 1931; served as New Jersey director Federal Housing Adminstrn., 1934-35, dept. adminstr., Washington, D.C., later asst. adminstr., 1935-38; pres. and dir. Edison-Splitdorf Corp., Edison Wood Products, Inc., Thomas A. Edison of Can., Ltd., Ediphone Corp. Dir. Thomas A. Edison, Ltd., of London, 1938. Apptd. U.S. Senator, Nov. 26, 1943 to serve until Dec. 7, 1944. Charter trustee, Rutgers U., 1945. Commr. Port of N.Y. Authority, 1943. Mem. N.J. Workmen's Compensation Investigation Commn. Dir. Am.-Russian C. of C., 1943. Mem. N.J. Bd. of Regents, 1941-42. Served in U.S. Marine Corps during World War I; lt. U.S.N.R., 1929-32; col. N.J. Nat. Guard, 1941. Mem. Nat. Assn. Mfrs. (dir.; v.p., 1946), Alpha Kappa Psi, Beta Gamma Sigma. Democrat. Roman Catholic. Elk. Clubs: Baltusrol Golf (Springfield, N.J.); Essex (Newark, N.J.); Traffic, Metropolitan (New York, N.Y.). Contbr. to business papers. Home: 332 Redmond Rd. Office: West Orange, N.J. Died Dec. 13, 1947.

WALSH, GERALD POWERS lawyer; b. Dover, Mass., Jan. 10, 1910; s. Nicholas and Catherine (Powers) W.; B.A., Harvard, 1931, LL.B., 1934; m. Marguerite Shepard, Oct. 12, 1939; children—Kathleen M., Gerald Powers. Admitted to Mass. bar, 1934, since practiced in New Bedford. Served to lt. (s.g.) USNR, World War II. Fellow Am. Coll. Trial Lawyers; mem. Am. (Ho. of Dels.), Mass. (pres. 1959-60), New Bedford (past pres.) bar assns. Club: Wamsutta (dir.) (New Bedford). Died Aug. 1, 1960.

WALSH, MATTHEW JAMES clergyman, educator; b. Chgo., May 14, 1882; s. David and Joanna (Clogan) W.; Litt.B., U. Notre Dame, 1903; Ph.D., Catholic U. Am., 1907; studied Columbia U., Johns Hopkins. Joined Congregation of Holy Cross, 1903; ordained priest R.C. Ch., 1907; prof. history, U. Notre Dame, 1907-22, 28-47, v.p., 1912-22, pres., 1922-28; asst. provincial U.S. Province, Congregation of Holy Cross, 1929-33. Has specialized in European history. Chaplain 135th Machine Gun Batt., Camp Sheridan, Ala., 1917-18; capt. chaplain 30th Inf., 3d Div., AEF; discharged 1919. Mem. Am. Cath. Hist. Assn., State Hist. Commn. Ind. Home: Notre Dame, Ind. Died Jan. 19, 1963; buried Cemetery of Holy Cross, Notre Dame.

WALSH, RAYCROFT aircraft mfg.; b. Boston, Mass., Nov. 14, 1888; s. James Lawrence and Rose (Raycroft); Walsh; student Mechanic Arts High Sch., Boston, 1902-05, Mass. Inst. Tech., 1908-09, Columbia U., 1909-10; m. Emma L. Wupperman, Sept. 14, 1920; children—Mary Louise, Raycroft, Jr., Emmy Lu. Commd. second lt., U.S. Army, and advanced through grades to maj., 1910-26; resigned as maj., Air Corps, with rating as airplane pilot from Sept. 1917; lt. col. Air Reserve, U.S. Army, since 1932; with McGraw-Hill Pub. Co., 1926-28, Cheney Bros., silk mfrs., 1928-30; with United Aircraft Corp. since 1930, dir. since 1936, vice pres., 1936-43, senior vice pres., 1942; vice chairman, 1943; gen. mgr. Hamilton Standard Propellers Division, 1930-40; director of the United Aircraft Export Corporation. Member Institute Aeronautical Sciences, Phi Kappa Psi. Roman Catholic. Clubs: Hartford (Conn.); Hartford Golf (West Hartford, Connecticut). Home: 35 Westwood Rd., West Hartford 5, Conn. Office: United Aircraft Corp., East Hartford 8, Conn. Died Aug. 17, 1952; buried Arlington Cemetery, Washington.

WALSH, RAYMOND JAMES publisher; b. Paterson, N.J., Aug. 27, 1917; s. Raymond James and Elizabeth O. (von Niedermayer) W.; B.A., Wesleyan U., 1938; m. Dorothy Joslin Gay, Apr. 17, 1942; children—Robert Lawrence, Elizabeth Gay, Catherine Thompson. Asst. to dean of freshmen Wesleyan U., 1938-40, teaching fellow social sci. and phys. edn., 1939-40; personnel mgr. Coro, Inc., Providence, 1940-42; mediator War Labor Bd., Washington, 1942; labor cons. Austin M. Fisher Assos., N.Y.C., 1942-47; personnel dir. James McCreery & Co., N.Y.C., 1947-50; asso. Booz, Allen & Hamilton, N.Y.C., 1950-54; exec. v.p. Wesleyan U. Press, Inc., 1954-56, pres., 1956—. Trustee Wesleyan University, 1952-59. Served as lt., USNR, 1942-45. Member of Eclectic Soc. Club: University. Home: 116 Mt. Vernon St. Office: 356 Washington St., Middletown, Conn. Died Dec. 16, 1960; buried Middletown.

WALSH, ROBERT DOUGLAS army officer; b. in Calif., Oct. 14, 1860; grad. U.S. Mil. Acad., 1883; Army War Coll., 1912. Commd. 2d lt. 22d Inf., June 13, 1883; promoted through grades to col. 8th Cav., July 1, 1916; brig. gen. N.G., Aug. 5, 1917. Duty at Ft. Bowie, Ariz., Ft. Walla Walla, Jefferson Barracks, Mo. Boisé Barracks, Vancouver Barracks; in Philippine Islands, 1899-1902; at Ft. Leavenworth, Kan., 1908; apptd. comdr. 178th Inf. Brigade, Camp Beauregard, Alexandria, La., Aug. 25, 1917; comdg. gen. Base No. 1, St. Nazaire, France, Dec. 1, 1917-July 28, 1919; dep. dir. gen. transportation, to Nov. 7, 1918; comdg. gen. Base No. 2, Bordeaux, France, to Mar. 31, 1919; comdr. 164th Inf. Brigade to May 31, 1919; retired at his own request, after 41 yrs.' service, June 30, 1919. Awarded D.S.M.; Comdr. Legion of Honor, France. Bvtd. 1st lt., Feb. 27, 1890, "for gallant service in action against Indians" in Terrace Mountains, Mexico, Sept. 22, 1885, and Patagonia Mountains, Ariz., June 6, 1886. Died Aug. 15, 1928.

WALSON, CHARLES MOORE army officer; b. Delaware, Aug. 24, 1883; s. George W. and Minnie S. (Collins) W.; M.D., Jefferson Med. Coll., Phila., 1906; grad. Army Med. Sch., 1912; m. Bonnie Miller, June 2, 1915; children—Charles W. (officer U.S. Army), Elizabeth W. (wife of Lt. Col. George W. Bixby). Commd. 1st lt., Med. Corps, U.S. Army, 1912, and advanced through the grades to brig. gen., 1945; surgeon, Expeditionary Forces, Vera Cruz, Mexico, 1914; during World War I served successively at Honolulu and Schofield Barracks, T.H.; camp surgeon, Camp Lewis, Wash.; div. surgeon, 15th Div., Camp Logan, Houston, Tex.; comdg. officer, Gen. Hosp. 33, Fort Logan H. Roots, Little Rock, Ark.; asst. to chief surgeon, A.E.F., France; at station hosp. Am. Forces in Germany, Coblenz, Germany; hosp. inspector and exec. officer, Walter Reed Gen. Hosp., 1922-26; asst. to corps area surgeon, 7th Corps Area Surgeon's Office, Omaha, Neb., 1926-31; surgeon, Station Hosp., Fort Benjamin Harrison, Ind., 1931-35; in Surgeon Gen.'s Office, Washington, D.C., 1935-39; asst. to corps area surgeon, II Corps Area, 1939, corps area surgeon, 1940-42; Service Command surgeon Aug. 1942-June 1946, surgeon of 1st Army since consolidation of 1st and 2d Service Commands. With St. Joseph Infirmary, Fort Worth, Texas, 1906-07, St. John's Hospital, St. Louis, Mo., 1907-08; asst. to clinical professor surgery, St. Louis U., 1908-11; assts. to city health officer, St. Louis, 1909-11; lecturer on vital statistics Creighton U., 1926-30, on tropical medicine, Indiana U. Med. Sch., 1930-34. Adminstr. Am. Red Cross Blood Program, Greater N.Y., 1947-51, Washington, 1951—. Decorated Mexican Service, Victory, Army Occupation of Germany medals, Am. Defense Ribbon, Am. Theater Campaign Medal, Victory Medal World War II, Legion of Merit, Army Commendation Ribbon. Fellow Am. Coll. Surgeons; mem. A.M.A., Assn. Mil. Surgeons of U.S.A., Am. Hosp. Assn., Phi Rho Sigma. Mason. Club: Army-Navy Country (Washington). Home: Washington, D.C. Died May 14, 1959.

WALTER, FRANCIS EUGENE congressman; b. Easton, Pa., May 26, 1894; s. Robley D. and Susie E. W.; student Princeton Prep. Sch., 1910-12, Lehigh Univ., 1912-14; A.B., George Washington U.; LL.B., Georgetown U., 1919; LL.D. (honorary), Norwich University, 1960; married May M. Doyle, Dec. 19, 1925; children—Barbara, Constance. Admitted Pennsylvania bar, 1919; in practice at Easton; solicitor Northampton County, 1928-33; mem. 73rd-87th Congresses, 15th Pennsylvania District. Vice president Board St. Trust Company Philadelphia; director Easton National Bank. Lt. Commander, Naval Aviation Reserve Corps. Trustee Easton Hosp. Member Phi Delta Theta, Phi Alpha Delta, Pi Gamma Mu. Democrat. Lutheran. Mem. Elks, I.O.O.F., Jr. Order United Am. Mechanics, Eagles. Home: 806 Hamilton St. Office: Drake Bldg., Easton, Pa., also House Office Bldg., Washington 25. Died May 31, 1963; buried Arlington Nat. Cemetery.

WALTERS, JACK EDWARD mgmt. cons., author; b. Croydon, Ind., Mar. 19, 1896; s. John Edward and Julia Mary (Bulleit) W.; student Ind. U., 1914-17, U. Dijon, France, 1919; B.S. in Mech. Engring., Purdue U., 1922,

M.S. in Mech. Engring., 1923; Ph.D., Cornell U., 1934; m. Agnes Wilson Ayres, July 28, 1925. Gen. mgr. Purdue Meml. Union, 1922-26; dir. personnel, prof. personnel adminstrn. Prudue U., 1926-40; personnel cons. to indsl. firms, 1928-—; personnel and labor relations cons. Revere Copper & Brass, Inc., 1940-41, v.p. personnel and labor relations, 1941-43; mgmt. cons., personnel relations, prin. McKinsey & Co., 1943-45; pres. Alfred (N.Y.) U., 1945-48; prof. mgt. and indsl. relations Amos Tuck Sch. Bus. Adminstrn., Dartmouth, 1948-54; prof., chmn. engring. adminstrn. dept. Coll. Engring., Rutgers U., 1954-55; prof. engring. adminstrn. Sch. Engring., George Washington U., 1955-61, emeritus, 1961-—, dir. engring. adminstrn. program, 1956-61; mgmt. cons. Chmn., Leland Inst. Leisure, 1964-66. Served as 1st lt., Ordnance Department, U.S. Army, 1917-19; with AEF, 1 yr.; capt. Ordnance Res., 1919-29. Sec. Ross-Ade Lafayette, Ind., 1923-40, pres. Assn. U. Unions, 1924. Mem. Am. Coll. Personnel Assn. (pres. 1930-33), Ind. Personnel Assn. (sec. 1933-40), Assn. Am. Coll. (mem. commn. on Art 1946), Am. Soc. M.E., Tau Beta Pi, Pi Tau Sigma, Sigma Chi. Presbyn. Author books, pamphlets, articles and bulls. relating to field; latest books include: Human Relations, 1962; The Management of Research and Development, 1965; Joy of Painting Pictures, 1962; Democratic Capitalism, 1963; Basic Administration, 1962; The Joy of Cutting Stones into Gems and Jewelry. Qualified witness before NLRB, 1939; mem. Nat. War Labor bd. panels, 1942-45. Address: Box 41, 708 Indiana Woods Rd., Leland, Mich. 49654. Died Feb. 1, 1967; buried Springvale Cemetery, Lafayette, Ind.

WALTHALL, EDWARD CARY army officer, senator; b. Richmond, Va., Apr. 4, 1831; s. Barrett White and Sally (Wilkinson) W.; m. Sophie Bridges, 1856; m. 2d, Mary Lecky Jones, 1859; 1 adopted dau. Dep. clk. Circuit Ct. of Miss.; admitted to Miss. bar, 1852; dist. atty. 10th Jud. Dist. Miss., 1856-61; elected 1st lt. Yalobusha Rifles (volunteer co.), Confederate Army, 1861; commd. col. 29th Miss. Inf., 1862, in command at Battle of Corinth; promoted brig. gen., 1863; served in battles of Chickamaugua, Lookout Mountain and Missionary Ridge, in fighting around Atlanta; in command inf. of rear-guard cooperating with Gen. Nathan Forrest's cavalry in retreat from Nashville; commd. maj. gen., 1864; a leader in overthrow of Carpet-bag govt. in Miss.; del. to all Nat. Democratic convs., except one, 1868-84; mem. U.S. Senate from Miss., 1885-Jan. 24, 1894, 1895-98, chmn. com. on mil. affairs, mem. coms. on public lands and Mississippi River improvement. Died Washington, D.C., Apr. 21, 1898; buried Holly Springs, Miss.

WALTON, JAMES HENRY chemist; b. Deer Isle, Me., Feb. 26, 1878; s. James Hume and Florence Strode (Hewlett) W.; B.S., Mass. Inst. Tech., 1899; Austin traveling fellow from M.I.T., 1901-03; Ph.D., U. of Heidelberg, Germany, 1903; m. Dorothy Brockway Dana, Apr. 20, 1918; children—Marcia Dana, Judith Dana. Asst. in chemistry, U. of Ill., 1899-1900, Mass. Inst. Tech., 1900-01; instr. chemistry, 1903-06, asso., 1906-07, U. of Ill.; asst. prof. chemistry, 1907-12, asso. prof., 1912-19, prof. since 1919, U. of Wis. Commd. capt. Sanitary Corps, Sept. 20, 1917; maj. engrs., May 3, 1918; in charge training in gas defense in U.S., Sept. 1917-July 1918; 1st army gas officer, A.E.F., Aug. 1918-Jan. 1919; hon. disch., Jan. 25, 1919; lt. col. C.W. Res., May 8, 1926-May 8, 1931. Mem. Am. Chem. Soc. (ex-pres. Wis. sect.), Zeta Psi, Sigma Xi, Alpha Chi Sigma, Phi Lambda Upsilon, Scabbard and Blade. Unitarian. Club: University. Author: (with A. T. Lincoln) Elementary Quantitative Chemical Analysis, 1907; (with L. Kahlenberg) Qualitative Chemical Analysis, 1911; (with F. C. Krauskopf) A Laboratory Manual of General Chemistry, 1921; (with C. H. Sorum) Introduction to Qualitative Analysis, 1937; An Introduction to General Chemistry (with F. C. Krauskopf), 1943; numerous papers in scientific jours. Collaborated with Lt. Col. S. J. M. Auld, of Brit. Mil. Mission in preparation of 4 monographs on gas warfare, used in training troops in U.S. and in A.E.F. Home: 2122 Vims Av., Madison, Wis. Died June 6, 1947.

WALTON, THOMAS CAMERON naval officer; b. Cumberland, Eng., May 31, 1838; s. Thomas and Ann (Watson) W.; came to America, 1847; ed. Toronto Acad. and McGill Univ., Canada, 1860; M.D., Univ. of New York, 1862; m. Kate Lane Lynch, Feb. 1871. Apptd. asst. surgeon U.S.N., Oct. 5, 1861; advanced through the various grades and retired May 31, 1900, with rank of rear admiral. Served during Civ. War and Spanish-Am. War and at all the important naval stas.; senior med. officer at Naval Acad. and in Naval Laboratory, 1883-1900. Episcopalian. Home: Annapolis, Md. Died 1909.

WALTZ, MILLARD FILLMORE army officer; b. in Md., Feb. 13, 1857; grad. U.S. Mil. Acad., 1878. Commd. add. 2d lt. 12th Inf., June 14, 1878; 2d lt., June 28, 1878; 1st lt., Oct. 15, 1884; capt., Jan. 9, 1896; maj. 1st Inf., July 5, 1901; a.a.g., July 8, 1902; assigned to 16th Inf., July 13, 1906; lt. col. 27th Inf., Mar. 26, 1907; col. of inf., Mar. 11, 1911; assigned to 19th Inf., July 14, 1911. Comd. company, Battle of El Caney, Cuba, July 1, 1898; participated in Battle of San Juan, July 2 and 3, 1898, also bombardment and siege of Santiago; at Surrender of Santiago, July 17, 1898; ordered to Philippine Islands, 1899; duty Gen. Staff, Washington, D.C., 1906-10; duty Ft. Sam Houston, Tex., 1916-17. Address: War Dept., Washington, D.C.

WAMBAUGH, EUGENE lawyer; b. nr. Brookville, O., Feb. 29, 1856; s. Rev. A. B. and Sarah (Sells) W.; A.B., Harvard, 1876, A.M., 1877, LL.B., 1880; LL.D., State U. of Iowa, 1892, Western Reserve U., 1908, Dartmouth Coll., 1908; m. Anna S. Hemphill, Apr. 7, 1881 (died 1938); children—Sarah, Miles. Admitted to Ohio bar, 1880; practiced at Cincinnati, 1880-89; prof. law, State U. of Ia., 1889-92, Harvard, 1892-1925, prof. law emeritus. Mem. bd. editors Am. Polit. Science Review, 1906-13; special atty. U.S. Bur. of Corps., 1908-12; spl. counsel U.S. State Dept., for war problems, 1914; U.S. mem. permanent internat. commn. under treaty with Peru, 1915-—. Commd. maj., Judge Advocate's Section, O.R.C., U.S.A., Nov. 8, 1916; called to service and assigned to Northeastern Department, Boston, Mass., July 3, 1917; office of the judge advocate gen., Washington, Sept. 13, 1917 (chief of constl. and internat. law div.); lt. col. N.A., Feb. 13, 1918; col., July 19, 1918; hon. discharged, July 11, 1919. Del. Pan-Am. Scientific Congress, 1915-16 (chmn. sub-sect. on jurisprudence). Hon. prof. law, Western Reserve U., 1909-—; lecturer, U. of Wis., 1909, Harvard Sch. of Pub. Health, 1913-25, Yale, 1921, U. of Cambridge (for bd. of history), 1923, U. of Oxford (for faculty of law), 1923. Counsel of Peruvian Government on Tacna-Arica plebiscite (at Arica and Washington), 1925-26; member Petersburg National Military Park Commn., Department of the Interior, 1934-37. Fellow Am. Acad. of Arts and Sciences. Author: The Study of Cases, 1892, 94; Cases for Analysis, 1894; Cases on Agency, 1896, 1925; Cases on Insurance, 1902; Littleton's Tenures, 1903; Cases on Constitutional Law, 1915; Guide to Articles of War, 1917. Home: Cambridge, Mass. Died Aug. 6, 1940.

WANLASS, RALPH PAGE, lawyer; b. at Provo, Utah, Sept. 17, 1912; s. William L. and Eva (Page) W.; A.B., Utah State U., 1936; LL.B. with distinction, George Washington U., 1936; m. Kathryn Caine, June 15, 1939; children—George R., Kathryn Ellen, Elizabeth Caine. Admitted to D.C. bar, 1935, Ohio bar, 1965; practice in Washington, 1935-52; mem. firm Mayle & Wanlass, 1940-52; with Champion Papers, Inc., Hamilton, O., 1952-65, sec., 1960-65, legal counsel, 1960-65; partner firm Frost & Jacobs, Cin., 1965-68. Mem. bd. edn. Wyoming, O., 1958-65, pres., 1960. Served to capt. AUS, 1943-46. Mem. Am. Bar Assn., Order of Coif, Phi Kappa Phi, Phi Delta Phi. Club: Maketewah Country (Cin.). Home: Cincinnati OH Died Apr. 7, 1968.

WANTLAND, WAYNE W(ARDE), univ. prof.; born Sheridan, Ill., Sept. 5, 1905; s. Hosmer Vorhees and Elma Maude (Burgess) W.; student North Central Coll., Naperville, Ill., 1923-24, Northern Ill. State Teachers Coll., DeKalb, 1924-25 and summers of 1925, 1926 and 1927; B.S., Northwestern U., Evanston, Ill., 1930, M.A., 1932, Ph.D. 1935; m. Edna Marie Lohmeyer, Aug. 19, 1928 (deceased September 11, 1963); 1 son, William Stanley; m. second, Evelyn Kendrick Kinney, Apr. 29, 1964. Principal of Newark (Ill.) High Sch., 1925-27, supt., 1927-29; asst. in zoology, Northwestern U., 1930-34, instr., 1934-37; prof. biology, DePaul U., Chicago, 1935-37; instructor zoology, Eastern Ill. State Teachers Coll., Charleston, Ill., 1937-38; dir. biol. sci., Stephens Coll., Columbia, Mo., 1938-42; fellow Am. Council on Edn., U. of Chicago, 1940-41; prof. and head dept. of biology, Ill. Wesleyan U., Bloomington, 1944-45, dean of men, 1944-45, chmn. div. natural sciences, 1945-71, and George C. and Ella Beach Lewis prof. of biology, 1947-71, dir. Cancer Research Program, 1948-51, dir. Biol. Research Lab., 1951-71, dir. U.S. Pub. Health Research on mouth protozoa, 1956-64, also bd. dirs. Ill. Wesleyan U. Served as lt. administration and malariology, USN, 1942-44. Fellow A.A.A.S.; mem. Internat. Assn. Dental Research, Am. Soc. Zoologists, Am. Inst. Biol. Scis., Am. Soc. Parasitologists, Am. Cancer Soc., Ill. Acad. Sci., N.E.A., Research Soc. Am., Soc. Protozoologists, Am. Legion, Sigma Xi, Phi Kappa Phi. Republican. Methodist. Mason. Club: College Alumni (Bloomington). Contbr. profl. jours. Home: Bloomington IL Died Mar. 4, 1971; buried Bloomington IL

WANZER, H. STANLEY dairy product distbr.; b. Chgo., Nov. 26, 1894; s. Howard Hill and Elma (Bridge) W.; B.S., U. Wis., 1918; m. Marion Lewis; children—Jane, Sally, Catherine. With Sidney Wanzer & Sons, Chgo., 1919-—, v.p., dir., 1922-50, pres., 1951-61, chmn. bd., 1961-—; dir. Chgo. Fed. Savs. & Loan Assn. Dir. Hosp. Planning Council, Met. Chgo.; mem. U. Chgo. Citizen Com. Pres. bd. trustees Provident Hosp., 1946-50; dir. Milk Found. (pres. 1945-47), U. Chgo. Cancer Research Found. Served as lt. F.A., U.S. Army, 1918-19; AEF. Mem. Nat. Dairy Council, Asso. Milk Dealers (pres. 1935-37, dir.), Am. Dairy Assn. Ill. (dir.), Chgo. Plan Commn., Mil. Order World Wars, Chi Psi. Methodist. Mason. Clubs: University (Chgo.); Quadrangle, Dairymen's Country, Rotary. Home: 5811 Dorchester Av., Chgo. 60637. Office: 130 W. Garfield Blvd., Chgo. 9. Died Nov. 25, 1966.

WARBURG, JAMES PAUL, author; born Hamburg, Germany, Aug. 18, 1896; s. Paul M. and Nina J. (Loeb) W.; brought to U.S. in infancy; grad. Middlesex Sch., Concord, Mass., 1913; A.B., Harvard U., 1917; m. Jean Melber, Aug. 28, 1948; children—James Paul, Jennifer Joan, Philip Neff, Sarah Neff; April, Andrea, Kay (by previous marriage). With B.&O. Railroad Company, 1916, National Metropolitan Bank, Washington, D.C., 1919, First Nat. Bank of Boston, 1919-21; v.p. Internat. Acceptance Bank, N.Y. City, 1921-29, pres., 1931-32; pres. Internat. Manhattan Co., 1929-31; vice chmn. of bd. Bank of the Manhattan Co., 1932-35; director of The Bydale Co., Fontenay Corp.; dir. Polaroid Corporation. Special assistant to coordinator of information, 1941-42; deputy director, Overseas Branch, Office of War Information, July, 1942-Feb. 1944; stationed London and Washington. Seaman 2d class, later lt. j.g. Navy Flying Corps, 1917-18. Financial advisor World Econ. Conf., London, 1933. Chmn. bd. Julliard School of Music. Member Am. Acad. Polit. and Social Sci. (dir.), Phi Beta Kappa. Democrat. Hebrew religion. Clubs: Econ., Harvard (N.Y.); Cosmos (Washington); Authors' (London). Author: Wool & Wool Manufacture, 1920; Cotton & Cotton Manufacture, 1921; Hides and Leather Manufacture, 1921; Acceptance Financing, 1922; Three Textile Raw Materials, 1923; And Then What (verse), 1931; Shoes, Ships and Sealing Wax (verse), 1932; The Money Muddle, 1934; It's Up to Us, 1934; Hell Bent for Election, 1935; Still Hell Bent, 1936; Peace in Our Time?, 1940; Our War and Our Peace, 1941; Man's Enemy and Man (verse) 1942; Foreign Policy Begins at Home, 1944; Unwritten Treaty, 1945; Germany, Bridge or Battleground, 1947; Put Yourself in Marshall's Place, 1948; Last Call for Common Sense, 1949; Faith, Purpose and Power, 1950; Victory Without War, 1951; How to Co-exist, 1952; Germany-Key to Peace, 1953; The United States in a Changing World, 1954; Turning Point Toward Peace, 1955; Danger and Opportunity, 1956; Agenda for Action—Peace Through Disengagement, 1957; The West in Crisis, 1959; Reville for Rebels, 1960; Disarmament-the Challenge of the 1960s, 1961; The Liberal Papers, 1962; Toward a Strategy of Peace, 1964; The Long Road Home (autobiography), 1964; Time for Statesmanship, 1965; The U.S. in the Postwar World, 1966; Western Intruders, 1967; Crosscurrents in the Middle East, 1968. Home: Greenwich CT Died June 3, 1969.

WARD, AARON rear admiral U.S.N.; b. Philadelphia, Oct. 10, 1851; s. Gen. Ward Benjamin and Emily (Ward) Burnett; ed. Cannstatt, Germany, and Lycee Bonaparte, Paris; grad. U.S. Naval Acad., 1871; m. Annie Cairns Willis, Apr. 20, 1876. Served on California, Pacific Sta., 1871-73; Brooklyn in W.I., 1874; Franklin, European Sta., 1875-76; Naval Acad., 1876-79; Constitution, training squadron, 1879-82; Hartford and Monongahela, Pacific Sta., 1885-88; naval attaché, Paris, Berlin, St. Petersburg, 1889-92; served on New York, in W.I. and Brazil, 1893-94; San Francisco, in Mediterranean, 1894-96; comd. Wasp during Spanish-Am. War, and advanced in grade for eminent and conspicuous service in battle; comd. Panther, in W.I., 1898-99; as comdr. and capt. served on Asiatic Sta. as chief-of-staff, also comd. Yorktown, Don Juan de Austria and Pennsylvania, 1901-08; surpervisor New York Harbor, 1908-09; aid to Sec. of the Navy, head of Inspection Dept., 1909-11; rear admiral, 1910; 2d in command Atlantic Fleet, flagship Minnesota and Florida, 1911-12; retired Oct. 10, 1913. Episcopalian. Officer Legion of Honor, France. Editor: Luce's Seamanship, revised edit., 1884. Home: Roslyn, L.I., N.Y. Died July 5, 1918.

WARD, ARTEMAS army officer, congressman; b. Shrewsbury, Mass., Nov. 26, 1727; s. Nahum and Martha (How) W.; grad. Harvard, 1748; m. Sarah Trowbridge, 8 children. Established gen. store, Shrewsbury, 1750, held various town offices including assessor, clk., selectman, moderator, treas.; commd. col. 3d Regt., Mass. Militia, 1758; justice Worcester County Ct. of Common Pleas, 1762, chief justice, 1775; mem. Mass. Gen. Ct. from Shrewsbury for many years; mem. convs. held in Worchester County to champion colonial rights; mem. 1st and 2d Mass. provincial congresses; commd. gen., comdr.-in-chief Mass. Militia, 1775, directed siege of Boston; commd. maj. gen., 2d-in-command Continental Army by Continental Congress, 1775, resigned commn., 1776; mem. Mass. Exec. Council, 1777-80, Continental Congress, 1780-81; mem. Mass. Legislature, 1782-87; mem. U.S. Ho. of Reps. (Federalist) from Mass., 1st-2d congresses, 1791-95; homestead now property of Harvard, maintained as meml. Died Oct. 28, 1800; buried Mountain View Cemetery, Shrewsbury.

WARD, FRANKLIN WILMER soldier; b. Phila., Pa., Dec. 4, 1870; s. Thomas P. and Sarah Elizabeth (Reeves-Stoy) W.; grad. Horace Binney Sch., Phila.; m. Mabel Loretta Downs, Jan. 9, 1898; 1 son, John Franklin. Enlisted as pvt. N.G. Pa., 1888; commd. 2d lt. N.G.N.Y., 1898; with 6th div. Mexican Border, 1916; chief of staff, adj. 27th Div., World War I, 1917-19; promoted col., comdg. 27th Trains and Mil. Police; comd. 106th U.S. Inf. at battles, St. Souplet, Arbre Guernon, St. Maurice River, France; assigned to War Dept. Gen. Staff, Washington, 1920-22; apptd. The Adj. Gen. of N.Y., 1926; maj. gen., 1930. Decorated with D.S.M. and Silver Star medal (U.S.); Officer Legion of Honor (France); Cross of War with Palm (Belgium); Grand Officer Order of Crown (Roumania); Comdr. Order of Polish Restitution; Conspicious Service Medal of State of N.Y. Mem. United Spanish War Veterans,

Mil. Order World War, Am. Legion, N.Y. Soc. Mil. and Naval Officers of World War, S.R., S.C.V. Co-author: The Service of Coast Artillery (with Gen. Frank T. Hines), 1910. Author: Between the Big Parades, 1932. Home: Albany, N.Y. Died Mar. 17, 1938.

WARD, FREDERICK KING brig. gen. U.S.A.; b. Newark, O., Mar. 19, 1847; s. Pruden Alling and Julia Bunnell (Ward) W.; grad. U.S. Mil. Acad., 1870; m. Lizzie Bell Dunn, June 26, 1873. Commd. 2d lt. 1st Cav., June 15, 1870; 1st lt., Nov. 11, 1875; capt., Feb. 11, 1887; maj. 10th Cav., July 11, 1899; transferred to 1st Cav., Aug. 2, 1899; lt. col. 14th Cav., Jan. 24, 1903; transferred to 1st Cav., Apr. 24, 1903; detailed insp. gen., Nov. 30, 1904; col. 2d Cav., June 23, 1905; detailed insp. gen., Oct. 1, 1906; assigned to 7th Cav., May 3, 1907; brig. gen. U.S.A., Feb. 11, 1910; retired by operation of law, Mar. 19, 1911. Home: Seattle, Wash. Died Oct. 25, 1933.

WARD, GEORGE EHINGER, lawyer; b. Roswell, N.M., Mar. 3, 1932; s. Charles Francis and Emily (Stephens) W.; B.S., N.M. Mil. Inst., 1954; LL.B., Washington and Lee U., 1959; m. Mary Lane Reed, Jan. 2, 1960; one son, George Ehinger. Admitted to N.M. bar, 1959; practiced in Roswell, N.M., 1959-67. Mem. Chaves County Safety Council. Dep. sheriff, Chaves County, 1967-67; mem. N.M. Republican Central Com. Chmn. bd. dirs. Chaves County Heart Assn.; bd. regents N.M. Mil. Inst., 1967. Served to 1st lt. AUS, 1954-56. Mem. N.M. Mil. Inst. Polo Assn. (v.p.), American, Chaves County bar assns., State Bar N.M., S.C.V., S.A.R. (pres. Southeastern N.M.), N.M. Mil. Inst. Alumni Assn. (pres. Roswell), Aqualantes, Sojourners (sec.), Delta Kappa Epsilon, Phi Alpha Delta. Mason, Rotarian. Home: Roswell NM2Died Apr. 7, 1967.

WARD, GEORGE GRAY gynecologist; b. London, Eng., Aug. 15, 1868; s. George Gray and Marianne (Smith) W.; brought to America, 1874; ed. Bklyn. Collegiate and Poly. Inst., Holbrook Mil. Acad. (Ossining, N.Y.); M.D., L.I. Coll. Hosp., 1891; studied U. Berlin, 1892-93, also London and Paris; m. Edith Wigham, June 23, 1898. Prof. diseases of women, N.Y., Post-Grad. Med. Sch., 1905-16, sec. faculty, 1910-16; prof. obstetrics and gynecology, Cornell U. Med. Coll., 1916-34, emeritus; chief surgeon Woman's Hosp., 1918-38, emeritus; prof. clin. obstetrics and gynecology, Columbia; formerly attending gynecologist, Bellevue Hosp.; con. gynecologist, N.Y. Post-Grad. Hosp., N.Y. Hosp., Monmouth Meml. Hosp., Lawrence Hosp., Home for Incurables, Booth Meml. Hosp. Mem. 7th Regiment, Nat. Guard, N.Y., 8 yrs.; capt., asst. surgeon, 12th Regt., 1895-98; maj. surgeon, 1898-1902; maj. surgeon 12th Regt. Inf., N.Y. Vols., Spanish-Am. War. Founder, fellow A.C.S.; fellow Am. Gynecology Soc. (ex-pres..), N.Y. Acad. Medicine; hon. fellow Edinburgh Obstet. Soc., Royal Coll. Obstetricians and Gynecologists, Royal Med. Soc. Budapest; hon. mem. British Congress Obstetrics and Gynecology; mem. A.M.A. (chmn. sect. obstetrics and gynecology), Med. Soc. State N.Y., N.Y. County Med. Soc. (ex-pres.), N.Y. Obstet. Soc. (ex-pres.), Hosp. Grads.' Club (ex-pres.), Phi Alpha Sigma, Alpha Omega Alpha, Mil. Order Fgn. Wars, Naval and Mil. Order Spanish-Am. War. Rep. Episcopalian. Clubs: Union, Century, Riding, Racquet (New York); Rumson Country; Army and Navy (Washington), Travellers (Paris). Co-author: Gynecology in Operative Therapeusis, 1915; Kelly's Gynecology, 1928; Lewis Practice of Surgery, 1928; Curtis Obstetrics and Gynecology, 1933; Davis Gynecology and Obstetrics, 1933; and numerous monographs on gynecology and obstetrics. Home: 1175 Park Av. Office: 101 E. 80th St., N.Y.C. Died Dec. 21, 1950; buried Greenwood, Bklyn.

WARD, HENRY CLAY brig. gen. U.S.A.; b. Worcester, Mass., Sept. 10, 1843; s. Artemus, 2d, and Huldah (Reed) W.; ed. pub. schs., Worcester, and army service schs.; m. Susie M. Denny, Feb. 12, 1867; m. 2d, Frances Crutcher, Dec. 6, 1876. Sergt. maj. 15th Mass. Inf., 1861; 2d lt., Apr. 9, 1863; hon. mustered out, Sept. 4, 1863; 1st lt. 57th Mass. Inf., Mar. 9, 1864; capt., July 31, 1864, until mustered out of vol. service, July 30, 1865. In regular army, 2d lt. and 1st lt. 11th Inf., Feb. 23, 1866; promoted through grades to brig. gen., Oct. 30, 1905, and retired. Served throughout Civil War in Army of Potomac, in battles of Ball's Bluff, siege of Yorktown, Fair Oaks, battles before Richmond, Va., June 1862; Seven Days' battles, and battle of the Wilderness; wounded at Antietam; participated battles of Fredericksburg, campaign under Gen. Grant from Rapidan to Petersburg; Spottsylvania (wounded); siege of Petersburg, Yellow Tavern, Va., Ft. Stedman, Va., where was taken prisoner; confined in Libby Prison, Mar. 25, 1865, until capture of Richmond, Va., then joined regt. until surrender of Lee's army. Bvtd. capt. U.S.A., "for bravery at battle of Ft. Stedman, Mar. 24, 1865." Served in Indian campaigns, 1880, and later, and in Philippines; with N.G. Tenn., 1892-96, and elected brig. gen. comdg., 1895. Mason. Episcopalian. Home: Wellesley Hills, Mass. Died Nov. 16, 1925.

WARD, HENRY HEBER, b. W. Haven, Conn., July 20, 1871; s. Israel Kimberly and Katharine Louise (Hannah) W.; apptd. U.S. Naval Acad. from N.J., and grad. 1893; m. Mary Minturn Hartshorne, of Highlands, N.J., Nov. 9, 1898; children—Katharine L., Julia, Mary Minturn, Henrietta, Henry H. Commd. ensign U.S.N., 1895; lt. jr. grade, 1899; advanced 10 numbers and commd. lt., 1901. On U.S.S. Baltimore, Asiatic Sta., 1893-95; U.S.S. Maine, 1895-97; Navy Dept., Washington, 1897; served as spy in Spanish-Am. War, 1898, and awarded medal for "extraordinary heroism" during the war; asst. to judge advocate on Schley Court of Inquiry, 1901; sec. Gen. Bd. of the Navy, and flag lt. European Sta.; resigned from Navy, 1903. Sec. Navy League of U.S., 1907-12, v.p., 1912-16. Officer and dir. various corpns. Clubs: Union, Brook, New York Yacht, University (New York); Metropolitan (Washington); Graduate (New Haven). Author: Naval Operations of the War with Spain, 1898. Address: 1 E. 51st St., New York NY

WARD, JAMES HARMON naval officer; b. Hartford, Conn., Sept. 25, 1806; s. James and Ruth (Butler) W.; grad. Am. Literary, Scientific and Mil. Acad., Norwich, Vt.; studied science Trinity Coll., Hartford, 1828; m. Sarah Whittemore, Apr. 11, 1833, 3 children. Commd. midshipman U.S. Navy 1823, served on ship Constitution in Mediterranean, 1824-28; became a recognized authority on ordnance and naval tactics; exec. officer U.S. Naval Acad., Annapolis, Md., 1845-47, head dept. of ordnance and gunnery; in command ship Cumberland, 1847; stationed at Bklyn. Navy Yard, at start of Civil War; commanded small fleet called Potomac Flotilla, 1861, silenced Confederate batteries at Aquia Creek, Va., 1861. Author: An Elementary Course of Instruction on Ordnance and Gunnery (adopted as U.S. Naval Acad. textbook), 1845; A Manual of Naval Tactics, 1859; Steam for the Million, 1860. Killed while leading attack on batteries at Matthias Point, Va., June 27, 1861; buried Hartford.

WARD, JOHN CHAMBERLAIN bishop; b. Elmira, N.Y., Aug. 27, 1873; s. Hamilton and Mary Adelia (Chamberlain) W.; A.B., Harvard, 1896; B.D., Gen. Theol. Sem., 1899, S.T.D., 1923; D.D., Kenyon, 1924; unmarried. Deacon, 1899, priest, 1900, P.E. Ch. Rector St. Stephen's Ch., Buffalo, 1899-1902, Grace Ch., Buffalo, 1902-21; consecrated bishop of Erie, Pa., September 22, 1921, retired June 1, 1943; member Special Committee on Budget and Program, P.E. Church. Mem. Pennsylvania State Commn. on Healing Arts, 1927; chmn. Citizens Relief Com., Erie, 1933. Chaplain 74th Inf., Nat. Guard N.Y., on Mexican border, 1916; chaplain same, local guard duty and Wadsworth, S.C., 1917; chaplain 105th Machine Gun Batt., 107th Inf., and 108th Inf., 27th Div., A.E.F., 1918, serving 9 mos. overseas; wounded in action; hon. disch. Mar. 1918, rank of capt.; later, lt. col. Reserves. Awarded D.S.C., Purple Heart (U.S.); M.C. (British). Mem. Am. Legion, Phi Beta Kappa. Republican. Clubs: Harvard, University. Home: 388 Delaware Av., Buffalo 2, N.Y. Died Feb. 15, 1949.

WARD, JOHN HENRY HOBART deputy co. clerk New York County, b. New York, June 17, 1823; ed. Collegiate Sch. of Trinity Ch.; in Mexican war as sergt. maj. 7th U.S. inf., from Corpus Christi to Cerro Gordo; asst. commissary gen. State of N.Y., 1850, commissary gen., 1850-59; col. 38th N.Y. vols., 1860; brig. gen. vols., Oct. 2, 1862; comd. 2d brigade, 1st div., 3d corps; comd. 1st div., 3d corps, at Gettysburg, Manassas Gap and Kelly's Ford, Army of Potomac. Mem. Supreme Council 33 deg. Masonry. Home: New York, N.Y. Died 1903.

WARD, ORLANDO, army officer; b. Macon, Mo., Nov. 4, 1891; s. Ethelbert and Ada (Smith) W.; B.S., U.S. Mil. Acad., West Point, N.Y., 1914; attended Field Arty. Sch., 1923-24; distinguished grad. Command and Gen. Staff Sch., 1925-26; attended Army War Coll., 1936, Army Gen. Staff Coll., Langres, France, 1919; D.Sc. (honorary), University of Denver, 1946; married Edith Hanington, June 16, 1915; children—Katherine Hanington (dec.), Edith Hanington, Ada Smith. Commd. 2d lt., Cav., U.S. Army, advanced through ranks to major general, 1942; served on Mexican border and with Punitive Expdn. in Mexico, 1916-17; transferred F.A., 1917, in 10th F.A., 3d Div., France, Army of Occupation, Germany, 1917-19; on R.O.T.C. duty, U. of Wis., 1919-23; Ft. F.E. Warren, Wyo., 1926-29; gen. staff, Philippines, 1929-31; instr. and dir., gunnery dept., Ft. Sill, Okla., 1931-35; comdg. 1st Batln., 83d F.A., Ft. Benning, Ga., 1936-38; on Gen. Staff, War Dept., 1938-41; sec. Gen. Staff, 1939-41; brig. and comdg. gen. 1st Armored Div., Ft. Knox, Ky., 1941-42; comdg. gen. 1st Armored Div., 1942-43; comdg. gen. Tank Destroyer Center, Camp Hood, Tex., June 1943-Jan. 1944; comdt. Field Arty. Sch., Ft. Sill, Okla., Jan.-Oct., 1944; comdg. gen. 20th Armored Div., Germany, Oct. 1944-July 1945; comdg. Inf. Advanced Replacement Tng. Center, Camp Gordon, Ga., 1945; with War Dependency Bd., Washington, 1945; mem., then pres. Confidential Personnel Bd., 1946; comdg. V Corps, Ft. Jackson, S.C., 1946, Replacement Sch. Command, Ft. Bragg, N.C., 1946; In command of 6th Div., Korea, 1946-49; chief historical div., Dept. of the Army 1949-53. Awarded D.S.C., Legion of Merit with oak leaf cluster, Silver Star with oak leaf cluster, Purple Heart, D.S.M., Bronze Star Medal. Home: Denver CO Died Feb. 4, 1972; buried Fairmount Cemetery Denver CO

WARD, ROBERT WILLIAM army officer; b. Cin., Mar. 2, 1905; s. Robert G. and Katie (Enderes) W.; student mech. engring., U. Cin., 1924-25; B.S., U.S. Mil. Acad., 1929; student Inf. Sch. 1932, Command and Gen. Staff Coll., 1942, Armed Forces Staff Coll., 1947, Nat. War Coll., 1951, Command Mgmt. Sch. 1956. Guided Misseles Sch., 1956; m. Marjorie II. Leward, June 7, 1930; 1 dau., Marjorie (Mrs. Frederick L. Munds, Jr.). Commd. 2d lt. inf., U.S. Army, 1929, advanced through grades to maj. gen., 1955; task force operations officer North African landings, 1942; comdr. 135th Inf. Regt., 34th Inf. Div., Tunisian, Italian campaigns, 1943-44; chief plans and policy, orgn. and tng. div. War Dept. Gen. Staff, 1945-47; staff Office Sec., Def., 1951; chief SHAPE Tng. Mission to Royal Netherlands Army, 1952-55; comdg. gen. Army Replacement Tng. Center, Ft. Dix, N.J., 1955; dep. chief staff for plans Hdqrs. Far East Command, 1956-57. Decorated Legion of Merit with cluster, Bronze Star medal, Purple Heart, Combat Infantryman's badge; comdr. Order Orange Nassau (Netherlands). Club: Army-Navy (Washington). Home: 2301 River Rd., West Point Pleasant, N.J. Office: Detachment of Patient, Walter Reed Army Hosp., Washington. Died Apr. 1, 1960.

WARD, SAMUEL army officer, mcht.; b. Westerly, R.I., Nov. 17, 1756; s. Gov. Samuel and Ann (Ray) W.; grad. R.I. Coll. (now Brown U.), 1771; m. Phoebe Greene, Mar. 8, 1778, 10 children including Samuel. Commd. capt. 1st R.I. Regt., Continental Army, 1775, taken prisoner at siege of Quebec, 1775, released, 1776; commd. maj., 1777, wintered at Valley Forge, 1777-78; lt. col., 1779, ret., 1781; founded firm Samuel Ward & Brother. N.Y.C.; one of 1st Americans to visit Far East; mem. Soc. of Cincinnati, 1784; del. Annapolis Conv., 1786; pres. N.Y. Marine Ins. Co., 1806-08; a rep. from R.I. to Hartford Conv., 1814. Died N.Y.C., Aug. 10, 1832.

WARD, THOMAS brig. gen. U.S.A.; b. West Point, N.Y., Mar. 18, 1839; s. Bryan and Eliza W.; grad. U.S. Mil. Acad., 1863; hon. A.M., Union Coll., 1878; m. Katharine L. Mott, Apr. 20, 1870; father of Philip R., colonel F.A.; and of Thomas, Jr., midshipman U.S.N., killed Apr. 13, 1904, aboard battleship Missouri; and of John M., 1st lieutenant A.E.F. Commd. 2d lieut., 1st U.S. Arty., June 11, 1863; 1st lt., July 18, 1864; capt., Nov. 1, 1876; maj. a.a.g., June 28, 1884; lt. col. a.a.g., Aug. 31, 1893; col. a.a.g., Sept. 11, 1897; brig. gen., July 22, 1902; retired at own request after over 40 yrs.' service, July 22, 1902. Bvtd.: 1st lt., June 3, 1864, "for gallant and meritorious services in battle of Cold Harbor, Va."; capt., Mar. 13, 1865, for same during the war. Prof. mil. science and tactics, Union Coll., 1873-77; pres. Bd. of Visitors to U.S. Mil. Acad., 1907. Home: Rochester, N.Y. Died Mar. 25, 1926.

WARD, THOMAS JOHNSON banker, broker; b. Balt., June 28, 1886; s. Francis Xavier and Ellen Topham (Evans) W.; ed. high sch., Balt.; m. Pansy Beale Bloomer, June 3, 1911; 1 son, Thomas Johnson. Began in banking and brokerage bus. with H. W. Noble & Co., Phila., 1906; with Cassatt & Co., bankers and brokers, Phila., 1911-—, partner 1913-35; pres. Cassatt & Co., Inc., 1935-40; v.p. Merrill Lynch & Co., Inc., N.Y., 1938-40; gen. partner Merrill, Lynch, Pierce, Fenner & Beane, 1940-56, ltd. partner, 1956-—; cons. Merrill, Lynch, Pierce, Fenner and Smith, Inc., 1959-—. Mem. exec. com. first 2 Liberty Loan drives 3d Fed. Res. Dist.; maj. U.S. Army, Gen. Staff, 1918-19; dep. dir. WPB, Region 3, 1942-43. Republican. Episcopalian. Clubs: Racquet (Phila.). Home: Merion, Pa. Office: 1422 Chestnut St., Phila. 2. Died Mar. 3, 1966.

WARD, WILLIAM THOMAS congressman, lawyer; b. Amelia County, Va., Aug. 9, 1808; attended St. Mary's Coll., nr. Lebanon, Ky.; studied law. Admitted to bar, began practice of law, Greensburg, Ky.; served as maj. 4th Ky. Volunteers in Mexican War, 1847-48; mem. Ky. Ho. of Reps., 1850; mem. U.S. Ho. of Reps. (Whig) from Ky., 32d Congress, 1851-53; commd. brig. gen., 1861, served throughout Civil War, brevetted maj. gen., 1865. Died Louisville, Ky., Oct. 12, 1878; buried Cave Hill Cemetery.

WARDER, WALTER lawyer; b. Maysville, Mason Co., Ky., Apr. 7, 1851; s. Joseph and Ann Thomas (Kirkham) W.; brought to Ill. by parents in infancy; ed. pub. schs. and U. of Ill.; m. Daro Bain, of Vienna, Johnson Co., Ill., May 25, 1874. Admitted to Ill. bar, 1874; practiced at Marion, Ill., 1874-80, since at Cairo. Apptd. state's atty. Alexander Co., Ill., 1883; master in chancery, Alexander Co. Circuit Ct., most of time, 1885-—; mem. Ill. Ho. of Rep., 1891-95, Senate, 1896-1901 (pres. pro tem., 1899-1900); acting gov. of Ill. for 2 mos., 1899-1900, successfully dealing with labor strike troubles at Virden and Caterville. Maj. privisional regt. Ill. Vols. Spanish-Am. War, 1898; commr. for Ill. to St. Louis Expn. and chmn. com. mines and minerals, 1904; pres. Bd. of Edn., Cairo, 1907-10. Republican. Episcopalian. Clubs: Alexander, Commercial. Address: Cairo, Ill.

WARDLE, ROBERT, JR., power co. exec.; b. Bklyn., Oct. 14, 1911; s. Robert and Margaret (Lang) W.; B.S. in Civil Engring., Ga. Inst. Tech., 1934; m. Elizabeth Collier, July 3, 1935; children—Margaret Elizabeth, Charles Collier, Robert III. With Ga. Power Co., 1934-41, 45-58, asst. to v.p. and gen. mgr., 1951-53, asst. to v.p. charge finance, 1953-58; v.p. Southern Co., Atlanta, 1958-62, Southern Services, Incorporated, 1963-69. Consultant Office Energy and Utilities, Exec. Office of

President, Nat. Security Resources Bd., 1948-50; cons. to adminstr. Def. Prodn. Adminstrn., 1951. Served to lt. col., C.E., AUS, 1941-46; col. Res. Decorated Bronze Star. Mem. Soc. Am. Mil. Engrs., Ga. Engring. Soc., Illuminating Engring. Soc., Am. Legion, Ga. Inst. Tech., Alumni Assn., Phi Gamma Delta. Clubs: Cherokee Town and Country (Atlanta); Civitan. Home: Atlanta GA Died June 27, 1969; buried Westview Cemetery, Atlanta GA

WARFIELD, AUGUSTUS BENNETT army officer; b. Prattsburgh, N.Y., July 24, 1878; s. Myron Franklin and Helena (Green) W.; grad. Hamilton Coll., Clinton, N.Y., 1900; m. Mary Lillian Dougherty, Nov. 15, 1905; children—Ellen Louise (wife of Col. L. H. Tull), Charles L. (officer U.S. Army). Entered U.S. Army, 1898; commd. 2d lt., 1900, and advanced through grades to brig. gen., 1936; served with 322d F.A. and 158th F.A. Brigade, 83d Div., 1918-20; with AEF, Saint Mihiel-Meuse-Argonne, 18 mos.; Army of Occupation, Coblentz, Germany, 8 mos.; comdg. officer Transp. Corps depots, Stockton, Cal., 1942-45; ret., 1945. Active in civil affairs, Stockton. Mem. Sigma Phi. Republican. Mason (32 deg.). Home: 433 S. Tuxedo Av., Stockton, Cal. 95204. Died Mar. 3, 1960.

WARFIELD, HARRY RIDGELY, JR., engineer, research dir.; b. Morgantown, W.Va., Aug. 17,21904; s. Harry Ridgely and Susan Elizabeth (Sadtler) W.; B.Engring., Johns Hopkins, 1928; m. Juliet Linn Reaney, June 17, 1932 (dec. Apr. 1968); children—Harry Ridgely III, Susan Linn; m. 2d, Helen Gardner Howard, Oct. 31, 1968. With works mgmt. course Westinghouse Electric Co., 1928; application engr. Silica Gel Corp., 1930; dist. engr. Frigidaire div. Gen. Motors Corp., 1932; partner Fonda and Warfield, cons. engrs., 1938-41; mem. Inst. Coop. Research, Johns Hopkins, 1947-69, research engr., 1948-50, asst. dir., 1950-53, dir., 1953-69. Mem. Md. N.G., 1931-53; served from 2d lt. to col. F.A., AUS, 1941-45, ETO. Decorated ETO Service Medal with Assault Arrowhead, Normandy, No. France, Rhineland and Central Germany battle stars, Legion of Merit, B.S.M. (U.S.); Legion of Honor, Croix de Guerre with palm (France); Order of Leopold, Croix de Guerre with palm (Belgium). Mem. Soc. Colonial Wars, Alpha Delta Phi. Tau Beta Pi, Omicron Delta Kappa. Episcopalian (exec. council Diocese Md. 1951-57). Home: Baltimore MD Died Oct. 3, 1969.

WARFIELD, HENRY MACTIER ins. exec.; b. Baltimore, Md., July 1, 1867; s. Henry M. and Anna (Emory) W.; ed. pvt. and pub. schs., Baltimore; m. Rebecca Carroll Denison, of Baltimore, Feb. 10, 1892; 1 dau., Mrs. Zachary R. Lewis. Began as clk. with wholesale dry goods house, 1884; clk., Continental Ins. Co. of N.Y., 1884-85, Royal Ins. Co. of Liverpool, 1885-96, resident mgr., 1896-1923; president of Henry M. Warfield-Roloson Company, mgrs. Royal Insurance Company and ins. brokers; dir. Md. Trust Company, Eutaw Savings Bank, Baltimore Steam Packet Co., Chesapeake & Potomac Telephone Co. Mem. Md. N.G., 1885-1920, col., 1903-08, adj. gen., 1908-12, 1916-20; served as maj., Md. Vol. Inf., Spanish-Am. War. Democrat. Episcopalian. Clubs: Maryland, Merchants, Bachelors Cotillon. Home: Timonium, Md. Office: 201-203 E. Redwood St., Baltimore, Md.

WARFIELD, WILLIAM b. Easton, Pa., Dec. 4, 1891, s. Ethelbert Dudley and Eleanor Frances (Tilton) W.; A.B., Lafayette Coll., 1911; post-grad. work, Princeton, 1911-13; Columbia Law Sch., 1913-14; m. Corinne Wendel, Jan. 29, 1920; 1 son, William; m. 2d, Marguerite Ruth, June 24, 1944. Made expeditions for scientific research and as consulting mining geologist to British Guiana and Trinidad, 1912, Mesopotamia and Arabia, 1913, India, 1912-13; mem. Am. expdn. to Sardes, Asia Minor, 1913, Serbian relief, 1914-15; attaché Am. Embassy, Petrograd, 1915-16; chargé d'affaires, Sofia, Bulgaria, 1916-17; dir. for Standard Oil Co. of N.J. in Argentina, Venezuela and Bolivia, 1920-26; pres. Trinidad Oil Fields, Inc., 1926-27; cons. petroleum engr., 1927-32; with Sperry Gyroscope Co., Inc., 1932-34, Am. Cyanamid Co., 1934-38, Davison Chemical Corp., Baltimore, 1938; dir. Standard Aircraft Products, Dayton, O., 1940-42; consultant to War Production Bd., Washington, D.C., 1942, Bd. of Economic Warfare, 1942-43. Commissioned captain, C.A.C., August 1917; transferred to Tank Corps, 1918; served in Meuse-Argonne offensive, 1918; promoted to maj. and lt. col., 1919. Dep. commr. of Am. Red Cross to Balkan States and commr. to Albania, 1919-20. Mem. Zeta Psi, Phi Beta Kappa; fellow Am. Geog. Soc., Am. Inst. Mining and Metall. Engrs. Several fgn. decorations. Clubs: University, Nat. Arts (New York); Royal Automobile (London). Author: The Gate of Asia, 1916. Address: National Arts Club, 15 Gramercy Park, New York. Died March 16, 1947; buried at Lexington, Ky.

WARLICK, HULON OTIS JR. govt. official; b. Humboldt, Tenn., Jan. 18, 1903; s. Hulon Otis and Chessie Mae (Dunlap) W.; B.S. in C.E., Univ. of Tenn., 1926; LL.B., Univ. of Memphis, 1941; m. Frances Smith, June 15, 1930; children—Hulon, Katharine (Mrs. W. R. Martin), Frances (Mrs. J. P. Leake), Ann. Admitted Tenn. bar, 1941. Civil engr. on flood control, Memphis, Tennessee, Mississippi River Commn. and United States Engineer dept., 1926-40; instr. in contracts and specifications, Univ. of Tenn. Extension Sch., 1939-40; dir. shipping and storage br., Prodn. and Marketing Adminstrn., U.S. Dept. of Agr., Washington, 1945-49, chief processing plants staff Office of Administrator, 1949-53; chief materials division ARO, Incorporated, 1955-—; consultant Hoover Commn., 1954-55; Eastern representative for Encinal Terminals of Cal., 1954-55. Served capt. to col. War Dept. gen. staff, office chief of engrs. and hdqrs. Army Service Forces, 1941-45; arranged for constrn., trained personnel, and supervised operation of all army engr. depots in U.S., 1942-43; supervised storage operations of all army service forces depots in U.S., 1944-45. Recipient commendation ribbon for orgn. and operation of Army Engrs. Depots U.S. Mem. Nat. Soc. Profl. Engrs., Soc. Am. Mil. Engrs., Am. Ordnance Assn., Am. Legion, U. Tenn. Alumni Assn. (dir. 1961-63), Coffee County Bar Assn., Sigma Alpha Epsilon. Episcopalian. Clubs: Army and Navy (Washington); Tullahoma Country. Home: 312 Oak Park. Office: ARO, Inc., Tullahoma, Tenn. Died Sept. 24, 1964; buried Humboldt, Tenn.

WARMOTH, HENRY CLAY governor; b. McLeansboro, Ill., May 9, 1842; s. Isaac Saunders and Eleanor (Lane) W.; ed. pub. and pvt. schs., Fairfield and Salem, Ill.; admitted to bar, Lebanon, Mo., 1861; m. Sally, d. James M. Durand, May 30, 1877. Apptd. dist. atty. 18th Jud. Dist., Mo., 1862; resigned to become lt. col. 32d Mo. Inf.; wounded in battles Chickasaw Bayou and Arkansas Post; assigned to staff Maj. Gen. John A. McClernand; served during campaign below and around Vicksburg, including assault of May 19-22, 1863; later on staff Maj. Gen. E. O. C. Ord, 13th Army Corps; comd. his regt. during campaigns against Gens. Forrest and Stephen D. Lee; joined Grant's army in attack on Missionary Ridge and Lookout Mountain, his regt. leading in assault and capture of Rossville Gap; again on staff Gen. McClernand, 1864; served in Gen. Banks' Tex. campaign; assigned as judge mil. court, Dept. of Gulf, with jurisdiction over mil., civil and criminal cases, serving till end of war. Del. Phila. Conv., 1866; one of co. which followed President Johnson on his "swing around the circle" through Eastern and Northern States; elected gov. of La., 1868; Gen. Grant made him mil. gov. until new constitution of state was accepted by Congress; after that was inaugurated and served until 1873; became sugar planter Plaquemines Parish, La.; mem. La. Legislature, 1876-77; del. La. Constl. Conv., 1879; collector customs, port of New Orleans, 1889-93; del. Rep. Nat. convs., 1896, 1900; built, 1890, and pres. New Orleans, Fort Jackson & Grand Isle R.R. Died Sept. 30, 1932.

WARNER, ADONIRAM JUDSON congressman; b. Wales, N.Y., Jan. 13, 1834; s. Levi and Hepsibah (Dickinson) W.; ed. Beloit, Wis., and New York Central Coll.; m. Susan E. Butts, Apr. 5, 1856. Prin. Lewiston Acad., and supt. public schs. of Mifflin County; served for a time on Roger's geol. survey of Pa.; prin. Mercer Union (Pa.) schs., 1856-61; capt. 10th Pa. Reserves, July 21, 1861; lt. col. May 14, 1862; served throughout the Peninsular campaign under McClellan; last field officer to leave Harrison's landing, subsequently ordered by Burnside to conduct detachments of troops arriving at Fredericksburg too late to cross to Bull Run, to Alexandria, by river, thence to join main army. Joined own command and participated in battles of South Mountain and Antietam under Hooker, Reynolds and Meade; severely wounded at Antietam; recommended for promotion to brig. gen.; col., Apr. 25, 1863; rejoined regt. and, with wound unhealed and unable to walk without supports, went through the battle of Gettysburg; heard Lincoln's Gettysburg speech and served as pallbearer at his funeral services, held in Indianapolis; col. Vet. Reserve Corps, Nov. 15, 1863; sent to Indianapolis; resigned Nov. 17, 1865; bvtd. brig. gen., Mar. 13, 1865. Began building steam and electric rys. opening coal and iron mines and developing water power for generating electricity. Mem. 46th (1879-81) and 48th and 49th (1883-87) Congresses; pres. Bimetallic Union from its organization. Author: Appreciation of Money, 1877; Source of Value in Money, 1882; also numerous pamphlets and monographs on various subjects. Died 1910.

WARNER, ALBERT LYMAN, radio news corr., editor; b. Bklyn., Mar. 1, 1903; s. Edwin G. and Euphemia Jane Gray (Lawson) W.; Bachelor of Arts, Amherst College, 1924, Master of Arts (honorary), 1954; student Columbia, 1925-26; m. Harriet West Rowe, Apr. 27, 1929;children—Edwin Gaylord II, Albert Lyman, Jr.; reporter Daily Eagle, 1924; legislative corr., N.Y. Times, Albany, 1926-29; asst. chief Washington Bur., N.Y. Herald-Tribune, 1930-36, chief of bur., 1936-39; covered Presdl. campaigns, 1928-56, World Econ. Conf., London, 1933, Inter Am. Conf., Havana, 1940. Washington Corr. and Commentator, C.B.S., March 1939-42; chief Washington news bur. Mutual Broadcasting Co., 1945-49, Am. Broadcasting Company, 1949-50, 54-56, NBC Three Star Extra, 1950-53; asso. editor U.S. News and World Report, 1956-71. Mem. White House Com. on Employment Physically Handicapped, 1946-56. Commd. major in Army the U.S., July 2, 1942, col., chief War Intelligence Div., Bur. Public Relations; temporary duty, ETO; broadcast Army Hour review of military operations; pioneered boradcasting of Congressional hearings. Received the first annual award for radio newswriting, Sigma Delta Chi, 1940; Legion of Merit, 1945; Headliners Radio News award, 1948. Mem. Amherst Alumni Council, 1925. Mem. White House Corr. Assn. (v.p. 1933-34, pres. 1935-36), Radio Corr. Assns. (v.p. 1939-40; pres. 1940-41 and 1948-49), Delta Kappa Epsilon, Phi Beta Kappa. Conglist. Clubs: Nat. Press, Gridirion, Cosmos, Overseas Writers (Washington). Contbr. mags. Home: McLean VA Died Jan. 11, 1971; buried Burdett NY

WARNER, MILO JOSEPH lawyer; b. Lime City, O., Nov. 11, 1891; s. Smith and Mary Ellen (Brownsberger) W.; A.B. Ohio State U., 1913, LL.B., 1916; m. Dorothy Casad Bennett, June 1, 1917; children—Milo Joseph, Donald W., and Carolyn B. (Mrs. Charles A. Harrison, Jr.). Admitted to Ohio bar, 1916; with Doyle, Lewis & Warner, Toledo, Ohio, since 1919, mem. firm since 1924, specializing insurance and R.R. law; spl. asst. to atty. gen. of Ohio, 1942-44. Pres. Toledo Legal Aid Society, 1957-59. Mem. Ohio Judicial Council, 1948-51, U.S. Regional Loyalty Bd. Mem. drafting com. Council State Govts.; mem. Ohio Defense Council, Ohio Nat. Defense Savings Com., 1941-44; civilian aide (Ohio) to secretary of army. Served with Ohio Nat. Guard cavalry, 1910-17; commd. 1st lt., O.N.G., Mar. 1917; commd. U.S. Army, June 3, 1917, and served as capt., 1917-18, comdg. Bat. B, 76 F.A., 3d Div.; now capt. retired. Awarded Purple Heart; Legion of Honor (France). Mem. Toledo Industrial Peace Bd., 1935-44. Mem. Am., Ohio State, Toledo (pres. 1935) bar assns., Am. Legion (nat. comdr. 1940; mem. mission to Eng. 1941), Pi Kappa Alpha, Phi Delta Phi. Honorary dominion pres. Canadian Legion of British Empire Service League; dir. Boys Club of Toledo, Toledo council Boy Scouts Am. Mason (32 deg.). Republican. Methodist. Clubs: Toledo, Inverness (Toledo); University (Columbus, O.); Army and Navy, Capitol Hill (Washington); Ohio Society of N.Y. (v.p. 1941-43). Home: 4250 Brookside Rd. Office: Nat. Bank Bldg., Toledo 4. Died Jan. 1968.

WARNER, RAWLEIGH, corporation exec.; b. Chgo., Ill., May 14, 1891; s. Samuel Rohrer and Mary Belle (Rawleigh) W.; student Lawrenceville (N.J.) School; Litt.B., Princeton University, 1913; LL.D., Marietta Coll., 1955; m. Dorothy Haskins, October 14, 1914; children—Mary (Clifford), Dorothy (Ryburn), Rawleigh, Suzanne (Kenly). Treas. Central Sugar Co., 1915-17; with Dawes Bros. Inc., 1919-39, as v.p., dir.; v.p., treas., dir. Pure Oil Co., 1926-47, chmn. bd., 1947-63, dir., chmn. exec. com., 1963-65. Spl. adviser to sec. of Navy, World War II; mem. Hoover Commn. Life trustee Northwestern U., Crerar Library, Chgo.; bd. dirs. Soc. Prevention Blindness; trustee Lawrenceville Sch., 1938-52. Served as 1st lt. U.S. Army, 1917-18. Recipient Distinguished Service award Dept. Navy. Mem. 25 Year Club Am. Petroleum Industry (pres. 1952-53). Conglist. Clubs: Commercial, Chicago, Old Elm Country, Indian Hill, Lake Geneva Country. Home: Winnetka IL Died Jan. 8, 1971; buried Winnetka Congl. Ch. Churchyard, Winnetka IL

WARNER, RICHARD AMBROSE Naval officer; b. Washington, D.C., July 4, 1878; s. John and Katherine Theresa (Keating) W.; student, Lehigh U., 1896-97; M.D., Georgetown U., 1901; m. Mary Cathcart Ransdell, Sept. 26, 1907; 1 dau., Mary Cathcart. Practicing physician and surgeon, Washington, (D.C.); Pekin (Peiping, China). Commd. M.C., U.S.N., 1905, commodor, M.C., U.S.N. 1944-—. Fellow Am. Coll. Surgery. Clubs: Army and Navy (Washington, D.C.), 1901-05. Home: 3716 49th St. N.W. Office: Navy Dept., Washington 25, D.C. Died Jan. 5, 1955.

WARNER, SETH army officer; b. Roxbury, Conn., Apr. 25, 1795; s. Dr. Benjamin and Silence (Hurd) W.; m. Hester Hurd, 1765, 3 children. Leader (with Ethan Allen and others) people of Vt. in resisting attempts of N.Y. to control Colony of Vt.; outlawed by N.Y. Gen. Assembly, 1772; aided Ethan Allen and Benedict Arnold in capture of Ticonderoga, 1775, Crown Point, 1775; obtained authorization of Continental Congress (with Allen) for creation of regt. called Green Mountain Boys, elected lt. col., commandant, 1775; brought up rear forces during Am. retreat from Can. and collected reinforcements in Vt., 1776; arrived with regt. during latter part of Battle of Bennington, responsible for Am. victory, 1777; promoted brig. gen. by Vt. Assembly, 1778. Died Roxbury, Dec. 26, 1784.

WARNER, WILLARD senator; b. Granville, O., Sept. 4, 1826; s. Willard and Eliva (Williams) W.; grad. Marietta Coll., 1845, LL.D. Served in army, 1861-65, as maj. and lt. col. 76th Ohio vol. inf.; col. 180th O. vol. inf., and insp. gen. on staff Gen. Wm. T. Sherman; bvtd. brig. gen. and maj. gen.; went to Ala., 1865, and to live in 1867; removed to Chattanooga, 1890. Mem. Ohio senate, 1866-67; mem. Ala. legislature, 1868; elected to U.S. Senate from Ala., 1868; collector port of Mobile, Ala., 1871-72; apptd. and confirmed gov. of New Mexico, 1872, but declined; mem. Tenn. legislature, 1897-98; mfr. of pig iron in Ala., 1873-90; built two blast furnaces at Nashville, Tenn., 1887-88, and one at Tecumseh, Ala., 1873-74; and Richmond Spinning Mill, Chattanooga, Tenn., in 1899; pres. Chattanooga Coffin & Casket Co.; dir. Chattanooga Savings Bank, Richmond Spinning Co. and Chattanooga Wagon Co.;

1st v.p. Chattanooga Mfrs.' Assn. Del. Rep. Nat. convs., 1860, 68, 76, 80 and 88. Home: Chattanooga, Tenn. Died 1906.

WARNER, WILLIAM EVERETT, educator; b. Roanoke, Ill., Aug. 22, 1897; s. Issac and Eva (Redmon) W.; diploma Wis. State U., Platteville, 1917; B.S., U. Wis., 1923, M.S., 1924; Ph.D. in Ednl. Research, Columbia, 1928; m. Ellen A. Todd, Aug. 14, 1920. Tchr. and prin. pub. and vocational schs., Wis. and N.Y., 1917-24; from asst. prof. to grad. prof. edn. Ohio State U., 1925-67, prof. emeritus, 1967-71; exec. dir. Civil Def. Ohio, 1950-53; cons. U.S. Office edn., 1934, Tuskegee Inst., 1936-37, 68, U.S. Office Civil Def., 1943, Am. Legion, 1946, Nat. Safety Council, 1948-51, Indonesia In-Service Indsl. Tng. Program, 1957-59, Philippine Indsl. Arts Assn., 1962, Canadian Indsl. Arts Assn., 1964-71, So. Assn. Colls. and Schs., 1965-71; pres. Adv. Com. Indsl. Safety, 1948. Served as pvt. F.A.C.O.T.S., World War I; as lt. col. World War II at SHAEF. Member International Executive Service Corps. Decorated Bronze Star, Purple Heart; Order Leopold II, Mil. Cross, Premier medal Nat. Red Cross (Belgium); named Colonel in Kentucky and Oklahoma; recipient Distinguished Alumnus award Wis. State U. and Inst. Tech., Platteville, 1963; Distinguished Service citation Ohio State U. Seminar, 1966; citation eminence Kent State U., 1967; registered Coll. of Arms, London, Eng., 1944. Fellow Internat. Inst. Arts and Letters: mem. Newcomen Soc. Eng., Am. Legion, Am. Vocational Assn., Am. Indsl. Arts Assn. (founder 1939, pres. 1939-41), Res. Officers Assn. (pres. Ohio 1948-49, security officer 1947-56), Am. Council Indsl. Arts Tchrs. Edn. (hon.), Mil. Order Purple Heart, Phi Delta Kappa, Kappa Delta Pi, Omicron Delta Kappa, Epsilon Pi Tau (hon.; founder 1929, exec. sec. 1929-71). Republican. Rotarian. Clubs: Faculty (Columbus); Army and Navy (Washington). Author 2 books, other writings. Editor Epsilon Pi Tau brochure series, 1929-71), Western Arts Assn. publs., 1932-37; cons. editor Arts and Industries series. A pioneer indsl. arts edn., speaker, lectr. before numerous groups in field. Address: Columbus OH Died July 12, 1971; buried Forest Cemetery, Stevens Point WI

WARNICK, SPENCER K(ELLOGG), banker; b. Amsterdam, N.Y., Sept. 14, 1874; s. Middleton and Marion (Kellogg) W.; A.B. cum laude, Yale, 1895; m. Jane M. Greene, June 1, 1898; children—Spencer K., Henry G. Admitted to N.Y. State bar, Nov. 1897; in pvt. practice, Amsterdam, N.Y., 1897-1925; asst. dist. atty., Montgomery County, N.Y., 1900-02; exec. vice pres. Montgomery County, N.Y., 1900-02; exec. vice pres. Montgomery County Trust Co., 1925-36, pres. since 1936, dir. since 1912. Dir. Mohawk Carpet Mills. Served as mem. N.Y. State Senate, 1902-06, chmn. com. on public instrn., 1902-06; appointed mem. commn. authorized by legislature of State of N.Y. to investigate and revise tax laws of state, June 7, 1906. Post master Amsterdam, N.Y., 1921-25. Commd. major, J.A.G.D., N.G. N.Y., July 31, 1917; disch. rank of maj., U.S. Army, 1919. Dir. and enrollment officer N.Y. State Mil. census, 1916. Trustee: Amsterdam Free Library Assn., Green Hill Cemetery Assn. Trustee Montgomery County Hist. Soc., Mem. Zeta Psi. Republican. Presbyterian (trustee). Elk. Mason (Shriner). Club: Antlers Country. Home: 21 Grant Av. Office: Six Market St., Amsterdam NY

WARNOCK, WILLIAM ROBERT ex-congressman; b. Urbana, O., Aug. 29, 1838; s. Rev. David and Sarah (Hitt) W.; A.B., Ohio Wesleyan U., 1861, A.M., 1864 (LL.D., 1901); capt. Co. G, 95th Ohio Vols., July, 1862; maj., Aug., 1863, "for gallantry at siege of Vicksburg"; bvtd. lt.-col., Mar. 9, 1865, "for gallantry at battle of Nashville, Dec. 16, 1864"; m. Kathryn Murray, of Springfield, O., Aug. 20, 1868. Admitted to bar, 1866; practiced at Urbana. Pros. atty. Champaign Co., O., 1867-72; mem. Ohio Senate, 1876-77; judge Ct. of Common Pleas, 2d Jud. Dist., 1879-89; mem. 57th, 58th Congresses (1901-05), 8th Ohio Dist.; U.S. pension agt. at Columbus, O., 1906-10. Republican. Comdr. Ohio Commandery Mil. Order Loyal Legion, 1898-1900; comdr. Dept. of Ohio G.A.R., 1913-14; del. Gen. Conf. M.E. Ch., 1876, 1900, 1904. Home: Urbana, Ohio.

WARREN, CHARLES ELLIOTT banker; b. N.Y. City, Apr. 9, 1864; s. George William and Mary Elizabeth (Pease) W.; prep. edn., St. Paul's Sch., Garden City, N.Y.; student U. of Calif.; m. Anna Margaret Geissenhainer, Apr. 19, 1892. Began in banking business in N.Y. City, 1882; pres. Lincoln Nat. Bank, 1910-20; v.p. and chairman advisory board, Lincoln office of Irving Trust Co.; pres. Erie & Kalamazoo R.R. Co., Lake Shore & Mich. Southern R.R. Co., Lessee; pres. Nestor Mfg. Co.; treas., dir. Luth. Cemetery (New York). Vice-gov. War Credits Bd., Washington, 1917-18. Served in 7th Regt., later in 12th Regt., N.Y. Nat. Guard, beginning as pvt., advanced to lt. col. brigade and div. staff; major, 3d N.Y. inf. brigade, Spanish-Am. war; maj., lt. col. and col. Ordnance Corps, U.S. Army, World War I; col. 514th Coast Arty., U.S. Army; brig. gen., N.Y. Nat. Guard; comdt. Vet. Corps Arty., N.Y. City; col. Coast Arty., Reserve U.S. Army. Medal N.Y. Nat. Guard, also for Spanish-Am. war, State of N.Y. and Mexican Border service; Victory medal, Conspicuous Service Cross, D.S.M. (U.S.); Médaille de la Reconnaissance and Legion of Honor. Mem. N.Y. State Bankers Assn. (pres. 1915-16), Pilgrims, N.Y. Hist. Soc., Mayflower Soc., Soc. Colonial Wars, Colonial Order of the Acorn, S.R., Soc. of the Cincinnati, Soc. War of 1812, Loyal Legion, Army Ordnance Assn. (treas., dir.), Vets. of 7th Regt., N.Y. (107th U.S. Inf.), Am. Legion, Mil. Order Fgn. Wars, Soc. Am. Wars, N.Y. Soc. Mil. and Naval Officers World War, Mil. Order World Wars, Am. Tract Soc. (treas.), Order of the Runnemede. Republican. Episcopalian. Clubs: Military and Naval, Metropolitan, St. Nicholas Society (New York); Rockaway Hunting, Lawrence Beach. Home: Hewlett Neck Rd., Hewlett, L.I., N.Y. Office: 100 E. 42d St., New York, N.Y. Died Dec. 25, 1945.

WARREN, FRANCIS EMROY senator; b. Hinsdale, Mass., June 20, 1844; s. Joseph S. and Cynthia Estella (Abbott) W.; acad. edn. in Mass.; pvt. and noncommd. officer 49th Mass. Vols., 1862-63; received Congressional Medal of Honor "for gallantry on battlefield at siege of Port Hudson"; later capt. Mass. Militia; m. Helen M. Smith, Jan. 26, 1871 (died 1902); m. 2d, Clara Le Baron Morgan, June 28, 1911. Engaged as farmer and stockraiser in Mass.; moved to Wyo., then part of Ty. of Dak., 1868; became interested in real estate, mercantile, live stock and lighting business in Cheyenne; mem. territorial Senate, 1873-74 (pres.) and 1884-85; mem. City Council, Cheyenne, 1873-74, and again, 1883-85; mayor of Cheyenne, 1885; apptd. territorial treas. 1876, 79, 82, 84; del. Rep. Nat. Conv., Chicago, 1888; chmn. Wyo. delegation to Rep. Nat. Conv., Phila., 1900, Chicago, 1904, 08, 12; chmn. Rep. Territorial Central Com., and Rep. State Central Com. of Wyo., 1896; apptd. gov. of Wyo. by President Arthur, Feb. 1885, and removed by President Cleveland, Nov. 1886; again apptd. gov. by President Harrison, Mar. 1889, and served until the territory was admitted as a state into the Union. Elected first gov. of Wyo., 1890; elected as a Republican to U.S. Senate, Nov. 18, 1890, and served until Mar. 4, 1893; resumed stock raising, farming, merchandising, etc.; again elected to Senate, 1894, and regularly reëlected to 1931. Home: Cheyenne, Wyo. Died Nov. 24, 1929.

WARREN, GOUVERNEUR KEMBLE army officer, engr.; b. Cold Spring, N.Y., Jan. 8, 1830; s. Sylvanus Warren; grad. U.S. Mil. Acad., 1850; m. Emily Forbes Chase, June 17, 1863, 2 children. Brevetted 2d lt. Corps Topog. Engrs., 1850, commd. 2d lt., 1854, 1st lt., 1856; engaged in making map and reconnaissances of Dakota Territory, 1856-59; asst. prof. mathematics U.S. Mil. Acad., 1859-61; lt. col. 5th N.Y. Volunteers, 1861; col. of a regt. of engrs. U.S. Army, 1861, capt., 1861; brevetted lt. col. for service in Battle of Gaine's Mill, 1862; brig. gen. U.S. Volunteers, 1862; chief topographic engr. Army of Potomac, 1863; brevetted col. U.S. Army for services in Battle of Gettysburg; commd. maj., 1864, brevetted maj. gen., 1865; resigned volunteer commn. 1865, re-entered Corps Engrs., U.S. Army; superintending engr. of surveys and improvements of upper Mississippi River; commd. lt. col. Corps Engrs., 1879; mem. Am. Philos. Soc., Nat. Acad. Sciences. Author: An Account of the Operations of the Fifth Army Corps, 1866; Report on Bridging the Mississippi River between St. Paul, Minnesota and St. Louis, Missouri, 1878. Died Newport, R.I., Aug. 8, 1882.

WARREN, JAMES GOOLD army officer; b. at Buffalo, Sept. 12, 1958; s. Joseph and Jane Vail (Goold) W.; grad. U.S. Mil. Acad., 1881; m. Sarah Clifton Wheeler, of West Point, N.Y., July 6, 1881 (died May 4, 1901). Commd. additional 2d lt. engrs., June 11, 1881; 2d, lt., Apr. 5, 1882; 1st lt., Mar. 26, 1883; capt., Apr. 12, 1894; maj., May 3, 1901; lt.-col., Nov. 15, 1907; col., Feb. 27, 1912. Service with engr. troops at Engr. Sch. and U.S. Mil. Acad.; in charge of constrn. of fortification and river and harbor works at various points; now div. engr. Lakes Div., in charge divs. of water for power purposes at Niagraa Falls. Mem. Am. Soc. C.E., Western Soc. Engrs., Mil. Service Instn. U.S. Episcopalian. Clubs: Army and Navy (Washington and New York), Buffalo, Saturn, University (Buffalo). Office: Federal Bldg., Buffalo, N.Y.

WARREN, MINTON M(ACHADO) cons. engr.; b. Salem, Mass., Aug. 7, 1888; s. Minton and Salome A. (Machado) W.; desc. in 10th generation from Richard Warren of the Mayflower, 1620; prep. edn., Browne and Nichols Sch., Cambridge, Mass.; A.B. cum laude, Harvard, 1910, M.C.E., 1912; m. Sarah Ripley Robbins, Sept. 17, 1927; children—Minton, William Bradford. Began engring. service under Hugh L. Cooper, on dam across Miss. River at Keokuk, Ia.; with Stone & Webster, constrn. engrs., 10 yrs., in design, constrn. and management; after World War I, served as chief engr. Technicolor Motion Picture Corp., also starting prodn. of several indsl. plants, in New England and Calif.; organized Aero Supply Co., mfrs. of hardware and fittings for airplane cos., in 1925; went to England, 1928, arranged for manufacture of the De Havilland Moth plane in the U.S. and was apptd. pres. of co. in U.S. and in charge of factory in Lowell, Mass.; v.p., mgr. and dir. Curtiss-Wright airplane mfg. plant at St. Louis, later sec. Curtiss-Wright Corp., Wright Aeronautical Corp., etc., until 1931; cons. practice N.Y. City and Boston since 1920; dir. research, Van Alstyne, Noel & Co., N.Y.; pres. and dir. Aeronautical Securities, Inc.; dir. Hercules Steel Products Corp. Commd. 1st lt. engrs., U.S. Army, Aug. 1917, capt., Aug. 1918; with 26th Div. in France; organized the first Am. topographical sect. participated in actions at Chemin-des-Dames, Chauteau Thierry, St. Mihiel, and Meuse-Argonne, at Verdun. Known for original research work in "water hammer," and discovery of formulas in hydraulics now largely adopted. Mem. Am. Soc. C.E., Harvard Engring. Soc. (pres. 1941-42), Soc. Mayflower Descendants. Republican. Episcopalian. Clubs: Harvard, City Midday Church Club (New York); Harvard (Boston). Home: 55 E. 86th St. Died Nov. 4, 1947.

WARREN, SIR PETER naval officer; b. Warrenstown, County Meath, Ireland, Mar. 10, 1703; m. Susannah De Lancey, July 1731, 6 children including Anne (Warren) Fitzroy, Susannah (Warren) Skinner, Charlotte (Warren) Abingdon. Entered Brit. Navy as midshipman, 1715; served in West Indies and off N.Am. coast in ship Rose, 1718; served in N.Y. Harbor as capt., comdr. H.M.S. Solebay, 1730; purchased tract of 14,000 acres in Mohawk Valley, N.Y., 1736, established Warren Farm (now Greenwich Village, N.Y.C.); commanded gunboats Squirrel, 1735-42, Launceton, 1742-45, Superbe, promoted to rear adm. of Blue fleet, 1745; took part in capture of Louisbourg, 1745; gov. of Louisbourg and Cape Breton Island, 1745; mem. Gov.'s Council of N.Y.; led Brit. naval force to victory over French off Cape Finistere, 1747; knighted with Cross of Bath, 1747; vice adm. of White fleet, 1747, Red fleet, 1748; Warren Street (N.Y.C.) named for him. Died Dublin, Ireland, July 29, 1752; buried church at Knockmark, nr. Warrenstown, Ireland.

WARREN, WILLIAM HOMER chemist; b. Charleston, S.C., Nov. 4, 1866; s. George William and Harriet (Strong) W.; A.B., Harvard, 1889, A.M., 1891, Ph.D., 1892; studied U. of Heidelberg, 1905, 06; m. Lucy Ellen Sargeant, of East Saugus, Mass., Dec. 20, 1894; children—Katharine, Priscilla, Juliet. Chemist, E. R. Squibb & Sons, Brooklyn, N.Y., 1892-96, New York Quinine & Chem. Works, Brooklyn, 1896-97; prof. chemistry, Washington U. Med. Sch., St. Louis, 1898-1911, sec. faculty, 1901-08, dean 1908-10; asst. prof. chemistry, Clark Coll., Worcester, Mass., 1911-12; univ. docent, Clark U., 1911-12; prof. chemistry, Wheaton Coll., Norton, Mass., 1912-17; chemist Peerless Color Co., 1919-22, Noil Color and Chem. Works, 1922-25; prof. chemistry, Clark U., since 1925. Commd. capt., Q.M.R.C., and on active duty at Camp Hancock, Augusta, Ga., and Washington, D.C., 1917-18; capt. Chem. Warfare Service, with A.E.F. in France; with Am. Commn. to Negotiate Peace, Paris. Mem. Am. Chem. Soc., Am. Inst. Chemists, Mil. Order World War, Deutsche Chemische Gesellschaft, Phi Beta Kappa. Translator: Autenrieth's Auffindung der Gifte, 1905. Home: 166 Woodland St., Worcester, Mass.

WARRINGTON, LEWIS naval officer; b. Williamsburg, Va., Nov. 3, 1782; attended Coll. William and Mary; m. Margaret Cary King, Mar. 3, 1817. Apptd. midshipman U.S. Navy, 1800; cruised West Indies in Chesapeake; participated in war with Barbary corsairs in ships President, Vixen and Enterprise, 1802-07; promoted lt., 1805; attached to Siren, 1809; 1st lt. in Congress during War of 1812; commd. master comdt., 1813; took command of sloop-of-war Peacock, 1813; forced Brit. brig Epervier to surrender, 1814; awarded gold medal by Congress, sword by State of Va., took many prizes during War of 1812; commanded the Macedonian, 1816, Java, 1819-20, Guerriere of Mediterranean Squadron, 1820-21; commr. of Navy bd. charged with adminstrn. of naval materiel, 1826-30, 40-42; chief Bur. Yards and Docks, 1842-46; U.S. sec. of navy ad interim, 1844; chief Bureau of Ordnance, 1846-51. Died Washington, D.C., Oct. 12, 1851.

WARWICK, HERBERT SHERWOOD, JR., educator, historian; b. Columbus, O., Mar. 4, 1910; s. Herbert Sherwood and Hazel (Hain) W.; A.B., Princeton, 1930, M.A., Ohio State U., 1931, Ph.D., 1934; student Louisville Presbyn. Sem., 1950-55; m. Bertella Mae Lee, Aug. 30, 1941; 1 dau., Judith Lee (Mrs. Derek Thompson). Successively univ. scholar, fellow, asst. history Ohio State U., 1930-33; mem. faculty U. Louisville, 1934-70, prof. history 1951-70, head dept., 1964-70. Sec. Atlantic Union Com., 1949-62. Served to capt. USAAF, 1942-45. Mem. Am. Hist. Assn., Orgn. Am. Historians, English Speaking Union. Democrat. Episcopalian. Mason. Home: Louisville KY Died 1970.

WASH, CARLYLE HILTON army officer; b. Minneapolis, Minn., Oct. 15, 1889; s. James Alexander and Helen (Turnbull) W.; B.S., U.S. Mil. Acad., West Point, N.Y., 1913; m. Constance Rogers, May 14, 1919; 1 dau., Elizabeth Patricia (Mrs. Samuel Knox Eaton). Commd. 2d lt., Cav., 1913, advanced through ranks to brig. gen., 1940; with Pershing Expdn., Mexico, 1916; transferred to Air Corps, 1917; served in World War, 1917-18; comdg. gen., 2d Interceptor Command, since 1940. Clubs: Army and Navy (Washington, D.C.); Seattle Country (Seattle, Wash.); University (Tacoma, Wash.). Address: War Dept., Washington, D.C. Died Jan. 26, 1943.

WASHBURN, F(RANK) S(HERMAN) chem. co. exec.; b. Somers, N.Y., Sept. 13, 1895; s. Frank Sherman and Irene (Russell) W.; student Morristown Sch., Hill Sch., Cornell U.; m. Evalyn Nesbitt, Apr. 30, 1919; 1

dau., Evalyn Nesbitt. Joined Am. Cyanamid Co., 1918, div. sales mgr., 1924, asst. dir. fertilizer sales, 1938, dir. 1939, dir. agrl. chemicals, 1947—, dir. co., 1946—; dir. Goodman Mfg. Co.; pres. N.Am. Cyanamid, Ltd., 1951-59. Served as lt. (j.g.) USN, 1917-18. Mem. Fla. Phosphate Rock Producers Industry Adv. Com., WPB, 1943-45; chmn. phosphate rock industry adv. com. of OPA, 1944-46; dir. Am. Food Plant Food Council, Inc., 1945-48, 49-50. Mem. Nat. Agrl. Chems. Assn., Delta Phi. Republican. Mason. Club: University (Larchmont). Home: Larchmont, N.Y. Office: 30 Rockefeller Plaza, N.Y.C. 20. Died Apr. 1963.

WASHBURN, FREDERIC AUGUSTUS physician; b. New Bedford, Mass., Nov. 22, 1869; s. Frederic Augustus and Mary Jane (Swan) W.; A.B., Amherst, 1892, M.A., 1928; M.D., Harvard, 1896; m. Amy Silsbee Appleton, Jan. 10, 1911; 1 dau., Amy (Mrs. Thomas Stewart Hamilton, Jr.). Asst. dir., Mass. Gen. Hosp., 1898-99 and 1903-08, dir., 1908-34, dir. emeritus since 1934; and dir. Mass. Eye and Ear Infirmary, 1915-34; commr. institutions, City of Boston, 1934-37; dir. Cambridge Hosp., 1937-40, cons. dir. 1940-47; director during World War II. Assistant surgeon and surg. U.S. Vols., 1898-1903; served in Puerto Rico, 1898, Philippines, 1899-1903; major comdg. Base Hosp. 6, A.E.F., in France, 1917; lt. col. Med. Corps, in charge hospitalization, Am. Hosps. in Gt. Britain; col., chief surgeon, Base Sect. 3, A.E.F., London, Oct. 1918, Mar. 1919. Awarded D.S.M.; Companion Order St. Michael and St. George (British), award of merit and medal American Hospital Association, 1941. Trustee Gardner State Hospital, 1923-38, chairman, 1923-35; ex-president Truro Neighborhood Association. Member A.M.A. (council med. edn. and hosps. 1932-38), Am. Hosp. Assn. (pres. 1912-13), Mass. Med. Soc., Mil. Order World War (comdr. Greater Boston Chapter 1923-24), Mass. Soc. Mayflower Descendants (gov. 1923-27). Club: Medical Superintendents (pres. 1921-33). Home: 190 Bay State Rd., Boston 15, Mass. Died Aug. 20, 1949.

WASHBURN, HENRY DANA congressman; b. Windsor, Vt., Mar. 28, 1832; attended common schs.; grad. N.Y. State and Nat. Law Schs. A tanner, currier and sch. tchr., in youth; admitted to bar, 1853, began practice of law, Newport, Ind.; county auditor, 1854-61; commd. lt. col. 18th Regt., Ind. Volunteer Inf., 1861, promoted col., 1862; brevetted brig. gen. Volunteers, 1864, maj. gen., 1865; mem. U.S. Ho. of Reps. (Republican, contested election) from Ind., 39th-40th congresses, Feb. 23, 1866-69; surveyor gen. Mont., 1869-71, headed expdn. to find headwaters of Yellowstone River, 1870, discovered Yellowstone Park; Mt. Washburn (Mont.) named for him. Died Clinton, Ind., Jan. 26, 1871; buried Riverside Cemetery.

WASHBURN, HOMER CHARLES coll. dean; b. Greenwich, O., Jan. 8, 1876; s. William Irving and Almira Bendora (Salsbury) W.; Ph.C., U. Mich., 1902, B.S. in Pharmacy, 1904; m. Mary Lavina Beckley, Dec. 14, 1902 (dec.); 1 dau., Helen. Began teaching, U. Okla., 1904, dean Sch. Pharmacy, 1905-11; organizer, 1911, and prof. Coll. Pharmacy, U. Colo., also dean, 1913-43; ret., 1943. Mem. 32d Mich. Vol. Inf., Spanish-Am. War, 1898; mem. inf. Mich. N.G., 1900-01; mem. 1st Cav., Colo. N.G., 1915-17, capt., 1915; in. Fed. Service, 1916, maj., 1917; maj. 157th inf. U.S. Army, World War I; grad. Army Small Arms Firing Sch., Camp Perry, O., and Army Sch. of the Line, Langres, France, lt. col. Inf. Res. Corps, U.S. Army, 1920; promoted col., 1923; ret. with rank of col., 1954, with credit for 24 yrs. and 6 months of service. Fellow A.A.A.S.; mem. Am. Geog. Soc., Am. Pharm. Assn., 157th Inf. Assn., Res. Officers' Assn. U.S., Res. Officers' Assn. Colo. (pres. 1928-29), United Spanish War Vet., Am. Legion, Kappa Sigma, Acacia, Alpha Chi Sigma, Phi Delta Chi, Omega Upsilon Phi. Mason. Author: (with Walter H. Blome) Textbook on Pharmacognosy and Materia Medica; (with Carl J. Klemme) Textbook on Beginning Pharmacy. Address: 1291 Paseo El Mirador, Palm Springs, Cal. 92262. Died Jan. 7, 1964.

WASHBURN, STANLEY war corr., author; b. Minneapolis, Feb. 7, 1878; s. U.S. Senator William Drew and Elizabeth M. (Muzzy) W.; A.B., Williams Coll., 1901, hon. Dr. Humane Letters, 1921; attended Harvard Law Sch., 1901; m. Alice Langhorne, Nov. 27, 1906; children—Fawan, Stanley, Langhorne. Attached Minneapolis Journal, 1901-02; on staff Minneapolis Times, 1902-04; war corr. Chicago Daily News, 1904-06. Covered Russo-Japanese War, operated dispatch boat "Fawan" 4 mos., at fall of Port Arthur; with Nogi's army before Port Arthur; served with 3d Japanese Army until end of war; organized news service in Far East and India; operated dispatch boat in Black Sea, Dec. 1905, carrying British and U.S. Govt. official dispatches, mail and refugees; covered Russian Revolution, 1905; went again to Europe, Aug. 1914, as corr. Collier's Weekly, to Russia, Sept. 1914, as spl. corr. London Times, attached to Russian Army for 26 mos., only Am. having access to whole Russian front; also with French at Verdun, Apr. 1916, and attached to Roumanian Army 2 mos., 1916. Wrote foreign policy of Russia for Russian Govt., 1916; wrote case of Roumania for King, 1916; attached to Sec. of State Lansing as mil. advisor, 1917. Commd. maj. Minn. N.G., Apr. 1915, col., Feb. 1916, as aide on gov.'s staff; apptd. maj., cav., O.R.C., May 5, 1917; active duty May 9, as mil. aide to John F. Stevens, adv. railroad mission to Russia; transferred at Vladivostok to Root diplomatic mission to Russia as mil. aide and asst. sec. of mission; G2 of 26th Div., in France, Apr. 1, 1918; served in Toul and Chateau-Thierry sectors with that div.; invalided home, Sept. 1918; hon. disch., Jan. 27, 1919; lt. col. Mil. Intelligence Dept., June 10, 1931; mil. aide to Queen Marie of Roumania during visit U.S., 1926. Before leaving for France, by request Russian Embassy, detailed by State and War depts. to make speaking tour through 35 states presenting case of Russia in the war. Decorated by Emperor of Japan, Order Imperial Crown, 1907; by Czar, Order of St. Anna, 1915; by Gen. Brossilov, Order of St. George, 1916; by King of Roumania, Comdr. Order of Crown; awarded Am. Service Ribbon with 2 silver stars, 1919. Hon. mem. Japanese Red Cross Soc. Del. Rep. Nat. Conv., Chicago, 1912. Apptd. by State Dept. to secretariat of Am. Delegation to Disarmament Conf., to do liaison between Am. and Japanese delegations, Washington, 1921. Pres. Washburn Lignite Coal Co., Wilton, N.D., 1926-29. Pres. N.D. Coal Operators Assn., 1925-35; v.p. and nat. councilor Greater N.D. Assn.; dir. Nat. Security League; chmn. Russian com. Nat. Civic Fedn., 1920-35; trustee Am. Defense Soc. Mason, Elk. Pres. Willkie Club of Lakewood, 1940; chmn. affiliated Rep. Clubs, Lakewood, 1936. Clubs: University, Century (N.Y.C.); Delta Psi. Member of the American Legion, also member of the Veterans Foreign Wars. Made 1000 speeches in 42 different states since 1917; war corr. or soldier with 20 armies; covered approximately 100 battles since 1904. Author: The Cable Game, 1911; Nogi—The Man Against the Background of a War, 1913; Field Notes from the Russian Front, 1915; The Russian Campaign, April to August, 1915; The Russian Offensive, 1917. Writer of propaganda for British, Russian and French, 1939-40; speaker and broadcaster on morale, mil. and naval intelligence, etc. Contbr. to newspapers. Home: Inverfirs, Lakewood, N.J. Died Dec. 14, 1950; buried Arlington Nat. Cemetery.

WASHBURN, VICTOR DUKE med. dir.; b. N.Y.C. July 16, 1882; s. Charles H. and Carlotta (Sorino) W.; M.D., Atlantic Med. Coll., Balt., 1905; Dr. Pub. Service, U. Del., 1953; m. 2d, Margaret A. Elliott, Oct. 26, 1915 (dec. Jan. 1960); children—(by 1st marriage) Ruth, (by 2d marriage) Elliott Sorino; m. 3d, Helen G. Northwood, Feb. 4, 1961. Urologist, 1905-51; cons. urology Meml. Hosp., Wilmington, Del., 1951—, med. dir., 1951-59. Mem. Wilmington Bd. Edn., 1915-27, pres., 1923-27; dir. Pub. Safety, 1927-30, pres., 1928-30; pres. Bd. Health, 1946-47; health commr., 1948-52; state dir. Selective Service, 1948-50. Served as 1st lt. MRC., U.S. Army, 1917-19; col. AUS, World War II; now brig.-gen. Del. N.G. (ret.). Awarded Del. N.G. Conspicuous Service Cross, 1941. Mem. A.M.A., Assn. Mil. Surgeons, S.A.R. Republican. Unitarian. Mason. Club: University. Home: 702 Blackshire Rd., Wilmington 19805. Office: 822 Washington St., Wilmington 1, Del. Died Sept. 24, 1966; buried Osceola, Pa.

WASHINGTON, GEORGE 1st Pres. U.S.; b. Bridges Creek, Westmoreland County, Va., Feb. 22, 1732; s. Augustine and Mary (Ball) W.; ed. privately; m. Mrs. Martha (Dandridge) Custis, Jan. 6, 1759, 2 stepchildren. Aided in survey of Shenandoah Valley, Va., 1748; apptd. county surveyor Culpeper County (Va.), 1749; inherited estate "Mt. Vernon" from half-brother Lawrence, 1752; apptd. by Gov. Robert Dinwiddie dist. adj. for S. Va., 1752; apptd. by Dinwiddie to carry ultimatum to French to leave English lands in Ohio country, 1753, received unconciliatory reply, also instructed to strengthen ties with the Six Nations, his report to Dinwiddie printed as Journal of Major George Washington . . ., 1754; commd. lt. col. Va. Militia, 1754; recommended establishment of post on site of present Pitts., found French entrenched there; erected Ft. Necessity, Great Meadow, Pa.; surprised and defeated French force, May 27, obtained generous terms in parley with French after 10-hour battle, July 3, 1754; served in unsuccessful expdn. under Gen. Braddock against Ft. Duquesne, 1755; apptd. col. and comdr.-in-chief of all Va. forces, 1755, responsible for defending 300 miles of mountainous frontier with about 300 men, 1755-58; accompanied British under Gen. Forbes who occupied Ft. Duquesne, 1758; resigned and became gentleman farmer, Mt. Vernon, 1759; contbr. to instns. including Washington Coll., Md., Liberty Hall (later Washington and Lee Coll.), Lexington, Va.; urged establishment of nat. univ. in nation's capitol and provided endowment for it in his will; mem. Va. Ho. of Burgesses, 1759-74; justice of Fairfax County (Va.); a leader colonial opposition to Brit. policies in Am.; acted as chmn. meeting in Alexandria which adopted Fairfax Resolutions, July 18. 1774; mem. Continental Congress from Va., 1774-75, mem. com. for drafting army regulations and planning defense of N.Y.C.; elected comdr.-in-chief Continental Army, June 15, 1775, took command at Cambridge, Mass., July 3, 1775; forced Brit. evacuation of Boston, May 17, 1776; defeated at Battle of L.I., 1776; crushed Hessians at Battle of Trenton, Dec. 25, 1776, dislocated entire line of Brit. posts along Delaware River; won Battle of Princeton, forced Brit. retirement to Brunswick, N.J.; characterized militia with phrase "they . . . come in you cannot tell how, go, you cannot tell when; and act, you cannot tell where; consume your Provisions, exhaust your Stores, and leave you at last in a critical moment"; defeated at Battle of Brandywine, Sept. 11, 1777; lost Battle of Germantown, Oct. 3-4, 1777; endured hardships with Continental Army at Valley Forge, winter 1777-78; heartened by French alliance, 1778; overtook British at Monmouth (N.J.), held field while British retired to N.Y.C., June 28, 1778; pursued siege of Yorktown (Va.) with aid of French under de Grasse and Rochambeau, Oct. 19, 1781; held army together until British evacuated N.Y.C., Apr. 19, 1783; bade his officers farewell at Fraunces Tavern, N.Y.C., Dec. 4, 1783; resigned commn., Dec. 23, 1783; retired to "Mt. Vernon," 1783; held meeting at Mt. Vernon on navigation rights on Potomac River, 1785 (indirectly led to U.S. Constl. Conv.); pres. U.S. Constl. Conv., Phila., 1787; unanimously elected 1st Pres. U.S. under new constn., 1788, took oath of office on balcony of U.S. Bldg. N.Y.C. (site of Washington statue at old Sub-Treasury Bldg.), Apr. 30, 1789; unopposed for reelection, 1792; stated Am.'s position regarding French Revolutionary War in Proclamation of Neutrality (issued 1793); strong nationalist; demonstrated power of U.S. Govt. by crushing Indians and suppressing Whiskey Rebellion, firmly fixed govtl. credit through Alexander Hamilton's policies, desired rise of U.S. to internat. importance; strongly backed Pinckney Treaty with Spain and Jay Treaty with Gt. Britain (1795) though neither was completely satisfactory; during his adminstrn. certain fundamental patterns of Am. politics developed including: formation of polit. parties (which he opposed), establishment of basic functions and rights of different branches of govt. (such as method of treaty ratification, presdl. consent for use of exec. documents in Congress), even patterns of patronage (such as having each major sect. of country represented in cabinet); made farewell address, Sept. 1796; served as lt. gen. and comdr.-in-chief U.S. Army (being raised in expectation of war with France), 1798-99. Died "Mt. Vernon," Dec. 14, 1799; buried "Mt. Vernon."

WASHINGTON, JOHN MACRAE army officer; b. Windsor Forest, Stafford County, Va., Oct. 1797; s. Baily and Euphan (Wallace) W.; grad. U.S. Mil. Acad., 1817; m. Fanny Macrae, 3 children. Commd. 3d lt. of arty., 1817, 2d lt. and battalion q.m. of arty., 1818, 1st lt., 1810, sent to Fla. frontier; served at Savannah Harbor, 1821-22, Ft. Moultrie, 1822-24, Augusta, Ga., 1824; instr. mathematics at arty. sch., Ft. Monroe, Va., 1824-26, ordnance officer, 1828-33; brevetted capt., 1830, commd. capt., 1832; fought against Seminoles in Fla., 1833-38; aided Gen. Winfield Scott in transporting Cherokee Nation to Okla., 1838-39; detailed to assist Scott in peacefully quelling Canadian border disturbances, 1840-42; served at Battle of Buena Vista in Mexican War, 1847, positioned at critical pass of La Angostura, largely responsible for maintaining Am. position and securing Am. victory; promoted maj., 1847, brevetted lt. col., 1847; civil and mil. gov. of N.M., 1848-49; served at Ft. Constitution, N.H., 1850-52. Drowned at sea nr. mouth of Delaware River, Dec. 24, 1853.

WASHINGTON, THOMAS naval officer; b. Goldsboro, N.C., June 6, 1865; s. James A. and Virginia N. W.; grad. U.S. Naval Acad., 1887; m. Genevieve F. Clement, June 12, 1900; children—John Clement, Primitive Secret Societies, 1908, rev. edit., 1932 Thomas. Commd. ensign, July 1, 1889; lt., jr. grade, Sept. 5, 1897; lt., Mar. 3, 1899; lt. commdr., July 1, 1905; commander, July 1, 1909; captain, April 9, 1914; rear admiral, August 10, 1918; admiral, October 11, 1923. Served on board Indiana, 1898-99, during Spanish-American war; on board Illinois, 1902. Hydrographer, in charge of Hydrographic Office, Washington, 1914-16; comdg. Florida, June 1916-Nov. 1918, serving with British Grand Fleet in the North Sea, Nov. 1917-Nov. 1918; comd. 3d Div. Atlantic Fleet, 1919; chief Bur. of Navigation, Navy Dept., 1919-23; comdr.-in-chief Asiatic Fleet, 1923-25; commanding 12th Naval Dist., San Francisco, Nov. 19, 1925; retired June 6, 1929; gov. U.S. Naval Home, Phila., 1931-37. Medals: Santiago, West India, Philippine, Nicaraguan (campaigns), D.S.M. (U.S.); Medaille Militaire (Belgium); Order of Bolivar (Venezuela). Mem. Order of the Cincinnati; Order of Washington, Baronial Order of Magna Charta. Episcopalian. Mason. Club: Army and Navy. Home: 1725 Monterey Av., Coronado, Cal. Died Dec. 15, 1954; buried Arlington, Va.

WASSERMAN, EARL REEVES, educator; b. Washington, Nov. 11, 1913; s. Samuel and Jennie (Applestein) W.; Ph.D., Johns Hopkins, 1937; m. Eleanor B. Franklin, Oct. 15, 1937. Instr., asst. prof., asso. prof. U. Ill., 1938-48; asso. prof. Johns Hopkins, 1948-53, prof., 1953-69, Caroline Donovan prof., 1969-73. Vis. prof. U. Wis., summer 1951, Columbia, 1959, 61, U. Wash., 1962, U. Colo., 1963, Harvard, 1966. Guggenheim fellow, 1967-68. Served as lt. (j.g.) USNR, 1944-46. Mem. Modern Lang. Assn., Am. Acad. Arts and Scis., Phi Beta Kappa. Clubs: Johns Hopkins, Tudor and Stuart (Balt.). Author: Elizabethan Poetry in the Eighteenth Century, 1947; The Finer Tone, Keats' Major Poems, 1953; The Subtler Language; Critical Reading of Neo-classic and Romantic Poems, 1959; Pope's Epistle to Bathurst, 1960; Shelley's Prometheus Unbound; A Critical Reading, 1965. Senior editor ELH aJour. English Literary History; editorial board Studies in English Literature. Contbr. prof. jours. Home: Towson MD Died Mar. 3, 1973.

WATERBURY, FREDERICK (MARTIN) b. Saratoga Springs, N.Y., May 1, 1868; s. Herman Lincoln and Louisa M. (Stover) W.; ed. Army War Coll., (div. adm. course), 1918; m. Mary P. Blackmur, Dec. 21, 1914; 1 dau., Mary B. Editor, pub. Saratoga (N.Y.) Eagle, 1889-1912; organizer, editor N.Y. Nat. Guardsman, 1924-32. Served to capt., 22d Separate Co., N.Y. N.G., Saratoga Springs, 1891-98, ordnance officer 2d regt., 1901-10, 3d Brigade, 1910-13, 27th div., 1913-19, chief ordnance officer State of N.Y., 1919-32, brig. gen. ordnance, 1932; ordnance officer 6th div. U.S. Army Mexican Border, 1916; insp. small rams practice 27th div. U.S. Army, 1917-18; ordnance officer corps and Army troops, U.S., 1918; ordnance officer 96th div. U.S. Army, 1918, 14th div., 1919; Raritan Arsenal, 1919; asst. ordnance officer gen. ordnance depot, 1919; comdg. officer gen. ordnance depot, Wingate, N.M., June-Oct.; comdg. officer Charleston Gen. Ordnance Depot, 1919. Mem. War Dept. Bd. for Promotion Rifle Practice 1921-46; capt. N.Y. State N.G. Rifle and Pistol Teams in nat. matches, Camp Perry, O., 1920-32. Awarded Distinguished Pistol Shot medal U.S.A. Mem. Nat. Rifle Assn. Am. (pres. 1926-27, life mem. bd. dirs. and exec. com.), N.G. Assn. U.S. (sec. 1928—), N.Y. Rifle Assn., Inc. (sec. 1932—), Am. Legion, Gen. Nathaniel Woodhull Post Heroes of '76, Mil. Order World Wars, N.Y. Soc. Mil. Order World Wars, Soc. Am. Wars, S.A.R., Nat. Council Boy Scouts. Republican. Episcopalian. Mason (Shriner, K.T.), Sojourner, Elk. Clubs: The Army and Navy (Washington); Military and Naval (N.Y.C.). Home: Carlton Apts., 109-15; Queens Blvd., Forest Hills, N.Y. Died June 8, 1960; buried Maple Grove Cemetery, Kew Gardens, L.I., N.Y.

WATERHOUSE, JOSEPH RAYMOND tobacco co. exec.; b. Perth Amboy, N.J., July 7, 1913; s. Joseph and Christine (Kallesen) W.; B.S., N.Y. U., 1936, M.B.A., 1939; m. Martha L. Hammerschmidt, Dec. 1, 1945; children—Janet C., Nancy E. With Am. Tobacco Co., N.Y.C., 1939—, asst. treas., 1950-62, dir., treasurer, 1962-64, vice pres., treas., 1964—, also dir. Served to lt. comdr. USNR, 1942-46. Recipient Sec. Navy commendation, 1945. C.P.A., N.J. Mem. Am. Inst. C.P.A.'s, N.J. Soc. C.P.A.'s. Clubs: Beacon Hill (Summit); Hartwood (Monticello, N.Y.). Home: 49 Templar Way, Summit, N.J. Office: 150 E. 42d St., N.Y.C. 17. Died Dec. 12, 1967.

WATERMAN, ALAN TOWER physicist; b. Cornwall-on-Hudson, N.Y., June 4, 1892; son Frank Alan and Florence (Tower) W.; A.B., Princeton, 1913, A.M., 1914, Ph.D., 1916; Doctor of Science (hon.), Tufts Coll., 1952, Northeastern U., 1953, U. Vt., 1955; LL.D., Cornell Coll., 1956, American University, University of Chattanooga, 1958; Sc.D., Bowdoin Coll., U. of Arizona, 1958; LL.D., U. Mich., 1959, U. Cin., 1959, U. Cal. at Berkeley, 1960, Ill. Inst. Tech., Mich. State U., 1962, Rockefeller Inst., 1963, Denison U., 1964; Sc.D., U. Notre Dame, U. Akron, 1960, U. So. Cal., Kenyon College, Norwich U., Poly. Inst. Bklyn., Loyola U., 1962, U. of Pitts., 1963; m. Mary Mallon, Aug. 1917; children—Alan Tower, Neil John, Barbara (Mrs. Joseph R. Carney), Anne (Mrs. William C. Cooley), Guy van Vorst. Instr. U. Cincinnati, 1916-17; instructor physics, Yale, 1919-22, assist. prof. of physics, 1923-30; National Research fellow, physics, King's Coll., London, 1927-28; asso. prof. of physics Yale univ., 1931-48; dep. chief and chief scientist Office Naval Research, Navy Dept., 1946-51; dir. NSF, 1951-63, cons., 1963—. Trustee of Atoms for Peace Awards; cons. President's Sci. Advisory Com.; mem. Nat. Aeros. & Space Council, 1958-59; mem. Fed. Council for Sci. and Tech., 1958-63, Def. Sci. Bd., 1956-63; mem. Distinguished Civilian Service Awards, Board, 1957-60; chmn. Interdependental com. on science Research and Development, 1958. Pvt. to first lt., Science and Research div. Signal Corps, U.S. Army, 1917-19; served as vice chmn. div. D, Nat. Research Defense Com., 1942-43; dep. chief office of field service, OSRD, 1943-45, chief, 1945. Chief reader, physics, coll. entrance examination board, 1935-41, chief examiner, physics, 1937-49. Recipient 1st ann. Capt. Robert Dexter Conrad award, 1957; Pub. Welfare medal Nat. Acad. Scis., 1960, Procter Prize, Sch. Research Soc. Am., 1960; Presdl. Medal of Freedom. Fellow A.A.A.S. (pres. 1963, chmn. bd. 1964), American Physical Soc., Am. Assn. Physics Tchrs.; mem. Am. Inst. E.E., Washington Acad. Sci., Philos. Soc. Washington, Washington Acad. of Medicine, Am. Assn. Univ. Profs. Scientific Research Soc. of America, Phi Beta Kappa, Sigma Xi. Clubs: Graduates, (New Haven), Cosmos (Wash.). Medal for Merit, 1948. Editor: Combat Scientists, 1947. Mem. editorial bd., Am. Jour. of Sci., 1934-42. Contbr. sci. papers to The Phys. Rev., Am. Jour. of Sci., Philos. Mag., Proc. Royal Soc. Home: 5306 Carvel Rd., Westmoreland Hills, Washington 16. Died Nov. 1967.

WATERMAN, JULIAN SESSEL prof. law; b. Pine Bluff, Ark., Sept. 9, 1891; s. Gus and Rachel U. (Sessel) W.; A.B., Tulane, 1912; A.M., U. of Mich., 1913; J.D., U. of Chicago, 1923; m. Evangeline Pratt, Sept. 5, 1927. Instr. dept. economics and sociology, U. of Ark., 1914-17, asso. prof. and chmn. dept. economics, 1923-24, prof. law and dean law sch. since 1924, chmn. athletic council since 1933, vice president of the University since 1937. Member Ark. Exec. Tax Com., 1924-25, Ark. Commn. on Business Laws and Taxation, 1927-28. Entered U.S. Army, 1917; camp transportation officer, Camp Pike, Ark., 1918-19. Vice-pres. Southwest Athletic Conf., 1937-41, pres. 1941-43. Mem. Am. Assn. Univ. Profs., Ark. Bar Assn., Am. Bar Assn., Nat. Tax Assn. (exec. com. 1929-32), Scabbard and Blade, Tau Kappa Alpha, Order of Coif; hon. mem. Phi Alpha Delta, Phi Beta Kappa. Democrat. Home: Fayetteville, Ark. Died Sep. 18, 1943.

WATERS, DANIEL naval officer; b. Charlestown, Mass., June 20, 1731; s. Adam and Rachel (Draper) W.; m. Agnes Smith, July 1759; m. 2d, Mary (Wilcox) Mortimer, June 8, 1779; m. 3d, Sarah Sigourney, July 29, 1802; 1 dau. Mem. Malden (Mass.) Minutemen, fought against British, 1775; requested by Malden Com. of Safety to prepare cannon of town; in command schooner Lee, 1776, captured 2 enemy vessels; commd. capt. Continental Navy, 1777; served on West Indies cruise in Continental sloop General Gates, 1779; commanded Mass. ship General Putnam; his most famous exploit occurred in privateer Thorn, 1779, defeated 2 enemy privateers of about equal armament but more heavily manned; captured the Sparlin, 1780; in privateer Friendship, 1781. Died Malden, Mar. 26, 1816.

WATERS, JAMES STEPHEN elec. engr.; b. Galveston, Tex., Sept. 15, 1894; s. James Stephen and Mary Violet (Hinkle) W.; B.S. in Elec. Engring., Rice Inst., 1917; m. Pauline O. Lackner, May 18, 1918. Instr. advancing to prof. elec. engring. Rice Univ., 1919-40, prof., 1941—, past head dept. elec. engring.; elec. engr. Humble Pipe Line Co., 1929-36; chief cons. Electro Geophysical Exploration Co., 1936-41; pres., chief cons. TGR Exploration Co., 1946-49; asso. R. R. Cookston and Assos., cons. engrs., Houston, 1949—. Served as 1st lt. Corps Engrs., U.S. Army, 1917-19, as col. USAF, 1941-46; col. Res. Decorated Legion of Merit. Registered profl. engineer, Texas. Fellow I.E.E.E.; mem. Am. Soc. Engring. Edn., Am. Soc. Profl. Engrs., Sigma Xi, Tau Beta Pi, Sigma Tau. Home: 6351 Vanderbilt St., Houston 77005. Office: Rice U., P.O. Box 1892, Houston 1. Died Dec. 28, 1964; buried Forest Park-Lawndale Cemetery, Houston.

WATIE, STAND Indian leader, army officer; b. at what is now Rome, Ga., Dec. 12, 1806; s. David and Susannah Vowatie or Uweti; m. Sarah C. Bell, 1843, 5 children. With brother published newspaper Cherokee Phoenix; co-signed treaty of New Echota, 1835; became leader minority or treaty party of Cherokee Indians; raised Cherokee co. of home guards, 1861, capt.; raised 1st Cherokee regt. of volunteers known as Cherokee Mounted Rifles, 1861; made col. by Confederate Govt.; served in battles of Wilson's Creek and Pea Ridge; commd. brig. gen., 1864; one of last Confederate officers to surrender, 1865; went to Washington (D.C.) as member of So. delegation of Cherokee, circa 1865. Died Sept. 9, 1871.

WATIES, JAMES RIVES brig.-general U.S.V.; b. at Charleston, S.C., Aug. 22, 1845; attended Charleston High School; married twice. Served in C.S.A. during Civil war; moved to Texas, 1867; clerk civil dist. court, Harris Co., Tex., 8 yrs.; col. 1st cav., Tex. Nat. Guard for 6 yrs. previous to Spanish-Am. war; apptd. col. 1st Tex. cav., May 9, 1898; promoted brig.-gen., May 28, 1898; lawyer. Address: Houston, Tex.

WATKINS, CHARLES W. insurance; b. East Salem, Washington County, N.Y.; s. Henry K. and Zina M. (Hanks) W.; attended common schs. and acad., Cambridge, N.Y.; moved to Allegan County, Mich., 1856; worked on farm; m. Mary Jane Gray, Sept. 19, 1867 (died 1895). Enlisted Co. B, 6th Mich. cav., Aug. 1862; promoted lt. 19th Mich. cav., 1864; bvtd. capt. for gallant service at Abbott's Creek, N.C., Apr. 1865; mem. Mich. legislature, 1871-73; moved to Grand Rapids, 1873; collector Internal Revenue 2 1/2 yrs. under President Arthur; defeated for Congress, 1890, and for mayor Grand Rapids, 1894; v.p. Peninsular Trust Co., Grand Rapids; mem. Insular Commn., Jan.-Aug. 1899; commn. visited Puerto Rico, Feb. 1899. Home: Grand Rapids, Mich. Died 1906.

WATKINS, FERRE C. lawyer; b. Bloomington, Ill., Jan. 24, 1893; s. Charles Sumner and Lucy (Ryburn) W.; grad. high sch., Bloomington, 1910; student Ill. Normal U., Normal, 1910-12; LL.B., Ill. Wesleyan U., 1917; LL.M., Kent Coll. Law, Chgo., 1921; m. Jean Elizabeth Angus, Honolulu, T.H., June 27, 1929. Admitted to Ill. bar, 1917; asso. in practice with Church & Shepard, Chgo., 1919-21, Church, Shepard & Lynde, 1921-22; mem. Watkins & Ten Hoor, attys. at law, 1928-40, Watkins & Meyers, 1955—; gen. counsel for Bur. Liquidations, Dept. Ins., 1941-49; spl. asst. atty. gen. for condemnations, 1956-57. Commd. 1st lt. inf., Ft. Sheridan, Ill., 1917; served 2 yrs. 86th Div. and 89th Div., AEF; maj. 341st Inf., O.R.C.; chmn. Ill. W.A.C. recruiting campaign, 1943-44. Decorated Distinguished Service Cross, Silver Star. Mem. Am., Ill., Chgo. bar assns., Am. Legion (comdr. Dept. Ill. 1926-27, mem. state exec. com. Am. Legion, 1922-24, judge advocate Dept. Ill., 1924-25; chmn. nat. legislative com. 1929-30). Chmn. exec. com. Green for Gov., 1940. Pres., Union League Club, 1941-42. Mem. Pi Kappa Delta, Phi Alpha Delta. Republican. Presbyn. Clubs: Casino, Economic, Saddle and Cycle (Chgo.). Home: 1500 Lake Shore Dr., Chgo. 60610. Died Sept. 3, 1966.

WATKINS, FRANK THOMAS naval officer; b. Provo City, Utah, Dec. 15, 1898; s. Charles Frederick and Mary Elizabeth (Kearney) W.; B.S., U.S. Naval Acad., 1922; m. Margaret Ruth Orem, July 11, 1925; children—Frank Thomas, John O. Commd. ensign, USN, 1922, advanced through grades to vice adm., 1957; chief staff to comdr. submarines Pacific Fleet, 1946-47; comdg. officer U.S. Naval Sch., Monterey, Cal., 1948-49; asst. chief naval personnel Navy Dept., Washington, 1949-51; comdr. cruiser div. 2 U.S. Atlantic Fleet, 1951; comdr. mine for Atlantic Fleet, 1952-53; dep. chmn. naval operations, 1953-54; comdr. submarines Atlantic Fleet, 1954-57, comdr. Anti-Submarine Force, Atlantic Fleet, 1957—. Decorated Legion of Merit, B.S.M. Mem. Phi Sigma Kappa. Home: 1549 N. Harvard Blvd., Hollywood, Cal. Office: Bureau of Naval Personnel, Navy Dept., Washington. Deceased.

WATMOUGH, JAMES HORATIO officer U.S.N.; b. Whitemarsh, Pa., July 30, 1822; s. John Godard and Ellen (Coxe) W.; ed. U. of Pa.; m. Emmeline Sheaff, Oct. 19, 1848 (died 1904); m. 2d, Annie Bowie Harris, July 15, 1907. Acting midshipman U.S.N., 1843-44; p.m., Dec. 12, 1844; served in Mexican War; at capture of Calif.; bombardment and capture of Guaymas; commandant Santa Clara and Don José; fleet p.m. S. Atlantic Squadron, 1864-65, serving in actions on Stone River, and on James and John islands; later gen. pay insp. and 1873-77, p.m. gen.; retired July 30, 1884; advanced to rank of rear admiral, June 1906. Died Jan. 18, 1917.

WATSON, ADOLPHUS EUGENE rear admiral; b. Norfolk, Va., Aug. 9, 1878; s. Rear Admiral Eugene Winslow and Virginia (Cruse) W.; grad. U.S. Naval Acad., 1899, Naval War Coll., 1925; m. Genevieve Gallagher, Jan. 10, 1907; 1 dau., Priscilla Winslow. Commd. ensign U.S. Navy, Feb. 1, 1901; promoted through grades to rank of rear adm., Sept. 1, 1932. Served on U.S.S. Montgomery, Spanish-Am. War and Philippine Campaign; exec. officer U.S.S. Florida with Grand Fleet in North Sea, World War; chief of Staff Naval Mission to Brazil, 1927-29; chief of staff U.S. Battleship Fleet, 1931-32; mem. General Board U.S. Navy, 1932; comdr. of Destroyer Squadrons, Scouting Force, 1933-35; then pres. Naval Examining Board; comdr. Battleship Div. 2, 1937-39; comdt. 4th Naval Dist. and Navy Yard, Phila., 1939-42; retired, 1942. Recalled to active duty in Navy Dept., 1943-45. Awarded Navy Cross for services in World War I, Legion of Merit for services World War II. Clubs: Army and Navy (Washington); Loyal Legion (Phila.); Chevy Chase. Address: 2126 Connecticut Av., Washington. Died Oct. 3, 1949; buried in Arlington National Cemetery.

WATSON, BENJAMIN FRANK lawyer; b. Warner, N.H., April 30, 1826; admitted to Mass. bar, 1850, and later to bar of Supreme Court of U.S.; counsel in leading case against the U.S. for the burning of Columbia, S.C., by Gen. Sherman, and as counsel for the owner, successfully presented the petition, under the Fugitive Slave Law, for the return to slavery of "The Slave Betty," before Chief Justice Lemuel Shaw at Boston, with John A. Andrew as counsel opposing. Editor and propr. Lawrence (Mass.) Sentinel, postmaster, city solicitor, and delegate to famous Democratic conventions (1860) at Charleston, S.C., and Baltimore. As major of 6th Mass. regt. offered the resolution passed by its col. and officers, tendering the regt., through Gov. Andrew, to President-elect Lincoln for service in case of need, thus distinguishing the regt. as the first to volunteer, as it was also the first in the field, in the Civil War, and the first to shed its blood and to force a way for the loyal troops through Baltimore to Washington; and as major, in command of one of the detachments of the regt. in Baltimore, April 19, 1861, ordered the shedding of the first blood in that war; elected lt. col. of 6th Mass. regt., and took command of it upon promotion of the col.; promoted to be bvtd. col. U.S.V.; declined command of another regt., and was apptd. and served as paymaster until became disabled in the service and retired from the army about Oct. 1864. Pres. Mass. Minute Men of 1861; apptd. by survivors of old 6th regt. to write the History of the Baltimore Campaign. In active practice of law in New York, 1867-1900, then retired. From that time devoted attention to benevolent work among working boys and young men. Pres. Church Temperance Legion. Died 1905.

WATSON, EARNEST CHARLES, physicist; born Sullivan, Ill., June 18, 1892; s. Charles Grant and Alice Bell (Smith) W.; Ph.B., Lafayette Coll., Easton, Pa., 1914; postgrad. U. Chgo., 1914-17; Sc.D., Lafayette Coll., 1958; m. Elsa Jane Werner, October 6, 1954. Asst. in physics Univ. of Chicago, 1914-17; asst. prof. of physics, Calif. Inst. Tech., 1919-20, associate professor, 1920-30, professor, 1930-62, emeritus, 1962-70, dean faculty, 1945-60 chairman faculty board, chmn. div. Physics, Mathematics and Astronomy, 1946-49, acting pres., 1956-57; cons. Ford Found. S. and S.E. Asia Program, 1964-70. Sci. attache to Am. Embassy New Delhi, India, 1960-62; del. to various confs. Served in

U.S.N.R.F., 1917-1919; member Division 3, National Defense Research Committee, 1941-44. Official Investigator, OSRD Contract OEMsr-418 (research and development work on artillery rockets, torpedoes, atomic bomb and other ordnance devices), 1941-45. Chmn. library adv. bd. City Pasadena, 1956-60. Fellow Am. Phys. Soc., A.A.A.S.; mem. Am. Assn. Physics Teachers, History of Science Soc., Am. Assn. Univ. Profs., Fgn. Policy Assn., Indian Internat. Centre, Phi Beta Kappa, Sigma Xi, Tau Beta Pi, Gamma Alpha. Clubs: Athenaeum. Author: Mechanics, Molecular Physics, Heat and Sound, 1937. Contbr. sci. jours. Home: Santa Barbara CA Died Dec. 5, 1970.

WATSON, EDWIN MARTIN sec. to the President, army officer; b. Eufaula, Ala., Dec. 10, 1883; s. Peter Penn and Addie (Martin) W.; B.S., U.S. Mil. Acad., 1908; m. Frances Nash, Aug. 31, 1920. Commd. 2d lt., U.S. Army, 1908, and advanced through the grades to brig. gen., Apr. 1939, major-gen., Oct. 1940; served with 11th Inf., Ft. Russell, Wyo., 1908-10; aide-de-camp to Brig. Gen. Frederick A. Smith, Dept. of Mo., Omaha, Neb., 1910-12; with 24th Inf., Philippines, 1912-15; 1st lt. 28th Inf., Galveston, Tex., 1915; mil. aide to President Wilson, 1915-17; maj. 12th F.A., with A.E.F. at Toulon-Troyon, Aisne, Aisne-Marne and St. Mihiel campaigns, 1918; lt. col. St. Mihiel and Meuse-Argonne offensives, with 15th F.A., 77th Div., 1918; junior aide to President Wilson at Paris and U.S. and chief of Mil. Sect., Peace Conf., Paris, in charge of all functions at the President's official residence, Paris, and the arrangements of all the President's visits to foreign countries, including England, Italy, and Belgium, 1918-20; attended French arty. schs., 1920-22; student office F.A. Sch., Ft. Sill, Okla., 1923-24; exec. officer F.A. group, Organized Reserves, 2d Corps, New York, 1924-26. Command and Gen. Staff Sch., Ft. Leavenworth, 1926-27; mil. attaché, Am. Embassy, Brussels, 1927-31; mil. aide to President Roosevelt, 1933-41, sec. since Apr. 1939. Decorated Silver Star with oak leaf cluster (U.S.); Chevalier of Legion of Honor, Croix de Guerre with palm (France); Comdr. Order of Crown, Officer Order of Leopold (Belgium); Comdr. Nat. Order of Southern Cross (Brazil); Silver Cross (Sweden); Star of Abdon Calderon (Ecuador); Order of Danilo I (Montenegro). Clubs: University (New York); Apawanis (Rye, N.Y.); Metropolitan, Army and Navy, Chevy Chase (Washington, D.C.). Home: 3133 Connecticut Av. Office: The White House, Washington, D.C. Died Feb. 20, 1945.

WATSON, EUGENE WINSLOW rear adm. U.S.N.; b. Northampton, Mass., Feb. 17, 1843; s. Adolphus Eugene and Elisa Hovey (Mellen) W.; ed. P.E. Acad., Phila.; m. Virginia Cruse, Apr. 14, 1869. Apptd. master's mate on board the Lancaster, May 2, 1859, served on that vessel until Oct. 1861, Rhode Island, 1862-63; promoted acting ensign, Sept. 18, 1863; commd. ensign in regular service, Mar. 12, 1868; master, Dec. 18, 1868; lt., Mar. 21, 1870; lt. comdr., Nov. 1883; comdr., Apr. 27, 1893; capt., Nov. 22, 1899; retired with the rank of rear adm., after 40 yrs.' service, June 2, 1902. Died Dec. 11, 1914.

WATSON, F(RANK) B(INGLEY) army officer (retired); b. Sharp's Wharf (now Sharps), Va., Feb. 9, 1870; s. Charles Clark and Mary (Wheeler) W.; B.S., U.S. Mil. Acad., 1895; grad. Army Sch. of the Line, 1912; grad. Army War College, 1921; married to Sara Maria Wetherill Dunn, November 1, 1898 (deceased May 10, 1952); one son, Numa Augustin. Apprentice and journeyman printer National Standard Printing office, Salem, New Jersey, 1886-91; commd. additional 2d lt. 19th inf., U.S. Army, 1895, and advanced through grades to brig. gen., Aug. 8, 1918; served in U.S., 1895-98, Puerto Rico, 1898-99 and Philippines, 1899-02, Alaska, 1904-06; Philippines, 1909-11, comd. 3d inf. detachment in expdn. against hostile natives, Mindanao, 1910; capt. Q.M. corps, asst. to contructing Q.M. and comdr. Army Service Detachment, West Point, N.Y., 1912-15; Mexican border, 26th Inf., 1915-17; 153d Depot Brig., Camp Dix, N.J., 1917; comd. 115th inf. 29th div., Camp McClellan, Ala., 1917-18; War Dept. gen. staff, 1918; comd. 13th div. and 26th brig., Am. Lake, Washington, 1918-19; comd. U.S. Troops, Butte, Mont., 1919; comdr. Presidio of San Francisco, Calif., 1919; col., asst. to constructing Q.M. and comdr. army service detachment, West Point, N.Y., 1919-20; comd. 52d inf., camp exec. and acting chief of staff 6th div., Camp Grant, Ill., 1921; comd. 2d inf., Ft. Sheridan, Ill., 1921-23; 1st corps area recruiting officer, Boston, 1923-27; sr. instr., Md. Nat. Guard, 1927-31; comd. 35th inf. Schofield Barracks, Hawaii, 1931-34; ret. brig. gen., Feb. 28, 1934. Mem. Assn. of Grads. of U.S. Mil. Acad. (sr. v.p., 1950), Army Athletic Assn., (U.S. Mil. Acad.), U.S. Inf. Assn., Am. Legion, 29th Div. Assn., Wash. chapt. No. 3, Nat. Sojourners Lodge 51 (charter mem., gov. 1940-50), Salem County Historical Soc., Heroes of 76 (New Eng.) D.C. chpt. Military Order World Wars, New Jersey State Society, Mil. Order of the Carabao. Republican. Presbyn. Clubs: Army and Navy (Boston, Washington). Mason (32 deg.). Home: 317 Atlantic St., Bridgeton, N.J. Died July 24, 1955; buried West Point, N.Y.

WATSON, JOHN B(ROADUS) psychologist; b. Greenville, S.C., Jan. 9, 1878; s. Pickens Butler and Emma K. (Roe) W.; A.M., Furman U., 1900; grad. student in psychology U. Chgo., 1900-03, Ph.D., 1903; LL.D., Furman U., 1919; m. Mary Ickes, Oct. 1, 1904; children—Mary I., John I.; m. 2d, Rosalie Rayner, Dec. 31, 1920; children—William Rayner, James Broadus. Prin. Batesburg Inst., 1899-1900; asst. in exptl. psychology U. Chgo., 1903-04, instr., 1904-08; prof. exptl. and comparative psychology, dir. psychol. lab., Johns Hopkins, 1908-20; became v.p. J. Walter Thompson Co., N.Y., 1924; v.p. William Esty & Co., N.Y., 1936. Editor Psychol. Rev., 1908-15, Jour. Exptl. Psychology, 1915-27. Commd. maj. Aviation Sect., Signal Corps, U.S.R., 1917; on duty, Washington, Mineola, and with A.E.F. Fellow Am. Acad. Arts and Scis.; mem. Am. Psychol. Assn. (pres. 1915), Am. Physiol. Soc., Sigma Xi, Phi Beta Kappa, Kappa Alpha (Southern). Author: Animal Education, 1903; Behavior, 1914; Homing and Related Activities of Birds, 1915; Suggestions of Modern Science Concerning Education, 1917; Psychology from the Standpoint of the Behaviorist, 1919; Behaviorism, 1925, rev. edit., 1930; Ways of Behaviorism, 1928; Psychological Care of Infant and Child, 1928. Contbr. on neurology, animal and infant psychology. Home: Park Rd., Woodbury, Conn. Died Sept. 25, 1958; buried Willowbrook Cemetery, Westport, Conn. Died Sept. 25, 1958, buried Willowbrook Cemetery, Westport, Conn.

WATSON, JOHN CRITTENDEN rear admiral U.S.N.; b. Frankfort, Ky., Aug. 24, 1842; s. Dr. Edward Howe and Sarah Lee (Crittenden) W.; apptd. to U.S. Naval Acad. from Ky., 1856, grad. 1860; m. his cousin, Elizabeth Anderson Thornton, May 29, 1873. Promoted midshipman, June 15, 1860; master, Aug. 31, 1861; lt., July 16, 1862; lt. comdr., July 25, 1866; comdr., Jan. 23, 1874; capt., Mar. 6, 1887; commodore, Nov. 7, 1897; rear admiral, Mar. 3, 1899; retired, Aug. 24, 1904. Served in Susquehanna, 1860-61; Richmond, 1861; Sabine, 1861; Hartford, W. Gulf Blockading Squadron, 1862-64; participated in bombardment and passage of Fts. Jackson and St. Philip, and Chalmette batteries, Apr. 1862; passage of Vicksburg batteries, June, July 1862; passage Port Hudson, Mar. 14, 1863; passage of Grand Gulf, Mar. 19 and 30, 1863; battle of Mobile Bay, Aug. 5, 1864; served in Colorado, Franklin and Canandaigua, European Squadron, 1865-69; Navy Yard, New York, 1869; spl. duty, Phila., 1869-70; Alaska, 1870-71; comdg. stationary store-ship Idaho, in harbor of Yokohama, 1871-73; on duty Navy Yard, New York, 1873-74, 1883-86, Navy Yard, Mare Island, 1874; aid to comdt., Navy Yard, Mare Island, 1874-77; comdg. Wyoming, 1878-80; torpedo instrn., 1880; light house insp. 11th dist., 1880-83; comdg. Iroquois, 1886-87; pres. Bd. of Inspection, San Francisco, 1888-90; capt. of yard, Navy Yard, Mare Island, 1890-92; comdg. San Francisco, 1892-94; mem. Naval Retiring Bd., 1894-95; gov. Naval Home, Phila., 1895-98; comdg. a div. of N. Atlantic Fleet, May-Sept., 1898, during war with Spain; comdr.-in-chief Eastern Squadron, July 1898, to threaten coast of Spain and reinforce Dewey's fleet; comdt. Navy Yard, Mare Island, 1898-99; commander-in-chief Asiatic Fleet, June 1899-Apr. 1900; pres. Naval Examining Bd., 1900-02; naval rep. to the coronation of King Edward VII, of England, 1902; pres. Naval Examining and Retiring Bds., 1902-04; spl. duty in Europe studying conditions for physical and moral betterment of enlisted personnel. Sr. v.comdr.-in-chief Loyal Legion, 1907-09. Mem. nat. council Boy Scouts of America. Home: Washington, D.C. Died Dec. 16, 1923.

WATSON, KENNETH NICOLL, investment banker, lawyer; b. Washington, Mar. 27, 1907; s. Walter Scott and Maude (Arthur) W.; A.B., George Washington U., 1928, LL.B., 1930; grad. student Harvard U. Bus. Sch., 1937; m. Diane G. Maitland (dec. Mar. 1949); m. 2d, Virginia Evans Carey, Dec. 1951; children—Nicole Carey, Diane Nicoll. Admitted to D.C. bar, 1930; atty. NRA, 1933-35, FTC, 1935-41; exec. WPB, 1941-43; mem. U.S. Tech. Mission to Brazil, 1942; pvt. practice law, Washington, also Europe, 1947-53; partner of Jones, Kreeger & Co., Washington, mem. N.Y. Stock Exchange, from 1953; dir. Allied Capital Corp., Peoples Bank, Buena Vista, Va. Vice chmn. President's Com. on Employment Handicapped; dir. U.S. Expn. Sci. and Industry, Washington. Trustee Washington chpt. Am. Cancer Soc. Served from lt. (j.g.) to lt. comdr., USNR, 1943-47; asst. naval and air attache Am. embassies, Colombia and Panama, 1945-47. Mem. Assn. Customers Brokers, Am., D.C. bar assns., Washington Bd. Trade, Soc. Cin., Washington Inst. Fgn. Affairs. Episcopalian. Clubs: Metropolitan (Washington and N.Y.C.); Burning Tree (Md.); City Tavern, Army Navy, 1925 F Street (Washington). Home: Washington DC Died June 4, 1970; buried Arlington Nat. Cemetery, Arlington VA

WATSON, MARK SKINNER journalist; b. Plattsburg, N.Y., June 24, 1887; s. Winslow Charles and Ella (Barnes) W.; A.B., Union Coll., Schenectady, 1908, hon. A.M., 1933, Litt.D. (hon.), 1948; m. Susan Owens, Sept. 24, 1921; children—Ellen Brashears (Mrs. Bainbridge Eager), Susan Ranies (Mrs. Charles Anthony Raven Crosland). Reporter, Plattsburg Press, 1908-09; reporter, traveling corr. Chgo. Tribune, 1909-14, 15-17, 15-17; dir. publicity San Diego Expn., 1914-15; mng. editor, Ladies' Home Jour., 1920; asst. mng. editor Balt. Sun, 1920-27, Sunday editor, 1927-41, mil. corr., 1941-—; historian hist. div. Spl. Staff, U.S. Army, 1946-50. Mem. U.S. (Wedemeyer) Mission to China and Korea, AEF (chiefly at G.H.Q.); officer-in-charge Stars 1947. Served to maj., U.S. Army, 1917-19; with and Stripes (AEF newspaper), 1919. Officer d'Academie (France). Recipient citation Dept. Def., 1961, Distinguished Pub. Service Award, USN, 1962, Pulitzer Prize, for internat. correspondence, 1945, Medal of Freedom (U.S. Army), 1946, Presdl. Medal of Freedom, 1963; Arts and Letters trophy Air Force Assn., 1964. Presbyn. Author: The Chief of Staff: Prewar Plans and Preparations. Author numerous mag. articles and revs. Occasional lectr. Nat. War Coll. Home: 1 Merryman Ct. Office: care Balt. Sun, Balt. Died Mar. 25, 1966; buried Port Kent, N.Y.

WATSON, ROBERT WALKER life insurance exec.; b. Paris, Tex., Oct. 21, 1894; s. Robert Gill and Susan Jane (Westerman) W.; student U. of Tex., 1911-13; m. Ola M. Smith, May 14, 1921. With Am. Nat. Bank, Paris, Tex., 1913-17; foreign dept., Nat. City Bank of N.Y., 1919-20; with Morris Plan Ins. Soc., New York, since 1920; successively asst. treas., treas., v.p., now pres.; dir. and mem. exec. com. Morris Plan Corp. America, Puritan Corp.; dir. Morris Plan Industrial Bank of New York; dir. of Morris Plan banks in Richmond, Va., Knoxville, Tenn., Atlanta, Ga., and Cleveland, O. Served as 1st O.T.C., Leon Spring, Tex.; commd. officer, U.S. Army, 1917-19. Democrat. Clubs: Uptown (N.Y. City); Sleepy Hollow Country (Scarborough, N.Y.). Home: Old Post Road S., Croton-on-Hudson, N.Y. Office: 420 Lexington Av., New York, N.Y. Died Dec. 1, 1944.

WATSON, SAMUEL NEWELL clergyman; b. Lyons, Ia., Feb. 27, 1861; s. George William and Hetty (Newell) W.; B.A., Trinity Coll., Conn., 1882, M.A., 1887; U. of the South, 1883-84; M.D., U. of Ia., 1893; (D.D., U. of Ia., 1889); m. Jeannette Grace Watkins, Jan. 7, 1885. Deacon, 1884, priest, 1885, P.E. Ch.; rector Trinity Ch., Iowa City, Ia., 1886-97, St. Paul's, Chillicothe, O., 1897-1903, St. Paul's, Akron, O., 1903-12; rector Am. Ch. in Paris, France, 1912-18, rector emeritus, 1918. Chaplain 3d Regt., Ia. Nat. Guard, 1886; relief work in France, World War, 1914-18. Pres. Council of Advice Am. Ch. in Europe. Decorated Officier Legion of Honor (French); Chevalier Order of Leopold (Belgium); Comdr. Order of St. Sava (Serbian). Mem. Alpha Delta Phi. Mason. Author: Those Paris Years, 1936. Home: 2321 State St. Address: P.O. Box 896, Santa Barbara, Calif. Died Mar. 27, 1942.

WATT, BEN H. state supt. pub. instrn.; b. Bruceville, Ind., Sept. 17, 1889; s. Robert Gordon and Hannah (Heitchecker) W.; A.B., Wabash Coll., 1913; A.M., Ind. State Tchrs. Coll., 1930; m. Vera Creel, Nov. 23, 1919; 1 dau., Patricia Ann (Mrs. William B. Bayer). Successively high sch. tchr., coach, high sch. prin., Macomb, Ill., 1913-17; high sch. prin. Princeton, Ind., 1920-21; supt. schs. Gibson County, 1921-25; coach Princeton High Sch., 1924-27; supt. schs., Owensville, Ind., 1927-31; high sch. prin., Noblesvill, 1931-33, supt. schs., 1933-41; adj. gen. State of Ind., 1945-47; state supt. pub. instrn., 1947-—; now prin. Danville (Ind.) Consol. Sch. Mem. Library bd., Noblesville. Commd. 2d lt. 1918, advanced to rank of 1st lt., F.A., U.S. Army, World War I; commd. capt. Ind. N.G., 1922, advanced through grades to col. gen. staff corps, World War II, serving overseas 38 months, apptd. maj. gen., 1946. Mem. Ind. State Tchrs. Assn., N.E.A., Beta Theta Pi. Republican. Presbyn. Mason (32 deg.), Elk. Club: Kiwanis (Noblesville). Home: Danville High Sch., Danville, Ind. Died Oct. 14, 1961.

WATT, RICHARD MORGAN naval officer; b. York, Pa., June 18, 1872; s. Andrew and Susan (Bahn) W.; grad. U.S. Naval Acad., 1891; B.S., U. of Glasgow, Scotland, 1893, D.Sc., 1911; m. Bessie Davis, Oct. 16, 1894; 1 son, Richard Morgan. Commd. in U.S. Navy, July 1, 1893; promoted through grades to rear adm., Feb. 1, 1934. Asst. to supt. of constrn. for U.S. Navy at Cramp's Shipyard, Phila., 1893-86; asst. to naval constructor, New York Navy Yard, 1896-1901; supt. constrn. Fore River Shipyard, Quincy, Mass., 1901-07; head dept. of constrn. and repair, Norfolk Navy Yard, 1907-10, mgr. indsl. dept., 1907-10 and 1915-21; chief constructor and chief Bur. of Constrn. and Repair, Navy Dept. (Washington, D.C.), 1910-14; mem. Claims Commn. U.S. Shipping Bd., 1921-23; mgr. indsl. dept. Phila. Navy Yard, 1924-30; insp. of material for U.S. Navy, Phila. Dist., 1930-—. Awarded Navy Cross (U.S.). Presbyn. Home: Merion, Pa. Died May 15, 1938.

WATT, ROBERT MCDOWELL utilities exec.; b. Charlotte, N.C., May 27, 1888; s. James B. and Emma (Wilson) W.; B.S. in Elec. Engring., U. N.C.; LL.D., Transylvania College, Centre College; m. Elizabeth Byers, Dec. 21, 1915; children—R. M., Malcolm K. With Tucker & Laxton, Charlotte, N.C., 1909-10, Commonwealth-Edison Co., Chgo., 1910-12, Ky. Traction & Terminal Co., Lexington, 1912-13; with Ky. Utilities Co., 1913-—, became pres., 1935, chmn., 1957-—; dir. Old Dominion Power Co., Lafayette Hotel Co., Electric Energy, Inc. Ky. del. Nat. Indsl. Conf. Bd. Pres. Ky. Independent Coll. Found.; dir. Southern States Indsl. Council; mem. bd. trustees Ind. Coll. Funds of Am. Served as capt. U.S. Army, World War I. Recipient Man of Year award Ky. Press Association. Member Ky. C. of C. (hon. chmn. area development com.), Soc. Mil. Engrs., Lexington C. of C., Newcomen Soc. Clubs: Filson, Pendennis (Louisville); Tower

(Chgo.); Idle Hour (Lexington). Home: 3543 Tates Creek Pike. Office: 120 S. Limestone St., Lexington, Ky. Died July 23, 1963.

WATTS, HERBERT CHARLES, physician; b. San Francisco, Calif., Mar. 1, 1874; s. Charles and Eliza Mills (Newman) W.; M.D., U. of Calif., 1900; m. Emily Cornelia Veirs, Apr. 26, 1905 (died June 30, 1908); 1 dau., Jessie (Mrs. Alan Scott); m. 2d, Silvia Josefa Varela, Oct. 10, 1914; children—Herbert Charles, George Joseph. House physician and surgeon City and County Hosp., San Francisco, 1900-01; surgeon Pacific Mail S.S. Co., 1902-04; resident surgeon Calif. Powder Works, Pinole, Calif., 1904-06; private practice, Modesto, Calif., 1906-08; physician and quarantine officer Panama Canal Service, 1909-20; commd. passed asst. surgeon U.S. Pub. Health Reserve, 1920, surgeon, 1921, sr. surgeon, 1923; transferred to Vets. Adminstrn. as chief med. officer, 1924; mgr. combined facility, Ft. Harrison, Mont., since 1929, retired Jan. 1, 1947. Served in Calif. Nat. Guard, 1893-1901, hosp. steward, 1898-1901; 1st lt. Med. Corps, U.S. Army, 1918-19; capt. Med. Sec., O.R.C., 1920. Mason (32 deg., Shriner). Home: 115 El Camino Real, Menlo Pk CA

WATTS, WILLIAM CARLETON naval officer; b. Phila., Pa., Feb. 14, 1880; s. Ethelbert and Emily (Pepper) W.; grad. with honors, U.S. Naval Acad., 1898; m. Julia F. Scott, Apr. 16, 1902. Ensign, Apr. 4, 1900; promoted through grades to rear adm., Apr. 1, 1931. Served on U.S.S. Columbia during Spanish-Am. War; judge advocate gen. of Navy, with rank of capt., Jan. 6, 1917-Apr. 15, 1918; apptd. comdr. U.S.S. Albany, Apr. 24, 1918; engaged on convoy escort duty to end of World War I; retired for physical disability, Dec. 1, 1940; served on active duty, Navy Dept., Jan. 1942-Aug. 1943. Episcopalian. Club: New York Yacht. Home: Ringwood Rd., Rosemont, Pa. Died Jan. 5, 1956; buried Arlington Nat. Cemetery.

WAUGH, SIDNEY sculptor; b. Amherst, Mass., Jan. 17, 1904; s. Frank Albert and Alice (Vail) W.; student Mass. Inst. Tech., 1920-23, Scuola delle Belle Arte, Rome, 1924; pupil Henri Bouchard, Paris, 1925-28; student Am. Acad. in Rome, 1929-32; hon. M.A., Amherst Coll., 1939; A.F.D., University of Massachusetts, 1950; married Elizabeth Lake, 1946. Principal works: group for Nat. Archives Bdlg., pediment group for U.S. P.O. Dept. Bldg., figure for U.S. atty. gen. conf. room, group for Fed. Res. Bd. Bldg., Lamar Monument (Richmond, Tex.), sculpture for Buhl Planetarium (Pittsburgh); Pres. Truman's gifts to Princess Elizabeth and Queen Wilhelmina; Pulaski Monument, Phila.; 4 statues, District Court of Appeals, Washington; Mellon Memorial Fountain, Washington; Presentation Medal to Pres. Gonzales Videla of Chile; group for Mead Art Bldg., Amherst Coll.; 9 sculptures for Bethlehem Steel Co.; 2 groups for Bank of Manhattan. Represented in Met. Mus., Chicago Art Inst., Cleveland Museum of Fine Arts, Toledo Mus., John Herron Inst., Johns Hopkins U., Victoria and Albert Mus. (London), Collections of the King of Italy, Shah of Iran, King of Egypt, Queen of Netherlands. Awarded bronze medal of Paris Salon de Printemps, 1928, silver medal, 1929; Prix de Rome, 1929. Served as captain, United States Army Air Forces, World War II. Awards: Bronze Star, Silver Star; 2 Croix de Guerre (French); Knight of Crown of Italy; recipient Saltus medal, also Herbert Adams Memorial medal. Mem. adv. com. Archtl. Sch. of Mass. Institute Tech.; commissioner City Art Commn., New York City, National Academecian, 1938. Fellow American, Numismatic Society, American Academy in Rome (trustee), American Geog. Soc.; mem. Nat. Inst. of Arts and Letters (1941), Nat. Sculpture Soc. (pres.; mem. council), Nat. Acad. (1st v.p.), Municipal Art Soc., Shakespeare Assn. of America, Kappa Sigma, Alumni Assn. of Am. Acad. in Rome (v.p.); hon. life member Nat. Arts Club. Clubs: Coffee House, Century Assn. (New York City). Director Rinehart School of Sculpture, Baltimore. Address: 101 Park Av., N.Y.C. Died June 30, 1963; buried Amherst, Mass.

WAUGH, WILLIAM HAMMOND, ex-army officer, civil engineer; b. Greenville, Pennsylvania, April 13, 1875; son John Harold and Ella Louise (Hammond) W.; educated Shattuck School, 1892-93; married Queen Scott Lawson, January 23, 1909; children—William Hammond (lieutenant colonel, C.A.C.), Dorothy Scott (Mrs. G. M. Watson). Began with Pecos Irrigation and Improvement Co., N.M., 1893; with Bessemer & Lake Erie Railroad, Greenville, Pa., 1895-98, locating engineer, same, 1903-04; contracting in Cuba, 1899-1902; chief engineer Shenango Traction Company, Greenville, Pennsylvania, 1904-07, Little Rock & Pine Bluff Traction Co., 1907-09; div. engr. Bur. Pub. Works, Manila, P.I., 1909-15; consulting practice, Riverside, Calif., 1915-17; pres. Alaska Road Commn., 1917-20, also acting district engr. Bur. Pub. Rds. and cons. engr., Ty. of Alaska, 1917-20. Corpl. Pa. Nat. Guard, 1897-98; corpl. 15th Pa. Vol. Inf., May-July 1898; 1st sergt. 3d Regt., U.S. Vol. Engrs., July 1898-April 1899; constructing engr. Q.-M. Dept. U.S. Army, Apr.-Oct. 1899; capt. Engr. Corps, Calif., 1916-June 1917; capt. engrs. U.S. Reserve, June 1917-June 1918; maj. engrs. U.S. Army, 1918-20; capt. Corps of Engrs., 1920-36, maj., 1936-39, retired; real estate dealer since 1940. Mem. Am. Soc. C.E., S.A.R. Republican. Episcopalian. Mason. Home: 345 Elmhurst Av., San Antonio TX

WAUL, THOMAS NEVILLE soldier, lawyer; b. in Sumter Dist., S.C., Jan. 5, 1813; s. Thomas and Anna (Mulcahy) W.; ed. at Charleston, S.C., 1825-28; S.C. Coll., Columbia, 1829-32; studied law in office of Sargent S. Prentiss, Vicksburg, Miss., 1834-35; m. Mary America Simmons, Nov. 25, 1837. Licensed to practice law in Miss., 1834; apptd. dist. atty. River Dist., Miss.; practiced law at Grenada, Miss., 1836-50; removed 1850 to Gonzales County, Tex.; Dem. candidate for Congress Western dist., Tex., 1859—defeated; elected from Tex. elector at large on Breckinridge ticket, 1860; mem. provisional Congress Confederate States, 1861-62, organized Waul's (Tex.) Legion (2,000 troops) for C.S.A., became its col. and with it served through war; comd. defenses of Yazoo and Tallahatchie Rivers, Miss., at Fort Pemberton; at siege of Vicksburg; promoted brig. gen.; comd. brigade under Kirby Smith in Trans-Miss. Dept., leading it at battles of Mansfield and Pleasant Hill, La.; comd. div. at battle of Saline, where he was severely wounded. Elected to reconstruction Conv. of Tex., 1865; established practice in Galveston; abandoned practice, 1896, retiring to farm in country. Home: Neyland, Hunt County, Tex. Died 1903.

WAVELL, ARCHIBALD PERCIVAL (The Earl Wavell), British Field Marshal; b. Colchester, Essex, Eng., May 5, 1883; s. Maj. Gen. Archibald Graham and Eliza (Percival) W.; ed. Winchester Coll.; Royal Mil. Coll., Sandhurst; Staff Coll., Camberley; m. Eugenie Marie Quirk, Apr. 22, 1915; children—Archibald John A. (Viscount Keren), Pamela (Lady Pamela Humphrys), Felicity (Lady Felicity Longmore), Joan (Lady Joan Gordon). Commd. 2d lt., May 8, 1901, apptd. to Black Watch (Royal Highland Regt.), 1901; served in S. African War, 1901-02, Indian frontier, 1908, World War I, 1914-18, Palestine, 1937-38, World War II, 1939-43; comdr. 6th Inf. Brigade, 1930-34, 2d Div., 1935-37, troops in Palestine, 1937-38; gen. officer So. Command, 1938-39; comdr.-in-chief Middle East, 1939-41, India, 1941-43; viceroy of India, 1943-47. Mem. Privy Council. Decorated: Knight Grand Gross of the Bath, Knight Grand Comdr. Star of India, Knight Grand Comdr. Indian Empire, Companion St. Michael and St. George, Mil. Cross constable of Tower of London, 1948, lord-lt. County of London, 1949 (Eng.); Comdr. Legion of Honour; Order of Nile; Order of El Nahda; Order of George I (Greece); Order St. Vladimir; Order St. Stanislas; Virtuti Militari (Poland); Czechoslovak Mil. Cross; Greek Mil. Cross; Seal of Solomon (Ethiopia); Order of Orange-Nassau (Holland); Comdr. Order of Merit; Star of Nepal, Chancellor Aberdeen Univ., 1945. Mem. Royal Soc. Lt. (pres.), Kipling Soc. (pres.), Ch. of England. Clubs: United Service, Athenaeum, Royal and Ancient, Marylebone Cricket. Author: The Palestine Campaign, 1928; Allenby: A Study in Greatness, 1941; Allenby in Egypt, 1943; Other Men's Flowers: An Anthology of Poetry, 1944; Generals and Generalship; Speaking Generally; The Good Soldier, 1947. Address: 23 Kingston House South, London, Eng. Died May 24, 1950; buried The Charity Garth, Winchester Coll.

WAYNE, ANTHONY army officer; b. Waynesboro, Pa., Jan. 1, 1745; s. Isaac and Elizabeth (Iddings) W.; m. Mary Penrose, Mar. 25, 1766, 2 children. Chmn. com. of Chester County (Pa.) to frame resolutions of protest against British, 1774; mem. Pa. Provincial Assembly from Chester County, 1775; col. of a Chester County regt., sent with Pa. brigade to reinforce Canadian expn., 1776; brig. gen. Continental Army, joined Washington at Morristown, N.J., 1777, took command Pa. troops; served in battles of Brandywine and Germantown, 1777; with Washington at Valley Forge, winter 1777-78; served in Battle of Monmouth, 1778; received medal from Congress for taking over 500 Brit. prisoners and munitions at Stony Point, 1779; sent to oppose British, Loyalists and hostile Indians in Ga., 1781; negotiated treaties of submission with Creek and Cherokee Indians, winter 1782-83; retired from active service as brevet maj. gen., 1783; mem. Pa. Gen. Assembly from Chester County, 1784, 85; mem. U.S. Ho. of Reps. from Ga., 2d Congress, 1791-92; maj. gen. in command U.S. Legion, 1791; defeated Indians at Fallen Timbers on Maumee River nr. what is now Toledo, O. Died Presque Isle (now Erie), Pa., Dec. 15, 1796.

WEAKLEY, CHARLES ENRIGHT, naval officer; b. St. Joseph, Mo., June 11, 1906; s. Lawrence O'Niel and Jeanette (Landis) W.; student U. Mo., 1924; B.S., U.S. Naval Acad., 1929; student U. Cambridge (Eng.), 1937-39; grad. Nat. War Coll., 1951; m. Geraldine Cullen, Mar. 31, 1934; children—Geraldine Louise, Linda Enright. Commd. ensign U.S. Navy, 1929, advanced through grades to vice adm., 1963, served at sea in cruisers, destroyers, anti-submarine ships, U.S.S. Omaha, 1929-33, U.S.S. Talbot, 1933-36, U.S.S. New Mexico, 1939-40, U.S.S. Sampson, 1940-41; comdr. U.S.S. Goff, 1941-42, Convoy Escort, 1941-44, anti-submarine warfare unit, Naval Operating Base, Norfolk, Va., 1944-45; assigned Office Chief Naval Operations, Washington, 1945-48; comdg. officer surface anti-submarine devel. detachment Atlantic, Key West, Fla., 1948-50; naval adviser NSC staff, internat. affairs div. Office Chief Naval Operations, 1951-53; comdr. U.S.S. Cambria, 1953-54, U.S.S. Northampton, 1954-55; asst. chief naval personnel for naval res., Navy Dept., 1955-56; with Office Chief Naval Operations, 1956-57, dir. undersea warfare div., 1957-58, anti-submarine warfare readiness exec., 1958-59; comdr. Destroyer Flotilla 2, 1959-60, Destroyer Force, U.S. Atlantic Fleet, 1960-61; asst. chief naval operations (devel.), 1961-63, dep. chief, 1963; comdr. Anti-submarine Warefare Force, U.S. Atlantic Fleet, 1963-67; asst. adminstr. mgmt. devel. NASA, Washington, 1967-72. Decorated Legion of Merit with combat V, Bronze Star, D.S.M., numerous campaign medals; U.S. Navy Destroyer Sch. at Newport, R.I. named Weakley Hall. Home: Chevy Chase MD Died Dec. 23, 1972; buried Arlington Nat. Cemetery.

WEATHERFORD, WILLIAM (INDIAN NAME RED EAGLE) Indian chief; b. nr. Montgomery, Ala., circa 1780; m. Mary Moniac (dec. 1804); m. 2d, Sapoth Thlanie; m. 3d, Mary Stiggins, 1817. Chief, Creek Indians; led followers in battle during Creek War, circa 1813; responsible for massacre at Ft. Mims (Ga.) in which 500 were put to death; a leader Creek Indians in Battle at Horseshoe Bend (Ala.), 1814. Died Mar. 9, 1824.

WEATHERRED, PRESTON ALONZO, lawyer; b. Oceola, Tex., Aug. 11, 1884; s. Thomas Preston and Elizabeth (King) W.; student Carlisle Mil. Acad., Arlington, Tex., 1901-03; LL.B., U. Tex., 1908; grad. Army War Coll., 1922, Inf. Sch., 1941; m. Irene Desole Warren, Oct. 14, 1907; children—Mary Elizabeth, Julia Augusta, Preston Alonzo. Practiced law, 1912-67, except for military service, 1916-25, 1940-42; specializes in indsl., administrative ins. and corporation practice; counsel Blanchette, Smith & Shelton, Dallas; gen. counsel Code Authority Ice Industry, Washington. 1934-35. Senior vice president, gen. counsel Internat. Fidelity Ins. Co.; dir. widespread coop. effort behalf conservation state govt.; dir. seminars labor relations, Arlington State Coll., oil industry, others. Served as maj. comd. 1st Battn. 2d Tex. Inf. Mexican Border, 1916-17; comd. 132d Machine Gun Battn., 36th Div., in France, 1918; lt. col., 1923, col., 1926, Tex. Nat. Guard; chief of staff, 36th Div., 1926-39; brig. gen. in command of 72d Inf. Brigade, 36th Div., 1939-42; transferred to inactive status, Sept. 26, 1942; recalled to active status as maj. gen. and assigned command 36th inf. div., Tex. Nat. Guard, April 29, 1946; made lt. gen., Tex. Nat. Guard, placed in commd. all Tex. N.G. Forces, 1948; ret. 1948. Mem. Bar Assn. of Dallas, Texas Bar Assn., Am. Bar Assn., Delta Chi. Clubs: Country, Executives' Dinner (1st pres.), Athletic, Rotary, Dallas, City, Imperial; Austin (Tex.). Contbg. editor: Ice and Refrigeration. Co-author: Pointers for Infantry Troop Leaders, 1940, 43, 50, 64. Author: Brochures on Labor-Management Relations and Fed. Wage and Hour Law; other publs. Home: Dallas TX Died Dec. 2, 1967; buried Tex. State Cemetery, Austin TX

WEATHERWAX, HAZELETT PAUL, retired naval officer, business executive; born at Honolulu, Hawaii, October 25, 1907; s. Charles Washington and Agnes May (Bookstaver) W.; student St. Louis Coll., Honolulu, 1923-27; B.S., U.S. Naval Acad., 1931; grad. U.S. Naval Postgrad. Sch., 1939, U.S. Naval War Coll., 1950; m. Alyce E. Hofmann, Apr. 15, 1933; children—Alyce Jean (Mrs. Robert A. Cornell), Susan Ann (Mrs. Clyde M. Walter). Commd. edsign U.S. Navy, 1931, advanced through grades to rear adm., 1959; assigned U.S.S. Childs, U.S.S. Leary U.S.S. Mississippi, U.S.S. Alexander J. Dallas, U.S.S. Massachusetts, 1941-43; ordance control officer staff comdr. Western Sea Frontier, 1943-46; comdr. U.S.S. Hanson, 1946-47; staff comdr. Second Task Fleet, 1947-49; asst. to dir. material div. Bur. Ordnance, Navy Dept., 1950-52. Comdr. U.S.S. Delta, 1952-53; asst. dir. research and devel. div., 1953-54, assigned Office Chief Naval Operations, 1954-56; comdr. Destroyer Sqdn. 5, 1956-57; asst. dir. surface type warfare div. Office Chief Naval Operations, Navy Dept., 1957-58; comdr. Destroyer Flotilla 1, 1958-59; insp. gen., asst. chief Bur. Naval Weapons for Adminstrn., Navy Dept., 1959-61; chief U.S. Naval Mission to Brazil, 1961-65; dir. Pan-Am. affairs Navy Dept., 1965-66, ret., 1966. Pres. Apito Assos. S.A., 1966-67. Decorated Commendation ribbon, numerous others. Home: Alexandria VA Died May 26, 1967; buried Arlington Nat. Cemetery, Arlington VA

WEAVER, AARON WARD rear admiral U.S.N.; b. Washington, July 1, 1832; s. Lt. William Augustus and Jane (Van Wyck) W.; apptd. midshipman from Ohio, 1848, grad. 1854; m. Ida, d. Alpheus Hyatt, Feb. 1864. Passed midshipman, June 15, 1854; master, Sept. 15, 1855; lt., Sept. 16, 1855; lt. comdr., July 16, 1862; comdr., July 25, 1866; capt., Aug. 8, 1876; commodore, Oct. 7, 1886; rear admiral, June 27, 1893; retired Sept. 26, 1893. Served in St. Louis and Congress, 1848-53; at Naval Acad., 1853-54; in Trenton, Fulton, and coast survey steamers Walker and Arctic, 1854-57; in Marion on African coast and returned home of prize slave bark Ardennes, 1857-59; Navy Yard, Philadelphia, 1859-60; during Civil War served in Susquehanna, at bombardment of Fts. Hateras, Clarke, Beauregard, Walker, and Port Royal, S.C.; in Winona and comd. Chippewa, in Mahopac, 1864-65; Navy Yard, Boston, 1865-66; comd. Tallapoosa, 1867; recruiting duty, Washington, 1867-68; spl. duty, 1869-70; comd. Terror and Severn, 1870-71; Navy Yard, Washington, 1872-73; in charge nitre depot, Malden, Mass., 1874-75; comd. Dictator, 1876-77; Navy Yard, Norfolk, 1879-

81; comd. Brooklyn, 1882-83; mem. Naval Examining and Retiring Bds., Washington, 1885-89; comdt. Navy Yard, Norfolk, 1890-92; pres. Naval Examining and Retiring Bds., 1893. Died Oct. 2, 1919.

WEAVER, ERASMUS MORGAN army officer; b. Lafayette, Ind., May 23, 1854; s. Erasmus Morgan and Fanny Mary (Bangs) W.; grad. U.S. Mil. Acad., 1875; studied in physical and elec. lab., Mass. Inst. Tech., 1895, 1896. Commd. 2d lt. U.S. Arty., June 16, 1875; 1st lt., Oct. 2, 1883; honor grad. Arty. Sch., 1888; capt. a.a.g. vols., May 12, 1898; capt. 1st U.S. Arty., May 14, 1898; lt. col. 5th Mass. Inf., July 1, 1898; hon. mustered out of vol. service, Mar. 31, 1899; maj. U.S. Arty. Corps, Aug. 4, 1903; maj. Gen. Staff, June 1905; lt. col. Arty. Corps, Jan. 25, 1907; lt. col. Gen. Staff, Oct. 1908; col. Coast Arty. Corps, Dec. 1909; col. Gen. Staff, Oct. 1910; brig. gen. chief of Coast Arty., Mar. 1911; maj. gen., July 6, 1916. Prof. mil. science and tactics, Western Reserve U., 1877-80, S.C. Mil. Acad., Charleston, S.C., 1883-86; instr. dept. chemistry, electricity, etc., U.S. Mil. Acad., 1888-91; instr. dept. of arty., U.S. Arty. Sch., 1900-03; chief, Div. Militia Affairs, Office Sec. of War, 1908-11; mem. Bd. Ordnance and Fortifications; mem. War Council of War Dept., Dec. 1917-May 1918; retired for age, by operation of law, May 23, 1918. Episcopalian. Author: Notes on Military Explosives, 1906. Died Nov. 13, 1920.

WEAVER, GEORGE CALVIN ret. naval officer; b. Mill Hall, Pa., Aug. 6, 1905; s. Jasper Daniel and Jessie Fremont (MacGregory) W.; B.S., U.S. Naval Acad., 1926; M.S., Mass. Inst. Tech., 1931; m. Irene Streeter, Sept. 7, 1930; children—Calvin George, Jeanne. Commd. ensign USN, 1926, advanced through grades to rear adm., 1954; submarine design, constrn., Navy Yard, Portsmouth, N.H., Electric Boat Co., Groton, Conn., Mare Island Navy Yard, Vallejo, Cal.; supr. shipbuilding, constrn. fleet-type submarines and LCT landing craft, Manitowoc, Wis., World War II; head submarine br. Bur. Ships, 1945-49; prodn. officer Phila. Naval Shipyard, 1949-52; comdr. Naval Shipyard, Long Beach, Cal., 1952-54; vice chief naval material Navy Dept., Washington, 1954-55, ret. Aug. 1956; asso. prof. mech. engring. George Washington U., 1957-—. Decorated Legion of Merit. Mem. Am. Soc. Naval Engrs. Home: 3709 Woodstock St. N., Arlington 7, Va. Office: George Washington U., Washington. Died Mar. 1960.

WEAVER, JAMES HARVEY, coll. athletic commr.; b. Rutherford, N.C., Mar. 29, 1903; s. Charles Clinton and Florence (Stacy) W.; student Emory and Henry Coll., 1919-21; B.S., Centenary Coll., Shreveport, 1925; m. Kate Speed Dunn, Aug. 16, 1938; 1 dau., Florence. Football coach Nacogdoches (Tex.) High Sch., 1926-27, Oak Ridge (N.C.) Acad., 1928-33; football coach Wake Forest (N.C.) Coll., 1933-36, athletic dir., 1937-54; commnr. Atlantic Coast Conf., 1954-70. Served to lt. comdr. USNR, 1942-45. Home: Greensboro NC Died July 11, 1970; buried Greensboro NC

WEAVER, WALTER REED army officer; b. Charleston, S.C., Feb. 23, 1885; s. Maj. Gen. Erasmus Morgan and Leize (Holmes) W.; educated Virginia Military Institute, 3 years; B.S., Military Academy, West Point, N.Y.; student Harvard, 1924, Army Industrial Coll., Washington, D.C., 1932-33; m. Elizabeth Ker Johnson, Sept. 30, 1911. Commd. 2d lt. U.S. Army, 1908, advanced through grades to maj. gen., 1941; assigned to 11th Inf. and served at Ft. D. A. Russell (now Francis E. Warren), Wyo., 1908; transferred to 28th Inf., Ft. Snelling, Minn., 1910; with 24th Inf., Philippines, 1912; with 15th Inf., Tientsin, China, Oct. 1914; recruiting at Columbus Barracks, O., 1915; with 22d Inf., Ft. Thomas, Ky., 1916; comdt. of flying cadets, Wilbur Wright Field, Dayton, O., 1917; organized U.S. Army Aviation Mech. Sch., St. Paul, Minn., 1917-18; chief of mech. training div., Supply Group, Office of Dir. of Air Service, Washington, D.C., 1919; received flying training, 1920; pilot, tech. observer, Kelly Field, Tex., 1921; chief of property requirements div., Supply Group, Office of Chief of Air Service, Washington, D.C., 1921; comdg. officer, Mitchel Field, N.Y., 1921-23; comdr., Boston Airport, 1923; comdr. air depot, Middletown, Pa., 1925-27; comdg. officer, Maxwell Field, Ala., 1927-31; chief of plans div., Office of Chief of Air Corps, 1932, chief of information div., 1933; rep. Air Corps Procurement Planning, N.Y. City, 1934-35; inspector, G.H.Q. Air Force, Langley Field, Va., 1935, post exec., Feb. 1936, comdg. officer 1st Air Base, June 1936; comdg. officer Langley Field, July 1937-39; comdt. Air Corps Tactical Sch., Maxwell Field, Ala., 1939; comdg. gen. Southeast Air Corps Training Center, Maxwell Field, Ala., 1940; acting chief of Air Corps, Washington, D.C., Dec. 1941-Mar. 1942; comdg. gen. of Army Air Forces Tech. Training Command, Knollwood Field, N.C., Mar. 1942-July 1943; retired, 1944; asst. to pres. for aviation, Aviation Corp. of Am. Received Distinguished Service Medal, 1943. Mem. Sigma Alpha Epsilon. Mason (Shriner). Clubs: Army and Navy (Washington); Metropolitan (New York); Kiwanis. Home: Fort Boykin, Smithfield, Va. Died Oct. 27, 1944; buried in Arlington National Cemetery.

WEBB, ALEXANDER STEWART educator; b. New York, Feb. 15, 1835; s. Gen. James Watson and Helen Lispenard (Stewart) W.; grad. U.S. Mil. Acad., 1855; 2d lt. 4th Arty., July 1, 1855; 2d lt. 2d Arty., Oct. 20, 1855; 1st lt., Apr. 28, 1861; capt. 11th Inf., May 14, 1861; maj. 1st R.I. Inf., Sept. 14, 1861; served in Army of Potomac; asst. chief of arty., insp. gen. 5th Corps; promoted brig. gen. U.S.V., June 1863; comdg. 2d Div., 2d Army Corps, 1 yr.; served with distinction at Gettysburg and was wounded there; afterward in Rapidan and Wilderness campaigns; severely wounded at Spottsylvania, May 12, 1864; awarded Congressional Medal of Honor "for distinguished personal gallantry in the battle of Gettysburg;" assigned as maj. gen. U.S.V. by President Lincoln, Dec. 1864; chief of staff, Army of the Potomac, to Appomattox C.H., and to May 1866; lt. col. 44th Inf., July 26, 1866, 5th Inf., Mar. 15, 1869; reached bvt. rank of maj. gen. in vol. and regular army. Assigned by President Grant as maj. gen. U.S.A., 1869, in command of 1st Mil. Dist. (state of Va.); discharged at own request, Dec. 3, 1870. Pres. Coll. of the City of N.Y. for 33 1/2 yrs., 1869-1903; retired and pensioned by state law. Comdr. gen. Mil. Order Foreign Wars. Mem. N.Y. Monuments Commn. Author: The Peninsula—McClellan's Campaign of 1862. Home: Riverdale-on-Hudson, N.Y. Died 1911.

WEBB, CHARLES M., judge circuit court 7th circuit Wis.; ed. U.S. Mil. Acad., West Point; served in Co. G, 12th Wis. regt., in Civil war; engaged in practice as lawyer until elected judge; voted for in Wis. legislature, 1899, as a Republican candidate for U.S. senator. Address: Grand Rapids Wood Co WI

WEBB, FRANK ELBRIDGE industrial engr., pub. works contractor; b. Calaveras County, Calif., Sept. 1, 1869; s. Elbridge and Annie E. (Settle); desc. of Mayflower ancestry; grad. Lincoln High Sch., San Francisco; studied law under John H. Dickinson, San Francisco; m. Elsa White Reid, Apr. 1928. Joined Nat. Guard of Calif., 1884; recruited regt. for Spanish-Am. War, but was sent on spl. mission around the world as confidential representative of President of U.S.; later served in Q.M. Dept. of the Army; engaged in handling gen. govt. supplies; with John A. Bensel, engr., 1906-16; made study of engring.; assisted in organ- ization Plattsburg training camps; purchased supplies for French, English and Belgians in earlier years of World War, also assisted in organization for Am. defense; actively identified with construction of ships and loading plants on Eastern Seaboard, after U.S. entered World War; name carried on confidential list of War Dept. under rank of col.; connected with bridge building on Pacific Coast in Calif. since 1923; engr. for Chelsea docks and canals for State of N.Y. Mem. S.A.R. Decorated Knight Comdr. of the Holy Sepulchre; Knight Comdr. of Crown of Charlemagne. Candidate of Farmer-Labor Party for President of U.S., 1928; nominated for Presidency by same party in spring of 1932, declined; nominated for Presidency by Liberty Party, July 4, 1932. Presbyterian. Home: Washington, D.C.; also San Francisco, Calif. Address: 815 15th St. N.W., Washington, D.C. Died June 15, 1949.

WEBB, GERALD BERTRAM physician; b. Cheltenham, Eng., Sept. 24, 1871; s. William John and Frances (Le Plastrier) W.; Guy's Hosp., London, 1890-93; M.D., U. of Denver, 1896; post-grad. work, Vienna and London, 1905-06; Sc.D., Colorado College 1936, University of Colorado, 1938; married Varina Howell Davis Hayes, July 30, 1904; children—Varina Margaret, Gerald Bertram (died), Frances Robine, Eleanor Constance Leila, Joel Addison Hayes. Came to the United States, 1893; in private practice at Colorado Springs since 1896; cons. physician Methodist, Sunnyrest, Glockner and St. Francis sanatoriums; chief of staff Union Printers Home; pres. Colo. Foundation for Research in Tuberculosis. Served as lt. col. Med. Corps U.S. Army, 1918; sr. consultant in tuberculosis, A.E.F., 1918-19. U.S. del. to Laennec-Centenary, Paris, Dec. 1926. Awarded Trudeau medal, Nat. Tuberculosis Assn., 1939. Fellow A.M.A., Am. Coll. Physicians, N.Y. Acad. of Medicine; mem. Assn. Am. Physicians (pres. 1939), Am. Clin. and Climatol. Assn. (pres. 1929-30), Am. Assn. Immunologists, Nat. Tuberculosis Assn. (pres. 1920; del. to Internat. Congress on Tuberculosis, Rome, 1912, Internat. Union Against Tuberculosis, Paris, 1920, London, 1921). Republican. Episcopalian. Club: Cheyenne Mountain Country. Author: (with C. T. Ryder) Overcoming Tuberculosis, 1927; Laennec—A Memoir, 1928; History of Tuberculosis, 1936; (with Desmond Powell) Henry Sewall, Physiologist and Physician. Home: 1222 N. Cascade Av. Office: Burns Bldg., Colorado Springs, Colo. Died Jan. 27, 1948.

WEBB, ULYS ROBERT naval officer; b. Jan. 18, 1874; grad. Naval War Coll. Entered U.S. Navy, Oct. 21, 1901; promoted through grades to rear admiral, Med. Corps, Feb. 1, 1933; retired Feb. 1, 1938. Deceased.*

WEBB, WILLIAM SNYDER educator; b. Greendale, Ky., Jan. 19, 1882; s. William and Gulielma (Snyder) W.; B.S., U. Ky., 1901, M.S., 1902; student U. Chgo., 7 quarters, 1911-15; Hon. D.Sc., U. Ala., 1937; m. Alleen P. Lary, June 8, 1910; children—William Lary, Jane Allen. Instr. physics U. Ky., 1904-08, asst. prof., 1908-14, asso. prof., 1914-17, prof., head dept. physics, 1919-—, prof., head dept., anthropology and archeology, 1929-—. Archeologist, TVA, 1934-37. Maj., F.A., U.S. Army, World War I, assigned to Ft. Sill Sch. Fire. Trustee Lees Collegiate Inst., 1920-29, 1943-—. Mem. council A.A.A.S.; sec. Am. Assn. Physics Tchrs.; mem. Com. on Basic Needs in Am. Archaeology, Div. Anthropology and Psychology; NRC; pres. Central Sect. Am. Anthropol. Assn.; v.p. Soc. for Am. Archaeology; v.p. Ky. Research Found.; chmn. com. for recovering archaeol. remains, rep. Am. Council Learned Socs.; mem. Am. Physicists Soc., Phi Beta Kappa, Sigma Xi, Pi Mu Epsilon, Sigma Pi Sigma, O.D.K. Presbyn. Author: Bulletins 119, 122 and 129, Bur. Am. Ethnology; also various reports and bulls. Home: Lexington, Ky. Died Feb. 15, 1964.

WEBER, JOHN mech. engr.; b. Pitts., Oct. 20, 1885; s. John and Emma Wilson (Beitler) W.; M.E., U. Pitts., 1909; D.Sc.; m. Blanche J. Martin, Mar. 21, 1912; children—John Martin, James Harold, Dorothy Ellen. With U. Pitts., 1909-—, except during war period, successively research asst., instr. in mech. engring., asst. prof., asso. prof., prof. and head of dept., 1922-25, bus. mgr., supervising engr. constructional work, 1926-36, sec. of univ., 1936-—. Served as capt. engrs., World War; mem. Vehicle Standardization Bd., also Automotive Products Com., War Industries Bd. Mem. Delta Tau Delta, Omicron Delta Kappa, Sigma Tau, Scabbard and Blade. Republican. Mem. United Presbyn. Ch. Club: University (Pitts.). Home: 1317 Dennison St., Pitts. 15217. Died Mar. 1, 1966.

WEBER, MAX soldier; b. Achern, Baden, Aug. 27, 1824; ed. Poly. Sch., and grad. Mil. Acad. Karlsruhe, 1843, as officer in the army; took part in revolution in support of German Parliament, 1849, and upon its failure came to U.S. Served in U.S. army, 1861-65, as col. 20th N.Y. vols. and brig. gen. after April 1862; after losing right arm at battle of Antietam, had command Harper's Ferry, which he defended successfully against attack of Gen. Early's forces. After war was 10 years assessor and collector internal revenue, New York City. Died 1901.

WEBER, RANDOLPH HENRY U.S. judge; b. St. Louis, Nov. 26, 1909; s. Henry P. and Lillian A. (Boelling) W.; student Westminster Coll., Fulton, Mo., 1928-30; LL.B., Washington U., 1933; LL.D., Culver-Stockton Coll., Canton, Mo., 1958; m. Lila H. Everts, Sept. 8, 1934; children—Phillip A., Randolph H. Admitted to Mo. bar, 1933; practiced in Poplar Bluff, 1933-57; city atty., Poplar Bluff, 1935-37; pros. atty., Butler County, Mo., 1937-38; rep. Butler County to Mo. Legislature, 1939-40; circuit judge 33d Jud. Circuit, Mo., 1943-57; U.S. dist. judge, Eastern Dist. of Mo., 1957-—. Dir. Poplar Bluff Loan & Bldg. Assn., 1950-57. Pres. Poplar Bluff Industries, 1947-56. Adv. bd. Salvation Army. Served as lt. col. Mo. Reserve Mil. Force, 1941-46. Recipient DeMolay Legion of Honor, 1957, Alumni Achievement award Westminster Coll., 1958. Mem. Am. Judicature Soc., Inst. Jud. Adminstrn., Poplar Bluff C. of C. (past pres.), Nat. Union Fraternal Beneficiary Assn. (v.p., dir.), Am., Mo. (gov. 1952-56), Butler County (past pres.) bar assns., Mo. Jud. Conf. (v.p., mem. exec. com. 1950-56), Sigma Phi Epsilon, Delta Theta Phi. Mem. Christian Ch. (elder). Mason (Shriner; past master; grand orator 1959). Odd Fellow; mem. Order Eastern Star. Club: Poplar Bluff Lions (past pres.). Home: 6340 Wydown, Clayton 5, Mo. Office: Federal Court House and Custom House, St. Louis 63101. Died Nov. 23, 1961; buried Meml. Gardens, Poplar Bluff, Mo.

WEBSTER, FRANK DANIEL army officer; b. Rolla, Mo., Sept. 11, 1866; s. Henry and Melinda (Burlingame) W.; grad. U.S. Mil. Acad., 1889, Inf. and Cav. Sch., 1897; Army War Coll., 1913; m. Anna G. Angell, Dec. 4, 1900. Commd. 2d lt. 25th Inf., June 12, 1889; trans. to 6th Inf., Oct. 3, 1889; 1st lt. 20th Inf., Dec. 7, 1896; capt. 18th Inf., Sept. 8, 1899; trans. to 20th Inf., Dec. 6, 1899; maj. inf., Mar. 11, 1911; assigned to 20th Inf., July 14, 1911; lt. col. 22d Inf., July 1, 1916; col., June 30, 1917; brig. gen. N.A., Dec. 17, 1917. A.d.c. to Brig. Gen. Loyd Wheaton, in Ala., Fla. and Ga., 1898, and in Philippine Islands, 1899-1902; again in P.I., 1904-06, 1909-11. Awarded life saving medal by Treasury Dept. for rescuing 2 persons from drowning, Jan. 18, 1893; recommended by Gen. Wheaton for bvt. of capt. "for gallantry" in Battle of Malinta, Mar. 26, 1899; for bvt. of maj. for charge at Santa Tomas, May 4, 1899; for bvt. of capt., U.S.A., by Gen. Lawton, "for services under fire," June 11, 1899. Comd. 17th Separate (regular) Brig., Jan.-Feb. 1918, 8th Brig., 4th (regular) Div., A.E.F., Feb.-July 27, 1918; retired as col. U.S.A., Dec. 3, 1918. Mason, Elk. Home: Leavenworth, Kan. Died Feb. 20, 1932.

WEBSTER, HARRIE rear admiral U.S.N.; b. Farmington, Me., Feb. 12, 1843; s. Nathan and Ellen Kilshaw (Whittier) W.; ed. pub. schs. and Farmington Acad.; m. Mary Simpson Hein, Nov. 20, 1870. Apptd. 3d asst. engr. in vol. service, U.S.N., Feb. 8, 1862; served under Farragut on Mississippi River and at Mobile Bay. Aug. 5, 1864; 3d asst. engr. U.S.N., May 20, 1864; 2d asst. engr., Jan. 1, 1868; passed asst. engr., Oct. 29, 1874; wrecked on U.S.S. Vandalia at Samoa, Mar. 15-16, 1889; promoted chief engr., Oct. 7, 1892; served on several vessels as chief engr., and was in recruiting service, 1898; afterward with Bur. Steam Engring., and under provisions of Personnel Bill (1899) transferred to line as comdr. on active list; served as insp. machinery and ordnance; promoted to capt., Jan. 4, 1903; retired on own application as rear admiral U.S.N., Feb. 9, 1903. Died Apr. 23, 1921.

WEBSTER, JOSEPH DANA engr., army officer; b. Hampton, N.H., Aug. 25, 1811; s. Josiah and Elizabeth (Wright) W.; grad. Dartmouth, 1832; m. Miss Wright, 1844, at least 3 children. Entered govt. service as civil engr., 1835; commd. 2d lt. Topog. Engrs., U.S. Army, 1838, 1st lt., 1849, capt., 1853; resigned, 1854; engaged in mfg. farming implements, Chgo.; mem. Chgo. Sewerage Commn., 1855; maj., paymaster in U.S. Volunteers, 1861; commd. col. 1st Ill. Light Arty.; chief of staff under U. S. Grant, in charge of all mil. rys. in Grant's area; commd. brig. gen. U.S. Volunteers, 1862; chief of staff under Gen. William T. Sherman at Battle of Nashville; brevetted maj. gen. volunteers, 1865; resigned commn., 1865; assessor internal revenue, 1869-72; asst. treasurer U.S., 1872-75; collector internal revenue, 1875-76. Died Chgo., Mar. 12, 1876.

WEBSTER, ROBERT MORRIS, air officer; b. Boston, Mass., Oct. 10, 1892; s. William Roland and Jennie Webster (Gorrie) W.; m. Flora Dorothy Bitzer, Mar. 19, 1921; children—Robert Morris, Roland Carl. Commd. 2d lt., Air Service, U.S. Army, 1918; promoted through the grades to major, Air Corps, U.S. Army, 1940; maj. gen., 1944; successively apptd. comdg. gen. 1st Air Support Command, Aug. 1942; 1st Tactical Air Force in France, Mar. 1945; Air Transport Command, Sept. 1946; 1st Air Force, 1947; East Air Defense Force, 1949; mem. Brazil-U.S. Mil. Com. 1950; Can.-U.S. Defense Bd., Mexico-U.S. Defense Com., Brazil-U.S. Defense Com.; Inter-Am. Defense Bd., 1953. Rated command pilot, combat observer. Awarded Victory Medal, Distinguished Flying Cross, Distinguished Service Medal, Silver Star, Legion of Merit, Comdr. Legion of Honor; Croix de Guerre with 3 palms; chief comdr. Order Aero Merit (Brazil). Mem. Order of Daedalians. Clubs: Wings, (N.Y.C.); Army and Navy (Washington). Address: Washington DC Died Mar. 6, 1972; buried Arlington Nat. Cemetery, Arlington VA

WEBSTER, WILLIAM, business exec.; b. Bel Air, Md., Dec. 6, 1900; s. Richard Henry and Harriet Archer (Williams) W.; grad. U.S. Naval Acad., 1920; B.S. and M.S., Mass. Inst. of Tech., 1923; D.Sc., Tufts Coll., 1950, Lowell Technol. Institute, 1961; LL.D., Bates College, 1950; D.S. in B.A., Bryant Coll., 1965; D. in C.S., Suffolk U., 1970; m. Eleanore Blodgett, April 21, 1924 (dec. April 1961); 1 son, Richard; m. 2d, Vollie Sanderson, November 29, 1963. Asst. to gen. mgr. New Eng. Power Assn., Boston, 1928-33, asst. to pres., 1933-35, asst. dist. mgr., 1935-42; pres. Narragansett Electric Co., Providence, past pres. United Electric Rys. Co.; vice pres. New Eng. Power Assn. and pres. Mass. Utilities Assos., 1942; exec. v.p., dir. N.E. Electric System, 1950-59, pres., 1959-63, chmn., chief executive, 1963-70; chmn., dir. Yankee Atomic Electric Company; v.p., dir. Vt. Yankee Nuclear Power Company, Maihe Yankee Atomic Co.; dir. Conn. Yankee Atomic Power Co., Huyck Corp., Arthur D. Little, Inc., State St. Bank & Trust, Mitre Corp., Fed. Res. Bank Boston; trustee Band Corp.; mgmt. cons. OPA, 1942-45; with Nat. Defense Research Com., 1943-46; appointed chairman Research and Development Board of U.S. Dept. of Defense, 1950; deputy sec. defense for atomic energy, chmn. mil. liaison com. Dir., v.p. Am. Inst. Counselling and Personnel Research; mem. gen. adv. com. AEC; dir. chmn. New Eng. Council; mem. NACA, 1950-51; mem. Sci. Adv. Bd., 1951-52, Army Sci. Adv. Panel, 1951-58; v.p., dir. Atomic Indsl. Forum; trustee Fund Peacetime Atomic Development; dir. Edison Electric Inst., Am. Transit Assn.; mem. Hudson Inst. Trustee Moses Brown Sch., 1940. Bates Coll., 1945, Sci. Engring. Inst., Woods Hole Oceanographic Institute, Baystate Sci. Found.; chairman advisory committee of Woodrow Wilson School, Princeton, 1959-66; life mem. corp. Mass. Inst. Tech. Served USN, 1917-28, naval constructor, 1922-28. Patriotic Civilian Service award; Exceptional Civilian Service award; New Eng. award Outstanding Engr., 1964, citation Atomic Energy Commission, 1967; John Fritz medal Am. Soc. M.E., 1971. Fellow Am. Academy of Arts and Scis.; mem. Am. Nuclear Soc. (charter mem.), Soc. Naval Architects and Marine Engrs., U.S.N. Acad. Grads. Assn., Delta Psi. Clubs: The Algonquin (Boston); Army and Navy, Cosmos (Washington). Home: Boston MA Died May 17, 1972; interred Bel Air MD

WEDEL, PAUL JOHN, accountant; b. Jersey City, Aug. 17, 1896; s. Fred Henry and Anna (Hunken) W.; student N.Y.U., 1914-16; m. Helen Agnes Cleary, Mar. 14, 1926; children—Paul George, Diana Clare (Mrs. John Joseph Riley, Jr.), Peter John. Sr. accountant J. H. Cohn Co., Newark, 1919-23; cons. accountant, Newark, 1923-34; sr. accountant Patterson, Teele & Dennis, C.P.A.'s, N.Y.C., 1934-38; utilities accountant SEC, 1939-40; accounting cons. Trustees Associates Gas & Electric Corp., 1940-43; chief accountant, bd. mem. Navy Price Adjustment Bd., 1943-47; mem. appeal bd. Office Contract Settlement, 1947-48; mem. Excess Tax Council, Internal Revenue Service, 1948-52; dir. office of accounting U.S. Renegotiation, Bd., 1952-57; became controller Craig Systems, Inc., 1957, retired. Served as 1st lt. USAAF, World War I; capt. USNR, World War II. Mem. Am. Inst. Accountants, Fed. Govts. Accountants Assn. Home: Ft Lauderdale FL Died Nov. 13, 1971.

WEED, FRANK WATKINS army officer; b. Baltimore, Md., Apr. 12, 1881; s. William Butler and Isabelle (Hall) W.; M.D., U. of Md., 1903; student Army Med. Sch., 1904-05; Army War Coll., 1928-29; m. Abigail S. Howell, Sept. 19, 1908; children—William Howell, Natalie Howell (Mrs. Robert Campbell Aloe). Served in the Med. Corps U.S. Army since 1904; editor in chief: The Medical Dept. of the U.S. Army in the World War (15 vols.), 1921-29. Promoted through grades to brig. gen., July 1942; surgeon, 1st Army, Governor's Island, N.Y., 1940-42; comdg. Letterman Gen. Hosp. since July 1942. Awarded Distinguished Service Medal (with Oak Leaf Cluster). Episcopalian. Address: Letterman General Hospital, San Francisco, Calif.* Died Oct. 1945.

WEED, JEFFERSON physician; b. N.Y.C., Oct. 12, 1907; s. LeRoy Jefferson and Mabel (Scott) W.; grad. St. Paul's Sch., 1925; A.B., Union Coll., Schenectady, 1929; M.D., Cornell U., 1935; m. Bettyanne Underwood, Aug. 5, 1939; children—Russell U., Leroy Jefferson II, Wyman W., Randolph, Elizabeth Anne. Intern Nassau Hosp., Mineola, N.Y., 1935-36; intern Bellevue Hosp., N.Y.C., 1936-38, clin. asst. physician gen. medicine, 1938-40, clin. asst. physician cardiology, 1945-47; asst. med. dir. Mut. Benefit Life Ins. Co., 1945-55, asso. med. dir., 1955-59, med. dir., 1959—. Trustee Glen Ridge (N.J.) Community Chest. Served to capt., M.C., AUS, 1941-45. Mem. A.M.A., Med. Soc. N.J., Essex County Med. Soc., Bd. of Life Ins. Medicine, Soc. Alumni Bellevue Hosp., Assn. Life Ins. Med. Dirs., Psi Upsilon, Nu Sigma Nu. Episcopalian. Clubs: Cornell (N.Y.C.); Glen Ridge Country. Home: 6 Hamilton Rd., Glen Ridge, N.J. Office: 520 Broad St., Newark 1. Died May 22, 1963.

WEEKS, ALANSON surgeon; b. Allegan, Mich., Sept. 15, 1877; s. Harrison S. and Julia (Shoemaker) W.; M.D., U. of Mich., 1899; m. Belle A. Harmes, June 7, 1905; 1 daughter, Leonie Belle. Became clinical professor of surgery, University of California Medical School, 1924, now emeritus; consultant in surgery St. Luke's Hosp., Children's, Marine and Emergency hosps.—all San Francisco. Served as maj. Med. Corps, U.S. Army, World War. Awarded D.S.M. (U.S.). Fellow Am. Coll. Surgeons; mem. Pacific Coast Surg. Assn., Am. Med. Assn., Calif. State and San Francisco County med. socs., Calif. Acad. of Medicine. Clubs: Pacific-Union, Family, Olympic (San Francisco); Country (Burlingame, Calif.); Country. Home: Pacific Union Club, San Francisco. Office: 384 Post St., San Francisco, Calif. Died Nov. 25, 1947.

WEEKS, EDGAR congressman; b. Mt. Clemens, Mich., Aug. 3, 1839; s. Aaron and Laura (Bingham) W.; ed. public schs.; m. Mary S. Campbell, 1867. Served in Civil War, sergt. Co. B, 5th Mich. inf.; promoted to capt. 22d Mich. inf.; later asst. insp. gen. 3d brigade, 2d div. reserve corps, army of the Cumberland. Practiced law, 1866—, prosecuting atty. Macomb County, 1867-70, probate judge, 1875-76; Congressman 7th Mich. dist., 1899-1903; mem. Com. on Pensions; Com. on Contested Elections, Com. on Claims. Republican; del. to Nat. Rep. Conv., 1888; asst. insp. gen. G.A.R., Companion Loyal Legion, Compatriot Sons of the Revolution. Home: Mount Clemens, Mich. Died 1904.

WEEKS, GEORGE H. brig. gen. U.S.A., retired, Feb. 3, 1898; b. Gifford, N.H., Feb. 3, 1834; s. Levi R. and Lydia Sleeper W.; entered army from Maine, July 1, 1853, as cadet in mil. acad.; grad. with bvt. 2d lt., 1st Arty., July 1, 1857; m. Laura, d. Gen. E. B. Babbitt, U.S.A., May 1859. Apptd. 2d lt. 4th arty., Feb. 10, 1859; 1st lt., May 14, 1861; capt. and asst. q.m., Mar. 24, 1862; maj. q.m., May 29, 1876; lt. col. dept. q.m. gen., Oct. 19, 1888; col. asst. q.m. gen., May 16, 1895; brig. gen. and q.m. gen., Feb. 16, 1897, until retired. Bvtd. maj. and lt. col., Mar. 13, 1865, for faithful and meritorious service in q.m.'s dept. during Civil War. Died 1905.

WEEKS, GRENVILLE MELLEN soldier, physician; b. New York, Nov. 22, 1837; s. Cyrus (M.D.) and M. L. (Child) W.; 7th in lineal descent from John Alden, of the Mayflower; student in New York Acad. (now Coll. City of New York), 1856-58, Coll. Phys. and Surg. (Columbia), 1859-60; M.D., Univ. Med. Coll. (New York U.), 1861; m. Helen Campbell Stuart, author, 1861; m. 2d, Maria Oberg; m. 3d, Pauline M. Sauer of Brooklyn, 1893. Apptd. asst. surgeon U.S.N., 1862; transferred from U.S. frigate Brandywine at scene of action between Monitor and Merrimac, Hampton Roads, 1862, and apptd. surgeon U.S. ironclad Monitor; saved the lives of a boatload of officers and men, having his right arm almost torn off at the shoulder; promoted by President Lincoln, and apptd. surgeon with rank of maj.; brigade surgeon and acting med. dir. Dept. of Fla., at close of war; reëntered mil. service 1865, as surgeon and acting Indian agent in Northwest during Indian troubles in Minn. and Dak.; returned East, 1871, and resumed practice. Author of resolution recognizing Cuban independence by Congress of U.S., 1898. Organized and pres., 1859, of the first Christian Union in the world that urged a universal peace union of all creeds, on doctrine of universal fatherhood of God and brotherhood of man. Died Apr. 26, 1919.

WEEKS, JOHN WINGATE sec. of war; b. Lancaster, N.H., Apr. 11, 1860; s. William D. and Mary Helen (Fowler) W.; reared on farm; grad. U.S. Naval Acad., 1881; m. Martha A. Sinclair, Oct. 7, 1885. Midshipman U.S.N., 1881-83; asst. land commr. Fla. Southern R.R., 1886-88; mem. Hornblower & Weeks, bankers and brokers, Boston, 1888-1912. Alderman, Newton, Mass., 1900. 01, 02, mayor, 1903-04; chmn. Rep. State Conv., 1905; mem. 59th to 62d Congresses (1905-13), 12th Mass. Dist.; U.S. senator, 1913-19. Sec. of War in Cabinets of Presidents Harding and Coolidge, Mar. 4, 1921-Oct. 1925 (resigned). Received 105 votes from 25 states (next to the nominee) for Presidential nomination in Republican Nat. Conv., Chicago, 1916. Comd. division of Mass. Naval Brigade, with rank of capt., 1890-98; comd. 2d div. auxiliary U.S. naval force on Atlantic Coast, 1898-99; mem. Mil. Advisory Bd. of Mass. and Mil. Bd. of Examiners, 1894-1900; mem. bd. of visitors U.S. Naval Acad., 1896. Home: West Newton, Mass. Died July 12, 1926.

WEEKS, SINCLAIR, former sec. of commerce; born at West Newton, Massachusetts, June 15, 1893; son of John Wingate and Martha A. (Sinclair) W.; student Newton (Massachusetts) High School, 1906-10; A.B., Harvard, 1914; m. Beatrice Dowse, Dec. 4, 1915 (Dec.);children—Frances Lee, John W., 2d, Martha S., Sinclair, William D., Beatrice; married 2d, Jane Tompkins Rankin, January 3, 1948; m. 3d, Alice Requa Low, August 22, 1968. In employ First Nat. Bank of Boston, Mass., as clerk to asst. cashier, 1914-23; hon. dir. United-Carr, Inc., 1 st Nat. Bank of Boston; chmn. Reed and Barton Corp.; dir. N.H. Ins. Co., Lancaster Nat. Bank; limited partner Hornblower & Weeks. United States Secretary of Commerce, 1953-58; appointed U.S. senator from Mass. to serve in place Henry Cabot Lodge, Jr., Feb.-Dec. 1944. Treas. Republican Nat. Com., 1941-44, chmn. finance com., 1949-52. Trustee U. of N.H., Fessenden Sch., Newton, Mass.; chmn. bd. trustees Wentworth Inst. Served as capt. F.A., U.S. Army, 1917-19, with A.E.F. in France. Unitarian. Home: Concord MA Died Jan. 27, 1972.

WEIGEL, GEORGE KIBLER, railroad ofcl.; b. New Rochelle, N.Y., Oct. 29, 1915; s. George Alexander and Ellen (Bourke) W.; B.A., Cornell U., 1936; M.B.A., N.Y.U., 1941; m. Marion Katherine Lyons, Aug. 17, 1946; children—George A., Paul H., Peter B. With investment dept. Met. Life Ins. Co., N.Y.C., 1947-56; controller N. Am. Car Corp., Chgo., 1957-62, v.p. finanace, controller, 1959-62, dir., 1960-62; joined M.P.R.R., 1963, became controller, 1964, v.p., 1965; later v.p. finance Ill. Central Industries, Chgo., until 1972. Served to capt. AUS, 1941-46; ETO. Mem. Assn. ICC Practitioners, Financial Execs. Inst., Financial Analysts Soc. (bd. govs. St. Louis from 1964), Delta Tau Delta. Clubs: Cornell (N.Y.C.); Union League (Chgo.); Press (st. Louis). Home: Olympia Fields IL Died Mar. 21, 1972; buried St. Catherine's Cemetery Sea Girt NJ

WEIGEL, WILLIAM army officer; b. New Brunswick, N.J., Aug. 25, 1863; s. Philip (Sr.) and Anna (Silzer) W.; grad. U.S. Mil. Acad., 1887; M.Sc., Rutgers Coll., 1919; unmarried. Commd. 2d lt. 11th Inf., June 12, 1887; 1st lt. 22d Inf., June 6, 1894; trans. to 11th Inf., June 22, 1894; capt. a.q.-m. vols., Nov. 26, 1898; hon. discharged vols., June 16, 1899; capt. U.S.A., Mar. 2, 1899; promoted through grades to brig. gen. N.A., Aug. 5, 1917; maj. gen., Aug. 8, 1918-June 15, 1919; remanded to regular rank of col., June 15, 1919; brig. gen. U.S.A., Mar. 6, 1921; maj. gen., Nov. 20, 1925. Served in Indian wars, Spanish-Am. War and Philippine Insurrection; brig. gen. N.A., comdg. 151st Depot Brig., Camp Devens, Mass., Sept.-Nov. 1917; comdr. 76th Div. and Cantonment, Camp Devens, Nov. 27-Feb. 13, 1918; comd. 56th Brig., 28th Div., Mar. 25-Sept. 8, 1918; comd. 88th Div., Sept. 10, 1918, to demobilization, June 15, 1919. In France, May 5, 1918-June 1, 1919; participated in Champagne-Marne defensive, July 15-18; Aisne-Marne offensive, July 18-Aug. 6; Oise-Aisne offensive, Aug. 18-Nov. 11; Center sector, Haute-Alsace, Oct. 12-Nov. 4; Meuse-Argonne, Sept. 26-Nov. 11, 1918. Thrice awarded Croix de Guerre, with palms, and Comdr. Legion of Honor (French); D.S.M. from U.S. "for exceptionally meritorious and distinguished services." Chief of staff Eastern Dept. Aug. 22, 1919-May 10, 1921; apptd. brig. gen. comdg. 2d Brig., 1st Div., July 1, 1921; dep. comdr. 12th A.C., Organized Reserves, Feb. 15, 1922-Nov. 20, 1924; comdg. Philippine Div. and Philippine Dept., Jan. 26, 1925-Feb. 16, 1927; retired as maj. gen. Aug. 25, 1927. Mem. Conservation and Development Bd. of State of N.J. Episcopalian. Mason. Died Mar. 4, 1936.

WEIL, RICHARD, JR., dept. store exec.; b. N.Y.C., Dec. 5, 1907; s. Richard and Minnie (Straus) W.; student Hotchkiss, 1921-25, Yale, 1925-38; m. Allene Hall, Jan. 5, 1935; children—Richard, III, Martha. With R. H. Macy & Co., 1928-36; v.p. L. Bamberger & Co., 1936-39, pres., 1939-45; v.p. R. H. Macy & Co., Inc., 1945-49, pres. Macy, N.Y., 1949-53; dir. E. J. Korvette, Inc., Intercultural Publs., Inc. Served as lt. col., AUS, World War II. Decorated Legion of Merit, 1945. Italian

Star of Solidarity, 1952. Clubs: Yale, Grolier, Regency. Author: The Art of Practical Thinking, 1940. Home: 540 Park Av., N.Y.C. Died May 10, 1958.

WEINBERG, BERNARD, educator; b. Chgo., Aug. 23, 1909; s. William and Anna (Goldstein) W.; Ph.B., U. Chgo., 1930, Ph.D., 1936; diploma U. Paris, 1931; study and research, Paris, London, Florence, Rome, 1930-31, 34-35, 38, 47-48, 50, 51-52, 57, 61, 63-64, 67-68. Asst. Romance langs. U. Chgo., 1932-37; instr. Washington U., St. Louis, 1937-39, asst. prof., 1939-46, asso. prof., 1946-49, prof., 1949; asso. prof. Northwestern U., 1949-51, prof., 1951-55; vis. prof. U. Chgo., summer 1947, prof., 1955, chmn. dept. Romance langs. and lit., 1958-67, William H. Colvin research prof., 1967-68, Robert Maynard Hutchins Distinguished Service prof., 1969-73; visiting prof. U. Ia., 1965, U. Minn., 1966; vis. Accademica dei Lincei prof. Scuola Normale Superiore di Pise, 1970. Chmn. Newberry Library Conf. Renaissance Studies, 1953, 62; mem. adv. council Renaissance Soc. Am., 1953, 63. Served to capt. USAAF, 1942-45. Am. Field Service fellow for France, 1934-35; Guggenheim fellow, 1947-48, 56-57, fellow Inst. Advanced Study, 1956-57; Fulbright sr. research award for Italy, 1951-52, for France, 1962-63. Fellow Am. Acad. Arts and Scis.; mem. Modern Lang. Assn. (1st v.p. 1963, exec. council), Accademia Toscana La Colombaria, Assn. Internationale des Etudes Francaises, Am. Assn. Tchrs. French, Am. Assn. U. Profs., Phi Beta Kappa. Author: French Realism: The Critical Reaction, 1830-1870, 1937; Critical Prefaces of the French Renaissance, 1950; Critics and Criticism, Ancient and Modern (with others), 1952; A History of Literary Criticism in the Italian Renaissance, 2 vols., 1961; The Art of Jean Racine, 1963; The Limits of Symbolism, 1966; Trattati di poetica e retorica del Cinquecento, vols. I and II, 1970. Editor: (with E. P. Dargan) The Evolution of Balzac's Comedie Humaine, 1942; French Poetry of the Renaissance, 1954. Editorial bd. Comparative Lit., 1964-66, Modern Philology, 1968-73; internat. editorial com. Rivista de leterature moderne, Florence, Italy. Author numerous articles and revs. to scholarly jours. in U.S., France, Italy, Switzerland. Home: Chicago IL Died Feb. 13, 1973.

WEINERMAN, EDWIN RICHARD, physician, educator; b. Hartford, Conn., July 17, 1917; s. David Tolner and Anna (Schwartz) W.; A.B., Yale, 1938; M.D., Georgetown U., 1942; M.P.H., Harvard, 1948; m. Shirley Basch, Dec. 23, 1940; children—Jeffrey Alan, Diane Lee. Med. house officer Beth Israel Hosp., Harvard and Tufts Services, Boston, 1942-43; resident communicable diseases Charles V. Chapin Hosp., Providence, 1942; resident internal medicine Drew Field Regional Hosp., Fla., 1943-44; spl. resident internal medicine San Francisco VA Hosp. U. Cal. Service, 1952-53; practice medicine, specializing in internal medicine, Berkeley, Cal. 1953-62; asst. chief med. officer health services div. FSA, Washington, 1946-47; asso. in med. care adminstrn. div. pub. health methods USPHS, 1947; asso. prof. med. econs., head div. med. care adminstrn. Sch. Pub. Health, U. Cal., 1948-50; med. dir. Permanente Health Plan, Oakland, Cal., 1950-51; med. dir. Herrick Meml. Hosp. Clinics, Berkeley, 1952-62; physician-in-charge Rheumatic Fever Clinic, Richmond, Contra Costa County Health Dept., 1953-62; dir. ambulatory services Yale-New Haven Hosp., Yale-New Haven Med. Center, 1962-66; prof. medicine and pub. health (med. care) Yale Sch. Medicine, 1962-70; cons., Group Health Corp. Puget Sound, Seattle, 1949; Am. fellow WHO, summer 1950; med. cons. San Francisco Labor Council, 1952; cons. med. group practice President's Commn. on Health Needs of Nation, 1952; med. plan adviser Sheet Metal Industry Welfare Fund, Oakland, 1956-62; med. cons Community Health Assn., Santa Rosa, Cal., 1961-62; cons. United Automobile Workers and Am. Motors Co., Milw., 1961, Office Econ. Opportunity, 1964-65; mem. adv. bd., cons. dept. univ. health Yale, 1964-70; cons. med. adv. com. Commn. on Delivery Personal Health Services, N.Y.C., 1966-70; mem. adv. com. on Medicaid, Conn. Dept. Welfare, 1967-70. Served to capt., M.C., AUS, 1943-46. Sr. faculty award Commonwealth Fund, 1967. Diplomate Nat. Bd. Med. Examiners, Am. Bd. Preventive Medicine. Fellow A.M.A., Am. Pub. Health Assn. (com. chmn.); mem. Conn., New Haven med. assns., Conn. Pub. Health Assn., Assn. Tchrs. Preventive Medicine, Am. Heart Assn., Internat. Acad. Legal Medicine and Social Medicine, Group Health Assn. Am., Am., Conn. hosp. assns., Assn. Am. Med. Colls., Royal Soc. Health (Gt. Britain), Nat. Rehab. Assn., Delta Omega (past nat. pres.). Contbr. articles profl. jours. Home: Hamden CT Died Feb. 20, 1970.

WEIR, JOHN M. (wer), army officer; b. Ind., Sept. 6, 1891; B.S. and LL.B., John B. Stetson U., 1914, A.M., 1917; grad. Inf. Sch., 1924. Commd. Capt. Inf., O.R.C., 1917; active duty, 1917-20; 1st lt. Inf., 1920; transferred to Judge Advocate Gen. Dept., 1928, and advanced through the grades to brig. gen., Sept. 1943. Address: Judge Advocate General's Dept., War Dept., Washington, D.C.* Died Nov. 21, 1948.

WEISS, LEWIS ALLEN (wis), business exec.; b. Chicago, Ill., May 8, 1893; s. Joseph Ignatius and Regina (Buchs) W.; student Kent Coll. of Law, 1912-15, U. of Southern Calif., 1926-29 (extension course in advanced economics); m. Sue C. Stephenson, April 22, 1922; 1 dau., Patricia Sue (Mrs. John Austin Armitage). Chairman board directors Mutual Broadcasting System; director and president of Don Lee Broadcasting System, Pacific Northwest Broadcasting Co.; pres., dir. Calif. Broadcasters, Inc.; pres. T. S. . Lee Enterprises; dir. Organic Chemicals. Asst. adminstr. Nat. Production Authority 1951-52. Mem. Los Angeles Airport Commn. Served as capt. 4th U.S. Cavalry, 1915-19. Dir. Los Angeles Chamber of Commerce (v.p.); mem. Hollywood Chamber of Commerce, Merchants and Mfrs. Assn. (dir.), Mil Order of the World War, Television Broadcasters Assn. (dir. 1944-45), Delta Theta Phi, Alpha Delta Sigma. Clubs: Los Angeles Rotary (dir., 1943-45), University (Los Angeles). Home: 9917 Durant Dr., Beverly Hills, Cal. Died June 15, 1953; buried Forest Lawn Cemetery, Los Angeles.

WEISSERT, AUGUSTUS GORDON lawyer; b. Canton, O., Aug. 7, 1843; grad. Racine (Wis.) High Sch.; admitted to bar, 1869; LL.B., U. of Mich., 1872; practiced at Milwaukee, Wis., since 1876. Served in 8th Regt. Wis. Vols., 1861-65; bvtd. capt. for bravery on battlefield; apptd. cadet U.S. Mil. Acad., but declined because of wounds received in battle. For a long time was a writer for the press. Mem. G.A.R. since 1866, comdr. dept. Wis., 1888, 1889, sr. vice-comdr.-in-chief, 1890, comdr.-in-chief, 1892. Rep. presdl. elector at-large for Wis., 1900, and was chosen pres. Electoral Coll. for Wis.; presdl. appointee on the Bd. of Visitors to the U.S. Mil. Acad., 1904; mem. Wis. Vicksburg Nat. Mil. Park Commn. Sch. commr. of Milwaukee, 4 yrs. Address: Wells Bldg., Milwaukee, Wis.

WEITZEL, GODFREY army officer, engr.; b. Cincinnati, Nov. 1, 1835; s. Louis and Susan Weitzel; grad. U.S. Mil. Acad., 1855; m. 2d, Louisa Bogen, circa 1864; at least 1 child. Brevetted 2d lt. engrs. U.S. Army, 1855, commd. 2d lt., 1856, 1st lt., 1860; served in fortification of New Orleans, 1855-59; asst. prof. engring. U.S. Mil. Acad., 1859-61; with an engr. co. on expdn. to Ft. Pickens (Fla.) to save it for Union, 1861; chief engr. fortifications of Cincinnati, 1861; chief engr. under Gen. Benjamin Butler in expdn. against New Orleans, 1862; asst. mil. comdr. New Orleans; commd. brig. gen. U.S. Volunteers, 1862; capt. Engr. Corps, U.S. Army, 1863, brevetted maj. and lt. col. for gallantry at battles of Thibodeaux and Port Hudson; chief engr. Second Div., XVIII Army Corps, 1864; brevetted maj. gen. volunteers; brevetted col. regular army for gallantry at capture of Fort Harrison (Va.); maj. gen. volunteers, 1864; brevetted brig. general, major general, U.S. Army for service in final operations against Richmond (Va.), 1865; commanded Rio Grande Dist., 1865; mustered out of U.S. Volunteers, 1866, returned to duty with Corps Engrs., promoted maj., 1866; asso. with constrn. of ship canals at falls of Ohio River, and Sault Sainte Marie (Mich.), lighthouse at Stannard's Rock in Lake Superior; commd. lt. col., 1882. Died Phila., Mar. 19, 1884.

WEITZMAN, ELLIS, psychologist, educator; b. Atlanta, Nov. 26, 1910; s. Nathan and Rachel (Stieffel) W.; A.B., Emory U., 1932; M.A., Creighton U., 1935; Ph.D., U. Neb., 1940; m. Ann Goldenberg, Aug. 23, 1934; children—Sandra Rae, Warren Ray. Social case investigator Douglas County Relief Adminstrn., Omaha, 1934-36; ednl. dir. Bellevue (Neb.) Vocational Sch., 1936-37; grad. asst. U. Neb., 1938-40; supr. spl. problems, occupational analysis sect. USES, 1940-42; dir. student personnel, univ. examiner Am. U., 1946-53, asso. prof. psychology, 1946-50, prof. psychology, 1950-67, chmn. dept., 1960-67, chmn. div. social scis., 1960-67; vis. prof. Mt. Vernon Jr. Coll., 1956-58; pres. Ellis Weitzman Assos., Inc., 1960-67. Psychol. stress research USPHS, 1961-62, cons. psychometrics heart dis. control program, 1962-63; cons. D.C. Dept. of Vocational Rehab., 1963-67. Served to lt. comdr. USNR, 1942-46. Diplomate Am. Bd. Examiners in Profl. Psychology. Fellow A.A.A.S., American Psychological Association, Royal Geographical Society; member Am. Personnel and Guidance Assn., Am. Assn. U. Profs. (chpt. pres.), D.C. Psychol. Assn., N.Y. Acad. Scis., Interam. Soc. Psychology, Phi Delta Kappa, Psi Chi. Author: Growing Up Socially, 1949; (with W.J. McNamara) Constructing Classroom Examinations, 1949; Guiding Children's Social Growth, 1951. Contbr. articles to psychol., ednl. jours. Home: Washington DC Died Aug. 17, 1967.

WELBORN, CURTIS R., fire prevention engr.; b. Ellisville, Miss., Jan. 10, 1894; s. Jefferson Lee and Lurline (Watson) W.; B.S. in Elec. Engring., Miss. State Coll., 1920; m. Ethel Len Privett, Aug. 17, 1920; 2 children. With Underwriters' Labs., Inc., Chicago, 1920-59, pres., 1948-59. Served as capt., A Co., 346th Regt., 87th Div., World War I. Mem. University Club, Tau Beta Pi. Home: Winnetka IL Died Apr. 1973.

WELBORN, IRA CLINTON, army officer; b. Laurel, Miss., Feb. 13, 1874; s. James L. and Tobitha (Welch) W.; grad. U.S. Mil. Acad., 1898; honor grad. Army Sch. of the Line, 1916; grad. Gen. Staff Sch., 1920; grad. Army War Coll., 1921; m. Margaret Sayles Kilbourne, of N.Y. City, Aug. 3, 1901; children—James Lawrence, John Clinton. Commd. 2d lt. 9th Inf., Apr. 26, 1898; promoted through grades to col., July 1, 1920. With expdn. to Cuba, Spanish-Am. War, 1898; participated in Battle of San Juan Hill, and engagements before Santiago; campaigned in Philippines, 1899-1900, and China Relief expdn., 1900; served on Mexican border, 1916; dir. Tank Corps, hdqrs. Washington, D.C., World War; mem. Gen. Staff, 1921-23. Awarded Congressional Medal of Honor "for distinguished bravery" at Battle of Santiago; D.S.M. "for especially meritorious and conspicuous service" in the organization and administration of the Tank Corps. Democrat. Clubs: Army and Navy (Washington, D.C.); New York Athletic. Address: War Dept., Washington DC

WELCH, E(DWARD) SOHIER lawyer; b. Boston, Mass., Jan. 27, 1888; s. Francis Clarke and Edith (Thayer) W.; A.B., Harvard, 1909; LL.B., and J.B., Boston U., 1911; m. Barbara Hinkley, June 3, 1909 (divorced, 1926); children—Barbara, Francis Clarke, Edward Sohier, Holmes Hinkley; m. 2d, Margaret Pearmain (Bowditch), Sept. 1, 1926. Began in father's office, 1908, succeeding to his business upon dis death, 1919; pres. Commercial Wharf Co., Lewis Wharf Co., Long Wharf Co., Metropolitan Storage Warehouse Co., Vermont & Mass. R.R. Co.; vice pres. Boston & Providence R.R. Co.; mng. trustee Bradlee & Francis, real estate trusts; trustee, South Terminal Trust, Boston Real Estate Trust, Tremont Building Trust; director Fifty Associates, Eastern Massachusetts Street Railway, Pepperell Mfg. Co., State Street Trust Co., Union Freight R.R. Co., State Street Exchange, United Elastic Corp.; mem. corp. Suffolk Savings Bank. Commd. lt. U.S.N.R.F., June 28, 1917; exec. and navigating officer U.S.S. Guinevere; attached to U.S. Naval Base, Brest, France, Oct. 16, 1917; resigned July 11, 1919. Clerk, proprs. of Louisburg Square. Trustee Masonic Edn. and Charity Trust, New Eng. Conservatory of Music, Soc. for Preservation of N.E. Antiquities, Member Boston and Massachusetts bar assns., Boston Real Estate Exchange, Bostonian Soc., Mass. Charitable Fire Society, A Republican Institution (treasurer), 250 Associates Harvard Business Sch., Mil. Order Fgn. Wars. Republican. Episcopalian. Mason (32 deg.); mem. National Grange. Clubs: Somerset, Boston Press, Essex County, Manchester Yacht, Millwood Hunt, Wine and Food; Harvard Travellers. Home: 20 Louisburg Sq. Office: 73 Tremont St., Boston, Mass. Died June 27, 1948.

WELCH, JOHN COLLINS publicist; b. at Angelica, N.Y., May 12, 1840; s. Joseph Bloomfield and Mary (Collins) W.; student Genesee Coll. (now Syracuse U.), 2 yrs.; A.B., Union Coll., 1860; m. Eliza Jane, d. Gen. Robert McNair, of Butler Co., Pa., Sept. 5, 1871. Served in Union Army, 1861-65; prisoner of war Apr.-Nov., 1864. Dealer in oil well materials and producer of petroleum in the oil country of Pa., 1865-74; established bureau of information in petroleum trade, 1874. Testified as an expert before the Hepburn railroad investigating com. of N.Y. legislature, 1879-82; gave testimony on interstate commerce on ry. management, rate making, etc., before Interstate Commerce Commission and U.S. Senate com., 1905. Contbr. to mags. and newspapers on interstate commerce, petroleum industry, common carriers, etc., and to vol. on petroleum industry of 10th Census. Home: Kansas City, Mo.

WELCH, WILLIAM ADDAMS park and cons. engr.; b. Cynthiana, Ky., Aug. 20, 1868; s. Ashbel Standard and Priscilla (Addams) W.; ed. high sch., Colorado Springs, Colo., Colorado Coll. (C.E. 1882), U. of Va. (M.E. 1886); m. Camille Beall, 1902; children—Jessie Elizabeth (Mrs. I. H. McAnally), William Addams. Engr. in railway location and constrn. in Eastern, Southern and Western states, Alaska, Mexico, and S. America; also engr. in reclamation, hydro-electric and harbor developments until 1900; gen. mgr. and chief engr. Palisades Interstate Park Commission, N.Y., since 1900; cons. engr. Bear Mountain Hudson River Bridge Corp. Served as chief engr. spruce production div., rank of maj., Air Service Production Div., U.S. Army, during World War; received commendation of chief of Air Service. Mem. Council Boy Scouts America (awarded the Silver Buffalo, also the Pugsley Medal, gold); dir. Nat. Council of State Parks; hon. pres. Appalachian Trail Conf. Mem. Am. Road Builders Assn., Am. Inst. Park Execs., Am. Soc. C.E., Adirondack Mountain Club, Audubon Soc., Nat. Park Soc., Am. Game and Protective Assn. Episcopalian. Clubs: Engineers, Camp Fire, Explorers (New York); Cosmos (Washington). Address: Bear Mountain, N.Y.* Died May 4, 1941.

WELCH, WILLIAM HENRY pathologist; b. Norfolk, Conn., Apr. 8, 1850; s. William Wickham and Emeline (Collin) W.; A.B., Yale, 1870; M.D., Coll. Phys. and Surg. (Columbia), 1875; univs. of Strassburg, Leipzig, Breslau and Berlin, 1876-78, 1884-85; hon. M.D., U. of Pa., 1894; LL.D., Western Reserve, 1894, Yale, 1896, Harvard, 1900, Toronto, 1903, Columbia, 1904, Jefferson Med. Coll., 1907, Princeton, 1910, Washington U., 1915, U. Chicago, 1916, U. of Southern Calif., 1930, Univ. State of N.Y., 1930; Sc.D., Cambridge, 1923, Western Reserve, 1929, U. of Pa., 1930; Doct., Strassburg, 1923. Prof. pathol. and anatomy and gen. pathology, Bellevue Hosp. Med. Coll., 1879-84; Baxley prof. pathology, 1884-1916, dean, med. faculty, 1893-98, dir. School of Hygiene and Public Health, 1916-26, professor history of medicine, 1926-30, emeritus, 1931, Johns Hopkins; pathologist Johns Hopkins Hosp., 1889-1916. Pres. Med. State Bd.

Health, 1898-1922, and mem. to 1929; pres. bd. dirs. Rockefeller Inst. for Med. Research, 1901—; mem. Internat. Health Bd. and China Med. Bd. of Rockefeller Foundation; trustee of Carnegie Instn., 1906—. Huxley lecturer, Charing Cross Hosp. Med. Sch., London, 1902. Pres. Med. and Chirurg. Faculty of Md., 1891-92, Congress of Am. Phys. and Surg., 1897, Assn. Am. Physicians, 1901, A.A.A.S., 1906-07, A.M.A., 1910-11, Nat. Tuberculosis Assn., 1910-11 (hon. pres.), Nat. Acad. Sciences, 1913-16, Am. Social Hygiene Assn., 1916-19, Nat. Com. Mental Hygiene (hon. pres.), History of Science Society, 1931; fellow Am. Acad. Arts and Sciences, Coll. of Physicians, Phila.; hon. fellow Royal Soc. Medicine, Royal Sanitary Inst., London, Royal Coll. of Phys., Edinburgh, Soc. Med. Officers of Health (Eng.). Commd. maj., Med. R.C., U.S.A., July 16, 1917; lt. col., Feb. 20, 1918; col., July 24, 1918; hon. discharged, Dec. 31, 1918; col. Med. Sect. O.R.C., U.S.A., Feb. 24, 1919; brig. gen. O.R.C., Dec. 23, 1921. Awarded D.S.M. (U.S.); Order of Rising Sun (Japan), 3d Class; Comdr. Order of St. Olav (Norway), 2d Class; Order of Mercy (Kingdom of Serbs, Croats and Slovenes); Officer Legion of Honor (France); gold medal, Nat. Inst. Social Sciences; medal of honor, U. of Vienna; Kober medal, 1927; Harbin gold medal, 1931. Author: General Pathology of Fever, 1888; The Biology of Bacteria, Infection and Immunity, 1894; Bacteriology of Surgical Infections, 1895; Thrombosis and Embolism, 1899; also numerous papers on pathol. and bacteriol. subjects, and addresses. Home: Baltimore, Md. Died Apr. 30, 1934.

WELD, FRANCIS MINOT banker; b. New York, N.Y., Feb. 18, 1875; s. Francis Minot and Fanny E. (Bartholomew) W.; grad. Roxbury Latin Sch., Boston, 1893; A.B., Harvard, 1897, A.M., 1898; m. Margaret Low White, Nov. 7, 1903; m. 2d, Mrs. Julia Tiffany Parker, Aug. 17, 1930. Partner in banking firm of Moffat & White, 1905-10, White, Weld & Co., New York and Boston, since 1910; dir. Internat. Minerals and Chem. Corp., Atlas Assurance Co., Pilgrim Exploration Company. Trustee Met. Museum of Art of N.Y., French Inst. Served as captain and major inf., 77th Div., A.E.F. World War I. Received Silver Star and Purple Heart. For two years, 1942-1944, served in New York City Patrol Corps as Lt. Col. and then Colonel commanding the Manhattan Division. Mem. Phi Beta Kappa. Clubs: Brook, Century, University, Union, Harvard (pres. 1936-38), Down Town, Racquet-Tennis. Home: 660 Park Av. Office: 40 Wall St., New York, N.Y. Died Nov. 1, 1949.

WELD, STEPHEN MINOT merchant; b. Jamaica Plain, Mass., Jan. 4, 1842; s. Stephen Minot and Sarah Bartlett (Balch) W.; A.B., Harvard, 1860, A.M., 1863; m. Eloise Rodman, June 1, 1869; m. 2d, Susan Edith Waterbury, May 26, 1904. Entered army as 2d lt. 18th Mass. Inf., Jan. 27, 1862; 1st lt., Nov. 1, 1862; capt., 1863; hon. discharged Dec. 25, 1863; apptd. lt. col. 56th Mass. Inf., Jan. 2, 1864; col., May 31, 1864; bvtd. brig. gen. vols., Mar. 13, 1865, for gallant and meritorious services; mustered out July 12, 1865. Head Stephen M. Weld & Co., cotton mchts., 1875—; also of Weld & Neville; dir. Old Colony Trust Co., Bay State Trust Co., West End St. Ry. Overseer, Harvard, 1899-1911. Home: Dedham, Mass. Died Mar. 16, 1920.

WELLDON, SAMUEL A. ret. banker; b. Lynn, Mass., Sept. 28, 1882; s. John W. and Janet (Turnbull) W.; B.A. magna cum laude, Harvard, 1904, LL.B., Law Sch., 1908; m. Julia M. Hoyt, Sept. 16, 1911 (div. 1949); children—Mary Appleton (Mrs. John McDougall), Angelica H. (dec.), Janet (Mrs. John M. Graham); m. 2d Emily Coster Morris, May 26, 1949. Dir. Am. Tel. & Tel., 1931-59, exec. com., 22 yrs.; retired chmn. of the board of directors 1st Nat. Bank of City of New York; director Bigelow Sanford, Inc., Bigelow-Sanford Carpet Co., Inc., Allied Chem. Corp.; honorary vice president of Community Service Society of N.Y. Served as capt., later major, F.A., A.E.F., 1918. Decorated Comdr. Order of British Empire. Mem. Phi Beta Kappa. Clubs: Harvard (pres. 1943-46), Knickerbocker, Piping Rock (pres. 1950-53). Home: 117 E. 72d St., N.Y.C. 10021. Office: 399 Park Av., N.Y.C. 10022. Died Apr. 13, 1962.

WELLER, JOHN B. senator, gov. Cal.; b. Montgomery, Hamilton County, O., Feb. 22, 1812; attended Miami U., Oxford, O., 1825-29; m. Miss Ryan; m. 2d, Miss Bryan; m. 3d, Susan McDowell Taylor; m. 4, Lizzie Brocklebank Stanton. Admitted to Ohio bar, 1832; pros. atty. Butler County (O.), 1833-36; mem. U.S. Ho. of Reps. (Democrat) from Ohio, 26th-28th congresses, 1839-45; served as col. U.S. Volunteers, Mexican War; chmn. commn. to determine boundary between U.S. and Mexico under Treaty of Guadalupe Hidalgo, 1849; opened law office, San Francisco, 1850; mem. U.S. Senate (Union Democrat) from Cal., 1851-57; gov. Cal., 1858-60; U.S. minister to Mexico, 1860-61; practiced law, New Orleans, 1867-75. Died New Orleans, Aug. 17, 1875.

WELLES, ROGER naval officer; b. Newington, Conn., Dec. 7, 1862; s. Roger and Mercy Delano (Aiken) W.; grad. U.S. Naval Acad., 1884; m. Harriet Ogden Deen, Oct. 17, 1908. Ensign, July 1, 1886; promoted through grades to rear adm. (temp.), July 1, 1918; rear adm. (perm.), July 1, 1919. Served in McArthur, Vermont and Wasp during Spanish-Am. War, 1898; exec. officer in warship New Hampshire, 1908-09; comd. New Orleans, 1909-10; mem. Bd. Insp. and Survey, Navy Dept., Washington, D.C., 1911; comd. Louisiana, 1911-13; comd. Naval Training Sta., Newport, R.I., 1913-15; comd. Oklahoma, 1916-17; dir. naval intelligence, Navy Dept., Washington, D.C., 1917-19; apptd. comdr. Div. 1, U.S. Fleet, Feb. 4-Aug. 28, 1919; comdr. Div. 4, Atlantic Fleet Flagship Minnesota, Sept. 1919. First comdt. 11th Naval Dist., 1921-23; comdt. 5th Naval Dist. and Naval Operating Base, Hampton Roads, Va., 1923-25; apptd. comdr. U.S. Naval Forces in European waters, Oct. 10, 1925, with rank of vice admiral; retired from active service December 7, 1926. Decorated Atlantic Battle Medal (Nipe Bay), Spanish-Am. War; Cuban and Philippine campaign medals; Comdr. Legion of Honor (French); Grand Officer Order of Leopold II (Belgian); 2d Order of the Rising Sun (Japanese); Grand Cross of Naval Merit and Efficiency (Spanish), 1926; Navy Cross (U.S.). Republican. Conglist. Mason. As a young man was sent as spl. commr., Columbian Expn., to Venezuela, etc., and made ethnol. collection (installed in Field Mus., Chicago), in interior of Venezuela, for which was awarded certificate and bronze medal; on duty at the expn., 1890-93. Died Apr. 26, 1932.

WELLMAN, SARGENT HOLBROOK lawyer; b. Malden, Mass., May 8, 1892; s. Arthur H. and Jennie L. (Faulkner) W.; A.B., Amherst, 1912; LL.B., Harvard, 1915; m. Mary Conover Lines, Oct. 1, 1919; children—Prudence H. (Mrs. Joseph L. Leonard), Howard L., Bradford S. Admitted to Mass. Bar, 1915, practiced in Boston since 1915; v.p. Danvers Savs. Bank; vice president ABCFM; member board directors Malden Trust Company. Served as 1st lt., then capt., U.S. Army with office of gen. purchasing agt. and S.O.S.; in France 1918-19. Moderator Town Topsfield, 1922-24, since 1949, chmn. finance com., 1931-46. Mem. Mass. House of Rep., 1925-26; govt. appeal agt. Topsfield draft bd., 1940-46; capt. and maj. Mass. State Guard, 1942-44. Mem. Am., Mass., Boston bar assns., Phi Beta Kappa, Chi Psi. Republican. Conglist. (president Am. Congl. Assn., vice president of Am. bd. of commrs. for fgn. missions, 1942-46, since 1947, pres. bd. of ministerial aid). Home: Wenham Rd., Topsfield, Mass. Office: 15 Congress St., Boston 9. Died Sept. 5, 1961; buried Topsfield Cemetery, Topsfield, Mass.

WELLS, ALMOND BROWN brig. gen. U.S.A.; b. in N.Y., June 16, 1842. Commd. 1st lt. 1st Battalion, Nev. Cav., July 13, 1863; capt., May 1, 1864; hon. mustered out, Nov. 18, 1865; apptd. from Nev., 2d lt. 8th U.S. Cav., July 28, 1866; 1st lt., July 31, 1867; capt., May 23, 1870; maj. 4th Cav., July 1, 1891; transferred to 8th Cav., July 8, 1891; lt. col. 9th Cav., Feb. 14, 1899; col. 1st Cav., Feb. 2, 1901; brig. gen.. Aug. 5, 1903; retired at own request, over 30 yrs.' service, Aug. 6, 1903. Home: Geneva, N.Y. Died Sept. 7, 1912.

WELLS, CHARLES RAYMOND dentist; b. Phila., Oct. 30, 1895; s. Dwight Sidney and Lillian Ida (Myers) W.; D.D.S., Northwestern U., 1918; D.Sc., Georgetown U., 1943; m. Clara Lillian Horn, Aug. 9, 1919; children—Steacy Raymond, Catherine Lillian (Mrs. John Mitchell Hoskiewicz). Pvt. practice dentistry, Bklyn., 1925—. Lt. on active duty with USN, 1918-25; entered as lt. comdr. Dental Corps, USNR, 1934; called to active duty as chief dental officer, also asst. chief med. div., Nat. Hdqrs. SSS, Washington, 1941; promoted comdr., 1942, capt., 1943, sr. dental officer; Naval Sta., Bklyn., and U.S. Naval Hosp., St. Albans, 1945; promoted to rear adm. USNR, 1954, ret. 1956; cons. Bur. Medicine and Surgery of Navy, 1955-57; impartial specialist Workmen's Compensation Bd. N.Y. State, 1956—; mem. dental adv. com. Dept. Welfare, N.Y.C., 1963—. Mem. Task Force, Med. Adv. Bd., Sec. Def., 1949-50. Dir. oral surg. Queens Gen. Hosp., Horace Harding Hosp., N.Y., now cons. dentistry Decorated Victory (World War I), Am. Def., Naval Res., Am. Theater, World War II, Selective Service, Legion of Merit medals. Recipient award of merit, Northwestern U., 1934, Pierre Fauchard medal, Pierre Fauchard Acad. (dental), 1943, Jarvie Fellowship award, medal, Dental Soc. N.Y., 1955. Diplomate N.Y. Bd. Oral Surgery. Fellow L.I. Acad. Odontology (ed. 1953), N.Y. Acad. Dentistry, Internat. Coll. Dentists (pres. 1941), Am. Coll. Dentists; mem. Am. Arbitration Assns. (nat. panel arbitrators), 2d Dist. (N.Y.), N.Y., Bklyn., Vt. state (hon.), Detroit (hon.), Costa Rica (hon.) State dental socs., Am. Dental Assn. (pres. 1944), S.R., Psi Omega, Am. Legion, Navy League; hon. mem. Omicron Kappa Upsilon. Methodist. Mason. Contbr. articles to profl. publs. Home: 86-56 Clio St., Hollis, N.Y. Office: 1 DeKalb Av., Bklyn. Died Dec. 9, 1966.

WELLS, CHESTER naval officer retired; b. Spring Hill, Pa., Oct. 15, 1870; s. Levi and Helen Louise (Jones) W.; student Pa. Normal Sch., Mansfield, 1885-86; B.S., U.S. Naval Acad., 1893; grad. U.S. Naval War Coll., 1921; m. Marion Leigh Dixson, Oct. 9, 1907; children—Christian Leigh, Helen Elizabeth. Entered U.S. Navy and promoted through grades to capt., 1917; retired in 1924 at own request after 36 years on active list; in Spanish-American War, Philippine Insurrection, North China Campaign, World War I. Pres. District Nat. Securities Corp.; mem. bd. dirs., chmn. trust com., Hamilton Nat. Bank (Washington). Awarded Sampson medal, 7 action clasps, Spanish-Am. War Medal, Philippine Insurrection medal, North China Campaign medal, Victory medal with convoy star, Navy Cross; Comdr. Order of Crown of Italy. Mem. Washington Nat. Monument Soc., Naval Hist. Foundation, Mil. Order of Carabao (past. comdr.), Naval and Mil. Order of Spanish-Am. War, Mil. Order of Dragon, (pres.), Am. Legion, Mil. Order Loyal Legion of U.S. Commandery of D.C. (past comdr.). Trustee, George Washington U.; pres. bd. dirs. Columbia Hosp.; past pres. Nat. Capital Area Council Boy Scouts America. Episcopalian. Republican. Clubs: Metropolitan, Army and Navy, Chevy Chase (Washington), N.Y. Yact. Home: "Woodend," 9320 Jones Mill Rd., Chevy Chase, Md.; (summer) Welbec Farms, Wyalusing, Pa. Office: Colo. Bldg., 14th and G St. N.W., Washington, D.C. Died Sep. 17, 1948.

WELLS, EBENEZER TRACY lawyer; b. Richland, N.Y., May 15, 1835; s. John H. and Julia (Tracy) W.; A.B., Knox Coll., Galesburg, Ill., 1855; admitted to bar, 1857; began practice at Rock Island, Ill.; m. Frances Sophia Pettitt, of Kenosha, Wis., Oct., 1858 (now deceased). Enlisted as pvt. Co. F, 89th Ill. Inf., May, 1862; mustered in as 1st lt.; promoted capt., Feb., 1863; apptd. by President Lincoln a.-a.-g. vols., Feb. 9, 1864; present at battles of Stone River, Liberty Gap, Chickamauga, Orchard Knob, Missionary Ridge, Resaca, New Hope Ch., Peach Tree Creek (severely wounded), etc.; bvtd. maj., lt.-col. and col. for gallantry. Removed to Colo. Ty., 1865; mem. Territorial Gen. Assembly of Colo., 1866; asso. justice Supreme Ct. of Colo. Ty., 1871-75; mem. Colo. Constl. Conv., 1876; elected asso. justice Supreme Ct. of Colo., Nov., 1876, resigned, Sept. 1,1877; reporter Supreme Ct. of Colo. since Feb. 15, 1909. Democrat. Mem. Beta Theta Pi, Loyal Legion. Author: Wells on Replevin (2nd edit.), 1906. Editor: Revised Statutes of Colo., 1868. Home: Hotel Metropole. Office: State House, Denver.

WELLS, FREDERICK BROWN corp. official; b. Am. parentage, Menton, France, Apr. 21, 1873; s. Thomas Bucklin and Annie Elizabeth (Jonas) W.; student U. Minn., 1889-90, Yale, 1890-93; m. Mary Drew Peavey, Sept. 19, 1898; children—Thomas B. (dec.), Mary (Staples) (dec.), Frank H. (dec.), Frederick Brown, Jr.; m. 2d, Grace Louise Broadfoot, June 17, 1936. Began career as clerk, 1891; pres. F. H. Peavey & Co.; dir. First National Bank & Trust Co. Served as colonel on general staff, U.S. Army, 1917-19. Awarded D.S.M., 1919. Dir. Minn. Inst. Arts, Mpls. Symphony Orchestra. Republican. Episcopalian. Clubs: Minneapolis; Cloister (Yale); Manitoba (Winnepeg); Woodhill Country. Home: Bloomington, Minneapolis. Office: Grain Exchange Bldg., Mpls. Died Aug. 3, 1953.

WELTY, BENJAMIN FRANKLIN, congressman; b. nr. Bluffton, O., Aug. 9, 1870; s. Frederick and Katherine (Steiner) W.; student Tri-State Normal Sch., Angola, Ind.; B.S., Ohio Northern U., Ada, O., 1894; LL.B., U. of Mich., 1896; m. Cora B. Gottschalk, of Berne, Ind., Sept. 28, 1903. Admitted to Ohio bar, 1896; city solicitor, Bluffton, O., 1898-1913; mem. Welty & Downing, Lima, since 1900; pros. atty., Allen Co., O., 1905-10; spl. asst. to atty. gen. of Ohio, 1910-12; spl. asst., Dept. of Justice, in charge of prosecutions under Sherman Anti-Trust Law, 1913-15; mem. 65th and 66th Congresses (1917-21), 4th Ohio Dist. Pvt. Co. C, 2d Regt. Ohio N.G., 1896, and served in 2d Regt. Ohio Vol. Inf., 1898, Spanish-Am. War; returned to Ohio N.G., 1898, and continued until 1913; retired as lt. col., commissary dept.; volunteered for World War but services refused because he was member of Congress. Democrat. Presbyn. Mem. Ohio State Bar Assn. Mason, Odd Fellow, K.P., Elk. Clubs: Lima, Shawnee Country. Home: 810 W. Spring St., Lima OH

WENDEL, HUGO CHRISTIAN MARTIN educator; b. Phila., Pa., Apr. 6, 1884; s. Hugo Rudolf and Louise (Freudenberger) W.; student Mt. Airy Sem., Phila., 1904-07; student philosophy and history, U. of Erlangen, 1907-08, U. of Leipzig, May-Aug. 1908; A.B., Princeton, 1910; Ph.D., U. of Pa., 1918; studied at Sorbonne, Paris, and L'Institut des Hautes Études Marocaines, Rabat, Morocco, 1925-26; m. Marie Theodora Petersen-Enge, Aug. 18, 1829; 1 dau., Marie Louise. Instr. in history Lankenau Sch. for Girls, Phila., 1910-14; Harrison fellow in history, U. of Pa., 1915-16, 1917-18, asst. in history, 1916-17; instr. in history, New York U., 1918-20, asst. prof., 1920-28, dir. Campus Concert Course, 1920-28; prof. history, chmn. Dept. History and Govt., L.I.U., since 1928; dir. summer schs., 1931-46; pres. Bronx Soc. Arts and Sciences, 1925-28. Vice pres. bd. education, United Lutheran Ch., 1926-32; mem. bd. edn., United Lutheran Synod, since 1944. Research and travel in Europe and North Africa, various periods. Mem. Internat. Law Seminar of Carnegie Endowment U. of Mich., summer 1936. Instr. in history S.A.T.C., New York U., 1918; later maj., staff specialist, U.S. Army Res. Mem. bd. dirs. Mt. Airy Sem., 1934-40. Mem. Am. Hist. Assn., Am. Philos. Assn., Foreign Policy Assn., Phi Beta Kappa, Delta Sigma Phi. Lutheran. Author: Democracy in the New German Constitution, 1920; The Evolution of Industrial Freedom, 1921; Mediterranean Menace, 1927; Proègé System in Morocco, 1930. Home: 5 Barry Pl., Fairlawn-Radburn, N.J. Address: Long Island University, Brooklyn, N.Y. Died Jan. 16, 1949.

WENGER, JOSEPH NUMA, naval officer; b. Patterson, La., June 7, 1901; s. Aloysius Bercthold and Frances Adele (Roussel) W.; B.S., U.S. Naval Acad., 1923; m. Mary Crippen, May 16, 1932; 1 son, Jeffrey Joseph. Commd. ensign U.S.N., 1923; promoted through grades to rear adm., 1951; various ship, shore and staff assignments, U.S. and abroad; specialist communications; dir. various naval communications research and operational activities; chmn. joint communications electronics com. Joint Chiefs of Staff; chmn. NATO communications-electronics bd., 1957. Decorated; D.S.M. (Navy); Comdr. Order of Brit. Empire; National Security Medal, 1953. Mem. Armed Forces Communications and Electronics Assn. (hon.), U.S. Naval Inst. Roman Catholic. Clubs: Chevy Chase; Army-Navy Town; Army-Navy Country (Arlington, Va.). Home: Washington DC Died Sept. 21, 1970; buried Arlington Cemetery, Arlington VA

WENTWORTH, EDWARD NORRIS livestock historian, specialist; b. Dover, N.H., Jan. 11, 1887; s. Elmer Marston and Elizabeth Tilton (Towne) W.; B.S., in Agr., Ia. State Coll. Agr. and Mechanic Arts, 1907, M.S., 1909; grad. study Cornell U. and Harvard; m. Alma B. McCulla, June 14, 1911; children—Edward Norris (dec.), Raymond Howard (dec.). Asst., asso. prof. animal husbandry, Iowa State Coll. Agr. and Mech. Arts, 1907-13; asso. editor Breeder's Gazette, also prof. zoötechny, Chicago Vet. Coll., 1913-14; prof. animal breeding, Kan. State Agrl. Coll., 1914-17; public relations dept., Armour and Co., Chgo., 1919-20, Bur. of Agrl. Research and Economics, 1920-23; ir. Armour's Livestock Bur., 1923-54, retired 1954; lectr. U. Chgo., 1923-31. Served as capt. F.A., U.S. Army, and mil. dir. Coll. Agr., A.E.F. Univ., Beaune, France, World War I; col., Honorary Reserve; mem. advisory com. to Q.M. General. Mem. Am. Farm Economics Assn., Am. Genetic Assn., Am. Soc. Animal Production, A.A.A.S., Am. Soc. Naturalists, Am. Econ. Assn., Am. Statis. Assn., S.A.R., Soc. of Piscataqua Pioneers, Am. Legion, Mil. Order World Wars (past commander in chief), Miss. Valley Hist. Assn., Reserve Officers' Assn. U.S., Sigma Alpha Epsilon, Alpha Zeta, Alpha Psi, Sigma Delta Chi, Phi Kappa Psi. Decorated Officer du Merite Agricole (French). Republican. Clubs: University, Saddle and Sirloin, Army and Navy Club, Army and Navy (Washington, D.C.); Town and Country Equestrian Assn. (pres.). Author: Portrait Gallery of Saddle and Sirloin Club, 1920; America's Sheep Trails, 1948. Co-author: Progressive Beef Cattle Raising, 1920; Progressive Hog Raising, 1922; Marketing Live Stock and Meats, 1924; Progressive Sheep Raising, 1925; Cattle Breeding, 1925. Co-author with Charles W. Towne, Shepherds' Empire, 1945; Pig's Progress, 1949. Home: R.R. 3, Box 285, Chesterton, Ind. Address: Armour and Co., Chgo. Died Apr. 21, 1959.

WERDEN, REED naval officer; b. Delaware County, Pa., Feb. 28, 1818; s. Col. William Werden. Commd. midshipman U.S. Navy, 1834; served with Brazil and Mediterranean Squadrons; on world cruise on ship Boston, 1840-43; commd. lt., 1847, in sloop Germantown in Mexican War; served in Minnesota at capture of Hatteras Inlet during Civil War, 1861; commanded some vessels in Albemarle Sound until 1862; comdr. in Conemaugh, 1862; fleet capt. of East Gulf Squadron, 1864, commanded Powhatan; blockaded Confederate ship Stonewall at Havana until surrender, 1865; commd. capt., 1866, commodore, 1871, rear adm., 1875; stationed at Mare Island (Cal.) Navy Yard, 1868-71; head New London (Conn.) Naval Station, 1872-74; commanded South Pacific Squadron, 1875-76; ret., 1877. Died Newport, R.I., July 11, 1886.

WESCOTT, ORVILLE DE WITT, physician; b. Gladbrook, Ia., July 21, 1871; s. Delos Gary and Mary Ruana (Dibble) W.; B.S., Cornell Coll., Ia., 1900; M.D., Rush Med. Coll., Chicago, 1904; m. Sue May Gailey, Alexandria, La., Oct. 8, 1910. Interne Muskoka Cottage Sanatorium for Consumptives, Gravenhurst, Ont., 1904-5; asst. phys., Agnes Memorial Sanatorium, Denver, 1905-9; in pvt. practice, specializing in diseases of chest, throat and nose, 1909—. Sec. Colo. State Assn. for Prevention and Control of Tuberculosis, 1908, dir., 1908-9-10; awarded gold medal for ednl. leaflet at Internat. Congress on Tuberculosis, Washington, D.C., 1908; mem. Nat. Assn. for Study and Prevention of Tuberculosis, A.M.A., Denver Med. Science Club, etc. Mem. Ia. Vol. Inf., Apr.-Nov., 1898, Spanish-Am. War; mem. Colo. N.G., 1910; commd. maj. and regtl. surgeon to 157th Inf., 40th Div., N.G., Camp Kearny, Cal., 1917. Republican. Mason (32 deg., Shriner). Clubs: University, Denver Athletic, Lakewood Country. Home: 2219 Ivy St., Denver CO

WESSELLS, HENRY WALTON JR. brig. gen. U.S.A.; b. Sacketts Harbor, N.Y., Dec. 24, 1846; s. Henry W. (U.S.A.) and Hannah (Cooper) W.; ed. Deer Hill Inst., Danbury, Conn.; m. Eliza Lane Meginnis, Mar. 24, 1869. Pvt. and sergt. cos. K and D, 7th U.F. Inf., Mar. 1-Aug. 16, 1865; apptd. 2d lt. and 1st lt. 7th Inf., July 21, 1865; transferred to 3d Cav., Jan. 1, 1871; capt., Dec. 20, 1872; major, Aug. 16, 1892; lt. col., May 8, 1899; col. unassigned, Feb. 2, 1901; retired for disability incurred in line of duty, Feb. 2, 1901; advanced to grade of brig. gen. U.S.A. retired, Apr. 23, 1904. Served in Indian wars, the Spanish-Am. War and the Philippines. Died Nov. 9, 1929.

WESSON, CHARLES MACON army officer; b. St. Louis, July 23, 1878; s. Charles Macon and Caroline Moye (Dancy) W.; B.S., U.S. Mil. Acad., 1900; grad. Ordnance Sch. of Technology, 1911, Army War Coll., 1925; Dr. Eng., Stevens Inst., 1941; married. Commd. 2d lt. cav., U.S. Army, 1900, and advanced through the grades to maj. gen., 1938; served in Cuba and Ft. Riley, Kan., with cav.; instr. in dept. of philosophy, West Point, 1903-07; served in ordnance dept. in Watertown and Watervliet arsenals and with A.E.F. in France; comdg. officer Aberdeen Proving Ground, 1925-29; chief of tech. staff. Office Chief of Ordnance, 1930-34; chief of ordnance, 1938-42; Office of Lend-Lease Adminstr. and Fgn. Econ. Adminstr., 1942-45. Decorated D.S.M. with 2 oak leaf clusters (U.S.); Officer Black Star (French); hon. comdr. British Empire. Clubs: Army and Navy, Chevy Chase (Washington, D.C.); St. Botolph (Boston). Home: The Westchester, Washington 16. Died Nov. 24, 1956; buried West Point, N.Y.

WEST, CHARLES, lawyer; b. Savannah, Ga., Mar. 16, 1872; s. Charles Nephew and Mary (Cheves) W.; A.B., Johns Hopkins, 1891; post-grad. work, U. of Leipzig, 1892-93, Johns Hopkins, 1893-94; m. Sophia Lovell Haskell, of Abbeville, S.C., Mar. 27, 1900. Admitted to bar Okla. Ty., 1894, and practiced at Pond Creek and Enid; atty.-gen. of Okla., 1907-15; practiced in Oklahoma City, 1915-17; mem. West, Hall & Hagan, then West & Petry, now alone. Democrat. Pres. Atty. Gen. Assn. 1911-12; member Nat. Tax Assn. Active in Territorial and State N.G., 1898-1910 (retired as lt. col.). Lecturer on law, Oklahoma U. Episcopalian. Mason (32 deg.), Elk, Redman. Commd. 1st lt., N.A., 1917; capt. inf., June 1918; with A.E.F. in France till Aug. 1919; col. inf. R.C. Home: 1635 S. Cheyenne St., Tulsa OK

WEST, CLIFFORD HARDY rear admiral U.S.N.; b. Brooklyn, Nov. 10, 1846; s. Edward Augustus and Ann (Peirce) W.; unmarried. Grad. U.S. Naval Acad., 1867; ensign, Dec. 18, 1868; master, Mar. 21, 1870; lt., Mar. 21, 1871; lt. comdr. Mar. 31, 1888; comdr., Oct. 11, 1896; capt., Sept. 22, 1901; rear admiral, June 17, 1902, and retired. On board steam sloop Wyoming, in W. Indies, during complications with Spain as to steamers Virginius and Edgar Stuart; lieut. and exec. officer on board Alliance during search for Lt. DeLong on E. coast of Greenland, Iceland and Spitzbergen; chief of staff to Admiral Sicard, flagship New York, at outbreak of Spanish-Am. War; comd. Princeton in Spanish-Am. War and in operations against insurgents in Philippines. Home: Brooklyn, N.Y. Died 1911.

WEST, PAUL BROWN pres. Assn. of Nat. Advertisers; b. Lake George, N.Y., Sept. 20, 1892; s. Elmer J. and Dora (Brown) W.; student Glens Falls Acad., 1906-10; A.B., Williams Coll., 1914; m. Lula Ren Swinney, June 21st, 1921; one son, Peter. Engaged in advertising work since 1914; sales and advertising Union Carbide Co., 1915-20; account exec. Murray Howe & Co., 1919-22; advertising mgr. Haynes Stellite Co., 1922-24; advertising and sales promotion mgr. Nat. Carbon Co., 1924-32; pres. and mem. bd. Assn. Nat. Advertisers, Inc. First lt., U.S. Army, World War. Founder and mem. bd. Advertising Research Foundation; founder and treas. Advt. Council, Inc. Member Board of Brand Names. Found. and Nat. Distbn. Council. Mem. Phi Delta Theta, Alpha Delta Sigma. Clubs: Metropolitan Advertising Golf Association, Advt., Williams, Uptown, Union League (N.Y.C.), Scarsdale Golf; Adcraft (Detroit). Home: 109 Old Army Road, Scarsdale, N.Y. Office: 155 E. 44th St., N.Y.C. 10017. Died May 5, 1960.

WESTBROOK, LAWRENCE research and development engineer, govt. ofcl.; b. Belton, Texas, August 23, 1889; s. Joel Whittsett and Margaret (Whitington) W.; student U. Tex., 1906-08; m. Martha Wooton, Mar. 22, 1937; children—Joel, Lawrence, Hirma. Dir. Tex. Relief Com., 1933-34; asst. adminstr. Fed. Emergency Relief Assn., 1934; dir. Nat. Rural Rehabilitation Progm., Drought Relief, rural settlements Matanuska, Alaska, Dyess, Ark., Pine Valley, Ga., and others, 1935; asst. adminstr. Work Projects Adminstrn., 1935-36, chmn. adv. bd., 1937-39, asst. commr. 1940; dir. mutual home ownership div. Fed. Works Agy., 1940-41. Cons. Rheinisch-Westfaeliches Inst. Fuer Wirtschaftforschung of Essen. Asst. chmn. Dem. Nat. Com. 1952. Pres. U.S. Joint Purchasing Bd., S. Pacific area; dir. Mil. Econ. Mission to New Zealand, 1942-43; mem. spl. planning div. Gen. Staff War Dept., 1944-45; mem. U.S. nat. commn. UNESCO, 1961—. Served from lieut. to maj., Signal Corps, U.S. Army, 1917-19; col., Army Services Forces, 1942. Decorated hon. officer mil. br., Order of Brit. Empire, 1946. Mem. Sigma Alpha Epsilon. Episcopalian. Clubs: Army and Navy, Nat. Press (Washington). Home: 1912 Jade Dr., San Angelo, Tex. Died Jan. 24, 1964; buried Ft. Sam Houston Mil. Acad., San Antonio.

WESTON, EUGENE, JR., architect; b. Bloomington, Cal., Jan. 12, 1896; s. Eugene and Margaret Hanna (Fegan) W.; student Los Angeles Poly. High Sch., 1911-14; m. Beatrice Stiles, May 17, 1921; children—Eugene, III, Russell Stiles, Jane Elizabeth. Archtl. draftsman, 1915-21; with Bertram G. Goodhue, N.Y.C., 1921-23; in practice Los Angeles, 1923-64. Served in California Field Artillery, United States Army, Mexican Border, 1916; capt., 20th F.A., 5th Div., A.E.F., 1917-19. Awarded A.I.A. honor award, 1929, 46, 51, 54, Certificate of Merit, 1936; Ceramics, 1940; bronze medal, Art Fiesta, 1931. Fellow A.I.A. (member emeritus); member of the Society of Mayflower Descendants, Southwest Museum, Am. Legion, Hist. Soc. of So. Cal., Los Angeles C. of C. Republican. Episcopalian. Home: Pauma Valley CA Died Dec. 23, 1969; buried El Camino Memorial Park, San Diego CA

WESTON, HAROLD, artist; b. Merion, Pa., Feb. 14, 1894; s. Samuel Burns and Mary (Hartshorne) W.; A.B. magna cum laude, Harvard, 1916; m. Faith Borton, May 12, 1923; children—Barbara (Mrs. Esty Foster, Jr.), Bruce, Haroldine (Mrs. William H. Sudduth II). With YMCA attached to Brit. Army in India, Mesopotamia, 1916-20; ofcl. artist London War Office, 1918; organizer, exec. sec. Reconstrn. Service Com., 1942-43; exec. dir. Food For Freedom, Inc., 1943-47. U.S. del. Internat. Assn. Plastic Arts, Vienna, 1960, N.Y., 1963, Tokyo, 1966, exec. com., 1957-63, v.p., 1961-62, pres., 1962-63, hon. pres., 1963-72, pres. U.S. com., 1961-67, hon. president, 1967-72; vice chmn. Nat. Council Arts and Govt., 1954-61, chmn., from 1961. Life fellow World Academy Arts and Sci.; mem. Soc. Am. Graphic Artists (honorary), National Society of Mural Painters (hon.), Fedn. Modern Painters and Sculptors (pres. 1953-57), Phi Beta Kappa. Recipient 3d prize for Am. painting Golden Gate Internat. Expn., 1939; Am. Soc. Contemporary Artists award, 1964. Works represented: War Mus. (London), Meml. Art Gallery (Rochester), Pa. Academy Fine Arts, Phillips Gallery (Washington), Yale Art Mus., San Francisco Mus. Art, Fogg Art Mus. (Cambridge, Mass.), Mus. Modern Art, Corcoran Gallery Art, Smithsonian Instn., Whitney Mus. of Am. Art, N.Y.U. Collection, Butler Inst. Am. Art (Youngstown, O.), Oakland Art Mus., Syracuse U. Art Mus., Purdue U., Fordham U., Everson Mus., Syracuse, St. Lawrence U.; portrait of Dr. Felix Adler, Butler Library, Columbia; executed murals (22 panels) U.S. General Services Bldg., Washington. Home: St Huberts NY Died Apr. 10, 1972; buried Norton Cemetery Keene NY

WESTON, JOHN FRANCIS major gen. U.S.A.; b. Louisville, Ky., Nov. 13, 1845; s. B. N. and Mary W.; ed. St. Mary's Coll., Ky.; m. Sally Garvin. Commd. 1st lt. 4th Ky. Cav., Nov. 26, 1861; capt., Jan. 9, 1863; maj., Nov. 1, 1864; hon. mustered out of vols., Aug. 21, 1865; apptd. from Ky. 2d lt. 7th U.S. Cav., Aug. 9, 1867; 1st lt., Nov. 27, 1868; grad. Arty. Sch., 1875; capt. commissary subsistence, Nov. 24, 1875; maj., Aug. 1, 1892; lt. col. asst. commissary gen., Nov. 15, 1897; col. asst. commissary gen., Apr. 30, 1898; brig. gen. vols., Sept. 21, 1898; hon. disch. from vols., Mar. 24, 1899; brig. gen. commissary gen. U.S.A., Dec. 6, 1900; maj. gen., Oct. 8, 1905; retired, Nov. 13, 1909. Awarded Congressional Medal of Honor, Apr. 9, 1898, "for gallantry at Wetumpka, Ala., Apr. 13, 1865," where, with 5 men, he swam the river, defeated a force of the enemy and captured steamboats loaded with supplies, lying in the river. Home: Briarcliff Manor, N.Y. Died Aug. 3, 1917.

WESTON, WILLIAM, physician; b. Eastover, S.C., Aug. 6, 1874; s. William and Caroline Elizabeth (Woodard) W.; prep. edn., Patrick Mil. Inst., Anderson, S.C., 1888-90; student U. of S.C., 1890-93; M.D., Med. Coll. of S.C., 1896, hon. Dr. P.H., 1929; student, U. of the South, 1896, hon. D.Sc., 1931; m. Elizabeth Vander Horst, June 16, 1896; children—Caroline (Mrs. Benjamin F. Few), William, Adele Allston (Mrs. Horace A. Steven). Practiced in Columbia, S.C., since 1896; founder of first uncinariasis clinic in U.S., 1901; chief of staff Columbia Hosp., 1919-25; chmn. S.C. Food Research Commn. since 1927. Maj. Med. Corps, U.S. Army, 1918-19, World War. Mem. A.M.A. (chmn. pediatric sect. 1930-31; mem. Ho. of Dels. same sect. since 1936), Southern Med. Assn. (chmn. pediatric sect. 1917-18), S.C. Med. Assn. (pres. 1913-14), Columbia Med. Soc. (pres. 1908), Am. Acad. Pediatrics, Sigma Alpha Epsilon. Democrat. Episcopalian. Club: Forest Lake (Columbia). Author: (brochure) Studies in Nutrition, 1926; also articles in med. jours. Home: 1231 Bull St. Office: 1428 Lady St., Columbia SC*

WESTOVER, OSCAR major general; b. Bay City, Mich., July 23, 1883; s. Emil and Kunigunde (Gaertner) W.; grad. U.S. Mil. Acad., 1906. Command and Gen. Staff Sch., 1928, also various air service schs.; m. Adelaide R. Bainbridge, 1907; children—Charles Bainbridge, Katherine Patricia. Pvt. U.S.A., 1901-02; 2d lt. inf., 1906; advanced through grades to major gen., Dec. 1935. Asst. exec. Bur. of Aircraft Production and in office of dir. Air Service, 1918-19; exec. Air Corps, Washington, D.C., and chmn. U.S. Claims Bd., 1919-20; dir. of aricraft production, U.S.A., 1922-28 and since 1932; asst. to chief of Air Corps, 1932-35, and chief of same from Dec. 1935. Winner Nat. Elimination Free Balloon RAce, June 1922; army entrant Internat. Balloon Race, Geneva, Switzerland, Aug. 1922. Awarded D.S.M. (U.S.). Presbyn. Mason. Died Sept. 21, 1938.

WESTOVER, WENDELL bus. exec.; b. Schenectady, N.Y., Aug. 29, 1895; s. Myron Fay and Lou Edna (Ham) W.; student Cornell, 1916-18; m. Gwen Childers, June 27, 1945; children—Lucy Scott, Wendell II. With advt. dept. Gen. Electric Co.; advt. mgr. Ludlum Steel

Co.; pres. Westover-Wolfe, Service, Inc.; president Westover-Wolfe Contracting Co., Inc.; director Monitor Equipment Corporation Exec., Reserve and R.O.T.C. affairs, Spl. Staff, Dept. of War, Washington. Served with U.S. Army, World Wars I and II; brig. gen. U.S. Army Res. ret. Mem. Res. Officers Assn. (pres. dept. N.Y., nat. exec. com.), Am. Soc. Heating and Ventilating Engrs., Albany C. of C., Chi Psi. Republican. Presbyn. Clubs: Rotary, Fort Orange, Albany Country (Albany); Lake Placid, Mohawk Golf (Schenectady); Lake George. Author: Suicide Battalions, 1927. Home: 17 Loudon Heights North, Loudonville, N.Y. Office: 21 Plaza, Albany 7, N.Y. Died Sept. 23, 1960; buried Vale Cemetery, Schenectady.

WETTACH, ROBERT HASLEY (wet'tak), prof. of law; b. Pittsburgh, Pa., Nov. 29, 1891; s. Theodore G. and Mary (Hasley) W.; A.B., U. of Pittsburgh, 1913, A.M., 1914, LL.B., 1917; S.J.D., Harvard, 1921; m. Helen Alpha Burkart, Aug. 28, 1924; children—Robert Hasley, Helen Jane, John Theodore. Admitted to Pa. bar, 1919, N.C. bar, 1928; asso. in practice with Arthur O. Fording, 1919-20; mem. law faculty, U. of N.C. since 1921, prof. since 1926, dean of the School of Law, 1941-49; visiting professor, summers, univs. of Pittsburgh, 1923, Kan., 1924, Minn., 1929, Northwestern, 1933, Texas, 1942, Western Reserve, 1946, Colorado, 1950, U. Fla., 59; asst. attorney general, North Carolina (on leave), 1938-39; dir. Orange County Bldg. and Loan Assn. Mem. bd. of Aldermen, Chapel Hill, N.C., 1935-38, 1942-45. Pub. Panel Mem. Nat. War Labor Bd., 1943-45. Chmn. Commn. to revise ins. laws of N.C., 1944-45, 1946-47. Served as ensign U.S. Naval Aviation, 1917-19. Mem. N.C. State Bar, Inc., Am. and N.C. bar assns., National Academy Arbitrators, Am. Arbitration Association, Sigma Alpha Epsilon, Delta Theta Phi, Omicron Delta Kappa, Order of Coif. Democrat. Mason (32 deg.). Contributor articles to law revs. Home: Chapel Hill, N.C. Died Aug. 29, 1964; buried Chapel Hill, N.C.

WEXLER, HARRY meteorologist, govt. ofcl.; born Fall River, Mass., Mar. 15, 1911; s. Samuel and Mamie (Starr) W.; S.B., Harvard, 1932; D.Sc., Mass. Inst. Tech., 1939; m. Hannah Paipert, Dec. 3, 1934; children—Susan Carol, Libby. Meteorologist U.S. Weather Bur., 1934-40, 41-42, chief sci. services, 1946-55; asst. prof. meteorology University Chicago, 1940-41; dir. meteorol. research, U.S. Weather Bureau, 1955-—; chief scientist U.S. Expdn. to Antarctic for International Geophys. Year, 1955-58; chairman meteorol. panel of Nat. Acad. of Science, com. to study biological effects of atomic radiation; mem. Nat. Acad. of Sci. space sci. bd., com. polar research, also chmn. com. meteorological aspects of satellites, U.S. nat. com. IGY. Served as capt. to lt. col. Weather Service, A.A.F., 1942-46, lt col. Res. Recipient Robert M. Losey award for outstanding services to aeronautics, Inst. Aeronautical Sci., 1945; Exceptional Service award, Dept. of Air Force, 1956, Dept. Commerce, 1958; Distinguished Pub. Service award, U.S. Navy, 1960; Nat. Civi.Civil Service League award, 1961. Fellow A.A.A.S., American Astronautical Society, also the American Acad. Arts and Scis.; mem. Am. Meteorol. Soc., Am. Geophys. Union, Royal Meteorol. Soc. Gt. Britain, Am. Vets. Com. Author sci. articles. Home: 204 S. Lee St., Falls Church, Va. Office: U.S. Weather Bureau, Washington 25. Died Aug. 11, 1962.

WEYLER, GEORGE LESTER, naval officer; b. Emporia, Kan., May 14, 1886; s. John William and Laura Amelia (Schmidt) W.; student Emporia (Kan.) Coll., 1904-05; B.S., U.S. Naval Academy, 1910; LL.B., George Washington Law Sch., Washington, D.C., 1922; grad. Naval War Coll., 1938; m. Laura Gertrude Pearks, Mar. 22, 1917; children—Mary Elizabeth (wife of Lt. Col. Harold Jones Mitchener, U.S.M.C. Ret.), Laura Therese Christian. Comd. ensign, U.S. Navy, 1912, advancing through the grades to rear admiral, 1942; retired with rank of vice admiral, 1946; sea duty, chiefly in Pacific area, includes service on all types of naval ships except submarines and carriers, totals 22 years; shore duty includes service in Navy yards, Navy Dept., Naval Acad., Naval War Coll., Naval Operating Base (Guantanamo, Cuba), and as naval attache, Peru and Ecuador. Decorated campaign badges, Mexican, World War I and World War II (with citation), Legion of Merit with gold star (U.S.), Orden El Sol del Peru, Knight Comdr., Navy Cross. Home: Coronado CA Died Aug. 6, 1971; buried San Francisco National Cemetery.

WHARTON, JAMES E. army officer; b. Elk, New Mexico, Dec. 2, 1894; commd. 2d lt. Inf., Officers Res. Corps, Aug. 1917, 2d lt. Regular Army, 1917, and advanced through the grades to brig. gen., Mar. 1942; on Civilian Corps Duty, Richmond, Mo., July 1933; at Fort Francis E. Warren, Wyoming, 1938; with Officers Branch Personnel Div., G-1, War Dept. Gen. Staff, Washington, D.C., June 1940; became chief of sect. Officers Branch, Sept. 1941; now attached to Hdqrs. Services of Supply, Washington, D.C.* Died Aug. 12, 1944.

WHARTON, JAMES PEARCE retired army officer, educator, portrait painter; b. Waterloo, S.C., Apr. 18, 1893; s. James Beauregard and Siddie (Pearce) W.; A.B., Wofford Coll., 1914; A.B., Duke, 1915; student Ecole des Beaux Arts, Dijon, France, 1919; grad. Tank Sch., 1922, Inf. Advanced Sch., 1933; grad. Maryland Art Inst., 1923; M.F.A., U. Guanajuato, 1952; m. Carol Forbes, Aug. 9, 1929 (dec. June 1958). Phys. dir. YMCA, 1915-16; enlisted as pvt., U.S. Army, 1917, advanced through grades to col., 1946; served with Tank Corps, World War I; with Tank Corps, Ft. G. G. Meade, Md., 1919-26; pub. relations officer Third Corps area, Balt., 1926-31, Inf. Sch., Ft. Benning, Ga., 1931-38, 31st Inf., Manila, P.I., 1938-41, 8th Inf., Ft. Jackson, S.C., 1941-42, Third Service Command, Balt., 1942-46; head Columbus Sch. Art, 1933-38, Manila Sch. Art, 1938-41; head dept. art U. Md., 1948-—; founder, dir. Flat Rock Summer Sch. Art, Hendersonville, N.C.; v.p. Art Found., Inc. Md.; one-man shows: Peale Mus., Balt., High Mus., Atlanta, Columbus, Cambridge and Bucknell univs.; represented numerous pub., pvt. collections, including U. Md.; commd. to paint portraits Maj. Gen. Milton A. Reckord, Glen L. Martin, Gov. McKeldin, Dr. Henry C. Byrd, others. Decorated Order Brit. Empire; Commendation medal U.S. Army; recipient art prizes Balt. Mus. Art, High Museum, Atlanta; alumni scholarship prize Maryland Inst., 1943. Mem. Retired Officers Assn., Wine and Food Soc. of Balt. (bd. govs.), Kappa Alpha. Methodist. Clubs: Water Color, Charcoal, University (Balt.). Home: 7727 Carroll Av., Takoma Park 12, Md. Office: A and S Bldg., College Park, Md. Died July 5, 1963; buried Arlington Nat. Cemetery, Washington.

WHARTON, VERNON LANE coll. dean; b. Handsboro, Miss., Sept. 29, 1907; s. Guy Verner and Fannie Henningham (Lane) W.; A.B., Millsaps Coll., 1928; A.M., U. N.C., 1931, Ph.D., 1940; student U. Mich., summer 1937, Yale, summer 1950; m. Beverley Dickerson, June 16, 1943; children—John Beverley, Vernon Lane. Tchr. Slidell (La.) High Sch., 1933-35; instr. social scis. Millsaps Coll., 1935-37, successively asso. prof., prof. history and sociology, head dept. sociology, 1939-42, 46-52; dean Coll. and Grad. Sch., Tex. Woman's U., 1952-56; dean Coll. Liberal Arts, Univ. Southwestern La., 1956-—. Mem. Gen. Conf. Bd. of World Peace, Meth. Ch.; 1948-52; exec. com. Miss. Assn. on Crime and Delinquency, 1949-52; pres. Miss. Conf. Social Work, 1950-51. Trustee Tougaloo So. Christian Coll., 1946-54. Served as lt. comdr. USNR, 1942-46. Mem. Am., So. hist. associations, American Association U. Profs., Pub. Affairs Research Council La., Phi Kappa Phi, Phi Beta Kappa, Phi Beta Kappa Assos., Omicron Delta Kappa, Pi Kappa Delta, Theta Chi, Phi Eta Sigma. Club: Rotary. Author: The Negro in Mississippi, 1865-1890, 1947. Contbr. to Reconstruction in the South, 1952. Contbr. articles profl. and bus. jours. Home: 112 Bellaire Rd. Lafayette, La. Died Sept. 7, 1964; buried Hollywood Cemetery, McComb, Miss.

WHARTON, WILLIAM H. army officer, diplomatic agt.; b. Albemarle County, Va., 1802; s. John Austin and Judith (Harris) W.; m. Sarah Ann Groce, Dec. 5, 1827; 1 son, John Austin. Planter, Eastern Tex., 1827; pres. Tex. Constl. Conv., 1833; judge advocate, col. Army of Texans organized at Gonzales, 1835, resigned, 1835; sent to U.S. for aid to Tex. Revolution, 1835; minister to U.S. (apptd. by Sam Houston), to negotiate recognition and eventual annexation of Tex. to U.S., 1836; mem. Tex. Senate, 1838-39; Wharton County (Tex.) named in his honor. Died Houston, Tex., Mar. 14, 1839; buried Eagle Island Plantation, Tex.

WHEAT, CARL IRVING lawyer; b. Holliston, Mass., Dec. 5, 1892; s. Frank Irving and Catherine Isabel (Pierce) W.; grad. Occidental Coll. Acad., Los Angeles, Calif., 1911; A.B., Pomona Coll., Claremont, Cal., 1915; LL.B., Harvard, 1920; Doctor of Letters (honorary), Pomona College, 1959; m. Helen Millspaugh, Sept. 22, 1919; children—Francis Millspaugh, Richard Pierce. Admitted to Calif. bar, 1920, and began practice at Los Angeles; atty. for R.R. Commn. of Calif., 1922-29, chief counsel, 1924-29; in practice at San Francisco, Calif., 1929-33; public utilities counsel for City of Los Angeles, associated with city attys. office, 1933-36; spl. telephone rate atty. FCC, Washington, D.C., 1936-37, counsel and dir. of telephone rate and research dept., 1937-38; practice at San Francisco and Los Angeles, 1938-39; cons. atty. Pub. Utilities Commn. of Hawaii, and Dept. Public Service, Washington, 1939; in practice in San Francisco, and Washington, 1940-57; sr. mem. firm Wheat, May & Shannon, 1940-57. Member adv. board on nat. parks, Dept. of Interior. Pres. Institute of Historical Cartography, 1957. With the American Ambulance Service in France, 1917; 1st lt., AS, U.S. Army, 1918-19. Trustee Pomona Coll. Recipient Henry R. Wagner Meml. Medal, Cal. Hist. Soc., 1959. Mem. nat., state and local bar assns. and legal socs., hist. socs. Republican. Congregationalist. Clubs: Bohemian (San Francisco); The Explorers Club, (N.Y.); Zamorano (Los Angeles); The Roxburghe (San Francisco); W.O.O.F.F.B. (Washington); Book (Calif.). Author numerous hist. works on western U.S., latest being: Mapping the American Transmississippi West, 1540-1804 Vol. I, 1957, II, 58, III, 59, IV, 60; editor of several jours. and collections hist. material. Contbr. to legal and hist. periodicals. Home: 332 Westridge Dr., Menlo Park, Cal. Died June 23, 1966.

WHEATON, FRANK maj. gen. U.S.A., retired, 1897; b. Providence, R.I., May 8, 1833; s. Dr. Francis L. W.; grad. Brown Univ., A.M.; became surveyor; went to Calif., 1850; employed as civil engr. on Mexican boundaries; commd. lt. 1st U.S. cav., 1855; served in Kan., Mo., and in Neb., against Indians, becoming capt., March 1861; lt. col. 2d R.I. vols., July 1861; brig. gen. vols., Nov. 1862, and by bvt. became maj. gen. vols. and U.S. army; comd. a div. at Gettysburg and Shenandoah Valley campaigns; was with Army of the Potomac from first Bull Run to Lee's surrender; particularly distingusihed himself in battles of the Wilderness, Cedar Creek and Petersburg. After war, served from lt. col. to maj. gen. regular army until age of retirement. Home: Washington, D.C. Died 1903.

WHEATON, LOYD maj. gen. U.S.A.; b. Pennfield, Mich., July 15, 1838; s. William G. and Amanda M. (Parker) W.; m. Mrs. Charlotte Flower Derby, Dec. 17, 1867 (died 1905), desc. of Flower family and of Gov. William Bradford, Plymouth. Enlisted as 1st sergt. Co. E, 8th Ill. Inf., April 20, 1861; discharged, July 24, 1861; commd. 1st lt. 8th Ill. Inf., July 25. 1861; capt., Mar. 25, 1862; maj., Aug. 28, 1863; lt. col., Nov. 25, 1864; hon. mustered out, May 4, 1866; apptd. from Ill., capt. 34th U.S. Inf., July 28, 1866; assigned to 20th Inf., Sept. 1, 1869; maj., Oct. 14, 1891; lt. col., May 31, 1895; transferred to 20th Inf., September 11, 1895; brig. gen. vols., May 27, 1898; transferred to 2d U.S. Inf., Dec. 30, 1898; col. 20th Inf., Feb. 6, 1899; hon. discharged from vol. service, Apr. 15, 1899; brig. gen. vols., Apr. 15, 1899; transferred to 7th U.S. Inf., Feb. 3, 1900; maj. gen. vols., June 18, 1900; brig. gen. U.S.A., Feb. 2, 1901; hon. disch. from vol. service, Feb. 28, 1901; maj. gen. U.S.A., Mar. 30, 1901; retired by operation of law, July 15, 1902. Bvtd.: maj., Mar. 2, 1867, "for gallant and meritorious services in siege of Vicksburg, Miss."; lt. col., Mar. 2, 1867, for same, in assault on Ft. Blakely, Ala.; col. vols., Mar. 26, 1865, for same during campaign against Mobile; maj. gen. vols., June 19, 1899, "for gallantry in action against insurgents nr. Imus, P.I."; awarded Congressional Medal of Honor, Jan. 16, 1894, 'for distinguished gallantry in assault on Ft. Blakely, Ala., Apr. 9, 1865, leading right wing of his regt. springing through an embrasure against a strong fire of artillery and musketry and first to enter enemy's works." Participated in many battles and engagements during Civil War; wounded at Shiloh; in service at western and other posts to 1898; comd. div. 7th Army Corps, Spanish-Am. War; participated in all principal battles and combats in P.I., 1899-1902; comd. depts. Northern Luzon and North Philippines, 1900-02, including army of 35,000 men. Home: Chicago, Ill. Died Sept. 17, 1918.

WHEELAN, JAMES NICHOLAS brig. gen. U.S.A.; b. Pa., Dec. 6, 1837. Served as 1st sergt. Co. A, 1st N.Y. Mounted Rifles, July 18-Dec. 6, 1861; commd. 2d lt., Dec. 7, 1861; capt., Feb. 7, 1862; maj., Aug. 13, 1862; bvt. col., Mar. 13, 1865; lt. col., 1st N.Y. Mounted Rifles, Aug. 17, 1865; hon. mustered out, Nov. 29, 1865; apptd. from N.Y., 2d lt. 2d U.S. Cav., Feb. 23, 1886; 1st lt., July 20, 1866; capt., Dec. 15, 1873; maj. 8th Cav., Mar. 7, 1893; lt. col. 7th Cav., June 9, 1899; col. 12th Cav., Feb. 2, 1901; retired by operation of law, Dec. 6, 1901; advanced to rank of brig. gen. retired, by act of Apr. 23, 1904. Bvtd.: col. vols., March 13, 1865, "for gallant and meritorious services during the war"; maj., Feb. 27, 1890, "for gallant services in action against Indians on the Rosebud, Mont., May 7, 1877." Was detailed as mil. attache to the courts of Netherlands, Belgium, and Berlin, temporarily. Died Nov. 30, 1922.

WHEELER, CHARLES BREWSTER army officer; born Matteson, Ill., May 3, 1865; s. Christopher and Mary J. (Safford) W.; grad. U.S. Mil. Acad., 1887; m. Zella Lentilhon, Apr. 3, 1893. Commd. 2d lt. 5th Arty., June 12, 1887; 1st lt. ordnance, Dec. 15, 1890; capt. July 7, 1898; maj. June 25, 1906; lt. col., June 13, 1909; col., Nov. 3, 1914; brig. gen., Oct. 6, 1917. Duty in Office Chief of Ordnance, Washington, 1896-1906; chief ordnance officer, Philippine Div., also comdr. Manila Ordnance Depot, 1906-07; comd. Watertown (Mass.) Arsenal, 1908-17; assigned duty Office Chief of Ordnance, Mar. 4, 1917; apptd. acting chief of ordnance, Dec. 19, 1917; chief ordnance officer A.E.F., Apr. 1918; retired from army, Sept. 3, 1919, to go into business; now v.p. Eaton, Crane & Pike Co., Pittsfield, Mass. Comdr. Legion of Honor (France); Companion Order of the Bath (Eng.). Episcopalian. Clubs: Army and Navy, Metropolitan (Washington); St. Botolph (Boston); University (N.Y. City). Home: Pittsfield, Mass. Died Wayland, Mass., Apr. 11, 1946.

WHEELER, DANIEL DAVIS brigadier gen. U.S.A.; b. Cavendish, Vt., July 12, 1841; s. Daniel Hosmer and Susan (Davis) W.; ed. Leland Sem; m. Nannie Phillips Smith, Jan. 16, 1896. Apptd. 2d lt. 4th Vt. Inf., Sept. 21, 1861; 1st lt., Apr. 21, 1862; hon. mustered out, Sept. 21, 1864; capt. a.a.g., June 30, 1864; maj. a.a.g., Dec. 27, 1864; lt. col. a.a.g., May 26, 1865-June 11, 1866; hon. mustered out, Oct. 19, 1866. Apptd. 2d lt. 1st Arty., May 11, 1866; 1st lt., Feb. 12, 1867; capt. a.q.m., July 2, 1879; maj. q.m., Sept. 6, 1893; lt. col. deputy q.m. gen., Nov. 11, 1898; col. a.q.m. gen., Oct. 2, 1902; brig. gen. U.S.A., Aug. 15, 1903, and retired Aug. 16, 1903, at own request after 40 yrs.' service. In Spanish War was lt. col. and chief q.m. U.S.V., May 9, 1898; col. q.m., Sept. 3, 1898-Mar. 1899. Bvtd.: capt., Mar. 2, 1867, for Salem Heights and Cold Harbor; maj. vols., Sept. 29, 1864, for campaign of 1864; col. vols., Dec. 1, 1865, "for faithful and meritorious services during war"; awarded Congressional Medal of Honor. Home: Fredericksburg, Va. Died July 27, 1916.

WHEELER, GEORGE MONTAGUE soldier, engr.; b. Grafton, Mass., Oct. 9, 1842; grad. West Point, 1866; assigned to engrs.; promoted 1st lt., Mar. 7, 1867; at head of Geog. Survey of U.S. west of 100th Meridian, as supt. engr., 1869-79; supervised the reports of that expdn.; promoted capt., 1879, and later maj. and retired, owing to illness, June 15, 1888; of late years has practiced as civ. engr.; mem. Am. Soc. Civ. Engrs. since 1894. Address: 930 16th St., N.W., Washington.

WHEELER, HARRIS ANSEL b. at Orrington, Me., July 30, 1850; s. John D. and Sarah J. W.; ed. in pub. schs. until 16 yrs. old; m. Anna M. Ayer, of Chicago, June 2, 1884. Clerk Bangor, Me., and Detroit, 1866-71; apptd. 2d lt. U.S.A., 1872, resigned 1874; financial management of the Mich. Mil. Acad., Orchard Lake, Mich., 1878-80; pres. Orchard Lake (Mich.) Mil. Acad., several yrs. from 1902. Invented the Wheeler coach and car seats; organized and pres. Northwestern Expanded Metal Co. A.-d.-c. on staffs of Govs. Cullom and Hamilton, 1881-84; later col. 2d Regt., Ill. N.G., until 1890; brig.-gen. comdg. 1st Brigade, Ill. N.G., 1893-98 (resigned); now Grand Recorder Grand Commandery of K.T. of Ill. Clubs: Union League, Chicago. Home: 1741 Monroe St. Office: 131 LaSalle St., Chicago.

WHEELER, HOMER WEBSTER soldier, author; b. Montgomery, Vt., May 13, 1848; s. Augustus Choto and Lucretia (Babcock) W.; ed. Vermont Acad. (Franklin, Vt.), New Hampton Inst. (Fairfax, Vt.), Eastman's Business Coll. (Poughkeepsie, N.Y.); grad. Inf. and Cav. Sch., Ft. Leavenworth, Kan., 1883; m. Isabella Dougherty, Aug. 10, 1886 (died 1888). Went to Ft. Wallace, Kan., 1868, and became connected with the post trader's store; guide to Capt. Bankhead's expdn. to the rescue of Maj. George Forsyth's command, besieged for 9 days, at Arickaree fork of Republican River, Kan., Sept. 1868; apptd. post trader, 1870, and later engaged in cattle raising, owning the only herd in Western Kan. for a number of yrs.; apptd. 2d lt. 5th Cav., U.S.A., Oct. 15, 1875, "for bravery and efficiency" in guiding Lt. Austin Henely, 6th Cav., in attacking a hostile Indian camp on Sappa Creek, Kan., Apr. 1875; promoted through grades to col., Mar. 11, 1911; retired Sept. 24, 1911. Organizer company of Indian scouts, and comdr. for 3 yrs.; in frequent combats with Indians through Sioux War of 1876; served with regt. in Puerto Rico, Spanish-Am. War; in Philippines, 1902-04, Cuba, 1906-09, Hawaiian Islands, 1910-11. Medal as marksman and sharpshooter. Republican. Mason. Author: The Frontier Trail, 1923; Buffalo Days, 1925. Home: Los Angeles, Calif. Deceased.

WHEELER, JOHN MARTIN ophthalmologist; b. Burlington, Vt., Nov. 10, 1879; s. Henry Orson and Elizabeth Lavinia (Martin) W.; A.B., U. of Vt., 1902, M.D., 1905, M.Sc., 1906. hon. D.Sc., 1928; hon. D.Sc., Middlebury (Vt.) Coll., 1933; m. Julia Warren Smith, May 15, 1912; children—Martha, Charles Smith, Edward Martin, Ann. Dir. eye service, Presbyn. Hosp., N.Y. City, 1928—; prof. ophthalmology, Columbia, 1928—; cons. ophthalmologist Bellevue Hosp., New York Eye and Ear Infirmary, 5th Avenue Hosp., Neurol. Inst., Babies Hosp., Sloane Maternity Hosp. Served as capt., advancing to maj., Med. Corps, U.S.A., World War I. Trustee U. of Vt.; dir. New York Eye and Ear Infirmary. Republican. Congregationalist. Home: New York, N.Y. Died Aug. 22, 1938.

WHEELER, JOHN SAMUEL, physician; b. Boston, Mass., Jan. 8, 1904; s. Rev. John Lewis and Tryphenia Halfyard (Garland) W.; student Univ. of N.H., 1923-26, Wesleyan Univ., Middletown Conn., 1924; M.D., Boston Univ., 1930; M.P.H., Johns Hopkins, 1938; m. Marion Ernestine Mitchell, June 22, 1929; children—John M. W., Harold H. C., Mark L. B., Michael L. L. Interne Bridgeport (Conn.) Hosp., 1930-31; gen. practice of medicine, Wolfeboro, N.H., 1931-37; dir. div. of epidemiology and local health N.H. State Dept. of Health, Concord, N.H., 1937-40; state health officer and sec. state bd. of health, N.H. State Dept. of Health, 1945-56, consultant in pub. health, staff Concord Gen. Hosp., 1947-56; staff physician and cons. pub. health Fairview Hosp. & Tng. Center, Salem, Ore., 1958-62, N.H. Hosp., Concord, 1962-67. Sec. state bd. funeral dirs. and embalmers, since Dec. 1945; sec. state bd. registration in medicine from Feb. 1946, in chiropody from 1946; chairman State Hospital Survey and Construction Commission. Mem. N.H. State water pollution commn., cancer commn., TB commn., commn. on alcholism. Trustee N.H. State Tb. Sanitarium, Glencliffe. Served in U.S. Army as N.H. state med. officer for Selective Service, Sept. 1940-Apr. 1945; med. insp. and hosp. insp. 31st gen. hosp., Lingayen Gulf, P.I., Sept. 1945, med. insp. Camp Wolters, Tex., May 1945; disch. as lt. col. Nov. 1945; served as state surg., staff N.H. Nat. Guard, Aug.-Oct. 1940; apptd. col., chief Selective Service Staff, 1951; col. m.c. ret. Fellow A.M.A., A.P.H.A. Mem. founders group Am. Bd. Preventive Med. and Pub. Health. Mem. State and Terr. Health Ofcrs. Assn., Assn. State and Provincial Health Authorities, N.H. Med. Soc. (chmn. pub. health commn.), Merrimack Co. Med. Soc., N.H. Tuberculosis Assn. (mem. exec. com.). N.H. Social Hygiene Soc. (mem. exec. com.), Alpha Chi Rho, Alpha Kappa Kappa. Rep. Episcopalian. Mason. Home: Contoocook NH Died Apr. 16, 1968; buried Blossom Hill Cemetery, Concord NH

WHEELER, JOSEPH brig. gen. U.S.A.; b. Augusta, Ga., Sept. 10, 1836; grad. West Point, 1859; LL.D., Georgetown Coll., 1899; m. Daniella Jones. Served as 2d lt. U.S. cav., 1859-61; 1st lt. Confederate arty.; col. inf.; brig. gen. cavalry, maj. gen. and corps commdr., lt. gen., wounded 3 times, 16 horses shot under him; eight of his staff officers killed and 32 wounded; received thanks of Confederate Govt. for skill and gallantry in battle, and specially thanked by State of S.C. for his brave and successful defense of the city of Aikin; distinguished and commended by his commdg. general for gallantry and skill in battles of Shiloh, Perryville, Murfreesboro, Tullahoma, Chickamauga, Ringgold, Dalton, Resaca, Adairsville, Cassville, Pickett's Mill, Kenesaw, Peach Tree Creek, Decatur, the several battles around Atlanta, battles of Averysboro and Bentonville; comd. in about 50 cavalry battles and hundreds of minor combats; comd. Confederate cavalary which daily fought Gen. Sherman in his campaign from Atlanta to Savannah and from Savannah through the Carolinas. After war lawyer and planter; congressman from 8th Ala. dist., 1881-99; reëlected for 56th Congress, but resigned. Senior mem. Congress on Dem. side; mem. 1887-93 and 1895, v.p. 1887, pres. 1895, Bd. of Visitors of Mil. Acad.; regent Smithsonian Instn., 1886-1900. Apptd., May 4, 1898, maj. gen. of vols., U.S.A., and assigned to the command of cav. div., 5th Corps. in Cuba. Planned and comd. in battle of Las Guasimas, Cuba, June 24, 1898; sr. officer in field at battle of San Juan, July 1-2, 1898; engaged in all conflicts in front of Santiago; sr. mem. of commn. which arranged the surrender of Santiago and Spanish Army to Am. Army; comd. troops at Montauk Point, L.I., 1898, of 4th Army Corps, Huntsville, Ala., 1898, en route to Manila, 1899; command 1st brigade, 2d div., Philippine Islands, Aug. 1899, to Jan. 24, 1900. Comd. troops in skirmishes with enemy under insurgent gen., Toma(s, Mascardo, at Santa Rita, Sept. 9 and 16, 1899; comd. force which carried enemy's entrenchments at Porac, Sept. 28, 1899; in immediate command on field in engagements at Angeles, Oct. 11 and 16, 1899; comd. brigade in advance upon Mabalacat, Nov. 8, in attack upon and capture of Bamban, Nov. 11, in advance upon Tarlac, Nov. 12-13, on expdn. to San Miguel de Camerling, Nov. 22-26, to San Ignacia and Moriones, Dec. 3-6; made inspection Island of Guam by direction of President, Feb. 8-12, 1900; brig. gen. U.S.A., June 16, 1900; comd. Dept. of Lakes, June 18 to Sept. 10, 1900. Author: Account of Kentucky Campaign, 1862; Cavalry Tactics, 1863; Military History of Alabama; History of the Santiago Campaign, 1898; History of Cuba, 1496 to 1899, 1899; 8 vols. of Congressional Speeches, 1883-98; History of the Effect Upon Civilization of the Wars of the Nineteenth Century. Also monographs upon the lives of Admiral Dewey, William McKinley, "Stonewall" Jackson and Theodore Roosevelt. Home: Wheeler, Ala. Died 1906.

WHEELER, RICHARD SMITH, govt. ofcl.; b. Chgo., Mar. 30, 1909; s. Herbert M. and Orra M. (Smith) W.; B.A., U. Mich., 1930; m. Dora L. Hughes, June 3, 1937; children—Douglas H., Richard M., David L. Exec. merc. establishments, N.Y.C., Washington, 1930-35; staff information statistics div., Nat. Emergency Council and successor agy. Office of Govt. Reports, Exec. Office of the President, 1936-38, chief information statistics div., 1938-40; fgn. affairs officer, div. internat. conferences Dept. State, 1946-49, asst. chief in charge program br., 1950-52, asso. chief div., 1953-54; dep. dir. Office Internat. Conferences, Bur. Internat. Orgn. Affairs, 1954-57, 59-60; exec. officer U.S. Mission to Internat. Atomic Energy Agency, Vienna, Austria, 1958-60; foreign service officer Department State, 1955-62; dir. advt. Arlington (Va.) Trust Co., 1964-70, asst. treas., asst. v.p. advt. and pub. relations, 1970-71. Mem. numerous U.S. delegations, ofcl. various internat. meetings. Served from 1st lt. to lt. col. Office Mgmt. Control, Hdqrs. USAAF, 1941-46. Decorated Military Legion of Merit; Commendation medal with 2 oak leaf clusters. Home: Arlington VA Died June 20, 1972; buried Ivy Hill Cemetery, Alexandria VA

WHEELER, WILLIAM REGINALD ch. ofcl.; b. Tidioute, Pa., July 10, 1889; s. Nelson P. and Rachel A. (Smith) W.; grad. Hill Sch.; A.B., Yale, 1911; B.D., Auburn (N.Y.) Theol. Sem., 1914; A.B., Harvard, 1915; D.D., Beaver Coll., 1938; m. Constance I. Hayes, May 16, 1914; children—Reginald K. (dec.), Alexander B., Nelson P. III. Ordained to the ministry Presbyn. Ch., 1914; missionary, Nanking, China, 1915-16, 1932-36; Hangchow, 1917-19; sec. Peking U., 1919-21; asst. sec. Presbyn. Bd. Foreign Missions, 1921-23, exec. sec., 1923-32; sec., 1938-42, research editor edn. and information div., 1946-47; v.p. bd. of founders U. Nanking 1937-38; exec. sec. Yale-in-China 1947-49; asst. dir. China Inst. in Am., 1949-50; research asst. Presbyn. Hist. Soc., 1952. Served from capt. to maj. AUS, 1942-46. Decorated Medal of Merit. Mem. Mil. Order of the World War. N.Y. Zool. Soc. (hon. life). Phi Beta Kappa, Psi Upsilon, Elihu. Clubs: National Arts; Yale. Author several books: 1st two, A Book of Verse of the Great War, 1917; China and the World War, 1919; the last two, A Man Sent From God: The Biography of Robert E. Speer, 1956; Pine Knots and Bark Peelers: The Story of Five Generations of American Lumbermen, 1960. Made aerial trip to China, 1948. Home: 230 E. 79th St., N.Y.C. Died 1963.

WHEELOCK, CHARLES DELORMA educator; born in Riverside, Calif., July 28, 1897; s. Arthur N. and Kate Dudley (Johnson) W.; B.S., U.S. Naval Acad., 1920; M.S., Mass. Inst. Tech., 1924; m. Beatrice Grace McLeish, June 6, 1922; children—Beatrice Jeanne (Mrs. Jeanne W. Lilly), Charles Arthur. Commd. ensign, U.S.N., 1920, and advanced through grades to rear adm., 1946; on duty in naval shipyards, 1924-34, at sea, 1934-36, in ship design, Bur. of Ships, 1936-43, head of design, 1943-44; prodn. officer, Mare Island, naval shipyard, 1944-46; prof. naval constrn., Mass. Inst. Tech., 1946; dep. and asst. chief, Bur. of Ships, Washington, 1946-51, insp. gen., 1951-53, ret.; research engr. Scripps Institution of Oceanography of U. Cal., LaJolla, Cal., 1953-58; prof. marine resources U. of Cal., La Jolla, Cal., 1958—. Dir. Inst. Marine Resources. Mem. Soc. of Naval Architects and Marine Engrs. (v.p.). Episcopalian. Home: 8355 Paseo del Ocaso, La Jolla, Cal., and Carmel, Cal.

WHELEN, TOWNSEND (hwe'len), army officer, author; b. Phila., Pa., Mar. 6, 1877; s. Dr. Alfred and Sarah Wurts (Smith) W.; grad. Drexel Inst., Phila., 1894; m. Mary Louise, d. Brig. Gen. Edward B. Pratt, United States Army, March 18th, 1905 (deceased March 17th, 1956); one daughter, Violet. Sergeant, Co. D, and sergt. maj. 1st Pa. Inf., May 11-Aug. 25, 1898; commd. 2d lt. same regt., Aug. 26, 1898, and hon. mustered out; commd. 2d lt. inf., regular army, Oct. 28, 1902; 1st lt., Oct. 2, 1908; capt., July 1, 1916; maj. of inf., N.A., Aug. 5, 1917; lt. col., July 30, 1918; maj. Ordnance Dept., regular army, July 1, 1920; promoted lt. colonel, Mar. 12, 1926, col., Oct. 1, 1934; retired from active service, Aug. 31, 1935; vice president Parker-Whelen Co., Washington, D.C.; associate editor of Sports Afield. In exploration in British Columbia, 1901; insp.-instr. on duty with Div. Mil. Affairs, Washington, D.C., 1912-15; explorations in Panama, 1915, 16, 17; assigned duty Gen. Staff, in charge inf. and small arms training, June 19, 1918. Mem. Nat. Bd. for Promotion Rifle Practice, 1918. Mem. Army Inf. Nat. Rifle Team, 1903, 05, 06, 07, 09; winner many army rifle competitions, regarded as authority on small arms instrn. and target practice, on mil. and commercial small arms and ballistics. Mem. Nat. Rifle Association (dir. 1918, life). Episcopalian. Clubs: Army and Navy (Washington, D.C.), Camp Fire Club America, Explorers; Wilderness (Philadelphia) (honorary member). Author: Suggestion to Military Riflemen, 1905; Trench Warfare (with Maj. J. A. Moss, 1917; The American Rifle, 1918; Big Game Hunting, 1923; Amateur Gunsmithing, 1923; Wilderness Hunting and Wildcraft, 1927; Telescopic Rifle Sights, 1936; The Hunting Rifle, 1940; Small Arms Design and Ballistics, 1945; Hunting Big Game, 1946; Why Not Load Your Own, 1950; On Your Own in the Wilderness, 1958. Home: 7408 Washington Av., St. Louis 63130; summer Woodstock, Vt. Died Dec. 23, 1961.

WHELESS, JOSEPH, author, lawyer; b. Nashville, Tenn., Nov. 13, 1868; s. Joseph and Ellen Thomas (Malone) W.; ed. Webb's Sch., Bellbuckle, Tenn., and under pvt. instructors; m. Mamie Willard Teasdale, June 17, 1904. Admitted to Tenn. bar, 1889, Mo. bar, 1895, N.Y. bar, 1920; practiced at Nashville and St. Louis; specialized, after 1910, in Latin-Am. law and represented Am. interests in Mexico; associated with Aldao, Campos & Gil, Argentine internat. firm, in New York office, 1919-24; mem. law staff of Western Union Telegraph Co., 1924-32; now in gen. practice, specialty of Mexican and foreign law. Sent to S. America by Carnegie Endowment for Internat. Peace, 1915, to report on the industrial and economic effects of the war in Argentina, Brazil and Paraguay. Speaks 5 modern langs. and has knowledge of 3 ancient langs. Maj., judge advocate, U.S. Army, on duty Central Dept., at Chicago, July 1917-Dec. 1918; instr. mil. law R.O.T.C., U. of Ark., 1918; Army Intelligence Service (Spanish and Italian), May 1942-Oct. 1943. Mem. Rep. County Com., N.Y. County, N.Y. Chmn. for Manhattan of Mayor's Com. on Tax Exemption and Tax Inequalities, author of its report, 1934-35. Mem. Am., N.Y. State and New York County bar assns., Am. Law Inst., Am. Arbitration Soc., A.A.A.S., New York Southern Soc., Mo. Hist. Soc., Science League America, Inc., New York County Am. Legion (legal com.), S.C.V.; mem. organization conv. of Am. Legion. Humanist, Freethinker. Mason. Club: Authors. Author: Compendium of the Laws of Mexico, 1910, revised edition, 1938; Is It God's Word? ("an exposition of fables and mythology of the Bible"), 1926; Forgery of Christianity, 1930; The Forgery Founded Church, 1931; Debunking the Laws of Moses. Translator: The Civil Code of Brazil, 1920. Asso. editor (sect. comparative law) Am. Bar Assn. Jour. Dir. and atty. for Freethinkers of America, Inc. Also lecturer. Home: 780 Riverside Drive, New York 32 NY

WHELPLEY, MEDLEY GORDON BRITTAIN, b. Bristol, New Brunswick, Can., Jan. 16, 1893; s. Charles Brown and Harriet (Brittain) W.; brought to U.S. in infancy; student Coe Coll., 1913-14, LL.D., 1947; student University of Pa., 1914-15; m. Katharine M. Dietz, Mar. 8, 1918; children—Gordon Brittain, Harriet (Mrs. Bruce C. Conklin), Katharine (Mrs. George

Atcheson). With Harris Forbes and Company, New York, 1915-17, Mechanics & Metals Nat. Bank, 1919-22, v.p., 1922-26; vice president Chase Nat. Bank, 1926-28, Chase Securities Corp., 1928-30; organized, 1930, and pres., dir. Am. Express Bank & Trust Co., 1930-31; partner Guggenheim Brothers, 1931-44, assisted in reorganization Chilean nitrogen industry; chairman Lautaro Nitrate Company, Ltd. (London), 1932-44; pres. and dir. Pacific Tin Consol. Corp., 1938-44, pres. and dir. Anglo-Chilean Nitrate Corp., 1932-44; dir. U.S. Rubber Co. Trustee Solomon R. Guggenheim Found. Chairman committee for Control of Nitrogen in Germany, National Engr. Council, 1945. President Bond Club of N.Y., 1926-27. Student Officers' Tng. Camp, Plattsburg, May-Aug. 1917; capt. 305th F.A., 77th Div., N.A., Aug. 1917-June 1919; with A.E.F., France, Apr. 1918-Mar. 1919; cited in gen. orders for gallantry in action. Certificate of Merit for activities, World War II. Republican. Episcopalian. Clubs: Links, Racquet and Tennis. Home: New York City NY Died Mar. 23, 1968; buried Kensico Cemetery, Valhalla NY

WHERRY, WILLIAM MACKEY brig. gen. U.S.A.; b. St. Louis, Sept. 13, 1836; s. Joseph A. and Amelia (Hornor) W.; ed. pub. schs., St. Louis County, Mo., and U. of Mo.; studied law; m. Alice W. Grammer, June 10, 1868 (died 1888). Served in Civil War, 1861-66, and on frontier against Indians, and war with Spain, 1898. Was a.d.c. to Gen. Nathaniel Lyon, July 19-Aug. 10, 1861; a.d.c. to Gen. Schofield, 1862-66, and 1867-85, and mil. sec., Feb. 11 to May 31, 1895; accompanied Gen. Schofield on spl. mission to France, Nov. 1865, to Jan. 13, 1866. Participated in battles of Wilson's Creek, Dug Spring, Rocky Face, Resaca, Dallas, Kennesaw Mt., Culp's Farm, Atlanta, Rough and Ready, Jonesboro, Franklin, Nashville, Ft. Anderson, capture of Wilmington, Kinston, and was present at surrender of Gen. J. E. Johnston. Bvtd.: capt., Sept. 1, 1864, for Atlanta campaign; maj., Dec. 16, 1864, for battles of Franklin and Nashville, Tenn.; lt. col. and col., Mar. 13, 1865, "for gallant and meritorious services during the war"; col. vols., Mar. 13, 1865, "for gallant and meritorious services during campaign in Ga. and Tenn."; brig. gen. vols., "for gallant and meritorious services"; awarded Congressional Medal of Honor, Oct. 30, 1895, "for distinguished gallantry at battle of Wilson's Creek, Mo., Aug. 10, 1861." Participated in battle on San Juan Hill and capture Santiago de Cuba, 1898; col. 8th Inf., Aug. 30, 1898; transferred to 17th Inf., Sept. 16, 1898; brig. gen. U.S.V., Sept. 21, 1898; brig. gen. U.S.A., Jan. 7, 1899; retired, Jan. 18, 1899. Mem. Mil. Service Instn. Wrote: Battle of Wilson's Creek, Mo., in Northwestern Review, 1878-79; Death of Gen. Lyon, Battles and Leaders of the Civil War, 1888-89; Lyon's Campaign in Missouri, Jour. Ohio Commandery, Loyal Legion, Vol. 3, 1896-97. Home: Cincinnati, O. Died Nov. 3, 1918.

WHIPPLE, ABRAHAM naval officer; b. Providence, R.I., Sept. 26, 1733; m. Sarah Hopkins, Aug. 2, 1761, 3 children. Commanded privateer Gamecock against French, 1759-60; commd. capt. Continental Navy, 1775; commodore of several vessels, captured, brought to port 8 East Indiamen with cargoes worth over $1,-000,000; participated in naval defense of Charleston, S.C., 1779; farmer in Ohio, after Revolutionary War. Died Marietta, O., May 27, 1819.

WHIPPLE, AMIEL WEEKS topog. engr., army officer; b. Greenwich, Mass., 1816; s. David and Abigail (Pepper) W.; grad. U.S. Mil. Acad., 1841; m. Eleanor Sherburne, Sept. 12, 1843. Mem. survey team established to settle Northeastern boundary of U.S., 1844-49; surveyed boundary between Mexico and U.S., 1849-53; surveyed route for railroad line to Pacific Ocean, 1853-56; supervised operation designed to open Gt. Lakes for large craft, 1856-61; chief topog. engr. at Battle of Bull Run, 1860; commd. maj. U.S. Army, 1861; promoted brig. gen. U.S. Volunteers, 1862; wounded 2d day of fighting at Battle of Chancellorsville, 1863; promoted maj. gen. U.S. Volunteers before his death. Died Washington, D.C., May 7, 1863.

WHIPPLE, CHARLES HENRY brig. gen., U.S.A.; b. Adams, N.Y., June 12, 1849; s. Rt. Rev. Henry Benjamin (bishop of Minn.) and Cornelia (Wright) W.; ed. St. Paul's Sch., Concord, N.H.; m. Evelyn E. McLean, Dec. 5, 1871. Cashier Citizens' Nat. Bank, Faribault, Minn., 1871-81; apptd. maj. p.m. U.S.A., Feb. 18, 1881; lt. col. deputy p.m. gen., May 3, 1901; col. asst. p.m. gen., Jan. 25, 1904; brig. gen. p.m. gen., Jan. 1, 1908; retired Feb. 15, 1912. Home: Alhambra, Calif. Died Nov. 6, 1932.

WHIPPLE, WILLIAM DENISON col. U.S.A.; b. Nelson, N.Y., Aug. 2, 1826; grad. West Point, 1851; same yr., 2d lt. 3d inf.; m. Caroline Mary Cooke, Dec. 16, 1854 (now deceased). Served in the Gila Expdn. against Apaches, 1857; Navajo Expdn., 1858, defense of Ft. Defiance, N.Mex., 1860; 1st lt., Dec. 1856; capt., 1861; served through Civil war. becoming brig. gen. vols., and bvt. brig. gen. and maj. gen. U.S.A.; during and after war in adjt. gen's. dept., reaching rank of col.; retired, 1890. Died 1902.

WHISENAND, JAMES FRANKLIN ret. air force officer; b. Bloomington, Ind., Feb. 9, 1911; s. Walter W. and Mary Katherine (Lipps) W.; B.S. in Archtl. Engring. with high honors, U. Ill., 1933; grad. Advanced Flying Sch., Kelly Field, 1935, Air War Coll., 1946; m. Hazel E. Waxler, Feb. 9, 1936. Commd. flying cadet USAAF, 1934, advanced through grades to maj. gen. USAF, 1957; various pilot and engring. assignments U.S., 1935-41; A-3 fighter wing, later chief staff 10th Air Force, CBI, World War II; mem. strategic Bombing Survey, Tokyo, Japan, 1945-46; mem. faculty Air War Coll., 1946-50; assigned Directorate Plans, Hdqrs. USAF, 1950-54; comdr. 388th Fighter-Bomber Wing, Clovis AFB, M.N. and Etain, France, 1954-55, 49th Air Div., Eng., 1955-56; dep. comdr. 3d Air Force, Eng., 1956-57; spl. asst. to chmn. Joint Chiefs Staff, 1957-60; chief planner Air Research and Devel. Command, 1960-62; asst. dep. chief staff, research and tech. Hdqrs. USAF, 1962-63, ret.; indsl. cons. The Martin Co., Balt., 1963—. Decorated D.S.M., Legion Merit with 3 cluster, D.F.C., Bronze Star, Air medal, Commendation medal with cluster; Order Cloud and Banner (China). Mem. Tau Beta Pi, Alpha Rho Chi, Phi Eta Sigma, Gargoyle. Home: 305 St. Ives Dr., Chartwell, Severna Park, Md. Office: The Martin Co., Balt. Died Apr. 1967.

WHISTLER, JOSEPH NELSON GARLAND army officer; b. Green Bay, Oct. 19, 1822; grad. West Point, 1846; entered army bvt. 2d. lt., 8th inf.; promoted Jan. 7, 1847, to 2d lt. 3d inf.; served through Mexican war; breveted for gallant conduct Battle of Centreros 1st lt., June 1852; captured in Texas by Confederates, 1861, and paroled as prisoner of war; promoted capt., May 1861; asst. instr. mil. tactics, West Point, 1861-63; col. 2d N.Y. arty., May 1863; served in Richmond campaign and defenses of Washington; bvtd. brig. gen.; lt. col. 5th inf., Feb., 1874; col. 15th inf. May 1883; retired, Oct. 19, 1886; m. Eliza C. Hall, dau. Maj. Nathaniel Nye Hall, U.S.A. Died 1899.

WHITAKER, JOHN THOMPSON journalist, war corr.; b. Chattanooga, Tenn., Jan. 25, 1906; s. Lawson Spires and Thulie (Thompson) W.; A.B., U. of the South, Sewanee, Tenn., 1927; unmarried. Began as reporter Chattanooga News; later with New York Herald Tribune, as City Hall reporter, Albany and Washington, D.C., corr., and foreign corr. at League of Nations, Geneva; war corr. Ethiopian and Spanish Wars; was corr. for Chicago Daily News in Europe, Near East and South America, now on leave of absence. Serving as colonel, Army of U.S. Decorated Legion of Merit, Croce di Guerra (Italy). Mem. Phi Beta Kappa. Author: And Fear Came, 1936; Americas to the South, 1939; We Cannot Escape History, 1943. Lecturer. Home: 412 Georgia Av., Chattanooga 3, Tenn. Died Sep. 11, 1946.

WHITAKER, SAMUEL ESTILL judge; b. Winchester, Tenn., Sept. 25, 1886; s. Madison Newton and Florence Jarrett (Griffin) W.; student Winchester (Tenn.) Normal Coll., 1902-05; U. Va., 1905-06; LL.B., U. Chattanooga, 1909; m. Lillian Nelson Chambliss, June 30, 1913; children—Nelson Chambliss (Mrs. Paul Campbell, Jr.). Samuel Estill. Admitted to Tenn. bar in 1909, and began practice in Chattanooga; atty. U.S. Dept. of Justice, 1919-20, Bur. Internal Revenue, 1920; in private practice of law in Chattanooga, 1921-37; city atty., Chattanooga, 1923; mem. firm of Whitaker & Whitaker, 1924-37; mayor of Riverview, Tenn., 1925-29; employed from time to time as special asst. to the U.S. atty. gen., 1933-37; U.S. asst. atty. gen., 1937-39; commd. judge U.S. Court of Claims, July 13, 1939. Served as capt. cavalry, later field arty., U.S. Army, 1917-19. Democrat. Presbyn. Home: 4921 Quebec St. N.W. Office: U.S. Court of Claims, Washington. Died Mar. 26, 1967; buried Chattanooga, Tenn.

WHITALL, SAMUEL RUCKER brig. gen. U.S.A.; b. in Mich., May 17, 1844. Commd. 2d lt. 2d N.Y. Arty., May 5, 1864; hon. mustered out, Sept. 23, 1864; apptd. from D.C., 2d lt. 11th U.S. Inf., Mar. 7, 1867; transferred to 16th Inf., Apr. 14, 1869; 1st lt., Mar. 4, 1879; capt., Apr. 14, 1887; maj., Mar. 2, 1899; lt. col. 27th Inf., July 11, 1901; col. 3d Inf., July 26, 1903; transferred to 27th Inf., Sept. 10, 1903; advanced to rank of brig. gen., June 15, 1906, and retired on account of disability received in line of duty. Died June 11, 1919.

WHITE, ALBERT EASTON educator; b. Plainville, Mass., Mar. 12, 1884; s. Albert Nelson and Martha (Easton) W.; A.B., Brown U., 1907, Sc.D., 1925; student Harvard, 1908; m. Margaret Belle Arnold, June 22, 1911 (dec. 1934); 1 son, Arnold Easton; m. 2d, Elsie Speckmann Hauswald, Aug. 2, 1935. In charge research, iron ores, flue dust and fire bricks, Jones & Laughlin Steel Co., 1908-11; instr. chem. engring. U. Mich., 1911-13, asst. prof., 1913-17, prof., 1919—, dir. engring. research, 1920—. Cons. metall. engr.; chmn. metall. com. NDRC, 1940-41; mem. war metallurgy com. OSRD, 1942-46. Served as capt. and maj., U.S. Army; with Insp. Div., Ordnance Dept., U.S. Army, 1917; head of metall. br. insp. sect., gun div., 1917-18; head of metall br. insp. gun div., 1918-19; head metall. br. Tech. Staff, 1919; now lt. col. Ordnance Res. Corps. Mem. Am. Chem. Soc., Am. Soc. Testing Materials (pres.), Am. Inst. Mining and Metall. Engrs., Am. Soc. Metals (pres.), Am. Soc. M.E. (soc. mgr. Engring. Found.), NRC, Sigma Xi, Tau Beta Pi, Phi Lambda Upsilon, Phi Delta Theta, Phi Kappa Phi. Republican. Methodist. Mason. Clubs: Mich. Union, University, Rotary, Barton Hills Country (Ann Arbor); Detroit Athletic; Engineers' Club (N.Y.). Wrote: An Investigation of Condenser Tubes, 1913. Contbr. about 100 tech. papers. Home: 2110 Dorset Rd., Ann Arbor, Mich. 48104. Died Dec. 18, 1956; buried Ann Arbor.

WHITE, CHARLES HENRY medical dir. with rank of rear admiral U.S.N.; b. Center Sandwich, N.H., Nov. 19, 1838; s. Dr. Charles and Sarah (French) W.; ed. in acads. there and at Northfield; M.D., Harvard, 1862. Asst. surgeon U.S.N., Dec. 26, 1861; served in S. Atlantic Blockading Squadron during Civil War; on many stas. and varied duties afterward. Promoted surgeon, Nov. 18, 1869; med. dir., June 8, 1895; retired Nov. 19, 1900, with rank of rear admiral. At Museum of Hygiene, 1897-1900. Home: Center Sandwich, N.H. Died July 25, 1914.

WHITE, DAVID congressman, lawyer; b. 1785; studied law. Admitted to bar, began practice of law, New Castle, Ky.; mem. Ky. Ho. of Reps., 1826; mem. U.S. Ho. of Reps. from Ky., 18th Congress, 1823-25. Died Franklin County, Ky., Oct. 19, 1834.

WHITE, DAVID STUART veterinarian; b. W. New Brighton, Staten Island, N.Y., Sept. 28, 1869; s. William Henry and Catharine Ann (Elliott) W.; gen. course Ohio State U.; Dr. Vet. Medicine, same, 1890; post-grad. study in Germany and Austria, 1890-93; m. Nellie Eliza Smith, June 24, 1896 (dec.); m. 2d, Mabel Elizabeth Moran, Dec. 21, 1925. Asst. in veterinary medicine, Ohio State U., 1893-95, head dept. of veterinary medicine and dean College Veterinary Medicine, 1895-1929 (retired). Mem. Ohio N.G., 1887-90. Mem. advisory bd. Vet. Corps of Med. Dept., U.S. Army; commd. maj., Vet. Corps N.A., 1917, lt. col. and col., 1918; chief veterinarian A.E.F., France; hon. discharged, 1919; ranking colonel, Veterinary Res., U.S. Army, since 1921. Officer Legion of Honor (France), 1918; Comdr. St. Michael and St. George (Gt. Britain), 1919. Mem. Am. and Ohio Vet. Med. assns.; hon. mem. Pa. State Vet. Med. Assn.; hon. asso. mem. Royal Coll. Vet. Surgs. (Eng.), Sigma Xi, Alpha Psi. Clubs: Faculty (O.S.U.); Torch (Columbus). Translator: Malkmus' Physical Diagnostics, 1901. Author: Principles and Practice of Veterinary Medicine, 1917. Home: 1490 Cardiff Rd., Columbus, O. Died Jan. 7, 1944.

WHITE, DUDLEY ALLEN publisher; b. New London, O., Jan. 3, 1901; s. Albert Union and Bertha (Triffit) W.; ed. pub. schs. of New London; hon. LL.D., 1940; m. Alice Davenport Snyder, June 28, 1924; children—Alice Mack, Dudley Allen. Pub. and editor Reflector-Herald, Norwalk, O.; pres. and gen. mgr. Sandusky Newspapers, Inc.; pub. The Register-Star-News, Sandusky, O.; pres. Sandusky Broadcasting Co.; dir. Citizens Nat. Bank, Norwalk; dir. The Northern Ohio Telephone Co.; mem. 75th and 76th Congresses (1937-41), 13th Ohio Dist. Mem. Ohio Citizens Narcotics Adv. Com., Gov.'s Traffic Safety Committee. Delegate National Republican Convention, 1928-48, alternate, 1932. Director Speakers Bureau, Rep. Nat. Committee, 1940. Exec. dir. U.S. Commn. on Intergovernmental Relations, 1953. Enlisted in USN, 1918; World War II as dir. recruiting and induction of U.S. Navy, rank of capt., USNR. Member New York Academy of Political Science, American Legion State comdr. 1929-30), Am. Newspaper Pubs. Assn. (chmn. postal com.), Ohio Newspaper Assn., Inter-Am. Press Association, Sigma Delta Chi. Republican. Episcopalian. Mason (32 deg.). Clubs: The Capitol Hill Club, Army-Navy Country, National Press (Washington, D.C.); Union (Cleveland, O.). Home: 27 Edgewood Dr., Norwalk, O. Address: The Register-Star-News, Sandusky, O. Died Oct. 14, 1957.

WHITE, EDWARD HIGGINS II astronaut; b. San Antonio, Nov. 14, 1930; s. Edward Higgins and Mary (Haller) W.; B.S., U.S. Mil. Acad., 1952; M.S. in Aero. Engring., U. Mich., 1959, Dr. Astronautics (hon.), 1965; grad. Air Force Test Pilot Sch., 1959; m. Patricia Eileen Finegan, Jan. 31, 1963; children—Edward, Bonnie Lynn. Commd. 2d lt. USAF, 1952, advanced through grades to lt. col., 1965; flight tng., Fla. and Tex., 1952-54; assigned fighter squadron in Germany, 1954-57; exptl. test pilot fighter div. aero. systems div., Wright Patterson AFB, O., 1960-66; became astronaut NASA, Oct. 1962; apptd. sr. pilot Apollo I; made 4 day orbital flight in Gemini-Titan 4, June 3, 1965; became first Am. to walk in space, first to propel self in space with maneuvering unit during extra vehicular activity. Active Scouting activities, Little League. Recipient Gen. Thomas D. White Space Trophy, 1966. Mem. Soc. Exptl. Test Pilots, Sigma Delta Psi, Tau Beta Pi; asso. mem. Inst. Aero. Scis. Home: Seabook, Tex. Office: Manned Spacecraft Center, NASA, Houston. Died Jan. 27, 1967.

WHITE, EDWIN rear admiral U.S.N.; b. Ohio, 1843; s. Lyman White; apptd. to U.S. Naval Acad., 1861; grad. as midshipman, 1864; promoted to ensign. 1866; master, same yr.; lt., 1868; lt. comdr., 1869; comdr., 1886; capt., 1898; performed duty at sea on the various stas.; last shore duty comdt. of cadets, U.S. Naval Acad., 1895-98; last sea duty in command of U.S.S. Philadelphia, flagship, Pacific Sta.; returned from Samoa with impaired health in Dec. 1899, from causes incident to the service incurred in the line of duty, retired as rear admiral by direction of President of U.S.; m. Antonia Thornton, d. Admiral George F. Emmons, 1870. Home: Princeton, N.J. Died 1903.

WHITE, FRANK treas. of U.S.; b. Stillman Valley, Ill., Dec. 12, 1856; s. Joshua and Lucy Ann (Brown) W.; B.S., U. of Ill., 1880 (LL.D., 1904); m. Elsie Hadley, Sept. 19, 1894. Mem. N.D. Ho. of Rep., 1891-93, Senate, 1893-99; maj. 1st N.D. Vol. Inf., May 2, 1898-Sept. 25, 1899; served in Philippines; col. of inf., 41st Div., July 18, 1917-June 12, 1919, 14 months in France. Gov. of N.D., 1901-05; treas. of U.S., 1921-28; pres. Middlewest Trust Co. Republican. Conglist. Past Grand Comdr. Knights Templars in N.D. Mem. S.A.R. Home: Chevy Chase, Md. Died Mar. 23. 1940.

WHITE, GEORGE ARED army officer; b. Longbranch, Ill., July 18, 1881; s. Ared and Mary A. (Murray) W.; student All Hallows Coll., 1896-97; m. Henrietta Diana White, Feb. 22, 1905; children—Henrietta Marion (Mrs. J. A. Routh; now dec.), Dorothy Diana (Mrs. George E. Emich, Jr.). Enlisted U.S. Field Artillery, 1898; promoted through grades to maj. gen., 1929. Awarded Etoile Noir, French Legion of Honor. Dir. Nat. Rifle Assn. of Am. Mem. of original founders of Am. Legion in France. Republican. Methodist. Mason, Shrine. Club: University (Tacoma, Wash.). Founder and first editor-mgr., Am. Legion Mag., New York, 1919. Contbr. of articles to mags. Home: Clackamas, Ore. Address: Fort Lewis, Wash.* Deceased.

WHITE, H. LEE, attorney; born Oswego, N.Y., Aug. 13, 1912; s. Walter A. and Frances (Baslow) W.; A.B., Hamilton Coll., 1934; LL.B., Cornell, 1937; Doctor of Laws, Syracuse University, 1954; married Betty F. Johnson, Apr. 1, 1939. Admitted to N.Y. bar, 1937; spl. asst. to gen. counsel U.S. Casualty Co., N.Y.C., 1937-38; staff Pearis & Resseguie, Binghamton, N.Y., 1938-39; asso. Mangan & Mangan, Binghamton, 1939-41, partner, 1941-43; asso. Cadwalader, Wickersham & Taft, N.Y.C., 1946-49, partner, 1949-53, 1954-71; dir. Day Assos., Inc.; assistant sec. air force, 1953-54; chairman of bd. Trinity Shipping Group, Oswego Shipping Group, Am. Steamship Company, Boland & Cornelius, Inc., Reiss S.S. Co., Gartland S.S. Company, chmn. bd., president Marine Transport Lines, Inc.; dir. Am. Inst. Mcht. Shipping, International Minerals & Chemical Corporation, American S.S. Owners Mutual Protection & Indemnity Assn., Inc. Member Def. Adv. Com. on Profl. and Tech. Compensation, 1956; mem. Pres.'s Maritime Adv. Com. Bd. mgrs. Am. Bur. Shipping. Comdr. USNR, 1943-46, Office Secretary of the Navy. Recipient of the Secretary of Navy's Commendation Ribbon, 1945, Air Force Exceptional Meritorious Civilian award, 1954. Mem. Council Fgn. Relations, Am. Law Inst., Assn. Bar City N.Y., Am., N.Y. State bar associations, New York Chamber of Commerce, also mem. Theta Delta Chi. Episcopalian. Clubs: Canoe Brook Country (Summit, N.J.); Army Navy Country (Washington); Down Town Assn., Recess. Home: Short Hills NJ Died 1971.

WHITE, JACOB LEE clergyman; b. Forsyth County, N.C., Sept. 6, 1862; s. Jacob and Martha Ellen (Grubbs) W.; prep. edn. Shelby (N.C.) Acad.; A.M., Wake Forest (N.C.) Coll., 1886; D.D., Mercer U., 1898, Wake Forest, 1900; hon. LL.D., John B. Stetson Univ., 1934; m. Dovie Zulia Poston, Sept. 22, 1886; children—Lee McBride, Hubert Taylor, Sarah Mabel (dec.), William Royall, James Livingston, Charles Marion, Russell Conwell, Edward Poston, Martha Elizabeth (Mrs. R. E. Kunkel). Ordained ministry Bapt. Ch., 1884; pastor successively First Ch., Raleigh, Durham, Asheville, N.C., Macon, Ga., Greensboro, N.C., Central Ch., Memphis, Tenn., Tabernacle, Atlanta, Ga., until 1916, First Ch., Miami, Fla., 1916-Apr. 1936; has received into membership of First Ch. more than 4,000; accepted pastorate of First Bapt. Ch., Madison, Fla., March 1938; retired as honorary pastor, Nov. 1940; now conducting Bible Conferences; conductor of Southern Bible Conf., Miami, since 1918. Chaplain 2d Regiment, Georgia Vols., Spanish-American War; camp pastor, Miami World War, also chmn. Home Service Committee Am. Red Cross. Trustee Mercer U., Bessie Tift Coll., Stetson U.; v.p. Foreign Mission Bd., Southern Bapt. Conv., 20 yrs.; mem. State Bd. Missions of Fla., 1916-27; pres. Fla. Bapt. State Conv., 1924-26. Democrat. Author of many published sermons and addresses; widely known as evangelist and orator. Home: 27 N.W. 47th St., Miami, Fla. Died Nov. 25, 1948.

WHITE, JAMES army officer, pioneer, legislator; b. Rowan County, N.C., 1747; s. Moses and Mary (McConnell) W.; m. Mary Lawson, Apr. 14, 1770, 7 children, including Hugh Lawson. Served as capt. N.C. Militia, 1779-81; began an exploration on French, Broad, Holston rivers, 1783; settled present site of Knoxville, Tenn., 1786; mem. N.C. Ho. of Commons from Hawkins County, 1789; justice of peace, 1790; maj. N.C., Militia, 1790; mem. Tenn. Constl. Conv., 1796; commd. brig. gen. Tenn. Militia, circa 1798; elected to Tenn. Senate from Knox County, 1796, presiding officers, 1801, 03; donor site for Blount Coll. (now U. Tenn.), trustee, 1794. Died Knoxville, Aug. 14, 1821; buried 1st Presbyn. Ch., Knoxville.

WHITE, JAMES A. anti-saloon leader; b. Bloomfield, Muskingum County, O., Oct. 13, 1872; Alexander H. and Christena (Hammond) W.; B.Pd., Muskingum (O.) Coll., 1898, B.S., 1905, M.S., 1906; LL.B., Ohio Northern U., Ada, O., 1906; LL.D., Muskingum Coll., 1921, Ohio Northern U., 1921; m. Myrtle Grow, Dec. 1, 1917; children—Thomas A., Mary Virginia (Mrs. R. W. Evans), Myrtle Jean, Marjorie Ruth. Law practice at Barnesville, O., 1900; mayor of Barnesville, 4 terms, 1898-1906, also justice of the peace, and mem. Bd. of Edn.; now U.S. referee in bankruptcy, Columbus Dist. Served 4 yrs., rank of capt., World War II. Pres. White Cross Hosp. Assn., Colored Rescue Mission (both Columbus); pres. bd. trustees Muskingum Coll., New Concord, Ohio. As mayor of Barnesville led attack with axes upon "blind tigers," and started the movement that later helped to place Ohio in the dry column; supt. Ohio Anti-Saloon League since 1915; leader in 5 state-wide elections to vote Ohio dry. Prosecuted about 250 saloon cases yearly for 10 yrs. up to 1919. Apptd. mem. Industrial Commn. of O., for 6 yr. term, Dec. 26, 1939. Republican. Lay del. to Gen. Conf. M.E. Ch. 4 times. Mason (32 deg., K.T., Shriner), K.P. Home: 44 12th Av. Office: 44 E. Broad St., Columbis, O. Died Mar. 14, 1949.

WHITE, JOHN BAKER lawyer, soldier; b. Romney, W. Va., Aug. 24, 1868; s. Capt. C.S. (of Confederate States Army) and Bessie J. (Schultze) W.; g.g.s. Judge Robert White, maj. Revolutionary Army; ed. high sch., Romney, W. Va. Chief clk. to sec. of State of W. Va., 1890-93; sec. to former Gov. William A. MacCorkle, 1893-1897; admitted to W. Va. bar, 1897, and practiced at Charleston; mem. Bd. of Affairs (governing bd. of Charleston), 1907-11; mem. W. Va. Board of Control since June 1932, now treas. of board; supt. of Law and Order League of Kanawha Co., W. Va., 1921-22. Enlisted as pvt. and advanced to maj., W. Va. N.G., 1887-98; mem. gov.'s staff, rank of col.; capt. Co. B, 1st W. Va. Regt., Spanish-Am. War, 1898-99; commd. maj. J.A.G.'s Dept., U.S.A., Dec. 6, 1917; lt. col., Apr. 1919; served as j.a.g. with Am. troops, Gt. Britain and Ireland, Dec. 1917-June 1919; sent to G.H.Q. and then to 3d Div. on the Rhine; hon. discharged, September 11, 1919; now col. J.A.G.O.R.C., U.S.A. Decorated British Distinguished Order; made hon. mem. Middle Temple and Gray's Inn and given privileges of Lincoln's Inn and Inner Temple and Athenaeum Club, all of London. Mem. Am. Bar Assn., Md. Hist. Soc., Am. Auto Assn., Nat. Travel Club, Order of the Cincinnati, S.A., Mil. Order Foreign Wars, Spanish War Vets., Am. Legion. Mason (K.T., 32 deg., Shriner). Club: Army and Navy (Washington, D.C.). Home: Charleston, W. Va.

WHITE, JOHN P., govt. ofcl.; b. Mass., Dec. 18, 1915; student Boston Coll., 1935-40; m. Elaine A. White. Atty., Mass. Ho. of Reps., 1935-40; sec. staff gov. of Mass., 1940, legislative sec., 1953-57; legislative counsel, 1946-53; Congl. liaison officer Dept. State, 1957-69, then dep. asst. sec. for Congl. relations. Served to capt. AUS, 1940-45. Home: Rockville MD Died Oct. 2, 1969; buried Gate of Heaven Cemetery, Rockville MD

WHITE, JOHN ROBERTS b. Reading, England, Oct. 10, 1879; s. Sydney Victor and Elizabeth (Roberts) W.; ed. pvt. schs.; Asso. of Arts, Oxford U., 1896; m. Fay Kincaid, Sept. 13, 1910; 1 dau., Phyllis Conway. Served in Greek Fgn. Legion, in battles of Milouna Pass, Pharsala, Domokos, etc., 1897; in British Columbia and Alaska salmon fishing, and with White Pass & Yukon Ry., 1897-99; 4th U.S. Inf., 1899-1901; Philippine Constabulary, 2d lt., 1901, col., Feb. 14, 1914; retired for physical disability in line of duty, Dec. 31, 1914. Supt. Iwahig Penal Colony, 1906-08; actg. gov. Agusan Province, P.I., 1911. Field service against insurgents in Cavite, Negros, Zamboanga, Cotabato, Jolo, etc. Medal for valor at Bud Dajo, Jolo, 1906 (severely wounded); hon. mention for rescuing drowning man, Iloilo, 1909. In Austria, Germany, Switzerland and Scandinavian countries for Am. Red Cross and Rockefeller Foundation, 1916-17. Candidate, R.O. T.C., Ft. Myer, Va., May-June 1917; commd. maj. adj. general R.C., May 27, 1917; promoted lt. col., Signal Corps, U.S. Army, Jan. 17, 1918. Qualified as pilot, Air Service, Mar. 1918; passed R.M.A. tests, Apr. 1918; A.E.F., France, 1918; dep. provost marshal gen., A.E.F., and provost marshal of Paris after Armistice; ranger and chief ranger, Grand Canyon Nat. Park, 1919-20; supt. Sequoia and Gen. Grant Nat. Parks, 1920-33; supt. Sequoia Nat. Park and Death Valley Nat. Monument, 1933-38, also supt. of Cabrillo Nat. Monument; chief of operations, gion 3, Nat. Park Service, Santa Fe, N.M., 1940; dir. Region 4, San Francisco, 1941, supt. Sequoia Nat. Park, Kings Canyon Nat. Park, 1943; ret., 1947. Life mem. Calif. Acad. Scis. Episcopalian. Clubs: Philippine, Adventurers (N.Y., hon.) Sierra (hon.). Author: Bullets and Bolos, 1928; Big Trees (with Walter Fry), 1930; Sequoia and Kings Canyon National Park, 1948; also articles on Philippines and nat. parks. Address: P. O. Box 104, St. Helena, Cal. Died Dec. 9, 1961; buried Arlington Nat. Cemetery, Washington.

WHITE, JOSEPH HILL, sanitarian; b. Milledgeville, Ga., May 4, 1859; s. Edward J. and M.A. (Hill) W.; pvt. and high schs.; M.D., Coll. Phys. and Surg., Baltimore, 1883; m. Emily H. Humber, Jan. 8, 1885; children—Emily H. (Mrs. R.A. Herring), Mary Roberta, Josephine H., Joseph H. Entered U.S. Marine Hosp. Service (since changed to U.S. Pub. Health Service), Oct. 2, 1884; passed asst. surgeon, Oct. 1887; surgeon, Aug. 1898; detailed to asst. surg.-gen., in charge of service quarantine div., 1899-1903; senior surgeon, 1915; asst. surgeon gen., 1920; first chmn. National Leprosy Commn. Lecturer on hygiene and tropical diseases, University of Alabama, 1903-05. Sanitary work as quarantine officer, 1885-91; in charge of smallpox epidemic in Southern Ga., 1891; sanitary rep. of U.S. at Hamburg during cholera epidemic, 1893; inspecting quarantine officer from Norfolk to Jacksonville, 1894; in charge smallpox epidemic, Key West, Fla., 1896, yellow fever epidemics in La. and Miss., 1897-98; inspected the troops returning from Cuba, 1898; eliminated the yellow fever out-break at Soldiers' Home, Hampton, 1899; disinfected San Francisco after plague, 1900; given full control by nat., state and city authorities to stamp out yellow fever epidemic, New Orleans, 1905 (epidemic fully started—wiped out before frost, for first time in history of yellow fever); dir. for Latin-America, Internat. Health Commn., 1914. On request of sec. of war was detailed to war service, July 1917, and served through the war as gen. insp. of anti-malarial work for army; commd. col., May 1918; eradicated epidemic of yellow fever in Guatemala, Sept. 1918; chief general inspector U.S.P.H.S., February 1919-23. Vice director International Sanitary Bureau, 1920-25, retired; member Yellow Fever Council since 1921. Lecturer on public health, U. of Tenn. Summer School, 1915-19, and Peabody Coll., Nashville, Tenn. Decorated Grand Officer of Order of Quetzai by Govt. of Guatemala for distinguished service with commendation by the president personally, Jan. 1943. Chmn. Section of Hygiene and Sanitary Science A.M.A., 1909; pres. Am. Soc. Tropical Medicine, 1911; hon. mem. Orleans Parish Med. Soc.; U.S. del. 6th Internat. Sanitary Conf., Montevideo, 1920. Pioneer proponent of total eradication yellow fever and director yellow fever campaigns for International Health Board in all Latin-America, 1921-27. Clubs: Mobile Round Table (hon. life); Egyptians (Memphis); Cosmos (Washington). Author of many papers on sanitary science. Contbr. to Nelson's System of Medicine, 1927-29. Home: 2955 Newark St., Washington DC

WHITE, KEMBLE, lawyer; b. Bellton, W.Va., Apr. 5, 1873; s. Henry Solomon and Loviah Fields (Kemble) W.; prep. edn., Trinity Hall, Washington, Pa., and Lindsley Inst., Wheeling, W.Va.; A.B., W.Va. U., 1894, LL.B., 1900; m. Jane Louise Ferguson, of Greenville, S.C., Oct. 4, 1904; children—Harriet Kemble, Kemble. Admitted to W.Va. bar, 1900, and began practice at Fairmont; counsel Standard Oil Co. interests in W.Va. since 1906. Served as capt., W.Va. Vol. Inf., Spanish-Am. War; chmn. Selective Draft Bd., Marion Co., W.Va. Mem. com. to cooperate with legislative commn. to codify laws of W.Va; mem. W.Va. State Constl. Commn. Mem. Am. Bar Assn., W.Va. State Bar Assn. (mem. exec. council 1920-28; pres. 1924-25), Am. Law Inst., Alumni Assn. W.Va. U. (pres. 1921-24), Phi Sigma Kappa. Republican. Methodist. Club: Clarksburg Country. Home: Stonewall Jackson Hotel. Office: Hope Natural Gas Co. Bldg., Clarksburg WV

WHITE, MICHAEL ALFRED EDWIN author; b. Ahmednugar, India, November 4, 1866; s. Capt. Alfred H. (British Army) and Mary Risdon (Davey) W.; ed. United Service College, Westward Ho, N. Devon, Eng.; m. Margaret Couper (artist), of Southampton, Eng., Nov. 3, 1880. Second lt. and capt. 3d Battalion, Scottish Rifles, 1884-89; traveled in Orient; finally settled at New York. Contbr. to mags. since 1900 of numerous fiction stories and articles on various topics. Episcopalian. Clubs: Authors' (New York). Author: Lachmi Bai, 1902; (collaboration with Philip V. Mighels) His Brother's Keeper (drama); The Garden of Indra, 1912. Also article, The Psychology of the Soldier, in Unpopular Review, Apr.-June 1916 (republished in Jour. Mil. Service Inst., May 1917). Editorial staff, Current History Mag., 1918-23. Home: 81 Morningside Av., New York, N.Y.

WHITE, S(OLON) MARX physician; b. Hokah, Minn., July 16, 1873; s. Solon C. and Anna (Amanda) Clayanna (Armstrong) W.; B.S., U. Ill., 1896 (as of 1894); M.D., Northwestern U., 1897; m. Sara Miner Abbott, July 25, 1900 (dec. Mar. 1931); children—Asher Abbott, Anna Elizabeth (Mrs. Herbert Wilson Rogers), Mary Grace (Mrs. James Lloyd Coffield, Jr.); m. 2d, Beulah S. Fuller, Jan. 22, 1944. Intern, Cook County Hosp., Chgo., 1897-98; instr. pathology and bacteriologh med. sch. U. Minn., 1898-1904, asst. prof., 1904-08, assoc. prof. medicine, 1908-15, prof., 1915-42, emeritus, 1942-—; chief dept. medicine, charge med. service U. Hosp., 1921-25; a founder, dir., chief dept. medicine, Nicollet Clinic. Mem. Hennepin County Sanatorium Commn., 1920-37, 40-55 (pres.); dir. Hennepin County Tb. Assn. Served as maj. M.C., U.S. Army, 1918; AEF. Recipient Francis E. Harrington award, 1956. Diplomate Am. Bd. Internal Medicine. Fellow A.C.P. (regents 1926-35; pres. 1931-32); mem. A.M.A., Assn. Am. Physicians, Am. Heart Assn., Minn., Hennepin County med. socs., Minn. (pres. 1931-32), Mpls. (pres. 1950-51) socs. internal medicine, Central Interurban Clin. Club, Central Soc. for Clin. Investigation, Nu Sigma Nu, Alpha Omega Alpha, Sigma Xi. Republican. Baptist. Clubs: Minneapolis, Six O'Clock, Skylight, Minneapolis Automobile (Mpls.). Contbr. chpts. to med. tests, also articles profl. publs. Home: 2216 Irving Av. S. Office: The Nicollet Clinic, 2001 Blaisdell Av., Mpls. Died Aug. 29, 1966.

WHITE, THOMAS DRESSER ret. air force officer, mil. analyst; b. Walker, Minn., Aug. 6, 1901; s. John Chanler and Katherine (Dresser) W.; student St. John's Mil. Acad., Delafield, Wis., 1914-18; B.S., U.S. Mil. Acad., 1920; LL.D., Bucknell U., 1958, Fairfield U., 1960; m. Constance Rowe, 1938; 1 dau., Rebecca Ann (by 1st marriage). Commd. 2d lt., inf., U.S. Army, 1920, advanced through grades to gen., USAF, 1953; vice chief staff USAF, 1953-57, chief staff, 1957-61, ret., 1961; bd. dirs. Eastern Air Lines, Bullock Fund, Carriers and Gen. Corp., Aeronca Mfg. Corp., FMA, Inc. Mem. gen. adv. com. U.S. Arms Control and Disarmament Agy. Bd. visitors U.S. Air Force Acad. Clubs: Nat. Press, Nat. Aviation, Army and Navy, Alfalfa (Washington); Anglers (N.Y.C.). Contbg. editor Newsweek. Home: 4527 Jamestown Rd. Office: 1750 Pennsylvania Av., Washington. Died Dec. 1965.

WHITE, (THOMAS) GILBERT, artist; b. Grand Haven, Mich., July 18, 1877; s. Thomas Stewart and Mary (Daniel) W.; grad. high sch., Grand Rapids, 1896; Columbia, 1896-98; Art Students' League New York, 1896-98; under Jean Paul Laurens and Benjamin Constant, Julian Acad., Paris, 1898-1902; also studied under Whistler and MacMonnies and Beaux Arts, Paris; m. Hertha Stenger, Aug. 21, 1928. Art dir. Goldwyn Films, 1921-22. Exhibited at Salon Des Artists Français, Paris, National Academy Design, Royal Academy. London, San Francisco Expn., Architectural League, Salon Interallié, Paris Expn., 1937, etc. Represented by murals in Ky. State Capitol, Utah State Capitol, World War Memorial, Okla. State Capitol, New Haven County (Conn.) Court House, Gadsden (Ala.) Federal Bldg., Peninsular Club, Grand Rapids, McAlpin Hotel, N.Y. City, Dept. of Agr., Washington, D.C.; portrait of Gov. McCreary, Pan-Am. Bldg., Washington, of Pres. Hine in N.Y. Clearing House, Jules Mastbaum, Locust Club Phila., Dr. Giraud, Hosp. les Andelys, France, Dr. Babcock, Carnegie Foundation, Paris, Welles Bosworth, University Club, Paris; pictures in collections of Houston (Tex.) Mus., Nat. Luxembourg Mus., Paris, U. of Okla., University of Utah, Brooklyn (N.Y.) Mus.. City of Paris Mus., Grand Rapids (Mich.) Mus., Locust Club (Phila.), Lithuanian Mus., Corcoran Mus. (Washington), St. Quentin Mus. (France), Paris Journal. Served as 1st lt., later capt. inf., U.S.A., 1917-19; citation for exceptional service from Gen. Pershing. Vice-pres. European chapter Am. Artists Professional League, 1932-33, pres., 1934-35; mem. Am. Mission to Negotiate Peace, 1919; U.S. del. 8th Internat. Art Congress, Paris; represented State Oklahoma Battle Monuments, 1937; mem. fine arts jury 1937 Paris Expn. Member Société Internat. de Peinture; founder mem. European commandery Mil. Order Foreign Wars (vice comdr. 1928; mem. council, 1929-30); mem. Am. Legion (sergt. at arms, Dept. of France, 1928-29; del. to conv. at San Antonio, Tex., 1928; exec. com. 1932-33; founder mem. Myron T. Herrick Post. v. comdr. 1935), Forty and Eight, Anglo-Am. Group of Paris. Officier de l'academie, 1914; Chevalier Legion of Honor (France), 1919, Officier, 1928, Comdr., 1935; awarded Verdun medal, order of the Purple Heart; awarded medals for drawing, Art Students League of New York, Julian Acad.; hon. citizen St. Quentin, France. Died Feb. 17, 1939.

WHITE, WELDON BAILEY state justice; b. Waxhachie, Tex., July 22, 1907; s. Richard C. and Ida (Cathey) W.; LL.B., Cumberland U., 1931; student U. Chgo., 1943-44; m. Ellen Wallace, Nov. 8, 1928; children—Ellen Wallace (Mrs. William W. Dillon III), Weldon Bailey. Admitted to Tenn. bar, 1931; practice of Law, Nashville, 1932-42, 47-—; sr. mem. firm White, Gullett, Phillips & Steele, Nashville, 1950-—; circuit judge 10th Jud. Dist. Tenn., 1942-47; asso. justice Supreme Court of Tenn., 1961-—. Mem. Tenn. Senate, 1940-42. Served as maj. AUS, World War II; PTO. Mem. Am. (ho. of dels. 1951-52, 56-58) Nashville (pres. 1951) bar assns., Bar Assn. Tenn. (pres. 1955-56), C. of C., Delta Theta Phi. Mem. Church of Christ. Mason (Shriner, 33 deg.). Clubs: Belle Meade Country, Cumberland (Nashville). Home: Jackson Blvd., Belle Meade, Nashville 37205. Office: Supreme Court Bldg., Nashville. Died Apr. 23, 1967.

WHITEAKER, ROBERT O. army officer; b. Texas, Dec. 16, 1882; enlisted Tex. Nat. Guard, Inf., July 1899; commd. capt. Cav. Tex. Nat. Guard, Mar. 1916 and entered Fed. service for Mexican border crisis, May 1916; commd. maj. Tex. Nat. Guard, F.A., Oct. 1922, and advanced to brig. gen. of the line, Apr. 1938; entered Fed. service, Nov. 1940, and in command of 72d Field Arty. Brigade, 36th Div. in training at Camp Bowie, Brownwood, Tex.; retired 1948. Address: 1716 Justin Lane, Austin, Tex. Died Apr. 26, 1959; buried Meml. Cemetery, Cleburne, Tex.

WHITEHEAD, ENNIS CLEMENT air force officer; b. Westphalia, Kan., Sept. 3, 1895; s. John Erastus and Celia (Dodd) W.; A.B., U. Kan., 1920; m. Mary Morse Nicholson, Sept. 25, 1920; children—Margaret, Ennis Clement. Flying cadet U.S. Army, 1917, advancing through the grades to lt. gen., 1945; became comdg. gen., Fifth Air Force, S.W. Pacific, 1945, Far East Air Forces, Pacific, 1945; retired, 1951; served as aviation cons. Decorated D.S.C., D.S.M., with 2 oak leaf clusters, Silver Star, D.F.C., Air Medal with oak leaf cluster, Victory medal (U.S.); Caballero Order Al Merito (Chile); Order of Sun (Peru); Order of Liberator (Venezuela); Order of Condor of Andes (Bolivia); Comdr. Order Brit. Empire (Gt. Britain); Special Necklet, Cloud and Banner (China); Comdr. Legion of Honor (France). Mason. Home: 11 Circle Dr., Newton, Kan. Died Oct. 12, 1964; buried Arlington Nat. Cemetery, Washington.

WHITEHEAD, HENRY C., army officer; b. Mar. 22, 1873; grad. U.S. Mil. Acad., 1896; distinguished grad. Army Sch. of the Line, 1911; grad. Army Staff Coll., 1912. Commd. add. 2d lt. cav., June 12, 1896; promoted through grades to col. Q.M.C., June 30, 1920; col. Signal Corps (temp.), Sept. 1917-Aug. 1919; apptd. asst. to q.m. gen. with rank of brig. gen. for 4 yrs. from Apr. 16, 1930; retired, Feb. 28, 1934. Home: Winchester KY*

WHITEHILL, HOWARD JOSEPH business exec.; born Knox, Pa., May 9, 1894; s. Benjamin Franklin and Catherine (Donovan) W.; student Ohio State Univ., 1912-14; A.B., Harvard, 1916; m. Ruth Allbritain, June 11, 1918; children—Benjamin Franklin II, Howard Joseph. In prodn. of crude oil since 1919; pres. Whitehill Oil Corp. since 1927; Mem. Petroleum Industry War Council, 1944-45; Crude Oil Adv. Com., 1944-45; vis. com. dept. geol. sciences, Harvard, 1946-50. Served as 1st lt., 323d field arty., 83d div., U.S. Army, World War I. Mem. Am. Petroleum Inst., Independent Petroleum Assn. of Am., Nat. Stripper Well Assn. of Am. (pres. 1944-45), Okla. Stripper Well Assn. (pres. and sec.), Phi Gamma Delta. Republican. Episcopalian. Mason (32 deg.). Clubs: Harvard (pres. 1942-46), Southern Hills Country, Tulsa (Okla.). Home: 7157 S. Evanston Av., Tulsa 5. Office: World Bldg., Box 867, Tulsa 1. Died Dec. 15, 1963; buried Meml. Park, Tulsa.

WHITELAW, JOHN BERTRAM, educator; b. N.Y. City, Oct. 3, 1905; s. Aubrey George and Norah Beatrix (Osborne) W.; Ph.B., Yale, 1929, Ph.D., 1935; m. Helen Chase Streeter, June 28, 1930; 1 son, John Streeter. Teacher Brooks Sch., North Andover, Mass., 1929-31; grad. fellow Yale, 1931-34; instr., asst. prof. Smith Coll., 1933-35; asst. prof. edn., acting dean School Edn. George Washington U., 1935-37; head, dept. edn. State Tchrs. Coll., Brockport, N.Y., 1937-41; gen. supervisor pub. schs., Newton, Mass., 1941-42; training adviser personnel div. War Manpower Commn., Washington, 1942-43; asst. dir. Fgn. Service Inst., Dept. State, 1946-47; prof. edn., chmn. dept. edn. Johns Hopkins, 1947-51; ednl. advisor CIA, Washington, 1951-55; specialist for tchr. edn. Office Edn., Dept. Health, Edn. and Welfare, 1955-66; consultant in education and mgmt., 1966-68; dir. instl. research and devel. Asheville-Biltmore Coll. (N.C.), 1967-68; regional training officer for Tropical Africa, Agy. Internat. Development, 1959-62; prof. U. Chgo. summers 1939-40; cons. Resettlement Adminstrn., summer 1935, Am. Council Edn., summer 1938; community study workshops Balt. Pub. Schs., 1948-50; member of U.S. Ednl. Mission to USSR, 1958. Served from lt. (j.g.) to lt. comdr. USNR, 1943-46. Mem. Am. Assn. School Adminstrs. (life), N.E.A. (life), Phi Delta Kappa. Clubs: Elihu, Elizabethan (New Haven); 14 W. Hamilton Street (Balt.); Mountain City (Asheville). Author: The School and Its Community, rev., 1951. Contbr. ednl. publ., jours. Home: Arden NC Died Aug. 5, 1968.

WHITELEY, JAMES GUSTAVUS, writer; b. nr. Baltimore, July 9, 1866; s. William Stevens and Elizabeth Emmeline (Holmes) W.; ed. at private schs. and under private tutors; m. Emily Baily Stone, December 16, 1896; 1 dau., Sophia Bainbridge (Mrs. S. Bainbridge Fonda); m. 2d, Bernadine Allen Miller. Unofficial representative of President of U.S. at The Hague, 1898, of Le Congres Internat. d'Histoire Diplomatique, of which was v.p. and a founder. Mem. Internat. Com. which organized Le Congres International d'Histoire Comparee, Paris, 1900; official del. of U.S. Govt. to same; apptd. consul of the Congo Free State by H.M. Leopold II, 1904, consol-gen., Sept. 1, 1905; apptd. consul of Belgium at Baltimore, Dec. 1916; attached to Belgian spl. mission to U.S. during its visit, June-Aug. 1917; hon. attache to Belgian Mil. Mission, 1918-19, Knighted by King Leopold, 1909, and created Chevalier de l'Ordre de la Couronne (Belgium); created Commander de l'Ordre de Leopold II, Nov. 1917, for service to Belgian mission, Chevalier de l'Ordre de Leopold, 1924; promoted Comdr. of Order of the Crown, 1931; Officer of Ordre de l'Etoile Africaine (Belgium). Fellow Royal Hist. Soc. (Eng.); mem. Inst. Internat. Colonial; v.p. Belgian League of Honor; mem. Am. Soc. Internat. Law; hereditary companion Mil. Order Foreign Wars; hon. mem. (with medal) Royal Zool. Soc. of Antwerp; pres. Consular Soc. of Baltimore. Sec. Nat. Com. of U.S. for the Restoration U. of Louvain; sec.-gen. of Central Com. of Belgian Relief Fund, which organized Belgian relief cons. in 33 states, 1914-18; consul gen. of Belgium, at Baltimore since 1928. Awarded Medaille Civique, for 25 yrs. service as Belgian consul general, 1945. Catholic. Extensive contbr. to principal American and foreign revs. on subjects of internat. law, diplomatic history and foreign affairs. Address: 223 W. Lanvale St., Baltimore 17 MD

WHITESIDE, HORACE EUGENE lawyer; b. Bell Buckle, Tenn., June 5, 1891; s. Samuel R. and Kate (Tune) W.; A.B., U. Chgo., 1912; LL.B., Cornell, 1922; S.J.D., Harvard, 1927; m. Esther Versey, Mar. 31, 1913 (died, 1950); children—Anne Esther (Mrs. Leo F. Wynd), Horace E. (dec. 1954); m. 2d, Ruth Kinyon, Jan. 20, 1951. Teacher, East Waterloo (Iowa) High School, 1912-14; athletic director, Earlham College, 1914-17; captain 67th Artillery, C.A.C., in France, 1918-19; lecturer and secretary, Cornell, Law School, 1922-24, assistant professor, 1924-27, professor, 1927-51, J. DuPratt White professor of law since 1951. Research consultant, New York State Law Revision Commn., on property, consideration and the seal; consultant with Whitman, Ransom, Coulson & Goetz, New York City, since 1939. Member of the American, New York State and Tompkins County bar assns., Order of Coif, Delta Theta Phi, Phi Kappa Phi. Republican. Clubs: Country (Ithaca, New York) also the Cornell (New York City). Author: Statutory Rules Against Perpetuities and Accumulations, 1957. Editor: Huffcut's Cases on Agency (3d edit.), 1925; Kales' Cases on Future Interests (2d edit.), 1936. Contbr. to legal jours. and N.Y. Annotations to Restatement of Contracts. Co-author: American Law of Property, 1951. Home: Highland Road, Ithaca, N.Y. Office: Myron Taylor Hall, Ithaca, N.Y. Died June 9, 1956; buried Arlington Nat. Cemetery.

WHITFIELD, JOHN WILKINS congressman; b. Franklin, Tenn., Mar. 11, 1818; attended local schs. Served in Mexican War, 1846; Indian agt. to Pottawatomies, 1853, to Arkansas Indians, 1855-56; del. U.S. Congress from Territory of Kan., 1855-56, 56-57; register land office, Doniphan, Kan., 1857-61; commd. capt. 27th Tex. Cavalry, 1861, promoted maj., 1862; engaged in battles of Pea Ridge and Iuka, 1862; promoted col.; served in cavalry battle nr. Spring Hill, 1863; received several citations for bravery; commd. brig. gen., 1863; settled in Lavaca County, Tex., 1865, engaged in farming and stock raising; mem. Tex. Ho. of Reps. Died nr. Hallettsville, Tex., Oct. 27, 1879; buried Hallettsville Cemetery.

WHITING, HENRY army officer; b. Lancaster, Mass., Nov. 28, 1788; son of John Whiting. Joined U.S. Army, 1808, commd. 2d lt., 1809, 1st lt., 1811; served on staff of Gen. J. P. Boyd during War of 1812, participated in capture of Ft. George in Upper Canada, 1813; promoted capt., 1817; served with 1st Arty., 1821-35, Q.M. Corps, from 1835; chief q.m. army under Gen. Taylor during Mexican War, 1846-47; brevetted brig. gen. for conduct at Buena Vista, 1847. Author: Life of Zebulon Pike; contbr. to N.Am. Review. Editor: George Washington's Revolutionary Orders, 1846. Died St. Louis, Sept. 16, 1851; buried St. Louis.

WHITING, WILLIAM HENRY rear admiral U.S.N.; b. New York, July 8, 1843; s. William Henry and Mary Jane (Christian) W. Apptd. to U.S. Naval Acad. from Wis., 1860, grad. 1863; ensign, Oct. 1, 1863; master, May 10, 1866; lt., Feb. 21, 1867; lt. comdr., Mar. 12, 1868; comdr., July 12, 1882; capt., June 19, 1897; rear admiral, Oct. 11, 1903. Served in the Hartford, W. Gulf Blockading Squadron, 1863-65; hon. mention by Admiral Farragut "for gallant conduct in burning of blockade-runner 'Ivanhoe' under guns of Ft. Morgan, July 5, 1864"; took part in battle of Mobile Bay, and, at surrender Ft. Gaines, hauled down the Confed. flag and hoisted U.S. flag; also at bombardment and surrender of Fort Morgan, Aug. 24, 1864; served on Kearsarge, Frolic and Ticonderoga, European Squadron, 1865-69; Swatara, 1869-71; Benicia, 1872-75; Navy Yard, New York, 1875-76, 1881-84, 1886-89, 1890-92; Torpedo Sch., Newport, 1876; Constitution, 1878-79; comd. training-ship Saratoga, 1884-6, Kearsarge, 1889, Alliance, 1892-93; comdt. Navy Yard, Pensacola, 1894-96, Naval Sta., Puget Sound, 1896-97; comd. Monadnock, 1897-98; took Monadnock from San Francisco to Manila; comd. Charleston, 1898-99, Boston, 1899; capt. of yard, Navy Yard, Mare Island, 1900; comd. receiving-ship Independence, 1900-02; comdt. Naval Sta., Honolulu, 1902-03, Naval Training Sta., San Francisco, 1903-05; retired, July 8, 1905. Home: Berkeley, Calif. Died July 26, 1925.

WHITING, WILLIAM HENRY CHASE army officer; b. Biloxi, Miss., Mar. 22, 1824; s. Levi and Mary Whiting; grad. Georgetown Coll., Washington, D.C. 1840; grad. U.S. Mil. Acad., 1845; m. Kate D. Walker. Apptd. 2d lt. U.S. Corps Engrs., 1845; supervised constrn. river and harbor improvements in North, also fortifications in Cal., 1845-61; worked on constrn. projects on Cape Fear River, N.C.; 1856-57; resigned from U.S. Army to join Confederate Army, 1861; planned defenses for Charleston (S.C.) harbor and Morris Island; commanded division which later joined Gen. Thomas J. Jackson's army in Shenandoah Valley, Va., 1862; mil. comdr. of Wilmington, N.C., 1862-64; apptd. maj. gen. Confederate States Army, 1863; sent to take command at Petersburg, Va.; 1864; mortally wounded in defense of Ft. Fisher, N.C., 1865. Died Ft. Columbus, Governor's Island, N.Y., Mar. 10, 1865.

WHITLOCK, ELLIOTT HOWLAND, mech. engr.; b. Brooklyn, N.Y., May 5, 1867; s. Elisha Schanck and Sarah Jane (Elliott) W.; student Agrl. and Mech. Coll. of Texas, 1886; M.E. Stevens Inst. of Tech., Hoboken, N.J., 1890, hon. M.Sc., 1933; m. Mrs. Charles H. Wellman, Oct. 24, 1907. With motive power dept. Pa. R.R. at Columbus, O., 1890-91; prof. mech. engring., Agrl. and Mech. Coll. of S.D., 1891-92; constrn. and operation of gas plants and in commercial business, 1892-96; with Nat. Carbon Co., Cleveland, 1896-1914; cons. practice, 1914-17; owner Whitlock Mfg. Co.; gen. mgr. Am. Fire Clay and Products Co.; mem. bd. dirs. Wellman-Seaver-Morgan Co.; commr. Division of Smoke Inspection, Cleveland, 1925-30; research prof. smoke abatement, Stevens Inst. Tech., 1930-32. Commd. maj. Engrs. R.C., U.S. Army, Feb. 23, 1917; called to active duty, May 7, 1917; assigned to 24th Engr. Regt. (Shop and Supply); sailed for France, Feb. 16, 1918; with Service of Supply, 2d and 3d armies; promoted lt. col. 24th Engrs., Dec. 31, 1918, and returned to U.S. in comd. of regt., June 1, 1919; commd. col. 112th Engr. Regt., 37th Div., Ohio Nat. Guard, June 1928. Mem. Am. Soc. Mech. Engrs. (v.p.), Soc. Am. Mil. Engrs., Cleveland Engring. Soc. (ex-pres.), S.A.R. Presbyterian. Club: University (Cleveland). Home: 3813 Euclid Av., Cleveland 15

WHITMAN, ARMITAGE orthopedic surgeon; b. Boston, Mar. 13, 1887; s. Royal and Julia Lambard (Armitage) W.; ed. St. Marks Sch., 1901-05; A.B., Harvard, 1909; M.D., Columbia U., 1912; m. m. Mary Lyman Sturgis, 1912 (div. 1933); children—Royal II, Robert Shaw Sturgis, Charlotte Armitage; m. 2d, Fraunziska Kaschewski, Sept. 4, 1933. Surg. interne Roosevelt Hosp., 1912-14; attending surgeon Ogdensburg (N.Y.) City Hosp., 1914, Hosp. for the Ruptured and Crippled, 1931-35; vis. surgeon N.Y. State Bd. Health, 1916-17; orthopedic surgeon Lincoln Hosp., Booth Meml. Hosp.; clin. prof. orthopedic surgery N.Y. U. Med. Sch.; asso. attending orthopedic surgeon U. Hosp.; cons. surgeon Hosp. for Ruptured and Crippled, N.Y. State Dept. Health and Tuxedo Meml., St. Joseph's, Mather Meml. hosps.; mem. med. adv. bd. Selective Service Act; awarded Congl. medal. Served as capt. M.C., U.S. Army, 1917-19; AEF. Awarded Victory medal with 7 bars. Diplomate Am. Bd. Orthopedic Surgeons. Fellow A.C.S., N.Y. Acad. Medicine; mem. Am. Orthopedic Assn., Am. Acad. Orthopedic Surgeons, Alpha Omega Alpha. Episcopalian. Club: Harvard (N.Y.). Author: From Head to Foot. Asst. lit. editor N.Y. State Jour. Medicine, 1946—. Contbr. to med. jours. Home: 433 E. 51st St., N.Y.C. 10022. Office: 71 Park Av., N.Y.C. Died Sept. 14, 1962; buried Arlington Nat. Cemetery, Washington.

WHITMAN, EZRA BAILEY cons. engr.; b. Balt., Feb. 19, 1880; s. Ezra B. and Belle Cross (Slingluff) W.; student Balt. City Coll.; C.E., Cornell U., 1901; m. Fanny Glenn, Oct. 15, 1906; children—Fanny Glenn (Mrs. T. Brian Parsons), Ezra B., John Glenn. Mem. Williams & Whitman, N.Y., 1902-06; div. engr. on design and constrn. Balt. Sewage Disposal Plant, 1906-11; chief engr. Balt. Water Dept. (design and constrn. Filtration Plant and Loch Raven Dem), 1911-14; mem. Greiner & Whitman, 1914-16, Norton, Bird & Whitman, 1916-25; mem. Whitman, Requardt & Smith, engrs., 1925-44; mem. Whitman, Requardt and Assos., 1944—. Mem., chmn. Pub. Service Com. Md., 1921-27; mem. Engring. Bd. Rev. Chgo. in lake level controversy, 1924-25; chmn. Efficiency and Economy Commn., apptd. by mayor to reorganize city govt. Balt.; chmn. Efficiency and Economy Commn., Pitts.; chmn. Md. State Roads Commn., 1939-45. Maj. constrn. div. U.S. Army, 1917-19; constructing q.m. and utilities officer, Camp Mead, Md. Whitman, Requardt and Assoc. were architect-engineers for three Chem. Warfare Service plants at Edgewood, Md., Huntsville, Ala., Denver, 1941-44. Trustee emeritus Cornell. Fellow Am. Soc. M.E.; mem. Am. Inst. Cons. Engrs. (past pres.), Am. Soc. C.E. (dir., pres.), Am. Inst. E.E., Am., N.E. water works assns., Am. Pub. Health Assn., Sigma Xi, Tau Beta Pi, Delta Upsilon. Democrat. Episcopalian. Mason. Clubs: Maryland, Elkrdige, Engineers', Merchants (Balt.); Cornell (N.Y.). Home: 139 W. Lanvale St. Office: 1304 St. Paul St., Balt. Died 1966.

WHITMAN, HENRY HAROLD banker; b. Marlboro, Mass., Sept. 7, 1897; s. Carmon Smith and Gertrude (Ruggles) W.; Ph.B., Brown U., 1919; m. Jean Mary Meyer, Sept. 14, 1931; children—Ralph Eugene, Charles Henry. Staff fgn. brs. Nat. City Bank, Brazil, Peru, Uruguay, 1919-41, Argentina, 1941-50, v.p., N.Y.C., 1950-62; dir. Central Bank Argentina, Argentine Trade Promotion Corp. Mem. adv. com. Export-Import Bank, 1960-61. Adv. com. Tinker Found.; trustee in N.Y., Ward Coll., Buenos Aires. Served as 2d lt., arty., U.S. Army, World War I. Mem. Am. C. of C. in Argentina (pres. 1943-45). Am. Soc. River Plate (pres. 1946-47). Council Fgn. Relations, Pan Am. Soc. U.S. (pres. 1959-62), Nat. Council Am. Importers (dir. 1951-62), U.S. Inter-Am. Council (vice chmn. 1954-62), Bankers' Assn. for Fgn. Trade (pres. 1960-61). Presbyn. Clubs: Metropolitan (treas.), Brown University (N.Y.C.); Pelham (N.Y.) Country; Metropolitan (Washington). Home: 311 Monterey Av., Pelham, N.Y. Office: 55 Wall St., N.Y.C. Died June 7, 1963; buried Huguenot Meml. Ch., Pelham.

WHITMAN, LEROY, editor; born at Washington, Sept. 14, 1902; s. Winfield Scott and Sarah Jane (Price) W.; student George Washington Univ., 1921-22; m. Lucetta Sabin, June 25, 1923; children—Jane Laura (Mrs. H. C. Patterson, Jr.), Lucetta Fay (Mrs. Donald D. Schneider), LeRoy Winfield. Reporter, picture editor, asst. city editor. The Washington Post, 1922-29; mng. editor, general mgr. Army, Navy Air Force Jour., Washington, 1929-30, editor, 1930-62, pub., 1958-62; editor Army Navy Airforce Jour. and Register, 1962-64; editorial cons. Air Force Mag. and Space Digest, 1964-68; v.p. Army and Navy Jour., Inc. Mem. exec. com. control of Periodical Press Galleries U.S. Senate and House of Rep., 78th, 79th and 80th Congresses. Served as lt. (j.g.) and lt., U.S.N.R., 1927-40; editor Army and Navy Jour. for period World War II (Jour. awarded certificate of achievement, Navy Dept.; certificate of appreciation, U.S. Coast Guard); vice pres. Army and Navy Journal, Inc., 1949-68. Mem. Robert J. Collier Trophy Com., 1954. Wright Bros. Meml. Trophy Committee, 1955. Member Aviation Space Writers Association (First vice president 1952-53, president 1954-55), White House Corrs. Association. Unitarian. Clubs: Overseas Writers, Nat. Aviation, Aero (Washington); Nat. Press. Editor U.S. at War (4 vols.), pub. annually during World War II. Contbg. editor Funk & Wagnalls New Internat. Year Book, 1940-60. Home: Silver Spring MD Died Oct. 17, 1968; buried Martha's Vineyard MA

WHITMAN, RALPH naval officer; b. Boston, Mass., Apr. 7, 1880; s. Kilborn and Ella May (Wightman) W.; S.B., Mass. Inst. Tech., 1901; diploma, Naval War Coll., 1923; m. Frances Guyon Seabrook, Dec. 12, 1916; 1 dau., Frances Guyon. Civil engr., Engring. Dept., City of Boston, 1901-05, Isthmian Canal Commn. (studies for Panama Canal), 1905-07; commd. ensign, Civil Engr. Corps, U.S. Navy, 1907, and advanced through ranks to rear adm., 1939; stationed successively at Navy Yard, Phila.; Navy Dept., Washington; Naval Station, Guatanamo, Cuba; Naval Acad.; aide on staff of U.S. Mil. Gov., Santo Domingo, Dominican Republic; Naval Ordnance Plant, South Charleston, W.Va.; Naval War Coll.; Norfolk (Va.) Navy Yard; Mare Island (Calif.) Navy Yard; Naval Operating Base, Norfolk, Va.; stationed at Headquarters, 3d Naval District, New York City, from 1939, to April, 1944; retired, May 1, 1944. Awarded Marine Corps' Commemorative Expeditionary medal; Victory medal with West Indies clasp, special letter of commendation with silver star. Member American Soc., C.E., Boston Soc. C.E., Soc. of Am. Mil. Engrs., A.A.A.S., Internat. Assn. of Navigation Congresses, U.S. Naval Inst. Club: Army and Navy (Washington). Address; 30 Deer Hill Av., Danbury, Conn. Died Feb. 3, 1946.

WHITMAN, ROGER B. author; b. New York, N.Y., June 22, 1875; s. Alfred and Sarah (Andrews) W.; student Columbia, 1894-95; m. Marian Curtis, Oct. 3, 1906; children—Roger C., Herbert S. Tech. dir. New York Sch. of Auto Engrs., 1905-08; sales manager, etc. Bosch Magneto Co., 1910-12; sec., dir. and mgr. Stromberg Motor Devices Co., 1913-14; architectural photographer, 1915-17. Commd. 1st lt. Photographic Div., Air Service, U.S. Army, Oct. 1917, capt., Apr. 1918. Asso. editor Country Life, 1920-25. Mem. N.Y. Naval Militia, 1897; voluntary sailor Spanish-Am. War, served aboard Yankee, Solace and Marblehead. Mem. Authors' League America, Phi Kappa Psi. Clubs: Dutch Treat and Players. Author: Motor Car Principles, fifth edition, 1915; Gas Engine Principles, 1912; Motor Cycle Principles and the Light Car, 1914; Tractor Principles, 1919; Beauty in Gardens, 1928; Home Owners' Fact Book, 1929; First Aid for the Ailing House, 1938. Contbr. articles on building to many mags. Editor of "Ailing House" column, daily in N.Y. Sun and in other newspapers through the Bell Syndicate. Writer and broadcaster under title "The House Detective." Home: 314 Nassau Blvd., Garden City, N.Y. Died July 21, 1942.

WHITMAN, ROSWELL HARTSON fgn. service officer; b. Tom's River, N.J., Apr. 12, 1908; s. Roswell Brown and Elizabeth Parmelee (Hartson) W.; A.B., Colgate U., 1928; Ph.D., U. Chgo., 1933; m. Mary Elizabeth McKeon, Oct. 14, 1933; children—Ruth Elizabeth, John Roswell. Instr. econs. Williams Coll., 1929-30; statistician Ill. Emergency Relief Commn., 1932-34; asso. research asst. U.S. Central Statis. Bd., 1934; mgr. research dept. Macy's Dept. Store, N.Y.C., 1934-41; br. chief OPA, 1941-43; asso. chief div. Japanese and Korean affairs State Dept., 1946-47, asso. chief. then acting chief div. occupied area econ. affairs, 1947-48, chief div. investment and econ. development, 1949-50, econ. orgn. affairs officer Office European Regional Affairs, 1950-51; attache, later counselor of embassy for econ. affairs, Oslo, Norway, 1951-53; assigned FOA, 1953-55; attache Am. embassy, Karachi, Pakistan, 1955-56, econ. counselor, ICA dep. dir., 1956-58; counselor embassy for econ. affairs, dir. ICA mission, Cairo, U.A.R., 1958-61; minister for econ. affairs Am. embassy, Tokyo, Japan, 1961—. Served to lt. (s.g.) USNR, 1943-46. Mem. Am. Econs. Assn., Am. Statis. Affairs Assn., Am. Fgn. Service Assn., Phi Beta Kappa. Home: 3973 Harrison St. N.W., Washington 20015. Office: Dept. of State, Washington 25. Died Nov. 27, 1962; buried Arlington Nat. Cemetery, Washington.

WHITNEY, ALFRED RUTGERS constructing engr.; b. New York, N.Y., June 16, 1868; s. Alfred R. and Adeline Peers (Nesbitt) W.; M.E., Stevens Inst. Tech., 1890, E.D., 1921; unmarried. With Portage Iron Co., Duncansville, Pa., 1890-91; gen. mgr., later v.p. Puget Sound Wire Nail and Steel Co., Everett, Wash., 1891-94, also gen. mgr. and elec. engr. Everett R.R. and Electric Co. and cons. engr. Puget Sound Pulp and Paper Co., Everett & Monte Cristo R.R., 1891-94; rep. Carnegie Steel Co., in Japan, 1894; mem. firm A. R. Whitney, iron and steel mfrs. and contractors, New York, 1894-96; organizer, 1896, A. R. Whitney, Jr. & Co., Inc., 1899, as The Whitney Co., of which was pres. and treas. until 1926, chmn. bd., 1926-29; retired from active business, 1929. Company constructors of Great Am. Ins. Co. Bldg., W. R. Grace & Co. Bldg., Iron Age Bldg., New York; Masonic Temple and Central Branch Y.M.C.A., Brooklyn; Stock Exchange Bldg., Baltimore; Wentworth Inst., Boston; Amherst (Mass.) Coll. Library; International Trust Co. Bldg., Denver; Smith Building, Seattle, Wash., etc. War corr. in Ethiopia, 1930. Dir. Morristown Trust Co. Mem. Squadron A, cav., N.Y. Nat. Guard, 1897; maj. staff Gov. Frank W. Higgins, 1905, and of Gov. John Alden Dix, 1911; brevet maj., 1911, successively capt. and regtl. adj., maj. and brigade adj. gen., 1912-16; aide to rear admiral Nathaniel R. Usher, 1913-17; aide Bur. of Naval Intelligence, World War. Mem. Am. Soc. C.E., New Eng. Soc., Am. Geog. Soc., S.R., Delta Tau Delta. Republican. Episcopalian. Clubs: Union League, University, Downtown Assn., Metropolitan Opera, Piping Rock, New York Yacht, Seawanhaka-Corinthian Yacht, Cruising Club of America, Anglers' (New York); Traveler, Explorer, Angler, Yachtsman and Navigator. Writer on engring., travel, cruising, fishing, etc. Designer and builder of the "Ruffhouse," original of now universally accepted type of Fla. houseboat. Home: Morristown, N.J.; also 277 Park Av., New York 17, N.Y. Died Oct. 7, 1946.

WHITNEY, COURTNEY, brig. gen., U.S. Army; now assigned duty with govt. section, G.H.Q., Supreme Comdr. Allied Powers, Tokyo, Japan. Home: Washington DC Died 1969.*

WHITNEY, HENRY HOWARD officer U.S. Army; b. Glen Hope, Pa., Dec. 25, 1866; s. Rev. Walter R. and Eliza (Kegerreis) W.; grad. (with honors) Dickinson Sem., Williamsport, Pa., 1884; grad. U.S. Mil. Acad., 1892; m. Ellen Wadsworth, d. Henry Whitney Closson, Feb. 25, 1897; children—Julie Eliza- beth (dec.) and Henry Wadsworth. Additional 2d lt. 4th Arty., June 11, 1892; 2d lt., Nov. 28, 1892; capt. asst. adj.-gen. vols., Hdqrs. of the Army, May 12, 1898-May 12, 1899; 1st lt., Mar. 2, 1899; capt. arty. corps, May 8, 1901, maj. Coast Arty. Corps, Apr. 14, 1909. Spl. duty mil. information div., War Dept., 1896-98; mil. attaché, Am. Legation, Buenos Aires, Apr. 12, 1898-Apr. 12, 1899; in May 1898, under orders Sec. of War, after visiting Cuba, incog. made mil. reconnaissance of Puerto Rico, disguised as an English sailor; furnished information which was basis of mil. campaign in P.R.; on Gen. Miles' staff during Spanish-Am. War; accompanied Gen. Miles on his tour around the world, 1902-03, as lt. col. and a.d.c. chief staff; grad. Sch. of Submarine Defense, 1907; detailed in adj.-gen.'s dept., Oct. 3, 1910; in Philippine Islands, Jan. 31, 1911-14, as adj. gen. dept. of Mindanao; adj. Western Dept., at San Francisco, Jan. 13, 1914; comdg. Presidio of San Francisco, 1915; comdg. Coast Arty. at Ft. Winfield Scott, San Francisco, 1916; promoted lt. col., Coast Artillery Corps. June 1916; re-detailed adj. gen.'s dept. and ordered to Mexican border as adj. gen. El Paso Dist.; to San Francisco, as dept. adj., Western Dept., Apr. 1917; promoted col.. July 1917; apptd. brig. gen. N.A., Aug. 5, 1917, and ordered to Camp Shelby, Miss.; apptd. comdr. 63d Field Arty. Brigade; apptd. mem. Gen. Staff A.E.F.; chief of staff, Dist. of Paris, France, 1918-19; retired June 30, 1920, at own request after more than 32 yrs.' service; brigadier general regular army, ret., June 21, 1930. Awarded D.S.C. and D.S.M.; Officier de la Legion d'Honneur (French); Commandeur de la Couronne de Roumanie avec Glaives (Rumanian); Commandeur de Danilo I (Montenegro). Mem. Loyal Legion, Am. Legion, Mil. Order World War, Mil. Order Foreign Wars; founder The Beloved Vagabonds, Inc., a society of wanderers and adventures. Mason (32 deg., Shriner). Clubs: St. Nicholas (New York); Racquet (Phila.); Bohemian (San Francisco); San Mateo Polo, California Yacht (Los Angeles); Pacific Coast (Long Beach); University (New York). Address: care War Dept., Washington, D.C. Died April 2, 1949.

WHITNEY, JAMES AMAZIAH lawyer. author; b. Rochester, N.Y., June 30, 1839; s. Amaziah and Margaret Scotland (Taylor) W. (7th in descent from John and Eleanor Whitney, who came from England 1635, settling, at Watertown, Mass.); removed in childhood to Otsego Co., N.Y.; common school edn. (A.M., Union Coll., N.Y., 1870; LL.D., Iowa Coll., 1880); worked on farm; self-taught in chemistry, mechanics and engring., 1860-65; m. Eda Annie, d. John Wickham Copley, Delaware Co., N.Y., Oct. 31, 1876 (died 1895). Adj. and later engr. with rank of capt. in 39th regt. Nat. Guard N.Y., 1862-66; writer of specifications for patent solicitors, 1865-68; editor of Am. Artisan, 1868-72; prof. agrl. chemistry in Am. Inst., 1869-72; established as patent solicitor, 1872; admitted to practice in U.S. circuit courts, 1876; makes splty. of equity practice and corporation, patent, trade-mark and copyright law. Author: The Relations of the Patent Laws to the Development of Agriculture, 1874; The Chinese and the Chinese Question, 1880; Sonnets and Lyrics, 1884; The Children of Lamech (poem); Poetical Works (2 vols.); Shobab, a Tale of Bethesda (verse), 1884; Sonnets and Lyrics, 1884; The Children of Lamech, 1886; Collected Poetical Works (2 vols.), 1886. Home: Maryland, Otsego Co., N.Y. Deceased.

WHITNEY, LOREN HARPER lawyer; b. Berlin, O., Sept. 12, 1834; s. James W. and Betsey (Harper) W.; left home at 16 and executed contract for a levee in Miss.; crossed plains to Calif., 1852, and engaged in gold mining; attended Mt. Morris (Ill.) Coll., 1856; studied law under Gen. Stephen A. Hurlbut, Belvidere, Ill., and Ind. Asbury U.; admitted to bar, 1858; m. Mary Munson, 1867. Entered army as capt. 8th Ill. Cav., Army of the Potomac; organized 140th Ill. Inf. and was col.; served in 12 battles and 40 or more skirmishes, and was twice wounded. In law practice in Chicago, 1865-—. Author: Parallels in Lives of Buddha and Jesus, 1906; Life and Teachings of Zoroaster, 1905; A Question of Miracles, 1908. Home: River Forest, Ill. Died 1912.

WHITNEY, PAUL CLINTON hydrographic engr.; b. Washington, D.C., Aug. 28, 1882; s. Arthur Pierce and Margaret Jane (Milburn) W.; student George Washington U., 1900-03; m. Jeannette B. Prescott, Dec. 17, 1908; 1 daughter, Margaret Jeannette (Mrs. Margaret Adams); married 2d, Barbara Schmitt, Sept. 24, 1932. With United States Coast and Geodetic Survey, 1902-—; commd. hydographic and geodetic engr., 1917; participated in and directed surveys, coasts of Alaska and Philippine Islands, and Pacific and Atlantic coasts, 1903-17; chief of Sect. of Coast Pilot, Washington, D.C., 1919-25; insp. San Francisco Field Sta., 1925-28; chief Div. of Tides and Currents, Washington, 1928-42, supervisor, S.E. District 1942-46. Magnetic observer on first magnetic cruise, Pacific Ocean, under auspices of Carnegie Instn., 1905. Served as lt. and lt. comdr. U.S. Navy, World War I; now capt. U.S. C. and G.S. (retired.). Mem. Washington Soc. Engrs., Philos. Soc. of Washington, Poetry Society of Virginia, American Geophysical Union A.A.A.S., Wash. Academy of Science. Author of various technical government publications, and articles on tides and ocean currents. Club: Cosmos. Home: 1306 Rockbridge Av., Norfolk, Va. Address: U.S. Coast and Geodetic Survey, Washington. Died June 9, 1954; buried Hillsboro, N.D.

WHITNEY, WILLIAM COLLINS, sec. of Navy of U.S.; b. Conway, Mass., July 15, 1841; s. Gen. James S. W.; grad. Yale, 1863 (LL.D., 1888); Harvard Law School, 1865; admitted to the bar and practiced in New York; assisted in organizing Young Men's Democratic Club, 1871; active in movement against Tweed ring; insp. schools, 1872; defeated for dist. atty., 1872; corp. counsel, 1875-82; sec. of Navy of U.S., 1885-89. Democrat. Home: New York, N.Y. Died 1904.

WHITSIDE, SAMUEL MARMADUKE brig. gen. U.S.A., retired June 9, 1902; b. Toronto, Can., Jan. 9, 1839; s. Hon. W. H. W., U.S. consul; ed. Normal School, Toronto, Can., and grad. Careyville Acad., N.Y., San Antonio, Tex.; m. Carrie McDowell McGavock, Nov. 24, 1868. Entered United States Army, 1858; served with 6th United States cav. in Civil War from 1861 to close, and in Indian wars for over 25 yrs. on western frontier. Captured Big Foot and his 400 Sioux warriors Dec. 1890, and comd. his regiment in the battle of Wounded Knee following day, in which 1 officer and 29 men were killed, and 2 officers and 37 were wounded, while of the Indians 195 were killed and all the others either captured or wounded. In command of Fort Riley, Kan., Fort Meyer, Va., Jefferson Barracks, Mo., Ft. Sam Houston, Tex., from 1891 to May 1898; in command of 5th U.S. cav. during Spanish war; took command 10th cav. Oct. 1898; accompanied regt. to Cuba. May 1899; in command Dept. of Santiago and Puerto Principe, 1900-02. Brig. gen. U.S.V., Jan. 3, 1901; brig. gen. U.S.A., May 29, 1902; retired from active service June 9, 1902. Home: Bethesda, Md. Died 1904.

WHITT, HUGH air force officer; b. Catlettsburgh, Ky., Aug. 3, 1888; s. John Bunyan and Julia (Ball) W.; m. Jewel Burnett, Apr. 14, 1935; 1 son, Hugh Pelham. Enlisted U.S. Army, 1907, advanced through grades to brig. gen., USAF, 1948; served in Mexican Punitive Expdn. under John J. Pershing; served in France, World War I; finance officer Tng. Command, USAAF, World War II; became dir. finance USAF, 1947; retired as brig. gen. USAF, 1948, and entered pvt. bus. in Atlanta as founder and pres. NAMAC Corp. Republican. Baptist. Mason, Sojourner; mem. Heroes of '76. Club: Army and Navy Country (founder mem.). Home: 1711 Westwood Av. S.W., Atlanta. Died Feb. 1, 1955; buried Greenwood Cemetery, Atlanta.

WHITTAKER, JAMES newspaper writer; b. Chgo., Jan. 23, 1891; s. James and Lydia (Lexau) W.; grad. in piano and composition, Conservatorium, Leipzig, Germany, 1906; studied music in Paris, 1906-11; m. Ina Claire, of Alexandria, W.Va., July 9, 1919. Began with Herald Examiner, Chgo., 1915; now drama critic N.Y. Daily News and drama corr. Chgo. Tribune. Served to 1st lt., F.A., U.S. Army, 1917-19, with AEF, in France, 1918. Club: Cliff Dwellers (Chgo.). Home: 64 E. 55th St. Address: The News, 25 Park Pl., N.Y.C. Died Mar. 1964.

WHITTEMORE, JAMES MADISON brig. gen. U.S.A.; b. Brighton, Mass., Mar. 5, 1836; s. Dr. James Madison and Sarah (Lancaster) W.; grad. U.S. Mil. Acad., 1860; m. Joanna Bontecou Peck, June 24, 1863. Bvtd. 2d lt. arty., July 1, 1860; promoted 2d lt. 3d Arty., Sept. 27, 1860; transferred to Ordnance Corps, May 5, 1861; 1st lt., July 1, 1861; capt., Mar 3, 1863; maj., June 23, 1874; lt. col., Aug. 2, 1879; col., Jan. 3, 1887; on duty at various arsenals and depots of ordnance dept. until retired, Mar. 5, 1900; advanced to brig. gen. U.S.A. retired, by act of Apr. 23, 1904. Served in defense of Ft. Pickens, Fla., Apr.-Oct. 1861; Washington Arsenal, Washington, D.C., winter of 1861-Aug. 1862; with Army of Potomac. Ordnance officer McDowell's Corps, spring of 1862. Bvtd. major, Mar. 13, 1865 "for meritorious service during war." Home: New Haven, Conn. Died Sept. 6, 1916.

WHITWORTH, PEGRAM, army officer; b. Mansfield, La., Aug. 5, 1871; s. William Thomas and Laura (Pegram) W.; student Thatcher Mil. Inst., 1886-89; grad. U.S. Mil. Acad., 1894, Army Sch. of the Line, 1915, Gen. Staff Sch., 1920, Army War Coll., 1921; m. Emeline Cole Smith, Apr. 18, 1899; 1 son, Pegram. Commd. 2d lt. Inf., June 12, 1894, and advanced through grades to temp. brig. gen., 1918, brig. gen. regular army, May 1933, retired, Aug. 31, 1935. Served in Philippine Insurrection, 1898-1900; again in Philippines, 1901-02 and 1906-08; construction q.m., Ft. Crockett, Galveston, Tex., 1909-12; in Panama Canal Zone, 1912-16; instr. and comdr. 1st Bn., 1st O.T.C., Presidio, San Francisco, 1917; col. 362d Inf., 91st Div., Aug. 1917; with A.E.F. in France, July 1918; brig. gen. comdg. 71st Brig., 36th Div., Aug. 1918-July 1919; chief of staff, 2d Div., 1932-33; comdr. 6th Inf. Brig., Ft. Douglas, Utah, 1933-35, also Civilian Conservation Corps of about 30 camps; apptd. member of the Bd. of Police Commrs. of the City of Los Angeles, Calif., June 1940. Awarded 3 silver stars for bravery against Spaniards in Manila, 2 citations for bravery against insurgents; cited by Marshal Petain, Apr. 1, 1919; Cross of Mil. Service (U.D.C. of La.). Republican. Christian Scientist. Mason (32 deg., Shriner). Home: 10950 Wellworth Av., W Los Angeles CA

WICK, SAMUEL, psychiatrist, hosp. adminstr.; b. Marinette, Wis., 1906; M.D., Rush Med. Sch., 1929. Intern Lutheran Meml. Hosp., Chgo., 1929-30; resident psychiatry, behavior clinic Criminal Ct. Cook County, Chgo., 1931-32; psychiatrist Elgin (Ill.) State Hosp., 1932-37; sr. psychiatrist Milw. County Hosp. Mental Diseases, 1937-42; chief acute intensive treatment VA Neuropsychiat. Hosp., Sawtelle, Cal., 1948-52; dir. edn. and research Ariz. State Hosp., Phoenix, 1952-53, supt., 1953-64; pvt. practice, Phoenix, from 1964. Served to capt., USAAF, 1942-46. Diplomate Am. Bd. Psychiatry and Neurology. Fellow Am. Psychiat. Assn.; mem. A.M.A. Home: Phoenix AZ Deceased.

WICKES,FORSYTH lawyer; b. N.Y.C., Oct. 26, 1876; s. Edward Allen and Mary (Forsyth) W.; grad. St. Marks Sch., 1894; A.B., Yale, 1898; A.B., Columbia, 1900; m. Marian Arnot Haven, Apr. 27, 1905; children—Fanny (Mrs. John E. Parsons), Marian (Mrs. T. F. Davies Haines), Kitty (Mrs. Ralph H. Poole, Jr.), Ann (Mrs. William C. Brewer, Jr.). Admitted to N.Y. bar, 1900, since practiced in N.Y.C.; director Shell Oil Company. Chmn. bd., trustee French Lycee, French Inst. N.Y.C.; 3d v.p., trustee N.Y. Hist. Soc. Served as maj. Inf., U.S. Army, World War I. Decorated D.S.M.; grand officer Legion of Honor (France); comdr. Order of Merit (Malagasy Republic). Clubs: Knickerbocker, Century (N.Y.C.); Newport (R.I.) Country. Home: Residence Starbord, Newport, R.I. Office: 1 Chase Manhattan Plaza, N.Y.C. 4. Died Dec. 20, 1964; buried Newburgh, N.Y.

WICKES, LAMBERT naval officer; b. Eastern Neck Island, Md., 1735; s. Samuel Wickes. Went to sea; master mcht. ships from Phila. and Chesapeake Bay ports, 1769; part owner of vessel, 1774; refused to carry East India tea from London, 1774; given command of armed ship Reprisal, 1776; carried William Bingham to Martinique, 1776, captured 3 prizes and H. M. S. Shark; transported Benjamin Franklin to France (becoming 1st Continental warship to enter European waters), 1776; raided English Channel and upturned 5 Brit. ships, 1777; commanded flotilla of 3 ships, 1777, took 18 Brit. prizes off Britain, 1777. Drowned when ship floundered off Newfoundland banks while returning to colonies (all drowned except cook) Oct. 1, 1777.

WIEGAND, CHARLES DUDLEY, ret. army ofer.; educator; b. Balt., Apr. 28, 1906; s. Charles List and Daisy Viola (George) W.; student St. Johns' Coll., 1924-25; B.S., U.S. Mil. Acad., 1929; grad. study Command and Gen. Staff Sch., 1942-43; Master of Arts, Colorado State University, 1957-59; m. Claire Elizabeth Baker, Mar. 14, 1931; children—Robert Dudley, Marguerite Claire. Commd. 2d lt., U.S. Army, 1929, advanced through grades to col., 1950; various army stas., U.S., Hawaii, Canal Zone, 1929-43; combat duty, Sicily and Italy, 1943-44; mil. missions, Guatemala, C.A., also founded Escuela de Aplicacion de Armas y Servicios, Escuela de Artilleria and Escuela de Caballeria, 1945-48; prof. mil. sci. and tactics Howe Mil. Sch., 1948-50, U. Mich., 1950-52, Colo. State U., 1957-59; asst. chief of staff, G4, U.S. Army, Alaska, 1952-54; chief of staff U.S. Army, Alaska, 1954; dep. post comdr. Ft. George G. Meade, Md., 1954-56, post comdr., 1956-57; ret.; with dept. of English, Colo. State U., 1961-72. Decorated Silver Star, Bronze Star (U.S.), Cruz de Merito Militar 2d class (Guatemala). Lion, Elk. Home: Fort Collins CO Died Mar. 7, 1972.

WIENER, MEYER, ophthalmologist; b. St. Louis, Mo., Jan. 10, 1876; s. Isidor Marcus and Julia (Meyer) W.; M.D., Mo. Med. Coll., 1896; grad. student U. of Berlin, 1897-98, U. of Heidelberg, summer, 1898, U. of Paris, 1898-99; m. Marguerite Edith Lesser, Dec. 28, 1915; children—Julia, Thomas Rodgers, Edith. Prof. of clin. ophthalmology, Washington University School of Medicine, 1910-46; emeritus professor since 1946; ophthalmic surgeon Missouri Pacific Hospital; retired from active practice 1936; now engaged in teaching research and writing. Formerly dir. of prevention of blindness, Mo. Commn. for the Blind. Commd. maj. Med. Corps, U.S. Army, 1918; organized and dir. Sch. of Ophthalmology, Med. Officers Training Group, Ft. Oglethorpe, Ga.; chief of eye dept. Gen. Hosp. No. 14, later chief plastic surgery of the eye, Gen. Hosp. No. 11; lt. col. Med. Reserve Corps.; now hon. consultant to Med. Dept., U.S. Navy. Certified by Am. Bd. Ophthalmic Examiners. Fellow Am. Coll. Surgeons; mem. A.M.A., Mo. State Med. Soc., St. Louis Med. Soc., St. Louis Acad. Science, Am. Acad. Ophthalmology and Otolaryngology (past exec. v.p.), St. Louis Ophthal. Soc. (past pres.); honorary mem. many socs., honorary asso. pres. Service Club for the Blind (St. Louis). Democrat. Unitarian. Author: Surgery of the Eye, 1939. Formerly editor St. Louis Med. Review, Annals of Ophthalmology, asso. editor Am. Jour. Ophthalmology, editor-in-chief Ophthalmology in the War Years, editorial board, Quarterly Review of Ophth. Home: 321 Alameda Blvd., Coronado CA

WIENER, PAUL LESTER city planner, architect; b. Leipzig, Germany, May 2, 1895; s. Julius and Helen (Goldmann) W.; grad. architect Royal Acad. Vienna; postgrad. Kunstgewerbe Acad. (Berlin); prof. honoris causa, Nat. U. San Carlos, Guatemala; m. Ingeborg A. E. Tenhaeff, July 13, 1948; children by previous marriage—Barbara Frank, Paul Lester. Came to U.S., 1913, naturalized, 1919. Co-founder Contempora, internat. art service, 1927; tech. adviser U.S. commn. Internat. Expn. in Paris, 1936-37; founder (with Jose Luis Sert), Town Planning Assos., N.Y.C., 1942; dir. tech. studies New Sch. Social Research, N.Y.C., 1943-45; cons. Office Prodn. Research and Devel., WPB, 1943-45; adj. prof. of urban planning Columbia, 1965-67; lectr. univs. U.S., France, Belgium, Netherlands, Chile, Brazil, Colombia, Peru, Cuba, Venezuela; U.S. specialist for Dept. of State, specialists div. Internat. Edn. Exchange Service; designer architecture and interior Am. Pavilion, Exposition Arts and Scis., Paris, 1937, also interior Brazilian Pavilion; Ecuadorian Pavilion, N.Y. World's Fair; consultant to government of Peru for founding of National Plan Office; cons. to government of Bahamas for planning of New Providence and Nassau; devel. pilot plan for numerous cities, Brazil, Colombia, Cuba, Peru, Venezuela; devel. plan for indsl. community, prefabricated and demountable housing project, Sydney, N.Y.; recent archtl. projects include pilot plan for urbanization of Island of Tierra Bomba, developed as an extension City of Cartagena, Colombia; cons. planner, designer Gateway Center devel., Mpls.; site planner, designer Downtown Community Devel., Syracuse, N.Y.; cons. planner, designer Washington Square Village residential devel., N.Y.C.; cons., planner designer for McCombs Bridge Urban Renewal project, N.Y.C.; master plan for Aspen, Colorado and Pitkin County, Colorado. Decorated chevalier Legion of Honor (France); Southern Cross (Brazil); recipient three grand prix for Pub. Architecture, Pvt. Architecture, Interior Design, Internat. Jury Arts and Scis., Paris, 1937; prize (with P. Bezy, J. Stedman, Jr.) Wheaton Coll. Art Center; prize Museum Modern Art, N.Y.C., 1939. Mem. American Society of Planning Officials, Pan-Am. Soc. (affiliate member), American Institute of Planners; hon. mem. archtl. socs. of Brazil, Peru, Belgium, Mexico, Colombia. Works published in profl. publis., U.S., S.A., Europe. Home: 25 Washington Sq. N., N.Y.C. Office: 119 E. 18th St., N.Y.C. 3. Died. Nov. 1967.

WIGGLESWORTH, RICHARD BOWDITCH ambassador; b. Boston, Mass., Apr. 25, 1891; s. George and Mary Catherine (Dixwell) W.; grad. Milton Acad., 1908; A.B., Harvard, 1912, LL.B., 1916; Dr. Public Administration, Suffolk University; Doctor of Jurisprudence, Portia Law Sch; m. to Florence Joyes Booth, Apr. 30, 1931; children—Ann Joyes, Mary Dixwell, Jane Booth. Asst. pvt. sec. to gov. gen. of P.I., 1913; admitted to Mass. bar, 1916, began practice at Boston; legal adviser to asst. sec. U.S. Treasury in charge foreign loans and ry. payments, and sec. of World War Debt Commn., Apr. 24, 1883; s. Richard Clark and Margaret Ann (Ingersoll) W.; student Harvard, 1900-01; B.S., U.S. Mil. Acad., 1905; grad. Army Engr. Sch., 1908, Sch. of Line, Ft. Leavenworth, 1922, Gen. Staff Sch., 1923, Army War Coll., 1924; D.Engring. (hon.), Clarkson Coll., 1943; m. Dorothy Langfitt, May 25, 1911 (dec. 1948): 1 son, Langfitt; m. Olive Emerson Payne, July 2, 1949. Commd. 2d lt., Engrs., 1905; advanced through grades to maj. gen. (temp.), 1941; dist. engr., Memphis, 1928-31; chmn. Fed. Bd. Surveys and Maps., 1931-35; mem. bd. mgrs. Fed. Barge Lines, 1935-38; sr. mem. Beach Erosion Bd.

Shore Protection Bd., 1938-39; chief staff, First Army, N.Y., 1939-41; supt. U.S. Mil. Acad., 1942-45; ret. with rank of maj. gen., 1946. Chmn., N.Y. State Power Authority. Mem. Miss. River Commn., 1935-38. Awarded D.S.M. (twice), Legion of Merit, various campaign medals (U.S.); Croix de Guerre (France). Mem. Soc. Am. Mil. Engrs., Am. Soc. C.E. Clubs: Army and Navy, Army-Navy Country (Washington). Office: Knappen Tippetts Abbett Engring. Co., 62 W. 47th St., N.Y.C.

WIGGLESWORTH RICHARD BOWDITCH ambassador; b. Boston, Mass., Apr. 25, 1891; s. George and Mary C Catherine (Dixwell) W.; grad. lfilton Acad., 1908; A.B., Harvard, 1912. LL.B., 1916; Dr. Public Administration. Suffolk University: Doctor of Jurisprudence, Portia Law Sch.; m. to Florence Joyes Booth, Apr. 30, 1931; children—Ann Joyes, Mary Dixwell, Jane Booth. Asst. pvt. sec. to gov. gen. of P.I., 1913; admitted to Mass bar. 1916, began practice at Boston; legal adviser to asst. sec. U.S. Treasury in charge foreign loans and ry. payments, and sec. of World War Dept. Commn., 1922-24; asst. to agt. gen. for reparation payments, Berlin, 1924-27; gen. counsel and Paris rep. for orgns. created under Dawes Plan, 1927-28. Mem. 70th Congress (unexpired term of late Louis A. Frothingham, 1928-29), also 71st and 72d Congresses (1929-33), 14th Mass. Dist., and 73d to 85th Congresses, 13th Massachusetts Dist.; United States ambassador to Canada, 1958—; chairman Rep. Nat. Speakers Bureau, New York. Alternate at large Rep. National Convention, 1948. In France as capt. Battery E. and comdg. officer 1st Batt., 303d Regt., F.A., 76th Div., U.S. Army, World War I. Mem. Am. and Mass. State bar assns., Am. Legion, 40 and 8. Vets. of Foreign Wars, Mil. Order World War. Mil. Order Foreign Wars. Republican. Unitarian. Home: Milton, Mass. ome: Mi ton Office: Am. Embassy, Ottawa, Can. Died Oct. 22, 1960.

WIGMORE, JOHN HENRY (wig'môr), prof. law; b. San Francisco, Calif., Mar. 4, 1863; s. John and Harriet (Joyner) W.; A.B., Harvard, 1883, A.M., LL.B., 1887; LL.D., U. of Wis., 1906, Harvard, 1909, Louvain, 1928, Northwestern, 1937, Lyon, 1939; m. Emma Hunt Vogl, Sept. 16, 1889. Practiced, Boston, 1887-89; prof. Anglo-American law, Keio Univ., Tokyo, 1889-92; prof. law since 1893, dean faculty of law, 1901-29 (emeritus), Northwestern U. Author: Digest of Decisions of the Massachusetts Railroad Commission, 1888; The Australian Ballot System, 1889; Notes on Land Tenure and Local Institutions in Old Japan, 1890; Materials for Study of Private Law in Old Japan, 1892, 1941; Treatise on Evidence (10 vols.), 1904-05, 1923, 1940; Pocket Code of Evidence. 1909, 1935, 1942; Principles of Judicial Proof, 1913, 1937; Student's Handbook of Evidence, 1935; Panorama of the World's Legal Systems, 1928, 36; Kaleidoscope of Justice, 1941. Editor: Greenleaf on Evidence (16th edit., Vol. I), 1899; Compiled Examinations in Law, 1900; Cases on Torts (2 vols.), 1911; Cases on Evidence, 1913. Co-Editor: Select Essays in Anglo-American Legal History, 1907; Evolution of Law Series, 1915; Modern Criminal Science Series, 1910-1915; Modern Legal Philosophy Series, 1911-1921; Continental Legal History Series, 1912-1920. Also extensive contributor to legal publications and magazines. Pres. Am. Inst. Criminal Law and Criminology, 1909-10, Am. Assn. Univ. Profs., 1916. Commd. mem. staff of judge advocate gen. U.S. Army, with rank of maj., Aug. 1916; commd. lt. col. Feb. 1, 1918; col., June 9, 1918; hon. discharged, May 8, 1919. Awarded D.S.M. Mem. U.S. Sect. Inter-Am. High Commn., 1915-19. Hon. mem. Asiatic Soc. of Japan, 1914, Soc. of Teachers of Law (Eng.); corr mem. Comité de Législation Etrangère (France); mem. Internat. Acad. of Comparative Law, League of Nations Com. on Intellectual Coöperation. Chevalier Legion of Honor (France), Aug. 1919; Order of Sacred Treasure (Japan), 1935; Am. Bar Assn. gold medal, 1932. Mem. Ill. Com. on Uniform State Laws, 1908-24 and since 1933. Home: 850 Lake Shore Drive. Address: 357 E. Chicago Av., Chicago, Ill. Died Apr. 20, 1943.

WILBER, HERBERT WRAY educator; b. Avoca, N.Y., Mar. 30, 1888; s. Herbert and Eliza Jane (McClure) W.; B.S., Rice Inst., 1916, M.S., 1917; m. Sarah Jane Stewart, June 17, 1922; 1 dau., Martha Jane. Prof. accounting Kent State U., 1939-—, head dept., 1940-—. Served as capt. USAAF, 1943-45. C.P.A., Pa. Mem. Am. Accounting Assn., Am. Assn. U. Profs., Delta Sigma Pi. Methodist. Mason. Home: 1423 S. Water St., Kent, O. Died Dec. 1, 1963.

WILCOX, CADMUS MARCELLUS army officer; b. Wayne County, N.C., May 29, 1824; s. Reuben and Sarah (Garland) W.; grad. U.S. Mil. Acad., 1846. Brevetted 2d lt. 4th U.S. Inf., 1846; promoted 2d lt., 7th Inf., 1847, trans. to Gen. Scott's army; served at Vera Cruz, Cerro Gordo; aide to Gen. John A. Quitman in advance on Mexico City; groomsman to Ulysses S. Grant at his wedding, 1848; commd. 1st lt., 1851; asst. instr. inf. tactics U.S. Mil. Acad., 1852-57; commd. capt., 1860; commd. col. 9th Ala. Inf., Confederate Army, after resigning from U.S. Army, 1861; served throughout war with Lees army; commd. brig. gen., 1861, maj. gen., 1864; chief railroad div. Gen. Land Office under Pres. Cleveland, 1886-90. Author: Rifles and Rifle Practice, 1859; History of the Mexican War, pub. posthumously, 1892. Died Dec. 2, 1890.

WILCOX, ELIAS BUNN, soldier, lawyer; b. Nash Co., N.C., June 28, 1869; s. Edward Warren and Mary (Bunn) W.; ed. pub. schs. and under pvt. instrn.; engaged in ednl. work; grad. in law, U. of N.C., 1895; m. Vardaman Cockrell, of New York, Nov. 5, 1910; children—Mary Winifred, Adah Louise. Admitted to Supreme Court of N.C., 1895, Supreme Court of U.S., 1907; capt. U.S. Vol. Inf. (Immunes), 1898; served at Santiago, Cuba; in comd. mil. forces of Dist. of Holguin, later comd. mounted troops to fight bandits, his reg. holding record for longest vol. service in Cuba. After being mustered out of mil. service was apptd. spl. insp. Pub. Instrn. for Cuba; formulated plan for grading of schs. of Cuba. In P.R., since Aug. 1902; was dist. supt. schs. of Guayama; spl. del. Govt. for inspection of elections of 1902; spl. asst. atty.-gen.; capt. Insular Constabulary and acting cheif same for several mos.; lt.-col. on governor's mil. staff; judge of Dist. Court of Ponce, P.R., 1903-04; asst. sec. of state; gen. supervisor of elections, Aug. 1, 1904-Jan. 14, 1905; spl. counsel of govt., prosecuting election fraud cases; dist. atty. Jud. Dist. of Guayama, 1905-08; dist. atty., 1909, resigned to practice law at San Juan, P.R. Prominently connected with citrus fruit culture in P.R.; pres. Rio Hondo Planters' Assn., Bayamon Fruit Growers' Assn. First comdr. Camp Spanish-Am. War Vets. in P.R. Hon. mention in Army and Navy Journal for mil. service in Cuba; medal of honor conferred for same by Nat. Congress of S.A.R., Nov. 26, 1917. Grad. as capt. N.A., and ranking officer from O.T.C., Henry Barracks, P.R.; served in world war with Porto Rico Brigade as ins. officer, judge advocate; comd. Development Battn.; detailed to organize, instruct and command Porto Rico Home Guard of 3,000 men and officers; bvtd. maj. just before armistice. Resumed practice of law, Feb. 18, 1919. Lt. col. Judge Advocate Gen's. Dept. Res., U.S.A. Revised and recorded titles of Federal property in Porto Rico, valued at O,000,000, without compensation, under appointment of sec. of war who officially referred to the work as "patriotic service." Author of article "Birth of English Civilization in America," dedicated to the lasting friendship of English Speaking Peoples as an important factor in the preservation and progress of world civilization, in the Town and Country Review of London, Sept. 1937. Home: San Juan PR

WILCOX, JOHN WALTER JR. naval officer; b. Milledgeville, Ga., Mar. 22, 1882; s. John Wesley and Anna Gray (Holmes) W.; ed. elementary and high sch., Macon, 1888-89; B.S., U.S. Naval Acad., 1905; grad. Naval War Coll., 1924; m. Caroline Manigault, Dec. 22, 1919; children—Arthur, Mary. Commd. ensign, U.S. Navy, 1905, and promoted through the grades to rear adm., 1938. Awarded special letter of Commendation by Navy Dept. for service in World War; decorated Mexican Campaign medal, World War medal with Silver Star, Am. Red Cross silver medal, Italian Croce Rossi silver medal. Mem. Sons of Confederate Vets. Episcopalian. Clubs: Army and Navy (Washington, D.C.); New York Yacht. Home: Kenwood, Chevy Chase, Md. Address: Navy Dept., Washington, D.C. Died Mar. 27, 1942.

WILCOX, REYNOLD WEBB M.D.; b. Madison, Conn., Mar. 29, 1856; s. Col. Vincent Meigs and Catherine Millicent (Webb) W.; B.A., Yale, 1878; M.D., Harvard, 1881; post-grad. med. study at Vienna, Heidelberg, Paris, Edinburgh, 1881-82; hon. M.A., Hobart, 1881; LL.D., Maryville, 1892; D.C.L., Wittenberg, 1915; m. Grace, d. Col. Floyd Clarkson, Dec. 12, 1917. Prof. medicine, New York Post-Grad. Med. Sch., 1884-1908; consultant in medicine, St. Mark's Hosp., 19-—; cons. physician, Ossining Hosp., 1910-—, Eastern Long Island Hosp., 1913-—; cons. internist, N.J. State Hospital, 1917-—. Major M.R.C., U.S.A., on duty as instr., Camp Greenleaf, Fort Oglethorpe, Ga., 1917; lt. col., 1924. Pres. Am. Therapeutic Soc., 1901-02, Am. Assn. Med. Jurisprudence, 1913-14, Am. Congress on Internal Medicine, 1915-17, Am. Coll. of Physicians, 1915-21, Harvard Med. Soc., 1894-95, Med. Assn. Greater City of N.Y., 1910-14, N.Y. Soc. Med. Jurisprudence, 1912-14, N.Y. div. Assn. of Med. Reserve Corps U.S.A., 1914-16; fellow A.A.A.S.; mem. Soc. American Wars (surgeon gen., 1915-27; comdr. N.Y. Comdry., 1919-20), Society Colonial Wars, S.R., War of 1812 (v.p. Pa. Soc. 1897-1925; v.p. gen. 1908-25; pres. gen. 1925). Author: System of Case Records, 1887; Materia Medica and Therapeutics, 1892 (12 edits.); Manual of Fever Nursing, 1904 (2 edits.); Treatment of Disease, 1907 (4 edits.); also (genealogical) The Descendants of William Wilcoxson, Vincent Meigs and Richard Webb, 1893; Madison—Her Soldiers, 1890; and numerous med. and hist. papers. Home: Princeton, N.J. Died June 6, 1931.

WILCOX, TIMOTHY ERASTUS brig. gen.; b. N.Y. State. Apr. 26, 1840; s. Rodney and Emily W.; A.B., Union Coll., N.Y., 1861, A.M., 1864; M.D., Albany Medical Coll., 1864; m. Clara B. Brown, Jan. 29, 1867; children—Victor Irving (dec.), Florence E.. Glover Brown (dec.). Asst. surgeon 6th N.Y. Heavy Arty., Jan. 4, 1865; asst. surgeon U.S.V., Apr. 25, 1865-June 4, 1866. In regular army, asst. surgeon, May 14, 1867-July 1, 1868; resigned, July 1, 1868; asst. surgeon, Nov. 10, 1874; capt. asst. surgeon, Nov. 10, 1879; maj. surgeon, Feb. 24, 1891; lt. col. deputy surgeon gen. May 7, 1902; col. asst. surgeon gen., Sept. 22, 1903; retired with rank of brig. gen., Apr. 26, 1904. Lt. col., chief surgeon vols., Nov. 12. 1898-May 12, 1899. Home: Washington, D.C. Died Dec. 10, 1932.

WILDE, GEORGE FRANCIS FAXON rear adm. U.S.N.; b. Braintree, Mass., Feb. 23, 1845; s. William Read and Mary Elizabeth (Thayer) W.; grad. U.S. Naval Acad., 1864; m. Emogen B. Howard, Dec. 13, 1868. Master, 1866; lt. comdr., Dec. 18, 1868; comdr., Oct. 1885; capt., Aug. 10, 1898; rear adm., Aug. 10, 1904; retired, Feb. 20, 1905. Served on flagship Susquehanna, 1864-67; went to Havana with fleet for Confederate ram Stonewall Jackson; later served on Albany, Tennessee, Wabash; comdr. U.S. monitor Canonicus, 1873-74; exec. officer U.S.S. Vandalia, 1878-82; comd. U.S.S., Dolphin, 1885-88, making cruise around the world—she being first steel vessel of U.S. Navy to circumnavigate the globe; sec. Lighthouse Bd., 1894-98; introduced gas buoys on Great Lakes; established electric light vessel off Diamond Shoal, Cape Hatteras, introduced telephone to light vessels from shore; comd. U.S. ram Katahdin in operations around Cuba, Mar.-Sept., 1898; ordered to command Boston; landed first marines ever landed in China and sent them to Peking, where they guarded legation, Nov. 1898-Apr. 1899; captured and occupied city of Ilolio, Feb. 11, 1899; captured Vigan, Feb. 18, 1900 (received thanks from Spanish Govt. for rescuing 160 Spanish officers and families at Vigan); comd. battleship Oregon, May 29, 1899-Jan. 16, 1901. Capt. Navy Yard, Portsmouth, N.H., 1901-02, Navy Yard, Boston, 1903-04; commandant Navy Yard, League Island, Pa., Feb.-May 1904, Navy Yard, Boston, May 1, 1904-Feb. 20, 1905. Chmn. Mass. Nautical Training Sch. Commn., 1906-—. Home: North Easton, Mass. Died 1911.

WILDER, JOHN THOMAS soldier; b. Hunter Village, N.Y., Jan 31, 1830; s. Reuben and Mary (Merritt) W.; ed. pub. schs., N.Y.; m. Martha Stewart, May 18, 1858 (died 1892); 2d, Dora E. Lee, 1904. Served 7 yrs. apprenticeship at iron business, as draughtsman, machinist, pattern-maker and millwright until 1842; built and operated gen-machine and millwright works until Civil War; enlisted in Ind. as pvt. 1st Independent Battery Arty., April 21, 1861, and elected capt. same day; made lt.-col. 17th Ind. Inf., June 12, 1861; col., Mar. 12, 1862; first in command brigade, Dec. 20, 1862; on June 24 cut his way through Confederate lines at Hoover's Gap, Tenn., against heavy odds, compelling Bragg to evacuate Tennessee; led Rosecrans army to Chattanooga; shelled latter place 18 days and entered city Sept. 9, 1863; began great battle of Chickamauga Sept. 18, and brigade lines were not broken during the 3-days' battle; bvtd. brig.-gen. and brigade named "Wilder's Lightning Brigade" by gen. order. Organized, 1867, Roane Iron Works; built and operated 2 blast furnaces at Rockwood, Tenn. (first in South); built rail mill, Chattanooga, 1870; has been active in mineral development of Tennessee ever since. Gen. mgr. Roane Iron Co.; pres. and propr. Wilder Machine Works; v.p. C., C. & C. R.R.; pres. Roane Mountain Hotel Co.; gen. mgr. Fentress Coal & Coke Co.; v.p. and gen. mgr. Knoxville, Power Co. Republican; U.S. Pension agt. at Knoxville, Tenn. Mem. Soc. Army of the Cumberland, Loyal Legion (Ohio), Nat. Geog. Soc., Iron and Steel Inst., Great Britain, Am. Inst. Mining Engrs. Address: Cherry Hill, Knoxville, Tenn. Died Oct. 20, 1917.

WILDER, RUSSELL MORSE physician, ret.; b. Cincinnati, O., Nov. 24, 1885; s. William Hamlin and Ella (Taylor) W.; grad. South Side Acad., Chgo., 1903; B.S., U. Chgo., 1907, Ph.D., 1912; M.D. Rush Med. Coll., 1912; grad. study U. of Chgo., 1913, Vienna, 1914; m. Lucy Elizabeth Beeler, Mar. 18, 1911; children—Russell Morse, Thomas Carroll. Instr. in anatomy and pathology, U. of Chgo., 1909-10; began practice at Chgo., 1912; resident Presbyn. Hosp., Chgo., 1915-17; instr. in medicine, Rush Med. Coll., 1915-17; mem. Mayo Clinic, 1919-29; asst. prof. medicine, Mayo Foundation, U. of Minn., 1919-22, asso. prof., 1922-29; prof. of med. and chmn. dept. of medicine, U. of Chgo., 1929-31; prof. med. and head dept. of med., Mayo Foundation, and mem. Mayo Clinic, Rochester, Minn., 1931-50; dir. Nat. Inst. Arthritis and Metabolic Diseases U.S. Pub. Health Service, 1951-53. Served as medical gas officer, A.E.F., 1918-19. Mem. Com. on Med., 1940-46, and chmn., 1940, also mem. Food and Nutrition Bd., 1940-50, and chmn., 1940-41—both of Nat. Research Council. Chief, Civilian Food Requirements Branch, Food Distribution Adminstrn., U.S. War Food Adminstrn., 1943. Recipient Howard Taylor Ricketts award, 1949; Joseph Goldberger award, 1954; Am. Bakers Assn. award, 1956. Member A.M.A. (mem. council on foods; Frank Billings Meml. lectr. 1950), A.C.P. (master 1957), Assn. Am. Physicians, Am. Soc. Clin. Investigation, Am. Physiol. Soc., Minn. Soc. of Internal Medicine, Chgo. Inst. Med., Inst. Nutrition, Am. Diabetes Assn. (pres. 1947), Minn., Washington acads. med. Central Interurban Clin. Club, Sigma Xi, Alpha Omega Alpha, Nu Sigma Nu, Delta Kappa Epsilon. Democrat. Episcopalian. Clubs: University. Author publs. relating to field, also collaborator on several med. books. Asso. editor profl. jours. Home: 705 Eighth Av. S.W. Address: Mayo Clinic, Rochester, Minn. Died Dec. 16, 1959.

WILDER, WILBUR ELLIOTT army officer; b. in Mich., Aug. 16, 1856; s. Elliott S. and Sylvia (Gilkey) W.; grad. U.S. Mil. Acad., 1877; m. Violet Blair Martin, 1884; children—Throop M., Wilbur E., Sylvia, Cornelia M., Violet B. Commd. 2d lt., 4th Cav., 1877, promoted through grades to col., 1911; ret., 1920; brig. gen. by spl. act. of Congress, 1927; served as big. gen. N.A., 1917-19; served on frontier until 1895, in many Indian campaigns and engagements. Adj. U.S. Mil. Acad., 1895-98; supt. Yellowstone Nat. Park, comdg. Ft. Yellowstone, Wyo., Mar.-June 1899; in Philippine Islands, comd. Macabebe Scouts 1899-1900 and supt. of police, Manila, 1901; comdr. 168th Inf., Brigade, Camp Taylor, Ky., 1917; in France, 1918-19. Bvtd. capt., 1890, for gallant service in action against Indians, at Horse Shoe Canyon, N.M., 1882. Decorated Congl. Medal of Honor for most distinguished gallantry in action. Mem. Soc. Indian Wars, Legion of Valor. Clubs: University (N.Y.C.); Army and Navy, Army and Navy Golf and Country (Washington). Address: University Club, 1. W. 54th St., N.Y.C. Died Jan. 30, 1952

WILDES, FRANK naval officer; b. Boston, June 17, 1843; s. Solomon Lovell and Sophia (Rice) W.; apptd. from Mass., 1860; grad. U.S. Naval Acad., 1863; apptd. ensign, May 28, 1863; apptd. steam sloop Lackawanna, West Gulf squadron, June 15, 1863; battle of Mobile and naval battery until surrender of Fort Morgan; monitor Chickasaw during operations in Mobile Bay, Mar. and Apr. 1865, till occupation of Mobile; m. Lucy A. Smith, Jan. 1, 1872. After war on various duties and stas.; master, 1866; lt., 1867; lt. comdr., Mar. 12, 1868; comdr., Apr. 1880; capt., July 1894; in command of cruiser Boston, Asiatic sta., 1895-—; took part in battle of Manila, May 1, 1898; capt. of the yard, Navy Yard, New York, Apr. 1, 1899; rear admiral. Address: Navy Yard, New York. Died 1903.

WILE, FREDERIC WILLIAM author, newspaper columnist and editorial writer; b. LaPorte, Ind.. Nov. 30, 1873; s. Jacob and Henrietta (Guggenheim) W.; ed. U. of Notre Dame, LL.D., 1924; LL.D., Ursinus, 1929; m. Ada Shakman, May 14, 1901; children—Frederic William, Helen Isabel. Reporter Chicago Record, 1898-1900; corr. for Chicago Record and Chicago Daily News in London during Boer War, 1900-01, in Berlin, 1902-06; chief corr. London Daily Mail and affiliated Northcliffe newspapers in Germany, and Berlin corr. New York Times and Chicago Tribune, 1906-14. During World War I. edited column in Daily Mail, London, entitled "Germany Day by Day." Specialist on German Affairs, Intelligence Sect., G.H.Q., A.E.F., 1917-18; lt. col. Res. Corps (staff specialist), U.S.A. Chief of Washington bur. of The Public Ledger, Phila., 1919-22; later conducted the Frederic William Wile column of news-correspondence from Washington; editorial staff writer Washington Evening Star. Polit. analyst for Nat. Broadcasting Co., 1923-28, Columbia Broadcasting System, 1929-38. First radio commentator on tra,nsatlnntic news events, at London Naval Conf., 1930; radio commentator from World Disarmament Conf., Geneva, 1932. Author: Our German Cousins, 1909; Men Around the Kaiser, 1913 (pub. in England, America and Germany); The Assault, 1916; Explaining the Britishers, 1918; Emile Berliner, Maker of the Microphone, 1926. Editor in chief: A Century of Industrial Progress, 1928; News Is Where You Find It (autobiography), 1939. Home: Washington, D.C. Died Apr. 7, 1941.

WILEY, HENRY ARIOSTO naval officer; b. Troy, Ala., Jan. 31, 1867; grad. U.S. Naval Acad., 1888. Ensign, July 1, 1890; promoted through grades to capt., Apr. 23, 1915. Served on Maple, Spanish-Am. War, 1898; comd. Standish, 1905; at U.S. Naval Acad., 1905-06; on Constellation, 1906-07; exec. officer, Kentucky, 1907-09; with Bur. of Navigation, Navy Dept., 1909-12; comd. Monterey, 1912, Saratoga, 1912-13; mem. Bd. Inspection and Survey Ships, Navy Dept., 1914-15; comd. New Jersey, 1916; apptd. comdr. Wyoming, June 17, 1916; served with 6th Battle Squadron Brit. Grand Fleet; temp. rear admiral, 1918; comdr. destroyers, Pacific Fleet, 1919-20; vice-admiral, 1923-25; Gen. Bd., 1925-27; comdr. U.S. Fleet with rank of admiral, 1927-29; retired Sept. 1929. Apptd. mem. Textile Labor Relations Bd., Sept. 1934; also mem. Steel Bd. Apptd. mem. U.S. Maritime Commn. 1936 for period of 4 yrs. Home: 1870 Wyoming Av. N.W., Washington, D.C. Died May 20, 1943.

WILEY, HERBERT V(ICTOR) naval officer (ret.); b. Wheeling, Mo., May 16, 1891; s. Joel Augustine and Minnie Alice (Carey) W.; B.S., U.S. Naval Acad., 1915; m. Marie F. Scroggie, Oct. 20, 1917 (dec. 1930); children—Gordon Scroggie, David Carey, Marie Elinor; m. 2d Charlotte Mayfield Weeden, Sept. 21, 1935. Commd. ensign U.S. Navy, 1915, and advanced through grades to rear adm., 1947; jr. officer, Pacific fleet, 1915-17; destroyer duty, 1917-21; instr., Dept. of Electricity, U.S. Naval Acad., 1921-23; service on lighter than air airships, Shenandoah and Los Angeles, 1923-30, battleship U.S.S. Tennessee, 1930-31, airship, Akron (only officer to survive crash of Akron), 1932-33; comdr. airship Macon, 1934-35; served on cruisers U.S.S. Cincinnati, Pensacola, and cargo transport Sirius, 1933-37; instr. English Dept., U.S. Naval Acad., 1937-39; served on U.S.S. Mississippi, 1940-41; comdr. destroyer squadron, Asiatic fleet, P.I., Java, Australia, 1941-42; head, dept. of electricity, U.S. Naval Acad., 1942-43; comdr. U.S.S. West Virginia, 1944-45, Atlantic fleet training unit, Guantanamo Bay, Cuba, 1945; ret. with rank of rear adm., Jan. 1, 1947; asst. to dean of engring., U. of Calif., 1947-—. Awarded Navy Cross, 1944, Bronze Star, 1945, Navy and Marine Corps medal (for saving life of fellow officer), 1935. Mem. U.S. Naval Inst. Episcopalian. Club: Union League (San Francisco) Pioneer in airship operations, developing mooring methods, airplane hook-on and carrying, 1923-30. Home: 43 Parkside Dr., Berkeley, Cal. Died Apr. 28, 1954; buried Golden Gate Nat. Cemetery, San Bruno, Cal.

WILEY, JOHN ALEXANDER brig. gen. U.S.V.; b. Allegheny County, Pa., Sept. 3, 1843; common sch. edn.; pvt. 8th Pa. reserves, vol. corps inf., in Army of Potomac, 1861-64; chief clerk q.-m.'s dept., 1864-65; extensive oil-producer after Civil War; mayor of Franklin, Pa., col. 16th regt., Pa. Nat. Guard; brig. gen. same, 1887-98; apptd., May 27, 1898, brig. gen., U.S.V.; served in war with Spain in command 1st brigade, 2d div., 1st army corps; 3d div., 1st army corps; 2d div., 1st army corps. Apptd. by gov. of Pa. to locate the lines of battle of the Pa. troops at Antietam battlefield. Home: Franklin, Pa. Died 1909.

WILKES, CHARLES naval officer; b. N.Y.C., Apr. 3, 1798; s. John De Ponthieu and Mary (Seton) W.; m. Jane Jeffrey Renwick, Apr. 16, 1826; m. 2d, Mary H. (Lynch) Bolton, Oct. 3, 1854; 4 children. Apptd. midshipman U.S. Navy, 1818; 1st cruised Mediterranean in ship Guerriere, later in Pacific in ship Franklin; engaged in surveying Narragansett Bay, 1832-33; in charge of Depot of Charts and Instruments, Washington, D.C., 1833; commanded Porpoise, engaged in survey St. George's Bank and Savannah River, 1837-38; on expdn. to explore coast of Antarctic continent, islands of Pacific Ocean, Am. N.W. coast, 1838-42; awarded Founder's medal Royal Geog. Soc. of London, 1847; tried by court martial and sentenced to public reprimand for illegal punishment of his men, 1842; commd. comdr., 1843, capt., 1855; overhauled Brit. mail steamer Trent in Bahama Channel, 1861, took from vessel Confederate commrs. James M. Mason and John Slidell, brought them to Boston, viewed as hero, congratulated by Sec. of Navy Gideon Welles, thanked by U.S. Ho. of Reps., event was actually act of war on Eng., case disallowed and Mason and Slidell sent on to Eng.; in command James River flotilla, 1862; transferred to Potomac flotilla; made acting rear adm., 1862; placed on ret. list as captain, 1862, commodore, 1863; court martialed, guilty of disobedience, disrespect, insubordination, conduct unbecoming an officer, sentenced to reprimand and suspended from duty 3 years, 1864; commd. rear adm. (ret.), 1866. Author: Narrative of the United States Exploring Expedition, 5 vols., 1844; Western America, 1849; Theory of the Zodiacal Light, 1857; On the Circulation of Oceans, 1859. Died Feb. 8, 1877.

WILKES, JOHN ret. naval officer; b. May 26, 1895; entered USN, 1912, grad. U.S. Naval Acad., Annapolis, 1916; m. Winifred Jarvis; 1 son, John. Advanced through grades to rear adm., 1943; stationed in Pacific at outbreak of World War II, escaped from Corregidor aboard submarine Swordfish, then reassembled U.S. underseas forces from base in Java; retired 1951. Decorated D.S.M., Legion of Merit. Address: Navy Dept., Washington 25. Died July 20, 1957; buried Arlington Nat. Cemetery.*

WILKINS, RAYMOND SANGER, judge; b. Salem, Mass., May 24,21891; s. Samuel Herbert and Marietta Burke (Rowell) W.; A.B., Harvard, 1912, LL.B., 1915; Doctor Juridicial Sci. (hon.), Suffolk U., 1951; LL.D., Northeastern U., 1952, Western N.E. Coll., 1956, Boston U., 1957, Tufts U., 1960, Am. Internat. College, 1963, Harvard, 1964; J.D., Portia Law Sch., 1960; m. Mary Louisa Aldrich, Sept. 22, 1923 (dec.); children—Raymond Sanger, David (dec.), Herbert Putnam; m. 2d, Katharine S. Choate, Nov. 18, 1956 (dec. Nov. 1959); m. 3d, Georgie E. Hebbard, August 7, 1965. Admitted to Mass. bar, 1915; and practiced in Boston, 1915-44, with Storey, Thorndike, Palmer & Dodge, later known as Palmer, Dodge, Wilkins & Davis; apptd. associate justice Supreme Judicial Ct. Mass., 1944; chief justice, 1956-70. Selectman, Winchester, Mass., 1935-37, moderator, 1940-43; mem. gov's council, Mass. 1941-43. Served as 2d lt., 1st lt., and capt., 301st F.A., A.E.F., 1917-19. Trustee Soldiers Home in Mass., 1942-44, Boston Athenaeum; Boston Symphony Orchestra, Peabody Mus. Former overseer Harvard; mem. corp. Northeastern University, Massachusetts Institute of Technology. Mem. council Am. Law Institute; member Harvard Law School Assn. (former pres.), Am. Antiquarian Soc., Am., Mass., Boston, Middlesex and Essex bar assns., Boston Legal Aid Soc. (hon. pres.), Colonial Soc. Mass., Mass. Hist. Soc., Vets. Fgn. Wars, Am. Legion, Phi Beta Kappa. Unitarian. Clubs: Harvard, Union, Odd Volumes, Somerset, Tavern (Boston); Myopia Hunt (Hamilton). Home: Boston MA Died May 1971.

WILKINSON, CHARLES FORE, JR., educator, physician; b. College Park, Ga., Mar. 30, 1912; s. Charles Fore and Martha Inez (Hardin) W.; B.S., Ga. Sch. Tech., 1932; grad. study U. N.C., 1932-33; M.D., Emory U., 1937; m. Frances Elizabeth Wallace, Apr. 22, 1939; children—Charles Fore, Martha Wallace, Robert Gage. Intern dept. internal medicine U. Mich. Hosp., 1937-38, asst. resident, 1938-39, resident, instr., Upjohn fellow clin. investigation, 1939-40; asst. prof. internal medicine, coordinator grad. med. edn. U. Mich., 1946-49; civilian cons. internal medicine Percy Jones Gen. Hosp., Battle Creek, Mich., 1946-49; asso. dir. div. medicine W. K. Kellogg Found., Battle Creek, 1948-49; prof., chmn. department of medicine, post-grad. med. sch. N.Y. U., N.Y. City, since 1949; vis. physician, dir. 4th Med. N.Y. U. div. Bellevue Hosp., med. service U. Hosp., 1949-—; cons. in internal medicine, Manhattan V.A. Hospital. Served as 1st lt. to col. with M.C., A.U.S., 1940-46. Diplomate Am. Bd. Internal Medicine. Fellow N.Y. Acad. Medicine, A.A.A.S., A.C.P.; mem. Harvey Soc., Am. Fedn. Clin. Research, Am. Genetic Assn., N.Y. Medico-Surgical Society, American Therapeutic Soc., Society for Experimental Biology and Medicine, American Society of Human Genetics, Am. Soc. Study of Arteriosclerosis, Am., N.Y. heart assns., Soc. Biol. Research, Sigma Xi. Author tech. and sci. articles med. jours. Home: 24 Ellery Lane, Westport, Conn. Office: New York University Post-Graduate Medical School, 550 First Av., N.Y.C. Died Sept. 29, 1959.

WILKINSON, HOWARD SARGENT clergyman; b. Philadelphia, Pa.; s. Zimri and Emma Frances (Garwood) W.; A.B. and A.M., Dickinson Coll.; S.T.B., Boston U. Sch. of Theol., B.D., Episcopal Theol. Sch., Cambridge, Mass.; D.D., U. of Southern Calif. and Dickinson Coll.; m. Helen Adams Treadwell; 1 dau., Madeleine. Deacon P.E. Ch., 1912, priest, 1912; asst. rector, St. Paul Ch., New Haven, Conn., 1912, minister in charge, 1912-13; rector Emmanuel Ch., West Roxbury, Boston, Mass., 1913-31; asst. to the dean, Cathedral of the Incarnation, Garden City, L.I., N.Y., 1931-36; rector St. Thomas' Ch., Washington, D.C., since Dec. 1936. Sec. of standing com., mem. exec. council, pres. of clericus and alternate deputy to Gen. Conv., all in Diocese of Washington. Served as captain, chaplain, U.S. Army, now maj., chaplain, O.R.C. Mason. Sojourner. Clubs: University, Torch, Cosmopolitan, Army and Navy Country Club. Contbr. to jours. Home: 1320 New Hampshire. Av. Office: 1772 Church St., Washington, D.C. Died Aug. 1, 1948.

WILKINSON, JAMES army officer, gov. La.; b. Calvert County, Md., 1757; s. Joseph Wilkinson; m. Ann Biddle; m. 2d, Celestine Laveau (Trudeau), Mar. 5, 1810; at least 3 children including 2 daus., 1 son, James B. Commd. capt. Continental Army, 1776; with Benedict Arnold in retreat from Montreal to Albany, 1776; a.d.c. to Gen. Gates in battles of Trenton and Princeton, 1776; served as lt. col. under George Washington, 1777; brevetted brig. gen. by Continental Congress, 1777; sec. bd. of war, 1778; involved in Conway cabal (intrigue in Continental Congress to remove George Washington as comdr.-in-chief of armed forces), forced to resign commn., 1778 brig. gen. Pa. Militia, 1783; elected to Pa. Assembly, 1783; involved in trading venture in Ky., 1784; took oath of allegiance to Spanish monarch to aid his own financial position; mem. Ky. Conv., 1788; led a force of volunteers against Indians, 1791; commd. lt. col. U.S. Army, 1791; brig. gen. under Gen. Wayne, 1792, took over Detroit from British, 1796; became ranking officer U.S. Army at death of Gen. Anthony Wayne, 1796; shared (with Gov. William C. C. Claiborne) honor of taking possession of La. Purchase, 1803; gov. La., 1805-06; chief witness against Aaron Burr at his trial for conspiracy with Spain, narrowly escaped indictment by grand jury, acquitted, stood 2d ct. martial trial, 1811, again acquitted; commd. maj. gen., 1813; commanded Am. forces on Canadian front, made a fiasco of campaign against Montreal, stood 3d ct. martial trial, circa 1814, acquitted; received honorable discharge, 1815; tried to collect claims for Mexico's creditors, also indirectly represented Am. Bible Soc. in Mexico, 1821. Author: Memoirs of my Own Times, 3 vols., 1816. Died Dec. 28, 1825; buried Ch. of Archangel San Miguel, Mexico City, Mexico.

WILKINSON, JOHN naval officer; b. Norfolk, Va., Nov. 6, 1821; s. Jesse Wilkinson. Commd. midshipman U.S. Navy, 1837. Ordered to South Atlantic in ship Independence; assigned to sloop Boston, 1840; passed midshipman, 1843; promoted lt., 1850; in command steamer Corwin collecting data for charts of waters on Fla. coast including Bahamas, 1859-61; resigned to enter Confederate Navy, 1861; ordered to ship Louisiana, 1861, as ranking officer ordered her destroyed when capture was certain, 1862; captured and exchanged, 1862; served spl. duty in England, purchased and commanded blockade-runner Giraffe (which he rechristened (Robert E. Lee), successful over Naussau to Wilmington (N.C.) route; assumed leadership in unsuccessful expdn. to capture Johnson's Island in Lake Erie and release Confederate prisoners, 1863; in command of ship Chickamauga; ended services with command blockade-runner Chameleon; engaged in business in Nova Scotia after Civil War. Author: Narrative of a Blockade-Runner, 1877. Died Annapolis, Md., Dec. 29, 1891.

WILKINSON, THEODORE S. naval officer; b. Annapolis, Md., Dec. 22, 1888; s. Ernest and Gulielina Caroline (Bostick) W.; student St. Pauls School, Concord, N.H., 1902-05; B.S., U.S. Naval Acad., 1909; M.S., George Washington U., 1912; m. Catherine

Dorsey Harlow, Dec. 17, 1918; children—Ann Harlow, Joan Susannah, Theodore S. Commd. ensign, U.S. Navy, 1911, and advanced through the grades to rear adm., Nov. 1941; served as experimental officer, Bureau of Ordnance, Navy Dept., World War I; sec. Navy General Board, 1931-34; chief of staff to comdt. Scouting Force and Hawaiian Detachment, 1939-41; comd. U.S.S. Mississippi, 1941; dir. of naval intelligence, Oct. 1941-July 1942, comdr. Battleship Div. Two, August 1942-Jan. 1943, deputy comdr. South Pacific, Jan. 1943-June 1943; comdr. Amphibious Force, South Pacific, July 15, 1943; comdr. 3d Amphibious Force, June 1944-Nov. 1945; mem. joint strategic Survey Com. Joint Chiefs of Staff, Jan.-Feb. 1946. Decorated Medal of Honor, D.S.M. (3); Companion of Bath (New Zealand). Sec. Navy letter of commendation for World War services. Mem. Am. Chem. Soc., Phi Sigma Kappa. Clubs: Metropolitan, Chevy Chase, Army and Navy, Army and Navy Country (Washington, D.C.); New York Yacht; Racquet (Phila.). Home: 3043 N. St., Washington. Died Feb. 21, 1946; buried in Arlington National Cemetery.

WILLARD, ARTHUR LEE naval officer; b. Kirksville, Mo., Feb. 21, 1870; grad. U.S. Naval Acad., 1891. Commd. ensign, July 1, 1893; promoted through grades to rear admiral, June 1924. Served on Machias, Spanish-Am. War, 1898, Maine, 1903-06; duty Naval Gun Factory, Washington, D.C., 1906-08; on Idaho, 1908-10; duty Navy Yard, Washington, D.C., 1910-13; comd. Hancock, 1913-15; apptd. capt. of yard, Navy Yard, Washington, D.C., June 3, 1915; later vice adm. comdg. scouting force, U.S. Fleet; retired, Mar. 1, 1934. Home: Kirksville, Mo. Died Apr. 7, 1935.

WILLARD, DEFOREST P. orthopedic surgeon; b. Phila., Feb. 20, 1884; s. Dr. DeForest and Elizabeth (Porter) W.; B.S., U. of Pa., 1905; M.D., 1908; m. Margaretta Miller, Dec. 11, 1926. Asst., orthopedic service, Univ. Hosp., also Orthopedic Hosp., Phila., 1910-17; orthopedic surgeon, Graduate, Bryn Mawr and Abington hosps., 1920-47; cons. in orthopedics, Pa., Babies and Chestnut Hill hosps.; vice dean orthopedics Grad. Med. Sch., U. of Pa., 1920-47, prof. orthopedics 1926-47, emeritus. Commd. 1st lt., M.C., U.S. Army, 1917-19; with A.E.F., France and England; disch. with rank lt. col., Army Res. Corps, 1935. Mem. Am. Orthopedic Assn. (sec. 1912-33; pres. 1935), Am. Surg. Assn., Am. Acad. Orthopedic Surgeons. Internat. Orthopedic Assn., A.M.A., Phila. Acad. Surgery, Phila. Coll. Physicians, Delta Psi. Clubs: Philadelphia, University (Phila.); Gulph Mills Golf. Contbr. numerous articles to med. jours. Home: "Redleaf," 514 Lancaster Av., Wynnewood, Pa. Office: 1726 Spruce St., Phila. 3. Died Dec. 1957.

WILLARD, IRA FARNUM banker, lawyer; b. Union, S.C., July 16, 1911; s. George and Mae (Sanders) W.; student N. Greenville Acad., 1925-29, U.S.C., 1930-34; LL.B., Southeastern U., 1938; m. Mary Lewis, Sept. 22, 1934; children—Elizabeth, Ira F., George J., Frances. With U.S. Geol. Survey, 1934-35, gen. accounting office U.S. Govt., 1935-41; admitted to S.C. bar, 1945; practiced in Spartanburg, 1947; city mgr., Hopewell, Va., 1948-52, Alexandria, 1952-56, Coral Gables, Fla., 1956-58; city mgr. Miami, Fla., 1959-60; pres. City Nat. Bank, Coral Gables, Fla., 1960-61, Key Biscayne Bank, Miami, Tom Wood Equipment Corp., Miami and Tampa. Chmn. health adv. bd. Dade County; Fla. dir. People to People Program. Served from 2d lt. to lt. col., Q.M.C., AUS, 1941-47. Deocrated Legion of Merit. Mem. League Va. Municipalities (past pres.), Internat. City Mgrs. Assn., Va., D.C., S.C. bar assns., Am. Soc. Pub. Adminstrn. (pres. So. Fla.), Am., Fla. bankers assns., Fla., Miami-Dade, Coral Gables chambers commerce, Am. Legion. Episcopalian. Mason (32 deg., Shriner, Jester), Rotarian. Home: 225 Sunrise Dr., Key Biscayne, Fla. Office: Key Biscayne Bank, Miami, Fla. Died Nov. 21, 1965; buried Arlington.

WILLCOX, CORNÉLIS DE WITT army officer, author; b. Geneva, Switzerland, Feb. 26, 1861; s. Cyprian Porter and Mary Frances (Smythe) W.; A.B., U. of Ga., 1880; grad. U.S. Mil. Acad., 1885; grad. U.S. Arty. Sch., 1892; U. of Grenoble, France. 1913; m. Mary Addison West, Oct. 31, 1888 (dec.). Commd. 2d lt. 2d Arty., U.S. Army, June 14, 1885; promoted through grades to maj., June 25, 1907; prof. U.S. Mil. Acad., with rank of lt. col., Sept. 28, 1910; promoted col., July 1, 1914; retired, Feb. 26, 1925. Capt. a.a.g. U.S. Vols.. May 12, 1898-Apr. 7, 1899; served in Santiago campaign, 1898; gen. staff corps, 1906-10; on mission to Germany, 1907, to witness fall maneuvers of German Army; chief of mil. information division, Manila, 1908-10. Serving with A.E.F. in France, 1917-18, as chief of Am. Mil. Mission at French Gen. Hdqrs. Episcopalian. Hon. mem. Soc. of the Cincinnati in Ga. Officier d'Académie, Officier de la Légion d'Honneur, Croix de Guerre with palm, 1918 (France); Comdr. Order of Sacred Treasure (Japan). Author: A French-English Military Technical Dictionary (pub. by War Dept.), 1900; Head Hunters of Northern Luzon, 1912; A Reader of Scientific and Technical Spanish, 1913; War French, 1917. Translator: (from the Spanish) Letters of Montiano, during siege of St. Augustine, 1909; Spanish Official Account of Attack on Colony of Georgia, 1913. Co-editor International Military Digest, 1915. Died Jan. 1938.

WILLCOX, ORLANDO BOLIVAR brig. gen. U.S.A., retired, April 16, 1887; b. Detroit, Mich., Apr. 16, 1823; s. Charles and Almira W.; grad. West Point, 1847; lt. 4th U.S. arty. and fought in Mexican, Seminole and other Indian campaigns and Civil war; col. 1st Mich. inf. vols.; was at the capture of Alexandria, Va., 1st Bull Run, South Mountain, Antietam, and subsequent battles with Army of the Potomac, in East Tenn., and elsewhere, becoming brig. gen. and bvt. maj. gen. vols. After war apptd. col. 12th and 29th inf. regulars; brig. gen., Oct. 13, 1886; received Congressional medal of honor, and comd. several mil. depts., the Soldiers' Home, etc. Author: Shoepac Recollections, by Walter March, 1854; Faca, an Army Memoir, by Maj. March, 1857. Home: Washington, D.C. Died 1907.

WILLETT, MARINUS army officer, mayor N.Y.C.; b. Jamaica, L.I., N.Y., July 31, 1740; s. Edward and Aletta (Clowes) W.; attended Kings Coll. (now Columbia); m. Mary Dearsee, Apr. 2, 1760; m. 2d, Mrs. Susannah Vardill, Oct. 3, 1793; m. 3d Margaret Bancker, circa 1799; at least 5 children. A wealthy mcht., N.Y.C.; served as 2d lt. Oliver De Lancey's N.Y. Regt.; leader Sons of Liberty, early supporter of Am. Revolution; helped seize arms from N.Y.C. arsenal, 1775; became 1st lt., 1st N.Y. Regt., 1775-76, lt. col. 3d N.Y. Regt., 1776; voted sword by Congress after courageous defense of Ft. Stanwix, 1777; joined Gen. Washington's army, 1778; sheriff City and County of N.Y., 1784-88, 92-96; concluded Creek Indian treaty, 1790; mayor N.Y.C., 1807-11. Died Cedar Grove, N.Y., Aug. 22, 1830.

WILLIAMS, ALBERT FRANK lawyer; b. Appleton City, Mo., July 18, 1876; s. Luke Allen and Jennie Jane (Wylie) W.; grad. high sch., Lamar, Mo., 1894; m. Kate Weisenbarker, Dec. 18, 1904; children—Margaret A. (dec.), June C. Admitted to bar, 1897; pracitìced, Columbus, Kan. Pres. Al. F. Williams Drug Corp. Co. atty. Cherokee Co., Kan., 1903-07; U.S. dist. atty. for Kan., by apptmt. of Pres. Harding, 1921, reapptd. by Pres. Coolidge, 1926. Mem. Am., Kan. State bar assns. Served as 1st lt. Co. F, 22d Kan. Vols., Spanish-Am. War. Republican. Methodist. Mason (32 deg., Shriner, life member Imperial Council); past president Internat. High Twelve Clubs (Masonic); K.P., Elk, Woodman. Home: 2506 W. 10th St., Topeka, Kan. Office: New England Bldg., Topeka, Kan. Died Sept. 11, 1958.

WILLIAMS, ALEXANDER ELLIOT army officer; b. Linden, N.C., Mar. 12, 1875; s. William L. and Mary Eliza (Elliot) W.; grad. U.S. Mil. Acad., 1898, Army War Coll., 1923; m. Janie McBryde, Dec. 29, 1899. Commd. 2d lt. inf., 1898; advanced through grades to col., detailed brig. gen., Q.M.C., 1920-21. In Santiago campaign, 1898, and in Cuba until 1900; in Philippines, 1900-02; detailed in Q.M.C., 1907, and in charge water transportation in Philippines; q.m. Militia Bur., Washington, 1916-17; in charge depot at Montoir, France, 1918-19; detailed as chief q.m. 3d Army, 1919, and went into Germany; asst. to q.m. gen., Washington, 1919-22; at War Coll., 1922-23, Field Arty. Sch., 1923-24; chief of staff, 82d Div., 1924-26; q.m. duties, 1926-30; handled pilgrimage of War Mothers, N.Y., 1930-31; apptd. asst. to q.m. gen. for 4 yrs. from 1931, with rank of brig. gen. Presbyn. Clubs: Army and Navy (Washington), Army and Navy (Manila). Author: Manual for Quartermaster, 1915; Company Supply Manual, 1916. Address: War Dept., Washington. Died Mar. 1948.

WILLIAMS, ALFORD JOSEPH, JR., aviator; b. N.Y.C., July 26, 1896; s. Alford Joseph and Emma Elizabeth (Madden) W.; A.B., Forham U., 1915; LL.B., Georgetown U., 1925; m. Alice Helen Ort Toomey; 1 foster son, John E. Pitcher N.Y. Giants, Nat. League baseball team, 1916-17; enlisted as aviator USN, 1917, research aviator, 1917-30, advanced through grades to lt.; tested planes, developed aerial acrobatics for air combat, specialized in hish speed research; Navy entrant Pulitzer Trophy Races, winner 1923, speed 243 mph; established world's absolute speed record of 266.7 mph in 1923; held Am. speed record 8 consecutive yrs.; unofcl. world's speed records, 302 mph in 1925, 322 mph in 1927; developed improvements for standard combat planes; performer Nat. Air Races, frequent winner Aerobatic trophy; headed 1st Internat. Aerobatic Team, Chgo., 1930; winner trophy for outstanding individual airmanship; Rickenbacker Airmanship trophy, Miami, 1935; inspected European Aero. centers, 1930-38; inaugurated ann. Lightplane Air Cavalcades to Miami Air Maneuvers, 1936-41; weekly commentator NBC radio Flying With Al Williams, 1933-36; pioneered establishment separate air force; pilot Gulfhawk aerobatic-fighter enshrined in Smithsonian Instn.; lectr. Nat. War Coll., NACA, Inst. Aero. Sci., the mil. univs., others; retired to cattle ranch The Eyrie, Elizabeth City, N.C., 1949; admitted to N.Y. bar, 1926; lectr. aero. engring. U. Pitts.; mgr. aviation dept. Gulf Oil Corp., 1933-49. Served as major U.S. Marine Corps Res., 1935-40. Decorated Distinguished Flying Cross (USN); trophy of Am. Soc. M.E., 1929. Comdr. Scripps-Howard Jr. Aviators numbering 485,-000; daily aviation columnist Scripps-Howard newspapers. Mem. N.Y. State Bar Assn., Nat. Aero. Assn. Author: Airpower, 1940; contbr. nat. periodicals and aero. jours. Inventor vertical dive-bombing, 1923. Address: The Eyrie, R.D. 1, Elizabeth City, N.C. Died June 15, 1958; buried Arlington Nat. Cemetery.

WILLIAMS, ALFRED HICKS, metals co. exec.; b. Nashville, Nov. 28, 1912; s. Alfred H. and Elise (Lipscomb) W.; student U. Va.; m. Virginia Nunn Eady, Dec. 30, 1944; children—Lawrence L., Keith L., Elizabeth Eady. Sales exec. Brown Williamson Tobacco Co., 1932-39; gen. mgr. Canada Dry Bottling Co., Louisville, 1939-42; v.p., dir., gen. sales mgr. Consider H. Willett Co., Louisville, 1946-54; v.p. Reynolds Metals Co., Richmond, Va., 1954-72. Mgr. industry and commerce div. Louisville Community Chest, 1955-56; mem. Louisville Met. Sewer Commn., 1955-58. Served to capt., Tank Corps, AUS, 1942-46. Decorated D.S.C., Bronze Star, Purple Heart. Clubs: Louisville Country, Pendennis, Harmony Landing Country, River, Wynn-Stay, Valley (Louisville); Country of Virginia, Deep Run Hunt, Commonwealth (Richmond). Home: Richmond VA Died 1972.

WILLIAMS, ALPHEUS STARKEY army officer, congressman; b. Saybrook, Conn., Sept. 20, 1810; s. Ezra and Hepzibah (Starkey) W.; grad. Yale, 1831, attended Yale Law Sch. 3 years; m. Jane Hereford (Lained) Pierson, Jan. 1838; m. 2d, Martha Ann (Conant) Tellman, Sept. 17, 1873; 7 children. Probate judge, Detroit, 1840-44; published Detroit Daily Advertiser, 1844-47; served as lt. col. 1st Mich. U.S. Volunteers, Mexican War, 1847-48; postmaster, Detroit, 1849-53; pres. Mich. Oil Co., 1853-61; apptd. brig. gen. Mich. Militia, in charge of camp instrn. Ft. Wayne, Detroit, 1861; commd. brig. gen. U.S. Volunteers, 1861; in charge of mil. dist in Ark. until 1866; minister resident to Republic of Salvador, 1866-69; mem. U.S. Ho. of Reps. (Democrat) from Mich., 44th-45th congresses, 1875-78, chmn. com. on D.C. Died Washington, D.C., Dec. 21, 1878.

WILLIAMS, ARCHIBALD HUNTER ARRINGTON congressman; b. nr. Louisburg, N.C., Oct. 22, 1842; attended Emory and Henry Coll. Enlisted as pvt. Confederate Army, during Civil War, served with Army of No. Va., 4 years, rose to capt. of his co.; wounded in Battle of Gettysburg; engaged in farming and retail trade, Oxford, N.C.; pres., Oxford & Henderson R.R.; mem. N.C. Ho. of Reps., 1883-85; mem. U.S. Ho. of Reps. (Democrat) from N.C., 52d Congress, 1891-93. Died Chase City, Va., Sept. 5, 1895; buried Elmwood Cemetery, Oxford.

WILLIAMS, BENJAMIN congressman; b. nr. Smithfield, N.C., Jan. 1, 1751; attended country schs. Engaged in farming; mem. N.C. Provincial Congress, 1774-75; served as 2d lt. Continental Army during Revolutionary War, promoted capt., 1776, promoted col. for gallantry at Guilford (N.C.), 1781; mem. N.C. Ho. of Commons, 1779, 85, 89; mem. N.C. Senate, 1781, 84, 86, 88; mem. U.S. Ho. of Reps. from N.C., 3d Congress, 1793-95; gov. N.C., 1799-1802, 07-08. Died Moore County, N.C., July 20, 1814; buried nr. Carbonton, N.C.

WILLIAMS, CHARLES MALLORY dermatologist; born Brooklyn, N.Y., Oct. 16, 1872; s. Charles Phelps and Fanny Elizabeth (Mallory) W.; A.B., Brooklyn Collegiate and Poly. Inst., 1890; Ph.B., Yale, 1892, post-grad. work, 1892-94; M.D., Coll. Physicians and Surgeons (Columbia U.), 1898; hon. D.Sc., U. of Vt., 1932; m. Margaret Dows Worcester, Feb. 25, 1904 (died March 30, 1941); children—Mary Low (wife of Dr. Macdonald Dick, of Duke U.), Margaret (wife of Billings B. Fairbrother); m. 2d, Edith Bramhall Cullis, Apr. 14, 1942. Intern Roosevelt Hosp., 1898-1900, Sloane Hospital 1900; specialized in dermatology since 1902; served in dispensaries Vanderbilt Clinic, North-Western Dispensary, and Bellevue Hospital, and New York Skin and Cancer Hospital; prof. dermatology, University of Vermont, 1913-30; attending physician New York Skin and Cancer Hospital, 1920-34, president med. bd. same, 1928-34; served as consulting dermatologist Memorial Hosp.; prof. clin. dermatology and syphilology, Post-Grad. Med. Sch. (Columbia), 1934-35; retired, 1935. Entered U.S. Army as 1st lt. M.C., 1917; advanced to lt. col., 1919; originated and put into practice segregation of venereal cases in separate battalion, in training camps; with 79th Div. in Meuse-Argonne; citation for services in World War I. Mem. A.M.A., Am. Dermatol. Assn. (pres. 1934-35; dir. 1935-39), New London County (Conn.) Medical Society, Medical Advisory Board (Connecticut), Society Colonial Wars, Century Assn. Republican. Episcopalian. Mason (32 deg.). Clubs: Yale (New York); Graduate, Beaumont Med. (New Haven); Wadawanuck Country (Stonington, Conn.). Contbr. on dermatology, especially in connection with fungus diseases. Home: Stonington, Conn. Died Nov. 12, 1951; buried Stonington, Conn.

WILLIAMS, CHARLES SUMNER naval officer; b. Saratoga Co., N.Y., Sept. 8, 1856; s. John F. and Anna E. W.; ed. U. of Wis. and U.S. Naval Acad. (non-grad.); m. Anna Emily Bayard, Dec. 9, 1885; 1 son, Charles Sumner. Apptd. asst. p.m., rank of ensign, June 16, 1880; promoted through grades to commodore, and retired Sept. 8, 1920; rear adm. (temp.), July 1, 1918. Served on battleship Newark, Spanish-Am. War, 1898; fleet p.m. in Newark, 1902-04; purchasing pay officer, Boston, 1904-07; gen. storekeeper, Navy Yard, Boston, 1907-10; Navy Pay Office, Boston, 1910-13; in charge Navy Disbursing Office, Washington, D.C., 1913-14; in charge Provisions and Clothing Depot, Navy Yard,

New York, 1914-17, South Brooklyn, N.Y., 1917-18; in comd. Fleet Supply Base, Brooklyn, 1918-Sept. 8, 1920. Home: Summit, N.J. Died Sept. 4, 1936.

WILLIAMS, CHARLES URQUHART lawyer; b. Henrico Co., Va., Dec. 27, 1840; s. Charles Bruce and Ann Mercer (Hackley) W.; ed. pvt. tutor and various schs. until 1857; in mercantile business, 1857-58; entered law class in U. of Va., 1860, but before graduation entered C.S.A., Apr. 1861, and served as pvt., lt. and capt. until surrender of Gen. R. E. Lee; admitted to Va. bar, Oct. 1865; m. Alice Davenport Williams, Aug. 27, 1867. In practice, 1865 to July 1, 1907. Mem. Va. Ho. of Rep., 1875-76, 1876-77. Home: Strawberry Hill, Va. Died 1910.

WILLIAMS, CLARENCE STEWART naval officer (ret.); b. Springfield, O., Oct. 7, 1863; s. Orson Bennett and Pamela (Floyd) W.; B.S., U.S. Naval Acad., 1814; m. Anna Marie Miller, June 6, 1888; 1 son, Edgar Miller. Commd. ensign, U.S. Navy, 1886, and promoted through grades to rear adm., 1918, vice adm. (temp), 1919, ret. with rank rear adm., 1927, vice adm. (ret.), 1930, adm. (ret.), 1942; pres. U.S. Naval War Coll., 1922-25; comdr. U.S. torpedo boat Gwin, 1898, U.S.S. Albany, 1910-11, U.S.S. Rhode Island (Mex. campaign), 1912-15; chief of staff, Battleship Force, Atlantic Fleet, 1916-17, Battleship Force 2, 1917; comdr. Battle Squadron 1, Pacific fleet, 1919, Battleship Force, Pacific Fleet, 1920; comdr. in chief U.S. Asiatic Fleet, 1925-27. Mem. party which pioneered hydrographic survey for cable sta. on Midway Islands, 1901. Decorated D.S.M., Spanish Campaign, Cuban Pacification, Mexican Campagn, Victory and Yangtze Service medals. Mem. U.S. Naval Inst. Club: Army-Navy (Washington). Address: Meadowbrook Heights, Charlottesville, Va. Died Oct. 24, 1951; buried Arlington Nat. Cemetery.

WILLIAMS, CLARK banker; b. Canandaigua, N.Y., May 2, 1870; s. George N. and Abigail Stanley (Clark) W.; A.B., Williams Coll., 1892; LL.D., 1939; LL.D., The Citadel, 1933; m. Anna Plater, April 29, 1897. With Guaranty Trust Co., New York, 1892-94; clerk, asst. treas., treas. and v.p. U.S. Mortgage & Trust Co., 1894-1905; organizer, 1905, mng. v.p., 1905-07, Columbia Trust Co.; supt. of banks State of N.Y., 1907-09; comptroller state of N.Y., 1909-11; pres. Winsor Trust Co., New York, 1911-13; apptd. pres. Industrial Finance Corp. (owner "Morris Plan" of industrial loans and investments), June 1914. Apptd. Am. Red Cross rep. with 1st Div. A.E.F., Apr. 1918; dir. army field service, Am. Red Cross, with A.E.F., rank of major, 1919. Mem. firm Clark Williams & Co. (financial), N.Y., 1919-39; mem. firm Winthrop, Mitchell & Co. since 1939. Commd. lt. col. O.R.C., U.S. Army, 1925. Decorated Chevalier French Legion of Honor; recipient Algernon Sidney Sullivan award, 1938. Trustee emeritus of Williams Coll. Congregationalist. Mem. S.R., Loyal Legion, Kappa Alpha (Williams). Clubs: Union, University, Union League, Williams, Recess, Midday. Author: The Story of a Grateful Citizen (an autobiography in 2 vols.). Home: Field Point Park, Greenwich, Conn.* Died Dec. 18, 1946.

WILLIAMS, CLIFTON CURTIS, JR., astronaut; b. Mobile, Sept. 26, 1932; s. Clifton Curtis and Gertrude (Medicus) W.; student Spring Hill Coll., 1949-51; B.M.E., Auburn U., 1954; m. Jane Elizabeth Lansche, July 1, 1964. Commd. 2d lt., USMC, 1954, advanced through grades to maj., 1963; naval aviator, 1956-60; test pilot Naval Air Test Center, Patuxent River, Md., 1960-63; astronaut Manned Space Flight Center, NASA, Houston, 1963-67. Home: Dickinson TX Died Oct. 5, 1967.

WILLIAMS, CONSTANT brig. gen. U.S.A.; b. Pittsburgh, May 25, 1843; s. W. H. and Ellen Pope (Barclay) W.; ed. Griggs and McDonald's Acad., Pittsburgh, Western Univ. of Pa., Kenwood Ch., New Brighton, Pa., and Webber's Acad., N. Sewickley, Pa.; m. Cornelia Peake De Camp, Sept. 7, 1865. Served during Civ. War as noncommd. officer and pvt. 82d Pa. Vols., and as pvt., 2d lt. and 1st lt. 7th Inf. U.S.A.; capt. 7th Inf., May 10, 1873, maj., Jan. 28, 1897; transferred to 17th Inf., Feb. 23, 1897, to 19th Inf., Oct. 21, 1898; lt. col. 15th Inf., Jan. 16, 1899; col. 26th Inf., Feb. 2, 1901; brig. gen. U.S.A., July 12, 1904; retired by operation of law, May 25, 1907. Served in Cuba, 1899-1900, in P.I., 1900-03; comd. Dept. of the Columbia, 1904-06, Dept. of the Colo., 1906-07. Bvtd. maj., "for gallant services in action against Indians at the Big Hole, Mont., Aug. 9, 1877," where was twice wounded. Episcopalian. Home: Schenectady, N.Y. Died Apr. 20, 1922.

WILLIAMS, DION, officer U.S.M.C., author; b. Williamsburg, O., Dec. 15,21869; s. Byron and Katherine (Park) W.; grad. U.S. Naval Acad., 1891; U.S. Naval War Coll., 1905-06; m. Helen M. Ames, Feb. 20, 1895. Commd. 2d lt. U.S.M.C., July 1, 1893; promoted through grades to brig. gen., June 3, 1924. Served on U.S.S. Atlanta, Baltimore, Olympia, Ore., Kearsarge, Me., Conn.; shore duty various posts in U.S., Cuba, Panama, Philippines and China. Comd. 1st co. that landed on Spanish soil after Battle of Manila Bay, and hoisted first U.S. flag on Spanish soil, May 2, 1898; fleet marine officer Atlantic Fleet, 1903-04, 1907-09; comd. Am. Legation guard, Peking, China, 1913-15; duty Gen. Bd. of Navy, Washington, D.C., 1915-18; comdr. 10th Regt. U.S.M.C., Quantico, Va., 1919; comdr. Northern Dist., Santo Domingo, 1919-21; U.S. Army War Coll., 1921-22, grad. 1922; comdg. 4th Brig., U.S. Marines, 1922-24; comdg. gen. Marine Barracks, Quantico, 1924; dir. Operations and Training, 1924-25; asst. to maj. gen. comdt. U.S.M.C., 1925-28; comdg. gen. Marine Corps Base, San Diego, Calif., 1928-29; comdg. gen. 2d Brigade of Marines in Nicaragua, 1929-30; apptd. pres. Marine Examining Bd. and Marine Retiring Bd., 1931; retired on account of age limit, Jan. 1, 1934. Mem. U.S. Naval Inst., Society Manila Bay, Mil. Order Foreign Wars, Mil. Order Carabao, United Spanish War Vets., S.R., Am. Legion. Awarded Congressional medal for Battle of Manila Bay, also medals Philippine Insurrection, Army of Cuban Pacification, Spanish-Am. War, Marine Expeditionary medal, Victory medal, Nicaraguan Presidential medal, Nicaraguan medal of merit, Nicaraguan campaign medal; also awarded D.S.M. (U.S.). Clubs: Army and Navy, Chevy Chase (Washington, D.C.); New York Yacht. Author: Naval Reconnaissance, 1906, 2d edit., 1917; Port Directory of Foreign Ports of the World, 1911; Army and Navy Uniforms and Insignia, 1918. Home: 1746 Q St. N.W., Washington 9 DC

WILLIAMS, ELIHU STEPHEN congressman, lawyer; b. New Carlisle, O., Jan. 25, 1835; s. Rev. Henry W.; ed. Linden Hill Acad.; m. Alice Gordon, May 31, 1866. Studied law, Dayton, O.; served in war, capt. Co. H, 71st Ohio vol. inf.; comd. post, Carthage, Tenn., 1863; atty. gen. 6th jud. dist. Tenn., 1865-67; mem. Tenn. legislature, 1867-69, removed to Troy, O., 1875; practiced law, 1875-87; mem. Congress, 1887-91, from 3d Ohio dist.; editor the Troy Buckeye. Home: Troy, O. Died 1903.

WILLIAMS, EPHRAIM army officer, philanthropist; b. Newton, Mass., Nov. 7, 1714; s. Ephraim and Elizabeth (Jackson) W. Represented Stockbridge in Mass. Gen. Ct., before 1745; commd. Capt., circa 1745, maj., 1753, col. of a regt., 1755; left bequest to establish free sch. chartered as Williams Coll., Williamstown, Mass., 1793. Killed in battle at Lake George, Sept. 8, 1755.

WILLIAMS, FRANCIS CHURCHILL editor; b. Phila., Apr. 23, 1869; s. Francis Howard and Mary B. (Houston) W.; B.A., U. of Pa., 1891; m. Grace Young, May 5, 1897 (died Oct. 12, 1920); 1 son, Francis Churchill; m. 2d, Marion Virginia Gormly, Apr. 4, 1923. Newspaper writer, corr. and editor, 1891-1900; literary adviser to J. B. Lippincott Co., pubs., 1902-06; associate editor Saturday Evening Post, 1907-27. Capt. Mil. Intelligence Div., Gen. Staff, 1918; grad. Army War Coll., G-2 course for the year 1923; maj., O.R.C., U.S.A., 1919, lt. col., 1924. Mem. Welcome Soc., Soc. of Colonial Wars, S.R., Hist. Soc. of Pa., Delta Phi. Clubs: Army and Navy. Author: J. Develin, Boss, 1901; Stories of the College (co-author), 1902; The Captain, 1903. Contbr. biog., critical and hist. articles and fiction to mags. Home: Spring Meadown Farm, Burks County, Pa. Died Apr. 11, 1945.

WILLIAMS, FRANKWOOD EARL M.D.; b. Cardington, O.. May 18, 1883; s. James Leander (M.D.) and Amanda Elizabeth (Wood) W.; Shortridge High Sch., Indianapolis. Ind.. 1903; A.B., U. of Wis., 1907; M.D., U. of Mich., 1912; hon. D.Sc., from Colgate U., 1927; unmarried. Res. physician State Psychopathic Hosp., U. of Mich., 1912-13; exec. officer. 1st asst. phys. Boston Psychopathic Hosp., 1913-15; med. dir. Mass. Soc. Mental Hygiene, 1915-17; chmn. Mass. Advisory Prison Bd., 1916-17; asso. med. dir. Nat. Com. for Mental Hygiene, 1917-22 (leave of absence during war) and med. dir. same, 1922-31; v. chmn. war work com. of Nat. Com. for Mental Hygiene, N.Y. City, and mem. various sub-coms. of war work com., 1917-19, also mem. com. of war work of Am. Psychiatric Assn., 1917-20; maj. U.S.A., 1918-19; 1st asst. and chief div. of neurology and psychiatry, Office of Surgeon Gen., Washington, D.C.; lt. col. Med. O.R.C., 1919-29. Editor Mental Hygiene, 1917-32, Mental Hygiene Bull., 1923-31; cons. editor Social Science Abstracts to 1932. Mem. teaching staff Smith Coll. Sch. for Social Work, 1921-26, and N.Y. Sch. Social Work, 1924; faculty New Sch. for Social Research; consultant in mental hygiene to the Univ. Dept. of Health, and lecturer in psychiatry, to Sch. of Medicine, Yale, 1926-29, Coll. Phys. and Surg. (Columbia), 1930-32. Chmn. mental hygiene sect., Nat. Conf. Social Work, 1917-19, 1922-24; mem. Internat. Conf. Social Work of Nat. Conf. Social Work, 1927; vice chmn. Nat. Health Council, 1922-23; member administrative bd. Inst. of Child Guidance of Commonwealth Fund, 1927-31; mem. advisory council N.Y. Health and Tuberculosis Demonstrations, also of Milbank Memorial Fund until 1931; mem. bd. dirs. N.Y. Psychoanalytic Inst. and of editorial bd. Psychoanalytic Quarterly; chmn. com. on program of First Internat. Congress on Mental Hygiene, 1930; editor Proceedings 1st Internat. Congress Mental Hygiene. Author: Adolescence—Studies in Mental Hygiene; Youth and Russia; Further Studies in Mental Hygiene. Co-Author: Med. Dept. U.S. Army in World War (Vol. X, Neuropsychiatry); Social Aspects of Mental Hygiene. Editor and contbr. Some Social Aspects of Mental Hygiene. Home: New York, N.Y. Died Sept. 24, 1936.

WILLIAMS, GEORGE FORRESTER journalist; b. on Rock of Gibraltar, 1837; s. of British Army officer; boyhood in E. and W.I. and Gold Coast of Africa; m. Marie Sophia Van Brunt, 1865. Joined staff New York Times, 1856; served in Civil War as pvt. to bvt. maj.; present at battles of Yorktown, Cold Harbor, Malvern Hill, Fredericksburg, Chancellorsville, Gettysburg, Thoroughfare Gap, Wilderness and other important engagements; severely wounded at Malvern Hill, and the Wilderness; acted as war corr., 1864-65; corr. during Franco-Mexican War, 1867, and saw Maximillian executed at Querétaro; vol. aid. col. Mexican Army, 1867; brig. gen. and chief of arty., Guatemalian and Peruvian armies, 1868; mng. editor New York Times, 1870-73; originated and conducted Poor Children's Picnics and Fresh Air Fund; mng. editor New York Herald, 1875-76; conducted the news-dealer war in 1883-84 when James Gordon Bennett fought for and compelled sale of the Herald at reduced price; later connected with New York World, Advertiser. Recorder, and Journal. Author: Bullet and Shell; Lucy's Rebel; The Memorial War Book; Unfair in Love and War; Across the Lines; Half a Century of New York Newspaper Life. Died Dec. 30, 1920.

WILLIAMS, GEORGE WASHINGTON naval officer; b. Yorkville, S.C., July 30, 1869; s. William B. and Mary E. W.; grad. U.S. Naval Acad., 1890; m. Susan M. Lyman, Feb. 6, 1895. Promoted ensign, July 1, 1892; lt. jr. grade, Mar. 3, 1899; lt., Mar. 26, 1899; lt. comdr., July 1, 1905; comdr., Mar. 3, 1911; capt. Aug. 29, 1916; rear admiral, June 3, 1922. Served on Columbia, Spanish-Am. War, 1898; Naval Torpedo Sta., 1900-1902; comdg. U.S.S. Bainbridge, 1903; comdg. first torpedo flotilla, 1904-05; U.S.S. Wisconsin, 1905-06; Bur. of Ordnance, Navy Dept., 1906-08; U.S.S. Montana, 1908-09; comdg. Atlantic Torpedo Fleet, 1910-11; in charge Naval Torpedo Sta., Newport, R.I., 1911-14; comdg. Cleveland, 1914-16, Oregon, 1916-17, Pueblo, 1917-18 (World War); War College, 1919-20; dir. of submarines, 1920-21; comdg. New Mexico, 1921-22; chief of staff U.S. Fleet, 1922-23; comdt. 6th Naval Dist., 1923. Methodist. Home: York, S.C. Died July 17, 1925.

WILLIAMS, HENRY EUGENE Weather Bur. official; b. Bethel, Conn., Apr. 3, 1844; s. Ira and Almira (Stowe) W.; ed. public schs. and acad., Bethel; m. Theresa A. Riopelle, Oct. 15, 1876. Entered U.S. weather service (then a branch of the Signal Corps of the Army), Mar. 24, 1876; instr. in Sch. of Instrn., Fort Myer, 1881-85; chief of Forecast Div., 1895-98; chief clk. Weather Bur., 1898-1903; asst. chief, July 1, 1903-June 30. 1914; meteorologist in charge Forecast Div., 1914-—. Enlisted in Co. C, 17th Conn. Inf., July 26, 1862; mustered out as 1st lt., Aug. 19, 1865. Trustee Universalist Gen. Conv., 1909-17. Mason. Wrote: Temperatures Injurious to Food Products in Storage and During Transportation (bull. 13), 1896. Home: Washington, D.C. Died 1930.

WILLIAMS, HERBERT OWEN army officer; b. Fulton, Miss., Aug. 5, 1866; s. John Dickson and Elizabeth (Marion) W.; grad. U.S. Mil. Acad., 1891, Inf. and Cav. Sch., Ft. Leavenworth, Kan., 1897, Army War Coll., 1912; m. Gertrude Ione Edwards, Nov. 22, 1919. Commd. 2d lt. inf., U.S.A., June 12, 1891; advanced through grades to col. (temp.), Aug. 5, 1917; col. regular army, Feb. 16, 1920; brig. gen., Sept. 24, 1926; retired. Awarded D.S.M. (U.S.). Died Aug. 13, 1936.

WILLIAMS, ISRAEL Loyalist; b. Hatfield, Mass., Nov. 30, 1709; s. Rev. William and Christian (Stoddard) W.; grad. Harvard, 1727; m. Sarah Chester, 1731, 7 or 8 children. Selectmen, Hatfield, 1732-63; 2d in command of Hampshire County Regt., Mass. Militia, 1744, apptd. col., 1748; responsible for defense of Western Mass. throughout French and Indian War; justice of peace, clk. Hampshire County Ct.; judge Hampshire County Ct. Common Pleas, 1758-74; mem. Mass. Legislature from Hatfield, intermittently, 1733-73; mem. Mass. Gov.'s Council, 1761-67; executor under will of Ephraim Williams, instrumental in founding "free school" (became Williams Coll.); considered Loyalist in Western Mass. during early years of Revolution, imprisoned for Loyalism, 1777, deprived of citizenship until 1780. Died Hatfield, Jan. 10, 1788.

WILLIAMS, JAMES MONROE army officer; b. Lowville, N.Y.. Sept. 12, 1833; s. Absalom and Fannie W.; moved to Wis., 1844; ed. pub. schs., N.Y., Wis., and acad.. Janesville, Wis.; read law Janesville, 1853-56; m. Mary E. Brawner, Jan. 30, 1868. Admitted to bar, Janesville, Wis., 1856; practiced law at Leavenworth, Kan. Capt. 5th Kan. Cav., U.S.V., July 1861, to Sept. 1862; lt. col. and col. 1st Kan. (afterwards 79th U.S.) Colored Troops, Sept. 1862, to May 1864; received 4 gun-shot wounds in engagement with Confederates at Elk Creek, Ind. Ty., July 17, 1863; comd. brigade May 1864, until Oct. 1865; bvt. brig. gen. U.S.V.; apptd. capt. 8th U.S. cav. (bvtd. maj. for conspicuous gallantry in engagements with Indians, 1867, on the Verde, in Yampa Valley, and nr. Music Mountain, Ariz.); seriously wounded in latter action; in hosp. and on nominal duty 2 yrs.; returned to regt., but resigned, 1871; retired as capt. cav. by spl. act of Congress, Jan. 1, 1891. Home: Washington, D.C. Died 1907.

WILLIAMS, JOHN senator; b. Surry County, N.C., Jan. 29, 1778; s. Joseph and Rebecca (Lanier) W.; m. Melinda White; children—Joseph Lanier, Margaret (Williams) Pearson, Col. John Admitted to Knoxville (Tenn.) bar, 1803; served as capt. 6th Inf., U.S. Army, 1779-1800, col. Tenn. Volunteers, 1812-14, col. 39th U.S. Inf., 1814; mem. U.S. Senate from Tenn., 1815 (apptd. to fill vacancy), 1817-23, chmn. com. mil. affairs; U.S. charge d'affaires (apptd. by Pres. Adams) to Fedn. of Central Am., 1825; elected to Tenn. Senate, 1827. Died Knoxville, Aug. 10, 1837.

WILLIAMS, JOHN FOSTER naval officer; b. Boston, Oct. 12, 1743; m. Hannah Homer, Oct. 6, 1774. Commd. capt. Mass. state sloop Republic, 1776; transferred to ship Massachusetts, 1776; made 2 cruises in Mass. state brig. Hazard, captured serveral prizes, 1778-79; forced Brit. brig Active (18 guns) to surrender off St. Thomas, W.I., 1779; commanded Protector (largest ship in Mass. navy); communicated an invention to distill fresh water from salt water with appropriate drawings to Boston Marine Soc., 1792; surveyed Nantasket Harbor, reported results to U.S. Govt., 1803; commanded U.S. revenue cutter Massachusetts, 1790-1814. Died June 24, 1814; buried Granary Buring Ground, Boston.

WILLIAMS, JOHN POWELL physician; born Richmond, Va., Oct. 25, 1894; s. William Reid, Sr. and Caroline (Henderson) P.; student McGuire's U. Sch., Richmond, Va., 1902-11, U. of Va., 1912-14, Med. Coll. of Va., Richmond, 1919-21; A.B., M.D., U. of Va., 1923; m. Virginia Pittman Marshall, July 15, 1928; 1 son, John Powell, Jr. Instr. mathematics and German, McGuire's U. Sch., 1914-16; resident physician St. Luke's Hosp., N.Y. City, 1923-25. Fellow McGuire Clinic, Richmond, 1925-28; mem. adjunct faculty Med. Coll. of Va., 1925, asst. prof. med., asst. physician to hosp. div., instr. physical diagnosis and clin. pathol., 1932. Pres. Richmond Acad. Med., 1940, chmn. bd. trustees, 1941; asso. prof. Medicine, Med. Coll. of Va., 1942, unit dir. and chief med. service of affiliated unit, 45th Gen. Hosp.; chief med. service Kennedy Gen. Hosp., Memphis, Tenn., 1945-46; prof. clin. medicine, Med. Coll. of Va., 1945; chief med. service, acting chief professional services, McGuire Vet. Adminstrn. Hosp., Richmond, 1946; col. and unit dir. comdg. officer Postwar 45th Gen. Hosp., since 1948. Served as pvt. Inf., 1914-15; lance corpl. 1st Va. Cavalry, Mexican border, 1916-17; instr. practical geometry and trigonometry, R.O.T.C., Fort Myer, Va., 1917; reconnaisance and telephone officer, F.A., Camp Lee, Va. and France; promoted to 1st lt. during combat, St. Mihel and Meuse-Argonne offensives, France; chief med. service 45th Gen. Hosp., Camp Lee, Va., N. Africa, Italy, 1942-46; promoted to col. Med Corps, 1944. Awarded Legion of Merit for outstanding clinical investigation in infectious hepatitis and trench foot. Diplomate Am. Bd. Internal Med. Fellow A.C.P., A.M.A., Am. Psychosomatic Soc.; mem. Richmond Acad. Med., Med. Soc. of Va. chmn. com. on emergency med. service), So. Med. Assn.; Phi Beta Kappa, Alpha Omega Alpha, Raven Hon. Soc. Contbr. sci. papers to med. jours. Instrumental in developing second liver extract produced for treatment of pernicious anemia. Active in developing Blue Cross Plan, Richmond and Va. (mem. bd. trustees, 1941). Democrat. Episcopalian. Home: 3614 Seminary Av., Richmond 22. Office: McGuire Veterans Adminstrn. Hosp., Richmond 19, Va. Died Sept., 1954; buried Holywood Cemetery, Richmond, Va.

WILLIAMS, JONATHAN army officer; b. Boston, May 26, 1750; s. Jonathan and Grace (Harris) W.; m. Marianne Alexander, Sept. 12, 1779. Joined Benjamin Franklin (his uncle), Paris, France, 1776; agt. of Continental Congress at Nantes to inspect arms and other supplies being shipped from that port; engaged in various business ventures in Europe, 1785; asso. judge Phila. Ct. of Common Pleas, 1796; insp. fortifications 1st supt. U.S. Mil. Acad. with rank of maj. U.S. Army, (apptd. by Thomas Jefferson) 1801-03, resigned, 1803, accepted reappointment with rank of lt. col. engrs. with complete authority over all cadets, 1805; resigned commn., 1812; a founder Mil. Philos. Soc. (to promote mil. science and history); mem. Am. Philos. Soc. Author: Theromometrical Navigation, 1799; The Elements of Fortification (translated from French), 1801; Manoeuvres of Horse Artillery (translation of work by Tadeuz Kosciuszko), 1808. Died May 16, 1815.

WILLIAMS, JOSEPH WHITE civil engr.; b. Milan, O., Oct. 20, 1879; s. Daniel Newton and Sophia E. (White) W.; grad. high sch., Milan, 1897; m. Eliza L. Hunt, Sept. 24, 1902; children—Joseph Hunt, Mary Elinor. On railroad location and constrn., N.M. and Calif., 1900-07; asst. chief engr. Northwestern Pacific R.R., 1907-14, chief engr. constrn., 1914-17, chief engr., 1919-21; chief engr. Western Pacific R.R., Aug. 1921-—. Served as pvt. 52d Ia. Vol. Inf., Spanish-Am. War; again entered military service, in Apr. 1917; maj., lt. col. 18th Engrs., U.S.A., World War I; in France, Aug. 1917-Apr. 1919; col. engrs. O.R.C. Republican. Home: Ross, Calif. Died Feb. 3, 1941.

WILLIAMS, KENNETH POWERS mathematician, historian, educator; b. Urbana, O., Aug. 25, 1887; s. John H. and Eva Augusta (Powers) W.; student Clark Coll., Worcester, Mass., 1905-06; A.B., Ind. U., 1908, A.M., 1909; Ph.D., Princeton, 1913; m. Ellen Laughlin Scott, Aug. 30, 1920. With Ind. U., 1909-—, instr. mathematics until 1914, asst. prof., 1914-19, asso. prof., 1919-24, prof., 1924-—, chmn. dept., 1937-44. Served as 1st lt. Indiana National Guard, Mexican Border, 1916; captain Field Artillery, United States Army, with A.E.F., 1917-19; maj. F.A., Ind. Nat. Guard, 1921-24, lt. col., 1924-31, col. and chief of staff, 38th Div., Nat. Guard, 1931-39, col., Q.M.C., comdg. 113th Q.M. Regt., and Q.M., 38th Div., in fed. service, 1941. Received Gold Medal Soc. of Libraries of N.Y. U., Diploma of Honor Lincoln Memorial U., and others. Fellow A.A.A.S.; mem. Am. Math. Soc., Math. Assn. Am. (mem. bd. govs., 1945-47, chmn. commn. on place of math. in secondary edn. 1934-40), Am. Astron. Soc., Société Astronomique de France, Am. Assn. Univ. Prof. (chmn. com. required courses in education 1931-35, council, 1946-48), Phi Beta Kappa, Sigma Xi, Scabbard and Blade. American Legion. Republican. Mason. Author: Dynamics of the Airplane, 1921; College Algebra, 1928; The Calculation of the Orbits of Asteroids and Comets, 1934; The Mathematical Theory of Finance, 1935, revised edit., 1947; Lincoln Finds a General, Vol. I, II, 1949, III, 1952; math. and astron. papers. Home: 702 E. 10th St., Bloomington, Ind. Died Sept. 25, 1958; buried Columbus, Ind.

WILLIAMS, LINSLY RUDD M.D.; b. N.Y. City, Jan. 28, 1875; s. John Stanton and Mary Maclay (Pentz) W.; A.B., Princeton, 1895; A.M., M.D., Columbia, 1899; m. Grace Kidder Ford, Jan. 18, 1908. Interne Presbyn. Hosp., New York, 1900-02, Sloane Maternity Hosp., 1902; asso. in practice with Dr. John S. Thacher, 1902-08; visiting phys. to House of Rest for Tuberculosis, Seton Hosp., and City Hosp.; instr. in histology, 1902-04, asst. in medicine, 1904-14, chief of med. clinic, 1906-11, Columbia; dep. commr. of health, N.Y. State, 1914-17 (resigned); assigned as 1st lt. Med. R.C. to investigate sanitary conditions in France and Eng., Aug. 1917; maj. asst. div. surgeon, Oct. 1917; later lt. col. M.C., U.S.A.; sanitary insp. 80th Div.; asst. sanitary officer Hdqrs. S.O.S.; service, Aug. 8, 1917-Apr. 12, 1919; dir. tuberculosis work in France for Rockefeller Foundation, 1919-22; mng. dir. Nat. Tuberculosis Assn., Oct. 1, 1922-28; mng. dir. N.Y. Acad. of Medicine; dir. Millbank Memorial Fund. Mem. board of mgrs. N.Y. Assn. for Improving Conditions of the Poor; trustee Columbia U. Democrat. Episcopalian. Home: New York, N.Y. Died Jan. 8, 1934.

WILLIAMS, OTHO HOLLAND army officer; b. Prince Georges County, Md., Mar. 1747; s. Joseph and Prudence (Holland) W; m. Mary Smith, 1786, 4 sons. Apptd. 1st lt. in company raised in Md., 1775; participated in siege of Boston, promoted capt.; commd. maj. Continental Army, 1776; wounded and taken prisoner, 1776; 1st parolled in N.Y.C., then thrown into provost's jail charged with secretly communicating mil. information to George Washington, exchanged, 1778; apptd. col. 6th Md. Regt., 1776; took part in battles of Monmouth and Camden; promoted brig. gen., 1782; naval officer of Balt. dist., 1783-89; founded town of Williamsport (Md.), 1787; collector Port of Balt., 1789-93. Died Miller's Town, Va., July 15, 1794; buried Riverview Cemetery, Williamsport.

WILLIAMS, RICHARD PETERS Marine Corps officer, (ret.); born Atlanta, Ga., June 20, 1879; s. Charles Wilson and Elizabeth (Overby) W.; ed. various pub. and pvt. schs. in U.S.; m. Agnes M. Miller, May 1909 (died Apr. 1913); m. 2d, Helen Strobhar, Oct. 21, 1921. Commd. 2d lt., U.S. Marine Corps, 1899, and advanced through the grades to brig. gen. 1934, retired Apr. 1, 1940; recalled to active duty Feb. 1, 1941, serving until Apr. 23, 1941 (retired); appointed secretary for defense, State of New Jersey, by Gov. Edison, June 3, 1941 (retired April 1, 1942). Served on various ships of United States Fleet and at shore stations in United States, P.I., China, Santo Domingo, Haiti; served as assistant chief of staff, G-3, attached to 6th Div. U.S. Army, in World War. Decorated Comdr. Order of Honor and Merit, Medaille Militaire and D.S.M. (Haiti); Naval D.S.M., Spanish-American War, Philippine Campaign, Cuban Pacification, Expeditionary (with 4 stars), Vera Cruz and Victory (with 2 bronze stars) medals (U.S.). Catholic. Clubs: Army and Navy (Washington, D.C.); University (Phila.); N.Y. Athletic (N.Y. City). Home: 1007 Whitaker St., Savannah, Ga. Died Mar. 14, 1950.

WILLIAMS, ROBERT brig. gen. U.S.A.; b. Culpeper County, Va., Nov. 5, 1829; grad. West Point, 1851; 2d lt., 1st dragoons; served in Oregon; asst. instr. tactics West Point, 1857-61; capt and asst. adj. gen., May 1861; col. 1st Mass. cav., Oct. 1861; maj., U.S.A., July 1862; on duty at War Dept. to end of Civil war; afterward asst. adj. gen. in various depts., and adj. gen., 1892; bvt. brig. gen., Mar. 1865; lt. col., 1869; col., 1881; brig. gen., 1892; retired, 1893. Died 1901.

WILLIAMS, ROBERT PARVIN, army officer; b. Greencastle, Ind., Aug. 29, 1891; s. Robert C(larence) and Arta (Parvin) W.; M.D., U. of Cincinnati, 1913; student Army Med. Sch., 1915-16; honor grad. Med. Field Service Sch., 1927; student, Command and Gen. Staff Sch., 1928-30; Army War Coll., 1934-35, Chem. Warfare Sch., 1935; m. Barbara Murray, July 21, 1917; 1 son, Charles Murray. Interne Ancon Hosp., Panama Canal Zone, 1912-13; Cincinnati Gen. Hosp., 1913-15; commd. 1st lt., Med. Corps, U.S. Army, 1915, promoted through grades to brig. gen., 1949. Army service; Mexican border, adjutant Camp Hosp., Douglas, Ariz., 1916-17; asst. div. surg., 1917-18; organized and comd. Gen. Hosp. No. 34, East Norfolk, Mass., 1918; camp surg. Camp Upton, N.Y., 1918; adj. Tripler Gen. Hosp., post surg. Ft. Kamehameha, Hawaii, 1919-22; duty in Post Hosp., attending surg. Vancouver Barracks, Wash., 1922-26; comdg. officer 1st Med. Squadron, 1st Cavalry div., Ft. Bliss, Tex., 1930-34; surg. No. Ariz. Dist., Civilian Conservation Corps, 1933-34; instr. The Inf. Sch., Ft. Benning, Ga., 1935-39; dir. training, Med. Field Service Sch., Carlisle Barracks, Pa., 1939-40; comdg. officer 1st Med. Regiment, march from Pa. to Calif., 1940; div. surg. 7th Inf. Div., Camp Ord, Calif., 1940; corps surg. IX Corps, Ft. Lewis, Wash., 1941-42; mem. Gen. Stilwell's Mil. Mission to China and Burma, Feb. 5, 1942; 1st Burma Campaign, liaison with Chinese armies, Feb.-May, 1942; surg. Gen. Stilwell's Column, retreat from Burma to India, May, 1942; 2d Burma Campaign, chief surg. Gen. Stilwell's China-Burma-India Theater and adv. to Chinese surg. gen., June 1942-44; chief surg. Gen. Dan I. Sultan's India-Burma Theater, 1944-45; Army surg. Fourth Army, 1945-July 1949; spl. asst. to surgeon gen., Sept.-Nov. 1949; chief surgeon Army Field Forces, Ft. Monroe, Va., 1949-56. Decorations: Legion of Merit, Bronze Star Medal with Oak Leaf Cluster, Army Commendation Ribbon, Order of Yin Whei (1st grade) (China), Chinese War Memorial Badge. Mem. Alpha Kappa Kappa, Theta Nu Epsilon, Assn. of Mil. Surgeons, Am. Med. Assn. Home: Carmel-by-the-Sea CA Died Nov. 20, 1967.

WILLIAMS, ROGER shipbuilding exec.; b. Chatham Centre, N.Y., Nov. 5, 1879; s. A. Ford and Katherine (Van Volkenburgh) W.; grad. U.S. Naval Acad., 1901; m. Frances McIlvaine, Nov. 7, 1906; children—Roger, Frances Randall (Mrs. William C. Chanler), Eveline Wilbor (Mrs. Saxon W. Holt, Jr.). Resigned commission U.S. Navy and joined Internat. Merc. Marine Co., N.Y.C., 1920-30; v.p. and dir. Newport News Shipbuilding & Drydock Company, 1930-46, chmn. exec. com., Aug. 1946-—. Served as officer, U.S. Navy, 1901-20. Awarded Sampson medal. Spanish-Am. War and Navy Cross, World War I. Trustee Mariners Mus. Mem. Soc. Naval Architects and Marine Engrs. Episcopalian. Clubs: Army and Navy (Washington); India House, N.Y. Yacht, Century (N.Y.C.). Home: Chatham Centre, N.Y. Office: 90 Broad St., N.Y.C. Died Nov. 1959.

WILLIAMS, ROGER D. army officer; b. Lexington, Ky., Aug. 29, 1856; s. Benjamin F. and Mary Gates (Massie) W.; student Transylvania U., Lexington, 1874-76; m. Minnie Lyle Sayre, Nov. 1887. War corr. attached to Gen. Crook's command throughout Gen. Custer's Sioux Indian campaign, 1876. Served in Ky. N.G., 1st lt. to brig. gen., 30 yrs.; comd. troops in all the Ky. feuds for 25 yrs.; comd. sector on Rio Grande from Fort Hancock, Tex., to Las Cruces, N.M., 1916; commd. brig. gen. N.A., Aug. 5, 1917; apptd. comdr. 76th Brigade, Camp Shelby, Hattiesburg, Miss., Sept. 1917; attached to Hdqrs. 1st Army in France, July 1918-Mar. 1919; retired as brig. gen. N.A., May 1919. Republican. Master of hounds Iroquois Hunt Club, 1882-1918. Author: Horse and Hound, 1905; Old Times in the Black Hills, 1906; Wolf Hunting and Coursing, 1908; Deer Hunting in the West Indies, 1909; The Foxhound, 1914. Home: Lexington, Ky. Died Dec. 12, 1925.

WILLIAMS, SETH marine corps officer (ret.); b. Foxboro, Mass., Jan. 19, 1880; s. Jarvis and Elizabeth (Plumridge) W.; B.S. (civil engring.), Norwich U., 1903; m. Mary Swift Baily, Sept. 11, 1907; 1 dau., Elizabeth Ray (wife of Comdr. John Remey Wadleigh, U.S. Navy). Commd. 2d lt. U.S. M.C., 1903, and advanced through grades to maj. gen., Apr. 1942; mem. War Industry Bd., World War I; ret. for age, 1944. Awarded Silver Star, 1919. Legion of Merit, 1944. Home: Washington. Died July 1963.

WILLIAMS, WILLIAM b. New London, Conn., June 2, 1862; s. Charles Augustus and Elizabeth H. W.; A.B., Yale, 1884 (A.M., 1906); LL.B., Harvard, 1888; A.M., Columbia, 1914. Practiced law at New York; U.S. commr. of immigration at New York, 1902-05, and May, 1909-July 1, 1913; commr. water supply, gas and electricity, New York City, by apptmt. of Mayor Mitchel, since Feb., 1914. Asso. counsel for U.S. during Behring Sea arbitration with Great Britain, 1892. Maj. U.S.V. during Spanish-Am. War, 1898. Republican. Clubs: University, Metropolitan, Century, Down Town, Republican, Yale. Home: 1 W. 54th St. Office: Municipal Bldg., New York. Died Feb. 8, 1947.

WILLIAMS, YANCEY SULLIVAN naval officer; b. Monetta, S.C., Apr. 7, 1876; s. Thomas Smith and America (Holston) W.; grad. U.S. Naval Acad., 1898; grad. U.S. Naval War Coll., 1924; m. Maude George Jackson, Jan. 5, 1906; 1 daughter, Evelyn Stuart (Mrs. Harry A. Guthrie). Commd. ensign U.S. Navy, 1898; promoted through grades to rear adm., June 1, 1931. Participated in Spanish-Am. War, 1898; at Samoa, 1899-1900; Hayti and San Domingo, 1914-15; on U.S.S. Delaware, World War, 1917-18; with Asiatic Fleet, 1925-27; Navy Dept., Washington, 1927-31; apptd. comdr. Yangtze Patrol, Asiatic Fleet, 1931. Awarded

Navy Cross, also West Indian, Spanish, Chinese, Haytian and Dominican campaign medals. and Victory medal, World War I. Died Nov. 1, 1938.

WILLIAMSON, ANDREW army officer; b. Scotland, circa 1730; m. Eliza Tyler, 4 children. Established as planter on Hard Labor Creek, Savannah, by 1765; commd. lt. S.C. Militia, 1760, promoted maj., 1775; served in "Snow Campaign," 1775; led 2d Cherokee expdn., 1776, ambushed as Essenecca; promoted col.; signed treaty which took large land cession from Indians, 1777; brig. gen. in command S.C. Militia in Robert Howe's Fla. expdn., 1778, shared blame for failure; sent troops home when it became obvious that British would take Charleston, S.C., 1779, accused of treason after fall of that city but not proved. Died St. Paul's Parish, nr. Charleston, Mar. 21, 1786.

WILLIAMSON, CHARLES SPENCER M.D.; b. Cincinnati, May 15, 1872; s. William F. and Mary Louise (Spencer) W.; M.S., U. of Cincinnati, 1893; M.D., Med. Coll. of Ohio, 1896; m. Josephine Gillette Stilwell, Oct. 15, 1903; children—Mary Josephine, Isabel Gillette, Elizabeth Spencer. Resident phys., Cincinnati Hosp., 1896-97; post-grad. study Leipzig, Berlin, Vienna and Paris, 1897-1900; removed to Chicago. 1901; adj. prof. medicine, 1901-03, prof. clin. medicine, 1903-12, Coll. Phys. and Surg.; asst. prof. diseases of stomach, 1901-07, prof., 1907-—, Chicago Polyclinic; prof. medicine and clin. medicine, and head of dept. of internal medicine, U. of Ill. Coll. of Medicine, 1912. Lt. col. M.C. U.S.A., and dir. dept. sanitation, Ft. Riley, Kan., and Ft. Oglethorpe, Ga.; also dir. Sch. of Mil. Hygiene and Sanitation, Ft. Oglethorpe, Ga. Awarded gold medal by A.M.A. for exhibit of research work, 1918. Mem. Assn. Am. Physicians. Episcopalian. Editor: French's Practice of Medicine, 1910. Contbr. several monographs containing results of original research in Am. and European publs. Home: Chicago, Ill. Died Feb. 16, 1933.

WILLIAMSON, JAMES ALEXANDER lawyer; b. Adair County, Ky., Feb. 8, 1829; s. William W.; academic edn.; m. Ann Whitfield Gregory, 1853. Enlisted, July 1861, 4th Ia. inf.; commissioned 1st lt. and adj.; promoted lt. col. March 9, 1862, col. March 18, 1862; later brig. gen. and still later bvt. maj. gen. Medal of honor for gallantry in action Chickasaw Bayou, Miss., Dec. 29, 1862. Commr. Gen. Land Office U.S., 1876-81; then land commr. and gen. solicitor Atlantic & Pacific R.R. Co., of which he later was pres. until road was sold to Atchison, Topeka & Santa Fe R.R. Republican. Died 1902.

WILLIAMSON, ROY ELISHA clergyman, ch. exec.; b. Carterville, Ill., May 12, 1890; s. James Franklin and Valura Etta (Jones) W.; A.B., Shurtleff Coll., Alton, Ill., 1918, D.D., 1932; B.D., Rochester (N.Y.) Theol. Sem., 1922; m. Loueva Harrell, June 30, 1910; children—William Franklin, Marie Louise. Newspaper reporter, 1910-12; pastor rural chs., 1913-18; student pastor, 1919-22; ordained to ministry Bapt. Ch., 1915; pastor First Ch., Waterloo, Ia., 1922-26, Grand River Av. Ch., Detroit, Mich., 1926-36; exec. sec. Bapt. Missionary Conv. of State of N.Y. since 1936; mem. administrative com. Council on Finance and Promotion, Northern Bapt. Conv.; v.p. and mem. bd. of dirs. N.Y. State Council of Churches and Christian Edn.; mem. bd. of trustees Kenka Coll. and of Cook Acad. Served as 1st lt., chaplain, U.S. Army, with 4th Div. A.E.F., 1918-19. Mem. Ministerial Assn. of Syracuse, N.Y., Ministers Council of Northern Bapt. Conv. Republican. Mason. Club: Rotary. Editor of The Baptist New Yorker since 1936. Home: 826 Westcott St. Office: 433 S. Salina St., Syracuse, N.Y. Died Dec. 23, 1944.

WILLIAMSON, SYDNEY BACON civil engr.; b. Lexington, Va., Apr. 15, 1865; s. Thomas Hoomes and Julia Anna (Lewis) W.; grad. Va. Mil. Inst., 1884; m. Helen C. Davis, May 20, 1890. Instr. mathematics, Kings Mountain (S.C.) Mil. Sch., 1884-86; with engring. depts. C.B. & Northern, St. Paul & Duluth, and N.P. rys., 1886-90; entered gen. engring., Montgomery, Ala., 1890; in employ U.S. Govt., on Tenn. River improvements, 1892-1900 (except during Spanish-Am. War), and at Newport, R.I., as asst. engr. on fortification work, 1900-04; in practice, New York, Baltimore and other cities, 1904-07; engr. in charge of Pacific Locks, and div. engr. Pacific Div., Panama Canal, 1907-12 (resigned); chief of constrn., U.S. Reclamation Service, Dec. 10, 1914-Jan. 1916 (resigned); apptd. cons. civil engr. for Guggenheim Brothers, 1916. Asso. with Gen. Geo. W. Goethals as cons. engr. for Port of Palm Beach, Fla.; apptd. by President of the U.S. mem. Interoceanic Canal Bd. to investigate and report on the Nicaragua Canal Bd. to investigate and report on the Nicaragua Canal route and other possible canal routes for connecting the Atlantic and Pacific oceans; retired May 1, 1935. Mem. of exec. com. Chile Exploration Company, Braden Copper Company. Served as capt. U.S. Volunteer Engrs., Spanish-Am. War; detailed as asst. to Col. George W. Goethals, chief engr. 1st Army Corps. Commd. col. engrs., and comd. 55th Engrs. A.E.F.; in France as sect. engr., intermediate Sect. West, and of the Paris Dist. Awarded D.S.M. (U.S.). Episcopalian. Home: Lexington, Va. Died Jan. 13, 1939.

WILLIAMSON, THOM chief engr. U.S.N.; b. Edenton, N.C., Aug. 5, 1833; s. William Price and Penelope Benbury (McDonald) W.; ed. Norfolk (Va.) Mil. Acad. and St. Mary's Coll., Baltimore, to 1850; m. Julia Price. Dec. 2, 1861. Apptd. 3d asst. engr. U.S.N., May 23, 1853; 2d asst. engr., June 27, 1855; 1st asst. engr., July 21, 1858; chief engr., Aug. 5, 1861; relative rank of capt., Jan. 30, 1889; retired on account of age, Aug. 5, 1895; chief engr. with rank of rear admiral, June 29, 1906. Offered a signed commn. as chief engr. in C.S.N. at outbreak of Civil War, but declined; sr. engr. officer with Admiral Farragut's fleet in fights at Fts. Morgan and Gaines and in operations in Mobile Bay; head of dept. of steam engring., U.S. Naval Acad., 1868-69; fleet engr. N. and S. Atlantic and Pacific stas. and acted as supt. State, War and Navy Depts. Bldg. under successive spl. orders from Presidents Harrison and Cleveland; mem. bd. to examine plans for coaling ships at sea during Spanish-Am. War; on duty in Navy Dept., Oct. 19, 1901-June 6, 1912. Awarded medal and diploma for collaboration, by Paris Expn., 1900, and diploma for distinguished services, by Buffalo Expn., 1901. Home: Annapolis, Md. Died Mar. 1918.

WILLIS, BENJAMIN ALBERTSON congressman; b. Roslyn, L.I., N.Y., Mar. 24, 1840; grad. Union Coll., Schenectady, N.Y., 1861; studied law. Admitted to N.Y. bar, 1862, began practice in N.Y.C.; enlisted in Union Army during Civil War, 1862, served as capt. 119th N.Y. Volunteers, later col. 12th Regt., N.Y. Volunteers, discharged, 1864; mem. N.Y. State Assembly, 1872-78; mem. U.S. Ho. of Reps. (Democrat) from N.Y., 44th-45th congresses, 1875-79; engaged in law practice, real estate bus. Died N.Y.C., Oct. 14, 1886; buried Friends Cemetery, Westbury, L.I., reinterred Woodlawn Cemetery, Westbury.

WILLISTON, EDWARD BANCROFT brig. gen. U.S.A.; b. Norwich, Vt., July 15, 1837; s. E. B. and Almira W.; B.S., Norwich U., 1856; m. Beatrice Moore, Jan. 20, 1868 (dec.); m. 2d, Florence Chatfield, of Detroit, 1902. Apptd. from Calif., 2d lt. 2d U.S. Arty., Aug. 5, 1861; 1st lt., Sept. 27, 1861; capt., Mar. 8, 1865; maj. 3d Arty., Mar. 22, 1885; lt. col., Feb. 12, 1895; col. 6th Arty., Mar. 8, 1898; brig. gen. vols., May 4, 1898; hon. discharged from vols., June 12, 1899; retired by operation of law, July 15, 1900; advanced to rank of brig. gen. retired, by act of Apr. 23, 1904. Awarded Congressional Medal of Honor, Apr. 6, 1892, "for distinguished gallantry in action at Trevillian Sta., Va., June 12, 1864"; bvtd.: capt.. May 3, 1863, "for gallant and meritorious services in action at Salem Heights, Va."; maj., July 3, 1863, for same in Gettysburg campaign; lt. col., Sept. 19. 1864, for same in battle of Winchester, Va.; col., Mar. 13, 1865, for same during the war. Home: Portland, Ore. Died Apr. 24, 1920.

WILLITS, ALBERT BOWER rear admiral U.S.N.; b. Phila., Mar. 7, 1851; s. Alphonso Albert and Eliza Jane (Street) W.; grad. U.S. Naval Acad., 1874; m. Anna Bain White, Sept. 28, 1876. Promoted asst. engr., Feb. 26, 1878; passed asst. engr., Oct. 12, 1881; chief engr., May 28, 1896; lt. comdr., March 3, 1899; comdr., Oct. 11, 1903; capt., Jan. 28, 1908; rear admiral, Sept. 14, 1911; retired on account of age, after service of 40 yrs., 5 mos., Mar. 7, 1913. Served at sea on the Montauk, Wyandotte, Adams, Powhatan, Hartford, Pensacola, Yorktown, Boston, Minneapolis, Marblehead, Iowa and Newark; on shore as asst. to engr.-in-chief, George W. Melville, at Navy Dept., 1898-1901; asst. insp. in bldg. the Minneapolis and Columbia, 1901-04; head dept. of engring. Norfolk Navy Yard, 1904-08; sr. insp. in bldg. the Utah and Arkansas, 1908-11; dir. of Navy Yards, Navy Dept., 1911-12. Insp. of machinery, Bayonne, N.J., 1917-19. Democrat. Presbyn. Contbr. numerous tech. articles to engring. mags. Home: Philadelphia, Pa. Died Jan. 7, 1926.

WILLITS, GEORGE SIDNEY naval officer; b. Phila., Feb. 21, 1853; s. George Sidney and Elizabeth (Githens) W.; Rutgers Coll., New Brunswick, N.J.; grad. U.S. Naval Acad., 1875; m. Sylvia B. Gaston, Aug. 3, 1876. Asst. engr. U.S.N., 1877; passed asst. engr., 1885; chief engr., 1896; lt. comdr., 1898; comdr., 1904; capt., 1908; rear admiral, Mar. 26, 1913; retired Feb. 21, 1915. Served at sea on Hartford, Vandalia, Huron, Tallapoosa, Enterprise, Marion, Boston, Trenton; on Marblehead during Spanish-Am. War, 1898; Solace, during Boxer rebellion in China; Baltimore, flagship Kearsarge, 1903-04. Holder of service medals for Cuban expdn. and Chinese expdn. Presbyn. Home: Philadelphia, Pa. Died May 3, 1917.

WILLKIE, WENDELL LEWIS (wil'ke), lawyer; b. Elwood, Ind., Feb. 18, 1892; s. Herman Francis and Henrietta (Trisch) W.; A.B., Indiana U., 1913, LL.B., 1916, LL.D., 1938; LL.D., Colgate U., 1939; Dartmouth Coll., 1941, Yale U., 1941, Bowdoin Coll., 1941, Rutgers University, 1941; Union Coll., 1942, Boston U., 1943, Oberlin Coll., 1943; Sc.D., Stevens Inst. of Technology, 1941; student Oberlin College, 1916; m. Edith Wilk, January 14, 1918; 1 son, Philip Herman. Admitted to Ind. bar, 1916, Ohio, 1919, N.Y., 1930; mem. law firm Willkie & Willkie, Elwood, 1916-19, Mather, Nesbitt & Willkie, Akron, O., 1919-29, Weadock & Willkie, N.Y. City, 1929-32; pres. Commonwealth & Southern Corp., 1933-40; mem. law firm Willkie, Owen, Otis, Farr & Gallagher; chmn. bd. 20th Century-Fox. Republican nominee for President of U.S., 1940. Trustee New York Hosp., Beekman Street Hosp., Hampton Inst. Enlisted as private, U.S. Army, Apr. 6, 1917 (the day war was declared); served as 1st lt., 325th F.A., A.E.F.; advanced to capt., 1918. Mem. Assn. of Bar City of New York. Republican. Episcopalian. Clubs: Century Assn., Lawyers Club, Downtown Assn. Author: One World, 1943. Home: 1010 5th Av. Office: 15 Broad St., New York, N.Y. Died Oct. 8, 1944.

WILLOUGHBY, CHARLES A., army officer; b. Heidelberg, Germany, March 8, 1892 (naturalized U.S. citizen, 1910); s. Freiherr T. von Tscheppe-Weidenbach and Emma (Willoughby) von T.; B.A., Gettysburg (Pa.) Coll., 1914; grad. student U. of Kan., 1933; grad. Inf. Sch., 1929, Command and Gen. Staff Sch., 1931, Army War Coll., 1936; commd. 2d lt. Inf., 1915; advanced through the grades to major general, 1945, reverted to brigadier general, 1946; served on Mexican Border, 1916-17; served with 1st Division, of A.E.F., 1917-18; chief of intelligence, Gen. MacArthur's staff, Philippine campaign, 1941, S.W. Pacific, 1942-46; veteran of Bataan and Corregidor; represented Gen. MacArthur to receive Imperial Japanese delegation for surrender negotiations, Aug. 15, 1945, Manila, P.I. Awarded D.S.C., D.S.M., both with oak leaf cluster, Silver Star, Legion of Merit (U.S.); Commander Order British Empire (Gr. Brit.); Medaille d'Honneur (Aff. Etr.); Legion of Honor (France); S. Maurizio e Lazzaro (Italy); Order of Bolivar (Venezuela); Al Merito and Star of Calderon (Ecuador). Member Phi Gamma Delta. Club: Army and Navy (Washington, D.C.). Mason. Author: United States Economic Participation World War, 1917-18, 1931; Maneuver in War, 1939. Columnist for Army-Navy Jour. Editor: General Staff Quarterly, 1931-35; editor in chief Gen. Intelligence Series, SWPA, prepared for Dept. of the Army. Home: Bronxville NY Died 1972.

WILLSON, LESTER SEBASTIAN soldier; b. Canton, N.Y., June 16, 1839; s. Ambrose and Julia A. (Hill) W.; acad. edn.; m. Emma D. Weeks, Mar. 2, 1869. Sergt. 60th N.Y. Inf., Sept. 9, 1861; 2d lt., Aug. 6, 1862; 1st lt. adj., Oct. 8, 1862; capt., Sept. 28, 1864; lt. col., Apr. 4, 1865; col., May 17, 1865; bvtd. col. and brig. gen. vols., Mar. 13, 1865, "for gallant and meritorious services in campaign resulting in the fall of Atlanta, Ga."; hon. mustered out, July 17, 1865. Asst. q.m. gen. State of N.Y., 1865-67; located in Mont., 1867, engaged in overland freighting, banking, mercantile pursuits. Mem. Territorial Legislature, 1868-69; q.m. gen. of Mont., 1883-87. Home: Bozeman, Mont. Died Jan. 26, 1919.

WILLSON, RUSSELL naval officer; b. Fredonia, N.Y., Dec. 27, 1883; s. Sidney Louis and Lucy Fenton (Staats) W.; student Mass. Inst. Tech., 1901-02; B.S., U.S. Naval Acad., 1906; student U.S. Naval War Coll., 1923-24; m. Eunice Westcott, June 3, 1911; children—Eunice Russell, Mary Westcott, Russell, Jr. (lt. U.S.N. deceased, 1945). Commd. ensign, U.S. Navy, 1908, and advanced through the grades to rear admiral, 1939, vice admiral, 1942; served on U.S.S. New York at Vera Cruz, 1914, and later as flag lieut. to adm. Mayo, Atlantic Fleet; organized and developed Code Signal Sect., Navy Dept., World War I; with 6th Battle Squadron of Grand Fleet at end of War; comd. destroyers at Greenland in connection with Army's around-the-world flight; mem. Naval Mission to Brazil, 1927-30; naval attaché Am. Embassy, London, 1937-38; comdr. Battleship Div. One, U.S. Fleet, 1939-40; supt. U.S. Naval Acad., 1941; chief of staff U.S. Fleet, Jan. 1942; vice adm., Mar. 1942, and dep. comdr-in-chief U.S. Fleet, Oct. 1942; retired Jan. 1943; duty with Joint Chiefs of Staff, 1944-46; now associate editor, "World Report"; member U.S. delegation at Dumbarton Oaks; mil. advisor, San Francisco Conf. Decorated Navy Cross, Distinguished Service Medal (Navy), Distinguished Service Medal (Army). Episcopalian. Club: Chevy Chase. Address: 107 Hesketh St., Chevy Chase, Md. Died July 6, 1948; buried in U.S. Naval Academy Cemetery, Annapolis, Md.

WILMER, WILLIAM HOLLAND M.D.; b. Powhatan Co., Va., Aug. 26, 1863; s. Richard Hooker (bishop Ala.), and Margaret (Brown) W.; prep. edn., Episcopal High Sch., Alexandria, Va.; M.D., U. of Va., 1885; studied New York Polyclinic, and hosps. of Europe; LL.D., Georgetown U., 1919; hon. Sc.D., Princeton, 1926, New York U., 1929; m. Re Lewis Smith, Oct. 6, 1891; 3 children—Richard Hooker, Mrs. Rebekah Scott, William Holland. Office asst. to Dr. Emil Gurening, N.Y. City, 1887-89; interne Mt. Sinai Hosp.; instr. N.Y. Polyclinic; outdoor dept. Bellevue Hosp., N.Y. City; practiced Washington, D.C., 1889-1925; prof. ophthalmology, Georgetown U., 1906-25; surgeon Episcopal Eye, Ear and Throat Hosp., Washington, D.C., 1895-1925; dir. Wilmer Ophthal. Inst. Johns Hopkins Hosp.; prof. ophthalmology Johns Hopkins University and ophthalmologist in chief to Johns Hopkins Hosp., 1925-34. Commd. lt. Med. R.C., U.S.A., Apr. 26, 1911; maj., 1917; lt. col. Med. Corps, N.A., Mar. 22, 1918; col. U.S.A., June 12, 1918; hon. disch., May 15, 1919; brig. gen. Med. R.C. Officer in charge Med. Research Lab., Air Serv., Mineola, L.I., until Aug. 1918; surgeon in charge Med. Research Labs., A.E.F., France, Aug. 1918-May 1919. Awarded D.S.M. (U.S.), Mar. 12, 1919. Comdr. Legion of Honor (France), Aug. 4, 1924. Mem. hygiene ref. bd. Life

Extension Inst.; mem. bd. of dirs., Nat. Com. for Prevention of Blindness, Advisory Com. Prevention Hereditary Blindness; fellow (a founder) Am. Coll. Surgeons; mem. numerous med. societies. Consulting oculist Episcopal Eye, Ear and Throat Hosp., Washington, D.C.; trustee Nat. Cathedral Foundation. Awarded decoration Angelo Secchi Acad. of Science, Georgetown U. Episcopalian. Home: Washington, D.C. Died Mar. 12, 1936.

WILSHIRE, WILLIAM WALLACE congressman; b. Shawneetown, Ill., Sept. 8, 1830; ed. country schs.; studied law. Gold miner, Cal., 1852-55; returned to Port Byron, Ill., 1855, engaged in coal mining, merc. bus.; admitted to Ill. bar, 1859; served as maj. 126th Regt., Ill. Volunteer Inf., Union Army, during Civil War, 1862-64; settled in Little Rock, Ark., began practice of law; apptd. solicitor gen. State of Ark., 1867; chief justice Ark. Supreme Ct., 1868-71; mem. U.S. Ho. of Reps. from Ark., as Republican, 43d Congress, 1873-June 16, 1874 (lost seat as result of contested election), as Conservative, 44th Congress, 1875-77; practiced law, Washington, D.C. Died Washington, Aug. 19, 1888; buried Mt. Holly Cemetery, Little Rock.

WILSON, CHARLES ERWIN ex-sec. of Defense; b. Minerva, O., July 18, 1890; s. Thomas Erwin and Rosalind (Unkefer) W.; E.E., Carnegie Inst. Technology, 1909; Sc.D., honorary, Columbia Univ., 1949; m. Jessie Ann Curtis, September 11, 1912; children—Thomas Erwin, Jessie Lucille, Jean Curtis, Edward Everett, Rosemary, Charles Erwin. Elec. engr. with Westinghouse Electric & Mfg. Co., 1909-19; chief engr., factory mgr. Delco Remy Co., 1919-26, pres., 1926-29; v.p. Gen. Motors Corp., 1929-39, dir. since 1934, exec. v.p., 1939-40, pres. 1941-53; designated chief exec. officer, 1946; secretary of Defense, 1953-57; director of the National Bank of Detroit. Member Society of Automotive Engrs. Republican. Episcopalian. Clubs: Detroit, Bloomfield Golf, Bloomfield Open Hunt. Home: Bloomfield Hills, Mich. Died Sept. 26, 1961.

WILSON, CHARLES IRVING brig. gen. U.S.A.; b. Washington, May 3, 1837; s. William and Huldah W.; ed. U. of Va.; m. Gertrude L. Houston, 1866. Apptd. from N.Y., asst. surgeon U.S.A., May 28, 1861; capt. asst. surgeon. May 28, 1866; resigned, Jan. 1, 1867; commd. capt. 16th Inf., Jan. 22, 1867; assigned to 14th Inf., Dec. 15, 1870; hon. disch. Dec. 31, 1870; apptd. maj. paymaster's dept., Mar. 3, 1875; lt. col. deputy p.-m.-gen., June 10, 1898; col. asst. p.-m.-gen., July 12, 1899; retired by operation of law, May 3, 1901; advanced to rank of brig. gen. retired, by act of Apr. 23, 1904. Bvtd.: capt., Mar. 13, 1865, .'for meritorious and distinguished services in battles of Todd's Tavern and Yellow Tavern, Va."; maj., Mar. 13, 1865, "for highly meritorious and distinguished services in 12 engagements in Shenandoah Valley, Va."; maj., Mar. 2, 1867, "for meritorious services in battle of Todd's Tavern." Home: New York, N.Y. Died Sept. 22, 1913.

WILSON, DUNNING STEELE M.D.; b. Louisville, Ky., Nov. 24, 1876; s. Samuel Ramsey (D.D.) and Anna Maria (Steele) W.; pub. schs., Louisville and St. Louis; Ph.G., Louisville Coll. Pharmacy, 1894; M.D., U. of Louisville, 1899; m. May Margaret Bonn, Sept. 8, 1903; children—Keith Singleton, Francis Edward. Med. practice at Louisville, Apr. 1, 1899—; supt. Eruptive Hosp., 1903; phys.-in-charge, Tuberculosis Dispensary, 1907-10; med. dir. and supt. Board of Tuberculosis Hosp., Sanatorium and Dispensary, Louisville, 1910-17; commd. capt. med. corps, Ky. N.G., 1910; maj. surgeon "Rainbow" Div., Ambulance Co., 1917, service in France; comdg. officer, Sanitary Train, 1st A.C., and lt. col. Med. Corps, Army of Occupation. Sch. trustee, Louisville, Ky., 1909-10. Mem. numerous med. societies. Med. dir. French Lick Spring (Ind.) Hotel. Citation from General Pershing and recommended for D.S.M. by chief surgeon 1st A.C., and chief surgeon of Army of Occupation. Colonel, O.R.C., U.S.A. Home: French Lick, Ind. Died Feb. 6, 1927.

WILSON, FLETCHER ALOYSIUS naval officer; b. Nottingham, Eng., Feb. 7, 1836. Apptd. 3d asst. engr. U.S.N., Aug. 26, 1859; 2d asst. engr., Oct. 21, 1861; 1st asst. engr., Oct. 1, i863; chief engr., Mar. 5, 1871; retired, Feb. 7, 1898; advanced to rank of rear admiral retired, June 29, 1906, for services during Civil War. Served on various vessels during Civil War; insp. machinery at San Francisco, 1887-90, Union Iron Works, 1894-98; mem. bd. Navy Yard, New York, 1893-94. Died 1907.

WILSON, FRANK ELMER bishop; b. Kittanning, Pa., Mar. 21, 1885; s. William White and Irene Mayhew (Ladd) W.; grad. Harvard Prep. Sch., Chicago, Ill., 1903; A.B., Hobart Coll., Geneva, N.Y., 1907, S.T.D., 1923; B.D., Gen. Theol. Sem., 1910; D.D., Nashotah House, 1929; S.T.D., Gen. Theol. Sem., 1929; m. Marie Louise Walker, Oct. 24, 1911 (died Nov. 1, 1924); 1 dau., Florence Harrington; m. 2d, Eleanor Lorinda Hall, 1929. Deacon, 1910, priest, 1910, P.E. Ch.; rector St. Ambrose Ch., Chicago Heights, Ill., 1910-13, St. Andrew's Ch., Chicago, 1913-15, St. Augustine's Ch., Wilmette, Ill., 1915-17, Christ Ch., Eau Claire, Wis., 1919-29; bishop, diocese of Eau Claire, since 1929. Served as chaplain A.E.F., 1917-18; maj., chaplain, U.S.R. Deputy, Gen. Conv. P.E. Ch., 1922, 25, 28. Pres. Trustees of Diocese of Eau Claire; trustee Nashotah House; trustee General Theological Seminary. Member Phi Beta Kappa, Sigma Phi fraternities. Decorated Italian Service Medal. Mason (33 deg.). Club: Country. Author: Contrasts in the Character of Christ, 1916; What a Churchman Ought to Know, 1920; Common Sense Religion, 1922; The Divine Commission, 1927; Outline History of the Episcopal Church, 1932; Outline of Christian Symbolism, 1933; Outline of the Old Testament, 1935; Outline of the New Testament, 1935; Outline of the Prayer Book, 1936; Outline of Personal Prayer, 1937; Outline of the Sacraments, 1937; Faith and Practice, 1939; Outline of the English Reformation, 1940; Outline of the Christian Year, 1941. Asso. editor The Witness. Home: 145 Marston Av., Eau Claire, Wis. Died Feb. 16, 1944.

WILSON, GEORGE BARRY naval officer; b. Norfolk, Va., Mar. 27, 1892; s. George Whitfield and Ada Maria (Maguire) W.; B.S., U.S. Naval Acad., 1914, student post grad. sch., 1919-20; M.S., Columbia, 1921; m. Mary Lawrence Stokes, Dec. 9, 1914; 1 dau., Mary Lawrence (Mrs. Desmond McTighe); m. 2d, Anna Ridout Tilghman, June 2, 1920; children—Anne Tilghman, George Barry, Ruth. Comd. ensign, U.S. Navy, 1914, advancing through the grades to rear adm., 1942; served in U.S.S. Delaware with British Grand Fleet during World War I; later assigned to Bureau of Aeronautics, then to U.S.S. Langley (first U.S. aircraft carrier); in destroyers of Battle Force (West Coast), 1923-25; aide to comdt. Navy Yard, Philadelphia, Pa., 1925-27; on staff of squadron comdr. of destroyers, Asiatic Sta., 1927-30; asst. inspector naval material, Philadelphia, Pa., 1930-32; gunnery officer, U.S.S. Mississippi, 1932-35; prodn. officer, Navy Yard, Pearl Harbor, 1935-38; exec. officer, U.S.S. Honolulu, 1938-40; various assignments Bureau of Naval Personnel, including dir. of officer personnel, 1940-42; comdg. officer, U.S.S. Alabama, 1942-43, chief of staff to comdr. U.S. Naval Forces in Europe, and naval attaché, London, Eng., since 1943. Home: 3420 39th St. N.W., Washington, D.C. Died Dec. 4, 1949.

WILSON, JAMES HARRISON soldier, railroad builder and manager; b. Shawneetown, Ill., Sept. 2, 1837; s. Harrison and Katharine (Schneider) W.; student McKendree Coll., Lebanon, Ill. (LL.D.), grad. U.S. Mil. Acad., 1860; m. Ella, d. Gen. J. W. Andrews, of Wilmington, Del., Jan. 3, 1866. Bvt. 2d lt. topographical engrs., July 1, 1860; 2d lt., June 10, 1861; promoted through grades to brig. gen. vols., Oct. 30, 1863; maj. gen. vols., May 6, 1865; bvtd.: maj., Apr. 11, 1862, "for gallant and meritorious services at Ft. Pulaski, Ga.,; lt. col., Nov. 24, 1863, for same at Chattanooga; col., May 5, 1864, for same, at the Wilderness, Va.; brig. gen., Mar. 13, 1865, for same at Nashville; maj. gen., Mar. 13, 1865, for same at Selma, Ala., and maj. gen., Oct. 5, 1865, for same during the war; hon. mustered out of vol. service, Jan. 8, 1866; lt. col. 35th U.S. Inf., July 28, 1866; hon. disch. at own request, Dec. 31, 1870; maj. gen. vols., May 4, 1898; brig. gen. vols., Apr. 12, 1899-Mar. 2, 1901; brig. gen. U.S.A. (by spl. act of Congress, Feb. 2, 1901), Feb. 11, 1901; retired, Mar. 2, 1901. Engr. and insp. gen. in Vicksburg and Chattanooga campaigns; chief of Cavalry Bur., War Dept., Feb.-Apr., 1864; comd. 3d div. Sheridan's cav., 1864; organized and comd. cav. corps Mil. Div. of the Miss., Oct. 1864; turned flank of Hood's army at Nashville, capturing many guns and prisoners and pursuing him to Tenn. River; comd. assault and capture of Selma and Montgomery, Ala., Columbus and Macon, Ga., and pursuit and capture of Jeff- erson Davis; in Spanish-Am. War, comd. 1st and 6th Army Corps in Ga. and the occupation of Cuba, also depts. of Matanzas and Santa Clara, and in P.R. campaign; joined China relief expdn.; comd. coöperating force of Am. and British troops in capture of the 8 temples, also Am. forces in Peking. Represented U.S. Army at coronation of King Edward VII. Largely engaged in r.r. and engring. operations for many yrs. Trustee Mut. Life Ins. Co., 1907—, and dir. in many corps. Author: Life of Andrew Alexander, 1868; Life of General Grant (with late Charles A. Dana), 1868; China—Travels and Investigations in the Middle Kingdom, 1887, 1900; Life and Services of Maj. Gen. William F. Smith; Life and Services of Maj. Gen. Alexander McD. McCook; Life and Services of Maj. Gen. John A. Rawlins; Life of Charles A. Dana, 1907; Under the Old Flag, 1912. Home: Wilmington, Del. Died Feb. 23, 1925.

WILSON, JOHN FRANKLIN lawyer; b. Pulaski, Tenn., May 7, 1846; academic edn.; m. 1890, Mrs. Robena Hamilton Nesby. Entered C.S. army, Aug., 1861; wounded 6 times; rose to lt.-col.; located in Ark., 1867; admitted to the bar, 1871; mem. legislature, 1877-79; pros. atty., 4th dist., 1884-87; removed to Ariz., 1887; atty.-gen., 1896-97; del. in Congress from Ariz., 1899-1901, and 1903-05. Democrat. Home: Phoenix, Ariz.

WILSON, JOHN MOULDER brig. gen. U.S.A.; b. in D.C., Oct. 8, 1837; grad. U.S. Mil. Acad., 1860; (LL.D., Columbian U., 1890). Bvt. lt. arty., July 1, 1860; 2d lt. arty., Jan. 28, 1861; 1st lt., May 14, 1861; transferred to engrs., 1862; capt. engrs., Mar. 3, 1863; maj., June 3, 1867; lt. col., Mar. 17, 1884; col., Mar. 27, 1895; brig. gen. chief of engrs. U.S.A., Feb. 1, 1897. In Civil war reached bvt. rank of col. in vols. and U.S.A. for gallantry in various battles; awarded Congressional Medal of Honor, July 3, 1897, "for most distinguished gallantry in action at Malvern Hill, Va., Aug. 6, 1862"; after war had charge of engring. works on rivers and harbors, canals, the building of the army med. museum and library, completion of Washington monument, etc.; supt. pub. bldgs. and grounds, 1885-89; supt. U.S. Mil. Acad., 1889-93; again supt. pub. bldgs. and grounds, 1893-97; chief of engrs. U.S.A., 1897-1901; retired at own request after 40 yrs.' service, Apr. 30, 1901. Pres. Washington Bd. of Trade, 1905-07; mem. Spanish War, Anthracite Coal Strike, Steamer Slocum Disaster commns. and Brownsville ct. of inquiry. Home: Washington, D.C. Died Feb. 1, 1919.

WILSON, JULIAN ALEXANDER, army officer; b. Lavonia, Ga., Nov. 11, 1909; s. Robert Marion and Nancy (Fleming) W.; B.S. in Commerce, Ga. Sch. Tech., 1933; postgrad. Clemson Coll., 1939, Mercer U., 1939; grad. Armed Forces Staff Coll., 1948, Air U., 1953, Air War Coll., 1953; m. Nancy West, June 26, 1935; children—Nancy L. (Mrs. James Barker), Julian Alexander, Valerie J., Robert M., John P. Commd. 2d lt. inf.-res., U.S. Army, 1933, called to active duty as 1st lt., 1940, advanced through grades to maj. gen., 1961; served in Hdqrs. ETOUSA, later with 12th Army Group, ETO, World War II; assigned War Dept. Gen. Staff, Washington, 1945-46, Office Adj. Gen., Washington, 1947-49; dep. adj. gen., later adj. gen., USARCARIB, Ft. Amador, C.Z., 1949-52; adj. gen. Armor Center, Ft. Knox, Ky., 1953-56; assigned officers assignment div. Dept. Army, 1956-61; adj. gen. Hdqrs. USAREUR, 1960-61; dep. adj. gen. Dept. Army, 1961-62, dep. chief personnel operations, then chief. Decorated Legion of Merit, Bronze Star, Commendation ribbon with metal pendant; Croix de Guerre with palm (Belgium); Croix de Guerre with palm, Legion of Honor (France); Order British Empire. Home: Falls Church VA Died Aug. 6, 1969; buried Arlington Nat. Cemetery, Arlington VA

WILSON, JULIAN MORRIS b. Beverly, N.J., July 22, 1866; s. John Jacob and Julia (Langdale) W.; ed. Van Rensselaer Inst. and under tutors; studied law in office of Southgate & Southgate, New York; m. Helen McNeely, June 2, 1897. Admitted to N.Y. bar, 1903, and began practice as patent atty. in N.Y. City; pres. Nat. Supply Co.; v.p. Fantail Boat Corp. Capt. U.S.A., World War; maj., 1919. Mem. Am. Legion; awarded N.Y. State Medal, World War Medal. Republican. Episcopalian. Home: New York, N.Y. Died June 6, 1931.

WILSON, LOUIS BLANCHARD pathologist; b. Pittsburgh, Pa., Dec. 22, 1866; s. Henry Harrison and Susan (Harbach) W.; M.D., U. of Minn., 1896, D.Sc., 1940; m. Mary Stapleton, Aug. 26, 1891 (died in 1920); children—Mrs. Alice Martin, Carroll Louis; m. 2d, Maud H. Mellish, Aug. 21, 1924 (died 1933); m. 3d, Grace G. McCormick, Jan. 2, 1935. Asst. prof. pathology and bacteriology, U. of Minn., 1896-1905; dir. Labs. of Mayo Clinic since 1905; prof. of pathology and dir. The Mayo Foundation for Medical Edn. and Research, U. of Minn., 1915-37; emeritus prof. pathology and dir., The Mayo Foundation, since 1937. Commd. Col. Medical R.C., U.S. Army, 1917. D.S.M. (U.S. Army), 1920. Mem. Assn. Am. Physicians, Am. Assn. Pathologists and Bacteriologists, Am. Anat. Soc., Am. Assn. Cancer Research, A.M.A. (council on edn. and hosps.), Assn. of American Med. Colleges (pres. 1931-33), Nat. Bd. of Med. Examiners, A.A.A.S., Adv. Bd. of Medical Specialties (pres. 1935-37), Minn. Hort. Society, Nat. Rifle Assn., Phi Beta Kappa, Sigma Xi (pres. 1932-33), Alpha Kappa Kappa, Alpha Omega Alpha. Unitarian. Clubs: University, Campus (Minneapolis); University, Commercial (Rochester). Contbr. various articles reprinted in "Collected Papers," by staff of Mayo Clinic, since 1910. Home: Rochester, Minn. Died Oct. 5, 1943.

WILSON, ORME foreign service, ret.; b. N.Y.C., Nov. 13, 1885; s. Marshall Orme and Caroline Schermerhorn (Astor) W.; A.B., Harvard, 1907; m. Alice Borland, June 8, 1910; 1 son, Orme. Mem. investment firm of R. T. Wilson & Co., New York, 1913-19; entered U.S. Diplomatic Service, 1920; has served as sec. in embassies at Brussels, Buenos Aires and Berlin and in legation at Berne; asst. chief Div. of Latin-Am. Affairs, Dept. of State, Washington, 1930-33; consul gen. and first sec. of legation, Prague, 1935-36; first sec. of Embassy, Buenos Aires, 1936-38, counselor of Embassy, 1938; counselor of Embassy, Brussels, 1938-40; liaison officer, Dept. of State with War and Navy departments, 1940-44; United States Ambassador to Haiti, 1944-46. Director of the Children's Hosp.; dir. Nat. Symphony Orchestra; 1st v.p., trustee Corcoran Gallery of Art. Served as 1st lt., U.S. Army M.I. Div., also with Council of Nat. Defense and Q.M.C., U.S. Army, World War I. V.p., bd. mgrs. Seamen's Ch. Inst., N.Y. Mem. Council Fgn. Relations. Episcopalian. Mason. Clubs: Harvard, Union, Knickerbocker, Tuxedo, Church, St. Nicholas, Pilgrims (N.Y.C.); Metropolitan, Chevy Chase (Washington). Address 760 Park Av., N.Y.C.; also 2406 Massachusetts Av., Washington. Died Feb. 13, 1966; buried Woodlawn Cemetery, N.Y.C.

WILSON, RICHARD HULBERT army officer; b. Hillsdale, Mich., June 10, 1853; s. Edward H. C. and Helen M. (Hulbert) W.; grad. U.S. Mil. Acad., 1877; m.

Grace A. Chaffin, of Cheyenne, Wyo., June 25, 1895. Commd. 2d lt. 8th Inf., June 15, 1877; 1st lt., Jan. 1, 1886; capt., July 31, 1894; maj., Feb. 28, 1901; lt. col. 16th Inf., Apr. 5, 1906; col. 14th Inf., June 12, 1910. Asst. instr. Inf. and Cav. Sch. until 1891; duty at Ft. McKinley, Wyo., 1891-94; Indian agt. Arapahoe and Shoshone Agency, Wyo., 1895-98; participated with regt. in battles of El Caney and San Juan, Cuba, and siege of Santiago, 1898; recommended for bvt. as maj. "for gallantry" at Battle of El Caney; comdr. Ft. Michael, Alaska, 1902-04; comd. Porto Rico Provisional Regt. of Inf., 1908-09; duty on Mexican border, 1917. Democrat. Methodist. Club: Rainier (Seattle, Wash.). Home: Amherst, Mass.

WILSON, THOMAS MURRAY fgn. service officer; b. Memphis, July 29, 1881; s. Thomas Edmiston and Ellen (Murray) W.; ed. mil. and pvt. schs. Engaged in cotton bus., banking and farming, 1899-1916; consul at Hankow, China, 1919-20, at Tientsin, Tsinan and Amoy, 1920-21, Madras, India, 1921-22, Bombay, 1922-23; with Fgn. Service Dept., Washington, 1923-25; fgn. service insp., 1925-33; consul at Kingston, Ont., temporarily, 1927; apptd. sec. in diplomatic service, consul gen., 1928; chief div. fgn. service personnel Dept. State, 1933-37; mem. bd. of examiners for fgn. service and fgn. service sch. bd., 1933-37; consul gen., at Sydney, Australia, 1937; consul gen. Calcutta, India, 1940-41; U.S. commr. to India, with rank of minister, 1941-42; State Dept., 1942; minister, consul gen., Bagdad, 1942-43; ret. from fgn. service, 1944. Served as 1st lt. and capt. ordnance, U.S. Army, World War I. Clubs: Metropolitan, University (Washington). Address: 3326 Reservoir Rd., Washington. Died 1967.

WILSON, WILLIAM army officer; b. Seneca, N.Y., June 16, 1855; s. James and Anna H. (Whitney) W.; A.B., Hobart Coll., Geneva, N.Y., 1876, A.M., 1879; m. Mary E. Hipple, Nov. 20, 1878; 1 son, James Whitney. In nursery business on own account, at Geneva, until 1899; entered hardware business, 1899; burned out Feb. 20, 1916 (retired). Enlisted as pvt. 34th Separate Co., N.G.N.Y., Jan. 21, 1880; commd. 1st lt., Feb. 28, 1882; promoted through grades to bvtd. brig. gen., Oct. 29, 1907; brig. gen. 4th Brigade, June 10, 1914; brig. gen. of the line, Mar. 1917; brig. gen. N.A., Sept. 5, 1917. Comd. 3d N.Y. Brigade, on Mexican border, June-Dec. 1916; comdr. Guards, Eastern Dept., Aug.-Nov. 1917; comdr. 78th Inf. Brigade, Camp Beauregard, Alexandria, La., Nov. 1, 1917-Jan. 3, 1918; comdr. 2d Prov. Brigade, Camp Wadsworth, Spartanburg, S.C., Jan.-Nov. 1918; comdg. Gen. Prov. Dept. for Corps and Army Troops, Nov. 1918-Mar. 1919; comdg. gen. Camp Wadsworth, Jan.-Apr. 1919; hon. disch., July 18, 1919; brig. gen. U.S.A., retired, June 21, 1928. Mem. staff of Gov. Theodore Roosevelt, N.Y., 1899-1900; mem. Militia Council of New York, 1912, 13; mem. State Bd. of Armory Commrs. of N.Y., 1914-19. Presbyterian. Home: Nobleton, Fla. Died Jan. 6, 1937.

WILSON, WOODROW twenty-eighth President of the United States; b. Staunton, Va., Dec. 28, 1856; s. Rev. Joseph R. and Jessie (Woodrow) W.; Scotch-Irish ancestry on both sides; Davidson Coll., N.C., 1874-75; A.B., Princeton, 1879, A.M., 1882; grad. in law, U. of Va., 1881; practiced law at Atlanta, Ga., 1882-83; post-grad. work at Johns Hopkins, 1883-85, Ph.D., 1886; (LL.D., Wake Forest, 1887, Tulane, 1898, Johns Hopkins, 1902, Rutgers, 1902, U. of Pa., 1903, Brown, 1903, Harvard, 1907, Williams, 1908, Dartmouth, 1909; Litt.D., Yale, 1901; m. Ellen Louise Axson, June 24, 1885 (died 1914); m. 2d, Edith Bolling Galt, Dec. 18, 1915. Asso. prof. history and polit. economy, Bryn Mawr College, 1885-88; prof. same, Wesleyan University, 1888-90; prof. Jurisprudence and political economy, 1890-95, prof. jurisprudence, 1895-97, prof. jurisprudence and politics, 1897-1910, pres., Aug. 1, 1902-Oct. 20, 1910, Princeton U.; gov. of N.J., Jan. 17, 1911-Mar. 1, 1913 (resigned); nominated for President in Dem. Nat. Conv., Baltimore, 1912, and elected Nov. 4, 1912, for term, Mar. 4, 1913-Mar. 4, 1917, receiving 435 electoral votes; Theodore Roosevelt, the Progressive nominee received 88 votes, and William Howard Taft, the Republican nominee received 8 votes. Renominated for President in Dem. Nat. Conv., St. Louis, 1916, and reëlected Nov. 7, 1916, for term Mar. 4, 1917-Mar. 4, 1921, receiving 277 electoral votes; Charles E. Hughes, the Republican nominee received 254 electoral votes. Left for France on the troopship George Washington, Dec. 4, 1918, at the head of Am. Commn. to Negotiate Peace; arrived at Brest, Dec. 13, at Paris, Dec. 14; visited Eng., Dec. 26-30, 1918, Italy, Jan. 2-6, 1919, Belgium, June 18-19, 1919; delivered many addresses and given hon. degrees by various univs. of allied countries; returned to U.S., arriving in Boston, Feb. 24, 1919; left New York on 2d trip to Europe, Mar. 5, after speaking at closing session of Congress and arrived in Paris, Mar. 14; signed Peace Treaty, June 28, 1919; returned to U.S., arriving in New York, July 8, 1919. Author: Congressional Government, a Study in American Politics, 1885; The State—Elements of Historical and Practical Politics, 1889; Division and Reunion, 1829-1889, 1893; An Old Master and Other Political Essays, 1893; Mere Literature, and Other Essays, 1893; George Washington, 1896; A History of the American People, 1902; Constitutional Government in the United States, 1908; The State-Elements of Historical and Practical Politics, new edit., 1911; Free Life, 1913; The New Freedom, 1913; When a Man Comes to Himself, 1915; On Being Human, 1916. Home: Washington, D.C. Died Feb. 3, 1924.

WINANS, EDWIN BARUCH (wi'nanz), army officer; b. Hamburg, Mich., Oct. 31, 1869; s. late Hon. Edwin B. (gov. of Mich.) and Elizabeth (Galloway) W.; grad. U.S. Mil. Acad., 1891; m. Edith May, d. Brig. Gen. William Auman, U.S. Army, June 1, 1892; died Feb. 8, 1920; children—Katherine Auman (wife of Russell L. Maxwell, U.S. Army), Elizabeth Galloway (wife of W. R. Grove, Jr., U.S. Army); m. 2d, Esther Walker, Sept. 5, 1943. Commd. 2d lt. 5th Cav., June 12, 1891; 1st lt. 4th Cav., Apr. 30, 1898, maj. 34th Mich. Inf., May 25, 1898; hon. mustered out vols., Nov. 26, 1898; capt. U.S. Army, Feb. 2, 1901; maj. of cav., Sept. 2, 1914; assigned to 7th Cav., Nov. 26, 1915; lt. col., Feb. 2, 1917; col. (temp.), Aug. 5, 1917; brig. gen. N.A., June 26, 1918; col. U.S. Army, Feb. 23, 1920; brig. gen., U.S. Army, Dec. 30, 1922. Served in Ind. Ty. and Tex., 1891-97; prof. mil. science and tactics, Mich. Mil. Acad., 1897-98; with regt. in Philippines, 1899-1900; with Punitive Expdn. in Mexico, 1916; apptd. comdr. 64th Brigade Inf., 32d Div., 1st Army Corps, A.E.F., 1918, and served therewith until close of war. Promoted col. cav., Feb. 23, 1920; brig. gen., Dec. 30, 1922; maj. gen., Oct. 18, 1927, and assigned as supt. U.S. Mil. Acad.; assigned as comdr. Hawaiian Div.; later in command 8th Corps Area, Ft. Sam Houston, Tex.; retired as maj. gen., Oct. 31, 1933. Mem. of League of Nations Commn. for the Government of Leticia, Jan. to July 1934. Awarded D.S.M. "for exceptionally distinguished and meritorious service" during three major offensives; Légion d'Honneur and Croix de Guerre with 2 palms, by French Govt. Address: Contemplation, Vienna, Va. Died Dec, 31, 1947; buried U.S. Military Academy Cemetery.

WINANS, HENRY MORGAN physician; b. Denver, Oct. 13, 1893; s. Henry Sample and Florence Adelaide (Morgan) W.; A.B., Leland Stanford U., 1916; M.D., John Hopkins, 1919; LL.D. (hon.), Baylor U., 1945; m. Judith Terrell Hawley, Dec. 19, 1918; children—Henry Morgan, Judith (Mrs. Carey Gray King), Sue Terrell (Mrs. Harold H. Young). Instr. medicine, Baylor U., the Coll. of Medicine, 1921-23, asst. prof., 1923-25, asso. prof., 1925-29, prof. medicine, chmn. dept., 1929-43; clin. prof. med. Southwestern Med. Coll., 1943-47, prof. since 1947, prof. med. hist., 1943-54, chmn. med. service, Baylor U. Hosp., 1929-54; chmn. med. bd., 1946-50; chief med. service, Brooke Gen. Hosp., 1945; cons. in medicine VA, since 1946. Organized 56th Evacuation Hosp.; served as col., M.C., U.S. Army, Africa, Naples-Foggia, and Rome-Arno campaigns; expert cons. in medicine to Surgeon Gen., 4th Army Area, 1946-47. Awarded Unit Citation and Army Commendation ribbon; Selective Service medal. Recipient Marchman award med. edn., 1957. Diplomate Am. Bd. Internal Medicine. Fellow A.C.P.; mem. Ho-Din Medical Soc., A.M.A., So. Med. Assn., Tex. Acad. Sci., Tex. Acad. Internal Medicine, Dallas So. Clin. Soc., Beta Theta Pi, Nu Sigma Nu, Phi Beta Kappa, Alpha Omega Alpha. Author and contbr. articles on medical subjects and on flying. Home: 3825 Beverly Dr., Dallas 75205. Office: 2703 Oak Lawn Av., Dallas 19. Died Mar. 14, 1965; cremated, Dallas.

WINANT, JOHN GILBERT (wi'nant), diplomat; b. New York, N.Y., Feb. 23, 1889; s. Frederick and Jeanette L. (Gilbert) W.; prep. edn., St. Paul's Sch., Concord, N.H.; M.A., Princeton, 1925, Dartmouth, 1925; LL.D., U. of N.H., 1926; m. Constance Rivington Russell, Dec. 20, 1919; children—Constance, John G., Rivington Russell. Mem. N.H. Ho. of Rep., sessions 1917, 23, Senate, 1921; gov. of N.H., 1925-26, 1931-34; chmn. Textile Inquiry Bd., 1934; asst. dir. Internat. Labor Office, Geneva, 1935 and 1937-39, dir. since 1939; chmn. Social Security Bd., 1935-37, apptd. ambassador to Great Britain, 1941. Apptd. U.S. rep. on European Advisory Commn., 1943. Enlisted in Paris as pvt. A.E.F., 1917; with 1st Aero Squadron; comdr. 8th Observation Squadron; hon. discharged as capt., Apr. 1919. Mem. N.E. Council, Nat. Recreation Assn. (v.p.), N.H. Tuberculosis Assn., (pres.), Nat. Consumers League (pres.), Am. Assn. Labor Legislation (v.p.). Trustee Internat. Y.M.C.A. Coll. Republican. Episcopalian. Clubs: Wonolancet (Concord); Odd Volumes (Boston); Century, Racquet and Tennis (New York). Home: 274 Pleasant St., Concord, N.H. Address: American Embassy, London, England.* Died Nov. 3, 1947.

WINCHESTER, JAMES army officer; b. Carroll County, Md., Feb. 6, 1752; s. William and Lydia (Richards) W.; m. Susan Black, 1803, 14 children including Marcus. Served with Md. Battalion of Flying Camp, Am. Revolution, 1776, wounded and captured, Staten Island, 1777, exchanged, 1778; captured again, Charleston, S.C., 1780; promoted capt., 1780, served at Yorktown, 1781; moved to Middle Tenn., 1785; mem. N.C. Conv. to ratify U.S. Constn., 1788; capt., col., brig. gen. of Mero dist., Tenn. Militia, famous for Indian campaigns; speaker Tenn. Senate, 1796; commd. brig. gen. U.S. Army, in command Army of N.W., War of 1812; commr. to run Chickasaw Boundary Line between Tenn. and Miss., 1819; a founder Memphis (Tenn.). Died July 26, 1826; buried "Cragfont," nr. Memphis.

WINDER, JOHN HENRY army officer; b. Rewston, Md., Feb. 21, 1800; s. William H. and Gertrude (Polk) W.; grad. U.S. Mil. Acad., 1820; m. Elizabeth Shepard, 1823; m. 2d, Mrs. Catherine Cox Eagle. Instr. tactics U.S. Mil. Acad., 1823; assigned to duty in Me. and Fla., 1827-45; brevetted maj., then lt. col. for conduct in Mexican War; commd. maj. arty. U.S. Army, 1860, resigned, 1861; commd. brig. gen. Confederate Army, 1861, provost marshal and comdr. Northern prisons, Richmond, Va.; in charge of mil. prison, Danville, Va., then all prisons in Ga. and Ala., 1864; commissary gen. all Confederate mil. prisons east of the Mississippi, 1864-65. Died Florence, S.C., Feb. 8, 1865.

WINDER, WILLIAM HENRY army officer, lawyer; b. Somerset County, Md., Feb. 18, 1775; s. John Winder; m. Gertrude Polk, 1799; 1 son, John Henry. Apptd. lt. col. 14th Inf., U.S. Army, 1812; promoted col., served on No. frontier, 1812; commd. brig. gen., 1813, captured in Battle of Stony Creek, released on parole; in command at Battle of Bladensburg (Va.), 1814, court martialed for ordering retreat resulting in abandonment of Washington (D.C.) to enemy, honorably acquitted; discharged from U.S. Army, 1815; practiced law. Balt., 1815-24. Died Balt., May 24, 1824.

WINDSOR, H. R. H., The Duke of (Edward Albert Christian George Andrew Patrick David); b. Richmond Park, England, June 23, 1894; s. H.M. King George V and H.M. Queen Mary; cadet R.N. Coll., Osborne, 1907-09, cadet, at Dartmouth, 1909-11, Oxford, 1912-14; m. Mrs. Wallis Warfield, June 3, 1937. Personal a.d.c. to King George V, 1919-36 served as a Counsellor of State; ascended the throne as King Edward VIII, Jan. 20, 1936, abdicated Dec. 1936 in favor of brother, Duke of York, as King George VI; lived on continent of Europe, 1937-39; gov. and comdr.-in-chief of the Bahama Islands, 1940-45. Apptd. midshipman, Royal Navy, 1911, and advanced through the grades to Admiral of the Fleet, 1936; apptd. 2d lt., 1st batn. Grenadier Guards, 1914; a.d.c. to comdr.-in-chief of British Expeditionary Forces and on active service, 1914; served in Italy, France and Egypt, 1916; decorated Knight of the Garter; Military Cross, (1916). Author: AKing's Story. Address: Paris France Died May 28, 1972; buried Frogmore, Windsor Eng.

WINDSOR, WILLIAM AUGUSTUS naval officer; b. in Va., Feb. 13, 1842; s. Griffith and Eliza (Fouchée) W.; ed. grammar and high schs., Baltimore; studied engring. in pvt. sch. of Richard C. Potts, Baltimore, and in drawing room and shops of B.&O. R.R. Co.; m. Rachel Josephine Noble, June 11, 1874. Apptd. 3d asst. engr., U.S.N., Sept. 16, 1862; 2d asst. engr., Aug. 8, 1864; promoted passed asst. engr., Jan. 1, 1868; chief engr. U.S.N. (rank lt. comdr.), June 17, 1889, and of relative rank of comdr., Feb. 26, 1897; made comdr. by Act of Congress, Mar. 3, 1899; promoted capt. U.S.N., Dec. 27, 1901; rear admiral U.S.N. and retired, Sept. 16, 1902. During Civ. War attached to U.S.S. Miami, N. Atlantic squadron, and U.S.S. Nyack, and after war served on various vessels and stas., last sea service being on U.S.S. Minneapolis, 1897-98; chief engr. (head dept. steam engring.) Navy Yard, New York, 1898-99; insp. machinery at Crescent Ship Yard, Elizabeth, N.J., and Babcock & Wilson Works, Bayonne, N.J., 1899-1903. Episcopalian. Died 1907.

WING, CHARLES BENJAMIN civil engr.; b. Willow Brook (now Clinton Corners), N.Y., Jan. 18, 1864; s. Phineas Rice and Mary (Sands) W.; prep. edn. Poughkeepsie Mil. Inst.; C.E., Cornell U., 1886; fellow civ. engring., Cornell, 1886-87; m. Anna Maria Paddock, Sept. 18, 1888 (died Feb. 1905); children—Sumner Paddock, Winchester Paddock, Charles Benjamin, Robert Lewis; m. 2d, Mrs. Marian (Colt) Browne, Feb. 20, 1908; step children—Ashley Colt Browne, Mrs. Frances Browne Wenzel. Instr. civil engring., Cornell, 1886-90; asst. prof., 1890-91, prof. bridge and hydraulic engring., 1891-92, U. of Wis.; prof. structural engring., 1892-1929, emeritus since 1929, exec. head dept. civil engring., 1923-29, Stanford U.; vice chmn. and exec. officer Calif. State Redwood Park Commn., 1911-26; chief of Div. of Parks of State Dept. of Natural Resources of Calif., 1928-35; chief State Park Authority and engr. in charge of Federal coöperative projects in Calif. State Parks, 1935-36; cons. civil engr. since 1936. Major and lt. col. 23d Engineers, on ry. constrn. and highway work and with 1st Army in Argonne-Meuse, in France, April 1918-June 1919. Cons. engr. bridges, wireless towers and spl. structures, among which are the 1,000 ft. towers for the Shanghai, China, station of the Federal Telegraph Co. Councilman Palo Alto, 1909-29. Mem. Am. Soc. C.E., Pacific Assn. Cons. Engrs., Am. Soc. Testing Materials, Sigma Xi. Clubs: Commonwealth, Engineers (San Francisco). Author: Freehand Lettering for Working Drawings, 1893; Manual of Bridge Drafting (with C. H. Wright,), 1896; also various papers in Trans. Am. Soc. C.E. and other tech. jours. Home and office: 345 Lincoln Av., Palo Alto, Calif. Died Aug. 22, 1945.

WINLOCK, HERBERT EUSTIS archeologist; b. Washington, D.C., Feb. 1, 1884; s. Wm. Crawford and Alice (Broom) W.; A.B., Harvard, 1906; hon. Litt.D., Yale, 1933, Princeton U., 1934; U. of Mich., 1936; Art D., Harvard, 1938; m. Helen Chandler, Oct. 26, 1912; children—Frances (dec.), William Crawford (dec.), Barbara. Engaged in archeol. excavations, 1906-31, at

Lisht, Oasis of Kharga, and Luxor, Egypt, for Met. Museum of Art, dir. Egyptian Expdn., 1928-32, curator Egyptian dept., 1929-39; dir. Metropolitan Museum of Art, 1932-39; dir. emeritus since 1939. Served as capt., later maj. C.A.C., World War. Hon. fellow Am. Numismatic Soc.; mem. Am. Oriental Soc., Am. Assn. Museums (pres. 1936-38), Am. Philosophical Society of American Academy Arts and Sciences, Royal Asiatic Society (hon.), Society of the Cincinnati. Decorated Chevalier Legion of Honor (France), Orders of Leopold and of the Crown (Belgium). Clubs: Century, Round Table (New York). Author: (with A. C. Mace) The Tomb of Senebtisi, 1916; Basreliefs from the Temple of Rameses I at Abydos, 1921; (with W. E. Crum) The Monastery of Epiphanius, 1926; The Tomb of Meryet-Amun, 1932; The Treasure of Lahun, 1934; The Oasis of ed Dakhleh, 1936; The Temple of Rameses I at Abydos, 1937; The Temple of Hibis in el Khargeh Oasis, 1941; Materials Used in the Embalming of Tutankhamen, 1941; Excavation at Deir el Behri: 1911-31, 1942; The Slain Soldiers of Neb-Hepet Re'Mentuhotpe, 1945; The Treasure of the Three Princesses, 1947; The Rise and Fall of the Middle Kingdom in Thebes, 1947. Contbr. to Bulletin of Metropolitan Museum Art, Met. Museum Studies, also Jour. Egyptian Archeology, Am. Jour. Semitic Languages, Am. Philosophical Soc., Scribner's Mag., Jour. Near Eastern Studies. Address: North Haven, Me. Died Jan. 26, 1950.

WINN, FRANK LONG army officer; b. Winchester, Ky.. Oct. 4, 1864; s. William and Carrie Sinclair (Hord) W.; student Centre Coll., Danville, Ky., 1880-81; grad. U.S. Mil. Acad., 1886, Army War Coll., 1916; m. Dora Boardman, Nov. 5, 1890 (died 1891); 1 dau., Dora (Mrs. Lovell Langstroth, dec.); m. 2d, Katharine McCord, Oct. 15, 1910. Commd. 2d lt. 1st Inf., July 1, 1886; promoted through grades to brig. gen. N.A., Aug. 5, 1917; maj. gen., Oct. 1, 1918; brig. gen. U.S.A., Oct. 2, 1921; promoted major general U.S.A., Dec. 2, 1922. In Sioux Indian Campaign, 1890-91; prof. mil. science and tactics, U. of Calif., 1893-97; in Cuba, Spanish-Am. War. 1898; nominated bvt. capt. "for gallantry in action" at El Caney, July 1, 1898; assisted in subduing Philippine Insurrection, 1899-1901; nominated bvt. maj. "for gallantry in action," at Angeles, Luzon, Aug. 16, 1899; Mexican Punitive Expdn., 1916; mil. sec. of Lt. Gen. Arthur MacArthur, 1907-09; in command of 177th Infantry Brigade, Camp Funston, Kansas, Sept. 5, 1917-May 1918 and Sept. 7-Nov. 11, 1918, 89th Division, Nov. 5-12, 1917. Nov. 26, 1917-Apr. 12, 1918, May 31-Sept. 6, 1918, and Nov. 12, 1918, till demobilization, June 1919; comd. Camp Custer, Mich., June, July 1919; remanded to regular rank of col. U.S.A., 37th Inf., July 31, 1919. In front line, sector northwest of Toul, St. Mihiel drive, Meuse-Argonne operations, and with Army of Occupation in Germany, D.S.M. "for exceptionally meritorious and distinguished services," 1919; Croix de Guerre, 2 palms; Comdr. Legion of Honor. Insp. gen., Aug. 20. 1920; insp., 2d Corps Area, Sept. 17, 1920-May 8, 1921; gen. staff, chief of staff, 2d Corps Area, May 9, 1921, Oct. 24, 1921; comd. 4th Coast Art. Dist., Ft. McPherson, Ga., Jan.-Dec. 1922, and 4th Training Camp, McClellan, Ala., Apr.-Sept. 1922; retired, Dec. 5, 1922. Citations by War Dept., 1924, for gallantry in Cuba in 1898 during Spanish-Am. War and in Luzon, 1899, during Philippine Insurrection. Mason. Home: Palo Alto, Calif. Died Feb. 24, 1941.

WINN, JOHN SHERIDAN army officer; b. in Ky., Nov. 26, 1863; grad. U.S. Mil. Acad., 1888. Commd. 2d lt. 2d Cav., June 11, 1888; 1st lt. 1st Cav., June 14, 1895; trans. to 2d Cav., Nov. 7, 1895; capt., Feb. 2, 1901; q.m., Apr. 9, 1907; assigned to 9th Cav., Apr. 9, 1911; maj. 4th Cav., July 23, 1911; trans. to 2d Cav., Aug. 31, 1911; insp. gen., Sept. 1, 1914; lt. col., July 1, 1916; nom. brig. gen. by Pres. Wilson, Jan. 4, 1918. Served at various southwestern posts until 1892; instr. mathematics, U.S. Mil. Acad., 1892-96; with regt. at Tampa, Fla., 1898, Matanzas, Cuba, 1902; duty in Philippine Islands, 1906-07; insp. gen. Southern Dept., 1917. Died Jan. 24, 1940.

WINN, RICHARD army officer, congressman; b. Fauquier County, Va., 1750; s. Minor and Margaret (O'Conner) W.; m. Pricilla McKinley, several children. Commd. 1st lt. 3d S.C. Regt., Continental Army, 1775; made justice of peace S.C., 1775; fought in Battle of Ft. Moultrie, 1776; as capt. in command defended Ft. McIntosh, Ga., 1777; took part in defense of Charleston, 1780; joined Thomas Sumter's guerrillas as maj., 1780; rep. to Jacksonborough Assembly, 1782; commd. brig. gen. S.C. Militia, 1783, maj. gen., 1800; surveyed Camden Dist., S.C., 1783; gave 100 acres to Mt. Zion Soc. (youth edn.), 1785; mem. S.C. Legislature; commr. to buy (later sell) lands for new state capital at Columbia, 1786; supt. Indian affairs for Creek Nation, 1788; mem. U.S. Ho. of Reps. (Democrat) from S.C., 3d-4th, 7th-12th congresses, 1793-97, Jan. 24, 1803-13; moved to Tenn., 1813, became planter and mcht. Died Duck River, Tenn., Dec. 19, 1818; buried Winnsboro, S.C.

WINSHIP, BLANTON army officer, b. Macon, Ga., Nov. 23, 1869; A.B., Mercer U., 1889; LL.B., U. of Georgia, 1893; LL.D., Mercer U., 1932, also U. of Puerto Rico. Served as capt., 1st Ga. Inf., in Spanish-Am. War, 1898; as 1st lt. U.S. Army, Philippine Insurrection, 1899-1901; promoted through grades and appointed maj. gen., judge advocate general of United States Army, Mar. 1, 1931; retired. Recalled to active duty as coordinator Inter-Am. Defense Bd., Washington, D.C., Nov. 30, 1933. Assistant secretary of state and justice, and member of advisory commn. for revision of laws of Cuba, 1906-09; with Gen. Funston at Vera Cruz, Mex., as officer in charge civil affairs, 1912; served in France, 1917-23, with 42nd, 1st and 28th divs., on staff of 1st Corps and 1st Army at their organization; comd. 112th and 110th Inf. of 28th Div.; went to Switzerland on special mission, 1918; dir. gen. of service for settlement of all claims in Europe arising out of U.S. mil. operations and in one year settled over 100,000 claims, 1918-19; judge advocate Army of Occupation in Germany; served on different coms. of Reparations Commn. for execution of peace treaties, 1920-23. Mil. aide to Pres. of U.S., May 1927-Jan. 1928; legal adviser to gov. gen. P.I., 1928-30; represented Philippine govt. at confs. of commissioners on uniform state laws, 1930-31; mem. delegation representing U.S. at unveiling of statue of Henry Clay in Venezuela, 1930; spl. commr. to Liberia, 1933, and designated as Am. mem. Com. of League of Nations on Liberian Affairs; gov. of Puerto Rico, Jan. 1934-Sept. 1939. Awarded Silver Star Citation, D.S.M., D.S.C.; also decorated Officer Legion of Honor; received Pan-Am. Society's insignia, the "Gold Award," for service to the Pan-Am. Union. Home: Macon, Ga. Died Oct. 9, 1947.

WINSLOW, CAMERON MCRAE naval officer; b. Washington, D.C., July 29, 1854; s. Comdr. Francis Winslow (U.S.N.) and Mary S. (Nelson) W.; grad. U.S. Naval Acad. (with high honors), 1875; m. Theodora Havemeyer, Sept. 18, 1899; children—Natalie, Cameron McRae, Theodora, Emilie, John Chilton, Arthur. Ensign, July 18, 1876; promoted through grades to rear adm., Sept. 14, 1911. Served on Nashville during Spanish-Am. War (wounded in action while in command of cable cutting expdn. off Cienfuegos, Cuba); advanced 5 numbers in rank for "extraordinary heroism" during Spanish-Am. War; served on U.S.S. Indiana, 1898; on staff of Admiral Sampson, 1899; at Brooklyn Navy Yard, 1899; in charge of branch hydrographic office, New York, 1900; on staff of Rear Admiral Higginson, N. Atlantic Fleet, 1901, 02, 04, 05; naval aide to Pres. Roosevelt, 1905; comd. Mayflower, 1905; comd. squadron for peace conf.; witness of signing Treaty of Portsmouth. Served with Bur. of Nav., 1902-05; comd. Charleston, 1905-07; with Sec. of State Root on bd. trip around S. America; with Bur. of Nav., 1907-08; comd. New Hampshire, 1908-09; supervisor of New York Harbor, 1909-11; comd. 2d Div., Atlantic Fleet, 1911-12, 3d Div., same, 1912-13, 1st Div., 1913; at Naval War Coll., Newport, 1914-15; comd. Spl. Service Squadron, 1914; comdr. in chief, Pacific Fleet, 1915-16; retired, July 29, 1916. Returned to active duty, Sept. 17, 1917, as insp. of naval dists., Atlantic Coast, Flagship Aloha. Died Jan. 2, 1932.

WINSLOW, E(BEN) EVELETH army officer; b. in D.C., May 13, 1866; grad. U.S. Mil. Acad., 1889, Engr. Sch. of Application, 1892. Commd. add. 2d lt. engrs., June 12, 1889; 2d lt., July 2, 1889; 1st lt., Apr. 12, 1894, capt., July 5, 1898; maj., Apr. 2, 1906; lt. col., Oct. 12, 1912; brig. gen., Oct. 2, 1917. Duty river, harbor and fortification works, Mobile, Ala., and vicinity, 1892-96; comd. co., Battle of San Juan, Cuba, July 2, 1898; in charge 1st and 2d dists., Miss. River Improvement, Memphis, Tenn., 1898-1902; at Wilmington, N.C., 1902-03, Norfolk, Va., 1903-06; assigned duty Office Chief of Engrs., 1907; mem. Bd. Engrs. for Rivers and Harbors. Died June 28, 1928.

WINSLOW, GEORGE FREDERICK naval officer; b. New Bedford, Mass., May 8, 1842; s. Giles and Elizabeth (Wilcox) W.; M.D., Harvard, 1864; m. Virginia Shearman, Jan. 14, 1875; children—George F., Virginia, Harold. Apptd. to U.S.N., July 26, 1862; advanced through grades to med. dir., Jan. 23, 1898; retired with the rank of rear admiral, Jan. 19, 1903, after over 44 yrs.' service. Received the thanks of Her Majesty's Govt. for taking care of distressed and suffering subjects in Patagonia during winter of 1869; also of Peruvian Congress for relief and surgical assistance rendered to suffering people of Arica, Peru, after the earthquake of Sept. 13, 1868. Died Sept. 3, 1928.

WINSLOW, HERBERT rear admiral; b. Roxbury, Mass., Sept. 22, 1848; s. Rear Admiral John Ancrum W. (who as capt. in command of old U.S.S. Kearsarge sank the Alabama off Cherbourg, France, June 19, 1864); grad. U.S. Naval Acad., 1869; m. Elizabeth, d. Lafayette Maynard, June 6, 1876 (died 1899). Ensign, 1870; master, 1872; lt., 1875; lt. comdr., 1897; comdr., 1900; captain, 1905; rear admiral, 1909. Wrecked in U.S.S. Saranac, in Seymour's Narrows, B.C., June 18, 1875; comd. U.S.S. Fern at Battle of Santiago, Spanish-Am. War; in the Pacific during Boxer rebellion, in command of U.S.S. Solace and landed the first detachment of marines at Taku, China; last command was the U.S.S. Kearsarge which was named, at launching, by his wife; retired. Died Sept. 24, 1914.

WINSLOW, JOHN army officer; b. Marshfield, Mass., May 10, 1703; s. Isaac and Sarah (Wensley) W.; m. Mary Little, 1725; m. 2d, Bethiah (Barker) Johnson; children—Pelham, Isaac. Apptd. capt. co. of Mass. Militia by Mass. Council, 1740, served in West Indian expdn.; entered Brit. Army, 1741, served at Cartagena; returned to Mass. for reinforcements; served in Phillip's Regt. Brit. Inf. in Nova Scotia, 1744-51; commd. maj. gen. Mass. Militia, served on Kennebec River, 1754; built Ft. Western as trading post for proprietors of Plymouth Colony, also Ft. Halifax; apptd. lt. col., commandant both New Eng. battalions, 1755; commanded provincial army raised in New Eng. and N.Y. in capture of Crown Point, 1775; mem. Mass. Gen. Ct. from Marshfield, 1757-58, 61-65; instrumental in surveying and supervising Kennebec River devel.; commr. on St. Croix Boundary, 1762; Town of Winslow (formerly Ft. Halifax, Kennebec County, Me.) named for him, 1771. Died Hingham, Mass., Apr. 17, 1774.

WINSLOW, JOHN ANCRUM naval officer; b. Wilmington, N.C., Nov. 19, 1811; s. Edward and Sara (Ancrum) W.; m. Catherine Winslow, Oct. 18, 1837, at least 3 children. Commd. midshipman U.S. Navy, 1827; decorated with sword-knot and pair of epaulettes Queen Victoria (of Eng.) for action in fire in hold of Cunard steamer in Boston Harbor, 1841; lost 1st command, schooner Morris, in gale while blockading Mexico, 1846; promoted comdr., 1855; served on Mississippi River, 1862; commd. capt., 1862, patrolled from Azores to English Channel in command ship Kearsage, 1863-64; defeated Confederate sloop Alabama commanded by Raphael Semmes, 1864; commanded Gulf Squadron, 1866-67; commd. rear adm., 1870, in command of Pacific fleet, 1870-72. Died Boston Highlands, Mass., Sept. 29, 1873.

WINSLOW, JOSIAH gov. Plymouth Colony; b. Marshfield, Mass., circa 1629; s. Edward and Susanna (Fuller) W.; attended Harvard; m. Penelope Pelham, circa 1657, 2 children including Isaac. Commanded militia, Marshfield, 1652; dep. to Gen. Ct., 1653, 57; asst. gov. Mass., 1657-73; Plymouth commr. for United Colonies, 1658-72; succeeded Myles Standish as comdr.-in-chief Plymouth Colony, 1659; captured Indian chief Alexander (son and successor of Massasoit), thus ending danger of Indian uprising, 1662; a signer Articles of Confederation of New Eng. Colonies, 1672; gov. New Plymouth (1st native-born gov. in Am.), 1673-80; established 1st public sch. in Plymouth, 1674; signed declaration of war and issued statement denying and legitimate grievance to Indians because Pilgrims had honestly bought their land, at beginning of Indian uprisings, 1675; comdr.-in-chief of forces of United Colonies (1st native-born comdr. Am. Army), 1675-76; won decisive battle against Narragansett Indians, 1675. Died Marshfield, Dec. 18, 1680.

WINT, THEODORE JONATHAN army officer; b. in Pa., Mar. 6, 1845; s. Jonathan R. and Euphemia (Johnston) W.; ed. Providence High Sch.; m. Lydia Porter Bullis, 1880. Served pvt. to 1st lt. Co. F. 6th Pa. cav., 1861-64; pvt. gen. mounted service, 1865. Apptd. in regular army, 2d lt., 4th cav., Nov. 24, 1865; 1st lt., May 9, 1866; capt. Apr. 21, 1872; maj. 10th cav., May 6, 1892; lt. col. 6th cav., Apr. 8, 1899; col., Feb. 23, 1901; brig. gen. U.S.A., June 9, 1902. Died 1907.

WINTER, FRANCIS ANDERSON surgeon U.S.A.; b. St. Francisville, La., June 30, 1867; s. William Drew and Sarah (Stirling) W.; ed. St. Vincents Coll. (Cape Girardeau, Mo.), Bethel Mil. Acad. (Va.) St. Louis U.; M.D., St. Louis Med. Coll., 1889; m. Mary Davenport Smith, Oct. 27. 1897. Apptd. asst. surgeon, U.S.A., Mar. 9, 1892; capt. asst. surgeon, Mar. 9, 1897; maj. surgeon 37th U.S. Inf., July 5, 1899; hon. discharged vols., Feb. 20, 1901; maj. surgeon U.S.A., Aug. 3, 1904; maj. Med. Corps, Aug. 3, 1904; lt. col., Apr. 13, 1912; col., May 15, 1917; brig. gen. (temp.), May 1, 1918. Chief surgeon, Line of Communications, A.E.F., July 1917-Mar. 1918; chief surgeon, A.E.F. in Eng., May-Oct. 1918; apptd. comdt. Army Med. Sch., Dec. 23, 1918. Roman Catholic. Died Jan. 11, 1931.

WINTERHALTER, ALBERT GUSTAVUS naval officer; b. Detroit, Mich., Oct. 5, 1856; s. of a Mexican War veteran; grad. Detroit high sch., 1873; grad. U.S. Naval Acad., 1877. Promoted ensign, July 11, 1880; lt. (j.g.), Dec. 14, 1886; lt., June 30, 1892; lt. comdr., Jan. 18, 1900; comdr., July 1, 1905; capt., July 1, 1909; rear admiral, May 5, 1915. Del. for U.S. Naval Obs. at Internat. Astrophotographic Congress, Paris, 1887; official report of its proceedings and of an inspection of European scientific instns. pub. as a quarto, XIV, 1889. Served on Philadelphia during Spanish-Am. War, 1898; flag lt. to Rear Admiral Joseph N. Miller and arranged naval share in transfer of Hawaiian sovereignty to U.S., Aug. 12, 1898; recorder Labor Bd., Phila. Navy Yard, 1898-1900; comd. div. of gunboats, Cavite to China, 1903; comd. Elcano, 1903; equipment and ordnance officer, Portsmouth (N.H.) Navy Yard, 1903-05; comd. Paducah, 1905-07; at Naval Obs., Washington, 1907-08; hydrographer, Navy Dept., 1908-09; comd. Louisiana, 1910-11; mem. Gen. Bd., Navy Dept., 1911-12; aid for material, Navy Dept., 1912-15; comd. Asiatic Fleet and Sta., 1915-17, with rank of admiral; on occasion of accession of Emperor of Japan, Nov.-Dec. 1915; mem. Gen. Bd., Navy Dept., May 11, 1917-—. Fellow A.A.A.S.; mem. U.S. Naval Inst. Home: Washington, D.C. Died June 5, 1920.

WINTHROP, JOHN (called Fitz-John Winthrop), gov. Conn., army officer; b. Ipswich, Mass., Mar. 14, 1629; s. John and Elizabeth (Reade) Winthrop II; attended Harvard, 2 years; m. Elizabeth Tongue, 1 dau. Had commn. in Parliamentary Army in England, served in mil. campaign in Scotland; returned to New London, Conn., 1663; dep. to Conn. Gen. Assembly, 1671, 78; apptd. chief mil. officer for New London County, 1672; comdr. Conn. troops in fight against Dutch on L.I., N.Y. (Dutch forced to retreat to New Amsterdam), 1673; fought in King Phillip's War, 1675-76; apptd. to Mass. Gov.'s Council by Joseph Dudley, 1686, also an assistant of Gov. Andros; apptd. maj. gen. and comdr. united force of colonists in unsuccessful invasion of Canada during King William's war, 1690, freed of blame for failure by Conn. Gen. Assembly; gov. Conn., 1698-1707. Died Boston, Nov. 27, 1707.

WIRZ, HENRY army officer; b. Switzerland. Confederate supt. of Andersonville (Ga.) Mil. Prison, where conditions were extremely unfavorable, resulting in death of many Union prisoners; after Civil War, was charged with having conspired with Jefferson Davis to deliberately murder some of prisoners; found guilty of charges at mil. trial, Aug. 1865; subsequent research has shown that many of accusations against Wirz were unfounded. Hanged Nov. 10, 1865.

WISE, HENRY ALEXANDER gov. Va., army officer; b. Drummondtown, Va., Dec. 3, 1806; s. Maj. John and Sarah Corbin (Cropper) W.; grad. Washington (Pa.) Coll., 1825; attended law sch., Winchester, Va.; m. Ann Jennings, Oct. 8, 1828; m. 2d, Sarah Sergant, Nov. 1840; m. 3d, Mary Lyons, 1853; 5 children including John Sergeant, Richard Alsop. Admitted to bar, Nashville, Tenn., 1828; practiced law, Nashville, 1828-30, Accomac County, Va., from 1830; supporter of Jackson, 1828, joined Whigs in Bank of U.S. controversy, 1832; mem. U.S. Ho. of Reps. from Va., 23d-28th congresses, 1833-Feb. 12, 1844; influential in nomination of Tyler as Whig candidate for vice pres. U.S., 1840; apptd. U.S. minister to France, rejected by Senate, 1843; U.S. minister to Brazil, 1844-47; Democratic presdl. elector, Va., 1848, 52; mem. Va. Constl. Conv., 1850-51; del. to Nat. Dem. Conv., 1852, worked for nomination of Franklin Pierce; gov. Va., 1856-60, sponsored internal improvement schemes, quelled John Brown's raid, 1859, destroyed influence of Know-Nothing Party in Va.; del. to Va. Secession Conv., 1861, opposed secession ordinance, but later was strong supporter of Confederacy; commd. brig. gen. Confederate Army, 1861, raised regt., served in Western Va. and Roanoke Island, N.C. Author: Seven Decades of the Union, 1872. Died Richmond, Va., Sept. 12, 1876; buried Hollywood Cemetery, Richmond.

WISE, WILLIAM CLINTON rear adm., U.S.N.; b. Lewisburg, Va., Nov. 8, 1842; s. James and Virginia F. (Caldwell) W.; m. Nellie Humphreys, May 18, 1875. Apptd. from Ky., and grad. U.S. Naval Acad., 1863; ensign, Oct. 1, 1863; master, May 10, 1866; lt., Feb. 21, 1867; lt. comdr., Mar. 12, 1868; comdr., Feb. 24, 1881; capt., Nov. 11, 1894; rear adm., June 14, 1902. Served in New Ironsides, S. Atlantic Blockading Squadron, 1863-64; participated in attacks on Charleston, and the Jacksonville expdn.; served in Minnesota, N. Atlantic Blockading Squadron, 1864-65; present at both attacks on Ft. Fisher; comdg. U.S.S. Malvern, 1865, flagship of Admiral Porter; served on Hartford, Asiatic Squadron, 1865-66; Wachusett, 1866-68; practice-ship Dale, 1869; Miantonomoh, 1869-70; Brooklyn, 1870-72; Ajax, 1873-74; receiving-ship Vermont, 1874-75; exec. officer Tennessee, 1875-76; comd. Palos, 1876-78; insp. ordnance Navy Yard, Norfolk, 1878-81; torpedo duty, 1882; comdg. Portsmouth, 1883-84; insp. ordnance Navy Yard, Portsmouth, 1884-87; comdg. Juniata, 1888-89; Navy Yard, Norfolk, 1889-90; light house insp. 15th dist., 1890-94; ordnance duty Navy Yard, Washington, 1894-95; comdg. Amphitrite, 1895-97, Texas, 1897; capt. of yard, Navy Yard, Norfolk, 1897-98; comdg. Yale, during war with Spain, 1898; comdg. receiving-ship Franklin, 1898-1902; mem. Gen. Bd. and comdt. Navy Yard, Pensacola, 1902-03; comdr.-in-chief of Atlantic Training Squadron, 1903-04; retired, Nov. 8, 1904; spl. duty in connection with steamboat inspection service, 1904-05. Hon. M.A., Yale, 1899. Died Nov. 23, 1923.

WISSER, JOHN PHILIP officer U.S.A.; b. St. Louis, July 19, 1852; s. Philip and Barbara (Weber) W.; grad. U.S. Mil. Acad., 1874, U.S. Arty. Sch., Ft. Monroe, 1878; studied Royal School of Mines, Freiberg, Saxony, 1883-84; m. Georgiana Hollister, June 15, 1893; children—Edward Hollister, John Philip. Apptd. 2d lt. 1st Arty., June 17, 1874; promoted through grades to brig. gen. U.S.A., May 26, 1913; retired July 19, 1916. Asst. prof. chemistry, mineralogy and geology, U.S. Mil. Acad., 1878-82 and 1886-94; instr. chemistry, U.S. Arty. School, 1882-84; represented U.S.A. at French maneuvers, 1884; editor Jour. U.S. Artillery, 1895-1902; inst. mil. science and mil. engring., U.S. Arty. Sch., 1895-1900; detailed to witness U.S. naval maneuvers, Caribbean Sea, 1902; detailed in Insp. General's Dept., 1904; acting insp. gen. Pacific Div. during and after the earthquake and fire in San Francisco, Apr. 18, 1906; mil. attaché at Berlin, 1906-09; comdg. arty. dist. of Savannah, 1909-11, arty. dist. of San Francisco, Feb. 6, 1911-Feb. 15, 1913; comdg. Presidio, San Francisco, Feb. 6, 1911-June 19, 1912; comdg. Dept. of Calif., Apr. 8-June 26, 1912; comdg. Ft. Winfield Scott, San Francisco, June 19, 1912-Feb. 13, 1913; comdg. Dept. of Calif., Jan. 2-30, 1913; comdg. Pacific Coast Arty. Dist., Feb. 15-Sept. 15, 1913; in comd. 4th Brigade, 2d Div., in camp at Texas City, Tex., Sept. 1913-Jan. 1914; comdg. Pacific Coast Arty. Dist., Ft. Miley, Calif., Jan. 4, 1914-Jan. 5, 1915; comdg. 1st Hawaiian Brigade and Schofield Barracks, H.T. to Nov. 5, 1915; comdg. Hawaiian Dept., H.T., Nov. 5, 1915-16. Author: Gun Cotton, 1886; Practical Problems in Minor Tactics and Strategy, 1888; By Land and Sea, 1891; articles Military Schools and Staff and Staff Schools, in Johnson's New Universal Cyclo., 1893; Explosive Materials, 1898; The Second Boer War, 1901; Tactics of Coast Defense, 1902; Practical Field Exercises, 1903; A Military and Naval Dictionary, 1905. Editor: International Military Series, 1902—. Contbr. to New International Ency., several articles on organization and tactics; a contributing, nominating and advisory editor, Nat. Cyclo. Am. Biography, 1921. Called into active service and comd. Hawaiian Dept., Aug. 1917-June 1918. Home: Berkeley, Calif. Died Jan. 19, 1927.

WITSELL, EDWARD FULLER, army officer; b. Charleston, S.C., Mar. 29, 1891; s. Edward Fuller and Rosa Ella (Oliveros) W.; B.S., The Citadel, Charleston, S.C., 1911, LL.D., 1947; grad. Chem. Warfare Sch., 1924, Army War Coll., 1929; m. Daphne Dow, Dec. 13, 1917; children—Edward F., Barbara D., Mary Ellen. Commd. 2d lieut., inf., U.S. Army, 1912, advancing through grades to maj. gen., 1945; served as officer of inf., Chem. Warfare Service, War Dept. Gen. Staff and Adj. Gen.'s Dept., Hawaii, Japan, Philippine Islands, Panama Canal Zone, and at various posts in U.S., also in War Dept.; chief of staff, Hawaiian Dept., U.S. Army, during World War I; dir. mil. personnel div. Adj. Gen.'s Office, War Dept., Washington, D.C., 1943-45, acting adj. gen., July 1945; apptd. adjutant gen., Feb., 1946, reapptd. 1950, ret. June 1951; dir., Army Emergency Relief, July 1951. Decorated Distinguished Service Medal, Army Commendation Ribbon, Victory, American Defense, American Theater and World War II medals. Japanese language student, and asst. mil. attache, Tokyo, Japan. Home: Washington DC Died Nov. 1969.

WITTENMYER, EDMUND army officer; b. in Ohio, Apr. 25, 1862; grad. U.S. Mil. Acad., 1887, Inf. and Cav. Sch., 1895. Commd. add. 2d lt. 9th Inf., June 12, 1887; 2d lt., June 15, 1887; 1st lt. 15th Inf., Nov. 27, 1894; capt. 10th Inf., Mar. 2, 1899; trans. to 15th Inf., July 3, 1899; p.m., Dec. 17, 1901; assigned to 5th Inf., Dec. 17, 1905; trans. to 6th Inf., Oct. 3, 1910; maj. 27th Inf., Feb. 15, 1911; lt. col., July 1, 1916; brig. gen. N.A., Aug. 5, 1917. Duty World's Fair, Chicago, 1893; at Puerto Principe, Cuba, 1898-99, Manila, P.I., 1900; adj. gen. 2d Brigade, China Relief Expdn., Aug.-Oct. 1900; in charge armed forces, provinces of Matanzas and Santa Clara, Cuba, 1907-09; gov. Province of Matanzas, Apr.-Oct. 1908; assigned duty Gen. Staff Corps, 1910; apptd. comdr. 153d Inf. Brigade, Camp Upton, Yaphank, L.I., N.Y., Sept. 1917. Died July 5, 1937.

WOFFORD, WILLIAM TATUM army officer; b. Habersham County, Ga., June 28, 1823; s. William Holingsworth and Nancy (Tatum) W.; m. Julia A. Dwight, 1859; m. 2d, Margaret Langdon, 1878; 6 children. Studied law in Athens, Ga.; admitted to Ga. bar; capt. volunteer cavalry under Gen. Winfield Scott in Mexican War, 1848; mem. Ga. Legislature, 1849-53, clk. lower house, 1853-54; edited (with John W. Burke) Athens Banner, 1852, later established Cassville (Ga.) Standard; del. to So. Comml. Conv., Knoxville, Tenn., 1857, Montgomery, Ala., 1858; mem. Ga. conv., 1861, voted against secession; commd. col. 18th Ga. Regt. at beginning of Civil War; served briefly in N.C, then transferred to Gen. John Hood's brigade, served around Richmond, Va.; led brigade at battles of 2d Manassas, South Mountain and Sharpsburg; served under Gen. Thomas Cobb, promoted brig. gen. after Cobb's death, 1863; after battles of Chancellorsville and Gettysburg sent to East Tenn. with Gen. James Longstreet; transferred back to Richmond after Knoxville; wounded at Spotsylvania and the Wilderness; in command of Dept. of Northern Ga., 1865, defended area with 7,000 troops, finally surrendered to Gen. H. M. Judah at Resaca, Ga., 1865; elected to Congress, 1865, refused seat by radical Republicans; an organizer Cartersville & Van Wert R.R., Atlanta & Blue Ridge R.R.; trustee Cherokee Baptist Coll., Cassville, Cassville Female Coll; contbd. land and money to Wofford Acad.; mem. Ga. Constl. Conv., 1877. Died nr. Cass Station, Ga., May 22, 1884; buried Cassville Cemetery.

WOGAN, JOHN B., army officer; b. New Orleans, La., Jan. 1, 1890; s. John A. and Marguerite H. (Beugnot) W.; A.B., Coll. of Immaculate Conception (now Loyola U.), 1908; student Spring Hill Coll., Mobile, Ala., 1906-07; B.S. U.S. Mil. Acad., 1915; grad. Command and Gen. Staff Sch., 1930, Army War Coll., 1933; m. Grace MacLain, July 7, 1921; children—Mary Patricia, John B. Commd. 2d lt., Coast Arty., U.S. Army, 1915, and advanced through the grades to brig. gen., Feb. 1942, major gen., Sept. 1942; served on Mexican Border Campaign, 1916; served as capt., later major, Coast Arty. Corps, France, Sept. 1917-Oct. 1920, taking part in Battles of St. Mihiel and Meuse-Argonne; transferred to Field Arty., Sept. 1920; served at Fort Sill, 1920-24; R.O.T.C., Harvard, 1924-28; comdg. 2d F.A. Batn., Panama Canal, 1930-32; Gen. Staff, War Dept., public relations, 1933-37; instr. Field Arty. Sch., 1937-40; comd. 68th F.A. Regt., 1940-41; chief of staff, 5th Armored Div., Aug. 1941-Jan. 1942, comd. Combat Command "B" 2d Armored Div., Fort Benning, Ga., Jan.-July 1942; Commanding 13th Armored Div., Camp Beale, Calif., 1942-44; served in European Theater, Dec. 1944-Apr. 1945; participated in battle of the Bulge and battle of the Ruhr; severely wounded in Ruhr battle, Apr. 15, 1945; retired as maj. gen. for combat wounds, Oct. 31, 1946. Mgr. Veterans' Hosp., Oteen, N.C. Feb. 15, 1947. Decorated D.S.M., Silver Star, Legion of Merit, Purple Heart; E.T.O. campaign ribbon with 2 battle stars; Legion of Honor, Croix de Guerre (French). Mem. Asheville Civitan Club, Mark Twain Soc., Soc. Promotion and Encouragement of Barber Shop Quartet Singing in Am., Inc., Am. Legion, Disabled Am. Vets. K.C. (4th deg.). Clubs: Biltmore Forest Country, Mens Garden, Executives. Home: Ashville NC Died Sept. 30, 1968; buried Arlington Nat. Cemetery, Arlington VA

WOHLENBERG, ERNEST T. F. cons. forestry; b. Lincoln, Neb., Sept. 9, 1889; s. Peter Jacob and Gretchen (Tychsen) W.; B.S., U. Neb., 1912, M.F., 1913; postgrad. forest econs. U. Cal. at Berkeley, 1933-35; m. Grace Shafer, Jan. 19, 1925 (dec.); dau., Joan Marie (Mrs. Joseph L. Eldredge). Forest examiner U.S. Forest Service, Ariz., N.M., 1913-17, prin. forester charge pvt. forestry, Western U.S., 1937-41; various positions lumber industry, Ore., Wash., 1919-22; valuation engr. lumber sect. U.S. Treasury Dept., Western half U.S., 1922-37; gen. mgr. Edward Hines Lumber Co., Burns, Ore., 1941-45; forest counsel Western Forestry and Conservation Assn., Portland, Ore., 1945-48; v.p., gen. mgr. Masonite Corp., 1948-54, retired; prof. indsl. forestry school of forestry Yale University, 1954-59, emeritus; consultant in forest industries, 1959—; adv. board Bank of Am., Ukiah; member board of directors Yokayo Land Co., Ukiah. First pres. Redwood Region Conservation Council, 1950-52, now dir. Trustee Found. for American Resource Management. Served as capt. 10th Engrs., A.E.F., 1917-19 Mem. Western Forestry and Conservation Assn. (pres.), Soc. Am. Mil. Engrs., Soc. Am. Foresters, Sigma Phi Epsilon. Episcopalian (vestry). Club: Faculty. Author articles on forestry. Address: P.O. Box 246, Ukiah, Cal. Died Sept. 11, 1963.

WOLCOTT, FRANK BLISS (woll'kut), industrial cons.; b. Cleve., Feb. 5, 1907; s. Frank Bliss and Mary Sheldon (Fox) W.; B.S., Princeton, 1930; m. Virginia Bogart, Aug. 5, 1929; children—Frank Bliss, III, Margery Schuyler. Mining engr. N.J. Zinc Co., Austinville, Va., 1930-33, supvr. mfr. zinc metal and allied products, Palmerton, Pa., 1933-41, charge various mfg. operations, Palmerton, 1946-51; gen. mfg. mgr. several plants Wyandotte Chemicals Corp., Mich., 1951-53, v.p. charge mfg., 1953-55, v.p. gen. mgr. research and engring. div., 1955-59; v.p. Mich. Brine Co., Wyandotte Transportation Co., 1954-59; exec. v.p., dir. Sawhill Tubular Products, Incorporated, 1959-60; indsl. cons., 1960—; v.p. Johnson Bronze Co., 1962—; dir. Ferra loy, Inc. Served from capt. to lt. col., F.A., U.S. Army, 1941-45. Decorated Bronze Star Medal. Mem. Engring. Soc. Detroit, Am. Inst. Mining and Metall. Engrs., American Ordnance Association, Armed Forces Chem. Assn., C. of C., Phi Beta Kappa. Clubs: Princeton (N.Y.C.). Home: 1235 Country Club Prado, Coral Gables, Fla. Office: 500 S. Mill St., New Castle, Pa. Died June 9, 1964; buried Coral Gables, Fla.

WOLF, GEORGE W. business exec.; b. Pittsburgh, April 15, 1892; grad. U.S. Naval Acad., 1913; grad. work Lehigh Univ. Entered Gen. Motors Overseas Operations Co., 1926, mng. dir. in Argentine, Poland, Germany, Spain, 1926-38; pres. U.S. Steel Export Co., N.Y.C., 1939-57; chmn. of Nat. Fgn. Trade Council, 1957—, dir. 1939—. Mem. Council on Fgn. Relations. Chmn. Mid Fairfield County com. on alcoholism. Trustee Miss Hewitt's Classes, N.Y. Served from ensign to lt. comdr. USN, 1913-26. Decorated Navy Cross, 1918; recipient Capt. Robert Dollar Award for advancement fgn. trade, 1955. Mem. Am. Iron and Steel Inst., Soc. Automotive Engrs., A.I.M. Clubs: Army and Navy (Washington); Metropolitan (gov.), Railroad and Machinery, India House (N.Y.C.); Duquesne (Pitts.); Lawyers. Office: 10 Rockefeller Plaza, N.Y.C. Died June 6, 1962; buried Shady Side Cemetery, Pitts.

WOLFE, JAMES army officer; b. Westerham, Kent, Eng., Jan. 2, 1727; s. Edward and Henrietta (Thompson) W. Commd. 2d lt. 44th Foot Inf., Brit. Army, 1741, served in European Wars, promoted maj., 1749; placed in command of Brit. regt. under Gen. Jeffrey Amherst in attack on Louisburg (Can.), 1758; maj.-gen., 1759, led attack on Quebec (held by French under Gen. Montcalm); made surprise attack by climbing poorly guarded path up high cliffs between river and city; defeated Montcalm's troops on Plains of Abraham in front of city, Sept. 12-13. Died in battle, Sept. 13, 1759; buried St. Albege, Greenwich, Eng.

WOLFE, KENNETH B., retired army officer and business executive; born in Denver, Colorado, August 12, 1896; son of George Frank and Selma Wilhelmena (Franzen) W.; grad. San Diego High Sch., 1915; grad.

U.S. Sch. Mil. Aeronautics, Berkeley, Calif., 1918, Air Service Flying Instrs. Sch., San Antonio, 1918; Air Corps Engr. Sch., Wright Field, 1931, Air Corps Tactical School, Maxwell Field, 1936, Command and Gen. Staff Sch., 1937; m. Edwina Ray, Jan. 14, 1922 (dec. Dec. 1964); 1 dau., Beverley Ray; m. 2d, Margaret Parker, Hall, August 7, 1965. Began as flying cadet, United States Army, January 14, 1918; commissioned 2d lieutenant July 1918, advanced through grades to lieutenant gen., Sept. 1949; comdg. gen. 20th Bomber Commd. (first B-29 orgn. to bomb Japan), June 5, 1943-July 8, 1944; comdg. gen. Materiel Command, July-Sept. 1944; comdg. gen. Fifth Air Force (occupational air force, Japan and Korea), 1945-48; dir. procurement indsl. planning, Air Material Command, U.S.A.F., Wright-Patterson Field, Dayton, 1948-49; became deputy chief of staff Materiel, Hdqrs. U.S. Air Force, Washington, 1949; retired from service; pres., Oerlikon Tool & Arms Corp., 1951-56; asst. to chem. Garrett Corp., 1956-57, sr. v.p., director, 1957-65; cons. Garrett Corp., Cohu Electronics, Inc.; dir. Automation Industries, Los Angeles, Cal. Mem. Nat. Security Indsl. Assn. (hon.), Order of Daedalians. Home: San Marcos CA Died Sept. 20, 1971; buried Arlington Nat. Cemetery, Arlington VA

WOOD, ABRAHAM army officer, colonial ofcl. Mem. Va. Ho. of Burgesses for Henrico County, 1644-46, for Charles City County, 1654; 56; mem. expdn. to Occoneechee Islands, 1650; mem. Va. Gov.'s Council, 1658-80; apptd. mem. spl. commn. of oyer and terminer for Va. following Bacon's Rebellion, 1676; capt. militia at Ft. Henry, 1646; commd. maj. gen.; maintained a fort and garrison at Ft. Henry, 1646; Col. Charles City and Henrico Regt., 1656; sent 1st party to cross Appalachian Mountains, 1671; sent group which reached what is now Tenn., 1673. Died 1680.

WOOD, CASEY ALBERT opthalmologist; b. of Am. parents, Wellington, Ont., Can., Nov. 21, 1856; s. Orrin Cottier and Rosa Sophia (Leggo) W.; ed. pvt. English and French schs.; grad. Ottawa (Can.) Collegiate Inst., 1874; C.M., M.D., Univ. Bishop's Coll., 1877, D.C.L., 1903; M.D., McGill U. 1906, LL.D., 1921; M.C.P.S., Ont., 1878; student N.Y. Eye and Ear Infirmary and Post-Grad. Med. Sch., 1886, also at many European hosps., 1886-1914; m. Emma Shearer, Oct. 28, 1886. Clin. asst. Royal London Ophthal. Hosp. (Moorfields), 1888-89; asst. Wm. Lang Eye dept., Middlesex Hosp., London, 1889; house surgeon Central London Ophthal. Hosp., Gray's Inn Rd., 1889; asst. surgeon West London Ophthal. Hosp., 1889; went to Chicago, 1900; attending ophthal. surgeon Alexian Bros., Passavant Memorial and St. Luke's hosps. (later consultant); cons. surgeon (eye) Cook County and St. Anthony hosps.; prof. chemistry and pathology, Univ. Bishop's Coll., 1878-85; prof. opthalmology, Chicago Post-Grad. Med. Sch., 1890-97; prof. clin. ophthalmology, Coll. Physicians and Surgeons, Chicago, 1898-1906; head prof. opthalmology, Northwestern U., 1906-08, U. of Ill., 1909-13 (now emeritus). Hon. collaborator on birds, Smithsonian Instn., 1927; hon. lecturer on ornithology, Stanford U., 1928; research asso. Calif Inst. Technology, 1932; retired from practice, 1917. Active service U.S. Army, as 1st lt., Nov. 1916-Feb. 1917, and later as maj.; head of exam. unit, at Chicago, of candidates for aviation and U.S. Signal Corps; in charge eye dept., Camp Sherman, O., Sept.-Dec. 1917; lt. col. on staff of surgeon gen., Washington, D.C., Dec. 1917-June 1919; now col. Med. Res. Corps, U.S. Army. Fellow Am. Acad. Medicine (pres. 1907), A.A.A.S., Mitglied d. ophthal. Gesellschaft (Germany), Am. Coll. Surgeons (foundation fellow), Acad. Medicine and of Medicolegal Soc. (Chicago), Am. Med. Assn. (chmn. sect. of ophthalmology 1889), Am. Acad. of Opthalmology and Otology (pres. 1905-06), Am. Geog. Soc., Zoöl. Soc. of London (del. to Centenary); mem. Assn. Military Surgeons, Calif. Acad. Science, Am., British and Royal Austral. Ornithol. unions; hon. mem. Am. Numismatic Soc. (New York), N.Y. Charaka Club, Peregrine Club (Phila.); ex-pres. Chicago Ophthal. Soc. Editor in chief Annals of Ophthalmology, 1894-1901; chief editor Ophthal. Record, 1902-08; editorial staff Anales de Oftalmologia (Mexico), Med. Standard (Chicago) and Annals of Med. History (New York); editor Am. Journal of Ophthalmology, 1908-14; editor eye sect. Practical Med. Series, 1908-15; contbr. to various "systems" and textbooks, also author of many mag. articles on medical and natural history, including numerous transls. from German, French, Italian, Spanish, Latin and Arabic treatises. Traveled 15 yrs. in Europe, 1919-34, also in the Far East (3 yrs. in India and Ceylon), Oceania, S. America (with Dr. Wm. Beebe, 2 winters in British Guiana), and in West Indies for zoölogic and medico. hist. research. Founder of Wood gold medal and of several spl. libraries at McGill Univ. Clubs: University (Chicago); Cosmos (Washington, D.C.); Authors (London); Athenaeum (Pasadena, California). Author: Lessons in Diagnosis and Treatment of Eye Diseases, 1895; Toxic Amblyopias, 1896; Commoner Diseases of the Eye (3d edit., 1907, with T. A. Woodruff); Primary Sarcoma of the Iris (with Brown Pusey), 1908; A System of Ophthalmic Therapeutics, 1909; A System of Ophthalmic Operations, 2 vols., 1911; American Encyclopedia of Ophthalmology, 17 vols., 1908-12; Fundus Oculi of Birds, 1917; A Physicians's Anthology (with Fielding Garrison), 1920; Birds of Fiji (with Alexander Wetmore), 1927-28; Introduction to the Study of Vertebrate Zoölogy (with annotated catalogue), 1931. Transl. (with notes) Benvenutus Grassius, De Oculis (A.D., 1474), 1930; transl. Tadhkirat, Arabic Note-Book of an Oculist (1000 A.D.), 1930; annotated transl. Notebook of a Tenth Century Oculist, 1936; transl. (with notes) of a Twelfth Century Codex, the De Arte Venandi cum Avibus by Emperor Frederick II (with Marjorie Fyfe), 1940. Home: Caltec, 551 S. Hill Av., Pasadena, Calif. Address: Hotel del Coronado, Coronado, Calif. Died Jan. 26, 1942.

WOOD, EDWARD EDGAR army officer; b. Lancaster County. Pa., Sept 17, 1846; s. Hon. Day and Eliza (Jackson) W.; student Pa. State Normal Sch., Millersville, 1860-62; grad. U.S. Mil. Academy, 1870; m. Elizabeth Wynn. August 2, 1870. Enlisted pvt. 17th Pa. Cav., Sept. 8, 1862; promoted sergt., 1st sergt., 1st lt., acting regimental adj. and staff officer on staff 1st Cav. Div., Army of the Potomac; hon. mustered out Aug. 7, 1865. Captured at Occoquan, Va., Dec. 27, 1862, and confined in Castle Thunder, Richmond, Va., exchanged May 1863, and thereafter present in all campaigns and battles of cav. corps, Army of the Potomac, including Gettysburg, Kilpatrick's Richmond Raid, Wilderness, Trevillian, Winchester, Five Forks and Appomattox. Apptd. cadet U.S. Mil. Acad., June 15, 1866; 2d lt. 8th Cav., June 15, 1870; 1st lt., July 1, 1873; capt., Jan. 20, 1886; a.-d.-c. to Gen. J. M. Schofield, U.S.A., 1879-82; asst. prof. French, U.S. Mil. Acad., 1876-79 and 1883-86; asst. prof. Spanish, 1889-92; lt. col. U.S.A. and prof. U.S. Mil. Acad., Oct. 1, 1892; col., Oct. 1, 1902; brig. gen. and retired, Sept. 17, 1910. Home: West Chester, Pa. Died June 21, 1924.

WOOD, ERIC FISHER architect, engr., army officer; b. N.Y. City, Jan. 4, 1889; s. William B. (M.D.) and Frances (Fisher) W.; Ph.B., Sheffield Scientific Sch. (Yale), 1910; A.B., Yale, 1910; studied Columbia U. Sch. of Architecture, and Ecole des Beaux Arts Paris; m. Vera de Ropp, Apr. 20, 1918; children—Eric Fisher (killed in action), Eleanor Morton (Mrs. Stanley M. Dye), Peter de Ropp, Alec Laughlin. Prop. Eric Fisher Wood & Co., architects and indsl. engrs.; with H. Hornbostel, won competition and selection as architects for Warren G. Harding Memorial at Marion, O. Attaché at the American Embassy, Paris, France, under Ambassador Herrick, 1914; officer Am. Ambulance Corps in France, 1915; maj. British Army, 1917, wounded at Battle of Arras; maj. U.S.N.A., Aug. 14, 1917, and asst. chief of staff, 83d Div.; lt. col. G.S. asst. chief of staff, 88th Div.; wounded in Meuse-Argonne; col. 107th U.S. Field Artillery, 1923; brig. gen., U.S. Army, Dec. 1940; on active duty, 1941-45; major general, 1949. Decorated Legion of Merit, Purple Heart with oak leaf; Knight-Officer of Polonia Restituta and White Lion (Bohemia); Croix de Guerre, 1918 and 1945, Comdr. Legion of Honor (France). V.p. National Security League, 1915-16; a founder Am. Legion, 1919, and elected its 1st nat. adj. past national, comdr.; mem. Beaux Arts Inst. Design, A.I.A. Chairman Pennsylvania Republican State Executive Committee, 1926-28; sec. Pa. Delegation to Republican National Convention, 1928. Clubs: Duquesne (Pittsburgh). Author: Note Book of an Attaché, 1915; The Writing on the Wall, 1916; The Note Book of an Intelligence Officer, 1918; Biography of Leonard Wood, 1920; Basic Manual Field Artillery, 1934; Troop Leading and Staff Procedure, 1941; also articles, Century Magazine, The Outlook, Saturday Evening Post. Home: R.D. 1, Bedford, Pa. Died Oct. 4, 1962; buried Arlington Nat. Cemetery, Washington.

WOOD, GEORGE author; b. Newburyport, Mass., 1799. Clk. in war dept., 1819-22; with treasury dept., 1822-40; contbr. to Knickerbocker Mag., 1846-47. Author: Peter Schlemihl in America, 1848; Modern Pilgrims, Showing the Improvements in Travel with the Newest Methods of Reaching the Celestial City. Died Saratoga, N.Y., Aug. 24, 1870.

WOOD, GEORGE HENRY b. Dayton, O., Nov. 3, 1867; s. Maj. Gen. Thomas J. (U.S. Army) and Caroline E. (Greer) W.; Ph.B., Yale, 1887; LL.B., Cincinnati Law Sch., 1889; m. Virginia Peirce, June 29, 1910; children—Thomas J., Peirce. Practiced law in Dayton, 1890-98; brokerage business, 1901-12. Enlisted as private, advanced to 2d lt., 3d Ohio Vol. Infantry, Spanish-Am. War, 1898; 1st lt. 28th U.S. Vol. Inf., Philippine Insurrection, 1899-1901; capt. and maj., Ohio Nat. Guard, 1901-12; adj. gen. of Ohio, 1913-15, 1917-19; in charge selective draft, State of Ohio. Recruited Ohio Nat. Guard from 8,000 to 25,000 men, making a complete div., which was drafted into the federal service as the 37th (Buckeye) Division. Commd. col. inf., June 24, 1918; joined 42d (Rainbow) Div. as comdr. of trains during 2d Battle of the Marne; served also at St. Mihiel and in the Argonne; mustered out, Jan. 18, 1919. Mem. Civ. Service Commn., Dayton, 1910-13; mil. comdr. Dayton, O., under martial law during great flood, 1913; sec. bd. mgrs. Nat. Home for Disabled Vol. Soldiers, Dayton, 1914-16, pres. since 1916; apptd. spl. rep. of administration covering Nat. Soldiers' Home activities, on consolidation of all veteran relief into Veterans' Administration, July 1, 1930; consultant to Administration of Veteran Affairs on Soldiers Home activities since July 1, 1933. Mem. nat. exec. com. of Am. Legion, 1919. Democrat. Presbyterian. Clubs: Buz Fuz, Dayton. Home: 25 Schantz Av., Dayton, Ohio.*

WOOD, HENRY CLAY brig. gen. U.S.A.; b. Winthrop, Me.. May 26, 1832; s. Gen. Samuel and Florena (Sweet) W.; A.B., Bowdoin Coll., 1854, A.M., 1857; B.S., Norwich (Vt.) U., 1874; read medicine, 1854; studied law; admitted to bar, Augusta, Me., Aug. 19, 1856. Apptd. maj. and a.d.c. to Maj. Gen. Samuel Wood, Me. militia, Mar. 28, 1856; 2d lt. 1st Inf. U.S.A., June 27, 1856; 1st lt., May 10, 1861; capt., Oct. 24, 1861; maj. a.a.g., June 24, 1864; lt. col. a.a.g., Feb. 28, 1887; col. a.a.g., Nov. 6, 1893; retired May 26, 1896; advanced to rank of brig. gen. retired, by act of Apr. 23, 1904. Bvtd. lt. col., "for gallant and meritorious services" in battle of Wilson's Creek, Mo., Aug. 10, 1861, also bvtd. col. and received Congressional Medal of Honor for "distinguished gallantry" in same battle. Died Aug. 30, 1918.

WOOD, JOHN ENOS naval officer; b. Newark, Del., Mar. 11, 1892; s. Alexander Jennings and Louisa Emma (Crossan) W.; student Pierce Coll. of Bus. Adminstrn., 1909-10; student U. Pa., 1922-24; m. Ruth Ball Filthian, Aug. 13, 1913; 1 son, John Enos; m. 2d, Charlotte Catherine Borm, June 12, 1924; 1 stepdau., Louise Carpenter Hall. Mem. advt. staff Phila. Evening Bull., 1912-15; mem. advt. staff Phila. Public Ledger and Evening Ledger 1915-17. Commd. ensign U.S. Navy, 1918, advanced through grades to rear adm.; aviation supply officer, supply officer in command Naval Aviation Supply Depot, dist. supply officer 4th Naval Dist. 1947, supply officer in command, Naval Supply Center, Pearl Harbor, Hawaii, 1949-51; comdg. officer Naval Supply Center, Norfolk, Va., also Dist. Supply Office 5th Naval Dist., 1951-54, ret., 1954. Received Legion of Merit for work as force supply officer on staff of comdr. Air Force, Atlantic Fleet; also Victory Medal, China Service Medal, Am. Def. Service Medal, Am. Area Campaign Medal, Asiatic-Pacific Area Campaign Medal, World War I Ribbon. Mem. Protestant Episcopal Church. Mason (Shriner). Clubs: Army-Navy Country (Arlington, Va.); Army-Navy (Manila, P.I.). Home: 7701 Washington Lane, Elkins Park, Pa. Died Feb. 1964.

WOOD, JOHN S. army officer; b. Jan. 11, 1888; B.S.C., U. Ark., 1907; B.S., U.S. Mil. Acad., 1912. Commd. 2d lt., 1912, advanced through grades to maj. gen., 1942; comd. arty. 2d Armored Div., 1941; assigned to 1st Armored Corps, Fort Knox, 1941, 5th Armored Div., 1941-42; assigned comdg. gen. 4th Armored Div. in tng. and battle, 1942-44. Campaigns in France, 1944 included liberation of Coutances, Avranches, Rennes, Brittany, Nantes, Orleans, Sens, Troyes, Vitry Francois, Chalons sur Marne, St. Dizier, Commercy; campaign across Mozelle, north and south of Nancy; def. of Avracourt sector, advance across Saar to Maginot Line; ret. as maj. gen., Army U.S., 1947; field dir. Austria and Germany Intergovtl. Com. on Refugees, 1946-47; spl. cons. Internat. Refugee Orgn., Germany, 1947—. Awarded D.S.C., D.S.M., Silver Star, Bronze Star with Oak Leaf, Air Medal with Oak Leaf (U.S.); Officer of Legion of Honor, Croix de Guerre with Palm (France). Address: Ardmore, Pa. Died 1966.

WOOD, JOSEPH Continental congressman; b. Pa., 1712. Moved to Sunbury, Ga., circa 1774; served as maj., lt. col., and col. 2d Pa. Battalion (became 3d Pa. Regt.) during Am. Revolution, on duty in Can., 1776; returned to Ga., engaged in planting; mem. Ga. Council of Safety; mem. Continental Congress from Ga., 1777-79. Died nr. Sunbury, Sept. 1791.

WOOD, LEONARD major gen. U.S.A.; b. Winchester, N.H., Oct. 9, 1860; s. Charles Jewett and Caroline E. (Hager) W.; attended Pierce Acad., Middleboro, Mass.; M.D., Harvard, 1884; LL.D., Harvard, 1899, Williams, 1902, U. of Pa., 1903, Princeton, 1916, U. of the South, 1917, U. of Ga., 1917, U. of Mich., 1918, Union Coll., 1918, Wesleyan, 1918, George Washington U., 1918, Abraham Lincoln U., 1919; Dr. Mil. Sc., Pa. Mil. Coll., 1913, and Norwich U., 1915; D.Sc., Rensselaer Poly. Inst., 1920; LL.D., U. of the Philippines, 1922; m. Louisa A. Condit Smith, Nov. 18, 1890; children—Leonard, Osborne Cutler, Louise Barbara. Apptd. from Mass. asst. surgeon U.S.A., Jan. 5, 1886; capt. asst. surgeon, Jan. 5, 1891; commd. col. 1st U.S. Vol. Cav. ("Rough Riders"), May 8, 1898; brig. gen., July 8, 1898, for services at Las Guasimas and San Juan Hill (1898); maj. gen., Dec. 7, 1898; hon. discharged from vol. service Apr. 13, 1899; brig. gen. vols., Apr. 13, 1899; maj. gen., vols., Dec. 5, 1899; brig. gen. U.S.A., Feb. 4, 1901; hon. discharged from vol. service, June 30, 1901; maj. gen. U.S.A., Aug. 8, 1903; retired, 1921, at his own request, after 30 years' service, to accept appmt. as gov. gen. of Philippine Islands. Mil. gov. of Cuba, Dec. 12, 1899, until transfer of the govt. of Cuba to the Cuban Republic, May 20, 1902; on duty in P.I., Mar. 1903; gov. of Moro Province, July 1903-Apr. 1906; comd. Philippines Div., 1906-08; comdg. Dept. of the East, 1908-09; spl. ambassador to Argentine Republic, Apr. 8-July 15, 1910; chief of staff U.S.A., July 16, 1910-Apr. 1914; comd. Dept. of the East, 1914-17, later assigned in command Southeastern Dept.; organized and trained the 89th N.A. Div. and 10th (reg. army) Div. and various spl. regts. and battalions, 1918-19; comd. Central Dept. hdqrs. Chicago, 1919-21; chmn. spl. mission from U.S. to P.I., visiting Japan and China, 1921; gov. gen. Philippine Islands, 1921—. Candidate for Rep. nomination for President, 1920. Awarded

Congressional Medal of Honor, Mar. 29, 1898, "for distinguished conduct in campaign against Apache Indians, in 1886, while serving as medical and line officer of Capt. Lawton's expdn."; D.S.M. for services during World War I; Grand Officer Legion of Honor (French); Grand Officer Order of the Rising Sun (Japanese); Grand Officer Order of S.S. Mauritius and Lazarus (Italian); Grand Officer Order of the Golden Grain (Chinese); Roosevelt Medal of Honor, "for distinguished service," 1923. Mem. Soc. Mayflower Descendants (gov. gen. 1915-19); fellow Royal Geog. Soc. Died Aug. 7, 1927.

WOOD, MARSHALL WILLIAM retired army officer; b. Watertown, N.Y., June 3, 1846; s. Benjamin and Eunice Augusta (Greenleaf) W.; M.D., Rush Med. Coll., Chicago, 1873; (hon. A.M., Bowdoin, 1894); m. at Chicago, Helen Jerene Hawes, Dec. 7, 1870. Commd. 1st lt. asst. surgeon U.S.A., June 26, 1875; capt., June 26, 1880; maj., June 28, 1894; chief surgeon 1st Div., 5th Army Corps (Santiago Campaign), 1898; retired, Aug. 12, 1902; lt. col. retired, by act of Apr. 23, 1904. Was three times officially commended "for distinguished services." Mem. Soc. Colonial Wars, S.A.R. (pres. Idaho Soc. since 1909, v.p.-gen. Nat. Soc. 1914-16), Soc. War of 1812, Loyal Legion, G.A.R. (dept. comdr. Ida. 1911-12). Mason (K.T., Past Potentate; 33 deg., Sovereign Grand Insp.-Gen. in Ida.). Mem. Am. Soc. Agronomy, A.A.A.S., etc. Clubs: Boisé University, Boisé Commercial. On active duty in Army during World War. Home: Boisé, Ida.

WOOD, MOSES LINDLEY commodore U.S.N.; b. Lexington, Mo., Aug. 12, 1854; s. William Thomas and Mary Evelyn (Broadwell) W.; grad. U.S. Naval Acad., 1875; m. Mary Elizabeth Green, of St. Louis, Oct. 25, 1887. Promoted through the various grades to capt.; comd. U.S.S. Eagle, Sept. 26, 1902-Aug. 31, 1904, Dixie, Nov. 20, 1906-Nov. 1, 1907, Maryland, July 22, 1908-July 29, 1909; retired at own request, June 30, 1909, with rank of commodore. Ordered to active duty, Apr. 8, 1917; pres. Naval Examining and Retiring Bds., 3d (New York) Naval Dist.; pres. Spl. Gen. Courts Martial, Navy Yard, New York. Clubs: Army and Navy (Washington), Army and Navy, New York Yacht (New York). Address: Army and Navy Club, New York, N.Y.

WOOD, MYRON RAY army officer; b. Salinas, Calif., Dec. 4, 1892; student U. of Colo.; enlisted as aviation cadet, 1918; commd. 2d lt. Aviation Sect. Signal Corps., Mar. 1918, 2d lt. Air Service, Regular Army, 1920, and advanced through the grades to brig. gen., June 1943; assigned to Wright Field, Dayton, O., as chief of Procurement Planning Br. Indsl. Planning Sect. Air Corps Material Div., June 1937; with Office of Chief of Air Corps, as asst. to the chief of Plans Div., Washington, D.C., July 1939; with Office of Asst. Sec. of War, Washington, D.C., Sept. 1939; became chief, Aircraft Div. Production Br. Office of Under Secretary of War, July 1940; named chief of Aircraft Sect. Production Br. Procurement and distribution Div., Hdqrs. Services of Supply (Army Service Forces), Washington, D.C., Apr. 1942; chief supply div. in charge Air Force Supply, European Theater of Operations since Sept. 1942. Rated command pilot, combat observer, aircraft observer.* Died Oct. 29, 1946.

WOOD, OLIVER ELLSWORTH brig. gen. U.S.A.; b. Hartford, Conn., June 6, 1844; s. Rev. George I. and Susan T. (Merwin) W.; ed. Hopkins Grammar Sch., New Haven, Conn.; m. Mary Wadsworth Norton, June 2, 1873. Pvt. Co. B, 1st Conn. Cav., July 29, 1862; discharged, Sept. 9, 1863; apptd. to U.S. Mil. Acad., Sept. 16, 1863, grad., 1867; commd. 2d lt. 5th U.S. Arty., June 17, 1867; grad. Arty. Sch., 1869 and 1888; 1st lt., June 11, 1870; capt., Aug. 27, 1896; lt. col. vols. chief commissary of subsistence, May 9, 1898; hon. discharged, Apr. 17, 1899; maj. commissary of subsistence, Apr. 17, 1899; maj. U.S. Arty. Corps, May 8, 1901; hon. discharged from vol. service, June 12, 1901; lt. col., Jan. 21, 1904; mil. sec., Apr. 14, 1905; col. Arty. Corps, June 8, 1906; advanced to rank of brig. gen., and retired at own request, over 40 yrs.' service, Oct. 1, 1906. Served in Army of Potomac in Fredericksburg campaign, 1862; 5th U.S. Arty., 1867-1898; 7th Army Corps and headquarters Div. of Cuba, at Havana, Oct. 1898-Aug. 1900; mil. attaché, Japan, 1901-05. Home: Washington, D.C. Died 1910.

WOOD, PALMER GAYLORD brig. gen. U.S.A.; b. in N.Y., June 2, 1843. Second lt. 7th Calif. Inf.. Oct. 28, 1864; 1st lt., Dec. 7, 1865; apptd. from Calif. 2d lt. 5th U.S. Inf., Feb. 23, 1866; hon. mustered out of vol. service, Apr. 26, 1866; 1st lt. U.S.A., Jan. 7, 1867; assigned to 12th Inf., July 14, 1869; resigned, May 24, 1873; apptd. 2d lt., 12th U.S. Inf., Mar. 1, 1877; 1st lt., Oct. 16, 1882; capt., Dec. 11, 1893; maj. 47th U.S. Vol. Inf., Aug. 17, 1899-Feb. 2, 1901; maj. 28th U.S. Inf., Feb. 2, 1901; transferred to 12th Inf., July 15, 1901; lt. col. 11th Inf., Oct. 30, 1905; brig. gen. U.S.A., Feb. 16, 1906; retired, Feb. 17, 1906, at own request, over 30 yrs.' service. Died July 18, 1915.

WOOD, ROBERT E., director Sears, Roebuck & Co.; b. Kansas City, Mo., June 13, 1879; s. Robert Whitney and Lillie (Collins) W.; grad. U.S. Mil. Acad., 1900; m. Mary Butler Hardwick, Apr. 30, 1908;children—Anne Hardwick, Frances Elkington, Sarah Stires, Robert Whitney, Mary Stovall. Served in the U.S. Army during Philippine Insurrection as 2d and 1st lt., 3d Cavalry, 1900-02; asst. chief quartermaster, chief quartermaster and dir. of Panama Railroad Co., on construction of Panama Canal, 1905-15; col. and brig. gen. N.A., World War I, acting quartermaster gen. U.S. Army, 1918-19. Entered business life, 1915; asst. to pres. Gen. Asphalt Co., 1915-17; v.p. Montgomery Ward & Co., Chicago, 1919-24; v.p. Sears, Roebuck and Co., 1924-28, pres., 1928-39, chmn. bd. 1939-54, chmn. finance com., 1954-57, also director. Awarded P.I. Insurrection medal, Panama Canal medal, D.S.M., Legion of Merit; Companion Order of St. Michael and St. George (Brit.); Knight Legion of Honor (French). Clubs: Univ., Chicago, Commercial (Chgo.); Army. and Navy (Washington); Old Elm, Onwentsia. Home: Lake Forest IL Died Nov. 6, 1969; buried Lake Forest Cemetery, Lake Forest IL

WOOD, SPENCER SHEPARD naval officer; b. Brooklyn, Aug. 7, 1861; s. John Wardell and Mary Garrison (Shepard) W.; grad. U.S. Naval Acad., 1882, Naval War Coll.; m. Mary Margaretta Fryer, June 12, 1895; children—Margaretta, Anne Elizabeth. Commd. ensign, July 1884; promoted through grades to rear adm., Oct. 15, 1917. Served in Iroquois, 1885-87; U.S. Coast Survey Steamer Patterson, Mar. 17-Oct. 26, 1888; in Monocacy, Omaha, Palos, Charleston, Marion, Asiatic station, 1889-92; flag lt. to Rear Adm. George E. Belknap; duty Navy Dept. and aide to Sec. of the Navy H. A. Herbert, 1892-93; flag sec. Rear Adm. J. G. Walker and R. W. Meade, 1894; duty U.S.S. Vermont and torpedo sta., Newport, R.I., 1895-97; comd. DuPont, 1897, and during Spanish-Am. War, 1898; in Battleship Massachusetts, 1898-99, Brooklyn and Baltimore, Asiatic sta., 1899-1900; flag sec. to Rear Adm. John C. Watson; asst. to the insp. 3d lighthouse dist., Tompkinsville, N.Y., 1900-02; on bd. San Francisco, European sta., Jan. 20-Aug. 19, 1902; on bd. Chicago, Aug. 21, 1902-Oct. 15, 1903; navigator on board Columbia, Oct. 15, 1903-Oct. 2, 1904; aide to Adm. Dewey, Oct. 17, 1904-Feb. 29, 1908; exec. officer Idaho, Apr. 1, 1908-Feb. 24, 1909; comd. New York, May 15, 1909-Mar. 4, 1910; sec. Gen. Bd., Mar. 4, 1910-Feb. 1912; comd. U.S.S. Nebraska, Feb. 20, 1912-Jan. 17, 1914; Naval War Coll., Jan. 1914-Dec. 22, 1914; Gen. Bd., Navy Dept., Dec. 28, 1914-Jan. 5, 1917; comdr. U.S.S. Oklahoma, Jan. 6, 1917-Jan. 1918; comdt. 1st Naval Dist., hdqrs. Boston, Jan. 1918-Apr. 30. 1919; comdr. Div. Two, cruisers, Pacific Fleet, to Oct. 4, 1919; comdr. Train, Pacific Fleet, 1919-20; pres. Naval Exam. and Retiring Bds., Oct. 3, 1920-Dec. 19, 1921, retired. Treas. and sec. Navy Relief Soc. Awarded Navy Cross and Sampson, Philippine Campaign, N.Y. State and Flushing (N.Y.) medals. Home: Washington, D.C. Died July 30, 1940.

WOOD, THOMAS JOHN maj. gen. U.S.A.; b. Munfordville, Ky., Sept. 25, 1823; grad. West Point, 1845; served Mexican war on staff Gen. Zachary Taylor; served 12 yrs. on Tex. and Kan. frontiers; at breaking out of Civil war was maj. 1st cav.; m. Caroline E. Greer, Nov. 29, 1861. Served throughout Civil war, 1861-65, in Army of the Cumberland, comd. div. 21st corps, div. 4th corps, and finally comd. the 4th corps. Took part in all battles of that army, including Shiloh, Perryville, Stone River, Chickamauga, Missionary Ridge, Atlanta Campaign, Franklin and Nashville; severely wounded at Stone River and again at Lovejoy's Sta.; promoted to maj. gen. vols.; retired, 1868, as maj. gen. U.S.A. for disabilities received in the line of duty. Home: Dayton, O. Died 1906.

WOOD, WILLIAM THOMAS army officer; b. Irving, Montgomery County, Ill., June 19, 1854; s. Preston and Jane K. W.; grad. U.S. Mil. Acad., 1877; m. Janet Judson Sanford, Sept. 27, 1877; 1 dau., Janet (wife of H. C. Pillsbury, U.S. Army). Commd. add. 2d lt. 4th Inf., June 15, 1877; promoted through grades to col., Mar. 12, 1910; retired on account of disability incurred in the line of duty, Apr. 3, 1913; brig. gen., June 21, 1930. Served at Ft. Clark, Tex., 1890-92, Fort Bliss, Tex., 1892-95; chief ordnance officer Dept. of Pacific, 1898-99; collector of customs, at Cebu, P.I., Mar.-Nov. 1899; treas. Philippine Archipelago and Island of Guam, 1899-1900; again in Philippines, 1905-07; insp. gen. Philippines Div., July-Aug. 1907; duty office of insp. gen., War Dept., 1907-09; insp. gen. Dept. of the East, Governors Island, N.Y., 1909-10; assigned 19th Inf., Mar. 12, 1910; comdg. 19th Inf. and post of Camp Jossman, P.I., 1910-11; comdg. recruit depot, Jefferson Bks., Mo., 1911-13; sec. U.S. Soldiers' Home, Washington, D.C., 1913-17; recalled to active service, May 16, 1917; brig. gen. (temp.), Feb. 18, 1918; duty Office of Insp. Gen., War Dept., May 24, 1917-May 25, 1919; spl. inspection tour, Europe, May 27, 1919-July 5, 1919; assigned Office of Insp. Gen., July 5, 1919; sec. bd. Soldiers' Home, Washington, D.C., 1920-30. Awarded D.S.M. by Pres. Wilson, "for exceptionally meritorious and conspicuous service" as sr. asst. to the insp. gen. of the Army, which was presented by Gen. Pershing, at Paris, France, June 14, 1919; cited in War Dept. orders "for gallantry in action," near Manila, P.I., during Spanish-Am. War, and authorized to wear silver star on ribbon of Spanish-Am. war medal. Mem. Loyal Legion, Am. Legion. Episcopalian. Club: Army and Navy (Washington, D.C.). Address: War Dept., Washington, D.C. Died Dec. 19, 1943.

WOODBURY, DANIEL PHINEAS army officer, engr.; b. New London, N.H., Dec. 16, 1812; s. Daniel and Rhapisma (Messenger) W.; attended Dartmouth; grad. U.S. Mil. Acad., 1836; m. Catherine Rachel Childs, Dec. 12, 1845, 4 children. Commd. 2d lt., 3d Arty., U.S. Army, 1836; transferred to Corps Engrs., commd. 1st lt., 1838; supervised constrn. of Ft. Kearny on Missouri River and Ft. Laramie (Wyo.), 1847-50; supervised constrn. Ft. Jefferson, Tortugas, W.I., also Ft. Taylor, Key West, Fla.; commd. capt., 1853; helped plan defenses of Washington, D.C., 1861; promoted maj. C.E., 1861; commd. lt. col. U.S. Volunteers, 1861, brig. gen., 1862; constructed seige works before Yorktown during Peninsular campaign, 1862; worked on defenses of Washington, 1862; in command of dist. including Tortugas and Key West, 1863. Author: (treatises) Sustaining Walls, 1845. Died Key West, Aug. 15, 1864.

WOODBURY, URBAN ANDRAIN governor; b. Acworth, N.H., July 11, 1838; s. Albert Merrill and Lucy Lestina (Wadleigh) W.; M.D., U. of Vt., 1859; m. Paulina Livonia Darling, Feb. 12, 1860. Enlisted Co. H, 2d Vt. Vols., May 25, 1861; sergt., June 19, 1861; lost right arm and taken prisoner in 1st battle of Bull Run, July 21, 1861; paroled, Oct. 5, 1861; commissioned capt. Co. D, 11th Vt. Vols., Nov. 17, 1862; transferred to Vet. Reserve Corps, June 17, 1863; resigned, Mar. 1865. Alderman, 1881-82 (pres. of bd. 1882), mayor, 1885-86, Burlington, Vt.; lt. gov. of Vt., 1888-90; gov., 1894-96. Mem. war investigation com., 1898. Republican. Dept. comdr. G.A.R., Vt., 1900. Died Apr. 15, 1915.

WOODCOCK, AMOS WALTER WRIGHT lawyer; b. Salisbury, Md., Oct. 29, 1883; s. Amos Wilson and Julia Ann Harris (Wright) W.; grad. Wicomico High Sch., Salisbury, Md., 1899; B.A., St. John's Coll., Annapolis, Md., 1903; LL.B., U. of Md., 1910; M.A., Harvard, 1912; LL.D., Washington, 1932, St. John's, 1937; unmarried. Began practice at Salisbury, 1912; mem. firm Woodcock & Webb, 1914-50; asst. atty. gen. of Md., 1920-22; U.S. atty., Dist. of Md., 1922-30; dir. of U.S. Bureau of Prohibition, 1930-33; apptd. special asst. to atty. gen. of U.S., Apr. 1, 1933, and continued to represent U.S. in various cases; atty. in prosecution of Japanese war criminals, Dec. 1, 1945, resigned March 31, 1946; president St. John's College, Annapolis, Md., 1934-37; mem. adv. bd. 1st Nat. Bank Md. Pres. Bd. Education, Wicomico Co., 1953-59. Served as captain Co. I, 1st Md. Inf., Mexican border, 1916; capt., maj., lt. col., 115th Inf., A.E.F., World War; participated in defense Centre Sector, Haute-Alsace, Aug. 13-Sept. 25, 1918; Meuse-Argonne, Oct. 8-29; comdr. batt. in capture Rechene Hill, North of Verdun, Oct. 10; cited "for gallantry in action"; brig. gen. comdg. 58th Brigade, Md. Nat. Guard, since Dec. 1, 1936; active service, Feb. 3, 1941-Aug. 25, 1942; ret. 1947, as brevet maj. gen. Mem. Am. and Md. bar assns., Am. Legion (dept. comdr. 1921-22), Phi Sigma Kappa. Republican. Methodist. Clubs: Nat. Press (Washington); Naval Acad. Officers. Author: Elizabeth W. Woodcock, A Story of a Good Life; Golden Days; To Hong Kong and Return; also articles in mags. and newspapers. Address: Chatillon, Sal-isbury, Md. Died Jan. 17, 1964; buried Parsons Cemetery, Salisbury, Md.

WOODFORD, STEWART LYNDON diplomat; b. New York, Sept. 3, 1835; s. Josiah Curtis and Susan (Terry) W.; A.B., Columbia, 1854, A.M., 1866; hon. A.M., Yale, 1866, Trinity, 1869; LL.D., Trinity, 1870, Dickinson, 1889, Marietta. 1908; D.C.L., Syracuse, 1894; m. Julia E. Capen, Oct. 15, 1857; m. 2d, Isabel Hanson, of New York, Sept. 26, 1900. Admitted to bar, 1857, in practice at New York, 1857—. Messenger presdl. electoral coll., 1860; asst. U.S. dist. atty., Southern Dist. of N.Y., 1861-62. Lt. col. 127th N.Y. Inf., Sept. 8, 1862; col. 103d U.S. C.T., Mar. 6, 1865; bvtd. brig. gen. vols., May 12, 1865, "for zeal, efficient and generally meritorious conduct"; resigned, Aug. 23, 1865; 1st Union mil. comdr. of Charleston, S.C., and Savannah, Ga. Lt. gov. of N.Y., 1866-68; nominee for gov., 1870; pres. electoral coll., 1872; elected 43d Congress (1873-75), resigned, July 1, 1874; U.S. dist. atty. Southern Dist. N.Y., 1877-83; mem. commn. to draft charter for Greater New York, 1896; E.E. and M.P. to Spain, 1897, until war was declared, 1898, when he returned to U.S.; mem. law firm Woodford, Bovee & Butcher, New York. Pres. Hudson-Fulton Commn., 1907; made speech placing Charles Evans Hughes in nomination for presidency, Rep. Nat. Conv., 1908. Decorated with Order of the Rising Sun, 2d Class (Japan), 1908; Crown Order of 1st Class by Emperor of Germany, 1910. Home: New York, N.Y. Died Feb. 14, 1913.

WOODFORD, WILLIAM army officer; b. Caroline County, Va., Oct. 6, 1734; s. Maj. William and Anne (Cocke) W.; m. Mary Thornton, June 26, 1762, 2 children. Justice of peace Caroline County, circa 1756-63; elected mem. Com. of Correspondence of Caroline County, 1774; sat as alternate to Edmund Pendleton in Va. Conv., 1775; col. 3d Va. Regt., Continental Army, 1775; defeated Brit. force of 300, 1775; apptd. by Continental Congress as col. 2d Va. Regt., 1776; commd. brig. gen., 1777; fought at battles of Brandywine, Germantown, Monmouth; relieved Charleston (S.C.) at Washington's order, 1779; besieged the British with 700 troops, 1780, taken prisoner when

Clinton took city, taken to N.Y.C., 1780; Woodford County (Ky.) named for him. Died N.Y.C., Nov. 13, 1780; buried Old Trinity Church Yard, N.Y.C.

WOODHULL, ALFRED ALEXANDER brig. gen. U.S.A.; b. Princeton, N.J., Apr. 13, 1837; s. Dr. Alfred A. and Anna Maria (Salomons) W.; A.B., Princeton, 1856. A.M., 1859, LL.D., 1894; M.D., U. of Pa., 1859; practiced in Kan.. 1859-61; m. Margaret, d. Elias Ellicott. Dec. 15, 1868. Assisted in raising co. vol. mounted rifles, 1861; commd. med. officer U.S.A., Sept. 19, 1861; med. insp. Army of the James, 1864-65; chief surgeon Dept. Pacific (Philippines), Apr.-Dec. 1899; bvtd. capt., maj. and lt. col. U.S.A., Mar. 1865, "for faithful and meritorious services" in war; commd. capt., asst. surgeon, July 28, 1866; maj. surgeon, Oct. 1, 1876; lt. col., deputy surgeon gen., May 16, 1894; col., asst. surgeon gen., Oct. 8, 1900; retired, Apr. 13, 1901; advanced to rank of brig. gen. retired, by act of Apr. 23, 1904. Lecturer on personal hygiene, and on gen. sanitation, Princeton U., 1902-07. Gold medalist, Mil. Service Instn., 1885; Seaman prize essayist, 1907. Mem. bd. mgrs. Geol. Survey N.J., 1904-15. Author: Surgical Catalogue Army Medical Museum, 1867; Studies, Chiefly Clinical, in the Non-Emetic Use of Ipecacuanha, 1876; Military Hygiene, 1890, 1898, 1904, 1909; Personal Hygiene. 1906; The Battle of Princeton (pamphlet), 1913. Home: Princeton, N.J. Died Oct. 18, 1921.

WOODHULL, MAXWELL VAN ZANDT author; b. Washington, D.C., Sept. 17, 1843; s. Comdr. Maxwell (U.S.N.) and Ellen Frances (Poor) W.; student Miami U., Oxford, O., 1859-62; studied law Columbian U., Washington, D.C., and in office of William B. Webb; hon. M.A., Miami U.; unmarried. Enlisted in U.S. vols., Dec. 22, 1862; commd. capt. a.d.c., Mar. 11, 1863; maj. a.a.g., July 2, 1864; lt. col. a.a.g., Feb. 17, 1865; bvtd. col., Mar. 13, 1865, "for faithful and meritorious services during recent campaigns"; brig. gen. vols., Mar. 13, 1865, "for faithful and efficient services" during the war; hon. mustered out, May 31, 1866. Served in Army of Va., Army of the Tenn. and on March to the Sea; adj. gen. at Battle of the Monocacy; adj. gen. 15th Army Corps during S. Carolina Campaign, and last adj. gen. Army of the Tenn. Asst. sec. Am. Legation, London, Eng., 1871-72 (resigned); chief of div., Consular Bur., Dept. of State, Washington, D.C., 1878-81 (resigned); admitted to bar but never practiced; dir. Utah Consol. Mining Co., Old Dominion Copper Co., Lanston Monotype Machine Co. Trustee George Washington U., Louise Home, Children's Hosp. Comdr. D. C. Commandery, Loyal Legion. Author: (brochure) A Glimpse of Sherman Fifty Years Ago, 1914; West Point in Our Next War—the Only Way to Create and to Maintain an Army, 1915. Home: Washington, D.C. Died July 26, 1921.

WOODHULL, NATHANIEL colonial legislator, army officer; b. Mastic, L.I., N.Y., Dec. 30, 1722; s. Nathaniel and Sarah (Smith) W.; m. Ruth Floyd, 1761, 1 child. Commd. maj. N.Y. Militia, 1758, col. 3d Regt., N.Y. Provincials, 1760; mem. N.Y. Colonial Assembly, 1768-75; represented Suffolk County in conv. which chose N.Y. dels. to 1st Continental Congress; apptd. brig. gen., 1775; mem. N.Y. Provincial Congress from Suffolk County, pres., 1775; assigned to remove supplies from L.I. (N.Y.) after Brit. landings, 1776; captured by British nr. Jamaica, N.Y. Died as result of ill treatment, New Utrecht, L.I., Sept. 20, 1776; buried Mastic.

WOODRUFF, CARLE AUGUSTUS brig. gen. U.S.A.; b. Buffalo, Aug. 8, 1841; s. Israel C. and Caroline A.W.; twice married. Apptd. from D.C., 2d lt. 2d U.S. Arty., Oct. 22, 1861; 1st lt., July 24, 1862; capt. 2d Arty., May 6, 1869; maj., Mar. 8, 1894; lt. col. 7th Arty., Feb. 13, 1899; col. Arty. Corps, May 8, 1901; brig. gen., Aug. 10, 1903; retired at own request after 40 yrs.' service, Aug. 11, 1903. Bvtd. capt., July 3, 1863, "for gallant and meritorious services in battle of Gettysburg, Pa."; maj., June 11, 1864, for same in battle of Trevillian Sta., Va.; lt. col., Mar. 13, 1865, "for good conduct and gallant services during the war"; awarded Congressional Medal of Honor, Sept. 1, 1893, "for distinguished gallantry in action at Newby's Cross Roads, Va., July 24, 1863." Home: Raleigh, N.C. Died July 20, 1913.

WOODRUFF, CHARLES ALBERT brig. gen. U.S.A.; b. Burke, Vt., April 26, 1845; s. Eratus and Eliza (Quimby) W.; grad. U.S. Mil. Acad., 1871; m. Louise V. Duff, July 2, 1874. Enlisted Co. A, 10th Vt. Vols., June 5, 1862; wounded 4 times, Cold Harbor, June 1 and 3, 1864. Cadet, 1867-71; 2d lt. 7th Inf., June 12, 1871; 1st lt., Aug. 9, 1877; wounded 3 times at Big Hole, Aug. 9, 1877; bvtd. capt. "for gallant services"; capt commissary, Mar. 28, 1878; maj., Dec. 27, 1892; lt. col., Feb. 4, 1898; col. asst. commissary gen., May 11, 1898; brig. gen. U.S.A. and retired, 1903. Served in Philippines; chief commissary Dept. of Calif., and purchasing commissary, San Francisco; mem. Bd. of Visitors U.S. Naval Acad., 1906; comdt. Veteran Home of Calif., 1909-14. Home: Berkeley, Calif. Died Aug. 13, 1920.

WOODRUFF, CHARLES EDWARD army medical officer; b. Philadelphia, Pa., Oct. 2, 1860; s. David Stratton and Mary Jane (Remster) W.; A.B., Central High Sch., Phila., 1879, A.M., 1884; U.S. Naval Acad., 1879-83; prof. higher mathematics, high sch.. Reading Pa., 1883-84; M.D., Jefferson Med. Coll., 1886; m. Stella M., d. Prof. John P. Caulfield, of Washington, Dec. 22, 1886. Asst. surgeon U.S.N., May 1886-Apr. 1887; 1st lt. asst. surgeon U.S.A., Apr. 14, 1887; capt., Apr. 14, 1892; maj., Apr. 13, 1901; lt. col., Jan. 1, 1910; retired from active service July 12, 1913. Served in the Spanish-Am. War, expdn. to P.I., 1898, Philippine insurrection, 1902, 3d tour in P.I., 1909-10; maj. brigade surgeon, June 4, 1898-Feb. 22, 1899. Awarded 2 medals for war service. Author: The Effects of Tropical Light on White Men, 1905; Expansion of Races, 1909; also Evolution of Numerals from Primitive Tally Marks (Am. Math. Monthly). Home: New Rochelle, N.Y. Died June 13, 1915.

WOODRUFF, JAMES ALBERT, army officer (ret.); b. Ft. Shaw, Mont., June 19, 1877; s. Charles Albert and Louise Virginia (Duff) W.; grad. U.S. Mil. Acad., 1899, U.S. Engr. Sch., 1901, Army Staff Coll., 1906, Army War Coll., 1917; m. Margarett Worth Hubbell, Oct. 8, 1904; children—Margarett Stafford, James Albert. Commd. 2d lt. Engr. Corps, Feb. 15, 1899, and promoted through grades to maj. gen., Mar. 1, 1938. Dept. dir. constrn. and forestry, A.E.F., 1918-19, World War; chief of staff Panama Canal Dept., 1924-27; div. engr. N. Atlantic Div., 1934-35; comdr. San Francisco Port of Embarkation, 1935-37, Hawaiian Coast Arty. Brigade, 1937-38, Hawaiian Div., 1938-39, First Corps Area, 1939-41; retired June 30, 1941, returned to active duty in Hawaii as pres. of mil. commn. under martial law, 1941-43; retired Aug. 1, 1943. Awarded D.S.M. (United States); Officer Legion of Honor (France); Officer Order of St. Michael and St. George (Eng.); Officer Order of Leopold (Belgium). Clubs: Army and Navy (Washington, D.C.), Army and Navy (San Francisco). Author: Applied Principles of Field Fortification, 1912. Home: Coronado CA Died Aug. 20, 1969.

WOODS, ALAN CHURCHILL ophthalmologist; b. Baltimore, Md., Aug. 20, 1889; s. Hiram and Laura (Hall) W.; prep. edn. Boys Latin Sch., Baltimore, 1900-06; A.B., Johns Hopkins, 1910, M.D., 1914; LL.D. (honorary), Hampden-Sydney, 1951; married Anne Powell Byrd, June 19, 1917; children—Alan Churchill, Anne Byrd, Jacquelin Ambler. House officer Peter Bent Brigham Hosp., Boston, 1914-15; fellow in research medicine and asst. in ophthalmology, U. of Pa., 1915-17; instr. in ophthalmology, Johns Hopkins Med. Sch., 1919-22, asso., 1922-26, asso. prof., 1926-34; acting prof. ophthalmology, 1934, dir. dept., 1937, prof., 1946-55, emeritus; ophthalmologist in chief Johns Hopkins Hosp., 1937-55, ophthalmologist in chief, 1955-60; visiting lectr., ophthalmology Harvard U., 1957. Member commission to review phys. standards for induction, 1944. Civilian consultant on ophthalmology to the surgeon general of the army, 1944. Member of com. on ophthalmology National Research Council, 1943, chmn., 1947, 58. Served as 1st lt. Med. Corps, U.S. Army, Mexican Punitive Expdn., 1916; capt. and maj., 1917-18; with A.E.F. Awarded A.M.A. Ophthal. Research Medal, 1948; Howe Research medal Am. Ophthal. Soc., 1953, Gonin medal, 1958. Hon. fellow Royal College of Surgeons (Edinburgh), 1950. Mem. Am. Ophthal. Society (president 1955), American Academy Ophthal. and Otolaryngol. (president 1947), Association American Immunologists, A.M.A., Ophthal. Soc. U.K. (honorary), Greek Ophthal. Soc. (hon.) Phi Kappa Psi, Sigma Xi. Presbyterian. Clubs: Maryland, Elkridge Hunt, Hamilton Street (Baltimore). Author: Allergy and Immunology in Ophthalmology, 1933; Endogenous Uveitis, 1956; Endogenous Inflammation of the Ureal Tract, 1961. Contbr. articles to ophthal. jours. Home: 103 Millbrook Rd., Balt. 18. Office: Johns Hopkins Hospital, Balt. 21205. Died Feb. 15, 1963.

WOODS, CHARLES ROBERT army officer; b. Newark, O., Feb. 19, 1827; s. Ezekiel S. and Sarah Judith (Burnham) W.; grad. U.S. Mil. Acad., 1852; m. Cecilia Impey, 1860. Commd. 2d lt., 1st Inf., U.S. Army, 1852; served in Indian warfare in 1850's; col. 76th Ohio Inf. Volunteers, 1861; participated in capture of Ft. Donelson, 1862, served at Battle of Shiloh; brig. gen. U.S. Volunteers, 1863; commanded expdns. on Mississippi River to destroy Confederate supply depots, 1863; participated in Atlanta campaign and "march to sea," 1864; with Sherman on march through Carolinas; brevetted maj. gen. volunteers, 1865; discharged from volunteer service, 1866, commd. col. infantry in regular army; served in West in Indian warfare, led expdn. against Indians in Kan., 1870; ret., 1874. Died Feb. 26, 1885.

WOODS, EDGAR LYONS naval med. officer; b. Charlottesville, Va., May 28, 1882; s. Samuel Baker and Lucretia Derrick (Gilmore) W.; M.D., U. Va., 1904; m. Grace Douglas Anderson, Apr. 14, 1910; 1 dau., Grace Douglas. Commd. lt. (j.g.) M.C., U.S. Navy, 1905, advanced through grades to rear adm., 1937; ret. Decorated Legion of Merit. Clubs: Army and Navy, Chevy Chase (Washington); University of Philadelphia, Pacific Union, Bohemian (San Francisco). Home: 2126 Connecticut Av., Washington 20008. Died Dec. 13, 1964; buried Arlington Cemetery.

WOODS, LOUIS EARNEST, Marine Corps officer; b. N.Y., Oct. 7, 1895; m. Evelyn Ninde; 1 dau., Marjorie (Williamson). Commd. 2d lt. Marine Corps, Apr. 1917, and advanced through the grades to brig. gen., 1942, major gen., 1944; asst. dir. Marine Corps Air Force; in command all Army, Navy and Marine Corps aviation units based on Guadalcanal, comdg. gen. Aircraft Fleet Marine Force, Atlantic, and 2d Marine Air Corps Wing, Cherry Point, N.C.; ret. 1951; v.p. First Nat. Bank Quantico (Va.), from 1951. Awarded D.S.M., Legion of Merit with a V, two Gold Stars and one Bronze Oak Leaf Cluster. Home: Washington DC Died Oct. 20, 1971; buried Arlington Nat. Cemetery.

WOODS, MICHAEL LEONARD lawyer; b. at Wood's Ferry, near Greeneville, Tenn., April 1, 1833; s. Dr. James and Martha (Harle) W.; ed. Panther Springs Acad., E. Tenn.; m. Montgomery, Ala., June 12, 1855, Martha, d. Col. Albert James Pickett. Mem. Ho. Reps., Ala., 1860-61; voted for calling Secession Conv., and later for joint resolution pledging support of Secession ordinance; served pvt. to col. Ala. inf. in C.S.A., 1861-65, surrendered with command at Salisbury, N.C., Apr. 10, 1865. Sec. Ala. senate, 1872-73; asst. examiner public accounts, Dec. 4, 1900, to Mar. 1, 1903; resigned. Democrat. Writer and newspaper contbr. on financial topics. Address: 13 Moulton St., Montgomery, Ala.

WOODS, WILLIAM WELLS, judge; b. Burlington, Ia., Jan. 24, 1841; s. James W. and Catherine (Chapin) W.; ed. Howe's Acad., Mt. Pleasant, Ia.; m. Melvina C. Whitney, 1874. Enlisted Pleyel's Ia. Lancers, Aug. 14, 1861; transferred to 4th Ia. Cavalry. Nov. 1861; 2d lt. Co. L, Nov. 17. 1861; 1st lt., June 9, 1862; capt.. Aug. 1, 1862; maj. 4th Ia. Cav., Sept. 27, 1864; mustered out, Aug. 24. 1865. Admitted to bar at Burlington, Ia., 1866; practiced law in Western Iowa to Jan. 1872, at Salt Lake City, 1872-84, Shoshone Co., Ida., 1884-—. Judge 1st Jud. Dist. of Ida., Jan. 1907-—. Mem. Constl. Conv., Ida., 1890; presdl. elector, 1896. Democrat. Home: Wallace, Ida. Died Nov. 1920.

WOODSON, WALTER BROWNE naval officer; b. Lynchburg, Va., Oct. 18, 1881; s. Edgar Alonzo and Roberta Virginia (Browne) W.; B.S., U.S. Naval Acad., 1905; LL.B., with distinction, George Washington U., 1914; grad. naval War Coll., 1922-23; m. Ruth Halford, Sept. 9, 1911; children—Ruth Halford, Walter Browne, Jr., Halford. Commd. ensign, U.S. Navy, 1907, and advanced through the grades to rear adm., judge advocate gen., June 20, 1938; admitted to bars of Dist. Court and Court of Appeals of U.S. for Dist. of Columbia, and U.S. Supreme Court; dir. ship movements, Office of Chief Naval Operations, Navy Dept., 1918-19; asst. judge advocate gen., 1921-22; exec. officer, U.S.S. Colorado, 1923-24; comdr. Destroyer Div. 34, U.S. Fleet, 1924-25; chief of staff Destroyer Force, Atlantic Fleet, 1929-31; asst. judge advocate gen., 1931-34; comdg. officer, U.S.S. Houston, 1934-35; chief of staff, Asiatic Fleet, 1935-36; naval aide to President, 1937-38; judge advocate general 1938-43. Retired 1 Sept. 1943 for physical disability. Clubs: New York Yacht; Army and Navy (Washington, D.C.); Army and Navy Country (Arlington, Va.); Army and Navy (Manila, P.I.). Home: 536 A Av., Coronado, Calif. Died Apr. 23, 1948.

WOODWARD, CALVIN MILTON university dean; b. Fitchburg, Mass., Aug. 25, 1837; s. Isaac Burnap and Eliza (Wetherbee) W.; A.B., Harvard, 1860; (hon. Ph.D., 1883, LL.D., 1905, Washington U.; LL.D., U. of Wis., 1908), m. Fanny Stone Balch, Sept. 30, 1863. Prin. Brown High Sch., Newburyport, 1860-65; capt. Co. A, 48th Mass. Vols., 1862-63, serving in La. Vice-prin. Smith Acad., St. Louis, 1865-70; prof. descriptive geometry, 1870-71, dean Sch. of Engring., 1871-96, dean Sch. of Engring. and Architecture, 1901-10, prof. mathematics and applied mechanics, 1871-1910 (emeritus), Washington University. Originator and director from organization, 1879, of St. Louis Manual Training Sch.; lecturer on manual training. Mem. St. Louis Bd. of Edn., 1877-79, and from 1897 (pres. of bd. 1899-1900, 1903-04); regent (pres. of bd.) Univ. of Mo., 1891-97. Pres. North Central Assn. Coll. and Secondary Schs.; fellow A.A.A.S. (pres. 1905-06). Author: History of St. Louis Bridge, 1881; The Manual Training School, 1887; Manual Training in Education, 1890; Applied Mechanics for Engineering and Architectural Students. Home: St. Louis, Mo. Died Jan. 12. 1915.

WOODWARD, CLARK HOWELL naval officer; b. 1877; entered U.S. Navy, 1895, and advanced through grades to rear adm., 1931; ret., 1941. Address: care Bureau of Naval Personnel, Navy Dept., Washington. Died May 29, 1967.

WOODWARD, GEORGE A. brig. gen. U.S.A.; b. Wilkes-Barre, Pa., Feb. 14, 1835; s. George W. (formerly chief justice Supreme Ct., Pa.) and Sarah Elizabeth (Trott) W.; B.A., Trinity Coll., Conn., 1855 (hon. M.A., 1895); m. Charlotte Treat Chittenden, Feb. 14, 1867. Admitted to bar and engaged in practice at Milwaukee, where was city atty., 1858-59; later practiced at Phila. Entered mil. service May 27, 1861, as capt. of 2d Pa. Reserves; maj., Apr. 2, 1862; lt. col., Feb. 20, 1863; hon. mustered out, Aug. 29, 1863; maj. Vet. Reserve Corps, Aug. 24, 1863; lt. col., Sept. 25, 1863; col., Dec. 4, 1863; hon. mustered out of vol. service, July 20, 1866; lt. col. 45th U.S. Inf., July 28, 1866; transferred to 14th Inf., Mar. 14, 1869; col. 15th Inf., Jan. 10, 1876; retired, Mar. 20, 1879; advanced to rank of brig. gen. retired, by act of Apr. 23, 1904. Bvtd. col., Mar. 2, 1867, for battle of Gettysburg. Participated in campaigns of Army of the Potomac; wounded and taken prisoner at battle of Glendale, Va., June 30, 1862; participated in battle of Gettysburg as lt. col. comdg. regt.; after entering regular service, served in Ky., Tenn., Dak., Wyo., Neb. and Utah. Mem. Phila. firm publishing mil. and naval books, 1879-87, and editor United Service Magazine during same period. Episcopalian. Democrat. Died Dec. 22, 1916.

WOODWARD, HAROLD CHRISTOPHER govt. ofcl.; b. Ottawa, Ill., Oct. 29, 1901; s. Charles E. and Lura (Hampson) W.; A.B., U. Ill., 1924; J.D., Northwestern U., 1926; m. Mabel A. Martin, Nov. 24, 1926; 1 dau., Ann (Mrs. James J. Kelly). Admitted to Ill. bar, 1926; practice in Chgo., 1926-62; partner firm Sider & Woodward, 1947-58, 60-61; master in chancery Superior Ct. Cook County, Ill., 1952-58, judge, 1959; hearings referee Ill. Commerce Commn., 1953-58; commnr. FPC, 1962—. Republican candidate for U.S. Ho. of Reps., 1946. Served to capt. USAAF, 1943-45. Mem. Am., Ill., Chgo. bar assns., Am. Legion, Delta Tau Delta, Phi Delta Phi. Mason. Home: 301 G St. S.W., Washington 24. Office: 441 G St. N.W., Washington 25. Died Aug. 4, 1964.

WOODWARD, JOSEPH JANVIER physician; b. Phila., Oct. 30, 1833; s. Joseph Janvier and Elizabeth Graham (Cox) W.; M.D., U. Pa., 1853; married twice; m. 2d, Blanche Wendell; at least 1 son, Janvier. Began practice of medicine, Phila.; became asst. surgeon Med. Corps, U.S. Army, 1861, served at 1st Battle of Bull Run; transferred to Surgeon Gen.'s Hdqrs., Washington, D.C., with duties of planning hosp. constrn., performing surgery, keeping med. records, 1862-65; asst. to curator Army Med. Museum; in charge of med. part of Medical and Surgical History of the War of the Rebellion, 1870-88; promoted maj. U.S. Army, 1876; mem. Nat. Acad. Scis., A.A.A.S., Washington Philos. Soc.; pres. A.M.A., 1881. Author various works including: Official Record of the Post-Mortem Examination of the Body of Pres. James A. Garfield, 1881. Died Wawa, Pa., Aug. 17, 1884.

WOODWARD, SAMUEL LIPPINCOTT brig. gen. U.S.A.; b. Burlington Co., N.J., Oct. 28, 1840; s. John E. and Elizabeth L. (Hornor) W.; ed. Phila. pub. schs., 1848-58; unmarried. Served in vol. army, from pvt. to maj., Feb. 1, 1862-Sept. 29, 1865; in regular army, 2d lt., June 18, 1867, to brig. gen., retiring from active service after more than 40 yrs.' service, July 9, 1904. Home: St. Louis, Mo. Died Apr. 17, 1924.

WOOL, JOHN ELLIS army officer; b. Newburgh, N.Y., Feb. 29, 1784; m. Sarah Moulton, Sept. 27, 1810. Raised co. o volunteers during War of 1812, Troy, N.Y.; commd. capt. 13th Inf., U.S. Army, 1812; promoted to maj. 29th Inf., 1813; brevetted lt. col. for gallant conduct in Battle of Plattsburg, 1814; col. and insp. gen. U.S. Army, 1816-circa 1841; brevetted brig. gen., 1826; personally assisted Gen. Winfield Scott in moving of Cherokee Indian nation to West, 1836; commd. brig. gen. U.S. Army, 1841; prepared and mustered 12,000 volunteers in 6 weeks at opening of Mexican War, 1846; 2d in command at Battle of Buena Vista for which he was brevetted maj. gen., 1846; commanded Eastern Mil. Div., 1848-53, Dept. of Pacific, 1854-57; commd. maj. gen. U.S. Army in command Middle Mil. Dept. and Dept. of East, 1862-63; ret. from active service, 1863. Died Troy, Nov. 10, 1869.

WOOLDRIDGE, EDMUND TYLER, naval officer; b. Lawrenceberg, Ky., Jan. 5, 1897; s. Dewell Henderson and Minnie Gray (Hawkins) W.; B.S., U.S. Naval Acad. 1919; m. Marion Lee Johnson, Nov. 18, 1921; children—Edmund Tyler, Marion Lee, Marshall Homer. Commd. ensign U.S. Navy, 1919, and advanced through grades to vice admiral, April 1954; assigned naval duties including commands of submarine, destroyer and battleship, 1916-41; chief of staff to task force comdr., North Atlantic, engaged in anti-submarine warfare, 1941-43; dir. naval officer personnel, hdqrs., Navy Dept., Washington, D.C., 1943-44; comd. U.S.S. New Jersey (flagship at various times for Admirals Halsey and Spruance), 1944-45; comd. naval forces, Northeastern Japan, 1945-46; comdg. cruiser div. Western Pacific, 1946-47; became asst. chief naval operations Mil.-Politico Affairs, Washington, 1947; now commander 2d Fleet and commander NATO Striking Fleet, 1954-55; comdt. The National War College, 1956-58. Decorated Distinguished Service medal, Legion of Merit, Bronze star, Commendation ribbon, Victory ribbon (World War I), Haitian Campaign ribbon, 1919, Am. Defense ribbon, European Theatre ribbon, Am. Theatre ribbon, Asiatic-Pacific Theatre ribbon, Victory (World War II); C.B.E.; Comdr. Order of Ayachucho, Peru, 1956. Presbyn. Club: Army-Navy-Marine Corps Country (Washington). Home: Annapolis MD Died Dec. 15, 1968; buried U.S. Naval Acad. Cemetery, Annapolis MD

WOOLLEY, ALICE STONE physician; b. Yankton, S.D.; d. Miles and Ellen (Stone) Woolley; B.S., Columbia, 1923; M.D., U. of Maryland, 1930. Dir. physical education, Poughkeepsie (N.Y.) Y.W.C.A., 1908-25; interne, Gallinger Municipal Hosp., Washington, D.C., 1930-31, Childrens Hosp., Washington, D.C., 1931-32; in practice of medicine, Poughkeepsie, N.Y., since 1932; mem. courtesy staff Vassar Brothers Hosp., St. Francis Hosp., Northern Dutchess Health Center; med. consultant Bard Coll. Annandale-on-Hudson, N.Y., since 1944. Served in France, World War I, 1918-19. Awarded Medaille de la Reconnaissance Française (for 2 yrs. service), 1920. Mem. bd. Dutchess County chapter Am. Red Cross, Girl Scouts America, Poughkeepsie Womens City and County Civic Club; mem. Dutchess County Womens Republican Club. Fellow A.M.A.; mem. Am. Med. Womens Assn. (pres. 1944-45), Womens Med Soc. of N.Y. State (pres. 1940-41), Dutchess County Health Assn., N.Y. State and Dutchess County med. assns., Womens Med. Assn. of N.Y. City, Am. Assn. Univ. women, Mahwenawasigh Chapter D.A.R., Womens Overseas Service League. Clubs: Tuesday Literary (Poughkeepsie); Cosmopolitan (New York). Home: "Stoneridge," Cedarcliff Manor, Poughkeepsie, N.Y. Died Nov. 16, 1946.

WOOLSEY, MELANCTHON TAYLOR naval officer; b. N.Y., June 5, 1780; s. Col. Melancthon Lloyd and Alida (Livingston) W.; m. Susan Cornelia Tredwell, Nov. 3, 1817, 7 children. Apptd. midshipmen U.S. Navy, 1800; participated in Barbary War, 1800-05; promoted lt., 1804; began tour of duty on Gt. Lakes, 1808, built ship Oneida on Lake Ontario; defeated superior Brit. force at Sackett's Harbor, Lake Ontario during War of 1812; participated in attack on Kingston and in combined army-navy siege of York (Ont.), 1813; commd. master comdt. in command of Sylph, 1813; on convoy duty from Oswego to Sackett's Harbor, 1814; commd. capt., 1816; commanded Constellation, 1825; on duty patrolling West Indies against pirates, 1825-26; in command of Pensacola Navy Yard, 1826-30; in command of Brazil squadron with rank of commodore, 1833-34. Died Utica, N.Y., May 19, 1838.

WOOLSEY, THEODORE SALISBURY forester; b. New Haven, Conn., Oct. 2, 1879; s. Theodore Salisbury and Annie Gardner (Salisbury) W.; B.A., Yale, 1901, M.F., 1903; m. Ruby Hilsman, d. Thomas H. Pickett, of Dawson, Ga., Mar. 15, 1908; children—Elizabeth P., Anne S., Edith, Sara P., Patricia. Insp., 1907-08, asst. dist. forester, 1908-15, U.S. Forest Service. Mem. Yale Forest Sch. Advisory Bd. and lecturer in 1912, on orgn. and management of national forests; also lecturer, 1916, apptd. asst. prof., 1917, but entered U.S.A.; commd. maj., 1917; lt. col. engrs., 1919; attached Paris hdqrs. staff, A.E.F. in France. Am. del. exec. com. Interallied War Wood Com., Paris, 1917-19. Cited by Gen. Pershing, 1919; Chevalier Legion of Honor, France; D.S.O., Eng.; Chevalier Order of Leopold, Belgium, 1919. Dir. New Haven Bank. Episcopalian. Asso. editor of "Forestry Quarterly," 1915-27. Made studies of the forestry movement in India, Austria and parts of Germany, France, Corsica, Algeria, Tunisia. Trustee and cons. forester, Middlebury (Vt.) Coll. Author: French Forests and Forestry, 1917; Studies in French Forestry, 1920; American Forest Regulation (textbook), 1922. Home: New Haven, Conn. Died July 10, 1933.

WOOSTER, CHARLES WHITING naval officer; b. New Haven, Conn., 1780; s. Thomas and Lydia (Sheldon) W.; m. Frances Stebbens, 1 child. Commanded ship Fair American, 1801; commanded privateer Saratoga, during War of 1812, captured 22 Brit. vessels including Rachel in Battle of La Guayra (Venezuela); commd. capt. of battalion of ships to protect N.Y. Harbor, 1814; commd. in Chilean Army in war of independence, 1817; commd. rear-adm. Chilean Navy; returned to U.S., 1835. Died San Francisco, 1848.

WOOSTER, DAVID army officer; b. Stratford, Conn., Mar. 2, 1711; grad. Yale, 1738; m. Mary Clap, Mar. 1746, 4 children. Apptd. lt. Conn. Colony, 1741; apptd. capt. of sloop Defense, to protect coast, 1742; served as capt. Conn. Militia, 1745; organizer Hiram Lodge (1 of earliest Free Mason lodges in Conn.), 1750; served as col. Conn. regt., Seven Years War, 1756-63; mem. Conn. Assembly from New Haven, 1757; apptd. by Conn. Assembly maj. gen. of 6 regts. and col. 1st Regt., 1775; in command of Continental Army before Quebec, Can., 1775; recalled by Continental Congress on charge of incompetence, 1776, acquitted of charge, retained rank of brig. gen. but was not given a command. Died May 2, 1777.

WOOTEN, RALPH H., army officer; b. Independence, Miss., Aug. 30, 1893; B.S., Agrl. and Mech. Coll. of Tex., 1916; commd. 2d lt. Inf. Aug. 1917, and advanced through the grades to major general, 1944; apptd. mil. attache, Santiago, Chile, Aug. 1938; on temp. duty in Mil. Intelligence Div., War Dept. Gen. Staff, July 1941-Sept. 1941, then on staff duty with Gen. Hdqrs. of the Army; later assigned to Army Air Forces Tech. Training Command, Miami, Fla.; commd. Sixth Air Force, Nov. 1943-May 1944; commd. U.S. Army Forces South Atlantic, Recife, Brazil, May 1944-November 1945, Duty with Foreign Liquidation Commn., State Dept., Washington, D.C., 1946; comdg. gen. Pacific Air Comd., Hawaii, 1947-48; ret. 1948; exec. v.p. Mid-South Chem. Co., Inc., Memphis, 1949-69. Home: Memphis TN2Died Nov. 19, 1969; buried Memphis Memorial Park.

WORDEN, JOHN LORIMER naval officer; b. Westchester County, N.Y., Mar. 12, 1818; s. Ananias and Harriet (Graham) W.; m. Olivia Taffey, 4 children. Apptd. midshipman U.S. Navy, 1834, commd., 1840; served at Naval Observatory, 1844-46, 50-S2; fought in storeship Southampton during Mexican War; captured at Pensacola, Fla., 1861, exchanged; apptd. comdr. in Monitor, 1862, wounded in Monitor-Merrimac fight; commd. capt., 1863; served in South Atlantic Blockade Squadron at battles of Ft. McAllister and Charleston; commd. commodore, 1868, rear adm., 1872; supt. U.S. Naval Acad., 1869-74; commanded European Squadron, 1875-77; pres. Navy Retiring Bd., 1878-86; ret., 1886. Died Washington, D.C., Oct. 18, 1897; buried Pawling, N.Y.

WORTH, WILLIAM JENKINS army officer; b. Hudson, N.Y., Mar. 1, 1794; s. Thomas Worth; m. Margaret Stafford, Sept. 18, 1818, 4 children. Apptd. 1st lt. 23d Inf., U.S. Army, 1813; served with Gen. Winfield Scott as a.d.c., 1818; brevetted capt. and maj.; comdt. U.S. Mil. Acad., 1820-28; brevetted lt. col., 1824; col. 8th Inf., 1838; brevetted brig. gen. by Pres. Polk for service in Seminole War of 1838, 1845; served in Mexican War, 1846, 1st to plant flag on Rio Grande; brevetted maj. gen., 1846, presented with sword by resolution of Congress, 1847; participated with distinction in engagements from Vera Cruz to Mexico City; involved him in dispute with Gen. Scott due to his ambition and tactlessness, 1847; in command of Dept. of Tex., 1848. Died May 7, 1849.

WORTH, WILLIAM SCOTT brig. gen. U.S.A., retired; b. Albany, N.Y., Jan. 6, 1840; s. Gen. Wm. Jenkins W.; U.S.A. (1794-1849); entered army as 2d lt., 8th inf., April 26, 1861; 1st lt., June 7, 1861 (bvtd. capt. and maj.); capt., Jan. 14, 1866; maj., 2d inf., Mar. 9, 1891; lt. col., 13th inf., Nov. 26, 1894; col., Sept. 1898; engaged in Santiago campaign; was severely wounded July 1, 1898, during the charge on San Juan Hill; promoted brig. gen., Nov. 2, 1898, and retired Nov. 9, 1898, on account of severe disabling wounds. In Civil war served on staff Gen. A. J. Smith during Corinth campaign; a.d.c. staff Gen. H. J. Hunt, chief of arty., Army of the Potomac, from summer of 1862 to the surrender, and took part in all engagements and campaigns of that army; on frontier duty, 1872-91. Home: New York, N.Y. Died 1904.

WORTHINGTON, WALTER FITZHUGH rear admiral; b. Baltimore, Md., Mar. 8, 1855; s. Nicholas Brice and Sophia Kerr (Muse) W.; A.B., Md. Agrl. Coll., 1873; grad. U.S. Naval Acad., 1875; m. Grace Winifred Macmillan, of Greenock, Scotland, Aug. 3, 1885. Apptd. to U.S. Naval Acad. from Md., 1873; rear admiral, Mar. 26, 1913—. Served on gunboats Alert, Castine and Vesuvius; transport Powhatan; frigate Lancaster; cruisers Atlanta, Chicago, Montgomery; battleships Illinois, Kearsarge; monitor Terror. Cruised on N. Atlantic, S. Atlantic, Mediterranean, Asiatic stas.; shore duty, Navy Dept., N.Y. Navy Yard and Pittsburgh, Pa.; instr. at U.S. Naval Acad.; adj. prof. Lafayette Coll., Pa.; prof. Clemson Coll., S.C.; was in charge erection and equipment U.S. Expt. Sta., Annapolis; insp. materials, Brooklyn dist., Mar. 26, 1913-Mar. 8, 1919; retired by operation of law, Mar. 8, 1919. Democrat. Episcopalian. Home: Santa Barbara, Calif. Died Aug. 1, 1937.

WOTHERSPOON, WILLIAM WALLACE maj. general U.S.A.; b. Washington, D.C., Nov. 16, 1850; s. Alexander S. and Louisa A. (Kuhn) W.; ed. at pvt. schs.; m. Mary C. Adams, Apr. 2, 1887. Apptd. from D.C., 2d lt. 12th U.S. Inf., Oct. 1, 1873; 1st lt., Mar. 20, 1879; capt., Apr. 28, 1893; maj. 30th Inf., Feb. 2, 1901; transferred to 6th Inf., June 26, 1902; lt. col. 14th Inf., July 12, 1904; transferred to 19th Inf., May 15, 1905; grad. Army War Coll., 1905; brig. gen. U.S.A., Oct. 3, 1907; maj. gen., May 12, 1912. Served on gen. staff, 1905-09; pres. Army War Coll., 1907-09; asst. to chief of staff, May 1909-10; pres. Army War Coll., 1910-12; comdr. Dept. of the Gulf, Atlanta, Jan.-Sept. 1912; asst. to the chief of staff, Sept. 1912-Apr. 1914; chief of staff U.S.A., Apr.-Nov. 1914; retired, Nov. 16, 1914. Home: Albany, N.Y. Died Oct. 21, 1921.

WRIGHT, ARTHUR MULLIN surgeon; b. Lyndonville, N.Y., Sept. 30, 1879; s. Richard Brainard and Ella Agatha (Mullin) W.; A.B., Cornell, 1903, M.D., 1905; D.Sc. (honorary), New York University, 1947; married Alice Stanchfield, Apr. 27, 1912; children—Richard Stewart, Stanchfield. Practiced in N.Y. City since 1905; teacher surgery since 1907; George David Stewart prof. surgery, Univ. and Bellevue Hosp. Med. Coll., Grove Farm, Earleville, Md., 1933-47, emeritus prof. surgery since 1947; emeritus director surgery, French Hospital, New York City; consulting surgeon, Bellevue and St. Vincent's hospitals (both New York City), St. Francis Hosp. (Port Jervis, N.Y.), Mount Vernon Hosp. (Mt. Vernon), Jamaica Hosp. (Jamaica, L.I.), St. Luke's Hosp. (Newburgh), Southside Hosp. (Bayshore), St. Agnes' Hosp. (White Plains), Central Islip Hosp. (L.I.). Served as capt. Med. Corp, U.S. Army, 1917; maj. lt. col., 1918-19, in charge Base Hosp. No. 1, A.E.F.; col. Res. Corps. Fellow Am. Coll. Surgeons, A.M.A.; mem. Acad. Medicine, Am. Surg. Assn., N.Y. Surg. Soc.; Internat. Surgical Assn., Am. Bd. of Surgery. Decorated Chevalier Legion of Honor; Order of the Jade (Chinese); awarded meritorious citation for army service. Clubs: Cornell University. Contbr. surg. articles. Home: Earleville, Md. Died June 24, 1948.

WRIGHT, CHARLES JEFFERSON president mil. acad.; b. St. Johnsbury, Vt., Oct. 21, 1839; g.g.s. Benjamin W., Minute Man who fought through Revolution; A.B., Hobart Coll., 1861; m. Margaret Worrall Bard, 1869. Entered Union Army in 16th N.H. Vols., 1861; bvtd. col., Mar. 13, 1865, "for gallant and meritorious services during war"; was severely wounded at Ft. Fisher and Petersburg. Prin. Peekskill, N.Y., Mil. Acad., 1872-87; was pres. N.Y. Mil. Acad., Cornwall, N.Y.; became pres. Matawan Mil. Acad. G.A.R. Home: Matawan, N.J. Died 1910.

WRIGHT, DANIEL BOONE congressman; b. nr. Mt. Pleasant, Tenn., Feb. 17, 1812; grad. Cumberland U., Lebanon, Tenn., 1837; studied law. Admitted to the bar, 1840, began practice in Ashland, Miss.; moved to Salem (later Hudsonville), Miss., 1850, practiced law, engaged in farming; mem. U.S. Ho. of Reps. (Democrat) from Miss., 33d-34th congresses, 1853-57; apptd. lt. col. 34th Regt., Miss. Inf., Confederate Army during Civil War; wounded at Battle of Perryville, 1862, captured and sent to Camp Chase, O., exchanged, 1863; resigned commn., 1863; apptd. col. of cavalry, 1864; judge mil. cts. Gen. N. B. Forrest's Cavalry Div.; captured, 1865, surrendered at La Grange, Tenn., later paroled. Died Ashland, Miss., Dec. 27, 1887; buried McDonald Cemetery, nr. Ashland.

WRIGHT, EDWARD EVERETT commodore U.S.N.; b. E. Bridgewater, Mass., Sept. 9, 1856; s. George Allen and Hannah (Litchfield) W.; grad. U.S. Naval Acad., 1877; m. Katherine Davis, Dec. 10, 1886 (died 1911). Promoted through the various grades to capt.; retired, July 1, 1910, with rank of commodore. Served on bd. Swatara, and Powhatan, N. Atlantic sta., 1877-79; Swatara and Monocacy, Asiatic sta., 1879-82; training sta., Newport, R.I., 1882-84; U.S. Coast Survey, 1884-87; Swatara and Alliance, S. Atlantic sta. and Yantic and Galena, N. Atlantic sta., 1887-90; Navy Yard, Boston, 1890-93; Newark, S. Atlantic Sta., 1893-96; Wabash, and Navy Yard, Boston, 1896-97; on bd. Minneapolis, Flying Squadron, Spanish War, 1898; Essex. apprentice training ship, 1898-1901; Navy Yard. Boston, 1901-03; Atlanta and Brooklyn, S. Atlantic Sta., 1903-05; comdg. prison ship Southery, Navy Yard, Portsmouth, N.H., 1905-06; insp. 2d lighthouse dist., Boston, 1906-07; comdg. flagship Rainbow and Chattanooga, Philippine Sta., 1907-09; capt. of yard, Navy Yard, Phila. and comdt. U.S. Naval Sta., Guantanamo Cuba, 1909-10; comdt. Naval Sta., Guantanamo Cuba, Sept. 4, 1917-Dec. 18, 1918. Home: Newton Center, Mass. Died Nov. 23, 1921.

WRIGHT, HORATIO GOVERNEUR army officer, engr.; b. Clinton, Conn., Mar. 5, 1820; s. Edward Wright; grad. U.S. Mil. Acad., 1841; m. Louise M. Bradford, Aug. 11, 1842, 2 children. Commd. 2d lt. Corps Engrs., U.S. Army, 1841, capt., 1855; asst. to chief engr., Washington, D.C., 1861, built defenses for Capitol; fought in Battle of Bull Run; chief engr. Port Royal expdn.; commd. brig. gen. U.S. Volunteers, 1861, maj. gen., 1864; chief engr. Dept. of Ohio, U.S. Army, 1862; fought in battles of Gettysburg, Mine Run, Wilderness; commanded VI Corps, U.S. Army, his troops were first to pierce Petersburg (Va.) defenses; commanded Dept. of Tex., 1865-66; returned to various constrn. assignments after Civil War; promoted brig. gen. U.S. Army, chief engrs., 1879; ret., 1884. Died Washington, July 2, 1899; buried Arlington (Va.) Nat. Cemetery.

WRIGHT, JOHN VINES lawyer; b. Purdy, Tenn., June 28, 1828; s. Capt. Benjamin W., U.S.A.; ed. Purdy and attended session of Univ. of Ky., Louisville; studied med. jurisprudence preparatory for law, taking whole med. course at Louisville; m. Georgia Hays, Nov. 23, 1858. Admitted to bar, 1852; defeated for mem. legislature, 1853, by one vote; mem. Congress, 1855-61. Entered 13th Tenn. regt., C.S.A.; elected capt. of co. and col. of regt.; was at battle of Belmont and had horse killed under him; served in army until elected mem. Confederate Congress, and served until surrender of Confederacy. After war, judge circuit court; chancellor and judge Supreme Court, Tenn.; chmn. Northwest Indian Commn., 1886-87; made more treaties with Indians than any other living man; also mem. commn. to Great Sioux Nation; nominated for gov. Tenn., 1880, but defeated by defection of faction of Democrats favoring repudiation of State bonds—Republican being elected. Is now in legal dept. of Gen. Land Office, Washington. Died 1908.

WRIGHT, JOSEPH JEFFERSON BURR physician, army officer; b. Wilkes-Barre, Pa., Apr. 27, 1801; A.B., Washington (Pa.) Coll., 1821; attended U. Pa. Sch. of Medicine, 1825-26; m. Eliza Jones; 3 children including Joseph P. Served as asst. surgeon U.S. Army, 1833-40, in Seminole War, 1840-41, 43; with 8th Inf. in occupation of Tex., 1846; served in battles of Palo Alto and Resaca de la Palma during Mexican War; in charge of hosp., Matamoras; wrote report on cholera epidemic published in So. Med. Reports, 1849; on field duty with troops in Kan., 1857, Utah expdn., 1858; served as med. dir. Dept. of Ohio on Gen. George B. McClellan's staff, Civil War; in battles of Rich Mountain, Carrick's Ford (W.Va.); surgeon Cavalry Recruiting Depot, Carlisle, Pa., 1862-76; brevetted col., 1864; promoted brig. gen., 1865; contbd. case reports to surg. vol. Medical and Surgical History of War of Rebellion, 6 vols., 1870-88. Died Carlisle, May 14, 1878.

WRIGHT, LUKE E. secretary of war; b. in Tenn., 1846; s. Hon. Archibald W. (chief justice of Tenn.); read law, and admitted to Tennessee bar; (LL.D., Hamilton, 1903); m. Kate, d. Admiral Semmes, C.S.N. Had 3 sons in service during Spanish-Am. War, 1898. Practiced law at Memphis; atty. gen. of Tenn., 8 yrs.; active in relief measures during yellow fever scourge, 1878. Mem. U.S. Philippine Commn., 1900-04 (pres. 1903-04); apptd. civil gov. of P.I., 1904, gov. gen. until 1906; ambassador extraordinary and plenipotentiary to Japan, 1906-07, resigned; sec. of war, U.S., in cabinet of President Roosevelt, July 1, 1908-Mar. 1909. Gold Democrat. Home: Memphis, Tenn. Died Nov. 17, 1922.

WRIGHT, RICHARD ROBERT educator, banker; b. Dalton, Ga., May 16, 1855; s. Robert Waddell and Harriet (Lynch) W.; A.B., Atlanta U., 1876, A.M., 1879; LL.D., Wilberforce, 1899; m. Lydia Elizabeth Howard, June 7, 1877; children—Richard Robert, Julia O., Mrs. Essie W. Thompson, Mrs. Lillian M. Clayton, Dr. Whittier H., Mrs. Edwina Mitchell, Emanuel C., Mrs. Harriet W. Lemon. Prin. Ware High Sch., 1880-91; pres. Ga. State Industrial Coll., 1891-1921; pres. Citizens & Southern Bank & Trust Co. of Phila. since 1921. Served in Spanish-Am. War as an additional paymaster with rank of major vols., Aug. 3-Dec. 1, 1898. Organizer and pres. Georgia State Agrl. and Industrial Assn.; anniversary speaker Am. Missionary Assn., 1907; trustee Atlanta Univ., 1880-98. Del. 4 Rep. nat. convs.; declined appointment E.E. and M.P. to Liberia, tendered by Pres. McKinley. Traveled extensively in Europe. Methodist. Mason (33 deg.), Elk. Mem. Am. Acad. Polit. and Social Science. Pres. Nat. Assn. of Presidents of A. and M. Colleges for Negroes; pres. Nat. Assn. Teachers in Colored Schools, 1900-06; pres. Nat. Negro Bankers Assn., 1908-12. Secured passage of an act by U.S. Senate for appropriation of $250,000 to promote Semi-Centennial Emancipation Exhbn., 1913. Apptd. by gov. Ga. chmn. Colored Assn. Council of Food Production and Conservation; apptd. by gov. of Ga. as Negro historian of enlisted colored troops in France, and visited Eng., France and Belgium to collect hist. data for the archives of Ga. and for a book on the Negro in the Great War. Mem. Spanish-Am. War Veterans, Phila. Business League (pres.). Apptd. by Gov. J. S. Fisher of Pa. mem. commn. to erect a statue in memory of the colored soldiers in all Am. wars. Promoter of Youths' Thrift Clubs, 1933-35. Promoted Good-Will Airplane trip to Haiti, 1939. Author and inspirer of the idea of first U.S. postage stamp named for a Negro (Booker T. Washington postage stamp). Founder and organizer Nat. Freedom Day, 1941, celebrating anniversary of adoption of 13th Amendment. Received Muriel Dobbins Vocational School 1946 Pioneers of Industry Award for service to community by Bd. of Edn. Home: 554 N. 58th St. Office; 1849 South St., Philadelphia, Pa. Died July 2, 1947.

WRIGHT, WALTER KING army officer; b. in N.Y., Sept. 19, 1858; grad. U.S. Mil. Acad., 1883; Army War Coll., 1909. Commd. 2d lt. 16th Inf., June 13, 1883; 1st lt., Oct. 1, 1888; capt. 7th Inf., Apr. 26, 1898; maj. com. subs. vols., June 7, 1898; hon. discharged vols., Apr. 12, 1899; maj. U.S. Army, Aug. 26, 1903; trans. to 8th Inf., May 11, 1906; lt. col., Mar. 10, 1911; trans. to 12th Inf., Feb. 1, 1913; col. of inf., Aug. 27, 1913; assigned to 23d Inf., July 7, 1914. Prof. mil. science and tactics, U. of Utah, 1891-94; riot duty, July-Aug. 1894; duty with gov. of Ky., Jan.-Apr. 1898; at Chickamauga Park, Ga., and camps Alger, Mead and Mackenzie; in Alaska, 1899-1901, Manila, P.I., 1903-05; comd. 23d Inf., on Mexican border, 1916-17. Address: War Dept., Washington, D.C.

WRIGHT, WILLIAM MASON army officer; b. Newark, N.J., Sept. 24, 1863; s. Edward H. and Dora M. W.; cadet U.S. Mil. Acad., July 1, 1882-Jan. 11, 1883; grad. Inf. and Cav. Sch., 1891; m. Marjorie Jerauld, June 1891; children—William Mason, Jerauld, Marjorie. Commd. 2d lt., 2d Inf., Jan. 19, 1885; 1st lt. 5th Inf., Dec. 17, 1891; trans. to 2d Inf., Feb. 9, 1892; capt. a.a.g. vols., May 20, 1898; hon. discharged vols., May 12, 1899; capt. U.S. Army, Mar. 2, 1899; promoted through grades to brig. gen. May 15, 1917; maj. gen. N.A., Aug. 5, 1917; maj. gen. regular army, Mar. 7, 1921. Participated in Santiago Campaign, 1898, later in subduing Philippine Insurrection; duty Gen. Staff, 1905-08; with Gen. Funston, at Vera Cruz, 1914; apptd. comdr. 35th Div., Sept. 1917; comd. 35th Div. with British, May 1-June 6, 1918, 3d, 5th and 7th corps A.E.F., in the Vosges, 89th Div. during the St. Mihiel and Meuse-Argonne offensives, and 1st Corps, Nov. 12, 1918-Mar. 22, 1919; dep. chief of staff, U.S. Army, Jan. 1920-July 1921; comdg. 9th Corps Area, July 1921; comdg. Philippine Dept., Feb.-Sept. 1922; retired Dec. 31, 1922. Awards: D.S.M., Knight Comdr. St. Michael and St. George, Comdr. Legion Honor, Grand Officier Order Leopold, Order Rising Sun, Croix de Guerre with Palm. Clubs: Union (New York); Metropolitan, Alibi (Washington). Address: War Dept., Washington, D.C. Died Aug. 16, 1943.

WULSIN, LUCIEN (wul'sin), piano mfr.; b. Cincinnati, O., Mar. 17, 1889; s. Lucien and Katharine E. (Roelker) W.; grad. St. George's Sch., Newport, R.I., 1906; A.B., Harvard, 1910, M.E.E., 1911; D.Litt. (hon.), Cincinnati Conservatory of Music, 1952; D.Sc., University of Cincinnati, 1957; married Margaret M. Hager, June 6, 1914; children—Katharine R., Lucien, John H., Eugene, Thomas M., Margaret M., Adele. Elec. engr. Stone & Webster, Boston, 1911, in statis. dept., 1911-12; with engring. dept. Baldwin Piano Co., Cincinnati, 1912-13, sec., 1913-19, treas., 1919-24, v.p., 1924-26, pres. The Baldwin Piano Company and subsidiaries, 1926-62, chairman of the board, 1962—. Served as 2d lt., later 1st lt., Engr. Res. Corps, 1917-18; capt. Engr. Corps, U.S. Army, 1918-19, office of chief engr. line of communications and engr. purchasing office, Paris, Oct. 1917-May 1919. Trustee and sec. Cin. Inst. of Fine Arts; mem. overseers com. Harvard. Mem. Hist. and Philos. Soc. of Ohio (president, trustee). Republican. Clubs: Queen City, Camargo, Cincinnati Country (Cin.); Harvard (N.Y.C. and Boston); Chicago; Century Assn. (N.Y.C.). Home: 2444 Madison Rd. Office: 1801 Gilbert Av., Cin. Died Jan. 13, 1964; buried Spring Grove Cemetery, Cin.

WURTSMITH, PAUL BERNARD army officer; b. Detroit, Mich., Aug. 9, 1906; s. Fred and Ella (Globensky) W.; student Holy Redeemer School; grad. Cass Tech. High Sch.; student U. of Detroit, 1925-27; m. Irene Catherine Gillespie Kloehr, June 6, 1933. Entered Army Air Corps, 1927; commd. 2d lt., 1928; promoted through grades to brig. gen., Feb. 1943; now maj. gen.; assigned to 50th Pursuit Group, Selfridge Field, Jan. 1941; assignment, Australia, Jan. 1942; returned to U.S., Aug. 1946; stationed MacDill Field, near Tampa, Fla. Decorated D.S.M. Home: 1318 Schley Av., San Antonio, Tex. Died Sept. 13, 1946; buried in Arlington National Cemetery.

WYATT, LEE B. judge; b. Franklin, Ga., July 13, 1890; s. Smitheul Franklin and Mary Elizabeth (Kent) W.; student Bowdon (Ga.) Coll., 1909-10; LL.B., Mercer U., Macon, Ga., 1914; m. Sara Baker, Dec. 25, 1939. Admitted to bar, 1914, engaged in general practice of law, LaGrange, Ga., 1914-31; city atty., City of LaGrange, 1923-31; mem. Gen. Assembly of Ga., 1917-22; judge of Superior Courts, Coweta Circuit, 1931-42; asso. justice Supreme Court of Ga., 1943-53, presiding justice, 1953—; apptd. mem. of mil. tribunals trying alleged major war criminals at Nürnberg, Germany, appointed for term of six months from Aug. 10th, 1947, on leave of absence from Georgia Supreme Court during this service; pres. LaGrange (Ga.) Theatre Co., Inc.; pres. Home Building Loan Assn.; v.p. LaGrange Banking Co. Mem. Am., Ga., Coweta and Troup Co. bar assns. Mason (Shriner), Elk, Woodmen of World. Home: Greenville Rd., LaGrange, Ga. Office: Judicial Bldg., Atlanta. Died Feb. 1960.

WYCKOFF, AMBROSE BARKLEY lieutenant U.S.N., retired; b. Delhi, Ill., Apr. 29, 1848; s. Ambrose Spencer and Sarah (Gelder) W.; grad. U.S. Naval Acad., 1868; m. Grace Traphagen, of Elsinore, Cal., Nov. 25, 1902. Lt., Oct., 1872; served during Spanish war in charge of light house dist.; had 14 yrs.' service at sea in all parts of the world; purchased the ground, established, and was first commandant Puget Sound Naval Sta., Bremerton, Wash.; retired, July 3, 1893, on account of ill health contracted in line of duty. Mem. Am. Philos. Soc.; hon. mem. Franklin Inst. Phila.; hon. mem. Seattle Chamber Commerce. Mem. Loyal Legion. Mason (32 deg.). Contbr. to jours. and proc. socs. on scientific subjects. Address: 402 Burke Blk., Seattle, Wash.

WYLIE, ROBERT H(OWARD) army officer; b. Huntington, W.Va., Feb. 24, 1899; s. Robert Danforth and Caroline (Gardner) W.; student, Greenbrier Mil. Sch., Lewisburg, W.Va., 1915-17; Va. Mil. Inst., Lexington, 1917-18; grad. Motor Transport Sch., 1922, Q.M. Sch., 1936, Army Indsl. Coll., 1937; spl. Navy Yard Course, 1927-29; m. Marjorie Leon Weir, Oct. 8, 1919 (div.); m. 2d, Elizabeth Salome Harris, Nov. 18, 1936; children—Robert Gardner, Carol Ann, Sarah Jean, Patricia Ruth. Commd. 2d lt. Inf., U.S. Army, 1918, advanced through grades to brig. gen., 1942; asst. supt. Army Transport Service, 1930-31, 38-41; asst. chief Transp. Corps., 1942-47; ret.; mgr. Bd. State Harbor Commrs. for San Francisco Harbor. Mason, K.T. Home: 39 Curtis Av., San Rafael, Cal. Died Dec. 1962.

WYLLIE, ROBERT (EDWARD) EVAN, army officer (ret.); b. Assam, India, Apr. 3, 1873; s. Henry Shaw and Emily (Cobb) W.; grad. arty. sch., sch. submarine defense, Army War Coll., Navy War Coll.; m. Marjorie Zoe Stuart, July 23, 1909; children—Zoe Roberta, Jean Louise (Mrs. O. Reeves Cross). Came to U.S., 1888, naturalized, 1896. Enlisted U.S. Army, 1895; 2d lt., arty., 1898; promoted through grades to col., ret. as brig. gen., 1930; established 1st coast defenses in Philippines; chief equipment br. War Dept., gen. staff, during World War I. Awarded Distinguished Service Medal. Author: Orders, Decorations and Insignia, 1920; contbr. to mags. Home: 59 Parkside Dr., Berkeley 5 CA

WYMAN, ROBERT HARRIS naval officer; b. Portsmouth, N.H., July 12, 1822; s. Thomas White and Sarah (Harris) W.; studied Phila. Naval Sch., 1842; m. Emily Madeline Dallas, Sept. 27, 1847, 3 children.

Apptd. midshipman U.S. Navy, 1837, assigned to steamer Independence, 1838; sailed in ship John Adams (commanded by his father) to East Indies, 1838-40; served under Commodore David Conner in Home Squadron in Mexican War; commanded expdn. up Rappahannock River, destroying Confederate property, 1862; took part in capture of Port Royal, S.C.; commanded gunboat Sonoma, 1863, captured Confederate ships Britannia and Lizzi; in charge of Hydrographic Office, Washington, D.C., 1871; commd. rear adm., 1878, in command of N.Am. Squadron. Author: Coasts of Chile, Bolivia and Peru, 1876; Navigation of Coasts and Islands in Mediterranean Sea, 1872. Died Washington, Dec. 2, 1882.

WYMAN, WILLARD GORDON, retired army officer; b. Augusta, Me., Mar. 21, 1898; s. John Monroe and Minnie (Haynes) W.; student Lincoln Acad., Newcastle, Me., 1912-15; grad. Coburn Classical Inst., Waterville, Me., 1916; student Bowdoin Coll., 1917, M.A. (hon.), 1951; B.S., U.S. Mil. Acad., 1919; grad. Coast Arty. Sch., Ft. Monroe, Va., 1920, Cav. Sch., Ft. Riley Kan., 1921, Signal Sch., Ft. Monmouth, N.J., 1926; student Chinese language Mil. Attache's Office, Peiping, China, 1928-32 (mem. Central Asiatic Expdn. under Roy Chapman Andrews, 1930); Command and Gen. Staff Sch., Ft. Leavenworth, Kan., 1937; m. Ethel Mae Megginson, Sept. 27, 1921; children—Patricia Anne (Mrs. Eugene Pinney), Nancy Lee (Mrs. Earl F. Geiger), Williard Gordon. Commd. 2d lt. Cav., 1918 and advanced through the grades to general, 1956; assistant commanding general of 1st U.S. Inf. Div., 1943-44; comdg. general 71st Inf. Div., 1944-45, G-2 Army Ground Forces 1945-46; chief of staff 1st U.S. Army, 1947-50, adminstrv. Dept. of Army, 1950-51, Comdg. Gen. IX U.S. Corps, 1951-52 Allied Land Forces Southeastern Europe, 1952-54; comdg. gen. 6th U.S. Army, Presido of San Francisco, 1954-55; deputy commanding general Continental Army Command, August 1955-March 1956; commanding general United States Continental Army Command, Ft. Monroe, Virginia, 1956-58, ret. Awarded Victory Medal, German Occupation Medal, Yangtze Service Medal (Naval), Nat. Defense Medal, Asiatic Theater Medal with 2 campaign stars, European Theater Medal with 7 campaign stars and arrowhead, Occupation Medal, Victory Medal World War II, Distinguished Service Cross, Silver Star, Legion of Merit, Bronze Star with oak leaf cluster (U.S.), Legion of Honor, Croix de Guerre with palm (France), Russian Order of Great War, 1st class, Distinguished Service Medal with 1st Oak Leaf Cluster. Mem. Assn. Grads. U.S. Mil. Acad., Lambda Chapter Zeta Psi, 1st Div. Soc., Sons of Cincinnati, Mayflower Soc., Explorers Club, Natural Resources Council, Nat. Rifle Soc. Club: Army-Navy (Washington). Contbr. to publication Am. Museum Natural History of "Topography of Mongolia." Home: Damariscotta ME Died Mar. 29, 1969; buried Arlington Nat. Cemetery, Arlington VA

WYNNE, CYRIL b. Oakland, Calif., Mar. 29, 1890; s. Ernest Philips and Carmelita (Mezes) W.; B.A., Harvard U., 1917, M.A., 1925, Ph.D., 1927; m. Louise French, Jan. 7, 1920; children—Edward Cyril, Mena Louise. Aide and asst. to dir. polit., territorial and economic intelligence, Am. Peace Commn., Peace Conf., Paris, Jan.-July. 1919; foreign service officer. 1919-20; 3d sec., Am. Embassy, Tokio, 1920-21, 2d sec., 1921-22; asst. solicitor, Dept. of State, 1922-24; with Inter-Dept. Radio Advisory Com., 1923-24; instr. and lecturer internat. relations and internat. govt., Harvard, 1927-29, also lecturer Harvard-Boston U. and Mass. State extension courses; asst. to sec. Am. Delegation to Internat. Radiotel. Conf., Washington, Aug.-Nov. 1927; asst. to solicitor Dept. of State, 1929; prof. constitutional law, 1929-36, prof. of legal history, 1936—, Columbus Univ. Law Sch., Washington, D.C.; apptd. asst. chief, Office of Historical Adviser, Dept. of State, July 22, 1929, acting historical adviser, May 7, 1933, mem. Bd. of Appeals and Review; chief div. of research and publication, 1933—. Commd. 2d lt., inf., U.S.A., Aug. 5, 1917; with 1st Army Hdqrs. Regt., 1917-18; with A.E.F. in France, 1918-19; Intelligence Service, Haute-Alsace sector; 1st lt., Sept. 1918; capt. Mil. Intelligence, O.R.C., 1924-28, maj., 1928-35, lt. col., 1936. Commended for gallantry; decorated Chevalier de l'Etoile Noire de Belin (France). Author: Department of State Publications, 1935. Review editor Am. Foreign Service Jour. Home: Washington, D.C. Died Sept. 26, 1939.

YATES, ARTHUR WOLCOTT army officer; b. in Wis., Feb. 14, 1865. Apptd. to U.S. Army from civil life; commissioned 2d lt. 9th Inf., Aug. 1, 1891; Inf. and Cav. Sch., 1895; 1st lt., Apr. 26, 1898; trans. to 4th Inf., July 28, 1900; capt. asst. q.m., Jan. 3, 1901; maj. q.m., Mar. 31, 1906; lt. col. Q.M. Corps, Feb. 1, 1913; col. (temp.) Oct. 9, 1917; col. June 27, 1920; brig. gen., July 9, 1926; retired, own request, Aug. 1, 1927. With A.E.F. and A.F.F. in France, returned to U.S., Jan. 1920. Died Sept. 25, 1930.

YEAGER, HOWARD AUSTIN naval officer; b. Chapman, Kan., Sept. 9, 1905; s. Harry Howard and Clara Jane (Hargett) Y.; B.S., U.S. Naval Acad., 1927; grad. Naval Postgrad. Sch., 1935, Nat. War Coll., 1953; m. Mary Jean Bailey, July 18, 1928; 1 son, Howard Bailey (USN). Commd. ensign U.S. Navy, 1927, advanced through grades to vice adm., 1960; jr. officer various ships, 1927-35; engr. instr. U.S. Naval Acad., 1935-37; jr. officer U.S.S. Tuscaloosa, 1937-41; with Bur. Ordnance, Washington, 1941-44; exec. officer U.S.S. Nevada, 1944-45; staff Office Chief Naval Personnel, 1945-47; staff Comdr. in Chief Pacific Fleet, 1947-48; aide to Chief Naval Operations, 1948-49; staff Office Chief Naval Personnel, 1949-50; comdr. Destroyer Squadron 1, Korea, 1950-51; chief staff Comdr. Cruiser Div. Four, 1951-52; comdg. officer U.S.S. Des Moines, 1953-54; staff Office Chief Naval Personnel, 1954-56; comdr. Amphibious Tng. Command, Atlantic Fleet, 1956-58; comdr. Amphibious Four, 1958; anti-submarine warfare readiness exec. Navy Dept., 1959-60; comdr. Amphibious Force, U.S. Pacific Fleet, 1960—. Decorated Legion of Merit. Bronze Star (2); Comdr. French Legion of Honor; Order Brit. Empire. Mem. Naval Order U.S. Naval Acad. Alumni Assn., Naval Acad. Found., Mil. Order World Wars. Mason, Lion. Clubs: Army-Navy (Washington). Home: 102 Overhill Rd., Salina, Kan. Office: Comdr. Amphibious Force, U.S. Pacific Fleet, San Diego 32. Died Mar. 1967.

YEATMAN, RICHARD THOMPSON brig. general, U.S.A.; b. Cincinnati, Nov. 27, 1848; s. Walker Merideth and Eva (Ammen) Y.; grad. Hughes High Sch., Cincinnati, 1868, U.S. Mil. Acad., 1872; m. F. L. Mulhall, Oct. 1, 1879. Second lt. 14th Inf., June 14, 1872; 1st lt., Mar. 15, 1883; capt., Mar. 28, 1892; maj. 22d Inf., Nov. 13, 1900; lt. col. 27th Inf., Aug. 14, 1903; col. 11th Inf., Mar. 26, 1907; brig. gen. U.S.A., June 5, 1909; retired for disability incurred in line of duty, June 26, 1909. Mem. Order of Indian Wars U.S. Home: Glendale, O. Died Apr. 1, 1930.

YOAKUM, CLARENCE STONE psychologist; b. Leavenworth County, Kan., Jan. 11, 1879; s. Hedges Conger and Lydia Isabel (Stone) Y.; A.B., Campbell Coll., Kan., 1901; Ph.D., U. of Chicago, 1908; m. Louise Branch Storey, July 29, 1919; 1 dau., Margaret Isabel. Teacher pub. schools, 1898-1900; instr. psychology and edn., Campbell Coll., 1901-03; instr. science and mathematics, Hiawatha (Kan.) Acad., 1903-05; fellow in psychology, U. of Chicago, 1906-08; prof. and head dept. philosophy and psychology, U. of Tex., 1908-17; prof. of applied psychology, and dir. bur. personnel research, Carnegie Inst. Tech., Pittsburgh, 1919-24; apptd. prof. personnel management, U. of Mich., 1924, and dir. Bur. of Univ. Research, 1927; dean, Coll. Liberal Arts, Northwestern U., 1929-30; v.p. U. of Mich. since July 1930, dean of Grad. Sch. since January, 1935. First lt., capt. and maj. psychol. service, U.S. Army, 1917-19; served at Camp Lee, later in Office of Surgeon Gen. and as supervisor psychol. service in army camps. Mem. Am. Psychol. Assn., A.A.A.S., Inst. of Management American Assn., Univ. Profs., Sigma Xi, Gamma Alpha, Phi Gamma Delta, Phi Kappa Phi. Conglist. Clubs: Pittsburgh Athletic; City (New York). Author: Army Mental Tests (Yoakum and Yerkes), 1920; Selection and Training of Salesmen (Yoakum and Kenagy), 1925. Home: 2017 Hill St., Ann Arbor, Mich. Died Nov. 20, 1945.

YOAKUM, HENDERSON army officer; b. Powell's Valley, Tenn., Sept. 6, 1810; s. George and Cally (Maddy) Y.; grad. U.S. Mil. Acad., 1832; m. Eveline Conner, Feb. 13, 1833. Brevetted 2d lt., 3d Arty., U.S. Army, 1832; commd. capt. Murphreesboro Sentinels, co. of Tenn. Mounted Militia, circa 1833; served as col. regt. Tenn. Inf. in Cherokee War, 1838; mem. Tenn. Senate, 1839-45; admitted to Republic of Tex. bar, 1845; served with regt. of Tex. Mounted Rifles during Mexican War, 1845-46, 1st lt. at Battle of Monterey; county in West Tex. named in his honor, 1876. Author: History of Texas from Its First Settlement in 1685 to Its Annexation to the United States in 1846 (1st history of Tex.), 1855. Died Houston, Tex., Nov. 30, 1856.

YODER, LLOYD EDWARD broadcasting exec.; b. Salem, O., July 13, 1903; s. Edward and Anna (Davis) Y.; B.A., Carnegie Inst. Tech., 1927; student Mt. Union Coll., Alliance, O., 1932, San Francisco Law Sch., 1935-37; m. Alma Cella, June 30, 1953. With NBC, Inc., 1927—, successively mgr. Western div. press dept., San Francisco, gen. mgr. KPO-KGO, San Francisco, KOA, Denver, KNBC, San Francisco, WTAM-WNBk, Cleve., 1927-56, v.p. NBC, gen. mgr. WRCV-WRCV TV, Phila., 1956-58, v.p. NBC, gen. mgr. WMAQ-WNBQ TV, Chgo., 1958—. Served at lt. comdr. USNR, World War II. Bd. trustees Carnegie Inst. Tech. Mem. Nat. Acad. Television Arts and Scis. (charter mem.; adv. council internat. assembly; hon. gov.), Nat. Better Bus. Bur. (dir.), Sigma Alpha Epsilon, Sigma Delta Kappa, Sigma Delta Chi. Mason (Shriner). Clubs: Rotary, Radio Pioneers; Press and Union League, Bohemian, Pacific Union (San Francisco); Radio Executives (N.Y.C.); Athletic, Federated Advertising, Broadcast Advertising, Chicago, Tavern, Edgewater Golf, Saddle and Cycle (Chgo.). Home: 179 E. Lake Shore Dr. Chicago, Ill.

YOUNG, CHARLES LUTHER soldier; b. Albany, N.Y., Nov. 23, 1838; s. Eli and Eleanor Y.; ed. Albany Acad., and (grad.) Prof. Charles H. Anthony's Classical Inst., Albany, 1858; L.L.D., Wilberforce U., Ohio; m. Cora M., d. Albert Day, M.D., of Boston, Jan. 18, 1871. Served throughout the Civil War, entering Apr. 1861, as Zouave cadet, and from May 1861, in Sickles' "Excelsior Brigade," U.S. vols.; comd. 1st Regt. 2d Bull Run campaign and last in command in the field; staff officer 2d and 3d Army Corps, Army of Potomac, with Generals Sickles, Hooker and Hancock; bvtd. lt. col. vols. at end of war; wounded at Chancellorsville, and again in the Wilderness, Va. Brig. gen., State of Ohio, 1878-80; charter companion Ohio Commandery Mil. Order Loyal Legion U.S.; senior vice comdr.-in-chief G.A.R., 1881-82. Mfr. and mcht. in lumber, Toledo, for 21 yrs.; park commr., Toledo, 18 yrs., and pres. bd.; trustee Toledo Med. Coll., 1888—; dir. Toledo U., 1898-1900; dir. Gettysburg Battlefield Memorial Assn., 1885-96; supt. Ohio Soldiers' and Sailors' Orphans' Home, Xenia, O., 1890-95, and 1900-04; first supt. Pa. Soldiers' Orphans' Industrial School, 1895-96. Home: Toledo, O. Died Sept. 18, 1913.

YOUNG, CLARENCE MARSHALL, aviation cons.; b. Colfax, Ia. s. Theodore G. and Ella (Foy) Y.; student Drake U.; LL.B., Yale, 1910; m. Lois Moran, Feb. 10, 1935; 1 son, Timothy Marshall. Admitted to Ia. bar, 1910, and began practice at Des Moines; served as exec. sec. Municipal Research Bureau, Des Moines, 1922-25; dir. aeros. U.S. Dept. Commerce, 1926-29, asst. sec. of commerce for aeros., 1929-33; mgr. Transpacific Div. Pan Am. Airways, 1934-45, v.p. Pan Am. World Airways, 1950-59; mem. CAB, Washington, 1946-50. Mem. Air Service, U.S. Army, 1917-19; overseas 18 mos., including 5 mos. as prisoner of war, Austria; col. U.S. Air Forces Res., ret. Decorated Comdr. Order Crown of Italy; named Elder Statesman of Aviation, Nat. Assn. Aeros; named to Aviation Hall of Fame Oxs Club Am. Asso. fellow Am. Inst. Aeros. and Astronautics, Royal Aero. Soc. London; mem. Acacia. Republican. Mason. Clubs: Yale (N.Y.C.); Family (San Francisco); Army and Navy (Washington). Home: Sedona AZ Died Apr. 10, 1973.

YOUNG, EVAN E. b. Kenton, O., Aug. 17, 1878; s. Sutton E. and Emma (Stickney) Y.; student Hiram (O.) Coll., 1895-96, S.D. State Sch. Mines, 1897; LL.B., U. of Wis., 1903; m. Dawn Waite, Aug. 23, 1905 (died January 9, 1943). Second lieutenant Company M, 1st S.D. Volunteer Infantry, April 25, 1898; mustered out as captain and adjutant, 11th Cavalry, U.S.V., Mar. 13, 1901. Practiced law, Sioux Falls, S.D., 1903-05; Am. consul at Harput, Turkey, 1905-08, at Saloniki, 1908-09; chief, Div. Near Eastern Affairs, Dept. State, 1909-11; E.E. and M.P. to Ecuador, 1911-12; apptd. foreign trade adviser of Dept. of State, 1912; consul gen., at Halifax, N.S., 1913-19, at Constantinople, 1920; Am. commr. to Baltic provinces of Russia, 1920-22; ordered to Washington, 1922; detailed to Dept. of State, Feb. 15, 1923; chief Div. of Eastern European Affairs, 1923-25; apptd. foreign service officer Class 1, July 1, 1924; E.E. and M.P. to Dominican Republic, 1925-30, to Bolivia, Jan.-Feb. 1930 (resigned); vice pres. Pan-Am. Airways, Inc., 1930-44 (retired Aug. 17, 1944), and became mem. board dirs. Mem. Sigma Alpha Epsilon, Phi Delta Phi. Home: Turnerhame, Loudonville, N.Y. Died Jan. 13, 1946.

YOUNG, LAURENCE W., ret. army officer; b. Swannanoa, N.C., Aug. 18, 1877; s. Robert H. and Pamelia (Gudger) Y.; student Warren Wilson Coll., 1896-97, Southern Bus. Coll., 1898; m. Hester Johnson, Sept. 19, 1900; children—Julia (Mrs. A. A. McNamee), Helen (Mrs. David D. Hedekin), Louise (Mrs. M. R. Kammerer). Commd. as 2d lt. Inf., N.C. Nat. Guard, 1905, advanced through grades to brig. gen., 1918; commd. maj., U.S. Army, 1918, promoted through grades to brig. gen., 1941; ret. 1941, recalled to active duty, relieved 1944. Democrat. Presbyterian. Home: 2085 E. Lake Rd. N.E., Atlanta 6 GA

YOUNG, LEON DECATUR clergyman; b. Highland, Kan., Dec. 2, 1872; s. John and Rachel F. (Nesbit) Y.; B.A., Highland Coll., 1897; student Princeton Theol. Sem., 1898-99; grad. McCormick Theol. Sem., 1900; D.D., Bellevue Coll., Omaha, Neb., 1910; LL.D., Hastings Coll., 1916; m. Dorothy Spriestersbach, May 6, 1902 (dec.); m. 2d, Mary B. Archibald, Aug. 2, 1938. Ordained Presbyterian ministry, 1900; pastor Charlestown, Ind., 1900-01, Washington, Ia., 1902-08, Beatrice, Neb., 1908-14, Lincoln, 1914-20, City Temple, Dallas, Tex., 1920-25. Abbey Presbyn. Ch., 1925-38, First Presbyn. Ch., Highland, Kan., 1939-41, pastor emeritus since Apr. 15, 1941. Trustee Highland Coll.; mem. Gen. Assembly Advisory Com. on Near East Relief; mem. Reorganization and Consolidation Com. of Gen. Assembly, 1920-23; vice moderator Gen. Assembly Presbyn. Church, U.S.A., 1932-33; Bible lecturer at Christian Workers Conferences, 1932-34; moderator Dallas Presbytery, Mar.-Sept. 1935; moderator Highland Presbytery, 1940; president United Forces Against the Liquor Traffic, Dallas County, Tex.; secretary United Texas Drys (State). Sec. Army Christian Commission, Camp Alger, Va., Spanish-Am. War; spl. preacher army camps, World War. Bible lecturer Mount Hermon Conf., 1934-37. Mem. Alpha Chi. Democrat. Clubs: Salesmanship, Dallas Writers, Lakewood, Kiwanis. Author: "Know Your Bible" Series (children's students', young men's and adults' edts.). Organized "Know Your Bible" Club of America. Lectures: America for Me; Ten Certainties of Life Insurance; If I Were a Salesman. Author of single budget plan of ch. finance; originator of "Sin Board," which has received wide recognition. Address: Box 502, Highland, Kan. Died March 13, 1947.

YOUNG, LUCIEN naval officer; b. Lexington, Ky., Mar. 31, 1852; s. Richard Bosworth and Jane Ellen Y.; apptd. to U.S. Naval Acad. from Ky., 1869, grad., 1873; s. Washington, Belle Parker, June 1895. Promoted midshipman, May 31, 1873; ensign, July 16, 1874; promoted through grades to rear admiral, Mar. 17, 1910. Served on Alaska and Hartford, 1873-75. While midshipman, July 23, 1873, and serving on the "Alaska," jumped overboard while under way at sea and saved life of seaman who had been knocked overboard. Served in Powhatan, 1875-76; Huron, Mar. 1876-Nov. 24, 1877, when she was wrecked off Nag's Head, N.C.; nominated by President and advanced to master by spl. act of Congress for extraordinary heroism. Served in Portsmouth, 1878-80; spl. duty Paris Expn., 1878; Bur. of Equipment, 1880-82; various ships, 1882-86; instr. in torpedoes and at Naval War Coll., 1887; Bur. of Equipment and aid to Sec. of the Navy, 1887-89; Library and War Records Office, 1889-91, 1893-96; Boston, 1891-93; took a prominent part in the protection of American interests in Hawaiian revolution; comd. Hist during Spanish War, June 1898-Jan. 1899; advanced 3 numbers "for eminent and conspicuous conduct in battles during Spanish War, while in command of Hist"; capt. port of Havana and commandantia de la marina of Cuba, 1899-1900; commandant U.S. Naval sta., Havana, 1900-01; insp. 9th lighthouse dist., 1902-04; comd. Bennington, 1904-05; Bennington, wrecked by explosion of boiler and beached at San Diego, Calif., July 21, 1905; Navy Yard, Mare Island, as capt. of yard and pres. of permanent court-martial, examining and retiring bds. on Pacific Coast; commandant Navy Station, Key West, Fla. Another of a standard work on navigation, Archaeological Researches in Peru; The Real Hawaii. Died Oct. 2, 1912.

YOUNG, PIERCE MANNING BUTLER diplomat, congressman; b. Spartanburg, S.C., Nov. 15, 1836; s. Robert Maxwell and Elizabeth Caroline (Jones) Y.; grad. Ga. Mil. Acad. at Marietta, 1856; attended U.S. Mil. Acad., 1857. Joined Confederate Army, 1861, commd. 2d lt. of arty., stationed Pensacola, Fla., 1861; promoted 1st lt., aide-de-camp to Gen. W. H. T. Walker; apptd. adj. T. R. R. Cobb's legion; promoted maj. for gallantry, 1862; commd. lt. col., 1862, commanded cavalry of legion under Wade Hampton; promoted col., served at Fleetwood or Brandy Station and Gettysburg; promoted brig. gen., 1863; in command of Hampton's Brigade, 1864; promoted maj. gen., 1864; mem. U.S. Ho. of Reps. (Democrat) from Ga., 40th, 41st-43d congresses, July 25, 1868-69, Dec. 22, 1870-75, opposed radical measures against South; del. Dem. nat. convs., Balt., 1872, St. Louis, 1876, Cincinnati, 1880; apptd. commr. to Paris Exposition, 1878; U.S. consul gen. to St. Petersburg (now Leningrad), Russia, 1885-87; U.S. minister to Guatemala and Honduras, 1893-96, developed friendship and comml. relations with Central Am. states. Died Presbyn. Hosp., N.Y.C., July 6, 1898; buried Oak Hill Cemetery, Catersville, Ga.

YOUNG, RICHARD WHITEHEAD lawyer; b. Salt Lake City, Utah, Apr. 19, 1858; s. Joseph Angell and Margaret (Whitehead) Y.; U. of Utah, 1874-77; grad. U.S. Mil. Acad., 1882; LL.B., Columbia, 1884; m. Minerva Richards, Sept. 5, 1882. Second lt. 5th U.S. Arty., 1882-89; capt. and acting judge-advocate U.S.A., on staff of Gen. W. S. Hancock, 1884-86; resigned, 1889; brig. gen. Utah N.G., 1894; capt. and maj. comdg. Utah Light Arty., Spanish-Am. War and Philippine insurrection, 1898-99; Congressional Medal of Honor for service in latter; recommended by army bd. for brevets of lt. col., col. and brig. gen. Admitted to bar, New York, 1884; in practice at Salt Lake City, 1889—. Latter Day Saint (Mormon). Mem. City Council, 1890-91, Bd. of Edn., 1890-94, 1898; superior provost judge, asso. justice and pres. criminal branch Supreme Ct. of P.I., 1898-1901; mem. bd. of visitors West Point, 1902; twice Dem. candidate for Supreme Ct. of Utah; regent U. of Utah, 1905-17; trustee Brigham Young U., Provo; pres. Internat. Irrigation Congress, 1912-14. V. chmn. Utah State Council Defense, 1917; col. 1st Utah and 145th Field Arty., June 17, 1917; brig. gen. National Army, Apr. 16, 1918. Author: Mobs and the Military, 1888. Home: Salt Lake City, Utah. Died Dec. 27, 1919.

YOUNG, ROBERT NICHOLAS army officer; b. Washington, Jan. 14, 1900; s. Robert Hall and Fanny Hempstone (Appleby) Y.; A.B., U. Md., 1922; grad., Inf. Sch., 1933, Signal Sch., 1934, Command and Gen. Staff Sch., 1938; m. Corinne Cameron Davis, Jan. 3, 1925; 1 dau., Corinne Francis. Commd. 2d lt. U.S. Army, 1923, advanced through grades to lt. gen., 1955; asst. sec., later sec. War Dept. Gen. Staff, 1942-43; apptd. asst. div. comdr. 70th Inf. Div., 1943, 3d Inf. Div., France and Germany, 1944; comdr. Mil. Dist. Washington, 1945-46; comdt. Sch. Combined Arms, Command and Gen. Staff Coll., 1946-49; asst. div. comdr. 82d Airborne Div., 1950-51; div. comdr. 2d Inf. Div., Korea, Sept. 1951; comdt. Inf. Sch., 1952-53; asst. chief of staff G-1, personnel, Dept. of Army, 1953-55; comdg. gen. Sixth Army, 1955-57. Decorated D.S.M. with 2 oak leaf clusters, Silver Star, Legion of Merit, Bronze Star, Purple Heart, French Croix de Guerre and Legion of Honor, Korean Legion of Honor. Mem. Kappa Alpha. Mason. Home: 17 Inglewood Rd., Ashville, N.C. Office: Hdqrs. Sixth Army, Presidio of San Francisco. Died Oct. 19, 1964; buried Arlington Nat. Cemetery, Washington.

YOUNG, SAMUEL BALDWIN MARKS lieutenant gen. U.S.A.; b. Pittsburgh, Jan. 9, 1840; s. Capt. John, Jr. and Hannah (Scott) Y.; ed. Jefferson Coll., Canonsburg, Pa.; m. Margaret McFadden, Sept. 1861. Enlisted as pvt. Co. K, 12th Pa. Inf., Apr. 25, 1861; discharged. Aug. 5, 1861; commd. capt. 4th Pa. Cav., Sept. 6, 1861; maj., Sept. 20, 1862; lt. col., Oct. 1, 1864; col., Dec. 29, 1864; bvtd. brig. gen., Apr. 9, 1865; hon. mustered out of vols., July 1, 1865; apptd. from Pa. 2d lt. 12th U.S. Inf., May 11, 1866; capt. 8th Cav., July 28, 1866; maj. 3d Cav., Apr. 2, 1883; lt. col. 4th Cav., Aug. 16, 1892; col. 3d Cav., June 19, 1897; brig. gen. vols., May 4, 1898; maj. gen. vols., July 8, 1898; hon. discharged from vols., Apr. 13, 1899; brig. gen. vols., Apr. 13, 1899; brig. gen. U.S.A., Jan. 2, 1900; maj. gen. U.S.A., Feb. 2, 1901; lt. gen. in command of the army, Aug. 8, 1903; chief of staff to the President, Aug. 15, 1903; retired by operation of law, Jan. 9, 1904. Bvtd.: maj., Mar. 2, 1867, "for gallant and meritorious services in action at Sulphur Springs, Va., Oct. 12, 1863"; lt. col., Mar. 2, 1867, for same in action at Amelia Spring, Va., Apr. 5, 1865; col., Mar. 2, 1867, for same in battle of Sailors Creek, Va., Apr. 6, 1865; brig. gen. vols., Apr. 9, 1865, for same during the campaign terminating with surrender of army under Gen. R. E. Lee. Comd. 2d Brigade, cav. div., 5th Corps, in Cuba; comd. 1st Div., 2d Corps, and later comd. 2d Army Corps until disbanded; served in P.I., 1899-1901, comd. cav. and inf. advance disintegrating Aguinaldo's army in Northern Luzon, Oct.-Dec., 1899; mil. gov. Northern Luzon; comdg. Dept. of Calif. to Mar. 15, 1902; 1st pres. War Coll., Washington, July 1, 1902-Aug. 8, 1903; was pres. Brownsville ct. of inquiry; gov. U.S. Soldiers' Home, Washington, D.C., 1910-20. Comdr. in chief Mil. Order Loyal Legion U.S., 1915. Home: Washington, D.C. Died Sept. 1, 1924.

YOUNG, THOMAS LOWRY congressman; b. Killyleagh, County Down, Ireland, Dec. 14, 1832; grad. Cincinnati Law Sch. Came to U.S., 1847; enlisted as musician U.S. Army, rose to 1st sgt. Co. A, 3d Arty., 1848-58; settled in Cincinnati, instr. Ohio State Reform Sch.; served as capt. Benton Cadets, Mo. Volunteers during Civil War, 1861; commd. maj. 118th Regt., Ohio Volunteer Inf., 1862, lt. col., 1863; col., 1864; brevetted brig. gen. U.S. Volunteers for meritorious service in Battle of Resaca (Ga.), 1865; resigned, 1865; admitted to Ohio bar, 1865, began practice in Cincinnati; asst. city auditor Cincinnati, 1865; mem. Ohio Ho. of Reps., 1866-68; elected recorder of Hamilton County (O.), 1867; apptd. supr. internal revenue, 1868; del. Republican Nat. Conv., Chgo., 1868; mem. Ohio Senate, 1871-73; lt. gov. Ohio, 1875; acting gov., 1877; mem. U.S. Ho. of Reps. (Rep.) from Ohio, 46th-47th congresses, 1879-93; mem. bd. pub. affairs Cincinnati, 1886-88. Died Cincinnati, July 20, 1888; buried Spring Grove Cemetery, Cincinnati.

YOUNGBERG, GILBERT A(LBIN), army officer (retired); b. Belle Creek, Minn., Feb. 12,21875; s. Par Nord and Kjerste (Branfelt) Y.; student Carleton Coll., 1893-95; grad. U.S. Mil. Acad., 1900, B.S., 1929; student Army Staff Coll., 1905-06, Army War Coll., 1909-10; m. Adele Harriett de Raismes, Apr. 22, 1903; children—Helen Biddle (Mrs. Charles E. Richheimer), Adele de Raismes (Mrs. Fleming W. Smith). Commd. 2d lt. arty. corps U.S. Army, 1900, transferred to C.E. as 2d lt., Feb. 2, 1901, and advanced through all grades to brig. gen., June 13, 1940; instr. engring., Army Service Schs., 1902-05; div. engr. Northern div., 1906-07; map making and highway constrn. in Cuba, 1907-09; prof. military engring., U.S. Mil. Acad., 1910-14; U.S. dist engr., Charleston, S.C., 1914-17; exec. officer for chief of engrs. A.E.F., 1917-18 and in charge engring. div. supply and constrn. sect., hdqrs. gen. staff, A.E.F., 1918-19; asst. to chief of engrs. U.S. Army, Washington, 1919-22; U.S. Dist. engr., Jacksonville, Fla., 1922-26; ret. 1926; cons. engr. on various river and harbor improvements, electric light and water plants, Jacksonville, Fla. since 1926; dir. Title & Trust Co. of Fla., since 1930. Awarded distinguished service medal U.S. Army; Companion of Distinguished Service Order of Great Britain; Officer of the Legion of Honor (France); Officer of the Order of Saints Mauricio and Lazaro (Italy). Fellow Fla. Engring. Soc.; mem. Am. Soc. Civil Engrs., Soc. Am. Mil. Engrs. (founder-mem. and past pres.), Am. Shore and Beach Preservation Assn. Episcopalian. Clubs: Engineering Professions, Jacksonville Rotary, Timuquana Country (Jacksonville). Author: Brief History of Engineer Troops, U.S. Army (1906); articles in engring. and mil. publs., also in 1920-21 edit. of Ency. Britannica. Home: 3519 Oak St., Jacksonville 5. Office: 712 Graham Bldg., Jacksonville FL

YOUNGER, THOMAS COLEMAN (Cole Younger), desperado; b. Jackson County, Mo., Jan. 15, 1844; s. Col. Henry and Busheba (Fristoe) Y. Served as Confederate guerilla under Quantrill and Anderson during Civil War; capt. Gen. Joseph O. Shelby's Iron Brigade; mem. Jesse James' gang, participated in attempted bank robbery in which 2 civilians were killed, Northfield, Minn., Sept. 7, 1876; captured, along with 2 of his brothers (3 other gang members killed), sentenced to life imprisonment, Nov. 1876; paroled by Minn. Bd. of Pardon, July 1901. Died Mar. 21, 1916.

YOUNGGREEN, CHARLES CLARK advertising; b. Topeka, Kan., Oct. 3, 1900; s. George and LaVinne (Dedrick) Y.; grad. high sch., Topeka, student U. of Kan.; m. Marjorie Eloise Martin, Aug. 13, 1918. Pub. Kansas Farmer, Topeka, 1916-18; advertising and sales mgr. J. I. Case Plow Works, Racine, Wis., 1918-22; advertising agency business, Milwaukee, 1922-30; now exec. vice-pres. Reincke-Ellis-Younggreen & Finn, Chicago. Served as 2d lt., later 1st lt. and capt. Aviation Corps, U.S. Army, World War; lt. Royal Flying Corps. Mem. Aviation Com., Milwaukee; gen. chmn. Milwaukee reception to Lts. Maitland and Hegenberger, Col Lindbergh, the Bremen flyers, Capt. Koehl, Maj. Fitzmaurice and Baron Von Huenefeld; mem. Wis. State Aviation Com. Formerly dir. Internat. Dry Farming Congress, Kan. State Fair, Am. Assn. Adv. Agencies, Audit Bur. of Circulations; mem. Internat. Advertising Assn. (ex-pres.), Advertising Fedn. America (dir.; ex-pres.), Nat. Better Business Bur. (dir.), Chicago Assn. Commerce (advt. com.), Advertising Council of Chicago (exec. bd.), Nat. Aeronautical Assn., Phi Kappa Psi; former pres. Alpha Delta Sigma (nat. advt. frat.); pres. Chicago Advertising Agency Assn.; hon. mem. Advertising Assn., Mexico, British Advertising Assn., Continental Advertising Assn. Past comdr. Cudworth Post, Am. Legion; hon. mem. Advertising Men's Post No. 209, Am. Legion, N.Y.; former pres. Kan. Alumni Assn. of Chicago. Republican. Methodist. Mason (32 deg.). Clubs: Advertising (ex-pres.; now hon. pres.), Mid-Day, Union League, Saddle and Cycle (Chicago); Advertising (New York). Ex-pres. Lions and Advertising clubs (Racine). Home: 1320 N. State St. Office: 520 N. Michigan Av., Chicago, Ill. Died Aug. 19, 1942.

YOUNT, BARTON K(YLE) army officer; b. Troy, O.; s. Noah and Ivy Caroline (Kyle) Y.; student Ohio State U., 1902-03; grad. U.S. Mil. Acad., 1907; m. Mildred Almy Parker, Sept. 29, 1914; 1 son, Barton Kyle. Commd. 2d lt.. U.S. Army, 1907; and advanced through the grades to brig. gen., 1936; asst. chief of Air Corps, Washington, D.C.; promoted maj. gen. Oct. 1, 1940, lt. gen., 1943; comd. S.E. Air Dist., Tampa, Fla., Nov. 1940-July 1941; comd. W. Coast Air Corps Training Center, Moffett Field, Calif., July 1941-Jan. 1942; assigned to Office of Chief of Air Corps, Jan.-Mar. 1942; comdg. gen. Army Air Forces Flying Training Command, Fort Worth, Mar. 1942-July 1943; apptd. comdg. gen. Army Air Forces Training Command, July 1943; retired with rank of lt. gen., June 30, 1946. Pres. American Inst. for Fgn. Trade, Phoenix, Ariz., since July 1, 1946. Decorated: D.S.M. with Oak Leaf Cluster, Legion of Merit, Air Medal; Knight Comdr. Order of British Empire; Officer Legion of Honor (France); Officer, Order Crown of Italy; Grand Officer Order Orange-Nassau (with swords; Netherlands); Grand Officer Nat. Order Southern Cross (Brazil); Order of Merit (1st Class; Mexico); Cloud Banner Decoration (Chinese). Clubs: Army and Navy, Columbia Country (Washington, D.C.). Address: 514 W. Rose Lane, Phoenix, Ariz. Died July 11, 1949; buried Arlington National Cemetery.

ZACHARIAS, ELLIS MARK naval officer; b. Jacksonville, Fla., Jan. 1, 1890; s. Aaron and Theresa (Budwig) Z.; grad. U.S. Naval Acad., 1912; student Japanese language and people, Japan, 1920-23; grad. sr. course U.S. Naval War Coll., 1933-34; m. Clara Evans Miller, June, 1925; children—Ellis Mark, Jerrold Matthew. Commd. ensign, 1912, and advanced through grades to rear adm.; served in various capacities aboard battleships; engring. officer in Atlantic, gunnery officer, World War I; attache to Am. Embassy, Tokyo, 1920-23; additional sea duty; officer in charge Far Eastern div. Office Naval Intelligence, 1928-31, 34-36; dist. intelligence officer 11th Naval Dist., San Diego, 1938-40; comdr. cruiser Salt Lake City, in bombardment of enemy bases, Gilbert and Marshall Islands, 1940-42; dep. dir. Naval Intelligence, 1942-43; comdr. battleship New Mexico, 1943-44; chief of staff 11th Naval Dist., 1944-45; temp. duty with comdr. in chief U.S. Fleet, conducting psychol. warfare against Japanese high command, 1945; author, lectr., since retirement, 1946. Decorated Legion of Merit (3), Commendation Ribbon, Mexican Service Medal, Victory Medal with Patrol Clasp, Yangtze Service Medal (U.S.); Am. Knight of Order of Dannebrog (Denmark). Clubs: Army and Navy (Washington); Army-Navy Country (Arlington, Va., charter mem.). Author: Secret Missions, The Story of an Intelligence Officer, 1946; (articles) Eighteen Words that Bagged Japan; Balance Sheet of Disaster, 1947; Absolute Weapons, 1947; The Bewildered American People; Behind Closed Doors; The Secret History of the Cold War, 1950. Lectr. on internat. affairs, past and future security, secret missions in Japan and Far East. Home: 4000 Cathedral Av. N.W., Washington 16. Died June 27, 1961; buried Arlington (Va.) Nat. Cemetery.

ZALINSKI, EDMUND LOUIS GRAY soldier, inventor pneumatic dynamite torpedo gun; b. Kurnich, Prussian Poland, Dec. 13, 1849, came with parents to U.S. when 4 yrs. old; settled at Seneca Falls, N.Y.; ed. pub. schs., Seneca Falls, Syracuse High School, 1861-63; entered army as vol. a. d. c. on staff Gen. Nelson A. Miles, 1864, served till close of war April 1865; promoted Feb. 1865, to 2d lt. in 2d New York heavy arty. for gallantry at battle of Hatcher's Run, Va. Mustered out of vol. service Sept. 1865; apptd. 2d lt.,

5th U.S. Arty., Feb. 1866; 1st lt., Jan. 1867; capt., Dec. 1887. Prof. mil. science Mass. Inst. Technology, 1872-76; grad. United States Artillery School, Fort Monroe, Va., and School of Submarine Mining, Willett's Point, N.Y., 1880. From 1883 to 1889 devoted time to development and perfecting of pneumatic dynamite torpedo gun. Traveled under orders in Europe, 1889-90 to obtain mil. information. Invented an intrenching tool, a ramrod bayonet, a telescopic sight for arty. and a system of range and position finding for sea-coast and arty. firing; on garrison duty at San Francisco, Calif., 1892; retired, Feb. 1894; promoted maj., Apr. 25, 1904. Home: New York, N.Y. Died 1909.

ZALINSKI, MOSES GRAY army officer; b. in New York, Jan. 23, 1863; grad. Arty. Sch., 1894. Served as pvt., corpl. and sergt., batteries G and H, 1st Arty., 1885-89; commd. 2d lt., 2d Arty., Feb. 11, 1889, promoted through grades to brig. gen., Apr. 19, 1925. and apptd. asst. to q.m. gen. for period of 4 yrs. Awarded D.S.M. Retired, Jan. 23, 1927. Died Aug. 28, 1937.

ZANE, ABRAHAM VANHOY naval officer; b. Phila., Aug. 14, 1850; s. Abraham V. and Mary R. (McNeir) Z.; grad. U.S. Naval Acad., 1874; m. Grace Helen Southgate, June 21, 1883. Promoted asst. engr., Feb. 26, 1875; passed asst. engr., Aug. 27, 1881; chief engr., Sept. 11, 1895; transferred to the line as lt. comdr., Mar. 3, 1899; comdr., Sept. 11, 1903; capt., Dec. 6, 1907; rear adm., Sept. 14, 1911. Mem. Jeannette relief expdn., 1881-82, Northern Alaska exploring expdn., 1885-86; served at works of Wm. Cramp & Sons Co., Phila., Pa., 1903-08; head Dept. Steam Engring., Navy Yard, Portsmouth, N.H., 1908-11; gen. insp. of machinery for Navy, 1911; pres. Bd. Inspections for Shore Stations, Navy Dept., 1911-12; retired on account of age, Aug. 14, 1912. Home: Washington, D.C. Died Jan. 2, 1919.

ZEILIN, JACOB marine officer; b. Phila., July 16, 1806; s. Jacob Zeilin; attended U.S. Mil. Acad.; m. Virginia Freeman, Oct. 23, 1845, 3 children including William F. Commd. 2d lt. U.S. Marine Corps, 1831; served in ship Erie off Brazil, 1835-37; promoted 1st lt., 1836; served aboard Congress in Mexican War, served in landings in Cal. and Mexico; brevetted maj., 1847; promoted capt., 1847; marine officer of E. India Squadron under Matthew Perry, served on ships Mississippi and Susquehanna; wounded at 1st Battle of Bull Run; promoted col., 1864; commandant of Marine Corps, 1864-76; promoted brig. gen., 1867, ret., 1876. Died Nov. 18, 1880; buried Laurel Hill Cemetery, Phila.

ZELIE, JOHN SHERIDAN (ze'le), clergyman; b. Princeton, Mass., May 3, 1866; s. Rev. John Sheridan and Caroline (Prescott) Z.; A.B., Williams, 1887, D.D.,

1904; B.D., Yale, 1890; Litt.D., Western Reserve, 1921; L.H.D., Lake Forest Coll., 1930; m. Henrietta S. Campbell; children—John S., Frances C. Doux. Pastor Congl. Ch., Plymouth, Conn., 1890-94, Bolton Av. Presbyn. Ch., Cleveland, O., 1894-1900, First Reformed Ch., Schenectady, N.Y., 1900-03, Crescent Av. Presbyn. Ch., Plainfield, N.J., 1903-17, First Presbyn. Ch., Troy, N.Y., 1919-27. Served as chaplain of 2d, 28th and 79th divs. field hosps. and ambulances and Base Hosp. 30, A.E.F., in France, 1918-19. On staff Am. Relief Administration, Russia, 1922. Mem. of Phi Beta Kappa, Delta Kappa Epsilon. Author: (with Carroll Perry) Bill Pratt, The Saw-Buck Philosopher, 1895; The Book of the Kindly Light (intimations from Cardinal Newman's hymn), 1909; Joseph Conrad the Man (with E. L. Adams), 1925; also articles in Atlantic Monthly, etc. Address: (summer) Cherryfield, Me.; (winter) Seabreeze, Daytona Beach, Fla. Died Nov. 9, 1942.

ZIEGEMEIER, HENRY JOSEPH naval officer; b. Allegheny, Pa., Mar. 27, 1869; s. Joseph and Regina (Meyer) Z.; grad. U.S. Naval Acad., 1890; m. Ida Wernet. Sept. 18, 1895 (died 1915); m. 2d, Jewel Ridings, Nov. 16, 1921; 1 dau., Rose Mary. Ensign, July 6, 1922. Served on Pensacola, 1890-91, Charleston, 1891-92, Philadelphia, 1892-94, Adams, 1894, Bennington, 1895; on duty at Naval Torpedo Sta., Newport, R.I., 1895-97; on Annapolis, Spanish-Am. War, 1898; at U.S. Naval Acad., 1905-06, 1906-08; exec. officer and navigator Arkansas, 1906; comd. Hartford, 1908; navigator West Virginia, 1908-09; exec. officer same, 1909-11; duty Gen. Bd., Navy Dept., 1911-12; sec. Gen. Board, 1912-13; comd. Annapolis, 1913-14, Denver, 1914-15; comd. Torpedo Flotilla, Pacific Fleet, 1915; duty Gen. Bd., 1915; sec. of same, 1915-17; assigned to comd. Virginia, June 13, 1917; comd. U.S.S. Virginia, June 13, 1917-July 18, 1919; operated with Atlantic Fleet until summer 1918, then in charge as convoy comdr., convoying U.S. transports with troops from the U.S. to France; after signing of armistice made 5 transport trips, bringing U.S. troops from France to U.S.; in charge orgn. and training of Naval Reserve Force, hdqrs. Washington, D.C., Aug. 15, 1919-July 5, 1921; detached Navy Dept. and ordered to comd. U.S.S. California when commissioned, Aug. 10, 1921; dir. naval communications, Washington, Aug. 1922-June 1923; comdt. Navy Yard, Norfolk, Va., June 1923-Jan. 19, 1925; comdr. 3d Div. Battleship U.S. Fleet; comdg. same on cruise to Australia and New Zealand, June-Nov. 1927; apptd. dir. Div. of Fleet Training, Navy Dept., Nov. 1927; then comdt. 9th Naval Dist. and Naval Training Sta., Great Lakes, Ill.; comdt. 13th Naval Dist. and Navy Yard, Puget Sound, Wash. Catholic. Home: Canton, O. Died Oct. 15, 1930.

ZIEGLER, DAVID army officer; b. Heidlberg, Palatinate (now part of Germany), Aug. 16, or July 13, 1748; s. Johann Heinrich and Louise Fredericka (Kern)

Z.; m. Lucy Sheffield, Feb. 22, 1789. Served with Russian Army against Turks on lower Danube and Crimea, promoted to rank of commissioned officer, 1768; came to U.S., settled in Carlisle, Pa., circa 1774; served as lt. Pa. battalion of riflemen led by William Thompson in siege of Boston, 1775; fought at L.I., Brandywine, Germantown, Paoli, Monmouth; commd. capt. Pa. Militia, 1778; commissary gen. Dept. of Pa. with hdqrs. at Waynesboro, 1779-80; mem. regt. which joined Lafayette in Va., 1781, attached to Gen. Nathanael Greene's Army, S.C., 1782; opened grocery store, Carlisle, 1783; commd. capt. in Josiah Harmer's expdns. against Indians, 1784, stationed at fts. Mackintosh (Beaver, Pa.), Harmer (Marietta, O.), Washington (Cincinnati); maj. 1st Inf., sent to Marietta, 1790, resigned from Army, 1792; pres. Cincinnati City Council (with duties of chief magistrate), 1802-04; 1st marshal Ohio Dist., 1803; adj. gen. Ohio, 1807; apptd. surveyor Port of Cincinnati, 1807. Died Sept. 24, 1811.

ZINN, GEORGE A. army officer; b. in Pa., Jan. 24, 1861; grad. U.S. Mil. Acad., June 13, 1883, Engr. Sch. of Application, 1886. Commd. 2d lt. engrs., June 13, 1883; 1st lt., June 2, 1884; capt., Feb. 3, 1895; maj., Apr. 13, 1903; lt. col., May 8, 1908; col., Aug. 12, 1913. Duty with Dept. of State, Washington, D.C., in connection with Internat. Am. Conf., 1889-90; asst. engr. officer, in charge of fortifications, Ft. Monroe, Va., 1891-94; sec. Mississippi River Commn., 1894-95; in charge improvements Fox River, etc., Mich., 1895-98, falls of Ohio River, 1898-1900; engr. officer, Dept. of Luzon, P.I., 1900-01; in charge constrn. locks and dams, Ohio River, at Wheeling, W.Va., and improvements other rivers, 1903-07; at Portland, Me., 1907; duty on Mexican border, 1916-17. Address: War Dept., Washington, D.C.

ZOLLICOFFER, FELIX KIRK editor, congressman, army officer; b. Maury County, Tenn., May 19, 1812; s. John Jacob and Martha (Kirk) Z.; attended Jackson Coll., Columbia, Tenn.; m. Louisa Gordon, Sept. 24, 1835, 11 children. Editor, part-owner Columbia Observer, Huntsville, Ala., 1834; an editor Southern Agriculturist, also Huntsville Mercury; state printer Tenn., 1835, 37; served as lt. U.S. Volunteers, Seminole War, 1836; apptd. editor Nashville (Tenn.) Republican Banner, Whig Party organ, 1843; adj. gen., comptroller Tenn., 1845-49; mem. Tenn. Senate, 1849-52; del. Whig Nat. Conv., Balt., 1852; mem. U.S. Ho. of Reps. (Whig) from Tenn., 33d-35th congresses, 1853-59; mem. Peace Conf., Washington, D.C., 1861; served as brig. gen. Confederate Army, in command of East Tenn. during Civil War; one of Tenn. gens. whose figures are carved in Stone Mountain, Atlanta, Ga. Died nr. Mill Springs, Ky., Jan. 19, 1862; buried Old City Cemetery, Nashville.